THE CONCISE
OXFORD DICTIONARY
OF CURRENT ENGLISH

Edited by
H. W. FOWLER AND F. G. FOWLER
based on
The Oxford Dictionary

FIFTH EDITION
Revised by
E. McINTOSH
Etymologies revised by
G. W. S. FRIEDRICHSEN

OXFORD
AT THE CLARENDON PRESS

Oxford University Press, Ely House, London W. 1

GLASGOW NEW YORK TORONTO MELBOURNE WELLINGTON
CAPE TOWN SALISBURY IBADAN NAIROBI DAR ES SALAAM LUSAKA ADDIS ABABA
BOMBAY CALCUTTA MADRAS KARACHI LAHORE DACCA
KUALA LUMPUR SINGAPORE HONG KONG TOKYO

FIRST EDITION 1911
NEW EDITION (*revised*) 1929
THIRD EDITION 1934
REPRINTED 1938, 1940, 1942
1944 (*with revised Addenda, etc.*)
1946, 1949 (*with revised Addenda, etc.*)
FOURTH EDITION 1951
REPRINTED (*with revised Addenda*) 1952, 1954
1955, 1956, 1958, 1959, 1960, 1961, 1962
FIFTH EDITION 1964
REPRINTED (*with corrections*) 1964, 1965, 1966
1967 (*twice*), 1968 (*twice*), 1969 (*thrice*)
1970 (*twice*)

PRINTED IN GREAT BRITAIN
AT THE UNIVERSITY PRESS, OXFORD
BY VIVIAN RIDLER
PRINTER TO THE UNIVERSITY

PREFACE TO THE FIFTH EDITION

IN this edition the etymologies have been thoroughly revised, and for the most part rewritten, by G. W. S. Friedrichsen, to whom I express my sincere thanks for undertaking a laborious task.

Numerous correspondents have sent in useful suggestions for improving the dictionary, all of which are gratefully acknowledged and many of which have been adopted in part or in full. Particular mention must be made of the contributions of P. B. M. Allan, R. W. Burchfield (who read through the proofs), the late Dr R. W. Chapman, L. F. Schooling, and G. C. Vanneck.

With regard to hyphening, some doubt is often felt when the hyphen in a word coincides with the end of a line. To clarify the matter a true hyphen is repeated at the beginning of the following line.

E. McI., 1963

PREFACE TO THE FOURTH EDITION

IN this completely revised and reset edition numerous corrections and additions have been made to bring the book up to date. Thanks are due to the many correspondents who have pointed out errors or suggested improvements. Especially must I express my gratitude to Dr Scholes, Dr Honeyman, and Mr J. M. Wyllie for the valuable assistance given for musical terms, chemical terms, and many technical terms. The officials of the Clarendon Press too, past and present, have throughout been most helpful.

In this edition the system of pronunciation devised for the *Pocket Oxford Dictionary* has been adopted, the senses have been usually numbered, the general abbreviations have been collected into an appendix, and the swung dash has been freely employed.

Swung dash (~).

To save space the 'swung dash' or 'tilde' is very frequently used in the body of the article or the list of derivatives. It represents either the complete word at the beginning of the article or the uninflected part of that word often marked by a vertical line. As, for example, in the article **repeat**, ~ stands for *repeat (or* repeat), ~*ed* for *repeated*, ~edLY² for repeatedLY², ~*ing* for *repeating*, ~ER¹ for repeatER¹; and in the article **reverber|ate** we have ~*ating*, ~ate, ~atoRY, ~ATION, ~ATIVE, ~ANT representing *reverberating*, reverberate, **reverberatoRY, reverber**ATION, **reverber**ATIVE, **reverber**ANT.

E. McI., 1950

From the
PREFACE TO THE THIRD EDITION

THE publication of the Supplement to the *Oxford English Diction-ary* in November 1933 makes important additions to the material which it is the aim of this book, as a dictionary of the living language, to present. Mr H. W. Fowler entrusted me with the preparation of this edition in February 1933, and until his death on the 26th December of that year I had the privilege of his guidance.

H. G. LE MESURIER, 1934

From the
PREFACE TO THE SECOND EDITION

WHEN we began, more than twenty years ago, the work that took shape as *The Concise Oxford Dictionary*, we were plunging into the sea of lexicography without having been first taught to swim. But lexicography for us was fortunately of the minor or dependent kind ; and, fortunately also, the time was one at which the major or firsthand kind was reaching greater excellence than ever before, and the *Oxford English Dictionary*, four-fifths completed, already pro-vided popularizers with unlimited material.

The object we set before us, hinted at by the word *current* on our title-page, was to present as vivid a picture as the small dictionary could be made to give of the English that was being spoken and written at the time. The vividness was to be secured by allotting space to words more nearly in proportion to the frequency and variety of their use, and consequently to their practical value, than had been the custom ; and further by an unprecedented abundance of illustrative quotation ; define, and your reader gets a silhouette ; illustrate, and he has it 'in the round'. That at least was our belief ; and we hailed as confirmation of it one or two letters from persons unknown congratulating us on having 'produced a live dictionary', or 'treating English at last as a living language'.

A living language, however, does not remain unchanged through twenty years and a great war ; our picture has needed, and received, a good deal of retouching before being again exhibited in public.

H. W. F., 1929

ACKNOWLEDGEMENTS

A DICTIONARY-MAKER, unless he is a monster of omniscience, must deal with a great many matters of which he has no firsthand knowledge. That he has been guilty of errors and omissions in some of these he will learn soon after publication, sometimes with gratitude to his enlightener, sometimes otherwise. The first letter we received after C.O.D. appeared was a demand for repayment of the book's cost, on the ground that it failed to give *gal(l)iot*, to settle the spelling of which it had been bought. Even for that announcement of an omission I am now grateful, as affording a good illustration of the less friendly form of correction, and reminding me to assure the public that to one revising for a new edition no correction is (ultimately) unwelcome; all is grist that comes to his mill. At the other end of the scale is the friend, known to me only by correspondence, who for years sent me fortnightly packets of foolscap devoted to perfecting a still contingent second edition—all this for love of the language not as a philological playground, but as the medium of exchange and bond of union among the English-speakers of the world. *Castigavit et emendavit Byron F. Caws* might have stood with justice at the foot of our title-page.

Other helpers have been many, some with systematic lists, others with a few isolated but valuable points; to all those in the list below I would fain offer—what some of them are no longer living to receive —my heartiest thanks:

Leslie J. Berlin Esq.; Major B. F. Caws; Dr R. W. Chapman; Mr S. K. N. Chaudhuri; *Sir Arthur Church K.C.V.O.; Rev. G. P. Ford; H. Gilbert-Carter Esq.; *Prof. Marcus Hartog; the Very Reverend Dr J. H. Hertz; Rev. J. Clare Hudson; Rev. F. E. Hutchinson; Lindsay Johnson M.D., F.R.S.; Rev. D. Evans Jones; Major C. V. N. Lyne; D. C. Macgregor Esq.; F. Morland Esq.; C. O. Ovington Esq.; George Pernet M.D.; Prof. Sir Flinders Petrie F.R.S.; Rev. S. de Saram; Kenneth Sisam Esq.; W. H. Thompson Esq.; B. H. Tower Esq.; F. F. Urquhart Esq.; *Rev. M. N. Walde; E. B. F. Wareing Esq.; *Dr F. H. P. van Wely; J. Beach Whitmore Esq.; Ernest W. Wignall Esq.; C. F. Williams F.G.S.; *Sir Dawson Williams C.B.E.

H. W. F.

---

* Those whose names are thus marked are known to me to be no longer living; and I fear the same may be true of some others, whom I have failed to reach by postal inquiries.

THE steady advance towards completion of the great *Oxford English Dictionary* has made it possible for the Delegates of the Clarendon Press to authorize the preparation and issue of this book, which in its own province and on its own scale uses the materials and follows the methods by which the Oxford editors have revolutionized lexicography. The book is designed as a dictionary, and not as an encyclopaedia ; that is, the uses of words and phrases as such are its subject matter, and it is concerned with giving information about the things for which those words and phrases stand only so far as correct use of the words depends upon knowledge of the things. The degree of this dependence varies greatly with the kind of word treated, the difference between cyclopaedic and dictionary treatment varies with it, and the line of distinction is accordingly a fluctuating and dubious one. It is to the endeavour to discern and keep to this line that we attribute whatever peculiarities we are conscious of in this dictionary as compared with others of the same size. One of these peculiarities is the large amount of space given to the common words that no one goes through the day without using scores or hundreds of times, often disposed of in a line or two on the ground that they are plain and simple and that everyone knows all about them by the light of nature, but in fact entangled with other words in so many alliances and antipathies during their perpetual knocking about the world that the idiomatic use of them is far from easy ; chief among such words are the prepositions, the conjunctions, the pronouns, and such 'simple' nouns and verbs as *hand* and *way*, *go* and *put*. Another peculiarity is the use, copious for so small a dictionary, of illustrative sentences as a necessary supplement to definition when a word has different senses between which the distinction is fine, or when a definition is obscure and unconvincing until exemplified ; these sentences often are, but still more often are not, quotations from standard authors ; they are meant to establish the sense of the definition by appeal not to external authority, but to the reader's own consciousness, and therefore their source, even when authoritative, is not named. A third and a fourth peculiarity are the direct results of the preceding ones ; if common words are to be treated at length, and their uses to be copiously illustrated, space must be saved both by the curtest possible treatment of all that are either uncommon or fitter for the encyclopaedia than the dictionary, and by the severest economy of expression—amounting to the adoption of telegraphese—that readers can be expected to put up with.

In attaching this great importance to illustration, by the need of which the relative length of articles, and our manner of expressing ourselves on every page, are governed, we are merely acting, with the exaggeration imposed on us by our limited space, upon the principles of the O.E.D. That may be said to be the first dictionary for which the ideal procedure has been possible, that is, the approaching of each article with an open mind and a collection of examples large enough to be exhaustive, and the extraction from these of classified senses—the first dictionary, to put it another way, in which quotations have served not merely to adorn or convince, but as the indispensable raw material. This procedure—first the collection of sentences from all possible sources as raw material, and then the independent classification—we have often followed even in that part of our book (A–R) in which the O.E.D., with senses already classified and definitions provided, was before us, treating its articles rather as quarries to be drawn upon than as structures to be reproduced in little; and in the later part (S–Z), where we had no longer the O.E.D. to depend upon, it has been our practice still more often; for many of the more difficult (i.e. especially the common and 'simple') words, we have collected the quotations given in the best modern dictionaries (the *Imperial*, the *Century*, the *Standard*, Cassell's *Encyclopaedic*, Webster, etc.), added to these what we could get either from other external sources or from our own heads, and then framed our articles, often without reference to the arrangement that we found in any of our authorities. Proceeding in this manner, it was almost inevitable that we should be very much alive to the inadequacy of mere definition and the need of constant illustration. That our examples have some general tendency to the colloquial, and include many usages for which room has not been found in dictionaries many times as large as this, is in harmony with our design of on the one hand restricting ourselves for the most part to current English, and on the other hand omitting nothing to which that description may fairly be applied.

VOCABULARY

The words, or senses of words, given are meant to be such only as are current; 'current', however, is an elastic term; we might, but we do not, stretch it to include all words and senses used by Shakspere or in the Bible, on the ground that the whole of Shakspere and the whole of the Bible are still commonly read; thus the archaic senses of *addition* (title), *buxom* (pliant), *owe* (own), *sad* (serious), *sort* (suit), and the archaic words *shend* (scold), *wood* (mad), familiar as they are to readers of Elizabethan literature, are not given. We do stretch it to include many words and senses that are fossilized, having in themselves no life or capacity for further development, but kept extant by being enshrined in perhaps a single proverb or phrase that is still in use; of this sort are *coil* (confusion), preserved by 'shuffled off this mortal coil', and *scotch* (wound), preserved by 'we have scotched the snake, not killed it'.

Again, of the many thousands of old or new scientific and technical terms that have a limited currency some are carried by accident into the main stream of the language and become known temporarily or permanently, vaguely or precisely, to all ordinarily well-informed members of the modern newspaper-reading public. For the purposes of a dictionary that is not to be bulky and yet is to give a fuller treatment than is usual in dictionaries of its size to the undoubtedly current words forming the staple of the language, selection among these intruders is a difficult but very necessary task. The most that can be hoped for is that every one conversant with any special vocabulary may consider us, though sadly deficient on his subject, fairly copious on others; the meaning of many learned words that have been omitted as having no pretence to general currency may easily be gathered by reference first to the stem, which is often the subject of an article, or to another word of which the stem is clearly the same, and secondly to the suffix.

In another class of words and senses the test of currency has led us to diverge in the opposite direction from the practice usual in dictionaries of this size; if we give fewer scientific and technical terms, we admit colloquial, facetious, slang, and vulgar expressions with freedom, merely attaching a cautionary label; when a well-established usage of this kind is omitted, it is not because we consider it beneath the dignity of lexicography to record it, but because, not being recorded in the dictionaries from which our word-list is necessarily compiled, it has escaped our notice; we have not, however, consulted slang dictionaries nor made any attempt at completeness in this respect.

SPELLING

The spelling adopted is for the most part, but not invariably, that of the O.E.D. Such generally established spellings as *judgment, rhyme, axe,* have not been excluded in favour of the *judgement, rime, ax,* preferred by the O.E.D., but are retained at least as alternatives having the right to exist. In dealing with verbs such as *level, rivet, bias,* whose parts and derivatives are variously spelt, the final consonant being often doubled with no phonetic or other significance, we have as far as possible fallen in with the present tendency, which is to drop the useless letter, but stopped short of recognizing forms that at present strike every reader as Americanisms; thus we write *riveted, riveter,* but not *traveling, traveler.* On another point of varying usage—the insertion of a mute e in derivatives in *-able, -age, -ish,* etc., to indicate the 'long' sound of the stem vowel (*likable* or *likeable, milage* or *mileage, latish* or *lateish*)—we have thought ourselves justified in taking a bolder line, and have consistently omitted the -e-; it is against all analogy (or why not *smileing, Romeish, doteage, tideal, indescribeable, desireable, exciteable?*), it is used chiefly in words not familiar or important enough to have their form respected as established, it obscures the different and more valuable use by which a soft g or c is indicated as in *manageable* and *serviceable,* and it tempts bad spellers to such monstrosities as *unpalateable, loveable,* and *moveable.* In words of the type *ardour, colour, favour,* where the O.E.D. recognizes both *-our* and *-or,* we have excluded the latter as being (except in particular words like *horror* and *torpor,* in which it is usually the only form) entirely non-British. Words in which -y- has intruded itself without completely dispossessing a more correct -i-, as *sylvan, tyro, tyre,* we have given with the -i- form either alone or placed first.

ORDER OF SENSES

From the order in which the senses of a word are here given no inference must be drawn as to their historical or other relations, the arrangement being freely varied according to the requirements or possibilities of the particular word. Sense-development cannot always be convincingly presented without abundant quotation from authorities, and the historical order is further precluded by the uniform omission of obsolete senses. Occasionally, when a rare but still current sense throws light on the commoner senses that follow or forms the connecting link with the etymology, it has been placed at the beginning; but more commonly the order adopted has been that of logical connexion or of comparative familiarity or importance.

DERIVATIVES

Hence introduces one or more of the direct derivatives of the word treated; *whence* introduces such derivatives under a particular sense to which they are restricted; *so* introduces words derived from another language; *hence or cogn.*, *whence or cogn.*, introduce groups of partly English and partly foreign derivation. The suffixes of such derivatives are commonly printed in small capitals, and are thus referred to the suffix article in its alphabetical place. The numbers enclosed in brackets indicate subdivisions of the suffix article, and are often used to distinguish among the possible senses of the derivative word those in which it is chiefly current.

REFERENCE BY SMALL CAPITALS

The use of small capitals for etymological purposes is explained above. In the same way reference is made:

(1) from the word treated to another word for the purpose of contrast, distinction, correlation, or the like. Of this kind are the references from *slander* to *libel* and *scandal*, from *creationism* to *evolution* and vice versa, and from *tenon* to *mortise* and vice versa;

(2) from any member of a group to the word under which the group is collected or further explained. *Ruby* (print.) is in this way referred to *type*; *order* (nat. hist.) to *class*[1]; and the *iron*[1], *golden*, and *silver ages* to *brazen*[1];

(3) from one or more words of a proverb or the like to that under which alone the proverb is explained. *Play*[1] and *drake*[2] contain such references to *duck*[1], *flesh* to *fish*[1];

(4) from a compound of the word treated to its other component for explanation. The sign (=) prefixed to such a reference indicates that the simple word treated is itself used in the sense of the compound. Thus, under *pie*[1], *sea-pie* is merely referred (SEA-∼) to *sea*, but *magpie*, besides being referred to the article *magpie*, is recorded (= MAGPIE) as one of the senses of *pie*.

June, 1911

ETYMOLOGY

The etymology is given in square brackets at the end of each article when it is certainly known or regarded as probable. .When, however, a proposed etymology rests on conjecture or hypothesis, it is ignored and the word is described as 'of unkn. orig.' or 'orig. unkn.'. References to other articles are in small capitals.

Words of Germanic (Gmc) origin that have come down from Old or Middle English are illustrated so far as possible by some or all of the forms recorded in the older stages of the cognate dialects, in the order Old Saxon (OS), Old High German (OHG), Old Norse (ON), and Gothic (Goth.). In Germanic inferred forms *th* and *dh* are used to denote the unvoiced and voiced dental spirants. In OE and ON words, as in OS and Gothic, the 'thorn' (þ) and the 'barred d' (ð) are represented by *th*, as hitherto. Thus OE *pæth* PATH, *thrāwan* THROW, ON *thveit* THWAITE, *garthr* GARTH. In OS words the plain b and d are used irrespective of their phonetic value in that dialect. The letters with superimposed macrons (*ā, ǣ*, etc.) in forms quoted from OE or other Gmc languages are long. For ON words the customary diacritic of length has been retained, as *á, ó*, etc.

'ME' includes the fifteenth century, no distinction being made between early and late ME. The use of this term will serve to distinguish words that were in use before 1500 from those whose documentation belongs to the sixteenth or later centuries.

Words of Romanic provenance are referred to their proximate origin, for the most part Old French, the earlier history of which, when known, is briefly indicated.

When OF or the like at the beginning of the etymology is not followed by the OF form, it is because the latter is identical in spelling with the English or differs from it only in some detail specified in brackets. Identity of ME and OF forms may be expressed as in 'ME *chartre* f. OF' (CHARTER[1]) or as in 'ME & OF *sidre*' (CIDER).

If the word is adopted from OF, the parent word is described as OF even though it survives in modern French in the same form, thus: 'ME *charge* f. OF'. Where the modern French differs appreciably from its OF form, this may be indicated as in 'ME & OF *prow* (mod. F *preux*)' (PROW[2]).

F, G, etc., must not be taken to imply that the word to which they are prefixed is current, or so spelt, in the modern language; nor does it follow from a word being given as OF that it is obsolete.

French nouns of Latin origin normally represent the Latin accusative case; nevertheless in this dictionary the Latin nominative is cited except when (e.g. in words ending in -*atio*) a change of stress is involved; thus, e.g., ORISON 'ME f. OF, f. L *orationem*'. For English words derived directly from Latin, the nominative case is cited, as in LIBATION 'f. L *libatio*'.

Many English words that have corresponding forms in both French and Latin present a special problem in that one cannot be certain whether the word was adopted from its French or from its Latin analogue. Sometimes, moreover, an earlier adoption from one source has been reinforced by a later adoption from, or conformation to, the other;

or, again, now one, now the other language has been laid under contribution by different individuals or groups of individuals. In such cases alternative origins have been given, which may mean either 'f. French or Latin' or 'f. French and Latin'.

In words derived from Latin, or from Greek through its latinized form, the age and standing of the Latin word are distinguished as Latin (L), late Latin (LL), medieval Latin (med. L), or modern Latin (mod. L). The dates here assumed are, for 'L', down to c. A.D. 200; for 'LL', from c. 200 to c. 600; for 'med. L', from c. 600 to c. 1500; for 'mod. L', from c. 1500.

The Latin form of a Greek word is usually omitted, and is to be inferred according to the rules of transliteration given below. Thus under PLEONASM 'f. L f. Gk *pleonasmos*' is to be read 'f. L *pleonasmus* f. Gk *pleonasmos*'.

A similar omission of a word in any other language implies identity of form.

Greek words are written with the corresponding English letters (φ, χ, ψ, ῥ, ῤῥ, = ph, kh, ps, rh, rrh, and ᾳ, η, ω = āi, ēi, ōi), and not according to the Latin transliteration, the rules for which are as follows: Greek k = Latin c; ai = ae, ou = u; u (except in diphthongs) = y; ei = i or e; oi = oe (but in nom. pl. = i); g (before g or k) = n; also, -ŏs (nom. masc.), -ŏn = -us, -um; -ēs, -ē (1st decl. nom.) = -a; -ōn (nom.) = -o; -ŏs (genit.) = -is; -a (accus. sing. masc. or fem.) = -em.

The first element of a compound word is often referred to a prefix article, and the remainder treated separately within brackets; meanings given within the bracket belong to the simple word, those of the compound being added if necessary outside it. Thus CONVENE is '[f. F *convenir* f. L CON(*venire* vent- come) assemble, agree, fit]'. The stem *vent-* and the sense 'agree, fit' are here added for the elucidation of CONVENTION and CONVENIENCE, which are referred to CONVENE.

The first element of a Greek compound similarly treated is sometimes written according to the current (Latin) transliteration, to facilitate reference to the prefix article; Greek *kakoepeia*, under CACOEPY, accordingly appears as CACO(*epeia*). Certain similar devices for saving needless repetition will, it is believed, explain themselves.

The etymological sections of all words, as also the prefix and the suffix articles, have been revised or redrafted for the present (fifth) edition. They are based in the first instance on the corresponding articles in the O.E.D., but we have also been privileged to make use of the proofs of the *Oxford Dictionary of English Etymology*, now nearing completion, by Dr. C. T. Onions, C.B.E. The great help and the many improvements afforded by this work are thankfully acknowledged.

G. W. S. F.

November, 1963

PRONUNCIATION

Phonetic respelling is placed in round brackets immediately after such words as require it, and the symbols in the PHONETIC SCHEME are primarily intended for this purpose. But respelling is often saved by employing the same symbols in the black type of the actual word; **bănǐsh**, for instance, has no respelling, and **dǐspōse** has only (-z).

Vowel symbols given in the Scheme with –, ◡, —, or ◠, are also used without these marks to denote a vague indeterminate sound, which is almost identical for all vowels and (except in studied elocution) has no clear relation to the corresponding vowel marked ¯ etc. (e.g., the a in *about* is like the o in *reason*, *proceed*, and is not like ā or ă). When so used in brackets, the indeterminates are printed in italics, thus: **ago** (*agō*), **proceed** (prosēd), **particular** (partĭkūl*ar*). Used in the actual word, they are recognized by the absence of the marks –, ◡, etc.; thus in **săcrament, cŏmmon, bĕggarly,** all the unmarked vowels (a; e; o; ar) are indeterminate. This does not apply to the last six symbols in the Scheme, which never have marks over them and are always distinct.

Indeterminate endings in -n, -m, -l or -le, when they require respelling, are also represented thus: **poison** (-zn), **fūsion** (-zhn), **tĕnsion** (-shn), **ōcean** (-shn), **listen** (-sn), **bosom** (boŏozm), **hŭstle** (-sl), **official** (-shl), **weasel** (-zl), the vowel sound being that similarly indicated by the actual spelling of *spasm*, *prism*, etc.

PHONETIC SCHEME

Consonants: b; ch (ch*i*n); d; dh (dhe = the); g (go); h; j; k; l; m; n; ng (*s*ing); ngg (*f*inger); p; r; s (s*i*p); sh (ship); t; th (th*i*n); v; w; y; z; zh (*vizhn* = vision).

Vowels: ā ē ī ō ū o͞o (mate mete mite mote mute moot)
ă ĕ ĭ ŏ ŭ o͝o (rack reck rick rock ruck·rook)
ār ēr īr ōr ūr (mare mere mire more mure)
ȧr ėr ȯr (part pert port)
ah aw oi oor ow owr (bah bawl boil boor brow bower)

Vowels marked ◡ may be pronounced either way, e.g. **pătriot** (pā- or pă-). In all vowel symbols with r (**ār, ȧr,** etc.), the r, besides influencing the vowel sound, has its consonantal value when followed by a vowel in the next syllable of the word or in the following word (in *fearing* but not in *fearful*, in *far away* but not in *far gone*).

ACCENT

The main accent is shown by the mark ′, usually placed at the end of the stressed syllable; but, division into syllables being arbitrary in English, positions for the accent that would disguise the pronunciation are avoided; thus **stărr′ў** but **că′rrў, woŏll′en** but **cool′lў, lōc′al** but **vělŏ′cĭtў, ōv′er** but **co′ver** (kŭ-), **mŭdd′ў** but **mŭd′dle.** The placing of two accents on a word means either (*a*) that the two marked syllables are equally stressed, as in ding′-dong′, or (*b*) that among good speakers the one accentuation has as many adherents as the other, or (*c*) that the stress varies according to position in the sentence as explained in the dictionary article -ED². In the thousands of compounds given under their first elements among the alphabetically arranged combinations, accent is thus shown: if there is no hyphen separating the parts, the accent is always given (back′bone, backslide′); if there is a hyphen, the regular usage is for the first of the compounded words to be stressed, and the accent is then usually omitted (so oak-apple); if the stress falls, contrary to this rule, on the second component, it is marked (head-on' adv.); if the stress is variable, each part has an accent (high-strung').

PRONUNCIATION WITHOUT RESPELLING

All the further information necessary for the pronunciation of any word or part of a word that is not respelt is contained in the following six paragraphs; the assumptions made in these hold unless the contrary is shown in brackets.

1. Any letter or combination in the Phonetic Scheme has the value there shown; e.g., aw as in *awl*, not as in **awake** (awāk'); and **ginger**, **linger**, would be required to rhyme with *singer* unless **ginger** were followed by (-j-), and **linger** by (-ngg-).

2. The following additional symbols are used in the black type:

ĕ = ĭ (nāk′ĕd, rĕlў′, cŏll′ĕġe, prĭv′ĕt)
ĭr, ûr, = er̄ (bĭr̄th, bûr̄n)
ȳ, ў, = ī, ĭ (implȳ′, sŭnn′ў).

3. Final e unmarked is not indeterminate, but mute (sāne, ĭndŭc′tĭve; cf. rĕcĭpĕ, dĭlĕttăn′tĕ).

4. A doubled consónant is pronounced as single (sĭll′ў, mănn′ĭsh, bŭtt′er), not as in cōōl′ly (-l-lĭ) or plain′nĕss (-n-n-).

5. The following combinations and letters have the values shown:

Vowels.

ae = ē (aegis)
ai = ā (pain)
air = ār̄ (fair)
au = aw (maul)
ay = ā (say)
ea, ee, = ē (mean, meet)
ear, eer, = er̄ (fear, beer)
eu, ew, = ū (feud, few)
ie = ē (thief)
ier = er̄ (pier)
oa = ō (boat)
ou = ow (bound)
oy = oi (coy)

Consonants.

c is 'hard' and = k (cob, cry, talc), but
c before e, i, y, is 'soft' and = s (ice, icy, city)
dg = j (judgement)
ġ before e, i, y, is 'soft' and = j (age, gin, orgy)
kn = n at beginning of word or element of compound (knot, unknot)
n before k, 'hard' c, q, x, = ng (zinc, uncle, tank, banquet, minx)
ph = f (photo)
qu = kw (quit)
tch = ch (batch)
wr = r at beginning of word or element of compound (wry, awry)
x = ks (fox)
χ is the sound in Scots and German loch.

6. The following terminations have the values shown:

-age = -ĭj (garbage)
-ate = -ĭt or -at (mandate)
-ey = -ĭ (donkey)
-ous = -us (furious)

-sm = -zm (atheism, spasm)
-tion = -shon (salvation)
-ture = -cher as well as- tūr̄, esp. in common words.

INFLEXION

The rules assumed, exceptions to which are noted in a bracket placed after a word's grammatical description, are given below. The term 'sibilants' stands for words ending in -s, -x, -z, -sh or soft -ch, '-o wds' for all that end in -o, '-e wds' for all that end in mute -e, and '-y wds' for all that end in -y not preceded by a vowel (e.g. *deny, puppy*, but not *bray, donkey*).

1. Plural of nouns. Sibilants add -es (*boxes, porches*); -y wds change -y into -ies (*puppies*); the plural of -o wds is usually stated thus, **photo** n. (pl. ~s), **potato** n. (pl. ~es); other nouns add -s (*books*).

2. **Possessive of nouns.** Singular nouns take apostrophe, s (*man's, James's*); plurals, if they do not end in s, form the possessive by the same rule (*men's, geese's*), but, if they end in s, take an apostrophe only (*boys'*).

3. **Comparative and superlative of adjectives and adverbs.** In monosyllables and some disyllables (e.g. those in -y) add -er and -est (*bolder*), -e wds dropping the -e (*bravest*), and disyllables in -y having -ier and -iest (*happier, luckiest*); in other cases prefix *more* and *most* (*more beautiful, most splendid*). Monosyllables double a final single consonant (except x and w) if preceded by a single vowel (*grimmer*). This may be stated in the dictionary.

4. **Third person singular present of verbs.** Sibilants and -o wds add -es (*pushes, goes*); -y wds change -y into -ies (*cries*); other verbs add -s (*sings*).

5. **Past and p.p. of verbs.** -e wds add -d (*moved*); -y wds change -y into -ied (*relied*); other verbs add -ed (*trusted, vetoed*); if the final consonant is doubled, it is stated in the dictionary, thus: **glut**, v.t. (-tt-); **revel**, v.i. & t. (-ll-).

6. **Participle of verbs.** All verbs add -ing (*fishing*), -e wds dropping the -e (*dancing*); monosyllables double a final single consonant (except x) if preceded by a single vowel (*grabbing*).

7. **Archaic 2nd and 3rd singular of verbs.** The forms in -(e)st and -(e)th, being archaic, need only be mentioned, without rules; -(e)st is 2nd sing. present and past, -(e)th is 3rd sing. present; examples are *playest, dost, hear'st, madest, wouldst, saith, goeth.*

ABBREVIATIONS USED IN THE DICTIONARY

(For list of general abbreviations see Appendix I)

a,, aa., adjective(s)
abbr./eviation etc.
abl./ative
abs./olute(ly)
acc., according, accusative
act./ive
adj./ective etc.
adjj., adjectives
adv./erb etc.
advv., adverbs
aeron./autics etc.
aesthet./ics etc.
AF, Anglo-French
Afr./ica(n)
AL, Anglo-Latin
alch./emy etc.
alg./ebra etc.
allus./ive etc.
alt./eration etc.
alw./ays
Amer./ica(n)
AN, Anglo-Norman
anal./ogy etc.
anat./omy etc.
Anglo-Ind./ian
anon./ymous etc.
ant./iquities
anthrop. ology etc.
ap./pendix
app./arently
Arab./ic
Aram./aic
arbitr./ary
arch./aic
archaeol./ogy etc.
archit./ecture etc.
arith./metic etc.

Ass./yrian
assim./ilated etc.
assoc./iated etc.
astrol./ogy etc.
astron./omy etc.
attrib./utive etc.
augment./ative etc.
Austral./ia(n)

b./orn
back form./ation
b e./ore
bibl./ical etc.
bibliog./raphy etc.
bill./iards
biog./raphy etc.
biol./ogy etc.
Boh./emian
bot./any etc.
Braz./il(ian)
Bret./on
Brit./ish
Bulg./aria(n)
Burm./ese
Byz./antine

c./entury
c./irca
cc., centuries
Celt./ic
cf., compare
chem./istry etc.
Chin./ese
chronol./ogy etc.
cinemat./ography etc.
cl./assical
cogn./ate

collect./ive(ly)
colloq./uial etc.
com./mon
comb./ination etc.
commerc./ial etc.
comp., compar./ative
compd, compound
compl./ement
compp., compounds
com./mon -Teut./onic
con./ics
conch./ology etc.
confus./ion
conj., conjunction, conjugation
conn./ect etc.
constr./uction etc.
contempt./uous etc.
contr./action etc.
cop./ulative
Copt./ic
Corn./ish
corr./ection etc.
correl./ative etc.
corresp./onding etc,
corrupt./ion
cp., compare
crick./et
cryst./allography
cu., cub., cubic
Cym./ric

d./ied
Da./nish
dat./ive
demonstr./ative
dent./istry

deriv./ative etc.
derog./atory etc.
dial./ect etc.
dict./ioriary
diff./erent
different./iate etc.
dim./inutive etc.
dimm., diminutives
diplom./acy
dir./ect etc.
dissim./ilate etc.
dist./inct etc.
distrib./utive etc.
disyl./labic etc.
Dor./ic
Du./tch
dynam./ics etc.

E, English
eccl./esiastical etc.
EFris., East Frisian
Egyptol./ogy
E. Ind., East Indian
electr./icity etc.
ellipt./ical etc.
embryol./ogy
engin./eering etc.
Engl., England, English
entom./ology etc.
erron./eous(ly)
eschat./ology etc.
esp./ecial(ly)
eth./ics etc.
ethnol./ogy etc.
etym./ology etc.
euphem./ism etc.
Eur./ope(an)
ex./ample
exagg./eration etc.
exc./ept
exch./ange
excl., exclamation etc., exclusive etc.
excll., exclamations
expl./ain etc.
expr./essing etc.
exx., examples

F, French
f./rom
facet./ious etc.
fam./iliar etc.
fem./inine etc.
fenc./ing
fig./urative etc.
Fl./emish
foll./owing (word)
footb./all
form./ation
fortif./ication
Fr./ench
Frank./ish
freq./uent(ly)
frequent./ative(ly)
Fris./ian
ft, foot, feet
fut./ure

G, German
Gael./ic
gal./lon(s)
gen., general etc., genitive
geog./raphy etc.
geol./ogy etc.
geom./etry etc.
Gk, Greek
Gmc, Germanic
Goth./ic
gr., gram./mar etc.
gym./nastics etc.

Heb./rew
ſier./aldry etc.
Hind., Hindi, Hindustani
hist./orical etc., history
hort./iculture etc.
Hung./arian, -ary
hydrost./atics etc.

i., intransitive
Icel./andic
illit./erate etc.
imit./ative etc.
imper., imperat./ive
imperf./ect
impers./onal
improp./er(ly)
incept./ive
incl./uding, -usive
Ind./ia(n)
ind., indicative, indirect
indecl./inable
inf./initive
infl./uence etc.
instr./umental (case)
int./erjection
interrog./ative(ly)
intr./ansitive
Ir./ish
iron./ical(ly)
irreg./ular(ly)
It., Ital./ian
ital./ics

Jam./aica(n)
Jap./an(ese)
Jav./anese
Jew./ish
joc./ose, -ular(ly)

L, Latin
lang./uage
Lat./in
lexicog./raphy etc.
LG, Low German
lit./eral(ly)
Lith./uania(n)
LL, late Latin
log./ic etc.

M, middle (with languages)
magn./etism etc.
manuf./acture etc.
masc./uline
math./ematics etc.
MDu., middle Dutch
ME, middle English (1200–
  1500)
mech./anics etc.
med./icine etc.
med.L, medieval Latin
metaph./or etc.
metaphys./ics etc.
metath./esis etc.
meteor./ology etc.
meton./ymy
Mex./ican
MHG, middle High German
mil./itary etc.
min./eralogy etc.
MLG, middle Low German
mod./ern
monosyl./labic etc.
morphol./ogy etc.
MSw., middle Swedish
mus./ic etc.
myth./ology etc.

n./oun
N. Amer., North American
nat. hist., natural history

nat. phil., natural philosophy
naut./ical etc.
nav./al etc.
neg./ative(ly)
neut./er
NFris., North Frisian
nn., nouns
nom./inative
Norm./an
north./ern
Norw./egian, -ay
N.T., New Testament
num./eral

O, old (with languages)
obj./ect etc.
obl./ique
obs./olete
obsc./ure etc.
obsolesc./ent
obstet./rics etc.
occas./ional(ly)
ODa., old Danish
OE, old English
OF, old French
OFris., old Frisian
OHG, old High German
OIr., old Irish
OLG, old Low German
ON, old Norse
ONF, old northern French
onomat./opoeic etc.
opp., (as) opposed (to)
OPr., old Provençal
opt., optative, optics etc.
ord./inary
orig./in(al(ly))
ornith./ology etc.
OS, old Saxon
OSl(av)., old Slavonic
OSp., old Spanish
O.T., Old Testament

p./age
paint./ing
Pal./estine
palaeog./raphy etc.
palaeont./ology etc.
parenth./etic etc.
Parl./iament(ary)
part., (present) participle
partic./ipial
pass./ive(ly)
path./ology etc.
pedant./ic(ally)
perf./ect (tense)
perh./aps
Pers./ia(n)
pers./on(al)
pert./aining
Peruv./ian
Pg., Portuguese
pharm./acy etc.
philol./ogy etc.
philos./ophy etc.
Phoen./icia(n)
phon., phonet./ics etc.
phonol./ogy etc.
photog./raphy etc.
phr./ase
phren./ology etc.
phrr., phrases
phys./ics etc.
physiol./ogy etc.
pl./ural
plup./erfect
poet./ical etc.
Pol./ish, -and

pol./itics etc.
pol. econ., political economy
polit./ics etc.
pop./ular etc.
Port./uguese
poss./essive, /ible etc.
p.p., past or passive participle
pp., pages
Pr./ovençal
pr./onounced etc.
prec., (the) preceding (word)
pred./icate etc.
pref./ix
prep./osition
pres./ent (tense)
pret./erite
print./ing
priv./ative
prob./able etc.
pron., pronoun etc., pronounced etc.
pronunc./iation
prop./er(ly)
pros./ody etc.
Prov./ençal
prov., proverb etc., provincial etc.
psych./ology etc.
psycho-an./alysis

R.-C., Roman Catholic
redupl./icated etc.
ref./erence
refash./ioned etc.
refl./exive(ly)
rel./ated, -ative
repl./acing etc.
repr./esent etc.
rhet./oric etc.
Rom., Roman, Romance, Romanic
Rom./an ant./iquities
Rom./an Cath./olic

Rom./an hist./ory
Russ./ia(n)

s./ingular
S. Afr., South Africa(n)
Sax./on
sb., substantive
Sc., Scotch, Scots, Scottish
Scand./inavia(n)
schol./astic
sci./ence etc.
Scot., Scotland, Scottish
sculp./ture
Sem./itic
sent./ence
Serb./ian
sing./ular
Skr., Sanskrit
sl./ang
Slav./onic
sociol./ogy etc.
Sp./anish
sp./elling
spec./ial(ly)
spirit./ualism etc.
sport./ing etc.
st./em
stat./ics etc.
subj., subject etc., subjunctive
subst./antive
suf./fix
sup., superl./ative
surg./ery etc.
surv./eying etc.
Sw./edish
syn./onym etc.

t., transitive
tech./nical(ly)
teleg./raphy etc.
term./ination
theatr./ical etc.
theol./ogy etc.
theos./ophy etc.

therm./ometry etc.
thr./ough
trans./itive etc.
transf., in transferred sense
transl./ation etc.
translit./eration etc.
trig./onometry etc.
Turk./ish, -ey
typ./ography etc.

ult./imate(ly)
uncert./ain
unexpl./ained
unkn./own
U.S., United States
usu./al(ly)

v./erb
var., variant, various
v. aux., verb auxiliary
vb, verb
vbl, verbal
v.i., verb intransitive
voc./ative
v.refl., verb reflexive
v.t., verb transitive
vulg./ar(ly)
vv., verbs

W, Welsh
w./ith
W. Afr., West Africa(n)
wd, word
wds, words
WFlem., West Flemish
WFris., West Frisian
WG, West Germanic
wh./ich
W.Ind., West Indian, -ies

yd, yard
yr(s), year(s)

zoogeog./raphy etc.
zool./ogy etc.

P = proprietary name. See below.
*, in etymologies, sign affixed to all forms not recorded but merely inferred.
*, other than in etymologies = (orig. or chiefly) U.S.
‖ = not U.S.
~ represents either the complete word at the beginning of the article or the uninflected part of that word often marked by a vertical line.

NOTE. The addition of etc. to the completion of an abbreviation means that it may be used not only for the exact form given, but for connected words or phrases; e.g. *bot./any etc.* means *botany*, *botanical*, *botanically*, *in botany*; *adv./erb etc.* means *adverb*, *adverbial*, *adverbially*; *transl./ation etc.* means *translated* as well as *translation*. Abbreviations given in the list with initial capital have always the capital in use; but those given with initial small letter have either form according to circumstances.

This dictionary includes some words which are or are asserted to be proprietary names or trade marks. Their inclusion does not imply either that they have acquired for legal purposes a non-proprietary or general significance or any other judgement concerning their legal status. In cases where the editor has some evidence that a word is used as a proprietary name or trade mark this is indicated by the symbol **P**, but no judgement concerning the legal status of such words is made or implied thereby.

A

A, letter (pl. *As*, A's, Aes). (Mus.) sixth note in scale of C major, & the corresponding scale. (In argument) first imaginary person or case. (Alg.) first known quantity. (Naut.) **A1** (ā wŭn), first-class vessel in Lloyd's Register of Shipping; (colloq.) excellent, best. (Naut.) Æ, third-class ship at Lloyd's.

a¹, **an**, (*a*, *an*; emphatic, ā, ăn), adj. (occas. called indefinite article. Before all consonants except silent *h*, use *a*; *a history*, *a historian*, though some still write *an* before *h* in unaccented syllable, but *an hour*: before all vowels except *eu*, *ū*, use *an*; *an ulcer*, but *a ūnit*, *a eulogy*; also *a one*. Placed after *many*, *such*, *what*, or any adj. preceded by *how*, *so*, *as*, *too*. Used with apparent plurals of number, *a dozen men* = a dozen of men; also with pl. adjj. *few*, *good many*, *great many*). (Unemphatic substitute for) one, some, any; one like *a Daniel*); (after *all of*, *many of*, etc.) the same (*all of a size*); (distrib.) each (*£40 a year*, where *a* is orig. = foll.). [weakening of OE *ān* ONE]

a², prep. On, to, towards, into, in. Mostly now written as pref., or oftener omitted than expressed, or confused w. A¹. On: *abed*, *afoot*. To: *ashore*. Towards: *aback*, *afar*, *aside*. Into: *apart*, *asunder*. In: *now-a-days*, *twice a day*; w. vbl nouns, passively, *a-building*, actively, *was* (*a-*)*fighting*, and esp. w. *go*, *set*, as *he went a begging*, *they set the bells a ringing*. [weakening of OE prep. *an*, ON]

a-, pref. f. various sources. **1.** OE *a-*, orig. *ar-*, away, on, up, out, as *arise*. Occas. confused w. OF *a-* f. L *ad-*, *ac-*, *ad-* etc. (No. 4), as *a*(*c*)*curse* etc. **2.** ME *a-* f. OE *an*, *on*, prep.; see prec. **3.** ME *a-* f. OE *of* prep., as *akin*, *a-clock*. **4.** ME *a-*, = OF pref. *a-*, f. L *ad* to, at, either directly, as *ascend*, or thr. F *a-* as *agree*; many wds derived in the latter way have been later assim. to L spelling, as *a*(*d*)*dress*, *a*(*g*)*grieve*. **5.** ME *a-*, = OF *a-*, f. L *ab* from, away, as *abridge*. **6.** ME, AF *a-* = OF *e-*, *es* f. L *ex* out, utterly, as *amend*, *affray*. **7.** Gk *a-*, *an-*, not, without; directly, as *amorphous*, thr. L, as *acatalectic*, or thr. L & F, as *adamant*; compounded chiefly w. Gk words, but also w. others, as *a-moral*.

-a, suf. **1.** Nn. f. Gk, L, & Rom. fem. sing., as *idea* (Gk), *arena* (L), *piazza* (It.), *duenna* (Sp.), esp. Nat. Hist. terms, ancient or latinized mod. (*hyena*, *dahlia*), geogr. names (*Africa*), & names of women,

ancient or latinized mod. (*Lydia*, *Hilda*). **2.** Gk & L neut. pl. nouns (*genera*, *phenomena*), esp. names, often f. mod. L, of classes of animals (*mammalia*).

aard-vark (ārd' värk), n. S.-African quadruped between armadillos & ant-eaters. [f. Du. *aarde* EARTH +*varken* pig; see FARROW]

aard-wolf (ārd' woolf), n. S.-African carnivore between hyenas & civets. [see prec.]

Aar'on's beard (ār-), n. Kinds of plant, esp. great St John's wort. [ref. to *Ps*. cxxxiii. 2]

Aar'on's rŏd (ār-), n. Kinds of plant, esp. great mullein & golden rod. [ref. to *Num*. xvii. 8]

aasvoġel (ah'sfōgl), n. S.-Afr. vulture. [S.-Afr.Du. (*aas* carrion +*vogel* bird)]

ab-, pref. repr. L *ab*, off, away, from, f. F, as *abuse*, or L, as *abduct*.

ăb'a, **abaya** (abā'ya), nn. Sack-like outer garment worn by Arabs. [Arab.]

abäck', adv. Backwards; (Naut.) of square sails pressed against mast by head wind; *taken* ~, of ship w. sails in that state, (fig.) surprised, discomfited. [Aᵖ + BACK¹]

ăb'acus, n. (pl. *-ci*, pr. -sī). **1.** Calculating frame w. balls sliding on wires, used before adoption of the nine figures & zero, & still in China etc., & in elementary teaching. **2.** (Archit.) upper member of capital, supporting architrave. [L *abacus* f. Gk *abax* *-akos* tablet]

Abăd'don, n. Hell; the devil (*Rev*. ix. 11). [Heb. word, destruction (*abad* he perished)]

abaft' (-ah-), adv. & prep. (naut.). In stern half of ship; nearer the stern than, aft of. [A² +*baft*, OE *beæftan* f. *be* BY +*æftan* AFT]

*ăbalō'nė, n. Californian edible mollusc with ear-shaped shell lined with mother-of-pearl, sea-ear. [Sp.]

abăn'don¹, v.t. Give up to another's control or mercy; yield *oneself* completely to a passion or impulse; give up (a possession or habit); forsake (a person, post). [ME, f. OF *abandoner* f. phr. *à bandon* under control f. Rom. **bandonem* f. med. L *bandum*, var. LL *bannus*, *-um* BAN²]

abăn'don² (or as F, see Ap.), n. Careless freedom, letting oneself go. [F; see prec.]

abăn'doned (-ond), a. Profligate. [p.p. of ABANDON¹]

abăndonee', n. (law). One to whom anything is relinquished. [ABANDON¹ +-EE]

abăn′donment, n. Giving up or forsaking; being forsaken; self-surrender; careless freedom of manner, impulsiveness. [f. ABANDON[1] +-MENT, or F *abandonnement*]

abāse′, v.t. Lower, humiliate, make base. Hence ~MENT (-sm-) n. [late ME *abesse* f. OF *abaissier* f. *a* (A- (4)) +*baissier* to lower f. Rom. **bassiare* f. LL *bassus* BASE[3], whence mod. form *abase*]

abăsh′, v.t. Put out of countenance; (chiefly in pass.) be confounded. Hence ~MENT n. [ME *abaiss(e)* f. OF *esbaïr* f. *es-* = A- (6) +*baïr* be astonished, of uncert. orig.; see -ISH[2]]

abask′ (-bah-), adv. In warm light. [A[2] + BASK]

abāte′, v.t. & i. **1**. Diminish (t. & i.). **2**. Do away with (nuisance); blunt (edge); lower (price); deduct (specified or unspecified part of price); mitigate (violence); weaken (energy). **3**. (In law) quash (writ or action). **4**. (Of flood or epidemic) grow less. So (f. OF) ~MENT (-tm-) n. [ME, f. OF *abatre* f. *a* = A (4) +*batre* beat f. Rom. **battere* for L *battuere*; cf. BATTLE[1]]

ăb′atis, **abătt′is**, n. Defence made of felled trees w. boughs pointing outwards. Hence **ăb′atisED**[2] (-st) a. [F, f. *abatre* fell; see prec.]

abattoir (see Ap.), n. Slaughter-house. [F]

abăx′ial, a. (bot.). Away from the axis. [AB-, AXIS, -AL]

ăbb, n. Woof. [A- (1) +WEB]

Abb′a (ă-), n. Father. Used w. *Father* in invoking God (*Mark* xiv. 36). [Aram.]

ăbb′acў, n. Office, jurisdiction, or tenure, of an abbot. [earlier *abbatie* (see -ACY) f. LL *abbatia* (*abbat-* ABBOT)]

abbā′tial (-shal), a. Of an abbey, abbot, or abbess. [F, f. med.L *abbatialis* (*abbatia* ABBACY,\-AL)]

abbé (ăb′ā), n. Frenchman (orig. abbot) entitled to wear ecclesiastical dress, esp. without official duties. [F, f. LL *abbatem* nom. *-as* ABBOT]

ăbb′ess, n. Superior of abbey of enclosed nuns. [ME, f. OF *ab(b)esse* f. LL *abbatissa* (ABBOT, -ESS)]

ăbb′ey, n. (pl. ~s). Building(s) occupied by monks or nuns under an abbot or abbess; the monks or nuns as a body; a church or house that was once an ~ or part of it (*the A*~, Westminster A~). [ME, f. OF *abbeie* etc. f. LL *abbatia* ABBACY]

ăbb′ot, n. Head of abbey of monks; *A*~ *of Misrule* or *of Unreason*, leader in medieval burlesque festivities. [OE *abbod*, f. LL *abbas* *-at-* f. Gk *abbas* (ABBA)]

abbrēv′iate[1], a. Relatively short (esp. in nat. hist.). [late ME f. LL *abbreviatus* p.p. of *-are* shorten (*ab* or *ad* +*brevis* short); cf. ABRIDGE]

abbrēv′i|āte[2], v.t. Make short (chiefly now of writing part of word for whole,

but also of visit, story, etc.). So (f. OF) ~ATION n. [f. as prec.; see -ATE[3]]

A B C (ābēsē′), n. The alphabet; rudiments of any subject; ‖ alphabetical railway guide.

Ab′derite (ă-), n. *The* ~, Democritus (see DEMOCRITEAN). [Gk *Abdēritēs* (*Abdēra*, a town, -ITE[1])]

ăb′dic|āte, v.t. Renounce formally or by default (a power, office, right; also abs., esp. of the crown). So (f. L) ~A′TION n., ~ā[1](2)ā. [f. L AB(*dicare* declare), -ATE[2]]

ăbdōm′ĕn (or ăb′do-), n. **1**. (anat.). Belly, including stomach, bowels, & other nutritive organs. **2**. (zool.). Hinder part of insects, spiders, etc. [L]

ăbdŏm′inal, a. Of the abdomen in either sense; (of fish) having the ventral fins under the belly. [f. *abdomin-* stem of prec. +-AL]

ăbdŏm′inous, a. Corpulent. [as prec. + -OUS]

abdū′cent, a. (anat.). Drawing away (of muscles that open or pull back the part they are fixed to). [f. L *abducent-* part. st. of AB(*ducere duct-* draw)]

abdŭct′, v.t. Kidnap; take away (esp. a woman) by force or fraud; draw (limb etc.) from its natural position. [f. L *abduct-* see prec.]

abdŭc′tion, n. Illegal carrying off, esp. of a child, ward; forcible carrying off of any one, as of a voter; withdrawal of limb from natural position; shrinking of sides of a wound, causing it to gape. [f. LL *abductio* (prec., -ION)]

abdŭc′tor, n. Person who abducts another; (also ~*muscle*) muscle that abducts a limb. [as ABDUCT +-OR]

abeam′, adv. On a line at right angles to the ship's or aircraft's length; ~ *of us*, opposite our centre, abreast. [A[2] +BEAM[1]]

abecedār′ian (ābīsī-), a. & n. **1**. Arranged alphabetically, as the 119th Psalm; elementary, ignorant. **2**. n. Pupil learning the alphabet (common in U.S.). [f. LL *abecedarius* (see -ARY[1]) +-AN]

aběd′, adv. In bed. [A[2] +BED[1]]

abele (abēl′, ā′bl), n. The white poplar. [f. Du. *abeel* f. OF *abel* earlier *aubel* f. med. L *albellus* dim. of *albus* white]

ā′belmŏsk, n. Malvaceous N.-Afr. evergreen shrub yielding musk-seeds. [ult. f. Arab. *ḥabbu-'l-misk* grain of musk]

Aberdeen′ (ă-), n. ~ *Angus*, Scottish breed of polled black cattle; ~ (*terrier*), rough-haired Scotch terrier. [*Aberdeen* in Scotland]

ăberdĕvine′, n. Bird-fancier's name for the siskin. [orig. unkn.]

Aberdōn′ian (ă-), a. & n. (Inhabitant, native) of Aberdeen. [f. med. L *Aberdonia* +-IAN]

aberglaube (ah′berglowbe), n. Excessive belief, superstition. [G]

Ab′ernĕthў (ă-), n. Hard biscuit flavoured with caraway seeds. [orig. unkn.]

abĕ′rr|ant, a. Straying from moral standard; (in nat. hist.) diverging from normal type. So ~ANCE, ~ANCY, nn. [f. L *aberrant-* part. st. of AB(*errare* stray)]

ăberrā'tion, n. **1.** A straying from the path, lit. & fig.; breaking of rules; moral slip; intellectual deficiency; temporary lapse of memory; deviation from type. **2.** (optics). Non-convergence of rays to one focus. **3.** (astron.). Displacement of heavenly body's true position to observer. [f. L *aberratio*; see prec., -ATION]

abĕt', v.t. (-tt-). Countenance or assist (offence or offender; esp. *aid & ~*), incite. So (f. AN) ~MENT, ~t'ER[1], ~t'OR, nn. ~*tor* is the legal & the commoner general form. [ME, f. OF *abeter* (à to +*beter* BAIT[1])]

ăb ex'tră, adv. From outside. [LL]

abey'ance (-bā-), n. State of suspension, dormant condition liable to revival, (of rights etc.; mostly in phrr. *be in* or *fall into ~*). [AF *abeiance* f. OF *abeer* f. *a* to +*beer* f. med.L *batare* gape]

abhŏr', v.t. (-rr-). Regard with disgust & hatred (*Nature ~s a vacuum*). [ME, f. L AB(*horrēre* shudder)]

abhŏ'rrence, n. Detestation; detested thing (*flattery is my ~*). [foll., -ENCE]

abhŏ'rrent, a. Inspiring disgust, hateful, of conduct, etc., often with *to* (person); inconsistent (*from*); (arch.) feeling disgust (*of*), as *the Greeks were ~ of excess*. [f. L *abhorrent-* part. st. see ABHOR]

abhŏ'rrer, n. (hist.). Nickname of those who signed addresses to Charles II in 1680. [ABHOR + -ER[1]]

abid'ance, n. Continuance, dwelling (*in*), abiding (*by* rules etc.). [ADIDE + -ANCE]

abide', v.t. & i. (past & p.p. *abōde*, occas. ~*d*). **1.** Remain over; continue; dwell (arch.); stand firm; (with *by*) remain faithful to, act upon (terms). **2.** Wait for; encounter, sustain; submit to, suffer; (negatively as *I cannot, who can, ~?*) put up with (noun or infinitive). [OE *abīdan* f. A-(1) +*bīdan* BIDE]

abid'ing, a. Permanent. Hence ~LY[2] adv. [part. of ABIDE]

ăbiĕt-, stem of several chemical terms. Of resin, or fir. [L *abiet-* nom. *abies* fir-tree]

ăb'ĭgail, n. Lady's-maid. [character in Beaumont & Fletcher's *Scornful Lady*, perh. w. ref. to 1 *Sam.* xxv. 24–31]

abil'itў, n. Sufficient power, capacity (*to do something*); legal competency (*to act*); financial competency to meet a demand; cleverness, mental faculty, (general in sing., special in pl.). [ME *ablete* f. OF f. L *habilitatem* (*habilis* deft, -TY[1]) to wh. mod. sp. conforms]

ăb ĭnĭt'ĭō, adv. From the beginning. [L]

ăb'iogĕn'ēsis, n. Spontaneous generation. (Allied words) **ăb'iogĕnĕt'ĭc** a., connected w. the doctrine; **ăb'iogĕnĕt'-ĬCALLY** adv., by spont. gen. or according to the doctrine; **ăbiŏ'gĕnĬST** (2) n., one who believes in it; **ăbiŏ'gĕnous** a., so produced; **ăbiŏ'gĕnў**[1] n., = abiogenesis. [f. Gk *abios* f. A-(7) +*bios* life +GENESIS]

ăb'jĕct, a. & n. **1.** Brought low, miserable; craven, degraded, despicable. **2.** n. (Bibl. & arch.) a person of the meanest condition. Hence ~LY[2] adv., ~NESS n. [ME, f. L *abjectus* p.p. of AB(*jicĕre* = *jacĕre* throw)]

abjĕc'tion, n. Abasement, low estate. [f. L *abjectio* (ABJECT, -ION)]

ăbjurā'tion (-joor-), n. Action or form of renunciation on oath, in all senses of ABJURE (in hist. esp. of the Stuart claim). [f. L *abjuratio* (ABJURE, -ATION)]

abjure' (-joor), v.t. Renounce on oath (an opinion, heresy, cause, claim, or claimant); swear perpetual absence from (one's country etc.) [f. F *abjurer* or L AB(*jurare* swear)]

ăblactā'tion, n. Weaning from the mother. [f. LL AB(*lactatio* f. *lactare* suckle f. *lact-* nom. *lac* milk)]

ăblā'tion, n. Removal (esp. in surgery, of any part of body); (Geol.) waste of a glacier or rock by melting or water action. [f. LL *ablatio* f. AB(*lat-* p.p. st. of *ferre* carry)]

ăb'lative, a. & n. The case in Latin nouns that expresses source, agent, cause, instrument, of action = *from* or *by* with the noun (usu. noun; adj. with *case, sense,* etc.); ~ ABSOLUTE, a construction of noun & particle in L Gram. giving time or circumstances. [ME, f. OF (-*if, -ive*) or L *ablativus* (prec., -IVE)]

ăb'laut (-ow-), n. Vowel changes in the parent Indo-European language, arising out of differences of accent & stress, & surviving e.g. in *drive, drove, driven.* [G]

ablāze', adv. & pred. a. On fire; glittering; excited. [A[2] +BLAZE]

ā'ble, a. Talented, clever; competent, having the means or power (*to*), esp. w. parts of *be* to supply the deficiencies of *can*; legally qualified; ~*-bodied seaman* (abbr. A.B.), of special class. Hence **āb'LY**[2] adv. [ME, f. OF *hable; able*, (now *habile*) f. L *habilis* handy (*habēre* to hold)]

-able, suf. f. F -*able* f. L -*a-* of first conjug. +-*bili-* see -BLE. In F extended to vbs of all conjugg. In E now appended even to native vbs as *bearable*, nouns as *clubbable*, & phrase vbs as *get-at-able*; prob. f. confusion w. the unrelated adj. *able*. Now always w. pass. sense (*eatable*), but in early wds freq. act. (*comfortable, suitable*); cf. -BLE; *salable* (where no vb exists) is on anal. of *debatable*.

|ăb'lĕt, ăb'lĕn, n. Name for the fresh-water fish bleak. [F *ablette* f. Rom. *abula* for *alb̄ula* dim. of *alba* white]

ăb'lings, āb'lins (-z), adv. (Sc. & north.). Possibly, perhaps. [ABLE + -LINGS]

ablōōm', adv. & pred. a. In or into bloom. [A[2] +BLOOM]

ablŭsh', adv. & pred. a. Blushing. [A[2] +BLUSH]

ablu'tion (-lōō-), n. (usu. pl.). Ceremonial washing of person, hands, or sacred vessels; ordinary personal washing; (sing.) water in which things have been washed, esp. in Catholic Ritual. Hence ~ARY[1] a. [ME, f. OF, or LL AB(*lutio* f. *lucre lut-* wash, -ION)]

ăb'něgāte, v.t. Deny oneself (something), renounce (a right or belief). [f. L AB(*negare* deny), -ATE[3]]

ăbněgā'tion, n. Denial; rejection (of doctrine); self-sacrifice (now oftener *self- -~*). [f. F, or LL *abnegatio* (prec., -ATION)]

abnōrm'al, a. Exceptional, irregular, deviating from type. Hence **ăbnormäl'ITY** n., the quality or an instance of it, ~LY[2] adv. [earlier & F *anormal* f. med. L *anormalus* corrupted f. Gk *anōmalos* ANOMALOUS; but now regarded as f. L *abnormis*, see foll.]

abnōrm'ĭtў, n. Irregularity; a monstrosity. [f. L AB(*normis* f. *norma* rule) see -TY]

aboard' (-ōrd), adv. & prep. On or into ship, train, etc. (*ship* etc. either expressed or omitted); alongside, near, esp. *close* or *hard*~. *Lay* (another ship)~, place one's own alongside of her to fight; *fall* ~, fall foul of (another ship). [A[2]+BOARD]

abōde', n. Dwelling-place, house; stay, habit of dwelling, as in *make* one's ~. [vbl n. of ABIDE; cf. *ride, rode, road*]

aboil', adv. & pred. a. A-boiling, boiling. [A[2]+BOIL[2]]

abŏl'ish, v.t. Do away with (customs, institutions). Hence ~ABLE a., ~ER[1], ~MENT, nn. [ME, f. F *abolir* (-ISH[2]) f. L *abolēre* destroy]

ăboli'tion, n. Abolishing, being abolished. In the 18th & 19th cc. w. ref. to Negro slavery & the movement against it, whence also ~ISM(3), ~IST(2), (-shon-), nn. [f. F *abolition* or L *abolitio* (prec., -ION)]

A-bomb (ā'bŏm), n. Atomic bomb. [*A* for ATOMIC]

abŏm'inab|le, a. Detestable, odious, morally or physically loathsome; (by conscious exaggeration) unpleasant. Hence ~leNESS (-ln-) n., ~LY[2] adv. [ME, f. OF, f. L *abominabilis* f. AB(*ominari* f. *omen* deprecate; early sp. *abh-* due to assoc. w. L *homo*]

abŏm'ināte[1], v.t. Loathe; (by exaggeration) dislike. [f. L *abominat-*; see prec.]

abŏm'ināte[2], a. (poet.). Abominated. [f. L *abominatus* p.p., see ABOMINABLE]

abŏminā'tion, n. Loathing; odious or degrading habit or act; an object of disgust (*to*). [ME, f. OF (ABOMINATE[1], -ATION)]

ăbori'ginal, a. & n. **1.** Indigenous, existing in a land at the dawn of history, or before arrival of colonists (of races & natural objects). **2.** n. (pl. ~*s,* but *aborigines* commoner). ~ inhabitant or (rarely) thing. Hence **ăboriginäl'ITY** n., ~LY[2] adv. [f. as ABORIGINES, +-AL]

ăbori'gĭnēs (-z), n. pl. (*aboriginal* usual for sing.; also the indefensible form *aboriginĕ,* & rarely *abŏ'rigin* or *-en*). First inhabitants, or those found in possession by colonists (also of native plants & ani-

mals). [L, f. phr. *ab origine* from the beginning]

abōrt', v.i. Miscarry, have premature delivery of a child; (Biol.) become sterile, remain undeveloped, shrink away, (of plants & animals—the race, the individual, or part of the body). Hence ~ĬFA'CIENT (-āshent) a. & n., (drug or other agent) causing abortion. [f. L *abort-* p.p. st. of AB(*oriri* be born) miscarry]

abōrt'ĕd, a. Untimely born, undeveloped; rudimentary (*thorns are* ~ *branches*). [ABORT +-ED[1] (2)]

abōr'tion, n. Miscarriage of birth: the procuring of this, whence ~IST (1) (-shon-) n.; arrested development of any organ; a dwarfed or mis-shapen creature; failure of a project or action. [f. L *abortio* (ABORT, -ION)]

abōr'tive, a. Premature (birth etc.); fruitless, unsuccessful; rudimentary (organ etc.), arrested in development. Hence ~LY[2] (-vl-) adv., ~NESS (-vn-) n. [ME, f. L *abortivus* (ABORT, -IVE)]

abou'lia (-ow-), **abū'lia,** n. Loss of will-power (as mental disorder). [f. Gk *a-* not +*boulomai* I will]

abound', v.i. **1.** (Orig.) overflow, either of vessel or of liquid. **2.** Be plentiful; be rich (*in*); teem or be infested (*with*). [ME, f. OF *abunder* etc. f. L AB(*undare,* f. *unda* wave); early sp. *hab-* due to assoc. w. L *habēre* have]

about'[1], adv. & prep. All round from outside, as *compass it* ~, *He is* ~ *my path, beat* ~ *the bush*; all round from a centre, as *look* or *lay* ~ *you*; somewhere round, as *lie* ~, *hang* ~ (the door), *the fields* ~ *Oxford, people* or *objects* ~ *us, have not a penny* ~ *me*; here and there (*in a place,* or abs.), as *smallpox is* ~, *move* or *order* ~, *he put the tale* ~, *I was much put* ~ (distracted), *out & ~,* restored to normal activity (after convalescence), *dotted* ~ *the fields, man* ~ *town*; near in number, scale, degree, etc., as ~ *half, fifty, right, tired, midnight, my size* (occas. *much* ~); facing round, as *right-* ~ *turn* (now ~ *turn!* as mil. word of command), *the wrong way* ~, *put* (the ship) or *go* ~; round a party, as *take turns* ~, *read verse* ~; occupied with, as ~ *my father's business, send* ~ *his business, what are you* ~*?, go* ~ *to do, am* ~ *to do* (so all fut. participles); in connexion with, as *quarrels* ~ *trade, something wrong* ~ *it*; circuitously, as *he went a long way* ~, *I brought it* ~, *it came* ~. [OE *on-būtan* f. *on* (A[2])+*būtan* BUT[1]]

about'[2], v.t. Change the course of (ship) to the other tack. [f. ABOUT adv.]

about'-slĕdge, n. Largest hammer used by smiths.

above' (-ŭv), adv., prep., a., & n. **1.** adv. At a higher point (w. spec. meaning acc. to context); overhead, on high; up stream, upstairs; in heaven; on the upper side; earlier in a book or article (*as was re-marked* ~; *the* ~*-cited passages; the* ~);

in addition (*over & ~*). **2.** prep. Over, on the top of, higher than (*~ par*; *~ one-self*, uppish, in unusual spirits etc.; *can't get ~ C*—in music), more than (*~ a hundred*), up stream from, projecting from (*head ~ water*; *heard ~ the tumult*; *~ ground* = alive), further north than, earlier in hist. than (*not traced ~ third century*), out of reach of (*~ criticism, measure, my understanding*), too great or good for (*~ meanness*, one's *station*), more important than (*~ all*), of higher rank than. **3.** adj. Preceding, previous, as *the ~ statements*. **4.** n. That which is *~*. [ME *abufan, abuven* f. A[2]+OE *bufan* (*be* by + *ufan* f. WG *ufana, *ubhana, f. *uf, *ubh UP)]

above'-board (-bōrd), adv. & pred. a. Undisguisedly; fair, open. [metaph. f. cards]

ăb ōv'ō, adv. (Relating tediously) from the very beginning. [L; Hor. *A.P.* 147]

ăbracadăb'ra, n. Spell, magic formula; gibberish. Cabbalistic word supposed when written triangularly, & worn, to cure agues etc. [L (3rd c.), of unkn. orig.]

abrāde', v.t. Scrape off, injure, (skin etc.) by violent rubbing. [f. L AB(*radere ras*- scrape)]

A'brahăm-măn (ā-), n. (hist.). Wandering beggar of the 16th c., either a lunatic or feigning lunacy; hence *to sham Abram*, to feign illness or madness. [*Luke* xvi]

abrănc'hial(-ngk-), **abrănc'hiate** (-ngk-), aa. Without gills. [A-(7)+Gk *bragkhia* gills+-AL & -ATE[2]]

abrā'sion (-zhn), n. Scraping off (of skin etc.); the wounded place that results. So **abrās'IVE** a. & n., (substance) capable of rubbing or grinding down, tending to graze the skin. [f. LL *abrasio* ABRADE, -ION]

ăbrĕăc'tion, n. (psycho-an.). The removal by revival & expression of the emotion associated with forgotten, or repressed ideas of the event that first caused it. [AB-, REACTION; after G *abreagierung*]

abreast' (-rĕst), adv. On a level & facing the same way; keeping up, not behind, (*of* or *with* progress, thought, etc., or as prep., *~ the times*). [A[2]+BREAST[1]]

abridge', v.t. Shorten (interview etc.); condense or epitomize (book etc.); curtail (liberty; of limbs etc. only now w. playful archaism); deprive (person *of*). [ME, f. OF *abregier* f. LL *abbreviare* ABBREVIATE[1].]

abridge'ment, -gment, (-jm-), n. Shortening (of time or labour), curtailment (of rights); epitome, abstract. [ME, f. OF *abregement* f. *abregier* (prec., -MENT)]

abroach', adv. & pred. a. Pierced, so as to let the liquor run (of casks). [A[2]+BROACH[2]]

abroad' (-rawd), adv. Broadly, widely, in different directions; in motion (*there is a rumour ~*; *the schoolmaster is ~*, education is now becoming generally accessible); out of doors, in or to foreign lands; in error (*all ~*). Also treated as a noun

in *from ~*. [A[2]+BROAD a.; cf. *along, at large*]

ăb'rogāte, v.t. Repeal, cancel, (law or custom). So **ăbroga'tion** n. [f. p.p. of L AB(*rogare* propose law); see -ATE[3]]

abrŭpt', a. Sudden, hasty, disconnected; steep, precipitous; (Bot.) truncated; suddenly cropping out (of geol. strata). Hence *~*LY[2] adv., *~*NESS n. [f. L *abruptus* p.p. of AB(*rumpere* break)]

abrŭp'tion, n. Breaking away of part from a mass. [f. L *abruptio* (ABRUPT, -ION)]

abs-, pref., variant, in L, of *ab*; see AB-.

ăb'scess (-sĕs), n. Collection of pus formed in a cavity of the body. [f. L *abscessus* a going away f. ABS(*cedere cess*- go)]

ăb'sciss(e) (-sĭs; pl. *-es*), **absci'ssa** (-sĭ-; pl. *-ae*), n. Portion of given line intercepted between fixed point within it & ordinate drawn to it from given point without it. [L *abscissa* (*linea*) p.p. of AB(*scindere sciss*- cut)]

absci'ssion (-sĭshn), n. (surg.). Cutting off, violent separation. [f. L *abscissio* (see prec., -ION)]

abscŏnd', v.i. Go away secretly, fly from the law. Hence *~*ENCE, *~*ER[1], nn. [f. L ABS(*condere* stow, f. *dare* put)]

ăb'sence, n. Being away from a place or person; time of being away; non-existence or want of; abstraction of thought (esp. *in* phr. *~ of mind*); ‖ roll-call. [ME, f. OF *absence* f. L *absentia* (*absent-* ABSENT[1])]

ăb'sent[1], a. **1.** Not present; not existing, **2.** Abstracted in mind, whence *~*LY[2] adv., *~*-**mĭn'dĕd[2]** a., *~*-**mĭn'dĕdly[2]** adv., *~*-**mĭn'dĕdnĕss**, *-*NESS, nn. [ME, f. OF *absent* f. L *absentem* part. of AB(*esse* be)]

absĕnt'[2], v.refl. Keep oneself away. [ME, f. *absenter* f. LL *absentare* f. *absent-* ABSENT[1]]

ăbsentee', n. A person not present; a person, esp. a landlord (& formerly parson), habitually living away from home. Hence *~*ISM (2) n., practice of being an *~*, practice of workers of absenting themselves from work, esp. frequently or without good reason. [ABSENT[2]+-EE]

ăb'sinth, n. Wormwood, the plant or its essence; a liqueur made (orig. at least) from wine & wormwood. [f. F *absinthe* f. L f. Gk *apsinthion*]

ăb'sĭt ōm'ĕn, sent. May no ominous significance attach to the words, may my fears not be verified. [L]

ăb'solute (-ōŏt, -ūt), a. Complete, perfect, pure (as *~ alcohol*), mere; unrestricted, independent; ruling arbitrarily; out of grammatical relation (*ablative ~* in L, *genitive ~* in Gk, *~ construction* in E, noun & participle used as adverbial clause, as *dinner being over we left the table*); real, not merely relative or comparative; unqualified, unconditional; self-existent & conceivable without relation to other things (*the ~*, as noun); *~ magnitude*

(Astron.), the magnitude of a star if at a standard distance of 10 parsecs: ~ *music*, self-dependent instrumental music devoid of literary suggestions; ~ *pitch* (Mus.), ability to recognize or reproduce the pitch of a note; ~ ZERO. Hence ~NESS (-tn-) n. [ME, f. L *absolutus* p.p. see ABSOLVE]

ăb'solutely (-ōōtlĭ, -ūt-), adv. Independently, in & by itself; arbitrarily, without external control; without qualification; without the usual accompaniments (as *a transitive vb used* ~, i.e. without its obj.); unconditionally; positively, though you would not believe it; conclusively, completely, quite; at all (w. negatives); ‖ (colloq.) quite so, yes. [f. prec. + -LY²]

ăbsolu'tion (-lōō-, -lū-), n. Formal setting free from guilt, sentence, or obligation; ecclesiastical declaration of forgiveness of sins; remission of penance; forgiveness. [ME, f. OF f. L *absolutionem* (ABSOLVE, -ION)]

ăb'solutism (-lōō-, -lū-), n. (Theol.) doctrine that God acts absolutely in the affair of salvation; (Pol.) principle of absolute government. [ABSOLUTE + -ISM (3)]

ăb'solutist (-lōō-, -lū-), n. Partisan of political absolutism (also adj., as ~ *principles*); a metaphysician who identifies subject & object. [ABSOLUTE + -IST (2)]

absŏlve' (-s-, -z-), v.t. Set, pronounce, free (*from* blame etc., *of* sin, *from* obligation etc., or abs.); acquit, pronounce not guilty. [f. L AB(*solvere, solut*- loosen)]

ăb'sonant, a. Discordant, alien (*from*), unreasonable. [f. AB-+*sonant*- part. st. of L *sonare* sound on anal. of *dissonant, consonant*, & L *absonus*]

absŏrb', v.t. Swallow up, incorporate (*be ~ed by*, lose one's identity in); engross the attention of; suck in (liquids); take in (heat, light, etc.) by chemical or molecular action. [f. F *absorber* f. L AB(*sorbēre sorpt*- suck in)]

absŏrb'|able, a. Easily sucked in. Hence ~ABIL'ITY n. [prec. + -ABLE]

absŏrbed' (-bd), a. Intensely engaged or interested. Hence ~LY² (-b'ĕdlĭ) adv. [p.p. of ABSORB]

absŏrbĕfā'cient (-shent), a. & n. Causing the absorption or drying up (e.g. of a tumour); agent that does this. [f. L *absorbēre* ABSORB +-FACIENT]

absŏrb'ent, a. & n. **1.** Having tendency to suck in (abs., or *of*). **2.** n. Substance of this kind; one of the vessels in plants & animals (e.g. root tips) that absorb nutriment. [f. L *absorbent*- part. st. of *absorbēre* ABSORB]

absŏrb'ing, a. Engrossing, intensely interesting. Hence ~LY² adv. [part. of ABSORB]

absŏrp'tion, n. Disappearance through incorporation in something else; natural or medical removal of tissues; mental engrossment; sucking in of fluid, light, etc., or nutriment. [f. LL *absorptio* (ABSORB, -ION)]

absŏrp'tive, a. Having a tendency to suck in. Hence ~NESS (-vn-) n. [f. L *absorpt*- (ABSORB, -IVE)]

absquat'ŭlāte (-ŏt-), v.i. Make off, decamp. [American-made jocular vb w. L pref. & suf.]

abstain', v.i. Keep oneself away, refrain, (*from*); refrain from alcohol, whence ~ER¹ n., ~ING² a. [ME, f. F *abstenir* f. L ABS(*tinēre tent*- = *tenēre* hold)]

abstēm'ious, a. Sparing, not self-indulgent, esp. in food and drink. Used of persons, habits, meals. Hence ~LY² adv., ~NESS n. [f. L *abstemius* +-OUS]

abstĕn'tion, n. Keeping off (abs., or *from* any pleasure); esp., not using one's vote. [F, f. L *abstent*- (ABSTAIN, -ION)]

abstēr'gent, a. & n. Cleansing; a cleansing substance. [f. L *abstergent*- part. st. of ABS(*tergēre ters*- wipe)]

abstēr'sion (-shn), n. Cleansing, purgation. [f. L *absters*- (see ABSTERGENT) +-ION; cf. LL *abstersio*]

abstēr'sive, a. Cleansing. [as prec., -IVE]

ăb'stinence, n. Refraining (*from* any pleasure, or abs. in sense of continence, fasting, or, usu. *total* ~, going without alcohol); occas. = foll. [ME, f. OF, or L *abstinentia* (ABSTINENT, -ENCE)]

ăb'stinency, n. Habit of refraining from pleasures, esp. food. [see prec. & -ENCY]

ăb'stinent, a. Practising abstinence. Hence ~LY² adv. [ME, f. OF, or L *abstinent*- (ABSTAIN, -ENT)]

ăb'străct¹, a. Separated from matter, practice, or particular examples, not concrete; ideal, not practical; abstruse; (with *the*, as noun) the ideal or theoretical way of regarding things (*in the* ~). Hence ~LY² adv., ~NESS n. [ME, f. L *abstractus* p.p. of ABS(*trahere* draw)]

ăb'străct², n. Essence, summary; abstraction or abstract term. [see prec.]

abstrăct'³, v.t. Deduct, remove, (an obj. *much* etc. is occas. omitted); (euphem.) steal; disengage (obj. *attention* etc. occas. omitted) *from*; consider apart from the concrete; summarize. [f. ABSTRACT¹]

abstrăct'ĕd, a. Withdrawn in thought, not attending. Hence ~NESS n. [-ED¹]

abstrăct'ĕdly̆, adv. In the abstract, ideally; separately (*from*—esp. after *consider*); in an absent-minded way. [-LY²]

abstrăc'tion, n. Taking away, withdrawal; (euphem.) stealing; process of stripping an idea of its concrete accompaniments; the idea so stripped, something visionary; absence of mind. [f. F, or L *abstractio* (ABSTRACT¹, -ION)]

abstruse' (-ōōs), a. Hard to understand, profound. Hence ~LY² (-sl-) adv., ~NESS (-sn-) n. [f. F, or L ABS(*trusus* p.p. of *trudere* push)]

absŭrd', a. Incongruous, unreasonable, ridiculous, silly. Hence ~LY² adv. [f. F, or L *absurdus* (ab-+*surdus* deaf, dull)]

absŭrd'ity̆, n. Folly, unreasonableness; an absurd statement or act. [f. F *absurdité* or LL *absurditas* (ABSURD, -ITY)]

abŭn'dance, n. Quantity more than sufficient, plenty; overflowing emotion (~ *of the heart*); many people (*there are* ~ *who*); affluence, wealth. [ME, f. OF *abundance* f. L *abundantia* (as foll., -ANCE)]

abŭn'dant, a. More than sufficient, plentiful; rich (*in*). Hence ~LY[2] adv. [ME, f. OF *abundant* f. L *abundant-* part. st. (ABOUND, -ANT)]

ăb urb'ě cŏn'dĭtā, adv. (abbr. A.U.C.). Counting from the foundation of Rome (753 B.C.). [L]

abŭse'[1] (-z), v.t. Misuse, make bad use of; deceive (arch., but still used esp. in pass.); maltreat (arch.); revile. [ME, f. OF *abuser* f. Rom. **abusare* f. AB(*us-* p.p. st. of *uti* USE[2])]

abŭs|e'[2] (-s), n. Misuse, perversion (*of*); an established unjust or corrupt practice; reviling, whence ~'IVE a., ~'iveLY[2] (-vl-) adv., ~'iveNESS (-vn-) n. [ME, f. OF *abus* or L *abusus* n. f. *abus-* see prec.]

abŭt', v.t.(-tt-). Have a common boundary with, border, (*upon*; or occas. without prep. as trans. vb; of estates or countries); end *on* or *against*, lean *on*, (of parts of a building). [sense 'border upon' f. OF *abouter* (*bout* end); sense 'end on' f. OF *abuter* (*but* end)]

abŭt'ment, n. A lateral support; (esp. in architecture) that on which an arch or bridge rests; point of junction between such support & thing supported. [ABUT + -MENT]

abŭtt'er, n. (In law) owner of the adjoining property. [ABUT + -ER[1]]

abȳ(e)', v.t. (arch.; past & p.p. *abought*). Redeem, pay the penalty of, (an offence; usu. w. *dearly*, *sore*). [OE *ábycgan*, f. A- (1) + BUY]

abȳsm' (-z-), n. Earlier form, still used in poetical style, of ABYSS. [ME *abime* f. OF f. med. L *abysmus* (L *abyssus* + -ISM) ABYSS, to which the sp. later conforms]

abȳs'mal (-z-), a. Bottomless, esp. fig., as ~ *ignorance*. Hence ~LY[2] (-z-) adv. [ABYSM + -AL]

abȳss', n. The primal chaos, bowels of the earth, lower world; a bottomless chasm, deep gorge; depth (~ *of light*). [f. LL *abyssus* f. Gk *abussos* bottomless]

abȳss'al, a. More than 300 fathoms below sea surface (water, zone, mud). [f. prec. + -AL: cf. F *abyssal*]

ac-, pref., assim. form of AD- before *c-*, *k-*, *qu-*. Occas. erron. for *a-* (of various orig.; see A-), as in *acknowledge*. See also AD- (2).

-ăc, suf. forming adjj., which are often also (if not only) used as nouns. From Gk *-akos*, the modification of adj. suf. *-kos* appended to nouns in *-ia*, *-ios*, *-ion*, & imitated in L. E wds in *-ac* may be f. Gk (*-akos*), L (*-acus*), or F (*-aque*).

acā'cia (-sha), n. Shrub or tree, of mimosa tribe, yielding gum arabic; the locust-tree or false~, grown for ornament; gum arabic. [L, f. Gk *akakia*]

ăc'adēme, n. (Prop.) = Academus (see ACADEMY); (used by mistake in poetic style for) the Gk Academy, a college, university. [Gk *Akadēmos* see ACADEMY; mistake perh. caused by Milton's 'grove of Academe', *P. R.* iv. 244]

ăcadēm'ic, a. & n. **1.** Belonging to or agreeing with the philosophic school of Plato (ACADEMY), (w. ref. to some of his successors' views) sceptical; an ancient Platonist. **2.** Scholarly, (& by implication) abstract, unpractical, cold, merely logical; (as sing. noun) member of a university, one too much enslaved to the principles (in painting etc.) of an academy; (as pl. noun) merely theoretic arguments, university robes. **3.** Of an academician or academy (~ *rank*). [f. L *academicus* (a. & n.); see ACADEMY; -IC]

ăcadēm'ical, a. Belonging to a college or university; (as pl. noun) college costume (commoner than *academics*). [prec. + -AL]

ăcadēm'ically, adv. Theoretically, unpractically; rarely also in any of the senses of the two prec. [prec. + -LY[2]]

acădemi'cian (-shn), n. Member of an Academy or art society, ‖ esp. of the Royal Academy of Arts. [f. F *académicien* f. L *academicus* ACADEMIC; see -IAN]

Acăděmȳ, n. **1.** The garden near Athens in which Plato taught; Plato's followers or philosophical system. **2.** (*a*~). A place of study, including universities, ‖ but occas. used pretentiously or depreciatingly of something between a school & a university. **3.** A place of training in a special art (Royal Military ~). **4.** A society for cultivating literature, art, etc., of which membership is an honour, ‖ esp. the Royal ~ of Arts; ‖ the R.A.'s annual exhibition. [f. F *académie* or f. L f. Gk *akadēmeia* (*Akadēmos* the man or demigod f. whom Plato's garden was named)]

Acād'ian, a. & n. Nova-Scotian. [f. F *Acadie* Nova Scotia + -AN]

ăc'ajou (-zhoo), n. CASHEW. [F, see CASHEW]

-acal, compd suf. = -AC + -AL. Adjj. in *-ac* being often used as nouns also, *-al* was appended to distinguish the adj. (*demoniac*, *-acal*), & even when there was no noun (*heliacal*). In adjj. *-acal* often differs f. *-ac* in suggesting looser connexion w. the orig. noun; e.g., *cardiac arteries* (*of the heart*), *cardiacal herbs* (*having influence on the heart*).

ăc'alĕph, -ephe (-ĕf), n. Jellyfish, medusa, sea-nettle. [Gk *akalēphē* nettle]

acăn'thus, n. Kinds of prickly-leaved plants, esp. bear's breech or brank-ursine; a conventional representation of its leaf used in Gk architecture. Hence **acanth**(o)- comb. form. [L, f. Gk *akanthos* (*akantha* thorn f. *akē* point)]

ăcărpĕll'ous, a. Without carpels. [A- (7), CARPEL, -OUS]

acărp'ous, a. (bot.). Not producing fruit. [A- (7) + Gk *karpos* fruit + -OUS]

acătalĕc′tic, a. & n. (A verse) not docked of a syllable, complete. [f. LL *acatalecticus* f. Gk *akatalēktos* (see A- (7), CATALECTIC)]

acăt′alēpsў, n. Incomprehensibility (philos. term), the quality in the object answering to agnosticism in the subject. So **acătalĕp′tic** a. [f. med. L f. Gk *akatalēpsia* f. A- (7) + *katalambanō* grasp]

acaul′ous, a. (also **-ĕs′cent, -ine, -ōse**). (bot.). Apparently stemless, having very short stem. [A- (7) + L *caulis* stem + -OUS]

Accăd′ian, a. & n. 1. Of Accad in Shinar (*Gen.* x. 10). 2. n. A language preserved in cuneiform inscriptions. [-IAN]

accēde′ (aks-), v.i. Enter upon an office; join a party; assent to an opinion or policy. Abs., or w. *to* if the office etc. is stated, in all senses. [f. L AC(*cedere* cesscome)]

accĕlerăn′dō (aks-), musical direction. Gradually increase speed. [It.]

accĕl′erāte (aks-), v.t. & i. Make quicker; cause to happen earlier; become swifter (of a motion or process); put on pace. [f. p.p. of L AC(*celerare* f. *celer* swift); see -ATE[2 3]]

accĕl′erātĕd (aks-), a. (phys.). Progressively quicker (~ *motion*). Hence ~LY[2] adv. [p.p. of prec.]

accĕl′erāting (aks-), a. Causing progressively quicker motion (~ *force*). [-ING[2]]

accĕlerā′tion (aks-), n. 1. Making quicker; being made quicker. 2. (phys.). Rate of increase of velocity per time unit, as with falling bodies. 3. (astron.). ~ *of stars*, time gained daily by them over sun; ~ *of planets*, increased velocity from aphelion to perihelion; ~ *of moon*, increase in speed of mean motion; ~ *of tides*, amount of local advance on calculated time. [f. L *acceleratio* (ACCELERATE, -ION) or F *accélération*]

accĕl′erātive (aks-), a. Tending to increase speed, quickening. [f. ACCELERATE + -IVE]

accĕl′erātor (aks-), n. Person or thing that increases anything's speed, esp. an attachment in motor-cars for this purpose; one of a class of nerves & muscles. [ACCELERATE + -OR]

ăc′cent[1] (äks-), n. 1: Prominence given to a syllable, whether by higher musical pitch (ancient Gk & L, Swedish & Norw.), or by stress (most mod. languages, but perh. not F). Three marks called *acute* (′), *grave* (`), & *circumflex* (^ or ᷄) accents (systematically employed in Gk, & to a less degree in F) used for various purposes; e.g. to indicate syllabic pitch (Gk), quality of vowel sound (F), etymological hist. (F, E), metrical stress, syllabic stress (dictionaries etc.), the fact of a letter's not being silent, or conventional distinction between homonyms (F). 2. Individual, local, or national mode of pronunciation; modulation to express feeling;

in pl., speech (poet.). 3. (In prosody) rhythmical stress. 4. (mus.). Stress recurring at intervals, regular or otherwise. 5. (fig.). Intensity, sharp distinction. [F, or f. L *accentus* (*cantus* song) repr. Gk *prosōidia* (PROSODY)]

accent′[2] (aks-), v.t. Pronounce with accent, emphasize (word or syllable); put the written accents on; heighten, make conspicuous. [f. obs. F *accenter* see prec.]

accĕn′tor (aks-), n. Kinds of bird (= WARBLER), esp. the hedge-sparrow, which name is now occas. avoided as misleading. [cf. LL *accentor*, f. *ad* to + *cantor* singer]

accĕn′tūal (aks-), a. Of accent; ~ *prosody* or *verse*, of which the principle is accent or stress, not quantity. Hence ~LY[2] adv. [f. L *accentus* ACCENT[1] + -AL]

accĕn′tūāte (aks-), v.t. = ACCENT[2], but more used than it in the fig. sense. [f. F *accentuer* or its source med. L *accentuare* (ACCENT[1], -ATE[3])]

accĕntūā′tion (aks-), n. Accenting (all senses from ACCENT). [f. as prec., -ION; cf. med. L *accentuatio*]

accĕpt′ (aks-), v.t. Consent to receive (gift), answer affirmatively (offer, invitation, suitor); regard with favour (esp. unfair favour, as ~ *the person of*, ~ *persons*); receive as adequate (~ *service of writ*), allow the truth of, believe; undertake (office); take responsibility for, agree to meet, (bill of exchange). *Of may be* added (exc. w. *service of writ, bill*) with a slight suggestion of formality or condescension. Hence ~ER[1] n. [ME, f. OF *accepter* or L *acceptare* frequent. of AC(*cipere* = *capere* take)]

accĕpt′|able (aks-), a. Worth accepting, pleasing, welcome. Hence or cogn. ~abLY[2] adv., ~abIL′ITY, ~ableNESS, nn. [ME, f. OF, or LL *acceptabilis* (ACCEPT, -ABLE)]

accĕpt′ance (aks-), n. Consent to receive (gift, payment, pleasure, duty); favourable reception (act. & pass.), approval, belief; ~ *of persons*, partiality; engagement to meet a bill; a bill so accepted. [F, see ACCEPT & -ANCE]

accĕptā′tion (äks-), n. A particular sense given to a word or phrase; its generally recognized meaning. [ME, f. OF, f. LL *acceptatio* (ACCEPT, -ATION)]

accĕpt′ĕd (aks-), a. Generally recognized or believed in (*Free & A~ Masons*, see FREE[1]-*mason*). Hence ~LY[2] adv. [-ED[1]]

accĕpt′or (aks-), n. One who accepts a bill (preferred to *accepter* in this sense). [f. ACCEPT; see -OR]

ăc′cĕss (-ks-; *also* aksĕs′), n. Approach; addition; right or means of approaching (*to*); being approached (*easy of* ~); advance (~ *& recess*); passage, channel, doorway; adhesion, growth, (usu. now *accession*); attack or outburst (*of illness*, anger, emotion). [ME, f. OF *aces, acces* or L *accessus* f. AC(*cedere* cess- come)]

accessarў (aksĕs′-, ăk′sĭs-), n. & pred. a.

(see also ACCESSORY). Helper in any act, one privy *to* it (as pred. a., *be* ~, *were made* ~); accompaniment, adjunct. [f. med. L *accessarius* (ACCEDE, -ARY¹); freq. confused w. *accessory*]

accĕss'i̇|ble (aks-), a. Able to be reached or entered (abs., or *to*); open to influence, to the influence of, (*to*). Hence ~BIL'ITY n., ~bLY² adv. [F, or LL *accessibilis* (ACCEDE, -BLE)]

accession (aksĕ'shn), n. Coming into presence or contact; coming into an office (esp. the throne) or condition (as manhood); being added; assent; thing added, addition; (in law) improvement or natural growth of property. [F, f. L *accessionem* (ACCEDE, -ION)]

accessor|y̆ (aksĕs'-, ăk'sĭs-), a. & n. (see also ACCESSARY). **1.** Additional, subordinately contributive (of things), adventitious. **2.** n. Thing of that character, esp. in pl. *the* ~*ies*. [f. med. L *accessorius* (ACCEDE, -ORY)]

acciaccatura (achahkatoor'a), n. (mus.). Grace-note performed quickly before an essential note of a melody. [It.]

ac'cĭdence (ăks-), n. The part of grammar, or a book, dealing with the variable forms of words; the elements of any subject. [f. L *accidentia* (tr. Gk *parepomena*) neut. pl. of *accidens* (ACCIDENT, -ENCE)]

ac'cĭdent (ăks-), n. Event without apparent cause, unexpected (so *chapter of* ~*s*, unforeseen course of events); unintentional act, chance, fortune, (*by* ~); mishap; irregularity in structure; a property not essential to our conception of a substance (so of material qualities of bread & wine after transubstantiation); a mere accessory. [ME, f. OF f. L *accident-* part. st. of AC(*cidere* = *cadere* fall)]

accidĕn'tal (ăks-), a. & n. **1.** Happening by chance, undesignedly, or unexpectedly; occasional; not essential to a conception (so also *an* ~ as n.); subsidiary. **2.** (mus.). ~ *sharps, flats, naturals,* & ~ as noun, signs attached to single notes, not in signature. **3.** (optics). ~ *colours,* those presented by subjective sensation, not external. **4.** (painting) ~ *lights,* & ~*s* as n., effects of other than ordinary daylight. [ME, f. OF (now -*el*), f. LL *accidentalis* (prec., -AL)]

accidĕn'tally̆ (ăks-), adv. By chance, unintentionally. [-LY²]

ac'cĭdie (ăks-). acĕd'ĭa, nn. Sloth, torpor; despair. [ME, f. AN *accidie* f. med. L *accidia* alt. f. LL *acedia* f. Gk *akēdia* (A- (7), *kēdos* care)]

accip'itral (ăks-), a. Hawklike; rapacious; keensighted. [f. L *accipitr-* nom. -*ter* hawk + -AL]

acclaim'¹, v.t. Applaud loudly or enthusiastically; (v. obj. & compl.) hail as (king, winner, saviour; ~*ed him king*). [ME, f. L AC(*clamare* shout), spelling assimilated to CLAIM]

acclaim'², n. Shout of applause. [f. prec.]

ăcclamā'tion, n. Loud & eager assent to a proposal (*voted, carried, by* ~); shouting in a person's honour (usu. pl.). [f. L *acclamatio* (prec., -ATION)]

ăcclimā'tion, n. = acclimatization (see foll.), or distinguished from it as a natural process, not imposed on animals by man. [irreg. f. *acclimate* (foll.)]

‖ **acclim'atize, -ise** (-īz; also, esp. U.S., ăcc'lĭmāte), v.t. & i. Habituate (animals, plants, one*self*) to new climate; (rarely) become so habituated. Hence ‖ **acclimatizA'tion** (also, esp. U.S., **acclimatā'tion**) n. [f. F *acclimater* (earlier adopted as *acclimate*) + -IZE]

accliv'ity̆, n. Upward slope of a hill (cf. DECLIVITY). [f. L *acclivitas* f. AC(*clivis* f. *clivus* slope)]

ăccolāde' (*or* -ahd), n. **1.** Sign at bestowal of knighthood, whether embrace, kiss, or stroke on shoulder with flat of sword. **2.** (mus.). Vertical line or brace coupling staves. [F, f. Prov. *accollada* n. from p.p. st. of Rom. **accollare* (AC- + L *collum* neck)]

accŏmm'odāte, v.t. Adapt (thing or person *to* another); prove such adaptation in, harmonize, (occas. w. implication of sophistry); reconcile, settle differences between; compose (quarrel); equip, supply, (person *with*); oblige, confer favour on; find lodging for. [f. p.p. of L AC(*commodare* -*at*- f. *commodus* fitting), -ATE²⸴ ³]

accŏmm'odāting, a. Obliging, easy to deal with, pliable, lax. Hence ~LY² adv. [-ING²]

accŏmmodā'tion, n. Adjustment (e.g. of eyes for various distances); adaptation of anything to a purpose or meaning different from the original; self-adaptation; settlement, compromise; serviceable thing, convenience (so in comp. as ~*-road*; ~*-ladder,* up ship's side); lodgings, entertainment; money loan (so in ~*-BILL*¹); ~ *unit,* a home. [F, or f. L *accommodatio* (ACCOMMODATE, -ION)]

accom'paniment (-ŭm-), n. **1.** Appendage, thing that attends another. **2.** (mus.). Subsidiary part, usu. instrumental, supporting solo instrument or voice, choir, etc. [f. foll. + -MENT, after F *accompagnement*]

accom'pan|y̆ (-ŭm-), v.t. **1.** Supplement (a thing *with,* as word w. blow); go with, escort, attend; coexist with (of things), characterize. **2.** (mus.). Support (singer, player, chorus) by performing subsidiary part, whence ~(ȳ)IST (-ŭm-) n. After pass., *by* has almost ousted older *with,* now only used when ~*ied* = combined. [ME, f. OF *acompagner* (*à* to + *compaing* COMPANION)]

accŏm'plice (*or* -ŭm-), n. Partner, usu. subordinate, in crime. [late ME, f. earlier & F *complice* (prob. by assoc. w. foll.), f. LL *complic-em*; see COMPLICITY]

accŏm'plish (*or* -ŭm-), v.t. **1.** Fulfil, perform, complete, finish. **2.** Perfect (a person) in graceful acquirements, whence ~ED¹ (-sht) a. [ME, f. OF *acomplir* f. L *complēre* COMPLETE; see AC-, -ISH²]

accŏm'plishment (*or* -ŭm-), n. Fulfilment, completion; thing done or attained, achievement; faculty that perfects a person for society, (derog.) merely superficial acquirement. [late ME, f. F *accomplissement*; see prec., -MENT]

accompt, -ant, arch. for ACCOUNT, -ANT.

accŏrd' ¹, v.t. & i. Be in harmony or consistent (abs., *or with*; chiefly of things); grant (indulgence, request, welcome, etc.). [ME, f. OF *acorder* f. Rom. *AC-(cordare* f. *cor cordis* heart)]

accŏrd' ², n. Consent (*with one* ~), mutual agreement; treaty of peace; harmonious correspondence in colour, pitch, tone; volition (*of* one's *own* ~). [ME, f. OF *acord* (prec.)]

accŏrd'ance, n. Conformity, agreement, esp. in phr. *in* ~ *with.* [ME, f. OF *acordance* (as prec., -ANCE)]

accŏrd'ant, a. In tune, agreeing, (abs., or *with*). Hence ~LY² adv. [ME, f. OF *acordant* (as prec., -ANT)]

accŏrd'ing, adv. (only now in the compd conj. ~ *as,* & the compd prep. ~ *to*). ~ *as*: in proportion as (of a process varying w. another); in a manner depending on which of certain alternatives is true. ~ *to*: in a manner consistent with or degree proportioned to; as stated by. [-ING²]

accŏrd'inglў, adv. As the (stated) circumstances suggest; therefore; ~ *as* = *according as.* [-LY²]

accŏrd'ion, n. Portable musical instrument having bellows, metal reeds, & keyboard &/or buttons. Hence ~IST (3) n. [f. G *akkordion*]

accŏst' ¹, v.t. Make up to & address, open conversation with; (of prostitute) solicit. [f. F *accoster* f. It. *accostare* f. Rom. *AC(costare* f. *costa* rib; see COAST)]

accŏst' ², n. Greeting, opening remark. [f. prec.]

accouchement (see Ap.), n. Lying-in, delivery in childbed. [F]

accoucheur (see Ap.), n. (fem. *-euse*). Man-midwife, midwife. [F]

account' ¹, v.t. & i. Consider, regard as, (followed by obj. & compl. or inf.; ~ *him a hero, wise, to be guilty*). *Be* ~*ed of,* be esteemed (alw. w. *little, much,* etc.). ~ *for,* give reckoning of (money held in trust); answer for (conduct, performance of duty); explain the cause of; serve as explanation of (*that* ~*s for it*); (sport) be responsible for the death of, kill. [ME, f. OF *aconter* f. *a-* AC- + *conter* COUNT²]

account' ², n. **1.** Counting, calculation, in phrr. *cast* ~*s* (reckon up), *money of* ~ (names not of coins, but of sums, as guinea). **2.** Reckoning of debit & credit, in money or service; statement of money received & expended, with balance;

so *open* or *close an* ~ *with, render* or *send in, pay* or *settle, an* ~; ~ *current* (whence a/c = account), one kept going w. occasional entries (now usu. *current* ~); ~ *rendered,* used when a bill previously sent in, but left unpaid, is sent again; *joint* ~*s,* in which two persons not otherwise partners count as one; *keep* ~*s,* enter all expenditure for comparison w. income; *balance* or *square* ~*s with* person, receive or pay the balance due; *cash, profit-&--loss,* etc., ~, headings of subdivision in ledger; ‖ *sale for the* ~, on the Stock Exch., not for cash, but payable at next periodic settlement; *A in* ~ *with B,* having credit relations with; *for* ~ *of,* to be sold for (person); *on* ~, as interim payment; *on* one's ~, for his service; *on* one's *own* ~, for & at one's own purposes & risk, whence generally *on* ~ *of,* because of, & *on no* ~, by no means, certainly not. A favourable result of the reckoning, profit; *find* one's ~ *in,* profit by, *turn to* ~, make useful. Statement of administration as required by creditor; *ask, demand, yield, render, an* ~, *call* or *bring to* ~, extended from money to conduct generally, so *the great* ~, Day of Judgement, *gone to his* ~, dead; *give* ~ *of,* find cause of, explain, (in sport) *give a good* ~ *of* one*self,* be successful. **3.** Estimation; person or thing *of,* or *held in, some* or *no* ~; *make little* ~ *of; take into, leave out of,* ~; *take* ~ *of; lay* one's ~ *with,* include in one's calculations, expect. **4.** Narration, report, description, of event, person, etc. [ME, f. OF *acont*; see prec. & COUNT¹]

accoun't|able, a. Bound to give account, responsible, (*for* things, *to* persons, or abs.); explicable (occas. followed by *for*), Hence ~ABIL'ITY, ~ableNESS, nn. [f. ACCOUNT¹ + -ABLE]

accoun'tant, n. **1.** (Law) one liable to render account; defendant in an action of account. **2.** Professional keeper & inspector of accounts; ~*-general,* chief ~ in public offices. Hence **accoun'tANCY** n., profession of an ~, ~SHIP n., office of an ~. [f. part. of OF *aconter* ACCOUNT¹; see -ANT]

accou'tre (-ōōter), v.t. (*-tring, -tred*). Attire, equip, esp. w. special costume (chiefly used in p.p.). [f. F *accoutrer* (OF *-coust-*) of uncert. orig.]

accou'trement (-ōōt-), n. (usu. in pl.). Equipment, trappings; (Mil.) soldier's outfit other than arms & garments. [F (prec., -MENT)]

accrĕd'it, v.t. Gain belief or influence for (adviser, advice); send out (ambassador etc.) with credentials *to* person, *to* or *at* a court or government; ~ thing (saying, policy) *to* person, or ~ person *with,* put it down to him. [f. F AC(*créditer* f. *crédit* CREDIT)]

accrĕd'itĕd, a. Officially recognized (persons); generally accepted, orthodox, (beliefs). [p.p. of prec.]

accrēte'[1], v.t. & i. Grow together or into one; form round or on *to*, as round a nucleus; attract (such additions). [f. L *accret-* p.p. st. of AC(*crescere* grow)]

accrēte'[2], a. (bot.). Grown into one with something else. [f.L *accretus* p.p. see prec.]

accrē'tion, n. Growth by organic enlargement; the growing of separate things (as particles) into one; the whole resulting from this; adhesion of extraneous matter to anything; the matter so added; (Law) = ACCESSION, also increase of legacy etc. by share of failing co-legatee. [f. L *accretio* (ACCRETE[1], -ION)]

accru|e' (-ōō), v.i. Fall (*to* one, *from* a thing) as a natural growth, advantage, result; esp. of interest on invested money. Hence ~ED[1] (-ōōd') a. [late ME, f. OF *accreu(e)*, p.p. of *acreistre* (mod. *accroître*) f. L *accrescere* ACCRETE[1]]

accŭm'ūlăte, v.t. & i. Heap up, gain by degrees, (usu. fig., a fortune, ill will, etc., or abs.), amass, make money; ‖ take (University degrees) by accumulation (obj. expressed, or abs.), i.e. more than one step at a time; grow numerous, form an increasing mass or heap (lit. & fig., as *dirt, disasters, had* ~*d*). [f. p.p. of L AC(*cumulare* f. *cumulus* heap), -ATE[2, 3]]

accūmūlā'tion, n. Collection (act. or pass.), amassing; money-making; growth of capital by continued interest; combination of distinct acts into one (degrees, see prec., or church services etc.); a mass (as snow, papers, property). [F, or f. med. L *accumulatio* (prec., -ION)]

accŭm'ūlative, a. Arising from accumulation (~ *proof, evidence*, now being ousted by *cumulative*); so arranged as to accumulate (sinking fund); acquisitive, given to hoarding. Hence ~LY[2] (-vl-) adv. [as prec. +-IVE]

accŭm'ūlātor, n. One who collects; money-maker; ‖ taker of degrees by accumulation; ‖ storage cell, battery. [L (as prec., -OR)]

ăcc'ūr|ate, a. Careful, precise, in exact conformity with a standard or with truth. Hence ~ACY n., ~ateLY[2] (-tl-) adv. [f. L AC(*curare* f. *cura* care), -ATE[2]]

accŭrs'ĕd, accŭrst', a. Lying under a curse, ill-fated; involving misery, execrable, detestable. [ME f. CURSE, with *a-* (= A- 1) as intensive, on anal. of *awake, arise*]

accūs'al (-z-), n. Sometimes used for foll. [f. ACCUSE + -AL (2)]

ăccūsā'tion (-z-), n. Accusing; being accused; a charge of offence or crime; indictment. [ME, f. OF, f. L *accusationem* (ACCUSE, -ION)]

accūs'ative (-z-), a. & n. ~ *case* (or ~ as n.), the grammatical case used in Gk & L for the goal of motion or obj. of action; in uninflected languages, applied to the wd that stands as obj., though with no mark of case. Hence **accūsatĭv'al** (-z-) adj., ~LY[2] (-z-; -vl-) adv. [ME, f. OF (-*if, -ive*)

or L (*casus*) *accusativus*, transl. Gk (*ptōsis*) *aitiatikē*]

accūsatōr'ial (-z-), a. ~ *procedure* etc., in which prosecutor & judge are not the same, opposed to *inquisitorial*. [as foll. +-AL]

accūs'atorў (-z-), a. ~ *language, manner*, etc., conveying or implying accusation. [f. L *accusatorius* (foll., -ORY)]

accūs|e' (-z), v.t. 1. Charge with a fault, indict, (person), whence p.p. as noun, *the* ~*ed*; blame, lay the fault on, (person or thing, as *the times*); ~*e as* offender, *of* offence. 2. Point to (subj. *evidence* etc., obj. a person). Hence ~'ER[1] (-z-) n., ~'ingLY[2] (-z-) adv. [ME *acuse* f. OF *acuser* f. L AC(*cusare* f. *causa* CAUSE)]

accūs'tom, v.t. Habituate (one*self*, person, or thing, *to* do or *to*; commoner in pass.). [late ME, f. OF *acostumer* f. *a-* AC- +*costume* CUSTOM]

accūs'tomed (-md), a. In vbl senses; also, usual. [p.p. of prec. in obs. sense *make usual*]

āce, n. 1. The one on dice (*ambs-*~, throw of two ones; *deuce* ~, throw of two & one, formerly two ones); the one on cards or dominoes; card etc. so marked. 2. One point at rackets, lawn tennis, etc.; (Tennis) service that beats opponent. 3. The smallest possible amount, hair's breadth, as *within an* ~ *of*. 4. (Orig. French) airman who has brought down 10 or more hostile aircraft; one who excels at something, champion; also attrib. [ME *as* f. OF f. L *as* unity]

-acea (-ā'sha), L suf. freely used to form names (neut. pl. agreeing w̃. *animalia*) for families of animals; the names are L & pl., the sing. being supplied by E adjj. in **-ACEAN** used as noun; so *the crustacea*, *a crustacean*. [f. L *-aceus* (-*ac-* + -*e-us*) compd adj. formative]

-aceae (-ā'sĭē), L suf. freely used to form names (fem. pl. agreeing w. *plantae*) for families of plants. [f. *-aceus* see prec.]

-acean (-ā'shan), a. & n. suf. As adj., = -ACEOUS; as n., see -ACEA. [f. L *-aceus* see -ACEA +-AN]

acēd'ia, n. See ACCIDIE.

Acĕl'dama (ak-), n. Field of bloodshed, scene of slaughter. [*Acts* i. 19]

-aceous (-ā'shŭs), suf. freely used to form adjj. to the Nat.-Hist. nouns in -ACEA, -ACEAE, as *crustaceous, rosaceous*. [f. L *-aceus* see -ACEA +-OUS]

acephal-, beginning of several bot., zool., & eccl. terms. Headless. [f. LL f. Gk *akephalos* f. A- (7) +*kephalē* head]

acĕph'alous (asĕf-), a. Headless; recognizing no chief; (Zool.) having no part of body specially organized as head; (Bot.) with head aborted or cut off; (in prosody), (verse) wanting the regular first syllable. [as prec. +-OUS]

ă'cerbāte, v.t. Sometimes used for EX-ACERBATE.

acĕrb' itў, n. Astringent sourness, harsh

taste; bitterness of speech, manner, or temper. [f. F *acerbité* or L *acerbitas* (*acerbus* sour-tasting, -TY)]

acĕrv′ate, a. Growing in compact clusters (of spines etc.). [f. L *acervare* (*acervus* a heap), -ATE²]

acĕs′cent, a. Turning sour, rather sour, lit. & fig. [F, or f. L *acescent*- f. *acēre* be sour, -ENT]

acet-, = ACETO-, before a vowel, as ~-*amide.*

ăcĕtăb′ūlum, n. (pl. -*la*). **1.** (Rom. Ant.) cup to hold vinegar. **2.** (Zool.) cup-shaped sucker of cuttle-fish etc.; socket of thigh-bone, or of joints in insects. [ME, f. L, f. *acetum* vinegar + -*abulum* dim. of -*abrum* receptacle]

ă′cĕtāte, n. Salt or ester of acetic acid. [f. ACET(IC) + -ATE¹ (3)]

acĕt′ĭc, a. Pertaining to vinegar; ~ *acid*, the acid contained in vinegar. [f. L *acetum* vinegar + -IC]

acĕt′ĭ|fȳ, v.t. & i. Convert into vinegar; become sour. Hence ~FICA′TION, ~fIER¹ (2), nn. [as prec. + -FY]

aceto-, chem. in comb., = ACETIC, ACETYL, before a consonant (cf. ACET-), as ~-*chloride.*

ă′cĕtōne, n. Colourless limpid liquid valuable as a solvent of organic compounds. [as prec. + -ONE]

ă′cĕtous, a. Having the qualities of vinegar; sour. [as prec. + -OUS]

ă′cĕtȳl, n. (chem.). The radical of acetic acid. [f. ACET(IC) + -YL]

acĕt′ȳlĕne, n. A colourless gas, burning with a bright flame. [as prec., see -YL & -ENE]

Achaean (akē′an), a. & n. (Inhabitant) of Achaea (district of the Northern Peloponnesus; also, in Homeric use, Greece generally). [f. L f. Gk *Akhaios*]

acharnement (see Ap.), n. Ferocity; gusto. [F]

Achates (akāt′ēz), n. Faithful friend of Aeneas (Virg. *Aen.*); any faithful friend.

ache¹ (āk), v.i. Suffer continuous or prolonged pain. [OE *acan*, ME *aken*; mod. sp. assim. to foll.]

ache² (āk), n. Continuous pain. [OE *æce*, ME *eche*, *ache*; mod. pronunc. assim. to prec.]

ache³ (āch), n. Name of letter H.

Acheulian (ashŭl′ĭan), a. Of the palaeolithic epoch represented by remains found at St Acheul in France. [-AN]

achiev|e′, v.t. Accomplish, carry out; acquire; reach (an end). Hence ~′ABLE a. [ME *acheve* f. OF *achever* f. phr. *a chief* to a head; see A- (4), CHIEF]

achieve′ment (-vm-), n. Completion, accomplishment; thing accomplished; escutcheon or ensign armorial in memory of a distinguished feat; = HATCHMENT. [f. prec. + -MENT, or f. F *achèvement*]

Achilles and Patrŏc′lus (akil′ēz), phr. Pair of devoted friends (in Homer's *Iliad*); TENDON *of Achilles.*

achīl′ous (ak-), a. (bot.). Without lips. [f. Gk *a*- A- (7) + *kheilos* lip + -OUS]

achlamȳd′éous (ăklam-), a. (bot.). Without calyx or corolla. [f. Gk *a*- A- (7) + *khlamus* -*udos* cloak + -EOUS]

ăchromăt′|ĭc (ăk-), a. (opt.). Free from colour; transmitting light without decomposing it. Hence ~ICALLY adv., ~i′CITY (ak-), ~ISM (2) (akrōm²), nn., ~IZE (3) (akrōm²) v.t. [f. Gk *akhrōmatos* + -IC; see A- (7), CHROMATIC]

ă′cĭd¹, a. Sour (~ *drops*, kind of sweeties); (Chem.) with the essential properties of an ACID². So **acid′ITY** n. [f. F *acide* or L *acidus* (*acēre* be sour)]

ă′cĭd², n. A sour substance; (Chem.) one of a class of substances that neutralize & are neutralized by alkalis, & are compounded of hydrogen & another element or elements, & of which the principal types are sour & turn vegetable blues to reds; ~ *test* (in which ~ is applied to test composition etc.; often fig. in morals etc.). Hence **acid′IC** a. (chem.). [f. prec.]

acid′i|fȳ, v.t. & i. Make, become, sour; (Chem.) convert into an acid, render acid. Hence ~fIABLE a., ~FICA′TION, ~fIER¹ (2), nn. [as ACID, see -FY]

ăcidim′ĕter, n. Instrument for measuring strength of acids. [as prec., see -METER]

ăcidōs′is, n. (path.). Acid condition of blood (esp. in diabetes). [hybrid formation f. ACID + -OSIS]

acid′ūlātĕd, a. Made somewhat acid. [f. as foll. + -ATE³]

acid′ūlous, a. Somewhat acid. [f. L *acidulus* (dim. of *acidus* sour) + -OUS]

ă′cĭnus, n. (pl. *acinī*). One of the small berries that make up a compound fruit such as the blackberry; the compound fruit itself; seed of a grape or berry; (Anat.) racemose gland. Hence **acin′i**-FORM a. [L, = berry, seed]

-acious (-ā′shus), suf. forming adjj. meaning 'inclined to', 'abounding in'. [f. L -*ax* -*acis*, added to vb stems to form adjj., + -OUS]

-ăcitȳ, suf. forming nouns of quality corresponding to adjj. in -ACIOUS directly f. L -*acitat*- or thr. F -*acité.*

ăck⟨ack′, a. (colloq.). Anti-aircraft (gun etc.). [formerly signallers' name for letters A.A.]

ăck ĕmm′a, adv. & n. (colloq.). *Ante meridiem*; air-mechanic. [formerly signallers' name for letters A.M.]

acknowledge (aknŏl′ij), v.t. Admit the truth of; own (person etc. *to be* something); own to knowing, take notice of; recognize the authority or claims of; recognize in legal form; express appreciation of; announce receipt of; reward (a service). [A- (2) + KNOWLEDGE; or from the obs. noun *acknowledge*]

acknowl′edgement, -ğment, (-nŏlijm-), n. Act of acknowledging; thing given or done in return for a service, message, etc. [prec. + -MENT]

aclin'ic, a. ~ *line*, magnetic equator, on which magnetic needle has no dip. [f. Gk *aklinēs* (*a*- not + *klinō* bend) + -IC]

ăc'mě, n. Highest point, point of perfection. [Gk, = point]

ăc'ně, n. Pimple; disease marked by pimples. [erron. for Gk *akme* (prec.)]

acŏck', adv. (Of the hat) in cocked fashion. [A prep. + COCK² v.]

ăc'olȳte, n. Inferior officer in the church; attendant, assistant; novice. [ME, f. med.L *acolit(h)us* corrupt. of LL *acoluthus* f. Gk *akolouthos* follower]

ăc'onite, n. Monk's-hood or wolf's-bane, a poisonous plant; extract from this. Hence **ăconit'ic** a., **acŏn'itine⁵** n. [f. F *aconit* or L *aconitum* f. Gk *akoniton*]

ăc'ŏrn, n. Fruit of the oak; ~-*shell*, multi-valve cirriped, allied to barnacles. [OE *æcern*, Gmc, of disputed orig. The mod. form by erron. assoc. w. *corn*¹]

acŏtȳlēd'on, n. Plant with no distinct seed-lobes. Hence ~OUS a. [f. mod. L *acotyledones*; see A- (7), COTYLEDON]

acou'chy (-ōōshī), n. Small rodent allied to guinea-pig. [f. F *acouchi*, perh. f. native name in Guiana]

acous't|ic (-ōō-, -ow-), a. Relating to the sense of hearing; (of a mine) that can be exploded by sound waves transmitted under water. Hence ~**ICAL** a., ~**ICALLY²** adv., ~**I'CIAN** (-shn) n., ~**ICS** n. pl., science of sound, ~ical properties of room). [f. Gk *akoustikos* (*akouō* hear)]

acquaint', v.t. Make (person, one*self*) aware (*of* or *with* facts, *that*, *how*, etc.); make one*self* familiar (*with* circumstances etc.); (pass.) have personal knowledge (*with* person or thing). [ME *acointe* etc., f. OF *acointer* f. med. L *accognitare* f. *cognit*-p.p. st. of CO(*gnoscere* come to know)]

acquain'tance, n. Knowledge of (*with*) person etc. more than mere recognition & less than intimacy; person(s) with whom one is acquainted (pl. now usu. ~*s* in this sense). Hence ~**SHIP** (-s-sh-) n. [ME, f. OF *acointance* (prec., -ANCE)]

acquĕst', n. Thing acquired; (Law) property gained otherwise than by inheritance. [f. OF *acquest* f. LL *acquistum* (whence Eng. var. *acquist*), f. L *acquisitum* (see ACQUIRE)]

ăcquiĕsc|e', v.i. Agree tacitly; ~*e in*, accept (arrangements, conclusions). So ~'**ENCE** n., ~'**ENT** a. [f. L AC(*quiescere* rest)]

acquīre', v.t. Gain by oneself & for oneself; (of qualities etc.) win (a person a good name etc.); come into possession of; *an ~d taste* (not natural). Hence ~**MENT** (-ïrm-) n., ~d mental faculty. [f. ME *acquere* f. OF *acquerre* f. Rom. *acquaerere for L AC(*quirere quisit*- = *quaerere* seek); mod. sp. after L & *require*]

ăcquisi'tion (-zi-), n. Act of acquiring; thing acquired, welcome addition. So **acquis'itive** (-zī-) a., **acquis'itiveness** (-zī-; -vn-) n. [f. L *acquisitio* (as prec., see -ION)]

acquit', v.t. (-tt-). Pay (a debt); declare (person) not guilty (*of* offence); discharge one*self of* (duty, responsibility); ~ one*self* (perform one's part) *well*, *ill*, etc. [ME, f. OF *aquiter* f. Rom. *acquitare (AC-, QUIT²)]

acquitt'al, n. Discharge from debt; deliverance from a charge by verdict etc.; performance (of duty). [prec. + -AL (2)]

acquitt'ance, n. Payment of debt; release from debt; receipt in full. [ME, f. OF *aquitance* (ACQUIT, -ANCE)]

ā'cre (-ker), n. Measure of land, 4,840 sq. yds; piece of tilled or enclosed land, field (only in special uses, as *broad ~s*, *God's A~*, *Long A~*). Hence (-)**ā'crED²** (-erd) a. [OE *æcer* = OHG *ackar*, ON *akr*, Goth. *akrs*, f. Gmc *akraz; cf. L *ager*, Gk *agros*]

ā'creage (-ker-), n. Amount of acres; acres collectively or in the abstract. [ACRE + -AGE]

ăc'rid, a. Bitterly pungent, irritating, corrosive; of bitter temper or manner. Hence **acrid'ITY** n. [irreg. f. L *acer -cris* + -ID, perh. after *acid*]

ăc'rimony, n. Bitterness of temper or manner. So **ăcrimōn'ious** a., **ăcrimōn'iousLY²** adv. [f. F *acrimonie* or L *acrimonia* (prec., -MONY)]

Ăc'rita (ăk-), n. pl. (zool.). Animals with no distinct nervous system. [mod. L f. Gk *akritos* undistinguishable]

ăcro- in comb. Highest, topmost, terminal; tipped with; at the point or extremity of. [f. Gk *akros* topmost, outermost]

ăc'robăt, n. Rope-dancer, tumbler; politician, reasoner, etc., who changes position nimbly. Hence **ăcrobăt'io** a., **ăcrobăt'icALLY** adv., ~**ISM** n. [f. F *acrobate* f. Gk *akrobatēs* (ACRO-, Gk *bainō* walk)]

ăc'rogĕn, n. (bot.). Cryptogamous plant having perennial stem with growing point at extremity, as ferns & mosses. Hence **acrŏ'gĕnous** a. [ACRO- + -GEN]

ăc'rolith, n. Statue with head & extremities of stone. [L f. Gk (ACRO-, -LITH)]

acrŏn'yc(h)al (-ĭk-), a. Happening at nightfall (esp. of rising or setting of stars). Hence ~**LY²** adv. [f. Gk *akronukhos* (ACRO- + *nux nuktos* night) + -AL]

ăc'ronym, n. Word formed from initial letters of other words (e.g. *Anzac*, *Nato*, *radar*). [ACRO- + Gk -*ōnum*- = *onoma* name]

acrŏp'ĕtal, a. Developing from below upwards. Hence ~**LY²** adv. [ACRO- + L *petere* seek + -AL]

ăcrophōb'ia, n. Morbid dread of heights. [ACRO-, -PHOBIA]

acrŏp'olis, n. Citadel or elevated part of a Greek city, esp. of Athens. [Gk *akropolis* (ACRO- + *polis* city)]

across' (-aws, -ō-), adv. & prep. In the form of a cross, as *with arms ~*; forming a cross with, making angles with, (object expressed or understood), as *a line drawn ~ (the road)*; into contact with, as *came ~*

a tiger, an instance; from side to side (of), as *run* ~ *(the road)*; on the other side (of), as *by this time he is* ~ *(the Channel)*. *Put it* ~ a person (sl.), get even with, impose on, deceive. [orig. adv. f. F *à croix, en croix*, later apprehended as f. A prep. + CROSS[1]]

acros'tic, n. Poem or other composition in which the initial (*single* ~), the initial & final (*double* ~), or the initial, middle, & final (*triple* ~) letters of the lines make words; word-puzzle so made; Hebrew poem of which the lines begin with the successive letters of the alphabet. Hence **acros'tic** a., **acros'TIC**ALLY adv. [f. Gk *akrostikhis* (ACRO-, Gk *stikhos* row, line of verse)]

act[1], n. Thing done, deed, this as outward sign of a condition etc. (~ *of faith, contrition*); process of doing, operation, as *in the very* ~ *of*, *Act of God* (operation of uncontrollable natural forces); *Acts (of the Apostles)*, N.T. book; decree passed by a legislative body etc.; ~ *& deed*, binding legal instrument (esp. *I deliver this as my* ~ *& deed* said at time of signing); main division of a play; one of a series of short performances in circus or variety programme (*put on an* ~, sl., show off, talk for display); || (formerly, in Universities) thesis maintained by candidate for degree etc. [ME, f. OF *acte* & L *actus, -um*; see foll.]

act[2], v.t. & i. Carry out (an incident or story) in mimicry, represent, perform a play or part; personate (character in a play or in life), as ~ *Othello,* ~ *the fool*; perform actions, behave, as ~ (behave) *generously,* ~ (serve) *as interpreter,* ~ *upon* (execute) *a suggestion,* ~ *up to* (put into practice) *a principle*; perform special functions, as *the policeman declined to* ~, *the brake refused to* ~, *alcohol* ~*s on the brain*. [partly f. L *act-* p.p. st. of *agere* do, partly f. prec.]

ac'ting, a. & n. In vbl senses, esp.: doing duty temporarily, as *A*~ *Captain*; doing alone duties nominally shared with others, as *A*~ *Manager, Trustee*; ~ *copy* (for players' use, with stage-directions & cuts). [ACT[2] + -ING[2,1]]

Actin'ia (ăk-), n. (pl. *-ae, -as*). Genus of zoophytes belonging to the family Actiniadae; (pop.) sea anemone. [mod. L f. Gk *aktis -inos* ray]

ac'tinism, n. That property of the sun's rays by which chemical changes are produced, as in photography. So **actin'ic** a. [as prec. + -ISM]

actin'ium, n. Radio-active element found in pitchblende. [as prec. + -IUM]

actino-, comb. form of Gk *aktis -inos* ray, as **actino̅m'eter** n., instrument for measuring intensity of sun's heating rays; **actino**THE'RAPY n., treatment of disease by light rays.

ac'tion, n., & v.t. 1. Process of acting, exertion of energy or influence, as *men of*

~, *put in* ~, ~ *of an acid*; thing done, act; (in drama) series of events represented; mode of acting, management of body, etc., as ~ *of a player, horse*; mechanism of piano or other instrument; legal process; engagement between troops etc.; ~ *committee*, one chosen to take active steps; ~ *stations*, positions taken up by troops etc. before going into ~. 2. v.t. Bring a legal ~ against. [ME, f. OF, f. L *actionem* (as ACT[2], see -ION)]

ac'tionab|le (-shon-), a. Affording ground for an action at law. Hence ~LY[2] adv. [ACTION + -ABLE]

ac'tivate, v.t. Make active (~*d carbon*, carbon, esp. charcoal, treated to increase its adsorptive power; ~*d sludge*, aerated sewage containing aerobic bacteria); (Phys.) make radio-active. [-ATE[3]]

ac'tive, a. 1. Given to outward action; working, effective; energetic, diligent; acting of one's own accord, acting upon others. 2. (gram.). The ~ *voice* comprises all forms of intransitive verbs, & those forms of transitive verbs that attribute the verbal action to the person or thing whence it proceeds (the logical subject), as *We punished him*; not, like the forms of the passive voice, to the person or thing to whom it is directed (the logical object), as *He was punished by us*. Less correctly, verbs are themselves called ~. Hence ~LY[2](-vl-) adv. [ME, f. OF *actif* & L *activus* (ACT[2], -IVE)]

activ'ity, n. Exertion of energy; quality of being active, diligence, nimbleness; (pl.) active forces, spheres of action. [f. F *activité* & med. L *activitas* (in LL also = active form of verb); see prec., -TY]

ac'ton, n. Jacket of quilted cotton worn under mail; mail-plated jacket of leather etc. [ME, f. OF *auqueton* (mod. *hoqueton*) padding, padded jacket, f. Sp. *alcoton* (mod. *algodon*) cotton f. Arab. *al-qutun* the cotton]

ac'tor, n. Dramatic performer, whence **ac'tr**ESS[1] n.; (rarely) doer. [L, = doer, actor (as ACT[2], see -OR)]

ac'tual, a. Existing in fact, real; present, current. [ME, f. OF *actuel* f. LL *actualis* (*actus* vbl n. f. *agere* ACT[2]; see -AL)]

actuál'ity, n. Reality; realism; (pl.) existing conditions. [f. as prec. + -ITY; in early use f. med. L *actualitas*]

ac'tualiz|e, -is|e (-iz), v.t. Realize in action; describe realistically. Hence ~A'TION n. [ACTUAL + -IZE]

ac'tually, adv. In actual fact, really; for the time being; even (strange as it may seem). [-LY[2]]

ac'tuary, n. Expert in theory & practice of statistics, esp. of mortality, sickness, retirement, & unemployment; (formerly) registrar, notary. Hence **actuar'ial** a. [f. L *actuarius* amanuensis, book-keeper (*actus*; see ACTUAL & -ARY[1])]

ac'tuate, v.t. Communicate motion to (a machine etc.); serve as motive to (person). Hence **ăctŭA'TION** n. [f. med. L *actuare* (*actus*, as prec., see -ATE³)]

acŭ'ĭtў, n. Sharpness, acuteness (as of needle, acid, disease, wit). [f. F *acuité* or med. L *acuitas* (*acus -ūs* needle; see -ITY)]

acŭl'éate, a. (Zool.) having a sting; (Bot.) prickly; pointed, incisive. [f. L *aculeatus* (ACULEUS, see -ATE²)]

acŭl'éus, n. (pl. *-ëi*). (Zool.) sting; (bot.) prickle. [L *aculeus* sting, dim. of *acus* needle]

acŭm'ĕn, n. Keen discernment, penetration. [L *acumen -minis* anything sharp (*acuere* sharpen)]

acŭm'ĭnate¹, a. (nat. hist.). Tapering to a point. [f. L *acuminare* (prec.), see -ATE²]

acŭm'ĭnāte², v.t. Sharpen, point; give poignancy to. Hence **acūmĭnA'TION** n. [as prec., see -ATE³]

‖**acu'shla** (-ŏŏ-), n. Darling. [f. Ir. *ā cuisle* O pulse (of my heart)!]

acūte', a. Sharp, pointed; (of angles) less than a right angle; (of diseases) coming sharply to a crisis, opp. to *chronic*; (of controversy, difficulty) critical, serious; (of sensations, senses, intellect) keen; (of sounds) high, shrill; (of letters) bearing the ~ ACCENT. Hence ~LY² (-tl-) adv., ~NESS (-tn-) n. [f. L *acutus* p.p. of *acuere* sharpen]

acūt'i- in comb. Sharp, as ~*foliate* sharp--leaved, ~*lobate* sharp-lobed. [L comb. form of *acutus* ACUTE]

-acў, branch of the wider suf. -CY forming nouns of state or quality from or modelled on L *-acia* or *-atia* or Gk *-ateia*. **1.** N. of quality f. L *-aci-a* f. adjj. in *-aci-*; *fall-* deceive *fallaci-* deceitful *fall-aci-a* fallacy. **2.** N. of state or quality f. L *-ati-a* f. nouns in *-at-* (nom. *-as*, *-i-* being part of stem or connecting link): med. L *primat- primati-a* primacy; & by analogy *supremacy*. **3.** N. of state f. med. L *-ati-a* f. nouns in *-atus*: *advocat-us advocat-ia* advocacy; & by analogy *curacy*. This formation was extended to adjj. [f. L *-atus* to form *accuracy*, *obstinacy*, from *accurate*, *obstinate*, where L has nouns in *-atio*; hence other L words in *-atio* appear in E with *-acy* where E has no corresponding adj. in *-ate*, as *conspiracy*; similarly, E *-acy* for L *-atus* (n. of 4th decl.), as *magistratus* magistracy, gives rise to *episcopacy* as if f. E *episcopate*; & *lunacy* is formed to match *lunatic* on anal. of *diplomacy* diplomatic. **4.** N. of state, through L, f. Gk *-ateia* f. nn. in *-atēs* or vbs in *-ateuein*; *peiratēs peirateia* piracy.

ăd, n. (colloq.). Advertisement; *ăd'man*, publicist, propagandist. [abbr.]

ad-, pref. **1.** f. L *ad* to, w. sense of motion or direction to, change into, addition, adherence, increase, or mere intensification. Assim. before *c*, *f*, *g*, *l*, *n*, *p*, *q*, *r*, *s*, *t*, & prob. before *b*; reduced to *a* before *sc*, *sp*, *st*. In OF, L *ad* was regularly reduced to *a*, *a-*. Later the spelling was refash.

after L, as also in E f. the 15th c. Subsequent adoptions conform to L spelling. (The use of *ad-*, *ab-*, in pairs like *adoral* & *aboral*, situated *at* & *away from* mouth, is unknown to L). **2.** The substitution of *ad-* (*ac-* etc.) for *a-* was occas. applied where *a-* repr. other preff., as L *ab* (*advance*), OF *es-*, L *ex-* (*affray*), OE *a-* (*accurse*), see A-. So *admiral* f. Arab. *amiral*.

-ad, suf. of nouns. **1.** f. Gk *-ad-* (nom. *-as*), in collective numerals (*monad*, *dyad*, *triad*, *chiliad*, *myriad*); in fem. patronymics (*Dryad*, *Naiad*); in names of poems (*Iliad*, & by anal. *Dunciad*, *Rosciad*); & in family names of plants (*liliad*). **2.** f. F *-ade*; see the more usual *-ADE*. **3.** suf. invented to form adjj. & advv. in the sense of 'towards' (the part indicated by main element of word), as *caudad* towards the tail [L *cauda* tail]

ăd'age, n. Traditional maxim, proverb. [F, f. L *adagium* (*ad* to + *agi-*, root of *aio* I say)]

adagio (adahj'yō), adv., a., n. (mus. & dancing). Slow(ly); (n-) ~movement. [It.]

Ad'am¹ (ă-), n. The first man (*not know* one *from* ~, have no knowledge of his looks); *old* ~ (unregenerate condition), ~*'s ale* or *wine* (water), ~*'s apple* (projection of the thyroid cartilage of the larynx). [Heb. *a-dam* man]

Ad'am² (ă-), a. (At first in pl.) of the decorative style created by the brothers Robert & James *Adam* in the 18th c.

ăd'amant, n. A thing impenetrably hard (*be* ~, stubbornly refuse compliance with requests); (formerly) loadstone; diamond. Hence **ădamăn'tĭNE²** a. [f. OF *adamaunt* f. L *adamantem* (nom. *-mas*) f. Gk *adamas -mantos* untamable (*a-* not + *damaō* I tame)]

Ad'amīte (ă-), n. Child of Adam, human being; unclothed man; (Eccl.) name of sects who imitated Adam in this respect; (pl.) a section of humanity supposed by some to be alone derived from Adam. [f. med. L *Adamita* (ADAM¹, -ITE)]

adăpt', v.t. Fit (a thing *to* another); make suitable (*to* or *for* a purpose); modify, alter, (~*ed for broadcasting*). Hence or cogn. ~ABIL'ITY, **ădapTA'TION**, ~ER¹, nn., ~ABLE, ~IVE, aa. [f. F *adapter* f. L AD(*aptare* f. *aptus* fit)]

ăd căptăn'dum (*vŭl'gus*), adv. & a. (Calculated) to take the fancy (of the rabble). [L]

ădd, v.t. & i. Join (one thing *to* another), as ~ *your entreaties to mine*, ~ *insult to injury*, *this* ~*s to* (increases) *our difficulties*, *he* ~*ed* (stated further) *that*—, ~ *up* or *together* (find the sum of), ~ (perform the process of summation) *correctly*, ~ *in* (include). [ME, f. L AD(*dere dit-* = *dare* put); see DO¹]

ădd'ăx, n. Large N.-African & Arabian antelope with twisted horns. [L, f. African wd]

addĕn'dum, n. (pl. *-da*). Thing to be added; appendix, addition. [L gerundive of *addere* ADD]

ădd'er, n. Small venomous snake, esp. common viper; *puff, death, horned*, ∼, species of Viperidae; *flying* ∼, dragon- -fly; ∼'s *tongue*, kind of fern. [f. OE *nǣdre*, Gmc = OS *nādra*, OHG *nātara*, ON *nathra*, Goth. *nadrs*; *n-* lost in ME by wrong division of *a naddre*; cf. APRON]

addict', v.t. Devote, apply habitually, (*to* a practice), as *his tastes* ∼ *him, he* ∼*s himself or his mind, he is* ∼*ed, to*; (Rom. Law) deliver over by sentence of a judge. So **ădd'ict** n., person ∼ed to a habit esp. the taking of a specified drug etc. (*opium* ∼), **addic'**TION n. [f. L AD(*dicere dict-* say) assign]

Add'ison's dĭsease' (ă-; -zĕz), n. Disease characterized by progressive anaemia & debility & brown discoloration of skin. [T. *Addison* discoverer, 1855]

addi'tion, n. Process of adding (*in* ∼ *to*, as well as); thing added (*a useful* ∼). [ME, f. OF, or L *additio* (as ADD, see -ION)]

addi'tional (-shon-), a. Added, supplementary. Hence ∼LY[2] adv. [prec. + -AL]

ădd'itive, a. & n. (Thing) to be added; characterized by addition (∼ *process*). [f. LL *additivus*, see ADD]

ăd'dle[1], a. ∼ *egg*, rotten one, one that produces no chicken; empty, vain; muddled, unsound, as ∼*-brained, -head, -pated*. [f. OE *adela* mire (cf. MLG *adele*, G *adel*); now used only as adj.]

ăd'dle[2], v.t. & i. Muddle, confuse; (of eggs) grow addle. [f. prec.]

ăd'dled (-ld), a. Made addle. [ADDLE a. assim. to p.p. form, apparently before ADDLE v. existed]

addrĕss'[1], v.t. Direct in speech or writing (∼ *remarks, a protest, petition*, etc. *to* person; ∼ *oneself to*, speak or write to); write directions for delivery on cover of (letter, parcel, etc.); speak or write to, esp. deliver a speech to, (person, audience); apply (*oneself to* a task); (Golf) adjust club head behind (ball) before playing stroke. [ME, f. OF *adresser* f. Rom. *AD(drictiare* f. **drictum* = L *directum* DIRECT)]

addrĕss'[2], n. Readiness, skill, dexterity, adroitness; superscription of letter, name of place to which person's letters are directed, whence ∼OGRAPH (2) n. **P**, machine for printing ∼es; act of dispatching a ship; manner, bearing, in conversation; discourse delivered to audience; (pl.) courteous approach, courtship (*pay* one's ∼*es to*). [f. prec. & f. F *adresse* n. f. *adresser*]

ăddrĕssee', n. Person to whom a letter is addressed. [ADDRESS[1] + -EE]

adduc|e', v.t. Cite as proof or instance. Hence ∼e'ABLE, ∼'IBLE, aa. [f. L AD-(*ducere duct-* lead)]

addū'cent, a. (physiol.). (Of muscles) drawing to a common centre. [as prec., see -ENT]

addŭct', v.t. (physiol.). Draw to a common centre. [as ADDUCE]

addŭc'tion, n. Act of adducing; act of adducting. [f. as ADDUCE; see -ION; cf. F *adduction*, LL *adductio*]

-āde, suf. of nouns. **1.** f. F *-ade*, the form in which Pr., Sp., or Port. wds in *-ada* f. L *-ata* (fem. sing. p.p. of verbs in *-are*) were adopted in F, often supplanting native F *-ée* direct f. L, as in *accolade* OF *acolée*. Now a living suf. both in F wds, many of which are borrowed by E (*tirade, gasconnade*), & in E (*blockade, orangeade*); E drops F *e* in *ballad, salad*. Meanings: action done (*tirade, fusillade*), body concerned in action or process (*ambuscade, cavalcade*), thing produced by action or from ·material (*masquerade, lemonade*). **2.** f. F *-ade* f. Gk *-ada* (nom. *-as*), as *decade*; but in E usu. -AD. **3.** f. Sp. or Port. *-ado*, masc. form corresp. to **1** above, with similar meaning (*brocade*), or that of the person concerned (*renegade*).

ăd'ĕnoids (-z), n. pl. Mass of spongy tissue between back of nose & throat, often hindering inflation of lungs. Hence **ădĕnoid'**AL a. [f. Gk *adēn -enos* acorn, gland; see -OID]

adĕpt', n. & a. (One who is) thoroughly proficient (*in* anything); skilled alchemist. [f. L *adeptus* p.p. of AD(*ipisci* attain)]

ăd'ĕqu|ate, a. Proportionate (*to* the requirements); sufficient, satisfactory. Hence ∼ACY n., ∼ateLY[2] (-tl-) adv. [f. L AD*aequare* make equal (*aequus*), see -ATE[3]]

adĕs'pota, n. pl. Literary works not attributed to (or claimed by) an author. [neut. pl. of Gk *adespotos* without owner (*a-* not +*despotēs* master)]

ăd ĕăn'dem, adv. *Admitted* ∼ (*gradum*), to the same (degree at another univ.). [L]

à deux (see Ap.), adv. & a. For two; between two. [F]

adhēre' (-h-), v.i. Stick fast, cleave, *to* (a substance, person, party, opinion). [f. F *adhérer* or L AD(*haerēre haes-* stick)]

adhēr'|ent (-h-), a. & n. Sticking (*to* substance); due *to*; connected with (*to*); (n.) supporter (*of* party etc.). So ∼ENCE (-h-) n. [f. F *adhérent* (as prec., see -ENT)]

adhē'sion (-hēzhn), n. Adhering (lit. & fig.); (Path.) unnatural union of surfaces due to inflammation. [f. F *adhésion* or L *adhaesio* (as ADHERE, see -ION)]

adhēs'ive (-h-), a. & n. Having the property of adhering; sticky; (n.) ∼ substance. Hence ∼LY[2] (-h-; -vl-) adv. [f. F *adhésif, -ive* (as ADHERE, see -IVE)]

adhĭb'it (-h-), v.t. Put on, affix; apply, administer, (remedies). So **ădhibi'**TION (-h-) n. [f. L AD(*hibēre hibit-* = *habēre* hold) employ]

ăd hŏc, a. Arranged for this purpose, special. [L]

ăd hŏm'ĭnĕm, adv. & a. To the man, personal; ARGUMENTUM ∼. [L]

ădiabăt′ic, a. (phys.). Impassable to heat; occurring without heat entering or leaving system. [f. Gk *adiabatos* impassable (a- not +*diabainō* pass)]

ădiăn′tum, n. Kinds of ferns including the true maidenhair; (pop.) black maidenhair. [L, f. Gk *adianton* maidenhair]

ădiăph′or|ism, n. Latitudinarianism. So ~IST n. [f. Gk *adiaphoros* (a- not +*diaphoros* different) +-ISM]

adieu (adŭ′), int. & n. (pl. ~s, ~x, pr. adŭz′). Good-bye; *make, take,* one's ~, say good-bye. [ME, f. OF (à to + *Dieu* God)]

ăd ĭnfīnī′tum, adv. Without limit, for ever. [L]

ăd ĭn′terĭm, adv. & a. For the meantime. [L]

ăd′ipocēre, n. Greyish fatty substance generated in dead bodies subjected to moisture. [f. F *adipocire* (L *adeps* -*ipis* fat +-o- +*cire* wax f. L *cera*)]

ăd′ipōse, a. & n. Pertaining to fat, fatty; (n.) animal fat. Hence **ădipŏs′ITY** n. [f. L *adeps* -*ipis* fat +-OSE]

ăd′it, n. Approach; (of mines) horizontal entrance; act of approaching. [f. L A*ditus* -*ūs* (*ire it-* go)]

adjā′c|ent, a. Lying near, contiguous. So ~ENCY n. [ME, f. L AD(*jacēre* lie), see -ENT]

ădj′ĕctive, a. & n. Additional, not standing by itself, dependent: ~ *colours* (not permanent without a basis); *Law* A~ (subsidiary part of law, procedure); (Gram.) ~, *noun* ~, the name of an attribute, added to the name of a thing to describe the thing more fully. Hence **ădjĕctiv′AL** a., **ădjĕctiv′alLY²,** ~LY² (-vl-), advv. [ME, f. LL *adjectivus* f. AD(*jicĕre ject-* = *jacĕre* throw), see -IVE]

adjoin′, v.t. Join, unite, (one thing *to* another); be contiguous with. [ME, f. OF *ajoindre, ajoign-* f. L AD(*jungere junct-* join)]

adjourn′ (ajẽrn′), v.t. & i. Put off, postpone; break off for later resumption; (intr., of persons met together) suspend joint proceedings & separate; change the place of meeting. Hence ~′MENT (ajẽr-) n. [ME, f. OF *ajorner* f. a AD- +*jorn* day f. LL *diurnum* day f. L *diurnus* DIURNAL; cf. JOURNAL, JOURNEY]

adjŭdge′, v.t. Adjudicate upon (a matter); pronounce judicially (*that* a thing *is* or a thing *to be*); condemn (person *to* penalty or *to* do); award judicially (thing *to* person). Hence ~′MENT (-jm-) n. [ME, f. OF *ajuger* (as foll.)]

adjŭd′ic|āte (ajōō-), v.t. & i. (Of a judge or court) decide upon (claim etc.); pronounce (person *to be* something); (intr.) sit in judgement & pronounce sentence. Hence ~A′TION, ~ātor, nn., ~ātive a., (ajōō-). [f. L AD(*judicare* f. *judex* -*icis* judge), see -ATE³]

ădj′ŭnct, n. Subordinate or incidental thing, accompaniment (*to, of*); (Gram.) amplification of the predicate, subject,

etc.; (Logic) non-essential attribute. Hence **adjŭnc′tIVE** a., **adjŭnc′tIVELY²** (-vl-) adv. [f. L as ADJOIN]

adjure (ajoor′), v.t. Charge (a person) under oath or penalty of curse (*to* do); request earnestly. Hence **adjurA′TION** (ăjoor-) n. [ME, f. L AD(*jurare* swear) in LL sense 'put person to an oath']

adjŭst′, v.t. Arrange, put in order; harmonize (discrepancies); adapt (*to* standard or purpose). Hence~ABLE a., ~MENT n. [f. F *adjuster* (now *ajuster*) a refashioning, after *juste* JUST, of OF *ajoster* (mod. *ajouter*, = obs. E *adjoust*) f. Rom. **ad*juxtare,* f. L *juxta* near]

adjutage, aj-, (ăj′ōō-), n. Mouthpiece of an artificial fountain. [f. F. *aj(o)utage* (*ajouter* add, join; see prec. & -AGE)]

adj′ut|ant (ăjōō-), a. & n. 1. Assistant; (Mil.) army etc. officer who assists superior officers by communicating orders, conducting correspondence, etc., whence~ANCY n. 2. Gigantic Indian stork. [f. L *adjutare* frequent. as foll., see -ANT]

adj′uvant (ăjōō-), a. & n. Helpful, auxiliary; person, thing, that helps. [f. L AD(*juvare jut-* help), see -ANT]

ăd līb′ĭtum, adv. (abbr. *ad lib.*). At pleasure, to any extent; *ăd′-lib,* v.i. (colloq.), speak extempore. [L]

ăd′măss, n. That section of the community easily influenced by mass methods of publicity and entertainment or considered as likely to be so influenced. [f. AD advertisement +MASS²]

admeasure (-mĕzh′er), v.t. Apportion, assign in due shares. [ME, f. OF *amesurer* f. med. L AD(*mensurare* MEASURE)]

admeasurement (-mĕzh′erm-), n. Process of admeasuring; comparison; dimensions. [f. OF *amesurement* (as prec., see -MENT)]

admin′icle, n. A help; (Law) corroboratory evidence. So **ădminic′ŭlAR¹** a. [f. L *adminiculum* prop; see -CULE]

admin′ister, v.t. & i. Manage (affairs); dispense (justice, sacraments, *to*); tender (oath *to*); furnish, give, (thing *to*); apply (remedies *to*); (intr.) act as administrator; contribute *to* (one's comfort etc.). Hence **admin′istRABLE** a. [ME, f. OF *aministrer* f. L AD(*ministrare* MINISTER)]

administrā′tion, n. Management (*of* business); management of public affairs, government; the ministry, the Government (chiefly U.S.); (Law) management of deceased person's estate; *Letters of A~,* authority to administer estate of an intestate, opp. to *probate;* dispensation (*of* justice etc.); tendering (*of* oath); application (*of* remedies). [ME f. OF, or L *administratio* (as prec., see -ATION)]

admin′istrātive, a. Pertaining to management of affairs; executive. Hence ~LY² (-vl-) adv. [f. L *administrativus* (as prec., see -IVE)]

admin′istrā|tor, n. Manager; one capable of organizing; one who performs

official duties (of religion, justice, etc.);
applier or giver (*of*); one authorized to
manage estates for legal owner during
minority etc., or estates of one who dies
without appointing competent executors.
Hence ~tor·SHIP n., ~TRIX n. (pl. ~*trices*,
pron. -ĭsĭz *or* -īs′ēz). [L, as ADMINISTER,
see -OR]

ăd′mirab|le, a. Surprisingly good, ex-
cellent; *A*~*le Crichton* (krīt′on), a prodigy,
one who excels in many things (from
James Crichton, 'The A~le Crichton',
1560–85, Scottish scholar, poet, athlete).
Hence ~LY[2] adv. [F, or f. L *admirabilis*
(as ADMIRE, see -ABLE)]

ăd′miral, n. Commander-in-chief of a
country's navy (in England, formerly
Lord High A~); naval officer of highest
rank, commander of fleet or squadron;
A~ *of the Fleet, A*~, *Vice-A*~, *Rear-A*~,
the four grades of A~ in British Navy;
privileged commander of fishing or
merchant fleet; ship that carries the ~,
Flagship; *Red A*~, *White A*~, two European species of butterfly. Hence ~SHIP n.
[ME *amyrayl* etc., *admirail* etc., f. OF
a(d)mira(i)l etc., med. L *a(d)miralis* etc.,
f. Arab. *amir* commander; see AMEER, EMIR]

ăd′miraltў, n. Office of admiral; the
department administering the Navy (in
Britain, *Lords Commissioners of A*~);
(Rhet.) command of the seas (esp. *the
price of* ~); *Court of A*~, tribunal for
trial & decision of maritime questions &
offences. [ME *a(d)myralte* etc. f. OF *ad-
miralte* (prec., -TY)]

ădmirā′tion, n. Pleased contemplation;
(formerly) wonder; *the* ~ *of*, admired by;
note of ~ (!). [F, or f. L *admiratio* (as
foll., see -ATION)]

admīre′, v.t. Regard with pleased surprise or approval; (also, colloq.) express
admiration of (*forgot to* ~ *her cat*); (formerly) wonder at. [f. F *admirer* or L
AD(*mirari* wonder at)]

admĭr′er, n. One that admires; lover.
[ADMIRE + -ER[1]]

admiss′i|ble, a. (Of idea or plan) worthy
to be entertained; (Law) allowable as
judicial proof; capable of being admitted
(*to* office or position). Hence ~BIL′ITY n.
[F, f. med. L *admissibilis* (ADMIT, -BLE)]

admĭs′sion (-shn), n. Admitting, being
admitted, (*to* society of persons or class of
things); acknowledgement (*of* thing as
true, *that* it is true). [late ME, f. L
admissio (as foll., see -ION)]

admĭss′ive, a. Tending to admit. [f.
med. L *admissivus* (as foll., see -IVE)]

admĭt′, v.t. & i. (-tt-). Allow (person etc.)
entrance or access (*to* place, class, privileges, etc.); accept as valid or true,
whence ~t′ĕdLY[2] adv.; acknowledge
(thing *to be*, *that* it is); (abs.) *this, I* ~,
was wrong; (of enclosed spaces) have
room for; ~ *of*, leave room for (doubt,
improvement). [ME, f. L AD(*mittere miss-
let go*)]

admĭtt′able, a. Capable of being admitted (usu. to a place). [prec. + -ABLE]

admĭtt′ance, n. Admitting, being admitted (usu. to a place). [ADMIT + -ANCE]

admĭx′, v.t. & i. Add as an ingredient;
mingle (*with* something). So ~TURE n.
[now f. AD- + MIX]

admŏn′ish, v.t. Exhort (person *to do*,
that he should do); give advice; warn (*of*
a thing); inform, remind, (*of* a thing,
that). Hence ~MENT n. [ME *amonest(e)* f.
OF *amonester* f. Rom. **admonestare* unexpl. alt. of L AD(*monēre monit*- warn);
mod. E form irreg. assim. to L *admonēre*
and -ISH]

admŏni′tion, n. Admonishing; warning,
reproof. So **admŏn′itorў** a. [ME, f. OF
amonition f. L *admonitionem* (as prec.,
see -ION)]

ăd naus′eăm, adv. To a disgusting extent. [L]

ădnŏm′inal, a. Belonging to an adnoun;
attached to a noun. [f. L *ad* + *nomen*
+ -AL, after PRONOMINAL; cf. foll.]

ăd′noun, n. Adjective, word added to a
noun substantive; adjective used sub-
stantively. [f. L *ad* to + NOUN on anal. of
adverb]

ado (adoo′), n. Action, business, fuss;
difficulty; *much ado* prop. = *much to do*;
but *much being* taken as adj., *ado* is
treated as n. [f. northern ME *at do* (= *to
do*) f. ON *at* AT as sign of infin. + DO]

-ado, suf. of nouns. **1.** f. Sp. or Port. *-ado*
f. L *-atus* p.p. of vbs in *-are*, as *desperado*
L *desperatus* (*desperare*); occas. changed
in E to *-ade*, as *renegado*, now *renegade*.
2. Ignorant refashioning of nouns in *-ade*
f. F *-ade* = Sp. *-ada* It. *-ata*, as *crusado*
Sp. *cruzada*, *scalado* Sp. *escalada*.

adōb′e (or -ōb′), n. Unburnt sun-dried
brick. [Sp.]

ădolĕs′c|ent, n. & a. (Person) growing
up, between childhood & manhood or
womanhood. So~ENCE,~ENCY, nn. [ME,
f. OF, f. L AD(*olescere ult*- grow up), see
-ENT]

Adōn′ĭs, n. Beautiful youth loved by
Venus; beau, dandy; (Bot.) genus including pheasant's eye; ‖ (Entom.) the
butterfly Clifden Blue. [Gk, f. Phoen.
adōn lord, title of a divinity]

ăd′onĭze, -ise (-īz), v. refl. & i. Adorn,
dandify, (one*self*), play the Adonis. [f. F
adoniser (prec., -IZE)]

adŏpt′, v.t. Take (person) into a relationship he did not previously occupy; take
(idea etc.) from some one else; choose.
Hence ~ABIL′ITY, adŏp′tION, nn., ~ABLE
a. [f. F *adopter* or L AD(*optare* choose)]

adŏp′tive, a. Due to adoption, as ~ *son,
father*; apt to adopt. Hence ~LY[2] (-vl-)
adv. [ME, f. OF (*-if, -ive*), f. L *adoptivus*;
see prec. and -IVE]

adŏr|e′, v.t. Regard with the utmost
respect & affection; (poet.) worship as
a deity; (in R. C. Church) reverence with
representative honours (the Host etc.).

So ∼'ABLE a., ∼'ABLY² adv., **ădor**A'TION n. [ME *aoure*, later *adoure*, f. OF *aorer*, later *adorer*, f. L *adorare* worship]

adōr'er, n. Worshipper; ardent admirer, lover. [prec. + -ER¹]

adōrn', v.t. Add beauty or lustre to; furnish with ornaments. So ∼MENT n. [ME *aourne*, later *adourne* f. OF *aourner*, later *adorner*, f. L AD(*ornare* furnish, deck)]

adown', adv. & prep. (arch., poet.). = DOWN³. [f. OE *of dūne* off the mount (A-(3), DOWN¹ n.)]

ăd rĕm, adv. & pred. a. To the point; to the purpose. [L]

ădrēn'alin, n. A hormone secreted by the adrenal ductless glands & affecting circulation & muscular action; this extracted from animals for medicinal use. [AD- + RENAL + -IN]

adrift', adv. In a drifting condition, at the mercy of wind & tide or of circumstances; (Naut.) unfastened. [A prep. + DRIFT¹]

adroit', a. Having address, dexterous. Hence ∼LY² adv., ∼NESS n. [F phr. *à droit* rightly]

ădsciti'tious (-sitishus), a. Adopted from without; supplemental. [f. L AD(*sciscere scit*-inceptive of *scire* know) + -ITIOUS]

ădscrip'tus glēb'ae, a. & n. (Serf) attached to the soil. [L]

adsōrb', v.t. (Of a solid) attract (molecules of a gas or liquid) to its surface (cf. ABSORB). So **adsōrp'**TION n. [f. AD- +L *sorbēre sorpt*- suck in]

ăd'sŭm, v.i. I am here. [L]

ăd'ŭl|āte, v.t. Flatter basely. So ∼A'TION, ∼ātoR, nn., ∼ātoRY a. [f. L *adulari* fawn on, see -ATE³]

Adŭll'amite, n. M.P. seceding from Liberal Party in 1866. [f. cave of *Adullam* (1 Sam. xxii. 1, 2) + -ITE]

adŭlt' (*or* ăd', *esp. as n.*), a. & n. (One who is) grown up; mature. [f. L *adultus* p.p. of *adolescere*; see ADOLESCENT]

adŭl'terant, a. & n. (Thing) employed in adulterating. [as foll., see -ANT]

adŭl'terate¹, a. Stained (in conduct or in birth) by adultery; (of things) spurious, counterfeit. [as foll., see -ATE²]

adŭl'ter|āte², v.t. Falsify by admixture of baser ingredients. So ∼A'TION, ∼ātoR, nn. [f. L *adulterare* corrupt (f. *adulter* adulterer), see -ATE³; replacing obs. vb *adulter* (f. F *adultérer* or L *adulterare*), itself replacing ME *avoutre* (f. OF *avoutrer* f. L *adulterare*)]

adŭl'ter|er, n. One guilty of adultery. So ∼ESS¹ n. [f. obs. *adulter* vb (orig. *avoutre*; see prec.) + -ER¹]

adŭl'terine, a. Of, born of, adultery; adulterated, counterfeit; illegal, unlicensed. [f. L *adulterinus* born of adultery, spurious (*adulter* adulterer, see -INE¹)]

adŭl'ter|y̆, n. Voluntary sexual intercourse of married person with one of the opposite sex other than his or her spouse. So ∼OUS a., ∼OUSLY² adv. [re-

placing ME *avoutrie* f. OF *avoutrie* etc., the mod. F *adultère* being, like E *adultery*, directly f. L *adulterium*]

adŭm'bral, a. Overshadowing, shady. [f. AD- +L *umbra* shade + -AL]

ăd'umbrāte (*or* adŭm'), v.t. Represent in outline; faintly indicate; typify, foreshadow; overshadow. Hence or cogn. **ădumbra'TION** n., **adŭm'bratIVE** a. [f. L AD(*umbrare* f. *umbra* shade), see -ATE³]

ăd ŭng'uem (-nggw-) (*făc'tus*), a. Highly finished. [L]

adŭst', a. Scorched, dried up, parched; sunburnt; atrabilious, gloomy. [f. F *aduste* or L *adustus* p.p. of AD-(*urere ust*-burn)]

ăd valōr'ĕm, adv. & a. (Of taxes) in proportion to estimated value of goods. [L]

advance'¹ (-vah-), v.t. & i. 1. Move or put forward; promote (plans, persons); bring forward (claims, suggestions); accelerate (events); pay (money) before it is due; lend; raise (price). 2. v.i. Move forward; make progress; rise (in price); (p.p.) far on in progress, as ∼d *studies, ideas*. So ∼'MENT (-ahnsm-) n. (esp. of promotion of plan or person). [ME *avaunce* f. OF *avancer* f. Rom. *abantiare* f. LL *abante* in front (*ab* away + *ante* before); see AD-]

advance'² (-vah-), n. Going forward; progress; personal approach, overture; rise in price; payment beforehand, loan; ∼ *copy* of book etc., supplied before publication; *in* ∼, before (of place or time). [f. prec. & f. F *avance* n. (as prec.)]

advan'tage¹ (-vah-), n. Better position, precedence, superiority; favourable circumstance, whence **ădvantā'geoUS** (-jus) a., **ădvantā'geousLY³** (-jus-) adv.; (in Tennis) next point or game won after deuce points or games; *have the* ∼ *of, gain an* ∼ *over*, have, acquire, a better position than (*you have the* ∼ *of me*, esp., you know me & I do not know you); *take* ∼ (avail oneself) *of a circumstance*; *take* ∼ *of* (over-reach) *a person*; *take a person at* ∼ (by surprise); *to* ∼, in a way to exhibit the merits (*was seen, heard, to* ∼); ∼-*ground* (usu. *vantage*-), position that gives superiority. [f. OF *avantage* f. *avant* (see ADVANCE¹) + -*age* -AGE, see -AD]

advan'tage² (-vah-), v.t. Be beneficial to; be an advantage to; further, promote. [late ME, f. prec. or F *avantager*]

Ad'vent (ăd-), n. Season before the Nativity; coming of Christ, Incarnation; second coming of Christ; (*a*∼) any (important) arrival. Hence ∼ISM (3) n., ∼IST (2) n., (tenets of) member of a sect holding millenarian views. [late OE, ME *advent* f. L *adventus* arrival f. AD(*venire vent*- come)]

ădventi'tious (-shus), a. ·Coming from without; accidental, casual; ‖ (Law, of property) coming from a stranger or by collateral, not direct, succession. Hence ∼LY² adv. [f. L *adventicius*; see prec. & -ITIOUS¹]

advěn'ture¹, n. Risk, danger; daring enterprise; unexpected incident; commercial speculation; hazardous activity. [ME *aventure* f. OF f. Rom. *adventura* (sc. *res* thing) about to happen (ADVENT); see AD-]

advěn'ture², v.t. & i. Hazard, imperil, (one*self*, thing); incur risk; dare to go or come (*into, in, upon*, a place); dare to enter *on, upon*, (undertaking). [ME, f. OF *aventurer* (as prec.)]

advěn'turer (-cher-), n. One who seeks adventures; soldier of fortune; speculator; one who lives by his wits. [f. F *aventurier* (as ADVENTURE¹, see -ER¹)]

advěn'turesome (-cher-), a. Given to adventures. [ADVENTURE¹ +-SOME]

advěn'turèss (-cher-), n. Female adventurer; woman who lives by her wits. [f. ADVENTURER, see -ESS]

advěn'turous (-cher-), a. Rash, venturesome; enterprising. Hence ~LY² adv. [ME, f. OF *aventuros* (as ADVENTURE¹, see -OUS)]

ăd'věrb, n. Word that modifies or qualifies an adjective, verb, or other adverb, expressing a relation of place, time, circumstance, manner, etc. (e.g. *gently, so, now, where, why*). [f. F *adverbe* or L *adverbium* (*verbum* word, VERB) transl. of Gk *epirrhēma*]

adverb'ial, a. Pertaining to an adverb; of the nature of an adverb. Hence ~LY² adv. [f. F, or LL *adverbialis*; see -AL]

ăd verb'um, adv. & a. Word for word. [L]

ăd'versary̆, n. Opponent, antagonist, enemy; the *A~*, the Devil. [ME, f. AF *adverser*, OF *adversier*, *-aire* f. L *adversarius*; see ADVERSE & -ARY¹]

advers'ative, a. (Of words etc.) expressing opposition or antithesis. Hence ~LY² (-vl-) adv. [f. LL *adversativus* (*adversari* oppose, see foll. & -IVE)]

ăd'věrse, a. Contrary, hostile, (*to*); hurtful, injurious, (*to*); placed opposite. Hence ~LY² (-sl-) adv. [ME, f. OF *adverse* (earlier *avers*) f. L *adversus* p.p. of AD- (*vertere vers-* turn)]

advers'ity̆, n. Condition of adverse fortune; misfortune. [ME, f. OF *adversite* (earlier *av-*) f. L *adversitatem* (as prec., see -TY)]

advěrt', v.i. Refer *to* (in speaking or writing). [ME *avert* f. OF *avertir* f. Rom. *advertire* for L *advertere* (ADVERSE) whence mod. form *advert*]

ăd'vertise (-z), v.t. & i. Notify, warn, inform, (person *of* thing, *that*); make generally known (thing *by* circular, *in* journal, also abs.); ~ *for*, ask for by public notice. [ME *avertise* f. OF *avertir* (st. -*iss*-); see ADVERT]

advěrt'isement (-zm-), n. Public announcement (usu. by placards or in journals). [earlier *avert-* f. F *avertissement* (as prec., see -MENT)]

advíce', n. Opinion given or offered as to action, counsel; information given, news; (pl.) communications from a distance; (Commerc.) formal notice of transactions. [ME *avis* f. OF f. Rom. *advisum* (*ad* to + *visum* p.p. of *videre* see; see AD-]

advís'|able (-z-), a. To be recommended; expedient. Hence ~ABIL'ITY, ~ableNESS, nn., ~abLY² adv. [f. foll. +-ABLE]

advise' (-z), v.t. & i. Offer counsel to; recommend (*the doctor ~s a change of air*); (Commerc.) inform, notify; take counsel *with*. Hence **advís'**ER¹(-z-)n., esp. person habitually consulted. [ME *avise* f. OF *aviser* f. Rom. **advisare* (see ADVICE)]

advised' (-zd), a. Deliberate, considered, whence ~LY² (-íz'édli) adv.; judicious; *ill-~*, injudicious. [p.p. of prec.]

advís'ory̆ (-z-), a. Giving advice; consisting in giving advice. [ADVISE +-ORY]

ăd rit'ăm aut cŭl'păm, adv. During good behaviour. [L]

ăd'vocacy̆, n. Function of an advocate; pleading in support *of*. [ME, f. OF *advocacie*, *-tie*, f. med. L *advocatia* (as foll., see -ACY)]

ăd'vocate¹, n. One who pleads for another; one who speaks in behalf *of* (proposal etc.); professional pleader in courts of justice; *Faculty of A~s*, Scots bar; *Lord A~*, principal law-officer of crown in Scotland; *Devil's ~* (also, L, *advocatus diaboli*), one who pleads against a candidate for canonization. Hence ~SHIP (-ts-) n., **ăd'voc**ātory a. [ME *avocat* f. OF f. L *advocatus* p.p. (as n.) of AD(*vocare* call)]

ăd'vocăte², v.t. Plead for, defend, recommend publicly. [f. prec.]

‖advows'on (-z-), n. Right of presentation to a benefice. [ME (AF) *avowesoun* etc. f. OF *avoeson* f. L *advocationem* (as prec., see -ION)]

ădy̆năm'ia, n. Want of vital force; physical prostration. Hence **ădy̆năm'ic** a. [Gk *adunamia* (a- not +*dunamis* power)]

ăd'y̆tum, n. (pl. -*ta*). Innermost part of a temple; private chamber, sanctum. [L f. Gk *aduton* not to be entered (a- not + *duton* vbl adj. of *duō* enter)]

ădze, n. & v.t. Tool for cutting away surface of wood, like axe with arched blade at right angles to handle; (vb) cut with ~. [OE *adesa* of unkn. orig.]

.æ, ae, symbol repr. a vowel sound betw. *a* & *e*. **1.** In OE short æ repr. orig. Teut. short *a*, the sound of '*a* in *man*; replaced after 1100 usu. by *a* sometimes by *e*. Long æ repr. same sound prolonged, & was replaced in 13th c. by *e* or *ee*. **2.** In 16th c. æ was reintroduced to repr. L *ae* & Gk *ai*; as, *ædify* (L *aedificare*), *æther* (Gk *aithēr*). In familiar wds æ gave place to *e*, (*edify, ether*), being kept (pron. *ē*) in some Gk & L proper names (*Æneas, Cæsar*, but *Judea, Etna*), in names of Gk & Roman antiquities (*ædile, ægis*), & ,in. some scientific terms (*ætiology, phænogamous*, but *phenomenon, museum*).

-æ, -ae, pl. suf. of L nouns of 1st decl. in *-a,* & L form of Gk *-ai* pl. of nouns of 1st decl. in *-ē, -a, -ēs, -as*; kept in non-naturalized words (*laminae, larvae*), esp. in proper names (*Heraclidae*) & names of animal & plant orders (*Felidae, Rosidae*); varying with *-as* in some wds acc. to degree of familiarity (*actiniae, -as*) or of technicality (mathematical *formulae,* theological *formulas*); familiar wds take *-as* (*areas, hyenas, Julias*).

aed'ile, n. Roman magistrate who superintended public buildings, shows, police, etc. Hence ∼SHIP (-lsh-) n. [f. L *aedilis* (*aedes* house, see -ILE)]

‖ **ae'ger,** n. (In Eng. univv.) note certifying that student is ill. [L, = sick]

ae'gis, n. Protection, impregnable defence; (Myth.) shield of Zeus or Athene. [L, f. Gk *aigis*]

‖ **aegrōt'āt,** n. (In Eng. univv.) certificate that student is too ill to attend examination etc. [L, = he is sick (*aeger*)]

Aeōl'ian, a. **1.** Of Aeōlis, district of Asia Minor colonized by ancient Greeks; (Mus.) ∼ *mode,* ancient Greek MODE, ninth of the church modes (with A as final & E as dominant). **2.** Of Aeolus, god of winds; ∼ *harp,* stringed instrument producing musical sounds on exposure to wind. [f. L *Aeolius* (1. *Aeolis* Gk *Aiolis*; 2. *Aeolus* Gk *Aiolos*)+-AN]

Aeōl'ic, a. & n. Aeolian (dialect). [f. L f. Gk *aiolikos* (as prec., see -IC)]

ae'olipȳle, -pile, (*or* ēŏl⁴), n. Instrument for showing force of steam escaping through narrow aperture. [f. F *æolipyle* f. L *Aeoli pylae* f. Gk *Aiolou pulai* gates of Aeolus, god of winds]

aeolŏt'ropȳ, n. Change of physical qualities consequent on change of position. [f. Gk *aiolos* changeful + *-tropia* turning]

ae'on, ē'on, n. An age of the universe, immeasurable period; eternity; (Platonic philosophy) a power existing from eternity, emanation or phase of the supreme deity. [LL *aeon* f. Gk *aiōn* age]

ā'erāte, v.t. Expose to mechanical or chemical action of air; charge with carbonic acid gas (formerly called *fixed air*). Hence **āerᴀ'TION** n. [f. L *aer* air + -ATE³, after F *aérer*]

āēr'ial (*or* āŭ⁴), a. & n. **1.** Of air, gaseous; thin as air, ethereal; immaterial, imaginary; of or in the atmosphere, atmospheric; existing, moving, in the air; ∼ *railway, ropeway,* system of overhead cables from which cars or containers are suspended, usu. driven electrically; ∼ *Derby,* annual air-race. **2.** n. (pron. āŭ⁴). ∼ wire or antenna as used in wireless. Hence ∼ITY (-ăl⁴) n., ∼LY² adv. [f. L f. Gk *aerios* (*aēr* air) + -AL]

aerie, aery, eyrie, eyry, (ā'erĭ, īr'ĭ), n. Nest of bird of prey, esp. eagle, or of raven or other bird that builds high up; human residence perched high on mountain; brood of bird of prey. [f. med. L

aeria, aerea, f. OF *aire* (= Prov. *agre* nest) f. L *ager* agri]

ā'erifórm (*or* āŭ⁴), a. Of the form of air, gaseous; unsubstantial, unreal. [f. L *aer* air + -FORM]

aero- (āŭr'o, ā'ero) in comb. Air, of aircraft, as: ∼*băt'ics,* feats of expert aviation [after *acrobatics*]; ∼*bĭŏl'ogy,* study of airborne micro-organisms or spores; ∼*dȳnăm'ĭcs,* the physics of gases in motion & their mechanical effects; ∼*dȳne,* heavier-than-air aircraft; ∼*foil,* aeroplane wing, tailplane, or fin; ‖∼*grăm,* wireless message; ∼*līte,* ∼*līth,* meteorite; ∼*naut,* one who navigates a (lighter-than-air) flying machine; ∼*naut'ĭc(al)* aa.; ∼*naut'ĭcs,* science, art, or practice of aerial navigation; ∼*plănk'ton,* collective name for all the forms of minute organic life drifting in the air; ∼*stăt,* lighter-than-air aircraft; ∼*stăt'ĭcs,* physics of gases in equilibrium, science of air-navigation. [Gk comb.-form of *aēr* air]

ā'erōbe, n. Any microbe that lives on free oxygen from the air. Hence **āerōb'iᴀN, āerōb'IC,** aa. [AERO-, Gk *bios* life]

‖ **aerodrōme** (āŭ⁴), n. Large tract of open level ground, including all buildings & fixtures, for the operation of aircraft. [AERO-, -DROME]

‖ **aeroplāne** (āŭ⁴), n. Mechanically driven heavier-than-air flying machine. [f. F *aéroplane* (AERO-, Gk *planos* wandering)]

aeru'ginous (ērōō-), a. Of the nature or colour of verdigris, or copper-rust. [f. L *aeruginosus* (*aerugo -inis* verdigris f. *aes aeris* brass, see -OUS)]

Aescūlāp'‖ius, n. God of medicine; physician. Hence ∼iᴀN a. [L]

aes'thēte, n. Professed appreciator of the beautiful. [f. Gk *aisthētēs* one who perceives (as foll.)]

aesthĕt'‖ic, a. Belonging to the appreciation of the beautiful; having such appreciation; in accordance with principles of good taste. Hence ∼ĭCAL a., ∼icᴀLLY² adv., ∼ĭcISM, ∼ĭCS, nn. [f. Gk *aisthētikos* (*aisthanomai* perceive, see -IC)]

aestho-physiŏl'ogȳ (-z-), n. Scientific study of the organs of sensation. [irreg. f. Gk *aisth-* perceive + PHYSIOLOGY]

aestival, (esp. U.S.) **estival** (ĕs'tĭval, ĕstĭv'al), a. Belonging to, appearing in, summer. [ME *estival* f. OF f. L *aestivalis* f. *aestivus* (*aestus* heat), see -IVE, -AL]

aes'tivāte (ēst-, ĕst-), v.i. Spend the summer, esp. (Zool.) in state of torpor. [f. L *aestivare,* see -ATE³]

aestivā'tion (ēst-, ĕst-), n. (Zool.) aestivating; (Bot.) arrangement of petals in flower-bud before expansion. [f. prec., see -ATION]

aetāt'ĭs, aet'ăt., aet. Of or at the age of (*aet.* 17); *anno* ∼ *suae* —, in the —th year of his age. [L]

aetiŏl'ogȳ, n. Assignment of a cause; philosophy of causation; (Med.) science of the causes of disease. So **aetiolŏ'gĭcᴀL**

a., **aetiŏlŏ′gicalLY²** adv. [f. LL f. Gk aitiologia (aitia cause, see -LOGY)]

af-, pref. = AD- before f.

afar′, adv. At, to, a distance (usu. ~ off; from ~, from a distance). [ME of feor, on ferr, see A- (2, 3), FAR]

ăff′able, a. Easy of address, courteous, complaisant. Hence or cogn. **ăffa**BIL′ITY n., **ăff′ab**LY² adv. [F, f. L affabilis f. AF(fari speak), see -BLE]

affair′, n. Thing to be done; concern, business, matter, as that is my ~; love ~; (pl.) ordinary pursuits of life; ~ of honour, duel; (colloq., of material things) a gorgeous etc. ~. ·[ME, f. OF afaire (à faire to do), cf. ADO]

affaire (de cœur) (see Ap.), n. Love affair. [F]

affĕct′¹, v.t. Practise, use, as ~ a costume; (of things) tend to assume (form, shape, etc.); assume (character), as ~ the free-thinker; pretend to have or feel (in-difference etc.); pretend (to do). [f. F affecter or L affectare aim at, frequent. of AF(ficere fect- = facere do)]

affĕct′², v.t. Attack (as disease); move, touch, (in mind), whence ~ingLY² adv.; produce (material) effect on; (pass., arch.) be assigned, allotted, (to particular service etc.). [f. F affecter or L affect- p.p. stem of afficere act on, influence; see prec.]

ăff′ĕct³, n. (psych.). Feeling, emotion, desire. [f. L affectus disposition f. afficere (prec.)]

ăffĕctā′tion, n. Studied display of; arti-ficiality of manner; pretence; (rare) de-clared occupation or employment (all ships, whatever their ~). [F, or f. L affectatio (as AFFECT¹, see -ATION)]

affĕc′tĕd, a. Artificially assumed or dis-played; pretended; (of persons) full of affectation, artificial, whence ~LY² adv., ~NESS n.; (with adv.) disposed, inclined, (towards or abs.); attacked (as by disease); moved in the feelings; acted upon physically. [AFFECT¹, ² + -ED¹]

affĕc′tion, n. Affecting; mental state, emotion, whence ~AL a.; disposition (towards); goodwill, love, (towards); bodily state due to any influence; malady, disease; mode of living; property, quality, attribute. [ME, f. OF f. L affectionem (as AFFECT², see -ION)]

affĕc′tionate (-shon-), a. Loving; fond; (of things) showing love or tenderness. Hence ~LY² (-tl-) adv., ~NESS (-tn-) n. [f. F affectionné or med. L affectionatus; see -ATE³]

affĕc′tive, a. Pertaining to the affections, emotional. [f. F affectif f. LL affectivus (as AFFECT², see -IVE)]

ăff′erent, a. Conducting inwards or to-wards, as ~ nerves, ~ vessels. [f. L AF-(ferre bring), see -ENT]

ăffĕttuŏ′sŏ (-tōō-), adv. (mus.). Feel-ingly. [It.]

affi′ance¹, n. Faith, trust (in); pledging of faith, esp. plighting of troth in mar-riage. [ME, f. OF afiancè f. after f. med. L AFfidare (fidus trusty), see -ANCE]

affi′ance², v.t. Promise solemnly in mar-riage (usu. pass.). [ME, f. OF afiancer f. afiance, see prec.]

affiche (àfèsh′), n. Notice-paper affixed to wall, poster. [F, f. afficher post up]

ăffĭdāv′it, n. Written statement, con-firmed by oath, to be used as judicial proof. (Strictly, deponent swears an ~, judge takes it; but in pop. use deponent makes or takes it). [med. L, = has stated on oath, f. AFfidare, see AFFIANCE¹]

affil′iāte, v.t. (Of an institution) adopt (persons as members, societies as branches); attach (persons, societies) to, connect (them) with, (a society); (Law) fix paternity of (illegitimate child on putative father) for purpose of main-tenance; ascribe (child) to its parent; father (a thing) upon, trace (it) to. So **affilia′tion** n. [f. med. L AFfiliare adopt (filius son), see -ATE³]

affined′ (-nd), a. Related, connected. [f. F affiné (affin f. L affinis, see foll.) + -ED¹; no vb in F or E]

affin′itȳ, n. Relationship, relations, by marriage; relations, kindred, in general; structural resemblance (between animals, plants, languages); (fig.) similarity of character suggesting relationship, family likeness; liking; attraction; (Chem.) ten-dency of certain elements to unite with others. [ME, f. OF afinite f. L affinitatem (AFfinis related, lit. bordering on, f. finis end, see -TY)]

affĭrm′, v.t. & i. Assert strongly, aver; make formal declaration, (Law) make AFFIRMATION; (Logic, Gram.) state in the affirmative; (Law) confirm, ratify, (judge-ment). Hence ~ABLE, ~atORY, aa. [ME af(f)erm(e) f. OF afermer f. L AFfirmare (firmus strong)]

affĭrmā′tion, n. Affirming, esp. (Law) solemn declaration by person who con-scientiously declines taking an oath. [F, or f. L affirmatio (as prec., see -ATION)]

affĭrm′ative, a. & n. Affirming, answer-ing yes; (Logic) expressing agreement of the two terms of a proposition; answer in the ~, answer yes, say that a thing is so. Hence ~LY² (-vl-) adv. [ME, f. OF affirmatif or LL affirmativus (as prec., see -IVE)]

affix′¹, v.t. Fix, fasten, (thing to, on); impress (seal, stamp); add in writing (signature, postscript); attach (censure, salary). [f. obs. F affixer or med. L affixare frequent. of L AF(figere fix- fix)]

ăff′ix², n. Appendage, addition; (Gram.) addition placed at the beginning or end of root, stem, or word, or in body of word, to modify its meaning. [f. F affixe f. L affigere (see prec.)]

affix′ture, n. Affixing. [f. AFFIX¹ after FIXTURE]

afflāt′us, n. Communication of super-natural knowledge; divine impulse, poetic or other; inspiration. [L vbl n. f. AF(*flare flat-* blow)]

afflict', v.t. Distress with bodily or mental suffering. [f. obs. *afflict* adj., f. OF *afflict*, earlier *afflit*, f. L AF(*fligere flict-*dash)]

afflic't|ion, n. Misery, distress; pain, calamity. So ∼IVE a. [ME, f. OF f. L *afflictionem* (as prec., see -ION)]

äff'lu|ent¹ (-lŏŏ-), a. Flowing freely, copious; abounding (esp. in riches), wealthy. Hence or cogn. ∼ENCE n., ∼entLY² adv. [ME, f. OF, f. L AF(*fluere flux-* flow), see -ENT]

äff'luent² (-lŏŏ-), n. Tributary stream. [f. prec., prob. after F]

äff'lūx, n. Flow towards a point, esp. of humours; accession. [f. F, or med. L *affluxus -ūs*, vbl n. as AFFLUENT¹]

affōrd', v.t. (With *can*) have the means, be rich enough, (*to* do), manage to spare; furnish, bestow; (of things) yield supply of. [OE *geforthian* further (f. Y- + *forthian* (FORTH), ME *i-forthen*, *aforthe*. Mod. sp. assim. to wds in AF-; for *-d-* cf. BURDEN]

affō'rĕst, v.t. Convert into forest or (formerly) hunting-ground. So ∼A'TION n. [f. med. L AF*forestare* (*foresta* FOREST)]

affrän'chīse (-z), v.t. Free from servitude or obligation. [f. F *affranchir*, as EN-FRANCHISE, with pref. A- (4)]

affray', n. Breach of the peace, caused by fighting or riot in a public place. [ME, f. OF *effrei* f. *esfreer*, vb f. Rom. *exfridare* (Rom. *fridus* f. Gmc *fridhu* peace); cf. AFRAID]

affreight'ment (-rāt-), n. The chartering of a ship to carry cargo (usu. *contract of* ∼). [f. F *affrétement*, with sp. alt. after FREIGHT]

äff'ricate, n. (phonet.). Combination of explosive consonant with an immediately following fricative or spirant, as G *pf*, *z*(= ts). So **affric'atIVE** a. & n. [f. L *affricatus*, cf. FRICATIVE]

affright'¹ (-īt), v.t. (arch.) Frighten. [late formation on FRIGHT v., partly due to obs. *affright* p.p. of OE *afyrhtan* (a-intensive)]

affright'² (-īt), n. (arch.). Alarm, terror. [f. prec.]

affront'¹ (-ŭnt), v.t. Insult openly: put to the blush, offend the modesty or self--respect of; face, confront. [ME, f. OF *afronter* slap in the face, insult, f. Rom. *AFfrontare* (*frons frontis* face)]

affront'² (-ŭnt), n. Open insult, as *put* ∼ *upon, offer an* ∼ *to, feel it an* ∼. [f. prec.]

affū'sion (-zhn), n. Pouring on, esp. of water on the body in one kind of baptism; (Med.) pouring of water, usually 50° to 70° Fahr., upon fever patients. [f. LL *affusio* f. L AF(*fundere fus-* pour), see -ION]

Afghan (äf'găn), n. Native, language, of ∼istan; (*a*∼) knitted woollen coverlet.

afield', adv. On or in the field (esp. of labour or battle); tŏ the fiel̃d; away from home, ät ạ distance, as *far* ∼. [OE, f. A²]

afīre', adv. & pred. a. On fire (lit. & fig.). [ME, f. A²]

aflame', adv. & pred. a. In flame, in a glow of light, (lit. & fig.). [f. A²]

afloat', adv. & pred. a. In a floating condition; at sea, on board ship, in naval service; full of water; floating in the air; out of debt, paying one's way; in full swing; in general circulation, current; (Commerc.) in currency as negotiable document; unsettled, adrift. [OE, f. A²]

à fond (see Ap.), adv. Thoroughly, fully. [F]

afŏŏt', adv. & pred. a. On one's own feet; astir, on the move; in operation or employment. [ME, f. A²]

afōre', adv. & prep. (Naut.) in front, in front of, as ∼ *the mast*; (arch.) previously. [OE, f. A² + FORE²]

afōre- in comb. Before, previously, as ∼*cited*, ∼*going*, ∼*named*, ∼*said*; ∼*thought*, premeditated, as *malice* ∼*thought*; ∼*time*, previously. [prec.]

ā fortiōr'ī, adv. With stronger reason, more conclusively. [L]

afraid', pred. a. Alarmed, frightened, (abs. or *of*); ∼ (of the consequences, & therefore unwilling) *to do* a thing, ∼ *of* a thing's *happening*, ∼ *lest it should happen*, ∼ *(that) it will happen*; *I'm* ∼ (colloq.), I have to admit with regret (*I'm* ∼ *I'm late*; *I'm* ∼ *there's none left*). [p.p. of obs. vb *affray* f. OF *esfreer*, see AFFRAY]

äf'reet, -rit, -rite, (-rēt), n. Evil demon in Mohammedan mythology. [Arab. *ifrīt*]

afrĕsh', adv. Anew, with fresh beginning. [A- (3) | FRESH]

Af'rican (äf-), a. & n. (Native) of Africa. Hence ∼ISM (4) n., ∼IZE (3) v.t. [see -AN]

Afrikaans' (äf-; -ahns), n. S.-African or Cape Dutch. [= Du. *Afrikaansch*]

Afrikän'der (äf-), n. S.-African breed of cattle; (formerly) Afrikaner. [f. Afrikaans *Afrikaander* alt. of Du. *Afrikaner* after *Hollander* etc.]

Afrika'ner (äfrīkahn-), n. Native of S. Africa born of European (esp. Dutch) settlers. [Du., = African]

Af'r(ō)- (äf-), comb. form of *African*.

aft (ahft), adv. (naut.). In or near stern of ship; towards the stern; *fore & ∼*, from stem to stern, lengthwise (also as adj. *fore-&-*∼). [hist. before 1600 obsc.; prob. alt. f. ME *baft* (see ABAFT) on anal. of *after*]

af'ter¹ (ah-), adv., prep., & conj. **1**. adv. Behind in place, later in time, (*Jill came tumbling* ∼; *look before & ∼*; *soon, a week,*∼). **2**. prep. In pursuit or quest of, as *run, inquire,* ∼ *him*; about, concerning, as *look* ∼ *him*, take care of, keep an eye on, *him*; for, as *hanker* ∼; following in point of time, later than, (∼ *you*, formula in yielding precedence; ∼ *you with*, colloq. request for next turn at; ∼ *six months,* when six months have or had elapsed); in view of, as ~ such behaviour; next in importance to; according to (~ a FASHION; ~ one's own heart, such as one loves); in imitation of (person), as a picture ~ Rubens; in allusion to, as named ~; ~ all, in spite of all that has happened or has been said etc. (~ all, what does it matter?) or of one's exertions, expectations, etc. (he tried for an hour & failed ~ all; so you have come ~ all!). **3.** conj. In, at, the time subsequent to that at which, as ~ he went, goes, has gone, had gone. [OE æfter, Gmc f. *af- (cogn. w. L ab, Gk apo) +compar. suf. *-ter (see -THER)]

af'ter² (ah-), a. Later, following, as ~ years; (Naut.) hinder, posterior, as ~ cabin, masts. [f. prec.]

af'terbirth, n. Membrane enveloping the foetus in the womb, so called because its extrusion follows that of the infant, placenta. [AFTER a.]

af'ter-care, n. Attention bestowed on an individual or class after a certain period of treatment etc.; freq. attrib., as ~ association. [AFTER a.]

af'terdamp, n. Choke-damp, gas left in mine after explosion of fire-damp. [AFTER a.]

af'ter-effect, n. Effect that follows after an interval. [AFTER a.]

af'terglow, n. Glow in the west after sunset. [AFTER a.]

af'ter-grass, n. Grass that grows after first crop has been mown for hay, or among stubble after harvest. [AFTER a.]

af'terlight, n. Light of what is known afterwards, hindsight. [AFTER a.]

af'termãth, n. After-grass; (fig.) consequences, fruits, results, as the ~ of war. [AFTER a. +math mowing, OE mǣth f. Gmc *mē- MOW]

af'termost (ah-), a. (naut.). Nearest the stern, most aft. [f. AFTER +-MOST]

afternoon', n. The time from noon to evening, as in, during, the ~, on Wednesday ~, (fig.) the ~ of life. [AFTER prep.]

af'terpiece, n. Farce or smaller entertainment after a play. [AFTER a.]

af'ters (ah-), n. pl. (colloq.). Course following main course esp. at midday meal. [AFTER a. or adv.]

af'terthought, n. Reflection after the act; later expedient or explanation. [AFTER a. or adv.]

af'terwards (ah-; -z), adv. Later, subsequently. [OE æftanweard, a. (æftan AFT +-WARD), late OE æfterweard, ME -ward(s): see -ES]

ag-, pref. = AD- before g.

aga (ǎʒ'a, agah'), n. Commander, chief officer in Mohammedan countries. [Turk. agha master]

again' (or agěn'), adv. Another time, once more; ~ & ~, time & ~, repeatedly; ever & ~, now & ~, occasionally; as much ~, twice as much; half as much ~, one-&-a- -half times as much; further, besides;

on the other hand, as these ~ are more expensive; back ~ (to the original position or condition); in return, as answer ~; in response, as rocks echoed ~, glasses rang ~; proportionately to specified act or condition, as the loaded table groaned ~. [OE ongēan, ongǣgn, etc., ME ayen etc., &c (orig. north.) again; Gmc f. ON + *gag-an- straight]

against' (or agěnst'), prep. & conj. **1.** In opposition to, as fight ~, I am ~ reform; in contrast to, as ~ a dark background; in anticipation of, as ~ his coming, ~ a rainy day; in preparation for, as warned ~ pickpockets; into collision with, as ran ~ a rock, (colloq.) ran ~ (chanced to meet) a friend; opposite to, as ~ the horsepond (usu. over ~). **2.** conj. (arch.). By the time that (be ready ~ he comes). [early ME ayenes etc., f. ayen (AGAIN) +-ES, with later (southern) inorganic -t as in amidst, amongst, betwixt, whilst]

ãg'ama, n. African & Indian lizard of the iguana type. [Carib]

ãg'ami, n. Tropical American bird, the trumpeter. [native name in Guiana]

agãm'ic, a. (zool.). Characterized by absence of sexual action. [as foll. +-IC]

ãgamo|gěn'ésis, n. Asexual reproduction. So ~gěnět'ic a., ~gěnět'ICALLY adv. [as foll. +genesis birth]

ãg'amous, a. (biol.). Without (distinguishable) sexual organs. [f. Gk agamos (a- not +gamos marriage) +-ous]

agãpe'¹, adv. & pred. a. On the gape; open-mouthed with wonder or expectation. [A prep.]

ãg'apē², n. Love-feast held by early Christians in connexion with Lord's Supper; (Theol.) Christian love, charity (opp. erōs earthly or sexual love). [Gk, = brotherly love]

Agapemon|e (ǎgapěm'onǐ), n. Love-abode (usu. with sinister implication). Hence ~ITE¹ n. & a., (member) of a sect or association founded in Somerset c. 1850, pop. believed to practise free love. [irreg. f. Gk agapē love +monē abode]

ãg'ãr(-ãg'ãr), n. Solidifying agent in culture-media for bacteria prepared from certain seaweeds. [Malay]

ãg'aric (or agǎ²), n. Mushroom; name of various fungi. [f. L f. Gk agarikon]

ãg'ate, n. Name of several varieties of precious stone (semipellucid variegated chalcedonies); burnishing instrument of gold-wiredrawers; *the printing-type called in England ruby. [f. F agate, -the, It. agata, -tha, f. L f. Gk akhatēs, whence earlier F achate, in ME achate]

Agãv'é, n. (bot.). Genus of plants, including American aloe. [f. L f. Gk Agauē, prop. name in myth.]

agãze', adv. On the gaze. [A prep.]

ãge'¹, n. Length of life or of existence; moon's ~, time elapsed since new moon; duration of life required for a purpose, as come of ~, full ~ (in Eng. Law, 21 years),

~ *of discretion* (14), *over* ~; latter part of life, as *peevishness of* ~, ~ *before honesty*, children must give precedence to their elders; a generation; ~ *of* CONSENT; BRAZEN [1] etc.~; (Hist., Geol.) great period, as *Patriarchal A*~, *Ice A*~; (colloq.) long time, as *waiting for*~s. [ME, f. OF f. Rom. **ætaticum* f. L *aetas -atis* age; see -AGE]

āge², v.t. & i. (part. ~*ing*, *aging*). (Cause to) grow old. [f. prec.]

-age, suf. OF f. L *-aticum*, neut. of adj. suf. *-aticus* -ATIC (e.g. L *viaticum* journeymoney, (later) journey). In Romanic greatly extended to form abst. nn. of appurtenance, & collectives, as **aelaticum* AGE, **coraticum* COURAGE. In med. L, the OF *-age* appears as *-agium*, e.g. OF *homage*, med. L *homagium*. Afterwards added as living suf. in F & in E. Meaning: (1) collective belongings or aggregate of (*cellarage*); (2) function, condition, (*baronage*, *bondage*); (3) action (*breakage*); (4) fees payable for, cost of using, (*cartage*, *demurrage*).

aged, a. 1. (āj'ĭd). Having lived long, old. 2. (ājd). Of the age of, as ~ *ten*; (of horses) over six years old. Hence **ā'gèd**-NESS n. [f. AGE v. +-ED[1]]

āge'lèss (-jl-), a. Never growing old. [AGE n. +-LESS]

ā'gencȳ, n. Active operation, action, as *moral*, *free*, ~; instrumentality, as *by the* ~ *of*; action personified, as *an invisible* ~; (Commerc.) office of agent; establishment for business purposes, as *Reuter's A*~. [f. med. L *agentia* (L *agere* do, see -ENCE)]

agĕn'da, n. Things to be done, (list of) items of business to be considered at a meeting; memorandum book. [L, neut. pl. of gerundive of *agere* do]

ā'gēne, n. Nitrogen trichloride, used for whitening flour. [P]

ā'gent, n. One who exerts power or produces an effect; (of things) efficient cause; a natural force acting on matter, as *chemical* ~; one who does the actual work, esp. one who represents a person or firm in business (*who is your* ~ *in Paris?*); *estate-*, *house-*, *land-*, ~. So **agĕn'tIAL** (-shl) a. [as ACT², -ENT]

agent provocateur (see Ap.), n. Person employed to detect suspected offenders by tempting them to overt action. [F]

agglŏm'er|āte¹, v.t. & i. Collect into a mass. Hence ~A'TION n., ~ātIVE a. [f. L AGglomerare (glomus'-meris ball), see -ATE²]

agglŏm'erate², a. & n. (Collected into a mass; (Geol.) mass of volcanic fragments united under heat, opp. to *conglomerate*. [as prec., see -ATE²]

agglut'ināte¹ (-lōō-), a. Glued together; consisting of simple words combined into compounds without change of form or loss of meaning. [f. L AGglutinare (gluten *-tinis* glue) see -ATE²]

agglut'in|āte² (-lōō-), v.t. & i. Unite with glue; combine simple words to express compound ideas; (t. & i.) turn into glue. Hence ~A'TION n., ~ātIVE a. [as prec., see -ATE³]

ăgg'randīze, -īse (-īz), v.t. Increase the power, rank, wealth, of (person, State); exaggerate, embellish. Hence **aggrăn'-**dizeMENT, **-īse-**, (-zm-) n. [f. F *agrandir* (st. *-iss-*) prob. f. It. AG(*grandire* f. L *grandis* large, the ending being assim. to vbs in -IZE)]

ăgg'rav|āte, v.t. Increase the gravity of (burden, offence, etc.); (colloq.) exasperate (person). So ~A'TION n. [f. L AGgravare make heavy (*gravis*) or F *aggraver*; see -ATE³]

ăgg'rëgāte¹, a. & n. 1. Collected into one body; collective, total; (Law) composed of associated individuals, as *corporation* ~. 2. Sum total; assemblage; broken stone etc. used in making concrete; (Phys.) mass of homogeneous particles; *in the* ~, as a whole. [f. L AGgregare herd together (*grex gregis* flock), see -ATE[1, 2]]

ăgg'rëg|āte², v.t. & i. Collect together; (trans.) unite (individual to company); amount to (specified total). Hence ~A'TION n., ~ātIVE a. [f. as prec., -ATE³]

ăgg'rëss, v.i. (rare). Begin a (or the) quarrel. So ~ION (-shn), ~OR, nn. [f. p.p. of L AG(*gredi gress-* = *gradi* step) or F *ag(g)resser*; later back-form. f. *aggression*]

ăgg'rëss'īve, a. & n. Of attack; offensive; disposed to attack; forceful; *assume the* ~, begin the quarrel. Hence ~LY² (-vl-) adv., ~NESS (-vn-) n. [as prec., see -IVE]

ăgg'rieve', v.t. Grieve, distress, oppress, (usu. pass.). [ME *agreve* f. OF *agrever* f. L *aggravare*, AGGRAVATE; mod. sp. after L, & GRIEVE]

aghast' (-gahst, -găst), a. Terrified; struck with amazement. [ME p.p. of obs. vb *agast* (A- (1) + *gasten*, obs. *gast* to alarm); sp. after *ghastly*]

ā'gīle, a. Quick-moving, nimble, active. Hence or cogn. **agil'ITY** n., ~LY² (-l-li) adv. [ME, f. OF f. L *agilis* (*agere* do)]

ā'giō, n. Percentage charged on exchange of paper-money into cash, or of one currency into another more valuable; excess value of one currency over another; exchange business. [It., = ease]

ā'giotage, n. Exchange business; speculation in stocks; stock-jobbing. [F, f. *agioter* (prec. + connecting *-t-*); see -AGE]

agist', v.t. Take in live stock to feed; charge (land or its owner) with a public burden. So ~MENT n. [f. OF *agister* (à to + *gister* lodge f. Rom. **jacitare* frequent. of *jacere* lie)]

ā'gitāte, v.t. Move, shake; disturb, excite, (feelings, persons); revolve mentally, discuss, debate, (plans etc.); (abs.) keep up an agitation (*for*). [f. L *agitare* or F *agiter*; see -ATE³]

ăgitā'tion, n. Moving, shaking; commotion, disturbance, (mental or physical); debate, discussion; keeping of a matter constantly before the public; public excitement. [F, or f. L *agitatio* (as prec., see -ATION)]

ăgĭtā'tō (-tah-)‚ adv. (mus.)‚ In an agitated manner. [It.]

ă'gĭtātor, n. One who agitates, esp. politically; apparatus for shaking or mixing. [L (see AGITATE & -OR)]

Aglaia (ăgli'a), n. One of the Graces. [Gk]

ăg'lĕt, aig'lĕt, n. Metal tag of a lace; spangle or other metallic ornament of dress; tagged point hanging from shoulder upon breast of some uniforms (usu. *aiguillette*); catkin of hazel, birch, etc. [ME, f. F *aiguillette* dim. of *aiguille* needle f. LL *acucula* dim. of *acus* needle]

agley' (-ē), adv. (Sc.). Askew, awry. [A prep. +Sc. *gley* squint]

aglow' (-ō), adv. & pred. a. In a glow. [A prep.]

ăg'nail, n. Torn skin at root of finger- -nail; (formerly) corn on toe or foot. [OE *angnægl* f. **ang-* (cf. Goth. *aggwus*) tight, painful, +*nægl* nail (of iron etc.), hard excrescence fixed in the flesh; mod. sense, & forms *hang-nail*, (Sc.) *anger-nail*, result from pop. etym., *nail* being taken as finger-nail]

ăg'nāte, n. & a. (One who is) descended by male links (also, by male or female links) from same male ancestor (cf. COGNATE); sprung from same forefather, of same clan or nation; (fig.) akin, of same nature. So **ăgnăt'ic** a., **ăgna'tion** n. [f. F *agnat* or L *agnatus* (ad to +*gnatus* born p.p. of (*g)nasci* f. stem *gen*-beget)]

ăgnōm'ĕn, n. A fourth name occas. given to Romans (cf. COGNOMEN); (loosely) nick- name. [L (*ad* to +(*g)nomen* name)]

agnŏs'tic, n. & a. **1.** One who holds that nothing is known, or likely to be known, of the existence of a God or of anything beyond material phenomena. **2.** adj. Pertaining to this theory. Hence ~ISM n. [f. Gk *agnōstos* unknown (*a-* not +*gnō*- know); see -IC]

Ag'nus Căs'tus (ă-), n. Tree once held a preservative of chastity. [L, f. Gk *agnos* (name of tree), confused w. *hagnos* chaste, whence L *castus* is added]

Ag'nus Dē'ī (ă-),‚n. Part of Mass begin- ning *Agnus Dei*; figure of lamb bearing cross or flag; cake of wax stamped with such figure & blessed by Pope. [L, = lamb of God]

agō', a. & adv. (Adj., always following noun) past, gone by, as *ten years* ~; (adv.) *long* ~, long since. [ME *ago*, *agone* p.p. of obs. vb *ago* (A-(1) +GO)]

agŏg', adv. & pred. a. On the move, eager, expectant. [perh. f. OF *en gogues* (*gogue* fun, orig. unkn.)]

agŏn'ic, a. Making no angle; ~ *line*, line of no magnetic variation. [f. Gk *agōnios* without angle (*a-* not +*gōnia* angle) +-IC]

ăgonis'tic, a. Pertaining to athletic con- tests (esp. of Ancient Greece); (Rhet.) polemic, combative; strained, aiming at effect. Hence ~AL a., ~alLY² adv. [f. Gk *agōnistikos* f. *agōnistēs* combatant (*agōnes* games); cf. LL *agonisticus*]

ăg'onīz|e, -is|e (-īz), v.t. & i. Torture; suffer agony, writhe in anguish; contend in arena, wrestle (lit. & fig.); make desperate efforts for effect. Hence ~ingLY² adv. [f. F *agoniser* or LL *agonizare* f. Gk *agōnizomai* contend (*agōn*, see prec.)]

ăg'onỹ, n. Mental anguish; ~ *column* (colloq.), = PERSONAL *column*; paroxysm of pleasure; pangs of death; extreme bodily suffering; struggle. [ME, f. OF *agonie* or LL *agonia* f. Gk *agōnia* f. *agōn* contest; see -Y¹]

ăgoraphōb'ia, n. Dread in and, of open spaces. [Gk *agora* assembly, -PHOBIA]

agou'tĭ, -tỹ, (-gōō-), n. Genus of rodents of cavy or guinea-pig family, esp.'a hare- like animal of W. Indies. [f. F *agouti* or Sp. *aguti* f. native Ind. *aguti*]

ăg'rapha, n. pl. Sayings of Christ not recorded in the Gospels. [Gk, = un- written things]

agrār'ian, a. & n. **1.** Relating to landed property; ~ *outrage* (arising from discord between landlords & tenants); relating to cultivated land. **2.** n. Advocate of re- distribution of landed property, whence ~ISM n., ~IZE v.t. & i. [f. L *agrarius* (*ager agri* land, see -ARY¹) +-AN]

agree', v.i. & t. Consent (*to* proposal, statement, *to* do); concur (*with* person *that*); become, be, in harmony (*with* per- son); (pl.) ~ *together, cannot* ~, get on with one another; suit the constitution of, as *work, lobster, does not* ~ *with him*; (Gram.) take some number, gender, case, person; (trans.) bring (balance, items of accounts) into harmony; consent to or approve of (proposal, terms, etc.). [ME, f. OF *agreer* f. Rom. **aggratare* make agreeable (*gratus*)]

agree'ab|le (-rīabl), a. Pleasing (*to* or abs.); (colloq., of persons) well-disposed (*to* a thing, *to* do, or abs.); conformable *to*, as ~*le to all experience*. Hence ~leNESS n., ~LY² adv. [ME, f. OF *agreable* (*agreer* AGREE, see -ABLE)]

agree'ment, n. Mutual understanding, covenant, treaty; (Law) contract legally binding on parties; accordance in opinion; (Gram.) concord in gender, number, case, person. [ME, partly OF, partly f. AGREE +-MENT]

agrément (agrā'mahň), n. pl. Agreeable qualities or surroundings; (Mus.) orna- mental notes embellishing a melody. [F]

agrĕs'tic, a. Rural, rustic; uncouth. [f. L *agrestis* (*ager* field) +-IC]

ăg'ricŭlture, n. Cultivation of the soil. Hence **ăgrĭcŭl'turAL** (-cher-) a., **ăgri- cŭl'tur(al)ıST** (-cher-) nn. [F, or f. L *agri cultura* (*ager agri* field +*cultura* CUL- TURE)]

ăg'rimonỹ, n. Kinds of plants, esp. *Agrimonia Eupatoria* with small yellow flowers. [ME *egrimoigne* etc. f. OF *aigremoine* f. L *agrimonia*, whence OE & mod. forms]

ăg'rimōtor, n. Agricultural motor tractor. [f. L *ager agri* field + MOTOR]

agrŏn'om|**y̆**, n. Rural economy, husbandry. So **ăgronŏm'ic**(AL) aa., **ăgronŏm'ics**, ~IST, nn. [f. Gk *agronomos* overseer of land (*agros* land + *-nomos* f. *nemō* dispense), see -Y¹]

aground', adv. & pred. a. Upon the bottom of shallow water, as *be, run, ~* (of ships). [ME, f. A prep. + GROUND]

ăg'ŭe, n. Malarial fever, with cold, hot, & sweating stages; shivering fit; quaking (lit. & fig.); ~*-cake*, enlargement of spleen or liver caused by ~. Hence **ăg'ŭED²** (-ūd) a. [ME, f. OF f. L *acuta* (sc. *febris* fever) ACUTE]

ăg'ŭish, a. Of the nature of ague; tending to produce ague; subject to ague; aguelike, quaking; coming by fits & starts. Hence ~LY² adv. [f. prec. + -ISH¹]

ah, int. expr. sorrow, regret, surprise, admiration, entreaty, remonstrance, dislike, contempt, mockery. [not in OE; ME has a, perh. f. OF *a, ah*]

aha¹ (ahhah'), int. expr. surprise, triumph, mockery, irony. [f. AH + HA¹; formerly written *a ha*]

aha², n. See HA-HA n.

ahead (ahĕd'), adv. & pred. a. In advance; in the direct line of one's forward motion, as *breakers ~*; straight forwards; forward at a rapid pace, as *go ~*; in advance *of* (lit. & fig.). [f. A prep. + HEAD¹]

ahem' (a-h-), int. used to attract attention or gain time. [lengthened form of *hem*]

ahimsa (a-hĭm'sah), n. Non-violence or non-killing acclaimed in Hindu Scriptures as the highest form of duty. [f. Skr. *a* without, *himsa* injury]

ahoy' (a-h-), int. Nautical call used in hailing. [obs. *a* int. + HOY²]

Ah'riman. See ZOROASTRIAN.

à huis clos (ah wē klō), adv. With closed doors, in private. [F]

ahŭll' (a-h-), adv. (naut.). With sails taken in & helm lashed on lee side. [f. A prep. + HULL²]

ai (ah'ī), n. Three-toed sloth of S. America. [f. Braz. *aí*, repr. its cry]

aiblins. See ABLINGS.

aid¹, v.t. Help (person *to* do, or abs.); promote (recovery etc.). [ME, f. OF *aid(i)er* f. L *adjutare* frequent. of AD-(*juvare jut*-)]

aid², n. Help; (Law) help claimed by defendant from one who has joint-interest; (hist.) grant of subsidy or tax to king, (later) exchequer loan; helper; material source of help (usu. pl.), as *~s & appliances*; *what's (all) this in ~ of?* (colloq.), what's your object? [ME, f. OF *aide* f. Rom. *adjuta fem. p.p. of *adjuvare* AID¹ used as n.; cf. LL *adjutus* help]

aide (ād), n. = foll. [abbr.]

aide-de-camp (ād'ekong, & see Ap.),

n. (pl. *aides-de-camp* pron. ăd'ekŏngz). Officer assisting general by carrying orders etc. [F]

aide-mémoire (ād'māmwahr), n. (Book, document, serving as) an aid to the memory (esp. in diplomatic use). [F, f. *aider* to help + *mémoire* memory]

aig'rĕtte, n. Lesser white heron (usu. EGRET); tuft of feathers or hair; spray of gems etc. [F, see EGRET]

aig'uill|**e** (-gw-), n. Sharp peak of rock, esp. in Alps. Hence ~ESQUE' a. [F, see AGLET]

aiguillette (āgwĭlĕt'), n. See AGLET.

ail, v.t. & i. Trouble, afflict, as *what ~s him?*; be ill. Hence **ail'MENT** n. [f. OE *eglan* (cogn. w. Goth. *agljan*) f. *egle* troublesome (Goth. *aglus*)]

ail'erŏn, n. (usu. pl.). Lateral-control flap(s) at rear of aeroplane's wingtip(s). [F]

aim¹, v.t. & i. Direct (blow, missile, *at*); point (gun etc.) towards (*at*); direct an act or proceeding against (*at*); (intr.) deliver blow, discharge missile, (*at*); take aim (abs.); form designs (abs.); *intend or try *to* do. [ME, prob. f. two vbs (1) Picard. *amer*, OF & Prov. *esmer*, f. L *aestimare* reckon, (2) OF *aësmer* f. Rom. *adaestimare; ME sense was *estimate*]

aim², n. Direction of a missile at an object, as *take ~*; design, purpose, object, whence **aim'LESS** a., **aim'lĕssly²** adv., **aim'lĕssNESS** n. [ME, f. prec.]

ain't. See BE.

air¹, n. **1.** Gaseous substance enveloping earth, mixture of oxygen & nitrogen, breathed by all land animals & plants; atmosphere; free space overhead, as *birds of the ~*; unconfined space, as *open ~*; *fresh ~*, also simply *~*, *~ not exhausted of its oxygen*; breeze, light wind; *take ~*, become known; (of projects etc.) *quite in the ~* (uncertain); (of opinions, feelings) *in the ~*, spreading about; *castles in the ~*, visionary projects; **give person the ~* (sl.), dismiss him; *on the ~*, broadcast(ing) by radio. **2.** Appearance, as *an ~ of absurdity*; mien, gesture, as *with a triumphant ~*; affected manner (esp. in pl.), as *gave himself ~s, ~s & graces*; (Mus.) melody, tune, esp., in harmonized composition, predominant (usu. soprano) part. **3.** Combb.: ~-*ball(oon)*, inflated toy; ~-*bed*, inflated mattress; ~-*bladder*, one filled with ~, in animals or plants; ~*'borne*: transported by ~; specially picked & trained for ~ operations, as *an ~borne division*; (of ~craft) in the ~, having taken off, as *the squadron was soon ~borne*; ~-*brake* (worked by ~ pressure); ~-*brick* (perforated for ventilation); ~-*bridge*, link between points provided by ~ transport; ~-*chamber* (in hydraulic machines, for equalizing pressure); *Air Chief Marshal, Air Commodore*, see *Air Force*; ~-*conditioned*, (of a room, building, etc.) having the ~ in it washed & brought to standard humidity (& temperature); ~-*cooled* (by a current of cool ~); ~'*craft*, aeroplane(s), ~ship(s), & balloon(s); ~*craft carrier*, ship that carries & serves as a base for aeroplanes; ~*craftman*, see *Air Force*; ~-*craftwoman*, lowest rank in Women's Royal Air Force; ~ *crew* (of an ~craft); ~-*cushion* (inflated with ~); *~'*drome*, aerodrome; ~-*engine* (actuated by heated ~); ~'*field*, aerodrome; *Air Force* (*the Royal Air Force*, abbr. *R.A.F.*), the ~craft service co-ordinate with Navy & Army, with officers as follows: *Marshal of the R.A.F.*, *Air Chief Marshal*, *Air Marshal*, *Air Vice-Marshal*, *Air Commodore*, *Group Captain*, *Wing Commander*, *Squadron Leader*, *Flight Lieutenant*, *Flying Officer*, *Pilot Officer*; the non-commissioned ranks are *warrant officer*, *flight sergeant*, *sergeant*, *corporal*, (*leading*)~*craftman*, ~-*mechanic*; ~-*frame*, body of ~craft as dist. from engine(s); ~'*graph*, system of transmitting letters etc. by ~ mail in the form of microfilms to save space, letter etc. so transmitted; ~-*gun* (using compressed ~ as propelling force); ~ *hostess*, stewardess on ~ liner; ~-*jacket* (inflated, to support wearer in water); ~-*lift*, transport of troops, supplies, etc. by ~; ~'*line*, line of ~craft for public service; ~ *liner*, large passenger ~craft; ~-*lock*, stoppage of flow in pump etc., caused by ~; ~ *mail* (carried by ~); ~'*man*, one who flies in an ~craft, esp. as pilot or member of crew; *Air Marshal*, ~-*mechanic*, see *Air Force*; ~-*minded*, interested in aviation; *Air Officer*, R.A.F. officer above the rank of Group Captain; *~'*plane*, aeroplane; ~-*pocket*, apparent vacuum in ~ causing ~craft to drop some distance; ~'*port*, aerodrome, esp. one fully equipped, usu. with customs-house, at which passengers by ~ liners embark or disembark; *~ post*, ~mail; ~-*pump* (for exhausting a vessel of its ~); ~ *raid*, attack by ~craft (freq. attrib., as ~-*raid precautions*, *warden*, *warning*); ~'*screw*, propeller of ~craft; ~'*ship*, flying machine lighter than ~; ~ *speed*, speed of ~craft relative to the ~ through which it is moving; ~-*stop*, helicopter passenger station; ~ *strip*, strip of ground used or usable for an ~field; ~ *thermometer* (with ~ instead of mercury); ~-*threads*, gossamer; ~-*tight* impermeable to ~; ~-*to*-~, from one ~craft to another; *Air Training Corps* (formed in 1941 for youths aged 15–18; abbr. *A.T.C.*); ~ *umbrella*, a force of ~craft used to give ~ protection to a military operation; ~'*way*: ventilating passage in mine; route regularly followed by ~craft; ~'*worthy*, (of ~craft) fit to fly; ~'*worthiness* n. [1. ME *eir*, *ayre* f. OF *air* f. L *āerem* f. Gk *āēr*. 2. developed in F, & taken into E about 1600]

air [2], v.t. Expose to open air, ventilate; dry at fire or in ~ing cupboard; (refl.) go

out into fresh air; parade (qualities, grievances, theories, fine clothes). [f. prec.]

Aire'dale (ārd-), n. Large rough-coated terrier. [place in Yorks.]

air'less, a. Stuffy; breezeless, still. [AIR[1] +-LESS]

air'ў, a. Aerial, lofty; breezy; immaterial; of thin texture; light in movement; sprightly; graceful, delicate; unsubstantial; superficial, flippant; ~-*fairy* (colloq.), delicate or light as a fairy. Hence **air'iLY**[2] adv., **air'iNESS** n. [AIR[1] +-Y[2]]

aisle (il), n. Division of church, esp. one parallel to & divided by pillars from the main nave, choir, or transept; passage between rows of pews. Hence **aisleD**[2] (ild) a. [ME *cle* f. OF f. L *ala* wing; later forms *i*(*s*)*le* by assoc. w. *island*; *aisle* after mod. F *aile*]

‖ **ait** (āt), n. Small isle, esp. in a river. [OE *iggath*, *igeoth*, perh. dim. of *ieg*, *ig* island; the ME *eyt* is unexpl.; mod. *eyet*, *eyot* artificial sp. after *islet* & F *ilot*]

aitch, n. = ACHE[3].

‖ **aitch'bône**, n. (Cut of beef lying over) buttock or rump bone. [orig. *nage-*, *nache*-bone (w. loss of *n*- as in ADDER), f. OF *nage*, *nache* buttock f. LL (pl.) *naticae* f. L *natis*, -*es* buttock(s); pop. etym. gives *H*-, *ice*-, *edge*-, bone]

ajär'[1], adv. (Of doors) slightly open. [A prep. +*char* (OE *cerr* a turn)]

ajär'[2], adv. In a jarring state. [A prep. + JAR[4] n.]

ajutage. See ADJUTAGE.

akim'bô, adv. (Of the arms) with hands on hips & elbows turned outwards. [in 15th c. *in kenebowe*, later *on kenbow*, *a kenbow*, of unkn. orig.]

akin', pred. a. Related by blood; (fig.) of similar or kindred character. [A prep.]

al-[1], pref. = AD- before *l*.

al-[2], pref. The Arab. article *the*, as in *alcohol* etc.

-al, suf. 1. Adj. f. L -*alis* (adj. suf. varying w. cogn. -*aris* -AR[1] which was always used when *l* preceded, as *regularis* but *generalis*) direct or through F -*el* (later refash. after L -*al*- in E); now appended freely to L nouns (*cordial*), Gk nouns (*colossal*), L adjj. (*individual*), & Gk adjj. in -*kos*, -*oïdēs*, (*comical*, *rhomboidal*); -*ical* indicates vaguer connexion w. the orig. n. than -*ic* (*comic* paper, *comical* story), cf. -ACAL; other suff. are occas. appended, as *generality*, *centralize*. 2. Nouns f. L -*alis*, -*al*, -*ales*, -*alia*, parts of above used as nouns (*rival*, *animal*, *annals*, *Saturnalia*), with new imitations (*cardinal*, *regimentals*). -*alia* became in F -*aille*, in E -*aille*, -*ail*, -*al* (L *sponsalia*, OF *espousaille*, E *spousaille* now *espousal*), the last now freely imitated to form vbl nn. (*reprisal*, *recital*, *bestowal*); in BRIDAL, BURIAL, the suf. is of diff. orig.

à la (ah lah), prep. After the manner of, as *à la Russe, à la Reform*. [F, for *à la mode*]

ăl'abaster (-bah-), n. & a. **1.** Name of several varieties of carbonate or sulphate of lime; (Min.) massive fine-grained sulphate of lime (*modern, gypseous, ~*), as distinct from the carbonates used by the ancients for holding unguents (*oriental, calcareous, ~*); box made of *~*. **2.** adj. Of *~*, like *~* in whiteness or smoothness. So **ălabas'trINE** [(-bah-) a. [ME, f. OF *alabastre* f. L *alabaster* f. Gk *alabast(r)os*]

à la carte (ah lah kärt), adv. By the bill of fare. [F]

alǎck', int. (arch.) expressing regret or surprise, esp. in phr. *~-a-day*. [prob. f. *a* int. + *lak* LACK]

alǎc'rĭtў, n. Briskness, cheerful readiness. [f. L *alacritas* (*alacer* brisk, see -TY)]

Alădd'in's lămp, n. Talisman enabling holder to gratify any wish. [*Arabian Nights*]

ă'lamōde, à la mode (ah lah mŏd), adv. & a. In the fashion, fashionable; *~ beef*, piece of beef larded & stewed; *~ silk* (also as n., *alamode*), a thin glossy black silk. [F (*à la mode*), = in the fashion]

ăl'ar, a. Pertaining to wings; winglike, wing-shaped; (Bot. & Physiol.) axillary. [f. L *alaris* (*ala* wing, see -AR[1])]

alărm' [1], n. Call to arms; warning sound giving notice of danger; warning, as *give, take, the ~*; excited anticipation of danger; (Fencing) stamp on ground made with advancing foot; *~-post*, place for troops to assemble at in case of *~*; mechanism that sounds the *~* (usu. *alǎ'rum*); *alarum- -clock*, one with apparatus that rings at appointed hour; *alar(u)ms & excursions* (joc.), noise & bustle. [ME, f. OF *alarme* f. It. *allarme* (*all' arme!* to arms); form *alarum* now only of *~*-signal]

alărm' [2], v.t. Arouse to sense of danger; disturb; agitate, excite with fear. Hence *~'ingLY* [2] adv. [f. prec.]

alărm'ｉst, n. One who raises alarms on slight grounds (often attrib., as *these ~ist reports*); panic-monger. So *~ISM* n. [ALARM + -IST]

alǎ'rum, n. See ALARM n.

ăl'arў, a. Pertaining to wings or winglike parts. [f. L *alarius* (*ala* wing, see -ARY[1])]

alas' (-ahs), int. expressing grief, pity, concern. [ME, f. OF (*h*)*a las* (mod. *hélas*) f. *ha* ah + *las*(*se*) wretched f. L *lassus* weary]

Alas'tor (-ahs-), n. Avenging deity, nemesis. [Gk (*a*- not + *last*- f. *lath*- forget)]

ăl'āte, ăl'ātĕd, a. Having wings or wing-like appendages. [f. L *alatus* (*ala* wing, see -ATE[2])]

ălb, n. White vestment reaching to feet, worn by priests, & by some consecrated kings. [OE, ME *albe* (later also *aube* f. F) f. LL *alba* white (sc. *tunica, vestis*)]

ăl'bacōre, n. Large species of tunny; other fish of same genus. [f. Port.

albacor (F *albicore*, also used in E) f. Arab. *al* the + *bukr* young camel, heifer]

Albān'ian (āl-), a. & n. (Native) of Albania; (native) of Scotland (hist.). [(1) f. med. Gk *Albania*; (2) f. med. L *Albania* Scotland (Ir. *Alban* gen. of *Albu*)]

albāt'a, n. White metal, German silver. [f. L *albata* whitened (*albus* white)]

ăl'batrŏss, n. Family of birds allied to petrels, inhabiting Pacific & Southern Oceans; esp. *wandering ~*, largest of sea-fowls. [alt., after L *albus* white, of obs. (17th c.) *alcatras* frigate-bird etc., f. Sp. & Pg. *alcatraz*, var. of Pg. *alcatruz* f. Arab. *alqadus* the bucket, Arab. name for the pelican, from its supposed water-carrying habit]

albē'it (awl-), conj. Though, as *~ that he failed, ~ he failed, he tried ~ without success*. [- all though it be that]

ăl'bert, n. (Also *A~ chain*) kind of watch- -chain. [f. Prince *Albert* consort of Queen Victoria]

Albert Hall, in Kensington, used for concerts, demonstrations, etc. [as prec.]

ălbĕs'cent, a. Growing white, shading into white. [f. L *albescere* (*albus* white), see -ENT]

Albigĕn'sēs (āl-, -z), n.pl. Heretics of 12th–14th cc. in S. France. [L *Albiga* Albi in S. France, -ESE]

ălbī'nŏ (-bē-), n. (pl. *-os*). Human being marked by congenital absence of colour-ing pigment in skin & hair, which are white, & eyes, which are pink & unable to bear ordinary light; any animal so distin-guished; plant lacking the normal colour-ing. Hence **ălbi'nESS** [1] (-bē-), **ăl'binISM**, nn. [Port., orig. of white Negroes, f. L *albus* white]

Al'bion (āl-), n. (poet.). (Greek & Roman name for) Britain. [F, f. L *Albion* of uncert. orig.]

ăl'bīte, n. White or soda feldspar. [f. L *albus* white + -ITE[1]]

ăl'bum, n. Book for insertion of auto-graphs, photographs, names, etc. [L, neut. sing. of *albus* white]

ălbūm'ｊĕn (or āl[2]), n. White of egg; a constituent of animal solids & fluids, of seeds, & of tuberous or fleshy roots, found nearly pure in white of egg; (Bot.) sub-stance found between skin & embryo of many seeds, usu. the eatable part. Hence *~iNOSE, ~iNOUS*, aa. [L *albumen -minis* white of egg (*albus* white) see -MEN]

ălbūm'ĕnīze, -ise (-īz), v.t. (photog.). Coat (paper) with an albuminous solution. [prec. + -IZE]

ălbūm'inoid, a. & n. Like albumen; (n. pl.) proteins, class of organic compounds forming chief part of organs & tissues of animals & plants. Hence **ălbūminoid'AL** a. [f. ALBUMEN + -OID]

ălbūminūr'ia, n. Presence of albumen in the urine, usu. as symptom of kidney disease. [ALBUMEN, URINE, -IA[1]]

ălbūrn'ｊum, n. Recently formed wood in

exogenous trees, sap-wood. Hence -ous
a. [L *alburnum* (*albus* white)]
‖ **alcahest**. See ALKAHEST.

Alcā′ic (ă-), a. & n. Pertaining to Alcaeus
(Gk lyric poet, 600 B.C.), or to the metre he
invented; (n. pl.)∼ strophes. [f. LL f. Gk
Alkaikos (*Alkaios*)]

alcalde (ahlkah′ldă), n. Magistrate or
mayor in Spanish, Portuguese, or Latin-
-American town. [Sp., ult. f. Arab. *qādi*
judge, CADI]

ălchĕm′ic (-k-), a. Pertaining to alchemy.
Hence ∼AL (-k-) a., ∼aLLY² (-k-) adv. [f.
med. L. *alchimicus* or F *alchimique*: see
ALCHEMY and -IC]

ăl′chemist (-k-), n. One who studies or
practises alchemy. Hence **ălchemis′tic**
(AL) (-k-) aa. [f. OF *alquemiste* or med. L
alchemista; see ALCHEMY and -IST]

ăl′chemīze (-k-), -ise (-īz), v.t. Change as
by alchemy; transmute. [back-forma-
tion on prec.]

ăl′chemў (-k-), n. Chemistry of the
middle ages; esp., pursuit of the transmutation of baser metals into gold (also
fig.). [ME, f. OF *alquimie* f. med. L *al-
chimia* f. Arab. *al-kimia*, *al* the +*kimia*,
apparently = *khemia* (Gk form of native
name of Egypt, but confused with Gk
khumeia pouring f. *khu-* perf. st. of *kheŏ*
pour, whence the spelling *alchymy*)]

ăl′cohŏl, n. Pure spirit of wine; any
liquor containing this; (Chem.) large
class of compounds of same type as
spirits of wine. Hence ∼ATE¹(3) (n.
[med. L, f. Arab. *al* the +*koh′l* powder
for staining eyelids (*kahala* v. stain)]

ălcohŏl′ic, a. & n. **1.** Of, relating to,
containing, caused by, alcohol. **2.** n.
Person addicted to excessive consumption of alcohol. [prec. +-IC]

ăl′cohŏlism, n. Action of alcohol on
human system. [ALCOHOL +-ISM]

ăl′cohŏl|īze, -ise (-īz), v.t. Saturate with
alcohol; subject to alcoholic influence.
Hence ∼īzA′TION n. [ALCOHOL +-IZE]

ălcohŏlŏ|m′ěter, n. Instrument for
measuring alcoholic strength of spirits.
Hence ∼M′ETRY n. [f. ALCOHOL +-o-+
METER]

Alcoran (ălkorahn′, ăl′-), n. Koran.
Hence ∼IC (-ăn²) a. [ME, f. OF f. Arab.
al-qoran the reading; see KORAN]

ăl′cōve, n. Vaulted recess in room-wall,
esp. (in Spain) recess for bed; recess in
garden wall or hedge; summer-house.
[F, f. Sp. *alcova*, *-ba*, f. Arab. *al-qobbah*
the vault (*qubba* v. vault)]

ăl′dėhȳde, n. Colourless volatile fluid of
suffocating smell, obtained by oxidation
of alcohol; class of compounds of this
type. Hence **ăldėhȳd′ic** a. [abbr. of
mod. L *alcohol dehydrogenatum* (deprived
of hydrogen)]

al′der (awl-), n. Tree related to birch;
other trees not related, as *black, white, red,*
∼. [OE *alor, aler* (cf. ON *ölr, elrir*, OHG
elira, mod. G *erle, eller*) w. phonetic *d*]

al′derman (awl-), n. Co-opted member
of an English county or borough council,
next in dignity to Mayor. Hence ∼IC
(-măn²) a.,∼SHIP n. [f. OE *aldor* patriarch
ald old +-*or* noun suf.)+-MAN]

al′dermanrў (awl-), n. Ward, district of
a borough having its own alderman; rank
of alderman. [prec. +-RY]

Al′derney (awl-), a. & n. **1.** Of cattle
bred in ∼ in the Channel Islands; (pop.)
of cattle bred in the Channel Islands.
2. n. Individual of either kind.

Al′dershŏt (awl-), n. (Used for) the
permanent military camp at ∼ in
Hampshire.

Al′dīne (awl-), a. Printed by Aldus
Manutius, Venetian printer of 16th cent.,
who ,introduced italic type; name of
certain style of type. [f. *Aldus*+-INE¹]

Al′dis (awl-), a. ∼ *lamp* (for signalling);
∼ *lens* (for hand cameras); ∼ *unit sight*
(for aircraft). [A. C. W. *Aldis*, inventor]

āle, n. Liquor made from an infusion of
malt by fermentation, flavoured with
hops etc.; ‖ merry-making at which ∼
was drunk; *alecost*, costmary; ∼-*house*,
one at which ∼ is retailed; ∼-*wife*,
woman who keeps an ∼-house; American
fish allied to herring. [OE *alu*, ON *öl*]

āl′éatorў, a. Depending on the throw of
a die or on chance. [f. L *aleatorius*
(*aleator* dice-player f. *alea* die)]

āle′cŏnner (ălk-), n. (hist.). Inspector of
ale & ale-measures (now a titular office
only). [ALE +CON¹ +-ER¹]

alee′, adv. & pred. a. On the lee or
sheltered side of ship; to leeward. [ME
(rare before 16th c.) f. A²+LEE]

āl′ēgar, n. Sour ale; malt vinegar. [f.
(after *vinegar*) ALE +*egre* (= F *aigre* sour,
see EAGER)]

alĕm′bic, n. Apparatus formerly used in
distilling; also fig., as ∼ *of fancy*. [ME
alambic f. OF f. med. L *alembicus* f. Arab.
al-anbiq the still f. Gk *ambix -ikos* cup,
cap of a still; *lembick, limbeck*, were usu.
in 15th–17th cc.]

alĕrt′, a., n., & v.t. **1.** Watchful, vigilant;
lively, nimble. **2.** n. Warning call,
alarm; (period of) air-raid warning; *on the*
∼, on the look-out. **3.** v.t. Make ∼, put
on the ∼. Hence ∼LY² adv., ∼NESS·n. [f.
F *alerte* f. It. *all′ erta* (*alla* to the +*erta*
watch-tower, fem. p.p. of *ergere* f. L
erigere ERECT)]

aleur′on, aleur′ōne, (-lūr-), n. Albuminoid substance found in seeds of plants
etc. [Gk *aleuron* flour]

Alĕxăn′drian (ăl-), a. Relating to the
late Greek civilization of Alexandria in
Egypt. [-AN]

Alĕxăn′drine (ăl-), a. & n. ∼ (*verse*),
iambic line of six feet or twelve syllables.
[f. F *alexandrin*, of disputed orig.]

alĕx′in, n. One of a class of substances
found in blood serum capable of destroying bacteria. [G, f. Gk *alexō* ward off,
-IN].

alĕxiphăr'mĭc, a. & n. (Having the quality of) an antidote. [earlier -ac f. F alexipharmaque f. Gk alexipharmakon remedy for poison (alexō ward off + pharmakon poison)]

ălfăl'fa, n. Lucerne. [Sp., f. Arab.]

ălfrĕs'cō, adv. & a. In the open air; open-air, as ~ lr̄nch. [f. It. al fresco in the fresh (air)]

ăl'g|a, n. (pl. ~ae, pr. -jē). Seaweed. Hence ~AL, ~OID, ~olō'gĭcAL, aa., ~IST (3) (-j-), ~ŏL'OGIST, ~ŏL'OGY, nn. [L]

ăl'gĕbr|a, n. Investigation of the properties of numbers & quantities by means of general symbols; quadruple~a, quaternions. Hence ~ā'IC(AL) aa., ~ā'icalLY[2] adv., ~(ā)IST nn. [It., f. Arab. aljebr reunion of broken parts (jabara reunite), bone-setting (obs. sense in E)]

ăl'gĭd, a. Cold, esp. of cold stage of ague. Hence **algĭd'ITY** n. [f. F algide or L algidus (algēre be cold, see -ID[1])]

ăl'gorĭsm, n. Arabic (decimal) notation; cipher in ~, 0, mere dummy. [ME augrim, later algorisme, f. OF augorime, algorisme, f. med. L algorismus f. Arab. al-Khowarazmi the man of Khiva, surname of a mathematician]

ălguazil' (-gw-), n. Spanish warrant-officer or sergeant. [Sp. (now -cil) f. Arab. al-wazir the VIZIER, minister (wazara)]

ăl'gum, n. Tree mentioned in Bible (2 Chron. ii. 8; in 1 Kings x. 11 wrongly given as almug), prob. a kind of sandal-wood. [Heb.]

Alhăm'bra, n. Palace of Moorish kings at Granada. Hence **ălhambrESQUE'** (-ĕsk) a. [f. Sp. f. Arab. al-hamra' the red (house)]

ăl'ias, adv. & n. (pl. ~es). (Name by which one is called) on other occasions. [L, = at another time, otherwise]

ăl'ibī, adv. & n. (The plea that when an alleged act took place one was) elsewhere; *excuse (colloq.). [L, = elsewhere]

ălicyc'lic, a. (chem.). Combining the properties of aliphatic & cyclic compounds. [f. aliphatic + cyclic]

ăl'idāde, -ăd, n. Index of astrolabe, quadrant, etc., showing the degrees cut off on the arc. [F; earlier allidatha (ME), alhidada, f. med. L, f. Arab. al-'idadah the revolving radius ('add upper arm)]

ăl'ien[1], a. & n. 1. Not one's own; foreign, under foreign allegiance; differing in nature (from); repugnant (to). 2. n. Stranger; non-naturalized foreigner; one excluded from; (Law) ~-friend, -enemy, alien owing allegiance to friendly, hostile, country. Hence ~ISM (2) n., study & treatment of mental diseases, ~IST n., specialist in such diseases. [ME, f. OF f. L alienus belonging to another (alius)]

ăl'ien[2], v.t. (Poet.) estrange; (Law) transfer ownership of. Hence ~ABLE a., ~abIL'ITY n. [ME, f. OF aliener f. L alienare (as prec.)]

ăl'ienāt|e, v.t. Estrange; transfer owner-

---

ship of; turn away, divert (from). Hence ~OR n. [ME, f. L as prec., see -ATE[2]]

ălienā'tion, n. Estrangement; transference of ownership; diversion to different purpose; (mental) ~, insanity. [ME, f. OF, or f. L alienatio (as prec., see -ATION)]

ălienee', n. One to whom transfer of property is made. [ALIEN[2] + -EE]

ăl'ĭfŏrm, a. Wing-shaped. [f. L ala wing + -FORM]

alĭght'[1] (-īt), v.i. Dismount (from horse), descend (from carriage); settle, come to earth, from the air. [OE ālĭhtan (A- (1) + lĭhtan LIGHT[5])]

alĭght'[2] (-īt), a. Kindled; on fire; lighted up. [p.p. of obs. alight kindle; now only used predicatively, on anal. of a-blaze & other adv. compds]

alĭgn' (-īn), **aline'**, v.t. & i. Place, lay, in a line; bring into line; esp. bring three or more points into a straight line, as ~ the sights (of rifle) & bull's-eye; (intr.) form in line (as troops). Hence ~MENT (-īn'm-) n. [f. F aligner f. phr. à ligne in a LINE[2]]

alike', pred. a. & adv. Similar, like; (adv.) in like manner. [ME ilike, alike, etc., combining OE gelic (Y- & LIKE[1]) & ON ālikr (= OE anlic, see A-(2))]

ăl'iment, n. Food; (fig.) support, mental sustenance. Hence **ălĭmĕn'tAL** a., **ălĭmĕn'talLY[2]** adv. [late ME, f. F, or f. L alimentum (alere nourish, see -MENT)]

ălĭmĕn'tarў, a. Nourishing; performing functions of nutrition, as ~ canal; providing maintenance. [f. L alimentarius (as prec., see -ARY[1])]

ălimentā'tion, n. Nourishment; maintenance. [f. med. L alimentatio (ulimentare, as ALIMENT, see -ATION)]

ăl'imonў, n. Nourishment; maintenance; allowance due to wife from husband's estate, on separation from certain causes. [f. L alimonia nutriment (alere nourish, see -MONY)]

ăl'ĭpĕd, a. & n. 1. Wing-footed. 2. n. ~ animal, e.g. bat. [f. L ala wing, pes pedis foot]

ălĭphăt'ĭc, a. (chem.). Of fat (as epithet of certain organic compounds). [f. Gk aleiphar -atos unguent, -IC]

ăl'iquŏt, a. & n. ~ (part), part contained by the whole an integral number of times, integral factor. [f. F aliquote f. L aliquot some, so many]

-ality, compd noun-suf. = -AL + -TY. Quality, or instance of it, as (a) generality.

alive', adv. & pred. a. In life, living; fully susceptible to (an idea etc.); active, brisk, as (colloq.) look ~, be brisk; swarming with, as river ~ with boats; any man ~ (whatever); man ~! (colloq. expletive). [OE on life, ME on live; see A[2] prep., LIFE]

alĭz'arĭn, n. Red colouring matter of madder. [f. F alizari madder prob. f. Arab. al the + 'açarah extract ('açara v. press); see -IN]

ăl′kahĕst, n. Alchemist's supposed universal solvent (also fig.). [sham Arab., prob. invented by Paracelsus]

ălkalēs′c|ent, a. & n. Incipiently or slightly alkaline (substance). Hence ~ENCE, ~ENCY, nn. [f. foll., see -ESCENT]

ăl′kali, n. (pl. ~s, ~es). (Chem.) series of compounds called bases, including soda, potash, & ammonia, highly soluble in water, producing caustic or corrosive solutions that neutralize strong acids, & turn vegetable yellows to brown, reds to blue, purples to green; (Commerc.) caustic soda, caustic potash, other alkaline products. Hence ~fi′ABLE a., ~FY v.t. [ME, f. med. L f. Arab. al-qaliy calcined ashes (qalay fry)]

ălkalim′ětrў, n. Measurement of strength of alkalis. [ALKALI + -METRY]

ăl′kaline, a. Of alkalis; of the nature of an alkali; ~ metals, those whose hydroxides are alkalis. [f. ALKALI + -INE[1], or f. F]

ăl′kaloid, n. Any nitrogenous base of vegetable origin. Hence **ălkaloid′AL** a. [f. G, as prec. + -OID]

ăl′kanĕt, n. (Plant whose root yields) a red dye. [ME, f. Sp. alcaneta, dim. of alcana f. Arab. al-henna the henna shrub]

all (awl), a., n., & adv. **1.** adj. (w. noun etc. expressed or understood). The whole amount, quantity, or extent of, as ~ day, ~ England, ~ his life, & ~ that, take it ~, ~ whom I saw; the greatest possible, as ~ speed; (w. pl.) the entire number of, as ~ men, ~ the others; ~ kind(s) of, every kind of; any whatever, as renounce ~ connexion; ~ the TIME[1]; ~-time high, (low), a record high, (low), level or figure. **2.** n. ~ men, as ~ were agreed; (in scoring at games) for both sides (the score was two ~; love ~, no score to either side); (w. of) the whole, every one, as ~ of it, ~ of us; everything (that is ~; ~ is lost); one's whole property, as he lost his ~; ~ along of (vulg.), owing to; ~ but, everything short of (used adv.), as ~ but impossible, he was ~ but drowned; ~-in, inclusive of ~, as ~-in wrestling, unrestricted style; ; ~ in ~, of paramount or exclusive importance; ~ one, just the same, as it is ~ one to me; ~-up, (of aircraft) total (weight) of machine, crew, passengers, cargo, etc. when in air; ~ very fine or well, colloq. formula of dissatisfaction, as ~ very fine, but I shall stand it no longer; at ~, in any way, as not at ~, did you speak at ~? (not in affirmative sent.); in ~, in total number; one & ~, ~ & some (arch.), ~ & sundry, ~ individually & collectively. **3.** adv. Wholly, quite, as dressed ~ (orig. an adj.) in white, ~ covered with mud, ~ the better, ~ at once, ~ too soon; All Blacks (colloq.), New Zealand rugby football international team; ~-clear, signal that danger is over, esp. from enemy aircraft; *~-fired (sl.), extreme(ly), excessive(ly); ~ in, exhausted; ~ out, involving ~ one's strength or resources, as he was going ~ out, at full speed; ~ OVER; ~-overish (colloq.), indisposed ~ over the body; ǁ ~-red, (of cable, line, etc.) British throughout; ~ right, (adv.) as desired, satisfactorily, certainly (that's the man ~ right), (pred. a.) safe & sound, in good state, satisfactory, (sent.) I consent, ~ is well, (also iron. in threats, as ~ right! you shall repent this); ~-round adj., having ability in many departments, as an ~-round sportsman, so ~-rounder, n.; ~ there (colloq.), sane, in one's senses, as he's not quite ~ there; ~ the same: just the same, making no difference, (it's ~ the same to me whether he comes or not; if it's ~ the same to you, if you don't mind); in spite of this, notwithstanding, however, (he was punished ~ the same, in spite of extenuating circumstances etc.; ~ the same I wish you hadn't done it). **4.** Combb.: All-father, Odin, God; All Fools' Day, first of April; All Hallows (arch.), All Saints' Day, general celebration of saints, November 1st; All Souls' Day, day of supplication for souls of faithful deceased, Nov. 2nd. All is prefixed to many adjj., as ~-bountiful, ~-righteous, ~-sufficient, & esp. to partt., as ~-sufficing, ~-seeing, ~-knowing. [OE all, eall, Gmc]

Allah (ăl′a) n. Name of God among Mohammedans. [Arab. allah contr. of al-ilah (al the + ilah god = Heb. eloah)]

allay′, v.t. Put down, repress; alleviate (pain etc.); diminish (pleasure etc.). [OE alecgan f. A- (1) + LAY[3]; ME alegge, aleye, alaye confused w. obs. allege alleviate & obs. allay ALLOY]

ăllĕgā′tion, n. Alleging; assertion (esp. one not proved). [ME, f. OF, or f. L allegatio (allegare allege, see -ATION)]

allĕg|e′, v.t. Affirm; advance as argument or excuse. Hence ~ed′ (-ĕjd) a., ~′ĕdLY[2] adv., (used in statements for which author disclaims responsibility). [f. AF alegier, OF esligier f. Rom. *ex-litigare clear at law; confused in sense w. L allegare (see prec.)]

allē′giance (-jans), n. Duty of subject to sovereign or government; loyalty (lit. & fig.). [ME var. (+ A- (4), by confusion of form w. obs. allegeance (prec.) allegation, or of form & sense w. med. L alligantia ALLIANCE), of ligeaunce f. OF f. lige (LIEGE, -ANCE)]

ăllĕgŏ′ric, a. Pertaining to, of the nature of, allegory. Hence ~AL a., ~ALLY[2] adv. [ME, f. F -ique or LL allegoricus f. Gk (as foll., see -IC)]

ăll′ĕgor|ize, -ise (-īz), v.t. & i. Treat as an allegory; make allegories. Hence ~IST n. [f. F -iser or LL allegorizare f. Gk (as foll., see -IZE)]

ăll′ĕgorў, n. Narrative description of a subject under guise of another suggestively similar; emblem. [ME, f. OF -ie or L f. Gk allēgoria (allos other + -agoria speaking)]

ăllégrĕtt′ō, adv. (mus.). Somewhat briskly. [It.]

ălleg′rō (-lā-), a., adv., n. (mus.). Lively, gay; (movement) in brisk time. [It.]

ăllêlu′ia (-lōōya), n. Song of praise to God. [f. LL f. (Septuagint) Gk *allēlouia* f. Heb. *halleluyah* praise ye Jehovah]

ăll′emănde, n. Name of several German dances; country dance figure. [F, = German]

ăll′ergў, n. (med.). Changed reactivity produced by a subsequent inoculation or treatment with the same thing, (more widely) sensitiveness to the action of particular foods, pollens, insect-bites, etc. Hence **allĕr′gic** a., relating to or characterized by ～, (colloq.) sensitive (esp. antipathetic) *to*. [in G *allergie*, f. Gk *allos* other, after *energie* ENERGY]

allēv′i|āte, v.t. Relieve, mitigate. Hence ～A′TION, ～ātOR, nn., ～ative, ～ātory, aa. [f. LL AL*leviare* lighten (*levis* light), see -ATE[3]]

ăll′ey, n. (pl. ～s). Walk, passage, esp. in park or garden; narrow street; *blind* ～, one closed at end, enclosure for skittles etc. [ME, f. OF *alee*, walking, passage, f. *aler* go]

Alleyn′ian (alĕn-), n. Member of Dulwich College. [E. *Alleyn*, founder (d. 1626)]

All-hăll′ow(s) (-ō, -ŏz), n. All saints (in heaven), as *All hallows' day*, *Allhallow-mass*. [ALL+HALLOW[1]]

ălliā′ceous (-shŭs), a. Of the genus *Allium*, including garlic, onions, & leeks; smelling, tasting, of garlic etc. [f. L *allium* garlic+-ACEOUS]

alli′ance, n. Union by marriage; relationship; confederation (esp. between States); community in nature or qualities; (Bot.) group of allied families. [ME, f. OF *aliance* (as ALLY[1], see -ANCE)]

ăll′igātor, n. Genus of saurian reptiles of crocodile family, found in America; other large American saurians; ～ *apple, pear, fruit* of W. Indian trees; ～ *tortoise*, snapping turtle. [16th c. (a)*lagarto*.f. Sp. *el lagarto* the lizard f. L *lacertus*]

allit′erāt|e, v.i. (Use words that) begin with the same letter or sound. Hence ～ive a., ～ively[2](-vl-) adv. [back-form. f. foll.]

allitera′tion, n. Commencement of words in close connexion (esp. in early Teut. poetry, of accented syllables) with the same letter or sound. [f. med. L (15th c.) *alliteratio*; cf. F *allitération*]

ăllo-, comb. form of Gk *allos* other.

ăll′oc|āte, v.t. Assign, devote, (*to* person or object); locate. Hence or cogn. ～ABLE a., ～A′TION n. [f. med. L AL*locare* (*locus* place), see -ATE[3]]

ăllocū′tion, n. Formal hortatory address (esp. one delivered by the Pope). [f. L *allocutio -onis* f. *alloqui* exhort]

al(l)ōd′i|um, n. Estate held in absolute ownership, without acknowledgement to a superior (opp. to *feudum*). Hence ～AL a., ～alLY[2] adv., ～alism, ～alist, nn. [f.

med. L f. Frankish *allōd* entire property (ALL+ōd estate); also anglicized *allod*, *allody*]

ăllŏg′amў, n. (bot.). Cross-fertilization. [f. ALLO-+-GAMY]

ăllŏp′ath|у, n. Curing of a diseased action by inducing another action of a different kind (opp. to *homoeopathy*). Hence **ăllopăth′ic** a., **ăllopăth′ically** adv., ～ist n. [in G *allopathie*, f. ALLO-+-*pathie* -PATHY]

ăllophўl′ian, a. & n. (One whose native tongue is) neither Aryan nor Semitic. [f. LL f. Gk *allophulos* (ALLO-+*phulē* tribe) +-IAN]

allŏt′, v.t. (-tt-). Distribute by lot or with authority; assign (*to*). [f. OF *aloter* f. *à* to+*lot*; see LOT]

ăll′othēism, n. Worship of strange gods. [f. ALLO-+Gk *theos* god+-ISM]

allŏt′ment, n. Apportioning; lot in life; share allotted to one; ‖ small portion of land let out for cultivation. [f. F *allotement* (*aloter*, see ALLOT & -MENT)]

ăllŏt′rop|ў, n. Variation of physical properties without change of substance. Hence **ăllotrŏp′ic(al)** aa., **ăllotrŏp′ical**LY[2] adv., ～ISM n. [f. Gk *allotropia* f. *allotropos* (ALLO-+*tropos* manner f. *trepō* turn)]

ăllŏttee′, n. One to whom allotment is made. [f. ALLOT+-EE]

allow′, v.t. & i. Admit (thing *to* be, *that*); permit (practice, person *to* do); (refl.) indulge one*self* in (conduct); (intr.) admit *of*; give (limited periodical sum), as ～ *him £200 a year*; add, deduct, in consideration of something; ～ *for*, take into consideration, make addition or deduction corresponding to; ～ *me* (formula in offering services). Hence ～ABLE a., ～abLY[2] adv.; ～êdLY[2] adv., admittedly. [ME, f. OF *alouer* f. (1) L AL*laudare* praise, (2) med. L AL*locare* place]

allow′ance[1], n. Permission; tolerance (*of*); a limited portion or sum esp. of money or food; deduction, discount; *make* ～ *for*, allow for. [ME, f. OF *alouance* (as prec., see -ANCE)]

allow′ance[2], v.t. Make allowance to (person); supply (thing) in limited quantities. [f. prec.]

alloy′[1] (*or* ăl′oi), n. Standard, quality, (of gold or silver); inferior metal mixed esp. with gold or silver (also fig.); mixture of metals. [f. F *aloi*, OF *alei* (whence obs. E *allay*), f. *aleier* combine f. L AL*ligare* bind]

alloy′[2], v.t. Mix with baser metal; mix (metals); debase; moderate. [f. F *aloyer*, OF *aleier*, see prec.]

all′seed (awl-), n. Name of various plants producing much seed.

all′spice (awl-), n. Jamaica pepper, pimento, supposed to combine flavour of cinnamon, nutmeg, and cloves; other aromatic shrubs, as *Carolina* ～, *Japan* ～, *wild* ～.

allude' (-ōō-, -ŭ-), v.i. Refer covertly, indirectly, to; (improp.) ~ to, mean. [f. L AL(ludere lus- play)]

allūre', v.t., & n. Tempt, entice, win over, (to, from, person, place, conduct); fascinate, charm; (n.) charm, attractiveness. Hence ~MENT (-ūr'm-) n. [ME, f. OF al(e)urer attract (a AD-+leurre LURE)]

allu'sion (-lōōzhn, -lū-), n. Covert, implied, indirect, reference (to). [f. F, or LL allusio (as ALLUDE, see -ION)]

allus'ive (-lōōs-, -lūs-), a. Containing an allusion (to); abounding in allusions; (Her.) ~ (canting) arms. Hence ~LY² (-vl-) adv., ~NESS (-vn-) n. [as prec., see -IVE]

alluv'ion (-ōō-, -ŭ-), n. Wash of sea, river, against shore, banks; flood; matter deposited by flood; (Law) formation of new land by water's action. [F, f. L ALluvionem (nom. -vio) f. luere wash]

alluv'i|um (-ōō-, -ŭ-), n. (pl. ~a, ~ums). Deposit of earth, sand, etc., left by flood. Hence~AL a. [LL, neut. of adj. ALluvius (luere wash)]

allȳ'¹ (or āl'ī), v.t. Combine, unite, for special object to, with, (esp. of marriage & alliance with foreign states); (of things) allied to, connected with. [ME, f. OF alier (aleier) f. L ALligare bind, cf. ALLOY¹]

āll'ȳ² (or ali'), n. Person, state, etc., allied with another. [f. prec.]

āll'ȳ³, *āll'ey, n. Choice playing-marble of marble or alabaster. [perh. dim. of alabaster]

āl'ma(h), n. Egyptian dancing-girl. [Arab. 'almah knowing ('alama know)]

āl'magĕst, n. Great astronomical treatise of Ptolemy; other books on astrology & alchemy. [ME, f. OF f. Arab. al the +majisti = Gk megistē greatest]

Al'ma Māt'er (ā-), n. Name used of Universities & schools. [L, = bounteous mother]

al'manăc, -ăck, (awl-), n. Annual calendar of months & days, with astronomical & other data. [14th c. almenak = 13th c. med. L almanac(h), F -ach, Sp. -que, It. -aceo, of unkn. orig.]

āl'mandīne, n. A garnet of violet tint. [F, alt. of obs. alabandine f. LL alabandina (Alabanda, city in Caria)]

almi'ghty (awlmīt'ī), a. & adv. All--powerful, esp. A~God, the A~; (sl.)great, (adv.) exceedingly. Hence **almi'ghti-NESS** n. [OE ælmiehtig (ALL adv.+ MIGHTY)]

almīr'ah (-a), n. (Anglo-Ind.). Wardrobe, movable cupboard. [Hind., f. Port. almario f. L armarium (see AMBRY)]

alm'ond (ahm-), n. Kernel of a stone--fruit borne by two trees (sweet, bitter, ~) allied to plum & peach; anything ~- -shaped. [ME almand(e) etc. f. OF f. med. L amandula f. L amygdala, Gk amugdalē]

almoner (ahm'oner, āl²-), n. Official distributor of alms; Hereditary Grand A~, Lord High A~, (officers in royal household

of Great Britain); medico-social worker attached to a hospital. [ME aumoner etc., f. AF aumoner, OF -ier, f. Rom. *almosinarius f. med. L eleemosynarius (as ALMS, see -ARY¹)]

al'mōst (awl-), adv. All but, very nearly (qualifying v., adv., adj.; also noun, as his ~ impudence). [f. ALL + MOST adv.]

alms (ahmz), n. (usu. as sing.). Charitable relief ' of the poor; donation; ~-folk, almsman, (supported by charity); ~- -giving; ~-house, ||one founded by charity for reception of poor. [OE ælmysse f. pop. L (Rom.) *alimosina, altered f. LL eleemosyna, elemosina, f. Gk elcēmosunē compassionateness (elcēmōn adj. f. elcos compassion)]

ăl'mŭg. See ALGUM.

ăl'ōe, n. Genus of plants with erect spikes of flowers & bitter juice; (pl.) purgative drug procured from juice of ~s; other plants, as American ~, Agave. [OE aluve f. L f. Gk aloē]

ălŏĕt'ic, a. & n. (Medicine) containing aloes. [f. Gk aloē aloe on false anal. of diuretic etc.]

alŏft' (or -aw-), adv. & pred. a. High up (lit. & fig.); upward. [ME, f. ON ā lopt (ā in, on, to, +lopt air); cf. LIFT, LOFT]

alōne', pred. a. & adv. Solitary; standing by oneself (in opinion etc.); LET, leave, ~, abstain from interfering with; (adv.) only, exclusively. [ME, f. ALL adv.+ ONE]

alŏng', adv. & prep. From end to end of; through any part of the length of; onward, as get~; ~ with, in company with, in conjunction with; all ~, all the time; (all) ~ of (vulg.), owing to; || ~-ships, directed fore & aft; ~-shore, ~ by the shore, ~ & on the shore; ~side, close to side of ship; ~side of, side by side with (lit. & fig.). [OE anªllang (and- against, facing, +lang LONG¹), orig. adj.]

alōof', adv. & pred. a. Away, apart, (lit. & fig.), as stand, keep, hold ~; (Naut.) away to windward, as spring~ (cf. LUFF). Hence ~NESS n. [f. A prep.+ LUFF]

ălōpē'cia, n. (med.). Baldness. [f. L, f. Gk alōpekia fox-mange f. alōpēx fox]

aloud', adv. Loudly; not in a whisper; (colloq.) noticeably, as reeks~. [f. A prep. + LOUD]

alow' (-ō), adv. (naut.). In, into, lower part of vessel. [f. A prep.+ LOW a.]

ălp, n. Mountain-peak; (in Switzerland) green pasture-land on mountain-side; Alps, mountain ranges separating France & Italy. [(pl.) f. F Alpes f. L]

ălpăc'a, n. Kind of llama with long woolly hair; its wool; fabric thence made. [f. Sp. f. paco, native Peruv. name]

ăl'penstŏck, n. Long iron-shod staff used in climbing Alps etc. [G, = Alp-stick]

ăl'pha, n. Greek letter A (A, a); A~ and Omega, beginning & end; (Astron.) chief star of constellation; ~ particles, rays, helium nuclei emitted by radio-active substances (orig. regarded as rays); ~

plus, superlatively good. [ME, f. Gk, f. Heb. *aleph* ox, leader]

ăl′phabĕt, n. Set of letters used in a language; first rudiments. Hence **ălpha-bĕt′ic** a. [f. LL *alphabetum* (Gk *alpha, bēta,* first two letters of alphabet)]

ălphabĕt′ical, a. Of the alphabet, as ~ *order.* Hence ~LY² adv. [as prec. +-ICAL]

Al′pine (ă-), ~LY² & n. Of the Alps or any lofty mountains; (n.) ~ plant. [f. L *Alpinus (Alpes,* see ALP & -INE¹)]

Al′pinist (ă-), n. Alpine climber. [f. F *alpiniste* (as prec., see -IST)]

already (awlrĕd′ĭ), adv. Beforehand; by this time, thus early. [f. ALL adv. +READY]

Alsati|a (ălsāsh′a), **Alsace** (ăl′săs), nn. Province west of Rhine, re-ceded by Germany to France 1919; White Friars in London, once sanctuary for lawbreakers. Hence ~AN (-shan) a.; ~an *(wolf-hound),* a breed of dog. [L form of G *Elsass,* F *Alsace*]

ăl′sike, n. Kind of clover. [*Alsike* in Sweden]

al′sŏ (awl-), adv. In addition, besides; ~*-ran* n., horse not placed in first three in race, person(s) that failed to win distinction. [comb. of ALL = altogether, wholly, +SO (OE *al* +*swā*)]

ălt, n. (Mus.) high note, esp. *in* ~, in octave above treble stave beginning with G; (fig.) *in* ~, in an exalted frame of mind; ~*-horn,* brass wind-instrument of saxhorn type. [f. It. *alto* ALTO f. L *altus* (cf. G *alt* 1540)]

al′tar (awl-), n. Flat-topped block for offerings to deity; Communion Table; *lead to the* ~, marry; ~*-cloth,* (prop.) linen cloth used at Communion or Mass, (loosely) silk frontal & super-frontal; ~*-piece,* reredos, esp. a painting. [OE *altar, -er* f. LL *altar(e), -ium (altus* high)]

al′tarwise (awl-), adv. In the manner of an altar.

ăltăz′imuth, n. Instrument for deter-mining altitude & azimuth of heavenly bodies. [*alt-* for *altitude* +AZIMUTH]

al′ter (awl-), v.t. & i. Change in character, position, etc. Hence or cogn. ~ABIL′ITY, ~A′TION, nn., ~ABLE a. [ME, f. OF *alterer* f. LL *alterare* (L *alter* other)]

al′terative (awl-), a. & n. Tending to alter; (n.) medicine, treatment, that alters processes of nutrition. [ME, f. med. L *alterativus* (prec., -ATIVE)]

al′terc|āte (ălt-, awlt-), v.i. Dispute hotly, wrangle, *(with).* So ~A′TION n. [f. L *altercari,* see -ATE³]

ăl′ter ĕg′ŏ, n. One's other self, intimate friend. [L, = second I]

altĕrn′ant (ălt-, awlt-), a. & n. Alterna-ting; (Min.) of alternating layers; (n.) ~ quantity. [F, part. of *alterner* f. L *alternare* ALTERNATE]

altĕrn′ate¹ (awl-), a. & n. **1.** (Of things of two kinds) coming each after one of the other kind; (Biol.) ~ *generation* (by ~ processes, as first by budding, next by

sexual reproduction); ~ *leaves, angles* (placed alternately on the two sides of stem, line). **2.** n. (awl²). *Deputy,* sub-stitute. Hence ~LY² (-tl-) adv. [f. L *alternare* do one thing after the other *(alternus* every other f. *alter* other), see -ATE²]

al′tern|āte² (awl-), v.t. & i. Arrange, perform, (two sets of things) alternately; interchange (one thing) alternately *with, by,* another; (of two things) succeed each other by turns; (of a whole) consist of alternate things; (of one class of things) appear alternately with another. So ~A′TION n.; ~ātor n., dynamo giving an ~*ating current* (reversing its direction at regular intervals). [f. prec.]

altĕrn′ative (awl-), a. & n. **1.** (Of two things) mutually exclusive. **2.** n. (Strictly) permission to choose between two things; (loosely) either of two possible courses, as *I had no (other)* ~; one of more than two possibilities. Hence ~LY² (-vl-) adv. [f. med. L *alternativus* (as prec., see -ATIVE)]

although (awldhō′), conj. Though. [ME, f. ALL adv. +THOUGH]

ăltim′ēter, n. Aeronautical aneroid for showing height above sea level. [L *altus* high, -METER]

ăl′titūde, n. Height; depth; (Geom.) length of perpendicular from vertex to base; height above sea level; (usu. in pl.) high place; (fig.) eminence. [ME, f. L *altitudo (altus* high), see -TUDE]

ăl′tŏ, n. (mus.). Highest male voice, counter-tenor; its musical part; female voice of similar range, contralto; its part; singer with ~ voice; tenor violin; ~*-clarinet, -trombone,* instruments similar to the clarinet, trombone. [It. *alto (canto)* high (singing); cf. earlier (16th c.) ALT]

altogether (awltogĕdh′er), adv. & n. Totally; on the whole; (n.) *an~,* a whole; *the* ~ (colloq.), the nude. [early ME f. ALL +TOGETHER]

ăl′tŏ-rĕliev′ŏ (-lē-), n. (sculp.). High relief. [It. *alto-rilievo*]

ăl′tru|ism (-rŏŏ-), n. Regard for others as a principle of action. Hence ~IST n., ~is′tic a., ~is′tICALLY adv. [f. F *altru-isme* f. It. *altrui* (= F *autrui*) somebody else; see -ISM]

ăl′um, n. A double sulphate of alumin-ium & potassium; series of salts including this; family of compounds including these; (Min.) various native minerals, alums proper & pseudo-alums. [ME, f. OF, f. L *alumen alumin-*]

alum′ina (-lŏŏ-), n. One of the earths, the only oxide of aluminium. [f. L *alumen* alum, on type of *soda* etc.]

ălūmin′ium, *alūm′inum, n. White light sonorous ductile malleable metal, not tarnished by air, used for instruments & as an alloy; ~ *bronze,* alloy of ~ & copper. [altered (after *sodium* etc.) f. *aluminum,* earlier *alumium;* see ALUM, -IUM]

alum'inous (-loo-), a. Of the nature of alum or alumina. [f. F *alumineux* or L *aluminosus* (*alumen* ALUM, see -OUS)]

alüm'n|us, n. (pl. ~ī; fem. ~a, pl. ~ae). (Former) pupil or student. [L, = foster--child]

ălvē'olate, a. Honeycombed, pitted with small cavities. [f. L *alveolatus* f. foll., see -ATE²]

ălvē'ol|us, n. Small cavity; socket of tooth, whence ~AR¹ a.; cell of honeycomb; conical chamber of a belemnite. [L, dim. of *alveus* cavity]

always (awl'wăz, -ĭz), adv. At all times; on all occasions (~ *excepting, provided,* etc., legal formulae). [OE (acc. case) *alne weg,* now (arch, or poet.) *alway*; superseded in ME by (gen. case) *alle(s) weis* always]

am. See BE.

ămadavăt', ăv-, n. Small Indian song--bird. [place-name]

ăm'adou (-oo), n. German tinder, prepared from fungi, used as a match & styptic. [F, f. Pr. f. L *amatorem* lover (*amare*, see -OR)]

amah (ah'ma), n. (S. India, formerly) wet-nurse; (China & Far East) child's (native) nurse. [f. Port. *ama* nurse]

amain', adv. (arch., poet.). Vehemently; in all haste. [A prep. +MAIN²]

amăl'gam, n. Mixture of a metal with mercury, as *gold* ~; plastic mixture of any substances (also fig.). [late ME, f. F *amalgame* or med. L *amalgama,* prob. f. L f. Gk *malagma* an emollient]

amăl'gamate¹, a. Combined, esp. of languages. [f. prec. +-ATE²]

amăl'gam|āte², v.t. & i. Mix; unite (classes, societies, companies, ideas, etc.); (of metals) combine with mercury. Hence ~A'TION n., ~ating or being ~ated, merging of two or more business concerns into one; ~ātoR n., ~ātIVE a. [f. prec., see -ATE³]

amănüěn'sĭs, n. (pl. -*nsēs*). One who writes from dictation or copies manuscript. [L, adj. used as n., f. (*servus*) *a manu* secretary +-*ensis* belonging to]

ăm'arănt(h), n. Imaginary unfading flower; genus, including prince's feather & love-lies-bleeding; purple colour. Hence **ămarăn't(h)INE¹** a. [f. F *amarante* f. L f. Gk *amarantos* everlasting (*a-* not +*marainō* wither); *h* by confusion with Gk *anthos* flower]

ămarўll'ĭs, n. Kinds of bulbous plant. [L, f. Gk *Amarullis,* name of a country girl]

amăss', v.t. Heap together; accumulate (esp. riches). [f. F *amasser* f. *a* (= A-(4)) +*masser* (f. *masse* MASS²)]

ăm'ateur (-tūr or ămatőr'), n. One who is fond *of*; one who cultivates a thing as a pastime. Hence **ămateur'ISH** (-tūr-) a., **ămateur'ishLY²** adv., **ămateur'ishNESS, ămateur'ISM**, nn. [F, f. L *amatorem* (*amare* love, see -OR)]

Amati (ahmah'tē), n. Violin or violoncello made by a member of the *Amati* family of Cremona (fl. *c.* 1570 onwards)

ăm'ative, a. Disposed to loving. Hence ~NESS (-vn-) n. [f. L *amare* love, see -ATIVE]

ăm'atŏl, n. High explosive made from TNT & ammonium nitrate. [irreg. f. AM(MONIUM)+(TRINITRO)TOL(UENE)]

ăm'atorў, a. Pertaining to a lover or to sexual love. Hence **ămatőr'IAL** a. [f. L *amatorius* (*amare* love, see -ORY)]

ămaur|ōs'is (-or-), n. Partial or total loss of sight from disease of optic nerve. Hence ~ŏT'IC a. [f. LL f. Gk, f. *amauroō* darken (*amauros* dark), see -OSIS]

amăz|e'¹, v.t. Overwhelm with wonder. Hence ~'ĕdLY², ~'ingLY², advv., ~e'-MENT (-zm-) n. [ME, perh. f. OE *āmasian* (once); see MAZE]

amăze'², n. (poet.). = AMAZEMENT. [f. prec.]

Am'azon (ă-), n. Fabulous race of female warriors in Scythia; female warrior (lit. & fig.); masculine woman. Hence **Amazōn'IAN** (ă-) a. [ME, f. L f. Gk (prob. foreign word, but explained by Greeks as *a-* not +*mazos* breast, from removal of right breast to facilitate use of bow)]

ămbā'ges (-jĕz), n. pl. Roundabout ways. [ME, f. OF f. L *ambages* circuits; in mod. use as direct f. L]

ăm'băn, n. Chinese resident official in Tibet. [Manchu, = minister]

ămbăss'ador, n. Minister sent by one sovereign or State on mission to another (usu. *A~ Extraordinary*); minister of highest rank permanently representing sovereign or State at foreign court or government (*Ordinary, Resident, A~*; formerly *A~ Leger*); *A~ Plenipotentiary* (with full power to sign treaties etc.); official messenger. Hence **ămbăssa-dőr'ial** a. [ME; many early forms; mod. sp. f. F *ambassadeur* f. Rom. *ambactiatorem f. *ambactiare f. med. L *ambactia* charge, office, f. L *ambactus* servant, of Celtic orig.]

ămbăss'adréss, n. Female ambassador; ambassador's wife. [f. prec. +-ESS¹]

ăm'ber, n. & a. **1.** Yellow translucent fossil resin, found chiefly on S. shore of Baltic; ~ *Fauna, Flora,* animals, plants, of which remains are found in ~; (of) the intermediate cautionary traffic light between red (= stop) and green (= go). **2.** adj. Made of, coloured like, ~. [ME, f. OF *ambre* or med. L *ambra* etc. f. Arab. '*anbar* ambergris, to which the name orig. belonged]

ăm'bergris (-ēs), n. Wax-like substance found floating in tropical seas, & in intestines of sperm-whale, odoriferous & used in perfumery, formerly in cookery. [late ME, f. OF *ambre gris* grey amber]

ămbidĕx'ter, a. & n. (Person) able to use left hand as well as right, double-

dealing. Hence **ămbĭdĕxtĕ′rĭty** n. [LL (*amb-* on both sides +*dexter* right-handed)]
ămbĭdĕx′t(e)rous, a. =prec. Hence ~LY² adv., ~NESS n. [as prec. + -OUS]
ăm′bĭent, a. Surrounding, circumfused. [f. L *ambiens -entis* part. of *ambire* go about (*amb-* on both sides + *ire* go)]
ămbĭgū′itў, n. Double meaning; expression capable of more than one meaning. [ME, f. OF *ambiguite* or L *ambiguitas* (as foll., see -TY)]
ămbĭg′ūous, a. Obscure; of double meaning; of doubtful classification; of uncertain issue. Hence ~LY² adv., ~NESS n. [f. L *ambiguus* doubtful f. *ambigere* (*amb-* both ways + *agere* drive) + -OUS]
ăm′bĭt, n. Precincts; bounds; compass, extent. [f. L *ambitus* a going round (*ambire*, see AMBIENT)]
ămbĭ′tion, n. Ardent desire for distinction; aspiration (*to* be, *to* do); object of such desire. [ME, f. OF f. L *ambitionem* (*ambire -it-*, canvass for votes, see AMBIENT & -ION)]
ămbĭ′tious (-shŭs), a. Full of ambition; strongly desirous (*of* a thing, *to* do); showing ambition, as *an* ~ *attempt*. Hence ~LY² adv., ~NESS n. [ME, f. OF *ambitious* or L *ambitiosus* (as prec., see -OUS)]
ămbiv′al|ence, n. Co-existence in one person of the emotional attitudes of love and hate towards the same object. So ~ENT a. [f. L *ambo* both, after *equivalence*]
ăm′ble¹, v.i. (Of horses etc.) move by lifting two feet on one side together; ride an ambling horse, ride at an easy pace; move in a way suggesting an ambling horse. [ME, f. OF *ambler* f. L *ambulare* walk]
ăm′ble², n. Pace of an ambling horse; easy pace. [ME, f. OF f. *ambler*, see prec.]
ămblў|ŏp′ia, n. Impaired vision. Hence ~ŏp′ɪc a. [Gk, f. *ambluōpos* a. (*amblus* dull + *ōps ōpos* eye)]
ăm′bō, n. (pl. ~*s*, ~*nes* pr. -ōn′ēs). Pulpit in early Christian churches. [med. L, f. Gk *ambōn* rim, (med. Gk pulpit)]
ămboy′na (wōŏd), n. Finely marked wood of an Asian tree. [*Amboyna* Island]
ămbrō′sia (-zĭa, -zhy*a*), n. (Myth.) food of the gods; anything delightful to taste or smell; bee-bread. [f. L f. Gk, elixir of life, f. *ambrotos* (*a-* not + (*m*)*brotos* mortal)]
ămbrō′sial (-zĭal, -zhyal), a. Divinely fragrant; divine. Hence ~LY² adv. [f. L f. Gk *ambrosios* divine + -AL]
ăm′brў, aum-, n. (arch.). Pantry; wall--press; dresser; closed recess in wall of church. [ME *ar-*, *almarie*, later *aumery*, *aumbry*, f. OF, f. med. L *ar-*, *almarium* (-*ia*) f. L *armarium* closet, chest]
ambs-ace (ămz ās′), n. Both aces, lowest throw at dice; bad luck; worthlessness. [ME, f. OF *ambes as* f. L *ambo* both: see ACE; also written *ames-*]

ăm′bŭlance, n. Moving hospital following army; conveyance for sick or wounded persons. [F (L *ambulare* walk, see -ANCE)]
ăm′bŭlant, a. (path.). (Of a disease) shifting from one part of the body to another, not confining patients to bed; (of treatment) involving exercise on part of patient. [f. part. of L *ambulare* walk, see -ANT]
ăm′bŭlatorў, a. & n. **1.** Pertaining to walking; adapted for walking; movable; not permanent. **2.** n. Place for walking; arcade, cloister. [f. L *ambulatorius* (as prec., see -ORY)]
ămbuscāde′¹, n. Ambush. [f. F *embuscade* f. It. *imboscata* or Sp. *emboscada* (*imboscare*, see AMBUSH v. and -ADE)]
ămbuscāde′², v.t. & i. Lie, conceal, in ambush. [f. prec.]
ăm′bush¹ (-ŏŏsh), n. Concealment of troops, troops concealed, in a wood etc.; (generally) lying in wait; *make, lay, an* ~, *lie in* ~. [earlier *en-*, *em-*, f. OF *embusche* (as foll.)]
ăm′bush² (-ŏŏsh), v.t. & i. Conceal (troops, only in p.p.); lie in wait for; attack from ambush; (intr.) lie in wait. [earlier *en-*, *em-*, etc. f. OF *embuscher*, *-buissier*, f. Rom. *IMBoscare* (*boscus* BUSH)]
âme damnée (see Ap.), n. Tool, devoted adherent. [F]
ameer′, amir′ (-ēr), n. Title of various Mohammedan rulers in Scinde & Afghanistan. [Arab. *amir* commander (*amara* command); cf. EMIR]
amēl′ior|āte, v.t. & i. (Cause to) become better. Hence ~A′TION, ~ātŏR, nn., ~ātɪve a. [f. earlier MELIORATE after F *améliorer* alt. f. OF *ameillorer* (*meilleur*, L *meliorem* better)]
amēn′ (ā-, ah-), int. So be it. [f. LL f. Gk f. Heb. *amen* certainty, certainly (*aman* strength)]
amēn′|able, a. (Of persons) responsible (*to* law etc. or abs.); (of things) liable *to*; capable of being tested by (*to*); responsive, tractable. Hence ~abɪL′ɪTY, ~able-NESS, nn., ~abLY² adv. [AF (Law Fr.), f. F *amener* bring to (*à* to +*mener* bring f. L *minare* threaten), see -ABLE]
amĕnd′, v.i. & t. Abandon evil ways; (arch.) improve in health; correct an error in (legal document), make professed improvements in (measure before Parliament); make better. Hence ~ABLE a., ~MENT n. [ME, f. OF *amender* f. Rom. **admendare* for L *emendare* EMEND]
***amende honorable** (see Ap.), n. Public apology & reparation. [F]
amĕnds′ (-z), n. Reparation, restitution, compensation, as *make* ~. [ME, f. OF *amendes* penalties, fine, pl. of *amende* reparation f. *amender* AMEND; pl. now treated in E as sing.]
amēn′itў, n. Pleasantness (of places, persons, etc.); (pl.) pleasant ways. [ME, f. OF

amenite or. L *amoenitas*, f. *amoenus* pleasant, see -TY]

ā měn'sā ět tŏr'ō, adv. From board & bed. [L]

amĕn'tia (-sha), n. Imbecility. [L, f. *amens* (*a* = *ab* + *mens mentis* mind)]

amĕn'tum, amĕnt', n. Catkin. Hence **ămentA'CEOUS, ămentīr'EROUS, amĕn'tiFORM,** aa. [L, = thong]

amĕrce', v.t. Fine; (loosely) punish. So **amēr'cIABLE** a., ~MENT (-sm-), **amēr'ciAMENT,** nn. [ME *amercy* f. AF *amercier* (*à* at + *merci* MERCY)]

Amē'rican, a. & n. 1. Belonging to continent of America or to United States; ~ *Beauty*, hybrid perpetual rose; || ~ *cloth, leather,* glazed cloth used for covering tables etc.; ~ *organ,* small organ with suction-operated reeds instead of blown pipes. 2. n. Native of America of European descent; citizen of United States. [-AN]

Amē'ricanism, n. Word or sense or phrase peculiar to or extending from United States; attachment to, sympathy with, United States. [prec. + -ISM]

Amē'ricanize, -ise (-īz), v.t. & i. Naturalize as an American; make American in character; become American in character; use Americanisms. [as prec. + -IZE]

ămeri'cium (-ĭsĭ-, -ĭshĭ-), n. Radio-active transuranic metallic element. [f. *Ameri-c(a)* + -IUM]

ames-ace. See AMBS-ACE.

ăm'ĕthy̆st, n. Precious stone, kind of quartz, purple or violet; *Oriental A~,* rare violet variety of sapphire. So **ămĕthy̆s'tINE[1]** a. [ME *ametist* f. OF *ametiste* f. L f. Gk *amethustos* not drunken, the stone being supposed to prevent intoxication]

Amhă'ric (ä-), n. Official & court language of Abyssinia. [f. *Amhara,* Abyssinian province]

ăm'iable, a. Feeling & inspiring friendliness; lovable. Hence **āmīaBIL'ITY,** ~NESS, nn., **ăm'iaBLY[2]** adv. [ME, f. OF, f. LL *amicabilis* AMICABLE; confused with OF *amable* (mod. F *aimable*) f. L *amabilis* lovable (*amare* love, see -BLE)]

ămiăn't(h)us, n. Mineral variety of asbestos, splitting into flexible fibres; green fibrous chrysolite. [L, f. Gk *amiantos* undefiled, i.e. purified by fire, being incombustible; for *-h-* cf. AMARANTH]

ăm'ic|able, a. Friendly; done in a friendly spirit. Hence ~aBIL'ITY, ~ableNESS, nn., ~abLY[2] adv. [f. LL *amicabilis* f. *amicus* friend, see -BLE]

ăm'ice[1], n., Square of white linen worn by celebrant priests, formerly on head, now on shoulders. [earlier *amyt* f. OF *anit* f. L *amictus* garment; *-ce,* or *-s,* perh. due to confus. w. foll.]

ăm'ice[2], n. Cap, hood, cape, of religious orders; badge worn by French canons on left arm. [ME, f. OF *aumusse* f. med.

L *almussa* etc. of unkn. orig.; early confused w. prec.]

amïc'us cūr'iae, n. Friend of the court, disinterested adviser. [L]

amid', amidst', prep. In the middle of (lit. & fig.); in the course of. [OE *on middan* etc. (i.e. *on* ON + oblique case of MID[1]), ME *amidde,* later *amiddes* (see -ES), & *amidst* with inorganic *-t* as in *against*]

ăm'īde, n. (chem.). Compound formed from ammonia by replacing one or more hydrogen atoms by an acid radical. [f. AM(MONIA) + -IDE]

ăm'idin, n. Soluble matter of starch; starch in state of solution. [f. *amid-* com.--Rom. form of L *amylum* starch (med. L *amidum,* F *amidon*) + -IN]

amid'ships, adv. In middle of ship. [f. AMID + SHIP + -ES]

ăm'ildār, n. Native revenue-collector in India. [f. Pers.]

ăm'ine, n. (chem.). Compound formed from ammonia by replacing one or more hydrogen atoms by alcohol or other base--radicals. [f. AM(MONIA) + -INE[5]]

amir', n. See AMEER.

amiss', adv. & pred. a. Not up to the mark; out of order; wrongly; untowardly, as *come* ~; *take* ~, take offence at; *not* ~, appropriate. [A prep. + MISS n.]

ăm'ity̆, n. Friendship, friendly relations. [ME, f. OF *amitie* f. Rom. *amicitatem* f. L *amicus* friend, see -TY]

ăm'mĕter, n. Instrument for measuring electric current in amperes. [f. AM(PERE) + -METER]

ăm'mō, n. (sl.). Ammunition. [abbr.]

ăm'monal, n. High explosive made from ammonium nitrate & aluminium. [f. AMMON(IUM) + AL(UMINIUM)]

ammōn'ia,· n. A colourless gas with pungent smell & strong alkaline reaction, spirit of hartshorn; *liquid* ~, (Chem.) liquefied ~; ~ *liquor,* solution of ~ in water. [f. foll.]

ammōn'iăc, a. & n. Of the nature of ammonia; *sal* ~, hard white crystalline salt, said to have been prepared from camels' dung near temple of Jupiter Ammon; (*gum*) ~, a gum resin used in medicine & as cement. Hence **ămmoni'acAL** a. [ME *armoniak* f. med. L *armoniacus, -um* f. L f. Gk *ammōniakon* belonging to Ammon]

ammōn'iātĕd, a. Combined with ammonia. [f. prec. + -ATE[1] (3) + -ED[1]]

ămm'onite, n. Fossil genus of Cephalopods. [f. mod. L *ammonites,* after med. L *cornu Ammonis,* L *Ammonis cornu* (Pliny), horn of (Jupiter) Ammon, see -ITE[1] (2)]

ammōn'ium, n. Univalent radical of ammonia salts; ~ *chloride, sal* AMMONIAC; ~ *carbonate,* rock ammonia (see SAL VOLATILE). [-IUM]

ămmūni'tion, n. Military stores (formerly of all kinds, now of bullets, shells, grenades, etc.); (fig.) facts, arguments, etc. used in attack or defence. [f. F (obs.)

amunition, an army corruption of (*la*) *munition* MUNITION]

ămnēs'ia, n. Loss of memory. [Gk, = forgetfulness]

ăm'nĕstў, n. & v.t. Intentional overlooking; act of oblivion, general pardon; (v.t.) give ~ to. [f. F *amnestie* or L f. Gk *amnēstia* oblivion f. *amnēstos* (-*mnē*- remember)]

ăm'niŏn, n. (pl. -*ia*). Innermost membrane enclosing foetus before birth. Hence **ămniŏt'ıc** a. [Gk, = caul (dim. of *amnos* lamb)]

amoeb'|a (-mē-), n. Microscopic animalcule perpetually changing shape. Hence ~iFORM, ~OID, aa. [f. Gk *amoibē* change]

amoebaean (ămēbē'*an*), a. Alternately answering, esp. of dialogue in verse. [f. L f. Gk *amoibaios* interchanging (*amoibē* change), see -AN]

amŏk'. See AMUCK.

among(st)' (-mŭ-), prep. In the assemblage of, surrounded by; in the number of; within the limits of (collectively or distributively), as *five shillings ~ us, divided ~ us*; in comparison with, as *one ~ many*; by joint action of, as *kill him ~ you*; reciprocally, as *quarrelled ~ themselves.* [OE *on gemang* (i.e. on ON +*gemang* assembly, cf. MINGLE), ME *among*(*c*), later *amonges* (see -ES), & *amongst* with inorganic -*t* as in *against*]

Amontillado (ahmŏntilyah'dō), n. (Formerly) a specially dry sherry; (now) sherry of a matured type; (fig., attrib.) of dry speech or manner. [Sp., f. *Montilla* (in Spain) + *ado* (= -ATE²)]

ămŏ'ral, a. Unconcerned with, out of the sphere of, morals, non-moral. [A- (7)]

‖ **amŏrce',** n. Priming charge; percussion cap for toy pistol. [F, f. OF *amordre* bite]

ăm'orist, n. One who professes (esp. sexual) love, a gallant. [f. L *amor* love +-IST]

ăm'orous, a. Inclined to love; in love; of, pertaining to, love. Hence ~LY² adv., ~NESS n. [ME, f. OF *amorous* (*amor* love, see -OUS)]

amŏrph'|ous, a. Shapeless; anomalous; (Min., Chem.) uncrystallized; unorganized. Hence ~ISM, ~OUSNESS, nn. [f. Gk *amorphos* shapeless (*a*- not +*morphē* form) +-OUS]

amŏrt'|ize, -ise (-īz), v.t. Alienate in mortmain; extinguish (debt, usu. by means of sinking fund), whence ~IZA'TION n. [ME, f. OF *amortir* (st. -*iss*-) f. Rom. *admortīre* (*ad* to +*mort*- death)]

amount'¹, v.t. Come to (so much); be equivalent (in significance) *to*. [ME, f. OF *amonter* f. *amont* upward (lit. uphill, f. L *ad montem*)]

amount'², n. Total to which a thing amounts; full value, significance, etc.; quantity, as *a considerable ~ (of).* [f. prec.]

amour' (-oor), n. Love-affair; intrigue. [F, = love f. L *amorem*]

amourĕtte' (-oor-), n. Petty love-affair. [F, dim. of *amour*]

amour-propre (ăm'oor-prŏp'r), n. Self-esteem. [F]

ămp, n. Ampere. [abbr.]

ămpĕlŏp'sis, n. Climbing plant allied to vine. [Gk *ampelos* vine, *opsis* appearance]

ăm'pere (-ēr, -ār), n. (electr.). Current that one volt can send through one ohm, unit of current. [name (*Ampère*) of physicist (d. 1836)]

ămpersănd', n. The sign & (*and*, L *et*). [corrupt. of '*and* per se (i.e. by itself) *and*' the old way of spelling & naming the character &]

amphi- in comb. Both, of both kinds, on both sides, around. [Gk, prep.]

Amphib'ia (ă-), n. pl. Division of Vertebrata, intermediate between reptiles & fishes, as frogs, newts, etc. [f. L f. Gk *amphibia* (*zōa*) (animals) living in both elements (AMPHI- +*bios* life)]

ămphib'ian, a. & n. (Animal) living both on land & in water; (Zool.) member of the Amphibia; (tank or other vehicle) adapted for both land & water; an aircraft designed to rise from & alight on either land or water. [as prec. +-AN]

ămphibiŏl'ogў, n. Branch of zoology treating of Amphibia. [as prec. +-LOGY]

amphib'ious, a. Living both on land & in water; connected with both land & water; (Mil.) involving co-operation of sea & land (& occas. air) forces organized for invasion, (of forces) trained for such action; having two lives, connected with two classes, etc. Hence ~LY² adv. [f. AMPHIBIA +-OUS]

ămphibŏl'ogў, n. Quibble; ambiguous wording. Hence **ămphibolŏ'gıCAL** a. [f. F *amphibologie* or LL -*logia*, f. L f. Gk AMPHI(*bolia* f. *ballō* throw); assim. to words in -LOGY]

ămphic'tўons, n. pl. Deputies from ancient Greek states forming council. So **ămphictўŏn'ıc** a. [f. Gk *amphiktuones* neighbours]

ăm'phigăm, n. (bot.). Plant with no distinct sexual organs. Hence **ămphig'-amous** a. [f. F *amphigame* (AMPHI- +Gk *gamos* marriage)]

ămphigour'i (-oorī), **ăm'phigorў,** n. Nonsensical composition. [F *amphigouri*, orig. unkn.]

ămphimix'is, n. (biol.). Mingling of two individuals, or of their germs, as in sexual reproduction. [AMPHI- +Gk *mixis* mingling]

ămphiŏx'us, n. The fish lancelet. [f. AMPHI- +Gk *oxus* sharp]

ămphip'od|a, n. pl. Order of Crustacea, with feet of two kinds. Hence **ăm'-phipŏd** n., ~AN, ~OUS, aa. [AMPHI- +Gk *pous podos* foot]

ămphip'rostўle, a. With portico at both

ends. [F, f. L f. Gk *amphiprostulos* (AMPHI- + *prostulos* PROSTYLE)]

ămphisbaen′a, n. Fabulous serpent with head at each end; (Zool.) genus of wormlike lizards. [L, f. Gk *amphisbaina* (*amphis* both ways + *bainō* go)]

ăm′phithĕatre (-*ater*), n. Oval or circular building, with seats rising behind & above each other round a central open space; large circular hollow; part of a theatre; (fig.) scene of a contest. Hence **ămphithĕăt′rical** a. [f. L f. Gk *amphitheatron* (see AMPHI- & THEATRE)]

Amphit′rÿon (á-), n. Host, entertainer. [Molière, *Amphitryon*, iii. 5]

ăm′phora, n. (pl. -*ae*, -*as*). Greek or Roman two-handled vessel. [L, f. Gk *amphoreus* for AMPHI(*phoreus* f. *pherō* bear)]

ămphŏ′rĭc, a. (med.). · Like the sound produced by blowing into large vessel with small mouth. [f. prec. + -IC]

ămphotĕ′rĭc, a. Acting both ways, esp. (Chem.) capable of reacting as acid & base, or as electropositive & electronegative. [f. Gk *amphoteros* both, + -IC]

ăm′ple, a.(-er, -est). Spacious; extensive; abundant; copious; quite enough. Hence **ăm′plY²** adv., ∼NESS (-ln-) n. [f. F f. L *amplus*]

ăm′pliative, a. (logic). Extending a simple conception. [f. L *ampliare* widen (*amplus*), see -ATIVE]

ămplifică′tion, n. Extension, enlargement; making the most of a thing. [F, or f. L *amplificatio* (as foll., see -ATION)]

ăm′plif|ȳ, v.t. & i. Enhance; enlarge (story, statement); expatiate. Hence ∼īER¹ n., (esp.) appliance increasing loudness of sounds, strength of wireless signals, etc. [ME, f. OF *amplifièr* or L *amplificare* (as AMPLE, see -FY)]

ăm′plitūde, n. Breadth; abundance; wide range; dignity; (Astron.) space by which celestial body rises, sets, wide of due east, west; (Phys.) extent of vibration or oscillation; (Electr.) maximum departure from average of alternating current or wave. [F, or f. L *amplitudo* (as AMPLE, see -TUDE)]

ăm′poule (-ōol), n. Small glass vessel for containing esp. hypodermic injection. [F, cf. foll.]

ămpŭll′a, n. (pl. -*ae*). Roman two-handled flask; vessel for sacred uses; (Biol.) dilated end of vessel, canal, duct, in an animal. Hence **ămpullA′ceous** (-āsh*u*s) a. [L]

ăm′pūt|āte, v.t. Cut off (part of animal body etc. or abs.). Hence ∼A′TION, ∼ātOR, ∼EE, nn. [f. L *amputare* (*amb*-about + *putare* prune), see -ATE³]

amŭck′, amŏk′, adv. *Run* ∼, run about in frenzied thirst for blood (also fig.). [f. Malay *amoq* rushing in frenzy]

ăm′ūlĕt, n. Thing worn as charm against evil (lit. & fig.). [f. L *amuletum*, orig. unkn.]

amŭs|e′ (-z), v.t. Divert from serious business (*with* trifles, *by* trifling); tickle the fancy of; *be* ∼*ed with*, *by*, *at*. So ∼′ABLE, ∼′IVE, aa. [ME, f. OF *amuser* cause to MUSE² (causal *à* to + *muser* stare)]

amŭse′ment (-zm-), n. Pleasant diversion; excitement of risible faculty; pastime. [f. F *amusement* (*amuser*, see prec. and -MENT)]

ămȳgdăl′ĭc, a. Of almonds, as ∼ *acid*. [f. L *amygdala* ALMOND + -IC]

amȳg′daloid, a. & n. (Igneous rock containing mineral nodules) of almond shape. [f. Gk *amugdalē* ALMOND + -OID]

ăm′ȳl, n. (chem.). The radical of various alcohols some of which are constituents of fusel oil. Hence **amȳl′ĭc** a. [f. L *am(ylum)* starch + -YL; named as discovered in distilling fusel oil from starch]

ămȳlā′ceous (-shus), a. Of starch, starchy. [f. L *amylum* starch + -ACEOUS]

ăm′ȳloid, a. & n. Starchy (food). [as prec. + -OID]

ămȳlŏp′sin, n. Ferment of the pancreatic juice that converts starch into sugar. [f. Gk *amulon* starch, after *pepsin*]

an¹, a. See A, adj.

an², conj. (arch., colloq., dial.). If. [weakening of *and*]

an-, pref. f. var. sources. **1.** OE, ME *an* = on, as in *anon*, *anent*. **2.** f. L *ad* before *n*, see AD-. **3.** f. L *an-* = *ambi-*, as in *anfractuosity*. **4.** f. Gk ANA-, as in *anode*. **5.** f. Gk *an-* = *a-* not (before vowel), as in *anarchy*.

-an, suf. of adjj. (often used as nn.), f. L -*anus* direct or through F -*ain*, -(*i*)*en*, the ME forms, (retained in *certain*, *captain*, *chaplain*), but later refashioned after L as -*an*, or It., Sp., Port., -*ano*, & freely used in new words; added esp. to names of place, system, zool. order, or founder (*Chilian*, *Anglican*, *reptilian*, *Lutheran*); often as E termination to L adjj. in -*ius*, giving -IAN as a mere phonetic variant (cf. *Christ-ian*, *Mohammed-an*). See also -ANE, -EAN.

ăn′a, n. (With pl. ∼*s*) collection of person's memorable sayings; (collect. pl.) anecdotes, lit. gossip, about a person. [= -ANA]

ăna-, pref. = Gk *ana* up, back, again, anew; before a vowel *an-*.

-ana, suf. Neut. pl. of L adjj. in -*anus* (see -AN) appended in 16th-c. F to names = the sayings of; in E from 18th c., now including anecdotes about, publications bearing on, places or persons, as *Tunbrigiana*, *Shakespeareana*.

ănabăp′tism, n. Re-baptism; doctrine of anabaptists. [f. LL f. Gk *anabaptismos* (ANA- + *baptismos* BAPTISM)]

ănabăp′t|ist n. One who baptizes over again; (opprobriously) = BAPTIST. Hence ∼is′tICAL a. [f. F *anabaptiste* or mod. L *anabaptista* (prec., -IST)]

ăn′abăs, n. Kinds of fishes that leave water & ascend trees. [Gk part. of *anabainō* walk up]

anăb'asis, n. Up-country march, esp. that of Cyrus the younger into Asia, narrated by Xenophon. [Gk, = ascent f. ANA(*bainō* go)]

ănabăt'ic, a. (meteor.). (Of winds) caused by air flowing upwards, cf. KATABATIC. [as prec. + -IC]

anăb'olism, n. (biol.). Constructive metabolism (opp. KATABOLISM). So **ănaböl'ic** a. [f. Gk *anabolē* ascent + -ISM]

ăn'abranch (-ahn-). n. A stream that turns out of, &, lower down, re-enters, a river. [ANA- + BRANCH]

ănachrŏn'ic (-k-), a. Involving anachronism, out of date. [f. ANA- + Gk *khronos* time + -IC]

anăch'ron|ism (-k-), n. Error in computing time; thing out of harmony with the present, esp. the relation of an event, custom, or circumstance to a wrong period of time; building etc. out of harmony with its surroundings in point of time. So ~**is'tic** a. [f. F *anachronisme* or Gk *anakhronismos* f. *anakhronizō* (as prec.)]

ănaclăs'tic, a. Pertaining to refraction; springing back with crackling sound, as ~ *glasses*. [f. Gk *anaklastos* refracted f. ANA(*klaō* bend)]

ănacolūth'on, n. (pl. -*tha*). Sentence, words, lacking grammatical sequence. [f. Gk *anakolouthon* (AN- (5) + *akolouthos* following)]

ănacŏn'da, n. Large snake of Ceylon; large S.-American Boa; any large snake that crushes its prey. [orig. unkn.]

anăcrĕŏn'tic, a. & n. (Poem) in the manner or metre(◡◡−◡|−◡−◡) of Anacreon's lyrics; convivial & amatory. [f. LL *Anacreonticus* (Gk *Anakreōn*, name of poet)]

ănacrus'ĭs (-ōō-), n. (pros.). Unstressed syllable at beginning of verse. [f. Gk *anakrousis* (ANA*krouō* strike up)]

anăd'romous, a. (Of fishes) ascending rivers to spawn. [f. Gk ANA(*dromos* running) + -OUS]

anaem'|ia, n. (med.). Lack of blood, unhealthy paleness; PERNICIOUS ~. Hence ~IC a. [f. Gk *anaimia* (AN- (5) + *haima* blood); see -IA[1]]

anaerobe (anā'erŏb), n. Minute organism that can live without free oxygen. Hence **anāerŏb'IAN, anāerŏb'IC**, aa. [f. AN- (5) + Gk *aēr* air + *bios* life]

ănaesthēs'ia, n. Insensibility (lit.). [f. Gk *anaisthēsia* (AN- (5) + *aisthēsis* sensation f. st. *aisthe-* perceive)]

ănaesthĕt'|ic, a. & n. (Agent) that produces insensibility. Hence ~ICALLY adv. [f. Gk *anaisthētos* insensible (as prec.) + -IC]

anaes'thet|ize, -ise (-īz), v.t. Render insensible (lit. & fig.). Hence ~IST (1), ~IZA'TION, nn. [as prec. + -IZE]

ăn'aglyph, n. Embossed ornament in low relief; (Photog.) composite stereoscopic picture printed in superimposed complementary colours. Hence **ănaglÿph'IC** a. [f. Gk ANA*gluphē* (*gluphō* carve); cf. LL *anaglyphus* a.]

ănagnŏ'risis, n. Recognition, dénouement in a drama. [Gk, f. *anagnōrizō* recognize]

ănagŏ'gē, n. Spiritual or allegorical interpretation. So **ănagŏ'gic**(AL) aa., **ănagŏ'gicalLY²** adv. [LL, f. Gk f. *anagō* lead up (AN- 4)]

ăn'agrăm, n. Transposition of letters of word or phrase, to form new word or phrase. Hence **ănagrammăt'IC(AL)** aa., **ănagrammăt'icalLY²** adv. [f. F *anagramme* after Gk *anagrammatizō* transpose letters; see -GRAM]

ănagrămm'at|ize, -ise (-īz), v.t. Form into an anagram. Hence -ISM, ~IST, nn. [f. Gk *anagrammatizō* (prec., see -IZE)]

ăn'al, a. Pertaining to, situated near, the anus. [f. ANUS + -AL]

ăn'alĕcts, ănalĕc'ta, n. pl. Literary gleanings. [f. Gk *analekta* things gathered (ANA*legō* pick up)]

ănalĕp'tic, a. & n. Restorative (medicine). [f. LL f. Gk *analēptikos* f. ANA(*lambanō* take) restore, see -IC]

ănălgēs'ia, n. Absence of pain. So **ănalgĕt'ic**, (irreg.) **ănalgēs'ic**, aa., giving ~, & nn., such drug. [Gk (-*gēs*-), f. *an*- (5), *algeō* feel pain]

ănalŏ'gic. a. Of analogy. [f. L f. Gk *analogikos* (as ANALOGY, see -IC)]

ănalŏ'gical, a. According to analogy; expressing an analogy. Hence ~LY² adv. [as prec., see -ICAL]

anăl'ogist, n. One occupied with analogies; philosopher who saw in words images of the things they expressed. [as foll., see -IST]

anăl'ogize, -ise (-īz), v.t. & i. Represent by analogy; show to be analogous; employ analogy; be in harmony (*with*). [f. ANALOGY + -IZE]

anăl'ogous, a. Similar, parallel, (*to*). Hence ~LY² adv., ~NESS n. [f. L f. Gk *analogos* (*ana* up to + *logos* proportion) + -OUS]

ăn'alogue (-ŏg), n. Analogous, parallel, word or thing. [F, f. Gk *analogon* neut. adj., see prec.]

anăl'ogy̆, n. (Math.) proportion; agreement, similarity, (*to, with, between*); analogue; (Logic) process of reasoning from parallel cases; (Lang.) imitation of inflexion or construction of existing words in forming inflexions or constructions of others, without intervention of the formative steps through which these at first arose; (Nat. Hist.) resemblance of form or function between organs essentially different. [f. F *analogie* or L -*ia* f. Gk *analogia* proportion (as ANALOGOUS)]

ăn'alÿs|e (-z), *-ÿz|e*, v.t. Examine minutely the constitution of; (Chem., Phys.) ascertain the elements of (a compound); find, show, the essence of (treatise etc.); (Gram.) resolve (sentence) into its grammatical elements. Hence ~ABLE a. [f. F *analyser* (*analyse*, as foll.); also *-yze* in E by assim. to vbs in -IZE].

anäl'ÿsis, n. (pl. *-ysēs*). Resolution into simple elements (in all senses of prec.); *bowling* ~, register of the result of each ball, ratio of balls bowled to wickets taken. [med. L f. Gk *analusis* f. ANA(*luō* loose)]

än'alÿst, n. One skilled in (usu. chemical) analysis. [f. F *analyste* f. *analyser* ANALYSE, on anal. of nouns in *iste* -IST f. vbs in *-iser* -IZE]

änalÿt'ic, a. Pertaining to analysis. Hence **änalÿt'ics** n. [f. LL f. Gk *analutikos* (as ANALYSIS, see -IC)]

änalÿt'ical, a. Employing the analytic method;~(co-ordinate) *geometry*; (Lang.) using separate words instead of inflexions. Hence ~LY² adv. [as prec., see -ICAL]

änamnēs'is, n. Recollection (esp. of a previous existence). [Gk (ANA*mimnēskō* remind)]

änamōrph'osis, n. Distorted drawing appearing regular from óne point; (Bot.) abnormal transformation. [Gk (ANA*morphoō* transform f. *morphē* form, see -OSIS)]

anän'as (*or* -ahn-), n. Pineapple. [F or Sp. *ananas, anana*; f. Guarani *nana*]

anän'drous, a. (bot.). Without stamens. [f. Gk *anandros* husbandless (AN- (5) + *anēr andros* male) + -OUS]

Anani'as (à-), n. A liar. [see *Acts* v. 1–5]

än'apaest, n. (Prosody) foot consisting of two short syllables followed by one long. Hence **änapaes'tic** a. [f. L f. Gk *anapaistos* reversed (ANA- + *paiō* strike)]

anäph'ora, n. Repetition of word or phrase in successive clauses. [LL, f. Gk *anaphora* = carrying back f. ANA(*pherō* bear)]

·än'ärch (-k), n. (poet.). Leader of revolt. [f. Gk *anarkhos* without ruler (AN- (5) + *arkhos*)]

anärch'ic(al) (-k-), aa. Lawless. Hence **anärch'icalLY²** adv. [as prec. + -IC, -ICAL]

än'arch|ist (-k-), n. Advocate of anarchy. So ~ISM (-k-) n. [as prec. + -IST]

än'archÿ (-k-), n. Absence of government; disorder; confusion. [f. med. L f. Gk *anarkhia* (as prec.)]

anär'throus, a. (Gk Gram.) used without the article; (Physiol.) jointless. [f. AN- (5) + Gk *arthron*, joint, article, + -OUS]

änasâr'c|a, n. A dropsical affection. Hence ~OUS a. [f. Gk *ana* up + *sarka* (nom. *sarx*) flesh]

änastät'ic, a. In relief; ~ *printing* (from reliefs on zinc plates). [f. Gk *anastatos* set up (ANA*sta*- stánd up) + -IC]

änastigmät'ic, a. Free from astigmatism (used esp. of photographic lenses in which this error is corrected). So (by back-formation thr. G) **anastig'mät** n., lens, or lens-system, so corrected. [AN- (5) + ASTIGMATIC]

anäs'tomōse (-z), v.i. Communicate by anastomosis. [f. F *anastomoser* (*anastomose* = foll.)]

anästomōs'is, n. (pl. *-osēs*). Cross connexion of arteries, branches, rivers, etc. [Gk,. f. *anastomoō* furnish with mouth (*stoma*), see -OSIS]

änäs'trophē, n. (rhet.). Inversion or unusual order of words or clauses. [Gk (ANA-, *strophē* turning f. *strephō* turn)]

anäth'ēma, n. Accursed thing; curse of God; curse of the church, excommunicating a person or denouncing a doctrine; imprecation. [eccl. L, = excommunicated person, excommunication, f. Gk *anathema* thing devoted, (later) accursed thing (ANA*lithēmi* set up)]

anäth'ēmatize, -ise (-iz), v.t. & i. Curse. [f. F *anathématiser* or LL f. Gk *anathematizō* (as prec., see -IZE)]

änatöm'ical, a. Belonging to anatomy; structural. Hence ~LY² adv. [f. F *anatomique* or LL f. Gk *anatomikos* (as ANATOMY); see -ICAL]

anät'omist, n. Dissecter of bodies; one skilled in anatomy; (fig.) analyser. [f. F *anatomiste*, as foll., see -IST]

anät'omize, -ise (-iz), v.t. & i. Dissect; (fig.) analyse. [f. F *anatomiser*, as foll., see -IZE]

anät'omÿ, n. Dissection; science of bodily structure; anatomical structure; analysis; (pop.) skeleton, mummy, emaciated creature. [f. F *anatomie* or LL f. Gk *anatomia* (ANA-, -TOMY)]

anät'ta, -tō, n. Orange-red dye, used for colouring cheese. [f. Carib *annoto*, name .of tree]

än'burÿ, ämb-, n. Soft tumour on horses & oxen; disease of turnips & allied plants. [perh. = *ang-berry* (OE *ang*-painful, cf. AGNAIL)]

-ance, suf. forming nn. of quality or action, chiefly thr. F *-ance* f. L *-antia* & *-entia* (see -ENCE) f. L pres. part. in *-ant-*, *-ent-* (nom. *-ans, -ens*). OF gave *-ance* both for existing L *-antia, -entia*, & for wds formed in F on same model; thus, *assistance, nuisance*, where L would have *-entia*. Later F followed L vowel; *élégance, tempérance* (L *-antia*), but *diligence, prudence* (L *-entia*). E adopted F forms of both kinds, & usu. retains F form; but after 1500 *-ence* was in some wds restored where L would have *-entia*, & mod. formations follow L vowel. F *-ance* also became living suf. in E on native vbs as *furtherance, forbearance, riddance*.

än'cèst|or, n. Any of those from whom one's father or mother is descended, forefather. Hence ~rESS¹ n. [ME, f. OF *ancestre, ancessor*, f. L. *antecessor, -orem*, f. ANTE(*cedere cess*- go), see -OR]

äncès'tral, a. Belonging to, inherited from, ancestors. [16th c., f. OF *ancestrel*, mod. F *-al*; see prec. & -AL]

än'cèstrÿ, n. Ancestral lineage; ancient

descent; ancestors. [ME, alt. f. OF *ancesserie* (as ANCESTOR, see -Y[1])]

anchithere (ăng'kĭthēr), n. Fossil animal, size of small pony, regarded as ancestor of the horse. [f. Gk *agkhi* near + *thērion* wild beast]

ănc'hor[1] (-k-), n. Heavy iron, composed of long shank, with ring at one end to which cable is fastened, & at other end two' flukes, used for mooring ship to bottom of sea etc.; *sheet, bower, kedge*, -~, (largest, middle, smallest size); (fig.) source of confidence; *cast, weigh*, ~, let down, take up, ~; *at* ~, anchored; *come to (an)* ~, anchor; *swallow the* ~ (Naut. sl.), retire from seafaring life; ~-*plate*, heavy piece of timber or metal serving as point of support for cables of suspension-bridge etc.; ~-*stroke* (Bill.), a kind of cannon; ~-*watch*, watch set while ship lies at ~. [OE *ancor* f. L *ancora* (not *anch-*) f.Gk *agkura* (st. *agk-* hook); later reinforced by OF *ancre*]

anc'hor[2] (-k-), v.t. & i. Secure (ship) with anchor; (fig.) fix firmly; (intr.) cast anchor, come to anchor. [ME, f. prec. or OF *ancrer*]

ănc'horage (-k-), n. Anchoring; lying at anchor; ~-*ground*; (fig.) thing to depend upon; ~-*dues*. [prec. + -AGE; cf. F *ancrage*]

ănc'horėss, ănc'rėss, (-k-), n. Female anchorite. [f. obs. *anchor* (OE *ancra*, short form of LL *anachoreta*, see foll.) + -ESS[1]]

ănc'horite, -rĕt, (-k-), n. Hermit; person of secluded habits. Hence **ănchorĕt'ic** (-k-) a. [f. LL *anachoreta* (med. L -*ita*) f. Gk *anakhōrētēs* (ANAkhōrcō retire, see -ETE), influenced by the forms of *anchor*, see prec.]

ăn'chŏvỹ (or ănchō[2]), n. Small fish of herring family; ~-*paste* & ~-*sauce*, ~--*toast*, (made, spread, with anchovies); ~-*pear*, W.-Indian fruit eaten like mango. [f. Sp., Pg. *anchova*, of disputed orig.]

anchusa (ăngkŭs'a), n. Kinds of hairy--stemmed plant, such as alkanet & bugloss. [L]

ănc'hylose (-kĭlōz), v.t. & i. (Of joints, bones) stiffen, unite. [f. foll.]

anchylōs'is (ăngkĭ-), n. Formation of stiff joint by consolidation of articulating surfaces. [f. Gk *agkulōsis* (*agkuloō* crook f. *agkulos*, see -OSIS); -*ch-* for -*c*- to preserve hard sound]

ancien régime (see Ap.), n. Time before French Revolution; (transf.) the old order. [F]

ăn'cient[1] (-shent), a. & n. Belonging to times long past (esp. before fall of Western Roman Empire); having existed, lived, long (~ *lights*, window that neighbour may not deprive of light by building); *the A*~ *of Days*, God; *the* ~*s*, civilized nations of antiquity. Hence ~LY[2] adv., ~NESS n. [ME *auncien* etc. f. OF *ancien* f. Rom. *anti-*, *anteanus* (*ante* before, see -AN); -*t* after wds in -ENT; cf. *tyrant*]

ăn'cient[2] (-shent), n. (arch.). = ENSIGN. [corrupt. due to confusion of early forms of ENSIGN & ANCIENT[1]]

ăn'cientrỹ (-shen-), n. Ancientness; old--fashioned style. [ANCIENT[1] + -RY]

ăncill'arỹ (or ăn[2]), a. Subservient, subordinate, (*to*). [f. L *ancillaris* (*ancilla* handmaid, see -ARY[2])]

ancon (ăng'kon), n. (Physiol.) elbow; (Archit.) quoin of wall or rafter, console, pretended support to cornice; *A*~ *sheep*, kind with long bodies & short legs, the fore-legs crooked. [L, f. Gk *agkōn* bend, elbow]

-ancỹ, suf., in mod. E f. L -*antia* (as -ENCY f. L -*entia*); used partly to form new wds direct f. L, partly to refashion earlier wds in -*ance*, to denote quality or state, as opposed to -*ance*, which has besides this meaning that of action or process. See -CY.

and (and, *emphat.* ănd), conj. connecting words, clauses, and sentences, as *cakes* ~ *buns, black* ~ *brown bread, buy* ~ *sell*. Special uses: *four* ~ *twenty* (but *twenty--four*); *two hundred* ~ *forty, two thousand* ~ *forty* (but *two thousand four hundred*); *two* ~ *ten pence, two pounds* ~ *ten pence* (but *two pound ten*); *miles* ~ (= innumerable) *miles*; *nice* ~ (= nicely) *thin*; *try* ~ (to) *come, mind* ~ (to) *bring*; *there are books* ~ (different kinds of, good & bad) *books*; *two* ~ *two, by twos*; *stir*, ~ (= if you stir) *you are a dead man*; *and/or*, formula allowing reader to take either or both of two expressions (*contributions in money and/or garments*). [OE *and*, *ond* (Gmc **anda*), *end* (Gmc **andi*)]

Andalu'sian (ăndălō[2]'shn), n. & a. (Native) of Andalusia, a province of Spain; || = *wool*, fine soft kind; ~ (*fowl*), bluish-black domestic fowl. [-AN]

ăndăn'tė, adv. & n. (mus.). (Movement) in moderately slow time. [It.]

ăndanti'nō (-tē-), adv. & n. (Movement) rather quicker (orig. slower) than *andante*. [It., dim. of prec.]

An'derson shĕl'ter (ăn-), n. Portable arched corrugated-steel air-raid shelter. [Sir J. *Anderson*, Home Secretary (1939–40)]

ăn'diron (-īrn), n. Firedog, for supporting burning wood on hearth. [ME *aundyre*, -*yrne*, f. OF *andier*, of unkn. orig.; assim. in form to *iron*]

ăndroe'cium (-rē-), n. (bot.). The stamens taken collectively. [f. Gk *andro-* male + *oikion* house]

ăn'drogen (-), n. Any substance (e.g. a male sex hormone) capable of developing & maintaining many male sexual characteristics. [f. Gk *andro-* male + -GEN]

ăndrŏg'ỹn|ous, a. Hermaphrodite, whence ~Y[1] n.; (Bot.). with stamens & pistils in same flower or on same plant. [f. L f. Gk *androgunos* (*anēr andros* male + *gunē* woman) + -OUS]

-āne, suf. **1.** Var. of -AN, usu. w. differentiation (germane, urbane, humane), but occas. alone (mundane). **2.** (Chem.) formed to give a series with Gk -ENE, -INE, -ONE, for naming hydrocarbon types.

ăn'ĕcdŏtage, n. Anecdotes; (joc.) garrulous old age. [-AGE]

ăn'ĕcdŏt|e, n. Narrative of detached incident; (pl. ~a) unpublished details of history. Hence ~IST n., ~AL, **ānĕcdŏt´IC(AL)**, aa. [orig. pl. f. F anecdotes f. Gk anekdota things unpublished (AN- (5) + ekdotos f. ekdidōmi publish)]

anēle', v.t. (arch.). Anoint; give extreme unction to. [ME anelien (AN- (1)+elien oil f. OE ele, n. f. L oleum)]

anĕm'o|graph (-ahf), n. Instrument for recording on paper the direction & force of wind. Hence ~grăph'IC a. [f. Gk anemos wind+-GRAPH]

anĕmŏm'ĕter, n. Instrument for measuring force of wind, whence **ănĕmomĕt'rIC** a., **ănĕmŏm'ETRY** n.; apparatus for showing wind-pressure in organ. [as prec. +-METER]

anĕm'onē, n. Kinds of plants, esp. ~ nemorosa (also called wind-flower); sea ~, popular name of various actinoid zoophytes. [f. L f. Gk anemōnē daughter of the wind (as prec.+-ōnē patronymic suf.)]

ănĕmŏph'ilous, a. Wind-fertilized. [f. Gk anemos wind, see -PHILOUS]

anĕnt', prep. (arch., Sc.). Concerning. [= OE on efen on a level with]

-ānēous, suf. f. L adjj. in -aneus (-an-+ -eo-)+-ous.

ăn'eroid, a. & n. ~ (barometer), one that measures air-pressure by its action on elastic lid of box exhausted of air, not by height of fluid column. [f. F anéroïde (Gk a- not+nēros wet, see -OID)]

ăn'eurўsm, -ism (-nūr-), n. Morbid dilatation of an artery; abnormal enlargement. Hence **ăneurўs'mAL**, **-ĭs'mAL** (-nūrĭz-), a. [f. Gk aneurusma (aneurunō widen out f. eurus wide); cf. LL -isma]

anew', adv. Again; in a different way. [A- (3)+NEW]

ănfrăctūŏs'itў, n. Circuitousness, intricacy, (lit. & fig.); (usu. pl.) winding passage. [f. F anfractuosité f. LL anfractuosus f. L anfractus a bending, see -OSE & -TY]

ăng'arў (-ngg-), n. (law). Belligerent's right (subject to compensation) of seizing or destroying neutral property under stress of military necessity. [f. F angarie or LL angaria f. Gk aggareia (aggaros Persian courier)]

ăn'gel (-j-), n. Divine messenger; visits, like those of ~s, short & far between; entertain an ~ unawares, do service to one who proves to be an important person etc. (Heb. xiii. 2); lovely or innocent being; minister of loving offices; (sl.) financial backer of enterprise; old English gold coin (in full ~-noble), from

6s. 8d. to 10s., showing Michael piercing dragon; good, evil, ~, attendant spirits; ~ (messenger) of death; ~-fish, kind of shark; ~s, devils, -on-horseback, savoury of oysters wrapped in slices of bacon. [OE engel (f. *angil) Gmc f. LL angelus f. Gk aggelos; in ME reinforced & superseded by OF angele, angle (mod. ange)]

ăngĕl'ic (-j-), a. Pertaining to angels; like an angel, of superhuman qualities; A~ Doctor, Thomas Aquinas. Hence ~AL a., ~alLY[2] adv. [f. F angélique or LL f. Gk aggelikos (as prec., see -IC)]

ăngĕl'ica (-j-), n. Aromatic plant, used in cooking & medicine; candied ~ root. [f. med. L (herba) angelica angelic herb]

ăn'gĕlus (-j-), n. Devotional exercise commemorating Incarnation, said by Roman Catholics at morning, noon, & sunset, at sound of bell (~-bell or ~). [f. opening words Angelus domini]

ăng'er[1] (-ngg-), n. Rage, hot displeasure. [ME, f. ON angr trouble (root *ang strait)]

ăng'er[2] (-ngg-), v.t. Make angry, enrage. [ME, f. ON angra vex (as prec.)]

An'gĕvin (ănj-), a. & n. Of Anjou, of the Plantagenets, including English kings from Henry II to Richard II; (n.) a Plantagenet. [F]

ăngī'na (-j-), n. Quinsy; ~ pĕc'torĭs, spasm of chest resulting from over-exertion when heart is diseased. [L, = quinsy, f. Gk agkhonē strangling]

ăn'gio- (-j-), comb. form of Gk aggeion vessel dim. of aggos chest, chiefly in terms relating to seed- or blood-vessels.

angle[1] (ăng'gl), n. Space between two meeting lines or planes; inclination of two lines to each other; ACUTE, OBTUSE, RIGHT, ~; corner; sharp projection; (fig.) point of view; ~-iron, L-shaped piece of iron to strengthen framework; ~-wise, angularly. Hence (-)anglED[2] (ăng'gld) a. [ME, f. OF angle or L angulus dim. of *angus, cf. Gk agkos bend]

angle[2] (ăng'gl), n., & v.i. Fish-hook (obs. exc. in brother of the ~, angler); (vb) fish with hook & bait (for or abs.), lit. & fig. [OE angul (= OHG angul, ON öngull) f. Gmc *ang-; cf. prec.]

Angle[3] (ăng'gl), n. (Pl.) Low-German tribe settled in Northumbria, Mercia, & E. Anglia. [f. L Anglus f. Gmc *angli- (OE Engle, cf. ENGLISH) f. Angul a district of-Holstein (as prec.)]

ăng'ler (-ngg-) n. One who angles; (Zool.) a British fish that preys upon small fish, attracting them by filaments attached to head & mouth. [f. ANGLE[2]+-ER[1]]

Ang'lican (ăngg-), a. & n. (Adherent) of the reformed church of England; ~ chant, short harmonized melody in two or more phrases each beginning with a reciting note, for singing to unmetrical words (psalms, canticles). Hence ~ISM n. [f. med. L Anglicanus (Magna Carta) f. Anglicus (Bede) f. Anglus ANGLE[3]]

Anglice (ăng'glĭsē), adv. In English. [L]

Ang'licism (ăngg-), n. English idiom; English political principles. [f. foll., see -ISM]

Ang'licize (ăngg-), **-ise** (-īz), v.t. Make English in form or character. [f. med. L *Anglicus* English + -IZE]

Ang'lo- (ăngg-) in comb. English, as ~- -*Catholic*; of English origin, as ~-*American*; half English & half —, as ~-*French* (*entente* etc.); ~-*Indian* a. & n., of British birth but living or having lived long in India, (in Eurasian use) Eurasian; ~- -*Norman* n., the French language of the Normans as used in England after the Conquest, also adj. [comb. form of L *Anglus* English]

Anglo-Căth'olic, a. & n. (Member) of the party that insists on the catholicity of the Church of England & repudiates the epithet *protestant*. [prec.]

Anglomān'ia (ăngg-), n. Excessive admiration of English customs. So **Ang'lo-** PHIL, **Ang'lo**PHOBE, **Anglo**PHOB'IA, (ăngg-), nn. [ANGLO- + -MANIA]

Anglo-Săx'on, n. & a. English Saxon (as distinct from Old Saxons of the continent), Old English (people, language) before Norman Conquest (in this dictionary called OE); of English descent (wherever found), whence ~DOM n. [f. mod. L *Anglo-Saxones* (Camden), app. after OE *Angul-Seaxan* (pl.), in med. L *Angli Saxones* (8th c.)]

Anglo-Săx'onism (ăngg-), n. Belief in claims of the Anglo-Saxon race. [prec. + -ISM]

ăngōl'a, **ăngōr'a**, (-ngg-), n. Fabric made from wool of angora goat; ~ *cat* (long-haired variety). [f. *Angora* (mod. form of ancient Gk *Agkura*, town in Asia Minor); *angola* is corrupt]

ăngostūr'a, **ăngŭs-**, (-ngg-), a. & n. Aromatic bark formerly used as febrifuge & tonic. [f. *Angostura*, town in Venezuela on the Orinoco, now Ciudad Bolivar]

ăng'r|y̌ (-ngg-), a. Enraged, wrathful, resentful, (*at*, *about*, thing, *at*, *with*, person); irritable, passionate; (of wound, sore, etc.) inflamed, painful. Hence ~ILY² adv. [ME, f. ANGER n. + -Y²]

Ång'ström (ăng'strĕrm or ŏng-) **ūn'it**, n. A hundred-millionth of a centimetre, used in expressing short wave-lengths (abbr. A.U.). [A. J. *Ångström*, Swedish physicist (d. 1874)]

ăng'uine (-nggw-), a. Snake-like. [f. L *anguinus* (*anguis* snake), see -INE¹]

ăng'uish (-nggw-), n. Severe bodily or mental pain. [ME *anguisse*, -*ish* f. OF *anguisse* choking f. L *angustia* tightness]

ăng'ular (-ngg-), a. Having angles; sharp--cornered; placed in, at, an angle; measured by angle, as ~ *divergence*; wanting plumpness; wanting suavity. Hence **ăngŭlă'rITY** (-ngg-) n., ~LY² (-ngg-) adv. [f. L *angularis* (*angulus* ANGLE¹, see -AR¹)]

ăng'ŭl|ate (-ngg-), a. Formed with corners. Hence ~ATE³ (-ngg-) v.t., ~A'-TION (-ngg-) n. [f. L *angulatus* (ANGLE¹, -ATE²)]

ăngŭs'ti- (-ngg-) in comb. With narrow —, as -*foliate*, -*rostrate*, (leaves, beak). [L *angustus* narrow]

ănhȳd'rous, a. (chem.). Without water of crystallization. [f. Gk *anudros* (AN- (5) + *hudōr* water) + -OUS]

ănĭcŏn'ic, a. (Gk ant.). (Of idols & symbols) not shaped in human or animal form. [AN- (5) + ICONIC]

ăn'icŭt, **ann-**, n. (Anglo-Ind.). River--dam in S. India built for irrigation purposes. [f. Tamil *anai-kattu* dam-building]

anigh (anī'), adv. & prep. Near. [mod. f. NIGH, after *anear*, *afar*]

ăn'il, n. Indigo (shrub & dye). [F or Pg. *anil* f. Arab. *an-nil* (*al* the + Arab.-Pers. *nil* f. Skr. *nili* indigo)]

ăn'ile, a. Old-womanish; imbecile. [f. L *anilis* (*anus* old woman, see -ILE)]

ăn'iline, n. A chemical base, the source of many dyes, obtained originally from indigo, now chiefly from coal-tar. [ANIL + -INE⁵]

anil'itȳ, n. Dotage. [f. L *anilitas* (ANILE, see -TY)]

ănimadvēr'sion (-shn), n. Criticism; censure. [f. L *animadversio* (*animadvertere* -*vers*-, see foll. and -ION)]

ănimadvert', v.i. Pass criticism or censure *on* (conduct, fault, etc.). [f. L *animadvertere* f. *animus* mind + AD(*vertere vers*- turn)]

ăn'imal, n. & a. **1.** Organized being endowed (more or less perceptibly) with life, sensation, & voluntary motion; other ~ than man; quadruped; a brutish man. **2.** adj. Pertaining to the functions of ~s, as ~ *spirits* (natural buoyancy), ~ *magnetism* (mesmerism); pertaining to ~s as opp. to vegetables; carnal. Hence ~LY² adv. [L, for *animale* neut. of *animalis* having breath (*anima* breath, see -AL); the adj. orig. f. L adj.]

ănimăl'cŭle, n. Microscopic animal. [f. L *animalculum* (*animal*, see prec. & -CULE)]

ănimăl'cŭl|ism, n. Reference of physiological phenomena to agency of animalcules. So ~IST n. [f. prec. + -ISM]

ăn'imalism, n. Animal activity; sensuality; doctrine that men are mere animals. [ANIMAL + -ISM]

ănimăl'itȳ, n. Animal nature or system; merely animal nature; the animal world. [f. F *animalité* (*animal* a., see -TY)]

ăn'imaliz|e, **-is|e** (-īz), v.t. Convert into animal substance, sensualize. Hence ~A'TION n. [ANIMAL + -IZE]

ăn'imate¹, a. Living; lively. [f. L *animare* quicken, see -ATE²]

ăn'imāt|e², v.t. Breathe life into; enliven, make lively, as *an ~ed discussion*; inspirit (esp. in p.p.); inspire, actuate. Hence or cogn. ~ēdLY² adv., **ănimA'TION** n., (esp.) ardour, vivacity, ~OR n., (also,

Cinemat.) artist who prepares ~ed cartoons. [f. prec., see -ATE³]

ǎn'imé (-mā), n. A W. Indian resin used in making varnish; other resins. [F, of unkn. orig.]

ǎn'im|ism, n. Doctrine of the *anima mundi* (that phenomena of animal life are produced by an immaterial soul); attribution of living soul to inanimate objects & natural phenomena; spiritualism (as opposed to materialism). Hence ~IST n., ~ĭs'TIC a. [f. L *anima* life, soul +-ISM]

ǎnimŏs'ĭtў, n. Active enmity (*against, between*). [ME, f. OF *animosite* or LL *animositas* (*animosus* spirited f. foll., see -OSE & -TY)]

ǎn'imus, n. (no pl.). Animating spirit; animosity. [L, = soul, mind, mental impulse]

ǎn'ion, n. Electro-negative element evolved at anode during electrolysis (opp. CATION). [f. ANA- +ION]

ǎn'ise, n. Umbelliferous plant with aromatic seeds. [ME, f. OF *anis* f. L f. Gk *anison* anise, dill]

ǎn'iseed, n. Seed of anise, used as a carminative.

ǎnisětte' (-z-), n. Liqueur flavoured with aniseed. [F, dim. of *anis* anise]

ǎnis|o- in comb. Unequal, as ~ŏm'erous, unsymmetrical, ~ŏp'ia, inequality of vision in the eyes. [f. Gk *anisos* (AN-(5) +*isos* equal)]

ǎnk'er, n. Measure of wine & spirits in Holland, N. Germany, Denmark, Sweden, Russia, & formerly in England (8¼ imp. gals); cask holding the quantity. [Du., of unkn. orig.]

ankh (ăngk), n. (Egypt. ant.). Key-like cross as symbol of enduring life & generative energy. [Egyptian, = life]

ankle (ăng'kl), n. Joint connecting foot with leg; slender part between this & calf. [ME *ankel* prob. f. ON (cf. OSw. *ankol*) f. Gmc **ank-* (Aryan **ang-* as in ANGLE¹), whence also, app., OE *ancléow*]

ǎnk'lět, n. Ornament or support for ankle. [prec. +-LET]

ǎnn'a, n. Formerly, a unit of currency in India and Pakistan, the sixteenth part of a RUPEE (now replaced by a decimal coinage); see PIE⁴, PICE. [Hind. *ana*]

ǎnn'alist, n. Writer of annals. Hence **ǎnnalis'tic** a. [f. foll. +-'IST]

ǎnn'als (-z), n. pl. Narrative of events year by year; historical records. [f. L *annales* (*libri*) yearly (books) f. *annus* year, -AL]

ǎnn'ātes (-ts), n. pl. (Rom. Cath.) first year's revenue of see or benefice, paid to Pope. [f. F *annate* f. med. L *annata* year's proceeds (*annus*, see -ADE)]

anneal' (-ēl), v.t. Toughen by gradually diminishing heat, temper (lit. & fig.). [OE *onǣlan* f. *on* AN- (1) +*ǣlan* burn, bake]

annĕc'tent, a. Connecting, as ~ *link*. [f. L as ANNEX, see -ENT]

Annĕl'ida, n. pl. (zool.). The class of segmented worms. Hence **ǎnn'elid³** n., **annĕl'id**AN a. [mod. L, f. F *annelés* ringed (OF *annel* ring f. L *a(n)nellus* dim. of *anulus* ring) +*ida*, cf. -ID³]

annĕx', v.t. Add as subordinate part; append (*to* book etc.); take possession of (territory etc.); attach as an attribute, addition, or consequence. Hence or cogn. ~'ABLE a., **ǎnnĕx**A'TION n. [ME, f. OF *annexer* f. *annexe* thing joined f. L AN-(*nectere nex-* bind)]

ǎnn'ĕx(e), n. Addition to a document; supplementary building. [F (-*xe*), see prec.]

anni'hilāt|e (-nī-), v.t. Blot out of existence. Hence ~OR n. [f. LL AN-*nihilare* (*nihil* nothing), see -ATE²]

annihilā'tion (-nī-), n. Utter destruction; (Theol.) destruction of soul as well as body, whence ~ISM, ~IST, nn. [F, or f. LL *annihilatio*, see prec. & -ATION]

ǎnnivĕrs'arў, n. Yearly return of a date; celebration of this. [ME, f. L *anniversarius* (*annus* year +*versus* turned, see -ARY¹)]

ǎnn'ō actāt'ĭs sū'ae, phr. In the — year of his or her age. [L]

Ann'ō Dŏm'ini (ă-), phr. In the year of our Lord, of the Christian era, (usu. A.D.); ‖ (colloq., as n.) advancing age (~ *is the trouble*). [L]

ǎnn'ot|āte, v.t. & i. Furnish with notes (book, author); (v.i.) make notes (*on*). So ~A'TION, ~ātOR, nn. [f. L AN*notare* (*nota* mark), see -ATE³]

announce', v.t. Proclaim; intimate the approach of; make known (without words) to senses or mind. Hence ~MENT (-sm-), **announ'cer**¹ (esp. of items broadcast), nn. [late ME, f. OF *anoncer* f. L AN*nunciare* (*nuntius* messenger)]

annoy'¹, n. (arch., poet.). Annoyance. [ME, f. OF *anui, anoi* f. Rom. *inodio* f. L phr. *in odio* in hatred, hateful]

annoy'², v.t. Irritate; molest, harass. [ME, f. OF *anuier* etc. f. Rom. *inodiare*, f. as prec.]

annoy'ance, n. Molestation; vexation; disgust. [ME, f. OF *anuiance, anoiance* (*anuier*, see prec. & -ANCE)]

ǎnn'ūal, a. & n. Reckoned by the year; recurring yearly; lasting for one year; (plant) that lives only for a year; (book etc.) published in yearly numbers. Hence ~LY² adv. [ME *annuel* f. OF f. LL *annualis* = cl. L *annalis* (*annus* year, see -AL)]

annū'itant, n. One who holds an annuity. [f. foll. +-ANT, by assim. to *accountant* etc.]

annū'itў, n. Sum payable in respect of a particular year; yearly grant; investment of money entitling investor to series of equal annual sums; *life, terminable, perpetual,* ~ (ceasing at death of investor, after specified term, on repayment of principal); *immediate, deferred* or *rever-sionary*, ~ (commencing at end of first interval of payment after investment, after specified interval or event). [ME, f. OF *annuite* f. med. L *annuitatem* (*annuus* yearly, see -TY)]

annul', v.t. (-ll-). Annihilate; abolish, cancel; declare invalid. Hence ~MENT n. [ME, f. OF *anuller* f. LL ANnullare (*nullus* none)]

ann'ular, a. Ring-like; ~ *space* (between inner & outer surface of cylinder); ~ *ligament* (girding wrist · & ankle); ~ *eclipse* of sun (when moon, projected on sun's disc, leaves ring of light visible). Hence ~LY[2] adv. [f. F *annulaire* or L *an(n)ularis* (*an(n)ulus* ring, see -AR[1])]

ann'ulate, -ātėd, aa. Furnished, marked, with rings; formed of rings. Hence **ann'ula'TION** n. [f. L *an(n)ulatus* (as foll., see -ATE[2])]

ann'ulėt, n. Small ring; (Archit.) small fillet encircling column. [f. L *an(n)ulus* ring +-ET[1]]

ann'uloid, a. Ring-like. So **ann'ulOSE[1]** a. [as prec. +-OID]

annun'ciāte (-shǐ-), v.t. Proclaim, intimate as coming or ready. [f. LL *annuntiare* ANNOUNCE, see -ATE[3]]

annuncia'tion (-sǐ-), n. Announcement; (A~) that of the incarnation, made by the angel Gabriel to the Virgin Mary, festival commemorating this, Lady-day, March 25th. [ME, f. OF *annonciation* or LL *annuntiatio* (as prec., see -ATION)]

annun'ciātor (-shǐ-), n. Announcer; indicator showing in which direction attendance summoned by bell or telephone is needed. [f. LL *annuntiator* (as prec., see -OR)]

ano-, pref. = Gk *ano* adv., upward; in scientific terms, as ~*car'pous*, (of ferns) having fructification on upper part of frond; ~*gĕn'ic*, developed upwardly or inwardly.

an'ōde, n. (electr.). Positive pole (cf. CATHODE). [f. Gk *anodos* way up (*ana* up +*hodos* way)]

an'odyne, a. & n. (Medicine, drug) able to assuage pain; (anything) mentally soothing. [f. L f. Gk *anodunos* painless (AN- (5) +*odune* pain)]

anoet'ic, a. (psych.). Characterized by **anoes'is**, consciousness with sensation but without thought. [f. A- (7) +Gk *noetos* perceptible +-IC]

anoint', v.t. Apply ointment, oil, to (esp. as religious ceremony at baptism or on consecration as priest or king); moisten, rub; *the Lord's Anointed*, Christ, (also) king by divine right. [f. obs. adj. *anoint* f. OF *enoint* p.p. of *enoindre* f. L IN(*unguere unct-*)]

anomalis'tic, a. (astron.). ~ *year*, time earth takes to pass from perihelion to perihelion; ~ *month*, time moon takes to pass from perigee to perigee. [f. Gk *anomalos* ANOMALOUS +-IST +-IC]

anom'alous, a. Irregular; abnormal. Hence ~LY[2] adv., ~NESS n. [f. LL f. Gk *anomalos* (AN-(5) +*homalos* even) +-OUS]

anom'alure, n. African scale-tailed squirrel. [f. Gk *anomalos* anomalous +*oura* tail]

anom'aly, n. Unevenness of motion etc.; irregularity; (Astron.) angular distance of planet or satellite from its last perihelion or perigee. [f. L f. Gk *anomalia* (*anomalos* see prec.)]

an'omo- in comb. Irregular, as ~*carp'ous*, bearing unusual fruit, ~*phyll'ous*, with leaves irregularly placed. [f. Gk *anomos* without law (*a*- not +*nomos*)]

anon', adv. Soon, presently; (of contrast) now again; *ever & ~*, every now & then. [OE *on an* into one, *on ane* in one (body, mind, state, way, movement, moment)]

anona'ceous (-ā'shŭs), a. Pertaining to the custard-apple family Annonaceae (formerly Anonaceae). [-ACEOUS]

an'onym, n. Person who remains nameless; pseudonym. [f. F *anonyme* (as foll.)]

anonym'ity, n. State of being anonymous. [as foll., see -TY]

anon'ymous, a. (abbr. *anon.*). Of unknown name; of unknown or undeclared authorship. Hence ~LY[2] adv., ~NESS n. [f. L f. Gk *anonumos* nameless (AN- (5) + *onoma* name)]

anoph'elēs (-z), n. Kinds of (esp. malarial) mosquito. [Gk, = hurtful (*an*- not, *opheleo* benefit)]

an'orak, n. Jacket of skin or cloth with hood attached, worn esp. in arctic regions. [f. Eskimo *anoraq*]

anos'mia, n. Loss of sense of smell. [mod. L f. AN- (5) +Gk *osme* smell +-IA[1]]

anoth'er (-ŭdh-), pron. & a. (pl. *other a.*, *others* pron.). An additional (one), as *try ~ pear, try ~*; ‖ unnamed additional party to legal action (*X versus Y & ~*); ‖ (in list of cricket eleven etc., written *A. N. Other*) anonymous player or one still to be selected; a counterpart to, as ~ *Solomon*; *such ~, ~* of the same sort; a different (one), as *take this towel away & bring me ~*; (contrasted or coupled with *one*) *one man's meat is ~ man's poison, taken one with ~*; ONE ~. [AN +OTHER; in ME superseding OE *other* used by itself]

anour'ous (-oor-), a. Tailless. [f. AN- (5) +Gk *oura* tail +-OUS]

anox'ia, n. (med.). Deficiency of oxygen. [f. AN-(5), OX(YGEN), -IA[1]]

anschluss (än'shlŏos), n. Union. [G]

an'serine, a. Of, like, a goose; silly. [f. L *anserinus* (*anser* goose, see -INE[1])]

answer[1] (ahn'ser), n. Reply; defence; solution; thing done in return. [orig.= solemn affirmation to rebut a charge, OE *andswaru* f. Gmc *andswarō (*and*-against + *swar- f. *swarjan, OE *swerian* swear)]

answer[2] (ahn'ser), v.t. & i. Reply to or *to*, as ~ *me, my question, to me, to my question*;

~ *to* (acknowledge, have) *the name of X*; ~ (summons to) *the door*; reply to (charge); be responsible (*for* person or thing); ~ (correspond to, also ~ *to*) *my hopes, your description*; ~ (fulfil) *my purpose*; *will not* ~ (do, succeed); ~ *back* (vulg.), ~ rebuke saucily. [OE *andswarian* (as prec.)]

answerable (ahn'ser-), a. Responsible (*to* person, *for* act); (arch.) corresponding (*to*). [prec.+-ABLE]

ant, n. A small social hymenopterous insect celebrated for industry, emmet, pismire; ~*-bear*, the great ~-eater; ~*-eggs*, larvae of ~s; ~*-catcher*, ~*-thrush*, bird of thrush family living on ~s; ~*-eater*, name of various animals that live on ~s; ~*-fly*, winged ~, used as bait in angling; ~*-hill*, mound over ~s'-nest, conical nest of termites; *White Ant*, termite, destructive social insect of neuropterous order. [OE *æmete, emete,* f. WG **ǎmaitjô* (ǎ off +*maitan* cut); *æmete* became *ant, emete* EMMET]

an't (ahnt). See BE.

ant- = ANTI- before unaspirated vowel.

-ant, suf. forming adjj. (& nn.) f. F *-ant* (or direct) f. L *-antem, -entem, -ēntem,* accus. of pres. part. (nom. *-ans, -ens*). OF levelled all L partt. under ending *-ant,* though later F preserved L *-ent-.* ME adopted OF *-ant* as *-aunt, -ant.* Most old wds retain *-ant,* but since 1500 some have been refash., universally (*apparent*) or partly (*dependent, -ant*); see -ENT. Mod. wds in *-ant* are f. L *-ant-,* direct or thr. F, or on L anal. (rarely where no vb exists, as *benignant* on anal. of *malignant*). Noun meanings: (1) personal agent, (2) thing, esp. drug, producing effect.

ăntă'cĭd, a. & n. Preventive of acidity (esp. in stomach). [ANT-+ACID]

ăntăg'onism, n. Active opposition (*to, against,* thing; *between* two; *come into* ~ *with*); opposing principle. [f. as foll., see -ISM (cf. F *-isme*)]

ăntăg'on|ĭst, n. Opponent, adversary; (Phys.) counteracting muscle. Hence ~ĭs'tĬc a., ~ĭs'tĬcALLY adv. [f. F *-iste* or LL *-ista* f. Gk *antagōnistēs* (as foll., see -IST)]

ăntăg'onize, -ise (-īz), v.t. (Of a force etc.) counteract, tend to neutralize, (another); evoke hostility in, provoke to opposition, make into an enemy; *oppose, resist. [f. Gk ANTAgōnizomai (*agōn* contest, see -IZE)]

ăntăl'kal|ĭ, n. Substance that counteracts an alkali. Hence ~ĬNE[1] a. [ANT-+ALKALI]

ăntăphrodĭs'ĭăc (-z-), a. & n. Preventive of venereal desire. [f. ANT-+APHRODISIAC]

ăntărc'tĭc, a. Southern, of south polar regions; *A*~ *Pole,* S. pole of earth or heavens; *A*~ *Circle,* parallel of 66° 32' S. [ME *antartik* f. OF *-ique* f. L f. Gk ANT-(*arktikos* ARCTIC)]

ăn'tĕ, n., & v.t. Stake put up by poker-player before drawing new cards; (v.t.) put up (an ~); *(transf.) to bet, stake, pay *up.* [L, = before]

ăn'tĕ-, pref. = L *ante* before, prep. & adv., used in E to form nn. & adjj. with or without adj. ending. **1.** nn. (main stress on *an'te*), as ~*-room.* **2.** adjj. (main stress not on *ante*), as ~*-reforma'tion(al);* ~*nup'tial;* ~*-Commun'ion* (*Service*), Anglican Communion Service to end of prayer for the 'Church militant'.

ăntĕcēd'ence, n. Precedence, priority, (in time or causal relation); (Astron.) retrograde motion. [f. L *antecedere,* see foll. & -ENCE]

ăntĕcēd'ent, a. & n. 1. Previous (*to*): presumptive, a priori. **2.** n. Preceding thing or circumstance; (Logic) the part of a conditional proposition on which the other depends; (Gram.) noun, clause, sentence, to which a following (esp. relative) pronoun or adverb refers; (Math.) first term of a ratio; (pl.) past history (esp. of persons). Hence ~LY[2] adv. [f. F, or L *antecedent-,* part. of ANTE-(*cedere* go), see -ENT]

ăn'tĕchāmber, n. Room leading to chief apartment. [earlier *anti-,* f. F *antichambre,* f. It. *anticamera* (ANTE-, CHAMBER)]

ăn'tĕchăpel, n. Outer part at west end of chapel. [ANTE-+CHAPEL]

ăn'tĕdāte[1], n. Date before the true time (esp. of writing). [ANTE-+DATE[2] n.]

ăntĕdāte'[2], v.t. Affix, assign, an earlier than the true date to (document, event); precede; anticipate. [f. prec.]

ăntĕdĭluv'ian (-lōō-), a. & n. Belonging, referring, appropriate, to the time before the flood; (colloq.) utterly out of date; (n.) old-fashioned person or thing, (also) very old person. [f. ANTE-+L *diluvium,* DELUGE+-AN]

ăn'tĕlōpe, n. Deer-like ruminant kinds of animals. [ME, f. OF *antelop* or med. L *ant(h)alopus* f. Gk *antholops* of unkn. orig.]

ăn'te mĕrĭd'ĭĕm, phr. (abbr. *a.m.*). Between midnight & noon, as 7.30 *a.m.* [L]

ăntĕmŭn'dāne, a. Existing, occurring, before creation of world. [f. ANTE-+L *mundus* world+-ANE]

ăntĕnāt'al, a. Previous to birth. [ANTE-+NATAL]

ăntĕnn'|a, n. (pl. ~*ae*). Sensory organ found in pairs on heads of insects & crustacea, feeler; (Bot.) irritable processes in male flower of some orchids; (Radio) = AERIAL n. Hence ~AL, ~ARY[1], ~ĬF'EROUS, ~ĬFORM, aa. [L, = sail-yard]

ăntĕnŭp'tial (-shl), a. Born, occurring, etc., before marriage. [f. LL ANTE(*nuptialis* NUPTIAL)]

ăntĕpĕn'dĭum, n. Veil for front of altar. [med. L (ANTE-, *pendēre* hang)] ĭtĕpĕnŭlt' (or -pēn²), a. & n. Last but two (orig. & usu. of syllables). [abbr. of LL (syllaba) antepaenultima, see foll.]

ăntĕpĕnŭl'timate, a. & n. = prec. [f. LL ANTE(paenultimus PENULT) + -ATE²]

ănte̅-pŏst', a. (Of racing bets) made before the runners' numbers are hoisted on the board. [ANTE-]

ăntĕprăn'dĭal, a.   Before-dinner. [f. ANTE- + L prandium + -AL]

ănter̅'ior, a. More to the front; prior (to). Hence ănter̅iŏ'rity n., ~LY² adv. [f. F antérieur or LL anterior, compar. f. ante ANTE-]

ăn'te-room, n.   Room leading to another; (Mil.) sitting-room in officers' mess. [ANTE- + ROOM, after earlier ANTECHAMBER.]

anth- pref. = ANTI- before aspirate.

ănthĕl'ion, n. (pl. -ia). Luminous ring projected on cloud or fog bank opposite to sun. [late Gk, neut. of anthēlios opposite to sun (ANTH- + hēlios sun)]

ănthĕlmin'tic, a. & n. (Medicine) of use against intestinal worms. [f. ANTH- + Gk helmins -minthos worm + -IC]

ăn'them, n.   Composition for church use sung antiphonally; non-metrical composition (usu. from Scriptures or Liturgy) set to sacred music; song of praise or gladness. [OE antefne f. med. L antefana f. LL antiphona, antefana ANTIPHON, E development being antef'ne, antem'ne, an'tem, an'them]

ăn'ther, n. (bot.). Part of stamen containing pollen; ~-dust, pollen; ~-valve, opening by which pollen is shed. Hence ~AL, ~IF'EROUS, ~OID, aa. [f. F anthère or mod. L anthera, in cl. L medicine extracted from flowers f. Gk anthēra flowery, fem. adj. f. anthos]

ănthŏl'og|y̆, n. A choice collection of passages from literature; the (Greek) A~y, a collection of about 4,500 poems, inscriptions, etc. by more than 300 writers 5th c. B.C.–6th c. A.D.). Hence ~IST n. [late Gk use of anthologia (anthos flower + -logia collection f. legō gather)]

ăn'thony̆ (ăn'to-), n.   St ~, patron of swineherds; ~, smallest pig of litter; (St) ~'s fire, erysipelas.

ăn'thracēne, n.   Complex hydrocarbon obtained in the distillation of coal-tar, the ultimate source of synthetic alizarin. [f. Gk anthrax -akos coal + -ENE]

ăn'thrac|ite, n.   Non-bituminous variety of coal. Hence ~it'IC, ~itOUS, aa. [f. Gk anthrakitis a kind of coal, or as prec. + -ITE¹]

ăn'thrăx, n.   Malignant boil; splenic fever of sheep & cattle; malignant pustule caused in man by infection from animals so affected. [L f. Gk, = carbuncle]

ănthrŏpo|- in comb. = Gk anthrōpos man, as: ~ocen'tric, centring in man; ~ŏg'eny, study of origin of man; ~ŏg'raphy, science of geographical distribution of mankind; ~olite, ~olith, (-ŏp²), fossil man; ~ŏm'etry measurement of human body; ~ŏph'agous, ~ŏph'agy, man-eating.

ăn'thropoid, a. & n.   Man-like; (n.) being that is human in form only, esp. ~ ape. [f. Gk anthrōpoeidēs (ANTHROPO-, see -OID)]

ănthropŏl'ogy̆, n.   Whole science of man; physiological & psychological science of man; study of man as an animal. Hence ănthropolŏ'gical a., ănthropolŏ'gicalLY² adv., ănthropŏl'OGIST n. [as prec. + -LOGY]

ănthropomŏrph'ic, a.   Of the nature of anthropomorphism. [as foll. + -IC]

ănthropomŏrph'|ize, -ise (-īz), v.t. Attribute human form or personality to (God etc. or abs.). Hence ~ISM, ~IST, nn. [as foll. + -IZE]

ănthropomŏrph'ous, a.   Of human form. [f. Gk ANTHROPOmorphos (morphē form) + -OUS]

anti-, pref. = Gk anti (before unaspir. vowel ant-, before aspirate unth-) opposite, against, in exchange, instead, rivalling. In wds f. Gk, or modelled on them, as -thesis, -climax. As living pref. in E (1) combining with nouns to form nouns, anti- having adj. force = rival (-pope, -king), opposing, counter, (-chorus, -league), reverse of (-climax); main stress is on an'ti-. (2) forming adjj. on nouns governed by anti- (-slavery society, -vaccination league) or on adjj. implying a noun so governed (-national, -ritualistic), with sense 'opposed to'; many of these are also nouns, esp. names of medicines (-dysenteric); main stress is not on ~. (3) forming derivative nouns & adjj. by addition of a suff., esp. -ist, (-alcoholist, -tobacconist, -sabbatarian) with sense 'one opposed to', also corresponding abstract nn. in -ism (-Darwinism); main stress is not on ~.

ănti-air'craft (-ah-), a. ~ gun etc. (for shooting down hostile aircraft). [prec.]

ăn'tiar, n.   Upas tree of Java; poison thence obtained. [Jav. antjar]

ăntibil'ious, a.   Of use against biliousness. [ANTI- (2)]

ăntibiŏt'ic, a. & n. 1. Capable of destroying or injuring living organisms, esp. bacteria. 2. n. ~ substance. [ANTI-(2), Gk biōtikos fit for life (bios life, -IC)]

ăn'tibŏdy̆, n. (physiol.). Kinds of substance in the blood tending to neutralize others that are harmful. [ANTI- (1)]

ăn'tic, a. & n. 1. (arch.). Grotesque, bizarre. 2. n. Grotesque posture (usu. pl.); (arch.) mountebank, clown. [f. It. antico f. L antiquus ancient, apparently from ascription of GROTESQUE work to the ancients]

ăn'tichrist (-k-), n.   Enemy of Christ; (A~, the A~) great personal opponent of Christ expected by early church to appear before end of world. [ME, f. LL antichristus f. Gk antikristos (ANTI- (1) + khristos CHRIST)]

ăntichris'tian (-k-), a.   Pertaining to Antichrist; opposed to Christianity.

Hence ~ism (-k-) n. [f. prec., with extended meaning]

ănti'cip|āte, v.t. Use in advance; forestall (person or thing); accelerate, as ~ate one's ruin; discuss, consider, realize, beforehand; (pop.) look forward to, expect, (event, that it will happen). Hence ~ant a. & n., ~ātive a., ~ātively² (-vl-) adv. [f. L anticipare (anti- for ANTE-+ -cipare f. capere take) see -ATE³]

ănticipā'tion, n. Action of anticipating (in senses of the vb); thanking you in ~, closing formula in letter of inquiry or request; (Med.) occurrence of phenomena before usual time; (Mus.) introduction beforehand of part of chord about to follow. [f. L anticipatio (as prec., see -ATION)]

ănti'cipāt|or, n. One who anticipates. Hence ~ORY a. [L (as prec., see -OR)]

ăn'ticlimăx, n. Opposite of climax, addition of a particular that weakens the effect; descent contrasting with previous rise. [ANTI-(1)]

ănticlin'al, a. (Geol.) forming ridge ou which strata lean against each other, & from which they slope down in opposite directions; (Anat.) with upright spine towards which spines on both sides incline. [f. ANTI-+Gk klinō lean +-AL]

ănticyc'lŏne, n. Rotary outward flow of air from atmospheric area of high pressure; whole system of pressure & outward flow. [ANTI-(1)]

ăn'tidŏt|e, n. Medicine given to counteract poison or disease (against, for, to); (fig.) something that counteracts an evil. Hence ~AL a. [f. L f. Gk antidoton neut. of ANTIdotos given against]

ăn'tigĕn, n. Substance introduced into the blood to stimulate production of antibodies. [ANTI(BODY)+-GEN (1)]

ăntigrŏp'ĕlŏs (-z), n. pl. Waterproof leggings. [perh. for anthygropelos (ANTI-(2)+Gk hugros wet +pēlos mud)]

ănti-Jăc'obin, a. & n. (One) opposed to the Jacobins (revolutionary party in France, 1789) or the French revolution. [ANTI-(2)]

ăntilŏg'arithm, n. Number to which a logarithm belongs, as 100 is the ~ of 2. [ANTI-(1)]

ăntil'ogy̆, n. Contradiction in terms. [f. Gk antilogia (ANTI-+-logia -LOGY)]

ăntimacăss'ar, n. Covering thrown over chairs etc., as protection from grease or as an ornament. [ANTI-(2)+MACASSAR]

ăn'timasque, -mask, (-mahsk), n. Grotesque interlude between acts of masque. [ANTI-(1)]

ăntimonărch'ical (-k-), a. Opposed to monarchy. [ANTI-(2)]

ăn'timony̆, n. Brittle metallic substance, bluish-white, of flaky crystalline texture. [late ME, f. med. L antimonium, of unkn. orig.]

ăntinŏm'ian, a. & n. **1.** Opposed to the obligatoriness of moral law; pertaining to A~s. **2.** n. (A~) one who maintains that the moral law is not binding on Christians. [f. med. L Antinomi, name of sect in Germany (1535) alleged to hold above opinion (ANTI-+Gk nomos law)+ -AN)]

ăntin'omy̆, n. Contradiction in a law, or between two laws; conflict of authority; paradox. [f. L f. Gk ANTInomia (nomos law)]

ăntipathĕt'ic, a. Opposed in nature or disposition (to). Hence ~AL a., ~ALLY³ adv. [f. Gk ANTIpatheō (as ANTIPATHY), see -ETIC]

ăntipăth'ic, a. Of contrary character (to); (Med.) having, producing, contrary symptoms. [f. F antipathique f. antipathie (as foll.)]

ăntip'athy̆, n. Constitutional or settled aversion (against, to, between persons). [f. F antipathie or L -pathia f. Gk -patheia f. ANTIpathēs opposed in feeling (pathos -eos)]

ănti-pĕrsonnĕl', a. (Of bombs etc.) designed to kill or injure human beings. [ANTI-(2)]

ăntiphlogĭs't|ic, a. & n. (Medicine, paste, etc.) reducing inflammation. So ~INE¹ n. P. [ANTI-(2)]

ăn'tiphon, n. Verse of psalm etc. intoned or sung responsively by alternating choirs during Divine Office before or after psalm; similar passage sung independently of psalm & not necessarily responsively. [f. LL antiphona, fem. sing., f. Gk ANTIphōna (neut. pl. of antiphōnos responsive) f. phōnē sound]

ăntiph'onal, a. & n. Sung alternately; responsive; (n.) collection of antiphons. Hence ~LY² adv. [as prec.+-AL]

ăntiph'onary̆, n. Book of antiphons. [f. med. L antiphonarium (as ANTIPHON, see -ARY¹)]

ăntiph'ony̆, n. Antiphon; antiphonal singing response, echo. [f. Gk antiphōnos, see ANTIPHON &-Y¹]

ăntip'od|ēs (-z), n. pl. Place(s) diametrically opposite (to each other), esp. region opposite to our own; (sing. ăn'tipŏde) exact opposite (of, to). Hence ~AL, ~ē'AN aa. [f. LL f. Gk antipodes having the feet opposite, pl. of ANTIpous adj. (pous podos foot)]

ăn'tipŏle, n. Opposite pole; direct opposite. [ANTI-(1)]

ăn'tipōpe, n. Pope elected in opposition to one (held to be) canonically chosen. [f. F antipape f. med. L antipapa; assim. to pope]

ăn'tiprōtŏn, n. Negative proton. [ANTI-(1)]

ăntipy̆rĕt'ic, a. & n. (Drug) allaying or preventing fever. So **ăntipȳr'in** n. P, a particular ~. [ANTI-(2); see PYRETIC]

ăntiquār'ian, a. & n. Connected with study of antiquities; large size of drawing paper; antiquary, whence ~ISM n., ~IZE v.i. [as foll.+-AN]

ăn'tiquary̆, n. Student, collector, of antiquities. [f. L *antiquarius (antiquus* ancient, see -ARY[1])]

ăn'tiquăte, v.t. Make obsolete (esp. in p.p.), abolish as out of date; make antique. [f. obs. adj. *antiquate* (L *antiquare* f. *antiquus* ancient, see -ATE[2])]

ăntique' (-ēk), a. & n. **1.** Of old times; existing since old times; old-fashioned; after the manner of the ancients; archaic. **2.** n. Relic of ancient art or of old times; *the* ~, ~ style. Hence ~NESS (-kn-) n. [F, or f. L *antiquus, anticus,* former, ancient (*ante* before); cf. ANTIC]

ănti'quitў, n. Ancientness; old times, esp. time before middle ages; the ancients; (pl.) customs, events, precedents, of ancient times; (usu. pl.) ancient relics. [ME, f. OF *antiquite* f. L *antiquitatem (antiquus,* see prec. & -TY)]

ăntirrhin'um (-rī-), n. Kinds of plant, snapdragon. [L, f. Gk *antirrhinon (anti* counterfeiting +*rhis rhinos* nose)]

ăntisăbbatār'ian, a. & n. (Person) opposed to observance of Sabbath. [ANTI-(3)]

ăntiscōrbūt'ic, a. & n. (Medicine) against scurvy. [ANTI- (2)]

ăntiscrip'tural (-chŏŏ-), a. Opposed to Scripture. [ANTI- (2)]

ănti-Sĕm'|ītе, a. & n. (Person) hostile to Jews. So **ănti-Sĕmit'ic** a., ~**itiSM** n. [ANTI- (2)]

ăntisĕp't|ic, a. & n. (Agent) counteracting putrefaction (lit. & fig.). Hence ~**ICALLY** adv. [f. ANTI- (3) +SEPTIC]

ăntisō'cial (-shl), a. Opposed to principles on which society is based. [ANTI-(2)]

ăntis'trophē, n. (Lines sung during) returning movement in Greek choruses (cf. STROPHE); inverse relation. [LL, f. Gk, = turning about (ANTIstrephō turn against)]

ăntistrŏph'ic, a. Pertaining to antistrophes. [f. Gk *antistrophikos* (as prec., see -IC)]

ăn'ti-tănk, a. (Of gun etc.) for use against tanks. [ANTI- (2)]

ăntithē'|ist, n. One opposed to belief in existence of a God. Hence ~**ISM** n. [ANTI-(3)]

ăntith'esis, n. (pl. *-theses*). Contrast of ideas expressed by parallelism of strongly contrasted words; opposition, contrast, (*of, between,* two things); direct opposite (*of, to*). [LL f. Gk (vbl n. f. ANTI*tithēmi* set against)]

ăntithĕt'ic, a. Of the nature of antithesis; contrasted; consisting of two opposites. Hence ~**AL** a., ~**alLY**[2] adv. [f. Gk *antithetikos* (as prec., see -IC)]

ăntitŏx'|in, n. A serum serving to neutralize a toxin. So ~**IC** a. [ANTI- (2)]

ăn'ti-trāde, a. & n. ~ (*wind*), one that blows in opposite direction to trade wind. [ANTI- (2)]

ăntitrīnitār'ian, a. & n. (One) opposed to doctrine of the Trinity. Hence ~**ISM** n. [ANTI- (3)]

ăn'titўpe, n. That which a type or symbol represents. Hence **ăntitўp'ICAL** a. [f. Gk ANTI*tupos* responding as an impression to the die (*typos* stamp)]

ăntivĕnēne', n. Antitoxin, esp. a snake--poison antidote. [f. ANTI- + L *venenum* poison]

ănt'ler, n. Branched horn, branch of a horn, of stag or other deer. Hence ~**ED**[2] (-lĕrd) a. [late ME *auntclere* f. OF *antoillier* (mod. *andouiller*) of unkn. orig.]

ăntonomās'ia (-z-), n. Substitution of epithet etc. for proper name (e.g. *the Iron Duke*); use of proper name to express general idea (e.g. *a Solomon*). [L f. Gk, f. ANTonomazō name instead (*onoma* name)]

ăn'tonўm, n. A word of contrary meaning to another, as *bad* to *good* (opp. *synonym*). [ANTI- +(SYN)ONYM]

ăn'trum, n. (pl. *-tra*). Cavity in the body (esp. one in the upper jaw-bone). [f. L, f. Gk *antron* cave]

Ant'wĕrp (ă-), n. ~ (*pigeon*), kind of homing or carrier pigeon. [*Antwerp* in Belgium]

ăn'us, n. Posterior opening of alimentary canal in animals. [L]

ăn'vil, n. Block (usu. iron) on which smith works metal; (Physiol.) a bone of the ear. [OE *onfilti, anfelle* (= OHG *anafalz*) of uncert. orig.]

anxi'etў (ăngz-), n. Uneasiness, concern; solicitous desire (*for* a thing, *to* do). [f. F *anxiété* or L *anxietas -atis* (as foll., see -TY)]

anx'ious (ăngk'shus), a. Troubled, uneasy (*about*); earnestly desirous (*for* a thing, *to* do); causing anxiety, as *an* ~ *business*. Hence ~**LY**[2] adv. [f. L *anxius (angere* choke) +-OUS; cf. LL *anxiosus*]

any (ĕn'ĭ), a., pron., & adv. (With interrog.) one, some, (no matter which), as *have you* ~ *wool? have you* ~ *of them? were* ~ *Frenchmen there?*; (after negative expr. or implied) *cannot see* ~ *difference, to prevent* ~ *loss, cannot find* ~ *of them*; (in affirmative sent.) whichever (of all) is chosen, every, as ~ *chemist will tell you, at* ~ *rate; anyone* (pron.), whatever individual is chosen; ~ *one* or *anyone* (adj.), ~ *person,* anybody; (adv., w. compar. in neg. or interrog. context) at all, in ~ degree, (*is that* ~ *better?*; *without being* ~ *the wiser*). [OE *ænig* (= OHG *einig*) f. *ān* ONE +*-ig* (see -Y[2])]

an'ybody (ĕn-), n. or pron. Any person; *if you wish to be* ~ (of any importance); *two or three anybodies* (ordinary people).

an'yhow (ĕn-), adv. & conj. In any way whatever; in any case, at any rate; at haphazard, as *does his work* ~, *things are all* ~.

an'ything (ĕn-), pron. & n. Whatever thing; a thing, no matter which; a thing of any kind.

an'yway (ĕn-), adv. & conj. = ANYHOW.

anywhere (ĕn'īwār), adv. In any place.

an'ywise (ĕn-; -z), adv. In any wise.

An′zac (ă-), n. & a. (Pl.) *the* Australian & New Zealand Army Corps in the war of 1914–18; (sing.) member of the ~s; (adj.) of the ~s. [= A. & N.-Z. A.C.]

ā′orist, a. & n. (Gram.) indefinite, implying no limitation; (Gk Gram.) ~ *(tense),* one denoting simply occurrence (in indicative, with AUGMENT[1], past), without limitations as to continuance etc. So **āoris′tic** a. [f. Gk *aoristos* indefinite (*a*- not+*horizō* limit)]

āort′|a, n. Great artery or trunk of the arterial system, issuing from left ventricle of heart. Hence ~IC a. [f. med. L f. Gk *aortē* that which is hung (*aeirō* lift)]

à outrance (see Ap.), phr. To the death, to the bitter end. [F]

ap-, pref. = AD- before *p*, & see APO-.

apāce′, adv. Swiftly, quickly. [A prep. +PACE[1]]

apache′ (-ahsh), n. Violent street ruffian in Paris; (*A*~, pr. *apäch′i*) member of N.-Amer. tribe. [F, f. native name, lit. = enemy]

ăp′anage, ăpp-, n. Provision for maintenance of younger children of kings etc., (orig. province or lucrative office); perquisite; (of territory) dependency; natural accompaniment or attribute. [F, f. med. L *appanagium* f. APpanare (*panis* bread) endow with means of subsistence, see -AGE]

apärt′, adv. Aside, separately, independently, (*from*); asunder; *set* ~, devote, reserve (*for*); *jesting* ~ (laid aside). [ME, f. OF *apart* (*à* to, *part* side)]

apärt′heid (-t-hät), n. (S. Afr.). Racial segregation. [Afrikaans (APART, -HOOD)]

apärt′ment, n. Single room of a house; (pl., & arch. & U.S. sing.) set of rooms (*~ house*, block of flats). [f. F *appartement* f. It. *appartamento* f. *appartare* separate]

ăpathēt′|ic, a. Insensible to emotion; indifferent. Hence ~ICALLY adv. [f. foll., after PATHETIC]

ăp′athy, n. Insensibility to suffering; passionless existence; indolence of mind. [f. F *apathie* f. L f. Gk *apatheia* f. *apathēs* without feeling (*a*- not+*pathos* suffering)]

āpe[1], n. Tailless monkey (gorilla, chimpanzee, orang-outan, gibbons); imitator, mimic; *play the* ~, mimic; *sea* ~, fish (sea fox). [OE *apa*, OHG *affo*, ON *api*, Gmc; ult. orig. unkn.]

āpe[2], v.t. Imitate, mimic. [f. prec.]

apeak′ (-ēk), adv. & pred. a. (naut.). Vertical, as *oars* ~. [f. F *à pic* (*à* to, at, *pic,* summit, see PEAK)]

apĕp′sў, n. Lack of digestive power. [f. Gk *apepsia* (*a*- not+*peptō* digest)]

aperçu (see Ap.), n. Summary exposition, conspectus. [F, p.p. of *apercevoir* perceive]

apē′rient (*or* -ĕr-), a. & n. Laxative (medicine). [f. L *aperire* open, see -ENT]

apē′ritif (*or* ahpărĕtēf′), n. Alcoholic appetizer. [F (-*ér*-), f. med. L *aperitivus*

variant of LL *aperitivus* (L *aperire* open, see -IVE)]

apē′ritive, a. & n. = APERIENT. [f. F *apéritif* (prec.)]

ăp′erture, n. Opening, gap; space through which light passes in optical instruments. [f. L *apertura* (as prec., see -URE)]

ăp′erў, n. Mimicry; apish performance; ape-house. [APE n.+-RY]

apĕt′alous, a. Without petals. [f. Gk *apetalos* leafless (*a*- not+*petalon* leaf)+ -OUS]

ăp′ĕx, n. (pl. -*icēs*, -*exes*). Tip, top, peak; vertex (of triangle, cone). [L, = peak, tip]

aph-. See APO-.

aphaer′ĕsis (-fēr-), n. (gram.). The taking away of a letter or syllable at the beginning of a word. [Gk (APH-, *haireō* take)]

aphās′ia (-zya), n. Loss of speech, as result of cerebral affection. Hence **aphās′ic** (-z-) a. & n. [Gk, f. *aphatos* speechless (*a*- not+*pha*- speak)]

aphĕl′ion, n. (pl. -*ia*). Point farthest from sun (of planet's or comet's orbit). [Graecized f. mod. L *aphelium* f. Gk *aph′ hēliou* from the sun, after *apogaeum* APOGEE]

aphēliotrŏp′|ic, a. (bot.). Turning from the sun. Hence ~ICALLY adv., **aphēliŏt′ropism** n. [f. Gk as prec.+*tropikos* turning (*trepō*)]

ăph′ĕsis, n. Gradual loss of unaccented vowel at beginning of word, as in (*e*)*squire*. [Gk, = letting go, f. *aphiēmi* (*apo* away+*hiēmi* send)]

aphĕt′ic, a. Pertaining to aphesis. Hence **ăph′ĕtIZE** v.t. [f. Gk *aphetos* vbl adj. (as prec.)+-IC]

ăph′is, n. (pl. *ăph′idēs*). Plant-louse, minute insect, the food of ladybirds, & tended by ants for the honey-dew it yields. Hence **aphid′IAN** a. [mod. L (Linnaeus) of unkn. orig.]

aphōn′ia, n. Total loss of voice. [Gk, f. *aphōnos* voiceless (*a*- not+*phōnē* voice)]

ăph′orism, n. Short pithy maxim. Hence or cogn. **ăphoris′mIC, ăphoris′tic** (-IST], aa., **ăphoris′tICALLY** adv. [f. F *aphorisme,* (obs.) *aff*-, or med. L f. Gk *aphorismos* definition, f. *aphorizō* (*horos* boundary), see -ISM]

ăphrodis′iăc (-z-), a. & n. Venereal; (drug) producing venereal desire. [f. Gk *aphrodisiakos* f. *aphrodisios* (*Aphroditē* Venus), see -AC]

aphўll′ous, a. (bot.). Naturally leafless. [f. Gk *aphullos* (*a*- not+*phullon* leaf)+ -OUS]

āpiār′ian, a. Pertaining to bee-keeping. [as foll.+-AN]

āp′iar|ў, n. Place where bees are kept. Hence ~IST n. [f. L *apiarium* (*apis* bee, see -ARY[1])]

āp′ical, a. Belonging to an apex; placed at the tip. Hence ~LY[2] adv. [f. L *apex -icis*+-AL]

ăp'ĭcŭlture, n. Bee-keeping. [f. L *apis* bee+CULTURE]

apiece', adv. Severally, each, as *five pounds~*. [orig. *a piece*]

ăp'ish, a. Of the nature, appearance, of an ape; ape-like in manner, silly. Hence ~LY² adv., ~NESS n. [f. APE n.+-ISH]

ăp'lanāt, n. (photog.). Symmetrical achromatic doublet lens comparatively free from spherical aberration. So **ăplanāt'ic** a., (of lens) free from certain aberrations. [G, f. Gk *a-* not+*planaō* wander; adj. f. Gk *aplanētos* free from error+-IC]

aplomb (see Ap.), n. Perpendicularity; self-possession. [F, = *à plomb* according to plummet]

ăpnoe'a (-nēa), n. Suspension of breathing. [mod. L f. Gk *apnoia* f. *apnoos* breathless (*a-* not+*pnoē* breath)]

ăpo-, pref. (before unaspirated vowel *ap-*, before aspirate *aph-*), = Gk *apo* prep. off, from, away, un-, quite; in compds f. Gk, & in mod. scientific wds with sense 'detached, separate'.

apŏc'alÿpse, n. Revelation, esp. that made to St John in island of Patmos; book recording this. So **apŏcalÿp'tic(al)** aa., **apŏcalÿp'ticalLY²** adv. [f. LL f. Gk *apokalupsis* (APOkaluptō uncover)]

apŏc'opė, n. Cutting off of last letter or syllable of word. [LL, f. Gk (APOkoptō cut off)]

apŏc'rÿpha, n. Books of Old Testament included in Septuagint & Vulgate, but not originally written in Hebrew, nor counted genuine by Jews, & excluded from Canon at Reformation; Christian gospels & epistles not admitted to the New Testament. [ME, f. LL *apocrypha* (*scripta*) hidden writings f. Gk *apokruphos* (APOkruptō hide away); treated in E as sing., with pl. *-as*]

apŏc'rÿphal, a. Of the apocrypha; of doubtful authenticity; sham, false. [as prec.+-AL]

ăp'ŏd, n. Bird, reptile, fish, without (or with undeveloped) feet or ventral fins. Hence **ăp'odAL** a. [f. Gk *apous* footless (*a-* not+*pous podos* foot)]

ăpodic'tic, **-deic'tic** (-dī-), a. Of clear demonstration; clearly established. Hence **ăpodic'ticalLY** adv. [f. L f. Gk *apodeiktikos* (APOdeiknumi show, see -IC)]

ăpŏd'osis, n. (pl. *-doses*). Concluding clause of sentence (cf. PROTASIS); consequent clause of conditional sentence, wherever placed. [LL, f. Gk (APOdidōmi give back)]

ăp'ogee, n. Point (in orbit of moon or any planet) farthest from earth; greatest distance of sun from earth when latter is in aphelion; (fig.) most distant spot, highest point. Hence **ăpogē'AN** a. [f. F *apogée* or med. L f. Gk APO*geion* away from earth (*gē* (*gai-, gei-*) earth)]

ăpolaus'tic, a. Self-indulgent. [f. Gk *apolaustikos* (APO*lauō* enjoy, see -IC)]

Apŏllinār'is, n. Mineral water exported from the ~ spring in Rhenish Prussia.

Apŏll'ō, n. (pl. *-os*). Greek sun-god; (poet.) the sun; man of great beauty. [L, f. Gk *Apollōn*]

Apŏll'yon (or *-ĭon*), n. The Devil. [LL (Vulg.), f. Gk *apolluōn* part. of *apolluō* (APO-+*olluō* destroy)]

apŏlogĕt'ic, a. & n. Regretfully acknowledging, excusing, fault or failure; vindicatory; (n., usu. pl.) argumentative defence, esp. of Christianity. Hence ~AL a., ~alLY² adv. [f. F *apologétique* f. LL f. Gk *apologētikos* (*apologeomai* speak in defence, see APOLOGY & -IC)]

ăpolŏ'gia, n. Written defence of the conduct or opinions of the writer. [Gk; see APOLOGY]

apŏl'ogist, n. One who defends (esp. Christianity) by argument. [f. F *apologiste* f. Gk *apologia*, see APOLOGY & -IST]

apŏl'ogize, **-ise** (-īz), v.i. Make an apology (*for*). [f. APOLOGY+-IZE]

ăp'ologue (-ŏg), n. Moral fable. [F, or f. L f. Gk *apologos* fable]

apŏl'ogÿ, n. Regretful acknowledgement of offence; assurance that no offence was intended; explanation, vindication; ~ *for*, poor or scanty specimen of (*this ~ for a letter*). [f. F *apologie* or L f. Gk *apologia* speech in defence]

ăp'ophthegm (-ofthĕm, -othĕm), n. Terse saying; pithy maxim. Hence ~ăt'IC (-ofthĕg-, -othĕg-) a., ~ăt'ICALLY adv. [f. Gk *apophthegma -matos* (APO*phtheggomai* speak out)]

ăpoplĕc't|ic, a. Pertaining to, causing, apoplexy; suffering from, tending to, apoplexy. Hence ~ICALLY adv. [f. F *apoplectique* or LL f. Gk *apoplēktikos* (APO*plēssō* strike completely, see -IC)]

ăp'oplĕxÿ, n. Malady arresting powers of sense & motion, usu. caused by effusion of blood or serum in brain. [ME, f. OF *apoplexie* or LL f. Gk *apoplēxia* (as prec.)]

ăposiopēs'is, n. (rhet.; pl. *-pēses*). Sudden breaking-off in speech. [L, f. Gk f. APO(*siōpaō* keep silent)]

apŏs'tasÿ, n. Abandonment of religious faith, vows, principles, or party. [ME, f. LL f. late Gk *apostasia* (APOsta- withdraw)]

apŏs'tate, n.&a. (One) guilty of apostasy. So **ăpostā'ICAL** a. [ME, f. OF, or LL *apostata* f. late Gk *apostatēs* (as prec.)]

apŏs'tatize, **-ise** (-īz), v.i. Become an apostate (*from one to* another). [f. as APOSTATE+-IZE; cf. LL *apostatare*, med. L *-izare*]

ā pŏstĕriōr'ī (or *-ĕr'-*), adv. & adj. phr. (Reasoning) from effects to causes; inductive. [L, = from what comes after]

apŏs'til, n. Marginal note. [f. F *apostille* f. *-iller* = med. L *-illare* (A-(4), POSTIL)]

apŏs'tle (-sl), n. Messenger, esp. any of the twelve whom Christ sent forth to preach Gospel; *A~s' Creed*, earliest form of Christian creed, anciently ascribed to the ~s; first successful Christian missionary in a country, as ~ *of Germany*; leader of reform, as ~ *of temperance*; ~ *spoons* (with figures of ~s on handles). Hence ~SHIP n. [OE *apostol* (ME *apostel*) f. LL f. Gk *apostolos* (APOStello send forth); later sp. (ME) f. OF *apostle* (mod. *apôtre*)]

apŏs'tolate, n. Apostleship; leadership in a propaganda. [f. LL *apostolatus* (as prec., see -ATE¹)]

ăpostŏl'ic, a. Pertaining to the Apostles; of the character of an apostle; of the Pope, papal, as *A~ See, succession*. Hence ~AL a., ~alLY² adv. [f. F -*ique* or LL f. Gk *apostolikos* (as APOSTLE, see -IC)]

apŏs'troph|ė¹, n. (rhet.). Exclamatory address, in course of public speech or in poem, to particular person (often dead or absent). Hence ăpostrŏph'IC a., ~IZE v.t. & i. [L f. Gk, lit. turning away (as foll.)]

apŏs'trophė², n. Sign of omission of letter, or of possessive case, (e.g. *can't*, *boy's*). Hence ăpostrŏph'IC a. [F, or LL f. Gk *apostrophos* adj. as n., accent of elision (APOstrephō turn away); assim. in pron. to prec.]

apŏth'ėcarȳ, n. (arch.). Druggist, pharmaceutical chemist, as *Apothecaries' Company*. [ME *apot(h)ecarie* f. OF *apotecaire* f. LL *apothecarius* f. L *apotheca* f. Gk *apothēkē* store-house (APOtithēmi lay away), see -ARY¹]

apŏthėŏs'is, n. (pl. -*osēs*). Deification (lit. & fig.); canonization; deified ideal; (loosely) release from earthly life. Hence apŏth'ėosIZE v.t. [LL, f. Gk (APOtheoō make a god of, f. *theos* god, see -OSIS)]

appal' (-awl), v.t. (-ll-). Dismay, terrify. Hence ~l'ingLY² adv. [ME, f. OF *apalir* wax pale; cf. PALL²]

appanage. See APANAGE.

ăpparāt'us, n. (pl. -*uses*). Mechanical requisites, *an* appliance, for doing something ⋅ organs by which natural processes are carried on; ~ *criticus*, list of variant readings, materials for textual study of document. [L (APparare make ready for, see -ATE¹)]

appă'rel¹, v.t. (-ll-). Attire, dress. [ME, f. OF *apareiller* f. Rom. *ADpariculare* make fit (*pariculum* dim. of *par* equal)]

appă'rel², n. Ornamental embroidery on ecclesiastical vestments; (arch.) clothing, dress. [ME, f. OF *aparail*, -*eil* f. *apareiller*, see prec.]

appăr'ent (*or* -ă'r-), a. Manifest, palpable; seeming; *heir* ~ (whose right cannot be superseded by birth of nearer heir, cf. PRESUMPTIVE). Hence ~LY² adv. [ME, f. OF *aparant* f. L as APPEAR, see -ENT]

ăppari'tion, n. Appearance, esp. of a supernatural being; ghost. [late ME, f. F, or f. L *apparitio* (as APPEAR, see -ION)]

appă'ritor, n. Public servant of Roman magistrate; officer of civil or ecclesiastical court; herald, usher. [L (as prec., see -OR)]

appeal'¹ (-ēl), v.i. & t. Call *to* (higher

tribunal) for deliverance from decision of lower (also abs.); ~ *to the country* (i.e. from parliament), dissolve parliament; remove (case) to higher court; call attention *to* (evidence); make earnest request (*to* person, *for* thing or *to* do); *pictures* ~ (address themselves) *to the eye, do not* ~ (prove attractive) *to me*. [ME, f. OF *apeler* f. L APpellare address]

appeal'² (-ēl), n. Act of appealing; right of appealing; *Court of A~* (hearing cases previously tried in inferior courts). [ME, f. OF *apel* (as prec.)]

appeal'able (-ēl-), a. That can be appealed against; that can be appealed *to*. [APPEAL v. + -ABLE]

appear', v.i. Become, be, visible; present oneself formally, publicly be published; be manifest; seem (occas. with implication of illusion). [ME, f. *aper-* st. of OF *aparcir* f. L APparēre -*rit*- come in sight]

appear'ance, n. Act of appearing (in vbl senses; *put in an* ~, show oneself); look, aspect; semblance; *to all* ~ (so far as can be seen); *save, keep up*, ~s (outward show etc.); apparition, phantom. [ME *aparaunce* f. OF -*ance*, -*ence*, f. LL *apparentia* (as prec., see -ENCE)]

appeas|e' (-z), v.t. Pacify, quiet, (strife, anger, person); try to conciliate or bribe (a potential aggressor) by making concessions, freq. with implication of sacrifice of principles; soothe; satisfy (appetite, prejudice). So ~'ABLE (-z-) a., ~e'MENT (-zm-) n. [ME *apese* f. OF *apeser, apaisier* (*à* to + *pais* PEACE)]

appĕll'ant, a. & n. 1. Appealing; (Law) concerned with appeals. 2. n. One who appeals to higher court. [late ME, f. F (as APPEAL¹, see -ANT)]

appĕll'ate, a. Taking cognizance of appeals, as ~ *jurisdiction*. [f. L as foll., see -ATE²]

ăppellā'tion, n. Name, title; nomenclature. [ME, f. OF, f. L as APPEAL¹, see -ATION]

appĕll'ative, a. & n. (Of words) designating a class, common (as opp. to *proper*); common noun, applicable to any member of a class; appellation. Hence ~LY² (-vl-) adv. [f. LL *appellativus* as APPEAL¹, see -ATIVE]

appĕnd', v.t. Hang on, annex; add in writing. [f. L APpendere]

appĕn'dage, n. Thing attached; addition; accompaniment. [prec. + -AGE]

appĕn'dant, a. & n. (Possession, thing, person) attached in subordinate capacity (*to* another). [F, part. of *appendre* f. L -*icis* (APpendĕre APPEND)]

appĕn'd|ix, n. (pl. ~*icēs*, ~*ixes*). Subsidiary addition (*to* book or document); small process developed from surface of any organ, esp. *vermiform* ~*ix* (of the intestine), whence~icIT'IS n. [L *appendix* -*icis* (APpendĕre APPEND)]

ăpperceive' (-sēv), v.t. (psych.). Unite and assimilate (a perception) to a mass of ideas already possessed, & so comprehend & interpret it. [ME, f. OF *aperceveir* (Rom. *appercipere f. AP-+L *percipere* PERCEIVE)]

äppercĕp'tion, n. Mind's perception of itself; mental perception; (Psych.) action or fact of becoming conscious by subsequent reflection of a perception already experienced; process by which the mind apperceives. [f. F *aperception* (as prec., see -ION)]

äppertain', v.i. Belong as possession or right *to*; be appropriate *to*; relate *to*. [ME, f. OF *apertenir* (mod. *appar-*) f. LL AP(*pertinēre* PERTAIN)]

äpp'étence, -cў, n. Longing after, desire, (*of, for, after*); affinity (*for*). [f. F *appétence* or L *appetentia* (AP*petere* seek after) see -ENCE, -ENCY]

äpp'étent, a. Eagerly desirous (*after, of*). [ME, f. L *appetere*, see prec. & -ENT]

äpp'étite, n. Desire, inclination, (*for*); desire to satisfy natural necessities, esp. hunger; relish. So **appĕt'itIVE** a. [ME *apetyte* f. OF *apetit* f. L *appetitus* (as prec., see -ITE²)]

äpp'étīz|e, -is|e (-īz), v.t. (Of things) give appetite (only in part. ~*ing*). Hence ~ER¹ (2) n. [f. F *appétissant* part. irreg. f. *appétit* (as prec.), assim. to vbs in -IZE]

applaud', v.i. & t. Express approval loudly, as by clapping hands; (v.t.) express approval of, praise. [f. L AP*plaudere -plaus-* clap hands]

applaus|e' (-z), n. Approbation loudly expressed: marked approval. Hence ~'IVE (-s-), a., ~'ivELY² (-sĭvlĭ) adv. [f. med. L *applausus, -ūs* (as prec.)]

äp'ple, n. Round firm fleshy fruit of a rosaceous tree; (Bot.) any inferior fleshy many-celled fruit; ~ *of discord*, golden ~ contended for by Juno, Minerva, & Venus; ~ *of Sodom, Dead Sea*~, fruit dissolving into ashes; ~ *of the eye*, the pupil, eyeball, any cherished object; ~ *brandy*, spirit distilled from cider; ~ *butter*, sauce of ~s stewed in cider; ~*-cart* (*upset* person's ~*-cart*, spoil his plans); ~ *cheese*, compressed ~ pomace; ~ *dumpling*, ~ cooked in paste; ~ *green*, a colour; ~ *pomace*, pulp remaining after juice is expressed; ~*-jack*, Amer. name for ~ brandy; ~*-john*, kind of ~ said to keep two years & to be best when withered; ~*-pie bed*, one with sheets so folded that one's legs cannot get down; ~*-pie order*, perfect order; *~ sauce* (sl.), insincere flattery (also as int. = nonsense!). ᵀOE *æppel*, OHG *apful*, ON *epli*, Gmc **aplu-*]

äppli'ance, n. Applying: thing applied as means to an end. [f. APPLY +-ANCE]

äpp'lica|ble, a. Capable of being applied; having reference, appropriate, (*to*). Hence ~BIL'ITY n, [f. L *applicare* (APPLY)+-ABLE; cf. F. *applicable*]

äpp'licant, n. One who applies (*for*). [as prec., see -ANT]

äpplica'tion, n. Putting of one thing *to* another; employment of means; (~ of) plaster, liniment, etc.; bringing (*of a* general rule etc.) to bear upon particular case; relevancy; diligence; making of a request; request made. [late ME, f. F, f. L *applicationem* (as APPLY, see -ATION)]

appliqué (äplē'kā), n., & v.t. Ornamental work cut out from one material & applied to the surface of another (esp. in dressmaking); (vb) ornament thus. [F p.p. of *appliquer* apply (L *applicare*)]

applỹ', v.t. & i. Put close (*to*); administer (remedy etc. *to*; lit. & fig.); devote (*to*); make use of; use as relative or suitable (*to*), set one*self* closely (*to* task, *to* do); have reference (*to*); attend closely (*to*); address oneself (*for* help etc. *to*); make application (*for* situation); *applied*, put to practical use, practical (opp. *theoretical* or *pure*). [ME, f. OF *aplier* f. L AP*plicare* fold, fasten to]

appoggiatur'a (-ōjatoora), n. (mus.). A grace consisting of the note above the principal note, interpolated before it & momentarily taking its place in the rhythm of the passage. [It.]

appoint', v.t. Fix (time, place, *for* purpose); prescribe (thing, *that*): (Law) declare the destination of (property, also abs.); nominate, as ~ *him governor, to govern, to be governor,* ~ *him*; (p.p.) *well, badly, ~ed,* so equipped. Hence ~EE' n. [ME, f. OF *apointer* (*à* point to the point)]

appoint'ment, n. Appointing; engagement, assignation; decree, ordinance; office assigned; (usu. pl.) outfit; *keep, break, an* ~, appear, fail to appear, at fixed place & time. [ME, f. OF *apointement* (as prec., see -MENT)]

appŏr'tion, v.t. Assign as due share (*to*); portion out. Hence ~MENT (-shon-) n. [f. OF *aportionner* (*à* to +*portionner* f. PORTION)]

äpp'osite (-z-), a. Well put; appropriate (*to*). Hence ~LY² (-tl-) adv., ~NESS (-tn-) n. [f. L AP(*ponere posit-* put)]

äpposi'tion (-z-), n. Application (of seal); placing side by side; (Gram.) placing of word in syntactic parallelism with another, esp. addition of one noun to another. Hence ~AL (-zĭsho-) a. [ME, f. F, or f. LL *appositio* (as prec., see -ION)]

apprais|e' (-z), v.t. (Esp. of official valuer) fix price for; estimate. Hence ~'AL (-z-), ~e'MENT (-zm-), nn., ~'ABLE (-z-) a. [f. PRAISE v. (formerly used in the same sense), on anal. of *prize, apprize*]

apprē'ciab|le (-sha-), a. Capable of being estimated; perceptible, sensible. Hence ~LY² adv. [as foll., see -BLE]

apprē'ci|āte (-shī-), v.t. & i. Estimate worth, quality, amount, of; estimate aright; be sensitive to; esteem highly; raise in value; rise in value. Hence ~atIVE, ~atORY, (-sha-), aa., ~atIVELY² (-vl-) adv. [f. LL AP*pretiare* appraise (*pretium* price), see -ATE³]

apprĕciā′tion (*or* -shĭ-), n. Estimation; judgement; perception; adequate recognition; rise in value; critique. [OF, f. LL *appretiationem* (as prec., see -ATION)]

ăpprĕhĕnd′, v.t. Seize, arrest; perceive (by senses or intellect); understand; fear (thing, *that*). [f. F *appréhender* or L AP(*prehendere -hens-* lay hold of), whence also F *apprendre* learn]

ăpprĕhĕn′si|ble, a. Capable of being grasped (by senses or intellect). Hence ~BIL′ITY n. [f. LL *apprehensibilis* (as prec., see -BLE)]

ăpprĕhĕn′sion (-shn), n. Seizure, arrest; grasping (of ideas), conception; understanding; dread. [F, or f. LL *apprehensio* (as prec., see -ION)]

ăpprĕhĕn′sive, a. Pertaining to sensuous or mental perception; perceptive (*of*); intelligent; uneasy, fearful, (of thing, *that* it may happen, *for* person, *for* his safety). Hence ~LY[2] (-vl-) adv., ~NESS (-vn-) n. [f. F *appréhensif* or med. L *apprehensivus* (as prec., see -IVE)]

apprĕn′tice[1], n. Learner of a craft, bound to serve, & entitled to instruction from, his employer for specified term; tiro. Hence ~SHIP (-ssh-) n. [ME, f. OF *aprentis* f. *apprendre* (see APPREHEND), suggested by words in *-tis, -tif*, f. L *-tivus* (see -IVE)]

apprĕn′tice[2], v.t. Bind as apprentice. [f. prec.]

apprise′ (-z), v.t. Inform; (pass.) be aware *of*. [f. F *appris -ise* p.p. of *apprendre* learn, teach, (see APPREHEND)]

apprize′, v.t. (arch.). Appraise; appreciate. [ME, f. OF *aprisier* (*à* to +*prisier* PRAISE, PRIZE)]

‖ ăp′prō, n. *On* ~, (of goods supplied) to be returned if not satisfactory. [= *approval* or *approbation*]

approach′[1], v.t. & i. Come near(er); (Golf) play the approach shot; approximate in character etc. *to*; come near to; approximate to; (Commerc.) make overtures or proposals to. Hence~ABIL′ITY n., ~ABLE a. [ME, f. OF *aprochier* f. LL AD*propiare* draw near (*propius* compar. of *prope* near)]

approach′[2], n. Act of approaching; approximation; access, passage, (lit. & fig.); (Golf) stroke, not from a tee, played for the green. [f. prec.]

*ăpp′robāte, v.t. Approve formally, sanction. [late ME, f. L AP(*probare* test f. *probus* good) see -ATE[3]]

ăpprobā′tion, n. Sanction; approval. So **ăpp′robātORY** a. [ME, f. OF f. L *approbationem* (as prec., see -ATION)]

apprŏp′riate[1], a. Belonging, peculiar, (*to*); suitable, proper, (*to, for*). Hence ~LY[2] (-tl-) adv., ~NESS (-tn-) n. [f. LL AP*propriare* (*proprius* own), see -ATE[2]]

apprŏp′ri|āte[2], v.t. Take possession of; take to oneself; devote to special purposes. Hence or cogn. ~A′TION, ~ātOR, nn., ~ATIVE a. [f. prec., see -ATE[3]]

approv′al (-ōō-), n. Approbation; sanction. [f. foll. +-AL (2)]

approve′ (-ōōv), v.t. & i. Give evidence of (quality); (refl.) show one*self* to be; confirm, sanction; commend; ~ *of*, pronounce, consider, good; (p.p.) pronounced satisfactory, accepted, (of persons, reasons, etc.; ~*d school*, State school for young offenders). [ME, f. OF *aprover* f. L as APPROBATE]

approv′er (-ōō-), n. One who approves; one who turns Queen's evidence. [f. prec. +-ER[1]]

approx′imate[1], a. Very near; closely resembling; fairly correct. Hence ~LY[2] (-tl-) adv. [f. LL AP*proximare* (*proximus*, very near), see -ATE[2]]

approx′im|āte[2], v.t. & i. Bring, come, near (*to* thing, esp. in quality, number, etc.). Hence ~A′TION n., ~ative a., ~ativeLY[2] adv. [f. prec., see -ATE[3]]

ăppui′ (-wē), n. (Mil.) defensive support; *point of* ~ (F *point d'*~), fixed object on which troops deploy into line, also fig. [F, f. *appuyer* support]

appŭrt′enance, n. Belonging; appendage; accessory. [f. AF *apurtenance* (OF *aper-, apar-*) f. Rom. *appertinentia (as APPERTAIN, see -ANCE)]

appŭrt′enant, a. & n. (Thing) belonging, appertaining, pertinent, (*to*). [ME, f. OF *apartenant* part. as APPERTAIN]

ăp′ricŏt, n. Orange-coloured stone-fruit allied to plum. [(earliest forms *abrecock, apricock*) f. Sp. *albar(i)coque* f. Arab. *al* the +*burquq* f. Gk *praikokion* prob. f. L *praecoquum* variant of *praecox* early-ripe; -*cot* by assim. to F *abricot*]

Ap′ril (ā-), n. Fourth month of year; ~-*fool*, one sportively imposed upon on ~-*fool-day* (April 1). [ME *averil* f. OF *avril*, & *aprille* dir. f. L *aprilis*]

ā priō′rī, adv. & a. (Reasoning) from cause to effect; deductively; (loosely) presumptively, as far as one knows. Hence **ā-priō′rITY** n. [L, = from what is before]

ăp′ron, n. Garment worn in front of body to protect clothes; official dress, as *bishop's, dean's, freemason's*, ~; leather covering for legs in open carriage; skin covering stuffing of roast goose or duck; *tied to* ~-*strings of* (wife, mother, etc.), unduly controlled by; hard-surfaced area on airfield, used for handling & (un)loading aircraft; (Theatr.) advanced strip of stage for playing scenes before curtain. Hence ~ED[2] (-nd) a., ~FUL (-ōōl) n. [ME *naperon* etc., f. OF dim. of *nape* table-cloth f. L *mappa* (cf. MAP[1]); for loss of *n-* (*a napron = an apron*) cf. ADDER]

ăpropos′ (-pō), adv., a., n. To the purpose; in respect *of*; appropriate(ness). [F, *à* to +*propos* PURPOSE]

ăpse, n. Semicircular or polygonal recess, arched or dome-roofed, esp. in church. [f. APSIS]

ăp'sidal, a. Of the form of an apse; of the apsides. [f. foll. +-AL]

ăp'sis, n. (pl. *ăp'sidēs, ăpsĭd'ēs*). Aphelion, perihelion, of planet; apogee, perigee, of moon; *line of apsides*, straight line joining these. [L, f. Gk *(h)apsis -idos* fastening, felloe of wheel, vault, *(haptō* join)]

ăpt, a. Suitable, appropriate; having a tendency *(to* do or be); quick-witted *(at).* Hence ~'LY[2] adv., ~'NESS n. [ME, f. L *aptus* fitted p.p. of *apere* fasten]

ăp'terous, a. Wingless; (Bot.) having no membranous expansions. [f. Gk *apteros* (a- not +*pteron* wing) +-OUS]

ăp'teryx, n. New Zealand bird with rudimentary wings & no tail. [f. Gk a- not +*pterux* wing]

ăp'titūde, n. Fitness; natural propensity *(for);* ability. [F, f. LL *aptitudinem* (as APT, see -TUDE)]

ā'qua, n. (chem.). Liquid, solution, as ~ *fort'is,* nitric acid, ~ *rē'gia,* mixture of nitric & hydrochloric acids, able to dissolve gold & platinum. [L, = water]

ā'qualŭng, n. Portable diving apparatus consisting of cylinders of compressed air strapped on back & feeding air automatically to diver as he requires it. [f. L *aqua* water+LUNG]

ăquamarine' (-ēn), n. Bluish-green beryl; bluish green (also as adj.). [f. L *aqua marina* sea-water]

ā'quaplāne, n., & v.i. (Ride on) plank towed behind speedboat. [f. L *aqua* water+PLANE[3]]

ăquarĕlle', n. Kind of painting with Chinese ink & thin water-colours. [F, f. It. *acquerella* water-colour dim. of *acqua* f. L *aqua* water]

aquār'ium, n. (pl. *-iums, -ia*). Artificial pond or tank for the keeping of live aquatic plants & animals; place of public entertainment containing such tanks. Hence ā'quarIST (3) n., keeper of an ~. [L *(aqua* water, see -ARIUM)]

Aquār'ius, n. Zodiacal constellation; eleventh sign of Zodiac. [L, = water--carrier (as prec., see -ARY[1])]

aquăt'ic, a. & n. (Plant, animal) growing, living, in or near water; (of sports) conducted in or upon water. [late ME, f. F *aquatique* or L *aquaticus (aqua* water, see -ATIC)]

ā'quatint, n. Method of engraving on copper by use of a resinous solution & nitric acid; engraving so made. [f. F *aqua-tinte* f. It. *acqua tinta*]

ăqua-vīt'ae, n. Ardent spirits, esp. of the first distillation. [L, = water of life]

ā'quĕdŭct, n. Artificial channel, esp. elevated structure of masonry, for conveyance of water; conduit; (Physiol.) small canal, esp. in head of mammals. [f. L *aquae ductus* conduit *(ducere duct-* lead)]

ā'quĕous, a. Of water, watery; (Geol.) produced by water, as ~ *rocks.* [irreg. f. L *aqua* water+-EOUS]

ăquilē'gia, n. (Kinds of) plant of buttercup type; columbine. [mod. L, etym. unkn.]

ā'quiline, a. Of an eagle; eagle-like, as ~ *nose* (hooked). [f. L *aquilinus (aquila* eagle, see -INE[1])]

aquŏs'itў, n. Wateriness. [f. L *aquosus (aqua* water), see -OSE & -TY; cf. LL *aquositas*]

ar-, pref. = AD- before *r.*

-ar[1], suf. (1) adj. suf. f. L -*aris* (varying w. cogn. -*alis* -AL) taken direct or thr. F, or formed on L nouns. The OF form of L -*arem* was -*er*, later -*ier*; ME adoptives had -*er* (see -ER[2]), later assim. to L with -*ar* (e.g. ME *scoler,* now *scholar*). For F learned adoptives in -*aire*, see -ARY[1]. (2) noun suf., f. L-*are, -ar,* neut. of above (e.g. *exemplar*) or thr. F (ME *piler,* now *pillar*).

-ar[2], suf. Occas. repr. L -*arius, -arium* (normally repr. by -ER[2], -ARY[1]). Generally, refash. (after -AR[1]) of earlier -*er* f. OF -*ier* (e.g. OF *mortier,* ME *morter,* now *mortar*), or after F -*aire* (e.g. *vicar,* ME *viker* & *vicary* f. OF *vicaire,* L -*arius*).

-ar[3], suf. Casual var. of -ER[1], -OR in nouns (e.g. *beggar, liar, pedlar*), prob. on anal. of *scholar, pillar, vicar* (see -AR[1, 2]).

A'rab (ă-), n. & a. One of the Semitic race inhabiting Saudi Arabia & neighbouring countries; ~ horse; *street arab,* homeless child; (adj.) Arabian. [f. F *Arabe* f. L *Arabem* (nom. -*bs*) f. Gk *Araps -abos*]

ărabĕsque' (-k), a. & n. 1. Arabian; fantastic. 2. n. Decoration in colour or low relief, with fanciful intertwining of leaves, scroll-work, etc.; (Mus.) florid melodic figure, composition based on such figures; ballet dancer's posture in which body is bent forward on one leg with the other leg extended horizontally backwards. [F, = Arabian, see -ESQUE]

Arāb'ian, a. & n. 1. Of Arabia; ~ *Nights' Entertainments* (or *The Thousand and One Nights*), collection of fabulous stories; ~ *bird,* phoenix. 2. n. = Arab. [f. *Arabia* +-AN]

A'rabic (ă-), a. & n. 1. Arabian; *gum* ~ (exuded by some kinds of acacia); ~ *numerals,* 1, 2, 3, etc. 2. n. Language of the Arabs. [ME, f. OF *Arabic* f. L *Arabicus (Arabs* ARAB, see -IC)]

A'rabist (ă-), n. Student of Arabic. [ARAB +-IST]

ā'rable, a. & n. (Land) fit for tillage. [f. F, or f. L *arabilis (arare* plough, see -BLE)]

ărăch'nid (-k-), n. (zool.). Member of the *Arachnida,* class comprising spiders, scorpions, & mites. [f. mod. L *arachnida* f. Gk *arakhnē* spider +-ID[3]]

arăch'noid (-k-), a. & n. 1.(bot.). Covered with long cobweb-like hairs. 2. n. Serous membrane lining the dura mater, & enveloping brain & spinal cord. [f. Gk *arakhnoeidēs (arakhnē* cobweb, see -OID)]

Aramā'ic (ă-), a. & n. (Language) of Aram or Syria; northern branch of

Semitic family of languages, including Syriac & Chaldee. [f. L f. Gk *Aramaios* of Aram +-IC]

Aranē′idan (ă-), a. & n. (Member) of the *Araneida* or spiders. [f. mod. L *araneida* (*aranea* spider), see -ID[3], -AN]

ărapai′ma (-pī-), n. S.-American food-fish (largest freshwater fish). [Brazilian]

Araucār′ia (ă-), n. Genus of trees including monkey-puzzle. [*Arauco*, name of province in Chile]

ărb′alĕst, ărb′last (-ah-), n. Crossbow. [f. OF *arbaleste* f. LL *arcuballista* (*arcus* bow + *ballista* military engine)]

ărb′iter, n. Judge; one appointed by two parties to settle dispute, umpire; one who has entire control (*of*); ~ *ĕlĕgăntiar′um* (-shi-), judge of taste (lit. of elegance). [L]

ărb′itrage, n. Traffic in bills of exchange or stocks to take advantage of different prices in other markets. [F, f. *arbitrer* as ARBITRATE, see -AGE]

ărb′itral, a. Pertaining to arbitration. [F, f. LL *arbitralis*, see ARBITER & -AL]

ărbit′rament, -ement, n. Deciding of dispute by arbiter; authoritative decision [ME, f. OF *arbitrement* (*arbitrer*, see ARBITRAGE & -MENT)]

ărb′itrar|y̆, a. Derived from mere opinion; capricious; unrestrained; despotic; (Law) discretionary. Hence ~iLY[2] adv., ~iNESS n. [f. L *arbitrarius* or F *arbitraire*, see ARBITER & -ARY[1]]

ărb′itrāte, v.t. & i. Decide by arbitration. [f. L *arbitrari* judge, see ARBITER & -ATE[3]]

ărbitrā′tion, n. Settlement of a dispute by an arbiter; ~ *of exchange*, determination of rate of indirect exchange between two currencies. [ME, f. OF, f. L *arbitrationem* (as prec., see -ATION)]

ărb′itrātor, n. (Now the legal term for) arbiter. Hence ~SHIP n. [ME, f. OF *arbitratour* f. LL *arbitratorem* (as ARBITRATE, see -OR)]

ărb′itrĕss, n. Female arbiter, mediatress; absolute mistress. [ME, f. OF *arbitresse* fem. of *arbitre* f. L ARBITER, see -ESS[1]]

ărb′or, n. Main support of machine; axle or spindle on which wheel revolves. [f. F *arbre* tree, axis, f. L *arbor*; refash. on L]

ărborā′ceous (-shŭs), a. Tree-like; wooded. [f. L *arbor* tree, see -ACEOUS]

Arb′or Day (ăr-), n. Day set apart annually in U.S., S. Australia, & elsewhere for public tree-planting. [L *arbor* tree]

ărbōr′ĕal, a. Of, living in, connected with, trees. [f. L *arboreus* (*arbor* tree, see -AL)]

ărbor′ĕous, a. Wooded; arboreal; arborescent. [as prec., see -OUS]

ărborĕs′c|ent, a. Tree-like in growth or general appearance; (Archit.) branching out. Hence ~ENCE n., ~entLY[2] adv. [f. L *arborescere* grow into a tree (*arbor*), see -ENT]

ărborĕt′um, n. (pl. *-ta*). A botanical tree-garden. [L, f. *arbor* tree]

ărb′ori|cŭlture, n. Cultivation of trees & shrubs. Hence ~cŭl′turAL a., ~cŭl′turIST n. [f. L *arbor* *-oris* tree + CULTURE]

ărborizā′tion, n. Tree-like appearance (Min., Chem.) in aggregation of crystals, (Anat.) from distension or injection of capillary vessels. [as prec. +-IZE +-ATION]

ărb′or vit′ae, n. Popular name of several evergreens. [L, = tree of life]

ărb′our (*-er*), n. Bower, shady retreat with sides & roof formed by trees or lattice-work covered with climbing plants. Hence ~ED[2] (*-erd*) a. [ME (*h*)*erber* f. OF (*h*)*erbier* grass lawn f. L *herbarium* (*herba* grass, herb, see -ARIUM), phonetic change to *ar-* being assisted by assoc. with L *arbor* tree]

Arb′ūtus (ăr-), n. Genus of evergreens including strawberry-tree. [L]

ărc, n. Part of circumference of circle or other curve; *diurnal, nocturnal*, ~, part of circle that a heavenly body appears to pass through above, below, horizon; belt contained between parallel curves; (Electr.) luminous bridge formed between two separate carbon poles; ~-*lamp, -light*, using this. [ME, f. OF, f. L *arcus* bow, curve]

ărcāde′, n. Passage arched over; any covered walk, esp. with shops along one or both sides; (Archit.) series of arches on same plane. Hence ărcād′ED[2] a. [F, f. Prov. *arcada* f. Rom. *arca ARCH, see -ADE]

Arcades ăm′bō (ärk′adēz), sent. Blackguards both (cf. Byron *D. Juan*, iv. 93). [joc. application of Virg. *Ecl.* vii. 4]

Arcād′ian (är-), a. & n. Ideal(ly) rustic. [f. L *Arcadius* (Gk *Arkadia* mountain district in Peloponnese) +-AN]

Arc′adў, Arcād′ia, (är-), n. (poet.). Ideal rustic paradise. [f. Gk *Arkadia*, see prec.]

ărcān′um (är-), n. (Usu. in pl. *-na*) mystery, secret. [L, neut. of *arcanus* (*arca* chest, see -AN)]

ărch[1], n. Curved structure supporting bridge, floor, etc., or merely ornamental; curve; curvature in shape of ~, as *fallen* ~ (of foot); vault; *Court of Arches*, ecclesiastical court of appeal for the province of Canterbury, orig. held in the church of St Mary-le-Bow (or 'of the Arches'); ~*way*, vaulted passage, arched entrance. Hence ~*wise* adv. [ME, f. OF *arche* f. Rom. *arca, n. pl. by-form of L *arcus* ARC]

ărch[2], v.t. & i. Furnish with an arch; form into an arch; overarch, span; (intr.) form an arch. [ME, f. OF *archer* (as prec.)]

ărch[3], a. (sup. *-est*). Chief, pre-eminent, as ~ *rogue, knave, impostor*, (but now usu. ~-); factiously serious, innocently roguish, whence ~′LY[2] adv., ~′NESS n. [= foll.]

ărch-, pref. = Gk *arkhi-, arkh-, arkhe-*, comb. form of *arkhos* chief. Hence L *archi-* whence OE *arce-*, ME *arche-*, coinciding w. OF *arche*. From these, *arch*-became a living formative. In mod. literary wds f. Gk or L directly, or thr. F, the form *archi-* is retained; cf. *archdeacon* but *archidiaconal*. Meaning: (1) in titles of office etc. 'chief, superior', as *archbishop*, *-duke*, esp. in titles of Holy Roman or German empire, as *-butler*, *-chamberlain*; (2) 'pre-eminent, leading', as *-antiquary*, *-builder*, *-prophet*, *-wag*; esp. 'extreme, worst', as *-buffoon*, *-knave*, *-liar*; (3) chiefly archaic = 'first, original', as *-founder*, *-messenger*; (4) of things, 'chief', as *-diocese*.

Arch'aean (ärk-), a. Of the earliest geological period. [f. Gk *arkhaios* ancient (*arkhē* beginning) +-AN]

archae|öl'ogў (-kǐ-), n. Study of antiquities, esp. of the prehistoric period. So ~olŏ'gIC(AL) (-kǐo-) aa., ~olŏ'gicaLLY² adv., ~öl'ogIST (-kǐ-) n. [f. Gk *arkhaiologia* (as prec., see -LOGY)]

archaeŏp'terўx (-k-), n. Oldest known (fossil) bird, a link between birds & reptiles. [f. Gk *arkhaios* ancient + *pterux* wing]

archā'|ic (-k-), a. Primitive, antiquated; (of language) no longer in common use, though retained for special purposes. Hence ~ICALLY adv. [f. Gk *arkhaïkos* (as prec., see -IC)]

arch'ā|ism (-k-), n. Retention, imitation, of what is old or obsolete (esp. in language & art); archaic word or expression. Hence ~IST n., ~īs'tIC a., (-k-). [f. Gk *arkhaïsmos* (*arkhaïzō*, see foll. & -ISM)]

arch'āize (-k-), -ise (-īz), v.t. & i. Imitate, affect, the archaic; (trans.) render archaistic. [f. Gk *arkhaïzō* copy the ancients (*arkhaios* ancient, see -IZE)]

arch'ăngel (-k-), n. Angel of highest rank; kind of dead-nettle; kind of pigeon. Hence archăngĕl'IC (-k-) a. [ME f. OF, or f. LL f. Gk *arkhaggelos* (see ARCH- & ANGEL)]

arch'bish'op, n. Chief bishop; metropolitan. Hence archBISH'OPRIC n. [OE *ærce-*, *erce-* (ME *erche-*) *biscop*, f. Rom. *arcebiscopo* f. LL *archiepiscopus* (see ARCH- & BISHOP)]

arch'deac'on, n. Ecclesiastical dignitary next below bishop, superintending rural deans & holding lowest ecclesiastical court, with power of spiritual censure. Hence archdeac'onSHIP n. [OE *ærce-*, *ercediacon*, f. LL *archidiaconus* (see ARCH- & DEACON)]

archdeac'onrў (-k-), n. Jurisdiction, rank, residence, of archdeacon. [prec. +-RY]

archdi'ocēse, n. See of an archbishop. [ARCH- (4)]

arch'dŭch'ĕss, n. (hist.). Wife of an archduke; daughter of Emperor of Austria. [f. F *archiduchesse* (see ARCH- & DUCHESS)]

arch'dūke, n. (hist.), Son of Emperor of Austria. So archDŪC'AL a., arch'DUCHY n. [f. OF *archeduc*, in med. L *archidux* (see ARCH- & DUKE)]

arch'-ĕn'ĕmў, n. Chief enemy; Satan. [ARCH- (2)]

arch'|er, n. One that shoŏts with bow & arrows; Sagittarius, ninth zodiacal constellation. So ~ERY (2) n. [AF, f. OF *archier* f. Rom. **arcarius* (*arcus* bow, see -ARY¹)]

arch'etўp|e (-k-), n. Original model, prototype. Hence ~AL a., ~alLY² adv. [f. L f. Gk *arkhetupon* (*arkhe-* ARCH- +*tupos* stamp)]

arch'-fiend', n. Satan. [ARCH- (2)]

archi-. See ARCH-.

‖ **arch'ibald** (-awld). See ARCHIE.

archidiäc'onal (-kǐ-), a. Pertaining to an archdeacon. [f. LL *archidiaconus* ARCH-DEACON +-AL]

‖ **ŭrch'ie**, **-ibald**, nn. (sl.). Anti-aircraft gun. [f. name in pop. song]

archiēpis'copal (-k-), a. Pertaining to an archbishop. [f. LL *archiepiscopus* ARCH-BISHOP +-AL]

arch'il (*or* -k-), n. (Violet dye from) various kinds of lichen. [corrupt. of ORCHIL]

archimăn'drite (-k-), n. Superior of monastery or convent in Greek church. [f. LL *archimandrita* f. late Gk *arkhimandritēs* (*arkhi-* ARCH- +*mandra* monastery)]

Archimēd'ēan (ärk-), a. Of Archimedes (Greek mathematician); ~ *screw*, instrument raising water by tube in form of screw ·wound round cylinder. [f. L *Archimedeus* +-AN]

archipĕl'agō (-k-), n. (pl. ~*s*). Aegean sea; sea with many islands; group of islands. [f. It. *arcipelago* (*arci-* ARCH- (4) +*pelago* gulf, pool, f. L f. Gk *pelagos* sea)]

arch'itĕct (-k-), n. Professor of building, who prepares plans & superintends work; designer of complex structure, esp. the Creator; (fig.) achiever, as ~ *of his own fortunes*. Hence ~IVE a. [f. F *architecte* or L *architectus* f. Gk *arkhitektōn* (*arkhi-* ARCH- +*tektōn* builder); some derivatives formed as if L *-tectus* were p.p. of *tegere* cover]

architĕctŏn'|ic (-k-), a. Of architecture or architects; constructive; controlling; pertaining to systematization of knowledge, whence ~ICS n., ~ICAL a. [f. F *-ique* or L *-icus* f. Gk. *arkhitektonikos* (as prec., see IC)]

arch'itĕcture (-k-), n. Art or science of building; thing built, structure; style of building; construction. Hence architĕc'-turAL (-k-; -cher-) a., architĕc'turaLLY² adv. [F, or f. L *architectura* (*architectus* ARCHITECT, see -URE)]

arch'itrāve (-k-), n. Epistyle, main beam resting immediately on the abacus on capital of column; the various parts surrounding doorway or window; moulding round exterior of arch. [F, f. It. *architrave* (*archi-* ARCH- +*trave* (f. L *trabs -abis*) beam)]

árch'íve (-k-), n. (usu. pl. ~s, pr. -kīvz). Place in which public records are kept; records so kept. [F (-if, -ive), f. LL archi(v)um f. Gk arkheion public office (arkhē government)]

árch'ivist (-k-), n. Keeper of archives. [f. prec. +-IST]

árch'ivòlt (-k-), n. Lowest member of arch from impost to impost; mouldings decorating this. [f. F archivolte or It. archivolto, arcovolta (arco f. L arcus arch +volta VAULT, volto arched)]

árch'on (-k-), n. One of nine chief magistrates in ancient Athens; ruler, president. Hence ~SHIP n. [Gk (-ōn), = ruler (part. of arkhō)]

árc'tic, a. Of the north pole, northern; A~ Circle (of earth), parallel of 66° 32' N. [ME artik f. OF artique f. L ar(c)ticus f. Gk arktikos (arktos bear, Ursa Major, see -IC)]

Arctúr'us (ár-), n. Brightest star in constellation Boötes. [ME, f. L, f. Gk arktouros (arktos bear+ouros guardian)]

árc'ūate, **-ātėd**, aa. Bent like a bow; arched. [f. L arcuatus (arcuare f. arcus bow; see -ATE²)]

árc'us sĕnīl'ĭs, n. Narrow yellowish-white band gradually encircling the cornea with advancing age. [L, = bow of old age]

-ard, suf. forming nouns, usu. of censure (sluggard, drunkard), but cf. standard (orig. stander, placard; also spelt -art (braggart). [ME & OF, f. Gmc *-hart, *-hard, hardy, in proper names]

árd'ent, a. Burning, red-hot; parching; ~ spirits (prop. = inflammable, but now understood of their taste), alcoholic spirits; eager, zealous; fervent (of persons & feelings). Hence árd'ENCY n., ~LY² adv. [ME, f. OF ardant f. L ardentem (ardēre burn, see -ANT]

árd'our (-der), n. Fierce heat; warm emotion; fervour, zeal, (for). [ME, f. OF, f. L ardorem (ardēre burn, see -OR)]

árd'ūous, a. Steep, hard to climb; hard to achieve, laborious, strenuous, energetic. Hence ~LY² adv., ~NESS n. [f. L arduus steep, difficult +-OUS]

are¹ (ár), n. French metric unit of square measure, square whose side is 10 metres (119·6 sq. yds). [F, f. L area]

are². See BE.

ár'ĕa, n. Vacant ground; level space; sunk court railed off from pavement & freq. giving access to basement of house, as ~ bell; superficial extent; region, tract; scope, range. [L, = vacant piece of ground in town]

ă'rėca, n. Kinds of palms; ~-nut, astringent seed of a species of ~. [Port., f. Tamil adaikay (aḍai close-clustering + kay nut)]

arēn'a, n. (pl. ~s). Central part of amphitheatre, in which combats take place; (fig.) scene of conflict, sphere of action. [L (h)arena sand, sand-strewn place of combat]

ărēnā'ceous (-shus), a. Sand-like; sandy. So **ărėnOSE'¹** a. [f. L arenaceus (as prec., see -ACEOUS)]

aren't (árnt). See BE.

arē'ol|a, n. (pl. ~ae). Very small area, as that between veins of a leaf; interstice in tissue; circular spot, as that surrounding the human nipple; (Biol.) cell-nucleus of plant. Hence ~AR¹, ~ATE², aa., ~A'TION n. [L, dim. of AREA]

Arėŏp'agīte (ă-, -jīt or -gīt) n. Member of the court of Areopagus. [f. L f. Gk areiopagītēs (see foll. & -ITE)]

Arėŏp'agus (ă-), n. Hill at Athens where highest judicial court sat. [L, f. Gk Areios pagos Mars' hill]

arête (árāt'), n. Sharp ascending ridge of mountain. [F, f. L arista ear of corn]

ár'gala, n. Adjutant-bird, gigantic Indian stork. [Hind. hargila]

ár'gali, n. Asian wild sheep. [Mongol]

ár'gand, n. Lamp with tubular wick; gas-burner on same principle. [inventor]

ár'gent, n. & a. Silver (colour, esp. in armorial bearings. [F, f. L argentum]

argentif'erous, a. Yielding silver. [f. L argentum+-FEROUS]

ár'gentine, a. & n. Of silver; silvery; imitation silver; silvery lamellae on scales of fish; (Zool.) kinds of small fishes; (Min.) slate-spar. [f. F argentin (L argentum+-in; see -INE¹)]

ár'gil, n. Clay (esp. potter's). So ~lA'CEous a. [f. F argille f. L argilla f. Gk argillos (argēs white)]

Argive (ár'gīv, -j-), a. & n. 1. Of Argos in ancient Greece, Greek. 2. n. An inhabitant of Argos, a Greek. [f. L Argivus f. Gk Argeios]

ár'gle-bár'gle, v.i., & n., (joc.). Debate [corrupt. & redupl. of argue]

ár'gol, n. Tartar deposited from fermented wines, which when purified becomes cream of tartar. [ME argoyle, of unkn. orig.]

ár'gon, n. (chem.). A gas, an inert constituent of the atmosphere. [neut. of Gk argos idle (A- (7), ergon work)]

Ar'gonaut (ár-), n. 1. (pl.). Legendary heroes who sailed with Jason in the Argo for the golden fleece. 2. Genus of cephalopod molluscs including paper nautilus. [f. L (-ta) f. Gk Argonautēs sailor in the Argō]

ár'gosy, n. (hist., poet.). Large merchant-vessel, esp. of Ragusa & Venice; (poet.) ship, venture. [earlier ragusye, prob. f. It. Ragusea (nave) Ragusan (vessel)]

ár'got (-gō), n. Jargon, slang, of a class, esp. of thieves. [F, of unkn. orig.]

ár'gūe, v.t. & i. Prove, indicate, as it ~s him (to be) a rogue, that he is a rogue, roguery in him; maintain by reasons (that), whence **ár'gūABLE** a.; treat (matter) by reasoning; ~ it away, get rid of it by argument; ~ (persuade) person into, out of; reason (with, against, person, for, against, about, thing). [ME, f. OF arguer f. L *argutare* frequent. of *arguere* make clear, prove, accuse]

ăr'gūment, n. Reason advanced (*for, against*, proposition or course); (Logic) middle term in syllogism; reasoning process; debate; summary of subject-matter of book; ~ (usu. *argumĕn'tum*) *ad hominem*, one that takes advantage of character or situation of particular opponent, *ad crumenam*, of his avarice, *ad ignorantiam*, of his ignorance of the facts, *ex silentio*, of his silence. [ME, f. F f. L *argumentum* (*arguere*, see prec. & -MENT]

ăr'gūmĕntā'tion, n. Methodical reasoning; debate. [f. F, or L *argumentatio* f. *argumentari* (as prec.), see -ATION]

ăr'gūmĕn'tative, a. Logical; fond of arguing. Hence ~LY² (-vl-) adv., ~NESS (-vn-) n. [F (-*if*, -*ive*), or f. LL *argumentativus*, as prec., see -ATIVE]

Ar'gus (ăr-), n. Fabulous person with a hundred eyes; watchful guardian; ~-*eyed*, vigilant; *argus-shell*, oculated porcelain-shell. [ME, f. L, f. Gk *Argos*]

ărgūte', a. Sharp, shrewd; (of sounds) shrill. [ME, f. L *argutus* p.p. of *arguere*, see ARGUE]

argyr-, argyro-, in comb. = Gk *arguros* silver, as *argyran'thous*, with silvery flowers, *argyrophyll'ous*, silvery-leaved.

ar'ia (ahr-), n. (mus.). Extended song in three sections common in 18th-c. opera & oratorio. [It.]

Ar'ian (ăr-), a & n. (Holder of the doctrine of Arius of Alexandria (4th c.), who denied consubstantiality of Christ. Hence ~ISM n., ~IZE v.t. & i. [f. LL *Arianus* (*Arius* f. Gk *Arios, Areios*, see -AN)]

-ăr'ian, suf. forming adjj. & nn., f. L *-arius* -ARY¹+-AN. First in 16th c. (*disciplin*~, *quinquagen*~, etc.), later (17th c.) & now chiefly denoting (member of a sect etc., as *millen*~, *Trinit*~, etc.

ă'rid, a. Dry, parched, (lit. & fig.); (of ground) barren, bare. Hence **arid'ITY**, ~NESS, nn. [f. F *aride* or L *aridus* (*arēre* be dry)]

ăr'iel, n. Species of gazelle in Western Asia & Africa. [f. Arab. *aryil* var. of *ayyil* stag]

Aries (ăr'ĭēz), n. The Ram, first zodiacal constellation. [ME, f. L, = ram]

aright' (-ĭt), adv. Rightly. [A prep.+ RIGHT n.]

ă'ril, n. Accessory seed-covering in certain plants. [f. mod. L *arillus* f. med. L *arilli* dried grapes]

-ăr'ious, compd adj. suf.=L *-arius*(-ARY¹) +-OUS.

arise' (-z), v.i. (*arōse, arĭsen*, pr. -z, -z-). (Arch.) rise, get up; (poet.) rise from the dead; (arch.) be heard (of sounds); originate; be born; come into notice; result (*from*); present itself. [A- (1)+ RISE v.]

aris'ta, n. (pl. *-ae*). Awn, beard, of grain & grasses. [L]

aris'tate, a. Awned, bearded. [f. L *aristatus* (ARISTA, see -ATE²)]

ăristŏc'racy̆, n. Government by the best citizens; supremacy of privileged order, oligarchy; state so governed; ruling body of nobles; class from which ruling body is drawn, nobles; the best representatives of (intellect etc.). [f. F *aristocratie* or f. LL f. Gk *aristokratia* (*aristos* best, see -CRACY)]

ă'ristocrăt, n. One of a ruling oligarchy; one of the class of nobles. Hence **ăristŏc'ratISM** n. [f. F *aristocrate* (as foll.)]

ăristocrăt'ic, a. Pertaining to, attached to, aristocracy; grand, stylish. Hence ~AL a., ~alLY² adv. [f. F *aristocratique* f. Gk *aristokratikos* (as ARISTOCRACY, see -IC)]

Aristotēl'ian (ă-), a. & n. (Disciple or student) of the Greek philosopher Aristotle. [f. L f. Gk *Aristotelēs* Aristotle +-IAN]

arith'mĕtĭc, n. Science of numbers; arithmetical knowledge, computation; treatise on computation. Hence **arithmĕti'CIAN** (-ĭshn) n. [ME, f. OF *arismetique* f. Rom. *arismetica* for L *arithmetica* f. Gk *arithmĕtikē* (*lekhnē*) (art) of counting f. *arithmeō* count (*arithmos* number), see -IC; corrupted in ME to *arsmetrike*, as if f. L *ars metrica* art of measure]

ărithmĕt'ical, a. Of arithmetic; ~.*progression*, (series of numbers showing) increase, decrease, by a constant quantity (e.g. 1, 2, 3, 4, etc., 9, 7, 5, 3, etc.). Hence ~LY² adv. [f. L *arithmeticus*+-AL]

-ăr'ium, noun suf. (= 'place for') f. L neut. of adjj. in *-arius* (-ARY¹), chiefly in antiquarian words as *sacrarium*, occas. popularized, as *aquarium*.

ărk, n. Chest, box; *Ark of the Covenant, Ark of Testimony*, wooden coffer containing tables of Jewish law; covered floating vessel in which Noah was saved at the Deluge; *Noah's* ~, toy ~ with animals. [OE *ærc*, OHG *archa*, ON *örk*, Goth. *arka*, Gme **arka* f. L *arca* chest]

arles (ărlz), n. pl. (dial.). Earnest-money. [see EARNEST²]

ărm¹, n. Upper limb of human body from shoulder to hand; *fore*~(from elbow to hand); fore limb of an animal; large branch of tree; sleeve; thing resembling ~, as ~ *of the sea*, ~'*chair*' (with side supports), ~ *of lever, balance* (part from fulcrum to point of application of power or weight); ~'*hole* in garment, hole, through which ~ is put; ~'*pit*, hollow under ~ at shoulder; ~-*in*-~ (of two persons with ~s interlinked); *infant in* ~*s* (too young to walk); *with open* ~*s*, cordially; *keep at* ~'*s length*, avoid familiarity with; *secular* ~, authority of secular tribunal. Hence **ărm'FUL** (-ŏŏl) n., **ărm'lĕss¹** [-LESS] a. [OE *earm, earm*, OHG *arm*, ON *armr*, Goth. *arms*, Gme **armaz*, cogn. w. L *armus* shoulder]

ārm², n. (usu. pl.). Weapon(s); *fire-~s* (requiring explosive); *small ~s*, portable fire-arms, esp. rifles, pistols, light machine guns, sub-machine guns, etc.; *stand of ~s*, set for one soldier; (sing.) particular kind of weapon; *take up ~s*, arm oneself (often fig.), *bear ~s*, serve as soldier; *lay down ~s*, cease hostilities; *in ~s*, armed; *up in ~s*, actively engaged in rebellion etc. (also fig.); *under ~s*, in battle array; military profession; (sing. & pl.) each kind of troops, infantry, cavalry, etc.; heraldic devices, as *coat of ~s*; *King-of-Arms*, Chief Herald. Hence **ārm'lèss²** [-LESS] a. [ME, f. OF *armes* f. L *arma* arms, fittings]

ārm³, v.t. & i. Furnish with arms; *~ed neutrality* (of nations prepared for war); furnish with tools or other requisites; plate (*with* anything); furnish (magnet) with an armature; (intr.) ~ oneself, take up arms. [ME, f. OF *armer* f. L *armare* (*arma*)]

ārmād'a, n. Fleet of ships of war, esp. *the* (*Invincible*) *A~* sent by Philip II of Spain against England in 1588. [Sp., f. L *armata* (*armare* ARM v., see -ADE)]

ārmadill'ō, n. (pl. *-os*). Burrowing animal of S. America, with body encased in bony armour, & habit of rolling itself into ball when captured; kinds of small terrestrial Crustacea with same habit, allied to wood-louse. [Sp., dim. of *armado* one armed f. L as ARM³, see -ADO]

Armagědd'on (ăr-, -g-), n. (Scene of) supreme conflict between the nations. [*Rev.* xvi. 16]

ārm'ament, n. Force (usu. naval) equipped for war; military equipments, guns on warship; process of equipping for war. [f. L *armamentum* (as ARM², see -MENT), partly through F *armement*]

ārm'ature, n. Arms, armour; defensive covering of animals or plants; piece of soft iron placed in contact with poles of magnet, increasing its power; essential part of a dynamo. [F, or f. L *armatura* (as prec., see -URE)]

arme blanche (see Ap.), n. Cavalry sword or lance; cavalry. [F,=white arm]

Armēn'ian (ăr-), a. & n. **1.** Of Armenia; ~ *bole*, red ~ earth, used medicinally; ~ *stone*, blue carbonate of copper. **2.** n. Native of Armenia; adherent of ~ church. [-AN]

ārm'igĕr, n. Esquire, one entitled to bear heraldic arms. [L, = bearing arms (*arma* arms + *gerere* bear)]

ārmill'arȳ, a. Pertaining to bracelets; ~ *sphere*, skeleton celestial globe of metal rings representing celestial equator, tropics, etc. [f. L *armilla* bracelet, see -ARY¹]

Armin'ian (ăr-), a. & n. (Adherent) of the doctrine of Arminius (d. 1609), Dutch protestant theologian, who opposed the views of Calvin, esp. on predestination. Hence ~ISM (ăr-) n. [f. *Arminius*, Latiniz. of *Harmensen* + -AN]

ārm'istice, n. Cessation from hostilities (lit. & fig.); short truce; *A~ Day*, 11th Nov., kept as anniversary of the ~ (1918) that ended hostilities in the war of 1914–·18. [F, or f. mod. L *armistitium* (*arma* arms + *-stitium* as in SOLSTICE)]

ārm'lėt, n. Band worn round arm; small inlet of sea or branch of river. [ARM¹ + -LET]

ārmōr'ial, a. & n. (Book) pertaining to heraldic arms. [ARMORY + -AL(1)]

ārm'or|ȳ, n. Heraldry. Hence ~IST n. [f. OF *armoirie* f. *armoier* blazoner f. *armoier* v. = It. *armeggiare* f. L *arma* arms] **ārm'our¹** (-mer), n. **1.** Defensive covering for the body worn in fighting (*~-bearer*, one who carries another's ~). **2.** Metal sheathing of ship of war, composed of *~-plates* (*~-clad*, furnished with this); steel plates etc. protecting cars, tanks, etc. from projectiles; armoured vehicles collectively, e.g. tanks, armoured cars, etc. **3.** Diver's suit. **4.** Protective covering of animals or plants. **5.** Heraldic insignia. [ME, f. OF *armēure* f. L *armatura* ARMATURE]

ārm'our² (-mer), v.t. Furnish with protective covering; *~ed* CRUISER; *~ed car, train*, etc., one supplied with protective plates of steel etc., & (usu.) guns; *~ed column, corps, division, force*, etc., one equipped with *~ed* cars, tanks, etc. [f. prec.]

ārm'ourer (-mer-), n. Manufacturer of arms; official in charge of ship's, regiment's, arms. [f. AF *armurer*, OF *-urier*, f. as above, see prec. & -ER²]

ārm'ourȳ (-mer-), n. Place where arms are kept, arsenal; *armourer's workshop. [perh. as ARMORY, but treated as f. ARMOUR + -Y¹]

ārm'ȳ, n. Organized body of men armed for war; *standing ~*, one of professional soldiers permanently in existence; *the ~*, the military service; vast host; organized body of men, as *Salvation A~, Church A~, Blue Ribbon A~*; ~ *broker, contractor* (carrying on business in connexion with the ~); ~ *corps*, main subdivision of ~ in the field consisting usu. of two or three divisions with technical, administrative, supply, etc. formations; *~-list*, official list of officers; *~-worm*, larva of cotton-moth. [ME, f. OF *armee* f. L *armata* fem. p.p. of *armare* arm; see -Y⁴]

ārn'ica, n. Kinds of plants including mountain tobacco; medicine, esp. tincture, prepared from this. [mod. L of unkn. orig.]

aroint', -oy-, v. or int. (arch.). ~ *thee*, begone. [ME, orig. unkn.]

arōm'a, n. (pl. *-as*). Fragrance, sweet smell; subtle pervasive quality. [ME *aromat* f. OF f. L *aromata* (pl.) f. Gk *arōma -atos*; later conform. to L *aroma*]

ărōmăt'ic, a. Fragrant; spicy; (of smell) pleasantly pungent. [ME, f. F *aromatique* f. LL f. Gk *arōmatikos* (AROMA, see -IC)]

arose. See ARISE.

around', adv. & prep. **1.** On every side, in every direction; *round, round about; *about. here & there, at random, as *fool* ~. **2.** prep. On, along, the circuit of; about, enveloping. [f. A-(2)+ROUND]

arouse' (-z), v.t. Awaken; stir up into activity. [A-(1)+ROUSE², on anal. of *rise, arise*]

ắrpe'ggio (-ĕjō), n. (pl. *-os*), (mus.). Striking of notes of chord in (usu. upward) succession; chord so struck. [It.]

arquebus. See HARQUEBUS.

ắ'rrack (*or* arăk'), n. Eastern name for any native spirituous liquor, esp. that distilled from the coco-palm, or from rice & sugar. [f. Arab. *'araq* juice]

ắ'rrah (-ra), int. An Anglo-Irish expletive.

arraign' (-ān), v.t. Indict before a tribunal; accuse; find fault with, call in question, (action, statement). So ~MENT (-ān-) n. [f. AF *arainer* f. OF *araisnier* f. Rom. *ADrationare* reason, talk reasonably (*ratio -onis* reason, discourse)]

arrắnge', v.t. & i. Put into order, adjust; draw up (army); (Mus.) adapt (composition) for new medium, instrumental or vocal; adapt (play etc.) for broadcasting; settle (dispute etc.); settle beforehand the order, manner, of; (intr.) take steps, form plans, give instructions, (~ *to be there, for the car to be there*; ~ *about it*); come to agreement (*with* person, *about* thing, *to* do, *that*, or abs.). [ME, f. OF *arangier* (*à* to+*rangier* RANGE¹)]

arrắnge'ment (-jm-), n. Arranging; thing arranged; settlement of dispute etc.; (pl.) plans, measures, as *make your own* ~*s*. [F, as prec. +-MENT]

ắ'rrant,a. Notorious,downright,thoroughpaced, as ~ *knave, dunce, hypocrite, nonsense.* Hence~LY² adv. [ME, variant of ERRANT, orig. in phrr. like ~ (= outlawed, roving) *thief*]

ắ'rras, n. Rich tapestry; hanging screen of this formerly hung round walls of rooms (often not too closely to admit person). Hence ~ED² (-st) a. [*Arras*, town in France famous for the fabric]

array'¹, v.t. Marshal, dispose, (forces); (Law) impanel (a jury); dress, esp. with display; (refl.) dress one*self* up; adorn; (fig.) clothe (in qualities etc.). [f. AF *arayer* = OF *areyer* f. Rom. *arredare* f. ad to+Gmc *rædh-* READY]

array'², n. Order, as *battle* ~; (hist.) arming of militia, as *Commission of A~*; military force; imposing series *of* persons or things; order of impanelling jury; (poet.) outfit, dress. [ME, f. AF *arai*= OF *arei* f. *areyer*, see prec.]

arrear', n. (Arch.) hinder part, esp. of procession; (pl.) outstanding debts, what remains undone (~*s of work*); *in* ~*s* or ~, behindhand, esp. in payment; *in* ~ *of*, behind. [ME, orig. adv. f. OF *arere* (mod. F *arrière*) f. Rom. *aretro* (*ab* from+ *retro* backwards); first used in phr. *in* ~]

arrear'age, n. Backwardness; unpaid balance; thing in reserve; (pl.) debts. [ME, f. OF *arerage* f. *arere*, see prec. & -AGE]

arrĕct', a. (arch. & poet.). (Of the ears) pricked up; (fig.) on the alert. [f. L *arrectus* p.p. of AR*rigere* raise up (*regere* straighten)]

arrĕst'¹, v.t. Stop (person, cannon-ball, decay); (Law) ~ *judgement*, stay proceedings after verdict, on ground of error; seize (person), esp. by legal authority; catch (attention); catch attention of. Hence ~IVE a., ~MENT, ~OR, nn. (~*or hook*, hook-like device for catching on cables on deck of aircraft carrier & checking speed of aircraft as they land). [ME, f. OF *arester* f. Rom. *ADrestare* remain, stop; see REST]

arrĕst'², n. Stoppage, check; ~ *of judgement* (see prec.); seizure; legal apprehension; imprisonment; *under* ~ (legal restraint). [ME, f. OF *arest* f. *arester*, see prec.]

arrêt (arā'), n. (hist.). Authoritative sentence or decree of the King or Parliament of France; (loosely) judgement, order. [F, f. OF *arest* (prec.)]

arride', v.t.(literary). Please, gratify. [f. L AR*ridere* smile upon, be pleasing to]

arrière-bắn (à'rĭer-), n. Summoning of vassals to military service by Frankish king; body thus summoned or liable to be summoned; noblesse; (improp.) summoning of inferior (*arrière-*) vassals. [F, f. OF *ariere-ban* for *herban, arban* f. Frankish *hari* army + *ban* edict, BAN (cf. OHG *heriban*), altered in form & sense by pop. etym., whence *ban* et *arrière-ban* summoning of superior & inferior vassals]

arrière-pensée (see Ap.), n. Ulterior motive; mental reservation. [F]

ắ'rris, n. Sharp edge formed by angular contact of two plane or curved surfaces, as ~*-gutter* (V-shaped), ~*-wise*, ridgewise. [corrupt. f. OF *areste*, mod. ARÊTE]

arriv'al, n. Act of coming to end of journey or destination (lit. & fig.); appearance upon scene; person, thing, that has arrived; (colloq.) new-born child; cargo to be delivered when ship arrives. [ME f. AF *arivaille* (*ariver*, see foll. & -AL (2))]

arrive', v.i. Come to destination (lit. & fig.) or end of journey (*at* Bath, *in* Paris, *upon* scene, *at* conclusion); (as Gallicism) establish one's repute 'or position; (of things) be brought; (of time) come; (of events) come about. [ME, f. OF *ariver* f. Rom. *arripare* come to shore (L *ripa*)]

arriviste (ărĕvēst'), n. Careerist, parvenu. [F]

ắ'rrog|ant, a. Overbearing; presumptuous; haughty. Hence or cogn. ~ANCE, ~ANCY, nn., ~antLY² adv. [ME, f. OF (as foll., see -ANT)]

ắ'rrogate, v.t. Claim unduly (thing, *to* one*self* a thing); claim unduly that one possesses (a quality); claim unduly for (to) some one else. [f. L AR(rogare ask), see -ATE³]

ărrogā'tion, n. Unjust claim (of or abs.); unwarrantable assumption. [f. L arrogatio (as prec., see -ATION)]

arrondissement (see Ap.), n. Administrative subdivision of French department. [F]

ă'rrow (-ō), n. Pointed missile shot from bow; index, pin, ornament, of similar shape; || broad ~, mark distinguishing British Government stores; ~-stitch, triangular set of stitches securing whalebone in stays; ~-headed characters, cuneiform; ~root, plant from which a nutritious starch is prepared. Hence ~Y² (-ōi) a. [OE earh, arwe, f. Gmc *arhw-, cf. Goth. arhwazna; cogn. w. L arcus bow]

ăr̄se, n. (not now in polite use). Buttocks, rump. [OF ærs, OHG, ON ars, Gmc *arsaz, cogn. w. Gk orrhos]

ăr̄s'enal, n. Public establishment for storage or manufacture of weapons & ammunition (also fig.). [f. It. arsenale, earlier arzenà f. Arab. dar accina'ah (dar house+al the+çina'ah art f. çana'a fabricate); d- dropped perh. by confus. w. de prep.; -ale added in It.]

ăr̄s'enic¹, n. (Chem.) brittle steel-grey semi-metallic substance, crystallizing in rhombohedrons, & volatilizing without fusion with odour of garlic; (pop.) trioxide of ~, white mineral substance, a violent poison; flowers of ~, same sublimed. Hence ăr̄sĕn'icAL a. [OF, f. L f. Gk arsenikon yellow orpiment (identified with arsenikos male, but in fact) f. Arab. az-zernikh the orpiment f. Pers. zerni (zar gold)]

ăr̄sĕn'ic², a. Of, belonging to, arsenic; esp. (Chem.) applied to compounds in which arsenic combines as a pentad. [f. prec., -ic being identified with -IC (1)]

ăr̄sĕn'ious, a. Containing arsenic; esp. applied to compounds in which arsenic combines as a triad. [f. ARSENIC n.+ -IOUS; see also -OUS]

ăr̄s'is, n. (pl. arsēs). Accented syllable in English scansion (cf. thesis). [f. L f. Gk, = lifting f. airō lift; in what sense, & whether orig. of voice or foot (in beating time), is disputed]

ăr̄s'on, n. Wilful setting on fire of another's house or similar property or one's own when insured. Hence *~IST n., incendiary. [legal AF arso(u)n (13th c.) = OF arson f. Rom. *arsionem f. L ardēre ars- burn]

art¹, v. See BE.

art², n. Skill, esp. human skill as opposed to nature; skilful execution as an object in itself; skill applied to imitation & design, as in painting etc.; (attrib.) of artistic design etc. (chiefly shop use: ~ needlework, carpet, curtain); thing in which skill may be exercised; esp. (pl.) certain branches of learning serving as

intellectual instruments for more advanced studies, as Bachelor, Master, of Arts, one who has obtained standard of proficiency in these; black ~, magic; practical application of any science; industrial pursuit, craft; guild, company of craftsmen; fine ~s, those in which mind & imagination are chiefly concerned; knack; cunning; stratagem; ~ & (or) part, design & (or) execution, as be ~ & part in (accessory in both respects). [ME, f. OF art f. L artem]

ărt'éfăct, ărt'ĭ-, n. A product of human art & workmanship; (Archaeol.) a product of prehistoric art as dist. from a similar object naturally produced. [f. L arte (abl. of ars art)+factum (neut. p.p. of facere make)]

ărtĕl', n. Collective enterprise of peasants or workers in the Soviet Union. [Russ.]

ărtēr'ial, a. Belonging to, of the nature of, resembling, an artery (now freq. of important main roads, & lines of transport or communication, as ~ railway, road, traffic). [F (artère ARTERY, see -AL)]

ărtēr'ializ|e, -is|e (-iz), v.t. Convert venous into arterial (blood) by exposure to oxygen in lungs; furnish with arterial system. Hence ~A'TION n. [prec.+-IZE]

ărtēriŏsclerōs'is, n. Hardening of the arteries, esp. as concomitant of old age. [see ARTERY, SCLER(O)-, -OSIS]

ărtēriŏt'omy̆, n. Opening of artery for blood-letting; dissection of arteries. [f. LL f. Gk artēriotomia (as foll., see -TOMY)]

ărt'er|y̆, n. Tube forming part of system by which blood is conveyed from heart (cf. VEIN) to all parts of body (also fig.). Hence ~IT'IS n. [ME, f. L f. Gk artēria prob. f. airō raise]

ărtē'sian (-zhn), a. ~ well, perpendicular boring into strata, producing constant supply of water rising spontaneously to surface. [f. F artésien (Artois, old French province)]

ărt'ful, a. Cunning, crafty, deceitful, (of persons & actions). Hence ~LY² adv., ~NESS n. [ART²+-FUL]

ărthr|it'is, n. Inflammation of joint; gout. So~it'ic a. [L f. Gk (arthron joint, see -ITIS)]

ărthro-, comb. form of Gk arthron joint, as in arthrŏp'athy, painful affection of joints, arthrōs'is, articulation.

ăr'thrŏpŏd, n. (zool.). Member of Arthrŏp'oda, consisting of animals with jointed body & limbs. [prec.+Gk pous podos foot]

Arthūr'ian (ăr-), a. Relating to King Arthur or his knights. [-IAN]

ărt'ichōke, n. Plant (of which bottom of flower & bases of its scales are edible) allied to thistles, native of Barbary; Jerusalem (corrupt. of girasole, sunflower) ~, species of sunflower with edible tuberous roots. [f. It. articiocco corrupt. of *alcarcioffo (mod. It. carciofo, OSp. alcarchofa) f. Arab. alkharshuf]

árt′ícle[1], n. Separate portion of anything written; separate clause (of agreement etc.) as *Thirty-nine A~s, A~s of war, Apprenticeship, Association*; literary composition forming part of magazine etc. but independent; *leading* ~ in newspaper, ~ expressing editorial opinion; particular; particular thing, as *the next* ~; (Gram.) *definite* ~, 'the', *indefinite* ~, 'a, an'; *in the* ~ (moment) *of death* (usu. *in artic′ulo mortis*). [ME, f. OF, f. L *articulus*, dim. of *artus* limb]

árt′ícle[2], v.t. Set forth in articles; indict; bind by articles of apprenticeship. [f. prec.]

ártic′ular, a. Pertaining to the joints. [ME, f. L *articularis* (as ARTICLE[1], see -AR[1])]

ártic′ulate[1], a. & n. Jointed; distinctly jointed, distinguishable, as ~ *speech*; (n.) ~ animal. Hence ~LY[2] (-tl-) adv., ~NESS (-tn-) n. [f. L *articulatus* (as prec., see -ATE[2])]

ártic′ulāt|e², v.t. & i. Connect by joints, mark with apparent joints (usu. pass.); divide into words, pronounce distinctly; (intr.) speak distinctly. Hence ~ORY a. [f. prec., see -ATE[3]]

ártículā′tion, n. Act, mode, of jointing; joint; articulate utterance, speech; consonant. [F, or f. L *articulatio* (*articulare* joint as ARTICLE[1], see -ATION)]

árt′ifice, n. Device, contrivance; address, skill. [F, f. L *artificium* (*ars artis* art + *-ficium* making f. *facere* make)]

ártif′icer, n. Craftsman; inventor (*of*). [ME, of uncert. orig.; OF had *artificien*, of which this may be an alteration]

ártifi′cial (-shal), a. Made by art; not natural; not real, as ~ *flowers*; real, but produced by art, as ~ *ice*; ~ *horizon*, device indicating attitude of aircraft to horizon; ~ *respiration*, inducing of respiration by manual or mechanical means. Hence **ártificiăl′ITY** (-shǐ-), ~NESS, nn., ~IZE v.t., ~LY[2] adv. [ME, f. F *-el*, or L *artificialis* (as ARTIFICE, see -AL)]

ártill′erў, n. Anti-aircraft, anti-tank, field, medium, heavy, & mountain guns used by an army; branch or arm of the service that uses these; ~-*train*, ordnance mounted on carriages & ready for marching. Hence **ártill′erIST**, ~**man**, nn. [ME, f. OF *artillerie* f. *artiller* equip, arm; see -ERY]

ártisăn′ (-z-), n. Mechanic, handicraftsman. [F, f. It. *artigiano* f. Rom. *artitianus (*artitus* p.p. of *artire* instruct in arts, see -AN)]

árt′ist, n. One who practises one of the fine arts, esp. painting; ~'s *proof*, copy of engraving taken for ~'s approval or correction & valued as fresher than ordinary copies; one who makes his craft a fine art (~ *in words* etc.). Hence **ártis′tIC**(AL) aa., **ártis′ticAL**LY[2] adv., ~RY n. [f. F *artiste* f. It. *artista* (*arte* ART, see -IST)]

ártiste′ (-tē-), n. Professional singer, dancer, etc. [F, see prec.]

árt′less, a. Unskilful, uncultured; clumsy; natural; guileless, ingenuous. Hence ~LY[2] adv., ~NESS n. [ART[2] + -LESS]

árt′ў, a. (colloq.). Pretentiously artistic; (of persons) aping the artistic; ~-& -*crafty*, (joc., usu. of furniture) remarkable rather for specially artistic style than for usefulness or comfort (after the *Arts & Crafts* Exhibition Society). [-Y[2]]

ār′um, n. Kinds of monocotyledonous plants including wake-robin; ~ *lily* (tall & white-spathed). [L, f. Gk *aron*]

-arў[1], suf. forming adjj. & nn. f. L *-arius*, *-arium* taken directly, or thr. later F learned adoptives in *-aire*, or formed in E on L nn.; adjj. as *arbitrary, contrary, primary*; nn. = *-arius*, as *actuary*, *adversary*, = *-arium*, as *dictionary*, = *-aria*, as *fritillary*. The popular forms in OF ended in *-ier* (*premier* PREMIER). OF *-ier* = AF *-er*, whence ME *-er* as in *danger, carpenter* (-ER[2]), *mortar, vicar* (-AR[2]).

-arў[2], suf. Occas. in adjj. f. L-*aris* instead of regular -AR[1], thr. F learned adoptives in *-aire*, which repr. both L *-arius* (e.g. L *contrarius*, F- *aire*, E -ARY[1]) & L *-aris* (e.g. L *militaris*, F *-aire*, E -ARY[2]).

Ar′yan (ār-), a. & n. **1.** Applied by some to family of languages (also called *Indo- -European, Indo-Germanic*) that includes Sanskrit, Iranian, Greek, Latin, Celtic, Germanic, Slavonic, with their modern representatives, by others only to the Indo-Iranian portion of these. **2.** n. Member of ~ family; in Nazi Germany esp. contrasted with SEMITE. [f. Skr. *arya* noble (in earlier use a national name comprising worshippers of the gods of the Brahmans); earlier *Arian* is f. L *Arianus* of Aria (f. Gk *Areia* eastern Persia)]

as[1] (ăz, az), adv., conj., rel. pron. **1.** adv. (in main sentence, foll. by as in subord. clause expressed or understood) in the same degree, as *I came as soon as I could, I know that as well as you, you might as well help me, as* FAR[1] *as*. **2.** rel. adv. or conj. in subord. clause, with or without antecedent *as, so*, expressing manner, degree, etc., of the principal sentence; (degree) *you are as good as he, it is not so* (or *as) easy as you think, quick as thought he jumped out, fair as* (= though) *she is*; (manner) *do as you like, according as we decide, he looks as if he had seen a ghost, treat him as a stranger, you are, as it were* (= as if it were actually so), *compromised, they rose as one man, late as usual, he smiled, as who should say* (= as a man would smile who); (time) *it struck me as I was speaking*; (reason) *as you are not ready, we must go on*; (result) *he so arranged matters as to suit everyone, be so good as to come*; (illustration) *cathedral cities, as Norwich.* **3.** rel. pron. That, who, which, as *I had the same trouble as you,* *such countries as Spain;* (with antecedent inferred from main sentence) *he was a foreigner, as* (which fact) *they perceived from his accent.* 4. Special phrases: *as for,* with regard to; *as from* (in formal dating, as *coal will be decontrolled as from 31st March*); *as regards,* so far as it concerns; *as to,* with respect to (*said nothing as to hours, as to when he would come; as to you, I despise you*); *as yet,* up to this time; *I thought as much,* I thought so; *as well* (*as*), in addition (to); *as good as dead,* practically dead. 5. Phrases in (*as*) . . . *as* expressing by reference to a proverbial type the highest or a high degree of some quality, & in alliterative or punning phrr. modelled on these: *bald as a coot, black as pitch, blind as a bat, bold as brass, brave as a lion, bright as a new pin, brown as a berry, busy as a bee, cold as charity, common as dirt, cool as a cucumber, cross as two sticks, dead as a doornail, deaf as a mutton, deaf as a post, drunk as a fiddler, drunk as a lord, dry as a bone, dull as ditchwater, easy as ABC, easy as lying, fit as a fiddle, flat as a pancake, good as gold* (of children's conduct), *good as a play* (amusing), *hard as nails, heavy as lead, hungry as a hunter, jolly as a sandboy, keen as mustard, large as life, light as air, mad as a hatter, mad as a March hare, meek as Moses, merry as a grig, old as the hills, pale as a ghost, plain as a pikestaff, pleased as Punch, plentiful as blackberries, plump as a partridge, proud as a peacock, proud as Lucifer, quick as thought, quiet as a mouse, right as a trivet, right as rain, safe as a house, sharp as a needle, silent as the grave, snug as a bug in a rug, soft as butter, soft as velvet, sound as a bell, stiff as a poker, straight as a die, strong as a horse, stubborn as a mule, sure as fate, thick as thieves, thin as a lath, tight as a drum, true as steel, ugly as sin, warm as* (a) *toast, weak as a rat, weak as water, white as a sheet.* [worn-down form of OE *al*(*l*)*swā* ALSO, later *alsa, als*]

ās², n. Roman copper coin, orig. weighing 12 oz., but finally reduced to ½ oz. [L]

as-, pref. = AD- before *s*.

ăsafoet′ida (-fĕt-) n. Concreted resinous gum with strong smell of garlic used in medicine and cookery. [med. L (*asa* f. Pers. *aza* mastic + FETID)]

asbĕs′tine (ăz-), a. Of, like, asbestos, incombustible (lit. & fig.). [f. L f. Gk *asbestinos* f. foll., see -INE²]

asbĕs′t|ōs (ăz-), n. Fibrous mineral that can be woven into an incombustible fabric (also fig.). Hence ~IC, ~OID, aa. [f. L f. Gk, = unquenchable (*a*- not + *sbestos* f. *sbennumi* quench)]

ascĕnd′, v.t. & i. Go, come, up; (of things) rise, be raised; slope upwards, lie along ~ing slope; rise in thought, rank, degree of quality; (of sounds) rise in pitch; go back in point of time; (trans.)

go up, climb; ~ *a river,* go along it towards its source; mount upon, as ~ *the throne.* [ME, f. L *ascendere,* AD(*scendere scens-* = *scandere* climb)]

ascĕn′dancȳ, -encȳ, n. Dominant control, sway, (*over*). [f. after foll., see -ANCY]

ascĕn′dant, -ent, a. & n. 1. Rising; (Astron.) rising towards zenith; (Astrol.) just above eastern horizon; predominant. 2. n. Horoscope; point of ecliptic or degree of zodiac that (esp. at birth of child) is just rising above eastern horizon; *house of the* ~ (from 5 degrees of zodiac above this point to 25 below it); *lord of the* ~, any planet within this; *in the* ~, supreme, dominating, (improp.) rising; supremacy; ancestor. [ME, f. OF (*-ant*) f. L as ASCEND, see -ENT]

ascĕn′sion (-shon), n. Act of ascending; ascent of Christ on fortieth day after resurrection; *A~-day,* Holy Thursday, on which this is commemorated; *A~tide,* period of ten days from A~-day to Whitsun Eve; rising of a celestial body, as *right* ~ (celestial longitude). Hence ~AL a. [f. L *ascensio* (as ASCEND, see -ION)]

ascĕn′sive, a. Rising, progressive; (Gram.) intensive. [as prec., see -IVE]

ascĕnt′, n. Act of ascending; upward movement, rise, (lit. & fig.); way by which one may ascend, slope, flight of steps. [f. ASCEND on anal. of *descent*]

ăscertain′, v.t. Find out (for certain), get to know. Hence ~ABLE a., ~MENT n. [ME, f. OF *accrtener,* st. *acertaine-* (*à* to + CERTAIN)]

ascĕt′ic, a. & n. Severely abstinent, austere; (n.) one who practises severe self-discipline, esp. (Eccl. Hist.) one who retired into solitude for this purpose. Hence ~AL a., ~alLY² adv., ~ISM (-sĭzm) n. [f. Gk *askētikos* f. *askētēs* monk (*askeō* exercise), see -ETE and -IC]

ascid′ium (asĭd-), n. Kinds of marine organism with leathery enveloping tunic, regarded as link in development of Vertebrata. [mod. L, f. Gk *askidion* dim. of *askos* wine-skin]

Asclēp′iad, n. (Gk and Lat. Prosody) verse consisting of a spondee, two or three choriambi, & an iambus. Hence ~ē′AN a. [f. LL f. Gk *Asklēpiadeios* (*Asklēpiadēs,* Greek poet, the inventor)]

As′cot (ă-), n. Racecourse on ~ Heath, Berks.; race-meeting at ~.

ascribe′, v.t. Attribute, impute, (*to*); consider as belonging (*to* person or thing). Hence or cogn. **ascrib′**ABLE a., **ascrip′**tion n., (esp.) preacher's words ascribing praise to God at end of sermon. [ME *ascrive* f. OF *ascriv-* st. of *ascrire* f. L AD(*scribere script-* write)]

As′dic (ăz-), n. Device for detecting submarine. [f. initials of *Allied Submarine Detection Investigation Committee*]

āse′itȳ, n. (metaphys.). Underived existence, the being uncreate. [f. med. L *aseitas* f. L *a se* from oneself; see -ITY]

asĕp′sĭs, n. Absence of putrefactive matter or harmful bacteria; the aseptic method in surgery. [A- (7)+Gk *sēpsis* decay (*sēpō*, see foll.)]

asĕp′tĭc, a. & n. Free from putrefaction or blood-poisoning; surgically sterile, sterilized, (of wounds, instruments, dressings); (of method etc.) seeking the absence (rather than counteraction, cf. *antiseptic*) of septic matter; (n.) non-putrescent substance. [A- (7)+Gk *sēptikos* putrefying (*sēpō* rot, see -IC)]

asĕx′ŭal, a. (biol.). Without sex. Hence **asĕxŭăl′**ITY n. [A- (7)+SEXUAL]

ăsh[1], n. Forest-tree with silver-grey bark,* pinnate foliage, & close-grained wood; wood of this; ∼-*fly*, ∼-*grub*, (found on ∼ & used by anglers); ∼-*key*, winged seed of the ∼; ∼-*leaf*, an early potato; *mountain* ∼, rowan-tree. [OE *æsc*, OHG *ask*, ON *askr*, f. Gmc **ask-az*]

ăsh[2], n. (usu. pl.). Powdery residue left after combustion of any substance; (pl.) remains of human body after cremation (lit. & fig.); *lay in* ∼*es*, burn to the ground; *sackcloth & ∼es* (symbol of repentance); ‖ *bring back the ∼es* (Crick.), wipe out defeat in series of test matches between England & Australia;* ∼′*can*, dustbin; ∼-*fire*, low fire used in chemical operations; ∼-*furnace* (used in glass-making); *Ash Wednesday*, first day of Lent (from Rom. Cath. custom of sprinkling ∼es on penitents′ heads). [OE *asce*, OHG *usca*, ON *aska*, Goth. *azgo*, f. Gmc **uzyon*]

ashāmed′ (-md), pred. a. Abashed, disconcerted, by consciousness of guilt; ∼ *of* (conduct); ∼ *for* (on account of) *you*; ∼ *to do* (implying reluctance, but not always abstention). [p.p. of obs. vb *ashame* (A- (1)+OE *scamian* SHAME)]

ăsh′en[1], a. Pertaining to an ash-tree; made of ash. [ASH[1]+-EN[5]]

ăsh′en[2], a. Of ashes; ash-coloured, pale. [ASH[2]+-EN[5]]

ăsh′ĕt, n. (Sc.). Big (usu. oval) plate. [f. F *assiette*]

Ashkenazim (ăshkĭnahz′ĭm), n. pl. Polish- -German Jews (as dist. from SEPHARDIM). [mod. Heb., f. *Ashkenaz* (Gen. x. 3)]

ăsh′lar, n. Square hewn stone(s); masonry constructed of this; similar masonry as facing to rubble or brick wall. [ME, f. OF *aisel(i)er* (-ER[2]) supporting beam, ult. f. L *axis*, *assis* axle, board; see -AR[2]]

ăsh′laring, n. Short upright boarding in garrets, cutting off acute angle formed by roof with floor; ashlar masonry. [prec. +-ING[1]]

ashōre′, adv. To, on to, on, shore. [A prep.]

ăsh′y̆, a. Of ashes; covered with ashes; ash-coloured, pale. [ASH[2]+-Y[2]]

Asian (āsh′an), a. & n. (Native) of Asia (now preferred to *Asiatic*). [f. L f. Gk *Asianos* (*Asia*, see -AN)]

Asiăt′ic (āshĭ-), a. & n. Asian. [f. L f. Gk *Asiaticus* (*Asiatēs* f. *Asia*, see -IC)]

aside′, adv. & n. **1.** To, on, one side,

away; **∼ (apart) *from*; *set* ∼, quash (verdict); *speak* ∼ (apart, in privacy). **2.** n. Words spoken ∼, esp. spoken by an actor & supposed not to be heard by other performers; indirect effort. [orig. *on side*, see A prep.]

ăs′inine, a. Pertaining to asses; stupid. Hence **ăsinĭn′**ITY n. [f. L *asininus* (*asinus* ass, -INE[1])]

-asis, suf. forming names of diseases. [L -*āsis* f. Gk -*āsis* in nouns of state f. vbs in -*aō*]

ask (ah-), v.t. & i. Call for an answer to, as ∼ (*him*) *a question*, ∼ (*him*) *this*, (*him*) *who it is*, ∼ *him the time*, ∼ *a question of a person*, ∼ *him about a thing*; make a request (for), as ∼ *a favour of him*, ∼ (*him*) *a favour*, ∼ (*him*) *for it*, *ask* (abs.), ∼ *him to do it*, ∼ *that it may be done*, ∼ *to have time given one*; invite (person *to* dinner etc., or *out*); (of things) demand, require, as *it* ∼*s* (*for*) *attention*; ∼ (publish) *the banns*; (pop.) *be ∼ed in church*, have one's banns called; ∼ *for trouble*, ∼ *for it* (sl.), court trouble; *if you∼ me*, in my opinion. [OE *āscian*, *ācsian*, OHG *eiscon*, f. WG **aiskojan*; *ax* was usu. literary form to 1600]

askănce′, **-ănt′**, adv. Sideways, asquint; with indirect meaning; *look* ∼ *at*, view suspiciously. [etym. unkn.]

ăskar′i (-ahr-), n. European-trained African native soldier. [Arab. ′*askari* soldier; pl. occas. as sing.]

askew′, adv. & pred. a. Obliquely; *look* ∼ (not straight in the face); (adj.) oblique. [A prep.+SKEW]

aslant′ (-ahnt), adv. & prep. Obliquely; (prep.) slantingly across, athwart. [A prep.+SLANT]

asleep′, adv. & pred. a. In, into, a state of sleep (lit. & fig.); (of limbs) benumbed; (of top) spinning without apparent motion. [A prep.+SLEEP]

aslōpe′, adv. & pred. a. Sloping, crosswise. [perh. f. OE *aslopen* p.p. of *aslupan* slip away]

ăsp[1], n. (also *aspen*). Kind of poplar with specially tremulous leaves. [OE *æspe*, OHG *aspa*, f. WG **aspōn*]

ăsp[2], n. Small venomous hooded serpent of Egypt and Libya; (poet.) any venomous serpent. [ME, f. L f. Gk *aspis*]

aspă′ragus, n. Plant, whose vernal shoots are a table delicacy. [L, f. Gk *asparagos*]

ăs′pĕct, n. Way of looking; a looking, fronting, in a given direction; side so fronting; phase; look, expression; appearance (esp. to the mind); (Gram.) a verbal form expressing action or being in respect of its inception, duration, or completion. [ME, f. L *aspectus -ūs* (AD-*spicere -spect-* look at)]

ăs′pĕn, a. & n. Of, like, the asp (tree); quivering; (n.)=ASP[1]. [ASP[1]+-EN; wrongly taken as noun used attrib. in *aspen leaf* etc.]

äspergill'um, n. Brush for sprinkling holy water. [med. L, f. *aspergere* (*ad* to + *spargere* sprinkle) + *-illum* dim. suf.]

äspĕ'rĭtў, n. Roughness; rough excrescence; severity (of weather); harshness, sharpness, (of temper). [ME *asprete* f. OF f. L *asperitatem* (*asper* rough, see -TY), whence mod. form]

aspĕrse', v.t. Besprinkle (*with*); bespatter (person, character, *with* damaging reports); calumniate. So **aspĕr'SION** (-shn) n. [f. L *aspergere* -*ers*-, see ASPERGILLUM]

äspersōr'ium, n. Vessel for holy water. [med. L (as prec., see -ORY)]

äs'phält¹, n. A smooth hard bituminous substance; mixture of bitumen, pitch, & sand, for pavements etc.; similar mixture of coal-tar with sand etc. Hence **äsphäl'TIC** a. [ME, ult. f. LL *asphaltus, -um,* f. Gk *asphaltos* of foreign orig.]

äs'phält², v.t. Lay (road) with asphalt. [f. prec.]

äs'phodĕl, n. Plant of lily family; (poet.) immortal flower in Elysium. [f. L f. Gk *asphodelos*; earlier *affodil,* whence DAFFODIL]

äsphўx'ĭ|a, -x'ў, n. Suspended animation due to lack of oxygen in blood, suffocation. Hence ~AL a., ~ATE³ v.t., ~A'TION n.⸜[mod. L f. Gk *asphuxia* (*a*-not + *sphuxis* pulse)]

äs'pĭc¹, n. (poet.). = ASP². [F, f. L *aspidem,* nom. -*is,* w. unexpl. -*ic*]

äs'pĭc², n. Savoury meat jelly with cold game, eggs, etc., in it. [F, of disputed etym.]

äspĭdis'tra, n. Foliage plant with broad taper leaves, freq. grown as a house plant. [mod. L f. Gk *aspis* shield]

äs'pirant (*or* aspīr'-), a. & n. (One) who aspires (*to, after, for*). [F, or f. L as foll., see -ANT]

äs'pirate¹, a. & n. (Consonant) pronounced with a breathing, blended with sound of *h*; the sound of *h*. [f. L *aspirare,* see ASPIRE and -ATE²]

äs'pirāte², v.t. Pronounce with a breathing; draw out (gas) from vessel. [as prec., see -ATE³]

äspirā'tion, n. Drawing of breath; desire (*for, after*); action of aspirating. [f. OF, or f. L *aspiratio* (as prec., see -ATION)]

äs'pirātor, n. Apparatus for drawing air, gas, through tube; instrument for drawing pus from abscesses; winnowing-machine. [f. L *aspirare,* see foll. and -OR]

aspīre', v.i. Desire earnestly (*to, after, at, to* do, or abs.); mount up (usu. fig.). [f. F, or L AD(*spirare* breathe)]

äs'pirin, n. An analgetic & febrifuge. [P]

asquint', adv. & pred. a. (With *look* or similar vb) obliquely, out at the corner of the eyes (esp. through defect in the eyes). [hist. & etym. unkn.; w. second element cf. Du. *schuinte* slant, slope]

äss (*or* ahs), n. Quadruped of horse family with long ears & tuft at end of tail (used esp. as type of ignorance, stupidity, etc.); *make an* ~ *of,* stultify (one*self,* or another); *asses' bridge* (*pons asinorum*), Euclid I, 5 'The angles at the base of an isosceles triangle are equal to one another'. [f. OE *assa,* not repr. outside OE, f. (thr. Celt.) L *asinus,* whence also OE *esol, eosol,* (OHG *esil,* Goth. *asilus*) which did not survive]

äss'agai, -sĕgai, (-gi), n. Slender spear of hard wood, esp. a missile of S. African tribes. [f. obs. F *azagaye* (mod. *zagaie*) f. Arab. *azzaghayah* (*al* the + Berber word *zaghayah*)]

assa'i (-ah-ē), adv. (mus.). Very. [It.]

assail', v.t. Make hostile attack upon (lit. & fig.); approach resolutely (task); overwhelm (*with* questions etc.). Hence ~ABLE a., ~ANT n. [ME, f. OF *asalir, asaillir,* f. med. L *assalire* f. L AS(*salire salt-* leap)]

assäss'in, n. One who undertakes to kill treacherously; (hist.) Moslem fanatic in time of Crusades, sent by the Old Man of the Mountains to murder Christians. [F, or f. med. L *assassinus* f. Arab. *ḥashshash, ḥashishiyy* hashish-eater]

assäss'in|āte, v.t. Kill by treacherous violence. Hence ~A'TION, ~ātOR, nn. [f. med. L *assassinare* (*assassinus*), see prec. and -ATE³]

assault'¹, n. Hostile attack (lit. & fig.); ~ *of, at, arms,* attack in fencing, display of military exercises; rush against walls of fortress etc., as *carry by* ~; (Law) unlawful personal attack (including menacing words), as ~ *& battery*; (euphem. for) rape (of woman). [ME, f. OF *asaut* f. Rom. **assaltus* (as ASSAIL)]

assault'², v.t. Make violent attack upon (lit. & fig.); assail; (euphem. for) rape (woman); attack (fortress) by sudden rush. Hence ~ABLE a. [ME, f. OF *asauter* f. Rom. **assaltare* spring at, for L ***AS(*sultare* frequent. of *salire salt-* leap)]

assay'¹, n. Trial of metals, esp. of fineness of coin or bullion; metal to be so tried; (arch.) attempt. [ME, f. OF *assai,* var. of *essai* (see ESSAY¹), f. LL *exagium* weighing (*exigere, -agere,* weigh, try)]

assay'², v.t. & i. Try the purity of (precious metals, also fig.); attempt (anything difficult, *to* do). Hence ~ABLE a. [ME, f. OF *asayer, essayer* (see ESSAY²) f. Rom. **exagiare* (*exagium,* see prec.)]

assĕm'blage, n. Bringing, coming, together; concourse of persons; collection. [F (*assembler,* see foll. and -AGE)]

assĕm'ble, v.t. & i. Gather together, collect; (Mech.) fit together the parts of (machine, structure). [ME, f. OF *asembler* f. L AS*simulare* in the (late) sense of bring together (*simul*)]

assĕm'blў, n. Gathering together, concourse, esp. deliberative body, legislative council; military call by drum or bugle; assembling a machine or its parts; ∼ *line*, group of machines & workers operating on some product to be assembled; ∼ *room*: room in which balls etc. are given; (also ∼ *shop*) place where a machine or its parts are assembled. [ME, f. OF *asemblée* fem. p.p. of *asembler*, see prec.]

assĕnt′¹, v.i. Agree (*to* proposal), defer (*to* a desire); express agreement (*to* statement or opinion, or abs.). Hence ∼OR n. [ME, f. OF *ascnter* f. L *assentari*, irreg. frequent. of ASsen*tiri* agree to (*sentire* think)]

assĕnt′², n. (Official) concurrence, sanction, as *royal* ∼ (of sovereign to bill passed by Parliament); mental acceptance. [ME, f. OF *asent*(*e*) (*asenter*, see prec.)]

assentā′tion, n. Obsequious concurrence. [F, f. L *assentationem* (as ASSENT, see -ATION)]

assĕn′tient (-shĭ-), a. & n. (Person) that assents. [f. L *assentient-* (*assentiri*, see ASSENT¹, -ENT)]

assĕrt′, v.t. Vindicate a claim to (rights); ∼ one*self*, insist upon one's rights; declare. Hence ∼ABLE, ∼IVE, aa., ∼ively² (-vl-) adv., ∼iveness (-vn-) n. [f. L AS(*serere sert-* join) put one's hand on slave's head to free him]

assĕr′tion, n. Insistence upon a right; *self-*∼, insistence on recognition of one's claims; affirmation, positive statement. [F, or f. L *assertio* (as prec., see -ION)]

assĕrt′or, n. One who asserts; champion, advocate, (*of*). [L (as prec., see -OR)]

assĕss′, v.t. Fix amount of (taxes, fine); fix amount of & impose (*upon* person or community); fine, tax, (person, community, property, *in*, *at*, so much); estimate value of (property) for taxation. Hence ∼ABLE a., ∼ably² adv., ∼MENT n. [ME, f. OF *assesser* f. med. L *assessare* frequent. of AS(*sidēre sess-* = *sedēre* sit)]

assĕss′or, n. One who sits as assistant, adviser, to judge or magistrate; one who assesses taxes or estimates value of property for taxation. [ME, f. OF *assessour* f. L *assessorem* assistant-judge (as prec., see -OR)]

ass′ĕts, n. pl. (sing. *-et*). (Law) enough goods to enable heir to discharge debts & legacies of testator; property liable to be so applied; effects of insolvent debtor; property of person or company that may be made liable for debts; (sing.) item of this in balance-sheet, (loosely) any possession, (colloq.) any useful quality. [f. AF *asetz* f. OF *asez* enough f. Rom. **assatis* (L *ad* to + *satis* enough)]

assĕv′er|āte, v.t. Solemnly declare. So ∼A′TION n. [f. L ASseverare (*severus* serious), see -ATE³]

assib′il|āte, v.t. Give a hissing sound to. Hence ∼A′TION n. [f. L ASsibilare hiss, see -ATE³]

ăssĭdū′itÿ, n. Close attention; (pl.) constant attentions. [f. L *assiduitas* (*assi-′duus*, see foll. and -TY)].

assid′ūous, a. Persevering, diligent. Hence ∼LY² adv., ∼NESS n. [f. L *assiduus* (as ASSESS) + -OUS]

assĭgn′¹ (-īn), v.t. Allot as a share (*to*); make over (esp. personal property, *to*); appoint (place etc. *to*); fix, specify; ascribe, refer, (event *to* date); ascribe (reason *to*, *for*, thing). Hence ∼ABLE (-īn-) a., **ăssĭgnor′** (-īn-) n. [ME, f. OF *assigner* f. L ASsignare mark out to (*signum* sign)]

assĭgn′² (-īn), n. One to whom property, right, is legally transferred. [ME *assigne* (three syllables) f. F *assigné* p.p. of *assigner* (see prec.) gives both *assign* & *assignee*]

ăss′ĭgnăt, n. Paper money issued by revolutionary government (1790-95) of France. [F, f. L *assignatum*, neut. p.p. of *assignare* assign]

ăssĭgnā′tion, n. Apportionment; formal transference; appointment (of time & place); *illicit love meeting. [ME, f. OF *assignacion* f. L *assignationem* (as ASSIGN¹, see -ATION)]

assĭgnee′ (-īn-), n. One appointed to act for another; assign; ∼*s in bankruptcy*, persons charged with management of bankrupt's estate. [ME, f. OF *a*(*s*)*signé*, see ASSIGN n.]

assĭgn′ment (-īn-), n. Allotment; legal transference; document effecting this; attribution; statement (of reasons); *task allotted to person. [ME, f. OF *assigne-ment* f. med. L *assignamentum* (as ASSIGN¹, see -MENT)]

assĭm′il|āte, v.t. & i. Make like (*to*, *with*); (now rare) compare (*to*, *with*); absorb into the system (lit. & fig.); (intr.) be so absorbed. Hence or cogn. ∼ABIL′ITY, ∼A^t TION, ∼ātOR, nn., ∼ABLE, ∼ātIVE, ∼ātORY aa. [f. L *assimilare*, by-form of *assimulare* (see ASSEMBLE) after *similis* like; see -ATE³]

assist′, v.t. & i., & n. **1.** Help (person, process, person *in* do*ing*), whence ∼ANT a. & n., ∼ANCE n. **2.** v.i. Take part (*in*); be present (*at*). **3.** n. *(Baseball) score credited to fielder who stops & throws in the ball to player nearest the base to which an opponent is running, so helping to put him out. [f. F *assister* f. L ASsis*tere* take one's stand by]

assīze′, n. Statutory price (of bread and ale); trial in which sworn assessors decide questions of fact, ‖esp. periodical sessions in each county of England & Wales for administration of civil & criminal justice; *great*∼, last judgement. [ME, f. OF *asise*, fem. sing. p.p. (as n.) of *aseëir* (mod. F. *asseoir*) sit at f. L *assidēre*, cf. ASSESS]

assō′ci|able (-sha-), a. That can be connected in thought (*with*). Hence ∼ABIL′ITY n. [F, f. associer (as foll., see -ABLE)]

assō′ciate¹ (-shī-), a. & n. **1.** Joined in companionship, function, or dignity; allied. **2.** n. Partner; companion; col-

league; subordinate member of a body, institute, etc.; thing connected with another. Hence ~SHIP n. [f. L ASsociare (socius sharing, allied), see -ATE²]

assō′ciāt|e² (-shĭ-), v.t. & i. Join (persons, things, or one with another); connect in idea; make oneself a partner in (a matter); (intr.) combine for common purpose; have intercourse (with). Hence ~IVE, ~ORY, aa., ~OR n. [as prec., see -ATE³]

associā′tion, n. Act of associating (in all senses); organized body of persons; ‖ deed of ~, document giving particulars of limited liability company; fellowship, intimacy; ~ of ideas, mental connexion between an object & ideas related to it; ‖ ~ football (abbr. soccer), kind played with round ball, which may not be handled except by goalkeeper (cf. RUGBY). [F, or f. med. L associatio (as prec., see -ATION)]

assoil′, v.t. (arch.). Absolve from sin, pardon; acquit; release; atone for. [ME, f. OF a(s)soil-, tonic stem of a(s)soldre f. L AB(solvere loose); Sc. has assoilzie (pron. -yī) still used in sense 'acquit']

ăss′on|ance, n. Resemblance of sound between two syllables; rhyming of one word with another in the accented vowel & those that follow, but not in the consonants (e.g. sonnet, porridge); partial correspondence. So ~ANT a. [F, f. L ASsonare respond to (sonus sound), see -ANCE]

assort′, v.t. & i. Classify, arrange in sorts; group with others; furnish (store, shop) with an assortment; (intr.) associate with; fall into a class; suit well or ill with. [f. OF assorter (à to +sorte SORT)]

assort′ment, n. Assorting; assorted set of goods of one or several classes. [-MENT]

assuāge′ (-sw-), v.t. Calm, soothe, (person, feelings, pain); appease (appetite, desire). Hence ~MENT (aswāj′m-) n. [ME, f. OF asouager f. Rom. *ASsuaviare (suavis sweet)]

assūm|e′, v.t. Take upon oneself (aspect, air); ~ing, taking much upon oneself, arrogant; undertake (office, duty); usurp; simulate; take for granted (thing, thing to be, that). Hence ~′ABLE a., ~′abLY² adv. [ME, f. L AS(sumere sumpt- take)]

assūmp′tion, n. Act of assuming (in all senses); (A~) reception of Virgin Mary into heaven, feast in honour of this; thing assumed; arrogance. [ME, f. L assumptio (as ASSUME, see -ION)]

assūmp′tive, a. Taken for granted; arrogant. [f. L assumptivus (as prec., see -IVE)]

assur′ance (ashoor-), n. Formal guarantee; positive declaration; (Law) securing of a title; compact securing value of property in the event of its being lost, or payment of specified sum on person's death (usu. life-~, fire-, marine-, insurance); certainty (make ~ double sure, remove all possible doubt, Shakesp.,

Macb. IV. i. 83); self-confidence; impudence. [ME, f. OF asĕurance (asĕurer, see foll. & -ANCE)]

assure (ashoor′), v.t. Make safe; ~ life (see prec.); make certain, ensure the happening etc. of; make (person) sure (of fact); tell (person) confidently (of a thing, of its being so, that it is so). Hence **assur′ĕdLY²** adv., **assur′ĕdNESS** n., (-shoor-). [ME, f. OF asĕurer f. Rom. *ASsecurare (securus safe)]

assūr′gent, a. Rising; (Bot.) rising obliquely; aggressive. [f. L ASsurgere rise, see -ENT]

Assȳrĭŏ|l′ogȳ, n. Study of language, history, antiquities, of Assyria. Hence ~L′OGIST n. [f. L f. Gk Assuria +-LOGY]

astăt′ĭc, a. Not tending to keep one position; ~ galvanometer, one in which the effect on the needle of the earth's magnetic field is greatly reduced; ~ needle (unaffected by earth's magnetism). [f. Gk astatos unstable (a- not +sta-stand) +-IC]

ăs′ter, n. Kinds of plants with showy radiated flowers; China ~, flower allied to this. [L, f. Gk astēr star]

-ăster, suf. expressing contempt, added to L and Rom. nn., as oleaster, poetaster, meaning 'petty, sham, would-be'. [L, as in philosophaster]

ăs′terisk, n., & v.t. Star (*) used to mark words for reference or distinction; (v.t.) mark with ~. [f. LL f. Gk asteriskos dim. as ASTER]

ăs′terism, n. Cluster of stars; three asterisks (*₊*), calling attention. [f. Gk asterismos (ASTER, see -ISM)]

astern′, adv. (naut.). In, at, the stern; away behind; ~ of, behind (a ship, boat); backwards. [A prep. +STERN²]

ăs′teroid, a. & n. 1. Star-shaped. 2. n. Name of small planets revolving round sun between orbits of Mars and Jupiter; kind of firework. Hence ~AL (-oid²) a. [f. Gk asteroeidēs (ASTER, see -OID)]

ăsthĕn′ia (or -ēnī′a), n. (med.). Loss of strength, debility. Hence **ăsthĕn′ic** a. & n. [mod. L f. Gk (A- (7) +sthenos strength) +-IA¹]

ăsth′ma (-sm-), n. A disease of respiration, characterized by difficult breathing, cough, etc. [ME asma f. med. L asma f. Gk asthma -matos]

ăsthmăt′ic (-sm-), a. & n. Pertaining to, suffering from, good against, asthma; (n.) person suffering from asthma. Hence ~AL a., ~aĭLY² adv. [f. L f. Gk asthmatikos (as prec., see -IC)]

‖ **asthōre′**, n. (voc.). Darling. [Ir., voc. of stōr treasure]

astig′matism, n. Structural defect in the eye or a lens, preventing rays of light from being brought to common focus. So **ăstigmăt′ic** a. [A- (7) +Gk STIGMA -matos point +-IC]

astir′, adv. & pred. a. In motion; out of bed; in excitement. [A prep. +STIR n.]

astonish

71

at

astŏn′ĭsh, v.t. Amaze, surprise; *astonied* (arch. p.p. of *astony*, see etym.), dazed, dismayed. Hence ~MENT n. [altered f. obs. *astony* unexpl. form of obs. *astone* apparently f. OF *estoner*, *estuner* (mod. *étonner*), stupefy, shock, f. Gallo-Rom. *EXtonare (alt. f. L *attonare* strike with thunderbolt, stun); relation to STUN and G *staunen* is uncertain]

astound′, v.t. Shock with alarm or surprise; amaze. [f. obs. *astound* a.=*astoned* p.p. of obs. *astone*, see prec.]

astrăd′dle, adv. & pred. a. In a straddling position. [A prep.+STRADDLE v.]

ăs′tragal, n. (Archit.) small moulding round top or bottom of columns; (Gunnery) ring round cannon near mouth. [f. foll.]

astrăg′alus, n. Ball of ankle-joint; kinds of leguminous plants including milk-vetch. [L, f. Gk *astragalos* huckle-bone, moulding, plant]

ăstrakhăn′ (-kăn), n. Skin of young lambs from Astrakhan in Russia, with wool like fur.

ăs′tral, a. Connected with, consisting of, stars; ~ *spirits* (supposed to live in stars); ~ *body*, spiritual appearance of the human form; ~ *hatch*, dome-shaped window in aircraft through which the navigator takes astronomical observations; ~ *lamp* (throwing no shadow on table below). [f. LL *astralis* (*astrum* star, see -AL)]

astray′, adv. or pred. a. Out of the right way (lit. & fig.). [ME, f. OF *estraié* p.p. of *estraier* f. Rom.*extravagare wander out of bounds; but confused w. forms like *a-float*, *a-sleep*; no early noun *stray*]

astrict′, v.t. (rare). Bind tightly; make costive; bind morally, legally; restrict (*to*). So **astric′tion** n. [f. L *astringere* -*ict*- (*ad* to +*stringere* bind)]

astric′tive, a. Tending to contract organic tissue; astringent, styptic. [as prec., see -IVE]

astride′, adv., pred. a., & prep. In stridling position; with legs on each side (*of*); ~ *of the road* etc., (Mil.) posted across it; (prep.) ~ of. [A prep.+STRIDE n.]

astringe′ (-nj), v.t. Bind together; compress; constipate. [as ASTRICT]

astrin′gent (-nj-), a. & n. Binding, styptic; severe; austere; (n.) ~ medicine. Hence ~LY² adv., **astrin′gency** n. [as prec., see -ENT]

astro-, in comb.=Gk *astron* star; in wds f. Gk, as ASTRONOMY, & mod. formations as *astrŏg′ony̆*, stellar cosmogony, *astrolĭthŏl′ogy̆*, study of meteoric stones; **ăs′trodōme**, **ăs′trohătch**, = ASTRAL *hatch*; **ăs′tronaut**, student or devotee of *astronaut′ics*, science of aerial navigation in space; *astrophy̆s′ics*, branch of astronomy dealing with the physics & chemistry of the heavenly bodies.

ăs′troïte, n. Gem known to the ancients; kind of madrepore. [f. L f. Gk *astroïtes* (see prec. and -ITE¹)]

ăs′trolābe, n. Instrument formerly used for taking altitudes etc. [ME, f. OF *astrelabe* f. med. L *astrolabium* f. Gk ASTRO- (*lab*- take)]

astrŏl′ogy̆, n. (Formerly) practical astronomy (also called *natural* ~); art of judging of reputed occult influence of stars upon human affairs (*judicial* ~). So **astrŏl′OGER** n., **ăstrolŏ′gĭc(AL)** aa., **ăstrolŏ′gĭcaLLY²** adv. [ME, f. OF *astrologie* f. L f. Gk ASTRO(*logia* -LOGY)]

astrŏn′om|y̆, n. Science of the heavenly bodies. So ~ER¹ (3) n., student of ~y, **ăstronŏm′IC(AL)** aa. (~*ical figures*, *distances*, as enormous as those familiar to ~ers), **ăstronŏm′icaLLY²** adv. [ME, f. OF *astronomie* f. L f. Gk *astronomia* f. ASTRO*nomos* a. star-arranging (*nemŏ* arrange)]

astūte′, a. Shrewd, sagacious; crafty. Hence ~LY² (-tl-) adv., ~NESS (-tn-) n. [f. obs. F *astut* or L *astutus* f. *astus* craft]

asŭn′der, adv. (Of two or more things) apart (in motion or position); *tear* ~, tear to pieces. [OE *on sundran*, see A prep. & SUNDER]

asȳl′um, n. Sanctuary, place of refuge, esp. for criminals or debtors; shelter, refuge; institution for shelter & support of afflicted or destitute persons, esp. lunatics (now *mental home*). [ME, f. L f. Gk *asulon* refuge]

asȳmm′etry̆, n. Want of symmetry. [A- (7)+SYMMETRY]

ăs′y̆mptōte, n. Line that approaches nearer & nearer to given curve but does not meet it within a finite distance. [f. Gk *asumptōtos* not falling together (*a-* not+*sum-* together+*ptōtos* falling f. *piptō*)]

asȳn′děton, n. (pl. -*ta*). A rhetorical figure esp. in Greek & Latin, omitting the particle that normally begins a sentence. [LL f. Gk *asundeton* unconnected (*a-* not+*sundetos* f. *sundeō* bind together)]

ăt¹ (*or* at), prep. **1.** Expressing exact, approximate, or vague position, lit. & fig., as *meet at a point*, *wait at the corner*, *at the top*, *at Bath* (or any town except London and that in which the speaker is, cf. IN¹), *at school*, *at sea*, *at a distance*, *at arm's length*, *out at elbows*, *at work*, *at dinner*, *play at fighting*, *good at repartee*, *at daggers drawn*, *at a disadvantage*, *at his mercy*, *at low price*, *at midday*, *at first*, *at least*, *at all events*, *annoyed at finding*, *impatient at delay*; *at 10 High Street*, = c/o Mr. A., 10 High Street. **2.** Expr. motion towards, lit. & fig., as *arrive at a place*, *get*, *rush*, *shoot*, *laugh*, *grumble*, *hint*, *snatch*, *aim*, *at*. **3.** *At all*, in any degree (in neg. context); *at best*, *worst*, assuming best, worst, result etc.; *at one*, in harmony or agreement (*with*); *at that*, at that estimate (*will take it at that*, accept that account of the matter), moreover, into the bargain (*lost an arm*, *& the right arm at that*). [OE *æt*, OHG *az*, ON, Goth. *at*, Gmc cogn. w. L *ad* to]

‖ **At²** (ăt), n. (colloq.). Member of the (Women's) Auxiliary Territorial Service (now W.R.A.C.). [f. initials A.T.S. ăts] treated as pl.]

at-, pref. = AD- before *t*.

ăt'arăxy, -ăx'ia, n. Stoical indifference. [f. mod. L f. Gk *ataraxia* (*a*- not +*tarassō* disturb)]

ăt'avism, n. Resemblance to remote ancestors, reversion to earlier type; recurrence of disease after intermission of some generations. Hence **ătavis'tic** [-IST, -IC] a. [f. F *atavisme* f. L *atavus* great-grandfather's grandfather, see -ISM]

atăx'ic, a. Characterized by ataxy; ~ *fever*, malignant typhus fever. [f. foll. + -IC]

atăx'y, n. Irregularity of animal functions; *locomotor* ~, morbid unsteadiness in use of legs, arms, etc. [f. mod. L f. Gk *ataxia* (*a*- not +*taxis* order f. *tassō* arrange)]

ate. See EAT.

-ate¹, suf. forming nn. orig. f. L -*atus* (gen. -*ūs*) in nouns of state from p.p. stems or nouns, or f. L -*atus*, -*ata*, -*atum* see -ATE²), which in OF became -*é* (-*ée*), but in learned words, & later in many reformed words, -*at*, as *prélat*, *primat*, *magistrat*. E having adopted -*at* afterwards added -*e* to mark quantity of *a*, & later words took -*ate* at once. E also formed wds either directly on L as *curate* or by anal. as *aldermanate*. Many such nn. in -*ate* are (1) nn. of office, as *marquisate*, *syndicate*, (2) participial nn., as *legate* one deputed, *precipitate* what is thrown down, (3) chem. terms denoting salts formed by action of an acid on a base, as *nitrate*, *sulphate*.

-ate², suf. forming adjj. (1) chiefly (thr. F) f. L p.p. in -*atus* (1st conjug.), which (cf. prec.) became successively -*at*, -*ate*, as *desolate*. Many such adjj. formed causative vbs (see foll.) & served as p.p. to them, till later the native -*ed* was added; -*ated* also appears without intervention of vb, as *annulated*, and as alternative form to -*ate*; (2) L participial adjj. were also formed on nn., as *caudatus* tailed, & on adjj. as *candidatus* white-robed; these were largely adopted in E, & others formed on anal. Many nouns in -ATE¹ were orig. adjj. In *cordate, ovate*, etc., the sense is 'shaped like'.

-ate³, suf. forming vbs to correspond to adjj. in -ATE², and subsequently to repr. the corresp. L vb in -*are* (p.p. -*atus*), as *separate, aggravate*. As these vbs usu. have F equivalents in -*er*, -*ate* was further used to form vbs on model of F vbs in -*er*, as *isolate* (F *isoler*). -*ate* was also used to form vbs that L might have formed, but did not, on nouns, as *felicitate* (L

felicitas -*atis*), & even vbs on nouns not of L orig., as *camphorate*.

atelier (see Ap.), n. Workshop, studio. [F]

ăt'elo- in comb. = Gk *atelēs* imperfect (*a*- not +*telos* end), as -*glossia*, -*gnathia*, -*stomia*, imperfect development of tongue, jaws, mouth.

Athanā'sian (ă-, -shn), a. Of Athanasius (archbishop of Alexandria in reign of Constantine); ~ *creed* (that beginning *Quicunque vult*, = *Whosoever will*). [f. LL *Athanasius*, see -AN]

āth'e|ism, n. Disbelief in the existence of a God; godlessness. So ~IST n., ~is'tic a., ~is'tICALLY adv. [f. F *athéisme* f. Gk *atheos* without God (*a*- not +*theos* God), see -ISM]

ăthēnae'um, n. Literary or scientific club (‖ esp. *the A*~, in London); reading--room, library. [L, f. Gk *Athēnaion* temple of *Athēnē*, goddess of wisdom]

athirst', pred. a. Thirsty; eager (*for*). [OE *ofthyrst* for *ofthyrsted* p.p. of *ofthyr-stan* be thirsty]

ăth'lēte, n. Competitor in physical exercises; robust, vigorous, man; ~'*s foot*, contagious skin-disease of the feet. [f. L *athleta* f. Gk *athlētēs* f. *athleō* contend for prize (*athlon*), see -ET²]

ăthlĕt'|ic, a. & n. Pertaining to athletes; physically powerful; (n. pl.) practice of physical exercises, ~ *sports*. Hence ~ICALLY adv., ~ICISM n. [f. L f. Gk *athlētikos* (as prec., see -IC)]

at-hōme', n. Reception of visitors within certain hours during which host or hostess or both have announced that they will be at home, a party.

athwart' (-ört), adv. & prep. Across from side to side (usu. obliquely); crosswise, perversely; in opposition to; (of ship) ~-*hawse*, across stem of another ship at anchor. [A prep.+THWART]

-atic, adj. suf. (= F -*atique*) f. L -*aticus* (orig. -*at*- of p.p. stems +-IC, but extended to nouns as *fanaticus* f. *fanum*), surviving phonetically in F & E -AGE; in many modern formations, as *lunatic, lymphatic*; but in many apparent exx. (*dramatic, piratic*) the suf. is -*ic*, & -*at*- part of the stem.

-atile, adj. suf. like -ATIC in orig. & use = -*at*-+-ILE, as *volatile, fluviatile*.

a-tilt', adv. Tilted; *run, ride*, ~ (in encounter on horseback with thrust of lance, usu. fig.). [A prep.+TILT]

-ation, suf. of nn. thr. F -*ation* (or direct) f. -*ationem* (nom. -*atio*), the particular form of the compd suf. -*tio* (-TION) f. L p.p. in -*at*- of 1st conj., +-*io* (-ION). The phonetic descendant of L -*ationem* in OF was -*aison*, -*eison*, surviving in E *orison, reason*, etc. All F wds in -*ation* are learned adoptions f. L, & may be paralleled by vbs ending in -*er*(= L -*are*), which far outnumber all other vbs & constitute the type of all new vbs in F. Hence F nouns in -*ation* exceed in number all the other members of the group (*-tion*, *-ition*, *-sion*), & so they do in E. Some of these have no accompanying vb in E use, as *lunation*, *constellation*; the great majority have a vb in *-ate*, as *create*, *creation*; some are formed on Gk vbs in *-ize* or their imitations, as *organize*, *-ation*; the remainder have a vb without suf., as *alteration*, *causation*, etc. These last having the appearance of being formed immediately on the vbs *alter*, *cause*, etc., *-ation* assumes the character of a living E suf., & is applied even to vbs not of F orig., as in *starvation*, *flirtation*. Meanings: (1) vbl action; (2) an instance of this; (3) resulting state; (4) concrete result (*plantation*).

-ative, adj. suf. f. F *-atif*, *-ative* f. L *-ativus* f. *-ivus* -IVE appended to p.p. stems in *-at-* (cf. -ATIC). The use of L *-ativus* was extended in LL & med. L, & its representatives are freely used in the mod. langg. In E, adjj, in *-ative* are usu. paired by vbs in *-ate*; the anal. of pairs such as *affirm*, *-ative* gave *talkative* f. *talk*; after such as *quality*, *-ative* (f. L *-itas*, LL *-ativus*), we have *authoritative* formed dir. on AUTHORITY.

atlăn'tes (-ēz), n. pl. (archit.). Sculptured male figures serving as pillars. [Gk, pl. of ATLAS]

Atlăn'tic, a. & n. **1.** Pertaining to mount Atlas in Libya; hence applied to sea near western shore of Africa, & later to whole ocean between Europe & Africa on east & America on west. **2.** n. ~ ocean. [f. L f. Gk *Atlantikos* f. ATLAS]

atlăn'tosaur'us, n. (palaeont.). (Kinds of) gigantic fossil reptile. [f. ATLAS + Gk *sauros* lizard]

ăt'las, n. Volume of maps; large size of drawing paper; (Physiol.) uppermost cervical vertebra, supporting skull. [*Atlas -antos* (1) Greek god of the older family, who held up pillars of universe; (2) the mountain in N. Africa, regarded as supporting the heavens]

atmo- in comp. = Gk *atmos* vapour, as *atmŏl'ogў*, science of aqueous vapour, *atmŏl'ўsis*, separation of vapours, *atmŏm'ēter* (for measuring evaporation).

ăt'mosphēre, n. Spheroidal gaseous envelope surrounding heavenly body; that surrounding earth; one surrounding any substance; mental or moral environment esp. artistic or emotional; air (in any place); (w. pl.) pressure of 15 lb. on square inch (that exerted by ~ on earth's surface). Hence **ătmosphĕ'ric**(AL) aa., **ătmosphĕ'ricalLY**[2] adv.; **ătmosphĕ'rics** n. pl., interference with wireless reception due to electric disturbance in~. [f. mod. L *atmosphaera*, see ATMO-, SPHERE]

atŏll' (*or* ăt'ŏl), n. Ring-shaped coral reef enclosing lagoon. [Maldive *atollon*, *atoll*, prob. = Malayalam *adal* closing]

ăt'om, n. **1.** Particle of matter indivisible

chemically; *physical* ~, supposed ultimate particle of matter (now held to consist of a positively charged nucleus, in which is concentrated most of the mass of the ~, round which revolve negatively charged electrons; *chemical* ~*s*, smallest particles in which elements combine with themselves or with each other; ~ *bomb*, ATOMIC *bomb*. **2.** Minute portion; small thing. [f. L f. Gk *atomos* indivisible (*a-* not + *-tomos* cut f. *temnō*), later reinforced by F *atome*]

atŏm'ic, a. Of, relating to, an atom or atoms; ~ *bomb* (deriving its destructiveness from the disintegration and partial conversion into energy of ~ nuclei); ~ *energy*, energy produced by changes in the ~ nuclei of uranium or similar metals; ~ *number*, (of a chemical element) number of unit positive charges carried by the nucleus of its atom; ~ *philosophy*, doctrine of formation of all things from indivisible particles endued with gravity & motion; (Chem.) ~ *theory* (that elemental bodies consist of indivisible atoms of definite relative weight, & that atoms of different elements unite with each other in fixed proportions, which determine the proportions in which elements & compounds enter into chemical combination); ~ *warfare* (in which ~ bombs are used); ~ *weight*, (now usu.) ratio between the weight of one atom of the element & $\frac{1}{16}$ of the weight of an atom of oxygen, (formerly) weight of an atom of the element as compared with that of an atom of hydrogen. Hence ~AL a., ~alLY[2] adv. [prec. + -IC]

ătomi'citў, n. The number of atoms in the molecule of an element; (formerly) = VALENCY. [f. prec., see -TY]

ăt'omism, n. Atomic philosophy; doctrine of action of individual atoms. [ATOM + -ISM]

ăt'om|ist, n. Holder of atomic theory or philosophy. Hence~**is'tic**a. [ATOM + -IST]

ăt'omiz|e, -is|e (-īz), v.t. Reduce to atoms. Hence ~A'TION n. [ATOM + -IZE]

ăt'omizer, n. Instrument for reducing liquids to fine spray. [prec. + -ER[1]]

ăt'omў[1], n. Skeleton; emaciated body. [f. ANATOMY, *an-* being taken as article]

ăt'omў[2], n. Atom, tiny being. [f. *atomi* pl. of L *atomus* ATOM]

atŏn'al, a. (mus.). Not conforming to any system of key or mode. [A- (7) + TONAL]

atōne', v.i. & t. **1.** Make amends (esp. ~ *for*, expiate). **2.** v.t. (arch.). Reconcile (enemies), compose (quarrel). [back form. f. foll.]

atōne'ment (-nm-), n. Atoning; expiation, reparation for wrong or injury; reconciliation of God & man, propitiation of God by expiation of sin; *Day of A*~, most solemn religious fast of Jewish year. [f. AT ONE + -MENT, after earlier *onement* f. obs. vb *one* unite]

atŏn'ĭc, a. & n. Unaccented, unstressed; (Path.) wanting tone; (n.) unaccented word (esp. in Gk Gram.). [f. med. L *atonicus* f. Gk *atonos* toneless (*a*- not + *tonos* TONE), see -IC]

atŏp', adv. On the top (*of*). [A prep.]·

ătrabil'ious (-*lyus*), a. Affected by black bile; melancholy; acrimonious. Hence ~NESS n. [f. L *atra bilis* (black bile, transl. Gk*melagkholia*MELANCHOLY)+-OUS]

atrip', adv. (Of anchor) just lifted from ground in weighing. [A prep.+TRIP]

āt'rium, n. (pl. -*a*, -*ums*). Central court of Roman house; covered portico, esp. before church door. [L]

atrō'cious (-*shus*), a. Heinously wicked; very bad, as ~ *pun*. Hence ~LY² adv., ~NESS n. [f. L *atrox* -*ocis* (*ater* black)+ -OUS]

atrō'cĭtў, n. Heinous wickedness; atrocious deed; bad blunder. [f. L *atrocitas* (as prec., see -TY)]

ăt'rophў, n. Wasting away through imperfect nourishment; emaciation (lit. & fig.). Hence **āt'rophў** v.t. & i. [f. LL f. Gk *atrophia* f. *atrophos* ill-fed (*a*- not + *trophē* food)]

ăt'ropine(-*ēn*), n. Poisonous alkaloid found in deadly nightshade. [f. mod. L *atropa* deadly nightshade f. Gk *Atropos* inflexible, name of one of the Fates, see -INE⁵]

ˈătt'aboy, int. Exclamation expressive of encouragement or admiration. [corrupt. of *that's the boy!*]

ăttăch', v.t. & i. Fasten (thing *to* another); join one*self* (*to* person, company, expedition); bind in friendship, make devoted, (*has the gift of* ~*ing people to him*; *is deeply* ~*ed to her*); affix (inmaterial things, name, liability, etc., *to*); attribute (importance etc. *to*); (Law) seize (person, property) by legal authority; adhere, be incident, as *no blame* ~*es to*. Hence ~ABLE a. [ME, f. OF *atachier* (mod. *attacher*, It. *attaccare*) f. *à to* + root found in Genevese *tache*, Sp. and Port. *tacha*, nail, TACK]

ăttaché (atăsh'ā), n. One attached to ambassador's suite; ~ *case*, small rectangular valise ostensibly for carrying documents. [F, p.p. of *attacher* (as prec.)]

ăttăch'ment, n. Act of attaching; thing attached; means of attaching; affection; legal seizure, esp. *foreign* ~ (of foreigner's goods, to satisfy his creditors). [ME, f. F *attachement* (*attacher* ATTACH, see -MENT)]

ăttăck'¹, v.t. Fall upon, assault, (lit. & fig.); (of physical agents or diseases) act destructively upon. Hence ~ABLE a. [f. F *attaquer* f. It. *attaccare*, see ATTACH]

ăttăck'², n. Act of attacking (lit. & fig.); offensive operation. [f. prec., or F *attaque* n.]

ăttain', v.t. & i. Arrive at, reach; gain, accomplish; (intr.) ~ *to*, arrive at. Hence ~ABIL'ITY n., ~ABLE a., ~ableness n. [ME, f. OF *ataign*- st. of *ataindre* f. L ATtingere (*tangere* touch)]

attain'der, n. Consequences of sentence of death or outlawry (forfeiture of estate, corruption of blood, extinction of civil rights). [AF, = OF *ataindre* ATTAIN used as n. (see -ER⁴); meaning influenced by confus. w. OF *taindre* TAINT]

attain'ment, n. Act of attaining; thing attained, esp. personal accomplishment. [ME, ATTAIN+-MENT]

attaint', v.t. Subject to attainder; (of diseases etc.) strike, affect; infect; sully. [f. obs. *attaint* a. f. OF *ataint* p.p. as ATTAIN; confused in meaning with TAINT]

ătt'ar, n. Fragrant essential oil from rose-petals. [f. Pers. *'aṭar(-gul)* essence (of roses) f. Arab. *'uṭūr* aroma f. *'aṭara* breathe perfume; see OTTO]

attĕm'per, v.t. Qualify by admixture; modify temperature of; soothe, mollify; accommodate *to*; attune *to*; temper (metal). Hence ~MENT n. [ME, f. OF *atemprer* f. L AT(*temperare* TEMPER)]

attĕmpt'¹, v.t. Try (thing, action, *to* do); try to master (mountain, fortress); ~ *the life of*, try to kill. Hence ~ABLE a. [f. OF *attempter*, f. L AT(*temptare* TEMPT)]

attĕmpt'², n. Attempting; endeavour. [f. prec.]

attĕnd', v.t. & i. Turn the mind *to*; apply oneself (*to* or abs.); be present (*at*); wait *upon*; (trans.) wait upon; escort, accompany; be present at (lecture etc.). [ME, f. OF *atendre* f. L ATtendere -*tent*- stretch]

attĕn'dance, n. Act of attending (*upon* person, *at* lecture); *dance* ~ *on*, attend the convenience of; body of persons present. [ME, f. OF *atendance* (as prec., see -ANCE)]

attĕn'dant, a. & n. **1.** Waiting (*upon*); accompanying, as ~ *circumstances*; present, as ~ *crowd*. **2.** n. Servant, satellite. [ME, f. OF, part. as ATTEND]

attĕn'tion, n. & int. Act of attending, as *pay*, *give*, ~; faculty of attending, as *attract*, *call*, ~; consideration, care; (pl.) ceremonious politeness (*pay* one's ~*s to*, court); *come to*, *stand at*, ~ (military attitude; *A*~*!*, order to assume it, also *'shun!*). [ME, f. L *attentio* (as ATTEND, see -ION)]

attĕn'tĭve, a. Heedful, observant; polite, assiduous. Hence ~LY² (-vl-) adv., ~NESS (-vn-) n. [F (-*if*, -*ive*), f. L as ATTEND, see -IVE]

attĕn'ū̆āte¹, v.t. Make slender; make thin in consistence; reduce in force or value. So ~A'TION n. [f. L ATtenuare (*tenuis* thin), see -ATE³]

attĕn'ū̆ate², a. Slender; rarefied. [as prec., see -ATE²]

attĕst', v.t. & i. Testify, certify (~*ed cattle*, certified free from the tubercle bacillus); put (person) on oath or solemn declaration; administer oath of allegiance to (recruit); (intr.) bear witness to. Hence ~OR n. [f. F *attester* f. L ATtestari (*testis* witness)]

ăttĕstā'tion, n. Act of testifying; testimony; evidence; formal confirmation by signature, oath, etc.; administration of an oath. [F, or LL *attestatio* (as prec., see -ATION)]

Att'ic (ă-), a. & n. Of Athens or Attica; ~ *(dialect)*, Greek spoken by the Athenians; ~ *salt, wit*, refined wit; ~ *order*, with square column of any of the five ORDERS. [f. L f. Gk *Attikos*]

ätt'ic², n. Structure consisting of small order placed above another of greater height (usu. *Attic*); highest storey of house; room in this. [f. F *attique*, as prec.]

ätt'ic|ism, n. Style, idiom, of Athens; refined amenity of speech; attachment to Athens. So ~IZE (2) v.i. [f. Gk *attikismos*]

attīre', v.t., & n. Dress, array. [ME, f. OF *atirer* f. *à* to + *tire*, of unkn. orig.; cf. TIRE³]

ätt'itūde, n. Disposition of figure (in painting etc.); posture of body, as *strike an* ~ (assume it theatrically); settled behaviour, as indicating opinion; ~ *of mind*, settled mode of thinking. [F, f. It. *attitudine* fitness, posture, f. med. L *aptitudinem* (*aptus* fit, see -TUDE)]

ätt'itūd'inize, -ise (-īz), v.i. Practise attitudes; speak, write, behave, affectedly. [f. prec. + -IZE]

attorn' (-ẽrn), v.t. & i. (law). Transfer; make legal acknowledgement of new landlord. Hence ~MENT n. [ME, f. OF *atorner* (*à* to + *torner* TURN)]

attorn'ey¹ (-tẽr-), n. One appointed to act for another in business or legal matters; barrister or solicitor (now joc. or derog., exc. in U.S.); *A~ General*, (in England & U.S.) legal officer empowered to act in all cases in which the State is a party; *abuse plaintiff's* ~ (iron. advice to lawyer with a weak case). Hence ~SHIP n. [ME, f. OF *atorné* p.p. as ATTORN; see -Y⁴]

attorn'ey² (-tẽr-), n. *Letter, warrant, of* ~ (by which person appoints another to act for him); *power of* ~, authority thus conferred. [ME, f. OF *atornée* fem. p.p., see prec.]

atträct', v.t. Draw to oneself (esp. of physical forces); excite the pleasurable emotions of (person); draw forth & fix upon oneself (attention etc.). Hence ~ABIL'ITY n., ~ABLE a. [f. L AT(*trahere tract-* draw)]

atträc'tion, n. Act, faculty, of drawing to oneself (lit. & fig.); drawing force; thing that attracts (fig.); ~ *of gravity* (existing between all bodies, & varying directly as their masses, inversely as the square of their distance apart); *magnetic* ~, action of magnet in drawing iron; *molecular* ~ (between molecules of bodies, acting only at infinitesimal distances); *capillary* ~ (by which liquid is drawn up through hairlike tube). [F, or f. L *attractio* (as prec., see -ION)]

atträc'tive, a. Attracting, capable of at-

tracting (esp. fig.). Hence ~LY² (-vl-) adv., ~NESS (-vn-) n. [F(-*if, -ive*), as prec., see -IVE]

ätt'ribute¹, n. Quality ascribed to anything; material object recognized as appropriate to person or office; characteristic quality; (Gram.) attributive word. [ME, f. F *attribut* or L *attributum* (ATtribuere -ut- assign)]

attrib'ūte², v.t. Ascribe as belonging or appropriate *to*; refer (effect *to* its cause); assign (*to* time or place). Hence ~ABLE a. [as prec.]

ättribū'tion, n. Act of attributing; authority granted (*to* a ruler etc.). [ME, f. OF, f. L *attributionem* (as prec., see -ION)]

attrib'ūtive, a. & n. **1.** (Logic) assigning an attribute to a subject; (Gram.) expressing an attribute (e.g. *old* in *the old dog* but not in *the dog is old*). **2.** n. Word denoting an attribute (usu. an adjective or its equivalent). Hence ~LY² (-vl-) adv. [F (-*if, -ive*), as ATTRIBUTE¹, see -IVE]

attrit'ed, a. Worn by friction. [f. L AT- (*terere trit-* rub)]

attri'tion, n. Friction; wearing out (*war* of ~, turning on which side can last longest); abrasion; (Theol.) sorrow for sin (short of *contrition*). [ME, f. LL *attritio* (as prec., see -ION)]

attūne', v.t. Bring into musical accord (*to*, lit. & fig.); tune (instrument). [AT- + TUNE v.]

atȳp'ical, a. Not conforming to type. [A- (7) + TYPICAL]

aubade (ōbahd'), n. Musical announcement of dawn; sunrise song. [F]

auberge (ōbãrzh'), n. Inn. [F]

aubergine (ō'bẽrzhēn), n. Purple fruit of egg-plant. [F]

aubrietia (ōbrēsh'a) (erron.) **-retia**, n. (Kinds of) spring-flowering dwarf perennial plant. [f. Claude *Aubriet* (French artist), see -IA¹]

aub'urn (-ern), a. Golden-brown (usu. of hair). [ME, f. OF *auborne* f. L *alburnus* whitish]

au courant (ō kōō'rahn), pred. a. Acquainted *with* what is going on; well-informed. [F]

auc'tion, n., & v.t. **1.** Public sale in which articles are sold to the highest of successive bidders; *Dutch* ~, sale in which price is reduced by auctioneer till a purchaser is found; ~ *bridge*, form of bridge in which players bid for right to play the hand. **2.** v.t. Sell by ~. [f. L *auctio* increase, auction (*augēre auct-*, see -ION)]

auc'tioneer' (-shon-), n., & v.i. (One whose business is to) conduct auctions. [-EER]

audā'cious (-shŭs), a. Daring, bold; impudent. Hence -LY² adv., ~NESS n., audA'CITY (-ăs-) n. [f. L *audax* (*audēre* dare, see -ACIOUS)]

aud'ib|le, a. Perceptible to the ear. Hence ~LY² adv., audiBIL'ITY, ~leNESS

(-ln-), nn. [f. LL *audibilis* (*audire* hear, see -BLE)]

aud'ience, n. Hearing; *give* ~, listen; formal interview; persons within hearing; assembly of listeners; (of a book) readers. [ME f. OF, f. L *audientia* (*audire* hear, see -ENCE)]

aud'ile, a. & n. (Usu. of supernormal phenomena) received through the auditory nerves; (person) specially sensitive to auditory impressions. [irreg. f. L *audire* hear + -ILE]

aud'iō-frē'quencў, n. & a. (Of, using) frequency comparable to that of sound. [f. L *audire* hear + -o- + FREQUENCY]

audiŏm'ĕter, n. Instrument for testing hearing-power. [f. L *audire* hear + -o- + -METER]

aud'iphōne, n. Instrument that, pressed against upper teeth, assists hearing. [improp. f. L *audire* hear + Gk *phōnē* sound, on *telephone*]

aud'it, n. Official examination of accounts; searching examination, esp. Day of Judgement; periodical settlement of accounts between landlord & tenants; ~ *ale* (of special quality, formerly brewed in English colleges, orig. for use on day of ~); ~-*house*, -*room* (attached to Cathedral for transaction of business). [ME, f. L *auditus* -*ūs* hearing (*audire* -*it*-)]

aud'it[2], v.t. Examine (accounts) officially. [f. prec.]

audi'tion, n., & v.t. & i. Power of hearing; listening; trial hearing of applicant for employment as singer etc.; (vb) give an ~ (to). [F, or f. L *auditio* (*audire* -*it*-, see -ION)]

aud'itive, a. Concerned with hearing. [F (-*if*, -*ive*), as prec., see -IVE]

aud'it|or, n. Listener; one who audits accounts. Hence ~orSHIP, ~TESS[1], nn. [f. AF *auditour* f. L *auditorem* (as prec., see -OR)]

auditōr'ial, a. Connected with an audit. [f. prec. + -IAL]

aud'itorў, a. & n. **1.** Connected with hearing; received by the ear. **2.** n. Assembly of hearers, audience; (now usu. auditōr'ium) part of building occupied by audience. [f. L *auditorius*, -*um* (as prec., see -ORY)]

au fait (ō fā'), pred. a. Conversant, instructed; *put a person* ~ *with*, instruct him in. [F]

au fond (see Ap.), adv. At bottom (cf. *à fond*). [F]

Augē'an, a. Filthy, like the stables of Augeas, which Hercules cleansed by turning river Alpheus through them. [f. L *Augeas* f. Gk *Augeias* + -AN]

aug'er (-g-), n. Tool for boring holes in wood, having long shank with cutting edge & screw point, & handle at right angles; instrument for boring in soil or strata, with stem that can be lengthened. [OE *nafugār* (*nafu* NAVE[1] + *gār* piercer), cf.

OHG *nabuger*, Du. *avegaar*; for loss of n-cf. ADDER]

aught (awt), n. & adv. Anything; (adv., arch.) in any degree or respect. [OE *āwiht* (*ā* ever + *wiht* wight, whit); OE contr. *āht*, gives mod. *ought*, now less usu. form]

aug'ment[1], n. Vowel (in Sanskrit *a*, in Greek *ĕ*) prefixed to past tenses in the older Aryan languages. [ME, f. OF, or f. LL *augmentum* increase (*augēre*, see -MENT)]

augmĕnt'[2], v.t. & i. Make greater, increase; prefix the augment to; (intr.) increase. [ME, f. F *augmenter* or LL *augmentare* increase; see prec.]

augmentā'tion, n. Enlargement; growth, increase; addition; (Mus.) repetition of a passage in notes longer than those of the original. [ME, f. OF, f. LL *augmentationem* (*augmentare*, see prec. and -ATION)]

augmĕn'tative, a. & n. Having the property of increasing; (Gram., of affixes or derived words) increasing in force the idea of the original word; (n.) ~ word. [F (-*if*, -*ive*), f. L as AUGMENT[2], see -ATIVE]

au grand sérieux (see Ap.), adv. Very seriously (*take* it, him, etc., ~). [F]

aug'ur[1] (-er), n. Roman religious official who foretold future events by omens derived from the actions of birds etc.; soothsayer. Hence ~SHIP n. [L, prob. f. *avis* bird; cf. AUSPICE]

aug'ur[2] (-er), v.t. & i. Forebode, anticipate; ~ *well*, *ill*, have good or bad expectations *of*, *for*; *it* ~s (promises) *ill*. [f. prec.]

aug'ūral, a. Pertaining to augurs; significant of the future. [f. L *auguralis* (AUGUR[1], see -AL)]

aug'ūrў, n. Divination by omens; augural ceremony; omen; presentiment; promise. [ME, f. OF *augurie* or L *augurium* (AUGUR[1])]

augŭst'[1], a. Majestic, venerable. Hence ~LY[2] adv., ~NESS n. [f. F *auguste* or L *augustus* consecrated, venerable]

Aug'ust[2], n. Eighth month of year, named after Augustus Caesar. [OE *august* f. L *augustus* (see prec.); in ME also *aust* f. OF *aoust*]

Augŭs'tan, a. & n. Connected with reign of Augustus Caesar, best period of Latin literature; (of any national literature) classical (in Eng. literature *c.* 18th c.); ~ *confession* (drawn up by Luther & Melanchthon at Augusta Vindelicorum or Augsburg); (n.) writer of the ~ age of any literature. [f. L *Augustanus*, see -AN]

Augŭs'tine (*or* awg[2]), n. An Augustinian monk. [f. L *Augustinus*, name of the Latin father]

Augŭstin'ian, a. & n. **1.** Of or relating to St Augustine (d. 430) or his doctrines; belonging to the order of Augustines. **2.** n. Adherent of the doctrines of St Augustine; one of the order of Augustines. Hence ~ISM (3) n. [f. L *Augustinus* (prec.) + -IAN]

auk, n. Kinds of black and white gregarious sea-bird, including the flightless and extinct *Great Auk*. [f. ON *álka* (cf. Sw. *alka*, Da. *alke*)]

aul'ic, a. Pertaining to a court; *A~ Council*, (in old German empire) personal council of emperor, (later) council managing Austrian war-department. [f. F *aulique* or L f. Gk *aulikos* (*aulé* court, see -IC)]

aum'brў, var. of AMBRY.

au naturel (see Ap.), adv. or pred. a. (Cooked) in the simplest way. [F]

aunt (ahnt), n. Father's, mother's, sister; uncle's wife; *A~ Sally*, game at fairs, in which players throw sticks at pipe in mouth of wooden woman's head, also fig. [ME, f. OF *aunte* f. L *amita*; E up to 17th c. had also *naunt* (my naunt = mine aunt), still used in dial.]

au pair (ō pār'), a. (Of arrangements between two parties) paid for by mutual services (no money passing). [F]

au pied de la lettre (ō pyā' de lah lĕt'r), adv. Literally. [F]

aur'a, n. Subtle emanation (from flowers etc.); atmosphere diffused by or attending a person etc. (esp. in mystical or spiritualistic use as a definite envelope of body or spirit); (Electr.) current of air caused by discharge of electricity from a sharp point; (Path.) sensation as of current of cold air rising from some part of body to head, premonitory symptom in epilepsy & hysterics. Hence **aur'al**[1] [-AL] a. [f. L f. Gk, = breeze, breath]

aur'al[2], a. Pertaining to organ of hearing; received by the ear. Hence ~LY[2] adv. [f. L *auris* ear + -AL]

aur'éate, a. Golden, gold-coloured; resplendent. [ME, f. L *aureatus* f. *aureus* golden f. *aurum* gold, -ATE[2]]

aurēl'ia, n. (Formerly) chrysalis, esp. of butterfly; (Zool.) kinds of phosphorescent marine animals. [It., = silkworm, fem. of *aurelio* golden f. L *aurum* gold]

aurēl'ian, a. & n. Of an aurelia; golden; (n.) collector, breeder, of insects. [prec. + -AN]

aurē'ola, n. Celestial crown won by martyr, virgin, doctor, by victory over world, flesh, or devil; = foll. [L (~ *corona*) golden (crown) fem. of *aureolus* f. *aureus* (*aurum* gold)]

aur'éōle, n. Aureola; (prop.) gold disc surrounding head in early pictures; circle of light depicted round head; oblong glory surrounding divine figures; actual halo, esp. that seen in eclipses. [OF, f. prec.]

au revoir (ō revwahr'), adv. (Good-bye) till we meet again. [F]

aur'ic, a. Pertaining to gold; (Chem.) in which gold is trivalent. [f. L *aurum* gold, see -IC]

aur'ic|e, n. External ear of animals; process shaped like lower lobe of ear; either of the two upper cavities of the heart. Hence ~ED[2] (-ld) a. [f. foll.]

auric'ŭla, n. Species of primula, bear's-ear; genus of molluscs. [L, = external ear, dim. of *auris* ear]

auric'ŭlar, a. Pertaining to the ear; told privately in the ear, as ~ *confession*; ~ *witness*, one who tells what he has heard; pertaining to auricle of heart; shaped like an auricle. Hence ~LY[2] adv. [f. LL *auricularis* (AURICULA, see -AR[1])]

auric'ŭlate, a. With ear-shaped projections. [as prec., see -ATE[2]]

aurif'erous, a. Yielding gold. [f. L *aurifer* (*aurum* gold); see -FEROUS]

aur'ifōrm, a. Ear-shaped. [f. L *auris* ear + -FORM]

Auri'ga, n. Northern constellation, the Waggoner. [L, = charioteer]

Aurigna'cian (-shn), a. Of the palaeolithic epoch represented by remains found in the Aurignac cave of the Pyrenees. [-AN]

aur'ilāve, n. Instrument for cleaning ears. [f. L *auris* ear + *lavare* wash]

aur'ist, n. Ear specialist. [as prec. + -IST]

aurochs (owr'ŏks, aw-), n. Extinct wild ox; (improp.) European bison. [f. G *aurochs* (mod. *auerochs*) f. OHG *ūr-ohso* f. *ūr*- URUS + *ohso* OX]

aurōr'a, n. Luminous atmospheric (prob. electrical) phenomenon radiating from earth's northern (~ *boreāl'is*) or southern (*austrāl'is*) magnetic pole; dawn; colour of sky at sunrise; *A~*, Roman goddess of dawn. Hence **aurōr'AL** a. [L, = dawn, goddess of dawn]

aur'ous, a. (chem.). In which gold is univalent. [f. L *aurum* + -OUS]

aur'um, n. Gold; ~ *fŭl'mĭnāns*, fulminate of gold; ~ *mosā'icum*, bisulphide of tin, bronze-powder. [L]

auscultā'tion, n. Act of listening, esp. (Med.) to movement of heart, lungs, etc. So **aus'cŭltātor** n., **auscŭl'tatory** a. [f. L *auscultatio* f. *auscultare* listen to, see -ATION]

Ausgleich (see Ap.), n. (hist.). Political agreement between Austria & Hungary, renewable every tenth year. [G]

aus'pĭcāte, v.t. & i. Inaugurate, initiate; (intr.) augur. [f. L *auspicari* (*auspex* -*icis* observer of birds for *avispex* f. *avis* bird + -*spec*- observe), see -ATE[3]]

aus'pĭce, n. Observation of birds for purposes of taking omens; prognostic; prosperous lead, patronage, as *under the ~s of*. [F. or f. L *auspicium* (*auspex*, see prec.)]

auspi'cious (-shŭs), a. Of good omen, favourable; prosperous. Hence ~LY[2] adv., ~NESS n. [as prec. + -OUS]

Auss'ie, n. (sl.). Australia(n). [abbr.]

austēre', a. Harsh, stern; stringently moral, strict, severely simple; harsh in flavour. Hence ~LY[2] (-rl-) adv., ~NESS (-rn-) n., **austē'rity** n. (also attrib., severely simple). [ME, f. OF, f. L f. Gk *austēros* drying, harsh (*auō* v. dry)]

Aus'tin, a. & n. Contr. f. AUGUSTINE.

aus'tral, a. Southern. [f. L *australis* (*Auster* south wind, see -AL)]

Australā'sian (-shn), a. & n. (Native) of Australasia (Australia & adjoining islands). [f. *Australasia* f. F *Australasie* (L *australis*, see prec. +*Asia*)+-AN]

Austrāl'ian, n. & a. Native of, resident in, Australia; (adj.) of Australia. [f. F *Australien* f. L as AUSTRAL]

aut'archy (-kǐ), n. Absolute sovereignty. Hence **autārch'IC**(AL) (-k-) aa. [f. Gk *autarkhia* (AUTO-, *arkhō* rule)]

aut'arkў, n. Self-sufficiency. Hence **autārk'IC**(AL) aa., **aut'arkIST** n. [f. Gk *autarkeia* (AUTO-, *arkeō* suffice)]

authěn't|ic, a. Reliable, trustworthy; of undisputed origin, genuine; (Mus., of ecclesiastical modes) having their sounds comprised within an octave from the final. Hence ~ICALLY adv., ~ĭ'CITY n. [ME, f. OF *autentique* f. LL f. Gk *authentikos* f. *authentēs* one who does a thing himself (AUTO-+*-hentēs*, cf. *sunentēs* fellow-worker), see -IC]

authěn'tic|āte, v.t. Establish the truth of; establish the authorship of; make valid. Hence ~A'TION, ~ātoR, nn. [f. med. L *authenticare* (*authenticus*), see prec. and -ATE³]

auth'or, n. Originator (*of* a condition of things, event, etc.); writer of book, treatise, etc.; (loosely) ~'s writings. Hence ~ESS¹ n., **authōr'IAL** a. [ME *autour* f. AF, OF *autor, -teur* f. L *auctor* (*augēre auct-* increase, originate, promote, see -OR); *auth-* appears as scribal var. of *aut-* in Eng. *c.* 1550]

authŏritār'ian, a. & n. (Esp. Pol.) favouring obedience to authority as opp. to individual liberty; (n.) supporter of this principle. [f. as foll.+-ARIAN]

authŏ'ritātive, a. Commanding, imperative; possessing authority; proceeding from competent authority. Hence ~LY² (-vl-)adv., ~NESS(-vn-)n. [f.foll.+-ATIVE]

authŏ'ritў, n. Power, right, to enforce obedience; delegated power (*to do, for* an act, or abs.); person or body having authority; personal influence, esp. over opinion; weight of testimony; book, quotation, considered to settle a question; evidence, declaration, that may be cited in support of a statement (*on the* ~ *of Plato*); person whose opinion is accepted, esp. expert in(*on*) a subject. [ME, f. OF *autorite* or L *auctoritas* (*auctor*, see AUTHOR and -TY)]

auth'oriz|e, -is|e (-ĭz), v.t. Sanction; give ground for, justify, (thing); give authority to, commission, (person *to do*). *Authorized Version* (abbr. A.V.), **King James's Bible* or *Version*, the Bible of 1611. Hence ~ABLE a., ~A'TION n. [ME, f. OF *autoriser* f. m ed. L *auctorizare* (*auctor*, see AUTHOR and -IZE)]

auth'orship, n. Occupation, career, as a writer; origin (of book). [-SHIP]

aut'ism, n. Morbid self-admiration,

absorption in phantasy. Hence **autĭs'tIC** a. [f. foll.+-ISM]

auto- in comp. = Gk *auto-* (*autos* self), in sense 'self, one's own, by oneself, independent(ly)', in wds f. Gk & ·new formations, as *-car'pous*, consisting of pericarp alone, *-gamy*, self-fertilization, *-genous*, self-producing, *-geny*, *-gony*, spontaneous generation, *-phagous*, *-phagy*, feeding on oneself (by absorption of tissues, during starvation), *-plasty*, repair of wounds with tissue from same body; *-sugges'tion*, hypnotic suggestion proceeding from the subject himself.

aut'obahn, n. (pl. ~*en*). German arterial road. [G (*auto* motor-car, *bahn* road)]

autobiŏg'rapher, n. One who writes his own history. [AUTO-]

autobiogrăph'ic, a. Pertaining to, engaged in, autobiography. Hence ~AL a., ~alLY² adv. [AUTO-]

autobiŏg'raphў, n. Writing the story of one's own life; story so written. [AUTO-]

aut'ocăr, n. Road vehicle driven by mechanical power. [AUTO-]

autocěph'alous, a. Having its own head; (of bishop, church) independent. [f. Gk *autokephalos*(AUTO-+*kephalē* head)+-OUS]

autŏch'thon (-k-), n. (usu. pl.; *-onēs, -ons*). Original, earliest known, inhabitants; aborigines. Hence ~AL, autochthŏn'IC, ~OUS, aa., ~ISM, ~Y¹, nn. [Gk, = sprung from that land itself (AUTO-+ *khthōn -onos* land)]

autŏc'racў, n. Absolute government; controlling influence. [f. Gk *autokrateia* (as AUTOCRAT)]

aut'ocrăt, n. Absolute ruler. So **autocrăt'IC**(AL) aa., **autocrăt'icalLY²** adv. [f. F *autocrate* f. Gk *autokratēs* (AUTO-+ *kratos* might)]

aut'o-da-fé' (-dahfā), n. (pl. *autos-da-fé*). Sentence of the Inquisition; execution of this, esp. burning of heretic. [Port., = act of the faith; also Sp. *-de-fé*]

aut'odidăct, n. Self-taught person. [AUTO-, DIPACT(IC)]

aut'o-ě'rotism, n. Spontaneous sexual emotion generated without external stimulus. [AUTO-+EROTISM]

autogī'ŏ, n. Kind of GYROPLANE. [patented name; AUTO-, GYRO-]

aut'ograph¹ (-ahf), n. Author's own manuscript; person's own handwriting, esp. signature; copy produced by autography. Hence **autŏgrăph'IC**(AL) aa., **autogrăph'icalLY²** adv. [F, or f. L f. Gk *autographon* neut. of *autographos* (AUTO-+*-graphos* written)]

aut'ograph²(-ahf), v.t. Write with one's own hand; copy by autography; sign. [f. prec.]

autŏg'raphў, n. Writing with one's own hand; author's own handwriting; reproduction in facsimile of writing or drawing. [as prec., see -Y¹]

(For other words in *auto-* see AUTO-.)

aut'ohárp, n. Kind of zither with mechanical contrivance making playing of chords possible. [AUTO-]

autŏl'ẏsis, n. Destruction of cells of the body by the action of its own serum. [f. AUTO- + Gk *lusis* dissolution]

***aut'omăt**, n. Café or restaurant in which meals etc. are provided in slot--machines. [G; see AUTOMATON]

automăt'ic, a. & n. 1. Self-acting; working of itself, (of a firearm) having mechanism for loading, firing, & ejecting until the ammunition is exhausted, or until the pressure on the trigger etc. is released; (n.) ~ firearm. 2. Mechanical, unconscious; unintelligent, merely mechanical. 3. (psych.). Performed unconsciously or subconsciously. Hence ~AL a., ~alLẏ[2] adv., **automati'city** n. [as AUTOMATON + -IC]

automã'tion, n. Automatic control of the manufacture of a product through successive stages, (loosely) use of machinery to save mental & manual labour. [irreg. f. prec.]

autŏm'atism, n. Involuntary action; doctrine attributing this to animals; unthinking routine; faculty of originating action or motion; (Psych.) action performed unconsciously or subconsciously. [f. foll. + -ISM]

autŏm'at|on, n. (pl. ~a, ~ons). Thing endued with spontaneous motion; living being viewed materially; piece of mechanism with concealed motive power; living being whose actions are involuntary or without active intelligence. Hence ~OUS a. [f. Gk (also L) AUTOmaton, neut. adj., acting of itself]

***automobile'** (-ŏl), n. Motor-car. [F]

autŏn'omous, a. Of, possessed of, autonomy. [f. Gk AUTO(nomos law) + -OUS]

autŏn'om|ẏ, n. Right of self-government; personal freedom; freedom of the will (in Kantian doctrine); a self-governing community. So **autonŏm'IC** a., ~IST n. [f. Gk *autonomia*, as prec., see -Y[1]]

autŏp'sẏ (or awt⁴), n. Personal inspection; post-mortem examination; (fig.) critical dissection. So **autŏp'tic**(AL) aa. [f. mod. L f. Gk *autopsia* f. *autoptos* (AUTO- + *op-* see); cf. F *autopsie*]

autostrad|a (owtostrah'dah), n. (pl. ~e, pr. -ā). Italian arterial road. [It., = motor-car road]

autotŏx'|in, n. Poisonous substance produced by changes within the organism. So ~IC a., ~ICA'TION n., poisoning by a virus generated within the body. [AUTO-, TOXIN, TOXIC]

aut'otẏpe, n. Facsimile; photographic printing process for reproducing in monochrome. Hence **aut'otẏpe** v.t. [AUTO-]

aut'umn (-m), n. Third season of the year, September–November (Astron., from autumnal equinox to winter solstice); (fig.) season of incipient decay. [ME *autumpne* f. OF f. L *autumnus*]

autŭm'nal, a. Of autumn; ~ *crocus*, MEADOW saffron; ~ *equinox*, time when sun crosses equator as it proceeds southward (Sept. 23); maturing, blooming, in autumn; past prime of life. [f. L *autumnalis* (as prec., see -AL)]

auxanŏm'ĕter, n. Instrument for measuring growth in plants. [f. Gk *auxanō* increase + -o- + -METER]

auxil'iar|ẏ (-lya-), a. & n. (One who is) helpful *to*; (Mil.) ~*y troops*, ~*ies*, foreign or allied troops in a nation's service; (Gram.) ~*y* (*verb*), one used to form tenses, moods, voices, of other verbs. [f. L *auxiliarius*(*auxilium* help, see -ARY[1])]

aux'in, n. Substance which stimulates growth, growth hormone. [f. Gk *auxanō* increase, -IN]

avadavat. See AMADAVAT.

avail'[1], v.t. & i. Afford help; be of value or profit; (trans.) help, benefit; ~ one*self of*, profit by, take advantage of. [ME; f. obs. *vail* vb f. OF *valoir* be worth f. L *valēre*]

avail'[2], n. Use, profit, only in phrr. *of* ~, *of no* ~, *without* ~, *to little* ~. [f. prec., cf. VAIL[2]]

avail'a|ble, a. Capable of being used, at one's disposal, within one's reach. Hence ~BIL'ITY, ~bleNESS (-ln-), nn., ~bLY[2] adv. [AVAIL v. + -ABLE]

ăv'alanche (-ahnsh), n. Mass of snow, earth, & ice, descending swiftly from mountain (also fig.). [F, dialect. form of *avalance* f. *avaler* descend, see -ANCE]

***ăvani'a** (-nêa), n. (hist.). (Extortionate) tax levied by Turks. [orig. unkn.; common in Levant]

avant-courier (avŏng'-kŏŏr'ĭer), n. One who runs, rides, before; esp. (pl.) scouts, advance-guard. [f. F *avant-coureur* (*avant* before + *coureur* runner, after COURIER]

avant-garde (avŏng'-gãrd'), n. The pioneers or innovators in any art in a particular period. [F, = vanguard]

ăv'arice, n. Greed of gain, cupidity; (fig.) eager desire to get or keep. Hence **ăvari'cious** (-shus) a., **ăvari'ciousLY**[1] adv. [ME, f. OF, f. L *avaritia* (*avarus* greedy, see -ICE)]

avast' (-ahst), int. (naut.). Stop; cease. [f. Du. *houd vast* hold fast]

ăv'atãr, n. (Hindu Myth.) descent of deity to earth in incarnate form; incarnation; manifestation, display; phase. [f. Skr. *avatara* descent (*ava* down + *tar-* pass over)]

avaunt', int. (arch., joc.). Begone. [ME, f. OF *avant* f. Rom. ***abante** before (L *ab* from + *ante* before)]

āv'e, int. & n. Welcome; farewell; shout of welcome or farewell; ~ *āt'que* VALE[2], hail & farewell; *Ave Maria* (Hail, Mary), devotional recitation (cf. *Luke* i. 28) & prayer to the Virgin; ~*bell*, rung when this is to be said. [L, 2nd sing. imper. of *avēre* fare well]

avĕnge′ (-j), v.t. Inflict retribution, exact satisfaction, on behalf of (person, violated right, etc.); *be ~d, ~* oneself; take vengeance for (injury). [ME, f. OF *avengier* (à to +*vengier* f. L *vindicare*)]

ăv′ens (-nz), n. *Wood ~*, herb bennet; *water~*, plant of same genus. [ME *avence* of OF (med. L *avencia* of unkn. orig.]

avĕn′tūrine, -in, n. Brownish glass with copper crystals, manufactured first at Murano near Venice; variety of quartz resembling this. [F, f. It. *avventurino* (*avventura* chance, from its accidental discovery)]

ăv′ĕnūe, n. Way of approach (usu. fig.); approach to country house bordered by trees; roadway marked by trees or other objects at regular intervals; (esp. in U.S.) wide street. [F, fem. p.p. (used as n.) of *avenir* f. L A*Dvenire* come to]

avĕr′, v.t. (-rr-). Assert, affirm; (Law) prove (a plea). Hence ~RABLE a. [ME, f. OF *averer* f. Rom. *A*Dverare* verify (*verus* true)]

ăv′erage¹, n. Generally prevailing rate, degree, or amount; ordinary standard; medial estimate, as *on the* or *an ~*; apportionment of loss of ship, cargo, or freight, through unavoidable accident (*particular ~*) or through intentional damage to ship or sacrifice of cargo (*general~*), among the owners or insurers; (Cricket) *batting ~,* aggregate number of runs made by batsman divided by the number of times he has been dismissed, *bowling ~,* cost of runs per wicket taken by bowler, calculated by dividing the number of runs scored off his bowling by the number of wickets he has taken. [Eng. *c.* 1500, corresp. to OF *avarie,* Cat., Sp. *averia,* Pg., It. *avaria,* Du. *avarij,* G *havarie;* ult. (thr. It.) f. Arab. *'awariya* damaged goods f. *'awār* damage; the Eng. form *-age* is by assoc. w. allied concepts, e.g. *damage, primage*]

ăv′erage², a. Estimated by average; of the usual standard. Hence ~LY² (-jl-) adv. [f. prec.]

ăv′erage³, v.t. Estimate the average of (by dividing the aggregate of several quantities by the number of quantities); estimate the general standard of; amount on an average to; *~* (work on an average) *six hours a day.* [as prec.]

avĕr′ment, n. Positive statement, affirmation; (Law) offer to prove, proof of, a plea. [ME, f. OF *averement* (as AVER)]

ăverrŭncāt′or (-ŭngk-), n. Instrument for cutting off branches of trees high above head. [f. obs. vb *averruncate,* f. L *averruncare* ward off (*a* off +*verruncare* turn), but wrongly explained as f. *eruncare* weed out]

avĕrse′, a. Opposed, disinclined, (*to, from*); unwilling (*to* do). Hence -NESS (-sn-) n. [f. L as AVERT]

avĕr′sion (-shn), n. Dislike, antipathy, (*to, from, for*); unwillingness (*to* do); ob-

ject of dislike, as *pet ~.* [F, or f. L *aversio* (as AVERT, see -ION)]

avĕrt′, v.t. Turn away (eyes, thoughts, *from*); ward off. Hence ~IBLE, ~ABLE, aa. [ME, f. L *avertere* (*a* AB- away +*vertere* vers- turn); partly f. OF *avertir* f. Rom. **avertire;* cf. ADVERT]

āv′ian, a. Pertaining to birds. [f. L *avis* bird +-AN]

āv′iarў, n. Place for keeping birds. [f. L *aviarium* (as prec., see -ARY¹)]

āv′iāte, v.i. Fly in or pilot an aircraft. [back form. f. foll.]

āviā′t|ion, n. Art or practice of operating a heavier-than-air aircraft. So ~OR n. [F, irreg. f. L *avis* bird, see -ATION]

āv′id, a. Eager, greedy (*of, for*). Hence ~LY² adv. [f. F *avide* or L *avidus* (*avēre* crave)]

avid′itў, n. Ardent desire, greed. [ME, f. OF *avidite* or L *aviditas* (as prec., see -TY)]

āv′ifauna, n. Birds (of district, country) collectively. [f. L *avis* bird +FAUNA]

avion (see Ap.), n. Aeroplane. [F]

avi′so (-ēzō), n. Boat for carrying dispatches. [Sp., f. L *advisum,* see ADVICE]

āvīzăn′dŭm, n. (Sc. Law). Private consideration. [med. L, gerund of *avizare* consider]

ăvocā′dō (-ah-), n. (pl. *~s*). (Also *~ pear*) pear-shaped tropical fruit, the ALLIGATOR pear. [Sp., =advocate (pop. rendering of Mex. *ahuacatl*)]

ăvocā′tion, n. Distraction; minor occupation; (loosely) vocation, calling. [f. L *avocatio* (*avocare* call away, see -ATION)]

ăv′ocĕt, -sĕt, n. Wading bird with upturned bill. [f. F *avocette* f. It. *avosetta*]

avoid′, v.t. Shun, refrain from (thing, doing); escape, evade; (Law) defeat (pleading), quash (sentence). Hence ~ABLE a. [f. AF *avoider* = OF *evuider* clear out, get quit of (*es* out +*vuidier* f. *vuit, vuide,* VOID)]

avoid′ance, n. Act of avoiding; vacancy (of office, benefice). [prec. +-ANCE]

avoirdupois (ăverdūpoiz′), a. & n. *~* (*weight*), system of weights used in English-speaking countries for all goods except precious metals & stones, & medicines; *~ pound* contains 7,000 grains; **weight,* heaviness. [ME *aver* (*avoir*) *de peis* (*pois*), f. AF, OF *aveir de pois* goods of weight (*aveir* f. L *habēre* + *peis, pois,* see POISE); sp. *-du-* from *c.* 1650]

avouch′, v.t. & i. Guarantee; affirm; confess. Hence ~MENT n. [ME, f. OF *avochier* f. L A*Dvocare* (in legal use) call upon as defender]

avow′, v.t. Admit, confess; (refl. & pass.) admit one*self* to be, as *~ed himself the author, the ~ed author.* Hence **avow′ABLE** a., **avow′AL** n., **avow′ĕdLY²** adv. [ME, f. OF *avouer* f. L *advocare;* see ADVOCATE]

avŭl′sion (-shn), n. Tearing away; (Law) sudden removal of land by flood etc. to another person's estate. [f. L avulsio (avellere -vuls- pluck away)]

avünc'ülar, a. Of, resembling, an uncle. [f. L avunculus maternal uncle (dim. of avus grandfather)+-AR¹]

await' (a-), v.t. Wait for; (of things) be in store for. [ME, f. ONF awaitier (à to+waitier, OF guaitier, see WAIT v.)]

awäke'¹ (a-), v.t. & i. (past awoke, p.p. awoke, ~d). Cease to sleep; (fig.) become active; ~ to, become conscious of; rouse from sleep (lit. & fig.). [(1) OE awæcnan, awōc, awacen, (a- prob. = on); of which present tense was early treated as weak vb, with past awæcnede, whence AWAKEN, awakened; (2) late OE awacian, awacode, in form a compd of wacian watch, but in sense = awæcnan; (3) in OE these were intr., the trans. sense being given, by awecc(e)an, ME awecche, Goth. uswakjan, G erwecken, ousted by awake, trans., before 1300; see WAKE¹]

awäke'² (a-), pred. a. Roused from sleep; not asleep; vigilant; ~ to, aware of. [short for awaken, orig. p.p. of prec.]

awäk'en (a-), v.t. & i. = AWAKE¹ (lit. & fig.) esp. (fig.) arouse (to a sense of). [see AWAKE¹ (1)]

award'¹ (awō̄rd'), v.t. Adjudge; grant, assign. [f. AF awarder f. ONF eswarder = OF esguarder, f. Rom. *EXwardare f. WG *ward-; see WARD, GUARD]

award'² (awō̄rd'), n. Judicial decision; payment, penalty, assigned by this. [AF, f. awarder; see prec.]

awäre' (a-), pred. a. Conscious, knowing, (of, that). Hence ~NESS (awār'n-) n., condition of being ~ (of something or that something is). [OE gewær (OS giwar, OHG gawar) f. ge- Y-, +wær WARE²]

awash' (-wō̆-), pred. a. Flush with or washed by the waves. [A- (2)]

away' (a-), adv. To, at, a distance from the place, person, thing, in question (lit. & fig.), as go ~, throw ~, give ~, he is ~, waste ~, fool ~, explain ~; out & ~, beyond comparison; constantly, continuously, as work ~, peg ~; without delay, as fire ~; = go away (imper.); ~ with (imper.), go ~ with, take ~; get ~ with it (colloq.), do something with impunity; make ~ with, destroy; quasi-adj. in ~ game, match, win. [OE onweg, later aweg on (the, his, one's) way; f. A² prep.+WAY]

awe¹, n. Reverential fear or wonder, as stand in ~ of, hold, keep, in ~; ~'struck, struck with ~. Hence ~'LESS (awl-), ~'SOME (aws-), aa. [ME age f. ON agi wh. replaced OE, ME ege, both f. Gmc *ag-; cf. Goth. agis fear]

awe², v.t. Inspire with awe. [f. prec.]

awe³, n. One of the float-boards of an undershot water-wheel. [orig. unkn.]

aweigh (awā'), adv. (Of anchor) just lifted from ground in weighing. [A² prep.+WEIGH]

awf'ul, a. Inspiring awe; worthy of profound respect; solemnly impressive;

(arch.) reverential; (sl.) notable in its kind, as ~ scrawl, bore, relief, something ~. Hence ~LY² adv., (also, sl.) extremely, ~NESS n. [AWE¹+-FUL]

awhile (awil'), adv. For a short time. [OE āne hwile a while]

awk'ward, a. Ill-adapted for use; clumsy (person, thing); bungling; embarrassing; difficult, dangerous, to deal with. Hence ~ISH¹ (2) a., ~LY² adv., ~NESS n. [f. obs. adj. awk backhanded, untoward (ME, f. ON afug turned the wrong way)+-WARD]

awl, n. Small tool for pricking, pricker, esp. that used by shoemakers. [OE æl, OHG ala, ON alr]

awn, n. Spinous process, beard, terminating grain-sheath of barley, oats, etc. Hence ~ed¹ (-nd) [-ED²], ~'LESS, aa. [ME, f. ON ögn pl. agnar, OHG agana, Goth. ahana]

awn'ing, n. Canvas roof, esp. above deck of vessel; (Naut.) poop-deck beyond bulkhead of cabin; shelter. Hence **awned²** (-nd) [-ED²] a. [orig. unkn.]

awry (ari'), adv. & a. Crookedly, askew; look ~, look askance (lit. & fig.); amiss, improperly; go, run, tread, ~, do wrong; (adj., usu. pred.) crooked (lit. & fig.). [A prep.+WRY]

äxe, äx, n., & v.t. Chopping-tool, usually iron with steel edge & wooden handle; put the ~ in the helve, solve a puzzle; (orig. U.S. pol.) an ~ to grind, private ends to serve; (vb) cut down (costs, services). [OE æx, OS akus, OHG ackus, ON öx, Goth. aqizi; cf. Gk axinē]

äx'ial, a. Forming, belonging to, an axis; round an axis. Hence **äxiäl'**ITY n., ~LY² adv. [f. AXIS+-AL]

äx'il, n. Upper angle between leaf & stem it springs from, or between branch & trunk. [f. L axilla armpit]

äx'īle, a. (bot., physiol.). Belonging to the axis. [f. AXIS, see -IL]

äx'illarÿ, a. Pertaining to the armpit; (Bot.) in, growing from, the axil. [f. F axillaire (see AXIL, -ARY)]

äx'iom, n. Established principle; (rare) maxim; self-evident truth (esp. in geom.). [f. F axiome or L f. Gk axiōma (axioō hold worthy f. axios, see -M)]

äxiomät'ic(al), aa. Self-evident; characterized by axioms; (rare) full of maxims, aphoristic. Hence **äxiomät'ical**LY² adv. [f: Gk axiōmatikos (axiōma -matos), see prec. & -IC, -AL]

äx'is, n. (pl. axēs). **1.** Imaginary line about which a body rotates, or by revolution about which a plane is conceived as generating a solid (sphere, cone, cylinder); line dividing regular figure symmetrically. **2.** Straight line from end to end of a body, as ~ of equator (polar diameter of earth). **3.** (bot.). Central column of inflorescence or other whorl of growth. **4.** (opt.). Ray passing through centre of eye or lens, or falling perpendicularly on it. **5.** (physiol.). Central core of organ or organism. **6.** (pol.). Agreement between two or more countries intended to form a centre round which like-minded nations may rally; *the Axis* (hist., orig. *the Rome--Berlin Axis*), (pact between) Germany & Italy, later extended to include Japan (*Rome–Berlin–Tokyo Axis*); attrib., as *Axis intrigues, powers, propaganda*. [L, = axle, pivot]

ä′xle, n. Spindle upon or with which wheel revolves; (in carriages, prop.) slender end of ~-*tree* (whole bar connecting wheels), (loosely) ~-tree; *wheel & ~*, a MECHANICAL power; ~-*box* (in which ends of ~s revolve); ~-*journal*, polished end of ~ revolving under bearing in ~-box. Hence **ä′xl**ED[2] (-ld) a. [earliest in ME *axel-tre* f. ON *öxul-tré*, replacing the native ME *ax-tre* f. OE *æx, eax*]

Ax′minster (ă-), a. ~ *carpet*, kind formerly hand-woven at ~, now made at Wilton.

äx′olötl, n. Newt-like amphibian found in Mexican lakes. [Aztec]

äx′ŏn, n. (zool.). Appendage of the nerve cell which carries signals from the cell. [f. Gk *axōn* axle]

ay (ī), int. & n. (pl. *ayes*). Yes; (n.) affirmative answer; *the ayes have it*, affirmative voters are in majority. [appears suddenly *c.* 1575; orig. unkn.]

ayah (i′a), n. Native Indian nurse or lady's maid. [Ind. vernacular *āya* f. Port. *aia* nurse, fem. of *aio* tutor]

aye (ā), adv. Ever, always; on all occasions; *for ~*, for ever. [ME *agg, ai, ei,* f. ON *ei, ey,* cogn. w. Goth. *aiw* f. Gmc *aiwaz*, cogn. w. L *aevum* age; cf. Gk *aei* always]

aye-aye (i′i), n. Squirrel-like animal of the size of a cat, found only in Madagascar. [F, f. Malagasy *aiay*]

Azäl′ëa, n. Genus of flowering shrubby plants, natives of northern*hemisphere. [mod. L, f. Gk *azalea* fem. of *azaleos* dry (from its dry wood or the dry soil in which it flourishes)]

Azil′ian, a. Of the transitional period between the palaeolithic & neolithic ages. [f. *Mas d'Azil* in French Pyrenees, where remains were found]

äz′imuth, n. Arc of the heavens extending from the zenith to the horizon, which it cuts at right angles; ~-*circle*, one of which this is a quadrant, passing through zenith & nadir; *true ~* of a heavenly body, arc of horizon intercepted between north (in Southern hemisphere, south) point of horizon & the point where the great circle passing through the body cuts the horizon; *magnetic ~*, arc intercepted between this circle & magnetic meridian. Hence **äzimüth′**AL a., **äzimüth′**ALLY[2] adv. [ME, f OF *azimut* f. Arab. *assumut* (*al* the +*sumut* pl. of *samt* way, direction)]

azŏ′ïc, a. Having no trace of life; (Geol.) containing no organic remains. [irreg. f. Gk *azōos* (*a*- not +*zōē* life) + -IC]

äz′öte, n. Former name of nitrogen. Hence **azŏt′**IC a., **äz′ot**IZE (3) v.t. [F, f. Gk *a*- not +*zōō* (for *zaō*) live, from its inability to support life]

Az′těc (ă-), a. & n. (One) of the Aztecs, the Mexican people dominant till the conquest of Cortes (1519).

ä′zure (-zher, -zhyer), n. & a., & v.t. **1.** Sky blue; (Her.) blue; unclouded vault of heaven; bright blue pigment; lapis lazuli. **2.** adj. Sky-blue, (fig.) cloudless, serene. **3.** v.t. Make ~. [ME, f. OF *azur* f. med. L *azura* f. Arab. *al* the +*lazward* f. Pers. *lazhvard* lapis lazuli]

äz′ÿgous (a. & n. (physiol.). (An organic part) not existing in pairs. [f. Gk *azugos* unyoked (*a*- not +*zugon* yoke) + -OUS]

B

B (bē), letter (pl. *Bs*, B's, Bees). (Mus.) seventh note in scale of C major (*B flat*, jocular euphem. for bug). (In argument) second hypothetical person or thing. (Alg.) second known quantity.

baa (bah), n., & v.i. (*baaing, baaed* or *baa'd*). = BLEAT. ~-*lamb*, nursery name for lamb. [imit.]

Bā′al, n. (pl. ~*im*). Phoenician god; (transf.) a false god. Hence ~ISM (3), ~IST (2), ~ITE (1), nn. [M̧E, f. Heb. *ba'al* lord]

baas (bahs), n. (S. Africa). Master (freq. as form of address). [Du., see BOSS[2]]

ba′bacōōte (bah-), n. Species of lemur (Madagascar). [Malagasy *babakoto*]

Băbb′itt-mět′al, n. Soft alloy of tin, antimony, & copper. [*I. Babbitt* inventor (d. 1862)]

băb′ble[1], v.i. & t. Talk half articulately, incoherently, or excessively; murmur (of streams etc.); repeat foolishly; let out (secrets). Hence ~MENT (-lm-) n. [imit. of infant's *ba, ba,* +-LE (3); cf. F *babiller*, MLG *babbelen*, G *pappeln*]

băb′ble[2], n. Imperfect speech; idle talk; murmur of water etc. [prec.]

băb′bler, n. Chatterer; teller of secrets; long-legged thrush. [-ER[1]]

bābe, n. (poet.). Young child, baby; inexperienced or guileless person (in pl. often ~*s & sucklings*). [ME, imit. of child's speech, cf. BABBLE]

băb′el, n. (*B~*) the tower in Shinar (*Gen.* xi); a high structure; visionary plan; scene of confusion, confusion of tongues, noisy assembly, meaningless noise. [ME, perh. f. Ass. *bab-ilu* gate of God]

băbirous′sa, -rus′sa, (-rōō-), n. E.--Asian wild hog with upturned horn-like tusks. [Malay *babi* hog +*rusa* deer]

Bab′ism (bah-), n. Doctrine of a Persian mystical & pantheistic sect (*Babi*) founded in 1844. [f. Pers. *Bab*-ed-Din, gate (= intermediary) of the Faith, whence the founder's usual title of (the) Bab]

baboon', n. Large African & S.-Asian monkey. [ME, f. OF babuin or med. L babewynus, f. unkn. orig.]

babouche' (-ōōsh), n. Oriental slipper. [F, f. Arab babush f. Pers. paposh (pa foot + posh covering); for p = b cf. pasha & bashaw]

ba'bu (bah'bōō), -bōō, n. (As Hindu title) Mr; Hindu (esp. Bengali) gentleman; Indian English-writing clerk, hence derog., ~ English. [Hind. babu]

babul' (-ōōl), n. Gum-arabic tree of India and Arabia. · [Hind. & Pers.]

bãb'ȳ, n. Very young child; childish person, whence ~ISH[1] a., ~ishNESS, ~ISM (2), nn.; thing small of its kind; *girl, sweetheart, (sl.); ~ car, motor-car of small size and power; *~ carriage, perambulator; ~-farmer, one who contracts to keep babies; ~ grand, small grand piano; ‖~-jumper, hanging frame in which child is fastened to exercise limbs; ~-sitter, person sitting with or looking after a ~ while its parents are out; hold the ~, carry the ~, (be left to) assume an undesired responsibility. Hence ~HOOD n. [ME, BABE, -Y[3]]

Bãb'ȳlon, n. Capital of Chaldean empire; any great empire or vicious city; Rome, the papacy (ref. to Rev. xvii etc.), London, etc. Hence **Bãbȳlõn'IAN** a. & n. [L, f. Gk Babvlõn f. Heb. Babel BABEL]

bãccalaur'êate, n. University degree of bachelor. [f. med. L baccalaureatus f. baccalareus BACHELOR; see -ATE[1]]

bãcc'ara(t) (-rah), n. Gambling card game. [F]

bãcc'ãte, a. (bot.). Bearing berries, berry-shaped. [f. mod. L baccatus berried (bacca berry, -ATE[2])]

Bãcc'hanal (-ka-), a. & n. **1.** Of, like, Bacchus or his rites; riotous, roistering. **2.** n. Priest, priestess, votary, of Bacchus; drunken reveller; dance or song in honour of Bacchus. [f. L bacchanalis (L f. Gk Bakkhos god of wine, -AL)]

Bãcchanãl'ia (-ka-), n. pl. Festival of Bacchus; drunken revelry. [L neut. pl. of bacchanalis = prec.]

Bãcchanãl'ian (-ka-), a. & n. Of Bacchanals; riotous, drunken; (n.) a Bacchanal, tippler. [f. L bacchanalis BACCHANAL + -AN]

Bãcc'hant (-ka-), n. masc. or fem., & a.; **Bacchante** (bãk'ant, bakãnt', bakãn'ti), n. fem. Priest, priestess, votary of Bacchus; Bacchus-worshipping, wine-loving. Hence **Bãcchãn'tic** (-kã-) a. [(-nte F) f. L bacchari (-ANT) f. Gk bakkhaō celebrate Bacchic rites]

Bãcc'hic (-kik), a. = BACCHANAL (adj. meanings). [f. L f. Gk bakkhikos of Bacchus]

Bãcc'hus (-kus), n. Greek god of wine. [L, f. Gk Bakkhos]

bãccif'erous, bãcc'ifõrm, bãcciv'orous, (bãks-), aa. Berry-bearing, -shaped, -eating. [L baccifer (-FEROUS); L bacca berry + -FORM, -VOROUS]

‖bãcc'ȳ (-k-), n. (colloq.) Tobacco. [abbr.]

bãch'elor, n. Young knight serving under another's banner (hist.); hence now, knight ~, simple knight not belonging to a special order; man or woman who has taken a university degree below Master; unmarried man. ~'s buttons, various button-shaped flowers esp. double buttercup, also small ratafia biscuits, also buttons attachable without sewing; ~ girl (unmarried and living independently); ~ (seal), young male fur-seal with no mate. Hence ~HOOD, ~SHIP, ~ISM(4), nn. [ME bacheler f. OF f. Rom. *baccalãris of unascert. orig. In the academic sense this was allied to baccalarius, & further (prob. by a word-play on bacca lauri laurel berry) to baccalaureus]

bacill'arȳ, a. Of little rods (tissue, membrane); connected with bacilli (disease, research). [BACILLUS + -ARY[1]]

bacill'ifõrm, a. Rod-shaped. [foll. + -FORM]

bacill'us, n. (pl. -lī). A rodlike bacterium, esp. one of the various types that cause disease by entering and multiplying in animal and other tissues. [LL dim. of L baculus stick]

bãck[1], n. & a. **1.** Hinder surface of human body (at the ~ of, behind in support, pursuit, or concealment; BEHIND one's ~; give, make, a ~, bend down at leapfrog; turn one's ~ upon, run away from, abandon; on one's ~, laid up; with one's ~ to wall, hard pressed); body as needing clothes (~ & belly, clothing & food) or as weight-carrier (~ equal to burden; have on one's ~, be burdened with; put, get, set, person's ~ up, make him angry; break one's ~, overburden him, & see BREAK[1] ~ of); surface of things corresponding to human ~ (less visible, active, or important; ~ of hand, leg, door, book, knife), side away from spectator; upper surface of animal's body, surface corresponding to this (ridge-shaped, etc.; ~ of hill, ship esp. in broke her ~; on the ~ of, in addition to); football player stationed behind (full, three-quarter, half, ~); the Backs, grounds on the Cam at the ~ of certain Colleges at Cambridge, of noted beauty; ~'band, over cart-saddle to keep shafts up; ~'board, as of cart, also strapped across child's ~ to straighten it; ~'bone, spine (whence ~bõnED[2] (-nd) a.; to the ~bone, thoroughly), main support, axis, watershed, chief strength, firmness of character; ~'fall, throw on ~ in wrestling; ~'sword, with only one edge, also singlestick. **2.** adj. (no comp., superl. ~'most). Situated behind, remote, inferior, (take ~ seat, humble oneself); overdue (~ rent); reversed, counter, (~ current); ‖~-bench(er), (occupant of) a seat in the House of Commons or similar assembly used by a member not entitled to a front-bench seat (~-*bench* freq. used attrib.); ||~-*blocks*, (Austral.) land in the remote & sparsely-inhabited interior; ~-*chat* (colloq.), retort(s), recrimination; ~-*cloth*, (Theatr.) painted cloth at ~ of stage as main part of scenery; ~'*door*, lit., & fig. secret means or approach, (adj.) clandestine, underhand; ~-*drop*, ~-*cloth*; ||~-*end*, late autumn; ~-*fire*, premature explosion in the cylinder of an internal-combustion engine (also as vb); ~ *formation*, making from a supposed derivative (as *lazy*, *banting*) of the non-existent word (*laze*, *bant*) from which it might have come; ~'*ground*, part of scene, picture, or description, that serves as setting to chief figures or objects & foreground, obscurity, retirement, (fig.) person's cultural knowledge, education, experience, etc.; ~'*hand(ed)*, delivered with ~ of hand or in direction counter to the usual, indirect, unexpected, (~'*hander*, such blow, indirect attack, extra glass got by bottle's travelling wrong way); ~'*log*, reserves, arrears of unfulfilled orders; ~-*marker*, scratch man in race etc.; ~ *number* (of magazine etc.), (sl.) out-of-date method or person; ~ *play* (Cricket), see BACK³; ~-*room boys* (colloq.), men engaged in (secret) research; ~-*seat driver*, one who attempts to control without responsibility; ~'*set*, counter-current, check, reverse; ~'*side*, posterior, rump; ~-*sight*, that nearer stock of rifle etc., (Surv.) sight taken backwards; ~ *slang*, form of low slang in which words are spelt & pronounced backwards (e.g. *ynnep* for *penny*); ~'*stage* adj. & adv., behind the curtain in a theatre (freq. in the wings or dressing-rooms), (fig.) behind the scenes; ~'*stairs* n. & a., ~'*stair* a., as ~'*door* above; ~'*stays*, ropes slanting abaft from mast-head to a lower point; ~'*stroke*, return or backhand stroke; ~'*wash*, motion of receding wave (lit. & fig.); ~'*water*, water dammed back, currentless water beside stream & fed by its backflow, stagnant condition of things, creek communicating with sea by barred outlets, water cast from ship's paddles, loss of power caused by this; ~'*woods* n. & a., ~'*wood* a., (connected with) remote uncleared forest land (so ~'*woodsman*); ~'*woodsman*, ||(also, fig.) peer who rarely or never attends House of Lords. [a. f. n., OE *bæc*, OS, ON *bak*, f. Gmc *bakam*; now almost confined to E; cf. BACON]

băck², v.t. & i. Put, or be, a back, lining, support, or background, to; assist with countenance, money, or argument, bet upon, whence ~'ER¹ n.; (of sporting dogs) follow suit to one that points; ~ *up*, help by subordinate action, esp. in cricket; ride upon, break in to the saddle; countersign, endorse; cause to move back (horse, boat, engine, etc.; ~ *a sail*,

yard, lay it aback, i.e. to face wind; ~ *water*, reverse boat's forward motion with oars); go backwards; (of wind) change counter-sunwise (cf. VEER); ~ *out (of)*, withdraw (from undertaking etc.); ~ *down*, abandon claim. [f. prec.]

băck³, adv. To the rear (often with omission of vb, esp. in imperative), away from what is considered the front (*push the bolt* ~); *play* ~ (Cricket), step ~ to play a defensive stroke; away from a promise (*go* ~ *from* or *upon* one's *word*); into the past, into or in an earlier position or condition, home; in return (*answer* ~ = retort; *pay* ~); at a distance (~ *from the road*); in a checked condition (*keep* ~); = ago; reckoning backwards (*for years* ~); behindhand; ~ *& forth* = to & fro; *~ of*, = behind; ~'*bite*, slander, speak ill of, whence ~'bitER¹ n.; ~'*lash(ing)*, irregular recoil of wheels in machinery due to defects or sudden pressure; ~'*pedal*, work pedal backwards, (fig.) check a forward movement, reverse one's action; ~*slide'* v.i., relapse into sin, whence ~slid'ER¹, ~slid'ING¹, n.; ~'*stitch* n. & v.t. & i., sew(ing) with overlapping stitches. [aphetic f. ABACK]

băck⁴, n. Shallow vat used in brewing, dyeing, etc. [f. Du. *bak* tub, = LG *back*; cf. also F *bac* tub, ferry-boat, punt, med. L *bac(c)us* ferry-boat, LL *bacca* tub, of uncert. relationships]

băckgămm'on, n. Game played on special double board with draughts & dice; most complete form of win in this. [BACK³ (because pieces go back or re-enter), GAME¹]

băck'ing, n. In vbl senses: esp.: body of supporters; material used to form thing's back or support. [BACK², -ING¹]

backsheesh. See BAKSHEESH.

băck'ward(s), adv., **băck'ward**, a. 1. Away from one's front (*look*, *lean*, etc.); back foremost (*walk* etc.); back to starting-point (*flow*, *roll*, etc.; not of living things exc. in ~ & *forwards*); into a worse state (*go* etc.); into the past (*reckon* etc.); the reverse way (*spell* etc.; *ring the bells* ~, from bass upwards). 2. adj. Directed to rear or starting-point; reversed; reluctant, shy, behindhand, dull, whence **băck'ward**NESS n. [aphetic f. *abackward*, later referred to BACK¹; see -WARD, -WARDS]

||**băckwardā'tion**, n. (St. Exch.). Percentage paid by seller of stock for right of delaying delivery (cf. CONTANGO). [f. prec. used as vb +-ATION]

bāc'on, n. Cured back & sides of pig (*save* one's ~, escape death or injury); *bring home the* ~ (sl.), succeed in one's undertaking. [ME, f. OF f. Frank. *bako* = OHG *bahho*, *bacho*, buttock, ham, flitch, f. Gmc *bakon-*; cf. BACK¹]

Bacōn'ian, a. & n. Of Francis Bacon or his philosophy, experimental, inductive; (n.) follower of Bacon; believer in ~

authorship of Shakespeare's plays. [*Bacon* (d. 1626)+-IAN]

băctēri|ŏl′y̆sis, n. Artificial liquefaction of solid sewage by bacterial agency; destruction of bacteria by a serum. So **~oly̆t′ic** a., capable of destroying bacteria. [f. BACTERIUM+Gk *lusis* dissolution]

băctēr′iophage (-fahzh, -fāj), n. Minute organism which destroys bacteria. [f. foll. +Gk *phagein* eat]

băctēr′|ium, n. (pl. *-ria*). Kinds of microscopic unicellular organism found almost everywhere, some of which cause disease. Hence ~IAL a., ~ĭŏL′OGY, ~ĭŏL′OGIST, nn. [mod. L, f. Gk *baktērion* dim. of *baktron* stick]

băc′ūline, a. Of the stick or flogging (esp. ~ *argument*). [f. L *baculum* stick +-INE[1]]

băd, a. (worse, worst), & n. **1.** (Negatively) worthless, inferior, deficient, of poor quality, incorrect, not valid, (~ *air*, corrupt; ~ *coin*, debased; ~ *debt*, not recoverable; ~ *food*, not nourishing; *•~ lands*, extensive barren uncultivable tracts; *go* ~, decay; *with* ~ *grace*, reluctantly; ~ *shot*, wrong guess; ~ *law*, not sustainable; ~ *form*, want of breeding; *in a* ~ *sense*, unfavourable); ~ *egg*, ~ *hat*, (sl.) person of ~ character. **2.** (Positively) noxious, depraved, vicious, offensive, painful (~ *blood*, ill feeling; ~ *for*, injurious to); in ill health, injured, in pain, (*she is* ~, *worse*, *today*; *a* ~ *leg*); (colloq. of things in no case good) notable, decided, pronounced, (~ *blunder*, *headache*, *falling-off*). **3.** n. Ill fortune (*take the* ~ *with the good*), wrong side of account (*£500 to the* ~), ruin (*go to the* ~). Hence **bădd′ISH**[1] (2) a. [ME *badde*, perh. f. OE *bæddel* hermaphrodite, womanish man; for loss of *l* cf. *mycel* MUCH]

bade. See BID[1].

bădge, n. Distinctive mark, formerly of knight, now worn as sign of office or licensed employment or membership of a society; symbol, something that betrays a quality or condition. [ME *bage*, cf. rare OF *bage*; orig. unkn.]

bădg′er[1], n. (dial.). Hawker, esp. of provisions. [orig. unkn.; cf. obs. vb *badge* to hawk]

bădg′er[2], n. Grey-coated strong-jawed nocturnal hibernating plantigrade quadruped between weasels & bears; fishing--fly, & painting or other brush, made of its hair; ~*-bailing*, *-drawing*, setting dogs to draw it from its burrow or a cask; ~--*legged*, with legs of unequal length (popular error). [16th c. (older *brock*, *bauson*, *gray*) perh. f. BADGE+-ARD (earlier forms *bageard*, *badgerd*) with ref. to its white forehead mark]

bădg′er[3], v.t. Bait like a badger, worry, tease. [f. prec.]

băd′ĭnage (-ahzh), n. Light raillery. [F]

băd′ly̆, adv. (worse, worst). Defectively, unsuccessfully, faultily, wickedly, cruelly,

dangerously, by much (*beaten*), very much (*want a thing* ~). [-LY[2]]

badmash (bŭd′mahsh), bŭd′, n. (Anglo--Ind.). Rascal, bad character. [Pers. & Urdu]

băd′minton, n. A summer drink (claret, soda, sugar); game with net, rackets, & shuttlecocks. [Duke of Beaufort's seat]

băd′nĕss, n. Poor quality or condition; faultiness, invalidity; wickedness, noxiousness, adverseness. [-NESS]

Baed′ēker (bād-), n. Guide-book published by firm founded by Karl *Baedeker*; ~ *raids*, German reprisal air-raids in 1942 on (cathedral) cities in England starred in ~.

bā′el, n. Indian tree, the orange-like fruit of which is a specific for diarrhoea etc. [f. Hind. *bel*]

băf′fle, v.t., & n. Foil, reduce to perplexity, bar progress of, (person, curiosity, faculties, efforts, ship); *baffling winds*, variable, preventing a straight course; (n.) ~ or ~*-plate*, plate hindering or regulating passage of fluid or gas through outlet or inlet (e.g. a damper); ~*-board*, *wall*, devices to prevent spread of noise. Hence ~**r** n., ~*-plate*. [hist. complex & uncert.; perh. f. obs. F *beffler*, mod. *bafouer* hoodwink etc.; also in obs. sense 'disgrace', cf. Sc. *bauchle*]

băff′y̆, n. Wooden golf club for lofting. [cf. Sc. *baff* a blow]

băg[1], n. Receptacle of flexible material with opening at top (‖*green* or *blue* ~, barrister's for briefs; hyphened with nouns showing contents or purpose etc., as *mail-*~, *travelling-*~, *hand-*~, VANITY ~; also alone for such compp., e.g. for money- ~, so ~*s* = wealth, or for game-~, also for game-~'s contents or all a sportsman has shot or caught; ~ *of bones*, lean creature; *whole* ~ *of tricks*, every device, everything, all the lot; *in bottom of* ~, as last resource; *in the* ~ (colloq.), in one's possession or power, (as good as) secured; *let cat out of* ~, reveal secret, esp. involuntarily; ~ *& baggage*, with all belongings, esp. of utter expulsion), whence ~**g′ING**[1] (3) n.; cow's udder; sac in body containing honey, poison, etc.; baggy place under eyes etc.; ‖(sl.) ~*s*, trousers; ~ *fox*, one brought, not found; ‖~*'man*, commercial traveller, also = ~ fox; ~*'pipe(s)*, reed-pipe wind instrument with bag as receptacle for air, melody pipe (chanter), & fixed-note pipes (drones), used in Scotland &, with variations, in Ireland & N. England; ~*-sleeve*, loose except at wrist; ~*-wig*, 18th-c. wig with back hair enclosed in ~. Hence ~*'FUL* (2) n. [ME *bagge*; cf. ON *baggi*, also OF *bague*, Pr. *bagua* baggage, med. L *baga* sack. The Engl. was possibly f. ON, but the source of this, & its relation to the Romanic, are unkn.]

băg[2], v.i. & t. (-gg-). Swell, bulge: ‖(Naut.) drop away from course; hang loosely;

put in a bag, secure (game, whether lit. bagged or not), take possession of, (euphem.) steal; ||(school sl.) claim on the ground of being first to claim (*I* ~, but usu. ~*s I* or ~*s, first innings!*). [prec.]

băg[3], v.t. (-gg-). Cut (wheat etc.) with a hook. [also *badge*; orig. unkn.]

bagâsse', n. Residue after extracting juice from sugar-cane & sugar-beet. [F]

băgatêlle', n. Trifle, negligible amount; short unpretentious piece of music; minor game of billiard kind. [F, f. It..*bagatella* dim. perh. f. *baga* BAGGAGE]

băgg'age, n. Belongings with which one travels (now ousted exc. in U.S. by *luggage*; *~ car*, luggage van; *~ room*, cloak-room; *~ tag*, luggage label); portable equipment of army; good-for-nothing woman (now only used playfully), saucy girl. [ME, f. OF *bagage* f. *baguer* tie up or *bagues* bundles pl. of *bague*=It. & med. L *baga* sack, chest, see BAG[1]]

băgg'|y̆ (-g-), a. Puffed out, hanging in loose folds. Hence ~**iNESS** n. [BAG[1] + -Y[2]]

bagnio (băn'yō), n. Bathing-house (now only in Italy & Turkey); oriental prison; brothel. [f. It. *bagno* f. L *balneum* bath]

băguette' (-gĕt), n. (Archit.) small moulding of semicircular section, like an astragal; gem cut in a long rectangular shape. [F]

bah, int. of contempt. [F]

Bahadur (bahahd'er), n. Title of respect appended in India to a person's name (& other titles). [Hind., = gallant]

baignoire (bēnwahr'), n. Box at theatre on level of stalls. [F, = bath]

bail[1], n. Security for prisoner's appearance, on giving which he is released pending trial (*forfeit* one's ~, fail to appear; *save* one's ~, appear); (joc.) *give leg* ~, run away; person(s) who become(s) surety for prisoner's appearance (*be, become, go,* ~; *go* ~ *for*, guarantee truth of anything; magistrate *accepts, admits to, allows, holds to, takes,* ~; prisoner *gives, offers, surrenders to his,* ~; his ~ *surrender, render, bring in, produce,* him). [ME, f. OF *bail* custody f. *baillier* take charge of f. L *bajulare* bear a burden (*bajulus* porter)]

bail[2], v.t. **1.** Deliver (goods) in trust. **2.** Admit to bail, release on security given for appearance, (of magistrate; arch.); secure liberation of, by becoming bail or security for (~ *out* if already in prison). [sense 1 f. F *bailler* deliver; sense 2 f. BAIL[1]]

bail[3], n. **1.** (hist.). Outer line of fortification formed of stakes; wall of castle court, or court itself (cf. BAILEY). **2.** (mod.). Bar separating horses in open stable; *swinging* ~, slung from manger to ceiling; (Cricket) one of the cross pieces (orig. one not two) over stumps. [ME, f. OF *bail, bail(l)e* perh. f. *bailler* enclose f. unkn. orig.]

bail[4], n. Half-hoop for supporting wagon-tilt etc.; hoop-handle of kettle etc.; ||(Australia) frame holding cow's head at milking. [ME *beyl* f. ON *beygla* sword-guard etc. (*beygya* = OE *bēgan* to bend)]

bail[5], v.t. Confine (arch.); || (Australia) ~ *up*, secure (cow; see prec.); (of bush-rangers) make hold up the arms to rob, (intr. of victim) throw up the arms. [app. f. OF *bailler* enclose, cf. BAIL[3]]

bail[6], **bāle**, v.t. & i. Throw water out of boat with pails etc. (~ *water out,* ~ *out boat,* or abs.); *bale out,* (of airman) make parachute descent esp. from damaged aircraft. Hence **bail'er**[1] [-ER[1] (2)] n. [f. obs. n. *bail* bucket f. F *baille* f. Rom. *bajula* fem. of L *bajulus* BAIL[1]]

bail'able, a. Admitting of bail (offence). [BAIL[1, 2] + -ABLE]

bailee', n. One to whom goods are entrusted for a purpose. [BAIL[2] + -EE]

bail'er[2], n. Ball that hits bails at cricket. [BAIL[3] + -ER[1]]

bail'ey, n. Outer wall of castle; also any of its inner defensive circuits, or any of the courts enclosed between these; *Old B*~, London Central Criminal Court, standing in ancient ~ of city wall. [ME variant of BAIL[3]]

Bail'ey bridge, n. Emergency bridge designed for rapid construction. [Sir D. *Bailey* (b. 1901), designer]

||**bail'ie** (-li), n. Scottish municipal magistrate = Eng. alderman. [ME *bailli* f. OF *baillis* BAILIFF]

bail'iff, n. (Orig.) King's representative in a district (including mayor, sheriff, etc.), esp. chief officer of a hundred (still in *High-B*~ *of Westminster, B*~ *of Dover Castle,* etc.; used as Eng. equivalent of F *bailli,* G *landvogt,* Channel-I. *bailly* or first civil officer); officer under sheriff for writs, processes, arrests; agent of lord of manor; landholder's steward. [ME, f. OF *baillif* obj. case of *baillis* f. *baillir* administer f. *bail* BAIL[1]]

bail'iwick, n. District, jurisdiction, of bailie or bailiff; (joc.) person's sphere of operations. [BAILIE + WICK[2]]

bail'ment, n. Delivery of goods in trust; bailing of prisoner. [OF *baillement* see BAIL[2] & -MENT]

bail'or, n. One who delivers goods to another for a stated purpose. [BAIL[2] + -OR]

bails'man (-z-), n. One who gives bail for another. [f. *bail's* (BAIL[1]) + MAN]

bain-marie (băn'marē'), n. Vessel of hot water in which stewpans are stood to warm. [F, transl. med. L *balneum Mariae,* whence earlier (15th c.) *balne, balneum*]

Bairam (bīrahm'), n. Mohammedan festival (twice a year, Lesser & Greater). [Turk. & Pers.]

bairn, n. Child (Sc. & N.-Eng. form now borrowed in literary Eng., the E *berne* having perished, & *barne* become dialectal). [OE *bearn,* Gmc **barn-* f. *beran* BEAR[3]]

bait[1], v.t. & i. (Orig.) cause to bite. **1.** Worry (chained animal) by setting dogs at it (*with* dogs, or abs.; also of the dogs), whence (*bear, bull*, etc.) **-baiting**[1] n.; torment (helpless person) with jeers etc. **2.** Give food to, take food, (of horses on journey); stop at inn (orig. to feed horses, then also for rest or refreshment). **3.** Put food (real or sham) on or in (hook, trap, fishing-place). [ME *beylen* f. ON *beita* causal of *bíta* BITE[1]; w. sense 1 cf. OF *beter* (f. ON); sense 3 prob. f. foll.]

bait[2], n. Food to entice prey (*live* ~, small fish so used); (fig.) an allurement, temptation; halt in journey for refreshment or rest. [partly f. ON *beita* food, partly f. prec.]

bait[3]. See BATE[3].

baize, n. Coarse woollen stuff with long nap used for coverings. [f. F *baies* pl. fem. of *bai* chestnut-coloured, BAY[6], treated as sing.; cf. BODICE]

bake, v.t. & i. Cook by dry heat in closed place or on hot surface (not by direct exposure to fire), whence **bak'ing**[1] (5) n.; harden by heat; *half*-~*d*, immature, half-witted; (of sun) ripen (fruit), tan (skin); (intr.) undergo the process, be cooked, hardened, tanned, by heat; ‖~' *house*, house or room for baking bread, or for making loaf-sugar; ~'*stone*, flat stone, slate, or iron plate, on which cakes are baked in oven; *baking-powder*, substitute for yeast. [OE *bacan*, OHG *bachan*, ON *baka*, f. Gmc **bak-*]

bak'elite, n. Widely-used synthetic resin or plastic made from formaldehyde & phenol. [G *bakelit*; f. L. H. *Baekeland* inventor (d. 1944); P]

bak'er, n. Professional breadmaker (*pull devil, pull* ~, encouragement to both sides; ~'*s dozen*, thirteen, 13th loaf being huckster's profit; ~'*legged*, knock-kneed); (Fishing) kind of artificial fly. Hence ~**ess**[1], **bak'ery** (3), nn. [OE *bæcere* (*bacan* BAKE +-ER[1])]

bak'sheesh, bakh'shish (-ēsh), n. Gratuity, tip, (article not used). [Pers., f. *bakhshidan* give]

Bāl'aam (-lăm). n. Di-appointing prophet or ally: ‖(Journalism) matter kept in stock to fill up gaps in newspaper (*Numb.* xxii. 28 or 38: ~-*box*, receptacle for this).

Bālaclav'a (-ahva), n. Site of Crimean battle; ‖~ *helmet*, woollen covering for head & shoulders worn esp. by soldiers etc. on active service.

balalaik'a (-lika), n. Triangular guitar-like musical instrument, popular in Slav countries. [Russ.]

bǎl'ance[1], n. **1.** Weighing-apparatus with central pivot, beam, & two scales; spring or lever substitute for this; regulating gear of clock or watch; zodiac constellation (usu. *Libra* or *The Scales*), & (not now corresponding) seventh sign of zodiac. **2.** The weighing of actions or opinions, the wavering of fortune or chance, power to decide (*hold the* ~); counterpoise, set-off; equilibrium (~ *of power*, no State greatly preponderant); (Art) harmony of design & proportion; steady position (*lose one's* ~, fall physically or be upset mentally; ~-*wheel*, in watch, regulating the beat); preponderating weight or amount (*the* ~ *of advantage lies with him*). **3.** (Accounts) difference between Cr & Dr, statement of this (*strike a* ~, determine it; ~-*sheet*, written statement of it with details); ~ *of payments*, difference of value between payments into & out of a country, including invisible items such as tourist expenditure etc.; ~ *of trade*, difference between exports & imports; ~ *in hand*, amount over after realizing assets & meeting liabilities; ~ *due*, deficiency; *on* ~, taking everything into consideration; *the* remainder of anything. [ME, f. OF f. Rom. **bilancia* f. LL (*libra*) bilanx *-lancis* two-scaled (balance)]

bǎl'ance[2], v.t. & i. **1.** Weigh (a question, two arguments etc. against each other); match (thing) *with, by, against*, another; bring (thing, one*self*) into, or keep in, equilibrium; equal or neutralize weight of, make up for; oscillate, waver; (Dancing) move conversely with one's partner. **2.** (Accounts) compare Dr & Cr, make the entry necessary to equalize them; *account* ~*s*, two sides are equal; settle (account) by paying deficit. [f. F *balancer* (*balance* = prec.)]

bǎl'as, n. Red spinel resembling ruby. [ME, f. OF *balais* f. med. L *balascus* ult. f. Pers. *Budakhshan* district of origin]

Bālbrig'gan, n. Knitted cotton fabric used in hose, underwear, etc. [~ in Ireland]

bǎl'con|y (-ĭ), n. Outside balustraded platform with access from upper-floor window; (Theatre) tier of seats generally between dress-circle & gallery. Hence ~**iED**[2] (-nĭd) a. [f. It. *balcone* f. Gmc **balkon* = BALK[1] +-*one* -OON]

bald (bawld), a. With scalp wholly or partly hairless (*go* ~-*headed* (sl.), stake everything, disregard consequences); (of animals etc.) hairless, featherless, treeless, leafless, napless; (of horses) marked with white, esp. on face (~-*faced*); (of style) meagre, dull, jejune, monotonous, (of bad qualities) undisguised, whence ~'**LY**[2] adv.; ~'*head*, ~'*pate*, (person) with ~ head, kinds of duck (*pate* only) & pigeon; ~'*ing* adj., becoming ~. Hence ~'**NESS** n. [ME *ballede* perb. f. obs. *ball* white spot (cf. W (*ceffyl*) *bàl* horse with white forehead, Ir. & Gael. *bal* spot), +-ED[2]]

bǎl'dachin (-k-), **-quin**, n. (Orig.) rich brocade; (now) canopy projecting, suspended, or on pillars, over altar, throne, etc. [f. F & Sp. *baldaquin* & It. *baldacchino*, in med. L *baldakinus*, f. *Baldacco*, It. form of *Bagdad*, place of origin]

bald'-coot, bald'icoot, (bawl-), n. The coot, from its bare white forehead (pop.); bald person.

bal'derdash (bawl-), n. (Formerly) frothy liquid, mixture of liquors; (now) jumble of words, nonsense. [orig. unkn.]

baldmoney (bawld'mŭni), n. Yellow--flowered umbelliferous plant. [orig. unkn.]

băl'dric (bawl-), n. Belt for sword, bugle, etc., hung from shoulder to opposite hip. Hence ~-WISE adv. [orig. & hist. obsc.; ME *baudry* f. OF *baudrei*; w. *baldric* cf. MHG *balderich* & med. L *baldringus*]

bāle¹, n. Evil, destruction, woe, pain, misery, (poet. & arch.). Hence ~'FUL (-lf-) a., ~'fulLY² adv. [OE, OS *balu*, OHG *balo*, ON *böl*, f. Gmc *balw-*]

bāle², n., & v.t. (Make up into) package of merchandise usu. done up in canvas & corded or metal-hooped. [ME *bale* f. MDu. *bale* (Du. *baal*) or its prob. source OF *bale* (mod. *balle*) f. Frank. *balla* f. Gmc *ballōn*; see BALL¹]

bāle³. See BAIL⁴.

baleen', n. & a. Whalebone. [ME *baleyne* f. OF *baleine* f. L *balaena* whale]

bāle'fīre (-lf-), n. Great fire in the open; funeral pyre; beaconfire (*fire* added only in 19th c.); bonfire. [f. ON *bál* (= OE *bǽl* great fire) + FIRE]

balk¹, baulk, (bawk), n. Ridge left un-ploughed; stumbling-block, hindrance; sanctuary area on billiard table; roughly squared timber beam; tie-beam of a house; headline of fishing-net. [OE *balc* f. ON *balkr* f. Gmc *balkuz*]

balk², baulk, (bawk), v.t. & i. Shirk, miss, (topic, turn, duty, chance); jib, shy, pull up; hinder, thwart, disappoint, discourage, startle. [f. prec.]

Bal'kan (bawl-), a. Of the peninsula bounded by the Adriatic, Aegean, and Black Seas, or of its peoples and countries. So ~IZE (3) v.t., divide (an area) into small antagonistic states.

ball¹ (bawl), n. Solid or hollow sphere; (with distinctive adj.) any of the heavenly bodies; hard or soft, inflated or solid, large or small, sphere used in games; (Cricket) single delivery of it by bowler (*no* ~, delivery breaking rules); solid missile (not always spherical) for cannon, rifle, pistol, etc. (*load with* ~, opposed to blank cartridge); (pl., vulg.) nonsense (*make a* ~ *s of*, do badly, make a mess of); = BALLOT n., & see BLACK¹; ~ *of eye*, eye within lids; material gathered or wound in round mass, as snow, medicine (veter-inary), wool, or string; ~ *of foot*, rounded part at base of great toe, so ~ *of thumb*. (Phrr.) *have the* ~ *at* one's *feet*, have one's opportunity; *keep up the* ~, *keep the* ~ *rolling*, do one's part in talk etc.; *the* ~ *is with you*, it is your turn; ~ *& socket*, joint with greatest possible freedom; ‖ *three* ~*s*, pawnbroker's sign; ~*-firing*, with ~ cartridge; ~*-PROOF*; ~*-bearings*, axle

fittings avoiding friction by use of small ~*s*; ~*-cock*, *-tap*, automatic cistern-tap with floating ~; ~*-flower*, archit. orna-ment resembling a ~ within a hollow flower; ~*-point*, (of fountain pen) having a tiny ~ as its writing point. [ME *bal* f. ON *böllr* f. Gmc *balluz*]

ball² (bawl), n. Social assembly for dancing (so ~*-room*; *give a* ~, of the entertainer; *open the* ~, lead first dance, fig. commence operations). [f. F *bal* f. obs. *baler, baller*, f. LL *ballare* to dance]

ball³ (bawl), v.t. & i. Squeeze or wind into a ball; ~ *up* (sl.), muddle; grow into a lump or lumps. [BALL¹]

băll'ad, n. Simple song, esp. sentimental composition of several verses, each sung to same melody, with accompaniment merely subordinate; poem in short stan-zas narrating popular story. Hence ~-MONGER, ~RY(5), nn. [ME & OF *balade* (F *ball-*) f. Pr. *balada* dancing-song f. *balar* (BALL²), -ADE (1)]

ballade' (balahd), n. Poem of one or more triplets of seven-lined or eight-lined stanzas, each ending with same refrain line, & envoy; poem of equal (usu. seven or eight line) stanzas; ~ *royal*, stanzas of seven or eight ten-syllable lines (also *rhyme royal*). [earlier spelling & pron. of prec., now used technically]

băll'ast¹, n. Heavy material placed in ship's hold to secure stability; *in* ~, in the hold, (of ship) laden with ~ only or unladen, (of material) as ~; experience, principles, etc., that give stability to character; slag etc. used to form bed of railroad or substratum of road. [of doubtful orig.; f. LG or OSw., ODa. *ballast*; earlier form of latter, *barlast* may be = *bar* bare + *last* load]

băll'ast², v.t. Furnish with, render steady by means of, ballast (lit. & fig.); fill in (railroad bed) with ballast. Hence ~ING¹(3) n. [f. prec.]

băllerin'a (-ēnah), n. Female ballet--dancer, esp. dancer taking one of the five leading classical female roles in ballet. [It.]

băll'et (-lā), n. Combined performance of professional dancers on the stage having a sustained continuous theme. Hence **băllêtomăne', băllêtoMAN'IA,** nn., enthusiast, enthusiasm, for ~ per-formances. [F, dim. of *bal* BALL²]

ballis'ta, n. (pl. *-ae*). Ancient military engine for hurling great stones etc. [L, f. Gk *ballō* throw]

ballis't|ic, a. Of projectiles. of hurling--power. Hence ~ICS n. [prec. + -IC]

ballon d'essai (see Ap), n. Experiment to see whether the public, or foreign States, will tolerate a new departure in policy etc., kite. [F]

băll'onĕt, n. Air compartment in envelope of balloon or airship. [F (*-nnet*) as foll.]

balloon'¹, n. (Archit.) large ball crowning pillar, spire, etc.; round or pear-shaped airtight envelope inflated with gas lighter than air & rising skywards, whence ~IST (3) n.; anything hollow & inflated; shape into which, or frame on which, trees & plants are trained; (colloq.) ~-shaped line enclosing words spoken by characters in strip cartoons etc.; ~ barrage, anti--aircraft barrier of steel cables supported in an almost vertical position each by a captive ~ (barrage ~); ~ tire, low--pressure tire of large section. [f. It. ballone large ball (balla see BALE² +-one see -OON)]

balloon'², v.t. Ascend in balloon, whence ~ER¹ n.; swell out like balloon (gowns etc.). [f. prec.]

ball'ot¹, n. (Small ball, ticket, or paper— also ~-paper—used in) secret voting; votes so recorded; lot-drawing (whether by balls or not); ~-box, used in voting or lot-drawing. [f. It. ballotta dim. of balla BALL¹]

ball'ot², v.i. Give secret vote; ~ for, select (officials etc.) by secret vote; draw lots (for precedence, esp. in H. of Commons for right of moving resolutions etc.). [f. It. ballottare (ballotta BALLOT¹)]

‖ ball'y̆, a. & adv. (sl.) expr. speaker's disgust or satisfaction (stung by a ~ wasp; too ~ tired; whose ~ fault is that?; won the ~ lot). [pronunciation of bl—y=bloody]

ballyhoo', n. (orig. U.S.). Trumped-up publicity of a vulgar or misleading kind; barker's harangue. [orig. unkn.]

ball'yrăg, v.t. & i. (sl.; -gg-). Maltreat by hustling, jeering, or playing practical jokes on; indulge in horseplay. Hence ~GING¹ (-g-) n. [orig. unkn.; also bully-rag]

balm (bahm), **n.** Fragrant & medicinal exudation from certain trees; ointment for anointing, soothing pain, or healing; perfume, fragrance; healing or soothing influence, consolation; tree yielding ~ (Asia & N. Africa); ~ gentle or ~-mint, bastard ~, field ~, fragrant herbs; ~ of Gilead or of Mecca, golden oleo-resin once much used as antiseptic, artificial imitation of this. [ME basme, ba(u)me, f. OF f. L balsamum BALSAM; sp. variously adjusted to the L, whence mod. -l-]

balm'-crickĕt (bahm-), n. Cicada. [earlier baum-; f. G baumgrille tree-cricket]

bălmŏ'ral, n. Kinds of laced boot, petticoat, Scotch cap. [B~ Castle, royal residence in Aberdeenshire, Scotland]

balm|y (bahm'ĭ), **a.** Yielding balm; fragrant, soft, mild, soothing, healing; (sl.) = BARMY. Hence ~ĭLY² adv., ~ĭNESS n. [BALM +-Y¹]

bălnĕŏl'ogy̆, n. Scientific study of bathing and medicinal springs. [f. L balneum bath +-O-+-LOGY²]

băl'sa (or bawl-), **n.** American tropical tree yielding light strong wood, cork-wood; raft or float. [Sp.]

bal'sam (bawl-), **n.** Resinous product= BALM; true ~ or ~ of Mecca = BALM of Gilead; other medicinal oleo-resins; Canada ~, used in mounting for microscope; artificial oily or resinous ointment, esp. various substances dissolved in oil or turpentine, e.g. ~ of aniseed; (fig.) healing or soothing agency; (Chem.) compounds of resins & volatile oils, insoluble in water; tree yielding ~; flowering plant of genus Impatiens; ~ apple, gourdlike plant with highly coloured fruit. Hence **balsăm'ĭc** (bawl- or băl-) a., **balsăm'ĭcALLY** adv., **balsamĭF'EROUS** a., ~Y² (bawl-) a. [f. L balsamum; from c. 1000 to 1600 either variants of basme were used, or the full L; balsam before & after those dates]

bal'timŏre (bawl-), **n.** N.-Amer. orange & black starling. [colours of Lord Baltimore's (proprietor of Maryland) coat of arms]

băl'uster, n. Short pillar, slender above, pear-shaped below; post helping to support rail; (pl.) set of these supporting handrail of staircase (now usu. banisters). [f. F balustre f. It. balaustro f. L f. Gk balaustion wild-pomegranate flower (from shape of its calyx-tube)]

bălustr|āde, n. Row of balusters with rail or coping as ornamental parapet to terrace, balcony, etc. Hence ~ăd'ED² a. [F, see prec., -ADE]

băm, v.t. & n. (sl., arch.). Hoax. [cf. BAMBOOZLE]

băm̆bin'ō (-ē-), **n.** (pl. -ni). Image of infant Jesus in swaddling-clothes shown in Italian churches at Christmas. [It., = baby]

bămbōō', n. (pl. -oos). Kinds of tropical giant grasses; the stem, used as stick or material. [16th c., app. unexpl. alt. f. Pg. f. Malay mambu]

bămbōō'zle, v.t. (sl.). Hoax, mystify, cheat into doing something or out of property etc. Hence ~MENT (-zelm-) n. [with BAM from c. 1700, of unkn. orig.]

băn¹, v.t. & i. (-nn-). Curse (t. & i., arch.); prohibit, interdict. [OE bannan summon, OHG bannan, ON banna interdict, curse, f. Gmc *bannan]

băn², n. Ecclesiastical anathema, interdict; curse supposed to have supernatural power; angry execration (arch.); formal prohibition; sentence of outlawry, esp. Ban of the (Holy Roman) Empire; tacit prohibition by public opinion (under a ~). [OF, f. LL bannum f. Gmc *ban proclamation with penalties; see prec. & cf. ABANDON]

băn³, n. (hist.). Viceroy of districts in Hungary, Croatia, etc., commanding in war. [Pers., = lord]

bānal' (-ahl, or băn'al, -ăl'), **a.** Commonplace, trite. [F. (BAN², -AL); orig. a feudal word; the use of the lord's mill was compulsory for all tenants (bannal mill), whence the sense common to all]

banăl'ity̆, n. Triteness; a commonplace. [f. F *banalité* f. prec., see -ALITY]

bana'na (-nah-), n. Tropical & subtropical fruit-tree; its fruit, finger-shaped with yellow rind, in clusters (*hand of* ~s, bunch). [Port. or Sp. f. the native name in Guinea]

banaus'ic, a. (derog.). Suitable for a mere mechanic, illiberal. [f. Gk *banausikos* (*banausos* working by fire f. *baunos* forge, -IC)]

‖ **Băn'bury̆ cāke**, n. Spiced cake made at Banbury, Oxfordshire.

banc (băngk), **banco** (băngk'ō), n. Used in phrases *in banc*, *in banco*, = on the bench, applied to sittings of a Superior Court of Common Law as a full court (not Nisi Prius or circuit). [*banco* L abl. of *bancus* bench; see BANK[5]]

bănd[1], n. 1. Thing that restrains, binds together, connects or unites (chiefly arch., now ousted by the orig. identical BOND); (Bookbinding) straps at back holding sheets together; ~-*stone*, one passing through dry-stone wall & binding it. 2. Flat strip of thin material; hoop round anything (of iron, elastic, etc.); strap forming part of a garment (shirt, waist, hat, etc.), (pl.) development of neckband or collar into two pendent strips (clerical, legal, academic); *reef*-~, strip sewn on sail at eyelet holes for strength; (Mech.) belt connecting wheels; stripe of colour or distinguishable material on object; ~'*box*, of paper-covered chip or cardboard for millinery (orig. for clerical ~s; *look as if* one *came out of* ~*box*, of extreme neatness); ~-*saw*, endless saw running over wheels; ~-*wheel*, worked by strap from another. 3. Organized company of armed men, robbers, persons with common object (*B*~ *of Hope*, total--abstinence association), body of musicians, esp. wind-instrument performers (*brass* ~; *military* ~; *dance* ~; ~'*master*, conductor; ~'*stand*, platform; ~*s'man*, member of ~); *~ wagon*, wagon for ~ of musicians esp. in circus parade, (fig.) imaginary vehicle regarded as carrying a ~ of political leaders likely to be successful (*climb on the* ~ *wagon*, strive to be on the winning side). [senses 1 & 2 ult. f. Gmc *bindan* BIND[1]. (1) (tie), ME *band* f. ON *band* f. Gmc *bandam*; (2) (strip), late ME *bande* f. OF *bande*, *bende* = Pr., It., med. L *benda* f. Gmc *bendōn*; (3) (company), 15th c. *bande* f. OF *bande* = Pr., Sp., It. *banda* ribbon f. WG *banda* cogn. w. Goth. *bandwa*; see BANNER]

bănd[2], v.t. Put a band on; mark with stripes; form into a league (usu. refl. or pass.). [f. F *bander* f. *bande*, see prec.]

băn'dag|e, n., & v.t. Strip of material for binding up limb, wound, etc., or anything used for blindfolding; (vb) tie up with ~e, whence ~ING[1] (3) n. [F, f. *bande* see prec., -AGE]

băndănn'a, -ăn'a, n. Richly coloured

yellow or white spotted (orig. always silk) handkerchief. [Hind. *bandhnu* method of spot-dyeing]

băndeau' (-dō), n. (pl. -*x*, pr. -z). Fillet for binding woman's hair; fitting-band inside woman's hat. [F]

băn'derŏl(e), n. Long narrow flag with cleft end flown at masthead; ornamental streamer on knight's lance; ribbon-like scroll (Archit., stone band) with inscription; sometimes = BANNEROL. [F *banderole* f. It. *banderuola* dim. of *bandiera* BANNER]

băn'dicoōt, n. (India) rat as large as cat; (Australia) insectivorous marsupial. [f. Telugu *pandi-kokku* pig rat]

băn'dit, n. (pl. -*its*, -*itt'i*). Outlaw; lawless robber, brigand, (usu. in organized gangs); *a banditti*, gang of brigands. [f. It. *bandito* pl. -*iti* p.p. of *bandire* = med. L *bannire* proclaim see BAN[1, 2]]

‖ **băn'dŏg**, n. Chained dog; mastiff, bloodhound. [earlier *band-dog* f. BAND[1]]

băndoleer', -ier' (-ēr), n. Shoulder-belt with cartridge-loops. [f. F *bandouillere* f. It. *bandoliera* or Sp. -*lera*, f. *bandola* dim. of *banda* BAND[1]; cf. Du. *bandelier*]

băndolēr'ō, n. Highwayman. [Sp.]

băn'doline, n. Gummy preparation for fixing the hair or moustache. [perh. f. BANDEAU]

băn'dy̆[1], v.t. Throw, strike, pass, to & fro (ball, or fig. stories, epithets, etc.); often ~ *about*; discuss (names etc.); give & take (blows etc.), exchange (something *with* some one). [orig. obsc.; cf. F *bander* 'bandie at Tennis' perh. f. *bande* side; *-y* unexplained]

băn'dy̆[2], n. (Orig.) special form of tennis; (now also ~-*ball*) hockey; the stick, curved at end, used in the game. [perh. f. prec.]

băn'dy̆[3], n. Indian cart or buggy. [f. Telugu *baṇḍi*]

băn'dy̆[4], a. Wide apart at the knees (of legs); ~-*legged*, (of persons or animals) having ~ legs. [perh. f. BANDY[2] curved stick]

bāne, n. Poison (lit. now only in comb., as *rat's*-~); cause of ruin, esp. *the* ~ *of*; ruin, woe, (poet.). Hence ~'FUL (-nf-) a., ~'fuI.Y[2] adv., ~'fuIness n. [OE *bana*, OHG *bano*, ON *bani*, f. Gmc *banon*-]

băng[1], v.t. & i. Strike (t. & i.) noisily; shut (t. & i. of door) with noise; make sound of blow or explosion; thrash; (sl.) surpass. [16th c., perh. f. Scand.; cf. ON *banga* to hammer, LG *bangen* strike]

băng[2], n. Sounding blow, sound of a blow, report of gun. [f. prec.]

băng[3], adv. & int. With sudden impact, abruptly, completely, explosively; *go* ~, explode; conventional imitation of gun-fire. [f. BANG[1]]

băng[4], v.t. & n. Cut (front hair) straight across forehead; (n.) fringe resulting; ~-*tail*, horse with tail cut straight across. [f. prec.]

bangl|e (băng'gl), n. Ring bracelet or anklet. Hence ~ED[2] (-ld) a. [f. Hind. *bangri*, glass wrist-ring]

băn'ian, băn'yan, n. Hindu trader; (Bengal) native broker to European house; Indian flannel jacket; (Naut.) ~-*day*, on which no meat is served out; ~-*hospital*, for animals; ~-*tree* (or ~), Indian fig, branches of which root themselves over great extent. [Port. *banian* f. Arab. *banyan* f. Gujarati *vaṇiyo* man of trading caste. ~ *day*, *hospital*, from caste reverence for animal life; ~ *tree*, E name used first of a specimen under which ~s had built pagoda]

băn'ish, v.t. Condemn to exile (person *from* place, or double obj. as ~*ed him the court*, or obj. of person only); dismiss from one's presence or mind. Hence ~MENT n. [ME, f. OF *banir* (-ISH[2]) f. Rom. **bannire* f. Gmc **bannjan* f. **bann-* BAN[1]]

băn'ister, n. (usu. pl.). Upright(s) supporting stair handrail (also in pl. for uprights & rail together). [corruption of BALUSTER]

băn'jō, n. (pl. *-os, -oes*). Stringed musical instrument with guitar neck & head, tambourine body, played with fingers. Hence ~IST (3) n. [Negro corruption of earlier *bandore* ult. f. Gk *pandoura*]

bănk[1], n. **1.** Raised shelf of ground, slope, elevation in sea or river bed; artificial slope enabling car etc. to maintain speed round a curve; flat-topped mass of cloud, snow, etc. **2.** Sloping margin of river, ground near river (*right, left,* ~, as seen looking down stream); edge of hollow place (e.g. top of shaft in mining). [ME *banke* f. ON; cf. OIcel. *bakki* in same senses f. Gmc **bankon* cf. BANK[5], BENCH]

bănk[2], v.t. & i. Contain as a bank, confine with bank(s); (of car or aeroplane or its occupant) travel with one side higher; confine watch-escapement (of ~ing-pins), strike against the ~ing-pins (or abs.; of escapement); ~ *up*, heap or rise into banks (of snow, clouds), pack tightly (fire, for slow burning). [f. prec.]

bănk[3], n. Establishment for custody of money, which it pays out on customer's order; ‖ *the B~*, B~ of England, managing the public debt, issuing legal-tender notes, & having the Government for chief customer; (Gaming) amount of money before keeper of table; ~-*bill*, drawn by one ~ on another; ~-*book*, containing customer's private copy of his account with ~; ~-*credit*, arrangement by which customer may overdraw on security given; ‖ ~ *holiday*, day on which ~s are legally closed, usu. kept as general holiday also in England; ‖~-*note*, banker's promissory note payable to bearer on demand & serving as money; ~-*rate*, announced percentage at which B~ of England is prepared to discount bills. [f. F *banque* or its source It. *banca* f. Gmc **bank* BENCH, see BANK[1, 5]]

bănk[4], v.t. & i. Keep bank, trade in money (~*ing-house*, commercial firm that does some ~ing); keep money at bank; deposit (money etc.) at bank; convert into money; (Gaming) hold table fund; ~ (*up*)*on*, base one's hopes on, count upon, reckon reliable. [f. prec.]

bănk[5], n. Galley-rower's bench; tier *of oars* in galley; row of organ keys; working-table in some trades. [ME, f. OF *banc* f. Gmc **bank-*; see BANK[1], BENCH]

bănk'able, a. That will be received at a bank (securities etc.). [BANK[3] + -ABLE]

bănk'er[1], n. Proprietor or partner of private bank, governor, director, etc., of joint-stock bank, (*let me be your~*, lend the money you need); (Gaming) keeper of the bank; dealer in some games of chance; a gambling game of cards. [BANK[5] + -ER[1], after F *banquier*]

‖ bănk'er[2], n. Labourer (Eastern counties); (Hunting) horse that jumps on & off banks too large to clear. [BANK[1] + -ER[1]]

bănk'er[3], n. Wooden or stone bench for trimming bricks or stone on; ~-*mark*, mason's sign manual (formerly engraved on a dressed stone before it left the ~). [perh. = It. *banco* statuary's bench]

bănk'ĕt, n. Auriferous conglomerate like pudding-stone found in S. Africa. [Du., = kind of hardbake (BANQUET)]

bănk'ing, n. In vbl senses of BANK[2, 4]; also, fishing on a sea bank (esp. Newfoundland). [BANK[1]]

bănk'rŭpt[1], n. (Law) insolvent person whose effects, on creditors' or his own petition to Bankruptcy Court, are administered & distributed for benefit of all creditors; (pop.) insolvent debtor. [16th c. *banke rota, bankrout,* etc. f. It. *banca rotta* broken bank (BANK[3], L *rupt-* p.p. of *rumpere* break); mod. sp. after L]

bănk'rŭpt[2], v.t. Reduce to bankruptcy. [f. prec.]

bănk'rŭpt[3], a. Under legal process because of insolvency; insolvent; bereft (*of* some quality etc.). [perh. the short p.p. of prec.]

bănk'ruptcў, n. Being declared bankrupt, being insolvent; utter loss (of something, e.g. reputation). [prec. + -CY, irreg. for *-rupcy*]

bănk'sia (-sha), n. Australian flowering shrub now grown in Europe. [Sir J. *Banks* (d. 1820), -IA[1]]

bănks'man, n. Coal-mine overlooker above ground. [BANK[1]]

bănn'er, n. Cloth flag on pole used as standard of emperor, king, lord, knight, for war; flag of a country etc. (*join, follow, the* ~ *of*; now chiefly fig.); ensign (esp. in frame, or with two poles) borne in religious or political demonstrations; anything used as symbol of principles; ~-*screen*, fire screen hung from standing pole or mantelpiece; (attrib.) preeminent, conspicuous, as ~ *headline* (in newspaper). Hence ~ED² (-erd) a. [ME, f. AF *banere*, OF *-iere*, f. Rom. *bandaria (cf. It. *bandiera*)˙f. med. L *bandum* standard (BAND¹), cf. Goth. *bandwa* sign]

bänn'erĕt, n. Knight having vassals under his banner; one knighted on the field for valour. [ME & OF *baneret* (*banicre* see prec. +-*et* = -ATE²) lit. bannered]

bänn'crŏl, n. Banner borne at great men's funerals & placed over tomb;= BANDEROLE. [var. of BANDEROLE]

bänn'ock, n. Scotch & N.-Eng. home--made loaf, usu. unleavened, flat, & round or oval; oatcake. [OE *bannuc*, 15th c. -*ok* etc.; cf. Gael. *bannach*]

bänns (-z), n. pl. Notice in church of intended marriage, thrice read to give opportunity of objection (*ask, publish, put up, forbid, the~*). [pl. of BAN²]

bän'quĕt¹, n. Sumptuous feast; dinner with speeches in celebration of something or to further a cause. [F, dim. of *banc* bench BANK³]

bän'quĕt², v.t. & i. Regale (person); feast, carouse, whence ~ER¹ n. [f. F *banqueter* (*banquet* = prec.)]

bänquette' (-kĕt), n. Raised way behind rampart etc. for firing from; bench behind driver in French diligence. [F, f. It. *banchetta* dim. of *banca* bench see BANK³]

bän'shee, n. Spirit whose wail portends death in a house (Irish & Scotch). [Ir. *bean sidhe* f. OIr. *ben side* woman of the fairies]

bänt, v.i. See BANTING.

bän'tam, n. Small kind of domestic fowl, of which the cock is very pugnacious; small but spirited person (~ *battalion*, of men below normal standard of height enrolled for the war of 1914–18); ~-*weight* (Boxing) see BOX²*ing weights*. [f. *Bantam* in Java whence they were perh. brought, though perh. orig. Japanese]

bän'ter, n., & v.t. & i. Humorous ridicule, good-humoured personalities; (vb) make fun of, rally; talk jestingly. [f. 17th c.; of unkn. orig.]

bän'ting, n. Treatment of obesity by abstinence from sugar, starch, & fat; bänt v.i., adopt this. [W. *B~*, d. 1878]

bänt'ling, n. Young child, brat. [late 16th c., perh. f. G *bänkling* (f. *bank* bench, cf. *bastard*)]

Bantu (bahntōō'), n. & a. Used to include many related African languages & races. [native, = people]

bänx'ring, n. Javanese squirrel-like insectivorous animal. [Javanese *bangsring*]

bän'yan. See BANIAN (used esp. for the tree).

bänzai' (-zī), int. Form of greeting by Japanese to their Emperor, cheer used in battle, etc. [Jap., = ten thousand years (of life to you)]

bä'obäb, n. African tree called also monkey-bread with enormously thick stem. [mentioned 1592]

bäp, n. (Sc.). Small loaf or roll of bread. [orig. unkn.]

bäp'tĭsm, n. Religious rite of immersing (person) in, or sprinkling with, water in sign of purification & (with Christians) of admission to the Church, generally accompanied by name-giving; (fig.) ~ *of blood*, martyrdom, ~ *of fire*, soldier's first battle; naming of church bells & mines. Hence **bäptis'mAL** (-z-) a., **bäptis-mALLy²** adv. [ME *bapteme* f. OF *baptesme* f. LL f. Gk *baptismos* (*baptizō* BAPTIZE)]

bäp'tist, n. One who baptizes, esp. John the B~; one of a sect (formerly called ANABAPTISTS by opponents) objecting to infant baptism, & practising immersion. [ME, f. OF *baptiste*, f. LL *baptista* f. Gk *baptistēs* (*baptizō* BAPTIZE)]

bäp'tĭst(e)rȳ, n. Part of church (or formerly separate building) used for baptism; (in Baptist chapel) immersion receptacle. [ME, f. OF *baptisterie* f. LL f. Gk *baptistērion* bathing-place (*baptizō* BAPTIZE)]

bäptīze', **-ise** (-īz), v.t. Immerse in or sprinkle with water, as sign of purification or initiation, esp. into the Christian Church; christen; (abs.) administer baptism; (fig.) purify, elevate; name or nickname. [ME, f. OF *baptiser* f. LL *baptizare* f. Gk *baptizō* bathe (*baptō* dip)]

bär¹, n. **1.** Long piece of rigid material (metal, wood, soap, etc.; ~-*bell*, iron ~ with ball at each end used in gymnastics; cf. *dumb-bell*; ~'*wood*, red wood from Gaboon imported in ~s for dyeing etc.). **2.** Slip of silver below clasp of medal as additional distinction; band of colour etc. on surface, (Her.) two horizontal parallel lines across shield (~ *sinister*, by mistake for BEND or BATON, supposed sign of illegitimacy). **3.** Rod or pole used to confine or obstruct (*window, door, grate, gate*, -~); barrier of any shape (*Temple Bar*, *toll'*~); sandbank or shoal at mouth of harbour or estuary. **4.** (Mus.) vertical line across stave dividing piece into sections of equal time-value, such sections; immaterial barrier; (Law) plea arresting action or claim; moral obstacle. **5.** Barrier with some technical significance, as, in lawcourt, place at which prisoner stands; hence ~ *of conscience, opinion*, etc.; ‖ *trial at* ~, in Queen's Bench division; a particular court (*practise at parliamentary, Chancery*, etc., ~); ‖ *be called to the* ~ (i.e. that in Inns of Court separating benchers), be admitted a barrister; ‖ *be called within the* ~ (i.e. that in courts within which Q.C.s plead), be appointed Queen's Counsel; *the* ~, barristers, profession of barrister. **6.** ‖ (Parl.) rail dividing off space to which non-members may be admitted on business. **7.** (In an inn etc.) counter across which refreshments are handed, space behind or room containing it; ‖ ~'*man*, ~'*maid*, **~ tender*, attendants at such counter. [ME *barre* f. OF f. Rom. *barra of unkn. orig.]

bar[2], v.t. (-rr-). Fasten (door etc.) with bar(s); keep (person) *in* or *out* (*~ring-out*, schoolboy rebellion); obstruct (path etc.); stay (process or party) by legal objection; exclude from consideration (esp. in imperative used as prep., e.g. *~ one* in betting); (sl.) object to, dislike, (person, habit, etc.); mark with stripe(s). [ME *barren* f. OF *barrer* (*barre* BAR[1])]

bar[3], n. Large European sea-fish. [F]

bărathĕ'a, n. Fine cloth made from wool (with or without silk or cotton). [orig. unkn.]

bă'rathrŭm, n. Pit at Athens into which criminals were thrown; abyss. [L, f. Gk *barathron*]

barb[1], n., & v.t. **1.** Beardlike feelers of barbel etc.; chin-piece of nun's head-dress; lateral filament branching from shaft of feather; subordinate recurved point of arrow, fish-hook, etc., (fig.) sting. **2.** v.t. Furnish (arrow etc.) with *~*; *~ed wire*, for fences & esp. as obstruction in war, with wire prickles at intervals. [ME, f. OF *barbe* f. L *barba* beard]

barb[2], n. Breeds of horse & pigeon imported from Barbary. [f. F *barbe* (*Barbarie*)]

barb'ara, first word of the scholastic mnemonic lines for figures & moods of the syllogism (some of these, esp. *barbara*, *barbara celarent*, are used allusively for logic or logical training).

barbār'ian, n. & a. (Foreigner) differing from speaker in language & customs, esp. in hist., (a) non-Greek, (one) outside the Roman Empire, (a) non-Christian; rude, wild, or uncultured (person). [f. obs. F *barbarien* f. *barbare* (BARBAROUS, -IAN)]

barbă'r|ic, a. Rude, rough, like or of barbarians & their art or taste. Hence *~*ICALLY adv. [ME, f. OF *barbarique* or L f. Gk *barbarikos* (*barbaros* BARBAROUS, & see -IC)]

barb'arism, n. Mixing of foreign or vulgar expressions in talk or writing; such an expression; absence of culture, ignorance & rudeness; instance of this. [f. F *barbarisme* or L f. Gk *barbarismos* (*barbarizō* speak like a foreigner f. *barbaros* BARBAROUS, -IZE)]

barbă'rity, n. Savage cruelty, instance of it; barbaric style or taste, instance of it, (usu. *barbarism*). [f. as foll., see -TY]

barb'ariz|e, -is|e (-īz), v.t. & i. Make or become barbarous; corrupt (language). Hence *~*A'TION n. [f. as foll., see -IZE]

barb'arous, a. (Lang.) not Greek, not Greek or Latin, not pure, illiterate; (people) non-Greek, beyond Roman Empire, non-Christian, outlandish; uncivilized; cruel; coarse. Hence *~*LY[2] adv., *~*NESS n. [f. L f. Gk *barbaros* foreign + -OUS]

Barb'ary āpe, n. Large tailless monkey of N. Africa and Gibraltar. [*Barbary*, old name of N. Africa]

barb'āte, a. (bot., zool.). Having hairy tufts. [f. L *barbatus* bearded (*barba* beard, -ATE[2])]

barb'ēcūe, n. Large wooden or iron framework for smoking or broiling; hog, ox, etc., roasted whole, whence **barb'ē-cūe** v.t.; **open-air party at which animals are roasted whole; floor for drying coffee-beans. [f. Sp. *barbacoa* f. Haitian *barbacòa* crate on posts]

barb'el, n. Large European fresh-water fish with fleshy filaments hanging from mouth; such filament in any fish, whence *~*(l)ED[2] a. [ME, f. OF *barbel* f. Rom. *barbellus dim. of *barbus* barbel (*barba* beard)]

barb'er, n. One who shaves & trims customers' beards & hair (now freq. *hair-dresser*); *~'s block*, for making & displaying wigs; *~'s itch*, skin disease caused by a fungoid organism communicated by (unsterilized) shaving apparatus; *~'s pole*, spirally painted & used as sign. [ME & AF *barbour* f. OF *barbeor* f. L *barbatorem (*barba* beard), see -OR]

barb'er(r)ў, bĕr-, n. Shrub with spiny shoots, yellow flowers, & oblong red berries; its berry. [late ME *barbere*, 16th c. *bar-*, *berbery*, f. OF *berbere*, *berberis*, of unkn. orig.]

barb'ĕt, n. Bird with bristle-tufts at base of bill. [cf. F *barbet* (*barbe* beard, see -ET[1])]

barbĕtte', n. Platform within fort or in ship from which guns fire over parapet etc. without embrasure. [F dim. of *barbe* beard; see -ETTE]

barb'ican, n. Outer defence to city or castle, esp. double tower over gate or bridge. [ME, f. OF *barbacane*, com.-Rom. of disputed orig.; cf. Pers. *barbār khānah* house on the wall]

barbitūr'|ic, a. (chem.). *~ic acid*, an acid from which various hypnotic and sedative drugs are derived. Hence *~*ATE[1] (3) n. [f. F (-*ique*) f. G *barbitur(säure)*]

Barb'izŏn, n. Village near Fontainebleau; *~ School*, coterie of French naturalistic painters (middle of 19th c.).

barbōl'a, n. (Also *~ work*) the embellishment of small articles by attachment of coloured models of flowers, fruit, etc. made from a plastic paste. [orig. unkn.]

barb'ūle, n. Filament branching from barb (of feather) as barb from shaft. [f. L *barbula* dim. of *barba* beard]

bărc'arōle, -ŏlle, n. Song of gondolier; imitation of it. [f. F *barcarolle* f. It. *barcaruola*, boatman's song (*barca* boat)]

Barcelōn'a, n. Spanish city, capital of Catalonia; *~* (*nut*), hazel-nut imported from Spain.

bard[1], n. Celtic minstrel, (Wales) poet recognized at Eisteddfod, whence *~'*IC a.; early poet; lyric poet; poet, whence *~'*LING[1] n. Hence *~*ŎL'ATRY n., worship of Shakespeare, the 'B~ of Avon'. [f. Gael. & Ir. *bàrd*]

bård², n. Armour for breast & flanks of warhorse. Hence ~'ED² a. [f. F *barde*, rel. to Pr. *aubarda*, Sp., Pg. *albarda*, f. Arab. *al-barda'ah* stuffed packsaddle]

båre¹, a. Unclothed, undisguised, uncovered, bald, unfurnished, unprotected, threadbare, unsheathed, ill-provided, empty, unadorned, scanty, mere; ~² *back* a. & adv., *-ed* a., with ~ back, on unsaddled horse; ~'*faced*, without beard etc., without mask, also undisguised, shameless, or impudent, whence **båre-fâ'cèdLY²** adv., **bârefâ'cèdNESS** n.; ~² *foot* a. & adv., ~'*footed* a., without shoes or stockings; ~-*headed*, without hat or cap. Hence **bâr'ISH¹**(2) a. [OE *bær*, OHG *bar*, ON *berr*]

båre², v.t. Uncover, unsheathe, reveal, strip. [f. prec.]

barège' (-äzh), n. & a. (Of) silky gauze. [orig. made at Barèges]

barely (bår'li), adv. Openly, explicitly; merely; only just; scarcely. [BARE¹+-LY²]

båre'nèss (-rn-), n. Lack of covering, unadorned state. [BARE¹+-NESS]

båre'sårk (-rs-), n. & adv. Wild Norse warrior; (adv.) without armour. [lit. bare shirt (SARK); mod. form embodying supposed etym. of BERSERKER]

bårg'ain¹ (-gĭn), n. Agreement on terms of give and take, compact, thing acquired by bargaining (*good, bad,* ~, result cheaply or dearly bought; *a* ~, thing acquired or offered cheap; *Dutch, wet,* ~, closed with drink; *into the* ~, beyond the strict terms, moreover; *strike a* ~, come to terms; *make the best of a bad* ~, take misfortune etc. cheerfully). [ME, f. OF *bargaine* f. *bargaigner*, see foll.]

bårg'ain² (-gĭn), v.i. & t. Haggle (*with* someone, or abs.) over terms of give & take; stipulate *with* person *for* thing or *to* receive, give, etc.; ~ *for*, be prepared for, expect, (usu. with neg. or *more than*); (trans.) ~ *away*, part with for a consideration. Hence ~ER¹ n. [ME, f. OF *bargaigner*, = Pr. *bargagnar*, It. *bargagnare*, med. L *barcaniare*, of disputed but undetermined orig.]

bårge, n., & v.i. 1. Flat-bottomed freight-boat for canals & rivers, with or without sails; second boat of man-of-war, for use of chief officers; large ornamental oared vessel for state occasions, house-boat (e.g. *College* ~); ~*-pole* (for fending; *would not touch with a* ~-*pole*, regard with loathing). 2. v.i. Lurch or rush heavily *into, against, about*; ~ *in*, intrude. [ME, f. OF *barge*, f. med. L *barga* var. of *barca* BARK³]

bårge-, comb. form in architecture = gable. ~-*couple*, two gable beams; ~*-course*, roof projecting beyond them; ~-*board*, ornamental screen to them; ~-*stones*, forming sloping or stepped line of gable. [f. med. L *bargus* gallows]

‖ **bårgee'**, n. Man in charge of barge; *swear like a* ~, fluently, forcibly; *lucky* ~ (colloq.), lucky fellow. [-EE]

bår'ic, a. Of or containing barium. [BARIUM+-IC]

barill'a, n. Plant (*Salsola Soda*) in Spain, Sicily, Canaries; impure alkali made by burning either this or kelp. [Sp.]

bå'ritòne, n. & a. (mus.). (Voice, singer with voice, music suited to voice) between tenor and bass; euphonium (or tenor tuba) or saxhorn in B flat or C. [var. of BARYTONE]

bår'ium, n. (chem.). White metallic element, basis of alkaline earth baryta. [BARYTA or obs. *baria*+-IUM]

bårk¹, n. Outer sheath of tree trunks & branches; tan; (arch.) quinine (also *Peruvian* or *Jesuits'* ~); (sl.) skin; ~-*bed*, hot-bed of tan; ~-*bound*, hindered in growth by tight ~; ~-*pit*, of ~ & water for tanning; ~-*tree*, E name of cinchona. [ME, f. Scand. *bark*- (ON *börkr*) f. Gmc **barkuz*]

bårk², v.t. Strip bark from (tree), kill (tree) by ring-cutting bark (also *ring-*~); abrade (one's knuckles etc.); encrust. [f. prec.]

bårk³, barque (-årk), n. Three-masted vessel with fore & main masts square-rigged, mizen fore-&-aft rigged (usu. *barque*); any ship or boat (poet., usu. *bark*). [f. F *barque* f. Pr., Sp., or It., *barca* f. LL *barca* ship's boat]

bårk⁴, n. Usual cry of dogs, foxes, squirrels; (fig.) sound of gunfire, or of cough; ~ *worse than bite*, of testy harmless person. [f. foll.]

bårk⁵, v.i. & t. Utter sharp explosive cry (of dogs & some other animals); speak (& ~ *out, say*) petulantly, imperiously; ~ *at*, abuse; ~ *up the wrong tree*, denounce wrong person etc.; (sl.) cough. [OE *beorcan*, repr. an earlier **berkan*, perh. metathetic var. of BREAK¹]

bårk'er, n. Noisy assailant; shop or auction or travelling-show tout; (sl.) pistol, cannon. [f. prec.]

bårl'ey, n. (pl. ~s). Hardy awned cereal used as food & in making malt liquors & spirits; its grain; *pearl* ~, the grain ground small: ~-*broth*, strong ale; ~*corn*, grain of ~ (*John Barleycorn*, malt liquor personified), its length as measure, ⅓ inch, top of fore-sight on rifle; ~-*mow*, stack; ~ *sugar*, twisted sweetmeat; ~-*water*, soothing decoction of pearl ~ for invalids. [OE *bærlic* adj. form; for *bær-* cf. obs. *bear* barley (f. Gmc **bariz*); so Goth. *barizeins* of barley); -*lic* = -LY¹]

*bårl'ow (-ō), n. (Also ~ *knife*) large single-bladed pocket-knife. [*B*~, orig. maker]

bårm, n. Froth on fermenting malt liquor, yeast, leaven. [OE *beorma*; cogn. w. Fris., LG *barm*]

Bårm'ècide, n. & a. (Giver of benefits that are) illusory, imaginary, disappointing. [name of Arabian-Nights prince whose feast to beggar was rich dish-covers with nothing below]

barm'ў, a. Full of barm; frothy; (sl., also ~ *on the crumpet*) wrong in the head, cracked. [-Y²]

barn, n. Covered building for storing grain etc.; (derog.) unadorned build-ing; ~ *dance*, (orig. U.S.) dance in which partners advance side by side & then dance a schottische step; ~*-door*, lit., & fig. target too large to be missed, also adj. of fowls = reared at the ~-door; ~*-owl*, = white, church, screech, -owl; ~*-stormer*, strolling player, ranting actor; ~*'yard*, farmyard. [OE *bern*, *berern*, f. *bere-ern* (*bere* barley +-*ærn* place)]

Barn'aby, n. (Saint) Barnabas; ~ *bright*, St Barnabas' day, 11th June (longest day in Old Style reckoning). [f. F *Barnabé* = LL (f. Heb.) *Barnabas*]

barn'acle¹, n. (Usu. pl.) pincers placed on horse's nose to coerce him into quiet for shoeing etc.; (sl.; pl.) spectacles. [ME *bernac*, *barnacle*, *ber-*, f. OF *bernac* muzzle, of unkn. orig.; later form app. Eng. dim., see -LE]

barn'acle², n. **1.** Arctic goose visiting Britain in winter (also *bernacle* for dis-tinction from 2). **2.** Stalked cirriped clinging by fleshy foot-stalk to ship's bottom; follower who cannot be shaken off. [hist. & etym. unkn.; ME *bernekke*, *bernake* = OF *bernaque*, med. L *bernaca*, *-eca*; later *ber-*, *barnacle* = mod. F *ber-*, *barnacle*, *bernicle*]

ba'rograph (-ahf), n. Self-recording aneroid. [f. Gk *baros* weight +-GRAPH(2)]

barŏm'eter, n. Instrument measuring atmospheric pressure used for forecasting weather & ascertaining height above sea-level; *siphon*, *wheel*, *aneroid*, ~, various systems; (fig.) ~ *of opinion* etc. Hence **bărŏmĕt'ric(AL)** aa., **bărŏmĕt'rically²** adv., **barŏm'ETRY** n. [as prec. +-METER]

bă'ron, n. **1.** (hist.). One who held by military or other honourable service from the king or other superior (restricted later to king's ~s, & again to those, *Great Barons*, attending Great Council or sum-moned to Parliament; hence, peer). **2.** (mod.). One of the lowest order of nobility; holder of foreign title (called *Baron* ——, not, like English ~, *Lord* ——); (orig. U.S.) a great merchant in a (designated) commodity, (*beef* ~; *beer* ~); ~ *of beef*, double sirloin undivided. [ME & AF *barun*, OF *baron* f. med. L *baronem* nom. *baro* man (as in *king's man*) etc., f. Frankish *baro* (Salic Law; cf. MHG *bar*)]

bă'ronage, n. Barons or great vassals of Crown collectively; the nobility; book with list of peers & comments. [ME & OF *barnage* (prec., -AGE)]

bă'roness, n. Baron's wife; lady holding baronial title in her own right. [ME, f. OF *barnesse*, *-onesse*, see BARON, -ESS¹]

bă'ronĕt¹, n. Member of lowest heredi-tary titled order, commoner with prece-dence of all knights exc. K.G.s; abbr. *bart*, added to name, as *Sir John Jones*, *Bart*. [ME, dim. of BARON; see -ET]

bă'ronĕt², v.t. Raise to rank of baronet. [f. prec. on anal. of *knight*]

bă'ronĕtage, n. Baronets collectively; book with list of them & comments. [-AGE; cf. BARONAGE].

bă'ronĕtcў, n. Baronet's patent or rank. [-CY]

barŏn'ial, a. Of, belonging to, befitting, baron(s). [foll. +-AL]

bă'rony, n. Baron's domain, rank, tenure; (Ireland) division of county; (Scotland) large manor. [ME, f. OF *baronie* (BARON, -Y¹); cf. med. L *baronia*]

baroque' (-ŏk), a. & n. **1.** (Of) certain stylistic tendencies in 17th-18th c. arts. **2.** Grotesque, whimsical. [F, f. Pg., It. *barroco*, Sp. *barrueco*, of unkn. orig.]

barouche' (-ōōsh), n. Four-wheeled car-riage with collapsible half-head, for four occupants & driver. [f. G (dial.) *bar-utsche* f. It. *barocchio* (Sp. *barrocho*) f. LL *birotus* (BI-¹a +*rota* wheel)]

bârque, n. See BARK³.

barquentine, bark-, (bark'entĕn), n. Ves-sel with foremast square-rigged, main & mizen fore-&-aft rigged. [f. BARK³ after BRIGANTINE]

bă'rrack, n., & v.t. **1.** Permanent build-ing(s) in which soldiers are lodged (usu. pl.); (transf.) building in which others (e.g. children) are similarly herded together; building of severely dull or plain ap-pearance. **2.** v.t. Place in ~s; hoot, jeer at, (players in cricket-match etc.). [f. F *baraque* f. It. *baracca* or Sp. *barraca* 'souldier's tent' (1617) orig. unkn.]

bă'rracōōn', n. Set of sheds or enclosure for slaves, convicts, etc. [f. Sp. *barracon* (as prec.; see -OON)]

bă'rracud'a (-ōŏd-), **-cōōt'a**, **-cout'a** (-ōŏt-), n. Large W.-Ind. sea-fish. [Sp.]

bă'rr'age, n. **1.** Damming; dam (esp. of those in Nile). **2.** (Mil., freq. bă'rahzh) barrier to offensive or defensive action on the part of an enemy usu. in the form of a line, area, or volume into which a large number of guns fire shells either continu-ously or for pre-arranged periods (*anti-aircraft* ~, barrier of shellfire against hostile aircraft; BALLOON ~; *box* ~, one laid down usu. on three sides so as to isolate a particular area; *creeping* ~, one laid down in front of & moving with one's own advancing troops); attrib., as ~ BALLOON. [F, f. *barre* BAR¹; see -AGE]

bă'rrator, **-er**, n. (legal). Vexatious liti-gant; malicious raiser of discord. [ME, f. AF *baratour*, OF *-eor* trickster f. *barat* (obs. Eng. *barrat*) of unkn. orig.]

bă'rratrỷ, n. (Marine law) fraud or gross negligence of master or crew to prejudice of ship's owners; (Law) vexatious litiga-tion or incitement to it. Hence ~ous a. [ME, f. OF *baraterie* (*barat* see prec., -ERY)]

barred (bård), a. In vbl senses; also [BAR¹] marked with bars, (of harbour) obstructed with sandbar.

bă′rrel¹, n. Flat-ended cylindrical wooden vessel of hooped staves, cask; varying measure of capacity (~-*bulk*, 5 cub. ft); revolving cylinder in capstan, watch, & other machines; cylindrical body or trunk of an object, belly & loins of horse, etc.; metal tube of gun; *barrel-*, cylindrical or semi-cylindrical, as ~-*drain*, *-vault*; ~-*organ*, with pin-studded cylinder turned by handle & mechanism opening the pipes as required. [ME, f. OF *baril* of unkn. orig.]

bă′rrel², v.t. (-ll-). Put in barrel(s); ~*led*, (also) = *barrel-shaped*. [f. prec.]

bă′rren, a. (-est), & n. Not bearing, or incapable of bearing, children, young, fruit, vegetation, or produce; meagre, unprofitable, dull; (n.) ~ tract of land; ~*wort*, purple-&-yellow-flowered wood plant. Hence ~LY² adv., ~NESS n. [ME *barain* etc. f. OF *baraine* (fem.) etc. of unkn. orig.]

bă′rret, n. Flat cap, esp. the biretta. [f. F *barrette* BIRETTA]

bă′rricăde′¹, (now rarely) -ā′dō, n. Hastily erected rampart across street etc. of barrels, carts, stones, furniture; any barrier, lit. or fig. [f. F *barricade* or Sp. *barricada* (whence earlier Eng. *barricado*; see -ADO) f. F *barrique* (Sp. *barrica*) cask]

bă′rricăde′², (now rarely) -ā′dō, v.t. Block (street etc.) with barricade; defend (place or person) with barricade. [f. prec].

bă′rrier¹, n. Fence barring advance or preventing access; (ancient chariot--races) barred starting-cells; (foreign towns) gate at which customs are collected; (tilting) the lists or enclosing palisade, also railing parallel to which, but on opposite sides, tilters charged reaching their lances across; any obstacle, boundary, or agency that keeps apart. [ME & AF *barrere*, OF *barrière* f. Rom. *barraria* (*barra* BAR¹) later assim. to F spelling]

bă′rrier², v.t. Close or shut in with barrier (usu. with *off*, *in*). [f. prec.]

bă′rring, prep. Except, not including. [part. of BAR²]

∥ **bă′rrister**, n. Law student called to bar & having right of practising as advocate in superior courts (in full, ~-*at-law*); *re-vising-*~, one appointed to revise lists of voters at parliamentary elections. [16th c. *bar(r)ester* f. BAR¹; second element unexpl.]

bă′rrow¹ (-ō), n. (In local names) hill; (Archaeol.) grave-mound, tumulus. [OE *beorg*, OS, OHG *berg*, f. Gmc **bergaz*]

bă′rrow² (-ō), n. (Also *hand-*~) rectangular frame with short shafts used by two or more men for carrying loads on, stretcher, bier; (also *wheel-*~) shallow box with shafts & one wheel for similar use by one

man; ∥ (also *coster's* ~) two-wheeled handcart (~-*boy*, coster); a ~ful. [ME *barewe* f. Gmc **barwā* f. *beran* BEAR³; cf. BIER]

bă′rrow³ (-ō), n. (dial.). Castrated boar. [OE *bearg*, = OS, OHG *baruh* (G *barch*) f. Gmc **barguz*, *-gwaz*]

bărt′er¹, v.t. & i. Exchange (goods or immaterial things) *for* other goods (occas. *away*); part with for a (usu. unworthy) consideration (usu. *away*), whence ~ER¹ n.; trade by exchange. [f. OF *barater* trick, exchange, f. *barat*; see BARRATOR]

bărt′er², n. Traffic by exchange, truck, (also fig., e.g. of talk); (Arith.) reckoning of quantity of one commodity to be given for another, values being known. [f. prec.]

bărtĭzăn′, n. Battlemented parapet, or overhanging battlemented corner turret, at top of church tower or castle. [spurious form (Scott) f. *bertisene* illit. spelling of *bratticing* see BRATTICE]

bărt′on, n. Farmyard; farm not let with rest of manor, but retained by owner. [OE *bere-tūn* (*bere* barley+*tūn* enclosure see TOWN)]

Bărt′'s, n. St Bartholomew's Hospital in London. [abbr.]

barȳt′|a, n. Oxide or hydroxide of barium. Hence ~IC a., ~O- comb. form. [f. foll.]

barȳt′ēs (-z), n. Native sulphate of barium, called also *heavy spar*, used in some white paints. [f. Gk *barus* heavy, partly assim. to mineral names in -ITES]

bă′rȳtōne, n. & a. (Gk gr.). (Word) with no or grave accent on last syllable. [f. F *baryton* or It. *baritono* & Gk *barutonos* (*barus* heavy+*tonos* TONE)]

bās′al, a. Of, at, or forming, the base; fundamental. [f. BASE¹+-AL]

basalt (băs′awlt, basawlt′), n. Dark green or brown igneous rock often in columnar strata, whence basal′tic, basal′tiform, (-sawl-), aa.; black porcelain invented by Wedgwood. [f. L *basaltes* (in MSS. of Pliny) var. of *basanites* f. Gk (*basanos* touchstone)]

bās′an (-z-), **băz′an**, n. Sheepskin tanned in oak or larch bark (also *basil*). [f. F *basane* f. Pr. *bazana* f. Sp. *badana* f. Arab. *bifanah* lining]

bas bleu (see Ap.), n. Bluestocking. [F]

băs′cūle, n. Lever apparatus used in ~--*bridge*, kind of drawbridge raised & lowered with counterpoise. [F, formerly *bacule* see-saw (*battre* bump+*cul* buttocks)]

bāse¹, n. **1.** That on which anything stands or depends, support, bottom, foundation, principle, groundwork, starting-point (~′*ball*, U.S. national game, more elaborate rounders, also ball used in it). **2.** (archit.). Part of column between shaft & pedestal or pavement. **3.** (bot. & zool.). End at which an organ is attached to trunk. **4.** (geom.). Line or surface on which plane or solid figure is held to stand. **5.** (chem.). Correlative of ACID, substance capable of combining with an acid to form a salt (including, but wider than, ALKALI). **6.** (mil.). Town or other area in rear of an army where drafts, stores, hospitals, etc., are concentrated (also ~ *of operations*). **7.** (surv.). Known line used as geometrical ~ for trigonometry. **8.** (math.). Starting-number for system of numeration or logarithms (as 10 in decimal counting). [F, or f. L f. Gk *basis* (*bainō* step, stand)]

bāse², v.t. Found (something) *on*; establish (with adv., as *firmly*); ~ *oneself on*, rely upon (in argument etc.). [f. prec.]

bāse³, a. (Orig.) of small height (now only in plant names as ~-*rocket*); morally low, cowardly, selfish, mean, despicable, whence ~'LY² (-sl-) adv.; menial; ‖ (Law) ~ *tenure, estate, fee*, not absolute, but determinable on fulfilment of contingent qualification; (Lang.) not classical (~ *Latinity*); ~-*born*, of low birth, illegitimate; ~-*court*, outer court of castle or court behind farmhouse; ~ *metals*, opposed to precious; ~ *coin*, spurious, alloyed. Hence ~'NESS (-sn-) n. [f. F *bas* f. LL *bassus* short (in L as cognomen)]

bāse'less (-sl-), a. Groundless, unfounded. Hence ~NESS n. [BASE¹, -LESS]

bāse'ment (-sm-), n. Lowest or fundamental part of structure; inhabited storey sunk below ground level. [BASE n. or v. +-MENT]

bǎsh, v.t., & n. **1.** Strike heavily so as to smash in (often *in*). **2.** n. Heavy blow; *have a ~ at it* (sl.), attempt it. [perh. init. cf. *bang, smash*; or = Sw. *basa* flog, Da. *baske* cudgel]

bashaw', n. Earlier form of PASHA.

bǎsh'ful, a. Shy; shamefaced, sheepish. Hence ~LY² adv., ~NESS n. [f. obs. *bash* vb for ABASH +-FUL]

bǎshi-bazouk' (-ōok), n. Mercenary of Turkish irregulars, notorious for pillage & brutality. Hence ~ERY (4, 5) n. [mod. Turk., lit. brain-turned]

bāsi-, stem of many adjj. in Physiol. Of, at, forming, the base of. [BASE¹, BASIS]

bǎs'ic, a. Of, at, forming, base; fundamental; (Chem.) having the properties of or containing a base; (Min.) slightly silicated (igneous rock); prepared by non-siliceous process (steel); ~ *English*, select vocabulary of 850 words; ~ *slag*, fertilizer containing phosphates produced as by-products in the ~ process of steel manufacture. [BASE¹+-IC]

basi'city, n. An acid's relative power of combining with bases. [prec.+-TY]

bǎs'il¹ (-z-), n. Kinds of aromatic herb, esp. *common* or *sweet* ~ & *bush* or *lesser* ~, both culinary. [ME, f. OF *basile* f. LL *basilisca* (*basiliscus* BASILISK), the Gk name *basilicon* (= royal) being misinterpreted as antidote for basilisk's venom]

bǎs'il² (-z-), n. Corruption of BASAN.

basil'ic, a. (Of vein) starting from elbow & discharging into axillary vein. [f. F *basilique* f. L f. Gk *basilikos* royal (as formerly thought of special importance)]

basil'ica, n. (Orig.) royal palace; hence, oblong hall with double colonnade & apse used for lawcourt & assemblies; such a building used as Christian church; (in Rome) one of the seven churches founded by Constantine. [L, f. Gk *basilikē* (*oikia*, *stoa*) royal (house, portico) f. *basileus* king, -IC]

basil'icon, -um, n. Kinds of ointment. [-*on* Gk, -*um* L, f. Gk *basilikos* as in prec.; so called as a 'royal' remedy]

bǎs'ilisk (-z-), n. Fabulous reptile (also *cockatrice*) hatched by serpent from cock's egg, blasting by its breath or look; (fig.) ~-*glance* etc., evil eye, person or thing that blasts (reputation etc.); (Zool.) small American lizard with hollow crest inflated at will. [f. L f. Gk *basiliskos* (dim. of *basileus* king) kinglet, serpent, golden-crested wren]

bǎs'in, n. Hollow round metal or pottery vessel, less deep than wide, & contracting downwards, for holding water etc., bowl; hollow depression; dock with flood-gates; land-locked harbour; tract of country drained by river & tributaries; circular or oval valley; (Geol.) formation with strata dipping towards centre, the deposit (e.g. coal) contained in this. Hence ~FUL (2) n. [ME & OF *bacin* (F *bassin*) f. Rom. **bac(c)hinus* f. LL *bacca* BACK⁴]

bǎs'inet, bǎs'net, n. Light steel head-piece. [ME *basnet, bacinet* f. OF *bacinet* dim. of *bacin* BASIN]

bās'is, n. (pl. *bāsēs*). = BASE¹ (chiefly in fig. senses); main ingredient, foundation, beginning, determining principle; common ground for negotiation etc.; military base. [L = BASE¹]

bask (bah-), v.i. Revel in warmth & light (usu. *in* the sun, firelight, etc.); ~-*ing* -*shark*, largest species of shark (also *sunfish* & *sailfish*). [app. f. ON *bathask* refl. of *batha* BATHE¹]

bas'ket¹ (bah-), n. Wicker vessel of osiers, cane, rushes, etc.; the quantity contained in it (also ~*ful*); wicker singlestick hand-guard; *pick of the* ~, best of the lot; ~-*ball*, game played with large inflated ball, a goal being scored when it is thrown into a ~ fixed 10 ft above ground at opponents' end; *basket*-, of ~ shape as ~-*hilt*, of ~ material or fashion as ~-*carriage, -work*. Hence ~RY(5)n. [orig. unkn.]

bas'ket² (bah-), v.t. Put in a basket, waste-paper or other. [f. prec.]

bās'on¹, n. (arch.). = BASIN.

bās'on², n., & v.t. Bench for felting hat material; (vb) felt. [perh. = BASIN]

basque (bahsk), n. & a. **1.** Biscayan, (native or language) of Western Pyrenees (*B*~). **2.** Short continuation of bodice below waist; bodice having this. [F, f. L *Vasco -onis*]

băs-rèlief', **băss-**, n. (Piece of) shallow carving or sculpture on background (less than half the true depth). [earlier *basse relieve*, f. It. *basso rilievo*, later alt. to F *bas-relief*]

băss[1], n. Common perch; *black* ~, perch of Lake Huron; European sea-fish (also *sea-wolf* and *sea-dace*). [earlier *barse* f. OE *bærs* = MHG *bars*, f. Gmc root **bars-*, **bors-* bristle]

băss[2], n. Inner bark of lime, used for mats, hassocks, & baskets, & for tying plants, flowers, etc.; ~*-broom*, coarse fibre broom for rough work; ~*-wood*, Amer. lime, its wood. [alt. f. BAST]

băss[3], a. & n. Deep-sounding; (of, suited to) lowest part in harmonized music; (man with) ~ voice; *thorough-*~, *figured* ~, ~ part with shorthand indications below of the proper harmony, hence theory of harmony; ~*-viol*, *viola da gamba* or violoncello. [ME *bas*, *base* see BASE[3]; now *bass* after It. *basso*]

băss'ět[1], n. Short-legged badger-dog. [F, dim. of *bas*, *basse* low; see BASE[3]]

băss'ět[2], n. Obsolete card-game. [f. It. *bassetta* f. *bassetto* dim. of *basso* BASE[3]]

băss'ět[3], n., & v.i. (geol.). Edge of stratum cropping out; (vb) crop out. [orig. unkn.]

băss'ět-hŏrn, n. Tenor clarinet. [transl. of F *cor de bassette* f. It. *corno di bassetto* see BASSET[2]]

băssinět', n. Hooded wicker cradle or perambulator. [F, dim. of *bassin* BASIN]

băss'ō, n. = BASS[3] (second and third senses); ~ *profundo* (or *-on-*), (singer with) specially deep bass voice. [It., = (deep) bass]

bassōōn', n. Wooden double-reed instrument used as bass to oboe; organ & harmonium stop of similar quality. Hence ~IST(3) n. [f. F *basson* (*bas* BASE[3] +*-on* see *-OON*)]

băssō-rĕliev'ō (*-lyä-*), n. (pl. *-os*). = BAS-RELIEF. [It.]

băst, n. Inner bark of lime (see BASS[2]); other flexible fibrous barks. [OE, *bæst*, MHG, ON *bast* f. Gmc **bastaz*]

băs'tard, n. & a. (Child) born out of wedlock or of adultery, illegitimate; (of things) unauthorized, hybrid, counterfeit; ~ *file* (with serrations of medium coarseness); ~ *slip*, sucker of tree (also fig., = *bastard* n.); (Bot.) nearly resembling another species (~ BALM); (Zool.) ~ *wing*, rudimentary extra digit with quill-feathers. [ME, f. OF f. *bast* (BAT-) pack-saddle (used as bed by mulcteer) + -ARD; cf. BANTLING]

băs'tardiz|e, **-is|e** (*-īz*), v.t. Declare illegitimate. Hence ~A'TION n. [prec. +*-IZE*]

băs'tardy̆, n. Illegitimacy; ~ *order*, for support of illegitimate child by putative father. [f. AF & OF *bastardie*; see BASTARD, -Y[1]]

băste[1], v.t. Stitch together, tack, (as prelim. to regular sewing). [ME, f. OF

bastir sew lightly f. Gmc **bastjan* (cf. OHG *besten* lace, tie) f. *bast-* BAST]

băste[2], v.t. Moisten (roasting meat) with fat to prevent burning; pour melted wax etc. on (wicks in candlemaking). [orig. unkn.]

băste[3], v.t. Thrash, cudgel. [perh. = Sw. *basa* (see BASH) thr. past or p.p. *baist*, *baist* in early exx.; cf. HOIST[1, 2]; or fig. use of prec. (cf. 'dry basting' Shakesp.)]

băstille' (*-ēl*), n. Fortress; Paris prison-fortress destroyed 1789; prison. [ME *bastcle*, *-ile*, *-el* f. OF *bastille*, for older *bastide* f. Pr. *bastida* fortification f. p.p. of *bastir* build]

băstinād'ō, n. (pl. ~*es*), & v.t. (Punish with) caning on soles of feet. [f. Sp. *bastonada* (*baston* BATON) see *-ADO*(2)]

băs'tion, n. Projecting part of fortification, irregular pentagon with its base in the line (or at an angle) of the main works. Hence ~ED[2] (*-nd*) a. [F, f. It. *bastione* f. *bastire* build; cf. BASTILLE]

băt[1], n. Nocturnal mouse-like quadruped with fingers extended as frame of membranous wings; *have* ~*s in the belfry*, be crazy or eccentric. [f. 1575, alt. of ME *bakke* f. Scand.; earlier wds were *rearmouse* (f. OE), *flittermouse* (f. Du.)]

băt[2], n., & v.i. & t. **1.** Implement for striking ball in cricket, baseball, etc. (*off one's own* ~, in cricket, also fig., unaided; *carry* one's ~, be not out at end of innings); ~*sman* (*a good* etc. ~); ~*s'man* (*-an*), performer with cricket etc. ~, also one who signals with ~s in his hands to guide aircraft landing on ship's deck. **2.** vb. (*-tt-*). Use ~, have innings; strike (as) with ~. [ME, f. OF *batte* club (*battre* strike, see ABATE)]

băt[3], n. (sl.). Pace of stroke or step (*went off at a rare* ~). [orig. unkn.]

băt[4] (*baht*), n. (Anglo-Ind., colloq.). *The* ~, spoken language (orig. of India, now extended); *sling the* ~ (Army sl.), speak the lingo (in this use freq. pron. băt). [Hind., = speech, word]

băt[5], v.t. To wink (*never* ~*ted an eyelid*, did not sleep a wink, betrayed no emotion). [var. of obs. *bate* to flutter]

băt-, **bât-** (*băt*, *baht*), comb. form. For officers' baggage on campaign; ~*-horse* (for carrying baggage); ~*-pay*, baggage allowance. [f. OF *bast*, mod. *bât* pack-saddle f. Rom. **bastum* perh. f. Gk *bastazō* lift]

batat'a (*-ahta*), n. W.-Indian plant, sweet or Spanish potato. [Sp. & Port. f. native American]

Batāv'ian, a. & n. (Inhabitant) of ancient Batavia (between Rhine & Waal) or of modern Holland, Dutch(man); of, inhabitant of, Batavia in Java. [f. L *Batavia* (*Batavi* pl.)]

bătch, n. Loaves produced at one baking; quantity or number of anything coming at once or treated as a set. [ME *bache* (*bacan* BAKE) cf. *wake*, *watch*, *make*, *match*] bāte[1], v.t. & i. Let down (~ *hope* etc.), restrain (~*d breath*); deduct (part of; usu. with neg., esp. *not ~ a jot of*); fall off in force. [apheitc f. ABATE]

bāte[2], n., & v.t. Alkaline lye for softening hides; (vb) steep in this. [cf. Sw. *beta* to tan, G *beize* maceration f. *beizen* cause to bite BAIT[1]]

|| bāte[3], bait[3], n. (sl.). Rage (*was in an awful* ~). [perh.=obs. *bate* var. of *debate*; or f. BAIT[1]=state of baited person]

bath[1] (bahth; *pl. pron.* -dhz), Bath, n. 1. Washing; immersion in liquid, air, etc. (*air-*~, *sun-*~, exposure of naked body to air, sun; *mud-*~, of mud for rheumatism; ~ *of blood*, carnage); water etc. for bathing, wash, lotion, surrounding medium; vessel (*sitz-*~, like HIP-~ but with broad flat bottom [G *sitzbad* sitting bath]; *sponge-*~, esp. of broad flat saucer shape to facilitate sponging), room (also ~-*room*), or building, for bathing in (see TURKISH); town resorted to for medical bathing; *~'robe*, dressing-gown. 2. Order of knighthood (*B*~; for C.B., K.C.B., G.C.B., see abbreviations) named from the ~ preceding installation. 3. Town in Somerset named from hot springs (*B~ bun*; *B~ Oliver*, biscuit invented by Dr W. Oliver of B~, d. 1764; *B~ brick*, preparation for cleaning metal; || *B~ chair*, wheeled for invalid; || *B~* CHAP[2]; *B~ stone*, oolite building-stone). [OE *bæth*, OHG *bad*, ON *bath*, f. Gmc *batham*]

bath[2] (-ah- *or* -ä- *in all parts*), v.t. Subject to washing in bath (child or invalid, of nurse etc.). [f. prec.]

băth|e[1] (-dh), v.t. & i. Immerse (in liquid, air, light, etc.); (of person, liquid, etc.) moisten all over; (of sunlight etc.) envelop; take a bath or bathe, so ~*ing-costume*, *-dress*, || *-drawers*, *trunks*; ~*ing-machine*, wheeled dressing-box drawn into sea for ~ing from. [OE *bathian*, OHG *badōn*, ON *batha*, f. Gmc *bathōn*]

bāthe[2] (-dh), băth'er (-dh-), nn. Taking, taker, of a bath, esp. in sea, river, swimming-bath. [f. prec. in intr. sense]

băthĕt'ic, a. Marked by bathos. [irreg. f. Gk BATHOS after *pathos*, *pathetic*]

bathōm'ēter, n. Instrument used to ascertain depth of water. [f. Gk *bathos* depth + -METER]

Bathōn'ian, a. & n. (Inhabitant) of Bath. [mod. L *Bathonia* Bath, -AN]

băth'ŏs, n. Fall from sublime to ridiculous; anticlimax; performance absurdly below occasion. [Gk, = depth]

bathy-, comb. form of Gk *bathus* deep.

bathȳb'ius, n. Slimy gelatinous substance dredged from great ocean depths (once believed to be protoplasmic, now known to be inorganic). [f. BATHY- + Gk *bios* life]

bathȳmĕtr-, stem of scientific words. Of depth-measurement. [f. BATHY- + -METER]

băth'ȳscaphe (-ăf), n. = foll. [f. BATHY- + Gk *skaphē* boat]

băth'ȳsphēre, n. Large strong submersible sphere for deep-sea observation. [f. BATHY- + SPHERE]

băt'ik, n. Method (orig. Javan) of printing coloured designs on textiles by waxing parts not to be dyed. [Javanese *'mbatik* drawing]

băt'ing, prep. Except. [part. of BATE[1]]

batiste' (-ēst), n. & a. (Of) fine light fabric like cambric in texture. [F, f. *Baptiste* of Cambrai, first maker]

|| băt'man, n. (mil.). An officer's servant, so *băt'woman*; (orig.) one who looked after a baggage animal. [BAT-]

băt'on, n., & v.t. Staff of office, esp. *Marshal's* ~; constable's truncheon (vb, strike with this); wooden tube carried in relay race; (Her.) truncheon in shield (~ *sinister*, badge of bastardy); (Mus.) conductor's wand for beating time. [F *bâton*]

batrā'chian (-k-), a. & n. Of frogs; (one) of the *Batrachia*, or animals that discard gills & tail. [f. Gk *batrakheios* (*batrakhos* frog) + -AN]

battăl'ion (-yon), n. Large body of men in battle array (*God is for the big* ~s, force prevails); unit of infantry composed of several companies & forming part of regiment or brigade. [f. F *bataillon* (now *bata-*) f. It. *battaglione* f. *bataglia* BATTLE[1]]

|| băt'els, n. pl. College account at Oxford for board & provisions supplied, or for all college expenses. [perh. f. obs. vb *battle* fatten f. obs. adj. *battle* nutritious cf. BATTEN[4]]

băt'ten[1], n. Piece of square-sawn softwood timber 2 in. to 4 in. thick & 5 in. to 8 in. wide; bar of wood used for clamping boards of door etc.; strip of wood carrying electric lamps; (Naut.) strip of wood nailed on spar to save rubbing, or securing hatchway tarpaulin. Hence ~ING[1](6) n. [var. of BATON]

băt'ten[2], v.t. Strengthen with battens; (Naut.) ~ *down*, close the hatches (see BATTEN[1]). [f. prec.]

băt'ten[3], n. Bar in silk-loom striking in the weft. [f. F *battant* (*battre* strike, -ANT)]

băt'ten[4], v.i. Feed gluttonously *on*, revel *in*, (often implying morbid taste); grow fat. [cf. ON *batna* get better (*bati* advantage cf. BETTER[1], BOOT[2]); see -EN[6]]

băt'ter[1], v.t. & i. Strike repeatedly so as to bruise or break (person, thing, or abs.; also with advv. *about*, *down*, *in*; & intr., ~ *at the door*); operate against (walls etc.) with artillery; (fig.) handle severely (theories, persons); beat out of shape, indent; (Printing) deface (type) by use; ~*ing-charge*, full charge of powder for cannon; ~*ing-ram*, swinging beam anciently used for breaching walls, sometimes with ram's-head end; ~*ing-train*, set of siege guns. [ME, f. *bat-* in OF *batre* (BAT[2]) + -ER[5]]

bătt′er², n. Mixture of ingredients beaten up with liquid for cooking; defect in printing-type or stereotype plate. [ME *batour, -owre* f. OF *bat(e)ure* beating]

bătt′er³, v.i. & n. (Have) receding slope from ground upwards (of walls narrower at top). [orig. unkn.]

bătt′ery, n. (Law) infliction of blows, or of the least menacing touch to clothes or person (esp. in phr. *assault & ~*); (Mil.) emplacement for one or more guns, artillery unit of guns & men & vehicles or horses consisting usu. of two sections & forming subdivision of regiment, (fig.) *turn a man's ~ against himself* (in argument); (in various sciences & arts) set of similar or connected cells, instruments, or utensils (electric, galvanic, optical, cooking); series of nesting-boxes, cages, etc., in which laying hens are confined for intensive laying or poultry reared & fattened; hammered brass or copper vessels. [f. F *batterie* (*battre* strike, & see -ERY)]

bătt′ing, n. In vbl senses; also, cotton fibre prepared in sheets for quilts etc. [BAT²+-ING¹]

băt′tle¹, n. Combat, esp. between large organized forces (*general's ~*, decided by strategy or tactics, *soldier's ~*, by courage & skill; *pitched ~*, fought by common consent; *~ royal*, in which several combatants or all available forces engage, free fight); victory (*the ~ is to the strong, youth is half the ~*); *join, give, refuse, accept, offer, do, ~*; *~-axe*, medieval weapon, (colloq.) formidable (usu. middle-aged) woman; *~-cruiser*, heavy-gunned ship of higher speed & lighter armour than ~ ship; *~ dress*, soldier's etc. uniform of belted blouse & trousers; *~-piece*, picture or literary description of a ~-scene; *line of ~*, troops or ships drawn up to fight; *line-of-~ ship*, (obs.) of 74 or more guns; *~-ship* (mod.), most heavily armed and armoured warship, designed to meet the most powerful ships in ~. [ME *batayle* f. OF *bataille* f. Rom. **battalia* f. LL *battualia* pl. gladiatorial exercises f. L *battuere* beat]

băt′tle², v.i. Struggle *with* or *against* (difficulties, the waves, etc.). [f. F *batailler* (*bataille* = prec.)]

băt′tledōre (-teld-), n. Wooden instrument like canoe paddle used in washing, baking, etc.; wooden, stringed, or parchmented bat used with shuttlecock in the game *~ & shuttlecock*. [from 1440; perh. f. Pr. *batedor* beater (*batre* beat+-*dor* = -TOR)]

băt′tlement (-tel-), n. (usu. in pl.). Indented parapet (raised parts, *cops* or *merlons*; gaps, *embrasures* or *crenelles*); parapet & enclosed roof. Hence ~ED² a. [Eng. formation (+-MENT) on OF *bataillier, bateillier* furnish with turrets of defence, also, furnish with ramparts or bastions (whence ME p.p. *batayld*)]

battue (see Ap.), n. Driving of game by beaters to the sportsmen's station; shooting party on this plan; wholesale slaughter. [F]

băt′y̆, a. (sl.). Crazy. [f. BAT¹+-Y²]

bau′ble, n. Showy trinket; court fool's emblem, a stick with ass-eared head carved on it; trifle, toy, thing of no worth. [ME *babel, babulle*, f. OF *babel, baubel* child's toy, of unkn. orig.]

baulk. See BALK.

baux′ite, n. (min.). Earthy compound containing varying proportions of alumina, the chief commercial source of aluminium. [f. *Les Baux* in France+-ITE¹(2)]

baw′bee, n. (Sc.). Halfpenny. [f. name of the laird of Sillebawby, mint-master under James V]

bawd, n. Procuress; obscene talk. [shortened form of ME *bawdstrot* f. OF *baudestrote, baudetrot* female pander]

bawd′|y̆, a. & n. Obscene (talk); *~y-house*, brothel. Hence ~iNESS n. [f. prec.]

bawl, v.t. & i. Say, speak, in a noisy way (often with *out*, also with *at, against*, etc.). [imit.; cf. med. L *baulare* bark, Icel. *baula* (Sw. *böla*) to low]

‖ **bawl′ey**, n. (dial.). Fishing smack peculiar to Essex and Kentish coasts. [orig. unkn.]

bawn, n. Court of a castle; cattlefold. [f. Ir. *bábhun*]

bay¹, n. Kind of tree or shrub; (pl.) wreath of its leaves worn by conquerors or poets, heroic or poetic fame; *~'berry*, a West Indian tree, (also) candleberry or its fruit; *~ rum*, a perfume distilled from bayberry leaves. [f. OF *baie* f. L *baca* berry]

bay², n. Part of sea filling wide-mouthed opening of land; recess in mountain range; *Bay State*, Massachusetts. [ME, f. OF *baie* f. Sp. *bahia* f. LL *baia*]

bay³, n. Division of wall between columns or buttresses; recess (*horse-~*, stall; *sick-~*, part of main deck used as hospital); space added to room by advancing window from wall line (*~ window*, filling such space); (Mil.) passing-place in a trench; ‖ railway platform having a cul-de-sac & acting as starting-point or terminus for a side-line, the cul-de-sac of such a platform, (*~-line*, side-line starting from this). [ME, f. OF *baée* f. *baer* to gape f. Rom. **batare*]

bay⁴, n. Bark of large dog, of hounds in pursuit, esp. the chorus raised as they draw close; (in phr. lit. of hounds & quarry, fig. of persecutors & victim, applied to the hunted animal) *stand* or *be at, turn to, hold hounds* etc. *at, ~*, show fight; (applied to hounds) *hold* or *have at, bring* or *drive to, ~*, come to close quarters with (quarry). [ME, f. (1) OF *tenir a bay* = It. *tenere a bada* hold agape or in suspense (see prec.) & (2) OF *abai*, in *tenir a bay* (mod. *aux abois*) f. *bayer*, foll.]

bay[5], v.i. & t. (Of large dogs) bark or howl; bark at, esp. ~ *the moon*. [ME, f. OF *bayer* (mod. *aboyer*) bark, (imit., of .uncert. orig.), later infl. by BAY[4]]

bay[6], a. & n. Reddish-brown (horse). [f. F *bai* f. L *badius*]

bayadère' (-dār'), n. Hindu dancing-girl (esp. one attached to a S.-Indian temple); striped textile fabric. [F, f. Port. *bailadeira* ballet-dancer]

Bay'ard, n. Chivalrous person. [French hero, 'chevalier sans peur et sans reproche', 1475–1524]

bay'onet[1], n. Stabbing blade attachable to rifle-muzzle; *the* ~, or ~*s*, military force; (with prefixed number) so many infantry (cf. SABRE); *Spanish* ~, a plant, kind of yucca. [f. F *baionnette* perh. f. *Bayonne* as made or first used there]

bay'onet, v.t. Stab with bayonet; ~ *into*, coerce by military force (or fig. by pressure) into. [f. prec.]

bayou (bī'ū), n. Marshy offshoot of river in southern N. America. [Amer. F, cf. Choctaw *bāyuk* branch in a delta]

bay'-salt (sawlt), n. Salt in large crystals obtained by evaporation. [f. BAY[2]]

bazaar' (-zār'), n. Oriental market; fancy fair in imitation of this, esp. sale of goods for charities. [f. Pers. *bazar* prob. through Turk. & It.]

*** bazook'a**, n. Anti-tank rocket-gun. [U.S., f. arbitr. name of comical mus. instrument]

bdell'ium (d-), n. Balsam-bearing tree; its resin. [L, f. Gk *bdellion* trans. of Heb. *b'dolakh* of uncertain meaning (carbuncle or crystal or pearl)]

be (bē, bǐ), v. substantive, copulative, & auxiliary (pres. ind.: *am*, pr. ăm, ạm; *art* arch., pr. ärt, art; *is*, pr. ĭz; pl. *are*, pr. är, ạr, & *be* arch.; past ind.: 1 & 3 *was*, pr. wŏz, woz; 2 *wast* arch., pr. wŏst, wost; pl. *were*, pr. wēr, wār, wẹr; pres. subj. *be*; past subj. *were*, exc. 2 sing. *wert* arch., pr. wārt, wert; imperat. *be*; part. *being*, pr. bē'ing; p.p. *been*, pr. bēn, bǐn; colloq. clipped forms '*m* = *am*, '*s* = *is*, '*re* = *are*, *Isn't*, *wasn't*, *aren't* pl., *weren't*, are legitimate in actual or printed talk; *ain't* is colloq. for *am not* & vulg. for *is* or *are not*. **1.** vb subst. Exist, occur, live, (often with *there*; *God is, there is a God*; *for the time being*, temporarily; *to be or not to be*, see *Haml.* III. i. 56—often joc. in trivial applications); remain, continue, (*let it be, do not be long*); (with advv. or adv. phrr.) occupy such a position, experience such a condition, have gone to such a place, busy oneself so, hold such a view, be bound for such a place, (*is in the garden, has been to Rome, be off, how is he?, what are you at?, I am for tariff reform, for London*); *been* colloq., called here, paid a visit, (*has anyone been?, has not been for orders*); *been and*, colloq. expletive of protest or surprise (*you have been & moved my papers!*); (with dat.) befall (*woe is me*). **2.** vb cop. (With nouns, adjj., or adj. phrr.) belong under such a description (*I am a man, sick, of good courage*); coincide in identity with, amount to, cost, signify, (*thou art the man, twice two is four, it is nothing to me, what are these pears?*). **3.** vb aux. With p.p. of trans. vbs forming passives (*this was done*); with p.p. of some intr. vbs, as *fall, come, grow*, forming perfects (*the sun is set, Babylon is fallen*); with prec. part. act. forming continuous tenses act. & pass. (*he is building a house, the house was building*); with pres. part. pass. forming continuous tenses pass. (*the house was being built*); with infin. expressing duty, intention, possibility, (*I am to inform you, he is to be there, the house is to let, he is to be hanged, it was not to be found*); *were* with infin. in hypotheses (*if I were*, or *were I, to tell you*). **4.** Parts used as adjj., advv., nouns: *may-be*, perhaps, a possibility; *the to-be*, the future; *might-have-beens*, past possibilities; *would-be*, that yearns, or fancies himself, to be; *be-all*, whole being, essence. [f. four roots (1) Aryan *es-*, Gk, L, & Gmc *es-*, Skr. *as-*, to be; (2) Gmc **wes-*, Skr. *vas-*, remain; (3) Skr. *bhu-*, Gk *phu-*, L *fu-*, Gmc **beo-*, become; (4) Gmc **ar-* (f. *or-*) of unkn. orig. From (1) come *am* (cf. Gk *esmi*); from (2) come *was, wast, wert, were*; from (3) come *be, being, been*; from (4) come *art, are*]

be- (bǐ-), pref. f. OE *be-*, weak or stressless form of prep. & adv. *bī* BY, accented form of which appears in *by-law, by-word, by-gone*, etc. The orig. meaning was *about*, the various developments of which may be seen in the following groups of uses. **1.** Adding notion of all over, all round, to trans. vb, as *beset, besmear*. **2.** Adding notion of thoroughly, excess, to trans. vb, as *bedrug, bescorch*. **3.** Making intr. vbs trans., as *bemoan, bestraddle*. **4.** Forming trans. vbs = *to make* from adjj. & nouns, as *befoul, bedim, bebishop*. **5.** Making trans. vbs = *to call so & so* from nouns, as *bedevil, bemadam*. **6.** Making trans. vbs = *to surround with, to affect with, to treat in the manner of*, from nouns, as *becloud, beguile, befriend*. **7.** Making adjj. in -ED[2], from nouns, as *bewigged, beflagged*, (usu. with some contempt).

beach[1], n. Water-worn pebbles or sand; sea-shore covered with these; shore between high & low water mark; ~*-comber*, white man in Pacific Islands etc. who lives by collecting jetsam, longshore vagrant; ~*-head*, fortified position established on ~ by landing forces [after *bridge--head*]; ~*-master*, officer superintending disembarkation of troops; ~*-rest*, chair--back for sitting against on ~. [16th c. *beach, bache*, of unkn. orig.]

beach[2], v.t. Run (ship, boat) ashore, haul up. [f. prec.]

‖ **beach-la-mār'** (-lah-), n. Jargon English used in Western Pacific. [corrupt. f. Port. *bicho do mar* BÊCHE-DE-MER]

beac'on¹, n. Signal, signal-fire on pole or hill; signal station; conspicuous hill (in names); lighthouse; guide or warning; BELISHA ~. [OE *bēacn*, OS *bōkan*, OHG *bouhhan* f. WG *baukn-*, cf. BECKON]

beac'on², v.t. Give light to, guide; supply (district) with beacons. [f. prec.]

bead¹, n. 1. (Orig.) prayer. 2. Small perforated ball for threading with others on string, used in counting one's prayers (*tell one's ~s*); the same used for ornament; drop of liquid, bubble; small knob in foresight of gun (*draw a ~ on*, take aim at); (Archit.) moulding like a bead series, or small one of semicircular section; *~-roll*, list of names, long series, (orig. of persons to be prayed for); *~s'man*, pensioner bound to pray for benefactor, almsman. [ME *bede* (f. *ibede*, OE *gebed* prayer), OS *beda*, OHG *beta*, Goth. *bida*, f. Gmc *beth-* see BID¹]

bead², v.t. & i. Furnish with beads; string together; form or grow into beads. [f. prec.]

bead'ing, n. In vbl senses; also, a bead moulding. [BEAD¹; see -ING¹]

‖ **bea'dle**, n. Ceremonial officer of church, college, city company, etc.; parish officer appointed by vestry; (Sc.) church officer attending on the minister. Hence ~SHIP (-dels-) n. [(a) ME *budel*, *bidel* f. OE *bydel* = OHG *butil* f. WG *buthilaz* (see BID¹); superseded by (b) ME *bedel*, f. OF *bedel* (med. L *bedellus*, *bidellus*) f. same Gmc source]

bea'dledom (-deld-), n. Stupid officiousness. [-DOM]

bead'y, a. (Of eyes) small & bright; covered with beads or drops. [BEAD¹]

bea'gle, n. The smallest English hound, used for hare hunting when field follows on foot; spy etc.; *beagling*, hunting with ~s. [ME, perh. f. OF *bé-gueule* open throat (*béer* gape)]

beak¹, n. Bird's bill (esp. in birds of prey, & when strong & hooked); similar mandible-end of other animals, as turtle; hooked nose; protection at prow of ancient warship; spout. Hence ~ED² (-kt) a. [ME *bec*, *bek* f. OF *bec* f. pop. L *beccus* of Gaulish origin]

‖ **beak²**, n.(sl.). Magistrate; schoolmaster. [orig. unkn.]

beak'er, n. Large drinking-cup; lipped glass vessel for scientific experiments; tall wide-mouthed pottery drinking-vessel found in Bronze Age graves (*~-folk*, *-people*) [ME *biker* f. ON *bikarr* = OS *bikeri*, OHG *behhāri*, f. Gmc *bikarjam*, f. med. L *bicarium* perh. f. Gk *bikos* drinking bowl. See PITCHER]

beam¹, n. Long piece of squared timber supported at both ends; cylinder in loom on which warp, cloth, is wound; chief timber of plough; bar of balance (*kick the~*, prove the lighter, be defeated); shank of anchor; lever in engine connecting piston-rod & crank; (pl.) horizontal cross-timbers of ship supporting deck & joining sides (*starboard*, *port*, ~, right & left sides, as *land on port ~* etc.); = ship's breadth (*on her ~-ends*, on her side, almost capsizing, in danger, at a loss); ray or pencil of light, or of electric radiation (~ *system*, wireless telegraphy in which transmission in a particular direction is achieved by reflecting a short--wave ~ from a parabolic arrangement of wires charged with static electricity), radiance, bright look, smile. [OE *bēam* tree, OS *bōm*, OHG *boum* f. WG *baumaz*; cf. ON *bathmr*, Goth. *bagms*]

beam², v.t. & i. Emit (light, affection, etc.); shine; smile radiantly. Hence ~'ING² a. [f. prec.]

beam'y, a. Radiant (rare); (poet., of spears etc.) huge; broad (of ships). [BEAM¹, -Y²]

bean, n. (Kinds of leguminous plants bearing smooth kidney-shaped seed in long pods; similar seed of other plants, as coffee; coin (sl.; *I haven't a ~*, I'm stony-broke); *full of ~s*, *~-fed*, in high spirits; ‖ OLD ~; *give one ~s* (sl.), punish or scold him; SPILL¹ *the ~s*. [OE *bēan*, OS, OHG *bōna*, ON *baun*, f. Gmc *baunā*]

‖ **bean-feast**, **bean'o** (sl., pl. *-os*), n. Employer's annual dinner to workpeople, fête, merry time. [f. prec. (beans & bacon being orig. considered an indispensable dish)]

bear¹ (bār), n. Heavy partly carnivorous thick-furred plantigrade quadruped; rough unmannerly person, whence ~'-ISH¹ a., ~'ishNESS n.; *Great Little*, *B~*, northern constellations; (St. Exch.) speculator for a fall, one who sells stock for future delivery hoping to buy it cheap meanwhile, & therefore tries to bring prices down (cf. BULL, & see foll.); heavy punching-machine: ~'s-breech, acanthus; ~'s-foot, kinds of hellebore; ~'garden, scene of tumult; ~'s-grease, pomade; ~'skin, (wrap etc.) of ~'s skin, Guards' tall furry cap; ~'leader, travelling tutor. [OE *bera*, OHG *bero*, f. WG *beron*]

bear² (bār), v.i. & t., & n. (St. Exch.). Speculate for a fall; produce fall in price of (stocks etc.); (n.) this operation. [f. prec., perh. w. ref. to selling the bear's skin before killing the bear]

bear³ (bār), v.t. & i. (*bore*, *borne* or *born*, see below†). **1.** Carry (poet. or formal, exc. in the senses or contexts following); ~ or ~ *away*, win (the palm, bell, prize); carry visibly, show, be known by, (banner, device, arms, the marks of, name, relation or ratio *to*; ~ *oneself well* etc., behave); bring at need (~ *witness*, *company*; ~ *a hand*, help); wield (office, rule); carry internally (~ *a grudge*; ~ *in mind*, remember); wear (~ *arms*, the *sword*); ~ *out*, confirm; *be borne away* (by external force or influence, or internal impulse); *is borne in upon* one, becomes one's conviction. **2.** Sustain (weight, responsibility, cost; ~ *a part in*, share); stand (test etc.), endure (*grin & ~ it*), tolerate, put up with (*cannot ~ him*), whence ~'ABLE a.; be capable of upholding weight (*ice ~s*); be fit for (*his language won't ~ repeating*); ~ *with*, treat forbearingly; ~ *up*, (trans.) uphold, (intr.) not despair; *borne on the books of*, paid by. **3.** Thrust, strive, apply weight, tend, (~ *down*, overthrow; ~ *hard on*, oppress; ~ *upon*, be relevant to; *bring to* ~, apply; ~ *to the right, away, off*, incline; ~ *down*, swoop; ~ *up*, keep ship farther away from wind; ~ *up for*, change ship's course so as to sail towards). **4.** Produce, yield, give birth to. †The p.p. is *borne*, exc. that *born* is used in pass. parts referring to human & other mammal birth; even then *borne* is used before *by* with the mother (*has borne a child*; *born 1901*; *born of, borne by, Eve*). [OE, OS, OHG *beran*, ON *bera*, Goth. *bairan*, f. Gmc **ber-*, Aryan **bher-* (L *ferre*, Gk *pherein*)]

beard[1], n. Hair of lower face (excluding usu. the moustache, & occas. the whiskers); chin tuft of animals; gills of oyster; attachment threads of some shellfish; beak-bristles of birds; awn of grasses; *old-man's ~*, = traveller's joy. Hence ~'ED[2], ~'LESS, aa., ~'lèssNESS n. [OE *beard*, OHG *bart* f. WG **bardaz*]

beard[2], v.t. Oppose openly, defy, (~ *the lion in his den*). [f. prec.]

bear'er (bār-), n. Person or thing that carries; part-carrier of coffin; (India) palanquin-carrier, body-servant; native carrier; bringer of letters or message, presenter of cheque; (with adj. *good* etc.) plant etc. that produces well etc.; ~ *company* (Mil.), medical unit organized to tend & bring in wounded on field service. [BEAR[3] + -ER[1]]

bear'ing (bār-), n. In vbl senses; also or esp.: outward behaviour; heraldic charge or device; relation, aspect, (*consider it in all its ~s*; *what is the ~ of this on the argument?*); (pl.) parts of machine that bear the friction; compass direction in which a place etc. lies, (pl.) relative position (*have lost my ~s*, do not know where I am); ~*-rein*, fixed rein from bit to saddle, forcing horse to arch its neck. [BEAR[3], ING[1]]

beast, n. Animal; quadruped; (Farming) bovine animal, esp. fatting-cattle (collect. pl. *beast*); animal for riding or driving; brutal man; person whom one dislikes; *The B~*, Antichrist; *the ~*, the animal nature in man. [ME, f. OF *beste* f. Rom. *besta* f. L *bestia*]

beast'linèss, n. Gluttony, drunkenness, obscenity; disgusting food or drink. [f. foll.]

beast'lў[1], a. Like a beast or its ways: unfit for human use, dirty; (colloq.) undesirable. [-LY[1]]

beast'lў[2], adv. (sl.). (Intensifying adjj.

& advv. used in bad sense; cf. JOLLY) very, regrettably, (~ *drunk, wet*; *raining ~ hard*). [-LY[2]]

beat[1], v.t. & i. (past *beat*; p.p. *beaten*, but *beat* in *dead-beat*, often in sense *surpassed*, & occas. in other senses). Strike repeatedly (t. & i.; ~ *the breast*, in mourning; ~ *black & blue*, bruise; ~ *the air*, strive in vain; ~ *at door*, knock loudly; ~ *path*, make it by trampling), inflict blows on, (of sun, rain, wind) strike (*upon* something, or abs.); ~ *up*, ~ (person) severely; overcome, surpass (~ *hollow*, easily; ~ *person to it*, get there first, lit. & fig.; ~*s cockfighting*, is extremely exhilarating), be too hard for, perplex; move up & down (t. & i. of wings); move rhythmically (*heart* etc. ~*s*, ~ *time, seconds*, etc.); (Phys. etc.) create pulsation (see foll.); shift, drive, alter, deform, by blows (~ *down, back, away, off*; ~ *in*, crush; ~ *down price* or *seller*, cheapen or bargain with; ~ *up eggs* etc., reduce to froth, powder, paste; ~ *or ~ out metal*, forge); (Naut.) ~ *up, about*, strive, tack, against wind; strike (bushes, water) to rouse game (~ *about the bush*, approach subject slowly, shilly-shally; ~ *up recruits* etc., collect; ~ *up the quarters of*, visit; ~ *one's brains*, search for ideas; || ~ *the bounds*, mark parish boundaries by striking certain points with rods); play on drum (~ *a parley, a retreat*, propose terms, retire); *~ it* (sl.), go away. [OE *bēatan*, OHG *bōzan*, ON *bauta*, f. Gmc **bautan*]

beat[2], n. Stroke on drum, signal so given; movement of conductor's baton; measured sequence of strokes or sounds; throbbing; (Phys. etc.) pulsation due to combination of two sounds or electric currents of (slightly) different frequencies; sentinel's or constable's appointed course; one's habitual round; sportsman's range. [f. prec.]

beat'en, a. In vbl senses; also or esp.: worn hard, trite; shaped by the hammer; exhausted, dejected. [p.p. of BEAT[1]]

beat'er, n. In vbl senses; esp.: man employed to rouse game; implement for beating flat. [BEAT[1] + -ER[1]]

bĕatif'ic, a. Making blessed. [f. F *béatifique* or L *beatificus* (*beatus* p.p. of *beare* bless, & see -FIC)]

bĕatifica'tion, n. Making or being blessed; (R.-C. Ch.) first step to canonization, announcement that dead person is in bliss. [F, or f. LL *beatificatio* (prec., -ATION)]

bĕat'ifў, v.t. Make happy; (R.-C. Ch.) announce in prec. [f. F *béatifier* or LL *beatificare* (prec., -FY)]

beat'ing, n. In vbl senses; esp.: a chastisement; a defeat. [f. BEAT[1]]

bĕat'itūde, n. Blessedness; (pl.) the blessings in *Matt.* v. 3–11. [F, or f. L *beatitudo* (*beatus* see BEATIFIC, -TUDE)]

beau (bō), n. (pl. *~x*, pr. bōz). Fop, dandy; lady's-man, admirer. [F]

Beauf'ort scāle (-bŏf-), n. Scale of wind velocity ranging from 0 (calm) to 12–17 (hurricane; 75 miles an hour or over). [Sir F. *Beaufort*, English admiral (d. 1857)]

beau geste (bōzhĕst'), n. A display of magnanimity. [F]

beau idē'al (bō), n. One's highest type of excellence or beauty. [F (*-éal*), = the ideal Beautiful (often misconceived in E as a beautiful ideal); see BEAU & IDEAL a.]

beau monde (see Ap.), n. Fashionable society. [F]

Beaune (bōn), n. A red Burgundy. [place]

beaut'ēous (bū-), a. (poet.). Beautiful. [ME *beaute* BEAUTY + -OUS; cf. *plenteous*]

beaut'iful (bū-), a. Delighting the eye or ear, gratifying any taste, (~ *face, voice, poem, picture, soup, batting*); morally or intellectually impressive, charming, or satisfactory (~ *patience, organization, specimen*). Hence ~LY² adv. [BEAUTY + -FUL]

beaut'if|ȳ (bū-), v.t. Make beautiful; adorn. Hence ~ĪER¹ (1, 2) n. [BEAUTY + -FY]

beaut'ȳ (bū-), n. Combination of qualities, as shape, proportion, colour, in human face or form, or in other objects, that delights the sight (~ *is but skin deep*, one cannot judge by appearances); combined qualities delighting the other senses, the moral sense, or the intellect; *a* ~, beautiful person or thing (often ironical), exceptionally good specimen (*here is a* ~); beautiful women; a beautiful trait or feature, ornament, (*that's the* ~ *of it*, the particular point that gives satisfaction); ~ *parlour* (orig. U.S.), establishment in which the art or trade of face-massage, face-lifting, applying cosmetics, etc. is carried on, whence *beauti'CIAN (bū-) n., one who runs a ~ parlour; ~-*sleep*, before midnight; ~-*spot*, small patch placed on lady's face as foil to complexion, beautiful scene. [ME *beaute* etc. f. OF f. Rom, *bellitatem* f. L *bellus* pretty; see -TY]

beaux yeux (bōzyē'), n. *For the* ~ *of*, just to gratify (person). [F, = fine eyes]

beav'er¹, n. Amphibious broad-tailed soft-furred rodent, building huts & dams; its fur; hat of this. [OE *beofor*, MDu. *bever*, OHG *biber*, ON *bjórr*, f. Gmc *bebruz*, cogn. w. L *fiber*]

beav'er², n. Lower face-guard of helmet. [ME & OF *bavière* bib (*bave* saliva)]

beav'erteen, n. Cotton twilled cloth with pile of loops. [f. BEAVER¹ after *velveteen*]

***bĕb'ŏp**, n. Kind of jazz music. [imit.]

bĕcall' (-kawl), v.t. (arch. or vulg.). Call (person) names. [BE-(2)]

bĕcalm' (-ahm), v.t. 1. Make calm (sea etc.). 2. Deprive (ship) of wind. [(1) BE-(2) + CALM v., (2) BE-(6) + CALM n.]

became. See BECOME.

bĕcause' (-ŏz, -awz), adv. & conj. For the reason (*that* & clause, arch.); by reason, on account, (*of* & noun); for the reason that, inasmuch as, since. [BY prep. + *cause* n., after OF *par cause de*; the conj. use arises by omission of *that*]

bĕccafic'ō (-fē-), n. (pl. *-os*). Small migrant bird eaten in Italy. [It. (*beccare* peck + *fico* fig)]

bĕ'chamĕl (-bĕsh-), n. Kind of white sauce. [inventor's name]

bêche-de-mer (see Ap.), n. Sea-slug, a Chinese dainty. [quasi-F of Eng. orig., alt. from *biche dé mer* f. Pg. *bicho do mar*, lit. sea-worm]

|| **bĕck¹**, n. Brook, mountain stream, (in northern England). [ME, f. ON *bekkr* cogn. w. OHG *bah*]

bĕck², n. Significant gesture, nod, etc.; the order implied (*have at* one's ~, *be at* person's ~ *& call*, of entire dominion & obedience). [f. foll.]

bĕck³, v.t. & i. (poet.). Make mute signal, signal mutely to. [f. dial. *beck* v., shortened f. BECKON]

bĕck'ĕt, n. (naut.). Contrivance for securing loose ropes, tackle, or spars, (rope-loop, hook, bracket, etc.). [orig. unkn.]

bĕck'on, v.t. & i. Summon, call attention of, by gesture; make mute signal (*to* person). [OE *biecnan, bēcnan*, OS *bōknian*, OHG *bouhhanjan* f. WG **bauknjan* f. *baukn-* BEACON]

bĕcloud', v.t. Cover with clouds; obscure. [BE-(6) + CLOUD n.]

bĕcom|e' (-ŭm), v.i. & t. (-came, -come). Come into being; *what has* ~*e of* (happened to) *him?*; (copulative) begin to be (followed by n., adj., or adj. phr.); suit, befit, adorn, look well on, whence ~'ING² a., ~'inglY² adv., ~'ingNESS n., (-kŭ-). [OE *becuman* (BE- + *cuman* COME) arrive, attain, = OHG *biquiman*, Goth. *biqiman*]

Becquerel rays (bĕk'rel rāz), n. pl. Rays emitted by radio-active substances (now usu. called *alpha, beta, gamma, rays*). [A. H. *Becquerel*, French physicist (d. 1878)]

bĕd¹, n. 1. Thing to sleep on, mattress (*feather* ~ etc.), frame-work with mattress & coverings; animal's resting place, litter; (elliptical for) use of ~, being in ~; ~ *& board*, entertainment, connubial relations; *narrow* ~, the grave; ~ *of down, flowers, roses*, easy position; ~ *of sickness*, invalid state; *brought to* ~, in child-birth, *of* child or abs.; *die in* one's ~, of natural causes; *go to* ~, retire for the night (imperat., sl., cease talking etc.); *take to, keep*, one's ~, become, be, ill; *make the* ~, arrange the coverings; *lie in the* ~ *one has made*, take consequences of one's acts; *got out of* ~ *on wrong side*, is bad-tempered for the day; ~'*chamber* (arch. exc. of royal, as *Groom, Lady*, etc., of *the* ~*chamber*), ~*room*; ~*clothes*, sheets, pillows, etc., of ~; ~'*fellow*, sharer of ~, (fig.) associate; ~*jacket* (for sitting up in ~); ~*key*, wrench for (un)fastening ~-*stead*; ~*lift*, appliance for raising invalid to sitting position; ‖~'*maker*, man tending college rooms at Oxf. & Camb.; ~--*pan*, invalid's chamber utensil for use in ~; ~'*post*, upright support of ~ (*in twinkling of* ~*post*, prob. transf. f. ~--*staff*, loose cross-piece of old ~steads often used as handy weapon; *between you & me & the* ~*post*, in confidence); ~'--*rid(den)*, confined to ~ by infirmity, decrepit. [OE *bedreda* (*rida* rider), -*en* by confusion w. p.p.]; ~'*room*, for sleeping in; ~'*side*, side of csp. invalid's ~ (*good* ~*side manner*, of tactful doctors); ~--*sitting room*, (colloq.) ~-*sitter*, combined ~room & sitting room; ~'*sore*, developed in invalid by lying in ~; ~'*spread*, coverlet; ~'*stead*, framework of ~; ~'*straw*, herbaceous plant once used as straw for ~s, esp. (*Our*) *Lady's* ~*straw*; ~'*lick*, quadrangular bag holding feathers etc. for ~; ~'*time*, hour for going to ~. 2. Flat base on which anything rests; ~--*plate*, metal plate forming base of machine; garden plot filled with plants, swamp with osiers; bottom of sea, river, etc. (~-*rock*, solid rock underlying alluvial deposits etc., fig. ultimate facts or principles of a theory, character, etc.); foundation of road or railway; slates etc. of billiard table; central part of gun--*carriage*; stratum; layer of oysters etc. [OE *bed(d)*, OS *bed*, *beddi*, OHG *betti*, Goth. *badi* f. Gmc **badjam*]

běd², v.t. & i. (-dd-). Put or go to bed (poet. or arch. exc. of horses etc.); plant (esp. ~ *out*); cover up or fix firmly in something; arrange as, be or form, a layer. [f. prec.]

bědăb'ble, v.t. Stain, splash, with dirty liquid, blood, etc. [BE-(1)+DABBLE]

bědăd', int. (Irish etc. for) by GAD¹.

bědaub', v.t. Smear with paint etc.; bedizen. [BE-(1)+DAUB v.]

bědd'er, n. In vbl senses; also, plant suited for flower-bed. [-ER¹]

bědd'ing, n. In vbl senses; also: mattress, bedclothes, etc.; litter for cattle; bottom layer; (Geol.) stratification. [-ING¹]

běděck', v.t. Adorn. [BE-(1)+DECK v.]

běd'ĕguar (-gär), n. Mosslike excrescence on rose-bush produced by insect's puncture. [f. F *bédeguar* f. Pers. *badawar* wind-brought]

‖ **běd'el(l)** (*or* bedĕl'), n. Official at Oxf. & Camb. with duties chiefly processional. [= BEADLE]

běděv'il, v.t. (-ll-, -l-). Treat with diabolical violence or abuse; possess, bewitch; spoil, confound; call devil. [BE-(5, 6)+DEVIL n.]

běděv'ilment, n. Possession by devil; maddening trouble, confusion. [prec.+ -MENT]

bědew', v.t. Cover with drops, sprinkle. [BE-(6)+DEW]

bědight' (-ĭt), v.t. (past & p.p. *bedight*). Array, adorn, (arch.; usu. in p.p.). [BE-(1)+DIGHT]

bědim', v.t. (-mm-). Make (eyes, mind) dim. [BE-(4)+DIM a.]

bědiz'en, v.t. Dress out gaudily. [BE-(2)+DIZEN]

běd'lam, n. (*B*~) hospital of St Mary of Bethlehem used as lunatic asylum; any madhouse; scene of uproar. [f. *Bethlehem*; hospital founded as priory 1247, converted to asylum 1547]

běd'lamite, n. & a. Lunatic. [-ITE¹ (1)]

Běd'lington, n. (Also ~ *terrier*) short--*haired*, narrow-headed sporting terrier. [~ in Northumberland]

běd'ouin (-ōō-; *or* -ēn), n. (pl. same) & a. (Arab) of the desert, wandering; gipsy. [ME *bedoyn* f. OF *beduin* f. Arab. *badawin* pl. of *badawiy* dweller in the desert (*badw* desert); -*n* is prop. the pl. sign]

bědrăb'bled (-ld), a. Dirty with rain & mud. [BE-(1), & see DRABBLE]

bědrăg'gle, v.t. Wet (dress etc.) by trailing it, or so that it trails or hangs limp. [BE-(1)+DRAGGLE]

bee, n. Four-winged stinging social insect (queen, drones, & workers) producing wax & honey; allied insects (*humble*, *mason*, *carpenter*, etc., ~); poet; busy worker; meeting for combined work or amusement (chiefly U.S., exc. *spelling*-~); *have a* ~ *in* one's *bonnet*, be obsessed on some point; ~-*bread*, (honey &) pollen used as food by ~s; ~-*eater*, kinds of foreign bird; ~HIVE; ~-*line*, straight between two places; ~-*master*, -*mistress*, keepers of ~s; ~ *orchis*, with ~-shaped flowers; ‖~-*skep*, straw hive; ~*s'wax*, secreted by ~s as comb material, (v.t.) polish with this. [OE *bēo*, OHG *bia*, ON *bý* f. Gmc **bīon*, cogn. w. OHG *bini* (G *biene*)]

beech, n. Smooth-barked glossy-leaved mast-bearing forest tree; its wood; ~--*fern*, kind of polypody; ~ *marten*, (also *stone marten*) white-breasted marten found in S. Europe; ~'*mast*, fruit of ~. Hence ~'EN⁵ a. [OE *bōece*, *bēce* f. Gmc **bōkjōn*, also **bōkā*-, whence OE *bōc* (cf. *buckmast*, *buckwheat*), ON *bók*, OHG *buohha*]

beef, n. (pl. -*ves*), & v.i. 1. Flesh of ox, bull, or cow; (in men) size, muscle; (usu. pl.) ox(en), esp. fattened, or their carcasses; ‖~'*eater*, yeoman of guard, warder of Tower of London, (f. obs. sense well-fed menial); ~ *tea*, stewed~ juice for invalids; ~STEAK; ~-*wood*, red timber of various trees. 2. v.i. *(sl.). Complain. [ME *boef*, *beef* f. OF *boef* f. L *bovem* nom. *bos* ox]

beef'|ў, a. Like beef; solid, muscular; stolid. Hence ~iNESS n. [-Y²]

Běěl'zěbŭb, n. The Devil; a devil. [OE, ME, f. L (Vulg.) f. Gk *beelzeboub* f. Heb. *ba'alz'bŭb* fly-lord]

been. See BE.

beer¹, n. Alcoholic liquor from fermented malt etc. flavoured with hops etc., including ale (pale) & porter (dark); other fermented drinks, as *nettle*-~;

GINGER-~; *small* ~, (lit.) weak~, (fig.) trifling matters (*think no small*~, of, have high opinion of); ~*-engine*, for drawing~ at a distance; ‖~*'house*, licensed for~, not spirits; ‖~*-money*, servant's allowance in lieu of ~; ~*-pull*, handle of ~*-engine. [OE *bēor*, MDu. *bēr*, OHG *bior*, com.-WG, whence prob. ON *bjórr*]

beer², n. One of the ends (so many threads) into which a warp is divided. [= BIER, cf. *porter* in same sense in Scotland]

beer'ȳ, a. Of, like, beer; esp., betraying influence of beer. [-Y²]

bees'tings (-z), n. pl. First milk after calving. [OE *bÿsting* f. OE *bēost* (obs. *beest*), OHG *biost*, of unkn. orig.]

bees'wing (-z-), n. Second crust in long-kept port; old wine. [BEE+WING, from its filmy look]

beet, n. Two plants with succulent root, *red* ~ used for salad, *white* ~ for making sugar; *~root*; ‖~*'root*, root of ~. [OE *bēte*, LG *beete*, OHG *bieza*, WG f. L *beta*]

bee'tle¹, n., & v.t. Tool with heavy head & handle for ramming, crushing, smoothing, etc. (vb, beat with this); *three-man*~, requiring three to lift it; ~*-brain* etc., blockhead. [OE *bīetel* f. Gmc *bautilaz* f. *bautan* BEAT¹; see -LE(1)]

bee'tle², n. Insect having upper wings converted to hard wing-cases (pop. only of the black & large varieties, also wrongly of insects like them, as the *black-~* or cockroach); short-sighted person (cf. ~*-eyed*, *blind as a* ~); ~*-crusher*, large boot or foot. [OE *bitula* biter f. *bītan* BITE¹]

bee'tle,³ a. Projecting, shaggy, scowling, (~ *brows*, ~*-browed*). [prob. f. prec. w. ref. to tufted antennae of some beetles]

bee'tle⁴, v.i. Overhang (of brows, cliffs), hang threateningly (of fate etc.). [f. prec.]

beeves. See BEEF.

beez'er, n. (sl.). Nose. [orig. unkn.]

befall' (-awl), v.t. & i. (-fell, -fallen). Happen; happen to (person etc.). [OE *befeallan* f. BE-(2)+*feallan* FALL; cf. OS, OHG *bifallan*]

befit', v.t. (-tt-). Suit, be fitted for; be incumbent on; be right for. Hence~t'ING² a..~t'ingLY² adv. [BE-(2)+FIT v.]

befog', v.t. (-gg-). Envelop in fog; obscure. [BE-(6)+FOG² n.]

befool', v.t. Dupe. [BE-(5)+FOOL¹ n.]

before', adv., prep., & conj. **1.** adv. Ahead (*go*~); on the front (~ *& behind*); previous to time in question, already, in the past, (*long* ~). **2.** prep. In front of (~ *the mast*, of common sailors berthed forward), ahead of; under the impulse of (~ *the wind, recoil* ~, *carry all* ~ *you*); in presence of (*appear* ~ *judge, bow* ~ *authority*; ~ *God*=as God sees me; *the question* ~ *us*); awaiting (*world all* ~ *them*); earlier than (~ *Christ*, usu. abbr. B.C., appended to dates reckoned back-

wards from birth of Christ); this side the coming of (future event); farther on than; rather than (*would die* ~ *lying*). **3.** conj. Previous to the time when; rather than (*would die* ~ *I lied*). [OE *beforan* (BE-+*foran* adv. f. Gmc **fora* FOR)]

before'händ (-rh-), adv. In anticipation, in readiness; *be* ~ *with*, anticipate, forestall; ~ *with the world*, having money in hand. [ME, orig. two wds; cf. L *prae manu, manibus* at hand]

befoul', v.t. Make foul (lit. or fig.); ~ one's *own* NEST. [BE-(4)+FOUL]

befriend' (-rĕnd), v.t. Help, favour. [BE-(6)+FRIEND n.]

beg, v.t. & i. (-gg-). Ask for (food, money, etc.); (abs.) ask alms; ask (*for* alms etc.); live by alms; (of dog) sit up with forepaws raised expectantly; ask earnestly or humbly (thing, *for* thing, *of* person, person *to* do, *of* person *to* do, *that* something may be done); (in formal & courteous phrr.) ~ *pardon, leave*; ~ *off*, get (person) excused penalty etc.; ~ *to* do, take leave to do, take the liberty of doing, (*I* ~ *to differ, enclose, announce*, etc.); ~ *the question*, assume the truth of matter in dispute; *go* (*a-*)*begging*, (of situations, opportunities, etc.) find no accepter. [of uncert. orig.; perh. shortened f. F *béguiner* be a *beghard* or *béguin*, lay brother of mendicant order named f. Lambert Bègue]

begäd', int. = by God (in fam. speech).

begän'. See BEGIN.

begĕt' (-g-), v.t. (-tt-, -got, arch.-gat, -gotten). Procreate (usu. of father, sometimes of father & mother, cf. BEAR³); give rise to, occasion. Hence ~t'ER¹ n. [OE *begitan*; see BE-(2) & GET; cf. Goth. *bigitan*]

begg'ar¹, n. One who begs; one who lives by begging; poor man or woman (~*s must not be choosers*, must take what is offered); (depreciatingly) fellow; (playfully) *little* ~, youngster etc.; *a good* ~ (= *begger*), good at collecting for charities etc. [perh.=*beghard* see BEG & -ARD]

begg'ar², v.t. Reduce to poverty; outshine, reduce to silence (~ *description*); ~*-my-neighbour*, card game. [f. prec.]

begg'ar‖ly, a. Indigent; intellectually poor; mean, sordid. Hence ~liNESS n. [BEGGAR¹+-LY¹]

begg'arẏ, n. Extreme poverty. [-Y¹]

begin' (-g-), v.t. & i. (-nn-, began, begun). Commence (*to* do, *doing, work*, etc., or abs.; in pass. sense either *it has begun to be done*, or *it has been begun*); be the first to do something; take the first step (~ *to* colloq., appear likely ever to, make any attempt to); start speaking; ~ *at*, start from; ~ *with*, take first; *to* ~ *with*, in the first place; ~ *upon*, set to work at; come into being, arise; have its commencement, nearest boundary, etc. (at some point in space or time); ~ *the world*, start in life,

[OE *beginnan*, OS, OHG *biginnan*, WG f. *bi-* BE + Gmc *-ginnan*, of unkn. orig.]

begĭnn'er (-g-), n. In vbl senses; also, tiro. [-ER¹]

begĭnn'ing (-g-), n. In vbl senses; also or esp.: time at which anything begins; source, origin; first part; *the ~ of the end*, first clear sign of final result. [-ING¹ (1)]

begĭrd' (-g-), v.t. (-irt). Gird round or encircle. [BE-(1) + GIRD¹]

begone' (-awn, -ŏn), vb imperat. = be gone (more peremptory than *go*).

begŏn'ia, n. Kinds of plant with coloured perianths but no petals. [Michel *Begon* (d. 1710), -IA¹]

begŏr'ra, int. (Irish corruption of) by God!

begŏt'(ten). See BEGET.

begrime', v.t. Soil deeply. [BE-(6) + GRIME]

begrŭdge', v.t. Feel or show dissatisfaction at (thing), envy (one) the possession of. [BE-(2) + GRUDGE v.]

beguil|e' (-gil), v.t. Delude; cheat (person *of*, *out of*, or *into doing*); charm, amuse; divert attention from (toil, passage of time). Hence ~'ER¹, ~e'MENT (-gĭlm-), nn. [BE-(2) + obs. vb *guile*, see GUILE]

beguinage (bĕg'ĭnahzh), n. House of beguines. [foll. + -AGE]

bĕg'uine (-gēn), n. Member of Netherlands lay sisterhood not bound by vows. [Lambert *Bègue*, founder 1180]

bĕg'um, n. Mohammedan princess or lady of high rank. [Hind. *begam* f. East Turk. *bigĭm* fem. of *big* prince (BEY)]

begŭn'. See BEGIN.

behalf' (-ahf), n. (Only in phrr. 'on *or* in 'my etc. ~', 'on *or* in ——'s ~', 'on *or* in ~ of ——') *on* the part *of*, *on* account *of*, (a person); *in* the interest *of* (person or principle etc.). [mixture of earlier phrr. *on his halve* & *bihalve him*, either = on his side; see HALF]

behave', v.i. & refl. (Intr., usu. with adv.) conduct oneself, act, (rarely abs., esp. to or of children) conduct oneself with propriety, ~ *towards*, treat (*well* etc.); (refl., freq. of or to children, & usu. without adv.) show good manners; (of machines etc., intr. or refl.) work (*well*, *badly*, etc.); ~*d* p.p. (with *well-*, *ill-*), having good, bad, manners or conduct. [BE-(2) + HAVE]

behav'iour (-yer), n. Deportment, manners; moral conduct, treatment shown to or towards others; *be on* one's *good* or *best ~*, do one's best under probation; way in which ship, machine, substance, etc., acts or works. [f. prec., the ending due to confusion w. obs. *aver*, *havour*, *havyoure*, possession, = F *avoir*]

behav'iourism (-yer-), n. (psych.). Doctrine that, given adequate knowledge, all human actions admit of analysis into stimulus & response, & that ability to predict them depends on exhaustive study of behaviour in that light. [f. prec. + -ISM]

behead' (-hĕd), v.t. Cut the head from; kill in that way. [OE *behēafdian* f. be-(from) about + *hēafod* HEAD n.]

beheld. See BEHOLD.

behĕm'oth (*or* bē'I-), n. Enormous creature. [perh. Egyptian *p-ehe-mau* water-ox (hippopotamus) assimilated to Heb. pl. (of dignity) of *b'hemah* beast, see *Job* xl. 15]

behĕst', n. Command (poet.). [OE *behǣs* (see HEST) f. *behātan* f. *be* BE- + *hātan* HIGHT]

behind', adv., prep., & n. In or to the rear (of), on the farther side (of), hidden (by), at one's back, towards what was one's rear, farther back in place or time (than), past in relation to, too late, in concealment, in reserve, in support of, in an inferior position (to), under the defence of, in the tracks of, outdone (by), in arrear (with); (n.) the posterior. Phrr.: *stay*, *leave*, ~, after others', one's own, departure or death; *fall ~*, not keep up; ~ *the scenes*, in private; *put ~* one, refuse to consider; *go ~* one's *words* etc., look for secret motives on his part; ~ one's *back*, without his knowledge; ~ *time*, unpunctual; ~ *the times*, antiquated. [OE *behindan* f. *be-* BE- + *hindan* HIND³]

behind'hănd, adv. & pred. a. In arrear (*with* payments etc.); out of date, behind time; ill-provided (*with*). [prec. + HAND, cf. BEFOREHAND]

behōld', v.t. (beheld). See, become aware of by sight; (abs. in imperat.) take notice, attend. Hence ~ER¹ n. [OE *bihaldan* f. BE-(2) + *haldan* HOLD]

behōl'den, pred. a. Under obligation (*to*). [p.p. obs. exc. in this use) of prec. = bound]

behōof', n. (arch.). (In phrr. *to*, *for*, *on* ~, or *the ~*, *of*) use, advantage. [OE *behōf*, OFris. *bihōf*, MHG *behuof* f. Gmc *bihafjan*; see HEAVE¹]

behōve', **-hōove'**, v.t. impers. Be incumbent on (person) *to* (do something). [OE *behōfian* f. prec.]

beige (bāzh), n. Kinds of fabric made of undyed and unbleached wool; colour of this. [F, of unkn. orig.]

be'ing, n. In vbl senses; also or esp.: existence (*in ~*, existing); constitution, nature, essence; anything that exists (*the Supreme B~*, God); a person. [BE-, -ING¹,²]

bĕl, n. Unit (= ten decibels) used in the comparison of two levels of power in an electrical communication circuit. [f. A. G. *Bell* (d. 1922), inventor of telephone]

belāb'our (-ber), v.t. Thrash (lit. & fig.). [BE-(3) + LABOUR v. (exert one's strength upon)]

belāt'ĕd, a. Overtaken by darkness; coming too late. [p.p. of obs. *belate* f. BE-(4) + LATE]

belaud', v.t. Load with praise. [BE-(2) + LAUD v.]

belay', v.t. Make fast (running rope) round cleat etc. to secure it; (sailor's sl.

in imperat.) stop!, enough!; ~*ing-pin*, wooden or iron pin for ~ing on. [in naut. sense f. LG, Du. *beleggen* (in OE *belecgan*) surround, f. BE- (1) + *lecgan* LAY³]

bĕl can'tō (kah-), n. Singing characterized by full rich broad tone & accomplished technique. [It., = fine song]

bĕlch¹, v.i. & t. Emit wind noisily from throat; utter noisily or drunkenly (abusive, blasphemous, or foul talk); (of gun or volcano) send out or up. [repr. OE *b(i)elcan*]

bĕlch², n. Eructation; sound of gun, volcano; burst of flame. [f. prec.]

bĕl'cher, n. Parti-coloured neckerchief. [Jim *B*~, pugilist]

bĕl'dam(e), n. Old woman, hag; virago. [an Eng. formation, in ME = 'grandmother', f. *bel-* (BEAU) as in *belsire* + *dame* DAM²]

bĕleag'uer (-ger), v.t. Besiege (lit. & fig.). [f. Du. *belegeren* camp round f. BE- (6) + *leger* a camp; see LEAGUER¹]

bĕl'emnīte, n. Tapering sharp-pointed fossil bone of extinct cuttlefish. [f. Gk *belemnon* dart + -ITE¹ (2)]

bĕl ĕsprit' (-rē), n. (pl. *beaux esprits* pr. bōz ĕsprē'). A wit. [F]

bĕl'fr|y̆, n. Bell tower, attached or separate; bell space in church tower; BATS *in the* ~*y*. Hence ~iED² (-Id) a. [ME *berfrey* f. OF *berfrei* f. Gmc *bergfrith* f. *bergan* protect + *frithuz* peace; mod. sp. chiefly due to assoc. w. *bell*]

bĕl'ga, n. Belgian unit of exchange. [L fem. of *Belgus* Belgian (sc. *pecunia*)]

Bĕl'gian, a. & n. (Native) of Belgium; ~ *hare*, kind of domestic rabbit. [-AN]

Bĕl'gic, a. Of the Netherlands or Belgium; of the ancient Belgae. [f. L *Belgicus* (*Belgae*, -IC)]

Bĕlgrăv'|ia, n. Fashionable residential part of London south of Knightsbridge containing Belgrave Square. Hence ~IAN a.

Bĕl'ial, n. The devil; the spirit of evil; *man of* ~, reprobate. [f. Heb. *b'li-ya'al* (*b'li* not + *ya'al* use) worthlessness]

bĕlie', v.t. (-lying). Give false notion of; fail to act up to (promise etc.); fail to justify (hope etc.). [OE *beléogan* f. BE-(3) + *léogan* LIE²]

bĕlief', n. Trust or confidence (*in*); acceptance of any received theology; acceptance as true or existing (of any fact, statement, etc.; *in*, or *of*, with nn., *that* with clause; *to the best of my* ~, in my genuine opinion); thing believed, religion, opinion, intuition; *The B*~, Apostles' Creed. [ME *bileafe* (f. OE *geléafa*; see foll.), = OS *gilôbho*, OHG *giloubo*, Goth. *galaubeins*]

bĕliev|e', v.t. & i. Have faith *in*, trust word of (person); put trust *in* truth of a statement, efficacy of a principle, system, machine, etc., existence of anything; give credence to (person, statement, etc., or *that*-clause; ~*e it or not*,

colloq., it is surprising but true); be of opinion *that*; *make* ~*e*, pretend. Hence ~'ABLE a., ~'ER¹ n., ~'ING² a. [early ME *bileven* f., by substitution of pref., OE *geléafan*, = OS *gilôbhian*, OHG *gilouben*, Goth. *galaubjan* f. Gmc *galaubhjan*, f same root as in LEAVE¹, LIEF, LOVE]

bĕlike', adv. (arch.). Probably, perhaps, (often iron.). [*be-*=BY prep. + LIKE a. (by what is likely)]

Belish'a (-ēsh-) beac'on, n. Post with yellow globe on top marking street crossing-place for pedestrians. [L. Hore-*Belisha*, Minister of Transport 1934]

bĕlit'tle, v.t. Make small, dwarf; depreciate. [BE-(4) + LITTLE]

bĕll¹, n. Hollow body of cast metal in deep cup shape widening at lip made to emit musical sound when struck; (Naut.) *one to eight* ~s, half hours of watch; ~-shaped object, as flower corolla (BLUE¹, CANTERBURY, ~). *Bear, carry away, the* ~, be first, win; ~, *book, & candle*, in allusion to eccles. cursing formula; *sound, clear, as a* ~, quite sound or clear (in other senses besides the acoustic); ~-*bird*, Brazilian and Austral.·kinds with ~-like note; ~-*buoy*, with warning ~ rung by waves' motion; ~-*flower*, any plant of genus *Campanula*; ~-*founder, -founding, -foundry*, caster, casting, & manufactory, of ~s; ~-*glass*, ~-shaped as cover for plants; ~-*hanger*, one who puts up ~s & wires; ~-*heather*, heath; *~-hop* (sl.), hotel page; ~-*metal*, alloy of copper & tin (more tin than in bronze) for ~s; ~-*pull*, cord or handle attached to ~-*wire*; ~-*ringer, -ringing* (of church ~s with changes etc.); ~-*wether*, leading sheep of flock with ~ on neck, ringleader. [OE *belle*, MDu., MLG *belle*, Du. *bel*; a LG wd perh. related to BELL³]

bĕll², v.t. Furnish with bell(s); ~ *the cat*, take the danger of a common enterprise on oneself (fable of cat & mice). [f. prec.]

bĕll³, n., & v.i. (Make the) cry of stag or buck at rutting-time. [OE *bellan* bark, bellow, OHG *bellan*; cf. ON *belja* & BELLOW¹]

bĕlladŏnn'a, n. (Bot.) deadly nightshade, a poisonous plant with purple flowers & purple-black berries; (Med.) drug prepared from this. [mod. L f. It., = fair lady, perh. because a cosmetic is made from it]

bĕlle, n. Handsome woman; reigning beauty (*the* ~ *of* any place). [F, f. L *bella* fem. of *bellus* pretty see BEAU]

belles-lettres (bĕl-lĕt'r), n. Studies, writings, of the purely literary kind. Hence **bĕllĕt'rist** (3) (-l-l-) n., **bĕllĕtris't-ic** (-l-l-) a. [F]

bĕll'ic|ōse, a. Inclined to fighting. Hence ~ōs'ITY n. [f. L *bellicosus* (*bellum* war, -IC, -OSE¹)]

bĕlli'gerency̆, n. Status of a belligerent. [f. foll., see -ENCY]

bĕlli'gerent, a. & n. (Nation, party, or

person) waging regular war as recognized by the law of nations; of such nation etc.; (loosely) any opponent engaged in conflict. [f. F *belligérant* or L *belligerare* wage war (*bellum* + *gerere*), -ANT]

Bĕllōn'a, n. War personified; woman of commanding presence. [L, = goddess of war f. *bellum* war]

bĕll'ow (-ō), v.i. & t., & n. **1.** Roar as a bull; shout, roar with pain; utter loudly and angrily (often *out*, *forth*); (of thunder, cannon, etc.) reverberate, roar. **2.** n. ~ing sound. [ME *belwe*, of uncert. orig.; perh. related to BELL[3]]

bĕll'ows (-ōz), n. pl. Portable or fixed contrivance for driving air into a fire or through pipes of organ, reeds of harmonium, etc.; *pair of* ~, two-handled for fire; means used to fan passion etc.; the lungs (~ *to mend*, of broken-winded horse); expansible part of photographic camera. [OE *blǣstbel(i)g*, later *bel(i)g*, whence ME *beli*, *bely*; see BELLY; also (north.) *belu*, *belw*, whence mod. *bellow(s)*]

bĕll'ў[1], n. Cavity of human body below diaphragm with stomach & bowels & other contents, abdomen; (externally) lower front of body; corresponding parts of animals; stomach; the body as food--consumer (cf. BACK[1]), appetite, gluttony; the womb; cavity of anything; bulging part (concave or convex); front, inner, or lower surface; surface of violin etc. across which strings pass; ~-*band* (below horse's ~, checking play of shafts); ~--*worship*, gluttony; ~-*timber*, food; ~--*pinched*, starving; ~-*ache*, (n.) colic, (v.i., sl.) complain bitterly. Hence -**bĕll'ied** (-ĭd) a. [ME *bali*, *bely* f. OE *belig*, earlier *belg* bag, skin, = ON *belgr*, OHG *balg*, Goth. *balgs* f. Gmc **balgiz* f. *balg*-, *belg*- to swell; cf. BELLOWS]

bĕll'ў[2], v.t. & i. Swell out (usu. of sails, & with *out*). [f. prec.]

bĕll'ўful (-ŏol), n. As much as one wants of anything, esp. of fighting. [-FUL(2)]

bĕlŏng', v.i. Pertain, be proper, *to* (as duty, right, possession, natural or right accompaniment, example in classification, characteristic, part, member, inhabitant, appendage); be rightly a member of club, coterie, household, grade of society, etc.; *be resident *in*, connected *with*; ~ *under* or *in*, be rightly classified among; ~ *here* etc., live here, be rightly placed under this heading etc.; *where it* ~*s*, in its proper place. [ME, app. an intensive, f. BE- (2), of ME *longen*, obs. in this sense; cf. OHG *bilangēn* in same sense]

bĕlŏng'ings (-z), n. pl. A person's property, relatives, or luggage; everything connected with a subject. [f. prec.]

bĕloved (*as adj.* or *n. usu.* -ŭv'ĭd; *as vb* -ŭvd'), p.p., a., & n. (Forming pass. parts of vb obs. in act.) dearly loved (followed by *of* or *by*, or abs.); (n.) darling (common

in voc., & with *my*, *his*, etc.). [BE-(2) + LOVE v.]

bĕlow' (-ō), adv. & prep. **1.** adv. At or to lower level; on earth; in hell; downstairs (esp. Naut. *go* ~, from deck); down stream; in lower rank (*the court* ~); at foot of page, or farther on in book. **2.** prep. Lower than (~-*stairs*, arch., downstairs); too low to be affected by (~ *flattery*); down stream from; on inferior side of dividing line (~ *par*, ~ *the gangway*); at or to greater depth than; covered by; lower in amount, degree, etc., than (~ one's *breath*, less audibly than); of lower rank etc. than; unworthy of. Cf. BENEATH, UNDER. [*be-* = BY + LOW a.]

bĕlt[1], n. Encircling strip of leather etc. worn round waist or baldric-wise to confine or support clothes or weapons etc. (*hit below the* ~, fight unfairly); cincture of earl or knight; strip of colour, special surface, trees, etc., round or on anything; zone (*cotton*, *wheat*, *fever*, ~); endless strap connecting wheels; row of armour plates under water-line; *Great & Little B*~, channels into Baltic. [OE *belt*, = OHG *balz*, ON *belti*, f. Gmc **baltjaz* f. L *balteus*]

bĕlt[2], v.t. Put belt round (~*ed cruiser*, with belt & metal-covered deck); fasten on with belt; mark with belt of colour etc.; thrash with belt. [f. prec.]

bĕl'tāne, n. (Ancient Celtic festival on) May-day. [ult. f. Gael. *bealllainn*]

bĕl'vedēre, n. Raised turret to view scenery from. [It. (*bel* beautiful, see BEAU, +*vedere* see)]

bĕlў'ing. See BELIE.

bēm'a, n. Platform in ancient Athenian public assembly. [Gk]

bĕmīre', v.t. Cover or stain with mud; (pass.) be stuck in the mud. [BE-(6) + MIRE n.]

bĕmoan', v.t. Weep or express sorrow for or over. [OE *bemǣnan* f. BE-(3) + *mǣnan* MOAN]

bĕmūse' (-z), v.t. Stupefy. [BE-(2) + MUSE v.]

‖ **bĕn**, n. (Sc.) Inner room (usu. of two--roomed cottage); *but & ~*, the outer & inner room. [ellipt. use of *ben* adv., within (OE *binnan*)]

bĕnch, n., & v.t. **1.** Long seat of wood or stone; boat-thwart; judge's seat, office of judge, law-court (*King's*, *Queen's*, *B*~); (collect.) judges, magistrates; ‖ (Parl.) seats appropriated to certain groups etc. (*Treasury*, FRONT[1], BACK[1], CROSS[3], *bishops'*, ~*es*); *be raised to*, *be on*, *the* ~, be (made) a judge or bishop; working-table of carpenter etc.; ledge in masonry or earthwork; ~-*table*, stone seat in cloister etc.; ~-*mark*, cut by surveyors to mark point in line of levels; ~-*warrant*, one issued by a judge (opp. justice's warrant). **2.** v.t. Exhibit (dog) at show. [OE *benc*, = OS *banc*, OHG *bank*, ON *bekkr*, f. Gmc **bankiz*; cf. BANK[1]]

‖ **běn'cher**, n. Senior member, sharing management, of Inn of Court. [-ER¹]

běnd¹, n. (Naut.) knot of various kinds (*fisherman's, weaver's*, etc.); (Her.) parallel lines from dexter chief to sinister base (~ *sinister* in opposite direction, sign of bastardy); shape (half BUTT) in which hides are tanned (~-*leather*, the thickest, used for soles). [OE *bend* band, bond, = OS *band*, OHG *bant*, Goth. *bandi*, f. Gmc **band*-, past stem of *bindan* BIND¹; see also BAND¹, BOND¹]

běnd², n. Bending, curve; bent part of anything; *the* ~s (colloq.), caisson disease. [f. foll.]

běnd³, v.t. & i. (past *bent*, p.p. *bent* exc. in ~*ed knees*). Force out of straightness, impart to (rigid object) or receive a curved or angular shape; arch (brows); tighten up, bring to bear, (energies etc. *on*, *to*); (pass.) be determined (*on* with gerund or noun); attach with knot (cable, sail); turn (t. & i.) in new direction (steps, eyes); incline (t. & i.) from the perpendicular (head), bow, stoop, submit, (*to* or *before*), force to submit (will etc.). Hence ~'ER¹ n., esp. (sl.) ‖ sixpenny bit, ~spree. [OE *bendan* bind, = ON *benda* join, strain f. Gmc **bandjan* f. *band*-, see BEND¹]

běneaped' (-pt), a. Left aground by neap--tide. [p.p. f. unused *beneap* see BE-(6) & NEAP]

běneath', adv. & prep. Below, under, underneath, (poetic, arch., & literary, but usual in) ~ *contempt* etc., not worth despising etc., ~ one, unworthy of him. [OE *beneothan* = BE-+*neothan* = OS *nithana*, OHG *nidana*, ON *nethan* f. Gmc **nith*-, cf. NETHER]

běnědi'cīte, n. Blessing invoked; grace at table; *the B*~, one of the canticles. [L, = *bless ye*, imperat. of *benedicere* -*dict*- bless (*bene* well + *dicere* speak)]

běn'ědick, n. Newly married man, esp. confirmed bachelor who marries. [Shakesp., *Much Ado*]

Běnědic'tine, a. & n. (Monk) of the order founded 529 by St Benedict, black monk; a liqueur. [f. F *bénédictin* f. L *benedictus* p.p. see BENEDICITE]

běnědic'tion, n. Utterance of a blessing, generally at table, at end of church service, or as special R.-C. service; a blessing, blessedness. [f. L *benedictio* (BENEDICITE, -ION)]

běnědic'tory, a. Of, expressing, benediction. [f. L *benedictus*, see prec. & -ORY, after *valedictory*]

běnědíc'tus, n. One of the canticles. [first word in L version; see BENEDICITE]

běnēfāc'tion, n. Doing good; gift for charitable purpose. [f. LL *benefactio* (BENEFIT¹, -ION)]

běn'ēfāct|or, n. Person who has given one friendly aid; patron of or donor to a cause or charitable institution. Hence ~TRESS¹ n. [ME, f. LL *benefactor* (BENEFIT¹, ͻ̄R)]

běn'ěfic|e, n. Church living; property held by an ecclesiastical officer esp. rector or vicar. Hence ~ED² (-st) a. [ME f. OF, f. L *beneficium* (*bene* well +-*fic*- f. *facere* do)]

běněf'icence, n., **běněf'icent**, a. Doing good, (showing) active kindness. Hence **běněf'icentLY²** adv. [f. F, or L *beneficentia* prec., -ENCE)]

běněfi'cial (-shl), a. Advantageous; (Law) of, having, the usufruct of property. Hence ~LY² adv. [ME, f. F *bénéficial* f. LL *beneficialis* (BENEFICE, -AL)]

běněfi'ciary (-sha-), a. & n. (Law) holder, holding or held, by feudal tenure; holder of a living; receiver of benefits. [f. L *beneficiarius*, see BENEFICE, -ARY¹]

běn'ěfit¹, n. Advantage (*for the* ~ *of*, on behalf of; *the* ~ *of the doubt*, assuming innocence rather than guilt); allowance, pension, attendance, to which person is entitled under Nat. Insurance Act or as member of benefit society etc. (*maternity, medical*, ~); exemption from ordinary courts by the privilege of one's order (~ *of* CLERGY, *peerage*); performance at theatre, game, etc., of which proceeds go to particular players (~*'s* ~, ~-*night*, ~-*match*); ~-*club*, -*society*, for mutual insurance against illness or age. [ME & AF *benfet* f. L *benefactum* neut. p.p. of *benefacere* do well]

běn'ěfit², v.t. & i. Do good to; receive benefit (*by* thing). [f. prec.]

Běn'ělŭx, n. Belgium, the Netherlands, & Luxembourg in association as a regional economic group; freq. attrib., as *the* ~ countries. [f. *Belgium*, *Nether*lands, *Lux*embourg]

běněv'olence, n. Desire to do good, charitable feeling; (Eng. Hist.) forced loan. [ME, f. OF *benivolence* f. L *benevolentia* f. *benevolens* -*entis* = foll.]

běněv'olent, a. Desirous of doing good, charitable. Hence ~LY² adv. [ME, f. OF *benivolent* f. L *bene volentem* nom. -*ens* well wishing (*velle* wish)]

Bengal' (běnggawl), a. ~ *light*, firework used for signals; ~ *stripes*, striped gingham, orig. from ~; ~ *tiger*, the tiger proper. [former Indian province]

Bengali (běnggawl'ĭ), n. & a. (Native, language) of Bengal. [f. native *Bangali*]

běnight'ěd (-nīt-), p.p. & a. (Forming pass, of vb obs. in act.) overtaken by night; involved in intellectual or moral darkness, ignorant. [BE-(6)+NIGHT]

běnign' (-īn), a. Gracious, gentle; fortunate, salutary; (of diseases) mild, not malignant. Hence ~LY² adv. [ME *benigne* f. OF f. L *benignus*; cf. *malign*]

běnig'n|ant, a. Kind, kindly, to inferiors; gracious; salutary. Hence ~ANCY n., ~antLY² adv. [recent formation f. prec. on anal. of MALIGNANT]

běnig'nity, n. Kindliness, kindness, (usu. in the old). [ME, f. OF *benignite* f. L *benignitatem* (BENIGN, -TY)]

bĕn'ĭson (-zn), n. (arch.). A blessing. [ME *beneysun* etc. f. OF *beneiçun* etc. f. L *benedictionem* BENEDICTION]

Bĕnj'amĭn¹, n. Youngest child, darling; ~'s *mess*, large share. [*Gen*. xliii. 4]

bĕnj'amĭn², n. = BENZOIN ; ~ *tree*, (a) that yielding benzoin, (b) a N.-Amer. shrub with aromatic bark. [corruption of BENZOIN]

bĕnn'ĕt, n. See HERB ~, & foll.

bĕnt¹, n. Stiff-stemmed grass of various kinds (with pl., or collect.); (also *bennet*) stiff flower-stalk, old stalk, of grasses; couch-grass; *way* ~, *stool* ~, etc., kinds of plant; heath, unenclosed pasture. [ME *bent*, repr. OE *beonet-* (in place-names), OS *binet*, OHG *binuz*, f. WG **binut-*]

bĕnt², n. Twist, inclination, bias, tendency; *to the top of* one's ~, *to heart's content*. [prob. f. BEND² on anal. of *descend*, *descent*, etc.]

bĕnt³. See BEND³.

Bĕn'tham|ism (-ta-), n. Greatest happiness of the greatest number as guiding principle of ethics. So ~ITE¹ (1) n. [Jeremy *Bentham*, 1748–1832; see -ISM (3)]

bĕn'thŏs, n. (biol.). Flora & fauna found at the ocean bottom. [Gk, = depth]

bĕn trŏva'tō (-ah-), a. Well invented, characteristic if not true. [It.]

bĕnŭmb' (-m), v.t. Make torpid, insensible, powerless, (usu. of cold); paralyse (mind, action). [OE *beniman* deprive, p.p. *benuman*, whence ME *benomen*, whence 16th c. *benum* vb, later *benumb* (cf. *dumb*, *limb*)]

bĕn'zédrine (-ēn), n. Drug used to relieve respiratory trouble by inhalation, and internally as a nerve stimulant. [P]

bĕn'zĕn|e, n. An aromatic hydrocarbon got from coal-tar & represented by derivatives in all coal-tar products (formerly, & still in trade use, called *benzol*, -*ole*). Hence ~OID- + -ENE] [BENZ(O)- + -ENE]

bĕn'zine (-ēn), n. Mixture of liquid hydrocarbons got from mineral oils & used for removing grease-stains (in trade use often called *benzoline* or *benzene*). [foll. + -INE⁵]

benz(o)-, forming derivatives of foll.

bĕn'zŏin (*or* -oin), n. (Also *gum* ~, *benjamin*) fragrant aromatic resin of Javanese tree. Hence **bĕnzō'ic** a. [earlier *benjoin* through F, Sp., It., f. Arab. *luban jawi* frankincense of Java (*lo-* being dropped in Rom. as if the article)]

bĕn'zŏl, -ōle, n. = BENZENE. [BENZ(O)- + -OL]

bĕn'zoline (-ēn, -ĭn), n. = BENZINE. [prec. + -INE⁵]

bĕqueath' (-dh), v.t. Leave (*to* person) by will (personalty; cf. DEVISE); transmit to posterity (example etc.). [OE *becwethan* f. BE-(3) + *cwethan* say, see QUOTH]

bĕquĕst', n. Bequeathing; thing bequeathed. [ME *biquyste* f. *bi-* BE- + *cwis* saying cf. prec.: for -*t* cf. BEHEST]

bĕrāte', v.t. Scold. [BE- + RATE³]

Bĕrb'er, n. & a. (Member) of the N.-African stock including the aboriginal races of Barbary, speaking allied languages. [f. Arab. *barbar* f. *barbara* talk confusedly, of unkn. orig.]

bĕrberry̆, n. See BARBERRY.

berceuse (bĕrsēr'), n. Cradle-song. [F]

|| bēre, n. Barley, esp. of six-rowed or four-rowed kinds. [OE]

bĕreave', v.t. (~*d* or *bereft*). Rob, dispossess, *of* (usu. of immaterial things, as life, hope); leave desolate (esp. in p.p., usu. ~*d* in this sense); (of death etc.) deprive of a relation, wife, etc., whence ~MENT (-vm-) n. [OE *bereafian*, see BE-(2), REAVE]

beret (bĕ'rā), n. Round flat cap worn by Basque peasants; similar cap worn by men & women with sports & holiday clothes; service military headdress. [F, f. Pr. *berret* f. med. L *birretum* cap, dim. of LL *birrus* cloak; see BIRETTA]

bĕrg¹, n. = ICEBERG.

bĕrg², n. (S. Africa). Mountain or hill (esp. in comb.); ~ *wind*, hot northerly wind blowing in Cape Colony in May & August. [Afrikaans f. Du.]

bĕrg'amŏt¹, n. Tree of the citrus family; perfume extracted from its rind; an aromatic herb. [f. *Bergamo* town in Italy]

bĕrg'amŏt², n. Kind of pear. [f. F *bergamotte* f. It. *bergamotta* f. Turk. *begarmudi* prince's pear]

bĕrg'mehl (-māl), n. Greyish-white flour-like geological deposit composed of infusorial shells, an abrasive & absorbent. [G, = mountain-flour]

berg'schrund (bāk'shrŏont), n. (mountaineering). Crevasse or gap at junction of steep upper slope with glacier or nevé. [G]

bĕrhyme' (-rīm), v.t. Write verses about, lampoon; put (matter) into rhymed form. [BE- (6) + RHYME n.]

bĕ'ribĕri, n. Deficiency disease common in the East. [Sinhalese, f. *beri* weakness]

Berkeleian (bārklē'an), n. & a. (Follower) of Berkeley or his philosophy, which denied the objective existence of the material world. [Bishop *Berkeley*, d. 1753; see -EAN]

bĕrkĕl'ium, n. Radio-active transuranic element. [f. *Berkel(ey)* in California + -IUM]

Bĕrlin', n. & a. Four-wheeled covered carriage with hooded seat behind (also *berline*); ~ *black*, iron-varnish; ~ *iron*, for casts; ~ *warehouse*, shop for ~ *wool*, fine dyed knitting wool; ~ *gloves*, knitted. [~ in Germany]

bĕrm, n. Ledge in fortification between ditch & base of parapet. [f. F *berme* f. Du. *berm*, prob. cogn. w. ON *barmr* brim]

Bĕrmūd'ian, a. & n. (Inhabitant) of the *Bermudas*; ~ *rigged*, fitted with a high tapering sail. [-IAN]

Bĕrn'ardine, a. & n. = CISTERCIAN.

bĕ'rry¹, n. (Pop.) any small roundish juicy fruit without stone; (Bot.) fruit with seeds enclosed in pulp; grain of wheat etc.; egg in fish-roe (*in* ~, of hen-lobster carrying eggs). Hence (-)bĕ'rri-ED[2] (-ĭd) a. [OE *beri(g)e*, OS *beri*, OHG *beri*, ON *ber*, Goth. (*weina*) *basi*, f. Gmc **basjam*, **bazjam*]

bĕ'rrў[2], v.i. Come into berry, fill out; go gathering berries. [f. prec.]

bersaglieri (see Ap.), n. pl. Crack Italian infantry, orig. riflemen. [It.]

bĕrs'ĕrk(er), n. Wild Norse warrior fighting with mad frenzy. [f. Icel. *berserkr* prob. = bear-sark, bear-coat]

bĕrth[1], n. Convenient sea-room (*give wide* ~ *to*, avoid); room for ship to swing at anchor; ship's place at wharf; proper place for anything; sleeping-place in ship, train, etc.; situation, appointment. [of uncert. orig.; prob. f. naut. use of BEAR[3] vb +-TH[1]]

bĕrth[2], v.t. Moor (ship) in suitable place; provide sleeping-place for. [f. prec.]

bĕrth'a, bĕrthe, n. Deep falling (usu. lace) collar to low-necked dress. *Big Bertha*, German gun of vast range used in bombarding Paris in the war of 1914–18. [F (-*e*), the woman's name]

Bĕrth'on boat, n. Collapsible boat. [E. L. *Berthon* inventor, d. 1899]

Bĕrtill'on sўs'tĕm, n. Method of identifying criminals by measurements. [A. *Bertillon*, French anthropologist, d. 1914]

bĕ'rўl, n. Precious stone, pale-green passing into light blue, yellow, & white; mineral species including also the emerald. [ME, f. OF f. L f. Gk *bērullos*]

bĕrўll'ium, n. Hard white metallic element. [prec. +-IUM]

bĕseech', v.t. (-*sought* pr. -sawt). Ask earnestly for (esp. *leave* etc.); entreat (person, person *that* or *to* do or *for* thing). [BE-(2) +ME *secen*, *sechen*, *seken*, SEEK]

bĕseech'ing, a. Suppliant (of look, tone, etc.). Hence ~LY[2] adv. [-ING[2]]

bĕseem', v.t. Suit; be fitting or creditable to, (abs., or with *well*, *ill*, etc.). Hence ~ingLY[2] adv. [BE-(2) +SEEM]

bĕsĕt', v.t. (-*tting*, past & p.p. -*set*). Hem in, set upon, (person); occupy & make impassable (road etc.); (of difficulties, temptations, etc.) assail, encompass. (~*ting sin*, that most frequently tempts one). [OE *besettan* (BE-(1), & see SET v.)]

bĕsĕt'ment, n. Besetting sin; being hemmed in. [prec. +-MENT]

bĕshrew' (-rōō), v.t. (Now only as mock-heroic imprecation) plague take (*me*, person, or thing). [BE-(2) +ME *schrewen* to curse f. SHREW]

bĕside', prep. (formerly also adv.=foll.). Close to, by, near; on a level with, compared with; wide of (*mark*, *question*, etc.); ~ *oneself*, out of one's wits. [OE *be sidan* (BY, SIDE n.)]

bĕsides' (-dz), adv. & prep. In addition (to), moreover; otherwise, else, (than); (neg. & interrog.) except. [prec. +-ES]

bĕsieg|e', v.t. Invest, lay siege to; crowd

round; assail with requests. Hence ~'ER[1] n. [f. ME *asege* by substitution of pref. BE-, f. OF *asegier* f. Rom. **assediare* f. **sedium* SIEGE]

bĕslāv'er, v.t. Cover with slaver; flatter fulsomely. [BE-(1) +SLAVER v.]

bĕslŏbb'er, v.t.=prec.; also, kiss effusively. [BE-(1) +SLOBBER v.]

bĕslŭbb'er, v.t. Besmear. [BE-(1) +SLUBBER]

bĕsmear', v.t. Smear with greasy or sticky stuff (also of the stuff as subj.). [OE *bismierwan* see BE-(1) & SMEAR v.]

bĕsmĭrch', v.t. Soil, discolour; dim brightness of. [BE-(1) +SMIRCH v.]

bĕs'om[1] (-z-), n., & v.t. (Sweep with) bundle of twigs tied round stick for sweeping, kind of broom. [OE *besema*, OHG *besamo*, f. WG **besmon*]

bĕs'om[1] (-z-), n. (Sc.). (Term of abuse for) woman. [orig. unkn.]

bĕsŏt', v.t. (-tt-). Stupefy mentally or morally (chiefly in p.p.). [BE-(4) +SOT]

bĕsought'. See BESEECH.

bĕspangle (-ăng'gl), v.t. Set about with spangles. [BE-(6) +SPANGLE]

bĕspătt'er, v.t. Spatter (object) all over; spatter (liquid etc.) about; cover with abuse or flattery. [BE-(1) +SPATTER]

bĕspeak', v.t. (past -*spoke*, p.p. -*spoke*, -*spoken*). Engage beforehand; order (goods); stipulate for; speak to (poet.); suggest, be evidence of; ‖ *bespoke bootmaker* etc. (prop. *bespoke-boot maker*), opposed to ready-made dealer. [OE, OS *bisprecan*, OHG *bisprehhan*, see BE-(3) & SPEAK]

bĕsprĕnt', p.p. (poet.). Sprinkled (*with*); scattered about. [f. OE *besprengan* f. BE-(1) +*sprengan* sprinkle f. Gmc **sprangjan* causal of *springan* v.]

bĕsprinkle (-ĭng'kl), v.t. Sprinkle or strew over (*with*; lit. & fig.; also with the liquid etc. as subj. or obj.). [ME *besprengil* frequent. of OE *besprengan*, see prec. & -LE]

Bĕss'ĕmer, a. & n. ~ *process*, for removing carbon, silicon, etc. from pig-iron by passing currents of air through it when molten & so making ~ *iron*, ~ *steel*, or ~. [Sir H. ~, inventor 1856]

bĕst[1], a. & adv. (superl. of *good*, *well*). Of, in, the most excellent kind, way (often, like *good*, *well*, used for specific adjj. & advv. as *kindest*, *most skilfully*). Phrr.: *the* ~ *part*, most; *had* ~, would find it wisest to; one's ~ *girl*, sweetheart; ~ *man*, bridegroom's supporter; ~ *seller*, (author of) popular book; *put* ~ *leg* or *foot foremost*, go at full pace, also fig.; *bad is the* ~, no good event possible; *with the* ~, as well as anyone; *do* one's ~, all one can; *be at* one's ~, in the ~ state; one's ~ or *Sunday* ~, ~ *clothes*; *have the* ~ *of it*, win in argument etc.; *make the* ~ *of things*, be contented; ~ *abused* (colloq.), most violently or generally abused (*the* ~ *abused book of the year*); *make the* ~ *of* one's *way*, go as fast as possible; *at* ~, on the most hopeful view; *did it for the* ~, with good intentions; *to the* ~ *of* one's *power* etc., as far as one's power etc. allows; *the* ~ *is the enemy of the good*, too high standard bars progress. [OE *betst*, OS *best*, OHG *bezzist*, ON *bazt*, *bezt*, Goth. *batist*, f. Gmc **batist-*; superl. of **bat-*; cf. BETTER & see -EST]

bĕst², v.t. (colloq.). Get the better of, circumvent, worst. [f. prec.]

bĕstead' (-ĕd), v.t. & i. Avail, help. [BE-(2) + *stead* v. f. STEAD]

bĕstĕd', p.p. (With *ill, hard, sore*, etc.) situated, circumstanced, pressed. [ME *bistad* f. BE-(2) + *stad* f. ON *staddr* p.p. of *stethja* place]

bĕs'tial, a. Of, like, a beast or beasts esp. quadrupeds; brutish, barbarous; depraved, lustful, obscene. Hence or cogn. ~ITY (-ăl²) n., ~IZE(3) v.t., ~LY² adv. [ME, f. OF f. LL *bestialis* (*bestia* BEAST + -AL)]

bĕs'tiarў, n. Medieval moralizing treatise on beasts. [f. med. L *bestiarium* f. L *bestia* beast]

bĕstir', v. refl. (-rr-). Exert, rouse, (one-*self*). [f. BE-(2) + STIR v.]

bĕstow' (-ō), v.t. Deposit; provide with lodging; confer (thing) *upon* (person) as gift. Hence ~'AL(2) (-ōal) n. [ME *bistowen*, see BE-(2), STOW]

bĕstrew' . (-rōō), v.t. (p.p. *~ed* or *~n*). Strew (surface) *with*; scatter (things) about; lie scattered over. [OE *bistrēowian* see BE-(1) & STREW; p.p. *-ewn* is recent, but now common]

bĕstride', v.t. (past *-ode*; p.p. *-idden, -id, -ode*). Get or sit upon (horse, chair) with legs astride; stand astride over (place or fallen friend or enemy; also fig. of rainbow etc.). [OE *bistrīdan*, see BE-(3), STRIDE v.]

bĕt, n., & v.i. & t. (*bet, ~ted*). (Engagement to) risk one's money etc., risk (an amount etc.) against another's on the result of a doubtful event (*on* or *against* result or competitor, *that* so-&-so will happen; *you* ~, you may take it as certain; ~*ting-book*, for entering ~s in. [of uncert. orig.; perh. f. ABET n., in sense 'instigation, support of a cause', w. *bet* vb f. *bet* n.]

bĕt'a, n. Second letter (B, β) of Gk alphabet, used as name of second star in a constellation, & in other numberings; ~ *plus, minus*, rather better, worse, than second-class; ~ *rays*, fast-moving electrons emitted by radio-active substances, orig. regarded as rays. [Gk]

bĕtāke', v. refl. (*-took, -taken*). Commit one*self to* (i.e. try) some course or means; convey one*self to* (i.e. go to) a place or person. [ME; BE-, TAKE]

bĕt'atrŏn, n. (phys.). Apparatus for accelerating speed of electrons. [f. BETA + (ELEC)TRON]

bĕt'el, n. Leaf of *Piper belle*, which In-

dians chew with areca-nut parings; (hence by mistake) ~*-nut*, the areca nut. [Port. f. Malayalam *veṭṭila*]

bête noire (bāt nwahr), n. (One's) abomination. [F]

bĕth'el, n. Hallowed spot (*Gen.* xxviii. 19); ‖ nonconformist chapel; seamen's church (ashore or floating). [Heb. *beth-el* house of God]

‖bĕthĕs'da (-z-), n. Nonconformist chapel, [*John* v. 2; Heb., = house of mercy]

bĕthink', v. refl. (*-thought*) (alw. with *self* or arch. refl. *me, him*, etc.). Reflect, stop to think; remind one*self of, how*, or *that*; take into one's head *to*. [OE *bethencan*, see BE-(3), THINK]

bĕtide', v.i. & t. (only in 3 sing. pres. subj.). Happen (*whate'er* ~); happen to (*woe* ~ *him* etc.). [ME *bitiden* see BE-(2), TIDE v.]

bĕtimes' (-mz), adv. Early in day, year, life, etc.; in good time. [*by time* (ME) + -ES]

bétise (bātēz'), n. Foolish, ill-timed, remark or action. [F]

bĕtŏk'en, v.t. Augur, indicate, suggest. [ME *bitacnen* see BE-, TOKEN]

bĕt'on, n. (Orig. lime, now any kind of) concrete. [f. F *béton* ult. f. L *bitumen* mineral pitch]

bĕt'onў, n. Purple-flowered plant. [ME, f. OF *betoine* f. pop. L **betonia* for L *betonica* f. L *vettonica* f. name of Spanish tribe]

betook. See BETAKE.

betray', v.t. Give up treacherously (person or thing *to* enemy); be disloyal to; lead astray; reveal treacherously; reveal involuntarily; be evidence or symptom of. Hence ~AL(2), ~ER¹, nn. [ME *betraien* f. BE-(2) + obs *tray* f. OF *traïr* f. L *tradere* hand over]

bĕtrŏth' (-ōdh), v.t. Bind with a promise to marry (usu. in p.p.). Hence ~AL(2) n., ~ED¹ a. & n. [ME *betreuthe, betrowthe* f. BE-(6) + *treulhe* TRUTH, later assimilated to TROTH]

bĕtt'er¹, a., adv., & n. (comp. of *good, well*). Of, in, a more excellent kind, way (often, like *good, well*, for specific wd as *more virtuous, more plentifully*). Phrr.: *no* ~ *than*, practically; *no* ~ *than she should be*, (usu.) of easy virtue; one's ~ *feelings*, higher self; ~ *part*, most; one's ~ *half*, wife; *for* ~ *for worse*, on terms of accepting all results (see Prayer Book, Marriage Service); ~ *than* (with number etc.), above; *had* ~, would find it wiser to; *be, get* ~, less unwell; ~ *than* one's *word*, more liberal than one promised to be; one's ~, more skilful person; one's ~s, people of higher rank; *get the* ~ *of*, defeat, outwit; *know* ~, refuse to accept statement, not be so foolish (as to do something); *think* ~ *of it*, change one's mind; *change for the* ~; ~ *off*, richer, more comfortable; *the* ~ *the day the* ~ *the deed* (retort to charge of Sabbath-

-breaking). [OE *betera*, OS *betiro*, OHG *beziro*, ON *betri*, Goth. *batiza*, f. Gmc *baṭizon* f. *bat-*, cogn. w. *bōt-* see BOOT³, -ER³]

bĕtt'er², v.t. & i. Amend, improve; surpass (a feat etc.); ~ one*self*, get better situation, wages, etc. Hence ~MENT n., (also) enhanced value (of real property) arising from local improvements. [ME f. prec.]

bĕtt'er³, **-or**, n. One who bets. [BET +-ER¹]

bĕtween', prep. & adv. (the orig. restriction to relations involving only *two* limits etc. still tends to be observed wherever AMONG is adequate for higher numbers). In, into, along, or across, a space, line, or route, bounded by (two or more points, lines, etc.); in, into, along, or across, an interval; separating; connecting; intermediately in place, time, or order (to); owing partly to, partaking of, shared by, (each); to & fro (*go-*~); to & from (*plies* ~ *London & Brighton*); reciprocally on the part of; confined to (~ *ourselves*, ~ *you & me*); by combination of; taking one & rejecting the other of (*choose* ~). *Far* ~, at wide intervals; ~ *cup & lip*, of dashed hopes; ||~-*maid* (now usu. *tweeny*), servant assisting two others, e.g. cook & housemaid; ~ *wind & water*, at a vulnerable point; ~ *the devil & the deep sea*, with no escape; *betwixt & ~*, half-&-half; *stand* ~, mediate, be protector; ~ *whiles*, in the intervals. [OE *betwēonum* (also, orig. acc., *betweon*) f. *be* BY + *twēonum*, dat. pl. (corresp. to Goth. *tweihnaim*, nom. *tweihnai*, distrib. num. formed w. *-n-* suff. (cf. L *bini*) on the cardinal num.)]

bĕtwixt', prep. & adv. (Poet., arch., or dial., for) BETWEEN. [ME *betwix*, later *betwixt*, OE *betweohs*, *betweox*, etc. (prob. shortened f. *betweoxum*, cf. prec.) f. *be* BY + *twisk-* (= OS *twisc*, OHG *zwiski* two each, G *zwischen*) f. *twā* TWO + *-isk- -ISH¹*]

|| **Beu'lah**, n. Nonconformist chapel. [*Is.* lxii. 4]

bĕv'el¹, n. Joiner's & mason's tool for setting off angles; a slope from the horizontal or vertical, surface so sloping; ~ *edge*, as in a chisel; ~*-gear*, working one shaft from another at an angle to it by ~-*-wheels*, cogged wheels with working face oblique to axis. [f. OF **bevel* (mod. *biveau*) of unkn. orig.; cf. OF *bever* (arch.) give bias to]

bĕv'el², v.t. & i. (-ll-). Reduce (square edge) to, take, a slope. [f. prec.]

bĕv'erage, n. Drinking-liquor. [ME, f. OF *bevrage* f. Rom. **biberaticum* f. L *bibere* drink, see -AGE]

bĕv'y̆, n. Company (prop. of ladies, roes, quails, larks). [orig. unkn.]

bewail', v.t. & i. Wail (over), mourn (for). [BE-(3) + WAIL v.]

bewāre', v.i. & t. (not inflected, & used only where *be* is the vbl part required, as *I will* ~, but not *I* ~). Be cautious, take heed; take heed *of*, *lest*, *how that not*. [f. BE v. + WARE²]

bewil'der, v.t. Lead astray, perplex, confuse. Hence ~**ing**LY² adv., ~MENT n. [f. BE-(3) + obs. WILDER lose one's way]

bewitch', v.t. Affect by magic, put a spell on; delight exceedingly, whence ~**ing**² a., ~**ing**LY² adv., ~MENT n. [ME *biwicchen* f. BE-(2) + OE *wiccian* enchant f. *wicca* WITCH n.]

bewray' (bǐrā'), v.t. (arch.). Reveal, esp. involuntarily. [ME *bewreien* f. BE- (2) + *wreien* (OE *wrēgan* accuse)]

bey (bā), **bey'lic** (bā-), nn. (*Bey*) Turkish governor; (*beylic*) his district; *Bey of Tunis*, ruler of Tunisia. [f. Osmanli *bey*, formerly *beg*; cf. BEGUM]

beyŏnd', adv., prep., & n. **1.** At, to, the farther side (of), past, outside, besides; later than; out of reach, comprehension, or range, of (~ *measure*, exceedingly); surpassing; more than (with objective case, as *you have prospered* ~ *me*); (neg. & interrog.) except. **2.** n. *The* ~, the future life, the unknown; *the back of* ~, the remotest corner of the world. [OE *begeondan* f. *be* BY + *geondan* f. Gmc **jand* (see YON, YONDER) + *-ana* adv. suff.]

bĕz'ant (or bĭzănt'), n. Gold coin current in Europe from 9th c.; also silver. [f. OF *besan* f. L *Byzantius* (*nummus* coin) of Byzantium]

bĕz'el, n. Sloped edge of chisel etc.; oblique faces of cut gem; groove holding watch-glass or gem. [f. OF **bezel* (mod. *biseau*) of unkn. orig.]

bēzique' (-ēk), n. Card-game for two or four; combination of queen of spades & knave of diamonds. [f. F *besigue* of unkn. orig.]

bēz'oar (-ōr), n. Concretion with hard nucleus found in stomach or intestines of certain animals (chiefly ruminants), formerly believed antidotal. [ult. f. Pers. *pādzahr* antidote, Arab. *bāzahr*]

bĕzŏn'ian, n. (arch.). Rascal, beggarly fellow. [earlier *besonio*, f. It. *bisogno* need, want]

bhăng (bă-). n. Indian hemp used as narcotic & intoxicant (smoked, chewed, eaten, & drunk). [earlier *bangue*, *bang*; f. Hind. etc. *bhang*]

bhis'tĭ, **bhees'ty̆** (bēs-), n. (Anglo-Ind.). Indian water-carrier. [Urdu *bhistī* f. Pers. *bihisht* paradise (prob. joc. origin)]

bī-, pref. f. L *bi-*, twice, doubly, having two-, two-, freely used in English, esp. with wds f. L, but also with E wds (*bi--weekly*); see also BIN-. **1.** Adjj., (a) having two ――, as *bilateral*, *bilingual*; (b) doubly, in two ways, as *bi-concave*; (c) in Bot. & Zool., twice over, i.e. divided into similarly divided parts, as *bipinnate*; (d) lasting for two ――, appearing every two ――, as *biennial*; (e) appearing twice in a ――, as *biannual*, *bi-monthly*; many wds are ambiguous between this & the last,

& *semi-*, *half-*, would be better here; (f) joining two ——, as *bi-parietal*. **2.** Nouns, double, as *bi-millionaire*. **3.** Chem. nouns & adjj., having twice the proportion of acid, base, etc., indicated by the simple wd, as *bicarbonate*. Now usu. superseded by *di-*.

bi′as¹, n. (In bowls) lopsided form of a bowl, its oblique course, the inserted plug of metal or influence deflecting, it; (metaph. from bowls) inclination, predisposition (*towards*), prejudice, influence; (Dressmaking etc.; as a., n., & adv.) *cut on the ~*, *cut ~*, cut obliquely across the texture, *~ band* etc., band so cut. [16th c., f. F *biais* = Pr. *biais*, Cat. *bialx*, *biais*, of unkn. orig.]

bi′as², v.t. (-s- *or* -ss-). Give a bias to, influence (usu. unfairly), inspire with prejudice. [f. prec.]

biăx′ial, a. With two (optic) axes. [BI- (1 a) + AXIAL]

bib¹, v.i. (-bb-). Drink much or often. [ME, perh. f. L *bibere* drink]

bib², n. Child's chin-cloth to keep dress-front clean; adult's apron-top (*best ~ & tucker*, best clothes). [perh. f. prec.]

bib³, n. A fish, the whiting-pout. [from an inflatable membrane on head resembling prec.]

bibb′er, n., **bibb′ing**, n. & a. Tippler, tippling, (usu. in comb., as *wine* etc. -~). [BIB v., -ER¹, -ING¹, ²]

bib′cŏck′, n. Tap or faucet with a bent nozzle fixed at the end of a pipe (dist. STOPCOCK. [perh. f. BIB²]

bibelot (bēb′lō), n. Small curio or artistic trinket. [F]

Bi′ble, n. Scriptures of the Old & New Testament, a copy of them, a particular edition of them (BREECHes, PRINTERS′, VINEGAR, WICKED, ~); authoritative book; *~-oath*, taken on the *~*; ‖*~-reader*, one employed to read the *~* from house to house; *~-Christian*, a member of sect so called; *~-clerk*, student at some Oxford colleges who reads lessons in chapel. [ME, f. OF f. LL f. Gk *biblia* books pl. of *biblion* dim. of *biblos*, *bublos* papyrus]

bib′lical, a. Of, concerning, contained in, the Bible. [f. med. L *ḅiblicus* (see -IC, -AL)]

bib′lico-, comb. of BIBLICAL, as *biblico-poetical*. [-O-]

bib′lio-, comb. form of *biblion* see BIBLE. Of books or the Bible.

bibliograph-. See foll. & -GRAPH, -GRAPHER, -GRAPHIC, -GRAPHY.

bibliŏg′raphy̆, n. History or description of books, their authorship, editions, etc.; book containing such details; list of books of any author, printer, country, subject. [f. Gk *bibliographia*; see BIBLIO-, -GRAPHY]

bibliŏl′ater, n., **bibliŏl′atrous**, a., **bibliŏl′atry̆**, n. Worshipper of, worshipping, worship of, books, a book, or the Bible. [BIBLIO-, -LATRY]

bibliomān′ia, **bibliomān′iăc**, nn. Rage for collecting, enthusiastic collector of,

books. [after F *bibliomanie*; see BIBLIO-, -MANIA]

bib′liophil(e), n. Book-fancier, -lover. Hence **bibliŏph′ilism**(3), **bibliŏph′ilist** (3), nn. [F *bibliophile* (BIBLIO-, -PHIL)]

bib′liopōle, **bibliŏp′oly̆**, nn. Seller, selling, of (esp. rare) books. [f. L (*-la*) f. Gk *bibliopōlēs* (BIBLIO-, *-pōlēs* -seller)]

bib′ūlous, a. Absorbent; addicted to drink. Hence ~LY² adv. [f. L *bibulus* freely drinking (*bibere* drink) + -OUS]

bicăm′eral, a. With two (legislative) chambers. [BI-(1 a) + L *camera* CHAMBER + -AL]

bicărb′onate. See BI-(3).

bīce, n. *~* or *blue ~*, *green ~*, pigments made from blue, green, hydrocarbonate of copper; similar pigment made from smalt etc.; dull shades of blue & green given by these. [f. F *bis* brownish-grey, of unkn. orig.]

bīcĕn′tēnary̆ (*also* -ĕntēn²-), a. & n. (Festival) of the two-hundredth anniversary. [BI-(1 a) + L *centenarius* CENTENARY; used of years by confusion with *centennial*]

bicĕntĕnn′ial, a. & n. Lasting, occurring every, two hundred years; (n.) = prec. [BI-(1 d) + CENTENNIAL]

bicĕph′alous, a. Two-headed. [BI-(1 a) + -CEPHALOUS]

bī′cĕps, n. (pl. ~*es*). Muscle with double head or attachment, esp. the upper-arm flexor; muscularity. [L, = two-headed f. BI-(1 a) + *-ceps* = *caput* head]

bĭchlŏr′ide (-kl-), n. Compound in which double proportion of chlorine combines with metal etc. (now usu. *dichloride*). [BI-(3)]

bĭchrōm′ate (-kr-), n. Salt with double proportion of chromic acid (now usu. *dichromate*). [BI-(3)]

bick′er, v.i. Quarrel; (of stream, rain, etc.) brawl, patter; (of flame, light, etc.) flash, glitter. [ME *biker*, *beker* of unkn. orig.; perh. a frequent. formation]

bīcŭs′pid, a. & n. (Tooth) with two cusps. [BI-(1 a) + L *cuspis -idis* point]

bī′cy̆cle, n., & v.i. (Ride on) two-wheeled pedal-driven vehicle. Hence **bī′cy̆clist**(1) n. [F, f. BI- (1 a) + Gk *kuklos* wheel]

bid¹, v.t. & i. (past *bad*, *bade*, *bid*, p.p. *bidden*, *bid*). Command to (usu. without *to*; now literary, arch., or poet., for *tell* with *to*; also abs., as *do as you are ~*); invite (esp. in *~den guest*); salute (person) with *welcome*, *farewell*, etc.; (esp. at an auction) offer price, offer (a certain price) *for* (past & p.p. *bid*), whence *~d′ER¹* n.; (Bridge) make a BID² of or in, make a bid; proclaim (*defiance*, the *banns*); *~ fair to do*, show promise of doing; ‖ *~ding-prayer*, inviting congregation to join. [(a) the standard forms are those of OE *biddan* beg, pray, etc., OS *biddian* OHG (G) *bitten*, ON *bithja*, Goth. *bidjan*, f. Gmc *•bidhjan*; (b) the meanings include some from OE *bēodan* offer, command, etc.,

OS *biodan*, OHG *biotan* (G *bieten*), ON *bjóða*, Goth. *biudan*, Gmc **beudhan*]

bid², n. Offer of price, esp. at auction; (Bridge) statement of number of tricks player proposes to win in specified suit or no-trumps; *make a ~ for*, (fig.) make an attempt to secure (favour, the prize, etc.). [f. prec.]

bidd'able, a. Obedient; (of hand or suit at cards) capable of being bid. [-ABLE]

bidd'ing, n. In vbl senses; esp. the offers at auction; a command. [-ING¹ (1)]

bidd'ȳ, n. (dial.). Chicken. [orig. unkn.]

bide, v.t. & i. (Arch. & poet. for ABIDE, but the regular wd in) ~ one's *time*, await best opportunity. [OE, OS *bidan*, OHG *bitan*, ON *biða*, Goth. *beidan* f. Gmc **bidan*]

bidet (bēd'ā), n. Raised narrow bath that can be bestridden. [F, = pony]

biénn'ial, a. & n. Lasting, recurring every, two years; (n., Bot.) plant that springs one year, & flowers, fructifies, & perishes, the next. Hence ~LY² adv. [f. L *biennis* f. BI-(1 d)+*annus* year+-AL]

bier, n. Movable stand on which corpse (or corpse) is taken to grave. [OE *bær*, OS, OHG *bāra* f. WG **bērō* f. *beran* BEAR³; mod. sp. app. after F *bière* f. same source]

biff, n., & v.t., (sl.). A smart blow; (vb) strike (person). [imit.]

‖ **biff'in**, n. Deep-red cooking-apple. [= *beefing* f. BEEF+-ING(3) with ref. to the colour]

bi'fid, a. Divided by a deep cleft into two parts. [f. L BI(*fidus* f. st. of *findere* cut)]

bifōc'al, a. & n. pl. 1. Having two foci (esp. of combined distant & near vision spectacles). 2. n. pl. ~ spectacles. [BI-(1 a)]

bifōl'iate, a. Of two leaves. [BI-(1 a)+L *folium* leaf+-ATE² (2)]

bi'furcāte¹ (-ferk-), v.t. & i. Divide into two branches, fork. [f. foll., first in p.p. *-ated*]

bi'furcāte² (-ferk-), a. Forked (esp. in Bot.). [f. med. L BI(*furcatus* f. *furca* fork, -ATE²)]

bifurcā'tion (-ferk-), n. Division into two branches; the point of division; the branches or one of them. [f. BIFURCATE¹]

big, a. & adv. Large; grown up; pregnant (~ *with young*, also ~-*bellied*, & esp. fig. as ~ *with fate, news*); important (*a* ~ *man*; *the Big Three, Five*, etc., the predominant few in any affair; *get, grow, too* ~ *for* one's *boots*, sl., become conceited, put on airs); boastful(ly) (~ *words, looks*; *look* or *talk* ~); (as distinctive epithet) ~ *drum, toe, game*; *Big Ben*, great bell in the Houses of Parliament; ~ *bug* (sl.), = ~*wig*; ~ *business*, commerce on the grand scale (freq. with sinister implication); ~ *end*, end of the connecting-rod that encircles the crank-pin; ~-*horn*, Rocky-Mountain sheep; **~ noise* (sl.), = ~*wig*; **~ stick*, display of force; ~'*wig*, person of importance. Hence ~'NESS n. [orig. unkn.]

big'amist, n. Man (woman) with two wives (husbands). [see BIGAMY, -IST]

big'amous, a. Guilty of, involving, bigamy. [f. as foll.+-OUS]

big'amy, n. Having two wives or husbands at once. [ME, f. OF *bigamie* (-Y¹) f. *bigame* bigamous f. LL *bigamus* (earlier *di-*, see BIGAMY)]

‖ **bigg**, **big**, n. Four-rowed barley. [f. ON *bygg*, corresp. to OE *bēow* grain, f. Gmc **beuwom*]

bight (bīt), n. Loop of a rope; curve, recess, of coast, river, etc., bay. [OE *byht*, MLG (G) *buchl* f. Gmc **bugan*, see BOW³]

big'ot, n. One who holds irrespective of reason, & attaches disproportionate weight to, some creed or view. Hence ~ED² a. [16th c. f. F; orig. unkn.]

big'otrȳ, n. Conduct, mental state, act, of a bigot. [f. F *bigoterie*; see BIGOT, -RY]

bijou (bēzh'ōō), n. (pl. *-oux*, pr. *-ōō*) & a. Jewel, trinket; small & elegant. [F]

bijouterie (bēzhōōt'erē), n. Jewelry, trinkets, etc. [F, see prec. & -RY]

bike, n., & v.i. (Colloq. abbr. for) BICYCLE.

bikin'i (-ēn'ē), n. Scanty two-piece beach garment worn by women. [f. *B~*, atoll in Marshall Islands in Pacific]

bilăt'eral, a. Of, on, with, two sides; affecting, between, two parties. Hence ~LY² adv. [BI-(1 a) + L *latus -eris* side +-AL]

bil'berrȳ, n. Fruit of dwarf hardy N.- -European shrub growing on heaths & in mountain woods (also *blaeberry*, *whortleberry*). [cf. Da. *böllebær*]

bil'bō, n. (hist.; pl. *-os*). Sword. [f. *Bilbao* in Spain]

bil'boes (-ōz), n. pl. Iron bar with sliding shackles for prisoner. [orig. unkn.]

bile, n. Brownish-yellow bitter fluid secreted by the liver to aid digestion; derangement of the ~; peevishness; ~-*stone*, calculus in gall-bladder. [F, f. L *bilis*]

bilge¹, n. Nearly horizontal part of ship's bottom, inside or out; the foulness that collects inside the ~; (sl.) nonsense, rot; belly of barrel; ~-*keel*, timber fastened under ~ to prevent rolling; ~-*water*, stinking water collected in ~. [prob. var. of BULGE]

bilge², v.t. & i. Stave in the bilge of, spring a leak in the bilge; bulge, swell out. [f. prec.]

bilhărz'i|a, n. Flat-worm parasitic in the blood & bladder of residents in tropical countries (esp. Egypt). Hence ~AS'IS n., chronic disease produced by its presence. [T. *Bilharz*, discoverer]

bil'iarȳ (-lya-), a. Of the bile. [f. F *biliaire*, see BILE, -ARY²]

biling'ual (-Inggwal), a. Having, speaking, spoken or written in, two languages. [f. L *bilinguis* f. BI-(1 a)+*lingua* tongue +-AL]

bil'ious (-lyus), a. Liable to, affected by, arising from, derangement of the bile;

peevish. Hence ~LY[2] adv., ~NESS n. [f. F *bilieux* f. L *biliosus*; see BILE, -OSE[1], -OUS]
-bility, suf. See -BLE.

bilk, v.t. Evade payment of (creditor, bill); cheat, give the slip to. [orig. uncert.; perh. = BALK[2]; earliest use in cribbage, = spoil opponent's score]

bill[1], n. Obsolete weapon, halberd; (also ~*'hook*) concave-edged lopping implement for pruning etc. [OE, OS *bil*, OHG *bill* f. WG **biljam*]

bill[2], n. Bird's beak (esp. when slender, flattened, or weak, & in pigeons & web-footed birds); muzzle of platypus; narrow promontory (*Portland B~* etc.); point of anchor-fluke. Hence ~ED[2] (-ld) a. [OE *bile* of unkn. orig.; not elsewhere in Gmc]

bill[3], v.i. Stroke bill with bill (of doves); exchange caresses (esp. ~ & *coo*). [f. prec.]

bill[4], n. Draft of proposed Act of Parliament; (Law) written statement of (esp. plaintiff's) case (*find a true ~, ignore the ~*, forms by which Grand Jury sends, does not send, case for trial); note of charges for goods delivered or services rendered; **bank or treasury note*; poster, placard, programme of entertainment; (also ~ *of exchange*) written order by drawer to drawee to pay sum on given date to drawer or to named payee (if drawn not against value received, but to raise money on credit, the ~ is known as an *accommodation ~*); ~ *of fare*, list of dishes to be served, menu, (fig.) programme; ~ *of health*, certificate regarding infectious disease on ship or in port at time of sailing (*clean ~ of health*, no disease); ‖ ~ *of lading*, ship-master's detailed receipt to consignor; ‖ ~ *of quantities*, detailed statement of work, prices, dimensions, etc., involved in the erection of a building; ~ *of sale*, transferring personal property, or authorizing its seizure by lender of money if payment is delayed; ~*s of mortality* (hist.), weekly return of deaths in London & district (*within the ~s of mortality*, in or near London); **~'board*, hoarding; ~*-poster*, *-sticker*, man who pastes up placards; ~*-broker*, *-discounter*, dealer in, discounter of, ~*s of exchange*. [ME, AF *bille*, AL *billa*, Eng. alt. of L *bulla* in medieval sense of *seal, sealed document*, BULL[3]; see BILLET[1]]

bill[5], v.t. Announce, put in the programme; ~*ed to appear* etc., announced as going to; plaster with placards. [f. prec.]

bill'abŏng, n. (Austral.). Branch of river that comes to a dead end. [native]

bill'ĕt[1], n. Order requiring person to board & lodge the soldier etc. bearing it (*every bullet has its ~*, hits only by providential order), place where troops etc. are lodged; destination; appointment, situation. [ME, AF *billette*, AL *billetta*, dim. of *billa* BILL[4]; cf. also OF *billele*, var. of *bullete*, med. L *bulletta*, dim. of *bulla*]

bill'ĕt[2], v.t. Quarter (soldiers etc.) *on* (town, householder, etc.), *in*, *at*; (of householder) provide (soldier etc.) with board & lodging. Hence ~EE, ~OR, nn. [f. prec.]

bill'ĕt[3], n. Thick piece of firewood; small bar of metal; short roll inserted at intervals in hollow moulding (Norman archit.). [ME, f. F *billette* & *billot* dim. of *bille* tree-trunk f. med. L *billa, billus* prob. of Celt. orig.]

billet-doux (bilidoo'), n. Love-letter (joc.). [F]

bill'iards (-lyardz), n. pl. Game played with cues & ivory balls on cloth-covered table; *billiard-marker*, attendant keeping the score. [f. F *billard* cue dim. of *bille* see BILLET[3]]

bill'ingsgate (-z-), n. Abuse, violent invective. [from the scolding of fish-women in *Billingsgate* market]

bill'ion (-yon), n. A million millions; (in U.S.) a thousand millions. [F, coined in 16th c. out of BI- & *million* to denote the second power of a million; meaning afterwards changed in France (so U.S.) but not in Britain]

bill'on, n. Alloy of gold or silver with a predominating amount of some base metal. [F, f. *bille* BILLET[3]]

bill'ow[1] (-ō), n. Great wave; (poet.) *the* sea; (fig.) anything that sweeps along, as sound, troops. Hence ~Y[2] (-ōi) a. [f. ON *bylgja* f. Gmc **belgan* swell]

bill'ow[2] (-ō), v.i. Rise, move, in billows. [f. prec.]

bill'ȳ, n. (Austral.). Tin can used as kettle etc. in camping out. [prob. the male name]

‖ **bill'ȳboy,** n. River or coasting trading barge. [orig. unkn.]

‖ **bill'ȳcŏck,** n. Round-crowned hard felt hat, bowler. [said to have been orig. designed for *William Coke* 1850]

bill'ȳ-goat, n. Male goat. [*Billy* male name]

bill'ȳ-(h)o, n. (Colloq., used in the intensive phr.) *like ~*; *raining like ~* (cats & dogs); *fighting like ~* (fiercely). [orig. unkn.]

bilŏb'ate, bi'lobed (-ōbd), aa. With two lobes. [BI- (1 a), & see LOBE, -ATE[2] (2), -ED[2]]

bil'tŏng, n. Strips of sun-dried meat. [Afrikaans f. *bil* buttock (from which it is cut) + *long* tongue (which it looks like)]

Bim, n. (colloq.). Inhabitant of Barbados.

bim'anal, bim'anous, aa., **bim'āne,** n. (Individual) of the *Bimana* or two-handed order of mammalia, two-handed. [*bimane* F f. BI- (1 a) + L *manus* hand, & see -AL, -OUS]

bimbash'i (-ah-), n. Turkish military captain or commander; (formerly) British officer in Egyptian service. [Turk., = head of a thousand]

bimĕtăll'ic, a., **bimĕt'allism,** n., **bimĕt'allist,** n. & a. Of, system of,

advocate of, using both gold & silver as legal tender to any amount at fixed ratio to each other. [f. F *bimétallique* 1869; see BI-(1 a), METALLIC, -ISM(3), -IST(2)]

bin, n. Receptacle (orig. of wicker, now usu. fixed, of wood) for corn, coal, dust, bottled wine, etc.; wine from a special ~; ‖ canvas receptacle used in hop--picking. [OE *binne* f. OBrit. **benna*, or f. med.L *benna* = OF *banne* f. Gaulish *benna*]

bin-, pref., treated as a euphonic form of BI- before vowels. Prob. orig. in F *binocle* (cf. BINOCULAR) & extended in E esp. to chem. compounds; cf. *bichloride*, *biniodide*.

bin'ary, a. Dual, of or involving pairs; (Mus.) ~ *measure*, of two beats to bar; ~ *form*, of movement in two sections; (Astron.) ~ *system*, two stars revolving round common centre or each other; (Chem.) ~ *compound*, of two elements; (Math.) ~ *scale*, with 2 (not 10) as base of notation. [f. LL *binarius* f. *bini* two together]

bin'ate, a. In pairs. [f. L *bini* two together + -ATE²(2)]

binaur'al, a. Of, used with, both ears, as ~ *stethoscope*. [BIN- + AURAL]

bind¹, v.t. & i. (*bound*, pr. bow-; also arch. p.p. in *bounden duty*). Tie; fasten, attach, *to*, *on*; put in bonds, restrain; fasten or hold together; be obligatory, exercise authority, impose constraint or duty, upon, (pass.) be required by duty *to* (do something); subject to legal obligation (esp. ~ *over to appear*, *to good behaviour*, *to keep the peace*; fig., *I'll be bound*, go bail for statement), indenture as apprentice; ratify (~ *the bargain*); make costive; bandage (usu. ~ *up*); wreathe (head etc.) *with*, (material) *round*, *about*, *on*; edge with braid, iron, etc.; cohere (of snow etc.); (Bookbind.) fasten (sheets) into stiff, orig. leather, vellum, etc., now usu. cloth, cover (*half-bound*, with leather at back & corners only), ~ *up*, together in one vol. [OE, OS *bindan*, OHG *bintan*, ON *binda*, Goth. *bindan* f. Gmc **bindan*]

bind², n. Indurated clay between coal strata; (Mus.) curved line between two notes to be held as one; = BINE. [f. prec.]

bin'der, n. In vbl senses; also or esp.: book~; obstetric apparatus; long fencing-withe; tie beam; through-stone in wall; wisp of straw, part of reaping--machine, for sheaf-binding; loose cover for unbound newspapers etc. [-ER¹]

bin'ding¹, a. Obligatory (*on*). [-ING²]

bin'ding², n. In vbl senses; also, book-cover; braid etc. for protecting raw edges. [-ING¹]

bind'weed, n. Kinds of convolvulus & other climbing plants. [BIND¹ + WEED]

bine, n. Flexible shoot; stem of climbing plant, esp. the hop. [orig. dial. form of, & now replacing, BIND²]

binge (-j), n. (sl.). Drinking-bout, spree. [orig. dial., = soak]

bing'o (-ngg-), n. Popular gambling game played with cards divided into numbered squares. [orig. unkn.]

binn'acle, n. Receptacle for ship's compass. [17th c. *bittacle* etc., f. Sp. or Pg. *bitácula* f. L *habitaculum* habitation]

binôc'ūlar, a. & n. (Field or opera glass) adapted for two eyes (n. now usu. pl.). [f. L *bini* two together + *oculus* eye + -AR¹]

binôm'ial, a. & n. Consisting of two terms; ~ *theorem*, formula for finding any power of a ~ without multiplying at length; (n.) algebraic expression of two terms joined by + or -. [f. mod. L *binomium* (+ -AL), a 16th c. application of med. L *binomius* having two personal names, irreg. f. BI- (1 a) + *nomen* name]

binôm'inal, a. Of two names (esp. ~ *system*, of scientific nomenclature by genus & species). [f. L *binominis* (BI- 1 (a) + *nomen -inis* name) + -AL]

bin'tŭrŏng, n. S.-Asian prehensile-tailed civet. [Malay]

bio-, comb. form of Gk *bios* (course of) life, which meaning it has in actual borrowings f. Gk, as *biography*; in mod. formations it is extended to include organic life (Gk *zōē*).

biochem'istry (-kĕ-), n. Study of the chemical or physico-chemical processes & products involved in the life phenomena of plants & animals. [prec.]

biogĕn'ésis, n. Hypothesis that living matter arises always from living matter. [BIO- + Gk GENESIS]

bi'ograph (-ahf), n. Early form of cinematograph. [trade name of U.S. machine exhibited in London in 1897]

biŏg'raphy, n. Written life of a person; branch of literature dealing with persons' lives; life-course of a living being. So **biŏg'RAPHER** n., **bIOGRAPH'IC**(AL) aa., **biŏgrăph'icaLLY²** adv. [f. mod. L f. med. Gk *biographia* see BIO-, -GRAPHY]

biŏl'ogy̆, n. Science of physical life, dealing with the morphology, physiology, origin, & distribution of animals & plants. So **biolŏ'gic**(AL) aa., **biolŏ'gicaLLY²** adv., **biŏl'ogIST** n. [f. F, G *biologie* see BIO-, -LOGY]

biŏm'ĕtry̆, n., **biomĕt'rics**, n. pl. Science of the application of statistical methods to biological facts. So **biomĕt'rIC**(AL) aa., **biomĕtri'cIAN** n. [BIO-, -METRY]

bionŏm'ĭcs, n. pl. Branch of biology dealing with the habits of life of organisms in their natural surroundings, relationship of forms of life to one another, etc. (cf. OECOLOGY). [f. BIO-, after ECONOMICS]

biophy̆s'ic|s (-z-), n. pl. Science of the application of the laws of physics to biological phenomena. Hence ~IST (-z-) n. [BIO-]

bi'oplăsm (-zm), **bi'oplăst**, nn. The

germinal matter, a small separate portion of it, from which all living things spring. [BIO- + Gk *plasma* see PLASMA]

bi′opsy̆, n. (surg.). Examination of tissue cut from the living body. [f. BIO-, & see OPTIC]

bi′oscōpe, n. = BIOGRAPH; (S.-Afr.) cinema. [BIO-, -SCOPE]

bipar̄tisăn′ (-z-; *or* -par̄t′-), a. Of or involving two (political) parties. [BI- 1 (a) +PARTISAN[1]]

bipar̄t′ite, a. 1. (Bot., of leaves) divided into two parts. 2. (Law, of treaties, contracts, etc.) drawn up in two corresponding parts. [BI-, PARTITE]

bi′pĕd, a. & n., **bi′pĕdal**, a. Two-footed (animal). [f. L *bipes* -*edis* f. BI-(1 a) +*pes pedis* foot]

bipinn′ate, a. Having lobes that themselves have lobes. [BI-(1 c) +PINNATE]

bi′plāne, n. Two-winged aeroplane. [BI-]

bipōl′ar, a. With two poles or extremities. [BI-(1 a)]

Bipŏn′tine, a. Printed at Zweibrücken (editions of classics). [BI- two +L *pons pontis* bridge (transl. of the name)+ -INE[1]]

biquadrăt′ic, a. & n. (Number) of the fourth power, square of a square; ~ (*equation*), in which there is a ~ variable. [BI-(1 b)]

bir̄ch[1], n. Kinds of smooth-barked slender-branched northern forest tree; (also ~-*rod*) bundle of its twigs used for flogging schoolboys etc. Hence ~′EN[5] a. [OE *bierce*, OHG *birihha* f. Gmc *berkjŏn*; also OE *berc* (whence north. dial. *birk*), ON *björk* f. Gmc *berkō*]

bir̄ch[2], v.t. Flog with a birch. [f. prec.]

bir̄d, n. Feathered vertebrate; game ~; (sl.) girl; *little* ~, unnamed informant; *old* ~, wary person; ~*s of a feather*, people of like character; *a* ~ *in the hand, in the bush*, certainty, contingency; ~ *is flown*, prisoner etc. escaped; *kill two* ~*s with one stone*, gain two ends at once; *give* one, *get, the* ~ (sl.), hiss him, be hissed; ~ *of Jove*, eagle, *of Juno*, peacock, *of paradise*, New Guinea family with beautiful plumage, *of passage*, migratory (also fig. of sojourner), *of prey*, member of orders *Raptores & Accipitres*, as hawk, eagle, owl; ~-*bath*, basin in garden etc. for ~s to bathe in; ~-*cage*, for ~ or ~s; ~-*fancier*, one who knows about, collects, breeds, or deals in, ~s; ~-*lime*, sticky stuff spread on twigs to catch ~s; ~-*seed*, special seeds given to caged ~s; ~′*s-eye*, kinds of plant with small bright round flowers as mealy primrose or germander speedwell, (tobacco) in which ribs are cut as well as fibre, ~′*s-eye view*, conspectus of town, district, etc., as seen from above, or résumé of subject, (of pattern etc.) marked with spots; ~′*s-foot*, kinds of vetch, fern, trefoil, & starfish; ~′*s mouth*, re-entrant angle cut in wood or stone; ~′*s nest*, ~-*nest*, nest of ~, kinds of plant

as wild carrot, ~-*nest* orchid, (v.i., esp. in gerund) hunt for nests, (of horse) turn head from side to side; ~-*table* (for wild ~s to feed on); ~-*watcher*, one who observes or identifies wild ~s, ~-*watching*, this practice; ~-*watch* v.i. [OE *brid* young bird, later superseding *fowl* in gen. sense ′(*any*) *feathered animal*; excl. E, etym. unkn.]

bir̄d′ie, n. (golf). Hole done in one under *par* or *bogey*. [prec. +-Y[3]]

bir̄′ēme, n. Ancient galley with two banks of oars. [f. L *biremis* f. BI-(1 a) + *remus* oar]

birĕtt′a, n. Square cap worn by R.-C. & some Anglican clerics. [f. It. *berretta* or Sp. *birreta* fem. forms corresp. to med. L *birretum*; see BERET]

Bir̄′rel(l)ism, n. Passing comment on life, pungent yet kindly, of a type characteristic of the writings & sayings of Augustine *Birrell*, English wit & essayist (d. 1933). [-ISM]

bir̄th, n. Bringing forth of offspring (so many *at a* ~); coming into the world (*give* ~ *to*); origin, beginning; parentage, descent, inherited position; noble lineage, high-born people; *new* ~, regeneration; ~-*control*, methods of preventing undesired sexual conception, practice of these; ~′*day*, (anniversary of) day of one's ~ (~*day present*, given on this; ~*day book*, for entering friends' ~days; ~*day suit* joc., one's skin; ~*day honours*, titles etc. given on sovereign's ~day); ~-*mark*, peculiar mark on one's body at or from ~, usu. an irregularly-shaped blotch of skin dark red in colour; ~-*place*, at which one was born; ~-*rate*, births per thousand of population; ~′-*right*, rights belonging to one as eldest son, as born in a certain station or country, or as a human being. [ME *burth(e)*, *byrth(e)* f. ON *burthr* = Goth. *gabaurths* f. Gmc ′(*ga*)*burthiz* f. stem of *beran* BEAR[3] +-TH[1]]

bis, adv. 1. (mus.). Over again, repeat. 2. Twice (calling attention to a double occurrence in references etc.). [F & It. f. L, = twice]

bis′cuit (-kit), n. & a. ‖ Piece of unleavened bread of various materials, usu. crisp, dry, hard, & in small flat thin cakes; *soft round cake; porcelain etc. after baking but before glazing & painting; ‖ half-piece or third of soldier's mattress; (of) light-brown colour; ~-*throw* (Naut.), short distance. [earlier *bisket* (now assim. to mod. F) f. OF *bescoit* (L BIS, *coctus* p.p. of *coquere* cook)]

bis dăt quī cit′ō dăt, sent. He gives twice who gives quickly. (formula in charity appeals.) [L]

bise (bēz), n. Keen dry N. wind in Switzerland, S. France, etc. [F]

bisĕct′, v.t. Cut or divide into two (prop. equal) parts. Hence **bisĕc′tion** n. [BI-, L *secare sect-* cut]

bisĕc′tor, n. Bisecting line. [-OR]

bisĕx'ūal, a. Of two sexes; having both sexes in one individual. [BI-(1 a)+ SEXUAL]

bish'op, n. Clergyman consecrated as eccl. governor of a diocese & possessing powers of confirming, instituting, & ordaining; ~ SUFFRAGAN; mitre-shaped piece in chess; mulled & spiced wine; *Bishops' Bible*, version of 1568; ~'s-*cap*, -*hat*, -*leaves*, -*weed*, various plants. [OE *biscop*, OS *biskop*, OHG *biscof*, ON *biskup* f. pop. L *biscopo* (cf. Pg. *bispo*, It. *vescovo*) f. LL f. Gk *episkopos* (whence Goth. *aipiskaupus*) overseer (EPI-+ -*skopos* -looking)]

bish'opric, n. Office of bishop. [OE *bisceoprice* (prec.+*rice* realm cf. G *reich*)]

bisk, n. Rich soup made by boiling down birds etc. [f. F *bisque* crayfish soup]

Bis'ley (-z-), n. (Used for) the ranges or the shooting competitions of the Nat. Rifle Association at ~ in Surrey.

Bismil'lah (-*a*), int. In the name of Allah! (common ejaculation of Moslems before action). [Arab. *bi-'sm-illāhi*]

bis'muth (-z-), n. A reddish-white metal. [f. mod. L *bisemutum*, latinization (1530) of G *wismut* of unkn. orig.]

bis'on, n. Wild ox of two species, (also *aurochs*) formerly over Europe, & still in Lithuania, (also *buffalo*) about Rocky Mountains. [f. L *bison* -*ontis* f. Gmc *wisand* cf. OE *wesend*, OHG *wisunt*]

bisque[1] (-k), n. (Tennis) right of scoring one point without winning it at any time in the set; (Croquet) right of playing extra turn; (Golf) stroke to be taken when desired. [F, etym. unkn.]

bisque[2] (-k), n. Unglazed white porcelain used in statuettes. [f. BISCUIT]

bissĕx'tile, a. & n. Leap(-year). [f. LL *bi(s)sextilis (annus)*, (year) containing the *bis sextus dies* or doubled 24th Feb. (the sixth day before the calends of March)]

bis'tört, n. Herb with cylindrical spike of flesh-coloured flowers. [f. med. L *bistorta* (*bis* twice+*torta* fem. p.p. of *torquēre* twist) w. ref. to twisted form of root]

bis'toury (-torï), n. Surgeon's scalpel. [f. F *bistouri*, orig. unkn.]

bis'tre (-ter), n. & a. Brown pigment prepared from soot; colour(ed) like this. [F, etym. unkn.]

bit[1], n. Something to eat (*a ~ & a sup*); boring-piece of drill, cutting-iron of plane, nipping-part of pincers etc., part of key that grips lock-lever; mouthpiece of bridle, (fig.) control, (*draw ~*, slacken pace; *take ~ between teeth*, reject control). [OE *bite*, OS *biti*, OHG *biz*, ON *bit* f. Gmc *bitiz* f. *bitan* BITE[1]]

bit[2], n. Morsel of food (*dainty ~*, *tit'~*); small piece of anything (~ *by ~*, gradually; *give a ~ of* one's *mind*, speak candidly; *do* one's ~, contribute service or money to a cause); piece of scenery actual or painted; short passage in book

etc.; ~*s & pieces* (colloq.), odds & ends; ~*s of*, poor little (*children, furniture*); *a ~ of a*, rather a (*coward* etc.); *a ~*, rather, *not a ~* (*of it*), not at all, *every ~ as*, quite as; *a short time* (*wait a ~*); small coin (U.S., of fractions of Spanish dollar; in Britain, *threepenny ~*, etc.). [OE *bita*, OHG *bizzo*, ON *biti* f. Gmc **biton* f. **bitan* BITE[1]]

bit[3], v.t. (-tt-). Put bit into mouth of (horse); accustom to the bit; restrain. [f. BIT[1]]

bitch, n. Female of dog, fox, wolf, (usu. ~ *fox*, & ~ *wolf*); (derog.) woman, esp. a lewd or catty or treacherous one. [OE *bicce*, ON *bikkja*, relation & etym. unkn.]

bite[1], v.t. & i. (past *bit*; p.p. *bitten* sometimes *bit*). Cut into or nip with the teeth; (with *off* etc.) detach with the teeth; snap *at*; (of serpents, fleas, etc.) sting, suck; accept bait (lit. & fig.); (of sword etc.) penetrate; cause glowing, smarting, etc., pain to (*frost-bitten*); corrode; (of wheels, anchor, etc.) grip; (now only in pass.) take in, swindle, (*were you bitten?*); ~ *the dust* or *ground*, fall & die; ~ one's *lips*, to control anger etc.; ~ *off more than* one *can chew*, attempt too great a task; *bitten with*, infected with (a mania, enthusiasm, etc.). [OE, OS *bitan*, OHG *bizan*, ON *bita*, Goth. *beitan* f. Gmc **bitan*]

bite[2], n. Act of, wound made by, piece detached by, biting; food to eat (~ *& sup*); taking of bait by fish; grip, hold, (lit. & fig.); herbage for cattle; (fig.) incisiveness, pungency. [f. prec.]

bit'er, n. In vbl senses; also, swindler (now only in *the ~ bit*). [-ER[1]]

bit'ing, a. In vbl senses; esp., pungent, stinging, sarcastic. Hence ~LY[2] adv. [part. of BITE[1]]

bitt'er, a., adv., & n. 1. Tasting like wormwood or quinine, opposite to sweet (~-*cup*, cup of quassia wood giving ~ tonic property to liquid drunk from it); unpalatable to the mind, full of affliction; virulent, relentless; biting, harsh; piercingly cold (also as adv., *it was ~ cold*); *to the ~ end*, last extremity; hence ~ISH[1] (2) a., ~LY[2] adv., ~NESS n. 2. n. ~*ness* (*the ~ with the sweet, the ~s of life*); (pl.) liquors impregnated with wormwood etc. taken as stomachics; = ~ *beer*, opp. *mild*; ~-*sweet*, sweet(ness) with ~ after-taste or element (lit. & fig.), woody nightshade. [OE *biter*, OS, OHG *bittar*, ON *bitr*, Goth. *baitrs*, prob. f. Gmc **bitan* BITE[1]; *the ~ end* may be f. Naut., where the wds mean the last part of a cable left round the BITTS when the rest is overboard, *bitter* being the turn at any moment on the bitts]

bitt'erling, n. Small carp-like freshwater fish of Central Europe. [G, f. *bitter* bitter +*ling* -LING[1]]

bitt'ern, n. Kinds of marsh bird allied to herons, esp. one known for its booming

note. [ME *botor* etc. f. OF *butor* f. Rom.
*butitaurus f. L *butio* bittern + *taurus*
bull]

‖ bitt′ock, n. (dial.). Little bit. [BIT² +
-OCK]

bitts, n. pl. Pair of posts on deck for
fastening cables etc. [ME (c. 1300), f. ON
biti cross-beam; cf. LG, Du. *beting*]

bit′ūm|én, n. Mineral pitch, asphalt;
kinds of native oxygenated hydrocarbon,
as naphtha, petroleum. Hence ~inif-
EROUS, bitūm′inous, aa. [L, genit.
-*minis*]

bitūm′iniz|e, -is|e (-ĭz), v.t. Convert
into, impregnate or varnish with, bitumen. Hence ~A′TION n. [prec. + -IZE
(3, 5)]

bi′valent, a. = DIVALENT.

bi′vălve, a. & n., bi′vălved (-vd), bivăl-
vūlar, aa. With two valves; (mollusc)
with hinged double shell; oyster. [BI-
(1 a) + VALVE, *valv*ED², & see -ULE, -AR¹]

biv′ouăc (-ŏŏ-), v.i. & n. (-*acking*, -*acked*).
(Remain, esp. for the night, in) temporary
encampment without tents; bivouacked,
in ~, see -ED¹ (2). [F, prob. f. G *beiwacht*
(BY, WATCH) additional guard at night (in
Argau & Zürich)]

biz, n. (colloq.). Business. [abbr.]

bizăr̄|re′, a. Eccentric, fantastic, gro-
tesque, mixed in style, half barbaric.
So ~′rerie (-rē) [-ERY] n. [F; cf. Sp.
bizarro handsome, brave, It. *bizzarro*
choleric perh. f. Basque *bizarra* beard]

blăb, v.t. & i. (-bb-), & n. 1. Talk or tell
foolishly or indiscreetly, reveal, let out,
(secrets etc., or abs.); hence ~b′ER¹ n.
2. n. Person who ~s. [imit., cf. BABBLE;
ME *blabbe* n., babbler (whence later *blab*
vb) & ME *blabber* vb; cf. OHG *blabbizōn*,
ON *blubbra*, G *plappern*]

blăck¹, a. 1. Opposite to white, colourless
from the absence or complete absorption
of all light; so near this as to have
no distinguishable colour; very dark-
-coloured (~ *in the face*, purple with
strangulation or passion); dark-skinned;
dark-clothed; (of sky, deep water, etc.)
dusky, gloomy; (of hands, linen) dirty;
(as specific epithet) ~ *bear, currant, snake,*
heart-cherry; deadly, sinister, wicked,
hateful, (~-*hearted*; ~ *ingratitude*; *crimes*
of ~*est dye*); dismal (~ *despair*); angry,
sulky, threatening, (~-*browed*; ~ *looks*;
look ~); implying disgrace or condemnation (~ *mark*, of discredit against one's
name; ~ *book, list*, of persons suspect,
tabooed, etc.; *deep in* one's ~ *books*, quite
out of his favour); (of goods etc.) not to
be handled by workers on strike. 2. ~ *&*
blue, discoloured with bruise; ~ *& tan*,
(dog) so coloured, B~ *& Tans*, ex-service
recruits of the R.I.C. against Sinn-Feiners
1921 named from mixture of military &
constabulary uniforms; ~ *& white*, ink
drawing (*down in* ~ *& white*, recorded in
writing or print); ~ *art*, magic [~ partly
in sense *wicked*, partly by assoc. w. med.

L *nigromantia* corrupt. of NECROMANCY];
~ *ball*, used to reject candidate in club
ballot, whence ~-**ball′** v.t.; ~-*beetle*,
cockroach; ~′*berry*, bramble or its fruit
(*plentiful as* ~*berries*, as can be; ~*berry-*
ing, gathering them); ~′*bird*, European
song-bird, kidnapped Negro on slave-ship
(~*birding*, trade in these); ~-*board*, in
lecture-room for demonstrations in chalk;
‖ ~ *cap*, put on by judge in sentencing to
death; ~′*cap*, kinds of bird, esp. the ~
warbler; ~ CATTLE; ‖ ~-*coat worker*, clerk
etc. (opp. industrial employee); ~′*cock*,
male (opp. *grey-hen*) of ~ grouse; ~ *coffee*
(without milk, usu. strong); ‖ B~ *Country*,
smoky district in Staffs. & War.; ~ *dog*,
sulks; ~ *draught*, an aperient; ~ *eye*, discoloured with bruise, also with dark iris
whence ~-eyED² (-id) a.; ~-*face*, dark-
-faced sheep; ~′*fellow*, Australian aboriginal; ~-*fish*, a species, also salmon just
after spawning; ~ *flag*, used by pirates,
also signal of execution completed;
Black′foot (pl. -*feet*), member of a tribe of
N.-Amer. Indians; ~ *friar*, Dominican;
~ *frost*, hard frost without snow or rime;
~ *game*, ~ grouse (& see ~*cock*); ~*guard*
(blăg′ärd), (n. & a.) scoundrel(ly), foul-
-mouthed (person), whence ~**guard**LY¹
(-ăg²) a., (v.t.) call ~guard, abuse scurri-
lously [orig. collect. n., applied at various
times to menials of royal household,
camp-followers, bodyguard, criminal
class, & vagrants]; B~ *Hand*, secret
organization of Italian ~*mailers & thugs*
in U.S.; ~-*head*, kinds of bird, esp.
kind of gull, (also) kind of pimple on the
skin; ~ *hole*, military lock-up (so B~
Hole of Calcutta); ~ *jack*, tarred-leather
wine-bottle, also pirates' ~ flag, also
flexible loaded life-preserver; ~-*lead*,
(polish with) PLUMBAGO [named from
marking like lead]; ~′*leg*, swindler esp.
on turf, ‖ workman who works for master
whose men are on strike (v.i. & t., act as
~*leg*, betray or injure thus) [orig. of
senses unknown]; ~ *letter*, old type like
the German; ~ *list* (of persons under
suspicion, liable to punishment, etc.);
~*list′* (v.t.), enter name of (person) on
~ list; ~*mail*, (hist.) tribute exacted by
freebooters for protection & immunity,
(mod., v.t. & n.) (force to make) payment
for not revealing discreditable secrets
etc., whence ~*mail*′ER¹ n. [obs. *mail*
rent, OE *māl* f. ON *māl* agreement perh.
= OHG *mahal* assembly]; ~ *Maria*,
vehicle for taking prisoners from & to
gaol; ~ *market*, illegitimate traffic in
officially controlled goods or currencies
or in commodities in short supply (~
marketeer, one who engages in this),
place where this traffic is carried on;
~ *mass*, travesty of the mass said to be
used in the cult of Satanism (also Eccl., a
Requiem Mass); ~ *monk*, Benedictine;
~ *pudding*, sausage-shaped of blood, suet,
etc.; ‖ B~ *Rod*, gentleman usher of Lord

Chamberlain's department, House of Lords, & Garter; ~ sheep, scoundrel; ~-shirts, fascists; ~'smith, smith working in iron (cf. WHITEsmith); ~'thorn, thorny shrub bearing white flowers before leaves & small plums or sloes (~thorn winter, time of its flowering, cold with NE winds), cudgel or walking-stick of this; ~ velvet, mixture of stout & champagne; || B~ WATCH¹, 42nd Highlanders [f. orig. uniform]; ~-water fever, tropical disease with bloody urine etc.; ~ widow, common Amer. spider, the female of which devours its mate. Hence ~'ISH¹ (2) a., ~'NESS n. [OE blæc, blac, OHG blah-, blach- (in comb.) of unkn. orig.]

black², n. Black colour; black paint, dye, varnish; black speck; fungus, smut, in wheat etc.; particle of soot; black cloth(es); Negro or negrito, whence ~'Y³ n. [f. prec.]

black³, v.t. Make black; polish with BLACKING; ~ out: obliterate or obscure; obscure (windows etc.) to prevent any light being seen from outside, esp. from the air, also abs.; ~-out n.: ~ing out or being ~ed out (also attrib., as ~-out material, offences, time); (fig.) condition of obscuration; temporary complete failure of memory; in flying, temporary blindness etc. resulting from centrifugal force when a sudden turn is made (v.i., suffer this). [f. BLACK¹]

black'amoor n. Negro; dark-skinned person. [BLACK¹+MOOR²]

black'avised (-ızd) a. (arch.). Dark-complexioned. [BLACK¹+F vis face]

black'en, v.t. & i. Make, grow, black or dark; speak evil of (person's character). [ME blaknen (BLACK¹, -EN³)]

black'ing, n. In vbl senses; also, paste or liquid for blacking boots. [-ING¹]

bladd'er, n. Membranous bag in human & other animal bodies (esp. the urinary ~, also gall, air, swimming, ~); the same or part of it prepared for various uses, inflated etc.; (fig.) anything inflated & hollow, wordy man, windbag; inflated pericarp or vesicle in plants & seaweeds (~-wrack, common seaweed with these in its fronds). Hence ~Y² a. [OE blǽdre, OS blādra, OHG blātara, ON blathra f. Gmc *blǽdram f. *blǽ- BLOW¹]

blade, n. (Vague & poet.) leaf; flat lanceolate leaf esp. of grass & cereals; whole of such plants before ear comes (in the ~); (Bot.) expanded part of leaf apart from foot-stalk; flattened part of instrument, as oar, bat, spade, paddle-wheel; cutting-piece of edged tool, as sword, chisel, knife; sword; (also ~-bone) flat bone, esp. shoulder-~ as joint of meat or otherwise; jovial, hectoring, gay, etc., fellow (usu. with epithet). Hence (-)blād'ED² a. [OE blǽd, OHG blat, ON blath f. Gmc *bladham f. *blō see BLOW³]

|| blae'berry (blā-), n. = BILBERRY. [f.

blae (Sc. & north. dial. f. ME blo f. ON blár; see BLUE)+BERRY]

blague (-ahg), n. Humbug, claptrap. [F]

*blah, n. (colloq.). Hyperbolic & frothy talk or writing. [orig. unkn.]

blain, n. Inflamed sore on skin, pustule. [OE blegen cf. Du. blein]

blâme¹, v.t. Find fault with (for offence etc.); fix the responsibility on; be to ~e, deserve censure. Hence ~'ABLE a., ~'ABLY² adv. [f. OF bla(s)mer, ult. f. LL blasphemare BLASPHEME]

blâme², n. Censure; responsibility for bad result (lay the ~ on, bear the ~). [f. OF bla(s)me cf. prec.]

blâme'ful (-mf-), a. (Rare) conveying, (usu.) deserving, censure. [-FUL]

blâme'less (-ml-), a. Innocent. Hence ~LY² adv., ~NESS n. [-LESS]

blâme'worth|ly̆ (-mwérdh-), a. Deserving blame. Hence ~INESS n.

blanch (-ah-), v.t. & i. Make white by withdrawing colour, peeling (almonds), or depriving of light (plants); make or grow pale with fear, cold, etc.; ~ over, palliate by misrepresentation. [ME, f. OF blanchir (blanc BLANK)]

blancmange (blamahnzh'), n. Opaque white jelly of isinglass, gelatine, or corn-flour, & milk. [ME blancmanger f. OF (blanc BLANK+manger eat f. L manducare MANDUCATE)]

blānd, a. Gentle, polite, in manner; ironical; balmy, mild. Hence ~'LY² adv., ~'NESS n. [f. L blandus]

blăn'dish, v.t. Flatter, coax. Hence ~MENT n. (usu. in pl.). [ME, f. OF blandir (-ISH²) f. L blandiri (blandus)]

blănk¹, a. Not written or printed on (of paper); (of document) with spaces left for signature or details (in ~, drawn in ~, so prepared; ~ cheque, with amount left for payee to fill in, hence = CARTE BLANCHE); empty, not filled, (~ space etc.; ~ cartridge, without ball); void of interest, incident, result, or expression; look ~, nonplussed; unrelieved, sheer; unrhymed (~ verse, esp. the five-foot iambic). Hence ~'NESS n. [f. OF blanc white f. Rom. *blancus f. Gmc *blankaz]

blănk², n. Lottery ticket that gains no prize; space left to be filled up in document, empty surface (one's mind, memory etc., is a ~, has no sensations etc.); *document having blank space(s) to be filled up; words printed in italics in Parl bills; time without incident, thing without meaning; coin-disc before stamping; = ~ cartridge (20 rounds of ~); dash written instead of word or letter, whence ~, ~y, ~ed, as substitutes for abusive nouns and adjs. [uses of prec.]

blănk'et¹ n. & a. 1. Large woollen sheet used for bed covering, for horse-cloth, & by savages for clothes; wet ~, person who extinguishes conversation; born on the wrong side of the ~, illegitimate. *2. adj. General rather than individual,

covering all cases or classes. [ME, f. OF
blanquette (*blanc* BLANK + -ETTE)]

blănk'ĕt², v.t. Cover with a blanket;
stifle, keep quiet, (scandal, question, etc.);
toss in a blanket as punishment; take
wind from sails of (another craft) by
passing to windward. [f. prec.]

blănk'lў, adv. Without expression, vacu-
ously, (*look* ~ etc.); flatly (*deny* ~ etc.).
[BLANK¹ + -LY²]

blanquette (blahṅkĕt'), n. (cookery).
White dish, such as a fricassee with white
sauce. [F]

blāre, v.i. & t., & n. (Make) sound of
trumpet; utter loudly. [ME *bleren*, imit.;
cf. MDu. *blaren*, MHG *blēren*, *blerren*, G
plärren]

blärn'ey, n., & v.t. & i. (Use, assail with)
cajoling talk. [*Blarney*, Irish castle near
Cork with stone conferring a cajoling
tongue on whoever kisses it]

blasé (-ahz'ā), a. Cloyed, tired of pleasure.
[F]

blăsphĕm|e', v.i. & t. Talk impiously;
utter profanity about, revile. So ~'ER²
(4), blăs'phĕmy¹, nn., blăs'phĕmous a.,
blăs'phĕmously² adv. [ME *blasfemen*
f. OF *blasfemer* f. LL *blasphemare* f. Gk
blasphēmeō ; cf. BLAME]

blast¹ (-ah-), n. Strong gust of wind;
sound of wind-instrument; current of air
in smelting etc. (*in, out of, ~*, of furnace
working or not); quantity of explosive
used in blasting operation; destructive
wave of highly compressed air spreading
outwards from an explosion; ~*-furnace*,
smelting furnace into which compressed
hot air is driven by engine. [OE *blǣst*,
OHG *blāst*, ON *blāstr* f. Gmc **blǣst-* f.
*blǣsan blow see BLAZE³]

blast² (-ah-), v.t. Blow up (rocks etc.)
with explosives; wither, shrivel, blight,
(plant, animal, limb, prosperity, character; esp., with subj. *God* understood, in
curses, whence ~*ed*, damnable). [f. prec.]

blasto-, first element in many biological
terms, meaning germ, bud. [f. Gk *blastos*
sprout]

blăs'todĕrm, n. Disc of cells found in
the early segmentation of a fertilized
ovum (as differentiated from *blastula*,
hollow ball of cells, & *morula*, solid ball).
[prec. + Gk *derma* skin]

blăt'ant, a. Noisy, vulgarly clamorous;
flagrant, palpable. Hence ~LY² adv.,
blăt'ANCY n. [a Spenserian wd (*blattant*)
of uncert. orig.; perh. after Sc. *b.aland* =
bleating]

blather(skite). See BLETHER.

blāze¹, n. Bright flame or fire (*in a ~*, on
fire); (sl.) ~*s* = hell (*go to ~s, what the
~s!; like ~s*, impetuously); violent outburst (~ *of passion* etc.); glow of colour,
bright display; full light (~ *of publicity*).
[OE *blase*, *blǣse* torch, f. Gmc **blasōn-*;
cf. MHG *blas* torch; ult. cogn. w. BLAZE³]

blāze², v.i. Burn with flame (~ *up*, burst
into blaze); be brilliantly lighted; burn

with excitement etc. (~ *up*, burst out
in anger); show bright colours; emit
light; ~ *away*, fire continuously with
rifles etc., work enthusiastically at anything; *blazing indiscretion*, rash &
conspicuous piece of candour; (Hunting)
blazing scent, very strong (opp. to *cold
scent*). [f. prec.]

blāze³, n. White mark on horse's or ox's
face, or made on tree by chipping bark
to mark route. [f. 17th c.; = ON *blesi*,
OHG *blassa* (G *blesse*), MDu. *blesse* in
same sense; stem *blas-* cogn. w. MHG
blas bald, G *blass* pale]

blāze⁴, v.t. Mark (tree, & so path) by
chipping bark, esp. ~ *a trail*, also fig.
[f. prec.]

blāze⁵, v.t. Proclaim as with trumpet,
esp. ~ *abroad*, spread (news) about. [ME
blasen blow prob. f. ON *blāsa* = OHG
blāsan, Goth. *-blēsan* f. Gmc **blǣsan* (cf.
BLAST) f. **blǣ-* (BLOW¹); later sense 'proclaim' f. MLG, MDu. *blāzen*]

blāz'er, n. Coloured jacket for boating,
golf, etc. [BLAZE² + -ER¹]

blāz'on¹, n. Heraldic shield, coat of
arms, bearings, or banner; correct
description of these; record, description,
esp. of virtues etc. [ME, f. OF *blason*
shield, of unkn. orig.]

blāz'on², v.t. Describe or paint (arms)
heraldically; inscribe (object) with arms,
names, etc., in colours or ornamentally;
give lustre to; set forth in fitting words;
proclaim. Hence ~MENT n. [f. prec.
partly confused in sense with BLAZE⁵]

blāz'onrў, n. (Art of describing or painting) heraldic devices, armorial bearings;
brightly coloured display. [prec. + -RY]

-ble, suf. Of F. L *-bilis* forming vbl adjj.
active or passive (*penetrabilis* penetrating or penetrable) f. vb or p.p. stems.
L has *-ab.*, *-eb.*, *-ib.*, or *-ib.*, acc. to conjug.
(*-ib.* also f. p.p. stems as *flexibilis*). Mod.
F in making new wds uses only *-able* ; E
vacillates between this & using *-ible*
wherever there was or might be a L
-ibilis; to this confusion is added that
between *-able* & *-eable*: *-eable* is necessary
after soft *-c, -g*, (cf. *navigable, manageable*); it is also used in some wds to affect
the vowel of the previous syllable (*tame-
able*). See also -ABLE, -IBLE. The E
meaning in new wds is always passive,
but some older wds (*capable, durable*)
have active meaning after the older F
(f. L) tradition. From adjj. in *-ble* are
formed nouns in *-bility* (L *-bilitas*, see -TY)
as well as in *-bleness*.

bleach, v.t. & i. Whiten by exposure to
sunlight or by chemical process; ~*ing-
-powder*, chloride of lime. Hence ~'ER¹ n. ;
one who ~es (esp. textiles); vessel or
chemical used in ~ing; *(usu. pl.) outdoor
uncovered plank-seat for spectators at
sports grounds. [OE *blǣcan*, ON *bleikja*,
OHG *bleichēn* f. Gmc **blaikjan* f. **blaik-*
white]

bleak[1], n. Small river fish, & allied sea-fish, of various species. [15th c. *bleke*; cf. ON *bleikja*, OHG *bleicha* f. Gmc *blaikjôn f. *blaik- white]

bleak[2], a. Wanting colour; bare, exposed, windswept; chilly; dreary. [16th c., of obsc. phonology; rel. to obs. *bleach*, obs. *blake* (= OE *blāc*, ON *bleikr*) pale, ult. f. Gmc *blaik-*; see BLEACH]

blear, a., & v.t. (Make) dim-sighted, dull, filmy, (eyes or mind); (make) indistinct in outline; ∼-eyed, having ∼ eyes or wits. Hence ∼'Y[2] a. [ME *blere* a. & vb, cogn. w. MHG *blerre* blurred vision, LG *blarr-*, *blerr-oged* blear-eyed]

bleat, v.i. & t., & n. (Make) sheep's, goat's, or calf's, cry; speak (&∼ *out*, say) feebly or foolishly or plaintively. [imit.; OE *blǣtan*, OHG *blāzen*, Du. *blaten*]

bleb, n. Small blister or bubble on skin, in water or glass. [imit. of making bubble with lips, cf. *blab*, *blob*, *blubber*]

bleed, v.i. & t. (*bled*). Emit blood (*heart* ∼s, is in acute distress); suffer wounds or violent death (often *for* cause etc.); (of plants) emit sap; part with money, pay lavishly, suffer extortion; draw blood surgically from; extort money from; ‖ (part., vulg. euphem., cf. *blinking*, *blooming*, for) bloody; ∼*ing heart*, pop. name of various plants, as wallflower. Hence ∼'ER[1] n., person inclined to ∼ excessively from a slight injury. [OE *blēdan*, ON *blætha* f. Gmc. *blōdhjan f. *blōdham BLOOD]

bleep, n., & v.i. 1. (Sound of) radio signal transmitted from Russian earth satellite launched in 1957. 2. v.i. Transmit this signal. [imit.]

blem'ish[1], v.t. Mar, spoil the beauty or perfection of, sully. [ME, f. OF *ble(s)mir* (-ISH[2]) f. *ble(s)me* pale, of Gmc orig.]

blem'ish[2], n. Physical or moral defect, stain, flaw. [f. prec.]

blench, v.i. & t. Start aside, flinch, quail; close the eyes to, disguise from oneself. [hist. obsc.; perh. f. OE *blencan*, ON *blekkja* deceive; w. later senses cf. BLINK]

blend[1], v.t. & i. (∼*ed* or *blent*). Mix (things) together (esp. sorts of tea, spirit, to get certain quality); mingle (t., & i. of element) intimately *with*; mix (components) so as to be inseparable & indistinguishable; become one, form harmonious compound; pass imperceptibly into each other (esp. of colours). [ME, f. ON *blanda* mix, not continuous w. cogn. OE (= OS, Goth.) *blandan*, OHG *blantan*]

blend[2], n. Mixture made of various sorts of tea, spirits, etc. [f. prec.]

blende, n. Native sulphide of zinc. [G *blende* f. *blenden* deceive, also *blendendes Erz* deceiving ore 'because while often resembling galena it yielded no lead']

Blen'heim (-ĕnĭm), n. & a. Kind of spaniel; ‖∼ *Orange*, golden-coloured apple. [Duke of Marlborough's seat at Woodstock]

blenno-, blenn-, stem of many wds in pathology. Of mucus. [Gk *blennos* mucus]

blenn'y̆, n. Small spiny-finned sea-fish. [as prec. (through L *blennius*) from mucous coating of its scales]

blent. See BLEND[1].

bleph'aro-, stem of pathological words. Of the eyelids. [f. Gk *blepharon* eyelid]

bles'bŏk, n. Large S.-African antelope. [Afrikaans, f. *bles* BLAZE[3] (from white mark on forehead)+*bok* goat]

bless, v.t. (past & p.p. ∼*ed*, sometimes *blest*, & see under BLESSED). Consecrate (esp. food; *not a penny to* ∼ *oneself with*, w. ref. to cross on silver penny); call holy, adore, (God); attribute good fortune to (esp. one's stars); pronounce words that bring supernatural favour upon (of father, priest, etc.); invoke God's favour on; make happy or successful (abs. or *with* something); *God* ∼ *me*, ∼ *me*, *God* ∼ *you*, ∼ *you*, ∼ *the boy*, ∼ *my soul*, *I'm blest*, exclamations of surprise or indignation; (euphem.)=damn, curse, etc. [excl. E; OE *blǣdsian*, *blēdsian*, *blētsian*, f. Gmc *blōdhisōjan f. *blōdham BLOOD (mark with blood, consecrate); meaning influenced (1) by the word's being used at the Eng. conversion to translate L *benedicere*, (2) by confusion with the independent BLISS]

bless'ed, blest, (for pronunc. see under etym.), a. Consecrated; revered; fortunate; ∼ *with*, fortunate in the possession of (esp. iron.); in paradise (esp. as n., *the* ∼); blissful, bringing happiness (∼ *ignorance* etc.); (euphem.) cursed. [p.p. of prec.; as p.p. & past tense *blessed* is usu. monosyl., as adj. disyl.; of the adj. forms *blessed* is the ordinary, *blest* the poet., also used in some phrr. as *Isles of the Blest*]

bless'edness, n. Happiness; enjoyment of divine favour; *single* ∼, jocular phr. for being unmarried (perversion of Shakesp. *M.N.D.*, I. i. 78). [prec.+-NESS]

bless'ing, n. Declaration, invocation, or bestowal, of divine favour; grace before or after food (*ask a* ∼); gift of God, nature, etc., thing one is glad of; ∼ *in disguise*, unwelcome but salutary experience etc. [BLESS+-ING[1]]

**bleth'er, blăth'er, (-dh-), v.i., & n. (Talk) loquacious nonsense. Hence blăth'er-skīte, blĕth'erskăte, nn. (dial.), blethering person. [ME *blather* f. ON *blathra* talk nonsense (*blathr* nonsense); *blether* is the Scots form adopted from Burns etc.]

blew, past of BLOW[1], [3].

blew'it (-ōō-), n. A late edible mushroom with lilac stem. [prob. f. *blue*, cf. dial. name *blue-legs*]

blight[1] (-īt), n. Disease of unknown or atmospheric origin affecting plants; plant disease caused by fungoid parasites, mildew, rust, smut; species of aphis; hazy close state of atmosphere;

any obscure malignant influence. [17th c., of unkn. orig.]

blight² (-īt), v.t. Exert baleful influence on, nip in the bud, wither, mar. Hence ~'ER¹ (-īt-) n., esp. (sl.) annoying person. [f. prec.]

‖ **Blight'y** (-īt-), n. (army sl.). England, home, after foreign service (a ~ one, wound that ensures return to ~). [Anglo-Ind. corruption of Hind. wilāyatī, bilātī, European, English (wilāyat country, cf. Turk. VILAYET)]

‖ **blim'ey**, int. (vulg.) of surprise etc. [= God blind me!]

blimp, n. 1. Small non-rigid airship. 2. (Col.) Blimp, character invented by the cartoonist David Low (b. 1891), representing a pompous, obese, elderly figure pop. interpreted as type of diehard or reactionary. Hence ~'ERY (4), ~'ishNESS, nn. [perh. f. LIMP²]

blind¹, a. Without sight (~ in one eye, ~ of an eye, having one eye ~; turn a or one's ~ eye to, affect not to see); without foresight, discernment, or moral or intellectual light (~ to, incapable of appreciating; one's ~ side, direction in which one is unguarded); reckless; mechanical, not ruled by purpose, (~ forces); hard to trace (~ track); (Post Office) ~ letter, man, reader, of ill-addressed letters & the officials dealing with them; concealed (~ ditch; ~-stitch, sewing visible only on one side, also as v.t. & i. sew thus); ~ door etc., walled up; closed at one end (~ alley; ~-alley occupations, such as fail to fit one for anything further); (sl.) drunk (also ~ drunk, ~ to the world); ~ flying, flying without sight of the ground, or guidance from (directional) wireless signals; ~ hazard, hookey, card-games; ~-man's-buff, game in which blindfold player tries to catch others, who push him about [f. obs. buff= buffet]; ~ stamping, tooling (in bookbinding without use of ink or goldleaf); ~-story, TRIFORIUM admitting no light; ~ man's holiday, time before candles are lighted; ~ coal, burning without flame, anthracite; ~-worm, = SLOW-worm (f. small size of eyes). [OE, OS blind, OHG blint, ON blindr, Goth. blinds f. Gmc *blindaz]

blind², v.t. & i. Deprive of sight permanently or temporarily; rob of judgement, deceive; (v.i., sl.) go blindly or heedlessly (chiefly of reckless motorists); ~ing (vbl. n.), process of covering newly made road with fine material to fill interstices, material used for this purpose. [f. prec.]

blind³, n. Obstruction to sight or light; screen for windows, esp. on roller (Venetian ~, of laths running on webbing); (Fortif.) = foll.; pretext, stalking-horse; (sl.) drinking-bout. [f. prec.]

blind'age, n. Screen for troops in fortification, sieges, etc. [-AGE]

blind'fōld¹, v.t. Deprive (eyes, person) of sight with bandage (also fig.). [replacing (through notion of folding) ME blind-fellen (FELL v.) strike blind, chiefly used in p.p. whence the -d, which helped the confusion]

blind'fōld², a. & adv. With eyes bandaged; without circumspection. [p.p., earlier blindfelled see prec.]

blind'ly, adv. Without seeing, gropingly; recklessly. [-LY²]

blind'nèss, n. Want of sight; want of intellectual or moral sense, folly, recklessness. [-NESS]

blink¹, v.i. & t. Move the eyelids; look with eyes opening & shutting; shut the eyes for a moment; shine with unsteady light, cast momentary gleam; ignore, shirk consideration of, (esp. the fact); (part., vulg. euphem., cf. bleeding, blooming, for) bloody. [hist. & relations obsc.; in ME a rare var. of northern blenk = BLENCH; common f. late 16th c., coinciding w. MDu., Du., G blinken]

blink², n. Momentary gleam or glimpse; (also ice-~) whiteness about horizon, reflection of distant ice-fields. [f. prec.]

blink'er, n. In vbl senses; also, (usu. pl.) screen(s) preventing horse from seeing sideways. [-ER¹]

bliss, n. Gladness, enjoyment; perfect joy, blessedness; being in heaven. Hence ~'FUL a., ~'fulLY² adv., ~'fulNESS n. [OE bliths, bliss, OS blīdsea f. BLITHE + suf. -sid-; sense 'heavenly joy' by assoc. w. BLESS]

blis'ter, n., & v.t. & i. 1. Vesicle on skin filled with serum, caused by friction, burning, etc.; similar swelling on surface of plant, metal, painted wood; (Med.) anything applied to raise a ~; ~ (almost pure) copper; ~ gas, poison gas causing ~s on skin. 2. vb. Raise ~ on; become covered with ~s. [ME blister, blester, of unkn. orig.; cf. OF blestre, blo(u)stre swelling, pimple]

blithe (-dh), a. Gay, joyous, (chiefly poet.). Hence ~'LY² (-dhl-) adv., ~'SOME (-dhs-) adj. [OE blithe, OS blīthi, OHG blīdi, ON blīthr, Goth. bleiths f. Gmc. *blīthiz]

blith'ering (-dh-), a. (colloq.). Senselessly talkative; consummate (~ idiot); contemptible. [part. of blither, var. of BLETHER]

blitz, n., & v.t., (colloq.). 1. Intensive (esp. air) attack. 2. v.t. Damage or destroy in ~ (esp. in pass., as ~ed areas, cities). [abbr. of foll.]

blitz'krieg (-krēg), n. A violent campaign intended to bring about speedy victory. [G, = lightning war]

blizz'ard, n. Blinding snow-storm. [U.S. 'violent blow' (1829), 'snow-storm' (1870), orig. unkn.; cf. blizz downpour (of rain, 1770)]

bloat¹, v.t., bloat'er, n. Cure (herring) by salting & smoking slightly into bloated herring or bloater. [f. obs. adj.

bloat, earlier *blote*; orig. obsc., rel. to foll. uncert.; w. 16–17th c. *blo(a)te* herring cf. ON *blautr fiskr* soft fish]

bloat², v.t. & i., **bloat'ĕd**, a. Inflate, swell (t. & i.); (chiefly in p.p. as adj.) puffed up, esp. with gluttony, overgrown, too big, pampered (esp. *bloated aristocrat, armaments*). [f. obs. adj. *blaute, blowt(e)*, later (? after prec.) *bloat*, perh. f. ON *blautr* soft, flabby; cf. prec.]

blŏb, n. Drop of liquid; small roundish mass; spot of colour; (Cricket) = duck's egg. [imit., cf. BLEB]

blŏbb'er-lipped (-ipt), a. With thick protruding lips. [imit., cf. BLEB; *blabber, blubber*, are found in same sense]

blŏc, n. Combination of parties to support a government; (transf.) combination of nations, groups, etc., to foster a particular interest, as *sterling* ~ (of countries with currencies tied to sterling). [F, = BLOCK¹]

blŏck¹, n. 1. Log of wood, tree-stump, (*chip of the old* ~, child like his father esp. in character; *cut* ~*s with razor*, waste ingenuity etc.); large piece of wood for chopping or hammering on (*the* ~, death by beheading) or mounting horse from; mound for shaping hats on, shape; *barber's* ~, wooden head for wigs. 2. Pulley, system of pulleys mounted in case. 3. Piece of wood (also *wood-*~) or metal engraved for printing. 4. Bulky piece of anything; unhewn lump of rock; prepared piece of building-stone. 5. Compact mass of buildings bounded by (usu. four) streets (~-*buster* sl., huge bomb capable of destroying this); *area in town or suburb. 6. Stolid or hard-hearted person, whence ~'ISH¹ a. 7. Obstruction, (Parl.) notice that a bill will be opposed, which prevents its being taken at certain times & so often kills it; ‖ (Traffic) jammed vehicles unable to proceed; ~ *system* on railways, by which no train may enter a section till it is clear. 8. (Cricket) spot on which batsman blocks ball & rests bat before playing. 9. Tract of land offered to individual settler by government. 10. Large quantity of shares etc. 11. (Austral.) fashionable city promenade. 12. ~-*chain*, kind of endless chain used in bicycle etc.; ~'*head*, dolt; ~'*house*, detached fort (orig. one blocking passage), occas. one of connected chain of posts, also one-storeyed timber building with loopholes, also house of squared logs; ‖ ~ *letters, writing* (with each letter separate as in print, & usu. in capitals); ~ *tin*, refined tin cast in ingots. [ME, f. OF *bloc* f. MDu. *blok* of unkn. orig.]

blŏck², v.t. Obstruct (passage etc.); put obstacles in way of (progress etc.; ~ *up, in*, confine; (Parl.) announce opposition to (bill; see prec.); restrict use or expenditure of (currency or other asset; chiefly in p.p.); (Cricket) stop (ball) with bat; shape (hats); emboss (book cover);

~ *out, in*, sketch roughly, plan, (work). Hence ~'AGE (3) n., a ~ed (up) state. [f. prec., or F *bloquer* f. *bloc* see prec.]

blŏckäde'¹, n. Shutting-up, total or on land or sea side, of a place by hostile forces in order to starve it into surrender or prevent egress & ingress (*paper* ~, one declared but not made effective; *raise* ~, cease blockading, compel blockaders to cease; *run* ~, evade blockading force; ~-*runner*, ship, captain, etc., doing this); imprisonment by snow etc. [f. prec. on anal. of F wds in -ADE]

blŏckäd|e'², v.t. Subject to blockade (see prec.); obstruct (door, view, etc.). Hence ~'ER¹ n. [f. prec.]

blŏke, n. (colloq.). Man, fellow, chap; dull or rustic person; *the* ~ (Nav. sl.), ship's commander. [etym. unkn.]

blŏnd, blŏnde (see etym.), a. & n. (Of hair) light-auburn-coloured; (of complexion) fair (n., person with such hair & skin); (also ~ *lace*) silk lace of two threads in hexagonal meshes (orig. of raw-silk colour, now white or black). [ME, f. F *blond*, fem. *blonde*, = Sp. *blondo*, It. *biondo*, med. L *blundus, blondus* perh. of Gmc orig.; *blonde* is used of the lace, & of the adj. & n. as applied to a woman, *blond* elsewhere]

blood¹ (blŭd), n. 1. Red liquid circulating in veins of higher animals, corresponding liquid in lower animals, (*flesh &* ~, the animal nature; *let* ~, surgically); (fig.) sap, grape-juice, etc. 2. Taking of life, murder, sacrifice, guilt of bloodshed. 3. Passion, temperament, mettle, (*bad* ~, ill feeling; *his* ~ *is up*, he is in fighting mood; ~ *out of a stone*, pity from the pitiless; *in cold* ~, deliberately). 4. Race (*blue* ~, high birth; *fresh* ~, new members admitted to family, society, etc.; ~ *royal*, royal family; *Prince* etc. *of the* ~ *royal* or *of the* ~, of royal race; *runs in the* ~, is a family trait). 5. Relationship, relations, (*own flesh &* ~; ~ *is thicker than water*, the tie of kindred is real); descent, good parentage, (of men, horses, etc.; *bit of* ~, ~-*horse*, thoroughbred). 6. Dandy, man of fashion, (*young* ~, either in this sense, or as personal form of *fresh* ~ above, =younger member of party). 7. ~ *& iron*, relentless use of force (esp. as motto of Bismarckian policy); ~-*&*-THUNDER; ~ *ally*, red-veined ALLY³; ~ *bank*, place where supply of ~ for transfusion is stored; ~ *count*, counting of the number of corpuscles in a definite volume of ~; ~-*curdling*, so horrific as to tend to curdle the ~; ~ *feud*, between families of which one has spilt the other's ~; ~ *group*, any one of the (usu. four) types into which ~ may be divided according to its compatibility in transfusion; ~-*guilty*, responsible for murder or death; ~-*heat*, ordinary heat of human ~ in health, 98·4° F.; ~'*hound*, large keen-scented dog with which cattle, slaves, etc., used to be tracked, detective, spy; ~-*letting*, surgical removal of some of patient's ~, (joc.) ~-*shed*; ~-*money*, reward to witness for securing capital sentence, fine paid to next of kin for slaughter of relative; ~ *orange*, with red juice; ~-*poisoning*, state resulting from introduction of septic matter into ~ esp. through wound; ~-*red*, red as ~; ~-*relation*, one related by ~, not marriage; ~'*shed*, spilling of ~, slaughter [f. phr. *to shed* ~]; ~'*shot*, (of eye) suffused, tinged, with ~ (*see things* ~*shot*, find incitements to slaughter or traces of ~ in them); ~ *sports*, those involving ~shed or the killing of animals; ~-*stained*, stained with ~, disgraced by ~shed; ~'*stone*, kinds of precious stone spotted or streaked with red, esp. heliotrope; ~'*stock*, thoroughbred horses collectively; ~-*sucker*, leech, extortioner; ~'*thirsty*, eager for~shed, whence~'thïrstiNESS n.; ~-*transfusion*, see TRANSFUSE; ~-*vessel*, flexible tube (vein or artery) conveying ~; ~'*worm*, bright-red kind used in fishing; ~-*wort*, kinds of plant with red roots or leaves, esp. bloody dock. [OE, OS *blōd*, OHG *bluot*, ON, Goth. *blōth*, f. Gmc *blōdham*]

blood² (blŭd), v.t. (Surg.) remove a little of the blood of (usu. *bleed*); allow first taste of blood to (hound; also fig. of inciting persons). [f. prec.]

blood′less (-ŭ-), a. Without blood; unfeeling; pale; without bloodshed, whence ~LY² adv. [-LESS]

bloody¹ (blŭd′ĭ), a. & adv. Of, like, running or smeared with, blood (~ *nose*, bleeding; ~ *flux*, dysentery); red (~ *hand*, armorial device of baronet); involving, loving, resulting from, bloodshed; (also ~-*minded*) sanguinary, cruel; ‖ (in strong language) = *damned* etc., or as mere intensive (*not a* ~ *one*); ‖ (similarly as adv.) = confoundedly, very; (in pop. plant names) ~ *finger*, *foxglove*. Hence **blood′iLY²** adv., **blood′iNESS** n. [OE *blōdig*, see BLOOD, -Y²]

bloody² (blŭd′ĭ), v.t. Make bloody, stain with blood. [f. prec.]

bloom¹, n. Flower, esp. of plants grown or admired chiefly for the flower, florescence (*in* ~); prime, perfection; flush, glow; powdery deposit on grapes, plums, etc., freshness, (*take the* ~ *off*, stale); kind of raisin. [ME *blom*, *blome* f. ON *blóm*, *blómi*, OS *blōmo*, OHG *bluomo*, -*ma*, Goth. *blōma* f. Gmc *blōmon*, -*ōn* f. *blō*- BLOW³; cf. BLOSSOM]

bloom², v.i. Bear flowers, be in flower; come into, be in, full beauty; culminate, flourish. [f. prec.]

bloom³, n. Mass of puddled iron hammered or squeezed into thick bar. [OE *blōma* in same sense]

bloom⁴, v.t. Make (puddled iron) into a BLOOM³. Hence ~'ERY (3) (also -*ary*) n. [f. prec.]

bloom′er¹, n. & a. (Obsolete female costume) of short skirt & trousers (as n., usu. pl.); (n. pl.) knickerbockers worn by girls & women for cycling, games, etc., with or without skirt. [Mrs *B*~, American editress, who advocated the use of the costume]

bloom′er², n. (sl.). Blunder. [= *blooming* (see foll.) *error*; -ER¹]

bloom′ing, a. In vbl senses (BLOOM²); also sl., euphemistic substitute for vulgar BLOODY. [-ING²]

Blooms′bury (-zberĭ), n. Part of London containing British Museum, formerly a fashionable residential (& later a literary) quarter.

bloss′om¹, n. Flower, esp. as promising fruit; mass of flowers on fruit-tree etc. (*in* ~); early stage of growth, promise; ~-*faced*, -*nosed*, bloated. Hence ~Y², ~LESS, aa. [OE *blōstm*, -*ma*, cogn. w. MDu. *bloesem*, MLG *blosem*, *blossem* (cf. also ON *blómstr*), prob. f. *blōs*-, extended form of *blō*-; see BLOOM]

bloss′om², v.i. Open into flower (lit., & fig., as ~ *out into a statesman*). [OE *blōstmian* cf. prec]

blot¹, n. Spot of ink etc., dark patch; disfigurement, blemish (esp. *on the scutcheon*), defect; disgraceful act or quality in good character. [14th c., of unkn. orig.; cf. ON *blettr* spot, stain]

blot², v.t. & i. (-tt-). Spot with ink (~ *one's copybook*, colloq., stain one's character, commit an indiscretion); smudge; (of pen, ink) make blots; cover with worthless writing; sully, detract from, (fair fame); ~ *out*, obliterate (writing), exterminate, destroy; dry with ~*ting-paper*, absorbent paper for drying wet ink-marks (~*ting-book*, -*case*, -*pad*, arrangements of this), whence ~t′ER¹ (2) n. (*also*, record, file). [f. prec.]

blot³, n. Exposed piece in backgammon; weak point in strategy etc. [16th c., of unkn. orig., possibly f. Du. *bloot* naked, exposed]

blotch, n. Inflamed patch, boil, etc., on skin; dab of ink or colour. Hence ~ED² (-cht), ~'Y², aa. [f. 1600; excl. E, perh. compounded f. *blot* & *botch* (obs. n.), *plotch* (obs.); cf. also SPLOTCH]

blottěsque′ (-sk), a. & n. (Piece of painting or description) done with heavy blotted touches. [-ESQUE]

blott′ō, a. (sl.). Fuddled with drink. [orig. unkn.]

blouse (-owz), n. Workman's loose linen or cotton upper garment usu. belted at waist (chiefly French); woman's loose light bodice visible only to waist, & there belted. [F, of unkn. orig.]

blow¹ (-ō), v.i. & t. (*blew* pr. bloo ; ~*n* &, in sense 'cursed', ~*ed*). (Of wind, air, 'it') move along, act as air-current, (~ *great guns*, violent gale); send strong air-current from mouth (~ *hot & cold*, vacillate), puff, pant; make or shape (bubble, glass) by ~ing; (of whales) eject air & water; (of electr. fuse) melt when over-loaded; cause air-current by means of (~ *bellows*); work bellows of (organ); exhaust of breath (esp. in pass.); send out by breathing (~ *air into*; ~ *off steam*, get rid of superfluous energy); (with advv. & prepp.) drive, be driven, by ~ing (~ *over*, pass off; ~ *in* sl., come in breezily, drop in); sound (wind instru-ment, note or signal *on* or *with* it, or with it as subject to *blow* t. or i.; ~ one's *own trumpet*, praise oneself); direct air--current at (~ *fingers, fire*; ~ *out*, extin-guish); clear by air-current (nose, egg); break *in* or send flying *off* or *out* or *up* by explosion (~ *out* one's *brains*, shoot him, or usu. oneself); ~ *up*, inflate, shatter or be shattered by explosion, reprove, lose one's temper, enlarge (map, print); (sl.) betray (~ *the* GAFF[2]); (of flies) deposit eggs in; (sl.) curse, confound, (*I'll be ~ed if* etc.; ~ *the expense*, spend recklessly); (sl.) squander, spend (sum) recklessly, cf. BLUE[3]; ~ *upon*, stale, discredit, tell tales of; ~ *ball*, seed-head of dandelion etc.; ~'*fly*, the meat fly; ~'*hole*, nostril of whale etc., vent for air, smoke, etc., in tunnel etc.; ~'*lamp* (for directing condensed heat on a selected spot); ~'*pipe*, tube for heating flame by blowing air or other gas into it, tube used in glass-blowing, Amer.-Ind. dart tube. [OE *blāwan*, OHG *blā(h)an, blājan*; not otherwise recorded in Gmc]

blow[2] (-ō), n. Blowing, taste of fresh air; blowing of flute, one's nose, etc.; =FLY[1]-*-blow*; ~*-out*, burst in a pneumatic tire, (Electr.) blowing of a fuse, (sl.) abundant meal or feed; ~*-up*, enlargement of picture etc. [f. prec.]

blow[3] (-ō), v.i. (*blew* pr. blōō, ~*n*). Burst into, be in, flower. [OE *blōwan*, OS *blōjan*, OHG *bluojan* f. *blō-*; see BLADE, BLOOM]

blow[4] (-ō), n. Blossoming (*in full* ~ etc.). [f. prec.]

blow[5] (-ō), n. Hard stroke with fist, instrument, etc.; disaster, shock; *come to, exchange, ~s*, fight; *strike a ~ for, against*, help, oppose; *at one ~*, in one operation. [f. 15th c., of unkn. orig.]

blow'er (-ōer), n. In vbl senses of BLOW[1,3]; also: apparatus for increasing a fire's draught, esp. sheet of iron before grate--front; escape of gas, or fissure allowing it, in coal mine. [BLOW[1], -ER[1]]

blow'y (-ōi), a. Windy, wind-swept. [BLOW[1], -Y[2]]

blowzed (-zd), **blowz'y** (-zi), aa. Red-faced, coarse-looking, dishevelled. [f. obs. n. *blouze* beggar's wench; orig. unkn.]

blub, v.i. (-bb-; sl.). Shed tears. [short for BLUBBER[3]]

blübb'er[1], n. Whale fat; jelly-fish (sailor's name); weeping. [ME *blober*; prob. imit. (obs. meanings *foaming, bubble*), cf. BLEB, BUBBLE]

blübb'er[2], a. Swollen, protruding, (of lips). [as prec.]

blübb'er[3], v.t. & i. Utter with sobs, weep noisily; wet, disfigure, swell, (face) with weeping. [as prec.]

bluchers (blōōk'erz), n. pl. Old-fashioned low boots or high shoes. [named after the Prussian Field Marshal *Blücher* (d. 1819)]

blüdg'eon (-ŭjn), n., & v.t. (Strike re-peatedly with) heavy-headed stick. [f. 18th c., of unkn. orig.]

blue[1] (blōō), a. Of the colour between green & violet in the spectrum, coloured like the sky or deep sea (also of things much paler, darker, etc., as smoke, dis-tant hills, moonlight, bruise; & qualified by or qualifying other colours etc., as ~*-black, deep ~*, NAVY ~, *Prussian ~*); *look ~*, nervous, depressed (*things looked ~*, depressing); ~ *funk*, uncontrollable fear; *true ~*, faithful; dressed in ~ (*Foot--Guards B~*); *the B~ (Squadron)*, one of three divisions (Red, White, B~) of Navy (hist.); belonging to a particular political party, usu. Tory; (of women) learned (see BLUESTOCKING); (of talk etc.) indecent; *drink till all 's ~*, to drunkenness. ~'*bell*, (Scotland & N. Eng.) light-blue-flowered *Campanula* growing in dry places & flowering in summer & autumn, harebell, (S. Eng.) wild hyacinth with ~ or white flower growing in moist places & flowering in spring; ~ *blood*, high birth; ~*-book*, ‖ Parliamentary or Privy-Council report, *book giving personal details of U.S. government officials; ~'*bottle*, ~ corn-flower, meat fly or blowfly; ~*-chip* attrib., (St. Exch. of shares) constituting a fairly reliable investment, though less secure than gilt-edged; ‖ ~*-coat boy*, scholar in charity school, esp. Christ's Hospital; ~ *devils*, depression; ~*-eyed boy* (colloq.), pet, favourite; ~ *gum*, kind of eucalyptus tree; ‖ ~'*jacket*, seaman in Navy; *~ laws*, severe Puritanic laws alleged to have been in force among early colonists of Connecticut; ~ *light*, flare with bluish light used for signals; *B~ Mantle*, one of four pursuivants of College of Arms; *once in a ~ moon*, very rarely; ~ *mould*, in certain cheeses when mature; ~ *murder* (colloq. in intensive phrr. as *like ~ murder*, at top speed); *B~-nose* (colloq.), Nova--Scotian; ~ *pencil*, used in marking correc-tions, obliterations, etc.; ~*-pencil* v.t., mark etc. with a ~ pencil, make cuts in, censor; *B~ Peter*, ~ flag with white square, hoisted before sailing; ~ *pill*, mercurial & antibilious; ~ *print*, ~ photo-graphic print representing final stage of engineering or other plans, (fig.) detailed plan of work to be done; ~ *ribbon*, ribbon of the Garter, greatest honour in any sphere, sign of teetotalism; ~ *rock*, kind of pigeon; ~ *ruin*, bad gin; ~*-stocking*, woman having or affecting literary tastes & learning [Blue Stocking Society (in sense 'not in full evening dress') name given to meetings about 1750 at houses of Mrs Montague etc. to talk on literature etc. instead of playing cards; blue-worsted, i.e. ordinary, stockings were worn by some of the men attending instead of black silk]; ~-*stone*, sulphate of copper; ~ *water*, open sea; ~'*throat*, kind of small bird allied to warblers; ~-*water school*, strategists regarding the fleet as sufficient defence for Gt Britain. Hence **blu'ISH**[1] (2) (bloō-) a., ~'NESS (-ōon-) n. [ME *blue, blew(e)* f. OF *bleu* f. Rom. **blāvus* f. Gmc **blǣwaz* (whence OE *blǣ-*, OHG *blao, blaw-*, ON *blár*)]

blue[2] (bloō), n. Blue colour (*Oxford* ~, dark; *Cambridge* ~, light; *the light, dark*, ~s, representatives or supporters of Cambridge, Oxford, in sporting contests); ~ pigment; ~ powder used by laundresses; ~ cloth etc.; *the sky* (BOLT[1] *from the* ~); *the* sea; (pl.) *the* Royal Horseguards; *the Blues* or *Blues trot*, dance of fox-trot kind; colour, member, of a political party; || one who has represented his university in athletics etc. (*win* one's ~, be chosen as representative); = BLUE[1] *stocking*; (pl.) *the* dumps; (pl.) kind of (usu. sad) song of Negro origin. [f. prec.]

blue[3] (bloō), v.t. Make blue; treat with laundress's blue; (sl.) squander (money). [f. BLUE[1]]

Blue'beard (bloō-), n. Husband of many wives. [hero of popular story, who hung up in locked chamber the bodies of his murdered wives]

bluff[1], a. With perpendicular broad front (of ship's bows, cliffs); (of person, manner) abrupt, blunt, frank, hearty. Hence ~'LY[2] adv., ~'NESS n. [17th c. naut. wd of unkn. orig.; obs. Du. *blaf*, in same senses, only in Kilian (1599)]

bluff[2], n. Headland with perpendicular broad face. [f. prec.]

bluff[3], v.t. & i. (Game of poker) impose upon (opponent) as to value of one's hand & induce him to throw up his cards; treat (political opponents or rival States) so; practise this policy. [orig. unkn.; w. earlier sense *blindfold*, goes w. foll.]

bluff[4], n. Act of bluffing (*call* person's ~, make him show his cards, also fig.); overbearing demeanour, threats designed to operate without action. [w. earlier senses *horse's blinker, excuse* (sl.), goes w. prec.]

blun'der[1], v.i. & t. Move blindly, stumble, (often *on, along*); ~ *upon*, find by fluke; make gross mistake; mismanage (a business etc.); ~ *out*, utter thoughtlessly; ~ *away*, waste by mismanagement. Hence ~ER[1] n., ~inGLY[2] adv. [ME *blondren, blundren*, of uncert. orig.; perh. frequent. (-ER[5]) of obs. *blond* (*bland*; see BLEND), or f. Icel. *blonda* doze, MSw. *blundra* ~but the eyes]

blun'der : Stupid or careless mistake. [prob. f. p. . . but found earlier]

blŭn'derbŭss, n. Ancient short gun with large bore firing many balls. [perverted f. Du. *donderbus* thunder gun]

blŭn'derhead (-hĕd), n. = DUNDERHEAD (cf. prec.)

blŭnge (-j), v.t. (Pottery) mix (clay, flint-powder, etc.) up with water by revolving machinery. [after *plunge, blend*]

blŭnt[1], a. & n. **1.** Dull, not sensitive; without edge or point; plain-spoken; hence ~'ISH[1] (2) a. **2.** n. Short thick needle; (sl.) ready money. [ME *blunt*, orig. unkn.]

blŭnt[2], v.t. Make less sharp or sensitive. [f. prec.]

blŭnt'lȳ, adv. Obtusely (shaped etc.); rudely, curtly. [-LY[2]]

blŭnt'ness, n. Dullness of point or edge; outspokenness. [-NESS]

blŭr[1], n. Smear of ink etc.; dimness, confused effect. [16th c.; orig. & relation to vb uncert.]

blŭr[2], v.t. & i. (-rr-). Smear (clear writing etc.) with ink etc.; sully, disfigure; make indistinct; efface; dim (perception etc.). [see prec.]

blŭrb, n. Publisher's (usu. eulogistic) description of book printed on jacket or in advertisements elsewhere. [orig. U.S. sl.]

blŭrt, v.t. Burst *out* with, utter abruptly. [imit. after *blow, spurt*, etc.]

blŭsh[1], v.i. Become red (in the face; also with *face* etc. as subj.) with shame or other emotion (*at* sight or word, *with* or *for* joy or shame, *for* another); be ashamed (~ *to own* etc.); be red, pink. Hence ~'inGLY[2] adv. [ME *blusche, blysche* f. OE *blyscan*, cf. MLG *bloschen*, LG *blüsken*; cf. also OE *-blysian* MDu. *blōzen*]

blŭsh[2], n. Glance, glimpse, (*at the first* ~, prima facie); reddening of face in shame etc. (*put to the* ~); rosy glow, flush of light; ~-, pink, rosy, (~-*rose*, ~-*tint*, etc.). [f. prec.]

blŭs'ter[1], v.i. & t. Storm boisterously (of wind, waves, persons); (trans. with *out, forth*) utter overbearingly; (refl.) storm (*oneself*) *into* (anger etc.). Hence ~ER[1] n., ~inGLY[2] adv. [c. 1500; imit., as on *blow, blast*, etc.]

blŭs'ter[2], n. Boisterous blowing, noisy self-asserting talk, threats. Hence ~ous, ~Y[2], aa. [f. prec.]

bō[1], **boh** (bō), int. used to startle (*can't say bo to a goose*, of shy or timid person).

*bō[2], n. (Hailing word corresponding to) mate, old chap. [orig. unkn.]

bō'a, n. S.-Amer. kinds of large non-poisonous snakes killing by compression (pop. extended to Old-World pythons; so also ~ *constrictor*, prop. a Brazilian species of ~); lady's long fur or feather throat-wrap. [L *boa* (Pliny)]

Bōanēr'gēs (-z), n. Loud-voiced preacher or orator. [Gk, f. Heb. *b'ney regesh* sons of thunder (*Mark* iii. 17)]

boar (bōr), n. Male uncastrated pig; its flesh; ~'s *head*, esp. as dish at Christmas or on festive occasion. [OE *bār*, OS *bērswīn*, OHG *bēr* (G *bär*) f. WG **bair-*, ult. orig. unkn.]

board[1] (bōrd), n. 1. Long thin usu. narrow piece of sawn timber (strictly, over 4 in. broad, under 2½ thick); wooden slab (of one or more breadths of ~ bare or covered with leather etc.) used for various purposes, as in games, for posting notices, etc.; (pl.) the stage (*on the* ~s, employed as actor); (also *straw-*~) thick stiff paper used in bookbinding (covered with paper, 'in ~s', or cloth, 'cloth ~s'), & for other purposes. 2. Table (only in spec. senses or contexts); *above* ~, open-(ly); *sweep the* ~, take all the cards or stakes; table spread for meals (*bed & *~, conjugal relations; *groaning* ~, plentiful meal); food served, daily meals provided at contract price or in return for services (~*-money*, *-wages*, servant's pay in lieu of food; esp. ~ *& lodging*); council-table, councillors, committee; ‖B~ *of Trade*, *B~ of Customs and Excise*, *B~ of Inland Revenue*, government departments; ~*-school* (before 1902), managed by ~ according to Elementary Education Act of 1870. 3. Ship's side (only in spec. phrases, cf. *over*~), *go by the* ~, (of masts etc.) fall over~, also fig., *on* ~ = ABOARD (in various senses), usu. now **on** or into ship (orig. meaning within the sides, not on the deck), train, coach, etc. 4. Tack (naut.). [OE *bord* combined two distinct Gmc words meaning (1) board (2) border, respectively f. Gmc **bordham* & **bordhaz*; the second was adopted in Romanic, &, thr. F, influenced the ME sense-development]

board[2] (bōrd), v.t. & i. 1. (f. prec.=wood) cover with boards (~ *up*, close with ~s). 2. (f. prec. = table) provide (lodger or daily guest) with, receive, stated meals at fixed rate; examine before a medical board (~*-out* v.t., invalid out of army etc.); ~ *with*, be entertained for pay in the house of. 3. (f. prec. = ship's side) come alongside (usu. to attack); force one's way on board (ship or abs.); embark on. 4. (Of ship) tack. [f. prec., with influence of F *aborder*]

board'er (bōr-), n. One who boards with someone (prec. 2), esp. boy or girl at boarding-school (opp. *day-boy*, *-girl*). [prec.+-ER[1]]

board'ing (bōr-), n. In vbl senses; also or esp.: erection of boards; ~*-house*, *-school*, in which persons, boys, board (BOARD[2], 2); ‖~*-out*, (intr.) feeding elsewhere than at home, (trans.) placing (destitute children) in families; ~*-ship* (examining neutrals for contraband). [BOARD[1,2]+-ING[1]]

boast[1], n. Vainglorious statement; self-exaltation in words; fact one is proud of; *make* ~ *of*, announce proudly. Hence ~'FUL a., ~'fulLY[2] adv., ~'fulNESS n.

[ME *bost* n., *bosten* vb; mutual relation & orig. unkn.]

boast[2], v.i. & t. Extol oneself (also refl.), brag *of* or *about*; vaunt, brag *of*, brag *that*; possess as thing to be proud of. Hence ~'ER[1] n. [see prec.]

boat[1], n. Small open oared or sailing vessel, fishing-vessel, mail packet, or small steamer (*take* ~, embark; *have an oar in everyone's* ~, of busybodies; *in the same* ~, with like risks etc.); ~*-shaped* utensil for sauce etc.; ~*-hook*, long pole with hook & spike; ~*-house*, shed at water's edge for keeping ~; *ship's* ~, carried on board ship; ~ *train*, timed to catch or meet ship; ~*-fly*, water-bug swimming on water on its back; ~*'man*, hirer-out or rower or sailer of ~ for hire; ~*-bill*, S.-Amer. heron; ~*-race*, between rowing ~s; ~*swain* (bō'sn), *bō's'n*, *bō'sun*, ship's officer in charge of sails, rigging, etc., & summoning men to duty with whistle [late OE *bātswegen*, cf. Icel. *sveinn* & see SWAIN]. Hence ~'AGE (4), ~'FUL (2), nn. [OE *bāt*, corr. to ON *beit* (ON *bátr* is f. OE), f. Gmc. **bait-* not otherwise represented; borrowed in other Gmc langg. f. these, & possibly in Rom. also (F *bateau* etc.)]

boat[2], v.i. & t. Go in a boat, amuse oneself so (~*ing man*); place, carry, in a boat. Hence ~'ER[1] n., hard straw hat (as worn in ~ing). [f. prec.]

bŏb[1], n., & v.t. (-bb-). Weight on pendulum, plumb-line, or kite-tail; knot of hair, tassel-shaped curl (~*-wig*, also ~, with short curls, opp. to full-bottomed; cf. CHERRY-*bob*); horse's docked tail; bunch of lob-worms; (Metre) short line at end of stanza; (vb) cut (woman's hair) to hang short of shoulders (*wear it* ~*bed*), (n.) ~bed hair. [f. 14th c.; orig. unkn.]

bŏb[2], v.i. (-bb-). Fish (*for* eels) with bunch (cf. prec.) of lob-worms.

bŏb[3], v.i. (-bb-). Move up & down, dance, rebound; ~ *up like a cork*, become active or conspicuous again after defeat; catch with the mouth (*for* cherries etc. floating or hanging); curtsy. [f. 14th c.; app. imit.]

bŏb[4], n. Jerk, bounding movement; curtsy; (Bellringing) kinds of change in long peals (*treble* ~ in which treble bell has a dodging course, ~ *minor* on 6 bells, *triple* on 7, *major* on 8, *royal* on 10, *maximus* on 12). [f. prec.]

‖ **bŏb**[5], n. *Dry*, *wet*,- ~, cricketing, boating, Etonian; *light-*~, soldier of light infantry. [prob. = *Robert*]

‖ **bŏb**[6], n. (sl.; pl. same). Shilling. [quoted f. 1812; orig. unkn.]

bŏb[7], v.t. (-bb-). Rap, jerk. [ME *boben*; orig. unkn.]

Bŏb'adil, n. Braggart. [Jonson, *Every Man in his Humour*]

bŏbb'erȳ, n. & a. 1. Disturbance, row, fuss. 2. adj. Noisy, troublesome, skittish, (~ *pack*, scratch pack of hounds &

dogs of various breeds, usu. for hunting jackals). [Hind. *bap re* O father! int. of dismay]

bŏbb′in, n. Cylinder for holding thread, yarn, wire, etc., & giving it off as wanted, reel, spool; small bar & string for raising door-latch. [f. F *bobine*]

bŏbb′inĕt, n. Machine-made cotton net imitating lace made with bobbins on pillow. [prec., *net*]

bŏbb′ish, a. (sl.). Brisk, well, (esp. *pretty* ~). [BOB[3] + -ISH[1]]

‖ **bŏbb′y̆**, n. (sl.). Policeman. [as BOB[5] + -Y[3] (Sir *Robert* Peel, Home Sec. 1828)]

***bŏbb′y̆-sŏx**, n. pl. Short socks covering ankle. Hence ~ER[1](3) n., adolescent girl, esp. in early teens, wearing ~. [orig. unkn.]

***bŏb′căt**, n. American lynx. [BOB[1] (from shortness of tail)]

bŏb′olĭnk, n. N.-Amer. songbird. [orig. *Bob* (o') *Lincoln*; imit.]

bŏb′-slĕd, -sleigh (slā), n. Two short sleighs coupled, used for drawing logs, & in tobogganing. [U.S. & Canadian wd, now also Anglo-Swiss]

bŏb′stay, n. Rope holding bowsprit down. [f. BOB (uncert. in what sense) + STAY[2]]

bŏb′tail, n. & a. Docked tail; with this; horse or dog with this; *raglay* (or *tagrag*) *&*~, the rabble. [BOB[1]]

Bŏche (-sh), n. & a. (sl.). (Contempt. for) German. [F, perh. abbr. of *Alboche* (*Allemand* German & *-boche* substituted in contempt for other endings)]

bŏck, n. Strong dark-coloured German beer; (loosely) a glass of (any) beer. [F, f. G *bock* (in full *bockbier* f. *Einbecker bier* f. *Einbeck* in Hanover]

bŏde, v.t. & i. Foresee, foretell, (evil); portend, foreshow; promise *well* or *ill.* Hence **bŏd′ing**LY[2] adv., ~′MENT(-dm-)n. [OE *bodian* f. *boda* messenger.]

bŏde′ful (-df-), a. Ominous. [mod. formation f. prec. or obs. n. *bode* omen + -FUL(1)]

bodēg′a, n. Cellar or shop selling wine. [Sp., f. L f. Gk *apothēkē* see APOTHECARY]

bŏd′ice, n. Close-fitting upper part of woman's dress, down to waist; also, inner vest over stays. [orig. *pair of bodies* (cf. pair of stays), being a whalebone corset; now spelt & understood as sing.; cf. BAIZE]

bŏd′ied (-dĭd), a. Possessed of body or a body, embodied; esp. in comb., as *full*-~, *able*-~. [BODY[1] + -ED[2]]

bŏd′ilĕss, a. Incorporeal; separated from the body. [-LESS]

bŏd′ily̆[1], a. Of, affecting, the human body or physical nature; ~ *fear*, of physical harm. [BODY[1] + -LY[1]]

bŏd′ily̆[2], adv. In the body, in person; with the whole bulk, as a whole. [BODY[1], -LY[2]]

bŏd′kin, n. Pointless thick needle with large eye for drawing tape etc. through hem; long pin for fastening hair; dagger;

person squeezed between two others (*ride, sit,* ~). [ME *boidekyn* etc.; orig. unkn.]

Bŏdleian (-lē′an), a. & n. The ~ (*library*), (also, colloq., *Bodley*) the Oxford University Library, founded by Sir Thomas *Bodley* (d. 1613). [-IAN]

bŏd′y̆[1], n. **1.** Man or animal as material organism (*keep* ~ *& soul together*, remain alive); corpse (~-*snatcher*, exhumer of corpses for dissection); ~ *of Christ*, sacramental bread; ~-*servant*, valet; ~-*guard*, (rarely, member of) dignitary's retinue, escort, personal guard. **2.** Trunk, main portion (stem, hull, nave, etc., acc. to context); upper garment (minus sleeves & collar, or = bodice); document minus preamble etc.; majority. **3.** Human being, person, (*heir of* one's ~, *good sort of* ~, *any* ~, etc.); ~-*line bowling* (Cricket), fast bowling delivered persistently on the leg side. **4.** Aggregate of persons or things (*in a* ~, all together; ~ *politic*, State); society, league, military force; collection *of* precepts, information, etc. **5.** Piece of matter (*heavenly* ~, sun, star, etc.), quantity; comparative solidity or substantial character (~-*colour*, opaque; *wine of good* ~), thing perceptible to senses. [OE *bodig*, corresp. to OHG *potah, botah* (Bav. dial. *bottech*); orig. unkn.]

bŏd′y̆[2], v.t. **1.** Provide with body (rare). **2.** (Usu. with *forth*) give mental shape to; exhibit in outward shape; typify. [f. prec.]

Boeotian (bēō′shn), a. & n. Crass, dull, (person). [of Gk nation derided by Athenians]

Bō′er (*or* boor), n. & a. (Of) Dutch or Dutch-descended S.-African(s). [Du., see BOOR]

bŏff′in, n. (sl.). Man engaged in research, scientist. [orig. unkn.]

Bŏf′ors ·(-orz), n. ~ (*gun*), light anti-aircraft gun. [~ in Sweden]

bŏg[1], n. (Piece of) wet spongy ground, morass (in many plant names as ~ *violet*, BUTTERwort, ~-*berry*, cranberry); ~ *butter*, fatty hydrocarbon found in Irish peat-~; ~ *oak*, ancient preserved in black state in peat; ~-*trotter*, Irishman. Hence ~g′Y[2] (-g-) a., ~g′iNESS (-g-) n. [16th c., f. Ir. or Gael. *bogach* (*bog* soft)]

bŏg[2], v.t. (-gg-). Submerge in bog (usu. in pass.).

bŏg′ey (-gĭ), **Colonel Bogey, n.** Score that good golf-player should do hole or course in. [f. BOGY as imaginary person?]

bŏgg′ard, -art, n. (dial.). Spectre, bogy; (fig.) bugbear. [orig. unkn.]

bŏg′gle, v.i. Start with fright, shy; hesitate, demur, *at* or *about*; equivocate; fumble. [var. of BOGLE used as vb]

‖ **bŏg′ie** (-gĭ), n. Under-carriage with two or more wheel-pairs, pivoted below end of locomotive or railway-car; ~-*car* etc., fitted on these. [northern dial. ¬wd of unkn. orig.]

bō′gle, n. Phantom, goblin; bugbear; scarecrow. [Sc. since 1500; cf. 16th c. (obs.) *bog*, north. *boggard*, ME *bugge* (BUGBEAR), but mutual relations & orig. unkn.]

bōg′us, a. Sham, fictitious. [U.S. wd, orig. unkn.]

bōg′y̆, **-gey**, (-gĭ), n. (pl. *-ies*, *-eys*). The devil; goblin (nursery, *the ~ man*); bugbear. [early 19th c., perh. southern var. of BOGLE]

bōhea′ (-hē), n. Black tea of lowest quality (last crop of season). [f. Chin. *Wu-i* name of district]

Bōhēm′ian, a. & n. **1.** (Native) of Bohemia, a former kingdom now part of Czechoslovakia, Czech. **2.** Socially unconventional (person); of free-&-easy habits, manners, & sometimes morals (esp. of artists etc.). Hence **bōhēm′ian-ISM** (2) n., **bōhēm′ianIZE** (4) v.i. [f. F *bohémien* gipsy]

boil¹, n. Hard inflamed suppurating tumour. [OE *bȳl*, *bȳle* (whence dial. *bile*), OS *būla*, OHG *būlla* (G *beule*) f. WG **būljā* f. **būl-*; mod. *boil* f. 16th c.]

boil², v.t. & i. Bubble up, undulate, (of liquid at the heat that converts it to gas; also of containing vessel); ~ *over* (of liquid or vessel), overflow or be overflowed thus; seethe, be agitated, like boiling water or its vessel (of sea etc., feelings, feeling person); bring (liquid, vessel) to heat at which it boils; subject to heat of ~ing water, cook thus; undergo cookery by ~ing; ~ *down*, *away*, reduce, convert to vapour, by ~ing; *keep the pot ~ing*, get a living; *~ing hot*, ~ing, (colloq.) very hot; *blood ~s*, with indignation; *~ed shirt* (sl.), cotton or linen shirt with starched front. [ME *boille* f. OF *boillir* f. L *bullire* (*bulla* bubble)]

boil³, n. = boiling, boiling-point, (esp. *on*, *at*, *to*, *the ~*). [f. prec.]

boil′er, n. One who boils; vessel for boiling, esp. large vessel of riveted wrought-iron plates for making steam in engine; tank attached to kitchen range; laundry vessel; vegetable etc. suited to boiling; *~-iron*, *-plate*, rolled iron ¼ to ½ in. thick; *~-tube*, internal air-pipe carrying heat through ~. [-ER¹]

boil′ing, n. In vbl senses; esp.: *the whole ~* (sl.), all the lot; *~-point*, temperature at which anything boils (water at sea-level, 212° F., 100° C.), high excitement. [-ING¹]

bois′terous, a. Violent, rough, (wind, sea, behaviour, speech, persons); noisily cheerful. Hence **~LY²** adv. [16th c. var. of ME (obs.) *boistous*, prob. thr. the later form *boisteous*, *-uous*, of unkn. orig.; deriv. f. AF *boistous*, OF *-eus* lame is semantically impossible]

‖ **bŏk′o**, n. (sl.). Nose. [orig. unkn.]

bōl′as, n. (sing. & pl.). S.-Amer. missile consisting of balls connected by a strong cord (when thrown bringing down quarry by entangling limbs). [Sp., pl. of *bola* ball]

bōld, a. Courageous, enterprising, confident; *make (so) ~ (as)*, presume, venture (*to* do); forward, immodest; vigorous, free, well-marked, clear, (imagination, drawing, description, features, headland, etc.); (of type, also *~-faced*) having a heavy or conspicuous face. Hence **~′LY²** adv., **~′NESS** n. [OE, OS, OHG *bald* (G *bald* soon), ON *ballr* f. Gmc **balthaz*; cf. Goth. *balthei* ~ness]

bōle, n. Stem, trunk. [ME, f. ON *bolr* cf. G *bohle* plank]

bolĕc′tion, a. & n. (Moulding) raised above panel etc. [orig. unkn.]

boler′o (-ār′ō), n. Spanish dance; (freq. pr. bŏl′erō) woman's short jacket with or without sleeves resembling zouave jacket. [Sp.]

bōl′ide, n. Large meteor, fire-ball. [F, f. L f. Gk *bolis -idos* (*ballō* throw)]

bōll, n. Rounded seed-vessel, as in flax or cotton; *~-weevil*, small destructive insect infesting cotton-plant. [f. MDu. *bolle*; see BOWL¹]

bŏll′ard, n. Post on ship or quay for securing ropes to; post on traffic island. [ME *bollarde* (c. 1300) f. ON *bolr* BOLE + -ARD]

bolōm′ĕter, n. Radiation-measurer. [Gk *bolē* ray +-o-+-METER]

*bolōn′ey, n. (sl.). Humbug, nonsense, trash. [orig. unkn.]

Bŏl′shĕv|ĭk, n. Advocate of proletarian dictatorship in Russia by soviets, Russian communist; (pop.) any revolutionary. Hence **~ISM** n., **~IST** n. & a., **Bŏl′shy̆** (sl.) n. & a. [f. Russ. *bolsheviki* n. pl. majority within the party]

bōl′ster¹, n. Long stuffed (esp. under-) pillow of bed or couch; pad or support in many machines & instruments. [OE *bolster*, OHG *bolstar*, ON *bolstr* f. Gmc **bolstraz* f. **bŭl-* swell]

bōl′ster², v.t. & i. (Usu. with *up*) support with bolster, prop, aid & abet, countenance, preserve from (merited) destruction; pad; (with schoolboys) belabour with bolster, (intr.) have bolster-fight. [f. prec.]

bōlt¹, n. Short heavy arrow of crossbow, quarrel, (*my ~ is shot*, I have done all I can); discharge of lightning (*~ from the blue*, complete surprise); door-fastening of sliding bar & staple, sliding piece of lock; headed metal pin for holding things together, usu. riveted or with nut; (as measure) roll of canvas etc., bundle of osiers; *~-line*, *-position*, (Mil.) defensive position at angle to main position to prevent a successful attack on some point of the main position from spreading farther; *~-rope* (round sail-edge to prevent tearing). [OE *boll*, MLG *bolte*, OHG *bolz*, ult. orig. unkn.]

bōlt², v.i. & t. Dart off or away, (of horse) break from control; gulp down unchewed; fasten (door etc.) with bolt, ~ *in* or *out*, shut in, exclude, by ~ing door; fasten together with bolts; *(Pol.) break away from (one's party), refuse to support one's party or a policy. [f. prec.]

bŏlt[3], n. Sudden start; running away. [f. prec.]

bŏlt[4], adv. (With *upright*) = as a bolt, quite.

bŏlt[5], **boult** (bōlt), v.t. Sift; investigate. [ME *bull(e)* f. OF *bulter, buleter,* thr. **bureter* = It. *buratlare,* of unkn. orig.]

bŏl′ter, n. In vbl senses of BOLT[2, 5]; esp.: horse given to bolting; (also *boulter*) sieve, sifting machine. [-ER[1]]

bŏl′us, n. Large pill. [mod. L, f. Gk *bōlos* clod]

bŏm′a, n. (Central Africa). Defensible enclosure; police or military post; magistrate's office. [Swahili]

bomb (-ŏm), n., & v.t. & i. **1.** A high--explosive or incendiary or smoke or gas etc. projectile fired from a mortar, or thrown or deposited by hand, or dropped from an aeroplane, & exploded by percussion or by time mechanism; ATOMIC, FLYING, ~; ~-*bay,* compartment in aircraft for holding ~s; ~-*disposal,* removal & detonation of unexploded & delayed-action ~s; ~-*load,* weight of ~s carried by aircraft; ~-*proof,* (shelter) strong enough to resist ~s; ~-*shell,* artillery ~ (now usu. *shell* exc. in similes, as *fell like a* ~-*shell* etc.); ~-*sight,* device in aircraft for aiming ~s. **2.** v.t. & i. Assail with ~s, throw ~s; ~ *out,* drive by ~s out of a building etc.; ~ *up,* load (aircraft) with ~s. Hence ~′ER[1] (-mer) n., soldier trained in, aircraft used for, ~ing (also attrib., as *Bomber Command*). [f. F *bombe* f. It. *bomba* f. L f. Gk *bombos* hum]

bŏmbărd′, v.t. Batter with shot & shell (esp. of warships attacking town); (Phys.) subject (atoms etc.) to a stream of high--speed particles; (fig.) assail persistently with abuse, argument, etc. Hence ~MENT n. [f. F *bombarder* f. *bombarde* f. med. L *bombarda* stone-throwing engine prob. f. L *bombus* hum]

bŏmbardier′ (or bŭm-), n. **1.** ‖ Artillery non-commissioned officer below sergeant. **2.** *Bomb-aimer in aircraft. [F, see prec. & -IER]

bŏm′bardon, n. Low-pitched brass instrument or organ stop imitating this. [It. (-*one*), f. *bombardo*+-*one,* see BOMBARD, -OON]

bom′basine (-ŏm- or -ŭm-; -zēn), n. Twilled dress-material of worsted with silk, with cotton, or alone, much used for mourning. [f. F *bombasin* f. LL *bombycinus* silken (*bombyx -ycis* silk or silk-worm f. Gk *bombux)*]

bŏm′bast, n. Turgid language, tall talk. Hence **bombăs′tıc** a., **bombăs′tıcALLY** adv. [alt. f. earlier *bombace* f. F f. LL *bombacem* alt. f. *bombyx* see prec.]

Bom′bay duck, n. Small fish of S.--Asian coasts, eaten dried with curry. [corrupt. of *bombil,* see BUMMALO]

bombe (bawǹb), n. (cookery). Any cone--shaped dish or confection, as *apricot, fish,* ~. [F]

bon, bonne, (F; see Ap.), a. French for *good,* common in some senses & phrases. [f. L *bonus]*

bŏn′a fĭd′ĕ, a. & adv. Genuine(ly), sincere(ly). [L abl. s. of foll.; as adj. it may be hyphened, not as adv.]

bŏn′a fĭd′ēs, n. (legal). Honest intention, sincerity. [L,=good faith; not hyphened]

bonăn′za, n. & a. (Prop.) prosperity, good luck; (pop.) greatly prospering, a large output (esp. of mines), worked with all best appliances (*a* ~ *farm),* a run of luck (*in* ~). [U.S. f. Sp., = fair weather f. L *bonus* good]

bon-bon (see Ap.), n. Sweetmeat. [BON]

‖ **bŏnce,** n. Large playing-marble. [orig. unkn.]

bŏnd[1], n. Thing restraining bodily freedom, imprisonment, (rare, only in pl., esp. *in.* ~s); faggot-withe; restraining or uniting force; binding engagement, agreement; deed by which A binds himself & his heirs etc. to pay a sum to B & his; government's or public company's documentary promise to pay borrowed money, debenture, (~*holder,* person holding such document); (Sc.) mortgage; (Customs, of goods) *in* ~, stored under charge of Customs in 'bonded warehouse' till importer pays duty (*take out of* ~); (Brick-laying) various methods (*English* ~, *Flemish* ~, etc.) of holding wall together by making bricks overlap; ~ (*paper*), superior kind of writing-paper (suitable for ~s & similar documents); ~-*stone,* stone or brick running through wall. [ME var. of BAND[1]]

bŏnd[2], v.t. Bind together (bricks etc., see prec.), put customable goods into bond (see prec.), whence ~′ER[1] n., person who puts goods into bond, binding stone or brick; encumber with bonded debt (see BONDED). [f. prec.]

bŏnd[3], n. League, confederation. [Du.]

bŏnd[4], a. In slavery, not free, (arch.). Hence ~′man, ~′maid, ~′servant, ~′ service, ~′slave, nn. [adj. use of ME *bonde* f. OE *bonda, bunda* husbandman f. ON *bóndi* = *bóandi,* part. of *búa, bóa* dwell; later infl. by BOND[1]]

bŏn′dage, n. Serfdom, slavery; confinement; subjection to constraint, influence, obligation, etc. [ME f. AF, or f. AL *bondagium;* see prec. & -AGE]

bŏnd′ĕd, a. (Of goods) placed in bond, (of warehouse) for such goods, (BOND[4]); (of debt) secured by bonds (BOND[1]). [BOND[1], -ED[2]]

bŏnds′man, n. Villein, serf; slave (lit. & fig.). [var. of *bondman* (BOND[4]) as though f. *bond's* genit. of BOND[1]]

Bŏnd Street, n. A London street, esp. as

resort of fashionable loungers (*a ~ exquisite*).

bōne[1], n. One of the parts making up vertebrate animal's skeleton; (pl. the body (*my old ~s* etc.), its remains (*his ~s were laid*); the body's hard, solid, or essential part (*flesh & ~; skin & ~*, thin person; *horse with plenty of ~*, well developed frame; *bred in the ~*, ineradicable; *to the ~*, penetrating, of cold, wound, etc.); material of which ~s consist; similar substance, as ivory, dentine, whalebone; thing made of ~, as (pl.) dice, castanets, stay-ribs; a small or nearly finished joint of meat (*knuckle-~, broiled ~s*); subject of dispute (*~ of contention, ~ to pick with someone*); *make no ~s of, about,* or *to*, not hesitate; *will never make old ~s*, live long; *feel in* one's *~s*, be quite sure; *~-dry*, quite dry, (of country etc.) teetotal; *~-head* (sl.), blockhead; *~-idle, -lazy*, utterly idle or lazy; *~-meal*, crushed or ground ~s used esp. as fertilizer; *~-setter*, one who sets broken or dislocated bones, esp. without being qualified surgeon; *~-shaker*, bicycle without rubber tires; *~-spavin*, callous growth in horse's leg becoming as hard as ~. [OE *bān*, OS *bēn*, OHG, ON *bein* f. Gmc *bainam*]

bōne[2], v.t. 1. Take out the bones from (meat, fish). 2. (sl.). Steal. [1 f. prec., & perh. 2 (as dog makes off with bone)]

bōne[3], v.t. (surv.). Take or test the level of (usu. as part.); *boning rod*, wooden rod used in levelling operations. [orig. unkn.].

bŏn'fīre, n. Large open-air fire in celebration of some event; fire for consuming rubbish (*make a ~ of*, destroy). [earlier *bonefire* f. BONE n., bones being the chief material formerly used]

bŏn'gō (-ngg-), n. Large striped African antelope. [native]

bonhomie (bŏn'omē), n. Geniality. [F, f. *bonhomme* good fellow + -*ie* = -Y[1]]

Bŏn'ifāce, n. Innkeeper. [Farquhar, *Beaux' Stratagem* (1707)]

bŏn'|ism, n. Doctrine that the world is good, but not the best possible. So ~IST (2) n. [f. L *bonus* good + -ISM, after OPTIMISM of which it is the positive form]

bŏnit'ŏ (-ē-), n. (Kinds of) large mackerel--shaped fish, the striped tunny. [Sp.]

bon mot (bawn̄ mō), n. (pl. *bons mots*), Witty saying. [F]

bŏnne, n. (French) nursemaid, maid. [BON]

bŏnne bouche (-ōōsh), n. Titbit, esp. to end up with. [F (BON, *bouche* mouth)]

bonnes fortunes (see Ap.), n. Ladies' favours, as a thing to boast of or pride oneself on. [F]

bŏnn'ĕt[1], n. (Man's) Scotch cap; woman's outdoor head-dress without brim, with strings, & covering no part of forehead; *~ rouge* (F, *pr*. bŏnā rōōzh), red cap as revolutionary symbol; (Naut.) additional

canvas laced to sail-foot; cowl of chimney etc., protective cap in various machines, ‖ hinged cover over motor of car; (Gaming, Auctions, etc.) accomplice, decoy; BEE *in ~*, an obsession; *~-laird* (Sc.), petty landowner (who wore a ~, & not the hat of the gentry). Hence ~ED[2] a. [ME, f. OF *bonet* short for *chapel de ~* cap of (med. L) *bon(n)etus* some kind of material]

bŏnn'ĕt[2], v.t. Put bonnet on (person); crush down hat over the eyes of (person). [f. prec.]

bŏnn'|ÿ, a. (chiefly Sc.). Comely, healthy--looking; satisfactory. Hence ~ILY[2] adv. [orig. unkn.; perh. f. BON]

bŏn'spiel, n. (Sc.). Curling-match (usu. between clubs). [perh. f. Du. *bond* league, *spel* game]

bon ton (see Ap.), n. Good breeding, the fashionable world, (arch.). [F]

bŏn'us, n. Something to the good, into the bargain; esp. extra dividend to shareholders of company, distribution of profits to insurance-policy-holders, gratuity to workmen beyond their wages. [jocular or ignorant use of L *bonus* good (thing)]

bon vivant (see Ap.), n. Gourmand. [F]

bŏn'ÿ, a. Of, like, bone(s); big-boned; with little flesh. [BONE[1] + -Y[2]]

bŏnze, n. Japanese or Chinese Buddhist priest. [F, f. Port. *bonzo* perh. f. Jap. *bonzô* f. Chin. *fan seng* religious person]

bŏn'zer, a. (Austral. sl.). Excellent, first-rate. [perh. f. BONANZA]

bōō, int., n., & v.t. & i. (Make) sound of disapproval or contempt; hoot (speaker, announcement, etc.). [imit. of cow's lowing]

*bōōb, n. Simpleton. [contr. of foll.]

bōōb'ÿ, n. Silly dull-witted fool, lout; kinds of gannet; *~ prize*, awarded to the last or lowest scorer in a contest of any kind; *~ trap*, things placed on top of door ajar to fall on first opener, (Mil.) kinds of apparently harmless device concealing an explosive charge designed to go off when tampered with; *~-trap* v.t. Hence ~ISH[1] a. [prob. f. Sp. *bobo* (both fool & bird) f. L *balbus* stammering]

bōō'dle, n. Crowd, pack, lot, (*the whole ~* or *caboodle*); money for political bribery etc.; a card-game. [now U.S.; 17th c. f. Du. *boedel* possessions, *the whole ~* = Du. *de heele boedel*, LG *de ganze bödel*; cf. CABOODLE]

bōō'gie-wōō'gie (-gǐ), n. Style of playing blues on the piano marked by a persistent bass rhythm. [orig. unkn.]

bōōhōō', n., & v.i. (Make) sound of noisy weeping. [imit.]

bōōk[1], n. 1. Portable written or printed treatise filling a number of sheets fastened together (forming roll, or usu. with sheets sewn or pasted hingewise & enclosed in cover); literary composition that would fill such a set of sheets (or several) if printed; (fig.) anything from which one may learn, also imaginary record, list, etc., (~ *of fate*; ~ *of life*, list of those who shall be saved); the Bible (esp. *swear on the* ~); main division of literary work (*Bk I* etc.), or of Bible (*B~ of Genesis*); = LIBRETTO; back-hinged set of blank sheets for writing accounts, notes, exercises, etc., in (pl., merchant's accounts); (Turf) one's bets on a race or at a meeting (*won't suit my* ~, transf., is inconvenient); set of tickets, stamps, cheques, tricks at cards, etc., bound up or collected. 2. ~ *of reference*, not read continuously but used intermittently for information; *speak like a* ~, in formal phrases, *by the* ~, with correct information; *take a leaf out of* ——*'s* ~, imitate him; *without* ~, without authority, from memory; *on the* ~*s*, entered in list of members etc. (so *take* one's *name off the* ~*s*); *in* ——*'s bad* or *black, good,* ~*s*, in disfavour or favour with him; *bring to* ~, call to account. 3. ~*'binder, -ding*, binder, binding, of ~*s*; ~*'case* (-k-k-), case containing ~shelves; ~ *ends*, pair of ornamental props used to keep a row of unshelved ~s upright; ~*-keeper, -ping*, one who keeps, art of keeping, the accounts of a merchant, public office, etc.; ~*-learning* or *-lore, -learnĕd*, mere theory, knowing ~s but not life, so ~'ISH[1] a., ~'ISHLY[2] adv.; ~'ishNESS n.; ~*-maker, -king*, compiler, compiling, of ~s (esp. for mercenary motives), also professional betting man or ~*'ie* [-Y[3]] n., his profession; ~*'man*, literary man; ~*-mark(er)*, thing to keep place in ~; ~*-muslin*, fine kind folded in ~like way when sold; ~*-plate*, label with owner's name, crest, etc., for pasting into ~s; ~*-rest*, adjustable support for ~ on table; ~*'seller*; ~*'slide*, expanding stand for a few ~s; ‖~*'stall* (of ~s exposed for sale out of doors);*~ token*, voucher for a sum of money to buy ~(s); ~ *value*, value of a commodity as entered in a firm's ~s (opp. *market value*); ~*-work*, study of rules or text~s (opp. to working sums, chemical analysis, etc.); ~*'worm*, maggot eating its way through ~s, person devoted to reading. Hence ~'LET n. [OE, OS *bōc*, OHG *buoh*, ON *bók*, Goth. *bokos* (pl.) f. Gmc **bōk-*, usu. identified w. BEECH]

book[2], v.t. Enter in book or list; engage (seat etc.) by previous payment, (guest, supporter, etc.) for some occasion; enter name of (person engaging seat etc.), issue railway ticket to; ‖ take railway ticket; give, take down, address of (goods to be transmitted); *I'm* ~*ed*, caught, cannot escape; ‖~*ing-clerk, -office*, person, place, for buying tickets from. [OE *bōcian* f. prec.]

book'land, n. (hist.). Part of common land granted by charter (under the sovereign's orders) to a private owner. [OE *bōcland*, f. *bōc* document]

boom[1], n. Long spar with one end attached stretching sail-foot; floating barrier of timber across river or harbour mouth. [Du., ⇒ BEAM]

boom[2], v.i. & n. (Make) deep resonant sound; hum, buzz; (make) bittern's cry. [imit.]

boom[3], v.t. & i., & n. (Show) sudden activity, development, (esp. of commercial ventures, prices, etc., cf. SLUMP); (win) sudden popularity for (an' invention, cause, etc.) by advertising etc., launch with éclat. [U.S. wd, perh. f. prec. (cf. *make things hum*)]

boom'er, n. Large male kangaroo; (trappers' name for) N.-Amer. mountain beaver. [orig. unkn.]

boom'erăng, n., & v.i. 1. Australian curved hardwood missile with convex edge returning to its thrower; (fig.) argument or proposal that recoils on its author. 2. v.i. Act as a ~, recoil. [native name, perh. modified]

boon[1], n. Request, thing asked for; favour, gift; blessing, advantage. [f. ON *bón*=OE *bén* prayer f. Gmc **bōniz* of unkn. orig.; the change f. prayer to gift prob. helped by confusion with foll.]

boon[2], a. Bounteous, benign, (poet.; of nature, air, life, etc.); congenial, jolly, (~ *companion*). [f. BON; from 14th c.]

boor, n. Peasant; clumsy or ill-bred fellow. Hence ~'ISH[1] a., ~'ishLY[2] adv., ~'ishNESS n. [f. LG *būr* or Du. *boer* peasant; cf. BOWER[1]]

boost, v.t., & n. 1. (colloq.). Shove, hoist. 2. Increase the reputation, value, etc. of (person, scheme, commodity, etc.) by advertising etc., boom. 3. (mech.). Raise the electromotive force in (electric circuit, battery, etc.), whence ~'ER[1] (2) n. 4. n. Scheme of advertisement; resulting advance in value etc. [U.S., orig. unkn.]

boot[1], n., & v.t. 1. Outer foot-covering, usu. all or partly of leather, coming above ankle; (hist.) instrument of torture, luggage-receptacle in coach under guard's & coachman's seat; luggage-receptacle at back of body of motor-car; *the* ~ *is on the other leg*, truth or responsibility just the other way round; *like old* ~*s* (sl.), tremendously; *over shoes over* ~*s*, as well risk much as little; *heart in* one's ~*s*, in terror; *die in* one's ~*s*, not in bed; ~ *& saddle* [perversion of F *boute-selle* 'place saddle'], cavalry signal to mount; ~*'jack*, for pulling ~s off; ‖~*'lace*, string or leather strip for lacing ~s; ~*'legger*, liquor-smuggler in U.S.; ~*'licker*, toady; ~*'maker*; ~*-trees*, moulds for keeping ~s in shape; (sl.) *get, give, the* ~, be dismissed, dismiss, from employment. 2. v.t. Kick; (sl.) kick (person) *out* (of the house, of employment, etc.). Hence~'ED[2] a. [ME, f. OF *bote* of unkn. orig.]

boot[2], n. Good, advantage, (now only in *to* ~, as well, to the good, additionally). [OE *bôt*, OS *bôta*, OHG *buoza*, ON *bót*,

Goth. *bōta*, f. Gmc **bōtā-* f. root **bat-* BETTER]

boot[3], v.t. (arch.; usu. impers. & abs.). Do good (*to*), avail, as, *what* ~*s* (*it*) *to*, (*it*) *little* ~*s*, (*it*) ~*s* (*me*) *not.* [ME *boten* f. *bot* BOOT[2]]

bootee', n. Kind of lady's boot; infant's wool boot. [cf. *coatee*, see -EE]

booth (-dh), n. Temporary shelter of canvas etc.; covered stall in market, tent at fair, etc.; *polling*-~, for voting at elections. [ME *bōthe* f. ODa. **bóth* (whence Sw., Da. *bod* stall) f. East Norse *bóa* dwell(cf. OIcel. *búth* f. *búa*),cf. BOWER[1]]

boot'less, a. Unavailing. [OE *bōtlēas*, see BOOT[2], -LESS]

boots, n. Hotel-servant who cleans boots, conveys luggage, etc.

boot'y̆, n. Plunder or profit acquired in common & to be divided; gain, a prize; *play* ~, act as decoy for confederates, practise collusion. [f. F *butin* f. *butiner* f. MLG *buyten* to plunder; ult. orig. unkn.]

booze, v.i., & n. Drink deeply, go on drinking; (n.) drink, a drinking-bout. [ME *bouse*, 16th c. *bowse*, f. MDu. *busen*, early mod. Du. *buizen* drink to excess]

booz'y̆, a. Addicted to drink; fuddled. [prec. +-Y[2]]

bo-peep', n. Game of hiding & suddenly appearing to child; *play* ~, of elusive politicians, arguers, etc. [BO +PEEP v.]

bōr'a[1], n. Cold dry N.-E. wind blowing seasonably in the upper Adriatic. [dial. It., f. L BOREAS]

bōr'a[2], n. Mohammedan trader or hawker. [Hind. *bohra*]

boră'cic, a. Of borax (~ *acid*, = BORIC acid). [-IC]

bo'rage (bŭ-), n. Blue-flowered hairy--leaved plant used to flavour claret-cup etc. [f. OF *bourrache* f. med. L *borrago* f. Arab. *abu -rashsh* 'father of sweat' from its use as a diaphoretic]

bōr'ăx, n. A native salt of BORON, in white powder or crystal when pure. [ME & OF *boras* f. med. L *borax* f. Arab. *buraq* prob. f. Pers. *burah*]

Bôrdeaux' (-dō), n. Wine from ~ in S.W. France, claret. [place]

*bôrděll'ō, n. Brothel. [It.]

bôrd'er[1], n. & a. Side, edge, boundary or part near it; frontier of country, (pl. after *within, out of*, etc.) territory; *the B*~, boundary & adjoining districts between England & Scotland, **frontier of civiliza-tion, (also *Border* adj. in these senses); continuous bed round garden or part of it, distinct edging for strength or orna-ment or definition round anything; ~*land*, district on either side of ~, (fig.) intermediate condition (as between sleep-ing & waking), debatable ground; ~ *line*, line of demarcation; ~(-)*line* adj., on the ~ line, as *a* ~-*line case*, (esp., Psych.) one verging on insanity. [ME *bordure*, f. OF f. Rom. **bordare* whence F *border*; see BOARD[1], -URE]

bôrd'er[2], v.t. & i. Put or be a border to, whence ~ING[1] (3) n.; adjoin (trans., or intr. with *on, upon*); ~ *upon*, resemble. [f. prec.]

bôrd'erer, n. Dweller on or near frontier, esp. that of England & Scotland. [BORDER n. +-ER[1] (4)]

bōre[1], v.t. & i. **1.** Make hole in usu. with revolving tool, hollow out evenly (tube etc.), whence **bōr'**ING[1] (2) n.; make (a hole, one's way), by boring, persistent pushing, or excavation. **2.** (Of horse) thrust the head out; (Racing) push (another) out of the course. [OE *borian*, OHG *borōn*, ON *bora* f. Gmc **borōn* f. **boraz* (whence OE, ON *bor* auger)]

bōre[2], n. Hollow of gun-barrel; diameter of this, calibre; small deep hole made in earth to find water etc. [partly f. prec., partly f., or cogn. w., ON *bora* bore-hole]

bōre[3], n. Nuisance (usu. as pred.); tire-some person, twaddler. [f. 1750, orig. unkn.; early quotations imply F deriv.]

bōre[4], v.t. Weary by tedious talk or dull-ness. [app. f. BORE[3], w. which it is contemporary, but relations uncert.]

bōre[5], n. Great tide-wave with precipi-tous front moving up some estuaries. [perh. f. ON *bára* wave]

bōre[6]. See BEAR[3].

bōr'eal, a. Of the North or north wind. [ME, f. LL *borealis* (foll., -AL)]

Bōr'ĕăs, n. (God of) the north wind. [L f. Gk]

bore'cōle (-ōrk-), n. = KALE. [f. Du. *boerenkool* peasant's cabbage']

bore'dom (-ōrd-), n. Being bored, ennui. [BORE[3] +-DOM]

bōr'er, n. Person, tool, or machine, that bores holes; horse that bores; kinds of boring insect. [BORE[1] +-ER[1]]

bŏ'ric, a. Of boron (~ *acid*, a preserva-tive & mild antiseptic. [-IC]

bôrn, p.p. & a. *Be*~, come into the world by birth; ~ *of*, owing origin to; ~ *again*, regenerate; (with compl.) destined to be (~ *rich, tired, to be hanged, a poet*; cf. also ~ *orator, an orator*, etc.); ~ *with a silver spoon in* one's *mouth, under a lucky star*, destined to wealth, good luck; *in all my* ~ *days*, my life; ~ *fool, idiot* (utter, hopeless); often in comb. with adjj. & advv., as *bare, first*, -~. [p.p. of BEAR[3]]

bôrne. See BEAR[3].

borné (bôrn'ā), a. Having limitations, of limited ideas, narrow-minded. [F]

boro-, comb. form of foll.

bōr'ŏn, n. Non-metallic solid element (a brown amorphous powder or yellow crystals). [f. BORAX with ending of *carbon*, which it resembles in some respects]

borough (bŭ'ru), n. ‖ (Munic.) town with corporation & privileges conferred by royal charter; (Parl.) town sending mem-ber(s) to parliament; *the B*~, of South-wark; (hist.) *own, buy*, ~, power of con-trolling election of member, *close, pocket*, ~, so controlled, *rotten* ~, no longer (before 1832) having real constituency. [OE *burg, burh*, OS *burg*, OHG *burug*, ON *borg*, Goth. *baurgs* f. Gmc **burgs* cogn. w. *bergan* shelter; cf. BURGH]

borough-Eng′lish (bŭ′ru ĭngg-), n. (hist.). Tenure in some parts of England, by which all lands & tenements fell to young-est son. [f. AF *tenure en Burgh Engloys* (i.e. not French, but existing in some English boroughs)]

bŏ′rrow (-ō), v.t. & i. Get temporary use of (money etc. to be returned; *of* or *from* person); adopt, use without being the true or original owner or inventor, derive from another, import from an alien source; (Golf) play ball up-hill to roll back, (also) allow for wind or slope; ~*ed light*, internal window; ~*ed* PLUMEs; ~*-pit* (from which material has been taken for filling or embanking). Hence ~ER[1], ~ING[1](2), nn. [OE *borgian* give a pledge (= OHG *borgēn* take heed, MHG, G *borgen* borrow) f. *borg, borh* (= OS *borg*, MHG *borc*) pledge, f. root of Gmc **bergan* protect (see BOROUGH)]

bŏrsch (-sh), n. Highly seasoned Russian soup of various ingredients including beetroot. [Russ. *borshch*]

Bŏrs′tal, n. ~ *system*, of imprisonment for young criminals, based on the INDE-TERMINATE sentence; ~ *Association*, for help of ~ prisoners on discharge; ~ *In-stitution*, formerly ~ *Prison*, at ~ in Kent.

bŏrt, n. Diamond fragments made in cutting; diamond malformed in the making. [f. Du. *boort*]

bŏrz′oi, n. Russian wolf-hound. [f. Russ. *borzoy* a. = swift, & n.]

‖ **bŏs, bŏss**, n., & v.t. & i., (sl.). (Also ~*-shot*) bad shot or guess, miss; bungle, mess; ‖~*-eyed* (sl.), blind in one eye, cross-eyed, crooked, one-sided; (vb; -ss-) miss, bungle. [orig. unkn.]

bŏs′cage, -kage, n. Masses of trees or shrubs. [ME, f. OF *boscage* f. *bosc* wood (see BUSH[1]) + *-age* -AGE]

bŏsh[1], n. & int. (sl.). Nonsense, foolish talk, folly. [Turk., = empty; introduced by Morier's novel *Ayesha* (1834)]

‖ **bŏsh**[2], v.t. (school sl.). Make a fool of, tease. [f. prec.]

bŏsh[3], n. Lower sloping part of blast--furnace shaft, from belly to hearth. [orig. unkn.]

bŏsk, bŏs′ket, -quèt (-k-), nn. Thicket, plantation. [(a) ME *bosk* var. of *busk* BUSH[1], in mod. use back form. f. BOSKY; (b) *bosket* f. F *bosquet* f. It. *boschetto* dim. of *bosco* wood; cf. BOUQUET]

bŏs′ky̆, a. Wooded, bushy. [f. ME *bosk* (prec.) + -Y[2]]

bo′s′n. See BOAT[1]*swain*.

bosom (bŏŏ′zm), n. Person's breast; en-closure formed by breast & arms (*wife of* one's ~); breast of dress, space between dress & breast, old equivalent of pocket (*put in* one's ~); **shirt-front; surface of lake, ground, etc.; the midst (~ *of* one's

family, *of the church*); the heart, thoughts, desires, etc. (*comes home to* one's ~, ~*-friend*). [OE *bōsm*, OS *bōsom*, OHG *buosam* f. WG **bōsm-* of unkn. orig.]

bŏss[1], n. Protuberance; round metal knob or stud on centre of shield or orna-mental work; (Archit.) carved or sculp-tured projection at intersecting-point of ribs; (Mech.) enlarged part of shaft. Hence ~ED[2] (-st), ~′Y[2], aa. [ME *boce* f. OF *boce* (mod. *bosse*) of unkn. orig.]

bŏss[2], n. (sl.). Master, person in authority; **manager of political organization; person or thing that is best at any thing, champion. [U.S. wd f. Du. *baas* master, of unkn. orig.]

bŏss[3], v.t. (sl.). Be master or manager of (~ *the show*, make all arrangements). [f. prec.]

Bŏs′ton, n. Variation of the waltz. [~ in U.S.]

bo′sun. See BOAT[1]*swain*.

Bŏs′well (-z-), n. Biographer like James ~ (1740–95), writer of Johnson's life. Hence **Boswell′IAN** a., ~ISM(3) n., ~IZE(4) v.i.

bŏt, bŏtt, n. Parasitic worm; *the botts*, horse disease caused by it; ~*-fly*, insect whose eggs produce the ~s. [16th c. *bottes* prob. of LG orig., cf. Du. *bot*, WFris. *botten* (pl.), WFlem. *botse*, of unkn. orig.]

bŏt′anist, n. Student of botany. [f. F *botaniste*, see BOTANY, -IST(3)]

bŏt′anize, -ise (-īz), v.i. Study plants, esp. by seeking them as they grow. [f. Gk *botanizō* gather plants, see BOTANY, -IZE]

bŏt′any̆[1], n. Science of plants. Hence **botăn′ICAL** a. (also **botăn′IC** in names of old societies), **botăn′ICALLY** adv. [(a) *botany* f. *botanic* on anal. of *astronomy -ic* etc., see -Y[1]; (b) *botanic* f. F *botanique* or LL f. Gk *botanikos* f. *botanē* plant, see -IC]

Bŏt′any̆[2], a. & n. ~ (*wool*), Australian wool; ~ *yarn*, yarn made from this. [f. ~ *Bay*, early convict settlement in N.S. Wales named from the variety of its flora]

botăr′gō, n. (pl. *-oes, -os*). Relish of mullet or tunny roe. [It., f. Arab. *bufarkhah* f. Copt. *outarakhon* (Copt. *ou-*indef. art. + Gk *tarikhion* pickle)]

bŏtch, n., & v.t. & i. (Make a) clumsy patch; bungle(d) work; repair badly. Hence ~′ER[1] n. [ME *bocche*, of unkn. orig.]

bŏth, a., pron., & adv. **1.** adj. The two ——s & not only one, as ~ (*the*) *brothers are dead* (*have it* ~ *ways*, choose now one now the other of alternatives or contra-dictories to suit one's argument etc.). **2.** pron. The two & not only one (a) with no n., as ~ *are dead*; (b) with *of* & n. or pron., as ~ *of them* (or *of the brothers*) *are dead*; (c) with n. or pron. as subj., & ~ in the pred. in apposition, as *they* (or *the brothers*) *are* ~ *dead, they were gentlemen* ~.

3. adv. With equal truth in two cases (a) where ~ might still be held pronominal, as ~ *brother & sister are dead*; (b) clearly adv., as *she is ~ dead & buried*; (c) of more than two nouns etc., as ~ *God & man & beast.* [ME *bathe* f. ON *báthar* (= OS *béthia*, OHG *bede, beide*), extended form of the simple wd repr. by OE *begen*, *bā* (ME *bō*), Goth. *bai, ba*]

both'er[1] (-dh-), v.t. & i. Pester, worry; be troublesome; worry oneself, take trouble; (subjunct. as mild imprecation) confound. [orig. unkn.; first in Irish writers, Sheridan, Swift, Sterne, & prob. of Anglo-Ir. orig.]

both'er[2] (-dh-), n. Worry, fuss, petty trouble. [f. prec.]

botherā'tion (-dh-), n. & int.=prec.; (int.) confound it! [BOTHER v. + -ATION]

both'ersome (-dh-), a. Annoying, troublesome. [-SOME]

both'ÿ, -ie, n. (Sc.). Hut, cottage; one-roomed building in which workmen are lodged. [orig. unkn.; perh. related to BOOTH]

bō'-tree, n. Sacred pipal tree of India, beneath which Gautama, by enlightenment, became the Buddha. [repr. Sinhalese *bogaha* f. *bo* = Pali & Skr. *bodhi* perfect knowledge + *gaha* tree]

bŏt'tle[1], n. Narrow-necked vessel, usu. of glass, for storing liquid; the amount of liquid in it; *the ~,* drinking, *over a ~,* while drinking; *bring up on the ~,* of child not fed from the breast; *~-brush,* cylindrical brush for cleaning ~s, kinds of plant as horsetail; *~-glass,* coarse dark-green glass; *~-green,* dark green; *~-holder,* pugilist's attendant at prizefight, second, supporter, understrapper; *~-neck,* narrow stretch or restricted outlet of road, (fig.) anything obstructing an even flow of production etc.; *~-nose,* swollen nose, *~-nosed whale; ~-party,* to which each guest brings a bottle of wine etc. (freq. extended to any gathering at which the licensing laws are defied); *~-washer* (colloq.), factotum, underling. [ME *botel, -ell(e)* f. OF *botele, bouteille* f. med. L *butticula* dim. of *butis, buttis* BUTT[1]]

bŏt'tle[2], v.t. Store in bottles; ~ *up,* conceal, restrain for a time, (resentment etc.). [f. prec.]

bŏt'tle[3], n. Bundle of hay or straw (*look for needle in ~ of hay,* of hopeless search). [ME, f. OF *botel* dim. of *botte* bundle]

bŏt'tle[4], n. *Blue, white, yellow,* ~, ~ *of all sorts,* kinds of plant. [partly corruption of *buddle* corn-marigold, partly from shape of ovary or calyx]

bŏtt'om[1], n. & a. **1.** Lowest part, part on which thing rests (*stand on own ~,* be independent; ~ *up,* upside-down); the posterior; seat (of chair); ground under water of lake etc. (*go, send, to the ~,* sink; *touch ~,* be at the lowest point or on firm facts; *lo, from,* ~ *of heart,* genuinely, pro-

foundly); river-basin etc., low-lying land; less honourable end of table, class, etc., person occupying this; farthest or inmost point (~ *of bay*); keel, horizontal part near keel, hull, ship esp. as cargo-carrier (*in British ~s*); foundation, basis, origin, (*be at the ~ of,* cause); essential character, reality, (*search to the ~, get to the ~ of; at* ~); stamina. **2.** adj. Lowest, last (*bet one's ~ dollar,* stake all); ~ *drawer,* drawer in chest of drawers etc., in which a woman stores clothes etc. in preparation for marriage; ∥~ GEAR; fundamental; hence ~MOST (-m-m-) a. [OE *botm,* OS *bodom,* OHG *bodam,* ON *botn* repr. Gmc **buthm-, *buthn-*]

bŏtt'om[2], v.t. & i. Put bottom to (saucepan, chair); base (argument etc.) *upon;* touch bottom of sea etc.; touch bottom of, sound, find the extent or real nature of. [f. prec.]

bŏtt'omless, a. Without bottom (chair etc.); unfathomable. [-LESS]

bŏtt'omry[1], n. System of lending money to shipowner for purposes of voyage on security of ship, lender losing the money if ship is lost. [BOTTOM n.=ship + -RY after Du. *bodmerij*]

bŏtt'omry[2], v.t. Pledge (ship; see prec.).

bŏt'ūlism, n. (med.). Sausage-poisoning or poisoning by infected tinned or other food. [f. L *botulus* sausage, -ISM]

boudoir (bōōd'wär), n. Lady's small private room. [F, lit. sulking-place f. *bouder* sulk]

Bou'gainvillae'a, -vil'ia, (bōōgan-), n. Tropical plant with large bright-coloured bracts. [*Bougainville,* French navigator, d. 1811]

bough (-ow), n. Tree-branch (if on tree, one of the chief branches). [OE *bōg, bōh,* OHG *buog,* ON *bógr* shoulder of an animal (the sense 'limb of a tree' is excl. Eng.) f. Gmc **bōguz*; see BOW[5]]

bought. See BUY. Var. ~en (baw'ten), (in dial. & U.S. use) purchased at a shop (opp. *home-made*).

bougie (bōōzh'ē), n. Wax candle; thin flexible surgical instrument for exploring, dilating, etc., the passages of the body. [F, f. Arab. *Bujiyah* Algerian town with wax trade]

bouillabaisse (bōōlyabäs'), n. French (esp. Marseilles) dish, rich fish-stew. [F]

bouilli (bōōyē'), n. Stewed or boiled meat. [F]

bouillon (see Ap.), n. Broth, soup; (Dress) puffed fold. [F, f. *bouillir* BOIL]

boul'der (bōl-), n. Water-worn rounded stone, cobble; large erratic block of weather-worn stone (in mining, of detached ore); *~-clay, -drift, -formation, -period,* geol. terms w. ref. to the Ice Age. [short for *boulderstone,* ME *bulderston* of Scand. orig.; cf. Sw. dial. *bullersten* large stone in a stream that makes a noise (Sw. *buller* noise, cf. G *bollern* rumble)]

Boule (bow'lē), n. Legislative council of

ancient Greece; modern Greek legislature. [Gk *boulē* senate (*boulomai* choose)]

boulevard (bōōl'vahr,* -ahrd), n. Broad street with rows of trees; *broad main road. [F, f. G *bollwerk* BULWARK orig. promenade on demolished fortification]

boul'ter (bōl-), n. Long fishing-line with many hooks. [orig. unkn.]

bounce[1], v.i. & t. (Cause to) rebound; (sl., of cheque) be returned to drawer when there are no funds to meet it; throw oneself about; burst noisily, angrily, etc., *into* or *out of* (room), *in* or *out*; talk big; hustle (person) by bluff or assumptions *into* doing or *out of* (something); *bouncing girl* etc., big, hearty, bustling, noisy. [ME *bunsen* beat, thump, of unkn. orig., perh. imit.; cf. however LG *bunsen*, Du. *bonzen* beat, thump, Du. *bons* thump]

bounce[2], n. Rebound; boast, exaggeration, swagger. [f. prec.]

bounce[3], adv. Suddenly, noisily, (*come ∼ against* etc. cf. BANG). [as prec.]

boun'cer, n. In vbl senses; also: unblushing lie; thing big of its kind; *chucker-out (sl.). [-ER[1]]

bound[1], n. Limit of territory or estate; (usu. pl.) limitation, restriction, (*out of ∼s*, beyond limits set by school etc. rules; *go beyond the ∼s of reason, put ∼s to*). [ME *bunne*, *bound*, etc. f. AF *bounde*, OF *bodne* etc., f. med. L *bodina* earlier *butina* of unkn. orig.]

bound[2], v.t. Set bounds to, limit, (esp. in pass. with *by*); be the boundary of. [f. prec.]

bound[3], v.i. (Of ball etc.) recoil from wall or ground, bounce; (of living thing, wave, etc.) spring, leap, advance lightly. [f. F *bondir* (orig. of sound) f. Rom. *bombitire* var. of LL *bombitare* (L *bombus* hum)]

bound[4], n. Springy movement upward or forward; (*advance by leaps & ∼s*, with startling speed); (of ball etc.) recoil (*on the first ∼*, between first two touchings of ground). [f. prec.]

bound[5], a. Ready to start, having started, *for* (or with preceding adv. as *homeward ∼*). [ME *bun(e)*, *boun(e)* f. ON *búinn* p.p. of *búa* get ready; -*d* phonetic, or partly after foll.]

bound[6], p.p. of BIND. In vbl senses; esp. *∼ up with*, having the same interests as, closely connected with; *∼ to win* etc., certain.

boun'darў, n. Limit-line; (Cricket) hit to limit of field scoring 4 or 6 runs. [BOUND[1]+-ARY[1]]

boun'den. See BIND[1].

boun'der, n. In vbl senses of BOUND[2, 3]; esp., (sl.) cheerfully or noisily ill-bred person. [-ER[1]]

bound'less, a. Unlimited. Hence ∼LY[2] adv., ∼NESS n. [BOUND[1]+-LESS]

boun'teous, a. Beneficent, liberal; freely bestowed. Hence ∼LY[2] adv., ∼NESS n. [ME *bontyvous* f. OF *bontif* (*bonté* BOUNTY)

+-OUS, altered later as though f. *bounté* BOUNTY+-OUS; cf. PLENTEOUS]

boun'tiful, a.=prec. (*lady ∼*, beneficent lady of a neighbourhood); also, ample. Hence ∼LY[2] adv. [foll.+-FUL]

boun'tў, n. Munificence, liberality in giving; gift (*king's*, *queen's*, *∼*, grant made to mother of triplets; *Queen Anne's ∼*, former fund for augmenting poor benefices); gratuity to soldiers etc. on joining etc.; sum paid to manufacturers & producers to encourage trade enterprise. [ME, f. OF *bonte* f. L *bonitatem* f. *bonus* good (BON, -TY)]

bouquet' (bōōkā'), n. Bunch of flowers; perfume of wine. [F, f. dial. var. of OF *bos*, *bois* wood; see -ET]

bouquetin (bōōk[2]), n. The Alpine ibex. [F]

***bour'bon**[1] (bŏr-, boor-), n. Kind of whisky distilled from Indian corn & rye. [f. *Bourbon* County, Ky, where first made]

***Bour'bon**[2] (boor-), n. Reactionary. [f. the ∼ family, whose descendants founded dynasties in France & Spain]

bour'don (boor-), n. Low-pitched (16 ft) stop in organ; similar stop in harmonium; lowest bell in peal of bells; drone pipe of bagpipes. [F, = bagpipe-drone]

bourgeois[1] (boorzh'wah), n. & a. (Member) of middle class, (person) of humdrum or conventional middle-class ideas. [F, see BURGESS]

bourgeois[2] (berjois'), n. & a. (Printing type) between long primer & brevier. [perh. a French printer's name]

bourgeoisie (boorzhwahzē'), n. The middle class. [F]

bourgeon. See BURGEON.

bourn[1] (boorn), n. Small stream. [southern var. of BURN[1]]

bourn(e)[2] (boorn), n. Limit, goal. [f. F *borne* f. OF *bodne* BOUND[1]]

bourse (boors), n. Foreign money-market, esp. that of Paris. [F]

boustrophēd'on, a. & adv. (Written) from right to left & from left to right in alternate lines. [Gk, adv. = as ox turns in ploughing (f. *bous* ox, -*strophos* turning, -*don* adv. suf.)]

bout, n. Spell of or turn at work or exercise; fit of drinking or illness; trial of strength; *this ∼*, on this occasion. [16th c. *bout*, *bout* app. same as obs. *bought* (*bout*) bending]

boutonnière (bōōtŏnyār'), n. (Spray of flowers worn in) buttonhole. [F]

bouts rimés (bōō rēmā'), n. pl. Rhymed ends; versifying to set rhymes. [F]

bōv'ine a. Of, like, an ox; inert, dull. [f. LL *bovinus* (*bos bovis* ox, see -INE[1])]

‖ **bōv'ril**, n. A meat extract used like beef tea. [P]

bow[1] (bō), n. Curve; rainbow; weapon for shooting arrows (*bend*, *draw*, *the ∼*; *two strings to* one's ∼, a second resource; *draw the long ∼*, exaggerate);=SADDLE-∼; rod with stretched horse-hair for playing violin etc., single passage of this across strings; = BAIL⁴; = BOW-WINDOW; slip--knot with single or double loop, ribbon etc. so tied; ~s, ~-compass(es), compass with jointed legs; ~-head, Greenland whale; ~-legged, bandy; ~-saw, narrow saw stretched like bowstring on wooden frame; ~-shot, distance to which ~ can send arrow; ~-string, (strangle with) string of ~ (former Turkish method of execution). [OE boga, OS, OHG bogo, ON bogi f. Gmc *bugon f. *bug- BOW³]

bow² (bō), v.t. Use the bow on (violin etc.; also abs.). [f. prec.]

bow³, v.i. & t. Submit (to the inevitable etc.), bend or kneel in sign of submission or reverence to or before (often with down); incline head in salutation, assent, etc. (~ing acquaintance, that stops at this, slight); express (thanks etc.), usher in or out, by ~ing; cause to bend (lit. & fig., knee, back etc. for burden, will); ~ down, crush, make stoop, (esp. ~ed down by care etc.). [OE būgan, cf. OHG biogan, ON *bjūga, Goth. biugan f. Gmc *beugan f. *beug-, *bug-, cf. BOW¹]

bow⁴, n. Bending of head or body in salutation, respect, consent, etc.; make one's~, retire. [f. prec.]

bow⁵, n. Fore-end of boat or ship from where it begins to arch inwards (often pl.); on the ~, of objects within 45° of the point right ahead; rower nearest the ~ (~-oar, his oar or himself); ~-chaser, see CHASE¹. [17th c. f. LG boog, Du. boeg, = Da. boug, Sw. bog, G bug, all = shoulder, ship's bow, the same wd as BOUGH; the naut. sense was developed in LG & Du.]

Bow bells (bō), n. Within the sound of ~, in City of London. [f. St Mary le Bow]

bowd'ler|ize, -ise (-īz), v.t. Expurgate (book, author). Hence ~ISM(3), ~IZA-TION, nn. [T. Bowdler (d. 1825), expurgator of Shakespeare, +-IZE(4)]

bow'el, n. Division of alimentary canal below stomach, intestine, gut, (sing. only in med. use); (pl.) entrails, inside of body; pity, tender feelings, (~s of mercy etc.); interior of anything. [ME buel, bouel f. OF buel f. L botellus dim. of botulus sausage]

bow'er¹, n. Dwelling, abode, (poet.); inner room, boudoir, (poet.); place closed in with foliage, arbour, summerhouse, whence ~Y² a.; ~-bird, Australian bird of the bird-of-paradise family constructing elaborate runs adorned with feathers, shells, etc. [OE (OS, OHG, ON) būr f. Gmc *būr- f. *bū dwell, cf. BOOR]

bow'er², n. (Also ~-anchor, -cable) either of two anchors (best & small) carried at ship's bow or of their cables. [BOW⁵ +-ER¹]

bow'er³, n. One of two cards (right ~, knave of trumps, left ~, knave of same colour) at euchre. [f. G bauer peasant, knave at cards, cogn. w. Du. boer; see BOOR]

*bow'ery, n. Farm, plantation; the B~, a wide street in New York City. [f. Du. bouwerij]

bow'ie-knife (bō'ī-), n. Long knife with 10–15 in. blade double-edged at point used as weapon in wild parts of U.S. [Col. J. Bowie (d. 1836)]

bowl¹ (bōl), n. Basin (hist., deep-shaped basin; now differing only as more dignified or poetic wd); drinking-vessel (the ~, conviviality); contents of a ~; ~-shaped part of tobacco-pipe, spoon, balance, etc. Hence~FUL(2) (bōl'fŏol) n. [ME bolle f. OE (OS, OHG) bolla, ON bolli f. Gmc *bŭl-swell; cf. BOLL]

bowl² (bōl), n. 1. Wooden ball made slightly out of spherical shape or weighted on one side to make it run curved course (BIAS). 2. Flattened or spherical wooden ball at skittles. 3. pl. Game played with ~s (sense 1) on grass, or with round balls in room. 4. pl. Skittles (dial.). [ME & F boule f. L bulla bubble; bowl² has taken its pronunc. f. bowl¹, & bowl¹ its spelling f. bowl²]

bowl³ (bōl), v.t. & i. Play bowls; trundle (ball, hoop, etc.) along ground; go along by revolving or by means of wheels, esp. ~ along, go fast & smoothly; (Cricket) deliver (ball, over, or abs.), knock off (bails) or down (wicket), dismiss (batsman; out or abs.), whence bowl'er¹ [-ER¹] n.; ~ over, knock down, (fig.) disconcert, render helpless. [f. prec.]

|| bowl'er² (bō-), n. = BILLYCOCK; ~-hat n., ~, v.t. (sl., -tt-), retire from the army etc. [f. B~, hatter, who designed it 1850]

bowline (bō'līn), n. Rope from weather side of square sail to bow; (also ~-knot) simple knot for forming a non-slipping loop at end of rope. [ME bouline etc. f. MLG bōline = MDu. boechlijne (BOW⁵, LINE²); early borrowing accounts for pronunc. diff. from that of BOW⁵; see also BOWSPRIT]

bowl'ing (bō-), n. In vbl senses; esp.: ~-crease, line from behind which bowler delivers ball; ~-alley, long enclosure for playing skittles; ~-green, lawn for playing bowls. [-ING¹]

bow'man¹ (bō-), n. (pl. -men). Archer. [BOW¹]

bow'man² (bō-), n. (pl. -men). Man stationed in bow of boat. [BOW⁵]

bow'sprit (bō-), n. Spar running out from ship's stem, to which forestays are fastened. [ME bouspret etc. f. MLG bōgsprēt = MDu. boechspriet (BOW⁵, SPRIT); see also BOWLINE]

Bow-street (bō-), n. & a. Street near Covent Garden with chief metropolitan police-court; B.-runner, -officer, old names for police officer.

bow win'dow (bō-; -dō), n. Curved (not angular) bay window; (sl.) large belly. Hence~ED² (-ōd) a. [BOW¹]

bow-wow' (bō-), int. & n. Dog's bark; imitation of it; (nursery talk etc.) dog; the (*big*) ~ *style*, dogmatic manner in talk or writing.

bow'yer (bō-), n. Maker, seller, of bows. [BOW[1] + -YER]

bŏx[1], n. Kinds of evergreen shrub, esp. one with small dark leathery leaves, much used in garden borders; (also ~*wood*) its wood, used by turners & engravers; (with qualification) similar plant (*bastard* ~ etc.). [OE *box* f. L *buxus*, Gk *puxos*]

bŏx[2], n. **1.** Receptacle (usu. lidded, rectangular or cylindrical, & for solids) of wood, cardboard, metal, etc. (*in the same* ~, i.e. predicament); driver's seat on carriage or coach (from the ~ under it); = ~*ful* as quantity; money-~ (*put in the* ~); separate compartment at theatre, in tavern, etc., in stable or railway truck for horse (*loose* ~, in which it can move about); = JURY-~, ‖ WITNESS-~; hut for sentry or signalman; *fishing, shooting,* etc., -~, small country house for such temporary uses; protective case in various machines; *in the wrong* ~, awkward position. **2.** ~ BARRAGE; ~ *bed*, with wooden roof & sides opening with sliding panels, also bed made to fold up & look like ~; ~-*cloth*, close-woven cloth like buff; ~-*coat*, heavy overcoat (for driving); ~-*drain*, of quadrangular section; ~-*iron*, for ironing, hollow for reception of heater; ~-*keeper*, attendant on theatre ~es; ~-*kite*, scientific kite consisting of two light rectangular ~es secured together horizontally; ~-*office*, in theatre etc. for booking seats; ~-*pleat*, double fold in cloth; ~ *spanner* (with socket head); ~-*wallah* (Anglo-Ind. colloq.), pedlar, (sl.) European commercial man in India (in derogatory sense). Hence ~'FUL(2) n. [OE *box* prob. f. *buxem* acc. (for *buxidem*) of LL *buxis* (whence OHG *buhsa* f. WG **buhsja*) f. L *pyxis* PYX]

bŏx[3], v.t. Provide with, put into, a box; ~ *up*, confine uncomfortably, squeeze together; ‖ lodge (document) in Law Court; divide off from other compartments; ~ *the compass*, (Naut.) rehearse the points in correct order, (fig.) make complete revolution & end where one began (in politics, argument, etc.). [f. prec.]

bŏx[4], n. Slap with hand *on the ear(s)*. [ME *box* of unkn. orig.]

bŏx[5], v.t. & i. Slap person's *ears*; fight (someone, or intr.) with fists (usu. in padded gloves & merely for exercise); ~*ing*-*glove*, padded glove worn in boxing; ~ing-weights (amateur given first, professional in brackets), *heavy-weight* over 12 st. 10 (over 12 st. 7), *light heavy* (or *cruiser*)-*weight* 12 st. 10 (12 st. 7), *middle*-*weight* 11 st. 11 (11 st. 6), *light middle*-*weight* 11 st. 2 (not a professional category), *welter-weight* 10 st. 8 (10 st. 7), *light welter-weight* 10 st. (not a professional category), *light-weight* 9 st. 7 (9 st. 9),

feather-weight 9 st. (9 st.), *bantam-weight* 8 st. 7 (8 st. 6), *fly-weight* 8 st. (8 st.). [f. prec.]

Bŏx and Cŏx, n. Two persons who are never together, never at home at the same time. [name of play adapted from the French in 1847 by J. M. Morton]

bŏx'calf' (-kahf), n. Chrome-tanned calfskin with hatched grain. [after Joseph *Box*, London bootmaker]

bŏx'er, n. Pugilist; (*B*~) member of Chinese anti-foreign secret society (hist.); medium-sized smooth-haired kind of dog derived from German bulldog. [BOX[5], -ER[1]]

bŏx'-haul, v.i. Veer ship round on her keel (for want of room). [BOX[3]]

‖ **Bŏx'ing-day**, n. First week-day after Christmas. [on which CHRISTMAS-*boxes* are given, f. obs. sense of BOX[3] f. (money)-BOX[2]]

boy, n. Male child (strictly till puberty, loosely till 19 or 20, 'the ~s' also of grown-up sons of a family); person who retains tastes or simplicity of boyhood; servant, slave, native labourer, male native, in various countries with subject races (cf. POST[2]-~ etc.); (familiar voc.) *old, my,* ~; ~, often = male (~-*friend*, girl's or woman's favourite ~), young (~-*husband*); ~ SCOUT[1]; ‖ ~'*s-love*, southernwood. [ME *boi, boy*, the orig. of which, subject of involved conjectures, remains unascertained]

boyc'ott, v.t., & n. **1.** Punish, coerce, (person, class, nation) by systematic refusal of social or commercial relations; combine in abstaining from (goods etc.) with this aim. **2.** n. Such treatment. [Capt. *B*~, Irish land-agent so treated; f. 1880]

boy'hŏod, n. Boyish age; boys. [-HOOD]

boy'ish, a. Proper to boys; as of a boy, spirited, puerile. Hence ~LY[2] adv., ~NESS n. [-ISH[1](1)]

bra (-ah), n. (colloq.), Brassière. [abbr.]

brăb'ble, v.t., & n., (arch.). (Engage in) paltry noisy quarrel. [orig. obsc.; cf. Du. *brabbelen* jabber, stammer]

brāce[1], n. Thing that clasps, tightens, unites, secures; ‖ (pl.) suspenders for trousers; thong for tuning drum; ‖ strap suspending carriage-body from springs; connecting mark in printing ({); pair, couple, (dogs, game, derog. persons; pl. *3, 20*, etc., *brace*); strengthening piece of iron or timber in building; ~ *& bit*, revolving tool for boring, screw-driving, etc.; (Naut.) rope attached to yard for trimming sail (*splice the* MAIN[3] ~). [ME, orig. f. OF *brace* the two arms, f. L *bracchia* (pl.) arms; some senses f. foll. the naut. meaning perh. f. F *bras* arm]

brāce[2], v.t. Fasten tightly, stretch, string up, give firmness to, (~ *oneself up*, ~ one's *energies*, etc.; *bracing air*, opp. *relaxing*); support; couple together, (Naut.) move (sail) by braces. Hence

*brā′cer[1] n. (sl.), pick-me-up. [ME, partly f. OF *bracier* embrace, partly f. prec.; the naut. perh. f. F *brasser*]

brāce′lĕt (-sl-), n. Ornamental band, chain, etc., for wrist or arm; (sl.) hand-cuff. Hence ~ED[2] a. [ME, f. OF, dim. of *bracel* f. L *bracchiale* f. *bracchium* arm, see -ET[1], -LET]

brā′cer[2], n. Wrist-guard in archery & fencing. [ME, f. OF *brasseüre* f. *bras* arm +-*eure* -URE]

brăch, n. (arch.). Bitch hound. [ME *braches* pl. f. OF *braches, -ez,* pl. of *brachet* (whence ME *brachet*) dim. of *brac* f. WG; cf. OHG *braccho,* med. L *braccus*]

bra′chĭal (-ăk-), a. Of the, like an, arm. [f. L *bracchialis* (*bracchium* arm) see -AL]

bra′chiate (-ăk-), a. (bot.). With branches in pairs at right angles to stem, each pair at right angles to the last. [f. L *bracchiatus* see prec. & -ATE[2] (1)]

brăchy- (-k-), comb. form of Gk *brakhus* short, in many scientific terms.

brăchycephăl′ĭc (-kĭsĕ-), a. Short-headed (of skulls with breadth at least four-fifths of length; or of person or race with such skull). [prec. +-CEPHALIC]

brăchyl′ogў (-kĭ-), n. Conciseness of speech, condensed expression, incorrect-ness of speech due to excessive condensa-tion. [f. Gk *brakhulogia,* see BRACHY-, -LOGY]

brăck′en, n. A fern abundant on heaths, hillsides, etc.; (collect.) mass of ferns. [northern ME f. ON **brakni* whence Sw. *bräken,* Da. *bregne* fern]

brăck′et[1], n. Flat-topped projection from wall serving as support to statue, arch, etc.; shelf with slanting under-prop for hanging against wall; wooden or metal angular support; side-piece of gun--carriage supporting trunnion; support projecting from wall of gas or other lamp; pairs of marks, ( ), [ ], { } (cf. BRACE), used for enclosing words, figures, etc. (~-*turn* in skating, like one of the third pairs); (Mil.) distance between two shots in ranging (see foll.); group bracketed together (**income-~,* class of tax-payers grouped according to income). [16th c. *bragget* f. F *braguette* or Sp. *bragueta* dim. of *brague, braga* f. L *braca* sing. of *bracae* breeches; sense-hist. obsc., perh. infl. by L *bracchium* arm]

brăck′et[2], v.t. Enclose in brackets as parenthetic, spurious, (Math.) having spec. relations to what precedes or follows, etc.; couple (names etc.) with a brace, imply connexion or equality between (~*ed,* equal); (Mil.) drop two shots one short of & one beyond (target) in range--finding. [f. prec.]

brăck′ish, a. Between salt & fresh (of water). [f. obs. adj. *brack* f. Du. *brak,* -ISH[1]]

brăct, n. Small leaf or scale below calyx. So **brăc′tĕAL, brăc′tĕATE**[2](2), aa. [f. L *bractea* thin plate, gold leaf]

brăd, n. Thin flat slightly-headed nail. [later var. of ME *brod* goad, pointed instrument, f. ON *broddr* (= OE *brord,* OHG *brort*) spike]

brăd′awl, n. Small non-spiral boring-tool. [perh. f. prec. +AWL]

‖ **Brăd′shaw,** n. (Used for) ~'*s Railway Guide,* a time-table of all passenger trains running in Great Britain. [orig. issued in 1839 by George *Bradshaw,* printer]

‖ **brae** (-ā), n. Steep bank, hill-side. [ME *brā* f. ON *brí* (= OE *brēw*) eyelid, = OS, OHG *brāwa* eyebrow f. Gmc **brēw-*; not related to BROW]

brăg, n., & v.i. & t. (-gg-). (Indulge in) boastful talk; boast of or *of,* boast *that*; card-game like poker. [ME, of unkn. orig.; cf. (16th c.) F *braguer* etc.]

brăggadŏ′cio (-shĭō), n. Empty vaunt-ing. [formed by Spenser (meaning *boaster*) on prec. & It. augmentative *-occhio*]

brăgg′art, n. & a. (Person) given to brag-ging. [f. 16th c. F *bragard* f. *braguer* BRAG +-ARD]

brahmaput′ra (-ŏŏt-), **brah′ma,** n. Kind of domestic fowl. [river *Brahmaputra,* whence brought]

brah′min, -man, n. Member of Hindu priestly caste; **Brahmin* (colloq., usu. derog.), highly cultured or intellectual person. Hence **brahmin′IC(AL), -man-´IC(AL), aa., brah′minISM(3), -manISM(3),** n. [f. Skr. *brahmaṇa* f. *brahman* wor-ship]

brah′minee, a. Belonging to brahmin caste etc.; ~ *bull, ox,* sacred (humped) cattle, immune from slaughter. [f. prec.]

Brah′mōism, n. Reformed theistic Hinduism. So **Brah′mō**(IST) n., adherent of ~. [f. *Brahmo* in *Brahmo Samaj* (religious society founded in 1830), -ISM]

braid[1], n. Entwined hair, plait; band etc. entwined with the hair; silk, thread, etc., woven into a band. Hence ~'ING[1] (3, 6) n. [see foll.]

braid[2], v.t. Plait, interweave, (hair, flowers, thread); arrange (hair) in braids; confine (hair etc.) with ribbon etc.; trim, edge, with braid. [OE, OS *bregdan,* OHG *brettan,* ON *bregtha* f. Gmc **bregdhan* move to & fro]

brail, n., & v.t. (Haul *up* with) small rope(s) on sail-edges for trussing sails be-fore furling. [ME, f. OF *brail, braiel* f. LL *bracale* (also *-ile*) girdle (*bracae* breeches) see -AL(2)]

braille, B-, (-āl), n., & v.t. 1. System of writing & printing for the blind, in which the characters are represented by raised dots. 2. v.t. Print or transcribe in ~ characters. [M. *Braille,* French in-ventor, 1834]

brain, n., & v.t. 1. Convoluted nervous substance in skull of vertebrates (sing. of the whole as an organ, pl. of the sub-stance; *blow out* one's ~*s,* shoot him in the head); centre of sensation, thought, etc. (usu. pl., sing. with dignified or exalted effect; *cudgel* etc. one's ~*s*, think hard; *have something on the* ~, be crazy about it; *turn* one's ~, make him vain & silly); intellectual power (*suck, pick*, one's ~, extract & use his ideas); ~*-fag*, nervous exhaustion; ~ *fever*, inflammation of the ~; ~*-fever bird*, Indian cuckoo (with maddeningly persistent cry sounding like '~fever'); ~*-pan* (colloq.), skull; ~ *sauce* (joc.), intelligence; ~*-sick*, mad; ~*-storm*, temporary mental upset marked by uncontrolled emotion & violent action; *Brains Trust*, *group of experts guiding or advising the government, (transf.) any group of experts, ‖ a body, consisting mainly of experts, broadcasting impromptu answers to selected questions from listeners; ~*-washing*, clearing the mind of established ideas by persistent suggestion & indoctrination; ~ *wave* (colloq.), sudden inspiration or bright idea; hence ~'LESS a. **2.** v.t. Dash out ~*s* of. [OE *brægen* = MDu., LG *bregen*, Du., Fris. *brein*, not elsewhere in Gmc]

brain'y, a. Clever. [-Y²]

‖ **braird**, n., & v.i. (Sc.).(Come up in) fresh shoots. [same wd as obs. (Sc.) *brerd* f. OE *brerd* brim; cf. OE *brord* point, see BRAD]

braise (-z), v.t. Stew (prop. with fire above & below) tender with bacon, herbs, etc. [f. F *braiser* (*braise* hot coals)]

brāke¹, n. = BRACKEN. [ME, perh. shortened f. *bracken*, -*en* being taken to be the pl. ending]

brāke², n. Thicket, brushwood. [10th c., orig. unkn.]

brāke³, n. Toothed instrument for braking flax & hemp; (also ~*-harrow*) heavy harrow; instrument for peeling off willow-bark. [15th c. = MLG, MDu. *brake*, flax-brake f. *breken* BREAK¹]

brāke⁴, v.t. Crush (flax, hemp) by beating. [f. prec.]

brāke⁵, n. Apparatus for checking wheel's motion; (also ~*-van*) railway-carriage from which ~*s* of a train can be controlled, guard's compartment. Hence ~'LESS (-kl-) a. [18th c., of uncert. orig.; perh. transferred use of obs. *brake* bridle, curb (15th c.), of uncert. orig.; cf. F *frein* curb, also brake, G. *bremse* barnacle, also brake]

brāke⁶, v.t. Apply brake to (wheel, car, train). [f. prec.]

brāke⁷. See BREAK³.

***brāke'man** (-km-), ‖ **brākes'man** (-ks-), n. Man in charge of BRAKE⁵.

Brăm'ah-. (Lock, press, pen, etc.) invented by J. *Bramah c.* 1790.

brăm'ble, n. Rough prickly shrub with long trailing shoots; blackberry-bush; blackberry. Hence **brăm'bly²** a. [OE *bræmbel* (for earlier *bræmel*, cf. *slumber*), f. WG *bræm-*, *bræm-* (see BROOM)+-LE (1); cf. OS *brāmalbusc*]

brăm'bling, n. The mountain finch. [prec.+-LING¹ (1)]

brăn, n. Husks of grain separated from flour after grinding; ~ *pie*, form of LUCKY¹-*bag*. [ME *bren*, *bran* f. OF f. Gaulish *brennos* bran]

brăn'card (-ngk-), n. A horse-litter. [F, = litter (foll., -ARD)]

branch¹ (-ah-), n. Limb springing from tree or bough (*bough*, ~, *twig*, is the order, but ~ occas. for either of the others); lateral extension or subdivision of mountain-range, river, road, family, genus, subject of knowledge, argument, legislature, bank or other business, etc.; *root-&-* ~ adj., *root & ~* adv., thorough(ly), radical(ly). Hence (-)~ED² (-cht), ~'LESS, aa., ~'LET n. [ME, f. OF *branche* branch f. LL *branca* paw]

branch² (-ah-), v.i. Put branches *out, forth*; spring *out*, spread *forth*, tend *away* or *off*, diverge *into*. [f. prec.]

brăn'chi|ae, **-ǐ|a** (-ngk-), n. pl. Gills. Hence ~AL, ~ATE²(2), ~F'EROUS, ~FORM, aa., ~o- comb. form. [L *branchia*, pl. *-ae*, f. Gk *bragkhia* pl.]

brăn'chy̆ (-ah-), a. With many branches. [-Y²]

brănd¹, n. Burning or charred log or stick (~ *from the burning*, rescued person, convert), torch (poet.); mark made by hot iron; stigma (*the ~ of Cain*, blood-guiltiness); trade-mark, particular kind of goods; iron stamp for burning a mark in; kind of blight (leaves etc. with burnt look); sword (poet.; perh. as flashing). [OE *brand*, OHG *brant*, ON *brandr* f. Gmc *brandaz* (*bran-* pret. st. of *brinnan* BURN²)]

brănd², v.t. Burn with hot iron (surgically, penally, or showing ownership or quality); impress on memory; stigmatize. [f. prec.]

brăn'dish, v.t. Wave about, flourish, (weapon, threat) as preliminary to action or in display. [f. OF *brandir* (-ISH²) f. Rom. *brandire* f. Gmc *brand-* BRAND¹ sword]

brănd'ling, n. Red worm with brighter rings used as bait. [BRAND¹+-LING¹(1)]

brănd'-new', **brăn-**, a. Conspicuously new. [f. BRAND¹, as if freshly stamped]

brăn'drĕth, n. Wooden stand for cask, hay-rick, etc. [ME, f. ON *brandreith* grate (*brandr* BRAND¹+*reith* carriage)]

brăn'dy̆, n. Strong spirit distilled from wine; ‖~*-ball*, kind of sweet; ‖~ *pawnee* [Hind. *pani* water], ~ & water; ~*-snap*, gingerbread wafer. [17th c *brandwine, brandewine*, f. Du. *brandew₁n* = burnt (distilled) wine]

brănk'-ûrs'ine (-ngk-), n. Bear's breech, acanthus. [f. med. L *branca ursina* bear's claw cf. BRANCH]

brăn-new. See BRAND-NEW.

brănt(-goose). See BRENT.

brăsh¹, n. Loose broken rock or ice; hedge refuse, clippings, etc. [of unkn. orig.; cf. Du. *bras* (G *brass*) heap, lot, rubbish]

*brăsh², a. (colloq.). Rash, cheeky, saucy. [orig. unkn.]

brass (-ahs), n., a., & v.t. & i. **1.** (Hist.) alloy of copper with tin, zinc, or other base metal; (mod.) yellow alloy of ⅔ copper with ⅓ zinc (cf. BRONZE); inscribed sepulchral table of ~; *the* ~, the ~ instruments of a band; (sl.) money; effrontery, shamelessness. **2.** adj. Made of ~; ~ *band*, set of musicians with ~ instruments; ~ *farthing*, least possible amount, esp. *don't care a* ~ *farthing*; ‖~ *hat*, (mil. sl.) officer of high rank with gold braid on his hat; ‖~ *plate*, on door, gate, or window-ledge, with name, trade, etc.; ‖~ *rags*, sailors' cleaning cloths, as *part* ~ *rags* (Naut. sl.), dissolve intimacy *with*; ~ *tacks*, (sl.) actual details, real business, esp. *get down to* ~ *tacks*. **3.** v.t. & i. (sl.). Pay *up*. [OE *bræs* of unkn. orig.; cf. MLG *bras* metal]

brăss´age, n. Mint-charge for coining money. [F, f. *brasser* stir melted metals together; see -AGE]

brăss´ard, n. Badge worn on arm. [F (*bras* arm & see -ARD)]

brăss´erĭe, n. Beer-saloon or beer-garden (usu. supplying eatables also). [F, = brewery (*brasser* brew)]

brassière (brăs´yār), n. Woman's undergarment worn to support breasts. [F]

brass´|ÿ (-ah-), a. & n. **1.** Like brass in colour, sound, taste; impudent; pretentious; hence ~ILY² adv., ~ĬNESS n. **2.** i. (Also ~ĭe) brass-soled golf-club. [-Y²]

brăt, n. Child (usu. derog.). [c. 1500 Sc., perh. short. f. Sc. *bratchart* = *bratchet* hound, child, dim. of BRACH]

brătt´ice, brătt´icing, nn. (Coal-mining) wooden partition or shaft-lining. [ME *brutaske* etc. temporary breastwork on parapet f. ONF *breteske* = OF *bretesche* (mod. -*èche*) f. med. L *brittisca* of unkn. orig.]

brava´dō (-vah-), n. (pl. -*oes*, -*os*). Show of courage, bold front. [f. Sp. *bravada*, F *bravade*; see foll., -ADO(2), -ADE(1)]

brāve¹, a. & n. **1.** Courageous (*the* ~, & men); (archaic-literary) finely dressed, showy, worthy, honest, admirable; hence ~´LY² (-vl-) adv. **2.** n. Red-Indian warrior. [ME, f. F, f. It. *bravo*, f. Rom. *brabus, f. *brabarus, f. L *barbarus* BARBAROUS]

brāve², v.t. Defy, encounter with courage; ~ *it out*, carry oneself defiantly under suspicion or blame. [f. F *braver* see prec.]

brāv´erÿ, n. Daring; splendour, ostentation, finery. [16th c. also = *bravado*, f. F *braverie* or It. -*ia* (prec., -ERY)]

bra´vō¹ (-ah-), n. (pl. -*oes*, -*os*). Hired assassin, desperado. [It., see BRAVE¹]

bra´vō² (-ah-), n. & int. Cry of approval, esp. to actors etc. (occas. *brava, bravi*, to actress, company; also *bravissimo* superl.). [It. = BRAVE¹]

*bravur´a (-oora), n. Brilliant or ambitious execution, forced display; style of (esp.

vocal) music requiring exceptional powers. [It.]

brawl, v. i., & n. Squabble, (engage in) noisy quarrel; (of streams) murmur. Hence ~´ER¹ n. [ME, of unkn. orig.]

brawn, n. Muscle; pickled or potted boar's flesh. [ME *braun(e)* f. AF *braun*, OF *braon* (Pr. *bradon*) f. WG *brādo (*brādan* = G *braten* roast); sense *boar's flesh* is excl. E]

brawn´|ÿ, a. Strong, muscular. Hence ~ĬNESS n. [-Y²]

brăx´ÿ, n. & a. (Sc.). Splenic apoplexy in sheep; (adj.) suffering from ~, (of meat) of a ~ sheep (also abs. as n., = ~ meat). [orig. unkn.; cf. OE *bræc* catarrh]

bray¹, n., & v.i. & t. (Make) the cry, or a sound like the cry, of ass or trumpet; ~ *out*, utter harshly. [ME. f. OF *braire*]

bray², v.t. Pound, beat small, esp. with pestle & mortar. [ME, f. OF *breier* (=Pr.-Sp. *bregar*, It. *brigare*) f. Gmc *brekan BREAK¹]

brāze¹, v.t. Colour like brass. [16th c., not continuous w. late OE *brasian* (*bræs* BRASS), but prob. formed anew on anal. of *glaze, glass*]

brāze², v.t. Solder with alloy of brass & zinc. [f. F *braser* solder]

brāz´en¹, a. Made of brass; strong, yellow, or harsh-sounding, as brass; (also ~-*faced*) shameless, whence ~LY² adv.; ~ *age*, third stage in human deterioration (golden, silver, ~, iron). [OE *bræsen* (*bræs* BRASS+-EN³)]

brāz´en², v.t. ~ *out*, carry off impudently ('it', matter, deed); make shameless. [f. prec.]

brā´zier¹ (-zher), n. Worker in brass. Hence **brā´zi**ERY(1) n. [f. BRASS+-*ier*, on anal. of *glass, glazier*]

brā´zier²(-zher), n. Pan for holding lighted coal. [f. F *brasier* (*braise* hot coal)]

Brazil´, n. & a. (Also ~-*wood*) kinds of hard red S.-Amer. wood yielding dyes; ~-*nut*, large three-sided nut. [ME *brasile*, orig. Sp., Port., & F name of E.-Ind. wood, transferred to S.-Amer. similar species & thence to the country]

breach¹, n. (Naut.) breaking of waves (*clear* ~, rolling over without breaking; *clean* ~, carrying away of masts & everything on deck); breaking or neglect (*of* rule, duty, contract, someone's privileged rights, or promise, esp. to marry); ~ *of close*, trespass, *of the peace*, riot or affray; breaking of relations, separation, alienation, quarrel; broken state; gap, esp. in fortifications made by artillery (*stand in the* ~, bear brunt of attack, lit. or fig.); whale's leap clear out of water. [ME *breche* f. OF *breche* f. Frank. *breka, Gmc *brekan BREAK; superseding OE *bryce*, ME *bruche* (Gmc *brukiz f. *brekan)]

breach², v.t. & i. Break through, make gap in; (of whale) leap clear out of water. [f. prec.]

bread (-ĕd), n. Flour moistened, kneaded, & baked, usu. with leaven (*white*, BROWN, *black*, ~; *standard* ~, wheaten or mixed flours; *break* ~, take food, join in Lord's supper; ~ *& butter*, ~ slices spread with butter, necessary food, a livelihood; ~-*&-butter letter*, ROOFER; ~-*&-butter miss*, school-girl; ~ *& scrape*, stingily buttered bread; *ship's* ~ (Naut.), hard biscuit; ~ *& cheese*, simple fare, a livelihood; ~ *& milk*, broken ~ in boiling milk; ~ *& wine*, Lord's supper; ~ *of life* (see *John* vi. 35); *know which side* one's ~ *is buttered*, where one's interest lies; ~ *buttered on both sides*, easy prosperity; *take the* ~ *out of* one's *mouth*, take away his living by competition etc.; *eat the* ~ *of idleness*, *affliction*, be idle, afflicted; *daily* ~, livelihood; *make* one's ~, earn a living); ~-*basket*, (sl.) stomach; ~--*crumb*, inner part of loaf, ~ crumbled for use in cooking; ~-*fruit*, -*tree*, South-Sea tree with farinaceous fruit; *&~-line*, queue of poor people waiting to receive food; ~-*stuffs*, grain, flour; ~-*ticket* (entitling to ration); ~-*winner*, person (also art, trade, tool) that supports a family. Hence ~'LESS a. [OE *brēad*, OS *brōd*, OHG *brōt*, ON *brauth* f. Gmc *braudh-* of unkn. orig., the orig. Gmc name for bread being LOAF]

breadth (-ĕd-), n. Broadness, measure from side to side, (*to a hair's* ~, exactly); piece (of cloth etc.) of full ~; extent, distance, room; largeness (*of* mind, view, etc.), liberality, catholicity, toleration; bold effect. Hence ~'WAYS, -WISE, advv. [16th c., f. obs. *brede*, OE *brǣdu*, +-TH[1] on anal. of *length* etc.]

break[1] (-āk), v.t. & i. (*broke* & in Bible *brake*; *broken* occas. *broke* see BROKE[2]). **1.** (Of a whole) make or become discontinuous otherwise than by cutting, divide into two or more parts, (~ BULK[1]; ~ *a set*, sell parts separately; ~ *a lance with*, argue against; ~ *bread with*, be entertained by; ~ *Priscian's head*, use bad grammar; ~ *person on wheel*, of medieval execution; ~ *butterfly on wheel*, waste power; ~ *ground*, plough, begin siege, or fig. any, operations; ~ *the ice*, get over initial shyness or reserve; ~ *the ranks*, disorder by leaving them; *troops* ~, disperse in confusion; *clouds* ~, show gap); crack, graze, (~ *a head*); shatter; dislocate (neck; ~ *the neck* or *back of*, kill, dispose of); make by separating obstacles (*a way* etc.); penetrate by ~ing (~ *open*); interrupt, change, (*gloom, spell, journey, silence*, one's *fast*; *voice* ~s, with emotion or at manhood; disrupt (*broken bonds* etc.); solve (a cipher); (Boxing, usu. as command from referee) come out of a clinch; ~ *out*, open up (receptacle) & remove contents (esp. Naut., of cargo). **2.** (Of a part) disconnect or depart from something otherwise than by cutting (~ *bough from* tree, person *of* habit; ~ *with*,

have breach or cease relations with; ~ *an officer*, dismiss; ~ *piece off*; *ball* ~s, changes from its course, *back* from off, *in* from leg, side). **3.** Make a way, come, produce, with effort, suddenness, violence, etc. (~ *into* house, *out of* prison, *through* obstacles; ~ *in*, intrude, interpose; *disease, war*, ~ *out*; ~ *out*, exclaim; ~ *news*, *a jest*, reveal it; ~ WIND[1]; *day* ~s; *abscess* ~s); escape, emerge from, (prison, bounds, covert; ~ *free* or *loose*; ~ *away from*). **4.** Make or become weak, disable, discourage, ruin, destroy, cease, exhaust, (~ *the heart, heart* ~s; *frost, weather*, ~s; ~ *bank*, exhaust its resources; *merchant* ~s, is bankrupt; ~ *blow, fall*, weaken its effect; tame, discipline, overpower, (with *in, to*, or abs.; ~ *a horse*, ~ *a horse to the rein*; ~ *in child*; ~ one's *will, spirit*; ~ *resistance, a rebellion, a strike*); make of no effect, transgress, violate, neglect, (*law, Sabbath, contract, promise*, one's *word*). **5.**~ *down*, collapse, fail; demolish; analyse (cost, total, etc.) into its component items; ~ *even*, emerge with neither gain nor loss; ~ *off*, detach by ~ing, bring to an end; cease; ~ *out*, burst from restraint or concealment, release (flag when run up) from its trussed state, open up (receptacle) & remove contents (esp. Naut., of cargo); ~ *up*, dismiss, depart, (small, (of person) become feeble, show signs of decay. Hence ~'ABLE a. (also as n. pl., things easily broken), ~'AGE(3) n. [OE *brecan*, OS *brekan*, OHG *brehhan*, Goth. *brikan* f. Gmc *brekan*]

break[2] (-āk), n. Breaking; ~ *of day*, dawn; (Cricket) deviation of ball on pitching (~-*back*, f. off side); (Billiards) points scored continuously; gap, broken place, interruption of continuity; short spell of recreation between lessons; (colloq.) a chance; (Mus.) point of separation between different registers of voice; irregularity; *a bad* ~ (colloq.), unfortunate remark or ill-judged action. [f. prec.]

break[3] (-āk), n. Carriage-frame with no body for breaking in young horses; large wagonette. [f. BREAK[1] or = brake framework, of unkn. orig.]

break'down (-āk-), n. Collapse, stoppage; failure of health or power; analysis of cost etc. into its component items; Negro dance. [f. BREAK[1], DOWN[3]]

break'er[1] (-āk-), n. In vbl senses (esp. in comb. as *horse*-~); also, heavy ocean-wave breaking on coast or over reefs. [-ER[1]]

break'er[2] (-āk-), n. (naut.). Small keg. [f. Sp. *barreca*, *barrica* cask]

break'fast (brĕk-), n., & v.i. & t. (Take, entertain at) first meal of day. Hence ~LESS a. [BREAK[1] interrupt + FAST n.]

break'neck (-āk-), a. Dangerous (~ *pace, road, climb*).

break-up (-āk-), n. Disintegration, decay, collapse, dispersal. [f. phr. *to break up*]

break'water (-åkwaw-), n. Object break-ing, mole etc. built to break, force of waves.

bream[1], n. Yellowish arch-backed fresh-water fish; (also *sea*-~) a salt-water variety of this. [ME *breme* f. OF *bre(s)me* f. WG, as OS *bressemo* (= OHG *brahsema*, G *brassen*)]

bream[2], v.t. Clear (ship's bottom) by singeing with burning furze etc. [perh. f. Du. *brem* BROOM, furze]

breast[1] (-ĕst), n. Either milk-secreting organ in woman, corresponding rudiment in man, (occas. of beast's dug); (fig.) source of nourishment; upper front of human body or of coat, dress, etc.; corresponding part of animals; heart, emotions, thoughts, (*make a clean ~ of*, confess); ~'*bone*, thin flat vertical bone in chest connecting ribs; ~-*drill*, -*hoe*, etc., pushed with ~; ~-*fed*, -*feeding*; ~-*harness*, with ~-band instead of collar; ~-*high*, high as the ~, (submerged) high the ~, (of scent) so strong that hounds race with heads up; ~-*pin*, jewelled etc,. worn in tie; ~'*plate*, piece of armour covering ~, lower shell of turtle, tortoise, etc., inscription-plate on coffin; ~ *stroke*, stroke made while swimming on the ~ by extending the arms in front & sweeping them back; ~-*wall*, confining a bank of earth; ~-*wheel*, water-wheel with water admitted near axle; ~'*work*, temporary defence or parapet a few feet high. Hence ~'ED[2] a. [OE *brēost*, OS *briost*, ON *brjóst* f. Gmc **breustam*, also OHG *brust*, Goth. *brusts* (Gmc **brusts*)]

breast[2] (-ĕst), v.t. Oppose the breast to, face, contend with, (waves, hill). [f. prec.]

breast'sŭmmer (-ĕst-), **brĕss'ŭmmer**, n. Beam across broad opening, sustaining superstructure. [BREAST[1] + SUMMER[2]]

breath (-ĕth), n. Exhalation as per-ceptible to sight or smell; slight move-ment of air; whiff of perfume etc.; air taken into and expelled from lungs (*draw* ~, breathe, live; *a ~ of fresh air*; *spend*, *waste*, ~, talk vainly; *keep ~ to cool porridge*, abstain from talk; ~ *of life*, *nostrils*, a necessity; *take away* person's ~, render him breathless with astonish-ment); respiration (*catch*, *hold*, one's ~, in fear or absorbing emotion); one re-spiration (*say inconsistent things in one or the same* ~); power of breathing (*out of* ~, not able to breathe quick enough; *take* ~, pause, rest); whisper, murmur, (*not a ~ heard*; also *below* one's ~, in a whisper). [OE *brǣth* f. WG **brǣth-*, whence OHG *brādam* (G *brodem*)]

breathe (-ēdh), v.i. & t. Use the lungs: live; seem alive; take breath, pause, (~ *again*, *freely*, recover from fear etc., be at ease); sound, speak, (of wind) blow, softly (~ *upon*, tarnish, taint); send out (*new life into*; *fragrance*; ~ one's *last breath* or *last*, die); take in (~ *foul*, *whole-some*, *air*); utter softly, also passionately

(~ *strife*), exhibit (~ *simplicity*); allow to ~, give rest to; force to ~, exercise, tire. [ME *brethen* f. prec.]

breath'er (-ĕdh-), n. In vbl senses; esp., short spell of exercise; brief pause for rest. [-ER[1]]

breath'ing[1] (-ĕdh-), n. In vbl senses; esp.: (Gk Gram.) *rough*, *smooth*, ~, signs ('), ('), indicating that initial vowel is or is not aspirated; ~-*space*, time to breathe, pause. [-ING[1]]

breath'ing[2] (-ĕdh-), a. In vbl senses; esp., lifelike (statue etc.) [-ING[2]]

breath'lĕss (-ĕth-), a. Lifeless; panting; holding the breath; unstirred by wind. [-LESS]

breath'lĕsslў (-ĕth-), adv. Pantingly; in suspense. [-LY[2]]

breath'|ў (-ĕth-), a. (Of singing-voice) not clear-cut at beginning of sound, using breath before vocal chords are tense. Hence ~iNESS n. [-Y[2]]

brĕc'cia (-cha), n. Rock of angular stones etc. cemented by lime etc. [It., whence F *brèche* f. Gmc = BREAK]

bred. See BREED[1].

breech, n., & v.t. 1. pl. ~*es* (-ĭch'ĭz) or *pair of* ~*es*, short trousers fastened below knee (*Breeches Bible*, Geneva Bible of 1560 with ~*es* for *aprons* in *Gen.* iii. 7) and (now) used esp. for riding or in court cos-tume etc. (cf. KNICKERBOCKERS); (loosely) trousers or knickerbockers; *wear the* ~*es*, of wife ruling her husband; (sing., arch.) posterior. 2. (Gunnery) part of gun behind bore, back part of rifle or gun barrel; ~-*block*, closing ~ aperture in guns; ~-*loader*, -*loading*, (gun) loaded at ~, not through muzzle; ~*es-buoy*, lifebuoy with canvas ~*es* for user's legs. 3. v.t. (arch.). Put (boy) into ~*es* instead of petticoats. Hence ~ED[2] a., (-ĭcht) wearing ~*es*, (-ēcht) having a ~. [OE *brēc* pl., OS *brōk*, OHG *bruoh*, ON *brók* f. Gmc **brōks*; relation to Gaul. *brāca*, whence L *braca*, doubtful; double pl. *breeches* since ME]

breech'ing (-ĭch-), n. Leather strap round shaft-horse's or wheeler's hind-quarters for pushing back; (Naut.) rope securing gun to ship's side. [f. prec. + -ING[1]]

breech'lĕss (-ĭch-), a. Without breeches. [-LESS]

breed[1], v.t. & i. (*brĕd*). Bear, generate, (offspring); cherish in womb or egg; propagate; be pregnant; yield, produce, result in; make propagate, raise, (cattle, domestic animals); train up; fit for being, adapt *to*, (~ *him a lawyer*, *bred to the law*), bring up; arise, spread; ~ *in & in*, always marry near relations; *what is bred in the bone*, hereditary traits. Hence ~'ER[1] n. (~*er reactor*, nuclear reactor that can create more fissile material than it con-sumes in the chain reaction). [OE *brēdan*, OHG *bruotan* f. WG **brōdjan* f. **brōd-* BROOD]

breed², n. Race, stock, strain; family with hereditary qualities. [f. prec.]

breed'ing, n. In vbl senses; esp., result of training, behaviour, good manners. [-ING¹]

breeze¹, n. Gad-fly. [OE *briosa* of unkn. orig.]

breeze², n., & v.i. 1. Gentle wind; wind off land, or sea, at certain hours; (sl.) quarrel, display of temper. 2. v.i. (sl.). Go like a ~, move *along* in lively manner. Hence ~'LESS (-zl-) a. [16th c. *brize*, *brieze*, app. f. OSp., Pg. *briza* NE wind, whence (18th c.) F *brise*; connexion w. F *bise* doubtful]

breeze³, n. Small cinders used with cement in making ~ *blocks* (light-weight concrete building blocks). [f. F BRAISE]

breez'|ly, a. Wind-swept; pleasantly windy; fresh, lively, jovial. Hence ~ILY² adv., ~INESS n. [-Y²]

Bré'hon, n. & a. Ancient Irish judge; ~ *law*, Irish code abolished under James I. [f. OIr. *brithem* judge]

Brĕn, n. (In full ~ *gun*) a light-weight machine-gun; ~ *carrier*, small bullet-proof tracked vehicle. [f. *Brno* in Czechoslovakia (where orig. made) + *En*-field in England]

brĕnt(-goose), **brănt-**, n. Smallest species of wild goose, visiting Britain in winter. [deriv. & orig. application uncert.; cf. ON *brandgás*, G *brandgans*]

brĕr, n. (U.S. Negro dial. contraction for) brother (esp. in beast-fable personifications, as *B~ Fox, Rabbit*).

brĕss'ümmer. See BREASTSUMMER.

breth'ren (-ĕdhrĭn). See BROTHER.

Brĕt'on, a. & n. (Native or language) of Brittany in France. [F, = BRITON]

Brĕtwal'da (-ŏl-), n. Lord of the Britons, title given to Egbert & Old Eng. kings of various States who held nominal or real supremacy over the rest.

brĕve, n. (Hist.) authoritative letter from sovereign or pope; (Mus.) note = two semibreves now rarely used (*alla* ~, time signature indicating 2 or 4 minim beats in bar); short prosody mark (˘) in printing. [var. of ME *bref(e)* BRIEF¹]

brĕv'ĕt, n., & v.t. Document conferring a privilege from sovereign or government, esp. rank without corresponding pay in army (~ *rank*, ~ *major*); honorary, nominal, position; (vb) confer ~ rank on. [ME f. OF, dim. of *bref* BRIEF¹]

brevi-, comb. form in scientific terms of L *brevis* short, as *brevirostrate* short-beaked.

brĕv'iary, n. (R.-C. Ch.) book containing the Divine Office for each day, to be recited by those in orders. [f. L *breviarium* summary (*brevis* short, -ARY¹)]

brĕvier', n. Printing-type size between bourgeois & minion. [f. Du. or G *brevier* f. L *breviarium* (prec.)]

brĕv'itў, n. Shortness of expression, conciseness; short span (*of* life). [f. AF

brevete f. L *brevitatem* (*brevis* short, -TY)]

brew¹ (-ōō), v.t. & i. Make (beer etc.) by infusion, boiling, & fermentation (*drink as you have ~ed*, take consequences); make (tea, punch) by infusion or mixture; undergo these processes; concoct, bring about, set in train, grow to ripeness, fester, gather force, (usu. of evil results; *mischief is ~ing, ~ rebellion*); ~-*house*, = brewery (but now less used). Hence ~'ER¹, ~'ERY (3), (-ōō-), nn. [OE *brēowan*, OS *breuwan*, OHG *briuwan*, ON *brugga* f. Gmc **breuwan*]

brew² (-ōō), n. Process of brewing; amount brewed at once; quality of stuff brewed (*a good strong* ~). [f. prec.]

brew'age (-ōō-), n. Concocted drink; process or result of concoction (lit. & fig.). [-AGE]

brew'is (-ōō-), n. Broth (arch. & dial.). [MF *browes* f. OF *brouez* nom. of *brouet* dim. of *bro, breu* f. WG **broth-*; see BROSE, BROTH]

‖ **Brew'ster Sĕ'ssions** (-ōō-; -shns), n. Sessions for issue of licences to trade in alcoholic liquors. [f. obs. *brewster* (orig. female) brewer, see -STER]

bri'ar. See BRIER.

Briär'eus, n. Many-handed person. [Gk mythol.]

bribe¹, n. Money etc. offered to procure (often illegal or dishonest) action in favour of the giver. [f. foll.]

brib|e², v.t. Pervert by gifts or other inducements the action or judgement of; (abs.) practise bribery. Hence ~'ER¹, ~EE', ~ABIL'ITY, ~'ERY(4), nn., ~'ABLE a. [ME, f. OF *briber, brimber* beg etc., of unkn. orig.]

bric'a-brăc, n. Curiosities, old furniture, china, fans, etc. [F, perh. = *de bric et de broc* by hook or by crook]

brick¹, n. & a. 1. Clay kneaded, moulded, & baked by fire or sun; block (usu. rectangular & about 9 in.×4⅜×2⅝) of this (*like a ton of* ~s colloq., with crushing weight or force); ~-shaped loaf, block of tea, etc.; child's toy building-block; (sl.), generous or loyal person; *drop a* ~ (sl.), commit an indiscretion; ~-*bat*, piece of ~, esp. as missile [BAT²]; ~-*dust*, powdered ~, colour like it; ~-*field*, -*kiln*, in which ~s are made, baked; ~-*layer*, workman building in ~; ~-*work*, building in ~; hence (rare) ~'EN⁵ a. 2. adj. Built of ~. [15th c., f. MLG, MDu. *bricke, brik(e)*, of unkn. orig., whence also F *brique*]

brick², v.t. ~ *up*, block (window etc.) with brickwork (& used with other advv.). [f. prec.]

brick'ў, a. Littered with, coloured or looking like, bricks. [-Y²]

bric'ole (-ĭkl), n. Stroke off wall or cushion in tennis & billiards. [16th c., F, of unkn. orig.]

brid'al, n. & a. 1. Wedding-feast, wedding. 2. adj. Of bride or wedding (~

cheer, veil); hence ~LY[2] adv. [=*bride* ALE or festivity; OE *brȳd-ealo*; the prevailing adj. use results f. confusion with -AL]

bride[1], n. Woman on her wedding-day & for some days or weeks before & after it; ~'*cake*, rich cake eaten at wedding, sent round to friends etc. [OE *brȳd*, OS *brūd*, OHG *brūt*, ON *brúthr*, Goth. *brūths* f. Gmc *brūdhiz*]

bride[2], n. Delicate network connecting the patterns in lace; bonnet-string. [F, = BRIDLE[1], f. Teut.]

bride'groom (-dg-), n. Man at or soon before or after his marriage. [OE *brȳd-guma*, f. BRIDE[1] +*guma* man, = OS *brūdi-*, OHG *brūtigomo*, ON *brúthgumi*; later assim. to GROOM]

brides'maid (-dz-), n. Unmarried woman (usu. one of several) attending bride at wedding. [16th c. *bridemaid*, cf. *bridegroom*]

brides'man (-dz-), n. Bridegroom's attendant, best man. [earlier *brideman*, cf. prec.]

|| **bride'well** (-dw-), n. House of correction, gaol. [St Bride's Well, near the London ~]

bridge[1], n. (northern form, in writers for local colour, *brig*). Structure carrying road or path across stream, ravine, road, etc. (~ *of boats*, over boats moored abreast; ~ *of gold*, golden ~, easy retreat provided for beaten enemy); (Naut.) raised platform from which ship is conned; upper bony part of nose; movable piece over which strings of violin etc. are stretched; (Billiards) support for cue formed with left hand; ~-*head*, post held on far side of river giving one access to enemy's position; ~-*train*, Mil. Engineers with material for building floating ~s. Hence ~'LESS (-jl-) a. [OE *brycg*, OS *bruggia*, OHG *brucca*, ON *bryggja* f. Gmc *brugjo*]

bridge[2], v.t. Span as, with, or as with, a bridge. [OE *brycgian* see prec.]

bridge[3], n. Card-game of Russian origin resembling whist, in which a player looks on while his exposed hand is played by his partner; AUCTION ~; CONTRACT[1] ~. [orig. unkn.]

bri'dle[1], n. Head-gear of harness, including head-stall, bit, & rein (*give horse the ~, lay ~ on his neck*, abandon control; *horse going well up to ~*, willing goer); restraint, curb; (Naut.) mooring--cable; (Physiol.) ligament checking motion of a part; ~-*bridge, -path, road*, etc., fit for riders but not for vehicles. [OE *bridel*, OHG *brittel*, f. Gmc *bregdan* see BRAID[2] +-LE(1)]

bri'dle[2], v.t. & i. Put bridle on (horse etc.); curb, hold *in*, bring under control; express offence, vanity, etc., by throwing up head & drawing in chin (often ~ *up*). [OE *bridlian* see prec.]

bridoon', n. Snaffle & rein of military bridle. [f. F *bridon* (BRIDE[2], -OON)]

Brie (brē), n. A soft cheese. [~, in northern France]

brief[1], n. Pope's letter on matter of discipline to person or community (less formal than bull); || (Law) summary of facts & law-points of a case drawn up for counsel (*hold ~ for*, be retained as counsel for, argue in favour of); size of writing -paper, typewriter, etc.; instructions given to air crews etc.; *watching-~*, of barrister who watches case for client indirectly concerned; || ~-*case*, small leather hand bag; || *a ~*, piece of employment for barrister, whence ~'LESS a. [ME & OF *bref* f. L *breve* dispatch, note, neut. of *brevis* short]

brief[2], v.t. (Law) reduce (facts etc.) to a brief; instruct (barrister) by brief, employ; instruct (air crews etc.) with regard to raid etc. (~-*ing-room*, where such in structions are given); instruct thoroughly in advance. [f. prec.]

brief[3], a. & n. Of short duration; concise, *be ~*, speak shortly; *in ~*, in short; (pl., colloq.) shorts, women's panties. Hence ~'LY[2] adv., ~'NESS n. [ME & OF *bref* f. L *brevis* short]

bri'er[1], **bri'ar**, n. (also *brere* arch.) Prickly bush, esp. of wild rose; *sweet ~*, wild rose with fragrant leaves & flowers, ~-*rose*, dog-rose. Hence ~-Y[2] a. [OE *brǽr*, *brēr*, of unkn. orig.; cf. *frere*, FRIAR]

bri'er[2], **bri'ar**, n. The white heath, of which the root is used for tobacco pipes, pipe made from this root. [orig. (c. 1859) *bruyer* f. F *bruyère* heath]

brig[1], n. Two-masted square-rigged vessel, but with additional lower fore-&--aft sail on gaff & boom to mainmast. [abbr. of BRIGANTINE]

brig[2]. Northern form of BRIDGE[1].

brigāde'[1], n. **1.** Subdivision of army, varying in different countries & times; infantry unit consisting usu. of 3 battalions (with freq. a regiment of field artillery) & forming part of a division, corresponding armoured unit; || *the B~* (of Guards). **2.** Organized or uniformed band of workers (*Boys', Church*, etc., *B~*, organizations on military model for disciplining & occupying boys etc.). [F, f. It. *brigata* company (*brigare* brawl, *briga* strife); see -ADE]

brigāde'[2], v.t. Form into brigade or brigades; join (regiment etc.) *with* others into a brigade. [f. prec.]

brigadier', n. (Formerly *Brigadier* -*General*) officer commanding a brigade, (titular rank granted to) staff officer of similar standing. [F, see -IER]

brig'and, n. Bandit, robber. Hence or cogn. ~AGE(3), ~ISM(2), nn., ~ISH[1] a. [ME f. OF, f. It. *brigante* (*brigare* see BRIGADE[1])]

brig'antine (-ēn), n. Two-masted vessel with square-sailed fore-mast & fore-&--aft mainmast. [16th c. -*din(e)* f. F

brigandin (now -tin) f. It. *brigantino* f.
brigante see prec.]

bright[1] (-it), a. Emitting or reflecting
much light, shining; lit up with joy,
hope, etc.; vivid (~ *red* etc.); illustrious,
vivacious, quick-witted, (often iron.;
~ *young things*). Hence ~'EN[5] v.t. & i.,
~'ISH[1] (2) a., ~'LY[2] adv., ~'NESS n., (-it·).
[OE *beorht*, OS, OHG *beraht*, ON *bjartr*,
Goth. *bairhts* f. Gmc *berhtaz*]

bright[2] (-it), adv.=brightly (*shine* ~, ~·
-beaming, etc.). [OE *beorhte* (prec.)]

Bright's disease' (-its; -zēz), n. Granular
degeneration of the kidneys. [Dr R.
Bright (d. 1858)]

brill, n. Flat-fish resembling turbot.
[orig. unkn.]

brill'i|ant[1] (-lya-), a. Bright, sparkling;
illustrious, striking; talented, showy.
Hence ~ANCE, ~ANCY, nn., ~antLY[2] adv.,
(-lya-). [f. F *brillant* part. of *briller* shine,
f. It. *brillare*, of unkn. orig.]

brill'iant[2] (-lya-), n. Diamond of finest
cut & brilliance (~ shape has two horizontal tables, joined by facets); a size
of TYPE. [f. F as prec. used as n.]

brill'iantine (-yantēn), n. Cosmetic for
hair. [f. F *brillantine* see BRILLIANT[1]
+-INE[4]]

brim[1], n. Edge or lip of cup, bowl, or
hollow; projecting edge of hat; ~-*full*,
to the ~. Hence ~'LESS, ~MED[2] (-md),
aa. [ME *brimme* of unkn. orig.; cf. ON
barmr brim, MHG *brem* (G *bräme*)
border]

brim[2], v.t. & i. (-mm-). Fill, be full, to the
brim (lit. & fig.); ~ *over*, overflow. [f.
prec.]

brimm'er, n. Full cup. [BRIM[2]+-ER[1]]

brim'stone, n. (Old name for) sulphur
(||~ & *treacle*, nursery medicine); fuel
of hell-fire; ~ *butterfly*, *moth*, sulphur-
·coloured species. Hence **brim'stony**[2] a.
[ME *brin-*, *bren-*, etc. (BURN[2]+STONE)]

brin'dled (-dld), **brin'dle**, a. Brownish
or tawny with streaks of other colour.
[*brindled* (whence back form. *brindle*) alt.
of *brinded* (also *branded*) f. (15th c.)
brended f. *brend*, perh. of Sc. orig.]

brine[1], n. Salt water; the sea; tears
(poet.); ~-*pan*, iron vessel or shallow pit
for getting salt by evaporation. Hence
brin'y[2] a. (*the briny*, sl., the sea). [OE
brȳne of unkn. orig.; cf. MDu. *brine*, Du.
brijn]

brine[2], v.t. Steep or pickle in, or wet
with, brine. [f. prec.]

bring, v.t. & i. (*brought*, pr. -awt). **1.**
Cause to come, come with or conveying
whether by carrying, leading, impelling,
or attracting, (*take* expresses the corresponding notions with *go* for *come*); cause,
result in; prefer (charge), adduce (argument); ~ *home to*, convict or convince
of; ~ *into play*, cause to operate; ~ *into
the world*, give birth to; cause to become
(~ *low*); ~ *to bear*, apply (influence etc.);
~ *to book*, exact account from (offender);

~ *to mind*, recall; ~ *to pass*, cause to
happen; persuade (*cannot ~ myself to
believe*). **2.** ~ *about*, cause to happen,
reverse (ship); ~ *back*, call to mind; ~
down, kill or wound, cause penalty to
alight *on*, abase, lower (price), continue
(record) *to* a point, (Theatr.) ~ *down the
house*, elicit tumultuous applause, ~
forth, give birth to, cause; ~ *forward*,
carry sum of page's figures to next page,
~ *in*, introduce (custom), produce as pro
fit, adduce, pronounce (*guilty*, *not guilty*),
~ *off*, rescue from wreck etc., conduct
(enterprise) to success; ~ *on*, lead to,
cause discussion of; ~ *out*, express,
exhibit clearly, introduce (girl) to society,
publish; ~ *over*, convert; ~ *round*,
restore to consciousness, win over (*to*
other person's opinion); ~ *through*, save
(sick person); ~ *to*, check motion of,
come to a stop, restore to consciousness;
~ *under*, subdue; ~ *up*, educate, rear,
sue in court, anchor (ship), come to a
stop, call attention to, cause (person) to
rise & speak, continue (accounts etc.)
to a further point; ~ *up the rear*, come
last. [OE, OS, OHG *bringan*, Goth.
briggan f. Gmc *brengan*]

brink, n. Edge of steep place or abyss (*on
~ of grave*, soon to die); border of water,
esp. when steep (*shiver on the* ~, hesitate
to plunge, usu. fig.); verge (*of* discovery,
ruin, eternity, etc.); ~'*manship*, art of
advancing to the very ~ of war but not
engaging in it. [ME also *brenk*, f. Scand.,
cf. OIcel. *brekka* slope (Sw., Da. *brink*),
MLG *brink* edge of field, MDu. *brinc*]

bri'o (-ēō), n. Vivacity. [It.]

briquette' (-kĕt), **bri'quet** (-kĕt), n.
Block of compressed coal-dust. [F (-*ette*),
dim. of *brique* BRICK]

brisk[1], a. Active, lively, (usu. of movement; ~ *pace*, *trade*, *wind*, etc.); enlivening, keen, (champagne, air, etc.). Hence
~'LY[2] adv., ~'NESS n. [16th c., f. F
BRUSQUE]

brisk[2], v.t. & i. Make or become brisk
(usu. with *up*). [f. prec.]

brisk'et, n. Breast of animals (esp. as
joint of meat). [15th c. *brusket(te)* f. OF
bruschet etc. (mod. *bréchet*)]

bri'stle[1] (-isl), n. One of stiff hairs on
hog's back & sides; short stiff hair of other
animals, man's short-cropped beard, or
plants; *set up* one's, another's, ~*s*, show
or rouse temper. Hence **bri'stly**[2] (-isli),
bri'stlED[2] (-isld), aa. [ME *brustel* f OE
byrst (= OHG, ON *burst*)+-LE (1)]

bri'stle[2] (-isl), v.i. & t. (Cause to) stand up
right (hair etc.), raise or rise like bristles
or into roughness, (often with *up*); show
temper, prepare for fight; be thickly set
with hair, difficulties, etc. [f. prec.]

bris'(t)ling, n. A small sardine-like fish
[Norw. *brisling* sprat]

Bris'tol, n. (attrib.). ~ *board*, kind of
cardboard for drawing on; (*shipshape &*)
~ *fashion* (Naut., & transf.), with all in

good order: ~ *cream, milk*, **P**, kinds of sherry.

Brit′ain (-ĭtn), n. (Also *Great* ~) England, Wales, & Scotland; *North* ~, Scotland; *Greater* ~ (descriptive, not official), Gt ~ & the colonies. [ME *Bretayne* f. OF *Bretaigne* f. L *Brittania*]

Britănn′ia (-ya), n. Personification of Britain; ~ *metal*, alloy of tin & regulus of antimony resembling silver. [L, anciently *Brittan(n)ia* = Gk *Brettania* f. *Brettanoi* Britons; see BRITISH]

Britănn′ic, a. Of Britain (chiefly in phr. *Her* or *His* ~ *Majesty*). [f. L *Britannicus* or F *britannique* (prec., -IC)]

Brit′icism, n. = BRITISHISM. [U.S. wd, f. *Brit*(ish) + -ISM(4), after *Gallicism*]

Brit′ish, a. Of the ancient Britons & their language; of Great Britain or its inhabitants (esp. in political or imperial connexion, & in botany etc.); *the* ~, ~ *soldiers, people*, etc.; ~ *Academy*, chartered body of 200 for promotion of historical, philosophical, & philological studies; ~ *Association* (for advancement of science); ~ COMMONWEALTH (*of Nations*); ~ *Expeditionary* Force (abbr. B.E.F.), any of the armies sent abroad in wartime, esp. Sir J. French's original force in France in 1914; ~ *Museum*, national museum of antiquities, books, natural history, etc., in London; ~ *warm*, kind of short military overcoat. [OE *Brettisc, Bryttisc.* f. *Bret, Bryt* (f. OCelt. **Brett-, *Britt-*) + -ISH¹]

Brit′isher, n. (U.S. etc. term for) British subject of British descent. [-ER¹; cf. *foreigner*]

Brit′ishism, n. Idiom used in Gt Britain & not in U.S. etc. [-ISM (4)]

Brit′on, n. One of the race found by Romans in England; native of Great Britain or the British Empire (poet., melodramatic, etc.). [ME & OF *breton* f. L *Brittōnem* nom. *Britto*, f. OCelt. name, see BRITISH]

brit′tle, a. Apt to break, fragile. Hence ~NESS (-ln-) n. [ME *britul* f. *brut-* stem of OE *brēotan* break]

brit′zka, -tzska, (-ĭtska), n. Open carriage with calash top & space for reclining. [f. Pol. *bryczka* dim. of *bryka* wagon]

brize (-ēz). = BREEZE¹.

broach¹, n. Roasting-spit; church spire rising from tower without parapet; boring-bit. [ME & OF *broche* f. Rom. *brocca spike f. L *brocc(h)us* in *brocci dentes* projecting teeth; see BROOCH]

broach², v.t. Pierce (cask) to draw liquor, begin drawing (liquor); open & start using (bale, box, cargo, etc.); begin discussion of, moot, (subject). [f. prec.]

broach³, v.t. & i. (Usu. ~ *to*) veer or cause (ship) to veer & present side to wind & waves. [c. 1700; orig. unkn.]

broad (-awd), a., n., & adv. **1.** Large across, wide, not narrow; = in breadth (*6 ft* ~); extensive (~ *acres*); full, clear, main, explicit, (~ *daylight, facts, distinction, hint*); coarse (~ *story*); downright in sound, not mincing, (~ *Yorkshire, Scotch*); generalized (~ *rule*); tolerant (B~ *Church*, churchmen favouring comprehension & not pressing doctrines); bold in effect or style; *as* ~ *as it is long*, indifferent; ‖ ~ ARROW; ~ *bean* (the common flat variety); ‖~′*cloth*, fine plain-wove double-width dressed black cloth [phr. in Act of Parl. 1482 kept as name for quality rather than width]; ~ GAUGE; ~′*mind′ed(ness)*, (the condition of) being tolerant in thought or opinion; ~′*sheet*, large sheet of paper printed on one side only; ~′*side*, ship's side above water between bow & quarter (~*side on, to*, with this presented), (discharge of) all guns on one side of ship, also = ~sheet; ~′-*silk, -weaver*, (of) silk in piece not in ribbons; ~′*sword*, ~-bladed cutting-sword. **2.** n. The ~ part (~ *of the back*); ‖ (E. Anglia) large piece of water formed by widening of river; (sl.) woman, prostitute. **3.** adv. = ~ly (*speak* ~, ~ *awake*); ~-*blown*, in full bloom. Hence ~′EN⁶ v.t. & i., ~′LY², ~′WAYS, ~′WISE, advv. [OE *brād*, OS *brēd*, OHG *breit*, ON *breithr*, Goth. *braiths* f. Gmc *braidhaz]

broad′cast (-awdkah-), a., adv., v.t. & i. (past -*casted*, p.p. -*cast*), & n. (Of seed) scattered freely, not in drills or rows, (adv.) in this manner, (v.i. & t.) sow thus, (all also fig. of information, propaganda, etc.); (Radio, v.t.) disseminate (news, music, any audible matter) by wireless telephony, (v.i.) speak, sing, play, etc., for such transmission, (n., esp. attrib.) the practice etc. of ~ing (*today's* ~ *programme*). [f. prec. + *cast* p.p.]

Broad′moor (braw-), n. Asylum in Berkshire for criminal lunatics.

broad′ness (-aw-), n. (Superseded by *breadth*, exc. in sense) indelicacy (of speech). [-NESS]

Brŏb′dĭngnăg, n. Land of giants. Hence ~IAN (-ăg²) a. [Swift, *Gulliver's Travels*]

brocade′¹, n. Fabric woven with raised patterns; Indian cloth of gold & silver. [f. Sp. & Port. *brocado* f. It. *broccato*]

brocade′², v.t. Work with raised pattern. [f. prec.]

brŏc′(c)olĭ, n. Cultivated cabbage with edible flower head, hardy variety of cauliflower. [It., pl. of *broccolo* cabbage-top dim. of *brocco* see BROACH¹]

‖ **broch** (-ŏχ), n. Prehistoric circular stone tower in the north of Scotland. [f. ON *borg* castle]

brō′ché (-shā), a. & n. (Of fabrics, esp. silk) embossed, woven with a pattern on the surface; (n.) such fabric. [F, p.p. of *brocher* stitch]

brŏchure′ (-shoor), n. Stitched booklet, pamphlet. [F]

brŏck, n. Badger; stinking fellow. [OE *broc* f. Celt.]

brŏck′ĕt, n. Second-year stag with

straight horns. [ME, f. AF *broquet* f. *broque* (= OF *broche* BROACH[1]) +-*et* -ET[1]; cf. F *brocard*]

broderie Anglaise (brŏd'rĭ ahṅglāz'), n. Open embroidery on white linen or cambric. [F, = English embroidery]

brogue[1] (-ōg), n. Rude Irish & Scotch--Highland shoe of untanned leather; *fishing-~s*, waterproof leggings with feet; nailed & goloshed shoe for golf etc. [f. Gael. & Ir. *brōg* f. OIr. *brōce* shoe]

brogue[2] (-ōg), n. Dialectal, esp. Irish, accent. [orig. unkn.; perh. allusively f. prec.]

broid'er, v.t., **broid'erȳ**, n. (Poet. & arch. for) EMBROIDER(Y).

broil[1], n. Quarrel, tumult. [f. obs. vb *broil* mix, quarrel (cf. EMBROIL) f. OF *brouiller*]

broil[2], v.t. & i. Cook (meat) or be cooked on fire or gridiron; make, be, very hot (of person in sun etc.). Hence ~*ER*[1] n., young chicken reared for ~ing. [ME *brule* f. OF *bruler*; ME *bruyle*, *broyle* corresp. formally to OF *bruillir* which, however, is intr.]

broil[3], n. Broiled meat. [f. prec.]

brōke[1], n. Short-stapled wool on certain parts of fleece. [OE *broc*·f. *brecan* BREAK]

brōke[2], p.p. of BREAK, still often used in some spec. senses, as = *ruined* (esp., sl., *stony-~*), & *dismissed the service*.

brōk'en, a. In vbl senses of BREAK[1]; also or esp., ~ *meat* etc., remains; ~ *tea*, siftings; ~ *water*, choppy; ~ *ground*, uneven; ~ *sleep*, intermittent; ~ *weather*, uncertain; ~ *English*, imperfect; ~--*hearted*, crushed by grief; ~ *man*, reduced to despair; ~ REED; ~ *time*, (esp. working) time which has been reduced by interruptions; ~-*winded*, (of horse) incapacitated for hard work by ruptured air--cells. [p.p. of BREAK]

brōk'enlȳ, adv. Spasmodically, by jerks, with breaks. [prec. +-LY[2]]

brōk'er, n. ‖ Dealer in second-hand furniture etc.; middleman in bargains; agent, commissioner; ‖ person licensed to sell or appraise distrained goods. Hence ~AGE(4) n. [ME & AF *brocour*= OF *brocheor* broacher, retailer of wine (BROACH[1])]

brōk'ing, n. Broker's trade, acting as broker. [f. obs. vb *broke* cf. prec.]

‖ **brŏll'ȳ**, n. (sl.). Umbrella. [abbr.]

brōm'al, n. Compound produced by action of bromine on alcohol. [BROM(INE) +*al-* of ALCOHOL]

brōm'ic, a. Containing bromine in chem. combination. Hence **brōm'ATE**[1](3) n. [BROMINE, -IC]

brōm'ide, n. Compound (see -IDE) of bromine, used in various preparations as sedative; a commonplace bore, trite remark, conventionalism, (orig. U.S. sl.); ~ *paper*, photographic printing & enlarging paper coated with silver ~ emulsion. [foll. +-IDE]

brōm'ine, n. Non-metallic element, a poisonous dark liquid with rank smell. Hence **brōm'IZE** (5) v.t., **brōm'ISM** (5) n. [f. F *brome* f. Gk *brōmos* stink +-INE[5]]

bromo-, brōm-, comb. forms of *bromine* as in *bromobenzoic, bromacetic*. [-O-]

brŏn'chĭ, brŏn'chĭa, (-ngk-), nn. pl. (From -*i*, with sing. -*us*) two main divisions of wind-pipe; (-*ia*) ramifications of these in lungs. Hence **brŏn'chĭ**AL a., **brŏn'chĭ**O-, **brŏn'cho**- (-ngk-) comb. forms, **brŏn'cho**- PNEUMONIA, **brŏnchŏT'OMIST**, -ŏT'OMY, nn. [LL; f. Gk *brogkhia*]

brŏnch|**it'ĭs** (-ngk-), n. Inflammation of bronchial mucous membrane. Hence ~**it'IC** a. [prec. +-ITIS]

brŏn'cō (-ngk-), n. (pl. -*os*). Wild or half--tamed horse of California etc.; ~-*buster* (sl.), breaker in of ~s. [Sp., = rough]

Brŏntosaur'us, n. Genus of huge prehistoric dinosaurian reptiles of the Jurassic & Cretaceous periods. [f. Gk *brontē* thunder +*sauros* lizard]

brŏnze[1], n. & a. 1. Brown alloy chiefly of copper & tin (about 8:1; *the ~ age*, in which weapons and tools were made of ~); work of art made of this; colour of ~; hence **brŏnz'Y**[2] a. 2. adj. Made of, coloured like, ~. [F, f. It. *bronzo*, = med. L *brundium*; orig. unkn.]

brŏnze[2], v.t. & i. Give bronze-like surface to; make or become brown, tan. [f. prec.]

brooch (-ō-), n. Ornamental jewelled, etc., safety-pin for fastening some part of female dress, esp. the neck. [ME *broche* = BROACH[1]]

brood[1], n. Hatch of young birds or other egg-produced animals; (usu. derog.) human family, children; swarm, crew, of men, animals, or things; ~-, for breeding (~-*mare*, -*hen*). [OE *brōd*, cogn. w. Du. *broed*, OHG *bruot* f. Gmc **brō-* warm, heat]

brood[2], v.i. Sit as hen on eggs; hang close *over* or *on* (of night etc.); meditate *on* or *over* (esp. insults, ill designs, etc.); meditate (often sullenly). [f. prec.]

brood'|ȳ, a. Wishing to sit or incubate (of hen). Hence ~iNESS n. [BROOD[1] +-Y[2]]

brook[1], n. Small stream; ~'*lime*, kind of speedwell common in ditches [OE *hleomoc* name of the plant]. Hence ~'LET n. [OE *brōc*, MLG *brōk*, OHG *bruoh* marsh, WG of unkn. orig.]

brook[2], v.t. Put up with, tolerate, (in neg. context). [OE *brūcan*, OHG *brūhhan*, Goth. *brūkjan* f. Gmc **brūk-* use]

broom, n., & v.t. Yellow-flowered shrub growing on sandy banks etc.; genus to which it belongs; sweeping-implement usu. on long handle (vb, sweep with this); *new ~*, newly appointed official eager to sweep away abuses; ~'*rape*, kinds of parasitic herbs on roots of broom etc.; ~'*stick*, handle of ~ (ridden on through the air by witches, & jumped over by parties to sham marriage). [OE *brōm*, OS *-brămio*, OHG *brămo* f. WG *brăm-* cf. BRAMBLE]

‖ **brōse** (-z), n. Dish of oatmeal with boiling water or milk poured on it; *Athole* ~, mixture of whisky & honey. [Sc. form of BREWIS]

broth (-ŏ-, -aw-), n. Water in which something, esp. meat, has been boiled, thin soup; (Irish) ~ *of a boy*, good fellow. [OE, *broth*, ON *broth*, OHG *brod* f. Gmc *brotham* f. *bru-* BREW +-TH¹]

brŏth'el, n. House of ill fame, bawdy--house. [ME *brothel* worthless man, prostitute, f. OE *brĕothan* go to ruin; hence 16th c. *brothel*(-*house*), confused w. & replacing ME *bordel* (OF f. *bord* BOARD)]

broth'er (-ŭdh-), n. (pl. ~*s* & in some senses *breth'ren* pr. -ĕdhrĭn, see below). Son of same parents or (strictly *half-*~) parent as another person (the latter usu. specified by *my* etc. or a possessive case; pl. abbr. *Bros*, in title of firm, as *Smith Bros & Co.*); (Bibl.) kinsman; close friend; fellow citizen, countryman, or man, equal, (*a man & a* ~, esp. of Negro slaves); fellow member of religious society (pl. *brethren*); fellow member of guild, order, profession, etc. (pl. *brethren*); official of certain companies etc. (*Elder B~*, *Brethren*, member(s) of Trinity House Corporation); companion, associate, (pl. ~*s* often with specification as ~ *in arms*, *of the angle*; member of religious order (as title; either pl.); ~ *german*, on both sides, ~ *uterine*, of same mother only; ~-*in-law*, ~ of one's husband or wife, husband of one's sister. Hence ~LESS a., ~LIKE a. & adv., ~LY¹² a. & adv., ~lINESS n. [OE *brōthor*, OS *-ar*, OHG *bruodar*, ON *brólhir*, Goth. *brōthar* f. Gmc *brōthar* cogn. w. L *frater*]

broth'erhŏŏd (-ŭdh-), n. Fraternal tie; companionship; (members of) association for mutual help etc.; community of feeling. [ME *brotherhede* alt. f. ME *brotherrede* (f. OE *brōthor-ræden*; cf. (KIND)RED) after wds in -HEAD]

brougham (-ōŏm, -ōŏ'am), n. One-horse (or electric) closed carriage. [Lord *B*~ (d. 1868)]

brought. See BRING.

brou'haha (-rōŏ-), n. Commotion, to-do, sensation; hubbub, uproar. [F]

brow¹, n. Arch of hair over eye (usu. in pl. & usu. *eye*~*s*; *knit*, *bend*, one's ~*s*, frown); forehead (~-*ague*, megrim); edge, projection, of cliff etc., top of hill in road. Hence -~ED² (-wd) a. [OE *brū* f. Gmc *brūs*, cf. ON *brún* eyebrow; not related to BRAE]

brow², n. (naut.). Gangway, inclined plane of planks. [app. f. Da., Sw. *bru* bridge]

brow'beat, v.t. Bully, bear down, with looks & words. [BROW¹]

brown¹, a. Of the colour given by mixing

orange & black or by toasting bread; as distinctive epithet of species etc. (~ *bear*, *willow*; ~ *coal*, lignite; ~ *bread*, of unbolted flour; ~ *paper*, coarse un-bleached kind used for parcels etc.; ~ *shirt*, a Nazi; ~ *sugar*, half refined; ~ *ware*, common sort of pottery); dark--skinned, tanned; ‖ (sl.) *do* ~, take in, cheat; ~ *study*, reverie. Hence ~'ISH¹ (2) a., ~'NESS (-nn-) n., ~y̆- comb. form. [OE *brŭn*, OS, OHG *brŭn*, ON *brúnn* f. Gmc *brūnaz*]

brown², n. Brown colour; brown pigment; (ellipt. for) brown butterfly, fishing-fly, clothes; ‖ (sl.) copper coin; ‖ *the* ~, brown mass of flying game-birds; ‖ *fire into the* ~, let fly into a covey without singling out a bird (also transf., fire, launch missile, indiscriminately into a mass). [f. prec.]

brown³, v.t. & i. Make or become brown by roasting, sunburn, or (gun-barrel etc.) chemical process; ‖ ~*ed off* (sl.), bored, fed up. [f. BROWN¹]

brown'ie, n. Benevolent shaggy goblin haunting house & doing household work secretly; junior member (ages 8–11) of GIRL *guides*. [BROWN¹ + -Y³]

Brown'ing, n. Kind of automatic rifle. [J. M. ~, Amer. inventor (d. 1926)]

*****brown'stŏne**, n. Kind of reddish-brown sandstone used for building (esp. in front elevation); ~ *district*, quarter occupied by the well-to-do. [BROWN¹]

browse¹ (-z), n. Twigs, young shoots, etc., as fodder for cattle; act of browsing. [16th c., f. F *broust* & foll.]

browse² (-z), v.i. & t. Feed *on*, crop, (leaves, twigs, scanty vegetation); (abs.) feed thus, (fig.) read for enjoyment. [16th c., f. F *brouster* (mod. *brouter*) f. *broust* (mod. *brout*) young shoot f. Frank. *brust*; cf. OS *brustian* sprout]

Bru'in (-ōŏ-), n. (Personifying name for) bear. [MDu., =BROWN¹, name in *Reynard the Fox*]

bruise¹ (-ōŏz), n. Injury by blow to body (also to fruit etc.) discolouring skin. [f. foll.]

bruise² (-ōŏz), v.t. & i. Injure by blow that discolours skin without breaking it or any bone, contuse, (human or animal body, also fruit, plant, etc.); dint, batter, (wood, metal); (fig.) disable; pound, bray, grind small; (Hunting) ride recklessly; (with *easily* etc.) show effects of blow. [ME *brise*, *bruse* f. OE *brŷsan* crush; reinforced by AF *bruser*, OF *bruisier* (mod. *briser*) break]

bruis'er (-ōŏz-), n. In vbl senses; esp., prizefighter. [-ER¹]

bruit¹ (-ōŏt), n. (arch.). Report, rumour. [F, = noise (*bruire* roar)]

bruit² (-ōŏt), v.t. (arch. & U.S.). Spread (report) *abroad*, *about*, make famous, celebrate. [f. prec.]

brŭmb'y̆, n. (Austral. colloq.). Unbroken horse. [orig. unkn.]

brume (-ōō-), n. (poet.). Mist, fog. [F, f. L *bruma* shortest day, winter]

Brümm'agém, n. & a. (Dial. & derog. form of) Birmingham; (article) made at ~ counterfeit, cheap & showy. [allusion to counterfeit groats made there in 17th c., & to its plated goods]

brum'ous (-ōō-); a. Wintry, foggy. [f. F *brumeux* f. LL *brumosus* rainy (*bruma* BRUME, see -OUS)]

brünch, n. (sl.). Single meal in lieu of breakfast & lunch. [portmanteau wd]

brunétte' (-ōō-), n. & a. Dark-skinned & black- or brown-haired (woman). [F, fem. of *brunet* dim. of *brun* BROWN[1] see -ETTE]

Brüns'wick (-z-), a. From ~ in Germany; esp., ~ *line*, of Eng. sovereigns from George I; ~ *black*, a varnish. [f. LG *Brunswik* = G *Braunschweig*]

brünt, n. Chief stress (usu. *of* the attack etc., & in phr. *bear the* ~ *of*). [ME, orig. unkn.]

brüsh[1], n. 1. (Arch. & U.S., Austral., etc.) brushwood or underwood, thicket, small trees & shrubs growing or (in U.S.) cut in faggots. 2. Implement of bristles, hair, wire, etc., set in wood etc. for scrubbing or sweeping; bunch of hairs etc. in straight handle, quill, etc., *for* painting etc.; *the* ~, art of painting; ~, painter's style, painter (*from the same* ~). 3. Tail, esp. of fox; ~-like tuft. 4. (electr.). ~-like discharge of sparks, piece of carbon or metal ending in wires or strips securing good metallic connexion, (also) movable strip of conductible material for making & breaking connexion. 5. (optics). Bright or dark figure with vague edge. 6. Application of ~, brushing, esp. ~ *up* [f. foll.]; short smart encounter, skirmish, graze, abrasion, [f. foll.]. 7. ~'*fire* (small frontier) *war*; ~-*pencil*, artist's colour-~; ~'*wood*, undergrowth, thicket; ~-*work*, painter's (style of) manipulation. Hence ~'Y[2] a. [(sense ~*wood*) ME *brusche* f. OF *brosse, broce*, (other senses) ME *brusshe* f. OF *brosse, broisse*; of uncert. orig.; *broce* & *broisse* have been identified, & related to Gmc *borst-, burst-* BRISTLE]

brüsh[2], v.t. & i. Move briskly, esp. *by, through, against*; sweep or scrub clean, put in order, with brush; ~ *up*, furbish, (fig.) renew one's memory of; ~ *over*, paint lightly; graze or touch in passing; remove (dust etc.) with brush; ~ *aside, away* (fig.), ignore, pass over; injure by grazing. [f. prec.]

brusque (-ŏŏsk, -ŭsk), a. Blunt, offhand, (of or in manner, speech). Hence ~'LY[2] (-kl-) adv., ~'NESS (-kn-), ~'rie (-ŏŏskerē') [-ERY], nn. [F, f. It. *brusco* sour]

Brüss'els (-z), a. Made or grown at, or adopted from, ~, as ~ *carpet, lace, sprouts* (edible buds of kind of cabbage).

brüt, a. (Of wines) unsweetened. [F]

brut'al (-ōō-), a. Sensual, rude, coarse, savagely cruel. Hence ~ISM(2), **brutăl-**

ITY, nn., ~LY[2] adv., (-ōō-). [f. F *brutal* or LL *brutalis* (*brutus* BRUTE, -AL)]

brut'alíz|e, -is|e) (-īz), v.t. & i. (-ōō-). Make (*rarely* grow) brutal. Hence ~A'TION n. [prec. +-IZE(3)]

brut|e (-ōōt), a. & n. (Beast) not gifted with reason; stupid, sensual, unspirited, beast-like, cruel, or passionate (person; & in same adj. senses of acts, motives, etc.); unconscious, merely material, (~ *force, matter*); lower animal; lower nature in man. Hence ~e'HOOD (-t-h-) n., ~'ISH[1](1) a., ~'ishLY[2] adv., ~'ishNESS n., ~'iFY v.t., ~'iFICA'TION n., (-ōō-). [15th c. (adj.) f. F *brut* f. L *brutus* stupid]

brut'um fǎl'měn (-ōō-) n. Empty threat, blank cartridge (fig.). [L]

Brut'us (-ōō-), n. Style of wig (19th cent.). [F name in honour of Roman hero]

bryŏl'ogĭst, -l'ogў, nn. Person learned in, the lore of, mosses. [Gk *bruon* kind of seaweed & +-LOGIST, -LOGY]

brý'onў, n. Kinds of climbing plants; *red* or *white* ~, common species; *black* ~, *bastard* ~, plants resembling but not belonging to the genus. [f. L f. Gk *bruōnia*]

būb'al,n. A N.-African antelope. [f. L f. Gk *boubalos* ox-like antelope]

būb'ble[1], n. Spherical or hemispherical envelope of liquid enclosing air etc.; air--filled cavity in solidified liquid, as glass, amber; unsubstantial or visionary project, enterprise, etc. (also adj. in this sense; *prick the* ~, unmask futility, pretension, etc.); SOUTH *Sea B~*; sound or appearance of boiling; ~-*&-squeak*, cold meat fried with chopped vegetables; ~-*car*, miniature motor-car with glass-like dome. Hence **būb'blY[2]** a. (also ‖ n., sl., champagne). [f. foll.]

būb'ble[2], v.i. & t. Send up, rise in, make the sound of, bubbles (lit., & fig. as ~ *over*, or ~, *with* laughter, wrath); delude (arch.). [14th c., imit.; cf. BLEB, BLUBBER, & obs. *burble*]

‖ **būb'blў-jŏck**, n. (Sc.). Turkey-cock. [*bubbly* (BUBBLE[1]) +*Jock* = *Jack*]

būb'|ō, n. (pl. -oes). Inflamed swelling in glandular part, esp. groin or armpit. Hence ~ŏn'ıc a. (esp. ~*onic plague*). [L, f. Gk *boubōn* groin]

būbŏn'ocele (-sĕl), n. Hernia of groin. [prec., -CELE]

būccaneer', n., & v.i. (Be a) sea-rover, pirate, esp. of the Spanish-American coasts; adventurer. Hence ~ISH[1] (-nēr-) a. [f. F *boucanier* f. *boucaner* cure meat on a *boucan* (i.e. barbecue) a Braz. wd]

buc'cĭnātor (bŭks-), n. Flat thin cheek--muscle. [L, f. *buccinare* blow the trumpet f. *buccina*, -TOR)]

Būcĕph'alus, n. Riding-horse (joc.). [charger of Alexander of Macedon]

Buch'man|ĭsm (bōōk-, bŭk-), n. Religious system, occas. called the *Oxford Group* (*Movement*) & (in U.S.) the *Moral Rearmament Movement*, introduced *c.* 1921

by F. *Buchman*. So ~ITE[1] a. & n.
[-ISM]

bŭck[1], n. Male of fallow-deer, reindeer,
chamois, antelope, hare, rabbit; dandy
(also *old* ~, vocative = old fellow), whence
~'ISH[1] a., ~'ishLY[2] adv.; (attrib., sl.)
male, of or for males, (~ *nigger* etc.);
~*-horn*, as material for knife handles etc.
(also ~-, as ~*-handled*); ~*-hound*, small
variety of staghound (not now used for
hunting); ~*-shot*, coarse shot; ~*'skin*,
(leather made of) ~'s skin, (pl.) breeches
of it; ~*'thorn*, thorny shrub with cathartic
berries; ~*-tooth*, one that projects. [OE
buc, OHG *bocch* (G *bock*), ON *bukkr*, f.
Gmc **bukkaz*]

bŭck[2], v.i. & t. (Of horse) jump vertically
with back arched & feet drawn together
(also ~*-jump*, whence ~'**jŭmp**ER[1] n.);
~ *off*, throw (rider) thus. Hence ~'ER[1] n.
[f. prec.]

bŭck[3], v.i. & t. (sl.). (With *up*) make
haste, become or make vigorous or
cheerful, (esp. intr. in imperat.). [f. BUCK[1]
in sense *dandy*]

‖ **bŭck**[4], n. Basket for trapping eels.
[orig. unkn.]

bŭck[5], n. Body of cart (chiefly in comb.
as ~*-board*, ~*-cart*, in various local
senses). [perh. f. obs. *bouk* belly, f. OE *būc*]

bŭck[6], n., & v.i., (orig. Anglo-Ind.). Conversation, boastful talk; (v.i.) chat,
swagger, brag (*about*); ~*'stick* (sl.),
braggart. [f. Hind. *baknā* talk freely]

*buck[7], n. (sl.). Article placed as a
reminder before a player whose turn it
is to deal at poker; *pass the* ~ *to*, shift
responsibility to (another), make a dupe
of (person). [orig. unkn.]

*buck[8], n. (sl.). Dollar. [orig. unkn.]

*buck[9], n. Frame on which wood is
cross-cut. [f. Du. *zaag-boc*]

bŭck'-bean, n. Water plant with pinkish
racemes. [transl. (1578) of Flem. *bocks
boonen* goats' beans]

bŭck'ĕt[1], n. Wooden or other vessel for
drawing or carrying water; piston of
pump; compartment of water-wheel,
scoop of dredging-machine or grain-
-elevator; socket for whip, carbine,
wooden leg, etc.; *kick the* ~ (sl.), die (but
perh. f. obs. *bucket* beam, yoke); ~*-shop*,
(orig. U.S.) office for gambling in stocks,
speculating on markets, etc. [accidental]
story connected with elevator of office
first so called]. Hence ~FUL(2) (-ŏŏl)
n. [ME, AF *buket*, *buquet*, perh. f. OE
būc pitcher]

bŭck'ĕt[2], v.i. & t. Ride hard (horse, or
abs.); ‖ (Rowing) hurry the forward
swing, row hurried stroke. [f. prec., cf.
pump = exhaust]

Bŭck'ingham Păl'ace, n. London
residence of the Sovereign. [place]

bŭc'kle[1], n. Metal rim with hinged spiked
tongue for securing strap, ribbon, etc.
[ME *bocle* f. OF *boucle* f. L *buccula* beaver
of helmet (*bucca* cheek, see -ULE)]

bŭc'kle[2], v.t. & i. Fasten with buckle
(often *up*, *on*, etc.); ~ *to* (with *to* prep.)
prepare for, set about, (with *to* adv.) get
to work, start vigorously; (cause to) give
way, crumple up, under longitudinal
pressure (t. & i. of wheel, saw, etc.). [f.
prec.; the last sense perh. f. F *boucler*
bulge]

bŭck'ler, n., & v.t. Small round shield
usu. held by handle; protection, protector, (vb, protect); also technically in
various naut., zool., & anat. senses. [ME
boc(e)ler f. OF *bocler* lit. 'having a boss'
f. *boucle* boss, see BUCKLE[1], -ER[2]]

bŭck'ō, a. & n. (naut. sl.). Swaggering
(fellow). [f. BUCK[1]]

bŭck'ra, a. & n. (Negro dial.). Characteristic of, belonging to, the white man;
(n.) white man, master. [f. Surinam
Negro patois *bakra* master]

bŭck'ram, n. & a. Coarse linen or cloth
stiffened with gum or paste; stiffness,
stiff, (of manner); strong, strength, in
appearance only; *men in* ~, ~ *men*, non-
existent (1 *Hen. IV*, II. iv. 210-50). [ME,
f. AF *bukeram*, OF *boquerant*, of unkn.
orig.]

‖ **bŭck'shee**, n., a., & adv., (sl., orig.
army). **1.** Something in addition to the
usual allowance, as extra rations. **2.** adj.
& adv. Gratuitous(ly), free. [corrupt. of
BAKSHEESH]

bŭck'wheat (-wēt), n. A cereal plant with
seed used for horse & poultry food, & in
U.S. for breakfast cakes. [f. MDu.
boecweite beech wheat]

būcŏl'ic, a. & n. Of shepherds, pastoral,
rustic; (usu. pl.) pastoral poems (*the
B~s*, those of Virgil). Hence **būcŏl'-
ICALLY** adv. [f. L f. Gk *boukolikos* f.
boukolos herdsman]

bŭd[1], n. Rudiment of branch, leaf-
-cluster, or flower; flower not fully open;
[Zool.] animal forming by GEMMATION,
anything still undeveloped; *in* ~,
putting forth buds; *nip in the* ~, destroy
at early stage (fig.). Hence ~'LESS a.,
~'LET n. [late ME *budde*, *bodde*, of unkn.
orig.]

bŭd[2], v.i. & t. (-dd-). Put forth buds,
spring forth; begin to grow or develop
(~*ding horns*, *lawyer*, *cricketer*); (Zool.)
produce, be produced, by GEMMATION;
(Gardening) ingraft (trans. or abs.) into
alien stock. [f. prec.]

bŭdd'ĕd, p.p. In vbl senses; esp., that
has budded, is in bud. [-ED[1](2)]

Buddh‖a (bŏŏd'a), n. The Enlightened,
title of successive teachers past & future
of the Asian religion ~ISM(3) (bŏŏd'ĭ-)
n., but applied esp. to Sakyamuni, Gautama, or Siddartha (5th c. B.C., in N.
India). Hence ~IST(2) (bŏŏd'ĭ-) n. & a.,
~is'TIC(AL) aa. [Skr., p.p. of *budh* know]

bŭdd'leia (-lĭa), n. Kinds of shrub with
lilac or yellow flowers of various forms.
[A. *Buddle*, botanist (d. 1715), -IA[1]]

*budd'y, n. (colloq.). (Usu. as familiar

form of address) brother, chum, mate. [dim. of *bud*, childish pronunc. of *brother*]

budge, v.i. & t. Make the slightest movement, force to do this, (in neg. sentences). [f. F *bouger* stir perh. (cf. Pr. *bolegar*)= It. *bulicare* f. Rom. *bullicare frequent. of *bullire* boil]

budg'erigar', n. The grass parakeet, or Australian love-bird. [native name]

budg'et, n., & v.i. Contents of a bag or bundle (mostly fig., esp. of news, & as title of newspapers); annual estimate of revenue & expenditure of a country (in Great Britain by Chancellor of Exchequer in House of Commons); private person's similar estimate; (v.i.) ~ *for*, allow or arrange for in ~. Hence ~ARY[1] a. [ME, f. OF *bougette* dim. of *bouge* leather bag f. L *bulga* (f. Gallic) knapsack; see BULGE]

buff[1], n. & a. (Of) stout velvety dull-yellow leather of buffalo or ox-hide; the human skin (*in* ~, naked); (of) dull-yellow colour (*the B~s*, East Kent Regt, from colour of the facings); (Path.) coagulated coating on blood drawn from fever patients, whence ~'Y[2] a.; ~-*coat*, -*jerkin*, formerly worn by soldiers as proof against sword-cut; ~-*stick*, -*wheel*, polishing tools covered with ~; ~-*tip*, kind of moth. [f. F *buffle* BUFFALO]

buff[2], v.t. Polish (metal) with buff; make (leather) velvety like buff. [f. prec.]

buff'alo, n. (pl. -*oes*). Kinds of ox (*Bos bubalus*, India, Asia, Europe, N. Africa; *Bos caffer*, S. Africa; American BISON); amphibious tank. [prob. f. Port. *bufalo*, f. LL *bufalus* f. L f. Gk *boubalos* antelope]

buff'er[1], n. Apparatus for deadening by springs or padding, or sustaining by strength of beams etc., a concussion, esp. of railway vans; ~ *State*, small State between two large ones diminishing chance of hostilities. [f. obs. vb *buff* (imit. of sound made by soft body struck, cf. PUFF & F *bouffer*) +-ER[1]]

buff'er[2], n. (sl.). (Usu. *old* ~) old-fashioned or incompetent fellow; (Nav.) chief boatswain's mate. [18th c., of obsc. orig.]

buff'et[1], n., & v.t. & i. (Strike with) blow of the hand; (of fate etc.) knock, hurt, plague; contend with (waves); contend *with*. Hence ~ING[1] (1, 2) n., beating, repeated blows, (Aeron.) irregular oscillation, caused by air eddies, of any part of an aircraft. [ME, f. OF, dim. of *buffe* blow (whence obs. E *buff* cf. BLIND[1]-*man's--buff*)]

buff'et[2], n. **1.** Sideboard, recessed cupboard, for china, plate, etc. **2.** (pr. bŏŏf'ā) refreshment bar. [18th c., F, of unkn. orig.]

buffo (bŏŏf'ō), n. & a. Burlesque, comic, (actor). [It.]

buffoon', n., & v.i. (Play the) wag, jester, mocker. Hence ~ERY(4) n. [f. F *buffon* f. It. *buffone* (*buffa* jest, *buffare* to puff), -OON]

bug, n. Flat ill-smelling blood-sucking insect infesting beds; (loosely) small insect (often with defining word as *harvest, May*, -~; ~-*hunter* etc., entomologist); *any insect; *big* ~ (sl.), person of importance. Hence ~G'Y[2] (-g-) a. [orig. unkn.]

bug'aboo, bug'bear (-bār), nn. Fancied object of fear; false belief used to intimidate or dissuade. [16th c. *bugbear* f. obs. *bug*+BEAR[1]; *bugaboo* undetermined; cf. BOGLE, BOGY]

bugg'er (-g-), n., & v.t. (Law) sodomite, man having unnatural intercourse with beast or man, whence **bugg'ery**(4) n.; (in foul or low talk, abusively or humorously): fellow, beggar, chap, beast; (v.t.) ~ *about*, hound from pillar to post. [f. F *bougre* f. med.L *Bulgarus* 11th-c. heretic from Bulgaria, supposed capable of any crime]

bugg'y (-g-), n. Light vehicle for one or two persons (esp. in U.S., India, colonies). [orig. unkn.]

bu'gle[1], n., & v.i. & t. Brass instrument like small trumpet used for military signals; (vb) sound ~, sound (call) on ~. Hence **bug'ler**[1] n. [ME, short for ~-*horn* f. OF *bugle*, f. L *buculus* dim. of *bos* ox]

bu'gle[2], n. Kinds of creeping plant with blue flowers. [F, f. LL *bugula*]

bu'gle[3], n. Tube-shaped glass bead sewn on dress etc. for ornament. [orig. unkn.]

bug'let, n. Small (cyclist's) bugle. [-ET[1]]

bug'loss, n. Kinds of plant allied with borage. [f. F *buglosse* or L f. Gk *bouglōssos* ox-tongued]

buhl (bŏŏl), n. & a. (Inlaid with) brass, tortoise-shell, etc., cut in ornamental patterns for inlaying. [Germanized f. *Boule* name of carver (d. 1732)]

build[1] (bĭl-), v.t. & i. (*built*). Construct by putting parts or material rightly together (house, ship, carriage, organ, engine, nest, or other structure large relatively to the builder); (abs.) be busy making one's house or nest; ~ *up, round, in*, surround (person, place, etc.) with houses etc., block up; (with material as obj.) lay *in(to* wall etc.)in~ing; establish, make gradually, (often with *up*) system, empire, reputation); base (hopes etc.) *upon*, rely *upon*; *built* (with preceding adv. etc.), of such & such a BUILD[2]. [ME *bulden* f. OE *byldan*, f. *bold* dwelling f. Gmc *bu- dwell, cf. BOWER[1], BOOTH]

build[2] (bĭl-), n. Style of construction, make; proportions of human body (*sturdy* ~ etc.); ~-*up* n., favourable publicity designed to popularize a person, product, etc. [prec.]

buil'der (bĭl-), n. In vbl senses; esp., master-builder, contractor for building houses. [-ER[1]]

buil'ding (bĭl-), n. In vbl senses; esp.: house, edifice; ~-*lease*, permitting lessee to build on the land; ‖~-*society*, of contributors to fund for loan to members when needing house. [-ING[1]]

bŭlb¹, n. Nearly spherical underground stem of lily, onion, etc., sending roots downwards & leaves etc. upwards; leaf--bud detaching itself from stem & becoming separate plant; (Anat.) roundish swelling of any cylindrical organ, as of hair-root or spinal cord; dilated part of glass tube (~-*tube*, ending in a ~); electric-light container. Hence ~ED² (-bd),~ĭr'EROUS, bŭl'bĬFORM, aa., bŭl'bo-comb. form. [f. L *bulbus* f. Gk *bolbos* onion]

bŭlb², v.i. Swell into bulb(s). [f. prec.]

bŭl'bous, a. Of, having, like, springing from, a bulb. [f. L *bulbosus* (BULB¹, -OUS)]

bulbul (bŏŏl'bŏŏl), n. Eastern song--thrush; singer, poet. [Pers. f. Arab.]

bŭlge¹, n. Convex part, irregular swelling, tendency to swell out, on flat or flatter surface; temporary increase in volume or numbers; =BILGE; (sl.) advantage (chiefly in phr. *have*, or *get*, *the* ~ *on*, have, get, the advantage over). Hence **bŭl'gY²** a., **bŭl'gĬNESS** n. [ME, f. OF *boulge*, *bouge*, or f. L *bulga* see BUDGET]

bŭlge², v.i. & t. Swell outwards irregularly & usu. faultily; extend (bag etc.) by stuffing it. [f. prec.]

bŭl'imy̆, bŭlĭm'ia, n. (Med.) morbid hunger; (fig.) voracity (for books etc.). [16th c. f. Gk *boulimia* (whence usu. mod. form) f. *bous* ox +*limos* hunger]

bŭlk¹, n. Cargo (*break* ~, begin unloading; ~ *not equal to sample*; *in* ~, loose, not in package; *load in* ~, put grain etc. in loose; *sell in* ~, in large quantities, as it is in the hold); large shape, person, body; size, magnitude; great size; mass, large mass; *the* greater part or number of; ~ *buying*, purchase by one buyer of all or most of a producer's output. [sense 'cargo' f. OIcel. *bulki*; sense 'mass' etc. perh. alt. f. obs. *bouk* (cf. BUCK⁵)]

bŭlk², v.i. & t. Seem in respect of size or importance (~ *large*, *larger*); ~ *up*, form considerable sum etc., amount *to*; pile in heaps (fish); (Customs) ascertain weight of (tea etc.) by emptying out of chest. [f. prec.]

bŭlk'head (-hĕd), n. Upright partition dividing ship's cabins or water-tight compartments; compartment, stall. [15th c. *bulke hede* f. *bulke* (loose) cargo (BULK¹) +HEAD¹]

bŭl'k|y̆, a. Large; too large. Hence ~ĬNESS n. [BULK¹+-Y²]

bull¹ (bŏŏl), n. & a. **1.** Uncastrated male of ox or any bovine animal (~ *in china shop*, reckless or clumsy destroyer; *take* ~ *by the horns*, meet not evade difficulty); male of whale, elephant, & other large animals (usu. ~ *whale* or *whale-*~ etc.); constellation & sign Taurus. **2.** (St. Exch.). Person trying to raise prices (see BEAR¹). **3.** = BULL'*s-eye* (of target). **4.** adj. Like that of a ~ (~ *head*, *neck*, *voice*; also ~ *operations* on St. Exch.). **5.** ~*-calf*, male calf, simpleton; ‖~*-corner* (local),

barred refuge, usu. at junction of fields, from ~'s attack; ~'*dog*, powerful & courageous large-headed smooth-haired breed of dog, tenacious & courageous (person), ‖ University proctor's attendant; *~'doze*, v.t. (sl.), cow, coerce; *~'dozer*, powerful caterpillar tractor pushing broad steel blade in front, used for removing obstacles, levelling uneven surfaces, etc.; ~'*fight*, Spanish sport of baiting ~ with horsemen etc.; ~'*finch*, strong-beaked handsome-plumaged song--bird, also [perh.=~ *fence*, cf. *minch* dial. for *mince*] quickset hedge with ditch; ~'*frog*, large Amer. species; ~'*head*, small big-headed fish = miller's thumb; ~--*headed*, obstinate, impetuous,blundering; ~*-of-the-bog*, bittern; ~*-puncher*, (Austral.) bullock-driver; ~*-pup*, *-bitch*, young, female, ~dog; ~'*ring*, arena for ~fight; ~'*roarer*, flat strip of wood tied to a string, making a roaring sound when whirled round; ~'*s-eye*, boss of glass formed at centre of blown glass sheet, hemispherical piece or thick disc of glass as light in ship's side, hemispherical lens, (lantern) with such lens, small circular window, centre of target, kind of sweet•meat; ~*-terrier*, cross between ~dog & terrier; ~'*trout*, fish of salmon tribe. [ME *bole* f. ON *boli* = MLG, MDu. *bulle*; see BULLOCK]

bull² (bŏŏl), v.i. & t. (St. Exch.). Speculate for the rise; try to raise price of (stocks). [f. prec.; BULL¹,² perh. merely correl. to the more explicable BEAR¹,²]

bull³ (bŏŏl), n. Papal edict. [ME, f. OF *bulle* f. L *bulla*. cf. BILL⁴]

bull⁴ (bŏŏl), n. (Often *Irish* ~) expression containing contradiction in terms or implying ludicrous inconsistency (often an intelligible statement made absurd by compression). [orig. unkn.]

bull⁵ (bŏŏl), n. Drink made of water flavoured in empty spirit cask. [orig. unkn.]

Bull⁶. = JOHN *Bull*.

bull⁷ (bŏŏl), n. Deck-game in which small flat sandbags are thrown on an inclined board marked with numbered squares. [orig. unkn.]

bullace (bŏŏl'ĭs), n. Wild (or semi-cultivated) plum tree or fruit. [ME *bolace* f. OF *beloce* f. Gaulish **bulluca* sloe]

bŭll'āte, a. (bot., physiol.). Puffy, blistered-looking. [f. L *bulla* bubble +-ATE²]

bull'ĕt (bŏŏ'-), n. Missile of lead etc., spherical or conical, used in rifles (*dum-dum*, *expanding*, *soft-nosed*, *explosive*, ~ varieties so shaped etc. as to inflict complicated wound); ~*-head*, *-headed*, (with) round & presumably thick head; ~--PROOF. [f. F *boulette* dim. of *boule* ball f. L *bulla* knob]

bull'ĕtĭn (bŏŏ'-), n. Short official statement of public event or news or of invalid's condition. [F, f. It. *bulletino* dim. of *bulletta* lottery ticket dim: of *bulla* seal, BULL³]

bullion¹ (bŏŏl'yon), n. & a. Gold or silver before (or as valued apart from) coining or manufacture; (made of) solid or real gold or silver. [f. AF *bullion* mint, formally = OF *bouillon* f. Rom. *bullionem* f. *bullire* BOIL²; meanings excl. E]

bullion² (bŏŏl'yon), n. Fringe of gold & silver thread twists. [f. F *bouillon*, see prec., in sense *bubble*]

bull'ock (bŏŏ-), n. Castrated bull, ox. [OE *bulluc*, dim. (-OCK) of *bulla* BULL¹]

bull'ȳ¹ (bŏŏ-), n. Blusterer, tyrant (esp. among boys), coward & tyrant; hired ruffian; man who lives on prostitute's earnings. [16th c. as term of endearment, gallant, etc., prob. f. MDu. *boele* (G *buhle*)]

bull'ȳ² (bŏŏ-), v.t. Persecute, oppress, tease, physically or morally; frighten *into* or *out of*; (abs.) play the bully; ~ *off*, perform preliminary crossing of clubs in hockey. [f. prec.]

bull'ȳ³ (bŏŏ-), a. & int. (esp. U.S.). Capital, first-rate; ~ *for you, him*, etc., = bravo. [f. BULLY¹]

‖ **bull'ȳ**⁴ (bŏŏ-), n. Scrummage in (prop. Eton) football.

bull'ȳ⁵ (bŏŏ-), n. (colloq.). (Also ~ *beef*) corned beef. [f. F *bouilli* boiled beef f. *bouillir* BOIL¹]

bull'ȳrăg (bŏŏ-). See BALLYRAG.

bul'rŭsh (bŏŏ-), n. Kinds of tall rush (pop. the cat's tail; in Bible, papyrus). [f. BULL¹, as in *bullfrog, bulltrout*, etc.]

bul'wark (bŏŏ-), n. Rampart, earthwork, etc.; mole, breakwater; person, principle, etc., that acts as a defence; ship's side above deck. [15th c., = rampart, corresp. to (prob. f.) MDu. *bolwerk*, see BOLE, WORK¹]

bŭm¹, n. Backside, buttocks; ‖ ~-*bailiff* (also ~), employed for arrests (from touching debtor on the back); ~-*boat*, plying with fresh provisions for ships (orig. scavenger boat). [ME *bom*, of unkn. orig.; prob. imit., cf. BUMP]

****bŭm**², n., a., & v.i. & t., (sl.). 1. Habitual loafer (*go on the ~*, sponge on the community). 2. adj. Of poor quality. 3. vb (-mm-). Loaf, sponge, wander *around*; obtain by sponging, scrounge. [perh. back-formation f. BUMMER]

‖ **bŭm'ble**, n. Beadle; consequential jack-in-office. Hence ~DOM (-ld-) n. [name of beadle in *Oliver Twist*]

bŭm'ble-bee, n. Large kind of bee. [f. obs. vb *bumble* (BOOM, or obs. var. *bum*, +-LE)]

bŭm'ble-pŭppȳ, n. Whist, tennis, etc., played unscientifically; game with tennis-ball slung to post. [orig. unkn.]

bŭm'bō, n. Cold rum-punch. [cf. It. *bombo* child's wd for drink]

bŭmm'alō, n. Small fish of S.-Asian coasts. [f. Mahratti *bombil(a)*]

‖ **bŭmmaree'**, n. Middleman at Billings-

gate fish-market; licensed porter at Smithfield meat-market in London. [orig. unkn.]

****bŭmm'er**, n. Idler, loafer. [cf. G *bummler*]

bŭmp¹, v.t. & i., & adv. 1. Push, throw down, (box etc.) *against* or *on* (wall, person, floor, etc.); hurt (one's head etc.) by striking it (*against, on*, or abs.); seize by arms & legs & strike the posterior of (person) against floor, wall, etc.; come with a bump *against*; go along with repeated bumps; (Boat-racing, see foll.) overtake; (of cricket-ball) rise abruptly on pitching; **~ off* (sl.), remove by violence, murder. 2. adv. With a bump, suddenly, violently, (*come, go*, etc., ~, cf. BANG, BOUNCE). [expressing sound of blow; by extension, the resulting swelling]

bŭmp², n. Dull-sounding blow, knock, collision; swelling caused by it; (Phrenol.) prominence on skull, faculty indicated by it; (Boat-racing) touching of boat by next, a win for latter (~-*supper*, in celebration of this); (Aviation) vertical air current causing irregularity in aircraft's motion, jolt experienced by aircraft in flight; ~-*ball* (Cricket; pr. bŭm'bawl) ball hit hard on ground close to bat, coming with a long hop to fieldsman (so looking like a possible catch). [f. prec.]

bŭmp³, n., & v.i. (Make) bittern's cry. [imit.]

bŭm'per, n. In vbl senses; also, brim-full glass of wine; anything unusually large or abundant (harvest, full theatre); (Whist) score of two games against nil; (Motoring) spring fender for mitigating collisions. [-ER¹]

bŭmp'kin, n. Country or awkward or bashful fellow. [perh. f. Du. *boomken* little tree or MDu. *bommekijn* little barrel]

bŭmp'tious (-shŭs), a. Self-assertive. Hence ~LY² adv., ~NESS n. [jocular form, on BUMP² & e.g. *fractious*]

bŭm'p|ȳ, a. Full of bumps, causing jolts, (esp. of road or cricket pitch or air in aviation). Hence ~ĭNESS n. [-Y²]

bŭn¹, n. Small soft round sweet cake with a few currants (the usu. Eng. sense, but with local variations); *hot cross ~*, marked with cross & eaten on Good Friday; hair dressed in ~ shape. [ME *bunne*, OF *bugne, buigne*; see BUNION]

‖ **bŭn**², n. (Personifying name of) squirrel, rabbit. [16th c., of unkn. orig.]

bŭn'a (or bŏŏ-), n. Synthetic rubber made by the polymerization of butadiene. [f. *bu(tadiene)*+*na(trium)* sodium]

bŭnch¹, n. Cluster of things growing or fastened together (flowers, grapes, keys), lot (*best of the ~*); (sl.) gang, group; ~ *grass*, kinds of N.-Amer. grass growing in tufts. Hence ~'Y² a. [orig. unkn.]

bŭnch², v.t. & i. Make into bunch(es), gather (dress) into folds; come or cling together, (Mil., of skirmishers) fail to keep intervals. [f. prec.]

•bŭnc'ō, n., & v.t., (sl.). (To) swindle (esp. by card-sharping or the confidence trick); ~-*steerer*, swindler. [cf. Sp. *banca* a card-game]

bŭn'combe. See BUNKUM.

bŭnd, n. (Anglo-Ind.). Embankment, causeway, quay. [Hind. *band*, of Persian orig.]

bŭn'der, n. (Anglo-Ind.). Landing-place, quay, harbour; ~-*boat* (used for coasting & harbour work). [Hind.]

bŭn'dle¹, n. Collection of things fastened together (esp. clothes & odds & ends in handkerchief); set of sticks, iron rods, etc., bound up; set of parallel fibres, nerves, etc.; 20 hanks of linen yarn. [ME *bundel* not continuous w. OE *byndele* a binding (Gmc **bund-* BIND) but f. MDu. *bondel*, LG, Du. *bundel*]

bŭn'dle², v.t. & i. Tie in, make *up* into, a bundle; throw confusedly *in* to any receptacle; go, put or send (esp. a person), in a hurry or unceremoniously *out, off, away*, etc. [f. prec.]

bŭng¹, n. Stopper, esp. large cork stopping hole in cask; ~-*hole*, for filling cask. [f. MDu. *bonghe* (= Du. *bom*)]

bŭng², v.t. Stop (cask) with bung; *eyes* ~*ed up*, closed with swelling from blow, or sealed with rheum; (sl.) throw (stones). [f. prec.]

bŭng'al|ow (-nggalō), n. One-storeyed house, orig. lightly built or temporary. Hence ~OID a., having the style or appearance of a ~ow. [f. Hind. *bangla* belonging to Bengal]

bungl|e (bŭng'gl), v.i. & t., & n. (Make) clumsy work, confusion; blunder over, fail to accomplish, (task). Hence ~ER¹ n; [imit., cf. obs. *bumble* in same sense]

bŭn'ion (-yon), n. Inflamed swelling on foot. [It. *bugnone* (*bugno* boil, lump) or OF *buignon* (f. *buigne*, mod. *bigne*) swelling]

bŭnk¹, n. Sleeping-berth. [orig. unkn.]

bŭnk², v.i., & n., (sl.). ~, *do a* ~, make off, vanish. [orig. unkn.]

•bŭnk³, n. (sl.). Humbug, balderdash. [contr. of BUNKUM]

bŭnk'er, n., & v.t. Ship's coal-bin; (Golf) sandpit on course constituting a HAZARD; (Mil.) underground shelter; (v.t., usu. in p.p.) entangle in ~, (fig.) bring into difficulties. [orig. unkn.]

bŭnk'um, -combe (-km), n. Humbug, claptrap, sophistry. [anecdotic; member for Buncombe in N. Carolina speaking needlessly in Congress (1819–21) to impress his constituents]

bŭnn'ia (-ya), n. (Anglo-Ind.). Indian (prop. Hindu) trader or shopkeeper. [Hind. *banya*; see BANIAN]

bŭnn'ỹ, n. Pet name for rabbit; ~-*hug*, an American dance. [BUN² + -Y³]

Bun'sen('s) (bŏŏn-, bŭn-), a. Invented by R. W. *Bunsen* (d. 1899), German chemist

(~ *burner*, *lamp*, burning air with gas for heating & blow-pipe work; ~ *battery*, *cell*, voltaic of spec. kind).

bŭnt¹, n. Cavity, baggy part, of fishing-net, sail, etc.; ~-*line* (confining ~ in furling sail). [orig. unkn.]

bŭnt², n. (Also *smut-ball*) disease of wheat. [orig. unkn.]

bŭnt³, v.t. & i., & n. 1. (Chiefly dial.) push with the head or horns, butt. 2. (In baseball) stop (ball) with bat without swinging. 3. n. Act of ~ing; (in baseball) a ~ed ball, hit made by ~ing. [orig. unkn.; cf. BUTT³]

bŭn'ting¹, n. Sub-family of birds including *common* or *corn* ~, *yellow* ~ (or *yellow-hammer*), *black-headed, reed, snow*, etc., ~; grey shrimp. [orig. unkn.]

bŭn'ting², n. (Open-made worsted stuff used for) flags. [orig. unkn.]

buoy¹ (boi), n. Anchored float showing navigable course or reefs etc.; (also *life*-~) something to keep person afloat; also fig. in both senses. [15/16th c. *boye, buie* f. MDu. f. OF *boie* (mod. *bouée*) f. Frank. **bōkan*; see BEACON]

buoy² (boi), v.t. 1. (Usu. with *up*) keep afloat; bring to surface of water; sustain (person, courage, etc.), uplift. 2. (Without *up*, sometimes with *out*) mark with buoy(s). [last meaning f. prec.; sense *float* etc. f. Sp. *boyar*; see BUOYANT]

buoy'age (boi-), n. Providing of buoys; series of buoys. [-AGE]

buoy'ancŷ (boi-), n. Floating power on liquid or in air; (Hydrost.) loss of weight by immersion in liquid; elasticity, recuperative power, (of spirits, also of prices, etc.). [f. foll.; see -ANCY]

buoy'ant (boi-), a. Apt to float, rise, keep up, or recover, springy; able to keep things up; light-hearted. Hence ~LY² adv. [16th c. f. Sp. *boyante* p.p. of *boyar* float (cf. obs. F *bouyant*) f. *boya* BUOY¹]

bûr, bûrr, n. (Any plant with) clinging seed-vessel or flower; female hop-catkin; person hard to shake off. [ME, = Da. *borre* bur, burdock, Sw. *kard-borre* burdock]

Bŭrb'errỹ, n. A kind of waterproof cloth, coat etc. of this, made by a company of that name. [P]

bûr'ble, v.i. Simmer (*with* rage, mirth). [19th c., imit.; but cf. ME (obs.) *burble* bubble]

bûrb'ot, n. Eel-like flat-headed bearded freshwater fish. [f. F *bourbotte*]

bûrd'en¹, bûrth'en (-dh-), n. (usu. -*den* exc. = *tonnage*). Load (lit., or of labour, duty, sorrow, etc.; ~ *of proof*, obligation to prove falling on maker of statement); obligatory expense; ship's carrying-capacity, tonnage; bearing of loads (*ship, beast, of* ~); (Bibl.) oracle, heavy fate; (= obs. senses of BOURDON) refrain, chorus, of song, chief theme or gist of poem, book, speech, etc. [OE *byrthen*,

OS *burthinnia* f. WG **burthi-* BIRTH + EN³; for *-d-* cf. *murder* etc.]

bŭrd'en², **bŭrth'en** (-dh-), v.t. Load (lit. & fig.), encumber, oppress, tax. [f. prec.]

bŭrd'ensome, a. Oppressive, wearying. Hence ~NESS (-mn-) n. [-SOME]

bŭr'dŏck, n. Coarse plant with prickly flower-heads (BUR) & dock-like leaves. [BUR + DOCK¹]

bureau (būrō', bū²), n. (pl. *-eaux*, pr. -ōz). ‖ Writing-desk with drawers, escritoire; *chest of drawers; office or department for transacting business, government department. [F, = desk, orig. the baize covering, f. OF *burel* f. *bure* coarse cloth]

bureau'|cracy̆ (-rō-), n. Government by bureaux, centralization; officialism; officials. Allied wds: ~CRAT (bū'ro-) n., ~crăt'IC a., ~crăt'ICALLY adv., ~'cratISM(2), ~'cratIST(2), nn. [f. prec. + -CRACY]

bŭrĕtte', n. Graduated glass tube for measuring small quantities of liquid. [F]

*bŭrg, n. (colloq.). Town or city. [see BOROUGH]

‖ **bŭr'gage**, n. An ancient tenure (*hold in* ~). [f. med. L *burgagium* (*burgus* see BOROUGH, -AGE)]

bŭrgee', n. Triangular flag bearing the colours or emblem of a yacht club or sailing club. [orig. unkn.]

bur'geon, bour'geon, (ber'jn), n., & v.i. (Put forth, spring forth as) young shoot(s), bud, begin to grow, (poet., & also in Zool. of GEMMATION). [ME, f. OF *bor-, burjon*, of unkn. orig.]

bŭr'gĕss, n. Inhabitant of borough with full municipal rights, citizen; (chiefly hist.) member of parliament for borough, corporate town, or university. [ME, f. OF *burgeis* f. Rom. *burgensis f. *burgus* f. Gmc *burgs BOROUGH]

burgh (bŭ'ru), n. (Sc.). Scots chartered town (used in E in writing of Scots borough). [Sc. form of BOROUGH]

burgher (ber'ger), n. Freeman or citizen of a burgh or borough; (S. Afr.) citizen of European descent, wherever resident. [16th c., f. G or Du. *burger* f. *burg* BOROUGH]

bŭrg'lar, n. One who breaks into house by night with intent to commit felony. Hence ~Y¹ n., **burglār'ious** a., **burg-lār'iousLY²** adv. [c. 1500 *burgular, burglour*, = AL *burg(u)lator*, f. earlier *burgator* (= AF *burgesour*, cf. OF *burgur* thief); formation & orig. obsc.]

bŭr'gle, v.i. & t. Commit burglary; enter or rob (house) burglariously. [19th c. back form. f. prec.]

bŭrg'omaster (-ah-), n. Mayor of Dutch or Flemish or German town. [f. Du. *burgemeester* (BOROUGH)]

bŭrg'onĕt, n. (hist.). Visored helmet; steel cap. [f. OF *bourguignotte* f. *Bourgogne* Burgundy]

bŭrgoo', n. (naut. sl.). Porridge. [orig. unkn.]

bŭrg'undy̆, n. Kinds of (usu. red) wine of Burgundy in France.

bŭ'r(h)el, n. Himalayan wild sheep. [f. Hind. *bharal*]

bu'rial (bĕ-), n. Depositing under earth, burying, esp. of dead body, funeral; ~*-ground*, cemetery; ~*-service*, religious form at funeral. [ME *buryel*, erron. formed as sing. of OE *byrgels* (cf. OS *burgisli*) f. **burg-* BURY + *-els* as in RIDDLE]

bŭr'in, n. Tool for engraving on copper. Hence ~IST(1) n. [F]

bŭrke¹, v.t. Avoid, smother, (publicity, inquiry); hush up, suppress, (rumour, book). [*Burke* executed 1829 for smothering people to sell bodies for dissection]

Bŭrke², n. (Used for) ~'s Peerage etc. [John ~, compiler (d. 1848)]

bŭrl, n., & v.t. Knot in wool or cloth; (vb) clear of ~s. [f. OF *bourle*]

bŭrl'ăp, n. Coarse canvas. [perh. f. Du. *boenlap* rubbing-cloth, confused w. *boer* BOOR]

bŭrlĕsque' (-k), a. & n., & v.t. Imitative, imitation, imitate, for purpose of deriding or amusing; bombast(ic), mock--serious(ness); caricature, parody, esp. (of) literary & dramatic work; *(vulgar) variety show freq. featuring comic strip--tease. [F, f. It. *burlesco* (*burla* mockery, -ESQUE)]

Bŭrl'ington House, n. Building in London used as headquarters of the Royal Academy, British Academy, British Association, Royal Soc., Geological Soc., Chemical Soc., & Linnean Soc.

bŭrl'|y̆, a. Sturdy, corpulent. Hence ~iNESS n. [ME *borlich* prob. f. OE *bŭrlīc (cf. OHG *bŭrlīh* exalted) fit for the BOWER¹, see -LY¹]

Bŭrmēse' (-z), a. & n. Of Burma; (n.) ~ native (pl. same) or language. **Bŭrm'an** a. & n., = ~. [*Burma* + -ESE, -AN]

bŭrn¹, n. (Sc., north., poet.). Small stream. [OE *burna*, MDu. *borne*, metathetic forms f. Gmc **brunnōn, -az*, cf. OS, OHG *brunno*, ON *brunnr*, Goth. *brunna*; cf. BOURN¹]

bŭrn², v.t. & i. (~*t*, occas. ~*ed*). **1.** Consume, waste, by fire (t. & i., the heat, heating person, or heated thing, being subject; ~ *away, out,* to nothing, to extinction; ~ *up,* get rid of by fire; ~ *out,* consume contents of; ~ one's *boats,* commit oneself irrevocably to a course); blaze, glow, with fire (~ *up,* flash into blaze; ~ *down, low,* less vigorously as fuel fails). **2.** Give, make to give, light (lamp, candles, gas, oil, etc.; ~ *blue* etc., give blue etc. light; ~ *candle at both ends,* not husband energy; ~ *daylight,* use artificial light by day; ~ *the midnight oil,* work late). **3.** Put, be put, to death by fire. **4.** Harden, produce, (bricks, lime, charcoal) by heat. **5.** Make (hole etc.) by heat (*money* ~s *hole in pocket,* clamours to be spent). **6.** Injure, be injured, by fire or great heat (~ one's *fingers*, suffer for meddling or rashness); char, scorch, in cooking (t. & i.), adhere to saucepan etc.; cauterize, brand, (~ *in, into*, impress indelibly); eat, make acid etc. eat, its way (*into* material, material, or abs.). **7.** Parch, freckle, tan, colour, (t. & i.; abs. or with *brown, dry*, etc.). **8.** Give, feel, sensation or pain (as) of heat (~*t child dreads fire*; *ears*~, when one is talked of; ~, get near discovery or truth, as in child's game). **9.** Make, be, hot or passionate, glow, blaze, rage, yearn. **10.** Utilize nuclear energy of (uranium etc.). **11.** ~ person *out*, expel him by fire; ~ *the water*, spear salmon by torchlight; ~*ing-glass*, convex lens or concave mirror concentrating sun's rays enough to ignite object at focus; ~*t almond* (enclosed in burnt sugar); ~*t ochre, sienna* (calcined); ~*t offering*, sacrifice made by ~*ing*. [OE *birnan* intr., *bærnan* trans., metathetic forms f. Gmc **brennan* (= OE, OS, OHG, Goth. *brinnan*), **brannjan* (= OS, OHG *brennan*, ON *brenna*, Goth. *brannjan*)]

burn³, n. Sore, mark, on body made by burning. [f. prec.]

burn'er, n. In vbl senses, esp. in comb. as *brick*~; also, part of lamp etc. that shapes the flame. [-ER¹]

burn'et, n. Kinds of brown-flowered plant. [f. obs. adj. *burnet* f. OF *burnete* see BRUNETTE]

burn'ing, a. In vbl senses; also; ardent (~ *desire*); flagrant (~ *shame, disgrace*); hotly discussed, exciting, (~ *question*); ~ *scent* (in hunting), strong. [-ING²]

burn'ish, v.t. & i. Polish by friction; (with *well* etc.) take a polish. Hence ~ER¹(2) n. [ME, f. OF *burnir* = *brunir* (*brun* BROWN), see -ISH²]

burnous(e)' (-ōōs, -ōōz), n. Arab, Moorish, & lady's, hooded cloak. [F (-s). f. Arab. *burnus*]

burp, n., & v.i. (sl.). Belch. [imit.]

burr¹, n. **1.** Nebulous disc round moon or star. **2.** Rough ridge left on cut or punched metal or paper (~*drill*, dentist's). **3.** Siliceous rock used for millstones; whetstone; kinds of limestone. **4.** Rough sounding of letter *r* as in Northumberland; whirring; sound. [(1) var. of earlier *burrow* (Sc. var. *brough*); (2) app. same wd as BUR]

burr², v.t. & i. Pronounce with sound of Northumbrian *r*, also of French *r*; speak without clear articulation. [cf. prec.]

*burro (bŏŏ'rō), n. (colloq.). Small donkey used as pack-animal. [Sp.]

bu'rrow (-ō), n., & v.i. & t. (Make, live in) hole excavated in earth, as of foxes, rabbits, etc.; make by excavating (hole, one's way); retire out of sight; (fig.) investigate mysteries etc. Hence ~ER¹ n. [ME, app. var. of = BOROUGH]

burs'|a, n. (pl. ~*ae*, ~*as*). (anat., zool.). A sac or saclike cavity to lessen friction. Hence ~AL a. [med. L]

burs'ar, n. Treasurer, esp. of a college; exhibitioner esp. in Scots University or school, whence ~Y¹ n. [f. med. L *bursarius* (*bursa* bag, see PURSE)]

burs̄ar'ial, a. Of bursar(y). [-AL]

burst¹, v.t. & i. (past & p.p. *burst*). **1.** Fly by expansion of contents, send (containing case), violently asunder, split, (powder, shell, etc.; exaggeratively, ~ *with food* or *emotion, heart* ~s). **2.** Get away from or through, make way *out* or *in*, express one's feelings, by force or suddenly (*river* ~s *banks*; ~ *in*, come into room, interrupt; ~ *out*, exclaim; ~ *into tears, out laughing*, break into tears, laughter). **3.** Open, come open, be opened, forcibly (*boil, bud, cloud*, ~; ~ *door, door* ~s, *in* or *open*). **4.** Fill, be full, to overflowing (*grain* ~s *granary, granary* ~*ing*; ~ *with joy, envy, pride, a secret*). **5.** Appear suddenly (~ *into flame, upon the view*; *sun, war, disease*, ~ *out*); suffer ~ing of (some part; ~ *a blood-vessel*, one's *heart, sides with laughing, buttons with food*); ~ *up*, explode, bring or come to utter collapse, (colloq., & often spelt *bust up*); *go bust* (colloq.), become bankrupt etc. [OE *berstan*, OS, OHG *brestan*, ON *bresta* f. Gmc **brestan*]

burst², n. Bursting, split; ~*up* (often *bust-* colloq.), collapse; sudden issuing forth (~ *of flame*), explosion, outbreak, (lit. & fig.); spurt; continuous gallop; bout of drunkenness etc. (often vulg. *bust*; *on the bust*). [f. prec.]

burth'en (-dh-). See BURDEN.

burt'on (-tn), n. Light handy two-block tackle. [1495 *Breton, Brytton* (*tackles*)]

bury (bĕ'rĭ), v.t. Deposit in, commit to, earth, tomb, or sea (corpse); (of relatives) *to have buried*, lost; perform burial rites over; put under ground (~ *alive*; ~ *the hatchet*, renounce quarrel); put away, forget; (chiefly refl. & pass.) consign to obscurity; hide in earth (treasure etc.), cover up, submerge; withdraw from view (face in hands, hands in pockets); (p.p.) immersed (*buried in sloth*); ~*ing-ground, -place*, graveyard, cemetery. [OE *byrgan* f. WG **burgjan* f. *burg-* st. of Gmc **bergan* shelter, protect, see BURIAL]

bus, n. (pl. ~*es*), & v.i. **1.** Omnibus; (sl.) aeroplane, motor-car, motor-cycle; *miss the* ~, lose an opportunity, fail in an undertaking; ~ *driver*, ~*man*, driver of an omnibus (~*man's holiday*, leisure time spent in the same kind of occupation as one's regular work). **2.** v.i. Go by ~. [abbr.]

‖ **bus'by** (-z-), n. Tall fur cap of Hussars & R.H.A. [orig. unkn.; cf. obs. *buzz*, see BUZZ⁴]

bush¹ (-ŏŏ-), n. Shrub, clump of shrubs; bunch of ivy as ancient vintner's sign (*good wine needs no* ~); luxuriant growth of hair, whisker, etc.; woodland, untilled district, (esp. of partly-settled countries;

take to the ~, become bush-ranger); BEAT[1] *about the* ~; ~ in many bird, beast, & plant names; ~*-fighter*, *-ing*, (person used to) fighting in the ~, guerilla warfare; ~*-harrow*, heavy frame with bars between which branches are inserted for harrowing grass land or covering seed, (vb) harrow with this; ~*'man*, aboriginal of a S.-Afr. tribe, dweller, farmer, or traveller in the Australian ~, whence **bush**′**man**SHIP(3) n. [after Du. *boschjesman* (*bosch* bush)]; ~*-ranger*, Australian brigand (at first escaped convict) living in the bush; ~*-rope*, tropical wild vine netting trees together; ~*-telegraph*, rapid spreading of information, rumour, etc. [ME *busk* f. ON *buskr* = OS, late OHG *busc*, f. Gmc *busk-*, whence med. L *buscus, boscus*, Rom. *bosco*, OF *bos, bosc, bois* wood]

bush[2] (-ŏŏ-), v.t. Set (ground) with bushes to frustrate net-poaching; bush-harrow (ground). [prec.]

bush[3] (-ŏŏ-), n., & v.t. Metal lining of axle-hole or other circular orifice, perforated plug; (vb) furnish with ~. [f. MDu. *busse* BOX[2]]

bush′**el** (-ŏŏ-), n. Measure of capacity (8 gal.) for corn, fruit, etc. (*not hide* one's *light or candle under a* ~, set example; *measure others' corn by* one's *own* ~, judge others by oneself). Hence ~FUL(2) n. [ME *boyschel* f. OF *boissel* of Gaulish orig.]

Bushido (bŏŏsh′ēdō), n. The code of honour & morals evolved by the samurai. [Jap., = military knight way]

bushveld (bŏŏsh′fĕlt), n. Veld composed largely of bush; low country of Transvaal. [f. Du. *boschveld*, sco BUSH[1] & VELD]

bush′**l̇y** (-ŏŏ-), a. Abounding in bushes; growing thickly. Hence ~iNESS n. [-Y[2]]

business (bĭz′nĭs), n. 1. Being busy (orig. sense, now obs., see BUSYNESS). 2. Task, duty, province, (*make it* one's ~ *to*, undertake); cause of coming (*what is your* ~?). 3. Habitual occupation, profession, trade; serious work (*means* ~, is in earnest; *on* ~, with definite purpose; ~ *as usual*, things will proceed in spite of disturbing circumstances; ~ *end* (of tool, weapon, etc.), operative part; ~ *hours*, *hours of* ~, of regular work, open shop or office, etc.). 4. Thing needing attention, agenda, (*the* ~ *of the day, meeting*, etc.); dealings with men & matters (~ *man*, one used to these, & see below; *man of* ~, agent, attorney). 5. Difficult matter (*what a* ~ *it is!*, *make a great* ~ *of it*). 6. Thing that concerns one, that one may meddle with, (*mind your own*, *go about your*, *send about his*, ~, reproof or dismissal; *has no* ~ *to*, no right). 7. (Contempt.) device, machine, process, concern, course of events, (*sick of the whole* ~; *a lath-&-plaster* ~). 8. (Theatr.) action, dumb-show. 9. Buying & selling, bargaining, (*doing a great* ~; *good stroke of* ~; ~*man*, engaged in commerce, also

see above). 10. Commercial house, firm. [OE *bisignis* (BUSY[1] + -NESS)]

business-like, a. Systematic, practical, prompt, well-ordered. [-LIKE]

busk, n. Rigid strip stiffening corset-front. [f. F *busc* f. It. *busco* splinter, rel. to F *bûche* log f. Gmc **busk-* see BUSH[1]]

bus′**ker**, n. Itinerant musician or actor. [f. *busk* peddle etc. (perh. f. obs. F *busquer* to prowl)]

bus′**kin**, n. Boot reaching to calf or knee; thick-soled boot lending height to tragic actor in ancient times; the tragic vein, tragedy, (see SOCK; *put on the* ~, write or act tragedy). Hence ~ED[2] (-nd) a. [c. 1500, f. OF *bouzequin*, var. of *brousequin*, = OSp. *boszegui*, of unkn. orig.]

büss, n., & v.t., (arch.). Kiss. [earlier *bass* n. & v.; cf. F *baiser*, f. L *basiare*]

büst[1], n. Sculpture of person's head, shoulders, & chest; upper front of body, bosom, esp. of woman. [f. F *buste* f. It. *busto* of unkn. orig.]

büst[2]. See BURST[1,2]. Hence **büs**′**tER**[1] (1, 2) n. (sl.), freq. in comb., as BLOCK[1]-, BRONCO-, TANK-, ~*er*.

büst′**ard**, n. Kinds of large swift-running birds. [late ME; perh. mixture of OF *bistarde, oustarde*, both f. L *avis tarda* slow bird (the inappropriate adj. unexplained)]

bü′**stle**[1] (-sl), v.i. & t. Bestir oneself; make show of activity, hurry *about*; make (others) hurry or work hard. [perh. var. of obs. *buskle* f. obs. *busk* prepare (ON *búask* refl. of *búa* prepare cf. BOUND[5])]

bü′**stle**[2] (-sl), n. Excited activity, fuss. [f. prec.]

bü′**stle**[3] (-sl), n. Pad or frame puffing out top of woman's skirt behind. [orig. unkn.]

busy[1] (bĭz′ĭ), a. & n. 1. Occupied, working, engaged, with attention concentrated, (~ *in, with, at*; also, prep. being dropped, with vbl n. now looking like part., as *he was* ~ *packing*); (of telephone line) engaged; unresting, ever employed, stirring, (~ *as a bee*); fussy, meddlesome, prying, mischievous; ~ *idle(ness)*, spending energy on trifles; ~*-body*, meddlesome person, mischief-maker. Hence busILY[2] (bĭz′-) adv. 2. n. (sl.). Detective. [OE *bisig*, ME *bisi* etc.; only E & MLG, MDu. *besich* (Du. *bezig*), of unkn. orig.]

busy[2] (bĭz′ĭ), v.t. Occupy (esp. one*self*, one's *hands, eyes*, etc.), keep busy, (*with, in, at, about*, or with *-ing*, or abs.). [OE *bisgian* see prec.]

busy̆nêss (bĭz′-), n. State or quality of being busy. [mod. form differentiated in spelling & pronunc. f. BUSINESS]

büt[1] (orig. adv. & prep. = outside, without; developed into conj., under which most mod. uses belong; but it is now adv., prep., negative rel. pron., subord. & co-ord. conj.; clear distinction of these is not here possible). 1. Only (*she is* ~ *a child, I can* ~ *do it*). 2. Except, if not,

short of, except that, if it were not that,
short of the condition that, (*they are all
wrong ~ he, him; no one ~ me, I; never ~
once; he all ~ did it; what can he do ~ die*;
nothing would content him ~ I must come).
3. Otherwise than (*cannot choose~, cannot
~, do it*). **4.** Who or that not (*no one ~
knows that*). **5.** Without the result etc.
that (*never rains ~ it pours; justice was
never done ~ someone complained*). **6.**
Rather than so-&-so shall prove untrue
(*it shall go hard ~ I will get there; ten to
one ~ it was you*); that not (*not such a
fool ~—also ~ that, ~ what—he can see
that; it is impossible ~ that offences will
come*). **7.** To say (that) not (*not ~
that—also what—he believed it himself*);
~ for this etc., were it not so, without
this; *~ then, ~* on the other hand (*it is
hot, no doubt, ~ then the heat is dry*). **8.**
(After neg.) that (*I don't deny, doubt, ~
that*). **9.** On the contrary, nevertheless,
however, on the other hand, moreover,
yet. [OE *be-ūtan, būtan, būta* (BE-, OUT)
outside, without, = OS *biūtan*, OHG
biūzan]

būt², n., & v.t. An objection; (vb) utter,
use, (~s; *~ me no~s*). [uses of prec.]

būtadi'ēne, n. (chem.). Gas used in
making synthetic rubber. [f. BUTA(NE)
+DI-²+-ENE; see BUNA]

būt'āne, n. (chem.). Hydrocarbon of the
methane series. [f. BUT(YL)+-ANE]

butch'er¹ (bŏŏ-), n. Slaughterer of animals for food; dealer in meat (*the ~, the
baker, the candlestick-maker*, people of all
trades); judge, general, etc., who has men
killed needlessly or brutally; a salmon-
-fly; *~-bird*, kind of shrike; *~'s-broom*, low
spiny-leaved evergreen; *~'s meat*, excluding poultry, game, & bacon etc. [ME
bocher f. OF *bochier* (*boc* BUCK¹) lit. dealer
in goat's flesh]

butch'er² (bŏŏ-), v.t. Slaughter (people)
wantonly or cruelly; ruin by bad reading
or editing, damage by harsh criticism. [f.
prec.]

butch'erly (bŏŏ-), a. Fit for, like, a
butcher, coarse, brutal, bloody. [-LY¹]

butch'ery (bŏŏ-), n. Shambles (in barracks, camp, ship, etc.); (attrib.) butcher's
trade (*~ trade, business*, etc.); needless or
cruel slaughter of people. [f. OF *boucherie*
(BUTCHER¹, -Y¹)]

būt'ler, n. Servant in charge of wine-cellar
& plate etc. principal manservant. [ME,
f. AF *buteler*, OF *bouteillier*, see BOTTLE¹,
-ER²(2)]

būtt¹, n. Wine or ale cask (108–140 gals);
any barrel. [15th c. *butt* (AF *but*) f. OF
bot (mod. *botte*) f. LL f. Gk *bytis* cask;
see BOTTLE¹]

būtt², n. Thicker end, esp. of tool or
weapon (*give fish the ~*, turn *~* of rod
towards him for firmer hold); trunk of
tree just above ground; *~* or *~-end*, remnant (*~-end* also = thicker end); base of
leaf-stalk; kinds of flat-fish, as sole,

plaice, turbot; hide of back & flanks
trimmed to rectangle, thickest leather
(cf. BEND¹); square end of plank meeting
a similar end (also *~-end*). [ME, (*a*) f.
MLG, MDu. *butt* (G *butte*) flat fish; see
HALIBUT, TURBOT; (*b*) = LG *but*, Du. *bot*
stumpy, Sw. *but* stump; see BUTTOCK]

būtt³, n. Mound behind target; grouse-
-shooter's stand screened by low turf or
stone wall; (pl.) shooting-range; target;
end, aim, object; object *of* (ridicule etc.);
object of teasing & ridicule. [14th c., f.
OF *but* goal, of unkn. orig.]

būtt⁴, v.i. & t., & n. Push (v. & n.) with
the head (*come ~* or *full ~ against*, run
into; *~ in*, fig., intervene, meddle); meet
end to end (*~ against, upon*); come, place
(timber etc.), with end flat *against* wall
etc. [ME, f. OF *boter* f. WG **buttan*
sprout (cf. MDu. *botten* strike, sprout)
see BUTTON; E senses partly infl. by ABUT,
BUTT²]

*butte (būt), n. Conspicuous isolated
hill, esp. one with steep or cliff-like sides.
[F, = knoll]

būtt'er¹, n. Fatty substance made from
cream by churning (*look as if ~ would not
melt in mouth*, demure; *melted ~*, sauce
of ~, flour, etc.); kinds of substance of
similar consistence or look, as *~ of almonds*; fulsome flattery; *~-&-eggs*, kinds
of plant with two yellows in flower, as
toadflax; *~-bean*, yellow-pod kind usu.
cooked in the pod unsliced, wax-pod,
(also) large dried haricot bean; *~-boat*,
sauce-boat; *~-knife*, blunt, of silver etc.,
for cutting ~; *~-scotch*, kind of toffee;
~bur, plant with large soft leaves; *~cup*,
kinds of yellow-flowered ranunculus;
~-fingers, -fingered, (person) unable to
hold things, esp. a catch at cricket;
~milk, liquid left after churning ~;
|| *~ muslin*, thin loosely woven cloth
with fine mesh, used primarily as a
wrapping for ~; *~-nut*, N.-Amer. oily
nut (-tree); *~-print*, wooden stamp for
marking ~; *~wort*, fleshy-leaved violet-
-flowered bog-plant. Hence *~Y²* a.,
~ĬNESS n. [OE *butere*, OS, OHG *butera*,
WG f. L *butyrum* f. Gk *bouturon*]

būtt'er², v.t. Spread, cook, sauce, with
butter (*fine words ~ no parsnips*, mere
professions are valueless); for other phrr.
see BREAD; (also *~ up*) flatter. [f. prec.]

|| **būtt'erbump**, n. = BITTERN. [see BUMP³]

būtt'erfly, n. & a. Diurnal erect-winged
insect with knobbed antennae; showy
or fickle (person), trifler; *~-nut, -screw*
(Mech.), with wings to be turned by
thumb & finger; BREAK¹ *~ on wheel*;
(colloq.) *butterflies* (nervous tremors) *in
the stomach* or *tummy*. [OE *buttor-flēoge* cf.
Du. *botervlieg*]

būtt'erine (-ēn), n. Imitation butter of
oleo-margarine & milk. [-INE¹]

būtt'eris, n. Farrier's tool for paring hoof.
[cf. F *boutoir* & obs. E *butter*]

būtt'ery, n. Place in colleges etc. where

bread & ale, butter, etc., are kept; ~-
-hatch, half-door over which provisions
are issued. [ME, = AF *boterie* butt-store,
f. BUTT¹+-ERY; cf. ME *botelerie* = OF
bouteillerie bottle-store]

bŭtt'ock¹, n. Half of rump (usu. in pl.);
manœuvre in wrestling (usu. *cross-~*,
running-~, etc.); *~-steak,* = rumpsteak.
[f. BUTT²+-OCK, but recorded much earlier]

bŭtt'ock², v.t. Throw by using buttock.
[f. prec.]

bŭtt'on¹, n. Knob.or disc sewn to garment to fasten it by passing through
~hole, or for ornament (*boy in* ~s, page;
take by the ~, detain, see ~*hole* below);
bud; unopened mushroom; in plant
names, as BACHELOR's ~; knob, handle,
catch, as in electric bell; small bar
revolving on pivot as door-fastening;
small rounded body; terminal knob (on
foil, making it harmless; also as ornament); ‖ ~*-boot,* fastened with ~s; ~*hole,*
slit made to receive fastening ~, (fig.)
small mouth, ‖ flower(s) worn in ~hole,
(vb) make ~holes (in), hold by a coat or
waistcoat ~, detain, (reluctant listener),
whence **bŭtt'onhōlēr¹** n. [last sense by
confusion with earlier ~*-hold*]; ~*hook,* for
pulling ~ into place; ~*-stick,* appliance
for ~-polishing. Hence (-)~ED² (-nd),
~LESS, aa., ~lĕssNESS n. [ME, f. OF
boton f. Rom. **bottonem* f. **bottare* f. WG
*buttan sprout; see BUTT⁴]

bŭtt'on², v.t. & i. Furnish with button(s);
fasten (t. & i.) with buttons (often *up*);
enclose within ~ed garment (person, or
object carried with one; usu. *up*). [f.
prec.]

bŭtt'ons, n. Liveried page. [pl. of
BUTTON¹]

bŭtt'onў, a. With many buttons. [-Y²]

bŭtt'rĕss, n., & v.t. Support built against
wall etc. (FLYING ~); prop (lit. & fig.); ~-
-like projection of hill; (vb) support (lit.
& fig., often with *up*) with ~, by argument, etc. [ME, f. OF (*ars*) *bouterez* (cf.
mod. F *arc-boutant*) pl. of *bouteret* f.
bouter BUTT⁴]

bŭtt'ў, n. (Colloq.) mate, chum, companion; (Mining) middleman between
mine-proprietor & miners; *~-gang* (of
men undertaking part of large job, sharing profits equally). [orig. unkn.]

būtyr-, būtyro-, st. & comb. form of
technical wds as *butyrA'CEOUS, butў'rIC,
butyroacĕt'ic*; of BUTTER, esp. in its chem.
aspect.

bŭx'om, a. Plump, comely. Hence
~NESS n. [earlier sense *pliant*; ME
buhsum f. st. of *būgan* BOW³+-SOME]

buy (bī), v.t. (*bought*, pr. bawt), & n. **1.**
Obtain by paying a (usu. money) price;
serve to procure (*money cannot* ~); get by
some sacrifice (*dearly bought*); gain over
(person) by bribery etc.; *I'll* ~ *it* (sl.),
I give it up, I don't know (in reply to a
riddle or question); ~ *in,* ~ a stock of,
withdraw at auction by naming higher

price than highest offered; ~ *into,* ~
stock or shares in (the Funds or a
company); ~ *off,* get rid by payment of
(claim, claimant, blackmailer); ~ *out,*
pay person to give up post, property,
etc.; ~ *over,* bribe; ~ *up,* ~ as much as
possible of, absorb (other firm etc.) by
purchase; *~ a pig in a poke,* commit oneself
inconsiderately. Hence ~'ABLE a., ~'ER¹
n., (esp.) agent who selects & purchases
stock for a large shop etc. (~*ers' market,*
one in which goods are plentiful & low
prices favour ~ers). **2.** n. A purchase (*a
good* ~, a bargain). [OE *bycgan,* OS
buggian, ON *byggja,* Goth *bugjan* of unkn.
orig.]

bŭz(z)¹, int. = Stale news!

bŭzz², v.i. & t. Make humming sound;
signal with buzzer; move, hover, *about*
(person or abs.) annoyingly like bluebottle; (sl.) go *off* or *away* quickly; (of a
company or place) sound confusedly;
circulate (t. & i. of rumour etc.); utter by
speaking together (~ *applause*); throw
hard (~ *stones*); interfere with by flying
very close to (aircraft). [imit.]

bŭzz³, n. Hum of bee etc.; sound of
people talking, stir, general movement;
*circular saw. [f. prec.]

bŭzz⁴, n. Downy beetle, fishing-fly like
it. [perh. as expressive, cf. FUZZY & obs.
buzz (large bushy) *wig*]

‖ **bŭzz⁵**, v.t. Finish (bottle of wine). [orig.
unkn.]

bŭzz'ard, n. Kinds of raptorial (*bald* ~ or
osprey, *honey* ~, *moor* ~, etc.). [ME, f.
OF *busard,* alt. f. *buson* f. L *buteonem*
falcon +-ARD]

bŭzz'er, n. In vbl senses; esp. steam-
-whistle, (also) electric buzzing-machine
for sending signals, (army sl.) signaller.
[BUZZ², -ER¹]

bwa'na (-ah-), n. (Africa). Master, sir.
[Swahili]

by¹, prep. & adv. **1.** prep. (bī, *sometimes*
bĭ). Near, at or to side of, in postal
district of, about person or in possession
of, in company of, in region of, slightly
inclining to, (*Bromley-by-Bow, Coniston-
-by-Ambleside; come here by me; stand by,*
be faithful to, help; *abide by,* accept,
observe; *have not got it by me; come by,*
obtain; *by* oneself, alone; *North by East,*
between N & NNE; *by the head, stern,*
deeper in water there; *by land & sea,
adventures by flood & field*). **2.** Along, in
passing along, through, via, avoiding;
passing, out-stripping, (*by nearest road;
by the way,* as one goes, parenthetically;
so *by the by,* esp. as formula introducing
digression; *travel by Bâle, Paris; pass
him by, go by him*). **3.** During, in the
circumstances of, (*by day, night, daylight;
by the space of,* biblical for *during*). **4.**
Through the agency, means, instrumentality, or causation, of, owing to, in
such a manner, with, (*by* oneself, without
help or prompting; *know, say, by* HEART;

multiply, divide, by; 3 ft by 2 ft; lead by the hand; set by the ears, egg on to quarrel; *go, be known, by the name of ——; what do you mean by that?; travel by rail; by all, no, means; live by bread; do it by one's deputy; have children by such a father, mother; authorized, hanged, made, by; no gas to read by; case goes by default; begin, end, by ——ing; by way of a joke; be by way of knowing everybody,* profess or be supposed to; *cautious by nature; by cheque, £6. 5. 4,* in Cr entries; *by chance; by dint of; by reason of).* 5. As soon as, not later than, (*by now, next week, tomorrow, the time—*with or oftener without—*that*); according to, after, from, (*by rote; by right; by rights,* if right were done; *take warning, ·example, by; by your leave; judge by appearances; sell, buy, by retail, measure, the yard, packet).* 6. With succession of, succeeding, (*by degrees, by hundreds, man by man, little by little).* 7ː To the extent of (*missed by a foot, too moral by half, better by far, much).* 8. Concerning, in respect of, (*do one's duty by; French by blood, Jones by name; pull up by the roots).* 9. As surely as I believe in (*by God); swear by all one holds sacred; swear by vegetarianism,* declare complete belief in it). 10. adv. (bī). Near (*stand by,* be inactive. also be ready for action, esp. Naut.). 11. Aside, in reserve, (*put, lay, set, by,* abandon or store up). 12. Past (*they marched by; all that is gone by).* 13. ~ *& large,* on the whole, everything considered, (orig. Naut., to the wind & off it). [OE *bī, bi, be,* OS, OHG *bī, bi,* Goth. *bi;* in OE the prep. was occas..*be;* in mod. E the adv. is always *bȳ,* the prep. usu. *bȳ* occas. *bȳ,* & the pref. either *bȳ-* or BE-]

bȳ², bȳe, a. Subordinate, incidental, secondary, side, out-of-the-way, secret, as *by(e) road,* the *by(e) effects, a by(e) consideration;* ~-ELECTION. [*by* adv. used attrib.; often hyphened with noun; usu. *by* when this is done, & *bye* as sep. wd]

bȳ³, n. = BYE (-*e* usu. exc. in *by the by*).

by-, the prep., adv., or adj. BY in composition. In mod. use chiefly (1) with adj. force; it may be written as separate wd (*by path* or *bye path*), hyphened (*by-path*), or, if the combination is often used, as one wd with the other (*bypath*); (2) with adv. force, as in *bystander, bygone.*

bȳ' and bȳ', adv. & n. Before long, presently; (n.) the future. [prob. f. BY prep. denoting succession (*one by one* etc.)]

bȳ-blow (-ō), n. Side blow at someone else than the main opponent; bastard child. [BY a.]

bȳe, n. Something subordinate (*by the by* or *bye,* incidentally, parenthetically); (Cricket) run scored for ball that passes batsman and wicket-keeper, *leg-~,* for one that touches batsman; (Golf) hole(s) remaining after decision of match & played as a new game; (in games where

competitors are paired off) odd man, being odd man. [BY¹ as n.]

bȳe'-bȳe¹, n. (Nursery word for) sleep, bed. [sound used in lullabies cf. *hushaby, lullaby, bye baby bunting*]

bȳe-bȳe'², int. = Good-bye. [colloq. & childish clipping of *good-bye*]

bȳ·ĕnd, n. Side or secret purpose. [BY a.]

bȳ'gone (-aw-), a. & n. Past, departed; antiquated; (pl. n.) the past, past offences (*let ~s be ~s,* forgive & forget). [BY adv.]

bȳ·lāne, n. See BY-.

bȳ·law, bȳe·law (bīl-), n. Regulation made by local authority or corporation, as town or railway company. [prob. f. obs. *byrlaw* local custom (ON *bújar* genit. sing. of *bȳr,* OE *bȳ* town, cf. *Derby* etc.), but associated with BY a.]

bȳ·nāme, n. Secondary name, sobriquet; nickname. [BY a.]

bȳ'pass (-ah-), n., & v.t. 1. Secondary gas-jet always alight from which main jet is lit when wanted. 2. Road usu. passing round, or through outskirts of, town etc., & designed to relieve traffic congestion by providing an alternative route for through traffic. 3. v.t. Furnish with a ~, make détour round (town etc.), also fig. [BY a.]

bȳ'past (-ah-), a. Gone by, elapsed. [BY adv.]

bȳ'path (-ah-), n. Retired path (lit., & fig. as ~*s of history*). [BY a.]

bȳ'play, n. Action apart from the main course of events; esp., dumb show of minor characters on stage. [BY a.]

bȳ·prŏduct, n. Thing produced incidentally in manufacturing something else. [BY a.]

bȳre, n. Cow-house. [OE *bȳre* perh. cogn. w. *būr* BOWER¹]

bȳ·road, n. Little-frequented road. [BY a.]

bȳss'|us, n. Fine ancient textile fibre & fabric of flax; tuft of silky filaments by which some molluscs adhere to rock. Hence ~A'CEOUS, ~AL, ~ĬF'EROUS, ~INE², ~OID, aa. [L, f. Gk *bussos*]

bȳ'stånder, n. Spectator. [BY adv.]

bȳ'street, n. Out-of-the-way street. [BY a.]

bȳ·way, n. Secluded road or track (often *highway & ~); short cut; less known department of any subject. [BY a.]

bȳ'word (-wĕrd), n. Proverb; person, place, etc. taken as type of some (usu. bad) quality (esp. *a ~ for iniquity* etc.). [BY a.]

bȳ·work (-wĕrk), n. Work done by the way, at leisure moments. [BY a.]

Bȳzăn't|ine, a. & n. (Inhabitant) of Byzantium or Constantinople (~*ine historians,* of Eastern Empire from 6th to 15th c.); of the style in architecture etc. developed in the Eastern Empire (round arch, cross, dome, circle, mosaic). Hence ~INĔSQUE' (-ĕsk) a., ~ĬNISM n., ~ĬNIZE(4) v.t. [f. LL *Byzantinus* f. L f. Gk *Buzantion*]

C

C (sē), letter (pl. *C*s, *C*'s, Cees). *C springs,* see CEE. (Mus.) first note of natural major scale. (In argument) third hypothetical person or thing. (Alg.) third known quantity.

Caaba (kah′aba), n. Sacred building at Mecca, Mohammedan Holy of Holies containing the black stone. [Arab. *ka′bah*]

căb, n., & v.i. (-bb-). (Go in a) hackney carriage or taxi; driver's shelter on locomotive; ~′*man*, driver of ~; ‖~-*rank*, row of ~s on ~′*stand*, where ~s are authorized to wait; ‖~-*runner, -tout*, men earning pay by fetching, or unloading luggage from, ~s. Hence ~′LESS a. [short for CABRIOLET]

căbăl′, n., & v.i. (-ll-). (Join in a) secret intrigue; clique, faction; (hist.) *the C~*, 'Committee for Foreign Affairs' under Charles II, esp. Clifford, Arlington, Buckingham, Ashley, & Lauderdale (1672), precursor of modern Cabinet. Hence ~l′ER[1] n. [f. F *cabale*(r) f. med. L *cabala* CABBALA; not f. initials of Clifford etc., being quoted from 1646]

căballer′o (-yȧr′ō), n. (pl. ~s). A Spanish gentleman. [Sp.; see CAVALIER]

căb′aret (-ā), n. French tavern; (in England, U.S., etc.) entertainment provided in restaurant etc. while guests are at table. [F]

căbb′age, n. Kinds of cultivated vegetable with round heart or head; *sea* ~, sea KALE′; ~ *butterfly, ~ white*, large white or small white; ~-*net*, for boiling ~ in; ~-*rose*, double red rose with large compact round flower; ~-*tree*, various trees, esp. certain palms with terminal bud eaten like ~. [15th c. *cabache, -oche* f. *caboche*, head, Picard form of OF *caboce* of unkn. orig.]

căb(b)′al|a, n. Jewish oral tradition; mystic interpretation, esoteric doctrine, occult lore. Hence ~ISM(3), ~IST(2), nn., ~is′tic a., ~is′tICALLY adv. [med. L, f. Heb. *qabbalah* tradition]

căbb′ȳ, n. (colloq.). Cab-driver. [-Y[3]]

căb′er, n. Roughly trimmed pine-trunk used in Sc. Highland sport of *tossing the* ~. [f. Gael. *cabar* pole]

căb′in, n., & v.t. Small rude dwelling; room or compartment in ship for sleeping or eating in, officer's or passenger's room; ~-*boy*, waiting on officers or passengers; ~ *cruiser*, power-driven vessel with ~ & living accommodation; (vb, chiefly in p.p.) confine in small space, cramp. [ME & OF *cabane* f. LL (Gaulisb) *capanna*]

căb′inėt, n. & a. **1.** Small private room, closet; case with drawers etc. for keeping valuables or displaying curiosities. **2.** ‖ (Pol.) council-room of inner circle of ministers controlling Government policy; those ministers collectively; ~ *council,*

one of their meetings; ‖ *C~ Minister*, one of them; ‖ ~ *crisis*, difficulties involving change of government or resignation of some member(s) of ~; *shadow* ~ (formed by Oppojition leaders from prospective holders of portfolios). **3.** ‖~ *edition*, between library & popular in cost etc.; ‖ ~ *photograph*, size larger than carte-de-visite; ~ *pudding*, made of sponge-cakes, eggs, milk, etc.; ~-*maker, -making*, skilled joiner, joinery, (also of prime minister forming new government). [CABIN + -ET[1], influenced also by F *cabinet*]

că′ble[1], n. Strong thick rope (Naut., 10 in. or more in circumf., cf. CABLET, HAWSER) of hemp or wire strands; (Naut.) rope or chain of anchor, (as measure) 100 fathoms; submarine or underground line containing insulated wires, also = CABLE-GRAM; (Archit. & goldsmith's work) rope-shaped ornament; ~-*car*, one moved by an endless ~; ~-*laid rope*, of three triple strands; ~ *railway, tramway*, one along which carriages are drawn by an endless ~. [ME, OF *cable* f. LL *capulum* halter]

că′ble[2], v.t. & i. Furnish, fasten, with cable; (Archit.) fill lower part of flutings of (column) with convex mouldings; transmit (message), communicate, inform (person), by cable. [16th c., f. prec.]

că′blegrăm (-lg-), n. Message by submarine cable. [CABLE[1] + -GRAM]

că′blėt, n. Cable-laid rope under 10 in. in circumference. [16th c., -ET[1]]

cabŏbs′, n. pl. Meat cooked in small pieces with ginger, garlic, etc. [Arab. *kabab*]

căbochŏn′ (-sh-), n. Gem polished but not shaped or faceted; *en* ~, (of a gem) so treated. [f. F *caboche*; see CABBAGE]

cabōō′dle, n. (sl.). *The whole* ~, all the lot (persons or things). [U.S., of unkn. orig.; cf. BOODLE]

cabōōse′, n. Cooking-room on ship's deck; *guard's van or car on goods train for workmen etc. [f. earlier Du. *cabuse* (*combuse*, cf. G *kabüse, kombüse*, F *cambuse*) mod. Du. *kabuis, kombuis*, of unkn. orig.]

căb′otage, n. Coasting-trade; reservation to a country of ground & surface & air traffic within its territory. [F, f. *caboter* to coast, of unkn. orig.]

căb′riōle, n. & a. Kind of curved leg characteristic of Queen Anne & Chippendale furniture (often attrib.). [as foll., from resemblance to goat's foreleg]

căbriolet′ (-lā), n. Light two-wheeled hooded one-horse chaise; motor-cab with fixed sides & folding top. [F, f. *cabriole* goat's leap; see CAPRIOLE]

ca′cănn′y (kah-). See CANNY.

cacā′o, n. & a. Seed of tropical Amer. tree, giving cocoa & chocolate; the tree (also ~-*tree*). [Sp., f. Mex. *caca*(*uatl* tree)]

căch′alot (-shalŏt, -shalō), n. Kinds of whale with teeth in lower jaw, esp.

common ~, sperm whale. [F, f. Sp., Pg. *cachalote*; ult. orig. unkn.]

cache (kåsh), n., & v.t. Hiding-place for treasure, provisions, ammunition, etc., esp. as used by explorers; the hiding (*make a* ~) or stores hidden; (vb) place in ~. [F, f. *cacher* to hide]

cachec'tic (-k-), a. Of, suffering from, CACHEXY. [f. L f. Gk *kakhektikos*; cf. F *cachectique*]

cách'et (-shā), n. Stamp (fig.), distinguishing mark, internal evidence of authenticity; (Med.) small case (made of gelatine etc.) enclosing dose of (nauseous) medicine. [F, f. *cacher* press]

cachěx'ÿ (-k-), n. Ill-conditioned state of body or mind. [f. LL *cachexia* f. Gk *kakhexia* (CACO- +*hexis* habit); cf. F *cachexie*]

căch'inn|āte (-k-), v.i. Laugh loudly. So ~A'TION n., ~ātoRY a. [f. L *cachinnare*, -ATE[3]]

căch'olŏng, n. Kind of opal. [f. Kalmuck *kaschtschilon* beautiful stone]

căch'ou (-shōō), n. = CATECHU; pill used by smokers to sweeten breath. [F, f. Malay *kachu*; see CATECHU]

cachu'cha (-ōō-), n. A Spanish solo dance. [Sp.]

cacique' (-sěk), n. W.-Indian & Amer.--Indian native chief; (Spanish pol.) political boss. Hence **caciqu'ISM** (-sěk²) n., local government on Tammany lines. [Sp., f. Haytian]

căc'kl|e, v.i. & t., & n. (Make) clucking of hen after laying; (indulge in) glib noisy inconsequent talk; boast; chuckle; ~e *out* etc., say ~ingly. Hence ~ER[1] n. [ME *cakelen*; imit., cf. Du. *kakelen*, G *gackeln*]

căco-, comb. form of Gk *kakos* bad, found in some wds taken direct or through L (& F) f. Gk; & prefixed in med. terms (=*disease of*, as *cacophthalmia* eye--disease, or *mal-*, as *cacomorphia* malformation) usu. to Gk components, rarely to L as *cacodorous* ill-smelling.

căcodēm'on, -aem'on, n. Evil spirit; malignant person. [f. Gk *kakodaimon* (prec. + *daimōn* spirit)]

căc'odýl, n. Stinking poisonous compound of arsenic & methyl. Hence **căcodýl'IC** a. [Gk *kakōdēs* stinking (CACO- + *od-* root of *ozō* to smell) + -YL]

cacŏ'ĕpý, n. Bad pronunciation (cf. ORTHO-EPY). [f. Gk CACO(*epeia* f. *epos* word, see -Y¹)]

căcoĕth'es (-ēz), n. Ill habit, itch for doing something unadvisable, usu. in *scribendi* ~, scribbling-mania. [f. L f. Gk *kakoēthes* neut. adj. (CACO- + *ēthos* disposition)]

cacŏg'raphý, n. Bad handwriting or spelling. Hence **cacŏg'RAPHER** n., **căco-GRAPH'IC**(AL) aa. [CACO-, after *orthography*]

cacŏl'ogÿ, n. Bad choice of words or pronunciation. [f. LL f. Gk *kakologia* vituperation (CACO-, -LOGY)]

cacōōn', n. Large flat polished bean of tropical shrub with 6–8 ft pods. [African?]

cacŏph'onous, a. Ill-sounding. [f. Gk *kakophōnos* (as foll.) + -OUS]

cacŏph'onÿ, n. Ill sound (cf. EUPHONY); discord (lit. & fig.). [f. Gk *kakophōnia* (CACO-, *phōnē* sound, see -Y¹)]

căc't|us, n. Kinds of succulent plant with thick fleshy stem, usu. no leaves, & clusters of spines. Hence~A'CEOUS (-shŭs), ~AL, ~OID, aa. [L, f. Gk *kaktos* cardoon]

cacūm'inal, a. (phonet.). (Of sounds) produced with the tip of the tongue inverted or curled upwards towards the hard palate. [f. L *cacumen -minis* top, extremity + -AL]

căd, n. Person of low manners; person guilty or capable of ungentlemanly conduct, blackguard, whence ~d'ISH¹ a.; (obs.) hanger-on employed about (esp. school & college) games; (obs.) omnibus conductor. [abbr. of CADET]

cadăs'tral, a. Of, showing, the extent, value, & ownership, of land for taxation (esp. ~ *survey*). [F, f. *cadastre* f. mod. Pr. *cadastro* f. It. *catast(r)o*, earlier *catastico* f. late Gk *katastikhon* list, register]

cădavě'ric, a. (med. & physiol.). Characteristic of a corpse. [f. L *cadaver* + -IC]

cadăv'erous, a. Corpse-like; deadly pale. [f. L *cadaverosus* (*cadaver* corpse) + -OUS]

cădd'ie, n. Golf-player's attendant for carrying clubs etc. [f. F *cadet* CADET]

cădd'is, n. ~*-fly*, feebly flying freq. nocturnal insect living near water; ~*-worm*, larva of ~*-fly* etc., living in water & making cylindrical case of sticks etc., used as bait. [of unkn. orig.]

cădd'ÿ, n. (Also *tea-*~) small box for holding tea. [f. Malay *kati* weight = 1⅓ lb.]

cād'ence, n. Rhythm; measured movement, esp. of sound; fall of voice, esp. at end of period; intonation; close of musical phrase. Hence (-)**căd'enc**ED² (-st) a. [F, f. It. *cadenza* f. pop. L *cadentia*; see CHANCE¹]

cād'encÿ, n. Descent of younger branch, cadetship. [as prec., -ENCY]

cadĕn'za (-tsa), n. (mus.). Flourish of voice or instrument at close of movement. [It.]

cadĕt', n. Younger son; student in naval or military or air force college, whence ~SHIP n.; ~ *corps*, company of schoolboys receiving elementary military training. [f. F *cadet* f. 15th-c. Gascon *capdet* = Prov. *capdel* f. LL *capitellum* dim. of L *caput* head = little chief]

cădge, v.i. & t. Go about peddling or begging; get by begging. [etym. unkn.]

cădg'er, n. Carrier; itinerant dealer in eggs, butter, etc., between remote farms & towns; street hawker; beggar, loafer. [-ER¹]

cad'ï (kah-, kā-), n. Civil judge, usu. of town etc., among Turks, Arabs, Persians. [f. Arab. *qadi* f. *qada* judge]

Cădmē′an. See VICTORY. [f. L f. Gk *Kadmeios*+-AN]

căd′mium, n. Bluish-white metal resembling tin; ~-*yellow*, intense yellow pigment. Hence **cădmiF′EROUS,** aa. [f. obs. *cadmia* CALAMINE f. L f. Gk *kadmia* (*gē*) Cadmean (earth), -IUM]

cadre (kah′dr), n. Framework, scheme; (Mil.) permanent establishment of unit forming nucleus for expansion at need. [F, f. It. *quadro* f. L *quadrus* SQUARE]

cadū′cěus, n. (pl. -*ěi*). Ancient herald's wand, esp. as carried by messenger-god Hermes or Mercury. [L, f. Gk *karukion* (*kērux* herald)]

cadū′cĭtў, n., **cadūc′ous,** a. Fleeting (nature); perishable(ness); (Zool. & Bot., of organs & parts) falling off (n. & a.) when work is done. [n. thr. F *caducité* (-TY), a. f. L *caducus* falling (*cadere* fall) + -OUS]

caec′|um (sē-), n. (pl. -*ca*). The blind gut, first part of large intestine in mammals etc.; any tube with closed end. Hence ~AL, ~ĬFORM, aa., ~aLĬY² adv., ~IT′IS n. [L, for *intestinum caecum* f. *caecus* blind]

Caesar (sēz′ar), n. Roman Emperor from Augustus to Hadrian; heir presumptive of later Roman Emperor; (loosely) any Roman Emperor; an autocrat; the civil power (*Matt.* xxii. 21); ~'s *wife*, person required to be above suspicion. [L, family name of C. Julius]

Caesǎ′rèan, -ĭan, (sīz-), a. & n. Of Caesar or the Caesars, imperial; ~ *birth, operation*, delivery of child by cutting walls of abdomen (from the improbable belief that Julius was so delivered); (n.) adherent of Caesar or an autocratic system. [f. L *Caesarianus* see -EAN]

Caes′arĭsm, -ĭst, (sēz-), nn. (Believer in) autocracy. [-ISM(3), -IST(2)]

caes′ious (sēz-), a. (bot.). Bluish or greyish green. [f. L *caesius*+-OUS]

caes′ium (sēz-), n. (chem.). An alkali-metal. [as prec. f. its spectrum lines]

caesūr′|a (sĭz-), n. (Cl. prosody) break between words within a metrical foot; (Eng. prosody) pause about middle of line. Hence ~AL a. [L (*caedere caes-* cut, -URE)]

café¹ (kăf′ā), n. Coffee-house, restaurant (esp. foreign; ~ *chantant* (see Ap.), with music & entertainments, often in open air). [F, = coffee(-house)]

café² (kafà′), n. Coffee; ~ *au lait* (ō lā), with milk; ~ *noir* (nwahr), without milk. [F]

căfētēr′ĭa, n. Restaurant in which customers fetch what they want from the counters. [Sp., = coffee-shop]

căffē′ic, a. (chem.). Of coffee (esp. ~ *acid*). [f. F *caféique,* see prec., -IC]

căff′ěine (-ēn), n. Vegetable alkaloid found in coffee & tea plants. [f. F *caféine* (CAFÉ², -INE⁵)]

Caffre. See KAFIR.

căf′tan (*also* kăftahn′), n. Eastern long under-tunic with waist girdle. Hence

~ED² (-nd) a. [f. Turk. *kaftan* (in earlier use thr. F)]

cāge, n., & v.t. Fixed or portable prison, of wire or barred, esp. for birds or beasts or prisoners of war; prison (lit. or fig.); (Mining) frame for hoisting & lowering cars; open framework of various kinds; (vb) place or keep in ~. [ME, f. OF f. L *cavea*]

***cā′gey** (-jĭ), a. Shrewd; not forthcoming, unapproachable, self-contained. Hence **cā′gĭLY²** adv. [orig. uncert.]

***cahoot** (ka-hŏŏt′), n. (sl.). Company, partnership; *go* ~s, go shares; *in* ~s, in collusion. [prob. f. F *cahute* cabin]

caiman. See CAYMAN.

Cain, n. Fratricide, murderer; *raise* ~, make a disturbance. [*Gen.* iv]

cainozō′ic (kĭn-), a. (geol.). Of the third geological period (= *tertiary,* cf. *palaeo-zoic, mesozoic*). [f. Gk *kainos* new +*zōon* animal (cf. ZOO-)+-IC]

caique (ka-ēk′), n. Light Bosporan row-boat; Levantine sailing-ship. [F, f. Turk. *kaïk*]

cairn, n. Pyramid of rough stones as memorial, sepulchre, landmark, etc.; (also ~ *terrier*) small short-legged long-bodied shaggy-coated terrier (from its being used to hunt among ~s). [f. Gael. *carn*]

cairngŏrm′, n. (Also ~ *stone*) yellow or wine-coloured semi-precious stone. [found on *C-*~, Scotch mountain (Gael. *carn gorm* blue cairn)]

caiss′on, n. Ammunition chest or wagon; large watertight case open at bottom, from which water is kept out by air pressure, used in laying foundations under water; boat-shaped vessel used as dock gate; ~ *disease* (of workers in compressed air, as in ~s etc.). [F (*caisse* f. L *capsa* CASE², -OON)]

cait′iff, n. & a. (poet. & arch.). Base, despicable, (person); coward(ly). [ME, f. ONF *caitif* f. L *captivus* CAPTIVE]

cajōl|e′, v.t. Persuade or soothe by flattery, deceit, etc. (also ~*e* person *into* doing, *out of*, something; or ~*e* something *out of* person). Hence ~e′MENT (-lm-), ~′ER¹, ~′ERY(4), nn., ~′ingLY² adv. [f. F *cajoler* of uncert. orig.]

cāke, n., & v.i. & t. **1.** Small flattish loaf of bread (arch., as in *King Alfred & the* ~*s*); thin oaten bread (Sc. & north.; also *oat*~; *land of* ~*s,* Scotland); (usu. Eng. sense) bread with other ingredients besides flour, as currants, spice, eggs, sugar —the substance (~) or (*a* ~) a portion of it baked in a thick disc or ornamental shape—; flattish compact mass of other food (*fish*~, *soap*~) or of any compressed substance (~ *of soap, wax, tobacco*); ~*s & ale,* merry-making; ~-*walk,* kinds of dance developed from Negro contest in graceful walking with ~ for prize; *a piece of* ~ (colloq.), something easy or pleasant; *take the* ~, carry off the honours; *cannot*

eat your ~ and have it, cannot enjoy the two alternatives; hence **cāk′y²** a.
2. v.t. & i. Form into compact flattish mass. [ME, prob. f. ON *kaka* (cf. OHG *kuocho*)]

călabăr′ bean, n. Poisonous seed of African climbing plant yielding an extract valuable in medicine & surgery. [*Calabar* on W. coast of Africa]

căl′abăsh, n. Kinds of gourd whose shell serves for holding liquid; fruit of American ~-tree, so used; pipe etc. made from these or of like shape. [f. F *calebasse* f. Sp. *calabaça*, Sicil. *caravazza*, perh. f. Pers. *kharbuz* melon]

căl′aber, -ar, n. Fur of grey squirrel. [ME, f. med. L *calabris, calebrum* f. Calabria]

***călaboōse′** (-s), n. Common prison, lock-up. [f. Sp. *calabozo* dungeon]

călaman′cō, n. Glossy Flemish woollen stuff much used in 18th c. [etym. unkn.; cf. Du. *kalamink*, F *calmande*]

călaman′der, n. Hard cabinet wood of Ceylon & India. [etym. unkn.]

căl′amarў, n. Kinds of cuttlefish with pen-shaped internal shell. [f. L *calamarius (calamus* pen, -ARY¹)]

căl′amine, n. A zinc ore found in England. [F, f. med. L *calamina* alt. f. L *cadmia* CADMIUM]

căl′amint, n. Kinds of aromatic herb. [ME, f. OF *calament* ult. f. Gk *kalaminthē*]

căl′amite, n. Fossil plant allied to mare's tail. [f. L *calamus* reed +-ITE¹(2)]

calăm′ĭtous, a. Marked by, causing, calamity. Hence ~LY² adv. [f. F *calamiteux* or L *calamitosus* see foll., & -ITOUS]

calăm′ĭtў, n. Adversity, deep distress; grievous disaster. [f. F *calamité* f. L *calamitatem* (-TY)]

***calăn′dō**, mus. direction. Diminish tone & pace gradually. [It.]

calăsh′, n. 1. Light low-wheeled carriage with removable folding hood; carriage hood. 2. (hist.). Woman's hooped silk hood. [f. F *calèche* f. Slav. (Czech *kolèsa* etc.)]

călc- comb. form=lime; ~-*sinter*, crystalline deposit from lime-springs; ~-*spar*, crystallized carbonate of lime; ~-*tuff*, porous calcareous deposit. [f. G *kalk* f. L *calx -cis*]

călcār′eous, -ious, a. Of, containing, carbonate of lime or limestone. Hence **călcār′ĕo-**, comb. form. [f. L *calcarius* (CALC-, -ARY¹)+-OUS; first spelling wrong but usu.]

călcĕolār′ia, n. Kinds of plant with slipper-shaped flower. [f. L *calceolus* dim. of *calceus* shoe, -ARY¹]

căl′cĕolāte, a. (bot.). Slipper-shaped. [as prec., -ATE²]

căl′cĭc, a. Of calcium. [-IC]

călcĭf′erous, a. Yielding carbonate of lime. [f. L *calx -cis* lime, +-FEROUS]

căl′cĭfў, v.t. & i. Convert, be converted,

into lime; replace by lime; harden by deposit of salts of lime; petrify. Hence ~ĭF′IC a., ~ĭFĬCA′TION n. [as prec. +-FY]

căl′cimĭne, n., & v.t. White or tinted wash for ceilings & walls; (vb) distemper with ~. [P; f. L *calx -cis* lime +factitious ending]

căl′cĭn|e, v.t. & i. Reduce to quicklime or friable substance by roasting or burning; desiccate; refine by consuming grosser part; burn to ashes; (intr.) suffer these processes. Hence ~A′TION, ~ER¹(2), nn. [ME, f. OF *calciner* or med.L *calcinare* f. LL *calcina* lime]

căl′cĭte, n. Native carbonate of lime. [f. L *calx -cis* lime +-ITE¹]

căl′cĭum, n. Chemical element, greyish white metal, the basis of lime (in many compd terms, as ~ *chloride*). Hence **căl′cĭo-** comb. form. [as prec. +-IUM]

căl′cŭl|able, a. That may be reckoned, measured, computed, or relied upon. Hence ~ABIL′ITY n. [f. as foll. +-ABLE]

căl′cŭl|āte, v.t. & i. Compute (w. noun or clause, or abs.) by figures (~*ating-machine*, that does sums automatically); ascertain beforehand (event, date, etc.) by exact reckoning; plan deliberately (t. & i., esp. in intr. part. & p.p.= cold-blooded, selfish); (usu. pass.) arrange, adapt, (conduct, apparatus, etc.) *for* (purpose), *to* (do); (in p.p.) fit, suitable, *to* do; rely *upon*; *(colloq.)* suppose, believe. Hence ~ATIVE a. [f. LL *calculare* (CALCULUS), -ATE³]

călcŭlā′tion, n. (Result got by) reckoning; forecast. [ME, f. OF f. LL *calculationem* (prec., -ATION)]

căl′cŭlātor, n. In vbl senses; also: set of tables for use in calculation; calculating-machine. [L (CALCULATE, -OR)]

căl′cŭlous, a. Of, suffering from, stone or calculus. [f. L *calculosus* (foll., -OUS)]

căl′cŭlus, n. (pl. -*li*, in math. sense freq. ~es). 1. (med.). Stone, concretion in some part of body (*renal* etc. ~ f. the particular part; *uric acid* etc. ~ f. its composition). 2. (math.). Particular method of calculation, as *differential, integral*, ~. [L, = small stone (-ULE) used in reckoning on abacus]

căldār′ĭum, n. (archaeol.). Roman hot bath room. [L, f. *calidus* hot, see -ARY¹]

caldron. See CAULDRON.

caldera (kahldār′a), n. (geol.). Deep cauldron-like cavity on summit of volcano. [Sp., = cauldron]

Călĕdōn′ian, a. & n. (Native) of ancient Scotland (also used in mod. titles of clubs etc., & joc.=Scotch or Scot). [f. L *Caledonia* northern Britain, -AN]

călĕfā′cient (-shent), a. & n. (Medical agent) producing warmth. [f. L *calefacere (calēre* be warm, *facere* make), -ENT, -ANT]

călĕfăc′torў, a. & n. Producing warmth; (Archaeol.) warm room in monastery. [f. LL *calefactorius* see prec., -TORY]

căl′endar¹, n. System by which beginning, length, & subdivision, of civil year are fixed, esp. the GREGORIAN ~, used in Engl. from 1752; JULIAN ~; table(s) with months, weeks, & festivals etc., of a given year, or with dates important for certain classes, as *Gardener's* ~; register, list, esp. of canonized saints, prisoners for trial, or documents chronologically arranged with summaries; ~ MONTH. [ME, f. AF *calender*, (OF *-ier*), f. L *calendarium* account-book (CALENDS, -AR²)]

căl'endar², v.t. Register, enter in list; arrange, analyse, & index (documents), whence ~ER¹ n. [15th c., f. prec.]

căl'ender¹, v.t., & n. Press (cloth, paper, etc.) in a ~ or roller-machine to smooth it; steam mangle; (arch.) person who ~s. Hence căl'endRY n. [f. F *calendre(r)*, f. med. L *ca-*, *celendra*, corr. of L f. Gk *kulindros*]

căl'ender², n. Mendicant dervish in Turkey or Persia. [f. Pers. *qalandar*]

căl'ends, k-, n. pl. First of month in Roman calendar; *on the Greek C~*, never. [ME, f. L *kalendae*, acc. *-as*, or OF *calendes*]

căl'enture, n. Tropical fever or delirium in which sailors etc. leap into sea. [F, f. Sp. *calentura* fever f. part. st. of L. *calēre* be hot, -URE]

calf¹ (kahf), n. (pl. *-ves*). Young of bovine animal, esp. domestic cow, for first year (*cow in*, *with*, ~, pregnant; *slip her* ~, suffer abortion); *golden* ~, wealth as object of worship (*Ex.* xxxii); *stupid fellow*; MOON-~; *child* (so ~*-love*, childish love affair); (also ~*skin*)=~*-leather*, esp. in bookbinding (~*-bound*) & shoemaking (*willow* ~, superior brown leather used in shoemaking; young of elephant, whale, deer, etc.; *sea-*~, seal; (Naut.) floating piece of ice; ~*-knee*, knock-knee; ‖ ~'s *teeth*, milk teeth; *calves-foot jelly*. Hence ~'HOOD n., ~'ISH¹(1) a. [OE *cælf*, OS *calf*, OHG *chalb*, ON *kalfr*, Goth. *kalbō* f. Gmc *kalbh-*]

calf² (kahf), n. (pl. *-ves*). Fleshy hinder part of leg-shank; ~ part of stocking. Hence ~'LESS, -calvED² (kahvd), aa. [f. ON *kálfi* of unkn. orig.]

Căl'iban, n. Man of degraded bestial nature. [Shakesp., *Tempest*, & see CANNIBAL]

căl'ibr|āte, v.t. Find calibre of; calculate irregularities of (tube, gauge) before graduating. Hence ~A'TION n. [foll. +-ATE³]

căl'ibre (*-er*), căl'iber, n. Internal diameter of gun or any tube; weight of character, standing, importance; ability. Hence -căl'ibrED²(*-erd*) a. [F (*-bre*), f. It. *calibro* or Sp. *-bre* f. Arab. *qalib* mould]

căl'icle, n. (biol.). Small cup-like body. So calic'ülAR¹ a. [f. L *caliculus* dim. of *calix* cup]

căl'icō, n. & a. (pl. ~*es*). ‖(Of) cotton cloth, esp. plain white unprinted, bleached or

unbleached (~*-ball*, dance at which only cotton dresses are worn); ~*-printer*, *-ting*, producer, production, of coloured patterns on ~. '[orig. *Calicut*-(etc.) *cloth* f. town on Malabar coast]

călifŏrn'ium, n. Radio-active transuranic element. [f. *Californ(ia)*+-IUM]

călĭŏl'ogy̆, n. Study of birds' nests. [f. Gk *kalia* hut, nest, -o-, -LOGY]

căl'ĭpăsh, căl'ĭpee, nn. Gelatinous substances in turtle regarded as dainties (*-ash*, dull green next upper shell; *-ee*, light yellow next lower shell). [perh. W.-Ind.; perh. *-ash* = CARAPACE]

căl'ĭph, *-if*, n. Successor (e.g. of Mohammed), (title of) Mohammedan chief civil & religious ruler. Hence căl'ĭphATE¹ n. [f. OF *caliphe* f. Arab. *khalifah* successor]

căl'ĭx, n. (anat.;: pl. *-ĭcēs*). Cup-like cavity or organ. [L, = cup, cf. CALYX]

calk¹ (kawk), v.t., & n. (Provide with) sharp iron to prevent horse-shoe or boot from slipping. [app. ult. f. L *calx calcis* heel, cf. CALKIN.]

calk² (kawk), v.t. Trace by colouring back of design & pressing along outlines. [f. F *calquer* f. It. & L *calcare* tread]

cal'kin (kaw-, *also* kăl-), n. Turned-down heels of horse-shoe, also turned edge in front, esp. when sharpened in frost; iron guards on boots or shoes. [f. OF *calcain* f. LL *calcaneum* (calx *-cis* heel); 15th c. *kakun* f. Du. *kalkoen*]

call¹ (kawl), v.t. & i. 1. Cry, shout, speak loudly, (lit. & fig. etc., as): (bird, trumpet, etc.) utter characteristic note; cry *out*; cry *to* (person); signal (*for* trumps); pay brief visit (*at* house, *on* person); read *over* (names to ascertain presence); ~ *for*, order, demand, need, go & fetch; ~ *on*, invoke, appeal to; ~ *off*, cancel (engagement etc.). 2. Summon (lit. & fig. etc., as): demand presence of (cab, witness, actor after curtain); broadcast (to); (Cards) direct opponent to play (exposed or other card); ~ *into being*, create; ~ *to* ACCOUNT²; ~ *into play*, give scope for; ~ *in question*, dispute; ~ *to mind* etc., also ~ *up*, recollect; ~ *away*, *off*, divert, distract; ~ *in* money lent, doctor etc. for advice; ~ *forth*, elicit; ~ *out*, elicit, challenge to duel, summon (troops) esp. to aid the civil authorities; ~ *over the* COALS; ~ *up*, imagine, summon to talk by telephone, summon to serve in army etc. (so ~*-up* n.); rouse from sleep; fix the moment for (~ *case* in law-court; ~ *a halt*; ~ *a meeting*); urge, invite, nominate, (*duty, pleasure, ~s*; *many are ~ed*; ‖ ~ *to* the BAR¹, *ministry*; ~ *attention to*; ~ *to witness*). 3. (With n. or adj. as compl.) name, describe as, (~ *a* SPADE *a spade*; ~ *him John*, ~ *him by the name of John*; ~ person *names*, abuse him; ~ COUSINS *with*); consider, regard as, (~ *that mean*; ~ *it a day*, regard the day's work as being finished); ~ (thing) one's *own*, possess; *~ down* (colloq.), reprimand, challenge.

[late OE *ceallian* f. ON *kalla*; cf. MLG, MDu. *kallen*, OHG *challōn*]

call² (kawl), n. Shout, cry; (also ~-*over* =ROLL-~; special cry of bird etc., imitation of this, instrument imitating it; signal on bugle etc., signalling-whistle; looking-in on business (so *house of* ~); short formal visit (*pay* ~, make one); invitation, summons, (to actor for applause; ‖ to the BAR¹; from God, conscience, or congregation, to be pastor); duty, need, occasion, (*no* ~ *to blush*); demand for money, esp. for unpaid capital from company shareholders (St. Exch.) option of claiming stock at given date; (Bridge) player's right or turn to make a bid, bid thus made, conventional signal to partner to lead trumps; a ring on or conversation over the telephone; ~-*loan*, ~-*money*, lent subject to recall without notice; *at*, *within*, ~, ready for orders; ~-*boy*, prompter's attendant summoning actors; ~-*day*, -*night*, at Inns of Court, for calling students to bar; ~-*girl*, prostitute accepting appointments by telephone; ~-*over*: (Betting) reading aloud a list of prices (in sporting club etc.); roll-~ at schools. [f.· prec.]

call'a, n. (bot.). (Also ~-*lily*) marsh plant of N. Europe. [orig. unkn.]

call'er¹ (kaw-), n. In vbl senses; esp., person who pays call or visit. [-ER¹]

call'er², a. (Sc.). Fresh, not decaying, (of herring etc.); cool (of air). [Sc. var. of ME *calver*; ult. hist. obsc.]

callig'raph|y̆, n. Beautiful handwriting; (improp.) handwriting. So calliG'RAPHER, ~IST(1), nn., **călliGRAPH'IC** a. [ult. f. Gk *kalligraphia* (*kallos* beauty, -GRAPHY)]

call'ing (kaw-), n. In vbl senses; also or esp.: divine summons to salvation or self-devotion; impulse to do something as right; occupation, profession, trade; persons following a particular business. [-ING¹]

Calli'opĕ, n. Muse of epic poetry; (*c*~) set of steam whistles played by a keyboard like that of an organ. [Gk *Kalliopē* beautiful-voiced]

căl(l)'iper, n. & a., & v.t. ~ *compasses* or ~*s*, compasses with bowed legs for measuring diameter of convex bodies, or with out-turned points for measuring calibre; ~ (*splint*), metal support for leg; ~-*square*, rule with movable cross-heads for taking internal or external diameters; (vb) measure with ~s. [app. = CALIBRE]

căllisthĕn'|ĭc, a. Suitable for producing strength with beauty (esp. of girls' gymnastics). Hence ~ICS n. [f. Gk *kallos* beauty+*sthenos* strength+-IC]

callŏs'it̆y, n. Abnormal hardness & thickness of skin; hardened insensible part, lump, (from friction, or natural as on horses' legs). [f. F *callosité* or L *callositas* (see foll., -TY)]

call'ous, a. (Physiol., Zool.) hardened, hard, (of parts of skin); (of person, heart,

etc.) unfeeling, insensible, whence ~NESS n. [f. L *callosus* (CALLUS, -OUS) or F *calleux*]

căll'ow (-ō), a. Unfledged; downy like young birds; raw, inexperienced; (Irish, a. & n.) low-lying, often flooded, (meadow). [OE *calu* f. WG *kalw*- (cf. G *kahl*) perh. f. L *calvus* bald]

căll'us, n.(physiol., path., bot.). Thickened part of skin or soft tissue; bony material formed while bone-fracture heals. [L]

calm¹ (kahm), n. Stillness,· serenity, (of weather, air, sea, the mind, social or political conditions); *a*~, windless period. [ME & OF *calme* f. It. (= Sp., Pg.) *calma*, app.· f. LL *cauma* f. (w. infl. of L *calor* heat) Gk *kauma* heat (*kaiō* burn)]

calm² (kahm), a., & v.t. & i. **1.** Tranquil, quiet, windless, (lit. & fig.); (colloq.) impudent (*pretty* ~ *of him*); hence ~'LY² adv., ~'NESS n. **2.** v.t. Make ~, pacify; (v.i.; alw. w. *down*) become ~. [f. F *calme* n. & a., see prec.]

căl'mative (*also* kahm-), a. & n. (med.). Calming (agent), sedative. [prec.+-ATIVE]

căl'omĕl, n. (med.). Mercurous chloride used as purgative. [F, f. Gk *kalos* fair, *melas* black (explained anecdotically in various ways)]

călores'cence, n. (physics). Change of heat-rays to light-rays. [irreg. f. L *calor* heat after wds in -*escence*]

calori-, comb. form of L *calor* heat in Physics & Physiol. Hence **calō'riFA'CIENT**, **călŏriF'IC**, **calŏ'riMET'RIC(AL)**, aa., **călŏriF'ICALLY** adv., **calŏ'riFICA'TION**, **călŏrĭM'ETER**, -METRY, nn., **calŏ'rĭFY** v.t.

calŏ'ric, n. Heat; ~-*engine*, driven by hot air. [f. F *calorique* (L *calor* heat, -IC)]

căl'orie, n. (physics). Unit of quantity of heat; amount of heat required to raise temperature of one gram (*small* ~) or one kilogram (*large* or *great* ~) of water 1° C. (the latter used as a unit in expressing energy value of foods). [F, irreg. f. L *calor* heat +-*ie* (-Y¹)].

calŏtte', n. Skull-cap of priests etc. [F]

călp, n. Irish dark-grey limestone. [orig. unkn.]

căl'trop, n. Four-spiked iron ball, formerly thrown on ground. to maim cavalry horses; kinds of plant with spined ~-like flower heads. [OE *calcatrippe*, ME *calketrappe*, corresp. to OF *kauke-trape* etc.; ult. referred to L *calx* -*cis* heel +TRAP, but hist. & interrelations obsc.]

căl'ŭmĕt, n. Amer.-Ind. clay-bowled reed-stemmed tobacco-pipe; symbol of peace; *smoke the* ~ *together*, make peace. [F (esp. Fr.-Canadian) dial. var. of mod. F *chalumeau* f. LL *calamellus* dim. of *calamus* reed]

calŭm'ni|āte, v.t. Slander. Hence or cogn. ~A'TION, ~ātOR, nn., ~ātORY a. [f. L *calumniari*, see -ATE³]

calŭm'nious, a. Given to, marked by, calumny. Hence ~LY² adv. [f. L *calumniosus* or F *calomnieux* (foll., -OUS)]

căl′umnў, n. Malicious misrepresentation; false charge; slanderous report. [f. L *calumnia* or F *calomnie*]

Căl′varў, n. Place, (R.-C. Ch.) representation, of Crucifixion. [OF, f. LL *calvaria* skull transl. of *Golgotha, Matt.* xxvii. 33]

calve (kahv), v.i. & t. Give birth to a calf; (esp. in pass. of calf) give birth to; (of iceberg etc.) throw off mass of ice. [OE *cealfian* (CALF[1])] **-calved.** See CALF[2].

Căl′vin|ĭsm, n. Calvin's theology (esp. the doctrines of particular election & redemption, moral inability in a fallen state, irresistible grace, final perseverance); adherence to this. So ~IST(2) n. & a., ~is′tic(AL) aa., ~is′ticalLY[2] adv., ~IZE(4) v.i. & t. [f. F *calvinisme* or mod. L *-ismus* (John *Calvin*, 1509-64)]

călx, n. (pl. *căl′cēs*). Powder or friable substance left when a metal or mineral has been burnt, residuum. [L *calx-cis* lime]

calyc-, calyci-, comb. form of CALYX. **călўcifl̄ōr′AL, -flōr′ATE[2], -flōr′ous,** aa., with stamens & petals inserted in calyx; **căl′ўcĭFORM** a.; **calўc′inAL, căl′ўcine[2],** aa., having a, on the calyx; **calўc′inAR[1]** a., = -al, also (of flower) double by increase of calyx-lobes; **căl′ўcoID, călў-coid′EOUS,** aa.

căl′ўcl|e, n. (bot.). Row of bracts surrounding calyx-base; adherent crown of seed. Hence or cogn. ~ED[2](-ld), **calўc′ū-lAR[1], calўc′ūlATE[2],** aa. [f. L *calyculus* dim. of CALYX (-ULE)]

calўp′sŏ, n. Spontaneous topical W.-Ind. song. [etym. unkn.]

calўptr-, st. of bot. terms=having, like, a hood. [f. Gk *kaluptra* veil (*kaluptō* to cover)]

căl′ўx, n. (pl. *-ycēs, -yxes*). (Bot.) whorl of leaves (SEPAL) forming outer case of bud (for derivatives see CALYC-); (Physiol. & Biol.) = CALIX. [L, f. Gk *kalux* (cf. *kaluptō* to cover) case of bud, husk]

căm, n. Projecting part of wheel etc. in machinery, grooved, toothed, or otherwise adapted to convert circular into reciprocal or variable motion. [f. Du. *kam* COMB, cf. Du. *kamrad* cog-wheel]

cămaraderie′ (-ahderĕ), n. The intimacy, mutual trust, & sociability, of comrades. [F]

cămarĭll′a, n. Cabal, clique, junto. [Sp.]

căm′aron, n. Large freshwater prawn resembling crayfish. [Sp., = shrimp]

căm′ber, n., & v.i. & t. Slight convexity above, arched form, (of beam, deck, road, etc.); (also ~*-beam*) slightly arched beam; small dock or tidal basin; (vb) have, impart to (beam etc.), such convexity. [f. F *cambre* f. L *camur* curved inwards; so F *cambrer* vb]

Căm′berwĕll Beaut′ў (bū-), n. A butterfly. [*Camberwell* in Surrey]

căm′bĭst, n. Expert in, manual of, exchangĕs; dealer in bills of exchange. [F (*-iste*) f. It. *-ista* f. *cambio* CHANGE]

căm′bĭum, n. Cellular tissue, below bark of exogens, in which annual growth of wood & bark occurs. [L, = (ex)CHANGE]

‖ căm′brel, n. Butcher's bent wood or iron for slinging carcasses by ankles. [orig. uncert.]

Căm′brian, a. & n. Welsh(man); (Geol.) (of) palaeozoic rocks lying above the Archaean in Wales & Cumberland. [f. L *Cambria* var. of *Cumbria* f. Celt. *Cymry* Welshman or *Cymru* Wales (OCelt. *Combroges* compatriots)]

căm′bric, a. & n. (Of) fine white linen; handkerchiefs. [f. *Kamerijk*, Flemish form of *Cambrai* in N. France, orig. place of making]

‖ Căm′bridge, n. University town in England; ~ *blue*, light blue; ~ *Platonists*, 17th c. group of philosophical divines at ~ University, influenced by aspects of (neo-) Platonism.

căme[1], n. Grooved slip of lead as used in lattice windows. [app.= Sc. *calm* casting-mould]

căme[2]. See COME.

căm′el, n. Large hornless ruminant long-necked cushion-footed quadruped with (Arabian) one hump or (Bactrian) two humps; thing hard to believe or put up with (*Matt.* xxiii. 24); machine for floating ship over shoals etc.; ‖ ~*-brown*, fishing-fly; ~*'s-hair*, made of ~'s hair or (paint-brushes) of squirrel's tail hairs. [late OE *camel(l)* f. L f. Gk *kamēlos* f. Semit. (cf. Heb. *gāmāl* camel); in ME reinforced by OF *cameil* etc.]

cămeleer′, n. Camel-driver. [-EER]

camĕll′ia, n. Flowering evergreen from China & Japan. [*Kamel*, 17th c. Jesuit & botanist, -IA[1]]

camĕl′opārd (*or* kăm[2]), n. = the now usu. GIRAFFE. [f. L *camelopardus* f. Gk *camēlo-pardalis* (CAMEL, PARD)]

căm′elrў, n. Troops on camels. [-RY]

Căm′embert (-ār), n. Small soft rich Normandy cheese. [name of village]

căm′éo, n. (pl. ~*s*). Piece of relief-carving in stone (sardonyx, agate, etc.) with colour-layers utilized to give background (cf. INTAGLIO). [f. It. *cam(m)eo*, whence F *camée*; OF also *cameu* (F *camaīeu*) whence earlier Eng. form, corresp. to med.L *cammaeus, camahutus*; ult. orig. unkn.]

căm′era, n. *In camera* (Lat.), in the judge's private room, not in open court; (orig. ~ *obscura*) photographing-apparatus; ~ *ŏbscūr′a, lū′cĭda* (L, = dark, light, chamber), two kinds of apparatus projecting on paper, for tracing, image of distant object. [L,=vault, f. Gk *kamara* anything with arched cover]

cămerling′o (-nggō), -lĕn-, n. The Pope's chamberlain & financial secretary; treasurer of the Sacred College. [It. (*-ingo*); see CHAMBERLAIN]

Cămerŏn′ian, a. & n. (Follower) of Richard Cameron or his doctrines; Scottish reformed presbyterian; ‖ (pl.) battalion(s) of the Scottish Rifles (formed in 1689 orig. of ~s). [-IAN]

‖ **cămi-knick'ers**, n. pl. Woman's under--garment of camisole & knickers combined. [*cami(sole)* + *knicker(bocker)*s]

căm'ĭon, n. Low flat four-wheeled horse or motor truck. [F]

căm'isŏle, n. Under-bodice, usu. embroidered etc. [F, f. Sp. *camisola* (*camisa* CHEMISE)]

căm'lĕt, n. Light cloth of various materials for cloaks etc. [orig. a costly Eastern stuff of silk & camel's hair; 15th c. *chamlett, -(e)lot* f. OF *cham-, camelot* perh. ult. f. Arab. *khaml* nap, in assoc. w. CAMEL]

cămm'ock, n. Rest-harrow; kinds of yellow-flowered plant. [OE *cammoc* of unkn. orig.]

căm'omile, ch- (pr. k-), n. Aromatic creeping composite plant with daisy-like flowers used as tonic; allied kinds of plant, *dog's, stinking, purple,* ~ ; ~ *tea,* infusion of the flowers. [ME, f. OF *camomille* f. LL *c(h)amomilla* f. Gk *khamaimēlon* earth-apple]

Camŏ'rra, n. Secret society in Naples etc. [It.]

căm'ouflage (-ŏŏflahzh), n., & v.t. Disguise of guns, ships, etc., effected by obscuring outline with splashes of various colours; use of smoke-screens, boughs, etc., for same purpose; (transf.) means of throwing people off the scent; (vb) hide by ~; [F, f. *camoufler* disguise]

camouflet (kahmŏŏflĕ'), n. Subterranean cavity formed by bomb exploding beneath surface of earth. [F]

cămp¹, n. Place where troops are lodged in tents etc.; army on campaign; military life (*courts & ~s*); temporary quarters of nomads, gypsies, travellers; camping--out; persons camping out; (S. Afr.) portion of natural veld fenced off for pasture on farms; adherents of a doctrine; ~*-bed, -chair, -stool,* folding & portable; ~*-colour,* flag used in marking out ~ ; ~*-fever,* esp. typhus; ~*- follower,* non-military hanger--on of camp, male or female; ~*-meeting,* American religious open-air or tent meeting lasting several days. [F, f. It. *campo* f. L *campus* level ground]

cămp², v.i. & t. Encamp, lodge in camp; (also ~ *out*) lodge in tent or the open, take ~ up quarters; station (troops) in camp. [f. F *camper* (prec.)]

Cămpagna (-ah'nya), n. The ~, Italian plain S.E. of Tiber. [It., f. L *Campania* (CAMP¹)]

cămpaign' (-ān), n., & v.i. **1.** Series of military operations in a definite theatre or with one objective or from taking the field to a temporary or final cessation of hostilities (*the Burma, Moscow, 1704,* ~); organized course of action, esp. (Pol.) attempt to rouse public opinion for or against a policy. **2.** v.i. Serve on or conduct a ~; hence ~ER¹ n. (*old ~er,* person practised in adapting himself to circumstances). [f. F *campagne* open country, campaign, f. It. CAMPAGNA]

cămpanil'ĕ (-nē-), n. Bell-tower, usu. detached, esp. in Italy. [It., f. *campana* bell]

cămpan|ŏl'ogў, n. The subject of bells (founding, ringing, etc.). Hence ~ŏl'OGER, ~ŏl'OGIST, nn., ~olŏ'gĭCAL a. [f. LL *campana* bell + -LOGY]

cămpăn'ūl|a, n. Kinds of plant with bell--shaped flowers, usu. blue or white, as Canterbury bell. Hence ~A'CEOUS a. [mod. L, f. as prec., + -*ula* -ULE]

cămpăn'ūlate, a. (zool. & bot.). Bell--shaped. [as prec. + -ATE²]

căm'phor, n. Whitish translucent crystalline volatile substance with aromatic smell & bitter taste. Hence **camphŏ'rĭc** a. [15th c. *camphire* etc., f. OF *camphore* or med. L *camphora,* f. Arab. *kafur*]

căm'phorāte, v.t. Impregnate or treat with camphor. [-ATE³]

căm'pĭon, n. Kinds of flowering plant, esp. the red & the white ~ & ragged robin. [etym. unkn.]

căm'pŏ săn'tō, n. Cemetery in Italy. [It., = sacred field]

‖ **cămp'shĕd**, v.t. Face with campshot, revet. [etym. unkn.]

‖ **cămp'shŏt**, n. ‖ **cămp'shĕdding**, ‖ **cămp'-sheeting**, nn. Facing of piles & boarding to resist water-action on, or out-thrust of, a bank, revetting. [etym. unkn.]

***căm'pus**, n. Grounds of a school or college; the college as a teaching etc. institution. [L, = field]

căm'pўlo-, comb. form in bot. terms = bent-. [f. Gk *kampulos*]

căm'wŏŏd, n. Hard red W.-African wood yielding dye. [perh. native *kambi*]

căn¹, n., & v.t. Vessel for liquids, usu. of metal, esp. tin, & with handle over top, whence ~'FUL(2) n.; *carry the* ~ (sl.), bear the responsibility; ~*-buoy,* large conical buoy over sands etc.; ~*-dock,* water-lily; (put in a) tin-plate box for hermetic sealing (meat, fish, fruit, etc.), whence (-)~n'ER¹ n., ~n'ERY (3) n., ~ning-factory; ~ned (sl.), drunk; ~ned *music* (sl.), music recorded for reproduction esp. on gramophone. [OE *canne* (once) = OHG *channa,* ON *kanna,* also LL *canna* f. Gmc; ME *canne, kan* prob. f. MDu. *kanne,* Du. *kan*]

căn², v. aux. (2 s., *canst* (poet.); 3 s., *can;* neg., *cannot, can't* (kahnt); past & condit., *could* (kŏŏd), (poet.) *couldst* or *couldest;* infin., part., & p.p., wanting; defective parts supplied f. *be able to*). Be able to; have the right to; be permitted to (*you ~ go;* also as mild imperat.); *could,* feel inclined to (*could laugh for joy; really couldn't think of it*); ~not AWAY *with;* (with ellipsis) *will do what I ~.* · [OE *cunnan* = OS *cunnan,* OHG *kunnan,* ON *kunna,* Goth. *kunnan,* pret.-pres. vbs. meaning *know,* cogn. w. KEN, KNOW, & w. L (*g)nosco,* Gk *gignōskō*]

Căn′aan (-nan), n. Land of promise, paradise. [O.-T. name of Palestine]

Căn′ada, a. Of, from, ~ (in names of plants, animals, products, as ~ BALSAM).

Canād′ian, a. & n. (Native) of Canada. [-IAN]

canaille (kanah′ē), n. The rabble. [F]

canăl′, n., & v.t. (-ll-). Duct in plant or animal body for food, liquid, air, etc.; artificial watercourse for inland navigation (~s *of Mars*, markings of doubtful nature on planet Mars); artificial irrigation channel; (Zool.) groove in shell for protrusion of breathing-tube; (v.t. ; rare) make ~ through; provide with ~s. [ME, f. OF canal f. L *canalis*; see CHANNEL]

cănăl′ĭcūlate, -ātĕd, aa. (nat. hist.). With longitudinal groove(s); striated. [f. L *canaliculus* dim. of CANAL*is* + -ATE[2,3]]

căn′alĭz|e, -is|e (-ĭz), v.t. = CANAL vb; convert (river) into canal by embanking, straightening course, locks, etc.; (fig.) give desired direction etc. to. Hence ~A′TION n. [prob. f. F *canaliser* (CANAL + -IZE)]

căn′apĕ (-ā), n. Piece of fried bread with anchovies etc. [F]

canǎrd′ (or kăn′ăr), n. False report, hoax. [F]

Canarese. See KANARESE.

canăr′y̆, a. & n. From the C~ Islands; (also ~-*bird*) yellow-feathered song-bird (green in wild state); (also C~-*wine*) a favourite wine in 16th–18th cc.; yellow fishing-fly; ~-*coloured*, bright yellow; ~ *convolvulus*, tree yielding RHODIUM[1]; ~ *creeper*, yellow-flowered climbing plant; ~-*seed*, used as food for the bird. [f. F *Canarie* f. Sp. & L *Canaria* (canis dog), one of the islands being noted in Roman times for large dogs]

canăs′ta, n. Card game of S.-Amer. origin resembling rummy. [Sp., = basket]

canăs′ter, n. Tobacco prepared by coarsely breaking the dried leaves. [orig. the rush basket container; f. Sp. *canastro*, ult. f. Gk *kanastron*; see CANISTER]

cancan (see Ap.), n. High-kicking dance. [F]

căn′cel[1], v.t. & i. (-ll-). Obliterate, cross out, annul, make void, abolish, countermand, neutralize, balance, make up for, (v.i., ~ *out* or ~, of items) neutralize each other; (Math.) strike out (same factor) from numerator & denominator, from two sides of equation, etc. Hence ~IA′TION n. [late ME, f. OF *canceller* f. L *cancĕllare* (cancelli cross-bars, lattice; see CHANCEL)]

căn′cel[2], n. Countermand; suppression & reprinting of leaf or leaves set up, the suppressed or the substituted leaf or leaves. [f. prec.]

căn′cellate, -ātĕd, aa. (bot. & zool.). Marked with crossing lines, reticulated; (of bone) formed of interlacing fibres & plates with cavities, porous. [f. L *cancellatus* (CANCEL[1], -ATE[2,3])]

căn′cellous, a. (Of bone) = prec. [-OUS]

căn′cer, C-, n. Zodiacal constellation the Crab (C~); fourth sign of zodiac (C~); TROPIC *of C~*; malignant tumour eating the part it is in, spreading indefinitely, & tending to recur when removed, (fig.) evil (sloth, bribery, etc.) acting similarly, whence ~ED[2] (-erd), ~OUS, aa. [ME, f. L *cancer* crab, cancer; see CANKER]

cănc′roid, a. & n. 1. Crab-like; like cancer. 2. n. Crustacean of crab family; disease like cancer. [as prec. + -OID]

căndĕlāb′rum (*also* -ă-, -ah-), n. (pl. -*bra*; also sing. -*bra*, pl. -*bras*). Large, usu. branched, candlestick or lampstand. [L (-*um*), f. candela CANDLE]

căndĕs′c|ent, a. Glowing (as) with white heat. Hence ~ENCE n. [f. L *candescere* (*candēre* be white, -ESCENT)]

căn′did, a. Unbiased; not censorious; frank; ~ *camera*, small camera for taking informal pictures of persons freq. without their knowledge; ~ *friend*, nominal friend glad to tell home-truths. Hence ~LY[2] adv., ~NESS n. [f. L *candidus* white, or F *candide*; see prec.]

căn′didate, n. One who puts himself or is put forward for appointment to an office or honour; person thought likely to gain any position; examinee. [f. L *candidatus*, as prec., -ATE[2] (2), orig. white-robed (Roman ~s wearing white)]

căn′did|āture, n. Standing for election, being candidate. So ~ACY n. [F, as prec. + -URE]

căn′died (-dĭd). See CANDY (p.p.).

căn′dle, n. Cylinder of wax, tallow, spermaceti, etc., enclosing wick, for giving light; (also ~-*power*) unit of light-measurement; *Roman* ~, firework, tube discharging coloured balls; *can't, is not fit to, hold a ~ to*, is not to be compared with; *sell by inch of* ~, by auction, last bid before small ~ expires winning (hist.); BELL, *book, & ~*; *game not worth the* ~, result not justifying the cost or trouble; BURN[2] *at both ends*; *hide* ~ *under* BUSHEL; ~-*berry-myrtle* (N.-Amer.), ~-*berry-tree* (Moluccas), yielding wax & nut-kernels used for ~s; ~-*ends*, remnants of ~; odds-&-ends hoarded by the stingy; ~-*light*, light of ~s, any artificial light, evening; ~-*stick*, support for (usu. single) ~; ~-*tree*, Amer., with ~-like fruit some feet long. [OE *candel* f. L *candela* (*candēre* shine), in ME reinforced by AN, OF *candel(l)e*]

Căn′dlemas (-lm-), n. Feast of purification of Virgin Mary, when candles are blessed; (as date) 2nd Feb.; quarter-day in Scotland. [OE *Candelmæsse* (CANDLE, MASS[1])]

căn′dour (-der), n. Open-mindedness, impartiality; freedom from malice; frankness. [f. L *candor* whiteness (*candēre* shine, -OR)]

căn′dy̆, n., & v.t. & i. 1. Crystallized sugar made by repeated boiling & slow

evaporation (also *sugar-~*); *(w. pl.)
sweets; ~-FLOSS, sweet confection, usu.
pink, of fluffy spun sugar; ~-*stripe(d)*,
pattern(ed) in alternate stripes of white
& colour. 2. vb. Preserve by coating with
~; form (t. & i.) into crystals; (p.p.)
glistening, (arch.) honeyed, flattering.
[for earlier (15th c.) *sugar candy* f. F *sucre
candi* f. Arab.-Pers. *sukkar qandi* (*qand*
sugar)]

căn′dўtüft, n. Plant with white, pink, or
purple flowers in flat tufts. [f. obs. *Candy*
(*Candia* Crete)+TUFT]

cāne¹, n. Hollow jointed stem of giant
reeds & grasses (bamboo, sugar ~) or
solid stem of slender palms (rattan,
Malacca, etc.) collectively & as material
(~), or with pl. (*a* ~, ~*s*) of the stem or
a length of it used for walking-stick or
instrument of punishment; ‖ any slender
walking-stick; stick of sealing-wax, sulphur, glass; ~-*apple*, strawberry-tree;
~-*brake*, kinds of grasses, (also) tract
of land overgrown with ~s; ~ *chair*, with
seat of woven~ strips; ~-*sugar* (obtained
from the sugar~). Hence **cān′y²** a. [ME
can(n)e, f. OF *cane* f. L f. Gk *kanna* reed
f. Semit. cf. Heb. *qaneh*]

cāne², v.t. Beat with cane, whence **cān′-
ING¹** (1) n.; drive (lesson) *into* (person)
with cane; insert cane into (chair-frame
etc.). [f. prec.]

canēph′orus, n. (pl. *-ī*). Sculptured
Greek youth or maid bearing basket on
head. [L, f. Gk *kanēphoros* (*kaneon*
basket, *pherō* carry)]

cangue (kǎngg), **cāng**, n. Heavy wooden
board worn round neck by Chinese
criminals. [F (*-gue*), f. Pg. *canga* yoke]

căn′īne (*also* kanīn′), a. & n. Of, as of, a
dog or dogs; ~ *tooth* or ~, one of the four
strong pointed teeth between incisors &
molars. [f. F *canin, -e* or L *caninus* (*canis*
dog, -INE¹)]

căn′ister, n. Small box usu. of metal for
tea, shot, etc.; (R.-C. Ch.) vessel holding
wafers before consecration; ~-*shot* or ~,
= CASE²-*shot*. [f. L *canistrum* f. Gk *kanastron* wicker basket (*kanna* CANE¹)]

cănk′er, n., & v.t. 1. Ulcerous disease of
human mouth; disease of horse's foot;
disease of trees; (fig.) corrupting influence,
rotten tendency; ~-*worm* or ~, caterpillar
or larva destroying leaves or buds;
~-*rash*, variety of scarlet fever with
ulcerated throat; hence ~OUS a. 2. v.t.
Consume with canker; infect, corrupt;
(p.p.) soured, malignant, crabbed. [ME
cancre f. ONF f. L *cancer* (whence OE
cancer); see CANCER, CHANCRE]

cănn′a, n. Plant with bright yellow, red,
or orange flowers & ornamental leaves.
[L (CANE¹)]

cănn′el, n. (Also ~-*coal*) bituminous coal
burning with bright flame & used in
making coal oils & gas. [orig. unkn.]

cănn′ibal, n. & a. 1. Man who eats human
flesh; animal feeding on its own species;

hence ~ISM(2) n., ~ĭs′tĭc a. 2. adj. Of,
having, these habits. [16th-c. E & Sp.
Canibales pl., var. of Carib name of W.-
-Ind. nation; *Caliban* is prob. another
variant]

cănn′ibalīze, -ise (-ĭz), v.t. Use (one of a
number of similar machines) to provide
spare parts for the others. [prec., -IZE (4)]

cănn′ikin, n. Small can. [-KIN]

cănn′on¹, n. 1. ‚Now *gun*) piece of ordnance, gun of the kind that needs mounting, (collect. sing. usu. instead of pl.);
aircraft's heavy automatic gun, firing
explosive shell; ~-*ball* (hist.), projectile;
~- *bone*, tube-shaped bone between hough
& fetlock; ~-*clock*, fired at noon by
burning-glass; ~-*fodder*, men regarded as
material to be consumed in war. 2.
(Mech.) hollow cylinder moving independently on shaft; watchkey barrel.
3. (Also ~-*bit*) smooth round bit for horse.
4. ‖ (Billiards) hitting of two balls successively by player's ball. 5. (Also ~-*curl*)
sausage-shaped, prop. horizontal, curl.
[f. F *canon* f. It. *cannone* great tube
(*canna* CANE¹, -OON); in sense 4 f. older
carom short for *carambole* (F, f. Sp.—*bola*)
in sense 5 f. Sp. *cañon*]

cănn′on², v.i. ‖ Make a cannon at billiards
(of player or ball); come into collision,
strike obliquely, *against, into, with*. [f.
prec.]

cănnonāde′, n., & v.t. & i. Continuous
gunfire; (vb) fire continuously; bombard,
fire fast at. [F, f. It. *cannonata* (prec.,
-ADE)]

cannot. See CAN².

cănn′ula, n. (surg.). Small tube for
inserting into a cavity or tumour to
allow fluid to escape. [L, dim. of *canna*
CANE¹]

cănn′|ў, a. Shrewd, worldly-wise; natural,
safe to meddle with, (esp. w. neg.);
(esp. of Scots) thrifty; gentle, quiet,
circumspect, (*ca′* ~*y*, Sc. for *drive* or *go
gently*, as name for trade-union policy
of limiting output); sly, pawky. Hence
~ĭLY² adv., ~ĭNESS n. [f. CAN² know + -Y²]

canoe′ (-ŏō), n., & v.i. (Go in, paddle)
boat propelled with paddle(s). Hence
~′ĬST(3) (-nŏō-) n. [f. Sp. & Haytian
canoa]

căn′on, n. Church decree; ~ *law*, eccl.
law; general law governing treatment of
a subject; criterion; list of Bible books
accepted by Church; list of recognized
genuine works of a particular author (*the
Shakespearian* ~); part of Mass containing words of consecration; (Mus.)
piece with different parts taking up same
subject successively in strict imitation;
(Typ.) largest size of type with specific
name; metal loop on bell for hanging it;
member of cathedral CHAPTER, whence
~RY(2) n.; MINOR ~. [OE, f. L f. Gk
kanōn rule (*kanna* CANE¹); in ME re-
-introduced f. AN, OF *canun, -on*; in last
sense short for CANONIC, in OE *canonic* f.

LL *canonicus*, whence OF *canonie*, *chanoine*, etc., whence ME *canun* etc.]

cañon. See CANYON.

canŏn'ical, a. & n., **canŏn'ic,** a. (arch.). Appointed by canon law (~ *hours*, for prayer, or for celebration of marriage, 8 a.m. to 3 p.m.; ~ *dress*, of clergy, also ~*s* as n. pl.); included in canon of Scripture; C~ *Epistles*, the seven of Peter, James, John, Jude; authoritative, standard, accepted; (Mus.) in canon form; of a cathedral chapter or a member of it. Hence **canŏn'ical**LY[2] adv. [f. OF *canonique* or LL *canonicus*, med. L *canonicalis*; see CANON, -IC, -AL]

canŏn'icate, n. = CANONry. [f. med. L *canonicatus* (as prec., -ATE[1])]

cănoni'cit̆y, n. Status as canonical book. [f. *canonicus* CANONICAL, -TY]

căn'on|ist, n.   Canon-lawyer.   Hence ~**ĭs'tic**(AL) aa. [f. F *canoniste* f. med. L *canonista*, see CANON, -IST]

căn'oniz|e, -is|e (-īz), v.t. Admit formally to calendar of saints; regard as a saint; recognize (book) as canonical; sanction by church authority. So ~A'TION n. [ME, f. LL *canonizare* (CANON, -IZE)]

***canŏŏ'dle,** v.i. & t. (sl.). Cuddle, fondle. [U.S., of unkn. orig.]

Canōp'ic, a. Of *Canopus*, town of ancient Egypt; ~ *jar*, *vase*, urn used for holding the entrails of an embalmed body in ancient Egyptian burial. [f. L *Canopicus*]

căn'op̆y̆, n., & v.t. Covering suspended or held over throne, bed, person, etc. (also fig. of any overhanging shelter, sky, etc.); (Archit.) roof-like projection over niche etc.; cover of cockpit in aircraft; (vb) supply, be, such a covering to. [ME *canape, -ope*, f. med. L *canopeum* f. L f. Gk *kōnōpeion* mosquito-net (*kōnōps* gnat)]

canōr'ous, a. Melodious, resonant. [f. L *canorus* (*canor* song f. *canere* sing) + -OUS]

cănt[1], n. Bevel, oblique face, of crystal, bank, etc.; push, toss, movement, that partly or quite upsets; tilted or sideways position; ~*-board*, sloping board. [app. f. MLG *kant, kante*, MDu. *cant*, point, side, edge, obsc. rel. to OF *cant* (mod. *chant, champ*), It., Sp. *canto* f. Rom. *canto* of obsc. orig.]

cănt[2], v.t. & i. (Trans.) bevel off; tilt; turn *over*, turn upside down; push, pitch, sideways; (v.i.) take inclined position; lie aslant; (Naut.) swing round; ~*-hook*, iron hook at end of long handle, used for rolling logs. [f. prec.]

cănt[3], n. & a., & v.i. **1.** Peculiar language of class, profession, sect, etc., jargon; temporary catchwords (esp. as adj., ~ *phrase* etc.); words used for fashion without being meant, unreal use of words implying piety; hypocrisy. **2.** v.i. Use talk of these kinds; (Her.) ~*ing arms*, *heraldry*, *coat*, containing allusion to name of bearer; hence ~*ER*[1] n. [earlier of musical sound, of intonation, & of

beggars' whining, perh. f. singing of religious mendicants; prob. f. L *cantus* song, *cantare* frequent. of *canere* sing]

can't (kahnt). See CAN[2].

Căn'tăb, n. (colloq.), **Căntabri'gian,** n. & a. (Member) of Cambridge University. [f. L *Cantabrigia* Cambridge + -AN]

căn'taloup (-ōōp), n. Kind of melon. [F, f. It. *Cantalupo* in Italy]

căntănk'erous, a. Cross-grained, quarrelsome. Hence ~LY[2] adv., ~NESS n. [perh. f. ME *contak* contention on anal. of *traitorous*, *rancorous*]

cănta'ta (-tah-), n. (mus.). Choral work, kind of short oratorio, or lyric drama set to music but not acted; (formerly) elaborate vocal solo. [It. (*cantare* sing, *-ata* -ADE)]

Cănta'te (-ahtĕ), n. Psalm xcviii (O sing—) as a canticle. [L, = sing ye]

căntatri'ce (-ē'chă, -ēs'), n. Professional woman singer. [It. & F]

cănteen', n. ‖ Provision & liquor shop in camp or barracks (*dry, wet, ~, without;* chiefly for, liquor); box of cooking--utensils for use in camp, soldier's mess-tin; soldier's water-vessel of tin, wood, etc.; bar, lunch-counter, etc. at outdoor entertainments & in large public & private institutions; case or chest of plate & cutlery for domestic use. [f. F *cantine* f. It. *cantina* cellar]

căn'ter, n., & v.i. & t. **1.** Easy gallop (*win in a ~*, easily). **2.** vb. Go at this pace (of horse or rider); make (horse) go thus. [short for *Canterbury pace, gallop, trot*, etc., f. easy pace of Canterbury pilgrims]

căn'terbur̆y̆, n. Stand with partitions for music etc.

Căn'terbur̆y̆ bĕll, n. Kind of campanula. [f. bells of Canterbury pilgrims' horses]

cănthă'rĭdēs (-z), n. pl. (med.). Dried Spanish fly. [L, pl. of L f. Gk *kantharis* blister-fly]

căn'thus, n. Outer or inner corner of eye, where lids meet. [L f. Gk *kanthos*]

căn'ticle, n. Little song, hymn; one of the Prayer-Book hymns, as the *Benedicite, Nunc Dimittis, Te Deum; Canticles*, Song of Solomon. [ME, f. OF *canticle*, var. of *cantique* f. L *canticum* (*cantus* song f. *canere* sing); in 16th c. reinforced by L dim. *canticulum*]

căn'tilĕver, n. Bracket (of length many times breadth & more than twice depth) projecting from wall to support balcony etc.; ~ *bridge*, with piers each of which has two ~s, with long girders connecting ~s of adjacent piers. [f. LEVER; the significance of the first element is unkn.]

căn'tle, n. ‖ Piece, slice, cut off; hind-bow of saddle. [f. ONF *cantel* dim. of CANT[1]]

căn'tō, n. (pl. *-os*). Division of long poem. [It., = song, as CANT[3]]

căn'ton[1] (*also* kăntōn'), n. Subdivision of country; State of Swiss confederation;

(Her.) square division less than a quarter in upper corner of shield. Hence ~AL a. [OF, = corner (CANT¹, -OON)]

canton'² (also -tōōn'), v.t. Divide into cantons (-tŏn); (-tōōn) quarter (soldiers). [f. F *cantonner*, partly prec.]

cănton'ment (-ōōn-, -ŏn-), n. Lodging assigned to troops (formerly in India also permanent military station). [f. F *cantonnement* (prec., -MENT)]

căn'tor, n. 1. Leader of singing in church, precentor. 2. Precentor in synagogue. [L]

cantŏr'ial, a. Of the precentor, of N. side of choir (cf. DECANAL). [f. L as foll. +-AL]

căntŏr'is, mus. direction. To be sung by cantorial side in antiphonal singing. [L, genit. of *cantor* precentor (*canere cantsing*, -OR)]

căn'trip, n. (Sc.). Witch's trick; piece of mischief, playful act. [orig. unkn.]

Canŭck', n. & a. (sl.). French Canadian; *Canadian. [U.S. word]

căn'vas, n. Strong unbleached cloth of hemp or flax, for sails, tents, painting on; open kind used as basis for tapestry & embroidery; *under* ~, in tent(s), with sails spread; racing-boat's covered end; picture; ~-*back*, N.-Amer. duck (f. colour of back feathers). [ME & ONF *canevas* f. Rom. *cannabaceus* (L f. Gk *kannabis* hemp, -ACEOUS)]

căn'vass, v.t. & i., & n. Discuss thoroughly; solicit votes, solicit votes from (constituency), ascertain sentiments of, ask custom of, whence ~ER¹ n.; (n.) ~ing for votes. [f. prec., orig. sense being toss in a sheet, & so shake up, agitate, etc.]

căn'yon, cañon (kăn'yon), n. Deep gorge freq. with stream. [f. Sp. *cañon* tube (*caña* f. L *canna* CANE¹)]

cănzonĕt', n. Short light song; kind of madrigal. [f. It. *canzonetta* (*canzone* f. L *cantionem* f. *canere* sing)]

caoutchouc (kowch'ōōk), n. & a. (Of) unvulcanized rubber. [F, f. Carib. *cahuchu*]

căp¹, n. Head-dress (woman's, esp. of muslin etc. worn indoors, but also now, like man's or boy's, for outdoor use, brimless & of cloth or soft material; ~ *in hand*, humbly; ~ *fits*, person feels that general remark is true of him; *set* one's ~ *at*, try to attract as suitor); special head-dress (*college* or *square* ~; *steel* ~, helmet; *Scotch* ~, part of Highland costume; *football* ~, of velvet etc., ‖ sign of inclusion in team; ~ *of* MAINTENANCE; ~ *of liberty*, conical, given to Roman slave on emancipation, now Republican symbol; ~ *& bells*, jester's insignia; FOOL's ~); caplike covering, natural (mushroom top, knee-~, etc.), or added for various purposes (windmill top, toe-~, inner watchcase; *percussion* ~, for igniting explosive in cartridges etc.); (Naut.) doubly pierced block for lengthening mast by extra spar; conical paper bag, cornet; (Fox-hunting etc.) recognized payment by non-subscriber for day's hunting (collected in ~), whence ~p'ER¹ n., the authorized collector; ~-*paper*, whity-brown for packing, also a size of writing-paper; ~-*stone*, top stone, coping. [OE *cæppe* f. LL *cappa*, of unkn. orig.; cf. CAPE¹, COPE¹]

căp², v.t. & i. (-pp-). Put cap upon; (Sc. Univv.) confer degree on; put percussion cap on nipple of (gun); protect (end of beam etc.) with metal etc., whence ~p'ING¹ (3) *b.*; lie (on top of, crown; award (a player) his cap for football etc.); outdo (~ *anecdote, quotation*, etc., produce a better or another apposite one; ~ *verses*, reply with one beginning with the last's last letter); touch or take off one's hat to (also intr. with *to*); injure at point (*horse* ~*s its hocks*). [f. prec.]

cāpabil'it|y̆, n. Power *of* (action etc., *acting* etc.), *for* (*being* done something *to*), *to* (do something); undeveloped faculty (*has* ~*ies*). [foll., -BILITY]

cāp'ab|le, a. Susceptible (*of*, or abs.); having the power or fitness for (*of*); wicked enough for (*of*); gifted, able. Hence ~LY² adv. [F, f. LL *capabilis* (L *capere* hold, -BLE)]

capā'cious (-shŭs), a. Roomy. Hence ~NESS n. [L *capax* (*capere* hold), -ACIOUS]

capā'citance, n. (electr.). 1. Ratio of the change in an electric charge to the corresponding change in potential. 2. Ability to store a charge of electricity, CAPACITY. [f. CAPACIT(Y)+-ANCE]

capā'citāte, v.t. Render capable (*for, to* do); make legally competent. [CAPACITY, -ATE³]

capā'citor, n. (electr.). Device for storing electric charges. [f. CAPACIT(Y)+-OR]

capā'cit̆y, n. Holding-power, receiving-power, (for happiness, heat, moisture; *filled to* ~, quite full; ~ *house*, packed theatre etc.); producing-power; cubic content (*measure of* ~, for vessels & liquids, grain, etc.); mental power, faculty; capability, opportunity, *to* do, *of doing*, etc. (rare); position, relative character, (*in a civil* ~; *in my* ~ *as critic*); legal competency; (Electr.) power of an apparatus to store electricity, CAPACITANCE. [f. F *capacité* f. L *capacitatem* (CAPACIOUS, -TY)]

căp-à-pie' (-apē), adv. From head to foot, (armed, ready, etc.). [f. OF *cap a pie*]

capā'rison, n. (freq. pl.), & v.t. Horse's trappings; equipment, outfit; (vb) put ~ upon. [f. F *caparasson* (now -açon) f. Pr. -*assoun* f. -*asso* ult. f. LL *cappa* CAP¹; cf. med. L *caparo* (*capa* CAPE¹)]

cāpe¹, n. Short sleeveless cloak, either as separate garment or as fixed or detachable part of longer cloak or coat. Hence cāpeD² (-pt) a. [16th c. f. F, f. Pr. *capa* (= OF *chape*) f. LL *cappa* CAP¹]

cāpe², C-, n. & a. Headland, promontory; *the C*~, of Good Hope, also = C~ Province (C~ *boy*, S.-African of mixed black

& white descent), & as adj. of its products (C~ *wine* etc.; C~ *doctor*, strong S.-E. wind peculiar to S. Africa; C~ *Dutch*, S.-Afr. Dutch, Afrikaans; C~ *gooseberry*, kind of winter cherry; C~ *smoke*, S.--African brandy). [14th c. *cape* f. F f. Pr. *cap* f. Rom. **capo* f. L *caput* head]

căp'(e)lin, n. Small smelt-like fish used as cod-bait. [F *cap(e)lan*, *-in*]

căp'er[1], n. Bramble-like S.-European shrub; (pl.) its flower-buds pickled (esp. ~ *sauce*); *English* ~*s*, seed vessels of nasturtium pickled. [ME *caperis*, *caperes*, (sing.) f. L f. Gk *kapparis*; for loss of *-s* cf. CHERRY, PEA]

căp'er[2], n., & v.i. (Give a) frisky movement, leap; fantastic proceeding; *cut a*~, ~*s*, = ~ vb. [short for CAPRIOLE]

căpercaill'ie, *-l'zie* (-lyi, -lzi), n. Wood--grouse, largest European gallinaceous bird (Scotland etc.). [f. Gael. *capull coille* horse of the wood]

cāp'erer, n. In vbl senses; esp., caddis-fly (from its flight). [CAPER[2], -ER[1]]

căp'ful (-ŏŏl), n. Enough to fill a cap; esp., ~ *of wind*, passing gust. [-FUL (2)]

căp'iăs n. Writ of arrest. [L, = arrest]

căpillä'ritў, n. (Power of exerting) capillary attraction or repulsion. [f. F *capillarité* see foll., -TY]

capill'arў (*also* căp'-), a. & n. Of hair; hair-like, thin as a hair; (tube, blood--vessel) of minute or hair-like diameter (e.g. one of ramified blood-vessels intervening between arteries & veins); so ~ ATTRACTION, REPULSION. [f. L *capillaris* (-ARY[2]) f. *capillus* hair; cf. F *capillaire*]

căp'ital[1], n. Head or cornice of pillar or column. [ME, f. OF *capitel* f. L *capitellum* dim. of *capitulum* dim. of *caput* head]

căp'ital[2], a. & n. Involving loss of life, punishable by death, (~ *sentence, offence*); vitally injurious, fatal, (~ *error*); standing at the head (~ *letter*, also ~ as noun); chief (~ *manor*, held in capite or direct from king; ~ *messuage*, occupied by owner of estate with several messuages; ~ *town* or *city*, or ~ as noun, head town of country, county, etc.); important, leading, first-class, (~ *ship*, battleship or battle cruiser); excellent, first-rate, (often as interj. of approval); original, principal, (~ *fund* or ~, stock with which company or person enters into business, accumulated wealth used in producing more, holders of this as a class, as C~ & *Labour*; ~ *goods*, goods (to be) used in producing commodities, opp. *consumer goods*; *fixed* ~, machinery etc., *circulating* or *floating* ~, goods, money, etc.; so fig., *make* ~ *out of*, turn to account). Hence ~LY[2] adv. [ME, f. OF f. L *capitalis* (*caput -itis* head, -AL)]

căp'italism, căp'italĭst, (*also* kapĭt[L]), nn. Possession or influence or system, possessor, of capital or fund used in production, (mod., Pol.) dominance of private capitalists (opp. *socialism*). Hence căpi-

talĭs'tic a. [prec., -ISM(3), -IST(3), after F *-isme, -iste*]

căp'italĭz|e, *-is|e* (-ĭz; *also* kapĭt[L]), v.t. Convert into, use as, capital; compute or realize present value of (income); (fig.) turn to account, make use of to one's advantage. Hence ~A'TION n. [-IZE(3); cf. F *-iser*]

căp'itāte, -ātĕd, aa. (nat. hist.). Having distinct head; with clustered flowers etc. [f. L *capitatus* headed (*caput -itis*, -ATE[2])]

căpitā'tion, n. (Levying of) tax or fee of so much a head; ~ *grant*, of so much for every person fulfilling conditions. [F, or f. LL *capitatio* poll-tax (*caput -itis* head, -ATION)]

Căp'itol, n. Roman temple of Jupiter on Tarpeian hill (later ~*ine hill* or ~*ine*); **Congress* or State legislature building. [ME, f. ONF *capitolie*, OF *-oile*, f. L *capitolium* (*caput* head), whence mod. sp.]

capit'ŭlar, a. Of a cathedral chapter; (Physiol.) of a terminal protuberance of bone. [f. med. L *capitularis* (L *capitulum* CHAPTER, -AR[1])]

capit'ŭlarў, n. Collection of ordinances, esp. of Frankish kings. [f. med. L *capitularius, -ium* (as prec., -ARY[1])]

capit'ŭlāte, v.i. Surrender esp. on terms. [f. med. L *capitulare* draw up under heads (*capitulum*), see -ATE[3]]

capitŭlā'tion, n. Stating heads of subject; agreement, conditions, (esp. *the C~s*, hist., by which foreign residents in Turkey had exterritoriality); surrender on terms, instrument containing these. [F, or f. LL *capitulatio* (prec., -ATION)]

căp'on, n. Castrated edible cock. Hence ~IZE(3) v.t. [late OE *capun* f. AN *capun*, *-on*, f. Rom. **cappone* f. L *caponem* (nom. *capo*)]

căponier', n. Covered passage across ditch of fort. [f. F *caponnière* f. Sp. *caponera* orig. a capon-cote (see prec.)]

căp'oral (-ahl), n. A French tobacco. [F]

capŏt', n., & v.t. (-tt-). (In piquet) winning of all tricks by one player; (vb) do this against (opponent). [F]

capōte', n. Soldier's, traveller's, etc., long cloak with hood. [F, dim. of *cape* CAPE[1]]

căp'ric, a. (chem.). ~ *acid*, obtained from butter, coco-nut oil, etc. [f. L *caper -pri* goat + -IC (from its goatlike smell)]

căpric'cio (-ĕchō), n. (mus.). Lively (usu. short) musical composition. [It., see foll.]

caprice' (-ēs), n. Unaccountable change of mind or conduct, fancy, freak; inclination to these; work of sportive fancy in art etc. [F, f. It. *capriccio* sudden start, orig. 'horror'; mod. sense f. *capra* goat]

capri'cious (-shŭs), a. Guided by whim, inconstant, irregular, incalculable. Hence ~LY[2] adv., ~NESS n. [f. F *capricieux* f. It. *capriccioso* (prec., -OUS)]

Căp'ricŏrn, n. Zodiacal constellation Goat; tenth sign of zodiac; TROPIC *of* ~. [f. OF *-corne* or L *capricornus* (*caper -pri* goat, *cornu* horn)]

căprĭfĭcā′tion, n. Hastening of ripeness in figs by subjecting them to puncture by wild-fig gall-insects. [f. L *caprificatio* f. *caprificus* wild fig (*caper* goat, *ficus* fig), -ATION]

căp′rine, a. Of, like, a goat. [f. L *caprinus* (*caper -pri,* -INE[1])]

căp′riŏle, n., & v.i. (Give a) leap, caper, esp. (in manège) horse's high leap & kick without advancing. [F (now *cab-*), or f. It. *capriola, capriolare* leap (L *capreolus* dim. of *caper* goat)]

caprō′ic, a. (chem.). ~ *acid,* found with capric & butyric acids in butter etc. [var. of CAPRIC for differentiation]

căps, abbr. of *capitals* (capital letters) in direction to printers etc.

căp′sicum, n. Kinds of plant with hot capsules & seeds; the prepared fruit. [mod. L, perh. f. L *capsa* CASE[2]]

căpsĭz|e′, n., & v.t. & i. Upset, overturn, (of ship, boat). Hence ~′AL(2) n. [f. *cap-* as in Pr. *capvirar* = F *chavirer* capsize (cf. It. *capovolgere,* Sp. *capuzar*); 2nd elem. unexpl.]

căp′stan, n. Revolving barrel, worked by men working round & pushing horizontal levers, or by steam etc., for winding cable in, hoisting heavy sails, etc. [f. Pr. *cabestan,* earlier *cabestran,* f. *cabestre* halter f. L *capistrum* f. *capere* hold]

căp′sŭl|e, n. (Physiol.) membranous envelope; (Bot.) dry seed-case opening when ripe by parting of valves; (Chem.) shallow saucer for evaporating etc.; (Med.) gelatine envelope enclosing dose; metallic top for bottle; detachable nose-cone of rocket or space missile containing instruments for recording & transmitting scientific data. Hence ~AR[1], ~īFORM, aa., ~ī- comb. form. [F, f. L *capsula* (CASE[2], -ULE)]

căp′tain[1] (-tĭn), n. Chief, leader; great soldier, strategist, experienced commander; (Army) OFFICER of rank next below major & above lieutenant, normally commanding a company or troop; (Navy) officer commanding man-of-war (also used; by courtesy, of commander); C~ *of the Fleet,* adjutant-general of a force, with rear-admiral's uniform; chief sailor of special gang (~ *of forecastle* etc.); Master of merchant ship; manager of Cornish mine; foreman; ‖ head boy or girl at school; leader of side in games; = grey GURNARD; ~'s *biscuit,* partly fermented ship's biscuit of superior quality. Hence ~CY, ~SHIP, nn., ~LESS a., (-tĭn-). [ME & OF *capitain* f. LL *capitaneus* chief (L *caput capit-* head); cf. CHIEFTAIN]

căp′tain[2] (-tĭn), v.t. Be captain of, lead. [f. prec.]

căptā′tion, n. Use of *ad captandum* arguments or appeals. [f. L *captatio* (*captare* catch at, frequent. of *capere* take, -ATION)]

căp′tion, n. ‖ Legal arrest; (Law) certificate attached to or written on document; heading of chapter, article, etc.; wording

on cinema screen, cartoon, etc. [f. L *captio* (*capere* take, -TION)]

căp′tious (-shŭs), a. Fallacious, sophistical; fond of taking exception, trying to catch people in their words. Hence ~LY[3] adv., ~NESS n. [f. F *captieux* or L *captiosus* (prec., -OUS)]

căp′tĭv|āte, v.t. Fascinate, charm. Hence ~A′TION n. [f. LL *captivare* take CAPTIVE, -ATE[3]]

căp′tive, a. & n. (Person, animal) taken prisoner kept in confinement, under restraint, unable to escape; of, like, prisoner (~ *state*); *lead, take, hold,* ~; ~ *balloon,* held by rope from ground. So **căptĭv′ITY** n. [ME, f. OF *captif* f. L *captivus* (*capere capt-* take, -IVE)]

căp′tor, n., **căp′trĕss,** n. fem. One who takes a captive or prize. [-*or* LL (as prec., -OR); & see -ESS[1]]

căp′tur|e, n., & v.t. Seizing, taking possession of; thing or person seized; (v.t.) take prisoner, seize as prize; hence ~ER[1] n. [F, f. L *captura* as prec., -URE]

Căp′ŭchin, n. & a. Franciscan (friar) of new rule of 1528; woman's cloak & hood; ~ *monkey, pigeon,* kinds with head hair or feathers like cowl. [F (now -*cin*), f. It. *capuccino* (*capuccio* cowl f. *cappa* CAP[1])]

căp′ut mŏr′tŭŭm, n. Worthless residue. [L, = dead head; alch. term for residuum of any substance after distillation or sublimation]

căpȳbăr′a, n. Large S.-Amer. rodent allied to guinea-pig. [Brazilian]

căr, n. Wheeled vehicle (chiefly poet. = chariot; ~ *of the sun, triumphal* ~, ~ *of Juggernaut,* etc.; or with specification as JAUNT[1]*ing-*~, MOTOR-~, *tramway-*~, *dining-*~; in U.S. of any railway carriage or van; in Engl. also of motor-car, of low two-wheeled truck for hogsheads etc., & of other low heavy carts; pendant of airship or balloon holding passengers; ~'*man,* driver of van or jaunting-~, carter, carrier. Hence ~′FUL(2) n. [ME & ONF *carre* f. Rom. **carra,* = L *carrus, -um* four-wheeled vehicle, f. Celt. **karrom, -os* (OIr., OWelsh *karr*)]

cărabineer′, cărb-, n. Soldier with carbine; *The C~s,* (now) the 3rd Dragoon Guards. [f. F *carabinier* (CARBINE, -EER)]

că′racăl, n. Kind of lynx. [F, f. Turk. *qarah-qulaq* black-ear]

că′racŏle, -ŏl, n., & v.i. (Execute) half-turn(s) to right or left (of horse or rider). [f. F *caracole(r)*]

că′racul (-ōōl), n. Kind of astrakhan fur; cloth imitating this. [Russ.]

carafe′ (-ahf), n. Glass water-bottle for table. [F, f. It. *caraffa* prob. f. Sp. *garrafa* f. Arab. *gharafa* draw water]

că′ramĕl, n. Burnt sugar used for colouring spirits etc.; a sweetmeat; the colour of ~, a light brown. [F, f. Sp. *caramelo*]

că′rapāce, n. Upper shell of tortoise & crustaceans. [F. f. Sp. *carapacho*]

că′rat, n. Measure of weight for precious

stones, about 3¼ grains; measure of purity of gold, pure gold being 24 ~. [F, f. It. *carato* f. Arab. *qirat* f. Gk *keration* fruit of carob (dim. of *keras* horn)]

că′ravăn (or -văn′), n. Eastern or N.-African company of merchants, pilgrims, etc., travelling together for safety, esp. through desert; covered cart or carriage, house on wheels. [16th-c. *carouan* f. Pers. *karwan*, later assim. to F *caravane*]

căravăn′serai (-rī), -sera, -sarȳ, n. Eastern quadrangular inn with great inner court where caravans put up. [f. Pers. *karwansarai* (prec., *sara* mansion)]

că′ravel, cărv′el, n. (hist.). Small light fast ship, chiefly Spanish & Portuguese of 15th-17th cc. [15th c. *carvel* etc. f. OF *carvelle* f. Pg. *caravela*, ult. f. LL f. Gk *karabos* crab, light ship; 16th c. *caravel* f. F -*velle* or It. -*vella*]

că′raway (-a-w-), n. Umbelliferous plant with fruit (~-*seeds*) used in cakes. [15th c., immediate source uncert.; f. OSp. *alcarahueya* f. Arab. *alkaraw̄iya*; in med. L, F, It., Sp. *carvi* (whence Sc. *carvy*); ult. orig. perh. L f. Gk. *karon, kareon* cummin]

cărb-, cărbo-, comb. forms of CARBON. Hence **cărb′IDE** n. (often for *calcium carbide* used in making acetylene gas).

cărb′ine, că′ra-, n. Short fire-arm for cavalry use. [f. F *carabine*, weapon of the *carabin* a mounted musketeer]

cărbōhȳd′rate, n. (chem.). Energy-producing organic compound of carbon with oxygen & hydrogen (starch, sugar, glucose).

cărbŏl′ic, a. (chem.). ~ *acid,* powerful antiseptic & disinfectant. Hence **cărb′o-lize**(5) v.t. [CARB-, -OL, -IC]

cărb′on, n. (chem.). Non-metallic element occurring as diamond, graphite, & charcoal, in carbonic acid gas, the carbonates, & all organic compounds; (Electr.) charcoal pencil used in one form of electric lighting; = ~ *copy* (made with ~ paper); ~ *dioxide,* carbonic acid gas; ~ *monoxide,* very poisonous, colourless, almost odourless gas formed during incomplete combustion of coke, charcoal, etc., occurring in coal-gas & in the exhaust fumes of motor engines; ~ *printing, process,* producing permanent prints in various colours; ~ *paper,* for taking copies of letters etc. Hence ~ATE[1](3) n. [f. F *carbone* f. L *carbonem* nom. -o charcoal]

cărbonā′ceous (-shus), a. Of, like, coal or charcoal; consisting of or containing carbon. [as prec., -ACEOUS]

cărbonā̆r′i (-rē), n. (hist.). Neapolitan secret society of republican revolutionists. [It. pl. of *carbonaro* charcoal-burner, the name assumed by the society]

cărb′onāte, v.t. (chem.). Form into a carbonate; impregnate with carbonic acid gas, aerate. [f. *carbonate* n. see CARBON, -ATE[3]]

cărbŏn′ic, a. (chem.). Of carbon; ~ *acid*

(*gas*), the gas formed in combustion of carbon, given out in breathing, & constituting choke-damp. [-IC]

cărbonif′erous, a. Producing coal; (Geol.) ~ *strata, system, formation,* palaeozoic next above old red sandstone; ~ *age, era, period,* in which these strata were deposited. [CARBON, -I-, -FEROUS]

cărb′oniz|e, -is|e (-īz), v.t. Convert into carbon; reduce to charcoal or coke; cover (paper) with carbon for taking copies. Hence ~A′TION n. [-IZE(3, 5)]

cărborŭn′dum, n. Silicon. carbide used for polishing by abrasion. [P; CARBON + CORUNDUM]

cărb′oy, ·n. Large globular glass bottle usually protected with a frame. [f. Pers. *qarabah*]

cărb′ŭncl|e, n. Red precious stone (formerly of many kinds, e.g. ruby; now garnet cut in boss shape); malignant tumour, anthrax, pimple on nose or face, whence ~ED[2] (-ld), **cărbŭnc′ŭlAR[1],** aa. [ME *charbucle* etc., f. OF f. L *carbunculus* small coal (CARBON, -UNCLE); mod. forms assim. to L]

cărbūrĕt′, v.t. (-tt-). Combine (any element) chemically with carbon; charge with carbon. Hence ~t′OR ·or ~t′ER[1] (2) n., apparatus mixing air with petrol vapour for combustion in motor engines. [CARBON, -URET]

căr′cajou (-jōō, -zhōō), n. American glutton, wolverene. [N.-Amer. F, app. of Ind. orig.]

căr̆c′ass, -ase, n. Dead body (of human body now only with contempt); (with butchers) beast's trunk without head or offal (~ *meat,* raw meat as dist. from corned or tinned meat); mere body, dead or alive (*to save* one's ~), worthless remains (*of*); skeleton, framework, (of house, ship, etc.); (Mil.) kind of fire-ball from gun for igniting buildings. [ME *carcois* etc. f. AF (OF *charcois*·etc.) = med. L *carcosium*; 16th c. *carcasse* f. F = It. *carcassa*; ult. orig. unkn.]

căr̆cin′ogĕn, n. (med.). Any cancer-producing substance. [f. Gk *karkinos* crab, cancer + -GEN]

căr̆cinōm′a, n. (pl. -*ata*). (med.). (A form of) cancer. [L, f. Gk *karkinōma* ulcer f. *karkinos* (prec.)]

cărd[1], n., & v.t. (Cleanse, comb. get into order, also scratch or torture, with) toothed instrument, wire-brush, or wire-set rubber or vulcanite strip, for raising nap on cloth or preparing wool, hemp, etc.; ~-*thistle,* teasel; ~-*ing-machine,* with card-strips fixed on rollers. [ME, f. OF *carde* f. Pr. *carda* f. *cardar* f. Rom. **caritare* f. L *carere* card; vb f. OF *carder* f. Pr. *cardar*]

căr̆d[2], n. (Also *playing-*~) one of pack of 52 oblong pieces of pasteboard used in games (COURT[1]-~; *house of* ~s, (lit.) child's game, (fig.) insecure scheme etc.; ~s, card-playing; *sure, safe, doubtful,* etc.,

~, such a plan, expedient; *knowing, queer,* ~, such a person; *put (all) one's ~s on the table,* disclose all one's resources, plans, etc.; *throw up, show,* one's ~s, give up, let out, one's plan; ~ *up* one's *sleeve,* plan in reserve; *on the*~s, likely, possible); flat piece of thick paper or pasteboard for various purposes (*speak by the*~, with precision, f. obs. use = mariner's compass; ‖ POST²~; (colloq.) an eccentric person, a character; *correspondence-*~, for short notes; = ticket of admission; = invitation; ~ or *visiting-*~, with name etc., sent or left in lieu of formal visit, so *leave a* ~ *on; wedding, Christmas,* etc., ~, sent in notification or compliment to friends; *collecting-*~, for entering subscribers to charities; programme of events at race-meetings etc., or of cricket scores, esp. *correct* ~; *the* ~, the correct thing, what is expected; printed or written notice, rules, etc., for hanging in window or on wall); ~-*case,* for carrying visiting-~s; ~-*basket, -rack,* for keeping visitors' ~s; ~-*board,* pasteboard for cutting ~s from or making boxes etc.; ~ *index* (in which each item is entered on separate ~); ~-*index* (v.t.), make a ~ index of; ~-*sharper,* swindler at ~-games; ‖~ *vote* (of delegates each counting for the number of his constituents). [f. F *carte* f. L *charta* f. Gk *khartēs* papyrus-leaf; -*d* for -*te* unexplained]

cărd'amom, n. Spice from seed-capsules of E.-Ind. plants. [f. L *cardamomum* or F *cardamome* f. Gk *kardamōmon* (*kardamon* cress, *amōmon* a spice plant)]

cărd'an, a. (engineering). ~ *joint,* UNIVERSAL joint; ~ *shaft* (with universal joint at one or both ends). [f. G. *Cardano,* Italian mathematician (d. 1576)]

cărd'iăc, a. & n. Of the heart (esp. path., as ~ *symptoms,* of heart-disease); of upper orifice of stomach; (n.) heart-stimulant, cordial. [f. L *cardiacus* (esp. in *cardiaca passio*), f. Gk *kardiakos* f. *kardia* heart; cf. F *cardiaque*]

cărd'igan, n. Knitted woollen jacket with or without sleeves. [named after Earl of C~ *c.* 1855]

cărd'inal, C~, a. & n. On which something hinges, fundamental, important, (~ *virtues,* the four natural & three theological, see VIRTUE; ~ *numerals,* the primitive ones, one, two, three, etc., as opp. to the ordinal ones, first, second, third, etc.; ~ *points* (of compass), N., S., E., W.; ~ *church,* hist., one of principal churches in Rome, to which others were subordinate, whence C~, noun, orig. person in charge of one of these, now one of seventy princes of R.-C. Ch., members of Pope's council of 6 ~ bishops, 50 ~ priests, & 14 ~ deacons, & electors of new Pope, whence ~ATE¹, ~SHIP, nn.; also prefixed to other titles, as C~-*Legate,* whence ~LY² adv.; of deep scarlet; woman's short hooded (orig. scarlet) cloak; small scarlet bird;

(Zool.) of the hinge of a bivalve; ~-*flower,* scarlet lobelia. [ME, f. OF f. L *cardinalis* (*cardo -inis* hinge, -AL); n. f. OF in later eccl. uses of the Latin]

cărdio-, comb. form of Gk *kardia* heart.

cărdōōn', n. Composite vegetable allied to artichoke. [f. F *cardon* f. *carde* artichoke (-OON) f. Pr. *carda, -do,* f. Rom. *carda* for L *cardu(u)s* thistle. See CARD¹]

cāre¹, n. Solicitude, anxiety; occasion for these; serious attention, heed, caution, pains, (*take, have a,* ~, be cautious); charge, protection, (*A, c/o* or ~ *of B,* in addresses; *have the, take,* ~ *of; in, under,* one's ~'); thing to be done or seen to (~*s of State* etc.; *that shall be my* ~); ~-*laden, -worn,* with anxieties; ~'*taker,* person hired to take charge, esp. of house in owner's absence, (adj.) exercising temporary control, as *a* ~*taker* (stopgap) *government.* [OE *caru,* OS *cara,* OHG *chara,* ON *kör,* Goth. *kara* f. Gmc *karō*]

cāre², v.i. Feel concern or interest *for* or *about;* provide food, attendance, etc., *for* (children, invalids, etc.); (w. neg. expressed or implied) feel regard, deference, affection, *for,* be concerned *whether* etc., (often with expletive *a pin, a damn, a farthing, a tinker's cuss; couldn't* ~ *less,* colloq., be utterly indifferent; *I don't* ~ *if I do,* am willing); be willing or wishful *to* (*should not* ~ *to be seen with him; do you* ~ *to try them?*). [OE *carian* f. Gmc *karō-jan* (prec.)]

careen', v.t. & i. Turn (ship) on one side for cleaning, caulking, etc.; (cause to) heel over; *(of vehicle etc.) career wildly. [ult. f. L *carina* keel]

careen'age, n. Careening a ship; expense of it; place for it. [f. prec. + -AGE]

career', n., & v.t. 1. Swift course, impetus, (*in full, mid,* etc., ~); course or progress through life; development & success of party, principle, nation, etc.; way of making a livelihood (*a* ~ *diplomat,* a professional); hence ~IST (3) n., one intent mainly on personal advancement & success in life. 2. v.i. Go swiftly or wildly (often *about*). [f. F *carrière* f. It. -*iera* f. Rom. **carraria* (*via*) carriage-(road) f. L *carrus* CAR¹]

care'ful (-ărf-), a. Concerned *for,* taking care *of;* painstaking, watchful, cautious, (*to do, that, what, whether,* etc.); done with or showing care. Hence ~LY² adv., ~NESS n. [OE *carful;* see -FUL]

care'less (-ărl-), a. Unconcerned, lighthearted; ' inattentive, negligent (*of*), thoughtless; inaccurate. Hence ~LY³ adv., ~NESS n. [OE *carlēas;* see -LESS]

caress', n., & v.t. 1. Fondling touch, kiss; blandishment. 2. v.t. Bestow these on; pet, make much of; hence ~ingLY² adv. [f. F *caresse(r)* f. It. *carezza(re)* f. L *carus* dear]

că'rĕt (or *kā̆r²*) n. Mark (∧) placed below line to show place of omission. [L, = is wanting]

cărg′ō, n. (pl. ~es). Freight of ship. [f. Sp. *cargo* f. *cargar* f. LL *car(ri)care* CHARGE²]

Că′rib, n. & a. (One) of aboriginal inhabitants of Southern W.-Ind. islands. So ~bē′an a. [f. Sp. *Caribe* cf. CANNIBAL]

cărĭbou′ (-ōō), -bōō′, n. N.Amer. reindeer. [-*ou* Canad. F, prob. f. native wd]

căricatūr|e′, n., & v.t. Grotesque representation of person or thing by over-emphasis on characteristic traits (pictorial, literary, or mimetic); hence ~ᶜ IST(1) n.; (v.t.) make, give, a ~e of; hence ~′ABLE a. [F, f. It. *caricatura* (in 17th c. Eng. use)]

căr′ĭēs (-z), n. Decay (of bones or teeth). [L]

că′rĭllon (-lyon, *or* karĭl′yon), n. Set of bells sounded either from keyboard or mechanically; air played on bells; instrument (or part of organ) imitating peal of bells. [F]

carĭn′|a, n. (zool. & bot.). Ridge-shaped structure. Hence ~AL, **căr′ĭnATE²**, aa., ~o- comb. form. [L, =keel].

căr′ĭous, a. Decayed(esp. of bones, teeth). [f. L *cariosus* CARIES, -OSE¹)]

cărk′ĭng, a. Burdensome (alw. with *care*). [f. obs. vb *cark* f. ONF *carkier* f. Rom. *carcare f. LL *carricare* CHARGE²]

‖ **cărl(e)**, n. (Sc.). Man, fellow. [OE in comb. as *hūs-carl* f. ON *karl* cogn. w. CHURL]

‖ **cărl′ine¹**, n. (Sc.). Old woman. [ME & ON *kerling* fem. of prec.]

cărl′ine², n. Kinds of composite plants allied to thistle. [F, f. med. L *carlina* for *Carolina* reputedly named f. *Carolus* Charlemagne]

Cărl′ism, Cărl′ĭst, nn. Spanish legitimism, legitimist, support(er) of Don Carlos (d. 1855) second son of Charles IV. [-ISM(3), -IST(2)]

Cărlovĭn′gĭan, Cărolĭn′gĭan, (-j-), a. & n. (One) of second French dynasty founded by Charlemagne (d. 814). [f. F *carlovingien* after *mérovingien* MEROVINGIAN]

Cărlȳl′|ism, n. Principles, literary manner, a mannerism, of Carlyle. So ~E′AN, ~IAN, aa., ~ESE′ a. & n. [Thomas *Carlyle* 1795–1881; -ISM(3, 4)]

Cărm′agnole (-anyōl), n. Song & dance among French revolutionists of 1793. [F]

Cărm′ėlite, n. & a. (Member) of mendicant order of friars (also *White Friars* f. their white cloak); fine woollen stuff, usu. grey. [F, or f. med. L *carmelita* (Mt *Carmel* in Palestine, place of foundation in 12th c., -ITE¹ (1))]

cărm′inative, a. & n. (Drug) curing flatulence. [F -*if* or med. L *carminativus* f. *carminare* heal (by incantation); see CHARM, -ATIVE]

cărm′ine, n. & a. (Coloured like, colour of) crimson pigment made from cochineal. [f. F or Sp. *carmin*, f. med. L *carminium*, f. *carmesinum* CRIMSON + *minium* cinnobar]

cărn′age, n. Great slaughter, esp. of

men. [F, f. It. *carnaggio* (L *caro carnis* flesh, -AGE)]

cărn′al, a. Sensual, fleshly; sexual (*have* ~ *knowledge of*, have sexual intercourse with); unsanctified, worldly. Hence ~ISM(2), **cărnăl′ĭTY**, nn., ~IZE(3) v.t., ~LY² adv. [f. LL *carnalis* (*caro* see prec., -AL)]

cărnā′tion¹, n. & a. (Of) rosy pink (orig. flesh-) colour. [F, f. LL *carnationem* (as prec., -ATION) fleshiness]

cărnā′tion², n. Cultivated kinds of clove pink. [in 16th c. also *coronation*, perh. the orig. form, later assim. to prec.]

cărnau′ba (-naōō-, -now-), n. Brazilian wax palm; (also *Brazilian wax*) its yellowish wax. [Braz. Port.]

cărnēl′ian. = CORNELIAN. [late 17th c. var. of CORNELIAN, after L *caro* etc., as flesh-coloured]

cărn′ĭ|fȳ, v.t. & i. (path.). Change (t. & i. of bone, lungs, etc.) to structure of flesh or muscle. Hence ~FICA′TION n. [L *caro carnis* flesh, -FY]

cărn′ĭval, n. Half-week or week before Lent; festivities usual during this in R.-C. countries; riotous revelry; reckless indulgence in something (*of*; ~ *of blood-shed* etc.). [16th c., f. It. *carne-*, *carnovale* f. med.L *carnelevarium* etc. Shrovetide, f. L *carn-* (*caro*) flesh + *levare* put away]

cărnĭv′ora, n. Large order of flesh-eating mammalia, including cats, dogs, etc. [L neut. pl. see CARNIVOROUS]

cărn′ĭvōre, n. Carnivorous animal or plant. [F, as foll.]

cărnĭv′orous, a. Feeding on flesh (esp. of the CARNIVORA, & of plants digesting animal substance). [f. L *carnivorus* (*caro carnis* flesh, -VOROUS)]

‖ **cărn′ȳ**, -ey, v.t.(colloq.). Coax, wheedle. [orig. unkn.]

că′rob, n. Horn-like pod of Mediterranean ~-tree. [16th c., f. F *carobe* (now -*oube*) f. Arab. *kharrubah* bean-pod]

că′rol, n., & v.t. & i. (-ll-). **1.** Joyous song, human or of birds, esp. Christmas hymn. **2.** vb. Utter, celebrate with, these; hence ~IER¹ n. [ME, f. OF *carole(r)* of unkn. orig.]

Că′roline, a. Of Charlemagne; of the time of Charles I & II of England. [f. L *Carolus* Charles + -INE¹]

Carolingian. See CARLOVINGIAN.

***că′rom**, n. Cannon at billiards. [see CANNON¹]

carŏt′ĭd, a. & n. Of, near, the two great arteries carrying blood to head; (n.) one of these. [f. F *carotide* f. Gk *karōtides* pl. (*karoō* stupefy, compression of these arteries being thought to do this)]

carous|e′ (-z), v.i., & n. (Have, engage in) a drinking-bout; drink deep. Hence ~′AL(2) n. [orig. as adv. = right out, in phr. *drink* ~ f. G *gar aus trinken*]

cărousĕl′ (-ōōz-), **cărr-**, n. Tournament (hist.); *roundabout, merry-go-round. [f. F *carrousel*]

carp[1], n. A freshwater fish usu. bred in ponds. [ME, f. OF *carpe* f. Pr. f. LL *carpa*, perh. of Gmc orig.; cf. OHG *karpfo*]

carp[2], v.i. Talk querulously, find fault, (usu. *at*); esp. ~*ing tongue*, *criticism*, captious. [obs. ME senses *talk*, *say*, *sing*, f. ON *karpa* to brag, but mod. sense (16th c.) f. or infl. by L *carpere* pluck at, slander]

carp'al, a. Of the CARPUS. [CARPUS, -AL]

carp'el, n. (bot.). Pistil-cell, whether pistil is one cell or several. Hence ~LARY[1] a. [f. F *carpelle* f. Gk *karpos* fruit, see -LE (2)]

carp'enter, n., & v.i. & t. 1. Artificer in woodwork (esp. of rough solid kinds as in ship or house building, cf. JOINER, CABINET-*maker*; *the* ~*'s son*, Jesus); ~-*ant*, -*bee*, kinds boring into trees; ~-*scene*, played before a painted scene (also ~-*scene*) to give ~ time for preparing elaborate scene behind; so **carp'entry** (2, 5) n. 2. vb. Do, make by, ~'s work. [ME & AF *carpenter* (OF -*ier*) f. LL *carpentarius* carpentum wagon f. Celt.)]

carp'et, n., & v.t. 1. Thick woven or felted fabric for covering floor & stairs (at first of table-covering, whence *on the* ~, under discussion; & as floor-covering long a boudoir luxury, whence ~-*knight*, stay-at-home soldier, ladies' man); *on the* ~, (also, colloq.) being reprimanded; smooth, soft, or bright expanse of grass, flowers, etc.; ~-*bed*, garden bed with dwarf plants arranged in pattern; ~-*dance*, informal; ~-*rods*, keeping stair-~ in place; ~-*snake*, variegated Australian kind; ~-*bag*, travelling-bag, orig. made of ~; ‖ ~-*bagger*, candidate for election or political agitator unconnected with district; hence ~LESS n. 2. v.t. Cover (as) with a carpet, whence ~ING[1] (3) n.; ‖ summon (servant etc.) into the room for reprimand, reprove. [ME, f. OF *carpite* or med. L -*ita*, corresp. to OF *charpie* lint, f. Rom. *carpire* f. L *carpere* pluck, pull to pieces]

carphol'ogy, n. Delirious fumbling with bed-clothes etc. [f. Gk *karphologia* (*karphos* twig, *legō* pick, -Y[1])]

carpo-[1], comb. form of CARPUS.

carpo-[2], comb. form of Gk *karpos* fruit. Hence **carpŏl'ogy** n.

carp'us, n. (anat.; pl. -*pī*). Part of skeleton that unites hand etc. to fore-arm, eight small bones in higher vertebrates (in man, wrist; in horse, knee). [f. Gk *karpos* wrist]

carrageen (kǎ'ragĕn), n. An edible seaweed found in N. Europe, Irish moss. [f. *Carragheen* in Ireland]

ca'rrel, n. 1. (hist.). Small enclosure or study in cloister. 2. Small cubicle in (stackroom of) library. [f. OF *carole*, med. L *carola*, of unkn. orig.]

ca'rriage (-rĭj), n. Conveying, transport; cost of conveying (~-FREE; ‖ ~-*forward*,

not prepaid); management (*of* enterprise etc.); passing (*of* Parl. motion etc.); manner of carrying (~ *of head*, *body*, etc.), bearing, deportment; wheeled vehicle for persons (*hackney*, *railway*, -~), esp. four--wheeled private vehicle with two (~ & *pair*) or more horses (~-*company*, -*folk*, who keep these), whence ~FUL (-rĭjf-) (2) n.; wheeled support of gun (usu. *gun*--~); wheeled framework of vehicle apart from body; (Mech.) sliding etc. part of machinery for shifting position of other parts; ~ *clock* (going in any position); ~-*dog*, spotted Dalmatian; ~-*drive*, road in parks etc.; ~-*way*, part of road intended for vehicular traffic. Hence ~LESS (-rĭjl-) a. [f. ONF *cariage* f. *carier* (CARRY, -AGE)]

ca'rriageable (-ĭja-), a. Available for carriages (of road). [-ABLE]

ca'rrick bĕnd, n. (naut.). Kind of knot or splice. [BEND[1]; *carrick* perh. f. obs. *carrack* armed merchant ship]

ca'rrier, n. In vbl senses; esp.: person undertaking for hire the conveyance of parcels (*common* ~, legal term including also railway and steamship companies etc.); part of bicycle etc. for carrying luggage; person or animal that without suffering from a disease conveys its germs; = *Bren* ~, *aircraft* ~, etc.; ~-PIGEON; ~-*nation* etc., conducting oversea trade for others; ~ *wave*, continuous electromagnetic wave motion emitted by radio transmitter. [CARRY + -ER[1]]

ca'rriōle, n. Small open carriage for one; covered light cart; Canadian sledge. [F]

ca'rrion, n. & a. Dead putrefying flesh; anything vile, garbage, filth; ~-*crow*, between raven & rook, feeding on ~, small animals, etc.; (adj.) rotten, loathsome. [ME, f. AN, ONF *caroine*, -*oigne* (F *charogne*), f. Rom. *caronia* f. L *caro* flesh]

ca'rronāde', n. (hist.). Short large--calibred ship's gun. [*Carron* (in Stirlingshire, Scotland) orig. place of making + -ADE]

ca'rrot, n. (Plant with) tapering orange--coloured edible root; (pl., sl.) red hair, red-haired person, whence ~Y[2] a. [f. F *carotte* f. L *carota* f. Gk *karōton*]

ca'rry[1], v.t. & i. 1. Convey in vehicle, ship, hand, or head (as *news*), or on person (also of vehicle etc., or water, wind, etc., as subject; ~ *corn*, from field to stack; *fetch & ~*, be underling; ~ *all before* one, succeed, overcome all opposition; ~ *weight*, be handicapped in horse-racing or fig.). 2. Conduct (*pipes* ~ *water*, *wires* ~ *sound*; ~ *into effect*; ~ one *back*, in fancy to earlier times; ~ *off to prison*, *to dine*). 3. Transfer (figures to column of higher notation; ~ *conviction*, implant one's own in other minds; ~ *over*, *forward*, entries to new page or account). 4. Propel to specified distance (of gun etc., with obj. usu. omitted; also intr.=*go* of missile).

5. Cause or enable to go *to* (of motive, journey-money, etc.). **6.** Bring *to* (of day's journey etc.). **7.** Prolong, continue, *to* (~ *tower to 500 ft, modestly to excess*). **8.** Win (prize; ~ *it, the day,* succeed; ~ *fortress* etc., capture; ~ *hearers with* one, persuade); win victory for (candidate; ~ one's *point, a motion, bill*). **9.** Wear, have with one, possess, involve, (arms, a watch, etc.; ~ one's BAT²; ~ *weight, authority,* be influential; ~ *with* one, remember; *loans* ~ *interest, principles* ~ *consequences*); stock (goods for sale). **10.** Hold in a certain way (~ one's *head, body,* one*self*; ~ *sword,* in saluting-position). **11.** Endure weight of, support, (*ships* ~ *sail, piers* ~ *dome*). **12.** ~ *away,* inspire, transport, deprive of self-control, (Naut.) lose (mast etc.) by breakage, break off or away; ~ *off,* remove from life, win, render passable, ~ *it off* (*well*), make brave show; ~ *on,* advance (process) a stage, continue, manage (business), (v.i.) go on with what one is doing, (colloq.) behave strangely, flirt or have amorous intrigue (*with*); ~ *out,* put (principles, instructions, etc.) in practice; ~ *over* (St. Exch.), keep over to next settling-day; ~ *through,* bring safely out of difficulties, complete. [f. ONF *carier* (*charrier*) f. *car* CAR]

câ′rry², n. (Mil.) *the* position of carrying sword; (Golf) ball's flight before pitching; portage between rivers etc.; range of gun etc.; ~-*over* (St. Exch.), process of carrying or amount carried over. [prec.]

cárt, n., & v.t. & i. **1.** Strong two-wheeled vehicle (cf. WAGON) used in farming & for heavy goods, (also *spring, mail, dog,* -~) light two-wheeled one-horse vehicle for driving in, (*put* ~ *before horse,* reverse order, take effect for cause); *in the* ~ (sl.), in a fix, in an awkward or losing position; ~-*horse,* thickset & fit for heavy work; ~-*ladder,* rack at sides or ends for increasing capacity; ~-*load,* = ~ful, also large quantity of anything; ~-*road, -way,* too rough for carriages; ~-*wheel,* wheel of ~, large coin as crown etc., lateral somersault (*turn* ~-*wheel*); ~-*whip,* long & heavy; ~-*wright,* maker of ~s; hence ~′AGE(4), ~′ER¹, ~′FUL(2) (-ŏŏl), nn. **2.** vb. Carry in a ~; work with a ~ [MÉ, f. ON *kartr* cart; relation to OE *cræt* is uncert.]

cárte, quarte (kärt), n. Fencing position (~ *& tierce,* sword-play). [F (*q*-), f. It. *quarta* fourth]

carte blanche (see Ap.), n. Blank paper given to person to write his own terms on; full discretionary power. [F, (CARD², BLANK)]

cárte-de-visite (vīzēt′), n. Photograph 3½ in. × 2¼. [F, = visiting card, its orig. purpose]

cártel′, n. Written challenge to duel; (agreement for) exchange of prisoners; (also *kartell*) manufacturers' union to control production, marketing arrangements, prices, etc. Hence ~IZE (3) v.t. &

i., combine to form a (business) ~. [F, f. It. *cartello* dim.·of *carta* CARD²]

Cârte′sian (-zhn), a. & n. (Follower) of Descartes or his philosophy or mathematical methods. Hence ~ISM (-zĭan-) (3) n. [*Cartesius* mod. L name of René Descartes, 1596–1650, -IAN]

Cârthū′sian (-zhn), a. & n. (Member) of order of monks founded by St Bruno 1086; (member) of Charterhouse school founded on site of ~ monastery. [f. med. L *carthusianus* f. L *Cart*(*h*)*usia* (*Chartreuse,* near Grenoble)+ -AN; see CHARTERHOUSE]

cârt′ilage, n. (Structure, part, in vertebrates, of) firm elastic tissue gristle, (*temporary* ~, in the young, changing later to bone). So **cârtila′ginoid** a. [F, f. L *cartilago* -*inis*]

cârtila′ginous, a. Of, like, cartilage (~ *fish,* with ~ skeleton). [f. F *cartilagineux* or L -*osus* (see prec., -OUS)]

cârtŏg′raphy, n. Map-drawing. So **cârtŏg′RAPHER** n., **cârtoGRAPH′IC**(AL) aa. [f. F -*ie,* see CARD², -GRAPHY]

cârtŏl′ogy, n. Study of maps & charts. So **cârtolŏ′gical** a. [f. F -*ie,* see CARD², -OLOGY]

cârt′omăncy, n. Fortune-telling by playing-cards. [f. It. *carta* CARD², -MANCY]

cârt′on, n. White disc within bull's-eye of target; cardboard box for holding goods or the cardboard used for these. [f. F as foll.]

cârtoŏn′, n., & v.i. & t. **1.** Drawing on stout paper as design for painting, tapestry, mosaic, etc.; full-page (or large) illustration, esp. on politics in a paper; hence ~IST(3) n.; *animated* ~, film made from a succession of drawings simulating a cinematographic film of living persons. **2.** vb. Draw ~, represent (person etc.) in a ~. [f. F *carton* or It. *cartone* (*carta* CARD², -OON)]

cârtouche′ (-ōōsh), n. (Archit.) scroll ornament, e.g. volute of Ionic capital; tablet imitating, or drawing of, scroll with rolled-up ends, used ornamentally or bearing inscription; (Archaeol.) oval ring containing hieroglyphic names & titles of Egyptian kings etc. [F, f. It. *cartoccio* augmentative of *carta* CARD²]

cârt′ridge, n. Charge of propellant explosive for fire-arms or blasting made up in case of paper, flannel, metal, etc. (small-arm *ball* ~, or ~, contains bullet also, *blank* ~ the explosive only); ~-*belt,* with sockets for ~s; ~-*paper,* thick & rough, used also for drawing & for strong envelopes. [16th c. *cartage* etc., corrupt. of prec.]

cârt′ulary, n. Collection of records; register. [f. med. L *c*(*h*)*artularium* f. L *chartula* dim. of *c*(*h*)*arta* CARD², -ARY¹]

că′runcle (*also* karŭ′-), n. Fleshy excrescence, as turkeycock's wattles. [F, f. L *caruncula* (*caro carnis* flesh, -UNCLE)]

cârve, v.t. & i. (p.p. -*ed,* arch. -*en*). Cut (in gen. sense now only fig., as ~ one's *way*); produce by cutting (statue, portrait, representation in relief or intaglio, inscription, design, *out of*, *in*, or *on*, material), change by cutting (material *into* something), cover or adorn (material) *with* figures cut in it, cut designs etc., whence **cārv'ING** [1](2) n.; cut up meat, cut up (meat etc.), at or for table (*carving knife*, long for this purpose); subdivide (usu. *up*); ~ *out*, take from larger whole, acquire esp. by the sword. [OE *ceorfan* f. WG **kerfan*]

cārv'el, = CARAVEL; ~-*built*, with planks flush (cf. CLINKER-BUILT).

cārv'er, n. In vbl senses; also, carving knife, (pl.) carving knife & fork. [-ER [1]]

cārÿǎt'id, n. Female figure used as pillar. [f. L f. Gk *karuatis -idos* priestess at Caryae]

cǎscāde', n., & v.i. (Fall like a) waterfall, or one section of large broken waterfall; wavy fall of lace etc. [F, f. It. *cascata* (*cascare* to fall f. L *cas-* see CASE [1])]

cǎscār'a (sagrā'da) (-ahd-), n. Laxative drug from the bark of a tree. [Sp., = sacred bark]

cāse [1], n. **1.** Instance of thing's occurring; actual state of affairs (*is*, *is not*, *the* ~, is true, false); position, circumstances, in which one is, plight, (*in good*, *evil*, ~, well, badly, off); (Med.) person's diseased condition; instance of any disease. **2.** (Law) cause, suit, for trial; statement of facts in cause *sub judice*, drawn up for higher court's consideration (*judge states a* ~); cause that has been decided & may be cited (*leading* ~, one often cited & governing subsequent decisions); sum of arguments on one side (*that is our* ~; *make out* one's ~, prove it); (fig.) ~ *of conscience*, matter in which conscience has to decide between conflicting principles. **3.** (Gram.) form of noun, adj., or pronoun, in inflected languages expressing relation to some other word in sentence (in uninflected languages, this relation itself apart from form). **4.** *In* ~, if, in the event that, lest; *in* ~ *of*, in the event of; *in the* ~ *of*, as regards (*in the* ~ *of Jones an exception was made*); *put* (*the*) ~ *that*, suppose; *in any* ~, whatever the fact is, whatever may happen; *in that* ~, if that is true, should happen; ~ *history*, record of person's ancestry, personal history, etc., for use in determining necessary treatment etc., ~-*law*, law as settled by precedent; ~-*work*, social work concerned with the individual. [ME & OF *cas* f. L *casus -ūs* fall (*cadere cas-* fall)]

cāse [2], n., & v.t. **1.** Enclosure of something, box, bag, sheath, etc.; glass box for showing specimens, curiosities, etc.; outer protective covering (of watch, sausage, seed-vessel, book, etc.); box with proper contents (*dressing-* ~); (Print.) receptacle with compartments (*upper* ~, capitals, *lower* ~, small letters); ~-*bottle*, square for fitting into ~ with others;

~-*harden* v.t., harden surface of, esp. give steel surface to (iron) by carbonizing, (fig.) render callous; ~-*knife*, worn in sheath; ~-*shot*, or ~ (hist.), bullets in tin box fired from cannon without fuse, also = SHRAPNEL; ~-*worm*, = CADDIS. **2.** v.t. Enclose in case, surround *with*, (also with *up*, *over*); hence **cās'ING** [1] (3) n. [f. ONF *casse* (F *châsse*) f. L *capsa* (*capere* hold)]

cās'ēin, n. Protein of milk, the basis of cheese. [L *caseus* cheese + -IN]

cāse'māt|e (-sm-), n. Vaulted chamber in thickness of wall of fortress, with embrasures; armoured enclosure for guns in warship. Hence ~ED [2] a. [16th c. *casamat(e)* f. It. *casamatta* or Sp.-*mata*, f. *casa* house (second element uncert.); mod. sp. f. F *casemate*]

cāse'ment (-zm-, -sm-), n. Metal or wooden hinged frame with glass forming (part of) window (often ~-*window*); (poet. etc.) window; ~ *cloth*, cotton cloth used for curtains & as dress material etc. [15th c., of unkn. orig.]

cās'ēous, a. Of, like, cheese. [f. L *caseus* cheese + -OUS]

casērn(e)' (-z-), n. (Usu. pl.) barracks. [F (-*e*), f. Pr. *cazerna* f. Rom. **quaderna* (place) for four f. L *quaterna*]

cǎsh [1], n. (no pl.), & v.t. **1.** Ready money (*in*, *out of*, ~, having, not having, money; ~ *down*, paid on the spot); || ~ *on delivery* (abbr. C.O.D.), forwarding of goods against ~ to be paid to postman; (Banking etc.) specie, or specie & bank-notes; (Book-keeping) ~-*account*, to which only ~ is carried, & from which all payments are made, ~-*book*, for record of ~ received & paid; ~ *payment*, in ready money; ~ *price*, lowest, for ready money; ~ *register*, mechanical till visibly recording amount of each purchase, totalling receipts, etc.; hence ~'LESS a. **2.** v.t. Give or obtain ~ for (note, cheque, etc.); ~ *in* (colloq.), die, ~ *in on*, realize profit on, (fig. use of poker phr.). [f. F *casse* (now *caisse*) box, or its source It. *cassa* f. L *capsa* CASE [2]]

cǎsh [2], n. (hist.; pl. *cash*). Kinds of E.-Ind. & Chinese small coin, esp. a former Chinese coin perforated for stringing = $\frac{1}{1000}$ of tael. [ult. f. Tamil *kasu* a small coin by confusion with CASH [1]]

cǎsh'ew (-ōō), n. W.-Ind. etc. tree with kidney-shaped nut (~-*nut*). [f Pg. *caju* (*acaju*, whence F *acajou* mahogany), f. Tupi (*a*)*caju*]

cashier' [1], n. Person in charge of bank's or merchant's cash. [f. Du. *cassier* or its source F *caissier* (CASH [1], -IER)]

cashier' [2], v.t. Dismiss from service, depose; discard. [c. 1600 *casseer* etc., f. Flem. *kasseren* disband, revoke, f. F *casser* = It. *cassare* quash f. LL *cassare* annul; see QUASH]

cǎsh'mēre, n. (Also ~ *shawl*) shawl of fine soft wool of Cashmere goat; the material; imitation of it. [f. *Kashmir* in N. India]

casi'nō (-sē-), n. (pl. -os). Public music or dancing or gambling room; old card--game. [It., dim. of *casa* house f. L *casa* cottage]

cask (-ah-), n. Wooden vessel (=BARREL[1]); this & its contents; varying measure of capacity. [16th c. *cask(c)* app. f. F *casque* helmet; sense 'barrel' is only Eng., & unexpl.]

cas'kėt (-ah-), n. Small box, often of precious material & workmanship, for jewels, letters, cremated ashes, etc. [15th c., in form a dim. of prec., of obsc. orig.]

Căs'lon (-z-), n. (typ.). ~ *type*, old-face type cut in the foundry established by William ~ (d. 1766), or in imitation of this.

casque (kǎsk), n. (hist., poet.). Helmet. [F, f. Sp. *casco*]

Cassăn'dra, n. Prophet of ill; unregarded prophet. [Trojan prophetess fated to prophesy truly & be unbelieved]

cassā'tion, n. Annulment; *Court of C~*, court of appeal in France. [F, f. *casser*; see QUASH, -ATION]

cassa'va (-sah-), n. W.-Ind. etc. plant with tuberous roots; its starch or flour, bread made from these. [16th c. *cas(s)avi* etc., f. Haytian]

căss'erōle, n. A heat-proof earthenware vessel in which meat etc. is cooked & served (*en~*, so served). [F]

că'ssia (*also* -sha), n. Inferior kind of cinnamon; kinds of plants yielding senna--leaves. [f. L f. Gk *kasia* f. Heb. *q'tsi'ah* (*qatsa'* cut off bark)]

căss'ock, n. Long close tunic worn by all clergy including seminarists and altar servers. Hence ~ED[2] (-kt) a. [f. F *casaque* long coat, f. It. *casacca* horseman's coat; ult. orig. uncert.]

căssolĕtte', n. Vessel for burning perfumes; perfume-box with perforated top. [F, dim. of *cassole* dim. of *casse* pan]

căss'owary (-o-w-), n. Kinds of large running bird related to ostrich. [f. Malay *kasuari*]

cast[1] (-ah-), v.t. & i. (*cast*). 1. Throw (poet. or arch. exc. in spec. uses, as: ~ *dice*; ~ *a vote*, give or deposit it; ~ LOTS; ~ *ashore*; ~ *net, hook, fly*; *~ing-net*, one thrown & at once drawn in; ~ *the* LEAD[1], in sounding; ~ *anchor*; ~ *in* one's *teeth*, reproach him with, *that*; ~ *an eye, glance, look*; ~ *a spell on*, bewitch; ~ *light, a shadow, on*; ~ *blame*, one's *cares, upon*;~ *into prison*). 2. Overthrow in a lawsuit. 3. Throw off, get rid of, lose, (~ *not a* CLOUT *till May be out*; ~ *aside*, give up using, abandon; *cow, tree,* ~ *calf, fruit,* drop prematurely; ~ *soldier, policeman, horse*, dismiss, reject; ~ *loose*, detach oneself). 4. Reckon, calculate, (~ *accounts*, do sums; ~ *a column of figures* etc., add up; ~ *a* HOROSCOPE *or nativity*). 5. Arrange (~ facts into such a shape; ~ actors *for* parts, parts *to* actors). 6. Form,

found, (molten metal) *into* some shape, (figure etc.) *of* metal, whence ~'ING[1](2) n. 7. ~ *about*, go this way & that in search, devise means, (*for, to do, how*); ~ *away*, reject, (pass., of ship) be wrecked; ~ *back*, revert; ~ *down*, depress; ~ *in* one's *lot with*, share fortunes of; ~ *off*, abandon, (Knitting) close loops & make selvedge, (Naut.) loose & throw off (rope etc.), (Printing) estimate space taken in print by MS. copy; ~ *up*, calculate. [ME, f. ON *kasta*; it displaced OE *weorpan*, & has been displaced in ordinary literary use by *throw*]

cast[2] (-ah-), n. 1. Throw of missile etc., distance so attained; throw, number thrown, at dice, whence chance or try; throw of net, sounding-lead, or fishing--line (also, in fishing, the fly with hook & gut; & *good, bad*, etc. place for casting). 2. Casual lift in cart etc. 3. Undigested food thrown up by hawk, owl, etc. 4. Calculation, adding of columns in account. 5. Set of actors taking the parts in play, or the distribution among them. 6. Form into which any work is thrown; model made by running molten metal or pressing soft material into mould (also the negative mould itself). 7. Twist, inclination, (~ *in eye*, slight squint). 8. Tinge, shade, of colour. 9. Type, quality, (esp. ~ *of features*, ~ *of mind*). [f. prec.]

Căs'talý, n. (poet.). Fount of poesy. So **Căstāl'iAN** a. [f. L f. Gk *Kastalia* fountain of the Muses]

căs'tanĕt (*or* -ĕt'), n. (Usu. pl.) hardwood or ivory instrument(s) used in pairs to rattle in time with dancing. [f. Sp. *castañeta* dim. of *castaña* f. L *castanea* chestnut]

cast'away (kahsta-), n. & a. Shipwrecked (person); reprobate. [p.p. of CAST[1], AWAY]

caste (-ah-), n. Hindu hereditary class, with members socially equal, united in religion, & usu. following same trade, having no social intercourse with persons of other ~s; hereditary more or less exclusive class elsewhere; this system, the position it confers (*lose, renounce, ~*, descend in social scale). Hence ~'LESS (-tl-) a. [f. Sp. & Port. *casta* lineage, race, breed, fem. of *casto* pure, CHASTE]

căs'tellan, n. Governor of castle. [ME & ONF *castelain* f. L *castellanus* (CASTLE, -AN)]

căs'tellātėd, a. Castle-like; battlemented; (of district etc.) having castles. [f. med. L *castellatus* (CASTLE, -ATE[2])]

căs'tig|āte, v.t. Chastise, punish with blows or words; correct & emend (book etc.). Hence ~A'TION, ~ātor, nn., ~ātory a. [f. L *castigare* (see -ATE[3])]

Căstile' (-ēl) soap, n. Hard soap, usu. mottled, made with olive oil & soda. [*Castile*, in Spain]

Castil'ian, a. & n. (Native or inhabitant) of Castile; language of Castile, standard Spanish. [f. as prec. +-IAN]

cast′ing-vōte (-ah-), n. Vote that decides between two equal parties. [part. of CAST¹ in obs. sense 'turn the scale']

cast iron, n., **cast-iron**, a. Iron shaped by being run into mould; (adj.) made of ~; hard, untiring, rigid, unadaptable.

castle¹ (kah′sl, kā′sl), n. Large fortified building or set of buildings, stronghold; mansion that was once such; (Ireland) *The C~* (hist.), government system (f. Dublin C~, seat of vice-regal court & government); *Englishman's house his ~*, none may force entrance; (Chess) piece made with battlemented top, also *Rook*; ~ *in the air*, ~ *in Spain*, visionary project, day-dream, (so ~*-builder*); ~*-nut*, one with notched extension for locking pin. Hence **ca′stlED²** (-ld) a., ~**WISE** (-lw-) adv. [late OE, ME *castel* stronghold f. ONF f. L *castellum* dim. of *castrum* fort]

ca′stle² (kah′sl, kā′sl), v.t. & i. (chess). Move castle next king and king round castle (~ *the king*, or abs.). [f. prec.]

cas′tor¹ (-ah-), n. Substance obtained from beaver used in medicine & perfumery; (sl.) hat. [F or L, f. Gk *kastōr* beaver]

cas′tor², **-er**, (-ah-), n. **1.** Condiment-bottle for table, (pl.)cruet-stand (~*sugar*, white, finely granulated. **2.** Small swivelled wheel on leg of chair, table, etc. [CAST¹+-OR, -ER¹; sense 1, 17th c.; sense 2, 18th c.]

cas′tor³ (-ah-), n. Horny external knob inside horse's leg (also *chestnut*). [orig. unkn.]

cas′tor oil (-ah-), n. Nauseous vegetable oil used as purgative (*cold-drawn* ~, expressed from seeds without heat) & lubricant. [orig. uncert.; perh. so called as having succeeded CASTOR¹ in med. use]

căstramĕta′tion, n. (archaeol.). Laying out of camps. [F, f. L *castra* camp, *metari* measure, -ATION]

căstr|āte′, v.t. Remove testicles of, geld; deprive of vigour; expurgate (book). Hence ~A′TION n. [f. L *castrare*, -ATE³]

căstra′tō (-rah-), n. (pl. *-ti*, pr. *-tē*). A male singer castrated in boyhood so as to retain a soprano or alto voice. [It.]

că′sual (-zhŏŏ-, -zū-), a. & n. Accidental; irregular; undesigned; unmethodical, careless; (colloq.) unceremonious; ~ *labourer*, who works when the chance comes; ǁ~ *poor*, who sometimes need poor-relief (also ~ as noun); ǁ~*ward*, for their relief in workhouse; ~ *water*, (Golf) temporary accumulation of water (i.e. not one of the recognized hazards of the course). Hence ~**LY²** adv., ~**NESS** n. [ME, f. OF *casuel* & L *casualis* (*casus* CASE¹, -AL)]

că′sualty̆ (-zhŏŏ-, -zū-), n. Accident, mishap, disaster, esp. (pl.) list or number of killed, wounded, & invalided, in a battle, march, war, etc., (sing.) wounded etc. person. [15th c. f. prec.+-TY; after *royalty* etc. (also 16th c. (obs.) *casuality*, f. F *casualité*, med. L *casualitas*)]

căsūarin′a (*also* -ĕn′*a*), n. (Kinds of) Australian & E.-Indian tree with jointed leafless branches resembling gigantic horse-tails. [f. mod. L *casuarius* cassowary (from resemblance between branches & feathers)]

că′suǀist (-zhŏŏ-, -zū-), n. Person, esp. theologian, who lays down application of ethical rules to special cases, weighs conflicting obligations, classifies exceptions, & draws distinctions; quibbler. Hence ~**is′tIC**(AL) aa., ~**is′ticaLLY²** adv., ~**istRY** n. [f. F *casuiste* f. L *casus* CASE¹, -IST(3)]

căs′us, L n. ~ *bĕll′ĭ*, act justifying war; ~ *foed′erĭs* (fēd-), circumstances contemplated in treaty as requiring the action of the parties when they arise.

căt¹, n. **1.** Small domesticated carnivorous quadruped (male, *Tom-*~); *wild* ~, larger native British kind; spiteful woman, scratching child; (Zool.) any member of genus *Felis*, as lion, tiger, panther, leopard (esp. *the Cats, the great Cats*); ~-like animal of other species (*civet, musk*, ~). **2.** (hist.). Pent-house in sieges. **3.** (also ~*head*) horizontal beam from each side of ship's bow for raising & carrying anchor. **4.** (Also ~*-o′-nine-tails*) rope whip with nine knotted lashes formerly used for flogging sailors & soldiers. **5.** Six-legged tripod always standing on three of its legs. **6.** Tapered short stick in game tip-~. **7.** *Turn ~ in pan*, change sides, be turncoat; *a ~ may look at a king*, rebuke to the exclusive; *care killed the ~* (for all its nine lives; therefore be cheerful); *wait for the ~ to jump, see which way the ~ jumps, cult of the jumping ~*, etc., of politician refusing to advise until public opinion has declared itself; *fight like Kilkenny ~s*, to mutual destruction; ·BELL² *the ~*; *not room to swing a ~*, confined space; ~*-&-dog life* etc., full of quarrels, esp. that of husband & wife; *rain ~s & dogs*, very hard. **8.** ~*head*, Amer. thrush; ǁ~ *burglar* (who enters by climbing); ~*′call*, shrill whistle (sound or instrument) expressing disapproval at theatre etc. (also as v.i. & t., use, reprove with, this); ~*-eyed*, able to see in dark; ~*′fish*, of various kinds, esp. large Amer. river-fish; ~*′head*, see sense 3; ~*-ice*, milky-looking, bubbly, not solid, irregular; ǁ~*-lap*, slops, tea, etc.; ~*-mint*, blue-flowered aromatic plant; ~*-nap, -sleep*, brief, in chair etc.; ~*′s-cradle*, child's game with transfers of string between fingers of two players; ~*′s-eye*, precious stone of Ceylon & Malabar, reflector stud on road; ~*′s-foot*, ground-ivy; ǁ~*′s-meat*, horse's or other flesh prepared & sold as food for ~s; ~*′s-paw*, person used as tool by another, slight breeze rippling water in places; ~*′s-tail*, various plants, as reed-mace; ~*-walk*, narrow footway along a bridge, among large engines, etc. Hence ~'HOOD n., ~'LIKE a. [OE *catte*, = OHG *kazza*, ON *köttr*, f. LL *cattus*, *catta*; ME *catt(e)* reinforced by ONF *cat* (F *chat*) f. same source]

căt², v.i. & t. (-tt-). ‖ Vomit (colloq.); (Naut.) raise (the anchor) from the surface of the water to the cathead. [f. prec.]

cata-, cat-, cath-, pref. in wds taken from Greek, & in others formed with Gk materials or on Gk analogy; meanings: down, away, wrongly, mis-, entirely, down upon, according to, alongside of, thoroughly. [f. Gk *kata* prep.]

catabolism. Var. of KATABOLISM.

cătachr|ēs'is (-k-), n. Perversion, improper use, of words. So ~ēs'tIC(AL) aa., ~ēs'ticaLLY² adv. [L, f. Gk CATA- (*khrēsis* f. *khraomai* use)]

căt'aclăsm, n. Violent break, disruption. [f. Gk CATA(*klasma* f. *klaō* to break)]

căt'aclÿsm, n. Deluge (esp. in Geol. as required by theory of school that believed in repeated destructions of all life followed by new creations); political or social upheaval. Hence ~AL, ~IC, aa., ~IST(3) n., (all -iz²). [f. F *cataclysme* f. Gk CATA(*klusmos* flood f. *kluzō* wash)]

căt'acomb (-kōm), n. Subterranean cemetery (orig. that under basilica of St Sebastian near Rome, supposed burying-place of Peter & Paul); (usu. pl.) the many Roman subterranean galleries with recesses excavated in sides for tombs; similar works elsewhere (in Paris; worked-out stone-quarries with bones from emptied churchyards); wine-cellar. [f. F *catacombes* f. LL *catacumbas* (name given to the cemetery of St Sebastian), of unkn. orig.; the ~s generally, while in use, were not so called]

catăd'romous, a. (zool.). Descending to lower river or sea to spawn. [f. Gk CATA- (*dromos* -running) + -OUS]

căt'afălque (-k), n. Decorated stage for coffin or effigy of distinguished person during funeral service; open hearse. [F, f. It. *catafalco* of unkn. orig.; see SCAFFOLD]

Căt'alan, a. & n. (Native, language) of Catalonia in Spain.

cătalěc'tic, a. Wanting a syllable in last foot (of verse). [f. LL f. Gk CATA(*lēktikos* ceasing f. *lēgō* cease)]

căt'alěpsÿ, n. Suspension of sensation & consciousness accompanied by rigidity of the body. [f. LL *catalepsia* f. Gk CATA(*lēpsis* seizure) see foll.]

cătalěp'tic, a. & n. Of, subject to, the disease catalepsy (n., ~ person); (Philos.) of mental apprehension. [f. LL *catalepticus* f. Gk CATA(*lēptikos* seizing f. *lambanō* seize)]

căt'alŏgu|e (-g), *-lŏg, n., & v.t. (Enumerate, enter, in a) complete list, usu. alphabetical or under headings, & often with particulars added to items; *university calendar; ~e *raisonné* (-zonā'), descriptive ~e arranged according to subjects or branches of subject. Hence ~ER¹ n. [F, f. LL f. Gk *katalogos* f. CATA- (*lēgō* choose) enrol]

catăl'pa, n. Kinds of tree with heart-shaped leaves & trumpet-shaped flowers. [N.-Amer. (Creek)]

catăl'ÿsis, n. (chem.). Effect produced by a substance that without undergoing change itself aids a chemical change in other bodies. So **căt'alÿst** n., agent in ~, **cătalÿt'IC** a. [f. Gk CATA(*lusis* loosing f. *luō* loose) dissolution] ᵥ

cătamarăn', n. Raft or float of logs tied side by side, longest in middle, used for communication with shore or short voyage; raft of two boats fastened side by side; quarrelsome woman. [f. Tamil *katta-maram* tied tree]

căt'amite, n. Sodomite's minion. [f. L *catamitus* f. Gk *Ganumēdēs* cup-bearer of Zeus]

cătamoun'tain (-tĭn), **căt-o'-m-**, n. Leopard; wild quarrelsome person. [15th c., of Eng. formation]

căt'aplăsm, n. (med.). Poultice. [F, or f. LL f. Gk *kataplasma* (*kataplassō* spread; smear over)]

căt'apŭlt, n., & v.t. & i. Ancient engine worked by lever & ropes for discharging darts, stones, etc.; ‖ boy's shooting contrivance of forked stick & elastic; mechanical contrivance for launching aircraft from deck of ship etc.; (vb) shoot or pepper (bird etc., or abs.) with ~, launch (aircraft). [f. F *catapulte* or L *catapulta* f. Gk *katapellēs* perh. f. CATA- + *pallō* hurl]

căt'arăct, n. Waterfall (prop. large & sheer, cf. CASCADE); downpour of rain, rush of water; (Path.) eye-complaint producing partial blindness; (Mech.) steam-engine governor acting by flow of water. [f. L *cataracta* f. Gk *katarrhaktēs* f. CAT(*arassō* dash): the path. sense prob. f. obs. sense *portcullis*]

catarrh' (-är), n. Inflammation of mucous membrane, a·cold. Hence **catăr'rhAL** (-ral) a. [f. F *catarrhe* f. LL *catarrhus* f. Gk *katarrhous* f. *katarreō* (CATA-, *rheō* to flow)]

căt'a(r)rhine (-rīn), a. & n. (zool.). (Monkey) having nostrils close together, oblique, & directed downwards, & opposable thumbs on all limbs. [f. Gk CATA-, *rhis rhinos* nostril]

catăs'troph|ė, n. Dénouement of drama; disastrous end, ruin; event subverting system of things, esp. in Geol. (cf. CATACLYSM, UNIFORMITARIAN), whence **cătastrŏph'IC(AL)** aa., ~ISM(3), ~IST(2), nn.; sudden, widespread, or signal disaster. [f. Gk CATA(*strophē* turning f. *strephō* to turn)]

Cataw'ba, c-, n. U.S. grape & wine. [river ~]

căt'boat, n. Sailing-boat with single mast

placed well forward, carrying one sail only. [prob. f. obs. *cat*(*t*), vessel formerly used on the N.-E. coast]

cătch[1], v.t. & i. (*caught* pr. kawt). **1.** Capture, ensnare (~ *a* CRAB[1]), overtake also ~ *up*; *caught in storm*), lay hold of (also ~ *hold of*; ~ *a* TARTAR; ~ *up habit* etc., adopt), be in time for (train etc.). **2.** Surprise, detect, (*at* or *in*, or *doing*; ~ *me!*, *him!*, you may be sure we shall not). **3.** Hit (usu. with part specified; *caught him on the nose*; also *caught him a blow* or *one*). **4.** (Of fire or combustible) ignite, be ignited, (~ *fire* or ~). **5.** Be entangled, take hold, (usu. ~ *in* a thing; *bolt* ~*es*; ~ *on*, become popular). **6.** Snatch (esp. ~ *up*, *away*; ~ *at*, often fig. = be glad to get). **7.** Intercept motion of (nail ~es dress; at cricket, ~ *ball*, prevent its touching ground off bat, also ~ or ~ *out* batsman, dismiss by doing this); ~ *out*, (fig.) ~ in a mistake etc., ~ napping. **8.** Check suddenly (~ one's *breath*; ~ *up* speaker, interrupt): **9.** Receive, incur, be infected with, (cold, a cold, a fever; a scolding, thrashing, or 'it'; enthusiasm, a habit, an accent; ~ one's DEATH; *pond* etc. ~*es*, is coated with ice). **10.** Grasp with senses or mind (meaning, sound, tune; ~ *a likeness*, see & reproduce it; ~ *a glimpse of*, see for a moment; *don't* ~ *on*, fail to see meaning). **11.** Arrest, captivate, (attention, eye, fancy; ~ *Speaker's eye*, succeed in being called on to speak in H. of Commons). **12.** ~-*as*-~-*can*, Lancashire wrestling style; ~-*drain*, along hillside to prevent water's running off; || ~-'*em-alive-o*, sticky flypaper; ~-*fly*, a sticky-stemmed plant; ~'*penny* (adj.), claptrap, intended merely to sell; ~'*weed*, goosegrass; ~'*word*, word so placed as to draw attention, e.g. first of dictionary article, rhyming word in verse, last word (cue) of actor's speech, first word of page anticipated at foot of previous one, also word or phrase caught up & repeated esp. in connexion with party politics, slogan. Hence ~'ABLE a., (·)~'ER (1, 2) n. [ME *cac*(*c*)*hen* f. ONF *cachier* (= OF *chacier*, whence CHASE[2]), f. Rom. **captiare* for L *captare* f. *capere capt-* seize; the gen. sense of *catch* (*take*, not *pursue*) is excl. E, the orig. meanings (still in Rom.) having been taken by the later adoption CHASE[2]]

cătch[2], n. **1.** Act of catching; amount of fish caught. **2.** Chance of, success in, catching at cricket (also *a good*, *safe*, ~, one skilful at it). **3.** Cunning question, deception, surprise; ~-*out*, act of catching out, circumstance that upsets calculations. **4.** Contrivance for checking motion of door etc. **5.** Thing or person caught or worth catching (*no* ~, bad bargain, unwelcome acquisition). .**6.** (mus.). Composition for three or more equal voices, occas. so devised as to produce punning or other humorous verbal combinations. [f. prec.]

cătch'ĭng, a. In vbl senses; esp.: infectious; attractive. [-ING[2]]

cătch'ment, n. ~-*basin*, -*area*, from which rainfall flows into river, reservoir, etc. [CATCH[1], -MENT]

cătch'pōle, -pōll, n. (hist.). Sheriff's officer, bum-bailiff. [late OE (once) *kæcepol*, ME *cachepol*, f. ONF **cachepol* (= OF *chacepol*) or AL *cacepollus* chase-fowl (CATCH[1], L *pullus* fowl)]

cătch'up, mis-spelling of KETCHUP.

cătch'ў, a. Attractive; easily caught up (of tune etc.). [CATCH[1]+-Y[2]]

cāte, n. (arch.; usu. pl.). Choice food. [for obs. *acate* f. OF *acat* purchase f. *acater* now *acheter* buy f. Rom. **AC*(*captare* frequent. of L *capere* take) catch at]

cătĕchĕt'ic(al) (-kĕ-), aa. Of, by, oral teaching; according to a, or the Church, catechism; consisting of, proceeding by, question & answer. Hence **cătĕchĕt'icaLLY**[2] adv. [f. Gk *katēkhētikos* f. *katĕkhētēs* oral teacher (foll.)]

căt'ĕchism (-k-), n. Instruction by question & answer; published example of this, esp. on religious doctrine (*Church* C~, the Anglican; *Longer* & *Shorter* C~, of Presbyterians); series of questions put to anyone. Hence **cătĕchis'mAL** (-k-) a. [f. LL *catechismus* (foll., -ISM)]

căt'ĕch|īze (-k-), -ise (-īz), v.t. Instruct by question & answer, or by use of Church Catechism; put questions to, examine. Hence or cogn. ~IST(1), ~ĪZER[1], (-k-), nn. [f. LL *catechizare* f. Gk *katĕkhizō* f. CAT(*ĕkheō* sound) make hear]

căt'ĕchu (-ōō), n. Astringent substances with much tannin from bark, wood, or fruits, of Eastern plants. [app. f. Malay *kachu*; cf. CACHOU]

cătĕchūm'ĕn (-kū-), n. A convert under instruction before baptism. [f. LL *catechumenus* (so F *catéchumène*) f. pass. part. of Gk *katĕkheō* CATECHIZE]

cătĕgŏr'ical, a. (Logic: of proposition) unconditional, absolute; explicit, direct, plain-speaking; (Ethics) ~ *imperative*, bidding of conscience as ultimate moral law. Hence ~LY[2] adv. [f. LL f. Gk *katĕgorikos* f. CAT(*ĕgoros* -speaking)+-AL]

căt'ĕgor|ў, n. (Orig. Gk meaning, *statement*) one of a possibly exhaustive set of classes among which all things might be distributed (the ~ies of Aristotle are: substance, quantity, quality, relation, place, time, posture, possession, action, passion); one of the *a priori* conceptions applied by the mind as frames to material supplied by sense; class, division. [f. LL f. Gk *katĕgoria* statement as prec.]

catĕn'a, n. Connected series. [L, = chain]

catĕn'arў, cătĕnār'ian, aa. & nn. (Like) curve formed by uniform chain hanging freely from two points not in one vertical line (~ *bridge*, suspension, hung from such chains). [f. L *catenarius* (prec., -ARY[1], -AN)]

căt'ĕn|āte, v.t. Connect like links. So ~A'TION n. [f. L *catenare* as prec., -ATE[3]]

cāt'er, v.i. Purvey food (usu. *for*); provide amusement etc. *for.* Hence ~ER[1] n. [f. obs. noun *cater* (now *caterer*), aphetic f. *acater* f. AN *acatour* buyer (CATE, -OR)]

cāt'eran, n. (hist.). Highland fighting-man, marauder, cattle-lifter. [f. Gael. *ceathairne* peasantry]

cāt'er-cousin (kŭz-), n. (arch.). Intimate; *be* ~s, on good or familiar terms. [perh. f. CATER as feeding together]

cāt'erpillar, n. Larva of butterfly or moth; rapacious person; (Mech.) endless articulated steel band passing round & worked by two wheels of a tank, tractor, or vehicle required to cope with rough ground. [perh. f. OF *chatepelose* lit. hairy-cat, with *-s* dropped as pl. sign, & spelling influenced by vb *pill* rob, strip]

cāt'erwaul, v.i., & n. (Make) cat's screaming; quarrel like cats. [of uncert. hist.; generally referred to CAT[1] & WAUL]

cāt'gŭt, n. Material used for strings of fiddle etc. made of twisted intestines of sheep, horse, or ass (not cat); stringed instruments. [reason for appellation (*cat-*) unkn.]

cath-. See CATA-.

cathār'sĭs, n. (Med.) purgation; outlet to emotion afforded by drama (ref. to Arist., *Poet.* 6). [f. Gk *katharsis* (*kathairō* cleanse f. *katharos* clean)]

cathārt'ĭc, a. & n. (med.). Purgative (medicine). [f. LL f. Gk *kathartikos* as prec.]

Cathay', n. (Arch. & poet. for) China. [f. med. L *Cat(h)aia*, f. *Kitah*, race name]

cathēd'ral, a. & n. (Orig. ~ *church*) principal church of diocese, with bishop's throne; ~ *utterance* etc., delivered EX CATHEDRA. [ME adj. f. OF *cathedral* or its source LL *cathedralis* f. L f. Gk CAT(*hedra* chair f. *hed-* sit), -AL]

Căth'erine-wheel, n. Circular spoked window or window-compartment; rotating firework; lateral somersault (*turn* ~s). [spiked wheel in St Catherine's martyrdom]

căth'ēter, n. (med.). Tubular instrument for passing into bladder. [LL, f. Gk *katheter* f. CAT(*hiemi* send)]

căth'ōde, n. (electr.). Negative pole of current; ~ *ray*, beam of electrons from ~ of high-vacuum tube under the impulse of an electron field. [f. Gk CAT(*hodos* way) descent]

căth'olic (*or* kah-), a. & n. **1.** Universal; of interest or use to all men; all-embracing, of wide sympathies, broad-minded, tolerant; C~ *Epistles*, encyclical (those of James, Peter, Jude, & John—2 & 3 *John* being irregularly included—; cf. CANONICAL). **2.** (Eccl.) C~ *Church*, whole body of Christians; ~, belonging (a) to this, (b) to the church before separation into Greek or Eastern & Latin or Western, (c) to the Latin church after that separation (cf. ORTHODOX), (d) to the part of the Latin church that remained under the

Roman obedience after the reformation, (e) to any church (as the Anglican) claiming continuity with (b); orthodox, in accord with the church in any of above senses, esp. = ROMAN CATHOLIC as (d) in contrast with Protestant, Reformed, Lutheran, etc.; C~ *King, his* C~ *Majesty,* of Spain (hist.); hence **cathŏl'ICALLY,** ~LY[2], advv., **cathŏl'ICISM**(2, 3) n., **cathŏl'ICIZE**(3), v.t., **cathŏl'ico-** comb. form. **3.** n. Member of Holy Catholic Apostolic and Roman Church accepting jurisdiction of Pope as supreme Head of that Church. [f. LL *catholicus* & F *catholique* f. Gk *katholikos* f. CATH- *holou* on the whole, universally]

cătholi'cĭty̆, n. Comprehensiveness, freedom from prejudice; wide prevalence; agreement with Catholic or R.-C. Church doctrine, catholicism. [prec., -ITY]

cathŏl'icŏn, n. Panacea. [F & med. L, f. Gk *katholikon* neut. CATHOLIC]

Căt'iline, n. Profligate conspirator. [*Catilina* Roman noble d. 63 B.C.]

căt'iŏn, n. Electro-positive element evolved at cathode in electrolysis (opp. ANION). [Gk, =going down (CAT-, *eimi* go)]

căt'kin, n. Downy hanging inflorescence of willow, hazel, etc. [f. Du. *katteken* (CAT[1], -KIN)]

căt'ling, n. Small cat; fine catgut; amputating knife. [-LING[1](2); surg. sense unexpl.]

catŏp'tr|ĭc, a. Of mirror, reflector, or reflexion. Hence ~ICS n. [f. Gk *katoptrikos* f. CAT(*optron* f.*op-* see, *-tron* instr. suf.)]

căt'sup. Var. of KETCHUP.

cătt'ĭsh, cătt'y̆, aa. Catlike; (esp. fig.) sly and spiteful. [CAT[1]]

căt'tle, n. Live-stock; oxen (as ~ & *sheep*); (occas.) horses; *black* ~, oxen of Scotch & Welsh highland breeds, orig. black; contemptible persons; ~*-feeder*, machine regulating amount of food for ~; ~*-leader*, nose-ring; ~*-lifter*, ~*-stealer*; ~-PEN[1]; ~*-piece*, picture with ~; ~*-plague*, contagious disease of ~, rinderpest; *~-rustler*, ~*-thief.* [ME & ONF *catel* (= OF *chatel*; see CHATTEL) f. med. L *capitale* CAPITAL[2]]

Caucā'sian (-shn), a. & n. (Member) of the white race, Indo-European; inhabitant of the Caucasus. [the *Caucasus,* supposed starting-place, +-IAN]

cauc'us, n., & v.t. & i. **1.** ‖ Local political usu. elective party committee for fighting elections, defining policy, etc. (gen. used only of opponents' organization); *the* ~, ~ system as a political power; hence ~DOM n. **2.** vb. Use the ~ system; organize, dictate to, by its means; hence ~ER[1] n. [U.S. wd (in sense *meeting*) of unkn. orig.]

caud'al, a. Of, at, like, tail. Hence or cogn.~LY[2] adv., **caud'ATE**[2] a. [f. L *cauda* tail +-AL]

caudillo (kowdēl'yō), n. (pl. ~s). (In Spanish-speaking countries) leader. [Sp.]

cau'dle, n. Warm gruel with spice, sugar, & wine, for invalids, esp. women in childbed. [f. ONF *caudel* (OF *chaudel*) f. LL *caldellum* dim. of L *caldum* hot drink (*calidus* warm)]

caught. See CATCH[1].

caul, n. Plain part at back of woman's cap; membrane enclosing foetus; portion of this occas. found on child's head (good omen, & charm against drowning); = OMENTUM. [ME *calle* perh. f. OF *cale* small cap]

caul'dron, căl-, n. Large boiling-vessel (usu. of deep basin shape with hoop handle & removable lid). [ME *caud(e)ron* f. ONF (OF *ch-*) augment. (see -OON) f. LL *caldaria* pot for boiling (L *calidus* warm, -ARY[1]); for the etymologizing -*l-* cf. FAULT]

caulĕs'cent, a. (bot.). With visible stem. [f. L *caulis* stalk after *arborescent* etc.]

caul'iflower (kŏl-), n. Cabbage with large fleshy flower-head. [16th c. *cole-florie* etc., f. F *chou-fleuri*; the first element was later assim. to COLE & L *caulis*, the second to FLOWER]

caul'ine, a. (bot.). Of, on, stem. [f. L *caulis* stem, -INE[1]]

caulk (kawk), v.t. Stop up seams of (ship), stop up (seams), with oakum & melted pitch (or, in iron ship, by striking plate-junctions with blunt chisel). Hence ~'ER[1] n. (in vbl senses, &, sl., = final dram). [f. OF *cauquer* tread, press with force, f. L *calcare* tread (*calx* heel)]

caulo-, comb. form of Gk *kaulos* or L *caulis* stem. [-O-]

caus'al (-z-), a. Of, acting as, expressing, due to, a cause or causes; of the nature of cause & effect. Hence ~LY[2] adv. [f. LL *causalis* (*causa*, -AL)]

causăl'itў (-z-), n. The being, having, or acting as, a cause; relation of cause & effect, doctrine that everything has cause(s). [prec., -ITY]

causā'tion (-z-), n. Causing, producing an effect; relation of cause & effect; doctrine that all things have causes, whence ~ISM(3), ~IST(2), nn. [f. LL *causatio* pretext etc., but w. sense f. med. L *causare* CAUSE[2], -ATION]

caus'ative (-z-), a. Acting as cause, productive *of*; (Gram.) expressing cause. Hence ~LY[2] (-vl-) adv. [ME, f. OF *causatif* or LL *causativus* (*causari* give as pretext, -IVE)]

cause[1] (-z), n. 1. What produces an effect; antecedent(s) invariably & unconditionally followed by a certain phenomenon; person who, agent that, occasions something; ground, reason, motive, for action; adequate motive or justification (esp. *show* ~); *efficient* ~, producing force, *material* ~, the requisite matter, *formal* ~, the idea or definition, *final* ~, purpose; *First C~*, the Creator. 2. (Law, & from law) matter about which person goes to law; his case (*plead a* ~); law-suit; side of any dispute espoused by person or

party, militant movement, propaganda (*make common* ~ *with*); ‖ ~-*list*, of cases awaiting trial. [ME, f. OF f. L *causa*]

cause[2] (-z), v.t. Effect, bring about, produce; induce, make, (person or thing *to* do, *to be* done something to). Hence **caus'ER**[1] n. [ME, f. med. L *causarc* (or OF *causer*) f. L *causa* CAUSE[1]]

cause célèbre (kōz sĕlĕ'br), n. (pl. *causes célèbres*, pr. as sing.). Law-suit that excites much attention. [F]

cause'lèss (-zl-), a. Fortuitous; without natural cause; unjustifiable, groundless, whence ~LY[2] adv. [-LESS]

causerie (kōzerē'), n. (pl. -*s*, pr. as sing.). Newspaper article (or spoken address) of an informal or conversational kind, esp. on literary subjects. [F]

cause'way (-zw-), **caus'ey** (-z-), n., & v.t. Raised road across low or wet place or piece of water; raised footway by road; (v.t.) provide with ~. [alt. (by assoc. w. WAY) f. ME *caucé* (mod. dial. *causey*) f. ONF *caucié(e)* (mod. F *chaussée*), f. Rom. *calciata* (sc. *via*) f. L *calx* -*cis* CHALK]

caus't|ic, a. & n. (Substance) that burns or corrodes organic tissue (*common* or *lunar* ~*ic*, nitrate of silver for surg. use; ~ *potash*, potassium hydroxide; ~ *soda*, sodium hydroxide); sarcastic, biting, whence ~ICALLY adv.; (Math.) (surface, curve) formed by intersection of rays reflected or refracted from curved surface. Hence ~**i'**CITY n. [f. F (-*ique*) or L f. Gk *kaustikos* (*kaustos* burnt f. *kaiō* burn), -IC]

caut'er|īze,·-ise (-īz), v.t. Sear with hot iron or caustic; (fig.) make callous. Hence ~**īzā'**TION n. [f. LL *cauterizare* f. Gk *kautērion* branding-iron (*kaiō* burn); cf. F *cautériser*]

caut'erў, n. Metal instrument for searing tissue; cauterizing. [f. L f. Gk *kautērion* see prec.]

cau'tion, n., & v.t. 1. Prudence, taking care, avoidance of rashness, attention to safety, (‖ ~ *money*, deposited as security for good conduct, esp. at Universities & Inns of Court), whence **cau'**tiOUS-(-shᵘs), a., **cau'**tiousLY[2] adv.; warning (in drill, preliminary word of command), fact that acts as warning, warning with reprimand (*dismissed with a* ~), whence ~ARY[1] (-sho-), a.; (colloq.) extraordinary thing, hideous or strange person. 2. v.t. Warn (person, often *against*, *to* or *not to* do); warn & reprove. [ME, f. OF f. L *cautionem* (*cavēre caut-* take heed, -ION)]

căvalcāde', n. Company of riders. [F, f. It. *cavalcata* f. *cavalcare* ride f. LL *caballicare* f. L *caballus* horse; see -ADE]

căvalier', n. & a. 1. Horseman; courtly gentleman, gallant, esp. as escorting a lady, whence **căvalier'** v.t.; 17th-c. royalist. 2. adj. Offhand, curt, supercilious, whence ~LY[2] adv. [earlier -*llero*, -*liero*, f. Sp.; present form F, f. It. *cavaliere*; see CHEVALIER]

cavăll'ў, n. Kinds of tropical fish, horse-mackerel. [f. Sp. *cavalla* mackerel]

căv'alrў, n. Horse-soldiers (usu. w. pl. vb). [f. F *cavallerie* f. It. *cavalleria* (*cavallo* f. L *caballus* horse, -ERY)]

căvati'na (-tē-), **n.** Short simple song; similar piece of instrumental music, usu. slow & emotional. [It.]

căve[1], n. Underground hollow usu. with horizontal opening, den; IDOLS *of the* ~; || (Pol.) secession of part of party on some question (ADULLAMITE), the seceders; ~-*dweller*, esp. of prehistoric men living in ~s; ~-*fish*, -*man*, -*rat*, -*spider*, -*swallow*, kinds living in ~s (also ~-*bear* etc. of extinct kinds whose remains are found in ~s); ~-*man*, (in modern use) man of primitive passions, instincts, & behaviour. Hence ~'LET (-vl-) n. [ME, f. OF f. L *cava* f. *cavus* hollow]

căve[2], v.t. & i. Hollow out, make into a cave; || form political CAVE[1]; ~ *in*: subside, recede, (of earth etc. over hollow; of wall yielding inwards cf. BULGE); yield to pressure, submit, withdraw opposition; smash in (esp. person's hat or head), spoil shape of. [f. prec.; but in ~ *in* may be f. U.S.~ *in*, app. f. E. Anglian dial. *calve in*; cf. Flem. *inkalven* Du. *af-kalven*, in similar sense]

|| căv'ē[3], int. (schoolboy sl.). Look out! (warning of master's approach). [L, = beware]

căv'ĕăt, n. 1. (Law) process to suspend proceedings (*enter*, *put in*, *a*~). **2.** Warning; proviso. [L, = let him beware]

căv'ĕăt ĕmp'tŏr, L sent. (= let the buyer see to it) disclaiming responsibility for buyer's disappointment.

căv'endish, n. Tobacco softened, sweetened, & pressed into cake, negro-head. [orig. unkn.]

căv'ẽrn, n. Underground hollow (rhet.). [ME, f. F *caverne* f. L *caverna* (*cavus* hollow)]

căv'ẽrned (-nd), **a.** Like, in, with, cavern(s). [-ED[2]]

căv'ẽrnous, a. Full of caverns; as of, huge or deep as, a cavern (~ *darkness*, *mouth*, *eyes*); porous. [f. L *cavernosus* (CAVERN, -OSE[1])]

căv'ĕ(s)son, n. Strong nose-band used in breaking in troublesome horses. [f. F *caveçon* f. It. *cavezzone* augment. of *cavezza* halter]

căviār(e)' (or kăv[1]-), n. Sturgeon-roe pickled, eaten as relish; ~ *to the general*, good thing unappreciated by the ignorant. [early forms represent It. *caviale* (obs. F *cavial*); later *caviar* etc., It. *caviaro* f., Pg. *caviar*, f. Turk. *khāvyār*; relations & ult. orig. uncert.]

căv'il, v.i. (-ll-), **& n.** (Raise) captious objection (*at*, *about*). Hence ~*lER[1]* n. [f. obs. F *caviller* f. L *cavillari* (*cavilla* mockery)]

căv'itў, n. A hollow place, a hollow. Hence **căvĬTA'TION n.**, formation of ~ in a structure, or of bubbles in a liquid, or of a vacuum. [f. F *cavité* or LL *cavitas* (L *cavus* hollow, -TY)]

*căvŏrt', v.i. (sl.). Prance. [orig. unkn.]

căv'ў, n. Amer. rodent. [f. *cabiai* native name in French Guiana]

caw, n. & int., & v.i. & t. (Make) rook's, crow's, raven's, cry; ~ *out*, utter in ~ing tone. [imit.]

Căx'ton, n. Book printed by W. ~ (first Engl. printer, d. 1492); printing-type in imitation of ~'s.

cay, n. Insular bank or reef of coral, sand, etc., cf. KEY[3]. [f. Sp. *cayo* shoal, reef; see KEY[3], QUAY]

cayenne (kăĕn'), **n.** (Also ~ *pepper*) pungent red pepper of capsicum. [f. Braz. *kyynha* assim. to *Cayenne* capital of French Guiana]

cay'man, cai'man, n. Kinds of large saurian of crocodile family (prop. an American genus with round short muzzle). [f. Sp., Pg. *caiman*, f. Carib *acayu-man*]

*cayuse (ki'ūs), **n.** Indian pony. [Amer.-Ind.]

|| cd, || cmd, = COMMAND[2] *paper*.

cē, = CEE.

cĕanŏth'us, n. A flowering shrub. [Gk]

cease[1], v.i. & t. Desist *from*; stop doing, being, etc., also w. inf.; (of feelings, actions) come to an end; bring to an end (strife, endeavours, etc.); (Mil.) ~ *fire*, discontinue firing. [ME, f. OF *cesser* f. L *cessare* frequent. of *cedere cess-* yield]

cease[2], n. Ceasing (obs. exc. in *without* ~, incessantly). Hence ~'LESS (-sl-) a., ~'lĕssLў[2] adv., ~'lĕssNESS n. [f. OF *ces* (*cesser* see prec.)]

cē'citў, n. Blindness (usu. fig.). [f. L *caecitas* (*caecus* blind, -TY)]

cēd'ar, n. Kinds of cone-bearing tree with fragrant durable wood including ~ of Lebanon, Atlas ~, & deodar; various trees resembling ~; *Japanese* ~, cryptomeria; = ~-*wood*. Hence (poet.) ~**n** [-EN[5]] a. [ME & OF *cedre* f. L (whence directly OE *ceder*) f. Gk *kedros*]

cēde, v.t. Give up, grant, admit, surrender (territory). [f. F *céder* or L *cedere* yield]

cĕdill'a, n. Mark (ꜱ) written under c to show that it is sibilant. [f. Sp. *cedilla*, *zedilla* (= It. *ze-*, *zediglia*, F *cédille*) dim. of *zeda* f. Gk *zéta* letter Z]

cee, n. The letter C; ~ *spring*, C-*spring*, spring so shaped supporting carriage body.

ceil (sēl), **v.t.** Line roof of (room). Hence **ceil'ING[1](2)** n.: such lining; (Aviation) maximum altitude a given aeroplane can attain, maximum altitude in particular weather conditions; upper limit of prices, wages, etc. [*ceiling* (14th c. *celynge*) f. *ceil* vb (in 15th c. cover w. wainscot, plaster, etc., cf. obs. *celure* canopy, hangings) + -ING[1](2); ult. orig. undetermined]

‖ **ceilidh** (kāl'ĭ), n. (Sc.). Informal gathering for song & story. [Gael.]

cĕl'adŏn, n. & a. Willow green; grey green glaze used on some pottery. [F, f. name of character in D'Urfé's *Astrée*]

cĕl'andine, n. Two yellow-flowered plants, *greater* ~, & *lesser* ~ (also PILE[6]-*wort*). [ME & OF *celidoine* f. LL *celidonia*, for L *chelidonia* f. Gk *khelidonion* (*khelidōn* swallow); for *-n-* cf. *passenger*]

cĕlanēse' (-z), n. Kind of artificial silk. [P]

-cele (sēl), in medical compound words, = tumour of the —. [f. Gk *kēlē* tumour]

cĕl'ĕbrant, n. Officiating priest, esp. at Eucharist. [F, or f. L *celebrare* (foll.), -ANT]

cĕl'ĕbr|āte, v.t. & i. Perform publicly & duly (religious ceremony etc.); officiate at Eucharist; observe, honour, with rites, festivities, etc. (festival, events); publish abroad, praise, extol, (p.p.) famous. So ~A'TION n. [f. L *celebrare* (*celeber* -*bris* frequented, renowned); see -ATE[3]]

cĕlĕb'ritў, n. Being famous; well-known person (also attrib., as ~ *concert*). [f. L *celebritas* (*celeber* see prec., -TY)]

cĕlĕ'riăc, n. Turnip-rooted celery. [f. CELERY, -*ac* unexplained]

cĕlĕ'ritў, n. Swiftness, dispatch (of living movement or agency). [ME & OF *celerite* f. L *celeritatem* (*celer* swift, -TY)]

cĕl'erў, n. Plant of which blanched stem is used as salad & vegetable. [f. F *céleri* ult. f. Gk *selinon* parsley]

cĕlĕste', n. & a. Sky blue; (also *voix* ~) organ & harmonium stop; (adj.) sky-blue. [f. F *céleste* f. L *caelestis* (*caelum* heaven)]

cĕlĕs'tial, a. & n. Of the sky (~ *globe, map*); heavenly, divine, divinely good, beautiful, etc., whence ~LY[2] adv.; *C~ Empire* (hist.), China (transl. of native title; so *C~* (joc.) = Chinese, a. & n.). [ME, f. OF f. L *caelestis* (see prec., -AL)]

cĕl'ibate, a. & n. (Person) not married, bound or resolved not to marry; unmarried (of life, habits). So **cĕl'ĭbACY** n., **cĕlibat**AR'IAN a. & n. [F, or f. L *caelibatus* unmarried state (*caelebs -ibis*); see -ATE[1]]

cĕll, n. 1. Dependent nunnery or monastery (hist.); anchoret's one-roomed dwelling; cottage (poet.); grave (poet.); single person's small room in monastery or prison (*condemned* ~, for one condemned to death); compartment in bees' comb; (Electr.) voltaic apparatus with only one pair of metallic elements, unit of battery. 2. Enclosed cavity in organism or mineral (~*s of brain*, imaginary compartments assigned to various faculties); (Biol.) portion of protoplasm usu. enclosed in membrane, ultimate element of organic structures; (Zoophytes) cup-like cavity of individual polype in compound polypidom; (fig., of persons) centre or nucleus of (revolutionary) activities. Hence (-)**cellED**[3] (-ld), ~'**ĭFORM**, aa. [ME *celle* f. OF, or L

cella small room; late OE *cell* perh. dir. f. L]

cĕll'ar, n., & v.t. (Put, store, in an) underground room; (also *wine-*~) place in which wine is kept, one's stock of wine (*keeps a good* ~); ~*-flap*, trapdoor into ~; ~*-plate*, in pavement over hole into coal-~. Hence ~AGE n. [ME *celer* f. AF, = OF *celier* f. LL *cellarium* (prec., -AR[2], -ARY[1])]

cĕll'arer, n. Monastic keeper of wine & provisions. [ME *cell(l)erer* f. AF, = OF *-ier* f. LL *cellerarius* (see prec., -ER[2] (2))]

cĕllarĕt', n. Case or sideboard for keeping winebottles in dining-room. [-ET[1]]

cĕll'|ō (ch-), 'c-, n. (pl. -*os*). (Short for) VIOLONCELLO. Hence ~IST (3) n.

cĕll'ophāne, n. Transparent wrapping material made from viscose. [P]

cĕll'ūlar, a. Of, having, small single rooms or compartments or cavities; ~ *shirt* etc. (of open texture); (Physiol.) consisting of cells (as ~ *tissue*); ~ *plant*, without distinct stem, leaves, etc. Hence **cĕllūlă'ritў** n. [f. F *cellulaire*, see foll., -AR[1]]

cĕll'ūl|e|e, n. (anat.). Cell or cavity (see CELL, 2; the derivatives are formed from *cellule*, not *cell*). Hence or cogn. ~ATE[2], -āted, =IF'EROUS, ~OUS, aa., ~A'TION n., ~O- comb. form. [f. L *cellula* (*cella* CELL, -ULE)]

cĕll'ūloid, a. & n. Like cells; (n.) plastic made from camphor & cellulose nitrate. [irreg. f. CELLULOSE[2] + -OID]

cĕll'ūlōse'[1], a. Consisting of cells. Hence **cĕllūlōs'ITў** n. [CELLULE, -OSE[1]]

cĕll'ūlōse'[2], n. (chem.). Substance forming solid framework of plants; (in pop. usage for) ~ acetate or ~ nitrate, solutions of which give the ~ finish used in varnishing metal, woodwork, etc., (also v.t., treat with ~). [F, f. L *cellula* CELLULE + -OSE[2]]

Cĕl'sius. See CENTIGRADE.

Cĕlt[1], **Kĕlt**, n. Member of one of the peoples akin to the ancient Gauls (Bretons, Cornish, Gaels, Irish, Manx, Welsh). [f. F *Celte* f. L *Celta*; cf. Gk *Keltoi, Keltai*, pl.]

cĕlt[2], n. (archaeol.). Bronze or stone (or iron) chisel-edged prehistoric implement. [wd founded on the reading of the Clementine Vulgate in *Job* xix. 24—*stylo ferreo, et plumbi lamina, vel celte* (v.l. *certe*) *sculpantur*]

Cĕl'tic, **K-**, a. & n. (Language) of the Celts; *the* ~ *fringe*, the Scots, Irish, Welsh, & Cornish, in relation to the U.K. Hence **cĕl'tICALLY** adv., **cĕl'tic**ISM(2, 4) n., **cĕl'ticIZE**(2, 3) v.i. & t. [f. L *cellicus* (CELT[1], -IC) or F *celtique*]

cĕlto-, comb. form of CELT[1]. Hence **cĕltŏL'OGIST**, **cĕltoMAN'IAC**, **cĕl'toPHIL**, nn. [-O-]

cĕmĕnt', n., & v.t. 1. Substance applied as paste & hardening into stony consistence for binding together stones or bricks &

for forming floors, walls, etc., strong mortar of calcinated lime & clay (*hydraulic* ~, hardening under water); any substance applied soft for sticking things together; (fig.) principle of union; substance for stopping teeth; bony crust of tooth-fang. **2.** v.t. Unite (as) with ~; apply ~ to, line or cover with ~. [ME *siment* f. OF *ciment* f. L *caementum* quarry stone (*caedere* cut, -MENT)]

cĕm'ĕtĕrў, n. Place for burials, not being a churchyard. [f. LL f. Gk *koimētērion* dormitory (*koimaō* put to sleep)]

cĕn'obite. See COENOBITE.

cĕn'otaph(-ahf), n. Sepulchral monument to person whose body is elsewhere; *the* C~, that in Whitehall commemorating the dead of the 1914–18 and 1939–45 wars; tomb from which one has risen. [f. F *cénotaphe* f. LL f. Gk *kenotaphion* (*kenos* empty, *taphos* tomb)]

cĕnse, v.t. Perfume, worship, with burning incense. [f. obs. *cense* noun (aphetic f. INCENSE[1]) or short for INCENSE[2]]

cĕn'ser, n. Vessel in which incense is burnt. [ME *censer* f. AF, = OF *censier* f. *encensier* f. *encense* INCENSE[1], -ER[2] (2)]

cĕn'sor, n., & v.t. **1.** Ancient-Roman magistrate drawing up register or census of citizens & supervising public morals; person expressing opinions on others' morals & conduct. **2.** Official licensing, or suppressing as immoral, seditious, or inopportune, books, plays, letters, news, or military intelligence (vb, exercise such control over, make excisions or changes in). **3.** Various university officials. **4.** (Psycho-anal.) ~(*ship*), a power by which elements of the Unconscious are inhibited from emerging into the consciousness. Hence or cogn. **cĕnsōr'IAL** a., ~SHIP n. [L, f. *censēre* tax, -OR]

cĕnsōr'ious, a. Fault-finding, over-critical. Hence ~LY[2] adv., ~NESS n. [f. L *censorius* (CENSOR, -ORY) + -OUS]

cĕn'sur|e (-sher), n., & v.t. **1.** Adverse judgement, expression of disapproval, reprimand. **2.** v.t. Blame, criticize unfavourably, reprove; hence ~ABLE a. [ME, f. OF *censure* f. L *censura* (*censēre* assess, -URE); vb f. F *censurer*]

cĕn'sus, n. Official numbering of population with various statistics (in Gt Britain taken every ten years); ~-*paper*, form left at 'every house to be filled up with names, ages, etc., of inmates. [L, f. *censēre* to rate]

cĕnt, n. *Per* ~, for, to, in, every hundred (in stating proportion, esp. of interest); *three* etc. *per* ~*s*, public securities at 3% etc.; ~ *per* ~, interest equal to principal; (U.S. etc.) hundredth of a dollar; typical small coin (*don't care a* ~). [f. F *cent*, or L *centum*, or It. *cento* hundred]

cĕn'tal, n. Weight of 100 lb. used for corn. [f. L *centum* hundred, perh. after QUINTAL]

cĕn'taur (-tŏr), n. Horse with human body, arms, & head, taking the place of its neck & head; hybrid creation, person or thing of double nature; (C~) name of a constellation; perfect horseman. Hence ~ESS[1] n. [f. L f. Gk *kentauros* of unkn. etym.]

cĕn'taurў, n. Name of various plants. [f. LL *centauria* f. L f. Gk *kentaurion* (*kentauros* see prec.)]

cĕnta'vŏ (-ah-), n. (pl. ~*s*). 1/100 of a peso or similar currency unit in some S.-Amer. republics; 1/100 of an escudo in Portugal. [Amer.-Sp.]

cĕntenār'ian, a. & n. (Person) a hundred years old. [as foll. + -AN]

cĕntēn'arў (*also* sĕn'tĕn-), a. & n. **1.** Of a hundred years. **2.** n. Space of a hundred years reckoned from any point in a century; centennial anniversary, celebration of it. [f. L *centenarius* (*centeni* a hundred each, -ARY[1])]

cĕntĕnn'ial, a. & n. Of, having lived or lasted, completing, a hundred years; (of) the hundredth anniversary. [f. L *centum* hundred, & as BIENNIAL]

cĕntēs'imal, a. Reckoning, reckoned, by hundredths. Hence ~LY[2] adv. [f. L *centesimus* hundredth (*centum* hundred) + -AL]

cĕn'ti-, comb. form of L *centum* hundred, = 1/100 of the denomination in the metric system. Hence ~GRAM, ~LITRE (-lēter), ~METRE (-mēter), nn.

cĕn'tigrāde, a. Having a hundred degrees (of Celsius's thermometer, with freezing-point of water 0° & boiling-point 100°). [F, f. L *centum* a hundred + *gradus* step]

‖ **cĕntill'ion** (-yon), n. Hundredth power of a million (1 with 600 ciphers). [*centum* (prec.), BILLION]

centime (sahntēm'), n. (hist.). French & Swiss coin = 1/100 of a franc. [F]

cĕn'tipēde, n. Many-footed wingless crawling animal. [f. L *centipeda* (*centum* hundred, *pes pedis* foot) or F *centipède*; earlier *centipie*, *centapee* prob. f. Sp.]

cĕnt'ner, n. German weight, about 1 cwt. [G, f. L *centenarius* CENTENARY]

cĕn'tŏ, n. (pl. -*os*). Composition made up of scraps from other authors. [L, = patchwork garment]

cĕn'tral, a. Of, in, at, from, containing, the centre; leading, principal, dominant; C~ *Empires*, *Powers*, (hist.), Germany & Austria-Hungary; ~ *heating*, method of warming a building by hot water or hot air or steam conveyed by pipes from ~ source. Hence **cĕntrăl'ITY** n.,~LY[2] adv., ~NESS n. [f. L *centralis* (*centrum* CENTRE, -AL) or F *central*]

cĕn'tralism, cĕn'tralist, nn. (Upholder of) a centralizing system. [prec. + -ISM(3), -IST(2)]

cĕn'traliz|e, -is|e (-īz), v.i. & t. Come, bring, to a centre; concentrate (administration) at single centre; subject (State etc.) to this system. Hence ~A'TION n. [CENTRAL, -IZE(3), or f. F *centraliser*]

cĕn'tre[1] (*-ter*), **cĕn'ter**, n. & a. **1.** Middle point (strictly, equidistant from ends of line measuring along it, or from extremities of regular surface or body, or from all points in circumference of circle or sphere, & at mean distance from all points in periphery of irregular surface or body). **2.** Point, pivot, axis, of revolution (of machine tool, short rod with cone-shaped point and tapered shank, one of pair between which rotating workpiece may be supported). **3.** Point of concentration or dispersion, nucleus, source. **4.** (Fenians etc.) organizer, leader, (esp. *head-~*). **5.** = INNER. **6.** (Archit.) wooden mould for arch or dome while building. **7.** (Mil.) main body of troops between wings. **8.** (Pol.; orig. f. French) the *C~*, men of moderate opinions (*left-~*, *left*, radical grades; *right-~*, *right*, reactionary). **9.** (Assoc. footb., Hockey) middle player in forward line (also ~ *forward*), kick or hit from wing to ~. **10.** ~ *of attraction*, (Physics) to which bodies tend by gravity, (fig.) drawing general attention; ~ *of gravity*, that point in body which being supported body remains at rest in any position; ~ *of mass*, point (in relation to body) any plane passing through which divides body into two parts of equal weight; DEAD ~; ~*-piece*, ornament for middle of table; ~*-rail*, third rail on mountain railways for cogged wheel etc.; ~*-second(s)*, seconds hand mounted on centre arbor of clock or watch; ~*-bit*, boring-tool with ~ point & side cutters; ~*-board*, (flat-bottomed boat with) board for lowering through keel to prevent leeway: hence ~LESS, **cĕn'trIc(AL)**, aa., **cĕn'trIcalLY**[2] adv., **cĕntri'cITY** n. **11.** adj. At, of, the ~; hence ~MOST (*-erm-*) a. [ME, f. OF *centre* or L *centrum* f. Gk *kentron* sharp point]

cĕn'tre[2] (*-ter*), **cĕn'ter**, v.i. & t. Be concentrated in, on, at, round, about; place in centre; mark with a centre; concentrate *in* etc.; find centre of; (Assoc. footb., Hockey) kick or hit (ball) from wing to centre. [f. prec.]

cĕn'tr(e)Ing (*-ter-*), n. Temporary framing used to support arch, dome, etc., while under construction. [CENTRE[1] + -ING[1]]

cĕntrif'ūgal, a. Flying, tending to fly, from centre; ~ *force*, with which body revolving round centre tends to fly off, inertia; ~ *machine* etc., in which ~ force is utilized; (Bot.) ~ *inflorescence*, in which end flower opens first & side ones in downward order. Hence ~LY[2] adv. [f. L *centrum* CENTRE[1] + *-fugus* -fleeing (*fugere* flee) + -AL]

cĕn'trifūge, n. Centrifugal machine rotating at very high speed, designed to separate solids from liquids, or liquids from other liquids (e.g. cream from milk). [F; see prec.]

cĕntrĭp'ĕtal, a. Tending towards centre; ~ *force*, *machine* etc., *inflorescence*, opposite of CENTRIFUGAL. Hence ~LY[2] adv. [f. L *-petus* -seeking (*petere* seek) & as CENTRE[1]]

cĕn'tro-, comb. form of L *centrum* & Gk *kentron* CENTRE[1], = centre-, central, centrally.

cĕn'tŭple, a., n., & v.t. Hundredfold; (vb) multiply by a hundred. [f. F *centuple* or LL *centuplus* for L *centuplex* (*centum* hundred, *-plic-* fold)]

cĕntŭp'licate, a. & n. (*-at*), & v.t. (*-āt*). = prec., esp. *in* ~, of things of which a hundred copies are produced. [f. L *centuplicare* as prec., -ATE[2,3]]

cĕntŭr'ion, n. Commander of century in Roman army. [ME, f. L *centurio -onis* (foll.)]

cĕn'tŭrў, n. **1.** (Rom. hist.) company in army, orig. of 100 men; political division for voting. **2.** A hundred of something (esp., 100 runs at cricket); one of the hundred-year periods counting from a received epoch, esp. from birth of Christ (*first* ~, 1–100, *nineteenth* ~, 1801–1900, etc.); any hundred successive years, centenary. [f. L *centuria* (*centum* hundred)]

cĕphăl'ic, a. Of, in, the head. [f. F *céphalique* f. L f. Gk *kephalikos* (*kephalē* head, -IC)]

-cĕphăl'ic. = -CEPHALOUS.

cĕph'alo-, comb. form = head-, head- & ——. [see CEPHALIC, -O-]

cĕph'alopŏd, n. Mollusc with distinct tentacled head. [prec. + Gk *pous podos* foot]

cĕphalothō̆r'ăx, n. Coalesced head & thorax of spider, crab, etc. [CEPHALO-, THORAX]

-cĕph'alous, last element esp. of anthropological terms = -headed, as *brachy~*, with short head. [f. Gk *kephalē* head + -OUS]

cĕrăm'|ĭc, k-, a. Of the art of pottery. Hence ~ICS, **cĕ'ramIST(2)**, nn. [f. Gk *keramikos* (*keramos* pottery, -IC)]

cĕrăs'tes (*-ēz*), n. The horned viper of N. Africa. [L f. Gk *kerastēs* (*keras* horn)]

cĕrăs'tium, n. Kinds of herb with horn-shaped capsules. [mod. L, f. Gk *kerastēs* horned (*keras* horn)]

cĕ'rato-, comb. form of Gk *keras -atos* horn, = horn-&- ——, horny-, & esp. of the cornea.

Cĕrb'erus, n. Three-headed dog guarding entrance to Hades (*sop to* ~, something to propitiate an official, guard, etc.). [L, f. Gk *Kerberos*]

cēre, n. Naked wax-like membrane at base of some birds' beaks. [f. L *cera* wax]

cĕr'ĕal, a. & n. Of corn or edible grain; (n., usu. pl.) kind(s) of grain used for human food; article of diet made from wheat, maize, or other ~ (usu. as breakfast dish). [f. L *Cerealis* (*Ceres* goddess of corn, -AL)]

cĕ́rĕbĕll'um, n. Little or hinder brain. [L, dim. of CEREBRUM]

cĕ'rĕbral, a. Of the brain; (of literature, music, etc.) appealing to intellectual appreciation; ~ *letter*, consonant sounded by turning tongue-tip to top of palate. [CEREBRUM + -AL; cf. F *cérébral*]

cĕrĕbrā'tion, n. Working of the brain, esp. *unconscious* ~, of results reached without conscious thought. [CEREBRUM + -ATION]

cĕ'rĕbrum, n. The brain proper, in front of & above the cerebellum. Hence **cĕ'rĕbro-** comb. form; *cerebro-spin'al*, of brain & spine (*cerebro-spinal meningitis*, spotted fever). [L]

cere'cloth (sĕ́rklaw-), n. Cloth impregnated with wax etc., used as waterproof covering or (esp.) winding-sheet. [15th c. *cered cloth* f. *cere* to wax f. L *cerare* f. *cera* wax]

cere'ment (sĕ́rm-), n. (hist.; usu. pl.). Grave-clothes. [app. a Shakespearian alt. of prec. (-MENT)]

cĕrĕmōn'ial, a. & n. **1.** With or of ritual or ceremony, formal; hence ~ISM(3), ~IST(2), nn., ~LY² adv. **2.** n. System of rites; formalities proper to any occasion; observance of conventions; (R.-C. Ch.) book of ritual. [f. LL *ceremonialis* (CEREMONY, -AL)]

cĕrĕmōn'ious, a. Addicted or showing addiction to ceremony, punctilious. Hence ~LY² adv., ~NESS n. [f. F *cérémonieux* or LL *ceremoniosus* (foll., -OUS)]

cĕ'remon|ў, n. Outward religious rite or polite observance; empty form; stately usage; formalities; punctilious behaviour (*without* ~y, offhand; *stand upon* ~y, insist on conventions, keep one's distance); *Master of the C~ies*, superintending forms observed on state or public occasions. [ME, f. OF *cerimonie* or L *caerimonia*]

cĕ'riph, (now rare for) SERIF.

cerise' (-ēz), a. & n. (Of) a light clear red. [F, = CHERRY]

cer'ium, n. A metallic element. Hence **cer'ic**(1), **cer'ous,** aa. [f. planet *Ceres*, discovered (1801) just before, + -IUM]

cēro-, comb. form of L *cera* or Gk *kēros* wax.

cēroplăs't|ic, a. Modelled, of modelling, in wax. Hence ~ICS n. [f. Gk *kēro-* = CERO(*plastikos* adj. f. *plassō* to mould)]

cĕrt, n. (sl.). Event or result certain to happen. [abbr. *certain*]

cĕrt'ain (-tn, -tin), a. Settled, unfailing; unerring, reliable; sure to happen; indisputable; convinced (*of, that*); destined, undoubtedly going, *to* do; that might but need not or should not be specified (*a* ~ *person, lady of a* ~ *age*), some though perhaps not much (*felt a* ~ *reluctance*), existing but probably unknown to hearer (*a* ~ *John Smith*); *for* ~, assuredly. [ME, f. OF f. Rom. *certanus* f. L *certus* f. *cernere* decide, -AN]

cĕrt'ainlў (-tn-), adv. Indubitably; infallibly; confidently; admittedly; (in answers) I admit it, no doubt, yes. [prec. + -LY²]

cĕrt'aintў (-tn-), n. Undoubted fact (*bet on a* ~, usu. dishonestly with secret knowledge of result), indubitable prospect; thing in actual possession; absolute conviction (*of, that*); *to, for, a* ~, beyond possibility of doubt. [ME & AF *certainte*, OF *-ete* (CERTAIN, -TY)]

cĕrt'ĕs (-z), adv. (arch.). Assuredly, I assure you. [ME, f. OF (*a*) *certes*, prob. f. Rom. *(ad) certas* of a certainty]

certif'icate, n., & v.t. **1.** (-it). Document formally attesting a fact; esp. the bearer's status, acquirements, fulfilment of conditions, right to company shares, etc.; ‖ *bankrupt's* ~, stating that he has satisfied legal requirements & may recommence business. **2.** v.t. (-āt). Furnish with, license by, ~; hence **cĕrtifica'TION** n. [f. F *certificat* or its source med. L *certificatum* neut. p.p. (foll.)]

cĕrt'if|ў, v.t. Attest formally, declare by certificate; ‖ (of doctor) officially declare (person) insane, whence ~IABLE a.; inform certainly, assure; ~*ied milk*, guaranteed free from tubercle bacillus. Hence ~IER¹ n. [ME, f. OF *certifier* f. med. L *certificare* f. L *certus* CERTAIN (-FY)]

cĕrtiorār'ī (-shi-), n. Writ from higher court for records of case tried in lower. [L, = L *certiorem facere* inform]

cĕrt'itūde (-ōōs), n. Feeling certain, conviction. [F, or f. LL *certitudo* (CERTAIN, -TUDE)]

cerul'ean (-ōō-), a. Deep-blue. [f. L *caeruleus* + -AN]

cerum'ĕn (-ōō-), n. Ear-wax. So **cerum'inous** (-ōō-) a. [f. L *cera* wax on anal. of *albumen*]

cēr'use (-ōōs), n. (Also *white lead*) a white paint from carbonate & hydrate of lead, esp. as cosmetic. [ME, f. OF *ceruse* or L *cerussa*]

cĕrv'ical (or sĕrvīk²-), a. (physiol.). Of the neck. So **cĕrvic'o-** comb. form. [F, or mod. L, f. L *cervix -icis* neck + -AL]

cĕrv'ine, a. Of, like, deer. [f. L *cervinus* (*cervus* deer + -INE¹)]

Cēsa'rĕvitch, -witch, (-z-), n. Tsar's eldest son (hist.); ‖ (-w-) horse-race run annually at Newmarket. [Russ.]

‖ **cĕss,** n. Tax, rate, (now displaced by *rate* in Engl., but used in various senses in Ireland & Scotland). [prop. *sess* for obs. *assess* n. see ASSESS]

cĕssā'tion, n. Ceasing; pause. [f. L *cessatio* (*cessare* CEASE¹, -ATION)]

cĕss'er, n. (legal). Coming to an end, cessation, (*of* term, liability, etc.). [F (CEASE¹, -ER⁴)]

cĕ'ssion (-shn), n. Ceding, giving up, (of rights, property, or esp. of territory by State). [F, or f. L *cessio* (*cedere cess-* go away, -ION)]

cĕ'ssionarў (-shon-), n. = ASSIGN². [f. LL *cessionarius* as prec. + -ARY¹]

cĕss'pit, n. Midden. [see foll.]

cĕss'pool, n. Well sunk for soil from water-closet etc., retaining solids & letting liquid escape (also fig., as ~ *of iniquity*). [alt., after POOL[1], f. 16th c. *cesperalle, susprall* ~, = 15th c. *suspiral* vent, water-pipe, f. OF *souspirail* (SUS-PIRE, -AL(2)]

cĕs'toid, a. & n. (zool.). Ribbon-like (intestinal worm, as tapeworm). [f. L f. Gk *kestos* girdle + -OID]

cĕs'tus, n. Loaded bull-hide hand--covering worn by Roman boxers. [L *caestus* (*caedere* strike)]

cĕt-, comb. form=of spermaceti, in chem. names. [f. L f. Gk *kētos* whale]

cĕtā'cean (-shn), a. & n. (Member) of the mammalian order containing whales. So **cĕtā'CEOUS** (-āshus) a. [as prec., -ACEAN]

cĕt'ĕosaur (-ŏr), ⸱**saur'us,** n. Fossil saurian. [f. Gk *kētos -eos* whale & *sauros* lizard]

cĕt'erăch (-k), n. Kinds of fern with frond-backs covered with scales. [med. L, prob. f. Arab.]

cĕt'erĭs pā'rĭbus, adv. Other things being equal. [L]

Chablis (shăb'lē), n. A French white Burgundy. [~ in France]

Chăd'bănd, n. Unctuous hypocrite. [person in Dickens's *Bleak House*]

chāfe, v.t. & i., & n. 1. Rub (skin, to restore warmth); make, become, sore by rubbing; (of beast, river) rub itself *against* (bars, rocks); irritate; show irritation, fume, fret. 2. n. (Sore made by) friction; state of irritation, pet, (*in a* ~). [ME *chaufe* f. OF *chaufer* f. Rom. **calefare* f. L *facere* (*calēre* be hot, *facere* make)]

chāf'er, n. Kinds of beetle, usu. the COCK-CHAFER. [OE *ceafor*; also OE *cefer*, OS *kever*, OHG *chevar*; f. WG **kabhr-, **kebhr-*, prob. cogn. w. JOWL]

chaff (-ahf), n., & v.t. 1. Separated grain--husks; chopped hay & straw; bracts of grass-flower; spurious substitute (*caught with* ~, easily deceived or trapped); worthless stuff; ~-*cutter*, machine chopping fodder; hence ~'y[2] (-ahf-) a.; (vb) chop (straw etc.). 2. Banter (n. & v.t.). [OE *ceaf*, OHG *cheva* husk, prob. f. Gmc **kaf-, **kef-* gnaw (prec.); sense 2 of sl. uncert. orig.]

chăff'er, v.i. & t., & n. 1. Haggle, bargain (~ *away*, = BARGAIN *away*); hence ~ER[1] n. 2. n. = ~ing. [ME *ch(e)apfare* f. OE *cēap* see CHAPMAN + *faru* FARE]

‖ **chăff'inch,** n. Common British small bird. [ME, f. CHAFF (f. haunting barndoor) + FINCH]

chāf'ing-dish, n. Vessel with burning charcoal etc. inside for keeping warm things placed on it. [f. obs. sense of CHAFE = warm]

chagrin (shagrēn'), n., & v.t. (Affect with) acute disappointment or mortification. [f. F *chagrin(er)*, of uncert. orig.]

chain, n., & v.t. 1. Connected series of metal or other links (ENDLESS ~); fetters, confinement, restraining force; necklace, watchguard, etc. 2. Sequence, series, set, (*of* proof, events, posts, mountains; *ladies'* ~, movement in quadrille). 3. Jointed metal-rod measuring-line, its length (66 ft). 4. (Also ~-*shot*) two balls or half balls joined by ~ for cutting masts etc. (hist.). 5. (naut.). Fastening for shrouds below CHANNEL[2] (also ~-*plate*), *the* ~*s*, whole contrivance (channel, ~--plate, & DEAD-eyes) for widening basis of shrouds; (pl.) leadsman's platform. 6. ~ *armour, mail,* made of interlaced rings; ~ *bridge,* = suspension; ~ *coupling,* extra coupling of railway vans in case of accident to screw coupling; ~-*gang* (of convicts ~ed together, or forced to work in ~s); ~-*letter,* a letter of which the recipient is asked to make copies to be sent to a (named) number of others (these doing the like in their turn); ~ *moulding,* archit. ornament with link carving; ~ *reaction,* chem. reaction forming intermediate products which react with the original substance & are repeatedly renewed; ~--*smoker* (who lights another cigarette or cigar from the stump of the one last smoked); ~-*stitch,* ornamental sewing like ~, (sewing machine) simple sewing (cf. LOCK[3]-*stitch*); ***~-*store,* one of a series of shops owned by one firm & selling the same goods; ~-*wale,* = CHANNEL[2]; ~-*wheel,* transmitting power by ~ fitted to its edge; hence ~'LESS a., ~'LET n. 7. v.t. Secure, confine, with chain (lit. & fig.). [ME *chayne* f. OF *chaeine* f. L *catena*]

chair, n., & v.t. 1. Separate seat for one, of various forms (ARM[1] or *elbow*, BATH[1], CURULE, DECK[1], EASY[1]; *take a* ~, sit down). 2. Seat of authority; professorship; ‖ mayoralty (*past* or *above the* ~, *below the* ~. of alderman who has, has not, been mayor). 3. Seat, office, of person presiding at meeting, public dinner, etc. (*take, leave, the* ~, begin, end, the proceedings); chairman (*address, appeal to, the* ~; '*chair! chair!*', protest against disorder). 4. (Railway) iron or steel socket holding rail in place. 5. (hist.). = SEDAN. 6. ***ELECTRIC ~. 7. v.t. Install in CHAIR of authority; ‖ place in ~ & carry aloft (winner of contest, election, etc.); act as chairman of, preside over, (meeting). [ME, f. OF *chaïère* f. L f. Gk *kathedra* (CATHEDRAL)]

chair'man, n. (pl. -*men*; fem. *chair⸱ -woman*). Person chosen to preside over meeting, permanent president of committee, board, etc. (*C*~ *of Committees*, in Houses of Parl., presiding instead of Lord Chancellor & Speaker when House is in Committee), whence ~SHIP n.; one who keeps or propels a Bath chair; (hist.) one of two sedan-bearers.

chaise (shāz), n. Pleasure or travelling carriage of various shapes, usu. now low, four-wheeled, & open, with one or two ponies; ~ *longue* (lŏngg; F, = long chair), kind of sofa with a rest for the back at one end only; POST-~. [F, var. of *chaire* f. OF *chaïre* CHAIR]

chălcĕd'onў (k-), **cal-**, n. Precious stone of quartz kind with many varieties as agate, cornelian, chrysoprase. [f. L *c(h)alcedonius* f. Gk *khalkēdōn*]

chălco- (k-), comb. form esp. in mineralogical terms = copper-, brass-. [f. Gk *khalkos*]

chălcŏg'raphў (k-), n. Art of engraving on copper. [prec., -GRAPHY]

chălcopyr'ite (k-; -ī-), n. A copper ore, yellow or copper pyrites. [CHALCO-, PYRITE]

Chaldē'an, **Chaldee'**, (kăl-), a. & n. (Native) of Chaldea or Babylon; soothsayer, astrologer. [f. L f. Gk *khaldaios* + -AN]

chald'ron (-awl-), n. Coal measure, 36 bushels. [f. OF *chauderon*, w. -*l*- as in CAULDRON]

chalet (shăl'ā), n. Swiss mountain dairy-hut; Swiss peasant's wooden cottage; small villa. [Swiss-F]

chăl'ice, n. Goblet; eucharistic wine-cup (*mixed*~, with water ceremonially added); (poet.) flower-cup, whence **chăl'iced²** (-st) a. [ME, f. OF (now *calice*), f. L CALIX]

chalk¹ (-awk), n. White soft earthy limestone used for burning into lime & for writing & drawing; coloured preparation of like texture used in crayons for drawing; *as like as* ~ & *cheese*, unlike in essentials; *by a long* ~, by far (f. use of ~ to score points in games); ~-*bed*, stratum of ~; ~-*pit*, quarry in which ~ is dug; ~-*stone*, gouty concretion like ~ in tissues & joints esp. of hands & feet. [OE *cealc*, OS *calc*, OHG *kalk* f. L *calx* -*cis* lime]

chalk² (-awk), v.t. Rub, mark, draw, write, write *up*, with chalk; ~ *it up*, put it down to·my account; ~ *out*, sketch, plan as thing to be accomplished (often *for one*self). [f. prec.]

chalk'|ў (-awk-), a. Abounding in, white as, chalk; like or containing chalk-stones. Hence ~INESS n. [-Y²]

chăll'enge¹ (-j), n. Calling to account (*sentry's* ~, 'Who goes there?'); exception taken (e.g. to juryman); summons to trial or contest, esp. to duel, defiance; signal requiring recognition signal to be displayed by ship, aircraft, etc. [ME & OF *ca-*, *chalenge*, -*lange*, f. L *calumnia* CALUMNY]

chăll'eng|e² (-j), v.t. Call to account (of sentry, & fig.); take exception to (evidence, juryman), dispute, deny; claim (attention, admiration, etc.); invite to contest, game, or duel, defy. Hence ~eABLE a., ~ER¹ n. [f. OF *ca-*, *chalenger* f. L *calumniari* (CALUMNY)]

chăll'is, n. Lady's-dress fabric. [perh. f. surname]

chalȳb'eate (ka-), a. Impregnated with iron (of mineral water or spring). [irreg.

for *chalybate* f. L f. Gk *khalups* -*ubos* steel + -ATE²]

cham (kăm), n. Great ~, autocrat (of dominant critic etc., esp. Dr Johnson). [f. earlier F & ·med. L form of KHAN¹]

chamade (shamahd'), n. Signal for retreat on drum or trumpet. [F, f. Port. *chamada* (*chamar* f. L *clamare* call, -ADE)]

chamâr', n. Member of the very low Indian caste of leather-workers: tanner, shoemaker. [Hind.]

chăm'ber, n. Room, esp. bedroom (poet. or arch.; but ~ *music*, for small instrumental combinations; ~ *concert*, of such music; ~ *orchestra*, *organ*, small); (pl.) set of rooms in larger building, esp. in Inns of Court, let separately, judge's room for hearing cases not needing to be taken in court; (hall used by) deliberative or judicial body, one of the houses of a parliament (esp. *second* ~); *C*~ *of Commerce*, *Agriculture*, board organized to forward these in a district; *C*~ *of* HORRORS; (also ~-*pot*) vessel for urine; ~ *counsel*, lawyer giving opinions in private, not practising in court; ~-*maid*, housemaid at inn or hotel, *housemaid; enclosed space in body of animal or plant, or in machinery etc. (esp. part of gun-bore, of larger diameter in some guns, separate in revolver, that contains charge). Hence (-)~ED² (-erd) a., ~ING¹ n. (arch.), licentiousness. [ME & OF *chambre* f. L *camera* vault]

chăm'berlain (-lĭn), n. Officer managing household of sovereign or great noble; *Lord Great C*~ *of England*, hereditary holder of ceremonial office; *Lord C*~ *of the Household*, with part management of Royal Household, & licenser of plays. Hence ~SHIP n. [ME, f. OF *chamberlain* etc., = med. L *camerlingus*, f. OFrank. *kamarling* (= OHG *chamarlinc*) f. *kamara* CHAMBER, -LING¹]

chamēl'é|on (ka-), n. Small prehensile-tailed long-tongued lizard with power of changing colour & of living long without food; inconstant person. Hence ~ŏn'IC a., ~on-LIKE, a. & adv. [f. L f. Gk *khamaileōn* (*khamai* on ground, *leōn* lion)]

chăm'fer, v.t., & n. Bevel symmetrically (right-angled edge or corner); (n.) surface so given (*hollow* or *concave* ~, made as with gouge instead of chisel); channel, flute, (v.t. & n.). [ult. f. F *chanfraindre* (lit. break-corner; CANT¹, L *frangere*); perh. back form. f. *chamfering*, f. F *chanfrain* etc. f. -*fraindre*]

chamois (shăm'wah, *in sense 2* shăm'ĭ), n. **1.** Wild mountain antelope of goat size. **2.** (Also ~-*leather*, *shammy*, *shammy-leather*) soft pliable leather from sheep, goats, deer, etc. [F, = LL *camox*; ult. orig. unkn.]

chăm'omile, = CAMOMILE.

chămp, v.t. & i., & n. Munch (fodder) noisily; work (bit) noisily in teeth; (make) chewing action or noise. [prob. imit.]

champagne (shămpān'), n. Kinds of wine from E. France (usu. white & sparkling). [name of province, cf. foll.]

chăm'paign (-ān), n. (Expanse of) open country. [ME, f. OF *champagne, -paigne* f. L *Campania*; see CAMPAIGN]

chăm'pert|y̆, n. (law). The offence of assisting a party in a suit in which one is not naturally interested with a view to receiving a share of the disputed property. So ~ous a. [ME & AF *champartie*, f. OF *champart* feudal lord's part of produce, f. L *campus* field, *pars* part]

chăm'pion, n. & a., & v.t. 1. Person who fights, argues, etc., for another or for a cause (*King's, Queen's, C~*, or *C~ of England*, hereditary official at coronations). 2. Athlete etc., animal, plant, etc., that has defeated all competitors (often as adj., ~ *boxer*, ~ *turnip*); (as adj. or adv., dial. or vulg.) first-class, prime, top-hole, splendidly. Hence ~LESS a., ~SHIP n. 3. v.t. Maintain the cause of. [ME, f. OF f. med. L *campionem* fighter (L *campus* CAMP¹)]

champlevé (shămp'levă), a. & n. ~ *enamel* or ~, enamel in which the colours are filled into hollows made in the surface (cf. CLOISONNÉ). [F, = raised field]

chance¹ (-ahns), n. & a. 1. Way things fall out, fortune; undesigned occurrence; opportunity; (Cricket) opportunity of dismissing a batsman given to a fieldsman (esp. in phr. *give a* ~); possibility; probability (esp. in pl., as *the* ~*s are against it*); absence of design or discoverable cause; course of events regarded as a power, fate; *by* ~, as it falls or fell out, without design; *on the* ~, in view of the possibility (*of, that*); *take* one's ~, let things go as they may, consent to take what comes; *the main* ~, that of getting rich; *stand a* (*good, fair*) ~, have a prospect; *chance-*, = *by* ~, as ~-*sown tree*. 2. adj. Fortuitous (*a* ~ *companion, meeting*). [ME & OF *cheance* f. *cheoir* fall (Rom. *cadēre f. L *cadere*+-ANCE)]

chance² (-ahns), v.i. & t. Happen (arch. in abs. use, getting rare in constr. *it* ~*d that, he* ~*d to* do); ~ *upon*, happen to find, meet, or come upon; (colloq.) risk (esp. ~ *it*); ~ one's *arm* (colloq.), take one's chance of doing something successfully (prob. orig. Army sl., from a N.C.O.'s risking the loss of his stripes). [f. prec.]

chan'cel (-ah-), n. Eastern part of church reserved for clergy, choir, etc., & usu. railed off. [ME, f. OF f. LL *cancellus* f. L *cancelli* lattice-bars]

chan'cellery (-ah-), **-ory̆**, n. Position, staff, department, official residence, of a chancellor; office attached to embassy or consulate. [f. OF *chancelerie* (*chancelier* see foll., -RY)]

chan'cellor (-ah-), n. State or law official of various kinds; *Lord C~* (also *C~ of England, Lord High C~*), presiding in H. of Lords & in Court of Appeal; *C~ of* EXCHEQUER; *C~ of Duchy of Lancaster*, member of government (legally representative of King as Duke of Lancaster), often Cabinet minister employed on extra-departmental work; *C~ of bishop* or *diocese*, bishop's law officer; *C~ of Garter* or other order, who seals commissions etc.; non-resident head of university (Vice-*C~* performing most duties); (Germany, Austria) chief minister of State. Hence ~SHIP n. [ME, f. AF c(h)*ancelcr*, OF -*ier* (-OR) f. LL *cancellarius* law-court usher (*cancelli* CHANCEL)]

chance₸měd'ley (-ah-), n. (Law) action, esp. homicide, mainly but not entirely unintentional; inadvertency. [AF *chance medlée* (see MEDDLE) mixed chance]

chan'cery (-ah-), n. (*C~*) Lord Chancellor's court, a division of High Court of Justice (formerly a separate court of equity for cases with no remedy in common-law Courts, whence the meaning, still in U.S. & in literature, of court of equity); office for public records; (Boxing) *in* ~, with head held under opponent's arm being pommelled (from difficulty of getting clear of old Court of *C~*). [contracted f. CHANCELLERY]

chancre (shănk'er), n. Venereal ulcer. [16th c., F, f. L CANCER]

chan'cy̆ (-ah-), a. Uncertain, risky. [CHANCE¹, -Y²]

chăndelier' (sh-), n. Branched hanging support for several lights. [F, see foll.]

chand'ler (-ah-), n. Dealer in candles, oil, soap, paint, & groceries (*corn-* ~, in corn; *ship-*~, in cordage, canvas, etc.). Hence chand'lERY(1) (-ah-) n. [ME & AF *chandeler*, OF -*ier* (CANDLE, -ARY¹, -ER²)]

chănge¹ (-j), n. Alteration; substitution of one for another, variety (*for a* ~); whence ~'FUL(1) (-jf-). ~'LESS (-jl-), aa.; *Change* (now freq. but wrongly '*Change*), place where merchants meet (*on C~*, engaged there); arrival of moon at fresh phase (prop. at new moon only); ~ (*of clothes*), second outfit in reserve; ~ *of life*, MENOpause; SEA ~; money given for money of a different value or currency; money returned as balance of that tendered for article (*take* one's, *the*, ~ *out of*, avenge oneself on); *get no* ~ *out of* (a person), fail to get the better of him (in business, argument, etc.); (Bell--ringing, usu. pl.) different orders in which peal can be rung (*ring the* ~*s* fig., vary ways of putting or doing thing); ~-*over*, alteration from one working system to another, reversal (of the situation in affairs, of opinions, etc.). [ME, f. AF *chaunge*, OF *change*, f. *changer* (foll.)]

chănge² (-j), v.t. & i. Take another instead of (~ one's *coat*); resign, get rid of, *for*; give or get money change for; put on different (esp. evening) clothes; go from one to another of (*thing* ~*s hands*, passes to different owner; ~ *houses*, *trains*; also abs. = ~ trains, boats, etc.); give & receive, exchange, (~ *places with*, *we ~d places*); make or become different (often *to*, ·*into*, *from*), (moon) arrive at fresh phase, esp. become new moon; ~ *colour*, turn pale or blush; ~ one's *feet* (colloq.), put on other shoes etc.; ~ *front*, take new position in argument etc.; ~ one's *condition*, marry; ~ one's *mind*, adopt new plan or opinion; ~ one's *note* or *tune*, become more humble, sad, etc.; ~ *step*, *foot*, *feet*, time other foot to drum in marching; ~ *up*, *down*, (Motoring) engage a higher, lower, gear. [ME, f. AF *chaunger*, OF *changer* f. L *cambiare*, *cambire* barter, of Celt. orig.]

change'a|ble (-ja-), a. Irregular, inconstant; alterable. Hence or cogn. ~BIL'ITY (-ja-), ~bleNESS (-ja-; -ln-), nn. [OF, as prec., -ABLE]

change'ling (-jl-), n. Thing or child substituted for another by stealth, esp. elf--child thus left by fairies. [CHANGE² + -LING¹]

chănn'el¹, n., & v.t. (-ll-). 1. Natural or artificial bed of running water; (Geog.) piece of water, wider than strait, joining two larger pieces, usu. seas (‖ *the C~*, English C~); tubular passage for liquid; course in which anything moves, direction, line; medium, agency (esp. *through the usual ~s*); (Radio & Television) narrow band of frequencies sufficiently wide for transmission; groove, flute; ~ *iron* (or *bar*), rolled iron bar or beam flanged to form a ~ on one side. 2. v.t. Form ~s in, groove; cut out (*way* etc.). [ME & OF *chanel* f. L *canalis* CANAL]

chănn'el², n. Broad thick plank projecting horizontally from ship's side abreast of mast to broaden base for shrouds; (mod., sing. or pl.) level of deck (*rolling ~s under*). [for *chainwale* (WALE) cf. *gunnel* for *gunwale*]

chant (-ah-), n., & v.i. & t. 1. Song; (Mus.) short musical passage in two or more phrases each beginning with reciting note, for singing to psalms & canticles (*single*, *double*, *quadruple*, as one, two, four, verses are sung to it); measured monotonous song; sing-song intonation in talk. 2. vb. Sing; utter musically; intone, sing to a ~; ~ *the praises of*, constantly praise; ~ *horses*, sell fraudulently. [f. OF *chant(er)* song, sing, f. L *cantus -ūs*, *cantare*, (*canere cant·* sing)]

chan'ter (-ah-), n. In vbl senses; also: melody-pipe, with finger-holes, of bag-pipe; (also *horse-~*) swindling horse--dealer. [-ER¹]

chanterĕlle' (-ah-), n. Yellow edible fungus. [F, dim. f. L f. Gk *kantharos* drinking-cup]

chan'ticleer (-ah-), n. (Personal name for) domestic cock. [ME, f. OF *chantecler* (CHANT, CLEAR), name in *Reynard the Fox*]

chan'trĕss (-ah-), n. Female singer (arch.

or poet.). [f. OF *chanteresse*, see CHANTER, -ESS¹]

chan'trÿ (-ah-), n. Endowment for priest(s) to· sing masses for founder's soul; priests, chapel, altar, so endowed. [ME, f. OF *chanterie* (*chanter* CHANT, -ERY)]

chan'tÿ (-ah-) -tey. Varr. of SHANTY².

chā'ŏs (kā-), n. Formless void or great deep of primordial matter (*C~*, this personified as eldest of the gods); utter confusion. Hence (irreg.) **chāŏt'IC** a., **chāŏt'ICALLY** adv. (kā-). [L, f. Gk *khaos*; -*otic* after *erotic* etc.]

chăp¹, v.t. & i. (-pp-), & n. 1. Crack (t. & i.) in fissures (usu. of skin, by wind etc., also of dried-up earth etc.). 2. n. (Usu. pl.) crack(s), open seam(s), esp. in skin; hence ~**p'ÿ²** a. [vb & n. 14th c.; rel. & etym. obscure]

chăp², **chŏp**, n. (Pl.) jaws, esp. of beasts (*lick* one's ~*s*, w. relish or anticipation), cheeks (*fat-chops*, fat-faced person); (sing.) lower jaw or half of cheek, esp. of pig as food (*Bath chap*; ~*-fallen*, with jaw hanging down, dispirited, dejected); *chops of the Channel*, entrance from Atlantic to Channel. [16th c. var. of CHOP³; etym. & hist. obscure]

chăp³, n. (colloq.). Man, boy, fellow. [short for CHAPMAN cf. *customer*]

***chaparejos** (chahparā'hŏs), n. pl. Cowboy's leather or sheepskin overalls for legs. [Mex. Sp.; freq. abbr. as **chăps** (ch- or sh-)]

chăparrāl', n. (Thicket of) dwarf evergreen oak; ~·*cock*, fast-running bird. [Sp., f. *chaparra* evergreen oak]

chăp'-bŏŏk, n. (bibliog.). Specimen of popular literature (usu. small pamphlet of tales, ballads, tracts) formerly hawked by chapmen. [19th c., see CHAPMAN]

chāpe, n. Metal cap of scabbard-point; back-piece of buckle attaching it to strap etc.; ‖ sliding loop on belt or strap. [ME, f. OF *chape* cope, hood; see CAPE¹]

***chapeau-bras** (shapō-brah'), n. (hist.). Three-cornered flat silk hat of 18th c. carried under arm. [F]

chăp'el, n. Place of Christian worship other than parish church or cathedral, esp. one attached to private house or institution (~ *royal*, of royal palace); oratory in larger building, with altar, esp. compartment of cathedral etc. separately dedicated (*Lady-~*, dedicated to Virgin, usu. E. of high altar); subordinate Anglican church, esp. ~ *of ease*, for convenience of remote parishioners; ‖ place of worship of certain nonconformist bodies; ~ *service* or *attendance at* ~ (*keep a* ~, be present, in colleges); (Print.) printing--office, journeyman printers' association or meeting. [ME, f. OF *chapele* f. med.L *cappella* dim. of *cappa* cloak (CAPE¹); first ~ was sanctuary in which St Martin's sacred cloak was kept by *cappellani*]

***chapelle ardente** (shăpĕl' ărdahnt'), n. Chamber prepared for lying-in-state of great personage & lit up with candles, torches, etc. [F]

chǎp′elrў, n. District served by chapel. [-RY]

chǎp′erōn (sh-), n., &.v.t. **1.** Married or elderly woman in charge of girl on social occasions; hence ∼AGE n. **2.** v.t. Act as ∼ to. [F, = hood, chaperon, dim. of *chape* cope (CAP¹)]

chǎp′iter, n. (bibl.). Capital of column. [earlier form of CHAPTER]

chǎp′lain (-lǐn), n. Clergyman officiating in private chapel of great person or institution, on board ship, or for regiment etc.; nun reciting inferior services in nunnery. Hence ∼CY (-lǐn-) n. [ME, f. OF *chapelain* f. med. L *cappellanus* (CHAPEL, -AN)]

chǎp′lět, n. Wreath of flowers, leaves, gold, gems, etc., for head; string of beads for counting prayers (one-third of rosary number), or as necklace; string of eggs in toad etc.; bead-moulding. Hence ∼ED² a. [ME & OF *chapelet* dim. of *chapel* f. Rom. **cappellus* dim. of LL *cappa* CAP¹]

chǎp′man, n. (hist ; pl. *-men*). Pedlar. [OE *cēapmann* (= OHG *koufman*) f. *cēap* barter; see CHEAP]

chǎpp′ie, -ў, n. (colloq.). Exquisite, man about town. [CHAP³ +-Y³]

chǎp′ter, n. Main division of a book (abbr. *cap*, *ch.*, *c.*), (fig.) limited subject, piece of narrative, etc.; ‖ Act of Parl. numbered as part of session's statutes for reference (5 & 6 Will. IV. cap. 62 = Statutory Declarations Act 1835); general meeting, whole number, of canons of collegiate or cathedral church or members of monastic or knightly order (∼-*house*, used for such meetings); ∼ & *verse*, exact reference to passage, exact authority *for* statement; *to end of* ∼, for ever; ∼ *of* ACCIDENTS. [ME & OF *chapitre* · f. L *capitulum* dim. of *caput -itis* head]

chǎr¹, n. Hill trout of Wales etc. [etym. unkn.]

chǎr², n., & v.i. (-r-, -rr-). **1.** Odd job(s) of housework (usu. pl., & now usu. *chore*); (colloq.)· ∼woman; ∼′*woman*, woman hired by the hour or day to do housework. **2.** v.i. Work by the hour or day at housecleaning, do odd jobs as ∼woman. [OE *cerr*, *cerran* turn]

chǎr³, v.t. & i. (-rr-). Burn (t. & i.) to charcoal, scorch, blacken with fire. [app. back formation f. CHARCOAL]

‖ **chǎr⁴,** n. (sl.). Tea. [f. Chin. *ch′a*]

char-à-banc(s) (shǎ′rabǎng, or as in Ap.), n. Long vehicle, with many seats looking forward, for holiday etc. excursions. [F *char à bancs* = benched carriage]

chǎ′racter (kǎrǐk-), n.; & v.t. **1.** Distinctive mark; (pl.) inscribed letters or figures; style of writing-symbols (*in the Roman*, *German*, ∼); person's handwriting. **2.** Characteristic (esp. of species etc. in Nat. Hist.); collective peculiarities, sort, style; person's or race's idiosyncrasy, mental or moral nature. **3.** Moral strength, backbone; reputation, good reputation; description of person's qualities; testimonial; status. **4.** Known person (usu. *public* ∼); imaginary person created by novelist or dramatist; actor's or hypocrite's part (*in*, *out of*, ∼, appropriate to these or not, also more widely of actions that are in accord or not with person's ∼). **5.** Eccentric person (∼ *actor*, who devotes himself to eccentricities).. **6.** v.t. (poet. & arch.). Inscribe; describe. [ME *ca-* f. OF *caractere* f. L f. Gk *kharaktēr* stamp, impress]

chǎracteris′t|ic (kǎ-), a. & n. Typical, distinctive, (trait, mark, quality), whence ∼ICALLY adv.; (Math.) index of logarithm. [f. F *charactéristique* f. Gk *kharaktēristikos* (prec., -IST, -IC)]

chǎ′racteriz|e (kǎ-), **-is|e** (-īz), v.t. Describe character of; describe *as*; be characteristic of, impart character to. Hence ∼A′TION n. [f. F or med. L f. Gk *kharaktērizō* (CHARACTER, -IZE)]

chǎ′racterlèss (kǎ-), a. Ordinary, undistinguished; without testimonial. [-LESS]

charade (sharahd′), n. Game of guessing word from written or acted clue given for each syllable & for the whole. [F, f. Pr. *charrado* (*charrà* chatter)]

chǎr′coal, n. Black porous residue of partly burnt wood, bones, etc., form of carbon (occas. w. allus. to use of the fumes as method of suicide); ∼-*burner*, maker ·of this. [perh. f. CHARE + COAL in sense (*wood*) *turned coal*]

chāre, n., & v.i. (Now rare var. of) CHAR².

chärge¹, n. **1.** Material load; right quantity to put into thing, esp. of explosive for gun; figurative load. **2.** (Her.) device, bearing. **3.** Expense (*at his own* ∼); price demanded for service or goods (*are his* ∼*s reasonable?*). **4.** Task, duty, commission; care, custody, (*of*; *nurse in* ∼ *of child*, *child in* ∼ *of nurse*; CURATE *in* ∼; ‖ *give* person *in* ∼, hand over to police); *take* ∼, (colloq., of things) get out of control (esp. with disastrous results); thing or person entrusted, minister's flock. **5.** Exhortation, directions, (*parting* ∼, *bishop's* ∼, *judge's* ∼ *to jury*). **6.** Accusation (*lay* to one's ∼, accuse him of; ‖ ∼-*sheet*, record of cases at police station). **7.** Impetuous attack (*bayonet* ∼), rush, (*return to the* ∼, begin again, esp. in argument); (Mil.) signal sounded for such attack. [ME, f. OF *charge* f. Rom. **carrica* f. LL *car(ri)care* (foll.)]

chärge², v.t. & i. **1.** Load, fill to the full or proper extent, (vessel, gun with explosive); saturate (air with vapour, water with chemicals, accumulator with electricity, memory with facts). **2.** Entrust *with* (∼ one*self with*, undertake). **3.** Command *to* do, exhort. **4.** Accuse, impute, (person *with* action, fault *upon* person); saddle *with* liability), place (liability) *on*; debit (∼ *it to my account*). **5.** Demand (price) *for* (also ~ *person price for*). **6.** Attack (t. & i.) impetuously, esp. on horseback. **7.** Place (weapon) in position for use. [ME, f. OF *charg(i)er* f. LL *car(ri)care* load f. L *carrus* CAR]

chárge'able (-ja-), a. **1.** Expensive (arch.). **2.** Liable to be charged *with* (accused of); subject to a money demand; liable to be made an expense; imputable to (*on*); proper to be added *to* an account. Hence **chárgea**BIL'ITY (-ja-) n. [1 f. CHARGE[1], 2 f. CHARGE[2], +-ABLE]

chargé (*d'affaires*) (shärzh'ā dafär'), n. (pl. -*yés* pr. as sing.). Diplomatic agent; representative at minor court or government. [F, = diplomatic representative]

chár'ger[1], n. (arch.). Large flat dish. [ME *chargeour* f. AF; see CHARGE[2], -OR]

chár'ger[2], n. In vbl senses; esp., (Mil.) officer's horse. [-ER[1]]

chá'riot, n., & v.t. Stately vehicle, triumphal car, (poet. & esp. fig. of sun's ~ etc.); (hist.) four-wheeled carriage with back seats only; (hist.) car used in ancient fighting & racing, whence **chárioteER'** n.; (vb) convey as or in ~. [ME, f. OF, augment. of *char* CAR]

chá'ritab|le, a. Liberal in giving to the poor; connected with such giving; wont to judge favourably of persons, acts, & motives. Hence ~**leNESS** (-ln-), n., ~**LY**[2] adv. [OF (*charité* = foll., -ABLE)]

chá'rity, n. Christian love of fellow men (*in, out of,* ~ *with*); kindness, natural affection, (~ *begins at home*, is due first to kith & kin—freq. an excuse for not subscribing etc.); candour, freedom from censoriousness, imputing of good motives when possible, leniency; beneficence, liberality to the poor, alms-giving (pl., acts of this), alms; trust for advancement of education; institution for helping the helpless, help so given, (*cold as* ~, in allusion to mechanical administration; ~-*boy, -girl,* brought up in such place); *Brother, Sister, of C*~, member of religious society devoted to relieving poor; *C*~ *Commission(ers),* board created 1853 to control charitable trusts. [ME, f. OF *charite* f. L *caritatem* in its later sense (*Christian) love,* f. *carus* dear +-TY]

chárivár'i (sh-), n. Medley of sounds, hubbub (prop. a serenade of pans, trays, etc., to unpopular person). [F, of unkn. etym.]

chárk'a, n. Country-made Indian spinning-wheel. [Hind. *charkha*]

|| **chár'lädy**, var. of CHARWOMAN.

chárl'atan (sh-), n. & a. Impostor in medicine, quack; (of, as of) empty pretender to knowledge or skill. Hence ~**ISH**[1](1) a., ~**ISM**(2), ~**RY**, nn. [F, f. It. *ciarlatano* (*ciarlare* patter)]

Chárles's Wain (-lzīz), n. (Also *Plough, Great Bear*) constellation *Ursa Major* or its seven bright stars. [OE *Carles wægn* the wain of Carl (Charles the Great, Charlemagne)]

Chárles'ton (-lz-), n., & v.i. An American dance with side-kicks from the knee; (vb) dance this, kick thus. [f. ~ in S. Carolina]

|| **Chárl'ey,** n. (old colloq.). Night-watchman. [dim. of *Charles*]

chárl'ock, n. Field mustard, a common yellow-flowered weed. [OE *cerlic*]

chárl'otte (sh-), n. Kinds of pudding made of stewed fruit with casing or layers or covering of bread, biscuits, sponge-cake, or bread-crumbs; ~ *russe,* custard enclosed in sponge cake. [F]

chárm[1], n. Verse, sentence, word, act, or object having occult power (*against*), spell; thing worn to avert evil etc., amulet; trinket on watch-chain etc.; quality, feature, exciting love or admiration (~*s,* beauty); attractiveness, indefinable power of delighting. [ME & OF *charme* f. L *carmen* song]

chárm[2], v.t. Bewitch, influence (as) by magic, (abs. or with pred. as ~ *asleep, away*); ~ (secret, consent, etc.) *out of*; endow with magic power (*bear a* ~*ed life*); captivate, delight; (~*ed with*); give pleasure to (*I shall be* ~*ed* as polite formula); (part.) delightful, whence ~'ingLY[2] adv. [f. OF *charmer* f. *charme* (prec.)]

chárm'er, n. In vbl senses; esp., beautiful woman (now joc. or arch.). [ER[1]]

charmeuse (shärm'ērz), n. Soft smooth silk dress-fabric. [F]

chárn'el-house, n. House or vault in which dead bodies or bones are piled. [ME & OF *charnel* burying-place f. med. L *carnale* f. LL *carnalis* CARNAL]

Chár'on (k-), n. Ferryman conveying souls across Styx to Hades in Gk mythol. (~*'s boat, ferry,* etc., phrr. for hour of death). [f. Gk *Kharōn*]

chár'poy, n. (Anglo-Ind.). Light Indian bedstead. [f. Hind. *charpai*]

chárt, n., & v.t. **1.** Navigator's sea map, with coast outlines, rocks, shoals, etc.; outline map with conspectus of special conditions, as *magnetic* ~; record by curves etc. of fluctuations in temperature, prices, etc.; sheet of tabulated information; hence ~'LESS a. **2.** v.t. Make ~ of, map. [f. F *charte* & its source L *c(h)arta* CARD[2]]

chárt'er[1], n. Written grant of rights by sovereign or legislature, esp. creation of borough, company, etc. (*Great C*~, MAGNA CHARTA); deed conveying land; = CHARTER--PARTY; privilege, admitted right; ~--*member,* original member of society, incorporation, etc. [ME *chartre* f. OF f. L *chartula* dim. of *charta* CARD[2]]

chárt'er[2], v.t. Grant charter, give privilege, to (||~*ed accountant,* member of Institute of Accountants with royal charter; ~*ed libertine,* one allowed to take liberties); hire (ship) by ~-*party,* (loosely) hire (vehicle etc.), whence ~ER[1] n. [f. prec.]

Chárt'erhouse, n. Alms-house in London for aged pensioners on site of Carthusian monastery; (also ~ *School*) public school of same foundation now at Godalming. [alt. f. AF *Chartrouse* = OF *Chartreuse*, earlier *Charteuse* Carthusian monastery f. L *Cart(h)usia*; see CARTHUSIAN]

chart'er-party, n. Deed between shipowner & merchant for hire of ship & delivery of cargo. [f. F *charte partie* f. med. L *charta partita* divided charter]

chart'ism, -ist, nn. (hist.). Principles, adherent, of reform movement of 1837–48. [f. L *charta* + -ISM(3), -IST(2), name taken from the democratic manifesto 'People's Charter']

chartŏg'raphỹ (k-), etc. See car-.

chartreuse (see Ap.), n. Carthusian monastery; kinds (*green, yellow,* ~) of liqueur; pale apple-green colour. [made at La Grande *Chartreuse* (Carthusian monastery near Grenoble) f. place-name L *Cart(h)usia*; see CHARTERHOUSE]

chart'ulary (k-). See car-.

‖ **char'woman** (-woŏ-), n. Woman hired by the day or hour for housework. [CHAR²]

char'ỹ, a. Cautious; shy *of*, sparing *in*, doing; stingy *of* (~ *of praise*). Hence **char'ILY²** adv., **char'INESS** n. [OE *cearig*, OS *carag*, OHG *charag* f. Gmc **karō* CARE¹ + -Y²]

Charỹb'dis (ka-), n. See SCYLLA.

chāse¹, n. Pursuit (*in* ~ *of*, pursuing; *give* ~, go in pursuit), hunting (*the* ~, hunting as sport); (also *chace*) unenclosed park-land; hunted animal or pursued ship; (Hist.) ~, ~-*port*, ~-*gun*, *chaser, bow*-~, *stern*-~, *bow, stern, -chaser*, gun, port, in bow or stern for use while chasing or being chased; (Tennis) a certain stroke. [ME & OF *chace* f. Rom. **captia* f. **captiare* CHASE²]

chāse², v.t. Pursue; drive *from, out of, to,* etc.; ~*r* (colloq.), tot of spirit taken after coffee, small quantity of water taken after drinking neat spirits (also fig.). [ME, f. OF *chacier* f. Rom. **captiare* for L *captare* f. *capere* take; see CATCH¹]

chāse³, v.t. Emboss, engrave, (metal). [app. f. syn. *enchase* f. F *enchâsser* (EN-, CASE²)]

chāse⁴, n. Part of gun enclosing bore; groove cut to receive pipe etc. [f. F *chas* enclosed space f. L *capsus* enclosure etc., or f. *capsa* (CASE²)]

chāse⁵, n. Iron frame holding composed type for page or sheet. [f. F *châsse* CASE²]

chasm (kǎ'zm), n. Deep fissure; break of continuity, hiatus; wide difference of feeling, interests, etc., between persons or parties; void, blank. Hence (poet.) ~Y² a. [f. L f. Gk *khasma*]

chasse (shahs), n. Liqueur after coffee etc. (also ~-*café*). [F]

chassé (shǎs'ā), n., & v.i. (Make) gliding step in dancing; ~ *croisé* (see Ap.; pl. -*s* -*s*), double ~, (fig.) idle manœuvring. [F]

chassis (shǎs'ē), n. (pl. the same). Base-frame of gun-carriage, motor-car, etc. [f. F *châssis* rel. to *chásse* (CHASE⁵)]

chāste, a. Abstaining from unlawful or immoral (also from all) sexual intercourse, pure, virgin; decent (of speech); restrained, severe, pure in taste or style, unadorned, simple. Hence ~'LY² (-tl-) adv. [ME, f. OF f. L *castus*]

chā'sten (-sn), v.t. Discipline, correct by suffering, (usu. of God, Providence, etc., or of trouble etc.); make chaste in style etc., refine; temper, subdue, (esp. in p.p.). Hence ~ER¹ (-sener) n. [f. obs. *chaste* vb (f. OF *chastier* f. L *castigare* CASTIGATE) + -EN⁶]

chăstīs|e' (-z), v.t. Punish; beat. Hence **chăs'tiseMENT** (-zm-), ~'ER¹, nn. [ME, app. irreg. f. obs. vbs *chaste, chasty* (see prec.) + -IZE]

chăs'titỹ, n. Continence; virginity, celibacy; simplicity of style or taste. [f. OF *chastete* f. L *castitatem* (*castus* CHASTE, -TY)]

chăs'ūble (-z-), n. Sleeveless vestment of celebrant at Mass or Eucharist with colour regulated by the feast of the day. [ME. & OF *chesible*; later -*uble* f. F *chasuble* f. LL *casub(u)la* irreg. f. LL *casula* hooded cloak, dim. of *casa* house]

chăt¹, v.i. (-tt-), & n. (Indulge in) easy familiar talk. Hence ~t'Y² a., ~t'INESS n. [short for CHATTER]

chăt², n. Kinds of bird, chiefly thrushes (usu. in comb. as *stone, whin,* -~). [f. prec.]

chặteau (shah'tō), n. (pl. -*x*, pr. -z), Foreign country house; *C*~, used attrib. in names of French wines made near certain ~*x*. [F]

chặt'elaine (sh-), n. Set of short chains attached to woman's belt for carrying keys, watch, pencil, etc.; mistress of country house; (esp. in journalistic use) hostess. [f. F *châtelaine*, fem. of -*ain* lord of a castle, f. L *castellanus* f. *castellum* CASTLE]

chặtt'el, n. Movable possession (usu. pl., esp. *goods & ~s*); ** ~ mortgage*, conveyance of ~s by mortgage as security for debt. [ME & OF *chatel* see CATTLE]

chặtt'er, v.i., & n. **1.** (Of birds) utter quick series of short notes; (of persons) talk quickly, incessantly, foolishly, or inopportunely; (of teeth) rattle together (also of ill-adjusted parts of machine). **2.** n. Any of these sounds; ~*box*, child etc. given to ~. [ME *chater* etc., imit., see -ER⁵]

chaud-froid (shō'frwah'), n. Dish of filleted poultry etc. served cold in jelly or sauce. [F, lit. hot-cold]

chauff'er, n. Metal basket holding fire; portable furnace with air-holes. [19th c., also (18th c.) *choffer*, of uncert. orig.; cf. (obs.) ME *chafer, chaufer,* & OF *chaufoire*; see CHAFING-DISH]

chauffeur (shŏf'er, shōfĕr'), n. Professional driver of a motor-car. Hence **chauffeuse** (shōfĕrz') n., female ~. [F]

chaulmoō'gra, n. East-Indian tree; ~

oil, fat obtained from its seeds & used in treatment of leprosy. [native name]

chauv'in|ism (shŏv-), n. Bellicose patriotism, foreign jingoism. So ~IST(2) n. & a., ~IS'TIC a. [*Chauvin,* Napoleonic veteran, person in Cogniard's *Cocarde Tricolore* 1831]

chaw, v.t., & n. (now vulg.). Chew; *~ *up,* utterly defeat; ~-*bacon,* bumpkin; (n.) quid of tobacco. [var. of CHEW]

cheap, a. Inexpensive (of thing, price, shop, dealer; ~ *& nasty,* of low cost & bad quality); worth more than its cost; easily got; worthless, of little account, staled, (*hold* ~, despise); (as pred.) = cheaply (*got it* ~ etc.); *dirt* ~, very ~; *feel* ~ (sl.), be out of sorts; *on the* ~, in ~ manner; *C~ Jack,* travelling hawker; ‖~ *trip(per),* excursion(ist) by rail etc. at reduced fares. Hence ~'LY² adv., ~'ISH¹(2) a., ~'NESS n. [f. phr. *good cheap* f. obs. *cheap* n. f. OE *cēap* barter, OS *kôp,* OHG *kouf,* ON *kaup* (cf. Goth. *kaupōn* vb) f. L *caupo* innkeeper]

cheap'en, v.t. & i. Haggle for (arch.); make or become cheap, depreciate. [-EN⁶]

cheat, n., & v.t. & i. **1.** Trick, fraud; swindler, deceiver; card-game in which undetected cheating is licensed. **2.** vb. Deceive, trick (person *out of* thing); deal fraudulently; while away (time, fatigue). [ME *chete* vb, aphetic f. *achete,* var. of ESCHEAT]

check¹, int. & n. **1.** (Announcement of) exposure of chess king to attack. **2.** Sudden arrest given to motion, rebuff, repulse; slight military reverse. **3.** (hunt.). Loss of the scent. **4.** Stoppage, pause; restraint on action (*keep in* ~, under control); person or thing that restrains. **5.** Control to secure accuracy; token of identification for left luggage, seat-holder, etc.; bill in restaurant. **6.** *Counter at cards (hence colloq., *hand in* one's ~*s,* die). **7.** ~-*action* in piano, restraining hammer from striking string twice; ~-*nut,* screwed on over nut to prevent its working loose; ~-*rein,* attaching one horse's rein to other's bit, also rein preventing horse from lowering head; ~-*string,* in carriage for signalling to driver to stop; ~-*taker,* collector of pass tokens in theatre etc.; ~-*till,* in shop, recording receipts. [ME *chek, chak* f. OF *eschec* ult. f. Arab. f. Pers. *shah* king]

check², v.t. & i. **1.** Threaten opponent's king at chess. **2.** Suddenly arrest motion of. **3.** (Of hounds) stop on losing scent, or to make sure of it. **4.** Restrain, curb, (of superior) find fault with, rebuke. **5.** Test (statement, account, figures, employees) by comparison etc., examine accuracy of. [ME *chek(e)* f. OF *eschequier* play chess, check, as prec.]

check³, n. Cross-lined pattern; fabric woven or printed with this. So ~ED² (-kt) a. [prob. short for CHEQUER]

check⁴, n. = CHEQUE.

check'er. See CHEQUER¹˒².

check'ers, n. pl. The game of draughts. [see CHEQUER¹]

checkmāte', int. & n., & v.t. (also *mate,* now more usu. in chess but not in fig. sense). (Announcement to opponent of) inextricable check of king at chess, final defeat at chess or in any enterprise; (vb) defeat, frustrate. [ME *chck mat(e)* f. OF *eschec mat* (see CHECK¹) f. Arab. *shah mata* king is dead]

Chĕdd'ar, n. Kind of cheese. [~ in Somerset]

chee'-chee', n. (Anglo-Ind.). The affected English accent attributed to Eurasians; a Eurasian. [f. Hind. *chhī-chhī* filth, fie!]

cheek, n., & v.t. Side-wall of mouth, side of face below eye, (~-*tooth,* molar; ~-*bone,* that below eye; ~ *by jowl,* close together, intimate; *to* one's *own* ~, not shared with others); saucy speech (vb, address saucily), whence ~'Y² a., ~'ILY² adv., ~'INESS n.; cool confidence, effrontery, (*have the* ~ *to*); side post of door etc.; (pl.) jaws of vice, side-pieces of various parts of machines arranged in lateral pairs. [ME *chek(e)* f. OE *cēce, cēace,* cogn. w. MDu. *kāke,* MLG *kāke, kēke* f. WG *kækōn-*]

cheep, v.i., & n. (Utter) shrill feeble note as of young bird. Hence (of young bird esp. of game) ~'ER¹ n. [imit.]

cheer¹, n. Frame of mind (*what* ~?, how do you feel? ; *be of good* ~, stout-hearted, hopeful); food, fare, (*make good* ~, feast; *the fewer the better* ~, more to eat); shout of encouragement or applause (*three* ~*s,* successive united hurrahs, often *for* person or thing honoured). [ME *chere* face etc. f. AF, = OF *chiere* f. LL *cara* face f. Gk *kara* head]

cheer², v.t. & i. Comfort, gladden; incite, urge *on,* esp. by shouts; applaud (t. & i.), shout for joy; ~ *up,* comfort, take comfort. [f. prec.]

cheer'ful, a. Contented, in good spirits, hopeful; animating, pleasant; willing, not reluctant. Hence ~LY² adv., ~NESS n. [CHEER¹ +-FUL]

cheer'less, a. Dull, gloomy, dreary, miserable. Hence ~LY² adv., ~NESS n. [CHEER¹ +-LESS]

cheer'ly, adv. (naut.). Heartily, with a will. [formerly adj. & adv. (see -LY²) f. CHEER¹]

cheer'|y, a. Lively, in spirits, genial. Hence ~iLY² adv., ~iNESS n., ‖~iŏ (sl.), int. of encouragement. [-Y²]

cheese¹ (-z), n. Food made of pressed curds; *a* ~, complete cake or ball of this within rind; *green* ~, immature, not yet dried; BREAD *&* ~; CHALK *&* ~; fruit of mallow; the heavy flat wooden ball used in skittles; *damson, guava,* ~, conserve of the fruit pressed into consistency of ~; ~-*cloth,* butter muslin; ~-*cutter,* with broad curved blade; ~-*cake,* tartlet filled

with sweet yellow compound of curds etc.;
~-*hopper*, maggot of ~-*fly*; ~-*monger*,
dealer in ~, butter, etc.; ~-*paring*, stingy,
stinginess, (pl.) worthless odds & ends;
~-*plate*, 5 or 6 in. in diameter, also large
coat-button; ~-*rennet*, name for Lady's
bedstraw; ~-*scoop*, -*taster*, instrument for
extracting piece; ~-*straws*, savoury of
grated cheese etc. made up into thin
strips. [OE *cēse*, OS *kāsi*, *k*(*i*)*ēsi*, OHG
chāsi, WG f. L *caseus*]

cheese² (-z), n. (obs. sl.). The ~, the correct
thing. [f. Hind. & Pers. *chiz* thing]

cheese³ (-z), v.t. (sl.). ~ *it*, stop, give over,
(only as imperat.). [orig. unkn.]

chees'|ў (-z-), a. Like, tasting of, cheese;
(sl.) stylish. Hence ~**ĭNESS** n. [CHEESE¹,²,
-Y²]

cheet'ah, n. Kind of leopard, tamed in
India & trained to hunt deer. [f. Hind.
chita f. Skr. *chitraka* speckled]

chef (sh-), n. Head cook (male). [F]

chef-d'œuvre (shādēr'vr), n. (pl. *chefs*-,
same pronunc.).~A, one's, masterpiece. [F]

cheil(o)- (kī-). = CHIL(O)-.

cheir(o)- (kīr-). = CHIR(O)-.

cheirŏp'teran, n., & **cheirŏp'terous**, a.,
(kīr-). (Member) of mammal order with
membraned hands serving as wings, the
bats. [prec. +Gk *pteron* wing + -AN,
-OUS]

chek'a (chā-), n. (Earlier name of) OGPU.
[Russ., f. initials (*che*, *ka*) of *Chresvy-
chainaya Kommissiya*, extraordinary
commission]

chel'a¹ (chā-), n. Novice qualifying for
initiation in esoteric Buddhism. [Hind.,
= pupil]

chel'|a² (kē-), n. (pl. -*lae*). The prehensile
claw of crabs, lobsters, scorpions, etc.
Hence ~**ATE²**, ~**ĭFORM**, aa. [f. Gk *khēlē*
claw]

Chĕll'ĕan (sh-), a. (archaeol.). Of the
palaeolithic epoch represented by remains found at Chelles in France. [-AN]

Chĕl'sea (-sĭ), n. Artistic quarter of
London; ~ *bun*, kind of rolled currant-
-bun; ||~*pensioner*, inmate of the~ Royal
Hospital for old or disabled soldiers; ~
ware, kind of porcelain made at ~ in
18th c. [place]

Chĕltŏn'ian, a. & n. (Member) of
Cheltenham College. [-IAN]

chĕm'ical (kĕ-), a. & n. Of, made by,
relating to, chemistry; ~ COMBINATION;
(usu. pl.) substance obtained by or used
in ~ process; *heavy* ~*s*, bulk ~*s* used
in industry & agriculture (prop. only of
manufactured ~*s*). Hence or cogn. ~**LY²**
adv., **chĕm'ico**- comb. form. [16th c.
chimicall f. F *chimique* or mod. L *chi-
chymicus* (for *alchimicus*; see ALCHEMIC)
+-AL]

chemin de fer (shemăn' defēr'), n. A form
of baccarat. [F, = railway]

chemise (shĭmēz'), n. Woman's body
under-garment. [ME, f. OF f. LL *camisia*
shirt; earlier *kemes* dir. f. LL]

chemisĕtte' (shĕmĭz-), n. Bodice with
upper part like chemise; lace, muslin,
etc., filling up opening of dress below
throat. [F, dim. of prec.]

chĕm'ist (kĕ-), n. Person skilled in
chemistry; || dealer in medical drugs,
apothecary. [16th c. *chym*-, *chimist* f. F
-*iste* f. mod.L -*ista* for *alchimista* AL-
CHEMIST]

chĕm'istrў (kĕ-), n. Science of the elements & compounds & their laws of
combination & behaviour under various
conditions; *applied* or *practical* ~, art of
utilizing this knowledge; (IN)ORGANIC ~;
(fig.) mysterious change or process.
[prec., -RY]

chĕm'itype (kĕ-), n. (Process for getting) relief cast of engraving. [CHEMICAL
etc. +TYPE]

chĕmothĕ'rapў (kĕ-), n. Treatment of
disease by chemical means. [f. CHEM-
(ICAL) +-O- +-THERAPY]

chenille (shĭnēl'), n. Velvety cord used in
trimming dresses & furniture. [F, =
caterpillar f. L *canicula* small dog]

chèque (-k), *check**, n. Written order
to banker to pay named sum on drawer's
account to bearer or (order of) named
person; BLANK¹ ~; CROSS²*ed* ~; ~-*book*,
number of stamped & engraved forms
for drawing ~*s* bound & issued to customer. [var. of CHECK¹ formerly used of
counterfoils for checking forgery]

chĕ'quer¹ (-ker), **chĕck'er**, n. (Pl.) chess-
board as inn-sign; (often pl.) pattern
made of squares or with alternating
colours, whence **chĕ'quer**-WISE (-ker-)
adv.; || *Chequers*, Prime Minister's official
country house in Bucks. [ME, aphetic
f. EXCHEQUER]

chĕ'quer²(-ker), **chĕck'er**, v.t. Mark with
squares, esp. of alternate colours; variegate, break uniformity of, (often fig.,
esp. in p.p. as *chequered lot, fortunes*).
[f. prec.]

chĕ'rish, v.t. Foster, nurse, keep warm;
value, hold in one's heart, cling to, (esp.
hopes, feelings, etc.). [ME, f. OF *cherir*
(see -ISH²) f. *cher* f. L *carus* dear]

cheroot' (sh-), n. Cigar with both ends
open. [f. F -*route* f. Tamil *shuruṭṭu* roll]

chĕ'rrў, n. & a. Small stone-fruit; tree
bearing this (also ~-*tree*), its wood (also
~-*wood*); *cornelian* ~, cornel; *make two
bites at a* ~, boggle, be unenterprising or
formal; || ~-*bob*, two cherries with joined
stems (BOB¹); ~ *brandy*, dark-red liqueur
of brandy in which cherries have been
steeped; ~-*pie*, garden heliotrope; ~ *ripe*,
fruit hawker's cry; (adj.) red (~ *lips*,
ribbon; || ~-*breeches*, 11th Hussars). [ME
chiri(*e*), *chery*(*e*) f. ONF *cherise* (treated as
pl.; cf. PEASE) = OF *cerise*, f. Rom.
*ceresia f. L f. Gk *kerasos*; OE *ciris*, *cyrs*
f. WG dir. f. pop. L]

chĕr'sonese (k-; -ēs), n. Peninsula. [f. L
f. Gk *khersonēsos* (*khersos* dry, *nēsos*
island)]

chert, n. A flint-like quartz. [orig. 'unkn.]

che'rub, n. (pl. -s, -im). Angelic being; one of the second order of ninefold celestial hierarchy, gifted with knowledge as the first (seraphim) with love; (Art) winged (head of) child; beautiful or innocent child. Hence **cheru'b**IC (-ōō-) a. [OE, ME *cherubin*, ME & mod. *cherub*, f. F f. L f. Gk f. Heb. *k'rub* pl. *k'rubim*]

che'rv'il, n. Garden herb used in soup, salad, etc. [OE *cerfille*, = OHG *kervola* f. L f. Gk *khairephullon*]

Chesh'ire (-er), n. ~ *cheese*, made in ~; ~ *cat*, person with fixed grin. [place in England; prov. *grin like a ~ cat* unexpl.]

chess[1], n. Game for two players with thirty-two pieces or ~-*men* on ~-*board* chequered with sixty-four squares. [ME *ches* f. OF *esches* pl. of *eschec* CHECK[1]]

chess[2], n. One of the flooring planks of a pontoon bridge. [orig. unkn.]

chess'el, n. Cheese-making mould. [app. f. CHEESE[1]+WELL[1]]

chest, n. 1. Large strong box; box for sailor's belongings; *carpenter's, medicine,* etc., ~, holding special requisites; treasury, coffer, of institution (usu. fig. for the sums in it); case of some commodity, esp. *tea* (& so as variable measure); ~ *of drawers,* (esp.) frame with drawers for keeping clothes in bedroom. 2. Part of human or lower animal's body enclosed in ribs (*get thing off* one's ~ sl., say & be quit of it), whence -~'ED[2] a.; ~-*note, -voice,* of lowest speaking or singing register; ~-*protector,* flannel etc. worn on ~; ~-*trouble,* lung disease esp. chronic. Hence ~'Y[2] a. (colloq.), inclined to, marked by, symptomatic of, ~ disease. [OE *cest, cist,* OHG, ON *kista* f. L f. Gk *kistē*]

ches'terfield, n. Kind of overcoat, also of couch. [19th-c. Earl of C~]

chest'nut (-sn-), n. & a. Tree (also ~-*tree,* *Spanish* ~, or *sweet* ~) or its edible fruit; =~-*wood;* = HORSE[1]-~; = CASTOR[3]; stale anecdote; (of) ~-*colour,* deep reddish--brown; horse of this colour. [f. obs. *chesten* (f. OF *chastai(g)ne* f. L f. Gk *kastanea*) +NUT]

cheval'-glass (sh-; -ahs), n. Tall mirror swung on uprights. [f. F *cheval* horse, frame]

chevalier' (sh-), n. Member of certain orders of knighthood, & of French Legion of Honour etc.; (hist.) *The C*~ or *C*~ *de St George,* Old Pretender, *The Young C*~, Young Pretender; soldier cadet of old French noblesse; ~ *of industry* (oftener in F form ~ *d'industrie,* see Ap.), adventurer, swindler. [ME & AF *chevaler* (OF *-ier*) f. med. L *caballarius* f. L *caballus* horse, see -IER, -EER; mod. form f. F; cf. CAVALIER]

chevaux de frise (shevō'defrēz'), n. pl. Iron spikes set in timber etc. to repel cavalry etc. in war, or to guard palings in peace; natural protective line of hair in plants, eyelashes, etc. [F, lit. horses of Friesland, invented by 17th-c. Frisians who had no cavalry]

chevet (shevā'), n. Apse; group of apses. [F, f. L *capitium* (*caput* head)]

chev'iot, n. & a. (Wool cloth) got, made, from sheep of C~ hills in Northumberland.

chev'ron (sh-), n. Bent bar of inverted V shape, in escutcheons, as archit. ornament (~-*moulding,* consisting of series of these), & on sleeve of Service uniform indicating *rank (3 bars for sergeant, 2 for corporal, etc.), or ‖ length of service. [ME, f. OF *chevron* f. Rom. **capronem* (nom. **capro*) f. L *caper* goat]

chev'rotain, -tin, (sh-), n. Small musk deer. [F, dim. f. OF *chevrot* (*chèvre* goat)]

chev'y̆, chi̇(v)v'y̆, (usu. spelt -e- & pron. -i̇-), n., & v.t. & i. Chase (n. & v.), scamper (n. & v.); game of prisoners' base. [prob. f. ballad *Chevy Chase* (place-name)]

chew (-ōō), v.t. & i., & n. 1. Work about between teeth, grind to pulp or indent with repeated biting; (abs.) ~ tobacco, whence ~'ER[1] n.; turn over in mind; meditate *upon* or *over;* ~ *the cud,* bring back half-digested food into mouth for further chewing, (fig., usu. with *of* reflection, fancy, etc.) meditate; ~ *the rag* or *the fat* (sl.), reiterate an old grievance, grouse; ~-*ing-gum,* preparation of sweetened & flavoured gums (esp. CHICLE), used for prolonged ~ing. 2. n. Act of ~ing; quid of tobacco. [OE *cēowan,* OHG *kiuwan,* ON *tyggva, -ja* f. Gmc **keuw(j)an*]

Chian'ti (kiah-), n. Dry red Ital. wine. [~ in Tuscany, Italy]

chiaroscuro (kyȧroskoor'ō), n. & a. Treatment of light & shade in painting; light & shade effects in nature; variation, relief, handling of transitions, use of contrast, in literature etc.; (adj.) of ~; half-revealed. [It., see CLEAR; OBSCURE]

chias'mus (kiăz-), n. Inversion in second phrase of order followed in first (*I cannot dig, to beg I am ashamed*). Hence **chias'tio** (ki̇-) a.. [f. Gk *khiasmos* crosswise arrangement (KHI)]

chib'ol, n. (dial.). Spring onion with green stalk attached. [ME *chibol(l)e* f. OF **chiboule* (mod. *ciboule*), ult. f. L *c(a)epa* onion; see CHIVE]

chibouk', -que, (-ōōk), n. Long Turkish tobacco pipe. [f. Turk. *chibuk* tube]

chic (sh-), n. & a. Skill, effectiveness, style, stamp of superiority; (adj.) stylish, in the fashion. [F]

chicane' (sh-), v.t. & i., & n. Use chicanery; cheat (person) *into, out of,* etc.; (n.) chicanery; (holding of) hand without any trumps in bridge. [f. F *chicane(r)*]

chican'ery (sh-), n. Legal trickery, pettifogging; sophistry. [f. F *chicanerie* (prec., -ERY)]

chichi (shē'shē'), a. & n. Frilly (thing), fussy or effeminate (person). [F]

chick[1], n. Young bird before or after hatching; *the ~s*, children of a family (so *~'abĭdd'ў*, term of endearment of or to child); *~-weed*, small plant. [ME *chike* short for CHICKEN[1]]

chick[2], **chik**, n. (Anglo-Ind.). Screen-blind of finely-split bamboo laced with twine. [Hind. *chik*]

chick'ĕn, n. (pl. *~s*, *~*). Young bird, esp. of domestic fowl, flesh of this; youthful person (esp. in *no ~*); *Mother Carey's ~*, stormy petrel; *count* one's *~s before they are hatched*, be over-sanguine, precipitate; *~-breast(ed)*, (having) malformed projection of breast-bone; **~-feed*, food for poultry, (fig.) poor or trifling stuff; *~ hazard*, game at dice; *~-heart(ed)*, (with) no courage; *~-pox*, mild eruptive disease esp. of children. [OE *cicen*, cogn. w. COCK[1], cf. MDu. *kieken*, MLG *küken*, ON *kjúklingr*]

chick'ling, n. Common cultivated vetch. [16th c. *chicheling* dim. of ME & OF *chiche* ult. f. L *cicer*]

chick'-pea, n. Dwarf-pea. [16th c. *chich-pease* as prec. + PEASE]

chi'cle (-kl or -klē), n. Milky juice of the sapodilla, the basis of chewing-gum. [f. Mex. *tzictli*]

chic'orў, n. Blue-flowered plant cultivated for its salad leaves & its root; its root ground for use with or instead of coffee. [late ME *cicoree* f. OF *cichoree* (now *chico-*) f. med. L *cic(h)orea* f. L f. Gk *kikhorion* SUCCORY]

chide, v.t. & i. (literary; *chĭd*, *chidden* or *chid*). Make complaints, speak scoldingly, (esp. fig. of hounds, wind, etc.); scold, rebuke. [OE *cīdan*, of unkn. orig.]

chief[1], n. (Her.) upper third of shield; leader, ruler; head man of tribe, clan, etc., whence *~'ess*[1] n.; head of a department, highest official; *C~ of Staff*, senior staff officer of a commander; || *C~ of the Imperial General Staff*, senior military member of the Army Council; *in ~*, most of all, especially, (*for many reasons, & this one in ~*); *-in-~*, supreme, as *Commander, Colonel, -in-~*. Hence *~'DOM*, *~'SHIP*, nn., *~'LESS* a. [ME & OF *chef*, *chief* f. Rom. **capum* f. L *caput* head]

chief[2], a. & adv. (*-er*, *-est*, now rare). First by title (*C~ Justice* etc.); first in importance, influence, etc.; prominent, leading; (adv.) chiefly, especially, (*but ~ or ~est of all, forget not*). [orig. CHIEF[1] used in apposition]

chief'ly[1], a. Proper for a chief. [CHIEF[1] + -LY[1]]

chief'ly[2], adv. Above all; mainly but not exclusively. [CHIEF[2] + -LY[2]]

chief'tain (-tĭn), n. Military leader (poet.); captain of robbers; chief of Highland clan or uncivilized tribe. Hence *~CY*, *~ESS*[1], *~RY*, *~SHIP*, (-tĭn-), nn. [ME

chevetaine etc. (later assim. to CHIEF) f. OF, f. LL *capitaneus* CAPTAIN]

chiff'-chaff, n. Bird of warbler family. [imit.]

chiffon (see Ap.), n. (Usu. pl.) adornments of female dress; (sing.) thin gauze. [F, f. *chiffe* rag]

chiffonier' (sh-), n. Movable low cupboard with sideboard top. [F (prec. -IER)]

chĭgg'er (-g-), n. = CHIGOE.

chignon (see Ap.), n. Mass of hair on pad at back of head. [F, orig. = nape of neck]

chig'ōe, n. Tropical flea, burrowing into skin. [W.-Ind.]

Chihuahua (chĭwah'wah), n. Very small breed of dog, originating in Mexico. [Mex. state & city]

chil'blain, n. Itching sore on hand, foot, etc., from exposure to cold. Hence *~ED*[2] (-nd), *~Y*[2], aa. [CHILL + BLAIN]

child, n. (pl. *chil'dren*). Unborn or new-born human being (pronoun *it*, or *he*, *she*); boy or girl (*from a ~*, from childhood on); childish person; (sl.) *this ~*, I, me; son or-daughter (at any age) *of* (or with *my* etc.), offspring; descendant lit. or fig. or follower or adherent of (*~ of God, of the devil*; *~ren of Izaak Walton*, anglers; *fancy's ~*; *~ of nature*); result *of*; (in arch. form *childe*) youth of noble birth (*Childe Harold*, *Roland*); *with ~*, pregnant; *~'s-play*, easy task; BURN[1] *~ dreads fire*; *~'bed*, *~'birth*, parturition; *~ wife*, very young wife. Hence *~'LESS* a., *~'less-*NESS n. [OE *cild* cogn. w. Goth. *kilthei* womb]

Chil'dermas, n. Festival of Holy Innocents, 28th Dec. [OE *cildra* gen. pl. CHILD + MASS[1]]

child'hōod, n. Child's state; time from birth to puberty; *second ~*, dotage. [-HOOD]

child'ish, a. Of, proper to, a child; puerile, improper for a grown person. Hence *~LY*[2] adv., *~NESS* n. [-ISH[1]]

child'like, a. Having good qualities of child, as innocence, frankness, etc. [-LIKE]

child'lў, a. & adv. (poet.). Like a child. [mod. revival of obs. wd; -LY[1,2]]

chil'ĕ, ***chil'i**. Var. of CHILLI.

chil'iad (k-), n. A thousand; a thousand years. [f. LL f. Gk *khilias*, -AD(1)]

chil'iăsm, **chil'iăst**, (k-), nn. Doctrine of or belief in, believer in, the millennium. Hence **chiliăs'TIC** a. [f. mod. Gk *khilias-mos*, LL f. Gk *-astēs* (prec.)]

chill[1], n. Cold sensation, lowered temperature of body, feverish shivering, (*catch a ~*; also of special part as *liver-~*); unpleasant coldness of air, water, etc. (*take ~ off water* or *claret*, warm slightly); depressing influence (*cast a ~ over*); coldness of manner. [OE *cele* cogn. w. COLD; but the noun, after giving CHILL[2,3], was dormant 1400–1600, & revived as deriv. of CHILL[3]]

chill[2], a. Unpleasantly cold to feel;

feeling cold; unfeeling, unemotional, abstract. Hence ~'NESS n. [app. f. prec.]

chill³, v.t. & i. Make, become, cold; deaden, blast, with cold; depress, dispirit; harden (molten iron) by contact of cold iron; (colloq.) take the chill off (liquid); ~ed beef etc., beef etc. preserved at moderately low temperature in cold storage (as distinct from frozen meat). [app. f. CHILL¹]

chill'i, -ȳ, n. Dried pod of capsicum (as relish, or made into cayenne). [f. Sp. *chile*, *chili* f. Mex.]

chill'|ȳ¹, a. Rather cold to feel; feeling rather cold; sensitive to cold; not genial, cold-mannered. Hence ~ĭNESS n. [CHILL¹ + -Y²]

chil'ly² (-l-lĭ), adv. (rare). In cold manner (lit. & fig.). [CHILL² + -LY²]

chil(o)-, **cheil(o)-**, (k-), comb. form of Gk *kheilos* lip, in zool. terms as *chilopod* (having feet serving as jaws).

‖ **Chil'tern Hŭn'drĕds** (-z), n. pl. *Apply for*, *accept*, *the* ~, resign seat in House of Commons. [a Crown manor, administration of which, being titular office under Crown, requires the member to vacate his or her seat]

chime¹, n. Set of attuned bells; series of sounds given by this; harmony, melody, rhythm, sing-song; agreement, correspondence. [ME *chymbe* ult. f. L f. Gk *kumbalon* CYMBAL]

chime², v.i. & t. Make (bell) sound; ring chimes (of person or bells); ring chimes on (bells); show (hour) by chiming (also of hour, = sound); summon by bells *to*; repeat mechanically; be in rhyme, make to rhyme; be in agreement (*together*, *with*, or abs.); join *in*, express eager agreement. [as prec.]

chime³, **chimb**, (-m), n. Projecting rim at ends of cask. [ME *chimbe*; cf. MDu., MLG (G) *kimme*]

chimēr'a, -aer'a, (kī-), n. 1. Monster with lion's head, goat's body, & serpent's tail. 2. Bogy; thing of hybrid character; fanciful conception; whence **chimē'r-ICAL** a., **chimē'ricaLY²** adv., (kī-). [ME & OF *chimere* f. L f. Gk *khimaira* she-goat, chimera, (*khimaros* goat); later assim. to L form]

chimēre', n. Bishop's robe. [ME *chemer*, *chymer*, rel. to OF *chamarre*, F *simarre*; see CYMAR]

chim'ney, n. Flue carrying off smoke or steam of fire, furnace, engine, etc.; (also ~-stalk, -top) part of flue above roof; glass tube providing draught for lamp-flame; natural vent, e.g. of volcano; (Mountaineering) narrow cleft by which cliff may be climbed; ~-corner, warm seat within old-fashioned fire-place; ~-jack, rotating cowl; ~-piece, = MANTEL; ~-pot, earthenware or metal pipe added to ~-top (‖ ~-pot hat, tall silk hat); ~-stack, united group of ~-stalks; ‖ ~-

-stalk, see above, also = tall factory ~; ‖~-swallow, common swallow; ~-sweep man who sweeps ~s; ~-sweeper, = ~-sweep, also = jointed ~-cleaning brush. [ME *chimenee* etc. f. OF *cheminee* f. LL *caminata* (?sc. *camera*) fireplaced (chamber) f. L *caminus* oven f. Gk; see -Y⁴]

chimpänzee', n. African ape resembling man. [native name in Angola]

chin, n. Front of lower jaw; *up to the* ~, ~-deep, deeply immersed. Hence ~nED³ (-nd) a. [OE *cin*, OS, OHG *kinni*, ON *kinn*, Goth. *kinnus* f. Gmo *kinn-* cogn. w. L *gena*, Gk *genus*]

Chin'a, a., **chīn'a**, n. & a. 1. (C~). From China (C~ *crape*, C~ ASTER, etc.; C~ *orange*, common orange, orig. from China; *Chin'aman*, (derog. for) a Chinese; *China-town*, section of a town (esp. a seaport) in which the Chinese live as a colony). 2. (c~). (Made of) a fine semi-transparent earthenware, porcelain; things made of this; whence ~MAN'IA(c) nn.; ~-closet, for keeping or displaying one's ~; ~-clay, KAOLIN; ~man, (Cricket) left-handed bowler's off-break to right-handed batsman. [ult. orig. unkn.; not native name; found in Skr. about 1st c.]

chinchill'a, n. Small S.-Amer. rodent; its soft grey fur. [Sp., dim. of *chinche* bug f. L *cimex* -*icis* (from supposed smell)]

‖ **chin'-chin'**, int. of greeting & farewell (Anglo-Chin.; also as n. & vb). [Chin. *ts'ing ts'ing*]

‖ **chine¹**, n. Deep narrow ravine (now only in Isle of Wight & Hampshire). [OE *cinu* chink etc., = MDu. *kēne* chap f. root *ki*- burst open; cf. CHINK¹]

chine², n. Backbone; animal's backbone or part of it as joint; ridge, arête. [f. OF *eschine* f. OFrank. *skina* SHIN]

Chinee', n. (sl.). Chinese; *the heathen* ~, (joc., w. ref. to Bret Harte's *Truthful James*, for) the typical Chinese. [due to taking *Chinese* for pl.]

Chinēse' (-z), a. & n. (pl. the same). (Native, language) of China; ~ *lantern*, collapsible of paper used esp. in illuminating; ~ *white*, a pigment, white oxide of zinc. [*China* + -ESE]

chink¹, n. Crevice; long narrow opening, slit, peep-hole. [16th c., obsc. rel. to CHINE¹, which it replaced]

chink², n., & v.i. & t. 1. Sound as of glasses or coins striking together; (sl.) ready money. 2. vb. Make this sound; cause (coin etc.) to make it. [imit.]

Chink³, n. (sl.). A Chinese. [abbr.]

Chino-, comb. form of *China*, = SINO-. [-O-]

chinook', n. Warm dry wind which blows over the Rocky Mountains. [native name]

chintz, n. & a. (Of) cotton cloth fast-printed with particoloured pattern & usu. glazed. [earlier *chints* pl. f. Hind. *chint* f. Skr. *chitra*; for sing. use cf. BAIZE]

chip[1], n. Thin piece cut from wood or broken from stone etc.; thin slice of potato, fruit, etc.; (pl., colloq.) potato-~s fried (*fish & ~s*); wood split into strips for making hats etc. (~ *bonnet, basket*); *dry as a ~*, flavourless, uninteresting; ~ (scion) *of*, esp. ~ *of old block*, son resembling father; place in china etc. from which a ~ has been knocked off; (sl.) counter, piece of money; *have a ~ on* one's *shoulder*, be quick to take offence; ~*-shot* (Golf), short lofted approach-shot on to putting-green. [14th c., belongs to CHIP[2]; rel. obsc.]

chip[2], v.t. & i. (-pp-). Cut (wood), break stone, crockery, at surface or edge; shape thus; cut or break (piece etc.) *off, from*; be susceptible to breakage at edge; carve (inscription); crack (egg-shell; esp. of chickens); (colloq.) banter (a person); (colloq.)~ *in*, interrupt. [1407 in *chip-ax*, prob. repr. OE *cippian*; cf. EFris. *kippen* cut, MDu. *kippen* chip eggs, hatch; in mod. senses apprehended as dim. of CHOP[1], cf. *drip drop, tip top*]

chip[3], n., & v.t. (-pp-). Wrestling-trick; (vb) trip up. [18th c., north.; etym. obsc.; cf. Du. *kippen* ensnare]

chip'muck, -ünk, n. North-American squirrel. [Amer.-Ind.]

Chipp'endāle, n. A fine and solid style of furniture. [T. ~ (d. 1779), cabinet--maker]

chipp'ly, a. (sl.). Dry, uninteresting; parched & queasy after drunkenness etc.; irritable. Hence ~iNESS n. [CHIP[1]+-Y[2]]

Chips, n. (naut. sl.). Ship's carpenter. [pl. of CHIP[1], cf. BUTTONS]

chir(o)-, cheir(o)-, (kīr-), comb. form of Gk *kheir* hand, as *chirō͝o'*RAPHY handwriting, *chir'*OMANCY palmistry.

chir'ograph (kīr-; -ahf), n. Document of various kinds formally written or signed. [f. F *chirographe* f. L f. Gk *kheirographon* (prec., -GRAPH)]

chirŏp'odist, chirŏp'odỹ, (kīr-), nn. Treater, treatment, of feet, toe-nails, corns, bunions, etc. [1785, app. f. CHIRO-, Gk *pous podos* foot, -IST(3)]

chiroprāc't|ic (kīr-), n. Manipulation of spinal column as method of curing disease. Hence ~OR n., one who practises~ic. [f. CHIRO- + Gk *praktikos* (*prassō* do, see -IC)]

chīrp, v.i. & t., & n. (Make) short sharp note (as) of small bird; utter (song), express (joy etc.); thus; talk merrily; speak feebly. [imit.; late ME modification of earlier *chirk, chirt*]

chīrp'|ỹ, a. Lively, cheerful. Hence ~iNESS n. [prec., -Y[2]]

chīrr, v.i., & n. (Make) prolonged trilling sound (as) of grasshopper. [imit.]

chi'rrup, v.i., & n. (Make) series of chirps, twittering; (make) imitative chirping to baby etc. [extension of CHIRP]

chis'el (-zl), n., & v.t. (-ll-). (Cut, shape, with) tool with square bevelled end for shaping wood, stone, or metal (*cold ~*, all of steel or iron for trimming cold iron; ~*led features* etc., clear-cut); *the ~*, sculptor's ~, (art of) sculpture; (sl.) defraud, unfair treatment. [ME, f. ONF *chisel*, OF *cisel*, f. Rom. **cisellum* (L *caedere caes-* cut, see -LE(2))]

chit[1], n. Young child; young, small, or slender woman (depreciatingly, esp. ~ *of a girl*). [14th c. = whelp, cub, kitten; etym. unkn., but cf. Ches. dial. *chit*, Sc. *cheet* puss, *chilly, cheety* cat]

chit[2], **chitt'ỹ,** n. (orig. Anglo-Ind.). Note or written paper, esp. character given to servant; note of sum owed for drink etc.; ~*-system* (of giving vouchers in payment instead of cash down). [f. Hind. *chiṭṭhī* f. Skr. *chitra* mark]

chit'al (-ĕt-), n. The Indian spotted deer. [Hind.]

chit'-chăt', n. Light conversation; subjects of it, gossip. [redupl. of CHAT[1]]

chit'in (kī-), n. Substance forming horny cover of beetles & crustaceans. Hence ~OUS a. [f. F *chitine* irreg. f. Gk *khitōn* tunic + -IN]

chitt'ack, n. Indian weight corresponding to the ounce. [Bengali *chhaṭāk*]

chitt'erling, n. (usu. pl.). Smaller intestines of beasts, esp. as cooked for food. [13th c., of unkn. orig.]

chitt'ỹ. See CHIT[2].

chiv'alrous, (poet. etc.) chiv'alric (also -āl[2]-), (see foll.), a. Of, as of, the Age of Chivalry; of, as of, the ideal knight, gallant, honourable, courteous, disinterested; quixotic. Hence **chiv'alrously**[2] adv. [ME, f. OF *chevalerous* (CHEVALIER, -OUS); *chivalric* f. foll. + -IC]

chiv'alrỹ (formerly ch-; now usu. sh-, as though a recent F importation), n. Horsemen, cavalry, (arch.); gallant gentlemen; knightly skill (arch.); medieval knightly system with its religious, moral, & social code; ideal knight's characteristics; devotion to service of women; inclination to defend weaker party; *flower of ~*, pattern knight, élite of nation's soldiers. [ME & OF *chi-, chevalerie* etc. f. med. L *caballerius* for LL *caballarius* horseman (CAVALIER, -ERY)]

chive, cive (s-), n. Small herb allied to onion & leek. [ME *cive, chive* f. OF *cive*, f. L *cepa*; see CHIBOL]

chiv(v)'ỹ. See CHEVY.

chlor-[1,2]. = CHLORO-[1,2], used before vowel.

chlōr'al (kl-), n. ~ *hydrate* or ~, a hypnotic & anaesthetic. Hence ~ISM(5) n., ~IZE(5) v.t. [F *chloral* f. CHLOR(INE) + AL(COHOL)]

chlōr'ide (kl-), n. (Chem.) compound of chlorine (-IDE); (pop.) kinds of bleaching agent, as ~ *of lime, soda, potash.* [CHLOR-[2], -IDE]

chlōr'in|āte (kl-), v.t. Impregnate with chlorine. Hence ~A'TION n., treatment with chlorine (esp. in the extraction of gold from certain ores). [CHLORINE + -ATE[3]]

chlŏr'ĭne (kl-), n. (chem.). Non-metallic element, a yellowish-green heavy ill--smelling gas. [f. Gk *khlōros* green + -INE[5]]

chlŏro-[1], **chlŏr-**, comb. form in bot. & mineral. terms of Gk *khlōros* green.

chlŏro-[2], **chlŏr-**, comb. form in chem. terms of CHLORINE etc. Hence **chlŏr'ATE**[1] (3) n., **chlŏr'IC**(2), **chlŏr'OUS** (chem.) aa., (kl-).

chlŏr'odyne (kl-), n. Patent medicine, narcotic & anodyne. [foll. + Gk *odunē* pain]

chlŏr'ofŏrm (kl-), n., & v.t. 1. Anaesthetic, thin colourless liquid whose inhaled vapour produces insensibility. 2. v.t. Treat (person) with, render insensible by, ~, whence ~IST (1) n.; soak (thing) in ~. [f. F *chloroforme* f. CHLORO-[2] + *form(yl)* see FORMIC]

chlŏromȳ'cĕtĭn (kl-), n. An antibiotic used in some diseases, e.g. typhus. [f. CHLORO-[2], Gk *mukēs -ētos* fungus, -IN]

chlŏr'ophȳll (kl-), n. Colouring-matter of green parts of plants. [F CHLORO[1](*phylle* f. Gk *phullon* leaf)]

chlŏr|ōs'ĭs (kl-), n. (Hist.) green sickness, anaemic disease of young women, with greenish complexion; (Bot.) blanching of green parts, or turning green of petals etc. Hence ~OT'IC a. [CHLOR-[1], -OSIS]

chŏck[1], n. Block of wood, esp. wedge for stopping motion of cask or wheel, also in various senses on ship esp. of wedges supporting boat on deck; (Turning; earlier form of) CHUCK[4]. [w. CHUCK[4] prob. f. ONF *choque* etc. repr. by mod. Pic. *choke*, Norm. *chouque* (- F *souche*)]

chŏck[2], v.t., & adv. Make fast with chocks; place (boat) on chocks; ~ *up*, wedge in tightly, encumber (room etc.) with furniture etc.; (adv.) closely, tightly, close up; ~-*a-block*, jammed together, crammed *with*. chock-full *of* (orig. naut., of two blocks brought close together in a tackle); ~-*full*, stuffed. [f. prec.; the var. *choke-full* for ~-*full* is prob. an etym. guess & misrepresents pronunc.]

chŏc'olate, n. & a. (Cake) of cacao-seed paste; drink of this in hot milk or water; dark brown (n. & a.); ~ *cream*, sweetmeat of ~ enclosing sweet paste. [f. F *chocolat* or Sp. -*ate* f. Mex. *chocolatl* (not f. *cacao* or *cocoa*)]

Chŏc'taw, n. 1. (Member of) N.-Amer. Indian tribe, now in Oklahoma. 2. (*c*~; skating). Step from either edge to edge on other foot in opposite direction. [native; cf. MOHAWK]

choice[1], n. Choosing, selection, (*make* ~ *of*, select; *take* one's ~, decide between possibilities; *the girl of* one's ~; *for* ~, by preference, if one must select); power, right, faculty, of choosing (*at* ~, at pleasure; *have* one's ~; *have no* ~, have no alternative, not care which; *Hobson's* ~, to take or leave the one offer); élite, flower, *of*; variety to choose from; thing

or person chosen; alternative (*have no* ~ *but*). [ME *chois* f. OF f. *choisir* f. Rom. **causire* f. Gmc **kausjan* choose]

choice[2], a. Of picked quality, exquisite; carefully chosen, appropriate. Hence ~'LY[2] (-sl-) adv., ~'NESS (-sn-) n. [f. prec.]

choir (kwīr), **quīre** (arch.), n., & v.t. & i. 1. Band of singers performing or leading in musical parts of church service; chancel of cathedral, minster, or large church; choral society, company of singers (also of birds, angels, etc.); band of dancers; ~-*organ* (corruption of *chair*-), softest of three parts (*great*, *swell*, ~, *organ*) making up large compound organ, with lowest of three keyboards; ~ *school*, school maintained by a cathedral or church for ~boys & other pupils. 2. vb. Sing in chorus (intr., or with *strain*, *hymn*, etc., as obj.). [ME *quer(e)* f. OF *cuer* (mod. *choeur*) f. L CHORUS. The sp. *choir* after F-L; for pr. *quire* cf. ME *frere* FRIAR]

chōke[1], v.t. & i., & n. Stop breath of, suffocate, temporarily or finally, by squeezing throat from without, blocking it up within, or (of water, smoke, etc.) being unbreathable; (fig., of emotion) paralyse (~-*pear*, fact, reproof, etc., hard to swallow); suffer temporary stoppage of breath, become speechless from anger etc., (n., this condition); smother, stifle, kill, (plant, fire, etc.) by deprivation of light, air, etc.; suppress (feelings); block up wholly or partly (tube by narrowing part of it; as n., the narrowed part, whence ~-*bore*, of gun with bore narrowing towards muzzle; also of channel with sand, stones, etc., *stones* ~ or ~ *up channel*, *channel* ~*s*), fill chock-full; ~ *down*, swallow (food), conceal (emotion), with difficulty; ~ *off*, make (person) relinquish an attempt; ~-*damp*, carbonic acid gas in mines, wells, etc.; *choking coil* (Electr.), (also ~) inductance coil used to prevent the passage of an alternating current or to alter its phase. [ME *cheke*, *choke* (= *acheke*, *achoke*), f. late OE (once) *ācēocian*, f. *cēace*, *cēce* CHEEK]

chōke[2], n. Centre part of artichoke. [prob. confusion of ending w. prec.]

chōk'er, n. In vbl senses; esp. clerical or other stand-up collar. [-ER[1]]

chōk'ra, n. (Anglo-Ind.). Boy (esp. one employed as domestic servant). [Hind. *chhokra*]

‖ **chōk'ȳ**, n. (orig. Anglo-Ind., sl.). Prison, lock-up. [Hind. *chaukī* shed]

chŏl(ē)- (k-), comb. form in med. & chem. wds repr. Gk *kholē* gall, bile.

chol'er (kŏ-), n. (Hist.) one of the four HUMOURS, bile; (poet., arch.) anger, irascibility. [ME & OF *colre*, *colere* bile, anger f. L f. Gk *kholera* diarrhoea, in LL = bile, anger (Gk *kholē* bile)]

chol'era (kŏ-), n. (Also *English*, *bilious*, *summer*, ~, or in L ~ *nostras* = of our country) bilious summer & autumn disorder with diarrhoea & vomiting; (also

Asian, epidemic, malignant, ~) non-
-bilious often fatal disease endemic in
India & epidemic in Europe; *chicken ~*,
infectious disease of fowls; *~-belt*,
flannel or silk waistband worn as
preventive. Hence **cholerā′ic** (kŏ-) a.
[ME, f. L f. Gk *kholera*; see prec.]

chol′eric (kŏ-), a. Irascible; angry. [ME
colerik(e) etc. f. OF f. L f. Gk *kholerikos*
(see CHOLER, -IC)]

chol′erine (kŏ-; *also* -ēn), n. Summer
cholera; diarrhoea often prevalent at
same time as Asian cholera. [F (-é-), f.
choléra CHOLERA]

chol′iamb (kŏ-), n. = SCAZON. Hence
~IC (-ăm²) a. [f. LL f. Gk *khōliambos*
(*khōlos* lame, *iambos* IAMBUS)]

chondri-, -o-, (kŏ-), comb. form of Gk
khondros, in Med. & Physiol.=cartilage-.

chōose (-z), v.t. & i. (*chōse, chōsen*, pr.
-z-). Select out of greater number;
(Theol., esp. in p.p.) destine to be saved
(*the chosen people, race*, Jews); decide (*to
do one thing rather than another*); think
fit, be determined, *to do*; make choice
between; *cannot ~ but*, must, have to,
(arch.); (with compl.) select as (*was chosen
king*); *pick & ~*, select carefully, be
fastidious; *nothing etc. to ~ between them*,
of things nearly equal. Hence **chōos′ER¹**
(-z-) n., **chōos′(e)Y²** (-z-) a. (colloq.),
fastidious. [OE *cēosan*, OS, OHG *kiosan*,
ON *kjósa*, Goth *kiusan*, f. Gmc **keusan*]

chŏp¹, v.t. & i. (-pp-). Cut by a blow, usu.
with axe (*~ up, ~ into small pieces*,
mince; often *~ off, away, down*); deliver
such blow *at*; make one's way by such
blows *through*; mince (esp. in p.p.); (fig.)
cut (words etc.) short or into distinct
parts; *~ in* (colloq.), intervene in talk; *~
back*, reverse one's direction suddenly,
double; (of strata) *~ up, out*, come to surface. [ME, var. of CHAP¹, etym. unkn.; in
sense approx. = MDu., LG *kappen* lop
off, sever]

chŏp², n. Cutting stroke with axe etc.;
thick slice of meat, esp. mutton or pork,
usu. including rib (*~-house*, cheap restaurant); broken surface of water usu. due
to action of wind against tide, so ~p′ȳ¹
[-Y²] a. [f. prec.]

chŏp³. See CHAP². [16th c.; var. of CHAP²;
rel. & etym. obsc.]

chŏp⁴, v.t. & i. (-pp-), & n. ~ & change
(emphatic for *change*, usu. intr.), vacillate,
be inconstant, (n., *~s & changes*, variations); *~ round, about*, (esp. of wind)
change direction suddenly; *~ logic*,
bandy arguments. Hence ~p′ȳ² [-Y²]
a. [vb 1391 in *choppe-church*; etym.
obsc.]

‖ **chŏp⁵**, n. (India, China) seal, licence,
passport, permit; (China) trade-mark, a
brand of goods; (Anglo-Ind. & colloq.)
first, second, -~, first, second, -class. [f.
Hind. *chhāp* stamp]

chŏp′-chŏp′, adv. & int. (pidgin Eng.).
Quick, quickly. [f. Chin. *k'wai-k'wai*]

chŏpp′er, n. One who chops; large-
-bladed short axe; butcher's cleaver.
[CHOP¹+-ER¹]

chŏp′stick, n. Small slip of ivory etc.
of which two held in one hand are used
by Chinese as fork. [pidgin Eng. (*chop*
= quick +STICK) equivalent of Chin.
k'wai-tsze nimble ones]

chŏp-sū′ey, n. Dish of fried or stewed
meat or chicken flavoured with sesame
oil & served with rice, onions, etc. (in
Chinese restaurant). [Chin., =mixed bits]

chŏr′al¹ (k-), a. Of, sung by, choir (*~
service*, with canticles, anthems, etc., so
sung; *full ~ service*, with versicles &
responses also sung); of, with, chorus.
Hence~LY² adv. [f. F, or med. L *choralis*
(CHORUS, -AL)]

choral(e)²(korahl′), n. (Metrical hymn to)
simple tune usu. sung in unison, orig.
in German reformed church. [f. G
choral(gesang)]

chŏr′alist (k-), n. Chorus singer. [CHORAL¹,
-IST]

chŏrd¹ (k-), n. String of harp etc. (poet.;
also fig., as *touch the right ~*, appeal skilfully to emotion); (Anat.) obs. spelling of CORD, as *vocal ~, spinal ~*,
(Math.) straight line joining ends of arc.
[16th-c. refash. of CORD¹ after L *chorda*]

chŏrd² (k-), n. (Mus.) group of notes
sounded together, combined according to
some harmonic system (*common ~*, any
note with its major or minor third, perfect
fifth, & octave; *break* or *spread ~*, play
its notes successively); harmonious combination of colours. [orig. *cord* for
ACCORD² later altered after CHORD¹]

chŏrd′al (k-), a. Of, like, etc., CHORD¹,²
[-AL]

chōre, n. Odd job, (pl.) household tasks.
[U.S. form of CHAR²]

chorē′a (k-), n. St Vitus's dance. [L]

chŏr′ee (k-), n. = TROCHEE. [f. L f. Gk
khoreios]

cho′regraph etc. See CHOREOGRAPH etc.

chorē′ic (k-), a. Of, having, chorea; of,
marked by, chorees. [-IC]

chŏ′reograph (kŏ-; -ahf), n. Designer of
ballet. So **choreŏg′RAPHER, choreŏg-
RAPHY,** nn., **choreoGRAPH′IC** a., (kŏ-). [f.
Gk *khoreia* dancing (*khoros* dancing-
-company)+-GRAPH]

chori- (kŏ-), bef. a vowel **choris-** (kŏ-),
f. Gk *khōri(s)* asunder, apart, used in bot.
terms etc.

cho′riamb, choriăm′bus (kŏ-), n. Metrical foot (– ∪ ∪ –). Hence **choriăm′bic**
(kŏ-) a. [f. LL f. Gk *khoriambos* (CHOREE,
IAMB)]

chŏr′ic (k-), a. Of, like, chorus in Greek
play. [f. LL f. Gk *khorikos* (CHORUS, -IC)]

chŏr′ion (k-), n. Outer membrane of
foetus. [f. Gk *khōrion*]

cho′rister (kŏ-), n. Member of choir, esp.
choir-boy (also fig. of angels, birds).
[ME *querestre, -istre* prob. f. AF **cueristre*
(= OF *-iste*) f. *cuer* CHOIR; 16th c. refash.

after (now obs.) *chorist* (F *choriste*, med. L *chorista*)]

chorog′raphy (kŏ-). n. Describing, description, of districts (more limited than *geography*, less than *topography*). Hence or cogn. **chorŏg′rapher** n., **choro-GRAPH′IC(AL)** aa., **chorogrăph′ical**LY[2] adv., (kŏ-). [f. F *-graphie* or L *-graphia* f. Gk (Gk *khōra* land, -GRAPHY)]

chŏr′oid (k-), a. & n. Like chorion in shape or vascularity, esp. ~ *coat* (or ~ as noun), membrane lining eyeball. [f. Gk *khoreidēs* for *khorio-* (CHORION, -OID)]

chorŏl′ogy (kŏ-), n. Local distribution of species etc. Hence **chorolŏg′ical** a. [f. Gk *khōra* land + -LOGY]

chŏr′tle, v.i., & n. (Utter) loud chuckle. [portmanteau wd (Lewis Carroll) app. f. *chuckle* + *snort*]

chŏr′us (k-), n., & v.t. & i. 1. (Gk Ant.) band of dancers & singers in religious ceremonies & dramatic performances (also representing interested spectators in play; so in some Eng. plays); (one of) their utterances. 2. Personage speaking prologue & commenting on action in Elizabethan plays. 3. Band of singers, choir; thing sung by many at once; any simultaneous utterance of many (*in* ~, all speaking etc. together). 4. (Mus.) composition in several (oftenest four) parts each sung by several voices; refrain of song in which audience joins. 5. vb. Sing, speak, say, in ~. [L, f. Gk *khoros*]

chose jugée (see Ap.), n. Thing it is idle to discuss, as already settled. [F]

chose(n). See CHOOSE.

chŏt′a haz(i)ri (hahz′rī), n. (Anglo-Ind.). Light early breakfast. [Hind. (*chh-*), = little breakfast]

chou (shōō), n. Rosette or ornamental knot of ribbon, chiffon, etc., on woman's hat or dress. [F, f. L *caulis* cabbage]

chough (chŭf), n. Red-legged crow. [ME *choghe* unexpl.; w. forms *c(h)owe* etc. cf. MDu. *kauwe*, ONF *cauwe*, OF *choue*]

chouse, v.t., & n.,(colloq.). Swindle, trick. [usu. supposed to be the same wd as Turk. *chiaus* official messenger, in allusion to one of these who is alleged to have defrauded Turkish merchants in England 1609, but there is some doubt about the account]

chow, n. Dog of a Chinese breed; (sl.) food. [pidgin Eng.]

chow⸗chow, n. Chinese preserve of orange-peel, ginger, etc. [pidgin Eng.]

chow′der, n. Newfoundland & New England dish, stew of fresh fish or clams with bacon, onions, biscuit, etc. [app. orig. in Brittany, in phr. *faire la chaudière* supply a pot etc. for cooking a stew of fish etc.]

chrēmatis′t|ic (k-), a.(derog.). Of money-making, economic. Hence -ICS n. [f. Gk *khrēmatistikos* of money-making]

chrēstŏm′athy (k-), n. Collection of choice passages. [f. F -*mathie* or Gk

khrēstomatheia f. *khrēstos* useful + -*matheia* learning]

chri′sm (k-), n. Consecrated oil, unguent, anointing, esp. in sacred rites. [(a) OE *crisma*, ME *crisme*, f. LL *c(h)risma* f. Gk *khrisma* unction, later *chrism(e)* after the L sp.; (b) ME *creme* f. OF *cresme*, mod. F *chrême* (f. same source), became obs. in 17th c.; see CREAM[1]]

chris′om (k-), n. (hist.). (In full, ~-*cloth*, -*robe*, etc.) child's white robe at baptism, used as shroud if it died within a month; ~-*child*, in its first month. [a different., pop. pr. of CHRISM]

Christ (k-), n. Messiah or Lord's anointed of Jewish prophecy; (title, now treated as name given to) Jesus as fulfilling this; divine ruler, saviour, inspirer, (esp. *the* or *a* ~); *the* ~-*child*, ~ as a child. Hence ~′HOOD n., ~′LESS, ~′LIKE, ~′LY[1], aa., ~′léssNESS, ~′likeNESS (-k-), nn., ~′WARD(S) adv. [OE *crist* = OS, OHG *Krist*, Goth. *Xristus* f. L *Christus* f. Gk *khristos* anointed one(*khriō* anoint) transl. of Heb.; see MESSIAH]

Christ-cross-row, criss-, (krĭs⸗krawsrō), n. (arch.). The alphabet. [*Christ's cross*, a cross before alphabet in horn-books, + ROW (of letters)]

christen (krĭ′sn), v.t. & i. Admit as Christian by baptism; administer baptism; give name to (person at baptism, or as nickname; ~ *him*, ~ *him John*; also ships, bells, etc., with analogous ceremony). [OE *cristnian* (ME *crist(n)en*) make Christian f. OE *cristen* adj. Christian, f. WG **cristin* f. L *Christianus* CHRISTIAN]

Christendom (krĭ′sn-), n. Christians; Christian countries. [OE *cristendom* f. *cristen* adj., see prec., + -DOM]

Christian (krĭs′tyan), a. & n. (Person) believing in, professing, or belonging to, the religion of Christ (also as adj. of communities); of Christ or his religion; (person) showing character consistent with Christ's teaching, of genuine piety, Christlike, (also as adj. of conduct, feelings, communities, etc.); human (person) as opposed to *brute, brutal*; (sl.) civilized, decent, (person); ~ *burial* (with the ceremonies of the church); ~ *name*, given (as) at baptism, personal name (cf. SURNAME); ~ *era*, reckoned from birth of Christ; ~ *Science, Scientist*, (adherent of) a system of combating disease etc. without medical treatment by mental effect of patient's ~ faith. Hence or cogn. ~IZE (2, 3) v.i. & t., ~īzA′TION n., ~LIKE a., ~LY[1, 2] a. & adv. [16th c., f. L *Christianus* (CHRIST, -IAN), replacing earlier *cristen* adj.; see CHRISTEN]

Christian′ia (k-; -ahn-), n. A turn in skiing, in which the skis are kept parallel (abbr. **Chris′tie**). [~ in Norway (now Oslo)]

Christiăn′ity (k-), n. The Christian faith,

doctrines of Christ & his apostles; a Christian religious system; being a Christian, Christian quality or character. [ME *cristianite* replacing (after LL *christianitas*) earlier *cristiente, cristente* f. OF *crestiente* f. *crestien* CHRISTIAN; see -TY]

Christie's (krĭs'tĭz), n. A sale-room in London esp. for art sales.

Christmas (krĭs'm-), n. (abbr. *Xmas*). (Also ~-*day*) festival of Christ's birth, 25th Dec., devoted esp. to family reunion & merrymaking, & a quarter-day (*Father* ~, personification of family festivity); (also ~-*tide*) week or more beginning 24th Dec. (~ *eve*); (attrib.) appropriate to ~, as ~ *book, card* (of greeting by post), *number* (of magazine), *present, pudding*; ‖ ~-*box* (cf. BOXING-DAY), money given at ~ to postman etc. in general acknowledgement of indefinite or continuous services; ~-*tree*, evergreen tree set up in room or in the open & hung with candles, presents, etc.; ~ *rose*, white-flowered hellebore blooming Dec.–Feb. Hence ~Y[2] a. [late OE *Cristes mæsse* (MASS[1])]

Christo- (k-), comb. form of L *Christus* or Gk *Khristos* CHRIST, as ~*phany* (-ŏf[i]-), manifestation of Christ. Hence **Christŏ-L'ATRY**, **Christŏman'IAC** (-mā-), **Christŏ-L'OGY**, **Christŏl'OGIST**, nn., **Christo-LO'GICAL** a.

Chris'tў min'strels (k-; -z), n. pl. Negro-song troupe with blacked faces. [E. P. *Christy* (d. 1862), originator]

chrŏm'āte (k-), n. (chem.). A salt of chromic acid. [-ATE[1] (3)]

chromăt'ic (k-), a. **1.** Of. produced by, full of bright, colour (~ *printing*, from blocks inked with various colours; ~*s*, science of colour). **2.** (mus.). Of, having, notes not included in diatonic scale; ~ *scale*, proceeding by semitones; ~ *semitone*, interval between note & its flat or sharp. Hence **chromăt'ICALLY** adv. [f. L *chromaticus* or Gk *khrōmatikos* (*khrōma* -*atos* colour, -IC)]

chrŏm'atin (k-), n. (biol.). Tissue that can be stained. [as CHROMATO- + -IN]

chrŏm'ato-, chrŏm'o-, (k-), comb. forms of Gk *khrōma* -*atos* colour, as in *chromatop'sy*, abnormally coloured vision, *chromophotograph(y)*, photograph(y) in the natural colours, *chrom'osphere*, red gaseous envelope of sun.

chrŏm'atrōpe (k-), n. Lantern slide of two circular discs, one rotating in front of other, giving kaleidoscopic movement of colours. [irreg. f. prec. + Gk -*tropos* (*trepō* turn)]

chrōme (k-), n. (Also ~ *yellow*) yellow pigment & colour got from chromate of lead; ~ *green, orange, red*, pigments from other compounds of chromium. [F, orig. name of *chromium*, f. Gk *khrōma* colour]

chrŏm'ic (k-), a. Of chromium. [prec. + -IC]

chrŏm'ium (k-), n. (chem.). Metallic ele-

ment. Hence **chrŏm'ATE[1]**(3) n. [CHROME + -IUM]

chromo-[1], comb. form of prec.

chromo-[2]. See CHROMATO-.

chrŏm'ograph (k-; -ahf), n., & v.t. (Reproduce with) gelatine copying-apparatus in which aniline dye is used for ink. [CHROMO-[2], -GRAPH]

chrŏmolith'ograph (-ahf), **chrŏm'ō** (pl. -*os*), (k-), n. Picture printed in colours from stone. So **chrŏmolithŏg'RAPHER**, **chrŏmolithŏg'RAPHY**, nn., **chrŏm'olithoGRAPH'IC** a. [CHROMO-[2] + LITHOGRAPH]

chrŏm'osōme (k-), n. (biol.). Rod-like or thread-like structure occurring in the nucleus of animal and plant cells, carrying genetic material. [f. G *chromosom* (CHROMO- + Gk *sōma* body)]

chrŏn'ic (k-), a. Lingering, lasting, inveterate, (of disease, cf. ACUTE; ~ *invalid*, with ~ complaint; also of other states as ~ *doubt, rebellion*); ‖ (vulg.) bad, intense, severe. Hence **chrŏn'ICALLY** adv., **chrŏni'ciTY** n. [f. F *chronique* f. L *chronicus* (in LL of disease) f. Gk *khronikos* (*khronos* time, -IC)]

chrŏn'icle (k-), n., & v.t. (Enter, relate, in a) continuous register of events in order of time; *Chronicles*, two books of O.T.; narrative, account; C~, newspaper name. Hence **chrŏn'iclER[1]** n. [ME *cronikle* f. AF -*icle* var. of OF *cronique* f. LL *chronica* sing. f. L f. Gk *khronika* neut. pl. (prec.); *ch*- after L sp.]

chronique scandaleuse (see Ap.), n. Body of scandalous gossip current at any time & place. [F]

chrŏn'ogrăm (k-), n. Phrase etc. of which the Roman-numeral letters added give a date, as LorD haVe MerCIe Vpon Vs = 50 + 500 + 5 + 1000 + 100 + 1 + 5 + 5 = 1666. Hence **chrŏnogrammăt'IC** a. [f. Gk *khronos* time + -GRAM; -*matic* after Gk *grammatikos* adj. f. *gramma*]

chrŏn'ograph (k-; -ahf), n. Instrument recording time with extreme accuracy; stop-watch. Hence **chrŏnoGRAPH'IC** a. [as prec. + rGRAPH]

chron|ŏl'ogў (k-), n. Science of computing dates; arrangements of events with dates, table or treatise displaying this. Hence or cogn. ~**ŏl'OGER**, ~**ŏl'OGIST**, nn., **chrŏnolo'GICAL** a., **chrŏnolŏ'gicalLY[2]** adv., ~**ŏl'ogIZE**(3) v.t. [as prec. + -LOGY]

chronŏm'éter (k-), n. Time-measuring instrument, esp. one with complete provision against disturbance by temperature, used for navigation by astronomical sights at sea. [as prec. + -METER]

chronŏm'étrў (k-), n. Scientific time-measurement. So **chrŏnoMET'RIC(AL)** aa., **chrŏnomĕt'ricalLY[2]** adv. [as prec. + -METRY]

chrŏn'oscōpe (k-), n. Apparatus measuring velocity of projectiles. [as prec. + -SCOPE]

chrўs- (k-), comb. form of Gk *khrusos* gold, = yellow in chem. & mineral. wds, of gold, golden, yellow, etc., in general wds.

chrỹs'alĭs, -ĭd, (k-), n. (pl. -ĭscs, -ĭds, chrysăl'ĭdēs). Form taken by insect in the torpid stage of passive development between larva (caterpillar etc.) & imago (butterfly etc.); case then enclosing it; (fig.) preparatory or transition state. [f. L f. Gk khrusallis -idos (khrusos gold)]

chrỹsăn'thĕmum (k-), n. (Bot.) genus including corn marigold; (Gardening) cultivated varieties of this brought from Japan & blooming from Sept. to Dec.; land of the ~, Japan. [f. L f. Gk khrusanthemon (CHRYS-, anthemon flower)]

chrỹsĕlĕphăn'tine (k-), a. Overlaid with gold & ivory as by ancient Greek sculptors. [f. Gk khruselephantinos (CHRYS-, ELEPHANT, -INE²)]

chrỹso- (k-). = CHRYS-.

chrỹsobĕ'rỹl (k-), n. Yellowish-green gem. [f. L f. Gk khrusobērullos (CHRYSO-, BERYL)]

chrỹs'olīte (k-), n. (Formerly) green gem of various kinds; (now) olivine. [ME & OF crisolite f. (med. L cri-) L f. Gk khrusolithos (CHRYSO-, lithos stone)]

chrỹs'oprāse (k-; -z), n. (N.T.) prob. a golden-green variety of beryl; (now) apple-green variety of chalcedony. [ME crisopace, -pase f. OF -pace f. L chrysopassus var. of L f. Gk khrusoprasos (CHRYSO-, prason leek)]

chŭb, n. Thick coarse-fleshed river fish of the carp family, dusky green above. [late ME chubbe, of unkn. orig.]

chŭbb'|ỹ, a. Round-faced, plump. Hence ~ĭNEES n. [CHUB + -Y²]

chŭck¹, int., n., & v.i. (Make) call of fowl or person calling fowls or urging horse. [imit.]

chŭck², n. Term of endearment. Hence ~Y³ n. [prob. var. of CHICK]

chŭck³, v.t., & n. Jerk under the chin (n. & v.); fling, throw, (n. & v.) with contempt, carelessness, ease, (the ~, sl., dismissal, as give one the ~); ~ away, waste, lose (chance etc.); ~ up the sponge, give up contest or attempt; ~ up, abandon in disgust; ~ out, expel (troublesome person) from meeting, music-hall, etc., whence ||~ER¹-out n.; (sl.) ~ it, cease; ~-farthing, kind of quoit game with coins, also pitch and toss. [in 16th c. chock, of uncert. orig.; perh. f. F choquer to knock]

chŭck⁴, n., & v.t. Contrivance in lathe & the like for holding work to be operated on; (vb) fix (wood etc.) to this. [var. of CHOCK¹]

chŭck⁵, n. (sl.). Food, grub; hard ~ (Naut.), ship's biscuit; *~-wagon, provision-cart accompanying pioneers etc. [orig. unkn.]

chŭc'kle, v.i., & n. (Indulge in) suppressed laughter, laugh with closed mouth, (show) signs of glee; exult over; (make) hen's call. [f. CHUCK¹, -LE(3)]

chŭc'kle-head (-hĕd), n., **chŭc'kle-headĕd** (-hĕd-), a. Dolt(ish); stupid (fellow). [f. chuckle blockish, prob. rel. to CHUCK⁴]

chŭdd'ar, n. (Anglo-Ind.). Large sheet, worn as shawl or head-covering by Indian women. [Hind. chadar]

chŭg, n. Characteristic sound of oil-engine or small petrol-engine when running slowly (also as v.i., esp. of exhaust gases). [imit.]

chŭkk'er, chŭkk'a, n.(polo). Each of the periods into which the game is divided. [Hind. chakar]

chŭm, v.i. (-mm-), & n. **1.** Occupy rooms together, whence ~m'ERY(3) n.; be intimate; ~ up (colloq.), form intimacy (with). **2.** n. Familiar friend (esp. now among boys); (Australia) new ~, recent immigrant, greenhorn. [from 1684; prob. short for chamber-fellow (1580), esp. at Oxford]

chŭmp, n. Short thick lump of wood; || thick end, esp. of loin of mutton (so ~ chop); (colloq.) head, || esp. off one's ~, mad with excitement etc.; (sl.) fool, blockhead. [mod. form, combining perh. chunk + lump etc.]

chŭnk, n. (colloq.). Thick lump cut off (wood, bread, cheese, etc.). [prob. var. of CHUCK¹]

chupătt'ỹ, n. (Anglo-Ind.). Small flat cake of coarse unleavened bread. [Hind. chapāti]

church¹, n. Building for public Christian worship, || esp. according to established religion of country; all Christians (C~ militant, Christians on earth warring against evil); an organized Christian society of any time (primitive C~), country (C~ of Scotland), or distinguishing principle (reformed C~); C~ of England, English or Anglican C~, English branch of Western or Latin Church rejecting Pope's supremacy since reformation; Established C~, recognized by State, as C~ of England, Scotland; organization, clergy & other officers, of a religious society or corporation; clerical profession (go into the C~, take holy orders); HIGH, LOW¹, BROAD, ~, parties with different views of doctrine & discipline, whence ~'man, ~'ISM(3), nn.; public worship (go to, after, ~; ~-time; ~-goer, -going); C~ Army, C.E. mission to working classes founded by Preb. Carlile in 1882; C~ Commissioners, body administering the assets & revenue of C~ of England; ~'man, ~'woman, ~'manship, member, membership, of ~; poor as a ~ mouse, of poor person; ||~-rate, levied by vestry for maintenance of parish ~ & its services; ~ service, public worship, || book with Common Prayer, proper lessons, etc.; ~-text, black letter in monumental inscriptions; ~ward'en, elected lay representative of parish (usu. one of two, elected one by incumbent, one by parishion**ér**s), ‖ also long clay pipe; ~'*yard*, enclosed ground in which ~ stands, sometimes used for burial (‖~-*yard cough*, heralding death; *fat* ~*yard*, many deaths). Hence~'LESS**a**., ~'WARD(S) adv. [OE *cir(i)ce*, OS *kirika*, OHG *kirihha* f. WG *kirika* f. med. Gk *kurikon* f. Gk *kuriakon* (sc. *dōma*) Lord's (house) f. *kurios* lord; see KIRK]

church[2], v.t. Bring (woman) to church to have thanks offered for delivery of child. [f. prec.]

church'|ly, a. Obtrusively or intolerantly devoted to church or opposed to dissent. Hence ~IFY v.t., ~INESS n. [-Y[2]]

churl, n. Person of low birth (*gentleman or* ~); peasant, boor; ill-bred fellow; cross-grained or niggardly person, whence ~'ISH[1] a., ~'ishLY[2] adv., ~'ishNESS n. [OE *ceorl*, MLG *kerle* f. WG *kerl*- man, cogn. w. CARL(E)]

churn, n., & v.t. & i. (Agitate *milk* or *cream*, produce *butter*, in) butter-making machine; work this machine; stir (liquid) about, make it froth; (of sea etc.) wash to and fro, foam, seethe; ‖ large milk-can of ~ shape; ~-*dash(er)*, -*staff*, appliance for agitating milk in ~; *a* ~*ing*, amount of butter made at once. [OE *cyrin*, MDu., MLG *kerne*, ON *kirna* f. Gmc *kernjōn*]

churr, v.i., & n. (Make) deep trill as of nightjar. [imit., cf. CHIRR]

chut, int. of impatience. [imit.]

chute (shōōt), n. Smooth rapid descent of water over slope; sloping channel, slide, with or without water, for conveying things to lower level (also *shoot*); slope for shooting rubbish down; toboggan--slide. [conflation of F *chute* fall (of water etc.) w. some senses of SHOOT]

chut'ney (pl. ~*s*), -**nee**, n. Hot Indian condiment of fruits, chillies, etc. [f. Hind. *chatni*]

chyle (kīl), n. White milky fluid formed by action of pancreatic juice & bile on chyme. [f. LL *chylus* f. Gk *khulos* juice (*khu-* pour)]

chylo- (kī-), comb. form of Gk *khulos* CHYLE.

chyme (kīm), n. Food converted by gastric secretion into acid pulp. [f. LL f. Gk *khumos* juice (*khu-* pour); *khumos* & *khulos*, synonyms, were differentiated by Galen]

chym'ist(ry). Old spelling of CHEMIST(RY).

chymo- (kī-), comb. form of Gk *khumos* CHYME.

cibor'ium, n. (Archit.) canopy, canopied shrine; receptacle for reservation of Eucharist, shaped like shrine, or cup with arched cover. [f. LL f. Gk *kibōrion* seed-vessel of water-lily, cup so shaped]

cicād'a, cica'la, cigā'la, (-ah-). n. Transparent-winged shrill-chirping insect. [L *cicada*, It.-*cala*, F-*gale*]

cic'atrice, cicāt'rix, n. (-*ix*, pl. -*īcēs*, L form in scientific use). Scar of healed wound; scar on tree bark; (Bot.) mark

left on stem by fall of leaf etc., hilum of seed. Hence **cicatri'ci**AL (-shl), **cicāt'-ric**OSE[1], aa. [ME, f. OF *cicatrice* or L *cicatric-* (nom. -*ix*)]

cicāt'ric(ū)le, n. (Biol.) germ of chick, round white spot on yolk, tread; (Bot.) = prec. [f. L *cicatricula* (prec., -ULE)]

cic'atriz|e, -**is|e** (-īz), v.t. & i. Heal, skin over, (t. & i.); mark with scars. Hence ~A'TION n. [f. F *cicatriser* f. LL *cicatricare* (CICATRICE) w. assim. to -*iser*, -IZE]

ci'cely, n. Kinds of umbelliferous plant (sweet, wild, rough, ~). [f. L f. Gk *seselis* SESELI w. assim. to the woman's name (= *Cecilia*)]

ciceron'ě (sīse-, chīche-), n. (pl. -*oni* pr. -ōnē), & v.t. (Conduct *traveller* etc. as) guide who understands & explains antiquities etc. [It., f. L *Ciceronem* nom. -*e* the Roman orator]

Ciceron'ian, a. & n. Eloquent, classical, or rhythmical, as Cicero's style; (n.) person learned in or admiring Cicero. Hence ~ISM(3, 4) n. [f. L *Ciceronianus* (prec., -IAN)]

cicisbeo (chichīzbā'ō), n. (pl. -*bei* pr. -bāē). Recognized gallant of married woman. So *cicisbe'ism*(3) n. [It.]

Cid, n. The ~, title (lord) of Ruy Diaz, 11th-c. Christian champion against Moors, & of epic relating his deeds. [Sp., f. Arab. *sayyid*]

-cīde, suf. forming nouns meaning (1) slayer of (F, f. L -*cida*) or (2) slaughter of (F, f. L -*cidium*) both f. L *caedere* kill; taken f. L as *parricide*, or formed on L nn. as *regicide* or Gk nn. as *dendricide* or joc. on E nn. as *birdicide*.

cid'er, n. Fermented drink from apple--juice; ~-CUP; ~-*press*, for squeezing juice from apples. [ME & OF *sidre* f. LL f. Gk *sikera* f. Heb. *shekar* strong drink]

ci-devant (see Ap.), a. or adv. Former(ly), that has been (with the earlier name-or state). [F]

cigala. See CICADA.

cigā'r, n. Roll of tobacco-leaf for smoking; ~-*shaped*, cylindrical with pointed end(s); ~-*holder*, mouthpiece holding ~. [f. Sp. *cigarro*]

cigarétte', n. Small cylinder of cut tobacco or of narcotic or medicated substance rolled in paper for smoking. [f. F dim. of *cigare*, -ETTE]

cil'i|a, n. pl. Eyelashes; similar fringe on leaf, insect's wing, etc.; (Physiol.) hair-like vibrating organs on animal & vegetable tissue, serving many lower water animals for locomotion. Hence ~ARY[1], ~ATE[2], ~ātĕd, aa., ~A'TION n. [pl. of L *cilium* eyelash]

cil'ice, n. (Garment of) hair-cloth. [F, or f. L Gk *kilikion* (*Kilikia* Cilicia); OE *cilic* f. L]

Cimmē'rian, a. Thick, gloomy, (of darkness, night, etc.). [f. L f. Gk *kimmerios* (of Cimmerii, people in perpetual night) + -AN]

*cinch, n., & v.t. **1.** Saddle-girth used in Mexico etc.; (sl.) sure thing, a certainty. **2.** v.t. Put ~ on. [Sp. *cincha*]

cinchōn'a (-kō-), n. Kinds of evergreen tree yielding cinchona bark or Peruvian bark & quinine; the bark, drug made from it & highly esteemed as tonic & febrifuge. Hence **cinchonA'ceous** a., **cin'chonINE⁵**, **cin'chonISM**(5), nn., **cin'chonIZE**(5) v.t., (-ko-). [Countess of *Chinchon*, introducer of drug in Spain 1640]

Cincinnāt'us, n. Great man in retirement who can be called upon in a crisis. [Roman hero called from plough to dictatorship (5th c. B.C.)]

cinc'ture, n., & v.t. (Surround with or as with a) girdle, belt, fillet, border. [f. L *cinctura* (*cingere cinct-* gird, -URE)]

cin'der, n. Slag; residue of coal, wood, etc., that has ceased to flame (whether cold or not) but has still combustible matter in it; (loosely in pl.) ashes; ~-*path*, running-track laid with fine ~s; ~-*sifter*, for separating ~s from ashes. Hence~Y² a. [OE *sinder*, (= OHG *sintar*, ON *sindr*), w. assim. to the unconnected F *cendre* & L *cinis*]

Cinderěll'a, n. Person of unrecognized merit or beauty; ~ *dance* or ~, dance closing at twelve o'clock. [allusions to fairy-tale]

cin'ě-, comb. form of CINEMA; so: ~-*camera* (for taking. cinematographic photographs); ~-*film*; ~-*projector*; ~-*variety*, vaudeville entertainment including a cinema show.

cin'ěma, n. Cinematograph theatre; *the* ~, cinematography, moving pictures. Hence **ciněmāt'IC** a., relating to, having the qualities characteristic of, the ~. [abbr. of foll.]

ciněmāt'ograph (-ahf), n., & v.t. & i. **1.** Apparatus producing pictures of motion by the rapid projection on a screen of a great number of photographs taken successively on a long film; = prec. **2.** v.t. Make ~ film of (scene), film; (v.i.) use ~ a. Hence **ciněmātográph'IC** a., **-icalLY²** adv., **ciněmātŏg'raphY¹** n. [f. F *cinématographe* f. Gk *kinēma -atos* movement (*kineō* move), see -GRAPH]

cinerār'ia, n. Bright-flowered composite plant, grown chiefly under glass. [f. L *cinerarius* of ashes f. *cinis -eris* ashes (ash-coloured down on leaves)]

cinerār'ium n. Recess in which a cinerary urn is deposited. [as prec.]

cin'erarў, a. Of ashes (esp. ~ *urn*, holding ashes of dead after cremation). [as prec.]

cinēr'ěous, a. Ashen-grey (esp. of birds or plumage). [f. L *cinereus* (*cinis -eris* ashes)+-OUS]

Cingalēse' (-nggalěz), a. & n. See SINHALESE.

cing'ŭlum (-ngg-), n. Belt (used technically in Surg., Anat., Zool., etc.). [L]

cinn'abăr, n. & a. Red mercuric sulphide, vermilion (n. & a.). [f. L *cinnabaris* f. Gk *kinnabari* f. Oriental source]

cinn'amon, n. & a. (E.-Ind. tree with) aromatic inner bark used as spice; ~-colour(ed), (of) yellowish-brown; ~ *bear*, ~-coloured variety of the common N.-American black bear; ~-*stone*, brown or yellow garnet. Hence or cogn. **cinn'a-mATE¹**(3) n., **cinnamōm'IC**, **cinnamōn'IC**, aa. [ME *cin-*, *sinamome* f. OF *cinnamome* f. L f. Gk *kinnamōmon* f. Semit. (Heb. *qinnamom*); mod. form after later Gk (L) *kinnamon*]

cinque, cinq, (sĭnk), n. The five at dice & cards. [f. OF *cink* f. L *quinque* five]

cinqueceh'tō, cinquecen'tist, (chĭnk-wĭ-chĕ-), nn. Italian style of art, artist, of the 16th c. (15-) with reversion to classical forms. [It. (-*o*, -*ista*) with omission (in It.) of *mil*]

cinq(ue)'foil (sĭnkf-), n. Kinds of plant with compound leaf of five leaflets; (Archit.) five-cusped ornament in circle or arch. [thr. OF f. L *quinquefolium* five-leaf]

Cinque Pŏrts (sĭnk), n. pl. Certain ports (orig. five only) on SE coast with ancient privileges. [ME *sink pors* repr. OF *cink porz*, L *quinque portus* five ports]

ciph'er¹, cў-, n. Arithmetical symbol (0) of no value in itself but multiplying number it is placed after, and dividing decimal number it is placed before, by ten; person or thing of no importance; any Arabic figure; secret writing, thing so written, key to it; interlaced initials of person, company, etc., monogram; continued sounding of organ-note owing to defective valve. [ME, f. OF *cyfre* f. Arab. *çifr* ZERO]

ciph'er², cў-, v.i. & t. Do arithmetic; work (usu. *out*) by arithmetic, calculate; put into secret writing (cf. DECIPHER); (of organ-note) go on sounding when not pressed. [f. prec.]

cip'olin, n. Italian white-&-green marble. [F, or f. .its source *cipollino* (*cipolla* onion)]

cîr'ca, cîr'cĭter, prepp. (abbr. *c.* or *circ.*). About (with dates). [L]

Circă'ssian (-shn), a. & n. (Member, language) of a group of tribes of Caucasian race living in the Kuban province of Russia. [f. *Circassia* f. Russ. *Tcherkess*]

Cîr'cě, n. Enchantress, temptress. Hence **Cîrcē'AN** a. [proper name in Gk myth.]

cîr'cinate, a. (bot.). (With leaves) rolled up from apex to base, as in most ferns. [f. L *circinare* make round (*circinus* compasses, -ATE²)]

cîr'cle¹, n. **1.** (Line enclosing) perfectly round plane figure (*square the* ~, find square of same area as given ~, attempt impossibilities; *great*, *small*, ~, ~ on surface of sphere whose plane passes, does not pass, through sphere's centre; POLAR, ARCTIC, ANTARCTIC, ~); (loosely) roundish enclosure; orbit of planet; ring;

road, railway, etc. whose ends meet, allowing traffic to circulate continuously; curved tier of seats at theatre etc. (*dress ~, upper ~*, more & less expensive); (Archaeol.) ring of stones as at Stonehenge; *run round in ~s* (colloq.), be fussily busy with little result. **2.** Period, cycle, round, (*come full ~*, end at starting-point); circling-feat in gymnastics; complete series. **3.** (Logic, often *vicious* ~) fallacy of proving proposition from another that rests on it for proof. **4.** Action & reaction that intensify each other (often *vicious* ~). **5.** Persons grouped round centre of interest; set, coterie, class, (*first, upper, ~s; ~s in which* one *moves*). **6.** Area of influence, action, etc., sphere. Hence ~WISE (-lw-) adv. [ME & OF *cercle* f. L *circulus* dim. of *circus* ring; OE *circul*, & mod. sp., f. L]

cîr'cle², v.t. & i. Encompass (poet.); encompass *round, about*; move in a circle *round, about*; (Gym.) revolve round bar in various ways; be passed round (of wine etc.); (Mil.) sweep round on moving flank (of cavalry, cf. WHEEL²); (p.p.) rounded, marked with circles. [ME, f. prec., or OF *cercler*]

cîr'clet, n. Small circle; circular band, esp. of gold, jewelled, etc., worn on head or elsewhere. [f. F *cerclet* (CIRCLE¹, -ET)]

cîrcs, n. pl. (colloq.). Circumstances. [abbr.]

cîr'cuit (-kĭt), n. Line enclosing an area, distance round; area enclosed; roundabout journey; sequence of changes, acts, etc.; chain of theatres, cinemas, etc., under a single management; journey of judge in particular district to hold courts, this district (eight in Eng. & Wales), the barristers (*member of a ~*) making the ~; group of local Methodist churches forming a minor administrative unit (*~ rider*, itinerant preacher serving a ~); (Electr.) path of current (*short ~*, faulty shortening of a ~ by defective insulation). [ME, f. OF or L *circuitus* f. CIRCUM(*ire it-go*)]

circu'itous, a. Roundabout, indirect. Hence ~LY² adv., ~NESS n. [f. LL *circuitosus* (CIRCUIT, -OSE¹)]

cîr'cular, a. & n. Round in superficies; moving in a circle (|| ~ *tour*, ending where it began by different route, ~ *ticket*, for this); (Logic) of, using, the *vicious* CIRCLE¹; addressed to a circle of persons, customers, etc. (~ *note*, banker's letter of credit in traveller's favour to several foreign bankers; ~ *letter* or ~, notice, advertisement, etc., reproduced for distribution; of, like, the geometrical circle; ~ *saw*, toothed disc revolving by machinery for sawing. Hence cîrcu-lā'rity n., ~LY² adv. [ME *circuler* f. AF -*er* (OF -*ier*) f. LL *circularis* (CIRCLE, -AR¹)]

cîr'cularize, -ise (-īz), v.t. Send circulars to. [-IZE(1)]

cîr'cŭlāt|e, v.i. & t. Go round (blood ~es through veins, water in pipes, wine on table, newspaper to circle of readers); (of decimals) = RECUR; send round, give currency to, (book, report, scandal, etc.); ~*ing library*, with books taken by subscribers in succession; ~*ing medium*, notes, gold, etc., used in exchange. [f. L *circulare* (CIRCLE¹), -ATE³]

cîrcŭlā'tion, n. Movement of blood from and to heart, similar movement of sap etc.; movement to and fro (~ *of water, atmosphere*, etc.); transmission, distribution, (of news, books, etc.); number of copies sold, esp. of newspapers; currency, coin, etc. [F, or f. L *circulatio* (*circulare* see prec., -ATION)]

cîr'cŭlātive, a. Inclined to, promoting, circulation. [as prec., -IVE]

cîr'cŭlātor, n. One who circulates news, coin, etc. [as prec., -OR; earlier also f. L *circulator* peddler, quack]

cîr'cŭlātory, a. Of circulation of blood or sap. [f. L *circulatorius* (as prec., -ORY)]

cîrcum-, pref. = L adv. & prep. *circum* round, about, used (1) adverbially, as *circumvagant* wandering round or about; (2) prepositionally, as *circumocular* surrounding the eye. E wds are some f. L (direct, as *circumscribe*, or thr. F as *circumcise*), & some formed in E on L elements as *circumambient*.

cîrcŭmăm'bi|ent, a. Surrounding (esp. of air or other fluid). Hence ~ENCY n. [CIRCUM-(1)+AMBIENT]

cîrcŭmăm'bŭl|āte, v.t. & i. Walk round (place etc.); walk about; beat about the bush. Hence ~A'TION n., ~ătORY a. [f. LL CIRCUM(*ambulare* walk), -ATE³]

cîrcŭmbĕn'dibus, n. (joc.). Roundabout method; circumlocution. [CIRCUM-(1), BEND, ending of L abl. pl. case]

cîr'cŭmcise (-z), v.t. Cut off foreskin of (as Jewish or Mohammedan rite, or surgically); purify (~ *the heart, passions*, etc.). [ME, f. OF *circonciser*, or *circoncis*-stem of *circoncire*, f. L CIRCUM(*cidere* -*cīs*- = *caedere* cut)]

cîrcŭmci'sion (-izhn), n. Act or rite of, spiritual purification by, circumcising; (Bibl.) *the* ~, the Jews; (Eccl.) festival of C~ of Christ, 1st Jan. [ME, f. OF f. LL *circumcisionem* (as prec., -ION)]

cîrcŭm'ference, n. Encompassing boundary, esp. of figure enclosed by curve, as circle; distance round. So cîrcum-ferĕn'tiAL (-shl) a. [ME, f. OF f. L CIRCUM(*ferentia* f. *ferre* bear, -ENCE)]

cîr'cŭmflĕx, a. & n., & v.t. ~ (*accent*), mark (^ or ~ in Gk, ^ elsewhere) placed over vowel to indicate contraction, length (e.g. *viâ*), or special quality (vb, mark thus); (Anat.) curved, bending round something else, (~ *artery, muscle*, etc.). [f. L CIRCUM (*flexus* p.p. of *flectere* bend) transl. of Gk *perispōmenos*; see PERISPOMENON]

cîrcŭm'flu|ent (-lōō-), a. Flowing round,

surrounding. Hence ~ENCE n. [f. L CIR-
CUM (fluens f. fluere flow, -ENT)]

circŭm'fluous (-lōō-), a. = prec.; surrounded by water. [f. L CIRCUMfluus
flowing or flowed round (fluere flow) + -OUS]

cĭrcumfū|se' (-z), v.t. Pour (fluid) about
or round (object); surround, bathe,
(object with, or of fluid as subj.). So
~'SION (-zhn) n. [f. L CIRCUM(fundere fus-
pour)]

cĭrcum|gy̆r'āte, v.i. Turn, wheel, travel,
round. Hence ~gy̆rA'TION n. [CIRCUM-(1)
+GYRATE]

cĭrcumjā'cent, a. Situated around. [f.
L CIRCUM(jacent- part. st. of jacēre lie)]

cĭrcumlitt'oral, a. Bordering the shore.
[CIRCUM-(2) +L lit(t)us -oris shore + -AL]

cĭrcumlocū'tion, n. Use of many words
where few would do; evasive talk; a
roundabout expression; C~ Office, dilatory Government office. Hence ~AL,
~ARY[1], (-shon-), cĭrcumlŏc'ŭtORY, aa.,
~IST(1) (-shon-) n. [F, or f. L CIRCUM-
(locutio LOCUTION)]

cĭrcumnăv'igāt|e, v.t. Sail round (esp.
the globe or world). Hence ~OR n. [f. L
CIRCUM (navigare NAVIGATE)]

cĭrcumnūt'|āte, v.i. (bot.). Bend towards
all points of compass successively (of
growing parts of plant). Hence ~A'TION n.
[CIRCUM-(1), NUTATE]

cĭrcumpōl'ar, a. (Astron.) ~ star, motion,
etc., above horizon throughout diurnal
course; (Geog.) about, near, one of the
earth's poles. [CIRCUM-(2), L polus POLE[2],
-AR[1]]

cĭrc'umscrĭbe, v.t. Draw line round;
(Geom.) describe (figure) round another
touching it at points, but not cutting it;
lay down limits of, confine, restrict;
define logically; sign (round robin),
whence cĭrcumscrĭb'ER[1] n. [f. L CIR-
CUM(scribere script- write)]

cĭrcumscrip'tion, n. Having, marking
out, or imposing, of limits; boundary;
limited district; definition; (Geom.) cir-
cumscribing (see prec.); inscription round
coin etc. [f. L circumscriptio (prec.),
-ION]

cĭrcumsōl'ar, a. Revolving round, being
near, the sun. [CIRCUM-(2), SOL[1], -AR[1]]

cĭrc'umspĕct, a. Cautious, wary, taking
everything into account. Hence or cogn.
cĭrcumspĕc'tION, ~NESS, nn., ~IVE a.,
~LY[2] adv. [f. L CIRCUM(spicere spect-
= specere look)]

cĭrc'umstance, n. 1. (pl.). Time, place,
manner, cause, occasion, etc., surroundings, of an act; external conditions
affecting or that might affect an agent
(in, under, the ~s, owing to or making
allowance for them; under no ~s, not
whatever happens, never); material
welfare (in good, bad, easy, reduced,
straitened, ~s). 2. (sing.). Full detail in
narrative; ceremony, fuss, (without ~,
unceremoniously; pomp & ~); incident,
occurrence, fact (esp. the ~ that). Hence

cĭrc'umstancED[2] (-st) a. [ME f. OF, or
f. L CIRCUM(stantia f. part. of stare stand)]

cĭrcumstăn'tial (-shl), a. Depending on
subordinate details (~ evidence, establishing the doubtful main fact by inference from known facts otherwise hard to
explain); adventitious, incidental; with
many details (~ story). Hence cĭrcum-
stăntiăl'ITY (-shĭ-) n., ~LY[2] (-shal-) adv.
[as prec. +-AL]

cĭrcumvăll'āte, v.t., cĭrcumvallā'tion,
n. (Surround with) rampart or entrench-
ment; process of doing this. [f. L
CIRCUM(vallare f. vallum rampart), see
-ATE[3], -ATION]

cĭrcum|vĕnt', v.t. Entrap; overreach,
outwit. So ~vĕn'tION n. [f. L CIRCUM-
(venire vent- come)]

cĭrcumvolu'tion (-lōō-), n. Rolling
round; coil; period; sinuous movement.
[f. L CIRCUM(volvere volut- roll), -ION]

cĭrc'us, n. Rounded or oval arena lined
with tiers of seats for equestrian & other
exhibitions; amphitheatre of hills; ‖ open
circle with streets converging on it;
travelling show of horses, riders, etc.
[L, = ring]

cĭrque (-k), n. Arena, natural amphitheatre, (chiefly poet. & rhet.). [F, f. L
as prec.]

cirrhōs'is (sĭrō-), n. Disease of liver,
chiefly alcoholic. [Gk kirrhos tawny,
-OSIS]

cirri-, cirro-, comb. form of CIRRUS.
Hence cĭrrif'EROUS, ci'rriFORM, aa., &
names of cloud-forms as cirro-cŭm'ŭlus.
[-I-, -O-]

ci'rripĕd, -ēde, n. Marine animal in
valved shell attached to other bodies,
with legs like curl of hair. [f. F CIRRI(pĕde
f. L pes pedis foot)]

ci'rrus, n. (pl. -ri). (Bot.) tendril; (Zool.)
slender appendage, as beard of fishes,
feet of cirripeds; (Meteor.) form of cloud
with diverging filaments like lock of hair
or wool. Hence cirrOSE'[1], ci'rrous, aa.
[L, = curl]

cis-, pref.=on this side of, opp. to trans-
or ultra-, retaining in some orig. L wds
the Roman sense (cispadane, cisalpine,
S. or Rome-wards of Po, Alps), but usu.
w. ref. to speaker's or majority's position
(cismontane, N. of Alps or non-Italian;
cis-Leithan, W. of Leitha, Austrian, non-
-Hungarian; cis-pontine, in London, on
northern or better-known side of bridges
or Thames); prefixed to the adj. form of
the second element; often used in wds
made for the nonce in opposition to
wds in trans- or ultra- (transatlantic &
cisatlantic); also of time as cis-Eliza-
bethan. [L prep.]

*cĭss'y̆, sĭ-, n. (sl.). Effeminate person.
[ult. f. SISTER]

cist, n. (archaeol.). Prehistoric stone or
hollowed-tree coffin; round receptacle
used esp. for sacred purposes. [f. L f. Gk
kistē box]

Cister′cian (-shn), n. & a. (Monk) of order founded 1098 at Cistercium or Citeaux, stricter offshoot of Benedictines, also called *Bernardine* as patronized by St Bernard of Clairvaux. [-AN]

cis′tern, n. Reservoir for storing water, esp. one on upper storey or level with pipes supplying taps on lower levels (also fig., of pond). [f. OF *cisterne* f. L *cisterna* (*cista* see CIST) cf. *caverna*]

cis′tus, n. Kinds of shrub with large white or red flowers. [f. L f. Gk *kistos*]

cit, n. (arch.). Citizen (usu. in derogatory sense). [abbr. of *citizen*]

cit′adel, n. Fortress, esp. one guarding or dominating city; last retreat of hard--pressed party, belief, etc. [f. F *citadelle* f. It. *cittadella* dim. of *cittade* f. L *civitatem* CITY]

cite, v.t. Summon to appear in law-court; quote (passage, book, author) in support of a position; mention as example. Hence or cogn. **cit′ABLE** a., **cita′TION** n., (also) *mention in an official dispatch. [f. F *citer* f. L *citare* f. *ciēre* set moving]

cith′er, n. (arch. or poet.) = foll. [f. F *cithare* or G *zither*; see foll.]

cith′ern, **citt′ern**, n. (arch. or poet.). Wire-stringed lute-like instrument usu. played with plectrum. [16th c. Eng. form, w. assim. to GITTERN, of L *cithara*, Gk *kithara* harp]

cit′izen, n. Burgess, freeman, of city; townsman; *civilian; member, native or naturalized, of a State (usu. *of*; ~ *of the world*, cosmopolitan); inhabitant *of*. Hence ~HOOD, ~RY, ~SHIP, nn. [ME *citesein* f. AF alt. (perh. after DENIZEN) of OF *citeain* (CITY, -AN)]

citôle′, n. (hist.). = CITHERN. [ME, OF, app. as CITHERN with dim. ending]

citr-, comb. form of foll. Hence **cit′rATE¹** (3) n.

cit′ric, a. (chem.). Of citron (esp. ~ *acid*). [f. F *citrique* f. L *citrus* CITRON + -IC]

cit′rine, a. Lemon-coloured. [ME & OF *citrin* f. LL *citrinus* (CITRON, -INE¹)]

citro-. = CITR-.

cit′ron, n. (Tree bearing) lemon-like but larger, less acid, & thicker-skinned fruit. [F, f. L *citrus*, after *limon* LEMON]

citronëll′a, n. Fragrant ethereal oil obtained from a tropical grass, used for keeping insects away. [mod. L, as CITRON]

Cit′rus, n. The genus including the citron, lemon, lime, orange, etc. [L]

cittern. See CITHERN.

cit′ÿ, n. (Loosely) important town; ‖ (strictly) town created city by charter, esp. as containing cathedral (but not all cathedral towns are cities, nor vice versa); *municipal corporation occupying a definite area; ~ *of* REFUGE; *Holy C~*, Jerusalem, Heaven; *Eternal C~*, *C~ of the Seven Hills*, Rome; *Celestial C~*, *Heavenly C~*, *C~ of God*, Paradise; ‖ *the*

C~, part of London governed by Lord Mayor & Corporation, business part of this, commercial circles, ‖ (*C~ man*, in commerce or finance; *C~ article*, in news-paper on these; *C~ Company*, corporation representing ancient trade-guild); *C~ editor*, one who deals with the financial news of a daily or weekly journal; ~ *state*, a city that is also an independent sovereign state. Hence (-)**citiED²** (-tïd), ~LESS, aa., ~WARD(S) adv. [ME *cite* f. OF f. L *civitatem* (*civis* citizen, -TY)]

civ′et, n. (Also ~-*cat*) carnivorous quad-ruped between fox & weasel in size & look; strong musky perfume got from anal glands of this. [f. F *civette* ult. f. Arab. *zabad*]

civ′ic, a. Of, proper to, citizens (~ *crown*, oak-garland, Roman honour to one who saved fellow-citizen's life in war); of city, municipal (~ *guard*, policeman, -men, in Eire); of citizenship, civil, (~ *virtues*, *activity*), whence **civ′ICS** n. Hence **civ′ICALLY** adv. [f. L *civicus* (*civis* citizen, -IC)]

civ(v)′ies (-vïz), n. pl. (sl.). Civilian clothes. [abbr.]

civ′il, a. 1. Of gregarious men (~ *society*, *life*); of a citizen community (~ *institu-tions*; ~ *war*, confined to this, between fellow-citizens, *The C~ War*, in Engl., be-tween Charles I & Parliament, in U.S., War of Secession); ~ *disobedience* (India), refusal to pay taxes, obey laws, etc., as part of a political campaign; of, becom-ing, a citizen (~ *rights*, *liberty*; ~ *spirit*). 2. Polite, obliging, not rude, whence (with pl. = favours) **civil′ITY** n. 3. Not naval, military, etc. (~ *defence*, civilian organization for dealing esp. with air raids; ~ ENGINEER¹; *C~ Service*, all non--warlike branches of State administration, *C~ Servant*, member of one of them). 4. Not ecclesiastical (~ *magistrates*, & formerly ~ *law*; ~ *marriage*, solemnized as ~ contract without religious ceremony). 5. Not criminal (~ *law*, concerning ques-tions of private rights merely). 6. Not natural or astronomical (~ *day*, *year*, as recognized for dating etc.). 7. *C~ Law*, Roman law (so D.C.L.; & see above); ‖ ~ *list*, Parliamentary allowance for sovereign's household & royal pensions. Hence ~LY² adv. [F, f. L *civilis* (*civis* citizen, -IL)]

civil′ian (-yan), n. & a. (Person) not in or of navy or army or air force. Hence ~IZE(3) v.t., convert (Service post) into a ~ one, ~IZA′TION n. [f. CIVIL+-IAN; earlier (ME) ‘one learned in Civil Law’ f. OF *civilien*]

civiliza′tion, **-is-** (-ïz-), n. Making or becoming civilized; stage, esp. advanced stage, in social development; civilized States. [f. foll. + -ATION]

civ′iliz|e, **-is|e** (-ïz), v.t. Bring out of barbarism, enlighten, refine; ~*e away*, get rid of (barbarous habits etc.). Hence

~ABLE a., ~ER¹ n. [f. F *civiliser*, see CIVIL, -IZE(3)]

Civv'ỹ Street, n. (sl.). Civilian life. [abbr.]

clăck, n., & v.i. **1.** Sharp sound as of boards struck together; flap-valve in pumps etc.; clatter of tongues. **2.** v.i. Chatter loudly; make sound as of clogs on stone. [ME *clack* to chatter, prate prob. f. ON *klaka* chatter, twitter; of imit. orig.; cf. OHG *klecken*, Du. *klakken*, F *claquer*]

clad. See CLOTHE.

clăd(o)-, comb. form of Gk *klados* young shoot, in bot. terms as *cladocarp'ous* with fruit on lateral branchlets.

claim¹, v.t. Demand as one's due (recognition etc., *to* be, *that* one should be, recognized etc.); represent oneself as having (~ *the victory, accuracy*); profess *to* (*be* the owner, *have* told the truth); demand recognition of the fact that; contend, assert; (of things) deserve (esp. *attention*). Hence ~'ABLE a., ~'ANT(1) n. [ME, f. OF *claim-*, tonic stem of *clamer* f. L *clamare* call out]

claim², n. Demand for something as due (*lay* ~ *to*); right, title, *to* thing, right to make demand *on* person; (Mining etc.) piece of land allotted; *~-jumper*, one who appropriates a mining ~ already taken by another. [ME, f. OF *claime* f. *clamer* see prec.]

clairvoy'ance, n. Faculty of seeing mentally what is happening or exists out of sight; exceptional insight. [F, f. *clairvoyant* (-ANCE, -ANT) f. *clair* CLEAR + part. of *voir* see]

clairvoy'ant, n. (occas. fem. *-te*), & a. (Person) having clairvoyance. [F, = clear-sighted, see prec.]

clăm¹. var. of CLAMP¹ in tech. senses. [ME f. OE *clam* bond, fetter = OHG *klamma* (G dial. *klamm*), also MHG, G *klemme*, f. Gmc *klam-* press or squeeze together]

clăm². n. Various bivalve shellfish, esp. the N.-Amer. hard or round, & soft or long, ~, used for food. [16th c. ~-*shell*, app. f. prec.]

clăm'ant, a. Noisy, insistent; urgent. [f. L *clamare* cry out, -ANT]

clăm'ber, v.i., & n. Climb with hands & feet; climb with difficulty or labour. [prob. f. *clamb* (obs. past tense of CLIMB) + -ER²; cf. obs. (16–17th c.) *climber*]

clămm'|ỹ, a. Moist, usu. cold, & sticky or slimy (of the hand, ill-baked bread, any surface). Hence ~ĭLY² adv., ~ĭNESS n. [f. obs. or dial. *clam* (vb smear, adj. 'clammy') + -Y²; cf. OE *clām* clay]

clăm'our(-mer), n., & v.i. & t. Shout(ing); (make) loud appeal, complaint, or demand (abs., or *for, against, to* do); also as v.t., ~ *down*, silence, ~ *out of, into,* force *by* ~); (make) continued noise. So clăm'orous a., clăm'orousLY² adv. [ME, f. OF f. L *clamorem* (*clamare* CLAIM¹)]

clămp¹, n., & v.t. (also *clam* in some technical uses of n.). **1.** Brace, clasp, or band, usu. of iron, for strengthening other materials or holding things together; various appliances or tools with opposite sides connected by screw for holding or compressing. **2.** v.t. Strengthen, fasten together, with ~ or ~s. [14th c., prob. f. MDu., MLG *klamp(e)*, alt. f. same root as CLAM¹]

clămp², n., & v.t. **1.** Pile (of bricks for burning, potatoes etc. under straw & earth, turf, peat, garden rubbish, etc.). **2.** v.t. Pile (bricks etc.) *up*. [16th c., f. Du. *klamp* heap, in brick-making]

clăn, n. Scottish Highlanders with common ancestor, esp. while under patriarchal control (~*s'man*, member, fellow member, of ~); tribe; family holding together, whence ~n'ISH¹ a., ~n'ishLY² adv., ~n'ishNESS n.; party, coterie; genus, species, class. [f. Gael. *clann* f. L PLANT*a*]

clăndĕs'tine, a. Surreptitious, secret. Hence ~LY² (-nl-) adv. [f. L *clandestinus* (*clam* secretly)]

clăng, n., & v.i. & t. Loud resonant metallic sound (esp. of trumpet, arms, large bell, some birds); (vb) make, cause (thing) to make, this. [imit., but infl. by L *clangere* resound, *clangor* (of trumpets, birds)]

clăng'our (-ngger), n. Succession, prevalence, of clanging noises. Hence clăng'orous a., clăng'orousLY² adv., (-ngg-). [f. L *clangor* (prec., -OR)]

clănk, n., & v.i. & t. Sound as of heavy chain rattling; (vb) make, cause (bucket, chain, etc.) to make, this. [imit.; cf. CLANG, CLINK, Du. *klank*]

clăn'ship, n. The clan system; division into mutually jealous parties; devotion to a leader. [-SHIP]

clăp¹, n. Explosive noise (*of* thunder, of hand-palms struck together); slap, pat, (arch.). [ME, app. f. foll.]

clăp², v.i. & t. (-pp-). ~ one's *hands, ~* (t. & i.), applaud by striking palms together loudly (also, usu. w. *hands*, strike them for warmth, as signal etc.); flap (wings) audibly; ~ *on the back,* slap so in encouragement or congratulation; put, place, quickly or energetically (spurs *to* horse, person *in* prison, duty *on* goods; ~ *on all sail*; ~ *up peace, bargain,* make hastily or carelessly; ~ *eyes on,* catch sight of, esp. w. neg.); *~-net,* fowler's or entomologist's, shut by pulling string. [ME *clappe(n)*, OE *clappian*, OHG *klapfôn*, ON *klappa* f. Gmc *klapp-* of imit. orig.]

clăp³, n. (not in decent use). Venereal disease, gonorrhoea. [orig. uncert.; cf. OF *clapoir*, obs. Du. *klapoore* bubo]

*clăp'board (-bōrd), n. = WEATHER-*board*. [anglicized f. LG *klappholt* cask-stave]

clăpp'er, n. Tongue or striker of bell; hand or wind rattle for scaring birds. [CLAP² + -ER¹]

clăpp'erclaw, v.t. (arch.). Scratch & hit; abuse, criticize spitefully. [prec., CLAW]

clăp'trăp, n. & a. Language, sentiment, meant to catch applause; showy. [CLAP[1], TRAP]

claque (-ahk), **claqueur'** (-kër), nn. Hired body of applauders, hired applauder. [F]

clă'rabĕlla (-ahr-), n. Fluty organ-stop. [f. L clarus clear, bellus pretty]

clă'rence, n. Four-wheeled close carriage with seats for four inside & two on box, four-wheeler cab. [Duke of C~ (William IV)]

Clă'renc(i)eux (-sū), n. Second KING[1] of Arms. [AF (-ceux), f. Clarence (Clare in Suffolk), dukedom of Lionel son of Edw. III]

clă'rendon, a. & n. (typog.). Thick-faced (type), thus, of various sizes.

clă'ret, II. & a. Kinds of red French wine imported from Bordeaux (usu. blends of light wine with Benicarlo); (sl.) blood (tap one's ~, make his nose bleed with blow of fist); ~-colour(ed), reddish--violet; artificial salmon-fly so coloured; ~-CUP[1]. [ME, f. OF (vin) claret (orig. of wines of light red colour) f. clair CLEAR]

clă'rifў, v.t. & i. Make clear (obscure subject, mind, sight); free from impurities, make transparent, (liquid, butter, air, etc.); become transparent (lit., & fig. of literary style etc.). Hence **clărific-A'TION** n. [ME, f. OF clare-, clarifier or LL clarificare (clarus CLEAR, -FY)]

clă'rinĕt (also -ĕt'), n. Wood-wind instrument with single-reed mouthpiece, holes, & keys; organ-stop of like quality. So **clărinĕtt'IST(3)** n. [f. F clarinette dim. of clarine kind of bell]

clă'rion, n. & a. Shrill narrow-tubed trumpet formerly used in war; rousing sound; organ-stop of ~ quality; (adj.) clear & loud. [ME clarion, -ioun, var. of OF claron (ult. f. L clarus CLEAR, see -OON), cf. med. L clario(n-), claro(n-)]

clărionĕt', n. = CLARINET. [alt. f. CLARINET, after CLARION]

clă'ritў, n. Clearness. [ME & OF clarte f. L claritatem (clarus clear, -TY)]

clărk'ia, n. Kinds of plant with showy flowers. [W. Clarke, U.S. explorer, -IA[1]]

clă'rў, n. Kind of pot-herb. [15th c. clary, somehow repr. med. L sclarea whence OE slarege, -ie]

clăsh, v.i. & t., & n. (Make) loud broken sound as of collision, striking weapons, cymbals, bells rung together; encounter, conflict, (v.i., & n.); disagree(ment); be at variance with; colours ~, are discordant; rush or charge (vb) into, against, upon; ring (bells) all together. [imit.; cf. clack, clash, crack, crash]

clasp[1] (-ah-), n. Contrivance of interlocking parts for fastening, buckle, brooch; metal fastening of book-cover; embrace, reach; grasp, handshake; bar of silver on medal-ribbon with name of occasion (in campaign commemorated by medal) at which wearer was present; ~-knife, folding, with catch fixing blade when open. [ME clasp, clapse, etym. unkn.; cf. hasp, (hapse)]

clasp[2] (-ah-), v.t. & i. Fasten (clasp); fasten (t. & i.) with or as clasp; encircle, hold closely, embrace; grasp (another's hand; ~ hands, shake hands emotionally; make common cause; ~ one's hands, interlace fingers). [partly f. prec.; w. some senses cf. grasp, grip, clasp, CLIP[1]]

clas'per (-ah-), n. In vbl senses; esp., (pl.) appendages of some male fish & insects for holding the female. [-ER[1]]

class (-ah-), n., & v.t. **1.** Rank, order, of society (higher, upper, middle, lower, working,~es; the~es, the rich or educated, opp. the masses); ~-con'scious(ness), esp. realizing & taking part in the conflict between the labouring & other~es; caste system. **2.** Set of students taught together, their time of meeting, their course of instruction, *all college students of same standing, (~-fellow, -mate, present or past member of same ~ with one; ~-book, used by ~; ~-room, where ~ is taught). **3.** (In foreign armies) all the recruits of a year (the 1960 ~). **4.** ‖ Division of candidates after examination (take a~, gain honours; so ~'man opp. to pass-man; ‖~-list, issued by examiners). **5.** Division according to quality (so high, low, first, second, etc., -~, as adjj. of praise or depreciation, & first, second, ~, of railway carriages etc.; no ~, sl., quite inferior). **6.** Number of individuals having common name as like in any respect. **7.** (Nat. Hist.) highest division (~, order, family, genus, species) of animal, vegetable, or mineral kingdom. **8.** Distinction, high quality (also attrib.). **9.** v.t. Place in a ~; hence ~'ABLE a. [f. F classe f. L classis assembly]

clăss'ic, a. & n. **1.** Of the first class, of allowed excellence; of the standard ancient Latin & Greek authors, art, or culture; of Latin & Greek antiquity; in the ~ style, simple, harmonious, proportioned, & finished (cf. ROMANTIC); having literary associations (~ ground); ‖~ races, Two & One Thousand Guineas, Derby, Oaks, St Leger. **2.** n. Writer, artist or work, example, of admitted excellence; ancient Greek or Latin writer; Latin and Greek scholar; follower of ~ models (cf. ROMANTIC); (pl.) classical studies. [f. F classique or L classicus; see -IC]

clăss'ical, a. Standard, first-class, esp. in literature; of ancient Greek or Latin standard authors or art; learned in these; based on these (~ education); in, following, the restrained style of ~ antiquity (as prec., cf. ROMANTIC). Hence ~ISM(3), ~ITY (-ăl²), nn., ~LY² adv. [f. L classicus +-AL]

clăss'icĭsm,-ĭst, nn. Following, follower,

of classic style; classical scholar(ship); advocacy, advocate. of classical education; (*-ism*) a Latin or Greek idiom. [-ISM(3, 4), -IST(2, 3)]

clǎss'icize, -ise (-iz), v.t. & i. Make classic; imitate the classical style. [-IZE (2, 3)]

clǎssico-, comb. form of L *classicus* w. senses of CLASSIC. Hence **clǎssicŏl'ATRY** n.

clǎss'if|ȳ, v.t. Arrange in classes; assign to a class; ~*ied*, *officially designated as secret. So ~IABLE, ~icātORY, aa., ~ICA'TION, ~iER[1], nn. [f. L CLASSis +-FY]

class'ȳ (-ah-), a. (sl.). Superior. [-Y[2]]

clǎs'tic, a. (geol.). Composed of broken pieces of older rocks; ~ *rocks*, conglomerates etc. [f. Gk *klastos* (*klaō* break)]

clǎtt'er, v.i. & t., & n. (Make) dry confused sound as of many plates struck together; (resound with) noisy talk; ~ *along*, *down*, etc., move, fall, with a ~; (v.t.) cause (plates etc.) to ~. [ME *clater*, OE *clatrian*, of imit. orig.; cf. Du. *klateren*]

clause (-z), n. Short sentence; (Gram.) distinct member of a sentence including subject & predicate; single proviso in treaty, law, or contract. [ME, f. OF f. med. L *clausa* = L *clausula* conclusion (*claudere claus-* shut, -ULE)]

claus'tral, a. Of the cloister, monastic, narrow. [f. LL *claustralis* (CLOISTER, -AL)]

claustrophōb'ia, n. Morbid dread of closed places. [f. L *claustrum* (see CLOISTER) +-PHOBIA]

clǎv'āte, a. (bot.). Club-shaped. [f. L *clava* club +-ATE[2]]

clǎv'ichŏrd (-k-), n. Predecessor of piano, first string-instrument with keyboard. [f. med. L *clavichordium* (L *clavis* key, CHORD[1])]

clǎv'icle, n. Collar-bone. So **clavic'ūlAR**[1] a. [f. L *clavicula* dim. of *clavis* key]

clǎv'ifŏrm, a. Club-shaped. [L *clava*, -FORM]

claw[1], n. Pointed horny nail of beast's or bird's foot (*pare, cut, the* ~*s of*, disarm); foot so armed, pincers of shellfish; (contempt.) hand; contrivance for grappling, holding, etc. (~*-hammer*, with bent split end for extracting nails; ~*-hammer coat*, dress coat). Hence (-)**clawED**[2] (-awd) a. [OE *clawu* f. obl. cases of *clēa* (whence dial. *clee*), with OS *clāuua*, OHG *klāwa* f. Gmc **klawō*, **klǣwō*]

claw[2], v.t. & i. Scratch, tear, seize or pull towards one, with claws or hands (~ *me & I'll* ~ *thee*, of mutual flattery f. obs. sense, still Sc., *scratch gently*); (Naut.) beat to windward, esp. ~ *off*, away from shore. [OE *clawian*, OHG *klāwen*, f. prec.]

clay, n. Stiff tenacious earth, material of bricks, pottery, etc.; (material of) human body (*wet, moisten*, one's ~, drink); (also ~ *pipe*) tobacco-pipe made of ~ (*yard of* ~, long one); ~*-cold*, cold as ~ (usu. of

the dead). Hence (with *-e-* to separate *yy*, & comp. *more, most*) ~'EY[2] a. [OE *clǣg*, (M) Du., (M)LG *klei*, f. Gmc **klai-* (whence OE *clām* clay; see CLAMMY), **klei-*, **kli-* to stick, cogn. w. Gk *gloios*, L *glus*, *gluten*]

clay'mōre, n. Ancient Scottish two--edged broadsword; (incorrectly) basket--hilted often single-edged broadsword introduced in 16th c. [f. Gael. *claidheamh mōr* great sword]

clean[1], a. 1. Free from dirt, unsoiled, clear, (land of weeds, ship of barnacles, paper of writing, printing-proof of corrections; ~ BILL[4]; ~ *hands*, ~*-handed*, ~*-handedness*, innocence, innocent; ~*-fingered*, unbribed; ~ *slate*, fig., freedom from all commitments; ~ *tongue*, abstinence from foul talk; ~ BREAST[1]; *come* ~ sl., own up, confess everything; *show a* ~ *pair of heels*, escape by speed; ~*-bred*, thoroughbred); (Bibl.) free of ceremonial defilement or of disease; (of beasts etc.) fit for food (esp. ~*fish*, not at or soon after spawning). 2. Hostile to dirt (~ *servant*), cleanly. 3. Well-formed, shapely, (joints, figure, so ~*-limbed*; ~ *ship*, with tapering lines). 4. Smart, adroit, not bungling, (~ *fielding*). 5. Even, unobstructed, clear--cut, complete, (~ *sweep*, complete riddance; ~ *timber*, without knots). 6. Free from impropriety, esp. *keep it* ~ (colloq.). Hence ~'NESS n. [OE *clǣne*, OS *klēni*, OHG *kleini* f. WG **klain-*, perh. f. **klai-* CLAY]

clean[2], adv. Completely, right, outright, altogether, simply, absolutely. (~ *gone*, ~ *bowled, cut* ~ *through*, ~ *mad*, ~ *wrong*); ~*-cut*, sharply outlined. [OE *clǣne* adv. f. prec.]

clean[3], v.t., & n. 1. Make clean (*of* dirt etc.); empty (one's plate); make one*self*, make oneself, become, clean (also ~ *up*); ~ *up*, put things tidy, put (things) tidy, clear (mess) away, (colloq.) acquire as gain or profit; ~ *out*, empty, strip, (esp. sl., person of his money); ~ *down*, ~ by brushing or wiping; hence ~'ABLE a., (-)~'ER[1](1, 2), n. 2. n. ~ing (*give it a* ~). [f. CLEAN[1]]

clean'lȳ[1], adv. In clean way. [OE *clǣnlīc* (CLEAN[1] +-LY[2])]

clean'l|ȳ[2] (-ĕn-), a. Habitually clean, attentive to cleanness. Hence ~ILY[2] adv., ~INESS n., (-ĕn-). [OE *clǣnlīc* (CLEAN[1] +-LY[2])]

cleanse (-ĕnz), v.t. Make clean (now formal or arch. for *clean* in lit. sense); purify (*of* sin etc., or with *sin* etc. as obj.); (Bibl.) cure (leper etc.). [OE *clǣnsian* (*clǣne* CLEAN[1])]

clear[1], a. & adv. 1. Unclouded, transparent, not turbid, lustrous, unspotted, (so ~*-starch* v.t., = starch well; ~ *conscience*, feeling that one is innocent); distinct, unambiguous, intelligible, not confused, manifest, (*in* ~, not in cipher or code); discerning, penetrating, (so ~-

-*sighted*, ~-*sightedness*, usu. fig.); confident, decided, certain, (*on* point, *of* fact, *that*); easily audible; without deduction, net; rid *of*; complete (*three* ~ *days*); open, unobstructed, (*coast is* ~, no one about to see or interfere); unengaged, free, unencumbered by debt. **2.** adv. Clearly (*speak loud & ~; ~-cut*, well defined; *show, shine, ~*); quite (~ *away, off, out, through*; *three feet ~*); apart, without contact, (*stand, hang, steer, get, ~*). [ME & OF *cler* (F *clair*) f. L *clarus*]

clear², v.t. & i. Make, become, clear (*of; ~ the air*, lit. of sultriness, fig. of suspicion, constraint, sulks, etc.; ~ one's throat, by slight coughing); show or declare innocent (*of*); free from or *of* obstruction (~ *the decks for action*, make ready to fight; ~ *land*, cut down trees etc. before cultivating); remove (obstruction, esp. ~ *out of the way*); melt away (also sl. of persons, go away); empty, become empty; pass over or by without touching (esp. in jumping, ~ *6 ft, 22 ft, a gate*); (Naut.) free (ship) by paying all dues, (intr. of ship) sail; defray (prospective charges) by single payment; make (sum) as net gain; ~ *away*, remove, remove meal from table, (of mist etc.) disappear; ~ *off*, get rid of, melt away, (of intruders) go away; ~ *out*, empty, make off; ~ *up*, solve (mystery), make tidy, (of weather etc.) grow clear. [ME, f. prec.]

clear′ance, n. Making clear; removal of obstructions; passing of cheques through Clearing-House; (certificate of) clearing of ship at Custom-House; permit to leave government employ; (Mech.) space allowed for the passing of two parts; ‖ ~ *sale* (held to effect ~ of superfluous stock). [prec. + -ANCE]

clear′côle, n., & v.t. (Paint with) size and whiting or white-lead as first coat in house-painting. [f. F *claire colle* clear glue]

clear′ing, n. In vbl senses; esp.; piece of land in primeval forest cleared for cultivation; C~ *Hospital*, field hospital for temporary reception and treatment of sick and wounded; C~-*House*, banker's institution in London at which cheques & bills are exchanged, the balances only being paid in cash; ~-*house* fig., agency for collecting & distributing. [CLEAR², -ING¹]

clear′ly, adv. Distinctly to, with, senses or mind; manifestly; undoubtedly, (in answers) yes, no doubt. [CLEAR¹, -LY²]

clear′nĕss, n. Transparence; distinctness to, of, senses or mind; freedom from obstruction. [CLEAR¹, -NESS]

cleat, n. Wedge; projecting piece bolted on spar, gangway, etc., to give footing or prevent rope from slipping; piece of wood or iron bolted on for fastening ropes to. [OE **clēat*, cogn. w. OHG *klōz* lump, Du. *kloot* ball, f. WG **klaut-*; see CLOT]

cleav′age, n. Way in which thing

(mineral, party, opinion, State) tends to split (esp. *lines, planes, of* ~). [foll. + -AGE]

cleave¹, v.t. & i. (*clove* or *cleft; cloven* or *cleft*). Split (often *asunder, in two*); chop, break, or come, apart, esp. along the grain or line of cleavage (*cleft palate*, malformation in mouth; *in a cleft stick*, in tight place allowing neither retreat nor advance; *cloven hoof*, of ruminant quadrupeds, of god Pan, & so of devil, whence *show the cloven hoof*, reveal an evil nature); make way through (water, air); hold (ground, persons) apart (of chasm lit. & fig.). Hence cleav′ABLE a. [OE *clēofan, clīofan*, OS, OHG *klioban*, ON *kljúfa* f. Gmc **kleubh-*]

cleave², v.i. (~*d* or *clave; ~d*). Stick fast, adhere, *to* (arch. exc. in fig. sense of *be faithful*). [OE *cleofian, clifian*, = OS *clibōn*, OHG *klebēn*; OE *clifan* = OS, OHG *kliban*, ON *klifa*; Gmc **klĭbh-* f. **kli-* stick; see CLAY]

cleav′er, n. In vbl senses; esp. butcher's chopping-tool for carcasses. [CLEAVE¹ + -ER¹]

cleav′ers (-z), **cliv′**, n. (used as sing. or pl.). Goose-grass, creeper sticking to clothes. [OE *clīfe*, OS, OHG *klība*; ME *clivre* etc., f. CLEAVE² + -ER¹]

cleek, n. Iron-headed golf-club with almost straight narrow face. [15th c. Sc. *cleke*, rel. to north. dial, *cleek*, south. dial. *cleach, cleech* to grasp]

clĕf, n. One of the three symbols (*C, tenor*, or *alto; G* or *treble; F* or *bass*) indicating pitch of stave in music. [F, f. L *clavis* key]

clĕft¹, n. Fissure, split. [ME *clift* f. OE **clyft* (cf. OHG, ON *kluft*) f. Gmc **klubh-* f. **kleubh-* CLEAVE¹, w. assim. to foll.]

clĕft², see CLEAVE¹.

‖ **clĕg**, n. Large grey fly, horse-fly. [15th c., f. ON *kleggi*]

cleistogăm′ic (klī-), a. (bot.). Permanently closed & self-fertilizing (of certain flowers). [Gk *kleistos* closed (*kleiō*) + -*gamos* -married]

‖ **clĕm**, v.t. & i. (northern; -mm-). Starve. [16th c., repr. OE -*clemman*, OHG -*klemmen* (G *klemmen*) f. Gmc **klam-* see CLAM¹]

clĕm′atis, n. Kind of climbing shrub (British wild species, traveller's joy or old man's beard). [L, f. Gk *klēmatis*]

clĕm′encў, n., **clĕm′ent**, a. Mild(ness) of temper or weather; (showing) mercy. [f. L *clementia, clemens -entis*]

clĕnch, clinch, v.t. & i., & n. (choice between *e* & *i* as indicated). **1.** Secure (nail, rivet) by driving point sideways when through (i, e); close (t. & i. of teeth or fingers) tightly (e); grasp firmly (e); (of boxers) come to quarters too close for full-arm blow (i); (Naut.) fasten (rope) with special bend (i); confirm, settle (argument, bargain) conclusively (i). **2.** n. Any of above actions or the resulting state. [ME *clenche* (16th c. var. *clinch*) f.

OE *clenc(e)an*, OHG *klenkan*, f. Gmc *klankjan* f. *klink-, *klank-, *klunk-, parallel to *kling-* see CLING]

clĕn'cher. See CLINCHER.

Clēopăt'ra's nee'dle, n. Egyptian obelisk on Thames embankment.

clĕp'sȳdra, n. Ancient time-measuring device worked by flow of water. [L, f. Gk *klepsudra* (*kleptō* steal, *hudōr* water)]

clere'stōrȳ (-cīs-), n. Part of wall of cathedral or large church, with series of windows, above aisle roofs. [ME, f. CLEAR[1]+STOR(E)Y]

clĕr'gȳ, n. The clerical order, all persons ordained for religious service (*the ~* usu. has pl. vb; *a ~*, i.e. the *~* of a country or church, has usu. sing. vb); *~men* (*30 ~ were present*); (hist.) membership of, learning proper to, *~* (*benefit of ~*, exemption from trial by secular court, & later from sentence for first conviction, enjoyed by all who could read); *~man*, ordained minister, esp. of Established Church; *~man's week, fortnight*, holiday including all weekdays before & after 1, 2, Sundays; *~woman*, wife, daughter, etc., of *~man*, esp. if dominating parish. [ME *clergy*, *-gie*, *-ge*, partly f. OF *clergié* f. LL *clericatus*, partly f. OF *clergie* f. *clerc* CLERK + *-ie* = -Y[1], after *clergié*]

clē'ric, a. (arch.), & n. Clergyman; of clergy. Hence **clē'rico-** comb. form. [f. LL f. Gk *klērikos* (*klēros* lot, allus. to *Acts* 1. 17)]

clē'rical, a. & n. Of clergy, clergyman, or clergymen; of, made by, .clerk(s) (*~ error*, in writing out; *~ duties, staff*); (n.) member of *~* party in a parliament etc. Hence *~*ISM(3), *~*IST(2), nn., *~*IZE(3) v.t., *~*ITY (-ăl-) n., *~*LY[2] adv. [f. LL *clericalis* (prec., -AL)]

clē'rihew, n. Short witty, comic, or nonsensical verse, usu. in four lines of varying length. [E. *Clerihew* Bentley (d. 1958)]

clerk (∥ klärk, *klûrk), n. (Also *~ in holy orders* clergyman (arch., legal & sometimes appended to signature to show status of writer); lay officer of parish church with various duties; (*no*) *great ~*. (no) scholar (arch.); officer in charge of records etc., secretary, man of business, of town (*Town C~*), corporation, etc. (usu. a lawyer); person employed in bank, office, shop, etc., to make entries, copy letters, keep accounts, etc.; *shop-assistant; C~ of the Weather*, personification of meteorology; *~ of the works*, overseer of materials etc. in buildings done by contract. Hence *~*DOM, *~*ESS[1], *~*SHIP(1, 3). nn., *~*LY[1] a. [OE *cleric, clerc*, merging w. ME *clerc, clerk(e)* f. OF *clerc*, f. LL *clericus* CLERIC]

clĕv'er, a. Adroit, dexterous, neat in movement (*~ horse*, good fencer); skilful, talented; ingenious (of doer or thing done); *~-~*, excessively *~*. Hence *~*ISH[1](2) a., *~*LY[2] adv., *~*NESS n. [early

hist. obsc., orig. unkn.; corresp. in form & sense to LG *klöver, klever*, MDu. *klever* sprightly, brisk, smart, suggests LG orig.]

clĕv'is, n. U-shaped iron at end of beam for attaching tackle. [etym. unkn.]

clew (-ōō), n., & v.t. **1.** Ball of thread or yarn; this as used in mythol. story to guide through labyrinth; = CLUE. **2.** (naut.). Small cords suspending hammock; lower or after corner of sail. **3.** v.t. *~ up*, draw lower ends of (sails) to upper yard or mast ready for furling. [ME *clyw(e), clew(e)*, OE *cliwen, cleowen*, = Du., MLG *kluwen*; prob. dim. of a wd corresp. to OHG *kliu, kliuwi* (whence G *knäuel* clew); loss of *-en* as in *eve, game*]

cliché (klēsh'ā), n. Metal cast esp. stereo or electro duplicate; hackneyed literary phrase. [F]

click, n., & v.i. (Make) slight sharp sound as of cocking gun; catch in machinery acting with this sound; (of horse) touch shoes of fore & hind feet (n., this fault); (S.-Afr. langg.) (make) sharp non-vocal sucking sound as articulation; (sl.) secure one's object, come to an agreement. So *~'ER[1]* n., foreman shoemaker who cuts out the leather and gives out work, ∥ (Printing) foreman of a companionship of compositors who distributes the copy etc. [imit., cf. Du. *klikken*, F *cliquer*]

cli'ent, n. (Rom. Ant.) plebeian under protection of noble; (arch.) dependant, hanger-on; employer of lawyer; employer of any professional man, customer. Hence *~*AGE, *~*SHIP, nn., *~*LESS a. [f. L *cliens -entis* (*cluere* hear, obey, -ENT)]

cli'entēle, n. **1.** Person's dependants, following. **2.** Customers, supporters, (of physician, shop, theatre, etc.). [f. L *clientela* clientship; later reintroduced f. F *clientèle*]

cliff, n. Steep rock-face, usu. overhanging sea; *~s'man*, skilled climber. [OE *clif*, OS, ON *klif*, OHG *klep*, f. Gmc *klibhom*]

climăc'tĕric (or -ĕ'r-), a. & n. **1.** Constituting a crisis, critical; (Physiol. & Med.) occurring at period of life (45–60) at which vital force begins to decline. **2.** n. Critical period in life (multiples of 7, odd multiples of 7, etc.; *grand ~*, 63rd year). [f. L (& partly f. F *climatérique*) f. Gk *klimaktērikos* f. *klimaktēr* rung of ladder (*klimax*), -IC]

clim'ate, n. (Region with certain) conditions of temperature, dryness, wind, light, etc.; (fig.) trend or attitude of community or era, character of something. Hence **climăt'ic** a., **climăt'ic-ALLY** adv., **climătŏl'ogy** n., **clim'ato-LO'GICAL** a. [ME f. OF *climat* f. L f. Gk *klima -at-* (*klinō* slope, -M)]

clim'ăx, n., & v.i. & t. **1.** Ascending scale; series of ideas or expressions so arranged; last term in these; culmination, apex; hence (irreg.) **climăc'tic** a. **2.** vb. Come, bring, to a *~*. [LL, f. Gk *klimax -akos* ladder, climax]

climb (-ĭm), v.t. & i. (past ~ed & arch. *clomb* pr. -ōm), & n. **1.** Ascend, mount, go *up*, (t. & i.) esp. with help of hands; ~ *down* (t. & i.), descend (cliff etc., or abs.) similarly, (intr.) retreat from position taken up, give in; (of sun, aeroplane, etc.) go slowly up; (of plants) get support by tendrils or twining from tree, trellis, etc.; slope upwards; rise by effort in social rank, intellectual or moral strength, etc.; ~*ing-iron*, spikes attachable to boot for ~ing trees or ice slopes; hence **clĭ'mb-ABLE** (-ma-) a. **2.** n. Piece of ~ing (~- *down*, abandonment of declared intention), place (to be) ~ed. [OE *climban*, (M)Du., (M)LG *klimmen*, OHG *klimban* (G *klimmen*), f. WG **klimban* f. nasalized var. of **klibh*- CLEAVE[2]]

clĭ'mber (-ĭmer), n. In vbl senses; esp.: climbing plant; kinds of bird, usu. with two forward & two backward toes; person climbing socially. [-ER[1]]

clime, n. (poet.). Tract, country, (with or without ref. to climate). [f. L *clima*; see CLIMATE]

clinch. See CLENCH.

clin'cher, clĕn'cher, n. In vbl senses; esp., remark, argument, that triumphantly settles a question; *clincher-built*= CLINKER-BUILT. [prec. +.-ER[1]]

cling, v.i. (*clung*). ~ *together*, remain in one body or in contact, resist separation; stick, adhere *to*, (whether by stickiness, suction, grasping, or embracing; ~*ing garments*, showing form of body or limbs); remain faithful *to* (friend, habit, idea); ~*'stone*, kind of peach or nectarine in which flesh adheres to stone. [OE *clingan*, MDu. *klingen* stick, f. Gmc **kling*-, **klang*-, **klung*- parallel to **klink*-, see CLENCH]

clin'ic, n. Teaching of medicine or surgery at the hospital bedside; class, institution, so taught, conducted; **SEMINAR* (last two senses). [f. F *clinique* f. Gk *klinikē* (*lekhnē*) CLINICAL (art)]

clin'ical, a. (med.). Of, at, the sick-bed (esp. of lectures, teaching, so given; ~ *thermometer*, for taking patient's temperature). Hence ~LY[2] adv. [f. prec.+ -AL]

clink[1], n., & v.i. & t. (Make, cause *glasses* etc. to make) sharp ringing sound; ‖ ~*ing* (sl. as a. & adv.), exceedingly (good, fine), as *a* ~*ing*, or ~*ing good, race*; ~*'stone*, kinds of felspar (f. ringing like iron when struck). Hence ‖ ~*'er*[1] [-ER[1]] n. (sl.), ~ing specimen. [ME, perh. f. MDu. *klinken*; cf. CLANG, CLANK]

clink[2], n. (sl.). Prison, lock-up, (esp. *in* ~). [16th c., orig. unkn.]

clink'er[2], n. Very hard yellow Dutch brick; brick with surface vitrified by great heat; mass of bricks fused together or of slag or lava. [17th c. *clincard* etc. f. Du. *klinkaerd* (now *klinker*) f. *klinken* CLINK[1]]

clink'er-built, a. (Of boats) made with external planks overlapping downwards & fastened with clinched copper nails. [f. *clink* north. var. of *clinch*; see CLENCH]

clinŏm'éter, n. Instrument for measuring slopes. [f. Gk *klinō* to slope, -O-, -METER]

Clī'ō, n. (The Muse of) history. [f. Gk *Kleiō* (*kleiō* celebrate)]

clip[1], v.t. (-pp-), & n. **1.** Surround closely, grip tightly. **2.** n. Appliance for holding things together or for attachment to object as mark; brooch; set of attached cartridges for magazine rifle. [OE *clyppan* embrace, = OFris. *kleppa*, f. WG **klupp-jan*]

clip[2], v.t. (-pp-), & n. **1.** Cut with shears or scissors, trim thus, take away part of (hair, wool) thus, remove hair or wool of (sheep, person) thus, (~ one's *wings*, disable him from pursuing his ambition); remove small piece of (railway, bus, etc. ticket) to show that it has been used, whence ~*p'ie* [-Y[3]] n. (colloq.), bus conductress; pare edge of (coin); omit letters or syllables of (words); omit (letter etc.; ~ *his* gs). **2.** n. Operation of shearing or hair-cutting; quantity of wool clipped from sheep, flock, etc.; smart blow with the hand, cut with the whip, etc. [ME *clippen* f. ON *klippa*]

clipp'er, n. In vbl senses; also or esp.: instrument for clipping hair; swift mover (esp. of horse or ship); ship with forward-raking bows & aft-raking masts; transoceanic flying-boat **P**; (sl.) thing excellent of its kind. [CLIP[2], -ER[1]]

clipp'ing[1], n. In vbl senses; esp., piece clipped off, *newspaper cutting. [CLIP[2], -ING[1]]

clipp'ing[2], a. In vbl senses; esp., (sl.) first-rate. [CLIP[2], -ING[2]]

clique (-ēk), n. Small exclusive party, set, coterie. Hence **cli'quish**[1] (-ēk-), **cli'qu(e)y**[2] (-ēki), aa., **cli'quishness**, **cli'quism**(2), (-ēk-), nn. [F, f. *cliquer* CLICK[1]]

clit'oris, n. Rudimentary internal part of female genitals analogous to penis. [Gk *kleitoris*]

clivers. See CLEAVERS.

cloā'ca, n. (pl. *-ae*). Sewer; excrementory cavity in birds, reptiles, etc.; gathering-place of moral evil. Hence **cloā'cal** a. [L]

cloak, (arch.) **clōke**, n., & v.i. & t. **1.** Loose usu. sleeveless outdoor upper garment; covering (~ *of snow*); pretence, pretext, (*under the* ~ *of*); ~*-room*, for leaving ~s, hats, etc., or any luggage. **2.** vb. Put on one's ~; put ~ on (*oneself* or another); conceal, disguise. [ME, f. OF *cloke*, dial. var. of *cloche* bell, cloak (from its bell shape) f. med. L *clocca* bell; see CLOCK[1]]

clŏbb'er, n. Black paste used to hide cracks in leather; (sl.) clothing, gear. [orig. unkn.]

cloche (klōsh), n. ~ (*hat*), woman's bell-shaped hat; (orig. bell-shaped) glass cover

for forcing or protecting outdoor plants.
[F, = bell]

clŏck¹, n., & v.i. & t. **1.** Time-measuring instrument periodically wound up, kept in motion by springs or weights acting on wheels, & recording hours, minutes, etc., by hands on a dial (*o'clock* now usu. only appended to the actual hour, as *six o'clock*, but *quarter to six, six fifteen*, 7.25; *what o'clock is it?*, what is the time?; *of the clock* still in formal or facetious use; *put back the* ~, fig., go back to a past age); ~like device showing readings on a dial (*range* ~); (colloq.) stop-watch; downy head of dandelion etc.; ~'*wise, counter- -*~'*wise*, moving in curve from left to right, right to left, as seen by spectator at centre; ~'*work*, mechanism on ~ principle (*like* ~*work*, regularly, automatically), (attrib.) regular, mechanical. **2.** v.i. (Of factory hands etc.) ~ *in, on, out, off*, register one's entry or exit by means of an automatic ~; (v.t.; colloq.) time (race) with stop-watch. [f. MDu., MLG *klocke* (= OS *glogga*, OHG *glocka*, ON *klokka*) f. med. L *clocca*, see CLOAK; ult. f. Celt., cf. OIr. *cloc*]

clŏck², n. (shop pl., formerly, *clox*). Pattern worked in silk etc. on side of stocking. Hence (-)~ED² (-kt) a. [16th c.; orig. unkn.]

clŏck'ing, a. ~ *hen*, one sitting on eggs. [Sc. & north. var. of CLUCK*ing*]

clŏd, n., & v.t. (-dd-). Lump of earth etc.; lump of earth (vb, pelt with ~s); *the* ~, soil, land, mere matter; (also ~'*hopper*, ~'*pole*) bumpkin, lout, (so ~'*hopping*, loutish), whence ~**d'**ISH¹ a., ~**d'**ishNESS n.; coarse part of neck of ox as meat. [in ME syn. var. of CLOT (now different.), corresp. to OE *clod*- f. Gmc **klud*-, cogn. w. **klut*- CLOT; see CLOUD]

clŏg¹, n. Block of wood fastened to leg to impede motion; impediment, encumbrance; woman's wooden-soled overshoe for wet ground; wooden-soled shoe with metal rim; ~-*dance*, performed in ~s. [ME, of unkn. orig.]

clŏg², v.t. & i. (-gg-). Confine (animal) with clog; be an encumbrance to, burden; impede, hamper; choke up, obstruct by stickiness; fill up with choking matter; stop or act badly from being choked up. [f. prec.]

clŏgg'y̆ (-g-), a. Lumpy, knotty; sticky. [-Y²]

cloisonné (klwahzŏnā'), a. & n. ~ *enamel* or ~, enamel in which colours of pattern are kept apart by thin outline plates. [F]

clois'ter, n., & v.t. (Enclose, shut *up*, in) convent, monastic house, (*the* ~, monastic seclusion); covered walk, often round quadrangle with wall on outer & colonnade or windows on inner side, esp. of convent, college, cathedral buildings, whence ~ED² (-erd) a. Hence **clois'trAL** a. [ME & OF *cloistre* f. L *claustrum, clostrum*]

clōke. See CLOAK.

clōne, n. A group of plants produced vegetatively from one original seedling or stock. Hence **clōn'AL** a. [f. Gk *klōn* twig, slip]

clōn'us, n. (path.). Spasm with violent successive muscular contractions & relaxations. Hence **clōn'IC** a. [f. Gk *klonos*]

clŏŏp, n., & v.i. (Make) sound (as) of cork being drawn. [imit.]

clōse¹, a. & adv. **1.** Shut; (of vowels) pronounced with lips or mouth cavity contracted (e.g. *o* in *not* is open, in *note* ~); narrow, confined, contracted, stifling (~ *siege, prisoner, air*); covered, concealed, secret, given to secrecy, (*keep, lie*, ~, be in hiding; ~-*stool*, chamber-pot mounted in stool with cover); niggardly (so ~ᴸ -fist'ED² a., ~-fist'ĕdNESS n.); restricted, limited, (~ *corporation* etc.; || ~ *scholarship*, not open to all; ~ BOROUGH); under prohibition (|| ~ *season, time*, in which something is forbidden, esp. killing of game etc.). **2.** Near; dense, compact, with no or slight intervals, (~ *texture, thicket, writing*; ~ *order, combat*; ~ *quarters*, immediate contact; ~ *reasoner, argument, analysis*, leaving no gaps or weak spots, coherent; also adv., as *shut* ~, ~ *ranked*; ~-*grainĕd*, without visible interstices; *stand, sit*, ~); in or nearly in contact (~ *proximity*; *a* ~ *shave*, near the skin, also fig., narrow missing of collision etc.; ~-*hauled*, with sails hauled aft so as to sail ~ to the wind; SAIL ~ *to the wind*; esp. in adv. or prep. phrr. ~ *by*, ~ *to*, ~ *upon*, as *he was* ~ *by*, ~ *to the road*, ~ *upon two hundred*); fitting exactly (~ *cap*, ~ *resemblance*); near & dear; nearly equal (~ *.contest*); concentrated (~ *examination, attention*); ~ *call* (colloq.), a near thing, something almost fatal; ~-*up* n., part of cinema film taken at short range and showing person(s) etc. on large scale. Hence ~'LY² (-sl-) adv., ~'NESS (-sn-) n. [ME & OF *clos* f. L *clausus* p.p. of *claudere* shut]

clōse², n. Enclosed place (*break* one's ~, legal, trespass on his land); precinct of cathedral; school playground; (Sc.) entry from street to court at back. [ME & OF *clos* f. L *clausum* enclosure (prec.)]

clōse³ (-z), v.t. & i., & n. **1.** Shut (t. & i. of lid or box, door or room or house; lit., or = declare or be declared not open, of place of business etc.; *closing-time*, at which shops etc. stop business; ~ *upon*, of hand, box, etc., grasp or imprison, also of eyes, lose sight of by shutting); ~*d shop*, a trade etc. restricted to members of a (particular) trade union. **2.** Be the boundary of, conclude, bring or come to an end, complete, settle, (~ one's *days*, die; ~ *bargain*; abs. stop speaking, often *with* the remark etc.). **3.** Bring or come into contact (~ *the ranks* or, intr., ~ *up*; ~ *electric current* or *circuit*, give it continuity), come within striking distance, grapple *with*, (Naut., as v.t.) approach or come alongside of (other ship etc.); (Mil., as v.i., to men in rank) *right ~*, *left ~*, move sideways to right, left. **4**. Express (often eager) agreement *with* (offer, terms, or person offering them). **5**. *~ in*, enclose, come nearer, (of days) get successively shorter; *~ up*, block, fill, coalesce. **6. n**. Conclusion, end; grappling of combatants; (Mus.) cadence. [ME *close(n)* f. OF *clos-* st. of *clore* f. L *claudere* shut]

clŏs′ĕt (-z-), n., & v.t. Private or small room, esp. for private interviews (so vb, *be ~ed with, together*, hold consultation) or for study (*~ play*, to be read not acted; *~ strategist* etc., theoretical); cupboard, as *china-~*; = WATER-*~*. [ME, f. OF dim. of *clos* CLOSE², -ET¹]

clō′sure (-zher), n., & v.t. **1**. Closing, closed condition. **2**. (Parl.) decision by vote of House of Commons, under certain restrictions, to put the question without further debate; (v.t.) apply *~* to (motion, speakers, etc.). [ME, f. OF, f. L *clausura* (*claudere claus-*, -URE)]

clŏt, n., & v.i. & t. (-tt-). **1**. Mass of material stuck together; semi-solid lump of coagulated liquid, esp. of blood (*~ of blood*, pop. name for THROMBOSIS); (sl.) stupid person. **2. vb.** Form (t. & i.) into *~s* (*~ted hair*, stuck together in locks; *~ted cream*, got by scalding milk; *~ted nonsense*, utter absurdity). [OE *clot(t)* f. WG **klutt-* (= MHG *kloz*) f. **klut-*, weak grade of **klaut-* CLEAT]

cloth (-awth, -ŏth, *pl.* -awdhz, -ŏths), n. (pl. *~s*, & in differentiated sense CLOTHES). (Piece, used for any purpose, of) woven or felted stuff; (also *table-~*) covering for table, esp. of linen at meals (*lay the ~*, prepare table for meal); woollen woven fabric as used for clothes; each of the breadths of canvas in a sail; duster; *~ of gold, silver*, tissue of gold or silver threads interwoven with silk or wool; ‖ *American ~*, enamelled *~* like leather; *cut coat according to ~*, adapt expenditure to resources; profession as shown by clothes, esp. clerical (*respect due to his ~*; also *the ~*, clergy); *~-binding*, cover of book in linen or cotton *~*; *~-yard shaft* (hist.), arrow a yard long. [OE *clǎth* of unkn. orig.; Gmc cognates only since 12th c., cf. G *kleid*]

clōthe (-dh), v.t. (*~d* or, arch. & literary, *clad*). Provide with clothes, put clothes upon; cover like or as with clothes or a cloth (*leaves ~ trees*; *~d with righteousness, with plantations*; *body ~s soul*; also *~ face in smiles, ideas in words*). Hence **clōth′ING¹**(4) (-dh-) n. [OE *clǎthian*, *clǎthan*, f. *clǎth* CLOTH]

clothes (-ōz, -ōdhz), n. pl. Wearing-apparel; BED¹-*~*; linen etc. to be washed (*~-bag, -basket*, for conveying this; *~-horse*, for airing it on; *~-line, -post*,

‖ *-prop*, ‖ *-peg*, rope, supports of rope, wooden clip on rope, for drying it after washing); *~-brush*; *~-moth*, destructive to *~*; *~-press*, cupboard with shelves for *~*; (*old-*)*~-man*, dealer in usu. old *~*. [repr. OE *clǎthas*; *cloths* (since c. 1600) completely different. in 19th c.]

clŏth′ier (-dh-), n. (Formerly) maker of cloth; dealer in cloth or clothes. [ME *clother*, see -ER¹, -IER]

clou (kloo), n. Point of greatest interest, chief attraction, central idea. [F, = nail]

cloud, n., & v.t. & i. **1**. (Mass of) visible condensed watery vapour (see CIRRUS, CUMULUS, NIMBUS, STRATUS) floating high above general level of ground (*~-drift*, *~* in motion), *~-rack*, pile of broken *~s*; *~-burst*, violent rainstorm; *~-capped*, of hill with top hidden by *~*; *~-scape*, picture, picturesque grouping, of *~s*; *~-kissing*, of high hill or building); unsubstantial or fleeting thing; mass of smoke or dust; local dimness or vague patch of colour in or on liquid or transparent body; great number *of* birds, insects, horsemen, arrows, moving together; light woollen scarf; obscurity (*under~ of night*; *a ~ of words*); *in the ~s*, mystical, unreal, imaginary, (so *~-castle*, daydream); *~-land*, *~-world*, utopia, fairyland), (of person) abstracted, inattentive; state of gloom, trouble, suspicion, louring or depressed look, (*~ on brow*; *under a ~*, out of favour, discredited); *~-berry*, mountain shrub with white flower & orange-coloured fruit; *C~-cuckoo-land*, *-town*, ideal realm [transl. of Gk *Nephelokokkugia* (*nephelē* cloud + *kokkux* cuckoo) in Aristophanes' *Birds*]; hence *~′LESS* a., *~′lĕssLY²* adv., *~′lĕssNESS*, *~′LET*, nn., *~′Y³* a., *~′iLY²* adv., *~′iNESS* n., *~′WARD*(s) adv. **2. vb.** Overspread, darken, with *~s*, gloom, or trouble; variegate with vague patches of colour; become overcast or gloomy (*~ up, over*). [ME *clud, clod, cloud*, app. same wd as OE *clǔd* mass of rock or earth, prob. cogn. w. CLOD]

clough (klŭf), n. Ravine, steep valley usu. with torrent bed. [OE *clōh*, rel. to OHG *klinga*, G dial. *klinge*]

clout n., & v.t. Patch (n. & v.); a cloth (esp. *dish-~*); piece of clothing; hit, cuff, (n. & v., esp. with open hand); iron plate on boot etc. to save wear, (also *~-nail*) broad-headed nail for attaching *~*; (hist.) canvas on frame as mark at archery (*in the ~*, a hit!). [OE *clǔt*, f. Gmc **klǔt-* cogn. w. CLOT, CLEAT]

clōve¹, clōven. See CLEAVE¹.

clōve², n. One of small bulbs making up compound bulb of garlic, shallot, etc. (usu. *of*). [OE *clufu* cogn. w. CLEAVE¹]

clōve³, n. (Pungent aromatic dried bud of) tropical tree (*oil of ~s*, extracted from *~s* & used in medicine); (also *~-gilly-flower*) *~*-scented pink, original of carnation & other double pinks. [ME *clou(e)* f. F *clou (de girofle)*; *girofle* (see GILLYFLOWER) was orig. name of the spice; *clou* (f. L *clavus* nail) *de girofle* (in Eng. ~*-gillyflower*) was used of it w. ref. to its shape, transferred to the similarly shaped bud of pink, & later divided into *clove* for the spice, & *gillyflower* for the pink]

clŏve hĭtch, n. Hitch by which rope is secured at any intermediate part round spar or rope that it crosses at right angles. [old p.p. of CLEAVE[1], as showing parallel separate lines]

clŏv′er, n. Kinds of trefoil used for fodder (*be*, *live*, *in* ~, in ease & luxury). [OE *clǣfre* = MLG *klāver*, first syll. corresp. to OS *klē*, OHG *klēo* (G *klee*) f. WG **klaiw-*]

clown, n., & v.i. **1.** Rustic; ignorant or ill-bred man, whence ~′ISH[1] a., ~′ĭshLY[2] adv., ~′ĭshNESS n.; jester, esp. in pantomime or circus, whence ~′ERY(4) n. **2.** v.i. Play the ~. [16th c., of obsc., perh. LG orig.; cf. NFris. *klönne*, *klünne* clumsy fellow]

clŏx. See CLOCK[2].

cloy, v.t. Satiate, weary, by richness, sweetness, sameness, excess, of food or pleasure (usu. *with*). [f. obs. *accloy* f. OF *encloyer* f. Rom. **inclavare*; cf. EN-CLAVE]

clŭb[1], n. **1.** Stick with one thick end as weapon (*Indian* ~s, pair swung to develop muscles; ~*-law*, rule by physical force); kinds of stick used in games, esp. golf; structure or organ in Bot. etc. with knob at end; ~*-foot(ed)*, (with) congenitally distorted foot; ~*-moss*, kind with upright spikes of spore-cases; ~*-root*, disease of turnips etc.; playing-card of suit bearing black trefoil (~s, the suit). **2.** Association of persons united by some common interest, meeting periodically for co-operation (*Alpine*, *golf*, *yacht*, BENEFIT, ~) or conviviality; body of persons with cooperation by ballot combined for social purposes & having premises (~*-house*) for resort, meals, temporary residence, etc. (‖ ~′*land*, St James's in London, where ~s cluster), whence ~′DOM n., ~′LESS a. [ME *clubbe*, *clobbe* f. ON *klubba* assim. form of *klumba* club, rel. to CLUMP]

clŭb[2], v.t. & i. (-bb-). Beat with club; use butt of (gun) as club; bring, come, into a mass; contribute (money, ideas) to common stock; (v.i.) combine *together*, *with*, for joint action, making up a sum, etc.; (Mil.) get (one's men) into a confused mass. [f. prec.]

clŭb′able, a. Fit for membership of a club. [CLUB[1], -ABLE]

clŭb′haul, v.t. Tack (*ship*, or abs.) by anchoring & cutting cable, as device for getting off lee-shore when there is not room to wear. [orig. unkn.]

clŭck, n., & v.i. (Make) guttural cry of

hen. Hence ~′Y[2] a., = CLOCKING. [early 17th c.; cf. obs. & dial. *clock* f. OE *cloccian*; imit.]

clue (-ōō), n. Fact or principle that serves as guide, or suggests a line of inquiry, in any problem, investigation, or study; thread of story, train of thought; (also rarely in other senses of) CLEW. Hence ~′LESS (-ōō-) a. [different. sp. of CLEW]

clŭm′ber, n. Kind of spaniel. [C~ in Notts.]

clŭmp, n., & v.i. & t. **1.** Cluster of trees or shrubs (usu. *of*); (also ~*-sole*) extra thickness of leather added to sole, usu. nailed on. **2.** vb. Tread heavily; heap or plant together; provide (boot) with ~. [16th c., f. MLG *klumpe* (LG *klump*, Du. *klomp*, G *klumpen*); see CLUB[1]]

clŭm′s│y̆ (-z-), a. Awkward in movement or shape, ungainly; ill-contrived; without tact. Hence ~ĭLY[2] adv., ~ĭNESS n. [c. 1600, app. f. north. dial. *clumse* (14th c.) benumbed with cold, +-Y[2]; prob. of Scand. orig., cf. Sw. dial. *klumsen*, *klumsig*]

clŭnch, n. Soft white limestone used for internal carving-work. [orig. unkn.]

clŭng. See CLING.

clŭs′ter, n., & v.t. & i. **1.** Group of similar things, esp. such as grow together, bunch; swarm, group, of persons, animals, etc. **2.** vb. Bring or come into, be in, a ~ or ~s (~*ed columns*, *pillars*, *shafts*, several close together, or disposed round or half detached from pier). [OE *clyster* app. f. Gmc **klut-*; cf. CLOT]

clŭtch[1], v.t. & i. Seize eagerly, grasp tightly; snatch *at*. [ME *clucche* var. of *clicche* (dial. *clitch*) f. OE *clyccan* f. Gmc **klukjan*]

clŭtch[2], n. Tight grasp; (pl.) grasping-hands, cruel grasp; a grasping *at*; (Mech.) arrangement for throwing working parts into or out of action, gripping-piece of crane. [f. prec., but hist. obsc.; ME *cloke*, *cloche* claw; later *clutch* f. vb]

clŭtch[3], n. Set of eggs; brood of chickens. [18th c., south. var. of north. *cletch* f. *cleck* to hatch f. ON *klekja*, assoc. w. CLUTCH[1]]

clŭtt′er, n., & v.i. & t. (Bustle, run, with) confused noise or movement, loss of self-possession; confused mass, untidy state, litter n. & (esp. in ~*ed up with*) v.t. [late 16th c.; in part, phon. var. of *clotter* (f. *clot*) coagulate; in part assoc. w. *cluster*, *clatter*]

Clydesdale (klīdz′dāl), a. & n. (Of) a breed of heavy draught-horses (orig. from *Clyde* district in Scotland).

clȳp′e│ŭs, n. Shield-like part of insect's head. Hence ~AL, ~ATE[2], ~ĭFORM, aa., ~o- comb. form. [L, = shield]

clȳs′ter, n., & v.t., (med., now rare). =EN-EMA; (vb) treat with ~. [ME, f. OF *clystere* or L. f. Gk *klustēr* syringe]

‖ **cmd**, = CD.

co-, pref. L short form of *com-* (*cum* prep. with), used in L only before vowels, h, gn, & (in the correct classical form) n, but in E as living pref. before any letter. **1.** Prefixed to vbs,=with other subjects (*co-operate*) or objects (*co-adjust*); to adjj. & advv., = jointly, together, mutually, (*coeternally, coadjacent*); & to nouns, = joint, mutual, (*coheir, coequality*). **2.** In some math. words, short for *complement*, = 'of the complement', 'complement of' as *cosine, co-declination*.

coäcervā′tion, n. Heaping together, pile. [f. L CO(*acervatio* f. *acervare* f. *acervus* heap, see -ATION)]

coach, n., & v.i. & t. **1.** State carriage; (also *stage-*~) large four-wheeled & usu. four-horsed close carriage with seats inside and on the roof carrying passengers at fixed rates & times with stoppages for meals & relays of horses; HACKNEY-~; MOURNING-~; SLOW-~; (official name for) railway carriage; long-distance bus; (Naut.) room near stern of man-of-war; private tutor; trainer of athletic team etc.; *drive* ~ *& six through Act of Parliament*, stultify it; ~-*box*, driver's seat; ~-*built*, (of motor-car bodies) built of wood by craftsmen; ~-*dog*, = CARRIAGE-~*dog*; ~-*house*, outhouse for carriages; ~′*man*, driver of any carriage, whence ~′*man*SHIP(3) n.; hence ~′FUL(2) n. **2.** vb. Travel in, go by, stage-~ (*in the old* ~*ing days*); tutor, train, (pupil for examination, crew for race); give hints to, prime with facts; (intr.) read with tutor. [f. F *coche* f. Hung. *kocsi* adj. f. *Kocs* place-name]

coädj′utor (-ŏŏ-; *also* -aĵŏŏ⁴-), n. Assistant esp. to bishop or other ecclesiastic. [ME, f. OF *coadjuteur* f. L CO(*adjutorem* f. ADjuvare -jut- help, -OR)]

coäd′ūnate, a. (physiol. & bot.). Congenitally united. [f. LL CO(*adunatus* p.p. of ADunare make one f. *unus* one)]

coăg′ūl|āte, v.t. & i. Change (t. & i.) from fluid to more or less solid state, clot, curdle, set, solidify. Hence or cogn., ~A′TION, ~ātor, ~ANT(2), nn. [f. L *coagulatus* p.p. of -*are*; see -ATE², ³]

coai′ta (kŏī-), n. Small S.-Amer. monkey (red-faced spider-monkey). [f. Braz. *coatá*]

coal, n., & v.t. & i. **1.** Hard opaque black or blackish mineral or carbonized vegetable matter found in seams or strata below earth's surface & used as fuel & in manufacture of gas, tar, etc. (~*s*, pieces of it ready for supplying fire; chief kinds, ANTHRACITE, BITUMINOUS, LIGNITE; *heap* ~*s of fire*, return good for evil, cf. *Rom*. xii. 20; *blow the* ~*s*, fan flame of passion etc.; *haul, call, over the* ~*s*, reprimand; ~*s to Newcastle*, superfluous action); ~-*bed*, -*seam*, stratum of ~; ~-*black*, quite; ~-*box, -scuttle*, receptacle for ~ to supply

room fire (~-*scuttle bonnet*, with front projection as of inverted ~-box); ~-BUNKER; ~-*dust*, small ~s; || ~-*factor*, middleman between ~-owners & customers; ~-*field*, district with series of ~ strata; ~-*fish*, black cod; || ~-*flap*, -*plate*, cover of ~-cellar opening in pavement; ~-*gas*, mixed gases extracted from ~ & used for lighting & heating; ~-*heaver*, man employed in moving~, whence~′ie [-Y³]n.; ~-*hole*, || small ~-cellar; ~-*master*, -*owner*, owner or lessee of ~-*mine* or ~-*pit* = COLLIERY; ~-*measures* (Geol.), series of rocks formed by seams of ~ & intervening strata; *~-oil*, paraffin; ~-*sack*, black patch in Milky Way (esp. one near Southern Cross); ~-*screen*, frame for parting large from small ~s; ~-*tar*, TAR extracted from bituminous ~, & yielding paraffin, naphtha, benzene, creosote, & aniline dyes; ~-*tit*, = COALMOUSE; ~-*whipper*, man, machine, raising ~ from ship's hold; hence ~′LESS (-l-l-), ~′Y², aa. **2.** vb. Put ~ into (ship etc.); take in supply of~. [OE *col*, MDu. MLG *kole*, OHG *kol(o)*, ON *kol*, f. Gmc **kolom*]

coales|ce′, v.i. Come together & form one (of material or immaterial things); combine in a coalition (of statesmen, parties). So ~′CENCE n., ~′CENT a. [f. L CO(*alescere alit*- grow f. *alere* nourish)]

coali′tion, n. Union, fusion; || (Pol.) temporary combination for special ends between parties that retain distinctive principles. Hence ~IST(1) (-sho-) n. [f. med. L *coalitio* (prec., -ION)]

coal′mouse, cōle-, n. Small dark-coloured bird (also COAL-*tit*). [ME *colmose* f. OE *colmāse* (*col* coal+*māse* f. WG **maisa* kind of small bird)]

coam′ing, n. Raised border round hatches etc. of ship to keep out water. [orig. unkn.]

coarse (kôrs), a. Common, inferior, (~ *fish, fare*); rough, loose, or large, in texture, grain, or features; not delicate in perception, manner, or taste, unrefined; rude, uncivil, vulgar; obscene (of language); ~-*fibred*, -*grained*, lit. of things, also fig. of persons = without delicacy. Hence ~′LY² (-sl-) adv., **coars′EN⁴** v.t. & i., ~′NESS (-sn-) n., **coars′ISH(2)** a. [15th c., of unkn. orig.; the suggested connexion w. *course* is unsubstantiated]

coast¹, n. (Also *sea-*~) border of land near sea, sea-shore; CLEAR¹~; (U.S. & Canada) toboggan slide; (hence through COAST²) downhill run on bicycle with feet up or still; ~′*guard(sman)*, Admiralty ~ police-(man); ~′*line*, the line of the sea-shore esp. with regard to its configuration (*the rugged ~line of the island*); ·||~ *waiter*, custom-house officer who deals with goods carried ~wise. Hence ~′AL a., ~-WARD(S) adv., ~′WISE a. & adv. [ME & OF *coste* f. L *costa* rib, flank, side]

coast[2], v.i. Sail along coast, trade between ports on same coast; slide down hill on toboggan, bicycle down hill without pedalling. Hence ~'ER[1] n., ~ing vessel, silver tray for decanter, rest for the foot on front fork of bicycle. [ME *costay, -ey, -ie* f. OF *costeier* f. *coste* (prec.)]

coat, n., & v.t. **1.** Man's sleeved usu. cloth body garment (*dress-~*, with swallow tails for the evening; ~ *of* MAIL; FROCK-~; *great~, top-~*, outdoor, worn over another; *red ~*, traditional uniform of British soldier; so *red'~*, soldier; ~ *of arms*, herald's tabard, gentleman's heraldic bearings or shield; ~ *armour*, blazonry, heraldic arms; ~*-card*, now *court-*, playing-card with coated figure, king, queen, or knave; *trail* one's ~*-tails*, for someone to tread on, = seek to pick quarrel; *dust* one's ~, beat him; *turn* one's ~, change sides, desert); woman's outer garment, (also, esp. in ~ *& skirt*) overcoat, or short tailored jacket worn with skirt; petticoat (arch. & dial.; in literature esp. in KILT one's ~s). **2.** Covering compared to garment; beast's hair, fur, etc.; (Physiol.) investing membrane etc. of organ; skin, rind, husk, layer of bulb etc.; covering of paint etc. laid on at once; hence (-)~'ED[2], ~'LESS, aa. **3.** v.t. Put or (with *paint* etc. as subj.) be ~ of paint, tin, etc., upon, (p.p.) covered over *with* dust etc. [ME, f. OF *cote* f. WG **kotta* (= OS *cot*, OHG *kozza, kozzo* (garment of) shaggy woollen stuff, in med. L *cotta*)]

coatee, n. Short-tailed coat. [-EE]

coa'ti (-ah-), n. American carnivorous mammal like civet & racoon with long flexible snout. [Braz. (*cua* cincture, *tim* nose)]

coat'ing, n. Layer of paint etc.; material for coats. [-ING[1]]

coax, v.t. & i. Persuade by blandishments (*to* do, *into* do*ing* or good temper etc.; ~ thing *out of* person; ~ *fire to light, key into lock*, etc.); ~ *away, out*, etc., entice; practise wheedling. Hence ~'ER[1] n. [16th c., 'make a cokes of', f. obs. *cokes* (16th c.) simpleton, of unkn. orig.]

coäx'al, -ial, a. (math.). Having common axis. [CO-, AXIS, -AL]

cob[1], n. Male swan; stout short-legged riding-horse, whence ~**b'Y**[2] a.; (also ~*-nut*) large kind of hazel-nut; roundish lump of coal etc.; round-headed loaf; CORN-~. [orig. unkn.]

|| **cob**[2], n. Composition of clay, gravel, & straw, used for building walls. [orig. unkn.]

cob'alt (-awlt), n. Silvery-white metal similar in many respects to nickel; deep--blue pigment made from it. Hence **cobal'tic**, ~**if'EROUS, cobal'tous** (chem.), aa., **cobal'to-** comb. form., (-awl-). [G, prob. = *kobold* goblin of mines]

cobb'er, n. (Austral. colloq.). Chum, pal. [orig. unkn.]

cob'ble[1], n., & v.t. (Also ~*-stone*) water--worn rounded stone of size used for paving (vb, pave with these); (pl.) coals of this size. [f. COB[1] + -LE]

cob'ble[2], v.t. Put together roughly; mend, patch *up*, (esp. shoes). [c. 1500, app. back form. f. foll.]

cobb'ler, n. Mender of shoes; clumsy workman; (often *sherry ~*) iced drink of wine, sugar, lemon, sucked through straw (orig. unkn.; from U.S.); **fruit* pie; ~'s *wax*, resinous substance used for waxing thread. [ME, of unkn. orig.]

Cob'den|ism, n. Policy based on Free Trade, international cooperation, & retrenchment, peace, non-intervention, and opposition to Empire. Hence ~ITE[1](1) a. & n. [R. *Cobden*, d. 1865, -ISM]

co'ble, n. Kinds of fishing-boat in Scotland & N.E. England. [ME *coble, -ill* cf. W *ceubal*, Bret. *caubal*]

cob'ra (dè capèll'ō), n. The venomous hooded snake of India, with neck dilated like hood under irritation. [Port.; *cobra* f. L *colubra* snake, *capello* hood f. med. L *capellus* f. *cappa* CAPE]

cob'web, n. & a. Spider's network, material of it, thread of this; thing of flimsy texture (so adj., thin, flimsy), subtle fanciful reasoning; musty rubbish (esp. fig. as ~*s of the law, of antiquity*; *blow away the ~s*, take an airing); entanglement, mesh. Hence ~**bED**[2] (-bd), ~**b'Y**[2], aa., ~**bERY**(5) n. [ME *cop(pe)web* f. (obs.) *coppe* spider + WEB]

cōc'a, n. (Leaves of) Bolivian shrub (chewed as stimulant). [Sp., f. Peruv. *cuca*]

*cōc'a-cōl'a, n. Aerated non-alcoholic drink. [P]

cocain|e', n. Drug from coca producing local insensibility. Hence ~'IZE(5) v.t., ~IZA'TION, ~'ISM(5), nn. [-INE[5]]

cŏc'cagee (-gē), n. A cider apple, cider from it. [f. Ir. *cac a ghéidh* goose dung (so coloured)]

cŏc'cyx (-ks-), n. Small triangular bone ending spinal column in man; analogous part in birds etc. Hence *or* cogn. **cŏccy̆'gèAL** a., **cŏccy̆'gèo-**, **cŏc'cy̆g**(o)-, (-ks-), comb. forms. [L, f. Gk *kokkux -ugos* cuckoo (like its bill)]

cŏch'in-chīn'a, n. & a. (Fowl) of Cochin China breed. [place]

cŏch'ineal, n. Dried bodies of insect reared on cactus in Mexico etc., used for making scarlet dye & carmine. [f. F *cochenille* f. Sp. *cochinilla* or It. *-iglia* (*coccino* f. L *coccinus* scarlet f. *coccum* scarlet, orig. berry)]

cŏch'lea (-k-), n. (pl. *-leae*). Spiral cavity of internal ear. [L, = snail]

cŏck[1], n. **1.** Male bird (alone of domestic fowl, as below, also of BLACK-~; of other birds only when aided by context; in comb. in bird-names, as PEACOCK, WOOD-~, & prefixed = male as ~ *robin*; ~

sparrow, male sparrow, small lively pugnacious person; ~ *of the wood*, capercaillie; ‖ ~ *of the north*, brambling; ~-*nest*, built by some ~s, as wren, to roost in); (short for) woodcock (w. collect. sing. for pl.); male of domestic fowl (~-*a-doodle-doo*, its crow, child's name for ~); GAME[1]-~; ~-&-*bull story*, idle invention, incredible tale; ~-*crow*, -*crowing*, dawn; ~-*fighting*, setting ~s to fight as sport; *this beats* ~-*fighting*, is inexpressibly delightful; *live like fighting* ~s, on best of fare; *that* ~ *won't fight*, that plea, plan, will not do; ~ *lobster*, *salmon*, male; ~-*shot*, -*shy*, object set up to be thrown at with sticks, stones, etc., as formerly ~s at Shrovetide, a throw at this; ~s'-*comb*, crest of ~, yellow rattle & other plants, & see COXCOMB; ~s'*foot*, a pasture grass; ~s'*head*, kinds of trefoil; ~'*spur*, ~'s spur, gas-burner of same shape; ~ *of the walk*, dominant person (so ~ *of the school* among boys); *old*~, familiar vocative. **2.** Tapped spout, tap, (~-*metal*, two parts copper to one of lead); (not decent) penis; lever in gun raised ready to be released by trigger (*at half, full*, ~, of gun half-ready or ready to be let off); indicating-tongue of balance. [OE *coc*(*c*), prob. f. med. L *coccus*(imit.), in ME reinforced by OF *coq* f. same source]

cŏck², v.t. & i. Erect, stick or stand *up*, jauntily or defiantly (~ *the ears*, in attention; ~ one's *nose*, in contempt; ~ *a* SNOOK; ~ one's *eye*, glance knowingly, wink); ~ one's *hat*, set it on aslant, also turn up the brim (~*ed hat*, formerly, with brim fixed so, now, brimless triangular hat pointed before, behind, & above, of various uniform costumes; *knock into a* ~*ed hat*, out of shape or recognition); raise cock of (gun) in readiness for firing. [f. prec. w. ref. to cock's comb, crowing-attitude, etc.]

cŏck³, n. Upward bend (of nose etc.); significant turn (of eye); way of cocking hat; cocked state of gun (see COCK¹). [f. prec.]

cŏck⁴, n., & v.t. (Heap *hay*, rarely *corn*, into) small conical heap(s) in the field. [14th c., perh. of Scand. orig., cf. Norw. *kȯk* heap, ON *kȯkkr* lump, G dial. *kocke* heap of hay]

cŏckabon'dỹ (-ŭn-), n. Kind of fishing-fly. [f. W *coch a bon ddu* red with black trunk]

cockăd|e', n. Rosette etc. worn in hat as badge of office or party or part of livery, esp. black leather rosette (badge of House of Hanover) worn by servants of persons serving Crown. Hence ~'ED² a. [earlier *cockard* f. F *cocarde* orig. in *bonnet à la coquarde*, f. fem. of *coquard* pert (*coq* COCK¹, -ARD)]

cŏck-a-hōōp', a. & adv. Exultant(ly), with boastful crowing. [of unkn. orig.]

Cockaigne' (-ăn), **-ayne'**, n. Imaginary land of idleness and luxury; (punningly w. ref. to COCKNEY) London. [ME *cokaygn*(*e*) f. OF (*pais de*) *cocaigne* (mod. *cocagne*) lit. 'land of cakes' f. MLG *kokenje* sweet cake]

‖ **cŏck-a-leek'ie.** = COCKY-LEEKY.

cŏckalōr'um, n. (colloq.). Self-important little man; ‖ *high* ~, boy's game of leap-frog type. [arbitrary form, f. COCK¹]

cŏckatōō', n. Kinds of parrot with movable crest. [f. Malay *kakatúa* w. assim. to COCK¹]

cŏck'atrice, n. = BASILISK. [ME *cocatris*, -*ice* f. OF *cocatris* etc. f. med. L *calcatricem* (L *calcare* tread, track) rendering Gk *ikhneumōn* tracker (see ICHNEUMON)]

cŏck'boat, n. Small ship's boat. [f. obs. *cock* small boat (f. OF *coque*) + BOAT¹]

cŏck'chāfer, n. Greyish-chestnut beetle flying with loud whirring sound. [perh. f. COCK¹ as expr. size or vigour + CHAFER]

cŏck'er¹, v.t. Indulge, pamper, coddle, (child, invalid, etc.; usu. *up*). [orig. obsc.; perh. f. obs. *cock* vb in same sense; cf. also obs. *cockle* fondle]

Cŏck'er², n. *According to* ~, exact, correct. [E. ~, famous teacher of arithmetic d. 1675]

cŏck'er³, n. Breed of spaniel. [a 'cocking-dog', as starting woodcock etc.; see -ER¹]

cŏck'erel, n. Young cock; pugnacious youth. [dim. of COCK¹, cf. *pickerel*, *mongrel*]

cŏck'-eyed (-īd), a. (sl.). Squinting; crooked, set aslant, not level; stupid. [COCK³]

cŏck'-hŏrse, adv. (Also *a-cock-horse*, see A²) astride, mounted. [in 16th c. = toy horse]

cŏc'kle¹, n. (Also *corn*-~) purple-flowered plant growing among corn, esp. wheat; disease of wheat turning grains black. [OE *coccul*; excl. E.; perh. f. a-dim. of L *coccum* berry]

cŏc'kle², n. An edible bivalve; its shell; small shallow boat (also ~-*shell*, ~-*boat*); ~s *of the heart*, one's feelings (*delight*, *warm, the* ~s etc.) [ME & OF *cokille* f. med. L *cochilia* for *conchylia* (pl.)]

cŏc'kle³, v.i. & t., & n. (Make to) bulge, curl up, pucker; (n.) bulge or wrinkle in paper, glass, etc. [f. F *coquiller* blister (of bread) f. *coquille*; see prec.]

cŏc'kle⁴, n. Radiating-stove for heating room. [perh. f. Du. *kakel*, *kachel* f. G *kachel* stove-tile]

cŏck'-loft (-aw-), n. Small upper loft. [orig. uncert.; perh. f. COCK¹ + LOFT]

cŏck'ney, n. & a. (pl. ~s). (Characteristic of a) native of London (usu. contemptuous, esp. ~ *accent*). Hence ~DOM (-nĭd-), ~ESE' (-nĭez'), nn., ~FY (-nĭf-) v.t., ~ISH¹ a., ~ISM(2, 4) n., (-nĭi-), ~IZE(3) (nĭi-) v.t. & i. [ME *coken-ey* cock's egg (*coken* gen. pl., *ey* f. OE *æg*); orig. sense prob. small or ill-shaped egg (still *cock's egg* in dial., cf. G *hahnenei*); obs. senses are 'child that sucketh long', 'one made a wanton or nestle-cock of', townsman, the limitation to London being later]

cŏck′pit, n. Place made for cockfights; arena of any struggle (~ *of Europe*, Belgium); (hist.) after part of man-of-war's orlop deck, quarters of junior officers, used in action as hospital; (Aeronaut.) space for pilot etc. in fuselage of aeroplane.

cŏck′roach, n. Nocturnal voracious dark-brown beetle-like insect (also *black-beetle*) infesting kitchens. [f. Sp. *cucaracha* w. assim. to COCK[1], ROACH[1]]

cŏck-sure′ (-shoor), a. Certain to happen, undoubtedly about *to* do; quite convinced *of, about*; self-confident, dogmatic, presumptuous, whence ~NESS (-rn-) n. [COCK[1] used intensively, SURE]

cocksy, coxy, coxiness. = COCKY etc.

cŏck′tail, n. & a., cŏck′tailed (-ld), a. (Horse) with docked tail, of racing stamp but not thoroughbred; (person) placed above his birth or breeding; kind of beetle; drink of spirit with bitters, sugar, etc. (origin doubtful; from U.S.). [tail like that of cock, or that cocks up; sense *half-bred* f. docking of hunters & stage-coach horses]

cŏck′ŭp, n. (typog.). Initial letter much taller than the rest. [COCK[2]]

cŏck′y̆, cŏck′sy̆, cŏx′y̆, a. Conceited, pert. Hence cŏck′ILY[2], cŏx′I-, adv., cŏck′INESS, cŏx′I-, n. [COCK[1], -Y[2]]

cockў-leek′y̆, n. Scotch soup of cock boiled with leeks.

cŏc′ky̆ŏll′y̆ bĭrd, n. (Nursery phr. for) bird.

cŏc′ō (pl. *-os*), cŏc′oa[1] (-kō), cŏk′er, n. (Also ~*nut*, ~*-tree*, ~*nut-tree*) tropical palm-tree; coconut, its large ovate brown hard-shelled seed with edible white lining enclosing whitish liquid (~*nut milk*), (sl.) human head; *that accounts for the milk in the* ~*nut*, (joc.) now all is explained;~*nut butter*, the solid oil obtained from the lining of a ~*nut*, used in soap, candles, ointment, etc.; ~*nut matting*, made from fibre of nut's outer husk; *double* ~*nut*, much larger two-lobed seed of Seychelles palm. [f. Port. & Sp. *coco* grimace; *cocoa* esp. since Dr Johnson's dictionary (1755), in which the article *coco* was run together with the article *cocoa* (= *cacao*); *coker* (17th c.) still in commerc. use]

cŏc′oa[2] (-kō), n. Powder made from crushed cacao seeds often with other ingredients; drink made from this or from the seeds; ~ *bean*, cacao seed;~ *nib*, cotyledon of this; ~ *powder*, kind of gunpowder. [alt. of CACAO]

cocoon′, n., & v.t. & i. Silky case spun by larva to protect it as chrysalis, esp. that

of silkworm, whence ~ERY(3) n.; similar structure made by other animals; (vb) form, wrap (one*self*, thing etc.) in, ~; spray with plastic material. [f. F *cocon* f. Pr. *coucoun* dim. of *coca* shell]

cŏcŏtte′, n. Member of the Parisian demi-monde; fashionable prostitute. [F]

cŏd[1], n. Large sea fish (also ~*'fish*); ~-*bank*, submarine bank frequented by it; ~-*liver oil*, used as medicine. [ME, of unkn. orig.]

cŏd[2], v.t. & i. (sl.; -dd-). Hoax, fool. [orig. unkn.]

cŏd′a, n. (mus.). Independent and often elaborate passage introduced after the natural conclusion of a movement (also fig.). [It., f. L *cauda* tail]

cŏd′dle, v.t., & n. Treat as invalid, keep from cold & exertion, feed *up*; (n.) person who coddles himself or others. [etym. uncert.; perh. same wd as CAUDLE, or (16th c.) *coddle* boil gently, stew]

cōde, n., & v.t. 1. Systematic collection of statutes, body of laws so arranged as to avoid inconsistency & overlapping, whence cŏd′IFY v.t., cŏd′IFIER[1], cŏDIFICA′TION, nn.; set of rules on any subject; prevalent morality of a society or class (esp. ~ *of honour*); system of mil. etc. signals; (Telegr.) set of letter or figure or word groups with arbitrary meanings for brevity or secrecy. 2. v.t. (Also *codify*) put (message) into ~ words, whence cōd′ER[1] n. [ME, f. OF f. L CODEX]

cō-dĕclīnā′tion, n. (astron.). Complement of the declination, North-Polar distance. [CO-(2)]

cŏd′eine (-ēn, -ĭēn), n. Alkaloid in opium used as hypnotic. [f. Gk *kōdeia* poppy-head +-INE[5]]

cŏd′ĕx, n. (pl. *-ĭcēs*). Manuscript volume, esp. of ancient Bible or classical texts. [L, earlier *caudex* tree-trunk, tablet, book]

cŏdg′er, n. (colloq.). Fellow, buffer, queer old person. [perh. var. of CADGER]

cŏd′icil, n. Supplementary addition, esp. modifying or revoking will. So cŏdicill′-ARY[1] a. [f. L *codicillus* (usu. pl.) dim. of CODEX]

cŏd′ling[1], n. Small codfish. [-LING[1](2)]

cŏd′lin(g)[2], n. Kinds of apple of long tapering shape; ~*s-&-cream*, willow-herb. [15th c. *querd(e)lyng(e)* f. AN *quer de lion* lion-heart; cf. the surname *Querdelioun, Querdling*, wh. survives as *Guadling, Guodling* (C.T.O.)]

cŏd′piece, n. (hist.). Bagged appendage to the front of men's breeches. [f. OE *codd* bag + PIECE[1]]

*cō′-ĕd′, n. (colloq.). Girl or woman student at *co-educational* institution. [abbr.]

cō-ĕdūcā′tion, n. Education of boys & girls together. Hence ~AL (-sho-) a. [CO-]

coĕffi′cient (-shnt), n. Joint agent or factor; (Alg.) number placed before and multiplying another quantity known or unknown; (Physics) multiplier that measures some property (~ *of friction, expansion,* etc.); *differential* ~, quantity measuring rate of change of a function of any variable with respect to that variable. [CO-]

coel'acănth (sēl-), a. & n. (Fish) having a hollow spine. [f. COEL(O)-, Gk *akantha* spine, thorn]

coel'iăc (sēl-), a. (physiol.). Of the belly. [f. L f. Gk *koiliakos* (*koilia* belly)]

coel'(o)- (sēl-), in scientific wds, f. Gk *koilos* hollow & L *coelum* heaven.

coen'(o)- (sēn-), in comb. = Gk *koinos* common.

coen'obite (sēn-), cĕn²-, n. Member of monastic community. Hence **c(o)eno-bit'ic**(AL) aa., **c(o)en'obītism**(3) n., (sēn-). [f. LL *coenobita* f. LL f. Gk *koinobion* convent (COENO-, *bios* life)]

cōē'qual, a. & n. (Arch., theolog., or emphatic, for) equal. Hence **cōĕqual'ITY** (-kwŏl-) n., ~LY² adv. [15th c., f. L *coaequalis* (CO-, EQUAL)]

cōĕrce', v.t. & i. Forcibly constrain or impel (person) into quiet, obedience, or any course (*into*, rarely *to* do, or abs.); use force, secure by force (*a~d obedience*). Hence **cōĕr'CIBLE** a. [f. L CO(*ercēre ercit-* = *arcēre* shut up)]

cōĕr'cion (-shn), n. Controlling of voluntary agent or action by force; government by force. Hence ~ARY¹ a., ~IST(2) n. & a., (-sho-). [f. OF *cohercion, -tion* f. L *coer(c)tionem* (COERCE, -ION)]

cōĕr'cive, a. Of, acting by, exercising, coercion. Hence ~LY² (-vl-) adv., ~NESS (-vn-) n. [irreg. f. COERCE+-IVE]

cōĕssĕn'tial (-shl), a. Of the same substance or essence. [f. LL *coessentialis*, alternative rendering, with *consubstantialis*, of Gk *homoousios* (Gk *ousia* = L *substantia, essentia*)]

cōĕtăn'ĕous, a. = COEVAL a. [f. LL CO(*aetaneus* f. L *aetas* age)+-OUS]

cōĕtĕrn'al, a. Alike eternal. So ~LY² adv. [f. LL *coaeternus*+-AL]

cōĕv'al, a. & n. (Person) of same date of origin, of same age, existing at same epoch, of same duration. Hence ~ITY (-ăl²-) n., ~LY² adv. [f. LL CO(*aevus* f. *aevum* age)]

cō-ĕxĕc'ūtor, cō-ĕxĕc'ūtrix, (-gz-), nn. Joint executor, executrix. [CO-]

cōĕxĭs|t', v.i. Exist together or *with*. So ~'TENT a., ~'TENCE n. (*peaceful ~tence*, of peoples with different political & social systems, living in mutual toleration). [CO-]

cōĕxtĕn'sĭve, a. Extending over same space or time. [CO-]

cŏff'ee (-fĭ), n. Drink made from seeds of a shrub roasted & ground; light meal with ~, ~ as final course at dinner; the shrub, its seeds raw, roasted, or ground; ~-*bean*, the seed; ~-*cup*, of special shape or size; ~-*grounds*, sediment after infusion; ~-*house*, -*palace*, refreshment house; ~-*mill*, for grinding seeds; ~-*pot*, for making or serving ~ in; ~-*room*, public dining-room of hotel; ~-*tavern*, temperance refreshment house. [f. Turk. f. Arab. *qahweh* the drink]

cŏff'er, n. Box, esp. for valuables; (pl.) treasury, funds; sunk panel in ceiling etc.; ~-*dam*, watertight case in bridge-building, caisson. [ME & OF *cofre* f. L f. Gk *kophinos* basket]

cŏff'in, n., & v.t. **1.** Chest in which corpse is buried; *drive nail into* one's ~, hasten his, one's, death by annoyance, intemperance, etc.; unseaworthy ship; horse's hoof below coronet (~-*bone*, last phalangeal bone of foot; ~-*joint* at top of hoof); ~-*plate*, of metal in lid with deceased's name etc.; hence ~LESS a. ''**2.** v.t. Put in ~, store away (e.g. books) inaccessibly. [ME, f. OF *cof(f)in* little basket etc. f. L *cophinus* (prec.)]

cŏff'le, n. Train of beasts, slaves, etc., fastened together. [f. Arab. *qâfilah* caravan]

cŏg¹, n. One of series of projections on edge of wheel or side of bar transferring motion by engaging with another series; *hunting* ~, extra ~ on one wheel etc. securing constant variation in the ~s engaged; ~-*wheel*, with ~s. Hence ~GED² (-gd) a. [ME *cogge*, app. rel. to Sw. *kugge*, Norw. *kug*]

cŏg², v.t. (-gg-). ~ *dice*, fraudulently control the way they fall (~*ged dice* for loaded dice is a mistake of modern archaists. [16th c. cant of unkn. orig.]

cō'gent, a. Forcible, convincing, (of argument, &, usu. now playfully as though by transf. from this, of motive, compulsion, etc.). Hence **cō'gENCY** n., ~LY² adv. [f. L *cogent-* part. st. of *cogere* compel]

cō'gitable, a. Able to be grasped by reason, conceivable. [f. L *cogitabilis* (foll., -ABLE)]

cō'git|āte, v.i. & t. Ponder, meditate; devise; (Philos.) form conception of. Hence or cogn. ~A'TION n., ~ATIVE a., ~ātiveLY² adv., ~ātiveNESS n. [f. L *cogitare* = CO(*agitare* AGITATE) think, -ATE³]

cognac (kŏn'yăk), n. French brandy, prop. that distilled from ~ wine. [place-name]

cŏg'năte, a. & n. **1.** Descended from common ancestor (cf. AGNATE), akin in origin, nature, or quality; a relative. **2.** (philol.). Of same linguistic family; representing same original word; of parallel development in different allied languages (*father* is ~ with L *pater, paternal* is derived from it); a ~ word. **3.** (gram.). ~ *object* or *accusative*, one of kindred meaning to vb, used adverbially, not as true object (in *die the death, death* is ~, in *he slew death* it is object). Hence ~NESS

For compounds of *co-* not given consult CO-.

(-tn-) n. [f. L co(*gnatus* born usu. *natus*
f. *gn*-, *gen*-, *gon*-, beget)]

cōgnā'tion, n. Cognate relationship, now
esp. in philology. [ME, f. L *cognatio*
(prec., -ION)]

cōgni'tion, n. (philos.). Action or faculty
of knowing, perceiving, conceiving, as
opposed to emotion & volition; a perception, sensation, notion, or intuition. So
~AL (-sho-), **cŏg'nĭtIVE**, aa. [f. L *cognitio*
f. co(*gnoscere -gnit-* apprehend f. *gno-*
KNOW, usu. *noscere*)]

cŏg'nizab|le (*also* kŏn²), -**is**- (-ĭz-), a.
Perceptible; recognizable; within the
jurisdiction of a court etc. Hence ~LY²
adv. [f. foll.+-ABLE]

cŏg'nizance (*also* kŏn²), -**is**- (-ĭz-), n. **1.**
Being aware, notice, sphere of observa-
tion, (*have*~ *of*, know, esp. in a legitimate
or official way; *take* ~ *of*, attend to, not
allow to go unobserved; *fall within, be
beyond*, one's~, of things that fairly concern, do not concern, one). **2.** (Right of)
dealing with a matter legally or judicially
(with phrr. as above in legal sense). **3.**
Distinctive mark, as crest, coat of arms,
badge. [ME, f. OF *conis(s)aunce* f. Rom.
*connoscentia f. L *cognoscent-* part. st. of
cognoscere see COGNITION, -ANCE]

cŏg'nizant (*also* kŏn²), -**is**- (-ĭz-), a. Having knowledge, being aware, *of*; (Philos.)
having cognition. [f. prec., see -ANT]

cŏgnize', -**ise'** (-ĭz), v.t. (philos.). Have
cognition of. [on anal. of COGNIZANCE &
RECOGNIZE & of vbs rightly ending in -IZE]

cŏgnōm'ĕn, n. Nickname; surname;
name; (Rom. Ant.) third or family name,
as Marcus Tullius *Cicero*, or fourth name
or personal epithet, as Publius Cornelius
Scipio *Africanus* (also called *agnomen*).
[L, co-, (g)*nomen* name f. st. of (g)*noscere*
KNOW]

cognoscente (kŏnyoshĕn'tĭ), n. (pl.-*ti*).
Connoisseur. [It., lit., one who knows]

cŏgnōs'cible, a. Capable of being known
(esp. Philos.). [f. LL *cognoscibilis* f. L
cognoscere see COGNITION +-IBLE]

cŏgnōv'ĭt, n. (legal). Defendant's acknowledgement, to save expense, that
plaintiff's cause is just. [L, = he has
acknowledged]

cohăb'ĭt, v.i. Live together, esp. as
husband & wife (usu. of persons not
married). So ~A'TION n. [f. LL *cohabitare*
f. L co(*habitare* dwell frequent. of *habēre*
hold); cf. F *cohabiter*]

coheir', **coheir'ĕss**, (kōār-), nn. Male,
female, joint heir. [co-]

cohēre', v.i. Stick together, remain
united, (of parts or whole); be consistent,
well knit (of arguments, style, etc.).
Hence **cohēr'ER¹** n., detector of electric
waves consisting of a glass cylinder containing metal filings which ~ when struck
by a wave. [f. L co(*haerēre -haes-* stick)]

cohēr'|ent, a. Cohering; consistent, easily
followed, not rambling or inconsequent,
(of argument, narration, etc.). So ~ENCE,

~ENCY, nn.,~entLY² adv. [f. L *cohaerent-*
part. st. of *cohaerēre* (prec., -ENT)]

cohē'ritor, n. = COHEIR. [co-]

cohē'sion (-zhn), n. Sticking together,
force with which molecules cohere;
tendency to remain united. So **cohēs'ivE**
a., **cohēs'ivELY²** (-vl-) adv., **cohēs'ive-
NESS** (-vn-) n. [f. L *cohaes-* (see COHERE,
-ION), after *adhere, adhesion*]

cō'hŏrt, n. Division of Roman army;
band of warriors; persons banded together. [f. L *cohors -hort-* or F *cohorte*]

coif, n. (hist.). Close cap covering top,
back, and sides, of head; serjeant-at-
-law's white cap. [ME, f. OF *coif(f)e* f.
LL *cofia, cufia*, of uncert. orig.]

coiffeur (see Ap.) n. Hairdresser. [F]

coiffure (see Ap.), n. Way one's hair is
dressed. [F]

coign (koin), n. ~ *of vantage*, place
affording good view of something. [old
form of COIN, QUOIN, preserved by *Macb.* I.
vi. 7]

coil¹, v.t. & i. Dispose (rope etc.) in
concentric rings; twist (t. & i., often *up*)
into circular or spiral shape; move
sinuously. [f. OF *coillir* (mod. *cueillir*,
also in same sense; cf. Pg. *colher un cabo*
coil a cable) f. L *colligere* COLLECT²]

coil², n. Length of coiled rope, spring,
etc.; arrangement, thing arranged, in
concentric circles; single turn of coiled
thing, e.g. snake; lock of hair twisted &
coiled; wire, piping, etc., in circles or
symmetric curves; (Electr.) spiral wire
for passage of current. [f. prec.]

coil³, n. (arch. & poet.). Disturbance,
much ado, noise, (*this mortal* ~, turmoil
of life). [orig. unkn.]

coin¹, n. Piece of metal made into money
by official stamp; metal money; money;
false ~, imitation in base metal etc.,
(fig.) anything spurious; *pay one in his
own* ~, give tit for tat. Hence ~'LESS
a. [ME, f. OF *coi(g)n* wedge, stamping-
-die, f. L *cuneus* wedge]

coin², v.t. Make (money) by stamping
metal (~ *money*, get money fast); make
(metal) into money; make money by
means of (one's *brains* etc.); invent,
fabricate, (esp. new word). [ME, f. OF
coignier f. *coin* see prec.]

coin'age, n. Coining; coins; system of
coins in use (*decimal* ~, in which each
value is ten times the next below);
fabrication (*the* ~ *of* one's *brain*), invention, coined word. [ME, f. OF *coigniage*
see prec., -AGE]

cōincīde', v.i. Occupy same portion of
space; occur at and occupy same time;
agree together or *with*; concur in opinion
etc. [f. med. L *coincidere* (used unchanged
in Eng. contexts in 17th c.), or F *coincider*]

cōin'cidence, n. (Instance of) being co-
incident; notable concurrence of events
or circumstances without apparent causal
connexion. [f. as prec. (see -ENCE) or F
coïncidence]

coin'cident, a. Coinciding. Hence ~LY[2] adv. [f. as prec. (see -ENT) or F *coïncident*]

coïnciden'tal, a. Of the nature of (a) coincidence. [f. prec. +-AL]

coin'er, n. In vbl senses; esp., maker of counterfeit coin. [COIN[2]+-ER[1]]

coïnstantān'eous, a. Exactly at the same moment. [CO-]

coir (koi'er), n. Coconut fibre, used for ropes, matting, etc. [f. Malayalam *kayar* cord]

coï'tion, n. Sexual copulation. [f. L *coitio* f. CO(*ire it-* go)]

cōke, n., & v.t. (Convert *coal* into) solid substance left when volatile parts have been distilled from coal. [prob. f. north. dial. *colk* core, of unkn. orig.]

coker(nut). See COCO.

cŏl, n. Depression in mountain-chain. [F, = neck, col, f. L *collum* neck]

cŏl-, form taken by COM- before *l*.

cŏl'a, k-, n. W.-Afr. tree; (also ~-*nut*, -*seed*), its seed, used as condiment, tonic, and antidote to alcohol. [W.-Afr.]

col'ander (kŭ-), **cŭll'ender,** n., & v.t. (Pass through a) perforated vessel used as strainer in cookery; similar appliance for casting shot. [15th c., perh. f. Pr. *colador* (Sp. *colador*) f. Rom. *colatorem* f. *colare* -*at*- f. *colum* strainer (-OR); cf. LL *colatorium*; for intrusive -*n*- cf. *passenger*]

cō-lăt'ĭtŭde, n. (astron.). Complement of latitude, difference between it & 90°. [CO-(2)]

‖ **cŏlcănn'on,** n. Irish dish of cabbage and potatoes pounded and stewed. [orig. unkn.]

cŏl'chicum (*or* -kĭ-), n. Meadow-saffron; drug extracted from it used for gout. [L, f. Gk *kolkhikon* neut. adj. (*Kolkhis* on Black Sea, -IC)]

cŏl'cothar, n. Red peroxide of iron used in polishing glass etc. [f. Arab. *qolqotar*]

cōld[1], a. **1.** Of low temperature, esp. when compared with human body or with that usual in things like the one in question (*ice, key, stone,* -~-, ~ as these; ~-*blooded*, of fish & reptiles, also fig. of sluggish persons, & see below; ~-*livered*, unemotional; ~ *steel*, sword, bayonet, etc., opposed to fire-arms, *inch* or *few* etc. *inches of* ~ *steel*, thrust). **2.** Not heated or having cooled after heat (~ *water*; throw ~ *water on plan*, discourage it; ~ *in death* or ~, dead; ~ *pig*, water thrown on sleeper to wake him, also ~-*pig* as v.t.; ~-*hammer*, work metal in ~ state; ~- -CHISEL; ~ *without*, ~ sugarless spirit & water; ~ *meat*, that has cooled after cooking; ~ *shoulder*, of roast mutton, *give the* ~ *shoulder to*, entertain poorly, show distaste for company of, also ~- -*shoulder* as v.t.; *in* ~ *blood*, without the excuse of heat or excitement, of cruelty etc., whence~'blood'ED[2]a.,~'blood'ĕd-NESS n.); feeling ~; slow to absorb heat

(of clayey soil). **3.** Without ardour, friendliness, or affection, undemonstrative, apathetic, (so ~'heart'ED[2] a., ~'heart'ĕdNESS n., ~'heart'ĕdLY[2] adv.; *idea leaves* one ~, unmoved, not impressed). **4.** Chilling, depressing, uninteresting, (~ *comfort, counsel, news*). **5.** Faint (of scent in hunting). **6.** ~ *colours*, blue, grey, etc., opp. red, yellow, etc.; ~-*drawn* CASTOR OIL; ~ *coil*, tube coiled round inflamed part with ~ water running in it; ~ *blast*, of ~ air forced into furnace; ~ CREAM; ~ *feet*, (orig. army sl.) funk, disinclination to fight or go to or remain at the front; ~ *snap*, sudden spell of ~ weather; *have* person ~ (at one's mercy; ~ WAR. Hence ~'ISH[1](2) a., ~'LY[2] adv., ~'NESS n. [OE, OS *cald*, OHG *kalt*, ON *kaldr*, Goth. *kalds* f. Gmc **kaldaz* cogn. w. L *gelu*]

cōld[2], n. Prevalence in atmosphere, or rarely in any object, of low temperature (*left out in the* ~, not looked after); inflamed state of mucous membrane, with hoarseness, running at nose, sore throat, etc. (CATCH[1] ~; often ~ *in the head*). Hence ~'PROOF a. [OF *cald* neut. adj. see prec.]

cōld'-shŏrt, a. Brittle in its cold state (of iron). [f. Sw. *kallskör* (= Norw., Da. *koldskjör*) f. *kallr* COLD+*skjör* brittle, w. assim. to SHORT (sense 6); cf. *red-short*]

cōle, n. (Old name, now rare exc. in comb., for) kinds of cabbage etc., as rape, sea kale; ~-*seed*, plant from which colza oil is got. [ME *col(e)*, north. *cal* (KALE), f. ON *kál* (= OE *cawel*, OHG *kōl(i)*), f. L *caulis* cabbage]

cŏleŏp'terous, a. Of the order of *Coleoptera* or beetles, with front wings converted into sheaths for hinder. [f. Gk *koleopteros* (*koleos* sheath, *pteron* wing)+ -OUS]

*cōle-slaw (-ls-), n. Salad of sliced cabbage. [f. Du. *koolsla* = *kool-salade* (*kool* cabbage)]

cŏl'ĭc, n. Severe griping pains in belly. Hence ~KY[2] a. [15th c., f. LL f. Gk *kolikos* (COLON[1], -IC)]

Coliseum. Var. of COLOSSEUM.

colī'tis, n. Inflammation of the lining of the colon. [COLON[1]+-ITIS]

collăb'or|āte, v.i. Work in combination (*with*, or abs.) esp. at literary or artistic production; co-operate treacherously with the enemy. So ~A'TION, ~ātoR, nn. [f. F *collaborer* or L COL(*laborare* LABOUR[2]), -ATE[3]]

cŏllage' (-ahzh), n. An abstract form of art in which photographs, pieces of paper, matchsticks, etc. are placed in juxtaposition & glued to the pictorial surface. [F]

collăpse', n., & v.i. (Undergo, experience, a) falling in, sudden shrinking together, giving way, prostration by loss of nervous or muscular power, breakdown of mental energy, loss of courage. [vb back form. f. *collapsed* f. L *collapsus* p.p. of COL(*labi laps-* slip); n.f. medical *collapsus* n.]

collăp'sible, **-able**, a. So made as to collapse when required for packing etc. [-BLE]

cŏll'ar[1], n. Neckband, upright or turned over, of coat, dress, shirt, etc.; band of linen, lace, etc., completing upper part of costume; ‖ neck-chain of order of knighthood; ‖ ~ *of SS* or *esses*, formerly badge of House of Lancaster, still in some officials' costume; leather or metal band round dog's or prisoner's neck; roll round horse's neck bearing weight of draught (~-*harness*, opp. BREAST[1]-*harness*; ~-*work*, hard pulling esp. up hill, & fig. of severe effort, so also *against the* ~); restraining or connecting band, ring, pipe, in machines etc.; arrangement connecting several fishing-flies; coloured stripe round animal's neck; piece of meat, brawn, fish, tied in roll; ~-*beam*, horizontal beam connecting two rafters and forming with them an A-shaped roof--truss; ~-*bone*, joining breast-bone & shoulder-blade, clavicle. Hence (-)~ED[2] (-rd), ~LESS, aa. [ME & AF *coler* (OF -*ier*) f. L *collare* (*collum* neck, -AR[1])]

cŏll'ar[2], v.t. Seize (person) by the collar, capture; (Rugby footb.) lay hold of and stop (opponent holding ball); (sl.) appropriate; press (meat etc.) into roll. [f. prec.]

cŏllarĕt(te)', n. Woman's collar of lace, fur, etc. [f. F *collerette* (*collier* COLLAR[1], -ETTE)]

collāt|e', v.t. Compare in detail (copies of text or document, one copy *with* another); (Bibliog.) verify order of (sheets) by signatures; put together; appoint (clergyman) to benefice (only of the Ordinary). So ~'OR n. [f. L COL(*lat*-p.p. st. of *ferre* bring)]

collăt'eral, a. & n. Side by side, parallel; subordinate but from same source, contributory, connected but aside from main subject, course, etc.; of common descent but by different line (so as noun =~ kinsman); ~ *security* or ~, property pledged as guarantee for repayment of money (opp. *personal* giving right of action for recovery). Hence ~LY[2] adv. [ME, f. med. L COL(*lateralis* LATERAL)]

collā'tion, n. In vbl senses of COLLATE; also: (R.-C. Ch.) light repast in evening of fast-day; light meal (usu. *cold* ~) often at exceptional time. [ME, f. OF f. L *collationem* (COLLATE, -ION); sense *repast* from Benedictine monastery readings of Lives of the Fathers (*collationes patrum*; *collatio* also of the reading & debate on it) followed by light repast]

cŏll'eague (-ĕg), n. One of two or more holders of joint office or (loosely) of position in a profession or business (usu. with *my* etc.). [f. F *collègue* f. L COL(*lega*)]

cŏll'ĕct[1], n. Short prayer of Common Prayer Book, esp. one of those appropriated to days or seasons & read before Epistle & in morning & evening prayer. [ME & OF *collecte* f. med. L *collecta* in similar senses = L *collecta* fem. p.p. of *colligere* COLLECT[2]]

collĕct'[2], v.t. & i. Assemble, accumulate, bring or come together; get (taxes, contributions) from a number of people; (colloq.) call for, fetch; secure (specimens, books, etc.) for addition to a set; regain control of, concentrate, recover, (one*self*, one's thoughts, energies, courage; ~*ed*, not distracted, cool, whence ~ĕdLY[2] adv.; ~ *a horse*, keep him in hand, not let him sprawl); infer, gather, conclude. Hence ~ABLE, -IBLE, a. [f. (partly) OF *collecter* (f. *collecte* n. COLLECT[1]), or LL *collectare*, or obs. E *collect* adj. f. L *collectus* p.p. of COL(*ligere* = *legere* pick)]

cŏllĕctăn'ĕa, n. pl. Collected passages, miscellany. [L, neut. pl. adj.]

collĕc'tion, n. Collecting; collecting of money, money collected, at meeting or Church service for charitable or religious purpose; accumulation *of* water, dust, etc.; group of things collected & belonging together (literary materials, specimens, works of art, etc.); ‖ (pl.) college terminal examination at Oxford etc. [ME, f. OF f. L *collectionem* (COLLECT[2], -ION)]

collĕc'tive, a. & n. Formed by, constituting a, collection, taken as a whole, aggregate, (~ *fruit*, resulting from many flowers, as mulberry); of, from, many individuals, common, (~ *note*, signed by several States; ~ *ownership*, of land, means of production, etc., by all for benefit of all, whence **collĕc'tiv**ISM, col**lĕc'tiv**IST, nn.); (Gram. & Log.) ~ *noun*, ~ *idea*, or~, used in sing. to express many individuals, as *cattle*, *troop*, *duck*; ~ *security*, (Pol.) policy or principle of the alliance of several countries in order to guarantee the security of each one. Hence ~LY[2] (-vl-) adv., **collĕctiv'**ITY n. [f. F *collectif* or L *collectivus* (as prec., -IVE)]

collĕc'tor, n. One who collects (specimens, curiosities, railway tickets at station, money due, esp. taxes, rent, & subscriptions); collecting-apparatus in various machines; in India, chief official of district collecting revenue & holding magisterial powers, whence (office & district) ~ATE[1] n. Hence ~SHIP n. [ME & AF *collectour* (F -*eur*) f. med. L *collectorem* (as prec., -OR)]

‖ cŏlleen', n. (Anglo-Ir.). Girl. [Ir. *cailín*, dim. of *caile* country-woman)]

cŏll'ége, n. Body of colleagues with common functions & privileges (*Sacred C*~, ~ *of cardinals*, the Pope's council of 70; *Heralds' C*~, or *C*~ *of Arms*; *C*~ *of Physicians*, *Preceptors*, etc.); ‖ independent corporation of scholars in university, usu. with master, fellows, scholars, & students not on foundation; ‖ similar foundation outside university (as Eton, Dulwich); small degree-giving university; institution for higher education affiliated to university; place of professional study (army, naval, or agriculture, etc.); ‖ large public secondary school (Marlborough); (pretentious name for) private school; buildings of any of these; ‖ ~ *living*, benefice in gift of a ~; ~ *pudding*, small plum pudding for one person. Hence **collĕ′gIAL** a. [ME, f. OF *colege* or L (*collegium* (*collega* COLLEAGUE).

‖ **cŏll′ĕger**, n. One of seventy foundation scholars at Eton. [-ER¹]

collē′gian, n. Member of a college; ‖ (old sl.) inmate of a prison. [f. med. L *collegianus* (*collegium*, -AN)]

collē′giate¹, a. Constituted as, belonging to, a college or body of colleagues, corporate; ~ *church*, endowed for chapter but with no see, (Sc. & U.S.) under joint pastorate; ~ *school*, of high pretensions. Hence ~LY² (-tl-) adv. [f. LL *collegiatus* (COLLEGE, -ATE²)]

collē′giate², v.t. Make collegiate. [as prec., -ATE³]

cŏll′ĕt, n. Encompassing band, ferrule, socket, flange holding gem, bezel. [F, dim. of COL]

collĭde′, v.i. Come into collision; be in conflict. [f. L COL(*lidere lis-* = *laedere* hurt)]

cŏll′ie, -ў, n. Scotch sheep-dog. [perh. f. *coll* COAL + -Y³ (as orig. black)]

cŏll′ier (-yer), n. Coal-miner, whence **cŏll′iERY(3)** (-ye-) n.; coal-ship; sailor on this. [ME *colier* f. COAL + -IER]

cŏll′ig|āte, v.t. Bring into connexion (esp. isolated facts by a generalization). So ~A′TION n. [f. L COL(*ligare* bind), see -ATE³]

cŏll′im|āte, v.t. Adjust line of sight of (telescope etc.), make parallel (telescopes, rays). Hence ~A′TION n. [*collimare* false reading in Cicero for COL(*lineare* f. *linea* line)]

cŏll′imātor, n. Small attached telescope for collimating an instrument; tube in spectroscope throwing parallel rays on prism. [-OR]

collin′ear, a. In same straight line. [COL-]

‖ **Cŏll′ins** (-z), n. (colloq.). = ROOFER. [Jane Austen, *P. & P.*, ch. xxiii]

colli′sion (-zhn), n. Dashing together, violent encounter of moving body, esp. ship or railway train, with another; (fig.) harsh combination (of consonants); clashing of opposed interests etc. (esp. *in* ~, *come into* ~ *with*); (Naut.) ~*mat*, ready for putting over hole made by ~. [f. LL *collisio* (COLLIDE, -ION)]

cŏll′oc|āte, v.t. Place together; arrange; station, set in particular place. So ~A′TION n. [f. L COL(*locare* f. *locus* place); see -ATE³]

cŏll′ocūtor, n. Partaker in talk, as *my* ~ *said*. [LL, f. COL(*loqui locut-* talk), -OR]

collŏd′ion, n. Solution of gun-cotton in ether filming when exposed, used in photography & surgery. Hence ~ED² (-nd) a., ~IZE(5) v.t., **collŏd′io-** comb. form. [f. Gk *kollōdēs* (*kolla* glue, -ODE)]

collōgue′ (-g), v.i. Talk confidentially (with suggestion of plotting, an obs. sense). [orig. obsc.; perh. f. F *colloque* conference assoc. w. L *colloqui* converse & obs. *colleague* vb plot]

cŏll′oid, a. & n. Gluey (substance); (Path.) ~ *tissue* etc., degenerated into homogeneous gelatinous consistence (also ~, such substance); (Chem.) non-crystalline substance with very large molecules; when dissolved the solution is viscous & sticky, e.g. starch, gelatine, & plastics. Hence **colloid′AL** a. [Gk *kolla* glue, -OID]

cŏll′op, n. Slice of meat; (Bibl.) fold of skin in fat person or animal. [14th c. (= fried bacon & eggs), of Scand. orig.; cf. Sw. *kalops* (dial. *kollops*) slices of beef stewed, OSwed. *kolhuppadher* roasted on coals (*kol* COAL, *huppa* leap)]

collō′quial, a. In or of talk, oral; belonging to familiar speech, not used in formal or elevated language. Hence ~ISM(3, 4), ~IST(1), nn., ~LY² adv. [f. L *colloquium* COLLOQUY, -AL]

cŏll′oquist, n. = COLLOCUTOR. [foll., -IST(1)]

cŏll′oquŷ, n. Converse; a conversation; judicial and legislative court in Presbyterian Church. [f. L COL(*loquium* f. *loqui* speak)]

cŏll′otype, n. Thin plate of gelatine etched by actinic rays & then printed from (~ *plate*, *process*, etc.). [f. Gk *kolla* glue + TYPE]

collūde′ (-ōō-), v.i. (arch.). Practise collusion. [f. L COL(*ludere lus-* play)]

collu′sion (-ōōzhn), n. Fraudulent secret understanding, esp. between ostensible opponents as in law-suit. Hence **collus′-IVE** (-ōō-) a., **collus′iveLY²** adv. [ME, f. OF, or f. L *collusio* (prec., -ION)]

collý′rium, n. (pl. -*ia*). Eye-salve; suppository. [f. L f. Gk *kollurion* poultice]

cŏll′ўwŏbbles (-lz), n. pl. (colloq.). Rumbling in the intestines. [imit.]

cŏl′ocynth, n. Bitter-apple, gourd plant with bitter-pulped fruit used as purgative drug; the drug. [f. L f. Gk *kolokunthis*]

cōl′on¹, n. (anat.). Greater part of larger intestine, from caecum to rectum. Hence **colōn′IC** a., ~IT′IS n. [ME, f. L f. Gk *kōlon*]

cōl′on², n. Punctuation-mark (:) ranking between period and semicolon, & used esp. to mark antithesis, illustration, or (often with dash : —) quotation; in Greek (·). [f. L f. Gk *kōlon* limb, clause]

colōn′ate, n. Serf system in later Roman Empire. [f. LL *colonatus* (L *colonus*, see COLONY, -ATE¹)]

colonel (kẽrn′el), n. Highest regimental

officer; (short for) lieutenant-~; C~
BLIMP; C~ *Commandant*, honorary rank of
senior officers of R.A., R.E., etc. Hence
~CY (kẽrn²) n. [16–17th c. also *coronel* f.
obs. F *coronel* (now *colonel*) f. It. *colonnello*
(*colonna* COLUMN)]

colonelship (kẽrn²), n. Being a colonel
(cf. *colonelcy*, ordinary word for the office),
[-SHIP]

colōn'ial, a. & n. (Inhabitant) of a colony,
esp. of a British Crown Colony; C~ *Office*,
State department in charge of the
Colonies. Hence ~ISM(2, 4) n., (freq.
derog.) alleged policy of exploitation of
backward or weak peoples, ~LY² adv. [F,
or f. L *colonia* COLONY + -AL]

cŏl'onist, n. Settler in, part-founder or
inhabitant of, a colony. [COLONIZE, -IST]

cŏl'oniz|e, -is|e (-īz), v.t. & i. Establish
colony in; establish in a colony; establish
or join a colony; *(Pol.) plant voters in
a district for party purposes. Hence
~A'TION, ~ER¹, nn. [f. L *colon-us, colon-ia*,
COLON-Y + -IZE]

cŏlonnād|e', n. Series of columns with
entablature; row of trees. Hence ~'ED²
a. [F (*colonne* COLUMN, -ADE)]

cŏl'onȳ, n. (Gk hist.) independent city
founded by emigrants; (Rom. hist.)
settlement usu. of veterans in conquered
territory acting as garrison; settlement,
settlers, in new country forming community fully or partly subject to mother
State; their territory; people of one
nationality or occupation in a city, esp.
if living more or less in isolation or in a
special quarter (so of animals, ~ *of
sparrows* etc.); (Biol.) aggregate of
animals as in coral. [f. L *colonia* (*colonus*
farmer f. *colere* till)]

cŏl'ophon, n. Tail-piece in old books,
often ornamental, giving information
now placed on title-page (*from title-page
to* ~, from cover to cover). [LL, f. Gk
kolophōn summit]

cŏlŏph'onȳ, n. Dark resin distilled from
turpentine & water. Hence **cŏlŏph'on-
ATE**¹(3) n., **coloph-, colophon-,** comb.
forms. [f. L *colophonia* (*resina* resin) of
Colophon in Lydia]

cŏloquin'tida, n. = COLOCYNTH.

Cŏlora'dō bee'tle(-rah-), n. Yellow black-
-striped beetle, destructive to potatoes.
[*Colorado* in U.S.]

colo(u)rā'tion (kŭ-, kŏ-), n. Colouring,
method of putting on or arranging
colour: natural, esp. variegated, colour
of living or other things. [F, or f. LL
coloratio f. *colorare* COLOUR², -ATION]

cŏloratura (-ahtoor'a), n. Florid passages
in vocal music (often attrib., as ~*soprano*).
[It.. f. L *colorare* to colour]

cŏlorif'ic (*also* kŭ-), a. Producing colour;
highly coloured. [f. F *colorifique* (COLOUR¹,
-I-, -FIC)]

cŏlorim'ēter (*also* kŭ-), n. Instrument
measuring intensity of colour. [L *color*,
-I-, -METER]

colŏss'al, a. Of, like, a colossus; gigantic,
huge; (colloq., f. G) remarkable, splendid,
delightful. Hence ~LY² adv. [F, or f.
COLOSSUS + -AL]

Cŏlossē'um, Cŏlīsē'um, nn. Amphitheatre in Rome begun by Vespasian in
A.D. 72; scene of gladiatorial combats &
the martyrdom of many Christians. [L]

colŏss'us, n. (pl. -ī, -*uses*). Statue of
much more than life size; gigantic
person or personified empire etc., esp.
conceived (like C~ of Rhodes) as astrid-
ing astride over dominions. [L, f. Gk
kolossos]

colŏt'omȳ, n. (surg.). Incision in COLON¹
to provide artificial anus in stricture
etc. [COLON¹, -TOMY]

colour¹ (kŭl'er), n. 1. Sensation produced
on eye by rays of decomposed light (cf.
black, effect produced by no light or by
surface reflecting no rays, & *white*, effect
produced by rays of undecomposed light).
2. A particular hue, one, or any mixture,
of the constituents into which light
decomposes as in spectrum, including
loosely black, white (ACCIDENTAL ~;
complementary ~, that combined with
given ~ makes white; *fundamental,
primary, simple*, ~s, red, green, & violet,
or with painters red, blue, & yellow,
giving all others by mixture; *secondary*
~, mixture of two primary; ~-*blind*,
unable to distinguish certain colours, see
DALTONISM, also fig. in U.S., impartial
between whites & blacks, whence
~-*blind*NESS n.; ~ *scheme*, ~-design on
which the furnishing and decoration of
a room or the planting of a flower garden
is based; ~-*wash*, coloured distemper
(also as v.t.); *see the* ~ *of* one's *money*,
receive some payment from him); *man,
woman*, etc., *of* ~, of non-white race, esp.
Negro (~ *bar*, legal or social distinction
between whites & people of ~). 3. Ruddi-
ness of face (*lose, gain,* ~; *change* ~, turn
pale or red). 4. Appearance, light, (*paint
in bright, dark*, ~s; *see in its true* ~s; *put
false* ~s *upon*). 5. (Art) colouring, ~-
-system, -perception, effects as of ~ got
by light and shade in engraving, whence
~IST(3) (kŭl'er-) n., ~IS'TIC a.; pigment,
paint, (~-*box*, of assorted artists' paints;
WATER-~s; ~-*man*, dealer in paints).
6. (Pl.) coloured ribbon, dress, etc., worn
as symbol of party, membership of club,
etc. (|| *get* one's, *give* one *his*, ~s, of
inclusion in athletic team; *show* one's ~s,
one's party or character); flag of ship,
pair of silken flags (*King's* or *Queen's* ~,
regimental ~) carried by regiment (TROOP-
ing of the ~ or ~s; *with the* ~s, serving in
army; *sail under false* ~s, fig. of hypocrite
or impostor; *come off with flying* ~s, win
credit; *nail* ~s *to mast*, persist, refuse to
climb down; ~-*sergeant*, senior sergeant
of infantry company, now *Company
Sergeant-Major* or *Quartermaster Sergt,*
with duty of guarding ~s); coloured

dresses. **7.** Show of reason. pretext, false plea, (give no ~ for saying; under ~ of). **8.** (Mus.) timbre, quality, also variety of expression. **9.** (Gen.) character, tone, quality, mood, shade of meaning, (take one's ~ from). **10.** (Literature) picturesqueness, ornate style, (local ~, use of details giving verisimilitude, background, or atmosphere). Hence ~FUL (kŭler-) a., full of ~, bright, gay (often fig.). [ME, f. OF color, -our f. L colorem]

colour² (kŭl'er), v.t. & i. Give colour to; paint, stain, dye; disguise; misrepresent (highly ~ed details); imbue with its own colour (motive ~s act); take on colour; blush; ~ed person (not wholly of white descent, of mixed blood). [ME, f. OF colo(u)rer f. L colorare (color COLOUR¹)]

col'ourab|le (kŭler-), a. Specious, plausible; counterfeit. Hence ~LY² adv. [ME, f. COLOUR²+-ABLE or OF colorable]

col'ouring (kŭler-), n. In vbl senses; esp., style in which thing is coloured, or in which artist employs colour. [-ING¹]

col'ourless (kŭler-), a. Without colour; pale; dull-hued; wanting in character or vividness; neutral, impartial, indifferent. Hence ~LY² adv., ~NESS n. [-LESS]

col'oury (kŭl'erĭ), a. (commerc.). Having the colour that goes with good quality (of hops, coffee, etc.). [-Y²]

colporteur' (-tẽr; also kŏl'-), n. Book-hawker, esp. one employed by society to distribute Bibles. [F]

colt¹, n., & v.t. Young male of horse from when it is taken from dam to age of 4 (with thoroughbreds 5); inexperienced person, || esp. cricket professional in first season; (Naut.) rope used for chastisement (vb, thrash with ~); ~'s'foot, common large-leaved yellow-flowered weed; ~'s tail, ragged-edged cloud. Hence ~'HOOD n., ~'ISH¹ a. [OE colt of unkn. orig., but cf. Sw. kult etc. applied to half-grown animals & boys]

Colt², n. (Used for) ~ revolver, automatic gun, or pistol. [S. ~, inventor (d. 1862)]

*****col'ter**. See COULTER.

col'ubrine, a. Snake-like; esp., of, like, the Coluber (genus of harmless snakes). [f. L colubrinus (coluber snake)]

columbar'ium, n. (pl. -ia). (In mod. use) building with tiers of niches for reception of cinerary urns. [L, = pigeon-house]

col'umbine¹, n. Garden plant with flower like five clustered pigeons, kind of aquilegia. [ME, f. OF f. LL columbina (herba) f. L columba dove, -INE¹]

Col'umbine², n. Mistress of Harlequin in pantomime. [f. F Colombine or It. -ina f. colombino dovelike]

columb'|ium, n. (chem.). = NIOBIUM. Hence ~ITE¹ n., native ore of ~ium. [f. Columbia in United States, -IUM]

col'umn(-ŭm), n. **1.** (Archit.) long vertical often slightly tapering cylinder usu. supporting entablature or arch, or alone as monument, (fig.) support; ~-shaped object, organ in Anat. or Bot., part of machine, etc. (~ of water, mercury, confined vertical cylindrical mass; ~ of smoke, rising straight). **2.** Vertical division of page for figures etc., or to reduce length of lines esp. in newspapers (also part of newspaper, sometimes more or less than ~, devoted to special subject, as AGONY ~, advertisement ~s; our ~s, the ~s of The Times, contents of newspaper), whence ~IST n., journalist who regularly contributes to a newspaper a ~ of miscellaneous comment on people and events. **3.** Narrow-fronted deep arrangement of troops in successive lines (in ~ of sections, platoons, companies, with one section etc. forming each line & one section's etc. length between lines; quarter ~, with 6 paces between lines); FIFTH ~; body of ships, esp. following one another. Hence or cogn. **colum'nar¹**, ~ED² (-ŭmd), **colum'niform**, aa. [15th c. & OF colompne f. L columna pillar; mod. sp. f. L]

colure', n. One of two great circles intersecting rectangularly at poles & dividing equinoctial & ecliptic into four equal parts, one passing through equinoctial, & one through solstitial, points of ecliptic. [f. LL f. Gk kolouros truncated]

col'za, n. = COLE-seed; ~-oil, made from it & used in lamps. [F, f. LG kōlsāt COLE-seed]

com-, pref. = L cum in comb., retained as com- before b, p, m, & rarely before vowels, changed to cor- before r, col- before l, co- before vowels, h, & gn, & con- before other consonants; com- occurs in E also before f (comfort). Meaning, with, together, altogether, completely.

com'a¹, n. Unnatural heavy sleep, stupor, lethargy. Hence ~TOSE a. [f. Gk kōma -atos deep sleep]

com'a², n. (pl. -ae). (Bot.) tuft of silky hairs at end of seed; (Astron.) nebulous envelope round nucleus of comet. [L, f. Gk komē hair of head]

comb¹ (-m), n. Toothed strip of horn, metal, ivory, etc., for arranging, cleaning, or confining the hair; = CURRY²-comb; thing of same shape, look, or purpose, in many machines, esp. for dressing wool, or collecting electricity, or in animal structure; red fleshy crest of fowl esp. cock, analogous growth in other birds, (cut the ~ of, humiliate); crest of hill or wave; = HONEYCOMB¹; ~-out, process or instance of COMB²ing out. Hence (-)COMBED²(-md) a. [OE, OS camb, OHG kamb, ON kambr f. Gmc *kambaz]

comb² (-m), v.t. & i. Draw comb through (hair), curry (horse), dress (wool, flax) with comb; search (place) thoroughly; (of wave) curl over; ~ out, secure or get rid of (as) by ~ing (esp. of getting recruits from among those previously exempted from service). [ME f. prec., replacing *kemb*; see UNKEMPT]

com'bat (kŭ- *or* kŏ-), n., & v.t. & i. (Do) battle; *single* ~, duel; (engage in) contest, struggle; oppose, strive against. [f. F *combat* & *combattre* f. LL (COM-, *battere, batuere*, fight), cf. BATTLE]

com'batant (kŭ- *or* kŏ-), a. & n. Fighting, fighter. [OF part. as prec.]

com'bative (kŭ- *or* kŏ-), a. Pugnacious. Hence ~LY² adv., ~NESS n. [COMBAT v. +-IVE]

combe. See COOMB.

cŏmb'er (-mer), n. In vbl senses; esp.: machine for combing cotton or wool very fine; long curling wave, breaker. [-ER¹]

cŏmbinā'tion, n. Combining; combined state (*in* ~ *with*); combined set of things or persons; (Math., pl.) different collections possible of given number of individuals in groups of given smaller number; (Chem.) union of substances in compound with properties differing from theirs; united action; ‖ (pl.) single under-garment for body & legs; motor-cycle with side-car attached (in full *motor-cycle* ~); ~ (*lock*), complicated locking arrangement used for safes, strong-rooms, etc.; ~-*room*, at Cambridge = COMMON¹-*room*. [16th c., f. obs. F *combination* or LL *combinatio* (COMBINE, -ATION)]

combine', v.t. & i., & n. **1.** Join together (persons or things material or other); possess (esp. qualities usu. separate) together; (cause to) coalesce in one substance, form chemical compound; co-operate; ~*d operation* (in which the fighting services co-operate); *combining form* (Gram.), special form of word used in combinations (e.g. *Anglo-* repr. *England* or *English*). **2.** n. (*usu.* kŏm²). Combination of persons, esp. to raise prices or obstruct course of trade; (pr. kŏm'-) ~d reaping and threshing machine. So **cŏm'binā**TIVE a. [ME, f. OF *combiner* or LL COM(*binare* f. L *bini* two together)]

cŏmb'ing (-mī-), n. In vbl senses; esp., (pl.) hairs combed off. [-ING¹]

combŭs'ti‖ble, a. & n. (Matter, thing) capable of or used for burning; excitable. Hence ~BIL'ITY n. [f. F, or med. L *combustibilis* (foll., -IBLE)]

combŭs'tion (-schn), n. **1.** Destruction by fire (SPONTANEOUS ~). **2.** (Chem. etc.) development of light & heat going with chemical combination; oxidation of organic tissue. [OF, or LL *combustio* f. L *comburere* -*ust*- burn]

come¹ (kŭm), v.i. (*came, come*). **1.** Start, move, arrive, towards or at a point, time, or result (often not specified because obvious, while point of departure, if it matters, is always specified; cf. GO; ~ *into world*, be born; ~ *of* AGE; ~ *to an end*, cease; ~ *to hand*, of letter etc., be delivered; ~ SHORT; ~ *to a point*, taper;

~ *to blows*, fight; ~ *home to*, be realized by; ~ *& go*, pass to & fro, pay brief visit, be transitory; *let 'em all* ~ *!*, sl. announcement of readiness; *light* ~ *light go*, what is easily won is soon lost; *coming nineteen*, in nineteenth year; *two years* ~ *Christmas*, including time from now to Christmas). **2.** Be brought (*the dinner came*; ~ *under notice, before judge*). **3.** Fall, land, on (*came on my head*). **4.** Move relatively by motion of beholder etc. towards one (~ *into sight*, to one's *knowledge*, in one's *way*; ~ *to light*, be revealed). **5.** Reach point with hand, instrument, or missile. **6.** Occur, fall *to* lot of, (~*s on such a page*; *one* ~*s before, after, another*; ~ *into* one's *head*; *the work, ill luck,* ~*s to me*). **7.** Happen (*how* ~*s it that* —*?*; *to* ~ pred. adj., future; *for a year to* ~; *the to-*~, the future; ~ *what may*, whatever happens). **8.** Become present from future (~ *to pass*; *the time will* ~ *when*). **9.** Spring *of*, be the result *of*, (*that's what* ~*s of grumbling*; ~ *of noble parents*). **10.** Enter, be brought, *into* (collision, play, prominence; ~ *to harm*, be injured). **11.** Amount *to* (~*s to 2/6*; *it* ~*s to this, that*—, is as much as to say that). **12.** Take form (*the butter will not*~). **13.** Find oneself under compulsion or in a position *to* (*have* ~ *to believe, has* ~ *to be used*). **14.** (With cogn. obj.) traverse, accomplish, (*have* ~ *3 miles, a long way*). **15.** Play a part (sl.; ~ *the bully over*; ~ *it strong*, show vigour; ~ *it too strong*, overdo something, exaggerate). **16.** Become, get to be, prove, (*string* ~*s untied, things* ~ *right, he came alive*; ~*s expensive, easy, true, natural*). **17.** (Imperat. as exclamation) now then (encouraging), think again, don't be hasty. **18.** ~ *about*, happen; ~ *across*, meet with; ~ *along*, (colloq.) make haste; ~ *at*, reach, discover, get access to; ~ *away*, get detached; ~ *back*, recur to memory, *retaliate or retort (sl.)*; (as n., ~-*back*) return to, reinstatement in, one's former position (*stage a* ~-*back*); ~ *by* (prep.) obtain, (adv.) pass; ~ *clean*, confess; ~ *down*, extend downwards *to*, be handled down by tradition, fall, be humbled (esp. *in the world*, lose caste); ~ *down upon*, rebuke, punish, exact reparation from; ~ *down with*, pay (money); ~ *forward*, present oneself, answer appeal; ~ *in*, enter house or room, begin innings, take such a place in race etc. (~ *in third*), be elected, come to power, be received as income, become seasonable or fashionable, serve a purpose (esp. ~ *in useful*), find a place (*where does the joke* ~ *in?*; *where do I* ~ *in?* how are my interests advanced?); ~ *in for*, get share of, get; ~ *into*, receive possession of; ~ *near doing*, narrowly escape or fail; ~ *off*, be detached, extricate oneself from contest etc. in such state (*with flying* COLOURS, *badly*), be accomplished, fulfilled; ~ *off it* (colloq.), stop acting or talking like that, change your tune; ~ *on*, (prep.) = ~ *upon*, (adv.) continue coming, advance esp. to attack, progress, thrive, supervene (of wind, storm, disease), arise to be discussed, appear on stage, begin to bowl, (imperat.) follow me, I defy you; ~ *out*, go on strike, emerge from examination etc. with such success, emerge from clouds, be found out, be solved, show itself (of photograph, smallpox, arrogance), be published (~*s out on Saturdays*), make début on stage or in society; ~ *out with*, utter; ~ *over*, (prep.) master as an influence, (adv.) ~ from some distance or across obstacle (*came over with the Conqueror, over from London to see us*), change sides or opinion; ~ *round*, look in for casual visit, recover from ill temper, swoon, anaesthetic, etc., be converted from one view to its opposite; ~ *to*, (prep.) inherit, return to (one*self*, one's *senses* from fainting-fit or from folly), (adv.) cease moving, revive; ~ *under*, be classed as or among, be subjected to (influence); ~ *up*, ‖ join university, approach person for talk, get abreast *with*, spring out of ground, become fashionable, be mooted, be equal *to* standard etc., (imperat., to horse) go faster; ~ *upon*, attack by surprise, strike or lay hold of (mind), make demand on, be a burden to, meet by chance with. [OE, OS *cuman*, OHG *queman*, ON *koma*, Goth. *qiman* f. Gmc **kweman*, *kuman*, cogn. w. L *venire*, Gk *bainō*]

come² (kŭm), n. ~-*&-go*, passing to & fro; ~-*down*, downfall, degradation. [f. prec.]

come-ăt'-able (kŭm-), a. Accessible. [-ABLE]

comēd'ian, n. Actor, writer, of comedies. [f. F *comédien* f. *comédie* COMEDY]

comēdiĕnne', n. Comedy actress. [F]

cŏm'ēdist, n. Writer of comedies. [foll., -IST(3)]

cŏm'ēdў̆, n. Stage-play of light, amusing, & often satirical character, chiefly representing everyday life, & with happy ending (cf. TRAGEDY); branch of drama concerned with ordinary persons & employing familiar language; life, or an incident in it, regarded as a spectacle; *Old, Middle, New, C~*, classification of ancient Greek ~, the first farcical & largely political, the last corresponding to modern ~, & the second transitional. [ME, f. OF *comedie* f. L f. Gk *kōmōidia* f. *kōmōidos* comic poet f. *kōmos* revel]

come'lɪ̣y (kŭm'li), a. Pleasant to look at (usu. of personal appearance, sometimes of behaviour or conduct). Hence ~**i-**NESS n. [ME *cumelich*, *cumli* prob. f. *becumelich* (BECOME + -LY); cf. MHG *komlich* suitable, G *bequem* (C.T.O.)]

com'er (kŭ-), n. One who comes (usu. qualified, as *first* ~); *all* ~*s*, any one who applies, takes up a challenge, etc. [-ER¹]

comĕs'tĭble, n. (usu. pl.). Thing to eat. [F, f. med. L *comestibilis* f. L *comedere* eat up]

cŏm'ĕt, n. A hazy-looking object, occas. with a star-like nucleus, & occas. with a tail, moving in an elliptical or nearly parabolic path about the sun; ~-*year*, in which conspicuous ~ comes; ~-*wine*, made in ~-year, supposed of superior quality. Hence ~ARY¹, **cŏmĕt'ic**, aa. [ME & OF *comete* f. L f. Gk *komētēs* long-haired (star); OE *cometa* f. L (-*ta*)]

com'fĭt (kŭ-), n. Sweetmeat, sugarplum. [ME f. OF *confit* f. L CON(*fectum* = *factum* neut. p.p. of *facere* make)]

com'fort (kŭ-), n., & v.t. 1. Relief in affliction, consolation, being consoled; person who consoles one or saves one trouble; cause of satisfaction; conscious well-being, being comfortable; possession of ~*s*, things that make life easy; *creature* ~*s*, good food, clothes, etc.; **eiderdown quilt*; **~ station*, public lavatory. 2. v.t. Soothe in grief, console; make comfortable; ~ *the king's enemies* (arch.), give them aid. [ME *confort* etc. f. OF *confort*(er) f. LL *confortare* strengthen f. L *fortis* strong]

com'fortable (kŭ-), a. & n. 1. Such as to obviate hardship, save trouble, & promote content, ministering to comfort; at ease, free from hardship, pain, & trouble; tranquil, with easy conscience; *the C~ Words*, the four scriptural passages following the Absolution in the Communion Office. 2. **n. Eiderdown quilt. Hence **com'fortabLY²** (kŭ-) adv. [ME, f. AF *confortable* (prec., -ABLE); cf. LL *confortabilis*]

com'forter (kŭ-), n. One who comforts (*the C~*, Holy Ghost); *Job's* ~, professed consoler who depresses); ‖ baby's dummy teat; ‖ woollen scarf; **eiderdown quilt. [ME, f. AF *confortour*, OF -*eor* (as prec., -ER¹)]

com'fortless (kŭ-), a. Dreary, without provision for comfort. [-LESS]

cŏm'frey (kŭ-), n. (pl. ~*s*). Tall rough-leaved ditch plant with clusters of whitish or purplish bells. [f. AF *cum-*, OF *confirie* of obsc. orig.]

com'fў̆ (kŭ-), a. (colloq.). Comfortable. [abbr.]

cŏm'ic, a. & n. 1. Of comedy (~ *opera*, with ~ treatment & much spoken dialogue, also mere burlesque set to music); mirth-provoking, laughable or meant to be so, facetious, burlesque, funny, (~ *song, paper*; ~ *history of Rome* etc.; ~ *strip*, set of drawings, forming part of a series, appearing regularly in a journal, usu. broadly humorous). 2. n. (colloq.). Music-hall comedian (also, in F form, *comique*); ~ *paper*. Hence ~**o-** comb. form. [f. L f. Gk *kōmikos*]

cŏm'ical, a. Mirth-provoking, laughable;

odd, queer. Hence ~ITY (-ăl²) n., ~LY²
adv. [as prec.+-AL]

Cŏm'infŏrm, n. International Communist organization (1947–56) established to
carry on the propaganda formerly conducted by the Comintern. [f. first
elements of Russ. forms of *Com(munist)
Inform(ation Bureau)*]

Cŏm'intērn, n. Third INTERNATIONAL. [f.
first elements of Russ. forms of *Com-
(munist) Intern(ational)*]

cŏmĭtädj'ĭ, n. Member of band of irregular soldiery in the Balkans. [common
Balkan form = Turk. *komita*, f. F *comité*
committee, +-*dji*; lit. 'member of a
(revolutionary) committee']

cŏm'ĭtў, n. Courtesy; ~ *of nations*,
friendly recognition as far as practicable
of each other's laws & usages. [f. L
cōmitas (*cōmis* courteous)]

cŏmm'a, n. Punctuation-mark (,) of the
least separation indicated between parts
of sentence, also used to separate figures
etc.; (Mus.) definite minute interval or
difference of pitch; *inverted* ~*s*, raised or
superior ~*s* used to begin & end a quotation, the first (or first pair) inverted (he
said 'no' or "no"); ~ *bacillus*, ~-shaped
found in cholera; ~ *butterfly*, one with a
white ~-shaped mark on the underside of
the hind wing. [f. L f. Gk *komma* clause]

command'¹ (-ah-), v.t. & i. Order, bid,
(*what God* ~*s*, ~*s us*, ~*s us to do*, ~*s that
we should do*, ~*s to be done*; also ellipt.,
let us do as God ~*s*; & abs., *God* ~*s & man
obeys*); have authority over, control of;
be supreme; be in command; be in command of (ship, forces, etc.); ~ *in chief*, be
commander-in-chief of, or abs.; restrain,
master, (passions, one*self*); have at disposal or within reach (sum, skill, person;
so *yours to* ~, obediently); deserve &
get (sympathy etc.); dominate (strategic
position) from superior height, look down
over. [ME, f. OF *comander* f. LL
commandare COMMEND]

command'² (-ah-), n. Order, bidding,
(*word of* ~, customary order for movement
in drill; *at* or *by* one's ~, in pursuance of
his bidding); ∥ ~ *paper* (usu. abbr. *Cmd*,
formerly *Cd*, with register number, as *Cd
5723*), paper laid by ~ of the Crown before
Parliament etc.; exercise or tenure of
authority, esp. naval or military (*in* ~
of, commanding; *under* ~ *of*, commanded
by); control, mastery, possession, (*great
~ of language*, skill in speech; *at* ~, ready
to be used at will; ~ *of the passes* etc.);
body of troops etc., district, under commander (*the Nore, Southern, Bomber, C*~);
~-*in-chief*, supreme ~; ∥ ~ *night*, with
theatrical etc. performance given by royal
~; ∥ ~ *performance*, theatrical etc. performance given by royal ~; *the* HIGH(*er*) ~.
[f. prec.]

cŏmmandănt', n. Commanding officer,
esp. governor of fortress. Hence ~SHIP n.
[17th c., F (COMMAND¹, -ANT)]

cŏmmandeer', v.t. Impress (men), seize
(stores), for military service. [f. S.-Afr.-
-Du. *kommanderen* (-ār-) f. F as prec.]

comman'der (-ah-), n. In vbl senses; also
or esp.: *C~ of the Faithful*, title of Caliph;
C~, Lieut.-C~, naval OFFICERS; *Wing
C~*, AIR¹-*force* officer; member of higher
class in some Orders of Knighthood; large
wooden mallet; *C~-in-Chief*, (Army) of
all military land-forces of State, of
portion of them quartered in colony, or
of expedition in foreign country, (Navy)
of all ships on a station. Hence ~SHIP(1)
n. [ME, f. OF *comandere, -eor* (COMMAND¹,
-ER¹)]

comman'ding (-ah-), a. In vbl senses;
esp.: exalted, impressive, (of persons,
looks, ability, etc.); with wide view (of
hill, position). [-ING²]

command'ment (-ah-), n. Divine command (*the ten* ~*s*, Mosaic decalogue;
eleventh ~, any precept jestingly classed
with these). [ME, f. OF *comandement*
(COMMAND¹, -MENT)]

comman'dō (-ah-), n. (pl. ~*s*). Party
called out for military service, body of
troops; (*C~*) unit of British & Imperial
amphibious shock-troops raised orig. in
the 1939–45 war, member of such unit.
[Port., f. *commandar* COMMAND¹, wd used
by S.-Afr. Dutch, & familiarized in Boer
war]

comme il faut (kŏm ēl fō), pred. a. Well-
-bred. [F]

commĕm'orāt|e, v.t. Celebrate in speech
or writing; preserve in memory by some
celebration; (of things) be a memorial of.
Hence ~IVE a. [f. L commemorare bring to
remembrance, see -ATE³]

commĕmorā'tion, n. Act of commemorating; service, part of service, in memory
of saint or sacred event; ∥ (Oxford Univ.)
annual celebration in memory of founders.
[ME, f. L *commemoratio* (as prec., see
-ATION)]

commĕnce', v.t. & i. Begin (work, doing,
to do); (arch.) start, set up, as (lawyer
etc.); ∥ take the full degree of (M.A. etc.).
[ME, f. OF *comencer* f. Rom. *cominitiare*
(COM-, *initiare* INITIATE)]

commĕnce'ment (-sm-), n. In vbl
senses; also, ceremony when degrees of
Master & Doctor are conferred at Cambridge, Dublin, & U.S. Univv. [ME, f.
OF (prec., -MENT)]

commĕnd', v.t. Entrust for safe keeping
(arch. exc. in ~ one's *soul to God*, ~ thing
to person's *care*); praise; (arch.) ~ *me to*,
remember me kindly to (person); ~ *me
to*, give me by choice (often iron.). [ME,
f. L COM(*mendare*=*mandare* entrust, see
MANDATE)]

commĕn'dab|le, a. Praiseworthy. Hence
~leNESS (-ln-) n., ~LY² adv. [ME, f. OF
f. L *commendabilis* (prec., -BLE)]

commĕn'däm, n. Tenure of benefice in
absence of regular incumbent. [med. L
(*dare in*) *commendam* give in trust]

cŏmmĕndā′tion, n. Praise; act of commending person to another's favour. [ME, f. OF f. L *commendationem* (as COMMEND, see -ATION)]

commĕn′datorў, a. Commending, holding, held, in commendam. [f. LL *commendatorius* (as prec., see -ORY)]

commĕn′sal, a. & n. (One) who eats at the same table; (animal, plant) living as another's tenant & sharing its food (cf. PARASITE). Hence ~ISM, cŏmmĕnsăl′-ITY, nn. [ME, f. OF, or f. med. L *commensalis* f. *mensa* table, see -AL]

commĕn′sur|able (-sher-), a. Measurable by the same standard (*with*, *to*); (of numbers) divisible without remainder by the same quantity; proportionate *to*. Hence ~ABIL′ITY, ~ableNESS, nn., ~abLY² adv., (-sher-). [f. LL COM(*mensurabilis*, as MEASURE, see -BLE)]

commĕn′surate (-sher-), a. Coextensive (*with*); proportionate (*to*, *with*). Hence ~LY² (-tl-) adv., ~NESS (-tn-) n. [f. LL COM(*mensuratus*, prec., see -ATE²)]

cŏmm′ĕnt¹, n. Explanatory note or remark; criticism; (fig., of events etc.) illustration. [f. L *commentum* contrivance (in LL also = interpretation) neut. p.p. of *comminisci* devise]

cŏmm′ĕnt², v.i. Write explanatory notes (*upon* a text); make (esp. unfavourable) remarks (*upon*). [f. prec., or F *commenter*]

cŏmm′entarў, n. Expository treatise; set of running comments on a book or remarks on a speech or performance; comment. [f. L *commentarius*, -*ium*, sb. use of adj. (COMMENT¹, -ARY¹)]

cŏmmentā′tion, n. Making of comments. [f. L *commentatio* (*commentari* discuss, see COMMENT & -ATION)]

cŏmm′ĕntātor, n. Writer of commentary; eyewitness whose description of a ceremony, sporting event, etc., is broadcast. [L (as prec., see -OR)]

cŏmm′ĕrce, n. Exchange of merchandise, esp. on a large scale; CHAMBER *of* ~; intercourse (esp. sexual); card game. [F, or f. L COM(*mercium* f. *merx mercis* merchandise)]

commĕr′cial (-shl), a. & n. Of, engaged in, bearing on, commerce; ~ (*traveller*), trader's agent, showing samples & soliciting orders; ~ announcement or programme; ||~ *room* (in hotel for ~ travellers). Hence ~ISM, ~IST, (-sha-), ~ITY (-shiăl²), nn., ~IZE v.t., ~LY² adv., (-sha-). [f. prec. + -AL]

Cŏmm′ie, n. (colloq.). Communist. [abbr.]

cŏmminā′tion, n. Threatening of divine vengeance; recital of divine threats against sinners in Anglican Liturgy. [ME, f. L *comminatio* f. *comminari* threaten; see -ATION]

cŏmm′inatorў, a. Threatening, denun-

ciatory. [f. med. L *comminatorius* (as prec., see -ORY)]

commin′gle (-nggl), v.t. & i. Mingle together. [COM-]

cŏmm′inūte, v.t. Reduce to small fragments; divide (property) into small portions. So cŏmminū′tion n. [f. L COM(*minuere* -*ut*- f. *minor* less)]

commis′er|āte (-z-), v.t. & i. Feel, express, pity for; condole *with*. Hence or cogn. ~A′TION n., ~ātive a., ~ātiveLY³ adv. [f. L *commiserari* f. *miser*; see MISER¹, -ATE³]

cŏmmissăr′, n. (Former name of) head of a government department of the U.S.S.R. [Russ. *kommissar* f. F *commissaire* (as COMMISSARY)]

cŏmmissār′ial, a. Of a commissary. [-AL]

cŏmmissār′iat, n. Department (esp. Mil.) for supply of food etc.; a department of the Soviet Republic Civil Service. [as foll., see -ATE¹]

cŏmm′issarў, n. Deputy, delegate; representative of a bishop in part of his diocese, or of absent bishop; officer charged with supply of food etc. for body of soldiers; C~ *general*, chief ~, esp. (Mil.) chief of a commissariat service. Hence ~SHIP n. [ME, f. med. L *commissarius* person in charge (COMMIT, -ARY¹)]

commi′ssion¹ (-shn), n. 1. Command, instruction; authority, body of persons having authority, to perform certain duties; ||~ *of the peace*, (authority given to) Justices of the Peace; *on the*~, having this; *royal* ~, ~ of inquiry or committee appointed by the Crown at the instance of the Government. 2. Warrant conferring authority, esp. that of officers in the army, navy, and air force from lieutenant or pilot officer upwards. 3. *In* ~, (of persons) having delegated authority, (of an office) placed by warrant in charge of a body of persons instead of the constitutional administrator, (of ship of war) manned, armed, & ready for sea. 4. Entrusting of authority etc. to a person; charge, matter, entrusted to person to perform. 5. Authority to act as agent for another in trade, as *have goods on* ~; pay of a ~-agent, percentage on amount involved. 6. Committing (*of* crime etc.); ||~-*day*, opening day of assizes, when judge's ~ is read. [ME, f. OF f. L *commissionem* (as prec., -ION)]

commi′ssion² (-shn), v.t. Empower by commission; give (officer) command of ship; order (ship) for active service; (of officer) assume command of (ship); give (artist etc.) a commission for piece of work. [f. prec.]

commissionaire′ (-shonăr, n. || Member of the *corps of C*~s organized in London for employment as messengers etc.; uniformed door attendant at theatres, cinemas, large shops, etc. [F, see COM-MISSIONER]

commi'ssioned (-shond), a. Authorized; (of officers) holding rank by commission; (of ships) put in commission. [-ED[1]]

commi'ssioner (-sho-), n. One appointed by commission; member of a commission, esp. of government boards etc., as *Charity, Civil Service, C~*; representative of supreme authority in a district, department, etc.; *High C~*, chief representative in London of Commonwealth countries, also chief United Kingdom representative in Commonwealth countries; *Lord High C~*, representative of the Crown at the General Assembly of the Church of Scotland. Hence ~SHIP n. [ME, f. med. L *commissionarius* (COMMISSION, -ARY[1], -ER[2](2))]

commi'ssure, n. Juncture, seam; joint between two bones; line where lips, eyelids, meet; bands of nerve substance connecting hemispheres of brain, two sides of spinal cord, etc. So **commissur'AL** a. [f. L *commissura* junction (as foll., see -URE)]

commit', v.t. (-tt-). Entrust, consign, for treatment or safe keeping (*to* person, his care, his judgement, *to* writing, memory, earth, the flames); ~ (*to* prison), consign officially to custody; refer (bill) to committee; perpetrate (crime, blunder), whence ~t'ABLE a.; compromise, involve, (character, honour, one*self*); bind one*self to* (a course). Hence ~t'AL n. (~ting to prison, reference to committee, ~ting of oneself), ~MENT n. (esp., engagement that restricts freedom of action). [ME, f. L *committere* join, entrust, f. *mittere* miss- send]

committ'ee (-tǐ), n. Body of persons appointed for special function by (& usu. out of) a (usu. larger) body, as (Parl.) *C~ of Supply, Ways & Means, House resolves itself into a C~*, goes into *C~, is in C~, C~ of the whole House; Standing C~* (permanent during existence of appointing body); *Joint C~* (of members nominated by different bodies); ~-*man*, member of a ~; (Law, pron. kŏmĭtē') person entrusted with charge, as ~*s for lunatics*. [f. prec. + -EE]

commix', v.t. & i. (arch., poet.). Mix. So ~TURE n. [back formation f. *commixt*, as MIX f. MIXED]

commode', n. Chest of drawers; chiffonier; (esp. *night*-~) close-stool. [F, f. L COM(*modus* measure) convenient]

commod'ious, a. Roomy; (arch.) handy. Hence ~LY[2] adv., ~NESS n. [f. F *commodieux* or med. L *commodiosus* f. L *commodus*; see prec.]

commod'ity, n. Useful thing; article of trade (*staple* ~); (arch.) convenience. [ME, f. OF *commodite* or L *commoditas* (COMMODE, -TY)]

commo'dore, n. Naval officer above captain and below rear-admiral (in Brit.

navy a temporary rank); *Air C~*, officer of AIR[1] *Force*; (courtesy title) senior captain when three or more ships cruise together, captain of pilots, president of yacht-club; senior captain of a shipping line; ~'s ship. [17th c. *comma(n)dore*, prob. f. Du. *kommandeur* commander; present form unexpl.]

comm'on[1], a. (-er, -est). **1.** Belonging equally to, coming from, or done by, more than one, as *our ~ humanity, ~ cause, ~ consent*. **2.** Belonging to, open to, affecting the public, as ~ *crier, jail, alehouse, nuisance, scold*. **3.** Of ordinary occurrence, as *a ~ experience* (~ *or garden*, sl., of the familiar kind); ordinary, of ordinary qualities, as ~ *honesty, no ~ mind*; without rank or position, as ~ *soldier, the ~ people*; of the most familiar type, as ~ *nightshade, snake*. **4.** Of inferior quality; vulgar. **5.** (Math.) belonging to two or more quantities, as ~ *factor, multiple*; (Gram.) ~ *noun*, name applicable to any one of a class, ~ *gender*, masculine or feminine; (Pros.) of variable quantity; (Mus.) ~ *time, measure*, (two or four beats in bar), ~ CHORD. **6.** ~ FORM[1]; ~ *ground*, basis for argument etc. accepted by both sides; ~ *law*, unwritten law of England, administered by the Queen's courts, purporting to be derived from ancient usage (~-*law wife*, concubine); ~ *metre*, hymn stanza of 4 lines (with 8, 6, 8, 6 syllables); *Court of C~ Pleas* (for trial of civil causes, abolished 1875); *C~ Prayer*, liturgy set forth in Book of C. P. of Edward VI; ||~-*room*, (in some colleges, schools, etc.) room to which the members have ~ access for business or social purposes; ~ *sense*, normal understanding, good practical sense in everyday affairs, general feeling (of mankind or community), *philosophy of ~ sense* (accepting primary beliefs of mankind as ultimate criterion of truth); ~*sens'ical*, possessing, marked by, ~ sense; ~ *weal*, ~*weal*, arch., public welfare, (also) = COMMONWEALTH. Hence ~NESS (-n-n-) n. [ME & OF *comun* f. L *communis*]

comm'on[2], n. Land belonging to a community, esp. unenclosed waste land; (*right of*) ~, a man's right over another's land, as ~ *of pasturage; out of the* ~, unusual; *in* ~, in joint use, shared; *in* ~ *with*, in the same way as (*in* ~ *with all sensible people I hold that . . .*). [prec. as n.]

comm'onable, a. (Of animals) that may be pastured on common land; (of land) that may be held in common. [f. obs. vb *common* f. OF *comuner* (as COMMON[1]) + -ABLE]

comm'onage, n. Right of common; land, condition of land, held in common; commonalty. [-AGE]

comm'onalty, n. The common people; general body (of mankind etc.); body corporate. [ME & OF *communalte, -aute,* **f. med.** L *communalitatem*; see COMMON[1], -AL, -TY]

‖ **cŏmm′oner,** n. One of the common people (below rank of peer); (rarely) member of House of Commons, esp. *the great C~,* elder Wm Pitt, *First C~,* the Speaker; (at Oxford University) student not on foundation; one who has right of common. [ME, f. COMMON[2] & obs. vb *common* (see COMMONABLE)+-ER[1]]

cŏmm′oney, n. Inferior playing-marble. [COMMON[1]+-Y[3]]

cŏmm′onlў, adv. Usually; to an ordinary degree, as ~ *honest*; meanly, cheaply. [-LY[2]]

cŏmm′onplăce[1], n. & a. **1.** Notable passage, entered for use in a ~-*book*; ordinary topic; everyday saying; platitude; anything common or trite. **2. adj.** Lacking originality, trite. Hence ~NESS (-sn-) n. [=L *locus communis*=Gk *koinos topos* general theme]

cŏmm′onplăce[2], v.t. & i. Extract commonplaces from; enter in commonplace-book; utter commonplaces. [f. prec.]

cŏmm′ons (-z), n. pl. The common people; third estate in English or other similar constitution, represented by Lower House of Parliament (*House of C~*); provisions shared in common; common table, as DOCTORS' COMMONS; ‖ (Oxf., Camb.) definite portion of food supplied at fixed charge; daily fare, as *short ~*. [ME, pl. of COMMON[2]]

cŏmm′onwealth (-wĕl-), n. Body politic, independent community; republic (also fig., as ~ *of learning*); republican government in England, 1649-60; title of federated Australian States; *British C~ of Nations,* (term coined by Gen. Smuts in 1919 for) British Empire, now usu. (*British*) *C~* (*C~ Institute,* building in London devoted to promoting wider public knowledge of the life, scenery, & industries of the C~; *C~ Relations Office,* Government department responsible for relations between Britain & the various countries of the C~); company of actors sharing receipts; (formerly) public welfare. [also *commonweal,* f. COMMON[1]+ WEALTH, WEAL; cf. F *bien public,* L *res publica*]

·commŏ′tion, n. Physical disturbance; bustle, confusion; tumult, insurrection. [ME, f. OF *comocion* or L *commotio* (as foll., see -ION)]

commove′ (-ōōv), v.t. Move violently (lit. & fig.); excite. [ME *comm(o)eve,* f. strong st. of OF *commo(u)voir* f. L COM-(*movēre mot-* MOVE)]

cŏmm′ūnal, a. Of a commune; of the Paris Commune; of the commonalty, of or for the community, for the common use; (India) of the antagonistic religious and racial communities in a district (~

voting, elections, disturbances, etc.). [F, **f.** LL *communalis* (as COMMUNE, see -AL)]

cŏmm′ūnal|ism, n. Theory of government by local autonomy. So ~IST n., ~IS′TIC a. [prec.+-ISM]

cŏmm′ūnalĭz|e, -is|e (-ĭz), v.t. Make (thing) the property of a local community. Hence ~A′TION n. [-IZE]

cŏmm′ūne[1], n. French territorial division, smallest for administrative purposes; similar division elsewhere; *The C~* (*of Paris*), (1) usurping body during the Reign of Terror, (2) communalistic government in 1871. [F, f. med. L *commūna* for *communia* neut. pl. of L *commūnis* COMMON[1]]

commūne[2] (*or* kŏm′), v.i. Hold intimate intercourse (*with* person, one's own heart, *together*); *receive Holy Communion. [f. OF *comuner* f. *comun* COMMON[1]]

commūn′ic|able, a. That can be imparted; communicative. Hence ~ABIL-ITY, ~ableNESS, nn., ~abLY[2] adv. [f. LL *communicabilis* (as foll., see -BLE); cf. F *communicable*]

commūn′icant, n. One who (esp. regularly) receives Holy Communion; one who imparts information. [as foll., see -ANT]

commūn′icăte, v.t.& i. Impart, transmit, (heat, motion, feeling, news, a discovery, *to*); share (a thing) *with*; receive, administer, Holy Communion; hold intercourse *with*; (of rooms etc.) have common door (*with*). [f. L *communicare* (as COM-MON[1] +-*ic-* factitive suf.), see -ATE[3]]

commūnicā′tion, n. Act of imparting (esp. news); information given; intercourse; common door or passage or road or rail or telegraph or other connexion between places, (Mil., pl.) connexion between base & front. [ME, f. OF *comunicacion* f. L *communicationem* (prec., -ATION)]

commūn′icătive, a. Ready to impart; open, talkative. Hence ~LY[2] adv., ~NESS n. [f. OF *-if, -ive,* as COMMUNICATE, see -IVE]

commūn′icātor, n. Person, thing, that communicates; part of telegraph instrument used in sending message; contrivance for communicating with guard or driver of train. [L (as prec., see -OR)]

commūn′ion (-yon), n. Sharing, participation; fellowship (esp. between branches of Catholic Church); body professing one faith; intercourse; participation in Lord's Supper (also *Holy C~*); *close, open*ₜ *~,* exclusion from, admission to, ~ of persons not baptized according to Baptist principles; ~-*cloth, -cup* (used at Holy C~); ~-*rail* (in front of ~-table in some churches); ~-*table* (used for Holy C~). [ME, f. L *communio* (as COMMON[1], see -ION) or OF *communion*]

commūn′ionist (-yon-), n. *Close, open, ~,*

adherent of close, open, communion; *fellow-~,* member of same communion. [-IST]

communiqué (see Ap.), n. Official intimation. [F]

cŏmm'ŭn|ĭsm, n. Vesting of property in the community, each member working according to his capacity and receiving according to his wants; (usu. *C~ism*) movement or political party advocating ~ism, party affirming need for a dictatorship of the proletariat, associated with the Comintern (1919–43) & the Cominform (1947–56). Hence ~IST n., ~ĭs'tĬO a. [f. F *communism* f. *commun* COMMON[1]; see -ISM]

commūnĭtār'ĭan, n. Member of community practising communism. [f. foll. + -ARIAN]

commūn'ĭtў, n. Joint ownership, as ~ *of goods*; identity of character; fellowship (~ *of interest* etc.; also attrib., as ~ *singing,* in which all present join); organized political, municipal, or social body; body of people living in same locality (~ *centre,* place providing social & other facilities for a neighbourhood); body of men having religion, profession, etc., in common, as *the mercantile ~, the Jewish ~; the ~,* the public; monastic, socialistic, or other, body practising ~ of goods. [ME & OF *comunete* f. L *communitatem* (as COMMON[1], see -TY)]

cŏmm'ŭnīz|e, -is|e (-īz), v.t. Make (land etc.) common property. Hence ~A'TION n. [f. L *communis* COMMON[1] +-IZE]

commūt'|able, a. Exchangeable; that can be compounded for. Hence ~ABIL'ITY n. [f. L *commutabilis* (as foll., see -BLE)]

cŏmmūtā'tion, n. Commuting; money paid by way of ~; *C~ Act* (for ~ of tithes in England, 1836); *~ ticket,* season ticket. [F, or f. L *commutatio* (as foll., see -ATION)]

commūt'ative (also kŏm'ūtăt-), a. Relating to or involving substitution. [f. med. L *commutativus* (as foll., see -ATIVE)]

cŏmm'ūtātor, n. Person, thing that commutes; contrivance for altering course of electric current. [as foll., see -OR]

commūt|e', v.t. & i. Interchange (two things); buy off (one obligation) by (*for, into*) another; change (punishment *into* another less severe); change (one kind of payment *into, for,* another); **buy and use a season (commutation)* ticket for travelling, esp. daily to and from work in a city, whence **~'ER[1]* n. [f. L COM*mutare -mutat-* exchange]

cŏmōse', a. Having a COMA[2]; hairy, downy. [f. L *comosus* (COMA[2], see -OSE[1])]

cŏmp, n. (colloq.). Compositor. [abbr.]

cŏm'păct[1], n. Agreement between parties; *general ~,* common consent; FAMILY, SOCIAL, ~. [f. L COM(*pacisci pact*-covenant); cf. PACT]

compăct'[2], a. & n. **1.** Closely or neatly packed together; (of style) condensed,

terse. Hence ~LY[2] adv., ~NESS n. **2.** n. (kŏm'păkt). Miniature flat vanity case, or refill for it. [f. L COM(*pingere pact- = pangere* fasten)]

compăct'[3], v.t. Join firmly together; condense; make up, compose, (*of*). [f. prec.]

compā'gēs, n. Framework, complex structure (lit. & fig.). [L COM(*pages* f. *pangere* fix)]

compā'gin|āte, v.t. Join firmly together. So ~A'TION n. [f. LL *compaginare* (*compago -ginis* = prec.), see -ATE[3]]

compăn'ion[1] (-yon), n., & v.t. & i. One' who accompanies another; associate *in,* sharer *of,* as ~ *in arms,* fellow-soldier, ~ *of his retreat*; title of handbooks, as *Gardener's C~*; ‖ member of lowest grade of some orders of knighthood, as *C~ of the Bath*; *C~ of Honour* (of the order of *C~s* of Honour); person (usu. woman) paid to live with another; thing that matches another (also adj., as ~ *volume*); (v.t.) accompany; (v.i.) consort *with.* Hence ~ATE[2] a. (*~ate marriage,* marriage with birth-control & provision for divorce by mutual consent). [ME, f. OF *compai(g)non* f. Rom. **companionem* f. L *panis* bread]

compăn'ion[2] (-yon), n. (naut.). Raised frame on quarter-deck for lighting cabins etc. below; *~ hatch,* wooden covering over *~-way;* ~ *hatchway,* opening in deck leading to cabin; *~-ladder* (from deck to cabin); *~-way,* staircase to cabin. [f. Du. *kompanje* (now *kam-*) quarter-deck, corresp. to OF *compagne,* It. (*camera della*) *compagna* pantry, caboose, ult. rel. to prec.]

compăn'ionab|le (-nyo-), a. Sociable. Hence ~LY[2] adv., ~leNESS (-ln-) n. [COMPANION[1] +-ABLE]

compăn'ionship (-nyo-) n. State of being companion(s); (Printing) company of compositors working together. [-SHIP]

com'panў (kŭm-), n., & v.t. & i. Companionship; *in ~,* not alone; *bear, keep, a person ~,* accompany him; *part ~* (*with*), part (from); *weep for ~* (because one's companion weeps); *keep ~,* associate as lovers; number of persons assembled; one's usual associates, as *addicted to low ~; he is good, bad, ~* (a pleasant, dull, companion); social party; guests; *I sin in good ~,* better men have done the same; *~ manners,* the artificial behaviour put on before strangers; body of persons combined for common (esp. commercial) object, as JOINT[2] *Stock C~,* ‖ *Limited Liability C~* (liability of each member limited usu. to amount subscribed by him), *John C~* (*East India C~*); partner(s) not named in title of firm, as *Smith & Co.*; party of players; subdivision of infantry battalion usu. commanded by major or captain (cf. TROOP, BATTERY; ~ *officer,* captain or lower commissioned officer; ~ *sergeant-major,* senior non-comd officer of ~); unit of R.A.S.C., R.E., etc.; *ship's*

~, entire crew; (v.t., arch.) accompany; (v.i.) consort *with*. [ME, f. OF *compaignie* f. Rom. *compania* f. *companio* (COM-PANION[1], -Y[1])]

cŏm'parable, a. That can be compared (*with*); fit to be compared (*to*). [ME, f. OF f. L *comparabilis* (as COMPARE[1], see -BLE)]

compă'rative, a. & n. **1.** Of or involving comparison, as *the ~ method*, esp. of sciences, as ~ *anatomy*; (Gram.) ~ *adjective, adverb*, one in the ~ degree; expressing a higher degree of the quality denoted by the simple word; estimated by comparison, as *the ~ merits of*; perceptible by comparison, as *in ~ comfort*. **2.** n. ~ degree. Hence ~LY[2] (-vl-) adv. [ME, f. L *comparativus* (foll., -ATIVE)]

compāre'[1], v.t. & i. Liken, pronounce similar, (*to*), esp. with negative, as *not to be ~d to*; estimate the similarity of (one thing *with, to*, another; two things together); observe the similarity or relation between (passages of book etc.; abbr. *cp.*); ~ *notes*, exchange views; (Gram.) form comparative & superlative degrees of (adjective, adverb); (v.i.) bear comparison, as *no lady can ~ with Sally*. [ME, f. OF *comperer* (later -*par*-) f. L COM*parare* (*par* equal)]

compāre'[2], n. Comparison, as *beyond, without, past*, ~. [app. f. (*without*) *compare* (obs. var. of COMPEER) being referred to COMPARE[1]]

compă'rison, n. Act of comparing; simile, illustration; *in ~ with*, compared to; *degrees of ~*, positive, comparative, superlative, (of adjectives & adverbs). [ME, f. OF *compareson* f. L *comparationem* (as COMPARE[1])]

compărt', v.t. Divide into compartments. [f. OF *compartir* or L COM*partiri* (*pars partis* part)]

compărt'ment, n. Division separated by partitions esp. of railway carriage; watertight division of ship; ‖ (Pol.) separate portion of a bill, or business in hand, for discussion of which a limit of parliamentary time is allotted by Government. [f. F *compartiment* f. It. -*mento* (as prec., see -MENT)]

com'pass[1] (kŭm-), n. (*Pair of*) ~*es*, instrument for describing circles, with two legs connected at one end by movable joint; *beam-~es* (with sliding sockets, for large circles); *bow-~es* (with legs jointed to bend inwards); circumference, boundary; area, extent, (also fig., as *beyond my* ~); range of a voice; roundabout way, as *fetch, go, a ~*; instrument of navigation showing magnetic or true north & bearings from it (*mariners'* ~, *gyro-*~); BOX[3] *the ~*; ~-*plane* (convex, for planing concave surfaces); ~-*saw* (with narrow blade, for curves); ~ *window*, semicircular bay window. [ME, f. OF *compas*, the relation

of wh. to Rom. collaterals & OF *com-passer* (see foll.) is obsc.]

com'pass[2] (kŭm-), v.t. Go round; hem in; grasp mentally; contrive; accomplish. Hence ~ABLE a. [ME, f. OF *compasser*, f. Rom. *compassare* measure (COM-, *passus* PACE)]

compă'ssion (-shn), n. Pity inclining one to spare or help, as *have ~ on us*. [ME & OF *compassion*, f. LL *compassionem* f. LL COM(*pati pass*- suffer), see -ION]

compă'ssionate[1] (-sho-), a. Sympathetic, pitying; ‖ ~ *allowance* (granted when an ordinary pension or allowance is not admissible under official rules); ‖ ~ *leave* (granted out of compassion). Hence ~LY[2] (-tl-) adv., ~NESS (-tn-) n. [latinized f. F *compassionné* (-ATE[2])]

compă'ssionāte[2] (-sho-), v.t. Regard, treat, with compassion. [f. prec.]

compăt'i|ble, a. Consistent, able to co-exist, (*with*). Hence or cogn. ~BIL'ITY n., ~BLY[2] adv. [F, f. med. L *compatibilis* (COM*pati* suffer with, -BLE)]

compăt'ri|ot, n. Fellow-countryman. Hence ~ŏt'IC a. [f. F *compatriote* f. LL COM(*patriota* PATRIOT)]

compeer', n. Equal, peer; comrade. [ME & OF *comper*; see COM-, PEER[1]]

compĕl', v.t. (-ll-). Constrain, force, (*to* do, *to* a course); bring about (an action) by force, as ~ *submission*; (poet.) drive forcibly; ~*ling* a., rousing strong interest or feeling of admiration. Hence ~l'ABLE a. [ME, f. L COM(*pellere puls*- drive)]

cŏm'pend, n. = COMPENDIUM.

compĕn'dious, a. Brief but comprehensive (of works & authors). Hence ~LY[2] adv., ~NESS n. [ME, f. LL *compendiosus* (foll., see -OUS)]

compĕn'dium, n. (pl. -*ums, -a*). Abridgement; summary; abstract. [L, lit. what is weighed together f. COM(*pendĕre* weigh)]

cŏm'pĕnsāt|e, v.t. & i. **1.** Counterbalance; make amends (*for* thing, *to* person, *with, by*, another thing, *or* abs.); recompense (person *for* thing). **2.** (mech.). Provide (pendulum etc.) with mechanical compensation. Hence **cŏmpĕn'sative** a. & n., ~OR n., **cŏmpĕn'satORY** a. [f. L COM(*pensare* frequent. of *pendĕre pens*-weigh)]

compĕnsā'tion, n. Compensating; thing given as recompense; ~-*balance*, ~-*pendulum*, of chronometer (neutralizing effect of temperature). Hence ~AL a. [ME, f. OF, or f. L *compensatio* (as prec., see -ATION)]

cŏm'père (-pār), n., & v.t. **1.** Organizer of cabaret or broadcast entertainment who introduces the artistes, comments on the turns, etc. **2.** v.t. Act as ~ to. [F, = gossip]

compēte', v.i. Strive (*with* another *for* thing, *in doing*, or abs.); vie (*with* another *in* a quality). [f. L COM(*petere -tit-* seek), in post-class. sense 'strive after or contend for (something)']

cŏm'pĕtence, -cў, nn. Sufficiency of means for living, easy circumstances; ability (*to do, for* a task); (of court, magistrate, etc.) legal capacity, right to take cognizance. [f. L *competentia* (as prec., see -ENCE, -ENCY)]

cŏm'pĕtent, a. Properly qualified (*to do, for* a task); legally qualified (judge, court, witness); (of things) belonging, permissible, *to,* as *it was ~ to him to refuse.* Hence~LY² adv. [ME, f. OF *competent* or L *competent-* (as COMPETE, see -ENT)]

cŏmpĕti'tion, n. Act of competing (*for*), by examination, in market, etc. [f. LL *competitio* (as foll., see -ION)]

compĕt'itive, a. Of, by, offered for, competition. Hence ~LY¹ (-vl-) adv. [f. p.p. st. of L *competere* (COMPETE) +-IVE]

compĕt'it|or, n. One who competes, rival. Hence~ORY a., ~rESS¹ n. [f. F *compétiteur* or L *competitor* (as prec., see -OR)]

cŏmpilā'tion, n. Compiling; thing compiled. [ME, f. OF f. L *compilationem* (foll., -ATION)]

compile', v.t. Collect (materials) into a volume; make up (volume) of such materials; (Cricket sl.) score (so many runs). [ME, f. OF *compiler* or app. source, L COM*pilare* plunder]

complā'cence, -cў, nn. Tranquil pleasure; self-satisfaction. [f. med. L *complacentia* f. L COM(*placēre* please), see -ENCE, -ENCY]

complā'cent, a. Self-satisfied. Hence ~LY¹¹ adv. [f. L *complacent-* part. st. of *complacēre,* see prec., -ENT]

complain', v.i. Express dissatisfaction with (*of*); announce that one is suffering from (*of* a headache etc.); state a grievance (*to* an authority *of* offender or offence), whence ~ANT (1) n., plaintiff in certain suits; (poet.) emit mournful sound. [ME, f. OF *complaindre* (st. *-aign-*) f. Rom. *COM(*plangere* planct-*beat the breast) bewail; see PLAIN²]

complaint', n. Utterance of grievance; formal accusation; *plaintiff's case in civil action; subject, ground, of ~;* bodily ailment. [ME, f. OF *complainte* (prec., COM-, PLAINT²)]

complais'|ance (-z-; *or* kŏm'plīz-**), n.** Obligingness, politeness; deference. So ~ANT a. [F, formally = med. L *placentia* COMPLACENCE; see PLEASANCE]

cŏm'plĕment¹, n. That which completes; (Gram.) ~ of (words completing) *the predicate;* full number required (to man ship, fill conveyance, etc.); (Math.) ~ *of an angle,* its deficiency from 90° (cf. SUPPLEMENT). Hence **cŏmplĕmĕn'tAL a., cŏmplĕmĕn'taLY²** adv. [ME, f. L *complementum* (COMPLETE, -MENT)]

cŏmplĕmĕnt'², v.t. Complete, form complement to. [f. prec.]

cŏmplĕmĕn'tary, a. Serving to complete; ~ *angles* (making up 90°); ~ COLOURS. [-ARY¹]

complēte'¹, a. Having all its parts, entire; finished; unqualified, as ~ *surprise;* (arch. of persons) accomplished, as ~ *horseman.* Hence ~LY² (-tl-) adv., ~NESS (-tn-) n. [ME, f. OF *complet* or L *completus* p.p. of COM*plēre* fill up]

complēte'², v.t. Finish; make whole or perfect; make up the amount of. So **complē'tion n., complēt'ive a.** [f. prec.]

cŏm'plĕx¹, n. Complex whole; (Psych.) kind of mental abnormality set up by suppressed tendencies or experience; (loosely) obsession. [f. L *complexus -ūs* embrace etc. (as foll.)]

cŏm'plĕx², a. Consisting of parts, composite; complicated; ~ *sentence,* one containing subordinate clause(s). Hence **complĕx'ITY n., ~LY²** adv. [f. F *complexe* or L *complexus* p.p. of *complectere* (-*i*) embrace; in some uses referred to *complexus* plaited]

complē'xion (-kshn), n. Natural colour, texture, & appearance, of the skin (esp. of face); (fig.) character, aspect, as *his conduct wears another ~.* Hence ~ED² (-kshond), ~LESS, aa. [OF, f. L *complexio-nem* (as prec., see -ION); orig. = combination of supposed qualities determining nature of a body]

compli'ance, n. Action in accordance with request, command, etc.; *in ~ with,* according to (wish etc.); base submission. [COMPLY, -ANCE]

compli'ant, a. Disposed to comply, yielding. Hence ~LY² adv. [-ANT]

cŏm'plicacў, n. Complexity; complicated structure. [f. L as foll., see -ACY]

cŏm'plicāte, v.t. Mix up (*with* other things); make intricate (esp. in p.p.). [f. L COM(*plicare* fold), see -ATE³]

cŏmplicā'tion, n. Involved condition; entangled state of affairs; complicating circumstance, as *here is a further ~.* [f. LL *complicatio* (as prec., see -ATION)]

compli'citў, n. Partnership in an evil action. [f. F *complicité* or *complice* (see ACCOMPLICE) +-TY]

cŏm'pliment¹, n. Polite expression of praise, as *pay, make, a ~; act* implying praise; (pl.) formal greetings, as *make, pay, send,* one's *~s,* (as accompaniment to message, note, present, etc.) *with Mr —'s ~s; ~s of* (greetings appropriate to) *the season;* (arch.) gift, gratuity. Hence ~ARY¹ (-ĕn²) a. [F, f. It. *complimento* f. Sp. *cumplimiento* fulfilment of the duties of courtesy f. L as COMPLEMENT¹; cf. COMPLY]

cŏm'plimĕnt'², v.t. Pay a compliment to (person *on* thing); present (person *with* thing) as mark of courtesy. [f. F *complimenter* (prec.)]

cŏm'plin(e), n. (Eccl.) last service of the day. [ME *cumplie* f. OF *complie* (mod.

complies) repr. LL *completa* (*hora*) COM-PLETE; forms *-in*, *-ines* after *matin*, *-in(e)s*]

comply′, v.i. Act in accordance (*with* wish, command, etc., or abs.). [f. It. *complire* ult. f. L *complēre* COMPLETE]

cŏm′pō, n. (pl. *-os*). Abbr. of COMPOSITION, esp. = stucco, plaster.

compōn′ent, a. & n. 1. Contributing to the composition of a whole. 2. n. ∼ part. [f. L COM(*ponere* put), -ENT]

compōrt′, v.t. & i. Conduct, behave, one*self*; ∼ *with*, suit, befit. [f. L COM-(*portare* carry) & F *comporter*]

compōs|e′ (-z), v.t. (Of elements) make up, constitute, (esp. pass., *be* ∼*ed of*); construct in words, produce in literary form, (poem etc., or abs.); (Mus.) invent & put into proper form; set (words) to music; (Print.) set up (type) to form words & blocks of words, set up (article etc.) in type; put together, arrange, artistically; adjust (dispute etc.); arrange in specified or understood manner, or for specified purpose, as ∼*e yourself to write*, ∼*e your countenance*, ∼*e your thoughts for action*; tranquillize (one*self*, passions, etc.), esp. in p.p., whence ∼′ĕdLY² adv., ∼′ĕdNESS n., (-z-). [f. F *composer*; see POSE¹]

compōs′er (-z-), n. One who composes (usu. music). [prec. + -ER¹]

compōs′ing (-z-), n. In vbl senses; ∼-*machine* (for setting up type); ∼-*stick*, metal instrument of adjustable width in which type is set. [-ING¹]

cŏm′posite (-zĭ- or -zī-), a. & n. (Thing) made up of various parts; (Archit.) fifth classical ORDER, Ionic & Corinthian mixed; (plant) of the Natural Order *Compositae*, in which the so-called flower is a head of many flowers (as daisy, dandelion, etc.); (of ships) built of both wood and iron; ‖∼ (railway) *carriage*, one with compartments of different classes; ∼ *candle* (of stearic acid & stearin of coconut oil); ∼ *photograph* (produced by accurately superimposing several portrait-heads). Hence ∼LY² adv., ∼NESS n. [f. F *composite* or L *compositus* p.p. of L COM(*ponere posit*- put)]

cŏmposi′tion (-z-), n. 1. Act of putting together; formation, construction; formation of words into a compound word; construction of sentences, art of literary production; act, art, of composing music; setting up of type. 2. Mental constitution, as *a touch of madness in his* ∼. 3. Arrangement (of the parts of a picture etc.); thing composed, mixture; piece of music or writing. 4. Agreement for cessation of hostilities; compromise. 5. Compound artificial substance, esp. one serving the purpose of a natural one (often attrib., as ∼ *billiard-balls*. 6. Agreement for payment of sum in lieu of larger sum or other

obligation, as *made a* ∼ *with his creditors*. [ME, f. OF, f. L *compositionem* (prec., -ION)]

compŏs′itive (-z-), a. Combining. [f. LL *compositivus* (as prec., see -IVE)]

compŏs′itor (-z-), n. Type-setter. [f. AF *compositour* f. L *compositorem* (as prec., see -OR)]

cŏm′pŏs (*mĕn′tĭs*), a. In one's right mind; *non* ∼, not in one's right mind. [L]

compŏss′ible, a. Able to coexist (*with*). [F, f. med. L COM(*possibilis* POSSIBLE)]

cŏm′pŏst¹, n. Compound manure; combination. [ME, f. OF, f. L *compositum*, as COMPOSITE]

cŏm′pŏst², v.t. Treat with, make into, compost. [ME, f. OF *composter* (prec.)]

compō′sure (-zher), n. Tranquil demeanour, calmness. [f. COMPOSE + -URE]

cŏmpotā′tion, n. Tippling together. So **cŏm′potātor** n. [f. L *compotatio* (COM-, POTATION)]

cŏm′pōte, n. Fruit preserved in syrup. [F, f. OF *composte*, fem. form of *compost* COMPOST]

compound′¹, v.t. & i. 1. Mix (ingredients, lit. & fig.); combine (verbal elements) into a word; make up (a composite whole). 2. Settle (matter by mutual concession, debt by partial payment, subscription by lump sum, or abs.). 3. Condone (liability, offence) for money etc.; ∼ *a felony*, forbear prosecution on private motive. 4. v.i. Come to terms (*with* person *for* forgoing claim etc., *for* offence). Hence ∼ABLE a. [ME *compoun(e)* f. OF *compondre* f. L COM(*ponere* put), whence obs. *compone*; *-d* as in EXPOUND]

cŏm′pound², a., & n. 1. Made up of several ingredients; consisting of several parts; combined, collective; ∼ *fracture* (complicated with skin wound); ∼ *addition*, *subtraction*, etc. (dealing with various denominations); ∼ INTEREST¹; (Zool., Bot.) consisting of a combination of organisms, or simple parts, as ∼ *animal*, ∼ *flower*; ‖∼ *householder* (whose rates are paid by landlord & included in rent). 2. n. Mixture of elements, ∼ thing, esp. ∼ word; (Chem.) substance consisting of two or more elements chemically united in definite proportions by weight. [orig. p.p. of *compo(u)ne*, see prec.]

cŏm′pound³, n. (In India, China, etc.) enclosure in which house or factory stands. [perh. f. Malay *kampong*]

cŏmpradōr′, n. (In China) chief agent or factotum in European house of business. [Port., = buyer, f. LL *comparatorem* f. COM(*parare* furnish), see -OR]

cŏmprĕhĕnd′, v.t. Grasp mentally, understand, (person, thing); include, take in. [ME, f. L COM(*prehendere -hens-* grasp) or OF *comprehender*]

cŏmprĕhĕn′s|ible, a. That may be understood; that may be comprised. Hence

~ĭBĬL'ĬTY n., ~ĭBLY² adv. [ĭ. L comprehensibilis (as prec., see -BLE)]

cŏmprĕhĕn'sion (-shn), n. Act, faculty, of understanding; inclusive power, as a term of wide ~; toleration of divergent opinions (esp. Eccl.). [f. L comprehensio (as prec., see -ION) or F compréhension]

cŏmprĕhĕn'sĭve, a. Of understanding, as ~ faculty; including much, as ~ term, ~ grasp (fig. & lit.); ~ school, large secondary school providing courses of varied kinds & lengths. Hence ~LY² (-vl-) adv., ~NESS (-vn-) n. [f. LL comprehensivus (as prec., see -IVE) or F compréhensif]

comprĕss'¹, v.t. Squeeze together; condense (air, language, thoughts). Hence ~IVE a. [ME, f. OF compresser or LL compressare f. COM(primere press- = premere press)]

cŏm'prĕss², n. Soft pad of lint etc. for compressing artery etc.; piece of wet cloth covered with waterproof bandage, for relief of inflammation. ·[f. F compresse f. L fem. p.p. as prec.]

comprĕss'|ible, a. That may be compressed. Hence ~ĭBĬL'ĬTY n. [-IBLE]

comprĕ'ssion (-shn), n. Squeezing together, condensation, (lit. & fig.). So comprĕss'OR n. [ME, f. OF f. L compressionem (as COMPRESS¹, see -ION)]

comprĭs|e' (-z), v.t. Include, comprehend; consist of, as the house ~es 9 bedrooms etc.; condense (within limits etc.). Hence ~'ABLE (-z-) a. [ME, f. OF comprise fem. p.p. of comprendre COMPREHEND, on anal. of SURPRISE (F surprise, surprendre)]

cŏm'promĭse¹ (-z), n. Settlement of dispute by mutual concession; adjustment of (between) conflicting opinions, courses, etc., by modification of each. [f. OF compromis f. L compromissum p.p. of COM(promittere PROMISE)]

cŏm'promĭse² (-z), v.t. & i. Settle (dispute) by mutual concession; (v.i.) make a compromise; bring (person, oneself) under suspicion by indiscreet action. [f. prec.]

cŏmprovĭn'cial (-shl), a. & n. (Person, esp. bishop) of the same (esp. archiepiscopal) province. [f. LL comprovincialis (COM-, PROVINCE, -AL)]

comptrŏll'er (kont-), n. Spelling of CONTROLLER (by erron. assoc. w. LL computus, see COUNT¹), introduced c. 1500, & surviving in some titles, as C~ and Auditor General.

compŭl'sion (-shn), n. Constraint, obligation; under, upon, ~, because one is compelled. [ME, f. OF f. LL compulsionem (as COMPEL, see -ION)]

compŭl'sĭve, a. Tending to compel. Hence ~LY² adv. [f. L compuls- as COMPEL, -IVE]

compŭl'sor|y̆, a. (Of action, agent) enforced; compelling (~y legislation etc., opp. permissive). Hence ~ĭLY² adv., ~ĭNESS n. [as prec., -ORY]

compŭnc't|ion, n. Pricking of conscience; slight regret, scruple, as without ~ion. Hence ~IOUS (-shus) a., ~iousLY² (-shus-) adv. [ME, f. OF f. LL compunctionem f. COM(pungere punct- prick), see -ION]

compŭrgā'tion, n. Clearing from a charge, vindication, esp. (Eng. Hist.) trial & purgation by oath. So cŏm'pŭrgātor n., compŭrg'atORY a. [f. LL compurgatio f. COM(purgare purify) see -ATION]

compŭt|e', v.t. Reckon (number or amount often at figure, that, or abs.). So ~'ABLE (or kŏm²-), ~'ATIVE (or kŏm²-), aa., compŭta'TION n., ~'ER¹ n., calculator, electronic calculating machine. [f. F computer or L COM(putare reckon)]

comrade (kŭm'rĭd, kŏ-), n. Mate or fellow in work or play or fighting, equal with whom one is on familiar terms, (usu. of males, cf. companion); (as prefix) fellow member of trade union, communistic society, etc. (C~ Smith). Hence ~SHIP (-dsh-) n. [16th c. cama-, camerade f. F, f. Sp. camarada room-mate, lit. roomful (CHAMBER, -ADE)]

*Cŏm'stŏckery̆, n. Opposition to naked realism in art or literature. [A. Comstock, U.S. neo-Puritan (d. 1915)]

Cŏm't|ism, n. = POSITIVISM. So ~IST n. [Auguste Comte, founder (d. 1857), +-ISM]

cŏn¹ (-nn-), v.t. ~ (over), study, learn by heart. [different. form of cun, ME cunn CAN²]

cŏn³, *cŏnn, v.t. (-nn-). Direct steering of (ship, or abs.); conning-tower, armoured pilot-house of warship, superstructure of submarine from which steering, firing, etc., are directed when it is on or near the surface. [app. weakened form of cond (17th c.) f. F conduire f. L conducere CONDUCT v.]

cŏn³, prep. (It.). With (esp. Mus.), as ~ brio (spirit), espressione (expression), fuoco (fire), moto (spirited movement).

cŏn⁴. See CONTRA.

*cŏn⁵, n., & v.t. (In attrib. use) confidence (~ game, CONFIDENCE trick); (v.t.) swindle, dupe. [abbr.]

con-, pref. = L cum (see COM-) before c d f g j n q s t v.

cŏn'acre (-ker) n. (In Ireland) letting by tenant of small portions of land prepared for crop. [CORN¹+ACRE]

cŏn amor'e, adv. Zealously. [It.]

conā'tion, n. (philos.). The exertion of willing that desire or aversion shall issue in action. Hence cŏn'atĭve a. [f. L conatio (conari to try, -ATION)]

concăt'en|āte (-n-k-), v.t. Link together (fig.). So ~A'TION n. [f. L CON(catenare f. catena chain), see -ATE³]

cŏnc'āve, a. & n. With outline or surface curved like interior of circle or sphere (cf. CONVEX); (n.) ~ surface, esp. vault of heaven. Hence or cogn. ~LY² (-vl-) adv., concăv'ITY n. [f. L ·CON(cavus hollow) or F concave]

concăv'ō-, in comb. Concavely, concave & —, as ~-*concave*, concave on both sides, ~-*convex*, concave one side, convex the other. [-O-]   -   -

conceal', v.t. Keep secret (*from*); hide. Hence ~MENT n. [ME, f. OF *conceler* f. L CON(*celare* hide)]

concēde', v.t. Admit, allow, (statement, *that*); grant (right, privilege, points or start in game etc.; *to* person); (Sport. sl.) lose (game etc.). [f. F *concéder* or L CON(*cedere, -cess-* yield)]

conceit'[1] (-sēt), n. Personal vanity; fanciful notion, far-fetched comparison or other euphuism; *in my own* ~ (judgement); *out of* ~, no longer pleased *with*. [ME, f. CONCEIVE on anal. of *deceit, deceive*, etc.]

conceit'[2] (-sēt), v.t. (arch.). Imagine; persuade one*self* (*that*). [f. prec.]

conceit'ĕd (-sēt-), a. Vain (orig. *self-*~). Hence ~LY[2] adv. [CONCEIT[1]+-ED[2]]

conceiv'|able (-sēv-), a. That can be (mentally) conceived. Hence ~ABIL'ITY, ~ableNESS, nn., ~abLY[2] adv., (-sēv-). [f. foll. + -ABLE]

conceive' (-sēv), v.t. & i. Become pregnant with; become pregnant; form in the mind, imagine, (also ≃ *of*); fancy, think, (*that*); formulate, express, (usu. pass., as ~*d in plain terms*). [ME, f. OF *conceiv-* stressed st. of *conceveir* f. L CON(*cipere cept-* = *capere* take)]

concĕl'ébr|āte, v.i. (R.-C. Ch., of newly ordained priest) celebrate mass with ordaining bishop. Hence ~A'TION¯ n. [f. L CON(*celebrare* CELEBRATE)]

cŏn'centrāt|e, v.t. & i., & n. **1.** Bring together to one point (troops, power, attention); (Chem.) increase strength of (liquid etc.) by contracting its volume, (fig. in p.p. of hate etc.) intense; (v.i.) employ all one's power or attention (*upon*). **2.** n. ~ed form of something, product of ~ion. Hence cŏncentrA'TION n. (~*ion camp*, for the accommodation of political prisoners, internees, etc.); ~iveNESS, ~OR, nn., ~IVE a. [f. after CONCENTRE; see -ATE[3]]

concĕn'tre (-ter), v.t. & i. Bring, come, to a common centre. [f. F *concentrer*, f. con-CON-+centre CENTRE[1]]

concĕn'tr|ic, a. Having a common centre (*with* or abs.). Hence ~ICALLY adv., cŏncĕntri'CITY n. [ME, f. OF *concentrique* f. med. L CON(*centricus*, as CENTRE)]

cŏn'cĕpt, n. Idea of a class of objects, general notion. [f. LL *conceptus* f. *concept-* (CONCEIVE)]

concĕp'tion, n. Conceiving (in all senses); thing conceived, idea. Hence ~AL (-shō-) a. [ME, f. OF f. L *conceptionem* (as prec., -ION)]

concĕp'tive, a. Conceiving (mentally), of conception. [f. LL *conceptivus* (as prec., see -IVE)]

concĕp'tūal, a. Of mental conceptions. [f. med. L *conceptualis* (*conceptus -ūs* as prec., -AL]

concĕp'tūal|ism, n. Doctrine that universals exist as mental concepts (only); doctrine that the mind can form ideas corresponding to abstract terms. So ~IST n. [-ISM]

concĕrn'[1], v.t. Relate to, affect; interest one*self* (*with, in, about*, matter, *to* do); *be* ~*ed* (take part) *in*; *I am not* ~*ed*, it is not my business (*to*); (in p.p.) troubled, as *a* ~*ed air, am* ~*ed to hear, at, for* person, *about*; ~*ing* (prep.), about. [f. F *concerner* & med. L sense 'regard, concern' of LL CON(*cernere* sift, discern) mix]

concĕrn'[2], n. Relation, reference, (*with*); *have no* ~ (nothing to do) *with*; *have a* ~ (interest, share) *in*; anxiety, solicitous regard, as *asked with deep* ~; matter that affects one, as *no* ~ *of mine*; (pl.) affairs, as *meddling in my* ~*s*; business, firm, as a *flourishing* ~; (colloq.) thing, as *smashed the whole* ~. [f. prec.]

concĕrn'ment, n. Affair, business; importance, as *of vital* ~; being concerned (*with*); anxiety. [-MENT]

cŏn'cert[1], n. Agreement, union, as *work in* ~ (*with*); combination of voices or sounds, as *voices raised in* ~; musical entertainment; ~ *grand*, grand piano of largest size for ~s; ~ *pitch* (slightly higher than the ordinary; transf., state of unusual efficiency or readiness). [f. F *concert* f. It. *concerto* f. *concertare*; see foll.]

concĕrt'[2], v.t. Arrange (by mutual agreement, also of one person). [f. F *concerter* f. It. *concertare* of obsc. orig.]

concĕrt'ĕd, a. In vbl senses; also (Mus.) arranged in parts for voices or instruments. [-ED[1]]

cŏncerti'na (-tē-), n. Portable musical instrument consisting of a pair of bellows with a set of studs at each end. [CONCERT[1]+-INA[1]]

concert'ō (-chĕr-), n. (pl. -*os*). Composition (usu. in three movements) for solo instrument(s) accompanied by orchestra. [It., see CONCERT[1]]

concĕ'ssion (-shn), n. Act of conceding; thing conceded, esp. (Diplom.) grant to CONCESSIONAIRE, piece of territory of which the occupation & use are granted to a State, company, or person. Hence ~ARY[1] (sho-) a. [F, or f. L *concessio* (as CONCEDE, see -ION)]

concĕssion(n)aire' (-sho-), n. Holder of concession, grant, etc., esp. of monopoly given by government to foreigner. [F (-*nn*-), prec., -ARY[1]]

concĕss'ive, a. Of, tending to, concession; (Gram.) expressing concession. [f. LL *concessivus* (as CONCEDE, see -IVE)]

concett'ism (-chĕt-), n. Use of fanciful turns (It. *concetti*) in literature. [-ISM] cŏnch (-ngk), n. Shellfish; shell of a mollusc, esp. (Rom. Myth.) as trumpet of a Triton; (Archit.) domed roof of semicircular apse; also 'concha) external ear, its central concavity. [f. L *concha* shell f. Gk *kogkhē* mussel etc.]

cŏnchif'erous (-ngk-), a. (zool., geol.). Shell-bearing. [as prec., see -FEROUS]

cŏnchŏl'og|ў (-ngk-), n. Study of shells & shellfish. So cŏncholŏ'gical a., ~IST n. [as CONCH, see -LOGY]

‖ cŏn'chў (*or* -shǐ), n. (sl.). Conscientious objector. [abbr.]

concierge (see Ap.), n. (In France etc.) door-keeper, porter, (esp. of flats etc.). [F]

concil'īar, a. Of ecclesiastical councils. [f. L *concilium* COUNCIL + -AR[1]]

concil'i|āte, v.t. Gain (esteem, goodwill); pacify; win over (*to* one's side etc.); reconcile (discrepant theories). Hence or cogn. ~atIVE, ~atORY, (-lya-), aa., ~ātOR, ~atorǐNESS (-lya-), nn. [f. L *conciliare* (as prec.), see -ATE[3]]

concilīā'tion, n. Reconcilement; use of conciliating measures; *Court of* ~ (offering parties a voluntary settlement). [f. L *conciliatio* (as prec., see -ATION)]

concinn' itў, n. Elegance, neatness, of literary style. [f. L *concinnitas* (*concinnus* well-adjusted, see -TY)]

concise', a. Brief in expression (of speech, style, person). Hence ~LY[2] (-sǐ-) adv., ~NESS (-sn-) n. [f. F *concis* or L *concisus* p.p. of CON(*cidere cis-=caeders* cut)]

conci'sion (-zhn), n. Mutilation (in *Phil.* iii. 2, = circumcision, contemptuously); conciseness. [ME, f. L *concisio* (as prec., see -ION)]

cŏnc'lāve, n. Meeting-place, assembly, of cardinals for election of Pope; private assembly, as *in* ~. [ME, f. OF f. L CON(*clave* lock-up place f. *clavis* key)]

conclude' (-n-klōōd), v.t. & i. Bring to an end, make an end, (~ one's *speech* etc., or ~, *with* remark etc., *by* saying etc.); (of things) come to an end; infer (*from* premisses etc.); settle, arrange, (treaty etc.); resolve (*to* do). [ME, f. L CON(*cludere clus-* = *claudere* shut)]

conclu'sion (-n-klōōzhn), n. Termination; final result; *in* ~, lastly, to conclude; inference; decision; (Logic) proposition deduced from previous ones, esp. last of three forming a syllogism; *try* ~*s with*, engage in a trial of skill etc. with; settling, arrangement, (*of* peace etc.). [ME, f. OF or f. L *conclusio* (as prec., see -ION)]

conclus'ive, (-n-klōō-), a., Decisive, convincing. Hence ~LY[2] (-vl-) adv., ~NESS (-vn-) n. [f. LL *conclusivus* (as prec., see -IVE)]

concoct', v.t. Make up of mixed ingredients (soup, drink, story, plot). Hence or cogn. concŏc'tION, concŏc'tOR, nn., concŏc'tIVE a. [f. L CON(*coquere coct-* cook)]

concol'orous (-kŭl-), a. (nat. hist.). Of uniform colour. [f. L CON(*color* colour) + -OUS]

concŏm'ǐtance, -cў̆, (-n-k-), n. Coexistence, esp. (-*ance*) of body & blood of Christ in each of the eucharistic elements. [f. med. L *concomitantia* (as foll., see -ANCE, -ANCY)]

concŏm'ǐtant (-n-k-), a. & n. Going together, as ~ *circumstances*; (n.) accompanying thing. Hence ~LY[2] adv. [f. LL CON(*comitari* f. *comes -mitis* companion), see -ANT]

cŏnc'ōrd, n. Agreement, harmony, between persons or things; treaty; (Mus.) chord satisfactory in itself without others to follow; (Gram.) agreement between words in gender, number, etc. [ME & OF *concorde* f. L *concordia* f. CON(*cors* f. *cor cordis* heart) of one mind]

concŏrd'ance (-n-k-), n. Agreement; alphabetical arrangement of chief words (*verbal* ~) or subjects (*real* ~) occurring in a book (esp. the Bible) or author, with citations of the passages concerned. [ME, f. OF, f. med. L *concordantia* (foll., -ANCE)]

concŏrd'ant (-n-k-), a. Agreeing, harmonious, (*with* or abs.); in musical concord. Hence ~LY[2] adv. [ME, f. OF, f. L *concordare* (*concors*), see CONCORD and -ANT]

concŏrd'at (-n-k-), n. Agreement between Church & State esp. one between Roman See (or Pope) and a secular government. [F, or f. its source L *concordatum* (Engl. since 17th c.) neut. p.p. as prec.]

cŏnc'ourse (-ōrs), n. Crowd; confluence of things, as *fortuitous* ~ *of atoms*. [ME, f. OF *concours* f. L *concursus -ūs* (as CONCUR)]

concrēs'cence, n. (biol.). Coalescence, growing together. [f. L *concrescentia* (as foll., see -ENCE)]

cŏnc'rēte[1], a. & n. 1. (Gram., of noun) denoting a thing as opposed to a quality, state, or action, not ABSTRACT; existing in material form, real; *in the* ~, in sphere of reality. 2. n. ~ thing; composition of gravel, cement, etc., for building, (attrib.) made of this. Hence ~LY[2] (-tl-) adv. [f. L *concretus* p.p. of CON(*crescere cret-* grow)]

concrēte[2], v.t. & i. (-n-krēt') form into a mass, solidify; (kŏnk[L]) treat with concrete. [f. prec.]

concrē'tion (-n-k-), n. Coalescence; concrete mass, esp. (Path.) morbid formation in the body, stone, (Geol.) mass formed of solid particles, whence ~ARY[1] (-n-krĕsho-) a.; embodiment in concrete form. [f. L *concretio* (CONCRETE[1], -ION)]

concŭb'inage (-n-k-), n. Cohabiting of man and woman not legally married; having, being, a concubine. [ME, f. OF, as CONCUBINE, see -AGE]

concŭb'inarў (-n-k-), a. & n. (Person) living in concubinage; of, sprung from, concubinage. [f. med. L *concubinarius* (as foll., see -ARY[1])]

cŏnc'ūbine, n. Woman who cohabits with a man, not being his wife; (among polygamous peoples) secondary wife. [ME, f. OF f. L CON(*cubina* f. *cubare* lie)]

concŭp'iscence (-n-k-), n. Sexual appetite; (N.T.) desire for worldly things. [ME, f. LL *concupiscentia* (as foll., see -ENCE)]

concŭp'iscent (-n-k-), a. Lustful, eagerly desirous. [f. L *concupiscere* inceptive of CON(*cupere* desire), see -ENT]

concŭr' (-n-k-), v.i. (-rr-). Happen together, coincide; (of circumstances etc.) co-operate (*with* or abs.); agree in opinion (*with*). So **concŭr'rENCE** (-n-k-) n. [f. L CON(*currere curs-* run)]

concŭr'rent (-n-k-), a. & n. Running together, as parallel lines; existing together; co-operating; agreeing; ~ *lease* (made before the former expires); ~ *fire insurance* (of which the risk is definitely proportioned among several companies); (n.) ~ circumstance. Hence ~LY[2] adv. [as CONCUR, see -ENT]

concŭss' (-n-k-), v.t. Shake violently, agitate, (usu. fig.); intimidate. [f. L CON(*cutere cuss-* = *quatere* shake)]

concŭs'sion (-n-kŭshn), n. Violent shaking; shock; (Surg.) injury to brain etc. caused by heavy blow etc.; ~-*bellows*, self-acting reservoir regulating wind in organ; ~-*fuse* (in shell, ignited by ~). [f. L *concussio* (as prec., see -ION)]

condĕmn' (-m), v.t. Censure, blame; give judgement against; bring about conviction of, as *his looks* ~ *him*; doom (*to* death, *to* be beheaded; also fig. *to* toil etc.); ~*ed cell* (for ~ed persons); pronounce forfeited (smuggled goods etc.), unfit for use, incurable. Hence **condĕm⸗ nABLE** (-mn-) a. [ME *condemp*, *-n(e)* f. OF *condem(p)ner* f. L CON(*demnare* = *damnare* DAMN)]

cŏndĕmnā'tion, n. Censure; judicial conviction; ground for condemning, as *his own conduct is his* ~. [f. L *condemnatio* (as prec., see -ATION)]

condĕm'natorў, a. Expressing condemnation. [f. L as CONDEMN, see -ORY]

cŏndĕnsā'tion, n. Act of condensing (t. & i.); condensed mass; abridgement. [f. LL *condensatio* (as foll., see -ATION)]

condĕns|e', v.t. & i. Compress; ~*ed milk* (reduced by evaporation); concentrate (rays of light); increase intensity of (electricity); reduce, be reduced, from gas or vapour to liquid; compress into few words, make concise. Hence or cogn. ~ABIL'ITY n., ~'ABLE a., ~'ERY (3) n., factory for ~ed milk. [f. F *condenser* or L CON(*densare* f. *densus* thick)]

condĕn'ser, n. In vbl senses; esp.: chamber in steam-engine in which steam is condensed on leaving cylinder; (electrical) CAPACITOR; lens, system of lenses, concentrating light. [-ER[1]]

cŏndĕscĕnd', v.i. Deign, stoop, (*to* an act, *to* do); waive one's superiority (*to* a

person); ‖ (Sc.) ~ *upon*, specify (particulars). [ME, f. OF *condescendre* f. LL CON- (*descendere* DESCEND)]

cŏndĕscĕnd'ing, a. Showing condescension, esp. patronizing. Hence ~LY[2] adv. [prec. +-ING[2]]

cŏndĕscĕn'sion (-shn), n. Affability to inferiors; patronizing manner.' [f. LL *condescensio* (as CONDESCEND, see -ION)]

condīgn' ('-īn), a. Severe & well-deserved (usu. of punishment). Hence ~LY[2] (-īnlī) adv. [ME, f. OF *condigne* f. L CON(*dignus* worthy)]

cŏn'diment, n. Thing used to give relish to food. Hence ~AL (-ĕn⸗) a. [f. L *con- dimentum* (*condire* pickle, see -MENT)]

condi'tion[1], n. Stipulation, thing upon the fulfilment of which depends that of another, (~ *precedent*, that must be fulfilled before a bequest etc. becomes valid); *on* ~ *that*, if, provided that; (Gram.) clause expressing a ~; (pl.) circumstances, esp. those essential to a thing's existence, as *the* ~*s of equilibrium, favourable* ~*s, under existing* ~*s*; state of being, as *eggs arrived in good* ~, *persons of humble* ~; *in, out of,* ~, in good, bad, ~; *change* one's ~, marry. [ME, f. OF *con- dicion* f. L *condicionem* f. CON(*dicere* say) agree upon, see -ION]

condi'tion[2], v.t. Stipulate (*that*); agree by stipulation (*to* do); *the size is* ~*ed by* (depends on) *the requirements*; *the two things* ~ (are essential to) *each other*; *they* ~ *the universe* (impose conditions on it) *anew*; (Commerc.) test the condition of (material); bring into desired state or condition; make fit (esp. dogs, horses, etc.). [f. OF *condicionner*, see prec.]

condi'tional (-sho-), a. & n. Not absolute, dependent (*on* or abs.); (Gram.) ~ *clause*, one expressing a condition, PROTASIS, ~ *mood* in French and Italian verbs, that used in the' apodosis; (n.) ~ word, conjunction, mood, clause. Hence ~ITY (-shonăl⸗) n., ~LY[2] adv. [ME & OF *con- dicionel* or f. LL *condicionalis* (as CONDI- TION[1], see -AL)]

condi'tioned (-shond), a. 1. Having a (specified) disposition, as *ill, well,* ~; in a (specified) condition, as *well-* ~ *ground, cattle*; circumstanced. 2. Subject to conditions. 3. ~ *reflex*, reflex action responding, through habit or training, to a stimulus not naturally connected with it, e.g. watering of dog's mouth at sound of feeding-bell. [CONDITION[1, 2] +-ED[2, 1]]

condōl'atorў, a. Expressing condolence. [f. foll. on anal. of *consolatory* etc.]

condōle', v.i. Express sympathy (*with* or abs., *upon* loss etc.). Hence **condōl'ENCE** n. [f. LL CON(*dolēre* suffer)]

cŏn'dom, n. Contraceptive sheath. [inventor]

cŏndomīn'ium, n. (diplom.). Joint control of a State's affairs vested in two or more other States. [CON-, L *dominium* DOMINION]

condōne', v.t. Forgive, overlook, (offence, esp. matrimonial infidelity); (of actions) atone for (offence). So **condonA'TION** n. [f. L CON(*donare* give)]

cŏn'dor, n. Large S.-Amer. kind of vulture; *California C~*, great vulture of California. [Sp., f. Peruvian *cuntur*]

cŏndŏttier'e (-tyärī), n. (pl. *-ri*, pron. -rē). Leader of troop of mercenaries. [It. f. *condotto* CONDUCT[1]]

condūce', v.i. (Usu. of events, rarely of persons) lead, contribute, *to* (result). Hence **condū'cive** a., **condū'civeness** (-vn-) n. [f. L CON(*ducere* lead)]

cŏn'duct[1], n. Leading, guidance, (cf. SAFE-*conduct*); ~-*money* (paid to a witness for travelling expenses); manner of conducting (business etc.); (Art) mode of treatment; behaviour (esp. in its moral aspect, as *good, bad, ~*); *regimental, company, ~ sheet*, record of a soldier's offences and punishments. [ME & OF *conduit*(e) f. L *conductus* (f. p.p. st. of *conducere*), also Rom. *conducta*; *conduct* (15th c.) after L]

conduct'[2], v.t. & i. Lead, guide, *to* (of road) lead *to*; command (army); direct (orchestra, choir, concert, or abs.); direct, manage, (business etc.); ~ *oneself*, behave (*well, with* judgement, etc.); (Physics) transmit (heat etc.). Hence ~ANCE n. (electr.), ~*ing* power of specified conductor. [ME & OF *conduit*(e) p.p. of *conduire* f. L CON(*ducere duct-* lead); later assim. to L; see prec.]

‖ **cŏn'duct**[3], n. An Eton chaplain. [f. L *conductus* hired (p.p. of *conducere* see prec.)]

condūc'ti|ble, a. Capable of conducting (heat etc.) or (rarely) being conducted. Hence ~BIL'ITY n. [f. L *conduct-*; see prec. & -BLE]

condūc't|ion, n. Transmission (of heat by contact etc.); conducting (of liquid through pipe etc., esp. of natural processes). So ~IVE a., **cŏnductiv'ITY** n. [F, or f. L *conductio* (CONDUCT[2], -ION)]

condūc'tor, n. Leader, guide; manager, director of orchestra, choir, etc.; official in charge of passengers on omnibus, tram, or (U.S.) train; thing that conducts or transmits (esp. heat etc., as *good, bad, non-, ~*); *lightning~*, rod at top of building, conducting electricity away into earth. Hence ~SHIP, **condūc'tress**[1], nn. [ME & OF *conduitour* f. L *conductorem* (CONDUCT[2], -OR); later assim. to L]·

conduit (kŭn'dit, kŏn[4]), n. Channel or pipe for conveying liquids (or fig.); tube or trough for protecting insulated electric wires, length of this; ~ *system*, (electr. traction) with conductor in underground ~, (house-lighting) with conducting wires in lead piping. [ME, f. OF *conduit* (= med. L *conductus* in same sense) CON-DUCT[1]]

condūp'licate, a. (bot.). Folded length-

wise along middle. [f. L CON(*duplicare* DUPLICATE)]·

cŏn'dўl|e, n. (anat.). Rounded process at end of bone, forming articulation with another bone. Hence ~OID a. [F, f. L f. Gk *kondulos* knuckle]

Cŏn'dў('s fluid), n. A solution of potassium (per)manganate as disinfectant. [H. B. *Condy*, Engl. physician]

cōne, n., & v.t. & i. 1. Solid figure with circular (or other curved) base, tapering to a point (generated by straight line that always passes through a fixed point, and describes any fixed curve); fruit of pine or fir; marine shell of genus *Conus*; ~-shaped thing, esp. (Meteorol.) foul--weather signal; ~*s*, fine flour used by bakers for dusting troughs. 2. v.t. Shape like ~; (pass., of aircraft) be picked up or illuminated by many (hostile) search-lights simultaneously; (v.i.) bear ~*s*. [f. F *cône* or L f. Gk *kōnos*]

cŏn'ey. See CONY.

confāb', n., & v.i. Colloq. abbr. of CON-FABULATION or foll. -

confāb'ŭl|āte, v.i. Converse, chat, (*with* or abs.). Hence or cogn. ~A'TION n., ~atORY a. [f. L CON(*fabulari* f. *fabula* tale), see -ATE[3]]

confěc'tion, n., & v.t. Mixing, compounding; thing compounded, esp. preserve, sweetmeat, whence ~ARY[1] (-sho-) a.; ready-made article of (usu. female) dress, mantle, wrap, etc.; (v.t.) prepare, make, (a ~). [ME, f. OF f. L *confectionem* f. CON(*ficere fect-* = *facere* make), see -ION]

confěc'tion|er'(-sho-), n. Maker of sweet-meats, pastry, etc. (usu. for sale). Hence ~ERY(1, 2) n. [-ER[1]]

confěd'eracy, n. League, alliance; conspiracy; collusion; body of confederate persons or States, as *Southern C~*, Confederate States of America. [ME & AF *confederacie* f. st. of LL *confoederatio*, as foll.; see -ACY(3)]

confěd'erate[1], a. & n. 1. Allied (lit. & fig.); *C~ States* of America (seceding from the Union, 1860–5). 2. n. Ally, esp. in bad sense, accomplice. [f. LL CON(*foederare* f. *foedus -eris* league), see -ATE[2]] ·

confěd'er|āte[2], v.t. & i. Bring (person, State, one*self*), come, into alliance (*with*). So ~A'TION n. [as prec., see -ATE[3]]

cŏn'fěr', v. (imperat.). Compare (abbr. *cf.*). [L]

confěr'[2], v.t. & i. (-rr-). Grant, bestow, (title, degree, favour, etc., *on*); (v.i.) converse, take counsel, (*with* or abs.). Hence ~MENT n., ~rABLE a. [f. L CON-(*ferre* bring)]

cŏn'ference, n. Consultation; (esp. annual) meeting of any organization, association, etc. for consultation etc.; annual assembly of Methodist Church. So **cŏnferěn'tiAL** (-shal) a. [f. F *conférence* or med. L *conferentia* (as prec., see -ENCE)]

confěss', v.t. & i. Acknowledge, as *I ~ my fault, that I did it, to doing it, to having*

done it, to a dread of spiders; formally declare one's sins, esp. to a priest, whence
~ANT n.; (of priest) hear (penitent) ~.
Hence ~êdLY² adv. [ME, f. OF *confesser*
f. Rom. *confessare* frequent. of L CON-
(*fitĕri fess-* = *fatĕri* declare, avow)]
confe'ssion (-shn), n. Acknowledgement
(of offence, fact, etc.); *auricular* ~ (of sins
to priest), whence ~ARY¹ (-sho-) a.; thing
confessed; ~ *of faith*, declaration of
religious doctrine, creed, statement of
one's principles in any matter; (formerly)
tomb of CONFESSOR. [ME, f. OF f. L
confessionem (as prec., see -ION)]
confe'ssional (-sho-), a. & n. Of confession; (n.) stall in which priest hears confession, as *secrets of the* ~. [(adj.) prec.
+-AL; (n.) F, f. med. L *confessionale*
(neut. adj. as n.)]
confe'ssionist (-sho-), n. Adherent of a
creed, esp. of the Augsburg Confession
(Lutheran). [f. F *confessioniste* (-IST)]
confess'or, n. One who confesses; one
who avows his religion in face of danger,
but does not suffer martyrdom; *The C~*,
King Edward the C~; priest who hears
confession. [ME, f. AF *confessur*, OF
-our, f. L *confessorem* (as CONFESS, see -OR)]
confett'i, n. pl. Plaster bonbons, bits of
coloured paper, used as missiles in the
carnival, at weddings, etc. [It., = sweet-
meats]
cŏnfidănt', n. (fem. ~*e*, pron. -ănt).
Person trusted with private (usu. love)
affairs. [18th c.; perh. meant to repr.
sound of F *confidente* (as foll., see
-ANT)]
confide', v.t. & i. Repose confidence *in*,
(part.) unsuspicious; impart (secret *to*);
entrust (object of care, task, *to*). [f. L
CON(*fidere* trust)]
cŏn'fidence, n. Firm trust; assured expectation; boldness; impudence; im-
·parting of private matters (*in* one's ~,
allowed to know his private affairs);
thing so imparted; *told in* ~ (as a secret);
‖~ *trick*, persuading victim to entrust
valuables to one as sign of ~. [ME, f.
L *confidentia* (as prec., see -ENCE)]
cŏn'fident, a. & n. Trusting, fully assured
(*that*, *of*, or abs.), bold; impudent; (n.)
confidant, sharer *of* (secret). Hence
~LY² adv. [as CONFIDE, see -ENT]
cŏnfidĕn'tial (-shl), a. Spoken, written,
in confidence; entrusted with secrets;
charged with secret service. Hence ~ITY
(-shiǎl²-), ~NESS, nn., ~LY² adv., (-sha-).
[as CONFIDENCE +-AL]
configūrā'tion, n. Mode of arrangement,
conformation, outline; (Astron.) relative
position of planets etc. [f. LL *configuratio*
(foll., -ATION)]
config'ure (-ger), v.t. Give shape to (usu.
fig.). [f. L CON(*figurare* FIGURE)]
cŏn'fine¹, n. (usu. pl.). Border-land, esp.
(fig.) between two classes of ideas etc. [f.

F *confins* pl. f. L CON(*finia* (neut. pl.) f.
finis end, limit)]
confine'², v.t. & i. Keep (person, thing,
oneself, *within*, *to*, limits); imprison;
(pass.) be in childbed, be brought to bed.
[f. F *confiner* f. *confins*, obs. *-ines*; see
prec.]
confine'ment (-nm-), n. Imprisonment;
being confined, esp. in childbed; limitation. [F (-MENT)]
confirm', v.t. Establish more firmly
(power, possession, person *in* possession);
ratify (treaty; possession, title, *to* person); corroborate (statement, evidence),
whence ~ATIVE, ~atORY, aa., ~ativeLY²
adv.; establish, encourage, (person *in*
habit, opinion, etc.); administer religious
rite of confirmation to, whence cŏnfirm-
ănd' [-ND¹] (candidate for ~ation), cŏn-
firmEE', nn.; *a~ed* (inveterate) *drunkard*,
disease. [ME *conferme* f. OF *confermer*
f. L CON(*firmare* f. *firmus* FIRM); later
assim. to L]
cŏnfirmā'tion, n. Act of confirming; corroboration; rite administered to baptized
persons in various Christian Churches.
[ME, f. OF f. L *confirmationem* (as prec.,
see -ATION)]
cŏn'fiscăt|e, v.t. Appropriate to the
public treasury (by way of penalty);
seize as by authority. So confis'cABLE,
confis'catORY, aa., ~OR n. [f. L CON-
(*fiscare* f. *fiscus* treasury), see -ATE³]
cŏnfiscā'tion, n. Act of confiscating;
(colloq.) legal robbery with sanction of
ruling power. [f. L *confiscatio* (prec.,
-ATION)]
confît'ĕor n. (eccles.). Form of prayer or
confession of sins. [L, = I confess (*con-*
fitĕri)]
cŏnflagrā'tion, n. Great & destructive
fire (lit. & fig.). [f. L *conflagratio* (CON-
flagare burn up, see FLAGRANT)]
conflā'tion, n. Fusing together esp. fig. of
two variant texts or readings into one.
[f. LL *conflatio* fusion f. L CON(*flare* blow),
see -ATION)]
cŏn'flict¹, n. Fight, struggle, (lit. & fig.);
collision; clashing (*of* opposed principles
etc.); *in* ~, discrepant (often *with*). [ME,
f. L *conflictus -ūs* (as foll.)]
conflict'², v.i. Struggle (*with* or abs., usu.
fig.); clash, be incompatible, whence
conflic'tION n. [ME, f. L CON(*fligere flict-*
strike)]
cŏn'fluent (-ŏoent), a. & n. **1.** Flowing
together, uniting, (of streams, roads, etc.,
& fig.), so cŏn'fluENCE (-ŏoens) n.; ~
smallpox (when vesicles run together).
2. n. Stream flowing with another (prop.
of same size). [f. L CON(*fluere flux-* flow),
-ENT]
cŏn'flŭx, n. Confluence. [f. LL *con-*
fluxus -ūs (as prec.)]
conform', v.t. & i. Form according to a
pattern, make similar (*to*); adapt one*self*

to; (v.i.) comply with (*to*), be conformable (*to* or abs.). Hence ~ANCE n. [ME, f. OF *conformer* or, esp. in bibl. contexts, L CON(*formare* f. *forma* shape)]

confŏrm'|able, a. Similar (*to*); consistent, adapted, (*to*); tractable. Hence ~ABIL'ITY n., ~ably² adv. [-ABLE]

cŏnformā'tion, n. Manner in which a thing is formed, structure; adaptation (*to*). [f. L *conformatio* (as CONFORM, see -ATION)]

confŏrm'ist, n. One who conforms to a practice or usage, esp. ‖ one who conforms to usages of Church of England. [-IST]

confŏrm'itŷ, n. Likeness (*to*, *with*); compliance (*with*, *to*). [ME, f. OF *conformite* or LL *conformitas*, see CONFORM, -TY]

confound', v.t. Defeat (plan, hope); (mild oath) ~ *it, you*, (= God ~), esp. in p.p. whence ~ĕdly³ adv.; (Bibl.) put to shame; throw into perplexity; throw (things) into disorder; mix up; confuse (in idea). [ME, f. OF *confondre* f. L CON-(*fundere fus-* pour) mix up]

cŏnfratẽrn'itŷ, n. Brotherhood (esp. religious or charitable); body, gang. [ME, f. OF *confraternite* or med. L CON(*fraternitas* FRATERNITY)]

confrère (see Ap.), n. Fellow member of profession, scientific body, etc. [OF, later f. F *confrère*]

confront' (-ŭnt), v.t. Meet face to face, stand facing; be opposite to; face in hostility or defiance; (of difficulties etc.) oppose; bring (person) face to face *with* (accusers etc.); compare. Hence cŏnfrontA'TION n. [f. F *confronter* f. med. L CON(*frontare* f. *frons -ntis* face)]

Confū'cian (-shn), a. & n. (Follower) of Confucius, the Chinese Philosopher. Hence ~ISM (-sha-) n. [f. *Confucius*, latiniz. of *K'ung Fŭ tsze* K'ung the master, +-AN]

confūs|e' (-z), v.t. Throw into disorder; mix up in the mind; abash, perplex, (usu. pass.). Hence ~ĕdly³ adv., ~'ĕdness n., (-z-). [19th c. back form. of *confused* (14th c.) f. F *confus* or its L source; see CONFOUND]

confū'sion (-zhn), n. Act of confusing; confused state; tumult; (as imprecation) ~ *!, drink* ~ *to*; ~ *worse confounded*, made worse than it was. [ME, f. OF, or f. L *confusio* (as prec., see -ION)]

confūte', v.t. Convict (person) of error by proof; prove (argument) false. So cŏnfūtA'TION n. [f. L *confutare*]

congé (see Ap.), cŏn'gee (-jĭ), n. Dismissal without ceremony; (arch.) bow, esp. at parting, (F) *congé d'élire* (dālēr'), royal permission to elect bishop. Hence con'gé, -gee, v.t. & i. [ME *congye* f. OF *congie* f. L *commeatus -ūs* leave of absence f. COM(*meare* go) go & come: now usu. treated as mod. F]

congeal' (-j-), v.t. & i. Freeze, solidify by cooling; coagulate t. & i. of blood etc. or

fig.). Hence ~ABLE a., ~MENT n. [ME *congele* f. OF *congeler* f. L CON(*gelare* f. *gelu* frost)]

cŏngēlā'tion (-j-), n. Congealing; con- ·gealed state; congealed substance. [ME, f. OF, or L *congelatio* (as prec., see -ATION)]

cŏn'gener (-j-), n. & a. One of the same kind as (*of*) another; (adj.) akin, allied, (*to*). ·[f. L *congener* f. *genus -eris* kind]

cŏngĕnĕ'ric (-j-), a. Of same genus, kind, race; allied in nature or origin. [as prec., -IC]

congĕn'erous (-j-), a. Of same genus or (loosely) family; of same kind; ~ *muscles* (concurring in same action). [f. L *congener* CONGENER +-OUS]

congĕn'ial (-j-), a. (Of persons, characters, etc.) kindred, sympathetic, (*with*, *to*); suited, agreeable, (*to*). Hence ~ITY (-ăl⁴) n., ~LY² adv. [app. f. CON-+ GENIAL]

congĕn'ital (-j-), a. Belonging to (*with*) one from birth (esp. of diseases, defects, etc.). Hence ~LY² adv. [f. L CON-(*genitus* p.p. of *gigno* beget)+-AL]

cŏng'er (-ngg-), n. Large sea eel (also ~ *eel*). [ME, f. OF *congre* f. L *conger -gri* f. Gk *goggros*]

congē'ries (-jĕrĭēz), n. (pl. same). Collection, mass, heap. [L (as foll.)]

congĕst' (-j-), v.i. & t. (Intr.) accumulate to excess (esp. in p.p.); affect with congestion; ~*ed district*, area of land too crowded to support its population; (Med.) ~*ed organ* (overcharged with blood). Hence congĕs'tive a. [f. L CON(*gerere gest-* bring)]

conges'tion (-jĕschon), n. Abnormal accumulation of blood in a part of the body (fig. of population, traffic, etc.). [F, f. L *congestionem* (as prec., see -ION)]

cŏn'glob|āte (-n-g-), v.t. & i., & a. Form into a ball; (adj.) so formed. So ~A'TION n. [f. L CON(*globare* f. *globus*), see -ATE², ³]

conglōbe' (-n-g-), v.t. & i. = prec. [f. F *conglobe* or L *conglobare*, see prec.]

conglŏm'erate¹ (-n-g-), a. & n. Gathered into a round mass; (Geol.) (pudding-stone, water-worn fragments of rock) cemented into a mass (cf. AGGLOMERATE). [f. L CON-(*glomerare* f. *glomus -eris* ball), see -ATE²]

conglŏm'er|āte² (-n-g-), v.t. & i. Collect into a coherent mass (lit. & fig.). So ~A'TION n. [as prec., see -ATE³]

conglū'tin|āte (-n-glōō-), v.t. & i. Stick together (as) with glue. So ~A'TION n. [f. L CON(*glutinare* (*gluten -inis* glue), see -ATE³]

cŏng'ou (-nggōō, -ō), n. Kind of black Chinese tea. [f. Chin. *kung-fu*(-*ch'a*) labour (tea)]

congrăt'ul|āte (-n-g-), v.t. Address (person) with expressions of sympathetic joy (*on* an event); ~*ate* oneself, think oneself happy (*on*). Hence ~ANT a. & n., ~ātive, ~ātory, aa., ~ātor n., (-n-g-). [f. L CON(*gratulari* f. *gratus* pleasing), see -ATE³]

congrătulā'tion (-n-g-), n. Congratulating; (pl.) congratulatory expressions. [F, or f. L *congratulatio* (prec., -ATION)]

cŏn′grĕgāte (-ngg-), v.t. & i. Collect, gather, into a crowd (of persons) or mass (of things). [ME, f. L CON(*gregare* f. *grex gregis* flock), see -ATE³]

cŏngrĕgā′tion (-ngg-), n. Collection into a body or mass; assemblage; ‖ general assembly of (qualified) members of university; (Bibl.) collective body of Israelites in wilderness, also, public solemn assembly of the nation; (Bibl.) *C~ of Saints, the wicked*, etc., (whole body); body assembled for religious worship; permanent committee of Roman College of Cardinals, as *the C~ de propaganda fide*. [ME, f. OF, or f. L *congregatio* (as prec., see -ATION)]

cŏngrĕgā′tional (-ngg-; -sho-), a. Of a congregation; (*C~*) of, adhering to, Congregationalism. [-AL]

Cŏngrĕgā′tional‖ism (-ngg-; -sho-), n. System of ecclesiastical polity that leaves legislative, disciplinary, and judicial functions to the individual church & congregation. So ~IST n., ~IZE v.t. [prec. + -ISM]

cŏng′rĕss (-ngg-), n. Coming together, meeting; formal meeting of delegates for discussion, esp. of persons engaged in special studies, as *Church C~*, annual meeting of Church of England, *Social Science C~*, etc.; (*C~*) national legislative body of U.S. or S. & Central Amer. republics; its session; *C~-man*, member of C~. [f. L *congressus -ūs* f. CON(*gredi gress-=gradi* walk)]

congrĕ′ssional (-nggrĕsho-), a. Of a congress. [f. L *congressio* (as prec., see -ION) + -AL]

Cŏng′rĕve (-ngg-), a. & n. ~ (*match*), kind of friction match; ~ (*rocket*), kind formerly used in war. [Sir W. ~, inventor (d. 1828)]

cŏng′ruence (-nggrŏŏens), -cў, n. Agreement, consistency, (*of* one *with* another, *between* two). [ME, f. L *congruentia* (as foll., see -ENCE, -ENCY)]

cŏng′ruent (-nggrŏŏ-), a. Suitable, accordant, (*with*); (Geom., of figures) coinciding exactly when superposed. [ME, f. L *congruens -ent-* part. of *congruere* agree]

cŏng′ruous (-nggrŏŏ-), a. Accordant, conformable, (*with*); fitting. Hence or cogn. **congru′ITY** (-nggrŏŏ-) n., ~LY² adv. [f. L *congruus* (as prec.) + -OUS]

cōn′ĭc, a. & n. Cone-shaped; of a cone, as ~ *section*; (n. pl.) study of plane ~ sections. Hence ~AL a., ~alLY² adv., ~alNESS n. [f. Gk *kōnikos* (CONE, -IC)]

cōn′ĭco-, in comb. With a conical tendency, as ~-*cylindrical*. [as prec.]

cōn′ifer, n. Cone-bearing plant. Hence **conĭf′EROUS** a. [L (as CONE, see -FEROUS)]

cōn′ĭfōrm, a. Cone-shaped. [CONE, -FORM]

cōn′īne, cōn′iīne, n. An alkaloid, the poisonous principle of hemlock. [f. LL *conium* f. Gk *kōneion* hemlock + -INE⁵]

conjĕc′tural (-kcher-), a. Involving, given to, conjecture. Hence ~LY² adv. [F, or f. L *conjecturalis* (as foll., see -AL)]

conjĕc′ture¹, n. Formation of opinion without sufficient grounds, guessing, esp. in textual criticism, of a reading not in the text; *a ~*, a guess, proposed reading. [OF, or f. L *conjectura* f. CON(*jicere ject- = jacĕre* throw), see -URE]

conjĕc′tur‖e², v.t. & i. Guess; propose (a conjectural reading); (v.i.) make a guess. Hence ~ABLE a., ~abLY² adv., (-kcher-). [ME, f. OF -*er* or LL -*are* (prec.)]

conjoin′, v.t. & i. Join (t. & i.); combine. [ME, f. OF *conjoign-* pres. st. of .*conjoindre* f. L CON(*jungere junct-* join)]

conjoint′, a. United; associated. Hence ~LY² adv. [OF, p.p. as prec.]

cŏn′jugal (-ŏŏ-). a. Of marriage, as ~ *rights*; of husband and/or wife, as ~ *affection*. Hence ~ITY (-ăl²) n., ~LY² adv. [f. L *conjugalis* f. CON(*jux -jugis* f. root of *jungere* join) consort, see -AL]

cŏn′jugāte¹ (-ŏŏ-), v.t. & i. (Gram.) inflect (verb) in voice, mood, tense, number, person; (v.i.) unite sexually; (Biol.) become fused. [f. L CON(*jugare* f. *jugum* YOKE) yoke together, see -ATE³]

cŏn′jugate² (-ŏŏ-), a. & n. Joined together, esp. coupled; (Gram.) derived from same root; (Math.) joined in a reciprocal relation; (Biol.) fused; (n.) ~ word or thing. [as prec., see -ATE²]

cŏnjugā′tion (-ŏŏ-), n. Joining together; (Gram.) scheme of verbal inflexion; (Biol.) fusion of two (apparently) similar cells for reproduction. Hence ~AL (-ŏŏ-; -sho-) a. [f. L *conjugatio* (as prec., see -ATION)]

conjŭnct′, a. & n. Joined together; combined; associated, joint; (n.) ~ person or thing. Hence ~LY² adv. [ME, f. L *conjunctus*, see CONJOIN]

conjŭnc′tion, n. 1. Union, connexion; *in* ~, together (*with*). 2. (astrol., astron.). Apparent proximity of two heavenly bodies. 3. Combination of events or circumstances; number of associated persons or things. 4. (gram.). Uninflected word used to connect clauses or sentences, or to co-ordinate words in same clause. Hence ~AL a., ~LY² adv., (-sho-). [ME, f. OF f. L *conjunctionem* (as prec., see -ION)]

cŏnjuncīī′v′a, n. Mucous membrane connecting inner eyelid & eyeball. Hence **conjŭnctīyIT′IS** (-ītĭs) n. [mod. L (for *membrana* ~) as foll.]

conjŭnc′tive, a. & n. 1. Serving to join, as ~ *tissue*. 2. (gram.). Of the nature of a conjunction; uniting sense as well as construction, cf. DISJUNCTIVE; ~ *mood* of verb, one used only in conjunction with another verb, cf. SUBJUNCTIVE. 3. n. ~

word or mood. Hence ~LY² (-vl-) adv. [f. LL *conjunctivus* (as CONJOIN, see -IVE)]

conjunc′ture, n. Combination of events, posture of affairs. [app. f. F *conjoncture* f. L as CONJOIN, see -URE]

conjura′tion (-ŏŏ-), n. Solemn appeal; incantation. [ME, f. OF f. L *conjurationem* (foll., -ATION)]

conjure, v.t. & i. **1.** (konjoor′). Appeal solemnly to (person *to* do). **2.** (kŭn′jer). Constrain (spirit) to appear by invocation (also ~ *up, down, out of* person); effect, bring *out,* convey *away,* by juggling; juggle, produce magical effects by natural means, perform marvels (*a name to* ~ *with,* of vast influence); *~ man, woman,* witch (-doctor); ~ *up,* cause to appear to the fancy. [ME, f. OF *conjurer* f. L CON- (*jurare* swear) band together by oath]

con′jurer, -or, n. One who practises legerdemain, juggler; unusually clever person, as *he is no* ~. [(-er, 14th c.) f. prec.+-ER¹; (-or, 15th c.) f. AF *conjurour* (OF -eor) f. L *conjuratorem* (as prec., see -OR)]

cŏnk¹, n. (sl.). Nose. Hence ~′Y² a. & n., big-nosed (person). [perh. = CONCH]

|| **cŏnk²,** v.i. (colloq.). Break down, give *out* (usu. of mechanism etc.). [orig. unkn.]

|| **cŏnk′ers** (-z), n. pl. Boys′ game played with horse-chestnuts (orig. with snail--shells) through which a string is threaded, the object being to break that held by opponent. [dial. *conker* snail-shell]

cŏnn′āte, a. Born with a person, innate; (of two or more qualities etc.) born together, coeval in origin; (Bot., Zool.) congenitally united (of leaves united at base etc.). [f. L *connatus* var. of *cognatus* COGNATE]

connä′tural (-cher-), a. Innate, belonging naturally, (*to*); of like nature. Hence ~LY² adv. [f. LL *naturalis* NATURAL)]

connĕct′, v.t. & i. Join (two things, one *to* another); make coherent (arguments etc.); (pass.) have practical relations *with*; associate mentally *with*; unite *with* others in relationship etc. (usu. pass. or refl.); (v.i.) join on (*with*). Hence ~ER¹(2), ~OR, nn., ~IBLE a. [f. L CON(*nectere nex-* bind)]

connĕc′tĕd, a. In vbl senses, esp.: joined in sequence, coherent, whence ~LY² adv., ~NESS n.; related, as *well* ~ (with persons of good position). [-ED¹]

connĕc′tive, a. Serving, tending, to connect; ~ *tissue* of the body, fibrous tissue connecting & supporting the organs. [-IVE]

connĕ′xion (-kshon), **connĕc′tion,** n. Act of connecting; state of being connected (*cut the* ~, separate things, have no more to do with something); relation of thought, as *in this* ~; connecting part, as *hot water—s*; connecting train, steamer, etc. as *miss the* ~; personal intercourse; sexual relation, as *criminal* ~ (abbr. *crim. con.*); family relationship; relative;

religious body, whence ~AL (-sho-) a.; body of customers etc., as *business with a good* ~; *in* ~ *with,* connected with, esp. of trains, boats, etc., taking on passengers from others. [f. L *connexio* (as CONNECT, see -ION)]

conning tower. See CON².

*****connip′tion,** n. (sl.). (Usu. ~ *fit*) fit of rage or hysteria. [orig. unkn.]

conniv′ance, n. Conniving (*at, in*); tacit permission, as *done with his* ~. [f. F *connivence* or L *conniventia* (as foll., see -ENCE, -ANCE)]

connive′, v.i. Wink *at* (what one ought to oppose). [f F *conniver* or L *connivēre* shut the eyes (to)]

conniv′ent, a. (nat. hist.). Gradually convergent. [as CONNIVE, see -ENT]

connoisseur (kŏnaser′), n. Critical judge (*of, in,* matters of taste). Hence ~SHIP n. [F (now -aiss-), f. pres. st. of *connoître* (now -aître) +-eur -OR; cf. RECONNOITRE]

connōt|e′, v.t. (Of words) imply in addition to the primary meaning; (of facts etc.) imply as a consequence or condition; (Logic) imply the attributes while denōting the subject; (loosely) mean. Hence or cogn. **connotA′tion** n., ~′ative a., ~′atively² adv. [f. med. L CON(*notare* f. *nota* mark) mark in addition]

connūb′ial, a. Of marriage; of husband and/or wife. Hence ~ITY (-ăl-) n., ~LY² adv. [f. L *connubialis* f. CON(*nubium* f. *nubere* marry), see -AL]

cŏn′oid, a., & n. Cone-shaped; (n.) solid generated by revolution of a conic section about its axis, also, any more or less cone--shaped body. Hence **conoid′**AL a. [f. LL f. Gk *kōnoeidēs* (as CONE, see -OID)]

cŏn′quer (-ngker), v.t. & i. Overcome by force; get the better of (habit, passion, etc.); *stoop to* ~, use indirect means for gaining one′s end; acquire, subjugate, (land). Hence ~ABLE a. [ME, f. OF *conquerre* f. Rom. *conquerere* f. L CON-. (*quirere* = *quaerere* seek, get)]

cŏn′queror (-ngke-), n. One who conquers; *the C*~, William I; (colloq.) *play the* ~ (decisive game); || horse-chestnut that has broken others in boys′ game of CONKERS. [ME, f. AF *conquerour* (OF -eor) f. *conquerre*; see prec. & -OR]

cŏn′quĕst, n. Subjugation (of country etc.); *the* (*Norman*) *C*~, acquisition of English crown by William of Normandy, 1066; conquered territory; person whose affections have been won; *make a* ~ (*of*), win (person′s) affections. [ME, f. OF *conquest*(e) f. p.p. of Rom. *conquerere*; see CONQUER]

cŏnquist′ador, n. Conqueror, esp. one of the Spanish conquerors of Mexico & Peru in 16th c. [Sp.]

consâng′uine (-nggwĭn), a.=foll. [F (-in, -ine), as foll.]

consânguin′eous (-nggw-), a. Of the same blood, akin. [f. L CON(*sanguineus* f. *sanguis -inis* blood) +-OUS]

cŏnsănguĭn'itў (-nggw-), n. Blood-
-relationship (also fig.). [ME, f. L *con-
sanguinitas* (as prec., see -TY)]

cŏn'science (-shens), n. Moral sense of
right & wrong; *good* or *clear, bad* or *guilty,*
~, consciousness that one's actions are
right, wrong; *have on* one's ~, feel guilty
about; *in all* ~, *upon* one's ~, (forms of
asseveration); *have the* ~ *to,* have the impudence to; *for* ~ (or ~') *sake,* to satisfy
one's ~; ~ *clause* in act, one ensuring
respect for the ~s of those affected; ~
money (sent to relieve the ~, esp. in payment of evaded income-tax). Hence
~LESS a. [ME, f. OF f. L *conscientia* f.
CON(*scire* know) be privy to, see -ENCE]

cŏnsciĕn'tious (-shĭ-; -shus), a. Obedient
to conscience, scrupulous, (of persons or
conduct); ~ *objector,* person who avails
himself of CONSCIENCE *clause,* man (often
abbr. *c.o.*) who pleads conscience &
objects to military service. Hence ~LY²
adv., ~NESS n., (-shus-). [f. F *conscienti-
eux, -euse,* f. med. L *conscientiosus* (as
prec., see -OUS)]

cŏn'scious (-shus), a. Aware, knowing,
(*of* fact, *of* external circumstances, *that,*
or abs.); with mental faculties awake; (of
actions, emotions, etc.) realized by the
actor etc. (*with* ~ *superiority*; *a hardly* ~
movement); = SELF-CONSCIOUS. Hence
~LY² (-shus-) adv. [f. L *conscius* f.
CON(*scire* know) be privy to +-OUS]

cŏn'sciousnĕss (-shus-), n. State of being
conscious; totality of a person's thoughts
& feelings, or of a class of these, as *moral*
~; perception (*of, that*). [-NESS]

conscribe', v.t. (now rare). Enlist by
CONSCRIPTION. [f. L CON(*scribere* script-
write) enrol]

conscript'¹, v.t. = prec. [orig. U.S.,
back form. f. CONSCRIPTION]

cŏn'script², a. Enrolled or formed by
conscription; ~ *fathers* [L *patres conscripti,* orig. *patres et conscripti*], collective title of Roman senators. [f. L
conscriptus, see CONSCRIBE]

cŏn'script³, n. One enrolled by conscription. [after F *conscrit*]

conscrip'tion, n. Compulsory enlistment
for military or naval or air force service
(esp. enrolment by lot); ~ *of wealth,*
taxation or confiscation of property for
war purposes to impose equality of
sacrifice on non-conscripts. [after F
conscription repr. L *conscriptionem,* see
CONSCRIBE]

cŏn'sĕcrāte¹, a. Consecrated. [ME, f. L
CON(*secrare* f. *sacer* sacred), see -ATE²]

cŏn'sĕcrāt|e², v.t. Set apart as sacred
(*to*); devote *to* (purpose); sanctify. So
~OR n., ~ORY a. [prec., -ATE³]

cŏnsecrā'tion, n. Act of consecrating,
dedication, esp. of church, churchyard,
etc., by bishop; ordination to sacred
office, esp. of bishop; devotion *to* (a pur-

pose). [ME, f. L *consecratio* (as prec., see
-ATION)]

consĕc'tarў, n. Deduction, corollary. [f.
L *consectarium* (neut. adj. as n.) f. *con-
sectari* frequent. as foll.]

cŏnsĕcū'tion, n. Logical sequence; sequence of events; (Gram.) sequence of
words, tenses, etc. [f. L *consecutio* f. CON-
(*sequi secut-* pursue) overtake, see -ION]

consĕc'ūtive, a. Following continuously;
(Gram.) expressing consequence, as ~
clause; (Mus.) ~ *intervals* (of the same
kind, occurring adjacently between the
same two parts, esp. fifths or octaves).
Hence ~LY² (-vl-) adv., ~NESS (-vn-) n.
[f. F *consécutif, -ive* f. med. L *consecutivus*
(as prec., see -IVE)]

cŏnsĕnĕs'cence, n. General decay by age.
[f. L CON(*senescere* grow old f. *senex*),
-ENCE]

consĕn'sual (-sū-, -shōŏ-), a. (physiol.).
Caused by sympathetic action. [f. foll.
+-AL]

consĕn'sus, n. Agreement (*of* opinion,
testimony, etc.); (Physiol.) agreement of
different organs in effecting purpose. [L
(as foll.)]

consĕnt'¹, v.i. Acquiesce, agree, (*to* a
thing, *to* do, *that,* or abs.). [ME, f. OF
consentir f. L CON(*sentire sens-* feel)
agree]

consĕnt'², n. Voluntary agreement, compliance; permission; *age of* ~ (at which ~,
esp. of girl to seduction, is valid in law);
(prov.) *silence gives* ~; *with one* ~, unanimously. [ME, f. OF *consente* f. *consentir*
(prec.)]

cŏnsĕntān'ĕous, a. Accordant, suited,
(*to, with*); unanimous, concurrent. Hence
consĕntanĕ'itў, ~NESS, nn., ~LY² adv.
[f. L *consentaneus* (as CONSENT¹) +-OUS]

consĕn'tient (-shnt), a. Agreeing; concurrent; consenting (*to*). [f. L as CON-
SENT¹, see -ENT]

cŏn'sĕquence, n. Result (of something
preceding; *take the* ~s, accept whatever
results from one's choice or act); logical
inference; *in* ~, as a result (*of*); importance; *of* (*no*) ~, (un)important; social
distinction, rank, as *persons of* ~. [ME,
f. OF f. L *consequentia* (as foll., -ENCE)]

cŏn'sĕquent¹, n. Event that follows
another; second part of conditional proposition, dependent on the antecedent;
(Math.) second of two numbers in a ratio,
second & fourth of four proportionals.
[as foll.]

cŏn'sĕquent², a. Following as a result
(*on*); following logically; logically consistent. [f. F *conséquent* f. L CON(*sequi*
follow), see -ENT]

cŏnsĕquĕn'tial (-shl), a. Following as a
result or inference; following or resulting
indirectly, as ~ *damages*; self-important.
Hence ~ITY (-shĭăl¹), n., ~LY² (-shal-) adv.
[f. L *consequentia* CONSEQUENCE+-AL]

For compounds of *co-* not given consult CO-.

cŏn'sĕquentlў, adv. & conj. As a result; therefore. [-LY²]

‖ **consĕrv'ancў,** n. Commission, court, controlling a port, river, etc., as *Thames C~*; official protection (of forests etc.). [18th c. alt. of (obs.) *conservacy* (16th c.) f. AF f. med. L *conservatia* (CONSERVE², -ACY)]

cŏnservā'tion, n. Preservation; ~ *of energy,* principle that total quantity of energy of any system of bodies (including the universe) is invariable. [ME, f. OF, or f. L *conservatio* (CONSERVE², -ATION)]

consĕrv'ative, a. & n. **1.** Preservative (a. & n.); (*C~ party,* English political party) disposed to maintain existing institutions; (of estimate) moderate, cautious, purposely low. **2.** n. One so disposed, (*C~*) member of the C~ party. So **consĕrv'atism** n. [ME, f. OF *conservatif* (CONSERVE², -IVE), f. LL *conservativus*]

consĕrvatoire' (-twahr), n. Public school of music & declamation (on Continent). [18th c. *-orio* f. It., whence F *-oire* (19th c. in Eng.)]

cŏn'servātor, n. Preserver; official custodian (of museum etc.); ‖~*s of the peace,* the King, Lord Chancellor, etc.; ‖~*s of a river* (see CONSERVANCY). [f. AF *-atour* (OF *-ateur*) f. L *conservatorem* (as foll., see -OR)]

consĕrv'atorў, n. Greenhouse for tender plants; = CONSERVATOIRE. [f. LL *conservatorius*; partly f. F *-toire* (as foll., see -ORY)]

consĕrve'¹, n. (usu. pl.). Confection, preserve. [f. OF, = med. L *conserva* as foll.)]

consĕrve'², v.t. Keep from harm, decay, or loss. [ME, f. OF *conserver* or L CON-(*servare* keep)]

consĭd'er, v.t. & i. Contemplate mentally; weigh the merits of (course, claim, etc.); reflect (*that, whether,* etc., or abs.), reckon with, make allowance for; be of opinion (*that*); regard as, as *I ~ him* (*to be*) *a knave,* ~ *yourself under arrest;* (arch.) ~ *of,* think over. [ME, f. OF *considerer* f. L *considerare* examine]

consĭd'erab|le, a. Worth considering; (of persons) notable, important; (of immaterial things) much, no small, (trouble, annoyance, pleasure), whence ~LY² adv. [f. med. L *considerabilis* (prec., -ABLE)]

consĭd'erate, a. Thoughtful for others; (arch.) careful. Hence ~LY² (-tl-) adv., ~NESS (-tn-) n. [as prec., -ATE²]

considerā'tion, n. Act of considering; meditation; *take into ~,* consider; *under ~,* being considered; *in ~ of,* in return for, on account of; fact, thing, regarded as a reason, as *that is a ~, on no ~;* compensation, reward, as *for a ~;* (Law) thing given, done, as equivalent by person to whom a promise is made; thoughtfulness for others; importance (now rare). [OF, f. L *consiterationem* (as prec., see -ATION)]

consĭd'ering, prep. In view of, as *it is excusable ~ his age, how young he is,* (*that*)

he has no experience; (ellipt.) *that is not so bad,* ~ (the circumstances). [-ING²]

consign' (-īn), v.t. Hand over, deliver, *to* (misery, watery grave, person, person's care); transmit, send by rail etc., *to* (person), whence **cŏnsignEE', cŏnsignOR',** (-īn-), nn.; deposit (money *in* bank). Hence ~ABLE (-īn-) a. [f. F *consigner* or L *consignare* mark with a seal (*signum*)]

cŏnsignā'tion, n. Formal payment of money to person legally appointed; act of consigning goods; *to the~ of,* addressed to. [f. L *consignatio* (as prec., see -ATION)]

consign'ment (-īn-), n. Consigning; goods consigned. [-MENT]

consil'i|ent, a. (Of inductions from different phenomena) accordant. Hence ~ENCE n. [f. mod. L CON(*silire* = *salire* jump), see -ENT]

consist', v.i. Be composed *of* (esp. material things); be comprised *in,* as *virtue ~s in being uncomfortable;* harmonize *with;* (Bibl., *Col.* i. 17) exist. [f. L CON(*sistere* stop) exist]

consis'tence, -cў, n. Degree of density, esp. of thick liquids; firmness, solidity, (lit. & fig.); (-*cy*) state of being consistent, esp. of persons. [f. F *consistence* (now *-ance*) or LL *consistentia,* see prec., -ENCE, -ENCY]

consis'tent, a. Compatible, not contradictory, (*with*); (of person) constant to same principles. Hence ~LY² adv. [as prec., -ENT]

cŏn'sistorў (*also* konsĭs⁴), n. Senate composed of Pope & Cardinals; (also *C~ Court*) bishop's court for ecclesiastical causes & offences; Lutheran clerical board; court of presbyters. So **cŏnsistōr'iAL** a. [f. ONF *consistorie* (OF *-oire*) f. L *consistorium* (as CONSIST, see -ORY)]

consō'ciate¹ (-shǐ-), a. & n. Associate(d). [f. L CON(*sociare* f. *socius* fellow), see -ATE²]

consō'ciāte² (-shǐ-), v.t. & i. Associate. So **consōciā'TION** n. [as prec., see -ATE³]

cŏnsolā'tion, n. Act of consoling; consoling circumstance; ~ *race, prize, stakes* (open to competitors unsuccessful in former events). [ME, f. OF f. L *consolationem* (as foll., see -ATION)]

cŏnsŏl'ator|ў, a. Tending, meant, to console. Hence ~ILY² adv. [ME, f. L *consolatorius* (as foll. see -ORY)]

cŏnsōl'e'¹, v.t. Comfort. Hence ~'ABLE a. [f. F *consoler* f. L CON*solare,* *-ri*]

cŏn'sōle², n. (Archit.) kind of bracket or corbel; frame containing keyboards, stops, etc., of organ; ~*-table, -mirror* (supported by bracket against wall). [F, of unkn. orig.]

cŏnsŏl'idāt|e, v.t. & i. Solidify (t. & i.); strengthen (usu. fig., power etc.); combine (territories, estates, companies, statutes, debts) into one whole; ‖ ~*ed annuities, consols,* Government securities of Great Britain, ~ed in 1751 into a single stock at 3% (now 2½), *C~ed Fund,* united product of various taxes etc., whence interest of national debt etc. is paid. Hence **consŏlidáʹtion**, ~OR, nn., ~ORY a. [f. L CON(*solidare* f. *solidus*), see -ATE³] ‖ **consŏls'** (-z), n. pl. See prec. [abbr.]

consommé (see Ap.), n. Strong meat soup [F]

cŏn'sonance, n. Recurrence of same or similar sounds in words, assonance; sounding of two notes in harmony; (Mus.) consonant interval, concord; (fig.) agreement, harmony. [ME, f. OF, or f. L *consonantia* (as foll., see -ANCE)]

cŏn'sonant¹, a. Agreeable *to*, consistent *with*; harmonious; agreeing in sound; (Mus.) making concord. Hence~LY² adv. [ME, f. F f. L CON(*sonare* sound f. *sonus*), see -ANT]

cŏn'sonant², n. Alphabetical element other than vowel; sound that in forming a syllable is combined with vowel. Hence **cŏnsonänʹtAL** a. [ME, f. OF f. L *consonantem* (*litteram* letter) sounding with another (as prec.)]

cŏn'sŏrt¹, n. **1.** Husband or wife; *queen* ~, king's wife; *king, prince,* ~, queen's husband. **2.** Ship sailing with another. [OF, f. L CON(*sors -rtis* lot) sharer, comrade]

consŏrt'², v.t. & i. Class or bring together, keep company, (*with*); agree, harmonize, (*with*). [f. prec.; sense 'agree' prob. f. SORT²(2)]

consŏr'tium (-shǐum), n. Temporary co-operation of several powers or large interests to effect some common purpose. [L,=partnership (*consors* sharing, sharer)]

conspĕc'tus, n. General view of subject, scene, etc.; tabulation of details, synopsis. [L, vbl n. f. CON(*spicere* look at)]

conspic'ūous, a. Clearly visible, striking to the eye; attracting notice, remarkable, as ~ *by its absence, for his loyalty.* Hence **cŏnspicū'ITY** (now rare), ~NESS, nn., ~LY² adv. [f. L *conspicuus* (as prec.) +-OUS]

conspi'racỹ, n. Act of conspiring (in good or bad sense); combination for unlawful purpose; plot. [ME, f. AF *conspiracie*, alt. f. OF *-ation* (whence ME *-ation*) f. L *conspirationem* (CONSPIRE, -ATION)]

conspi'rat|or, n. One engaged in a conspiracy. Hence ~RESS¹ n. [ME, f. AF *-tour*, OF *-teur*, f. as foll., see -OR]

conspire', v.i. & t. Combine privily for unlawful purpose, esp. treason, murder, sedition; combine, concur, (*to* do); plot, devise, as ~ *his ruin,* ~ *an attack.* [ME, f. OF *conspirer* f. L CON(*spirare* breathe) agree, plot]

conspūe', v.t.(rare). Express detestation, clamour for the abandonment or abolition, of (person, policy, etc.). [f. F *conspuer* f. L CON(*spuere* spit) spit upon]

con'stable (kŭn-), n. (Also *police* ~)

policeman; ‖ *Chief C*~, head of police force of county etc.; *special* ~, person sworn in to act as ~ on special occasion; *outrun the* ~, run into debt; *C*~ *of France,* principal officer of household of early French kings, commander-in-chief in king's absence; *C*~ *of England, Lord High C*~, similar officer in English Royal household (now temporary officer on special occasions). [ME, f. OF *conestable* f. LL *comes stabuli* (med. L *conestabulus*) count of the stable]

constăb'ūlarỹ, a. & n. (Organized body) of constables. [f. med. L *constabularia* f. *-arius* (prec., -ARY¹)]

cŏn'stancỹ, n. Firmness, endurance; faithfulness; unchangingness. [f. L *constantia* (as foll., see -ANCY)]

cŏn'stant, a. & n. **1.** Unmoved, resolute; faithful (*to*); unchanging; unremittent, as ~ *attention, chatter.* **2.** n. (Math.) quantity that does not vary; (Phys.) number expressing a relation, property, etc., that remains the same for same substance in same conditions, as ~ *of friction.* [ME, f. OF f. L CON(*stare* stand), see -ANT]

Constăn'tia (-sha), n. Wine from the ~ farm near Cape Town.

cŏn'stantlỹ, adv. Always; often. [-LY²]

cŏn'stellāte, v.t. & i. Form into a constellation. [f. LL *constellatus* f. L *stella* star, see -ATE³]

cŏnstellā'tion, n. Number of fixed stars grouped within an imaginary outline (also fig.). [OF, or f. LL *constellatio* (as prec., see -ATION)]

cŏn'sternāte, v.t. Dismay (usu. pass.). [f. L CON(*sternare, -sternere,* throw down), see -ATE³]

cŏnsternā'tion, n. Dismay. [F, or f. L *consternatio* (as prec., see -ATION)]

cŏn'stipāte, v.t. Confine (bowels); render costive. [f. L CON(*stipare* press), see -ATE³]

cŏnstipā'tion, n. Costiveness. [ME, f. OF, or f. LL *constipatio* (as prec., see -ATION)]

constit'ūencỹ, n. Body of voters who elect a representative member; (division of) county or (division of) borough returning an M.P.; place, body of residents in place, so represented; body of customers, subscribers, etc. [f. foll., see -ENCY]

constit'ūent, a. & n. **1.** Composing, making up, a whole; appointing, electing; able to frame or alter a (political) constitution, as ~ *assembly, power.* **2.** n. One who appoints another his agent; component part; member of a constituency. [f. L *constituent-* (partly thr. F *-ant*), as foll., see -ENT]

cŏn'stitūte, v.t. Appoint, as ~ *him president,* ~ *oneself a judge;* establish, found; give legal form to (assembly etc.); frame, form, (esp. pass. of bodily or mental constitution); make up, be the components of. [f. L CON(*stituere -ut-*=*statuere* set up)] cŏnstĭtū'tion, n. Act, mode, of constituting; character of the body as regards health, strength, etc.; mental character; mode in which State is organized; body of fundamental principles according to which a State is governed; *written* ~, document embodying these; (hist.) decree, ordinance, as *C*~*s of Clarendon* (1164). [ME, f. OF,, f. L *constitutionem* (as prec., see -ION)]

cŏnstĭtū'tional (-sho-), a. & n. **1.** Of, inherent in, affecting, the bodily or mental constitution; essential; of, in harmony with, authorized by, the political constitution, as ~ *sovereign, government* (limited by ~ forms), whence ~ITY (-shonăl²) n.; adhering to the political constitution. **2.** n. ~ walk, for health's sake. Hence ~LY² adv. [-AL]

cŏnstĭtū'tionalĭsm (-sho-), n. Constitutional government; adherence to constitutional principles. [-ISM]

cŏnstĭtū'tionalĭst (-sho-), n. Writer on the political constitution; adherent of constitutional principles. [-IST]

cŏnstĭtū'tionalĭze (-sho-), -ĭse (-īz), v.t. & i. Make constitutional; (intr.) take a constitutional. [-IZE]

cŏn'stĭtūtive, a. Constructive, formative; essential; component. Hence ~LY² (-vl-) adv. [f. LL *constitutivus* (see CONSTITUTE, -IVE); cf. F *constitutif*]

cŏn'stĭtūtor, n. Person that constitutes. [L (as CONSTITUTE, see -OR)]

constrain', v.t. Compel (person *to do, to* course or state, or abs.); bring about by compulsion; confine forcibly, imprison (lit. & fig.); (p.p.) forced, embarrassed, as ~*ed voice, manner*, whence ~ĕDLY² adv. [ME, f. OF *constreindre* f. L CON(*stringere strict-* tie)]

constraint', n. Compulsion (*under* ~); confinement; restraint of natural feelings, constrained manner. [f. OF *constreinte*, fem. p.p. as n., see prec.]

constrict', v.t. Contract, compress; cause (organic tissue) to contract. So constric'TION n., constric'TIVE a. [f. L as CONSTRAIN]

constric'tor, n. Muscle that draws together or narrows a part; compressor (surgical instrument); BOA-~. [mod. L (as prec., see -OR)]

constrin|ge' (-j), v.t. Compress; cause (organic tissue) to contract. Hence ~'ğENCY n., ~'ğENT a., (-j-). [f. L con*stringere* CONSTRAIN]

construct', v.t. Fit together, frame, build, (also fig.); (Gram.) combine (words) syntactically; draw, delineate, as ~ *a triangle*. [f. L CON(*struere struct-* pile, build)]

construc'tion, n. Act, mode, of constructing; thing constructed; syntactical connexion between words; construing, explanation, (of words); interpretation (of conduct etc.), as *put a good, bad,* ~

upón his refusal; ~ *train* (conveying materials for the ~ or upkeep of a railway). Hence ~ISM (-sho-) n., artistic expression by means of mechanical structures (chiefly Theatr.). [ME, f. OF or L *constructio* (as prec., see -ION)]

construc'tional (-sho-) a. Of construction; structural, belonging to the original structure. [-AL]

construc'tive, a. Of construction; tending to construct, esp. opposed to *destructive* as *positive* to *negative*, as ~ *criticism*; belonging to the structure of a building; inferred, not directly expressed, virtual, as *a* ~ *denial, permission, blasphemy, treason*. Hence ~LY² (-vl-) adv. [17th c., f. CONSTRUCT +-IVE; cf. F *constructif*, LL *-ivus*]

construc'tor, n. One who constructs, esp. supervisor of naval construction. Hence ~SHIP n. [-OR]

cŏn'strue (-ōō, *also* konstrōō'), v.t. & i., & n. **1.** Combine (words *with* others) grammatically, as '*rely*' *is* ~*d with* '*on*'; analyse (sentence), translate word for word; admit of grammatical analysis, as *this passage does not* ~; expound, interpret, (words, actions). **2.** n. (kŏn²-). Passage to be translated word for word. [ME, f. L *construere* CONSTRUCT]

cŏnsŭbstăn'tial (-shl), a. Of the same substance, esp. of the three Persons in the Godhead. Hence ~ITY (-shiăl²-) n. [ME, f. LL *consubstantialis* (Tert.); see SUBSTANCE & -AL]

cŏnsŭbstăn'tiāte (-shī-), v.t. & i. Unite in one substance. [f. LL *consubstantiatus* (as prec., see -ATE², ³)]

cŏnsŭbstăntiā'tion (-shī-), n. (Doctrine of) real substantial presence of body & blood of Christ together with bread & wine in Eucharist (cf. TRANSUBSTANTIATION). [f. LL *consubstantiatio* (as prec., see -ATION)]

cŏn'suĕtūde (-sw-), n. Custom, esp. as having legal force; social intercourse. [ME, f. L *consuetudo*, see CUSTOM]

cŏnsuĕtūd'inarў (-sw-), a. & n. Customary, as ~ *law*; (n.) manual of customs, esp. of monastic house, cathedral, etc. [ME, f. LL *consuetudinarius* (as prec., see -ARY¹)]

cŏn'sul, n. Title of two annual magistrates exercising supreme authority in Roman republic; title of three chief magistrates of French Republic 1799–1804 (*First C*~, Napoleon); State agent residing in foreign town and protecting subjects there. Hence ~SHIP n. [ME, f. L *consul*; cf. CONSULT]

cŏn'sūlar, a. & n. Of a consul; (Roman) of ~ rank. [ME, f. L *consularis* (as prec., see -AR¹)]

cŏn'sūlate, n. Office, establishment, of a (modern) consul; (period of) consular government in France; office of (Roman) consul. [ME, f. L *consulatus* (as prec., see -ATE¹)]

consult', v.t. & i. Take counsel (with person or book, or abs.); seek information or advice from (person, book); ~ one's pillow, take a night for reflection; take into consideration (feelings, interests); ~ing physician, ⌐who is called in by colleagues or applied to by patients for advice in special cases). Hence **consŭl'tABLE, consŭl'tATIVE, aa., cŏnsultEE'** n. [f. F consulter or L consultare frequent. of consulere -sult-; cf. CONSUL]

consŭl'tant, n. One who consults; consulting physician. [as prec., see -ANT]

cŏnsultā'tion, n. Act of consulting; deliberation; conference. [ME, f. OF, or f. L consultatio (as prec., see -ATION)]

consŭm|e', v.t. & i. Make away with; use up; eat, drink, up; spend, waste, (time, trouble, etc.); (p.p.) eaten up (with envy); (v.i.) waste away. Hence ~'ABLE a. & n. (usu. pl.), (article) intended for consumption (~able ledger, register of receipt and issue of such items). [ME, f. L cŏn-(sumere sumpt- take up); partly thr. F consumer]

consŭm'ĕdlў, adv. Excessively. [prec., -LY²]

consŭm'er, n. In vbl senses, esp. (Pol. Econ.) user of an article, opp. to producer; ~(s') goods, things which directly satisfy human wants and desires, e.g. food and clothing; ~ resistance, = SALES resistance. [-ER¹]

consŭmm'ate¹, a. Complete, perfect, as ~ general, skill, ass. Hence ~LY² (-tl-) adv. [f. L CON(summare complete f. summus utmost), see -ATE²]

cŏn'summāt|e², v.t. Accomplish, complete, esp. marriage (by sexual intercourse). Hence~IVE a., ~OR n. [as prec., see -ATE³]

cŏnsummā'tion, n. Completion (esp. of marriage, see prec.); desired end, goal; perfection; perfected thing. [ME, f. OF consommation or L consummatio (as prec., see -ATION)]

consŭmp'tion, n. Using up; destruction; waste; amount consumed; wasting disease, esp. pulmonary~, phthisis. [ME, f. L consumptio (as CONSUME, see -ION), or OF consumption]

consŭmp'tive, a. & n. Tending to consume; tending to, affected with, consumption, whence ~LY² (-vl-) adv., ~NESS (-vn-) n.; (n.) ~ patient. [17th c., f. CONSUMPT(ION) + -IVE, after presumption, presumptive, etc.]

cŏntabĕs'c|ence, n. (bot.). Suppression of pollen formation in anthers of flowers. So ~ENT a. [f. L CON(tabescere waste away f. tabes consumption), see -ENCE]

cŏn'tact, n., & v.t. 1. State, condition, of touching, as be in ~ with; (fig.) come into ~ with, come across, meet; make, break, ~, complete, interrupt, electric circuit (so ~-maker, -breaker); (Math.) touching of straight line & curve, two curves, or two surfaces; (Med.) person likely to carry contagion through ~ with infected person; ~ lenscs, glasses fitting inside eyelids; ~ man, intermediary esp. between a government department & the public. 2. v.t. (also kontăkt'), Get into touch with (person). [f. L contactus -ūs vbl n. f. CON(tingere tact- = tangere touch)]

contadi'no (-ahdē-), n. (fem. -na; pl. -ni pr. -nē, fem. -ne pr. -nä). Italian peasant. [It.]

contā'gion (-jn), n. Communication of disease from body to body; contagious disease; moral corruption; contagious influence (fig.). [ME, f. OF, or f. L CON(tagio f. tangere touch, -ION)]

contā'gionist (-jon-), n. One who thinks a disease (plague, cholera, etc.) contagious. [-IST]

contā'gious (-jus), a. Communicating disease by contact (lit. & fig.); (of diseases) so communicable (fig.) catching, infectious. Hence ~LY² adv., ~NESS n., (-jus-). [ME, f. OF contagieus or LL contagiosus (as CONTAGION, see -OUS)]

contain', v.t. Have, hold, as contents; comprise, include; (of a measure) be equal to, as a pound ~s 16 ounces; (pass.) be included (within a space, between limits); (Geom.) enclose, form boundary of; (of numbers) be divisible by (number) without remainder; restrain, as could not ~ himself for joy, ~ your anger; (Mil.) keep (enemy force) from moving, esp. with a view to operations elsewhere. Hence ~ABLE a., ~ER¹ n., (esp.) vessel, box, etc., designed to ~ some particular article(s), ~MENT n., (esp.) policy of building up strength against a possible enemy in the hope of eventual agreement with him. [ME, f. OF contenir f. L CON(tinere tent-= tenēre hold)]

contăm'inate, v.t. Pollute, infect. So **contăminA'TION** n. (also, in literary criticism, the blending of two plays, tales, etc., into one). [f. L contaminare, see -ATE³]

‖ **contăng'ō** (-ngg-), n. (pl. -os). Percentage paid by buyer of stock for postponement of transfer (cf. BACKWARDATION); ~ (also continuation)-day, second day before settling-day. [etym. unkn.]

conte (kawñt), n. Short story (as a form of literary composition). [F]

contĕmn' (-m), v.t. (literary). Despise, treat with disregard. Hence ~ER¹ (-mn-) n. [ME, f. OF contemner or L CON(temnere tempt- despise)]

cŏn'templ|āte, v.t. & i. Gaze upon; view mentally; expect; intend, purpose; (v.i.) meditate. So ~A'TION n. (in ~ation, intended), ~ātOR n. [f. L contemplari, see -ATE³]

cŏn'templătive (also kontĕm'pla-), a. Meditative, thoughtful; (of life in middle ages) given up to religious contemplation, opp. to *active.* Hence ~LY² (-vl-) adv., ~NESS (-vn-) n. [ME, f. OF -*if*, f. L *contemplativus* (prec., -IVE)]

contĕmporān´eous, a. Existing, occurring, at the same time (*with*); covering the same time; of the same period. Hence **contĕmporanē´ITY,** ~NESS, nn., ~LY² adv. [f. L CON(*temporaneus* f. *tempus -oris* time, see -ANEOUS)]

contĕm´poraryˇ, a. & n. (Person) belonging to the same time; (person) equal in age; (newspaper) published during same period. [CON-+TEMPORARY; in 18th c. *cotemporary* was preferred]

contĕm´porize, -ise (-īz), v.t. Make contemporary, cause to agree in time. [f. st. of prec. +-IZE]

contĕmpt´, n. Act, mental attitude, of despising; condition of being despised; *have, hold, in* ~, *bring, fall, into* ~; (Law) disobedience to sovereign's lawful commands or to authority of Houses of Parliament or other legislative body, esp. ~ *of court,* disobedience to, interference with administration of justice by, courts of law. [ME, f. L *contemptus -ūs* (as CONTEMN)]

contĕmp´tible, a. Deserving contempt, despicable; *Old C*~*s,* Sir J. French's army of 1914 (w. ref. to Kaiser's alleged 'French's ~ little army'). Hence **contĕmptiBIL´ITY,** ~NESS, nn., **contĕmp´tiBLY²** adv. [ME, f. LL *contemptibilis* (as CONTEMN, see -BLE)]

contĕmp´tŭous, a. Showing contempt (*of*); scornful; insolent. Hence ~LY² adv., ~NESS n. [as CONTEMPT+-OUS]

contĕnd´, v.i. & t. Strive, fight, (*with* person *for* thing; struggle *with* (feelings, natural forces); compete, be in rivalry, as ~*ing passions;* argue (*with*); (v.t.) maintain (*that*). [f. OF *contendre* or L CON(*tendere tent*-stretch, strive)]

cŏn´tĕnt¹ (*formerly, & still occas.,* kontĕnt´), n. 1. (pl.) ~*s of,* what is contained in (vessel etc., book, document); (*table of*) ~*s,* summary of subject-matter of book. 2. Capacity (of vessel), volume (of solid). 3. (sing. only). Constituent elements of a conception; substance (of cognition, art, etc.), opp. *form;* amount (of some particular constituent) contained (the *ester*~ of an oil), or yielded (the *sugar* ~ per acre of beet). [ME, repr. med. L *contentum, -ta* (as CONTAIN)]

contĕnt´², n. Contented state, satisfaction, esp. *to* one's *heart's* ~. [immed. source obsc.; perh. f. CONTENT v. or a.]

contĕnt´³, a. & n. Satisfied; willing (*to* do); *well*~, well pleased; ‖ (House of Lords ~, *not* ~, (= *ay, no,* in House of Commons); ‖ (n. pl.) those who vote '~'. [ME, f. OF f. L *contentus,* as CONTENT¹]

contĕnt´⁴, v.t. Satisfy; ~ one*self,* be satisfied (*with* thing, *with* do*ing*). Hence ~ĕdLY² adv., ~ĕdNESS, ~MENT, nn. [ME, f. OF *contenter* (as prec.)]

contĕn´tion, n. Strife, dispute, contro-

versy; emulation; point contended for in argument. [ME, f. OF, or f. L *contentio* (as CONTEND, see -ION)]

contĕn´tious (-shŭs), a. Quarrelsome; involving contention. Hence ~LY² adv., ~NESS n., (-shŭs-). [ME, f. OF *contentieux* f. L *contentiosus* (as prec., see -IOUS)]

contĕrm´inal, a. Having a common boundary. [as foll. +-AL]

contĕrm´inous, a. Having a common boundary (*with, to*); (of two things) meeting at their ends; coextensive (in space, time, meaning). Hence ~LY² adv. [f. L CON(*terminus* boundary)+-OUS]

cŏn´tĕst¹, n. Debate, controversy; strife; (friendly) competition. [f. foll., or F *conteste*]

contĕst´², v.t. & i. Debate, dispute (point, statement, etc.); strive in argument (*with, against*); strive *for;* dispute with arms (field, victory, issue, battle); contend or compete for (seat in Parliament etc.). Hence **contĕs´tABLE** a. [f. F *contester* f. L CON(*testari* f. *testis* witness)]

contĕs´tant, n. One who contests. [F (-ANT)]

cŏntĕstā´tion, n. Disputation; assertion contended for; *in* ~, in dispute. [f. L *contestatio* (as CONTEST², see -ATION), & partly f. F -*ation*]

cŏn´tĕxt, n. Parts that precede or follow a passage & fix its meaning; *in this* ~ (connexion). So **contĕx´tŭAL** a., **contĕx´tŭALLY²** adv. [f. L *contextus -ūs* f. CON(*texere text*- weave)]

contĕx´ture, n. Act, mode, of weaving together; structure; fabric; mode of literary composition. [F (as prec., see -URE)]

cŏntigū´ityˇ, n. Contact; proximity; (Psych.) proximity of ideas or impressions in place or time, as principle of association. [f. LL *contiguitas* (as foll., see -TY), or F *contiguité*]

contig´ŭous, a. Touching, adjoining, (*to*); next in order (*to*); neighbouring. Hence ~LY² adv. [f. L *contiguus* f. CON(*tingere*= *tangere* touch)+-OUS]

cŏn´tinent¹, a. Temperate; chaste. Hence or cogn. **cŏn´tinENCE** n., ~LY² adv. [ME, f. L as CONTAIN, see -ENT; cf. OF *continent*]

cŏn´tinent², n. Continuous land, mainland; ‖ *the C*~, mainland of Europe; one of the main continuous bodies of land (Europe, Asia, Africa, N. & S. America, Australia). [15th c. *continent land,* = F *terre continente,* L *terra continens* (as prec.)]

cŏntinĕn´tal, a. & n. 1. Of a continent; ~ *drift,* (Geol.) supposed slow movement of the continents on a deep-seated plastic substratum; belonging to, characteristic of, the Continent, whence ~ISM, ~IST, nn., ~IZE v.t., ~LY² adv. 2. n. Inhabitant of the Continent; *(sl.)* currency note of an early issue that rapidly depreciated (*I don't care a* ~). [-AL]

contĭn'gencў (-j-), n. Uncertainty of occurrence; chance occurrence; thing that may happen hereafter; thing dependent on an uncertain event; thing incident to another, incidental expense etc. [f. LL *contingentia* as foll., see -ENCY]

contĭn'gent (-j-), a. & n. **1.** Of uncertain occurrence; accidental; incidental *to*; true only under existing conditions; non--essential; conditional. **2.** n. Force contributed to form part of army etc. (or fig.). Hence ~LY² adv. [f. L CON(*tingere= tangere* touch), see -ENT]

contĭn'ūal, a. Always going on; very frequent. Hence ~LY² adv. [ME & OF *continuel* f. L as CONTINUOUS, see -AL]

contĭn'ūance, n. Going on, duration; *of long* ~, lasting long; remaining, stay, (*in* place, condition, etc.). [OF (CONTINUE, -ANCE)]

contĭn'ūant, a. & n. (Consonant) of which the sound can be prolonged (as *f v s r*), opp. of stop or check. [F, or f. L as CONTINUE, see -ANT]

contĭnūā'tion, n. Carrying on, resumption, (of an action, course, story, book, etc.); ǁ (Stock Exch.) carrying over an account to next ~ (or CONTANGO) *-day*; that by which a thing is continued, additional parts; gaiters continuous with knee--breeches; ~ *school* (for additional teaching in leisure time of those who have left primary and other schools). [ME, f. OF f. L *continuationem* (as prec., see -ATION)]

contĭn'ūātive, a. Tending, serving, to continue. [f. LL *continuativus* (as prec., see -IVE)]

contĭn'ūātor, n. One who writes continuation to another's work. [f. mod. L as foll., -OR]

contĭn'ū|e, v.t. & i. Maintain, keep up, (action etc.); retain (person *in* office etc.); take up, resume, (narrative etc. or abs.); (Law) adjourn; remain in existence; stay (*in*, *at*, place, *in* a state); *if you* ~*e* (are still) *obstinate*; not cease (*doing*, *to* do). Hence ~ABLE a. [ME, f. OF *continuer* f. L *continuare* as CONTINUOUS]

contĭnū'itў, n. State of being continuous; (Cinemat.) scenario; *law of* ~ (that all changes in nature are continuous, not abrupt). [f. F *continuité* f. L *continuitatem* (as foll., see -TY)]

contĭn'ūous, a. (Of material things) connected, unbroken; uninterrupted in time or sequence; ~ *brake* of train, ~ series of carriage brakes controlled from one point; (Archit.) ~ *style* (with mullions of window continued in tracery); ~ *voyage*, one which, though interrupted, is regarded as a single voyage in ref. to the object with which it was undertaken. Hence ~LY² adv., ~NESS n. [f. L *continuus* f. CON*(tinēre = tenere* hold) + -OUS]

contĭn'ūum, n. (philos.). An unbroken mass or tissue or course of or *of* matter,

sensation, events, etc. (SPACE-*time* ~). [L, neut. of *continuus*, see prec.]

cŏnt'-line, n. Spiral interval between strands of rope; space between casks stowed side by side. [etym. unkn.]

contōr'iate, a. & n. (Medal) with deep furrow round disc within edge. [f. It. *contorniato*, f. *contorno* CONTOUR; so F *-iate*]

contōrt', v.t. Twist, distort. [f. L CON-(*torquēre tort-*)]

contōr'tion, n. Twisting; twisted state (esp. of face or body). [f. L *contortio* (prec. -ION)]

contōr'tionist (-sho-), n. Artist whose work, gymnast whose body, exhibits contortions. [-IST]

cŏn'tour (-oor), n., & v.t. Outline; line separating differently coloured parts of design; artistic quality of outline; outline of coast, mountain mass, etc.; ~ *line*, one representing horizontal ~ of earth's surface at given elevation, as in a ~ *map*; (v.t.) mark with ~ lines, carry (road) round ~ of hill. [F, f. It. *contorno* f. *contornare* draw in outline f. *tornare* TURN]

cŏn'tra, prep. & n. *Pro & ~* (usu. *con*), for & against; *pros & cons*, arguments for & against; (Bookkeeping) opposite side of account, esp. credit side. [L, as foll.]

contra-, pref. f. L adv. & prep. *contra* against, opposite, etc. In many E wds f. or after L or It. In names of mus. instruments & organ-stops, denoting a pitch of an octave below.

cŏn'trabănd, n. & a. **1.** Prohibited traffic, smuggling; smuggled goods; ~ *of war*, anything forbidden to be supplied by neutrals to belligerents (*absolute, conditional*, ~, things that may under no, *some*, circumstances be supplied, as, *absolute* ~, weapons, *conditional* ~, cotton). **2.** adj. Forbidden to be imported or exported, as ~ *goods*; concerned with these, as ~ *trade*(r). [f. Sp. *contrabanda* f. It. CONTRA(*bando* proclamation), cf. BAN]

cŏn'trabăndist, n. Smuggler. [f. Sp. *contrabandista* (as prec., see -IST)]

cŏn'trabăss, n. = DOUBLE¹-*bass*. [f. It. CONTRA(*basso* BASS)]

cŏntracĕp'tive, a. & n. Preventive of uterine conception. So **cŏntracĕp'tion** n., use of ~s. [CONTRA- + (CON)CEPTION]

cŏn'trăct¹, n. Agreement between parties, States, etc.; business agreement for supply of goods or performance of work at fixed price; agreement enforceable by law (NUDE ~); accepted promise to do or forbear; formal agreement for marriage; conveyance of property; (Bridge) undertaking to make so many tricks; ~ *bridge*, a form of auction bridge in which only tricks bid and won count towards game. [ME, f. OF f. L *contractus* contract (as foll.)]

contrăct'[2], v.t. & i. Enter into business or legal engagement (*to* do, *for doing*, *for* piece of work, or abs.); ~ one*self out of*, ~ *out of*, or abs. ~ *out*, for exemption or exclusion from provisions of (law etc.); ~ (enter into) *marriage*; form (friendship, habit); incur (debt); draw together (muscles, brow, etc.); make smaller, whence **contrăctibil'ity** n., **contrăc't-ible** a.; restrict, confine, (lit. & fig.); (Gram.) shorten (word) by combination or elision; shrink, become smaller; (p.p.) narrow, mean, (of ideas etc.). [f. L CON-(*trahere tract*- draw)]

contrăc'tile (-il, -il), a. Capable of or producing contraction, as ~ *muscles, metal, force*. So **contrăctil'ity** n. [F (as prec., see -ILE)]

contrăc'tion, n. Shrinking, contracting; restriction, confinement; shortening of word by combination or elision; contracted word; contracting (*of* debt, disease, habit). [F, f. L *contractionem* (as prec., see -ION)]

contrăc'tive, a. Serving to contract. [-IVE]

contrăc'tor, n. Undertaker of contract; contracting muscle. [LL (as CONTRACT[2], -OR)]

contrăc'tūal, a. Of (the nature of) a contract. [as CONTRACT[1] + -AL]

contradict', v.t. Deny (statement); deny the words of (person); be contrary to, as *these rumours ~ each other*. Hence or cogn. **contradic'table** a., **contradic'tor** n. [f. L CONTRA(*dicere dict-* say)]

contradic'tion, n. Denial; opposition; statement contradicting another; inconsistency; ~ *in terms*, plainly self-contradictory statement or words as '*almost quite ready*' *is a* ~ *in terms*. [ME, f. OF, f. L *contradictionem* (as prec., -ION)]

contradic'tious (-shŭs), a. Inclined to contradict; disputatious. Hence ~LY[2] adv., ~NESS n. [-IOUS]

contradic'tor|ў, a. & n. Making denial; mutually opposed or inconsistent; contradictious; (n.) ~y assertion. Hence ~ILY[2] adv., ~INESS n. [f. LL *contradictorius* (as prec., see -ORY)]

contradistinc'tion, n. Distinction by contrast. [CONTRA-]

contradisting'uish (-nggw-), v.t. Distinguish (things, one *from* another) by contrast. [CONTRA-]

contrăl'tō, n. & a. (pl. -os). (Part assigned to, singer with) lowest female voice. [It. (CONTRA- + ALTO)]

contraposi'tion (-z-), n. Opposition, contrast; (Logic) a mode of conversion (*if all A is B, then by* ~ *all not-B is not-A, or no not-B is A*). So **contrapŏs'itive** (-z-) a. [f. LL *contrapositio* (Boeth.)]

cŏn'traprŏp, n. Coaxial, oppositely rotating airscrew. [CONTRA-, PROP(ELLER)]

contrăp'tion, n. (sl.). Queer machine, makeshift contrivance. [perh. f. *contrive*, cf. *conceive, -ception*]

cŏntrapŭn'tal, a. Of or in counterpoint. [f. It. *contra(p)punto* COUNTERPOINT + -AL]

cŏntrapŭn'tist, n. One skilled in counterpoint. [f. It. *contra(p)puntista* (as prec., -IST)]

contrār'iant, a. Opposed (*to*). [ME, f. OF, f. LL *contrariare* (as CONTRARY), see -ANT]

contrari'ety, n. Opposition in nature, quality, or action; disagreement, inconsistency. [ME, f. OF *contrarete* f. LL *contrarietatem* (as CONTRARY, see -TY)]

contrār'ious, a. (arch.). Opposed; perverse; (of things) adverse. [ME, f. OF f. med. L *contrariosus* (as prec., see -OUS)]

cŏn'trariwise (-z; *also* kontrār'-), adv. On the other hand; in the opposite way; perversely. [foll. + -WISE]

cŏn'trary (see below), a., n., adv. **1.** Opposed in nature or tendency (*to*); (of wind) impeding, unfavourable; *the* opposite (of two things); (pop., pron. kontrār'ĭ) perverse, self-willed, whence **contrār'i-ness** n.; opposite in position or direction. **2.** n. *The* opposite; *on the* ~ (corroborating a denial expressed or understood, as *Have you nearly done?—On the* ~, *I have only just begun*); interpret *by contraries*, understand Yes for No etc.; *to the* ~, to the opposite effect, as *there is no evidence to the* ~. **3.** adv. In opposition *to*, as *act* ~ *to* nature. Hence **cŏn'trarily**[2] adv. [ME, f. AF *contrarie* (OF *-aire*) f. L *contrarius* (CONTRA, see -ARY[1])]

contrast'[1] (-ah-), v.t. & i. Set (two things, one *with* another) in opposition, so as to show their differences; show striking difference on comparison (*with*). [f. F *contraster* f. It. f. med. L CONTRA(*stare* stand)]

cŏn'trast[2] (-ah-), n. Juxtaposition (esp. of forms, colours, etc.) showing striking differences (*between*; *in* ~ *with*); thing showing such a difference (*to*). Hence **contras'tй**[2] (-ah-) a., exhibiting strong ~s (esp. of photographic negatives). [f. F *contraste* f. It. *contrasto* (see prec.)]

cŏn'trate, a. ~ *wheel*, one with teeth at right angles to its plane. [CONTRA- + -ATE[2]]

cŏntravallā'tion, n. Chain of redoubts and breastworks placed by besiegers between their camp and the town. [f. F *contre-*, It. *-vallazione* (CONTRA-, see CIRCUMVALLATION)]

cŏntravēne', y.t. Infringe (law); dispute (statement); (of things) conflict with. [f. F *contrevenir* or LL CONTRA(*venire vent-* come)]

cŏntravĕn'tion, n. Infringement (*in* ~ *of*, violating). [F (as prec., see -ION)]

contretemps (see Ap.), n. Unlucky accident; hitch. [F]

contrib'ute, v.t. & i. Pay, furnish, (*to* common fund etc.); supply (literary article etc.); (v.i.) ~ *to*, help to bring about. [f. L CON(*tribuere -ut-* bestow)]

cŏntribū'tion, n. Act of contributing; thing, help, literary article, contributed;

imposition levied for support of army in the field; *lay under* ~, *exact* ~s from. [ME, f. OF, or f. LL *contributio* (prec., -ION)]

contrib'utor, n. One who contributes (esp. literary articles). [f. AF *contributor* (as CONTRIBUTE, -OR)]

contrib'utory, a. & n. That contributes (~ *negligence*, of injured person who has failed to take proper precautions against accident); (n.) person liable, when a company fails, to share in paying off its debts. [f. med. L *contributorius* (as prec., -ORY)]

con'trite, a. Broken in spirit by sense of sin, completely penitent; (of actions) showing a ~ spirit. Hence ~LY² (-tl-) adv. [ME, f. OF *contrit* or eccl. L *contritus* f. L CON(*terere trit-* rub) bruise]

contri'tion, n. Being contrite, penitence. [ME, f. OF, or f. eccl. L *contritio* (prec., -ION)]

contriv'ance, n. Act of contriving; deceitful practice; invention; mechanical device; inventive capacity. [-ANCE]

contriv|e', v.t. Invent, devise; bring to pass, manage, (thing, *to* do; also of undesired event, as ~*e to make matters worse*); (abs.) manage household affairs (*well* etc.), whence ~'ER¹ n. Hence ~'ABLE a. [ME *controve, -eve,* f. OF *controver* find, imagine; mod. *contrive* unexpl.]

control'¹, n. Power of directing, command; restraint; means of restraint, check; standard of comparison for checking inferences deduced from experiment; (Spirit.) personality actuating a medium; station at which aeroplanes, motors, etc., in races are allowed time to stop for overhauling etc.; section of road in which a (racing) motor vehicle has to observe certain instructions (as to speed etc.); (pl.) various devices in aircraft used to control altitude, direction, speed, etc. [corresp. to F *contrôle,* earlier *contrerolle* copy of a roll, as med. L CONTRA(*rotulus* see ROLL¹); in Eng. prob. f. foll.]

control'², v.t. (-ll-). Dominate, command; hold in check (*oneself,* one's anger); check, verify; regulate (prices etc.). Hence ~l'ABLE a., ~MENT n. [ME, f. AF (= OF) *contreroller* keep copy of roll of accounts, in mod. F *contrôler;* see prec.]

controll'er, n. In vbl senses; also one who checks expenditure, steward, ǁ esp. of royal household, Mint, Navy, etc. (often spelt *compt-*). Hence ~SHIP n. [ME *counterroller* f. AF *contrerollour* (as prec., see -OR)]

controver'sial (-shl), a. Of, open to, given to, controversy. Hence ~ISM, ~IST, nn., ~LY² adv., (-sha-). [f. LL *controversialis* (as foll., -AL)]

con'troversy, n. Disputation; *without, beyond,* ~, unquestionably. [ME, f. L

controversia (as foll., see -Y¹); cf. obs. F *controversie*]

con'trovert (*also* -vert'), v.t. Dispute about, discuss; dispute, deny. Hence ~IST n. [c. 1600 formed on contemporary *controverse* vb (f. L *controversus* disputed), on anal. of *convert, pervert,* etc.; cf. LL *controvertere* invert]

contumā'cious (-shus), a. Insubordinate, disobedient, esp. to order of court. Hence or cogn. ~LY² adv., ~NESS, **con'tumacy,** nn. [f. L CON(*tumax -acis,* see -ACIOUS]

contumēl'ious, a. Opprobrious; insolent. Hence ~LY² adv. [ME, f. OF *contumelieus* f. L *contumeliosus* (as foll., see -OUS]

con'tumely, n. Insolent, reproachful, language or treatment; disgrace. [ME, f. OF *contumelie* f. L *contumelia*]

contūse' (-z), v.t. Injure by blow without breaking skin, bruise. So **contū'sion** (-zhn) n. [f. L CON(*tundere tus-* thump)]

conun'drum, n. Riddle; hard question. [orig. unkn.]

conurbā'tion, n. Aggregation of urban districts. [CON-, L *urbs urbis* city, -ATION]

convalésce', v.i. Regain health. [ME, f. L CON(*valescere* incept. of *valēre* be well)]

convalés'c|ent, a. & n. (Person) recovering from sickness; ~*ent hospital* (for ~ents). So ~ENCE n. ['as prec., see -ENT]

convéc't|ion, n. Transportation of heat or electricity, by movement of heated or electrified substance. Hence ~OR n., heating apparatus for circulating warm air. [f. LL *convectio* f. CON(*vehere vect-* carry), see -ION]

convenance (see Ap.), n. (usu. pl.). Conventional propriety. [F]

conven|e', v.t. & i. Assemble (t. & i.); convoke (assembly); summon (person *before* tribunal). Hence ~'ABLE a. [ME, f. OF *convenir* or L CON(*venire vent-* come) assemble, agree, fit]

conven'ience, n. Suitableness, commodiousness; material advantage, as *marriage of* ~; personal comfort, as *at your* ~, in a way, at a time, convenient to you; advantage, as *a great* ~; *make a* ~ of one, utilize him unconscionably, abuse his good nature; useful appliance; ǁ water-closet; (arch.) vehicle; (pl.) material comforts. [f. L *convenientia* (as prec., see -ENCE)]

conven'ient, a. Suitable, commodious; not troublesome, as *if it is* ~ *to you.* Hence ~LY² adv. [as CONVENE, see -ENT]

con'vent, n. Religious community (usu. women, cf. MONASTERY) living together; building occupied by this. [ME & AF *covent* = OF *convent* f. L *conventus* (as prec.), to wh. later (16th c.), sp. conforms]

ǁ **conven'ticle,** n. (hist.). Clandestine religious meeting, esp. of Nonconformists or Dissenters; building used for this. [f. L *conventiculum* (place of) assembly, dim. as prec.]

convĕn′tion, n. Act of convening; formal assembly, esp. (Eng. Hist.) of Parliament without summons of King, 1660 & 1688; agreement between parties; general (often tacit) consent; practice based on this; accepted method of play (in leading, bidding, etc.) in various card games. [ME, f. OF or f. L *conventio* (as CONVENE, see -ION)]

convĕn′tional (-sho-), a. Depending on convention, not natural, not spontaneous; (Art) following traditions; (of bombs, weapons, etc.) other than atomic. Hence ~ISM, ~IST, ~ITY (-ăl²), nn., ~IZE v.t., ~LY² adv. [f. F *conventionnel* or LL *conventionalis*]

convĕn′tionarў (-sho-), a. & n. (Tenant, tenure) on terms orig. fixed by convention, not by custom. [f. med. L *conventionarius* (as prec., -ARY¹)]

convĕn′tŭal, a. & n. (Member, inmate) of a convent; (member) of the less strict branch of Franciscans, living in large convents. [f. med. L *conventualis* (as CONVENT, see -AL; cf. F *conventuel*)]

convērge′, v.i. & t. (Of lines) tend to meet in a point (also fig.); (Math., of series) approximate in the sum of its terms towards a definite limit; (trans.) cause to ~. So **convēr′gENCE, -ENCY**, nn., **convēr′gENT** a. [f. LL CON(*vergere* VERGE)]

convērs′ab|le, a. Easy, pleasant, in conversation; fit for social intercourse. Hence ~leNESS n., ~LY² adv. [F, f. med. L *conversabilis* (as foll., see -BLE)]

cŏn′versance, -cў, n. Familiarity, acquaintance, (*with*). [as foll., see -ANCE]

cŏn′versant, a. Having frequent intercourse, well acquainted, (*with* person, subject, etc.); (of things) concerned (*in, about, with*). [ME, f. OF f. L *conversari* CONVERSE¹, see -ANT]

cŏnversā′tion, n. Talk, whence ~IST (-sho-) n.; ~ (*piece*), kind of genre painting of group of figures; sexual intercourse, as *criminal* ~ (*crim. con.*, cf. CONNEXION). [OF, f. L *conversationem* (as prec., see -ATION)]

cŏnversā′tional (-sho-), a. Fond of, good at, pertaining to, conversation. Hence ~IST n., ~LY² adv. [-AL]

cŏnversaziōn′e (-äts-), n. (pl. *-nes, -ni* pr. -nē). Soirée given by learned or art society. [It., f. L as CONVERSATION]

convērse′¹, v.i. Talk (*with* person, *on, about,* subject). [f. OF *converser* f. L *conversari* keep company (with), frequent. as CONVERT¹]

cŏn′vērse², n. (arch.). Discourse; intercourse. [f. prec.]

cŏn′vērse³, a. & n. **1.** Opposite, contrary. **2.** n. (Logic) converted proposition; form of words produced by transposition of some terms of another (*he had learning without wealth* is the ~ of *he had wealth without learning*); (Math.) *this proposition is the* ~ *of the former* (assumes its conclu-

sion & proves its datum). Hence ~LY³ (-sl-) adv. [f. L p.p. *conversus*, see CONVERT¹]

convēr′sion (-shn), n. Transposition, inversion, esp. (Logic) of subject & predicate (*if no A is B, then by* ~ *no B is A*); bringing over (*to* an opinion, party, faith, etc.); turning of sinners to God; changing (*to, into*); change (of debentures, stocks, etc.) into others of different character. [ME, f. OF, f. L *conversionem* (foll., -ION)]

convērt′¹, v.t. Change (*into*); cause to turn (*to* opinion, faith, etc.), cf. PERVERT; turn to godliness; (Stocks etc.) see prec.; (Logic) see prec.; (Rugby football) complete (a try) by kicking goal (also abs.). Hence ~ER¹ n., (esp.) large retort used in Bessemer steel process. [ME, f. OF *convertir* f. Rom. **convertire* for L CON(*vertere vers-* turn) turn about; in some senses dir. f. L]

cŏn′vērt², n. Person converted, esp. to religious faith or life. [f. prec.]

convērt′ible, a. & n. **1.** That may be converted; (of terms) synonymous; (of currency etc.) that may be converted into gold or dollars; (of motor-car etc.) capable of being converted from one class or type to another; ~ *husbandry*, rotation of crops. **2.** n. A ~ motor-car etc. Hence **convērtiBIL′ITY** n., **convērt′-ibLY²** adv. [OF, f. L *convertibilis* (as prec., see -BLE)]

cŏn′vĕx, a. Curved like the outside of circle or sphere (cf. CONCAVE). Hence or cogn. **convĕx′ITY** n., ~LY² adv. [f. L *convexus*]

convĕx′o- in comb. Convex and —, as ~*-concave*. [as prec., see -o-]

convey′ (-vā), v.t. Transport, carry; transmit (sound, smell, etc.); impart, communicate, (idea, meaning); (Law) make over (property *to,* or abs.). Hence ~ABLE (-ā′a-) a. ~ER¹ (-ā′er), ~OR (-ā′or), nn., (esp.) mechanical contrivance for ~ing heavy articles or materials (*coal--er; ~or belt*). [ME, f. OF CON*veier*, mod. *convoyer* CONVOY¹ (*veie, voie,* f. L *via* way)]

convey′ance (-ā′a-), n. Carrying; transmission; communication (of ideas etc.); (document effecting) transference of property; carriage, vehicle. [-ANCE]

convey′ancer (-ā′a-), n. Lawyer who prepares documents for conveyance of property. [-ER¹]

convey′ancing (-ā′a-), n. Work of prec. [-ING¹]

cŏn′vict¹, n. Condemned criminal undergoing penal servitude. Hence ~ISM(3) n. [f. obs. adj. *convict* (as foll.)]

convict′², v.t. Prove guilty (*of* offence); declare guilty by verdict of jury or decision of judge; impress (person) with sense of error. Hence **convic′tIVE** a. [ME, f. L CON(*vincere vict-* conquer)]

convic′tion, n. Proving or finding guilty; summary ~ (by judge or magistrates without jury); act of convincing; settled belief; (Theol.) awakened consciousness of sin. [f. LL *convictio* (as prec., see -ION)]

convinc|e', v.t. Firmly persuade (*of, that*; esp. pass.); produce in (person) a moral conviction (*of* sin etc.). Hence ~e'MENT (-sm-), ~'ingNESS, nn., ~'ingLY² adv. [as CONVICT²]

convin'cible, a. Open to conviction. [f. LL *convincibilis* (as prec., see -IBLE)]

conviv'ial, a. Of, befitting, a feast; festive, jovial. Hence~IST, **convivial'ITY**, nn., ~LY² adv. [f. L *convivialis* f. *convivium* feast]

convoca'tion, n. Calling together; assembly; || (Ch. of Eng.) synod of clergy of province of Canterbury or York; || legislative assembly of Oxford or Durham Univ. Hence~AL(-sho-)a. [ME, f. L *convocatio* (as foll., -ATION)]

convoke', v.t. Call together, summon to assemble. [f. L CON(*vocare* call)]

cŏn'volute (-ōōt), a. & n. (bot., conch.). Rolled together, coiled; (n.) coil. [as CONVOLVE]

cŏn'volutĕd (-ōōt-), a. (zool.). Coiled, twisted. [f. vb *convolute* (as prec.), otherwise rare]

convolu'tion (-ōō-), n. Coiling, twisting; fold, twist. [as foll., see -ION]

convŏlve', v.t. & i. Roll together, roll up, (esp. in p.p.). [f. L CON(*volvere volutroll*)]

convŏl'vŭlus, n. (pl. *-luses*). Kinds of twining plant including bindweed. [L, as prec. with dim. suf.]

convoy'¹, v.t. (Of ship or war) escort (merchant or passenger vessel); escort with armed force; (arch.) conduct (guests, lady, etc.). [ME, f. OF *convoier*, var. of *conveier* CONVEY]

cŏn'voy², n. Act of convoying; protection; escort (for honour or protection); company, supply of provisions, etc., under escort; number of merchant ships sailing in company under escort. [f. F *convoi* f. *convoier* (prec.)]

convulse', v.t. Shake violently (lit. & fig.); throw into convulsions (usu. pass.); cause to be violently seized with laughter (usu. pass.). [f. L CON(*vellere vuls-* pull)]

convul'sion (-shn), n. Violent irregular motion of limb or body due to involuntary contraction of muscles (usu. pl., & esp. as a disorder of infants); (pl.) violent fit of laughter; violent social or political agitation; violent physical disturbance. Hence ~ARY¹ (-sho-) a. [F, or f. L *convulsio* (as prec., see -ION)]

convul'sive, a. Attended or affected with, producing, convulsions (lit. & fig.). Hence~LY² (-vl-) adv. [CONVULSE, -IVE]

cŏn'ȳ, **-ney**, n.·(pl. *-ies, -eys*). Rabbit (now used only in statutes etc., & as shop name for the fur); (Bibl.) hyrax; (arch.) ~-*catcher*, sharper. [ME *cunin* f. OF *conin-*, parallel form of *conil* (f. L *cuni-*

culus), pl. *coniz, conis*, whence ME *conies* (pl.), whence sing. *cony*]

cōō, v.i. & t., & n. (Make) soft murmuring sound of or as of doves & pigeons; *bill & ~*, converse amorously; say ~ingly. [imit.]

cōō'ee, **cōō'ey**, n., & v.i. (Make) sound adopted as signal by Australian settlers from the aborigines. [imit.]

cŏŏk¹, n. One whose business is to cook food; *too many ~s spoil the broth*, one director is enough; **~-book*, cookery book; ~-*house*, camp kitchen, outdoor kitchen in warm countries, (on ship, also ~-*room*) galley; ~-*shop*, eating-house. [OE *cōc* f. pop. L *cōcus* for L *cŏquus*]

cŏŏk², v.t. & i. Prepare (food or abs.) by heat; (v.i.) undergo ~ing; (also ~ *up*) concoct (fig.); (colloq.) tamper with (accounts etc.); || (sl., of exertion etc.) exhaust (runner etc., esp. in p.p.); ~ *his goose*, do for him, settle his hash. [prec.]

cŏŏk'er, n. Cooking-apparatus, -stove; vessel food is cooked in; fruit etc. that cooks well; one who cooks (accounts etc.) or concocts. [-ER¹]

cŏŏk'erȳ, n. Art, practice, of cooking; ~-*book* (dealing with ~). [-ERY]

cŏŏk'ie, n. (Sc.) plain bun; **small flat cake, biscuit. [f. Du. *koekje* dim. of *koek* cake]

cŏŏk'ȳ, n. (colloq.). (Usu. female) cook. [-Y³]

cōōl¹, a. & n. Moderately cold; (Hunt.) ~ *scent* (faint, weak); unexcited, calm; lacking zeal, lukewarm; wanting cordiality; calmly audacious, as *a ~ hand* (person); (complacently or emphat. of large sums of money) *it cost me a ~ thousand*; (n.) ~ air, ~ place, ~ness; ~-*headed*, not easily excited; ~ *tankard*, ~ing drink of wine, water, lemon-juice, etc. Hence ~'ISH¹ a., ~'LY² (-l-li) adv., ~'NESS n. [OE *cōl* f. Gmc **kōluz* f. **kōl-*, ablaut f. **kal-*, see COLD]

cōōl², v.i. & t. Become cool (lit. & fig.; also ~ *down*); make cool (lit. & fig.); ~ one's COPPERS; ~ one's *heels*, be kept waiting. [OE *cōlian* (f. prec.)]

cōōl'ant, n. Liquid applied to edge of cutting tool etc. to lessen friction. [COOL¹, -ANT]

cōōl'er, n. Vessel in which a thing is cooled, as *wine, butter*, ~; **refrigerator; (sl.) prison cell. [-ER¹]

cōōl'ie, **-lȳ**, n. Indian or Chinese hired labourer. [f. Hind. *quli*]

cōōlth, n. (now colloq. or joc.). Coolness. [f. COOL¹, after *warmth*]

|| **coomb**, || **combe** (kōōm), n. Valley on flank of hill; short valley running up from coast; CWM. [OE *cumb*; cf. W *cwm* valley]

*****cōōn**, n. = RAC(C)OON; sly fellow; (contempt.) a Negro; *gone ~*, one whose case is hopeless. [abbr.]

For compounds of co- not given consult CO-.

cōon'-căn', n. (Also *conquian*) simple two-handed card-game (orig. Mexican). [f. Sp. *con quien* with whom?]

cōop [1], n. Basket placed over sitting or fattening fowls; fowl-run; ‖ basket used in catching fish. [ME *cupe* basket f. MDu., MLG *kūpe*, ult. f. L *cūpa* cask]

cōop [2], v.t. Put in coop; confine (persons; also ~ *up*, *in*). [f. prec.]

‖ **cō-ŏp'**, n. (colloq.). Co-operative society or store. [abbr.]

cōop'er [1], n., & v.t. Maker of casks for dry goods (*dry* ~) or liquids (*wet* ~); *white* ~, maker of pails, tubs, etc.; (on ship) repairer of casks etc.; (also *wine*-~) one who samples, bottles, or retails wine; equal mixture of stout & porter; (v.t.) repair (cask), stow in casks, furbish *up*. [f. MDu., MLG *kūper* f. *kūpe* COOP [1]; see -ER [1]]

cooper [2], see COPER [2].

cōop'erage. n. Cooper's work or workshop. So **cōop'ERY(3)** n. [-AGE]

cō(-)ŏp'er|āte, v.i. Work together (*with* person *in* a work, *to* an end); (of things) concur in producing an effect. So ~ANT a. & n., ~ātor n. [f. LL CO(*operari* f. *opus operis* work), see -ATE [3]]

cō(-)ŏperā'tion, n. Working together to same end; (Pol. Econ.) co-operative combination. [ME, f. L *cooperatio* (as prec., see -ION); partly thr. F -*tion*]

cō(-)ŏp'erative, a. Of, tending to, co-operation; (Pol. Econ.)~ *society* (for production or distribution of goods, profits being shared by members), ~ *store* (belonging to ~ society). Hence ~LY [2] (-vl-) adv. [f. LL *cooperativus* (as prec., see -IVE)]

cō-ŏpt', v.t. Elect into body by votes of existing members. So **cō-ŏptA'TION** n. [f. L CO(*optare* choose)]

cō-ōrd'inate [1], a. & n. **1.** Equal in rank, esp. (Gram.) of clauses of compound ·sentence (cf. SUBORDINATE); consisting of ~ things. **2.** n. ~ thing, esp. (Math.) each of a system of magnitudes used to fix position of point, line, or plane. Hence ~LY [2] (-tl-) adv. [f. CO-+L *ordinare* (*ordo* -*inis* or.ier), see -ATE [2]]

cō-ōrd'in|āte [2], v.t. Make co-ordinate; bring (parts) into proper relation. Hence ~A'TION n., ~ātIVE a. [prec., -ATE [3]]

cōot, n. Name of several swimming & diving birds, esp. the *bald* ~, web-·footed bird with base of bill extended to form white plate on forehead, whence *bald as a* ~. [ME *cote*, *coote*, corresp. to Du. *koet*; ult. orig. unkn.]

cōot'ie, n. (Army sl.). Body-louse. [perh. f. Hind. *khuthi* scab]

cŏp [1], n. (spinning). Conical ball of thread wound upon spindle. [OE *cop* top]

cŏp [2], n. (sl.). Policeman. [cf. foll., COPPER [2]]

cŏp [3], v.t. (-pp-), & n., (sl.). **1.** Catch (~ *it*, catch it, be punished). **2.** n. Capture (chiefly in phr. *a fair* ~). [etym. unkn.]

copai'ba, -**va**, (-pī-, -pä-), n. Aromatic balsam used in medicine & the arts. [(-*ba*) Sp., f. Braz. *cupauba*]

cŏp'al, n. Kinds of resin used for varnish. [Sp., f. Mex. *copalli* incense]

cōpăr'cĕnary̆, -**ery̆**, **cōpăr'CENER**, nn. = PARCENARY, PARCENER. [CO-]

cōpărt'ner, n. Partner, sharer, associate. Hence ~SHIP n. (*labour* ~*ship*, system designed to interest workmen in their business by means of profit-sharing). [CO-]

cōpărt'nery̆, n. Copartnership. [f. prec., see -ERY(2)]

cōpe [1], n. (Eccl.) long cloak worn by ecclesiastics in processions; (fig.) ~ (cloak) *of night*, ~ (canopy) *of heaven*; (Founding) outer portion of mould; = COPING; ~-*stone*, head stone of building, finishing touch. [ME *cāpe*, *cŏpe*, repr. OE -*cāp*, *cāpe* (= ON *kápa*), f. med. L *cāpa* var. of LL *cappa* CAP [1], CAPE [1]]

cōpe [2], v.t. & i. Furnish with a cope; cover (wall etc.) with COPING; cover as with a vault; (v.i.) ~ *over*, project like a coping. [f. prec.]

cōpe [3], v.i. Contend evenly, grapple successfully, *with* (person, task). [f. OF *coper*, *colper*, (mod. F *couper*); see COUP]

cŏp'ĕck, n. Russian copper coin (the hundredth part of a rouble). [f. Russ. *kopeika* dim. of *kopyé* lance]

‖ **cŏp'er** [1], n. (Also *horse*-~) horse-dealer. [f. obs. *cope* buy, f. MDu., MLG *köpen* (cogn. w. CHEAP), +-ER [1]]

cŏp'er [2], **coop'er** [2] (kō-), n. Floating grog-shop for North Sea fishers. [f. Flem. & Du. *kooper* f. *koopen* buy (prec.)]

Copĕr'n'ican, a. ~ *system*, *theory*, (that the planets, including earth, move round sun). [f. *Copernicus* latinized f. *Kopper-nik*, astronomer (d. 1543)+-AN]

cŏp'ing, n. Top (usu. sloping) course of masonry in wall; overhanging ledge protecting wall-fruit; ~·*stone* (used for ~). [COPE [2] +-ING [1]]

cŏp'ious, a. Plentiful; abounding in information; profuse in speech; (of languages) having large vocabulary. Hence ~LY [2] adv., ~NESS n. [ME, f. OF *copious* or L *copiosus* (*copia* plenty, see -OUS)]

cŏpŏl'y̆mer, n. Compound analogous to a polymer but with units of more than one kind. So ~IZE(3) v.t., ~īZA'TION n. [CO-, POLYMER]

cŏpp'er [1], n., a., & v.t. **1.** Reddish malle-able ductile metal; bronze (formerly ~) coin, penny, halfpenny, farthing; cooking or laundry boiler of iron or ~; *hot* ~*s*, mouth & throat parched by drinking; *cool* ~*s* (by drinking); ~ *beech* (kind with ~-coloured leaves); ~-*bit*, soldering tool pointed with ~; ~-*bottom* v.t., sheathe bottom of (ship) with ~ (esp. in p.p.);‖~*captain*, sham captain; ~ *Indian*, red Indian of N. America; ~*head*, venomous American snake; ~*plate*, polished ~ plate for engraving or etching, print from this, (adj., of writing) neat; ~-*smith*, one who works in ~. **2. v.t.** Cover (ship's bottom etc.) with ~. Hence ~Y² a. (esp., ~-coloured). [OE *coper*, ON *kopar* f. **kupar* (also **kuppar* whence OHG *kupfar*) f. LL *cuprum* for L *cyprium aes* Cyprian metal]

‖ **cŏpp'er²**, n. (sl.). Policeman. [cf. COP²]

cŏpp'eras, n. Sulphate of iron, green vitriol. [15th c. *coperose* f. OF *couperose* f. med. L *cup(e)rosa* perh. = *aqua cuprosa* copper water]

cŏpp'ice, n. Small wood of underwood & small trees, grown for periodical cutting; ~-*wood*, underwood. [f. OF *copeiz* f. Rom. **colpaticium* f. **colpare* cut f. med. L *col(a)pus* f. L f. Gk *kolaphos* blow, cuff]

cŏp'ra, n. Dried kernels of coconut. [Port., prob. f. Malayalam *koppara* coconut]

cŏp'ro- in comb. = Gk *kopros* dung, as: -*lite*, fossil dung, so -*lit'ic* a.; -*logy* (-ŏl²), treatment of filthy subjects in literature etc.; -*phagous* (-ŏf²), (of beetles) dung-eating.

‖ **cŏpse**, n., & v.t. = COPPICE; ~'*wood*, underwood; (v.t.) treat as ~wood, cover with ~s. Hence **cŏp'sY²** a. [syncop. form of COPPICE]

Cŏpt, n. Native Egyptian Christian of Jacobite sect of Monophysites. [f. F *copte*; earlier (*c.* 1600) *Coptie, Cophl(i)e* f. Arab. *quft, qufti*, f. Copt. *gyptios, kyptaios*, f. Gk *Aiguptios* Egyptian]

Cŏp'tic, a. & n. (Language) of the Copts. [-IC]

cŏp'ŭl|a, n. (Logic, Gram.) verb *be* (as mere sign of predication); (Anat.) connecting part (bone, cartilage, ligament); (Mus.) short connecting passage. Hence ~AR¹ a. [L]

cŏp'ŭl|āte, v.i. Unite sexually. Hence ~atORY a. [f. L *copulare* fasten together (prec.), see -ATE³]

cŏpŭlā'tion, n. Sexual union; grammatical or logical connexion. [ME, f. OF or L *copulatio* (as prec., see -ION)]

cŏp'ŭlātive, a. & n. Serving to connect; (Gram.) connecting words or clauses that are connected in sense (cf. DISJUNCTIVE); also, connecting subject & predicate; (Zool., Anat.) relating to sexual union; (n.) ~ conjunction or particle. Hence ~LY² (-vl-) adv. [ME, f. OF (-*if*, -*ive*), or LL *copulativus* (as prec., see -IVE)]

cŏp'ȳ¹, n. Reproduction (of writing, picture, etc.); imitation; page written after model (of penmanship); ‖ (Law) transcript of manorial court-roll, containing entries of admissions of tenants to land hence called COPYHOLD; written or printed specimen (of book etc.); *rough, foul,* ~, original draft; *fair, clean,* ~ (transcribed from rough ~); ~ *of verses,* short set as school exercise; *fair* ~, model version of this; *model* to be copied; manuscript or matter to be printed (*in-*

cident etc. *will make good* ~, lends itself to interesting narration in newspapers etc.); ~-*book*, one containing copies for learners to imitate (BLOT² one's ~-*book*); ~-*book maxims, morality* (commonplace); ~-*writer*, one who writes or prepares advertising ~ for publication. [ME, f. OF *copie* f. L *copia* abundance &c., in med. L = transcript, from phr. *facere copiam describendi* give permission to transcribe]

cŏp'ȳ², v.t. & i. Transcribe (*from* original), whence ~IST n.; make copy of; imitate; crib from neighbour in examination; ~-*cat* (colloq.), slavish imitator. [ME, f. OF *copier* f. med. L *copiare* (as prec.)]

‖ **cŏp'ȳhōld**, n. & a. Tenure by COPY¹; (land) so held. Hence ~ER¹ n.

cŏp'ȳright (-rīt), n. & a., & v.t. Exclusive right given by law for term of years to author, designer, etc., or his assignee to print, publish, or sell, copies of his original work; (adj.) protected by ~ (of books etc.); (v.t.) secure ~ for (book etc.).

coque (kŏk), n. Small loop of ribbon; (in mod. use, pr. kŏk, attrib.) applied to feathers used in trimming, in boas, etc. [F, = a shell]

coquet'¹ (-kĕt), a. Coquettish. [F (orig. noun, dim. of *coq* cock)]

coquet'², coquette', (-kĕt), v.i. (-tt-). Play the coquette; flirt (*with*); dally, trifle, *with* (matter, proposal, etc.). [f. F *coqueter* f. prec.]

co'quetrȳ (-kĭt-), n. Coquettish behaviour or act; (fig.) trifling; attractive prettiness as result of art. [f. F *coquetterie* (*coqueter*, as prec., see -ERY)]

coquett|e' (-kĕt), n. Woman who trifles with man's affections; crested humming-bird. Hence ~'ISH¹ a., ~'ishLY² adv., (-kĕt-). [F, fem. of COQUET]

coqui'tŏ (-kē-), n. Chilian palm-tree yielding palm-honey. [Sp., dim. of *coco* coconut]

cor-, pref. = COM- before *r*.

‖ **cŏ'racle**, n. Wicker boat covered with watertight material used on Welsh & Irish lakes & rivers. [f. W *cwrwgl* f. *cwrwg* = Ir. *curach* boat]

cŏ'raco- in comb. (anat.). Of the *coracoid process* (beak-shaped process extending from shoulder-blade towards breast-bone). [f. Gk *korax -akos* crow]

cŏ'ral, n. & a. Hard calcareous substance (red, pink, white, etc.) secreted by many tribes of marine polyps for support & habitation; ~-*reef*, accumulation of this; toy of polished ~ for children cutting teeth; unimpregnated roe of lobster; (adj.) like ~, esp. red; ~-*island* (formed by growth of ~); ~-*rag*, limestone containing beds of petrified ~s. [ME, f. OF f. L *corallum* f. Gk *korallion*]

coralli- in comb. Coral, as -*ferous, -form,* bearing, shaped like, coral. [as prec., see -I-]

For compounds of *co-* not given consult co-.

cŏ'ralline[1], n. Kinds of seaweeds with calcareous jointed stem; (pop.) name of various plant-like compound animals; ~ zone of sea-depths, that in which these abound. [f. It. *corallina* dim. of *corallo* CORAL]

cŏ'ralline[2] (-ĭ-, -ĭ-), a. Coral-red; ~ *ware*, Italian red-paste pottery (17th–18th c.); like, composed of, coral. [F, or f. L *corallinus* (CORAL, -INE[1])]

cŏ'rallite, n. Fossil coral; coral skeleton of polyp; coralline marble. [-ITE[1]]

cŏ'ralloid, a. & n. (Organism) like, akin to, coral. [-OID]

cŏr'ăm prep. (w. abl. case). In the presence of (*judice*, (jōōd'ĭsĭ), a judge, *pŏp'ŭlō*, the public, etc.). [L]

cor anglais (kŏr ahng'glā), n. The alto oboe. [F, = English horn]

cŏrb'el, n., & v.t. & i. (-ll-). (Archit.) projection of stone, timber, etc., jutting out from wall to support weight, whence ~lED[2] (-ld) a.; (also ~-*block*) short timber laid on wall or pier longitudinally under beam; ~-*table*, projecting course resting on ~s; (v.t. & i.) ~ *out*, *off*, (cause to) project on ~s. [ME, f. OF dim. of *corp* (foll.); see -LE[2]]

cŏrb'ie, n. (Sc.). Raven; carrion crow; ~-*steps*, step-like projections on sloping sides of gable. [ME, f. OF *corbet*, -*in* (dim. of *corp* f. L *corvus* crow) + -Y[3]]

cŏrd, n., & v.t. Thin rope, thick string; (Anat.) ~-like structure in animal body, as SPINAL, UMBILICAL, ~, VOCAL ~s; ~-like rib on cloth; ribbed cloth, esp. corduroy; ~-s, corduroy breeches or trousers; measure of cut wood (usu. 128 cub. ft); (fig.) ~s of discipline, fourfold ~ of evidence, etc.; (v.t.) bind with ~. [ME, f. OF *corde* f. L f. Gk *khordē* gut, string of musical instrument]

cŏrd'age, n. Cords, ropes, esp. in rigging of ship. [F (as prec. + -AGE)]

cŏrd'āte, a. Heart-shaped. [f. L *cor cordis* heart, see -ATE[2]]

cŏrd'ĕd, a. Bound with cords; furnished with cords; (of cloth etc.) ribbed. [-ED[2,1]]

cŏrdèlier', n. Franciscan friar of strict rule (wearing knotted cord round waist). [ME, f. OF *cordeler*, -*ier* (*cordele* dim. as CORD, see -IER)]

cŏrd'ial, a. & n. (Medicine, food, drink) that stimulates the heart, esp. (Commerc.) aromatized & sweetened spirit; hearty, sincere; warm, friendly, whence ~ITY[1] (-ăl[t]) n., ~LY[2] adv. [ME, f. med. L *cordialis* (*cor cordis* heart, -AL)]

cŏrdiller'a (-lyā'ra), n. Mountain ridge (one of parallel series), esp. of the Andes & same system in Central America & Mexico. [Sp.]

cŏrd'ite, n. A smokeless explosive. [f. CORD (from its appearance) + -ITE[1](2)]

cŏrd'on, n., & v.t. Projecting course of stone in wall; chain of military posts; line or circle of police etc.; (also *sanitary*

~) guarded line between infected & uninfected districts; ornamental cord or braid; (pron. as F) ribbon of knightly order (~ *bleu*, see Ap., joc., first-class cook); fruit-tree pruned to grow as single stem; (v.t., also ~ *off*) enclose with (military, police, etc.) ~. [16th c. *cordone* f. It.: later f. F *cordon* (as CORD, see -OON)]

cŏrd'ovan, a. & n. (Leather) of Cordova. [f. Sp. *cordovan(o)*]

cŏrd'uroy, n. & a. Coarse thick ribbed cotton stuff, orig. worn chiefly by labourers; (pl.) ~ trousers; *~ road*, of tree-trunks laid across swamp. [late 18th c., app. f. *cord* ribbed fabric; remainder uncert.]

cŏrd'wain, n. (arch.). Spanish leather formerly used for shoes. [ME *cordewan(e)*, *corduan(e)*, f. OF *corduan*, -*ewan* of Cordova]

cŏrd'wainer, n. Shoemaker (now only as guild-name etc.). [AF *cordewaner*, OF *cordouanier* (prec., see -ER[2])]

cōre, n., & v.t. Horny capsule containing seeds of apple, pear, etc.; central part cut out (esp. of rock in boring); bar of soft iron forming centre of electro-magnet or induction coil; internal mould filling space to be left hollow in a casting; central strand of rope; innermost part, as (fig.) *rotten at the ~, English to the ~*; heart; a disease, tumour, in sheep; (v.t.) remove ~ from, whence cōr'ER[1](2) n. Hence ~'LESS (-rl-) a. [ME *core*, of unkn. orig.]

cō'rela'tion. See CORRELATION.

cō-rēli'gionist (-jo-), n. Adherent of same religion. [-IST]

cŏreŏp'sis, n. Plant with rayed usu. yellow flowers. [mod. L, f. Gk *koris* bug, *opsis* appearance, w. ref. to shape of seed]

cō-rĕspŏn'dent, n. Person proceeded against together with the RESPONDENT in divorce suit. [CO-]

‖ **cŏrf**, n. Large basket formerly used in mining; basket in which fish are kept alive in water. [f. MDu., MLG *korf* (= G *korb*) f. L *corbis*]

cŏrg'i (-gĭ), -**gў**, n. Small Welsh dog. [W]

cŏriā'ceous (-shus), a. Like leather, leathery. [f. LL *coriaceus* (*corium* leather, see -ACEOUS)]

cŏriăn'der, n. Annual plant with aromatic fruit (pop. called ~ *seed*) used for flavouring. [ME, f. OF *coriandre* f. L *coriandrum* f. Gk *koriannon*]

Corin'thian, a. & n. (Native) of Corinth; (arch.) man of fashion & pleasure; *Epistles to the ~s*, books in N.T.; (Archit.) ~ *order*, one of the three Grecian ORDERS, having bell-shaped capital with rows of acanthus leaves, whence ~ESQUE' a. [f. L f. Gk *Korinthios* (*Korinthos*) + -AN]

cŏrk, n. & a., & v.t. **1.** Bark of ~-oak (~-*tree*) of W. Europe; piece of ~ used as float for fishing line etc. (*like a ~*, buoyant, recovering quickly from depression etc.); bottle-stopper of ~; (Bot.) inner division of the bark in higher plants; (adj.) made of ~, as ~ *jacket* (for supporting person in water); ~*screw*, steel screw for drawing ~ from bottle, ~*screw curl* (spirally twisted), (v.t. & i.) move spirally; ~'*wood*, name of various light porous woods. **2.** v.t. Stop, stop *up*, (as) with ~, blacken with burnt ~. [ME, f. Du., LG *kork*, f. Sp.-Arab. *alcorque*, of unkn. orig.]

cōrk'age, n. Corking, uncorking, of bottles; hotel-keeper's charge for serving wine etc. not supplied by himself. [-AGE]

cōrked (-kt), a. Stopped with, blackened with burnt, cork; (of wine) gone bad from defective corking. [-ED[1]]

cōrk'er, n. (sl.). Something that puts an end to a discussion, something astonishing, e.g. a monstrous lie, a 'whopper'. [-ER[1]]

cōrk'ў, a. Cork-like; (colloq.) frivolous, lively, skittish, restive. [-Y[2]]

cōrm, n. (bot.). Bulb-like subterraneous stem, solid bulb. [f. Gk *kormos* trunk with boughs lopped off (*keirō* cut)]

cormo- in comb. Trunk, stem, (in terms referring to evolution of races etc.). [as prec.]

cōrm'orant, n. Large lustrous-black voracious sea-bird; rapacious person. [ME, f. OF *cormaran* f. med. L *corvus marinus* sea-raven; for ending -*ant* cf. *peasant, tyrant*]

cōrn[1], n. A grain, seed, esp. of cereals (also of pepper etc.); (collect. sing.) grain, also cereal plants while growing; *maize, Indian ~; ‖~-*chandler*, retail dealer in ~; ~-*cob*, part to which grains are attached in ear of maize; ~-*cob pipe* (made of this); ~-COCKLE[1]; ~'*crake*, the bird landrail; ~-*exchange* (for trade in ~); ‖~-*factor*, dealer in ~; ~-*flag*, plant of genus Gladiolus; ‖~'*flour*, fine-ground Indian~, also, flour of rice or other grain; ~'*flower*, name of various plants growing among ~; ‖~-*laws* (regulating ~-trade, esp. the English laws restricting importation, and repealed in 1846); ~ *marigold*, yellow-flowered ~field weed; ‖~-*rent* (paid in ~ or varying with price of ~); ‖~-*stalk* (colloq.), tall person (applied as nickname to persons of European descent born in Australia, esp. in N.S.W.). [OE *corn*, OS, OHG, ON *korn*, Goth. *kaurn* f. Gmc *kurnam cogn. w. L *granum*]

cōrn[2], v.t. Sprinkle, preserve, with salt (esp. in p.p.). [f. prec.]

cōrn[3], n. Horny place esp. on feet; *tread on my* ~s, hurt my feelings; ~-*plaster* (for application to ~s). [ME, f. OF f. L *cornu* horn]

cōrn'brăsh, n. (geol.). Coarse calcareous sandstone. [f. CORN[1]+BRASH[1]]

cōrn'ĕa, n. Transparent horny part of anterior covering of eyeball. [med. L *cornea* (*tela*) horny (web)]

cōrn'el, n. Genus including cornelian cherry & *common* ~ or dogwood. [ult. f. L *cornus*]

cōrnĕl'ian, cār-, n. Dull red or reddish-white chalcedony. [ME & OF *corneline*, refash. after med. L *cornelius*, earlier *corneolus*; cf. CARNELIAN]

cōrn'ĕous, a. Horn-like, horny. [f. L *corneus* (*cornu* horn) + -OUS]

cōrn'er, n., & v.t. & i. **1.** Place where converging sides or edges meet; projecting angle, esp. where two streets meet; *turn the* ~, pass round it into another street, (fig.) pass critical point (in illness etc.); *cut off a* ~, avoid it by a short cut; ‖ (sl.) *the C*~, Tattersall's betting-rooms (orig. near Hyde Park C~); hollow angle enclosed by meeting walls etc.; *put* (child) *in the* ~ (as punishment); (fig.) *drive into a* ~ (difficult position from which there is no escape). **2.** Secret or remote place, as *done in a* ~, *hole-&-*~ *transactions* (underhand); region, quarter, as *all the* ~*s of the earth*. **3.** (Commerc.) buying up the whole of any stock in the market, so as to compel speculative sellers to buy from one to fulfil their engagements, (loosely) any combination to raise price by securing monopoly. **4.** (Association football and Hockey) free kick, hit, from the ~-*flag* given when the ball has been kicked, hit, over his own goal-line by an opponent. **5.** ~-*chisel*, -*punch*, etc. (angular, for cutting, etc., ~s); ‖~-*boy*, -*man*[1], street rough, loafer; ‖~-*man*[2] (at either end of row of nigger minstrels, playing bones or tambourine & contributing comic effects); ~-*stone*, one in projecting angle of wall, foundation stone, (fig.) indispensable part, basis. **6.** v.t. Furnish with ~s, set in ~, drive into ~ (esp. fig.), force (dealers) or control (commodity) by means of ~. **7.** v.i. Form ~ (in commodity). [ME, f. AF *corner* (OF -*ier*, -*ierc*) f. Rom. *cornarium, -*ia* f. L *cornu* horn, see -ER[2](2)]

cōrn'ĕt[1], n. (Also *cornet-à-piston*(*s*), *cornopean*) brass musical instrument of trumpet class, with valves operated by pistons; ~-*player*, also ~IST n.; conically-rolled piece of paper for groceries etc.; conical wafer filled with ice-cream; *solo* ~, *echo* ~, organ-stops. [ME, f. OF *cornet*, dim. of Rom. *corno f. L *cornu* horn]

cōrn'ĕt[2], n. White head-dress of Sister of Charity; ‖ (formerly) fifth commissioned officer in cavalry troop, who carried the colours (from obs. sense *pennon, standard*), whence ~CY n. [f. F *cornette* dim. of *corne* f. Rom. *corna f. L *cornua* horns]

cōrn'ic|e, n. (Archit.) horizontal moulded projection crowning a building etc., esp. uppermost member of entablature of an

For compounds of *co-* not given consult CO-.

order, surmounting frieze; ornamental moulding round wall of room just below ceiling; (Mountaineering) overhanging mass of hardened snow at edge of precipice. Hence ~ED[2] {-st) a. [*cornice, -ish* f. F (16th c. *-ice, -isc, -iche*), f. It. *cornice*, prob. f. L *cornix -ic-* crow]

cŏrnif'erous, a. (geol.). Producing or containing hornstone. [f. L *cornifer* horn-bearing (*cornu* horn, see -FEROUS)]

Cŏrn'ish, a. & n. **1.** Of Cornwall; ~ *boiler*, cylindrical flue-boiler; ~ CHOUGH, PASTY[1]; ~ *Riviera*, coastal region of Cornwall, esp. the south coast. **2.** n. The ~ language (extinct since 18th c.). [-ISH[1]]

cŏrnōp'ēan. See CORNET[1].

cŏrn'stōne, n. Mottled red and green limestone, subordinate bed in Old Red Sandstone formation. [CORN[1]]

cŏrnŭcōp'ï|a, n. (pl. *-as*). Horn of plenty; goat's horn represented in art as overflowing with flowers, fruit, and corn; ornamental vessel shaped like this; overflowing store, whence ~AN a. [LL, f. L *cornu copiae* horn of plenty]

cŏrnŭt'ĕd, a. Having horns or horn-like projections. [f. obs. *cornute* f. L *cornutus* (*cornu* horn) + -ED[1]]

cŏrn'ÿ[1], a. Of, abounding in, corn. [-Y[2]]

cŏrn'ÿ[2], a. Of, having, corns; (sl., of jokes etc.) out of date, old-fashioned. [CORN[1] + -Y[2]]

corŏll'a, n. (bot.). Whorl of leaves (petals), separate or combined, forming inner envelope of flower. Hence **cŏrollA'ceous** (-ā'shŭs) a. [L, dim. of *corona* crown]

corŏll'arÿ, n. Proposition appended to one already demonstrated, as inference from it; immediate deduction; natural consequence, result. [f. L *corollarium* money paid for chaplet, gratuity, neut. adj. f. prec., -ARY[1]]

corōn'a[1], n. (pl. *-ae*). **1.** Small disc of light round sun or moon; similar disc opposite sun, ANTHELION; halo of white light seen around disc of moon in total eclipse of sun (now. known to belong to sun). **2.** Circular chandelier hung from roof of a church. **3.** (archit.). Member of cornice, with broad vertical face, usu. of considerable projection. **4.** (anat.). Various crown-like parts of body. **5.** (bot.). Appendage on top of seed or inner side of corolla. **6.** Brush discharge of electricity. [L, = crown]

corōn'a[2], n. A brand of Havana cigar. [Sp.; P]

‖ **cŏ'ronach** (-ăχ), n. Funeral-song, dirge, in Scottish Highlands and Ireland. [Ir., = Gael. *corranach* (*comh-* together + *ranach* outcry)]

cŏ'ronal[1], n. Circlet (esp. of gold or gems) for the head; wreath, garland. [ME, app. f. AF *coro(u)nal* f. *coroune* CROWN[1] + -AL]

corōn'al[2] (*also* kŏ̆²), a. (Anat.) ~ *suture*, transverse suture of skull separating frontal bone (~ *bone*) from parietal bones; of the crown of the head; (Bot.) of a

corona. [F, or f. L *coronalis* (CORONA[1], see -AL)]

cŏ'ronarÿ, a. (anat.). Resembling, encircling like, a crown (~ *arteries*, those that supply the tissues of the heart with blood; ~ THROMBOSIS). [f. L *coronarius* (*corona* crown, -ARY[1])]

cŏ'ronate, -ātĕd, aa. (bot. & zool.). Furnished with a corona or crown-shaped part. [f. L *coronare* (CORONA[1], see -ATE[2])]

cŏronā'tion, n. Ceremony of crowning sovereign or sovereign's consort; ~-*oath*, taken by sovereign at ~. [ME, f. OF f. med. L *coronationem* (as prec., -ATION)]

cŏ'roner, n. Officer of county, district, or municipality, holding inquest on bodies of persons supposed to have died by violence or accident; ~*'s inquest*, inquiry held by ~'s court as to cause of death; official holding inquiry in cases of treasure trove; (orig.) officer charged with maintaining rights of private property of crown. Hence ~SHIP n. [ME, f. AF *cor(o)uner* f. *coroune* CROWN, see -ER[2](2)]

cŏ'ronĕt, n. Small crown (implying dignity inferior to that of sovereign); fillet of precious materials, esp. as decorative part of woman's head-dress; garland; (Anat.) lowest part of horse's pastern. [f. OF *coronette* dim. of *corone* CROWN]

cŏ'ronĕtĕd, a. Wearing a coronet (esp. as belonging to peerage). [-ED[2]]

corōn'oid, a. (anat.). Curved like crow's beak (of processes of bones). [f. Gk *korōnē* crow + -OID]

coroz'ō, n. (pl. *-os*). S.-American tree, allied to palms; ~-*nut*, its seed, from which vegetable ivory is made. [native]

cŏrp'oral[1], a. Of the human body, as ~ *punishment*; personal; (arch.) ~ *oath*, one ratified by touching a sacred object. Hence ~LY[2] adv. [ME, f. OF f. L *corporalis* (*corpus -oris* body, see -AL)]

cŏrp'oral[2], -as, n. Cloth on which consecrated elements are placed during celebration of mass. [14th c. *-al*, f. med. L *corporale* (sc. *pallium*) body cloth (as prec.); so OF *corporaus*, whence ME *-aus*, later *corporas*]

cŏrp'oral[3], n. Non-commissioned officer ranking below sergeant (*the little C~*, Napoleon I); ‖ *ship's ~*, officer attending to police matters under master-at-arms. [obs. F, var. of *caporal* f. It. *caporale* prob. f. L *corporalis* (as prec.) confused w. *capo* head]

cŏrporăl'itÿ, n. Material existence; body; (pl.) bodily matters, wants, etc. [ME, f. LL *corporalitas* (as CORPORAL[1], see -TY)]

cŏrp'orate, a. Forming a body politic or corporation, as ~ *body, body ~*; ~ *town* (having municipal rights); forming one body of many individuals; of, belonging to, a body politic. Hence ~LY[2] (-tl-) adv. [f. L *corporare* form into a body (*corpus -oris*), see -ATE[2]]

cŏrporā'tion, n. United body of persons,

esp. one authorized to act as an individual; artificial person created by charter, prescription, or act of the legislature, comprising many persons (~ *aggregate*) or one (~ *sole*); *municipal* ~, civic authorities of borough, town, or city; (colloq.) abdomen, esp. when prominent. [f. LL *corporatio* (as prec., see -ATION)]

cŏrp'orative, a. Of a corporation. [f. CORPORATE + -IVE]

cŏrp'orātor, n. Member ŏf a corporation. [as CORPORATE, see -OR]

cŏrpŏr'ĕal, a. Bodily; material; (Law) tangible, as ~ *hereditament* (of material objects). Hence ~ITY (-ăl-) n., ~LY² adv. [f. LL *corporealis* f. L *corporeus* (*corpus* -*oris* body) + -AL]

cŏrporē'itў, n. Quality of being or having a material body; bodily substance. [f. med. L *corporeitas* (as prec., see -TY)]

cŏrp'osant (-z-), n. Ball of light sometimes seen on ship during storm, St Elmo's fire. [f. OSp., It. *corpo santo* = L *corpus sanctum* holy body]

corps (kōr), n. (*pl. same, pr.* kōrz). **1.** = ARMY ~. **2.** Body of troops for special (medical, ordnance, intelligence, etc.) service. **3.** A students' society in a German university. **4.** ~ *d'armée* (ărmä'), army ~; ~ *de ballet* (see Ap.), the company of dancers in a ballet; C~ *diplomatique* (dĕplōmahtĕk'), all the ambassadors & attachés of foreign states at a Court ŏr capital. [F (as foll.)]

cŏrpse, n. Dead (usu. human) body; ~-*candle*, lambent flame seen in churchyard or over grave, regarded as omen of death. [ME *corps*, var. sp. of *cors* (CORSE), f. OF *cors* (mod. *corps*) f. L *corpus* body]

cŏrp'ŭl|ent, a. Bulky (of body); fat. So ~ENCE, -ENCY, nn. [ME, f. L *corpulentus* (*corpus* body, see -ULENT)]

cŏrp'us, n. (pl. -*pora*). Body, collection, of writings; ~ *juris* (joor'ĭs), body of law; ~ *delicti* (dĭlĭk'tī), all that goes to make a breach of law; (Physiol.) structure of special character in the animal body; C~ *Christi* (krĭs'tī), Feast of the body of Christ (Thursday after Trinity Sunday). [L, = body]

cŏrp'ŭscle (-sl), **cŏrpŭs'cule** (-kŭl), n. Minute body forming distinct part of the organism, esp. (pl.) those constituting large part of the blood in vertebrates; atom (esp. of electricity). [f. L *corpusculum* (as prec., see -CULE)]

cŏrpŭs'cŭlar, a. Of corpuscles or atoms; ~ (EMISSION) *theory of light*. [as prec. + -AR¹]

corrăl', n., & v.t. (-ll-). **1.** Pen for horses, cattle, etc. (in U.S. & Span. Amer.); defensive enclosure of wagons in encampment; enclosure for capturing wild animals. **2.** v.t. Form (wagons) into ~, confine in ~; *(colloq.)* get hold of. [f. Sp. *corral*; cf. KRAAL]

correct'¹, v.t. Set right, amend; substitute right for (wrong); mark errors in (proof-sheet etc.) for amendment; admonish (person); cure (person) of fault; punish (person, fault); counteract (hurtful quality); bring into accordance with standard (reading of barometer etc.). [ME, f. L COR(*rigere rect-* = *regere* guide)]

correct'², a. True, accurate; right, proper, (of conduct, manners, etc.); in accordance with a good standard (of taste etc.). Hence ~LY² adv., ~NESS n. [F, as prec.]

correc'tion, n. Correcting; *I speak under* ~, I may be wrong; thing substituted for what is wrong; punishment, as *house of* ~ (bridewell). Hence ~AL (-sho-) a. [ME, f. OF f. L *correctionem* (as prec., see -ION)]

correc'titūde, n. Correctness esp. of conduct. [mod., = *correct* + *rectitude*]

correc'tive, a. & n. (Thing) serving, tending, to correct or counteract what is harmful. Hence ~LY² (-vl-) adv. [F as CORRECT¹, see -IVE; cf. LL *correctivus*]

correc'tor, n. One who corrects; censor, critic; ‖ ~ *of the press*, proof-reader; one who punishes. [ME, f. AF *corectour* f. L *correctorem* (as CORRECT¹, see -OR)]

cŏ'rrĕlāte¹, n. Each of two related things (esp. so related that one implies the other). [f. as foll.]

cŏ'rrĕlāte², v.i. & t. Have a mutual relation (*with, to*); bring (thing) into such relation (*with* another). [app. suggested by earlier *correlation, correlative* (16th c.)]

correl'ative, a. & n. Having a mutual relation (*with, to*); analogous; (Gram., of words) corresponding to each other & regularly used together, e.g. *either* & *or*; (n.) ~ word or thing. Hence or cogn. (n.) ~ word or thing. Hence or cogn. **cŏrrĕlā'tion** n., ~LY² (-vl-) adv., **corrĕlativ'ity** n. [f. med. L *correlativus* (-IVE); cf. F *corrélatif*]

cŏrrĕspŏnd', v.i. Be in harmony (*with, to*); be similar, analogous, (*to*); agree in amount, position, etc. (*to*); communicate by interchange of letters (*with*); ~ing *member* (of learned society etc.), honorary non-resident member with no voice in the society's affairs. Hence ~ĭngLY² adv. [f. F *correspondre* f. med. L COR(*respondere* RESPOND)]

cŏrrĕspŏn'dence, n. Agreement, harmony, (*with, to; between* two); communication by letters; letters; ~ *school* (instructing by~, and conducting~ courses). [ME, f. OF f. med. L *correspondentia* (as prec., see -ENCE]

cŏrrĕspŏn'dent, n. & a. One who writes letters (to person or newspaper, esp. one employed for that purpose, as *our New York* ~, *war*-~); person, firm, having regular business, relations with another esp. in another, country; (adj.) corresponding (*to, with*, or abs.), whence ~LY² adv. [ME, f. OF, or f. med. L as prec., see -ENT]

For compounds of *co-* not given consult *co-*₊

cŏ'rridŏr, n. Main passage in large building, on which many rooms open; outside passage connecting parts of building; (Pol.) strip of a State's territory that runs through that of another & secures access to the sea etc.; ‖ ~ *train* (with narrow passage from end to end). [F, f. It. *corridore* corridor for *corridoio* (*correre* run + -*orio* -ORY) by confus. w. *corridore* runner]

‖ cŏ'rrie, n. (Sc.). Circular hollow on mountain side. [f. Gael. *coire* cauldron]

cŏrrigĕn'dum, n. (pl. -*da*). Thing to be corrected (esp. fault in printed book). [L (as CORRECT[1])]

cŏ'rrigible, a. Capable of being corrected; (of persons) submissive, open, to correction. [ME, f. OF (as CORRECT[1], see -BLE)]

corriv'al, n. = RIVAL. [F (as COR-, RIVAL)]

corrŏb'orant, a. & n. Strengthening (medicine); corroborating (fact). [F, or as foll., see -ANT]

corrŏb'or|āte, v.t. Confirm formally (law etc.); confirm (person, statement) by evidence etc. Hence or cogn. ~ative, ~atory, aa., ~ātor n. [f. L COR(*roborare* f. *robur* -*oris* hard wood) strengthen, -ATE[3]]

corrŏborā'tion, n. Confirmation by further evidence. [F, or f. LL *corroboratio* (as prec., see -ATION)]

corrŏb'oree, n. Native dance of Australian aborigines. [native]

corrōde', v.t. & i. Wear away, destroy gradually (of rust, chemical agents, diseases, & fig.); (v.i.) decay. So cor-rō'SION (-zhn) n. [ME, f. L COR(*rodere ros-gnaw*)]

corrōs'ive, a. & n. (Thing) tending to corrode (lit. & fig.); ~ *sublimate*, (Commerc.) mercuric chloride, a strong acrid poison. Hence ~LY[2] (-vl-) adv., ~NESS (-vn-) n. [ME, f. OF *corosif*, -*ive*, as CORRODE, see -IVE]

cŏ'rrugāte (-ŏŏ-), v.t. & i. Contract into wrinkles or folds (t. & i.); mark with, bend into, ridges, as ~*d iron*. Hence or cogn. cŏrrugā'TION (-ŏŏ-) n. [f. L COR(*rugare* f. *ruga* wrinkle), -ATE[3]]

cŏ'rrugātor (-ŏŏ-), n. Muscle that contracts the brow in frowning. [mod. L as prec., see -OR]

corrŭpt'[1], a. Rotten; depraved, wicked; influenced by bribery; (of language, texts, etc.) vitiated by errors or alterations; ~ *practices*, forms of bribery esp. at elections. Hence ~LY[2] adv., ~NESS n. [ME, f. OF *cor(r)upt* or L COR(*rumpere rupt-* break)]

corrŭpt'[2], v.t. & i. Infect, taint, (lit. & fig.); bribe; destroy purity of (language); become corrupt. So corrŭp'tIVE a. [ME, f. prec., replacing (now obs.) *corrump*]

corrŭp'ti|ble, a. Liable to corruption, perishable; capable of moral corruption. Hence or cogn. ~BIL'ITY n., ~bLY[2] adv. [ME, f. LL *corruptibilis* (CORRUPT[1], -BLE)]

corrŭp'tion, n. Decomposition; moral deterioration; use of corrupt practices (bribery etc.); perversion (of language etc.) from its original state; deformation (of word); (Law) ~ *of blood*, effect of attainder upon person attainted. [ME, f OF, or f. L *corruptio* (as prec., see -ION)]

cŏrs'ăc, -ăk, n. (zool.). Tartar fox. [Turki]

cŏrs'age (-ahzh or -ij), n. Bodice or waist of woman's dress; *bouquet (to be) worn, orig. at waist. [ME, f. OF (*cors* body, see CORPSE & -AGE)]

cŏrs'air, n. Privateer, privateering vessel, esp. of Barbary; a pirate. [f. F *corsaire* f. med. L *cursarius* (*cursus* -*ūs* inroad, f. *currere* run, -ARY[1])]

cŏrse, n. (arch., poet.). See CORPSE.

cŏrs'ĕt, n. Woman's closely fitting inner bodice stiffened with whalebone & fastened by lacing, stays. Hence ~ED[2] a. [ME, f. OF, dim. of *cors* body, see CORPSE]

cŏrs'lĕt, -selĕt (-sl-), n. Piece of armour covering body; garment (usu. tight-fitting) covering body as distinct from limbs; (Zool.) insect's thorax, part between head & abdomen. [OF, as prec., see -LET]

cortège (kŏrtāzh'), n. Train of attendants; (esp. funeral) procession. [F]

Cŏrt'ĕs, n. pl. Two chambers making legislative assembly of Spain or Portugal. [Sp., Port.]

cŏrt'ĕx, n. (pl. -*tĭcēs*). Bark; outer grey matter of brain, outer part of kidney. [L *cortex* -*icis* bark]

cŏrt'ical. a. (Bot.) of the bark or rind; (Anat., Zool.) forming the outer part of animal body or organ. [f. as prec. + -AL]

cŏrt'icate, -ātĕd, aa. Having bark; bark-like. [f. L *corticatus* (as prec., see -ATE[2])]

cŏrt'isōne, n. One of a group of hormones produced by the cortex of the suprarenal gland. [P]

corŭn'dum, n. Crystallized mineral of same species as sapphire & ruby, blue, grey, brown, black; mineral species of crystallized alumina. [f. Tamil *kurun-dam*]

cŏ'ruscāte, v.i. Sparkle, flash, (lit., & fig. of wit etc.). So corŭs'cANT a., cŏruscA'TION n. [f. L *coruscare* (as -ATE[3]]

corvée' (-vä), n. (feudal). Day's work of unpaid labour due by vassal; statute labour, e.g. that exacted of French peasants before 1776. [ME, f. OF f. med. L *corrogata* (sc. *opera*) f. COR(*rogare* ask)]

cŏrvĕtte', n. (naut.). Flush-decked war-vessel with one tier of guns (hist.); small fast naval escort-vessel. [F, f. MDu. *korf* kind of ship, + dim. -ETTE]

cŏrv'ine, a. Of, akin to, the raven or crow. [f. L *corvinus* (*corvus* raven, see -INE[1])]

Cŏ'rybănt, n. (pl. -*s*, -*ēs*). Priest of Phrygian worship of Cybele, performed with extravagant dances. Hence CŏrybăntIAN, **Cŏrўbăn′tIC, Cŏrўbăn′tINE**, aa. [ME, f. L f. Gk *Korubas -bant-*]

Cŏ′rўdon, n. Typical rustic in pastoral poetry. [L, f. Gk *Korudōn*]

cŏ′rўmb, n. (bot.). Species of inflorescence; raceme in which lower flower--stalks are proportionally longer. Hence ～OSE′[1] a. [f. L f. Gk *korumbos* cluster]

cŏrўphae′us, n. (pl. *-aei* pr. -ē′ī). Leader of a chorus (also fig.). [L, f. Gk *koruphaios* (*koruphē* head)]

cŏ′rўphée (-fā), n. A leading dancer in a ballet. [F, as prec.]

corŷz′a, n. Catarrh. [LL, f. Gk *koruza* running at nose]

cŏs[1], n. (Also *Cos lettuce*) kind of lettuce introduced from Cos (now Stanchio). [f. Gk *kōs*]

cŏs[2], n. Abbr. of COSINE,

cŏse (-z), v.i. Make oneself cosy. [back formation on COSY, cf. LAZE f. *lazy*]

cŏsĕc′ant, n. (trig.). Secant of complement of given angle (abbr. *cosec.*). [CO-]

cŏseis′mal (-sīz-), a. & n. (Line or curve connecting points) of simultaneous shock from earthquake wave. [CO-]

∥ **cŏsh**, n., & v.t., (sl.). Bludgeon, life--preserver (～*boy*, youth or man armed with ～); (v.t.) strike with～. [orig. unkn.]

cŏsh′er, v.t. Pamper, cocker *up*. [orig. unkn.]

cŏ-sig′natorў, a. & n. (Person) signing jointly with others. [CO-]

cŏ′sine, n. (trig.). Sine of complement of given angle (abbr. *cŏs*). [CO-]

cŏsmĕt′ic (-z-), a. & n. (Preparation) designed to beautify hair, skin, or complexion. [f. Gk *kosmētikos* (*kosmeō* adorn f. *kosmos* order, adornment, see -ETIC)]

cŏs′mic (-z-), a. Of the universe or COSMOS (esp. as distinguished from the earth); ～ *philosophy*, = foll.; ～ *rays*, radiations that reach the earth equally from all directions, characterized by enormous voltages and high penetrative power. Hence ～AL a., ～alLY[2] adv. [f. Gk *kosmikos* (*kosmos* world, see -IC)]

cŏs′mism (-z-), n. Conception of the cosmos as a self-acting whole. So **cŏs′m-IST** n. [COSMOS[1] + -ISM]

cosmo- in comb. = Gk *kosmos* universe, as *-geny*, evolution of the universe, *-logy*, *-logist*, *-lo′gical*; science of, student of, concerned with, the universe, *-plas′tic*, moulding the universe.

cŏsmŏg′on∣ў (-z-), n. (Theory of) the creation of the universe. So **cŏsmŏgŏn⌐IC(AL)** aa., ～IST(3) n., (-z-). [f. Gk *kosmogonia* (COSMO- + -*gonia* f. -*gonos* -begetting)]

cŏsmŏg′raphў (-z-); n. Description, mapping, of general features of universe or earth. So **cŏsmŏg′RAPHER** n., **cŏsmo-GRAPH′IC(AL)** aa., (-z-). [f. Gk *kosmographia*, see COSMO-, -GRAPHY]

cŏsmŏp′olĭs (-z-), n. A cosmopolitan city. [f. COSMO- + Gk *polis* city]

cŏsmŏpŏl′itan (-z-), a. & n. Belonging to all parts of the world; (person) free from national limitations. Hence ～ISM n., ～IZE v.t. & i., (-z-). [f. foll. + -AN]

cŏsmŏp′olit∣e (-z-), n. & a. Citizen of the world; (adj.) free from national prejudices. Hence ～ISM n. [f. Gk *kosmopolitēs* (COSMO- + *politēs* citizen)]

cŏsmopolit′ical (-z-), a. Belonging to universal polity. [f. prec: + -ICAL]

cŏsmora′ma (-z-; -ah-), n. Peep-show illustrating all parts of the world. Hence **cŏsmorăm′IC** a. [f. COSMO- + Gk *horama* spectacle (*horaō* see)]

cŏs′mŏs[1] (-z-), n. The universe as an ordered whole; ordered system of ideas, etc., sum-total of experience. [f. Gk *kosmos*]

cŏs′mŏs[2] (-z-), n. Plant bearing single dahlia-like blossoms of various colours. [f. Gk *kosmos* ornament]

Cŏss′ăck, n. Member of a people of south--eastern Russia, esp. as light horse in Russian army; ～ *post*, military outpost of a few mounted men. [f. F *cosaque* f. Turki *quzzaq* adventurer]

cŏss′ĕt, n., & v.t. Pet lamb; (v.t.) pet, pamper. [(ỹb f. n.) perh. = OE *cotsæta* cot-sitter (i.e. animal brought up in house)]

cost[1] (kaw-, kŏ-), n. Price (to be) paid for thing; *prime* ～ (also ～ *price*), that at which merchant buys; (pl.) law expenses, esp. those allowed in favour of winning party; expenditure of time, labour, etc.; *at* ～, at the initial ～; *at all* ～*s*, cost what it may; *at the* ～ *of*, at the expense of losing; *count the* ～, consider the risks before action; *to* a person's ～, to his loss; ～ *accountant, clerk*, one who records every item of (esp. overhead) expenses in a business concern (with a view to checking wasteful expenditure); ～*-book* (showing expenses, profit, etc., of mine). Hence ～LESS a. [ME, f. OF *cost, coust* f. Rom. *costo f. *costare (foll.)]

cost[2] (kaw-, kŏ-), v.i. & t. (*cost*). Be acquirable at, involve expenditure of, as ～ *him five shillings*, ～ *the writer infinite labour*; result in the loss of, as ～ *him his crown*; ～ *him dear(ly)*, involved a heavy penalty; (Commerc.) fix price of. The person is indirect object, the price is expressed adverbially, *in* being understood. [ME, f. OF *coster, couster* f. Rom. *costare f. L CON(*stare* stand) stand firm, stand at a price]

cŏs′tal, a. Of the ribs. [F, f. L *costa* rib; see -AL; cf. LL *costalis*]

cŏs′tard, n. ∥ Large kind of apple; (arch.) head. [ME, perh. f. OF *coste* rib (as prec.,) + -ARD]

cŏs′tate, a. Ribbed, having ribs. [f. L *costatus* (*costa* rib, see -ATE[2])]

‖ **cŏstean'**, **-een**, v.i. (mining). Sink pits down to rock to find direction of lode. [f. Corn. *cothas stean* dropped tin]

‖ **cŏs'ter(monger)** (-ŭngg-), n. Man who sells fruit, fish, etc., from barrow in street. [COSTARD, MONGER]

cŏs'tive, a. With confined bowels, constipated; (fig.) niggardly. Hence ~NESS (-vn-) n. [ME *costif* f. OF *costive* f. L *constipatus* CONSTIPATED]

cost'l|ȳ (kaw-, kŏ-), a. Of great value; expensive. Hence ~iNESS n. [-LY¹]

cŏst'mārȳ, n. Aromatic perennial plant, formerly used in medicine & for flavouring ale. [OE *cost* f. L f. Gk *kostos*+(St) *Mary*]

cŏst'ūme (*also* -tūm'), n., & v.t. Style, fashion of dress or attire (including way of wearing hair); complete set of outer garments; ~ *jewellery*, artificial jewellery worn for decorative purposes; ~ *piece*, play in which actors wear historical ~; (v.t.) provide with ~. [F, f. It. *costume* f. L *consuetudinem* CUSTOM]

cŏstūm'ier, **-ūm'er**, n. Maker of, dealer in, costumes. [F (-*ier* as prec., see -EER]

cŏs'ȳ (-z-), **-zȳ**, a. & n. Comfortable, snug, (of person or place); (n.) canopied corner seat for two (cf. F *causeuse*); *tea, egg*, ~, quilted covering to retain heat in teapot, egg. Hence **cōs'iLY²** adv., **cōs'iNESS** n., (-z-). [etym. unkn.]

cŏt¹, n., & v.t. (-tt-). Small erection for shelter, as *bell-, sheep-*, ~; (poet.) cottage; (v.t.) put (sheep) in ~. [OE *cot*, = MDu., MLG, ON *kot*, f. Gmc *kutom*, cogn. w. COTE]

cŏt², n. (Anglo-Ind.) light bedstead; (Naut.) swinging bed for officers, sick persons, etc.; ‖ small (usu. swinging) bed for child; bed in children's hospital. [Anglo-Ind., f. Hind. *khaṭ* bedstead, bier]

cŏt³, n. Abbr. of foll.

cŏtăn'gent (-j-), n. (trig.). Tangent of complement of given angle (abbr. *cŏt*). [CO-]

cōte, n. Shed, stall, shelter, esp. for animals as *dove-, hen-, sheep-*, ~. [OE *cote* = MLG *kote*, f. Gmc. *kutōn*, cogn. w. COT¹]

co-temporary etc. See CONTEMPORARY etc.

cō-těn'ant, n. Joint tenant. [CO-]

cŏt'erie, n. Circle, set, of persons associated by exclusive interests; select circle in society. [F, orig. = association of country people, f. *cotier* COTTAR, see -ERY]

cōtěrm'inous, a. Var. of CONTERMINOUS. [CO-]

cothŭrn'us, n. (pl. *-nī*). Buskin, thick-soled boot of Athenian tragic actor (also fig., of elevated style etc.). [L, f. Gk *kothornos*]

cō-tid'al, a. ~ *line* on map (connecting places at which high water occurs at same time). [CO-]

cotill'ion, **-llon**, n. Name of several dances; music for these. [F (-*llon*), = petticoat]

cŏtōněăs'ter, n. (Kinds of) small tree or shrub of N. Europe, resembling hawthorn and bearing rose-red berries. [f. L *cotonea* quince+-ASTER]

cŏtt'a, n. Short surplice. [It., see COAT]

cŏtt'age, n. Labourer's or villager's small dwelling; small country residence; ~ *hospital* (in ~, without resident medical staff); ~ *loaf* of bread (of two round masses, smaller on top of larger); ~ *piano* (small upright). [ME, f. AF *cotage*, f. COT¹, COTE, see -AGE]

cŏtt'ager (-tĭ-), n. Inhabitant of a cottage. [-ER¹]

‖ **cŏtt'ar**, **-er¹**, n. Scots peasant occupying cottage on farm, and labouring on farm at fixed rate when required; = COTTIER. [partly f. med. L *cotarius* (see COTTIER), partly (16th c.) f. COT¹, see -AR², -ER²]

cŏtt'er², n. Key, wedge, bolt, for securing parts of machinery etc.; esp., split pin that opens after passing through hole; ~-*pin*, pin to keep ~ in place. [also, earlier, *cotterel*; orig. unkn.]

‖ **cŏtt'ier**, n. Cottager; Irish peasant holding under ~ *tenure* (letting of land in small portions at rent fixed by competition). [ME, f. OF *cotier*, in med. L *cotarius* f. *cota*; see COT¹, COTE, -IER, -ER²]

cŏtt'on¹, n. White downy fibrous substance clothing seeds of ~-*plant*, used for making cloth, thread, etc.; ~-*plant*; thread spun from ~ yarn (also *sewing-*~); cloth made of ~; GUN-~; ~-*cake*, compressed ~ seed as food for cattle; ~-*grass*, kinds of plant with white silky hairs; ‖~-*lord*, magnate of ~ trade; ~-*spinner*, workman who spins ~; owner of ~ mill; ~-*tail*, common American rabbit, with white fluffy tail; ~ *waste*, refuse yarn used for cleaning machinery etc.; ‖~ *wool*, raw ~, esp. as prepared for wadding; ~ *yarn*, ~ prepared for weaving into fabrics. Hence ~Y² a. [ME *coto(u)n* f. OF *coton* f. Arab. *qutun*]

cŏtt'on², v.i. Agree, harmonize, (*together, with* each other); ~ *up*, make friendly advances (*to* or abs.); become attached *to*; ~ *on to* (person, thing), take to him, it; ~ *on* (*to*), (sl.) understand. [f. prec.]

cŏttonŏc'racȳ, n. The magnates of the cotton trade. So **Cŏttonŏp'olis** n. (joc.), Manchester. [COTTON¹+-O-+-CRACY, Gk *polis* city]

cŏtȳlēd'on, n. Primary leaf in embryo of higher plants, seed-leaf; kinds of plants including navelwort or pennywort. [L, f. Gk *kotulēdōn* cup-shaped cavity (*kotulē* cup)]

cŏtȳlēd'onous, a. Having cotyledons. [-OUS]

cŏt'ȳloid, a. (anat.). Cup-shaped. [f. Gk *kotuloeidēs* (*kotulē* cup, see -OID)]

couch¹, n. Bed; thing one sleeps on; lounge like sofa, but with half-back and head-end only; (Malting) bed in which grain germinates after steeping. [ME & OF *couche* f. *coucher* (foll.)]

couch², v.t. & i. Lay one*self* down (now only in p.p.); (Malting) lay (grain) on floor to germinate; lower (spear etc.) to position of attack; remove (cataract; also ~ person, person's *eye*, for cataract); express (thought etc. *in* words); veil (meaning *under* words); (of animals) lie (esp. in lair); crouch, cower; lie in ambush. [ME, f. OF *coucher* f. L COL(*locare* place)]

ˈcouch³ (kow-, kooͩ-), n. (More usu. ~-*grass*) kind of grass with long creeping roots, a common weed. [var. of QUITCH]

couchˈant, a. (her.). (Of animals) lying with body resting on legs and head raised. [F, part. as COUCH²; see -ANT]

Couéism (kooͩˈäizm), n. Systematic auto-suggestion of a sanguine kind. [Émile *Coué*, French psychologist (d. 1926), +-ISM]

cougˈar (kooͩ-), n. Large American feline quadruped, puma. [f. F *couguar* repr. Guarani *guazu ara*]

cough¹ (kawf, kŏf), n. Act of coughing; tendency to cough, diseased condition of respiratory organs; ~-*drop*, *-lozenge*, medicated sweet to relieve ~. [f. foll.]

cough² (as prec.), v.i. & t. Expel air from lungs with violent effort and noise produced by abrupt opening of glottis; (trans.) ~ *out*, *up*, eject by, say with, cough; ~ *down*, silence (speaker) by ~ing; ~ *up* (sl.), blurt out, say with reluctance, bring out, produce. [ME *coghe*, *cowhe*, rel. to OE *cohhetan*, MDu. *cuchen*, MHG *küchen* (G *keuchen*), of imit. orig.]

could. See CAN².

couleurˈ de rōseˈ (koolêˈr; -z), a. & n. = ROSE-*colour*(*ed*). [F]

coulisse (kooͩlēs'), n. (Usu. pl.) wings in theatre; space between two of these; groove in which sluice-gate moves. [F]

ˑcouloir (koolˈwahr), n. Steep gully on mountain side. [F]

coulomb (kooͩlŏm'), n. Quantity of electricity conveyed in one second by current of one ampere. [*de C*~, French physicist (d. 1806)]

coulˈter (kōl-), *cŏl-, n. Iron blade fixed in front of share in plough. [OE *culter* f. L *culter*]

coumˈarin (kooͩ-), n. Aromatic crystalline substance found in seeds of Tonka bean etc. [f. F *coumarine* (*cumarú*, name in Guiana of Tonka bean, see -IN)]

ˈcounˈcil, n. Ecclesiastical assembly, as *oecumenical*, *diocesan*, ~; (N.T.) Jewish Sanhedrin; advisory or deliberative assembly, as (hist.) *Great C*~, ~ of tenants-in-chief & great ecclesiastics (last summoned in 1640), CABINET ~; body of councillors, ‖ as PRIVY ~ (*the King*, *Queen*, *Crown*, *in C*~, Privy C~ as issuing

Orders in C~ or receiving appeal petitions from colonies etc.), *C*~ *of State* (of foreign countries); ‖ body assisting governor of British crown colony or dependency; local administrative body of town, city, or administrative county, as *County C*~; *C*~ *of War*, assembly of officers called in special emergency, (in some foreign countries) permanent military board; ~-*board*, table at which ~ sits, ~ in session; ~-*chamber*, room in which ~ meets; ~-*house*, building in which ~ meets, (also) house built by a municipal ~. [This form represents OF *cuncile* f. L *concilium* convocation, assembly, f. *calare* summon (cf. Gk *kalein*); the form COUNSEL repr. OF *cunseil* f. L *consilium* advice. From ME both spellings were interchangeable; in 16th c. began the different. acc. to wh. *council* = any deliberative body, *counsel* = act of counselling, advice, &c.]

counˈcillor, n. Member of a (town etc.) council. Hence ~SHIP n. [16th-c. different. f. COUNSELLOR; see COUNCIL]

counˈsel¹, n. Consultation; *take* ~, consult (*with* or abs.); advice; (Theol.) ~ *of perfection*, injunction (orig. of Christ or Apostles) not regarded as universally binding (*Matt*. xix. 21); plan; *keep* one's (*own*) or *another's* ~ (secret); body of legal advisers in cause; barrister; *Queen's*, *King's*, *C*~ (abbr. *Q.C.*, *K.C.*), ~ to the crown, taking precedence of other barristers. [ME, repr. OF *con-*, *cunseil* f. L *consilium* consultation, advice, rel. to *consulere* (cf. CONSUL), *consultare* CONSULT. See COUNCIL]

counˈsel², v.t. (-ll-). Advise (person to do); recommend (thing, *that*). [ME *conseil* f. OF *conseiller* f. L *consiliari* (as prec.)]

counˈsellor, n. Adviser; (also ~-*at-law*) advising barrister (now arch. in England). [ME *counseiller*, *-our*, f. OF *conseillere*, *-eor*, f. as COUNSEL¹ + -ER², -OR; cf. med. L *consiliaris*, *-ator*]

count¹, n. Counting; one's reckoning (*keep*, *lose*, ~, be aware, fail to know, how many there have been); sum total; (Law) each charge in an indictment; ~-*down*, counting of seconds before a missile etc. is fired; ‖ (H. of Commons) ~-*out*, ~, adjournment when fewer than 40 members are present; ~-*out* (Boxing), counting of 10 sec. to give fallen man time to rise, failing which he loses the match. [ME, f. OF *conte* f. LL *computus* (as foll.)]

count², v.t. & i. Enumerate, reckon up; repeat numerals in order; ~ *up*, find the sum of; ~ *out*, ~ while taking from a stock; (of boxer) *be* ~*ed out*, fail to rise in time (see prec.); ‖ ~ *out the House*, procure adjournment (as prec.); include in reckoning; consider (a thing) to be (so & so); ~ *on*, *upon*, expect confidently; be included in reckoning, as *that does not* ~;

For compounds of *co-* not given consult CO-.

~ *for*, be worth (much etc.); (Sc.) ~ *kin* (*with*), be demonstrably related (to). [ME, f. OF *conter* f. L *computare* COMPUTE]

count[3], n. Foreign noble corresp. to earl; ~ PALATINE. Hence ~'SHIP n. [f. OF *conte* f. L *comitem* (nom. *-mes*) companion]

count'énance[1], n. Expression of face, as *change* (one's) ~ (from emotion), *keep* one's ~, maintain composure, esp. refrain from laughing; face; composure, as *put out of* ~, disconcert, *keep* (person) *in* ~ (usu. by show of support). [ME, f. OF *contenance* f. L *continentia* (as CONTAIN, see -ENCE)]

count'énance[2], v.t. Sanction (act); encourage (person, practice, person *in* practice). [f. prec.]

coun'ter[1], n. **1.** Small (usu. round) piece of metal, ivory, etc., used for keeping account in games, esp. cards; imitation coin. **2.** Banker's table; table in shop on which money is counted out & across which goods are delivered; ~*-jumper*, (derog.) shopman. [f. AF *cont(e)our*, OF *-(e)oir*, f. med. L *computatorium* (as COMPUTE, see -ORY(2))]

coun'ter[2], n. Part of horse's breast between shoulders and under neck; curved part of stern of ship. [orig. unkn.]

coun'ter[3], n. (fencing). Circular parry in which hand retains same position while point describes a circle. [f. F *contre* COUNTER-]

coun'ter[4], n. (shoemaking). Back part of shoe or boot round heel. [abbr. of COUNTERFORT]

coun'ter[5], a. Opposed; opposite; duplicate; ~ (*rocking turn* or *rocker*), skating figure (see ROCK[3]). [arising f. combb. w. COUNTER-]

coun'ter[6], v.t. & i. Oppose, contradict; (Chess) meet with counter move; (Boxing) give (opponent, or abs.) return blow while parrying. [ME, partly f. ENCOUNTER, partly f. COUNTER-]

coun'ter[7], adv. In the opposite direction, as *hunt, run, go,* ~ (i.e. to direction taken by game); contrary, as *act, go,* ~ (*to* instructions etc.). [ME, f. F *contre* COUNTER-]

coun'ter[8], n. (Abbr. for) counter rocking turn (see ROCK[3]).

coun'ter-, pref. in ME *countre-* f. OF f. L *contra* against, in return, orig. in words f. OF, F, or It., but now a living prefix of vbs, nouns, adjj., and advv., with sense (1) reciprocation, opposition, frustration, rivalry, (2) opposite position or direction, (3) correspondence, match, (of things having naturally two opposite parts), (4) duplicate, substitute.

counter|ăct', v.t. Hinder, defeat, by contrary action; neutralize. Hence ~ăc'tION n., ~ăc'tIVE a. [COUNTER(1)]

counter-ā'gent, n. Counteracting agent or force. [COUNTER-(1)]

coun'ter-approach, n. (mil.). Work constructed by besieged outside permanent fortifications to check besiegers. [COUNTER-(1)]

coun'ter-attăck', n., & v.t. & i. Sortie, charge, etc., in reply to attack by enemy; (v.t. & i.) make ~ (upon). [COUNTER-(1)]

coun'ter-attrăc'tion, n. Attraction of contrary tendency; rival attraction. [COUNTER-(1)]

coun'terbăl'ance, n., & v.t. Weight balancing another; (v.t.) act as ~ to. [COUNTER-(1)]

coun'terblast (-ah-), n. Energetic declaration against something. [COUNTER-(1)]

counterchănge' (-j), v.t. & i. Interchange; chequer (-j), (v.i.) change places or parts. [f. F *contrechanger* (see COUNTER-(1) and CHANGE v.)]

coun'tercharge, n. Charge in opposition to another, charge against accuser. [COUNTER-(1)]

coun'tercheck, n. Check that opposes a thing; check that operates against another; (arch.) retort (*the* ~ *quarrelsome*, see *As You Like It*, v. iv. 85). [COUNTER-(1)]

coun'ter-claim, n. Claim set up against another; claim set up by defendant in suit. [COUNTER-(1)]

counter-clŏck'wise (-z). See CLOCK[1].

coun'ter-ĕs'pionage (*or* -ahzh'), n. Spying directed against the enemy's spy system. [COUNTER-(1)]

coun'terfeit[1] (-fĭt, -fēt), a. & n. (Thing) made in imitation, not genuine, (of coins, writings, persons, etc.). [ME, f. OF *contrefet, -fait*, p.p. of *contrefaire* f. Rom. *CONTRA-* (*facere* make)]

coun'terfeit[2] (-fĭt, -fēt), v.t. Imitate; forge (coin, bank-notes, handwriting); simulate (feelings); (fig.) resemble closely. Hence ~ER[1] n. [ME, f. prec.]

coun'terfoil, n. Complementary part of bank cheque, official receipt, etc., with note of particulars, retained by drawer. [COUNTER-(3)]

coun'terfŏrt, n. Buttress supporting wall or terrace. [f. F *contrefort* or It. *contraforte* (COUNTER-, FORT)]

counter-i'rritant, n. Thing used to produce surface irritation and thus counteract disease (also fig.). So **counter-irritā'tion** n. [COUNTER-(1)]

countermand' (-ah-), v.t., & n. Revoke (command); recall (person, forces, etc.) by contrary order; cancel order for (goods etc.); (n.) order revoking previous one. [ME, vb f. OF *contremander* f. med. L *CONTRA*(*mandare* order)]

coun'termarch, v.i. & t., & n. (Cause to) march in the contrary direction. [COUNTER-(2)]

coun'termark, n. Additional mark, for greater security etc.; additional mark on bale of goods belonging to several merchants; hallmark added to that of the maker. [f. F *contremarque*, see COUNTER-(3) & MARK]

coun'termine, n., & v.t. & i. (Mil.) mine made to intercept that of besiegers; submarine mine sunk to explode enemy's mines by its explosion; (fig.) counterplot; (v.t.) oppose by ~; (v.i.) make a ~. [COUNTER-(1); cf. F *contremine(r)*, It. *contramina(re)*]

coun'termūre, n. Wall raised within or behind another as reserve defence. [f. F *contremur* (It., Sp. *contramuro*)]

coun'terpane (-īn, -ān), n. Outer covering of bed, coverlet, quilt. [alt. (w. assim. to PANE in obs. sense *cloth*) f. (now obs.) *counterpoint* f. OF *contrepointe* alt. f. *cou(l)tepointe* f. med. L *culcita puncta* quilted mattress]

coun'terpârt, n. Duplicate; person, thing, forming natural complement to another; opposite part of INDENTURE. [COUNTER-(3), after OF *contrepartie*]

coun'terplŏt, n., & v.t. & i. (-tt-). Plot contrived to defeat another; (vb) frustrate by ~, devise ~ (against). [COUNTER-(1)]

coun'terpoint, n. (mus.). Melody added as accompaniment to given melody; art, mode, of adding melodies as accompaniment according to fixed rules; *double*, *triple*, etc. ~, invertible ~, in which the melodies can be changed in position above and below one another; *strict* ~ (acc. to code of rules as academic exercise, not as actual composition). [f. OF *contrepoint* f. med. L CONTRA*punctum* pricked opposite, i.e. to the original melody (*pungere punct-* prick)]

coun'terpoise[1] (-z), n. Counterbalancing weight; thing of equivalent force etc. on opposite side; equilibrium. [ME & OF *countrepeis* f. *contre* COUNTER- (1)+*peis*, later *pois*, f. L *pensum* weight; cf. POISE]

coun'terpoise[2] (-z), v.t. Counterbalance; compensate; bring into, keep in, equilibrium (lit. & fig.). [ME *countrepeise*, *-pese*, f. OF *contrepeser* (as prec.); later Eng. *-poise* assim. to prec.]

coun'ter-rĕformā'tion, n. Reformation running counter to another, esp. that in Church of Rome following on Protestant Reformation. [COUNTER-(1)]

coun'ter-rĕvolu'tion (-lōō-, -lŭ-), n. A revolution opposed to a former one or reversing its results. Hence ~ARY[1] (-shon-) a. & n. [COUNTER-(1)]

coun'terscârp (n. (fortif.). Outer wall or slope of ditch, supporting covered way. [f. F *contrescarpe* f. It. CONTRA(*scarpa* SCARP)]

coun'tershaft (-ah-), n. Intermediate shaft driven from main shaft to transmit motion to particular parts of a system of machinery. [COUNTER- (1)]

coun'tersign[1] (-īn), n. Watchword, password, given to all men on guard (cf. PAROLE); mark used for identification etc.

[f. F *contresigne* f. It. *contrasegno* (COUNTER-(3) & SIGN)]

coun'tersign[2] (-īn), v.t. Add signature to (document already signed); ratify. [f. F *contresigner* (as prec.)]

countersink', v.t. Bevel off (top of hole) to receive head of screw or bolt; sink (screw-head) in such hole. [COUNTER-(3)]

counter-tĕn'or, n. (mus.). (Part for, singer with) male voice higher than tenor, alto. [f. OF *contre-teneur* f. It. *contra-tenore* (see CONTRA- & TENOR)]

countervail', v.t. & i. Counterbalance (esp. in ~*ing duty*, one put on imports that are bounty-fed to give home goods an equal chance); avail against. [ME, f. OF *contrevaloir* f. L CONTRA *valēre*]

coun'terweight (-wāt), n. Counterbalancing weight. [COUNTER-(1)]

coun'terwork (-ẽrk), n., & v.t. & i. (Mil.) work raised in opposition to those of enemy; (gen.) opposing work; (v.t.) counteract, frustrate; (v.i.) work in opposition. [COUNTER-(1)]

coun'tèss, n. Wife, widow, of count or earl; lady ranking with count or earl in her own right. [ME & OF *contesse* f. Rom. *comitissa* fem. of *comes* COUNT[3], see -ESS]

‖ **coun'ting-house**, n. Building, room, devoted to keeping accounts; office.

count'lèss, a. Too many to count. [-LESS]

coun'trified, **-rŷfied**, (kŭn-; -īd), a. Rural, rustic, in appearance, manners, etc. [p.p. of *countrify*, else little used (COUNTRY +-FY)]

coun'trŷ (kŭn-), n. Region; territory of a nation; land of a person's birth, citizenship, etc., fatherland; rural districts as opp. to towns, esp. the rest of a land as opp. to the capital; (Cricket sl.) *in the* ~, far from the wickets; ‖ APPEAL[1] *to the* ~ (body of electors); ~ *club* (orig. U.S.), club with its quarters in a rural district for the sake of outdoor sports; ~ *cousin*, relation or person of countrified manners or appearance; ~*-house*, *-seat*, residence of ~ gentleman; ‖~ *note*, bank-note issued by local bank; ~ *party*, political party supporting agricultural against manufacturing interests; ~*side*, particular rural district, its inhabitants. [ME, f. OF *contree*, *cuntree*, f. med. L (Rom.) *contrata* (land) lying opposite (CONTRA); see -Y[4]]

coun'try dance, n. Any rural or native English dance, esp. those in which couples stand face to face in two long lines. [COUNTRY + DANCE; perverted to *contre-dance* etc.]

coun'tryman, n. (fem. *coun'trywoman*). Man of one's own (or a specified) country; person living in rural parts.

coun'tŷ, n. Territorial division in Great Britain and Ireland, chief unit for administrative, judicial, and political purposes; administrative division in most British colonies; *political and administrative division next below State; people of a ~; ~ PALATINE; ‖ ~ corporate, city, town, ranking as administrative ~; ‖ ~ borough, large borough ranking as ~ for administrative purposes; ~ council, representative governing body of administrative ~; ~ court, ‖ judicial court for civil action, whence ~-court (v.t. colloq.), sue in this; ‖ ~ family (with ancestral seat in a ~); ~ town, one in which business of ~ is (or was orig.) transacted; ‖ the ~, ~ families, so ~ attrib. [ME, f. AF counte f. L comitatus (as COUNT³, see -ATE¹)]

coup (koo͞), n. Notable or successful stroke or move; (Billiards) direct holing of ball; ~ d'état (dětah'), violent or illegal change in government; ~ de grâce (de grahs), finishing stroke; ~ de main (see Ap.), sudden vigorous attack; ~ d'œil (dŭ'ĕ), comprehensive glance, general view; ~ de théâtre (tăah'tr), dramatically sudden or sensational act. [F, f. med. L col(a)pus f. L f. Gk kolaphos blow]

coupé (koo͞p'á), n. Four-wheeled closed carriage for two inside & driver; ‖ half--compartment at end of railway carriage; covered motor-car seated for two. [F, p.p. of couper cut, as noun]

cou'ple¹ (kŭ-), n. Leash for holding two hounds together, whence (fig.) go, hunt, run, in ~s; pair, brace, esp. of hunting dogs (collect. sing. for pl., as 15 ~); approximately two, a few; wedded or engaged pair; pair of partners in dance; a ~ of, two; pair of rafters; (Dynam.) pair of equal and parallel forces acting in opposite directions. [ME, f. OF cople f. L COPULA]

cou'ple² (kŭ-), v.t. & i. Fasten, link, together (esp. dogs in pairs); connect (railway carriages) by a coupling; unite, bring together, (persons); marry (t. & i.); associate in thought or speech (two things together, one with another); (v.i.) unite sexually. [ME, f. OF copler (as prec.)]

coup'ler (kŭ-), n. In vbl senses; esp. contrivance for connecting two manuals, or manual with pedals, or notes with their octaves above or below (octave ~), as organ. [prec. + -ER¹]

coup'let (kŭ-), n. Pair of successive lines of verse. [F, dim. of COUPLE]

coup'ling (kŭ-), n. In vbl senses; esp.: link connecting railway carriages; contrivance for connecting parts of machinery. [-ING¹]

coup'on (koo͞-), n. Detachable ticket entitling holder to periodical payments of interest, services of excursion agency, ration of food, cloth, clothes, etc. when controlled; ‖ (Pol. sl.) party leader's recognition of parliamentary candidate as deserving election; voucher given with retail purchase, a certain number of which entitle holder to a 'free gift' (so ~

system). [F, = piece cut off (couper, see COUPÉ, -OON)]

cou'rage (kŭ-), n. Bravery, boldness, as take, pluck up, lose, ~; take one's ~ in both hands, nerve oneself to a venture; Dutch ~ (induced by drinking); ~ of one's opinions, ~ to act up to them. [ME & OF corage f. Rom. *coraticum f. L cor heart; see -AGE]

cou'rageous (kŭrāj'us), a. Brave, fearless. Hence ~LY² adv., ~NESS n. [ME & AF corageous (OF -eus), f. prec., see -OUS]

cou'rier (koo͞-), n. Servant employed to make travelling arrangements on continent; title of newspapers, as Liverpool C~; running messenger. [(1)ME corour f. OF coreor f. Rom. *curritorem (L currere run); (2) 16th c. currior, -ier f. F, f. It. corriere (med. L ci rrerius)]

cour'lan (koor-), n. Long-billed rail-like wading bird of tropical America, noted for its dismal cry; limpkin. [F]

course¹ (kōrs), n. **1.** Onward movement; pursuit of game esp. of hares with (grey)-hounds; direction taken, as hold, take, change, one's ~, ship's ~, a dangerous ~ (line of conduct), ~ of events, ~ of nature (ordinary procedure); (pl.) evil ~s (behaviour). **2.** Ground on which race is run (also race-~); channel in which water flows; golf links. **3.** ~ of EXCHANGE. **4.** Career; series (of lectures etc.); rota for duty among members of cathedral body. **5.** Each of successive divisions of meal (esp. soup, fish, joint, etc.). **6.** Continuous layer of stone etc. in building. **7.** (naut.). Fore, main, -~, fore, main, -sail. **8.** In the ~ of, during; by ~ of, according to ordinary procedure of (law etc.); in due ~, in the natural order; of ~, naturally, as was to be expected; matter of ~, natural thing. [ME & OF co(u)rs f. L cursus (currere curs- run); later reinforced by corresp. fem. form OF course]

course² (kōrs), v.t. & i. Pursue (game, as prec.); run about, run (esp. of liquids); give (horse) a run; use (hounds) in coursing. [f. prec.]

cours'er (kōr-), n. (poet.). Swift horse. [ME, f. OF corsier f. Rom. *cursarius (cursus COURSE, see -ARY¹); orig. = war-horse, charger]

court¹ (kōrt), n. **1.** (Also ~'yard) space enclosed by walls or buildings; ‖ (Camb. Univ.) college quadrangle; subdivision of an Exhibition building, museum, etc., open to the general roof; ‖ confined yard opening off street; (in a town) yard surrounded by houses & communicating with street by an entry. **2.** Enclosed quadrangular area, open or covered, for games, as tennis, fives, -~; plot of ground marked out for lawn-tennis. **3.** ‖ Sovereign's residence; his establishment and retinue; the body of courtiers; ‖ sovereign and his councillors as ruling power, as C~ of St James's (British sovereign's ~); assembly held by sovereign, state recep-

tion; *High C~* (assembly) *of Parliament.*
4. Assembly of judges or other persons
acting as tribunal, as ~ *of law, law-~, ~
of justice,~ of judicature,* COUNTY, *criminal,*
POLICE, ~; place, hall, in which justice
is administered; *out of ~,* (of plaintiff, and
fig. of arguments) not entitled to be heard.
5. (Meeting of) qualified members of company or corporation; (in some friendly
societies) = LODGE[1]. **6.** Attention paid to
one whose favour, affection, interest, is
sought, as *pay* ~ *to.* **7.** || ~*-card,* king,
queen, knave; || ~ *circular,* daily report
of ~ doings published in newspapers; || ~
guide, directory containing (theoretically)
names of those who have been presented
at ~; ~ *martial,* judicial ~ of naval,
military, or air force officers, (v.t., ~-
-martial) try by this; *drumhead* ~ *martial*
(held round upturned drum in time of
war); ~ *plaster,* sticking-plaster for cuts
etc. (formerly used by ladies at ~ for
face-patches); ~ *roll,* manorial-court
register of holdings (see COPY[1]). [ME, f.
OF *cort* f. LL, med. L *cortis, curtis, -us* f.
L *cohortem* (nom. *-ors*), yard, COHORT; the
senses of military, assembly, judicial court, by
confus. in F with L *curia*]

court[2] (kōrt), v.t. Pay court to; make love
to (also abs.) with a view to matrimony;
entice (person, *into, to, from,* etc.); seek
to win (applause etc.); invite (inquiry
etc.; *you are ~ing disaster*). [prec.]

court'éous (kŏr-, kĕr-), a. Polite, kind,
considerate, in manner or address. Hence
~LY[2] adv., ~NESS n. [ME & OF *cort-,
curteis* f. Rom. **cortensis* (prec., -ESE)
assim. to wds in -OUS]

courtesan, -zan (kŏrtĭzăn'), n. Prostitute. [f. F *courtisane* f. It. *cortigiana,*
fem. adj. as n. (as prec. + -*ana* -AN)]

court'ésȳ (kŏr-, kĕr-), n. Courteous
behaviour or disposition; *by* ~, by
favour, not of right; || ~ *title,* one held by
~, having no legal validity; || (Law) ~ *of
England, Scotland,* husband's tenure after
wife's death of certain kinds of property
inherited by her; = CURTSY. [ME, f. OF
curt-, cortesie f. *corteis* COURTEOUS; see -Y[1]]

court'ier (kŏr-), n. Attendant at, frequenter of, sovereign's court. [ME
courteour, app. f. AF **corte(i)our,* f. OF
cortoyer vb f. *cort* COURT[1]]

court'l|ȳ (kŏr-), a. Polished, refined, in
manners; obsequious, flattering. Hence
~ĭNESS n. [-LY[1]]

court'ship (kŏr-), n. Courting, wooing,
with view to marriage. [-SHIP]

couscous(sou) (kōō'skōōsōō), n. African
dish of granulated flour steamed over
broth, freq. with meat added. [F, f. Arab.
kuskus (*kaskasa* bruise)]

cous'in (kŭzn), n. (Also *first* ~, ~ *german*)
child of one's uncle or aunt; *my second* ~,
my parent's first ~'s child; *my first
(second* etc.) ~ *once* (*twice* etc.) *removed,*

my first (second etc.) ~'s child (grandchild etc.), also, my parent's (grandparent's etc.) first (second etc.) ~; *call
~s,* claim kinship (*with*); title used by
sovereign in addressing another sovereign
or a nobleman of same country. Hence
~HOOD,~SHIP, nn.,~LY[1] a., (kŭzn-). [ME,
f. OF *cosin, cusin,* f. L *consobrinus* cousin
by the mother's side]

coûte que coûte (kōōtkekōōt'), adv. At
all costs. [F]

coutur|e (kōō'tūr), n. Dressmaking.
Hence ~*ier* (kōōtūr'ĕā), fem. ~*ière*
(kōōtūryār'), nn., dressmaker. [F]

couvade (kōōvahd'), n. Primitive people's
custom by which husband feigns illness
and is put to bed when his wife lies in.
[obs. F, f. *couver* hatch]

cōve[1], n. Small bay or creek; sheltered
recess; (Archit.) concave arch, curved
junction of wall with ceiling or floor.
[OE *cofa,* MLG *cove,* MHG *kobe,* ON *kofi*
f. Gmc **kubhon*]

cōve[2], v.t. Arch (esp. ceiling at junction
with wall); slope (fireplace sides) inwards.
[prec.]

cōve[3], n. (sl.). Fellow, chap. [16th c. *cofe,*
cant of unkn. orig.]

|| **co'ven** (kŭ-), n. (Sc.). Assembly of
witches. [var. of AF *covent,* see CONVENT]

co'vĕnant (kŭ-), n., & v.t. & i. Compact,
bargain; (Law) contract under seal, clause
of this; (Bibl.) compact between God and
the Israelites, as ARK *of the* ~, *land of the*
~ (Canaan); *Solemn League and C*~
(establishing Presbyterianism in England
and Scotland, 1643); *C*~ *of the League of
Nations,* document constituting the
League, incorporated in the Treaty of
Versailles & other treaties concluding
the first world war (1919); (v.t. & i.) agree
(*with* person *for* thing, *to* do, *that*). [ME,
f. OF, part. of *co(n)venir,* see CONVENE]

co'vĕnantĕd (kŭ-), a. Bound by a
covenant. [-ED[1]]

co'vĕnanter (kŭ-), n. One who covenants,
esp. (Sc. Hist.) adherent of the National
Covenant (1638) or Solemn League &
COVENANT. [-ER[1]]

Cŏv'ent Gård'en (*also* kŭ-), n. (Used for)
the ~ fruit and vegetable market in
London.

Cŏv'entrȳ (*also* kŭ-), n. Town in Warwickshire; *send* person *to* ~, refuse to
associate with him.

co'ver[1] (kŭ-), v.t. Overspread, overlay,
(*with* cloth, lid, etc.,·also fig. *with* disgrace
etc.); strew thoroughly (*with*); lie over,
be a covering to; extend over, occupy
the surface of; protect; ~*ing letter,*
explanatory one with enclosure; (of
fortress, guns, etc.) command (territory);
conceal (feelings etc.); ~ *with gun,* present
gun at; (Mil., Cricket) stand behind
(front-rank man, another player to stop
balls he misses; ~*-point,* fielder ~ing

point, his place); include, comprise; deal with (subject); (Journalism) report (proceedings of a meeting, public dinner, etc.); suffice to defray (expenses); protect by insurance; (of stallion) copulate with; ~ *in*, complete the covering of, fill in (grave etc.) with earth; ~ *up*, conceal, esp. by wrapping up. Hence ~ING¹(3) n. [ME, f. OF *covrir, cuvrir* f. L CO(*operire opert-*)]

co'ver² (kŭ-), n. Thing that covers; lid; binding of book; either board of this, as *from* ~ *to* ~; wrapper, envelope, of letter, as *address* person *under* ~ *to another*; case of bicycle tire; hiding-place, shelter, (*take* ~, Mil., utilize lie of ground for protection); protection from attack (*cloud* ~); a force of aircraft for protecting a land or sea operation (*air, fighter,* ~); screen, pretence, as *under (the)* ~ *of humility*; woods or undergrowth sheltering game, COVERT² ; (Commerc.) funds to meet liability or secure against contingent loss; plate, napkin, etc., laid for each person at table; ~ *girl*, girl or woman whose picture illustrates ~ of magazine etc. [f. prec.]

co'verage (kŭ-), n. Area or amount covered, section of community reached by a particular advertising medium, risk covered by insurance policy. [-AGE]

co'verlet, -lid, (kŭ-), n. Counterpane, quilt; covering. [ME *coverlite* etc. app. repr. OF **covre-lit* (as COVER¹ +*lit* bed)]

co'vert¹ (kŭ-), a. (Of threat, glance, etc.) secret, disguised. Hence ~LY² adv. [ME, f. OF, p.p. of *covrir* COVER¹]

co'vert² (kŭ'vert, -cr), n. Shelter, esp. thicket hiding game; ~ *coat*, short light overcoat. [ME, f. OF *covert* p.p. as n. (COVER¹)]

co'verture (kŭ-), n. Covering, cover; shelter; condition of married woman under husband's protection. [ME, f. OF as prec., see -URE]

co'vet (kŭ-), v.t. Desire eagerly (usu. what belongs to another). Hence ~ABLE a. [ME, f. OF *cu-, coveitier* f. Rom. **cupiditare* (as CUPIDITY)]

co'vetous (kŭ-), a. Eagerly desirous (*of* another's property etc.); grasping, avaricious. Hence ~LY² adv., ~NESS n. [ME, f. OF *coveitous* (as prec., see -OUS)]

co'vey (kŭ-), n. (pl. ~s). Brood of partridges; family, party, set. [ME, f. OF *covee* p.p. of *cover* hatch f. L *cubare*, see -Y⁴]

co'vin (kŭ-), n. (legal, arch.). Conspiracy, collusion. [ME, f. OF *covin(e)* f. med. L *convenium, -ia* f. *convenire* (as CONVENE)]

cō'ving, n. Arched piece of building; (pl.) curved sides of fire-place. [COVE² +-ING¹]

cow¹, n. (pl. ~s, arch. *kine*). Female of any bovine animal, esp. of the domestic species; female of elephant, rhinoceros, whale, seal, etc.; ~*-bane*, water hemlock; ~*-boy*, boy in charge of ~s, *man in charge of grazing cattle on ranch; *~-

-catcher, apparatus fixed in front of locomotive engine to remove cattle & other obstructions; ~*-fish*, (1) sea-cow, (2) Indian & American fish with horn-like spines over eyes; ~*-grass*, wild species of trefoil; ~*-heel*, foot of ~ or ox stewed to jelly; ~*-herd*, one who tends ~s at pasture; ~*-hide*, (leather, whip, made of) ~'s hide, = COWAGE; *~-puncher, = ~-boy*; ~*-shot* (Cricket sl.), violent pull made in crouching position; ~*-tree*, S.-American tree with milk-like juice. Hence ~'ISH¹ a. [OE *cū*, OS *kō*, OHG *kuo*, ON *kȳr*, Gmc **kōuz, *kōz*, cogn. w. L *bos*, Gk *bous*]

cow², v.t. Intimidate. [perh. f. ON *kuga*]

cow'age, cowh-, n. Tropical plant with stinging hairs on pod. [f. Hind. *kawanch*]

‖ cow'an, n. (Sc.). Working but unqualified mason; (hence) intruder on a freemasons' lodge. [orig. unkn.]

cow'ard, n. & a. Faint-hearted, pusillanimous, (person). Hence ~LINESS n., ~LY¹ a., ~LY² adv. [ME, f. OF *coart* (= It. *codardo*), f. L *cauda*; see -ARD]

cow'ardice, n. Faint-heartedness; moral ~, fear of disapprobation. [ME, f. OF *couardise* (as prec., see -ICE)]

cow'er, v.i. Stand, squat, in bent position; crouch, esp. from fear. [ME, f. MLG *kūren* lie in wait, of unkn. orig.]

cowl¹, n. Monk's hooded garment; hood of this; hood-shaped covering of chimney or ventilating shaft. Hence cowlED² (-ld) a. [(1) OE *cugele* f. LL *cuculla* f. L *cucullus* hood of cloak; (2) OE *cufle* cogn. w. Du. *keuvel*, conn. w. Icel. *kofl* cowl]

‖ cowl², coul (-ow-), n. Tub for water, esp. one with two ears, carried by two men on ~*-staff*. [ME *cuvel(e)* app. f. OF *cuvele* f. L *cupella* dim. of *cupa* barrel]

cow'-pŏx, n. Disease on teats of cows, communicated to human beings by vaccination.

cowr'ie, -y̆, n. Shell of small gastropod found in Indian Ocean, used as money in Africa & S. Asia; the animal; kinds of gastropod including common ~ of British coast. [f. Hind. *kauri*]

cow'slip, n. ‖ Wild plant growing in pastures, with fragrant yellow flowers; ‖ ~ *tea, wine* (made from these). [OE *cū-slyppe* f. *cū* cow+*slyppe* slimy substance (i.e. cow-dung)]

cŏx, n., & v.t. & i., (colloq.). = COXSWAIN, esp. of racing boat; (vb) act as ~ (of). [abbr.]

cŏx'a, n. (pl. *-ae*). Hip. Hence cŏx'AL a. [L]

cŏx'comb (-ōm), n. Conceited showy person. Hence cŏxcomb'ICAL (-mĭ-) a. [= *cock's comb*; orig. (cap worn by) professional fool]

cŏx'combry (-komrĭ), n. Foppery, behaviour of a coxcomb. [-RY]

cŏx'swain (-kswān, -ksn), n. (abbr. COX). Helmsman of boat; person on board ship permanently in charge of, & (unless superior officer is present) commanding, boat & crew. Hence ~LESS a., ~SHIP n. [ME, f. *cock* (see COCKBOAT)+SWAIN; cf. BOATSWAIN]

coxy. See COCKY.

coy, a. Modest, shy, (usu. of girl); (of place) secluded; ~ *of*, backward, reserved, in (speech etc.). Hence ~'LY[2] adv., ~'NESS n. [ME, f. OF *coi* (fem. *coite*) f. Rom. **quetus* f. L *quietus* QUIET]

coyŏt'é (ko-, *also* ki'ŏt), n. N.-American prairie-wolf. [Mex. Sp., f. Mex. *coyotl*]

coypu (koi'pōō), n. S.-American aquatic beaver-like rodent (cf. NUTRIA). [native name]

coz (kŭz), n. (arch.). Abbr. of COUSIN.

cōze, v.i., & n. (Have a) chat. [(vb) prob. f. F *causer*], n. perh. influenced by COSY]

co'zen (kŭ-), v.t. & i. (literary). Cheat, defraud, (*of*, *out of*); beguile (*into* do*ing*); act deceitfully. Hence~AGE(3) n. [16th c. cant, of unkn. orig.]

cōz'ў, a. See COSY.

crăb[1], n. Kinds of ten-footed crustacean, esp. edible species found near most sea--coasts; zodiacal constellation, CANCER; machine (orig. with claws) for hoisting heavy weights; (pl.) lowest throw at hazard, two aces, whence *turn out* ~s, end in failure; *catch a* ~ in rowing, get oar jammed under water by faulty stroke; ~'s *eyes*, round concretion of carbonate of lime, found in stomach of crayfish; ~(-*louse*), parasitical insect infesting human body; ~-*pot*, wicker trap for ~s. Hence ~'LET n., ~'LIKE a. & adv. [OE *crabba*, MDu., MLG *krabbe*, ON *krabbi*, rel. to OS *krebit* etc., see CRAYFISH]

crăb[2], v.t. & i. (-bb-). (Of hawks) scratch, claw, fight with, (each other or abs.); (colloq.) cry down, pull to pieces. [f. MLG *krabben*, rel. to prec.]

crăb[3], n. (Also ~-*apple*) wild apple (fruit & tree); sour person. [perh. alt. (after CRABBED) of 15th c. (now Sc. & north.) *scrab*, of Scand. orig.; cf. Sw. dial. *skrabba* wild apple]

crăbb'ĕd, a. Cross-grained, perverse; churlish, irritable; (of writings or authors) ruggedly intricate, difficult to make out; (of handwriting) ill-formed & hard to decipher; sour, harsh. Hence ~LY[2] adv., ~NESS n. Also (in first two senses only) **crăbb'ў** a. [ME; CRAB[1] +-ED[2], influenced in sense by CRAB[3]]

crăck[1], n. & a. Sudden sharp noise (of whip, rifle, thunder); ~ *of doom*, thunder--peal of Day of Judgement; sharp blow, as *a* ~ *on the head*; *in a* ~, in a moment; (arch., sl.) boast, lie; ‖ (Sc. & North.) brisk talk, (pl.) news; (sl.) = WISE[1] ~; fissure formed by breakage; partial fracture (the parts still cohering); good player, horse, etc.; burglar, house--breaking; (adj., colloq.) first-rate; ~-

brained, crazy. [ME *crak*, goes w. foll.; so OHG *krach*]

crăck[2], v.t. & i. (Cause to) make sharp noise, as ~ *a whip*, *whips* ~; (utter) *a joke*; chat;* ~ *down on* (sl.), take severe measures against; ~ *up*, praise; break (nut, skull, etc.) with sudden sharp report; ~ *a bottle*, empty, drink it; (sl.) ~ *a crib*, break into a house; break (t. & i.) without complete separation of parts; *voice* ~s, *is* ~*ed* (becomes dissonant, esp. at age of puberty); damage, ruin, (credit etc.); decompose (heavy oils) by heat and pressure to produce lighter hydrocarbons (such as petrol); (p.p., colloq.) crazy, insane; ~-*jaw* (colloq.), (word) difficult to pronounce. Hence ~'ABLE a. [OE *cracian*, Du. *kraken*, OHG *krahhōn* f., WG **krakōjan*]

crăck'er, n. In vbl senses; also or esp.: firework exploding with sharp report; explosive bon-bon; instrument for cracking, as *nut-*~s; thin hard biscuit; *biscuit; smash, breakdown; (school sl.) lie; *~-*jack* (sl.), exceptionally fine or expert (thing or person); ~s, pred. a. (sl.), crazy, mad. [-ER[1]]

crăc'kle, v.i., & n. Emit slight cracking sound; (n.) such sound, (also ~-*china*, -*glass*, -*ware*) china, glass, with appearance of minute cracks. [f. CRACK[2]+-LE(3)]

crăck'ling, n. In vbl senses; also, crisp skin of roast pork. [-ING[1]]

crăck'nel, n. Light crisp kind of biscuit. [f. F *craquelin* f. MDu. *krākeling* f. *krāken* CRACK[2]]

crăcks'man, n. Burglar. [CRACK[1], MAN]

crăck'ў, a. Full of cracks; apt to crack; (colloq.) crazy. [-Y[2]]

-cracў, noun suf. added to Gk stems (and as -*ocracy* to E wds), meaning 'rule of, ruling body of, class influential by'; thus *demo*~=popular government, *the demo*~ = the lower classes as political power; *pluto*~ = government by the rich, *the pluto*~, those whose wealth gives them power; so *cottono*~ etc. [f. F -*cratie* f. Gk -*kratia* (*kratos* power); see -CY]

crā'dle, n., & v.t. **1.** Bed, cot, for infant, mounted on rockers; *from the* ~, from infancy; (fig.) place in which thing is nurtured in earliest stage, as ~ *of an art*, *of a nation*; framework resembling ~, esp. (Naut.) that on which ship or boat rests during construction or repairs; frame attached to scythe to lay corn evenly; (Engraving) kind of serrated chisel, rocking-tool; (Mining) trough on rockers in which auriferous earth is shaken in water; CAT's-~. **2.** v.t. Place in (child's, ship's) ~, contain or shelter as ~; mow (corn) with ~-scythe. [OE *cradol* cogn. w. OHG *kratto* basket]

crā'dling, n. In vbl senses; also (Archit.) wood or iron framework. [prec.+-ING[1]]

craft (-ah-), n. Skill; cunning, deceit; art,

trade, (esp. in combb., as *handi*~, *priest*-~, *state*~); *the gentle*~, angling; members of a ~; *the C*~, brotherhood of Freemasons; boat, vessel, (pl. *craft*); ~*-brother*, *-guild*, workman, guild of workmen, of same trade; ~*s'man*, one who practises a ~, whence ~s'manSHIP(3) (-ah-) n., (also) private in the R.E.M.E. [OE *cræft*, OS, OHG *kraft*, ON *kraptr* strength]

craf't| y̆ (-ah-), a. Cunning, artful, wily. Hence ~ĭLY[2] adv., ~ĭNESS n. [f. prec. +-Y[2]]

crăg[1], n. Steep or rugged rock; ~*s'man*, skilled climber of ~s. Hence ~g'ED[2], ~g'Y[2], aa., ~g'ĕdNESS, ~g'ĭNESS, nn., (-g-). [of Celt. orig.]

|| **crăg**[2], n. (geol.). Deposits of shelly sand found in Norfolk, Suffolk, Essex. [orig. unkn.]

crāke, n., & v.i. Kinds of bird including CORN~; cry of the corn~; (v.i.) utter this. [ME; n. f. ON *kráka* crow, or f. the vb (imit., cf. CROAK)]

crăm, v.t. & i. (-mm-), &n. 1. Fill overfull; force (thing *into*, *down*); ~ *down* one's *throat*, tell him repeatedly); stuff (poultry etc. *with* food); eat greedily; (fig.) prepare (t. & i.) for examination; learn, get up, (subject) for special purpose; ~*-full*, as full as ~ming can make it. 2. n. Crowd, ~ming for examination; (sl.) lie. [OE *crammian* (=ON *kremja* squeeze), cogn. w. *crimman* cram, OHG *krimman* press etc.]

crăm'bō, n. Game in which one player gives word to which each of the others must find rhyme; *dumb* ~, game in which one side must guess word, a rhyme to which is given, by representing other rhymes to it in dumb show. [16th c. *crambe*, app. allus. L *crambe repetita* cabbage served up again]

crămm'er, n. In vbl senses, esp.: one who crams (esp. pupils); lie. [-ER[1]]

crăm'oisy̆, -m'esy̆, (-z-), a. & n. (arch.). Crimson (cloth). [15th c. *cremesi* &c., f. early It. *cremesi* & OF *crameisi* (mod. *cramoisi*) f. Arab. *qirmazi* of the KERMES; see CRIMSON]

crămp[1], n. Contraction of muscles from sudden chill, strain, etc.; ~*-fish*, electric ray, torpedo. [ME, f. OF *crampe* f. MDu., MLG *kramp* f. same root as CRAM]

crămp[2], n. (Also ~*-iron*) metal bar with bent ends for holding masonry etc. together; portable tool for pressing two planks etc. together; restraint. [f. MDu. *krampe*, as prec.]

crămp[3], a. Hard to make out, as ~ *word*, *handwriting*; contracted, cramped. Hence ~'NESS n. [perh. f. CRAMP[1], [4], but cf. F *crampe* curved]

crămp[4], v.t. Affect with CRAMP[1]; confine narrowly (also ~ *up*); (fig.) restrict (energies etc.); fasten with CRAMP[2]. Hence ~'ĕdNESS n. [f. CRAMP[1,2]]

crăm'pon, n. Metal hook, grappling--iron; iron plate with spikes for walking

on ice etc. [ME; F, f. as CRAMP[2], see -OON]

|| **crăn**, n. (Sc.). Measure for fresh herrings (37½ gal.). [= Gael. *crann* of unkn. orig.]

crān'age, n. Use of crane; dues paid for this. [CRANE[1]+-AGE]

crăn'berry̆, n. Small dark-red acid berry, fruit of dwarf shrub native of Britain, N. Europe, N. America, etc. [17th c., named by Amer. colonists f. G *kranbeere*, LG *kranebere* crane-berry]

crāne[1], n. Large wading bird with long legs, neck, and bill; machine for moving heavy weights; siphon; (also *water*-~) tube for supplying water to locomotive; ~*-fly*, daddy-long-legs; ~*'s-bill*, various species of geranium. [OE *cran*, OS, OHG *krano*; w. suff., OE *cranoc*, OHG *chranuh* (G *kranich*)]

crāne[2], v.t. & i. Move with crane; stretch (neck), stretch neck, like crane; ~ *at*, pull up at, shrink from, (hedge, difficulty). [f. prec.]

crāniŏ- in comb. = foll., as *cranio*LO'GICAL, -LOGIST, -LOGY (-ŏl[2]), -METRY (-ŏm[2]).

crān'ium, n. (pl. *-ia*, *-iums*). Bones enclosing the brain; bones of the whole head, skull. Hence **crān'iAL** a. [med. L, f. Gk *kranion* skull]

crănk[1], n., & v.t. 1. Part of axle or shaft bent at right angles for. converting reciprocal into circular motion, or vice versa; elbow shaped connexion in bell--hanging; revolving disc turned by criminals as punishment. 2. v.t. Bend into ~ shape, furnish or fasten with ~; ~ *up*, set (engine of motor-car) going by turning a ~ (also abs.). [OE *cranc*, app. f. *crincan* by-form of *cringan* fall in battle, orig. 'curl up']

crănk[2], n. Fanciful turn of speech; eccentric idea or act; eccentric person. [different. f. prec.]

crănk[3], a. Weak, shaky, (usu. of machinery). [f. CRANK[1]]

crănk[4], a. (naut.). Liable to capsize. [perh. rel. to prec.]

crankle (-ăng'kl), v.i., & n. Bend in and out, twist; (n.) bend, twist. [f. CRANK[1] +-LE]

crănk'|y̆, a. Sickly; shaky; crazy; capricious; crotchety, eccentric; full of twists; (Naut.) = CRANK[4]. Hence ~ĭLY[2] adv., ~ĭNESS n. [CRANK[1,2,3,4]+-Y[2]]

crănn'og, n. Ancient lake-dwelling in Scotland or Ireland. [Ir. (*crann* tree, beam)]

crănn'|y̆, n. Chink, crevice, crack. Hence ~ĭED[2] (-ĭd) a. [15th c., perh. rel. to OF *cran*, *cren* notch; cf. CRENEL]

crāpe, n., & v.t. Gauze-like fabric with wrinkled surface, usu. of black silk or imitation silk (of other colour or material now usu. CRÊPE), used for mourning dress; band of this round hat etc. as sign of mourning; ~*-cloth*, ~*-like* woollen material; (v.t.) cover, clothe, drape, with ~. Hence **crăp'Y[2]** a. [anglicized sp. of CRÊPE]

craped (-pt), a. In vbl senses; also, crisped, crimped. [CRAPE + -ED²,¹]

*craps, n. pl. Game of chance played with dice; *shoot* ~, play this. [orig. unkn.; cf. *crabs* (CRAB¹)]

crap′ul|ent, a. Given to, suffering from effects of, resulting from, intemperance. Hence or cogn. ~ENCE n., ~OUS a. [f. LL *crapulentus* f. L *crapula* inebriation, see -LENT]

crash¹, v.i. & t., & n. 1. Make a ~ (see n.); move, go, with a ~, (of aircraft or airman) fall to earth; (v.t.) dash in pieces, throw, force, drive, with a ~; *go, fall*, ~ (with a ~). 2. n. Noise as of broken crockery, thunder, loud music, etc., violent percussion or breakage, (fig.) ruin, collapse of mercantile credit; ~-*dive*, (of submarine) dive hastily and steeply in an emergency (also as n.); ~-*helmet*, protective helmet of motor cyclist etc.; ~-*land*, (of aircraft or airman) land hurriedly with a ~, usu. without lowering undercarriage. [imit., cf. CLASH]

crash², n. Coarse linen for towels etc. [f. Russ. *krashenina* coloured linen]

cras′is, n. (Gk gram.). Combination of the vowels of two syllables (as *kagō* for *kai egō*). [Gk, = mixture (*kerannumi* mix)]

crass, a. Thick, gross; (fig.) gross, as ~ *stupidity*; grossly stupid. Hence ~′LY² adv., ~′NESS n. [f. L *crassus* solid, thick]

crass′itūde, n. Grossness; gross stupidity. [f. L *crassitudo* (as prec., see -TUDE)]

-crat, noun suf. = supporter, member, of a -CRACY, & used & appended similarly (-*crat*, -*ocrat*). Hence -**crăt′**IC(AL) adj. suff. [f. F -*crate* formed f. adjj. in -*cratique* (on anal. of Gk *autokratēs* or independently) f. Gk -*kratia* -CRACY]

crătch, n. Rack for feeding beasts out of doors. [ME *crecche* f. OF *creche* f. Rom. *creppja f. WG *krippja CRIB]

crāte, n. Large open-work case or basket for carrying glass, crockery, fruit, etc. Hence ~′FUL (-tf-) n. [perh. f. Du. *krat* basket etc.]

crāt′er, n. Mouth of volcano; bowl-shaped cavity, esp. that made by explosion of shell or bomb. Hence ~ĪFORM a. [L, f. Gk *kratēr* mixing-bowl]

cravăt′, n. Neckcloth, tie (now arch. or shop). Hence ~t′ED² a. [f. F *cravate* f. Croatian *Hrvat* Croat]

crāve, v.t. & i. Beg for; long for; beg, long, *for*. Hence **crāv′**ING¹ n., strong desire, intense longing, (*for*). [OE *crafian*, rel. to ON *krefja*]

crāv′en, a. & n. Coward, abject, (person); *cry* ~, surrender. Hence ~LY² adv. [ME *cravant, -and(e)*, of unkn. orig.]

craw, n. Crop of birds or insects. [ME *crawe* f. OE *craga, cogn. w. MDu. *crāghe*, MLG *krāge*, MHG *krage* neck, throat]

crawfish. See CRAYFISH.

crawl¹, n. Pen in shallow water for fish, turtles, etc.; = KRAAL. [f. Du. KRAAL]

crawl², v.i., & n. 1. Move slowly, dragging body along close to ground, or on hands & knees; walk, move, slowly; creep abjectly; (of ground etc.) be alive *with* crawling things; feel creepy sensation, whence ~′Y² a. 2. n. ~ing; *the* ~, a high-speed swimming stroke. [ME *creule, croule*, later *crawle*, of unkn. orig.; cf. Da., Norw. *kravle*, G *krabbeln* crawl]

crawl′er, n. In vbl senses; esp.: baby's overall; louse; cab moving slowly in search of fare. [-ER¹]

cray′fish, crawʟ, n. Small lobster-like freshwater crustacean; spiny lobster. [ME & OF *crevice* f. WG *krabitja, *krebitja, whence OS *krebit*, OHG *krebiz* (G *krebs*); see CRAB]

cray′on, n., & v.t. Stick, pencil, of coloured chalk or other material for drawing; carbon point in electric arc lamp; (v.t.) draw with ~s, (fig.) sketch. [F, f. *craie* chalk, see -OON]

crāze, v.t. & i., & n. Render insane (usu. in p.p.); produce small cracks on (pottery); (v.i.) have such cracks; (n.) insane fancy, mania, crazy condition, (*be the* ~, be generally sought or affected). [ME; (n. f. vb) orig. = break, shatter, perh. f. ON *krasa (Sw. *krasa* crunch, *slå i kras* dash to pieces)]

crāz′ing, n. In vbl senses; ~-*mill* (for crushing tin ore). [-ING¹]

crāz′|y̆, a. (Of ship, building, etc.) unsound, shaky; sickly; insane, mad; (colloq.) extremely enthusiastic (*about*); (of paving, quilts, etc.) made of irregular pieces fitted together; ~-*y bone*, funny bone. Hence ~ĪLY² adv., ~ĪNESS n. [CRAZE + -Y²]

creak, n., & v.i. Harsh strident noise, as of unoiled hinge, new boots, etc.; (v.i.) make this. Hence ~′Y² a. [ME, imit., cf. CRAKE, CROAK]

cream¹, n. Oily part of milk, which gathers on the top, & by churning is made into butter; CLOTted (also *Devonshire* or *Cornish*) ~; fancy dish, sweet, like or made of ~; best part of anything, esp. the point of an anecdote; part of a liquid that gathers at the top; ~ *of tartar*, purified & crystallized bitartrate of potassium, used in medicine etc.; ~ *of lime* (pure slaked); ~-like preparation, as *cold* ~ (cooling unguent); ~-coloured horse; ~ *cheese*, soft rich kind made of unskimmed milk & ~; ~-*fruit*, a ~-like fruit of Sierra Leone; ~-*coloured*, yellow-ish white; ~-*laid*, ~-*wove*, *paper*, laid, wove, paper of ~ colour; ~ *separator*, machine for separating ~ from milk. Hence ~′Y² a., ~′ĪNESS n. [ME *creme* f. OF *cresme* (mod. F *crème* f.), a pop. application of the orig. sense CHRISM (mod. F *chrême* m.); see CHRISM]

cream², v.i. & t. (Of milk & liquids) form cream or scum; cause (milk) to ~; take cream from (milk); take the best part of (anything); add cream to (tea etc.). [f. prec.]

cream'er, n. Flat dish for skimming cream off milk; machine for separating cream. [-ER¹]

cream'erў, n. Butter-factory; shop where milk, cream, etc., are sold. [-ERY]

crease, n., & v.t. & i. Line caused by folding, fold, wrinkle; (Cricket) line defining position of bowler & batsman, as *bowling* ~ (from behind which bowler delivers ball); POPPING ~; (v.t.) make ~s in (material); (v.i.) fall into ~s. Hence **creas'ў²** a. [in 16th c. form *creast*(e) the same wd as CREST (in 15th c. also *creast*); cf. obs. *crest* (of cloth), middle line of fold]

creāt|e', v.t. & i. Bring into existence, give rise to; originate, as (of actor) ~*e a part*; invest (person) with rank, as ~*e a man a peer*, ~*e a peer*; (v.i., sl.) make a fuss. Hence ~'IVE a., ~'IVELY² adv., ~'IVENESS n. [ME, f. L *creare*, see -ATE³]

crē'atine, n. An organic base found in the juice of flesh. [f. Gk *kreas -atos* meat +-INE⁵]

creā'tion, n. Act of creating (esp. the world); investing with title, rank, etc. (~ *of peers*, ultimate means of overcoming resistance of House of Lords to will of Commons); all created things; a production of the human (esp. dressmaker's, actor's) intelligence, esp. of the imagination. [ME, f. OF f. L *creationem* (as CREATE, see -ATION)]

creā'tion|ism (-sho-), n. Theory that God creates a soul for every human being at birth; theory that attributes origin of matter & species to special creation (not EVOLUTION). So ~IST n. [-ISM]

creā'tor, n. *The C~*, the Supreme Being; one who creates, whence **creāt'ress¹** n. [ME, f. OF *creator, -ur, -our*, f. L *creatorem* (as CREATE, see -OR)]

crea'ture, n. Created thing; animate being; animal (often as distinct from man); human being, person, (often expr. admiration, contempt, patronage, etc.); one who owes his fortune to another; mere instrument; *the* ~ (often spelt as Ir., *cratur* etc.), whisky or other intoxicant; ~ COMFORTS. [ME, f. OF f. LL *creatura* (as prec., see -URE)]

crea'turelў (-rl-), a. Of creatures. [-LY¹]

crèche (krāsh), n. Public nursery for infants; model of the manger-scene at Bethlehem. [F (as CRATCH)]

crēd'ăt Judae'us (Apěll'a) (joo-), sent. expressing incredulity. [L, = let the Jew Apella believe it, see Hor. *Sat.* I. v. 100]

crēd'ence, n. Belief; *give* ~ *to*, believe; *letter of* ~ (introduction); small side table for eucharistic elements before consecration. [ME, f. OF or f. med. L *credentia* (*credere* believe, see -ENCE)]

crēděn'tial, n. (usu. pl.; -shalz). Letter(s) of introduction (also fig.). [f. med. L *credentialis* (as prec., see -AL)]

crěd'i|ble, a. (Of persons or statements) believable, worthy of belief. Hence or cogn. ~BIL'ITY n., ~bLУ² adv. [ME, f. L *credibilis* (as CREDENCE, see -BLE)]

crěd'it, n. Belief, trust; *give* ~ *to*, believe (story); good reputation; power derived from this; acknowledgement of merit, as *have the* ~ *of, get* ~ *for*; source of honour, as *a* ~ *to the school, it does him* ~; trust in person's ability & intention to pay, as *give* ~, *deal on* ~, *long* ~; reputation of solvency & honesty; sum placed at person's disposal in books of a bank etc.; *letter of* ~ (authorizing person to draw money from writer's correspondent in another place); (Bookkeeping) acknowledgement of payment by entry in account, sum entered on ~ side of account (cf. DEBIT), this side; *give* person ~ *for*, enter (sum) to his ~, (fig.) ascribe (quality) to him. [f. F *crédit* f. It. *credito* f. L *credere -it-* believe, trust]

crěd'it², v.t. Believe; carry to credit side of account (~ *amount to* person, person *with* amount); (fig.) ~ person *with*, think he has a quality). [f. prec.]

crěd'itab|le, a. That brings credit or honour (*to*). Hence ~LУ² adv. [-ABLE]

crěd'itor, n. One to whom a debt is owing; (Bookkeeping) ~ (abbr. *Cr*) side of account, right-hand side. [ME & AF *creditour* (OF *-eur*) f. L *creditorem* (as CREDIT¹, see -OR)]

crēd'ō, n. (pl. *-os*). Creed (esp. Apostles' & Nicene, beginning in Latin with ~); musical setting of Nicene Creed. [ME; L, = I believe]

crěd'ūlous, a. Too ready to believe; (of things) showing such readiness. Hence or cogn. **crēdūl'ITY,** ~NESS, nn., ~LУ² adv. [f. L *credulus* (*credere* believe)]

creed, n. Brief formal summary of Christian doctrine, esp. *Apostles'* (also *the C~*), *Nicene, Athanasian, C~*; system of religious belief; set of opinions on any subject. Hence ~'LESS a. [OE *crēda*, f. L CREDO]

creek, n. ‖ Inlet on sea-coast; small harbour; short arm of river; (U.S. & Colon.) tributary river; narrow plain between mountains. [(1) ME *crike* f. ON *kriki* (or partly f. OF *crique*, f. ON); (2) ME *crēke* f. MDu. *krēke* (or f. *crike* by lengthening); ult. orig. unkn.]

creel, n. Large wicker basket for fish; angler's fishing-basket. [orig. Sc., of unkn. orig.]

creep, v.i. (*crěpt*), & n. **1.** Move with body prone & close to ground; move timidly, slowly, or stealthily; ~*ing* BARRAGE; insinuate oneself *into*, come *in, up*, unobserved; proceed, exist, abjectly; (of plants) grow along ground, wall, etc.; *flesh* ~*s*, feels as if things were ~*ing* over it (result of fear, repugnance, etc.). (Naut.) drag with creeper at bottom of water; ~*-mouse* (adj.), timid, shy. **2.** n. ~*ing*; shrinking horror, as (colloq. pl.)

gave me the ~s; low arch under railway embankment; opening in hedge etc.; (Geol.) gradual movement of disintegrated rock due to atmospheric changes etc. [OE *crēopan*, OS *criopan*, ON *krúpja* f. Gmc **kreupan*]

creep'er, n. In vbl senses, esp.: plant that creeps along ground or up wall; grapnel for dragging bottom of water. [-ER[1]]

creep'y̆, a. Having a creeping of the flesh; productive of this; given to creeping. So **~-crawl'y̆** a. [-Y[2]]

creese, crease, kris (-ēs, -is), n. Malay dagger with wavy blade. [Malay (*keris, kres*)]

crĕm|āte', v.t. Consume (esp. corpse) by fire. So **~A'TION**, **~ā'tion**IST(2) (-sho-), nn. [19th c. back form. f. *cremation* (17th c.) f. L *crematio* f. *cremare* burn]

crĕmāt'or, n. Person, furnace, cremating corpses or rubbish. Hence **crĕmatŏr'ium** (pl. -s, -ia), **crĕm'atory**(2), nn. [f. as prec., see -OR]

crème (-ām), n. *~ de menthe* (demahnt), peppermint liqueur; *~ de la ~* (-dlah-), the very pick, élite. [F]

crĕmōn'a, n. Violin made at C~; cromorne. [place]

crĕn'ate, -āted, a. (bot., zool.). With notched or toothed edge. Hence **crĕnA'-TION** n. [f. mod. L *crenatus* f. pop. L (= It.) *crena* notch, see -ATE[2]]

crĕn'ature, n. Rounded tooth on edge of leaf etc. [as prec. see -URE]

crĕn'el, crĕnĕlle', n. Open space in embattled parapet, for shooting through etc. [ME, f. OF *crenel*, dim. of *cren, cran*; cf. It. f. pop. L *crena* notch; see CRANNY, CRENATE]

crĕn'e(l)lāte, v.t. Furnish with battlements or loopholes. Hence **crĕnellA'TION** n. [f. F *créneler* (as prec.), see -ATE[3]]

crē'ōle, n. & a. (Descendant of) European (also *~ white*) or Negro (*~ Negro*) settler in W. Indies, Mauritius, etc.; (adj.) of such descent, (of animals etc.) naturalized in W. Indies etc. [F *créole* f. Sp. *criollo*, app. ult. f. *criar* breed (cf. Sp. *criado* domestic), f. L *creare* CREATE]

crē'osŏte, n. Colourless oily liquid distilled from wood-tar, a strong antiseptic; (Commerc.) carbolic acid. Hence **crēs'OL** n., caustic liquid obtained by distillation of coal tar. [f. Gk *kreas* meat + *sōzō* save]

crêpe (-āp), n. Crapy fabric other than black mourning crape; *~ de Chine* (deshēn), of silk kind; *~ rubber*, very durable rubber used for shoe soles etc. [F, f. L *crispa* curled; see CRAPE]

crĕp'it|āte, v.i. Make crackling sound; (of beetles) eject pungent fluid with sharp report. So **~ANT** a., **~A'TION** n. [f. L *crepitare* frequent. of *crepare* creak, see -ATE[3]]

crĕpon (krĕp'ŏn), n. Stuff like crape, but of firmer substance. [F (as CRÊPE, see -OON)]

crĕpt. See CREEP.

crĕpŭs'cūlar, a. Of twilight; (Zool.) appearing, active, in twilight; dim, not yet fully enlightened. [f. L *crepusculum* twilight + -AR[1]]

crescĕn'dō (krĕsh-), adv., n., & a. (mus.). (Passage of music to be played) with gradually increasing volume (abbr. *cres.*, *cresc.*); (fig.) progress towards a climax. [It., part. of *crescere* grow (as foll.)]

crĕs'cent, n. & a. **1.** Increasing moon, figure of moon in first or last quarter; this as badge of Turkish Sultans; the Turkish power; the Moslem religion; any figure of ~ shape, ‖ esp. row of houses. **2.** adj. Increasing, ~-shaped. [ME & AF *cressant*, OF *creissant*, f. L *crescere* grow, see -ENT]

crĕss, n. Name of various plants usu. with pungent edible leaves, as *garden ~*, WATER[1]~; *Indian ~*, tropaeolum. [OE *cresse, cressa* = OHG *kressa*, -o, f. WG **krasjō*- creep]

crĕss'ĕt, n. Metal vessel for holding grease or oil for light, usu. mounted on pole; (mod.) fire-basket for lighting wharf etc. [ME, f. OF *cresset, craisset*, f. *craisse = graisse* GREASE]

crĕst, n., & v.t. & i. **1.** Comb or tuft on animal's head; *~'fallen*, with drooping ~, dejected, abashed; plume, tuft, of feathers; (apex of) helmet; head, top, esp. of mountain; surface line of neck in animals; mane. **2.** (anat.). Ridge along surface of bone, as *frontal, occipital, ~ of skull.* **3.** (her.). Device above shield & helmet on coat of arms, or separately, as on seal, notepaper, etc. **4.** v.t. Furnish with ~, serve as ~ to, reach ~ of (hill, wave); (v.i., of waves) form into a ~. [ME, f. OF *creste* f. L *crista* tuft]

crētā'ceous (-shus), a. Of (the nature of) chalk; *C~ system* (Geol.), third & final system of the Mesozoic group of rocks. [f. L *cretaceus* (*creta* chalk, see -ACEOUS)]

crĕt'ic, n. Metrical foot (– ∪ –). [f. L f. Gk *Krētikos* (*Krētē* Crete, see -IC)]

crĕt'in, n. Deformed idiot of a kind found esp. in Alpine valleys. Hence **~ISM** (2) n., **~IZE** v.t., **~OUS** a. [f. F *crétin* f. Swiss F *creitin, crestin* f. L *Christianus* CHRISTIAN in mod. Rom. sense 'human creature']

crĕt'ŏnne (*also* -ĕtŏn'), n. Stout unglazed cotton cloth with pattern printed on one or both sides. [F]

crĕvăsse', n. Deep fissure in ice of glacier. [F, readopted as different. f. foll.]

crĕv'ice, n. Chink, fissure. [ME *crevace*, -*isse* f. OF *crevace* (mod. -*asse*) f. *crever* burst (L *crepare*) + -*asse* = L -*aceo*, see -ACEOUS]

crew[1] (-ōō), n. Whole body of men manning ship or boat; associated body, company, of persons; set, gang, mob; *~ cut*, man's hair cut short all over. [ME *crue* f. OF *crue* increase fem. p.p. (as n.) of *croistre* grow f. L *crescere*]

crew[2]. See CROW[3].

crew'ĕl (-ōō-), n. Thin worsted yarn for

tapestry & embroidery; ~-*work*, design in worsted on linen or cloth ground. [15th c. *crule*; orig. unkn.]

crib[1], n. Barred receptacle for fodder; hovel, hut; small bed for child, with barred sides; wicker salmon-trap; framework lining shaft of mine; (also ~-*work*) heavy crossed timbers used in foundations in loose soil etc.; *bin for maize, salt, etc.; set of cards given to dealer at cribbage, taken from other players' hands; (colloq.) plagiarism; translation for (esp. illegitimate) use of students; CRACK[2] *a* ~; ~-*biting* (of horses), habit of seizing manger in teeth & at same time noisily drawing in breath. [OE *crib*(*b*), OS *kribbia*, OHG *kripp*(*e*)*a* f. WG **kribjōn*]

crib[2], v.t. (-bb-). Confine in small space; furnish (cowshed etc.) with cribs; pilfer; copy unfairly or without acknowledgement. [f. prec.]

cribb'age, n. Card game for two, three, or four persons. [f. CRIB[1] + -AGE]

crib'rifórm, a. (anat., bot.). Having small holes, like a sieve. [f. L *cribrum* sieve + -FORM]

crick, n., & v.t. Spasmodic affection of muscles of neck, back, etc., sudden stiffness; (v.t.) produce ~ in (neck etc.). [15th c., of unkn. orig.]

crick'ét[1], n. (Also *house-*~) a jumping chirping insect. [ME, f. OF *criquet* f. *criquer* creak etc.; imit.]

crick'ét[2], n., & v.i. Open-air game played with ball, bats, & wickets, between two sides of 11 players each (‖ *not* ~ colloq., infringing the codes of fair play between honourable opponents in any sphere); (v.i.) play ~. Hence ~ER[1] n. [from 1598, of uncert. orig.; cf. OF *criquet* stick to aim at in the game of bowls; cf. Flem. *krick*(*e*) stick]

cric'oid, a. & n. Ring-shaped (cartilage of larynx). [f. Gk *krikoeidēs* (*krikos* ring, -OID)]

cri de cœur (krē' de kȇr'), n. A passionate appeal, complaint, or protest. [F, = cry from the heart]

cri'er, n. One who cries; officer who makes public announcements in court of justice or (*town* ~) in a town. [ME & OF *criere*, nom. of *crieur* (*crier* CRY, see -OR)]

crik'ey, int. (sl.), expr. astonishment. [euphem. for *Christ*]

crime, n., & v.t. 1. Act (usu. grave offence) punishable by law; evil act, sin; ~-*sheet*, record of soldier's offences against regulations. Hence ~'LESS (-ml-) a. 2. v.t. (mil.). Charge with or convict of military offence. [ME, f. OF f. L *crimen -minis* judgement, offence]

crime passionnel (krēm' păsyŏnȇl'), n. Crime due to jealousy. [F, = crime of passion]

crim'inal, a. & n. Of (the nature of) crime; ~ CONVERSATION, CONNEXION; (person) guilty of crime. Hence or cogn.

criminăl'ITY n., ~LY[2] adv. [ME, f. OF *criminel* f. LL *criminalis* (as CRIME, see -AL)]

crim'inăte, v.t. Charge with crime; prove (one*self* etc.) guilty of crime; censure. Hence or cogn. ~A'TION n., ~ătive, ~ătory, aa. [f. L *criminari* (*crimen* CRIME), see -ATE[3]]

crim'inĕ, -nȳ, int. (arch.), expr. astonishment. [euphem. for *Christ*]]

criminŏl'ogȳ, n. Science of crime. [f. L *crimen -minis* CRIME + -O- + -LOGY]

crim'inous, a. Guilty of crime, only in phr. ~ *clerk* (clergyman). [f. AF *criminous* (OF -*eux*) f. L *criminosus* (as prec., see -OUS)]

crimp[1], n., & v.t. Agent who entraps men for seamen or soldiers (also fig.); (v.t.) entrap thus, impress, (seamen, soldiers). [17th c., of unkn. orig.]

crimp[2], v.t. Compress into plaits or folds, frill; make flutings in, corrugate; contract (flesh of freshly-caught fish) by gashing; mould, bend, into shape. [prob. f. MDu., MLG *krimpen*, = MHG *krimpfen*; cogn. w. CRAMP[1, 2]]

crim'son (-z-), a. & n., & v.t. & i. Deep-red (colour); ~ RAMBLER; (v.t. & i.) turn ~. [15th c. *cremesin* = early Sp. *cremesin*, early It. -*ino*, med. L -*inus*, metathetic alt. (+ -*in*(*o*) -INE[1]) of *ker-*, *car-* f. Arab. *qirmazi*: see CRAMOISY]

cringe (-j), v.i., & n. Cower; bow servilely; behave obsequiously (*to*); (n.) fawning obeisance, cringing. [ME *crenge*, causal deriv. of OE *cringan*, *crincan*, see CRANK[1]]

cringle (krĭng'gl), n. (naut.). Eye of rope containing thimble for another rope to pass through. [f. LG *kringel* dim. of *kring* ring f. root of CRANK[1]]

crin'ite, a. (bot., zool.). Hairy. [f. L *crinitus* (*crinis* hair)]

crinkl|e (krĭng'kl), v.t. & i., & n. Twist, wrinkle. Hence ~Y[2] a. [ME, frequent. f. st. of OE *crincan*, see CRINGE, CRANK[1], -LE(3)]

crink'um-crănk'um, n. & a. (Thing) full of twists & turns (lit. & fig.). [playful f. CRANK[1]]

crin'oid, a. & n. (zool.). Lily-shaped (echinoderm). Hence **crinoid'AL** a. [f. Gk *krinoeidēs* (*krinon* lily, see -OID)]

crinolĕtte', n. Contrivance for distending back of woman's skirt. [dim. f. foll.]

crin'oline (*also* -ēn), n. Stiff fabric of horsehair etc. formerly used for skirts; hooped petticoat; netting round warship as defence against torpedoes. [F (L *crinis* hair + *linum* thread)]

crio-, comb. form of Gk *krios* ram, as -*sphinx* (ram-headed), -*ceratite*, ram's-horn ammonite.

crip'ple, n., & v.t. & i. Lame person; staging for cleaning windows etc.; (v.t.) lame, (fig.) disable, impair; (v.i.) hobble, walk lamely, (*along* etc.). Hence ~DOM (-ld-), ~HOOD (-lh-), nn. [OE *crypel*, MHG *krüppel*, ON *kryppill* f. Gmc **krup-* (**kreupan* CREEP)]

cris. = CREESE.

cris′is, n. (pl. *cris′es,* pr. -ēz). Turning-point, esp. of disease; moment of danger or suspense in politics, commerce, etc., as *cabinet, financial,* ~. [L, f. Gk *krisis* decision (*krinō* decide)]

crisp, a., n., & v.t. & i. Hard but fragile, brittle; bracing, as ~ *air*; brisk, decisive, as ~ *manner, style,* etc.; (of hair etc.) curly; ‖ (n. pl.) thin fried and dried slices of potato (marketed in packets); (v.t. & i.) curl in short stiff folds, make or become ~. Hence ~′LY[2] adv., ~′NESS n. [OE *crisp* adj. f. L *crispus* curled]

cris′pāte, a. Crisped, (Bot., Zool.) with wavy margin. [f. L *crispare,* -ATE[2]]

crispā′tion, n. Curling; undulation; contraction (esp. = GOOSE-*skin*). [as prec., -ATION]

crisp′ỹ, a. Curly; brittle; brisk. [-Y[2]]

criss′-cross (-aws), n., a., adv., & v.i. & t. 1. Crossing lines, currents, etc. (for ~ *row* see CHRIST-CROSS-ROW). 2. adj. In cross lines (~ *pattern, traffic*), (of persons or temper) peevish. 3. adv. Crosswise, at cross purposes (*everything went* ~). 4. vb. Move crosswise, work with ~ pattern. [orig. (15th c.) f. *Christ's Cross*; later apprehended as redupl. of *cross*]

cris′tāte, a. (nat. hist.). Having a crest. [f. L *cristatus* (as CREST, see -ATE[2])]

critēr′ion, n. (pl. *-ia*). Principle, standard, a thing is judged by. [f. Gk *kritērion* as foll.]

crit′ic, n. One who pronounces judgement; censurer; judge of literary or artistic works; one skilled in textual criticism. Hence ~ASTER n. [f. L f. Gk *kritikos* (*kritēs* judge f. *krinō,* see -IC)]

crit′ical, a. Censorious, fault-finding; skilful, engaged, in criticism; belonging to criticism; involving risk or suspense, as ~ *condition, operation*; (Math., Physics) marking transition from one state etc. to another, as ~ *angle, temperature.* Hence ~LY[2] adv. [-AL]

crit′icism, n. Work of a critic; critical essay or remark; *textual* ~ (dealing with text of an author); *the higher* ~ (dealing with origin, character, etc., of texts, esp. of Biblical writings). [-ISM]

crit′iciz|e, -is|e (-īz), v.t. Discuss critically (often abs.); censure. Hence ~ABLE a. [-IZE]

crit′ico- in comb. = critically, critical & —, as *-historical.* [CRITIC+-O-]

critique′ (-ēk), n. Critical essay or notice; art of criticism. [alt., after F *critique,* of CRITIC in obs. sense *criticism*]

croak, n., & v.i. & t. Deep hoarse sound of frog or raven; (v.i.) utter ~, forebode evil, (sl.) die; (v.t.) utter dismally, *(sl.) kill. Hence ~′Y[2] a. [16th c. (cf. 15th c. *crok*), imit.; cf. CRAKE, CREAK]

croak′er, n. In vbl senses; esp., prophet of evil. [-ER[1]]

Crō′at, n. Member of the people from which Croatia is named. [Slav.]

crō′ceāte (-sī-), a. Saffron, saffron-coloured. [f. L *croceus* (CROCUS), see -ATE[2]]

crō′chet (-shī), n., & v.t. (*-cheted* pr. -shīd). Knitting (material or work) done with hooked needle; (v.t.) make (shawl etc. or abs.) in ~. [F, dim. of *croc* hook]

crō′cidolīte, n. A fibrous silicate of iron & sodium, blue asbestos; yellow mineral produced from this, used for ornament. [f. Gk *krokis -idos* nap of cloth + -LITE]

crock[1], n. Earthen pot or jar; ‖ (dial.) metal pot; broken piece of earthenware used for covering hole in flowerpot. [OE *croc, crocca,* rel. to ON *krukka*; also rel. to OE *crōg* (G *krug*), OE *crūce* (MHG *krūche*)]

crock[2], n., & v.i. & t. (Sl.) inefficient or broken-down or worn-out person; broken-down horse; ‖ (Sc.) old ewe; (v.i. sl.) ~ *up,* break down; (v.t.) disable (usu. in p.p.). [orig. Sc., cf. Norw. *krake* sickly beast, MDu. *kraecke* broken-down horse or house; app. cogn. w. CRACK]

crock′ery, n. Earthenware vessels. [f. obs. (14th c.) *crocker* potter (CROCK[1]), see -ERY]

crock′et, n. Small ornament (usu. bud or curled leaf) on inclined sides of pinnacles etc. [f. AF *croket,* = OF CROCHET; see CROQUET, CROTCHET]

croc′odile, n. Large amphibious saurian reptile (esp. the Nile species); ~ *tears* (hypocritical, from belief that the crocodile wept while devouring, or to allure, its victim); ‖ (colloq.) schoolgirls walking two & two. Hence **crocodil′IAN** (-yan) a. [ME & OF *cocodrille* f. LL *cocodrillus* f. L f. Gk *krokodeilos*]

croc′us, n. Kinds of dwarf bulbous plants with brilliant (usu. yellow or purple) flowers; ~ *sativus,* species of this yielding saffron; AUTUMNAL ~; a peroxide of iron used for polishing. [L, f. Gk *krokos* crocus, saffron]

Croes′us (krēs-), n. Wealthy person. [~, king of Lydia]

‖ **croft** (-aw-, -ŏ-), n. Enclosed piece of (usu. arable) land; small holding of CROFTER. [OE *croft,* of unkn. orig.]

‖ **crof′ter** (-aw-, -ŏ-), n. One who rents a small holding, esp. joint tenant of Scotch divided farm. [-ER[1]]

Crō-Magnon (-măn′yon), a. Of a prehistoric tall long-headed European race, remains of which were found in ~, a cave in Dordogne, France.

crŏm′lech (-k), n. (In Wales & now rarely in England) megalithic tomb; (in France) circle of upright prehistoric stones; (formerly in England) megalithic tomb or stone circle. [W (*crom* bent, *llech* flat stone)]

cromōrne′, crêmōn′a, n. An organ reed-stop. [F, f. G *krummhorn* crooked horn]

crōne, n. Withered old woman; old ewe. [ME, f. ONF *carogne* CARRION or MDu. *c(a)roonje,* f. same source]

crōn′ỹ, n. Intimate friend. [17th c.,

Camb. Univ. sl., f. Gk *khronios* of long standing, chronic, f. *khronos* time]

crŏŏk, n. & a., & v.t. & i. Shepherd's, bishop's, hooked staff; anything hooked; hook; bend, curve; act of bending; (sl.) rogue, swindler; *by* HOOK *or by* ~; (sl.) *on the* ~, dishonestly; ~-*back(ed)*, hunchback(ed); (adj.) = CROOKED; (v.t. & i.) bend, curve. [ME *crŏc* f. ON *krókr* hook etc.]

crŏŏk′ĕd, a. Not straight, bent, twisted; deformed; bent with age; (fig.) not straightforward, dishonest; (of stick, pr. -ŏŏkt) having a cross handle, crutched. Hence ~LY² adv., ~NESS n. [ME, f. prec. +-ED¹]

Crŏŏkes (-ks), n. Name of Sir William ~ (d. 1919), English scientist, used attrib. (or in gen.) to designate apparatus invented by him etc. So: ~ *rays*, cathode rays; ~'*s tube*, glass vacuum tube for illustrating high rarefaction phenomena; ~'*s vacuum* (extremely high one).

crŏŏn, v.t. & i., & n. (Hum, sing, mutter, in) low undertone. Hence ~'ER¹ n., soft singer of highly sentimental songs. [ME, orig. Sc. & north., f. MDu., MLG *krōnen* groan, lament, (Du. *kreunen*)]

crŏp¹, n. Pouch-like enlargement of gullet in birds, where food is prepared for digestion; stock, handle, of whip; (also *hunting*-~) short whipstock with loop instead of lash; produce of cultivated plants, esp. cereals; *in, under, out of,* ~ (cultivation); season's total yield (of cereal etc.); entire hide of animal tanned; cropping of hair; style of wearing hair cut short; piece cut off end; various cuts of meat; NECK *& ~*; ~*-eared*, with ears (also, hair) cut short; ~*-over*, annual junketings at end of the W.--Indian sugar-cane harvest. [OE *crop(p)*, MDu., MLG *kropp*, OHG *kropf*, ON *kroppr*]

crŏp², v.t. & i. (-pp-). Cut off; (of animals) bite off (tops of plants); gather, reap; cut short (ears, tail, hair, nap of cloth, edges of book); sow, plant, (land *with* barley etc.); (v.i.) bear a crop; turn *up* unexpectedly; ~ *out, forth,* appear; (Geol.) ~ *up, out,* come to surface. [f. prec.]

crŏpp′er, n. Person, thing, that crops; pigeon with large crop, pouter; *good, heavy, light,* ~, plant yielding good etc. crop; (sl.) heavy fall, as *came a* ~. [CROP¹,² +-ER¹]

crŏpp′y̆, n. Person with short cropped hair, esp. (hist.) Irish rebel, sympathizer with French revolution, in 1798. [CROP¹ +-Y²]

cro′quet (-kā, -kĭ, *krokā′*), n. Game, played on lawn, in which wooden balls are driven with mallets through hoops; act of croqueting a ball. [perh. North. F, dial. form of CROCHET]

cro′quet² (-kĭ), v.t. (~*ing,* ~*ed,* pr. -kĭing, -kĭd). (In game of croquet) drive away (opponent's ball or abs.) by placing the two together & striking one's own (cf. ROQUET). [f. prec.]

croquette′ (-kĕt), n. Seasoned & fried ball of rice, potato, meat, etc. [F (*croquer* crunch)]

crōre, n. (Anglo-Ind.). Ten millions, one hundred lakhs (usu. of rupees). [f. Hind. *kror*]

cro′sier, -zier, (-zhyer), n. Bishop's, abbot's, pastoral staff; (improp.) archbishop's cross. [orig.=bearer of a crook, ME *croser*, f. OF *crossier* f. *crosse* CROOK; confused w. OF *croisier* (ME *croiser*) cross-bearer, f. *croiz* CROSS +-IER; mod. *crosier* = ~'*s staff* (16th c.)]

cross¹ (-aw-, -ŏ-), n. **1.** Stake (usu. with transverse bar) used by the ancients for crucifixion, esp. that on which Christ was crucified; model of this as religious emblem; sign of ~ made with right hand as religious act; staff surmounted with ~ & borne before archbishop or in processions, ~-*bearer*, person who carries this; monument in form of ~, esp. (also *market*-~) one in centre of town; Christian religion. **2.** Trial, affliction; annoyance. **3.** ~-shaped thing; (*Southern*) C~, a constellation; *Greek* ~ (✝); *Latin* ~ (†); *St Andrew's* ~ (✕); *Tau* ~, ~ *of St Anthony,* (T); *Maltese* ~ (✠); *fiery* ~, Scots signal (orig. two bloody sticks) sent through district to rouse inhabitants. **4.** Decoration in orders of knighthood (*Grand C*~, highest degree of this); decoration for personal valour, as *Victoria, George, Distinguished Service, Military, Distinguished Flying, C*~. **5.** Intermixture of breeds; animal resulting from this; mixture, compromise, *between* two things; (sl.) fraud, swindle; *on the* ~, diagonally. Hence ~'LET n., ~'WISE adv. [(a) This (surviving) form is OE *cros* f. ON *kross* f. OIr. *cros*; there were also (b) OE *crūc,* ME *cr(o)uche, =* OHG *krūzi;* (c) ME *croiz* f. OF *croiz;* (d) later Norse *cors* surviving in Sc., all ult. f. L *crux crucis*]

cross² (-aw-, -ŏ-), v.t. & i. Place crosswise, as ~ *swords* (in fighting, also fig.); ~ *one's fingers, keep* one's *fingers* ~*ed,* crook one finger over another to bring good luck; make sign of cross on or over (esp. one*self,* as sign of awe, to invoke divine protection, etc.); ~ *fortune-teller's hand with,* give her (coin); draw line across, as ~ *out, off,* cancel, ‖~ *cheque* (with two lines usu. filled up with *& Co.* or name of bank through whom alone it may be paid); write across (what is already written, a letter); go across (road, river, sea, or abs.); bestride (saddle, horse); carry, move, across; meet and pass (*each other* or abs.; *two persons' letters* ~ (each being dispatched before receipt of the other); ~ *one's mind,* occur to one; ~ *the path of,* meet with, thwart; thwart (person, will, plans); (cause to) interbreed; cross--fertilize (plants). [f. prec.]

cross[3] (-aw-, -ŏ-), a. Passing from side to side, transverse, (||~ *bench*, in the House of Lords, for independent members who do not vote with the Government or the official Opposition; so ~-*bench*, adj., impartial, as *the* ~-*bench mind*; ~ *voting*, when in Parliamentary divisions etc. some of either or each side vote against their own party, as *there was no* ~ *voting*); intersecting; contrary, opposed, (*to* a purpose etc., or abs.); (colloq.) peevish, out of humour, as *be* ~ *with* one, *as* ~ *as two sticks*, whence ~'LY[2] adv., ~'NESS n.; ~-*patch*, ill-natured person; ~ *reference* (from one part of book to another for further information); (Bookkeeping) ~ *entry* (transferring amount to different account or neutralizing previous entry); ~-*bred*, hybrid; (sl.) dishonest, dishonestly got. [partly f. CROSS[1], partly thr. (obs.) *cross* adv.]

cross- in comb. **1.** f. CROSS n., objectively, as ~-*bearer*, or attrib. = having a transverse part, as CROSS-BOW, marked with a ~, as ~-BUN. **2.** f. CROSS a. = crossing, transverse, as ~-*bar*, -*beam*, -*keys*, -*piece*, CROSS-SECTION, CROSS-BONES. **3.** Adv., in vbs as ~-*breed*, -*fertilize* (animals, plants, from individuals of different species), CROSS-EXAMINE, CROSS-QUESTION; in vbl nouns as ~-*fire*, firing in two crossing directions. **4.** Prep. = across, as ~-*country*, adj., across fields, not following roads.

cross'belt, n. Belt for cartridges etc. from shoulder to opposite hip. [CROSS-(2)]

cross'bill, n. Bird the mandibles of whose bill cross when bill is closed. [CROSS-(2)]

cross'bones, n. pl. Figure of two thigh--bones laid across each other, usu. under skull as emblem of death. [CROSS-(2)]

cross'bow (-bō), n. Bow fixed across wooden stock, with groove for the missile (stone, arrow, etc.) and mechanism for holding and releasing string. [CROSS-(1)]

cross'butt'ock, n., & v.t. Throw over the hip, in wrestling. [CROSS-(4)]

cross'coun'ter, n. (boxing). Blow at head delivered across opponent's lead-off with the other hand. [CROSS- (4)]

cross'cut, n. & a. Diagonal cut, path, etc.; figure in skating; (adj.) adapted for cutting across the grain (chiefly in ~ *saw*). [CROSS-(2)]

crŏsse, n. Long racquet-like implement used in LACROSSE. [F, f. OF *croce*, *croc*, hook]

cross-exam'ine, v.t. Examine (esp. witness in legal action) minutely, with a view to checking previous examination or eliciting suppressed facts. Hence **cross--examin**A'TION n. [CROSS-(3)]

cross'garnet, n. T-shaped hinge, fixed to door etc. by the long shank. [CROSS-(1) +*garnet* kind of tackle or purchase]

cross'grain, n. Grain running across the regular grain. [CROSS-(2)]

cross'grained (-nd), a. (Of wood) with grain running irregularly or in crossing

directions; (fig.) perverse, intractable. [-ED[2]]

cross'hatch, v.t. Engrave with intersecting series of parallel lines. [CROSS-(3)]

cross head(ing), n. (In newspaper etc.) indication of the contents of the following passage inserted here & there across the column for the reader's guidance in an article or report. [CROSS-(2)]

cross'ing (-aw-, -ŏ-), n. In vbl senses; also or esp.: intersection of two roads, railways, etc., as || *level* ~ (of road and railway, or two railways, on same level); place where street is crossed; ~-*sweeper*, one who sweeps this. [-ING[1]]

cross'legged (-gd), a. (Of person squatting) with legs crossed; (of person sitting on chair) with one leg laid across the other. [CROSS-(3)]

cross'light, n. Light that crosses another; (fig.) illustration of subject from another point of view. [CROSS-(2)]

cross purposes, n. pl. Contrary or conflicting purposes; name of a game; *be at* ~, misunderstand one another, (also) have conflicting plans with same object. [CROSS-(2)]

cross question, n. Question asked in CROSS-QUESTIONing; ~*s & crooked answers*, game in which each question gets answer written for another.

cross-ques'tion, v.t. Question in order to elicit details or test accuracy. [CROSS-(3)]

cross'road, n. Road that crosses another or joins two main roads; (also *cross roads*) intersection of two roads; *at the* ~*s* (fig.), at a critical turning-point (in person's life etc.). [CROSS-(2)]

cross'ruff, n., & v.i. (Whist, Bridge). Alternate trumping by partners (see RUFF[4]); (vb) play a ~. [CROSS-(3)]

cross'sec'tion, n. A transverse section, (fig.) a comprehensive representative sample. [CROSS-(2)]

cross'stitch, n. Stitch formed of two crossing each other; kind of needlework characterized by these. [CROSS-(2)]

*****cross'tie**, n. Railway sleeper. [CROSS-(2)]

cross'trees, n. pl. Two horizontal cross--timbers bolted to head of lower mast to support mast above. [CROSS-(2)]

cross'word, n. Puzzle in which words crossing vertically & horizontally according to a chequered pattern have to be filled in from clues. [CROSS[2]]

crŏtch, n. Bifurcation, fork (esp. of the human body). [perh. = ME & OF *croche*, *croc* hook f. ON *krókr* CROOK]

crŏtch'ĕt, n. || (Mus.) black-headed note with stem, half of minim; whimsical fancy, whence ~EER', ~iNESS, nn., ~Y[2] a.; hook. [ME, f. OF, dim. of *croc* hook (prec.), see CROCKET]

Crŏt'on, n. Genus of plants, from one species of which *c*~ *oil*, a drastic purgative, is obtained. [f. Gk *krotōn* tick, croton]

crouch, v.i., & n. Stoop, bend, esp. timidly or servilely; (n.) ~ing. [ME, perh. f. OF *crochir* be bent, f. *croc* CROOK]

croup[1], -pe (-ōō-), n. Rump, hindquarters, (esp. of horse). [ME & OF *croupe* f. WG *krupp*- rel. to CROP[1]]

croup[2] (-ōō-), n. Inflammatory disease in larynx & trachea of children, marked by sharp cough. [f. (now dial.) vb *croup* croak (imit.)]

croup'ier (-ōō-), n. Raker in of money at gaming table; assistant chairman at public dinner. [F, orig.=rider on the CROUP[1]]

croûton (krōōt'awn), n. Small piece of fried bread served with soups. [F]

crow[1] (-ō), n. Kinds of birds, esp. *carrion* ~, large black bird; *white* ~, a rarity; *as the* ~ *flies*, straight; **eat* ~, submit to humiliation; ~ (-*bar*), bar of iron (usu. with beak-like end) used as lever; ~'-*berry*, fruit of a small heath-like shrub; ~-*bill*, forceps for extracting bullets etc.; ~'*foot*, name of various plants, esp. species of buttercup, (Naut.) arrangement of small ropes for suspending awning, (Mil.) also ~'s-*foot* caltrop; ~'s-*footed*, marked with ~'s-feet; ~'-*quill*, ~'s quill or steel pen for fine writing; ~'s-*foot*, wrinkle at outer corner of eye; ~s-*nest*, barrel fixed at mast-head of whaler etc. as shelter for look-out man; ~-*toe*, ‖ bluebell (& other flowers, as buttercup). [OE *crāwe*, OS *krāia*, OHG *krāja* etc., f. CROW[3]]

crow[2] (-ō), n. Crowing of cock; joyful cry of infant. [ME, f. foll.]

crow[3] (-o), v.i. (past *crew* pr. krōō, or ~*ed* pr. krōd, p.p. ~*ed*). Utter loud cry of cock; (of child) utter joyful cry; exult loudly; ~ *over*, triumph over. [OE *crāwan*, OHG *krājan*, *krāen*, WG of imit. orig.]

crowd[1], n. Throng, dense multitude, (*would pass in a* ~, is not conspicuously defective); *the* ~, the masses; (colloq.) company, set, lot; large number (of things); (Naut.) ~ *of sail*, large number of sails hoisted. [f. foll.]

crowd[2], v.i. & t. Collect (t. & i.) in a crowd; fill, occupy, cram, (space etc. *with*); fill (place etc.) as a crowd does; force one's way *into*, *through*, etc. (confined space etc. or abs.); force (thing, person) *into* etc.; ~ *out*, exclude by ~ing; (Naut., of ship or crew) hasten on; ~ *sail*, hoist unusual number of sails. [OE *crūdan* press, drive, corresp. to MDu., MLG *crūden* press, push]

crown[1], n. 1. Wreath of flowers etc. worn on head, esp. as emblem of victory, (also fig. as *martyr's* ~, *no cross no* ~). 2. Monarch's head-covering of gold etc. & jewels; (fig.) king or queen, regal power, supreme governing power in a monarchy. 3. Any ~-shaped ornament. 4. (British coin worth) five shillings; foreign coin, esp.=KRONE. 5. Top part, esp. of skull; whole head; upper part of cut gem above girdle; highest or central part of arch or arched structure, as ~ *of the causeway*; top of hat; part of tooth projecting from gum. 6. Size of paper, 15″×20″. 7. ~ & *anchor*, popular gambling game played with dice marked with ~s, anchors, etc., and a corresponding board; ~-*glass*, made in circular sheets without lead or iron and used chiefly for windows; ‖ ~-*land* (belonging to the C~); C~ *Colony* (controlled by the C~); ~ *Derby*, kind of china made at Derby & often marked with ~ surmounting D; ‖ ~ *law*, criminal law; ‖ ~ *lawyer* (in service of the C~); C~ *office* (transacting common law business of Chancery); C~ *prince*, heir-apparent or designate to a sovereign throne; C~ *princess*, his wife; ~-*wheel*, CONTRATE wheel. [ME *corune*, *crune*, etc., f. ONF *corune* (OF *corone*) f. L *corona*]

crown[2], v.t. 1. Place crown on (person, head); invest (person) with regal crown or dignity (~ *him*, ~ *him king*; ~*ed heads*, kings & queens); (fig.) reward; occupy the head of, form chief ornament to, (lit. & fig.); put finishing touch to, as *to* ~ *all*; bring (efforts) to happy issue. 2. (Draughts) make (piece) a king. 3. (Dent.) ~ *a tooth*, protect its remains with a gold etc. cap cemented on. [ME *c(o)rune* etc., f. AF *coruner* (OF *coroner*) f. L *coronare*]

crowned (-nd), a. In vbl senses; (of hat) *high*, *low*, ~, with high, low, crown. [-ED[1,2]]

‖ **crown'er**, n. (obs. or dial.). = CORONER. [pop. by-form of CORONER, assim. to CROWN]

cru'cial (-ōōshl), a. Decisive, critical, (case, point, test, etc.); (Anat.) cross-shaped, as ~ *incision*. [F, f. L *crux crucis* cross + -AL]

cru'cian, -**sian**, (-ōōshn), n. Yellow fish allied to carp. [f. LG *karusse* + -AN]

cru'ciate (-ōōsh-), a. (zool., bot.). Cross-shaped. [f. L *crux crucis* cross; see -ATE[2](2)]

cru'cible (-ōō-), n. Melting-pot (usu. of earthenware); (fig.) severe trial. [ME, f. med. L *crucibulum* night-lamp, crucible, app. f. *crux crucis* CROSS]

cruciferous (-ōō-), a. Wearing, adorned with, a cross; (Bot.) of the family *Cruciferae*, having flowers with four equal petals arranged crosswise. [f. LL *crucifer* (as CRUCIAL, see -FEROUS)]

cru'cifix (-ōō-), n. Image of Christ on the cross; (improp.) cross. [ME, f. LL *crucifixus* f. *crux crucis* cross; see FIX]

crucifi'xion (-ōō-; -kshon), n. Crucifying; *the* C~ (of Christ); picture of this. [f. LL *crucifixio* (as prec., see -ION)]

cru'ciform (-ōō-), a. Cross-shaped. [f. L *crux crucis* cross, see -FORM]

cru'cify (-ōō-), v.t. Put to death by fastening to a cross; (fig.) mortify (passions, sins, flesh); (Mil.) tie up (soldier) with arms out in field punishment. [ME, f. OF *crucifier* f. Rom. **crucificare* (see -FY) for LL *crucifigere* (see CRUCIFIX)]

crude (-ōō-), a. In the natural or raw state; (of food etc.) not digested; unripe; (of diseases etc.) not matured; (fig.) ill-digested, unpolished, lacking finish; rude, blunt, (action, statement, manners); (Gram., of form of word) uninflected. Hence or cogn. ~'LY² (-dl-) adv., ~'NESS (-dn-), crud'ITY, nn., (-ōō-). [ME, f. L *crudus* raw]

cru'el (-ōō-), a. Indifferent to, delighting in, another's pain; (of actions) showing such · indifference or pleasure; painful, distressing. Hence or cogn.~LY² adv., ~TY n., (-ōō-). [ME, f. OF, f. L *crudelis*]

cru'et (-ōō-), n. Small glass bottle with stopper for vinegar, oil, etc., for table; small vessel for wine or water in celebration of Eucharist; ~-stand (for ~s & castors). [ME *cruet(t)e* app. f. AF **cruet(e)* dim. OF *crue, cruie* pot, f. OLG *cruca* (CROCK¹)]

cruise (-ōōz), v.i., & n. 1. Sail to & fro on look-out for ships, for protection of commerce in time of war, for plunder, or for pleasure, making for no particular port (also fig.); (of aircraft) fly at *cruising speed* (economic travelling speed, less than top speed). 2. n. Cruising voyage. [f. Du. *kruisen* (f. *kruis* CROSS); cf. Sp., Port. *cruzar*, F *croiser*]

cruis'er (-ōōz-), n. Warship of high speed & medium armament; *armoured* ~ (with lighter armour than battleship); BATTLE¹, BELT²*ed*, ~; (*un*)*protected* ~, one with(out) protective deck; ~ *weight* (Boxing), 'light-heavy' weight, 12 st. 10 lb. (amateur), 12st. 7lb. (professional). [f.Du. *kruiser* (as prec., see -ER¹)]

‖ **cruive** (-ōōv), n. (Sc.). Wicker salmon-trap. [15th c., of unkn. orig.]

*crüll'er, n. A small cake made of dough containing eggs, butter, sugar, etc., twisted or curled & fried in fat. [f. Du. *krullen* curl]

crümb (-m), n., & v.t. Small fragment, esp. of bread; (fig.) small particle, atom, (*of* comfort etc.); soft inner part of bread; ~-*cloth* (laid over carpet, esp. under table); (v.t.) cover, thicken, with ~s, break into ~s. Hence ~'Y² (-mI) a. [OE *crūma*, MDu. *crūme*, MDu., MLG *crōme*, Icel. *krumr, kraumr*]

crüm'ble, v.t. & i. Break, fall, into crumbs or fragments (lit. & fig.). [earlier *crimble* f. OE *crūma*; assim. to CRUMB]

crüm'blў, a. Apt to crumble (intr.). [CRUMB + -LY¹; now treated as f. prec. + -Y²]

crümp, v.t., & n. (colloq.). Hit (esp. cricket-ball) hard; (n.) hard hit, heavy fall, (army sl.) bursting shell; sound of bursting bomb or shell. [imit.]

crüm'pĕt, n. Soft cake of a yeast mixture, baked on iron plate; (sl.)·head (BARMY *on the* ~). [17th c., of unkn. orig.]

crüm'ple, v.t. & i. Crush together or *up* into creased state; ruffle, wrinkle; become creased; (fig.) collapse, give way (usu.

with *up*). [f. obs. *crump* v. & a. (make, become) curved + -LE(3)]

crünch, v.t. & i., & n. 1. Crush with teeth, esp. noisily; grind under foot (gravel etc.); make one's way (*up, through*, etc.) thus. 2. n. ~ing (noise). [replaces *cra(u)nch*, imit.]

crüpp'er, n. Strap buckled to back of saddle & looped under horse's tail; hindquarters of horse. [ME, f. AF *cropere* (OF *-iere*), f. WG **kropp-* CROP¹; see CROUP¹, -ER²]

crur'al (-oor-), a. (anat.). Of the leg. [f. L *cruralis* (*crus cruris* leg, see -AL)]

crusāde' (-ōō-), n., & v.i. (Hist.) Christian expedition to recover Holy Land from Mohammedans; war instigated by Church for alleged religious ends; (fig.) aggressive movement against public evil etc., as *Temperance* ~; (v.i.) engage in ~. Hence **crusād'ER¹** n. [in 16th c. *croisade* (F, f. *croix*), later *crusado, -ada* (Sp., f. *cruz*), 18th c. *crusade*; see CROSS, -ADE]

crusād'ō (-ōō-), n. Portuguese coin. [f. Port. *cruzado* marked with cross]

cruse (-ōōs, -ōōz), n. (arch.). Pot, jar, of earthenware (WIDOW'S ~). [15th c. *crowse* corresp. to OE *crūse* (cf. OHG *krūselin*, MHG *krūse*); *cruse* perh. f. MLG *krūs*]

crüsh¹, v.t. & i. Compress with violence, so as to break, bruise, etc.; crumple (dress etc.) by rough handling; (fig.) subdue, overwhelm, as *a* ~*ing defeat, reply*; ~ *out*, extinguish, stamp out; ~ *a cup of wine*, drink it; (v.i.) squeeze one's way (*into* etc.). [ME, f. OF *croissir, cruissir*, of unkn. orig.]

crüsh², n. Act of crushing; crowded mass (esp. of persons); (colloq.) crowded social gathering; (Austral.) fenced passage with funnel-shaped end along which cattle are driven in single file for branding; similar but shorter closed passage for dealing with single animal; ~-*room* in theatre etc. (for promenade during intervals); ~ *hat*, collapsible opera hat with spring; *have a* ~ *on* (sl.), be in love with. [f. prec.]

crüst, n., & v.t. & i. 1. Hard outer part of bread; similar casing of anything, e.g. harder layer over soft snow (~-*hunt* n. & v.t. & i., of hunting elks etc. over a ~ that supports hunters but not quarry); hard dry·scrap of bread; pastry covering pie; hard dry formation, scab, on skin; (Geol.) outer portion of earth; coating, deposit, on surface of anything; ~ *of wine*, deposit on sides of bottle; hard external covering of animal or plant; (fig.) anything superficial; (sl.) impudence. 2. v.t. Cover with, form into, ~; (v.i.) become covered with ~. [ME *crouste, cruste*, partly f. OF *crouste*, partly f. its source, L *crusta*]

Crüstā'cea (-sha), n. pl. Large class of animals, mostly aquatic, with hard shell, as crabs, lobsters, shrimps. Hence **crüstA'CEAN** (-āshn) a. & n.; **crüstā-**

cĕŏL'OGY n [neut. pl. of mod. L CRUST-
(*aceus* -ACEOUS)]

crŭstā'ceous (-shŭs), a. Crust-like; (of
animals) having a hard covering, esp.
(Zool.) belonging to the *Crustacea*. [f.
mod. L *crustaceus* (CRUST, -ACEOUS)]

crŭs'tĕd, a. Having a crust; (of wine)
having deposited a crust; (fig.) antiquated, venerable, as ~ *prejudice, theory*.
[-ED²]

crŭs't|ў̆, a. Crust-like, hard; irritable;
curt. Hence ~ĭLY² adv., ~ĭNESS n. [-Y²]

crŭtch, n. Staff (usu. with crosspiece at
top) for lame person (usu. *pair of ~es*)
support, prop, (lit. & fig.); forked rest for
leg in a side-saddle; fork of the human
body (cf. CROTCH); (Naut.) various forked
contrivances; crosspiece, whence ~ED²
(-cht) a. [OE *crycc*, OS *krukka*, OHG
krucka ON *krykkja* f. Gmc. *kruk-* bend]

Crŭtch'ĕd Fri'ars, n. pl. Minor order of
friars wearing a cross; site of their convent in London. [f. ME *crouch* CROSS¹+
-ED²]

crŭx, n. Difficult matter, puzzle; ~
ănsāt'a, ANKH (lit. = handled cross). [L,
= cross]

cruzeiro (kro͞ozār'ŏ), n. The monetary
unit of Brazil. [Pg., f. *cruz* cross]

crȳ¹, n. Loud inarticulate utterance of
grief, pain, fear, joy, etc.; loud excited
utterance of words; appeal, entreaty;
proclamation of wares to be sold in
streets; rumour; voice of the public;
watchword, as *war-~, battle-~*; fit of
weeping; yelping of hounds (also fig.), as
full ~ (pursuit); *within ~*, within calling
distance (*of*); *a far ~*, a long way; *~-baby*,
one who cries childishly; *follow in the ~*,
be in the following crowd of nobodies;
much ~ & little wool, fuss to no purpose,
as when pigs are shorn. [ME & OF *cri* f.
crier CRY²]

crȳ², v.t. & i. (*cried*). Utter loudly, exclaim, (with sentence as object, or *that*);
make loud utterance, as ~ *out*, ~ *to*
(person etc.); announce for sale, as ~
muffins; ~ *stinking fish*, condemn one's
own wares; weep (*bitter tears*), one's *heart
out*, oneself *to sleep*, or abs.; ~ *over spilt
milk*, waste regrets; (of animals, esp.
birds) make loud call; (of hounds) yelp;
ask *for* (esp. ~ *for the moon*); ~ *down*,
disparage; ~ *off*, withdraw *from* bargain;
~ *up*, praise, extol; ~ CRAVEN; ~ *halves*,
claim share (*in*); ~ QUARTER, QUITS; ~
shame upon, protest against (act, person).
[ME *crie* f. OF *crier* f. L *quiritare*]

crȳ'ing, a. In vbl senses; esp. (of evils)
calling for notice, flagrant. [-ING²]

crȳ'ogen, n. (chem.). Freezing-mixture;
thing mixed with ice to make this. [f.
Gk *kruos* frost + -GEN(1)]

crȳ'olite, n. Lustrous mineral of considerable industrial value found abundantly in Greenland, consisting mainly
of sodium-aluminium fluoride. [f. Gk
kruos frost + -LITE]

crȳpt, n. Underground cell, vault, esp.
one beneath church, used as burial-place.
[f. L f. Gk *krupte* (*kruptē* hide)]

crȳptaesthēs'ia, n. Supernormal knowledge, whether telepathic or clairvoyant.
[CRYPTO- + Gk *aisthēsis* perception + -IA¹]

crȳp'tic, a. Secret, mystical. [f. LL f. Gk
kruptikos (as CRYPT, see -IC)]

crȳp't|(ō)-, comb. form of Gk *kruptos*
hidden, secret, as ~*obranchiate* with concealed gills, ~*o-Communist* secret sympathizer with Communism, ~*ŏl'ogy* enigmatical language.

crȳp'tō, n. (colloq.). Person owing secret
allegiance to a political creed etc.; esp.
short for ~-*Communist*. [as prec.]

crȳp'togăm, n. Plant having no stamens
or pistils, & therefore no proper flowers.
Hence crȳptogăm'ic, crȳptŏg'amous,
aa., crȳptŏg'amIST(3), crȳptŏg'amy¹,
nn. [f. F *cryptogame* (CRYPTO- + Gk *-gamos*
wedded), after Linnaean class-name
Cryptogamia]

crȳp'tográm, -graph (-ahf), nn. Thing
written in cipher. So crȳptŏg'RAPHER,
crȳptŏg'RAPHY, nn., crȳptoGRAPH'IC a.
[CRYPTO- + -GRAM, -GRAPH]

crȳptomer'ia, n. Evergreen tree of the
cypress type; Japanese cedar. [CRYPTO-
+ Gk *meros* part (because the seeds are
enclosed by scales)]

crȳs'tal, n. & a. 1. A clear transparent ice-
-like mineral; *rock-~*, a form of pure
quartz; piece of this; ~ *set*, simple form
of receiving apparatus in broadcasting
using a ~ rectifier; (poet.) any clear transparent thing, esp. water; ~*-gazing*, concentration of one's gaze on ball of rock-
~*, pool of ink, etc., for the purpose
of inducing a hallucinatory picture of
future or distant events (~, colloq., view
of the future thus obtained, prophetic
utterance); (also ~ *glass*) glass of very
transparent quality; vessel etc. of this;
C~ Palace, building of glass & iron built
in Hyde Park for the 1851 Exhibition &
re-erected at Sydenham & destroyed by
fire in 1936; (Chem., Min.) aggregation of
molecules with definite internal structure
& external form of solid enclosed by symmetrically arranged plane faces. 2. adj.
Made of, like, clear as, ~. [ME, f. OF
cristal f. L f. Gk *krustallos* ice, crystal]

crȳs'talline, a. Made of, clear as, like,
crystal; ~ *heaven* (in Ptolemaic system,
between primum mobile & firmament,
assumed to explain precession of equinox
etc.); ~ *lens* of eye, transparent body in
membranous capsule behind iris. [ME, f.
OF *-in* or L f. Gk *krustallinos* (as prec., see
-INE²)]

crȳs'talliz|e, -is|e (-īz), v.t. & i. Form
into crystals or (fig.) definite or permanent
shape; ~*ed fruit* (preserved by impregnation with sugar, and coated with sugar
crystals). Hence ~ABLE a., ~A'TION n. [-IZE]

crȳs'tall|o-, comb. form of Gk *krustallos*
CRYSTAL, as ~*ogen'ic, ~ŏ'geny*, forming,

formation of, crystals, ~*ŏg'rapher*, ~*o-graph'ic*, ~*ŏg'raphy*, student of, pertaining to, science of, crystal structure.

crȳs'talloid, a. & n. Crystal-like; (body) of crystalline structure (cf. COLLOID). [-OID]

ctēn'oid (t-), a. & n. (Fish with scales or teeth) like a comb. [f. Gk *ktenoeidēs* (*kteis ktenos* comb, see -OID)]

cŭb, n., & v.t. & i. (-bb-). **1.** Young of fox, as ~-*hunting*; young of bear or other wild beast; unpolished youth (usu. *unlicked* ~); (colloq., short for) ~ *reporter*, young or inexperienced newspaper reporter; = WOLF-~ (junior boy scout). **2.** vb. Bring forth (~s, or abs.). Hence ~b'ISH[1] a., ~'HOOD n. [of unkn. orig.]

cŭb'age, n. (Finding of) cubic content. [CUBE+-AGE]

cŭb'ature, n. = prec. [f. CUBE after QUADRATURE; cf. F *cubature*]

cŭbb'ing, n. CUB-hunting. [CUB+-ING[1]]

cŭbb'y, n. Snug place (usu. ~-*hole*). [f. obs. or dial. *cub*, stall, pen; cf. LG *kübje* linhay]

cūbe, n., & v.t. **1.** Solid contained by squares; block of anything so or similarly shaped; product of a number multiplied by its square (~ *of 2*, alg. symbol 2^3, = *8*, ~ *root of 8*, alg. symbol $^3\sqrt{8}$, = 2). **2.** v.t. Find ~ of (number); find cubic content of (solid); pave with ~s. [F, or f. L f. Gk *kubos*]

cūb'ĕb, n. Pungent berry of a Javan shrub, used in medicine & cookery, & when crushed in medicated cigarettes. [ME, f. OF *cubebe, quibibe*, f. Arab. *kababah*]

cūb'ic, a. Cube-shaped; of three dimensions; ~ *foot, inch*, volume of a cube whose edge is one foot, inch; ~ *content* of solid, its volume expressed in ~ feet etc.; involving the cubes of quantities, as ~ *equation*. Hence ~AL a., ~alLY[2] adv. [f. F *cubique* or L f. Gk *kubikos* (as CUBE, see -IC)]

cūb'icle, n. Small separate sleeping compartment in schools etc. [f. L *cubiculum* (*cubare* lie down)]

cūb'ifŏrm, a. Cube-shaped. [-I-, -FORM]

cūb'ism, n. A style in art in which objects are so presented as to give the effect of an assemblage of geometrical figures. So cūb'IST n. [CUBE, -ISM]

cūb'it, n. Ancient measure of length, 18 to 22 in. [ME, f. L *cubitum* elbow, length of forearm]

cūb'ital, a. Of the forearm or corresponding part in animals. [ME, f. L *cubitalis* (prec. -AL)]

cūb'oid, a. & n. Cube-shaped, like a cube, as ~ *bone* (of the foot); (n.) rectangular parallelepiped. Hence cūboid'AL a. [f. Gk *kuboeidēs* (as CUBE, see -OID)]

cŭck'ing-stool, n. (hist.). Chair in which disorderly women etc. were ducked as punishment. [ME; orig. also *cuck-stool*, f. obs. *cuck* f. ON *kúka* void excrement]

cŭck'old, n., & v.t. Husband of unfaithful wife; (v.t.) make a ~ of. [ME *cukeweld, -wold*, f. OF *cucuault* (*cucu* CUCKOO)]

cu'ckōō (kŏō-), n. & pred. a. **1.** Migratory bird reaching British Islands in April & depositing its eggs in nests of small birds; simpleton; ~ *clock* (striking with sound like ~'s note); ~-*flower*, meadow plant with lilac-white flower, lady-smock; ~-*pint*, common arum, wake-robin; ~-*spit*, froth exuded by the larvae of certain insects as a protection. **2.** adj. (sl.). Crazy, barmy. [ME *cuccu* etc. (superseding OE *gēac*, ME *geke*) f. OF *cucu*]

cŭc'ŭllate, -ātĕd, a. (bot., zool.). Shaped like, covered with, a hood. [f. LL *cucullatus* (*cucullus* hood, see -ATE[2])]

cŭc'ŭmber, n. (Creeping plant with) long fleshy fruit eaten in thin slices as salad; *cool as a* ~, quite cool, self-possessed. [14th c. *cucumer* f. L; 15th c. *cocomber* etc. f. OF *cocombre* f. L *cucumerem* (nom. *-mis*)]

cūcūrb'it, n. Gourd. Hence ~A'CEOUS (-āshus) a. [f. L *cucurbita*]

cŭd, n. Food that ruminating animal brings back from first stomach into mouth & chews at leisure; (fig.) *chew the* ~, reflect, ruminate. [OE *cwidu, cudu*; app. cogn. w. OHG *chuti, quiti*, glue]

cŭd'bear, n. (-bâr). Purple or violet dyeing-powder prepared from various lichens; kind of lichen. [named by *Cuthbert* Gordon, patentee]

cŭd'dl|e, v.t. & i., & n. **1.** Hug, embrace, fondle; lie close & snug; nestle together; curl oneself *up*. **2.** n. Hug, embrace. Hence ~ESOME (-ls-), ~Y[2], aa., given to ~ing or tempting to ~e. [orig. unkn.]

cŭdd'y[1], n. Cabin of half-decked boat, (hist.) saloon of large ship; closet, cupboard. [perh. f. early mod. Du. *kajute*]

|| **cŭdd'y[2],** n. (Sc.). Donkey; fool, ass; young of the coal-fish; lever on tripod for lifting stones etc. [perh. f. pet form of *Cuthbert*, as DICKY, NEDDY]

cŭd'gel, n., & v.t. (-ll-). **1.** Short thick stick used as weapon; ~-*play*, contest with ~s; (fig.) *take up the* ~*s for*, defend vigorously. **2.** v.t. Beat with ~, esp., fig., ~ *one's brains for*, try to think of. [(vb f. n.) OE *cycgel*, of unkn. orig.]

cŭd'weed, n. Composite plant with chaffy scales round flower-heads, given to cattle that had lost their cud. [f. CUD]

cūe[1], n. Last words of a speech in a play, serving as signal to another actor to enter or speak; (Mus.) similar guide to singer or player; hint how to act; proper course to take. [orig. unkn.]

cūe[2], n. Pigtail (also QUEUE); long straight tapering leather-tipped rod for striking ball in billiards etc. [f. F *queue* QUEUE]

cue'ist (kū'ist), n. Billiard-player. [prec. +-IST(3)]

cŭff[1], n. Ornamental bottom part of sleeve; separate band of linen worn round wrist; *trouser turn-up*; *off the* ~

extempore, without preparation. Hence (-)cŭffED² (-ft) a. [orig. unkn.]

cŭff², v.t., & n. 1. Strike with open hand. 2. n. Such blow. [orig. unkn.; cf. Sw. *kuffa* thrust, G *kuffen* thrash]

Cŭf'ĭc, K-, a. & n. (Of) rude form of the Arabic alphabet found chiefly in inscriptions. [f. *Cufa*, city S. of Bagdad, -IC]

cui bŏn'ŏ?(kī), sentence. Who profited by it? (i.e. who is most likely to have brought it about?); (pop.) to what purpose? [L]

cuirăss' (kw-), n. Body armour, breast-plate & back-plate fastened together; woman's close-fitting sleeveless bodice. [ME, f. OF *cuirasse* f. It. *corazza* f. Rom. *coriacea* f. LL *coriaceus* (*corium* leather, see -ACEOUS)]

cuirassier (kwīrasēr', kūr-), n. Horse-soldier wearing cuirass. [F (as prec., see -EER)]

cuisine (kwĭzēn'), n. Kitchen arrangements; style of cooking. [F, f. L *coquina* (*coquere* cook)]

cuisse (kwĭs), cuish (kw-), n. (hist.). Thigh armour (usu. pl.). [14th c. *quyssewes*, *cuissues*, f. OF pl. of *cuissel* f. LL *coxale* (*coxa* hip)]

cul-de-sac (see Ap.), n. Blind alley; (Anat.) tube etc. open at one end only. [F]

-cule, dim. suf. = F -*cule* f. L -*culus*, -*cula*, -*culum*; the L suf. appears in E as -*cle*, as -*cule*, or in full: *article, corpuscule, corpuscle, fasciculus, Auricula, vasculum*.

cŭl'ĭnarў, a. Pertaining to a kitchen or cooking; fit for cooking, as ~ *plants*. [f. L *culinarius* (*culina* kitchen, see -ARY¹)]

cŭll, v.t., & n. Pick (flower etc.); select; (n.) animal removed from flock (& usu. fattened) as inferior or too old for breeding. [ME, f. OF *cuillir* etc., ult. f. L *colligere* COLLECT]

cullender. See COLANDER.

cŭll'ĕt, n. Refuse glass with which crucibles are replenished; broken glass. [later form of COLLET now disused in this sense]

‖ cŭll'ў, n. (sl.). Dupe, simpleton; mate, pal. [prob. cant, of unkn. orig.]

cŭlm¹, n. Coal-dust (esp. of anthracite). [orig. unkn.]

cŭlm², n. (bot.). Stem of plant (esp. of grasses). So ~ĭF'EROUS a. [f. L *culmus*]

cŭl'mĭnant, a. At, forming, the top; (of heavenly body) on the meridian. [foll., -ANT]

cŭl'mĭn|āte, v.i. Reach its highest point (*in*; lit. & fig.); (Astron.) be on the meridian. Hence ~A'TION n. [f. LL *culminare* (*culmen* summit) see -ATE³]

cŭl'pab|le, a. Criminal, blameworthy, as ~*le negligence, hold him ~le*. Hence cŭlpABIL'ITY, ~leNESS (-ln-), nn., ~LY² adv. [ME & OF *coupable* f. L *culpabilis* (*culpa* blame, see -ABLE); later assim. to L]

cŭl'prĭt, n. Offender; prisoner at the bar. [17th c.; orig. in formula *Culprit, how will you be tried?*, said by Clerk of Crown

to prisoner pleading Not Guilty; abbr. of *Culpable: prest d'averrer* etc. (You are) guilty: (I am) ready to prove etc.]

cŭlt, n. System of religious worship; devotion, homage, to person or thing (*the ~ of*). [f. F *culte* or L *cultus -ūs* worship (*colere cult-* till, worship)]

cŭl'tĭvāte, v.t. Till, whence cŭl'tĭvABLE, cŭltĭvāt'ABLE, aa.; (fig.) improve, develop, (person, mind, manners; esp. in p.p.); pay attention to, cherish, (faculty, art, person, his acquaintance); prepare (ground) with CULTIVATOR. [f. med. L *cultivare* f. *cultiva* (*terra*) tilled (land), as prec., -IVE, -ATE³]

cŭltĭvā'tion, n. Cultivating, cultivated state, (lit. & fig.). [F (as CULTIVATE, see -ATION)]

cŭl'tĭvātor, n. One who cultivates; implement for breaking up ground & up-rooting weeds. [-OR]

cŭl'trate, a. (nat. hist.). Knife-edged. So cŭl'trĭFORM a. [f. L *cultratus* (*culter -tri* knife, -ATE²)]

cŭl'tur|e, n., & v.t. Tillage; rearing, production, (of bees, oysters, fish, silk, bacteria); set of bacteria thus produced; improvement by (mental or physical) training; intellectual development; (v.t.) cultivate (lit. & fig., chiefly in p.p. ~ed pr. -cherd). Hence ~AL a., ~IST(2) n., (-cher-). [ME, f. OF, or f. L *cultura* (as CULT, see -URE); vb (16th c.) f. n., or F *culturer*]

‖ cŭl'ver, n. (dial.). Wood-pigeon; ~*keys*, cowslip, other plants. [OE *culfre*, of unascert. orig.]

cŭl'verin, n. (hist.). Large cannon, small firearm. [ME, f. OF *coulevrine* snake (L *colubra*, -INE¹)]

cŭl'vert, n. Channel, conduit, carrying water across under road, canal, etc.; channel for electric cable. [c. 1770, of unkn. orig.]

cŭm, prep. With; ~ *grano* (*salis*) (grān'ŏ sāl'ĭs), with caution or reserve (lit. with a grain of salt); ~ *dividend* (abbr. ~ *div.*), including dividend about to be paid; also in names ˑf combined parishes, as *Stow-~-Quy*. [L]

cŭm'ber, v.t., & n. Hamper, hinder; burden; (n.) hindrance, obstruction. [ME, prob. aphetic f. ENCUMBER or obs. *acumber*]

cŭm'bersome, a. Unwieldy, clumsy. Hence ~LY² (-ml-) adv., ~NESS (-mn-) n. [-SOME]

Cŭm'brian, a. & n. (Native) of Cumberland; of the ancient British kingdom of Cumbria. [-AN]

cŭm'brous, a. = CUMBERSOME. Hence ~LY² adv., ~NESS n. [CUMBER+-OUS]

cŭm'in, -mm-, n. Umbelliferous plant like fennel, with aromatic seed. [ME, f. OF *cumin, comin* f. L f. Gk *kuminon*; OE *cymen* (OHG *kumin, -il*, G *kümmel*) dir. f. L]

‖ cŭmm'er, kimm'er, n. (Sc.). Godmother of one's child or godchild; female companion; woman. [ME, f. OF *commere* f. LL *commater*]

cŭmm'erbŭnd, n. (Anglo-Ind.). Waist sash. [f. Hind. & Pers. *kamar-band* loin band]

cŭm'quat (-ŏt), n. Plum-sized orange--like fruit with sweet rind and acid pulp, used in preserves. [dial. form of Chin. *kin kü* golden orange]

cŭm'shaw, n. (pidgin-Eng.). Present, tip, baksheesh. [dial. form of Chin. *kan hsieh* grateful thanks]

cŭm'ūlate¹, a. Heaped up, massed. [as foll., see -ATE²]

cŭm'ūl|āte², v.t. & i. Accumulate. Hence ~A'TION n. [f. L *cumulare* (*cumulus* heap), see -ATE³]

cŭm'ūlātive, a. Tending to accumulate; increasing in force etc. by successive additions, as ~ *evidence*; ~ *voting*, system in which each voter has as many votes as there are representatives, & may give all to one candidate; ~ *preference shares* (entitling holder to arrears of interest before other shares receive any on current year). Hence ~LY² (-vl-) adv., ~NESS (-vn-) n. [f. prec. + -IVE]

cŭm'ūlus, n. (pl. *-li*). Heap; set of rounded masses of cloud heaped on each other & resting on horizontal base. So **cŭm'ūlo-** comb. form, **cŭm'ūlous** a. [L]

cŭn'ēate, a. Wedge-shaped. [f. L *cuneare* (*cuneus* wedge), see -ATE²]

cŭn'eifŏrm (*also* kūnē'ĭ-), a. & n. 1. Wedge-shaped. 2. n. ~ writing in ancient inscriptions of Persia, Assyria, etc. [f. L *cuneus* wedge, -FORM]

cŭnĕtte', n. (fortif.). Central trench sunk in fort ditch, serving as drain. [F, f. It. *cunetta*, aphetic f. *lacunetta* dim. of *lacuna* ditch etc., see LACUNA]

cŭnn'ing¹, n. Artfulness, craft; (arch.) ability, dexterity. [ME (not in OE), app. f. ON *kunnandi* f. *kunna* know, see CAN²]

cŭnn'ing², a. Artful, crafty; (arch.) skilful, ingenious; able. Hence ~LY² adv. [ME (not in OE), f. ON as prec.; see -ING²]

cŭp¹, n. Drinking-vessel, with or without handle & stem, as *tea, coffee, -~*; *challenge* ~ (prize for race etc., usu. of gold or silver, esp. one held by winner only until next race etc.); rounded cavity, esp. calyx of flower, socket of some bones, etc.; cupful, as ~ *of tea, half a* ~; one's ~ *of tea* (colloq.), what interests or suits one; chalice used, wine taken, at Communion; fate, portion, experience, as *a bitter* ~, *his* ~ *was full* (happiness, misery, was complete); *the* ~*s that cheer but not inebriate*, tea (Cowper *Task* iv. 39); *in* one's ~*s*, while (getting) drunk; wine, cider, etc., with various flavourings, as *claret-~*; ~ *& ball*, ~ at end of stem, with attached ball to be thrown & caught in ~ or on spiked end of stem; ~*-bearer*, one who serves wine, esp. officer of royal or noble

household; ~*-moss*, lichen with ~*-*shaped processes arising from the thallus; ~*-shake*, opening between two concentric layers of timber. Hence ~FUL (-ŏŏl) n. (pl. *-ls*). [OE *cuppe* f. pop. L *cuppa* cup, different. f. L *cūpa* cask]

cŭp², v.t. (-pp-). Bleed (person) by means of a ~*ping-glass*. [f. prec.]

cupboard (kŭb'erd), n. Shelved closet or cabinet for crockery, provisions, etc.; SKELETON *in the* ~; ~ *love* (simulated for sake of what one can get by it). [CUP¹ + BOARD]

cŭp'el, n., & v.t. (-ll-). Small flat circular vessel used in assaying gold or silver with lead; (v.t.) assay in ~. Hence ~lA'-TION n. [f. F *coupelle* dim. of *coupe* CUP¹]

Cūp'ĭd, n. Roman god of love; beautiful boy; ~*'s bow*, (upper edge of) upper lip, which is shaped like the conventional double-curved bow carried by ~. [f. L *Cupido* (*cupere* desire)]

cūpid'itў, n. Greed of gain. [ME, f. OF *cupidite* or L *cupiditas* (*cupidus* desirous, see -TY)]

cūp'ola, n. Small rounded dome forming roof; ceiling of dome; (also ~*-furnace*) furnace for melting metals; revolving dome protecting mounted guns on warship; (Anat., Zool.) dome-like organ or process. [It., f. LL *cupula* dim. of *cūpa* cask, see CUP¹]

cŭp'rēous, a. Of or like copper. [f. LL *cupreus* (LL *cuprum* COPPER) + -OUS]

cŭp'ric, a. Containing divalent copper. So **cūpriF'EROUS**, **cŭp'rous**, aa., **cŭp'ro-** comb. form. [f. LL *cuprum*, -IC(1)]

cŭp'ūle, n. (bot., zool.). Cup-shaped organ, receptacle, etc. [f. L as CUPOLA]

cŭr, n. Worthless, low-bred, or snappish dog; surly, ill-bred, or cowardly fellow. [ME *curre*, earlier *kur-dogge*, = MDu. *korre*; perh. ult. f. ON *kurra* grumble]

cūr'açao, **-çoa**, (-sō), n. Liqueur of spirits flavoured with peel of bitter oranges. [Du. island in Caribbean sea; *-çoa* is E mis-spelling]

cūr'acў, n. Curate's office; benefice of perpetual curate. [f. CURATE, see -ACY(3)]

cūrār'e̍, -i, n. Resinous bitter substance from some S. American plants, paralysing the motor nerves, used by Indians to poison arrows. Hence **cūr'arINE⁵** n.; **cūr'arIZE**(5) v.t. [native *wurali* etc.]

cūr'assow (-ō), n. Turkey-like bird of Central & S. America. [= CURAÇAO]

cūr'ate, n. Assistant to parish priest; ~*-in-charge*, clergyman appointed to take charge of parish during incapacity or suspension of incumbent. [f. med. L *curatus* f. *cura* CURE]

cūr'ative, a. & n. (Thing) tending to cure (esp. disease). [F (*-if*, *-ive*), f. L *curare* CURE², see -ATIVE]

cūrāt'or, n. Person in charge, manager; keeper, custodian, of museum; ‖ member of board managing property or having general superintendence in University;

‖ (Sc. law; kūr'a-) guardian of minor, lunatic, etc. Hence **cūrātōr'**IAL a., ~SHIP n. [ME, f. AF *curatour* (OF *-eur*) or L *curator* (as prec., -OR)]

cûrb, n., & v.t. **1.** Chain, strap, passing under lower jaw of horse, used as a check; (fig.) check, restraint; hard swelling on horse's leg, whence ~'Y² n.; frame round top of well; timber or iron plate round edge of circular structure; = KERB; ~ *roof*, one of which each face has two slopes, the lower one steeper. **2.** v.t. Put ~ on (horse), (fig.) restrain. [ME, f. OF *courbe* adj. & *courber* vb f. L *curvus* bent]

cûrc'ūma, n. Turmeric, substance used in curry-powder, as test for alkalis (~ *paper*), etc.; kinds of tuberous plants yielding this & other commercial substances. [med. or mod. L, f. Arab. *kurkum* saffron, turmeric]

cûrd, n. Coagulated substance formed (naturally or artificially) by action of acids on milk, and made into cheese or eaten (often pl.; ~*s & whey*, junket); fatty substance found between flakes of boiled salmon; ~ *soap* (white, of tallow & soda). Hence ~'Y² a. [ME *crud(de)*, *crod(de)*, of unkn. orig.]

cûr'dle, v.t. & i. Congeal, form into curd; (fig.) ~ *the blood* (with horror). [f. curd vb (f. prec.) +-LE(3)]

cūre¹, n. Remedy; course of medical or other treatment (esp. of specified kind, as *grape*, *milk*, -~), success with this; spiritual charge, as ~ *of souls*; vulcanization. Hence ~'LESS (kūrl-) a. [ME, f. OF f. L *cura* care]

cūre², v.t. & i. Restore to health (also fig.); remedy (an evil); preserve (meat, fruit, tobacco) by salting, drying, etc. (also intr.); vulcanize (rubber), (of rubber) become vulcanized. Hence **cūr**ABIL'ITY n., **cūr'**ABLE a. [ME, f. OF *curer* f. L *curare* take care of (*cura*)]

cūre³, n. (sl.). Odd or eccentric person. [abbr. of CURIOUS]

curé (see Ap.), n. Parish priest in France etc. [F]

curětte', n., & v.t. & i. Surgeon's small · scraping-instrument; (vb) scrape with ~. [F, f. *curer* cleanse (CURE²)]

cûrf'ew, n. Medieval regulation for extinction of fires at fixed hour in evening; hour for this; (also ~-*bell*) bell announcing it; ringing of bell at fixed evening hour, still surviving in some towns; (under martial law etc.) signal or time after which inhabitants may not be abroad. [ME, f. OF *coeverfu*, = OF *cuevrefeu*, f. imper. of *covrir* COVER+*feu* fire]

cûr'ia, n. One of the ten divisions of any of the three ancient Roman tribes; its place of worship; Roman senate-house; senate of ancient Italian towns; court of justice (esp. under feudal organization); the Papal court. [L]

cûr'ial, a. Of a curia; of the Papal court, whence ~ISM n. [OF, f. L *curialis* (CURIA, see -AL)]

cūr'iō, n. (pl. *-os*). Curious object of art. [19th c. abbr. of foll.]

cūriŏs'itў, n. Desire to know; inquisitiveness; strangeness; *a* ~, strange or rare object. [f. OF *curiosete* f. L *curiositatem* (as foll., see -TY)]

cūr'ious, a. Eager to learn; inquisitive; minutely careful, as ~ *inquiry*; strange, surprising, odd; erotic, pornographic (as euphemism in booksellers' catalogues). Hence ~LY² adv., ~NESS n. [ME, f. OF *curios* f. L *curiosus* f. *cura* care, see -IOUS(1)]

cūr'ium, n. (chem.). Radio-active transuranic element. [f. Marie & Pierre *Cur(ie)*, French scientists, +-IUM]

cûrl¹, n. Spiral lock of hair; ~-*paper* (used for twisting hair into ~s); anything spiral or incurved; act of curling, as ~ *of the lip* (expressing scorn); state of being curled, as *keep the hair in* ~; disease of potatoes etc. in which shoots or leaves are curled up. [f. foll.]

cûrl², v.t. & i. Bend, coil, into spiral shape (t. & i.); ~ *up*, roll up into a curl, (intr., sl.) collapse; move in spiral form (of smoke etc.); play at CURLING; ~*ing-irons*, *-tongs*, instruments (heated before use) for ~ing the hair; ~*ing-pins*, folding clips used (cold) for similar purpose. [earliest in 14th c. *crolled*, *crulled*, f. obs. adj. *crolle*, *crulle* curly, f. MDu. *krul*; cf. vbs G *kröllen*, *krollen*, LG, Du., EFris. *krullen* curl]

cûrl'ew, n. Wading bird with long slender curved bill. [ME *curlu* f. OF *corlieu*, *corlio*, orig. imit., but assim. to OF *corlieu* courier]

cûrl'ing, n. In vbl senses; esp.: Scots game played on ice with large round stones; ~*-irons*, *-tongs*, *-pins*, see CURL². [-ING¹]

cûrl'ў, a. Having, arranged in, curls; ~·*pate*, ~-headed person. Hence **cûrl'i**NESS n. [-Y²]

cûrmŭdg'eon (-jn), n. Churlish or miserly fellow. Hence ~LY¹ (-jn-) a. [orig. unkn.]

cŭ'rrach (-ra), n. Coracle. [f. Ir. *curach*, cf. CORACLE]

cŭ'rrant, n. Dried fruit of a seedless variety of grape grown in the Levant, much used in cookery; *red*, *white*, *black*, ~, (fruit of) species of Ribes; *flowering* ~, grown for ornament. [ME *raisins of Corauntz* (Corinth), f. AF, as in mod. F *raisins de Corinthe*]

cŭ'rrencў, n. Time during which a thing is current; (of money) circulation; money current in actual use in a country (‖ ~ *note*, inconvertible legal-tender note for £1 or 10s. issued by Treasury during & after the 1914–18 war, replaced in 1928 by Bank of England notes); prevalence (of words, ideas, reports). [f. foll., see -ENCY]

cŭ'rrent¹, a. In general circulation or use

(of money, opinions, rumours, words); pass, go, run, ~, be generally accepted as true or genuine; (of time) now passing, as ~ week, month; belonging to the ~ time, as ~ issue (of journal); ~ handwriting, cursive. Hence ~LY² adv. [ME cora(u)nt f. OF part. of corre (courir) f. L currere run]

cǔ′rrent², n. Running stream; water, air, etc., moving in given direction; course, tendency, (of events, opinions, etc.); transmission of electric force through a body. [prec. as n.]

cǔ′rricle, n. Light two-wheeled carriage (usu. for two horses abreast). [f. foll. L]

currǐc′ul|um, n. (pl. ~a). Course (of study). Hence ~AR¹ a. [L, = course, race-chariot, f. currere run]

cǔ′rrier, n. One who dresses & colours tanned leather. [ME & OF corier f. L coriarius (corium leather, see -ARY¹, -ER²)]

cǔr′rish, a. Like a cur; snappish; mean-spirited. Hence ~LY² adv., ~NESS n. [-ISH¹]

cǔ′rry¹, n., & v.t. 1. Dish of meat etc. cooked with bruised spices & turmeric; ~-paste, -powder, preparations of turmeric etc. for making ~. 2. v.t. Prepare, flavour, with ~-powder. [f. Tamil kari sauce]

cǔ′rry², v.t. Rub down or dress (horse etc. with ~-comb; dress (tanned leather); (fig.) thrash; ~ favour (orig. favel f. OF faveau, favel, the chestnut horse), ingratiate oneself (with person) by officiousness etc. [ME, f. OF correier f. Rom. *conredare f. Gmc (cf. Goth. garaidjan prepare); see READY]

cǔrse¹, n. Utterance of deity or person invoking deity, consigning person or thing to destruction, divine vengeance, etc. (~s come home to roost, injure the curser; under a ~, feeling or liable to its effects); sentence of excommunication; profane oath, imprecation; accursed object; evil inflicted in response to a ~; great evil, bane; (Cards) ~ of Scotland, nine of diamonds. [late OE curs, isolated & of unkn. orig.]

cǔrse², v.t. & i. Utter curse against; excommunicate; blaspheme; afflict with (esp. in pass.); (v.i.) utter curses. [late OE cursian, f. prec.]

cǔrs′ĕd, -st, a. & adv. In vbl senses; also: damnable, abominable; (arch.; usu. curst) cantankerous; (adv.) cursedly. Hence **cǔrs′ĕd**LY² adv., **cǔrs′ĕd**NESS n. [ME, p.p. of prec.]

cǔrs′ive, a. & n. Running (writing in manuscript), opp. to UNCIAL. [f. med. L (scriptura) cursiva (L currere curs- run, see -IVE)]

cǔrs′or, n. Transparent slide engraved with hair-line forming part of slide-rule. [L, as CURSIVE]

cǔrsōr′ial, a. Having limbs adapted for running (~ birds etc.). [as CURSORY, -AL]

cǔrs′or|y̆, a. Hasty, hurried, (~y inspec-

tion). Hence ~ILY² adv., ~INESS n. [f. L cursorius of a runner (as CURSIVE, see -ORY)]

cǔrs′us, n. Race-course; stated order of daily prayer; course of studies. [L]

cǔrt, a. Discourteously brief; terse, concise; (literary) short. Hence ~′LY² adv., ~′NESS n. [f. L curtus short]

cǔrtail′, v.t. Cut short (lit. & fig.); deprive of. Hence ~MENT n. [f. obs. curtal horse with docked tail f. F courtault (OF cortald, f. court short (CURT) + Gmc. suff. *-ald); assim. to tail]

cǔrt′ail-stĕp, n. Lowest step of stair, with outer end carried round. [orig. unkn.]

cǔrt′ain (-tn), n., & v.t. 1. Suspended cloth used as screen; draw the ~ (back or aside to reveal objects, forward to conceal them); screen separating stage of theatre from auditorium (~ falls, drops, is dropped, at end of action, rises, is raised, at beginning; also fig.; ~ !, narrator's word drawing attention to dramatic situation just described, = tableau); fire-proof ~ in theatre, metal sheet cutting off stage; plain wall of fortified place, connecting two towers etc.; piece of plain wall not supporting a roof; partition, cover, in various technical senses; ~-fire, = BARRAGE (Mil.); ~ lecture, wife's reproof to husband in bed; ~-raiser in theatre, short opening piece. 2. v.t. Furnish, cover, shut off, with ~s. [ME & OF cortine f. LL cortina rend. Gk aulaia (aulē court)]

cǔrtā′na (or -ah-), n. Pointless sword borne before kings of England at Coronation, as emblem of mercy. [ME, f. Anglo-L curtana (sc. spatha sword) f. curtus CURT, see -AN]

cǔrt′ilage, n. (law, dial.). Area attached to dwelling-house. [ME, f. AF f. OF cortil small COURT +-AGE]

cǔrt′sy̆, -sey, n., & v.i. 1. Feminine salutation made by bending knees & lowering body; make, drop, a ~. 2. v.i. Make ~ (to person). [var. of COURTESY]

cǔr′ule (-ōol), a. Pertaining to any high civic dignity; (Rom. Ant.) ~ chair, one like camp-stool, inlaid with ivory; ~ magistrate, one entitled to this. [f. L curulis f. currus chariot]

cǔrv′ature, n. Curving; curved form; (Geom.) deviation (of curve) from straight line. [f. L curvatura (as foll., see -URE)]

cǔrve¹, v.t. & i. Bend so as to form a curve. [f. L curvare (as foll.)]

cǔrve², n. Line of which no part is straight; curved form or thing; (Statistics etc.) line presenting diagrammatically a continuous variation of quantity, force, etc., graph. [f. L curvus bent]

cǔrvĕt′ (also kĕrv′ĭt), n., & v.i. (-tt-, -t-). Horse's leap with fore-legs raised together & hind-legs raised with spring before fore-legs reach ground; (v.i.; of ~-horse or rider) make ~. [(vb f. It. cor-

vettare) f. It. *corvetta* dim. of *corva* curve as prec.)]

cūrvi-, comb. form of L *curvus* curved, as *-caudate*, *-costate*, *-dentate*, *-rostral*, with curved tail, ribs, teeth, beak; *-foliate*, with leaves bent back; *-form*, of curved shape; *-nervate* (of leaves), with veins diverging from mid-rib & converging towards margin.

cūrvilin′ear, a. Contained by, consisting of, curved line(s). Hence~LY² adv. [prec. +-LINEAR]

cŭs′cŭs, n. Aromatic root of an Indian grass, used for fans etc. [f. Hind. *khas khas*]

cū′sĕc, n. (Flow of) one cubic foot (of water) per second (unit in irrigation engineering). [abbr. of 'cubic foot per second']

cŭsh′at, n. (Sc., dial.). Wood-pigeon, ring-dove. [OE *cūscute*, of unkn. orig.]

cushion¹ (kŏŏ′shn), n. **1.** Mass of soft material stuffed into cloth or silk covering, for sitting, kneeling, reclining, on; PIN-~. **2.** Pad worn by woman under hair; pad beneath skirt of woman's dress. **3.** Elastic lining of sides of billiard table; steam left in cylinders as buffer to piston; fleshy part of buttock (of pig etc.); frog of horse's hoof; sweet in ~ shape; ~-*tire* of bicycle (rubber tubing stuffed with rubber shreds). Hence ~Y² (-sho-) a. [(a) 14th c. *cuisshin* etc. f. OF *coissin*; (b) 14th c. *cusshin* etc. f. OF *coussin*; OF forms of uncert. orig.; ult. f. L *culcita*]

cushion² (kŏŏ′shn), v.t. Furnish with cushions; protect with cushions (also fig.); suppress quietly (complaints etc); (Billiards) place, leave, (ball) against cushion. [f. prec.]

cush′y (kŏŏ-), a. (sl.). (Of a post, task, etc.) easy, pleasant, comfortable. [Anglo-Ind., f. Hind. *khush* pleasant]

cŭsp, n. Apex, peak; (Geom.) point at which two branches of curve meet & stop; (Archit.) projecting point between small arcs in Gothic tracery; (Bot.) pointed end, esp. of leaf. Hence ~ED² (-pt) a. [f. L *cuspis -idis* point]

cŭs′pid|al, a. Of (the nature of) a cusp. So ~ate, ~āted, [-ATE²(2)] aa. [as prec., -AL]

*cŭs′pidōr, n. Spittoon. [Port., = spitter (*cuspir* f. L CONspuere, see -OR)]

*cŭss, n. Curse; person, creature, (often disparaging). [vulg. pron. of CURSE¹]

cŭss′ĕdnĕss, n. Perversity, esp. *pure* ~. [vulg. pron. of *cursedness*]

cŭs′tard, n. Mixture of eggs & milk, baked or served liquid; ~-*apple*, W. Indian fruit with pulp like ~. [in ME a kind of pie; alt. f. obs. *crustade*, f. AF, f. *cruste* CRUST, see -ADE]

cŭstōd′ial, a. Relating to custody. [-AL]

cŭstōd′ian, n. Guardian, keeper. So **cŭstōd′ier¹** n. [as foll. +-AN]

cŭs′todȳ, n. Guardianship, care, (*parent has* ~ *of child, child is in the* ~ *of father*);

imprisonment, esp. *take into* ~, arrest. [f. L *custodia* (*custos -odis* guardian, see -Y¹)]

cŭs′tom, n. Usual practice; (Law) established usage having the force of law; (pl.) duty levied upon imports from foreign countries; ~-*house*, office (esp. in seaport) at which ~s are collected; business patronage or support; *the C~s*, department of the Civil Service that deals with the levying of ~s; *~ *clothes* (made to measure; so ~-*built*, -*made*, etc.) [ME & OF *custume* (see COSTUME) f. Rom. *costumne f. *costudne f. L *consuetudinem*]

cŭs′tomar|ȳ, a. & n. Usual; (Law) subject to, held by, custom (of the manor etc.); (n., also -*tumary*) written collection of the customs of a country. Hence ~ILY² adv., ~INESS n. [f. med. L *custumarius* f. *custuma* f. AF *custume* (as prec., see -ARY¹)]

cŭs′tomer, n. Buyer; client of bank; (colloq.) *queer, awkward,* etc., ~ (person to deal with). [ME, f. as prec.; in mod. senses f. CUSTOM +-ER¹]

cŭs′tŏs, n. Guardian, keeper; ~ *rōtŭlōr′um*, keeper of the rolls, principal justice of the peace in a county. [L]

cŭt¹, n. Act of cutting; stroke, blow, with knife, sword, whip; ~ *& thrust*, hand-to-hand struggle; excision (of part of a play etc.); act, speech, that wounds the feelings; particular stroke in cricket, lawn tennis, croquet, etc.; refusal to recognize an acquaintance (*give one the* ~ *direct*); *short* ~, crossing that shortens the distance; fashion, style, (of clothes, hair, etc.; *the* ~ *of one's* JIB¹); *a* ~ (degree, stage) *above*; wound made by cutting; railway cutting; narrow opening in floor of stage of theatre, by which scenes are moved up & down; = WOOD-*cut*; piece (esp. of meat) cut off; reduction (in wages, prices, etc.); *draw* ~s, draw lots with sticks of unequal length (a different word, of unkn. orig.); ~-*off*, device to prevent feeding of cartridges from magazine of rifle; ~-*out*, device in motor-car for releasing gas rapidly without passage through silencer. [f. foll.]

cŭt², v.t. & i. (*cŭt*). **1.** Penetrate, wound, with edged instrument, as *the knife* ~ *his finger, he* ~ *his finger with a knife*, (fig.) *argument* ~s *both ways* (tells for both sides); (fig.) *a* ~*ting wind*, ~*ting retort, it* ~ *him to the heart*, whence ~t′ingLY² adv.; divide with knife etc., *in two, in* or *into* pieces (~ *the knot*, fig., solve problem in irregular but efficient way, cf. GORDIAN); (fig.) ~ (renounce) *a connexion*; detach by ~ting; carve (meat); cross, intersect, as *two lines* ~ *each other*; (intr.) pass *through, across,* etc., (sl.) run (~ *& run*, run away); reduce by ~ting (hair etc.); reduce (wages, prices, time, etc.; ~ *it fine*, allow only the minimum; ~ *a loss*, abandon losing speculation in good time; ~ *the record*, reduce the recorded shortest time for race etc., or surpass record otherwise); shape, fashion, by ~ting (coat, gem, etc.); perform, execute, make, as ~ *a* CAPER, DASH, FIGURE, *joke*; divide (pack of cards, or abs.) to select dealer, prevent cheating, etc.; hit (ball, or abs.) in certain way, in cricket etc.; renounce acquaintance of (person), decline to recognize him, esp. ~ *him dead*; absent oneself from, avoid, renounce, as ~ *a lecture*, ~ *the whole concern*; ~ *a tooth*, have it appear through gum (~ one's *eye* or *wisdom teeth*, fig., develop insight or wisdom); ~ *short*, shorten by ~ting (lit. & fig.), also interrupt; ~ one's *stick*, go; ~ *coat according to* CLOTH. **2.** ~ *back* (Cinemat.), repeat, for dramatic reasons, portions of scenes already shown on screen (also as n., ~*-back*); ~ *down*, lining or throw down by ~ting, (fig.) reduce (expenses); ~ *in* (intr.), enter abruptly, interpose (in conversation), (Cards) join in game by taking place of player who ~s out, (Motoring) obstruct path of vehicle one has just overtaken by returning to one's own side of the road too soon; ~ *no ice* (sl.), effect little or nothing; ~ *off*, remove by ~ting, bring to abrupt end or (esp. early) death, intercept (supplies, communications), exclude (*from* access etc.); ~ *off with a shilling*, disinherit by bequeathing a shilling; ~ *out*, remove by ~ting, stop doing or using (something), (fig.) out-do or supplant (rival), fashion or shape (lit. & fig.), *de*tach (animal) from the herd, (Cards, intr.) be excluded from game as result of ~ting, (Nav.) capture (enemy ship) by getting between it & shore, (Motoring) obstruct path of oncoming vehicle by moving out from one's own side of the road, esp. in order to overtake another vehicle; ~ *up*, ~ in pieces, destroy utterly, (fig.) criticize severely, (usu. pass.) distress greatly, ~ *up* (*well*), leave (large) fortune, ~ *up rough*, show resentment; ~*-&-come-again*, abundance; ~ *& dried* or *dry* (of opinions etc.), ready-made, lacking freshness; ~'*purse*, thief; ~'*throat*, murderer, (adj., of competition) intensive, merciless, (of bridge, euchre, etc.) three-handed. [ME *cutte*, *kitte*, *kette*, without cogn. in WG or Rom.; cf. however, Swed. dial. *kåta*, (*kulå*), from source of which the ME wd may derive]

cūtān'ĕous, a. Of the skin. [f. mod. L *cutaneus* (*cutis* skin, see -ANEOUS)]

cŭt'away, a. & n. (Coat) with skirt cut back from the waist.

cŭtch'a, a. (Anglo-Ind.). Of poor quality; makeshift (opp. PUCKA); (of bricks) sun-dried. [Hind. *kachcha* raw]

cutchĕ'rry, cŭtch'ery, n. (Anglo-Ind.). Public office, court-house; office of planter etc. [f. Hind. *kachahri*]

cūte, a. (colloq.). Clever, shrewd; inge-

nious; *attractive. Hence ~'LY² (-tl-) adv., ~'NESS (-tn-) n. [for ACUTE]

cŭt'icle, n. Epidermis or other superficial skin; (Bot.) superficial film of plants. Hence **cūtic'ūlAR¹** a. [f. L *cuticula* dim. of CUTIS]

cŭt'is, n. (anat.). True skin, underlying the epidermis. [L, = skin]

cŭt'lass, n. Short sword with wide slightly curved blade, esp. that used by sailors. [f. F *coutelas* augment. of *couteau* (*coutel*; see foll.)]

cŭt'ler, n. One who makes or deals in knives & similar utensils. [ME, f. OF *coutelier* f. *coutel* (f. L *cultellus* dim. of *culter* COULTER), see -ER²(2)]

cŭt'lerў, n. Trade of the cutler; things made or sold by cutlers. [ME, f. OF *coutelerie* (as prec., see -ERY)]

cŭt'lĕt, n. Neck-chop of mutton, small piece of veal, broiled or fried in bread-crumbs; imitation of mutton-~ in minced fish etc. [f. F *côtelette* double dim. of *côte* rib f. L *costa*]

cŭtt'er, n. Person, thing, that cuts; superior kind of brick that can be cut; boat belonging to ship of war, fitted for rowing & sailing; small single-masted vessel rigged like sloop, but with running bowsprit. [-ER¹]

cŭtt'ing, n. In vbl senses; ‖ esp. excavation of high ground for railway, road, etc.; ‖ *press* ~, paragraph etc. cut from newspaper. [-ING¹]

cŭt'tle, n. (Usu. ~*-fish*) mollusc ejecting black fluid when pursued; ~*-bone*, its internal shell, used for polishing. [OE *cudele*, of uncert. orig.]

‖ **cŭtt'ў**, a. & n. (Sc. & north.). Cut short, abnormally short; (n.) short pipe; ~*-stool*, seat in Sc. churches where unchaste women sat to receive public rebuke during service. [CUT², -Y²]

cŭt'water (-waw-), n. Knee of head of ship, dividing water before it reaches bow; forward edge of prow; wedge-shaped end of pier of bridge.

cŭt'worm (-wĕrm), n. Caterpillar that cuts off young plants level with the ground.

cwm (kōōm), n. Var. of COOMB.

-cў, suf., special form of the abstract suf. -Y¹, repr. L -*cia*, -*tia*, & Gk -*kia*, -*keia*, -*tia*, -*teia* (in E occurring chiefly in the combined forms -ACY, -ANCY, -ENCY, -CRACY, -MANCY). On anal. of wds in -*acy*, -*ncy*, with corresp. nn. in -*ate*, -*nt*, as *advocacy*, *advocate*, *infancy*, *infant*, -*cy* was extended to wds in -*n*, as *chaplaincy*, *captaincy*, after *incumbency*, *lieutenancy*, &, being thus regarded as independent suf. = -*ship*, to other wds as *colonelcy*; it is even added to wds ending in -*t* (where -*c*- should have been substituted for -*t*-), as *bankruptcy*, *idiotcy*, normal form being *idiocy* f. Gk *idiōteia*.

cўăn'ic, a. Blue; (Chem.) of, containing, cyanogen. [as foll. +-IC]

cȳan|(o)-, comb. form of Gk *kuanos*, a dark-blue mineral. *kuaneos* dark-blue. Meaning (1) dark-blue, as ~*ōm'eter*, instrument for measuring blueness of sky; (2) of, containing, cyanogen.

cȳăn'ogĕn, n. (chem.). Compound of two radicals each consisting of one atom of nitrogen and one of carbon. Hence **cȳ'an**IDE n. (*cyanide process*, method of extracting a precious metal from its ore by treatment with a dilute solution of potassium cyanide). [f. F *cyanogène* (as prec. +-GEN)]

cȳanōs'is, n. Blue discoloration, due to circulation of imperfectly oxygenated blood. [f. Gk *kuanōsis* (as prec., see -OSIS)]

cȳbernĕt'ics, n. Study of system of control & communications in animals & electrically operated devices such as calculating machines. [f. Gk *kubernētēs* steersman, -ICS]

cȳ'cad, n. (bot.). Kinds of palm-like plant. [f. mod. L *cycas cycad*-f. supposed Gk *kukas*, scribal error for *koïkas*, pl. of *koïx* Egyptian palm]

cȳc'lamĕn, n. Kinds of plant cultivated for their early-blooming flowers. [L, irreg. f. Gk *kuklaminos*]

cȳ'cle, n., & v.i. 1. Recurrent period (of events, phenomena, etc.); *Metonic* or *Lunar~*, one of 19 years, used for finding date of Easter; period of a thing's completion; complete set or series; series of poems or songs (*song~*) collected round a central event or idea; bicycle, tricycle, or similar machine; ~*car*, very light motor vehicle of simplified design with 3 (rarely 4) wheels, usu. fitted with chain drive & engine of 1 or 2 cylinders. 2. v.i. Revolve in ~s; ride ~. [ME, f. OF or f. LL f. Gk *kuklos* circle]

cȳc'lic, -ical, aa. Recurring in cycles; belonging to a chronological cycle; (*-ic*) of a cycle of poems, as ~ *poet*; (Gk Ant., *-ic*) ~ *chorus*, dithyrambic chorus, danced in ring round altar; (Bot., of flower) with its parts arranged in whorls; (Org. Chem., *-ic*) with the constituent atoms in a ring formation. [f. F *cyclique* or L f. Gk *kuklikos* (prec., -IC)]

cȳc'list, n. Rider of a cycle. [CYCLE +-IST]

cȳclo-, comb. form of Gk *kuklos* circle, as ~*graph*, instrument for tracing circular arcs, ~*meter* (-ŏm²), instrument for measuring (1) circular arcs (2) distance traversed by bicycle etc., ~*stomous* (-ŏs²), with round mouth, ~*ra'ma* (-ah-), circular panorama.

cȳc'loid, n. Curve traced by a point on a radius of a circle within (*prolate* ~), on (*common* ~), or without (*curtate* ~), its circumference, as the circle rolls along a straight line. Hence **cȳcloid'**AL a. [f. Gk *kukloeidēs* (as CYCLE, see -OID)]

cȳc'lōne, n. System of winds rotating round a centre of minimum barometric pressure; violent hurricane of limited diameter. Hence **cȳclŏn'IC** a. [as *cyclome*

prob. repr. Gk *kuklōma* wheel, coil of snake, f. *kuklos* CYCLE]

cȳclop(a)ed'|ia (-pĕd-), n. = ENCYCLOPAEDIA. Hence ~IC a. [abbr. of ENCYCLOPAEDIA]

Cȳclope'an, -clŏp'ian, a. Of, like, a Cyclops; huge; ~ *masonry*, an ancient style made with huge irregular stones. [f. L *Cyclopeus, -pius*, f. Gk *kuklōpeios, -pios*, (as foll.)]

Cȳc'lŏp(s), n. (pl. *-ops, -opses, -ōp'ēs*). (Gk Myth.) one-eyed giant; one-eyed person. [L (*-s*), f. Gk *kuklōps* (*kuklos* circle +*ōps* eye)]

cȳc'lostȳle, n., & v.t. Apparatus printing copies of writing from stencil-plate cut by pen with small toothed wheel; (v.t.) reproduce with this. [CYCLO-]

cȳc'lotrŏn, n. (phys.). Apparatus for electro-magnetic acceleration of charged atoms, atomic nuclei, etc. [f. CYCLO-+ (ELEC)TRON]

cȳd'er. See CIDER.

cȳg'nĕt, n. Young swan. [ME, f. OF *cygne* or L *cygnus* +-ET¹]

cȳl'inder, n. (Geom.) solid generated by straight line moving parallel to itself and describing with its ends any fixed curve, esp. circle; roller-shaped body, hollow or solid; barrel-shaped object of baked clay covered with cuneiform writing and buried under Babylonian or Assyrian temple; stone of similar shape used as seal by Assyrians; cylindrical part of various machines, esp. chamber in which steam acts upon piston; metal roller used in printing. [f. L f. Gk *kulindros* (*kulindō* roll)]

cȳlin'drical, a. Cylinder-shaped. [mod. L, f. Gk *kulindrikos* (as prec., see -IC) +-AL]

cȳl'indroid, a. & n. (Figure) like a cylinder. [f. Gk *kulindroeidēs* (as prec., -OID)]

cȳm'a, n. (pl. *-mas*). Ogee moulding of cornice (~ *recta* with concave, ~ *reversa* with convex, curve uppermost); = CYME. [mod. L, f. Gk *kuma* wave, anything swollen]

cȳmār', n. Woman's loose light garment esp. under-garment. [f. F *simarre*; see CHIMERE]

cȳm'bal, n. One of a pair of concave brass or bronze plates, struck together to make ringing sound. Hence ~IST n. [ME, f. OF *symbale* or L f. Gk *kumbalon* (*kumbē* cup)]

cȳm'balō (pl. *-os*), -lŏn, nn.=DULCIMER. [f. It. *cembalo*, as prec.]

cȳm'bifōrm, a. (anat., bot.). Boat-shaped. [f. L *cumba, cymba* f. Gk *kumbē* boat +-FORM]

cȳme, n. (bot.). Inflorescence in which primary axis bears single terminal flower that develops first, system being continued by axes of secondary and higher orders (cf. RACEME). Hence **cȳ**MOSE'¹ a. [F *cyme*, var. of *cime* summit, f. pop. L *cima*, L f. Gk *kuma* CYMA]

Cȳm′rĭc (k-), a. Welsh. [f. W *Cymru* Wales]

cȳn′ĭc, a. & n. **1.** Of, characteristic of, the Cynic philosophers; = foll. **2.** n. (C~) philosopher of sect founded by Antisthenes, marked by ostentatious contempt for pleasure. **3.** Sneering fault-finder. Hence ~ISM n. [f. L f. Gk *kunikos* (*kuŏn kunos* dog, nickname for Cynic)]

cȳn′ĭcal, a. Churlish; captious; incredulous of human goodness; sneering. Hence ~LY² adv. [-AL]

cȳno- = Gk *kuno-*, comb. form of *kuŏn* dog, as ~*phob′ia*, dread of dogs.

cȳnocĕph′alus, n. Fabulous dog-headed man; (Zool.) dog-faced baboon. [L, f. Gk *kunokephalos* (prec. +*kephalē* head)]

cȳn′osūre (*or* -shoor), n. (Constellation containing) Pole-star, Little Bear; guiding star; centre of attraction or admiration. [F, or f. L f. Gk *kunosoura* dog's tail, Little Bear]

cypher. See CIPHER.

cy pres (sēprā′), adv., n., & a. (Law) as near as possible (to testator's intentions); (adj.) approximate; (n.) approximation. [AF, = F *si près* so near (as etc.)]

cȳp′rĕss, n. Coniferous tree with hard wood and dark foliage; branch of this as symbol of mourning. [ME, f. OF *cipres* f. LL *cypressus* (= L *cu-*) f. Gk *kuparissos*]

Cȳp′rian, a. & n. (Inhabitant, native) of Cyprus; licentious (person). [f. L *Cyprius* (*Cyprus*) +-AN]

Cȳp′riot, -ōte, a. & n.=prec. (first sense). [-OT²]

Cyrēnā′ĭc (sīr-), a. & n. (Philosopher) of the hedonistic school of Aristippus of Cyrene. [f. L f. Gk *Kurēnaikos* (*Kurēnē*)]

Cȳrill′ĭc, a. ~ *alphabet*, that used by Slavonic peoples of the Eastern Church. [St *Cyril*, reputed author, +-IC]

cyrto- (sẽr-), comb. form of Gk *kurtos* curved, as ~*meter* (-ŏm′-), instrument measuring chest.

cȳst, n. (Biol.) hollow organ, bladder, etc., in animal or plant, containing liquid secretion; (Path.) sac containing morbid matter, parasitic larva, etc.; cell containing embryos etc. [f. LL & med. L *cystis* (so in 16th c. Eng.), f. Gk *kustis* bladder]

cȳst-, cȳsti-, cȳsto-, comb. form of Gk *kustis*, *kustē*, bladder, as *cystiform*, bladder-shaped, *cysto*CELE, -SCOPE, -TOMY.

cȳs′tĭc, a. Of the urinary bladder; of the gall-bladder; of the nature of a cyst. [f. as CYST +-IC]

cȳstīt′ĭs, n. Inflammation of the bladder. [CYST-, -ITIS]

-cȳte, suf. in biol. wds meaning *cell*, as LEUCO*cyte*. [f. Gk *kutos* vessel]

cȳto-, comb. form of Gk *kutos* vessel, as ~*blast*, protoplasmic nucleus of a cell; ~*plasm*, protoplasmic content of cell other than the nucleus.

cȳtŏl′ogȳ, n. (biol.). Study of cells. Hence **cȳtŏl′OGIST** n. [CYTO-]

czar etc. See TSAR etc.

Czech, -kh, (chĕk), n. & a. (Native or language) of Bohemia. [f. Boh. *Cech*]

Czechoslovak (chĕkŏslōv′ăk), a. & n. (Native) of the State called *Czechoslovakia*, including Bohemia, Moravia, part of Silesia, Slovakia, and formerly Carpathian Ruthenia. [*Czech, Slovak,* native race-names, -O-]

D

D (dē), letter (pl. *Ds*, *D's*, *Dees*); *D block, trap, valve,* shaped like the letter; also D=DEE; (Mus.) second note of natural major scale.

'd. Colloq. clipping of *had* & *would*, chiefly after *I*, *we*, *you*, *he*, *she*, *they*.

-d, p.p. suf. (*heard* etc.); see -ED¹.

da. See DAD.

dăb¹, v.t. & i. (-bb-). Strike lightly or undecidedly, hit feebly *at*, tap, peck; press but not rub (surface) with sponge etc., whence ~b′ER¹(2) n.; press (brush, dabber, etc.) against surface. [f. 1300, of unkn. orig.]

dăb², n. Slight or undecided but sudden blow, tap, peck; brief application of sponge, handkerchief, etc., to surface without rubbing; moisture, colour, etc., so applied. [f. prec.]

dăb³, n. Kind of flat-fish. [16th c., of unkn. orig.]

dăb⁴, n. & a. (colloq.). Adept (*at* games etc., *doing*); *he is a* ~ *hand* (*at*). [f. 1690, of unkn. orig.]

dăb′ble, v.t. & i. Wet intermittently, slightly, or partly, soil, moisten, splash; move the feet, hands, bill, about in water; engage *in* or *at* pursuit etc. as a hobby, whence **dăb′blER¹** n. [16th c., f. Du. *dabbelen*]

dăb′chick, n. Water-bird, the little grebe. [16th c. *dap-, dop-,* later *dip-*; perh. cogn. w. DIP]

dăb′ster, n. = DAB⁴; = DAUB*ster*. [-STER]

da ca′pō (dahkah-), mus. direction. Repeat from the beginning. [It.]

dāce, n. Small freshwater fish. [ME *darse* f. OF *dars* f. med. L (8th c.) *darsus*, of Gaulish orig.]

dachs′hund (dahks-hŏont), n. Short-legged breed of dog. [G, = badger-dog]

dacoit′, n. Member of Indian or Burmese armed robber band. [f. Hind. *ḍakait* f. *ḍaka* gang-robbery]

dacoit′ȳ, n. (Act of) gang-robbery. [f. Hind. *ḍakaiti* as prec.]

dăc′tȳl, n. Metrical foot ~⌣⌣. [f. L f. Gk *daktulos* finger]

dăctȳl′ĭc, a. & n. Of dactyls; (noun. usu. pl.) ~ verse(s). [f. L f. Gk *daktulikos* (prec., -IC)]

dăd, da (dah), **dăd′a, dădd′ȳ**, nn. (colloq.). Father (esp. as voc.); *daddy--long′legs*, crane-fly. [f. 16th c.; infantile sound]

dãd'ō, n. (pl. *-os*). Cube of pedestal between base & cornice; lower few feet of room-wall when faced with wood or coloured differently from upper part. Hence ~ED² (-ōd) a. [It., = DIE¹]

daed'al, a. (poet.). Skilful, inventive; mazy; manifold, complex, mysterious. [f. L f. Gk *daidalos* skilful, variegated]

Daedāl'ian, -ean, a. In the manner of Daedalus the Greek artificer; intricate; labyrinthine. [f. L *Daedaleus* of Daedalus (cf. Gk *daidaleos* cunningly wrought) + -AN]

daemonic. See dem-.

daff (dah-), v.t. (arch.). Put aside, waive. [var. of DOFF, preserved by 1 *Hen. IV*, IV. i. 96]

dãff'odil (also dãffodill'y̆, dãff'adowndill'y̆, in poetry etc.), n. & a. Lent lily, pale-yellow-flowered narcissus (alternative to leek a*s* Welsh national emblem); pale yellow (n. & a.). [f. earlier *affodill* (*d*- unexplained) f. L f. Gk *asphodelos* ASPHODEL]

daft (dah-), a. (esp. Sc.). Foolish, reckless, wild, crazy. [ME *daffte* = OE *gedæfte* mild, meek; orig. sense (cf. Goth. *gadaban* be fit) fitting, suitable (cf. DEFT); for change of meaning cf. SILLY]

dãgg'er (-g-), n. Stabbing-weapon with short pointed and edged blade (*at ~s drawn*, on the point of fighting, in strained relations, *with* person, or abs.; *look, speak, ~s* bitterly, so as to wound); (Print.) (*double*) ~, = (*double*) OBELISK. [ME, app. an E form.; prob. related to *dag* stab (14th c.) & OF, F *dague* dagger]

ᵗdãg'ō, n. (pl. *~s, ~es*). (Term of contempt for) a Spaniard, Portuguese, or Italian. [f. Sp. *Diego* = James]

dague'rreoty̆pe (-g̃ĕro-), n. (Portrait taken by) early photographic process. [*Daguerre* 1839 inventor, -O-, TYPE]

dah, n. Burmese sword-knife. [Burmese]

dahabee'yah (dah-ha-), **-bi'ah** (-bē-), n. Nile sailing-boat. [Arab., = the golden, orig. sense *gilded barge*]

dahl'ia (dāl-), n. Mexican composite plant cultivated in Europe for its many-coloured single & double flowers (*blue ~*, impossibility); shade of red. [*Dahl* d. 1789, botanist, -IA¹]

dai (dī), n. (Anglo-Ind.). Wet-nurse. [Hind.; cf. Pers. *dāyah*]

Dail (Eireann) (doil(y̆ĕ'ran)), n. Chamber of Deputies in the Irish Republic legislature. [Ir., = assembly of Ireland]

dail'y̆, a., adv., & n. **1.** (Recurring, appearing, done) every day or week-day, from day to day, constant, often; ~ *bread*, one's necessary food or livelihood. **2.** n. A ~ newspaper (pl. *dailies*); ‖ (colloq.) non-resident maid-servant. [OE *-dæglic* (DAY, -LY¹)]

dai'miō (dī-), n. (pl. *-os*). Japanese feudal vassal, noble, (hist.). [Jap., f. Chin. *dai* great, *myo* name]

dain'ty̆,¹ n. Choice morsel, dish, etc.,

delicacy, tit-bit, (lit. & fig.). [f. OF *dainte, -tie* f. L *dignitatem* (*dignus* worthy, -TY)]

dain't|y̆², a. Delicate, choice; tasteful, pretty, of delicate beauty, scrupulously clean; particular, nice, of delicate tastes & sensibility, fastidious; inclined to luxury. Hence ~ILY² adv., ~iNESS n. [f. prec.]

ᵗdaiquiri (dīk'ĭrĭ, dăk'-), n. Kind of cocktail. [Cuban]

dair'y̆, n. Room or building for keeping milk & cream & making butter etc. (~*maid*, in charge of this); the milk department in farming; shop for milk etc. (~*man*, dealer in milk etc.); cows of a farm. Hence (f. rare vb) ~ING¹ n. [ME *deierie* f. obs. *dey* (OE *dǣge* 'kneader of DOUGH') dairymaid + -ERY]

dais (dās), n. Raised platform, esp. at end of hall for high table, throne, etc., or terrace. [ME, f. OF *deis* f. L *discus* DISC, DISH, in med. L sense *table*]

dais'y̆ (-z-), n. Small European wild & garden flower; other plants resembling it, esp. the larger ox-eye ~; (sl.) first-rate specimen of anything; ~*-chain*, string of daisies fastened together; ~*-cutter*, horse lifting feet very little, ball travelling along ground at cricket. Hence **dais'iED²** (-zĭd) a. [OE *dæges êage* day's eye]

dak, dâk. See DAWK.

dal (dahl). See DHAL.

dāle, n. Valley (esp. in north; also in poet. use, as *hill & ~*); ~*s'man*, inhabitant of ~s in north. [OE *dæl*, OS *dal*, OHG *tal*, ON *dalr*, Goth. *dal(s)* f. Gmc *ᵗdal-*; see DELL]

dăll'y̆, v.i. & t. Amuse oneself, make sport; toy amorously (*with* or abs.); coquet *with* temptation etc.; be evasive *with* person or business; idle, loiter, delay; ~ *away*, consume (time, opportunity) to no purpose. Hence **dăll'iANCE** n. [f. OF *dalier* chat]

Dălmā'tian (-shn), n. (Also ~ *dog*) spotted dog kept to run with carriage. [*Dalmatia*, -AN]

dălmăt'ĭc, n. Wide-sleeved loose long vestment with slit sides worn by deacons & bishops on some occasions, & by kings & emperors esp. at coronation. [ME, f. OF *dalmatique* or LL *dalmatica* (*vestis* robe) of Dalmatia]

dăl segno (sān'yō), mus. direction (abbr. *D.S.*). Repeat from point indicated. [It.]

dalt'onĭsm (dawl-), n. Colour-blindness, esp. inability to distinguish green from red. [f. F *daltonisme* f. John *Dalton*, Eng. chemist so affected, d. 1844, -ISM(2)]

dăm¹, n., & v.t. **1.** Barrier constructed to hold back water & raise its level, to form a reservoir, or to prevent flooding; causeway; water confined by ~. **2.** v.t. (-mm-). Furnish or confine with ~ (usu. *up*); block *up*, obstruct, (lit. & fig.). [12th c., app. f. MLG, MDu. *dam* (= OFris. *dam*, MHG *tam*, ON *dammr*), cf. (f. same stem but not directly related) OE *fordemman* (ME *demme*), = Goth. *faurdammjan* stop up, shut off]

dăm², n. Mother (usu. of beast); *the devil & his ~*, the powers of evil. [ME; var. DAME]

dăm'age, n., & v.t. **1.** Harm (*to* one's *great ~*), injury impairing value or usefulness; (Law; pl.) sum of money claimed or adjudged in compensation for loss or injury; (sl.) cost (*what's the ~?*). **2.** v.t. Injure (usu. thing) so as to diminish value; detract from reputation of (person etc.; *trying to ~ the Government*; *a damaging admission*); hence ~ABLE (-IĮa-) a. [ME, f. OF *damage(r)* f. *dam* loss f. L *damnum* + -AGE]

dămascēne', **-skeen'**, v.t. Ornament (metal) with inlaid gold or silver; ornament (steel) with watered pattern produced in welding. [f. *Damascus*, *-cene* thr. L f. Gk *damaskēnos*,*-keen* thr. F & It.]

dăm'ask, n. & a., & v.t. **1.** *~ rose*, old variety brought from Damascus; its colour; figured woven material (prop. of silk); twilled table-linen with woven designs shown by reflection of light; steel of or as of Damascus, with wavy surface-pattern due to special welding of iron & steel together. **2.** adj. Coloured like *~ rose*, blush-red; made of or resembling the silk, linen, or steel. **3.** v.t. Weave with figured designs; = DAMASCENE; ornament with pattern; make (cheek etc.) red. [ME, f. AF *damasc* f. L *Damascus*]

dāme, n. (Arch., poet., or joc., for) lady; ‖ keeper, male or female, of Eton boarding house; (Law; ‖ prefixed title of) wife of knight or baronet (*Lady* in ordinary use; cf. *D~ Fortune*, *D~ Nature*); ‖ lady member of Order of British Empire (also as prefix corresp. *Sir*); *D~ Commander*, *D~ Grand Cross*, (ranks in Order of B.E. & in R.V.O.); ‖ higher female member of Primrose League; ‖*~-school*, primary school of the kind formerly kept by old women; *~'s violet*, cruciferous plant with pale lilac flowers that have no scent until evening. [ME, f. OF f. L *domina* mistress]

dămm'ar, n. Resin obtained from certain Indian and Australasian coniferous trees, used in varnish-making. [Malay *damar*]

dămn (-m), v.t. & i., & n. **1.** Condemn, censure, (*~ a person's character*); (Theatr., of audience) receive coldly, secure the withdrawal of, (play); bring condemnation upon, be the ruin of; *~ with faint praise*, commend so frigidly as to suggest disapproval; doom to hell (so in optative, often *d~*, = *may God ~* person or thing, or with object omitted; *~ed*, or *I'll be ~ed, if I know* etc., colloq. negation); cause the damnation of; curse (person or thing, or abs.; esp. *~ your eyes*, or *impudence!*). **2.** n. An uttered curse; a

negligible amount (*don't care, not worth, a~*). [ME, f. OF *damner* f. L *damnare* (*damnum* loss, harm)]

dăm'nab|le, a. Subject to, deserving, damnation; hateful, confounded, annoying. Hence ~LY² adv. [ME, f. OF f. LL *damnabilis* as prec., -ABLE]

dămnā'tion, n. & int. Damning of play; (condemnation to) eternal punishment in hell; (int.) = *may ~ take* a person or thing. [ME, f. OF f. L *damnationem* (DAMN, -ATION)]

dăm'natory̆, a. Conveying, causing, censure or damnation. [f. L *damnatorius* (*damnare* DAMN, -ORY)]

dămned (-md), a. & adv. In vbl senses; also or esp.: *the ~*, souls in hell; damnable, infernal, unwelcome; confoundedly, extremely, (*~* or *d—d* or *damn' hot, funny*, etc.). [-ED¹]

dăm'ni|fy̆, v.t. (legal). Cause injury to. Hence ~FICA'TION n. [f. OF *damnifier* f. LL *damnificare* (*damnum* loss, -FY)]

dămn'ing¹ (-mǐ-), n. In vbl senses; esp., cursing. [-ING¹]

dămn'ing² (-mn-, -mǐ-), a. In vbl senses; esp., *~ evidence*, that secures conviction. [-ING²]

dămnōs'a herĕd'ĭtăs, n. Inheritance that brings more burden than profit. [L]

Dăm'oclēs (-z), n. *Sword of ~*, imminent danger in midst of prosperity. [Greek who was feasted with sword hung by a hair over him]

Dăm'on and Py̆th'iăs, n. & a. (As of) devoted friends (*~ friendship*). [Gk tale]

dăm'osĕl (-z-), **-zĕl**, n. (arch.). Var. of DAMSEL.

dămp, n., a., & v.t. & i. **1.** = CHOKE¹-*~* (also *black~*); = FIRE¹-*~*; moisture in air, on surface, or diffused through solid; dejection, chill, discouragement, (*cast* or *strike a ~ over* or *into*); *~(-proof) course*, layer of slate etc. in wall to keep *~* from rising; hence ~²PROOF n. **2.** adj. Slightly wet; hence ~'EN³ v.t. & i. (chiefly U.S.), ~'ISH¹(2) a., ~'LY² adv., ~'NESS n. **3.** vb. Stifle, choke, dull, extinguish, (*~ down a fire*, heap with ashes etc. to check combustion); (Mus.) stop vibration of (string); discourage, depress, (zeal, hopes); moisten; (Gardening) *~ off*, rot, & fall off from *~*. [late 15th c., f. MLG *damp* vapour etc., = OHG *dampf*]

dăm'per, n. Person or thing that depresses; (Piano) pad silencing string except when removed by pedal or by note's being struck; metal plate in flue controlling combustion; contrivance for wetting paper, stamps, etc.; (Austral.) unleavened cake baked in wood ashes. [-ER¹]

dăm'sel (-zl), n. (arch. & literary). Young unmarried woman. [ME, f. OF *dameisele* f. Rom. *domnicella* dim. of L *domina* mistress]

dăm'son (-z-), n. & a. Small dark-purple plum (*~ plum*, larger but similar); tree bearing it; ~ *cheese*, solid conserve of ~s & sugar; (adj.) ~-coloured. [ME *damascene* f. L *damascenum* (*prunum* plum) of Damascus]

dan, n. (Also ~ *buoy*) small buoy used as a mark in deep-sea fishing; steel canister attached to a long flagged pole showing limits of area cleared by mine--sweepers (~*n'er*, ~*-layer*, vessel laying these). [orig. unkn.]

Danaos. See TIMEO.

dance[1] (dah-), v.i. & t. Move with rhythmical steps, glides, leaps, revolutions, gestures, etc., usu. to music, alone or with a partner or set (~ *to* one's *tune* or *pipe*, follow his lead); jump about, skip, move in lively way (of heart, blood, etc.); bob up and down on water etc. (~ *upon nothing*, be hanged); perform (minuet, waltz, etc.); ~ *attendance* (*upon* person), be kept waiting (by), follow about; cause to ~ (bears etc.); toss up & down, dandle, (baby); ~ *away, off, into,* etc., lose, bring, etc., by dancing (*his head off, his chance away, herself into favour*). [ME, f. OF *danser* f. Rom. **dansare* of unkn. orig.]

dance[2] (dah-), n. Dancing motion (see prec.); some special form of this; single round or turn of one; tune for dancing to, or in ~ rhythm; dancing-party; *lead* (person) *a* ~, cause him much trouble; *D~ of Death* or *of Macabre*, medieval picture-subject of Death leading all ranks to grave; *St Vitus's* ~, disorder chiefly in children with convulsive involuntary movements. [ME, f. OF f. *danser* (prec.)]

dan'cer (dah-), n. In vbl senses; esp.: one who dances in public for money; ‖ *merry* ~*s*, aurora borealis. [-ER[1]]

dan'dèlion, n. Yellow-flowered composite plant with widely toothed leaves. [f. F *dent de lion* lion's tooth]

dan'der, n. (colloq., esp. U.S.). Temper, anger, indignation, (*get* one's ~ *up*, grow, make him, angry). [orig. unkn.]

Dan'die Din'mont, n. Breed of terrier. [character in *Guy Mannering*]

dan'dle, v.t. Dance (child) on knee or in arms; pet. [16th c., of unkn. orig.; cf. It. *dandolare* waggle]

dan'druff, -iff, n. Dead skin in small scales among the hair, scurf. [also *-riff, -raff, dander*, of unkn. orig.]

dan'dy[1], n. & a. (Person) devoted to smartness esp. of costume, neat, smart, decorated, whence **dàndi**'ACAL a., **dàn'diFY** v.t., **dàndi**FICA'TION n., ~ISH[1] a., ~ISM(2) n.; ***(colloq.) very good of its kind, splendid, first-rate; sloop with special rig; ‖ (also ~*-cart*) spring-cart used by milkmen; ~*-brush*, of whalebone etc. for cleaning horse. [1780 in Scotland, where *Dandy* also stands for *Andrew*]

dan'dy[2], n. = DENGUE. [W.-Ind. Negro corrupt.]

dan'dy[8], n. (Anglo-Ind.). Strong cloth hammock slung from bamboo pole, car-

ried shoulder-high by two or more men (a common means of transport in hilly districts). [Hind. *ḍaṇḍī* (*ḍaṇḍ* staff)]

Dāne, n. Native of Denmark; (hist.) Northman invader of England; (also *Great* ~) powerful short-haired breed of dog. [ME, f. ON *Danir* (in OE *Dene*, as in *Denmark*), LL *Dani*]

Dāne'gĕld, -gĕlt, (-ng-), n. (Hist.) annual tax prob. imposed orig. in 10th c. to provide funds to protect England against the Danes, & later continued as a land tax; (transf.) appeasement by bribery. [f. prec. +ON *gjeld* payment]

dān'ger (-j-), n. Liability or exposure to harm, risk, peril, (*of* one's *life, of* death or other evil; *in* ~ *of*, likely to incur etc.); position of railway signal directing stoppage or caution (*signal is at* ~); thing that causes peril (*a* ~ *to the peace of Europe, to navigation*). So ~OUS a., ~OUSLY[2] adv., (-j-). [earlier sense *power* f. OF *dangier* f. Rom. **dominiarium* f. L *dominus* lord]

danġl|**e** (dang'gl), v.i. & t. Be suspended & sway to & fro; hold or carry (thing) swaying loosely; hold (hopes etc.) as temptation *before* person, *in* his sight, etc.; hover *after, round, about,* person as a follower, lover, etc., whence ~ER[1] n. [16th c., of unkn. orig.; cf. Da. *dangle*]

Dǎn'iel (-yel), n. Upright judge, person of infallible wisdom. [*Dan.* i–vi, & *Merchant of Venice*, IV. i. 223, 333]

Dǎn'ish, a. & n. (Language) of Denmark or the Danes. [OE *Denisc* (-ISH[1]), altered after DANE]

dǎnk, a. Soaked, oozy; unpleasantly or unwholesomely damp (of air, weather, etc.). [ME, prob. f. Scand.; cf. Sw. *dank* marshy spot]

Dǎnte'an, a. & n. (Student) of Dante; in Dante's style or recalling his descriptions. So **Dǎnt**ESQUE' a., **Dǎn'tIST**(3) n. [-AN]

dǎp, v.i. & t. (-pp-), & n. Fish by letting bait bob on water; dip lightly; make (ball) bounce, (of ball) bounce, on ground; (n.) bounce of ball. [cf. DAB[1]]

dǎph'nè, n. Kinds of flowering shrub. [Gk (-*ē*) = laurel]

dǎpp'er, a. Neat, smart, in appearance or movement. [ME, f. MDu. *dapper* strong, stout, cogn. w. OHG *tapfar*]

dǎp'ple, v.t. & i., & n. Variegate, become variegated, with rounded spots or patches of colour or shade; (n.) ~d effect; ~*-grey*, (horse) of grey with darker spots. [of unkn. orig; ON *apalgrár*, G *apfelgrau*, F *gris-pommelé*, & other parallels, suggest some connexion with *apple*]

dárb'ies (-biz), n. pl. (sl.). Handcuffs. [allus. use of *Father Darby's bands*, some rigid form of band for debtors (16th c.)]

Dárb'y and Joan, n. Devoted old married couple. [perh. f. poem 1735 in *Gentleman's Mag.*]

dāre, v.t. (before expressed or implied infin. without *to*, the 3 sing. pres. is usu.

~, the past & conditional often *durst*; otherwise ~*s*, ~*d*; infin. without *to* is usual only after the sense *venture* in negative or virtually negative sentence), & n. **1.** Venture (to), have the courage or impudence (to), (*I ~ swear*, feel sure that; *~ he do it? he ~s to insult me*; *I would if I durst* or ~*d*; *they ~d* or *durst not come*, *did not ~ to come*); attempt, take the risks of, (~ *all things, a leap, the event*, person's *anger*); defy (*person*); challenge (person) *to do, to it*, etc.; *I ~ say* (rare exc. in 1st person; 3rd sing. in reported speech, *he ~s to say*, past *he ~d say* or *to say*), am prepared to believe, do not deny, = very likely (often iron.); ~'*devil*, reckless (person). **2.** n. Act of daring, challenge. [a Gmc preterite-present (cf. CAN); OE *durran*, OS *gidurran*, OHG *giturran*, Goth. *gadaursan*, f. Gmc. *ders-*, *dars-*, *durs-*; cf. Gk *tharseō* be bold]

‖ **darg**, n. (Sc.). A day's work, a definite amount of work. [contr. f. *daywerk* or *daywark* day-work]

dar'i, n. = DURRA.

dar'ing[1], n. In vbl senses; esp., adventurous courage. [-ING[1]]

dar'ing[2], a. In vbl senses; esp., adventurous, bold. Hence ~LY[2] adv. [-ING[2]]

dark[1], a. With no or relatively little light, unilluminated (~ *lantern*, that can have its light covered), gloomy, sombre; of colour more or less near black (esp. as pref. to adj. of colour as ~*-brown*; ~ BLUE[2]*s*); brown-complexioned, not fair; evil, atrocious; cheerless (~ *side of things*); sad, sullen (*a ~ humour*), frowning; obscure (~ *saying*, ~ *oblivion*); secret (*keep* thing ~; *keep ~*, remain in hiding); little known of (~ *horse*, one of whose racing form little is known, & fig. of persons); unenlightened (*in the ~est ignorance*; *the ~ ages*, Middle Ages, also, & esp., the period between the break-up of the Roman Empire (A.D. 395) & the end of the 10th c.); *the D~ Continent* (in last two senses), Africa; ~ *room*, with actinic rays excluded for treating photographic films. Hence ~'ISH[1](2) a., ~'LY[2] adv., ~'NESS n. (*Prince of ~ness*, the Devil). [OE *deorc*; as adj. exclusively E, but cf. OHG *tarchanjan* to hide]

dark[2], n. Absence of light (esp. *in the ~*); nightfall (*at ~*); dark colour (esp. in art, *the lights and ~s of a picture*); want of knowledge (*am in the ~ about it*; *leap in the ~*, rash step or enterprise). Hence ~'SOME a. (poet.). [f. prec.]

dark'en, v.t. & i. Make or become DARK[1]; ~ *one's door*, pay him a visit (usu. neg.); ~ *counsel*, make perplexity worse. [-EN[3]]

dark'le, v.i. Lie concealed; grow dark. [mod. back formation f. foll. misunderstood as part.]

dark'ling, adv. & a. In the dark. [-LING[2]]

dark'y, -ey, n. (colloq.). Negro. [-Y[3]]

darl'ing, n. & a. Loved, best loved, lovable, (person or animal). [OE *dēorling* (DEAR, -LING[1])]

darn[1], v.t., & n. **1.** Mend (esp. knitting) by interweaving yarn with needle across hole, whence ~'ING[1](5) n.; ~'*ing-ball*, *-last*, for stretching work during operation. **2.** n. Place so mended. [*c.* 1600, perh. f. MDu. *dernen* stop holes in (a dike)]

darn[2], v.t. (sl.). Damn (as imprecation). [deformation of DAMN]

darn'el, n. Kind of grass growing as weed among corn. [prob. f. Walloon *darnelle*]

dart, n., & v.t. & i. **1.** Pointed missile, esp. light javelin, ‖ (pl.) indoor game with toy ~s & target; sting of insect etc.; sudden rapid motion; act of throwing missile. **2.** vb. Throw (missile), throw missile; emit suddenly (glance, flash, anger); start rapidly in some direction. [ME, f. OF *dart* (mod. *dard*) f. Frank. **daroth*]

dart'er, n. In vbl senses; also: web-footed bird of pelican tribe; (pl.) order of birds including kingfishers & bee-eaters; kinds of fish. [-ER[1]]

dart'le, v.t. & i. Keep on darting. [-LE(3)]

Dart'moor, n. (Used for) ~ convict prison near Princetown, Devon.

Dart'mouth (-mu-), n. (Used for) Royal Naval College, ~, Devon.

dar'tre (-ter), n. Kinds of skin disease, esp. herpes. So **dar'trous** a. [F, in OF *dertre*, med. L *derbita* f. Gaulish **dervita*]

Dar'win'ian, a. & n. Of, person believing in, Charles Darwin.(d. 1882) or his doctrines esp. on evolution of species. So **Dar'winism**(3) n., **Dar'winist**(2) n. & a., **Dar'winis'tic** a., **Dar'winite**[1](1) n. & a., **Dar'winize**(2, 4) v.t. & i.

dash[1], v.t. & i. Shatter *to pieces* (rarely abs., as *flowers ~ed by rain*); knock, drive, throw, or thrust, *away, off, out, down*, etc.; fling, drive, splash, (thing or person) *against, upon, into*; bespatter *with* water etc. (~'*board*, of wood or leather in front of vehicle to keep out mud, board beneath motor-car windscreen containing instruments; ~*ed with colour*); dilute, qualify, (water *with* spirit, joy *with* pain); frustrate (~ one's *hopes*), daunt, discourage, confound; write *down* or throw *off* rapidly (composition, sketch); underline, (sl.) = *damn* as mild imprecation; fall, move, throw oneself, with violence; come into collision *against, upon*; ride, run, or drive *up*, move about, behave, with spirit or display, whence ~'ING[3] a., ~'ing LY[2] adv. [ME *dasse, dasche*, prob. imit.; cf. Sw. *daska* to beat]

dash[2], n. Sound of water striking or struck; splash of colour; infusion (~ *of brandy, of good blood*); hasty pen-stroke; horizontal stroke in writing or printing to mark a break in sense, a parenthesis (two ~es), omitted letters or words, etc.; rush, onset, sudden advance; (capacity for) vigorous action; showy appearance or behaviour (cut a ~, make a brilliant show). [f. prec.]

dash'er, n. In vbl senses; esp., contrivance for agitating cream in churn. [-ER¹]

das'tard, n. Coward skulker, esp. one who commits brutal act without endangering himself. Hence ~LY¹ a., ~lINESS n. [prob. f. dazed p.p. +-ARD]

da'syūre, n. (Kinds of) small ferocious arboreal cat-like carnivorous marsupial found in Australia and Tasmania. [Gk dasus rough +oura tail]

dat'a. See DATUM.

‖ **dāt'aller, day'-taler**, n. Workman engaged and paid by the day. [DAY, TALE in sense reckoning, -ER¹]

dāte¹, n. W.-Asian & N.-Afr. tree (also ~-palm), or its fruit, an oblong single--seeded berry. [ME, f. OF, f. L f. Gk daktulos finger]

dāte², n. Statement in document, letter, book, or inscription, of the time (& often place) of execution, writing, publication, etc.; time at which thing happens or is to happen; *(colloq.) engagement, appointment; period to which antiquities etc. belong; person's age, duration, term of life, (arch. or poet.); (go) out of ~, (become) obsolete; up to ~ (f. book--keeping phr. for accounts completed to current day, now as adj. & adv.), meeting, according to the latest requirements or knowledge; ~-line, meridian 180° from Greenwich, east & west of which the ~ differs, line in newspaper at head of message, special article, etc., giving ~ & place of dispatch. [ME, f. F f. L data fem. p.p. of dare = (letter) given (at such a time & place)]

dāte³, v.t. & i. Mark (letter etc.) with date (~d from London), whence **dāt'ER¹**(2) n.; refer (event) to a time;* (colloq.) make an appointment with; count time, reckon, (dating from the Creation); bear date, be ~d; have origin from (church ~s from the 14th c.); (of art, style, etc.) become recognizable as of a past or particular period; be or become out of date. Hence **dāt'ABLE** a. [f. prec.]

dāte'less (-tl-), a. Undated; endless; immemorial. [f. DATE², ³, -LESS]

dāt'ive, a. & n. ~ (case), the case in nouns, pronouns, & adjj., proper to the remoter object or recipient. So **dativ'AL** a., ~LY² (-vl-) adv. [f. OF (-if, -ive) or L dativus (dare dat- give, -IVE)]

dāt'um, n. (pl. -ta). Thing known or granted, assumption or premiss from which inferences may be drawn; fixed starting-point of scale etc. (ORDNANCE ~); (pl.) facts of any kind, notes. [L, neut. p.p. of dare give]

datūr'a, n. Kinds of poisonous plant, including stramonium, yielding strong narcotic. [f. Hind. dhatura]

daub, v.t. & i., & n. Coat (wall etc.) with plaster, clay, etc. (n., the material); smear (surface; n., a smear), lay on

(greasy or sticky stuff); soil, stain; paint (t. & i.) inartistically, lay (colours) on so, (n., a coarse painting), whence ~'ER¹, ~'STER, nn., ~'Y² a. [ME, f. OF dauber f. L DE(albare f. albus white) whitewash]

daught'er (dawt-), n. One's female child; female descendant, female member of family, race, etc.; woman who is the spiritual or intellectual product of person or thing; product personified as female (Carthage ~ of Tyre; Fortune and its ~ Confidence; ~-language, as French of Latin); ~-in-law, son's wife, (loosely) step~. Hence ~HOOD n., ~LY¹ a. [OE dohtor, OS -ar, OHG tochter, ON dóttir, Goth. dauhtar, cogn. w. Gk thugatēr]

daunt, v.t. Discourage, intimidate; press (herrings) down in barrel. [ME, f. OF danter (now dompter) f. L domitare frequent. of domare tame]

daunt'less, a. Intrepid, persevering. Hence ~LY² adv., ~NESS n. [perh. f. obs. daunt a check f. prec. +-LESS]

dauph'in, dauph'iness, nn. (hist.). (Wife of) King of France's eldest son. [ME; family name (f. L delphinus DOLPHIN) of lords of Dauphiné, last of whom ceded it on condition of dauphin's being accepted as French heir-apparent's title]

‖ **dăv'enpôrt**, n. Escritoire with drawers & hinged writing-slab. [prob. maker's name]

Dāv'id and Jŏn'athan, n. Any pair of devoted friends. [1 Sam. xviii etc.]

dăv'it, n. Crane on board ship used for hoisting anchor, torpedo, etc. inboard or outboard; one of pair of cranes for suspending or lowering ship's boat. [ME, f. OF daviot (mod. davier), dim. of OF Davi David]

Dāv'y (lămp), n. Miner's wire-gauze safety lamp. [Sir H. Davy (d. 1829), inventor]

dāv'y, n. (sl.). Take one's ~, swear (that, to fact). [short for AFFIDAVIT]

Dāv'y Jones's lock'er (jōnziz), n. The deep, a watery grave (in the sea). [f. 1751; allusion unkn.]

daw, n. = JACKDAW. [ME, corresp. to OE *dawa, OHG tāha (G dohle)]

daw'dl|e, v.i. & t., & n. Idle, dally; ~e away (time etc.), waste; hence ~ER¹ n.; (n.) ~ing person. [cf. dial. daddle, doddle, in same sense]

dawk, dâk, dak, (dawk), n. (Anglo-Ind.). Post or transport by relays of men or horses; relay; ~ bungalow, house for travellers at ~ station. [Hind.]

dawn, v.i., & n. 1. Begin to appear or grow light (of day, daylight, morning, country shone upon, things becoming evident to mind, intelligence, civilization, etc.); first ~ings etc., beginning; ~ing, the East; ~ upon, begin to be perceptible to. 2. n. First light, daybreak, rise or incipient gleam of anything. [dawn vb (whence the n.) deduced f. dawning (c. 1300), app. f. ON (cf. OSw. daghning);

these wds replaced older *daw* vb (OE *dagian*), *dawing* (OE *dagung*)]

day, n. **1.** Time while sun is above horizon, (loosely) including twilights (~ *& night*, adv., throughout these or in both alike; *all* ~, *all the* ~, adv., throughout it; ~'*break*, *break of* ~, *dawn*; ~*-dream*, *-ing*, *-er*, reverie or castle in air, indulgence, indulger, in them); *dawn* (*before*, *at*, ~); *daylight* (*by* ~; *was broad* ~; *clear as* ~). **2.** Twenty-four hours (*solar* or *astronomical* ~, from noon; *civil* ~, from midnight; *sidereal* ~, between two meridional transits of first point of Aries, about 4′ shorter than *solar*; *natural* ~, = *sidereal*, also in first sense above). **3.** Civil ~ as point of time, date, etc. (*one* ~, adv., on an unspecified date past or future; *the other* ~, on a ~ not long ago; *one of these* ~*s* or *fine* ~*s*, before long, in prophecy or promise; *some* ~, adv., in the future; *on* one's ~, when he is at his best; ~ *of* GRACE). **4.** Date of specified festival etc. (*first* ~, Sunday; *Christmas* ~, *birth*~, *pay*~, *last Day* or *Day of* JUDGEMENT). **5.** Date agreed upon (*keep* one's ~, be punctual; one's ~, for being at home to guests, esp. once a week). **6.** Victory (*carry*, *win*, *lose*, *the* ~). **7.** Period (often pl., *in the* ~*s of*, *the* ~*s of old*, *in* ~*s to come*, *men of other* ~*s*; *better* ~*s*, when one was or will be better off; *fallen on evil* ~*s*, in misfortune; sing., *at*, *to*, *this* ~; *present*~, adj. = modern; *these*~*s*, adv., nowadays; *the* ~, the current ~; *sufficient for the* ~ *is the evil thereof*, do not anticipate trouble; *men of the* ~, persons of importance at any time; *creature of a* ~, short-lived). **8.** One's ~, lifetime, period of prosperity, activity, power, etc., (also pl. *end* one's ~*s*, die; *every dog has his* ~, no one always unlucky). **9.** *This* ~ *week*, *month*, *year*, reckoning forward or back from to~; ~ *about*, on alternate ~*s*; ~ *by* ~, ~ *after* ~, *from* ~ *to* ~, *every* ~, advv. of daily repetition or progress; *twice* etc. *a* ~, in each ~ (see A²); *call it a* ~, consider that one has done a ~'s work; *know the time of* ~, be wide awake, knowing; *the* ~ *before*, *after*, *the fair*, advv., too early, late, for opportunity. **10.** ‖~*-boarder*, schoolboy feeding but not sleeping at school; ~*-book* in book-keeping, book in which esp. sale transactions are entered at once for later transfer to ledger; ‖~*-boy*, schoolboy living at home; ~*-fly*, ephemerid; ~*-labourer*, hired by ~ at fixed wage; ~*-long* a. & adv., (lasting) for whole ~; ~*-owl*, hawk-owl hunting by ~; ~*-room*, used by ~ only, esp. common living-room at schools; ~*-school*, opp. Sunday, evening, or boarding school; ~*-spring*, dawn (poet.); ~*-ticket*, covering return on same~; ~*-time*, not night, esp. *in the* ~*-time*. [OE *dæg*,

OS *dag*, OHG *tac*, ON *dagr*, Goth. *dags* f. Gmc **dagaz*]

day'light (*-lit*), n. Light of day (BURN³ ~); openness, publicity; *let* ~ *into* (sl.), stab or shoot; *dawn* (*before*, *at*, ~); visible interval as between boats in race, wine & glass-rim (*no* ~, fill up), or rider & saddle; ~*-saving*, use of fictitious time in summer prolonging ~ working hours.

dāze, v.t., & n. **1.** Stupefy, bewilder; dazzle; hence **dāz′ĕdLY²** adv. **2.** n. Stupefaction, bewilderment. [ME *dasen* f. ON; cf. Icel. *dasask* refl. vb become weary]

dăz′zl|e, v.t., & n. **1.** Confuse or dim (sight, eye, person) with excess of light, intricate motion, incalculable number, etc.; confound or surprise (mind, person) by brilliant display lit. or fig.; ~*ed with* or *by*; ~*e lamps* or *lights* (over-bright, on motor-car); ~*e paint* (so patterned on ship as to deceive enemy about her type or course); hence ~*e*MENT (*-lm-*) n., ~*e*ingLY³ adv. **2.** n. Glitter. [f. prec. + -LE(3)]

D-Day, n. Day (6 June 1944) on which British and American forces invaded N. France. [*D* for *day*]

de-, pref. f. L adv. & prep. *de*. As an etymological element: (1) in senses down (*depend*), away (*defend*, *deduce*), completely (*declare*, *denude*), in a bad sense (*deceive*, *deride*); (2) repr. L *dis-* (in privative sense, largely replacing *de-*), thr. Rom., OF *des-*, later *de-* (mod. F *dé-*). Early adoptives in E retained OF *des-*, later refash. *dis-* (as in *disarm*); later wds have *de-* wh. was treated as identical with *de-* f. L *de-*; hence (3) as a living pref. with privative force forming compd vbs (with derivatives) as *de-acidify*, *decentralize*, *demoralize*, *denazify* (*-ication*).

deac′on, n. (Primitive Church) appointed minister of charity (*Acts* vi. 1–6); (Episcopal) member of third order of ministry below bishop & priest; (Baptist, Congregational, Presbyterian) officer attending to congregation's secular affairs. Hence ~SHIP n. [OE, f. LL f. Gk *diakonos* servant]

deac′onĕss, n. Woman in primitive & some modern Churches with functions analogous to deacon's. [f. LL *diaconissa* (prec., -ESS¹)]

dead (dĕd), a., n., & adv. **1.** That has ceased to live (*the* ~, n., ~ person or persons, or all who have ever died; *from the* ~, from among these; ~ *men tell no tales*, argument for killing possessor of secret; ~*-house*, mortuary; ~ *march*, march-like funeral music; ~*-office*, funeral service; ~ *as a doornail*, quite ~; ~ *& gone*; *wait for* ~ *men's* SHOES; FLOG ~ *horse*; ~ *men* or *marines*, empty bottles; ~ *man's finger*, *hand*, *thumb*, kinds of orchid; ~ *man's handle*, the controlling handle in electric trains which must be held and pressed down for current to pass, so that slackening by death or illness cuts the current & stops the train). **2.** Benumbed, insensible, (of hands etc.; also ~ *to*, unconscious or unappreciative of, hardened against). **3.** Without spiritual life. **4.** Obsolete, past, not effective, (~ *language*, one no longer in ordinary use, e.g. ancient Gk; ~ *letter*, law no longer observed, unclaimed or undelivered letter at post office). **5.** Inanimate (~ *fence*, of timber etc., opp. *quickset*; ~ *matter*); extinct, dull, lustreless, without force, muffled, (~ *brand*, *coal*; ~ *gold*, unburnished; ~ *colour*, first layer in picture, cold & pale; ~-*nettle*, non-stinging weed like nettle; ~-*alive*, spiritless; ~ *sound*, not resonant). **6.** Inactive, motionless, idle, (*D~ Sea*; ~ *point* or ~ *centre*, least & greatest extension of piston or crank, where it exerts no effective power; ~ *weight*, inert, of lifeless matter, also fig. of debt etc.; ~ *pull*, *lift*, at thing too heavy for one to move; ~ *freight*, sum paid in chartering ship for part not occupied by cargo; ~ *arch*, *window*, etc., sham; ~ *end*, terminus of branch line of railway etc.; ~ *hand*, = MORTMAIN, usu. implying protest; ~ *hours*, still, in night; ~ *season*; ~ *stock*, unemployed capital, unsaleable goods; ~ *ball*, out of play; *wind falls* ~, as n., = ~ *time*, *at* ~ *of night*, *in the* ~ *of winter*). **7.** Abrupt, complete, unrelieved, exact, (*come to* ~ *stop*; *a* ~ *faint*; *on a* ~ *level*; ~ *heat*, exact equality in race, ~-*heat* v.i. & t.; ~ *spit* (colloq.), very counterpart *of*; *a* ~ *calm*; ~ *loss*, without compensation; *be in* ~ *earnest*; *a* ~ *certainty*; ~ *on the target*, quite straight, so ~ *shot*, unerring; ~'*lock*, utter standstill, also as v.t.). **8.** (Golf, of ball) very close to hole, within certain holing distance. ~-*alive*, (of place, occupation, etc.) dull, tedious, monotonous; ~-*eye* (Naut.), round flat three-holed block for extending shrouds; ~-*fire*, St Elmo's fire, as presaging death; ~ *ground*, *water* (out of reach of a fort's guns, infantry fire, etc.); ~'*head*, non-paying theatre-goer or passenger; ~'*light* (Naut.), shutter inside porthole to prevent light showing out; ~ (·) *line*, line beyond which it is not permitted or possible to go, fixed limit of time, (U.S. prisons) painted line across exercise-yard on crossing which a prisoner is liable to be shot; ~ *man's* (or *men's*) *fingers*, finger-like divisions of gills in lobster or crab; *~ pan* (sl.), expressionless immobile face; ~ *reckoning* (Naut.), of ship's position by log, compass, etc., when observations are impossible; *D~-Sea* APPLE; hence ~'NESS n. **10.** adv. Profoundly, absolutely, completely, (~ *asleep*, *level*, *straight*, *tired*, *drunk*; ~-*beat*, tired out, (Mech.) without recoil, *(n., sl.) worthless sponger; CUT² ~; ~ *against*, directly opposite to). [OE *dēad*, OS *dōd*, OHG

tōt, ON *dauthr*, Goth. *dauths* f. Gmc *dauthaz* f. *dau- DIE²]

dead'en (dĕd-), v.t. & i. Deprive of or lose vitality, force, brightness, feeling, etc.; make insensible *to*. [-EN⁶]

dead'ly¹ (dĕd-), a. Causing fatal injury; of poisonous nature (~ *nightshade*); entailing damnation (~ *sin*); implacable, internecine; deathlike (~ *paleness*, *faintness*, *gloom*); intense (*in* ~ *haste*; ~ *dullness*). Hence **dead'liNESS** n. [OE *dēadlīc* (DEAD, -LY¹)]

dead'ly² (dĕd-), adv. As if dead (~ *white*, *faint*); extremely (~ *tired*, *dull*). [OE *dēadlīce* (DEAD, -LY²)]

deaf (dĕf), a. Wholly or partly without hearing (*the* ~, ~ *people*; ~ *of an*, or *in one*, *ear*; ~ *as an adder* or *a post*; *none so* ~ *as those that won't hear*); insensible *to* harmony, rhythm, etc.; not giving ear *to*, uncompliant, (*turn a* ~ *ear to*); ~ *nut*, with no kernel; ~-*&-dumb alphabet*, *language*, etc., signs for communication by the ~; ~ *mute*, ~ & dumb person. Hence ~'LY² adv., ~'NESS n. [OE *dēaf*, OS *dōf*, OHG *toup*, ON *daufr*, Goth. *daufs* f. Gmc *daubhaz*]

deaf'en (dĕf-), v.t. Deprive of hearing by noise; make (sound) inaudible by louder one; make (floor etc.) impervious to sound. [-EN⁶]

deal¹, n. *A great*, *good*, ~, large, considerable, amount; (sl.) *a* ~, = *a great* ~; (same phrases used adv.) to a large, considerable, extent, (esp. with comparative or superl.) by much, considerably. [OE *dǣl*, OS *dēl*, OHG *teil*, Goth. *dails*, f. Gmc *dailiz*; cf. DOLE¹]

deal², v.t. & i. (~*t* pr. dĕlt), & n. **1.** Distribute, give *out*, (gifts etc.) among several; deliver as his share or deserts to person (esp. of Providence etc.; ~*t him happiness*, *good measure*; of persons, esp. ~ *a blow*, abs. or with *at*, lit. & fig.). **2.** Distribute cards to players for a game or round (n., such distribution, player's turn for it, as *my* ~, or round played after it), give (card, hand, etc.) to player. **3.** Associate *with* (esp. neg. as *refuse to* ~ *with*); do business *with* person, *in* goods (n., colloq., a bargain or transaction; also dishonest job); *New D*~, the programme of social and economic reform planned by the Roosevelt administration of 1932 and subsequent years; *raw* ~ (colloq.), unfair treatment; *square* ~ (colloq.), justice, fair treatment. **4.** Occupy oneself, grapple by way of discussion or refutation, take measures, *with*; (with adv.) behave (~ *honourably*, *cruelly*, esp. *with* or *by* person). Hence ~'ING¹(1) n. [OE *dǣlan* as prec.]

deal³, n. Piece of sawn fir or pine wood between 7 & 9 in. broad & 6 ft long, & 3 in. thick; a quantity of these; fir or pine wood. [c. 1400; f. MLG *dele* plank; see THILL]

deal'er, n. In vbl senses; esp.: player

dealing at cards; trader, usu. in comb. as *corn-*~. [-ER[1]]

dĕămbūlā'tion, n., **dĕăm'būlatŏry̆**, a. Walking. [f. L *deambulatio, deambulatorium*, f. DE(*ambulare* walk), -ATION, -ORY]

dean[1], n. Head of cathedral or collegiate--church chapter; ‖(also *rural*~) clergyman exercising supervision over group of parochial clergy within division of archdeaconry; (colleges) resident fellow, or one of several, with disciplinary & other functions; (foreign, Scots, & modern universities) president of a faculty; = DOYEN; *D*~ *of Faculty*, president of the Faculty of Advocates in Scotland. [ME *deen, dene*, f. OF *deien* f. LL *decanus* f. Gk *dekanos* one set over ten]

dean[2], **dēne**, n. Vale (esp. in names ending in *-dean, -dene, -den*). [OE *denu*, cogn. w. DEN]

dean'ery̆, n. Office, house, of dean; ‖ group of parishes presided over by rural dean. [-ERY]

dear, a., n., adv., & int. **1.** Beloved (often as merely polite or even ironical form in talk, esp. *my* ~ *sir, my* ~ *Jones*, & now used at beginning of most letters not intended to be markedly business-like; as n., ~ or ~'*est*, esp. in voc., = ~ *one*; *a* ~, esp. in coaxing formulae). **2.** Precious *to*; one's cherished (*for* ~ *life*, as though life were at stake). **3.** High-priced, costly, (as adv., *sell, buy, pay*, COST[2] one, ~; ~ *year, shop*, in which prices run high); hence ~LY[2] adv., ~'NESS n. **4.** int. ~, ~'*!*, ~ *me!, oh* ~'*!*, expressing surprise, distress, sympathy, etc. [OE *dēore*, OS *diuri*, OHG *tiuri*, ON *dȳrr* f. Gmc *°deurjaz*]

dearth (dẽr-), n. Scarcity & dearness of food; scanty supply *of*. [ME *derthe* (prec., -TH[1])]

dear'y̆, -ie, n. (usu. voc.). Dear one. [-Y[3]]

death (dĕth), n. **1.** Dying (DIE[2] *the* ~; ~'*-bed*, on which one dies, ~*bed repentance*, fig., change of policy made too late to bear fruit; ~*-rattle*, sound in dying person's throat; ~*-roll*, list of the killed or dead; ~*-watch*, kinds of insect whose ticking portends ~). **2.** End of life (*civil* ~, ceasing to count as citizen by outlawry, banishment, etc.; *catch one's* ~, i.e. fatal chill etc.; ~*-duties*, tax levied before property passes to heir; ~*-rate*, yearly number of ~s to 1,000 of population; ~*-trap*, unwholesome or dangerous place). **3.** Being killed or killing (*field of* ~, battlefield etc.; *be the* ~ *of*, kill; *do, put, stone*, etc., *to* ~; *war to the* ~, ~*-feud*, till one kills or is killed; *it is, we make it*, ~ *to*, ~ *is* the penalty; *be in at the* ~, see fox killed, or fig. any enterprise ended; *be* ~ *on* (sl.), skilful at killing game etc., or fig. at doing anything; *sick unto, tired to*, ~, to utmost limit; ~*-adder*, kinds of venomous snake; ~*-blow*, mortal,

lit. & fig.; ~*-warrant*, for criminal's execution, abolition of custom etc.). **4.** Ceasing to be, annihilation, personified power that annihilates, (*at* ~'*s door*, soon to die; ~'*s-head*, skull as emblem of mortality, also kind of moth with skull marked on back; *sure, pale, as* ~; *hold on like grim* ~; *on rats*, good rat-killer, of dogs; ~*!*, archaic imprecation). **5.** Being dead (~*-mask*, cast taken of dead person's face; *eyes closed in* ~). **6.** Want of spiritual life (*everlasting* ~, damnation). **7.** *Black D*~, (mod. name, transl. f. G for) great pestilence of Oriental Plague in Europe in 14th c. Hence ~'LESS a., ~'lĕssLY[2] adv., ~'lĕssNESS n., ~'LIKE a. & adv., ~'LY[1] a. & adv., ~'WARD(s) a. & adv., (dĕth-). [OE *dēath*, OS *dōth*, OHG *tōd*, ON *dauthr*, Goth. *dauthus* f. Gmc *°dau-* DIE[2], -TH[1]]

°dĕb, n. (colloq.). Débutante. [abbr.]

débâcle (dĭbah'kl), n. Break-up of ice in river; (Geol.) sudden rush of water carrying along blocks of stone and other debris; confused rush, rout, stampede; collapse, downfall, e.g. of a government. [F]

dĕbăg', v.t. (sl.; -gg-). Remove the 'bags' (= trousers) from. [DE-, BAG[1]]

dĕbăr', v.t. (-rr-). Exclude *from* admission or right (also ~ person *the crown* etc.); (rare) prevent, bar, (entrance etc.). [ME, f. F *débarrer* (OF *des-*), f. des- DE- + *barrer* BAR[2]]

dĕbărk', v.t. & i. = DISEMBARK. Hence **dĕbărka'TION** n. [f. F *débarquer* (DE-, BARK[3])]

dĕbāse', v.t. Lower in quality, value, or character; adulterate (coin). Hence ~MENT (-sm-) n. [DE- + obs. *base* for ABASE]

dĕbāt'able, a. Questionable, subject to dispute, (~ *ground* lit. or fig., for which parties contend, borderland). [OF (foll., -ABLE)]

dĕbāt'e|e, v.t. & i., & n. **1.** Contest, fight for, (*long* ~*ed the victory*); dispute about, discuss, (a question); hold argument, esp. in Parliament or public meeting (~*ing--society*, for practice); consider, ponder, (t. & i.); hence ~'ER[1] n. (esp. of one skilled rather in argument than in oratory). **2.** n. Controversy, discussion, public argument. [ME, f. OF *debat, debattre* f. Rom. *°debattere* (DE-, see BATTLE)]

dĕbauch', v.t., & n. **1.** Pervert from virtue or morality; make intemperate or sensual; seduce (woman); vitiate (taste, judgement); hence ~ABLE a. **2.** n. Bout or habit of sensual indulgence; hence ~ERY(4) n. [f. F *débaucher*, of unkn. orig.]

débauchee' (-bosh-), n. Viciously sensual person. [f. F *débauché* p.p. see prec., -EE]

dĕbĕn'ture, n. **1.** ‖(Arch. or techn.) voucher given to person supplying goods to Royal Household or Government Office, entitling him to payment, Custom--House certificate to exporter of amount due to him as drawback or bounty. **2.** ‖ (Ord. sense) sealed bond of corporation or company acknowledging sum on which interest is due till principal is repaid, esp. fixed interest constituting prior charge on assets; ‖ ~ *stock*, ~s consolidated or created as stock whose nominal capital represents debt of which interest only is secured as perpetual annuity. [ME; early sp. *-ur*, app. = L *debentur* are owing]

dĕbil′itāte, v.t. Enfeeble (constitution etc.). [f. L *debilitare*, see foll., -ATE[3]]

dĕbil′itў̆, n. Feebleness (of health, purpose, etc.). [ME, f. OF *debilite* f. L *debilitatem* (*debilis* weak, -TY)]

dĕb′it, n., & v.t. **1.** Entry in account of sum owing; side of account (left-hand) in which these entries are made (cf. CREDIT). **2.** v.t. Charge (person) *with* sum; enter (sum) *against* or *to* person. [f. L *debitum* DEBT]

dĕbonair′, a. Genial, pleasant, unembarrassed. [ME, f. OF *debonaire* = *de bon air* of good disposition]

dĕbŏshed′ (-sht), a. (Arch. for) debauched.

dĕbouch′ (-sh; *also* -ōōsh), v.i. Issue from ravine, wood, etc., into open ground (of troops; also of stream). So ~MENT (-ōōsh-) n. [f. F *déboucher* f. *dé-* DE- + *bouche* mouth]

Dĕbrĕtt′, n. (Used for) ~'s Peerage etc. [John ~, compiler]

debris, dé-, (dĕb′rē), n. Scattered fragments, wreckage, drifted accumulation. [F (*dé-*), f. obs. *débriser* break down]

debt (dĕt), n. Money, goods, or service, owing (~ *of honour*, not legally recoverable, esp. of sum lost in gambling; ‖ ~-*collector*, one whose business it is to collect ~s for creditors; ~ *of nature*, death; *National D~*, money owed by State in its corporate capacity; *funded ~*, the part of this converted into fund of which interest only is to be paid; *floating ~*, part of it repayable on demand, annuity, at stated time; *small ~*, of limited amount recoverable in County Court); being under obligation to pay something (*in*, *out of*, *get into*, ~ or person's ~). [ME & OF *dette* f. Rom. **debita* f. L *debitum* p.p. of *debēre* owe]

debt′or (dĕt-), n. One who owes money or an obligation or duty; (Book-keeping) *Debtor, Dr*, heading of left-hand or debit side of account. [ME & OF *dettour* f. L *debitorem* (prec., -OR)]

*dĕbŭnk′, v.t. (colloq.). Remove the false sentiment from (person, reputation, institution, cult, etc.); remove (celebrity) from his pedestal. [DE-, BUNK[3]]

‖ **dĕbŭs′**, v.t. & i. (-ss-). Unload (men, stores) or alight from motor vehicles. [DE- + BUS, after *detrain*]

début (see Ap.). n. First appearance in society, or on stage etc. as performer. [F] **débutant, débutante** (see Ap.), nn. Male or female performer making début; (fem.) girl coming out or being presented. [F]

dĕca-, dĕc-, pref. f. Gk *deka* ten in many technical terms as *decăg′ynous* with ten pistils, *decahĕd′ral* ten-sided (*-hedron*, such solid), *decăn′drous* with ten stamens, *dĕc′astyle* ten-columned (portico); esp. in French metric system = ten of the specified unit (cf. DECI-), whence **dĕc′-agrăm, dĕc′alitre** (*-ēter*), **dĕc′amètre** (*-ter*).

dĕc′ade, n. Set, series, of ten; ten years; ten books (1-10, 11-20, etc.) of Livy. So **dĕc′adAL, dĕcăd′ic**, aa. [F *décade* f. LL *decas -ad-* (also *decada* fem.) f. Gk *deka* ten), see -AD, -ADE(2)]

dĕc′adence, n., **dĕc′adent**, a. & n. Falling away, declining, deteriorating, (used esp. of a period of art or literature after culmination); (literary sl.) *decadent*, (writer or artist) affecting certain vices, obscurities, & turgidities of style. [F, f. med. L *decadentia* f. med. L *decadēre* (DECAY), see -ENCE]

dĕc′agon, n. Plane figure with ten sides and angles. So **dĕcăg′onAL** a. [f. med. L *decagonum* (DECA-, -GON)]

dĕcăl′cify, v.t. Deprive (bone etc.) of its lime. [DE-]

dĕc′alogue (-ŏg), n. The ten commandments. [ME, f. OF, or LL f. Gk *dekalogos* (after *hoi deka logoi* the ten precepts)]

dĕcăm′eron, n. Collection of tales like the D~ of Boccaccio (100 tales told by a company in ten days). [f. It. *decamerone* after med. L *Hexameron*]

dĕcămp′, v.i. Break up or leave camp; go away suddenly, take oneself off, abscond. So ~MENT n. [f. F *décamper* (DE-, CAMP[1])]

dĕcăn′al (*or* dĕk′a-), a. Of dean, deanery, or south side, on which dean sits, of choir. [f. LL *decanus* DEAN[1] + -AL]

dĕcān′i, mus. direction. To be sung by decanal side in antiphonal singing (cf. CANTORIS). [L genit. as prec.]

dĕcănt′, v.t. Pour off (liquid of solution) by gradual inclination of vessel without disturbing sediment; pour (wine) similarly from bottle into decanter; (fig.) move or transfer as if by pouring. [f. med. L DE(*canthare* f. L. f. Gk *kanthos* CANT[1] used of lip of beaker)]

dĕcăn′ter, n. Stoppered glass bottle in which wine or spirit is brought to table. [-ER[1]]

dĕcăp′it|āte, v.t. Behead (esp. as legal punishment); cut the head or end from. So ~ABLE a., ~A′TION n. [f. F *décapiter* or LL DE(*capitare* f. *caput -itis* head)]

dĕc′apŏd, n. Ten-footed crustacean. [f. F *décapode* f. Gk DECA(*pous -podos* foot)]

dĕcărb′onize, -ise (-īz), v.t. Deprive of its carbon or carbonic acid. [DE-]

dĕcă′sualiz|e (-zhōŏ-, -zū-), -is|e (-īz), v.t. Do away with the casual employment of (labour). Hence ~A'TION n. [DE-, -IZE]

dĕcasȳllăb'ĭc, a. & n., dĕcasȳll'able, n. & a. (Line) of ten syllables. [DECA-]

dĕcay'¹, v.i. & t. Deteriorate, lose quality, decline in power, wealth, energy, beauty, etc.; rot (t. & i.); cause to deteriorate. [ME, f. OF *decair* f. Rom. *DE(cadēre for L *cadēre* fall)]

dĕcay'², n. Decline, falling off; ruinous state, wasting away (*phonetic* ~, wearing down of word-forms); break-up of health, decomposition; rotten tissue (*remove the* ~). [f. prec.]

dĕceas|e', n., & v.i. (Esp. in legal and formal use for) death, die, depart(ure) from life. Hence ~ED'¹(2) (-ēst') a. and n. (with or without *the*). [ME, f. OF *deces* f. L DE(*cessus* n. f. *cēdere cess-* go)]

dĕceit' (-sēt), n. Misrepresentation, deceiving; trick, stratagem; the vice of deceitfulness; misleading appearance. Hence ~FUL a., ~fuLLY² adv., ~fulNESS n. (-sēt-). [ME, f. OF *deceite* n. f. fem. p.p. of *deceveir* f. L DE(*cipere -cept-* = *capere* take) deceive]

dĕceiv|e' (-sēv), v.t. & i. Persuade of what is false, mislead, (~e one*self*, juggle with one's own convictions, also be mistaken); use deceit; disappoint (esp. *hopes*). So ~'ABLE a., ~'ER¹ n., (-sēv-). [ME, f. OF *deceveir* f. L as prec.]

dĕcĕl'erāte, v.t. Diminish speed of, cause to slow down (also abs.). [DE-, after ACCELERATE]

Dĕcĕm'b|er, n. Twelfth month of year. Hence ~RIST n., member of Russian revolutionary conspiracy in ~er 1825. [ME, f. OF *decembre* f. L *December* (*decem* ten) orig. tenth month of Roman year]

dĕcĕm'vir (-er), n. (pl. ~s, ~ī). (Rom. Hist.) member of board of ten acting as council or ruling power, esp. that appointed 451 B.C. to draw up laws of Twelve Tables; member of any ruling body of ten, as at Venice. So ~AL a., ~ATE¹ n. [L, f. *decem viri* ten men]

dĕ'cenc|ȳ, n. Propriety of behaviour; what is required by good taste or delicacy; avoidance of obscene language & gestures & of undue exposure of person; respectability; *the* ~*ies*, decorous observances, requirements of a decent life. [f. L *decentia* (*decēre* be fitting, -ENCY)]

dĕcĕnn'arȳ, a. & n. '(Of) period of ten years. [f. L *decennis* (*decem, annus*) ten- -year + -ARY¹]

dĕcĕnn'iad, dĕcĕnn'ium (pl. -*ia*), n. Ten-year period. [-*ad* irreg. f. L (-*um*) f. *decennis* (prec.); see -AD]

dĕcĕnn'ial, a. Of ten-year period; recurring in ten years. Hence ~LY² adv. [f. L *decennium* see prec. + -AL]

dĕ'cent, a. Seemly, not immodest or obscene or indelicate; respectable; passable, good enough, tolerable, whence

~ISH¹(2) a.; ‖ (school sl.) kind, not severe or censorious. Hence ~LY² adv. [f. L *decēre* beseem, -ENT]

dĕcĕn'traliz|e, -is|e (-īz), v.t. Undo the centralization of; confer local government on. Hence ~A'TION n. [DE-]

dĕcĕp'tion, n. Deceiving, being deceived; thing that deceives, trick, sham. [ME, f. OF, or LL *deceptio* (*decipere* see DECEIT, -ION)]

dĕcĕp'tive, a. Apt to deceive, easily mistaken. Hence ~LY² (-vl-) adv., ~NESS (-vn-) n. [f. F *déceptif* (prec., -IVE); cf. LL *deceptivus*]

dĕchris'tianize (-krĭscha-), -ise (-īz), v.t. Divest of its christianity. [DE-]

dĕci-, pref. shortened from L *decimus* tenth, used (as *déci-* in F) esp. in French metric system in sense $\frac{1}{10}$ of specified unit. So dĕ'cibĕl (unit for measuring relative intensities of sounds), dĕ'cigrăm, dĕ'cilitre (-ēter), dĕ'cimĕtre (-er), nn.

dĕcide', v.t. & i. Settle (question, issue, dispute) by giving victory to one side; give judgement (*between, for, in favour of, against*, or abs.); bring, come, to a resolution (*that* ~s *me*; ~ to do, *on, for*, or *against* doing). Hence dĕcid'ABLE a. [ME, f. OF *decider* or L DE(*cīdere cis-* = *caedere* cut]

dĕcid'ĕd, a. In vbl senses; also: definite, unquestionable, (*a* ~ *difference*); (of persons) of clear opinions or vigorous initiative, not vacillating. Hence ~LY³ adv. [-ED¹]

dĕcid'er, n. In vbl senses; also, (Racing) heat in which tie is run off. [-ER¹]

dĕcid'ūous, a. Shed periodically or normally (of leaves, teeth, horns, etc.); shedding its leaves annually; shedding its wings after copulation (of ants etc.); fleeting, transitory. [f. L *deciduus* f. DE-(*cīdere* = *cadere* fall) + -OUS]

dĕcill'ion (-yon), n. ‖ Tenth power of million (1 with 60 ciphers). Hence ~TH³ a. & n. [f. L *decem* ten & *million*, see BILLION]

dĕ'cimal, a. & n. Of tenths or ten, proceeding by tens, (~ *numeration*, ordinary counting-system with ten for basis, reckoned by decades; ~ *system*, of weights and measures, with denominations rising by tens; ~ *notation*, counting in tens; ~ *arithmetic*, using this notation, also in narrower sense that, also called ~*s*, treating of ~ fractions; ~ *fraction* or ~, one whose denominator is a power of ten, esp. when expressed by figures written to right of the ~ *point* or dot placed after the unit figure, & denoting tenths, hundredths, etc., according to their place; RECURRING ~, ~ COINAGE); of ~ coinage, whence ~IST(2) n. Hence ~IZE(3) v.t., ~ĪZA'TION n., ~LY² adv. [*c.* 1600 (math.) f. L *decimus* tenth, -AL]

dĕ'cimāte, v.t. Put to death one in ten

of (mutinous or cowardly soldiers); destroy tenth or large proportion of (esp. of epidemic or other visitation). So **děcĭmĀ'TION** n. [f. L *decimare* take the tenth man (*decimus*), see -ATE[3]]

dĕ'cĭmō-sĕx'tō. = SEXTODECIMO.

dĕ'cĭmus. See PRIMUS[1].

dĕcĭph'er, v.t., & n. Turn into ordinary writing or make out with key (thing written in cipher); make out meaning of (bad writing, hieroglyphics, anything perplexing); (n.) interpretation of cipher document. Hence ~ABLE a., ~MENT n. [DE-]

dĕcĭ'sion (-ĭzhn), n. Settlement (*of* question etc.), conclusion, formal judgement; making up one's mind, resolve; resoluteness, decided character. [ME, f. OF, or L *decisio* (DECIDE, -ION)]

dĕcĭs'ive, a. Deciding, conclusive, (esp. ~ *battle*); = DECIDED (~ *character*, ~ *superiority*). Hence ~LY[2] (-vl-) adv., ~NESS (-vn-) n. [F (DECIDE, -IVE)]

dĕcĭv'ĭlīze, -ise (-īz), v.t. Divest of civilization. [DE-]

dĕck[1], n. 1. Platform of planks or wood--covered iron extending from side to side of ship or part of it (in large ships *main*, *middle*, *lower*, ~*s*, also *upper* or *spar* ~ above *main*, & ORLOP below *lower*; *poop* & *forecastle* ~*s*, short ones in stern & bow); (sl.) the ground; CLEAR[2] *the* ~*s*; *on* ~, not below; ~-*chair*, camp-stool, also long-armed reclining chair, used in passenger steamers; ~-*hand*, man employed on vessel's ~ in cleaning and odd jobs; ~-*house*, room erected on ~. 2. Pack of cards (now chiefly U.S.). [15th c. 'covering' f. MDu. *dec* (cf. foll.); naut. use (c. 1500) app. an Eng. development]

dĕck[2], v.t. Array, adorn; furnish with, cover as, a deck. [c. 1500 f. MDu. *dekken* cover; see THATCH]

dĕc'kle, n. Contrivance in papermaking--machine for limiting size of sheet (~-*edge*, rough uncut edge). [f. G *deckel* dim. of *decke* cover]

dĕclaim', v.i. & t. Speak rhetorically (often *against*, = inveigh), practise speaking or recitation; deliver impassioned rather than reasoned speech; utter rhetorically. Hence ~ER[1] n. [16th c. *declame* f. F *declamer* or L *declamare*; see CLAIM]

dĕclamā'tion, n. Act or art of declaiming; rhetorical exercise, set speech; impassioned speech, harangue. So **dĕclăm'atORY** a. [f. F, or L *declamatio* (prec., -ATION)]

dĕclăr'ant, n. One who makes legal declaration. [f. L *declarare* DECLARE, -ANT]

dĕclarā'tion, n. Stating, announcing; positive, emphatic, solemn, or legal assertion, announcement, or proclamation (~ *of war*, before beginning hostilities, not now usual; ~ *of the poll*, of vote-totals of election-candidates); manifesto, written announcement of

intentions, terms of agreement, etc. (*D*~ *of* INDULGENCE; *D*~ *of* RIGHTS; *D*~ *of Independence*, of 4th July 1776 by N.--Amer. British colonies; *D*~ *of Paris* 1856, *of London* 1909 unratified by Gt Britain, international agreements on maritime law); (Law) plaintiff's statement of claim, affirmation in lieu of oath, Custom--House statement (see foll.); (Cards) a bid, pass, double, etc., the winning bid. [ME, f. L *declaratio* (foll., -ATION)]

dĕclāre', v.t. & i. 1. Make known, proclaim publicly, formally, or explicitly, (~ *war*, *a dividend*); (abs.) *Well. I* ~ (excl. of incredulity, surprise, or vexation). 2. Pronounce (person etc.) to be something, as ~ *him* (*to be*) *an enemy to humankind*; ~ *oneself*, avow intentions, reveal character; ~ *for*, *against*, side with, against; ~ *innings closed*, or ~, elect to cease batting as though all were out; ~ *off*, break off (bargain etc., or abs.). 3. (Customs) name (dutiable goods) as in one's possession. 4. (Bridge) name the trump suit, or call 'No trumps'; (other card games) announce that one holds (certain combinations of cards etc.). Hence or cogn. **dĕclă'rATIVE, dĕclă'ratORY**, aa., **dĕclă'ratĭveLY**[2], **dĕclār'ĕdLY**[2], advv., **dĕclār'ER**[1] n. (esp. at cards). [ME, f. L DE(*clarare* f. *clarus* clear)]

déclassé (dāklás'ā), a. (fem. -ée). That has lost caste or sunk in social scale. [F]

dĕclăss'ĭfy, v.t. Remove from classified or secret list. [DE-]

dĕclĕn'sion (-shn), n. Deviation *from* uprightness etc.; deterioration, decay; (Gram.) case-inflexion, (one of the noun--classes distinguished by their different methods of case-inflexion, declining. [irreg. f. OF *declinaison* f. L *declinationem*, whence obs. E *declination* in same sense]

dĕclinā'tion, n. Downward bend; (Astron.) angular distance of star etc. north or south of celestial equator, celestial latitude; (Compass) angular deviation of needle, E. or W., from true north. Hence ~AL (-sho-) a. [ME, f. OF or f. L *declinatio* (foll., -ATION)]

dĕclĭne'[1], v.i. & t. Slope downwards (usu. intr.); bend, droop, (i., & also t. as *with head* ~*d*, ~*s its blossoms*); (of day, life, etc.) draw to close; sink morally (~ *on*, descend to); fall off, decay, decrease, deteriorate; turn away from, refuse, (discussion, challenge, battle; ~ *to do*, *doing*, *to be* treated in such a way); say one 'cannot accept (invitation etc., or abs.; ~ *with thanks* freq. iron., reject scornfully); (Gram.) inflect, recite the cases of, whence **dĕclĭn'ABLE** a. [ME, f. OF *decliner* or L DE(*clinare* bend)]

dĕclĭne'[2], n. Sinking, gradual loss of vigour or excellence, decay, deterioration; phthisis, consumption; fall in price; setting, last part of course, (of sun, life, etc.). [ME, f. prec. & OF *declin*]

dĕclĭnŏm'ĕter, n. Instrument for measuring magnetic declination. [irreg. f. L *declinare* see DECLINE + -METER]

dĕcliv'it|y̆, n. Downward slope. Hence ~OUS a. [f. L *declivitas* f. DE(*clivis* f. *clivus* slope), -TY (cf. DEFORMITY)]

dĕcliv'ous, a. Sloping down (esp. in Zool. of profile). [f. L *declivis* see prec., + -OUS]

dĕclŭtch', v.i Disengage clutch esp. of motor-car. [DE-]

dĕcŏc'tion, n. Boiling down so as to extract essence; liquor resulting. [ME, f. OF or L DE(*coctio* f. *coquere coct-* boil, -ION)]

dĕcōde', v.t. Decipher (code telegram etc.). [DE-]

dĕcŏll'āte, v.t. Behead, truncate (p.p., of spiral shell without apex). So **dĕcoll-A'TION** n. [LL DE(*collare* f. *collum* neck), -ATE³]

dĕcolletage (dākŏl'tahzh), n. (Exposure of neck and shoulders by low-cut neck of bodice. [F (DE-, *collet* collar of dress)]

dĕcolleté (dākŏl'tā), a. (fem. *-ée*). Low--necked (of dress); wearing low-necked dress. [F, as prec.]

dĕcol'o(u)rīz|e (-kŭler-), -is|e (-īz), v.t. Deprive of colour. Hence ~A'TION, ~ER¹(2), nn. [DE-, COLOUR¹, -IZE(3)]

dē'cŏmplĕx, a. Doubly complex, having complex parts. [DE-]

dĕcompōs|e' (-z), v.t. & i. Separate into its elements (substance, light, etc.); analyse (thought, motive); rot (t. & i.). Hence ~'ABLE a., ~'ER¹(2), dĕcŏmposi'-TION, nn., (-z-). [f. F *décomposer* (DE-, COMPOSE)]

dĕcŏm'posĭte (-z-), a. & n. (Substance, word, etc.) made by compounding a compound with another element, further composite. [f. LL *decompositus* transl. of Gk *parasunthetos* used of words derived from compounds; see DE-]

dē'compound, a. & n. = DECOMPOSITE (esp. in Bot.). [DE-]

dĕcomprĕss', v.t. Relieve pressure on (underwater or other worker) by means of an air-lock. Hence **dĕcomprĕ'ssion** (-shn) n., ~OR n., contrivance for relieving pressure in motor engine. [DE-]

dĕcŏn'sĕcrāte, v.t. Secularize. [DE-]

dĕcontăm'in|āte, v.t. Remove contamination from (esp. areas, clothes, etc., affected by poison-gas or radio-activity). Hence ~A'TION n. [DE-]

dĕcontrōl', v.t. (-ll-), & n. Release from (esp. war-time) control by Government etc. [DE-]

dĕcor (dĕkôr'), n. All that makes up the appearance of a room or the stage. [F]

dĕc'orāt|e, v.t. Furnish with adornments (esp. church with flowers etc.); serve as adornment to; invest with order, medal, etc.; ~*ed* as adj. or n., (of) third English STYLE of architecture. Hence ~IVE a.

[f. L *decorare* (*decus -oris* beauty), -ATE³]

dĕcorā'tion, n. In vbl senses; esp.: (pl.) flags, wreaths, etc., put up on occasion of public rejoicing; medal, star, etc., worn as honour. [F, or f. LL *decoratio* (prec., -ATION)]

dĕc'orātor, n. In vbl senses; esp., tradesman who papers, paints, etc., houses. [-OR]

dĕc'orous (or dĭkōr'-), a. Not violating good taste or propriety, dignified and decent. Hence ~LY² adv. [f. L *decōrus* (*decor* f. *decēre* be fit, -OR) + -OUS]

dĕcôrt'icāte, v.t. Remove the bark, rind, or husk from. [f. L DE(*corticare* f. *cortex* bark), -ATE³]

dĕcōr'um, n. Seemliness, propriety, etiquette; particular usage required by politeness, or decency. [L, neut. adj. as DECOROUS]

dĕcoy', n., & v.t. (Entice, esp. by help of trained bird etc., into) pond with narrow netted arms into which wild duck may be tempted and caught; allure *into, out of, away,* etc., ensnare; bird etc. trained to entice others; (also ~*-duck*) swindler's confederate, tempter; bait, enticement. [17th c., f. MDu. *de kooi* 'the coy', whence also, without the article, obs. (now dial.) E *coy*; *kooi* f. WG *ca(u)wia* f. L *cavea* CAGE]

dĕcrease', v.i. & t., **dĕc'rease,** n. 1. Lessen, diminish, (i. & t.); hence **dĕcreas'ingLY²** adv. 2. n. Diminution, lessening. [ME *dis-, de-*, f. OF *de(s)creiss-*, pres. stem of *de(s)creistre* f. Rom. **discrescere* (in LL w. sense 'grow in different directions') f. L DE(*crescere cret-* grow); n. f. OF *de(s)creis*]

dĕcree', n., & v.t. 1. Ordinance or edict set forth by authority; decision (in other courts called *judgement*) in Admiralty cases, (in Divorce cases) order declaring nullity or dissolution or giving judicial separation (∥~ *nis'ĭ*, order for divorce unless cause to the contrary is shown within a period, orig. six months, later six -weeks); will, as shown by result, of God, Providence, Nature, etc. 2. v.t. Ordain by ~. [ME, f. OF *decre* f. L DE(*cretum* neut. p.p. of *cernere* sift) thing decided]

dĕc'rèment, n. Decrease, amount lost by diminution or waste, (esp. as scientific term opp. INCREMENT). [f. L *decrementum* (DECREASE, -MENT)]

dĕcrĕp'it, a. Wasted, worn out, enfeebled with age & infirmities, (of persons or institutions). So **dĕcrĕp'ITUDE** n. [ME, f OF *decrepit* or L DE(*crepitus* p.p. of *crepare* creak)]

dĕcrĕp'it|āte, v.t. & i. Calcine (mineral or salt) till it ceases to crackle in fire; crackle under heat. Hence ~A'TION n. [DE-, L *crepitare* frequent. of *crepare* creak]

decrescĕn'dō (dākrĕsh-). = DIMINUENDO. [It.]

For compounds of *de-* not given consult DE-.

décrĕs'cent, a. Waning, decreasing, (usu. of moon). [f. L *decrescens* (DECREASE, -ENT)]

dĕcrēt'al, n. Papal decree; (pl.) collection of these, forming part of canon law. [ME, f. OF *decretal* f. LL *decretalis* (letter) of DECREE, -AL]

dĕcry', v.t. Disparage, cry down. [f. F *décrier* (DE-, CRY²)]

dĕc'ūman, a. Especially large or power-ful (usu. of wave lit. or fig.). [f. L *decu-decimanus*, used of main gate of camp where tenth cohort was quartered (*decimus* tenth, -AN)]

dĕcŭm'bent, a. (bot. & zool.). Lying along ground or body (of plant, shoot, bristles). [f. L DE(*cumbere* lie), -ENT]

dĕc'ūple, a., n., & v.t. & i. Tenfold (amount); (vb) multiply by ten. [F (*dé-*), f. LL *decuplus* (*decem* ten, *-plus* cf. *duplus* DOUBLE)]

dĕcŭss'ate, a. (-*at*), & v.t. & i. (-ăt). 1. X-shaped, intersecting; (Bot.) with pairs of opposite shoots, each at right angles to pair below; (Rhet.) marked by chiasmus. 2. vb. Arrange in these ways; intersect; hence **dĕcŭssA'TION** n. [f. L *decussare* (*decussis* number ten, X), -ATE², ³]

dedans (dedahň'), n. (tennis). Open gallery at end of service-side of a court; (transf., *the* ~) spectators watching a tennis match. [F, = inside]

dĕd'icāt|e, v.t. Devote with solemn rites (*to* God or *to* sacred use; of church etc. esp. without certain forms necessary for legally consecrating ground or buildings); give up (*to* special purpose); inscribe (book etc.) *to* patron or friend. So ~OR, ~EE', nn., ~IVE, ~ORY, aa. [f. L DE(*dicare* declare), -ATE³]

dĕdicā'tion, n. In vbl senses; also, dedi-catory inscription on building etc. or in book. [ME, f. OF, or f. L *dedicatio* (prec., -ION)]

dĕdūc|e', v.t. Bring down (annals etc.) *from* or *to* a time; trace descent of (person etc.) *from*; infer, draw as conclusion, *from*. So ~'IBLE a. [f. L DE(*ducere duct-* lead)]

dĕdŭct', v.t. Take away, put aside, (amount, portion, etc., *subtract* being now used of numbers) *from* (or abs.). [f. L *deduct-* see prec.]

dĕdŭc'tion, n. Deducting; amount de-ducted; deducing, inference from general to particular, *a priori* reasoning, (cf. INDUCTION); thing deduced. [ME, f. OF, or L *deductio* (DEDUCE, -ION)]

dĕdŭc'tive, a. Of, reasoning by, deduc-tion, *a priori*. Hence ~LY² (vĭ-) adv. [f. L *deductivus* (DEDUCE, -IVE)]

dee, n. Letter D; D-shaped harness-ring.

deed, n. Thing done intentionally; brave, skilful, or conspicuous act; actual fact, performance, (*in word & ~*; *in ~ & not in name*, whence INDEED; *in very ~*); (Law) written or printed instrument

effecting legal disposition & sealed & delivered by disposing party (in practice now always signed also but not always delivered); ~-*poll*, deed made & exe-cuted by one party only (paper polled or cut even, not indented). Hence ~'LESS a. [OE *dǣd*, OS *dād*, OHG *tāt*, ON *dáth*, Goth.-*deths* f. Gmc **dǣdiz*, cogn. w. DO¹]

deem, v.t. Believe, consider, judge, count, (abs. in parenthesis, as *it was, I ~ed, time to go*; ~ *highly of*, have high opinion of; ~ *it* one's *duty*; *was ~ed sufficient, to suffice*; ~*ed that this would do*). [OE *dēman*, OS *dōmian*, OHG *tuomen*, ON *dœma*, Goth. *domjan* f. Gmc **dōmaz* DOOM]

deem'ster, n. One of two justices of Isle of Man. [prec., -STER]

deep¹, a. 1. Going far down from top (~ *hole, water, draught, drink, drinker, gambling, gambler*; *go (in) off the* ~ END¹; *in* ~ *waters*, plunged in grief etc.); going far in from surface or edge (~ *wound, shelf, border*; ~ *mourning*, expressed by wide crape etc.; ~ *plunge*; ~ *reader, thinker*). 2. Hard to fathom, profound, not superficial, penetrating, (~ *dissimu-lation*; *a* ~ *one*, sl., cunning or secretive; *the* ~*er causes*; ~ *learning, study*; ~ *influ-ence*; ~ *insight*). 3. Heartfelt, absorbing, absorbed, (~ *feelings, interest, curses*; ~ *in a pursuit*, dead to everything else). 4. Intense, vivid, extreme, heinous, (~ *disgrace, sleep, night, sin, colour*; ~-*red* etc.). 5. Going or placed (so) far down, back, or in (*water 6 ft* ~; *ankle-* ~ *in mud*; *drawn up six* ~; *ship* ~ *in the water, hands* ~ *in pockets*; ~ *in debt*; ~ *in the human heart*, fully versed in it). 6. Brought from far down (~ *sigh*); not shrill, low-pitched, full-toned, (note, bell, voice; ~-*mouthed*, of dog). Hence ~'EN⁶ v.t. & i., ~'LY² adv., ~'MOST a., (rare, for *depth*) ~'NESS n. [OE *dēop*, OS *diop*, OHG *tiuf*, ON *djúpr*, Goth. *diups* f. Gmc **deupaz* cogn. w. DIP¹]

deep², n. The ~ (poet.), the sea; (Cricket, *the* ~) position of fieldsmen stationed behind the bowler at or near boundary (*the* ~ *field*); (usu. pl.) deep part(s) of the sea; abyss, pit, cavity; mysterious region of thought or feeling. [as prec. (neut. adj. in OE)]

deep³, adv. Deeply, far in, (*read* ~ *into the night*; *still waters run* ~, real feeling or knowledge not showy); esp. in comb. as ~-*drawn* (of sighs), ~-*laid* (of scheme, secret & elaborate), ~-*rooted* (esp. of prejudice), ~-*seated* (of emotion or disease). [OE *dīope, dēope*, (DEEP¹)]

deep'ing, n. Section, one fathom deep, of fishing-net. [-ING³]

deer, n. (collect. sing. usu. for pl.). Kinds of ruminant quadruped with deciduous branching horns (*small* ~, insignificant animals or things collectively, cf. *King Lear* III iv. 144); ~-*hound*, large rough greyhound; ~-*forest*, normally treeless wild land reserved for stalking ~; ~·*lick*, spring or damp spot impregnated with salt etc. where ~ come to lick; ~·*neck*, horse's thin neck; ‖ ~'*s-foot*, a fine grass; ~'*skin*, (made of) ~'s skin; ~'*stalker*, sportsman stalking ~, cloth cap peaked before and behind. [OE *dēor*, OS *dior*, OHG *tiur*, ON *dȳr*, Goth. *dius* f. Gmc **deuzom*]

dèfāce', v.t. Mar appearance or beauty of, disfigure; discredit; make illegible. Hence ~ABLE (-sa-) a., ~MENT (-sm-) n. [ME, f. OF *def-, desfacer* (DE-, FACE[1])]

dē fāc'tō, a. & adv. In fact, whether by right (DE JURE) or not (*king* ~, *the* ~ *king*). [L]

dĕf'alcāt|e, v.i. Commit defalcations, misappropriate property in one's charge. So ~OR n. [f. med. L DE(*falcare* lop f. L *falx -cis* scythe), -ATE[3]]

dĕfalcā'tion, n. Defection, shortcoming; fraudulent deficiency of money owing to breach of trust, misappropriation, amount misappropriated. [f. med. L *defalcatio* (prec., -ATION)]

dèfāme', v.t. Attack the good fame of, speak ill of. So **dèfam**A'TION n., **dèfām'a-** TORY a. [ME *dif-, de-*, f. OF *diffamer* f. L *diffamare* spread abroad (DIS-, *fama* report), see DE-; form *de-* after L *defamis, -atus* infamous]

dèfătt'ĕd, a. Deprived of its fat. [DE-]

dèfault'[1], n. Want, absence, (*in* ~ *of*, if or since such a thing is wanting); failure to act or appear, neglect, (*make* ~; *judgement by* ~, given for plaintiff on defendant's failure to plead); failure to pay, defaulting. [ME, f. OF *defaute* f. *defaillir* see foll. & cf. FAULT]

dèfault'[2], v.i. & t. 1. Make, be guilty of, default; fail to appear in court; not meet money calls, break; hence ~ER[1] n., (also Mil.) soldier guilty of military offence (~*er sheet*, record of such offences, now *conduct sheet*). 2. Declare (party) in default & give judgement against him. [ME, f. prec. & OF *defaillir* (3 sing. *default*) f. DE-, L *fallere* deceive]

dèfeas'ance (-fēz-), n. Rendering null & void. [ME, f. OF *defesance* f. *de(s)faire* undo, DEFEAT, -ANCE]

dèfeas'i|ble (-fēz-), a. Capable of annulment, liable to forfeiture. Hence ~BIL'ITY n. [AF, as prec., -IBLE]

dèfeat', v.t., & n. Frustrate, frustration; (Law) annul(ment); (arch.) disappoint of; overthrow (v. & n.) in contest esp. in battle. [ME; n. prob. f. vb, which is f. OF *defait* p.p. of *desfaire* f. med. L *disfacere* (DE-, L *facere* do)]

dèfeat'|ism, n. Conduct tending to bring about acceptance of defeat, esp. by action on civilian opinion. So ~IST n. & a. [f. F *défaitisme* (as prec., -ISM)]

dĕf'ĕc|āte, v.t. Clear of dregs, refine, purify, (lit. & fig.); get rid of (dregs, ex-

crement, sin). Hence ~A'TION, ~ātOR, nn. [f. L DE(*fecare* f. *faex -cis* dregs), -ATE[3]]

dèfĕct', n., & v.i. Lack of something essential to completeness; shortcoming, failing, (*has the* ~*s of his qualities*, the particular ones that often accompany his particular virtues); blemish; amount by which thing falls short; (v.i.) desert. [f. L *defectus* n. f. DE(*ficere fect-* = *faccre* do) desert, fail]

dèfĕc'tion, n. Falling away from allegiance to leader, party, religion, or duty; desertion, apostasy. [f. L *defectio* (prec., -ION)]

dèfĕc'tive, a. & n. 1. Having defect(s), incomplete, faulty, wanting or deficient (*in* some respect); (Gram.) not having all the usual inflexions. 2. n. A ~ person. Hence ~LY[2] (-vl-) adv., ~NESS (-vn-) n. [ME, f. OF *defectif* or LL *defectivus* as prec., -IVE]

‖ dèfĕnce', ***dèfĕnse'**, n. Defending from, resistance against, attack (cf. OFFENCE; *best* ~ *is offence*, advantage goes with the initiative; in cricket, guarding of one's wicket, also batting as opposed to bowling; *science* or *art of* ~, boxing or fencing); (Mil., pl.) fortifications (also *line of* ~, series of fortified posts); ~ *in depth*, system of ~ comprising successive areas of resistance; thing that protects; justification, vindication, speech or writing used to this end; (Law) accused party's denial, pleading, & proceedings, counsel for the ~; ‖ *D*~ *of the Realm Act* (abbr. D.O.R.A., joc. *Dŏr'a*), Act of August, 1914, providing Government with wide powers during war. Hence ~LESS (-sl-) a., ~lĕssLY[2] adv., ~lĕssNESS n. [ME *defens, defense*, f. OF f. LL *defensum, -a*, p.p. see foll.]

dèfĕnd', v.t. & i. Forbid, avert, (arch.; still in *God* ~*!*); ward off attack from, keep safe, protect (*against, from*); uphold by argument, vindicate, speak or write in favour of; (Law) make defence in court (~ *oneself*, conduct one's own defence), (of counsel) appear for defendant, conduct defence of. [ME, f. OF *defendre* f. L DE(*fendere -fens-* FEND)]

dèfĕn'dant, n. Person sued in law-suit (cf. *plaintiff*); (attrib.) holding this relation (*the* ~ *company*). [ME, f. OF *defendant* part. (prec., -ANT)]

dèfĕn'der, n. One who defends; *D*~ *of the Faith*, title of Eng. Sovereigns from Henry VIII, who received it from Pope for writing against Luther; (Sport) holder of championship etc. defending the title (opp. *challenger*). [ME & AF *defendour*, OF *-eor* (DEFEND, -OR)]

dèfĕnĕstrā'tion, n. Action of throwing out of a window. [DE-, L *fenestra* window, -ATION]

defense. See DEFENCE.

For compounds of de- not given consult DE-.

defĕn'si|ble, a. Easily defended (in war or argument); justifiable. Hence ~BIL'ITY n., ~bLY² adv. [ME -*able* f. OF f. LL -*abilis*; later -*ible* f. LL -*ibilis*; see DE-FEND, -ABLE, -IBLE]

defĕn'sive, a. & n. 1. Serving, used, done, for defence, protective, not aggressive; hence ~LY² (vI-) adv. 2. n. State or position of defence (esp. *be, stand, act, on the* ~). [ME, f. F *défensif* f. med. L *defensivus* (DEFEND, -IVE)]

defĕr'¹, v.t. & i. (-rr-). Put off, postpone, (~*red* ANNUITY; ~*red pay*, part of soldier's pay formerly held over to be paid at discharge or death; ~*red* SHARE¹s); procrastinate, be dilatory. Hence ~MENT n. [later, differentiated form of ME *differre*; see DIFFER]

defĕr'², v.i. (-rr-). Submit or make concessions in opinion or action *to* (person). [f. F *déférer* f. L DE(*ferre* bring)]

def'erence, n. Compliance with advice etc. of one superior in wisdom or position (*pay* etc. ~ *to*); respect, manifestation of desire to comply, courteous regard, (*in* ~ *to*, out of respect for authority of). Hence defĕrĕn'tIAL (-shl) a., defĕrĕn'tIALY² (-shal-) adv. [f. F *déférence* (prec., -ENCE)]

def'erent, a. (Physiol.) conveying to a destination (of ducts etc.); (rare for) deferential. [first sense (f. F or direct) f. L *deferens* part. of DE(*ferre* carry); second f. DEFER², -ENT]

defi'ance, n. Challenge to fight or maintain cause, assertion, etc.; open disobedience, setting at nought, (*bid* ~ *to, set at* ~, *in* ~ *of*). [ME, f. OF (DEFY, -ANCE)]

defi'ant, a. Openly disobedient; rejecting advances, suspicious and reserved. Hence ~LY² adv. [f. F *défiant* (DEFY, -ANT)]

defi'ciency (-Ishn-), n. Being deficient; want, lack; thing wanting; amount by which thing, esp. revenue, falls short; ~ *disease* (caused by lack of some essential element in the diet). [f. LL *deficientia* (*deficere* see DEFECT, -ENCY)]

defi'cient (-Ishnt), a. Incomplete, defective, wanting *in* specified quality; insufficient in quantity, force, etc.; half--witted. Hence ~LY² adv. [f. L *deficiens* (*deficere* see DEFECT, -ENT)]

def'icit, n. Amount by which esp. sum of money is too small; excess of liabilities over assets. [f. F *déficit* f. L *deficit* 3 sing. pres. of *deficere* see DEFECT]

dē fīd'ē, pred. a. Required to be held as article of faith. [L]

defi'er, n. One who defies. [DEFY, -ER¹]

defilā̆de', v.t. & n. Secure (fortification) against enfilading fire; (n.) this precaution or arrangement (also *defilement*). [Eng. formations after ENFILADE vb & n.]

defile'¹, v.i., def'ile, n. 1. March by files, in file. 2. n. Narrow way through which troops can only march so, gorge. [f. F *défiler* & *défilé* p.p. (DE-, *file* FILE³)]

defile'², v.t. Make dirty, befoul; pollute,

corrupt; desecrate, profane; make ceremonially unclean. Hence ~MENT (-lm-) n. (see DEFILADE). [ME *defoul* f. OF *defouler* trample down, outrage (DE-, *fouler* FULL²); altered after obs. *file, befile* f. OE (*be*)*fȳlan* f. *ful* FOUL]

defin|e', v.t. Settle limits of; make clear. esp. in outline (*well-*~*ed image*; ~*e* one's *position*, state it precisely); set forth essence of, declare exact meaning of, (also abs., frame definitions); (of properties) make up total character of. Hence ~'ABLE a. [ME, f. OF *definer* f. Rom. **definare* for L DE(*finire* f. *finis* end)]

def'inite, a. With exact limits; determinate, distinct, precise, not vague; (Gram.) ~ *inflexions*, those of German and early E adjj. used after ~ article & similar wds; ~ *article*, the; *past* or *preterite* ~, simple past tense in French, as *il vint* he came. Hence ~LY² (-tl-) adv. (also, in loose colloq. use, yes, certainly), ~NESS (-tn-) n. [f. L *definitus* p.p. see prec.]

defini'tion, n. Stating the precise nature of a thing or meaning of a word; form of words in which this is done; making or being distinct, degree of distinctness, in outline (esp. of image given by lens or shown in photograph); degree of accuracy of sound reproduction in radio or of picture reproduction in television. [ME, f. OF (-*cion*) or L DE(*finitio* f. *finire* f. *finis* end, -ION)]

defin'itive, a. Decisive, unconditional, final, (of answer, treaty, verdict, etc.). Hence ~LY² (-vl-) adv. [ME, f. OF *definitif* f. L *definitivus* (prec., -IVE)]

dē'flagr|ā̆te, v.t. & i. Burn away with rapid flame. Hence ~A'TION, ~ā̆tOR, nn. [f. L DE(*flagrare* blaze), -ATE³]

def"lā̆te', v.t. Let inflating air etc. out of (pneumatic tire etc.); (Finance) reduce the inflation of (State's currency), (abs.) adopt this policy. Hence dēflā̆'tION n. [f. DE- +(IN)FLATE]

dēflĕc|t', v.t. & i. Bend aside or (rarely) down, (make) deviate (*from*). Hence ~'tOR n. [f. L DE(*flectere flex*- bend)]

dēflĕ'xion (-kshn), -ĕc'tion, n. Lateral or downward bend, deviation, (lit. & fig.; in Electr. & Magn., of needle from its zero). [f. L *deflex*- (prec., -ION)]

deflora'tion, n. Deflowering. [ME, f. OF f. LL *deflorationem* (foll., -ATION)]

deflow'er, v.t. Deprive of virginity, ravish; ravage, spoil; strip of flowers. [ME, f. OF *desflorer* f. Rom. **disflorare* f. LL DE*florare* (*flos floris* flower)]

dē'fluent (-lōō-), a. & n. Down-flowing (part; e.g. lower end of glacier). [f. L DE(*fluere* flow), -ENT]

defő'rĕst, v.t. = DISFOREST. [f. DE- + FOREST]

defőrm', v.t. Make ugly, deface; put out of shape, mis-shape, (esp. in p.p. of person with mis-shapen body or limb). [ME, f. OF *deformer* f. L DE(*formare* f. *forma* shape)]

deförmä'tion, n. Disfigurement; change for the worse (esp. as opponent's name for Reformation); perverted form of word (*dang* for *damn* etc.); (Physics) changed shape *of.* [ME, f. OF f. L *deformationem* (prec., -ATION)]

deförm'ity, n. Being deformed, ugliness, disfigurement, (physical or moral); a malformation esp. of body or limb. [ME, f. OF (*-te*) f. L *deformitatem* f. DE(*formis* f. *forma* shape), -TY]

defraud', v.t. Cheat (person, person *of*, or abs.). [ME, f. OF *defrauder* or L *defraudare* (DE-, *fraus* FRAUD)]

defray', v.t. Settle, discharge by payment, (cost, expense). Hence ~ABLE a., ~AL(2) n. [f. F *défrayer* f. *frai*(*t*) (now pl. *frais*) cost, f. LL *fritus, fretus, fredus* f. OFrank. *frithu* peace; cf. AFFRAY]

defröck', v.t. = UNFROCK.

deft, a. Dextrous,'skilful, handling things neatly. Hence ~'LY[2] adv., ~'NESS n. [ME; var. of DAFT]

defünct', a. Dead (*the* ~, way of mentioning a particular dead person), no longer existing. [f. L DE(*functus* p.p. of *fungi* perform) dead]

defÿ', v.t. Challenge to combat or competition (arch. or joc.); challenge *to* do or prove something; resist openly, set at naught; (of things) present insuperable obstacles .to (*defies definition, capture, attack,* etc.). [ME, f. OF *defier* f. Rom. *DIS(*fidare* trust f. *fidus* faithful)]

dégagé (see Ap.), a. (fem. *-ée*). Easy, unconstrained. [F]

dégauss' (*-gows*), v.t. Neutralize the magnetization of (ship etc.) with an encircling current-carrying conductor (~*ing belt*), esp. as precaution against magnetic mines. [DE-, GAUSS]

dégen'erate[1], a. & n. **1.** Having lost qualities proper to race, sunk from former excellence; (Biol.) having reverted to lower type; hence **dégen'er**ACY n. **2.** n. ~ person or animal. [f. L p.p. see foll., -ATE[2]]

dégen'erāte[2], v.i.' Become degenerate (see prec.). [f. L *degenerare,* f. DE(*gener* f. *genus -eris* race) ignoble, -ATE[3]]

dégenerā'tion, n. Becoming degenerate; (Path.) morbid disintegration of tissue or change in its structure (esp. *fatty* ~ *of heart*). [f. F, or LL *degeneratio* (prec., -ION)]

dégluti'tion (*-gloo-*), n. Swallowing. [f. F *déglutition* f. L DE(*glutire* swallow), -ION]

dégrāde', v.t. & i. Reduce to lower rank; depose as punishment; lower in estimation, debase morally, whence **dégrād'**ING[2] a.; reduce (Biol.) to lower organic type, (Physics) to less convertible form (energy), (Geol.) to disintegration (rocks etc.); degenerate; || (Camb. Univ.) put off entering for honours examination

for a year beyond regular time. So **dégrada'**TION n. [ME, f. OF *degrader* f. LL DE*gradare* (*gradus* step)]

dégree', n. **1.** Step (as) of staircase (arch.; perh. so in 2 *Kings* XX. 9, & in Psalm-title *Song of D~s,* Ps. 120–134); thing placed like step in series, tier, row; stage in ascending or descending scale or process (*by* ~*s,* gradually; *fine by* ~*s* & *beautifully less,* see Prior, *Henry & Emma,* 431; often misquoted *small by* etc.); step in direct genealogical descent (*prohibited* ~*s,* number of these too low to allow of marriage, i.e. first, second, & third, reckoning from one party up to common ancestor & down to the other). **2.** Social or official rank; relative condition (*each good in its*~); stage in intensity or amount (*to a high* or *the last* ~, also colloq. in latter sense *to a* ~; in law, *principal in the first, second,* ~). **3.** Academic rank conferred as guarantee of proficiency, or (*honorary* ~) on distinguished person; masonic rank. **4.** (Gram.) stage (POSITIVE, COMPARATIVE, SUPERLATIVE) in comparison of adjj. & advv. **5.** (Geom. etc.) unit of angular or circular-arc measurement, 1/90 of right angle or 1/360 of circumference (symbol °, as 45°; ~ *of* LATITUDE, about 69 miles); (Therm.) unit of temperature in any scale. **6.** *Third*~, severe and protracted examination of accused person by the police to extract information or confession (also attrib.). Hence ~LESS a. [ME, f. OF *degre* f. Rom. *DE(*gradus* step)]

dégré'ssion (*-shn*), n. A going down; (esp. decrease in the rate of taxation on sums below a certain limit. [in mod. use after *pro-, regression*]

de haut en bas (see Ap.), adv. In a condescending or superior manner. [F]

déhis|ce' (*-Is*), v.i. Gape, burst open, (esp. in Bot. of seed-vessels, & in Physiol.). So ~'CENCE n., ~'CENT a. [f. L DE(*hiscere* incept. of *hiare* gape)]

déhört'ative, a. & n. Dissuasive; thing meant to dissuade. [f. LL DE(*hortativus* f. *hortari* exhort, -IVE)]

déhüm'anize, -ise (*-Iz*), v.t. Divest of human characteristics. [DE-]

déhÿd'rāte, v.t. (chem.). Deprive (substance) of water or its elements. [f. DE- + HYDRATE]

déhÿp'notize, -ise (*-Iz*), v.t. Rouse, release, from hypnotic state. [DE-]

dé-i'cer, n. Composition applied to aircraft's wings to prevent formation of ice, or any mechanical or electrical device for the same purpose. So **dé-ice'** v.t., free (aircraft) from ice. [DE-]

dé'icide, n. Killer, killing, of a God. [f. LL *deicida* (*deus* god, -I-, -CIDE)]

deic'tic (*dik-*), a. (philol., gram.). Pointing, demonstrative. [f. Gk *deiktikos* (*deiktos* f. *deiknumi* show, -IC)]

---

dē'ifōrm, a. Godlike in form or nature. [f. med. L *deiformis* (*deus* god, -I-, -FORM)]

dē'ifȳ, v.t. Make a god of; make godlike; regard as a god, worship. Hence **dēi-FICA'TION** n. [ME, f. OF *deifier* f. LL *deificare* (*deus* god, -FY)]

deign (dān), v.t. Think fit, condescend, *to* do; condescend to give (answer etc.). [ME, f. OF *degnier* f. L *dignare*, -*ari* deem worthy]

dē'ī grā'tiā (-shĭ-), adv. By God's grace. [L]

dē īn'tĕgrō, adv. Afresh. [L]

dē'ism, dē'ist, nn. Belief, believer, in the existence of a god without accepting revelation; (adherent of) natural religion. Hence **dēis'tic**(AL) aa. [f. F *déisme*, *déiste*, f. L *deus* god + -ISM(3), -IST(2)]

dē'itȳ, n. Divine status, quality, or nature; a god; *the D~*, the Creator, God. [ME, f. OF *deite* f. LL *deitatem* (*deus* god, -TY)]

dejěct', v.t. Dispirit, depress (usu. in p.p.). Hence **~edLY²** adv. [ME, f. L DE(*jicĕre* -*ject-* = *jacĕre* throw)]

dejěc'ta, n. pl. Person's or animal's excrements. [L, neut. pl. p.p. as prec.]

dejěc'tion, n. Downcast state, low spirits; (Med.) evacuation of bowels, excrement. [ME, f. OF, or L *dejectio* (prec., ION)]

déjeuner (dĕ'zhonä), n. Breakfast; lunch, esp. of ceremonial kind. [F]

dē jure (joor'ī), a. & adv. Rightful, by right, (king etc. ~; *the ~ king*; cf. DE FACTO). [L]

děkk'ō, n. (sl.). A look (*let's have a ~*). [Hind. *dekho* imp. of *dekhnā* look]

dèlaine', n. Light dress-fabric. [f. F (*mousseline*) *de laine* woollen (muslin)]

dèlāte', v.t. Inform against, impeach, (person); report (offence). So **dèlā'tION, dèlāt'ōR**, nn. [f. L DE(*lat-* p.p. st. of *ferre* carry)]

dèlay', v.t. & i., & n. Postpone(ment), defer(ring), put(ting) off, loiter(ing), be(ing) tardy, wait; hinder, hindrance. [ME; (n. f. OF *delai*) f. OF *delaier* f. *laier* leave]

dĕl cred'erĕ (-ād-), a., adv., & n. (commerc.). Under, charge made for, selling agent's guarantee that buyer is solvent. [It.]

dēl'ē, printing direction (abbr. *d*). Delete indicated letter, word, or passage (written in margin). [L, imperat. of *delēre* DELETE]

dèlěc'table, a. Delightful, pleasant. [ME, f. OF f. L *delectabilis* f. *delectare* DELIGHT]

dělěctā'tion, n. Enjoyment (usu. *for* one's ~). [ME f. OF (prec., -ATION)]

dèlěc'tus, n. School reading-book of selected passages. [L, n. f. DE(*ligere lect-* = *legere* choose)]

dēl'ĕgacȳ, n. System of delegating; appointment as delegate; body of delegates. [foll., -ACY]

dēl'ĕgate¹, n. Deputy, commissioner;

elected representative sent to conference. [ME, f. OF *delegat* f. L *delegatus* (foll., -ATE²)]

dēl'ĕgāte², v.t. Depute (person), send as representative; commit (authority etc.) to *or* to agent; ~*d legislation*, delegation to Ministers, by Acts of Parliament, of the power to make orders & regulations which have the force of law. [f. L DE-(*legare* depute), -ATE³]

dēlĕgā'tion, n. Entrusting of authority to deputy; body of delegates (**Congress* representatives of a single State; Austro-Hungary, *the D~s* (hist.), two bodies appointed by Austrian & Hungarian Parliaments to deal jointly with imperial questions). [f. L DE(*legatio* LEGATION)]

dèlēte', v.t. Strike out, obliterate, (letter, word, passage; also fig.). So **dèlē'tion** n. [f. L *delēre* -*let*-]

dèlēt'ērious, a. Noxious physically or morally, injurious. Hence **~LY²** adv. [f. Gk *dēlētērios* f. *dēlētēr* destroyer (*dēleomai* injure) + -OUS]

dēlf(t), n. Glazed earthenware made at Delft (earlier *Delf*) in Holland. [place]

dèlib'erate¹, a. Intentional; considered, not impulsive; slow in deciding, cautious; leisurely, not hurried, (of movement etc.). Hence **~LY²** (-tl-) adv., **~NESS** (-tn-) n. [f. L *deliberatus* (foll., -ATE²)]

dèlib'erāte², v.i. & t. Consider, think carefully, (intr., or with indirect question *how it might be done, what to do*); take counsel, consult, hold debate. [f. L DE(*liberare* = *librare* weigh f. *libra* balance), -ATE³]

dèliberā'tion, n. Weighing in mind, careful consideration; discussion of reasons for & against, debate; care, avoidance of precipitancy; slowness of movement. [ME, f. OF *deliberation* f. L *deliberationem* (prec., -ATION)]

dèlib'erative, a. Of, appointed for purpose of, deliberation or debate (usu. *~ assembly* or *functions*). Hence **~LY²** (-vl-) adv. [F (-*if*, -*ive*) or f. L *deliberativus* (DELIBERATE², -IVE)]

dēl'icacȳ, n. Fineness of texture, graceful slightness, tender' beauty; weakliness, susceptibility to disease or injury, need of care, discretion, or skill; nicety of perception, sensitiveness, (of persons, senses, or instruments); consideration for others' feelings; shrinking from, avoidance of, the immodest or offensive; choice kind of food, dainty; a nicety. [ME; foll., -ACY]

dēl'icate, a., Delightful (poet.); palatable, dainty, (of food); sheltered, luxurious, effeminate, (*~ living, nurture, upbringing*); fine of texture, soft, slender, slight; of exquisite quality or workmanship; subdued (of colour); subtle, hard to appreciate; easily injured, liable to illness; requiring nice handling, critical, ticklish; subtly sensitive (of persons or instruments); deft (*a ~ touch*); avoiding the offensive or immodest; considerate (esp. of actions). Hence ~LY² (-tl-) adv. [ME, f. OF *delicat* or L *delicatus*]

⁕dèlicatèss'en, n. pl. (Shop selling) delicacies or relishes for the table. [G *delikatessen* f. F *délicatesse*]

dèli'cious (-shŭs), a. Highly delightful, esp. to taste, smell, or the sense of humour. Hence ~LY² adv., ~NESS n. [ME, f. OF f. LL *deliciosus* f. L *deliciae* delight f. DE(*licere* = *lacere* allure), -OUS]

dèlict', n. Violation of law, offence, (*in flagrant ~*, = IN FLAGRANTE DELICTO). [f. L *delictum* neut. p.p. of DE(*linquere* leave) come short]

dèlight' (-īt), v.t. & i., & n. **1.** Please highly (*shall be ~ed to*, in accepting invitation; *was ~ed with* or *at the result*); take, find, great pleasure *in* (so in p.p., *the books ~ed in by the many*), be inclined and accustomed *to* do. **2.** n. High pleasure, thing that causes it; hence~FUL a., ~fuLY² adv., ~SOME a. (literary), (-ĭt-). [ME *deliten* f. OF *delitier* f. L *delectare* see DELECTABLE; sp. *-gh-* since 16th c., after *light* &c.]

Dèlil'ah (-la), Da-, n. Temptress, false & wily woman. [*Judges* xvi]

dèlim'it(āte), vv.t. Determine limits or territorial boundary of. So **dèlimit-A'TION** n. [*-it* thr. F *délimiter*, *-itate* direct, f. L DE(*limitare* f. *limes -itis* boundary), -ATE³]

dèlin'é|āte, v.t. Show by drawing or description, portray. So~A'TION, ~ātor, nn. [f. L DE(*lineare* f. *linea* line), -ATE³]

dèlīnèāv'ĭt, *-v⁻'unt*, L vb sing. & pl. (usu. abbr. *del.*). So-&-so drew this. [f. L as prec.]

dèlin'quencỹ, n. Neglect of duty; guilt; a sin of omission; misdeed. [f. L *delinquentia* f. *delinquens* part. (DELICT, -ENCY)]

dèlin'quent, a. & n. **1.** Defaulting, guilty. **2.** n. Offender. [f. L *delinquens* (prec. -ENT)]

dèliquĕs|ce', v.i. Become liquid, melt, (fig.) melt away; (Chem.) absorb enough water from the air to dissolve itself. So ~'CENT a., ~'CENCE n. [f. L DE(*liquescere* incept. of *liquēre* be liquid)]

dèli'rious, a. Affected with delirium, temporarily or apparently mad, raving; wildly excited, ecstatic; betraying delirium or ecstasy. Hence ~LY² adv. [as foll. +-OUS]

dèli'rium, n. Disordered state of mind with incoherent speech, hallucinations, & frenzied excitement; great excitement, ecstasy; ~ *trēm'ĕns* (abbr. *d.t.*), special form of ~ with terrifying delusions to which heavy drinkers are liable. [L, f. DE*lirare* (*lira* furrow)]

dèlitĕs'cent, a., **dèlitĕs'cence**, n. Latent (state). [f. L DE(*litescere* incept. of *-litēre* = *latēre* lie hid), -ENT, -ENCE]

dèliv'er, v.t. Rescue, save, set free *from*;

disburden (woman in parturition) *of* child (usu. pass.; also fig. *was ~ed of a sonnet*); unburden one*self* (*of* esp. a long-suppressed opinion etc.) in discourse; (of judge) pronounce (judgement); give *up* or *over*, abandon, resign, hand on *to* another; distribute (letters, parcels, ordered goods) to addressee or purchaser (~ *the goods*, fig., carry out one's part of agreement); present, render, (account); (Law) hand over formally (esp. sealed deed to grantee, so *seal & ~*); launch, aim, (blow, ball, attack; ~ *battle*, accept opportunity of engaging); recite (*well-*-~*ed sermon*). Hence~ABLE a. [ME, f. OF *delivrer* f. LL *deliberare* (DE-, L *liberare* f. *liber* free)]

dèliv'erance, n. Rescue; emphatically or formally delivered opinion, (in jurors' oath) verdict. [ME, f. OF *delivrance* (prec., -ANCE)]

dèliv'erer, n. In vbl senses; esp., saviour, rescuer. [ME, f. DELIVER +-ER¹]

dèliv'erỹ, n. Childbirth; surrender *of*; delivering of letters etc., a periodical performance of this (*the first, the two-o'clock, ~*); (Law) formal handing over of property, transfer of deed (formerly essential for validity) to grantee or third party; sending forth of missile, esp. of cricket-ball in bowling, action shown in doing this (*a good, high, ~*); uttering of speech etc. (*its ~ took two hours*), manner of doing this (*a telling ~*). [ME, f. AF *delivree* fem. part. used as n. of *delivrer* DELIVER, -Y⁴]

dèll, n. Small hollow or valley usu. with tree-clad sides. [ME *delle*, MLG, MDu. *delle*, MHG *telle* f. WG ⁕*daljō* (as in Goth. *ibdalja* slope); cf. DALE]

Dèll'a Crüs'can, a. & n. (Member) of the Florentine Academy della Crusca, a society for purifying the Italian language, which issued an authoritative dictionary; following artificial literary methods; member of a late 18th-c. artificial English school of poetry. [f. It. (*Accademia*) *della Crusca* (Academy) of the bran (i.e. sifting) +-AN]

dèlouse', v.t. Rid of lice, & fig. of booby-traps, mines, etc. [DE-]

Dèl'phĭan, Dèl'phĭc, aa. (As) of the oracle of Delphi; obscure, ambiguous. [*-ic* f. L f. Gk *Delphikos*, *-ian* f. L f. Gk *Delphoi* +-IAN]

Dèl'phin, a. *The ~ classics* or *text*, in an edition prepared for the Dauphin, son of Louis XIV. [L f. Gk, = dolphin; see DAUPHIN]

dèl'phinine, n. (chem.). A poisonous alkaloid used medically. [f. bot. L f. Gk *delphinion* (dim. of *delphin* dolphin) larkspur +-INE⁵]

dèlphin'ium, n. (Kinds of) ranunculaceous plant, including the larkspur. [as prec.]

For compounds of *de-* not given consult DE-⁕

dĕl'phinoid, n. & a. (Member) of the family including dolphins, porpoises, grampuses, etc. [f. Gk *delphin* dolphin, -OID]

dĕl'ta, n. Letter D (Δ, δ) of Greek alphabet; triangular alluvial tract at mouth of river enclosed or traversed by its diverging branches, esp. that of Nile, whence dĕltā'IC a.; ~ *metal*, alloy of copper, zinc, and ferro-manganese; ~ *rays*, rays of low penetrative power emitted by radium, polonium, uranium, etc., consisting of low-velocity electrons knocked from an atom during a collision with some other particles; ~ *wing*, triangular swept-back wing of aircraft [Gk]

dĕl'toid, a. & n. Triangular; ~ *muscle* or ~, muscle of shoulder lifting upper arm; like a river delta. [f. F *deltoide*, mod. L *deltoides* (prec., -OID)]

dĕlude' (-ōōd, -ūd), v.t. Impose upon, deceive. [ME, f. L DE(*ludere lus*- play)]

dĕl'ūge, n., & v.t. 1. Great flood, inundation, (*the D*~, Noah's flood); heavy fall of rain; flood of words etc. 2. vb. Flood, inundate, (lit. & fig.). [ME, f. OF f. L *diluvium* (*diluere* DILUTE)]

dĕlu'sion (-ōōzhn, -ū-), n. Imposing or being imposed upon; false impression or opinion, esp. as symptom or form of madness, whence ~AL a. (DELUDE, -ION)]

dĕlus'ive (-ōō-, -ū-), a. Deceptive, disappointing, unreal. Hence ~LY[2] adv., ~NESS n. [DELUDE, -IVE]

de luxe (lōōks), a. & adv. Luxurious(ly), sumptuous(ly); of superior kind. [F]

dĕlve, v.t. & i., & n., (arch., poet., & dial.). 1. Dig; make research in documents etc.; (of road etc.) make sudden dip. 2. n. Cavity; depression of surface, wrinkle. [OE *delfan*, OS *-delban*, OHG *-telban* f. WG *delbh*-]

dĕmăg'nĕtiz|e, -is|e (-īz), v.t. Deprive of magnetic quality. Hence ~A'TION n. [DE-]

dĕm'agŏg|ue (-g), n. Popular leader; political agitator appealing to cupidity or prejudice of the masses, factious orator. Hence or cogn. dĕmagŏg'IC (-gĭk) a., ~ISM(2), ~Y[1] nn., (-g-). [f. Gk *dēmagōgos* (DEMOS, *agōgos* leading)]

dĕmand'[1] (-ah-), n. Request made as of right or peremptorily, thing so asked, (*payable on* ~, as soon as the ~ is made); call of would-be purchasers *for* commodity (*laws of supply and* ~ in Pol. Econ.; *in* ~, sought after); urgent claim (*many* ~s *on my time*). [ME, f. OF *demande* f. *demander* see foll.]

dĕmand'[2] (-ah-), v.t. Ask for (thing) as a right or peremptorily or urgently (*of or from* person; obj. a noun, infin., or *that*-clause); require, need (*piety* ~s *it*; *task* ~s *skill*); ask to be, insist on being, told (~ one's *business*, what he wants). Hence or cogn. ~ABLE a., ~ANT(1) n. [ME, f. AF, OF *demander* f. L DE(*mandare* order cf. MANDATE)]

dēmârcā'tion, n. Marking of boundary, esp. *line of* ~. Hence (by back formation) dē'mârcāte v.t. [Sp. (-*cion*), f. *demarcar* mark bounds of (DE-, MARK)]

dēmârche (dēmârsh'), n. (In E diplomatic journalese) political step or proceeding. [F]

dēmatēr'ialize, -ise (-īz), v.t. & i. Make, become, non-material, spiritual. [DE-]

dēme, n. (Gk hist.) township of ancient Attica. [f. Gk *dēmos*]

dēmean'[1], v. refl. ~ *oneself*, behave, conduct oneself, (always w. adv. or adv. phr.). [ME, f. OF *demener* f. DE-+*mener* lead f. post-class. L *minare* drive cattle f. *minari* threaten]

dēmean'[2], v.t. (usu. refl.). Lower in dignity. [DE-, MEAN[3]]

dēmean'our (-ner), n. Bearing, outward behaviour. [f. DEMEAN[1]; earlier -*ure*, -*er*]

dēmĕnt', v.t. Drive mad, craze, (usu. in p.p.). Hence dēmĕn'tĕdLY[2] adv. [f. LL *dementare* f. DEmens out of one's mind (*mens mentis*)]

dēmenti (see Ap.), n. Official denial of rumour etc. [F]

dēmĕn'tia (or -sha), n. (med.). Species of insanity consisting in feebleness of mind. [L (*demens* see DEMENT)]

dēmerār'a (or -ah'ra), n. Kind of brown raw cane sugar in large crystals from Demerara. [place]

dēmĕ'rit, n. Ill desert; fault, defect. Hence ~ōr'IOUS [-ORY, -OUS] a. [OF *de(s)merite* or f. L *demeritum* neut. p.p. of *demereri* deservo; orig. sense desert (good or bad, like *merit*); the two have now been fixed to opposite senses]

dēmesne' (-ēn *or* -ān), n. 1. (Law) possession (of real property) as one's own (esp. *hold in* ~); an estate held in ~, all of an owner's land not held of him by freehold tenants, or all that he actually occupies himself; *Royal* ~, Crown lands; *State* ~, land held by State. 2. Sovereign's or State's territory, domain; landed property, estate; region, sphere, *of*. [ME, f. AF, OF *demeine* (later AF *demesne* perh. by assoc. w. MESNE or *mansio*) f. L *dominicus*; see DOMAIN]

dĕm'i-, pref. usu. written with the hyphen, still used as living pref. to form temporary words, but largely superseded by SEMI-. Half-size, half, imperfect, partial(ly), semi-; ~-*tâsse* (F), small cup (of black coffee). [F, f. L *dimidius*, -*um*]

dĕm'igŏd, n. Partly divine being, son of god and mortal, or deified man. [prec.]

dĕm'ijohn (-jŏn), n. Bulging narrow--necked bottle of 3–10 gal., usu. cased in wicker & with wicker handles. [corrupt. of F *dame-jeanne* Dame Jane; found in many langg., but earliest in F, prob. as playful personification]

dēmil'itarize, -ise (-īz), v.t. Take away the military organization from (frontier, zone, etc.). [DE-]

dĕm'ilune (-ōōn), n. (fortif.). Outwork

protecting bastion or curtain. [F, = half moon]

dĕm'ĭ-mŏnd|e, n. Class of women on outskirts of society, of doubtful reputation & standing. Hence ~*aine'* n., woman of the ~e. [F, = half world]

dĕm'ĭ-rĕp, n. Woman of suspected chastity. [abbr. for *demi-reputable*]

dĕmīse' (-z), v.t., & n. Convey, grant, (estate) by will or lease (n., this process); transmit (title etc.) by death or abdication (n., this event, esp. ~ *of the Crown*; transf., death). Hence **dĕmīs'ABLE** (-z-) a. [vb f. n., AF use of p.p. of OF *desmettre* DISMISS, in refl. abdicate]

dĕm'ĭsĕmĭquāv'er, n. (mus.). Note, with three-hooked symbol, equal to half a semiquaver. [DEMI-]

dĕmi'ssion (-shn), n. Resigning, abdication, *of*. [f. F *démission* f. L DI(*missionem* f. *mittere miss-* send, -ION)]

dĕmit', v.t. & i. (-tt-). Resign (office, or abs.).. [f. F *démettre* f. L DE(*mittere* send)]

dĕm'iŭr̄ge, n. Creator of world (in Platonic philosophy; also of Christian God, & of supposed subordinate agents in creation). Hence **dĕmiŭr̄'gɪc** a. [f. LL f. Gk *dēmiourgos* craftsman (*dēmios* f. DEMOS, -*ergos* working)]

dĕmŏb', v.t. (-bb-). Demobilize (esp. in p.p. of individuals released by demobilization). [abbr.]

dĕmŏb'ilĭz|e, -is|e (-ĭz), v.t. Release from mobilized state, disband, (troops, ships). Hence ~A'TION n. [DE-]

dĕmŏc'racy̆, n. (State practising) government by the people, direct or representative; *the* politically unprivileged class. [f. F *démocratie* f. LL f. Gk *dēmokratia* (DEMOS, -CRACY)]

dĕm'ocrăt, n. Advocate of democracy; *(D~)* member of Democratic party. Hence **dĕmŏc'ratISM**(3) n. [f. F *démocrate* (prec.)]

dĕmocrăt'ic, a. Of, like, practising, advocating, democracy; *D~party*, opposed to REPUBLICAN & supporting State, local, & individual liberty against federal powers. So **dĕmocrăt'ICALLY** adv., **dĕmŏc'ratIZE**(3) v.t. & i., **dĕmŏcratīzA'TION** n. [f. F *démocratique* (as prec.)]

Dĕmŏc'rĭtē'an, a. Of Democritus, his humour, or his theory of atoms. [f. L f. Gk *Dēmokriteios* of Democritus (Gk philosopher of 5th c. B.C. called the laughing philosopher, & an atomistic physicist) +-AN]

démodé (dāmōd'ā), a. Out of fashion. [F]

Dēmogŏrg'on, n. A mysterious & terrible infernal deity. [LL; perh. assim. of some Oriental name to Gk DEMOS, *gorgos* grim]

dēmŏg'raphy̆, n. Vital statistics, illustrating condition of communities. Hence

dēmŏg'RAPHER n., **dēmOGRAPH'IC** a. [DEMOS, -GRAPHY]

demoiselle (dĕm'wazĕl'), n. The Numidian crane. [F, = DAMSEL]

dĕmŏl'ish, v.t. Pull or throw down (building), destroy; overthrow (institution, theory); eat up. So **dĕmoli'TION** n. [f. F *démolir* (-ISH²) f. L DE(*moliri* construct *f. moles* mass)]

dēm'on, dae-, n. (Gk myth.; often *dae-*) supernatural being, inferior deity, spirit, ghost, indwelling or attendant spirit, genius; evil spirit (as in demoniacs); heathen deity; devil; malignant supernatural being; cruel, malignant, destructive, or fierce person (~ *bowler*, very fast; *is a ~ for work*, works strenuously); personified vice or passion. Hence **dēmono-** comb. form, **dēmonŏl'ATRY, dēmonŎL'OGY**, nn. [f. L f. Gk *daimōn* deity, w. sense also of L f. Gk *daimonion* divine (power etc.) neut. adj.]

dēmŏn'ĕtīze, -ise (-ĭz; *or* -mŭ-), v.t. Deprive (metal etc.) of its status as money. [f. F *démonétiser* (DE-, L *moneta* MONEY, -IZE)]

dēmŏn'ĭăc, a. & n. (Person) possessed by an evil spirit; of such possession; devilish; fiercely energetic, frenzied. [ME, f. LL *daemoniacus* (Gk *daimonion* see DEMON, -AC)]

dēmonī'acal, a. = prec. adj. (esp. in phr. ~ *possession*, & in sense *devilish*). [prec. +-AL]

dēmonī'ic, dae-, a. = prec, inspired, of supernatural genius or impulses. [f. LL f. Gk *daimonikos* (DEMON, -IC)]

dēm'onISM, n. Belief in the power of demons. [-ISM(3)]

dēm'onīze, -ise (-ĭz), v.t. Make into or like, represent as, a demon. [f. med. L *daemonizare* (DEMON, -IZE)]

dēmŏn'stra|ble (*or* dēm'on-), a. Capable of being shown or logically proved. Hence ~BIL'ITY n., ~BLY² adv. [ME, f. OF or L *demonstrabilis* (foll., -ABLE)]

dĕm'onstrāte, v.t. & i. Show (feelings etc.); describe & explain by help of specimens or experiments, teach as a demonstrator; logically prove the truth of; be a proof of the existence of; make a military demonstration; take part in a demonstration by public meeting, whence **dĕmŏn'strANT**(1) n. [f. L DE-(*monstrare* show, see MONSTER), -ATE³]

dĕmonstrā'tion, n. Outward exhibition of feeling etc.; logical proving, clear proof, (*to ~*, conclusively); thing serving as proof; exhibition & explanation of specimens or experiments as way of teaching; show of military force to intimidate, to mask other operations, or in peace to show readiness for war; exhibition of opinion on political or other question, esp. public meeting or procession, whence ~IST(1) (-sho-) n. Hence

~AL (-sho-) a. [ME, f. OF, or L *demonstratio* (prec., -ION)]

dĕmŏn′strative, a. & n. Serving to point out or exhibit (esp. in Gram., ~ *pronoun* or *adjective*, or ~ as noun, this etc.); giving proof *of*; logically conclusive; concerned with proof; given to or marked by open expression of feelings (~ *person*, *behaviour*, *affection*, etc.). Hence ~LY[2] (-vl-) adv., ~NESS (-vn-) n. [f. F *démonstratif* or L *demonstrativus* (as prec., -IVE)]

dĕm′onstrātor, n. One who demonstrates; teacher by demonstration, assistant to professor doing practical work with students; partaker in demonstration by public meeting. [L (DEMONSTRATE, -OR)]

dĕmō′ralīz|e, -is|e (-īz), v.t. Corrupt morals of, deprave; destroy the discipline, cohesion, courage, or endurance of (esp. troops; see MORALE). Hence ~A′TION n. [f. F *démoraliser* (DE-, MORAL, -IZE)]

dē mŏr′t′ŭĭs nĭl nĭs′ĭ bŏn′um, sent. Nothing but good should be spoken of the dead. [L]

Dēm′ŏs, n. Personification of the populace or democracy. [Gk, = people]

Dĕmŏsthĕn′ĭc, a. Like Demosthenes or his oratory; eloquent, patriotic, denunciatory, (of speech). [f. Gk *Dēmosthenikos* of Demosthenes (Attic orator 4th c. B.C.)]

*dĕmōte′, v.t. Reduce to lower rank or class. Hence dĕmō′tion n. [f. DE- +(PRO)MOTE]

dĕmŏt′ic, a. Popular, vulgar; (Archaeol.) in the popular form (opp. *hieratic*) of ancient Egyptian writing. [f. Gk *dēmotikos* (*dēmotēs* one of the DEMOS +-IC)]

dĕmŭl′cent, a. & n. Soothing (medicine). [f. L DE(*mulcēre* soothe), -ENT]

dĕmŭr′, v.i. (-rr-), & n. 1. Make difficulties, raise scruples or objections *to* or *at*; (Law) put in a demurrer, whence dĕmŭ′rrant(1) n. 2. n. Objecting, objection, (usu. *without, no,* ~). [f. OF *demorer* f. Rom. *DE(*morare* f. L -*i* delay]

dĕmūre′, a. Sober, grave, composed; ironically reserved; affectedly coy, prudish. Hence ~LY[2] (-rl-) adv., ~NESS (-rn-) n. [ME; perh. f. AF *demuré* f. OF *demorer* (prec.), w. sense-development as *staid*; infl. by obs. *mure* in same sense f. OF *meur* f. L *maturus* ripe]

dĕmŭ′rrable, a. That may be demurred to, open to objection, (esp. legal). [DEMUR, -ABLE]

dĕmŭ′rrage, n. Rate or amount payable to shipowner by charterer for failure to load or discharge ship within time allowed, similar charge on railway trucks; detention, delay; charge (1½*d.* per oz) of Bank of Engl. deducted in giving notes or gold for bullion. [f. DEMUR +-AGE]

dĕmŭ′rrer, n. Legal objection to relevance of opponent's point even if granted, which stays action till relevance is settled; exception taken. [f. AF *demurrer* infin. = DEMUR; -ER[4]]

dĕmў′, n. (pl. *-ies*, pr. -īz). Size of paper (printing, 17½ x 22½; writing, 15½ x 20); ‖ scholar of Magd. Coll., Oxford (orig. w. half fellow's allowance), whence ~SHIP n. [var. of DEMI-]

dĕn, n. Wild beast's lair; lurking-place of thieves etc.; small room unfit to live in; room in which person secludes himself to work etc. [OE *denn*, MLG *denne*, OHG *tenni*, f. WG *dannja, -jō*; cogn. w. DEAN[2]]

dēnār′ĭus, n. (pl. -ĭī). Ancient-Roman silver coin (orig. about 8*d.*), whence Engl. *d.* for penny. [f. *deni* ten each, -ARY[1]; *denarius* (*numus*) = (coin) of ten (asses)]

dĕn′arў, a. Of ten, decimal. [f. L (prec.)]

dĕnă′tionalīz|e, -is|e (-īz; -sho-), v.t. Deprive (nation) of its status or characteristics, (person) of membership or characteristics of his nation, (institution) of its position as national property. Hence ~A′TION n. [f. F *dénationaliser* (DE-, NATIONAL, -IZE)]

dĕnă′turalīz|e, -is|e (-īz; -cher-), v.t. Change nature of, make unnatural; (usu. refl.) divest of citizenship or membership of State. Hence ~A′TION n. [DE-, NATURAL, -IZE(3); also DE- +NATURALIZE]

dĕnă′ture, v.t. Change nature or essential qualities of (esp. tea or alcohol by adulteration). So dĕnā′turant (-chŏŏ-) n., substance used in denaturing. [f. F *dénaturer* (DE-, NATURE)]

dĕna′zi|fў (-ahts-), v.t. Rid of Nazism & its influence. Hence ~FICA′TION n. [DE-]

dĕn′drite, n. (Stone or mineral with) natural tree-like or moss-like marking. Hence dĕndrit′ic a. [F, f. Gk *dendritēs* adj. (*dendron* tree), -ITE[1]]

dĕndr(o)-, -i-, comb. forms, f. Gk *dendron* tree. Hence dĕn′drIFORM, dĕn′drOID, aa., dĕndrŏL′OGY, dĕndrŏL′OGIST, nn., dĕn′drOPHIL(E), dĕn′drOPHOBE, aa. & nn.

‖ dēne[1], n. Bare sandy tract, low sandhill, by sea. [perh. related to LG, Fris. *düne*, Du. *duin*, F *dune*]

dēne[2]. See DEAN[2].

dēnĕgā′tion, n. (arch.). Denial. [F (*déné-*), f. LL DE(*negationem* f. *negare* deny, -ATION)]

dēne-hōle, dāne-, n. (archaeol.). Artificial cave in chalk entered by vertical shaft often 60 ft deep. [orig. uncert.; perh. f. DANE]

dĕng′ue (′-nggĭ), n. Infectious eruptive fever causing acute pains in joints. [prob. f. Swahili name, w. assim. to Sp. *dengue* prudery, w. ref. to stiffness of patient's neck & shoulders]

dĕnī′able, a. That one can deny. [-ABLE]

dĕnī′al, n. Refusal of request; = SELF- -~; statement that thing is not true (*meet charge with flat* ~) or existent, contradiction; disavowal of person as one's leader etc. [DENY, -AL(2)]

dĕnī′er[1], n. One who denies. [DENY, -ER[1]]

denier'[2] (-nēr), n. **1.** (arch. or obs.). Very small sum or coin. **2.** (commerc.; *also* dĕn'yer, dĕn'iā). Unit of weight by which silk & rayon yarn is weighed & its fineness estimated. [OF, 1/12 of sou, f. DENARIUS]

dĕn'igr|āte, v.t. Blacken; defame, whence or cogn. ~ātor, ~a'tion, nn. [f. L DE(*nigrare* f. *niger* black)]

dĕn'im, n. Twilled cotton fabric used for overalls etc. [for *serge de Nim* (*Nîmes* in France)]

denīt'rāte, **denīt'rifȳ**, vv.t. Free of nitric or nitrous acid or nitrates. [DE-]

dĕn'izen, n., & v.t. **1.** Inhabitant, occupant, (*of* place); foreigner admitted to residence & certain rights; naturalized foreign word, animal, or plant; hence ~SHIP n. **2.** v.t. Admit as ~ (usu. pass.). [ME, f. AF *deinzein* (*deinz* = F *dans* f. L DE-, *intus* within, -*aneus* see -ANEOUS)]

denŏm'inate, v.t. Give name to, call or describe as so-&-so (w. obj. & compl.). [f. L DE(*nominare* NOMINATE)]

denŏmina'tion, n. Name, designation, esp. characteristic or class name; class of units in numbers, weights, money, etc. (*reduce to the same* ~; *money of small* ~s); class, kind, with specific name; religious sect, whence ~AL (-sho-) a. (~*al education*, according to principles of a Church or sect, whence ~alIZE(3) (-sho-) v.t.). [ME, f. OF, or L *denominatio* (prec., -ATION)]

denŏm'inative, a. Serving as, giving, a name. [f. F-*if*, or L *denominativus* (as prec., -ATIVE)]

denŏm'inātor, n. Number below line in vulgar fraction, divisor; *common* ~, (least) common multiple of the ~s of a number of fractions, also fig. [f. F -*teur*, or LL *denominator* (as prec., -OR)]

denota'tion, n. Denoting; expression by marks or symbols; sign, indication; designation; meaning of a term; (Log.) aggregate of objects that may be included under a word (cf. CONNOTATION), extension. [f. F, or L *denotatio* (DENOTE, -ATION)]

denōt'ative, a. Indicative *of*; (Log.) merely designating, implying no attributes, (cf. CONNOTATIVE). Hence ~LY[2] (-vl-) adv. [DENOTE, -ATIVE]

denōte', v.t. Mark out, distinguish, be the sign of; indicate, give to understand, (esp. *that*-clause); stand as name for; (Log.) be a name for, be predicated of, (*the word* white ~s *all white things, as* snow, paper, foam). Hence ~MENT (-tm-) n. [f. F *dénoter* or L DE(*notare* mark f. *nota* NOTE[1])]

denouement' (see Ap.), n. Unravelling of plot or complications, catastrophe, final solution, in play, novel, etc. [F (*dénouer* unknot, f. DE-, L *nodare* f. *nodus* knot, -MENT)]

denounce', v.t. Prophesy (woe, vengeance); inform against; openly inveigh

against; give notice of termination of (armistice, treaty). Hence ~MENT (-sm-) n. [ME, f. OF *denoncier* f. L DE(*nuntiare* f. *nuntius* messenger)]

de nouveau (de nōōvō'), adv. Afresh, starting again. [F]

dē nŏv'ō, adv. = prec. [L]

dĕnse, a. Closely compacted in substance; crowded together; crass, stupid. Hence ~'LY[2] (-sl-) adv., ~'NESS (-sn-) n. [f. F, or L *densus*]

dĕn'sitȳ, n. Closeness of substance; (Physics) degree of consistence measured by ratio of mass to volume or by quantity of matter in unit of bulk; crowded state; stupidity. [f. F *densité* or L *densitas* (prec., -TY)]

dĕnt, n., & v.t. (To mark with a) surface impression (as) from the blow of a blunt-edged instrument. [ME; var. of DINT]

dĕn'tal, a. & n. Of tooth, teeth, or dentistry; ~ *letter* or ~, made with tongue-tip against upper front teeth (as *th*) or front of palate (as *d*, *t*), whence ~IZE(3) v.t. [f. med. L *dentalis* f. L *dens dentis* tooth +-AL]

dĕn'tāte, a. (bot. & zool.). Toothed, with tooth-like notches. So **dĕnta'tion** n., **dĕntāt'o**- comb. form. [f. L *dentatus* (prec., -ATE[2])]

dĕn'ti-, comb. form of L *dens dentis* tooth, as ~*lingual* formed by teeth & tongue. Hence ~FORM, **dĕnti'gerous, aa.**

dĕn'ticle, n. Small tooth or tooth-like projection; = DENTIL. So **dĕntic'ūlar**[1], **dĕntic'ūlāte**[2] (-at) or -**āted**, aa., **dĕnticūla'tion** n. [f. L *denticulus* (prec., -CULE)]

dĕn'tifrice, n. Powder, paste, etc., for tooth-cleaning. [F, f. L DENTI(*fricium* f. *fricare* rub)]

dĕn'til, n. One of series of small rectangular blocks under bed-moulding of cornice in classical architecture (often ~-*cornice, -band, -moulding*). [f. obs. F *dentille* dim. of *dent* tooth f. L *dens dentis*]

dĕn'tine, n. Hard dense tissue forming main part of teeth. [f. L as prec. +-INE[4]]

dĕn'tist, n. One whose profession it is to treat diseases of the teeth, extract them, insert artificial ones, etc. Hence ~RY n. [f. F *dentiste* f. *dent* see DENTIL, -IST(3)]

dĕnti'tion, n. Cutting of teeth, teething; characteristic arrangement of teeth in animal. [f. L *dentitio* (*dentire* to teethe, -ION)]

dĕn'ture, n. Set of (usu. artificial) teeth. [F, f. *dent* tooth (see DENTIL) +-URE]

denūde' v.t. Make naked; strip of clothing, covering, possession, attribute; (Geol.) lay (rock, formation) bare by removal of what lies above. Hence **denūda'tion** n., **denūd'ative** a. [f. L DE(*nudare* f. *nudus* naked)]

denŭncia'tion, n. Denouncing; invective. So **denŭn'ciative, denŭn'ciatory**,

(-sha-) aa., **dĕnŭn'ciātoR** (-shI-) n. [F, or f. L *denuntiatio* (DENOUNCE, -ATION)]

dĕnÿ', v.t. Declare untrue or non-existent (~ *the charge, the possibility, that it is so, this to be the case*; rarely with *but* after neg., *I don't ~ but he may have thought so*); disavow, repudiate, (~ one's *word, signature, faith, leader*); refuse (person, thing, person a thing, thing *to* person; *I was denied this, this was denied me* or *to me*); ~ *oneself*, be abstinent; report as not at home, refuse access to, (person visited). [ME, f. OF *denier* f. L DE(*negare* say no)]

‖ **dĕ'odănd**, n. (hist.). Thing forfeited to Crown to be used in alms etc. as having caused a human death. [f. L *deo dandum* thing to be given to God]

dĕ'odār, n. Himalayan cedar. [f. Hind. *de'odar* f. Skr. *deva-dara* divine tree]

dĕŏd'oriz|e (*or* -ōd-), -**is|e** (-ĭz), v.t. Deprive of odour, disinfect. Hence ~A'TION, ~ER[1](2), nn. [DE-, L *odor* smell, -IZE]

dĕŏntŏl'ŏgy̆, n. Science of duty, ethics. So **dĕŏntoLO'GICAL** a., **dĕŏntŏl'OGIST** n. [f. Gk *deont-* part. st. of *dei* it is right, -O-, -LOGY]

Dĕ'ō ŏp'tĭmō măx'ĭmō, phr. To God the best & greatest (in dedications). [L]

Dĕ'ō volĕn'tĕ adv. (abbr. D.V.). God willing; if nothing occurs to prevent it. [L]

dĕpärt', v.i. & t. (Poet., arch., etc.) go away (*from*), take one's leave; set out, start, leave, (esp. in time-tables, as *dep. 6.30 a.m.*); die, leave by death, (~ *from life*, ~ *this life*); diverge, deviate, (~ *from received account, custom*). [ME, f. OF DE(*partir* f. L *partire* divide)]

dĕpärt'ĕd, a. & n. Bygone (~ *greatness*); deceased (person; esp. *the ~*). [-ED[1](2)]

dĕpärt'ment, n. Separate part of complex whole, branch, esp. of municipal or State administration; French administrative district; *~ *store*, large shop supplying all kinds of goods. So **dĕpärtmĕn'tAL** a., **dĕpärtmĕn'taLy̆[2]** adv. [f. F *département* (DEPART, -MENT)]

dĕpär'ture, n. Going away; deviation *from* (truth, standard); starting, esp. of train (*the ~ platform*); setting out on course of action or thought (esp. *new ~*); (Naut.) amount of ship's change of longitude in sailing. [f. OF *-ēure* (DEPART, -URE)]

dĕpa'stur|e (-ah-), v.t. & i. (Of cattle) graze upon, graze; put (cattle) to graze; (of land) feed (cattle). Hence ~AGE n. [DE-]

dĕpaup'erize, -**ise** (-ĭz), v.t. Raise from, rid of, pauperism. [DE-, PAUPER, -IZE]

dĕpĕnd', v.i. Hang down (poet., arch., etc.); be contingent (*it ~s upon himself*, i.e. upon his efforts, skill, wisdom, etc.; also abs. in *that ~s*, i.e. can only be answered conditionally); be grammatically dependent (*up*)on; rest for maintenance etc. *upon* (*she ~s upon her own efforts, her pen, her mother, my help*); reckon confidently *upon* (esp. in imperat.,

~ *upon it*, you may be sure); be waiting for settlement (of lawsuit, Bill, etc.). [ME, f. OF DE(*pendre* f. L *pendēre* suspend but with sense of *pendēre* be suspended)]

dĕpĕn'dab|le, a. That may be depended on. Hence ~leNESS (-ln-) n., ~LY[2] adv. [-ABLE]

dĕpĕn'dant, -**ent[1]**, n. One who depends on another for support, retainer, servant. [f. F *dépendant* part. (DEPEND, -ANT)]

dĕpĕn'dence, n. Depending (*upon*), being conditioned or subordinate or subject; living at another's cost; reliance, confident trust; thing relied on. [f. F *dépendance* (prec., -ANCE)]

dĕpĕn'dency̆, n. Something subordinate or dependent, esp. country or province controlled by another. [as prec., -ANCY, -ENCY]

dĕpĕn'dent[2], a. Depending (*on*), contingent, subordinate, subject; maintained at another's cost; (Gram. of clause, phrase, or word) in subordinate relation to a sentence or word. [earlier *-ant* = DEPENDANT]

dĕpic|t', v.t. Represent in drawing or colours; portray in words, describe. Hence or cogn. ~'tER[1], ~'toR, ~'tION, nn., ~'tIVE a. [f. L DE(*pingere pict-* paint)]

dĕpic'ture, v.t. Picture, depict. [DE-+PICTURE n.]

dĕp'il|āte, v.t. Remove hair from. Hence ~A'TION, ~ātoR, nn., **dĕpil'atORY** a. & n. [f. L DE(*pilare* f. *pilus* hair), -ATE[3]]

dĕplĕt|e', v.t. Empty out, exhaust; relieve of congestion. So **dĕplē'tION** n., ~'IVE a. & n., ~'ORY a. [f. L DE(*plēre -plet-* fill)]

dĕplōr|e', v.t. Bewail, grieve over, regret; be scandalized by. Hence ~'ABLE a., ~'abLY̆ adv., ~ABIL'ITY, ~'ableNESS, nn. [f. F *déplorer* or L DE(*plorare* bewail)]

dĕploy', v.t. & i., & n., (mil.). 1. Spread out (t. & i. of troops) from column into line; so ~MENT n. 2. n. Doing this. [f. F *déployer* f. L DIS(*plicare* fold), cf. DISPLAY]

dĕplume' (-ōō-), v.t. Pluck, strip of feathers. [ME, f. OF *deplumer* or med. L *deplumare* (DE-, L *pluma* feather)]

dĕpŏl'ariz|e, -**is|e** (-ĭz), v.t. (Opt.) change direction of polarization of (ray); (Electr. & Magn.) deprive of polarity; (fig.) disturb, shake loose, dissolve, (convictions, prejudices). Hence ~A'TION, ~ER[1](2), nn. [DE-]

dĕpōn'ent, a. & n. 1. (L & Gk gram.) (verb) passive (or, in Gk, middle) in form but active in sense (named from notion that they had laid aside the pass. sense). 2. Person making deposition under oath or giving written testimony for use in court etc. [f. L DE(*ponere posit-* place), -ENT]

dĕpŏp'ŭl|āte, v.t. & i. Reduce population; decline in population. So ~A'TION n. [f. L DE(*populari* lay waste f. *populus* people), -ATE[3]; see DISPEOPLE]

dĕpŏrt′, v.t. **1.** Bear or conduct one*self* in such a manner. **2.** Remove, esp. into exile, banish, whence **dēpŏrtA′tion** n., **dēpŏrtEE′** n., person who is or has been ~ed. [sense 1 f. OF *deporter* (DE-, *porter* carry f. L *portare*); sense 2 f. F *déporter* f. L DE(*portare* carry)]

dĕpŏrt′ment, n. Bearing, demeanour, manners; way a thing (e.g. metal in chem. experiment) behaves. [F (-*ement*), as prec. 1, -MENT]

dĕpŏs|e′ (-z), v.t. & i. Remove from office, esp. dethrone, whence ~′ABLE (-z-) a.; bear witness *that*, testify *to*, esp. on oath in court. [ME, f. OF *deposer* (DE- +*poser*); cf. LL *deponere* in same sense & see POSE[1]]

dĕpŏs′it[1] (-z-), n. Thing stored or entrusted for safe keeping; sum placed in bank, ‖ usu. at interest & not to be drawn on without notice (*on* ~, so disposed of; *has a current & a* ~ *account*); sum required and paid as pledge or earnest or first instalment; layer of precipitated matter, natural accumulation. [f. L DE(*positum* neut. p.p. of *ponere* place)]

dĕpŏs′it[2] (-z-), v.t. Lay down in a (usu. specified) place; lay (eggs; usu. with adv. etc.); (of water or natural agency) leave (layer of matter) lying; store or entrust for keeping (esp. sum at interest in bank); pay as pledge for fulfilment of contract or further payment. [f. obs. F *dépositer* or med. L *depositare* frequent. of L *deponere* see prec.]

dĕpŏs′itary (-z-), n. Person to whom thing is committed, trustee. [f. LL *depositarius* (DEPOSIT[1], -ARY[1])]

dĕposi′tion (-z-), n. (Picture of) taking down of Christ from the cross; deposing from office, esp. dethronement; (giving of) sworn evidence, allegation, (usu. dĕ-); depositing. [ME, f. OF, f. L *depositionem* f. *deponere* (DEPOSIT[1], -ION), used as n. of action of *depose, deposit*]

dĕpŏs′itor (-z-), n. Person who deposits money, property, etc.; apparatus for depositing some substance. [f. DEPOSIT + -OR]

dĕpŏs′itory (-z-), n. Storehouse (lit. & fig.); = DEPOSITARY. [f. LL *depositorium* (DEPOSIT[1], -ORY)]

dĕp′ot (-ō), n. **1.** (Mil.) place for stores; headquarters of regiment; recruit- -drilling station; ‖ part of regiment not on foreign service. **2.** Storehouse, emporium; *(pr. dē′pō) railway station. [f. F *dépôt* f. L as DEPOSIT[1]]

dĕprāve′, v.t. Make bad, deteriorate, pervert, corrupt, esp. in moral character or habits. So **dĕpravA′tion** n. [ME, f. OF *depraver* or L DE(*pravare* f. *pravus* crooked)]

dĕprăv′itў, n. Moral perversion, viciousness; (Theol.) innate corruption of man. [DE- +obs. *pravity* f. L *pravitas* (prec., -TY)]

dĕp′rĕcāt|e, v.t. Plead against (~*e* one's

anger, beseech him not to be angry); express wish against or disapproval of (~*e war, hasty action, panic*). Hence or cogn. ~**ingLY**[2] adv., **dĕprĕcA′tion** n., ~**ive**, ~**ory**, aa. [f. LL DE(*precari* pray), -ATE[3]]

dĕpre′ciāt|e (-shĭ-), v.t. & i. Diminish (t. & i.) in value; lower market price of; reduce purchasing power of (money); disparage, belittle. Hence ~**ingLY**[2] adv., ~**ory** (-sha-) a. [f. L DE(*pretiare* f. *pretium* price), -ATE[3]]

dĕprēciā′tion (-ēsĭ-, -ēshĭ-), n. Depreciating or being depreciated; allowance made in valuations, estimates, and balance sheets, for wear & tear. [prec., -ATION]

dĕprĕdā′tion, n. (usu. pl.). Spoliation, ravages. [F (dé-), f. LL DE(*praedationem* f. *praedare* f. *praeda* prey, -ATION)]

dĕp′rĕdātor, n. Spoiler, pillager. [f. LL *depraedator* (prec., -OR)]

dĕprĕss′, v.t. Push or pull down, lower; bring low, humble; reduce activity of (esp. trade); lower (voice) in pitch; dispirit, deject; ~*ed classes* (Indian pol.), persons of the lowest Indian castes, untouchables. So ~**IBLE** a. [f. OF *depresser* f. LL DE(*pressare* frequent. of *premere* PRESS[2])]

dĕprĕss′ant, a. & n. (med.). Lowering, sedative, (medicine). [prec. + -ANT]

dĕprĕss′ion (-shn), n. Lowering, sinking; (Astron.) angular distance of star etc. below horizon; sunk place, hollow, on surface; reduction in vigour (esp. of trade), in pitch (of voice), vitality, or spirits; (Meteorol.) lowering of barometer or atmospheric pressure, esp. centre of minimum pressure or system of winds round it. [ME, f. OF, or LL DE(*pressio* f. *premere* press- press, -ION)]

dĕprĕss′or, n. (anat.). ~ *muscle* or ~, one pulling down some organ etc. [LL (prec., -OR)]

dĕprivā′tion (*or* -ī-), n. Loss, being deprived, *of*; deposition from esp. ecclesiastical office; felt loss (*that is a great* ~). [f. med. L *deprivatio* (foll., -ATION)]

dĕpriv|e′, v.t. Strip, bereave, debar from enjoyment, *of*; depose (esp. clergyman) from office. Hence ~′**ABLE** a., ~′**AL**(2) n. [ME, f. OF *depriver* f. med. L DE(*privare* f. L *privare* deprive)]

dē profŭn′dis, n. & adv. (Cry) from the depths of sorrow etc. [initial L wds of *Ps*. cxxx]

dĕpth, n. Being DEEP; measurement from top down, from surface inwards, or from front to back; abstruseness; sagacity; intensity of colour, darkness, etc.; (pl.) deep water, deep place, abyss, lowest or inmost part; middle (*in the* ~ *of winter*); deep or mysterious region of thought, feeling, etc. (*cry from the* ~*s*, ~ *of inspiration*, ~*s of degradation*); *out of* one's

For compounds of de- not given consult DE-**.**

~, in water too deep to stand in, (fig.) engaged on too hard a task or subject; **~-charge**, bomb for dropping on submerged submarine, set to explode at desired **~**. [ME; DEEP, -TH[1]]

dĕp'ūr|āte, v.t. & i. Make, become, free from impurities. So **~A'TION**, **~ātor**, nn., **dĕpūr'ative** a. & n. [f. med. L DE-(*purare* f. L *purus* pure)]

dĕpūtā'tion, n. Body of persons appointed to represent others. [f. LL *deputatio* (foll., -ATION)]

dĕpūte', v.t. Commit (task, authority) to substitute; appoint as one's substitute. [ME, f. OF *deputer* f. L DE(*putare* think) regard as, allot]

dĕp'ūtize, -ise (-īz), v.t. Act as deputy or understudy (*for*), esp. in musical engagements. [foll. + -IZE]

dĕp'ūtў, n. Person appointed to act for another or others (*by* ~, by proxy; ~ *lieutenant*, abbr. D. L., ~ of Lord Lieutenant of county); member of deputation; parliamentary representative (*Chamber of Deputies*, lower house in French & other Parliaments); || manager of doss-house; **~-**, deputed, acting-. Hence **~SHIP**(1) n. [ME, f. OF *depute* p.p. of *deputer* DEPUTE, -Y[4]]

dĕrā'cināte, v.t. Tear up by the roots. [f. F *déraciner* (DE-, *racine* f. LL *radicina* dim. of *radix* root), -ATE[3]]

dĕrail', v.t. & i. Cause (train etc.) to leave the rails (usu. pass.); (rarely) leave the rails. So **~MENT** n. [f. F *dérailler* (DE-, *rail* rail)]

dĕrânge' (-j), v.t. Throw into confusion or out of gear, disorganize, cause to act irregularly; make insane (esp. in p.p.); disturb, interrupt. So **~MENT** (-jm-) n. [f. F *déranger* (DE-, *rang* rank)]

dĕrāte', v.t. Remove proportion of rates incident on (*derating scheme, bill*). [DE-]

dĕrā'tion, v.t. Remove (food etc.) from rationed category. [DE-]

Der'bў (där-), n. **1.** Annual horse-race at Epsom; ~ *day*, of the race; ~ *dog*, any dog straying on course, (fig.) trivial untimely interruption. ***2.** (*d*~; pron. dĕr-) bowler hat. [Earl of ~ founder 1780]

Der'bўshire (där-; -sher), a. ~ *neck*, goitre, bronchocele; ~ *spar*, fluor-spar.

de règle (rā'gl), pred. a. Customary, proper. [F]

dĕ'rĕlict, a. & n. Abandoned, ownerless, (esp. of ship at sea); abandoned property, esp. ship; person abandoned by society. [f. L DE(*relict-* see RELINQUISH)]

dĕrĕlic'tion, n. Abandoning, being abandoned; retreat of sea exposing new land; neglect *of duty*; failure in duty, short-coming. [f. L *derelictio* (prec., -ION)]

dĕrĕquisi'tion (-z-), v.t. Free (requisitioned property). [DE-]

dĕrīde', v.t. Laugh to scorn. [f. L DE(*ridēre ris-* laugh)]

de rigueur (rēgĕr'), pred. a. Required by etiquette (*evening dress is* ~). [F]

dĕrī'sion (-zhn), n. Ridicule, mockery, (*hold, have, in* ~, mock at; *be in* ~, be mocked at; *bring into* ~); laughing-stock. [ME, f. OF, f. LL *derisionem* (DERIDE, -ION)]

dĕrī'ive, dĕrīs'orў, aa. Scoffing (~ *cheers*, ironical); (-*ory* only; of offer etc.) ridiculously futile, not to be taken seriously. Hence **dĕrīs'ively**[2] (-vl-) adv. [f. L *deris-* see DERIDE, + -IVE, -ORY]

dĕrivā'tion, n. Obtaining from a source; extraction, descent; formation of word from word or root, tracing or statement of this (cf. COGNATE); theory of evolution, whence **~IST**(2) n. [f. F, or L *derivatio* (DERIVE, -ATION)]

dĕriv'ative, a. & n. (Thing, word, chemical substance) derived from a source, not primitive or original. Hence **~LY**[2] (-vl-) adv. [f. F *dérivatif* f. LL *derivativus* (foll., -IVE)]

dĕriv|e', v.t. & i. Get, obtain, (*from* a source, or ·with the source present in thought); have one's or its *origin* etc. *from*; gather, deduce, (knowledge, truth, ideas, etc.) *from*; (pass., refl., & intr.) be descended or have one's origin *from*; (pass., of words) be formed *from*; trace, show, or assert, descent, origin, or formation, of (person, thing, word) *from*. Hence **~'ABLE** a. [f. OF *deriver* or L *derivare* (DE-, *rivus* stream) divert, derive]

dĕrm, n. Skin; true skin or layer of tissue below epidermis. Hence or cogn. **~'AL**, **~'IC**, aa., **~'at**(o)-, **~o-**, comb. forms, **~atīt'is** n., inflammation of the skin, **~atŏl'ogy**, **~atŏl'ogist**, nn. [f. Gk *derma* skin (*derō* flay, -M)]

dern. = DARN[3].

dernier ressort (dĕrnyā' resŏr'), n. Last resort, desperate expedient. [F]

dĕ'rogate, v.i. Detract, take away part, *from* (a merit, right, etc.); sink in the scale, do something derogatory. [f. L DE(*rogare* ask), -ATE[3]]

dĕrogā'tion, n. Lessening or impairment *of* law, authority, position, dignity, etc.; deterioration, debasement. [ME, f. OF, or L *derogatio* (prec., -ATION)]

dĕrŏg'atorў, a. Tending to detract *from*, involving impairment, disparagement, or discredit, *to*; lowering, unsuited to one's dignity or position; depreciatory. [f. LL *derogatorius* (DEROGATE, -ORY)]

dĕ'rrick, n. Contrivance for moving or hoisting heavy weights, kind of crane with adjustable arm pivoted at foot to central post, deck, or floor; framework over oil-well or similar boring. [obs. senses *hangman*, *gallows*, f. name of hangman *c.* 1600]

dĕ'rring-dō', n. (pseudo-arch.). Desperate courage. [f. Chaucer's *In dorryng don that longeth to a knyght* (in daring to do that which belongeth etc.) misinterpreted by Spenser]

dĕ'rringer (-j-), n. Small large-bore pistol. [U.S. inventor's name] dĕ´rris, n. Kinds of tall tropical woody climbers; insecticide made from the powdered tuberous root of some of these. [Gk, = leather covering]

dĕ´rv, n. Fuel oil used in heavy road vehicles. [f. *Diesel*-engined *r*oad *v*ehicle]

dĕr´vish, n. Moslem friar vowed to poverty & austerity (*dancing* or *whirling* ~, *howling* ~, according to the practice of his order). [f. Pers. *darvesh* poor]

dĕs´cant[1], n. (Poet.) melody, song; (Mus.) melodic independent treble accompaniment. [ME, f. OF *deschant* f. med. L DIS(*cantus* CHANT)]

dĕscănt´[2], v.i. Talk at large, dwell freely, *upon* (esp. in praise, ~ *upon the beauties of*). [f. OF *deschanter* f. med. L *discantare* (prec.)]

dĕscĕnd´, v.i. & t. Come or go down, sink, fall, (~*ing letter* in Typ., with tail below line); slope downwards; make sudden attack *upon*; proceed in narrative etc. from earlier to later time, from greater to less (so Math., ~*ing series* of numbers), from general to particular; stoop *to* do; (rare) be DESCENDED *from*; be transmitted by inheritance *from* of qualities, property, privileges, pass (*to* heir, or abs.); go down (hill, stairs). Hence ~ER[1] n., ~ing letter. [ME, f. OF *descendre* f. L DE(*scendere* = *scandere* climb)]

dĕscĕn´dant, n. Person or thing DE-SCENDED (*of*, or with *his* etc.) [F (prec., -ANT)]

dĕscĕn´dĕd, p.p. Sprung, having origin, *from* ancestor or stock (*is* ~ etc. usual instead of the rare *descends* etc.). [-ED[1](2)]

dĕscĕn´dible, -able, a. Transmissible by inheritance. [OF (-*able*); see -BLE]

dĕscĕnt´, n. Descending, downward motion; downward slope; way down; sudden attack, esp. from sea; decline, sinking in scale, fall; being descended, lineage; single generation (*lineal succession of four* ~s); transmission of property, title, or quality, by inheritance. [ME, f. OF *descente* (*descendre* DESCEND)]

dĕscrīb|e´, v.t. Set forth in words, recite the characteristics of; qualify *as* (*should* ~*e him as a scoundrel*); mark out, draw, (esp. geom. figure); move in (such a line, curve); (abs.) deal in, give a, description. Hence ~´ABLE a. [f. L DE(*scribere script*-write)]

dĕscrip´tion, n. Describing, verbal portrait(ure), of person, object, or event (*answers to the* ~, has the qualities specified), more or less complete definition; sort, kind, class, (*no food of any* ~, *tyrant of the worst* ~). [ME, f. OF, f. L *descriptionem* (DESCRIBE, -ION)]

dĕscrip´tive, a. Serving to describe (~ *touches*), fond of describing (~ *writer*). Hence ~LY[2] (-vl-) adv. [f. LL *descriptivus* (DESCRIBE, -IVE)]

dĕscrȳ´, v.t. Catch sight of, succeed in discerning (lit. & fig.). [ME; prob. var. of obs. *descrive* f. OF *descrivre* DESCRIBE, & confused in early use with DECRY]

dĕs´ēcr|āte, v.t. Deprive of sacred character; outrage, profane, (sacred thing); dedicate *to* (evil). Hence ~A´TION, ~āTOR, nn. [DE- +(CON)SECRATE]

*dĕsĕg´rēgāte, v.t. Abolish racial segregation in (schools etc.). [DE-]

dĕsĕn´sitize, -ise (-īz), v.t. Reduce or destroy the sensitiveness of (photographic plates etc.). [DE-]

dĕsĕrt´[1] (-z-), n. Deserving, worthiness of recompense good or bad; character that deserves good, virtue, whence ~LESS a.; deserving people; (pl.) acts or qualities deserving good or bad recompense, such recompense, (*reward him according to, give him, he has got, his* ~s). [ME, f. OF obs. p.p. of *deservir* DESERVE]

dĕs´ert[2] (-z-), a. & n. **1.** Uninhabited, desolate; uncultivated, barren. **2.** n. Waterless & treeless region, (fig.) uninteresting or barren subject, period, etc.; ~ *rat* (colloq.), soldier of 7th (British) armoured division, which had a jerboa's figure as divisional sign, & which fought in the ~ campaign in N. Africa (1941-2). [ME; OF a. f. LL p.p. see foll.; n. f. LL *desertum* (cl. L *deserta* neut. pl.)]

dĕsĕrt´[3] (-z-), v.t. & i. Abandon, give up, (thing); depart from (place, haunt); forsake (person or thing having claims on one, as *wife, post, the colours, ship*); fail (*his presence of mind* ~*ed him*); run away (esp. from service in armed forces), whence ~ER[1] (-z-) n. So dĕsĕr´tION (-z-) n. [f. F *déserter* f. LL *desertare* frequent. of L DE(*serere sert*- join)]

dĕsĕrv|e´ (-z-), v.t. & i. Be entitled by conduct or qualities to (good or bad); have established a claim to be *well* or *ill* treated at the hands *of*. Hence ~´edLY[2] (-z-) adv. [ME, f. OF *deservir* f. L DE-(*servire* serve)]

dĕsĕrv´ing (-z-), a. Meritorious; worthy (*of* praise, censure, etc.). [-ING[2]]

déshabillé(see Ap.), n. = DISHABILLE. [F]

dĕs´icc|āte, v.t. Dry, dry up, (esp. milk etc. for preservation). So ~A´TION, ~-ātOR, nn., ~ATIVE a. [f. L DE (*siccare* f. *siccus* dry), -ATE[3]]

dĕsid´erāte, v.t. (pedant.). Feel to be missing, regret absence of, wish to have. [f. L DE(*siderare* see CONSIDER), -ATE[3]]

dĕsid´erative, a. & n. (gram.). (Verb, conjugation, etc.) formed on another verb etc. & expressing desire of doing the action. [f. LL *desiderativus* (prec., -IVE)]

dĕsiderāt´um, n. (pl. *-ta*). Thing missing, felt want. [L (neut. p.p. see DESIDERATE)]

dĕsign´[1] (-zīn), n. Mental plan; scheme of attack *upon* (*has* ~*s upon me*); purpose (*whether by accident or* ~); end in view; adaptation of means to ends (*the argu*-

ment from ~, maintaining existence of a God by pointing to such adaptation); preliminary sketch for picture etc.; delineation, pattern; artistic or literary groundwork, general idea, construction, plot, faculty of evolving these, invention. [f. 15th-c. F *desseing* f. *desseigner* see foll.]

desiġn'² (-zīn), v.t. & i. Set (thing) apart *for* person; destine (person, thing) *for* a service; contrive, plan; purpose, intend, (~*s an attack, to* do, *doing, or that* —, thing or person *to* be or do something), whence ~**ĕdLY²** (-zīn-) adv.; make preliminary sketch of (picture); draw plan of (building etc. to be executed by others); be a designer; conceive mental plan for, construct the groundwork or plot of, (book, work of art). [f. F *désigner* appoint f. L *designare* DESIGNATE², with senses also of obs. F *desseigner* purpose & mod..F *dessiner* draw]

dĕs'iġnate¹ (-z-), a. (placed after its noun). Appointed to office but not yet installed (*bishop* ~ etc.). [f. L p.p. (foll., -ATE²)]

dĕs'iġnāte² (-z-), v.t. Specify, particularize; serve as name or distinctive mark of; style, describe as; appoint to office (*as, to, for*). [f. L DE(*signare* f. *signum* mark), -ATE³]

dĕsiġnā'tion (-z-), n. Appointing to office; name, description, title. [f. L as prec., -ATION]

dĕsiġn'er (-zīn-), n. In vbl senses; esp. draughtsman who makes plans for manufacturers. [-ER¹]

dĕsiġn'ing (-zīn-), a. In vbl senses; esp. crafty, artful, scheming. [-ING²]

dĕsip'ience, n. Trifling, silliness. [f. L *desipientia* f. DE(*sipere = sapere* be wise)]

dĕsīr'a|ble (-z-), a. Worth wishing for. Hence ~**BIL'ITY**, ~**bleNESS**, nn., ~**bLY²** adv., (-z-). [ME, f. OF (DESIRE², -ABLE)]

dĕsīre'¹ (-z-), n. Unsatisfied appetite, longing, wish, craving; request; thing desired. [ME, f. OF *desir*, f. vb (foll.)]

dĕsīre'² (-z-), v.t. Long for, crave, wish, (noun, infin., noun & infin., or *that*-clause); (abs.) feel desire; ask for; pray, entreat, command, (~ *him to wait*; *she* ~*d we would wait*). [ME, f. OF *desirer* f. L *desiderare* DESIDERATE]

dĕsīr'ous (-z-), pred. a. Wishful *to* do, ambitious *of* (success etc.), having the desire *of* doing, wishful *that*. [f. AF *-ous*, = OF *-eus*, f. Rom. *desiderosus* (prec., -OUS)]

dĕsist' (-zī-, -sī-), v.i. Cease (*from doing, from* sin). [f. OF *desister* f. L DE(*sistere* stop)]

dĕsk, n. Fixed or movable piece of furniture or box having (often in combination with drawers, seat, etc.) a board usu. sloped serving as rest for writing or reading at; *the* ~, clerical, office, or literary work. Hence ~'**FUL²** n. [ME, f. med. L *desca* f. L *discus* disc]

dĕs'man, n. Aquatic insectivorous shrewlike mammal of Russia and the Pyrenees. [F & G, f. Sw. *desman-råtta* musk-rat]

dĕs'olate¹, a. Left alone, solitary; uninhabited; ruinous, neglected, barren, dreary; forlorn, disconsolate, wretched. Hence ~**LY²** (-tl-) adv., ~**NESS** (-tn-) n. [ME, f. L DE(*solare* f. *solus* alone). -ATE²]

dĕs'olāt|e², v.t. Depopulate; devastate; make (person) wretched. Hence ~**OR** n. [ME, f. prec., see -ATE³]

dĕsolā'tion, n. Desolating; neglected, ruined, solitary, or barren state; being forsaken, loneliness; dreary sorrow. [ME, f. LL *desolatio* (as prec., -ATION)]

dĕspair', n., & v.i. 1. Loss, utter want, of hope; thing that causes this, whether by badness or unapproachable excellence. 2. v.i. Lose, be without, hope (*of, or* abs.; *his life is* ~*ed of*); hence ~**inġLY²** adv. [ME, f. OF *despeir*- stressed st. of *desperer* f. L DE(*sperare* hope)]

|| **despatch**. See disp-.

dĕsperad'ō (-ahd-, -ād-), n. (pl. *-oes*). Person ready for or given to reckless, esp. criminal, undertakings. [OSp.(adj. only), f. L *desperatus* see foll.]

dĕs'perate, a. Leaving no or little room for hope, extremely dangerous or serious, utterly impracticable; reckless from despair, violent, lawless, staking all on a small chance, so **dĕsperA'TION** n.; extremely bad (*a* ~ *night, storm,* etc.); very great (~ *fear, a* ~ *fool*). So ~**LY²** (-tl-) adv., ~**NESS** (-tn-) n. [ME, f. L DE(*sperare* hope), -ATE²]

dĕs'picab|le, a. Vile, contemptible. Hence ~**LY²** adv. [f. LL *despicabilis* f. DE(*spicari* cf. *specere* look at), -BLE]

dĕspīse' (-z), v.t. Look down upon, contemn. [ME; f. *despis-* st. of OF *despire* f. L DE(*spicere = specere* look at)]

dĕspīte', n. & prep. Outrage, injury, contumely, (arch.); malice, spite, offended pride (*died of mere* ~); *in* ~ *of,* ~ *of,* ~, notwithstanding the opposition of, in the teeth of, in spite of, (also *in my* etc. ~, in spite of my etc. efforts, arch.). Hence ~**FUL** a., ~**fulLY²** adv., (-tf-). [ME, f. OF *despit* f. L *despectus -ūs* f. *despicere* see prec.]

dĕspoil', v.t. Plunder, spoil, rob, deprive, (person or place; often *of*). Hence or cogn. ~**ER¹**, ~**MENT**, **dĕspoliā'TION**, nn. [ME, f. OF *despoiller* (now *dépouiller*) f. L DE(*spoliare* spoil)]

dĕspónd', v.i., & n. 1. Lose heart, be dejected; so ~**ENCY** n., ~**ENT** a., ~**entLY²**, ~**inġLY²**, advv. 2. n. (Arch., only in SLOUGH *of D*~) dejection. [ME, f. L DE(*spondēre* promise) give up, resign]

dĕs'pot, n. Absolute ruler, whence ~**IST**(2) n.; tyrant, oppressor. So **dĕspŏt'IC** a., **dĕspŏt'ICALLY** adv. [f. F *despote* f. med. L *despota* f. Gk *despotēs*]

dĕs'potism, n. Arbitrary rule; State under a despot. [f. F *despotisme* (prec., -ISM)]

dĕs'quam|āte, v.i. Come off in scales. Hence ~**A'TION** n., **dĕsquăm'ative**, dèsquăm′atORY, aa. [f. L DE(*squamare* f. *squama* scale)]

dèssêrt′ (-z-), n. ‖ Course of fruit, sweets, etc., at end of dinner; ∼-SPOON. [F, f. *desservir* (des- f. L dis-, *servir* SERVE) clear the table]

dèstĭnā′tion, n. Place for which person or thing is bound. [OF, or f. L *destinatio* (foll., -ATION)]

dĕs′tĭne, v.t. Appoint, fore-ordain, devote, set apart, (person or thing to do, *to* or *for* a service, achievement, etc.; of God, Fate, etc., or of persons; but chiefly in pass.); *was* ∼*d to*, was, as we now know, to. [ME, f. F *destiner* f. L DE(*stinare* prob. causative of *stare* stand)]

dĕs′tĭnў, n. Predetermined events; person's, country's, etc., appointed or ultimate lot; power that fore-ordains, invincible necessity. [ME, f. OF *destinee* (prec., -Y⁴)]

dĕs′tĭtūte, a. Without resources, in want of necessaries; devoid *of*. So dĕstĭtū′tION n. [f. L DE(*stituere -tut-* = *statuere* place) forsake]

dĕs′trĭer, n. (hist.). War-horse. [OF, f. Gallo-Rom. *dextrarius hand-led(DEXTER, -ARY¹)]

dèstroy′, v.t. Pull down, demolish, undo, make useless, kill, annihilate, nullify, neutralize effect of. Hence ∼ABLE a. [ME, f. OF *destruire* f. Rom. *destrugere f. L DE(*struere struct*- build)]

dèstroy′er, n. In vbl senses; esp. (orig. *torpedo-boat* ∼) a warship designed to attack the enemy with torpedoes and to protect her own fleet from attacks by enemy light surface craft and submarines. [-ER¹]

dèstrŭc′tĭ|ble, a. Able to be destroyed. Hence ∼BIL′ITY n. [f. LL *destructibilis* (DESTROY, -BLE)]

dèstrŭc′tion, n. DESTROYing or being destroyed; what destroys, cause of ruin, (*is our* ∼). [ME, f. OF f. L *destructionem* (DESTROY, -ION)]

dèstrŭc′tive, a. & n. **1.** Destroying; deadly *to*, causing destruction *of*; (of criticism or policy) merely negative, refuting etc. without amending, not constructive; hence ∼LY² (-vl-) adv., ∼NESS (-vn-) n. **2.** n. Person, thing, that aims at or effects destruction. [ME, f. OF (-*if*, -*ive*), f. LL *destructivus* (DESTROY, -IVE)]

‖ dèstrŭc′tor, n. Refuse-burning furnace. [LL, = destroyer (DESTROY, -OR)]

dĕs′uetŭde (-swĭ-), n. Passing into, state of, disuse. [f. F *désuétude* or L DE(*suetudo* f. *suescere suet*- be wont, -TUDE)]

dèsŭl′phurīz|e (-fer-), -is|e (-ĭz), v.t. Free from sulphur. Hence ∼A′TION n. [DE-]

dĕs′ultor|ў, a. Skipping from one subject to another, disconnected, unmethodical. Hence ∼ĭLY² adv., ∼ĭNESS n. [f. L

desultorius f. desultor circus-rider f. DE(*sult-* = *salt-* p.p. st. of *salire* leap)]

dēsўnŏn′ўmīze, -ise (-ĭz), v.t. Differentiate in sense (synonymous words). [DE-, SYNONYM, -IZE]

dètăch′, v.t. Unfasten & remove (*from*, or abs.; ∼*ed mind, view*, etc., regarding things impartially, free from prejudice; ∼*ed house*, not joined to another on either side); (Mil. & Nav.) send (ship, regiment, etc.) on separate mission. Hence ∼ABLE a., ∼èdLY² adv., ∼èdNESS n. [f. F *détacher*; see DE-, ATTACH]

dètăch′ment, n. Detaching; portion of army etc., or large body, separately employed; standing aloof from or unaffected by surroundings, public opinion, etc., independence of judgement, selfish isolation. [f. F *détachement* (prec., -MENT)]

dĕt′ail¹, n. Dealing with things item by item (*in* ∼; *go into* ∼, give the items separately; minute account, number of particulars; item, small or subordinate particular, (*but that is a* ∼, often iron. to call special attention), whence ∼ED² (-ld) a., with particulars; minor decoration in building, picture, etc., way of treating this; (Mil.) distribution of orders of the day, small detachment. [f. F *détail* f. *détailler* see foll.]

dètail′², v.t. Give the particulars of, relate circumstantially; (Mil.) tell off for special duty.` [f. F *détailler* (DE-, *tailler* cut, see TAILOR)]

dètain′, v.t. Keep in confinement; withhold (money due etc.); keep waiting, hinder. Hence ∼EE n., person ∼ed in custody, usu. on political grounds. [f. OF *detenir* f. Rom. *detenēre f. L DE(*tinēre -tent-* = *tenēre* hold)]

dètain′er, n. (legal). Detaining of goods taken from owner for distraint etc.; keeping of person in confinement; writ by which person already arrested may be detained on another suit. [f. AF *detener* f. OF *detenir* see prec., -ER⁴]

dètĕct′, v.t. Find out (guilty person, person *in doing*); discover existence or presence of. Hence or cogn. dètĕc′tABLE a., dètĕc′tION n. [f. L DE(*tegere tect-* cover)]

dètĕc′tive, a. & n. **1.** Serving to detect. **2.** n. Policeman employed to investigate special cases (*private* ∼, person undertaking special inquiries for pay; *amateur* ∼, person who sets up theories on police cases); ∼ *story* etc. (that tempts readers to solve ∼ problems). [prec., -IVE]

dètĕc′tor, n. In vbl senses; also or esp.: coherer used in wireless telegraphy; valve in wireless receiving set. [-OR]

dètĕnt′, n. Catch by removal of which machinery is set working, (in clocks etc.) catch that regulates striking. [f. F *détente* f. *détendre* slacken (DE-, L *tendere* stretch)]

For compounds of de- not given consult DE-.

détente (see Ap.), n. Easing of strained relations esp. between States. [F, as prec.]

dêtên'tion, n. Detaining, being detained; arrest, confinement, (*House of D*~, lock-up); compulsory delay; (at schools) keeping in as punishment; ~ *barracks*, military prison. [F, or f. LL *detentio* (DETAIN, -ION)]

détenu (dātenoō'), n. Person detained in custody. [F, p.p. of *détenir* detain]

dēter', v.t. (-rr-). Discourage or hinder (*from*, or abs.) by or as fear, dislike of trouble, etc. Hence **dēter'rrENT**(2) a. & n., **dětě'rrENCE**, ~**MENT**, nn. [f. L DE(*terrēre* frighten)]

dēter'gent, a. & n. Cleansing (agent). [f. L DE (*tergēre* ters- wipe), -ENT]

dētēr'ior|āte, v.t. & i. Make, grow, worse. Hence or cogn. ~A'TION n., ~ātīvE a. [f. L *deteriorare* (*deterior* worse f. *de* down), -ATE[3]]

dětěrm'inant, a. & n. Determining, decisive, conditioning, defining, (agent, factor, element, word). [DETERMINE, -ANT]

dětěrm'inate, a. Limited, definite, distinct, finite, definitive. Hence ~LY[2] (-tl-) adv., ~NESS (-tn-) n. [ME, f. L p.p. (DETERMINE, -ATE[2])]

dětěrminā'tion, n. (Law) cessation of estate or interest; conclusion of debate; judicial sentence; fixing of date etc.; delimitation, definition; exact ascertainment *of* amount etc.; fixed direction, decisive bias, (~ *of blood to* some part, tendency to flow there); settling of purpose, fixed intention; resoluteness. [ME, f. OF, or L *determinatio* (DETERMINE, -ATION)]

dětěrm'inātive, a. & n. (Thing) that impels in a certain direction; (attribute, mark, symbol) serving to define or qualify. [f. F *déterminatif* (foll., -IVE)]

dětěrm'in|e, v.t. & i. Bring, come, to an end (esp. in law); limit in scope, define; fix beforehand (date); settle, decide, (dispute, person's fate, *what* is to be done, *that* —, *whether*, etc.), come to a conclusion, give decision; be the decisive factor in regard to (*demand* ~*es supply*); ascertain precisely, fix; give an aim to, direct, impel *to*; decide (person) *to do*; resolve (*to do, that* —, *on doing, on* a course; *be* ~*ed*, have resolved). Hence ~ABLE a. [f. OF *determiner* f. L DE(*terminare* f. *terminus* end)]

dětěrm'ined (-nd). a. In verbal senses; also, resolute, unflinching. [-ED[1]]

dětěrm'in|ism, n. Theory that human action is not free but determined by motives regarded as external forces acting on the will. So ~IST(2) n. & a., ~is'tIC a. [f. F -*isme* or G -*ismus* (Kant)]

dětěrs'īve, a. & n. Cleansing (substance). [f. F *détersif* (DETERGENT, -IVE)]

dětěst', v.t. Abhor, dislike intensely. Hence or cogn. ~ABLE a., ~ableNESS (-ln-) n., ~ablY[2] adv. [f. L DE*testari* call·God to witness against]

dětěstā'tion, n. Abhorrence (*have, hold, in* ~, abhor); detested person or thing. [F, or f. L *detestatio* (prec., -ATION)]

dēthrōne', v.t. Depose (ruler, dominant influence). Hence ~MENT (-nm-) n. [DE-]

dět'inūe, n. (legal). *Action of* ~, suit for recovery of thing wrongfully detained. [f. OF *detenue* f. p.p. of *detenir* DETAIN]

dět'on|āte (*or* dē-), v.i. & t. (Cause to) explode with loud report. Hence or cogn. ~A'TION n., ~ātīvE a. [f. L DE(*tonare* thunder), -ATE[3]]

dět'onātor, n. Detonating contrivance, esp. as part of bomb or shell; railway fog-signal. [-OR]

detour (dītoor'), **détour** (F), n. Deviation, roundabout way, digression, (esp. *make a* ~). [F (*dé-*), f. *détourner* (DE-, TURN)]

dětrăct', v.t. & i. Take away (*much, something*, etc., or abs.) *from* a whole (esp. in sense *reduce the credit due to, depreciate*). Hence or cogn. **dětrăc'tION**, **détrăc'tOR**, nn., **dětrăc'tīvE** a. [f. L DE(*trahere tract*- draw)]

dětrain', v.t. & i. Discharge, alight, from train (troops etc.; cf. ENTRAIN). [DE- + TRAIN n.]

dětrib'aliz|e, -is|e (-īz), v.t. (anthrop.). Break up (tribal organization), also abs. So ~A'TION n. [DE-]

dět'riment, n. Harm, damage, (esp. *without* ~ *to*). [ME, f. OF or L DE(*trimentum* f. *terere trit*- rub, wear, -MENT]

dětrimĕn'tal, a. & n. Harmful, causing loss, whence ~LY[2] adv.; (n., sl.) undesirable suitor, e.g. younger son. [-AL]

dětrīt'ĕd, a. (geol.). Disintegrated, formed as detritus. [DETRITUS as p.p. + -ED[1]]

détri'tion, n. Wearing away by rubbing. [f. L *detrit*- see DETRIMENT, -ION]

dětrīt'|us, n. Matter produced by detrition, as gravel, sand, silt; debris. Hence ~AL a. [L *detritus -ūs* = wearing down, see DETRIMENT]

de trop (de trō'), pred. a. Not wanted, unwelcome, in the way. [F]

deuce[1], n. The two of dice or cards; (Tennis) state of score (40 all, games all) at which either party must gain two consecutive points or games to win. [f. OF *deus* (mod. *deux*) f. L *duos* nom. *-o* two]

deuce[2], n. Plague, mischief; the devil (~ *take it*; *who, where, what*, etc., *the* ~? ; *the* ~ *is in it if I cannot*, I certainly can; *play the* ~ *with*, spoil, ruin; *the* ~ *to pay*, trouble to be expected; *a* ~ *of a mess*; ~ *knows*; ~ *a bit*, not at all; *the* ~ *he isn't*, it is incredible that he is not). [f. LG *duus*, = G *daus*, f. as prec., the two at dice being the worst throw]

deu'cĕd (dū-, doō-), a. & adv. Confounded(ly); great (*in a* ~ *hurry*). Hence ~LY[2] adv. [-ED[2]]

dē'us ĕx măch'īnā (-k-), n. Power, event,

that comes in the nick of time to solve difficulty, providential interposition, esp. in novel or play. [L, = god from the machinery (by which in ancient theatre gods were shown in air)]

dē′us misĕrĕāt′ur (-z-), n. The canticle God be merciful, Psalm 67. [L]

deuterăg′onist, n. Person of next importance to PROTAGONIST in drama. [f. Gk *deuteragōnistēs* (DEUTERO-, *agōnistēs* actor)]

deutĕr′ium, n. Heavy isotope of hydrogen with mass about double that of ordinary hydrogen; so **deut′eron** n., nucleus of the ∼ atom. [DEUTERO- + -IUM; *deuteron* after PROTON]

deut′ero-, comb. form of Gk *deuteros* second, as ∼-*Isaiah*, supposed later author of *Isaiah* xl–lv, ∼-*canŏn′ical* of Bible books, admitted later to Canon, *deuterŏg′amў*, second marriage.

Deuterŏn′omist, n. Author, joint--authors, or compiler, of *Deuteronomy.* [-IST]

Deuterŏn′omў, n. Fifth book of Pentateuch. Hence **Deuteronŏm′ic(AL)** aa. [f. LL f. Gk DEUTERO(*nomion* f. *nomos* law) second book of law]

deut′zia (*also* doit²), n. White-flowered shrub. [J. *Deutz* d. 1781, -IA¹]

deux-temps (see Ap.), n. Kind of waltz more rapid than the trois-temps. [F, = two-time]

dĕvăl′ū|e, v.t. Reduce the value of. Hence ∼A′TION n. [DE-]

dĕv′ast|āte, v.t. Lay waste, ravage. Hence or cogn. ∼A′TION, ∼ātoR, nn. [f. L DE(*vastare* f. *vastus* waste), -ATE³]

dĕvĕl′op, v.t. & i. Unfold (t. & i.), reveal, bring or come from a latent to an active or visible state; (Mil.) open (an attack); make or become fuller, more elaborate or systematic, or bigger; (Photog.) treat (plate, film) so as to make picture visible; make progress; exhibit (*has* ∼*ed a tendency to*), come or bring to maturity. Hence ∼ABLE a., ∼ER¹ (1, 2) n. [late 16th c. *dis-* f. F *de(s)velopper* f. Rom. **volup-*, **velup-* of unkn. orig.]

dĕvĕl′opment, n. Gradual unfolding, fuller working out; growth; evolution (of animal & plant races); well-grown state; stage of advancement; product; more elaborate form; developing of photograph; ‖ ∼ *area*, one suffering from or liable to severe unemployment. [f. F (prec., -MENT)]

dĕvĕlopmĕn′tal, a. Incidental to growth (∼ *diseases*); evolutionary. Hence ∼LY² adv. [-AL]

dĕv′iāte, v.i. Turn aside, diverge, (*from* course, rule, truth, etc., or abs.), digress. [f. LL DE(*viare* f. *via* way), -ATE³]

dĕviā′tion, n. In vbl senses; esp.; deflexion of compass-needle by iron in ship etc.; divergence of optic axis from normal position. Hence ∼IST (-sho-) n.,

one who departs from strict Communist doctrine. [f. F, or LL *deviatio*]

dĕvīce′, n. Make, look, (arch.: *things of rare, strange,* ∼); (pl.) fancy, will, (*left to* one's *own* ∼*s*); plan, scheme, trick; contrivance, invention, thing adapted for a purpose; drawing, design, figure; emblematic or heraldic design; motto. [ME & OF *devis, devise,* f. L *divisum, -a,* neut. & fem. p.p. of *dividere* DIVIDE]

dĕv′il¹, n. **1.** *The D*∼, supreme spirit of evil, tempter of mankind, enemy of God, Satan. • **2.** Heathen god; evil spirit possessing demoniac; superhuman malignant being. **3.** Wicked or cruel person; mischievously energetic, clever, knavish, or self-willed person, luckless or wretched person (usu. *poor* ∼); vicious animal. **4.** Junior legal counsel working for a leader (*Attorney-General's* ∼, junior Counsel to Treasury). **5.** Literary hack doing what his employer takes the credit and pay for; *printer's* ∼ (hist.), errand--boy in printing-office. **6.** Personified evil quality (*the*∼ *of greed* etc.); fighting-spirit, energy or dash in attack. **7.** (Name of) kinds of animal, bird, firework, & implement; violent S.-African dust-storm (also *dust* ∼); highly seasoned dish, esp. devilled bones. **8.** Phrases (see also those in DEUCE², in all of which ∼ may be substituted): *a* ∼ *of a* ∼, one of an unwelcome or remarkable or amusing kind; *— in the* ∼, a great difficulty or nuisance; *like the* ∼, with great energy etc.; *go to the* ∼, be ruined, (imperat.) be off; *the* ∼*!*, excl. of annoyance or surprise; ∼ *a one*, not one; *the* ∼ *& all*, everything bad; *between the* ∼ *& the deep sea*, in a dilemma; ∼*s-on-horseback*, see ANGEL; ∼ *take the hindmost* (motto of selfish competition); *give the* ∼ *his* DUE; *the* ∼ *to pay*, trouble ahead; *talk of the* ∼ (*& he will appear*), said when one comes just after being mentioned; ‖ *the* ∼ *among the tailors*, row, disturbance; ∼*'s advocate*, *-acy* (one who puts) the ∼*'s* case against canonization, (transf.) depreciator, depreciation; ∼*'s bones*, dice; ∼*'s books*, cards; ‖ *D*∼*'s Own*, 88th Foot, Inns of Court Volunteers; ∼*'s* TATTOO; ∼*'s* in many plant-names, esp. ∼*'s-bit*, kind of scabious; ∼*'s coach-horse*, large cocktail beetle; ‖∼*'s dust*, shoddy. **9.** ∼-*dodger*, preacher, parson; ∼-*fish*, name of many kinds; ∼-*may-care*, reckless, rollicking. Hence ∼DOM, ∼HOOD, nn., ∼WARD(S) adv. [OE *dēofol*, OS *diubul*, OHG *tiufal*, ON *djöfull*, Goth. *diabaulus* f. LL f. Gk *diabolos* slanderer, in LXX rendering Heb. *sātān* SATAN]

dĕv′il², v.i. & t. (-ll-). Work as lawyer's or author's devil (usu. *for* principal); grill with hot condiments. [f. prec.]

dĕv′ilish, a., & adv. **1.** Like, worthy of, the devil, damnable; hence ∼LY² adv.,

~NESS n. **2.** adv. (colloq.). Very. [-ISH[1]]

děv'ilism, n. Devilish quality or conduct; worship of devils. [-ISM]

děv'ilment, n. Mischief, wild spirits; devilish or strange phenomenon. [-MENT]

děv'ilry, -**try,** n. Diabolical art, magic; the devil and his works; wickedness, cruelty; reckless mischief, daring, or hilarity; demonology; devils. [-RY]

děv'ious, a. Remote, sequestered; winding, circuitous, erratic; erring. Hence ~LY[2] adv., ~NESS n. [f. L DE(*vius* f. *via* way)+-OUS]

děvīs|e' (-z), v.t., & n. (Law) assign, give (realty; cf. BEQUEATH) by will (n., this act, clause effecting it), whence ~'OR, ~EE', (-z-), nn.; plan, contrive, invent, plot, scheme, (thing, *how*, or abs.). Hence or cogn. ~'ABLE a., ~'ER[2] (4) n., (-z-). [ME, f. OF *deviser* f. Rom. **divisare* frequent. of L *dividere* -*vis*- DIVIDE]

děvīt'aliz|e, -**is|e** (-īz), v.t. Make lifeless or effete. Hence ~A'TION n. [DE-]

děvit'ri|fȳ, v.t. Deprive of vitreous quality, make (glass or vitreous rock) opaque & crystalline. Hence ~FICA'TION n. [DE-]

děvoid', a. Destitute, empty, *of*. [ME; short p.p. of obs. *devoid* f. OF DE(*voidier* f. *voide* VOID)]

děv'oir (-vwȧr), n. Duty, one's best, (*do* one's ~); (pl.) courteous attentions (*pay* one's ~*s to*). [ME & AF *dever* = OF *deveir* f. L *debēre* owe]

děv'olute (-ōōt), v.t. Transfer by devolution, depute, (work). [f. L p.p. st. see DEVOLVE]

děvolu'tion (-lōō-), n. Descent through a series of changes; descent of property by due succession; lapse of unexercised right to ultimate owner; (Biol.) degradation of species (cf. EVOLUTION); deputing, delegation, of work or power (esp. by House of Parliament to its committees). [f. LL *devolutio* (foll., -ION)]

děvolve', v.t. & i. Throw (duty, work), (of duties) be thrown, fall, descend, *upon* (deputy, or one who must act for want of others); descend, fall by succession, (*to*, *upon*, or abs.). [f. L DE(*volvere volut*-roll)]

Děvōn'ian, a. & n. (Native) of Devonshire; (Geol.) (of) the formation lying above the Silurian & below the Carboniferous. [-IAN]

Děv'onshire (-er), n. ~ (i.e. clotted) *cream*.

děvōte', v.t. Consecrate, dedicate, give up exclusively, (one*self*, another, thing, esp. abilities etc.) *to* (God, person, pursuit, purpose); give over to destruction etc. Hence ~MENT (-tm-) n. [f. L DE(*vovēre vot*- vow)]

děvōt'ěd, a. In vbl senses; esp.: zealously loyal (~ *friend*), whence ~LY[2] adv.; doomed (esp. ~ *head*). [-ED[1]]

děvotee', n. Votary *of*, one devoted *to*; zealously or fanatically pious person. [-EE]

děvō'tion, n. Devoutness; devoting;

divine worship, (pl.) prayers, praying, (*was at his* ~*s*), whence ~AL a., ~alLY[2] adv., ~alISM(3), ~alIST(2), nn., (-sho-), enthusiastic addiction or loyalty (*to*, or abs.). [ME, f. OF, f. L *devotionem* (DEVOTE, -ION)]

děvour' (-owr), v.t. Eat (of beasts); eat like a beast or ravenously; (Bibl.) consume recklessly, waste, destroy, pillage, (substance, property, or its owners); kill, decimate, (of fire, sword, plague, etc.), engulf; take in greedily with ears or eyes (book, story, beauty or beautiful person); absorb the attention of (~*ed by anxiety*); (poet.) ~ *the way* etc., go fast, esp. of horses. Hence ~inglY[2] adv. [ME, f. OF *devourer* f. L DE(*vorare* swallow)]

děvout', a. Reverential, religious, pious, (of person, act, etc.), whence ~NESS n.; earnest, hearty, genuine. Hence ~LY[2] adv. [ME, f. OF *devot* f. L p.p. (DEVOTE)]

dew[1], n. Atmospheric vapour condensed in small drops on cool surfaces from evening to morning; freshness, refreshing or gently stealing influence, (usu. *of* sleep, eloquence, youth, music, etc.); any beaded or glistening moisture, esp. tears, sweat; *mountain* ~, illicitly distilled whisky; ~'*berry*, kind of blackberry; ~-*claw*, rudimentary inner toe of some dogs; ~-*drop*; ~-*fall*, time when ~ begins to form, evening; ~-*point*, temperature at which it forms; ‖~-*pond*, shallow, usu. artificial, pond fed by atmospheric condensation, (chiefly) found or constructed on English downs; ~-*rake*, for surface of grass or stubble; ~-*ret* v.t., RET by exposure to ~ instead of steeping in water; ~-*worm*, large garden worm. Hence ~'LESS, ~'Y[2], aa., ~'iLY[2] adv., ~'iNESS n. [OE *dēaw*, OS *dau*, OHG *tou*, ON *dǫgg* f. Gmc **dawwa-*]

dew[2], v.t. & i. (Impers.) form or fall as dew (*it is beginning to* ~); (poet.) bedew, moisten. [ME *dewen* as prec.]

děwan' (-wahn), n. Head financial minister of Indian state; prime minister of a native state. [Arab. & Pers. *dīwān* (= *devan*, see DIVAN)]

dew'lăp, n. Fold of loose skin hanging from throat of cattle (& transf. of other animals or men). Hence ~pED[2] (-pt) a. [ME; f. LAP[1]; first element of unkn. orig.; cf. Da., Norw. *doglæp*, Sw. *dröglapp*]

děx'ter, a. Of or on the right-hand side (in Her., to the spectator's left). [L]

děxtě'rity, n. Manual or mental adroitness, skill, neatness of handling; right-handedness, using of right hand. [f. F (-*té*) or L DEXTER(*itas* -ITY)]

děx'trin, n. (chem.). Soluble gummy substance obtained from starch & used on adhesive stamps etc. [as foll.+-IN]

děx'tro-, comb. form of L DEXTER, esp. in terms concerned w. chem. property of causing plane of polarized light ray to rotate to right (opp. LAEVO-, which see for compounds).

dĕx'trōse, n. (chem.). Dextro-rotatory form of glucose. [prec., -OSE²]

dĕx'trous, -ter-, a. Neat-handed, deft; mentally adroit, clever; using right hand by preference. Hence dĕx't(e)rousLY² adv. [DEXTER+-OUS; -tr- correct but less common]

Dey (dā), n. (hist.). Commander of janizaries at Algiers; governor of Algiers or Tripoli. [F, f. Turk. dāī maternal uncle]

d(h)al (dahl), n. Split pulse, a common foodstuff in India. [Hind.]

dhar'ma (dăr-, dĕr-), n. (India). Right behaviour, virtue; (in Buddhism) the law. [Skr., = a decree, custom]

dharmsala (dărmsah'la), n. (India). Building devoted to charitable uses (esp. a travellers' rest-house). [Skr., f. dhárma custom, sālā house]

dhōb'i (dō-), n. Indian native washerman; ~('s) itch, troublesome oriental form of eczema. [Hind., f. dhōb washing]

dhōt'i (dō-), n. Loin-cloth worn by male Hindus. [Hind.]

d(h)ow (dow), n. Single-masted Arabian--Sea ship of about 200 tons; any Arab ship, esp. as used in E.-Afr. slave-trading. [in Arab. dāw, but orig. lang. unkn.]

d(h)u'rrie (dŭr-), n. A thick coarse durable Indian cotton cloth fringed square used for floor-coverings etc. [f. Hind. dari]

di-¹, pref. Form of L DIS- (which see for meaning) used before b, d, l, m, n, r, s+cons., v, usu. g, & sometimes j. In LL & Rom. often replaced by dis- (so dismiss), in OF & ME often varying with de- (so defer¹ f. L differre). Not a living pref. in E.

di-², pref. f. Gk di- for dis twice, two-, double-. In many E wds, & as living pref. in Chem. with various special uses.

di-³, pref. = foll. before vowel.

di(a)-, repr. Gk dia-, di-, the prep. dia through, thorough(ly), apart, across. In Gk words taken direct, or through L or F & L; also in many scientific words made with Gk elements or on Gk analogy.

diabēt'ēs (-z), n. Disease with excessive glucose-charged urine, thirst, & emaciation. [LL f. Gk, f. DIA(bainō go)]

diabēt'ic, a. & n. Of diabetes; (person) suffering from diabetes. [f. prec.+-IC]

dia'blerie (-ahblerē), n. Devil's business; sorcery; wild recklessness; devil-lore. [F (diable f. L diabolus DEVIL, -RY)]

diabŏl'ic(al), aa. Of, having to do with, proceeding from, externally like, the devil (usu. -ic); fiendish, atrociously cruel or wicked, (usu. -ical). Hence diabŏl'icalLY² adv. [ME, f. OF diabolique or LL f. Gk diabolikos (DEVIL, -IC) +-AL]

diăb'olĭsm, n. Sorcery; devilish conduct

or nature; belief in or worship of the devil. [f. Gk diabolos DEVIL+-ISM]

diăb'olize, -ise (-īz), v.t. Make into, represent as, a devil. [as prec.+-IZE]

diăb'olō (or dī-), n. Game with two-headed top & sticks. [fancy formation]

diachrŏn'|ic (-k-), a. (Of the approach to the study of a subject, esp. linguistics) historical (opp. synchronic, which seeks to describe it as it is found to exist). Hence ~ical, ~ist'ic, diăch'ronous (-k-), aa. [DIA-+Gk khronos time+-IC]

diăch'ỹlon, -hỹlum, (-k-), -ŭlum, n. Sticking-plaster of litharge, olive oil, & water, on linen. [ME, f. OF diaculon etc. or LL diachylon f. Gk dia khulōn by juices]

diăc'onal, a. Of a deacon. [f. LL diaconalis (DEACON, -AL)]

diăc'onate, n. Office of, one's time as, deacon; deacons. [f. LL ◁(-tus), as DEACON, -ATE¹]

diacrit'ical, a. Distinguishing, distinctive, esp.~marks used to indicate different sounds of a letter, accents, diaeresis, cedilla, etc.; capable of seeing distinctions. [f. Gk DIA(kritikos see CRITIC)+-AL]

diăctin'ic, a. Transmitting, transparent to, the actinic rays. [DI-³, Gk aktis -inos ray, -IC]

diadĕl'phous, a. (bot.). With stamens united in two bundles (cf. MONADELPHOUS, POLYadelphous). [DI-³, Gk adelphos brother]

di'adĕm, n. Crown, or plain or jewelled fillet, as badge of sovereignty; wreath of leaves or flowers worn round head; sovereignty; crowning distinction or glory. Hence ~ED² (-md) a. [ME, f. OF diademe f. L f. Gk DIA(dēma f. deō bind, -M)]

diaer'esĭs, n. (pl. -esēs). Mark (as in aërate) over second of two vowels indicating that they are not one sound. [LL, f. Gk diairesis (DI-³, haireō take) separation]

diagnōse' (-z), v.t. Determine from symptoms the nature of (a disease). [f. foll.]

diagnōs'ĭs, n. (pl. -osēs). Identification of disease by means of patient's symptoms etc., formal statement of this; classification of person's character, assignment of species etc. [f. Gk (DIA-, gignōskō recognize)]

diagnŏs't|ic, a. & n. Of, assisting, diagnosis; (n.) symptom. Hence ~ics n., ~ically adv., ~i'cian (-shn) n. [f. Gk DIA(gnōstikos f. gnōstos known, prec., -IC)]

diăg'onal, a. & n. (Straight line) joining two non-adjacent angles of rectilineal figure or solid contained by planes; obliquely placed like the ~ of a parallelogram (~ row or ~, as of the squares of the same colour on chess-board); inclined at other than a right angle, having some part so inclined (~ cloth or ~, twilled with ridges oblique to the lists). Hence ~LY² adv. [f. L *diagonalis* f. Gk DIA(*gōnios* f. *gōnia* angle), -AL]

di′agram, n. (Geom.) figure made of lines used in proving etc. ; sketch showing the features of an object needed for exposition; symbolic representation, by lines, of process, force, etc. Hence or cogn. **diagrammăt′IC** a., **diagrammăt′ICALLY** adv., **diagrăm′atIZE**(1) v.t. [f. F *diagramme* or L f. Gk DIA(*gramma -atos* f. *graphō* write, -M)]

di′agraph (-ahf), n. Instrument for drawing projections, enlarging maps, etc., mechanically. [f. F *diagraphe* (prec., -GRAPH)]

di′al, n., & v.t. & i. (-ll-). **1.** (Usu. *sun*-~) instrument showing hour by sun's shadow on graduated plate; (also ~-*plate*) face of clock or watch; plate in steam-gauge, gas-meter, etc., on which pressure, consumption, etc., are indicated by index--finger; (sl) face. **2.** vb. Measure, indicate, (as) with ~ ; (automatic telephony) make a call by moving disc from successive numbers or letters to fixed point and letting it return, ring up (number etc.) thus. [ME, f. med. L *dialis* f. L *dies* day; ult. hist. obsc.]

di′alĕct, n. Form of speech peculiar to a district, class, or person, subordinate variety of a language with distinguishable vocabulary, pronunciation, or idioms. Hence **dialĕc′tAL** a., **dialĕc′talLY²** adv., **dialĕctŏL′OGY**, **dialĕctŏL′OGIST**, nn. [f. F *dialecte* or L f. Gk *dialektos* f. DIAlegomai converse]

dialĕc′tic¹, n. (often in pl.). Art of investigating the truth of opinions, testing of truth by discussion, logical disputation; (Mod. Philos.; not in pl.) criticism dealing with metaphysical contradictions & their solutions. So **dialĕctr′CIAN** (-shn) n. [f. OF *dialectique* or L f. Gk *dialektikē* (*tekhnē* art) of debate (prec., -IC)]

dialĕc′tic², a. & n. Logical, of disputation; (person) skilled in critical inquiry by discussion; = DIALECT*al*. [f. L or Gk *dialektikos* (-IC)]

dialĕc′tical, a. = DIALECTIC² (adj.); = DIALECT*al*; belonging to DIALECTIC¹ in mod.-philos. sense. Hence ~LY² adv. [-AL]

dialŏ′gic, a. In, of, dialogue. [f. LL *dialogicus* (DIALOGUE, -IC)]

diăl′ogist, n. Speaker in, writer of, dialogue. [f. LL f. Gk *dialogistēs* (foll., -IST)]

di′alogue (-ŏg), n. Conversation; piece of written work in conversational form, this kind of composition (*written in* ~); the conversational part in a novel. [ME, f. OF *dialoge* L f. Gk *dialogos* (DIAlegomai converse)]

diăl′ysis, n. (pl. *-ysēs*). Parting of colloid from crystalloid parts of mixture by filtration through parchment floating in

water. Hence **di′alyse** (-z) v.t. · [f. Gk DIA(*lusis* f. *luō* loose)]

dialy̆t′ic, a. (chem.). Of, by, dialysis. [f. Gk DIA(*lutikos* f. *lutos* loosed f. *luō* loose, -IC)]

diamăgnĕt′|ic, a. & n. Tending to lie E. & W., across the magnetic axis, when suspended freely & acted on by magnetism; of ~ic bodies or diamagnetism; a ~ic body or substance. Hence ~ICALLY adv., **diamăg′nĕtIZE**(3) v.t. [DIA-]

diamăg′nĕtism, n. Diamagnetic tendency; the diamagnetic branch of magnetism. [DIA-]

diamanté (dĕamahň′tā), a. & n. (Material) scintillating with powdered crystal etc. [F, see DIAMOND]

diamăntif′erous, a. Diamond-yielding. [f. F *diamant* DIAMOND, -I-, -FEROUS]

diăm′ĕt|er, n. Straight line passing from side to side of any body or geom. figure through centre (with special geom. applications for curves), transverse measurement, width, thickness; unit of linear measurement of magnifying-power (*lens magnifying 2000* ~*ers*). So ~rAL a., ~ralLY² adv. [f. OF *diametre* f. L f. Gk DIAmetros (*grammē* line) measuring across f. *metron* measure]

diamĕt′rical, a. Of, along, a diameter, diametral; (of opposition, difference, etc.) direct, complete, like that between opposite ends of diameter. Hence ~LY² adv. [f. Gk *diametrikos* (prec., -IC) +-AL]

di′amond, n., a., & v.t. **1.** Colourless or tinted precious stone of pure carbon crystallized in octahedrons & allied forms, harder than any other known substance (cut into TABLE, ROSE, & BRILLIANT²; *Bristol, Cornish*, etc., ~, kinds of rock crystal; *black* ~, dark--coloured ~, coal; *rough* ~, not·yet cut, person of intrinsic worth but rough manners; ~ *cut* ~, of persons well matched in wit or cunning). **2.** Glittering particle or point. **3.** (Usu. *glazier's* or *cutting* ~) tool with small ~ for glass--cutting. **4.** Figure shaped like section of ~, rhomb (~ *panes*, small panes so shaped set in lead), playing-card bearing this (~*s*, the suit; *a small* ~, one of lower cards). **5.** A printing TYPE. **6.** ~-*back*, kinds of moth & turtle; ~ *cement*, for setting ~s; ~-*drill*, set with ~s for boring hard substance; ~-*field*, tract yielding ~s; ~--*point*, ~-tipped stylus used in engraving, (usu. pl.) place where two lines or rails intersect obliquely; ~-*snake*, Australian python; ~ *wedding*, 60th anniversary; hence ~iF′EROUS a., ~-WISE adv. **7.** adj. Made of, set with, ~ or ~s, rhomb-shaped. **8.** v.t. Adorn with ~s, dewdrops, etc. [ME & OF *diamant* f. med. L *diamas -mant-* var. of L f. Gk *adamas* ADAMANT]

Diăn′a, n. Horsewoman, lady who hunts; woman bent on remaining single. [L, goddess of hunting & chastity]

diapās′on (-zn), n. Combination of notes

or parts in harmonious whole; melody; strain, esp. grand swelling burst of harmony; compass of voice or instrument; range, scope; fixed standard of musical pitch; *open, stopped, ~,* two chief foundation-stops in organ. [L, f. Gk DIA-*pasōn (khordōn)* through all (strings) f. *pas* all]

di'aper, n., & v.t. Linen fabric with small diamond pattern; baby's napkin of this; sanitary towel; ornamental design of diamond reticulation for panels, walls, etc. (vb, decorate with this). [ME, f. OF *diapre* f. med. L f. Byzant. Gk *diaspros* adj. f. DIA-, *aspros* white]

diäph'anous, a. Transparent. [f. med. L *diaphanus* f. Gk DIA(*phanēs* -showing f. *phainō* show) + -OUS]

diaphorĕt'ic, a. & n. (Drug, treatment) productive of perspiration. [f. LL f. Gk *diaphorētikos* f. DIA(*phoreō* carry f. *pherō*), -ETIC]

di'aphragm (-ăm), n. Muscular & tendinous partition separating thorax from abdomen in mammals; partition in shellfish, plant tissues, & various instruments, esp., in optics, telephony, & wireless, disc pierced with circular hole: So diaphrăgmăt'ic a. [ME, f. LL f. Gk DIA(*phragma -atos* f. *phrassō* hedge in, -M)]

di'archy (-kĭ), dȳ-, n. Government by two independent authorities, esp. the reformed Indian constitution started in 1921. [DI-², Gk *archō* rule; *dy-* less correct]

di'arist, n. One who keeps a diary. Hence diaris'tic a. [DIARY + -IST]

di'arize, -ise (-ĭz), v.i. & t. Keep, enter in, a diary. [DIARY, -IZE]

diarrhoe'|a (-rēa), n. Excessive evacuation of too fluid faeces. Hence ~'AL, -IC, aa. [f. LL f. Gk DIA(*rrhoia* f. *rheō* flow)]

di'arȳ, n. Daily record of events, journal; book prepared for keeping this in; calendar with daily memoranda esp. for persons of a particular profession. Hence diăr'IAL a. [f. L *diarium (dies* day, -ARY¹)]

Diăs'pora, n. The DISPERSION (of the Jews). [Gk, f. DIA(*spora* f. *speirō* scatter)]

di'astāse, n. (chem.). A ferment converting starch to glucose, important in digestion. So diastăt'ic, (irreg.) -ăs'ic, aa. [F, f. Gk *diastasis* separation (DIA-, *histēmi* set)]

diăs'tolė, n. Dilatation of heart or artery alternating with systole, & with it forming pulse (*systole & ~* often fig. of reaction, fluctuation, etc.). [LL f. Gk, f. DIA(*stellō* send)]

diatĕss'arŏn, n. Harmony of the four gospels. [f. LL f. Gk *dia tessarōn* composed of four]

diathĕrm'ancȳ, n. diathĕrm'anous, diathĕrm'ic, aa. (Having the) quality of transmitting radiant heat. [f. F *diathermansic, diathermane* + -OUS, *diathermique*, f. Gk DIA(*thermansis* f. *thermainō* f. *thermos* warm)]

di'athermȳ, n. Application of electric

currents to produce heat in the deeper tissues of the body. [DIA- + Gk *thermē* heat + -Y¹]

diäth'ėsis, n. (med.; pl. -*esēs*). Constitutional predisposition, habit. [Gk, f. DIA-(*tithēmi* place)]

di'atŏm, n. Member of genus *Diatoma*, microscopic unicellular algae found esp. at bottom of sea & forming fossil deposits. So diatoma'ceous (-āshŭs) a. [f. Gk DIA(*tomos* f. *temnō* cut) alluding to the cells' being connected in easily separable chains]

diatom'ic, a. (chem.). Consisting of two atoms; having two replaceable atoms of hydrogen. [DI-², ATOM, IC]

diatŏn'ic, a. (mus.). (Of scale) proceeding by notes proper to key without chromatic alteration; (of melodies & harmonies) constructed from such a scale. [f. F *diatonique* or LL f. Gk DIA(*tonikos* TONIC) with intervals of a tone]

di'atribe, n. Piece of bitter criticism, invective, denunciation. [F, f. L f. Gk (-*ē*) = wearing away of time, discourse, f. DIA(*tribō* rub)]

dib, v.i. (-bb-). = DAP. [var. of DAB¹, whence also *dap*]

dibăs'ic, a. (chem.). Having two bases or two atoms of a base. [DI-², BASE¹]

dibb'er, n. Instrument for dibbling, dibble. [f. DIB, now used thus only in *dibbing-stick*]

dib'ble, n., & v.t. & i. 1. Instrument for making holes in ground for seeds etc. 2. vb. Prepare (soil) with this; sow or plant thus; use a ~. [ME; perh. f. DIB + -LE(1), but found much earlier]

dibs (-z), n. pl. (Child's game with) sheep's knuckle-bones; counters at cards; (sl.) money. [prob. f. DIB; cf. earlier *dib-stones*]

dic'ăst, dicăs'terȳ, nn. (Gk Ant.). (Member of) Athenian jury (-*ery*), which gave both verdict & sentence. [f. Gk *dikastēs, dikastērion, (dikazō* I judge f. *dikē* right)]

dice¹, n. pl. See DIE¹.

dice², v.i. & t. Play DICE¹, whence di'CER¹ n.; gamble *away* at dice; chequer, mark with squares; (Cookery) cut (meat) into small squares. [f. prec.]

dice-box, n. Box of hour-glass shape from which dice are thrown; ~ *insulator*, piece of porcelain so shaped supporting telegraph wire.

dichlor'ide (-kl-), n. (Now usu. chem. form of) BICHLORIDE. [DI-²]

dichŏg'amous (-k-), a. (bot.). Having stamens & pistils that mature at different times, so that self-fertilization is impossible. [f. Gk *dikho-* asunder, -*gamos* -married]

dichŏt'om|ȳ (-k-), n. Division into two; binary classification; (Bot. & Zool.) repeated bifurcation. So dichotŏm'ic, ~ous, aa., ~ist(1) n., ~ize (1, 3) v.t. & i., ~ously² adv., (-k-). [as prec., -TOMY]

dichrō'ic (-k-), a. Showing two colours

(esp. of doubly refracting crystals). [f. Gk DI¹(khroos f. khrōs colour)+-IC]

dichrōm'ate (-k-), n. (Now usu. chem. form of) BICHROMATE. [DI-²]

dichromät'ic (-k-), a. Two-coloured (esp. of animal species of which individuals show different colorations). [DI-² +Gk khrōmatikos (khrōma -atos colour, -IC)]

dichrōm'ic(-k-), a. With only two colours (esp. of colour-blind vision seeing two of three primary colours). [Gk dikhrōmos (prec.)+-IC]

dick¹, n. (sl.). Take one's ~ that or to it, swear, affirm. [short for declaration]

*dick², n. (sl.). Detective.

dick'ens (-z), n. (colloq.). Devil, deuce. [from 1598; prob. use of Dickon= Richard, or the surname Dickens, as alliterative substitute for devil]

dick'er¹, n. (commerc.). Half-score, ten, esp. of hides. [ME dyker f. WG *decura f. L decuria set of ten (decem)]

*dick'er², v.i. Trade by barter, chaffer, haggle. [prob. f. prec. through the barter in skins with Indians]

dick'y¹, -ey, n. (colloq. & sl.). Donkey; (also ~-bird) small bird; false shirt- -front; pinafore or apron; driver's seat; ‖ servant's seat at back of carriage. [some senses f. the male name]

‖ dick'y², a. (sl.). Unsound, shaky. [orig. unkn.]

dicōtylēd'on, n. Flowering plant with two cotyledons. Hence ~ous a. [DI-²]

dic'taphōne, n. Machine recording, for subsequent reproduction in type, what is spoken into it. [P, f. foll.+PHONE¹]

dic'tāte¹, n. Authoritative direction (usu. of reason, conscience, nature, etc.; often pl.). [f. L dictatum neut. p.p. see foll.]

dictāte'², v.t. & i. Say or read aloud (matter to be written down, often to writer; also abs.); prescribe, lay down authoritatively, (terms, thing to be done; of person, also of motive etc.); lay down the law, give orders, (will not be ~d to). So DICTA'TION n. [f. L dictare frequent. of dicere dict- say, -ATE³]

dictāt'or, n. Absolute ruler, usu. tem- porary or irregular, of a State, esp. one who suppresses or succeeds a democratic government; person with absolute autho- rity in any sphere; one who dictates to writer. Hence ~SHIP, dictāt'rESS¹, nn. [ME; L (prec., -OR)]

dictatōr'ial, a.. Of dictator; imperious, overbearing. Hence ~LY² adv. [f. L dictatorius f. prec. +-AL]

dic'tion, n. Wording & phrasing, verbal style. [f. F, or L dictio (dicere dict- say, -ION)]

dic'tionary (-sho-), n. Book dealing, usu. in alphabetical order, with the words of a language or of some special subject, author, etc., wordbook, lexicon, (French- -English etc. ~, of French etc. words with English etc. explanation; ~ of archi- tecture or the Bible, Shakespeare ~, etc.);

walking or living ~, well-informed person; ~ English, style, etc., over- -correct, pedantic. [f. med. L dictionarium (prec., -ARY¹)]

dic'tograph (-ahf), n. Apparatus repro- ducing in one room the sounds made in another, loud-speaking internal telephone. [P, irreg. f. foll. +-GRAPH]

dic'tum, n. (pl. -a, -ums). Formal saying, pronouncement; (Law) judge's expres- sion of opinion not having legal validity; maxim, current saying. [L, neut. p.p. of dicere say]

did. See DO¹.

didăc't|ic (or dī-), a. Meant to instruct; having the manner of a teacher. Hence ~ICALLY adv., ~ĪCISM n. [f. Gk didaktikos (didaskō teach)]

did'apper, n. Small diving water-fowl. [for dive-dapper f. earlier divedap f. OE dufedoppa (dūfan dive+doppa cf. dip)]

did'dle, v.t. (sl.). Cheat, swindle. [perh. back formation f. Jeremy Diddler in Kenney's Raising the Wind, 1803]

didgeridoo', -ydoo', n. Australian aboriginal musical instrument of tubular shape. [native]

*did'ō, n. (colloq.). (pl. -oes). Antic, caper, prank (esp. in phr. cut (up) ~es). [orig. unkn.]

didst. 2 sing. past of DO¹.

didym'ium, n. (chem.). A rare metal. [f. Gk didumos twin+-IUM (from its being always found with lanthanum)]

die¹, n. (pl. dice, ~s). 1. (Pl. dice) small cube with faces bearing 1–6 spots used in games of chance; dice, game played with these; the ~ is cast, course irre- vocably decided; upon the ~, at stake; as straight, true, as a ~. 2. (Pl. ~s); (Archit.) plinth, cubic part of pedestal between base & cornice; engraved stamp for coining, striking medal, embossing paper, etc.; ~-sinker, engraver of ~s. [ME & OF de f. L datum neut. p.p. of dare give; sp. dice as in mice, ice]

die², v.i. (dỹ'ing). Cease to live, expire, (of illness, hunger, etc., by violence, the sword, one's own hand, from wound etc., through neglect, on scaffold, at the stake, in battle, for friend, cause, etc., in poverty; ~ a beggar, martyr; ~ a glorious, dog's, death; ~ the death, be put to death, arch. or jocular; ~ game, fighting, not tamely; ~ hard, not without struggle; ~ in one's bed, of age or illness, in one's boots or shoes, by violence, in harness, while still at work, in last ditch, desper- ately defending something; never say ~, not give in, keep up courage); (Bibl.) suffer as in death (I ~ daily), suffer spiritual death, ~ unto, escape thraldom of (sin); be dying for, to do, have great desire; ~ of laughing, laugh to exhaustion; (of plants etc.) lose vital force, decay; come to an end, cease to exist, go out, dis- appear, be forgotten, fade away, (of flame, fame, sound, etc.; secret ~s with one; often *away, down, off, out*); ~-*away* adj., languishing; ~-*hard*, person who dies hard or resists compulsion etc. to the last, obstinate politician etc. to the last, obstinate politician etc.; || *Die--hards*, 57th Regiment of Foot. [ME *deghen*, prob. f. ON *deyja* = OS *dōian*, OHG *touwan*, f. Gmc *dawjan; cf. DEAD]

dĭĕlĕc′tric, a. & n. Insulating (medium or substance), non-conductive, non-conductor. [DI-[3] +ELECTRIC = through which electricity is transmitted (without conduction)]

dies′el (dēz-), n. (attrib.). ~ *engine*, type of oil-engine invented by Dr R. *D*~ of Munich (d. 1913), in which ignition of fuel is produced by the heat of air suddenly compressed. [person]

di′ēs (-z) ī′r′ae n. Day of Judgement; Latin hymn beginning so. [L, = day of wrath]

di′ēs (-z) *nŏn*, n. (Law) day on which no legal business is done; (transf.) day that does not count or cannot be used. [L, short for ~ *juridicus* non-judicial day]

di′et[1], n., & v.t. 1. Way of feeding; prescribed course of food, regimen, whence **dĭĕti′tian, -i′cian**, (-shn), n., one versed in or practising dietetics (prop. *-ician*, after *physician*); one's habitual food. 2. v.t. Feed (person, one*self*) on special food as medical regimen or punishment. [ME, f. OF *diete(r)* f. L f. Gk *diaita* way of life]

di′et[2], n. Conference, congress, on national or international business; meeting of the estates of the realm or confederation (esp. as Engl. name for foreign parliamentary assemblies. [ME, f. med. L *dieta* day's work, assembly, etc.; prob. f. *diaita* DIET[1] confused with *dies* day]

di′ĕtarў, n. & a. (Course) of diet; allowance or character of food in large institutions. [ME f. med. L *diaetarium* (DIET[1], -ARY[1])]

dĭĕtĕt′|ĭc, a. Of diet. Hence ~ICS n., ~ICALLY adv. [f. LL f. Gk *diaitētikos* DIET[1], -IC)]

dif-, pref. = DIS- before *f* in L wds. Repr. in OF by *de-* (mod. F *dé-*), which occas. survives in E, as in *defer, defy*.

diff′er, v.i. Be unlike; be distinguishable from; be at variance, disagree, (*from, with*, or abs.; *agree to* ~, give up attempt to convince each other). [ME *differre* f. OF *differer* f. L DIF(*ferre* bear, tend), all used in senses (a) *differ*, (b) *defer*; in E, sense (b) was differentiated as DEFER[1] esp. since 1500]

diff′erence, n., & v.t. Being different, dissimilarity, non-identity (DISTINCTION *without* ~); point in which things differ; quantity by which amounts differ, remainder after subtraction, (*split the* ~, come to compromise); change in price of stocks etc. between certain dates (*pay, meet, the* ~); disagreement in opinion, dispute, quarrel; characteristic mark distinguishing individual or species,

differentia (vb, serve as distinguishing mark of, differentiate); *make a* ~ *between*, treat differently; *it makes a great* ~, is important. [ME, f. OF *difference* f. L *differentia* (foll., -ENCE)]

diff′erent, a. Not the same, unlike, of other nature, form, or quality, (*from, to, than*, all used by good writers past and present, *than* chiefly where a prep. is inconvenient). Hence ~LY[2] adv. [ME, f. OF *different* f. L *different-* part. st. (DIFFER-ENT)]

differen′tia (-shĭa), n. (pl. *-ae*). Distinguishing mark, esp. of species within a genus. [L, see DIFFERENCE]

differĕn′tial (-shl), a. & n. 1. Of, exhibiting, depending on, a difference (~ *duties, charges, tariff*, that differ according to circumstances). 2. Constituting a specific difference, distinctive, relating to specific differences (~ *diagnosis*). 3. (Phys., Mech.) concerning the difference of two or more motions, pressures, etc. (~ *gear*, or ~ as n., gear enabling car's hind-wheels to revolve at different speeds in rounding corners). 4. n. (Math.) infinitesimal difference between consecutive values of continuously varying quantity (~ *calculus*, method of calculating this); difference in wage between industries or between skilled & unskilled workers in same industry. Hence ~LY[2] (-sha-) adv. [f. mod. L *differentialis* (DIFFERENCE, -AL)]

differĕn′ti|āte (-shĭ-), v.t. & i. Constitute the difference between, of, or in; develop (t. & i.) into unlikeness, specialize, (species, organs, functions, synonyms); discriminate, discriminate between. Hence ~A′TION (-sĭ-) n. [f. DIFFERENCE; see -ATE[3]]

dĭff′ĭcile (-ēl), a. Unaccommodating, exigent, hard to deal with, persuade, etc. [F]

diff′icult, a. Hard to do or practise, troublesome, perplexing, (often ~ *of access, to answer*, etc.); = prec. [back formation f. foll.]

diff′icult|ў, n. Being hard to do (*with* ~*y*, often as adv. = not easily) or obscure; something hard or obscure; hindrance; embarrassment of affairs, esp. want of money; reluctance, demur, objection, (*make* ~*ies*, be unaccommodating). [ME, f. OF *difficulte* or L DIF(*ficultas* = *facultas* FACULTY)]

diff′idence, n. Self-distrust, excessive modesty, shyness. [f. (obs.) F, or L *diffidentia* (foll., -ENCE)]

diff′ident, a. Wanting in self-confidence, bashful. Hence ~LY[2] adv. [f. L DIF(*fidere* trust), -ENT]

diff′luence, n., **diff′luent**, a., (-lŏŏ-). Flowing apart, becoming fluid; deliquescence, deliquescent. [f. L DIF(*fluere* flow), -ENT, -ENCE]

diffrăct′, v.t. (opt.). (Of edge of opaque body) break up (beam of light) into series of dark and light bands or coloured spectra. So **diffrăc′tion** n, **diffrăc′tive** a., **diffrăc′tively**[2] (-vl-) adv. [f. L DIF(*fringere* = *frangere fract*- break)]

diffuse′[1] (-s), a. Spread out, diffused, not concentrated, (of light, inflammation, etc.); not concise, long-winded. Hence ~LY[2] (-sl-) adv., ~NESS (-sn-) n. [ME, f. OF *diffus* or L DIF(*fundere fus*- pour)]

diffus|e′[2] (-z), v.t. & i. Send forth, shed abroad, (light, particles, heat. geniality, knowledge, rumour); (Phys.) intermingle (t. & i. of gases or fluids) by diffusion, whence ~′IBLE (-z-) a., ~IBIL′ITY (-z-) n. Hence or cogn. **diffu′sion** (-zhn) n., ~′IVE (-s-) a., ~′ively[2] (-sĭvl-) adv., ~′iveness n. [f. L *diffus*- see prec.]

dig, v.t. & i. (*dug*, formerly also ~*ged*; -*gg*-), & n. 1. Use spade or mattock, claws, hands, or snout, in excavating or turning over ground; make research (*for* information, *into* author etc.); make way by ~ging *into, through, under*; excavate or turn up (ground) with spade etc.; make (hole etc.) by ~ging (~ *a pit for*, fig., try to entrap); get by ~ging (potatoes); thrust (spurs, one's nails, feet, point of weapon) *into* something or *in*; poke (person *in the ribs*); ~ (-*self, -selves*, or abs.) *in*, prepare defensive trench or pit; ~ *out*, get, find, make, by ~ging; ~ *up*, break up (fallow land). 2. n. Piece of ~ging; (colloq.) archaeological excavation; thrust, poke, (esp. *in the ribs*; also fig. ~ *at*, remark directed against). [14th c. *digge*; deriv. f. OE *dícian* (f. DIKE) presents phonological, connexion w. F *diguer* semantic, difficulties]

digămm′a, n. Sixth letter (ϝ, in sound = w) of original Gk alphabet, later disused, but important in philology from correspondences with cognate languages. [L f. Gk (DI-[2], GAMMA, i.e. double gamma (ϝ) from its shape)]

dig′am|ў, n. Taking, having, a second spouse. Hence or cogn. ~IST(1) n., ~OUS a. [f. LL f. Gk DI[2](*gamia* f. -*gamos* -married)]

digăs′tric, a. & n. (anat.). With two swelling ends (of muscles); muscle of lower jaw. [DI-[2], Gk *gastēr* -*tr*- belly, -IC]

di′gĕst[1], n. Methodical compendium or summary, esp. of a body of laws (the *D*~, that compiled by order of Justinian); periodical synopsis of current literature or news. [ME, f. L *digesta* neut. pl. p.p. see foll.]

digĕst′[2], v.t. & i. Reduce into systematic form, classify; summarize; think over, arrange in the mind; prepare (food) in stomach and bowels for assimilation (intr. of food, admit of digestion; ~*s well, will not* ~); (of drugs, wine, etc.) promote digestion of; assimilate (conquered territory etc.); brook, endure, be reconciled to, (insult, opinion); get mental nourishment from. Hence ~IBLE a., ~ĭBIL′ITY n., ~ĭBLY[2] adv. [ME, f. L DI[1](*gerere gest*- carry) sort]

digĕs′ter, n. In vbl senses; esp. in cookery, stock-pot (cf. foll.). [-ER[1]]

digĕs′tion (-schon), n. Digesting (*hard, easy, of* ~) of physical or mental food; power of digesting (*a good, weak*, ~); long steeping in hot fluid to extract essence, stewing. [ME, f. OF f. L *digestionem* (DIGEST[2], -ION)]

digĕs′tive, a. & n. Of, promoting, digestion; substance aiding digestion; ointment to promote suppuration. Hence ~LY[2] (-vl-) adv. [ME, f. OF (-*if*, -*ive*), f. LL *digestivus* (DIGEST[2], -IVE)]

digg′er (-g-), n. In vbl senses; also or esp.: (also *gold*-~) one who digs or searches for gold in gold-fields; (sl.) Australian; *D*~s, N.- Amer. Indians living on roots; digging-part of various machines; (also ~-*wasp*) division of Hymenoptera. [-ER[1]]

digg′ing (-g-), n. In vbl senses; also or esp.: (pl., occas. *a* ~*s*) mine or goldfield; ‖ (pl., colloq., also abbr. *digs*) lodgings. [-ING[1]]

dight (dīt), v.t. (arch., & chiefly in p.p. *dight*). Clothe, array, adorn; make ready. [OE *dihtan* f. L *dictare* DICTATE, = OHG *tihtōn*, ON *dikta*; obs. in 18th c., revived by Scott etc.]

di′git, n. Finger or toe (joc., or in zool. or anat.); finger's breadth; any numeral from 0 to 9; (Astron.) twelfth part of sun's or moon's diameter (in measuring eclipse). So ~AL a. [ME, f. L *digitus*]

digitāl′is, n. Medicine prepared from foxglove. [L, naming the foxglove (1542) after its G name *fingerhut* thimble (DIGIT, -AL)]

di′gitate, -āted, a. (zool., bot.). With divided fingers or toes; with deep radiating divisions. Hence **digita′tion** n., **digĭta′to**- comb. form. [f. L *digitatus* (DIGIT, -ATE[2])]

di′gitigrade, a. (zool.). Walking on toes, not touching ground with heel, (cf. PLANTIGRADE). [F (L *digitus*, -I-, -*gradus* -walking)]

dig′nif|ў, v.t. Make worthy; confer dignity upon, ennoble; make stately (p.p., marked by dignity, self-respecting, stately); speak of by high-flown title (*school* ~*ied with name of college*). [f. OF *dignifier* f. LL *dignificare* (*dignus* worthy, -FY)]

dig′nitary, n. Person holding high office, esp. ecclesiastical. [f. foll. + -ARY[1]]

dig′nity, n. True worth, excellence, (*the* ~ *of labour*); high estate or estimation (*beneath* one's ~, unfit for one to do); honourable office, rank, or title; elevation of manner, proper stateliness; ~ *ball*, Negro public dance (from its elaborate formality). [ME & OF *dignete* f. L *dignitatem* (*dignus* worthy, -TY); cf. DAINTY]

dig′răph, n. Group of two letters expressing one sound, as *ch, ea*. [DI-[2], Gk *graphē* writing]

digrĕss′ (or dī-), v.i. Diverge from the

track, stray; depart from or *from* the main subject temporarily in speech or writing. .Hence or cogn. digrĕ'ssion (-shn) n., ~ive a. [f. L DI¹(*gredi* = *gradi* walk *gress*-)]

dihĕd'ral, a. Having or contained by two plane faces; ~ *angle*, (esp.) angle formed by wing pairs of an aeroplane. [f. DI-² + Gk *hedra* seat, base, +-AL (1)]

dike, dȳke, n., & v.t. **1**. Ditch; ‖ natural watercourse; ‖ low wall esp. of turf; embankment, long ridge, dam, against flooding, esp. those in Holland against sea; causeway; (fig.) barrier, obstacle, defence; (Mining & Geol.) fissure in stratum filled with deposited matter, this matter; ‖ ~-*reeve*, officer in charge of drains, sluices, & sea-banks, of fen district. **2**. v.t. Provide, defend, with ~(s). [ME, f. ON *dik* & MLG *dik* dam, MDu. *dijc* ditch, dam; see DITCH]

dilăp'idāte, v.t. & i. Bring, come, into disrepair or decay (building, furniture, clothing, estate, fortune). [f. L. DI¹-(*lapidare* f. *lapis* stone) squander; the E sense based on a peculiarly E application of the L]

dilăpidā'tion, n. Squandering; bringing or coming into, being in, disrepair; ‖ sum charged against incumbent etc. for wear & tear during his tenancy; falling away of cliffs etc., debris resulting. [ME, f. LL *dilapidatio* (prec., -ATION)]

dilāt|e' (dī-, dĭ-), v.t. & i. Make or become wider or larger, expand, widen, enlarge, (*with ~ed eyes*, whence ~'ABLE a., ~abil'ity n., dilatA'tion (& irreg. dilā'tion) n.; expatiate, speak or write at large (usu. *upon*). [ME, f. OF *dilater* f. L DI¹(*latare* f. *latus* wide)]

dilāt'or, n. (anat.). (Also ~ *muscle*) muscle that dilates an organ (cf. CONSTRICTOR). [irreg. for less used *dilatator*; see prec., -OR]

dil'ator|ȳ, a. Tending to; designed to cause, given to, delay. Hence ~iLȳ adv., ~iNESS n. [f. LL *dilatorius* (DI¹*lat*-p.p. st. of *differre* DEFER¹, -ORY)]

dilĕmm'a (or dĭ-), n. Argument forcing opponent to choose one of two alternatives (*horns of the ~*) both unfavourable to him; position that leaves only a choice between equal evils. So dilĕmmăt'ic a. [LL, f. Gk DI²(*lēmma -atos* assumption f. root of *lambanō* take, -M)]

dilĕttăn'|tè, n. (pl. *-ti*, pr. -tē) & a. **1**. Lover of the fine arts; amateur; smatterer, one who toys with subject or concentrates on nothing; hence ~tisH¹ a., ~tism(1) n. **2**. adj. Trifling, not thorough, amateur. [It., f. *dilettare* f. L *delectare* DELIGHT, -ANT]

dil'igence¹, n. Persistent effort or work; industrious character. [ME, f. OF (DILIGENT, -ENCE)]

dil'igence² (*occas.* dĕlĕzhahǹs'), n. Foreign public stage-coach. [F, as prec.]

dil'igent, a. Hard-working, steady in application, industrious, attentive to duties. Hence ~LY² adv. [ME, f. OF, f. L DI¹(*ligere lect*- = *legere* choose) love, take delight in, -ENT]

dill, n. Umbelliferous annual yellow-flowered herb. [OE *dile*, OS *dilli*, OHG *tilli*, ON *dylla*, of unkn. orig.]

dill'ȳ-dăllȳ, v.i. (colloq.). Vacillate; loiter. [redupl. of DALLY]

dil'üent (or -ōō-), a. & n. Diluting (agent); (substance) increasing proportion of water in the blood etc. [f. L *diluere* DILUTE², -ENT]

dil'üte¹, a. Weakened by addition of water; (of colour) washed-out, faded; (fig.) watery, watered down. [f. L *dilutus* p.p. see foll.]

dilüte'², v.t. Reduce strength of (fluid) by adding water; diminish brilliance of (colour); water down (doctrine, zeal); ~ *labour*, substitute a proportion of women or unskilled men (*dilutees'*) for skilled men. So dilu'TION (-ōō-) n. [f. L DI(*luere lut*- wash)]

dilu'vial (-ōō-, -ū-), a. **1**. Of a flood, esp. of the Flood in Genesis. **2**. (Geol.) ~ *theory, changes*, etc., depending on general deluge or catastrophic water-action, whence ~IST(2) n.; of the drift formation now called Glacial Drift. [f. LL *diluvialis* (*diluvium* DELUGE, -AL)]

dim, a., & v.i. & t. (-mm-). **1**. Faintly luminous or visible; not bright, clear, or well-defined; obscure; seeing or seen, hearing or heard, apprehending or apprehended, indistinctly; *take a ~ view of* (colloq.), regard with pessimism; hence ~'LY² adv., ~m'isH¹ (2) a., ~'NESS n. **2**. vb. Become or make~, becloud, outshine. [OE *dim(m)*, ON *dimmr*, cogn. w. OHG *timbar*, of unkn. orig.]

*dīme, n. Silver coin, 1/10 of dollar (~ *novel*, cheap shocker). [obs. sense *tithe*, f. OF *disme* f. L *decima* fem. of *decimus* tenth]

dimĕn'sion (-shn), n. Measurable extent of any kind, as length, breadth, thickness, area, volume, (usu. pl.; *of great ~s*, very large); *the three ~s*, length, breadth, & thickness (point has no ~s, line one, surface two, body three; *fourth ~* in math. speculations, property of matter that should be to solids as solids are to planes); (Alg.) number of unknown quantities contained as factors in a product (*x*³, *x*²*y*, *xyz*, all of three ~s). Hence ~AL, ~LESS, aa., (-sho-). [ME, f. OF f. L DI¹(*mensionem* f. *metiri mensus* measure, -ION)]

dim'erous, a. (bot., entom.). With two parts. [DI-², -MEROUS]

dim'ēter, n. Verse of two measures (measure in some metres has one foot; in others two). [f. LL f. Gk DI²(*metros* f. *metron* measure)]

dimid'iate, a. Halved, split in two. [f. L (-*diare*) f. DI(*midium* f. *medius* mid), -ATE²]

dimin'ish, v.t. & i. Make or become,

actually or in appearance, less (*hide* one's ~ed *head*, i.e. reduced power etc.; in Mus., ~ed, of intervals less by a chromatic semitone than the full, as ~ed *fifth* etc.); (t. & i.); ~ed *responsibility* (Law), limitation of criminal responsibility on the ground of mental weakness or abnormality. Hence ~ABLE a., ~INGLY² adv. [ME; conflation of MINISH & obs. *diminue* f. OF *diminuer* f. L DI¹*minuere* -*minut-* cf. *minor* less]

dĭmĭn'ŭĕn'dō, mus. direction (abbr. *dim.*) & n. Gradually decrease loudness (cf. CRESCENDO); gradual decrease, musical passage marked by it, (also fig.). [It.]

dĭmĭnū'tion, n. Diminishing, amount of it; (Mus.) repetition of passage in notes shorter than those previously used. [ME, f. OF f. LL *di-* (cl. L *de-*) *minutionem* (DIMINISH, -ION)]

dĭmĭn'ūtĭve, a. & n. (Gram.) (word) describing small specimen of the thing denoted by corresponding primitive word; remarkably small, tiny. Hence **dĭmĭn'ūtĭv'AL** a. (gram.), ~LY² (-vl-) adv., ~NESS (-vn-) n. [ME, f. OF f. LL *di-* (*de-*)*minutivus* (DIMINISH, -IVE)]

dĭm'ĭssōrў, a. Sending away; permitting to depart; *letters* ~ (Eccl.), bishop's authorization of a candidate's ordination outside his own see. [f. LL *dimissorius* (*dimittere* send away)]

dĭm'ĭtў, n. Stout cotton fabric woven with raised stripes or fancy figures used for bedroom hangings etc. [ME, f. It. *dimito* or f. med. L *dimitum* f. Gk DI²(*mitos* warp-thread)]

dĭmŏrph'ĭc, dĭmŏrph'ous, aa. (bot., zool., chem., mineral.). Exhibiting, occurring in, two distinct forms. So **dĭmŏrph'ISM**(2) n. [f. Gk DI²(*morphos* f. *morphē* form)+-IC, -OUS]

dĭm'ple, n., & v.t. & i. 1. Small hollow esp. in cheek or chin; ripple in water, hollow in ground; hence **dĭm'plў²** a. 2. vb. Produce ~s in, show ~s. [c. 1400, formally corresp. to OHG *tumpfilo* (G *tümpel*) pool]

dĭn, n., & v.t. & i. (-nn-). 1. Continued confused stunning or distracting noise. 2. vb. Assail with ~; repeat ad nauseam *into* person or person's *ears*; make a ~. [vb f. n., OE *dyne*, OHG *tuni*, ON *dynr*]

dĭnâr' (dē-), n. Unit of currency in Iraq & Jugoslavia. [Arab. *dīnār* f. L DENARIUS]

dĭne, v.i. & t. Take dinner (~ *out*, away from home; ~ *off* or *on*, have for dinner; ~ *with Duke Humphrey*, go without dinner—perh. w. allusion to those who walked during dinner-time in Duke Humphrey's Walk in St Paul's); entertain (persons) at dinner, (of room etc.) provide dining-accommodation for (some number); *dining-room*, used for meals. [ME, f. OF *di*(*s*)*ner* f. Rom. *dis*(*je*)*junare* f. DIS- + LL *jejunare* f. *jejunus* fasting]

dĭn'er, n. One who dines; railway dining-car; ~-*out*, one who often dines from home, esp. one much invited for his social qualities. [-ER¹]

dĭng'-dŏng', adv., n., & a. (With) alternating strokes as of two bells (*hammer away at it* ~; ~ *race*, *game*, etc., in which each has the better alternately); sound of bell(s); jingle of rhyme. [imit.]

dĭnghy, dingey, (dĭng'gĭ), n. Small ship's--boat; small pleasure rowing-boat; air-craft's small inflatable rubber boat. [orig. native rowing-boat on Indian rivers, f. Hind. *ḍeṅgi*]

dĭngle (dĭng'gl), n. Deep dell, usu. shaded with trees. [orig. unkn.]

dĭng'ō (-ngg-), n. (pl. ~es). Wild or half--domesticated Australian dog. [native]

dĭn'gʹlў (-j-), a. Dull-coloured, grimy, dirty-looking. Hence ~ILY² adv., ~INESS n. [perh. f. DUNG+-Y²]

|| **dĭnk'um**, a. & n. (Austral. dial. or sl.). Genuine, real (~ *oil*, the honest truth); (n.) work, toil. [orig. unkn.]

dĭnk'ў, a. (colloq.). Pretty, neat, of engaging appearance. [f. 16th c. Sc. *dink* trim (of unkn. orig.)+-Y²]

dĭnn'er, n. Chief meal of day, whether at midday or evening (formal meal with distinct courses); public feast in honour of person or event; ~-*bell*, -*hour*, -*time*, -*party*; || ~-*jacket*, tailless dress coat; ~-*set*, of plates, dishes, etc.; ~-*wagon*, movable tray on castored legs. Hence ~LESS a. [ME, f. OF *di*(*s*)*ner*; see DINE, -ER⁴]

dĭnō'ceras, n. Extinct elephant-sized ungulate mammal with three pairs of horns. [f. Gk *deinos* terrible + *keras* horn]

dĭnôrn'ĭs, n. Extinct ostrich-sized New Zealand flightless bird, the moa. [f. Gk *deinos* terrible + *ornis* bird]

dĭn'osaur (-ôr), n. Extinct gigantic reptile. Hence **dinosaur'IAN** (-ôr'-) a. & n. [f. Gk *deinos* terrible + *sauros* lizard]

dĭn'othēre, n. Huge extinct proboscidean quadruped. [f. Gk *deinos* terrible + *thērion* wild beast]

dĭnt, n., & v.t. 1. (Arch.) stroke, blow, (whence, mod.) *by* ~ *of*, by force or means of; mark made by blow or pressure, dent. 2. v.t. Mark with ~s, dent. [OE *dynt*, & partly f. cogn. ON *dyntr*; ult. orig. unkn.]

dĭō'cĕsan (-zn), a. & n. 1. Of a diocese. 2. n. Bishop in relation to diocese or clergy; || member of diocese in relation to bishop (corresp. to *parishioner*). [ME, f. OF *diocesain*, LL *diœcesanus* (foll., -AN)]

dĭ'ocese (-ĕs, -ēs), n. Bishop's district. [ME & OF *diocise* f. L f. Gk DI³(*oikēsis* f. *oikeō* inhabit) administration]

dĭ'ōde, n. Electronic valve having two electrodes. [DI-², Gk *hodos* way]

dĭoe'cious (-ēshŭs), a. (Bot.) having the male & female flowers on separate plants; (Zool.) with the two sexes in separate individuals. [DI-², Gk -*oikos* -housed, -OUS]

Dionys'ian, -iăc, a. Of *Dionysus*, the Greek god of wine, or his worship. [*-ian* f. L *Dionysius*+-AN; *-iac* f. LL f. Gk *Dionusiakos* f. *Dionusia* the feast of Dionysus]

diŏp'ter, -tre (-*ter*), n. Refractive power of a lens having a focal length of one metre (used as unit of refractive power; thus a lens of +5 ~s is a positive lens with a focal length of 20 cm.). [f. F *dioptre* f. L f. Gk *dioptra* (see foll.)]

diŏp'tr|ic, a. & n. 1. Serving as medium for sight, assisting sight by refraction, (~*ic glass, lens, system*); of refraction, refractive; of ~ics; hence ~ICALLY adv. **2.** n. Unit of refractive power, power of lens with focal distance one metre; (pl.) part of optics dealing with refraction (cf. CATOPTRICS). [f. Gk *dioptrikos* f. DI³(*optra* f. *op*- see +instr. suf. *-tra*) optical instrument, -IC]

diora'ma (-rah-), n. Spectacular painting in which, by changes in the colour & direction of light thrown on or through it, effects of such natural processes as sunrise are produced. Hence (irreg.) **diorăm'ic** a. [DI-³, Gk *horama* -*atos* (*horaō* see, -M)]

diŏx'ide, n. (chem.). Oxide formed by combination of two atoms of oxygen with one of metal or non-metal (*carbon* ~ etc.). [DI-²]

dip¹, v.t. & i. (-pp-). **1.** Put or let down into liquid, immerse, (~ one's *pen in gall,* write bitterly); dye thus; make (candles) by immersing wick in hot tallow; wash (sheep) in vermin-killing liquid; take *up* (liquid, grain, etc.) in scoop, pan, etc. **2.** Lower (flag, sail, scale of balance) for a moment. **3.** Involve in debt (colloq.). **4.** Go under water & emerge quickly; put hand, ladle, etc., *into* to take something out (~ *into* one's *purse* etc., spend freely); go below any surface or level (*sun* ~*s below horizon; bird'*~*s & rises in flight; scale* ~*s*). **5.** Extend downwards; have downward slope (esp. of magnetic needle, & of strata; ~*ping-needle,* one so mounted as to measure magnetic dip). **6.** Make investigations (~ *deep into the future*): look cursorily or skippingly *into* (book). [OE *dyppan* f. Gmc *dupjan* cogn. w. DEEP]

dip², n. 1. A dipping (see prec.); quantity dipped up; (colloq.) bathe in sea etc.; amount of submergence. **2.** (Astron., Surv.) apparent depression of horizon due to observer's elevation; angle made by magnetic needle with horizon. **3.** Downward slope of stratum; depression of skyline etc. **4.** Tallow candle. **5.** Washing-preparation for sheep etc. **6.** ~*-needle,* = dipping-needle (see prec.); ~*-net,* small fishing-net with long handle; ~*-pipe,* || *-trap,* arranged to cut off communication of gas etc. by downward bend in which liquid stands; ~*-stick,* rod for measuring depth of liquid. [f. prec.]

diphthēr'ia, dĭphtherīt'ĭs, (-fth-), nn. Acute infectious disease with inflammation of a mucous membrane esp. of throat, & exudation forming a false membrane. Hence **diphthēr'IAL, diphthĕ'rIC, diphtherit'IC, diph'therOID,** aa. [f. F *diphthérie, diphthérite* (earlier name), f. Gk *diphthera* hide, -Y¹, -ITIS]

diph'thŏng (-fth-), n. Union of two vowels pronounced in one syllable (ou, oi); two vowel characters representing sound of single vowel (ea in *feat*), digraph; compound vowel character, ligature, (œ). Hence **diphthŏng'AL** a., ~IZE (3) v.t., (-ngg-). [f. F *diphthongue* f. LL f. Gk DI²(*phthoggos* -sounded f. *phthoggos* voice)]

dĭpl(o)-, comb. form of Gk *diplous* double, in many scientific words as *diploblas'tic* with two germinal layers, *diplocard'iac* with right & left sides of heart separate.

diplŏd'ocus, n. Gigantic extinct N.-American herbivorous dinosaur. [f. prec. +Gk *dokos* wooden beam]

diplōm'a, n. (pl. -s, rarely *-ta*). State paper, official document, charter; document conferring honour or privilege, esp. University or College certificate of degree, whence ~'d, ~ED² (-mad), ~LESS, aa. [L f. Gk (-ō-), f. *diploō* (*diplous* double), -M; orig. folded paper]

diplōm'acў, n. Management of, skill in managing, international relations; DOLLAR ~; adroitness, artful management, tact. [f. F *diplomatie* f. *diplomate* see foll., -Y¹]

dip'lomăt, n. = DIPLOMATIST. [f. F *diplomate* back formation f. *diplomatique* see foll.]

diplomăt'ĭc, a. & n. (Palaeographic examination) of official or original documents, charters, etc. (freq. pl. in n.); of diplomacy (~ *body,* ambassadors & legation-officials at a court; ~ *agent, service*); skilled in diplomacy; proceeding by negotiation; (of statements, dealings, persons) uncandid, subtle. Hence **diplomăt'ICALLY** adv. [f. mod. L *diplomaticus* & F *-ique* f. Gk DIPLOMA -*atos,* -IC]

diplōm'atist, n. One officially engaged in diplomacy; adroit negotiator. [DIPLOMAT, -IST]

diplōm'atīze, -ise (-īz), v.i. Act as diplomatist; use diplomatic arts. [DIPLOMAT, -IZE]

dip'nŏan, a. & n. (Fish) having both gills and lungs. [f. Gk *dipnoos* with two breathing-apertures (DI-²+*pnoē* breath)]

di'pōle, n. (phys. & chem.). Object oppositely charged at two points or poles; molecule in which centre of action of positive portions (protons) does not coincide with that of negative portions (electrons). Hence **dipōl'AR¹** a., having two poles, as a magnet. [DI-², POLE²]

dipp'er, n. In vbl senses; also or esp.: Anabaptist or Baptist; kinds of bird, esp. water ouzel; kind of ladle; (Photog.)

apparatus for immersing negatives; *the D~*, the Great Bear. [DIP[1], -ER[1]]

‖ **dipp′y**, a. (sl.). Crazy. [orig. unkn.]

dipsomān′ia, n. Morbid craving for alcohol. Hence **dipsoMAN′IAC** n. [Gk *dipso-* (*dipsa* thirst, -o-), -MANIA]

dip′teral, a. With double peristyle. [f. L f. Gk DI[2](*pteros*-winged f. *pteron* wing), -AL]

dip′terous, a. (Entom.) two-winged, belonging to the order *Diptera* (insects with one pair of membranous wings); (Bot.) with two wing-like appendages. [as prec. +-OUS]

dip′tych (-ĭk), n. Ancient hinged two-leaved writing-tablet with inner sides waxed; painting, esp. altarpiece, of two leaves closing like book. [f. LL *diptycha*, *-um* f. Gk DI[2](*ptukha* neut. pl. of *-ptukhos* -folding)]

dīre, a. Dreadful, calamitous, (~ *sisters*, the Furies). Hence ~′LY[2] (-ĭrĭ-) adv. [f. L *dirus*]

dirèct′[1], v.t. & i. Address (letter, parcel, *to* person or place); utter or write *to* or to be conveyed *to* (*I ~ my remarks to you*); control, govern the movements of, (*soul, ~s body, commander troops*); turn (thing, person, eyes, attention) straight *to* something; tell (person) the way (*to; ~ing-post, = FINGER-post*); guide as adviser, principle (*duty ~s my actions*), etc.; order (person) *to* do, thing *to be* done; give orders (*that* or abs.). So **dirèc′tIVE** a. (also n., general instruction for the carrying out of military etc. operations). [f. L DI[1](*rigere rect-=regere* put straight)]

dirèct′[2], a. & adv. Straight, not crooked(ly) or round about, (*the ~ road; went ~ to heaven*; ~ *action*, exertion of pressure on the community by strikes instead of on Parliament by votes to force political measures on the Government; ~ *ray*, not reflected or refracted; ~ *shot, hit*, without ricochet; (Astron.) proceeding from W. to E., not retrograde; (of descent) lineal(ly), not collateral(ly); (of argument) following uninterrupted chain of cause & effect etc.; diametrical (~ *opposite, contrary, contradiction*); (Mus.) not inverted (of interval, chord), not contrary (of motion); straightforward, frank, going straight to the point, not ambiguous; immediate(ly), personal(ly), not by proxy; (Gram.) ~ *speech* or *oration*, the words as actually spoken, not modified (cf. OBLIQUE, INDIRECT) in reporting; ~ *current*, electric current flowing always in the same direction; ~ *method*, method of teaching a language through use of the language itself without translation & without study of formal grammar; ~ *tax*, levied originally (income tax etc.) on person who bears the burden ultimately (cf. INDIRECT). Hence ~NESS n. [f. L *directus* p.p. see prec.]

dirèc′tion, n. Directing, aiming, guiding, managing; = DIRECTORATE; instruction what to do, order, (usu. pl.); address on letter or parcel; course pursued by moving body, point to which one moves or looks, (*in the ~ of London*, Londonwards); scope, sphere, subject, (*new ~s of inquiry, improvement in many ~s*); ~*-finder*, wireless receiving device for finding bearings of transmitting stations. Hence ~AL (-shon-) a. (esp. of wireless transmitted over a narrow angle). [ME, f. OF, or L *directio* (DIRECT[1], -ION)]

dirèct′ly, adv. & conj. In a DIRECT[2] manner; at once, without delay; presently, in no long time; (colloq.) as soon as (*went ~ I knew*). [-LY[2]]

Dirèc′toire (-twǎr), a. (Dressmaking) in imitation of styles prevalent during the French Directory. [F; see DIRECTORY[2]].

dirèc′tor, n. Superintendent, manager, esp. member of managing-board of commercial company; (Cinemat.) stage-manager and producer of a film; (Fr. Hist.) member of Directory; (Eccl.) priest acting as spiritual adviser; apparatus controlling direction in instruments etc.; elaborate gun-sight for co-ordinating fire of several guns. Hence **dirèctōr′IAL** a., ~SHIP, **dirèc′trEsS**[1], nn. [f. AF *directour*, OF *-eur*, f. LL *director* (DIRECT[1], -OR)]

dirèc′torate, n. Office of director; board of directors. [-ATE[1]]

dirèc′tory[1], a. Directive, advisory, (esp. of part of law advising procedure omission of which does not invalidate action). [ME, f. LL *directorius* (DIRECT[1], -ORY)]

dirèc′tory[2], n. Book of rules, esp. for public or private worship; book with lists of inhabitants of district, members of professions, etc., with various details; (Fr. Hist.) revolutionary executive of five directors in power 1795–9 (*D~*). [f. LL *directorium* neut. adj. see prec.]

dirèc′trix, n. (pl. *-ices*). = DIRECTRESS; (Geom.) fixed line used in describing curve or surface. [DIRECTOR, -TRIX]

dire′ful (-ĭrf-), a. Terrible, dread. Hence ~LY[2] adv. [DIRE, -FUL(1)]

dīrge, n. Song sung at burial, or in commemoration of the dead; lament. [ME, f. L *dirige* imperat. of *dirigere* DIRECT[1], first wd. in Latin antiphon in Matins part of Office of the Dead]

di′rigible, a. & n. Capable of being guided (esp. of balloons); (n.) ~ balloon or airship as opp. *aeroplane*. [as DIRECT[1], -IBLE]

dirigisme (dērĕzhĭzm′), n. Policy of State direction & control in economic & social matters. [F *diriger* DIRECT[1])]

di′riment, a. Nullifying (~ *impediment*, making marriage null & void from the first). [f. L *dirimere* (DIS-, *emere* take), -ENT]

dĭrk, n., & v.t. Kind of dagger (esp. of Highlanders); (vb) stab with this. [17th-18th c. *durk*, of unkn. orig.]

dĭrn′dl, n. Kind of dress imitating Alpine peasant costume with bodice & full skirt;

(also ~ *skirt*) full skirt with tight waist-band. [G, dim. of *dirne* girl]

dirt, n. Unclean matter that soils, wet mud (~ *pie*, made by children in gutters etc.); anything worthless (*yellow* ~, gold; ~, scornful name for land; ~-*cheap*, very cheap); earth, soil; dirtiness; foul talk; *fling* ~, talk abusively or slanderously; *eat* ~, put up with insult etc.; ~-*eating*, disease with morbid craving to eat earth; ~ *track*, a course made of rolled cinders, brickdust, etc., for motor-cycle racing, or of earth for flat-racing; *~ wagon*, dust-cart. [ME *drit* f. ON *drit* excrement]

dirt'ў̆, a., & v.t. & i. **1.** Soiled, foul, mixed with or like or connected with dirt, (*D*~ *Shirts*, 101st Foot, from fighting in shirt-sleeves at Delhi); unclean, obscene; sordid, mean, despicable; *do the* ~ (sl.), play a shabby trick; ~ *work*, esp. dis-honourable proceedings, (also) drudgery (*do* person's ~ *work for him*); ill-gotten, esp.~*money*; (of weather) rough, squally; (of colour) not pure or clear; *D*~ *Allan*, sea-bird getting food by forcing gulls etc. to disgorge; hence **dirt'ily²** adv., **dirt'i-NESS** n., ~**ISH¹**(2) a. **2.** vb. Make, become, ~. [-Y²]

dirz'i, n. (Anglo-Ind.). Indian native tailor. [Hind. f. Pers. *darzi* (Pers. *dari* sewing)]

dis-, pref. f. L *dis-* (which was changed to DI-¹ or DIF- before certain letters; see also DE-) related to *bis* (orig. **dvis* = Gk *dis* twice) & *duo* two. In E, *dis-* appears (1) in wds taken direct f. L or f. F wds similarly adopted; (2) as repr. OF *des-* (mod. F *dé-, des-*) the inherited form of L *dis-*; (3) as repr. LL *dis-* for L *de-* (see DE-); (4) as a living pref. with privative force. Meanings: asunder, away, apart or be-tween, one by one, utterly (in wds already negative, as *disannul*), un-, not, the re-verse of, deprivation of, expulsion from.

disabil'itў̆, n. Thing, want, that prevents one's doing something, esp. legal dis-qualification. [f. obs. adj. DISAble (= un-*able*), -BILITY]

disa'ble, v.t. Incapacitate *from doing* or *for* work etc.; cripple, deprive of power of acting; disqualify legally, pronounce in-capable, hinder. Hence ~MENT (-blm-) n. [DIS-, ABLE]

disabuse' (-z), v.t. Undeceive, disillusion. [DIS-]

disaccord', n., & v.i. Disagree(ment), (be at) variance. [ME; DIS-]

disadvan'tage (-vah-), n. Unfavourable condition (*taken at a* ~); loss, injury. [f. F *désavantage* (DIS-, ADVANTAGE)]

disăd'vantā'geous (-*j*us), a. Involving disadvantage or discredit, derogatory. Hence ~LY² adv. [DIS-]

disaffec'tĕd, a. Estranged, unfriendly, disloyal, esp. to Government. [p.p. of vb DISaffect, dislike]

disaffec'tion, n. Political discontent, dis-loyalty. [as prec. after AFFECTION]

disaffirm', v.t. (legal). Reverse (previous decision); repudiate (settlement). Hence **disaffirma'tion** n. [DIS-]

disaffo'rest, v.t. ‖ Reduce from legal state of forest to ordinary land. Hence ~A'TION n. [f. AL DIS(AFFORESTare)]

disagree', v.i. Differ, be unlike, not correspond; differ in opinion, dissent, quarrel; (of food, climate, etc.) prove un-suitable, have bad effects, (*with* person, his health, digestion, etc.). Hence ~MENT n. [ME, f. OF *desagreer* (DIS-, AGREE)]

disagree'ab|le (-grīa-), a. & n. **1.** Not to one's taste, unpleasant; unamiable, bad--tempered; hence ~leness (-ln-) n., ~LY² adv. **2.** n. (Usu. pl.) unpleasant experi-ence(s), trouble(s), worries. [ME, f. OF *desagreable* (DIS-, AGREEABLE)]

disallow', v.t. Refuse to sanction or accept as reasonable or admit, prohibit. [ME, f. OF *desalouer* (DIS-, ALLOW)]

disannul', v.t. (-ll-). Cancel, annul. [DIS-]

disappear', v.i. Cease to be visible, vanish, die away from sight or exist-ence, be lost. Hence ~ANCE n. [DIS-]

disappoint', v.t. Not fulfil desire or ex-pectation of, break appointment with, (person; ~*ed at, in, of, with; agreeably* etc. ~*ed*, glad to find one's fears groundless); belie, frustrate, (hope, purpose, etc.). Hence ~ING² a., ~ĕdLY², ~ingLY², advv., ~MENT n., event etc. that ~s, distress re-sulting. [f. F *désappointer* (DIS-, APPOINT)]

disăpprobā'tion, n. Disapproval. So **disăpp'robātIVE, disăpp'robātORY, aa.** [DIS-]

disapprov|e' (-ōōv), v.t. & i. Have, express, unfavourable opinion of or *of*. Hence ~'AL(2) n., ~'ingLY² adv., (-ōō-). [DIS-]

disarm', v.t. & i. Deprive *of* weapons; deprive of weapons (esp. in fencing, jerk foil etc. out of hand of); dismantle (city, ship), reduce, be reduced, to peace foot-ing (of army), abandon or cut down military establishment, whence **disARM'A-MENT** n.; deprive of power to injure; pacify hostility or suspicions of. [ME, f. OF *desarmer* (DIS-, ARM³)]

disarrange' (-j), v.t. Put into disorder, disorganize. Hence ~MENT (-jm-) n. [DIS-]

disarray', n., & v.t. (Throw into) dis-order; (poet.) unclothe. [ME; DIS-]

disartic'ul|āte, v.t. Separate, undo the articulation of, take to pieces. Hence ~A'TION n. [DIS-]

disassimilā'tion, n. (physiol.). Conver-sion of assimilated into less complex or waste substances. [DIS-]

disassōciā'tion, n.=DISSOCIATION (esp. in psych. senses: ~ *of a personality*). [DIS-]

disas'ter (-zah-), n. Sudden or great mis-fortune, calamity; ill luck (*a record of* ~*er*). So ~ROUS a., ~ROUSLY² adv., (-zah-).

[f. F *désastre* (DIS-, *astre* f. L f. Gk *astron* star)]

disavow', v.t. Say one does not know or approve of, repudiate. Hence ~AL(2) n. [ME, f. OF *desavouer* (DIS-, AVOW)]

disband', v.t. & i. Break up, disperse, (tt. & i. of troops etc.). Hence ~MENT n. [f. 16th-c. F *desbander* see DIS-, BAND[1] (3)]

disbar', v.t. (-rr-). Expel from membership of the bar, deprive of status of barrister. Hence ~MENT n. [DIS-, BAR[1]]

disbelieve', v.t. & i. Refuse credence to (person or statement etc.); be a sceptic; have no faith *in*. So **disbelief'** n. [DIS-]

|| **disbench'**, v.t. Deprive of status of bencher. [DIS-, BENCH n.]

disbranch' (-ah-), v.t. Strip of branches. [DIS-]

disbud', v.t. (-dd-). Remove (esp. the superfluous) buds of. [DIS-]

disburd'en, v.t. Relieve of or of a burden; get rid of, discharge, (load, thoughts). [DIS-]

disburse', v.t. & i. Expend, defray; pay money. Hence ~MENT (-sm-) n. [f. OF *desbourser* (DIS-, BOURSE)]

disc, disk, n. Thin circular plate (e.g. coin); round flat or apparently flat surface (*sun's* ~) or mark; round flattened part in body, plant, etc.; gramophone record (*~jockey* sl., compère of radio programme of gramophone records). [f. L f. Gk *diskos* DISCUS]

discal'ceate, a. & n., **discal'ceated, discalced'** (-st), aa. Barefooted or only sandalled (friar, nun). [(-*ed* anglicized) f. L DIS(*calceatus* p.p. of *calceare* f. *calceus* shoe)]

discard', v.t. & i., & n. 1. Throw out or reject from hand at cards (specified card, or abs. of playing non-trump that does not follow lead); cast aside, give up, (clothes, habit, belief, etc.); dismiss, cashier. 2. n. (dis'-). ~ing at cards, ~ed card. [DIS-, CARD[2]]

discarn'ate, a. Parted from the flesh, disembodied. [DIS-, (IN)CARNATE]

discern' (-s-, -z-), v.t. & i. 1. (arch.). Distinguish, see the difference between, (good & bad, good *from* bad, *between* good & bad). 2. Perceive clearly with the mind or senses, make out by thought or by gazing, listening, etc.; so ~IBLE a., ~IBLY[2] adv. [ME, f. OF *discerner* f. L DIS(*cernere cret*- sift)]

discern'ing (-s-, -z-), a. Having quick or true insight, penetrating. [-ING[2]]

discern'ment (-s-, -z-), n. Discerning; keenness of perception, penetration, insight. [-MENT]

discerp'ti|ble, a. That can be plucked apart, not indestructibly one. Hence ~BIL'ITY n. [f. LL DIS(*cerpere* -*cerpt*-= *carpere* pluck) +-IBLE]

discerp'tion, n. Pulling apart, severance; severed piece. [f. LL *discerptio* (prec., -ION)]

discharge'[1], v.t. & i. Relieve of load

(ship etc.; ~ *gun*, fire it off; ~ *bankrupt*, relieve him of further liability), withdraw electricity from; dismiss, cashier, (*was ~d from*, or rarely ~*d*, *the service*); release (prisoner), let go (patient, jury); put forth, get rid of, send out, emit, unload from ship, (cargo, missile, liquid, purulent matter, abuse; also abs., as *ship, abscess, has ~d*); (of river, refl. or intr.) disembogue; (Law) cancel (order of court); acquit oneself of, pay, perform, (duty, debt, vow); (Dyeing) remove (colour), undye (fabric). [ME, f. OF *descharger* (DIS-, CHARGE[2])]

discharge'[2], n. Unloading (*of* ship or cargo); firing off of gun etc. (*a ~ of arrows*, several arrows shot); emission (of liquid, electricity, purulent matter); release, exoneration, exemption, acquittal, written certificate of these; dismissal; liberation; payment (*of* debt); performance (*of* obligation); (Dyeing) process of, composition used in, discharging. [ME, f. prec.]

dischar'ger, n. In vbl senses; esp., appliance for producing electric discharge. [-ER[1]]

disci'ple, n. One of Christ's personal followers, esp. one of the Twelve; any early believer in Christ; follower, adherent, of any leader of thought, art, etc. Hence ~SHIP (-lsh-) n., **discip'ular**[1] a. [OE *discipul* (ME *deciple* f. OF) f. L *discipulus* (*discere* learn)]

disciplinar'ian, n. Maintainer of discipline (*strict, good, poor, no,* ~). [as foll. +-AN]

dis'ciplinary (*also* -lin'-), a. Of, promoting, discipline; of the nature of mental training. [f. med. L *disciplinarius* (foll., -ARY[1])]

dis'cipline[1], n. Branch of instruction; mental & moral training, adversity as effecting this; military training, drill, (arch.); trained condition; order maintained among schoolboys, soldiers, prisoners, etc.; system of rules for conduct; control exercised over members of church; chastisement; (Eccl.) mortification by penance. So **dis'ciplinal** (*or* -lin'-) a. [ME, f. OF f. L *disciplina* (*discipulus* DISCIPLE, -INE[2])]

dis'ciplin|e[2], v.t. Bring under control, train to obedience & order, drill, whence ~ABLE a.; chastise. [ME, f. LL (-*nare*) as prec.]

disclaim', v.t. & i. Renounce legal claim to, renounce claim; disown, disavow, (authorship, character). [AF *desclamer* (DIS-, CLAIM[1])]

disclaim'er, n. Act of disclaiming; renunciation, disavowal. [AF (= prec. as n., -ER[4])]

disclose' (-z), v.t. Remove cover from, expose to view, make known, reveal. [ME, f. OF *desclore* (DIS-, L *claudere claus*-shut)]

disclo'sure (-zher), n. Disclosing; thing disclosed. [-URE]

discŏb'olus, n. (pl. *-lī*). Ancient quoit--thrower; statue of one in act of throwing. [L, f. Gk *diskobolos* (*diskos* stone or metal quoit, *-bolos* -throwing f. *ballō* throw)]

discŏg'raphў, n. Catalogue raisonné of gramophone records. [DISC, -O-, -GRAPHY]

dis'coid, a. Disc-shaped. [f. LL f. Gk *diskoeidēs* (prec., -OID)]

discol'our (*-ŭler*), v.t. & i. Change or spoil the colour of, stain, tarnish; become stained etc. Hence or cogn. **dĭscolo(u)rA͟-** TION, ~MENT, (*-ŭler-*), nn. [ME, f. OF *descolorer* or LL DIScolorare = L DE- (*colorare* COLOUR)]

discom'fĭt (*-ŭm-*), v.t. Defeat in battle; thwart, disconcert. So ~URE n. [ME *disconfit* f. OF p.p. of *desconfire* (DIS-, COMFIT)]

discom'fort (*-ŭm-*), n., & v.t. Uneasiness of body or mind; want of comfort; (vb) make uneasy. [ME, f. OF *desconfort*(*er*) (DIS-, COMFORT)]

discommōde', v.t. Put to inconvenience. [DIS- + obs. *commode* f. L *commodare* (*commodus* see COMMODE)]

discŏmm'on, v.t. ‖ Debar (tradesman) from serving undergraduates; enclose (common land). [DIS-, COMMON[1], [2]]

‖ **discŏmm'ons** (*-z*), v.t. Deprive (member of college) of commons; discommon (tradesman). [DIS-, COMMONS]

discompōs|e' (*-z*), v.t. Disturb composure of, ruffle, agitate. Hence ~'ĕdLY[2], ~'ĭngLY[2], (*-z-*), advv., **dĭscompō'sURE** (*-zher*) n. [DIS-]

disconcêrt', v.t. Derange, spoil, upset, (plan, concerted measures); disturb self--possession of, ruffle, fluster. Hence ~MENT n. [f. obs. F DIS(*concerter* CON-CERT[2])]

disconnect', v.t. Sever the connexion of (thing *from, with,* another) or between. [DIS-]

disconnĕc'tĕd, a. In vbl senses; esp. (of speech or writing) incoherent, with bad connexion or transitions, whence ~LY[2] adv., ~NESS n. [-ED[1]]

disconnĕ'xion, -ction (*-kshn*), n. Disconnecting; want of connexion, disconnectedness. [DIS-]

discŏn'solate, a. Forlorn, inconsolable, unhappy, disappointed. Hence ~LY[2] (*-tl-*) adv. [ME, f. med. L DIS(*consolatus* p.p. of L *consolari* CONSOLE[1])]

discontĕnt', n., a., & v.t. **1.** Dissatisfaction, want of contentment; grievance. **2.** adj. (rare). Not content, dissatisfied, (*with*). **3.** v.t. (Usu. in p.p.) make dissatisfied; hence ~ĕdLY[2] adv.,~ĕdNESS, ~MENT, nn. [DIS-, CONTENT[2], [3], [4]]

discontig'uous, a. (With parts) not in contact. [DIS-]

discontin'u|e, v.t. & i. (Cause to) cease; cease from, give up, (do*ing,* habit etc.); cease taking, paying (newspaper, subscription). So ~ANCE n. [ME, f. OF *dis-*

continuer f. med. L DIS(*continuare* CON-TINUE)]

discontin'ūous, a. Wanting continuity in space or time, having interstices, intermittent. Hence or cogn. **dĭscŏntinū'-** ITY n., ~LY[2] adv. [f. med. L DIS(*continuus* . CONTINUOUS) + -OUS]

dis'cŏrd[1], n. **1.** Disagreement, variance, strife; harsh noise, clashing sounds; whence or cogn. **discŏrd'ANT** a., **discŏrd'-** ANCE n., **dĭscŏrd'antLY[2]** adv. **2.** (mus.). Want of harmony between notes sounded together; chord unpleasing or unsatisfactory in itself & requiring to be resolved by another; any interval except unison, octave, perfect fifth and fourth, major & minor third & sixth, & their octaves; single note dissonant with another. [ME, f. OF *discord* (foll.)]

discŏrd'[2], v.i. Disagree, quarrel, be different or inconsistent, (*with, from*); be dissonant, jar, clash. [ME, f. OF *desorder* f. L *discordare* f. DIS (*cors-* cord- -hearted f. *cor* *-dis* heart)]

dis'count[1], n. Deduction from amount due or price of goods in consideration of its being paid promptly or in advance; deduction from amount of bill of exchange etc. by one who gives value for it before it is due; discounting; allowance for exaggeration in accepting story; *at a* ~, below par, depreciated, not in demand. [17th c., f. F *descompte, -conte* (foll.)]

discount'[2], v.t. Give or get present worth of (bill not yet due); leave out of account; lessen, detract from; part with for immediate but smaller good; allow for exaggeration in; use up effect of (news etc.) beforehand, stale by anticipation. Hence ~ABLE a. [f. OF *desconter, -comp-ter,* f. med. L DIS(*computare* L = COMPUTE)]

discount'ĕnance, v.t. Refuse to countenance, discourage, show disapproval of. [partly f. obs. F *descontenancer* (DIS-, COUNTENANCE[2])]

discou'rag|e (*-kŭ-*), v.t. Deprive of courage, confidence, or energy; deter *from;* discountenance. Hence ~eMENT n., ~ĭngLY[2] adv., (*-kŭrĭj-*). [ME, f. OF *descoragier* (DIS-, COURAGE)]

dis'course[1] (*-ōrs*), n. Talk, conversation, (arch.); dissertation, treatise, sermon. [ME, f. OF *discours* f. L DIS(*cursus* COURSE[1])]

discourse'[2] (*-ōrs*), v.i. & t. Talk, converse; hold forth in speech or writing on a subject (*of, upon,* or abs.); give forth (some kind of music; ref. to *Hamlet* III. ii. 374). [f. prec., partly f. F *discourir*]

discourt'eous, a., **discourt'esў,** n., (*-kĕr-, -kōr-*). Rude(ness), uncivil, incivility. Hence **discourt'eousLY[2]** adv. [DIS-]

disco'ver (*-kŭ-*), v.t. Disclose, expose to view, reveal, make known, exhibit, manifest, betray; (Chess) ~ *check,* check by removing piece or pawn; find out (fact etc., *that* etc., unknown country), suddenly realize, whence or cogn. ~ABLE a., ~ER[1] n. [ME, f. OF *descovrir* f. LL DIS-(*cooperire* COVER[1])]

disco'vert (-kŭ-), a. (legal). Unmarried or widowed (of woman). [f. OF *descovert* p.p. (prec.)]

disco'very (-kŭ-), n. Revealing, disclosure, (in Law, compulsory disclosure by party to action of facts or documents on which he relies; in play, poem, etc., revelation unravelling plot); finding out, making known; thing found out. [f. DISCOVER on anal. of *recover, recovery*]

discrĕd'it[1], n. Loss of repute, thing involving this; doubt, lack of credibility, (*throws* ~ *upon*); loss of commercial credit. [DIS-]

discrĕd'it[2], v.t. Refuse to believe; bring disbelief or disrepute upon. [DIS-]

discrĕd'itab|le, a. Bringing discredit, shameful. Hence ~LY[2] adv. [DIS-]

discreet', a. Judicious, prudent, circumspect, not speaking out at inopportune times. Hence ~LY[2] adv. [ME, f. OF *discret* f. L DIS(*cretus* p.p. of *cernere* sift) separate, with LL sense f. its derivative *discretio* discernment]

dis'crĕpant (*or* -rĕp'-), a. Different, inconsistent, (of stories etc.). So **discrĕp'-ANCY** n. [f. L DIS(*crepāre* sound), -ANT]

dis'crēte, a. Separate, individually distinct, discontinuous; (Metaphys.) abstract, not concrete. Hence ~NESS (-tn-) n. [ME, f. L *discretus* see DISCREET]

discrē'tion, n. Liberty of deciding as one thinks fit, absolutely or within limits (*it is within* one's ~ *to*; *at the* ~ *of*, to be settled or disposed of by the wish of; *at* ~, at one's own pleasure; *surrender at* ~, unconditionally), whence ~ARY[1] (-sho-) a.; discernment, prudence, judgement, (*years, age, of* ~, time at which one is fit to manage oneself—in Eng. law, 14; ~ *is the better part of valour*, used as joc. excuse for cowardice). [ME, f. OF *discrecion* f. L *discretionem* (DISCREET, -ION)]

discrim'in|āte, v.t. & i. Be, set up, or observe, a difference between (also intr. with *between*), distinguish *from* another; make a distinction (~*ate against*, distinguish unfavourably, of taxes etc.), observe distinctions carefully. So ~A'TION n., ~ATIVE a. [f. L *discriminare* (*discrimen* distinction f. *discernere* DISCERN), -ATE[3]]

discrim'ināting, a. In vbl senses; esp.: discerning, acute; ~ *duty, rate*, varying in amount according to country sending goods or person rated, differential. [-ING[2]]

discrown', v.t. Take crown from, depose, (sovereign lit. or fig.). [DIS-]

discūrs'ive, a. Rambling, digressive, expatiating; proceeding by argument or reasoning, not intuitive. Hence ~LY[2] (-vl-) adv., ~NESS (-vn-) n. [f. med. L *discursivus* f. L DIS(*currere curs-* run), -IVE]

dis'cus, n. Heavy disc thrown in ancient Roman & Greek athletic exercises & modern Olympic Games & other sports. [L f. Gk *diskos* quoit]

discŭss', v.t. Examine by argument, debate, whence ~IBLE a.; consume with enjoyment (food, wine, meal). [ME, f. L DIS(*cutere -cuss- = quatere* shake)]

discŭss'ion (-shn), n. Examination by argument; a debate; consumption with enjoyment of food. [ME, f. OF f. LL *discussionem* (prec., -ION)]

disdain', n., & v.t. Scorn, (regard with) contempt; think beneath oneself (*to do, doing*, or noun) or one's notice. Hence ~FUL a., ~fuLY[2] adv. [ME, f. OF *desdeign(er)* f. L DE(*dignari* f. *dignus* worthy)]

disease' (-zēz), n. Morbid condition of body, plant, or some part of them, illness, sickness; any particular kind of this with special symptoms & name; deranged or depraved state of mind or morals. [ME, f. OF *desaise* (DIS-, EASE n.)]

diseased' (-zēzd), a. Affected with disease; morbid, depraved. [ME; p.p. of *disease* vb (now rare) f. OF *desaaisier* as prec.]

disĕmbȧrk', v.t. & i. Put, go, ashore. Hence **disĕmbȧrkā'TION** n. [f. F *désembarquer*, or It., or Sp. (DIS-, EMBARK)]

disĕmbȧ'rrass, v.t. Free from embarrassment, rid or relieve (*of*); disentangle (*from*). Hence ~MENT n. [DIS-]

disĕmbŏd'|y̆, v.t. Separate, free, (soul, idea) from body or the concrete; disband (troops). Hence ~ĭMENT n. [DIS-]

disĕmbōgue' (-g), v.i. & t. (Of river etc.) pour forth at mouth (intr., or *itself*, waters, etc.); (fig.) discharge, pour forth, (t. & i. of speech, crowd, etc.). [f. Sp. *desembocar* (DIS-, *en* in, *boca* mouth)]

disĕmbos'om (-ŏoz-), v.t. & i. Disclose, reveal; unburden oneself, make confidences. [DIS-]

disĕmbow'el, v.t. (-ll-). Remove entrails of, rip up so as to cause bowels to protrude. Hence ~MENT n. [DIS-]

disĕmbroil', v.t. Extricate from confusion or entanglement. [DIS-]

disĕnchant' (-ah-), v.t. Free from enchantment or illusion. Hence ~MENT (-ah-) n. [f. F *désenchanter* (DIS-, ENCHANT)]

disĕncŭm'ber, v.t. Free from encumbrance. [f. F *désencombrer* (DIS-, ENCUMBER)]

disĕndow', v.t. Strip (esp. Church) of endowments. Hence ~MENT n. [DIS-]

disĕngāge', v.t. & i., & n. Detach, liberate, loosen; (Fencing) pass point of sword to other side of opponent's (n., this movement); come apart, break contact. [DIS-]

disĕngāged' (-jd), a. In vbl senses; esp.: at leisure to attend to any visitor or business that comes; vacant, not bespoken. [-ED[1]]

disĕngāge'ment (-jm-), n. Disengaging; liberation (of chem. component); freedom from ties, detachment; easy natural manner; dissolution of engagement to marry; (Fencing)=DISENGAGE n. [-MENT]

disentail', v.t. (legal). Free from entail, break the entail of. [DIS-]

disentang'le (-nggl), v.t. & i. Extricate, free from complications; unravel, untwist; come clear of tangle. Hence ~MENT (-nggelm-) n. [DIS-]

disenthral(l)' (-awl), v.t. (-ll-). Free from bondage. Hence **disenthral'**MENT (-awl-) n. [DIS-]

disentomb' (-ōōm), v.t. Take out of tomb; unearth, find by research. [DIS-]

disequilib'rium, n. Lack or loss of equilibrium, instability. [DIS-]

disestab'lish, v.t. Undo establishment of; deprive (Church) of State connexion, depose from official position. Hence ~MENT n. [DIS-]

diseur (dēzĕr'), n. (fem. *-euse*, pr. *-ĕrz'*). Artiste entertaining with monologue. [F, = talker]

disfav'our (-ver), n., & v.t. Dislike, disapproval; being disliked (*fall into, be in,* ~); (vb) regard, treat, with ~. [DIS-]

disfea'ture, v.t. Mar features of, disfigure. [DIS-]

disfig'ure (-ger), v.t.* Mar beauty of, deform, deface, sully. Hence **disfigūra**ʟ TION, ~MENT (-germ-), nn. [ME, f. OF *desfigurer* (DIS-, L *figurare* f. *figura* FIGURE[1])]

disfo'rest, v.t. = DISAFFOREST; clear of forests. [f. OF *desforester* (DIS-, FOREST)]

disfran'chise (-īz), v.t. Deprive of citizen rights; deprive (place) of right of sending, (person) of right of voting for, parliamentary representative. Hence ~MENT (-īzm-) n. [DIS-, obs. *franchise* vb = ENFRANCHISE]

disfrock', v.t. Deprive of clerical (garb &) status. [DIS-]

disgorge', v.t. & i. Eject (as) from throat (esp. fig., trans. or abs., of giving up ill-gotten gains, booty, etc.); (of river etc., trans., refl., or intr.) disembogue, discharge (waters). [ME, f. OF *desgorger* (DIS-, GORGE[1])]

disgrace'[1], n. Loss of favour, downfall from position of honour; ignominy, shame; thing involving dishonour, cause of reproach. Hence ~FUL a., ~fulLY[2] adv., ~fulNESS n., (-sf-). [f. F *disgrâce* f. It. *disgrazia* (DIS-, GRACE)]

disgrace'[2], v.t. Dismiss from favour, degrade from position; bring shame or discredit upon, be a disgrace to. [f. F *disgracier* as prec.]

disgrun'tled (-ld), a. Discontented, moody. [from 17th c.; DIS-, *gruntle* obs. frequent. of GRUNT]

disguise'[1] (-gīz), v.t. Conceal identity of (~ *oneself*, person or thing, *as* someone or something else, *by doing, with* false beard etc., *in* costume etc.); misrepresent, show in false colours; conceal, cloak, (~ one's *intention, opinion*). Hence ~MENT (-īzm-) n. [ME, f. OF *desguisier* (DIS-, Rom. *guisa* GUISE)]

disguise'[2] (-gīz), n. Use of changed dress or appearance for concealment's sake, disguised condition (*blessing in* ~, one that seems to be a misfortune); garb used to deceive; artificial manner, deception. [ME, f. prec.]

disgust'[1], n. Loathing, nausea, repugnance, strong aversion, (*at, for, towards, against*). [f. OF *desgout* or It. *disgusto* (DIS-, GUST[2])]

disgust'[2], v.t. Excite loathing, aversion, or indignation, in (~ *ed with, at, by*). Hence ~édLY[2], ~ingLY[2], advv. [f. OF *desgouster* or It. *disgustare* (prec.)]

disgust'ful, a. Disgusting, repulsive; (of contempt, curiosity, etc.) inspired by, full of, disgust. [-FUL]

dish[1], n. Shallow flat-bottomed usu. oval or oblong vessel of earthenware, glass, or metal, for holding food at meals; food so held, particular kind of food (SIDE-~; *made* ~, of various ingredients; *standing* ~, that appears daily, also fig.); || (arch.) cup, esp. ~ *of tea*, tea-drinking, whence ~ *of gossip*, a chat; ~-shaped receptacle used for any purpose; ~-*cover*, of metal etc. for keeping food in ~ hot; ~-*cloth* & (arch.) -*clout*, for washing ~es & plates; ~-*wash*, -*water*, in which ~es have been washed; ~-*washer*, water wagtail. [OE *disc*, OS *disk*, OHG *tisc*, ON *diskr* f. L *discus* DISC]

dish[2], v.t. & i. Put (food) into dish ready for serving; ~ *up*, serve meal, (fig.) present (facts, argument) attractively; make concave or dish-shaped; (of horse) move fore-feet not straight but with scooping motion; circumvent, outmanœuvre, (esp., Pol.) defeat (opponents) by adopting their policy (~*ing the Whigs,* of Reform Bill 1867). [f. prec.]

dishabille' (-sabĕl), n. Being negligently or partly dressed, undress, (usu. *in* ~); undress garment or costume. [f. F *déshabillé* p.p. of *déshabiller* (DIS-, *habiller* clothe)]

dishabit'ūate (-s-h-), v.t. Make (person) unaccustomed (*for* etc.). [DIS-]

disharm'onize (-s-h-), **-ise** (-īz), v.t. Put out of harmony, make discordant. [DIS-]

disharm'onў (-s-h-), n. Discord, dissonance. So **disharmōn'ious** a. [DIS-]

disheart'en (-s-har-), v.t. Make despondent, rob of courage. Hence ~MENT n. [DIS-]

|| **dishe'rison** (-s-h-), n. Disinheriting. [ME, f. OF *desheritcisun* f. *desheriter* (ME *disherit*) f. DIS- +LL *hereditare* INHERIT]

dishev'elled (-ld), a. With disordered hair; (of hair) loose, flung about, unconfined; (of person) untidy, ruffled, unkempt. Hence **dishev'el**MENT n. [ME *dischevel, -ee*, f. OF *deschevelc* (DIS-, *chevel* hair f. L *capillus*) +-ED[1]]

dishon'est (-sŏ-), a. Fraudulent, knavish, insincere, (of person, act, statement),

For compounds of *dis-* not given consult DIS-.

Hence ~LY[2] adv. [ME, f. OF *deshoneste* (DIS-, HONEST)]

dishon'esty (-sŏ-), n. Want of honesty, knavery, deceitfulness, fraud. [ME, f. OF *deshoneste* (prec., -Y[1])]

dishon'our[1] (-s-ŏner), n. State of shame or disgrace, discredit; thing that involves this; refusal to honour cheque, bill of exchange, etc. [ME, f. OF *deshonor* (DIS-, L *honorem* HONOUR[1])]

dishon'our[2] (-s-ŏner), v.t. Treat with indignity; violate chastity of; disgrace; refuse to accept or pay (cheque, bill of exchange). [ME, f. OF *deshonorer* f. LL DIS(*honorare* L = HONOUR[2])]

dishon'ourab|le (-s-ŏner-), a. Involving disgrace, ignominious; unprincipled, base, against dictates of honour. Hence ~leNESS n., ~LY[2] adv. [DIS-]

dishŏrn' (-s-h-), v.t. Cut off horns of. [DIS-]

disillu'sion, n., & v.t., **disillu'sion|ize**, -ise (-iz), v.t., (-ōozho-). Disenchant-(ment), free(dom) from illusions. Hence ~MENT n. [DIS-, -IZE]

disincĕn'tive, a. & n. Deterrent. [DIS-]

disinclinā'tion, n. Want of liking or willingness (*for* or *to* course, *to* do). [DIS-]

disincline', v.t. Make indisposed (*to* do, *for* or *to* course). [DIS-]

disincŏrp'orāte, v.t. Dissolve (corporate body). [DIS-]

disinfĕct', v.t. Cleanse (room, clothes, etc.) of infection. Hence or cogn. **disinfĕc'tANT(2)** a. & n., **disinfĕc'tION** n. [DIS-]

disinflā'tion, n. (econ.). Deflation. Hence ~ARY[1] (-sho-) a. [DIS-]

disingĕn'ūous (-j-), a. Insincere, having secret motives, not candid. Hence ~LY[2] adv., ~NESS n. [DIS-]

disinhĕ'rit, v.t. Reject as heir, deprive of inheritance. Hence ~ANCE n. [ME; DIS-, *inherit* in obs. sense *make heir*]

disin'tĕgr|āte, v.t. & i. Separate into component parts, deprive of or lose cohesion. Hence ~A'TION, ~āTOR, nn. [DIS-]

disintĕr', v.t. (-rr-). Unbury, exhume; unearth. Hence ~MENT n. [f. F *désenterrer* (DIS-, INTER[1])]

disin'terest, v.t. & refl. To divest of interest, (refl.) cease to concern one*self* (esp., in Diplom., renounce intention or right of intervening etc.). [DIS-]

disin'terestĕd, a. Not biased by self--seeking, impartial; ~ *management* (of public house by manager who does not profit by sale of liquor). Hence ~LY[2] adv., ~NESS n. [DIS-]

disinvĕst'ment, n. Realization of a country's assets. [DIS-]

dĭsjĕc'ta mĕm'bra, n. pl. Fragments, scattered remains. [L]

disjoin', v.t. Separate, disunite, part. [ME, f. OF *desjoindre* f. L DIS(*jungere junct-* join)]

disjoint', v.t. Dislocate, disturb working or connexion of (p.p., esp. of talk, inco-

herent, desultory, whence ~ĕdLY[2] adv., ~ĕdNESS n.); take in pieces at the joints. [ME, f. obs. *disjoint* adj. f. p.p. of OF as prec.]

disjŭnc'tion, n. Disjoining, separation. [ME, f. OF or L *disjunctio* (DISJOIN, -ION)]

disjŭnc'tive, a. & n. Disjoining, involving separation; (Log., Gram.) alternative (adj.), involving choice between two words etc., (n., ~ proposition or conjunction). Hence ~LY[2] (-vl-) adv. [f. L *disjunctivus* (DISJOIN, -IVE)]

disk. See DISC.

dislike', v.t., & n. 1. Not like, have aversion or objection to. 2. n. Aversion (*to*, *of*, *for*). [DIS-]

dis'locāte, v.t. Put out of joint (limb, or fig. machinery, affairs); (Geol.) make (strata) discontinuous; displace. So **dislocA'TION** n. [f. med. L DIS(*locare* L = place), -ATE[3]]

dislŏdĝ|e', v.t. Remove, turn out, (esp. fortified enemy) from position. Hence ~(e)'MENT (-jm-) n. [ME, f. OF *desloger* (DIS-, LODGE v.)]

disloy'al, a. Unfaithful to or *to* friendship etc.; untrue to allegiance, disaffected to government, whence ~IST(2) n. .& a. Hence or cogn. ~LY[2] adv., ~TY n.· [ME, f. OF *desloial* (DIS-, LOYAL)]

dis'mal (-z-), a., **dis'mal|s**, n. pl. Depressing, miserable, sombre, dreary; hence ~LY[2] adv., ~NESS n.; *the* ~ *science*, political economy; *the* ~*s*, low spirits, dumps. [orig. noun = unlucky days f. AF *dis mal* f. L *dies mali* ill days; these were two special days in each month in medieval calendars]

dismăn'tle, v.t. Strip *of* covering, protection, etc.; deprive (fortress, ship, etc.) of defences, rigging, equipment. Hence ~MENT (-lm-) n. [f. obs. F *desmanteller* (DIS, MANTLE n.)]

dismast' (-ah-), v.t. Deprive (ship) of mast(s). [DIS-]

dismay', v.t., & n. (Fill with) consternation, discourage(ment). [ME, f. OF *desmaier* (cf. Pr. *desmaiar*) f. Rom. *dismagare* f. DIS-+Gmc *mag-*; cf. MIGHT[1]]

dismĕm'ber, v.t. Tear or cut limb from limb; partition (empire, country), divide up. Hence ~MENT n. [ME, f. OF *desmembrer* (DIS-, L *membrum* limb)]

dismiss', v.t., & n. Send away, disperse, disband, (assembly, army; Mil., imperat., word of command closing drill, also as n., *the* ~, release at end of drill); allow to go; discharge, cashier, from service or office (*was* ~*ed the*, or *from the*, *army*); send away from one's presence; put out of one's thoughts, cease to feel; treat (subject) summarily; (Law) send out of court, refuse further hearing to, (case); (Cricket, of batsman) send (ball), send ball of (bowler), usu. *to boundary* or *for four* etc., (of fielding side) put (batsman, side) out (usu. *for score*). Hence ~AL(2), (now rare)

dismi'ssion (-shn), nn., ~IBLE a. [ME; superseding obs. *dismit*, after OF *desmis* (p.p. of *desmettre*) or its source, med. L *dismissus* (DIS-, L *mittere miss-* send)]

dismount', v.i. & t., & n. Alight, cause to alight, from or *from* horseback etc. (n., alighting); unseat, unhorse, (of horse, enemy, or stumble etc.); remove (thing) from its mount (esp. gun from carriage). [DIS-]

disobēd'ience, n., **disobēd'ient**, a. Disobeying (~ *to* orders, master, etc.), rebellious(ness), rule-breaking. Hence **disobēd'iently**[2] adv. [ME, f. OF (*des*-), see DIS-, OBEDIENCE, OBEDIENT]

disobey' (-bā), v.i. & t. Disregard orders, break rules; not obey (person, law). [ME, f. OF *desobeir* (DIS-, OBEY)]

disoblig|e', v.t. Refuse to consult convenience or wishes of. Hence ~'ING[2] a., ~'ingLY[2] adv., ~'ingNESS n. [f. F *désobliger* (DIS-, OBLIGE)]

disōrd'er[1], n. Want of order, confusion; tumult, riot, commotion; ailment, disease. [f. F *désordre* (DIS-, ORDER)]

disōrd'er[2], v.t. Disarrange, throw into confusion; put out of health, upset. [ME; assim. to ORDER v. of earlier *disordain* f. OF *desordener* (DIS-, ORDAIN)]

disōrd'erl|ȳ, a. **1.** Untidy, confused; irregular, unruly, riotous; hence ~iNESS n. **2.** Constituting public nuisance (~*y house*, bawdy, gaming, or betting, -house) [DISORDER[1], -LY[2]]

disōrg'aniz|e, -is|e (-īz), v.t. Destroy system etc. of, throw into confusion. Hence ~A'TION n. [f. F *désorganiser* (DIS-, ORGANIZE)]

disō'rient|āte, v.t. Place (church) with chancel not directly eastwards; confuse (person) as to his bearings (lit. & fig.). Hence ~A'TION n. [DIS-]

disown' (-ōn), v.t. Refuse to recognize, repudiate, disclaim; renounce allegiance to. [DIS-]

dispa'rag|e, v.t. Bring discredit on, lower; speak slightingly of, depreciate. So ~EMENT (-ĭjm-) n., ~ingLY[2] (-ĭj-) adv. [ME, f. OF *desparagier* marry unequally (DIS-, *parage* equality f. L *par* equal, -AGE)]

dis'parate, a. & n. **1.** Essentially different, diverse in kind, incommensurable, without relation; hence ~LY[2] (-tl-) adv., ~NESS (-tn-) n. **2.** n. (usu. pl.). Thing(s) so unlike that there is no basis for comparison. [f. L DIS(*paratus* p.p. of *parare* provide) separate, influenced in sense by L *dispar* unequal]

dispā'ritȳ, n. Inequality, difference, incongruity. [f. F *disparité* f. LL *disparitatem* (DIS-, PARITY)]

dispärk', v.t. Convert (park-land) to other uses. [DIS-]

dispärt'[1], n. (gunnery). Difference between semidiameters of gun at base-ring and at muzzle, to be allowed for in aim-

ing; sight making the allowance. [orig. unascertained: cf. foll.]

dispärt'[2], v.t. & i. (poet.). Separate, part asunder, (t. & i.); go in different directions; distribute. [f. L DIS(*partire* f. *pars part*) distribute]

dispä'ssionate (-sho-), a. Free from emotion, calm, impartial. Hence ~LY[2] (-tl-) adv., ~NESS (-tn-) n. [DIS-]

dispätch'[1], dĕs-, v.t. & i. Send off to a destination or for a purpose; give the death-blow to, kill; get (task, business) promptly done, settle, finish off; eat (food, meal) quickly; (arch.) make haste. [f. It. *dispacciare* or Sp. *despachar* expedite; not connected w. F *dépêcher*]

dispätch'[2], dĕs-, n. Sending off (of messenger, letter, etc.); putting to death (*happy* ~, suicide as practised by Japanese); prompt settlement of business, promptitude, efficiency, rapidity; written message, esp. official communication on State affairs (~-*box*, for carrying these & other documents); (*D*~) title of newspaper; agency for conveying goods etc.; ~-*rider*, esp. motor-cyclist or horseman carrying military messages. [f. prec., or It. *dispaccio*, Sp. *despacho*]

dispĕl', v.t. (-ll-). Dissipate, disperse, (fears, darkness). [f. L DIS(*pellere* drive)]

dispĕn'sable, a. That can be relaxed in special cases (canon, law, oath); not necessary, that can be done without. [f. med. L *dispensabilis* (DISPENSE, -ABLE)]

dispĕn'sarȳ, n. Place, esp. charitable institution, where medicines are dispensed. [f. med. L *dispensarius*; see -ARY[1]]

dispensā'tion, n. Distributing, dealing out; ordering, management, esp. of the world by Providence; arrangement made by Nature or Providence; special dealing of Providence with community or person; religious system prevalent at a period (*Mosaic, O.T., Christian,* ~); exemption from penalty or duty laid down in esp. eccl. law (*with, from*); doing without (*with*). [ME, f. OF, or L *dispensatio* (foll., -ATION)]

dispēnse', v.t. & i. **1.** Distribute, deal out; administer (sacrament, justice); make up & give out (medicine); grant dispensations; release *from* obligation. **2.** ~ *with*: relax, give exemption from, (rule); annul binding force of (oath); render needless (usu. *the need of* etc.); do without. So **dispĕn'ser**[1] n., (esp.) professional maker-up of medical prescriptions. [ME, f. OF *despenser* f. L *dispensare* frequent. of DIS(*pendĕre pens-* weigh)]

dispeo'ple (-pēp-), v.t. Depopulate. [ME, f. OF *despeupler* (DIS-, PEOPLE)]

dispĕrs|e, v.t. & i. Scatter (t. & i.), drive, go, throw or send, in different directions, rout, dispel, be dispelled; send to or station at separate points; put in circulation, disseminate; (Opt.) divide (white light) into its coloured rays. Hence ~'AL(2) n., ~'ĕDLY² adv., ~'IVE a., ~'ive-LY² adv., ~'iveNESS n. [ME, f. OF *disperser* f. L DI¹(*spergere -spers-* = *spargere* scatter)]

disper'sion (-shn), n. Dispersing (see prec.); *the D*~, the Jews dispersed among Gentiles after Captivity. [ME, f. LL *dispersio* (prec., -ION) transl. Gk *diaspora*]

dispi'rit, v.t. Make despondent, depress. Hence ~ĕdLY² adv. [DIS-]

dispit'éous, a. Pitiless. [19th-c. revival with changed sense as if f. DIS-, PITEOUS, of 16th-c. *despiteous* (DESPITE)]

displăce', v.t. Shift from its place (~*d person*, one who has been expelled or has escaped from his native country as a result of annexation, transfer of population, etc.; abbr. D.P.); remove from office; oust, take the place of, put something else in the place of, replace. [f. OF *desplacer* (DIS-, PLACE n.)]

displăce'ment (-sm-), n. Displacing, being displaced; amount by which thing is shifted from its place; ousting, replacement by something else; amount or weight of fluid displaced by solid floating or immersed in it (*a ship with a* ~ *of 11,000 tons*). [prec., -MENT]

display'¹, v.t. Exhibit, expose to view, show; show ostentatiously; reveal, betray, allow to appear. [ME, f. OF *despleier* f. L DIS(*plicare* fold) cf. DEPLOY]

display'², n. Displaying; exhibition, show; ostentation; (Print.) arrangement of type with a view to calling attention. [f. prec.]

displeas|e' (-z), v.t. Offend, annoy, make indignant or angry, be disagreeable to; *be* ~*ed* (*at, with*, or abs), disapprove, be indignant or dissatisfied. Hence ~'ING² a., ~'ingLY² adv., (-zī-). [ME, f. OF *desplaisir* (DIS-, L *placēre* PLEASE)]

displea'sure (-lĕzher), n., & v.t. Displeased feeling, dissatisfaction, disapproval, anger; (vb) cause ~ to, annoy. [ME, f. OF as prec., assim. to PLEASURE]

displume' (-ōō-), v.t. (poet.). Strip of feathers, lit. & fig. [DIS-]

dispŏrt', v. refl. & i., & n. 1. Frolic, gambol, enjoy one*self*, display one*self* sportively. 2. n. (arch.). Relaxation, pastime. [ME, f. OF *desport*(*er*) f. DIS-, *porter* carry; see SPORT]

dispōs'a|ble (-za-), a. That can be disposed of, got rid of, made over, or used; at disposal. Hence ~BIL'ITY n. [DISPOSE, -ABLE]

dispōs'al (-zl), n. Disposing of, getting rid of, settling, dealing with, bestowal, assignment; sale; control, management, (*at* one's ~); placing, disposition, arrangement. [foll., -AL(2)]

dispōse' (-z), v.t. & i. 1. Place suitably, at intervals, or in order; bring (person, mind) into certain state (esp. in p.p. *well-, ill-, ~d*); incline, make willing or desirous, *to* something or *to* do; give (thing)

tendency *to*; determine course of events (*man proposes, God* ~*s*). 2. ~ *of*: do what one will with, regulate; get off one's hands, stow away, settle, finish, kill, demolish (claim, argument, opponent), dismiss (cricket XI *for* certain score), consume (food); sell. [ME, f. OF DIS-(*poser* see POSE¹) confused with L *disponere* thr. such derivatives as foll.]

disposi'tion (-zǐ-), n. Setting in order, arrangement, relative position of parts; (usu. pl.) plan, preparations, stationing of troops ready for attack, defence, etc.; ordinance, dispensation, (*a* ~ *of Providence* etc.); bestowal by deed or will; control, disposal, (*at* one's ~); bent, temperament, natural tendency; inclination *to*. [ME, f. OF f. L DIS(*positionem* f. *ponere posit-* place)]

dispossĕss' (-oz-), v.t. Oust, dislodge, (person); deprive *of*; rid (person) of or of evil spirit (obs.). Hence **dispossĕ's-**sion (-shn), ~OR (-oz-), nn. [f. OF *despossesser* (DIS-, POSSESS)]

dispraise' (-z), v.t., & n. Disparagement), censure. [ME; n. f. vb, f. OF *despreisier* f. LL DE*pretiare* DEPRECIATE]

disproŏf', n. Refutation; thing that disproves. [DIS-]

dispropor'tion, n. Want of proportion; being out of proportion. Hence ~ED⁸ (-shond) a. [DIS-]

dispropor'tionate (-sho-), a. Wanting proportion; relatively too large or small. Hence ~LY² (-tl-) adv. [DIS-]

disprove' (-ōōv), v.t. (p.p. ~*d*, rarely ~*n*). Prove false, show fallacy of, refute. [ME, f. OF *desprover* (DIS-, PROVE)]

dis'pŭtab|le, a. Open to question, uncertain. Hence ~LY² adv. [F, or f. L *disputabilis* (DISPUTE¹, -ABLE)]

dispŭt|ā'tion, n. Argument, controversy. Hence ~ā'tIOUS (-shus) a., ~ā'tiousLY² adv., ~ā'tiousNESS n., (-shus-). [ME, f. OF, or L *disputatio* (foll., -ATION)]

dispūte'¹ v.t. & t. Argue, hold disputation, (*with, against*, person, *on, about*, subject), whence **dis'pŭtANT**(1) n. & a.; quarrel, have altercation; discuss (*whether, how*, etc.; point, question); controvert, call in question, (statement, fact); resist (landing, advance, etc.); contend for, strive to win, (pre-eminence, victory, every inch of ground). [ME *despute* f. OF *desputer* f. L DIS(*putare* reckon)]

dispūte'², n. Controversy, debate, (*in* ~, being argued about; *beyond, past, without,* ~, certainly, indisputably); heated contention, quarrel, difference of opinion. [f. prec.]

disqualificā'tion (-ŏl-), n. In vbl senses; esp., thing that disqualifies. [foll., -FICATION]

disqual'ifỹ (-ŏl-), v.t. Unfit, disable, (*for* some purpose or office); incapacitate legally, pronounce unqualified; debar from competition because of infringement of rules. [DIS-]

disqui'et, v.t., a., & n. Deprive of peace, worry; (adj.) uneasy, disturbed, whence **disqui'ĕtude**, ~NESS, nn.; (n.) anxiety, unrest. [DIS-]

disquisi'tion (-zĭ-), n. (Arch.) Investigation, inquiry; (mod.) long or elaborate treatise or discourse *on* subject. Hence ~AL a. [f. L DIS(*quisitio* f. *-quirere -quisit-* = *quaerere* seek, -ION)]

disrāte', v.t. (naut.). Reduce to lower rating or rank. [DIS-]

disrĕgārd', v.t.; & n. **1.** Pay no attention to, ignore, treat as of no importance. **2.** n. Indifference, neglect (*of*, *for*). [DIS-]

disrĕl'ish, n., & v.t. Dislike, (regard with) distaste, aversion. [DIS-]

disrĕmĕm'ber, v.t. (dial. etc.). Fail to remember. [DIS-]

disrĕpair', n. Bad condition for want of repairs (usu. *is* etc. *in* ~). [DIS-]

disrĕp'ūtab|le, a. Discreditable; of bad repute, not respectable in character or appearance. Hence ~leNESS (-ln-) n., ~LY² adv. [DIS-]

disrĕpūte', n. Ill repute, discredit. [DIS-]

disrĕspĕct', n. Rudeness, want of respect. So ~FUL a., ~fulLY² adv., ~fulNESS n. [DIS-]

disrōbe', v.t. & i. Divest of robe or garment (also fig.); undress (refl. or intr.). [DIS-]

disrōot', v.t. Uproot; dislodge. [DIS-]

disrŭpt', v.t. Shatter, separate forcibly. [19th-c. vb f. L *disrupt-* see foll.]

disrŭp'tion, n. Bursting asunder, violent dissolution, rent condition; *the D~*, split in Church of Scotland 1843. So **disrŭp'tive** a. [f. L DIS(*ruptio* f. *rumpere rupt-* break, -ION)]

dissăt'isfȳ, v.t. Fail to satisfy, make discontented (*dissatisfied with*, *at*). So **dissatISFAC'TION** n. [DIS-]

dissāve', v.i. Spend one's savings. [DIS-]

dissēat', v.t. Unseat. [DIS-]

dissĕct', v.t. Cut in pieces; anatomize, cut up, (animal, plant) to show its structure etc.; examine part by part, analyse, criticize in detail. Hence or cogn. **dissĕc'tion**, **dissĕc'tor**, nn. [f. L DIS(*secare sect-* cut)]

disseise', -ze, (-sēz), v.t. Oust, dispossess, *of* estates (or fig.). [ME, f. AF = OF *dessaisir* (DIS-, SEIZE)]

disseis'in, -zin, (-sēz-), n. (legal). Disseising, wrongful dispossession of real property. [ME, f. AF = OF *dessaisine* (DIS-, SEIZIN)]

dissĕm'bl|e, v.t. & i. Cloak, disguise, conceal, (character, feeling, intention, act); pretend not to see, ignore, (insult etc.; arch.); fail to mention (fact); conceal one's motives etc., be a hypocrite, whence ~ER¹ n. [perh. assim. to *resemble* of obs. *dissimule* f. OF *dissimuler* f. L DIS(*simulare* SIMULATE)]

dissĕm'in|āte, v.t. Scatter abroad, sow in various places, (lit., seed; usu. fig., doctrines, sedition, etc.); ~*ated sclerosis*, disease of central nervous system resulting in various forms of paralysis. So ~A'TION, ~ātor, nn. [f.'L DIS(*seminare* f. *semen -inis* seed), -ATE³]

dissĕn'sion (-shn), n. Discord arising from difference in opinion. [ME, f. OF f. L DIS(*sensionem* f. *sentire sens-* feel, -ION)]

dissĕnt'¹, v.i. Refuse to assent; disagree, think differently or express such difference (*from*), ǁ esp. in religious doctrine from an established church (~*ing minister*, nonconformist clergyman). Hence ~ingLY² adv. [ME, f. L DIS(*sentire* feel)]

dissĕnt'², n. (Expression of) difference of opinion; ǁ refusal to accept doctrines of established church, nonconformity, (collect.) dissenters. [f. prec.]

dissĕn'ter, n. One who dissents, esp. from a national church; ǁ member of a sect that has separated itself from the Church of England. [-ER¹]

dissĕn'tient (-shĭ-, -shnt), a. & n. (One) disagreeing with a majority or official view. [f. L DIS(*sentire* feel), -ENT]

dissĕp'iment, n. (bot. & zool.). Partition, septum. [f. L DIS(*saepimentum* f. *saepire* f. *saepes* hedge, -MENT)]

dissĕrt', **diss'ertāte**, vv.i. Discourse, give an exposition, disquisition, or dissertA'TION n. [f. p.p. stems of L DIS-(*serere sert-* join) & its frequent. *dissertare*, -ATE³]

dissĕrve', v.t. Do an ill turn to. So **disSERV'ICE** n. [DIS-]

dissĕv'er, v.t. & i. Sever, divide. [ME, f. AF f. OF *desevrer* f. LL *disseparare* (DIS-, SEPARATE)]

diss'idence, n. Disagreement, dissent. [f. L *dissidentia* (foll., -ENCE)]

diss'ident, a. & n. Disagreeing, at variance; dissentient (a. & n.); dissenter. [F, or f. L DIS(*sidēre* = *sedēre* sit), -ENT]

dissim'ilar, a. Unlike (*to*, also rarely *from*, *with*). Hence **dissimilā'rITY** n., ~LY² adv. [DIS-]

dissim'il|āte, v.t. (philol.). Make unlike (sounds repeating each other, as in cinnamon, orig. cinnamom). Hence ~A'TION n. [f. L DIS(*similis* like), after ASSIMILATE]

dissimil'itūde, n. Unlikeness. [f. L *dissimilitudo* (prec., -TUDE)]

dissim'ūl|āte, v.t. & i. Pretend not to have or feel (cf. SIMULATE); dissemble, be hypocritical. So ~A'TION, ~ātor, nn. [f. L DIS(*simulare* SIMULATE), -ATE³]

diss'ipāt|e, v.t. & i. Disperse, dispel or disappear (cloud, vapour, care, fear, darkness); dissolve to atoms, bring or come to nothing; squander (money); fritter away (energy, attention); engage in frivolous or dissolute pleasures (*people go there to* ~*e*). Hence ~IVE a. [f. L DIS(*sipare* throw), -ATE³]

For compounds of *dis-* not given consult DIS-.

diss'ipāted, a. In vbl senses; esp., given to dissipation, dissolute. [-ED[1]]

dissipā'tion, n. Scattering, dispersion, disintegration; wasteful expenditure *of*; distraction, want of concentration, *of* faculties etc.; frivolous amusement; intemperate or vicious living. [f. F, or L *dissipatio* (DISSIPATE, -ION)]

dissō'cialize (-sha-), **-ise** (-īz), v.t. Make unsocial, disincline for society. [DIS-, SOCIAL, -IZE]

dissō'ci|āte (-shī-), v.t. Disconnect, separate, in thought or in fact (*from*); (Chem.) decompose, e.g. by heat; (Psych.) cause (person's mind) to develop more than one centre of consciousness (~*ated personality*, co-existence of two or more distinct personalities in the same person). So ~A'TION (-sī-), n., ~ABLE, ~atIVE, (-sha-), aa. [f. L DIS(*sociare* f. *socius* comrade), -ATE[3]]

diss'olu|ble (-ŏobl; *or* dīsŏl'ŭbl), a. That can be disintegrated, untied, or disconnected. Hence ~BIL'ITY (-lŏo-) n. [f. F, or L DIS(*solubilis* SOLUBLE)]

diss'olute (-ŏot), a. Lax in morals, licentious. Hence ~LY[2] (-tl-) adv., ~NESS (-tn-) n. [f. L *dissolutus* p.p. (DISSOLVE)]

dissolu'tion (-lŏo-), n. Disintegration, decomposition; liquefaction (of ice or snow); undoing *of* bond, partnership, marriage, or alliance; dismissal of assembly, ‖ esp. ending of a Parliament with a view to fresh election; death; coming to an end, fading away, disappearance. [ME, f. OF, or L *dissolutio* (foll., -ION)]

dissōlv|e' (-z-), v.t. & i. Decompose (t. & i.); make or become liquid esp. by immersion in liquid (~*ed in tears*, weeping copiously), relax, enervate; vanish (~*ing views*, of magic lantern, one fading while another replaces it); disperse (t. & i.), ‖ esp. ~*e Parliament* or ~*e*, declare DISSOLUTION; put an end to (partnership etc.), annul. Hence ~'ABLE a. [ME, f. L DIS(*solvere solut-* loosen)]

dissōl'vent (-z-), a. & n. (Thing) that dissolves something (usu. *of*). [-ENT]

diss'onant, a. Discordant, harsh-toned, incongruous. Hence or cogn. **diss'o**nANCE n., ~LY[2] adv. [ME, f. OF, or L DIS(*sonare* sound), -ANT]

dissuade' (-swād), v.t. Advise against, deprecate, (action); give advice to hinder, divert, (person *from*). So **dissua'**sION (-wāzhn) n., **dissua'**sIVE (-sw-) a. [ME, f. L DIS(*suadēre suas-* persuade)]

dissyllable etc. See disy- etc.

dissymmet'rical, a., **dissymm'etry̆**, n. Symmetrical, symmetry, in opposite directions, as in the two hands (esp. of crystals with two corresponding forms). [DIS-]

dis'taff (-ahf), n. Cleft stick about 3 ft long on which wool or flax was wound for spinning by hand; corresponding part of spinning-wheel; woman's work; ~ *side*, female branch of family (cf. *spear-side*

for the male). [OE *distæf*, f. STAFF[1], the first element being app. = LG *diesse* bunch of flax; cf. DIZEN]

dis'tal, a. (anat., bot.). Away from centre of body or point of attachment, terminal. [irreg. f. DISTANT, -AL]

dis'tance, n., & v.t. 1. Being far off, remoteness; extent of space between, interval, (*within striking-*~, near enough to deliver blow); avoidance of familiarity, reserve, (esp. *keep* one's ~); distant point (*at, to, from, a* ~); remoter field of vision (*in the* ~; *middle* ~, in painted or actual landscape, between foreground & far part); space of time (*at this* ~ *of time*); (in adv. phrr.) *a good* etc. ~ *off*; (Racing) a length of 240 yds (i.e. the ~ of the ~-*post*, used in (obs.) heat-racing, from the winning-post); *beaten by a* ~ (by about that ~). 2. v.t. Place or make seem far off; leave far behind in race in competition. [ME, f. OF *destance* f. L *distantia* (DI[1]*stare* stand apart)]

dis'tant, a. Far, or a specified distance, away or *from* (*three miles* ~); remote, far apart, in position, time, resemblance, etc. (*a* ~ *likeness, connexion*; ~ *ages*; ~ *signal* on railway, one in advance of home signal to give warning); not intimate, reserved, cool. Hence ~LY[2] adv. [ME, f. OF, or L *distant-* part. st. see DISTANCE]

distāste', n. Dislike, repugnance, slight aversion, (*for*). [DIS-]

distāste'ful (-tf-), a. Disagreeable, repellent, (*to*). Hence ~NESS n. [-FUL]

distem'per[1], v.t. (arch., usu. in p.p.). Upset, derange, in health or sanity (*a* ~*ed fancy*). [ME, f. LL DIS(TEMPER*are* L)]

distem'per[2], n. Derangement, an ailment, of body or mind; dog-disease with catarrh, cough, & weakness; political disorder. [f. prec.]

distem'per[3], n., & v.t. 1. Method of painting on plaster or chalk with colours mixed with yolk of egg, size, etc., instead of oil, used for scene-painting & internal walls (*paint in* ~). 2. v.t. Paint (wall etc., or abs.) thus. [n. f. vb, f. OF *destemprer* f. LL as DISTEMPER[1]]

distend', v.t. & i. Swell out by pressure from within (balloon, vein, nostrils, etc.). So **disten'sible** a., **distensibIL'ity**, **distěn'sION** (-shn), nn. [f. L DIS(*tendere tens-* stretch)]

dis'tich (-k), n. Pair of verse lines, couplet. [f. L f. Gk DI[2](*stikhon* f. *stikhos* line) next incl. adj.]

dis'tichous (-k-), a. (bot.). (Having fruit etc.) arranged in two vertical lines on opposite sides of stem. [f. L f. Gk *distikhos*, as prec., -OUS]

distil', v.i. & t. (-ll-). Trickle down; come or give forth in drops, exude; turn to vapour by heat, condense by cold, & recollect (liquid); extract essence of (plant etc., or fig. doctrine etc.); drive (volatile constituent) *off* or *out* by heat; make (whisky, essence) by distillation; undergo distillation. So ~lA'TION n., ~l'aTORY a. [ME, f. OF distiller, or L DI¹(stillare drop)]

distil'l

distil'late, n. Product of distillation. [as prec., -ATE²]

distill'|er, n. One who distils, esp. alcoholic spirit, whence~ ERY(3) n.; apparatus for distilling salt water at sea. [-ER¹]

distinct', a. Not identical, separate, individual, different in quality or kind, unlike, (from, or abs.); clearly perceptible, plain, definite; unmistakable, decided, positive. Hence ~LY² adv., ~NESS n. [ME, f.' L distinctus p.p. see DISTINGUISH]

distinc'tion, n. Making of a difference, discrimination, the difference made (~ without a difference, a merely nominal or artificial one); being different; thing that differentiates, mark, name, title; showing of special consideration, mark of honour; distinguished character, excellence, eminence; (of literary style) individuality. [ME, f. OF f. L distinctionem (DISTINGUISH, -ION)]

distinc'tive, a. Distinguishing, characteristic. Hence ~LY² (-vl-) adv., ~NESS (-vn-) n. [f. LL distinctivus; see -IVE]

distingué (see Ap.), a. Of distinguished air, features, manners, etc. [F]

disting'uish (-nggw-), v.t. & i. Divide into classes etc.; be, see, or point out, the difference of (thing, thing from another; also intr. with between), differentiate, draw distinctions; characterize, be a mark or property of; make out by listening, looking, etc., recognize; make oneself prominent (often by gallantry etc.). Hence ~ABLE a., ~abLY² adv. [f. F distinguer or L DI¹(stinguere stinct- extinguish) with irreg. use of -ISH²]

disting'uished (-nggwisht, a. In vbl senses; esp.: remarkable (for or by quality etc.), eminent, famous, of high standing; = DISTINGUÉ. [-ED¹]

distort', v.t. Put out of shape, make crooked or unshapely, (actually or, as by curved mirror etc., apparently); misrepresent (motives, facts, statements). Hence or cogn. ~édLY² adv., distor'tion n., (also) lack of clearness and correctness in sounds transmitted by telephone or wireless, distor'tionAL (-sho-) a. [f. L DIS(torquēre tort- twist)]

distor'tionist (-sho-), n. Caricaturist; acrobat who distorts his body. [-IST]

distract', v.t. Divert, draw away, (attention, the mind, usu. from); draw in different directions, divide or confuse the attention of, (often p.p. with between) bewilder, perplex; (chiefly p.p.) drive mad or infuriate (~ed with, by, at). Hence ~édLY², ~ingLY², advv. [ME, f. L DIStrahere tract- draw)]

distrac'tion, n. Diversion of, thing that diverts, the mind; interruption; lack of concentration; amusement, relief from over-absorption; confusion, perplexity, internal conflict, dissension; frenzy, madness, (to ~, to a mad degree). [f. L distractio (prec., -ION)]

distrain', v.i. (legal). Levy a distress (upon person or his goods, or abs.), seize chattels to compel person to pay money due (esp. rent) or meet an obligation, or to attain satisfaction by sale of the chattels. Hence~ER¹, ~OR, ~EE', ~MENT & (in same sense) distraint', nn. [ME, f. OF destreindre f. L DI¹(stringere strictsqueeze)]

distrait' (-rā), a. (fem. -te, pr. -āt). Absent-minded, not attending. [F]

distraught' (-awt), a. Violently agitated; crazy. [ME; alt. of obs. distract a. after straught, p.p. of stretch]

distress'¹, n. Severe pressure of pain, sorrow, etc., anguish; want of money or necessaries; straits, dangerous position; exhaustion, being tired out, breathlessness; (Law) = DISTRAINT; ~-gun, -rocket, signals from ship in danger; ~-warrant, authorizing distraint. Hence ~FUL a. [ME, f. OF destrece f. Gallo-Rom. *districtia (= LL districtio DISTRAIN, -Y¹)]

distress'², v.t. Subject to severe strain, exhaust, afflict; cause anxiety to, vex, make unhappy. Hence ~ingLY² adv. [ME, f. AF destresser, OF -ecier, f. prec.]

distrib'utary, n. River branch that does not return to main stream after leaving it (as in a delta). [foll. +-ARY¹]

distrib'ut|e, v.t. Deal out, give share of to each of a number; spread abroad, scatter, put at different points; divide into parts, arrange, classify; (Print.) separate (type that has been set up) & return each letter to its proper box in the case; (Log.) use (term) in its full extension so that it includes every individual of the class. Hence (orig. -er) ~OR n., ~ABLE a. [ME, f. L DIS(tribuere tribut-assign)]

distribu'tion, n. Distributing, apportionment; (Pol. Econ.) dispersal among consumers effected by commerce, also extent to which individuals or classes share in aggregate products of community; spreading abroad, dispersing, scattered situation or arrangement; division into parts, arranging, classification; (Print.) act or process of distributing type; (Log.) application of term to all individuals of the class. Hence ~AL (-sho-) a. [ME, f. OF, or L distributio (prec., -ION)]

distrib'utive, a. & n. 1. Of, concerned with, produced by, distribution; (Log., Gram.) referring to each individual of a class, not to the class collectively. 2. n. (Gram.) ~ word (as each, neither, every). Hence~LY² (-vl-) adv. [ME, f. F (-if, -ive), or LL -ivus (DISTRIBUTE, -IVE)]

dis'trict, n., & v.t. 1. Territory marked

off for special administrative purpose; ‖ division of parish with its own church or chapel & clergyman; ‖ urban or rural division of county with D~ Council; assigned sphere of operations; tract of country with common characteristics, region; *~ *attorney*, prosecuting officer of a ~; ‖ ~ *visitor*, person working under clergyman's direction in section of parish. **2.** v.t. Divide into ~s. [F, f. med. L *districtus* jurisdiction f. L *district-* see DISTRAIN]

distring'ăs (-ngg-), n. (law). Writ bidding the sheriff or other officer distrain in certain cases. [L, = thou shalt DISTRAIN]

distrŭst'¹, n. Want of trust, doubt, suspicion. Hence ~FUL a. (*of*), ~fulLY² adv. [DIS-]

distrŭst'², v.t. Have no confidence in, doubt, not rely on. [DIS-]

distŭrb', v.t. Agitate, trouble, disquiet, unsettle; perplex. [ME, f. OF *destorber* f. L DIS(*turbare* f. *turba* crowd)]

distŭrb'ance, n. Interruption of tranquillity, agitation; tumult, uproar, outbreak; (Law) molestation, interference with rights or property. [ME, f. OF *destorbance* (prec., -ANCE)]

disûn'ion (-yon), n. Separation, want of union, dissension. So **disûnite'** v.t. & i. [DIS-]

disûse'¹ (-s), n. Discontinuance, want of use or practice, desuetude. [f. foll.]

disûse'² (-z), v.t. Cease to use. [f. OF *desuser* (DIS-, USE)]

disyl'|able, diss-, n. Word, metrical foot, of two syllables. So ~ab'ic a., ~ăb'ically adv. [f. F *dissyllabe* (DI-², SYLLABLE); -ss- in F as sign of hard sound]

ditch, n., & v.i. & t. **1.** Long narrow excavation, esp. to hold or conduct water or serve as boundary; watercourse; *the D~*, English Channel or North Sea (R.A.F. sl.); DIE² *in last* ~, *~-water*, stagnant in ~ (esp. *dull as ~-water*). **2.** vb. Make or repair ~es (esp. *hedging & ~ing*), whence ~'ER¹ (1, 2) n.; provide with ~es, drain; (sl.) leave in the lurch; (sl., of airman) make forced landing on sea, bring (aircraft) down thus; (pass., of vehicle) stick in a ~. [OE *dic*, OS *dik*, MHG. *lich*, ON *diki*, of unkn. orig., see DIKE]

di'theïsm, n. Religious dualism, belief in independent principles of good & evil. [DI-²]

dith'er (-dh-), v.i., & n. Tremble, quiver; vacillate. [imit.]

dith'yramb (-ăm), n. Greek choric hymn of wild character; Bacchanalian song; vehement or inflated poem, speech or writing. So **dithyrăm'bic** a. & n. [f. L f. Gk *dithurambos*]

ditt'anỹ, n. A herb, formerly of medicinal repute. [ME, f. OF *ditan* f. L f. Gk *diktamnon* perh. f. *Diktē* in Crete]

ditt'ō, a. & n. (*abbr.* d°, do; pl. *-os*). The aforesaid, the same, (in accounts, inventories, & commerc. or colloq. talk, instead of repeating word); duplicate, similar thing, (~ *suit*, *suit of ~s*, clothes all of one material); *say* ~ *to*, agree with, endorse opinion of. [It. (now *detto*), f. L *dictus* p.p. of *dicere* say]

dittŏg'raphỹ, n. Copyist's mistaken repetition of letter, word, or phrase, cf. HAPLOGRAPHY. Hence **dittogrăph'ic** a. [f. Gk *dittos* double, -GRAPHY]

ditt'ỹ, n. Short simple song. [ME, f. OF *dite* f. L *dictatum* neut. p.p. of *dictare* DICTATE²]

ditt'ỹ-băg, -bŏx, nn. Sailor's, fisherman's, receptacle for odds & ends. [orig. unkn.]

diûrĕt'ic, a. & n. (Substance) exciting discharge of urine. [ME, f. OF *-ique*, or LL f. Gk *diourētikos* f. DI³(*oureō* make water), -IC]

diûrn'al, a. (Astron.) occupying one day; (arch.) daily, of each day; of the day, not nocturnal. Hence ~LY² adv. [ME, f. LL *diurnalis* (*dies* day)]

div (dĕv), n. Evil spirit in Persian mythology. [Pers., = Skr. *deva* god]

di'va (dē-), n. Great woman singer, prima donna. [It. f. L, = goddess]

div'ag|āte, v.i. Stray, digress. Hence ~A'TION n. [f. L DI¹(*vagari* wander), -ATE³]

di'valent, a. Combining with two atoms of hydrogen etc., having two combining equivalents. [DI-², L *valēre* be worth, -ENT]

dīvăn', n. Oriental council of State, esp. Turkish privy council; oriental council-chamber, court of justice; long seat against room-wall; smoking-room, cigar-shop. [Turk., f. Pers. *dewan* brochure, account-book, custom-house (see DOUANE), tribunal, senate, bench]

dīvā'ric|āte (or di-), v.i. Diverge, branch, (of roads, branches, etc.). Hence or cogn. ~A'TION n., ~ATE² (-at) a. (bot., zool.). [f. L DI¹(*varicare* f. *varicus* straddling), -ATE³]

dīve, v.i., & n. **1.** Plunge, esp. head foremost, into water etc.; (of aircraft) plunge steeply downwards, (of submarine) submerge; go down or out of sight suddenly; put one's hand *into* water, vessel, pocket; penetrate or search mentally *into*; *diving-bell*, open-bottomed box or bell in which person can be let down into deep water. **2.** n. Plunge, header, swim under water; submerging of submarine, aircraft's steep descent; sudden dart out of sight; *drinking-den*; a basement or underground room in which some particular commodity is sold (*oyster* ~); *hiding-place or sanctuary for the disreputable; ~-bomber*, aircraft specially designed to aim bombs at target by diving towards it and release them while diving, so ~-bomb v.t. & i. [repr. OE *dūfan* (intr.) dive, sink, & *dyfan* (trans.) immerse; f. Gmc *dūbh-*, cogn. w. DEEP, DIP]

dīv'er, n. In vbl senses; esp.: person who dives for pearls, to examine sunk ships, etc.; kinds of diving bird. [-ER¹]

diver|ge' (*or* dĭ-), v.i. & t. Proceed in different directions from point or each other; go aside *from* track; differ, deviate; make ~ge, deflect. Hence ~'**gENCE**, ~'**gENCY**, nn., ~'**gENT** a., ~'**gENTly**[2] adv. [f. med. L *divergere* f. DI-[1], L *vergere* VERGE v.]

div'ers (-z), a. (arch. or joc.). Sundry, several, more than one. [ME, f. OF f. L DI[1] (*versus* p.p. of *vertere* turn) = foll.]

diverse' (*or* dĭ-), a. Unlike in nature or qualities; varied, changeful. Hence or cogn. ~LY[2] (-sĭ-) adv., **divers'ıFORM** a. [ME, as prec.]

divers'ı|fy (*or* dĭ-), v.t. Make diverse, vary, modify, variegate. So ~**FICA'TION** n. [ME, f. OF *diversifier* f. med. L *diversificare* (prec., -FY)]

diver'sion (*or* dĭ-; -shn), n. Deflecting, deviation; diverting of attention, manœuvre to secure this, feint; recreation, pleasant distraction, pastime. [f. LL *diversio*. (DIVERT, -ION)]

divers'ıty (*or* dĭ-), n. Being diverse, unlikeness; different kind; variety. [ME, f. OF *diversite* f. L *diversitatem* (DIVERS, -ITY)]

divert' (*or* dĭ-), v.t. Turn aside, deflect, (stream etc., *from*, *to*, or abs.); turn elsewhere, get rid of, ward off; draw off attention of (*from* one thing *to* another), distract; entertain, amuse, whence ~ING[2] a., ~**ıNGly**[2] adv. [f. OF *divertir* f. L DI[1]*vertere* & DEvertere -*vers*- turn in different directions, turn away]

divertissement (dēvertēs'mahn), n. Short ballet etc. between the acts of a play. [F]

Div'ēs (-z), n. (Typical name for) rich man; || (Law) ~ *costs*, costs on higher scale (opp. *pauper costs*). [L, = rich, ref. to *Luke* xvi. 19, where Vulgate has ~]

divest' (*or* dĭ-), v.t. Unclothe; strip *of* garment etc.; deprive, rid, *of* (~ one*self* of, abandon). Hence ~**MENT**, ~**ıTURE**, nn. [16th c. *devest* f. OF *desvestir* (DIS-, L *vestire* f. *vestis* garment)]

|| **div'ı**, **divv'y̆**, n. (Co-op. societies' sl.). Dividend. [abbr.]

divide'[1], v.t. & i. Separate (t. & i.) into or in(*to*) parts, split or break up; sunder, part, cut off, (things, thing *from*); cause to disagree, set at variance, distract; distribute, deal out, (*among*, *between*); share *with* others; (Math.) see how often number contains another (~ 20 *by* 3), do **DIVISION**, (of number) go into (number) without remainder; part (t. & i. of House of Parliament, meeting, etc.) into two sets in voting. (*Mr X did not* ~ *the House*; *the House* ~ *d*). [ME, f. L DI[1](*vidēre* -*vis*-)]

divide'[2], n. (U.S. etc.). Watershed. [f. prec.]

div'idend, n. (Math.) number to be divided by **DIVISOR**; sum payable as interest on loan or as profit of joint-stock company (EX ~, CUM ~) or to creditors of insolvent estate; individual's share

of it (|| ~-*warrant*, order to pay this); ~ *stripping*, evasion of tax on ~s by an arrangement between a company liable to pay tax and another able to claim repayment of tax. [f. F *dividende* or L *dividendum* (DIVIDE[1], -ND[1])]

divid'er, n. In vbl senses; esp., (pl.) measuring-compasses, esp. those provided with screw for setting to small intervals. [-ER[1]]

div'ı-div'ı, n. Curved pods of a small tropical-American tree, used in tanning; this tree. [Carib]

divid'ual, a. Separate; separable. Hence ~LY[2] adv. [f. L *dividuus* +-AL]

divinā'tion, n. Divining, insight into or discovery of the unknown or future by supernatural means; skilful forecast, good guess. [ME, f. OF f. L *divinationem* (DIVINE[2], -ATION)]

divine'[1], a. (-er, -est), & n. 1. Of, from, like, God or a god (~ *right of kings*, independent of their subjects' will); devoted to God, sacred, (~ *service*, public worship); superhumanly excellent, gifted, or beautiful; hence ~LY[2] (-nĭ-) adv. 2. n. Person (usu. cleric) skilled in theology. [ME, f. OF *devin* f. L *divinus* f. *divus* godlike]

divin|e'[2], v.t. & i. Make out by inspiration, magic, intuition, or guessing, foresee, predict, conjecture; practise divination; ~*ing-rod*, see **DOWSING**. Hence ~**ER**[2] (4) n. [ME, f. F *deviner* f. L *divinare* (*divinus* DIVINE[1])]

divin'ıty̆, n. Being divine, godhood; a god, godhead; *the D*~, God; adorable or adored person; theology, University theological faculty; (Bookbind.) ~ *calf* (dark brown with *blind* **TOOLING**). [ME, f. OF *divinite* f. L *divinitatem* (DIVINE[1], -TY)]

div'inīz|e, -is|e (-īz), v.t. Deify. Hence ~**A'TION** n. [f. F *diviniser* f. *divin* DIVINE[1]]

divis'ible (-z-), a. Capable of being divided actually or in thought; (Math.) ~ *by*, containing (a number) some number of times without remainder. Hence **divisıBIL'ITY** (-z-) n. [f. F, or LL *divisibilis* (DIVIDE[1], -IBLE)]

divi'sion (-zhn), n. 1. Dividing or being divided, severance; distribution, sharing, (~ *of labour*, time-saving arrangement giving different parts of manufacturing process etc. to different persons). 2. Disagreement, discord. 3. (Math.) process of dividing number by another (*long*, *short*, ~, methods usual with divisors greater, not greater, than 12; *symbol of* ~, ÷, as 3÷4 = ¾). 4. (Log.) classification, enumeration of parts, distinction of meanings. 5. (Parl.) separation of House into two sets for counting votes. 6. Dividing line, boundary; part, section. 7. Administrative etc. district, definite part, under single command, of army or fleet, esp. (Mil.) formation of an army, commanded by a Major-General, and (*infantry* ~) usu. consisting of three infantry brigades, with cavalry (now armoured car regiment), artillery, engineers, signals, R.A.S.C., R.A.M.C., and R.A.O.C.; *airborne, armoured, parachute,* ~; ‖ part of county or borough returning a Member of Parliament. **8.** (Nat. Hist.) section of kingdom, order, genus, etc. **9.** ‖ (Prison) 1*st,* 2*nd,* 3*rd,*~, lenient, medium, severe, treatment in prison prescribed by judge. Hence ~AL (-zho-) a., ~aILY² adv. [ME, f. OF f. L *divisionem* (DIVIDE¹, -ION)]

divis'or (-z-), n. (math.). Number by which another (the DIVIDEND) is to be divided; number that divides another without remainder. [ME, f. F *diviseur* or L *divisor* (DIVIDE¹, -OR)]

divōrce'¹, n. Legal dissolution of marriage (~ *ā vin'cŭlō matrimōn'iī,* i.e. from the bonds of marriage) opp. to judicial separation of married pair (~ *ā men'sā et tho'ro,* i.e. from board and bed); (loosely) decree of nullity of marriage; (fig.) severance, sundering. [ME, f. OF f. L *divortium* f. DI¹(*vortere* later *vertere* turn)]

divōrce'², v.t. Legally dissolve marriage between; separate (spouse) by divorce *from*; put away, repudiate, (spouse); dissolve (union); sever (things, thing *from*). Hence **di-** or **divōrcEE'** (also F *divorcé* masc., *-ée* fem.), ~MENT (-sm-), nn. [ME, f. OF *divorcer* f. LL *divortiare* (prec.)]

div'ot, n. (Sc., north.). ‖ A turf, sod; (Golf) piece of turf cut out in making a stroke. [orig. unkn.]

divŭl|ge' (-j), v.t. Let out, reveal. Hence or cogn. **divŭlgâ'TION, ~ge'MENT** (-jm-), ~'ǵENCE, nn. [f. L DI¹(*vulgare* publish f. *vulgus* people)]

‖ **divv'y̆,** n. Var. of DIVI.

Dix'ic('s länd), n. The U.S.A. south of Mason & Dixon's line, the former slave States. [corrupt. of *Dixon,* surveyor]

dix'y̆, dix'ie, n. Large iron pot in which stew, tea, etc., are made or carried on campaign. [f. Hind. *degchī* cooking pot]

diz'en (*or* dī-), v.t. (rare). Array with finery, deck *out* or *up,* bedizen. [dress (distaff) with flax (1530): app. identical with first element in DISTAFF]

dizz'|y̆, a., & v.t. **1.** Giddy, dazed, unsteady, tottering, confused; making giddy; (of mountain, tower, etc.) very high; (of stream, wheel, etc.) whirling rapidly; hence ~ILY² adv., ~INESS n. **2.** v.t. Make ~y, bewilder. [OE *dysig,* OFris. *dusig,* MDu. *dosech,* LG *dusig, dösig,* OHG *tusic* f. WG **dus-*]

djibba(h). See JIBBA(H).

do¹ (dōō), v.t. & i. & aux. (sing. pres. 2, *doest* pr. dōō'ĭst as t. & i., *dost* pr. dŭst as aux.; 3, *does* pr. dŭz & arch. *doth* pr. dŭ-, *doeth* pr. dōō'ĭth; past *did,* *dĭdst;* p.p. *done* pr. dŭn; *dōn't, didn't,* are common for *do not, did not; doesn't,* & vulg. *dōn't,* for *does not*). **1.** v.t. Put (arch.; now only in *do to death*); bestow, impart, grant, render, give, (*does him credit, does credit to his intelligence; does me good, harm; did a service to his country; do*

justice to); perform, carry out, effect, bring to pass, (thing, work, good, right, wrong, duty, bidding, penance; *it isn't done,* is bad form), whence do'ING¹(1) (dōō-) n., (esp., pl.) what happens on an occasion or is done by or befalls a person, (sl.) adjuncts, things needed; (p.p. & perf.) complete, bring to an end, (*it is, I have, done*); exert, use, (*do* one's *endeavour,* one's *best,* &, sl., one's *damnedest*); produce, make, (*have done six copies*); operate on, deal with, repair, set in order, (*does the French books for the Athenaeum;* *paper-hanger does a house, housemaid a room; do* one's *hair*); cook, roast, etc., to the right degree (*chop done to a turn; well, over, under, -done*); solve (sum, problem); translate *into* English etc.; work at (lesson); play the part of (*did Lear, the cicerone;* hence *do the polite* etc.); exhaust, tire out; (sl.) cheat (also *do in the eye*); traverse (such a distance); (colloq.) see the sights of (city, museum); (sl.) undergo (term of punishment); (with noun of action as compd vb) *do battle* etc., fight etc.; ‖(sl.) provide food etc. for (*they do you very well; do* oneself *well,* make liberal provision for one's own comfort). **2.** v.i. (With adv. or advl phr.) act, proceed, (*do as they do at Rome; would do wisely to withdraw*); perform deeds (*do or die*); make an end (*have done!,* cease; *let us have done with it*); fare, get on, (well, badly, etc.; of person or thing; *how do you do?* or *how d'ye do?*); be suitable, answer purpose, serve, suffice. **3.** v. substitute: (a) replacing vb and taking its construction, as *I chose my wife as she did her gown;* (b) replacing vb & obj. etc., as *if you saw the truth as clearly as I do;* (c) as elliptical auxiliary, as ‘*did you see him?* ’ ‘*I did*’; (d) with *so, it, which,* etc., as: *I wanted to see him, & I did so; in passing through the market, which he seldom did; if you want to tell him, do it now.* **4.** v. aux. Used with infin. for simple pres. & past (a) when special emphasis is to be laid on a fact, as *I do so wish I could,* esp. in contrast with what has preceded, as *but I did see him;* also for imperat. in urgent petitions, as *do tell me, do but think;* or when the pronoun is inserted & emphasized, as *do you go rather;* (b) when inversion is desired, as *rarely does it happen that;* (c) the usual form in questions except with *have, be,* & some monosyl. vbs, as *did you recognize her?, do you dare?* or *dare you?;* (d) usual in *not* statements except with *be, have, dare, need,* etc.; also in *not* commands. **5.** Phrr. etc.: *a to-do,* bustle, fuss; *well--to-do,* rich enough, thriving; *have to do with,* be concerned or connected or have dealings with; *nothing doing,* going on; *done,* used in accepting offer or bet; *do--nothing,* a. & n., idle(r). n. **6.** With prepp.: *do by,* treat, deal with, in such a way; *do for* (colloq.), ‖ act as housekeeper etc. for, ruin, destroy, kill; *do to, unto,* = do by; *do with,* get on with, tolerate (joc., *could do with a drink*), find sufficient; *do without,* dispense with. 7. With advv.; *do away (with),* abolish; *do in* (sl.), kil'; *do up,* restore, repair, wrap up (parcel), tire out. Hence do′ABLE (dōō-) a., do′ER¹ (dōō-) n. [OE & OS *dōn,* OHG *tuon,* f. WG *dō- cogn. w. Gk *tithĕmi*]

do² (dōō), n. (sl.). Swindle, imposture, hoax; ∥(colloq.) entertainment, jollification (*there's a big do on at No.* 2), (in pl.) share (*fair do's!* share fairly). [f. prec.]

do³, doh, (dō), n. (mus.).· Key-note of scale (*movable do*); the note C (*fixed do*). [arbitrary]

dō⁴, abbr. of DITTO.

doat. See DOTE.

dŏbb′in, n. Draught or farm horse. [pet-name = Robert]

Docĕt′ic, a., Docĕt′ist, Docĕt′ism, nn. (Of, holder of) the heresy that Christ's body was not human but phantasmal or of celestial substance. [med. L f. Gk *dokētai* (*dokeō* seem) + -IC, -IST, -ISM]

doch-an-dō′ris (dŏx, see Ap., dŏk-), n. Stirrup-cup, last drink. [f. Gael. *deoch-an-doruis* a drink at the door]

doch′miăc (dŏk-), a. & n. Composed of dochmii (dochmius, ∪−−∪−); (n., usu. pl.) line(s) so composed. [f. L f. Gk *dokhmiakos* f. *dokhmios* oblique]

dō′cile, a. Teachable; submissive; easily managed. So docil′ITY n. [ME, f. OF, or L *docilis* (*docēre* teach, -IL)]

dŏck¹, n. Kinds of coarse weedy herb, popular antidote for nettle stings. [OE *docce,* cf. MDu. *dockeblaederen*]

dŏck², n. Solid fleshy part of animal's tail; crupper of saddle or harness. [ME, = mod. Icel. *dockr*; ult. orig. unkn.]

dŏck³, v.t. Cut short (animal in tail, person in hair; or tail etc.); lessen, deprive *of,* put limits on (person, supplies); (Law) ~ *the entail,* cut it off; ~-*tailed,* with tail ~ed. [f. prec.]

dŏck⁴, n., & v.t. & i. 1. Basin with flood-gates in which ships may be loaded, unloaded, or repaired (*dry* or *graving* ~, for repairing or building, water being pumped out; *wet* ~, with water kept at high-tide level; *floating* ~, floating structure usable as dry ~); (usu. pl.) range of ~ basins with wharves and offices, dockyard; *ship's berth, wharf; (Railway) ∥ platform-enclosure in which line terminates; ~*dues,* charge for use of ~, also ~′AGE(4) n.; ~-*glass* (large, for wine-tasting); ~-*master,* superintendent of ~′yard or enclosure with ~s & all shipbuilding & repairing appliances, ∥ esp. in connexion with Navy. 2. vb. Bring (ship), (of ship) come, into ~; furnish with ~s. [c. 1500, f. MDu. *docke,* of unkn. orig.]

dŏck⁵, n. Enclosure in criminal court for prisoner; ∥~ *brief* (undertaken gratis by barrister in court selected by poor

prisoner in ~). [16th c., prob. = Flem. *dok* cage, of unkn. orig.]

dŏck′er, n. Labourer in DOCK⁴. [-ER¹]

dŏck′ĕt, n., & v.t. ∥(Law) register of legal judgements (vb, enter in this); endorsement on letter or document showing its contents or subject (vb, endorse thus); ∥ Custom-House warrant certifying payment of duty; ∥ certificate of cotton clearing-house entitling presenter to delivery; ∥ permit to buy controlled or scarce goods. [15th c., of unkn. orig.]

dŏck′iz|e, -is|e (-īz), v.t. Make (river) into range of docks. Hence ~A′TION n. [-IZE]

dŏc′tor¹, n. (Arch.) teacher, learned man, (*D*~*s of the Church,* certain, esp. four Eastern & four Western, early fathers; *who shall decide when* ~*s disagree?*); holder of the highest university degree in any faculty (often honorary; used as prefix to surname, usu. abbr. *Dr*), esp. ~ of medicine male or female (also pop. of any medical man, M.D. or not, esp. in voc.); (Naut. sl.) ship's cook; kinds of mechanical appliance for regulating etc.; artificial fly; ~*'s stuff,* physic. Hence or cogn. ~AL, dŏctŏr′IAL, ~LESS, aa., ~ATE¹, ~SHIP(1, 3), ~HOOD, dŏc′trESS¹ (joc. etc. for usu. ~ fem.), nn. [ME, f. OF f. L (*docēre doct-* teach, -OR)]

dŏc′tor², v.t. & i. Confer degree of doctor on; treat (patient, oneself) medically; castrate; patch up (machinery etc.); adulterate, falsify; practise as physician (esp. in gerund). [f. prec.]

Dŏc′tors' Cŏmm′ons, n. pl. Common table, buildings (in which certain courts were held), of former College of Doctors of Civil Law in London (frequent literary allusions to probate, marriage-licence, & divorce business once transacted there). [COMMONS]

dŏctrinaire′, dŏctrinār′ian, nn. & aa. 1. Pedantic theorist, person who·applies principle without allowance for circumstances; hence dŏctrinair′ISM(2), dŏctrinār′ianISM(2), nn. 2. adj. Theoretic and unpractical. [-*aire* F (L *doctrina* DOCTRINE, -ARY¹) name of French political party 1815; -ARIAN]

dŏc′trinal (or dŏktrīn²), a. Of, inculcating, doctrine(s). Hence ~LY² adv. [f. LL *doctrinalis* (foll., -AL)]

dŏc′trin|e, n. What is taught, body of instruction; religious, political, scientific, etc., belief, dogma, or tenet (*Monroe* ~*e,* U.S. policy foreshadowed by President Monroe 1823 discountenancing European State interference in America). Hence ~ISM(1), ~IST(1), nn., ~IZE(2) v.i. [ME, f. OF f. L *doctrina* (DOCTOR¹, -INE³)]

dŏc′ūment, n., & v.t. 1. Thing, esp. deed, writing, or inscription, that furnishes evidence (*human* ~, description, incident, etc., illustrating human nature); hence dŏcūmĕn′tARY¹ a., (also n., film dealing with a natural history, archaeological, industrial, travel, or similar subject, usu. accompanied by an explanatory talk). **2. v.t.** Prove by, provide with, ~s or evidence; so **dŏcŭmĕntá′tion** n. [ME, f. OF f. L *documentum* (*docēre* teach, -MENT)]

dŏdd′er[1], n. Kinds of slender leafless threadlike parasitic plant. [ME *doder* = MLG *dod(d)er*, MHG *toter* (G *dotter*)]

dŏdd′er[2], v.i. Tremble, nod, with frailty, palsy, etc. (~*grass*, quaking-grass); totter, potter, be feeble. Hence ~ER[1] n., infirm, feeble, or inept person. [orig. unkn.; cf. obs. (15th c.) *dadder*]

dŏdd′ered (-erd), a. Having lost the top or branches (of oaks & other trees). [prob. f. frequent. of obs. vb *dod* poll, lop]

dŏdec(a)-, comb. form = twelve-, as *dŏdĕc′agon*, plane figure of twelve sides, *dŏdĕcahĕ′dron*, solid figure of twelve faces, *dŏdĕcasyll′able*, verse of twelve syllables. [f. Gk *dōdeka* twelve]

dŏdge[1], v.i. & t. **1. v.i.** Move to & fro, change position, shuffle; move quickly *round*, *about* or *behind*, obstacle so as to elude pursuer, blow, etc.; play fast & loose, quibble, prevaricate; (of bell in chime) sound one place out of the normal order. **2. v.t.** Baffle by finesse, trifle with; elude (pursuer, opponent, blow) by sideward deviation etc.; move (thing) to & fro; ask (person) questions in unexpected order. [orig. unkn.]

dŏdge[2], n. Piece of dodging, quick side-movement; trick, artifice; (colloq.) clever expedient, mechanical etc. contrivance; sounding of bell out of normal place in chimes. Hence **dŏdg′y**[2] a. [f. prec.]

dŏdg′er, n. In vbl senses; esp., artful or elusive person; (colloq.) screen on ship's bridge as protection from spray etc.; *small handbill; *Indian-meal cake (*corn*~). [-ER[1]]

dŏd′ō, n. (pl. -oes, -os). Large extinct bird of Mauritius. [f. Port. *doudo* simpleton]

doe (dō), n. Female of fallow deer (cf. BUCK[1]), hare or rabbit; ~′*skin* (-ōs-), skin of ~, leather of this, fine cloth resembling it. [OE *dā*, of unkn. orig.]

does, doest. See DO[1].

dŏff, v.t. Take off (hat, clothing); (rarely) abandon, discard, (custom, condition). [ME, = *do off*]

dŏg[1], n. **1.** Quadruped of many breeds wild & domesticated; hunting-dog (fig., ~*s of war*, havoc, rapine); male of ~, wolf (also ~*wolf*), (fem. *bitch*), or fox (also ~*fox*). **2.** Worthless or surly person; fellow (*sly*, *lucky*, *jolly*, ~; SEA-~). **3.** (astron.). *Greater* or *Lesser Dog*, constellations, also Sirius or Procyon, chief star in either (also ~*star*, usu. Sirius; ~*days*, hottest part of year in July & Aug., variously dated with ref. to rising of Sirius). **4.** Kinds of mechanical device for gripping etc.; short iron bar with upturned spike at each end in common use for joining heavy timbering; (pl., also *fire*-~s) pair of

metal supports for burning wood, or for grate, or for fire-irons. **5.** (Also *sea*-~) light near horizon portending storm; *sun*-~, parhelion. **6.** Phrr.; *go to the* ~*s*, be ruined; *throw to the* ~*s*, throw away, sacrifice; *not have* WORD[1] *to throw at* ~; *every* ~ *has his* DAY; *love me, love my* ~, accept my friends as yours; *rain* CATS *& ~s*; *die like a* ~, *a* ~*'s death*, miserably, shamefully; *not a* ~*'s chance*, not even the least chance; *take hair of* ~ *that bit you*, drink more to cure effects of drink; *help lame* ~ *over stile*, be friend in need; *lead, lead one, a* ~*'s life*, a life of misery or of miserable subserviency; *give* ~ *ill name & hang him*, of power of nickname or slander; *let sleeping* ~*s lie*, let well alone; *put on* ~ (colloq.), assume airs of importance; || *the* ~*s* (colloq.), greyhound race-meeting; ~ *in the manger*, one who prevents others enjoying what is useless to him; ~ *in a blanket*, rolled currant dumpling or jam pudding. **7.** ~′*berry*, fruit of ~*wood*; ~*biscuit*, for feeding ~s; || ~*box*, railway van for ~s; ~′*cart*, two-wheeled driving-cart with cross seats back to back; ~*cheap*, very; ~*collar*, lit., & fig. of person's straight high collar divided at back, clerical collar; ~*faced*, epithet of kind of baboon; ~*fall*, in which wrestlers touch ground together; ~*fennel*, stinking camomile; ~′*fight*, a fight (as) between ~s, (colloq.) a fight between aircraft; ~′*fish*, kinds of small shark & other fish; ~('s)*grass*, couch-grass; ~*hole*, *hutch*, mean room; ~′*house* (*in the* ~*house*, sl., in disgrace); ~ *latin*, incorrect, mongrel; ~*lead*, string etc. for leading ~; ~*leg(ged)* staircase, going back & forward without well-hole; ~′*rose*, wild hedge rose; ~('s)*earn*. & v.t., corner of page turned down with use, fill (book) with these; ~'s*body*, (Naut. sl.) dried pease boiled in a cloth, a junior officer, drudge; ~′*shore*, wooden prop supporting ship's weight during building and cut away before launching; ~′*skin*, leather of or imitating ~'s skin used for gloves; ~*sleep*, light & fitful; ~'s *letter*, r (f. snarling sound); ~'s*meat*, horseflesh, offal; ~'s*nose*, mixed drink of beer & gin; ~('s)*tail*, kind of grass; ~'s*tongue*, plants of borage kind; ~'s*tooth*, plant with speckled leaves & flowers; ~*tired*, tired out; ~*tooth*, small pyramidal ornament esp. in Norman & Early English architecture; ~*violet*, scentless kind; ~*watch* (Naut.), short half watch of two hours (4–6, 6–8, p.m.); ~*whip*, for keeping ~s in order; ~′*wood*, wild cornel, *kind of flowering shrub. Hence ~g′ISH[1], ~′LESS, ~′LIKE, aa., ~g′ў[1] or ~g′ie (-g-) [-Y[3]], ~′HOOD, nn. [late OE *docga*, of unkn. orig.]

dŏg[2], v.t. (-gg-). Follow closely, pursue, track, (person, his *steps*; of person or calamity etc.); (Mech.) grip with dog. [f. prec.]

dōg′āte, n. Office of doge. [f. F *dogat* f. It. *dogato* (foll., -ATE[1])]

dōge (-j), n. (hist.). Chief magistrate of Venice, Genoa. [F f. It., f. L *ducem* nom. *dux* leader]

dŏgg′ĕd (-g-), a. Obstinate, tenacious, persistent, unyielding, (*it's* ~ *does it*, persistency succeeds). Hence ~LY[2] adv., ~NESS n. [ME; -ED[2]]

dŏgg′er (-g-), n. Two-masted bluff--bowed Dutch fishing-boat. [ME, f. MDu. *dogger* fishing-boat, cf. *ten dogge varen* to go to the cod-fishing]

dŏgg′erel (-ge-), a. & n. Trivial, mean, halting, or irregular, (verse). [ME, app. f. DOG[1] (as in *dog latin* etc.)]

dŏgg′ō, adv. (sl.). *Lie* ~ (motionless, making no sign). [*dog*]

dŏgg′|ўˊ[2] (-g-), a. (for *doggy*[1] see DOG[1]). Of dogs; devoted to dogs. Hence ~iNESS n. [-Y[2]]

dŏg′ma, n. (pl. ~s, rarely ~ta). Principle, tenet, doctrinal system, esp. as laid down by authority of Church; arrogant declaration of opinion. [L f. Gk (*dogma* *-mat-* opinion, f. *dokeō* seem, -M]

dŏgmăt′|ic (rarely ~ical), a. Of dogma(s), doctrinal; based on *a priori* principles, not on induction; (of person, book, etc.) authoritative, laying down the law, arrogant. Hence ~ICS n., ~ICALLY adv. [f. LL f. Gk *dogmatikos* (prec., -IC)]

dŏg′mat|ize, -t|ise (-iz), v.i. & t. Deal in positive unsupported assertions, speak authoritatively; express (principle etc.) as a dogma. So ~ISM(1), ~IST (1), nn. [f. F *dogmatiser* or LL f. Gk *dogmatizō* (DOGMA, -IZE)]

do′-gŏŏd′er (dŏŏ-), n. (colloq., freq. derog.). Earnest, idealistic, would-be reformer. [-ER[1]]

doh. See DO[3].

doil′ў, n. Small napkin placed below finger-glass etc. [fabric named from 17th--c. London linen-draper]

do′ing (dŏŏ-). See DO[1].

doit, n. Very small sum or coin; merest trifle (esp. *don't care a*~). [16th c., f. MLG *doyt*, MDu. *duit*, of unkn. orig.]

‖ **doit′ĕd**, a. (Sc.). Crazed, esp. with age. [ME; orig. unkn.]

dŏl′ce fär nĭĕnt′ė (-chā), n. Pleasant idleness. [It., = sweet doing nothing]

dŏl′drums (-z), n. pl. Dullness, dumps, depression; (of ship, usu. *in the* ~) becalmed state; region of calms & light baffling winds near equator. [prob. formed on *dull*, cf. *tantrums*]

dōle[1], n., & v.t. 1. (arch.). Lot, destiny, (*happy man be his* ~, may he be happy). 2. Charitable distribution; charitable (esp. sparing, niggardly) gift of food, clothes, or money; ‖ *the* ~ (colloq.), relief claimable by the unemployed. 3. v.t. Deal *out* sparingly, esp. as alms. [OE *dāl*, f. Gmc *dailaz*, see DEAL[1]]

dōle[2], n. (poet.). Grief, woe; lamentation.

[ME *dol* etc. f. OF *dol*, *doel*, etc. f. Rom. *dolus* f. L *dolēre* grieve]

dōle′ful (-lf-), a. Dreary, dismal; sad, discontented, melancholy. Hence ~LY[2] adv., ~NESS n. [ME; prec., -FUL]

dŏl′erite, n. Coarse basaltic rock much used as road-metal. [F (-é-), f. Gk *doleros* deceptive (because easily confused with true greenstone)]

dŏl′ichocĕphăl′ic (-ko-), a. Long-headed (of skull with breadth less than ⅘ of length; or of person or race with such skull). [f. Gk *dolikhos* long + -CEPHALIC]

dŏll, n., & v.t. & i. 1. Toy baby, puppet; (~'s *house*, miniature toy house for ~s, diminutive dwelling-house); pretty silly woman (so ~'s *face*). Hence ~'ISH[1] a., ~'ishLY[2] adv., ~'ishNESS n. 2. v.t. & i. (colloq.). Dress *up* smartly, deck up. [short for *Dorothy*]

dŏll′ar, n. (Orig.) English name for German thaler, also for Spanish piece of eight; unit of U.S. gold & silver coinage = 100 cents (symbol or ~ *sign*, $; *the almighty* ~, money, mammon); corresponding coin in Canada, etc.; ‖ (sl.) five-shilling piece, crown; *half a* ~ (sl.), half a crown; ~ *area* (in which currency is linked to U.S. ~); ~ *diplomacy* (that seeks to further the commercial and financial interests of a country abroad and to extend its influence in international relations by means of these interests). [16th c. *daler* etc. f. LG & early mod. Du. *daler* f. G *taler* f. *Joachimstaler* coin from silver mine of the *Joachimstal*]

dŏll′op, n. (colloq.). Clumsy or shapeless lump of food etc. [orig. obsc.; cf. Norw. dial. *dolp* lump]

dŏll′ў, n. (Pet-name, esp. in voc., for) doll; kinds of appliance in ·clothes--washing, ore-washing, pile-driving, iron--punching, polishing, etc.; ~-*shop*, marine store. [-Y[3]]

Dŏll′ў Vărd′en, n. Kinds of woman's hat & dress. [character in *Barnaby Rudge*]

dŏl′man, n. Long Turkish robe open in front; hussar's jacket worn with sleeves hanging loose; woman's mantle with flaps for sleeves. [ult. f. Turk. *dolaman*]

dŏl′mĕn, n. Megalithic tomb. [F, perh. f. Cornish (*doll* hole, *men* stone)]

dŏl′omite, n. Kind of rock (double carbonate of lime & magnesia); *The D*~s, mountains of this, esp. those in Tyrol. Hence dŏlomit′ic a. [*Dolomieu*, French geologist 1794, -ITE[1]]

dŏl′orous, a. (usu. poet. or joc.). Distressing, painful; dismal, doleful; distressed. Hence ~LY[2] adv. [ME, f. OF f. LL *dolorōsus* (DOLOUR, -OUS)]

dolōse′, a. (legal). Having criminal intent; intentionally deceitful. [f. L *dolosus* (*dolus* guile, -OSE[1])]

dŏl′our (-ler), n. (poet.). Sorrow, distress. [ME, f. OF, f. L *dolorem* nom. *-or*]

dŏl′phin, n. Sea animal of the whale order resembling porpoise but larger &

with beak-like snout; the fish dorado, which changes to many colours in dying; curved fish in heraldry, sculpture, etc.; bollard or mooring-post or buoy. [ME also *delphin* f. L *delphinus* f. Gk *delphis -inos*; cf. DELPHIN]

dōlt, n. Dull fellow, blockhead. Hence ~ISH[1] a., ~'ishNESS n. [app. related to *dol, dold,* obs. var. of DULL, *dull..d*]

Dŏm, title prefixed to names of R.-C. dignitaries, and Benedictine & Carthusian monks, and in Portugal & Brazil to Christian names of persons of the royal family, cardinals, bishops, etc. [abbr. of L *dominus* lord]

-dom, suf. forming nouns expressing rank, condition, domain, f. nn. or adjj. (*earldom, freedom, kingdom*), & (f. nouns) used collectively for the pl. or = the ways of (*officialdom*). [OE, OS *-dōm,* OHG *-tuom* (G-*tum*), orig. an independent n. = DOOM[1]]

domain', n. Estate, lands, dominions; district under rule, realm, sphere of influence; scope, field, province, (of thought or action; (Internat. & U.S. law) *Eminent D~,* lordship of sovereign power over all property in State, with right of expropriation. So **doman'IAL** a. [f. F *domaine,* earlier OF *demeine* DEMESNE]

dōme, n., & v.t. **1.** Stately building, mansion, (poet.); rounded vault as roof, with circular, elliptical, or polygonal base, large cupola; natural vault, canopy, (of sky, trees, etc.); rounded summit of hill etc.; hence ~ED[2] (-md), dōm'IC(AL), ~'LIKE (-ml-), dōm'Y[2], aa. **2.** v.t. Cover with, shape as, ~. [F, f. It. *duomo* cathedral, dome, (& direct) f. L *domus* house]

Domes'day (Bŏŏk) (dōŏmz-), n. Record of Will. I's Great Inquisition of lands of England made 1086. [ME, = DOOM[1]*sday,* pop. name given to the book as final authority]

domĕs't|ic, a. & n. **1.** Of the home, household, or family affairs; of one's own country, not foreign; native, home-made; (of animals) kept by or living with man; home-keeping, fond of home; hence ~ICALLY adv. **2.** n. Household servant. [f. F *domestique* f. L *domesticus* (*domus* home)]

domĕs'tic|āte, v.t. Naturalize (colonists, animals); make fond of home (esp. in p.p.); bring (animals) under human control, tame; civilize (savages). So ~ABLE a., ~A'TION n. [f. med. L *domesticare* (prec., -ATE[3])]

dŏmĕsti'cit|y (*or* dō-), n. Domestic character; home life or privacy; homeliness; *the* ~*ies,* domestic affairs; domesticated state. [-ITY]

dŏm'ĕtt, n. Fabric of wool & cotton used for shrouds etc. [orig. unkn.]

dŏm'icile (*or* -ĭl), n., & v.t. & i. **1.** Dwelling-place, home; (Law) place of perman-

ent residence, fact of residing; place at which bill of exchange is made payable (v.t., make payable *at* a place). **2.** vb. (Also **dŏmicil'IATE[3])** establish, settle (t. & i.), in a place; so **dŏmiciliA'TION** n. [ME, f. OF f. L *domicilium* f. *domus* home]

dŏmicil'iarЎ (-lya-), a. Of a dwelling- -place (~ *visit,* of officials to search or inspect private house). [as prec., -ARY[1]]

dŏm'inant, a. & n. **1.** Ruling, prevailing, most influential; (of heights) outstanding, overlooking others. **2.** (mus.). Fifth note of scale of any key (adj., of this, as ~ *chord, seventh,* etc.); reciting note in eccles. modes, usu. fifth from final. **3.** (Mendelism) main characteristic appearing in the first generation of hybrids inherited from one only of the parents (adj., of this). Hence **dŏm'inANCE** n., ~LY[2] adv. [F, f. L *dominari* see foll., -ANT]

dŏm'ināte, v.t. & i. Have commanding influence over (also intr. with *over*); be the most influential or conspicuous (of person, power, sound, feature of scene); (of heights) overlook, hold commanding position *over.* [f. L *dominari* (*dominus* lord), -ATE[3]]

dŏminā'tion, n. Ascendancy, sway, control; (pl.) angelic powers of fourth rank (see ORDER[1] 1). [ME, f. OF f. L *dominationem* (prec., -ATION)]

dŏmineer', v.i. Act imperiously, tyrannize, be overbearing. Hence ~ingLY[2] adv. [f. Du. (-*neren*) f. F *dominer* DOMINATE]

domin'ical, a. Of the Lord (Christ; ~ *year,* date A.D.); of the Lord's day, Sunday-, (~ *letter,* the one of the seven A-G denoting Sundays in any year). [f. LL & med. L *dominicalis* f. LL *dominicus* (L *dominus* lord, -IC) +-*alis* -AL]

Domin'ican, a. & n. **1.** Of St Dominic or his order of preaching friars. **2.** n. Black or ~ friar. [f. med. L *Dominicanus* f. *Dominicus* L name of *Domingo* de Guzman +-AN]

|| **dŏm'inie,** n. (Sc.). Schoolmaster. [later sp. of (16th c.) *domine* sir voc. of L *dominus* lord]

domin'ion (-yon), n. Lordship, sovereignty, control; domains of feudal lord; territory of sovereign or government (*D~ of Canada,* name given to Canadian colonies united 1867; *D~ of New Zealand,* title given 1907; *D~ of Ceylon* 1948); (Law) right of possession. [ME, f. OF f. med. L *dominionem* nom. -*o* f. L *dominium* (*dominus* lord)]

dŏm'inō, n. (pl. ~*es*). **1.** Loose cloak with half-mask worn to conceal identity esp. at masquerade, whence ~ED[2] (-ōd) a.; person wearing this ~. **2.** One of 28 small brick-shaped pieces marked with pips used in game of ~es. [F, prob. f. L *dominus* lord, but unexplained]

dŏn[1], n. **1.** Spanish title prefixed to

Christian name (*Don Juan*, rake, libertine; *Don* QUIXOTE); Spanish gentleman, Spaniard. **2.** Distinguished person; adept *at* something. **3.** Head, fellow, or tutor, of college, whence ~n'ISH¹ a., ~n'ishNESS n. [Sp., f. L *dominus* lord]

dŏn², v.t. (-nn-). Put on (garment). [= *do on*]

dŏn'a(h), n. (sl.). Woman; sweetheart. [f. Sp. *doña* or Port. *dona* f. L *domina* lady]

donā'tion, n. Bestowal, presenting; thing presented, gift (esp. of money given to institution), whence ***donāte'** v.t., present. [ME, f. OF f. L *donationem* (*donare* give, -ATION)]

dŏn'ative (*or* dō-), a. & n. (Benefice) given directly, not involving presentation to or investment by the Ordinary; gift, present, esp. official largess. [ME, f. L *donativum* gift (OF *donatif*); adj. use later (L *donare* give, -ATIVE)]

dŏn'atory̆, n. Recipient of donation. [f. med. L *donatorius* (*donare* give, -ORY)]

done (dŭn), p.p. of DO¹. ~ *brown*, duped, swindled; ~ *up*, tired.

dŏnee', n. Recipient of gift. [as DONOR, -EE]

‖ **dŏn'ga** (-ngga), n. Gully, ravine. [S.-Afr.]

dŏn'jŏn (*also* dŭ-), n. Great tower of castle, keep. [arch. spelling of DUNGEON]

dŏnk'ey, n. (pl. ~s). (Usual word for) ass; stupid person; ~*-engine*, hauling or hoisting steam-engine on ship's deck; ~*'s years* (sl.), a very long time. [18th c., perh. f. DUN¹, or proper name *Duncan* (cf. *dicky*, *neddy*)]

dŏnn'a, n. Italian or Spanish or Portuguese lady. [It., f. L *domina* mistress]

Dŏnn'y̆brŏŏk (Fair), n. Scene of uproar, free fight. [*Donnybrook* in Ireland]

dŏn'or, n. Giver (esp. of blood for transfusion). [ME, f. OF *doneur* f. L *donatorem* (*donare* give, -OR)]

dŏn't¹. See DO¹.

dŏn't², n. (joc.). Prohibition. [use of prec.]

dŏŏ'dle, v.i., & n. **1.** Scrawl or draw absent-mindedly. **2.** n. Scrawl or drawing so made; ~*-bug*, *(larva of) tiger beetle, *unscientific device for locating minerals, ‖ flying-bomb (colloq.). [orig. unkn.]

dŏŏl'ie, -y̆, n. Simple form of Indian litter used as army ambulance. [f. Hind. *doli* (Skr. *dul-* to swing)]

dŏŏm¹, n. (Hist.) Statute, law, decree; (arch.) decision, sentence, condemnation; fate, destiny, (usu. evil); ruin, death; the Last Judgement (now only in *crack*, *day*, *of* ~, & in ~*s'day*; *till* ~*sday*, for ever; cf. DOMESDAY). [OE, OS *dōm*, OHG *tuom*, ON *dómr*, Goth. *dōms* f. Gmc **dōmaz* f. **do-* DO¹]

dŏŏm², v.t. Pronounce sentence against, condemn *to* some fate, *to* do; consign to misfortune or destruction (esp. in p.p.); (arch.) decree (~*ed his death*). [f. prec.]

door (dōr), n. **1.** Hinged or sliding barrier usu. of wood or metal for closing entrance to building, room, safe, etc. (*front* ~, *chief* ~ from house to street etc.; *lives* etc. *next* ~, in next house or room; so *three* ~*s off* etc.; *next* ~ *to* fig., nearly, almost, near to; so *at death's* ~). **2.** Entrance, access, exit, (*show one the* ~, expel him; *open a* ~ *to*, *close the* ~ *upon*, make possible, impossible). **3.** *Out of* ~*s*, abroad, in the open air; *within* ~*s*, in the house; *lay*, *lie*, *at the* ~ *of*, impute, be imputable, to; DARKEN ~. **4.** ~*'bell*, inside bell worked by handle or button outside ~; ‖ ~*-case*, *-frame*, structure in which ~ is fitted; ‖ ~*-keeper*, porter; ~*'mat*, for rubbing off mud from shoes; ~*-money*, taken at ~ of place ·of entertainment; ~*'nail*, with which ~s used to be studded (*dead*, *deaf*, etc., *as a* ~*nail*); ~*-plate*, usu. of brass bearing occupant's name; ~*-post*, upright of ~*-case*; ~*'step*, leading up to usu. outer ~; ~*-stone*, slab in front of ~; ~*'way*, opening filled by ~. Hence (-)~ED² (-ōrd), ~'LESS (-ōrl-), aa. [OE, OS *duru* (dor), OHG *turi* (tor), ON *dyrr*, Goth. *daur* f. Gmc **dur-* cogn. w. L *fores*, Gk *thura*]

dŏp, n. Cheap S.-Afr. brandy; a dram of liquor. [Du., = shell, husk]

dōpe, n., & v.t. **1.** Thick liquid used as food or lubricant; kinds of varnish esp. in aeroplane manufacture; narcotic, stupefying drink; drug etc. given to horse or greyhound to try to make it win; *(sl.) information about a racehorse's past performances or form, information of use to journalists etc. **2.** v.t. Administer ~ to, drug, (cf. NOBBLE). [f. Du. *doop* sauce (*doopen* to dip)]

doppel-gänger. See DOUBLE¹-*ganger*.

dŏpp'er, n. (Derog. for) member of the Gereformeerde Kerk of S. Afr., in communion with the Christian Reformed Church of Holland. [f. Du. *dooper* baptist, f. *doopen* dip]

dōr, n. Insect flying with loud humming noise; black dung-beetle, cockchafer, rose-beetle, etc. [OE *dora* orig. unkn.]

‖ **Dōr'a**, n. See DEFENCE.

dora'dō (-ah-), n. (pl. ~s). Splendidly coloured sea-fish, dolphin. [Sp., f. L DE(*auratus* gilt f. *aurum* gold. -ATE²)]

Dŏrc'as, n. Meeting of ladies to make clothes for the poor. [*Acts* ix. 36]

Dōr'ïan, a. & n. (Inhabitant) of Doris, district of ancient Greece; (member) of one of three divisions (*Aeolian*, *Ionian*, ~) of ancient Greeks (~ *mode*: ancient Greek MODE, reputedly simple & solemn in character; first of eccles. modes, with D as final & A as dominant). [f. L f. Gk *Dōrios* (*Dōris* as above) + -AN]

Dŏ'ric, a. & n. **1.** = prec. adj.; ~ ORDER (also ~ as n.); (of dialect) broad, rustic. **2.** n. Dialect of ancient Greece (cf. *Attic*, *Ionic*, *Aeolic*), rustic English or esp. Scots. [f. L f. Gk *Dōrikos* (prec., -IC)]

Dork'ing, a. & n. (Fowl) of the ~ breed. [~ in Surrey]

dorm'ant, a. Lying inactive as in sleep (of some animals through winter, undeveloped buds, potential faculties); (Her., of beast) with head on paws; not acting, in abeyance, (often *lie* ~; ~ *warrant* etc., drawn in blank; ~ *partner*, sleeping). Hence **dorm'ancy** n. [ME, f. OF (*dormir* f. L *dormire* sleep, -ant)]

dorm'er, n. (Also ~*-window*) projecting upright window in sloping roof. [f. OF *dormeor* f. L *dormitorium* (prec., -ory)]

dorm'itory, n. Sleeping-room with several beds & sometimes cubicles; suburban or country district of city people's residences. [ME, f. L (DORMER)]

dorm'ouse, n. (pl. *-mice*). Small hibernating rodent between mouse and squirrel. [ME; orig. obsc.; pop. referred to F *dormir* & MOUSE since 16th c.]

dorm'y, a. (golf). (Of player or side) as many holes ahead as there are holes to play (~ *one*, *five*, etc.). [orig. unkn.]

‖ **do'rothy bag**, n. Lady's open-topped handbag slung by loops from wrist. [fem. name]

Do'rothy Perk'ins (-z), n. Climbing rose bearing clusters of double pink flowers. [personal name]

dorp, n. (S. Africa). Village, small township. [Du.; see THORP]

dors'al, a. (Anat., Zool., Bot.) of, on, near, the back; ridge-shaped. Hence ~LY[2] adv. [F, or f. LL *dorsalis* (foll., -AL)]

dors(o)-, comb. form = back-&-, as in *dorsabdom'inal* of back & belly, *dorsolat'eral* of back & sides. [L *dorsum* back, -o-]

dort'our (*-ter*), **-ter**, n. (hist.). Bedroom, dormitory, esp. in monastery. [ME, f. OF (*-our*), as DORMER]

dor'y[1], n. (Also *John D*~) sea-fish used as food. [ME, f. OF *doree* fem. p.p. of *dorer* gild, as DORADO]

dor'y[2], n. Flat-bottomed skiff, esp. fishing-vessel's boat in U.S. [orig. unkn.]

dos'age, n. Giving of medicine in doses; size of dose. [-AGE]

dose, n., & v.t. 1. Amount of medicine to be taken at once (also fig. of flattery, punishment, etc.). 2. v.t. Give physic to (person), adulterate, blend, (esp. wine with spirit). [vb f. noun, F, f. LL f. Gk *dosis* (*didōmi* give)]

‖ **doss**, n., & v.i., (sl.). Bed in ~*-house* or common lodging-house; (v.i.) sleep in this; hence ~'ER[1] n. [18th c. *dorse* f. L *dorsum* back; cf. dial. *hoss* for *horse*]

doss'al, n. Hanging behind altar or round chancel. [f. med. L *dossale* f. LL *dorsalis* DORSAL]

doss'ier (-syā, -sier), n. Set of documents, esp. record of person's antecedents. [F, so called f. label on back (*dos*); see -ER[2](2)]

dost. See DO[1].

dot[1], n. Small spot, speck, roundish penmark; (Orthogr.) period, point over *i* or *j*, point used as diacritical mark; (Mus. writing) point used with various meanings; small child, tiny object; ~*-&-dash*, using ~s & dashes, as in Morse code; ~*-wheel*, used for making dotted line; ‖ *off* one's ~ (sl.), half-witted, (temporarily) crazy; *on the*~, exactly on time. [16th c., perh. repr. OE *dott* head of boil, cogn. w. OHG *tutto* nipple]

dot[2], v.t. (-tt-). Mark with dot(s); place dot over (letter *i*; ~ *the is & cross the ts*, fill in details, make meaning quite clear); (Mus.) ~*ted crotchet* etc., with time value increased by half; diversify as with dots (*sea* ~*ted with ships*); scatter (*about*, *all over*) like dots; ‖ (sl.) hit (~*ted him one in the eye*); ~ *& carry* (*one*), child's formula for remembering to carry in addition sum; ~ *& go one*, n., a., & adv., limp, limping(ly). [f. prec.]

dot[3], n. Woman's marriage portion. [F]

dot'ard, n. One in his dotage. [foll., -ARD]

dote, **doat**, v.i. Be silly, deranged, infatuated, or feeble-minded, esp. from age, whence **dot'age**(2) ñ.; concentrate one's affections, bestow excessive fondness, (*up*)*on*. Hence **dot'ingly[2]** adv. [ME *doten* corresp. to MDu. *doten* be silly, whence OF *redoter* (mod. *ra-*)]

doth. See DO[1].

dot'(e)rel, n. Kind of plover. [ME; DOTE + -REL, named from the ease with which it is caught]

dot'tle, **-tel**, n. Plug of tobacco left unsmoked in pipe. [DOT[1], -LE]

dott'y, a. Dotted about, sporadic, marked with dots; (colloq.) shaky of gait (~ *on his legs*), feeble-minded, half idiotic. [DOT[1] + -Y[2]]

Dou'ai, **-ay**, (doo'ā, dow'ā), n. ~ *version*, *Bible*, English translation of the Bible used in the R.C. Church. The Old Testament was completed at ~ in France early in the 17th c.

dou'ane (doo'ahn), n. Foreign custom-house. [F, f. Arab. *diwan* DIVAN]

dou'ble[1] (dŭ-), a. & adv. 1. adj. Consisting of two members, things, layers, etc., forming a pair, twofold (~ *chin*, with roll of fat below chin proper); folded, bent, stooping much; with some part ~ (~ *axe*, with two edges, ~ *eagle*, with two heads); (of flowers) with petals multiplied by conversion of stamens etc.; having twofold relation, dual, ambiguous (~ *meaning*, = DOUBLE ENTENDRE); twice as much or many (*of*, or, with prep. omitted, seeming to govern following wd); of twofold or extra size, strength, value, etc. (~ *ale*, ~ *florin*); (Mus.) lower in pitch by an octave (~ *bassoon* etc.; ~ *bass*, lowest-pitched stringed instrument); (Mil.) ~ *time* (also formerly, & still in general use, ~*-quick time*), regulation running pace; deceitful, hypocritical; ~ ENTRY; ‖ (~ *first*, (person who has taken) first-class University honours in two subjects; ~ *star*, two stars so close as to seem one, esp. when forming connected pair; *work* ~ TIDES; hence ~NESS (-ln-) n., doub'LY² adv. **2.** adv. To twice the amount etc. (~ *as bright*; *see* ~, two things when there is only one, esp. of drunken man); two together (*ride* ~, two on horse); *sleep* ~, two in bed). **3.** ~-, a. or adv., is freely used in new or obvious compounds, as well as in the following: ~-*acting*, in two ways, directions, etc., esp. of engine in which steam acts on both sides of piston; ~-*banking*, leaving a vehicle alongside another stationary vehicle; ~-*barrel*, = ~- -barrelled, or~-barrelledgun;~-*barrelled*, with two barrels (also fig. = ambiguous, of compliment etc.; & of compound surname); ~-*bass*, lowest-pitched stringed instrument; ~-*bedded*, with two beds or ~ bed; ~-*bitt* v.t. (Naut.), pass (cable) twice round bitts or round two pairs of bitts; ~-*breasted*, (of coat or waistcoat) made to button on either side; '~-*cross*' (sl.), (v.t.) cheat (each of two parties, usu. by pretended collusion with both), (n.) act of this nature; hence ~-*cross'er*; ~-*dealer*, -*ling* n. & a., deceiver, deceit-(ful); ~-*dyed* usu. fig., deeply stained with guilt (~-*dyed scoundrel*); ~-*edged*, with two cutting edges, (of argument, sarcasm, etc.) telling against as well as for one; ~-*faced*, insincere; ~-*gänger* (-ng-), wraith of living person [f. G *doppel-gänger* double-goer]; ~ *harness* (fig.), matrimony; ~-*jointed*, having joints that allow unusual bending movements to limb; ~-*leaded* (-lĕd-), of printed matter with wide spaces between lines to draw attention; ~-*lock* v.t., turn key of (some locks) twice; ~-*quick* (see ~ *time* above; also) adv., very quickly; ~-*reef* v.t. (Naut.), contract spread of (sail) by two reefs; ~-*refine*, refine twice over. [ME, f. OF f. L *duplus* (*duo* two)]

dou'ble² '(dŭ-), n. Double quantity, double measure of spirits etc., twice as much or many (~ *or quits*, game, throw, toss, deciding whether person shall pay twice his loss or debt or nothing); counterpart of thing or person; wraith; (Mil.) *at the* ~, running; (Bridge) doubling of a bid; score (short whist) of five to less than three, (long whist) of ten to nothing, (stake being doubled); (Lawn-tennis etc.) game between two pairs; (Darts) a throw on the narrow space enclosed by the two outer circles of a dartboard; (Racing) a bet on two horses etc. in different races, the winnings & stake from one race being carried forward & bet on the second; sharp turn of hunted animal, or of river. [f. prec. & foll.]

dou'ble³ (dŭ-), v.t. & i. **1.** Make double, increase twofold, multiply by two; (Bridge) ~ value of points to be won or lost on (adversary's bid); amount to

twice as much as; (Mus.) add same note in higher or lower octave to; (of actor) ~ *part*(s), play two in same piece. **2.** (mil.). Move in double time, run. **3.** Put (passenger etc.) in same quarters with another (also ~ *up*). **4.** Bend, turn, (paper, cloth) over upon itself (often *up*). **5.** ~ *up*, bend one's body into stooping or curled-up position, cause (another) to do this by blow, (of paper, leaf, etc.) become folded. **6.** Clench (fist). **7.** (billiards). Rebound, make to rebound. **8.** (naut.). Get round (headland). **9.** Turn sharply in flight, pursue tortuous course. [ME, f. OF *dobler*, *dubler* f. LL *duplare* (L *duplus* DOUBLE¹)]

double entendre (see Ap.), n. Ambiguous expression, phrase with two meanings, one usu. indecent; use of such phrases. [from 1673; obs. F (now *double entente*, which is often needlessly substituted in E for the established ~)]

doub'let (dŭ-), n. **1.** (hist.). Close-fitting body-garment worn by men with or without sleeves & short skirts (~ *& hose*, masculine attire, also light attire without cloak). **2.** One of a pair, esp. one of two words of same derivation but different sense (*fashion* & *faction*). **3.** pl. Same number on two dice thrown at once. **4.** Two birds killed with double-barrel. **5.** (Microscope etc.) combination of two simple lenses. [ME, f. F (DOUBLE¹, -ET)]

dou'bleton (dŭ'blton), n. Two cards only of a suit (dealt to a player). [f. DOUBLE¹, after *singleton*]

doubloon' (dŭ-), n. (hist.). Spanish gold coin, double pistole (orig. 33–36s., later slightly over £1). [f. F *doublon* or Sp. *doblon* (DOUBLE¹, -OON)]

doublure (dooblūr'), n. Ornamental usu. leather lining inside book-cover. [F]

doubt¹ (dowt), n. Feeling of uncertainty (*about*), undecided frame of mind, inclination to disbelieve (*of*, *about*; *have no* ~ *that* . . .), hesitation; uncertain state of things, want of full proof (*give one the benefit of the* ~, assume his innocence rather than guilt) or of clear signs of the future; *make no* ~, feel sure; *nó* ~, certainly, admittedly; *without* ~, certainly. [ME, f. OF *doute* f. *douter* DOUBT²]

doubt² (dowt), v.i. & t. Feel uncertain (about); waver; be undecided about or *about*, hesitate to believe or trust, call in question, (person, fact expressed by noun or by clause with *whether*, *if*, or, in negative or interrog. sentences, *that*, *but*, *but that*; *I* ~ *whether*, *I don't* ~ *that*, *can you* ~ *that*, *he will win*); have doubts of (esp. w. neg., as *never* ~*ed of success*); ‖ (arch. & dial.) be afraid, rather think, suspect, that (*I* ~ *we are late*). [ME *dute* f. OF *doter*, *duter* f. L *dubitare*; mod. sp. after L]

doubt'ful (-owt-), a. Of uncertain meaning, character, truth, or issue, undecided, ambiguous, questionable, (~ *syllable*, *letter*, that can be either long or short); unsettled in opinion, uncertain, hesitating. Hence ~LY² adv., ~NESS n. [-FUL]

doubt'less (-owt-), adv. Certainly, no doubt, I admit, (usu. concessive, cf. UN-DOUBTEDLY). [-LESS]

‖ **douce** (doos), a. (Sc.). Sober, gentle, sedate. [ME, f. OF *doux* fem. *douce* f. L *dulcis* sweet]

douceur (see Ap.), n. Gratuity; bribe. [F]

douche (doosh), n., & v.t. & i. **1**. Jet of water applied to body externally or internally as form of bathing or for medicinal purpose. **2**. vb. Administer ~ to, take ~. [F, f. It. *doccia* pipe f. L *ductio* conduit (*ducere* lead)]

dough (dō), n. Kneaded flour, bread-paste; pasty mass; (sl.) money; ~'boy, boiled dumpling, (sl.) U.S. infantryman; ~'nut, cake of ~ sweetened & fried. Hence ~'Y² (dō'ĭ) a., ~'INESS (dō'ĭ-) n. [OE *dāg*, OHG *teic*, ON *deig*, Goth. *daigs* f. Gmc *daigaz*]

dought'ly (dowt-), a. (arch. or joc.). Valiant, stout, formidable. Hence ~ILY² adv., ~INESS n. [OE *dohtig* var. of *dyhtig* = MLG, MDu. *duchtich*, MHG *tühtic* f. Gmc *dugan* be strong]

Dou'khobŏrs (dōoko-), n. pl. Religious sect, with some likeness in doctrines to Quakers, of which large numbers migrated from Russia to Canada after persecutions for refusing military service. [f. Russ. = spirit-fighters]

doum (dowm, dōom), n. (Also ~-*palm*) Egyptian palm-tree. [f. Arab. *daum*, *dum*]

‖ **dour** (-oor), a. (Sc.). Severe, stern, obstinate. Hence ~'LY² adv., ~'NESS n. [ME; poss. f. L *durus* hard]

douse, dowse, v.t. (Naut.) lower (sail), close (port-hole); extinguish (light; ~ *the glim*, arch., put out the light); throw water over, drench. [orig. uncert.]

dove (dŭv), n. Kinds of pigeon (*cushat*, *ground*, *ring*, *rock*, *stock*, *turtle*, *wood*, ~~); the Holy Spirit; type of gentleness or innocence (so ~-*eyed*); messenger of good news or peace (*Gen.* viii); darling (esp. *my* ~); ~-*colour(ed)*, (of) warm grey; ~'s-*foot*, kinds of crane's-bill; ~-*hawk*, hen-harrier (from its colour); ~ *cot(e)*, pigeon-house (*flutter the* ~*cots*, alarm quiet people). Hence ~'LIKE (dŭvl-) a. [ME *duve*, OS *dūba*, ON *dúfa*, OHG *tūba*, Goth *dūbo* f. Gmc *dūbhōn*]

Dōv'er's powd'er, n. (pharm.). Preparation of opium, ipecacuanha, and sulphate of potash or sugar of milk, an anodyne diaphoretic. [Dr. Thos. *Dover* (d. 1742)]

dove'tail (dŭvt-), n., & v.t. & i. **1**. Tenon shaped like dove's spread tail or reversed wedge, fitting into corresponding mortise & forming joint; such a joint. **2**. vb. Put together with ~s; (fig.) fit together (t. & i.) compactly.

dow. See D(H)OW.

dow'ager, n. ‖ Woman with title or pro-

perty derived from her late husband (often in comb. as *Queen* ~, ~ *countess* or *countess* ~; ~ *duchess*); (colloq.) dignified elderly lady. [f. OF *douagere* f. *douage* DOWER, -ER²(2)]

dowd' (ĭy, n. & a. (Woman) shabbily, badly, or unfashionably dressed; (of dress etc.) unattractive, unfashionable. Hence ~ILY² adv., ~INESS, ~YISM(2), nn., ~ŸISH¹ a. [f. obs. *dowd* slut, of unkn. orig.]

dow'el, n., & v.t. Headless pin of wood, metal, etc., for keeping two pieces of wood, stone, etc., in their relative position; (vb) fasten with ~. [ME, f. MLG *dovel* (whence G *döbel*), = OHG *tubili*; see THOLE²]

dow'er, n., & v.t. **1**. Widow's share for life of husband's estate; property or money brought by wife to husband, dowry; endowment, gift of nature, talent. Hence ~LESS a. **2**. v.t. Give dowry to; endow *with*'talent etc. [ME; vb f. n., OF *douaire* f. med. L *dotarium* (L *dos dotis*, -ARY¹)]

‖ **dowl'as**, n. Kind of strong calico or linen. [*Doulas* in Brittany]

down¹, n. Open high land, ‖ esp. (pl.) treeless undulating chalk uplands of S. England used for pasture; = DUNE; ‖ *The* D~s, part of sea (opposite North D~s) within Goodwin Sands. [OE *dūn*, OS *dūna* (MDu. *dūne*); see DUNE]

down², n. First covering of young birds; bird's under plumage, used in cushions etc.; fine short hair, esp. first hair on face, also on fruit etc.; fluffy substance. [ME f. ON *dúnn*, whence LG *dūne*, G *daune*]

down³, adv. (superl., a. or adv., ~'*most*). **1**. (Motion): from above, to lower place, to ground, (*come* ~, from bedroom; *knock*, *fall*, ~; *sun*, *ship*, *goes* ~, sets, sinks; *food goes* ~, is swallowed; *get* ~, swallow, alight; *book* etc. *goes* ~, finds acceptance; *get*, *set*, ~, from carriage etc.; *brought* ~ *by river*; *money* ~, *pay* ~, at once, as though on counter; *write*, *set*, *put*, *take*, *copy*, ~, on paper; so *Bill* ~ *for second reading today*); to place regarded as lower, into helpless position, with current or wind, southwards, ‖ from capital or university, (*Lords' amendments sent* ~ *to Commons*; *bear* ~, sail to leeward; *run*, *ride*, *hunt*, ~, bring to bay; *shout*, *hiss*, ~, silence; ~ *to Norfolk* from Scotland, to *Scotland* or *the country* from London; ‖ *go* ~, for vacation or at end of university life; ‖ *send* ~, university punishment; *up & ~*, to & fro); (ellipt. for imperat. of) lie, get, put, etc., ~ (~, *Ponto!*; ~ *helm*, put the HELM ~; & with *with*, ~ *with the aristocrats!*). **2**. (Station): in lower place (*blinds were* ~; *is not* ~ *yet*, i.e. out of his bedroom); ‖ not up in capital or university; in fallen posture, prostrate, at low level, in depression, humiliation, etc., (*hit man who is* ~; *many* ~ *with fever*; *sun*, *tide*, *are* ~; ~ *in* *the mouth* or ~ or ~-*hearted*, dispirited; *are we* ~-*hearted?*, sl. assertion of confidence; *bread is* ~, cheaper). **3.** (Order, time, quality): inclusively of lower limit in series (*from King* ~ *to cobbler*); from earlier to later time (*custom handed* ~); to finer consistence (*boil, grind, wear, thin,* ~); into quiescence (*calm*~). **4.** (Phrases): *be* ~ *on*, pounce upon, treat severely; ~ *to the ground*, completely; ~ *at* HEEL; ~ *on* one's LUCK; ~ *& out*, unable to resume the fight in boxing, beaten in the struggle of life, done for; ~-*&-out* n.; ~ *under*, at the antipodes, in Australia etc. [OE *dūne* aphetic f. *adūne* ADOWN]

down[4], prep. Downwards along, through, or into; from top to bottom of; at a lower part of (*situated* ~ *the Thames*); *up & ~*, to & fro along; ~ *town*, into the town from higher or outlying part, *to or in the business part of a city; ~ *the wind*, with it (*let go* ~ *the wind*, abandon, discard). [f. prec.]

down[5], a. (not compared). Directed downwards (~ *leap, look;* ~ *grade*, descending slope in railroad, fig. deterioration); ~ *draught*, downward draught, esp. one driving down chimney into room; ~ *payment*, made in cash; ~ *train*, going, coming, from London, ~ *platform*, for such train's departure or arrival. [f. DOWN[3]]

down[6], v.t. (colloq.). Put, throw, knock, (usu. person or aeroplane) down; ~ *tools*, cease work for the day etc., go on strike. [f. DOWN[3]]

down[7], n. Reverse of fortune (usu. *ups & ~s*; (Dominoes) = POSE[1]; *have a ~ on*, dislike, tend to be down on, (colloq.). [f. DOWN[3]]

down'cast[1] (-ah-), n. (Also ~-*shaft*) shaft for introducing fresh air into mine. [DOWN[3] + CAST[2]]

down'cast[2] (-ah-), a. (Of looks) directed downwards; dejected.

down'fall (-awl), n. Great fall of rain etc.; fall from prosperity, ruin.

downhill, n., adj. & adv. (N., down'hĭl') downward slope, decline, (~ *of life*, later half); (adj., down[2]) sloping down, declining; (adv., -hĭl') in descending direction, on a decline.

Down'ing Street, n. Street in London containing important government offices, esp. the Prime Minister's official residence (No. 10), the Government of the day (*does not find favour in* ~; ~ *disapproves*).

down'pour (-pōr), n. Heavy fall of rain etc.

down'right (-rīt; downrīt' *if placed late*), a. & adv. **1.** (Arch.) vertical; plain, definite, straightforward, blunt, whence ~NESS (-rīt[.]) n.; not short of, out-&-out, (*a* ~ *lie, atheist;* ~ *nonsense*). **2.** adv. Thoroughly, positively, quite, (~ *scared, insolent*). [ME; DOWN[3] + RIGHT a. & adv.]

downstairs', adv., down'stair(s), a. Down the stairs; to, on, of, a lower floor.

down'throw (-ō), n. (geol.). Depression of strata on one side of fault.

down'trŏdden, a. Oppressed, kept under.

down'ward, a. & adv., down'wards (-z), adv. (Moving, pointing, leading) towards what is lower, inferior, or later. [OE *adūnweard* (DOWN[3], -WARD)]

down'ÿ[1], a. Like, of, downs. [DOWN[1], -Y[2]]

down'|ÿ[2], a. Of, like, covered with, down; (sl.) wide awake, knowing. So ~ĭLY[2] adv., ~ĭNESS n. [DOWN[2], -Y[2]]

dowr'ÿ, n. Portion woman brings to her husband; talent, natural gift. [ME, f. AF *dowarie*, OF *douaire* DOWER]

dows'ing (-z-), n. Searching for latent water or minerals with the ~- (or *divining*-) *rod*, a forked twig held by the **dows'er** (-z-) & dipping over the right spot. [orig. unkn.]

dŏxŏl'ogÿ, n. Liturgical formula of praise to God, as *Glory be to* etc. [f. med. L f. Gk *doxologia* (*doxa* glory, -LOGY)]

dŏx'ÿ[1], n. Beggar's wench, paramour. [16th c. cant, of unkn. orig.]

dŏx'ÿ[2], n. Opinion, esp. on theology. [joc. use of end of *orthodoxy, heterodoxy*]

doyen (see Ap.), n. Senior member *of* a body, esp. senior ambassador at a court. [F, f. L as DEAN[1]]

doyley. See DOILY.

dōze, v.i. & n. **1.** Sleep drowsily, be half asleep; ~ *off*, fall lightly asleep. **2.** n. Short slumber. [cf. ON *dúsa* doze, Da. *döse* make drowsy]

do'zen (dŭ-), n. (Pl. ~, used adjectivally or as noun, when with numeral or equivalent except *some*) twelve, as *a, three, several, how many,* ~ *figs* or *of the best figs*, of *these*, but *some* ~s of *people*, cf. *some* (about a) ~ (*of*) *people*, ~s of (= many) *times*; (pl. ~s) set of twelve, as *pack them in* ~s; *baker's, devil's, long, printer's,* ~, thirteen; || *talk nineteen to the* ~, incessantly. [ME, f. OF *dozeine* (L *duodecim* twelve)]

drăb[1], n., & v.i. (-bb-). Slut, slattern; prostitute; (vb) whore. [perh. related to LG *drabbe* mire, Du. *drab* dregs]

drăb[2], a. & n. (Of) dull light brown colour; dull, monotonous; monotony. [prob. f. obs. & F *drap* cloth]

|| **drăbb'ĕt**, n. Drab twilled linen used for smock-frocks. [prec., -ET[1]]

drăb'ble, v.i. & t. Go splashing *through*, make dirty and wet with, water or mud. [ME, f. LG *drabbelen* paddle in water or mire; cf. DRAB[1]]

Dracaen'a (-sēn-), n. Genus of liliaceous trees, including the *dragon tree* (yielding DRAGON's-blood). [mod. L f. Gk *drakaina* fem. of *drakōn* dragon]

drachm (-ăm), n. Ancient Greek silver coin, drachma; (Apoth. wt) 60 grains, ⅛ oz; (Avoird.) 27½ grains, ₁₆ oz; small quantity. [ME *dragme* f. OF, or f. LL *dragma* f. L f. Gk *drakhmē*]

drăch'ma (-k-), n. (pl. ~s, ~e). Ancient

Greek coin (see prec.); modern Greek coin. [L, f. Gk *drakhmē* (*drassomai* grasp)]

Dracon'ian, Dracon'ic, aa. (Of laws) rigorous, harsh, cruel. [*Drakōn* Athenian legislator 621 B.C. +-IAN, -IC]

draff (-ahf), n. Dregs, lees; hog's-wash; refuse of malt after brewing. [ME, = MLG, Icel., Sw. *draf*, OHG pl. *trebir* (G *treber*)]

draft[1] (-ah-), n. **1.** (Selection of) detachment of men from larger body for special duty, contingent, reinforcement; *(Mil.) call-up, conscription. **2.** Drawing of money by written order (*make a ~ on fund* etc., also fig. *on* person's confidence, friendship, etc.), bill or cheque drawn, esp. by one branch of bank on another. **3.** Sketch of work to be executed; rough copy of document. **4.** (masonry). Chisel--dressing along margin of stone's surface. [var. of DRAUGHT[1]]

draft[2] (-ah-), v.t. **1.** Draw off (part of larger body, esp. of troops) for special purpose; *conscript. **2.** Prepare, make rough copy of, (document, esp. Parliamentary Bill), whence ~'ER[1] n. **3.** (masonry). Cut draft on (stone). [f. prec.]

drafts'man (-ahf-), n. One who makes drawings or designs; one who drafts documents or Parliamentary Bills. [= DRAUGHTSMAN]

drag[1], v.t. & i. (-gg-). Pull along with force, difficulty, or friction; allow (feet, tail, etc.) to trail; ~ one's *feet*, (fig.) be slow or reluctant to do something; *ship ~s her anchor*, *anchor ~s*, anchor fails to hold; ~ *in*, introduce (subject) needlessly (*why ~ in Velasquez?*; also ~ *in by the head & shoulders*); (Mus.) go too slowly, be wanting in life; trail, go heavily; ~ *on*, continue (t. & i.) tediously; ~ *out*, protract; use grapnel or drag (often *for* drowned person or lost object), dredge, search bottom of, (river etc.) with grapnels, nets, etc.; harrow (land) apply drag to (wheel, vehicle); (colloq.) ~ *up* (child), rear roughly. [ME, f. OE *dragan* or ON *draga* DRAW]

drag[2], n. Heavy harrow; rough sledge; four-horsed private vehicle like stage coach; (also ~-*net*) net drawn over bottom of river etc. or surface of field to enclose all fish or game; *(sl.) influence, pull; apparatus for dredging or recovering drowned persons etc.; muckrake; iron shoe for retarding vehicle downhill; obstruction to progress; strong-smelling lure for hounds in lieu of fox (so ~--*hounds*), club for pursuing this sport; slow motion, impeded progress;~-*anchor*, floating frame on hawser to check leeway of drifting ship; ~-*chain*, used to retard vehicle by fixing wheel, (fig.) impediment. [f. prec.]

dragée (drah'zhā), n. Sugar-coated almond, small silver ball for decorating cake, sweet (often one serving as vehicle for a drug). [F, see DREDGE[2]]

drag'gle, v.t. & i. Make wet, limp, & dirty, by trailing; hang trailing; lag, straggle in rear; ~-*tail*(*ed*), (woman) with ~*d* or untidily trailing skirts. [f. DRAG[1] + -LE(3)]

drag'oman, n. (pl. -*ans*, -*en*). Interpreter, esp. in Arabic, Turkish, or Persian. [f. F f. O Arab. *targuman*, cf. TARGUM]

drag'on, n. Mythical monster like crocodile or snake with wings & claws & often breathing fire; (with allusion to legends) guardian of treasure etc. or of female chastity, watchful person, duenna; (Bibl.) whale or shark, serpent, crocodile, jackal; *the old D~*, Satan; kinds of lizard & pigeon; ~-*fly*, neuropterous insect with long slender body & two pairs of large wings; ~'*s-blood*, bright red gum exuding from kind of palm fruit (~ *tree*); ~'*s teeth*, anti-tank obstacles resembling teeth pointed upwards. [ME, f. OF f. L *draconem* nom. -*o* f. Gk *drakōn* serpent]

dragonnade', n., & v.t. (Pl.) persecutions of Protestants under Louis XIV by quartering dragoons on them; persecution carried on by means of troops; (vb) persecute thus. [F (*dragon* DRAGOON, -ADE)]

dragoon', n., & v.t. **1.** Cavalryman (orig. mounted infantryman armed with carbine called ~; later of certain cavalry regiments that were formerly mounted infantry); rough fierce fellow; kind of pigeon (also *dragon*). **2.** v.t. Set ~s upon, persecute (see prec.), force *into* a course by persecution. [f. F *dragon* carbine, so named as breathing fire (DRAGON)]

drail, n. Fish-hook & line weighted with lead for dragging at depth through water. [app. f. TRAIL, infl. by *draw* etc.]

drain[1], v.t. & i. Draw (liquid) *off* or *away* by conduit, ~-*pipes*, etc. (also fig., ~ *the wealth of England*); drink (liquid), empty (vessel), to the dregs; dry (land etc.) by withdrawing moisture; (of river) carry off superfluous water of (district); deprive (person, thing) *of* property, strength, etc.; trickle *through*, flow *off* or *away*; (of wet cloth, vessel, etc.) get rid of moisture by its flowing away (*set it there to ~*). [OE *drēahnian* cogn. w. DRY]

drain[2], n. Channel carrying off liquid, artificial conduit for water, sewage, etc.; (Surg.) tube for drawing off discharge from abscess etc.; constant outlet, withdrawal, demand, or expenditure (*a great ~ on my resources*); (sl.) small draught, drink; ~-*pipe*, pipe for carrying off surplus water or liquid sewage from a building, (attrib., colloq., of trousers) very narrow; ~-*pipes* (colloq.), such trousers. [f. prec.]

drain'age, n. Draining; system of drains, artificial or natural; ~-*basin*, district drained by river; what is drained off, sewage. [-AGE]

G

drain′er, n. In vbl senses; esp., vessel in which things are put to drain. [-ER¹]

drāke¹, n. Kinds of ephemeral fly used in fishing (green ~, common day-fly). [OE *draca*, MLG, MDu. *drake*, OHG *trahho*, WG f. L *draco* DRAGON]

drāke², n. Male duck (*play* DUCK¹*s & ~s*). [ME; corresp. to LG *drake*, G. dial. *drache, trech,* repr. second element in OHG *anutrehho* (G *enterich*) f. *anut* (G *ente*); ult. orig. unkn.]

drăm, n. A weight (see DRACHM); small draught of spirit etc. (*~-drinker, -ing,* tippler, -ing; *~-shop,* public-house). [ME; for DRACHM]

dra′ma (-ah-), n. Stage-play; *the ~,* the dramatic art, composition & presentation of plays; set of events having the unity & progress of a play & leading to catastrophe or consummation. [LL f. Gk (gen. *-atos*), f. *draō* do, -M]

dramăt′|ic, a. Of drama; as of a play-actor, theatrical; fit for theatrical representation, sudden, striking, impressive; (of utterances etc.) not to be taken as one's own, representing another person's thoughts. Hence ~ICALLY adv. [f. LL f. Gk *dramatikos* (prec., -IC)]

drăm′atis persōn′ae, n. pl. (often with sing.·constr.). (List of) characters in a play. [L]

drăm′atist, n. Playwright. [DRAMA, -IST]

drăm′atīz|e, -is|e (-īz), v.t. & i. Convert (novel etc.) into a play, admit of such conversion; make a dramatic scene of. Hence ~A′TION n. [DRAMA, -IZE]

drăm′atūrg|e, n. Playwright. So **drămatūr′gic** a., ~IST(1), ~Y¹, nn. [F, f. Gk *dramatourgos* (DRAMA, *-ergos* -working)]

drank. See DRINK¹.

drāpe, v.t., & i. 1. Cover, hang, adorn, with cloth etc.; arrange (clothes, hangings) in graceful folds. 2. n. Piece of drapery, curtain. [ME, f. OF *draper* (*drap* f. LL *drappus* cloth)]

drāp′er, n. Dealer in cloth, linen, etc. [ME, f. AF *draper* (OF *-ier*), see prec., -IER]

drāp′er|y̆, n. Cloth & linen & cotton fabrics; draper's trade; arrangement of clothing, in sculpture etc.; clothing or hangings disposed in folds, whence ~IED² (-ĭd) a. [ME, f. OF *draperie* (*drap* cloth, -ERY)]

drăs′t|ic, a. Acting strongly, vigorous, violent, esp. (Med.) strongly purgative. Hence ~ICALLY adv. [f. Gk *drastikos* (*drastos* vbl adj. of *draō* do, -IC)]

drăt, v.t. 3 sing. subjunct. (vulg.). Confound, curse, bother, (as woman's imprecation). Hence ~t′ED¹ a. [for *'od* (God) *rot*]

draught¹ (-ahft), n. (also *draft* in some senses, as stated). 1. Drawing, traction, (*beast of ~, ~-horse,* etc., for drawing cart; plough, etc.). 2. Drawing of net for fish etc., take of fish at one drawing. 3. Single act of drinking, amount so

drunk, (also fig. of joy, love, pain, etc.); dose of liquid medicine (*black* ~, a purgative). 4. (naut.). Depth of water ship draws or requires to float her. 5. pl. ‖ Game with 24 similar pieces on ~ (same as *chess*) *-board*. 6. Current of air in room, chimney, etc. (*forced* ~, of furnace, made by rarefying air above or compressing it below; ‖ *feel the* ~, sl., suffer from adverse, usu. financial, conditions), whence ~′Y² a., ~′INESS n., (-ahf-). 7. Outline, preliminary drawing for work of art; plan of something to be constructed (also *-ft*); rough copy, first conception, of document (usu. *-ft*). 8. (Selection of) military detachment, party, reinforcement, (usu. *-ft*). 9. (Written order for) withdrawing of money from fund in bank etc., cheque, bill of exchange, (now *-ft*). 10. Drawing of liquor from vessel (*beer on* ~, in tapped cask; so ‖ *~ beer,* opp. *bottled*). [ME *draht,* f. unrecorded OE, or f. ON *drahtr, drattr,* = MDu. *dragt,* OHG *traht* f. Gmc *dragan* DRAW]

draught² (-ahft), v.t. Draw off (party for military service etc.) from larger body (now *draft*); make plan or sketch of (also *-aft*). [f. prec.]

draughts′man (-ahft-), n. (pl. -men). One who makes drawings, plans, or sketches (*good, bad, no,* ~, one who draws well etc), whence ~SHIP(3) n., **draughts′woman (-ahftswŏŏ-) n.** fem.; (usu. *draftsman*) person who drafts document, esp. Parliamentary Bill; piece in game of draughts. [*draught's* +*man*]

Dravid′ian, a. & n. (Member, language) of one of the non-Aryan races of Southern India and Ceylon (including Tamils & Kanarese). [f. Skr. *Dravida,* a province of S. India]

draw¹, v.t. & i. (*drew, drawn*). 1. Pull (boat up from water, hat over face, belt tighter, pen across paper, friend aside); pull after one (plough, cart, cartload, etc.); drag (criminal) on hurdle etc. to execution; contract, distort, (*with ~n face*); haul in (net); bend (bow; ~ *a* BEAD¹ *on*); pull at (~ *bit, bridle,' rein,* check horse, & fig. oneself); pull (curtain, véil) open or shut; ~ *cloth,* clear table after meal; (Cricket) divert (ball) to on side with bat; (Golf) drive (ball) too much to left (of right-handed player). 2. Attract, bring to one, take in, (*drew a deep breath*; & abs., *chimney, pipe,* ~*swell,* promotes, allows, draught; *I felt* ~*n to him*; *drew my attention*; ~ *him into talk, out of temptation*; ~*s customers,* & abs., attracts attention or custom); induce *to* do; be attracted, assemble, *round* or *about* some centre (*drew round the table*); bring about, entail, (*drew after it great consequences*; ~ *ruin upon* oneself). 3. Extract (cork, tooth, gun-charge, nail, cricket-stumps from ground, card from pack; pistol, sword from sheath, also abs.= ~ one's sword or pistol; ~ one's *sword against*, attack; ~ LOTS, also abs. = ~ lots, & trans. = obtain by lot, as *drew the winner*); drag (badger, fox) from hole; haul up (water) from well; bring out (liquid, blood) from vessel, body (~ *it mild*, i.e. orig. beer, now = be moderate, not exaggerate); extract essence of (~ *the tea*, also intr. *the tea* ~s); (of poultice) drain (gathering etc.); take, get from a source (~ *inspiration*, one's *salary; tax* ~s *well*, ~s *from the rich only*); (Cards) cause to be played (~ *all the trumps*); bring (person) out, make him reveal information, talent, irritation, etc.; deduce, infer, (conclusion); extract something from, empty, drain (*calf* ~s *cow*), disembowel (*hanged*, ~n, & *quartered*, of criminal; ~ *fowl* before cooking); (Hunt.) search (covert) for game (~ *blank*, find none). 4. Protract, stretch, elongate, (*long*-~n *agony*); ~-*plate*, hard steel plate pierced with graduated apertures through which rods or wires are ~n during manufacture; ~ *wire*, make it by pulling piece of metal through successively smaller holes); (Naut., intr. of sail) swell out with wind. 5. Trace (furrow, figure, line; ~ *the line at*, refuse to go as far as or beyond) delineate, make (picture), represent (object), by ~ing lines, (abs.) use pencil thus; describe in words; practise delineation; frame (document) in due form, compose, (often *up, out*); formulate, institute, (comparisons, distinctions); write out (bill, cheque, draft, *on* banker etc.), (abs.) make call *on* person or his faith, memory, etc., *for* money or service. 6. Make way, move, *towards, near, off, back*, etc. (~ *to an end* or *close*); (Racing) get farther *away* to the front, come *level*, gain *on*. 7. (Of doubtful origin); (of ship) require (such a depth of water) to float; ~ *game* or *battle*, part without deciding it. 8. (With advv. in special senses); ~ *back*, withdraw from undertaking; ~ *in*. entice, persuade to join, (of day) close in, (of successive days) become shorter; ~ *off*, withdraw (troops; or intr. of troops etc.); ~ *on*, lead to, bring about, allure, approach (intr.); ~ *out*, lead out, detach, or array (troops), prolong, elicit, induce to talk, write out in proper form, (of days) become longer; ~ *up*, (refl.) assume stiff attitude, (intr.) come up *with* or *to* = overtake, come to a stand, (t. & i. of troops) bring or come into regular order, (trans.) compose (document etc.). [OE, OS *dragan*, OHG *tragan*, ON *draga*, Goth. *gadragan*]

draw², n. Act of DRAWing; esp.: strain, pull; attractive effect, person or thing that draws custom, attention, etc.; drawing of lots, raffle; drawn game; remark etc. meant to elicit information or set person off on pet subject; act of whipping out revolver in order to shoot (*quick on the* ~); *movable part of drawbridge. [f. prec.]

draw'băck, n. Amount of excise or import duty paid back or remitted on goods exported; deduction *from*; thing that qualifies satisfaction, disadvantage; ~ *lock*, with spring bolt that can be drawn back by inside knob. [DRAW¹]

draw'bridge, n. Bridge hinged at one end for drawing up to prevent passage or to open channel. [ME; DRAW¹]

Drawcăn'sir (-*er*), n. & a. (Person) formidable both to friend and foe; fierce swashbuckler. [name of character in Villiers's *Rehearsal*]

drawee', n. Person on whom draft or bill is drawn. [-EE]

draw'er, n. In vbl senses; also or esp. (arch.) tapster; receptacle sliding in & out of special frame (~s or *chest of* ~s) or of table etc., for holding clothes, papers, etc., whence ~FUL(2) n.; (pl.) two-legged (usu. under-) garment suspended from waist. [-ER¹]

draw'ing, n. In vbl senses; esp.: art of representing by line, delineation without colour or with single colour, (*out of* ~, incorrectly drawn); product of this, black-&-white or monochrome sketch; ~-*block*, of detachable leaves of ~-paper adhering at edges; ~-*board*, for stretching ~-paper on; ~-*compass(es)*, with pen or pencil substituted for one point; ‖~-*pin*, for fastening ~-paper to ~-board. [-ING¹]

draw'ing-rŏŏm, n. Room for reception of company, to which ladies retire after dinner; levee, formal reception esp. at court. [for 16th c. *withdrawing*-]

drawl, v.i. & t., & n. **1.** Speak, utter (often *out*), with indolent or affected slowness; (of words, esp. in part.) be so uttered; hence ~'ing**LY** adv. **2.** n. Slow utterance. [16th c. cant; f. LG, Du. *dralen* delay, linger, EFris. *draulen* loiter]

drawn, p.p. of DRAW¹; ~-*work*, fancy work in linen etc. done by drawing out threads.

draw'well, n. Deep well with rope and bucket. [ME; DRAW¹]

dray, n. Low esp. brewer's cart without sides for heavy loads (~-*horse*, large & powerful; ~'*man*, brewer's driver). [ME, f. OE *dragan* DRAW¹; cf. MLG *drage* litter, Sw. *drög* dray]

dread¹ (-ĕd), v.t., & n. **1.** Be in great fear of; shrink from, look forward to with terror; fear greatly (*that, to* learn etc.), be afraid (*to* do). **2.** n. Great fear, awe, apprehension; object of fear or awe. [n. f. vb, ME *dreden* f. OE *a*-, *ondrædan*, OS *antdrādan*, OHG *inttrātan*, ult. orig. unkn.]

dread² (-ĕd), a. Dreaded, dreadful; awful, revered. [ME p.p. of DREAD¹]

dread'ful (-ĕd-), a. Terrible, awe-inspiring (‖ *penny* ~ ellipt., hist., story-book full of horrors); troublesome, disagreeable, boring, very bad or long, horrid. Hence ~**LY**² adv. [-FUL]

dread'nought (-ĕdnawt), n. (Cloth used for) thick coat for stormy weather; (*D*~) early type of 20th-c. battleship greatly superior in tonnage & power to all predecessors (f. name of first built in 1906).

dream[1], n. Vision, series of pictures or events, presented to sleeping person; act, time, of seeing such vision; *waking* ~, similar experience of one awake; conscious indulgence of fancy, reverie, castle in the air, (also *day*-~); thing (ideal, person, dress, dish, etc.) of~like goodness, beauty, or refinement; ~*-reader*, interpreter of ~s; ~*-world*, *-land*, region outside the laws of nature. Hence ~'LESS, ~'LIKE, aa. [ME *dream* corresp. to OE *drēam*, OS *drōm*, OHG *troum*]

dream[2], v.i. & t. (~*t* pr. -ĕmt, or ~*ed*). Have visions in sleep; see, hear, etc., in sleep (~*t a dream, did you* ~ *it?*, ~ *that* . . .); imagine as in a dream, think possible; (with negative etc.) think of even in a dream, so much as contemplate possibility *of*, have any conception *of*; fall into reverie; form imaginary visions *of*; be inactive or unpractical (& trans. ~ *away* one's *time*). Hence ~'ER[1] n. [ME; as prec.]

dream'-hole, n. Hole left in wall of tower etc. to admit light. [perh. f. OE *drēam* mirth, music (the holes letting sound of bells issue)]

dream'|y̆, a. Full of dreams (rare or poet.); given to reverie, fanciful, unpractical; dreamlike, vague, misty. Hence ~ILY[2] adv., ~iNESS n. [-Y[2]]

drear'|y̆, (poet.) **drear**, a. Dismal, gloomy, dull. Hence ~(i)LY[2] adv., ~(i)NESS n. [OE *drēorig* (*drēor* gore). cogn. w. *drēosan* to drop & G *traurig* sad]

drĕdge[1], n., & v.t. & i. 1. Apparatus for bringing up oysters, specimens, etc., or clearing out mud etc., from river or sea bottom. 2. vb. Bring *up*, clear *away* or *out*, with ~; clean out (harbour, river) with ~; use ~; hence **drĕdg'er**[1] [-ER[1] (1, 2)] n. [15th c. Sc. *dreg*, perh. rel. to MDu. *dregghe*, or to DRAG[1]]

drĕdge[2], v.t. Sprinkle with flour or other powder; sprinkle (flour etc.) *over*; *dredging-box*, = foll. [16th c., f. obs. *dredge* sweetmeat, f. OF *dragee* f. L f. Gk *tragēma* (*trōgō* chew)]

drĕdg'er[2], n. (for *dredger*[1] see DREDGE[1]). Box with perforated lid for sprinkling flour etc. [prec., -ER[1]]

‖ **dree**, v.t. (arch.). Endure (still in ~ one's *weird*, submit to one's lot). [OE *drēogan*]

drĕg, n. (usu. pl.). Sediment, grounds, lees, (*drink, drain, to the* ~*s*, leaving nothing); worthless part, refuse; (sing.) small remnant (esp. *not a* ~). Hence ~g'y̆[2] (-g-) a. [ME; prob. f. ON: cf. Icel. *dreggjar*, Sw. *drägg* pl., lees]

Dreibund (drī'bŏŏnt), n. = TRIPLE Alliance (3). [G (*drei* three, *bund* league)]

drĕnch[1], n. Draught or dose administered to animal; (arch.) large, medicinal, or poisonous draught; a soaking or downpour. [OE *drenc* f. Gmc **drank*- f. **drinkan* DRINK]

drĕnch[2], v.t. Make to drink largely; force (animal) to take draught of medicine; (Sheep-washing, Tanning) steep, soak; wet all over with falling liquid (or of the liquid; ~*ed with, by*). [OE *drencan* f. Gmc **drankjan* causative of **drinkan* DRINK]

drĕn'cher, n. In vbl senses; esp.: drenching shower; apparatus for giving drench to beast. [-ER[1]]

Drĕs'den (-z-), n. ~ *china, porcelain*, kind produced in Saxony esp. in 18th c.

drĕss[1], v.t. & i. 1. (mil.). Correct the alignment of (companies etc. in relation to each other, or men in line), (intr.) come into correct place in line etc. (*up*, i.e. forward, *back*, or abs.). 2. Array, clothe. (~*ed in black, serge*, etc.); provide oneself with clothes (~ *well* etc.); put on one's clothes; put on evening dress (esp. ~ *for dinner*); ~ *up*, attire oneself, attire (another), elaborately or in masquerade; ~ *out*, attire conspicuously. 3. Deck, adorn, (ship with flags, shop-window with 'tempting wares); provide (play) with costumes. 4. Treat (wound, wounded man) with remedies, apply dressing to. 5. Subject to cleansing, trimming, smoothing, etc.; brush, comb, do up, (hair); curry (horse, leather; & fig., often ~ *down*, thrash, scold). 6. Finish surface of (textile fabrics, building-stone). 7. Prepare, cook, (food); prune (plant); manure. [ME, f. OF *dresser* f. Rom. **directiare* f. L *directus* DIRECT]

drĕss[2], n. 1. Clothing, esp. the visible part of it, costume (*full* ~, that worn on great occasions; *evening* ~, or ~, that worn at dinners or evening parties; *morning* ~, ordinary; *a* ~, lady's gown, frock). 2. External covering, outward form. (*birds in their winter* ~, *French book appearing in English* ~). 3. ‖ ~ *circle*, first gallery in theatres, in which evening-~ was once required; ~ *coat*, swallow-tailed for evening ~; ~*-guard*, on bicycle etc. to protect ~; ~*-improver*, = BUSTLE[3]; ~*'maker*, *-king*, (woman) making women's ~es; ~ *rehearsal*, final one in costume: ~*-shield*, *-preserver*, piece of waterproof material fastened under the arms of a bodice. [f. prec.]

drĕss'age (-ahzh), n. Training of horse in obedience & deportment. [F, f. *dresser* train]

drĕss'er[1], n. Kitchen sideboard with shelves for dishes etc.; **dressing-table.* [ME, f. OF *dresseur* (*dresser* DRESS[1]); cf. med. L *directorium*]

drĕss'er[2], n. In vbl senses; esp.: surgeon's assistant in hospital operations, whence ~SHIP(1) n.; one who helps to dress actors or actresses, looks after costumes, etc. [-ER[1]]

drĕss′ing, n. In vbl senses; esp.: scolding or thrashing (usu. with *down*); sauce, stuffing, etc.; manure; bandages, ointments, etc., for wound; stiffening used in finishing fabrics; ~-*bell* etc., signal to dress for dinner; ~-*case*, of toilet necessaries; ~-*gown*, worn while making toilet or in dishabille; ~-*room*, attached to bedroom for toilet; ~-*table*, for looking-glass etc. [-ING¹]

drĕss′|ў, a. Fond of, smart in, dress; (of clothes) stylish. Hence ~ĭNESS n. [-Y²]

drew. See DRAW¹.

drey (drā), n. Squirrel's nest. [orig.unkn.]

drĭb′bl|e, v.t. & i., & n. **1.** Flow, let flow, in drops or trickling stream (n., such flow); (of child, idiot, etc.) run at the mouth. **2.** (Football) work (ball) forward with slight touches of alternate or different players' feet (n., piece of ~ing). **3.** (Billiards) make (ball) just roll (or intr. of ball) into pocket. Hence ~ER¹ n. [frequent. of obs. *drib* vb. var. of DRIP; see -LE(3)]

drĭb(b)′lĕt, n. Small quantity, petty sum, (esp. *by* ~s). [f. *drib* see prec.+-LET]

dried, drier. See DRY², ¹.

drift¹, n. **1.** Being driven by current; slow course or current; ship's deviation due to currents (~-*anchor*, = DRAG²-*anchor*). **2.** Projectile's deviation due to rotation. **3.** ‖ (Forest Law) driving of cattle to one place on appointed day to determine ownership etc. **4.** Natural or unperceived progress, tendency. **5.** Waiting on events, inaction, (esp., contempt., *the policy of* ~). **6.** Purpose, meaning, tenor, or scope, of person or his words. **7.** Shower, driving mass; snow, sand, etc., accumulated by wind; (also ~-*ice*, -*wood*, etc.) matter driven by water; (Geol.) superficial deposit made by current of water or air (*D*~-, Pleistocene ice detritus, boulder clay). **8.** (Also ~-*net*) large net for herrings etc. allowed to drift with tide. **9.** (Mining) horizontal passage following mineral vein. **10.** S.-Afr. ford. **11.** Tool for enlarging or shaping hole in metal. **12.** The horizontal component of the aerodynamic pressure on all exposed surfaces of an aeroplane in flight (cf. LIFT). [ME, vbl n. f. DRIVE¹]

drift², v.i. & t. Be carried (as) by current of air or water, (of current) carry; go passively or aimlessly; pile, be piled, by wind into drifts; cover (field, road) with drifts; form or enlarge hole (see prec.). Hence ~′AGE(1) n., ~′ER¹ n., (esp.) boat used in drift-net fishing (much also in mine-sweeping during the 1914–18 war). [f. prec.]

drill¹, n., & v.t. & i. **1.** Pointed steel etc. tool, or machine, for boring holes (vb, bore, of person or tool, with *metal* etc., or *hole* etc., as obj.; also intr., ~ *through*, perforate); boring shellfish. **2.** Instruction or exercise in military evolutions (~-*sergeant*, instructor in ~, also fig.), rigorous discipline, exact routine, (vb,

subject to, or undergo, such discipline; *B Company will* ~ *tomorrow*; ~ *him in what he is to say, in Latin Grammar*). [f. MDu. *drillen* vb, *dril* n., of unkn. orig.]

drill², n., & v.t. Small furrow for sowing seed in, ridge with such furrow on top, row of plants so sown; machine for furrowing, sowing, & covering seed; (vb) sow (seed) thus, plant (ground) in ~s. [perh. f. obs. *drill* rill, of unkn. orig.]

drill³, n. Kind of baboon. [prob. W.-Afr.]

drill⁴, n. Coarse twilled linen or cotton fabric. [earlier *drilling* f. G *drillich* f. L *trilicem* nom. -*ix* (*tri*- three-, *licium* thread)]

dril′ў. See DRY¹.

drink¹, v.t. & i. (*drănk*; *drŭnk* & poet. *drŭnk′en*). Swallow (liquid); take (*the waters* at a spa) medicinally; ~ *off*, *up*, ~ the whole of at once; (of plants, porous things, etc.) absorb (moisture; often *up* or *in*); (fig.) ~ *in*, contemplate, listen to, with delight; empty (vessel, *the cup of* pain or joy); spend (wages etc.) on drink; swallow liquid, take draught, (often of a source; ~ *deep*, take large draught, or be great ~er as in next sense); take spirituous liquor esp. to excess, tipple, be a drunkard, (~ *hard*, *heavily*, *like a fish*; ~*ing*-BOUT; ~-*ing*-*water* (reserved, pure enough, for ~ing); ~ *oneself drunk*, *to death*, *out of a situation*; ~ *down* or *under the table*, outlast in retaining control of oneself while ~ing); ~ *to*, pledge, toast; wish good etc. to in ~ing (~ *one's health*, ~ *success* or *confusion to*). Hence (-)~′ER¹ n. [OE *drincan*, OS *drinkan*, OHG *trinkan*, ON *drekka*, Goth. *drigkan* f. Gmc *drenk-*]

drink², n. Liquid swallowed or absorbed; beverage; intoxicating liquor (also *strong* ~), excessive indulgence in it, intemperance (*on the* ~, giving way to this; *in* ~, drunk); glass etc. or portion of liquor (STAND¹ ~s *round*); ~-*offering*, libation; *the* ~ (R.A.F. sl.), the sea. Hence ~′LESS a. [OE *drinc* & *drinca* f. *drincan*= prec.]

drink′able, a. & n. Good to drink; (n., esp. in pl.) thing(s) to drink. [-ABLE]

drip, v.i. & t. (-pp-). Fall, let fall, in drops; let drops fall, be so wet (*with* blood etc.) as to shed drops (~*ping wet*, very wet). [cogn. w. DROP, but of uncert. hist., poss. f. Scand., cf. MDa. *drippe*]

drip², n. Act of dripping; dripping liquid; (sl.) boring person; (Archit.) projection keeping rain from parts below (so ~-*moulding*, ~′*stone*); ~-*drop*, persistent dripping. Hence ~p′Y² a. [f. prec.]

dripp′ing, n. In vbl senses; also: fat melted from roasting meat, & used for frying or as food; ~s, water, grease, etc., dripping from anything. [-ING¹]

drive, v.t. & i. (*drŏve*, *driven*). **1.** Urge in some direction by blows, threats, violence, etc. (usu. with adv. or prep. as *away*, *back*, *in*, *out*, *from*, *to*, *through*; ~

out, oust, take place of); chase or frighten (game, wild beasts, enemy esp. in guerrilla warfare) from over large area into small in order to kill or capture. **2.** Scour (district), ‖ (Forest Law) hold a DRIFT¹. **3.** (Urge &) direct course of (animal drawing vehicle or plough, vehicle etc., or locomotive); convey in vehicle; act as driver of vehicle; travel, go, in car or carriage at one's disposal (cf. *ride* in omnibus, tram, train). **4.** Impel forcibly, constrain, compel, (*to, into, to* do; *~ mad, out of* one's *senses*); overwork (*was very hard ~n*). **5.** Impel, carry along (of wind, water), throw, propel, send in some direction, (inanimate things); (Cricket) return (ball) from freely swung bat to or past bowler; (Golf) strike (ball, or abs.) with DRIVER from tee (also *~ off*). **6.** Force (stake, nail, etc.) *into* ground etc. with blows; bore (tunnel, horizontal cavity); (also *let ~*) aim blow or missile (*at*). **7.** (Of steam or other power) set or keep (machinery) going (also of person, *~ a quill, pen*, write). **8.** Carry on, effect, conclude, (*drove a roaring trade, good bargain*). **9.** Defer (*~ it to the last minute*). **10.** Dash, rush, hasten; work hard *at*. **11.** Float along, drift, tend, (*driving rain; ~ at*, seek, intend, mean; *what is he driving at?*). [OE *drīfan*, OS *drīban*, OHG *trīban*, ON *drīfa*, Goth. *dreiban* f. Gmc **drībhan*]

drive², n. Excursion in vehicle (see prec.); driving of game or enemy (see prec.); stroke at cricket, golf, etc. (see prec.); energy, push; tendency; organized effort to achieve a special purpose; carriage-road, ‖ esp. private road to house; WHIST³·*~*. [f. prec.]

driv′el, v.i. & t. (-ll-), & n. **1.** Run at mouth or nose like child; talk childishly or idiotically; fritter *away*; hence *~*IER¹ n. **2.** n. Silly nonsense, twaddle. [ME *drevele, dravele*, OE *dreflian*, perh. cogn. w. DRAFF]

driv′er, n. One who drives (DRIVE¹), coachman (also *cab·~, engine·~*, etc.; *slave·~*, overseer of slave gang); (Golf) straight-faced wooden club for driving from tee; (Mech.) driving-wheel or other part that receives power directly; *front, rear, ·~*, bicycle in which power is applied to front, rear, wheel; QUILL·*~*. Hence *~*LESS a. [-ER¹]

driv′ing-wheel, n. Wheel communicating motion to other parts of machine; large wheel of locomotive; cycle wheel that is directly worked.

driz′zle, v.i., & n. (Fall in, be wet with) spray-like rain (subj., *the day, rain, it*). Hence **driz′zly²** a. [16th c.; perh. f. ME *drese* (OE *drēosan* fall)+-LE(3)]

drō′gher (-ger), n. W.-Ind. coasting vessel; slow heavy craft. [18th c., f. F *drogeur* f. Du. *drogher* (*droogen* to dry) named from drying herrings]

drōgue (-ōg), n. Buoy at end of harpoon line; sea anchor, a bag-like contrivance used to retard the drifting of a boat & keep her head to the wind; = WIND¹*sock*. [perh. var. of DRAG²]

droit (or drwah), n. Right, due, legal perquisite, (esp. *~s of Admiralty*, proceeds of enemy's ships, wrecks, etc.). [ME, f. OF f. L *directum* DIRECT²]

drŏll, a., n., & v.i. Facetious, amusing; queer, odd, surprising; hence **drŏl′ly²** (-ŏl-li) adv., *~′*NESS n.; (n. now rare) jester, wag; (v.i., now rare) play the buffoon, jest *with, at, on*. [f. F *drôle(r)* of unkn. orig.]

drŏll′erў, n. Jesting; a facetious composition; quaint humour. [-ERY]

drōme, n. (colloq.). Aerodrome. [abbr.] **-drōme**, suf. repr. Gk *dromos* course, used in Gk compounds such as *hippodrome*, in modern words such as *aerodrome*, and (loosely) in *picturedrome*.

drŏm′edarў (*also* -ūm-), n. Light fleet usu. Arabian or one-humped camel bred for riding. [ME, f. OF *dromedaire* f. LL *dromedarius* f. L f. Gk *dromas -ados* runner, -ARY¹]

drŏm′ond, n. (hist.). Large medieval ship for war or commerce. [ME, f. OF *dromon(t)* f. LL f. Byz. Gk *dromōn*]

drōne, n., & v.i. & t. **1.** Male of honey-bee, which does not work; idler; deep humming sound; monotonous speech or speaker; bass-pipe of bagpipe; fixed continuous note emitted by this. **2.** vb. Buzz like bee or bagpipe, talk or utter monotonously, whence **drōn′ingly²** adv.; idle; idle *away* (life etc.). [OE *drān, drāen*, OS *drān*, OHG *treno*, of obsc. phonology; f. WG **dran-, dren-, drun-*, boom]

drōol, v.i. (U.S. & dial). Drivel, slobber. [contr. f. DRIVEL]

drōop, v.i. & t., & n. **1.** Hang down, slope, incline, as in weariness; (of eyes) look downwards; (poet., of sun etc.) sink; languish, decline, flag, lose heart; let (head, face, eyes) fall forward or down; hence *~′*ingly² adv. **2.** n. *~*ing attitude, loss of spirit, fall of tone. [ME, f. ON *drūpa* vb cogn. w. foll.]

drŏp¹, n. **1.** Round, pear-shaped, or hemispherical portion of liquid such as hangs or falls separately or adheres to surface (*of* water, tears, sweat, dew, rain, blood, or abs. in these senses); (Med.) smallest separable quantity of a liquid (in pl., liquid medicine to be measured by *~*s); minute quantity (*~ in bucket* or *ocean*, infinitesimal factor); glass etc. of intoxicating liquor (*take a ~; has taken a ~ too much*, is drunk; *have a ~* in one's *eye*, show signs of having drunk); pendant, hanging ornament, (*ear-~*s, ear-rings; *~*s of glass chandelier); sugarplum (*acid, pear* etc., *~*s); hence *~*′LET n. **2.** Act of dropping, fall, social come-down, descent in prices, temperature, etc.; thing that drops or is dropped, as

(Theatr.) painted curtain let down between acts (also ~-*curtain*), (in gallows) platform withdrawn from under feet of condemned (also, distance he is allowed to fall, as ~ *of 3 ft*); abrupt fall in level of surface, amount of this; (also ~-*kick*) kick at football made by dropping ball and kicking it as it rises (~-*off*, -*out*, such kick to start play after goal, try, or touch- -down). **3.** ~-*forging* (also *die-forging*), the system of forcing a piece of white-hot metal through an open-ended die of the required shape; ~-*hammer* (also ~-*press*), forging-machine using the power of a dropped weight; ~-*shot* (Lawn Tennis), shot dropping abruptly after clearing net; ~-*shutter*, appliance for giving instantaneous exposure in photography; ~-*sulphur*, -*tin*, granulated by being dropped molten into water; ~-*wort*, kinds of plant with tuberous root fibres. [OE *dropa*, OS *dropo*, ON *dropi*, cogn. w. OHG *tropfo*; f. Gmc **dreup-*, **draup-*, **drup-*, whence DRIP, DROOP]

drŏp², v.i. & t. (-pp-). **1.** Fall in drops; give off moisture in drops. **2.** Fall by force of gravity from not being held etc., (fig.) be uttered casually (*the remark* ~*ped from him*), disappear (*a letter has* ~*ped out*). **3.** Sink to ground exhausted, wounded, etc. (~ *on one's knee*, kneel), (of setter) crouch at sight of game. **4.** Fall naturally *asleep*, (*back*) *into* habit etc.; die; cease, lapse, (*affair was allowed to* ~; *the correspondence* ~*ped*). **5.** Fall in direction, condition, amount, degree, pitch, (*prices, voices,* ~); go *down* stream; fall *behind*, *to the rear*, etc. **6.** Come or go casually *in* as visitor, *into* place, *across* person; ~ *on* or *across*, reprimand or punish; **7.** Let fall (liquid, tears) in drops, shed; let go, relinquish, cease to hold, (~ *anchor*, anchor ship); give birth to (esp. lambs). **8.** Utter casually as if unconsciously (esp. ~ *a hint*; so ~ *a postcard, line, note*). **9.** Lose (money, esp. in gaming). **10.** Fell with axe, blow of fist, or bullet. **11.** Set down (passenger, parcel). **12.** Omit (*letter*, one's *h*s, *syllable*) in speech. **13.** Let (eyes) droop; lower (voice); ~ CURTSY. **14.** (Football) send (ball), make (goal), by drop-kick (see prec.; also intr. = take drop-kick). **15.** Cease to associate with, have done with (~ *it!*, stop that). **16.** ~ *away*, *in*, depart, enter, one by one; ~ *off*, = ~ *away*, also fall asleep. [OE *dropian*, see prec.]

drŏpp'ings (-z), n. pl. What falls or has fallen in drops, e.g. wax from candles; dung of beasts or birds. [-ING¹]

drŏp-'scène, n. = drop-curtain (DROP¹); final scene, finale, of drama in real life.

drŏp'sǁý, n. Disease in which watery fluid collects in cavities or tissue of body, (fig.) overswollen state. Hence ~ICAL a., ~icALLY² adv. [ME, aphetic form of HYDROPSY]

drŏs(h)'kў, n. Russian low four-wheeled

carriage; cab in German towns. [f. Russ. *drozhki* dim. of *drogi* wagon (*droga* shaft)]

Drosŏph'ila, n. Genus of flies, used extensively in genetic research; common fruit-fly. [mod. L, f. Gk *drosos* dew, moisture, -PHIL]

drŏss, n. Scum thrown off from metals in melting; foreign matter mixed with anything, impurities; refuse, rubbish. Hence ~'Y² a. [OE *drŏs*, MDu. *droese* dregs; cf. MLG *drōsem*, OHG *truosana* (G *drusen*)]

drought (-owt), (poet., Sc., U.S.) drouth, n. (Arch.) dryness, lack of moisture, also thirst; continuous dry weather, want of rain. Hence **drought'**Y² (-owt-), **drouth'**Y², a. [OE *drūgath* (*drȳge* DRY¹, -TH¹)]

drōve¹, n. **1.** Herd, flock, being driven or moving together; crowd, multitude, shoal, large number, esp. as moving together. **2.** Mason's broad chisel. [OE *drāf* (*drīfan* DRIVE¹)]

drōve². See DRIVE¹.

drōv'er, n. Driver of droves to market, cattle-dealer. Hence **drōve³** v.t., **drōv'**ING¹ n. [ME; DROVE¹+-ER¹]

drown, v.i. & t. **1.** Suffer death by suffocation in liquid (now usu. *be* ~*ed*; but ~*ing man* etc.); suffocate (person, animal) by submersion (subj., person etc., or the liquid); submerge, flood, drench, (esp. fig. ~*ed in tears, sleep, wine; like* ~*ed rat*, in soaked condition; ~ *out*, drive out by flood). **2.** Deaden (grief etc.) with or *in* drink; overpower (esp. of louder sound making voice etc. inaudible). [ME (orig. north.) *drun, droune*, pointing to an OE **drūnian*; orig. obsc.]

drowse (-z), v.i. & t. & n. Be dull & sleepy, half asleep; be sluggish; make drowsy; pass *away* (time) in drowsing; (n.) half-asleep condition. [back form. f. foll.]

drow'sǁý (-z-), a. Sleepy, half asleep, dozing; lulling, soporific; sluggish; ~*y*- -*head*, sleepy person. Hence ~iHEAD (arch.), ~iNESS, nn., ~ilý² adv. [early 16th c., prob. rel. to OE *drūsian* sink, become slow, cogn. w. *drēosan*, see DREARY]

drŭb, v.t. (-bb-). Cudgel, thump, belabour; beat in fight; beat (notion) *into*, *out of*, person. Hence ~b'ING¹ n. [earlier sense *bastinado*, perh. f. Arab. *darb* beating]

drŭdgǁe, n., & v.i. Servile worker, slave, hack; hence ~'ERY(2, 5) n. **2.** v.i. Work slavishly at distasteful work; hence ~'ingLY² adv. [orig. unkn.]

drŭg, n., & v.t. & i. (-gg-). **1.** Original simple medicinal substance, organic or inorganic, used alone or as ingredient (*the* ~ *habit*, of taking opiates etc.); unsalable commodity, thing no longer in demand (usu. ~ *in the market*); **-store*, chemist's shop; hence ~'gY² (-g-) a. **2.** vb. Adulterate with ~, esp. with narcotic or poison; administer ~s, esp. narcotics, to; indulge in narcotics etc.; nauseate, cloy. [ME, f. OF *drogue* of unkn. orig.]

drŭgg′ĕt (-g-), n. (Over-carpet or floor-cloth of) coarse woollen stuff used for floor or table coverings. [f. F *droguet* of unkn. orig.]

drŭgg′ist (-g-), n. Dealer in drugs, pharmaceutical chemist. [f. F *droguiste* (DRUG, -IST)]

Dru′id (-ōō-), n. Priest, magician, soothsayer, among Celts of ancient Gaul & Britain; officer of Welsh Gorsedd or national assembly. Hence ~ESS[1], ~ISM (3), nn., Druid′IC(AL) aa., (-ōō-). [f. F *druide* or L pl. *druidae*, *-des*, f. OCelt. *druid-* magician]

drŭm[1], n. **1.** Musical instrument sounded by striking & made of hollow cylinder or hemisphere with parchment stretched over opening(s) (*bass, tenor, big,* KETTLE, etc., ~). **2.** (zool.). Natural organ giving resonance, as howling monkey's hyoid bone. **3.** Sound (as) of ~, bittern's cry; player of ~, drummer. **4.** Cylindrical structure (~ *of ear,* hollow part of middle ear) or object, cylinder or barrel in machinery on which something is wound or for other purposes; solid part of Corinthian or composite capital; stone block forming section of shaft; cylindrical receptacle for packing dried fruit, holding oil, etc. **5.** Evening or afternoon-tea party (hist.). **6.** (Also ~*-fish*) kinds of American fish able to make drumming noise. **7.** ~′*fire,* heavy continuous rapid artillery fire usu. heralding infantry attack; ~′*head,* skin or membrane across ~ (~*head* COURT[1] *martial*), membrane across ~ of ear, circular top of capstan; ~ *major,* N.C.O. commanding drummers of regiment; ~′*stick,* stick with knob or pad for beating ~, lower joint of cooked fowl's leg. [f. 16th c. (obs.) *drombeslade, drombyllsclad,* f. LG *trommelslag* drum- beat f. *trommel* f. *trum*(b)*e,* Du. *trom*]

drŭm[2], v.i. & t. (-mm-). Play the drum, whence ~**m′ER**[1] n., player of drum, *commercial traveller; beat, tap, or thump, continuously on something (*on* piano, *at* door; *feet* ~ *on floor*; *a* ~*ming in the ears*); (of birds, insects) make loud hollow noise with quivering wings; summon, beat *up,* as by ~ming; ~ *out,* cashier by beat of drum; drive (person) *into* apathy etc., (lesson) *into* person, by persistence; strike (hands etc.) repeatedly (*up*)*on* something; play (tune etc.) on or as on drum. [f. prec.]

drŭm[3], **drŭm′lin,** nn. (geol.). Long oval mound of drift or diluvial formation. [f. Gael. & Ir. *druim* ridge; *-lin* perh. for -LING[1]]

Drŭmm′ond light (lĭt), n. Limelight or oxyhydrogen light. [Capt. T. *Drummond,* inventor *c.* 1825]

drŭnk, pred. a. & n. (also p.p. of DRINK[1]). **1.** Intoxicated, overcome with liquor, (*beastly, blind, dead, half,* etc., ~; ~ *as a*

fiddler or *lord*; also fig., ~ *with joy, success, rage*); hence ~′ARD n. **2.** n. (sl.). Drinking-bout, drunken fit; (from police charge-sheets) case of drunkenness (hence gen.) man charged with drunkenness, drunken man. [p.p. of DRINK[1]]

drŭnk′en, a. (rarely pred., cf. prec.). Intoxicated; given to drinking, often drunk; caused by or exhibiting drunkenness (~ *frolic, brawl*). Hence ~LY[2] adv., ~NESS n. [as prec., see -EN[1]]

drupe (-ōō-), n. Stone-fruit, fleshy or pulpy fruit enclosing stone or nut with kernel, as olive, plum, cherry. Hence **drup**A′CEOUS (-ōōpā′shŭs) a. [f. L f. Gk *druppa* over-ripe (olive)]

drup′el (-ōō-), **drupe′lĕt** (-ōōpl-), nn. Small drupe in compound fruit, as blackberry. [-EL, -LET]

druse[1] (-ōōz), n. Crust of crystals lining rock-cavity, cavity so lined. [G]

Druse[2] (-ōōz), n. Member of political & religious sect of Mohammedan origin about Mt Lebanon. [Ismail al-*Darazi,* founder 1040]

drȳ[1], a. (*drier, -est*). **1.** Without moisture (~ *eyes,* free from tears; ~ SHAMPOO): not rainy, with deficient rainfall. **2.** Parched, dried up, (colloq.) thirsty, (of liquid) having disappeared by evaporation, draining, wiping, etc.; (of country, state, legislation, etc.) teetotal, prohibiting sale of intoxicants (*go* ~, accept such legislation). **3.** Not yielding water, milk, etc. (*cow, well, is* ~). **4.** Without butter (~ *bread, toast*). **5.** Solid, not liquid, (~ *goods,* see below; ~ *measure,* measure of capacity for these). **6.** (Of wine) free from sweetness & fruity flavour. **7.** Unconnected with liquid (*die a* ~ *death,* not by drowning or bloodshed; ~ *cough,* without phlegm; ‖ ~-BOB[3]). **8.** Impassive, unsympathetic, stiff, hard, cold, (~ *jest, sarcasm, humour,* expressed in matter-of-fact tone with show of unconsciousness). **9.** Meagre, plain, bare, not enlarged upon, (~ *facts, thanks*); uninteresting, dull, unprofitable. **10.** Untinged by prejudice or interest (~ *light*). **11.** ~*-bulb thermometer,* one of pair in hygrometer with wet & ~ bulbs; ~*-clean,* clean (clothes etc.), by means of spirit etc., without using water, so ~*-cleaner, -cleaning*(~; ~ *cooper,* maker of casks for ~ goods; ~*-cure,* cure (meat etc.) without pickling in liquid; ~-DOCK[4]; ~*-fly* a. & v.i., (fish) with fly floating lightly on water; ~ *goods,* non-liquid goods, as corn, also (esp. U.S.) drapery, mercery, haberdashery; ~ *lodging,* without board; ~*-nurse,* tending but not suckling child, (v.t.) bring up by hand; ~ *pile,* electric pile or battery in which no ‖liquid is used; ~*-plate,* photographic plate with sensitized film hard & ~ for convenience of keeping, developing at leisure, etc.; ~*-point,* needle for engraving without acid on bare copper plate (also v.i. use this process, & n., engraving produced so); ~*-rot*, decayed state of wood not exposed to air caused by fungi, also the fungi, (fig.) unsuspected moral or social decay; ~*-salt* v.t., = ~*-cure*; ~*-salter*(y), dealer, dealing or shop that deals, in drugs, dyes, gums, oils, pickles, tinned meats, etc.; ~*-shod* a. or adv., without wetting the feet; ~*-walling* without mortar). Hence ~'ISH¹ (2) a., dri'LY² (or ~'lỹ) adv. (esp. in fig. senses), ~'NESS n. [OE *drȳge*, rel. to MLG *dröge*, MDu. *druge*, *dröghe*, Du. *droog* f. WG *drȳg-, whence also G *trocken*]

drȳ², v.t. & i. Make or become dry by wiping, evaporation, draining, etc.; cause (cow) to cease giving milk; ~ *up*, make utterly dry, (of moisture) disappear utterly, (of well etc.) cease to yield water, (colloq., esp. in imperat.) cease talking or doing something, (Theatr.) forget one's lines. Hence dri'ER¹ (1, 2) (or ~'er) n., (also) substance mixed with oil-paints to expedite~ing. [OE *drȳgcan* (*drȳge* DRY¹)]

drȳ'ăd, n. Nymph inhabiting tree, wood--nymph. [f. L f. Gk *druas -ados* (*drus* tree)]

Drȳ'asdŭst (-*az*-), n., d-, a. Dull laborious antiquary or historian; (adj.) very dry, uninteresting. [Dr ~, fictitious person (*dry as dust*) to whom Scott dedicated]

'dst, clipping of *wouldst, hadst*.

dū'ăd, n. (Incorrect for) DYAD.

dū'al, a. & n. **1**. Of two, twofold, divided in two, double, (~ *ownership, skirt*); the *D*~ *Monarchy*, former Austro-Hungarian Empire; shared by two, joint, as ~*control*. **2**. (gram.). ~ *number* or ~, inflected form proper to two persons or things (additional to *singular & plural*). So **dūal'ITY** n., ~IZE(3) v.t., ~LY² adv. [f. L *dualis* (*duo* two, -AL)]

dū'alin, n. Powerful explosive of nitre, nitroglycerin, & sawdust. [prec. (dual nitre) +-IN]

dū'al|ism, n. Duality; use of dual number; theory recognizing two independent principles (mind & matter, cf. *idealism & materialism*); good & evil in the universe; two personalities in Christ), so ~IST (2) n., ~is'TIC a., ~is'TICALLY adv. [DUAL+-ISM]

¶ **dŭb¹**, n. Deep pool in northern streams; a puddle (sl.). [16th c. Sc., orig. unkn.]

dŭb², v.t. (-bb-). **1**. Make (person) into *a knight* by striking shoulders with sword; invest with (new title), name, nickname, (person or thing, with complement; ~*bed me Doctor, quack, a scribbler*). **2**. Dress (artificial fishing-fly). **3**. Smear (leather) with grease. [late OE *dubbian*, aphetic f. OF *aduber, adober*, com.-Rom. of unkn. orig.]

dŭb³, v.t. (-bb-). Make another recording of sound-track of (film) esp. in a different language, add (sound effects or music) to a film, or to a radio or television production. [abbr. of *double*]

dŭbb'ing, n. In vbl senses; esp., prepared

grease for leather (also *dŭbb'in*). [-ING¹]

dūbi'etȳ, n. Feeling of doubt; doubtful matter. [f. LL *dubietas* (*dubius* doubtful, -TY)]

dūb'ious, a. Indistinct (~ *light*), vague, unreliable (~ *friend*), of questionable value or truth (*a ~ compliment*); of doubtful issue (~ *undertaking, struggle*); of suspected character (~ *gains, company*); hesitating, doubting. Hence ~LY² adv., ~NESS n. [f. L *dubiosus* (*dubium* doubt, -OSE¹)]

dūbitā'tion, n. Doubt, hesitation. [ME, f. OF, or L *dubitatio* (*dubitare* DOUBT², -ATION)]

dūb'itātive, a. Of, expressing, inclined to, doubt or hesitation. Hence ~LY² (-vi-) adv. [f. LL *dubitativus* as prec. +-IVE]

dūc'al, a. Of, like, bearing title of, duke. [F, f. LL *ducalis* (*dux* DUKE, -AL)]

dūc'at, n. Gold coin, formerly current in most European countries; coin, (pl.) money. [ME, f. It. *ducato* f. med. L *ducatus* DUCHY (prob. named from Duke of Apulia 1140)]

Duce (doo'chä), n. Chief (*Il*, or *the*, ~, Mussolini as Fascist leader). [It., f. L *dux ducis*]

dŭch'ĕss, n. Duke's wife or widow; lady holding a duchy in her own right; imposing woman; ‖ (sl.) costermonger's wife (abbr. *dŭtch*). [ME, f. OF (-*e*), f. med. L *ducissa* (DUKE, -ESS¹)]

duchesse (dōōshĕs'), n. Kind of satin; ~ *lace*, kind of Brussels pillow-lace. [F, = duchess]

dŭch'ȳ, n. Territory of reigning duke or duchess; royal dukedom of Cornwall or Lancaster, each with certain estates, revenues, & jurisdiction of its own. [ME, f. OF *duche(e)* f. med. L *ducatus* (DUKE, -Y⁴)]

dŭck¹, n. (pl. often ~ collective; also ~*s*). **1**. Kinds of swimming-bird, esp. the domesticated form of the mallard or wild-~ (like ~ in *thunderstorm*, with upturned eyes, looking flabbergasted, faint, etc.; *like water off ~'s back*, producing no effect; *take to anything like ~ to water*; *fine day for young ~s*, rainy weather; *lame ~*, disabled person, defaulter on Stock Exchange; *in two shakes of ~'s tail*, in an instant; female of this (cf. DRAKE²); its flesh. **2**. Darling (esp. in voc.), whence ~'Y³ n. (also ~*y diamond*). **3**. (Cricket; also ~*'s-egg*) batsman's score of 0. **4**. *Bombay ~*, BUMMALO; ~ *& drake*, game of making flat stone skip along water (*make ~s & drakes of, play ~s* etc. *with*, squander); ~*'bill*, = ~-billed PLATYpus or ORNITHO*rhynchus*; ~*-boards*, narrow path of wooden slats in trench or over mud; ~*-hawk*, marsh harrier; ~*-shot*, of size for shooting wild ~; ~*-weed*, plant that carpets surface of still water. Hence ~'LING¹(2) n. (UGLY ~*ling*). [OE *duce, dūce* f. *dūcan dive (foll.)]

dŭck², v.i. & t., & n. **1.** Plunge, dive, dip head, under water & emerge; bend quickly, bob, to avoid blow etc. or by way of bow or curtsy; plunge (person etc.) momentarily *in* water, or abs.; whence ~'ING¹(1) n. (~*ing-stool*, chair at end of oscillating pole, formerly used for ~ing scolds and other objectionable persons); lower (head) suddenly. **2.** n. Quick dip below water in bathing, or lowering of head. [ME *d*(*o*)*uke* f. OE **dūcan*, (=. MLG, MDu. *dūken*, OHG *tūhhan*)]

dŭck³, n. Strong untwilled linen or cotton fabric for small sails & outer clothing esp. of sailors; (pl.) trousers of this. [f. MDu. *doek*, = OS *dōk*, OHG *tuoh*, of unkn. orig.]

dŭck⁴, n. (colloq.). Amphibious landing craft. [f. DUKWS, official designation]

dŭck'er¹, n. Kinds of diving-bird, esp. dabchick & water ouzel. [DUCK², -ER¹]

dŭck'er², n. Breeder of ducks. [DUCK¹, -ER¹]

dŭct, n. Conduit, tube, for conveying liquid; tube or canal in body conveying chyle, lymph, or secretions (named from function, as *biliary* ~, or from discoverer, as *Eustachian* ~, ~*s of Bellini*); vessel of plant's vascular tissue holding air, water, etc. Hence ~'LESS a. (~*less glands*, of which the secretion is not carried off by a ~, but acts directly on the blood). [f. L *ductus* leading, aqueduct (*ducere duct-*lead)]

dŭc'tile, a. (Of metals) malleable, flexible, not brittle, (in technical use) capable of being drawn out into wire, tough; plastic (of clay etc., or of person or character), pliable, tractable, docile. Hence dŭctil'-ITY n. [ME, f. OF f. L *ductilis* (*ducere* see prec., -IL)]

dŭd, n. & a. (sl.). **1.** (Pl.) clothes, rags; (sing.) scarecrow (also ~'*man*), shell etc. that fails to go off, futile plan or person. **2.** adj. Counterfeit, useless, unsatisfactory, futile. [orig. unkn.]

*dŭde, n. (sl.). Fastidious aesthetic person, often imitating English speech, dress, & manners; dandy, swell. Hence .dŭd'ISH¹ a. [orig. unkn.]

dŭdg'eon (-jn), n. Resentment, feeling of offence, (usu. *in* ~). [orig. unkn.]

dud(h)een' (dōō-), n. (Ir.). Short clay pipe. [f. Ir. *dúidín*, dim. of *dúd* pipe]

dūe¹, a. & adv. **1.** Owing, payable, as a debt or obligation (*fall, become,* ~, as bill reaching maturity; that ought to be given *to* person (*first place is* ~ *to Milton, it is* ~ *to him to say*), merited, appropriate (*has his* ~ *reward*), rightful, proper, adequate (*after* ~ *consideration*), to be looked for, calculated or foreseen (*in* ~ *time*); to be ascribed *to* cause, agent, etc. (*the difficulty is* ~ *to our ignorance; the discovery is* ~ *to Newton;* the advl use for *owing,* as *I came late* ~ *to an accident,* is incorrect); under engagement *to* do something (*is* ~ *to speak tonight*) or to arrive

at certain time (*train* ~ *at 7.30, already* ~ *& over*~). **2.** adv. (Of points of compass) exactly, directly, (*went* ~ *east, a* ~ *N. wind*). [ME, f. OF *deü* (p.p. of *devoir* owe) f. Rom. **debutus* f. L *debitus* (*debēre* owe)]

dūe², n. Person's right, what is owed him, (*give* one, esp. *the devil, his* ~, not be unjust to him, even though he deserves little or is no friend); what one owes (*pay* one's ~*s*); (usu. pl.) toll, fee, legally demandable (*harbour, light, tonnage, university,* ~*s*); (Naut.) *for a full* ~, for good, thoroughly, completely. [f. prec., & OF *deu*]

dū'el, n., & v.i. (-ll-). **1.** Fight with deadly weapons between two persons, in presence of two seconds, to settle quarrel (*the* ~,' ~ling & its code of rules); any contest between two persons, animals, parties, causes; hence ~IST(1) n. **2.** v.i. Fight ~(s). [f. med. L (AL) *duellum* (arch. f. L *bellum* war) single combat; cf. LL *duellare* fight a duel]

dŭenn'a, n. Elderly woman acting as governess & companion in charge of girls (orig. & esp. in Spanish family); chaperon. [f. Sp. *dueña* f. L *domina* mistress]

dū̆et', -tt, n. Musical composition for two voices or performers; (fig.) dialogue, scolding-match; pair, couple. Hence dŭett'IST(1) n. [f. It. *duetto* dim. of *duo* duet f. L *duo* two]

‖ dŭff¹, n. (Dial. etc. for) DOUGH; PLUM-~.

dŭff², v.t. (sl.). Fake up (goods), give look of newness etc. to, (‖ ~*ing*, counterfeit); (Austral.) steal & alter brands on (cattle); (Golf) mishit (shot, ball). [perh. back form. f. DUFFER]

dŭff'el, dŭf'fle, n. Coarse woollen cloth with thick nap (~ *coat*, overcoat of ~ with toggle fastenings instead of buttons); *kit of sportsman or camper-out. [*Duffel* in Brabant]

dŭff'er, n. ‖ One who sells trash as valuable, pretending it to be smuggled, stolen, etc.; ‖ pedlar, hawker; faker of sham articles; counterfeit coin, picture, etc.; unproductive mine; thing of which no use can be made; inefficient, useless, or stupid person. [goes with DUFF²]

dŭg¹, n. Udder of female mammals, also teat, nipple, (not now used of women exc. contempt.). [orig. unkn.; cf. Sw. *dægga* suckle]

dŭg². See DIG¹.

dŭg'ŏng (dōō-), n. (pl. often ~). Large herbivorous mammal of Indian seas. [f. Malay *duyong*]

dŭg'out, n. Canoe made by hollowing tree-trunk; underground shelter esp. for troops in trenches; ‖ (sl.) retired officer etc. recalled to service.

duik'er, duy-, (dik-), n. Small S.-African antelope. [Du. *duiker* (in full *duikerbok*)]

dūke, n. **1.** (Hist.) provincial military commander under later Roman emperors; (Bibl.) chief of tribe. **2.** (In some parts of Europe) sovereign prince ruling duchy or small State; (Gt Britain & some other countries) person holding highest hereditary title or nobility outside royal family (also *royal* ~, ~ who is also royal prince, with precedence); DINE *with* D~ *Humphrey*. **3.** Kind of cherry. L *duke* (sl.). Hand, fist. [ME, f. OF *duc* f. L *dux ducis* leader]

duke′dom (-kd-), n. Territory ruled by, dignity of, duke. [-DOM]

Dūk′eries (-ĭz), n. pl. District in Notts. containing several ducal estates. [-ERY]

Dul′ag (dŏo-), n. Camp for prisoners of war in transit. [G abbr. of *Durchgangslager*]

dŭl′cĕt, a. Sweet, soothing, (esp. of sounds). [15th c. also *doucet* f. OF dim. of *doux* f. L *dulcis* sweet]

dŭl′ci|fȳ, v.t. Sweeten, make gentle. Hence ~FICA′TION n. [f. LL *dulcificare* (*dulcis* sweet, -FY)]

dŭl′cimer, n. Musical instrument with strings of graduated length over sounding board or box struck with hammers, prototype of piano. [f. OF *doulcemer* said to repr. L *dulce melos* sweet song]

Dŭlcinē′a (*or* -sĭn′ĭa), n. Idolized & idealized mistress. [name of Don Quixote's mistress]

dŭll, a., & v.t. & i. **1.** Slow of understanding, obtuse, stupid, whence ~′ARD n.; (of ears, eyes, etc.) without keen perception; (of inanimate things) insensible; (of pain etc.) indistinctly felt; sluggish, slow-moving, stagnant, (of person, animal, trade); (of goods, stocks) not easily salable, not in demand; listless, depressed; tedious, monotonous; blunt (esp. of edge); (of colour, light, sound, taste) not bright, vivid, or keen; (of weather) overcast, gloomy; hence ~′ISH a., dŭl(l)′NESS n., dŭl′LY² (dŭl-lĭ) adv. **2.** vb. Make ~ (~ *the edge of*, blunt, make less sensitive, interesting, effective); lose force, intensity, clearness, or keenness. [ME *dul*, also (obs.) *dil*, f. OE *dol* (*dyll*), corresp. to MLG, MDu. *dul*, OS (Du.) *dol*, OHG *tol* f. WG *dul-*]

dŭlse, n. Edible kind of sea-weed. [f. Ir. & Gael. *duileasg*]

dŭl′ȳ, adv. Rightly, properly, fitly; sufficiently; punctually. [ME; DUE¹+-LY²]

du′ma (dŏo-), n. Russian parliament, 1906-17. [previously name of elective municipal councils]

dŭmb¹ (-m), a. (compar. & superl., pron. -mer, -mĭst). Unable to speak, abnormally (of human beings; *the* ~, *the deaf & ~*, as nouns) or normally (~ *animals*, used in pity or contempt); inarticulate, having no voice in government etc., (*the ~ millions*); silenced by surprise, shyness, etc. (esp. *strike* ~; ~ *in mixed company*); taciturn, reticent, (*Nature is ~ on the point*; *English a ~ people*); *stupid; without speech (~ *crambo*; ~ *show*, significant gestures, part of play given in early drama without words);

unheard, giving no sound; without the voice, sound, or other property, usual in things of the name (~ *piano*, set of keys for exercising fingers; ~*-waiter*, ‖ an upright with revolving shelves enabling waiter to be dispensed with in dining-room, *food-lift; ‖~ *barge, craft*, without sails or motive power; ~*-bell*, short bar with weight at each end used in pairs for exercising muscles, (v.i.) use these; ~ *well*, sunk merely to carry off surface water); ~*-iron*, one of the two curved forward ends of the side-members of a motor-car chassis. Hence ~′LY² (-ml-) adv., ~′NESS (-mn-) n. [OE, OS *dumb*, OHG *tump* stupid, ON *dumbr*, Goth. *dumbs* mute, of unkn. orig.]

dŭmb², v.t. Make dumb. [f. prec.]

dŭmbfound′ (-mf-), v.t. Strike dumb, confound, nonplus. [*dumb, confound*]

‖ **dŭm′bledōre** (-ld-), n. (dial.). Bumblebee; cockchafer. [f. *dumble-* (cf. *bumble-*, *drumble-*; *humble-bee*)+DOR]

dŭm′dŭm, a. & n. ~ (*bullet*), kind of soft-nosed bullet that expands & inflicts laceration. [D~ in India, with cantonment & arsenal]

dŭmm′ȳ, n. & a. **1.** (Whist) imaginary fourth player whose hand is turned up & played by partner (~ *whist* or ~, game so played; *double* ~, game with two such hands); (Bridge) the partner of the player who makes the first call in the accepted declaration, or his (exposed) hand. **2.** Person taking no real part, or present only for show, figurehead, mere tool, man of straw; dolt, blockhead. **3.** Counterfeit object, sham package etc., clothes-block, lay figure, man's figure as target; baby's indiarubber teat; *sell the* ~ (Rugby football), deceive opponent by feigning to pass ball. **4.** adj. Sham. [DUMB¹+-Y³]

dŭmp¹, n. ‖ Short thick object of various kinds; ‖ leaden counter used in games; obs. Australian coin, (sl.) small coin (*not worth a* ~); ‖ kind of bolt in ship-building; rope quoit for game on board ship; kind of skittle; kind of sweetmeat; short stout person. [18th c., orig. unkn.; goes with DUMPY]

dŭmp², v.t. & n. **1.** Shoot, deposit, tilt down, (rubbish); let fall with a bump; (Commerc.) send (goods unsalable at high price in home market) to foreign market for sale at low price, to avoid lowering home price & capture new market; drop down (t. & i.) with a thud; land (superfluous immigrants) in foreign country; hence ~′ER¹ n. **2.** n. Dull blow, thud; heap of refuse, place for shooting this; (Mil.) temporary depot of munitions. [ME, perh. of Norse orig., cf. Da. *dumpe*, Norw. *dumpa*, Sw. dial. *dompa*, fall plump]

dŭmp′ling, n. Mass of dough boiled or baked either plain or enclosing apple etc. [c. 1600; in sense, as f. DUMP¹+-LING¹, but is recorded very much earlier]

dŭmps, n. pl. Depression, melancholy, (usu. *in the ~*). [16th c., of obsc. orig.; perh. f. MDu. *dump* exhalation, haze, mist]

dŭm′p|ў, a. & n. 1. Short & stout (*~y level*, kind used in surveying); hence *~*iNESS n. **2.** n. ‖ Short-legged Scotch breed of fowls. [18th c., orig. unkn.; goes w. DUMP[1]; for the sense, cf. DUMPLING]

dŭn[1], a. & n. (Of) dull greyish-brown colour as of ass or mouse (*~-bird*, ‖ pochard; *~ diver*, ‖ female or young male of goosander); (poet.) dark, dusky; *~* horse; kinds of artificial fishing-fly. [OE *dun*(*n*), = OS *dun* reddish brown]

dŭn[2] n., & v.t. (-nn-). **1.** Importunate creditor; debt-collector; demand for payment. **2.** v.t. Importune for payment of debt; pester. [perh. var. of DIN]

dŭnce, n. One slow at learning, dullard, (*~'s cap*, paper cone put on head of *~* at school). [f. John *Duns* Scotus, schoolman, d. 1308, whose followers were ridiculed by 16th-c. humanists and reformers as enemies of learning]

dŭn′derhead (-ĕd), n., **dŭn′der-headĕd** (-ĕd-), a. Blockhead; stupid (person). [17th c., orig. unkn.]

Dŭndrear′ў, n. *~ whiskers*, long side whiskers worn without beard. [*~*, character in T. Taylor's comedy *Our American Cousin*]

dūne, n. Mound or ridge of loose sand on coast. [f. F *dune* f. MDu. *dūne*; see DOWN[1]]

dŭng, n., & v.t. **1.** Manure; excrement of animals (rarely of man; *~-beetle*, whose larvae develop in *~*; *~-fly*, feeding in it; *~-worm*, found in cow-*~* & used as bait; *~-cart*, *-fork*, for conveying, loading, & spreading, manure); moral filth. **2.** v.t. Manure (land; of farmer, grazing animals, or the manure). [OE *dung*, OHG *tunga* (G *dung*, *dünger*), also Icel. *dyngja*]

dŭng′aree (-ngg-), n. Coarse Indian calico; (pl.) overalls etc. of *~*. [f. Hind. *dungrī*]

dŭn′geon (-jn), n., & v.t. (Now usu. *donjon*) great tower of castle in innermost court or bailey; strong subterranean cell for prisoners; (vb) shut *up*, imprison in *~*. [ME, f. OF *donjon* f. Gallo-Rom. **domnionem* f. L *dominus* lord]

dŭng′hill, n. Heap of dung or refuse in farmyard (*cock on his own ~*, household, parish, etc., tyrant or bully; *~ cock* etc., barn-door not game, whence *~* as adj., craven).

‖ **dun′iwassal** (dōō-), n. (Sc.). Highland gentleman of secondary rank. [Gael. *duine* man, *uasal* noble]

dŭnk, v.t. & i. Dip (bread, cake, etc.) into soup or a beverage while eating. [f. G *tunken* (var. *dunken*) dip]

Dŭnkĭrk′, n. (Scene of) evacuation of a defeated army by sea like that of the British from *~* in May 1940. [port in France]

dŭn′lĭn, n. Red-backed sandpiper. [-LING[1]]

dŭnn′age, n. Mats, brushwood, gratings, etc., stowed under or among cargo to prevent moisture & chafing. [17th c. *dinnage*; orig. unkn.]

‖ **dŭnn′ock**, n. Hedge-sparrow. [DUN[1], -OCK]

dŭnt, n. Blow given to aircraft by a vertical current of air suddenly encountered. [orig. Sc., prob. var. of DINT]

dū′ō, n. (In music-hall usage) pair of artistes (*comedy ~*). [L, = two]

dŭodĕ′cimal, a. & n. Of twelve or twelfths, proceeding by twelves; (n. pl.) cross-multiplication, method used for dimensions given in feet, inches, & twelfths of inch, used by quantity surveyors etc. [f. L *duodecimus* twelfth +-AL]

dŭodĕ′cimō, n. (usu. 12mo). Book-size in which each leaf is 1/12 of printing-sheet; book of this size; diminutive thing or person. [L (*in*) *duodecimo* abl. see prec.]

dŭodĕn′arў, a. Proceeding by twelves, in sets of twelve. [f. L *duodenarius* (*duodeni* twelve at once, -ARY[1])]

dŭodĕn′|um, n. (anat.). First portion of small intestine immediately below stomach. Hence *~*AL a., *~*IT′IS (-īt-) n. [ME, f. med. L (*duodeni* see prec., from its length of 12 in.)]

dū′ologue (-ŏg), n. Conversation between two persons, dramatic piece with two actors. [irreg. f. Gk *duo* two, after *monologue*]

duŏm′ō (dw-), n. (pl. *~s*). Italian cathedral. [It.]

dŭp|e, n., & v.t. **1.** Victim of deception, gull; hence *~*'ERY(2) n. **2.** v.t. Cheat, make a fool of; hence *~*'ABLE a., *~*ABIL′ITY, *~*'ER[1], nn. [F *dupe* (dial.) hoopoe, from the bird's stupid appearance]

dū′ple, a. Double (now only in: *~ ratio*, that of 2 to 1; *~ time*, *rhythm*, of two beats to the bar). [f. L *duplus* (*duo* two, *-plus* f. *ple-* fill)]

dūp′lex, a. Of two elements, twofold, (*~ gas-burner*, with two jets combining into one flame; *~ lamp*, with two wicks); *~ telegraphy*, by which one wire transmits messages both ways at once. [L, gen. *-plicis* (*duo* two, *plic-* fold)]

dūp′licate, a. & n. **1.** With two corresponding parts, existing in two examples; doubled, twice as large or many; *~ proportion*, *ratio*, proportion of squares in relation to that of their radicals; exactly like a thing already existing (of any number of copies or specimens). **2.** n. One of two things exactly alike, esp. that made after the other; second copy, with equal legal force, of letter or document; second copy of bill drawn in two parts, second of exchange; pawnbroker's ticket; one of two or more specimens of thing exactly or virtually alike; synonym; exact correspondence between two things (*made in ~*). [ME, f. L as foll., -ATE[2]]

dŭp'lĭc|āte², v.t. Double, multiply by two; make in duplicate, make exact copy of, produce copies of, whence ~ātoR n. Hence ~A'TION n. [f. L *duplicare* (DUPLEX, -ATE³)]

dŭpli'cĭtў̆, n. Double-dealing, deceitfulness; doubleness. [ME, f. OF *duplicite* or LL *duplicitas* (DUPLEX, -TY)]

dŭr'ab|le, a. Lasting, not transitory; resisting wear, decay, etc. Hence **dŭrabĬl'ĬTY**, ~leNESS (-ln-), nn., ~LY² adv. [ME, f. OF f. L *durabilis* (*durare* f. *durus* hard, -ABLE)]

dŭral'ūmĭn, n. An aluminium alloy remarkable for its strength and hardness, used for aircraft etc. [P, f. *Dür(en)* in the Rhineland + ALUMIN(IUM)]

dū'ra māt'er, n. (anat.). Tough outer membrane enveloping brain & spinal cord. [med. L, = hard mother, transl. of Arab. phrase]

dŭrām'ĕn, n. Heart-wood of exogenous tree. [L, f. *durare* harden]

dūr'ance, n. Imprisonment (usu. *in ~ vile*). [F (*durer* last f. L *durare* see DURABLE, -ANCE)]

dūrā'tion, n. Continuance in, length of, time; time for which thing continues (*for the ~*, phr. common in war-time contracts). [ME, f. OF f. med. L *durationem* (prec., -ATION)]

dŭrb'ar, n. Indian ruler's court; public levee of Indian prince or (hist.) Anglo-Ind. governor or viceroy. [f. Pers. & Hind. *darbar* court]

dūrĕss(e)' (*or* dū'rĕs), n. Forcible restraint, imprisonment; compulsion, esp. imprisonment, threats, or violence, illegally used to force person to do something (*under ~*; *plea of ~*, for voiding contract so made). [ME, f. OF *duresse* f. L *duritia* (*durus* hard, -ESS²)]

dŭr'ian (door²), n. S.-E. Asian tree bearing a large oval fruit containing pulp notable for its fetid smell and agreeable taste; its fruit. [Malay]

dūr'ĭng, prep. Throughout, at some point in, the continuance of. [ME (-ING²) f. OF *durant* after L abl. abs. constr., as *durante vita* (or *vita durante*)]

dŭrm'ast (-ah-), n. Kind of oak. [*dur-* (perh. erron. for *dun*) + MAST²]

dŭrn, v.t. = DARN².

dŭ'rra, dh-, (dŏŏ-), n. Indian millet. [f. Arab. *durah*]

dŭrst. See DARE.

dŭsk, n., a., & v.i. & t. **1.** Shade, gloom; darker stage of twilight. **2.** adj. (poet.). Shadowy, dim, dark-coloured, whence ~'ISH¹ a., & (in ordinary use) ~'Y² a., ~'ĬLY² adv., ~'ĬNESS n. **3.** vb. (poet.). Become, look, make, dim or dark or shadowy. [ME *dosk*, later *dusk*, f. OE *dox* swarthy; -*sk* is abnormal]

dŭst¹, n. **1.** Finely powdered earth or other matter lying on ground or on surfaces or carried about in clouds by wind (*shake off the ~ of one's feet*, depart indignantly; *throw ~ in one's eyes*, mislead him by misrepresentation or diverting attention from point; *bite the ~*, fall wounded or slain). **2.** ‖ Household refuse (~-*bin*, receptacle for this; ~-*man*, man who empties this & removes the ~ in ~-*cart*). **3.** Pollen. **4.** (With *a*) cloud of ~ (*what a ~!*, *a great ~*, *make or raise a ~*). **5.** Dead person's remains (*honoured ~*; also *in the ~*, dead); the human body, man. **6.** Humiliation (*humbled in, to, the ~*). **7.** Confusion, turmoil, excitement, row, contest, (~ & *heat*, the burden of a struggle). **8.** (sl.). Cash. **9.** *~-bowl*, area denuded of vegetation by drought & overcropping & so reduced to desert; ~-*brand*, disease of corn, smut; ~-*cloak*, -*coat*, -*gown*, -*wrap*, -*cloth*, worn or put over objects to keep off ~; ~-*colour*, dull light brown; ~-*cover*, -*jacket*, book's jacket; ~-*guard*, in machine, or on bicycle to protect dress; ~'*man*, = SAND-*man*; ~'*pan*, into which ~ is brushed from floor; ~- *shot*, smallest-sized shot. Hence ~'LESS a. [OE *dūst*, MDu. *dūst* (LG *dust*, Du. *duist* fine flour), ON *dust* f, Gmo *dunst-* (whence G *dunst* vapour)]

dŭst², v.t. & i. Sprinkle with dust or powder (intr., of birds, take dust-bath; ~ *the eyes* of, deceive, take in); make dusty; sprinkle (dust, powder); clear of dust by brushing, wiping, or beating (~ one's *jacket*, beat him); clear away (dust etc.), clear furniture of dust. [f. prec.]

dŭs'ter, n. Cloth for dusting furniture etc.; person who does this. [-ER¹]

dŭs'tĭng, n. In vbl senses; esp. (sl.), thrashing, tossing in storm at sea. [ING¹]

dŭs't|ў̆, a. Full of, strewn with, finely powdered like, dust; dry as dust, uninteresting; vague, indefinite, (~*y answer*; ‖ (sl.) *not so* ~*y*, fairly good; ~*y miller*, plant auricula (from white dust on leaves & flowers), artificial fishing-fly. Hence ~'ĬLY² adv., ~'ĬNESS n. [-Y²]

Dŭtch¹, a. & n. **1.** (hist.). Of Germany including Netherlands (*High ~*, of Southern Germans; *Low ~*, of Germans of sea coast, Netherlands, & Flanders). **2.** Of the language or people of Holland & Netherlands (~ *school*, of painters distinguished by artistic treatment of everyday subjects; *the ~*, people of Holland & Netherlands). **3.** Coming from Holland, made or invented by the ~, (~ *clock*, *chair*, *cheese*, HOE, OVEN). **4.** Characteristic of or attributed to the ~ (~ AUCTION, COURAGE; *talk to one like a ~ uncle*, lecture him paternally; ~ *wife*, frame of cane etc. for resting the limbs in bed, long bolster similarly used). **5.** n. The German language in any of its forms (*High ~*, German; *Low ~*, Low German including language of Holland & other northern varieties) (hist.). **6.** Language of Holland & Netherlands (*double ~*, gibberish). [f. MDu. *dutsch* Hollandish,

Netherlandish, German, = OE *thēodisc,* OS *thiudisc,* OHG *diutisc* (G *deutsch* German) national, f. Gmc **theudā* people + -ISH[1]]

‖ **dŭtch**[2], n. See DUCHESS.

Dŭtch′man, n. (pl. *-men,* fem. *-woman*). Hollander or Netherlander (*or I'm a* ~, *I'm a* ~ *if*—, forms of positive & negative asseveration); Dutch ship (*Flying* ~, spectral ship).

dūt′eous, a. Dutiful, obedient, (of person or conduct). Hence ~LY[2] adv., ~NESS n. [irreg. f. DUTY + -OUS (cf. *beauteous*) after *bounteous, plenteous*]

dūt′iable, a. Liable to customs or other duties. [-ABLE]

dūt′iful, a. Regular or willing in obedience & service. Hence ~LY[2] adv., ~NESS n. [foll. + -FUL]

dūt′y, n. **1.** Behaviour due to superior, deference, expression of respect. **2.** Payment to public revenue levied on import, export, manufacture, or sale, of goods (CUSTOMS, EXCISE, *duties*), transfer of property (DEATH, PROBATE, *succession, stamp, duties*), licences, legal recognition of documents, etc. (~ is levied on article or transaction, tax usu. on persons). **3.** Moral or legal obligation, what one is bound or ought to do (~ *call,* visit one would rather not but feels bound to pay). **4.** Binding force of what is right. **5.** Business, office, function, performance of or engagement in these (*on, off,* ~, actually so engaged or not), (Eccl.) performance of church services (*look my* ~ *for me*). **6.** (mech.). Measure of engine's effectiveness in units of work done per unit of fuel. **7.** *Do* ~ *for,* serve or pass for (something else); ~*-paid, -free,* of goods on which customs or excise ~ has been paid or is not leviable. [f. AF (not in OF) *duete,* see DUE[1], -TY]

dūūm′vir (*-er*), n. (pl. ~*s,* ~*ī*). Member of board of two equal officials. Hence ~ATE[1] n. [L, lit. man of the two‍]

duvet (see Ap.), n. Eider-down quilt. [F]

‖ **dŭx,** n. (no pl.). Top pupil in class (chiefly Sc.). [L, = leader]

dwāle, n. Deadly nightshade. [prob. f. Scand. (ON *dvöl* delay, Sw. *dvala* trance)]

dwarf (*-ôrf*), n., a., & v.t. **1.** Person, animal, or plant, much below ordinary size of species, whence ~′ISH[1]a., ~′ishLY[2] adv., ~′ishNESS n., (*-ôrf-*). **2.** Small supernatural being in esp. Scandinavian mythology skilled in metal-working. **3.** adj. Undersized (in many plant names); puny, stunted. **4.** v.t. Stunt in growth, or in intellect etc.; make look small by contrast or distance. [OE *dweorg,* MLG, MDu. *dwerch,* OHG *twerg,* ON *dvergr* f. Gmc. **dwergaz*]

dwĕll, v.i. (*dwĕlt*), & n. **1.** Keep one's attention fixed, write or speak at length, (*up*)on subject (~ *upon note, syllable,* etc.,

prolong it). **2.** Make one's abode, spend one's time, live, *in, at, near, on,* etc. (now usu. *live* in talk). **3.** (Of horse) be slow in raising feet, pause before taking fence. **4.** n. Slight regular pause for some purpose in motion of machine. [OE *dwellan,* OS *-ian,* OHG *twellan,* ON *dvelja* delay etc., f. Gmc **dwaljan*]

dwĕll′er, n. Inhabitant, resident *in, on,* etc.; horse that DWELLS at fence. [-ER[1]]

dwĕll′ing, n. In vbl senses; also : place of residence, house; ~*-house,* used as residence, not as office, warehouse, etc.; ~*-place;* = ~. [-ING[1]]

dwin′dle, v.i. Become smaller, shrink, waste away; lose importance, decline, degenerate. [16th c., f. (now dial.) *dwine* fade away f. OE *dwīnan,* ON *dvīna* + -LE(3)]

dy′ad, n. The number two; group of two, couple. Hence **dyăd′IC** a. [f. LL f. Gk *duas -ad-* (*duo* two, -AD)]

Dy′ăk, n. Aboriginal of Borneo. [Malay, = savage]

dyarchy. See DIARCHY.

dye[1], n. Colour produced by or as by dyeing, tinge, hue, (also fig., *crime, scoundrel, of blackest, deepest,* ~); matter used for dyeing, colouring-matter in solution; ~*-stuff, -ware, -wood,* yielding ~; ~*-house, -works,* where dyeing is done. [OE *dēag* (foll.)]

dye[2], v.t. & i. (~*d;* part. ~*ing*). Colour, stain, tinge; impregnate (tissue) with colouring-matter (~ *in the wool, in grain,* while material is in raw state, giving more permanent result); make (thing) such a colour (~ *cloth red, a rose colour,* etc.); (of material) take colour *well, badly,* etc. [OE *dēagian* of unkn. orig.]

dy′er, n. One who dyes cloth etc. (~'s in many names of plants yielding dye, as ~'s bugloss, broom, oak, weed). [-ER[1]]

dy′ing, n. In vbl senses of DIE[2]; esp. (attrib.) connected with, at time of, death (~ *bed, declaration, wish;* ~ *oath,* made at, or with solemnity proper to, death). [-ING[1]]

dyke. See DIKE.

dȳnăm′ic, a & n. **1.** Of motive force (cf. *static*); of force in actual operation (cf. *potential*); active, potent, energetic; of dynamics; (Med.) functional (cf. *organic*); (Philos.) accounting for matter or mind as being merely the action of forces, so **dȳn′amISM**(3), **dȳn′amist**[1] [-IST(2)] (& see DYNAMICS), nn. **2.** n. Energizing or motive force. [f. F *dynamique* f. Gk *dunamikos* (*dunamis* power, -IC)]

dȳnăm′ical, a. Of dynamics; of force or mechanical power actively operative; (Theol., of inspiration) endowing with divine power, not impelling mechanically; of dynamism (see prec.). Hence ~LY[2] adv. [-AL]

dȳnăm′ics, n. pl. used as sing. **1.** Branch of mechanics that treats of motion in itself, and of the motion of bodies or matter under the influence of forces (including KINEMATICS and KINETICS; opp. STATICS), whence **dȳn'amist²** [-IST(3)] (& see DYNAMIC) n.; branch (of any science) in which forces are considered (now often with a specific prefix, as in AERO*dynamics*). **2.** Moving forces, physical or moral, in any sphere. [-ICS]

dȳn'amite, n., & v.t. High explosive of nitro-glycerine mixed with inert absorbent; (vb) shatter with ~. [Gk *dunamis* force, -ITE]

dȳn'amit|er, n. User of explosive esp. for revolutionary purposes. So **dȳnamit'ic** a., ~ISM(1), ~IST(1), nn. [prec., -ER¹]

dȳn'amo-, comb. form of Gk *dunamis* power, as in ~-*electric*=of current (formerly *dynamic*) electricity, also = converting mechanical into electric energy.

dȳn'amō, n. (pl. -os). Machine converting mechanical into electric energy by rotating coils of copper wire in magnetic field. [short for ~-*electric machine*, see prec.]

dȳnamŏm'eter, n. Kinds of instrument measuring energy expended by animal, engine, or mechanical force; gauge for telescope's magnifying-power. [DYNAMO-, -METER]

dȳn'ast, n. Ruler, member of a dynasty. [f. L f. Gk *dunastēs* (*dunamai* am able)]

dȳn'astȳ, n. Line of hereditary rulers. So **dȳnăs'tic** a., **dȳnăs'tically** adv. [f. F *dynastie* or LL f. Gk *dunasteia* lordship (prec.)]

dȳne, n. (phys.). Unit of force (the amount that, acting for one second on one-gram mass, gives it velocity of one centimetre per second). [F, f. st. of Gk *dunamis* force]

dȳs-, pref.=Gk *dus-* bad-, opp. *eu-* good-, chiefly in medical or other scientific words taken f. Gk or made with Gk elements.

dȳs'enterȳ, n. Disease with inflamed mucous membrane & intestinal glands, griping pains, & mucous & bloody evacuations. So **dȳsentĕr'ic** a. [f. OF *dissenterie* or L f. Gk *dusenteria* (DYS-, *entera* bowels)]

dȳsgĕn'ic, a. Exerting a detrimental effect on the race (opp. EUGENIC). [f. DYS- + Gk *gen-* produce + -IC]

dȳslogis't|ic, a. Disapproving, opprobrious, (of sense in which term is used). Hence ~ICALLY adv. [DYS- + (EU)LOGISTIC]

dȳspĕp'sïa, n. Indigestion. So **dȳspĕp'tic** a. & n., (person) subject to ~ or the attendant depression. [L, f. Gk DYS(*pepsia* f. st. of *pessō* cook!)]

dȳspnoe'|a (-nĕa), n. (path.). Difficult breathing. Hence ~IC a. [L, f. Gk *duspnoia* (DYS-, *pneō* breathe)]

dȳsprŏs'ium (-zI-), n. (chem.). Element of rare-earth group. [mod. L, f. Gk *dusprositos* hard to get at]

dȳsūr'ia, n. Painful urination. [LL, f. Gk *dusouria* (DYS- + *ouron* urine)]

E

E, e, (ē), letter (pl. *Es*, E's). (Mus.) note, & corresp. scale; second-class ship in Lloyd's register.

e-, pref. Shortened form of EX-(1).

each, a. & pron. (Of two or more) every (one) taken separately, as ~ *man has two votes*, ~ *of us has two votes, we have two votes* ~, *they cost a penny* ~, ~ *is worse than the one before*; *they hate* ~ *other*, ~ *hates the other*; *sides of two triangles are equal* ~ *to* ~ (a side of one to the corresponding side of the other). [OE *ǣlc*, = LG, Du. *elk*, OHG *eogilih* (G *jeglich*) f. WG **aiwō galikaz* ever alike; see AYE, LIKE, ALIKE; OE had also *ylc* ILK; *gehwilc* = OHG *gihwelih* (see WHICH); *ǣghwilc* = OHG *eogihwelih*]

eag'er (-g-), a. Full of keen desire; strongly desirous (*to do, for, after, about,* etc.); (of passions etc.) keen, impatient; (arch.) ~ (cold) *air*. Hence ~LY² adv., ~NESS n. [ME, f. OF *aigre* keen, f. L *acrem* (nom. *acer*)]

ea'gle, n. **1.** Large bird of prey, with keen vision & powerful flight; figure of this, esp. as ensign of Roman or French army, or as lectern in church. **2.** (golf). Hole played in two strokes under par. **3.** **Double* ~, coin worth twenty dollars; ~-*eyed*, keen-sighted; ~-*owl*, largest European owl. [f. OF *aigle* f. L *aquila*]

eag'lĕt, n. Young eagle. [f. F *aiglette* (as prec., see -ET¹)]

eagre (āg'er, ē-), n. Large tidal wave, esp. in the Humber, Trent, and Severn. [orig. unkn.]

-ean, suf. of adjj. & nn. (also *-aean, -eian*), with sense ' of, belonging to, like '; = -AN w. end of stem, usu. Gk *-ai(os)*, L *-ac(us)*, or Gk *-ei(os)*, L *-ei(us)*; *-aean* chiefly in unfamiliar wds as *Ascraean, Achaean*; *-eian* (apart from Gk & L as *Pompeian* etc.) is used w. E names in *-cy, -y*, as *Bodleian, Rugbeian*; *-ean* is pron. with ē (*Tacitēan, empyrēan,* exc. in familiar adjj. as *Prŏt'ean, Hercŭl'ean,* (-Ian), but cf. *pygmēan*; some have *-ean* incorrectly for *-ian-*(*antipodean*), & some vary betw. the two (*Aristotelean, -ian*).

ear¹, n. **1.** Organ of hearing, esp. external part of this; faculty of discriminating sound, as *an* ~ *for music*; ~-shaped thing, esp. handle of pitcher; *bring* (storm, hornets' nest, etc.) *about* one's ~s; *prick up* one's ~s, assume expectant attitude; *I would give my* ~s, make any sacrifice (*for* a thing, *to* do); *over head and* ~s, deeply immersed *in* (lit. & fig.); *set* (persons), *be, by the* ~s (at variance); *a word in your* ~s (in private); *be all* ~s (deeply attentive); *it goes in at one* ~ *& out at the other*, it leaves no impression; *give* ~, listen *to*; *have* a person's ~ (favourable attention); *were your* ~s *burning last night?* (we were talking about you); *sent* him away with a flea in his ~, told him some home truths etc. **2.** ~-*ache*, pain in drum of ~; ~*mark*, (n.) mark on ~ of sheep etc. as sign of ownership, (fig.) mark of ownership, (v.t.) mark (sheep etc.) with this, (fig.) assign (fund etc.) to definite purpose; ~-*phone*, = HEAD-*phone*; ~-*ring* (worn in lobe of ~ for ornament); ~*shot*, hearing distance, as *within, out of,* ~*shot*; ~-*trumpet*, tube used by persons partly deaf; ~-*wax*, viscid secretion in ~. Hence (-)~ED[2] (-rd), ~'LESS, aa. [OE *ēare*, OS, OHG *ōra*, ON *eyra*, Goth. *auso*, cogn. w. L *auris*, Gk *ous*]

ear², n. Spike, head, of corn, containing its flowers or seeds. [OE *ēar*, OS *ahar*, OHG *ahir*, ON *ax*, Goth. *ahs* cogn. w. L *acus -eris* husk]

ear'ing, n. (naut.). Small rope (one of several) fastening upper corner of sail to yard. [EAR[1]+-ING[1]; or = *ear-ring*]

earl (ĕrl), n. (fem. *countess*). Nobleman ranking between marquis & viscount (cf. COUNT[3]); E~ *Marshal*, officer presiding over Heralds' College etc. Hence ~'DOM (ĕr-) n. [OE *eorl*, OS, OHG *erl*, ON *earl*, JARL, of unkn. orig.]

earl'ў (ĕr-), a. & adv. Absolutely or relatively near to the beginning of a portion of time, as *an* ~ *visit*, ~ *risers, rise* ~, *keep* ~ *hours* (rise & go to bed ~), ~ *peaches* (maturing ~ in the year), E~ *English* STYLE, *fix an* ~ *date* (not long hence), *at your earliest convenience* (as soon as you conveniently can), *the* ~ *part* (beginning) *of the century; the* ~ *spring, morning,* etc., the ~ part of spring etc.; ~ *bird*, (joc.) ~ riser (w. ref. to proverb *the* ~ *bird gets the worm*); ~-*Victorian* a. & n. (writer etc.) of or characteristic of Victoria's ~ reign; ~ *door*, theatre door admitting audience before usual hour and at enhanced price; *earlier on,* at an earlier stage, previously (after *later on*). Hence **earl'**ıNESS (ĕr-) n. [(adj. f. adv.) OE *ārlīce* (ar posit. degree of *ǣr* ERE, -LY²)]

earn (ĕrn), v.t. (Of person, action, conduct, etc.) obtain as reward of labour or merit. [OE *earnian* = OHG *arnen* f. WG *aznōjan*, cf. OE *esne*, Goth. *asneis* labourer, Goth. *asans* (cf. G *ernte*) harvest]

earn'est¹ (ĕr-), a. & n. Serious, zealous, not trifling; ardent (*desire* etc.); *in* ~, serious(ly), not jesting(ly). Hence ~LY² adv., ~NESS n. [(a.f.n.) OE *eornust* = OHG *ernust* (G *ernst*) f. *ern-* as in ON *ern* vigorous]

earn'est² (ĕr-), n. Money paid as instalment, esp. to confirm contract etc.; foretaste, presage, betokening, (*is an', in,* ~ *of what is to come*). [ME *ernes* prob. var. of *erles, arles* f. OF **erles* f. Rom. **arrulas* pl. dim. of L *arr(h)a* pledge]

earn'ing (ĕr-), n. In vbl senses, esp. (pl.) money earned. [-ING[1]]

earth¹ (ĕr-), n. (pl. only as below). **1.** The ground, as *it fell to* ~; (w. pl.) hole (of

---

badger, fox, etc'; the dry land; land & sea opp. the sky; this planet; this world opp. heaven or hell (*why* etc. *on* ~? why EVER?); (w. pl.) soil, mould; (Chem., w. pl.) any of certain metallic oxides, uninflammable, & having little taste or smell; || (Electr., w. pl.) connection with ~ as completion of circuit. **2.** ~-*born*, of mortal race, (Myth.) emerging from ~ at birth; ~-(substitute for WATER¹-) *closet; ~-light, -shine,* partial illumination of dark part of moon by light from ~; ~-*nut*, (roundish tuber of) an umbelliferous woodland plant, other plants; ~'*work*, bank of ~ used in fortification; ~-*worm*, worm living in ground, (fig.) grovelling person. Hence ~'WARD(S) adv. [OE *eorthe*, OS *ertha*, OHG *erda*, ON *jörth*, Goth. *airtha* f. Gmc **erthō*]

earth² (ĕr-), v.t. & i. Cover (roots of plants) with heaped-up earth; drive (fox) to earth; (intr., of fox) run to earth; (Electr.) = GROUND². [f. prec.]

earth'en (ĕr-), a. Made of earth; made of baked clay. [-EN⁵]

earth'enwāre (ĕr-), n. (often attrib.). Vessels etc. made of baked clay; baked clay. [WARE¹]

earth'l|ў (ĕr-), a. Of the earth; terrestrial; (colloq.) *no* ~*y use, reason, chance,* no use etc. at all; || *not an* ~*y* (sl.), no chance whatever. Hence ~INESS n. [-LY¹]

earth'quāke (ĕr-), n. Volcanic convulsion of earth's surface; (fig.) social or other disturbance.

earth'l|ў (ĕr-), a. Like, of, earth or soil; (fig.) grossly material. Hence ~INESS n. [-Y²]

ear'wig, n., & v.t. (-gg-). Insect once held to get into the head through the ear; (v.t.) influence (person) by secret communications. [OE *ēarwicga* (*ēare* EAR¹ + *wicga* ~)]

ease¹ (ēz), n. Freedom from pain or trouble; freedom from constraint, as *at one's* ~; (Mil.) *stand at* ~ (in relaxed attitude, with feet apart); relief from pain; CHAPEL *of* ~; facility, esp. *with* ~. Hence ~'LESS (-zl-) a. [ME, f. OF *eise, aise* (cf. Prov. *aize,* It. *agio*) f. Rom. **adjaces* f. L *adjacens* ADJACENT]

ease² (ēz), v.t. & i. Relieve from pain etc.; give mental ease to (person, one*self,* one's *mind*); (joc.) rob (person *of* his purse etc.); relax, adjust, (what is too tight); (Naut.) slacken (rope, sail, *away, down, off*), ~ *her,* reduce speed of engine; (v.i.) ~ *off,* become less burdensome. [ME, f. OF *a(a)isier* (prec.)]

ease'ful (ēzf-), a. Comfortable, soothing; at rest; slothful. Hence ~LY² adv., ~NESS n. [-FUL]

eas'el (-z-), n. Wooden frame to support picture,·blackboard, etc. [f. Du. *ezel* = G *esel* ASS]

ease'ment (-zm-), n. (Law) right of way or similar right over another's ground; supplementary building, shed, etc.;

(arch.) relief from pain or burden. [ME, f. OF *aisement* (as EASE², -MENT)]

east, adv., n., & a. (Towards, at, near) the point of the horizon where the sun rises (90° to right of North); *to the ~ (of)*, in an eastward direction (from); *~ (wind)*, wind blowing from the *~*; eastern part of the world, orient; altar-end of church (whether truly oriented or not); **the E~*, (esp.) north-*~* region of the U.S.; *Far E~*, China, Japan, etc.; *Middle E~*, (esp.) countries from Egypt to Iran inclusive; *Near E~*, Turkey & Balkan States; || *E~ End*, eastern part of London; **E~ Side*, eastern part of New York. Hence *~'WARD* a. & n., *~'WARD(S)* adv. [OE *ēast*, OS, OHG *ōst-*, ON *aust-* f. Gmc **aus-to-*, **aus-tro* f. Aryan **aus* (L *aurora*, *auster*)]

Eas'ter, n. Festival of Christ's resurrection, corresponding to Passover, & observed on 1st Sunday (*~ day*, *Sunday*) after the first full moon on or after March 21 (also arch. *~tide*); (also *~-week*) week commencing with *~* day; *~ eggs* (painted & presented to friends at *~*); *~ eve*, day before *~* day; *~ offering(s)*, customary payments made to the incumbent on *~* day (now usually the collection proceeds). [OE *ēastre*, pl. *ēastron*, OHG *ōstarūn* app. f. *Eostre*, dawn-goddess (*aus-*, see prec.)]

eas'terly, a. & adv. In an eastern position or direction; (coming) from the east, as *~ wind*. [f. obs. *easter* (perh. compar. of EAST) |-LY¹]

eas'tern, a. & n. Of, dwelling in, the east part of the world; *E~ Church* (Greek); lying towards the east; (n.) inhabitant of the East, member of E~ Church. Hence *~MOST* a. [OE *ēasterne* (see EAST & -ERN)]

eas'ting, n. (naut.). Distance to the eastward; easterly direction. [-ING¹]

eas'y (-z-), a., adv., &n. 1. Free from pain, discomfort, annoyance, anxiety, etc.; *~ circumstances*, affluence; free from embarrassment or stiffness, as *~ manners*, *free & ~* (not stiff, not strict); not difficult (*to do*, or abs.; *~ of access*, easily got at); easily persuaded, compliant, (*woman of~ virtue*, unchaste); (Commerc., of commodity) not much in demand, (of market) not showing eager demand, (cf. TIGHT). 2. adv. In *~* manner, as *take it ~*, proceed comfortably; (as command) *~ !*, move gently, *~ all!*, stop (prop. rowing), whence *an ~*, a short rest; || *stand ~!* (Mil.), permission to squad standing at ease to relax attitude further. 3. *~ chair*, one designed for comfort, usu. with arms; *~-going*, (of horse) having an *~* gait, (of person) fond of comfort, indolent, taking things easily; *~ mark* (colloq.), simpleton; *~ money* (not hard to earn). Hence **eas'ILY²** adv., **eas'INESS** n., (-z-). [ME, f. OF *aisie* p.p. of *aisier* EASE²]

eat, v.t. & i. (past *ate*, *eat*, pron. ět; p.p. *eaten*, pron. ětn). Masticate & swallow (solid food); swallow (soup); *~* one's *words*, retract them in humiliating manner; || *~* one's *terms* or *dinners*, be studying for the bar; *~* HUMBLE *pie*; *~* (person) *out of house & home*, ruin him by *~ing* (lit. & fig.) all he has; *horse* etc. *~s its head off*, costs more to feed than it is worth; *well, don't ~ me!*, joc. reply to vehement protest etc.; (intr. as pass.) *the cakes ~ crisp*; destroy, consume, as *~* one's *heart out*, suffer bitterly; *~ away*, destroy gradually (lit. & fig.); *~ up*, consume completely, waste, (lit. & fig.), absorb, as *~en up with pride*. Hence **eat'ABLE** a. & n. (usu. pl.), *~'ER¹* n., one who or that which *~s* (*he is a big ~er, an opium~er*), fruit that may be *~en* raw. [OE, OS *etan*, OHG *eȝȝan*, ON *eta*, Goth. *itan* f. Gmc **etan* f. Aryan **ed-* (L *edere*)]

eat'ing, n. in vbl senses; *~-house*, restaurant. [-ING¹]

*eats, n. pl. (sl.). Food. [pl. of obs. *eat*, something edible (OE *æt*), or fresh formation f. vb]

eau (ō), n. *~-de-Cologne* (ōd'ekolōn'), perfume made at Cologne; *~-de-Nil* (-denēl'), greenish colour (supposed to resemble Nile water); *~-de-vie* (-devē'), brandy; *~ sucrée* (see Ap.), water and sugar. [F, = water]

eaves (ēvz), n. (now pl.). Overhanging edge of roof or thatch; *~'drop*, stand under this to listen to secrets, listen secretly to private conversation; *~'dropper*, one who does this (usu. fig.). [OE *efes*, cf. OHG *obasa* (G dial. *obsen*), f. same root as OVER; *-s* being now taken as pl. *eave* is occas. used for sing.]

ebb, n., & v.i. 1. Reflux of tide, as *~ & flow*, *~-tide*; decline, decay, as *at a low ~*. 2. v.i. Flow back, recede, decline, decay. [OE (*ebbian* vb f.) *ebba* (Du. *eb*, *ebbe*), f. WG **abhjon*, *-ōn* f. **abh* OFF]

E'-boat, n. Enemy high-speed motor torpedo-boat. [E abbr. of *enemy*]

ĕb'on, a. (poet.). Made of, black as, ebony. [15th c. *eban* f. med. L *ebanus* f. L f. Gk *ebenos*]

ĕb'onite, n. = VULCANITE. [f. foll. + -ITE¹]

ĕb'on|y, n. & a. 1. Kinds of hard black wood. 2. adj. Made of, black as, this. Hence *~IZE(3)* v.t. [16th c., irreg. var. of *ebon*, perh. after *ivory*]

ēbrī'ĕt|y, n. (now rare). Drunkenness. [f. F *ébriété* or L *ebrietas* (as foll., see -TY)]

ĕb'rious, a. (now rare). Drunk; given to, of, drunkenness. [f. L *ebrius* (-OUS]

ĕbŭll'i|ent, a. Boiling; exuberant. So *~ENCE*, *~ENCY*, nn. [f. L E(*bullire* *-it*-boil), -ENT]

ĕbulli'tion, n. Boiling; effervescence; (fig.) sudden outburst (*of* passion, war, etc.). [f. L *ebullitio* (as prec., see -ION)]

écarté (ākȧr'tā), n. Card-game for two persons in which cards may be discarded for others. [F (*écarter* discard)]

Ec'ce Hōm'ō (ĕksĭ), n. Picture of Christ

wearing crown of thorns. [L, = behold the man (*John* xix. 5)]

eccen'tric (-ks-), a. & n. **1.** Not concentric (*to* another circle); not placed, not having its axis etc. placed, centrally; (of 'orbit) not circular; (of heavenly body) moving in an ~ orbit; irregular; odd, whimsical. **2.** n. (Mech.) ~ contrivance for changing rotatory into backward-&-forward motion, esp. for slide-valve of steam-engine; odd, whimsical person. Hence **eccen'trically** adv., **eccentri'city** n. [f. LL *eccentricus* f. Gk *ekkentros* (*ek* out of + *kentron* CENTRE[1]), see -IC]

eccles'ia (-z-), n. (Gk Ant.). General assembly (esp. of Athenian citizens), cf. BOULE. [L, f. Gk *ekklēsia* (*ekkaleō* call out); in later Gk & LL = church]

eccles'iast (-z-), n. Member of Athenian ecclesia; ' the Preacher ', Solomon (regarded as author of *Eccles.*). [f. LL, Gk *ekklēsiastēs* (as prec.)]

Ecclesias'tes (-ī-, -zī-, -z), n. An O.T. book. [as ECCLESIAST]

ecclesias'tic (-zī-), n. & a. Clergyman; (adj., now rare) = foll. [f. F -*ique* or LL f. Gk *ekklēsiastikos* (as prec.)]

ecclesias'tic|al (-zī-), a. Of the church or the clergy; ‖ *E~al Commission*(ers), body formerly administering part of Church of England revenues. Hence or cogn. ~**ally**[2] adv.; ~**ism** n. [-AL]

Ecclesias'ticus (ī-, -zī-), n. A book of the Apocrypha. [as ECCLESIASTIC, = of (i.e. to be read in) church]

ecclesiol'og|y (-zī-), n. Science of churches, esp. of church building & decoration. Hence **ecclesiolo'gic**(AL) aa., ~**ist** n., (-zī-). [f. ECCLESIA + -O- + -LOGY-]

ec'dysis, n. (pl. -*sēs*). Casting off (esp. of slough in serpents etc.; also fig.); slough. [f. Gk *ekdusis* (*ekduō* put off)]

e'chelon (-sh-), n., & v.t. Formation of troops in parallel divisions, each with its front clear of that in advance; *in* ~, so drawn up; (v.t.) draw up thus; grade in civilian organization. [(vb f. n.) f. F *échelon* (*échelle* ladder f. L *scala*, see -OON)]

echid'na (-k-), n. Australian toothless burrowing animal like hedgehog. [f. Gk *ekhidna* viper]

ech'inite (-k-), n. Fossil echinoderm or sea-urchin. [f. ECHINUS + -ITE[1]]

echinoderm (ikin-, ek'in-), n. Class of animals including sea-urchins. [as foll. + DERM]

echin'us (-k-), n. Sea-urchin, animal inhabiting spheroidal prickly shell. [f. L f. Gk *ekhinos* hedgehog, sea-urchin]

ech'o[1] (-k-), n. (pl. ~*es*). Repetition of sound by reflexion of sound-waves (*cheer* person etc. *to the* ~, loudly); *E*~, cause of this personified; close imitation; obsequious imitator or adherent; artifice by which last syllables of one verse are taken up by next; conventional indication given to partner at bridge or whist of

the number of cards held in suit led etc.; ~*gram*, record of ~-*sounder* (sounding apparatus for determining depth of sea beneath ship). Hence ~**LESS** a. [ME, f. L f. Gk *ēkhō*, conn. w. *ēkhē* sound]

ech'o[2] (-k-), v.i. & t. (Of places) resound with an echo; (of sounds) be repeated, resound; (Bridge etc.) play the echo (see prec.); (v.t.) repeat (sound) by echo; repeat (another's words), imitate the words or opinions (of person). [f. prec.]

ech'o|ism (-k-), n. = ONOMATOPOEIA. So ~**IC** a. [-ISM]

éc'lair (āk'lār), n. Small finger-shaped cake filled with cream and iced. [F]

éclaircissement (see Ap.), n. Clearing up, explanation, (of conduct etc.). [F]

éclamp'sia, n. Kind of epileptic convulsions caused by anatomical lesion to which pregnant women are specially liable. [ult. f. Gk *eklampō* shine forth (visual hallucination being a symptom)]

éclat (ēklah'), n. Conspicuous success, general applause, as *with great* ~; social distinction. [F]

eclec't|ic, a. & n. (Ancient philosopher) selecting such doctrines as pleased him in every school; (person) borrowing freely from various sources, not exclusive in opinion, taste, etc. Hence ~**ICALLY** adv., ~**ICISM**(3) n. [f. Gk *eklektikos* (*eklegō* pick out, see -IC)]

éclipse[1], n. Interception of the light of a luminous body (sun, moon, etc.), by intervention of another body between it & the eye or between the luminous body and what illuminates it; ANNULAR, PARTIAL, TOTAL, ~; deprivation of light; loss of brilliance or splendour (*in* ~, of birds, having lost the courting plumage); periodical obscuration of lighthouse light. [ME: f. OF f. L f. Gk *ekleipsis* vbl n. f. *ekleipō* fail to appear, be eclipsed (*leipō* leave)]

éclipse[2], v.t. (Of a heavenly body) obscure (another) by passing between it & spectator or between it and the source of its light; intercept (light, esp. of lighthouse); (fig.) deprive of lustre, outshine, surpass. [f. prec.]

éclip'tic, a. & n. Of eclipse; (n.) sun's apparent orbit. [f. L f. Gk *ekleiptikos* (ECLIPSE[1], -IC)]

éc'logue (-g), n. Short poem, esp. pastoral dialogue, such as Virgil's Bucolics. [f. L f. Gk *eklogē* selection (*eklegō* pick out)]

écol'ogy, oec- (ē-), n. Branch of biology dealing with living organisms' habits, modes of life, and relations to their surroundings. [f. G *ökologie* f. Gk *oikos* house, -LOGY]

économ'ic, a. & n. **1.** Of ~s; maintained for profit, on a business footing, paying expenses, (of rent) high enough to compensate builder, owner, etc.; connected with industrial arts; ~ *botany, geography,* etc., botany etc. studied from the utilitarian standpoint. **2.** n. pl. Practical science of the production & distribution of wealth, (also) condition of a country as to material prosperity. [f. F *-ique* or L f. Gk *oikonomikos* (see ECONOMY & -IC)]

ĕcŏnŏm'ical, a. Saving, thrifty, not wasteful (*of*); relating to economics or to political economy. [-AL]

ĕcŏnŏm'icallў, adv. Thriftily; from an economic point of view. [-LY²]

ĕcŏn'omist, n.. Manager (*of* money etc.); thrifty person; writer on economics or political economy. [as ECONOMY + -IST]

ĕcŏn'omiz|e, **-is|e** (-īz), v.t. & i. Use sparingly; turn to the best account; (v.i.) practise economy, cut down expenses. Hence ~A'TION n. [as foll. + -IZE]

ĕcŏn'omў, n. **1.** Administration of concerns & resources of a community; *Political E~*, theory of production & distribution of wealth. **2.** Frugality; (w. pl.) instance of this. **3.** (theol.). Judicious handling of doctrine, whence (with play on sense *frugality*) ~ *of truth*. **4.** Organization; organized body, society, etc. [f. F *économie* or L f. Gk *oikonomia* f. *oikonomos* steward (*oikos* house + *-nomos* f. *nemō* manage)]

ĕcru' (-ōō, or as F *écru*), n. Colour of unbleached linen. [F, = unbleached]

ĕc'stasīze, **-ise** (-īz), v.t. & i. Throw, go, into ecstasies. [f. foll. + -IZE]

ĕc'stasў, n. Exalted state of feeling, rapture, (esp. of delight); (Med.) morbid state of nerves in which mind is occupied solely by one idea; trance; poetic frenzy. [ME, f. OF *extasie* f. LL f. Gk *ekstasis* vbl n. f. *existēmi* put (person) out of (his senses)]

ĕcstăt'|ic, a. Of, subject to, producing, ecstasies (esp. of joy). Hence ~ICALLY adv. [f. F *extatique* f. Gk *ekstatikos* (as prec., see -IC)]

ĕc'to- in comb., f. st. of Gk *ektos* outside, as, ~*blăst*, (Biol.) outer membrane of cell; ~*plăsm*, (Biol.) outer layer of protoplasm, supposed viscous substance exuding from body of spiritualistic medium during trance; ~*zōon*, external parasite.

ĕc'todĕrm, n. (biol.). Outer cellular membrane investing a multicellular animal. [ECTO-, DERM]

-ectomy, suf. f. Gk *ektomē* excision, in surgical terms denoting operations in which some part is removed, as *colectomy*, excision of part of the colon.

ecumenical. See OECUMENICAL.

ĕc'zèma, n. Inflammation of the skin, of several kinds. [f. Gk *ekzema* (*ek* out + *zeō* boil, see -M)]

-ed¹, (1) suf. forming p.p. of weak vbs (also *-d*, *-t*, as in *sold, bought*); *-ed* (now reduced in sound to *-d* or *-t* except in *-ded, -ted*, in some bibl. wds, as *blessed*, & in *learned*) was in OE *-ed, -ad, -od*, acc. to vb class, *-d* alone being the participial element, f. Gmc -*dha*- f. Aryan *-to- (cf..Gk vbl adj. *-tos*, L p.p. *-tus*); *-t* is used in vbs that

shorten in p.p. a long vowel of stem, as *crept, dreamt* (*dreamed* if pronounced with ē), and in some ending in *-d* after *l, n, r*, as *gilt, sent, girt*. (2) p.pp. in *-ed* (and *-en*) are used (rarely f. intr., commonly from trans. vbs) as adjj., meaning when intr. 'that has done so-&-so' (*vanished hand, fallen idol, escaped convict*); a special use, w. resultant force, is seen in *outspoken, well-read*; occas. it is doubtful whether adjj. in *-ed* are trans. (or intr.) p.pp. or belong to foll.: *decayed* may be *that has been decayed, that has decayed*, on the *affected with decay*; reference to -ED¹(2) is made only for the rare intr. p.p. adjj.

-ed² (as prec.), suf., distinct f. prec. in OE *-ede*, OS *-ōdi*, f. Gmc type -*°ōdhja*- (functioning as L *-tus* in *caudatus*), appended to nn. to form adjj. meaning possessed of, affected with, etc., as *talented, wooded, diseased*; esp. used to make adj. out of adj. & n., usu. stressed (apart from demands of context) in attrib. use on first component (*a quick-witted lad, met'al-cornered chest*), in pred. use on second (*he seems quick-witt'ed enough*) exc. where this is more or less otiose (*ru'by, coff'ee*, etc., *-coloured* attrib. & pred.); occas. = ' having the ways of ' instead of simply ' having ', as *bigoted, crabbed, dogged*; occas. indisting. f. prec. (2).

ĕdā'cious (-shŭs), a. (pedant.). Of eating; greedy. So **ĕdĂ'CITY** n. [f. L *edax -acis* (*edere* eat, see -ACIOUS)]

Ed'ăm (ē-), n. Spherical Dutch cheese. [~, in Holland]

Edd'a (ĕ-), n. (*Older, Poetic*, ~) collection of ancient Icelandic poems; (*Younger, Prose*, ~) miscellaneous handbook (c. 1230) to Icelandic poetry. [perh. f. a name in an ON poem]

ĕdd'|ў, n., & v.t. & i. **1.** Small whirlpool; wind, fog, smoke, moving like this. **2.** v.t. & i. Whirl round in ~ies. [orig. obsc.]

edelweiss (ād'elvīs), n. Alpine plant with white flower, growing in rocky places. [f. G *edel* noble + *weiss* white]

Ed'en (ē-), n. Abode of Adam & Eve at their creation; delightful abode; state of supreme happiness. [ME, f. LL f. Gk f. Heb. *'eden* orig. = delight]

ĕdĕn'tāte, a. & n. (Animal) without incisor & canine teeth; toothless (animal). [f. L E(*dentatus* f. *dens -ntis* tooth, see -ATE²)]

ĕdge¹, n. Sharpened side of blade of cutting instrument or weapon; sharpness of this, as *the knife has no ~*; *take the ~ off*, blunt, weaken, dull, (appetite, argument, etc.); *be on ~*, be excited or irritable; *set* (person's) *teeth on ~*, jar his nerves, affect him with repulsion; ~-shaped thing, esp. crest of a ridge; (fig.) critical position or moment; meeting-line of two surfaces of a solid; (Skating) *do the inside, outside, ~*, skate on the inner, outer, ~ *of skates*; boundary-line of surface; brink (of precipice); *have the ~*

on (sl.), have the advantage of ; ~·*bone*, see AITCH-BONE ; ~·*tool*, cutting-tool (in fig. sense also *edged tool*). Hence ~'LESS (-jl-) a. [OE *ecg*, OS *eggia*, OHG *ekka*, ON *egg* f. Gmc *agja cogn. w. L *acies* edge]

ĕdge², v.t. & i. Sharpen (tool etc., also fig.) ; ~ *on*, =EGG²*on* ; furnish with border, form border to ; insinuate, push, (thing, one*self*) *into*, *in*, *out*, *off*, etc. ; (v.i.) advance obliquely. [f. prec.]

ĕdge'ways, **-wise**, (-jwāz, -jwīz), adv. With edge uppermost or foremost ; (fig.) *get a word in* ~ (in talkative person's silent interval) ; (of two things) edge to edge. [-WAYS, -WISE]

ĕdg'ing, n. In vbl senses, esp. border, fringe ; ~·*shears* (for trimming edges of lawn). [-ING¹]

ĕdg'y̆, a. Sharp-edged ; (of painting) of too sharp outline ; having one's nerves on edge, irritable. [-Y²]

ĕd'ible, a. & n. (Thing) fit to be eaten. Hence ĕdiBIL'ITY n. [f. LL *edibilis* (*edere* eat, see -BLE)]

ĕd'ict, n. Order proclaimed by authority ; *E*~ *of Nantes*, issued by Henry IV of France to grant toleration to Protestants, and revoked by Louis XIV. Hence ĕdic'tAL a. [ME ; f. L *edictum* f. E(*dicere dict*- say) proclaim]

ĕd'ifice, n. Building (esp. large one ; also fig.). [ME, f. OF *edifice* f. L *aedificium* (*aedis* temple + -*ficium* f. *facere* make)]

ĕd'ify, v.t. Benefit spiritually ; improve morally (often iron.). So ĕdIFICA'TION n. [ME, f. OF *edifier* f. L *aedificare* (as prec., see -FY)]

ĕd'it, v.t. Prepare an edition of (another's work) ; set in order for publication (material chiefly provided by others), garble, cook, (dispatches etc. in newspaper) ; act as editor of (paper etc.). [(1) f. F *éditer* f. L (*dere dit-* = *dare* give) put out ; (2) back formation f. EDITOR]

ĕdi'tion, n. Form in which a literary work is published (*library, cabinet, popular*, ~) ; whole number of copies of book, newspaper, etc., issued from same types & at same time (see also IMPRESSION) ; (fig.) production of the same type, person etc. resembling another (*a more charming* ~ *of her sister*). [f. F *édition* f. L *editionem* (as EDIT, see -ION)]

édition de luxe (see Ap.), n. Handsome edition. [F]

ĕdī'tĭŏ prīn'cĕps (-shĭŏ,), n. First printed edition of a book. [L]

ĕd'itor, n. One who prepares the work of others for publication ; one who conducts a newspaper or periodical. Hence ~SHIP, ĕd'itRESS¹, nn. [L (as EDIT, see -OR)]

ĕditŏr'ial, a. & n. 1. Of an editor. 2. n. Newspaper article written by or under responsibility of the editor. Hence ~LY² adv. [-IAL]

ĕd'ŭclate, v.t. Bring up (young persons) ; give intellectual & moral training to ; provide schooling for ; train (person,

one*self*, a faculty, *to* do) ; train (animals). Hence ~ABIL'ITY, ~ātoR, nn., ~ABLE, ~ātive, aa. [f. L *educare* conn. w. EDUCE, see -ATE³]

ĕdŭcā'tion, n. Bringing up (of the young) ; systematic instruction ; course of this, as *classical, commercial, art*, ~ ; development of character or mental powers ; training (of animals). Hence ~AL a., ~(al)IST(3) nn., ~alLY² adv., (-shon-). [f. F, or L *educatio* (as prec., see -ATION)]

ĕdūce', v.t. Bring out, develop, from latent or potential existence ; (Chem.) disengage (substance) from a compound ; infer (number, principle, *from* data). Hence ĕdū'CIBLE a. [f. L E(*ducere duct*-lead)]

ĕd'ŭct, n. (chem.). Body disengaged from another in which it previously existed ; inference. [as prec.]

ĕdŭc'tion, n. Educing ; (in steam-engine) ~·*pipe*, -*valve*, etc., EXHAUST¹-pipe etc. [f. L *eductio* (as prec., see -ION)]

ĕdŭl'corlāte, v.t. Free from acid properties or from soluble particles, purify. Hence ~A'TION n. [f. med. L *edulcorare*, f. L *dulcorare* (*dulcor* sweetness f. *dulcis*), see -ATE³]

Edward'ian (ĕdwŏrd-), a. & n. 1. Of the time of any of the Edwards, Kings of England ; (esp.) characteristic of Edward VII's reign (1901-10). 2. n. Person belonging to this period. [-IAN]

-ee, suf. forming nn. expr. the person affected by the vbl action, corresp. to agent nn. in -*or*, prop. in legal terms on anal. of AF, as *appellor, appellee*, but extended to the indirect obj., as *lessee, vendee* ; now also in non-techn. wds, & without corresp. -*or*, as *employee, payee* ; & without consciousness of its meaning, as *bargee, absentee* ; a few wds are adoptions f. mod. F -*é*, -*ié*, as *debauchee, refugee*. In *committee* (orig. a person), accent has changed with meaning. *Epopee* is not an instance ; in *coatee*, -*ee* perh. = -Y³ ; in *settee, goatee*, -*ee* is unexplained. [AF -*é* of p.p. f. L -*atus*]

eel, n. A snake-like fish ; (fig.) slippery creature ; (pop.) minute animal found in vinegar & in sour paste ; ‖~·BUCK⁴ ; ~·*spear* (for transfixing ~s). Hence ~'Y² a. [OE *æl*, OS, OHG *āl*, ON *áll* f. Gmc *ælaz of unkn. orig.]

e'en. See EVEN¹,³.

-eer, Anglicized form of F suf. -*ier* f. L -*arius* -ARY¹, expr. person concerned with ; F -*ier* is retained in the less familiar wds (*muleteer* but *bombardier*) ; -*eer* is freely used for new nn., as *auctioneer, mountaineer*, often derog., as *sonneteer*. Vbs are also formed (*electioneer*) by back formation on *auctioneering* etc. See -IER.

e'er. See EVER.

eer'|ie, -r|y̆, a. Superstitiously timid ; strange, weird. Hence ~iLY² adv., ~iNESS n. [ME *eri*, of unkn. orig.]

ef-, pref. = EX-(1) before *f*.

efface′, v.t. Rub out; (fig.) obliterate, wipe out; utterly surpass, eclipse; treat, regard, one*self* as unimportant. Hence ~ABLE a., ~MENT (-sm-) n. [f. F *effacer* f. *ef*- EF-+*face* FACE]

effect′¹, n. Result, consequence (*cause and* ~, causation); efficacy, as *of no* ~; combination of colour or form in picture etc., as *a pretty* ~; (pl.) property, as *personal* ~*s*, *no* ~*s* (written by banker on dishonoured cheque); *give* ~ *to*, *take* ~, make, become, operative; impression produced on spectator, hearer, etc., as *calculated for* ~; *bring to*, *carry into*, ~, accomplish; *in* ~, for practical purposes. Hence ~LESS a. [ME, f. OF, or L *effectus -ūs* f. EF(*ficere fect-* = *facere* make)]

effect′², v.t. Bring about, accomplish; ~ (take out) *a policy* (of insurance). [f. prec.]

effec′tive, a. & n. 1. Having an effect; ~ *range* (of weapon), range within which it is ~; powerful in effect; striking; (of soldiers, sailors, etc.) fit for service; actual, existing. 2. n. ~ soldier, ~ part of army. Hence ~LY² (-vl-) adv., ~NESS (-vn-) n. [f. OF (-*if*, -*ive*) or L *effectivus* (as EFFECT¹, see -IVE)]

effec′tual, a. Answering its purpose; valid. Hence ~LY² adv., ~NESS n. [ME, f. OF *effectuel* f. med. L *-alis* (EFFECT¹, -AL)]

effec′tuāte, v.t. Bring to pass, accomplish. Hence ~A′TION n. [f. med. L *effectuare* (as EFFECT¹)]

effem′in|ate, a. Womanish, unmanly. Hence ~ACY n., ~ately² (-tl-) adv. [ME, f. L EF(*feminare* f. *femina* woman), see -ATE²]

effen′di, n. Turkish title of respect applied to government officials & members of learned professions. [f. Turk. *efendi* lord, corrupt. of Gk *authentēs* (see AUTHENTIC)]

eff′erent, a. (physiol.). Conveying outwards, discharging. [f. L EF(*ferre* carry), see -ENT]

efferves|ce′, v.i. Give off bubbles of gas, bubble, (often fig. of persons); (of gas) issue in bubbles. Hence ~′CENCE, ~′CENCY, nn., ~′CENT a. [f. L EF(*fervescere* incept. of *fervēre* be hot)]

effête′, a. Exhausted, worn out; feeble, incapable. Hence ~NESS (-tn-) n. [f. L EF*fetus* worn out by breeding (*fetus*)]

effica′cious (-shŭs), a. (Of thing) producing, sure to produce, desired effect. Hence or cogn. ~LY² adv., ~NESS, **eff′icACY**, nn. [f. L *efficax* (as foll., -ACIOUS)]

effi′cient (-shent), a. Productive of effect; (of persons) competent, capable; ~ CAUSE¹, that which makes a thing what it is. Hence or cogn. **effi′ciENCY** n. (also, Mech.) the ratio of useful work performed to the total energy expended, ~LY² adv., (-shen-). [ME, f. L *efficient-*, as EFFECT¹, see -ENT]

eff′igy̆, n. Portrait, image; *hang, burn,*

(person) in ~, hang, burn, his image. [f. L *effigies* (EF*fingere* fashion)]

efflores|ce′, v.t. Burst out into flower (lit. & fig.); (Chem., of crystalline substance) turn to fine powder on exposure to air, (of salts) come to the surface & there crystallize, (of ground or wall) become covered with saline particles. So ~′CENCE n., ~′CENT a. [f. L EF(*florescere* FLOURISH)]

eff′luence (-lōō-), n. Flowing out (of light, electricity, etc., or fig.); what flows out. [foll., -ENCE]

eff′luent (-lōō-), a. & n. 1. Flowing forth. 2. n. Stream flowing from larger stream, lake, sewage tank, etc. [f. L EF(*fluere flux*- flow), see -ENT]

effluv′ium (-lōō-), n. (pl. -*ia*). Exhalation affecting lungs or sense of smell; (supposed) stream of minute particles emitted by magnet etc. [L, as prec.]

eff′lux, n. Flowing out (of liquid, air, gas; also fig.); that which flows out. Hence **efflŭ′xion** (-kshon) n. [f. L *effluxus -ūs* (as prec.)]

eff′ort, n. Strenuous exertion; (of oratory etc.) display of power; (colloq.) something accomplished involving concentration or special activity (*that's a pretty good* ~). [F, f. *efforcer* f. Rom. *EX(fortiare* f. *fortis* strong)]

eff′ortless, a. Making no effort, passive; (of skill etc.) without effort, easy. [-LESS]

effron′tery (-ŭnt-), n. Shameless audacity. [f. F ¬*erie* f. *effronté* f. Rom. *exfrontatus* f. LL EF(*frons -ntis* forehead) shameless; see -ATE², -ERY]

efful′g|ent, a. Radiant. Hence ~ENCE n., ~entLY² adv. [f. L EF(*fulgēre* shine), see -ENT]

effuse′¹ (-s), a. (Bot., of inflorescence) spreading loosely; (Conch.) with lips separated by groove. [as foll.]

effuse′² (-z), v.t. Pour forth (liquid, air, light, smell; also fig.). [ME, f. L EF(*fundere fus*- pour)]

effū′sion (-zhn), n. Pouring forth (lit. & fig.); unrestrained utterance (often contempt., of literary work). [ME, f. OF, or L *effusio* (as prec., see -ION)]

effūs′ive, a. (Of speech or emotions) exuberant, demonstrative; (Geol., of an igneous rock) poured out when molten and later solidified. Hence ~LY² (-vl-) adv., ~NESS (-vn-) n. [as EFFUSE², see -IVE]

eft, n. Newt. [OE *efeta* NEWT, of unkn. orig.]

‖ **eftsōōn(s)′**, adv. (arch.). Soon afterwards. [OE *eftsōna* (see AFT & SOON); *-s* = -ES]

egăd′, int. By God. [prob. orig. *a* ah +*God*]

egălitār′ian, a. & n. 1. Of, relating to, holding, the principle of the equality of mankind. 2. n. ~ person. Hence ~ISM n. [f. F *égalitaire* f. *égal* equal]

Egēr′ia (ij-), n. A person's tutelary divinity. [name of a prophetic nymph of Roman legend, Numa's instructress]

ĕgg¹, n. Spheroidal body produced by female of birds etc. esp. of domestic fowl, containing germ of a new individual; ADDLE, WIND¹, ~; *bad* ~, person, scheme, that comes to no good; *good* ~ (sl.), excellent person or thing (also as commendatory exclamation); *as sure as* ~*s is* ~*s*, undoubtedly; *teach your grandmother to suck* ~*s*, offer advice to persons more experienced than yourself; *have all your* ~*s in one basket*, risk all on a single venture; ~ *& anchor, dart, tongue,* (Archit.) kinds of moulding; ~*-&-spoon race* (in which runners carry ~ in spoon); ~ *cleavage* (Biol.), process of cleavage in fertilized ~*-shell*; ~*-cup* (for holding ~ boiled in shell); ~*-dance*, dance blindfold among ~s, (fig.) intricate task; ~*-flip*, *-nog*, hot beer, cider, wine, etc., with ~s stirred in; *°*~*-head* (sl.), intellectual; ~*-plant*, (fruit of), white-fruited *Solanum esculentum*; ~*-shell*, shell of ~, fragile thing (~*-shell china*, very thin kind); ~*-slice*, utensil for taking omelette from pan; ~*-spoon*, small spoon for eating boiled ~s; ~*-tooth*, protuberance on bill-sheath of embryo bird for cracking shell; ~*-whisk*, utensil for beating ~s. [ME *ey* f. OE *ǣg* (= OS, OHG *ei*) superseded by ME *eg* f. ON *egg*]

ĕgg², v.t. Urge (person) *on* (*to* an act, *to* do). [f. ON *eggja* = EDGE v.]

ĕgg'er, n. Kind of large moth common in Great Britain (also ~*-moth*, *oak* ~*-moth*). [prob. f. EGG¹ + -ER (owing to egg-like appearance of cocoon)]

ĕg'lantine, n. Sweetbriar. [ME, f. OF *eglantine* f. OF *aiglent* prob. f. L *acus* needle, see -LENT]

ĕg'ō, n. (metaphys.). The conscious thinking subject, opp. to the non-ego or object. [L, = I]

ĕgocĕn'tric, a. Centred in the ego; (loosely) self-centred, egoistic. [EGO + *centric* (CENTRE¹ + -IC), after *geocentric* etc.]

ĕg'ō|ism, n. (Ethics) theory that treats self-interest as foundation of morality; systematic selfishness; self-opinionatedness; = foll. Hence ~ɪST n., ~ɪs'tɪc(AL) aa., ~is'ticalLY² adv. [f. F *égoïsme* (as EGO, see -ISM)]

ĕg'ot|ism, n. Too frequent use of 'I' & 'me'; practice of talking about oneself; self-conceit; selfishness. Hence ~ɪST n., ~is'tɪc(AL) aa., ~is'ticalLY² adv., ~ɪZE v.i. [f. EGO + -ISM; *-t-* perh. on F *idiotisme* etc.]

ĕgrē'gious (-jus), a. (Arch.) surpassing, (mod.) shocking, as ~ *folly, blunder, ass.* Hence ~LY² adv., ~NESS n. [f. L E(*gregius* f. *grex gregis* flock) lit. towering above the flock]

ĕg'rĕss, n. (Right of) going out; (Astron.) end of eclipse or transit; way out (lit. & fig.). [f. L *egressus -ūs* f. L E(*gredi gress-* = *gradi* step)]

ĕgrē'ssion (-shn). Going out or forth. [f. L *egressio* (as prec., see -ION)]

eg'rĕt (ĕg- *or* ēg·), n. Lesser white heron; feathery down on seeds of dandelion, thistle, etc. [ME; var. of AIGRETTE]

Egyp'tian (ĭjĭp'shn), a. & n. (Native) of Egypt; ||~ *printing-type* (thick-stemmed); = GIPSY (obs.). [-IAN]

Egyptŏl'ogy (ē-), n. Study of Egyptian antiquities. So ~L'OGIST n. [-O-, -LOGY]

eh (ē), int. expr. inquiry or surprise, or inviting assent. [ME *ey*]

eid'er (ī-), n. A northern species of duck; ~ (*-down*), small soft feathers from breast of this (~*-down*, also, quilt stuffed with ~-down). [ult. f. Icel. *ǣðr*]

eid'ograph (ī-; -ahf), n. Instrument for enlarging or reducing drawings. [f. Gk *eidos* form + *graphō* write]

eidōl'on (ī-), n. (pl. *-ons*, *-a*). Spectre, phantom, cf. IDOL. [Gk, see IDOL]

eight (āt), a. & n. One more than seven (8, viii); (Skat.) figure of two adjacent circles; crew of ~ in rowing-boat; || *the E~s*, boat-races at Oxford & Cambridge between such crews; || *have one over the* ~ (sl.), get rather drunk. Hence **eighᴛʜ²** (ātth) a. & n., ~h'LY² (ātth·) adv. [OE *eahta* OS, OHG *ahto*, ON *átta*, Goth. *ah'tau* f. Gmc *°ahtō-* cogn. w. L, Gk *oktō*]

eighteen' (āt-), a. & n. One more than seventeen (18, xviii); ~*mo*, = OCTODECIMO. Hence ~ᴛʜ² a. & n. [OE *e*(*a*)*htatȳne*, *-tēne* (as prec., see -TEEN)]

eight'some (āt-), n. & a. ~ (*reel*), lively Scottish reel for eight dancers. [-SOME]

eight'y (āt-), a. & n. Eight times ten (80, lxxx). Hence **eight'**ɪᴇᴛʜ (āt-) a. & n. [OE *eahtatig* (as EIGHT + -*tig* -TY²)]

eirēn'icŏn (īr-)ʻ n. Proposal tending to make peace. [Gk, neut. adj. (*eirēnē* peace, see -IC)]

eisteddfod (āstĕdh'vod), n. (pl. ~*au*). Congress of Welsh bards; local gathering for musical competitions etc. [W, lit.= session f. *eistedd* sit]

eis wool (is), n. (Also *ice wool*) very fine glossy worsted wool of two-thread thickness. [G *eis* ice]

ei'ther (īdh-, ē-), adj., pron., & adv. (conj.). 1. Each of two, as *at* ~ *end was a lamp*, ~ *view is tenable*, ~ *is tenable*; one or other of two, as *put the lamp at* ~ *end*, *there is no lamp at* ~ *end*, ~ *of you can go*. 2. adv. or conj. On one or other supposition, which way you will, as *he is* ~ *drunk or mad*, ~ *come in or go out*, (w. neg. or interrog.) any more than the other, as *if you do not go, I shall not* ~. [OE *ǣghwæther*, OHG *eogihwedar* f. WG *°aiwō gihwatharaz* ever each of two; cf. AYE, EACH, WHETHER]

ĕjăc'ŭl|āte, v.t. Utter suddenly (words or abs.); eject (fluids etc.) from the body. Hence ~A'TION n., ~ātORY a. [f. L E(*jaculari* f. *jaculum* javelin) dart]

ĕjĕct'¹, v.t. Expel (*from* place, office, property), dispossess (tenant) by legal process; dart forth, emit. Hence *or* cogn. **ĕjĕc'tion**, ~MENT, **ĕjĕc'tor**, nn. [f. L E(*jicĕre ject-* = *jacĕre* throw)]

ēj'ĕct², n. Something inferred, not an actual nor a conceivable object of our own consciousness. [f. L *ejectum* neut. p.p. of *ejicere* (see prec.)]

ĕjĕc'tive, a. Tending to eject; pertaining to an eject. Hence~LY² (-vl-) adv. [-IVE]

ēke¹, v.t. ~ *out*: supplement (defective means etc. *with*); (improp.) contrive to make (livelihood) or support (existence). [OE *ēacan*, OS *ōkian*, OHG *ouhhōn*, ON *auka*, Goth. *aukan* f. Gmc *aukan* cogn. w. L *augēre*]

ēke², adv. (arch.). Also. [OE *ēac*, OS *ōk*, OHG *ouh*, ON, Goth. *auk*; of disputed orig., perh. cogn. w. prec.]

ĕkk'a, n. (Anglo-Ind.). Small one-horse Indian vehicle; similar cart drawn by bullock. [Hind.]

-el. See -LE(1) & (2).

ĕlăb'orate¹, a. Carefully or minutely worked out; highly finished. Hence ~LY² (-tl-) adv., ~NESS (-tn-) n. [f. L E(*laborare* f. *labor* work), see -ATE²]

ĕlăb'or|āte², v.t. Produce by labour; work out (invention, theory, etc.) in detail; (of natural agencies) produce (substance etc.) from its elements or sources. Hence or cogn. ~A'TION n., ~ATIVE a. [as prec., -ATE³]

ĕlaeo-, comb. form of Gk *elaion* oil, as ~*meter*, instrument for determining purity of oils.

ĕlan (see Ap.), n. Vivacity; impetuous rush. [F]

ĕl'and, n. S.-African antelope of heavy build. [Du., = elk]

ĕlăpse', v.i. (Of time) pass away. [f. L E(*labi laps-* glide)]

ĕlăs'tic (or -lah-), a. & n. 1. Spontaneously resuming its normal bulk or shape after contraction, dilatation, or distortion (of solids, liquids, & gases); springy; (of feelings or persons) buoyant; flexible, adaptable, as ~ *conscience*; ~*-side boots* or ~*-sides*, 19th-c. boots with ~ web at sides instead of buttons or laces. 2. n. ~ cord or string, usu. woven with india-rubber. Hence **ĕlăs'tically** adv., **ĕlăsti'city** n. [f. Gk *elastikos* impulsive (*elaunō* drive)]

ĕlāte', v.t., & a. 1. Inspirit, stimulate, (esp. in p.p.); make proud. 2. adj. (arch.). In high spirits, exultant, proud. So **ĕlā'tion** n. [ME, f. L E*fferre* E*lat-* raise]

ĕl'bow¹ (-ō), n. Outer part of joint between fore & upper arm; ~*-shaped* bend or corner; *at* one's ~, close at hand; *lift* one's ~, drink too much; *up to the* ~*s*, busily engaged *in*; *out at* ~*s*, (of coat) worn-out, (of person) poor; ~*-grease*, vigorous polishing, hard work; ~*-room*, plenty of room. [OE *elnboga*, OHG *elinbogo*, ON *ǫlnbogi* f. Gmc *alino-bogan* (see ELL & BOW¹)]

ĕl'bow² (-ō), v.t. & i. Thrust, jostle, (person, one*self*, *into*, *in*, etc.; also intr.). [f. prec.]

ĕl'chee (-ǐ), n. Ambassador. [f. Turk. *ilchi* representative of a tribe (*il*)]

‖ **ĕld**, n. (arch., poet., dial.). Old age; the olden time. [OE *eldo*, OS *eldi*, OHG *elti*, ON *elli* f. Gmc *althi* f. *althaz* OLD]

ĕl'der¹, a. & n. 1. (The) senior (of relations, or of two indicated persons), as *his* ~ *brother*, *which is the* ~?; (Cards) ~ *hand*, first player; ‖ ~ *brother of Trinity House*, each of thirteen senior members of this corporation who sit as Nautical Assessors in navigation cases (usu. pl., ~ *brethren*); *E*~ STATESMAN. 2. n. (Pl.) persons of greater age, as *respect your* ~*s*; person advanced in life; member of a senate; official in early Christian Church (= Gk *presbuteros*), & in some Protestant (esp. Presbyterian) churches, whence ~SHIP n. [OE *eldra*, comp. of OLD, see -ER³]

ĕl'der², n. Low white-flowered tree; ~(*-berry*) *wine* (made from fruit of this). [OE *ellærn*, MLG *ellern*, *elderne*]

ĕl'derly, a. Getting old. [ELDER¹ + -LY¹]

ĕl'dĕst, a. First-born or oldest surviving (member of family, son, daughter, etc.). [OE *eldest* superl. of OLD, see -EST]

El Dorad'o (ĕldorahd'ō), n. (pl. ~*s*). Fictitious country or city abounding in gold. [Sp., = the gilded]

ĕl'dritch, a. (Sc.). Weird, hideous. [orig. unkn.]

Elĕăt'ic (ĕl-), a. & n. 1. Relating to Elea, an ancient Greek city in S.W. Italy, or the school of philosophers who were born or lived there about the 6th c. B.C., esp. Zenophanes, Parmenides, & Zeno. 2. n. An~ philosopher. [f. L *Eleaticus* f. *Elea*]

ĕlĕcămpāne', n. Plant with bitter aromatic leaves & root; sweetmeat flavoured with this. [corrupt. of med. L *enula* (for L' *inula*) *campana* (prob. = of the fields)]

ĕlĕct'¹, a. Chosen; select, choice; (Theol.) chosen by God, as *the* ~; chosen to office etc., as *bride* ~. [ME, f. L E(*ligere lect-* = *legere* pick)]

ĕlĕct'², v.t. Choose (thing, *to* do); choose (person) by vote, as ~ *a magistrate*, ~ *him to the magistracy*, ~ *him* (*to be*) *magistrate*; (Theol., of God) choose (persons) in preference to others for salvation. [as prec.]

ĕlĕc'tion, n. Choosing, esp. by vote; *general* ~ (of representatives, esp. members of House of Commons, throughout the country), ‖ *by*~ (of M.P. to fill vacancy); (Theol.) see prec. [ME, f. OF f. L *electionem* (as prec., see -ION)]

ĕlĕctioneer' (-shon-), v.i., & n. Busy oneself in political elections; (n.) one who ~*s*. [prec. + -EER]

ĕlĕc'tive, a. (Of official, office, authority) appointed by, filled up by, derived from, election; having power to elect; (Chem.) ~ *affinity*, tendency to combine with some substances rather than others. Hence ~LY² (-vl-) adv. [f. F *électif -ive* f. LL *electivus* (as ELECT¹, -IVE)]

ĕlĕc'tor, n. One who has right of election (esp. of M.P.); (hist.) German Prince entitled to share in election of Emperor, Hence ~AL a., ~SHIP n. [ME; L (as ELECT¹, -OR)]

ĕlĕc'torate, n. Dignity, dominions, of German Elector; body of electors. [-ATE¹]

ĕlĕc'trĕss, n. Female elector; wife of German Elector. [as prec. +-ESS¹]

ĕlĕc'tric, a. & n. 1. Of, charged with, capable of developing, electricity; ~ *blanket* (heated by ~ current); ~ *blue*, steely blue; ~ *chair* (used in an electrocution); ~ *eel*, one able to give ~ shock; ~ *light* (produced by electricity); ~ *shock*, effect of sudden discharge of electricity; ~ *storm*, violent disturbance of the earth's electrical condition; ~ *torch*, portable ~ lamp operated by a dry battery in its holder. 2. n. Substance in which ~ force can be excited by friction. Hence **ĕlĕc'trICALLY** adv., **ĕlĕctrI'CIAN** (-shn) n. [f. mod. L *electricus* f. L f. Gk *ēlektron* amber, see -IC]

ĕlĕc'trical, a. Relating to electricity (rare in other senses of prec.). [-AL]

ĕlĕctri'cĭtў, n. 1. (Prop. *static*~) abnormal condition of the atoms or molecules of a body usu. due to an excess or deficiency of electrons; various kinds were formerly distinguished by the methods of production, as *frictional* ~ (by friction), *galvanic* ~ (by chemical action), *thermal* ~ (by heat), *magnetic* ~ (by magnetism), or by the substances in which they were produced, as *vitreous* ~ (in glass), *resinous* ~ (in resin); but only two kinds are now recognized in ordinary use, *positive* ~, a deficiency of electrons, and *negative* ~, an excess of electrons. 2. Movement of electrons or electrons moving along a conductor. 3. Science of static ~ or of electric currents. [-ITY]

ĕlĕctrificā'tion, n. Electrifying; conversion of steam railway into electric. [as foll., see -FICATION]

ĕlĕc'trifў, v.t. Charge (body) with electricity; subject (person etc.) to electric shock; convert (railways, transport, manufactures, etc.) to electric working; (fig.) startle, excite. [f. ELECTRIC + -FY]

ĕlĕc'trīz|e, -is|e (-īz), v.t. = prec. Hence ~A'TION n. [as prec. +-IZE]

ĕlĕc'trō, n., & v.t., (colloq.). = ELECTRO- *plate, type.* [abbr.]

ĕlĕc'tro-, comb. form of Gk *ēlektron*, taken as meaning 'electricity'. Of, pertaining to, caused by, electricity, as: ~*biol'ogy*, science of the electrical phenomena of living beings; ~*card'iogram*, record of the sequence of electrical waves generated at each heartbeat, used in diagnosis of heart disorders, recorded by an ~*card'iograph*; ~*chem'istry*, electricity as applied to chemistry; ~*dynām'ics*, dynamics of electricity; ~*kĭnĕt'ics*, science of electricity in motion; ~*logy* (-ŏl²), electric

science; ~*lўsis* (-ŏl²), chemical decomposition by electric action, science of this, (Surg.) breaking up of tumours or calculi by electric agency; ~*lўse* (-z), decompose thus; ~*lўtc*, any liquid or solution chemically changed by passage of electric current, any substance forming such a solution with water or another liquid; ~*magnĕt'ic*, having both electrical and magnetic character or effects (applied esp. to waves or radiations which travel with the same velocity as light); ~*mǎg'netism* production of magnetism by electric current; ~*meter* (-ŏm²), instrument measuring electricity; ~*mō'tion*, motion of electric current, mechanical motion produced by electricity; ~*mōt'ive*, producing, tending to produce, an electric current; ~*mōt'or*, machine for using electricity as motive power; ~*nĕg'ative*, ~*pos'itive*, of negative, positive, electricity; ~*pathy* (-ŏp²), electrical treatment of disease; ~*phōre*, ~*phorus* (-ŏf²), instrument for generating statical electricity by induction; ~*plāte*, (v.t.) coat with silver by ~lysis, (n.) ware thus produced; ~*scōpe*, instrument indicating presence or quality of electricity; ~*stăt'ics*, science of statical electricity; ~*thĕ'rapy*, cure of diseases by electrical treatment (hence ~*thĕ'rapist*); ~*therm'al*, relating to heat electrically derived; ~*tonus* (-ōt²), condition of motor nerve under electric current; ~*tўpe*, (n.) model, copy, formed by deposition of copper on a mould by electrolytic action, esp. for printing, (v.t.) copy thus.

ĕlĕctrocū'tion, n. Killing by electricity (as capital punishment); (transf.) death caused in any way by electricity. Hence **ĕlĕc'trocūte** v.t. [f. prec., suggested by *execution*]

ĕlĕc'trōde, n. Conductor through which electricity enters or leaves an electrolyte, gas, vacuum, or other medium. [ELECTRO- + Gk *hodos* way]

ĕlĕctrolier', n. Cluster of electric lamps. [f. ELECTRO- on *chandelier*]

ĕlĕc'trŏn, n. (phys., chem.). Indivisible unit of negative electricity and one of the fundamental constituents of matter, normally rotating (in numbers constant for each element) about the positive nucleus of every atom. Hence **ĕlĕctrŏn'ic** a., also n. pl., branch of physics and technology dealing with behaviour of ~s esp. in a vacuum, e.g. in radio valves, X-ray tubes, etc. [f. ELECTRO- or ELECTRIC, with Gk -*on* appended]

ĕlĕc'trum, n. Alloy of silver & gold used by the ancients; (Mineral.) native argentiferous gold ore. [L, f. Gk *ēlektron* amber, ~]

ĕlĕc'tūarў, n. Medicinal powder etc. mixed with honey or syrup. [ME, f. LL *electuarium* perh. corrupt. of Gk *ekleikton* (*ekleikhō* lick out)]

ĕlēēmŏs'ўnarў (*or* -z-), a. Of, dependent

on, alms; charitable; gratuitous. [f. med.
L *eleemosynarius* (as ALMS, see -ARY¹)]

ĕl'ĕgant, a. & n. (Of movements, style,
author, manners) graceful; tasteful;
refined; (of modes of life etc.) of refined
luxury; (vulg.) excellent; (n.) person
with pretensions to taste & fashion.
Hence or cogn. **ĕl'ĕgANCE** n., **~LY²** adv.
[f. F *élégant* or L *elegant-*, cf. ELECT¹]

ĕlĕgí'ăc, a. & n. 1. (Of metre) suited to
elegies, esp. ~ *couplet*, (usu. Gk or Lat.)
dactylic hexameter & pentameter;
mournful. 2. n. pl. ~ verses. [f. LL f. Gk
elegeiakos (as ELEGY, see -AC)]

ĕl'ĕgīze, –ise (-īz), v.i. & t. Write an elegy
(*upon*); write in mournful strain; write an
elegy upon. [-IZE]

ĕl'ĕgy̆, n. Song of lamentation, esp. for
the dead (often vaguely used of other
poems); poem in elegiac metre. [f. F
élégie f. L f. Gk *elegeia* (*elegos* mournful
poem)]

ĕl'ĕment, n. 1. Component part, as *reduced to its ~s*, analysed, *the ~s of national
wealth*, *there was an ~ of cant, cant was a
notable ~, in his style*. 2. (chem.). Any of
the substances that cannot be resolved by
chemical means into simpler substances.
3. Any of *the four ~s*, viz. earth, water,
air, fire (hist.); one of these as a being's
abode or sphere, as (usu. fig.) *in, out, of,
his ~*. 4. Atmospheric agencies, as *war of
the ~s*. 5. (electr.). Resistance wire in an
electric heater; electrode. 6. pl. Rudiments of learning (i.e. the A B C) or of an
art or science; *Euclid's E~s* (of Geometry). [ME, f. OF, f. L *elementum*]

ĕlĕmĕn'tal, a. & n. 1. Of the four elements; of the powers of nature, as ~
worship; comparable to these, as ~
grandeur, tumult; uncompounded; essential. 2. n. (theosoph.). Spirit of earth, air,
etc. [prec. +-AL]

ĕlĕmĕn'tar|y̆, a. Rudimentary, intro-
ductory; (Chem.) not decomposable.
Hence **~ĭLY²** adv., **~ĭNESS** n. [f. L *ele-
mentarius* (as ELEMENT, see -ARY¹)]

ĕl'ĕmĭ, n. A stimulant resin used in ointments, varnish, etc. [= F *élémi*, Sp.
elemi, f. Arab. *al-lami*]

ĕlĕn'chus (-ngk-), n. (pl. *-chī*). Logical
refutation; *Socratic ~*, mode of eliciting
truth by short question & answer. [L, f.
Gk *elegkhos*]

ĕlĕnc'tic (-ngk-), a. Of, given to, refutation or cross-examination. [f. Gk
elegktikos (*elegkhō* refute, as prec., see
-IC)]

ĕl'ĕphant, n. 1. Huge four-footed pachy-
derm with proboscis & long curved ivory
tusks; *white ~*, burdensome possession
(from cost of maintenance). 2. Size of
paper (28 × 23 in.; *double ~*, 40 × 26½).
Hence **ĕlĕphăn'toID** a. [ME *oli-, ele-
faunte* f. OF *oli-, elefant*, f. L *elephan-
tus, -ntem* (nom. *-phas*), f. Gk *elephas
-antos*]

ĕlĕphăntī'asĭs, n. Skin disease causing

part affected to resemble elephant's hide.
[L f. Gk (as prec., see -ASIS)]

ĕlĕphăn'tine, a. Of elephants; ~ *epoch*
(when large pachydermata abounded);
clumsy, unwieldy, as ~ *movements,
humour, task*. [f. L f. Gk *elephantinos* (as
prec., -INE²)]

Eleusĭn'ĭan (ĕ-), a. ~ *mysteries* (of
Demeter, celebrated at Eleusis in Attica).
[f. L f. Gk *Eleusinios* (*Eleusis -inos*) +-AN]

ĕleuth'ero– in comb. = Gk *eleutheros* free,
as **~mān'ia**, mad zeal for freedom,
~phy̆ll'ous, with distinct leaves.

ĕl'ĕvāt|e, v.t. Lift up; hold up (the Host)
for adoration; raise (one's eyes, voice,
hopes); raise axis of (gun); exalt in rank
etc.; raise morally or intellectually (aims,
style; esp. in p.p.); (p.p., colloq.) slightly
drunk. Hence **~ORY** a. [f. L E(*levare* lift
f. *levis* light), see -ATE³]

ĕlĕvā'tion, n. Elevating, being elevated,
(in all senses); angle (esp. of gun) with
the horizontal; height above given (esp.
sea) level; drawing made in projection on
vertical plane, flat drawing of front, side,
or back, of house etc.; grandeur, dignity.
[f. OF, or L *elevatio* (as prec., see -ATION)]

ĕl'ĕvātor, n. Person, thing, device, that
elevates; muscle that raises limb etc.;
machine for hoisting grain etc.; *lift.
[L (as prec., see -OR)]

ĕlĕv'en, a. & n. One more than ten (11, xi,
XI); *an ~*, ~ persons forming side at
cricket etc.; *the E~* (disciples, without
Judas); ∥ ~*s(es)* n. (colloq.), light refreshment about 11 a.m. So **~TH²** a. & n. (*the
~th* HOUR). [OE *endleofon*, OS *elleban*,
OHG *einlif*, ON *ellifu*, Goth. *ainlif* f.
Gmc *ainas* ONE +-*lif* (perh. = one *left
over* (ten))]

ĕlf, n. (pl. *elves*). (Teut. Myth.) a supernatural being; mischievous creature;
dwarf; little creature; ~*-bolt*, flint arrow-
-head; ~*-lock*, tangled mass of hair; ~*-
-struck*, bewitched. Hence **ĕl'fISH¹, ĕl'v-
ISH¹**, aa. [OE *elf* (= MHG *elbe*) & *ælf*
= OS *alf*, MHG *alp*, ON *álfr* f. Gmc
albh-]

ĕl'fin, a. & n. Of elves, elfish; (n.) dwarf,
child. [f. prec., *-in* unexpl.]

ĕli'cit, v.t. Draw forth (what is latent,
usu. fig.); educe (truths *from* data), draw
out, evoke, (admission, answer *from*
person). [f. L E(*licere licit-* for *lacere*
entice)]

ĕlide', v.t. Omit (vowel, syllable) in pronunciation. [f. L E(*lidere lis-* = *laedere*
dash)]

ĕl'ĭgĭ|ble, a. Fit to be chosen (*for* office
etc.); desirable, suitable. Hence **~BIL'ITY**
n., **~bLY²** adv. [f. F *éligible* or LL *eligi-
bilis* (ELECT¹, -BLE)]

ĕlĭm'ĭn|āte, v.t. Remove, get rid of;
(Physiol., Chem.) expel (waste matter
from tissues, substance *from* a compound); ignore (part of question etc.);
(Alg.) get rid of (quantities) from equation; (improp.) extract (desired element

from compound, also fig.). So ~ABLE a., ~A'TION n., ~ātoR n., (esp.) apparatus enabling a wireless set to use current from electric main, so ~ating any or all of its batteries. [f. L E(liminare f. limen -minis threshold), see -ATE³]

éli'sion (-zhn), n. Suppression of vowel or syllable in pronouncing, (rarely) of passage in book etc. [f. LL elisio (as ELIDE, see -ION)]

élite (ēlēt'), n. The choice part, the best, (of). [F]

élix'ir (-er), n. Alchemist's preparation designed to change metals into gold or (also ~ of life) to prolong life indefinitely; sovereign remedy; PAREGORIC ~. [ME, f. med. L, f. Arab. aliksir the elixir (iksir prob. f. late Gk xērion desiccative powder)]

Elizabeth'an (I-), a. & n. (Person, writer) of the time of Queen Elizabeth I. [-AN]

élk, n. Large animal of the deer kind found in N. Europe and (also moose) N. America; species of deer & antelope; ~-hound, large Scandinavian shaggy-coated hunting dog. [15th c. elke prob. repr. OE elh, eolh; further hist. obsc.]

éll, n. Measure of length (English ~, = 45 in.; now obs. as measure); give him an inch (a little) & he'll take an ~ (much). [OE eln, OHG elina, ON ölnₗ Goth. aleina f. Gmc *alinā cogn. w. L ulna]

éllipse'¹, n. Regular oval; figure produced when a cone is cut by a plane making smaller angle with the base than the side of the cone makes, whence éllipti'cITY n.; = foll. Hence or cogn. éllip'tic(al¹) aa., -ically¹ adv. [f. Gk elleipsis f. elleipō come short (en in + leipō leave)]

éllip'sis, éllipse'², n. (pl. -pses, pron. -psēz). Omission from sentence of words needed to complete construction or sense. So éllip'tical² a., -ically² adv. [as prec.; cf. ECLIPSE¹]

éllip'soid, n. Solid of which all plane sections through one axis are ellipses & through the other ellipses or circles. [-OID]

élm, n. Tree with rough doubly serrated leaves. Hence ~'Y² a. [OE, OHG elm, cogn. w. ON almr, L ulmus]

El'mō (ě-), n. St ~, pop. name for St Peter Gonzalez (d. 1246), Spanish Dominican preacher who became patron saint of seamen; St ~'s fire, CORPOSANT, interpreted as a sign of his protection, though occas. of impending disaster (dead-fire).

élocū'tion (ē- or ě-), n. Manner, style, art, of oral delivery. Hence ~ARY¹a., ~IST(3) n., (-shon-). [f. L elocutio f. E(loqui locutspeak), see -ION]

éloge (ělōzh'), n. Discourse in honour of deceased person (esp. member of French Academy, pronounced by his successor). [F]

Elō'hist (ē-), n. Author(s) of the elohistic parts of the Hexateuch, marked by use

of Elohim for Yahveh (Jehovah). [f. Heb. elohim God+-IST]

él'ŏngate (-ngg-), v.t. & i., & a. 1. (-āt). Lengthen, prolong; (Bot.) be of slender or tapering form. 2. adj. (-at; Bot., Zool.) long, slender, tapering. [f. LL E(longare f. longus long), see -ATE³,²]

élŏngā'tion (-ngg-), n. Lengthening; the part (of line etc.) produced; (Astron.) angular distance of planet from sun. [f. LL elongatio (as prec., see -ATION)]

élōpe', v.i. (Of woman) run away from husband or home (with paramour, lover); abscond. Hence ~MENT (-pm-) n. [AF aloper perh. f. ME *alope p.p. of *aleapen (a- = and- against+LEAP), cf. G entlaufen run away]

él'oquence, n. Fluent, forcible, & apt use of language; rhetoric. So él'oquENT a., él'oquentLY² adv. [ME, f. OF f. L eloquentia f. E(loqui speak), see -ENCE]

élse, adv. (Following indef. or interrog. pron.) besides, in addition, as any one, anybody, anything, ~, who ~? who ~'s?, whose ~?; (same constr.) instead, as what ~ could I say?; otherwise, if not, as run, (or) ~ you will be late; ~'where, in, to, some other place. [OE, OHG elles, OSw. äljes gen. sing. cogn. w. Goth. aljis other, L alius]

élu'cid|āte (-ōō-, -ū-), v.t. Throw light on, explain. Hence ~A'TION, ~ātoR, nn., ~ātIVE, ~ātoRY, aa. [f. LL E(lucidare f. lucidus bright f. lux lucis light)]

élude' (-ōōd, -ūd), v.t. Escape adroitly from (blow, danger, difficulty, person's grasp, person, inquiry, observation); avoid compliance with (law, request) or fulfilment of (obligation); escape from, baffle, (the understanding). So élu'sIon (-lōōzhn or -lū-), élus'ivENESS, nn., élus'ivE, élus'ORY, aa., élus'ivELY² adv., (-lōō- or -lū-). [f. L E(ludere lus- play)]

él'van, n. Hard rock of igneous origin; broad vein or dyke of this. [perh. f. Corn. elven spark]

él'ver, n. A young eel. [var. of eel-FARE³ = brood of young eels]

elvish. See ELF.

Élysée (ālēzā'), n. Official residence of French President. [F]

Élys'i|um (ĭlĭz-), n. (Gk Myth.) abode of the blessed after death; place, state, of ideal happiness. Hence ~AN a. [f. L f. Gk Elusion (ē-) (pedion plain)]

él'ytron, n. (pl. -ra). Outer hard wing-case of coleopterous insect; the vagina. [f. Gk elutron sheath (eluō roll round)]

El'zevir (ě-; -er), a. & n. (Book) printed by Elzevier family at Amsterdam, The Hague, etc. (1592-1680); a printing type.

ěm, n. The letter M; (Typog.) unit for measuring amount of printed matter in line.

'em pron. (colloq.). Them. [orig. a form of ME hem, dat. & acc. 3rd pers. pl.; now regarded as abbr. of them]

em-, pref. = EN- before b, p, & (freq.) m.

Nearly all E wds with this pref. have (or formerly have had) alternative forms in IM-.

ĕmă'ci|āte (-shĭ-), v.t. Make lean, waste, (esp. in p.p.); impoverish (soil). So ~A'TION (-sĭ-) n. [f. L E(*maciare* f. *macies* leanness), see -ATE[3]]

ĕm'anāte, v.i. Issue, originate, (*from* source, person, etc.); (of gases, light, etc.) proceed, issue, (*from*). [f. L E(*manare* flow), see -ATE[3]]

ĕmanā'tion, n. Issuing (*from*); thing proceeding from a source (esp. fig., of virtues, qualities, moral powers); person, thing, proceeding from the Divine Essence. So **ĕm'anātIVE** a. [f. LL *emanatio* (as prec., see -ATION)]

ĕmăn'cĭpāt|e, v.t. (Rom. Law) release (child, wife) from power of *pater familias*; free from legal, social, political, intellectual, or moral restraint. Hence ~OR n., ~ORY a. [f. L E(*mancipare* f. *manceps* purchaser f. *manus* hand +*capere* take), -ATE[3]]

ĕmăncipā'tion, n. Setting free, esp. from slavery or from legal disabilities, whence ~IST (-shon-) n.; setting free, freedom, from intellectual or moral fetters. [f. L *emancipatio* (prec. -ATION)]

ĕmăn'cĭpist, n. (Austral.; hist.). Ex-convict who has served his term. [f. EMANCIPATE +-IST]

ĕmăs'cŭlāte[1], a. Castrated; effeminate. [f. L E(*masculare* f. *masculus* dim. of *mas* male), see -ATE[2]]

ĕmăs'cŭl|āte[2], v.t. Castrate; weaken, make effeminate; impoverish (language); weaken (literary composition) by excisions. Hence ~A'TION n., ~ātIVE, ~ātORY aa. [as prec., see -ATE[3]]

ĕmbalm' (-ahm), v.t. Preserve (corpse) from decay orig. with spices, now by means of arterial injection; preserve from oblivion; endue with balmy fragrance. Hence ~MENT (-ahm-m-) n. [ME *embaume* f. OF EM(*baumer*, as BALM)]

ĕmbănk', v.t. Shut in, confine, (river etc.) by banks, raised stone structure, etc. Hence ~MENT n., (also) structure of earth etc. to carry a railway, road, etc. [EM-]

ĕmbärg'ō, n. (pl. ~*es*), & v.t. 1. Order forbidding ships of a foreign power to enter, or any ships to leave, the country's ports; suspension of (a branch of) commerce, as *be under, lay on, an* ~; impediment. 2. v.t. Lay (ships, trade) under ~; seize (ship, goods) for State service. [Sp., f. *embargar* f. Rom. *IMbarricare* (*barra* BAR[1])]

ĕmbärk', v.t. & i. Put, go, on board ship (*for* destination), whence **ĕmbärka'TION** n.; engage (*in, upon*, undertaking, war, etc.). [f. F *embarquer* f. *en* EM- +*barque* BARK[3]]

embarras de choix, de richesse (ahṅbahrah' de shwah', de rĕshĕs'), n. More alternatives, wealth, than one knows how to deal with. [F]

ĕmbă'rrass, v.t. Encumber, impede; (p.p.) encumbered with debts; complicate (question etc.); perplex. Hence ~ingLY[2] adv.,~MENT n. [f. F *embarrasser* f. Sp. *embarazar* (EM-, BAR[2])]

ĕm'bassy, n. Ambassador's function or office; his residence; deputation to a sovereign etc. [f. OF *ambassee* f. med. L *ambasciata* (LL *ambascia* order, duty), f. Rom. *ambactiare* see AMBASSADOR]

ĕmbăt'tle[1], v.t. Set (army) in battle array. [ME, f. OF EM(*bataillier* f. *bataille* BATTLE)]

ĕmbăt'tle[2], v.t. Furnish (building, wall) with battlements. [ME, f. EM- +OF *batailler* (-*eill*-), see BATTLEMENT]

ĕmbay', v.t. Lay (vessel) within a bay; (of wind) force (vessel) into a bay; enclose as in a bay, shut in. Hence ~MENT n. [EM-]

ĕmbĕd', **im-**, v.t. (-dd-). Fix firmly in surrounding mass (esp. in p.p.); (of the mass) surround thus. [EM-]

ĕmbĕll'ish, v.t. Beautify, adorn; heighten (narrative) with fictitious additions. Hence ~MENT n. [ME, f. OF EM(*bellir* f. *bel* f. L *bellus* handsome), see -ISH[2]]

ĕm'ber[1], n. (usu. pl.). Small piece of live coal or wood in dying fire (& fig.). [OE *æmerge*, OHG *eimuria* pyre, ON *eimyrja* embers; -*b*- as in *slumber*]

ĕm'ber[2], a. ~ *days*, days of fasting and prayer, the Wed., Fri., & Sat., after (1) 1st Sun. in Lent, (2) Whitsunday, (3) Holy Cross Day (Sep. 14), and (4) St Lucia's day (Dec. 13). [OE *ymbren* n. perh. f. *ymbryne* period (*ymb* about +*ryne* course)]

ĕm'ber[3], n. (Usu. ~-*goose, -diver*) an Orkney sea fowl, the loon. [f. Norw. *emmer*]

ĕmbĕz'zle, v.t. Divert (money etc., also abs.) fraudulently to one's own use. Hence ~MENT (-zelm-) n. [f. AF *enbesiler* f. OF *besillier* maltreat, ravage, of unkn. orig.]

ĕmbitt'er, v.t. Make bitter (fig.); aggravate (evil); exasperate (person, feeling). Hence ~MENT n. [EM-]

ĕmblāz'on, v.t. Portray conspicuously, as on heraldic shield; adorn (shield) with heraldic devices (also fig.); celebrate, extol. Hence ~MENT n. [EM-]

ĕmblāz'onrỹ, n. = BLAZONRY. [EM-]

ĕm'blēm, n., & v.t. 1. Symbol, typical representation; (arch.) pictorial parable; (of person) type of (a quality); heraldic device. 2. v.t. Symbolize, show forth by ~. [(vb f. n.) f. L f. Gk *emblēma* -*matos* insertion f. EM(*ballō* throw)]

ĕmblĕmăt'ic(al), aa. Serving as a type (*of*). Hence **ĕmblĕmăt'icalLY**[2] adv. [prec., -IC]

ĕmblĕm'atist, n. Maker of emblems or of allegories. [as prec. +-IST]

ĕmblĕm'atize, -ise (-īz), v.t. Serve as emblem of; represent by an emblem. [as prec. +-IZE]

ĕm'blĕment, n. (legal; usu. pl.). Profits

of sown land; natural products of soil. [f. OF *emblaement* f. *emblaer* f. med. L ɪᴍʜ*ládare* sow with wheat (*bladum*), see -ᴍᴇɴᴛ]

ĕmbŏd′|y̆, v.t. Clothe (spirit) with body; give concrete form to (ideas etc.); express tangibly (principles *in* actions etc.); (of things) be an expression of (ideas etc.); form into a body; include, comprise. Hence ~ɪᴍᴇɴᴛ n. [ᴇᴍ-]

ĕmbŏg′, v.t. (-gg-). Plunge into, hamper in, a bog (lit. & fig.). [ᴇᴍ-]

ĕmbŏl′den, v.t. Make bold, encourage (often *to* do). [ᴇᴍ-+ʙᴏʟᴅ+-ᴇɴ⁶]

ĕm′bolĭsm, n. Obstruction of artery etc. by clot of blood etc., esp. as cause of paralysis. [14th c. 'intercalation' f. LL f. Gk *embolismus*; in medical sense f. *embolus* (L f. Gk 'peg', 'stopper')+ -ɪsᴍ]

embonpoint (see Ap.), n. Plumpness (chiefly of women; usu. euphem.). [F, f. phr. *en bon point* in good condition]

ĕmbos′om (-ŏŏz-), v.t. Embrace; (p.p.) enclosed *in*, surrounded *with*, (trees, hills, etc.). [ᴇᴍ-]

ĕmbŏss′, v.t. Carve, mould, in relief; cause figures etc. to stand out on (surface); make protuberant. Hence ~ᴍᴇɴᴛ n. [ᴍᴇ; prob. f. OF *ᴇᴍ*bocer* (see ʙᴏss¹)]

embouchure (see Ap.), n. Mouth of river; opening of valley; (Mus.) part of musical instrument applied to mouth, mode of applying this. [F]

ĕmbow′ĕl, v.t. (-ll-). Remove the bowels from (body). [f. OF ᴇɴ*boweler* for *es-boueler* (*es-* = ᴇx-+*bouel* ʙᴏᴡᴇʟ)]

ĕmbow′er, v.t. Enclose as in bower. [ᴇᴍ-]

ĕmbrāce′, v.t., & n. **1.** Fold (person etc.; in pl. abs. = ~ one another) in the arms, usu. as sign of affection; clasp, enclose; accept eagerly (offer, opportunity, etc.); adopt (course of action, doctrine, party, cause); (of things) include, comprise; (of persons) comprise (thing *in* a formula, report, etc.); take in with eye or mind. **2.** n. Folding in the arms, (euphem.) sexual intercourse. Hence ~ᴀʙʟᴇ a., ~ᴍᴇɴᴛ (-sm-) n. [ᴍᴇ; (n. f. vb) f. OF ᴇᴍ(*bracer* f. L *bracchium* arm)]

ĕmbranch′ment (-ah-), n. Branching out (of arm of river etc.). [ᴇᴍ-+ʙʀᴀɴᴄʜ n.+-ᴍᴇɴᴛ]

ĕmbrăng′le (-nggl), **ĭm-**, v.t. Entangle, confuse. Hence ~ᴍᴇɴᴛ (-nggelm-) n. [ᴇᴍ-+obs. *brangle*]

ĕmbrā′sure (-zher; *also* ĕmbrazhoor′), n. Bevelling off of wall at sides of door or window, splaying; opening in parapet for gun, widening from within. [F, f. *embraser* splay, of unkn. orig.]

ĕm′brocāte, v.t. Bathe, foment, (limb etc.) to mitigate disease. [f. LL *embrocare* f. *embrocha* f. Gk *embrokhē* f. ᴇᴍ(*brekhō* wet)]

ĕmbrocā′tion, n. Liquid used for rubbing affected part. [as prec., see -ᴀᴛɪᴏɴ]

ĕmbroid′er, v.t. Ornament (cloth etc.,

or abs.) with needlework; embellish (narrative) with fictitious additions. [ᴍᴇ, f. AF *enbrouder* = OF *brouder* whence *broider*; -*er* perh. after foll.]

ĕmbroid′ery̆, n. Embroidering; embroidered work; adventitious ornament. [ᴍᴇ, f. AF *enbrouderie* (prec., -ᴇʀʏ)]

ĕmbroil′, v.t. Bring (affairs, narrative, etc.) into state of confusion; involve (person) in hostility (*with* another). Hence ~ᴍᴇɴᴛ n. [f. F ᴇᴍ(*brouiller*, see ʙʀᴏɪʟ¹)]

ĕmbrown′, v.t. Make brown. [ᴇᴍ-]

ĕm′bry̆ŏ, n. & a. (pl. -*os*). **1.** Offspring of animal before birth (or emergence from egg); thing in rudimentary stage; *in* ~, undeveloped. **2.** adj. Undeveloped. Hence **ĕmbry̆ŏn′ɪᴄ** a. [LL *embryo -onis* erron. f. Gk ᴇᴍ(*bruŏn* f. *bruŏ* swell, grow)]

ĕmbry̆o- in comb. = prec., as ~*ctony* (-ŏk⁴), destruction of foetus in womb, ~*gĕn′esis*, formation of embryo, ~*logy* (-ŏl⁴), science of the embryo, ~*tomy* (-ŏt⁴), cutting up of foetus in womb.

‖ **ĕmbŭs′**, v.t. & i. (mil. etc.; -ss-). Put (men, stores) or get into motor vehicles. [ᴇᴍ-+ʙᴜs, after *entrain*]

ĕmĕnd′, v.t. (Seek to) remove errors from (text of book etc.). Hence **ēmĕndᴀ′ᴛɪᴏɴ**, **ēm′ĕndātoʀ**, nn., ~ᴀᴛᴏʀʏ a. [f. L ᴇ(*mendare* f. *menda* fault)]

ĕm′erald, n. Bright-green precious stone; colour of this; size of ᴛʏᴘᴇ; *E*~ *Isle*, Ireland. Hence ~ɪɴᴇ¹ a. [ᴍᴇ, f. OF *emer-aude* f. com.-Rom. *smaralda* f. L f. Gk *smaragdos*]

ĕmĕrge′, v.i. Come up out of a liquid; come into view (*from* enclosed space etc.); issue (*from* state of suffering etc.); (of facts etc.) come out as result of inquiry; (of question, difficulty, etc.) crop up. So **ĕmĕr′gᴇɴᴄᴇ** n., **ĕmĕr′gᴇɴᴛ** a. [f. L ᴇ(*mergere mers-* dip)]

ĕmĕr′genc|y̆, n. Sudden juncture demanding immediate action; ~*y door*, *exit*, etc., for use in ~*ies* only, e.g., in case of fire. [f. LL *emergentia* (as prec., see -ᴇɴᴄʏ)]

ĕmĕ′ritus, a. Honourably discharged from service, as ~ *professor* (retired). [L, p.p. of ᴇ(*merēri* earn)]

ĕm′erŏds, n. pl. (bibl.). = ʜᴀᴇᴍᴏʀʀʜᴏɪᴅs.

ĕmĕr′sion (-shn), n. Emerging; reappearance of sun, moon, star, after eclipse or occultation. [f. LL *emersio* (ᴇᴍᴇʀɢᴇ, -ɪᴏɴ)]

ĕm′ery̆, n. Coarse corundum used for polishing metal, stones, etc.; ~*-cloth*, *-paper*, *-wheel* (covered with ~ powder). [f. F *émeri(l)* f. Rom. *smericulum* f. Gk *smēris* polishing powder]

ĕmĕt′ic, a. & n. (Medicine) that causes vomiting (also fig.). [f. LL f. Gk *emetikos* (*emeō* vomit, see -ᴇᴛɪᴄ)]

émeute (see Ap.), n. Popular rising. [F]

ĕm′igr|āte, v.i. & t. Leave one country to settle in another; (colloq.) change one's place of abode; (v.t.) assist (person) to emigrate. So ~ANT a. & n., ~A'TION n., ~ATORY a. [f. L E(*migrare* MIGRATE)]

émigré (ĕm'ĭgrā), n. French emigrant, esp. Royalist who fled at French Revolution. [F]

ĕm'inence, n. 1. Rising ground. 2. Distinguished superiority (social, intellectual, etc.); (E~) cardinal's title. [f. L *eminentia* (as EMINENT, see -ENCE)]

éminence grise (ā'mĕnahňs grēz'), n. Confidential agent, esp. one who exercises power unofficially (applied orig. to Cardinal Richelieu's private secretary). [F, = grey cardinal]

ĕm'inent, a. Exalted, distinguished; ~ DOMAIN; (of qualities) remarkable in degree, whence ~LY[2] adv. [f. L *eminēre* jut; see -ENT]

emir' (-ēr), n. Saracen or Arab prince or governor; descendant of Mohammed. [f. F *émir* f. Sp. *emir* f. Arab. *amir* AMEER]

ĕm'issary̆, n. Person sent on (usu.) an odious or underhand mission. [f. L *emissarius* (as EMIT, see -ARY[1])]

emi'ssion (-shn), n. Giving off or out (*of* light, heat, smell, etc.); thing thus given out; ~ *theory* (that light is ~ of streams of imponderable particles from luminous bodies). So **emiss'IVE** a. [f. L *emissio* (as foll., see -ION)]

emit', v.t. (-tt-). Give out, send forth, (stream, light, heat, sound, opinion, paper currency, etc.). [f. L E(*mittere miss-* send)]

ĕmm'ĕt, n. (dial.). Ant. [OE; see ANT]

ĕmŏll'ient (-lye-), a. & n. (Application) that softens living animal textures (also fig.). [f. L E(*mollire* f. *mollis* soft), see -ENT]

ĕmŏl'ūment, n. Profit from office or employment, salary. [ME, f. OF, or f. L *ēmŏlumentum, ēmŏli-*, f. E(*mŏlere* grind out), -MENT]

emō'tion, n. Agitation of mind, feeling; excited mental state. Hence ~LESS a. [F, f. *émouvoir*, after *mouvoir* MOVE, *motion* MOTION]

emō'tional (-shon-), a. Of the emotions; liable to emotion, whence ~ISM(1), ~IST(2), ~ITY (-shonăl'-), nn., ~LY[2] adv. [prec. + -AL]

emōt'ive, a. Of, tending to excite, emotion. Hence ~LY[2] (-vl-) adv. [f. L *emovēre*, see EMOTION & -IVE]

ĕmpăn'el, ĭm-, v.t. (-ll-). Enter on panel, enrol, (jury). [f. AF EM(*paneller* PANEL)]

ĕm'pathy̆, n. (psych.). The power of projecting one's personality into (and so fully comprehending) the object of contemplation. [rendering of G *einfühlung* (*ein* in + *fühlung* feeling) after Gk *empatheia*]

ĕm'peror, n. (fem. ĕm'press). Sovereign of Roman, Western, or Eastern Empire; head of Holy Roman Empire; sovereign (title superior in dignity to king); ~ *penguin*, largest known species of penguin of the Antarctic; *purple* ~, kind of butterfly. Hence ~SHIP n. [ME, f. OF *emperere*,

-pereor, f. L *imperator, -orem*, f. IM(*perare* = *parare* prepare, order) command, see -OR]

ĕm'phasis, n. Stress laid on word(s) to indicate special significance; vigour, intensity, of expression, feeling, action, etc.; importance assigned to a thing; prominency, sharpness of contour. [L f. Gk, f. EM(*phainō* show)]·

ĕm'phasize, -ise (-īz), v.t. Lay stress upon (word in speaking); bring (fact etc.) into special prominence. [f. prec. + -IZE]

ĕmphăt'|ic, a. (Of language, tone, gesture) forcibly expressive; (of words) bearing the stress; (of person) expressing himself with emphasis; (of actions) forcible, significant. Hence ~ICALLY adv. [earlier *-ical* (16th c.) f. LL f. Gk *emphatikos* (as EMPHASIS, see -IC)]

ĕmphy̆sēm'a, n. (path.). Enlargement of air vesicles of the lungs; swelling caused by presence of air in connective tissues of body. [f. LL f. Gk *emphusēma* (*emphusaō* puff up)]

ĕm'pīre, n. Supreme & wide (political) dominion; absolute control (*over*); government in which sovereign is called emperor; territory of an emperor; (hist.) *the E~*, (usu.) Holy Roman E~; *E~ Day* (now *Commonwealth Day*), May 24th, birthday of Q. Victoria; **E~ City, State* (of New York); (attrib., *E~*) denoting a style of furniture or dress fashionable during the first (1804-15) or second (1851-70) French E~. [ME, f. OF *empire* (earlier *emperie* whence E *empery*) f. L *imperium* conn. w. *imperare*, see EMPEROR]

empi'ric, a. & n. Based, acting, on observation & experiment, not on theory, whence ~IST(2) n.; (person) relying solely on experiment; quack. Hence ~AL a., ~alLY[2] adv., ~ISM n. [f. L f. Gk *empeirikos* f. *empeiria* experience]

emplāce'ment (-sm-), n. Situation; placing; platform for guns. [F (EM- + PLACE + -MENT)]

emplāne', v.i. & t. Go or put on board aeroplane. '[EM- + (AERO)*plane*]

employ', v.t., & n. 1. Use (thing, one's power, etc., *for, in, on, about*, an object); use services of (person); keep (person) in one's service; busy, keep occupied, (oneself, others, *doing, in*, etc.). 2. n. *In the ~ of*, ~ed by. Hence ~ABLE a., ~ER[1] n. [ME (n. f. F *emploi*) f. OF *employer* f. L IM(*plicare* fold), cf. IMPLY]

employé (ŏmploi'ā), n. (fem. -*ée*). Person employed for wages. [F p.p. (prec.)]

employee', n. = prec. [-EE]

employ'ment, n. In vbl senses; esp., one's regular trade or profession. [-MENT]

empois'on (-zn), v.t. Put poison into; taint; corrupt (fig.); embitter (person's mind *against*). [ME, f. OF EM(*poisonner* POISON)]

empŏr'ium, n. Centre of commerce, mart; shop. [f. L f. Gk *emporion* f. EMporos merchant (*por-* journey)]

empow'er, v.t. Authorize, license, (person *to* do); enable. [EM-]

ĕm'prĕss, n. Wife of emperor; woman governing an empire or (fig.) having absolute power. [ME, f. OF *emperesse* fem. of *emperere* EMPEROR, see -ESS¹]

empressement (see Ap.), n. Display of cordiality. [F]

‖ **ĕmprise'** (-z), n. (arch.). (Chivalrous) enterprise. [ME, f. OF fem. p.p. as n. of *emprendre* f. Rom. *IM(prē(he)ndre* take)]

ĕmp'tў¹, a. & n. **1.** Containing nothing; devoid *of* (qualities); (colloq.) hungry; (of house) devoid of furniture or inmates; (of van, ship, etc.) without load; (of persons, plans, etc.) lacking sense; meaningless. **2.** n. ~ truck, box, etc. **3.** ~-*handed*, bringing no gift, carrying nothing away; ~-*headed*, -*pated*, witless. Hence **ĕmp'tiNESS** n. [OE *ǣmetig* f. *ǣmetta* leisure +-Y²]

ĕmp'tў², v.t. & i. Remove contents of (vessel etc. *upon* etc.); transfer (contents of one thing *into* etc. another); (of river) discharge itself (*into*); (v.i.) become empty. [f. prec.]

ĕmpūr'ple, v.t. Make purple, redden. [EM-]

ĕmpўrē'an, a. & n. (Of) the highest heaven, as the sphere of fire or as the abode of God; (of) the visible heavens. So **ĕmpў'rèAL** a. [f. LL *empyreus* f. Gk EM(*puros* f. *pur* fire) + -AN]

ĕm'ū, n. Large Australian bird allied to the cassowary. [17th c. *emia*, *eme*, f. Port. *ema* crane, ostrich]

ĕm'ūl|āte, v.t. Try to equal or excel; rival; imitate zealously. So ~A'TION, ~ātoR, nn., ~ātiVE a. [f. L *aemulari* (as foll.), see -ATE³]

ĕm'ūlous, a. Zealously, jealously, imitative (*of*); desirous (*of* renown etc.), actuated by spirit of rivalry. Hence ~LY² adv. [f. L *aemulus* + -OUS]

ĕmŭl'sifў, v.t. Convert into an emulsion. [f. L E(*mulgēre muls-* milk) + -FY]

ĕmŭl'sion (-shn), n. Milky liquid with oily or resinous particles suspended in it; mixture of light-sensitive silver salts suspended in gelatine or collodion for coating photographic plates and films. Hence or cogn. ~IZE(3) v.t., **ĕmŭl'siVE** a. [F, or f. mod. L *emulsio* (as prec., see -ION)]

ĕmŭnc'torў, a. & n. Of nose-blowing; (organ, duct) conveying waste matter from the body. [f. L E(*mungere munct-*), see -ORY]

ĕn, n. Unit of width in printing, narrower than EM. [N]

en-¹, pref. The form assumed in F by L *in-* (see IN-¹); in E used chiefly in wds from F (*enamour*, *embarrass*, *engage*); before *b* & *p*, occas. before *m*, it is changed to *em-*; from 14th c. *in-* (*im-*) [or IN-(IM-¹)] has taken the place of *en-* (*em-*), & conversely; now used to form E vbs (a) on nouns, with sense 'put (the object) into

or on something' (*embed*, *engulf*, *entrust*) or 'put something into or on (the object)' (*enjewel*); (b) on nn. or adjj., w. sense 'bring into such condition' (*englad*, *enslave*); often with suf. -EN⁶ (*embolden*, *enlighten*); (c) on vbs with sense 'in', 'into', 'upon', (*enfold*) or w. intensive force (*encarnalize*).

en-², pref. The form assumed by Gk *en-* (*em-* before *b*, *m*, *p*, *ph*; *el-*, *er-*, before *l*, *r*), w. sense 'in' (*energy*, *enthusiasm*, *emphasis*).

-en¹, -n, suf. forming p.p. of strong vbs (*spoken*, *sworn*); often obs. or arch. (*gotten*, *graven*); freq. displaced by -*ed* (*shaped* for *shapen*); or surviving only in adj. sense (*drunken*, *lorn*). For adj. sense see -ED¹(2). [OE -*en*, OS, OHG -*an*, ON-*enn*, -*inn*, Goth. -*ans*, f. Gmc *-enaz*, *-anaz*]

-en², suf. forming dimm., as *chicken*, *maiden*. [Gmc *-īno(m)*, neut. of -*ino*- -EN⁵]

-en³, suf. forming femm. (now only in *vixen*), and found in some nouns, as *burden*. [f. WG* -*innja* f. Gmc *-inī*]

-en⁴, suf. seen in *oxen*; orig. part of stem in weak-decl. nouns, but retained only in pl., & added to other old plurals, as in *brethren*, *children*, *kine*, (earlier -*ther*, -*der*, *ky*). [OE -*an*]

-en⁵, -n, suf. forming adjj. f. nn., usu. expr. material; mostly obs. or arch. (*silvern*) or usu. in metaph. senses (*golden*), the noun being used as adj.; but *wooden*, *woollen*, & a few others, remain. [OE -*en*, OS, ON -*in*, OHG -*īn*, Goth. -*ein*- f. Gmc *-īno*- cogn. w. L -*īno*- see -INE]

-en⁶, suf. forming vv.t. & i. from adjj. (*deepen*, *moisten*) on anal. of a few in OE (*fasten*), & f. nouns as *listen* (OE), *happen* (14th c.), *heighten*, *hearten*, etc., (mod.).

enā'ble, v.t. Authorize, empower, (person *to* do); supply (person etc.) with means *to* (do); ‖ *Enabling Act*, esp. that of 1920 conferring on the Established Church a certain measure of autonomy subject to parliamentary veto. [EN-¹]

enăct', v.t. **1.** Ordain, decree, (thing, *that*), whence **enăc'tION**, ~MENT, nn., **enăc'tiVE**, **enăc'toRY**, aa.; ~*ing clauses* (containing new provisions). **2.** Play (scene, part, on stage or in life). [EN-¹ + ACT n. & v.]

enăm'el¹, n. Glass-like opaque or semi-transparent coating of metallic surfaces for ornament or as preservative lining (also fig.); any smooth hard coating; kinds of complexion-veneer; coating of teeth; painting done on ~; (poet.) smooth bright surface colouring, verdure, etc. [f. foll.]

enăm'el², v.t. (-ll-). Inlay, encrust, (metal etc., the face or skin) with enamel; portray (figures etc.) with enamel; adorn with varied colours. [ME, f. AF EN¹-*ameler*, -*aynailler*, f. OF *esmail*, alt. f. *esmaut* f. WG *small*- see SMELT¹]

ĕnăm'our (-mer), v.t. Inspire with love (*of*, esp. in p.p.); charm, delight. [f. OF EN¹(*amourer* f. *amour* love f. L *amorem*, nom. *-or*)]

ĕnăn'tiōmŏrph, n. Mirror image, form related to another as an object is to its image in a mirror. [f. Gk *enantios* opposite, *morphē* form]

ĕnăntiŏp'athў̆, n. = ALLOPATHY. [f. Gk *enantios* opposite + -PATHY]

ĕnăr̆thrōs'ĭs, n. (anat.). Ball-&-socket joint. [Gk, f. EN²(*arthros* f. *arthron* joint), -OSIS]

en blŏc (ahn), adv. In a lump, wholesale. [F]

ĕncaen'ĭa (-sēn-), n. Dedication festival; ‖(Oxf.) = COMMEMORATION. [L, f. Gk *egkainia* (EN-² + *kainos* new)]

ĕncāge', in-, v.t. Confine (as) in cage. [EN-¹]

ĕncămp', v.t. & i. (Of troops) settle (t. & i.) in camp; lodge (t. & i.) in the open in tents. [EN-¹]

ĕncămp'ment, n. In vbl senses; also, place where troops are encamped. [-MENT]

ĕncāse', in-, v.t. Put into a case; surround as with a case. Hence ~MENT (-sm-) n. [EN-¹]

‖ **ĕncăsh'**, v.t. Convert (bills etc.) into cash; receive in form of cash, realize. Hence ~MENT n. [EN-¹]

ĕncaus'tĭc, a. & n. (Painting, art of painting) by burning in; ~ *brick, tile*, (inlaid with coloured clays burnt in). [f. Gk *egkaustikos*, see EN-², CAUSTIC]

-ence, suf. forming nn. of quality or action f. F *-ence* or direct f. L *-entia* f. L pres. part. in *-ent-* (nom. *-ens*); also f. earlier (M)E & F wds in *-ance*, after 1500 refash. after L *-entia*; see -ANCE, -ENCY.

enceinte (see Ap.), a. & n. **1.** (Of women) pregnant. **2.** n. Enclosure (in fortification). [F]

ĕncĕphăl'ĭc, a. Of the brain. [f. Gk *egkephalon* brain (EN-² + *kephalē* head) + -IC]

ĕncĕph'al‖(o)-, comb form of Gk *egkephalon* (prec.); ~*it'is*, inflammation of the brain (see SICKNESS); ~*ogram*, an X-ray photograph of the brain; ~*ograph*, ~*ogram*, (also) instrument for recording brain waves; ~*ŏg'raphy*; ~*ŏt'omy*, dissection of the brain.

ĕncĕph'alon, n. (anat.). The brain. [mod. L f. Gk (see ENCEPHALIC)]

ĕnchain', v.t. Chain up, fetter; hold fast (attention, emotions). Hence ~MENT n. [f. F EN¹(*chainer* CHAIN)]

ĕnchant' (-ah-), v.t. Bewitch (lit. & fig.); charm, delight. Hence or cogn. ~ER¹, ~MENT, ~rESS¹, nn., ~ĭngLY² adv., (-ah-). [ME, f. F *enchanter* f. L IN(*cantare* sing, frequent. of *canere* cant-)]

ĕnchīrĭd'ion (-k-), n. Handbook. [f. LL f. Gk f. *en* in, *kheir* hand]

ĕncĭr'cle, v.t. Surround, encompass, (*with*); form a circle round. [EN-¹]

en clair (ahn), phr. (Of telegrams, official messages, etc.) in ordinary language (not in code or cipher). [F]

ĕnclasp' (-ah-), v.t. Hold in clasp or embrace. [EN-¹]

ĕnclāve', n. Territory surrounded by foreign dominion. [F, f. *enclaver* f. Rom. *IN(*clavare* f. *clavis* key)]

ĕnclĭt'‖ĭc, a. & n. (gram.). (Word) so unemphatic as to be pronounced as part of preceding word, esp. (Gk) throwing its accent back on preceding word. Hence ~ICALLY adv. [f. LL f. Gk *egklitikos* (EN-³ + *klinō* lean), see -IC]

ĕnclōse', in-, (-z), v.t. Surround, fence in, (land etc. *with, in*, walls etc.); shut up in receptacle (esp. something besides letter in envelope); bound on all sides, contain, (esp. Math.); hem in on all sides. [ME, f. OF *enclos* p.p. of *enclore*; see EN-¹, CLOSE³]

ĕnclō'sure (-zher), n. Enclosing (esp. of common land, to make it private property, as *E~ Act*); enclosing fence etc.; enclosed place; paper etc. enclosed with letter in envelope. [AF, OF *enclosure* (prec., -URE)]

ĕnclōthe' (-dh), v.t. Clothe. [EN-¹]

ĕncloud', v.t. Envelop in cloud. [EN-¹]

ĕncōde', v.t. Put (message) into code or cipher. [EN-¹]

ĕncōm'ĭăst, n. Composer of an encomium; flatterer. Hence **ĕncōmĭăs'tĭc** a. [f. Gk *egkōmiastēs* (*egkōmiazō*, as foll., *-ast* = -IST(1) w. vbs in *-azō*)]

ĕncōm'ĭum, n. Formal or high-flown praise. [L, f. Gk *egkōmion* (EN-² + *kōmos* revelry)]

ĕncom'pass (-ŭm-), v.t. Surround (esp. with friendly or hostile intention); contain. Hence ~MENT n. [EN-¹ + COMPASS n.]

encore (ŏngkōr', & see *Ap.*), int., n., & v.t. **1.** (Spectator's or auditor's demand for song etc. to be sung etc.) again, once more; further, item given in response. **2.** v.t. Demand repetition of (song etc.), summon (performer) for this. [(vb f. n.) F, = once again]

ĕncoun'ter, v.t., & n. **1.** Meet hostilely; fall in with. **2.** n. Meeting in conflict, falling in, (*with*). [ME; (n. f. OF *encontre*) f. OF *encontrer* f. Rom. *IN(*contrare* f. L *contra* against)]

ĕncou'rag‖e (-kŭ-), v.t. Embolden; incite, advise, (person *to* do); promote, assist, (commerce, opinion, etc.). Hence or cogn. ~eMENT (-kŭrĭjm-) n., ~ĭngLY² adv. [ME, f. OF EN¹(*coragier* f. as COURAGE)]

En'cratite (ĕ-), n. Member of early Christian heretical sect abstaining from meat, wine, & marriage. [f. LL f. late Gk *egkratitēs* (*egkratēs* continent, -ITE¹)]

ĕncrim'son (-z-), v.t. Make crimson. [EN-¹]

ĕncroach', v.i. Intrude usurpingly (*on* others' territory, rights, etc., or abs.). Hence ~MENT n. [f. OF EN¹(*crochier* f. *croc* hook); see CROOK]

ĕncrust', in-, v.t. & i. Cover with a crust; overlay (surface) with ornamental crust of precious material; (v.i.) form into a crust. Hence ~MENT n. [f. F *incruster* f. L IN(*crustare*, as CRUST); also f. EN-¹ + CRUST]

encŭm′ber, v.t. Hamper (person, movement, action, *with* burden, difficulty, etc.); burden (person, estate, *with* debts); fill, block, (place *with* lumber etc., lit. & fig.). Hence ~MENT n. [ME, f. OF EN¹- (*combrer* CUMBER)]

encŭm′brance, n. Burden; annoyance; impediment; *without* ~, having no children; claim, mortgage, etc., on property. [f. OF *encombrance* (as prec., see -ANCE)]

encŭm′brancer, n. One who has an encumbrance on another's estate. [-ER¹]

-ency̆, suf. f. L *-entia*, usu. denoting quality or state, not action; see -ANCE, -ANCY, -CY.

ency̆c′lic(al), aa. & nn. (Pope's letter) for extensive circulation. [f. LL *encyclicus*, for *-ius*, f. Gk *egkuklios* (EN-² + *kuklos* circle)]

ency̆clop(a)ed′|ia (-pĕ-), n. (pl. ~*ias*). Book giving information on all branches of knowledge or of one subject, usu. arranged alphabetically; esp. the French ~ia of Diderot, D'Alembert, and others; general course of instruction. Hence ~IC(AL) aa., ~ISM(3), ~IST(3), nn. [mod. L, f. pseudo-Gk *egkuklopaideia* for *egkuklios paideia* all-round education (as prec., *paideia* f. *paideuō* educate f. *pais paidos* boy)]

ency̆st′, v.t. Enclose in a cyst. Hence ~A′TION, ~MENT, nn. [EN-¹]

end¹, n. **1.** Limit, as *there is no* ~ *to it*; extremity (of line etc.); ‖ *East, West, End* (part of London); surface bounding a thing at either extremity, head of cask etc.; remnant, as *candle* ~*s*, *odds & ~s*; *rope's* ~, short piece bound at ~s with thread for flogging; *shoemaker's* ~, length of thread armed with bristle. **2.** Conclusion (of period, action, state, book, etc.); latter part; destruction; death. **3.** Result, purpose, as *to gain his ~s*, *to what* ~ *?*; object for which a thing exists, final cause. **4.** *Place on* ~ (upright); *turn* ~ *for* ~, reverse; *world without* ~, for ever; *placed* ~ *to* ~ (lengthwise, continuously); ~ *on*, with its ~ fronting one; *no* ~, much, many, *of*; *on* ~, continuously (*for three weeks on* ~); *be at, come to, an* ~, be, become, exhausted or completed; *in the* ~, finally, after all; *at* one's *wits'* ~, quite perplexed; *put an* ~ *to*, stop, abolish; *keep* one's ~ *up*, acquit oneself well in conversation, bargain, etc.; *go* (*in*) *off the deep* ~ (sc. of swimming-bath) fig., take risks, (also) lose one's temper; *make an* ~ *of*, put a stop to; *at a loose* ~, unoccupied; *make both* ~*s meet*, live within one's income; *is at the* ~ *of his tether*, knows, can do, no more; ~*-iron*, movable plate changing size of grate in range; ~*-paper*, blank leaf pasted down on

boards or wrappers of book; ~*-product*, final product of a number of operations. [OE *ende*, OS *endi*, OHG *enti*, ON *endir*, Goth. *andeis* f. Gmc **andja*-]

end², v.t. & i. Bring (action, speech, life, etc.) to an end; put an end to, destroy; come to an end; ~ *by doing*, eventually do (*will* ~ *by marrying a duke*); result *in*; ~ *up*, conclude, finish. [OE *endian* (as prec.)]

endăm′age, v.t. = DAMAGE. [EN-¹]

endăn′ger (-j-), v.t. Cause danger to. [EN-¹]

endear′, v.t. Render (person, thing, one*self*) dear (*to*). Hence ~ingLY² adv., ~MENT n. [EN-¹]

endeav′our (-dĕver), v.t. & i., & n. **1.** Try (*to* do); strive *after*. **2.** n. Attempt (*to* do, *at* doing). [ME; (n. f. vb) f. EN-¹ + DEVOIR]

endĕm′|ic, a. & n. **1.** Regularly found among (specified) people, in (specified) country. **2.** n. ~ic disease. Hence ~ICALLY adv., **endĕmi′city** n. [f. F *endémique* f. Gk EN-² + *dēmos* people + -IC; cf. *epidemic*]

endĕrm′|ic, a. Acting on the skin. Hence ~ICALLY adv. [EN-² + DERM + -IC]

end′ing, n. In vbl senses, esp. latter part (of word, story, etc.). [-ING¹]

en′dive, n. Species of chicory, with curled leaves, used as salad. [ME, f. OF f. LL *endivia* f. L *intibus*, *-um*, Gk *entubon*]

end′less, a. Infinite; eternal; incessant; (Mech.) ~ *band, cable, chain* (with ends joined for continuous action over wheels etc.). Hence ~LY² adv., ~NESS n. [OE *endelēas*, see END¹ and -LESS]

en′do- (before a vowel end-), comb. form of Gk *endon* within, as; ~*card′ium*, lining membrane of heart; ~*cardit′is*, inflammation of this; ~*carp*, inmost layer of pericarp; ~*crăne*, inner surface of skull; ~*crine*, secreting internally, ductless, of the ~crine glands, [Gk *krinō* sift]; ~*derm*, inner layer of blastoderm; ~*gamous*, ~*gamy*, (-ŏg′-), (of) marrying within the tribe; ~*gen*, plant that develops wood in interior of stem; ~*genous* (-ŏj²), growing from within; ~*lymph*, fluid in membranous labyrinth of ear; ~*metrit′is*, ~*mēt′rium*, (inflammation of) lining membrane of womb; ~*morph*, mineral enclosed in another; ~*pă′rasite*, internal parasite; ~*plasm*, ~*sarc*, inner soft layer of protoplasm; ~*scope*, instrument for viewing internal parts of body; ~*skĕl′eton*, internal framework of vertebrates; ~*smōse* (-ŏz′m-), ~*smōs′is* (-ŏzm-), passage of a fluid inwards through a porous septum; ~*sperm*, albumen enclosed with embryo in seeds; ~*spore*, inner coat of spore, spore formed in a case; ~*thĕl′ium*, layer of cells lining blood-vessels etc.

endôrse′, in-, v.t. Write on back of (document), esp. sign one's name on back of (bill, cheque, etc.); write (explanation, comment, *on* back of document); ~ *over*, make over one's rights in (bill etc. *to* another person, also fig.); confirm (statement, opinion), (vulg. in advertisements) confirm advertiser's praise of (—'s pills etc.); || motorist's, publican's, *licence is* ~*d*, has record of offence written on the back. Hence ~MENT (-sm-) n. [refash. on L; ME *endosse* f. OF *endosser* f. med. L IN(*dorsare* f. *dorsum* back)]

endow', v.t. Bequeath, give, permanent income to (person, institution); invest (person) *with* (privileges etc.); furnish (person) *with* (ability etc.; esp. in p.p.). Hence ~MENT n. (~*ment assurance*, payment of a fixed sum to an insured person on attaining an agreed age, or to his or her estate if death occurs earlier). [ME, f. AF *endouer* f. EN-¹ + OF *douer* f. L *dotare* (as DOWER)]

endūe', **in-**, v.t. Put on (clothes etc., also fig.); clothe (person) *with*; (usu. pass.) furnish (person *with* qualities etc.). [ME, f. OF *enduire* f. L IN(*ducere* lead, draw), associated in sense w. *induere* put on (clothes)]

endūr'ance, n. Habit, power, of enduring; enduring. [OF, see -ANCE]

endūr|e', v.t. & i. Undergo (pain etc.); submit to; bear (*to* do, esp. w. neg.); last. Hence ~'ABLE a., ~'ingLY² adv., ~'ingNESS n. [ME, f. OF *endurer* f. L IN (*durare* harden f. *durus*)]

end'ways, **-wise**, (-z), adv. With the end turned towards the spectator or uppermost or foremost; end to end. [-WAYS, -WISE]

-ēne, suf. forming names of hydrocarbons, as *benzene, camphene.*

en'ēma (or ĭnē⁴), n. Injection of liquid or gaseous substance into the rectum; the syringe used. [LL, f. Gk *ĕnĕma* f. *enĭĕmi* inject]

en'emy̆, n. & a. 1. Hostile person; opponent (*of, to,* another); *the E~*, the Devil; member of hostile army or nation; hostile force or ship; (colloq.) *how goes the* ~?, what is the time? 2. adj. Of, or belonging to, the ~ (~ *ships, aircraft, alien; destroyed by* ~ *action*). [ME, f. OF *enemi* f. L IN²(*imicus = amicus* friend)]

energĕt'|ic, a. & n. Strenuously active; forcible, vigorous; powerfully operative; (n. pl.) science of energy. Hence ~ICALLY adv. [f. Gk *energētikos* f. EN²(*ergō* work), see -IC]

enĕr'gic, a. (rare). = prec. [f. ENERGY + -IC]

en'ergize, **-ise** (-ĭz), v.t. & i. Infuse energy into (person, work); be in active operation. [-IZE]

energūm'ĕn, n. Demoniac; enthusiast, fanatic. [f. LL f. Gk *energoumenos* (pass. part., see ENERGETIC)]

en'ergy̆, n. 1. Force, vigour, (of speech, action, person, etc.); active operation; (pl.) individual powers in exercise, as *devote your energies to this*; (latent) ability. 2. (phys.). *Actual, kinetic, motive,*

~, a body's power of doing work by virtue of its motion (half product of mass into square of velocity); *potential, static, latent,* ~, body's power of doing work by virtue of stresses resulting from its relation to other bodies; CONSERVATION *of* ~; *mass* ~, ~ which all bodies possess in virtue of their mass (product of mass into square of velocity (of light), and of which a small portion is released (as radiations etc.) in radio-activity and other types of atomic disintegration. [f. LL f. Gk *energeia* f. EN²(*ergĕs* f. *ergon* work)]

enĕr'vate¹, a. Wanting in (physical, moral, literary, artistic) vigour. [f. L E(*nervare* f. *nervus* sinew), see -ATE²]

en'erv|āte², v.t. Weaken (physically etc. as prec.). So ~A'TION n. [as prec., -ATE³]

enfāce', v.t. Write, print, stamp (form of words) on bill etc.; do this to (bill etc.). Hence ~MENT (-sm-) n. [EN-¹]

en famille (ahn famē'ye), adv. At home, among one's family. [F]

enfant terrible (see Ap.), n. Child who asks awkward questions, repeats what it has heard, etc. [F]

enfee'ble, v.t. Make feeble. Hence ~MENT (-belm-) n. [ME, f. OF EN¹ (*feblir* as FEEBLE)]

enfeoff' (-fĕf'), v.t. Invest (person) with fief; (fig.) hand over. [ME, f. AF *enfeoffer,* OF *enfeffer* (FIEF)]

enfeoff'ment (-fĕf-), n. Enfeoffing; document effecting this; fief. [-MENT]

en fête (ahn fāt), adv. & pred. a. Engaged in, attired etc. for, holiday-making. [F]

enfĕtt'er, v.t. Bind in fetters (lit. & fig.); enslave (person *to*). [EN-¹]

enfilāde', n., & v.t. 1. Fire from guns etc. sweeping line of works or men from end to end. 2. v.t. Subject (troops, road, etc.) to ~. [(vb f. n.) F, f. EN¹(*filer* f. *fil* thread), see -ADE]

enfōld', **in-**, v.t. Wrap up (person etc. *in, with*); clasp, embrace; shape into folds. [EN-¹]

enfōrce', v.t. Urge, press home, (argument, demand); impose (action, conduct, *upon* person etc.); compel observance of (law etc.). Hence or cogn. ~ABLE a., ~dLY² (-sĕd-) adv., ~MENT (-sm-) n. [ME, f. OF *enforcier* f. Rom. *infortiare* f. *fortis* strong]

enfrāme', v.t. Set (picture etc.) in frame; serve as frame to. [EN-¹]

enfrăn'ch|ise (-z), v.t. Set free; invest (town) with municipal rights, || esp. that of representation in parliament; admit (person) to electoral franchise. Hence ~iseMENT (-zm-) n. [f. obs. F EN¹(*franchir* f. *franc* FRANK a.), see -ISH²]

engāg|e' (-n-g-), v.t. & i. 1. Bind by contract or promise (esp. of marriage, as ~*ed couple*). 2. Hire (servant); bespeak (seats, cab, etc.). 3. Pledge oneself (*to* do, *that*); ~*e for,* guarantee, promise. 4. Induce; attract, charm, (esp. in part.), whence ~'**ĭng**LY² adv. **5.** (archit.). Fasten (pillar) into wall; interlock (thing *with* another). **6.** Hold fast (attention); employ busily (usu. pass.). **7.** Embark *in* (politics etc.). **8.** Bring (troops) into conflict; enter into conflict with (also *with*). Hence ~e'MENT (-jm-) n. [f. F EN¹(*gager* f. GAGE¹)]

en garçon (see Ap.), adv. & pred. a. As a bachelor, unmarried. [F]

ĕngārl'and (-n-g-), v.t. Put a garland upon; wreathe (*with* flowers etc.). [EN-¹]

ĕngĕn'der (-j-), v.t. Beget (now only fig.); (of situation, condition, etc.) bring about. [ME, f. OF *engendrer* f. L IN(*generare* GENERATE)] ·

ĕn'gine (-j-), n., & v.t. **1.** Mechanical contrivance consisting of several parts; ⇒ STEAM-~; FIRE-~; machine, instrument, used in war; instrument, means; ‖~- *-driver* (of ~, esp. locomotive); ~*-lathe* (worked by machinery); ~*-turning*, engraving of symmetrical patterns on metals by machine. **2.** v.t. Fit (ship etc.) with ~(s). [(vb f. n.) f. OF *engin* f. L *ingenium* (see INGENIOUS)]

ĕngineer'¹ (-j-), n. **1.** One who designs & constructs military works; soldier of branch of army called E~s, trained to engineering. **2.** (Also *civil* ~) one who designs works of public utility, bridges, canals, gas-works, etc.; maker of engines. **3.** One who has charge of engine; *engine-driver. Hence ~SHIP n. [ME, f. OF *engineor* f. med. L *ingeniatorem* (*ingeniare*, as ENGINE, see -OR); ending later assim. to -EER]

ĕngineer'² (-j-), v.i. & t. Act as engineer; construct, manage, (bridge, work, etc.) as engineer; (colloq.) arrange, contrive, bring about. [f. prec.]

ĕn'ginerȳ (-j-), n. Engines; machinery (often fig.). [-ERY]

ĕngĭr'd(le) (-n-g-), vv.t. Surround with or as with girdle. [EN-¹]

‖ **Eng'lander** (ĭngg-), n. *Little* ~, one opposed to imperial policy. [-ER¹]

Eng'lish¹ (ĭngg-), a. & n. **1.** Of England; *the* ~ (people, soldiers, etc.); ~*man*, ~*woman*, one who is ~ by birth, descent, or naturalization. **2.** Of, written or spoken in, the ~ language. **3.** n. The ~ language (also *the king's, queen's,* ~, as *mishandle the queen's* ~); *Old* ~, (ending about 1150), *Middle* ~ (ending 1500); *in plain* ~, in plain words. **4.** Size of TYPE; *Early* ~ STYLE. [OE *englisc, ænglisc*, OS *engelsch*, MHG *engel(i)sch*, ON *enskr* f. Gmc *anglisko* (*angli-* ANGLE³)]

‖ **english**² (ĭngg-), v.t. (arch.), affected). Render into English. [f. prec.]

ĕngōrge', v.t. Devour greedily; (pass.) be crammed, (Path.) be congested with blood. Hence ~MENT (-jm-) n. [f. F EN-¹ (*gorger* GORGE)]

ĕngraft', **in-**, (-ah-), v.t. Insert (scion of one tree *into, upon*, another); implant (principles etc. *in* the mind etc.); incor-

porate (thing *into* another); add (adventitious thing *upon*). [EN-¹]

ĕngrail', v.t. Indent the edge of, give serrated appearance to, (esp. Her.). [ME, f. OF EN¹*gresler* f. *gresle* hail]

ĕngrain', **in-**, v.t. Cause (dye etc.) to sink deeply into a thing (usu. fig.); (p.p., cf. INGRAINED) inveterate, as *an* ~*ed rogue*. [ME, f. OF *engrainer* dye in grain (*en graine*); see GRAIN]

ĕngrāve', v.t. Inscribe, ornament, (hard surface *with* incised marks); carve (figures etc. *upon* surface); (fig.) impress deeply (*upon* memory etc.); cut (figures etc.) in lines on metal plates for printing. [EN-¹ + GRAVE²]

ĕngrāv'ing, n. In vbl senses, esp. copy of picture etc. from engraved plate. [-ING¹]

ĕngrŏss', v.t. Write (document) in large letters; express in legal form; (hist.) buy whole stock of (corn etc.) so as to get monopoly; monopolize (conversation etc.); absorb (person, his attention, time, etc.; esp. in p.p. ~*ed in* subject etc.). Hence ~MENT n. [ME; (1) f. AF EN¹*grosser* (*grosse* f. med. L *grossa* large writing); (2) f. phr. *in gross* wholesale]

ĕngŭlf', **in-**, v.t. Plunge into, swallow up (as) in a, gulf. Hence ~MENT n. [EN-¹]

ĕnhance' (-hah—, -hǎ-), v.t. Heighten, intensify, (qualities, powers, etc.); exaggerate; raise (price). Hence. ~MENT (-hahnsm-) n. [ME, f. AF *enhauncer* prob. alt. f. OF *enhaucer* f. Rom. *IN(*altiare* f. *altus* high)]

ĕnhǎrmŏn'ĭc, a. (mus.). Of, having, intervals smaller than semitone (esp. such intervals as that between G sharp & A flat). Hence ~ICALLY adv. [f. LL f. Gk EN²*armonikos* (*harmonia* HARMONY, see -IC)]

ĕnig'ma, n. Riddle; puzzling person or thing. Hence or cogn. **ĕnigmǎt'ic**(AL) aa., **ĕnigmǎt'icaL**LY² adv., ~TIZE(3) v.t. [f. L f. Gk *ainigma -matos* f. *ainissomai* speak allusively (*ainos* fable)]

ĕnisle', **in-**, (-īl), v.t. (poet.). Make into an isle; place on an isle; isolate. [EN-¹]

ĕnjāmb'ment (-m-m-; *or* ahńzhahń-bmahń'), n. (pros.). Continuation of sentence beyond second line of couplet. [f. F *enjambement* f. EN¹(*jamber* f. *jambe* leg), see -MENT]

ĕnjoin', v.t. Prescribe, impose, (action, conduct, *on* person); command (person *to* do); issue instructions (*that*); (Legal, esp. U.S.) prohibit by judicial order. [ME, f. OF *enjoindre* (st. *-joign-*) f. L IN(*jungere* join)]

ĕnjoy', v.t. ~ *oneself*, experience pleasure; take delight in, whence ~ABLE a., ~able-NESS n., ~abLY² adv.; have the use of (advantages etc.); experience, as ~ *poor health*. Hence ~MENT n. [ME, f. OF EN¹- (*joier* f. *joie* JOY) give joy to, (refl.) enjoy; or f. OF EN¹(*joir* f. L *gaudere* rejoice)]

ĕnkin'dle, v.t. Cause (flame, passions, war, etc.) to blaze up; inflame with passion. [EN-¹]

ênlāce′, v.t. Encircle tightly; enfold; entwine. Hence ~MENT (-sm-) n. [ME, f. OF *enlacier* f. Rom. **inlaciare* f. **lacius*; see LACE[2]]

ênlârge′, v.t. & i. Increase, extend; widen, expand, (mind, heart, ideas); (arch.) release; grow larger; expatiate upon; (Photog.) reproduce, be capable of reproduction, on larger scale. Hence ~MENT (-jm-) n., (esp.) such photographic reproduction, **ênlâr′**GER[1] n., apparatus for enlarging or reducing negatives or positives. [ME, f. OF EN[1]*larger* (LARGE)]

ênlight′en (-ît-), v.t. Instruct, inform, (person *on* subject); (poet.) shed light on (object), give light to (person); free (person) from prejudice or superstition (esp. in p.p.). Hence ~MENT (-ît-) n. [EN[1]+LIGHT n. +-EN[6]]

ênlink′, v.t. Link together, connect closely, (*with, to*; lit. & fig.). [EN[1]]

ênlist′, v.t. & i. Engage (t. & i.) for military service (*~ed man*, private soldier); secure the co-operation or support of (persons, feelings, natural forces, sciences, etc., *in* enterprise etc.). Hence ~MENT n. [EN[1]]

ênliv′en, v.t. Animate, inspirit, (persons, feelings, trade, etc.); brighten (picture, scene). [EN[1]+LIFE +-EN[6]]

en măsse (ahń), adv. In a mass; all together. [F]

ênmêsh′, v.t. Entangle in or as in a net. Hence **ênmêsh′**MENT n. [EN[1]]

ên′mîtỹ, n. Hatred; state of hostility. [ME, f. OF *enemistie* f. Rom. **inimicitatem* (as ENEMY, see -TY)]

ênn′ead, n. Set of nine (discourses, books, points). [f. Gk *enneas* nine, see -AD)]

ênnō′ble, v.t. Make (person) a' noble; make noble, elevate. Hence ~MENT (-belm-) n. [f. F EN[1] *noblir* (NOBLE)]

ennui (ŏn′wē, *& see Ap.*), n. Mental weariness from lack of occupation or interest. Hence~ED[2] (ŏnwēd′), **ennuyé** (see *Ap.*, fem. -*ée*, pl. -*és*, -*ées*), aa. [F, f. L *in odio*, cf. ANNOY[1]]

ênôrm′ity, n. Monstrous wickedness; crime. [f. F *énormité* f. L *enormitatem* (as foll., see -TY)]

ênôrm′ous, a. Huge, very large, as ~ *beast, difference*. Hence ~LY[2] adv., ~NESS n. [f. L E(*normis* f. *norma* pattern, stand-ard)+-OUS]

ên′osĭs, n. Union of Cyprus with Greece. [Gk *henōsis*]

enough′ (ênûf′), (poet.) **enow′**, a., n., & adv. Not less than the required number, quantity, degree, as: (adj.) *we have apples* ~, ~ *apples, beer* ~, ~ *beer, he made* ~ *noise* (to justify supposition etc.), ~ *noise to wake the dead, for his purpose*; (n.) *we have*~ *of everything except beer,* ~ *of* (stop) *this folly,* ~! (say no more), ~ *is as good as a feast, cry* ' ~ ' (acknowledge defeat), *I have had* ~ (am tired) *of him, I had* ~ *to do* (my work cut out) *to catch the train,*

you have done more than ~, ~ *and to spare*, (pred.; adj. or n.) *five men are* ~, *five quarts is not* ~; (adv.) *it is boiled* (just) ~, *he does not advertise* ~, *are you warm* ~ ?, *he does not* ~ (usu. *sufficiently*) *realize the difficulties, she sings well* ~ (tolerably), *you know well* ~ (quite well) *what I mean*; *oddly* ~ (to justify the term *oddly*), *he had lost his purse; sure* ~ (to satisfy rational doubt), *there it was*. [OE *genōg*, OS *gi-*, OHG *ginuog*, ON *gnógr*, Goth. *ganōhs* cogn. w. Gmc **-nah-* in OE *geneah* it suffices]

ênounce′, v.t. Enunciate; pronounce (words). Hence ~MENT (-sm-) n. [f. F *énoncer* (as ENUNCIATE)]

en passant (see Ap.), adv. By the way; (Chess) *take* (pawn that advances two squares at once) ~ (with your own pawn by which it could have been taken if it had advanced only one). [F]

en pension. See PENSION.

en prise (ahń prēz), phr. (Chess). In a position to be taken. [F]

‖ **enquire, enquiry.** See INQUIRE, INQUIRY.

ênrāge′, v.t. Make furious (~*d at, by, with*). [f. F EN[1]*rager* (RAGE)]

en rapport (ahń rapŏrr′), adv. In touch (*with*). [F, see RAPPORT]

ênrăp′ture, v.t. Delight intensely. [EN[1]]

ênrē′giment (-jm-), v.t. Form (men) into a regiment; discipline. [f. F EN[1](*régimenter* f. *régiment* REGIMENT)]

en règle (ahń rāgl), adv. In due form. [F]

ênrich′, v.t. Make rich; add to contents of (collection, museum, book); make richer in quality, flavour, etc. Hence ~MENT n. [ME, f. OF EN[1](*richir* f. *riche* RICH)]

ênrōbe′, v.t. Put a robe upon. [EN[1]]

ênrōl′, -ll, v.t. (-ll-). Write name of (person) on list, esp. of army; incorporate (person) as member (*in* society etc.); enter (deed etc.) among rolls of court of justice; record, celebrate. Hence **ênrōl′**MENT n. [ME, f. OF EN[1]*roller* f. *rolle* ROLL n.]

en route (ahń rōōt), adv. On the way (*to, for*, place etc. or abs.). [F]

ens (ĕnz), n. (pl. *entia*, pr. ĕn′shĭa). An entity (esp. as an abstract notion). [L, part. of *esse* be, suggested by *absens*; cf. ENTITY]

‖ **En′sa** (ĕ-), n. Organization for entertaining troops etc. [initials of *Entertainments National Service Association*]

ênsăm′ple, n. (arch.). = EXAMPLE. [ME, f. AF *ensa*(u)*mple* f. OF *essemple* EXAMPLE]

ênsăng′uined (-nggwĭnd), a. Blood-stained, bloody, (lit. & fig.) [EN[1]+L *sanguis -inis* blood +-ED[1]]

ênscônce′, v.t. Establish (oneself etc. in secret, safe, snug, etc., place). [EN[1]]

ensemble (see Ap.), n. (Also *tout* ~) thing viewed as a whole; general effect; (Mus.) concerted passage in which all performers unite (*good* ~, performance of such passage in which all performers are in tune & time with one another, with blend & balance of tone). [F]

ĕnshrīne', v.t. Enclose (relic etc.) in shrine; serve as shrine for (precious thing, lit. & fig.). Hence ~MENT (-nm-) n. [EN-¹]

ĕnshroud', v.t. Cover completely, hide from view. [EN-¹]

ĕn'sĭfŏrm, a. Sword-shaped; ~ *cartilage* (appended to the sternum). [f. L *ensis* sword +-FORM]

ĕn'sĭgn (-ĭn), n. **1.** Badge (of office etc.); banner, flag, ‖ esp. (Brit. naut.) white, blue, or red, flag with union in corner (*white* ~, of Royal Navy & Royal Yacht Squadron, *blue* ~, of naval reserve etc., *red* ~, of merchant service). **2.** Standard--bearer (formerly), lowest commissioned officer of foot, cf. ANCIENT²), whence ~CY (-ĭn-) n. [ME, f. OF *enseigne* f. L INSIGNIA]

ĕn'silage, n., & v.t. Preservation of green fodder in silo or pit without drying; fodder thus preserved; (v.t.) treat (fodder) by ~. [(vb f. n.) F (as foll., see -AGE)]

ĕnsīle', v.t. Put (fodder) into a silo: [f. F *ensiler* f. Sp. EN¹*silar* (SILO)]

ĕnslāve', v.t. Make (person etc.) a slave (lit., or fig. *to* habit, superstition, etc.). Hence ~MENT (-vm-) n. [EN-¹]

ĕnslāv'er, n. In vbl senses, esp. woman by whose charms a man is enslaved. [-ER¹]

ĕnsnāre', v.t. Entrap (lit. & fig.). [EN-¹]

ĕnsoul' (-sōl), in-, v.t. Infuse a soul into. [EN-¹]

ĕnsphēre', v.t. Encircle, enclose. [EN-¹]

ĕnsūe', v.i. & t. Happen afterwards: result (*from*, *on*); (Bibl.) seek after. [ME, f. OF *ensuivre* f. Rom. *IN(sequere* = L *sequi* follow)]

ĕnsure' (-shoor), v.t. Make (person, thing) safe (*against* risks); make certain (thing, *that* it shall happen); secure (thing *to*, *for*, person etc.); (formerly)=INSURE. [f. AF EN¹*seurer* f. OF *asseurer* ASSURE]

ĕnswāthe' (-dh), v.t. Bind, wrap, in bandage (lit. & fig.). Hence ~MENT (-dhm-) n. [EN-¹]

-ent, suf. forming adjj. & nn., f. F -*ent* (or direct) f. L -*entem*, acc. of pres. part. (nom. -*ens*) in 2nd, 3rd, & 4th conjj. Also f. earlier (M)E & F wds in -*ant*, refash. (since 1500) after L -*ent*-; see -ANT.

ĕntăb'lature, n. (archit.). The part of an order above the column, including architrave, frieze, & cornice. [f. It. *intavolatura* f. IN(*lavolare* f. *tavola* TABLE), see -URE]

ĕntā'blement (-belm-), n. Horizontal platform(s) supporting statue, above dado & base. [F, f. EN¹*tabler* (TABLE), see -MENT]

ĕntail'¹, n. Settlement of succession of landed estate so that it cannot be bequeathed at pleasure; estate so secured; (fig.) inalienable inheritance (of qualities, beliefs, etc.). [ME; f. foll.]

ĕntail'², v.t. Settle (land etc.) as in prec.; bestow (thing) as inalienable possession (*on* person); impose (expense, labour, *on*

person); necessitate. Hence ~MENT n. [ME; EN-¹+TAIL²]

ĕntăng'le (-nggl), v.t. Catch in snare or among obstacles; involve (person etc.) in difficulties; make (thing) tangled or intricate (lit. & fig.). Hence ~MENT (-nggelm-) n., (also, Mil.) barrier erected to impede the enemy's progress (esp. one formed of stakes and interlaced barbed wire). [EN-¹]

ĕn'tasis, n. (archit.). Slight convexity of a column shaft (introduced to correct the visual illusion of concavity). [Gk, f. *enteinō* to stretch]

ĕntĕl'echy (-kĭ), n. (philos.). Realization, the becoming or being actual of what was potential, developed perfection, (*Aristotle defines the soul, the Form or E~ of an organized body*);. what gives perfection, informing spirit. [f. LL f. Gk *entelekheia* (*en telei ekhein* tŏ be in perfection)]

ĕntĕll'us, n. (Also ~ *monkey*) the sacred Indian bearded monkey. [proper name (Virg. *Aen.* v. 437–72)]

entente (see Ap.), n. (diplom.). Friendly understanding between States; group of States in such relation; E~ *cordiale*, of Gt Britain & France 1904; *the* (*Triple*) E~, of these with Russia 1908. [F, = understanding]

ĕn'ter, v.i. & t. **1.** v.i. Go, come, in, (*into* place, room, etc., or abs.); (3rd pers. imperat. as stage direction) come upon stage, as E~ *Macbeth*; ~ *into*, engage in (conversation, relations, agreement, inquiry, etc.), sympathize with (person's feelings etc.), form part of (calculations, plans, etc.), bind oneself by (recognizances, treaty, contract); ~ (*up*)*on*, assume possession of (property), begin (process etc.), begin to deal with (subject). **2.** v.t. Go, come, into (place etc.); penetrate (flesh etc.); become member of (army, church, etc.); give initial training to (dog), break in (horse); write (name, details, etc., in list, book, etc.); record name of (person) as competitor *for* (contest, race, etc.; also intr., announce oneself as competitor); ~ *an appearance*, show oneself at a meeting etc.; (of minority in deliberative body, ‖ esp. House of Lords) ~ *a protest*, record it in journals or minutes, make it; admit, procure admission for, (pupil, member of a society); ~ *up*, complete series of entries in (account-books etc.). Hence ~ABLE a. [ME, f. OF *entrer* f. L *intrare* (*intra* within)]

ĕntĕr'ĭc, a. & n. Of the intestines; ~ (*fever*), typhoid. So **ĕnterī'tīs** n. [f. Gk *enterikos* (*enteron* intestine, see -IC)]

ĕn'tero- (before a vowel **ĕn'ter-**), comb. form of Gk *enteron* intestine, as ~*lite*, stony concretion of stomach etc., ~*tomy* (-ōt²) cutting open intestine.

ĕn'terprise (-z), n. Undertaking, esp. bold or difficult one; courage, readiness, to engage in ~*s*, as *he has no* ~. [ME, f.

OF *entreprise* f. *entreprendre* (*entre* between +*prendre* take f. L *pre(he)ndere*)]

ĕn′terprīsing (-z-), a. Showing enterprise. Hence ~LY² adv. [part. of arch. vb *enterprise* (f. prec.)]

ĕntertain′, v.t. Maintain (correspondence, discourse); amuse, occupy agreeably, (person etc., often iron.), whence ~ING² a., ~ingLY² adv.; receive hospitably (~ *angels unawares*, see *Heb.* xiii. 2; also abs., as *they ~ a great deal*); harbour, cherish, welcome or consider, (idea, feeling, proposal). [f. F *entretenir* f. Rom. *INTER(tenēre* hold)]

ĕntertain′ment, n. In vbl senses, esp.: amusement, as *much to my ~*; public performance or show (‖ ~ *tax*, one levied on attendance at these). [-MENT]

ĕnthral(l)′ (-awl), v.t. (-ll-). Enslave (usu. fig.); charm. Hence **ĕnthral′**MENT (-awl-) n. [EN-¹]

ĕnthrōne′, v.t. Place (king, bishop, etc.) on throne, esp. as formal induction (also fig.). Hence ~MENT (-nm-) n. [c. 1600, replacing *enthronize* (foll.)]

ĕnthrōnīzā′tion, n. Enthronement (lit. & fig.). [f. ME *en-*, *intronise* f. OF *introniser* f. LL (*in-*) f. Gk EN²(*thronizō* as THRONE, -IZE)]

ĕnthūse′ (-z), v.i. (colloq.). Show enthusiasm, gush. [back formation on foll.]

ĕnthū′siăsm (-zī-), n. Ardent zeal (*for*, *about*, an object, cause, etc.). [f. LL f. Gk *enthousiasmos* f. *enthousiazō* f. EN²(*theos* god) possessed by a god]

ĕnthū′siăst (-zī-), n. One who is full of enthusiasm (*for* cause etc.), whence ~IC a., ~ICALLY adv., (-zĭăs⁴); visionary, self-deluded person. [f. LL f. Gk *enthousiastēs* (as prec.)]

ĕn′thȳmēme, n. (logic). Syllogism in which one premiss is suppressed. [f. L f. Gk *enthumēma* f. EN²*thumeomai* consider (*thumos* mind)]

ĕntīce′, v.t. Allure (person etc. *from* place, course of conduct, etc., *into* another; *to* do). So ~MENT (-sm-) n. [ME, f. OF EN¹-*ticier* prob. lit. set on fire (L *titio* firebrand)]

ĕntīre′, a. & n. Whole, complete; not broken or decayed; not castrated; unqualified, as ~ *affection*; mere, as *an ~ delusion*; all of one piece, continuous; pure, unmixed; (n., hist., ‖ & on inn-signs) blend of former ale, beer, & two-penny. Hence ~NESS (-īīn-) n. [ME, f. OF *entier* f. L IN²(*teger*, f. *tag-*, *tangere* touch)]

ĕntīre′ly (-īrli), adv. Wholly; solely, [-LY²]

ĕntīre′t|y (-īrti), n. Completeness, esp., *in its ~y*; sum total (*of*); (Law) *possession by ~ies* (undivided). [f. OF *entierete* f. L *integritatem* (as ENTIRE, see -TY)]

ĕntī′tle, v.t. Give (book etc.) the title of (*Adam Bede* etc.); give (person) the title of (sultan etc.); (of circumstances, qualities, etc.) give (person etc.) a claim (*to* a

thing, *to* do). [ME, f. OF *entiteler* f. LL IN-(*titulare*, as TITLE)]

ĕn′tĭty, n. A thing's existence, as opp. to its qualities or relations; thing that has real existence. So **ĕn′tĭt**ATIVE a. [f. F *entité* or med. L *entitas*, see ENS, -TY]

ĕn′to-, comb. form of Gk *entos* within, as *-pa′rasite*, *-zo′on*, internal parasite, *-phyte*, plant growing inside a plant or animal.

ĕntomb′ (-ōōm), v.t. Place in tomb (lit. & fig.); serve as tomb for. Hence ~MENT (-ōōm-m-) n. [f. OF EN¹*toumber* (as TOMB)]

ĕntŏm′ĭc, a. Of insects. [as foll. +-IC]

ĕntomo- in comb. Insect, as : ~*lite* (-ŏm²), fossil insect, ~*phagous* (-ŏf²), insect-eating, ~*philous* (-ŏf²), (Bot.) fertilized by means of insects, ~*tomy* (-ŏt²), insect anatomy. [f. Gk EN(*tomos* f. *temnō* cut) cut up, in neut. pl. = insects]

ĕntomŏl′og|ȳ, n. Study of insects. Hence **ĕntomolŏ′gĭcal** a., ~ıST n., ~ıZE v.i. [f. F ENTOMO(*logie* -LOGY)]

entourage (see Ap.), n. Surroundings; attendant persons. [F]

en-tout-cas (ahn tōō kah), n. Umbrella-sunshade; kind of hard lawn-tennis court. [F, lit. in any case]

entr′acte (see Ap.), n. (Performance in) interval between acts of play. [F]

ĕn′trails (-z), n. pl. Bowels, intestines; (fig.) inner parts (*of* the earth etc.). [ME, f. OF *entrailles* f. med. L *intralia* alt. f. L *interanea* (neut. pl.) f. *inter* among]

ĕntrain′, v.t. & i. Put (esp. troops), get, into a train. [EN-¹]

ĕntrămm′el, v.t. (-ll-). Entangle, hamper. [EN-¹]

ĕn′trance¹, n. Coming or going in; coming of actor upon stage; entering *into*, *upon* (office etc.); right of admission; (in full ~ *fee*) fee paid on admission to club, school, etc.; door, passage, etc., one enters by. [OF (as ENTER, -ANCE)]

ĕntrance′² (-ah-), v.t. Throw into a trance; overwhelm (*with* joy, fear); carry away as in trance (*from*, *to*). Hence ~MENT (-ahnsm-) n. [EN-¹]

ĕn′trant, n. One who enters room, profession, etc., or *for* (race etc.). [F, part. as ENTER]

ĕntrăp′, v.t. (-pp-). Catch in or as in trap; beguile (person *to* destruction etc., *into doing*). [f. OF EN¹(*traper* TRAP¹)]

ĕntreat′, v.t. (Also ~ *of*) ask (person) earnestly (*to do*, *that*), whence ~ingLY² adv.; (Bibl.) *evil ~*, treat ill. [ME, f. OF EN¹(*traiter* TREAT)]

ĕntreat′y, n. Earnest request. [prec. +-Y⁴]

entrechat (ŏ′ntreshah), n. Striking together of the heels several times during leap from ground, in dancing. [F, f. It. (*capriola) intrecciata* complicated (caper)]

entrecôte (ŏ′ntrekŏt), n. (cookery). Steak cut off the ribs. [F]

entrée (ŏ′ntrā, *& see Ap.*), n. Right, privilege, of admission; ‖ made dish served between fish & joint. [F, = ENTRY]

entremets (see Ap.), n. A side dish or dainty. [F]

èntrench', **ìn-**, v.t. & i. Surround (post, army, town) with trench (also fig., esp., one*self*); (rarely) encroach, trespass, *upon*. Hence ~MENT n. [EN-[1]]

entre nous (see Ap.), adv. Between you & me. [F]

entrepôt (see Ap.), n. Storehouse for deposit; commercial centre for import & export, collection & distribution. [F]

entrepreneur (ahǹtreprenêr'), n. Person in effective control of commercial undertaking; contractor acting as intermediary. [F]

entresol (see Ap.), n. Low storey between first & ground floor. [F]

ĕn'tropў, n. (phys.). Measure of the unavailability of a system's thermal energy for conversion into mechanical work. [f. G *entropie* f. EN-[2] + Gk *tropē* transformation, after *energie* ENERGY]

èntrŭst', **ìn-**, v.t. Charge (person) *with* (duty, object of care); confide (duty, person, thing, its safety, *to* person). [EN-[1]]

ĕn'trў, n. **1.** Coming or going in; ceremonial entrance; (Law) taking possession; place of entrance, door, gate, lobby, mouth of river. **2.** Registration in records, account-books, etc.; item so entered; *bookkeeping by double, single,* ~ (in which each item is entered twice, once, in ledger); list of competitors for race etc. [ME *entre(e)* f. OF *entree* f. Rom. **intrata* (as ENTER, -Y[4])]

èntwine', **ìn-**, v.t. Interweave (lit. & fig.); wreathe (thing *with, about, round*, another); embrace. [EN-[1]]

èntwist', **ìn-**, v.t. Clasp with, form into, a twist; twist (thing) in *with* (another). [EN-[1]]

ènŭc'lė|āte, v.t. Explain, clear up; (Surg.) extract (tumour etc.) from shell etc. Hence ~A'TION n. [f. L E(*nucleare* f. NUCLEUS)]

ènŭm'er|āte, v.t. Count; specify (items). Hence or cogn. ~A'TION, ~ātOR, nn., ~ātIVE a. [f. L E(*numerare* NUMBER[2])]

ènŭn'ci|āte (-shǐ-), v.t. Express definitely (proposition, theory); proclaim; pronounce (words). So ~A'TION (-sǐ-), ~ātOR (-shǐ-), nn., ~ātIVE (-sha-) a. [f. L E(*nuntiare* announce f. *nuntius* messenger), -ATE[3]]

ènūre', v.i. (& t.). See INURE.

ènūrḗs'ìs, n. (path.). Incontinence of urine. [f. Gk *enoureō* urinate in (EN-[2] + *ouron* urine)]

ènvĕl'op, v.t. Wrap up (person, thing, subject, etc., *in* garment, flames, clouds, mystery, or w. *flame* etc. as subject); (Mil.) effect the surrounding of (enemy). Hence ~MENT n. [ME *envolupe* OF *envoluper* f. EN-[1] as DEVELOP]

ĕn'velōpe (*or* ŏn-), n. Wrapper, covering, (lit. & fig.), esp. folded & gummed cover of letter. [f. F *enveloppe* (as prec.)]

ènvĕn'om, v.t. Put poison on or into (weapon, air, etc.); infuse venom into (feelings, words, actions); corrupt (mind etc.). [ME *-im*, f. OF EN[1](*venimer* as VENOM)]

ĕn'viab|le, a. Calculated to excite envy (said of desirable thing or its possessor). Hence ~LY[2] adv. [f. ENVY v. +-ABLE]

ĕn'vious, a. Full of envy; feeling envy *of* (person, thing). Hence ~LY[2] adv. [ME, f. AF *envious*, OF *-eus*, f. L *invidiosus* (as ENVY[1], see -OUS)]

ènvīr'on, v.t. (Of persons or things) form a ring, be stationed, round; surround (person, place, etc.) hostilely, protectively, as attendants, etc.; surround (person, thing, *with* others). [ME, f. OF *environer* f. adv. as ENVIRONS]

ènvīr'onment, n. Surrounding; surrounding objects, region, or circumstances. [-MENT]

ènvīr'ons (-z; *or* ĕn'vīronz), n. pl. District surrounding town etc. [17th c. f. F, f. OF *environ* (n. f. adv.) f. *viron* circuit, neighbourhood, f. *virer* VEER]

ènvis'age (-z-), v.t. Look in the face of; face (danger, facts); contemplate, esp. under particular aspect. Hence ~MENT (-jm-) n. [f. F EN[1]*visager* (VISAGE)]

ĕn'voy[1], n. (arch.). (Author's parting words, esp.) short stanza concluding certain arch. forms of poem (also *-oi*). [ME, f. OF f. *envoier* send (*en voie* on the way f. L *via*)]

ĕn'voy[2], n. Messenger, representative; esp. minister plenipotentiary, ranking below ambassador & above *chargé d'affaires*. Hence ~SHIP n. [f. F *envoyé*, p.p. as prec., loss of *-é* as in ASSIGN[2]]

ĕn'vў[1], n. Grudging contemplation (*of* more fortunate persons, *of, at*, their advantages, or abs.; often playfully), object, ground, of this, as *she, her poodle, is the* ~ *of Bath*. [ME, f. OF *envie* f. L *invidia* f. *invidus* f. IN(*vidēre* see) envy]

ĕn'vў[2], v.t. Feel envy of, as *I* ~ *him,* ~ *his impudence,* ~ *him his impudence*. [ME, f. OF *envier* f. med. L *invidiare* (*invidia* ENVY[1])]

ènwind', v.t. (Of thing) wind itself round (another). [EN-[1]]

ènwomb' (-ōom), v.t. Enclose (as) in womb. [EN-[1]]

ènwrăp', **ìn-**, v.t. (-pp-). Wrap, enfold, (*in*; lit. & fig.). [EN-[1]]

ènwreathe' (-dh), v.t. Surround as or (as) with wreath; intertwine. [EN-[1]]

ĕnzoŏt'ic, a. & n. (Disease) regularly affecting cattle etc. in a particular district or at a particular season. [f. EN-[2], Gk *zōion* animal, -IC]

ĕn'zўme, n. (chem.). An organic catalyst formed by living cells but not depending on their presence for its action. [f. G *enzym*, f. EN-[2] + Gk *zumē*, see ZYMOSIS]

E'ocène (*or* ē-; a. (geol.). Of the lowest division of Tertiary strata. [f. Gk *eōs* dawn + *kainos* new]

ēolith'ic, a. Of the period preceding the

PALAEOlithic age. [Gk *ēōs* dawn, *lithos* stone]

eon. See AEON.

e'osin, n. Red fluorescent dye-stuff used (esp.) in microscopy and colour-photography [f. Gk *ēōs* dawn + -IN]

-eous, suf. = L *-eus* + -OUS, forming adjj. meaning ' of the nature of ', as *ligneous* like wood; in *righteous, courteous, gorgeous, -eous* is a corruption of another suf.; *bounteous, duteous* result from the addition of *-ous* to another suf.

ēozo'ic, a. (geol.). (Of strata) showing the earliest indications of animal life. [Gk *ēōs* dawn, *zōion* animal]

ep- in comb. = EPI- before unaspirated vowels.

ep'äct, n. Age of moon on Jan. 1; excess of solar over lunar year. [f. F *épacte* f. LL f. Gk *epaktai* f. EP(*agō* bring) intercalate]

ep'arch (-k), n. Governor, bishop, of an eparchy. [f. Gk EP(*arkhos* ruler)]

ep'archў (-k-), n. Subdivision of modern Greece; diocese in Russian (Greek) Church. [f. Gk *eparkhia*(as prec., see -Y[1])]

épaule'ment (-awlm-), n. (fortif.). Breastwork (esp. as flank protection). [F, f. *épauler* protect with ~, f. *épaule* (as foll.)]

ep'aulet(te) (-pol-), n. Ornamental shoulder-piece of uniform; (of private soldier) *win his ~s,* earn promotion to rank of officer. [f. F *épaulette* dim. of *épaulę* shoulder f. L *spatula*]

épée (āpā'), n. The sharp-pointed duelling-sword, used (blunted) in fencing. [F, = sword]

ēpeirogĕn'ĕsis (-pīr-), n. (geol.). Process of making continents. [f. Gk *ēpeiros* mainland, GENESIS]

epĕn'thĕsis, n. Insertion of a letter or sound within a word. Hence **ĕpĕnthĕt'IC** a. [Gk]

epergne (ĕpĕrn'), n. Centre ornament (esp. in branched form) for dinner-table to hold flowers or fruit. [orig. unkn.]

ĕpĕxĕg|ēs'is, n. Additional, addition of, words to make meaning clear (e.g. ' difficult *to do* '). So ~ĕt'IC(AL) aa., ~ĕt'icalLY[2] adv. [Gk (EP- + EXEGESIS)]

eph-, pref. = EPI- before *h*.

ĕphēbe', n. (Gk Ant.). Citizen aged 18 to 20. [f. L f. Gk EPH*ēbos* (*hēbē* early manhood)]

ĕphĕm'era (pl. *-ras*), **-eron** (pl. *-rons, -ra*), nn. Insect living only a day; kinds of insects including mayfly; short-lived thing. [f. Gk EPH*ēmeros* lasting only a day (*hēmera*)]

ĕphĕm'eral, a. (Of diseases) lasting only a day; (of insects, flowers, etc.) lasting a day or a few days; short-lived, transitory. Hence ~ITY (-ǎl[2]) n. [f. Gk as prec. + -AL]

ĕphĕm'er|is, n. (pl. ~*ides,* pr. -ĕ'rīdēz). Astronomical almanac or table. [LL f. Gk (-*ēm-*), = calendar (as prec.)]

ĕph'od, n. Jewish priestly vestment. [ME; Heb., f. *aphad* put on]

ĕph'or, n. One of five Spartan magistrates controlling the kings; (in mod. Greece) overseer. [f. Gk EPH*oros* (*horaō* see)]

ĕpi-, pref. = Gk *epi* upon, at, on the ground of, in addition.

ĕp'iblǎst, n. (biol.). Outermost layer of blastoderm. [f. EPI- + Gk *blastos* sprout, germ]

ĕp'ic, ˉa. & n. (Poem) narrating continuously achievements of one or more heroes, as the *Iliad & Odyssey;* fit for recital in an ~, of heroic type or scale; *E~ dialect,* form of Gk in which the ~ poems were written; *national~,* poem of, any form, embodying nation's conception of its past history. Hence ~AL a., ~alLY[2] adv. [f. L f. Gk *epikos* (EPOS, -IC)]

ĕpicĕd'ium, n. Funeral ode. [f. L f. Gk EPI(*kēdeion* f. *kēdos* care)]

ĕp'icēne, a. & n. (Lat. & Gk Gram.) denoting either sex without change of gender; for, used by, both sexes; (person) with characteristics of both sexes. [f. LL f. Gk EPI(*koinos* common)]

ĕpicĕn'trum, -tre (-*ter*), nn. Point at which earthquake breaks out. [f. Gk EPI(*kentros* a. as CENTRE)]

ĕpiclēs'is, -klēs'is, n. Invocation, esp. of the Holy Spirit to consecrate the elements in the Eucharist. [Gk (EPI-, *kaleō* call)]

ĕp'icūr|e, n. One who is choice & dainty in eating & drinking. Hence ~ISM (2) n. [f. med. L *epicurus,* appellative use of L f. Gk *Epikouros* Epicurus]

ĕpicūrē'an, a. & n. (Follower) of Epicurus, Athenian philosopher (300 B.C.) who taught that highest good was pleasure (i.e. practice of virtue); (person) devoted to pleasure, esp. refined sensuous enjoyment. Hence ~ISM(3) n. [f. L *epicurēus* (LL *-ius*) f. Gk *Epikoureios* (prec., -EAN)]

ĕp'icycle, n. (geom.). Small circle rolling on circumference of a greater. Hence **ĕpicyc'lIC** a. [ME, f. OF, or LL f. Gk EPI(*kuklos* circle)]

ĕpicyc'loid, n. Curve traced by point in circumference of a circle rolling on exterior of another. Hence ~AL (-oid[2]) a. [prec. + -OID]

ĕpideic'tic (-dīk-), a. Meant for display. [f. Gk *epideiktikos* f. EPI(*deiknumi* show), see -IC]

ĕpidĕm'ĭc, a. & n. (Disease, lit. & fig.) prevalent among community at special time, cf. ENDEMIC. Hence ~AL a., ~alLY[2] adv. [f. F *épidémique* f. *épidémie* f. LL f. Gk *epidēmia* f. *epidēmios* a. (*dēmos* people)]

ĕpidēmiŏl'ogў, n. Science of epidemics. [f. Gk as prec., -LOGY]

ĕpidĕrm'|is, n. Outer layer of skin of animals, cuticle; outer animal integument of shell; true skin of plant below cuticle. Hence ~AL, ~IC, ~OID, **ĕpidĕr-moid'AL,** aa. [LL, f. Gk EPI*dermis* (DERM)]

ĕpĭdĭ′ascōpe, n. Optical lantern projecting images of both opaque & transparent
objects. [EPI- + DIA- + -SCOPE]

′ĕpĭgăs′tr|ium, n. Part of abdomen im-
mediately over stomach. Hence ~IC a.
[LL, f. Gk EPIgastrion (gastēr stomach)]

ĕp′ĭgēne, a. (Geol.) produced on surface of earth; (of crystal) chemically
altered since its formation. [f. F épigène
f. Gk EPI(genēs born)]

ĕpĭgĕn′esis, n. Formation of organic
germ as a new product; theory of ~ (that
the germ is brought into existence, not
merely developed, in process of reproduction). [EPI-]

ĕpĭglŏtt′|ĭs, n. Erect cartilage at root of
tongue, depressed during swallowing to
cover glottis. Hence ~IC a. [Gk EPI-
(glōttis f. glōtta tongue)]

ĕp′ĭgōne, n. One of a later (& less distinguished) generation. [f. L f. Gk
epigonos (EPI- + root of gignomai be born]

ĕp′ĭgrăm, n. Short poem ending in witty
turn of thought; pointed saying or mode
of expression. So **ĕpĭgrammăt′IC** a.,
ĕpĭgrammăt′ICALLY adv., **ĕpĭgrămm′-
atIST**(3) n., **ĕpĭgrămm′atIZE**(1, 2) v.t.
& i. [f. F épigramme or L f. Gk EPI-
(gramma -GRAM)]

ĕp′ĭgraph (-ahf), n. Inscription on stone,
statue, coin, etc., whence **ĕpĭgrăph′IC** a.,
ĕpĭg′raphIST (2), **ĕpĭg′raphY**[1], nn.;
motto. [f. Gk EPI(graphē f. graphō
write)]

ĕp′ĭlĕpsy̆, n. Nervous disease in which
patient falls to ground unconscious, with
or without convulsions. [f. F épilepsie or
LL f. Gk epilēpsia f. EPI(lambanō take)]

ĕpĭlĕp′tic, a. & n. Of epilepsy; (person)
subject to epilepsy. [f. F épileptique or
LL f. Gk epilēptikos (as prec.)]

ĕpĭl′ogĭst, n. Writer, speaker, of epilogue.
[f. foll. + -IST]

ĕp′ĭlŏgue (-g), n. Concluding part of
literary work; speech, short poem, addressed to spectators by actor at end of
play; || (Radio) short religious service
towards the end of some B.B.C. programmes. [F, f. L f. Gk EPI(logos speech)]

ĕpĭph′any̆, n. Manifestation of Christ to
the Magi; manifestation of a superhuman
being. [ME; (1) f. OF epiphanie f. LL f.
Gk epiphania (neut. pl. adj.) f. EPI(phainō
show); (2) f. Gk epiphaneia manifesta-
tion]

ĕpĭphĕnŏm′ĕnon, n. (med., philos.; pl.
-ena). Secondary symptom, mere concomitant of something else not regarded
as its cause or result. [EPI-, PHENOMENON]

ĕp′ĭphy̆te, n. Plant growing on (usu. not
fed by) another; vegetable parasite on
animal body. Hence **ĕpĭphy̆t′AL**, **ĕpĭ-
phy̆t′IC**, aa. [f. EPI- + Gk phuton plant]

Epir′ot (I-), n. Inhabitant of Epirus. [f.
Gk ēpeirōtēs (ēpeiros, -OT[2])]

ĕpis′copacy̆, n. Government of church by
bishops; the ~, the bishops. [as EPISCO-
PATE, -ACY, after prelacy]

ĕpis′copal, a. Of bishop(s); ~ church,
constituted on principle of prec. Hence
~ISM(3) n., ~LY[2] adv. [f. F épiscopal or
LL episcopalis (as BISHOP, see -AL)]

ĕpiscopāl′ian, a. & n. (Adherent) of episcopacy; (member) of episcopal church.
Hence ~ISM(3) n. [f. L as prec. + -AN]

ĕpis′copate, n. Office, position, tenure, of
bishop; the ~, the bishops. [f. LL episco-
patus (episcopus BISHOP, see -ATE[1])]

ĕp′isōde, n. Part between two choric
songs in Gk tragedy (orig. interpolation);
incidental narrative or series of events.
Hence **ĕpĭsŏd′IC(AL)** aa., **ĕpĭsŏd′icalLY**[2]
adv. [f. Gk EPIeisodion f. eisodos entry (eis
into + hodos way)]

ĕpispăs′tic, a. & n. (med.). Blistering
(plaster, substance). [f. LL f. Gk epispas-
tikos f. EPI(spaō draw), see -IC]

ĕpistēmŏl′ogy̆, n. Theory of the method
or grounds of knowledge. [f. Gk epistēmē
knowledge + -O- + -LOGY]

ĕpis′tle (-sl), n. Letter (now only joc.
of ordinary modern letters), esp. one of
an apostle, part of the canon of Scripture;
the E~, extract from apostolical ~ read in
Communion service; literary work, usu.
verse, in form of letter. [ME, f. OF f. L
f. Gk epistolē f. EPI(stellō send)]

ĕpis′tolary̆, a. Of, carried on by, suited
to, letters. [f. F épistolaire or L episto-
laris (as prec., see -ARY[2])]

ĕpis′toler, n. (eccl.). Reader (cf. GOSPEL-
LER) of the Epistle. [f. OF epistolier or
med. L epistolarius as prec., -ER[2] (2)]

ĕpis′trophe, n. (rhet.). Ending of several
sentences or clauses with same word.
[Gk EPI(strophē turning f. strephō)]

ĕp′isty̆le, n. (archit.). = ARCHITRAVE. [f.
L f. Gk EPI(stulion f. stulos pillar)]

ĕp′itaph (-ahf), n. Words (supposed to be)
inscribed on tomb. [ME, f. OF epitaphe or
L f. Gk EPI(taphion f. taphos tomb)]

ĕpithalām′|ium, n. (pl. -iums, -ia). Nup-
tial song or poem. Hence ~IAL, **ĕpĭtha-
lăm′IC**, aa. [f. L f. Gk EPI(thalamion f.
thalamos bride-chamber)]

ĕpithĕl′|ium, n. Tissue forming outer
layer of mucous membrane; (Bot.) epidermis formed of young cells. Hence
~IAL a. [mod. L, f. EPI- + Gk thēlē teat]

ĕp′ithĕt, n. Adjective expressing quality
or attribute; significant appellation.
Hence ~IC(AL) aa., ~icalLY[2] adv., (-ĕt[4]).
[f. F épithète or L f. Gk epitheton f.
EPI(tithēmi place)]

ĕpit′om|e, n. Summary, abstract, of
book; condensed account; (fig.) thing
that represents another in miniature, as
man, the world's ~e. Hence ~IST(1) n.,
~IZE(3) v.t. [f. L f. Gk EPI(temnō
cut) abridge]

ĕpizō′ŏn, n. (pl. -oa). External parasite or
commensal. [EPI-, Gk zō(i)on animal]

ĕp′izoŏt′ic, a. & n. (Disease) temporarily
prevalent among animals (cf. ENZOOTIC,
EPIDEMIC). [prec., -IC]

ĕp′ŏch (-k), n. Beginning of era in history,

science, life, etc., as *this made an* ~, *an* ~- -*making event*; date; period in history or life marked by special events. Hence **ĕp'ochAL** (-k-) a. [f. med. L f. Gk *epokhē* stoppage f. EP(*ekhō* hold)]

ĕp'ōde, n. Form of lyric poem, used by Horace; third division of Greek choral ode (see STROPHE). [f. F *épode* or L f. Gk *epō(i)dos* f. EP(*a(i)dō* sing)]

ĕp'onȳm, n. One who gives his name to a people, place, or institution. So **ĕpŏn'ȳmous** a. [f. Gk EP(*ōnumos* f. *onoma* name)]

ĕp'opee, n. Epic poem or poetry. [f. F *épopée* f. Gk *epopoiia* (foll. +*poieō* make)]

ĕp'ŏs, n. Early unwritten epic poetry; epic poem. [L f. Gk *epos* word, song]

ĕpsīl'on, n. Greek letter (E, ε) ĕ (cf. ETA). [Gk (*psilos* bare)]

Ep'som (ĕ-), n. Town in Surrey; ~ *salt(s)*, magnesium sulphate; (used for) race- -course at ~, principal race-meeting there held, including Derby and Oaks.

ē'qua|ble, a. Uniform, even, not easily disturbed. Hence ~BIL'ITY n., ~bLY² adv. [f. L *aequabilis* (as EQUATE, -BLE)]

ē'qual¹, a. & n. **1.** The same in number, size, value, degree, etc. (*to, with,* or abs.), as *twice three is* ~ *to six, the totals are* ~, *talks French & Dutch with* ~ *ease, the two are* ~ *in ability*; having strength, courage, ability, etc., adequate *to* (*the occasion, a cup of tea, doing,* etc.); uniform in opera- tion etc., as ~ *laws*; evenly balanced (fight etc.); ~ TEMPERAMENT. **2.** n. Person ~ to another in rank etc., as *mix with your* ~*s*, or in power etc., as *he has no* ~; (pl.) ~ things, use *if* ~*s be added to* ~*s*. [ME, f. L *aequalis* (*aequus* even, see -AL)]

ē'qual², v.t. (-ll-). Be equal to (person, thing, *in* quality, number, etc.). [f. prec.]

ēqual'itȳ (-ŏl-), n. Condition of being equal (*between* two or more; *with* person etc. *in* quality etc.; usu. abs.); *is on an* ~ *with*, is on equal terms with. [ME, f. OF *equalite* f. L *aequalitatem* (as EQUAL¹, see -TY)]

ē'qualiz|e, -is|e (-īz), v.t. & i. Make (thing etc.) equal (*to, with*; (Footb. etc.) bring score to equality with opponent's. Hence ~A'TION n. [-IZE]

ē'qualiȳ, adv. In an equal degree; in equal shares; uniformly. [-LY²]

ēquanim'itȳ, n. Evenness of mind or temper; composure; resignation. [f. F *équanimité* or L *aequanimitas* (*aequus* even +*animus* mind), see -TY]

ēquāte', v.t. State equality of (thing *to, with*, another); treat as equivalent. [f. L *aequare* (*aequus* equal), see -ATE³]

ēquā'tion, n. **1.** Making equal, balancing, (of demand & supply etc.). **2.** (Amount or process of) compensation for inaccuracy, as (Astron.) *personal* ~, allowance for individual slowness in noting phenomena (also fig.), ~ (difference between mean & apparent places) *of the equinoxes*. **3.** (math.). Formula affirming equivalence of

two expressions connected by the sign=. Hence ~AL a., ~alLȳ² adv., (-shon-). [f. L *aequatio* (as prec., see -ATION)]

ēquāt'or, n. A great circle of the earth, equidistant from the poles; = EQUINOC- TIAL; *magnetic* ~, ACLINIC line. [ME, f. med. L (as prec., -OR)]

ēquatōr'ial, n. Of, near, the equator; ~ *telescope* (attached to axle revolving in direction parallel to plane of equator). Hence ~LY² adv. [-IAL]

‖ **ē'querrȳ** (*or* ĭkwĕ'rĭ), n. Officer of prince or noble charged with care of horses; officer of British royal household. [16th c. *esquiry* f. obs. F *escurie* stable (= med. L *scura, scuria*) perh. f. WG *skur* shed; confused in E w. L *equus* horse]

ēquĕst'rian, a. & n. **1.** Of horse-riding; ~ *statue* (of person on horse); (Rom. Ant.) of the order of Equites or Knights. **2.** n. Rider, performer, on horseback. [f. L *equestris* (*eques* horseman f. *equus* horse) +-AN]

ēquĕstriĕnne', n. Horsewoman; (esp.) female circus-rider. [pseudo-F, f. prec. with fem. suffix]

ēqui- = L *aequi-*, comb. form of L *aequus* equal, as ~*ăng'ūlar* (-ngg-), having equal angles.

ēquidis'tant, a. Separated by equal distance(s). [f. F *équidistant* f. LL *aequi- distantem* (see EQUI- & DISTANT)]

ēquilăt'eral, a. Having all the sides equal. [f. LL *aequilateralis* (see EQUI- & LATERAL)]

ēquilib'r|āte, v.t. & i. Cause (two things) to balance; balance (t. & i.); counter- poise. Hence ~A'TION n. [f. LL *aequili- brare*, see -ATE³]

ēquil'ibrist, n. Rope-walker, acrobat. [f. F *équilibriste* (*équilibre* EQUILIBRIUM)]

ēquilib'rium, n. State of balance (lit. & fig.); *a body in stable* ~ (tending to re- cover ~ after disturbance); neutrality of judgement etc. [L (EQUI-, *libra* balance)]

ēquimŭl'tiple, n. (usu. pl.). Number having a common factor with another. [EQUI-]

ē'quine, a. Of, like, a horse. [f. L *equinus* (*equus* horse, see -INE¹)]

ēquinŏc'tial (-shal), a. & n. **1.** Of equal day & night; ~ *line*, circle of celestial sphere whose plane is perpendicular to earth's axis; happening at or near time of equinox, as ~ *gales*; at, near, the (terres- trial) equator. **2.** n. ~ line, (pl.) ~ gales. [ME, f. OF, or L *aequinoctialis* (as foll., see -AL)]

ē'quinŏx, n. Time at which sun crosses equator & day & night are equal (*vernal* ~, about March 20; *autumnal* ~, about Sep. 22 or 23); (pl.) two points at which sun crosses equator; PRECESSION *of* ~*es*. [ME, f. OF *equinoxe* or med. L *equi- noxium* for L *aequinoctium* (*nox* -*ctis* night, EQUI-)]

ēquip', v.t. (-pp-). Furnish (ship, army, person, *with* requisites); provide (one*self* etc.) for journey etc. Hence ~MENT n. [f. F *équiper*, *esq-*, prob. f. ON *skipa* man (ship) f. *skip* SHIP]

ē′quipage, n. Requisites for an ·undertaking; outfit for journey etc.; carriage & horses with attendants. [f. F *équipage* (as prec., -AGE)]

ē′quipoise (-z), n., & v.t. **1.** Equilibrium (often fig.); counterbalancing thing. **2.** v.t. Counterbalance, hold (mind) in suspense. [EQUI-]

ēquipŏll′|ent, a. & n. Equal in power, force, etc.; practically equivalent; (n.) ~ent thing. So ~ENCE, ~ENCY, nn. [f. OF *equipolent* f. L *aequipollentem* (EQUI-, *pollēre* be strong)]

ēquipon′der|āte, v.t. Counterbalance. So ~ANT a. & n. [f. med. L *aequi(ponderare* weigh f. *pondus -eris* weight), see EQUI- & -ATE[3]]

ēquipotĕn′tial (-shl), a. (phys.). In which the potential of a force is the same· or constant at all points. [EQUI-]

ē′quitab|le, a. Fair, just, whence ~leNESS n., ~LY[2] adv.; (of claims etc.) valid in equity as opposed to law. [f. F *équitable* (as EQUITY + -ABLE)].

ēquitā′tion, n. (usu. joc.). Riding on horse; horsemanship. [F, or f. L *equitatio* f. *equitare* f. *eques -itis* horseman f. *equus* horse, see -ATION]

ē′quity, n. **1.** Fairness; recourse to principles of justice to correct or supplement law; system of law coexisting with and superseding common and statute law. **2.** ‖ (*E*~) actors' trade union. **3.** pl. ‖ Stocks and shares not bearing fixed interest. **4.** Net value of mortgaged property after deduction of charges. [ME, f. OF *equite* f. L *aequitatem* (*aequus* fair, see -TY)]

ēquiv′al|ent, a. & n. **1.** Equal in value (*to*); (of words) meaning the same; (Chem.) equal in combining value (*to*); having the same result; corresponding. **2.** n. ~ent thing, amount, word, etc. So ~ENCE, ~ENCY, nn. [ME, f. OF or f. LL *aequi-* (*valēre* be worth), see EQUI- & -ENT]

ēquiv′ocal, a. Of double meaning, ambiguous; of uncertain nature; ~ *generation* (spontaneous); undecided; (of persons, character, etc.) questionable, suspicious. Hence ~ITY (-ăl′-), ~NESS, nn., ~LY[2] adv. [f. LL *aequivocus* (EQUI-, *vocare* call), see -AL]

ēquiv′oc|āte, v.i. Use ambiguous words to conceal the truth, prevaricate. Hence or cogn. ~A′TION, ~ātOR, nn. [f. LL *aequivocare* (as prec., see -ATE[3])]

ē′quivŏque (-k), -ōke, n. Pun; ambiguity. [f. LL *aequivocus* EQUIVOCAL; later also f. F *équivoque*]

-er[1], suf. forming esp. agent nn. f. nn. & vbs. Orig. = ' one who has to do with ', OE *-ere* f. Gmc *-arjaz*, the relation of which to L *-arius* (-ARY[1]) is obsc.; so E wds as *hatter*, *slater*; a few as *cottager*, *villager*; also colloq. wds of action, as

header, *oul-&-outer*, and of number, as *fiver*, *tenner*; add *Londoner*, *foreigner*, etc. As many wds so formed correspond to vbs, -er took agent sense (*clothier* one connected with cloth, one who clothes), & can now be added to any vb unless otherwise provided, as *correspond(ent)*, *translat(or)*; *-or* (*-our*, *-ier*) & *-er* may coexist, with or without differentiation (*saviour*, *-er*; *assertor*, *-er*); some wds app. double *-er* (*caterer*, *fruiterer*, *poulterer*); -er is occas. used to anglicize L *-us* (*astronomer*, *biographer*, *chronologer*). Meanings: (1) person, animal, that does something; (2) instrument, machine, occurrence, etc. (*poker*, *paper-culter*, *deodorizer*, *eye-opener*); (3) person concerned with thing (*hatter*, *geographer*); (4) person belonging to place etc. (*Londoner*, *Brilisher*); (5) sl. distortion of word with other ending (*Rugger*, *Soccer*, *footer*, Rugby, Association, football).

-er[2], suf. in nn. & adjj. f. OF, of var. orig., esp.: (1) OF, ME -er f. L *-arem*; ME -er was later refash. w. *-ar*; see -AR[1]. (2) AF, ME -er (OF *-ier*) f. L *-arius*, *-arium*, as in *buller*, *carpenter*, *danger*; see -ARY[1]. (3) OF *-eure* f. L *-aturam* = -URE, as *border*. (4) For interchange of *-er*, *-or*, see -OR.

-er[3], suf. forming comparatives; now (exc. in poetry and mannered prose) only in adjj. of one syllable, or of two ending in *-y*, *-ly*, *-le*, *-er*, *-ow*, & a few others (esp. w. accent on last syllable; see -EST), & in advv., chiefly those identical with adjj., as *hard*; the vowel change seen in German etc. now remains only in *elder*, BETTER. [OE: (adj.) *-ra* f. Gmc *-izon-* & *-ozon-*; (adv.) *-or* f. Gmc *-ōz*]

-er[4], suf. esp. in Law terms, as *cesser*, *disclaimer*, *misnomer*, *user*; also *dinner*, *supper*. Meaning: (single instance of) the vbl action, document effecting this. [AF, OF inf.]

-er[5], suf. forming frequent. vbs f. others (*wander*, *waver*, f. *wend*, *wave*) or on sound-imitations (*twitter*); *batter*, *flicker*, *shimmer*, *slumber*.

ēr′a, n. System of chronology starting from some particular point of time, as *Christian* ~, ~ *of the* HEGIRA; historical or other period; date forming commencement of this. [f. LL *aera* number expressed in figures (pl. of *aes aeris* money, treated as fem. sing.)]

ērādiā′tion, n. Emission of rays. [E-]

ērăd′ic|āte, v.t. Tear up by roots; extirpate, get rid of. So ~ABLE a., ~A′TION n. [f. L E(*radicare* f. *radix -icis* root), -ATE[3]]

ērāse′ (-z), v.t. Rub out; obliterate. Hence ērās′ABLE a., ērās′ER[1](2), ērā′sURE (-zher), nn. [f. L E(*radere ras-*scrape)]

Erās′tian (I-), a. & n. (Adherent) of the supposed doctrines of Erastus, subordinating ecclesiastical to secular power. Hence ~ISM(3) n., ~IZE(3) v.t. & i. [f. *Erastus*, Heidelberg physician of 16th c., + -IAN]

E'ratō (ĕ-), n. Muse of lyric poetry. [Gk]

ere (ār), prep. & conj. (poet., arch.). Before (of time); ~ *long*, before long; ~*while'* (arch.), formerly. [OE ǣr, OS, OHG ēr, Goth: *airis* f. Gmc **airiz* compar. of *air* adv. early]

E'rebus (ĕ-), n. (Gk Myth.). Place of darkness between earth & Hades. [L, f. Gk *Erebos*]

ĕrĕct' [1], a. Upright, not stooping, (lit. & fig); vertical; (of hair etc.) set up, bristling. Hence ~**LY** [2] adv., ~**NESS** n. [ME, f. L E(*rigere rect-* = *regere* direct) set up]

ĕrĕct' [2], v.t. Raise, set upright, (oneself, body, etc.); build (lit. & fig.); form (persons, principles, etc.) *into* (class, system, etc.). [ME; as prec.]

ĕrĕc'tile, a. That can be erected; ~ *tissue* in animals (capable of being distended & becoming rigid under excitement). [f. F *érectile* (as ERECT [1], see -IL)]

ĕrĕc'tion, n. Erecting; building, structure, (lit. & fig.). [F, or f. L *erectio* (as prec., see -ION)]

ĕrĕc'tor, n. Person, thing, that erects, as ~*-muscle*. [-OR]

ĕ'rĕmite, ·n. Hermit (esp. of Christian solitaries from 3rd c. onwards). Hence **ĕrĕmit'IC**(AL) aa. [ME, f. OF or f. LL *eremita* HERMIT]

ĕ'rĕthism, n. (path.). Abnormal excitement (of organ or tissue, fig. of mind). [f. F *éréthisme* f. Gk *erethismos* (*erethizō* irritate, see -ISM)]

ĕrg, ĕrg'ŏn, n. (phys.). Unit of work or energy. (The work done by unit force, one dyne, on a body which moves 1 cm. in the direction of action of the force). [f. Gk *ergon* work]

ĕrgatŏc'racў, n. Rule of the workers. [Gk *ergatēs* worker, -O-, -CRACY]

ĕrg'ō, adv. (usu. joc.). Therefore. [L]

ĕrg'ot, n. Disease of rye etc. caused by fungus; diseased rye used as medicine. [F, f. OF *argot* cock's spur, f. appearance produced]

ĕrg'otism, n. = prec.; disease produced by bread made from flour affected by this. [-ISM]

ĕricā'ceous (-shŭs), a. Belonging to the heath genus *Eric'a* or its family *Ericā'-ceae*. [f. L f. Gk *ereikē* heath, see -ACEOUS]

E'rin (ĕ-), n. (Ancient name of) Ireland.

Erin'ўs (ĕ-), n. (pl. *Erinyes*, pr. ĕrĭn'ĭĕz). A Fury. [Gk]

ĕris'tic, a, & n. (Art) of disputation; (of argument or arguer) aimed or aiming at victory rather than truth. [f. Gk *eristikos* (*erizō* f. *eris* strife, see -IC)]

ĕrl'-king', n. Bearded golden-crowned giant of Teutonic folk-lore who lures little children to the land of death. [f. G *erl-kōnig* alder-king, a mistransl. of Da. *ellerkonge* king of the elves]

ĕrm'in|e, n. Animal of weasel tribe, whose fur is brown in summer & white (except black tail-tip) in winter; its fur, used in robes of judges & peers (often poet. as emblem of purity), whence ~**ED** [2] (-nd). a; (Her.) white marked with black spots. [ME, f. OF (*h*)*ermine* of unkn. orig.]

-ern, suf. in *northern* etc. f. Gmc **-rōnja-* (-*ro-*+-*ŏnja-* = L -*aneus*).

ĕrne, n. Sea eagle. [OE *earn*, OHG *arn*, ON *ǫrn* f. Gmc **arn-*]

|| **Ern'ie** (ĕr-), n. Device for drawing prize-winning numbers of premium bonds. [f. initial letters of *electronic random number indicator equipment*]

ĕrōde', v.t. (Of acids, currents, etc.) gnaw away, destroy gradually, wear out. So **ĕrō'SION** (-zhn) n., **ĕrōs'IVE** a. [f. F *éroder* or L E(*rodere ros-* gnaw)]

Er'ŏs (ēr-), n. Love, god of love, Cupid. [Gk *erōs*]

ĕrŏt'ic, a. & n. 1. Of love, amatory. 2. n. ~ poem or composition or person. Hence ~**a** n. pl., ~ literature, ~ISM n., ~ spirit or character. [f. F *érotique* or Gk *erōtikos* (*erōs -ōtos* sexual love, see -IC)]

ĕ'rŏtism, n. Sexual desire or excitement, eroticism. [f. Gk *erōs* (as prec.) + -ISM]

ĕrōt'omān'ia, n. (path.). Melancholy, madness, arising from love. [f. Gk *erōs* (as prec.) + -MANIA]

ĕrr, v.i. Make mistakes; (of statements etc.) be incorrect; sin. [ME, f. OF *errer* f. L *errare*]

ĕ'rrand, n. Short journey on which an inferior is sent to carry message etc., as *run, go*, (on) ~*s*, ~*-boy*; object of journey; purpose. [OE *ǣrende*, OS *ārundi*, OHG *ārunti*, of obsc. orig.]

ĕ'rrant, a. & n. Roaming in quest of adventure, esp. KNIGHT-~; itinerant; erring, deviating from correct standard; whence **ĕ'rrANCY** n.; (n.) KNIGHT-~. [ME; (1) f. OF *errer, edrer*, f. LL *iterare* (*iter* journey), (2) as prec.; see -ANT]

ĕ'rrantrў, n. Condition, conduct, notions, of a knight-errant. [-RY]

ĕrrāt'|ic, a. Uncertain in movement; (of diseases) moving from one part to another; irregular in conduct, habit, opinion; (Geol.) ~*ic blocks*, stray masses foreign to surrounding strata. Hence ~**ICALLY** adv. [ME, f. OF *erratique* f. L *erraticus* (as ERR), see -ATIC]

ĕrrāt'um, n. (pl. *-ta*). Error in printing or writing, esp. (pl.) errors noted in list attached to book. [L, neut. p.p. as prec.]

ĕrrŏn'ĕous, a. Mistaken, incorrect. Hence ~**LY** [2] adv., ~**NESS** n. [ME, f. OF *erroneus* or L *erroneus* (*erro -onis* vagabond, as ERR) + -OUS]

ĕ'rror, n. Mistake, as *make, commit, an* ~, CLERICAL~; condition of erring in opinion; wrong opinion; *in* ~, mistaken(ly), by mistake; ~ *of a planet*, difference between its observed & calculated positions; (Law) *writ of* ~ (to procure reversal of judgement on ground of~); transgression. Hence ~**LESS** n. [ME, f. OF f. L *errorem* (as ERR, -OR)]

ersätz' (ārz-), n. & a. Substitute. [G]

Erse (ĕrs), a. & n. Highland Gaelic

(dialect); (unused & disliked in Ireland for) Irish. [early Sc. form of *Irish*]

ĕrst, adv. (arch.). (Also ~*'while*) formerly, of old. [OE *ǣrest* superl. of *ǣr*, see ERE]

ĕrubĕs'cent (-rŏŏ-), a. Reddening, blushing. [f. L E(*rubescere* incept. of *rubēre*, see -ENT]

ĕrŭctā'tion, n. Belching (lit. & fig., esp. of volcano). [f. L *eructatio* (E*ructare*, see -ATION)]

ĕ'rudite (-rŏŏ-), a. (Of persons & writings) learned. Hence or cogn. ~LY² (-tl-) adv., **ĕrudi'tion** n., (-rŏŏ-). [ME, f. L E*rudire* -*it*- train (*rudis* rude)]

ĕrŭpt', v.i. (Of teeth) break through gums; (of volcano) break out. [f. L E(*rumpere rupt*- break)]

ĕrŭp'tion, n. Outbreak (of volcano, whence ~AL (-shon-) a.; also of geyser, disease, war, passion, mirth, wit); (Path.) breaking out (of rash, pimples, etc.); (of teeth) breaking through gums. [F, or f. L *eruptio* (as prec., see -ION)]

ĕrŭp'tive, a. Bursting forth; tending to burst forth; of, formed by, forced up by, volcanic eruption. Hence ~LY² adv., ~NESS, **ĕruptiv'ITY**, nn. [f. as ERUPT +-IVE, or F *éruptif*]

-erŷ, -rŷ, suf. forming nouns, orig. after F -*erie*: (a) f. com.-Rom. -*aria* = L -*ario*- (F -*ier*, -*er*) +-*ia* -Y¹; F wds in -*ier* usu. denote ocupation having some occupation, wds in -*erie* the class of goods he deals in, as *draperie*, his employment, as *archerie*, his place of work, as *boulangerie*; -*erie* was also used without existing wd in -*ier*, as *soierie* (*soie*) silk goods, *niaiserie* (*niais*) foolishness. (b) f. OF -*ere*, -*eor* (mod. F -*eur* f. L -*ator* +-*ie*. On anal. of wds thus formed, -*erie* was added to vb stems direct, w. sense class of actions (*tromperie* deceit), occupation (*confiserie* confectioner's business), place of this (*brasserie* brewery). Many E wds are f. F; others are formed on nn. in -*er* (*bakery*, *fishery*, *pottery*), or on others (*knavery*, *slavery*, *popery*). Meanings: (1) class of goods (*drapery*); (2) employment or condition (*archery*, *dupery*); (3) place of work or cultivation or breeding (*brewery*, *vinery*, *piggery*); (4) conduct (*foolery*); (5) all that has to do with (*popery*), things of the nature of.

ĕrŷsip'elas, n. (Also *St Anthony's fire*, *the rose*) local febrile disease producing deep red colour on skin. [f. L f. Gk *erusipelas*]

ĕrŷthĕm'a, n. Superficial inflammation of the skin in patches. [f. Gk *eruthēma* f. *eruthainō* be red (*eruthros*)]

-es, old genit. termination used to give adv. force; appearing as -*s* (*needs*), -*ce* (*once*), & (w. excrescent -*t*) -*st* (*against*); also in the emphatic absolute forms *ours*, *yours*, *hers*, etc.

ĕscalāde', n. Scaling of walls with ladders. [F, f. Sp. *escalada* f. med. L *scalare* (*scala* ladder), see -ADE]

ĕs'calātor, n. Moving staircase for carrying passengers up or down. [as ESCALADE, -OR]

ĕscallon'ia, n. S.-Amer. kinds of flowering shrubs. [*Escallon*, discoverer, -IA¹]

ĕscăll'op. See SCALLOP.

ĕscapāde', n. Breaking loose from restraint; flighty piece of conduct. [F, f. Sp. *escapada* (as ESCAPE², see -ADE)]

ĕscāpe'¹, n. Act of escaping; fact of having escaped (*a narrow, hairbreadth,* ~); (means of) mental distraction or relief from reality (also attrib., as ~ *literature, reading*), whence **ĕscāp'ISM** n., **ĕscāp'IST** n. & a.; leakage (of gas etc.); garden plant growing wild; = FIRE-~; ~ *clause*, one specifying conditions under which contracting party is free from obligations; ~-*pipe*, -*valve* (for ~ of steam or water); ~-*shaft* (for ~ of miners when other shaft is blocked). [f. foll.]

ĕscāpe'², v.i. & t. Get free (*from* prison, person, etc.); (of steam, fluids, etc.) find a way out; get off safely, go unpunished; (v.t.) get clear away from (person, his grasp, etc.), avoid (unpleasant thing, doing); elude notice or recollection of, as *his name had* ~*d me*; (of words) issue unawares from (person, his lips). Hence **ĕscapEE'** n., one who has ~d. [ME *escape* f. AF, ONF *escaper*; ME *eschape* f. OF *eschaper* f. Rom. *excappare f. cappa* cloak (see CAP)]

ĕscāpe'ment (-pm-), n. Outlet; (of watch or clock) mechanism connecting motive power & regulator. [-MENT]

ĕscārp', n., & v.t. **1.** Steep bank immediately in front of & below rampart; similar natural formation. **2.** v.t. Cut into form of ~, so ~MENT n. [(vb f. F *escarper*) f. F *escarpe* f. It. *scarpa* SCARP]

-ĕs'cent, suf. forming adjj. f. L part. of inceptive vbs (-*escens* -*ntis*), as *effervescent*, & thence in wds usu. describing play of colour, as *iridescent*, *opalescent*, or merely adjectival, as *alkalescent*.

eschalĕt' (ĕsh-). See SHALLOT.

eschat|ŏl'ogŷ (ĕsk-), n. Doctrine of death, judgement, heaven, & hell. Hence ~olŏ- gĭCAL a. [f. Gk *eskhatos* last +-LOGY]

ĕscheat'¹, n. Lapsing of property to crown or lord of manor on owner's dying intestate without heirs; property so lapsing. [ME, f. OF *eschete* p.p. of *escheoir* f. Rom. *excadēre*-f. L EX- (*cidere = cadere* fall)]

ĕscheat'², v.t. & i. Confiscate; hand over (property) as an escheat (*to* person, *into* his hands); revert by escheat (*to* or abs.). [prec.]

eschew' (-ŏŏ), v.t. Avoid, abstain from, (action, conduct, kind of food, etc.). [ME, f. OF *eschiver* f. Rom. *skivare* f. WG *skeuh*, see SHY¹]

eschscholt'zia (ĭshŏl-), n. A plant with usu. yellow flowers, Noah's nightcap. [*Eschscholtz*, explorer, -IA¹]

esclandre (ĕsklahn'dr), n. Scandal; disturbance. [F]

ĕs'cōrt¹, n. Body of armed men acting as guard to persons, baggage, etc.; person(s) accompanying another on journey for protection or guidance, or for courtesy's sake. [f. F *escorte* f. It. *scorta* f. *scorgere* conduct f. Rom. *EX(COR*rigere* f. *regere* direct)]

ĕscōrt'², v.t. Act as escort to; ~ *carrier*, aircraft carrier for ~ing convoys. [f. prec.]

ĕscrībe', v.t. (math.). Describe (circle) so as to touch one side of triangle exteriorly & the other two produced. [f. E-+L *scribere* write]

ĕs'critoire (-twahr), n. Writing-desk with drawers etc. for stationery. [F (now *éc-*), f. med. L *scriptorium* (as prec., see -ORY)]

ĕscrow' (-ō), n. Written legal engagement to do something, kept in third person's custody until some condition has been fulfilled. [AF *escrowe*, OF *escroe*, f. med. L *scroda* f. Gmc *skraudh-*, see SCROLL, SHRED]

ĕscūd'ō, n. (pl. *-os*). Portuguese monetary unit & silver coin (applied also to various Spanish-American gold & silver coins). [Sp. & Port., f. L *scutum* shield]

ĕs'cūlent, a. & n. (Thing) fit for food. [f. L *esculentus* (*esca* food, see -LENT)]

ĕscūtch'eon (-chon), n. Shield with armorial bearings; *a blot on his* ~ (stain on reputation); middle of ship's stern where name is placed; pivoted keyhole-cover. [f. ONF *escuchon* f. Rom. *scutionem* (L *scutum* shield, see -ION)]

-ēse, suf. forming adjj. (& nn.), f. OF *-eis* f. L *-ensis* local suf. (freq. now *-ian*, as *Atheniensis* Athenian); applied to some foreign countries & towns (*Japanese, Milanese*), either as adj. or meaning ' inhabitant ' (pl. *-ese*) or ' language '; also used spec. (adj. or n.) of diction of mannered writers (*Carlylese*), as though a non-English language.

ĕs'kar, -er, n. (geol.). Long ridge of post-glacial gravel in river valleys. [f. Ir. *eiscir*]

Eskimo, -quimau, (ĕs'kĭmō), n. (pl. *-os*, *-oes*, pr. *-mōz*; *-maux*, pr. *-mō*, *-mōz*). Member of a people in arctic coasts of America. [native]

ĕsotĕr'ic, a. (Of philosophical doctrines etc.) meant only for the initiated; (of disciples) initiated; private, confidential. Hence ~AL a., ~alLY² adv. [f. Gk *esōterikos* (*esōterō* compar. of *esō* within, see -IC)]

ĕspagnolette' (-ănyŏlĕt), n. Fastening of French window. [F, dim. of *espagnol* Spanish]

ĕspăl'ier, n. Lattice-work on which trees or shrubs are trained; tree so trained. [F, f. It. *spalliera* (*spalla* shoulder)]

ĕspărt'ō, n. (Also ~ *grass*) kinds of grass imported from Spain and N. Africa for paper-making. [Sp., f. L f. Gk *sparton* rope of the plant *spartos*]

ĕspē'cial (-shl), a. Pre-eminent, excep-tional, as *my* ~ *friend, thing of* ~ *importance*; particular (opp. to *ordinary*,. cf. SPECIAL); belonging chiefly to one case (*for your* ~ *benefit*). Hence ~LY² (-sha-) adv. [ME, f. OF, f. L as SPECIAL]

Esperän'tō (ĕ-), n. An artificial language designed as a medium for persons of all nations. [pen-name (f. L *spero* hope) of its inventor, Dr Zamenhof, 1887]

ĕspi'al, n. Acting as a spy; watching; espying. [ME, f. OF *espiaille*, as ESPY, see -AL(2)]

ĕspiègle'rie (see Ap.), n. Roguishness. [F]

ĕs'pionage (-ĭj, -ahzh'), n. Practice of spying or using spies. [F (*-nn-*) f. *espionner* f. *espion* SPY]

ĕsplanäde', n. Level piece of ground, esp. one used for public promenade; level space separating citadel of fortress from town. [F, f. Sp. *esplanada* f. *esplanar* f. L EXplanare make level (*planus*), see -ADE]

ĕspous'al (-zl), n. (arch.). (Usu. pl.) marriage or betrothal; (fig.) espousing of (a cause etc.). [ME, f. OF *espousailles* f. L *sponsalia* neut. pl. (*sponsus* p.p. as foll., see -AL)]

ĕspouse' (-z), v.t. (Usu. of man) marry; give (woman) in marriage (*to*); adopt, support, (doctrine, cause, etc.). [ME, f. OF *espouser* f. L *sponsare* (*sponsus* p.p. of *spondēre* betroth)]

ĕpréssiv'o (-ēvŏ), adv. (mus.). With expression. [It.]

ĕprĕss'ō, n. Apparatus for making coffee under pressure; coffee-bar equipped with this; also attrib. [It.]

ĕsprit (ĕsprē'), n. Sprightliness; wit; ~ *de corps* (de kōr), regard for honour & interests of body one belongs to; ~ *fort* (fōr), strong-minded person, free-thinker. [F, f. L as SPIRIT]

ĕspy', v.t. Catch sight of; detect (flaw etc.). [ME, f. OF *espier* f. com.-Rom. *spiare* f. Gmc *spehōn*, see SPY]

-ĕsque, suf. forming adjj., = F *-esque* f. It. *-esco* f. med. L *-iscus* in Gmc wds; cf. OHG *-isc* (mod. *-isch*) = -ISH¹; meaning ' after the manner of ', as *arabesque, burlesque, Dantesque*.

Esquimau. See ESKIMO.

ĕsquīre', n. ‖ Title appended to name of one regarded as gentleman by birth, position, or education, esp. in address of letter (abbr. *Esq.*); (arch.) = SQUIRE. [ME, f. OF *esquier* f. L *scutarius* shield-bearer (*scutum* shield, see -ARY¹)]

ĕss, n. S(-shaped thing); COLLAR¹ of ~es.

-ĕss¹, suf. forming female nn. f. F (*countess, lioness*) or on E wds (*goddess*); in 15th c. the OE fem. *-ster* (now only in *spinster*) came to be regarded as masculine, & could take fem. *-ess* (*seamstress*); agent nn. in *-ter, -tor*, regularly have *-tress* (*chantress*); other exx. are *authoress* etc. (*author* etc. now preferred), *giantess, quakeress; governess* (formed on vb) is irreg., perh. on anal. of *sorceress* (formed on old *sorcer* not on *sorcerer*, which has double agent suf.); euphony leads to same clipping in *adventuress, murderess*; *-tress* is now recognized angliciz. of F *-trice* (L *-trix -tricis*), though of diff. orig. [f. F *-esse* f. LL f. Gk *-issa*]

-**èss²**, suf. in abstr. nn. f. adjj., as *duress, largess*; *riches, laches*, are exx., mistaken for pl. [ME & OF *-esse* = It. *-ezza* f. L *-itia* -ICE]

èss′ay¹, n. Attempt (*at*); a literary composition (usu. prose & short) on any subject, whence ~IST(3) n. [f. F *essai*, see ASSAY¹]

èssay′², v.t. & i. Try, test, (person, thing); attempt (task, *to* do, or abs.). [refash. f. ASSAY² on F *essayer*]

èss′è, n. Essential being or nature (often contrasted with *bene esse* well-being). [L, = to be]

èss′enc|e, n. An existence or entity (spiritual or immaterial); absolute being, reality underlying phenomena; all that makes a thing what it is; intrinsic nature; indispensable quality or element; extract obtained by distillation etc. (lit. & fig.); perfume, scent, whence ~ED² (-st) a. [ME, f. OF f. L *essentia* f. *essens -ntis* fictitious part. of *esse* be, repr. Gk *ousia*]

Essēne′ (ĕ-), n. Member of an ancient Jewish sect, of mystical tenets & coenobitical life. [f. L f. Gk pl. *Essēnoi*]

èssèn′tial (-shl), a. & n. **1.** Of, constituting, a thing's essence; indispensable (*to*); ~ *proposition*, one that predicates of a subject what is implied in its definition; ~ *character* (of species, genus, etc.), marks that distinguish it from others included with it in next superior division; ~ *harmony* (belonging to one particular key); ~ *oil*, volatile oil, marked by characteristic odour etc. **2.** n. Indispensable element. Hence ~ITY (-shĭăl⁴) n., ~LY² (-shal-) adv. [ME, f. LL *essentialis* (as ESSENCE, -AL)]

-**èst**, suf. forming superl. adjj. & advv. (& FIRST, LAST); for limits of use see -ER³, but many adjj. can bear *-est* though not *-er*, as *awkward, barren, fragile, loyal, legible*, & many in *-id*, as *limpid*; in poetry & mannered prose *-est* is used w. almost any adj., & appended to advv. in *-ly*, as *quickliest*. [OE *-ost, -ust, -ast*, f. Gmc *-ōsto-*, & OE *-est, -st*, f. Gmc *-istaz* (compar. *-ōz-, -iz-*, +Aryan *-to-*), cf. Gk *-isto-*; *-iz-* required vowel change, now only in *eldest*, BEST]

èstăb′lish, v.t. Set up (government, house of business, etc.) on permanent basis; settle (person, one*self, in* office etc.); secure permanent acceptance for (custom, precedent, belief, etc.); place beyond dispute (fact, *that*); make (church) legally national. [ME, f. OF *establir* (st. *-iss-*, see -ISH²) f. L *stabilire* (as STABLE a.)]

èstăb′lishment, n. Establishing; *Church E~, the E~*, church system established by law; organized body of men maintained

for a purpose, as army, navy, civil service; *peace, war,* ~, reduced, increased, army etc. in time of peace, war; staff of servants etc.; public institution, house of business; household, as *separate* ~ (of man maintaining paramour). [-MENT]

èstăblishmentār′ian, a. & n. (Person) adhering to, advocating the principle of, an established church. [-ARIAN]

èstăm′ĭnet (-nā), n. French café selling wine, beer, & coffee, or cottage with bar-room. [F]

èstāte′, n. **1.** Order, class, forming part of body politic & sharing in government; ‖ *the Three E~s* (in England), Lords Spiritual, Lords Temporal, Commons; *third* ~, (usu.) French bourgeoisie before Revolution; ‖ (joc.) *fourth* ~, the press. **2.** Person's interest in landed property (*real* ~) or movables (*personal* ~), whence **èstāt′ED²** a.; a landed property (‖ ~ *agent*, steward or ~, go-between in sales of houses & land); ~ *car*, dual-purpose light saloon vehicle constructed or adapted for the carriage of both passengers & goods. **3.** One's collective estates & liabilities. **4.** (arch.). Condition, as *the holy* ~ *of matrimony*. [ME, f. OF *estat* f. L as STATE]

èsteem′, v.t., & n. **1.** Think highly of; consider, as *I shall* ~ *it* (*as*) *a favour*. **2.** Favourable opinion, regard, respect. [(n. f. vb) f. OF *estimer* f. L as ESTIMATE²; see AIM¹]

ès′ter, n. (chem.). Compound formed by replacing the hydrogen of an acid by a hydrocarbon radical of the ethyl type. [coined by the German chemist L. Gmelin (d. 1853)]

ès′timable, a. Worthy of esteem. [F, f. L *aestimabilis* (as ESTEEM, see -BLE)]

ès′timate¹, n. Approximate judgement (of number, amount, etc.); quantity assigned by this; ‖ *the E~s*, forecasts of national expenditure, presented annually to parliament; contractor's statement of sum for which he will undertake specified work; judgement of character or qualities. [f. foll. or L *aestimatus -ūs*]

ès′tim|āte², v.t. Form an estimate of; fix (number etc.) by estimate *at* (so much); form an opinion of. So ~ATIVE a., ~ātor n. [f. L *aestimare*, see -ATE³]

èstimā′tion, n. Judgement of worth, as *in my* ~; esteem, as *hold in* ~, *be in* ~. [ME, f. OF *estimacion* or L *aestimatio* (as prec., see -ATION)]

estival etc. See **aest-**.

èstŏp′, v.t. (law; -pp-). Bar, preclude, (*from* thing. *from* doing). Hence~p′AGE n. [f. AF, OF *estoper* f. *estoupe* f. L *stuppa* tow; see STOP¹]

èstŏpp′el, n. (law). The being precluded from a course by previous action of one's own. [f. OF *estoupail* bung f. *estoper* (prec., -AL(2))]

èstŏv′ers (-z), n. pl. Necessaries allowed by law (as wood for repairs or fuel taken by a tenant from his holding). [f. AF *estover*, OF -*eir* be necessary, f. L *est opus*]

éstrade' (-ahd), n. Raised platform, dais. [F, f. Sp. *estrado* f. L *stratum* neut. p.p. of *sternere* spread (with carpets)]

éstrānge' (-j), v.t. Alienate (person) in feeling (*from* another). Hence ~MENT (-jm-) n. [ME, f. OF *estranger* f. L *extraneare* (as STRANGE)]

éstreat', v.t. (law). Take out record of (fine, bail, etc.) & return it to Court of Exchequer to be prosecuted. [f. AF *estrete*, OF *estraite* fem. p.p. of *estraire* EXTRACT]

és'tŭar|ỹ, n. Tidal mouth of large river. Hence ~INE¹ a. [f. L *aestuarium* neut. adj. as n. (*aestus* -*ūs* tide, see -ARY¹)]

ésŭr'i|ent, a. (joc.). Hungry; needy & greedy. So ~ENCE, ~ENCY, nn. [f. L *esurire*, desiderative f. *edere es-* eat]

-ĕt¹, suf. forming (orig.) dimm., many not now realized as such; mostly in ME adoptions f. OF (*bullet, hatchet, sonnet*); double dim. -LET (F -*el* + -*et*) is living suf. [OF -*et* & -*ette* (dist. only in mod. E) = It. -*etto, -etta*, f. Rom. -*itto, -itta*, of unkn. orig.]

-ĕt², -ēte, suf. in agent nn. f. Gk, -*et* in older or more familiar wds, as *poet, comet, anchoret, -ete* in newer or learned ones, as *athlete, aesthete, exegete*. [f. Gk -*ētēs*; *epithet, paraclete*, are not exx.; *diabetes* retains full form]

ēt'a, n. Greek letter (H, η)=ē (cf. EPSILON). [Gk]

et'acism (ā-), n. Pronunciation of Gk ē as English ā (cf. ITACISM). [f. Gk *ēta* letter *ē*, -ISM]

état-major (ătah' mahzhōr'), n. (mil.). Staff, staff-office. [F]

ĕt cĕt'era, ĕtcĕt'era, phr. & n. (pl. -*as*). (Abbr. *etc., &c.*) & the rest, & so on, as *I remain yours etc.*; (n. pl.) extras, sundries. [L]

ĕtch, v.t. & i. Reproduce (pictures etc.), portray (subject), by engraving metal-plate etc. by means of acids or corrosives, esp. for purpose of printing copies; (v.i.) practise this art. [f. Du. *etsen* f. G *ätzen* etch f. OHG *azzen* cause to eat or be eaten f. Gmc **atjan* causative of **etan* EAT]

ĕtch'ing, n. In vbl senses, esp. copy from etched plate; ~-*needle*, used in ~. [-ING¹]

étĕrn'al, a. That always (has existed &) will exist, as ~ *life, punishment*; *the E*~, God; ~ CITY; (colloq.) incessant, too frequent, as *these*~ *bickerings*; *the*~ *triangle*, two males & a female or *vice versa*. Hence or cogn. étĕrn'(al)IZE(3) vv.t., ~LY² adv. [ME, f. OF f. LL *aeternalis* f. L *aeternus*, see -AL]

étĕrn'itỹ, n. Being eternal; immortal fame; (pl.) eternal truths; infinite time, esp. future; the future life. [ME, f. OF *eternite* f. L *aeternitatem* (*aeternus*, see prec. & -TY)]

Etesian (ĭtēzh'an), a. ~ *winds* (blowing annually in Mediterranean from N.W. for about 40 days in summer). [f. L f. Gk *etēsios* (*etos* year) + -AN]

-eth, suf. See -TH².

ĕth'āne, n. A colourless and odourless gas insoluble in water and burning with a pale flame, ethyl hydride. [f. ETH(ER) + -ANE]

ĕth'er, n. 1. Clear sky, upper regions beyond clouds. 2.(phys.). A medium assumed to permeate space & fill interstices between particles of air & other matter, medium in which electro-magnetic waves are transmitted, whence ~IC a. 3. (chem.). Colourless light volatile liquid produced by action of sulphuric acid & other acids on alcohol, an anaesthetic. [f. L f. Gk *aithēr* f. root of *aithō* burn, shine]

ĕthēr'ëal, -ial, a. 1. Light, airy; heavenly; of unearthly delicacy of substance, character, or appearance, whence ~ITY (-ăl'-), ~IZA'TION, nn., ~IZE(3) v.t., ~LY² adv. 2. (phys., chem.). Of, like, ETHER, so ĕth'erIFICA'TION n., ĕth'erIFY v.t.; ~ *oil*, essential or volatile oil. [f. L (-*eus, -ius*) f. Gk *aitherios* (as prec.) + -AL]

ĕth'erĭz|e, -is|e (-īz), v.t. Put (patient) under influence of ether. Hence ~A'TION n. [-IZE]

ĕth'ĭc, a. & n. 1. (Now usu. ~*al*) relating to morals, treating of moral questions, *moral; ~ *dative* (of person indirectly interested, as *knock* me *at the door*). 2. n. pl., & rarely sing. Science of morals, treatise on this, moral principles, rules of conduct, whole field of moral science. Hence ~AL a. (also, of drugs, conforming to a recognized standard), ~alLY² adv., ~IZE(3) v.t. [f. F *éthique* or L f. Gk *ēthikos* (ETHOS, -IC)]

Ethiōp'ian (ē-), a. & n. (Native) of Ethiopia, esp. (Anthropol.) as epithet of one of the races into which human species is divided. [-AN]

ĕth'moid, a. Sieve-like; ~ *bone*, square-shaped bone at root of nose, through the many perforations of which the olfactory nerves pass to the nose. [f. Gk *ēthmoeidēs* (*ēthmos* sieve)]

ĕth'nārch (-k), n. Governor of a people or province. So ~Y¹ (-kĭ) n. [f. Gk *ethnos* nation + -*arkhēs* ruler]

ĕth'nic, -ic|al, aa. Pertaining to race, ethnological, whence ~alLY² adv.; (~) gentile, heathen, whence ~alISM(2) n. [f. LL f. Gk *ethnikos* (*ethnos* nation, see -IC)]

ĕthnŏg'raphỹ, n. Scientific description of races of men. So ĕthnŏg'RAPHER n., ĕthnŏgrăph'IC(AL) aa., ĕthnŏgrăph'icalLY² adv. [f. Gk *ethnos* nation + -GRAPHY]

ĕthnŏl'ogỹ, n. Science of races & their relations to one another & characteristics. So ĕthnolŏ'gIC(AL) aa. (-*ic frontier*, corresponding to a division of races), ĕthnolŏ'gicalLY² adv., ĕthnŏl'oGIST n. [as prec. + -LOGY]

ĕt hŏc gĕn'us ŏm'nĕ, phr. And all that kind of thing (often as ornamental substitute for *et cetera*). [L]

ĕthŏl′ogў, n. Science of character-formation. Hence **ĕtholŏ′gICAL** a. [f. L f. Gk *éthologia* (ETHOS, see -LOGY)]

ĕth′ŏs, n. Characteristic spirit of community, people, or system. [Gk (ē-) = character, nature, disposition]

ĕth′ўl, n. (chem.). The hydrocarbon radical present in ordinary alcohol & ether. [f. ETH(ER), -YL]

-ĕt′ic, suf. of adjj. & nn. = Gk agent suf. *-ĕt-* or *-ēt-*+-IC, in wds f. Gk or on Gk models, as *emetic* (Gk *emĕtikos*), *ascetic* (Gk *askētikos*).

ĕt′iol|āte, v.t. Make (plant) pale by excluding light; give sickly hue to (person). Hence **~A′TION** n. [f. F *étioler* f. Norm. *étieuler* make into haûlm (*éteule* f. pop. L *stupila* f. L *stipula* straw)]

ĕtiology. See AETIOLOGY.

ĕtiquette′ (-kĕt), n. Conventional rules of personal behaviour in polite society; ceremonial of court; unwritten code restricting professional men in what concerns interests of their brethren or dignity of their profession, esp. *medical*, *legal*, ~. [f. F *étiquette* TICKET, ~]

ĕt′na, n. Vessel for heating small quantity of liquid by burning spirit. [f. the volcano]

Et′on (ē-), n. ~ *collar* (broad, stiff, worn outside coat-collar); ~ *crop*, cutting of woman's hair short like boy's; ~ *jacket*, boy's short coat reaching only to waist. [f. ~ College]

Etrŭs′can (I-) a. & n. (Native) of ancient Etruria. [f. L *Etruscus*+-AN]

ĕt sĕq(q).,* *sĕquĕn′tĕs (-z), **-***tĭa*, (in reference to books etc.). And the words, pages, etc., that follow. [L]

-ĕtte, suf. forming dim. nn. (rarely adjj.), repr. OF *-ette*, the fem. corresp. to *-ET*[1]. (1) Older adoptions now have *-et*; *-ette* appears chiefly in wds introduced since 17th c., as *cigarette, etiquette*. (2) A mod. commerc. use, = 'sham', is seen in *leatherette, Brusselette* (carpet). (3) A mod. fem. suf., as *usherette*.

étude (ātūd′), n. A short musical composition or exercise. [F]

ĕtui′ (-wē), **ĕtwee′,** n. Small case for needles, toothpicks, etc. [f. F *étui*]

ĕtўmŏl′ogīze, **-ise** (-īz), v.t. & i. Give, trace, the etymology of; suggest etymology for; study etymology. [16th c., f. F *-iser*, or med. L *ethimologizare* (as foll., -IZE)]

ĕtўmŏl′ogў, n. Account of, facts relating to, formation & meaning of word; branch of linguistic science concerned with this; part of grammar treating of individual words & their formation & inflexions. Hence or cogn. **ĕtўmŏL′OGER, ĕtўmŏL′O-GIST,** nn., **ĕtўmolŏ′gIC(AL)** aa., **ĕtўmo-lŏ′gicalLY**[2] adv. [f. OF *ethimologie* f. L f. Gk *etumologia* (as foll., -LOGY)]

ĕt′ўmŏn, n. Primary word that gives rise to a derivative. [L, f. Gk *etumon* (neut. of *etumos* true) literal sense, original form, of a word]

eu- in comb. = Gk *eu* well, cf. DYS-.

eucalŷp′tus, n. Kinds of plants including Australian gum tree; ~ *oil*, a disinfectant. [f. EU-+Gk *kaluptos* covered (*kaluptō*), flower being protected by cap]

eu′charis (ūk-), n. (Also ~ *lily*) S.-Amer. bulbous plant with white bell-shaped flowers. [Gk EU(*kharis* grace) pleasing]

Eu′charist (ūk-), n. Lord's Supper; consecrated elements, esp. the bread, as *give, receive, the* ~. Hence **~IC(AL)** (-is′-) aa. (~ *ic Congress*, international meeting of Roman Catholics in veneration of the Blessed Sacrament, originally held annually, later biennially. [ME, f. OF *eucariste* f. LL f. Gk *eukharistia* f. EU-(*kharistos* f. *kharizomai* offer willingly) grateful]

eu′chre (-ker), n., & v.t. **1.** American card game for 2, 3, or 4 persons. **2.** v.t. Gain advantage over (opponent) by his failure to take three tricks at ~ (also fig.). [orig. unkn.]

Eu′clid, n. Alexandrian mathematician (c. 300 B.C.); his *Elements* or treatise on geometry, a copy of this; (obs.) geometry as a science or subject; (mod.) the geometry of ordinary experience, accepting ~'s axioms as indisputable (cf. RELATIVITY). Hence **Euclid′EAN** a. [f. Gk *Eukleidēs*]

eud(a)em′on|ism (-dēm-), n. System of ethics basing moral obligation on tendency of actions to produce happiness. So **~IST**(2) n. [f. Gk EU(*daimōn* guardian genius) happy, -ISM]

eudiŏm′ēter, n. Graduated glass tube in which gases may be chemically combined by electric spark passing between metallic terminals at its closed end, used in chemical experiments. So **eudiomĕt′rIC**(AL) aa., **eudiomĕt′ricalLY**[2] adv., **eudiŏ-M′ETRY** n. [f. Gk EU(*dios*, st. of *Zeus*, gen. *Dios*, god of the sky) clear+-METER]

eugĕn′ic, a. & n. **1.** Of the production of fine (esp. human) offspring. **2.** n. pl. Science of this. So **eu′gĕn**IST(2)n., student of ~s. [f. EU-+Gk *gen*- produce +-IC]

euhēm′er|ism, n. Reference of myths to historical basis. So **~IST**(2) n., **~is′tIC** a., **~IZE**(4) v.t. & i. [f. *Euhemerus*, Sicilian author c. 316 B.C., +-ISM]

eul′og|īze, -ise (-īz), v.t. Extol, praise, in speech or writing. So **~IST**(1) n., **~is′tIC** a., **~is′tICALLY** adv. [f. foll. +-IZE]

eul′ogў, n. Speech, writing, in praise of person etc., as *pronounce his* ~, *pronounce a* ~ *on him*; praise. [f. med. L *eulogium* f. (app. by conf. w. L *elogium*) LL f. Gk *eulogia* (EU-, -LOGY)]

Eumĕn′ides (-ēz), n. pl. (Euphemistic name for) Furies. [Gk, = gracious ones]

eun′uch (-uk), n. Castrated male person. esp. one employed in harem, or (in Oriental courts & under Roman empire) employed in state affairs. [ME, f. L f. Gk *eunoukhos* lit. bedchamber attendant (*eunē* bed+*okh*- st. of *ekhō* hold)]

euon'ymus, n. Kinds of shrubs including spindle-tree. [f. L f. Gk EU(*ōnumos* f. *onoma* name) of lucky name]

eupep'tic, a. Of, having, good digestion. [f. Gk EU(*peptos* f. *pessō*, *peptō*, digest)+ -IC]

euph'em|ism, n. Substitution of mild or vague expression for harsh or blunt one; expression thus substituted, as ' *queer* ' *is a ~ism for* ' *mad* '. So ~is'TIC a., ~is'TICALLY adv., ~IZE(1, 2) v.t. & i. [f. Gk *euphēmismos* f. EU(*phēmos* f. *phēmē* speaking, fame), see -ISM]

euphōn'ium, n. (mus.). Bass instrument of saxhorn family. [mod. L, f. Gk *euphōnos* see foll.]

euph'ony, n. Pleasing sound; quality of having this (usu. of words, phrases, etc.); tendency to phonetic change for ease of pronunciation. So euphōn'IC, euphōn'i-OUS, aa., euphōn'ICALLY, euphōn'ious-LY², advv., euph'onIZE(3) v.t. [f. F *euphonie* f. LL f. Gk *euphōnia* f. EU*phōnos* (*phōnē* sound)]

euphōr'bia, n. (Kinds of) widely distributed herb or shrub of the spurge family. [L (-*ea*), f. *Euphorbus* physician to Juba II, -IA¹]

euphōr'ia, euph'ory, nn. Feeling of well-being. Hence euphō'ric a. [f. Gk EU- (*phoria* f. *pherō* bear]

euph'rasy, n. = EYEbright. [f. med. L f. Gk *euphrasia* cheerfulness f. EU*phrainō* gladden (*phrēn* mind)]

Euphrōs'ynē (*or* -z-), n. One of the Graces. [Gk]

euph'u|ism, n. Artificial or affected style of writing (prop., in imitation of Lyly's *Euphues*, 1580); high-flown style. So ~IST n.,~is'tic a.,~is'TICALLY adv. [-ISM]

Eurasian (ūrāsh'*an*), a. & n. (Person) of mixed European & Asian parentage; of Europe & Asia. [f. *Europe*+*Asia*+-AN]

eurēk'a (ūr-), int. & n. (The exulting exclamation) ' I have (found) it! ' [f. Gk *heurēka* 1st pers. perf. of *heuriskō* find]

eurhyth'mic (ūr-), a. In or of harmonious proportion (esp. in architecture). Hence ~s n. pl., harmony of bodily movement, esp. as developed with the aid of music into a system used in education. [f. L f. Gk *euruthmia* good rhythm (see EU-, RHYTHM)+-IC]

Europē'an (ūr-), a. & n. (Native) of Europe; happening in, extending over, Europe, as *a ~ reputation*. Hence ~ISM(2, 3, 4),~ĪZA'TION, nn.,~IZE(3) v.t., (ūr-). [f. F *européen* f. L *Europaeus* (L f. Gk *Europē* Europe)+-AN]

eurōp'ium (ūr-), n. (chem.). A rare-earth metallic element. [mod. L, f. L *Europa* Europe, -IUM]

Eurovision (ūr'ōvizhn), n. Television of European range. [*Euro(pean) (tele)vision*]

eu'sŏl, n. Antiseptic and bactericide prepared from bleaching powder. [f. initial letters of *E*dinburgh *U*niversity *sol*ution of *l*ime]

Eustach'ian (-āk-), a. Of Eustachius the Italian anatomist (d. 1574); ~ *tube*, canal leading from the pharynx to the cavity of the middle ear. [-AN]

eutĕc'tic, a. (chem.). ~ *mixture*, one in which the constituents are in such proportions as to solidify at one temperature (~ *temperature* or *point*) like a pure substance. [f. EU-+Gk *tēkō* melt+-IC]

Eutĕrp'ē, n. The MUSE¹ of music, whence ~AN a.; genus of palms. [Gk]

euthanās'ia (-z-, -s-), n. Gentle & easy death; bringing about of this, esp. in case of incurable & painful disease. [Gk (EU-+*thanatos* death)]

evăc'ū|āte, v.t. Empty (esp. stomach or bodily organ of contents), whence ~ANT(2) a. & n.; withdraw from (place; esp. of troops); remove (person) esp. from place considered to be dangerous, whence ~EE' n., person so removed; discharge (excrement etc.; also fig.). So ~A'TION n.- [f. L E(*vacuare* f. *vacuus* empty)]

evāde', v.t. Escape from, avoid, (attack, pursuit, designs, adversary, blow, obstacle, etc.); avoid doing (duty etc.), answering (question), yielding to (argument etc.); defeat intention of (law etc., esp. while complying with its letter); (of things) elude, baffle. Hence evād'ABLE a. [f. F *évader* f. L(*vadere vas-* go)]

evă'gin|āte, v.t. (physiol.). Turn (tubular organ) inside out. So ~A'TION n. [f. L E(*vaginare* f. *vagina* sheath), see -ATE³]

evăl'ū|āte, v.t. Ascertain amount of; find numerical expression for. So ~A'TION n. [f. F *évaluer* (é- EX, VALUE)]

evanĕsce', v.i. Fade out of sight; become effaced; disappear. [f. L E(*vanescere* VANISH)]

evanĕs'c|ent, a. (Of impression, appearance, etc.) quickly fading; (Math.) infinitesimal. Hence ~ENCE n., ~entLY² adv. [f. F *évanescent* (as prec., see -ENT)]

evăn'gel (-j-), n. (arch.). The Gospel; any of the Four Gospels; doctrine, principle, (of politics etc.). [ME, f. OF *evangi(l)le* f. eccl. L f. Gk EU(*aggelion* cf. ANGEL) good news]

evăngĕl'ic, -ic|al, (-j-), aa. & nn. **1.** Of, according to, the teaching of the Gospel or the Christian religion; esp. (usu. ~*al*) of the Protestant school maintaining that the essence of the Gospel consists in doctrine of salvation by faith, good works & sacraments having no saving efficacy, whence ~alISM(3) n. **2.** n. Member of this school. Hence ~alLY² adv. [f. LL f. eccl. Gk *euaggelikos* (as prec., see -IC, -AL)]

evăn'gelism (-j-), n. Preaching of the Gospel; = EVANGELICALISM. [-ISM]

evăn'gelist (-j-), n. One of the writers of the Four Gospels; preacher of the Gospel; layman doing home missionary work. [ME, f. OF *evangeliste* f. LL (-*ta*) f. Gk *euaggelistēs* (as EVANGELIZE, -IST)]

ĕvăngĕlĭs'tĭc (-j-), a. Of the Four Evangelists; of preachers of the Gospel; = EVANGELICAL. [-IC]

ĕvăn'gĕlīz|e (-j-), -is|e (-īz), v.t. Preach the Gospel to (persons, also abs.); win over (person) to Christianity. Hence ~A'TION n. [f. LL *evangelizare* f. Gk *euaggelizomai* (as EVANGEL)]

ĕvăn'ĭsh, v.i. (literary). Vanish; die away. Hence ~MENT n. [ME, f. OF *evanir* (-ISH²) f. Rom. **exvanire* = L *evanescere* EVANESCE]

ĕvăp'or|āte, v.t. & i. Turn (t. & i.) from solid or liquid into vapour (also fig.; esp. colloq. disappear, die); remove the liquid part of; (v.i.) exhale moisture. So ~ABLE, ~atIVE, aa., ~A'TION, ~ātOR, nn. [f. L *Evaporare* (as VAPOUR), see -ATE³]

ĕvā'sion (-zhn), n. Act, means, of evading; shuffling excuse. So ĕvās'IVE a., ĕvās'ĭvELY² (-vl-) adv., ĕvās'ĭveNESS (-vn-) n. [ME, f. OF *evasion* f. LL *evasionem* (as EVADE, see -ION)]

Eve¹ (ēv), n. The first woman; *daughter of* ~, woman (often w. allusion to feminine curiosity etc.). [f. Heb. *Havvah* orig. = life, living]

ēve², n. Evening or day before (*of*) a church festival or any date or event; time just before anything, as *on the* ~ *of an election*; (arch.) evening. [ME; = EVEN¹; for loss of -n cf. *maid*]

ĕvĕc'tion, n. Inequality in moon's longitude. [f. L *evectio* f. E(*vehere vect*- carry), -ION]

ē'ven¹, n. (poet.). Evening; ~*song*, evening prayer in Church of England; ~*tide*, evening. [OE *ǣfen*, OS, OHG * āband* of obsc. orig.]

ē'ven², a. (-er, -est). Level; smooth; uniform in quality; in same plane or line (*with*); equally balanced, as ~-*handed justice*; equal in number or amount; (Law, Commerc.) *of* ~ (same) *date*; (of temper etc.) equable, unruffled; ~ *money* (Betting), neither laying nor taking odds; (of numbers) integrally divisible by two, opp. to ODD; ODD & ~; *be* ~ *with*, have one's revenge on. Hence ~LY² adv., ~NESS n. [OE *efen*, OS, OHG *eban*, ON *jafn*, Goth. *ibns* f. Gmc **ebhnaz* of unkn. orig.]

ē'ven³, adv. inviting comparison of the assertion, negation, etc., made with a less strong one that might have been made, as *he disputes* ~ *the facts* (not merely the inferences from them), *I never* ~ *opened* (much less read) *it, does he* ~ *suspect* (not to say realize) *the danger?*, ~ *if my watch is right we shall be late* (later if it is slow), *this applies* ~ *more* (not merely equally) *to French* (*than to English*); (arch.) neither more nor less than, just, simply, as ~ (quite) *so*, (emphasizing identity) that is, as *God,* ~ *our own God.* [OE *efne*, as prec.]

ē'ven⁴, v.t. Make even; treat as equal or comparable (*to*); ~ *up*, to balance; **~ up on*, requite, make return to (a person). [OE *efnan*, as prec.]

ēve'ning (-vn-), n. Close of day, esp. sunset to bedtime; this 'time spent in particular way, as *musical* ~s; (fig.) decline of life, closing period; ~ *dress*, that prescribed by fashion to be worn in the ~; ~ *primrose* (with pale yellow flowers that open in the ~); ~ *star*, Jupiter, Mercury, or other planet, & esp. (*the* ~ *star*) Venus, when seen in West after sunset. [OE *ǣfnung* vbl n. f. *ǣfnian* (as EVEN¹)]

ĕvĕnt', n. Fact of a thing's happening, as *in the* ~ *of his death, his coming*, if he dies, comes; thing that happens, esp. important thing, as *quite an* ~, whence ~FUL, ~LESS, aa.; (in doctrine of chances) any of several possible but mutually exclusive occurrences; *double* ~, combined occurrence of two ~s, esp. as subject of bets; (Sport.) something on the issue of which money is staked; result, outcome; *in any* or *either* ~, *at all* ~s, in any case. [f. L *eventus -ūs* f. E(*venire* come)]

ĕvĕn'tūal, a. That will happen under certain circumstances; ultimately resulting, whence ~LY² adv. [f. prec., after *actual*]

ĕvĕn'tūăl'ĭtў, n. Possible event. [-ITY]

ĕvĕn'tūāte, v.i. Turn out (*well, ill,* etc.); result (*in* or abs.); **happen, come to pass. [f. L as EVENT, -ATE³]

ĕv'er, adv. Always, at all times, (arch. exc. as foll.); *for* ~ (& ~, & *a day*), for all future time, incessantly; ~*more'*, always; ~ *after*, ~ *since*; ~ *yours* (in ending a letter); (arch.) ~ & *anon*, now & then; (w. negative, question, condition, comparison) at any time, as *nothing* ~ *happens, did you* ~ *hear such stuff?, if I* ~ *catch him, the best thing I* ~ *heard, as good as* ~, *better than* ~; (strengthening *as*) *be as quick as* ~ *you can*; (emphasizing question, colloq.) *what* ~ (also *whatever*) *does he want?, who* ~ *can it be?, which* ~ *Brown do you mean?, when, where, how,* ~ *did I drop it?, why* ~ *didn't you say so?*; ~ *so* (earlier *never so*), very, as *it is* ~ *so much easier*; (appended to superl. as sl. ellipsis for *that* ~ was or were: *the back-benchers were the most docile* ~); *did you* ~? (as complete sentence), did you ~ see or hear the like? [OE *ǣfre*, of unkn. orig.]

*ĕv'erglāde, n. Marshy tract of land, esp. (pl.) swamp in S. Florida. [prec. +GLADE]

ĕv'ergreen, a. & n. Always green or fresh (lit. & fig.); (tree, shrub) having green leaves all the year round (cf. DECIDUOUS).

ēverlas'ting (-ah-), a. & n. **1.** Lasting for ever; lasting long; lasting too long, repeated too often; (of plants) keeping shape and colour when dried. **2.** n. Eternity, as *from* ~; ~ *flower*; strong twilled woollen stuff. Hence ~LY² adv., ~NESS n. [ME; EVER+LASTING]

èvèrt′, v.t. (Physiol.) turn (organ etc.) inside out; (arch.) overthrow (goverment etc.). So **èvèr′sion** n. [f. L E(*vertere vers-* turn)]

ĕv′erӯ (-vr-), a. Each, all (w. sing. vb), as ~ *word of it is false*, (w. possess. pron.) *it engaged his ~ thought*, (of succession or alternation) *he comes ~ day*, ~ *other* (i.e. second) *day*, ~ *three days*, ~ *third day* ; ~ *now & then*, ~ *now & again*, ~ *so often*, from time to time ; ~ *bit* (quite) *as much*; ~*body* (*else*), ~ (other) person ; ~*day′* (adj.), occurring daily, worn or used on ordinary days, commonplace ; ~ *one* each, as ~ *one of them is wrong* ; ~*one* (also ~ *one*), ~ *body*, as ~*one likes to have his way* ; ~*thing*, all things, as ~*thing depends on that*, thing of first importance, as *pace is* ~*thing*; ~ *time* (colloq.), without exception, without any hesitation ; ~ *way*, in ~ way, in ~ respect ; ~*where*, in ~ place. [OE *æfre ælc* EVER EACH]

Ev′erӯmän (ĕvr-), n. The ordinary or typical human being, the 'man in the street'. [character in 16th c. morality]

èvict′, v.t. Expel (person; esp. tenant *from* land etc.); recover (property, title to it, *of, from,* person) by legal process. So **èvic′tion, èvic′tor,** nn. [f. L E(*vincere vict-* conquer)]

ĕv′idence,n., & v.t. 1. Clearness, obviousness, esp. *in* ~, conspicuous. 2. Indication, sign, (*of* quality, treatment, etc.); testimony, facts, making *for* (also *of*) a conclusion, esp. (pl.) *the E~s of Christianity*; INTERNAL, EXTERNAL, ~. 3. (law). Information (given personally or drawn from documents etc.) tending to establish fact, as *call* (person) *in* ~ (as a witness), CIRCUMSTANTIAL, PRESUMPTIVE, *verbal* ~; ‖ *turn King's, Queen's* ~, (of accomplice in crime) give ~ against one's accomplices ; statements, proofs, admissible as testimony in court. 4. v.t. Serve to indicate, attest. So **ĕvĭdĕn′tiAL** (-shl), **ĕvĭdĕn′tiARY¹** (-sha-), aa., **ĕvĭdĕn′tialLY²** (-sha-) adv. [OF, or f. L *evidentia* (as foll., see -ENCE)]

ĕv′ident, a. Obvious (to eyes or mind). Hence ~LY² adv. [OF, or f. L E(*vidēre* see), see -ENT]

ēv′il (-vl, -vĭl), a., n., & adv. 1. Bad, harmful; *the E~ One*, the Devil; *of* ~ (bad) *repute, an* ~ (slanderous) *tongue* ; ~ *eye*, malicious look, pop. believed to do material harm. 2. n. ~ thing, sin, harm, (*of two* ~*s choose the less*) ; ~*-doer*; *Aleppo* ~, a disease of boils ; = KING's ~. 3. adv. In ~ manner, as *speak* ~ *of*, (Bibl.) ~ *entreat,* ~*-disposed.* Hence ~LY² adv. [OE *yfel*, OS, OHG *ubil*, Goth. *ubils* f. Gmc *ubhilaz*]

èvince′,v.t. Show, indicate, (quality etc., *that* etc.); show that one has (quality). Hence ~IVE a. [as EVICT]

ĕv′ir|āte, v.t. Castrate (male); (fig.) deprive of manly qualities. So ~A′TION n. [f. L E(*virare* f. *vir* man), see -ATE³]

èvis′cer|āte, v.t. Disembowel; (fig.) empty (thing) of vital contents. Hence ~A′TION n. [f. L *Eviscerare* (VISCERA), see -ATE³]

èvōke′, v.t. Call up (spirit from the dead, feelings, memories, energies); ‖ summon (cause) to higher court. So **èvoCA′TION** n., **èvŏc′atIVE, èvŏc′atORY** aa. [f. L E(*vocare* call), or f. earlier *evocation*]

ĕv′olute (-ōōt), a. & n. ~ (*curve*), locus of centres of curvature of another curve that is its INVOLUTE. [f. L p.p. as EVOLVE]

ĕvolu′tion (-lōō-), n. 1. Opening out (of roll, bud, etc.; usu. fig.); appearance (of events etc.) in due succession; evolving, giving off, (of gas, heat, etc.). 2. Unfolding of curve; (Math.) extraction of root from any given power (cf. INVOLUTION). 3. Development (of organism, design, argument, etc.); *Theory of E~* (that the embryo is not created by fecundation, but developed from a pre-existing form); origination of species by development from earlier forms, not by special creation (cf. CREATIONISM), whence ~ISM, ~IST, nn., ~is′tIC a., (-lōōshon-). 4. Formation of heavenly bodies by concentration of cosmic matter. 5. Change in disposition of troops or ships; wheeling about, movement, in dancing etc. Hence ~AL, ~ARY¹, aa., (-lōōshon-). [f. L *evolutio* (as EVOLVE, see -ION)]

ĕv′olutive (-lōō-), a. Tending to evolution. [-IVE]

èvŏlve′, v.t. & i. Unfold, open out, (fig.); set forth in due sequence; give off (heat etc.); develop, deduce, (theory, facts, etc.); develop (t. & i.) by natural process; ~ *from* one's *inner consciousness,* create imaginatively (often joc. of romancing etc.). Hence ~MENT (-vm-) n. f. L E(*volvere volut-* roll)].

èvŭl′sion, n. Forcible extraction. [f. L *evulsio* f. E(*vellere vuls-* pluck), see -ION]

ewe (ū), n. Female sheep; one's ~ *lamb*, one's most cherished possession (2 *Sam.* xii); ~*-necked*, (of horses) having a thin concave neck. [OE *ĕowu*, OS *ewwi*, OHG *ouwi*, ON *ær* f. Gmc *awi-* cogn. w. L *ovis*]

ew′er, n. Pitcher; water-jug with a wide mouth. [ME, f. AF *ewere* = OF *aiguiere* f. Rom. *aquaria*, fem. adj. as n. (*aqua* water, see -ARY¹)]

ewigkeit (ā′vĭgkĭt, n. (joc.). *Into, in, the* ~, into thin air, into the unknown. [G, = eternity]

ĕx, prep. (commerc.). (Of goods) out of, sold from, (*ship, store,* etc.); (of stocks or shares) *ĕx dĭv′idend* (abbr. *ĕx dĭv.* or *x.d.*), not including next dividend. [L]

ex-¹, pref. 1. = L *ex* before *h, c, p, q, s* (which is often dropped), and *t*; becoming *ef-* before *f, e-* before other consonants; forming vbs with sense ' out ', ' forth ', (*exclude, exit*), 'upward' (*extol*), 'thoroughly' (*excruciate*), 'make so-&-so' (*exasperate*), 'remove, expel, free, from' (*expatriate, -onerate, -coriate*), and adjj. w. sense ' not having ', esp. in form *e-* (*ecaudate* tailless). 2. L *ex* is prefixed to nn. and rarely adjj. (orig. to titles of office etc.) in sense ' formerly ', ' quondam ', as *ex-chancellor, ex-Prime-Minister*. **ex-²**, pref. repr. Gk *ex* (*ek* before vowels) out, as *exodus, ecdysis*.

ĕxä'cerb|āte, v.t. Aggravate (pain, disease, anger); irritate (person etc.). So **~A'TION** n. [f. L EX¹(*acerbare* f. *acerbus* bitter)]

ĕxăct'¹ (-gz-), a. Precise, rigorous, (rules, order, etc.); (of person, judgement, description, report, answer, etc.) accurate, strictly correct; ~ *sciences* (admitting of absolute precision). Hence or cogn. **ĕxăc'tiTUDE, ~NESS**, nn., (-gz-). [f. L p.p. as foll.]

ĕxăct'² (-gz-), v.t. Demand & enforce payment of (money, fees, etc., *from, of,* person), insist upon (act, conduct, *from, of*), whence **~ING²** a.; (of circumstances) require urgently. Hence or cogn. **ĕxăc't-ABLE** a., **ĕxăc'toR** n., (-gz-). [f. L EX¹-(*igere act- = agere* drive)]

ĕxăc'tion (-gz-), n. Exacting (*of* money etc.); sum, thing, thus exacted; illegal or exorbitant demand, extortion; arbitrary & excessive impost. [ME, f. L *exactio* (as prec., see -ION)]

ĕxăct'lÿ (-gz-), adv. In adj. senses, esp. (as answer or confirmation) quite so, just as you say. [-LY²]

exa'gger|āte (ĭgzăj-), v.t. Magnify (thing described, or abs.) beyond limits of truth; intensify, aggravate; make (physical features etc.) of abnormal size. Hence or cogn.**~ātédLY²,~ativeLY²**,advv.,**~A'TION**, **~ātoR**, nn.,**~ative** a., (ĭgzăj-). [f. L EX¹-(*aggerare* heap up, f. *agger* heap), see -ATE³]

exalt' (ĭgzawlt'), v.t. Raise, place high in rank, power, etc.; praise, extol, (often ~ *to the skies*); dignify, ennoble, (esp. in p.p.); intensify (colours etc.). [ME, f. L EX¹(*altare* f. *altus* high)]

ĕxaltā'tion (-awl-), n. Raising, lifting up, (usu. fig.); elation, rapturous emotion; intensification. [ME, f. OF, or f. LL *exaltatio* (prec., -ATION)]

ĕxăm' (-gz-), n. (colloq.). See foll.

ĕxăminā'tion (-gz-), n. Minute inspection (*of, into*); POST-MORTEM ~; (colloq. abbr. *exam*) testing of knowledge or ability (of pupils, candidates) by questions oral or written; ~*-paper*, series of such questions or of examinee's answers to them. Hence **~AL** (-shon-) a. [ME, f. OF, or f. L *exa-minatio* (as foll., see -ATION)]

ĕxăm'in|e (-gz-), v.t. & i. Investigate, scrutinize, (accounts, person *in* or *on* subject, organ, baggage for contraband goods, theory, statement, one's own conscience, *whether*); (intr.) inquire *into*. Hence **~ANT, ~EE', ~ER¹**, nn., **~atŏr'ial** a., (-gz-). [ME, f. OF *examiner* or L *examinare* (*examen*, for *exagmen*, tongue of balance, examination, as EXACT²)]

exam'ple (ĭgzah-), n., & v.t. Fact, thing, illustrating general rule; problem, exercise, designed to do this; specimen of workmanship, picture, etc.; warning to others, as *make an ~ of* (punish) *him*; precedent, as *beyond, without,* ~; conduct as object of imitation, as *give, set, a good* ~ (cf. EXEMPLARY); *take ~ by,* copy; (v.t., rare exc. in p.p.) exemplify. [ME; (vb f. n.) OF f. L *exemplum* (as EXEMPT¹)]

ĕxăn'imate (-gz-), a. Dead; lacking animation, spiritless. [f. L EX¹*animare* deprive of life (*anima*), see -ATE²]

ĕx ăn'ĭmō, adv. & a. Heartily, sincere(ly). [L, = from the soul]

ĕx'ărch (-k), n. (Under Byzantine emperors) governor of distant province; (in Eastern Church) patriarch, bishop, patriarch's deputy. So **~ATE¹** (-k-) n. [f. LL f. Gk *exarkhos* f. EX²(*arkhō* rule)]

ĕxăs'per|āte (-gz-), v.t. Make worse (ill feeling, disease, pain); irritate (person; ~*ated at, by*); provoke (person *to* ill, *to* do). Hence or cogn. **~ātingLY²** adv., **~A'TION** n., (-gz-). [f. L EX¹(*asperare* f. *asper* rough), see -ATE³]

ĕx cathĕd'rā, adv. & a. Authoritative(ly). [L, = from the (teacher's) chair]

ĕx'căv|āte, v.t. Make hollow; make (hole, channel) by digging; dig out (soil) leaving a hole; unearth, get out, by digging. Hence or cogn. **~A'TION, ~ātoR**, nn. [f. L EX¹(*cavare* f. *cavus* hollow), see -ATE³]

ĕxceed', v.t. & i. Do more than is warranted by (one's commission, rights, etc.); be greater than (quantity, thing, *by* so much); surpass (person etc. *in*); be pre-eminent, whence **~ING²** a. & (arch.) adv., **~ingLY²** adv.; be immoderate in feeding etc.; exaggerate. [ME, f. OF *exceder* f. L EX¹(*cedere cess-* go)]

ĕxcĕl', v.t. & i. (-ll-). Surpass (others *in* quality, *in* doing); be pre-eminent (*in, at,* thing, *in* quality, *in* doing). [ME, f. L EX¹(*cellere,* cf. *celsus* lofty)]

ĕx'cellence, n. Surpassing merit; thing in which person etc. excels. [ME, f. L *excellentia* (as prec., see -ENCE)]

ĕx'cellencÿ, n. Title (*Your, His, Her, E~*) of ambassadors, governors & their wives, & some other officers. [as prec., see -ENCY]

ĕx'cellent, a. Pre-eminent; very good. Hence **~LY²** adv. [OF (as prec., see -ENT)]

ĕxcĕl'sior, int. & n. Higher (as trade mark etc.); *soft shavings of wood for stuffing. [L, compar. of EX¹*celsus* lofty]

ĕxcĕpt'¹, v.t. & i. Exclude (thing) from enumeration, statement, etc., as *present company ~ed;* ~ *him from the general pardon;* make objection *against.* So **ĕxcĕp'tive** a. [f. L EX¹(*cipere cept- = capere* take)]

ĕxcĕpt'², **ĕxcĕp't|ing**, prep. & conj. (~*ing* is required only after *not, without,* as *we are all fallible, except the pope,* but *not excepting the pope;* ~*ing* is also usual after *always*). 1. Not including, but, as *we all* *failed* ~ *him, he is everywhere* ~ *in the right place, never to be found* ~ *in the wrong place, it is right* ~ *that the accents are omitted,* ~ *for the omission of accents.* 2. conj. (arch.). Unless, as ~ *he be born again.* [*except* ME; *except* orig. p.p. (f. L as prec.) in abs. constr. (~ *you*= *you being excepted*); ~*ing*, abs. use of part. of prec.]

excep′tion, n. Excepting; thing excepted, thing that does not follow the rule; *the* ~ *proves the rule,* the excepting of some cases shows that the rule exists, or that it applies to those not excepted; *with the* ~ *of,* except; *take* ~, object *to; subject, liable, to* ~ (objection), whence ~ABLE (-shon-) a. [ME, f. OF, or f. L *exceptio* (EXCEPT[1], -ION)]

excep′tional (-shon-), a. Forming an exception; unusual, as ~ *advantages.* Hence ~ITY (-ăl²) n., ~LY² adv. [-AL]

excerpt[1] (ĕk′serpt *or* ĭksĕrpt′), n. Extract from book etc., article from learned society's Transactions etc. printed off separately for private circulation. [as foll.]

excerpt′², v.t. Extract, quote, (passage *from* book etc., or abs.). Hence *or* cogn. ~IBLE a., **excerp′tion** n. [f. L EX¹(*cerpere cerpt-* = *carpere* pluck)]

excess′, n. (Usu. pl.) outrage; intemperance in eating *or* drinking; overstepping of due limits; fact of exceeding, esp. *in* ~ *of,* more than; amount by which one exceeds another; ~ *fare* on railway, payment due for travelling farther or in higher class than ticket warrants; ~ *luggage* (over the weight for free carriage); superabundance, extreme degree, (*of* cruelty etc.); exceeding of the proper amount or degree, esp. *in, to,* ~; ~ *profits duty, levy, tax,* tax on profits swollen by war conditions. So ~IVE a., ~IVELY² (-vl-) adv. [ME, f. OF *exces* f. L *excessus -ūs* (as EXCEED)]

exchange′¹, n. 1. Act, process, of exchanging (*of* goods, prisoners of war, blows, words, etc.; ~ *is no robbery,* joc. excuse for unfair ~). 2. Exchanging of coin for its equivalent in coin of same or another country; money-changer's trade; *par of* ~, standard value of coinage of one country in terms of that of another; (*rate, course, of*) ~, price at which bills drawn in a foreign currency may be bought, also, difference between this & par; system of settling debts between persons (esp. in different countries) without money, by *bills of* ~ (*first, second, third, of* ~, separate bills of even tenor & date as security against miscarriage). 3. Thing exchanged for another. 4. Building where merchants assemble to transact business, as STOCK-~. 5. ‖ Central telephone office of a district where connexions are made for local or trunk calls. [ME, f. AF *eschaunge* = OF *eschange* (EX-¹, CHANGE¹); later *ex-* after L]

exchange′², v.t. & i. Give, receive, (thing) in place of (*for*) another; inter-

change (blows, words, glances, etc.); (v.i., esp. of coin) be received as equivalent *for*; pass (*from* one regiment or ship *into* another) by exchange with another officer. [ME, f. OF *eschangier* (EX-¹, CHANGE²)]

exchan′gea|ble (-jabl), a. That may be exchanged (*for*); ~*ble value* (estimated by that of the goods for which a thing may be exchanged). Hence ~BIL′ITY (-jab-) n. [-ABLE]

exche′quer (-ker), n. ‖ Department of public service charged with receipt & custody of revenue; ‖ *Chancellor of the* E~, finance minister of United Kingdom; royal or national treasury; money of private person etc.; ‖ (also *Court of* E~) court of law, now merged in King's Bench Division (orig. using table with chequered cloth for accounts); ‖ ~ *bill* (issued by authority of Parliament, bearing interest at current rate). [ME, AF *escheker,* OF *eschequier* f. med. L *scaccarium* chess-board, CHEQUER; *ex-* by erron. assoc. w. EX-¹ in *exchange* etc.]

excise′¹ (-z), n., & v.t. 1. Duty or tax levied on goods & commodities produced or sold at home, & on various licences etc.; ‖ government office collecting ~ (now *Board of Customs & E~*); ‖ ~′*man,* officer collecting ~ & preventing infringement of ~ laws. 2. v.t. Force (person) to pay ~, overcharge (also fig.). Hence **excis′able** (-z-) a. [(vb f. n.) f. MDu. *excijs, accijs* f. OF *acceis* tax f. Rom. **accensum* f.· **accensare* tax (CENSUS)]

excise′² (-z), v.t. Cut out (passage of book, limb, organ, etc.); (Bot., Zool.) cut out, notch. So **exci′sion** (-zhon) n. [f. L EX¹(*cidere cis-* = *caedere* cut)]

excite|′e, v.t. Set in motion, rouse up, (feelings, faculties, etc.); provoke, bring about, (action, active condition); promote activity of (bodily organs etc.) by stimulus; move (person) to strong emotion; (colloq. ellipt.) *don't* ~*e!,* keep cool!; (Electr., Magnet.) induce activity in (substance), set (current) in motion, whence **excita′tion** n.; (Photog.) sensitize (plate). Hence *or* cogn. ~ABIL′ITY, ~e-MENT (-tm-), nn:, **ex′citant** a. & n., ~e-ABLE (esp., of persons, easily ~ed, unbalanced), ~′ATIVE, ~′atORY, aa., ~′edLY² adv. [ME, f. OF *exciter* or L *excitare* frequent. of EX¹(*ciēre* set in motion)]

exclaim′, v.i. & t. Cry out, esp. from pain, anger, etc.; utter (words quoted direct or with *that*) thus; ~ *against,* accuse loudly. [f. F *exclamer* or L *exclamare,* sp. after CLAIM]

exclama′tion, n. Exclaiming; words exclaimed; *note of* ~ (!). So **exclam′atORY** a. [ME, f. OF, or f. L *exclamatio* (prec., -ATION)]

exclude′ (-lōod), v.t. Shut out (person, thing, *from* place, society, privilege, etc.); prevent the occurrence of, make impossible, (doubt etc.); expel & shut out.

So **exclu'sion** (-loozhn) n. [ME, f. L EX¹(*cludere clus-* = *claudere* shut)]

exclus'ive (-loo-), a. Shutting out; not admitting *of*; desirous of excluding others, (of social circles etc.) chary of admitting members, select, whence **exclus'ivism**(2) (-loo-) n.; (shop, newspaper) not to be had, not published, elsewhere; (of terms etc.) excluding all but what is specified; employed, followed, to the exclusion of all else, as *his ~ occupation*; (quasi-adv.) not counting, as *20 men, ~ of our own*. Hence ~LY² (-loosivl-) adv., ~NESS (-loosiyn-) n. [f. med. L *exclusivus* (prec., -IVE)]

exco'git|āte, v.t. Think out, contrive. So ~A'TION n., ~ātive a. [f. L EX¹(*cogitare* COGITATE)]

excommūn'icāt|e, v.t. (eccl.). Cut off (person) from participation in sacraments, or from all communication with the Church. So **excommūnica'TION**, ~OR, n., ~IVE, ~ORY, aa. [f. LL EX¹(*communicare* f. *communis* COMMON, see -ATE³]

exco'ri|āte, v.t. Remove part of skin of (person etc.) by abrasion etc.; strip, peel off, (skin). So ~A'TION n. [f. L EX¹*coriare* (*corium* hide), see -ATE³]

ex'crement, n. Waste matter discharged from bowels, dung, (often pl.). Hence or cogn. ~AL (-ĕn²), ~I'TIOUS¹ (-ĭshus), aa. [f. F *excrément* or L *excrementum* (as EXCRETE, see -MENT)]

excrēs'cence, n. Abnormal or morbid outgrowth on animal or vegetable body (also fig.). So **excrēscĕn'tIAL** (-shal) a. [f. L *excrescentia* (as foll., see -ENCE)]

excrēs'cent, a. Growing abnormally; redundant; (Gram., of sound in word) due merely to euphony. [f. L EX¹(*crescere cret-* grow), -ENT]

excrēt'a, n, pl. Waste expelled from body, esp. faeces & urine. [L, p.p. as foll.]

excrēt|e', v.t. (Of animals or plants) separate & expel (waste matters, also abs.) from system. Hence or cogn. **excrē'tION** n., ~IVE, ~ORY, aa. [f. L EX¹(*cernere cret-* sift)]

excru'ciāt|e (-krooshi-), v.t. Torment acutely (person's senses; now esp. in part. as adj.); torture mentally (now rare). Hence or cogn. ~ingLY² (-krooshi-) adv., **excrucia'TION** (-kroo-) n. [f. L EX¹(*cruciare* torment f. *crux crucis* cross), see -ATE³]

ex'culpāte, v.t. Free from blame; clear (person *from* charge etc.). Hence **exculpA'TION** n., **excul'patORY** a. [f. med. L EX¹(*culpare, culpa* blame), see -ATE³]

excŭ'rrent, a. Running out; (of blood) flowing from heart, arterial; affording an exit; (Bot.) projecting. [as foll., see -ENT]

excŭrs|e', v.i. (rare). Wander, digress (usu. fig.); make an excursion. Hence ~'IVE a., ~'iveLY² (-vl-) adv., ~'iveNESS (-vn-) n. [f. L EX¹(*currere curs-* run)]

excŭr'sion (-shon). Journey, ramble, with intention of returning (also fig.);

pleasure trip of number of persons, whence ~IST (-shon-) n.; ~ *train* (for ~ists; usu. at reduced rates); (arch.) sortie (*alarms & ~s*); (Astron.) deviation from regular path. Hence ~AL, ~ARY¹, aa., (-shon-). [f. L *excursio* (as prec., see -ION)]

excŭrs'us, n. (pl. ~*es*). Detailed discussion of special point in book, usu. in appendix at end. [L vbl n. as EXCURSE]

excūs|e'¹ (-z), v.t. Attempt to lessen the blame attaching to (person, act); obtain exemption for (person, one*self, from* duty etc.); (of things) serve as exculpation of (person, act, person *for* act); release (person *from* a duty; also double obj., as *we ~e him the fee*); dispense with, as *we will ~e your presence*; ~*e me* (as apology for lack of ceremony, interruption, etc.; also as form of dissent). So ~'ABLE, ~'atORY, aa., ~'abLY² adv., (-z-). [ME & OF *es-, excuse(r)* f. L EX¹*cusare* (*causa* CAUSE¹)]

excūse'² (-s), n. Apology offered, exculpation (usu. *in ~ of*); ground of this; plea for release from duty etc. [ME, f. OF (as prec.)]

|| **ex'eăt**, n. (In schools, colleges, etc.) permission for temporary absence. [L, 3rd sing. subj. of EX¹(*ire* go)]

ex'ecrab|le, a. Abominable. Hence ~LY² adv. [f. L *execrabilis* (foll., -BLE)]

ex'ecrāt|e, v.t. & i. Express, feel, abhorrence for; (v.i.) utter curses. Hence or cogn. **execrA'TION** n., ~IVE, ~ORY, aa. [f. L EX¹(*s)ecrari* (*sacrare* devote f. *sacer* sacred, accursed), see -ATE³]

exĕc'ūtant (-gz-), n. One who executes, performer, (of music etc.). [f. F *exécutant*, part. as foll.]

ex'ecūt|e, v.t. Carry (plan, command, law, judicial sentence, will) into effect; carry out design for (product of art or skill); perform (action, operation, etc.); make (legal instrument) valid by signing, sealing, etc.; || convey (estate) in property; discharge (office, function); perform (musical composition); inflict capital punishment on. Hence ~ABLE a. [ME, f. OF *executer* f. med. L *executare* f. L EX¹(*sequi secut-* follow)]

exĕcū'tion, n. Carrying out, performance; dexterity in performing music; (of weapons) destructive effect, as *do ~* (also fig. of personal charms etc.); seizure of property or person of debtor in default of payment; infliction of capital punishment, whence ~ER¹ (-shon-) n.; || *E~ Dock* (hist.), place on bank of Thames near Wapping where pirates were formerly hanged. [ME, f. OF *execution* f. L *executionem* (as prec., -ION)]

exĕc'ūtive (-gz-), a. & n. 1. Pertaining to, having the function of, executing. 2. (Branch of government) concerned with executing laws, decrees, & sentences (cf. JUDICIAL, *legislative*). 3. *Person in ~* position in business organization etc. [-IVE]

execūtor, n. **1.** (ĕk'sĭ-). One who carries out or performs. **2.** (ĭgzĕk²-). Person appointed by testator to execute his will; *literary* ~, person charged with writer's unpublished works etc. Hence **èxècū-tŏr'ial** a., **èxèc'ūtor**ship, **èxèc'ūtrix** (pl. *-cūt'rĭces*), nn., (-gz-). [ME, f. AF *executour* f. L *executorem* (EXECUTE, -OR)]

èxèg|ĕs'ĭs, n. Exposition esp. of Scripture. So **~ĕt'ic**(AL) aa., **~ĕt'ical**LY² adv. [Gk *exēgēsis* f. EX²(*ēgeomai* lead)]

èxĕm'plar (-gz-), n. Model, pattern; type (of a class); parallel instance. [ME, f. OF *exemplaire* f. LL *exemplarium* (EXAMPLE, -ARY¹)]

èxĕm'plar|ў (-gz-), a. Fit to be imitated; typical; illustrative; serving as a warning (~*y damages* in law, exceeding amount needed for compensation). Hence **~ĭLY²** adv., **~ĭNESS** n. [f. L *exemplaris* (as EXAMPLE, see -ARY²)]

èxĕm'pli|fў (-gz-), v.t. Illustrate by example; be an example of; make. attested copy of (document) under official seal. So **~FICA'TION** n. [ME, f. med. L *exemplificare* (EXAMPLE, -FY)]

èxĕmpt'¹ (-gz-), a. & n. **1.** Free (*from* taxation, control, failings, etc.). **2.** n. Person exempted, esp. from tax; || one of four officers sometimes commanding Yeomen of Guard (now usu. *exon*). [ME, f. OF f. L EX¹(*imere empt-* = *emere* take)]

èxĕmpt'² (-gz-), v.t. Free *from* (as prec.). So **èxĕmp'tion** (-gz-) n. [prec.]

èxĕn'ter|āte, v.t. Disembowel (only fig.). So **~A'TION** n. [f. L EX¹*enterare* (Gk *enteron* intestine), see -ATE³]

èxèquāt'ur (-*er*), n. Recognition of a country's consul by a foreign government; temporal sovereign's authorization of bishop under Papal authority, or of publication of Papal bulls. [L, = he may perform]

èx'èquies (-kwĭz), n. pl. Funeral rites. [ME, f. OF f. L *exsequiae* f. EX¹(*sequi* follow)]

èx'ercīse¹ (-z), n. Employment of organ, faculty, power, right); practice (of virtues, profession, functions, religious rites); exertion of muscles, limbs, etc., esp. for health's sake; bodily, mental, or spiritual training; task set for this purpose; (pl.) military drill, athletics, etc.; academical declamation etc. required for degree; composition set to pupils: act of worship. [ME, f. OF *exercice* f. L *exercitium* f. EX¹(*ercēre -cit-* = *arcēre* restrain) keep at work]

èx'ercīs|e² (-z), v.t. & i. Employ (faculty, right, etc.); train (person etc.); tax the powers of; perplex, worry; discharge (functions); take, give (horse etc.), exercise. Hence **~ABLE** a. [ME; f. prec.]

èxèrcitā'tion (-gz-), n. Practice, training; literary or oratorical exercise. [f. L *exercitatio* f. *exercitare* frequent., as EXERCISE¹, -ATION]

ex'èrgue (-g; *also* ĕgzẽrg'), n. Small space

usu. on reverse of coin or medal, below principal device; inscription there. Hence **èxẽrg'ual** (-gl) a. [F, f. med. L *exergum* f. Gk EX-² + *ergon* work]

èxẽrt' (-gz-), v.t. Exercise, bring to bear, (quality, force, influence); ~ *oneself*, strive (*to* do, *for* object). So **èxẽr'tion** n. (-gz-). [f. L EX¹(*serere sert-* bind) put forth]

exes (ĕk'sĭz), n. pl. (colloq.). Expenses. [abbr.]

Ex'eter Hall (ĕ-; hawl), n. Building in Strand formerly used for May meetings etc. (see MAY).

ĕx'èŭnt, v.i. (Stage direction) they (two or more actors) leave the stage; ~ *om'nēs*, all leave the stage. [L, = they go out]

èxfōl'i|āte, v.i. (Of bone, skin, minerals, etc.) come off in scales or layers; (of tree) throw off layers of bark. So **~A'TION** n. [f. L EX¹(*foliare* f. *folium* leaf), see -ATE³]

ĕx grā'tia (-shĭa), phr. As an act of grace. [L]

exhalā'tion (ĕksa-), n. Evaporation; puff of breath; short burst (*of* anger etc.); mist, vapour; effluvium. [ME, f. L *exhalatio* (foll., -ATION)]

exhāle', v.t. & i. Give off (fumes etc., also fig.) in vapour; be thus given off, evaporate, (*from*, *out of*); (Path., of animal fluids) pass off in minute quantities through blood-vessel etc.; breathe out (life, soul, words, etc.); get rid of (anger etc.) as if by blowing. [ME, f. OF *exhaler* f. L EX¹(*halare* breathe)]

exhaust'¹ (ĭgzaw-), n. (In hydraulic, steam, or internal-combustion engines) expulsion or exit of motive fluid, steam, or gaseous products of combustion from cylinder after completion of power stroke by piston; similar exit of spent fluid or gases from turbine; ~-*pipe* etc. (for this); process of exhausting vessel of air; (apparatus for) production of outward current of air by creating partial vacuum. [f. foll.]

exhaust'² (ĭgzaw-), v.t. Draw off (air, also fig.); consume entirely; use, account for, the whole of; empty (vessel) of contents; say, find out, all that is worth knowing of (subject); drain (person, kingdom, etc.) of strength, resources, etc. esp. in p.p.); tire out. Hence **~ĭBIL'ITY** n., **~IBLE** a. [f. L EX¹(*haurire haust-* draw)]

exhaustion (ĭgzaws'chon), n. Exhausting (in all senses); total loss of strength; arrival at a conclusion by eliminating alternatives. [-ION]

exhaus'tive (ĭgzaw-), a. Tending to exhaust esp. a subject; comprehensive. Hence **~LY²** (-vl-) adv., **~NESS** (-vn-) n. [-IVE]

exhib'it¹ (ĭgzĭ-), n. Document or thing produced in lawcourt & referred to in written evidence; thing, collection of things, sent by person, firm, etc., to an exhibition; showing, display. [f. L neut. p.p. as foll.]

exhibit 424 **exorbitant**

exhĭb′ĭt² (ĭgzĭ-), v.t. Show, display; submit for consideration; manifest (quality); show publicly (for amusement, in competition, etc.). So ~OR n., ~ORY a. [f. L EX¹(*hibēre hibit-* = *habēre* hold)]

exhibĭ′tion (ĕksĭ-), n. **1.** Showing, display, (of thing); *make an* ~ *of* one*self*, behave so as to excite contempt; public display of works of art etc.; *the Great E*~, first ~ on large scale, London, 1851. **2.** ‖ Fixed sum given to student for term of years from funds of school, college, etc., whence ‖ ~ER¹ (ĕksĭbĭsh′on-) n.,· cf. SCHOLARSHIP. [OF, f. LL *exhibitionem* (as prec., see -ION); sense 2 f. LL use ' food, maintenance ']

exhibĭ′tion|ism (ĕksĭbĭsh′on-), n. Tendency towards display or extravagant behaviour; (Path.) perverted mental condition characterized by indecent exposure of the person. So ~IST n. & a. [-ISM]

exhil′ar|ate (ĭgzĭ-), v.t. Enliven, gladden, (person, spirits). So ~ANT(2) a. & n., ~A′TION n., ~ātIVE a., (ĭgzĭ-). [f. L EX(*hilarare* f. *hilaris* cheerful), see -ATE³]

exhort (ĭgzŏrt′), v.t. Admonish earnestly; urge (person *to* do, *to a* course); advocate (reform etc.). So ~′atIVE, ~′atORY, aa., (ĭgzŏrt′-). [ME, f. OF *exhorter* or L EX¹(*hortari* see HORTATORY)]

exhortā′tion (ĕksŏr-), n. Exhorting; formal, liturgical, address. [ME, f. OF, or f. L *exhortatio* (prec., -ATION)]

exhūm|e′, v.t. Dig out, unearth, (lit. & fig.). So ~A′TION n. [f. F *exhumer* f. med. L EX¹(*humare* f. *humus* ground)]

ex′igence, -cў, nn. Urgent need; emergency. [F, or LL *exigentia* (foll., -ENCY)]

ex′igent, a. Urgent, pressing; requiring much, exacting; ~ *of*, demanding. [f. L *exigere* EXACT², see -ENT]

ex′igible, a. That may be demanded or exacted (*against, from*, person). [as prec., -BLE]

exig′uous, a. Scanty, small. Hence or cogn. **exĭgū′ITY**, ~NESS, nn. [f. L *exiguus* (as prec.) + -OUS]

ex′ile¹, n. Penal banishment; long absence from one's country (also fig.). [ME, f. OF *exil* f. L EX¹*silium* (*salire* leap)]

ex′ile², n. Banished person (lit. & fig.). [ME, f. prec., or OF *exile*, & infl. by L *exul*]

ex′ile³, v.t. Banish (person *from*; lit. & fig.). [ME, f. OF *exilier* f. LL *exiliare* (as EXILE¹)]

exil′|ian, a. Of the Jews' exile in Babylon. So ~IC a. [f. L as EXILE¹ + -IAN]

exil′itў, n. (pedant.). Thinness; subtlety. [f. L *exilitas* (*exilis* thin, see -TY)]

exist′ (-gz-), v.i. Have place in the domain of reality; have being under specified conditions; ~ *as* (in the form of); (of circumstances etc.) occur, be found; live; continue in being. [c. 1600, back form. f. foll.; cf. F *exister*]

exis′tence (-gz-), n. Being, existing, esp. *in* ~; life, as *a wretched, precarious*, ~; mode of existing; existing thing; all that exists. [ME, f. OF, f. LL *existentia* f. L EX¹(*sistere* redupl. f. *stare* stand), see -ENCY]

exis′tent (-gz-), a. Existing, actual, current. [-ENT]

existĕn′tial (-gz-; -shl), a. Of or relating to existence; (Log., of a proposition) predicating existence. [f. LL *existentialis*, see EXISTENCE]

existĕn′tial|ism (-gz-; -shəl-), n. An anti-intellectualist philosophy of life holding that man is free & responsible, based on the assumption that reality as existence can only be lived but can never become the object of thought. Hence ~IST a. & n. [f. F *existentialisme*, see prec. & -ISM]

ex′it¹, n. Departure of player from stage (also fig.); death; going out or forth; liberty to do this; passage to go out by. [f. L *exilus -ūs* going out (as foll.); partly also from foll.]

ex′it², v.i. (Stage direction) — goes off stage, as *E*~ *Macbeth* (also fig.). [3rd sing. pres. of L EX(*ire it-* go)]

ex-lib′ris, n. Book-plate, label with arms, crest, etc., & owner's name pasted into book. [L *ex libris* from library (of So-&-so)]

ex′o- in comb. = Gk *exō* outside, as: ~*dĕrm*, outer layer of blastoderm; ~*gamous*; ~*gamy*, (-ŏg⁴), (of, following) custom compelling man to marry outside his own tribe; ~*gen* n., ~*genous* (-ŏj⁴) a., = DICOTYLEDON (*ous*), w. ref. to external growth of stem; ~*păth′ic*, (of disease) originating outside the body; ~*phagous*, ~*phagy*, (-ŏf⁴), not eating members of one's own tribe; ~*plasm*, outermost layer of protoplasm; ~*skĕl′eton*, external integument, bony or leathery; ~*smŏs′is*, passage of a fluid outwards through a porous septum.

ex′odus, n. Departure, going forth, (esp. of body of emigrants); departure of Israelites from Egypt; (*E*~) book of O.T. relating this. [LL, f. Gk EX²*odos* (*hodos* way)]

ex offi′cio (-shiō), adv. & a. In virtue of one's office, as ~ *members of committee*. [L]

‖ **ex′ŏn**, n. See EXEMPT¹. [repr. F pron.]

exŏn′er|āte (-gz-), v.t. Exculpate; free (person) *from* (blame etc.); release (person *from* duty etc.). Hence or cogn. ~A′TION n., ~ātIVE a., (-gz-). [f. L EX¹(*onerare* f. *onus -eris* burden), see -ATE³]

exŏphthăl′m|us, -ŏs, n. Protrusion of eyeball. Hence ~IC a. [f. Gk EX²(*ophthalmos* eye) adj.]

exŏrb′it|ant (-gz-), a. Grossly excessive (of price, demand, ambition, person). Hence ~ANCE n., ~antLY² adv., (-gz-). [f. LL EX¹*orbitare* go out of the wheel-track (ORBIT), -ANT]

ĕx'ŏrc̵|īze, -ise (-īz), v.t. Expel (evil spirit *from, out of*, person or place) by invocation or use of holy name; clear (person, place, *of* evil spirits). So ~ISM, -IST, nn. [f. LL *exorcizare* f. Gk EX²*orkizō* (*horkos* oath)]

ĕxŏrd'ĭ|um, n. (pl. -*iums*, -*ia*). Beginning, introductory part, esp. of discourse or treatise. Hence ~AL a. [L, f. EX¹(*ordiri* begin)]

ĕxotĕ'ric̵, a. & n. (Of doctrines, modes of speech, etc.) intelligible to outsiders (cf. ESOTERIC); (of disciples) not admitted to esoteric teaching; commonplace, ordinary, popular; (n. pl.) ~ doctrines or treatises. Hence ~AL a., ~alLY² adv. [f. LL f. Gk *exōterikos* (*exōterō* compar., see EXO-, -IC)]

ĕxŏt'ic̵ (-gz-), a. & n. **1.** (Of plants, words, fashions) introduced from abroad; strange, bizarre. **2.** n. ~ plant (also fig.). [f. L f. Gk *exōtikos* see EXO-, -IC)]

ĕxpănd', v.t. & i. Spread out flat (t. & i.); expound, write out, in full (what is condensed or abbreviated, algebraical expression, etc.); develop (t. &-i.) *into*; swell, dilate, increase in bulk, (t. & i.); become genial, throw off reserve; ~*ed* *metal*, sheet metal slit and stretched into a lattice, used (esp.) to reinforce concrete. So **ĕxpănsĭBIL'ITY** n., **ĕxpăn'SIBLE** a. [f. L EX¹(*pandere* pans- spread)]

ĕxpănse', n. Wide area or extent; expansion. [as prec.]

ĕxpăn'sile, a. (Capable of) expansion. [-IL]

ĕxpăn'sion (-shn), n. Expanding; (Commerc.) extension of transactions; ~ (increase) *of the currency, of territory*, whence ~ISM(3), ~IST(2), nn. (-shon-); increase in bulk of steam in cylinder of engine; *triple*-~ *engine* (in which steam passes through 3 cylinders). [f. LL *expansio* (prec., -ION)]

ĕxpăn'sive, a. Able, tending, to expand (t. & i.); extensive; comprehensive; (of persons, feelings, speech) effusive. Hence ~LY² (-vl-) adv., ~NESS (-vn-), **ĕxpănsĭv'ITY**, nn. [as prec., see -IVE]

ĕx pärt'e̽, adv. & a. (law, & transf.). On, in the interests of, one side only; (adj., *ex-parte*) made or said thus, as *an ex-parte statement*. [L]

ĕxpā'tǐ|āte (-shǐ-), v.i. Speak, write, copiously (*on* subject); wander unrestrained (usu. fig.). Hence ~A'TION (-sǐ-) n.; ~atORY (-sha-) a. [f. L EX¹(*spatiari* walk about, as SPACE), -ATE³]

ĕxpăt'rĭ|āte¹, v.t. Banish; (refl.) emigrate; (Law of Nations, refl.) renounce citizenship. Hence ~A'TION n. [f. med. L EX¹(*patriare* f. *patria* native land), see -ATE³]

ĕxpăt'rĭate², a. & n. Expatriated (person). [as prec., see -ATE¹,²]

ĕxpĕct', v.t. Look forward to, regard as likely, as *I ~ a storm, ~ to see him, ~ him to come, ~ (that) he will come, ~ him next* week, *don't ~ me, ~ payment today, not so bad as I ~ed (it to be), just what I ~ed of him; shall not ~ you till I* etc. *see you*, leave you to arrive when you please; look for as due, as *I ~ you to be punctual, that you will be punctual, do you ~ payment for this?*; (colloq.) think, suppose, (*that*); (abs.) *she is ~ing* (colloq.), she is pregnant. [f. L EX¹(*spectare* look, frequent. of *specere* see)]

ĕxpĕc'tancy, n. State of expectation; prospect, esp. of future possession; prospective chance (*of*). [c. 1600, f. foll., see -ANCY]

ĕxpĕc'tant, a. & n. **1.** Expecting (*of* or abs.; ~ *mother*, pregnant woman); having the prospect, in normal course, of possession, office, etc.; characterized by waiting for events, esp. (Med.) ~ *method*; (Law) reversionary. **2.** n. One who expects, candidate for office etc. Hence ~LY² adv. [14th c., f. L *exspectare* EXPECT; see -ANT]

ĕxpĕctā'tion, n. Awaiting; anticipation, as *beyond, contrary to*, ~; ground for expecting (*of*); (pl.) prospects of inheritance; thing expected; ~ *of LIFE*, probability of a thing's happening. [f. L *expectatio* (as prec., see -ATION)]

ĕxpĕc'tative, a. Of reversion of benefices, reversionary. [f. med. L *expectativus* (prec., -ATIVE)]

ĕxpĕc'torant, a. & n. (Medicine) that promotes expectoration. [as foll., see -ANT]

ĕxpĕc'tor|āte, v.t. Eject (phlegm etc.) from chest or lungs by coughing or spitting; (abs.) spit. Hence ~A'TION n. [f. L EX¹*pectorare* (*pectus -oris* breast), -ATE³]

ĕxpēd'ĭent, a; & n. **1.** (Usu. predic.) advantageous, suitable, as *do whatever is* ~, *it is ~ that he should go*; politic rather than just. **2.** n. Contrivance, device. Hence or cogn. **ĕxpēd'iENCE, -ENCY**, nn., ~iAL (-ĕn'shal) a., ~LY² adv. [ME, f. OF, or f. L *expedient*- (as foll., see -ENT)]

ĕx'pĕdite, v.t. Assist the progress of (measure, process, etc.); dispatch (business). [f. L EX¹*pedire -dit-* (*pes pedis* foot)]

ĕxpĕdī'tion, n. Warlike enterprise; journey, voyage, for definite purpose; men, fleet, sent on this; promptness, speed. Hence ~ARY¹ a., ~IST(3) n., (-shon-). [ME, f. OF, or f. L *expeditio* (as prec., see -ION)]

ĕxpĕdī'tious (-shus), a. Doing or done speedily; suited for speedy performance. Hence ~LY² adv., ~NESS n., (-shus-). [f. prec., see -IOUS(2)]

ĕxpĕl', v.t. (-ll-). Eject (person *from* place, bullet *from* gun, etc.) by force; turn out (person *from* a community, school, etc.; also w. *from* omitted *was* ~*ed the school*). Hence ~l'ENT a. [ME, f. L EX¹(*pellere puls-* drive)]

ĕxpĕnd', v.t. Spend (money, care, time, *on* object, *in doing*); use up; (Naut.) wind (spare rope) round spar etc. Hence ~ABLE a., likely to be or meant to be sacrificed or destroyed. [ME, f. L EX¹(*pendĕre pens-weigh*)]

expĕn'diture, n. Laying out (*of money* etc.); consuming; amount expended. [after earlier (obs.) *expenditor* f. as prec. (med. L irreg. p.p. *penditus*); see -URE]

expĕnse', n. Expenditure; cost; (pl.) outlay in execution of commission etc., reimbursement of this, as *he paid my ~s, offered me £10 & ~s; at the ~* (cost) *of,* esp. (fig.) by bringing discredit etc. on, as *you defend his veracity at the ~ of his understanding,* if what he says is true he is a fool; *a laugh at his ~* (at him). [ME, f. AF (= OF *es-*), f. LL *expensa* fem. p.p. (as EXPEND)]

expĕn'sive, a. Costly. Hence ~LY² (-vl-) adv., ~NESS (-vn-) n. [EXPEND, -IVE]

expēr'ience¹, n. Actual observation of or practical acquaintance with facts or events; knowledge resulting from this, whence **expēr'iencED²** (-st) a.; event that affects one, as *an unpleasant ~*; fact, process, of being so affected, as *I learnt by ~*; (usu. pl.) state, phase, of religious emotion; *~ table,* table showing expectation of life at different ages etc. compiled from the ~ of life-assurance offices. [ME, f. OF *experience* f. L *experientia* f. EX¹*periri pert-* try; see -ENCE]

expēr'ience², v.t. Meet with, feel, undergo, (pleasure, treatment, fate, etc.); learn, find; (*that, how,* etc.). [f. prec.]

expēriĕn'tial (-shal), a. Of experience; *~ philosophy* (treating all knowledge as based on experience), whence ~ISM, ~IST, nn., (-shal-). Hence ~LY² (-shal-) adv. [f. L as EXPERIENCE¹, see -AL]

expĕ'riment¹, n. Test, trial, (*of*); procedure adopted on chance of its succeeding or for testing hypothesis etc. [ME, f. OF, or L *experimentum* (as prec., see -MENT)]

expĕ'riment², v.i. Make experiment (*on, with*). Hence ~A'TION n. [prec.]

expĕrimĕn'tal, a. Based on experience, not authority or conjecture; based on experiment, as *~ philosophy,* whence ~-ISM, ~IST, nn.; tentative; used in experiments. Hence ~IZE(2) v.i., ~LY² adv. [-AL]

expĕrt'¹, a. Trained by practice, skilful, (*at, in*). Hence ~LY² adv., ~NESS n. [ME, f. OF, f. L as EXPERIENCE¹]

ĕx'pĕrt², n. Person having special skill or knowledge (*at, in*), as *mining ~,* (attrib.) *~ evidence.* [F (prec. as n.)]

ĕxpertise' (-ēz), n. Expert opinion or skill or knowledge. [F]

expĕrt'ō crēd'ē, sent. You may take my word for it, because I have tried. [L, = believe one who has tried]

ĕx'pĭ|āte, v.t. Pay the penalty of, make amends for, (sin). So ~ABLE, ~ātORY, aa., ~A'TION, ~ātOR, nn. [f. L EX¹(*piare* seek to appease f. *pius* devout), -ATE³]

ĕxpirā'tion (-per-), n. Breathing out (*of* air etc.); termination (*of* period, truce, etc.). [f. L *expiratio* (as foll., see -ATION)]

expīre', v.t. & i. Breathe out (air *from* lungs, or abs.), whence **expīr'atORY** a.; die; (of fire etc.) die out; (of period) come to an end; (of law, patent, truce, etc.) become void, reach its term; (of title etc.) become extinct. [ME, f. OF *expirer* f. L EX¹(*spirare* breathe)]

expīr'y̆, n. Termination (of period, truce, etc.) [f. prec. +-Y⁴]

|| **expis'cāte,** v.t. (Sc.). Find by scrutiny etc. [f. L *expiscari* (EX-¹, *piscari* to fish)]

explain', v.t. Make known in detail (thing, *that, how,* etc.); make intelligible (meaning, difficulty, etc., also abs.); account for (conduct etc.); *~ away,* modify, do away with, (esp. offensive language, awkward facts) by explanation; *~ oneself,* make one's meaning clear, (also) give an account of one's motives or conduct. Hence ~ABLE a. [f. L EX¹(*planare* f. *planus* flat)]

explanā'tion, n. Explaining, esp. with view to mutual understanding or reconciliation; statement, circumstance, that explains. [ME, f. L *explanatio* (as prec., see -ATION)]

explăn'atOr|y̆, a. Serving, meant, to explain. Hence ~iLY² adv. [as EXPLAIN, see -ORY]

• **ĕx'plĕtive** (*or* iksplē'), a..& n. **1.** Serving to fill out (esp. sentence, metrical line, etc.). **2.** n. ~ thing, word, etc., esp. oath or meaningless exclamation. [f. LL *expletivus* f. EX¹(*plēre* fill), -IVE]

ĕx'plic|āte, v.t.· Develop (notion, principle, etc.), whence ~A'TION n.; (arch.) explain, whence ~ABLE, ~ātIVE, ~ātORY, aa. [f. L EX¹(*plicare plicat-* or *plicit-* fold) unfold, see -ATE³]

ĕx'plĭcĭt¹, v.i. Here ends (formerly written at end of book), cf. INCIPIT. [LL; prob. abbr. of p.p. as prec., but treated as 3rd sing.]

explĭ'cĭt², a. Stated in detail, leaving nothing merely implied; definite; (of persons) outspoken; *~ faith,* acceptance of doctrine with clear understanding of all it involves (cf. IMPLICIT). Hence ~LY² adv., ~NESS n. [f. F *explicite* or L *explicitus* (as EXPLICATE)]

explōde', v.t. & i. Expose, bring into disrepute, (theory, fallacy, etc.); (of gas, gunpowder, boiler, etc.) go off· with loud noise; cause (these) to do this; *magneto ~r,* hand-operated portable electrical apparatus for detonating high-explosive charges. [f. L EX¹(*plodere plos-* = *plaudere* clap) hiss off stage]

ĕx'ploit¹, n. Brilliant achievement. [ME, f. OF *esploit(e)* f. L neut. & fem. p.p. as EXPLICATE]

exploit'², v.t.· Work, turn to account, (mine etc.); utilize (person etc.) for one's own ends, esp. derog. of *~ing* colonial possessions, the working classes, etc. Hence or cogn. ~ABLE a., ~AGE, **exploitA'-**TION, nn. [ME, f. OF *exploiter* f. Gallo--Rom. •*explicitare* frequent. as prec.]

explōr|e', v.t. Inquire into; examine (wound) by touch; examine (country etc.) by going through it. Hence or cogn. explorA'TION, ~'ER¹, nn., ~'ATIVE, ~'A-TORY, aa. [f. F explorer f. L explorare]

explō'sion (-zhn), n. Going off with loud noise; such noise; outbreak (of anger etc.). [f. L explosio (as EXPLODE, see -ION)]

explōs'ive, a. & n. 1. Tending to eject something with loud noise; (of consonant sound) produced by explosion of breath, stopped; tending to explode or cause explosion (lit. & fig.). 2. n. ~ agent or material, ~ letter; high ~ (abbr. H.E.), kinds having very violent shattering effect & used not as propellents but in shells, bombs, etc. Hence ~LY² (-vl-) adv., ~NESS (-vn-) n. [as EXPLODE, see -IVE]

expōn'ent, a. & n. (Person, thing) that sets forth or interprets; executant (of music etc.); type, representative; (Alg.) index, symbol indicating what power of a factor is to be taken, whence ex-ponĕn'tIAL (-shal) a. [f. L EX¹(ponere posit- put), see -ENT]

expōrt'¹, v.t. Send out (goods) to another country. Hence or cogn. ~ABLE a., ~A'TION n. [f. L EX¹(portare carry)]

ĕx'pōrt², n. Exported article; (usu. pl.) amount exported; exportation; ~ duty (paid on ~). [f. prec.]

expōse' (-z), v.t. Leave (person, thing) unprotected (esp. from weather); subject to (risk etc.); (Photog.) subject (film etc.) to light; turn (child) out of doors to perish (p.p.) open to (the East etc.); exhibit, display; put up for sale; disclose (secret, project, etc.); unmask (villain, villainy). [ME, f. OF EX¹(poser, see COM-POSE)]

exposé (ĕkspōz'ā), n. Statement of facts; showing up (of discreditable thing). [F, p.p. as prec.]

exposi'tion (-z-), n. Setting forth, description; explanation; commentary; = EXPOSURE; exhibition of goods etc. [ME, f. OF, or f. L expositio (as EXPONENT, see -ION)]

expŏs'it|ive (-z-), a. Descriptive; explanatory. So ~OR n., ~ORY a., (-z-). [as prec., see -IVE]

ĕx pŏst făc'tō, a. Acting retrospectively, as ~ law. [L, = from what is made (i.e. enacted) afterwards]

expŏs'tūl|āte, v.i. Make friendly remonstrance; remonstrate (with person about, for, on). Hence or cogn. ~A'TION n., ~ātORY a. [f. L EX¹(postulare POSTULATE)]

expō'sure (-zher), n. Exposing, being exposed, (to air, cold, danger, etc.); abandoning (of child); display, esp. of goods for sale; unmasking of imposture etc.; aspect, as southern ~; (Photog.) action of exposing plate or film to the light, duration of this action. [-URE]

expound', v.t. Set forth in detail (doc-

trine etc.); explain, interpret, (esp. Scripture). [ME expoune f. OF espondre (as EXPONENT)]

exprĕss'¹, a., adv., & n. 1. (Of likeness) exact; definitely stated, not merely implied; done, made, sent, for special purpose; ‖ ~ train (fast, stopping at few intermediate stations); ~ rifle (discharging bullet with high initial velocity & low trajectory); ~ bullet (expanding, for ~ rifle); ‖ ~ delivery (by special postal messenger). 2. adv. With speed, by ~ messenger or train. 3. n. ~ train, messenger, rifle. Hence ~LY² adv. [ME, f. OF expres, -esse (as foll.)]

exprĕss'², v.t. Squeeze out (juice, air, from, out of); emit, exude; represent by symbols, as (Math.) ~ (quantity) in terms of (another); reveal, betoken, (feelings, qualities); put (thought) into words; ~ oneself, say what one means (strongly etc. on subject, well, aptly, etc.). Hence ~IBLE a. [ME, f. OF EX¹(presser PRESS²)]

exprĕ'ssion (-shn), n. Expressing (in all senses); wording, diction, word, phrase; (Alg.) collection of symbols expressing a quantity; aspect (of face), intonation (of voice), whence ~LESS (-shon-) a.; (Art) mode of expressing character etc., whence ~IST(2) (-shon-) n.; (Mus.) execution that expresses the feeling of a passage, as ~-mark, sign, word, indicating~ required, ~-stop (in harmonium, producing ~ by varied air-pressure). [ME, f. OF f. L expressionem f. EX¹(primere = prĕmere PRESS², -ION)]

exprĕ'ssional (-shon-), a. Of verbal, facial, or artistic expression. [-AL]

exprĕ'ssionIsm (-shon-), n. Modern tendency among painters, dramatic authors, etc., to subordinate realism to the symbolic or stylistic expression of the artist's or character's inner experience; (Mus.) tendency to discard rules and conventions and thus obtain complete freedom for composer's self-expression (as in Schönberg). [-ISM]

exprĕss'ive, a. Serving to express (~ of motion etc.); (of word, gesture, etc.) significant. Hence ~LY² (-vl-) adv., ~NESS (-vn-) n. [F (-if, -ive), as EXPRES-SION, see -IVE]

exprobrā'tion, n. Reproachful language. [f. L exprobratio f. EX¹(probrare f. probrum shameful deed), see -ATION]

exprōp'ri|āte, v.t. Dispossess (from estate etc.); take away (property). So ~A'TION n. [f. med. L EX¹(propriare f. proprium property), see PROPER & -ATE³]

expŭl's|ion (-shon), n. Expelling. So ~IVE a. & n. (med.). [ME, f. L expulsio (as EXPEL, see -ION)]

expŭnge'(-j), v.t. Erase, omit, (name from list, passage from book, etc.). So expŭnc'-TION n. [f. L EX¹(pungere pung- prick)]

ĕx'purg|āte (-per-), v.t. Purify (book etc.) by removing matter thought objectionable; clear away (such matter). Hence

or cogn. ~A'TION, ~ātor, nn., **ĕxpūrga-**
tōr'IAL, ĕxpūrg'atORY, aa. [f. L EX¹-
(*purgare* cleanse), -ATE³]

ĕx'quisite (-z-), a. & n. **1.** Of consummate excellence or beauty; acute (~ *pain*,
pleasure); keen (~ *sensibility* etc.). **2.** n.
Coxcomb, fop. Hence ~LY² (-tl-) adv.,
~NESS (-tn-) n. [f. L EX¹(*quirere quisit-*
= *quaerere* seek)]

ĕxsāng'uināte (-nggwĭn-), v.t. Drain of
blood. [f. L EX¹(*sanguinatus* f. *sanguis*
-*inis* blood), see -ATE³]

ĕxsāng'uine (-nggwĭn), a. Lacking blood.
[EX-¹]

ĕxscind', v.t. Cut out, excise, (lit. &
fig.). [f. L EX¹(*scindere* cut)]

ĕxsērt', v.t. (biol.). Put forth. [= EXERT]

‖ **ĕx-sērv'ice**, a. That has been but is no
longer in one of the fighting services. [EX-¹]

ĕx'siccāte, v.t. Dry up; drain dry. [f. L
EX¹(*siccare* f. *siccus* dry)]

ĕx'tant (*or* ĭkstănt'), a. Still existing (esp.
of documents etc.). [f. L EX¹(*stare* stand),
see -ANT]

extasy. See ECSTASY.

ĕxtĕm'por|ĕ, adv. & a. (Spoken, done)
without preparation; off-hand; *speak* ~e
(without notes). Hence or cogn.~AN'EOUS,
~ARY¹, aa.,~ăn'ĕousLY²,~ariLY², advv.,
~ăn'ĕousNESS n. [L *ex tempore* (*tempus*
time) on the spur of the moment]

ĕxtĕm'poriz|e, -is|e (-īz), v.t. & i. Com-
pose, produce, extempore; (intr.) speak
extempore. Hence ~A'TION n. [f. prec.
+IZE]

ĕxtĕnd', v.t. & i. Lay out (esp. body,
limbs, etc.) at full length; write out
(shorthand 'etc.) at full length; (intr. &
refl.) reach (*to* point, *over*, *across*, etc.,
space); cause to do this; prolong (period);
enlarge (scope, meaning of word, etc.);
(Mil., of line etc.) spread out into open
order with regular intervals between men
(trans., cause to~); (Sport. sl.) tax powers
of (horse, athlete) to the utmost (usu.
pass.); stretch forth (hand, arm); accord
(kindness, patronage, *to*); (Law) value
(land etc.), seize (land etc.) for debt.
Hence or cogn. **ĕxtĕnsi**BIL'ITY n., **ĕx-**
tĕn'dible, ĕxtĕn'sible, aa. [ME, f. L
EX¹(*tendere tens-* or *tent-* stretch)]

ĕxtĕn'sile, a. . Capable of being stretched
out or protruded. [as prec., see -ILE]

ĕxtĕn'sion (-shn), n. Extending (in all
senses exc. Law); extent, range; prolongation; enlargement; additional part
(of railway, plan, theory, etc.); word(s)
amplifying subject or predicate; *University E~,* extramural instruction conducted by a university or college. [f. L
extentio, -sio, (as prec., see -ION)]

ĕxtĕn'sive, a. (Of space, purchase,
operation, etc.) large; far-reaching, comprehensive; (of agricultural production
etc.) depending on extension of area (cf.
INTENSIVE). Hence ~LY² (-vl-) adv.,
~NESS (-vn-) n. [f. LL *extensivus* (as prec.,
see -IVE)]

ĕxtĕn'sor, n. ~ (*muscle*), one that
straightens out part of the body. [as
EXTEND, see -OR]

ĕxtĕnt', n. Space over which a thing
extends; width of application, scope, as
to a great ~, *to the full* ~ *of his power*;
large space, as *a vast* ~ *of marsh*; (Law)
valuation (of land etc.); seizure, writ for
seizure (of land etc.). [f. AF *estente, ex-*,
p.p. of *estendre* (as EXTEND)]

ĕxtĕn'ūāt|e, v.t. Lessen seeming magni-
tude of (guilt, offence) by partial excuse,
as *we must not* ~*e*, *nothing can* ~*e*, *his
baseness*, whence ~ORY a.; (improp.)
lessen seeming guilt of, as *do not* ~*e
yourself*, *his conduct*; (arch.) make thin or
weak. Hence **ĕxtĕnūā'TION** n. [f. L
EX¹(*tenuare* f. *tenuis* thin), -ATE³]

ĕxtēr'ior, a. & n. **1.** Outer; situated or
coming from without; ~ *angle*, that
between side of rectilineal figure & adjacent side produced. **2.** n. Outward
aspect or demeanour. Hence ~ITY (-ŏ'r-)
n., ~LY² adv. [L, compar. of *exterus*
outside]

ĕxtēr'ioriz|e, -is|e (-īz), v.t. Realize (con-
ception) in outward form; attribute external existence to. Hence ~A'TION n.
[-IZE]

ĕxtērm'in|āte, v.t. Root out (species,
race, sect, opinion). Hence or cogn.
~A'TION, ~ātoR, nn., ~ātoRY a. [f. L
EX¹(*terminare* (TERMINUS), -ATE³]

ĕxtĕrn'al, a. & n. **1.** Situated outside; (of
remedies etc.) applied to the outside of
the body; (Theol.) consisting in outward
acts, whence ~ISM(2) n.; belonging to the
world of phenomena (~ *world*), outside
the conscious subject; ~ *evidence* (derived
from source independent of the thing
discussed). **2.** n. pl. Outward features or
aspect, ~ circumstances, non-essentials.
Hence **ĕxtĕrnăl'ITY** n., ~LY² adv. [f.
L *externus* outward +-AL]

ĕxtĕrn'aliz|e, -is|e (-īz), v.t. Give, attri-
bute, external existence to. Hence ~A'-
TION n. [-IZE]

ĕxtĕrritōr'ial, a. = EXTRATERRITORIAL.
So ~ITY (-ăl⁴-) n. [EX-¹]

ĕxtĭnct', a. (Of fire etc.) no longer burning; (of volcano) that has ceased eruption; (of life, hope, etc.) quenched; (of
family, class, species) that has died out;
(of office etc.) obsolete; (of title of nobility) having no qualified claimant. [ME,
f. L EX¹(*stinguere stinct-* quench)]

ĕxtĭnc't|ion, n. Extinguishing; making,
being, becoming, extinct; wiping out (of
debt); annihilation. . So ~IVE a. [f. L
extinctio (as prec., see -ION)]

ĕxtĭng'uish (-nggw-), v.t. Put out,
quench, (light, hope, life, faculties);
eclipse, obscure, (person) by superior
brilliancy; reduce (opponent) to silence;
destroy; wipe out (debt); annihilate.
Hence ~ABLE a., ~MENT n. [irreg. f. L
extinguere (as EXTINCT)+-ISH²; cf. *distinguish*]

extĭng'uĭsher (-nggw-), n. In vbl senses, esp. *fire* ~, apparatus with jet for discharging liquid chemicals or foam to extinguish fire. [-ER¹].

ĕx'tĭrp|āte, v.t. Root out, destroy, (tree, weed, species, nation, tumour, heresy, etc.). So ~A'TION, '~ātōr, nn. [f. L EX¹(*s*)*tirpare* (*stirps* stem), see -ATE³]

ĕxtŏl', v.t. (-ll-). Praise enthusiastically (~ *him to the skies*). [f. L EX¹(*tollere* raise)]

ĕxtŏrt', v.t. Obtain (money, promise, etc.) by violence, intimidation, importunity, etc. (*from*); extract forcibly (meaning, inference, *from* words, data). Hence ĕxtŏr'tĭVE a. [f. L EX¹(*torquēre tort*- twist)]

ĕxtŏr'tion, n. Extorting, esp. of money; illegal exaction. Hence ~ER¹ (-shon-) n. [ME, f. LL *extortio* (as prec., see -ION)]

ĕxtŏr'tionate (-shon-), a. Using, given to, extortion; (of prices etc.) exorbitant. [-ATE²]

ĕx'tra, a., adv., & n. 1. Additional; larger than its name indicates, as ~ *foolscap, octavo*; of superior quality, as *calf* ~. 2. adv. More than usually, as ~ *strong*; additionally; ||~*special* (latest) *edition* (of evening paper). 3. n. ~ thing, one for which ~ charge is made, as *dancing is an* ~; (Crick.) run not scored off bat; additional dance; (Cinemat.) person engaged temporarily for a minor part or to be one of a crowd. [prob. for EXTRAORDINARY, perh. f. F]

ĕx'tra- in comb. = L *extra* in senses 'situated outside of a thing', 'not coming within its scope'; chiefly in wds f. med. L or mod. L (L has only *extraordinarius*), as: ~*atmosphē'ric*, of the space beyond the atmosphere; ~*cos'mical*, acting outside the universe; ~*crān'ial*, outside the skull; ~*curric'ular*, not coming within the curriculum; ~*essēn'tial*, not included in the essence of a thing; ~*judi'cial*, not belonging to the case before the court, not legally authorized, (of confession) not made in court; ~*mun'dane*, outside of our world or of the universe; ~*mur'al*, outside the walls or boundaries (of town or city), outside the scope of university teaching or studies; ~*offi'cial*, not pertaining to an office; ~*parŏch'ial*, outside, not concerned with, the parish; ~*phys'ical*, not subject to physical laws; ~ *spĕc'tral*, lying outside the visible spectrum; ~*terrēs'trial*, outside the earth or its atmosphere.

ĕx'trăct¹, n. The tough or viscid matter got by treating a substance with solvents & then evaporating them; preparation containing the active principle of a substance in concentrated form; passage from book etc. [as foll.]

ĕxtrăct'², v.t. Copy out (passage in book etc.); make extracts from (book etc.); take out by force (teeth, anything firmly fixed); draw forth (money, admission, etc.) against person's will; obtain (juices etc.) by suction, pressure,

etc.; derive (pleasure etc. *from*); deduce (principle etc. *from*); (Math.) find (root of a number). Hence ĕxtrăc'tABLE a., ĕxtrăc'tOR n. [f. L EX¹(*trahere tract*- draw)]

ĕxtrăc'tion, n. Extracting; lineage (*of Indian* ~); ~ *rate*, proportion of total weight of unground wheat which is converted into flour, & not into bran or sharps, expressed as a percentage of the weight unground. [F, or f. LL *extractio* (prec., -ION)]

ĕxtrăc'tive, a. & n. (Thing) of the nature of an extract; ~ *industries* (depending on mining & oil). [-IVE]

ĕxtradit'able, a. Liable to, (of crime) warranting, extradition. [f. foll. + -ABLE]

ĕx'tradite, v.t. Give up (fugitive foreign criminal) to the proper authorities; obtain the extradition of. [back formation f. foll.]

ĕxtradi'tion, n. Delivery of fugitive criminal to proper authorities; (Psych.) localizing of sensation at distance from the centre of sensation. [F (EX-¹, see TRADITION)]

ĕxtrăd'ŏs, n. Upper or outer curve of arch. [F EXTRA(*dos* back f. L *dorsum*)]

ĕxtrān'ēous, a. Of external origin; foreign *to* (object to which it is attached etc.); not belonging (*to* matter in hand, class). Hence ~LY² adv., ~NESS n. [f. L *extraneus* (*extra* outside) + -OUS]

ĕxtraŏrd'inar|y̆ (-trŏr-, -traŏr-), a. & n. Out of the usual course; (of officials etc.) additional, specially employed; *envoy*~*y*, diplomatic minister of second class, ranking next to ambassador; exceptional, surprising; unusually great; (n. pl.) extra allowances to troops (arch.). Hence ~ILY² adv., ~iNESS n. [f. L *extraordinarius* (*extra ordinem* outside the usual order, -ARY¹)]

ĕxtrăp'olāte, v.t. & i. (math.). Calculate from known terms a series of other terms which lie outside the range of the known terms (also fig.). So ĕxtrapolA'TION n. [EXTRA-+(INTER)POLATE]

ĕxtraterrĭtōr'ial, a. (Of ambassadors etc.) free from jurisdiction of the territory in which one resides. So ~ITY (-ăl⁴) n. [EXTRA-]

ĕxtrăv'agance, n. Being extravagant; absurd statement or action. [F (foll., -ANCE)]

ĕxtrăv'agant, a. Immoderate; exceeding the bounds of reason; profuse, wasteful; (of price etc.) exorbitant. Hence ~LY² adv. [f. med. L EXTRA(*vagari* wander), see -ANT, & F *extravagant*]

ĕxtrăvagăn'za, n. Fantastic composition (literary, musical, dramatic), language, or behaviour. [f. It. *estravaganza* (prec., -ANCE)]

ĕxtrăv'agāte, v.i. (rare). Wander away (*from* right course, *into* error etc.); exceed due bounds. [as EXTRAVAGANT, see -ATE³]

ĕxtrăv'asāte, v.t. & i. Force out (fluid) from its proper vessel; flow out. Hence ĕx'trăvasa'tion n. [EXTRA-, L *vas* vessel, -ATE³]

ĕx'travĕrt, n. Var. of EXTROVERT.

ĕxtrēme', a. & n. **1.** Outermost, farthest from centre, situated at either end; *divided in~ & mean ratio* (the whole being to one part as that part to the other); utmost; last, as (R.-C. Ch.) ~ *unction*, anointing by priest of dying person; reaching a high degree, as ~ *old age, in* ~ *danger; an* ~ *case* (having some characteristic in the utmost degree); (of actions, measures) severe, stringent; (of opinions, persons, etc.) going to great lengths, opp. to *moderate*, whence ĕxtrēm'ISM, ĕxtrēm'IST, nn.; *in the* ~, ~ly. **2.** n. Thing at either end of anything, esp. (pl.) things as remote or as different as possible, as ~*s meet*; (Logic) subject or predicate in proposition, major or minor term in syllogism; (Math.) first, last, term of ratio or series; *run to an* ~, *go to* ~*s*, *taken an* ~ *course*. Hence ~LY² (-ml-) adv., ~NESS (-mn-) n. [ME, f. OF f. L *extremus* superl. of *exterus* outward]

ĕxtrēm'it|y̆, n. Extreme point, very end; *the~ies*, hands & feet; extreme adversity, embarrassment, etc., as *driven to* ~*y*, *what can we do in this* ~*y?*; (usu. pl.) extreme measure(s). [ME, f. OF *extremite* or L *extremitas* (prec., -TY)]

ĕx'tric|āte, v.t. Disentangle, release, (person, thing, *from* confinement, difficulty); (Chem.) liberate (gas etc.) from state of combination. Hence ~ABLE a., ~A'TION n. [f. L EX¹(*tricare* f. *tricae* perplexities), -ATE³]

ĕxtrin's|ic, a. Lying outside, not belonging, (*to*); operating from without; not inherent or essential. Hence~ICALLY adv. [f. LL adj. *extrinsicus*, f. L adv. *-secus* (*exter* outside + *-in* local suf. + *secus* beside)]

ĕxtrōrse', a. (bot.). (Of anthers) turned outwards. [F, f. L *extrorsus* outwards (EXTRA- +*versus* towards)]

ĕx'trovĕrt, n. (psych.). Person not given to introspection (chiefly in antithesis with INTROVERT n.). So ĕxtrovĕr'SION (-shn) n. [f. L *extra* outside (w. assim. to INTRO-) +*vertĕre* turn]

ĕxtrude' (-rōō-), v.t. Thrust out (person, thing, *from*). Hence ĕxtru'sION (-rōōzhn) n., ĕxtrus'IVE (-rōō-) a. [f. L EX¹(*trudere trus-* thrust)]

ĕxŭb'er|ant (-gz-), a. Luxuriantly prolific (lit. & fig.); growing luxuriantly, (of health, emotions, etc.) overflowing, abounding; (of persons, actions, etc.) effusive, overflowing with spirits; (of language) copious, lavish in ornament, abundant. Hence or cogn. ~ANCE n., ~antLY² adv., (-gz-). [F, or f. L EX¹(*uber-are* be fruitful f. *uber* fertile), -ANT]

ĕxŭb'erāte (-gz-), v.i. Abound, overflow; indulge freely *in*. [as prec., see -ATE³]

ĕxūde' (-gz-), v.i. & t. Ooze out, give off (moisture etc.), like sweat. Hence or cogn. ĕxūdA'TION n., ĕxūd'atIVE (-gz-) a. [f. L EX¹(*sudare* sweat)]

ĕxŭlt' (-gz-), v.i. Rejoice exceedingly (*at, in*, thing, *to* find etc.); triumph (*over* person). Hence or cogn. ĕxŭl'tancY (-gz-), ĕxulta'TION, nn., ĕxŭl'tANT a., ĕxŭl'tantLY² adv., (-gz). [f. F *exulter* or L EX¹(*sultare = saltare* frequent. of *salire salt-* leap)]

ĕxŭv'i|ae, n. pl. Animal's cast skin, shell, or covering, (recent or fossil, also fig.). Hence ~AL a. [L, = animal's skin, spoils of enemy, f. EX¹*uere* divest oneself of]

ĕxŭv'i|āte, v.t. & i. Shed (exuviae, also fig.), slough. Hence ~A'TION n. [prec., -ATE³]

ĕx vŏt'ŏ, adv. & n. (Offering made) in pursuance of a vow. [L (as adv. phr.)]

eyas (ī'as), n. Young hawk taken from nest for training, or not yet completely trained. [orig. *nyas* f. F *niais* f. Rom. **nid(i)acem* (nom. *-ax*) f. *nidus* nest; for loss of *n-* cf. ADDER]

eye¹ (ī), n. Organ of sight; iris of this, as *blue, brown,* ~*s*; region of the ~*s*, as BLACK¹ ~; ~ *of day*, sun; EVIL ~; *in the wind's* ~ (direction of the wind); (Mil.) ~*s right, left, front*, (turn them thus); *mind your*~, take care; (contempt.) *pipe, put one's finger in, one's* ~, weep; *beam, mole, in one's* ~ (*Matt.* vii. 3); ~ *for* ~, retaliation (*Exod.* xxi. 24); *clap, set,* ~*s on*, behold; *be all* ~*s*, watch intently; *up to the* ~*s*, deeply (engaged), as *up to the* ~*s in work, mortgaged up to the* ~*s*; *his* ~*s are bigger than his belly* (said of a person who has helped himself to more than he can eat); *made him open his* ~*s* (stare with astonishment); *open one's* ~*s to*, make him realize; *wipe the* ~ *of* (shooter), kill game he has missed; *all my* ~ (*& Betty Martin*), humbug, nonsense; *my* ~*(s)!*, int. expr. astonishment; *lose an* ~, (often) lose the sight of it; *if you had half an* ~ (were not wholly blind or dull); *saw with half an* ~ (at a glance); the NAKED ~; *have an* ~ *to*, have as one's object; *with an* ~ (a view) *to*; *keep an* ~ *on*, keep watch on (lit. & fig.); *have an* ~ *for* (a due sense of) proportion etc.; *in the* ~*s* (judgement) *of*; *in the* ~ (from the point of view) *of the law*; *in the mind's* ~, in anticipation or imagination; *see*~ *to* ~, agree entirely (*with*); *view with a friendly, jealous,* ~ (with such feelings); *throw* DUST *in the* ~*s of*; *make* ~*s* (look amorously) *at*; *cast* SHEEP's ~*s*; thing like an ~, as spot on peacock's tail, ~ *of needle* etc. (hole for thread etc.), *hook & ~* (kind of fastening for dress), loop of cord or rope, leafbud of potato; BULL¹'s-~; *glass* ~ (artificial, of glass etc.), APPLE *of the* ~; ~'ball, pupil of the ~, ~ itself within lids & socket; ~-*bath*, -*cup*, small glass for applying lotion etc. to ~; ~-*bolt*, bolt, bar, with ~ at end for hook etc.; ~'*bright* (also *euphrasy*), plant formerly used to cure weak ~*s*; ~'*brow*, fringe of hair over ~; ~-*glass*, lens for assisting defective sight, (pl.) pair of these held in position by hand or by spring on nose (cf. SPECTACLE); ~'*hole*, hole containing ~, hole to look through; ~'*lash*, hair, row of hairs, on edge of ~lid; ~'*lid*, upper or lower cover of ~, (fig.) *hang on by the* ~*lids*, have only slight hold; ~'*opener*, enlightening or surprising circumstance; ~'*piece*, lens(es) at ~-end of telescope etc.; ~-*servant* (working properly only under employer's ~); ~-*service* (performed only thus); ~'*shot*, seeing-distance, as *beyond, in, out of,* ~*shot* (*of*); ~'*sight*, power, faculty, of seeing; ~'*sore*, ugly object, thing that offends the sight; ~-*splice* (made by turning up end of rope & interlacing its strands with those of upper part); ~'*strings*, muscles, nerves, tendons, of ~; ~-*tooth* (canine, just under or next to ~, in upper or lower jaw); ~'*wash*, lotion for ~, (sl.) bunkum, mere professions; ~'*water*, tears, lotion for ~, aqueous or vitreous humours of ~; ~'*witness*, one who can bear witness from his own observation. Hence (-)eyED² (id), ~'LESS (il-), aa. [OE *ēage*, OS *ōga*, OHG *ouga*, ON *auga*, Goth. *augo* f. Gmc *augon]

eye² (i), v.t. (part. *eying* or ~*ing*). Observe, watch, (*jealously, narrowly, with disgust*, ASKANCE, etc.). [f. prec.]

eye'let (il-), n. Small hole in cloth, sail, etc., for lace, ring, rope, etc.; loophole; ~-*hole*, small hole to look or shoot through; small eye. [ME *oilet* f. OF *oillet* dim. of *œil* eye f. L *oculus*]

eyot. See AIT.

eyre (âr), n. (hist.). Circuit, circuit court, as *Justices in E*~. [ME, f. OF *eire* f. L *iter* journey]

eyrie. See AERIE.

F

F (ĕf), letter (pl. Fs, F's). (Mus.; also *fa*) fourth note in diatonic scale of C major. (In MSS. a capital F was freq. written as ff. Hence, by a misunderstanding, the spelling of certain family names as *ffolkes, fforde*, etc.).

fa (fah), fah, n. Fourth note of octave in solmization. [first syl. of *famuli*, see GAMUT]

Fāb'ian, a. Employing cautious & dilatory strategy to wear out an enemy (esp. ~ *policy*); ~ *Society* (of socialists following such policy). [f. L *Fabianus* (Q. Fabius Cunctator (= delayer), commander against Hannibal, -AN)]

fā'ble¹, n. Story, esp. of supernatural character, not founded on fact; (collect.) myths, legendary tales, idle talk (*old wives'* ~s); false statement, lie; thing only supposed to exist; short story, esp. with animals for characters, conveying a moral, apologue; plot of play etc. [ME, f. OF f. L *fabula* (*fari* speak)]

fā'ble², v.i. & t. (arch. & poet.). Romance, tell fictitious tales, whence fāb'lER¹ n.; state fictitiously; (p.p.) celebrated in fable, legendary, fictitious. [ME, f. OF *fabler* f. L *fabulari* see prec.]

fāb'liau (-lō), n. (pl. *-x* pr. -z). Metrical tale of early French poetry. [F]

fāb'ric, n. Thing put together; edifice, building; frame, structure, (lit. & fig.); (often *textile* ~) woven material; construction, texture, tissue. [f. F *fabrique* f. L *fabrica* (*faber* artificer)]

fāb'ric|āte, v.t. Construct, manufacture, (rare); invent (facts), forge (document). So ~A'TION, ~ātOR, nn. [f. L *fabricare* as prec., -ATE³]

fāb'ūlist, n. Composer of fables or apologues; liar. [f. F *fabuliste* (FABLE¹, -IST)]

fāb'ūlous, a. Given to legend (~ *historians*); celebrated in fable; unhistorical, legendary, incredible, absurd, exaggerated. Hence or cogn. fābūlos'ITY, ~NESS, nn., ~LY² adv. [f. F *fabuleux* or L *fabulosus* (FABLE¹, -OUS)]

façade' (-sahd), n. Face of building towards street or open space; frontal or outward appearance. [F (foll., -ADE¹)]

fāce¹, n. 1. Front of head from forehead to chin (*look one in the* ~, confront him steadily; *show* one's ~, appear; ~ *to* ~, confronted; ~ *to* ~ *with*, confronting; *set* one's ~ *against*, oppose; *with wind, sun, in* one's ~, straight against one; *fly in the* ~ *of*, openly disobey; *in* ~ *of*, opposite to; *in the* ~ *of*, or *in* ~ *of*, despite; *to* person's ~, openly in his presence; *in the* ~ *of day*, openly; *her* ~ *is her fortune*, beauty her only dower. 2. Expression of countenance (*pull, wear, a long* ~, look serious or dismal); grimace (*make, pull, a* ~ or ~s). 3. Composure, coolness, effrontery, (*have the* ~, be shameless enough; *save* one's ~, forbear from or evade shaming him or oneself openly). 4. Outward show, aspect, (*on the* ~ *of it*, to judge by appearance; *put a new* ~ *on*, alter aspect of; *put a good, bold,* ~ *on matter*, make it look well, show courage in facing it); *lose* ~, be humiliated, lose one's credit or good name [transl. of Chin. *tiu lien*]. 5. Surface (*from the* ~ *of the earth*); front, façade, right side, obverse, dial-plate of clock etc., working surface of implement etc. 6. ~-*ache*, neuralgia; ~ *card*, king, queen, or knave; ~-*lift*(*ing*), plastic surgery for making ~ firm, removing wrinkles, etc.; ~ *value*, nominal value as stated on coin, note, etc. Hence -fācED² (-st) a. [ME, f. OF f. Rom. *facia f. L *facies*]

fāce², v.t. & i. 1. Meet confidently or defiantly (~ *matter out*, carry it through; ~ *opponent down*, browbeat him); not shrink from (~ *up to*, confront), stand fronting, (~ *the music*, not quail at moment of trial); present itself to (*the problem that* ~s *us*). 2. Turn (card) face upwards. 3. (Of persons etc.) look, (of things) be situated, in a certain direction (on, to, or North, Eastwards, etc.). **4.** Front towards, be opposite to, (to ~ page 20). **5.** (Lacrosse, Ice hockey, etc.) place (ball, puck, etc.) between crosses, sticks, etc., of two opposing players as preliminary to commencement of game (so ~ off). **6.** (mil.). Turn in certain direction on one's ground (left, about, ~; also trans., he ~d his men about. **7.** Supply (garment) with FACINGS; cover (surface) with layer of other material; dress surface of; coat (tea) with colouring matter. [f. prec.]

fā′cer, n. Blow in the face; great & sudden difficulty. [FACE¹ + -ER¹]

fā′cèt, n. One side of a many-sided body, esp. of a cut gem; one segment of a compound eye. Hence ~ED² a. [f. F facette (FACE¹, -ETTE)]

facē′tiae (-shǐē), n. pl. Pleasantries, witticisms; (book catalogues) books of humorous or erotic character. [L (facetus urbane)]

facē′tious (-shŭs), a. Addicted to or marked by pleasantry, waggish. Hence ~LY² adv., ~NESS n., (-shŭs-). [f. F facétieux (facétie f: L facetia sing. of prec.)]

fā′cia (-sha), n. Plate over shop-front with occupier's name etc. [var. of FASCIA]

fā′cial (-shl), a. & n. **1.** Of the face (esp. in Anat., as ~ artery); ~ angle, that formed by two lines from nostril to (1) ear & (2) forehead. **2.** n. Face massage. [f. med. L facialis (FACE¹, -AL)]

-façient (-shnt), suf. forming adjj. representing L -facient- (facere make, -ENT) added to infin. in -ē(re), as calefacere, liquefacere, w. sense producing the action of the vb. E forms, on strict anal. w. L, absorbefacient etc., &, loosely, abortifacient, calorifacient, etc., where L would have vbs in -ficare, adjj. in -ficus -FIC.

fā′cile, a. Easily done or won (now usu. derog.); working easily, ready, fluent; of easy temper, gentle, flexible, yielding. [F, or f. L facilis (facere do)]

fā′cĭlè prīn′cĕps, pred. a. Easily first. [L]

facil′it|āte, v.t. Make easy, promote, help forward, (action or result). Hence ~A-TION n. [f. F faciliter (FACILE, -ATE³)]

facil′it|y̆, n. Being easy, absence of difficulty, unimpeded opportunity (give ~ies for, of doing); ease or readiness of speech etc., aptitude, dexterity, fluency; pliancy. [f. F facilité or L facilitas (FACILE, -TY)]

fā′cing, n. In vbl senses of FACE²; esp.: (pl.) cuffs, collar, etc., of soldier's jacket, differently coloured from rest; coating of different material, esp. of stone etc. on wall; turning in some direction (put person through his ~s, test his qualities, proficiency, etc.; go through one's ~s, be thus tested). [-ING¹]

facsim′ilè, n., & v.t. Exact copy, esp. of writing, printing, picture, etc. (reproduced in ~, exactly); (vb) make ~ of. [L fac

imperat. of facere make + neut. of similis like]

făct, n. Perpetration of act, occurrence of event, (now only in before, after, the ~, confess the ~); thing certainly known to have occurred or be true, datum of experience, (often with explanatory clause or phrase, as the ~ that fire burns, of my having seen him); the ~s of life (colloq.), details of animal reproduction, the realities of a situation; thing assumed as basis for inference (his ~s are disputable); (sing. without a) the true or existent, reality, (so matter of ~, independent of inference; MATTER¹-of-~; in ~; as a matter of ~; in point of ~; the ~ of the matter is); in ~, (also, in summarizing) in short; ~-finding adj., engaged in finding out ~s. [f. L factum neut. p.p. of facere do]

făc′tion, n. Self-interested, turbulent, or unscrupulous party, esp. in politics; prevalence of party spirit. Hence or cogn. ~AL (-shon-), **făc′tious** (-shŭs), aa., **făc′-tious**LY² adv., **făc′tious**NESS n., (-shŭs-). [F, f. L factionem (facere fact- do, -ION); see FASHION]

-faction, suf. repr. L -factio, forming nn. of action related to vv. in -FY, prop. only when -fy represents L -facere, F -faire, as in satisfaction, but also used (instead of -FICATION) when -fy represents L -ficare, F -fier, as in petrifaction.

factī′tious (-shŭs), a. Designedly got up, not natural, artificial. Hence ~LY² adv., ~NESS n. (-shŭs-). [f. L facticius (facere fact- make) + -OUS; see -ITIOUS]

făc′titive, a. (gram.). ~ verb, one with sense make, call, or think, that takes obj. & compl. (he thought her mad). [irreg. f. L facere fact- make, -IVE]

făc′tor, n. Agent, deputy; merchant buying & selling on commission, whence ~AGE(4) n.; ∥ (Sc.) land agent, steward; (Math.) one of the components that make up a number or expression by multiplication; (Biol.) physiological unit determining hereditary character; circumstance, fact, or influence, contributing to a result; ~ cost, cost of product to producer; ~ of safety (Engineering), ratio of a material's strength to the maximum load etc. it may have to sustain. [f. F facteur or L factor (prec., -OR)]

factōr′ial, n. & a. (math.). Product of series of factors in arithmetical progression; product of an integer & all lower integers (adj., ~ 4, symbol |4 or 4!, = 4×3×2×1). [-IAL]

făc′tory̆, n. Merchant company's foreign trading station (hist.); manufactory, workshop, (∥ F~ Acts, regulating management in interest of the hands). [16th c., repr. Pg. feitoria, Sp. factoria, obs. F factorie (FACTOR, -Y¹)]

factōt′um, n. Man or woman of all work; servant managing his master's affairs. [med. L, as FACSIMILE + neut. of L totus whole]

făc'tŭal, a. Concerned with, of the nature of, fact. Hence ~LY² adv. [f. FACT, after ACTUAL]

făc'tum, n. Statement of facts or points in controversy, memorial. [L, see FACT]

făc'ŭl|a, n. (astron.; pl. -ae). Bright spot or streak on sun. Hence ~AR¹, ~OUS, aa. [L, dim. of *fax fac-* torch]

făc'ultative, a. Permissive; optional; contingent; of a faculty. [F (-*if*, -*ive*); foll., -IVE]

făc'ult|y̆, n. Aptitude for any special kind of action; executive ability (chiefly U.S.); power inherent in the body or an organ; a mental power, e.g. the will, reason; ‖ branch of art or science, department of University teaching (*the four* ~*ies*, Theology, Law, Medicine, Arts), Masters or Doctors in any of these (‖ pop., *The F~y̆*, members of medical profession); *staff of university or college; liberty of doing something given by law or a superior, authorization, licence, (esp. eccl.). [ME, f. OF *faculté* or f. L *facultas* (*facilis* easy)]

făd, n. Pet notion or rule of action, craze, piece of fancied enlightenment. Hence ~d'ISH¹, ~d'Y², aa., ~d'iNESS, ~d'ish-NESS, ~d'ISM(3), ~d'IST(2), nn. [dial., of unkn. orig.]

fāde, v.i. & t. Droop, wither, lose freshness & vigour; (of colour etc.) grow dim or pale; cause to lose colour; disappear gradually; (Cinemat.) cause (picture) to pass gradually *in* or *out* (of view on the screen), (transf. of sound-films and broadcasting) increase or reduce (sound) from or to inaudibility, whence făd'ING¹ vbl n. Hence ~'LESS a., ~'lèssLY² adv., (-dl-). [ME, f. OF *fader* (*fade* dull, insipid)]

fae'cēs (-z), n. pl. Sediment; excrement of the bowels. Hence faec'AL a. [L, pl. of *faex*]

Fä'erie, -ry̆, n. & a. Fairyland, the fairies, esp. as represented by Spenser; (attrib.) visionary, fancied. [var. of FAIRY]

făg, v.i. & t. (-gg-), & n. **1.** Toil painfully; (of occupation) tire, make weary; ‖ (at schools, of seniors) use the service of (juniors), (of juniors) do service for seniors; (Cricket) ~ *out*, field; ~-*end*, inferior or useless remnant. **2.** n. ‖ Drudgery, unwelcome task (*what a* ~ *!*), exhaustion (*brain-*~); ‖ (at schools) junior who has to ~; (sl.) cigarette. [orig. unkn.; cf. FLAG⁵]

făg'g'ot, făg'ot, n., & v.t. & i. **1.** Bundle of sticks or twigs bound together as fuel; bundle of steel rods; ‖ dish of liver chopped, seasoned, & baked; ‖ ~-*vote* (hist.), manufactured by transferring sufficient property to unqualified person, so ~-*voter*. **2.** vb. Bind in ~s, make ~(s). [ME, f. OF *fagot*]

Fahr'enheit (-hīt), a. (*abbr.* F.). ~ *thermometer*, with 32° & 212° for freezing & boiling points of water. [Prussian inventor d. 1736]

faience (see Ap.), n. Decorated earthenware & porcelain. [f. F *faïence* f. *Faenza* Italian town]

fail¹, n. Failure, one who fails, in an examination; *without* ~, for certain, irrespective of hindrances, (emphasizing injunction or promise). [ME, f. OF *fail(l)e* (*faillir* FAIL²)]

fail², v.i. & t. (strictly intr. with ind. obj.). Be missing (see FAILING²) or insufficient, not suffice for needs of (person), run short, (*time would* ~ *me to tell*; *words* ~ *me*, I cannot adequately describe etc.; *his heart* ~*ed him*); neglect, not remember or not choose, *to* (*he* ~*ed to appear*; *don't* ~ *to let me know*); become extinct, die away; flag, break down; become weaker or less efficient; prove misleading, disappoint hopes of, (*the prophecy* ~*ed*; *the wind* ~*ed us*); be insufficiently equipped *in*, not succeed in the attainment *of*; not succeed (*in doing* or *to* do); miscarry, come to nothing; suspend payment, go bankrupt; be rejected as candidate; reject (candidate). [ME, f. OF *faillir* f. Rom. **fallire* = L *fallere* deceive]

fail'ing¹, n. In vbl senses; also, foible, shortcoming, weakness. [-ING¹]

fail'ing², prep. In default of (~ *this*, if this does not happen; *whom* ~ or *whom* in proxy appointments). [-ING²]

faille (fāl), n. A light glossless ribbed silk dress-material. [F]

fail'ure (-yer), n. Non-occurrence, non-performance; running short, breaking down; ill success; unsuccessful person, thing, or attempt; insolvency. [17th c. *failer* f. AF = OF *faillir* FAIL², cf. -ER⁴, -URE]

fain¹, pred. a., & adv. Willing under the circumstances *to*; left with no alternative but *to*; (adv.) *would* ~, would be glad to. [OE *fægen*, OS *fagan*, ON *feginn*, cogn. w. OE *gefēon*, OHG *gifehan* rejoice]

‖ **fain², fains** (-z), **fēn(s)** (-z),˙ child's formula (usu. *fains I* as v.t.) stipulating for exemption from unwelcome office etc. (~ *I wicket-keeping!*). [with *fen, fens*, f. FEND in obs. sense 'forbid']

fainéant (see Ap.), n. & a. Idle(r), inactive (official). [F, perversion on *faire* do, *néant* nothing, of OF *faignant* sluggard (*faindre* skulk, FEIGN)]

faint¹, a. Sluggish; timid (~-*heart*, coward; so ~-**heart'**ED² (-hŭrt-) a., ~-**-heart'éd**LY² adv., ~-**heart'éd**NESS n.); feeble (*a* ~ *show of resistance*); dim, indistinct, pale (~ or *feint lines, ruled*~ or *feint*, of paper with lines to guide writing; *a* ~ *idea*, inadequate); giddy or languid with fear, hunger, etc., inclined to swoon; (of air, scents, etc.) sickly, oppressive. Hence ~'ISH¹(2) a., ~'LY² adv., ~'NESS n. [ME, f. OF, p.p. of *faindre* FEIGN]

faint², v.i., & n. Lose courage, give way, (arch.); swoon (v. & n.; ~*ed away*; *in a dead* ~, utterly insensible. [f. prec.]

faints, n. pl. Impure spirit coming over at beginning & end of distillation. [f. FAINT¹]

H

fair[1], n. Periodical gathering for sale of goods, often with shows & entertainments, at place & time fixed by charter, statute, or custom (*a day after the* ~, too late); FANCY ~. [ME, f. OF *feire* (now *foire*) f. LL *feria* sing. f. L *feriae* holiday]

fair[2], a., n., & v.i. & t. **1.** Beautiful (*the* ~ *sex, the* ~, women; also arch. as n., *a* ~ = a woman); satisfactory, abundant, (*a* ~ *heritage*); specious (~ *speeches*); blond, not dark, (*a* ~ *man, complexion, hair*, whence ~-*hair*ED[2] a.); clean, clear, unblemished, (~ *water*; ~ COPY[1]; ~ *fame*); just, unbiased, equitable, legitimate, (~ *& square* a. & adv., without finesse, above-board; ~ *trade*, principle that reciprocity should be the condition of free trade; *a* ~ FIELD[1] *& no favour; all's* ~ *in love & war; by* ~ *means or foul;* ~ *play*, equal conditions for all); of moderate quality, not bad, pretty good, whence ~ISH[1](2) a.; favourable, promising, gentle, unobstructed, (~ *or foul weather*; ~*weather friends*, not good in a crisis; *in a* ~ *way to succeed; by* ~ *means*, without violence or fraud; ~'*way*, navigable channel, regular 'course or track of ship, prepared part of golf-links free from hazards between tee and green); ‖ ~-*light*, = TRANSOM *window*; ~-*maid*, = FUMADE; *February Fair-maids*, snowdrops. **2.** v.i. (Of weather) become ~; (v.t.) make ~ copy of (document); (Shipbuilding etc.) make smooth and regular. Hence ~'NESS n. [OE *fæger*, OS, OHG *fagar*, ON *fagr*, Goth. *fagrs* f. Gmc **fagraz*]

fair[3], adv. *Speak* one ~, address him courteously; ~-*spoken*, (of person) courteous, bland; *write out* ~, as FAIR[2] copy; *hit, fight*, ~, according to the rules; BID[1] ~; ~ *& softly*, gently, not so fast, (esp. as protest against assumptions etc.); (with *strike, fall*, etc.) straight, plump, clean. [OE *fægre* (prec.)]

fair'ing[1], n. Present bought at a fair. [-ING[1]]

fair'ing[2], n. The making of an aircraft's surface smooth and streamlined; any light structure added for this purpose. [f. FAIR[2] as v.t. + -ING[1]]

Fair Isle (īl), n. One of the Shetlands; ‖ ~ (*sweater, pull-over*, etc.), jersey knitted in designs said to be Moorish.

fair'ly, adv. In adj. senses; (also) utterly, completely, (~ *beside himself*; there is sometimes doubt between this sense & that of *rather, tolerably*, as in ~ *good*). [-LY[2]]

fair'ly, n. & a. **1.** Small supernatural being with magical powers; ~*y lamps, lights* (of glass, for esp. outdoor decoration); *Fairyland*, home of ~ies, enchanted region; ~*y ring*, circular band of darker grass caused by fungi & attributed to ~y dancing; ~*y tale*, about ~ies, also account of strange incident, coincidence, marvellous progress, etc., fabrication, fib; hence ~*ў*-

DOM, ~*ў*HOOD, ~*ў*ISM, nn. **2.** adj. Of ~ies; imaginary, fictitious; ~y-like, beautiful & delicate or small, whence ~ILY[2] adv. [ME, f. OF *faerie* (now *féerie*) f. *fae* FAY; see -ERY]

fait accompli (see Ap.), n. Thing done & no longer worth arguing against. [F]

faith, n. Reliance, trust, (*in*; belief founded on authority (*pin* one's ~ *to* or *upon*, believe implicitly); (Theol.) belief in religious doctrines, esp. such as affects character & conduct, spiritual apprehension of divine truth apart from proof; system of religious belief (*the Christian, Jewish*, ~; DEFENDER *of the F*~; *the* ~, the true religion); things (to be) believed; warrant (*on the* ~ *of*); promise, engagement, (*give, pledge, plight, keep, break, violate*, one's ~); loyalty, fidelity, (*good* ~, honesty of intention; *bad* ~, intent to deceive; *Punic* ~, treachery); ~-*cure*, -*curer, -healing, -healer*, acting by prayer, not drugs etc. [ME *feith*, f. OF *feid* (pron. *feith*), later *fei* (mod. *foi*) whence arch. (*by my*) *fay*, f. L *fidem*]

faith'ful, a. Loyal, constant, (*to* person, one's word), conscientious; trustworthy; true to fact, the original, etc., accurate; *the* ~ (pl.), true believers, esp. Mohammedans. Hence ~NESS n. [-FUL]

faith'fully, adv. In adj. senses; esp.: *yours* ~, customary formula for closing business or formal letter; *deal* ~ *with*, speak home truths to or of; *promise* ~, emphatically (colloq.). [-LY[2]]

faith'less, a. Unbelieving; perfidious, false to promises; unreliable. Hence ~LY[2] adv., ~NESS n. [-LESS]

fake[1], v.t., & n. (naut.). Coil (rope); (n.) one round of a coil. [orig. unkn.]

fake[2], v.t., & n. **1.** Do *up*, make presentable or specious, contrive out of poor material. **2.** n. Piece of faking, thing ~d up (esp. sham antique), dodge, cooked report. Hence ~'MENT (-km-) n., ~. [perh. f. obs. *feak, feague* thrash, prob. f. G *fegen* sweep, thrash]

fakir' (-ēr), n. Moslem (or Hindu) religious mendicant, devotee. [f. Arab. *faqir* poor man]

Falăn'gist, n. Member of a Spanish Fascist organization *Falăn'ge* (-ghä). [Sp. ~ f. *falange* phalanx]

făl'bala, n. Flounce, trimming. [17th c. f. F, of unkn. orig.; see FURBELOW]

făl'căte, a. (anat., bot., zool.). Hooked, sickle-shaped. [f. L *falcatus* f. *falx* sickle, -ATE[2](2)]

făl'cătĕd, a. (astron.). = prec. (of moon etc.). [as prec., see -ATE[2]]

falchion (fawl'chon), n. Broad curved convex-edged sword. [ME *fauchoun* f. OF *fauchon* f. Rom. **falcionem* (nom. -*cio*) f. L *falx* sickle]

făl'cifŏrm, a. (anat.). Sickle-shaped. [f. L *falx -cis* sickle + -FORM]

falcon (faw'kn, fawl'kn), n. Small diurnal bird of prey, esp. as trained to hawk for

sport (in ~ry the female only, cf. TERCEL).
So ~RY(2, 5) n. [ME, f. OF *faucon* f. LL *falconem*]

falc'oner (fawk-), n. Keeper and trainer of hawks; one who hunts with hawks. [f. OF *faulconnier*, see prec., -ER²(2)]

falc'onet (fawk-), n. 1. (hist.). Light cannon. 2. Species of shrike. [first sense f. It. *falconetto* dim. of *falcone* FALCON; last f. FALCON + -ET¹]

fälderäl', n. Gewgaw, trifle. [cf. the earlier *fal-lal*]

fald'stool (fawl-), n. Bishop's armless chair; ‖ movable desk for kneeling at; desk for litany to be said from. [f. med. L *faldistolium* f. WG *faldistōl* (*faldan* to fold, STOOL)]

Falẽrn'ian, n. A famous wine of ancient Campania. [f. L (*vinum*) *Falernum* Falernian (wine) + -IAN]

fall¹ (fawl), v.i. & (dial. & U.S.) t. (*fell*; ~*en* often conjugated with *be*, see -ED¹(2), & used as adj.). 1. Descend freely (~*ing star*, meteor), drop (*the remark fell from him*; *lambs* ~, are born), come down, lose high position (*statesmen* ~; ~*en angel*, one of those cast out of heaven), swoop (*vengeance fell*). 2. Become detached, hang down; sink to lower level (*barometer, prices*, ~), decline, slope; disembogue *into*; subside, ebb, abate; show dismay (*faces* ~), droop (*eyes* ~). 3. Cease to stand (~*ing sickness* arch., epilepsy), become prostrate, come to ground, sin, be overthrown, perish (~ *prostrate, flat*; *plans* ~ *to the ground*, are abandoned), fail; ~ *on* one's *sword*, in suicide; *wicket* ~*s*, batsman is out; *fortress* ~*s*, is taken; *woman* ~*s*, loses chastity; *many fell*, were killed in battle; *seven lions fell to his rifle*; ~*en on evil times*, in misfortune; ~ *a prey* or *sacrifice to*; ~ *into error*; *houses* ~, tumble in fragments; ~ *to pieces, in two, asunder*); (trans.) cause to ~, fell (tree). 4. Take such a direction (*his eye fell upon me*), have such a place (*accent* ~*s on first syllable*), alight, come by chance etc., (*the lot fell upon me*; *it fell to my lot to*; *cost* ~*s to you*; *it fell in my way*; ~ *amongst thieves*, *upon a corrupt age*; *subject* ~*s into three divisions*). 5. Pass into such a state (*fell into a rage, in love*), become so-&-so (~ *dumb, due*); lapse, revert, (*revenues* ~ *to the Crown*). 6. Occur, have date, (*Easter* ~*s early*), find place (*what now* ~*s to be described*). 7. With prepp.: ~ *a-* ~*ing*, begin; ~ *behind*, be passed by; ~ *for* (colloq.), be captivated by, admire, yield to the charms or merits of; ~ *into*, (line) take one's place in the ranks, combine with others, (*conversation with*) begin talking to, (*habit* etc.) adopt it; ~ (*up*)*on*, assault, come across, (one's *feet* or *legs*) get well out of difficulty; ~ *to* —*ing*, take to, begin, (also ~ *to work*); ~ *under*, be classed among, be subjected to (*observation* etc.); ~ *within*, be included in. 8. With advv.: ~ *astern*, (of ship) drop

behind; ~ *away*, desert, revolt, apostatize, decay, vanish; ~ *back*, retreat; ~ *back upon*, have recourse to; ~ *behind*, lag; (colloq.) ~ *down* (*on*), fail (in); ~ *foul of*, come into collision with, quarrel with, attack; ~ *in*, (Mil.) take or cause to take places in line, (of buildings etc.) give way inwards, (of debt etc.) become due, (of land etc.) become available, (of lease) run out; ~ *in with*, happen to meet, accede to (views), agree with (person), coincide with, humour; ~ *off*, withdraw, decrease, degenerate (so ~*ing off*, n.), (of ship) refuse to answer helm, (of subjects) revolt; ~ *on*, join battle, begin feeding; ~ *out*, quarrel, come to pass, result *well* etc., (Mil.) leave the ranks; ~ *out of*, give up (habit) etc.; (fig.) ~ (LEAN²) *over backwards*; ~ *short*, become insufficient, (of missile) not go far enough; ~ *short of*, fail to obtain; ~ *through*, miscarry, fail; ~ *to*, begin eating or fighting. [OE *feallan*, OS, OHG *fallan*, ON *falla*]

fall² (fawl), n. Act of falling (see prec.); also or esp.: amount of rain etc. that falls; (now chiefly U.S.; also ~ *of the year* or *leaf*) autumn; number of lambs born; cataract, cascade, (often pl.); downward trend, amount of descent; wrestling-bout, throw in this, (*try a* ~, lit. & fig.); rope of hoisting-tackle; amount of timber cut down; succumbing to temptation (*the F*~ *of man*, Adam's sin and its results); kind of woman's veil; ~*-out*, airborne particles of radio-active materials from explosion of atomic or hydrogen bomb. [f. prec.]

fäll'acy, n. Misleading argument, sophism, (Log.) flaw that vitiates syllogism, one of the types of such flaws; delusion, error, (PATHETIC ~); unsoundness, delusiveness, disappointing character, (of arguments, or beliefs). So fallA'cious (-āshus) a., fallā'ciousLY² adv., fallā'ciousNESS n., (-shus-). [f. ·L *fallacia* (*fallax* deceiving f. *fallere* deceive) see -ACY]

fäl-läl', n. Piece of finery. Hence fälläl(l)²-ERY(5) n. [contemptuous reduplication, cf. *gewgaw*, perh. f. FALBALA]

fäll'ible, a. Liable to err or be erroneous. Hence fälliBIL'ITY n. [f. med. L *fallibilis* (*fallere* deceive, -BLE)]

Fallōp'ian, a. Of Fallopius the Italian anatomist (d. 1562); ~ *tubes*, the human oviducts. [-AN]

fäll'ow¹ (-ō), n., a., & v.t. (Ground) ploughed and harrowed but left uncropped for a year; uncultivated (land); (vb) break up (land) for sowing or to destroy weeds. [ME *falwe*, rel. to OE *fealga* (pl.) harrows, *fealgian* break up land, MLG *valge*, G *felge*]

fäll'ow² (-ō), a. Of pale brownish or reddish yellow (now only in ~*-deer*, species smaller than red deer). [OE, OS *falu*, OHG *falo* (G *fahl, falb*), ON *fǫlr* f. Gmc *falwaz*]

false (fawls), a. & adv. **1.** Erroneous, wrong, incorrect, (~ *idea, verdict*; ~ *concord*, breach of agreement rules in grammar; ~ *quantity*, incorrect length of vowel in verse or pronunciation; ~ *note* in music; ~ *drawing*; ~ *imprisonment*, illegal; ~ *weights* etc.; ~ *pride, shame*, based on wrong notions; ~ *position*, one that tempts person to act against his principles; ~ *step*, stumble, transgression; ~ *start*, wrong start (in racing); lying, deceitful, treacherous, unfaithful *to*; deceptive (~ *mirror, medium*); spurious, sham, artificial, (~ *coin, god, prophet, hair, teeth*; ~ *colours*, flag one has no right to, lit. & fig.); improperly so called, pseudo-, (~ *acacia*; ~ *bottom*, horizontal partition in vessel, drawer, etc.; ~ KEEL[1]); ~ *alarm* (given without good cause, either to deceive or under apprehension of danger); ~ *card*, one played contrary to usual custom, in order to mislead opponents; ~ *pretences*, misrepresentations made with intent to deceive; hence or cogn. ~'LY[2] (-awlsl-) adv., ~'NESS (-awlsn-), **fal'SITY** (fawl-), nn. **2.** adv. *Play* person ~, cheat, betray.' [ME *fals(e)* f. OF *fals, faus* f. L *falsus* p.p. of *fallere* deceive; OE *fals* dir. f. L]

false'hood (fawls-h-), n. Falsity; something untrue, contrariety to fact; lying, lie(s). [-HOOD]

falsett'o (fawl-), n. (pl. *-os*). Head voice in men, as used by male altos (*in* ~, *a* ~ *tone*, etc., often of sham indignation). [It., dim. of *falso* FALSE]

fal'sif|y (fawl-), v.t. Fraudulently alter (document); misrepresent; make wrong, pervert; disappoint (hope, fear, etc.). So ~iCA'TION (fawl-) n. [f. F *falsifier* or LL *falsificare* (FALSE, -FY)]

Falstäff'ian (fawl-), a. Like or characteristic of Shakespeare's Falstaff, fat, jovial, & humorous. [-IAN]

fal'ter (fawl-), v.i. & t. Stumble, stagger, go unsteadily; stammer, speak hesitatingly, (~ *out*, utter, say, thus); waver, lose courage, flinch. Hence ~ingLY[2] adv. [orig. obsc.; perh. f. ME *falden* (FOLD[2]) in obs. sense *falter*, after *totter* etc.]

fame[1], n. Public report, rumour; reputation (*house of ill* ~, bawdy-house), good reputation; renown, celebrity. [ME, OF f. L *fama* = Gk *phēmē* (*fa*- speak)]

fame[2], v.t. (Pass.) be currently reported *as, for, to* be or do; (p.p.) famous, much spoken of, (*for valour* etc.). [ME, f. OF *famer* (prec.)]

famil'ial (-lyal), a. Of, occurring in, characteristic of, (member of) a family. [-IAL]

famil'iar (-lyar), a. & n. **1.** Of one's family (arch. for *family* attrib.); intimate (*with*), in close friendship (~ *spirit*, or ~ as n., demon attending & obeying witch etc.); closely acquainted *with* (some subject); well known, no longer novel, (*to*); common, current, usual; unceremonious, free, over-free; amorously or sexually intimate (*with*). **2.** n. (R.-C. Ch.) person rendering certain services in Pope's or bishop's household; intimate friend or associate; ~ spirit. Hence ~LY[2] adv. [ME, f. OF *familier* f. L *familiaris* (FAMILY, -AR[1])]

familiä'rit|y, n. Close intercourse, intimacy *with* person or some subject; amorous intimacy, (pl.) caresses etc.; unceremoniousness, treating of inferiors or superiors as equals, (~ *breeds contempt*). [ME, f. OF *familiarite* f. L *familiaritatem* (prec., -TY)]

famil'iariz|e, -is|e, (-lyarïz), v.t. Make (thing) well known; make (person, person's *mind* etc., one*self*) well acquainted or at home *with*. Hence ~A'TION n. [-IZE]

fam'ily, n. **1.** Members of a household, parents, children, servants, etc. (*happy* ~, animals of different kinds in one cage); set of parents & children, or of relations, living together or not (*Holy F*~, the Virgin, Jesus, St Joseph, & often St John Baptist & St Elizabeth, as grouped in pictures); person's children. **2.** All descendants of common ancestor, house, lineage, (*of* ~, well born); race, group of peoples from common stock. **3.** Brotherhood of persons or nations united by political or religious ties. **4.** Group of objects distinguished by common features. **5.** Group of allied genera, usu. subdivision of ORDER. **6.** ~ *allowance* (paid to employees or State-insured person in proportion to size of ~); ~ *butcher* etc., supplying families as opp. to the army etc.; ~ *hotel*, with special terms for families; *in a* ~ *way*, without ceremony; || *in the* ~ *way*, with child; ~ *Bible*, large Bible with fly-leaves for registering births etc.; || ~ *coach*, large closed carriage, a game of forfeits; ~ *likeness*, that between relations, vague resemblance; || ~ *living*, benefice in gift of head of ~; ~ *man*, one with ~, domestic person; ~ *planning*, birth control; ~ *tree*, genealogical chart. [f. L *familia* household (*famulus* servant, -Y[1])]

fam'ine, n. Extreme scarcity of food in a district etc.; dearth of something specified, as *water* ~ (~ *prices*, raised by scarcity); hunger, starvation, (*die of* ~). [ME, f. OF, f. *faim* f. L *fames* hunger, -INE[1]]

fam'ish, v.t. & i. Reduce, be reduced, to extreme hunger; (colloq.) be ~*ing*, feel hungry. [ME, f. *fame* (obs., f. OF *afamer* f. L *fames* hunger) +-ISH]

fam'ous, a. Celebrated (*for* quality etc.), well known; (colloq.) capital, excellent, whence ~LY[2] adv. [ME, f. AF *famous* f. OF *-eus* f. L *famosus* (FAME, -OSE[1])]

fam'ulus, n. (pl. *-li*). Attendant on magician. [L, = servant]

fan[1], n. Winnowing-machine; instrument, usu. folding & sector-shaped when spread out, on radiating ribs, for agitating air to cool face; anything so spread out, as bird's tail, wing, leaf, kind of ornamental vaulting (~ *tracery*); rotating apparatus giving current of air for ventilation etc.; (Naut.) (blade of) screw, propeller; (in windmill) small sail for keeping head towards wind; ‖ ~-*light*, ~-shaped window over door; ~-*tail*, ~-shaped tail or end, kind of pigeon, ‖ coal-heaver's hat or sou'-wester. [OE *fann* f. L *vannus* winnowing-basket]

fan², v.t. & i. (-nn-). Winnow (corn), whence ~n'ER¹(2) n.; winnow away (chaff), sweep *away* (as) by wind from fan; move (air) with fan; drive current of air (as) with fan upon, to cool (face etc.) or to kindle (flame; ~ *the flame*, increase excitement etc.); (of breeze) blow gently on, cool; spread out (t. & i.) in fan shape. [f. prec.]

fan³, n. (sl.). Devotee of a specified amusement, as *film* ~s, *football* ~s; ~ *mail*, letters from ~s. [abbr. of foll.]

fanăt'ĭc, a. & n. (Person) filled with excessive & mistaken enthusiasm, esp. in religion. Hence ~AL a., ~aLLY² adv., ~ISM n., ~IZE(2, 3) v.i. & t. [f. F (*-ique*) or L *fanaticus* (*fanum* temple, -ATIC)]

fan'cier, n. Connoisseur in some article or animal (of which the name is usu. prefixed, as *dog, rose*, -~). [FANCY², -ER¹]

fan'ciful, a. Indulging in fancies, whimsical, capricious; fantastically designed, ornamented, etc., odd-looking; imaginary, unreal. Hence ~LY² adv., ~NESS n. [-FUL]

fan'cý¹, n. & a. **1.** Delusion, unfounded belief; faculty of calling up things not present, of inventing imagery; mental image; arbitrary supposition; caprice, a whim; individual taste, inclination, (*take a ~ to, for; catch the ~ of*, please); *the ~*, those who have a certain hobby, = *-fanciers*, esp. the patrons of boxing; art of breeding animals with certain points of excellence; ~-*free*, not in love. **2.** adj. (not pred.). Ornamental, not plain, (~ *bread*; ~ *dress*, masquerade costume, so ~-*dress* or ~-*ball*; ~-*work*, ornamental sewing etc.; ‖ ~ *fair*, bazaar for sale of ~ goods); (of flowers etc.) particoloured; capricious, whimsical, extravagant, (*at a ~ price*; ‖ ~ *franchise*, based on complicated or arbitrary qualifications; ~ *dog, pigeon*, etc., bred for particular points of beauty etc.); based on imagination, not fact (~ *picture*); ~ *man*, sweetheart, (sl.) man living on earnings of a prostitute. [contraction of FANTASY]

fan'cý², v.t. Picture to oneself, conceive, imagine, (~ *oneself dead*; ~ *a blue dahlia*; ~ *him to be here, that he is here*; imperat. as excl. of surprise, ~*!*, ~ *his believing it!*); be inclined to suppose, rather think; (colloq.) have good conceit of (*oneself*, one's *game* etc.); take a fancy to, like; breed, grow, (animals, plants) with attention to certain points. [f. prec.]

făndangle (-ăng'gl), n. Fantastic ornament, tomfoolery. [perh. f. foll.]

făndang'ō (-ngg-), n. (pl. *-oes*). Lively Spanish dance; tune for this. [Sp.]

fāne, n. (poet.). Temple. [f. L *fanum*]

făn'fāre (& see Ap.), n. Flourish of trumpets, bugles, etc. [F]

fănfäronāde', n. Arrogant talk, brag; = prec. [f. F *fanfaronnade* f. *fanfaron* (prec., -OON), -ADE]

făng¹, n. Canine tooth, esp. of dogs & wolves; serpent's venom-tooth; spike of tool held in the stock; (prong of) root of tooth. Hence (~)~ED² (-gd), ~'LESS, aa. [late OE *fang* f. ON (= OS, OHG) *fang* f. Gmc vb *fanhan* to catch]

făng², v.t. Prime (pump) by pouring in water to start it. [f. prec.]

fän-tăn', n. Chinese gambling game in which the number of coins etc. hidden under a bowl has to be guessed; gambling game played with cards. [Chin.]

făntasia (-azē'a, -ā'zia, -ah²), n. Musical or other composition in which form is subservient to fancy. [It. = FANTASY]

făn'tăst, ph-, n. Visionary, dreamer. [f. med. L f. Gk *phantastēs* (*phantazomai* make a show f. *phainō* show)]

făntăs'tic, a. Fancied (rare); extravagantly fanciful, capricious, eccentric; grotesque or quaint in design etc. Hence (thr. obs. ~*al*) ~al'ITY, ~alNESS, ~ISM, nn., ~alLY² adv. [ME, f. OF f. med. L *fantasticus* f. LL f. Gk *phantastikos* (prec., -IC)]

făn'tasý, ph-, n. Image-making faculty, esp. when extravagant or visionary; mental image; fantastic design; = FANTASIA; whimsical speculation. [ME, f. OF *fantasie* f. L f. Gk *phantasia* (see FANTAST)]

Făn'tee, n. Member, language, of a Negro tribe inhabiting the territory of Ghana; *go ~*, (of European) conform to native habits. [native]

făntocci'ni (-ochēnē), n. pl. Mechanically worked puppets; marionette show. [It.]

faquir. See FAKIR.

fär¹, adv. (FARTHER, *-thest*, FURTHER, *-thest*), & n. **1.** At a great distance, a long way off, (often with *away, off, out*; also fig., as ~, *so ~, from doing, ~ from it*; ~ *be it from me to*, I would on no account); to a great distance or advanced point (*driven ~ into the ground*; ~ *gone*, advanced (see below also); *he will go ~*, do much; *go ~ to effect* etc., nearly do so; by a great interval, by much, (~ *different, better, the best*; also ~ *& away*); *so ~*, to such a distance, (also) up to now; *how ~*, to what extent; *as ~ as*, right to, not short of, (place); *as or so ~ as, in so ~ as*, to whatever extent. **2.** ~-*away*, remote, long-past, (of look etc.) absent, dreamy; ~-*between*, infrequent; ~ EAST; ~-*famed*, widely known; ~-*fetched*, (of simile, illustration, etc.) studiously sought out, strained; ~-*flung* (rhet.), widely extended; ~ FORTH; ~ *gone*, very ill or mad or drunk or much in

debt; ~ *off*, remote; ~-*reaching*, widely
applicable, carrying many consequences;
~-*seeing*, -*sighted*, prescient, prudent,
(-*sighted*) seeing distant things more clearly than near ones. **3.** n. A distance (*do you
come from* ~ ?); large amount (*by* ~, with
compar. & superl., *prefer, surpass*, etc.).
[OE *feor*(r), OS, OHG *fer*, ON *fjarri*,
Goth. *fairra* f. Gmc **fer-* cogn. w. Gk
peran beyond]
far², a. (*farther, -est, further, -est*). Distant,
remote, (*a* ~ CRY¹). [OE *feorr* f. prec.]
fa′rad, n. (electr.). Electro-magnetic unit
of capacity. [f. *Faraday*, physicist, d.
1867]
farada′ic, a. (electr.). Inductive, induced,
(of current). [as prec., -IC]
farce¹, n. Dramatic work merely to excite laughter; this species of drama;
absurdly futile proceeding, pretence,
mockery. Hence **far′CICAL** a., **far′ci-
caLLY²** adv., **farcicăl′ITY** n. [F, orig.=
stuffing, f. L *farcire* to stuff, used metaph.
of interludes etc.]
farce², v.t. (arch.). Season, spice, stuff,
(in cookery, & fig. of literary compositions). [ME f. OF *farsir* f. L as prec.]
farceur′ (-sēr), n. Joker, wag. [F]
far′cy, n. Disease, esp. of horses, allied to
glanders; ~ *bud, button,* small tumour in
this. [w. older *farcin* f. F *farcin* f. L
farciminum (*farcire* stuff)]
‖ **fard′el,** n. (arch.). Bundle, burden. [ME,
f. OF, dim. of *farde* burden f. Arab.
fardah]
fare¹, n. **1.** Cost of passenger's conveyance, passage-money; passenger in hired
vehicle. **2.** Food provided (usu. *good,
bad, plentiful*, etc., ~; BILL⁴ of ~). [OE
fær, = OHG, ON *far,* & OE *faru* = ON
for, f. st. of foll.]
fare², v.i. Journey, go, travel, (poet.; so
~ *forth,* start); happen, turn out, (*how
~s it?*); get on *well, ill,* etc., have such
luck; be entertained, be fed or feed oneself, *well* etc. [OE, OS, OHG, Goth., Gmc
faran, f. far- cogn. w. Gk *poros* ford]
farewell′ (-rw-), int. & n. **1.** Good-bye!,
Adieu!, (~ *to,* no more of). **2.** n. Leave-
-taking, parting good wishes. [ME;
imper. of prec. + *well*]
farin′a, n. Flour or meal of corn, nuts,
or starchy roots; powdery substance;
‖ (Bot.) pollen; (Chem.) starch. Hence
farinā′CEOUS (-āshŭs) a. [L (*far* corn,
-INE⁴)]
fa′rinōse, a. Mealy, sprinkled with
powder. [f. LL *farinosus* (prec., -OSE¹)]
‖ **fărl,** n. (Sc.). Thin cake, orig. quadrant-
-shaped, of oatmeal or flour. [for obs.
fardel quarter (FOURTH, DEAL), cf. FARTH-
ING]
farm¹, n. Tract of land used under one
management for cultivation (orig. only
of leased land; *home* ~, reserved &
worked by owner of ·estate containing
other ~s); (also ~-*house*) dwelling-place
attached to ~; tract of water used as a

preserve (*oyster-*~); place where children
are farmed (see foll.); ~-*hand,* worker on
~; ~′*stead,*~ with buildings on it; ~*yard′,*
yard or enclosure attached to ~-house.
[ME *ferme* f. OF f. med. L *firma* fixed
payment (L *firmare* fix f. FIRMus)]
farm², v.t. & i. **1.** Take proceeds of (tax,
office, etc.) on payment of fixed sum;
(also ~ *out*) let out proceeds of (tax etc.)
to person for fixed sum. **2.** Let the labour
of (persons) for hire; contract to maintain
and care for (persons, esp. children) for
fixed sum. **3.** Cultivate, till; till the soil,
be a farmer. Hence ~′ER¹, ~′ING¹, nn.
[f. prec.]
far′ō, n. Gambling card-game. [f. *Pharaoh*
(significance doubtful)]
farouche′ (-ōōsh), a. Sullen, shy. [F]
farra′gō (-rah-, -rā-), n. (pl. -*os*). Medley,
hotch-potch. Hence **farrā′ginous** a. [L
(genit. *-inis*), = mixed fodder (*far* corn)]
fa′rrier, n. Shoeing-smith; ‖ horse-doc-
tor; N.C.O. in charge of cavalry regiment's horses. Hence **fa′rriERY**(2) n.
[16th c. *ferrier* f. F f. L *ferrarius* f. *ferrum*
iron, -ER²(2)]
fa′rrow (-ō), n., & v.t. & i. **1.** Giving birth
to, litter of, pigs (*20 at one* ~). **2.** vb.
Produce (pigs), produce pigs. [vb f. n.,
OE *fearh,* OHG *farah* f. Gmc **farhaz*
cogn. w. L *porcus*]
fart, n., & v.i. (indecent). Emission of,
emit, wind from the anus. [Aryan, cf. Gk
perdomai]
farth′er (-dh-), adv. & a. (used as comp.
of FAR¹,², see etym.), & v.t. **1.** To or at a
more advanced point or greater extent or
distance (*I'll see you* ~ or FURTHER *first*);
in addition, also besides, moreover, (now
usu. *further*). **2.** adj. More extended, additional; more; more distant or advanced,
whence ~MOST a. **3.** v.t. (rare). =FURTHER.
[ME *ferther,* var. of FURTHER; both used
as comp. of *far,* but with tendency to
restrict ~ to lit. & *further* to secondary
senses]
farth′est (-dh-), a. & adv. **1.** Most distant
(*at the, at,* ~, at the greatest distance, at
latest, at most). **2.** adv. To or at the
greatest distance. [var., now more usu.,
of FURTHEST]
‖ **farth′ing** (-dh-), n. Quarter of a penny;
least possible amount (*doesn't matter a* ~).
[OE *fēorthing* (*feortha* FOURTH, -ING³)]
farth′ingāle (-dhingg-), n. (hist.). Hooped
petticoat. [16th c. (also *vard-, verd-*) f.
F *verdugale* f. Sp. -*ado* (*verdugo* rod,
-ADO)]
fart′lek, n. (athletics). Method of training
for middle & long-distance running, in
which the athlete runs over country,
mixing fast with slow work. [Sw.,
= speed-play]
fǎs′cēs (-z), n. pl. (Rom. hist.). Bundle of
rods with axe in the middle carried by
lictor before high magistrate; ensigns of
authority. [L (pl. of *fascis* bundle)]
fascia (fā′shia), n. (Archit.) long flat sur-

face of wood or stone under eaves or cornice, cf. FACIA; (Anat.) thin sheath of fibrous tissue; stripe, band, fillet, belt; (in full ~ *board*) instrument board of motor-car. [L]

fä'sciätěd (-shǐ-), a. (Bot.; of contiguous parts) compressed, growing, into one (so **fãsciA'TION** n.); striped. [f. L *fasciatus* p.p. of *fasciare* swathe (prec.), -ATE²]

fãs'cicle, -icůle, -ic'ůlus, (fãsǐ-), n. (Bot. etc.) bunch, bundle, whence **fãs'cicleD²** (-ld), **fascic'ůlAR¹, fascic'ůlATE², -ãtěd,** aa., **fascicůlA'TION** n.; one part of book published by instalments. [f. L *fasciculus* (FASCES, -CULE)]

fãs'cin|ãte, v.t. Deprive (victim) of power of escape or resistance by one's look or presence (esp. of serpents); attract irresistibly, enchant, charm, whence ~ãtINg³ a., ~ãtingLY² adv. Hence or cogn. ~A'TION, ~ãtOR (esp., = opera-hood), nn. [f. L *fascinare* (*fascinum* spell), -ATE³]

fãscine' (-sēn), n. Long faggot used for engineering purposes & esp. in war for lining trenches, filling ditches, etc.; ~ *dwelling,* prehistoric lake dwelling supported by cross layers of sticks sunk below surface. [F, f. L *fascina* (*fascis* bundle, -INE¹)]

Fãs'cism (fãshǐ-, fãsǐ-), *fasci'smo* (-shēzmō), n. Principles & organization of the patriotic & anti-communist movement in Italy started during the 1914–18 war, culminating in the dictatorship of Benito Mussolini (d. 1945), & imitated by Fascist or blackshirt associations in other countries. So **Fãs'cist** (fãshǐ-, fãsǐ-), **fasci'sta** (-shē-; pl. -*ti* pron. -*lē*), n. [It. *fascismo* (*fascio* bundle, group, f. L as FASCES, see -ISM)]

‖ **fãsh,** v.t. (or refl.), & n. (Sc.). Bother, trouble, inconvenience. [n. f. vb, f. OF *fascher* (now *fâcher*)]

fä'shion (-shn), n., & v.t. 1. Make, shape, style, pattern, manner, (*after the ~ of,* like; so -~ =-WISE, as *walk crab-~*); *after, in, a ~,* not satisfactorily, but somehow or other. 2. Prevailing custom, esp. in dress (~-*plate,* picture showing style of dress). 3. Conventional usages of upper--class society (*the~,* whatever is in accord with these for the time being; *set the ~,* give the example in changing them; *the ~,* (also) admired & discussed person or thing; *in, out of, ~* or *the ~,* agreeing or not with current usage; *man* etc. *of ~,* (hist. or joc.), of social standing, moving in & conforming with upper-class society); hence -~ED² (-ond) a. 4. v.t. Give shape to, form, mould, (*into, to,* or abs.). [ME *faciun, -soun* f. AF *fasun* (F *façon*), f. L *factionem* (*facere fact-* make, -ION)]

fä'shionab|le (-shon-), a. & n. 1. Following, suited to, the fashion; characteristic of, treating of, or patronized by, persons of fashion. Hence ~leNESS n., ~LY² adv. 2. n. ~le person. [prec. n., -ABLE]

fast¹ (fah-), v.i. 1. Abstain from all or some kinds of food as religious observance or in sign of mourning (~*ing-day,* = FAST²-*day*). 2. Go without food. [OE *fæstan,* OHG *fastēn,* ON *fasta,* Goth. *fastan* orig. = keep, observe, hold FAST³]

fast² (fah-), n. Act of fasting (prec., 1); season or (also ~-*day, fasting-day*) day appointed for fasting; going without food (*break* one's. ~ = BREAKFAST v.). [ME, f. ON *fasta* (OS, OHG *fasta*) as prec.]

fast³ (fah-), a. 1. Firmly fixed or attached (*stake ~ in the ground* ; ~ *friend* or *friendship,* steady, close; *ship ~ aground* ; ~ *asleep* ; *a ~ prisoner* ; ~ *colour,* unfading, not washing out; *make ~,* fasten; *play ~ & loose,* ignore obligations, be unreliable; *door is~,* locked etc.; *take~ hold of,* tight; ~ *with gout,* confined). 2. Rapid, quick--moving, producing quick motion, (~ *train* ; ~ *cricket-pitch, racquet-court, putting-green,* on which ball bounds or runs smartly; *watch is ~,* shows too advanced time; ~ *person,* dissipated, see foll.). Hence ~'ISH¹(2) a. [OE *fæst,* OS *fast,* OHG *festi,* ON *fastr,* Gmc **fast-,* same base as FAST¹]

fast⁴ (fah-), adv. (-er, -est). Firmly, fixedly, tightly, securely, (*stand, sit, stick,* ~; ~ *bind,* ~ *find,* lock up what you would not lose; *eyes ~ shut; sleep ~,* soundly); (poet. & arch.) close *beside, by, upon,* etc.; quickly, in quick succession; *live ~,* live in a dissipated way, expend much energy in short time. [OE *fæste* (prec.)]

fa'sten (fah'sn), v.t. & i. Make fast, attach, fix, secure by some tie or bond, (*to, upon, on* adv. or prep., *together, up, in* adv. or prep.; or abs.; ~ *parcel, garment, door,* etc., or *string, bolt,* etc.; ~ *off thread* etc., secure with knot or otherwise), whence ~ING¹(4) (fah'sn-) n.; direct (look, thoughts, etc.) keenly (*up*)*on*; fix (nickname, imputation, etc.) (*up*)*on*; ~*quarrel upon,* pick quarrel with; become fast (*door will not* ~); ~ (*up*)*on,* lay hold of, single out for attack, seize upon (pretext). Hence ~ER¹(2) (fah'sn-) n. [OE *fæstnian,* OS *fastnōn,* OHG *fastinōn,* f. Gmc **fastinōjan* f. **fast-* FAST³, -EN⁶]

fãs'tī, n. pl. Chronological register of events, annals. [L, = calendar]

fãstid'ious, a. Easily disgusted, carefully selective, hard to please. Hence ~LY² adv., ~NESS n. [f. L *fastidiosus* (*fastidium* loathing, see -OUS¹)]

fãsti'giãte, a.(bot.). With conical or tapering outline. [f. L *fastigium* gable +-ATE²]

fast'něss (fah-), n. In adj. senses (FAST³); also, stronghold, fortress. [OE *fæstnes* f. FAST³ +-NESS]

fãt, a., n., & v.t. & i. (-tt-). 1. Fed up for slaughter, fatted; well-fed, plump, (*cut up* ~, leave much money), corpulent; thick, substantial, (esp. of printing-type); greasy, oily, unctuous, (*cut it ~,* make a display); (of coal) bituminous; (of clay etc.) sticky; fertile, rich, yielding abundantly, (~ *lands, benefice, job* ; *a ~ lot,* sl.,

a great deal usu. iron. = very little); slow-
-witted, indolent, (~-*head*, dolt; ~-*witted*,
stupid); ‖ ~-*guts*, corpulent person; ~-
-*hen*, kinds of GOOSE-*foot*; ~ *lime*, nearly
pure lime, slaking easily; hence~**t′**ISN¹(2)
a., ~ ′NESS n. **2. n.** The~ part of anything
(*live on the ~ of the land*, have the best of
everything); oily substance composing
~ parts of animal bodies (*the ~ is in the
fire*, there will be an explosion); (Theatr.)
part of role that enables actor to show
off; (Chem.) natural ester of glycerol &
acid; hence ~′LESS a. **3.** vb. = FATTEN;
kill the fatted calf for, receive (returned
prodigal) with joy. [OE *fæt(t)* (whence
fættian vb), OFris. *fatt, fett*, OHG *feizzit*
(G *feist*) f. WG *faitidhaz*, p.p. f. Gmc
faitjan fatten f. Gmc *failaz* adj. fat]

fāt′al, a. Like fate, inevitable, necessary;
of, appointed by, destiny (~ *sisters*, the
Fates; ~ *thread*, allotted length of life;
~ *shears*, death); fateful, important,
decisive; destructive, ruinous, ending
in death, (*to*); deadly, sure to kill; (by
exagg.) mischievous, ill-advised. Hence
~LY² adv., ~NESS n. [ME, f. OF *fatal* or
L *fatalis* (FATE, -AL)]

fāt′al|ism, n. Belief that all events are
predetermined by arbitrary decree; submission to all that happens as inevitable.
So ~IST(2) n. & a., ~īs′tīc a., ~īs′tICALLY
adv. [-ISM]

fatăl′itў, n. Subjection to, supremacy of,
fate, predestined liability to disaster;
fatal influence; misfortune, calamity;
death by accident, in war, etc. [f. F
fatalité or LL *fatalitas*, see FATAL, -ITY]

fāt′alize, -ise (-iz), v.i. & t. Incline to
fatalism; subject to government by fate.
[-IZE]

fa′ta mŏrga′na (fah-, -gah-), n. Kind of
mirage seen esp. in strait of Messina. [It.
(*fata* FAY, *Morgana* female name)]

fāte, n., & v.t. **1.** Power predetermining
events unalterably from eternity; (Myth.)
goddess, one of the three Greek goddesses
(*Clō′thō, Lăch′esis* (-k-), *At′ropos*), of
destiny; what is destined to happen;
appointed lot of person etc.; person's
ultimate condition (*decide, fix, seal*, one's
~); death, destruction. **2.** v.t. (usu. pass.).
Preordain (*he was ~d to* do or be; *it was
~d that*); (p.p.) doomed to destruction.
[ME, f. L *fatum* neut. p.p. of *fari* speak]

fāte′ful (-tf-), a. Prophetic; fraught with
destiny, important, decisive; controlled
by, showing power of, fate. Hence ~LY²
adv. [-FUL]

fa′ther¹ (fahdh-), n. **1.** Male parent (also
fig.; *the wish is ~ to the thought*, one
believes because one wishes to; *the child
is ~ to the man*, lays down the lines of his
development); = ~-*in-law*; = step-~;
(also *adoptive* ~), one who has adopted a
child. **2.** Progenitor, forefather; originator, designer, early leader, (~ *of English
poetry*; *F~ of history*, Herodotus; *F~ of
lies*, the devil; *F~s of the Church* or *F~s*,

Christian writers of first five centuries).
3. One who deserves filial reverence (~ *of
his country*); religious teacher. **4.** God;
First Person of the Trinity. **5.** Confessor;
priest belonging to religious order,
superior of monastic house; *Right, Most,
Reverend F~ in God*, titles of bishop, archbishop; *The Holy F~*, the Pope; = *priest*
as prefixed title; venerable person, god,
(*F~ Christmas, Thames, Time*, personifications). **6.** Oldest member, doyen, (*F~
of House of Commons*, member with longest
continuous service); (pl.) leading men,
elders, (*City F~s*; *Conscript F~s*, Roman
senators). **7.** ~-*figure*, an older person
regarded as a trusted leader; ~-*in-law*, ~
of one's wife or husband; ~*land*, native
country. Hence~HOOD, ~SHIP, nn., ~LESS
a., ~LIKE, ~LY¹,², aa. & advv., ~LINESS n.,
(fahdh-). [OE *fæder*, OS *fadar*, OHG
fater, ON *father*, Goth. *fadar* f. Gmc
fader, cogn. w. L *pater*]

fa′ther² (fahdh-), v.t. Beget; be the father
of; originate (statement etc.); pass as,
confess oneself, the father, author, of
(child, book); govern paternally; fix
paternity of (child, book) *upon*. [f. prec.]

făth′om¹ (-dh-), n. (pl., with numbers,
often *fathom*). Measure of six feet, chiefly
used in soundings; ‖ quantity of wood 6 ft
square in section, whatever the length.
[OE *fæthm* the outstretched arms, cogn.
w. OS *fathmos*, OHG *fadum*, ON *fathmr*]

făth′om² (-dh-), v.t. Encircle with the
arms (arch.); measure with fathom-line,
sound, (depth of water); (fig.) get to the
bottom of, comprehend, whence ~LESS a.,
~lèssLY² adv. [OE *fæthmian* (prec.)]

fathŏm′ēter (-dh-), n. Instrument for
determining depth of sea by measuring
time taken by sound-wave to reach the
bottom and return. [FATHOM¹, -METER]

fatĭd′ical, a. Gifted with prophetic power.
[f. L *fatidicus* (FATE, *-dicus* -saying) + -AL]

fatigue′, (-ēg), n., & v.t. **1.** Weariness after
exertion; weakness in metals after re-
peated blows or long strain; task etc.
that wearies; soldier's non-combatant
duty (~-*party* or ~, party told off for this;
so ~-*dress*). **2.** v.t. Tire, exhaust, whence
~LESS (-ēgl-), fati′guING² (-ēgī-), aa.;
weaken (metal; see above). [f. F *fatigue(r)*
f. L *fatigare*]

făt′ling, n. Young fatted animal. [-LING¹]

fătt′en, v.t. & i. Make fat (esp. animals
for slaughter); grow fat; enrich (soil).
[-EN⁵]

fătt′ў¹, a. Like fat, unctuous, greasy;
consisting of fat, adipose; with morbid
deposition of fat (~ *degeneration* of heart
or kidney). [-Y²]

fătt′ў², n. ·Fat child etc. (usu. voc.). [-Y³]

făt′uous, a. Vacantly silly, purposeless,
idiotic. Hence or cogn. fatŭ′ITY n., ~LY²
adv., ~NESS n. [L *fatuus* + -OUS]

faubourg (fōb′oorg), n. Suburb, esp. of
Paris. [F]

fauc′al, a. & n. (phonol.)., Of the throat,

deeply guttural (sound). [f. L *fauces* throat + -AL]

fau'ces (-ēz), n. pl. (anat.). The cavity at the back of the mouth. [L]

fau'cet, n. (esp. U.S.). Tap for barrel etc.; any kind of tap. [f. OF *fausset* vent-peg]

faugh (faw), int. of disgust.

fault, n., & v. t. & i. **1.** Defect, imperfection, blemish, of character or of structure, appearance, etc. (*generous* etc. *to a* ∼, excessively; *with all* ∼s, at buyer's risk). **2.** Transgression, offence, thing wrongly done, (Racquets etc.) ball wrongly served; *find* ∼ (*with*), complain (of), whence ∼'findER[1] n., ∼'findING[1,2], n. & a. **3.** Responsibility for something wrong (*the* ∼ *was mine; it will be our own* ∼), defect that causes something (*the* ∼ *is in the patient*); *in* ∼, guilty, to blame, (*who is in* ∼?). **4.** (hunt.). Loss of the scent, check so caused, (*be at* ∼, also fig. = be puzzled, not know what to do). **5.** (geol.). Break in continuity of strata or vein. **6.** (telegr.). Imperfect insulation, leakage. **7.** vb. Find ∼ with, blame; (Geol.) break continuity of (strata or vein), show such break. Hence ∼'LESS a., ∼'lèssLY[2] adv., ∼'lèssNESS n., ∼'Y[2] a., ∼'ILY[2] adv., ∼'iNESS n. [ME & OF *fault(e)* f. Rom. *fallita* fem. p.p. of *fallere* FAIL[2]]

faun, n. One of a class of Latin rural deities with horns & tail. [ME, f. L *Faunus* Latin god identified w. Gk Pan]

faun'|a, n. (pl. ∼ae, ∼as). The animals of a region or epoch; treatise upon these. Hence ∼AL a., ∼IST(3) n., ∼is'tic(AL) aa. [mod. L, f. name of goddess sister of Faunus, see prec.]

fauteuil (see Ap.), n. Arm-chair; theatre stall. [F]

faux pas (fō pah), n. Act that compromises one's, esp. a woman's, reputation; an offence against social convention, an indiscreet speech or action. [F, = false step]

fāv'our[1] (-ver), n. **1.** Friendly regard, goodwill, (*find* ∼ *in the eyes of*, be liked by; CURRY[2] ∼), approval (*look with* ∼ *on*), good graces (*be, stand high* etc., *in* person's ∼); kindness beyond what is due (*should esteem it a* ∼; *by* ∼ *of* —, written on letter conveyed by friend; *do me the* ∼ *of* —*ing*; *have received your* ∼ *of yesterday*, letter; *woman bestows her* ∼s *on* lover, yields). **2.** Leave, pardon, (arch.; *by your* ∼; *under* ∼, if one may venture to say so). **3.** Partiality, too lenient or generous treatment (FEAR[1] *or* ∼). **4.** Aid, furtherance, (*under* ∼ *of night*); *in* ∼ *of*, on behalf or in support of, on the side of, to the advantage or account of, (*am in* ∼ *of a five-day week*; *cheques to be drawn in* ∼ *of the treasurer*). **5.** Thing given or worn as mark of ∼, knot of ribbons, rosette, cockade, badge. **6.** (arch.). Looks, countenance, whence *well, ill, hard*, etc., ∼ED[2] (-erd) a. [ME, f. OF, f. L *favorem* (*favēre* show kindness to, -OR)]

fāv'our[2] (-ver), v.t. **1.** Look kindly upon,

approve; treat kindly, countenance, (Journalism) choose to wear; oblige *with*. **2.** Treat with partiality, be unjust on behalf of. **3.** Aid, support; serve as confirmation of (theory etc.); prove advantageous to (person), facilitate (process etc.), whence ∼ING[2] (-ver-) a. **4.** Resemble in features (∼ *one's father*). **5.** (p.p.). Having unusual advantages (*most* ∼ed *nation*, to which a State accords lowest scale of import duties); ∼ed *by*, (of letter) by favour of. [ME, f. OF *favorer* f. med. L *favorare* as prec.]

fāv'ourab|le (-ver-), a. Well disposed, propitious; commendatory, approving; giving consent (∼*le answer*); promising, auspicious, (∼*le aspect*); helpful, suitable, (*to*). Hence ∼leNESS n., ∼LY[2] adv. [ME, f. OF *favorable* f. L *favorabilis* (FAVOUR[1], -ABLE)]

fāv'ourit|e (-ver-), n. & a. (Person or thing) preferred above others (*the* ∼*e of*, *a* ∼*e with* or *of*); (Racing) *the* ∼*e*, competitor generally expected to win; person chosen as intimate by king or superior & unduly favoured, whence ∼ISM(3) n. [f. obs. F *favorit* f. It. *favorito*, p.p. of *favorire* (= OF *favorir*) favour]

fawn[1], n., a., & v.i. & t. **1.** Young fallow deer, buck or doe of first year (*in* ∼, pregnant); ∼ or ∼-*colour(ed)*, (of) light yellowish brown. **2.** vb. (Of deer) bring forth (young, or abs.). [ME, f. OF *faon* f. Rom. *fetonem* nom. -o (FOETUS)]

fawn[2], v.i. (Of animals, esp. dog) show affection by tail-wagging, grovelling, etc. (∼ *on, upon*, lavish caresses on); (of persons) behave servilely, cringe (*upon* patron, or abs.), whence ∼'ING[2] a., ∼'ingLY[2] adv. [OE *fagnian, fægnian*, OS, OHG *faganon*, ON *fagna*, Goth. *faginōn* rejoice, cogn. w. FAIN[1]]

fay, n. (poet.). Fairy. [ME, f. OF *fae* f. Rom. *fata* sing. f. L *fata* pl. the fates]

fē'alty, n. Feudal tenant's or vassal's (acknowledged) obligation of) fidelity to his lord (*do, make, receive, swear*, ∼). [ME, f. OF *feaulte* f. L *fidelitatem* (*fidelis* f. *fides* faith, -TY)]

fear[1], n. Painful emotion caused by impending danger or evil, state of alarm (*was in* ∼), dread *of, that*, or *lest*; *for* ∼ *of*, (*that*), *lest*, in order that so-&-so may not occur; *without* ∼ *or favour*, impartially; dread & reverence (*the* ∼ *of God*); anxiety for the safety *of* (*in* ∼ *of his life*); *no* ∼, it is not likely. Hence ∼'LESS a. (*of danger* etc.), ∼'lessLY[2] adv., ∼'lessNESS n. [OE *fǣr*, corresp. to OS *vār*, OHG *fāra* (G *gefahr*), ON *fár* f. Gmc *fǣr-*]

fear[2], v.i. & t. Be afraid (also as arch. refl. in parenthesis, *I* ∼ *me*; *never* ∼, there is no danger of that); be afraid of; hesitate *to do*, shrink from *doing*; revere (God); apprehend, have uneasy anticipation of; be afraid *that* (or with *that* omitted; also *need not* etc. ∼ *but* or *but that*). [OE *fǣran* f. prec.]

fear'ful, a. Terrible, awful; (by exagg.) annoying etc. (in a ~ mess); frightened, timid; apprehensive of, lest, (that); wanting resolution to; reverential. Hence ~LY² adv., ~NESS n. [-FUL]

fear'nought (-awt), n. Stout woollen cloth used at sea for clothing & for protecting portholes etc. [FEAR², NOUGHT]

fear'some, a. Appalling, esp. in appearance (usu. joc.). Hence ~LY² (-ml-) adv., ~NESS (-mn-) n. [-SOME]

feas'i|ble (-z-), a. Practicable, possible; (loosely) manageable, convenient, serviceable, plausible. Hence ~BIL'ITY n. [ME, f. OF faisable, -ible f. fais- st. of faire f. L facere do +-IBLE]

feast, n., & v.i. & t. 1. Joyful religious anniversary (movable, immovable, ~, recurring on different, same, date); annual village festival; sumptuous meal, esp. one given to number of guests and of public nature; (fig.) gratification to the senses or mind (~ of reason, intellectual talk). 2. vb. Partake of ~, fare sumptuously, whence ~'ER¹ n.; pass (night etc.) away in ~ing; regale (guests, one's eyes on beauty etc.). [ME, f. OF feste(r) f. pop. L festa pl. of festum feast]

feat¹, n. Noteworthy act, esp. deed of valour (often ~ of arms); action shoying dexterity or strength, surprising trick. [ME faite, fete f. OF fait, fet FACT]

‖ **feat²**, a. (arch.). Adroit, smart, dextrous, neat. Hence ~'LY² adv. [ME fete f. OF fet (prec.)]

feath'er¹ (fĕdh-), n. 1. One of the appendages growing from bird's skin, consisting of quill, shaft, & two vanes of barbs (show the white ~, betray cowardice—white ~ in game-bird's tail being mark of bad breeding—; crop one's~s, humiliate him); (collect.) plumage (in high or full ~, in good spirits etc.; birds of a ~, people of one sort); feathered game (fur & ~, game beasts & birds). 2. Piece(s) of ~ attached to arrow; plume worn in hat etc. (a ~ in one's cap, something one may be proud of); very light object (could have knocked me down with a ~); ridge of upright hair; ~like flaw in gem. 3. (rowing). Action of feathering (see foll.). 4. ~ bed, mattress stuffed with ~s; ~-bed v.t. (-dd-), make things easy for, pamper; ~-edge, (n.) fine edge of wedge-shaped board, (v.t.) bring (board) to this; ~-head(ed), -brain(ed), -pate(d), silly (person); ~-stitch, ornamental zig-zag sewing; ~-weight, very light thing or person, esp. jockey not over 4 st. 7 lb., boxer 9 st. Hence (-) ~ED² (-erd), ~LESS, ~Y², aa., ~ÎNESS, ~LET, nn., (fĕdh-). [OE fether, OS fethara, OHG fedar, ON fjothr f. Gmc *fethrō]

feath'er² (fĕdh-), v.t. & i. 1. Furnish, adorn, line, coat, with feathers (~ an arrow; ~ one's nest, enrich oneself; TAR &~); form featherlike ornamentation for. 2. Float, move, or wave, like feathers. 3. Turn (oar), turn oar, so as to pass through the air edgeways; (Aeron.) make (propeller blades) rotate in such a way as to lessen air resistance. 4. (Shoot.) knock feathers from (bird) without killing. 5. (Hunt.; of hound) make quivering motion of body & tail while seeking scent. [OE gefithrian f. prec.]

feath'ering (fĕdh-), n. In vbl senses; esp.. plumage; feathers of arrow; feathery structure in animal's coat; (Archit.) cusps in tracery; featherlike marking in flower. -ING¹]

fea'ture, n., & v.t. 1. (Usu. pl.) part(s) of the face, esp. with regard to shape & visible effect; distinctive or characteristic part of a thing, part that arrests attention; distinctive or prominent article etc. in newspaper etc.; ~ film, ~ picture, cinema drama of some length in several reels. 2. v.t. Stand as distinctive mark upon; portray, sketch the prominent points of; *show on cinema screen, have as chief ~, give special prominence to. Hence -fea'turED² (-cherd), ~LESS (-cherl-), aa. [ME, f. OF fet-, faiture f. L factura (facere fact- make, -URE)]

fĕb'rifūge, n. Medicine to reduce fever, cooling drink. Hence **fĕbrif'ūg**AL a. [f. F fébrifuge or LL febrifuga, -ia (L febris fever, -FUGE)]

fĕb'rile, a. Of fever, feverish. [f. F fébrile or LL febrilis (febris fever, -ILE)]

Fĕb'ruary (-rŏŏ-), n. Second month of year (~ fill-dike, name referring to its rain & snow). [ME feverer, februar, f. OF feverier f. Rom. febrarius; mod. sp. after L februarius]

fē'cĭt, fēcēr'ŭnt (abbr. fec.), v. sing. & pl. 3rd pers. (So-&-so) made this picture etc. (used with artist's signature). [L, perf. of facere make]

fĕck'lĕss, a. Feeble, futile, inefficient. Hence ~LY² adv., ~NESS n. [Sc. feck (aphetic f. EFFECT) +-LESS]

fēc'ūl|ent, a. Turbid, fetid. So ~ENCE n. [F (fé-), or f. L facculentus (FAECES, -ULENT)]

fēc'ŭnd, a. Prolific, fertile; fertilizing. So **fēcŭn'dITY** n. [ME, f. OF fecond or L fecundus]

fēc'und|āte, v.t. Make fruitful; impregnate. Hence ~A'TION n. [L FECUNDare, -ATE³]

fed. See FEED¹.

fĕd'eral, a. 1. (theol.). Based on doctrine of Covenants. 2. (pol.). Of the polity in which several States form a unity but remain independent in internal affairs; concerning this whole & not the separate parts. 3. Relating to, favouring, central (as distinct from State) government. Hence ~ISM(3), ~IST(2), nn., ~IZE(3) v.t., ~ÎZA'TION n., ~LY² adv. [17th c. foederal f. L foedus -eris covenant +-AL]

fĕd'er|āte, v.t. & i. Band together (t. & i.) in league for some common object; organize (t. & i. of States) on a FEDERAL basis.

So ~ATE² (-*at*), ~ATIVE, aa., ~atively²
adv. [LL *foederare* (prec.), -ATE³]
federa'tion, n. Federating, whence
~IST(2) (-sho-) n.; federated society, esp.
federal empire or group of States; IM-
PERIAL~. [f. LL *foederatio* (prec., -ATION)]
fee, n., & v.t. (~'*d*, ~*d*). **1.** Fief, feudal
benefice, (hist.). **2.** Inherited estate (~
simple, without limitation to particular
class of heirs; ~-*tail*, with such limitation;
hold in ~ *simple* or ~, have as absolute
property). **3.** Sum payable to public
officer for performing his function;
remuneration of lawyer, physician, or
any professional man (RETAIN*ing*-~);
entrance money for examination, society,
etc.; terminal payment for instruction at
school; gratuity. **4.** vb. Pay ~ to, engage
for a ~. [ME, f. AF *fee* = OF *fe, fieu,* etc.
f. med. L *feodum, feudum,* prob. f. Frank.
*fehod cattle-property. See FEUD²,
FIEF]
fee'b|**le,** a. & n. **1.** Weak, infirm; deficient
in character or intelligence; wanting in
energy, force, or effect; dim., indistinct;
hence ~le**NESS** (-ln-) n., ~lish²(2) a., ~**LY**²
adv. **2.** n. (Fenc.) = FOIBLE. [ME, OF
feble f. L *flebilis* lamentable (*flëre*
weep)]
feed¹, v.t. & i. (*fĕd*). Supply with food (~
a cold, eat plentifully when you have a
cold); put food into mouth of (*cannot* ~
himself); graze (cattle); gratify (*vanity*
etc., also *eyes* etc.), comfort (person) *with*
hope etc.; take food, eat, (*at the high
table*; *well, high,* etc.; often ~ *on,* consume); serve as food for; nourish, make
grow, (~ *up,* fatten, and satiate; *fed up,*
sl., having had too much of something,
bored *with*); keep (reservoir, fire, etc.)
supplied; supply (machine) with material
(~-*pipe,* doing this); use (land) as pasture
(often ~ *down, close*); deal out (fodder) *to*
animals; supply (material) (*in*)*to* machine;
(Theatr. sl.) supply (actor etc.) with cues;
(Football) give a pass to; (of cattle) eat,
eat *down,* (pasture); ~*ing-bottle,* for hand-
-fed infants. [OE *fēdan,* OS *fōdean,* OHG
fuotan, ON *fœtha,* Goth. *fōdjan* f. Gmc
*fōdhon FOOD]
feed², n. Act of feeding, giving of food,
(*two biscuits at one* ~; *out at* ~, turned out
to graze; *off* one's ~, with no appetite;
on the ~, of fish, feeding or looking out for
food); pasturage, green crops; horse's
allowance of oats etc.; fodder; (colloq.)
meal, feast; feeding of machine, material
supplied, charge of gun; ~-*tank, trough,*
holding water **for** locomotive. [f. prec.]
feed³. See FEE.
feed'băck, n. (electr.). The return of a
fraction of the output signal from one
stage of a circuit, amplifier, etc. to the
input of the same or a preceding stage
(*positive, negative,* ~, tending to increase,
decrease, the amplification etc.); (transf.,
esp. of biol., psych., and social systems)
the carrying back of some of the effects

of some process to its source or to a
preceding stage so as to strengthen or
modify it; also attrib. [FEED², BACK³]
feed'er, n. In vbl senses; esp.: *large,
quick, gross,* etc., ~, one who eats much
etc.; child's feeding-bottle; || child's bib;
tributary stream (also fig.); (Rounders
etc.) player who tosses ball to striker;
hopper or feeding apparatus in machine;
~ *line, railway,* branch line linking up
outlying districts with main line. [-ER¹]
feed'ing, a. In vbl senses; also, ~ *storm,*
one that constantly increases. [-ING²]
fee-faw-fŭm', int. & n. Ogreish exclamation; (n.) nonsense fit only to terrify
child. [in *Jack the Giant-Killer*]
feel, v.t. & i. (*fĕlt*), & n. **1.** Explore by
touch (~ *the pulse of,* lit., & fig. = cautiously ascertain sentiments of; ~ one's *way,*
grope it out, proceed carefully); search
(*about*) with hand *after, for*; try to ascertain by touch *whether, if, how;* (Mil.)
reconnoitre (ground, enemy); perceive by
touch (~ *a hard substance, heat, pain,
a blow*; *I felt him move, moving, that he was
cold*; ~ one's *legs* or *feet,* find firm standing, also fig., be at ease); have sensation
of touch; be conscious of (sensation,
emotion, conviction; *a felt want,* desidera-
tum); be consciously (~ *well, warm, angry,*
CHEAP; ~ *quite* oneself, be fit, self-possessed, etc.; ~ UP *to work* etc.; ~ *like* do-
ing, have inclination to do); experience,
undergo, (*he shall* ~ *my vengeance*; *felt
the storm severely*), be affected by, behave
as if conscious of, (*ship* ~s *her helm*); be
emotionally affected by, have sympathy
with or compassion *for,* (~ *the censure
keenly*); have vague or emotional conviction (*that*; esp. ~ *in* one's *bones*);
(quasi-pass.) be realized as, seem, produce
impression of being, (*air* ~s *chilly*; ~s
like velvet). **2.** n. Sense of touch (*firm to
the* ~); testing by touch; sensation
characterizing something. [OE *fēlan,* OS
-*folian,* OHG *fuolen* f. WG *fōljan]
feel'er, n. In vbl senses; esp.: organ in
certain animals for testing things by
touch or searching for food; (Mil.) scout;
tentative proposal or hint, *ballon d'essai.*
[-ER¹]
feel'ing¹, n. In vbl senses; esp.: sense of
touch; physical sensation; emotion (often
of hope, fear, etc.); (pl.) susceptibilities,
sympathies, (*hurts my* ~s, offends me);
readiness to feel, tenderness for others'
sufferings, (*good* ~, avoidance of unkindness etc.); consciousness *of* (*had a* ~ *of
safety*), conviction not based solely on
reason; sentiment (*the general* ~ *was
against it*); (Psych.; differently used by
various writers) state of consciousness,
sensation or desire or emotion (not perception or thought), element of pleasure
or pain in any mental state, intuitive
belief; (Art) general emotional effect
produced. [-ING¹]
feel'ing², a. In vbl senses; esp.: sensitive;

sympathetic; showing emotion; heartfelt (*a ~ pleasure*). Hence ~LY[2] adv. [-ING[2]]

feet. See FOOT.

feign (fān), v.t. & i. Invent (excuse, story, accusation), forge (document), represent in fiction, imagine, (arch.); simulate, pretend, (~ *that one is mad, oneself mad, madness*); practise simulation. [ME, f. *feign-* st. of OF *feindre* f. L *fingere*]

feint[1] (fā-), n., & v.i. **1.** Sham attack (blow, cut, thrust, or military assault) to divert attention or deceive opponent; pretence (*make a ~ of doing*). **2.** v.i. Make ~ (*at, upon, against*). [f. F *feinte* (p.p. *feindre* FEIGN)]

|| **feint**[2] (fā-), a. & adv. ~ *lines, ruled ~*, = FAINT[1]. [old spelling often kept in this use]

fel(d)'spar, n. Kinds of crystalline white or flesh-red mineral. So **fel(d)spāth'IC** a. [f. G *feldspat(h)* f. *feld* field, *spat(h)* spar; spelling *fels-*, commoner but incorrect, due to false deriv. f. G *fels* rock]

fel'ibrist, n. Member of the *Félibrige*, a society of Provençal poets & writers (Mistral etc.). [f. F *Félibrige*, -IST]

fel'icīde, n. Cat-killing. [f. L *feles* cat + -CIDE]

fēlicif'ic, a. (eth.). Tending to happiness. [f. L *felix -icis* +-FIC]

fēli'cit|āte, v.t. Make happy (rare); congratulate (usu. *on*), whence (usu. pl.) ~A'TION n. [f. L *felicitare* (*felix* happy), -ATE[3]]

fēli'citous, a. Blissful (rare); (of expression, quotation, civilities, or person in these connexions) strikingly apt, pleasantly ingenious. Hence ~LY[2] adv. [foll., -OUS]

fēli'city, n. Being happy, intense happiness; a blessing; fortunate trait; happy faculty in expression, appropriateness; well chosen phrase. [ME, f. OF *felicite* f. L *felicitatem* (*felix* happy, -TY)]

fē'lid, n. One of the *Felidae* or cat-tribe. [f. L *feles* cat, -ID[3]]

fē'līne, a. & n. Of cats; catlike (~ *amenities*, veiled spite, women's innocent-seeming thrusts), whence **fēlin'ITY** n.; (n.) = prec. [f. L *felinus* (prec., -INE[1])]

fell[1], n. Animal's hide or skin with the hair (also transf. of human skin); thick or matted hair or wool, fleece, (~ *of hair*, unkempt hair of head); ~MONGER. [OE *fel(l)*, OS, OHG *fel*, ON *-fjall*, Goth. *-fill* f. Gmc **fellam* cogn. w. L *pellis*]

|| **fell**[2], n. Hill (in names, as *Sca F~*); stretch of N.-English moorland. [f. ON *fiall* cogn. w. OHG *felis* (G *fels*) rock]

fell[3], a. (poet.). Fierce, ruthless, terrible, destructive. [ME, f. OF *fel* f. Rom. **fello* FELON]

fell[4], v.t., & n. Strike (person, animal) down by blow or cut; cut down (tree; n., amount of timber cut); stitch down (projection of seam). [OE *fellan* f. Gmc **falljan* causative of **fallan* FALL[1]]

fell[5]. See FALL[1].

fell'ah (-*a*), n. (pl. ~*een*, ~*s*). Egyptian peasant. [Arab.]

fell'oe (-lī, -lō), **fell'ў**, n. Outer circle (or one piece of it) of wheel, attached by spokes. [OE *felg*, MLG, MDu. *velge*, OHG *felga* of unkn. orig.]

fell'ow (-ō), n. **1.** One associated with another, comrade, (usu. in pl., as *separated from his ~s*; *good ~*, boon companion; HAIL[3]*-~well-met*; ~*-feeling*, sympathy). **2.** Counterpart, match, other of pair, equal, one of same class, contemporary, *(stone dead hath no ~*, no keeper of secrets like a dead man; *shall never find his ~*; *passed all his ~s*). **3.** Co-opted graduate incorporated member of college & in some colleges re-elected at intervals (~ *commoner*, undergraduate privileged to dine at ~s' table); elected graduate holding stipend for certain years on condition of research. **4.** Member of governing body in some Universities; member of various learned Societies. **5.** Man, boy, (*poor ~!*, *my dear* or *good ~*, *old ~*; *a ~*, occas. = *one*, *I*, as *a ~ can't work all day long*; *the ~*, contemptuously). **6.** (In comb. with nn.; ~ or ~-) belonging to same class (~ *creature*, person or animal also created by God), associated in joint action (~ *soldier*), in same relation to same object (~ *citizen*, whence ~*-cit'izen-*ship n.; ~*-countryman*); ~*-traveller*, (also) non-Communist who sympathizes with aims and general policy of Communist party. [OE *féolaga* f. ON *felagi* f. *fé* (= OE *fcoh* FEE) +LAY[3]]

fell'owship (-lō-), n. Participation, sharing, community of interest; companionship, intercourse, friendliness, (often *good ~*); body of associates, company, (*right hand of ~*, sign of admission); guild, corporation; brotherhood, fraternity; dignity or emoluments of college fellow; *post-graduate scholarship. [-SHIP]

felly. See FELLOE.

fel'ō dē sē, n. (pl. *felonēs, felos*). Self-murderer, (no pl.) self-murder. [Anglo-L, = FELON about himself]

fel'on[1], a. (poet.), & n. **1.** Cruel, wicked, murderous. **2.** One who has committed felony. [ME, f. OF f. med. L *fellonem* nom. *-o* of unkn. orig.]

fel'on[2], n. Small abscess esp. under or near nail, whitlow. [perh. as prec.]

fēlōn'ious, a. Criminal; (Law) of, involving, felony; who has committed felony. Hence ~LY[2] adv. [FELONY +-OUS]

fel'onry, n. The class or body of felons. [-RY]

fel'ony, n. Crime of kind legally graver than misdemeanour. [ME, f. OF *felonie* (FELON, -Y[3])]

felspar. See FELDSPAR.

fel'stone (-ōn), n. Compact felspar occurring in amorphous rock masses. [f. G *felsstein* (*fels* rock, *stein* stone)]

felt[1], n., & v.t. & i. **1.** Kind of cloth made by rolling & pressing wool with lees or size; (attrib.) made of this (esp. ~ *hat*); hence~'Y² a. **2. vb.** Make into ~, mat together; become matted; cover with ~. [OE *felt*, OS *filt*, OHG *filz* f. WG **felta*, *-i*]

fĕlt². See FEEL.

fĕl'teric, n. A horse-disease. [orig. unkn.]

fĕlŭcc'a, n. Small Mediterranean coasting vessel with oars or lateen sails or both. [17th c. f. It., ult. f. Arab. *fulk* ship]

fēm'āle, a. & n. **1.** Of the offspring-bearing sex (~ *child, slave, dog*); (of plants or their parts) fruit-bearing, having pistil & no stamens, (also used of some plants by mere metaphor suggested by their colour etc., as ~ *fern, bamboo, myrtle*); of women (~ *sex, education, suffrage, weakness*). **2.** Of inferior vigour etc. (~ *sapphire*, pale variety). **3.** (In instruments etc.) fitted to receive corresponding male part (~ *screw*, as in nuts). **4. n.** ~ person (*the law is harsh to all ~s*) or animal; (vulg.) woman, girl, (*a young ~ has called*). [ME & OF *femelle* n. f. L *femella* dim. of *femina* woman, w. assim. to *male*]

feme co'vert (fēm kŭ-), **feme sōle**, nn. (legal). (*Covert*) married woman; (*sole*) spinster, widow, or married woman entirely independent of her husband as regards property. [AF *feme* woman, *covert* covered, *sole* single]

fĕminăl'itў, n. Female nature; female peculiarity; woman's knick-knack etc. [obs. *feminal* f. OF (L *femina* woman, -AL) +-ITY]

fĕminē'itў, n. Womanliness; womanishness. [f. L *femineus* (*femina* woman) +-ITY]

fĕm'inine, a. Of female sex (rare); of women; womanly; (Gram.) having the gender proper to women's names; (Pros.) ~ *rhyme*, of two syllables, the second being unstressed (orig. in F verse, of words ending in mute *-e*), ~ *ending*, of line with last accent on penult, ~ *caesura*, not immediately following stress. Hence ~LY² adv.,~NESS, **fĕminin'ITY**, nn. [ME, f. OF *feminin* or L *femininus* (*femina* woman, -INE¹)]

fĕm'in|ism, n. Advocacy, extended recognition, of the claims of women. So ~IST n. [f. L *femina* woman +-ISM]

fĕmin'itў, n. = FEMININITY. [ME, f. OF *feminite* (L *femina* woman, -ITY)]

fĕm'iniz|e, -is|e (-ĭz), v.t. & i. Make or become feminine. Hence ~A'TION n. [f. L as prec. +-IZE]

femme de chambre (see Ap.), n. Lady's maid; chambermaïd. [F]

fĕm'ur (*-er*), n. (pl. ~s, *fĕm'ora*). Thigh-bone; corresponding part of insect. So **fĕm'orAL**. [L]

fĕn¹, n. Low marshy or flooded tract of land (|| *the* ~s, low-lying districts in Cambs. etc.; ~*-berry*, cranberry; ~*-fire*, will-o'-the-wisp; ~*-man*, inhabitant of ~s; || ~*-pole*, for use in jumping ditches; || ~*-reeve*, officer in charge of ~-lands; ~-

-runners, kind of skates. Hence ~n'Y² a. [OE *fen(n)*, OFris. *fen(n)e*, OHG *fenna*, *-ni*, ON *fen*, Goth. *fani* f. Gmc **fanja-*]

fen², **fens**. See FAIN².

fence¹, n. Art of fencing, use of the sword, (*master of* ~, skilled swordsman, often fig. = good debater); (arch.) bulwark; hedge, wall, railing, etc., keeping out intruders from field etc. (*sunk* ~, placed along bottom of ditch; *sit on the* ~, remain neutral in contest, not take sides; *come* etc. *down on right side of* ~, join winner; PUT *horse at* ~); guard, guide, gauge, in various machines; receiver, receiving-house, of stolen goods; || ~*-month*, *-season, -time*, close time for game or fish. [ME, for DEFENCE]

fence², v.i. & t. Practise sword-play, use the sword scientifically, (~ *with question* or *questioner*, parry, evade answering); screen, shield, protect, (*from, against*); repel, keep *off* or *out*; surround (as) with fence, enclose, fortify, (~*d cities* in O.T.; often *about, in, round, up*); (of horse) leap fences; deal in stolen goods. Hence **fĕn'CER¹** n. (esp. of swordsman, also of horse). [f. prec.]

fĕnce'less (-sl-), a. Unenclosed; (poet.) unfortified, defenceless. [FENCE¹ +-LESS]

fĕn'cible, n. (hist.). Soldier liable only for home service. [for DEFENSIBLE]

fĕn'cing, n. In vbl senses; also : railing; fences; material for fences. [-ING¹]

fĕnd, v.t. & i. Ward *off*, keep *away*, repel *from*; provide *for* (usu. one*self*). [ME, for DEFEND]

fĕn'der, n. Thing used to keep something off, prevent collision, etc.; (naut.) piece of old cable, matting, etc., hung over vessel's side; guard, esp. metal frame for fire to keep coals from rolling into room; || ~*-stool*, long footstool before ~. Hence ~LESS a. [-ER¹]

fĕnĕstĕll'a, n. (archit.). Niche in wall S. of altar holding piscina & often credence. [L, dim. of *fenestra* window]

fĕnĕs'tra, n. (pl. *-ae*). Small hole or opening in bone etc., esp. one of two (~ *ovalis* and ~ *rotunda*) in internal ear. [L, = window]

fĕnĕs'tr|ate, a. (bot., zool.). With small window-like perforations. So ~**āt**ED² a., furnished with windows, pierced with hole(s), perforated. [f. L *fenestrare* (prec.), -ATE²]

fĕnĕstrā'tion, n. (Archit.) arrangement of windows in a building; (Bot. & Zool.) being fenestrate; (Surg.) operation of making a 'window' in medial wall of middle ear, performed in some cases of deafness. [prec., -ATION]

Fēn'ian, n. & a. **1.** One of a league among the Irish in U.S. founded in 1858 for promoting revolution & overthrowing English government in Ireland; hence ~ISM(3) n. **2.** adj. Of ~s or ~ism. [f. OIr. *féne* name of ancient Irish people confused w. *fiann* guard of legendary kings]

fĕnks, n. pl. Fibrous parts of whale's blubber, refuse of blubber when melted. [orig. unkn.]

fĕnn'ĕc, n. Small N.-African fox notable for its huge pointed ears. [Arab.]

fĕnn'el, n. Yellow-flowered fragrant umbelliferous herb used in sauces. [OE *finugl* f. L *faeniculum* (*faenum* hay, -CULE)]

fĕn'ŭgreek, n. Leguminous plant with seeds used in farriery. [ME, f. OF *fenugrec* f. L *faenugraecum* (*faenum* hay, *Graecus* Greek)]

feoff. See FIEF.

feoffee' (fĕfē'), n. Person to whom freehold estate in land is conveyed by a feoffment; ~ *in* or *of trust*, trustee invested with such estate. [f. AF *feoffe* p.p. f. OF *fieffer* (FEE), see -EE]

feoff'ment (fĕf-), n. Particular mode of conveying freehold estate. [as prec., -MENT]

feoff'or, -er, (fĕf-), n. One who makes feoffment to another. [as FEOFFEE, -OR]

fĕr'ae natŭr'ae, a. (pred. or placed after noun). Not domesticated, living in a wild state, (*hares are, the hare is*, ~; *animals*~). [L, = of a wild nature]

fĕr'al, a. Wild, untamed, uncultivated; brutal. [f. LL *feralis* (L *fera* wild beast, -AL)]

fer de lance (fărdelahǹs'), n. A large and peculiarly venomous snake of tropical S. America. [F, = iron head of lance]

fĕ'rĕtorў, n. Shrine for saint's relics, tomb; ‖ bier; chapel in which shrines were deposited. [ME *fertre* f. OF *fiertre* f. L *feretrum* f. Gk *pheretron* (*pherō* bear), w. assim. to -ORY]

fĕr'ial, a. (eccl.). (Of day) ordinary, not appointed for festival or fast (~ *service* etc., for use on ~ day). [ME, f. OF *ferial* or med. L *ferialis* (*feria* week-day + -AL)]

fĕr'ine, a. = FERAL. [f. L *ferinus* (*fera* wild beast, -INE[1])]

Fering'hee (-ĭnggi), n. (Indian term for) European, esp. Indian-born Portuguese. [corrupt. of FRANK[1]]

fĕrm'ĕnt[1], n. Leaven, fermenting-agent; fermenting, fermentation; agitation, excitement, tumult. [ME, f. OF, or L *fermentum* (*fervēre* boil, -MENT)]

fermĕnt'[2], v.i. & t. Suffer, subject to, fermentation; (make) effervesce; excite, stir up, foment. Hence ~ABLE a. [ME, f. OF *fermenter* or L *fermentare* (prec.)]

fĕrmĕntā'tion, n. Process like that induced by leaven in dough, with effervescence, heat, & change of properties; agitation, excitement. Hence **fermĕnt'ATIVE** a. [f. med. L *fermentatio* (prec., -ATION)]

fĕrn, n. One of a large group of vascular cryptogams many of which have feathery fronds (also collect., *go through heath &* ~); ~*owl*, nightjar. Hence ~'LESS, ~'Y[2], aa., ~'ERY(3) n. [OE *fearn*, MDu. *væren*, OHG *farn* f. WG **farna*]

ferō'cious (-shus), a. Fierce, savage,

cruel. Hence ~LY[2] (-shus-) adv. [f. L *ferox -ocis* + -OUS]

ferō'citў, n. Ferocious character or act. [f. F *férocité* or L *ferocitas* (prec., -TY)]

-ferous, suf. (in actual use *-iferous*, see -I-) forming adjj., f. L *-fer* -producing (*ferre* bear) + -OUS; in adjj. taken direct or thr. F *-fère* f. L as *auriferous*, & now a living suf., esp. in Nat. Hist., = -bearing, -having.

fĕ'rŏx, n. Great lake trout. [L name *Salmo ferox* fierce salmon]

fĕ'rrāte, n. A salt of ferric acid. [f. L *ferrum* iron + -ATE[1](3)]

fĕ'rreous, a. Of, containing, iron. [f. L *ferreus* (prec.) + -OUS]

fĕ'rrĕt[1], n. Half-tamed variety of polecat kept for driving rabbits from burrows, killing rats, etc.; searcher, detective. Hence ~Y[2] a. [ME, f. OF *fuiret*, *furet* alt. f. *fuiron*, *furon* f. LL *furionem*, *furonem* f. L *fur* thief]

fĕ'rrĕt[2], v.i. & t. Hunt with ferrets (*go* ~*ing*); clear out (holes, ground), take or drive away (rabbits etc.), with ferrets (*about, away, out*, etc.); rummage, search *about, (for)*; search *out* (secrets, criminals, etc.). [f. prec.]

fĕ'rrĕt[3], n. Stout cotton or silk tape. [f. It. *fioretti* floss-silk pl. of *fioretto* dim. of *fiore* f. L *flos -oris* flower]

fĕrri-, comb. form used to indicate presence of iron in ferric compounds; see -IC.

fĕ'rriage, n. Conveyance by, charge for using, ferry. [-AGE]

fĕ'rric, a. Of iron; (Chem.) containing iron in trivalent form (cf. FERROUS). [f. L *ferrum* iron + -IC]

fĕrrif'erous, a. Iron-yielding. [as prec. + -FEROUS]

Fĕ'rris wheel, n. Giant revolving vertical wheel supporting passenger cars on its periphery, an attraction at exhibitions etc. [G. W. G. *Ferris*, U.S. engineer]

fĕrro-, comb. form used to indicate presence of iron in ferrous compounds; see -OUS.

fĕrro-măgnĕt'ĭc, a. Magnetic as opp. to diamagnetic. [prec.]

fĕ'rrotỹpe, n. Positive photograph taken on thin iron plate; this process. [FERRO-, TYPE]

fĕ'rrous, a. Containing iron (~ *& non-*~ *metals*); (Chem.) containing iron in divalent form (cf. FERRIC). [f. L *ferrum* iron + -OUS]

ferru'ginous (-rōō-), a. Of, containing, iron-rust or iron as a chemical constituent; rust-coloured, reddish-brown. [f. L *ferrugo -ginis* rust (*ferrum* iron) + -OUS]

fĕ'rrule, -rel, n. Metal ring or cap strengthening end of stick or tube; band strengthening or forming joint. Hence **fĕ'rrul**ED[2] (-ld) a. [15th c. *vyrelle*, 17th c. *verrel*, f. OF *virelle* etc., f. L *viriola* dim. of *viriae* bracelet, assim. to *ferrum* iron]

fĕ'rrў, v.t. & i., & n. **1.** Convey or pass in boat, work (boat), (of boat) pass to &

fro, over river, canal, or strait; fly (air-craft) from factory to operational airfield (~ *pilot*, one who makes such flights). **2.** n. Place, provision, for ~ing; (Law) right of ~ing & levying toll for it; ~-*boat*; ~*man*; ~*-bridge*, large ~-boat transporting railway train entire. [vb OE, OS *ferian*, OHG *feren*, ON *ferja*, Goth. (= Gmc) *farjan* f. *far-* FARE²; n. (ME) f. ON *ferja* f. *far-*(prec.)]

fert'ile (-il, -il), a. Bearing abundantly, fruitful, (lit. & fig.; ~ *of*, *in*). So **fertil'ity** n. [ME, f. OF *fertil* f. L *fertilis* (*ferre* bear)]

fert'iliz|e, **-is|e** (-iz), v.t. Make fertile or productive (esp. soil); (Bot. etc.) fecundate (individual, organ). Hence ~ABLE a., ~A'TION, ~ER¹(1, 2), nn. [-IZE]

fe'rula (-ŏŏl-), **fe'rule** (-ŏŏl), nn. (Bot.) giant fennel (-*ula*); flat ruler with widened pierced end for punishing boys, whence **fe'rule** (-ŏŏl) v.t. [L (-*a*)]

ferv'ent, a. Hot, glowing; ardent, intense, (~ *soul*, *lover*, *hatred*), so **ferv'ency** n. Hence ~LY² adv. [ME, f. OF f. L *fervēre* boil, -ENT]

ferv'id, a. **1.** (poet.) Hot, glowing. **2.** Ardent, intense. Hence ~LY² adv. [f. L *fervidus* (prec.)]

ferv'our (-*er*), n. Glowing condition, intense heat; vehemence, passion, zeal. [ME, f. OF *fervor* f. L *fervorem* nom. -*or* (FERVENT, -OR)]

Fes'cennine, a. ~ *verses*, scurrilous lampoons. [f. L *Fescenninus* (*Fescennia* town in Etruria, -INE¹)]

fes'cue, n. Small stick, teacher's pointer; kinds of grass, including some valuable for pasture & fodder. [ME *festu(e)* f. OF *festu* f. Rom. **festucum* f. L -*a*; *fescue* f. 16th c.]

fesse, n. (her.). Two horizontal lines as bar across middle of field. [ME, f. OF, f. L FASCIA]

fes'tal, a. Of a feast; keeping holiday; gay. Hence ~LY² adv. [f. OF, or LL *festalis* (FEAST, -AL)]

fes'ter, v.i. & t., & n. **1.** (Of wound or sore) generate matter, ulcerate; (of poison, disease, grief) cause suppuration, rankle; putrefy, rot; cause festering in. **2.** n. ~ing condition. [ME; f. obs. n. *fester* f. OF *festre* f. L FISTULA]

fes'tival, a. (not pred.), & n. Festal day, celebration, merry-making; periodic musical performance(s) of special importance; (adj.) of a feast (-day). [ME (adj.) f. OF f. med. L *festivalis* (foll., -AL)]

fes'tive, a. Of a feast; joyous; fond of feasting, jovial. Hence ~LY² (-vl-) adv. [f. L *festivus* (*festum* FEAST, -IVE)]

festiv'ity, n. Gaiety, rejoicing; festive celebration, (pl.) festive proceedings. [ME, f. OF *festivite* or L *festivitas* (prec., -TY)]

festoon', n., & v.t. **1.** Chain of flowers or leaves, or ribbons etc., hung in curve between two points. **2.** v.t. Adorn (as)

with, form into, ~s. Hence ~ERY(5) n. [f. F *feston* f. It. *festone* f. *festa* feast + -OON]

fetch¹, v.t. & i., & n. **1.** (Go for &) bring back (person or thing; ~, or *go & ~*, a *doctor*; FAR¹-~*ed*; ~ *& carry*, run backwards & forwards with things, be a servant; cause to come, draw forth, (blood, tears; ~ *up*, vomit); bring in, realize, sell for, (a price); move the feelings of, delight (whence ~'ING² a.) or irritate; heave (sigh), draw (breath); deal (blow; usu. with ind. obj., ~ *him a box on the ears*; ~ *a* COMPASS¹; ~ *up*, come to a stand. **2.** n. Far-reaching effort (arch.); dodge, trick; (Naut.) line of continuous extent from point to point, e.g. of a bay or of open sea. [OE (*fecc(e)an* var. of *fetian* whence dial. *fet* in same sense]

fetch², n. Person's wraith or double. [orig. unkn.]

fête (fät), n., & v.t. **1.** Festival, great entertainment, (~-*day*, appointed for ~); day of saint after whom child is named, observed in R.-C. countries like birthday. **2.** v.t. Entertain, make much of, (person). [f. F *fête(r)* FEAST]

fête champêtre (see Ap.), n. Outdoor fête. [F]

fe'tial (-shl), a. & n. (Rom. ant.). **1.** ~ *law*, of declarations of war & treaties of peace. **2.** n. One of Roman college of priests who served as heralds. [f. L *fetialis*]

fet'id, **foe-** (fē-), a. Stinking. Hence ~LY² adv., ~NESS n. [f. L *fetidus* (*fetēre* stink)]

fet'ish, **-ch(e)** (-sb), n. Inanimate object worshipped by savages for its magical powers or as being inhabited by a spirit; principle etc. irrationally reverenced. Hence or cogn. ~EER', ~ER¹, ~ISM(3), ~IST(2), nn., ~is'TIC a. [f. F *fétiche* f. Port. *feitiço* charm, orig. adj. = FACTITIOUS]

fet'lock, n. Part of horse's leg where tuft of hair grows behind pastern-joint (~-*deep*, so as to cover ~s). [ME *fet(e)lak*, *fytlok*, corr. to MHG *vizzeloch*, G *fissloch*; rel. to G *fessel* & ult. to FOOT]

fet'or, n. Stench. [L, see FETID, -OR]

fett'er, n., & v.t. **1.** Shackle for the feet; bond, (pl.) captivity; check, restraint; ~*lock*, (heraldic representation of) D-shaped ~ for tethering horse by leg. **2.** v.t. Bind (as) with ~s, impede, restrain. Hence ~LESS a. [OE *feter*, OS *feteros*, OHG *fezzera*, ON *fjǫturr* f. Gmo **feter-* cogn. w. FOOT]

fet'tle, n. Condition, trim, (*in good* etc. ~). [f. ME (now dial.) vb *fettle* make ready, f. OE (now dial.) n. *fetel* girdle]

fetus. See FOETUS.

fet'wa, n. Decision given by Moslem judicial authority. [Arab.]

feu, n. (Sc.). Perpetual lease at fixed rent; piece of land so held. [var. of FEE]

feud¹, n. Lasting mutual hostility (*be at* ~ *with*), esp. (often *deadly* ~) between two tribes, families, etc., with murderous assaults in revenge for previous injury.

[ME *fede*, f. OF *faide*, *fede* f. Frank. *faida* = OHG *fêhida*, OE *fǣhthu* enmity; see FOE]

feud[2], n. Fief, feudal benefice, territory held in fee. [f. med. L as FEE]

feud'al, a. Of a feud or fief; ~ *system*, medieval European polity based on relation of vassal & superior arising from holding of lands in feud; of, resembling, according to, this system. Hence ~LY[2] adv., ~ISM(3), ~IST(2), nn., ~īs'tic a., ~IZE(3) v.t., ~īZA'TION n. [f. med. L *feudalis* (prec., -AL)]

feudal'itỹ, n. Feudal system or principles; feudal holding, fief. [f. F *feodalité* (prec., -TY)]

feud'atorỹ, a. & n. Feudally subject *to*, under overlordship; (n.) feudal vassal. [f. med. L *feudatorius* f. *feudare* (FEUD[2], -ORY)]

feu de joie (fĕrdezhwah'), n. Salute of guns fired on ceremonial occasions. [F]

feuilleton (see Ap.), n. Ruled-off portion at foot of (esp. French) newspapers, devoted to fiction, criticism, light literature, etc. [F, = leaflet]

fêv'er, n., & v.t. 1. Morbid condition with high temperature & excessive change & destruction of tissues; any of a group of diseases so characterized, each with distinctive name, as *scarlet*, *typhoid*, ~; nervous excitement, agitation; ~ *heat*, high temperature of body in ~; ~*-trap*, place that collects ~-germs. 2. v.t. Throw into ~ [OE *fēfor* = OHG *fiebar*, f. L *febris*]

fêv'erfew, n. A herb formerly used in medicine. [OE *fēferfuge* f. LL; see FEBRIFUGE]

fêv'erish, a. Having symptoms of fever; excited, fitful, restless; (of places) infested by fever, feverous. Hence ~LY[2] adv., ~NESS n. [-ISH[1]]

fêv'erous, a. Infested with or apt to cause fever; feverish. [-OUS]

few, a. & n. Not many (~ is opp. to *many*, *a* ~ to *none*, *only a* ~ = ~; *a man of* ~ *words*; *he spoke a* ~ *words*; ~ *have such a chance*; ~, *a* ~, *of his friends were there*; *a* ~ *know the truth*; *a faithful* ~ *remained*; *visitors are* ~); *in* ~ (arch.), in ~ words, briefly; *some* ~, no great number; *the* ~, the minority, the elect, etc.; *not a* ~, many; (colloq.) *a good* ~, fair number (*of*); *every* ~ *days* etc., once in every group of a ~ days. Hence ~'NESS n. [OE *fēawe*, OS, OHG *fao* (faw-), ON *fár*, Goth. *fawai* f. Gmc **faw-* cogn. w. L *pau-cus*]

fey (fā), a. (Sc.). ‖ Fated to die, at point of death; disordered in mind (often with over-confidence etc.) like person about to die. [OE *fǣge*, OS *fēgi*, OHG *feigi*, ON *feigr* f. Gmc **faigjaz*]

fêz, n. Turkish cap, a tasselled dull-red truncated cone. [f. Turk. *fes* perh. f. *Fez*, town]

fiacre (fē'ahkr), n. French four-wheeled cab. [f. the Hôtel de St *F*~, Paris]

fiancé, *-ée* (see Ap.), n. One's betrothed, (*-é*) male, or (*-ée*) female. [F]

Fianna Fail (fē'ana fawl), n. Eamon de Valera's party, which entered the Dail Eireann in August 1927. [nom. pl. of Ir. *fian* + gen. of *Fál* Ireland; lit. = armed men of Ireland]

fiăs'cō, n. (pl. *-os*). Failure or break-down (orig. in dramatic etc. performance), ignominious result. [It., = bottle (unexplained allusion)]

fi'at (*-at*, *-ăt*), n., & v.t. Authorization; decree, order, (n., & rarely vb = authorize); **~ money*, inconvertible paper-money made legal tender by Government decree. [L, = be it done]

fib[1], n., & v.i. (-bb-). (Tell) trivial or venial lie. Hence ~b'ER[1], ~'STER, nn. [perh. f. obs. *fible-fable* nonsense, redupl. of FABLE]

‖ **fib**[2], n., & v.t. (-bb-). A blow (vb, strike, hit about) in pugilism etc. [orig. unkn.]

fi'bre (*-ber*), n. Thread-like filament forming with others animal & vegetable tissue or textile substance; substance consisting of ~s; fibrous structure; structure, grain, character, (*man of coarse* ~); substance that can be spun, woven, or felted; small root or twig; ~*board*, building material made of wood or other plant ~s compressed into boards. Hence (-)fi'brED[2] (-berd), ~LESS (-erl-), fib'rīFORM, fib'rous, aa., fib'rouslỹ[2] adv., fib'rousNESS n., fibro- comb: form. [F, f. L *fibra*]

fib'ril, n. Small fibre; subdivision of fibre; ultimate subdivision of root. Hence ~IAR(Y), ~IATE[2], ~lātĕd, ~l'IFORM, ~lOSE[1], aa., ~lA'TION n. [also *fibrilla* mod. L dim. of prec.]

fib'rin, n. Coagulable lymph found in animal & vegetable matter. Hence ~o-comb. form, ~OUS a. [FIBRE + -IN]

fib'roid, a. & n. Of fibrous structure or appearance; (n.) ~ uterine tumour. [-OID]

fib'röin, n. Chemical substance of which silk & cobweb mainly consist. [FIBRO- + -IN]

fibrōm'a, n. (pl. *-ta*). Fibrous tumour. [mod. L (FIBRE, & cf. SARCOMA)]

fibrosīt'īs, n. (Rheumatic) inflammation of fibrous tissue. [f. mod. L *fibrosus* (FIBROUS) + -ITIS]

fib'ūl|a, n. (pl. *-ae*, *-as*). Splint bone on outer side of leg; (Ant.) brooch or clasp. Hence ~AR[1] a. [L]

-fic, suf. (in actual use, *-ific*, see -I-) repr. L *-ficus* f. weakened root of *facere* make, do, forming adjj. f. nn. as *pacificus* peace-making, f. adjj. as *magnificus*, f. vv. as *horrificus*, & f. the advv. *male*, *bene*. E adopted many L adjj. of this type thr. F; & later formations, arising in various langg., are usu. of international currency, as *acidific*, *morbific*.

-fica'tion, suf. (in actual use *-ification*, see -I-) repr. L *-fication-* (nom. *-tio*), which formed nn. of action f. vv. in *-ficare* -FY. E adopted many pairs of words, n. & vb, f. L thr. F or of F formation, as *purify*, purification; hence -*fication* has become the recognized means of forming nn. corresp. to vv. in -*fy* exc. when these repr. L vv. in -*facere* (see -FACTION); as a rule the formation is based only on possible L types; exceptions are *beauti~*, *Frenchi~*, *transmogri~*.

fice'lle', a. String-coloured. [F, = string]

fi'chu (-shoo), n. Woman's small triangular shawl of lace etc. for shoulders & neck. [F]

fic'kle, a. Inconstant, changeable. Hence ~NESS (-ln-) n. [OE *ficol* cf. *befician* deceive]

fic'tile, a. Made of earth or clay by potter, of pottery. [f. L *fictilis* (*fingere fict*- fashion, -IL)]

fic'tion, n. Feigning, invention, thing feigned or imagined, invented statement or narrative, literature consisting of such narrative, esp. novels, whence ~IST(3) (-shon-) n., conventionally accepted falsehood (esp. *legal*, *polite*, ~). Hence ~AL (-shon-) a. [F, f. L *fictionem* (prec., -ION)]

ficti'tious (-shus), a. Counterfeit, not genuine; (of name or character) assumed; imaginary, unreal; of, in, novels; regarded as what it is called by legal or conventional fiction. Hence ~LY² adv., ~NESS n., (-shus-). [f. L *ficticius* (prec.) +-OUS]

fic'tive, a. Creating, created, by imagination. [F -*if*, -*ive*, see FICTION, -IVE]

fid, n. 1. (naut.). Conical wooden pin used in splicing; (also ~*'pin*) square wooden or iron bar for supporting topmast. 2. Small thick piece or wedge of anything. [orig. unkn.]

fid'dle, n., int., & v.i. & t. 1. (Fam. or contempt. for) violin (*fit as a ~*, in good condition & spirits; *hang up* one's ~ *when* one *comes home*, be witty abroad & dull at home; *play first, second, ~*, take leading, subordinate, position; *face as long as a ~*, dismal). 2. (naut.). Contrivance for stopping things from rolling off table. 3. (sl.). An act of cheating. 4. ~-BOW¹, ~-*case*, for holding ~; ~-*de-dee'*, int. & n. nonsense, ~-*faddle*, (n.) trivial matters, idler, (adj.) petty, fussy, (int.) nonsense, (v.i.) fuss, trifle; ~-*head*, carving at ship's bows; ~ *pattern*, of spoons & forks with ~-shaped heads; ~*stick*, (n.) = ~-bow, (also, usu. pl., as int.) nonsense! 5. int. Nonsense! 6. vb. Play the ~, play (tune etc.) on ~, be idle or frivolous, make aimless movements, (*about, at, with*, etc.); fritter *away*; (sl.) cheat, swindle. [ME, f. OE **fithele*, OHG *fidula*, ON *fithla*, Gmc **fithulōn* f. pop. L **vitula* VIOL]

fidd'ler, n. Player on fiddle, esp. for hire (*F~'s Green*, sailor's Elysium); kind of small crab. [OE *fithelere* (prec., -ER¹)]

fidd'ley, n. (naut.; pl. ~*s*). Iron framework round opening of stokehole. [orig. unkn.]

fidd'ling, a. In vbl senses; esp., petty, futile, contemptible, inconsiderable. [-ING²]

fidel'ity, n. Faithfulness, loyalty, (*to*); strict conformity to truth or fact; exact correspondence to the original; (Radio etc.) clarity of reproduction. [f. F *fidélité* or L *fidelitas* FEALTY]

fidg'et¹, n. 1. Bodily uneasiness seeking relief in spasmodic movements (often *the ~s*); restless mood. 2. One who fidgets or causes others to; act of bustling etc. rustle of dress etc. Hence ~Y² a., ~iNESS n. [sense 1 f. obs. *fidge* to twitch sense 2 f. foll.]

fidg'et², v.i. & t. Move restlessly (often *about*); be uneasy, worry; make uncomfortable, worry, (person). [f. prec.]

fid'ibus, n. Paper spill for lighting candles, pipes, etc. [G students' slang]

Fid'o, n. Device for enabling aircraft to land by dispersing fog by means of petrol-fired flame burners heating air over runway. [initials of *Fog Investigation Dispersal Operation*]

fidu'cial (-shl), a. (surv., astron., etc.). ~ *line, point*, etc., one assumed as fixed basis of comparison. [f. LL *fiducialis* (*fiducia* trust, -AL)]

fidu'ciary (-sha-), a. & n. 1. Of trust or trustee(ship); held or given in trust; (of paper currency) depending for its value on public confidence or securities. 2. n. Trustee. [f. L *fiduciarius* (prec., -ARY¹)]

fid'us Achat'es (akātēz), n. Devoted follower, henchman. [L, =faithful Achates, follower of Aeneas in *Aeneid*]

fie (fi), int. expr. sense of outraged propriety, usu. iron. or to children (often ~ *upon you!*). [ME, f. OF f. L *fi* excl. of disgust at stench]

fief (fēf), feoff (fĕf), n. = FEUD².

fie-'fie (fi'fī), a. Improper, scandalous. [FIE]

field, n., & v.i. & t. 1. (Piece of) ground, esp. one used for pasture or tillage, & usu. bounded by hedges etc.; tract abounding in some natural product (*diamond, coal*, etc., ~~). 2. Ground on which battle is fought (often *battle-~*; also fig., *left his rival in possession of the ~*; *a fair ~ & no favour*, equal conditions in contest; *hold the ~*, not be superseded); scene of campaign (*in the ~*, campaigning; *take, keep, the ~*, begin, continue, campaign); battle (*hard-fought, stricken, ~*); *F~ of Cloth of Gold*, scene of meeting between Henry VIII & Francis I, 1520. 3. Ground for playing cricket, football, etc.; players, partakers, in outdoor contest or sport; all competitors or all except the favourite (*a good ~*, many & good competitors), (Cricket) side not batting, one of this side (see also LONG¹ ~). 4. Large stretch, expanse, of sea, sky, ice, snow, etc., also fig. (*the whole ~ of history*). 5. (Her.) surface of escutcheon or of one of its divisions; groundwork of picture, coin, flag, etc. 6. Area or sphere of operation, observation, intellectual activities, etc. (*each supreme in his own* ∼, *filled the* ∼ *of the telescope*, *wide* ∼ *of vision*, *outside the magnetic* ∼, not near enough to be attracted) 7. attrib. (In names of animals etc.) found in the open country (∼-*mouse*, ∼-*ash*). 8. ∼-*allowance*, to officer on campaign to meet increased expenditure; ∼-*artillery*, -*battery*, -*gun* or -*piece*, light & mobile for use with armies in the ∼, ∼-*book* (used in ∼ by surveyor for technical notes); ∼-*boot*, knee-length & close-fitting, ∼-*cornet*, magistrate of township in Cape Colony etc.; ∼-*day*, (Mil.) manœuvring-exercise or review, (fig.) great occasion, important debate; ∼ *dressing*, appliances for wound in battle, ∼ *events*, athletic sports such as weight-putting, jumping, discus-throwing, etc. (i.e. other than *races*); ∼-*glass*, binocular telescope for outdoor use, one of the lenses of astronomical telescope or compound microscope; ∼ *hospital*, ambulance, temporary hospital near battlefield; *F*∼ *Marshal*, army officer of the highest rank, ∼ *mustard*, charlock; ∼-*night*, = ∼-*day* (fig. sense); ∼-*officer*, above captain & below general; ∼-*preacher*, -*preaching*, in open air; ∼ *punishment* (Mil.), kinds of penal servitude for offences on campaign; ∼-*s′-man*, ∼-er at cricket; ∼-*sports*, outdoor, esp hunting, shooting, fishing; ∼ *telegraph*, movable for use on campaign; ∼-*work*, temporary fortification, outdoor work of surveyor etc., or of collector of scientific data; hence ∼′WARD(s) adv. 9. vb. Act as ∼sman in cricket, baseball, or rounders; stop (& return) ball; put into the ∼ (of football teams etc.); (Betting) back the ∼ against the favourite; hence ∼′ER[1] n. [OE, OS, OHG *feld* f WG *felthu*]

field′fāre, n. Species of thrush spending winter in Britain. [ME *feldefare* perh. f FIELD + FARE[2]]

fiend, n. The devil; evil spirit, demon; person of superhuman wickedness, esp. cruelty (often jocular, as *the interviewer-*∼), (with qualifying word) devotee or addict (*fresh-air* ∼, *dope* ∼, *morphia* ∼). Hence ∼′ISH[1] a., ∼′ishLY[2] adv., ∼′ish-NESS n, ∼′LIKE a. [OE *féond*, OS *fiond*, OHG *fiant*, ON *fjándi*, Goth. *fijands* part. of Gmc *fijējan* hate; cf. FRIEND]

fierce, a. Violent in hostility, angrily combative; raging, vehement; (of mechanism) violent, not smooth or easy in action, ardent, eager. Hence ∼′LY[2] (-sl-) adv. ∼′NESS (-sn-) n. [ME, f. OF *fiers* nom. of *fier* (F = proud) f. L *ferus* savage]

∥**fi′eri fā′ciăs** (-shī-), n. (legal; abbr. *fi. fa.*) Writ to sheriff for executing judgement. [L, = see that (the sum) is made]

fier′|l y̆ (fīr-), a. Consisting of, flaming with, fire; (of arrows etc.) fire-bearing; looking like fire, blazing-red; (of eyes) flashing, ardent; hot as fire; acting like fire,

inflaming, (∼y *taste* etc.), eager, pugnacious, spirited, irritable; (of horse) mettlesome; (of gas, mine, etc.) inflammable, liable to explosions; (of cricket-pitch) making ball rise dangerously, ∼y CROSS[1]. Hence ∼ĭLY[2] adv., ∼ĭNESS n [ME; FIRE[1] + -Y[1]]

fiesta (fē′ĕstah), n. Festivity, holiday [Sp., = feast]

fife, n., & v.i. & t. 1. Kind of small shrill flute used with drum in military music; = ∼r. 2. vb. Play the∼; play (air etc.) on the ∼; hence **fif′**ER[1] n. [f. G *pfeife* PIPE, or f. F *fifre*]

fife′-rail (-fr-), n. (naut.). Rail round mainmast with belaying-pins. [perh. f. prec. because fifer sat on it while anchor was weighing]

fifteen′ (*also* fif′t̲), a. & n. One more than fourteen, 15, XV; (Rugby football) side of 15 players; *the F*∼, Jacobite rising of 1715. Hence ∼TH[2] a. & n. [OE *fiftēne*, -*tÿne*, (FIVE, -TEEN)]

fifth, a. & n. 1. Next after fourth (*smite under the* ∼ *rib*, kill; ∼ *wheel* of coach etc., something superfluous, also as name of two horizontal half-circles sliding one over the other when a carriage-front turns); ∼ *part*, one of five equal parts into which thing is or might be divided. 2. n. = ∼ part; (Mus.) interval of which the span involves five alphabetical notes, harmonic combination of the notes thus separated; (pl.) ∼-rate material. 3. ∼ *column*, organized body sympathizing with and working for the enemy within a country at war etc., (loosely) traitors, spies; ∼-*column activities*, organized hindrance of the national effort by subversive propaganda on the part of ∼-*columnists*; *F*∼ *Monarchy*, last of the five great empires (*Dan*. ii. 44; ∼-*monarchy-man*, 17th-c. zealot expecting immediate second coming of Christ & repudiating all other government); *F*∼ REPUBLIC. [OE *fifta* (still *fift* in diall.); *fifth* f. 14th c. on analogy of FOURTH; see -TH[2]]

fifth′ly̆, adv. In the fifth place (in enumerations). [-LY[2]]

fif′t|y̆, a. & n. 1. Five times ten, 50, L, (∼y-*one*, -*seven*, etc.; ∼y-*first*, -*third*, etc.); ∼y-∼y, half & half, equal shares (*go* ∼y-∼y; *on a* ∼y-∼y *basis*); large indefinite number (*have*∼y *things to tell you*); hence ∼y̆FOLD a. & adv., ∼ĭETH a. & n. 2. n. Set of ∼y persons or things (*hid them by* ∼*ies in a cave*; *the* ∼*ies*, years between 49 & 60 in life or century). [OE *fiftig* (FIVE, -TY[2])]

fig[1], n. (Broad-leaved tree, usu. ∼-*tree*, bearing) soft pear-shaped many-seeded fruit eaten fresh (*green* ∼s) or dried (esp. *Turkey* or *Smyrna*∼s; *pulled*∼s, superior hand-picked Turkey ∼s); *under* one's *vine & ∼-tree*, safe at home; anything valueless (*don't care a* ∼ *for*; also *a* ∼ *for* —*!*, as excl.); ∼-*leaf*, device for fig   451   filaria

concealing private parts (*Gen.* iii. 7); ~-*wort*, brown-flowered herb. [ME, f. OF *figue* f. Pr. *figa* f. Rom. *fica f. L *ficus*]

fig², n. Dress, equipment, (*in full* ~); condition, form, (*in good*. ~). [f. foll.]

fig³, v.t. (-gg-). ~ *out* or *up* (horse), make lively, ~ *out* (person), dress up, bedizen. [var. of obs. *feague* f. G *fegen*; see FAKE²]

fight¹ (fīt), v.i. & t. (*fought*, pr. fawt). Contend in battle or single combat (*against*, *with*, *for*, on behalf of person or to secure thing); maintain (cause, suit at law, quarrel) against opponent, contend over (question), win one's *way* by ~ing; contend with in battle or duel, or with the fists; set on (cocks, dogs) to ~ (~*ing*-COCK¹); handle (troops, ship) in battle; ~ *off*, repel with effort; ~ (dispute etc., or *it*) *out*, settle by ~ing; ~ *shy of*, keep aloof from (person, undertaking, etc.); ~*ing chance*, a possibility of success if strenuous effort is made; ~*ing-top*, circular gun-platform fixed high up on warship's mast. Hence ~′ER¹ (fīt-) (esp.) n. & a., (fast aircraft) designed primarily for aerial ~ing (~*er-bomber*, such aircraft used as a bomber). [OE *feohtan*, OS, OHG *fehtan* f. WG *fehtan]

fight² (fīt), n. Act of fighting, (*give, make a*, ~, *valiant in* ~); battle; combat, esp. pugilistic or unpremeditated, between two or more persons, animals, or parties (*running* ~, kept up while one party flees & one pursues; || *sham* ~, between troops for practice or display; *stand-up* ~, open & formal); (fig.) strife, conflict; appetite or ability for fighting (*has* ~ *in him yet*; *show* ~, not yield tamely). [f. prec.]

fig′ment, n. Invented statement; thing that has no existence except in imagination. [f. L *figmentum* (*fig*- see FIGURE¹, -MENT)]

fig′ūrant masc., -*ante* fem., **fĭgŭrăn′tĕ** (pl -*ti*, pr. -tĕ), nn. Ballet-dancer. [F (first two forms) & It. (third)]

figūrā′tion (*also* -ger-), n. Determination to a certain form; the resulting form; shape, outline; allegorical representation; ornamentation by designs; (Mus.) use of florid counterpoint. [f. F, or L *figuratio* (FIGURE², -ATION)]

fig′urative (-ger-, -gūr-), a. Emblematic, typical; pictorial or plastic; metaphorical, not literal; metaphorically so called; abounding in, addicted to, figures of speech. Hence ~LY¹ (-vl-) adv., ~NESS n. [ME, f. OF (-*if*, -*ive*), or LL *figurativus* (as prec., -ATIVE)]

fig′ure¹ (-ger), n. **1.** External form, shape; (Geom.) superficial space enclosed by line(s), or three-dimensional space enclosed by surface(s), any of the classes of these, as triangle, sphere; bodily shape (*has a well-developed* ~; *keep* one's ~, not grow stout); a person as seen (*saw a* ~ *leaning against the door*; ~ *of fun*, grotesque person); a person as contem-

plated mentally (*the most terrible* ~ *in our history*); conspicuous appearance (*make* or *cut a brilliant, poor,* ~, produce such impression; *person of* ~, distinguished). **2.** Image, likeness; representation of human form, statue, person in picture; emblem, type, simile. **3.** Diagram, illustrative drawing, (abbr. for ref. *fig.*), esp. *text*-~, dist. from *plate*; horoscope; decorative pattern; evolution in dancing, division of set dance; (Skating) movement, series of movements, beginning & ending at centre. **4.** Numerical symbol, esp. one of the ten in Arabic notation (*double* ~s, number between 9 & 100; *income of five* ~s, between £10,000 & £100,000; *reach three* ~s, in cricket, get century; *got it at a low, high,* ~, cheap, dear). **5.** (rhet.; also ~ *of speech*) recognized form of abnormal expression giving variety, force, etc., e.g. aposiopesis, hyperbole, metaphor, (~ *of speech* only) piece of exaggeration. **6.** (gram.). Permitted deviation from rules of construction, e.g. ellipse. **7.** (log.). Particular form of syllogism according to position of middle term. **8.** (mus.). Short succession of notes producing single impression, brief melodic or rhythmic formula out of which longer passages are developed. **9.** ~-*dance*, dance or dancing exhibition with distinct divisions, ~-*dancer*, performer in this; ~-*head*, carving, usu. bust or full-length ~, over ship's cutwater, nominal leader or president without real authority, (joc.) person's face. Hence ~LESS (-gerl-) a. [ME, f. OF f. L *figura* (*fig*- st. of *fingere* fashion, -URE)]

fig′ure² (-ger), v.t. & i. Represent in diagram or picture; picture mentally, imagine, (often *to oneself*; *I ~ *it like this* colloq., this is my theory, explanation, etc.); be symbol of, represent typically, embellish with pattern (~*d satin*); mark with numbers or prices, do arithmetic, cipher (~ *up*, reckon amount of); ~ *out*, give result in figures (~*s out at £45*); make appearance, appear, (~ *as*, pass for, assume character of), be conspicuous. [ME, f. OF *figurer* f. L *figurare* (prec.)]

figūrine′ (-ēn), n. Statuette. [F, f. It. *figurina* dim. of *figura* FIGURE¹]

fil′ament, n. Slender thread-like body, fibre, (esp. in animal or vegetable structure); not easily fusible conductor in electric bulb or thermionic valve, heated or made incandescent by current; (of air, light, etc.) imaginary portion of stream, row of particles following each other, (Bot.) part of stamen that supports anther. Hence ~ARY¹ (-ĕn²), ~ED², ~OUS (-ĕn²), aa. [F or mod. L, f. LL *filare* spin f. L *filum* thread, -MENT]

filār′ia, n. (pl. ~*iae* pr. -iē). Parasitic worm introduced into the blood by certain flies and mosquitoes. Hence ~IAL a., filarī′ASIS n. [mod. L f. L *filum* thread (-AR¹, -IA¹)]

fil'ature, n. (Establishment for) reeling silk from cocoons. [F, as FILAMENT, -URE]

fil'bert, n. (Nut of) cultivated hazel. [short for ~-*nut* = dial. F *noix de filbert,* ripe about St *Philibert's* day (Aug. 22)]

filch, v.t. Steal, pilfer. [orig. unkn.]

file¹, n., & v.t. **1.** Instrument usu. of steel with roughened surface(s) for reducing or smoothing objects (*bite, gnaw,* ~, attempt vain task); (sl.) artful person, dodger, (usu. *old, deep,* etc., ~), person. **2.** v.t. Smooth, reduce surface of, with ~; elaborate to perfection (esp. literary work); ~ *away* (roughnesses etc.), remove with ~. [OE *féol, fil,* OS, OHG *fila* f. WG *fihala*]

file², n., & v.t. **1.** Stiff pointed wire on which documents etc. are run for keeping; folder for holding papers arranged for reference; set of papers so kept, esp. in court of law referring to a cause; series of issues of a newspaper in order. **2.** v.t. Place (papers) on ~ or among public records. [f. F *fil* f. L *filum* thread]

file³, n., & v.i. & t. **1.** (Mil.) a front-rank man & the man or men straight behind him (*in* ~, marching with the men of a double line faced towards one of its ends; *single, Indian,* ~, similar formation of single line; RANK¹ *& ~ ; a ~ of men,* two told off for some purpose); row of persons or things one behind another; (Chess) line of squares from player to player (cf. RANK¹). **2.** vb. March in ~; ~ *off, away,* go off by ~s; (v.t.) order (soldiers) to move *off* by ~s. [f. F *file* f. LL *filare* f. L *filum* thread]

fil'emöt, a. & n. Dead-leaf colour(ed), brownish yellow. [f. F *feuille morte* dead leaf]

filet (fēl'ā), n. Kind of net with square mesh (~ *lace,* ~ *net*). [F, = thread]

fil'ial, a. Of, due from, son or daughter. Hence ~LY² adv. [f. F, or LL *filialis* (L *filius, -a,* son, daughter, -AL)]

fil'iäte, v.t. (Rare for) AFFILIATE.

filiä'tion, n. Being some one's child; descent (*from*); formation of offshoots, branch of a society or language; genealogical relation or arrangement. [f. F, or LL *filiatio* f. L *filius* son, -ATION]

fil'ibĕg, n. (Sc.). Kilt. [f. Gael. *feileadh-beag* little fold]

fil'ibŭster, n., & v.i. **1.** One who engages in unauthorized warfare against foreign State, *obstructionist in legislative assembly **2.** v.i. Act as ~. Hence ~ER¹ n., a ~, one who ~s. [ult. f. Du. *vrij-buiter* FREEBOOTER affected by F *flibustier,* Sp. *filibustero,* mutual rel. uncert.]

fil'igree, fil'a-, n. Ornamental work of fine gold or silver or copper wire formed into delicate tracery, fine metal open-work anything delicate, light, showy, & frail. Hence **fil'igree**ED² a. [f. F *filigrane* f It. *filigrana* (L *filum* thread, *granum* grain)]

fil'ing, n. In vbl senses of FILE¹, also,

(usu. pl.) particle(s) rubbed off by file. [-ING¹]

fill, v.t. & i., & n. **1.** Make or become full (*with;* *sails* ~, are distended with wind); stock abundantly; occupy whole capacity or extent of, spread over, pervade, (~ *the bill,* be the only conspicuous item, also in U.S., do all that is required suffice); (of dentist) block up (hollow tooth, cavity) with gold etc., whence ~'ING¹(4) n.; satisfy, satiate, (esp. in part., of kinds of food); hold (position), discharge duties of (office); execute (an order, commission, etc.); occupy (vacant time); appoint holder of (vacant post); adulterate (esp. cotton fabrics; usu. in p.p.); ~ *in,* complete (outline), add what is wanted to complete (unfinished document, blank cheque, etc.); ~ *out,* enlarge, become enlarged, to the proper limit; ~ *up,* ~ completely, supply vacant parts or places or deficiencies in, do away with (pond·etc.) by ~ing, grow full; FEBRUARY ~-*dike;* hence ~'ER¹(1, 2) n. **2.** Full supply of drink or food (*drink, have,* etc., one's ~; also with intr. vbs, as *fret her* ~); enough to ~ something (*a ~ of tobacco*). [OE *fyllan,* OS *fullian,* OHG *fullen,* ON *fylla,* Goth. *fulljan* f. Gmc *fullaz* FULL¹]

fille (fē'ye), n. ~ *de chambre* (de shahn'br), chambermaid; ~ *de joie* (de zhwah), prostitute. [F, = daughter]

fill'ĕt, n., & v.t. **1.** Head-band, ribbon, string, or narrow band, for binding the hair or worn round head; band, bandage; thin narrow strip of anything; (pl.) animal's loins; fleshy detachable piece of meat near loins or ribs, undercut of sirloin; one of the thick slices into which a fish may be divided; middle part of leg of veal boned, rolled, & tied up; piece of beef, fish, etc., similarly prepared; (Archit.) narrow flat band separating two mouldings, small band between flutes of column; (Her.) horizontal division of shield, quarter of CHIEF¹ in depth; raised rim or·ridge on any surface; (Book-bind.) plain line impressed on cover. **2.** v.t. Bind (hair, person as to hair) with ~; encircle with ornamental band; divide (fish) into ~s. [ME, f. OF *filet* f. L *filum* thread + -ET¹]

fill'ip, n., & v.t. & i. **1.** Sudden release of finger or thumb when it has been bent & checked by thumb or finger; slight smart stroke thus given; stimulus, incentive; mere trifle (*not worth a* ~). **2.** vb. Propel (coin, marble, etc.) with a ~, stimulate (~ one's *memory* or *wits*); strike slightly & smartly; make a ~. [prob. imit., cf. FLIP]

fill'ister, n. Rabbeting-plane for window-·sashes etc. [orig. unkn.]

fill'ÿ, n. Female foal (cf. COLT); (sl.) young lively girl. [f. ON *fylja* f. Gmc *fuljón-* see FOAL]

film, n., & v.t. & i. **1.** Thin skin, plate, coating, or layer; (Photog.) coating of collodion, gelatin, etc., spread on photographic paper or plate, or used instead of plate, celluloid roll used in cinematography, its contents as shown (~-FAN³; ~ star, eminent cinema actor or actress; ~ test, photographic test of would-be ~ actor; the ~s, cinema show); dimness over eyes; slight veil of haze etc.; fine thread or filament; hence fil'mY² a., fil'miLY² adv., fil'miNESS n. 2. vb. Cover, become covered, (as) with ~; reproduce (scene etc.) for the cinema; be (well or ill) suited for reproduction on the ~s. [OE filmen membrane = OFris. filmene skin, cogn. w. FELL¹]

fil'osĕlle, n. Floss silk. [F, f. It. filosello perh. f. Rom. *follicellus cocoon, dim. of L follis bag, influenced by It. filo thread]

fils (fēs), n. The son, junior, (appended to name to distinguish between father & son of same names, cf. PÈRE). [F]

fil'ter, n., & v.t. & i. 1. Contrivance for freeing liquids from suspended impurities, esp. by passing them through stratum of sand, charcoal, etc.; (Photog.) screen (usu. of coloured glass or gelatine) for absorbing light of some colours; ~-bed, tank or pond with false bottom covered with sand etc. for ~ing large quantities; ~-tip, (of cigarettes) having a ~ at the mouth end. 2. vb. Pass (liquid), flow,. through ~; (of ~) purify (liquid); make way through, into, etc., percolate, (of news etc.) leak out or come through; join another line of traffic at road junction etc.; obtain by ~ing. [vb f. n., f. F filtre f. med. L filtrum f. Gmc st. whence FELT¹ (earliest ~ being of felt)]

filth, n. Loathsome dirt; uninviting food, garbage; vileness, pollution, obscenity; foul language. Hence fil'thY² a. (~y lucre, dishonourable gain, also joc., money), fil'thiLY² adv., fil'thiNESS n. [OE fȳlth, OS fūlitha, OHG fūlida (FOUL¹, -TH¹)]

fil'trāte¹, n. Filtered liquor. [FILTER v., -ATE¹(2)]

fil'tr|āte¹, v.t. & i. = FILTER v. So ~A'TION n. [f. mod. L filtrare (as prec., -ATE³)]

fim'br|iāte, -āted, aa. (bot., zool.). Fringed, bordered with hairs etc. [f. L fimbriatus f. fimbriae fringe; see +-ATE²]

fin, n. Organ for propelling & steering attached to fish & cetaceans at various parts of body (anal, caudal, dorsal, pectoral, ventral, etc.); sharp lateral projection on share or coulter of plough; small projecting surface on various parts of aircraft, for ensuring stability; (sl.) hand (tip us your ~, shake hands). Hence (-)~nED² (-nd), ~'LESS, aa. [OE finn, MLG, MDu. vinne]

fin'al, a. & n. 1. At the end, coming last, ultimate; putting an end to doubt, conclusive, definitive, unalterable; concerned with the purpose or end aimed at (~ CAUSE¹; ~ clause in Gram., introduced

by in order that, lest, etc.); hence ~LY² adv. 2. n. Last or deciding heat or game in athletics, whence ~IST n., competitor in this; (sing. or pl.) last of a series of examinations; ‖ (colloq.) edition of newspaper published latest in the day; (Mus.) principal note in any mode. Hence ~IZE v.t.,. complete, bring to an end. [ME, f. OF, or L finalis (finis end, -AL)].

fina'le (-nah-), n. (Mus.) last movement of instrumental composition, piece of music closing act in opera; close of drama etc.; conclusion, final catastrophe. [It., as prec.]

finăl'itў, n. Principle of final cause viewed as operative in the universe; being final; belief that something is final; final act, state, or utterance. [F (-lé), f. LL finalitatem (FINAL, -TY)]

finănce', n., & v.t. & i. 1. (Pl.) pecuniary resources of sovereign, State, company, or person; management of (esp. public) money, science of revenue. 2. vb. Furnish with ~s, find capital for; engage in financial operations. [ME, f. OF (finer settle debt f. fin end; -ANCE)]

finăn'cial (-shl), a. Of revenue or money matters (~ year, annual period for which public accounts are made up). Hence ~LY² (-sha-) adv. [prec.+-IAL]

finăn'cier¹ (*also finansēr'), n. One skilled in levying & managing public money; capitalist. [F (FINANCE, -IER)]

financier'² (-sēr), v.i. & t. Conduct financial operations (usu. contempt.); *cheat, swindle, (~ money away; ~ one out of). [f. prec.]

finch, n. Kinds of small bird (usu. with distinctive epithet or prefix, as mountain-~, BULL¹-~). [OE finc, OHG fincho f. WG *finkiz, *finkjon]

find, v.t. (found), & n. 1. Come across, fall in with, light upon, (was found dead; we ~ St John saying; administer the law as you ~ it; found a treasure); obtain, receive, (~ favour, mercy, one's ACCOUNT² in; ~ one's feet, get the use of them, develop one's powers); recognize as present, acknowledge or discover to be so-&-so, (I ~ no sense in it, ~ the terms reasonable; how do you ~ yourself?; must take us as you ~ us, put up with us as we are); discover by trial to be or do or (that) or to (has been found wanting; ~s rest agreeable; is found to pay; I ~ it pays, pay, or to pay, or that it pays; ~ it impossible, necessary, to —); discover by search; discover (game), discover game, in hunting; ~ oneself, discover one's vocation, & see below; succeed in obtaining (money, bail, sureties; can't ~ time to read; found courage to —; could ~ it in my heart to —, am inclined; ~ expression, place, vent); come home to, reach the conscience of; ascertain by study or calculation or inquiry (~ one's way to, contrive to reach, arrive at); (Law) determine & declare (it, i.e. the

offence, *murder*; person *guilty* etc.; *that*
—; ~ *true* BILL³), whence ~'ING¹(2) n.;
supply, provide, furnish, (*they found him
in clothes*; *hotel does not ~ tea*; *all found*,
with all necessaries provided, of servants'
wages; ~ one*self*, provide for one's own
needs, & see above); ~ *out*, discover,
devise, solve, detect in offence; hence
~'ABLE a. 2. n. ~ing of fox; discovery of
treasure, minerals, etc.; *sure* ~, place
where something (esp. fox) is sure to be
found. [OE, OS, OHG *findan*, ON *finna*,
Goth. *finthan*, Gmc **finthan*]

fin'der, n. In vbl senses; esp.: small
telescope attached to large one to find
object; contrivance for same purpose in
microscope & in photographic camera.
[-ER¹]

fin de siècle (see Ap.), a. Characteristic
of end of nineteenth century, advanced,
modern; decadent. [F, = end of century]

fine¹, n., & v.i. & t. **1.** End (now only in *in
~*, to sum up, finally, in short); ‖ sum
of money paid by in-coming tenant in
consideration of small rent; sum of money
fixed as penalty for offence. **2.** vb. Pay consideration *for* privilege or appointment;
punish by a ~, whence **fin'ABLE**-a. [ME
& OF *fin* settlement of dispute f. L *finem*,
nom. *finis* end]

fine², a., n., adv., & v.t. & i. **1.** Of high
quality; clear, pure, refined, (of gold or
silver) containing specified proportion
of pure metal, as *gold 22 carats ~, silver
11 oz ~*; delicate, subtle, exquisitely
fashioned, (of feelings) elevated; of
slender thread, in small particles, thin
(~ *pencil*, of hard lead for making ~
lines); sharp (~ *pen*, narrow-pointed);
(Athlet.) reduced to perfect condition;
capable of delicate perception or discrimination, perceptible only with difficulty (a ~ *distinction*); excellent, of
striking merit, good, satisfactory, fortunate, of good effect, (*had ~ sport*; *has
been a ~ thing for him*; often iron., as *a ~
friend you have been!*); well conceived or
expressed; of handsome appearance or
size, dignified, (~ *potatoes*; *a man of ~
presence*); free from precipitation or thick
fog & with some sunshine, (~ *weather*;
one ~ day, once upon a time; *one of these
~ days*, some day, in prophecies); ornate,
showy, smart, (~ *feathers*, gaudy plumage, lit. & fig., as ~ *feathers make ~ birds*);
fastidious, dainty, affecting refinement,
(of speech or writing) affectedly ornate;
complimentary, euphemistic, (*say ~
things about person*, call *things by ~
names*); ~ *arts*, those appealing to sense
of beauty, as poetry, music, & esp.
painting, sculpture, architecture; ~
chemicals, produced or used in small
quantities and in a state of comparative
purity (i.e. other than heavy chemicals,
dyestuffs, cellulose or sugar products,
etc.); ~*-draw*, sew together (two pieces of
cloth, rent, garment) so that the join is

imperceptible; ~*-drawn*, subtle, extremely thin, (Athlet.) trained down in
weight; ~ *gentleman, lady*, person of
fashion, person who thinks himself above
working; ~*-spun*, delicate, flimsy, (of
theories etc.) excessively subtle, unpractical; hence **fin'ISH**¹(2) a., ~'LY²
(-nl-) adv., ~'NESS (-n-n-) n. **2.** n. ~
weather (*in rain or* ~). **3.** adv. ~ly (*talk
~*). **4.** vb. Make (beer) clear (often *down*);
(of liquid) become clear; ~ *away, down,
off*, make or become ~r, thinner, less
coarse, (make) dwindle, taper. [ME, f.
OF *fin* f. Rom. **finus*, deduced f. *finire*
FINISH after *grossus, grossire* (GROSS)]

fine champagne (see Ap.), n. Liqueur
brandy. [F]

fin'ery¹, n. Smartness, stylishness, (rare);
showy dress or decoration. [FINE² adj.,
-ERY]

fin'ery², n. Hearth where cast iron is
made malleable or steel made from pig-
iron. [f. F *finerie* f. *finer* refine (FINE²4)]

finesse', n., & v.i. & t. **1.** Delicate manipulation, subtle discrimination; artfulness,
cunning strategy; (Cards) attempt to
take trick by inferior card, with higher
one in reserve. **2.** vb. Use ~; wheedle
into, trick *away*, manage by ~; (Cards)
make a ~, play (card) by way of ~. [F
(FINE², -ESS²)]

fing'er (-ngg-), n., & v.t. **1.** One of five
terminal members of hand (*thumb*, &
fore, middle, ring, & *little ~s*), or four
excluding thumb (usu. now numbered
thus, but cf. *fourth* ~, i.e. ring ~, in
marriage service), (*done by the* ~, i.e.
agency, *of God*; *more wit in his little* ~
than in your whole body; *lay, put, a ~
upon*, touch however slightly; *lay, put*,
one's ~ *on* ailing part or cause of evil,
point with precision to; *look through* one's
~*s at*, pretend not to see; *lift, stir, a ~*,
make the least effort; *turn* or *twist* person
round one's (*little*) ~, cajole him; *my ~s
itch*, I long, am impatient, *to do*; *his ~s are
all thumbs*, he is clumsy; *with a wet ~*, with
ease; BURN² one's ~s; CROSS² one's ~s;
have a ~ in the pie, take part in a matter;
let slip through one's ~s, lose hold of;
have at one's ~-*tips* or ~-*ends*, be versed
in, know familiarly; *to the* ~-*nails*, completely); part of glove that holds ~; ~-
-like object, esp. such part of a fruit etc.,
& in various machines; ~-*alphabet*,
-*language*, conventional signs for talking
with the deaf; ~-*bowl, -glass*, for rinsing
~s after dessert; ~-*fern*, kind of spleen-
wort; ~-*fish*, starfish; ~-*plate*, fastened
on door to prevent ~-marks; ~-*post*,
giving directions at parting of roads;
~-*print*, impression of person's ~, used
for identifying criminals etc.; ~-*stall*,
cover of leather or rubber to protect ~
in dissections etc. or when wounded;
hence ~LESS, (-)~ED² (-nggerd), aa. **2.** v.t.
Touch with, turn about in, the ~s; take
(bribes etc.); play upon (instrument) with

the ~s, play (passage) with ~s used in particular way, mark (music) with signs showing which ~s are to be used, whence ~ing¹ (-ngg-) [-ING¹] n. [OE *finger*, OS, OHG *-ar*, ON *fingr*, Goth. *figgrs* f. Gmc *fingraz*]

fing′ering² (-ngg-), n. (for *fingering¹* see prec.). Wool for stockings. [17th c. *fingram*, perh. f. F *fin grain*, as GROGRAM f. *gros grain*]

‖ **fing′erling** (-ngg-), n. Parr. [FINGER n., -LING¹]

fin′ial, n. (archit.). Ornament finishing off apex of roof, pediment, gable, tower-corner, canopy, etc. [14th c., var. of FINAL]

fin′ical, a. Over-nice, precise, fastidious; too much finished in details. Hence ~LY² adv., ~NESS, ~ITY (-ăl²), nn. [perh. f. FINE², or var. of foll.]

fin′icking, fin′ikin, a. = prec. [perh. f. MDu. *fijnkens* accurately, neatly; rel. to prec. undetermined]

fin′is, n. (no. pl.). (At end of book) the end; end of anything, esp. of life. [L]

fin′ish, v.t. & i., & n. 1. Bring to an end, come to the end of (often ~ *doing*; ~ *off*, provide with an ending), complete; consume, get through, the whole or remainder of (food, book); kill, dispatch, overcome completely; perfect, put final or ~ing touches to, (~ed *manners*, *gentleman*; also with *off*, *up*); complete education of; (v.i.) reach the end, cease, leave *off*; have done *with*; end *in* something or *by doing*. 2. n. Last stage, termination, esp. of a fox-hunt (*be in at the* ~, often fig.); *fight to a* ~, till one party is completely worsted; what serves to give completeness; accomplished or completed state; mode of ~ing (esp. furniture, as *mahogany* ~). [ME *fenys* etc. f. OF *fenir* f. L *finire* (*finis* end), -ISH²]

fin′isher, n. In vbl senses; esp.: workman or machine doing last operation in manufacture; discomfiting thing, crushing blow, etc. [-ER¹]

fin′ite, a. Bounded, limited, not infinite; (Gram.) limited by number and person, not infinitive. Hence ~NESS (-tn-) n. [f. L *finitus* p.p. of *finire* FINISH]

Fin(n), n. One of N.-Eastern European people who call their country *Suomi*. [OE *Finnas*, ON *Finnr*, L *Fenni*, Gk *Phinnoi*]

finn′an, n. (Also ~ *haddock*) haddock cured with smoke of green wood, turf, or peat. [f. *Findhorn* or *Findon*, Scotland]

finn′er, n. Kinds of whale, esp. rorqual, having dorsal fin. [-ER¹]

Finn′ic, a. Of the group of peoples allied to the Finns; Finnish. [-IC]

Finn′ish, a. & n. (Language) of the Finns; Finnic. [-ISH¹]

Finn′ō-Ug′ric (-ōog-), a. & n. (Belonging to) family of Ural-Altaic languages including Finnish, Estonian, Lapp, & Hungarian. So **Finn′ō-Ug′rian** (-ōog-) a. [UGRIAN]

finn′y̆, a. Having fins; like a fin; of, teeming with, fish. [FIN + -Y²]

fiŏrd, fjŏrd, (fy-), n. Long narrow arm of sea between high cliffs as in Norway. [Norw., ON *fjorthr*; see FIRTH]

fi′orin, n. Kind of grass. [f. Ir. *fiorthán*]

fir̄, n. (Also ~*-tree*) kinds of coniferous tree with needles placed singly on the shoots (*Scotch*, *silver*, *spruce*, ~); their wood; ~*-apple*, *-ball*, *-cone*, fruit of ~; ~*-needle*, its leaf. Hence ~r′Y² a. [ME *firr(e)* f. OE **fyre* or ON *fyri-* f. Gmc **furhjōn-*]

fire¹, 1. Active principle operative in combustion, flame, incandescence, (*set* ~ *to*, kindle; *strike* ~, elicit sparks by friction or blow; *no smoke without* ~, always some ground for rumour). 2. State of combustion (*on* ~, burning, fig. excited; *set on* ~, ignite, excite; *set the Thames on* ~, do something remarkable; *catch*, *take*, ~, be ignited). 3. Burning fuel in grate, furnace, etc. (*heap* COALS *of* ~; *burnt child dreads the* ~; *out of the* FRY*ing-pan into the* ~; FAT *is in the* ~), whence **fir̄′ing**¹(3) n. 4. Conflagration, destructive burning, (~!, call for aid at a ~; *pour oil on* ~, add to excitement; *go through* ~ *& water*, face all perils; ~ *& sword*, burning & slaughter); *Greek* ~ (hist.), combustible composition for igniting enemy's ships etc. 5. Luminosity, glow, (*St Elmo's* ~, corposant); burning heat, fever, *St Anthony's* ~, erysipelas). 6. Vehement emotion, fervour, spirit, lively imagination, vivacity, poetic inspiration. 7. Firing of guns (*open*, *cease*, ~; *running* ~, successive shots from line of troops etc., esp. fig. of criticism, objections, etc.; *between two* ~s, shot at from two directions; *line of* ~, path of bullet about to be shot; *under* ~, being shot at; HANG, MISS², ~). 8. ~*-alarm*, automatic arrangement for giving notice of ~; ~*-arm* (usu. pl.), rifle, gun, pistol, etc.; ~*-back*, Sumatran pheasant; ~*-ball*, large meteor, globular lightning, (Mil.) ball filled with combustibles (hist.); ~*-balloon*, made buoyant by heat of combustible burning at its mouth; ~*-bird*, kind of bee-eater; ~*-blast*, disease of plants; ~*-blight*, disease of hops; ~*-bomb*, incendiary; ~*-box*, fuel-chamber of steam-boiler; ~*-brand*, piece of burning wood, person or thing kindling strife; ~*-brick* (proof against ~, used in grates etc.); ‖ ~*-brigade*, organized body of ~men; **~-bug* (colloq.), incendiary, pyromaniac; ~*-clay* (kind used for ~-bricks); ~*-control*, system of regulating ~ of ship's or fort's guns; ~*-crest*, very small bird akin to wren; ~*-cross*, = *fiery* CROSS¹; ~*-damp*, miner's name for carburetted hydrogen, explosive when mixed in certain proportion with air; ~*-dog*, andiron; ~*-drake*, meteor, fiery dragon (in German myth.); ~*-eater*, juggler who eats fire, great fighter, duellist; ~*-engine*,

machine for throwing water to extinguish
~s; ~-escape, apparatus for saving people
in burning house; ~-eyed (poet.), with
glowing eyes; ~-flair, a fish, the sting-
-ray; ~-fly, winged insect emitting phosphorescent light; ‖~-guard, protective
frame or grating in front of ~ in room,
(also) = ~-watcher; ~-hose, hose-pipe for
extinguishing ~s; ~-insurance, against
losses by ~; ~-irons, tongs, poker, &
shovel; ~-light, light from ~-place; ~-
-lighter, prepared kindling-fuel; ~-lock,
antiquated musket in which priming was
ignited by sparks; ~'man, tender of
furnace or steam-engine ~, man employed
to extinguish ~s; ~-new (arch.), = brand-
-new; ‖~-office, insuring against ~; ~-
-opal, kind of opal with internal flame-
-coloured reflections, GIRASOLE; ‖~-pan,
brazier; ~-place, grate or hearth for
room-~; ~-plug (abbr. F.P.), connexion
in water-main for ~-hose; ~-policy, ~-
-insurance office's certificate guarantee-
ing compensation in case of ~; ~-raising,
arson; ~-screen, to keep off heat of ~;
~-ship (hist.), freighted with combustibles
and sent adrift to ignite enemy's ships
etc.; ~-side, space round ~-place, home
life (*~-side chat, radio talk by President
to the nation); ~-step, = firing-step
(FIRE²); ~-stone, kind that resists ~, used
for furnaces etc.; ~-teazer, stoker; ~-trap,
building without proper exits in case of
~; ~-walking, (religious) ceremony of
walking barefoot over white-hot stones,
wood-ashes, etc.; ~-watcher, person keeping watch for ~s esp. those caused by
~-bombs; ~-water, ardent spirits; ~-
wood, wood prepared for fuel; ~'work,
kinds of apparatus giving spectacular
effects by use of combustibles etc.,
squib, rocket, etc., (fig., pl.) display of wit,
passion, etc.; ~-worship, treatment of ~
as a deity. Hence ~'PROOF (-ĭrp-), ~'LESS
(-ĭrl-), aa. [OE fȳr, OS, OHG fiur, f. WG
*fūir, cogn. w. Gk pur]

fire², v.t. & i. Set fire to with intention
of destroying; kindle (explosives); (fig.)
stimulate (the imagination), fill (person)
with enthusiasm; (of explosives, mines)
catch fire; become heated or excited (~
up, show sudden anger); redden (t. & i.);
bake (pottery, bricks), cure (tea, tobacco)
by artificial heat; (Farriery) cauterize;
supply (furnace, engine) with fuel; cause
(explosive, gun) to explode (often off; ~
salute, discharge number of guns as salute;
~ broadside, discharge all guns on one
side of ship), (abs.) shoot, discharge gun
etc. (at, into, on, upon), (fig.) ~ away, begin, go ahead; (of gun etc.) go off; propel
(missile) from gun etc. (fig. ~ off a postcard, a remark); *~ out or ~, expel,
dismiss, reject, (person); firing-party,
-squad, squad detailed to ~ volleys at a
military funeral or carry out a military
execution; firing-step (on which soldier in
trench stands to ~). [f. prec.]

fir'er, n. In vbl senses; esp. single etc. ~,
gun that fires once etc. without reloading.
[-ER¹]

firkin, n. Small cask for liquids, butter,
fish, etc.; (as measure) half of kilderkin.
[15th c. ferdckyn prob. f. MDu (vierde
fourth, -KIN)]

firm¹, n. Partners carrying on business
(‖ long ~, set of swindlers who obtain
goods & do not pay). [in 16th, 18th c.
signature, style, f. Sp. & It. f. Rom. *firma
(L firmare confirm); cf. FARM¹]

firm², a., adv., & v.t. & i. 1. Of solid or
compact structure; fixed, stable; steady,
not shaking; established, immutable, (of
offer etc.) not liable to cancellation after
acceptance; steadfast, unflinching, resolute; constant to; (Commerce., of prices,
goods) maintaining their level or value;
hence ~'LY² adv., ~'NESS n. 2. adv. ~ly
(stand ~, hold ~ to). 3. vb. Solidify (t. &
i.), compact, (soil after planting etc.,
cheese); fix ~ly (plants in soil). [ME, f.
OF ferme f. L firmus]

firm'ament, n. Vault of heaven with its
clouds & stars. Hence ~AL (-ĕn²) a. [ME,
in med. L senses of L firmamentum (firmare
as prec., -MENT)]

firm'an, n. Oriental sovereign's edict,
grant, licence, passport. [f. Pers. ferman]

first, a., n., & adv. 1. Earliest in time or
order (at ~ sight, view, or blush, prima
facie; F~ CAUSE¹; come in ~, win race;
shall do it ~ thing, colloq., before anything
else; in the ~ place, to begin with; the two
etc. ~, the ~ two etc., lit., or = the ~ &
second etc.; often further defined, as the
~ man you meet, was the ~ to do it); foremost in position, rank, or importance
(head etc. ~, with the head etc. in front;
the ~ men in the country; ‖ F~ Lord of the
TREASURY; ‖ F~ Lord of the Admiralty,
parliamentary chief of Navy; ‖ F~ Sea
Lord, professional chief of Navy); coming
next after a specified or implied time
(shall take the ~ train; the ~ cuckoo); (with
the) even one (he doesn't know the ~ thing
about it); unsupported by others, sufficient by itself, (obeyed at her ~ word); basic
or self-evident (~ principles). 2. ~ aid,
help given to hurt person before doctor
comes; ~-born, eldest (child); ~-CHOP⁵;
~ class, set of persons or things grouped
together as better than others, ‖best
accommodation in railway train etc.,
‖ highest division in examination list,
place in this; ~-class, (adj.) belonging to
the ~ class, of best quality, very good,
(adv.) ‖ by the ~ class (travels ~-class);
~ coat, ~ layer of paint; ~ cost, cost
not including profit; ~-day, Sunday; ~
floor, ‖ the one above ground-floor,
*ground-floor; ‖ ~-foot (Sc.), ~ person to
cross threshold in the New Year (also as
vb); ~ form, lowest class in schools; ~-
-fruit (usu. pl.), ~ products of agriculture
for the season esp. as offered to God, ~
results of work etc., (hist.) payment to

some superior by new holder of office; ~-hand, direct, without intermediate agency (at ~ hand, directly); ~ name, Christian name; ~-night(er), (habitual frequenter of) ~ performance of plays; ~-offender (against whom no previous conviction is recorded); ~-rate, of the highest class (the ~-rate Powers, great States of ~-rate importance), excellent, very well, (a ~--rate machine, feeling ~-rate), (as n., Naut.) line-of-battleship of the old type, three--decker (hist.); ~ violin, one of the players taking the uppermost string part in orchestral music, the leader of such players, the leader of a string quartet. 3. n. The ~, person or thing ~ mentioned; from the ~, from the beginning; from ~ to last, throughout; at ~, at the beginning; = ~ day of June etc.; || the F~ (of September, when partridge-shooting begins); (Commerc.) ~ of exchange, ~ of set of bills of even tenor & date; place in ~ class in examination, person who takes this; ~ place in race, winner of it; (pl.) best quality of flour, butter, etc. 4. adv. Before anyone or anything else (often ~ of all, ~ & foremost; ~ come ~ served; ~ & last, taking one thing with another, on the whole; ~ or last, sooner or later); before some specified or implied event, time, etc. (must get this done ~); in preference, rather, (will you see him damned ~); for the ~ time (when did you see him ~?). [OE fyrst, OS, OHG furist, ON fyrstr f. Gmc *furist-, superl. f. *fur-, *for-; see FORE, FORMER, etc.]

first'ling, n. (usu. pl.). First result of anything, first-fruits; first offspring, first born of season. [-LING¹]

first'ly, adv. In the first place, first, (only in enumerating topics; & many writers still prefer first). [-LY²]

firth, frith, n. Arm of sea; estuary. [15 c. Sc., f. ON fjǫrthr FJORD]

fisc, fisk, n. Treasury of ancient Rome, Roman emperor's privy-purse; (rare) State treasury, exchequer. [f. L fiscus]

fis'cal, a. & n. 1. Of public revenue (*~ year*, financial year). 2. n. Legal official in some foreign countries; (Sc.) = PRO-CURATOR ~. Hence ~LY² adv. [f. F, or L fiscalis (prec., -AL)]

fish¹, n. (pl. often fish). 1. (Pop.) animal living in the water, (strictly) vertebrate cold-blooded animal having gills throughout life & limbs (if any) modified into fins, (pretty kettle of ~, confusion, muddle; ~ out of water, person out of his element; drunk, dull, mute, as a ~; drink like a ~, excessively; feed the ~es, be drowned, be seasick; all 's ~ that comes to his net, he takes all he can get; there 's as good ~ in the sea as ever came out of it, no fear of scarcity; FLAT, FLYING, GOLD, JELLY, SHELL¹, SUN, SWORD, etc., ~~); person who is angled for; (colloq.) person of specified kind (cool, loose, queer, etc., ~); the flesh of ~ (~, flesh, & fowl; neither ~,

flesh, nor good red herring, thing of indefinite character; other ~ to fry, more important business to attend to); the F~ or F~es, zodiac constellation. 2. ~-carver, knife for serving ~; ~-globe, for keeping gold~ etc. in; ~-glue, isinglass; ~-hook, used for catching ~, (Naut.) part of anchor-raising tackle; ~-kettle, oval, pan for boiling ~; ~-knife, of silver etc. for eating ~; ~'monger, dealer in ~; ~-pond, in which ~ are kept, (joc.) the sea; ~-pot, wicker trap for eels, lobsters, etc.; ~-slice, carving-knife for~, cook's implement for turning or taking out ~; ~-sound, ~'s swimming-bladder; ~-tail, shaped like ~'s tail (of jet of gas, whence ~-tail burner), ~-tail wind in rifle shooting, one blowing down range & varying in direction; ~-torpedo shaped like ~ & with automatic propulsion; ~-wife, woman selling ~. Hence ~'LET, || ~'MONGER, nn. [OE fisc, OS, OHG fisk, ON fiskr, Goth. fisks f. Gmc *fiskaz cogn. w. L piscis]

fish², v.i. & t. Try to catch fish (~ in troubled waters, make one's profit out of disturbances, whence ~'ERY(2, 3) n.; search for something in or under water; seek by indirect means for (secrets, compliments, etc.), whence ~'ING² a.; (rare) try to catch (fish) or get (coral etc.) from below water; draw out of water, pocket, etc., draw out; (Naut.) ~ the anchor, draw flukes up to gunwale; try to catch fish in (pool etc.; ~ out, exhaust the fish in), whence ~'ABLE a.; get (fact, opinion, secret) out; ~-ing-rod, long tapering usu. jointed rod to which ~-ing-line is attached. [OE fiscian f. Gmc *fiskōjan (prec.)]

fish³, n., & v.t. 1. (Naut.) piece of wood, convex & concave, used to strengthen mast etc.; flat plate of iron, wood, etc. strengthening beam or joint (so ~-plate, one of two holding rails together). 2. v.t. Mend or strengthen (spar etc.), join (rails) with ~. [(n. f. vb) 17th c. f. F ficher fix f. Rom. *figicare f. L figere]

fish⁴, n. Piece of ivory etc. used as counter in games. [f. F fiche f. ficher (prec.)]

fish'er, n. Fisherman (arch.; ~ of men, evangelist, see Matt. iv. 19); fishing animal; ~-man, man who lives by fishing, angler, fishing-boat. [OE fiscere (FISH¹, -ER¹)]

fish'y, a. Abounding in fish; like fish's (~-y eye, dull, vacant-looking); smelling or tasting like fish; consisting of fish (a ~-y repast); (sl.) of dubious character, questionable. Hence ~iLY² adv., ~iNESS n. [-Y²]

fisk. See FISC.

fissi-, fisso-, comb. forms of L fissus see FISSURE, as fissidác'tyl with digits divided, fissíp'arous reproducing by fission.

fiss'ile, a. Cleavable, tending to split. Hence fissil'ITY n. [f. L fissilis (FISSURE, -IL)]

fi'ssion (-shn), n. 1. (biol.). Division of cell etc. into new cells etc. as mode of reproduction. **2.** (phys.). Splitting of atomic nuclei (~ *bomb*, atom bomb). Hence ~ABLE (-sho-) a. [f. L *fissio* (foll., -ION)]

fi'ssure (-sher), n., & v.t. & i. Cleft made by splitting or separation of parts; (Bot., Anat.) narrow opening in organ etc., esp. depression between convolutions of brain; cleavage; (vb) split (t. & i.). [ME, f. OF, or L *fissura* (*findere fiss-* cleave, -URE)]

fist, n., & v.t. **1.** Clenched hand, esp. as used in boxing (~ *law*, the right of the strongest); (joc.) hand ·(*give us your ~*, shake hands), handwriting (*writes a good ~*; *I know his ~*); HAND[1] *over ~*. **2.** v.t. Strike with ~; (Naut.) handle (sail, oar, etc.). Hence ~'ED[2] a. [OE *fȳst*, MLG, OHG *fūst* f. WG *fūsti*]

fis'tic(al), aa. (joc.). Pugilistic. [-ICAL]

fis'ticuffs, n. pl. Fighting with the fists. [c. 1600, f. *fisty* + CUFF[2]]

fis'tul|a, n. Long pipe-like ulcer with narrow mouth; natural pipe or spout in whales, insects, etc. Hence ~AR[1], ~OUS, aa. [L *fistula* pipe, flute;· earlier *fystel* etc. f. OF]

fit[1], **fȳtte**, n. (arch.). Section of a poem. [OE *fitt*, orig. unkn.]

fit[2], n. Paroxysm of periodic ailment, sudden transitory attack of some illness; sudden seizure, with loss of consciousness or convulsions, of hysteria, apoplexy, fainting, paralysis, or epilepsy (*give one a ~*, surprise or outrage him; *beat one into*, *give* one, ~*s*, defeat him easily·); sudden transitory state (*a ~ of energy, idleness, devotion, indifference,* etc.,whence ~'FUL a., ~'fulLY[2] adv., ~'fulNESS n.; *by ~s* (*& starts*), spasmodically); caprice, mood, (*when the ~ was on him*). [ME *fitt* position of danger, perh. = OE *fitt* (once)? conflict; orig. unkn.]

fit[3], a. (-tt-). Well adapted or suited (*for* some purpose or status or *to* do or be; SURVIVAL *of the ~test*); good enough *for* (*a dinner ~ for a king*); becoming, proper, right, (*it is ~ that; see or think ~ to*, decide to); qualified, competent, worthy, *to* do (*not ~ to hold a* CANDLE *to*); in suitable condition, ready, *to* do or *for* (also vulg. as adv., *crying ~ to burst himself*); angry, troubled, or exhausted enough *to* (do something violent, sink to the ground, etc.); in good athletic condition or health (~ *as a* FIDDLE). Hence ~'LY[2] adv. [c. 1440, of unkn. orig.]

fit[4], v.t. & i. (-tt-), & n. **1.** Be in harmony with, become, befit; be of right measure, shape, & size for (esp. of dress; often abs., as *the* CAP[1]~*s*); fill up, exactly correspond to; (receptacle, fellow, etc., or abs.; often *in*, *into*, *in with*), make to do this; make suitable, adapt, *for*, *to* with n. or inf.; make competent *for* or *to*; ~ *on*, try on (garment); supply, furnish, (ship etc., rarely person) *with*; ~ *out*, *up*, equip; hence ~t'ER[1] n., esp.: (Tailoring and Dressmaking) one who supervises cut-

ting, ~ting, altering, etc., of garments; mechanic who ~s (up) all kinds of machinery. **2.** n. Adaptation, adjustment, style in which garment ~s (*a tight, bad, excellent, ~*); ~·*out*, equipment. [16th c., perh. f. prec.]

fitch, n. (Brush made of) polecat's hair. [16th c. = polecat, f. foll. or its MDu. source]

fitch'ew (-ōō), n. Foumart, polecat. [14th c., f. OF *fichau*, also *fissel*, f. MDu. *fisse, vitche*]

fit'ment, n. Piece of fixed furniture. [FIT[4], -MENT]

fit'ness, n. Being fit; moral worthiness; propriety (*the ~ of things*, what is right or appropriate). [-NESS]

fitt'ing[1], n. In vbl senses; esp.: (usu. pl.) fixture(s), apparatus, furniture; (Engin.) ~·*shop*, place where parts are put together. [-ING[1]]

fitt'ing[2], a. In vbl senses; esp. becoming, proper, right, whence ~LY[2] adv. [-ING[2]]

fit'·up, n. (Theatr. colloq). Temporary or portable stage and stage-fittings; ~ (*company*), minor travelling theatrical troupe carrying makeshift scenery. [FIT[4]]

five, a. & n. One more than four, 5, v, V, (*twenty-~*, ~*·&·twenty*); ~ *o'clock*; *How old are you?*—*F~*); the number ~ (*twice ~ is ten*); set of ~ things; card, die, or domino with ~ pips; (also fiv'ER[1] n.) hit at cricket for ~ runs, || £5 note; *bunch of ~s*, hand; (pl.) gloves, shoes, etc., of fifth size; (pl.) the ~-per-cents (colloq.); ~·*day week* (having ~ working days); ~·*finger exercise*, on piano for exercising all fingers, keeping them on same ~ notes all the time; ~·*finger*, kinds of plant (as cinquefoil, oxlip), also starfish; || ~·*line*(d) *whip*, urgent summons to attend in House of Parliament (now disused); ~·*o'clock tea*, light afternoon meal; ~'*penny* (*also pr.* fĭp-), costing, rated at, 5*d*; || ~·*per-cents*, stock or shares paying 5% ; ~·*year plan* (for the economic development of Russia in 5 years, inaugurated in 1928, later of other countries & repeated in Russia). Hence ~'FOLD (-vf-) a. & adv. [OE, OS *fíf*, OHG *fimf*, ON *fimm*, Goth. *fimf* f. Gmc *fimfi* cogn. w. L *quinque*, Gk *pente*]

fives (-vz), n. Ball-game played with hands or bat in court with two, three, or four walls. [pl. of *five* used as sing.; significance unknown]

fix[1], v.t. & i. Make firm or stable, fasten, secure, implant (principles, memory, etc.) (*in*, *on*, *to*, etc.); direct steadily, set, (eyes, gaze, affection, attention) *on* or *upon*; (of object) attract & hold (attention, eyes, etc.); make (eyes, features), or become, rigid; deprive of, lose, volatility or fluidity, congeal (t. & i.); make (colour, photographic image) fast, whence ~'ER(2) n.; single out (person) *with* one's eyes etc.; place definitely or permanently, station, establish; take up one's position; settle one's choice, decide, (up)on; assign precise position of; refer (thing, person) to definite place or time; determine incidence of (liability etc.); settle, determine, specify, (price, date, place); arrest changes or development in (language, literature); mend, repair; *(freq. up) arrange, organize, prepare; ~ed focus (Photog.), best position of lens for general snapshot work. [ME; ult. f. L fixus p.p. of figere fix; partly thr. obs. fix a. (OF fix), & med. L fixare]

fix², n. Dilemma, position hard to escape from; finding position, position found, by bearings or astronomical observations (radio ~, position of aircraft, ship, etc., found by radio). [f. prec.]

fixā'tion, n. Fixing, being fixed; process of rendering solid, coagulation; process of combining a gas with a solid; (Psycho-anal.) arrested mental development. [f. med. L fixatio (fixare see FIX¹, -ATION)]

fix'ative, a. & n. Tending to fix; (n.) substance used to fix colours or drawings. [-ATIVE]

fix'ature, n. Gummy preparation for fixing the hair. [as prec., -URE]

fixed (-kst), a. In vbl senses, esp.: ~ idea, one tending to become a monomania; ~ acid or oil, one not evaporable without decomposition; ~ point, where policeman is permanently stationed; ~ star, one seeming to keep same relative position to others (opp. planet); ~ CAPITAL²; ~ property, land & houses. [-ED¹]

fix'edly, adv. In fixed manner; esp. (of looking) intently. [-LY²]

fix'edness, n. Fixed state, immobility, permanence, steadfastness. [-NESS]

*fix'ings (-z), n. pl. Apparatus, equipment; trimming of dress or dish, adjuncts. [-ING¹]

fix'ity, n. Fixed state; (Phys.) property of enduring heat without being volatilized or losing weight; stability, permanence. [f. L fixus see FIX¹ +-ITY]

fix'ture, n. Thing fixed or fastened in position; (Law; pl.) articles of a personal nature annexed to house or land; person or thing confined to or established in one place (chiefly in pred., as seems to be a ~); (Athlet. etc.) (date appointed for) meet, race, etc. [changed f. obs. fixure f. LL fixura (figere fix-, -URE)]

fiz'gig (-g-), n. & a. Giddy flirtatious young woman; kind of small firework, cracker; (adj.) flighty. [prob. f. FIZZ+gig (obs. = flighty girl)]

fizz, v.i., & n. (Make) hissing or spluttering sound, whence ~'Y² a.; (sl.) champagne. [imit.]

fiz'zle, v.i., & n. Hiss or splutter feebly (n., this sound); ~ out, come to lame conclusion; (n.) fiasco. [f. as prec. +-LE(3)]

flăbb'ergast (-gah-), v.t. Dumbfound, so astonish as to incapacitate. [from 1722; perh. f. flabby, aghast]

flăbb'ily, a. Hanging down, flaccid, limp, (usu. of flesh); nerveless, feeble, (of language or character). Hence ~INESS n. [alt. f. earlier flappy (FLAP, -Y²)]

flabĕll'ate, flabĕll'iform, aa. (bot. & zool.). Fan-shaped. [f. L flabellum fan (flare blow)+-ATE², -FORM]

flăc'cid (-ks-), a. Hanging loose or wrinkled, limp, flabby, (usu. of flesh); relaxed, drooping; wanting vigour, feeble. Hence **flăccid'ITY** n. [f. F flaccide or L flaccidus (flaccus flabby)]

flăg¹, n. Kinds of plant with bladed leaf growing on moist ground, esp. various species of iris; ~s or ~ collect., kinds of coarse grass; long slender blade of a plant. Hence ~g'Y² (-g-) a. [ME; cf. Du. flag, Da. flæg]

flăg², n., & v.t. (-gg-). (Also ~'stone) flat slab of rock for paving, (pl.) pavement made of these, also ~g'ING¹(6) (-g-) n.; (vb) pave with ~s. [15th c. sod, cf. Icel. flag spot whence sod has been cut out, ON flaga slab of stone; cf. FLAW¹]

flăg³, n. (Also ~-feather) quill-feather of bird's wing. [perh. f. obs. flag drooping f. OF flac f. L flaccus flabby]

flăg⁴, n., & v.t. (-gg-). 1. Piece of bunting or other stuff, usu. oblong or square, attached by one edge to staff or halyard & used as standard, ensign, or signal (black ~, pirate's ensign, also ~ hoisted outside prison to announce execution of criminal; white ~, ~ of truce, ~ disclaiming hostile intention; yellow ~, displayed by ship with infectious disease on board, hospital ship, or ship in quarantine; ~ of convenience, foreign ~ under which a ship is registered to avoid taxation etc. at home; ~ of truce, white, indicating desire to parley; DIP¹~; hoist the ~, as claim to discovered territory; lower or strike one's ~, take it down as salute or sign of surrender); (Naut.) ~ carried by ~ship as emblem of admiral's rank afloat (hoist, strike, one's ~, assume, relinquish, command); tail of setter or Newfoundland dog; ~-boat, serving as mark in aquatic matches; ‖ ~-captain, captain of ~ship; ~-day ‖ (on which money is raised for a cause by sale to passers-by etc. of ~s to be worn as evidence of having given); *F~ Day, June 14, anniversary of the adoption of the Stars and Stripes in 1777; ~-lieutenant, admiral's A.D.C.; ‖ ~-list, roll of ~-officers, i.e. admirals, vice-admirals, or rear-admirals; ~-man, signaller at races etc.; ~-rank (of ~-officers); ~'ship, having admiral on board; ~'staff, pole on which ~ is hung; ~-station, where trains stop only if signalled; ~-wagging (sl.), signalling; ~-waver, agitator. 2. v.t. Place ~ on or over; mark out with ~s; inform (person), communicate (information, that), by ~-signals. [orig. unkn.; perh. as FLAG³, FLAG⁵; earliest in E (15th-16th c.) whence perh. in other Teut. langg.]

flăg[5], v.i. (-gg-). Hang down, flap loosely; droop, fade, become limp; lag, lose vigour, grow languid; fall off in interest. [15 c., rel. to obs. *flag* (FLAG³)]

flagĕll'ant (*also* flăj¹), n. & a. (One) who scourges himself; given to flogging. [f. L *flagellare* (FLAGELLUM), -ANT]

flă'gell|āte¹, v.t. Scourge. Hence or cogn. ~A'TION, ~ātoR, nn., ~ātoRY a. [as prec., -ATE³]

flagĕll'|um, n. (pl. ~a). (Bot.) runner, creeping shoot; (Zool. Biol.) lashlike appendage. Hence **flă'gellate²** [-ATE²], ~īFORM, aa. [L, = whip]

flăgeolĕt'¹ (-jol-; *also* flăj¹), n. Small flute blown at end. [F, dim. of OF *flag(e)ol* of unkn. orig.]

flăgeolĕt'² (-jol-; *also* -lā), n. Kind of kidney-bean. [F, = *fageolet* dim. of *fageol* f. L *faseolus*]

flagi'tious (-shŭs), a. Deeply criminal, atrocious, heinous, villainous. Hence ~LY² adv., ~NESS n., -(shŭs-). [ME, f. L *flagitiosus* (*flagitium* crime, -OUS)]

flăg'on, n. Large vessel usu. with handle, spout, & lid, to hold liquor for table; similar vessel for Eucharist; (Wine-trade) flattened globular glass bottle holding nearly two bottles. [ME *flakon* f. OF *flacon* (FLASK, -OON)]

flăg'rant, a. Glaring, notorious, scandalous, (of offence or offender). Hence or cogn. **flăg'RANCY** n., ~LY² adv. [f. L *flagrare* blaze, -ANT]

flail, n. Hand threshing-implement, wooden staff at end of which a short heavy stick hangs swinging. [OE **flegil*, OS *flegil*, OHG *flegel*, WG f. L *flagellum*]

flair, n. Selective instinct for what is excellent, paying, etc. [F (*flairer* to smell f. Rom. **flagrare* = *fragrare* see FRAGRANT)]

flăk, n. (German) anti-aircraft fire; ~ *ship*, German anti-aircraft vessel. [abbr. of *F'liegerabwehrkanone*]

flāke¹, n. Rack for storing oatcake etc.; stage for drying fish etc. [ME *fleke* f. ON *flake*, *fleke* hurdle]

flāke², n., & v.i. & t. 1. Light fleecy tuft, esp. of snow; portion of ignited matter thrown off; thin broad piece peeled off, chiplike piece (*corn*, *wheat*, ~); natural division of fish's flesh; layer; carnation with striped petals; ~*-white*, pigment made from white-lead in ~s; hence **flāk'y²** a. 2. vb. Fall like, sprinkle as with, snow; take, come, *away* or *off* in ~s. [ME, orig. unkn.; cf. ON *flakna* flake off]

flăm, n. Sham story, trick, deception. [17th c., goes with earlier FLIM-FLAM]

flăm'beau (-bō), n. (pl. -*s* or -*x*, pr. -z). Torch, esp. of several thick waxed wicks. [F, f. *flambe* FLAME¹ (= med. L *flambellum*)]

flămboy'ant, a. & n. 1. Marked by wavy flamelike lines (of French 15th & 16th c. Archit.); floridly decorated; gorgeously

coloured; ostentatious, showy. 2. n. Kinds of flame-coloured flower. [F, part. of *flamboyer* (*flambe* FLAME¹)]

flāme¹, n. (Portion of) ignited gas (*the* ~*s*, fire, esp. as consuming); visible combustion (*in* ~*s*; *burst into* ~ or ~*s*); bright light, brilliant colouring; passion, esp. of love (*fan the* ~, make it more intense); (joc.) sweetheart (*an old* ~ *of mine*); kinds of moth; ~*-projector* or *-thrower*, = FLAMEMENWERFER. Hence ~'LESS (-ml-) (poet.), **flām'y²**, aa. [ME *flame*, *flaum(b)e* f. OF *flame* (f. L *flamma*) & *flambe* (f. L *flammula* dim. of *flamma*)]

flāme², v.i. & t. Emit flames, blaze, (often *away*, *forth*, *out*, *up*); (of passion) burst out; (of persons, break *out*, blaze *up*, into anger; shine, gleam, (~ *up*, blush violently); move like flame; send (signal) by fire; subject to action of flame (*sterilized by flaming*). [ME *flam(b)e* f. OF *flam(b)er* (prec.)]

flām'ĕn, n. (Rom. Ant.). A god's priest. [L]

flām'ing, a. In vbl senses; esp.: very hot (*a* ~ *sun*); bright-coloured; exaggerated, over-laudatory (*a* ~ *description*); ~ *onions*, anti-aircraft projectile resembling a chain of fire-balls. [-ING²]

flamingō (-ngg-), n. (pl. ~*es*). Tall long-necked web-footed (sub)tropical bird with pink, scarlet, & black plumage. [Port. (-*engo*) perh. f. Rom. *flama* flame + -*enc* = -ING³]

flămm'able, a. (Rare, & chiefly in *non-*~, for) INFLAMMABLE.

flămm'enwerfer (-vārfer), n. Machine spouting liquid fire in war. [G, = flame-thrower]

flăn, n. Pastry spread with jam, conserves, etc. [F]

flânerie (flah'nrē), **flâneur** (flah'nēr), nn. Idling, idler. [F]

flănge (-j), n., & v.t. 1. Projecting flat rim, collar, or rib. 2. v.t. Provide with ~. [orig. uncert.; w. obs. *flanch* perh. rel. to OF *flanchir* (see FLANK), *flangir* bend]

flănk, n., & v.t. 1. Fleshy part of side between ribs & hip; side of building, mountain, etc.; right or left side of army or body of troops (*in* ~, at the side; TURN¹ ~ *of*). 2. v.t. Guard or strengthen on the ~, menace ~ of, take in ~, enfilade, rake; be posted or situated at ~ of; march past ~ of; OUT~. [ME, f. OF *flanc* (*flanche*) f. Gallo-Rom. **flancum* (-*ca*) f. OFrank. *hlanca* side]

flănk'er, n. Fortification guarding or menacing flank; (Mil., usu. pl.) flank skirmisher(s); thing that flanks anything [-ER¹]

flănn'el, n. & a. 1. Woven woollen stuff, usu. without nap (pl., kinds of this, ~ goods); (pl.) underclothing of ~, ~ bandages, garments esp. trousers of ~ whence ~IED² (-ld) a.; piece of ~ used in washing person or cleaning floor, whence **flănn'el** (-ll-) v.t.; hence ~ETTE² (2) n., ~LY² a. 2. adj. Made of ~. [perh. f. W *gwlanen* (*gwlân* wool)]

flăp, v.t. & i. (-pp-), & n. **1.** Strike with something broad, drive (flies etc.) *away or off*; (of birds) strike (something) with flat of wing; swing or sway about, flutter, oscillate; move (t. & i. of wings) up & down; beat the wings. **2.** n. Light blow with something broad; motion of wing etc.; (colloq.) state of excitement (*be in, get into, a ~*); broad hanging piece hinged or attached by one side only, e.g. trapdoor, pocket-cover, hat-brim, table-leaf, valve, fish's gill-cover, piece of skin left in amputations; open mushroom-top (cf. *button*). [ME, imit.]

flăpdoŏ'dle, n. Nonsense, bunkum. [orig. unkn.]

flăp'jăck, n. Small cake of flour fried in grease; flat vanity case for face-powder. [FLAP + JACK[1]]

flăpp'er n. Flat fly-killing instrument; bird-scaring clapper; young wild-duck or partridge; (sl.) girl in late teens; hinged or hanging piece, flap; broad fin; crustacean's tail; (sl.) hand; (w. ref. to Laputans) person, thing, that jogs one's memory or wits. [-ER[1]]

flāre, v.t. & i., & n. **1.** (Cause to) bulge gradually upwards (of ship's sides); spread outwards gradually (as the sides of a ship, a woman's skirt, etc.); blaze with bright unsteady flame, glow as with flame, (often *about, away, out*; part., gaudy, over-conspicuous); ~ *up*, burst into sudden blaze or anger. **2.** n. Dazzling irregular light, unshaded flame in open air; sudden outburst of flame; signal light used at sea; bright light used as signal; container of combustible material, dropped from aircraft to illuminate target area etc.; ~-*path*, area illuminated to enable aircraft to land or take off; ostentation; upward bulge in ship's sides; gradual widening (esp. of a skirt); ~-*up*, sudden breaking into flame, short brilliant popularity or display, burst of anger, uproarious merrymaking. [orig. unkn.]

flăsh[1], v.i. & t. Break suddenly into flame, give out flame or sparks, (~ *in the pan*, fail after showy start, like priming of old guns); emit or reflect light, gleam; send, reflect, (something) like a flash or in flashes (*eyes ~ fire, ~ back defiance*); burst suddenly into view or perception (~*ed upon me that* —); move swiftly; ~ *up* or *out*, show sudden passion; cause to gleam (~*ed his sword*; *had a torch ~ed in my face*); send by telegraph (*news was ~ed over England*); (Glass-making) spread out (t. & i.) into a sheet, cover (plain glass) with coloured film; (of water) rush along, rise & flow, fill or flood (stream etc.) with water; ~-*board*, for sending more water from mill-dam into mill-race; ~-*pipe*, extra pipe with line of holes for lighting high gas-lamp; ~*ing-point*, temperature at which vapour from oil etc. may be ignited. [in 14th c. of the sea etc., of imit. orig.; cf. *clash, plash*]

flăsh[2], n. Sudden transitory blaze (~ *in the pan*, abortive effort; see prec.), time occupied by it, instant, (*in a ~*); ostentation; sudden short access of feeling (*a ~ of hope*); (Cinemat.) exposure of a scene, recapitulation of an earlier scene (also ~'*back*); preparation for colouring spirits; rush of water let down weir to take boat over shallows, contrivance for producing this; (Mil.) coloured patch of cloth as distinguishing emblem of division etc.; ~-*light*, used for signals & in lighthouses, also for photographing by night etc., (also) electric torch; ~-*point*, (now more usu. for) FLASH[1]*ing-point*, also fig. [f. prec.]

flăsh[3], a. Gaudy, showy, counterfeit (~ *notes, money*); cant, slang; connected with thieves, tramps, etc. [f. prec.]

flăsh'ing, n. Strip of metal to obviate flooding or soaking at joint of roofing etc. [18th c., = obs. *flash* (16th c.)]

flăsh'|y̆, a. Brilliant but shallow or transitory, cheaply attractive; showy, gaudy; given to display. Hence ~ĭLY[2] adv., ~ĭNESS n. [-Y[2]]

flask (-ah-), n. (Also *powder-~*) leather or metal case for carrying sportsman's supply of gunpowder; Italian narrow-necked wickered wine or oil bottle; traveller's pocket bottle of metal or (usu. leather-covered) glass for wine, spirit, etc. [16th c. 'powder-flask' f. OF *flasque*, 17th c. 'bottle' f. It. *fiasco* f. LL *flasca, flasco*; ult. orig. unkn.]

flask'ĕt (-ah-), n. ‖ Long shallow basket (arch.); ‖ clothes-basket; small flask. [f. OF *flasquet* (*flasque* FLASK, -ET[1])]

flăt[1], n. Storey (now rare); suite of rooms on one floor as residence; *apartment; (Nav.) ship's compartment on to which cabins etc. open (*after cabin, wardroom, ~*). [alt. f. obs. *flet* = OE *flet* cogn. w. foll.]

flăt[2], a. & adv., n., & v.t. (-tt-). **1.** Horizontal, level; spread out, lying at full length, (*fell ~*; ~ *against the wall*; *with the ~ hand*); even, smooth, unbroken, without projection, (~ *tint*, uniform); with broad level surface & little depth; unqualified, plain, downright, (~ *denial, refusal*; ~ *nonsense, blasphemy*; *that's ~*, let there be no doubt about it); dull, lifeless, monotonous, (*fall ~*, prove a failure, not win applause; *market is, prices are, ~*, inactive, sluggish); slow-witted; dejected, without energy, (~ *beer*, that has lost its effervescence); (Mus.) below the true pitch (*B, D*, etc., ~, a semitone lower than B, D, etc.; *sings ~*); ~ *aback* (emphat. for ABACK naut. & fig.); ~-*boat*, with ~ bottom for transport in shallow water; ~ *candlestick*, with broad base & short stem for carrying about; ~-*fish*, family including sole, turbot, plaice, etc.; ~-*foot(ed)*, (having) foot not normally arched; ~-*iron*, for ironing linen etc.; ~ *out*, all out, at top speed, using all one's strength or resources; ~ *race*, over level ground (opp. hurdle-race or steeplechase); ~ *rate* (the same in all cases, not proportional etc.); hence ~'LY² adv., ~'NESS n., ~t'EN⁶ v.t. & i. (~*ten out*, bring aircraft parallel with ground), ~t'ISH¹(2) a., ~'WAYS, ~'WISE, advv. 2. n. What is ~ (*on, from, the* ~, of drawings etc. as opposed to sculpture), ~ part of anything (*the* ~ *of the hand, with the* ~ *of his sword*); level ground, plain, low land, swamp; ~-bottomed boat; shallow basket; (Theatr.) section of scenery mounted on frame (*join the* ~*s*, transf., make a thing into a coherent whole, preserve appearance of a consistent attitude); (sl.) duffer, dupe; (Mus.) note lowered a semitone below natural pitch, sign indicating this lowering, *sharps & ~s*, black notes on piano. 3. v.t. Make ~ (chiefly in manufacturing processes; elsewhere ~*ten*). [ME, f. ON *flatr* of unkn. orig.]

flătt'er, v.t. Court, fawn upon; compliment unduly, overpraise; gratify vanity of, make feel honoured; inspire with (esp. unfounded) hope; please one*self* with the belief (*that*); gratify (eye, ear, etc.); ~*ing unction*, salve one administers to one's own conscience or self-esteem (*Haml.* III. iv. 145); (of portrait, painter, etc.) exaggerate good looks of. Hence or cogn. ~ER¹, flătt'ERY(4, 5), nn., ~ingLY² adv. [ME; orig. obsc., ult. rel. to OF *flater* to smooth]

flăt'ŭl|ent, a. Generating gas in the alimentary canal; caused by, attended with, troubled with, accumulation of such gas; inflated, puffed up, windy, pretentious. Hence or cogn. ~ENCE, ~ENCY, nn., ~ently² adv. [F (foll., -ULENT)]

flăt'us, n. Wind in stomach or bowels. [L, vbl n. (*flare* blow)]

flaunt, v.i. & t., & n. 1. Wave (t. & i.) proudly; display oneself or one's finery; show off, parade, (one*self*, finery, etc.); hence ~'ingLY² adv., ~'Y² a. 2. n. ~*ing* motion. [orig. unkn.]

flaut'ist, n. Flute-player. [f. It. *flautista* (*flauto* FLUTE)]

flaves'cent, a. Turning yellow, yellowish. [f. L *flavescere* (*flavus* yellow, -ESCENT)]

flăv'in, n. Surgical antiseptic, & yellow dye, got from dyer's oak. [L *flavus* yellow, -IN]

flăv'ō-prōt'ĕin (or'-tēn), n. One of group of conjugated proteins which constitute the yellow oxidizable enzymes. [prec., PROTEIN]

flāv'our (-ver), n., & v.t. 1. Aroma, mingled sensation of smell & taste, distinctive taste; undefinable characteristic quality; hence flāv'orous, ~LESS, ~SOME, (-ver-), aa. 2. v.t. Give ~ to, season; hence ~ING¹(3) (-ver-) n. [ME, f. OF *flaur, fraor*, etc. (perh. f. L *fragrare* be FRAGRANT), w. assim. to *savour*]

flaw¹, n., & v.t. & i. 1. Crack, breach, rent; imperfection, blemish; (Law) invalidating defect in document, procedure, evidence, etc.; hence ~'LESS a., ~'lèssLY² adv., ~'lèssNESS n. 2. vb. Crack (t. & i.), damage, mar. [ME, perh. f. ON *flaga* slab cf. FLAG², FLAKE²]

flaw², n. Squall of wind; short storm. [16th c., prob. f. MDu. *vlāghe* (Du. *vlaag*), MLG *vlāge*]

‖ **flawn,** n. (arch.). Kind of custard. [ME, f. OF *flaon* (now *flan*) f. LL *fladonem* nom. -*o* f. OFrank. *flado* flat cake]

flăx, n. Blue-flowered plant cultivated for its textile fibre & its seeds called linseed; (with qualifying word prefixed or suffixed) kinds of similar plant, as *dwarf, toad, ~, ~-dodder*; fibres of ~, dressed or undressed; cloth of ~, linen; ~-*lily*, New Zealand plant of lily family yielding a valuable fibre; ~-*seed*, linseed. [OE *flæx*, OS, OHG *flahs*, f. WG **flahsa*]

flăx'en, a. Of flax; (of hair) coloured like dressed flax, pale yellowish-brown. [-EN⁵]

flay, v.t. Strip off skin or hide of; (fig.) criticize severely; pillage, plunder, (person); peel off (skin, bark, peel); pare off (turf); ‖ ~-*flint*, extortioner, miser. [OE *flēan*, MDu., *vlae(gh)en*, ON *flá* f. Gmc **flahan*]

flea, n. Small wingless jumping insect feeding on human & other blood (*send one away with a* ~ *in his ear*, discomfited by a reproof or repulse); *sand-~, water-~*, small jumping crustaceans; = ~-*beetle*; small or contemptible creature; ~-*bag* (sl.), sleeping-bag; ~-*bane, ~-wort*, kinds of plant supposed to drive away~s; ~-*beetle*, jumping beetle infesting hops; ~-*bite*, lit., & fig. slight inconvenience or expense, mere trifle, also small reddish spot in animal's colouration (~-*bitten*, sprinkled with these on lighter ground; also lit.); **~ circus*, a show of performing ~s; ~-*dock*, butterbur; ~-*louse*, jumping plant-louse; ~-*pit* (sl.), allegedly verminous place of public assembly, e.g. cinema. [OE *flēah*, MDu. *vlō*, OHG *flōh*, ON *fló* f. Gmc **flauh-* or **thlauh-* (FLEE)]

fleam, n. Lancet for bleeding horses. [f. OF *flieme* f. Rom. **fleutomum* f. LL *flebotomus* f. Gk *phlebotomon* see PHLEBOTOMY]

flèche (-āsh), n. Slender spire perforated with windows, esp. at intersection of nave & transept. [F, orig. = arrow]

flĕck, n., & v.t. 1. Spot in the skin, freckle; patch of colour or light; small particle, speck; hence ~'LESS a. 2. v.t. Mark with ~s, dapple, variegate. [f. ON *flekkr* n. *flekka* vb, or MLG, MDu. *vlecke*; cf. OHG *flec, fleccho* (G *fleck*)]

flĕck'er, v.t. Dapple, variegate; scatter in patches. [prec. + -ER⁵]

flĕd. See FLEE.

flĕdge, v.t. Provide with feathers or plumage, wing for flight, deck with feathers or down. Hence ~'LESS (-jl-) a. [f. obs. adj. *fledge* corresp. to late OE (*un*)*fligge*,

MDu. *vlugge*, OHG *flucchi* f. WG **fluggja* (**flug-* FLY²)]

fledg(e)'ling (-jl-), n. Young bird; inexperienced person. [as prec. +-LING¹]

flee, v.i. & t. (*fled*; *fly*, *flying*, are now usu. substituted for ~, ~*ing*; *is fled*, see ED¹(2), or *has fled*). Run away, seek safety in flight, (*from*, *before*); vanish, cease, pass away; run away from, leave abruptly; eschew, shun. [OE *fléon*, OS, OHG *fliohan*, ON *flý(j)a*, Goth. *thliuhan* f. Gmc **thleuhan*]

fleece, n., & v.t. **1.** Woolly covering of sheep or similar animal (*Golden F~*, Austrian & Spanish order of Knighthood); quantity of wool shorn from a sheep at once; rough, abundant, or woolly head of hair; thing like a ~, white cloud, falling snow, etc.; (Carding) thin sheet of cotton or wool fibre; hence (-)fleeceD³ (-ĕst), flee'cy², aa. **2.** v.t. Shear (sheep; rare); strip of money, property, etc. (also *of*), whence ~'ABLE a.; overspread as with ~ (*sky* ~*d with clouds*). [OE *fléos*, Du., MHG *vlies*, f. WG **fleus-*]

fleer, v.i., & n. **1.** Laugh impudently or mockingly, gibe, jeer, sneer. **2.** n. Mocking look or speech. [cf. Norw. & Sw. dial. *flira* to grin]

fleet¹, n. Naval armament, number of warships under one command-in-chief (*the* ~, the navy); number of ships or boats sailing in company; group of aircraft; ~ *of cabs, taxis*, etc., those owned by one proprietor; ‖ *F~ Air Arm*, aviation service of Royal Navy. [OE *fléot* ship, shipping (*fléotan* FLEET⁵)]

‖ **fleet²**, n. Creek, inlet; *The F~*, stream, now covered sewer, running into Thames E. of F~ Street, also the prison that stood near it (*F~ marriage*, performed by a *F~ parson* or disreputable clergyman in & about the F~ ready to marry clandestinely); *F~ Street*, (used for) the press, London journalism. [OE *fleot*, MLG *flēt*, MDu., LG *vliet*, MHG *vliez(e)*, ON *fljót* cogn. w. FLEET⁵]

fleet³, a. (poet. or literary). Swift, nimble. Hence ~'LY² adv., ~'NESS n. [f. ON *fljótr*, cogn. w. FLEET⁵]

‖ **fleet⁴**, a. & adv. Shallow (of water); at or to no great depth (*plough* or *sow* ~). [perh. repr. OE **fléat*, cogn. w. foll.]

fleet⁵, v.i. Glide away, vanish, be transitory; pass rapidly, slip *away*; move swiftly, fly. Hence ~'ING² a., ~'ingLY² adv. [OE *fléotan*, OS *fliotan*, OHG *fliozan*, ON *fljóta* f. Gmc **fleutan*, cogn. w. FLOAT²]

Flem'ing, n. Inhabitant of Flanders. [f. MDu. *Vlāming*, w. assim. to foll.]

Flem'ish, a. & n. (Language) of Flanders; ~ BOND¹. [f. MDu. *Vlaemisch* (prec., -ISH¹)]

flench, flinch¹, flense, v.t. Cut up (whale); flay (seal). [f. Da. *flense*, cf. Norw. *flinsa* flay]

flesh¹, n. **1.** Soft substance between the skin & the bones, esp. the muscular part of animal bodies (~ *& blood*, the body or its material, mankind, human nature with its emotions & infirmities; as adj., actually living, not supernatural or imaginary; one's *own* ~ *& blood*, near relations, descendants; ~ *& fell*, the whole body; as adv., entirely; *one* ~, united as one personality, see *Gen.* ii. 24; *proud* ~, overgrowth of granulations springing on wound; *make his* ~ *creep*, frighten or horrify him esp. with dread of the supernatural). **2.** Pulpy substance of fruit or plant. **3.** Plumpness, fat, (*lose, put on,* ~, grow thin, fat); *in* ~, fat. **4.** Tissue of animal bodies (excluding fish & sometimes fowls) as food, meat, (~-*feeding*, ~-*eater*, etc.; *neither* FISH¹, ~, *nor* etc.). **5.** Visible surface of human body (~-*colour*, -*ed*, yellowish pink); = ~ *& blood* above (*all* ~, whatever has bodily life; *the way of all* ~, the experience common to all men; *in the* ~, in bodily form, in life; *after the* ~, corporeally). **6.** The sensual appetites (*sins of the* ~, unchastity). **7.** ~-*brush*, -*glove*, for stimulating circulation by rubbing; ~-*fly*, depositing eggs or larvae in dead ~; ~-*pots* (w. ref. to *Exod.* xvi. 3), high living; ~ *side* or ~, side of a hide that adjoined the ~; ~ *tights*, fleshings; ~ *tints*, esp. painter's rendering of ~-colour; ~-*wound*, one not reaching bone or vital organ. Hence ~'LESS a. [OE *flǣsc*, OS *flēsk*, OHG *fleisc*, ON *flesk* f. Gmc **flaisk-*]

flesh², v.t. Incite (hound etc.) by taste of blood; initiate in bloodshed; inflame by foretaste of success; use *sword* etc. for first time on flesh (or fig. *pen, wit*, etc.). [f. prec.]

‖ **flesh'er**, n. (Sc.). Butcher. [f. FLESH +-ER¹]

flesh'ings (-z), n. pl. Close flesh-coloured garment usu. of silk worn on stage etc. to represent natural skin. [FLESH¹, -ING¹]

flesh'l|y̌, a. Carnal, lascivious, sensual, (esp. of appetites etc., rarely of persons); mortal, material, not divine or spiritual; worldly. Hence ~iNESS n. [OE *flǣsclic* (FLESH¹, -LIKE)]

flesh'|y̌, a. Plump, fat; of flesh, without bone; (of plant or fruit tissue) pulpy; like flesh. Hence ~iNESS n. [-Y²]

fleur-de-lis (flĕr'delē'); pl. *fleurs-* pr. as sing.), **flow'er-de-lūce'** (arch. & U.S.), n. Iris flower; heraldic lily; (sing. or pl.) royal arms of France, French royal family, France. [F (first form), = lily flower (*lis* lily); the arch. E form is unexpl.]

fleur'et (-oor-), n. Ornament like small flower. [f. F *fleurette* (*fleur* FLOWER, -ETTE)]

fleuron (flĕrawn'), n. Flower-shaped ornament in architecture or printing, on coins, etc. [F]

fleur'y (-oori), **flor'y̌**, a. (her.). Decorated with fleurs-de-lis. [f. F *fleuré*, OF *flore* (*fleur* FLOWER, -Y⁴)]

flew. See FLY².

flews (-z), n. pl. Hanging lips of blood-hound etc. [orig. unkn.]

flex[1], v.t. Bend (in scientific use of bend-ing limb etc. by flexor, or in Geol. of distorted strata). [f. L *flectere flex-*]

flex[2], n. Flexible insulated wire used for conveying electric current. [abbr. of foll.]

flex'i|ble, a. That will bend without breaking, pliable, pliant; easily led, manageable; adaptable, versatile; supple, complaisant. Hence or cogn. ~BIL'ITY n., ~bLY[2] adv. [f. OF, or L *flexibilis* (FLEX[1], -IBLE)]

flex'ile, a. Supple, mobile; tractable; versatile. Hence **flĕxil'**ITY n. [f. L *flexilis* (FLEX[1], -IL)]

fle'xion (-kshn), n. Bending, curvature, bent state, (esp. of limb or joint); bent part, curve; (Gram.)=inflexion, whence ~AL, ~LESS, (-kshon-), aa.; (Math.)=flexure. [f. L *flexio* (FLEX[1], -ION)]

flex'or, n. (Also ~ *muscle, tendon*) muscle that bends a part (opp. EXTENSOR). [FLEX[1], -OR]

flex'uōse, a. (bot.). Serpentine, undulating. Hence **flĕxuōs'**o- comb. form. [f. L *flexuosus* (*flexus -ūs* a bend see FLEX[1], -OSE[1])]

flex'uous, a. Full of bends, winding. Hence or cogn. **flĕxuōs'**ITY (-ŏs-) n., ~LY[2] adv. [as prec., -OUS]

fle'xure (-ksher), n. Bending, curvature, bent state; bend, curve, turn; (Math.) curving of line or surface or, in theory of elasticity, of surface or solid (~ *of a curve*, its bending to or from a straight line); (Geol.) bending of strata under pressure. [f. L *flexura* (FLEX[1], -URE)]

flibb'ertigibb'ĕt, n. Gossiping, flighty, frivolous, or restless person. [imit. of chatter]

flick, n., & v.t. **1.** Light sharp blow with whiplash etc. shot out and withdrawn, or with finger-nail; sudden movement, jerk; slight sharp cracking sound; (sl.) cinema film, (pl.) cinema performance; ~-*knife* (with blade springing out when button is pressed). **2.** v.t. Strike with a ~; dash or jerk (dust etc.) *away, off*; give a ~ with (whip, towel, etc.). [imit.]

flick'er, v.i., & n. **1.** Quiver, vibrate, wave to and fro, blow lightly & unsteadily, (of flags, leaves, serpents' tongues, wind, etc.); (of flame etc., & fig. of hope etc.) flash and die away by turns; hence ~ingLY[2] adv. **2.** n. ~ing movement or light. [OE *flicorian* imit.]

flier. See FLYER.

flight[1] (-īt), n., & v.t. **1.** Act or manner of flying through air (*take* one's or *a, wing* one's, ~, fly), pursuit of game by hawk; migration, migrating body, flock, of birds or insects; swift movement of projectiles etc.; passage of projectile from gun to target; (of time) swift passage; soaring, excursion, sally, (*of* wit, fancy, ambition, etc.); distance that bird, aircraft, or missile, can fly; series (*of* stairs between two landings, or *of* hurdles or rails for racing over); volley (*of* arrows etc.); *in the first* ~, taking a leading place; oat-chaff; R.A.F. unit consisting of a few machines; ~-*deck*, for taking-off from, and landing on, an aircraft-carrier; ~-*feather, -muscle*, used in flying; ~-*lieutenant, -sergeant*, see AIR[1] *Force*. **2.** v.t. Shoot (wildfowl; also abs.) in ~; vary trajectory and pace of (cricket-ball etc.). [OE *flyht*, OS *fluht*, f. WG **fluhti* f. **fleugan* FLY[2]]

flight[2] (-īt), n. Running away, hasty retreat, absconding, (*take, take to, betake* one*self to*, ~, run away; *put to* ~, rout). [OE **flyht*, OS, OHG *fluht*, ON *flótti* f. Gmc **thluhtiz* f. **thleuhan* FLEE]

flight'|ỹ (-īt-), a. Guided by whim or fancy, fickle; half-witted, crazy. Hence ~iLY[2] adv., ~iNESS n. [FLIGHT[1] + -Y[2]]

flim'flăm, n. Trifle, nonsense, idle talk; piece of humbug, deception. [16th c., imit. redupl.; cf. FLAM & foll.]

flim's|ỹ (-z-), a. & n. **1.** Easily destroyed, frail, slightly put together; paltry, trivial; frivolous, superficial; hence ~iLY[2] adv., ~iNESS n. **2.** n. Banknote(s) (sl.); thin paper, reporter's copy. [17th c., goes w. prec. & FLAM]

flinch[2] (for *flinch*[1] see FLENCH). v.i. Give way, draw back, (*from* duty, course, etc.); wince. [f. OF *flenchir* f. WG (OFrank.) **hlankjan*; see LANK]

flin'ders (-z), n. pl. Fragments, splinters, (*break, fly, in* ~). [15th c., cf. Norw. *flindra* splinter]

fling, v.i. & t. (*flŭng*), & n. **1.** Rush, go angrily or violently (~ *out of the room*; *flung away in a rage*); (of horse etc.) kick and plunge (often *out*), (of person; usu. *out*) break into invective; throw, hurl, (often *about, aside, away, by, out, up, at*; rejected thing, missile, flotsam, dice); throw one*self into* person's arms, a boat, etc., *on* person's compassion etc., or *into* an enterprise (i.e. take it up with all one's might); suddenly spread *out* (arms), kick *up* (heels); cast (one's eyes) carelessly (*up*)*on*; send, emit, (sound, smell, light); put (person) suddenly or violently *into* prison; launch (troops etc.) *on* enemy or *against* fortress or enemy; (of wrestler or ridden horse) throw to the ground; ~ (fact etc.) *in* one's *teeth*, reproach him with it; ~ (door etc.) *open* or *to*, open or shut violently. **2.** n. Throw, cast, (*have a* ~ *at*, make an attempt at, jeer at); impetuous dance (esp. *Highland* ~); violent movement, plunge; spell of indulgence in impulse (*have* one's ~). [ME, perh. f. ON **flinga*, whence *flengja* flog]

flint, n. Hard stone of nearly pure silica found in pebbly lumps steel-grey within & encrusted with white; anything hard and unyielding; piece of ~ used with steel to produce fire (~ *& steel*) esp. in ~-*lock gun*; piece of an alloy of rare-earth metals used in automatic petrol lighters as the spark-producing element; pebble of ~ (*wring water from a* ~), work miracles; *skin a* ~, be miserly or avaricious; *set one's face like a* ~, be determined); ~--glass, pure lustrous kind orig. made with ~; ~-*lock*, (lock of) gun discharged by spark from ~. Hence flin'ty² a., flin'ti-NESS n. [OE *flint*, MDu. *vlint*, OHG *flins*]

flip¹, v.t. & i. (-pp-), & n. 1. Put (pellet, coin) in motion with a fillip; fillip (person's ear, cheek, etc.), strike lightly; make a fillip with fingers; move (fan, whip, fishing-fly) about with sudden jerk(s); strike smartly *at* with whip etc. 2. n. Smart light blow, fillip, flick; (colloq.) a (short) flight in an aeroplane. [imit.]

flip², n. Beer and spirit mixed, sweetened, & heated with hot iron; EGG¹-~. [perh. f. prec. in sense *whip up*]

flip-flăp, n. Kind of somersault; kind of firework, cracker; (in places of amusement) machine with passenger cars hung at ends of long moving arms. [imit.]

flipp'ant, a. Lacking in gravity, treating serious things lightly, disrespectful. Hence flipp'ANCY n., ~LY² adv. [from 1605, orig. = nimble, voluble, perh. f. FLIP¹, -ANT]

flipp'er, n. Limb used to swim with, as in turtle & penguin; (sl.) hand. [FLIP¹ + -ER¹]

flipp'erty-flŏpp'erty, a. Loose, dangling.

flirt, v.t. & i., & n. 1. Fillip, send with a jerk; wave or move briskly (fan, bird's tail); play at courtship (*with*), pretend to make love, whence ~A'TION n., ~ā'tious (-shŭs) a. 2. n. Sudden jerk, quick motion quickly checked; man who pays, or usu. woman who invites or accepts, attentions merely for amusement, whence ~'ISH¹, ~'Y², aa. [imit.]

flit, v.i. (-tt-), & n. 1. Migrate, be gone, depart; change one's abode, move; pass lightly, softly, or rapidly (often *about, by, to & fro*); fly lightly, make short flights, (of birds & esp. bats). 2. n. Change of abode. [ME, f. ON *flytja* cogn. w. FLEET⁵]

flitch, n., & v.t. 1. Side of hog salted and cured (~ *of Dunmow*, there given yearly to any couple proving conjugal harmony for year and day); square of blubber; steak of halibut; ‖ slice (usu. outside one) of timber from tree-trunk; ~-*beam* (compound, esp. of iron plate between two slices of wood). 2. v.t. Cut (log or halibut) into ~es. [OE *flicce*, MLG *vli(c)ke*, ON *flikki*]

flitt'er, v.i. Flit about, flutter; ~-*mouse*, bat. [FLIT + -ER⁵]

•flivv'er, n. (sl.). Cheap motor-car. [orig. unkn.]

flix, n. Kinds of fur; beaver's down. [orig. unkn.]

float¹, n. ‖ Floating (rare; *on the* ~, afloat); mass of floating weeds, ice, etc.; raft; cork or quill used on fishing-line as indicator; cork supporting edge of fishing-net;

inflated part supporting fish etc.; hollow ball regulating cistern tap; (Theatr.; sing. or pl.) footlights; (also ~-*board*) one of the boards of water-wheel or paddle-wheel; kind of low-bodied cart; platform on wheels with show used in processions; tool for smoothing plaster (~-*stone*, for smoothing curved bricks, & cf. foll.); single-cut file; passing of weft-threads over part of warp without being interwoven, thread so passed; ~-*bridge*, of rafts; ~-*grass*, kind of aquatic grass. [partly f. OE *flot* floating state, OE *flota* ship, & foll.]

float², v.i. & t. Rest on surface of liquid; (of stranded ship) get afloat; move with moving liquid, drift; be suspended freely *in* liquid; move or be suspended in air as if buoyed up; hover *before* eye or mind; (Commerc., of acceptance) be in circulation, awaiting maturity; (Commerc.) bring (company, scheme) into favour, launch, (of scheme etc.) be launched; cover with liquid, inundate; (of water etc.) support, bear along, (buoyant object); set afloat; circulate (rumour); waft through air; ~-*stone*, kinds of light stone that ~ (& see prec.). [OE *flotian*, OS *flotōn*, ON *flota* cogn. w. FLEET⁵; in ME infl. by OF *floter*]

float'able, a. Capable of floating; (of stream) in which rafts etc. can float. [-ABLE]

float'age, n. Floating; ‖ (right of appropriating) flotsam; ships etc. afloat on river; floating masses; buoyancy; part of ship above water-line. [-AGE]

floatā'tion, flot-, n. Floating (*centre of* ~, of gravity in floating body); starting of company or enterprise. [*flot*- on anal. of *quotation* etc.; FLOAT², -ATION]

float'er, n. In vbl senses; esp. (St. Exch.) government stock certificate, railway bond, etc., recognized as security. [-ER¹]

float'ing, a. In vbl senses; esp. (Commerc.; of cargo) at sea (~ *trade, rates*, etc., concerned with cargoes at sea); ~ CAPI-TAL², DEBT, RIB; fluctuating, variable, (*the* ~ *population*); ~ *anchor* = DRAG²--*anchor*; ~ DOCK⁴; ~ *bridge*, kinds of bridge & ferry, also part of bridge that can be swung away on pontoon; ~ *kidney*, abnormal condition in which the kidneys are movable; ~ *light*, lightship, lifebuoy with lantern; ~ VOTE. [-ING²]

flŏcc'ōse, a. (bot.). Tufted. [f. LL *flocco-sus* (L *floccus* FLOCK¹, -OSE¹)]

flŏcc'ūle, n. Small portion of matter like flock of wool. [f. FLOCCULUS]

flŏcc'ūlent, -lōse, -lous, aa. Like tufts of wool; in, showing, tufts. Hence flŏcc'ŪLENCE n. [foll., -ULENT, -OSE¹, -OUS]

flŏcc'ūlus, n. (pl. -*lī*).= FLOCCULE; (Anat.) small lobe in under surface of cerebellum. [mod. L, dim. of foll.]

flŏcc'us, n. (pl. -*cī*, pr. -ŏksī). Tuft of woolly hairs or filaments. [L, = foll.]

flŏck¹, n. Lock, tuft, of wool, cotton, etc.;

(pl.) material for quilting & stuffing made of wool-refuse or torn-up cloth; (pl. or collect. sing) powdered wool or cloth for making ~-paper; (Chem.; pl.) light loose masses precipitated; ~-bed, stuffed with ~s; ~-paper, wallpaper sized & then powdered with ~ either all over or in patterns. Hence ~'Y² a. [f. OF floc f. L floccus]

flŏck², n., & v.i. **1.** Large number of people (chiefly in such phrr. as come in ~s); number of animals of one kind, esp. birds, feeding or travelling together; number of domestic animals, usu. sheep, goats, or geese, kept together (~s & herds, sheep &· cattle); the Christian body; a congregation esp. in relation to its pastor; family of children, number of pupils, etc.; ~-master, sheep-farmer. **2.** v.i. Congregate, go in great numbers, troop, (often about, after, into, to, in, out, together). [OE flocc, MLG vlocke, ON flokkr]

flŏe, n. Sheet of floating ice. [prob. f. Norw. flo, ON fló layer]

flŏg, v.t. (-gg-). Beat with birch, cane, whip, etc., whence ~g'ING¹(1) (-g-) n.; drive (learning, laziness, etc.) into or out of person; urge (horse etc.) on with whip (~ dead horse, waste energy); (sl.) defeat, excel; (sl.) sell; cast fishing-line repeatedly over (stream). [17th c. cant; imit., or f. L flagellare to whip]

‖ **flŏng**, n. Prepared paper for stereotyping. [f. F flan FLAWN]

flood (flŭd), n., & v.t. & i. **1.** (Also ~-tide) inflow of tide (opp. EBB); (poet.) river, stream, sea (~ & field, sea & land); irruption of water over land, inundation, (the F~, Noah's F~, that in Genesis), whence ~ŏm'ETER n.; outpouring of water, torrent, downpour, (~s of rain, a ~ of tears or words); ~-gate, opened & closed to admit or exclude water, esp. lower gate of lock, also sluice; ~-light, copious artificial light projected from many directions, eliminating all shadows in surface illuminated (so ~-lighting, ~-lit). **2.** vb. Inundate, cover with a ~ (also fig., was ~ed with letters); irrigate; deluge (burning house, mine) with water; (of rain) fill (river) to overflowing; come in great quantities (usu. in); have uterine haemorrhage. [OE, OS flōd, OHG fluot, ON flóth, Goth. flōdus f. Gmc *flōthuz]

floor (-ōr), n., & v.t. **1.** Lower surface of room, (also ~'ing) boards etc. of which it is made; bottom of sea, cave, etc.; part of House of Parliament where members sit and speak (take the ~, esp. U.S., speak in debate); set of rooms etc. on same level in house (‖ ground~, on ground level, first ~, ‖ above this), storey; level area; ~-lamp, mounted on metal etc. pillar standing on ~; ~-cloth, substitute for carpet; ~ show, entertainment presented not on stage but on ~ of night-club etc.; *~-walker, shopwalker; hence ~'LESS (-ōrl-) a. **2.** vb. Furnish with ~, pave; serve as

~ of; bring to the ~ or ground, knock down; confound, nonplus; ‖ (at school) tell (boy) to sit down as not knowing lesson; overcome, get the better of, (~ the paper, answer every question in it). [OE, ON flōr, MHG vluor f. Gmc *flōruz]

floor'er (-ōr-), n. Knock-down blow; disconcerting news or argument; paper or question hard to answer. [-ER¹]

flŏp, v.i. & t. (-pp-), n., int., & adv. **1.** Sway (intr.) about heavily; walk etc. in ungainly way; sit, kneel, lie, down awkwardly; throw down negligently or noisily; make dull sound of soft body falling or of flat thing slapping water; (sl., of book, play, etc.) fail, collapse; hence ~p'Y² a. **2.** n. ~ping motion, sound made by it; (sl.) failure (of book, play, etc.). **3.** int. & adv. With a ~. [var. of earlier FLAP]

flōr'a, n. (pl. -ae, -as). (List of) plants of particular region or epoch (cf. FAUNA). [L goddess of flowers (flos -oris flower)]

flōr'al, a. Of flora(s) (~ zone, tract of earth with special vegetable characteristics); of flower(s). [f. L floralis of Flora (prec.)]

Flō'rentine, a. & n. (Inhabitant) of Florence in Tuscany (~ iris, white or pale blue one); kind of twilled silk. [f. L Florentinus (Florentia Florence, -INE¹)]

florĕs'cence, n. Flowering time or state. [f. L florescere (florēre bloom, -ESCENT, -ENCE)]

flōr'ĕt, n. (Bot.) one of small flowers making up a composite flower (~ of the disc, the ray, of the flower's centre or circumference); small flower, floweret. [17th c., f. L flos -oris +-ET]

flōr'iāte, v.t. Decorate with flower-designs etc. [as foll., -ATE³]

flōr'iculture, n. Cultivation of flowers. Hence flōricul'turAL a., flōricul'turIST (3) n., (-cher-). [f. L flos -oris flower + CULTURE]

flŏ'rid, a. Profusely adorned as with flowers, elaborately ornate, (of literary, artistic, or musical style); ostentatious, showy; ruddy, flushed, high-coloured. Hence florid'ITY, ~NESS, n., ~LY² adv. [f. F floride or L floridus (flos FLOWER)]·

Flŏ'rida, n. State in U.S. (~ water, a perfume; ~ wood, kind used for inlaying).

florif'erous, a. (Of seeds or plants) producing many flowers. [f. L florifer (flos FLOWER, -FEROUS)]

flōrīlĕ'gium, n. (pl. -ia). Anthology. [transl. into mod. L (L flos FLOWER, legere gather) of Gk anthologion ANTHOLOGY]

flŏ'rin, n. Foreign coin of gold or silver current at different times; (hist.) English gold coin (6/8) of Edw. III; ‖ current English coin (2/-). [ME, f. OF f. It. fiorino dim. of fiore f. L florem nom. flos FLOWER (stamped with lily)]

flōr'ist (also flŏ'-), n. One who deals in, raises, or studies flowers. [L *flos -oris flower, -IST]

flōr'uit (-ŏŏ-), n. Period (failing exact birth and death dates) at which a person was alive. [L, = he flourished]

flory. See FLEURY.

flŏs'cŭlar, -lous, aa. Having florets, composite-flowered. [f. L *flosculus* (FLOWER, -CULE)]

flŏss, n. Rough silk enveloping silkworm's cocoon (~ *silk,* this used in cheap silk goods; CANDY ~. Hence ~'Y² a. [f. F (*soie*) *floche* floss (-silk), ult. f. L *floccus* FLOCK¹]

flotation. See FLOATATION.

flotill'a, n. Small fleet; fleet of boats or small ships. [Sp., dim. of *flota* fleet]

flŏt'sam, n. Wreckage found floating (cf. JETSAM); oyster-spawn. [f. AF *floteson* (OF *floter* = FLOAT²)]

flounce¹, v.i., & n. **1.** Go with agitated or violent motion, flop, plunge, throw the body about, (*away, out, about, down, up*). **2.** n. Fling, jerk, of body or limb. [16th c., of unkn. orig.; perh. imit., as *bounce, pounce*]

flounce², n., & v.t. **1.** Strip gathered & sewn by upper edge round woman's skirt, & with lower edge hanging, as ornament. **2.** v.t. Trim with ~(s). [alt. of ME *frounce* fold, pleat, f. OF *fronce* f. *froncir* wrinkle f. WG (OFrank.) *hrunkjan*; cf. FLANK, FLINCH]

floun'der¹, n. A small flat-fish. [late ME, f. AF *floundre,* OF *flondre* of Scand. orig.; cf. OSwed. *flundra*]

floun'der², v.i., & n. **1.** Struggle & plunge (as) in mud or wading; make mistakes, manage business badly or with difficulty. **2.** n. Piece of ~ing, staggering attempts to get on. [imit., perh. assoc. w. *founder, blunder*]

flour (-owr), n., & v.t. **1.** Finer part of meal obtained by bolting; wheat meal; fine soft powder; ~-*box,* tin box for dredging ~; hence ~'Y² (-owr-) a. **2.** v.t. Sprinkle with ~; *grind into ~. [different. sp. of FLOWER in sense *finest part*]

flou'rish¹ (flŭ-), v.i. & t. Grow vigorously; thrive, prosper, be successful; be in one's prime; spend one's life, be active, *in, at, about,* etc., a certain time (cf. FLORUIT); use flourishes in handwriting or literary work or speech; show ostentatiously; wave (weapon) about; throw (limbs) about; prelude fancifully in music etc. [ME, f. OF *florir* (-ISH²) f. L *florēre* (*flos* FLOWER)]

flou'rish² (flŭ-), n. **1.** Prosperity, vigour, (rare; *in full* ~). **2.** Ornament of flowing curves about letter or word in handwriting; rhetorical embellishment, florid expression; ostentatious waving of weapon, hand, etc. **3.** (mus.). Fanfare of brass instruments, florid passage, extemporized addition or prelude; hence ~'Y² a. [f. prec.]

flout, v.t. & i. Mock, insult, express contempt for by word or act; scoff *at.* [from 16th c.; perh. var. of FLUTE v.]

flow (-ō), v.i., & n. **1.** Glide along as a stream; (of blood) circulate; (of persons or things) come, go, in numbers; (of talk, literary style, etc.) move easily; (of garment, hair, etc.) hang easily, undulate; (Math.; of numbers) increase or diminish continuously by infinitesimal quantities; gush out, spring; (of blood) be split; result *from;* run full, be in flood (*ebb & ~*; *swim with the~ing tide,* be on the winning side); (of wine) be poured out without stint; be plentifully supplied *with* (arch.; *land ~ing with milk & honey*). **2.** n. ~ing movement in stream; amount that ~s; ~ing liquid; (of dress, figure, etc.) undulation; outpouring, stream, copious supply; rise of tide (*ebb & ~*); overflowing of Nile etc.; ~ *of spirits,* habitual cheerfulness; ~ *of soul,* genial conversation (as complement to FEAST *of reason*). [OE *flōwan,* cogn. w. ON *flóa,* Du. *vloeijen,* f. Gmc *flō-* (FLOOD)]

flow'er (*also* flowr), n., & v.i. & t. **1.** (Bot.) reproductive organ in plant containing one or more pistils or stamens or both, & usu. a corolla & calyx, (pop.) coloured (i.e. not green) part of plant from which fruit or seed is later developed, whence ~AGE(1) n.; (Old Chem.; pl.) powder left after sublimation (~s *of sulphur* etc.); scum formed by fermentation (~s *of tan*); a blossom apart from the plant (*No~s,* intimation that wreaths etc. are not desired at funeral); ~ing plant; (pl.) ornamental phrases (usu. ~s *of speech* often iron.); *the* pick or choice *of*; *the* best part, essence; *the* choicest embodiment *of*; state of blooming (*in ~*), prime (*in the ~ of his age*); ~-de-luce, see FLEUR-DE-LIS; ~-girl, who sells ~s; ~-piece, picture of ~s; ~-pot, usu. of red earthenware holding soil in which plant may be set; ~-show, competitive or other exhibition of ~s; hence (-)~ED² (-erd), ~LESS, aa., ~ET¹ n. **2.** vb. Produce ~s, bloom or blossom, whence ~ING² a. (~ing fern, osmund); (Gardening) cause or allow (plant) to ~; embellish with worked ~s or floral design. [ME & OF *flour, flur,* f. L *florem* nom. *flos*]

flow'erer, n. Plant that flowers at specified time etc. (*late, abundant,* ~). [-ER¹]

flow'er|ý, a. Abounding in flowers; full of fine words, compliments, figures of speech, etc., whence ~INESS (-owr-) n. [-Y²]

flow'ing (-ōǐ-), a. In vbl senses; also or esp.: (of style) fluent, easy; (of lines, curves, contour) smoothly continuous, not abrupt; (Naut.) *with ~ sheet* or *sail,* sailing with lee clews eased off when wind is nearly across course. Hence ~LY² adv. [-ING²]

flown¹ (-ōn), a. (arch.). Swollen, puffed up, (~ *with insolence and wine-* Milt.). [obs. p.p. of FLOW]

flown². See FLY².

flŭc'tū|āte, v.i. Move up & down like waves (rare); vary irregularly, rise & fall, be unstable; vacillate, waver. So ~A'TION n. [f. L *fluctuare* (*fluctus -ūs* wave f. *fluere* flow), -ATE³]

flue¹ (floo), n. Kind of fishing-net. [from 14th c.; cf. MDu. *vluwe*]

flue² (floo), n. Substance formed by loose particles of cotton etc., fluff. Hence ~'Y² (-oo'¹) a. [16th c., cf. Flem. *vluwe* in same sense]

flue³ (floo), n. Smoke-duct in chimney; channel for conveying heat, esp. hot-air passage in wall, tube for heating water in some kinds of boiler; ~-*pipes* (mus.), organ-pipes other than reed-pipes. [perh. rel. to FLUE⁵]

flu(e)⁴ (floo), n. (colloq.). (Short for) IN-FLUENZA.

flue⁵ (floo), v.i. & t. Splay, make (opening) widen inwards or outwards. [f. obs. adj. *flue* splayed, expanded, of obsc. orig.]

flu'ency (floo-), n. Smooth easy flow, esp. in speech; ready utterance. [f. LL *fluentia* (f. foll.; see -ENCY]

flu'ent (floo-), a. & n. Flowing (rare in lit. sense); ready to flow, liquid, (rare); fluid, not settled, liable to change, (rare); (of motion, curves, etc.) graceful, easy; (of speech or style) copious, coming easily, ready; expressing oneself quickly & easily; (Math., in fluxions) that FLOWs (n., the variable quantity that flows). Hence ~LY² adv. [f. L *fluere* flow, see -ENT]

fluff, n., & v.t. **1.** Light feathery stuff given off by blankets etc.; soft fur; soft downy mass or bunch; *bit of* ~ (sl.), girl, woman; soft short hair on lip or cheek; ‖ (sl.) theatrical part imperfectly known; hence ~'Y² a., ~'INESS n. **2.** v.t. Put soft surface on (flesh side of leather); make into ~; shake (one*self*), one's feathers etc.) *up* or *out* into ~y mass; ‖ (sl.) blunder in theatrical part. [perh. modification of FLUE²]

flu'id (floo-), a. & n. (Substance) consisting of particles that move freely among themselves & yield to the slightest pressure (including gases & liquids); moving readily, not solid or rigid, not stable; liquid constituent or secretion. Hence fluid'IFY v.t., fluid'ITY n., (floo-). [f. F *fluide* or L *fluidus* (*fluere* flow, -ID¹)]

fluke¹ (flook), n. Kinds of flat-fish, the flounder, (now rare); kinds of parasitic worm found in sheep's liver; ‖ kind of kidney potato. [OE *flōc*, cogn. w. ON *flóki* & G *flach* flat]

fluke² (flook), n. Broad triangular plate on arm of anchor; barbed head of lance, harpoon, etc.; (pl.) whale's tail. [perh. f. prec.]

fluk|e³ (flook), n., & v.i. & t. (Make) lucky accidental stroke; get, hit, etc., by ~e. Hence ~'Y² a., ~'ILY² adv., ~'INESS n., (floo-). [orig. unkn.; first in billiards]

*flume (floom), n., & v.i. & t. Artificial channel conveying water for industrial use; ravine with stream; (vb) build ~s,

convey down a ~. [ME, f. OF *flum* f. L *flumen* river (*fluere* flow)]

flŭmm'ery, n. Food made by boiling oatmeal down to a jelly (arch. or dial.); kinds of sweet dish made with milk, flour, eggs, etc.; empty compliments, trifles, nonsense. [f. W *llymru* of unkn. orig.]

flŭmm'ox, v.t. (sl.). Confound, bewilder, disconcert. [prob. dial., imit.]

flŭmp, v.i. & t., & n. Fall or move heavily, set or throw *down*, with a dull noise (n., the action or sound). [imit.]

flung. See FLING v.

flŭnk'ey, n. (pl. ~s). Liveried servant, footman, (usu. contempt.); toady, snob. Hence ~DOM (-kĭd-), ~ISM (-kĭizm), nn. [orig. Sc.; perh. f. FLANK, with sense *sidesman, flanker*]

fluo(r)-, fluoro-, (floo-), comb. forms of FLUORINE, as *fluoroó'ric*; *flu'oroSCOPE*, instrument with fluorescent screen used instead of dark room to show X-ray effects. [foll.]

flu'or (floo-), n. Kinds of gemlike readily fusible mineral containing fluorine; ~-*spar*, calcium fluoride. [mod. application of L, = flowing, flux (*fluere* flow, -OR)]

fluor|ĕs'cence (floo-), n. Coloured luminosity produced in certain substances by incident light or other electro-magnetic radiations of shorter wave-length, esp. violet and ultra- violet light and X-rays; property of absorbing light of short (invisible) wave-length and emitting light of longer (visible) wave-length. Hence ~ĕsce' v.i., exhibit ~escence, ~ES'CENT a., (floo-). [prec., -ESCENT, -ENCE]

flu'orine (floo-), n. Non-metallic element of the HALOGEN group. Hence flu'orIDE (floo-)·n.···[F, (FLUOR, -INE⁵]

flŭ'rry, n., & v.t. **1.** Gust, squall; commotion, excitement, nervous hurry, agitation; whale's death-throes. **2.** v.t. Confuse by haste or noise, agitate. [imit.; cf. earlier *flurr, hurry*]

flŭsh¹, v.i. & t., & n. **1.** Take wing & fly away; cause to do this, put up, (birds). **2.** n. Number of birds put up at once. [ME, imit.; cf. *fly, rush*]

flŭsh², v.i. & t. Spurt, rush out; cleanse (drain etc.) by flow of water; flood (meadow); (of plant) throw out fresh shoots (also causative, *rain—es the plants*); glow with warm colour; (of blood) rush into & redden face; (of face) become red or hot, blush; cause to glow or blush, suffuse with warm colour; inflame with pride or passion, encourage, (~*ed with exercise, joy, victory, insolence,* etc.). [perh.=prec. influenced by *flash & blush*]

flŭsh³, n. Rush of water; sudden abundance; stream from mill-wheel; rush of emotion, elation produced by it or by victory etc.; fresh growth of grass etc.; cleansing of drain by flushing; glow of light or colour; rush of blood to face, reddening caused by it; hot fit in fever; freshness, vigour. [f. prec.]

flush[4], a., & v.t. **1.** Full to overflowing, in flood; (usu. pred.) having plentiful supply of or of money etc., (of money) abundant; even, in same plane, level *with*, without projections or raised edges. **2.** v.t. Level; fill in (joint) level with surface. [prob. f. FLUSH[2]]

flush,[5] n. Set of cards all of one suit; *straight ~*, set of cards in a regular sequence; *royal ~* (Poker), a straight *~* headed by ace. [f. OF *flus, flux* = Flem. *fluys*, Sp. *flux*, f. L FLUX*us*]

flus'ter, v.t. & i., & n. **1.** Confuse with drink, half-intoxicate; flurry, make nervous; be agitated, bustle. **2.** n. Flurry, flutter, agitation. [orig. unkn.; cf. Icel. *flaustr(a)* hurry, bustle]

flus'tra, n. (pl. *-ae, -as*). Sea-mat, polyzoic species resembling seaweed. [arbitrary mod. L coinage by Linnaeus]

flute (floot), n., & v.i. & t. **1.** Musical wind--instrument, long wooden pipe with holes along it stopped by fingers or keys, & blow-hole in side near upper end, whence **flut'IST**(3) (floo-) n.; *~*-player; organ stop with *~*-like tone; semicylindrical vertical groove in pillar, similar groove elsewhere, e.g. in frills, whence **flut'ING**[1](6) (floo-) n. **2.** vb. Play *~*; whistle, sing, or speak, in *~*-like tones; play (air etc.) on *~*; make *~*s or grooves in. [ME, f. OF *fleüte, flaüte, flahute*, f. Pr. *flaüt*]

flutt'er, v.i. & t., & n. **1.** Flap wings, flap (wings), without flying or in short flights; come or go with quivering motion (usu. to the ground); go about restlessly, flit, hover; quiver, vibrate, (of pulse) beat feebly & irregularly; tremble with excitement, be agitated: move (flag etc.) irregularly, agitate, ruffle; throw (person) into confusion or agitation. **2.** n. *~*ing; tremulous excitement (*be, put, in a ~*); stir, sensation, (*make a ~*); vibration (*wing, tail, ~*, defects of aircraft in flight); (sl.) modest gambling venture, speculation. [OE *flotorian* frequent. form cogn. w. OE *fleotan* FLEET[5]]

flut'y (floo-), a. Like flute in tone, soft & clear. [-Y[2]]

fluv'ial (floo-), a. Of, found in, river(s). [f. L *fluvialis* (*fluvius* river, -AL)]

fluv'iatile (floo-), a. Of, found in, produced by, river(s). [f. F, or L *fluviatilis* (prec., -ATILE)]

fluv'io- (floo-), comb. form of L *fluvius* river, as *fluvio-marine, fluviom'eter*.

flux, n., & v.i. & t. **1.** Morbid or excessive discharge of blood, excrement, etc., (formerly) dysentery; flowing out, issue; flowing; inflow of tide (usu. *~ & reflux*, often fig.); flood of talk etc.; continuous succession of changes (*in a state of ~*); (Math.) continued motion (*line is the ~ of a point*); (Phys.) rate of flow of any fluid across given area, amount crossing area in given time; substance mixed with metal etc. to promote fusion. **2.** vb. Issue in a *~*, flow copiously; make fluid,

fuse, treat with a fusing *~*. [ME *flix(e), flux* f. OF *flux* or L *fluxus* (*fluere flux-* flow)]

flu'xion (-kshn), n. Flowing (rare); continuous change (rare); (Math.) rate or proportion at which a flowing or varying quantity increases its magnitude (*method of ~s*, the Newtonian calculus). Hence *~AL, ~ARY*[1], aa., (-kshon-). [f. F, or L *fluxio* (prec., -ION)]

fly[1], n. Two-winged insect (*~ in amber*, curious relic; *~ on wheel*, person who over-estimates his own influence; *break ~ on wheel*, expend disproportionate energy; *a ~ in the ointment*, trifling circumstance that mars enjoyment; *no flies on him* etc., sl. praise of person's or thing's efficiency; HESSIAN, TSETSE, *~*); kinds of plant-disease caused by various flies (*a good deal of ~ exists*); natural or artificial *~* used as fishing-bait; CATCH[1]*~*; *~-blow*, (n.) *~*'s egg in meat etc., (v.t.) deposit eggs in, taint, (*~-blown*, tainted, lit. & fig.); *~-book*, case for keeping fishing-flies in; *~-catcher*, trap for flies, kinds of bird; *~-fish* (v.i.), fish with *~*; *~-flap*, for driving away flies; *~-net*, net or fringe protecting horse from flies; *~-paper*, for catching or poisoning flies; *~-trap*, for catching flies, also kinds of plant esp. *Venus's ~-trap*; *~-weight* (BOX[5]); *~--whisk*, for driving away flies. [OE *flÿge, fleoge*, OS, OHG *flioga* f. WG **fleugon* (foll.)]

fly[2], v.i. & t. (*flew*, pr. floo, *flown* pr. flōn; *is, has flown*, see -ED[1](2); *fly* is preferred in talk & ordinary prose for *flee*, but not *flew* or *flown* for *fled*). Move through air with wings (*~ high*, be ambitious; *high-flown*, exalted, turgid, bombastic; *as the* CROW[1] *flies; the bird is flown*, person wanted has escaped; often *about, away, forth, off, out*) or in aircraft; direct flight of (aircraft), transport (passengers) in aircraft; make (pigeon, hawk) *~*; (Hawk.) soar by way of attack *at* (fg., *~ at higher game*, have nobler ambitions); pass or rise quickly through air; jump clear over or *over* fence etc.; make (kite) rise & stay aloft (*~ a kite*, raise money by accommodation bill, also try how the wind blows, feel one's way by *ballon d'essai*); (of flag, hair, garment, etc.) wave; set or keep (flag) *~*ing; travel swiftly, rush along, pass rapidly; spring, start, hasten, (*~ to arms*, take up arms eagerly; *~ in the* FACE[1] *of*; *~ at, upon*, attack violently; *~ into* a passion, raptures, etc.; *~ out*, burst into violent language or action); be driven or forced off suddenly (*made sparks ~*; *send ~*ing; make the money ~*, spend quickly; *door flew open; glass* etc. *flies*, breaks in pieces); *let ~*, discharge (missile), (abs.) shoot, hit, or use strong language, *at*; run away, flee, flee from (*must ~ the country*); *~-away*, (of garments) streaming, loose, négligé, (of persons) flighty; *~-by-night*, one who makes night excursions or decamps by night; ~-*over* n., procession of aircraft, (also ~-*over bridge*, *viaduct*) bridge for carrying vehicles over traffic-congested areas, esp. over main roads; ~-*past* n., ceremonial flight of aircraft past some person or place, cf. MARCH⁴ *past*; ~-*the- -garter*, kind of leap-frog. [OE *fléogan*, OS, OHG *fliogan*, ON *fljúga* f. Gmc *fleugan*]

flȳ³, n. Flying, distance flown, (*on the* ~, *on the wing*, in motion); ‖ one-horse hackney-carriage (obs.); lap on garment to contain or cover buttonholes, flap at entrance of tent; part of flag farthest from staff, also its breadth from staff to end; (Theatr.; pl.) space over proscenium; speed-regulating device in clock-work & machinery; ~-*leaf*, blank leaf at beginning or end of book, blank leaf of circular etc.; ~*'man*, ‖ driver of ~ = carriage (obs.), man stationed in flies of theatre to work rope etc.; ~-*sheet*, 2 or 4 page circular etc.; ~-*wheel*, heavy-rimmed on revolving shaft to regulate machinery or accumulate power. [f. prec.]

flȳ⁴, a. (sl.). Knowing, wide awake. [orig. unkn.]

flȳ'er, fli'er, n. Bird etc. that flies (usu. *high*, *poor*, etc., ~); (colloq.) ambitious person; animal, vehicle, etc., going with exceptional speed; airman; flying jump. [-ER¹]

flȳ'ing, a. In vbl senses; also or esp.: making movements like flight (~ *bed-stead*, experimental aircraft shaped like bedstead for testing methods of vertical take-off; ~ *boat*, form of SEAplane in which a boat serves as both fuselage & float; ~ *bomb*, aerial torpedo, pilotless aircraft with explosive war-head; ~-*dog*, kind of vampire-bat; ~ DUTCHMAN; ~*fish*, kinds rising into air by wing-like pectoral fins, also nickname for native of Barbados; ~ *fox*, kinds of fruit-eating bat; ~ *man*, airman; F~ *Officer*, rank in AIR¹ Force; ~ *saucer*, saucer-like object occas. reported as having been seen flying at great speed & height; ~ *squad*, police detachment with motor-cars etc. for rapid pursuit; ~ *squirrel*, kinds floating in air by skin connecting fore & hind legs); hanging loose, fluttering, (~ *jib*, light sail set before jib on ~ jib-boom; *with* ~ COLOUR¹s); done or taken in passing (~ *jump*, with running start; ~ *handicap*, *mile*, *start*, in which starting-post is passed at full speed); passing, hasty, (~ *visit*); temporary (~ *bridge*); designed for rapid movement (~ *squadron*, *column*); ~ *but-tress*, slanting from pier etc. to wall & usu. carried on arch. [-ING²]

foal, n., & v.t. & i. **1.** Young of horse, ass, etc., colt or filly, (*in*, *with*, ~, pregnant). **2.** vb. Give birth to (~), give birth to ~. [OE *fola*, OHG *foli*, ON *foli*, Goth. *fula* f. Gmc *folon* cogn. w. L *pullus*]

foam, n., & v.i. **1.** Collection of small bubbles formed in liquid by agitation, fermentation, etc.; froth of saliva or perspiration; (poet.) the sea; ~ *rubber*, ~-like rubbery substance used esp. in upholstery. **2.** v.i. Emit ~, froth at the mouth; (of water etc.) froth, gather ~, run ~ing *along*, *down*, *over*, etc., pass off or *away* in ~; (of cup etc.) be filled with ~ing liquor. Hence ~'LESS, ~'Y², aa. [OE *fām*, OHG *feim* f. WG *faima*]

fŏb¹, n., & v.t. (-bb-). Small pocket for watch etc. formerly made in waistband of breeches; (vb) put in one's ~, pocket. [17th c., cf. G dial. *fuppe* pocket]

fŏb², v.t. (-bb-). Cheat, take in; palm (something inferior) *off upon* (person); put (person) *off with* (something inferior). [16th c., cf. obs. *fop* to dupe & G *foppen* befool]

fŏc'al, a. Of, situated or collected at, a focus; (Opt.) ~ *distance* or *length*, distance between centre of mirror or lens & its focus. [FOCUS, -AL]

fŏc'aliz|e, -is|e (-iz), v.t. = FOCUS v.t. Hence ~A'TION n. [prec., -IZE]

fo'c's'le. See FORECASTLE.

fŏc'us, n. (pl. *-ci* pr. *-sī*, *-uses*), & v.t. & i. (-s-, -ss-). **1.** (Plane geom.) one of points from which distances to any point of given curve are connected by linear relation; (Opt., Heat, etc.) point at which rays meet after reflection or refraction, point from which rays appear to proceed, point at which object must be situated for image given by lens to be well defined (*in*, *out of*, *bring into*, ~), focal length of lens, adjustment of eye or eyeglass necessary to produce clear image; point to which sound-waves converge; principal seat (of disease, activity, etc.). **2.** vb. Converge, make converge, to a ~; adjust ~ of (lens, eye); bring into ~. [L, = hearth]

fŏdd'er, n., & v.t. **1.** Dried food, hay, straw, etc., for stall-feeding cattle; CANNON¹-~; hence ~LESS a. **2.** v.t. Give ~ to. [OE *fōdor*, OHG *fuotar*, ON *fóthr* f. Gmc *fōthram* (FOOD)]

foe, n. (poet. etc.). Enemy, adversary, opponent, ill-wisher; ~'man (arch.), enemy in war. [OE *gefā* n. f. *gefāh* adj. (= OHG *gafēh* at feud with, f. WG *gafaiha*; cf. FEUD¹)]

foet'us (fēt-), **fēt'us**, n. Fully developed embryo in womb. Hence **f(o)et'AL** a., **f(o)et'ICIDE**(2) n., (fē-). [L *fetus -ūs* offspring]

fŏg¹, n., & v.t. & i. (-gg-). **1.** Aftermath; long grass left standing in winter. **2.** v.t. Leave (land) under ~; feed (cattle) on ~. [14th c., of unkn. orig.; cf. Norw. *fogg*]

fŏg², n., & v.t. & i. (-gg-). **1.** Vapour suspended in atmosphere at or near earth's surface, obscurity caused by this (*in a* ~, puzzled, at a loss); abnormal darkened state of atmosphere; (Photog.) cloud on developed plate; ~-*bow*, like rainbow produced by light on ~; ~-*horn*, sounding instrument for warning ships in ~; ~- -*signal*, detonator placed on railway line in ~ to guide driver. **2. vb.** Envelop (as) with ~; bewilder, perplex; (Gardening) die *off* from damp; (Photog.) make (negative) obscure or cloudy; || (Railway) place ~-signals on line, whence || ~-g′ER¹ n. [perh. back form. f. FOGGY; from 16th c.]

fŏg′|l̄y (-g-), a. Thick, murky; of, like, infested with, FOG²; obscure, dull, confused, (*has only a ~y idea of it*; *not the ~iest*, colloq., sc. *idea*); beclouded, indistinct. Hence ~ĭLY² adv., ~ĭNESS n. [f. FOG¹+-Y; earlier senses *covered with coarse grass, boggy, flabby* (flesh), *murky* (air); hence, poss., FOG²]

fŏ′gle, n. (thieves' sl.). Silk handkerchief. [orig. unkn.]

fŏg′y̆, -gey, (-g-), n. (Usu. *old* ~) old- -fashioned fellow, old man behind the times. Hence fŏg′(e)yDOM, fŏg′y̆ISM, nn., fŏg′y̆ISH¹ a., (-g-). [18th c., abbr. of *fogram*, of unkn. orig.]

Föhn (fȫn), n. Hot southerly wind in the Alps. [G, ult. f. L *Favonius*]

foi′ble, n. Weak point, weakness of character, quality on which one mistakenly prides oneself; (Fenc.) part of sword-blade from middle to point (cf. FORTE). [F, obs. form of *faible* FEEBLE]

foil¹, n., & v.t. **1.** (Archit.) arc or space between cusps of window (vb, ornament with ~s, as ~*ed arch*). **2.** Metal hammered or rolled into thin sheet (usu. *gold, tin,* etc., ~); sheet of this, or now amalgam of tin & quicksilver, placed behind mirror-glass, backing; leaf of it placed under precious stone etc. to brighten or colour it or enhance its brightness by contrast (vb, supply with this). **3.** Anything that sets something off by contrast (vb, set off thus). [ME, f. OF f. L *folium* leaf]

foil², v.t. & i., & n. **1.** (Hunt.) run over or cross (scent, ground) so as to baffle hounds (also abs. of deer etc., spoil the scent thus); beat off, repulse, frustrate, parry, baffle. **2.** n. Track of hunted animal (*run, run upon, the ~*, over same track a second time); (arch.) repulse, defeat, check. [f. OF *fouler* full cloth, trample; f. Rom. **fullare* f. L *fullo* fuller]

foil³, n. Blunt-edged sword with button on point used in fencing. [16th c., of unkn. orig.]

|| **fois′on** (-zn), n. (arch.). Plenty. [ME, f. OF f. L *fusionem* (*fundere fus-* pour, -ION, -SON)]

foist, v.t. Introduce surreptitiously or unwarrantably *into* or *in* (adv.); palm (*off*) *on* or *upon*, father (composition) *upon*. [orig. of palming false die; prob. f. Du. dial. *vuisten* take in the hand (*vuist* fist)]

fōld¹, n., & v.t. **1.** (Usu. *sheep*-~) enclosure for sheep; (fig.) church, body of believers (also *true* ~). **2.** v.t. Shut up (sheep etc.)

in ~; place sheep in ~ or ~s on (land) to manure it. [OE *fald* = MLG *valt*; unconnected w. foll.]

fōld², v.t. & i., & n. **1.** Double (flexible thing) over upon itself (also *in, over, together*); ~ *up*, make more compact by (~ing); bend portion of (thing) *back, down*; become, be able to be, ~ed (~*ing door(s)*, in 2 parts, often themselves ~ing, hung on 2 jambs); wind, clasp, (arms etc.) *about, round*; lay together & interlace (arms), clasp (one's hands); swathe, envelop, (~ *it in paper*; *hills ~ed in mist*); embrace *in* arms or *to* breast. **2.** n. Doubling of ~ed object; hollow between two thicknesses (*carried it in a ~ of her dress*), hollow or nook in mountain etc.; coil of serpent, string, etc.; ~ing (*another ~ gives 32mo*); line made by ~ing; (Geol.) the ~ing or curvature of strata. [OE *fealdan*, OHG *faltan*, ON *falda*, Goth. *falthan*, Gmc **falthan*]

-fold, suf. (OE *-feald*, OS *-fald*, OHG *-falt*, ON *-faldr*, Goth. *-falths*) cogn. w. FOLD², Gk *-pallos, -plasios*, & *-plo-* in *haplos* single, & prob. L *-plex* (*simplex* etc.); added to cardinals to form adjj. w. sense *multiplied by* (orig. sense *folded in* —, *plaited in* — *strands*). Now largely superseded by wds f. L in *-ble, -ple*, (*treble, quadruple*), but retained in the advl use (*repaid tenfold*), & in adjj. when there is a plurality of things more or less different (*a twofold charm*).

fōld′er, n. In vbl senses; esp.: paper- -folding instrument; folded circular etc.; (pl.) folding eyeglasses. [-ER¹]

fōliā′ceous (-shus), a. Leaf-like; with organs like leaves; of leaves; laminated. [f. L *foliaceus* (*folium* leaf, -ACEOUS)]

fōl′iage, n. Leaves, leafage, (lit., or as represented in art; ~ *leaf*, excluding petals etc.; ~ *plant*, cultivated for ~, not for flowers). Hence (-)**fōl′iageD**(-ĕjd) a. [f. F *feuillage* f. *feuille* (f. L *folia* pl. of *folium* FOIL¹)+-AGE]

fōl′iar, a. Of leaves. [f. L *folium* leaf, -AR¹]

fōl′iate¹, a. Leaf-like; having leaves; having specified number of leaflets (*1, 5*, etc., ~~). [f. L *foliatus* (*folium* leaf, -ATE²)]

fōl′i|āte², v.i. & t. Split (intr.) into laminae; decorate (arch, door-head) with foils; number leaves (not pages) of (volume) consecutively. So ~A′TION n. [f. L *folium* leaf, -ATE³]

fōl′iō, n. (pl. *-os*). Leaf of paper, parchment, etc., numbered only on front; (Bookkeep.) two opposite pages of ledger etc. used concurrently, page of ledger etc. used for both sides of account; leaf- -number of printed book; number of words (72 or 90) taken as unit of reckoning length of document; sheet of paper folded once (*in* ~, of books on such paper), volume made of such sheets, largest- -sized volume, (also attrib., *a ~ book, in six volumes* ~). [L, abl. of *folium* leaf (abl. f. use in reff., = *on leaf 50* etc.)]

fōl'iōle, n. Division of compound leaf, leaflet. [F, f. LL *foliolum* dim. of *folium* leaf]

folk (fōk), n. (Arch.) a people, nation, race; (pl., the sing. being arch. or dial.) people in general, people of specified class, (now being ousted by *people*); ~, of the people (chiefly in compounds imitated f. German, as ~-*custom*, -*song*; ~ -*etymology*, perversion of word's form to make it significant; ~'*lore*, traditional beliefs etc., study of these, ~'*lōrist*, student of these); *~'*sў a., friendly, sociable. [OE, OS, OHG *folc*, ON *folk* f. Gmc *folkam*]

fōll'icle, n. Small sac or vesicle; cocoon. So **fōllic'ūlAR**[1], **fōllic'ūlātèd** [-ATE²], aa. [f. L *folliculus* (*follis* bellows, -CULE)]

fōll'ow (-ō), v.t. & i., & n. 1. Go or come after.(moving thing or person; ~ *the hounds*, hunt; ~ *my leader*, game in which each player must do as leader does; ~ one's *nose*, leave one's route to chance; ~ *the plough*, be ploughman); go along (path); come after in order or time; accompany, serve; go after as admirer or FOLLOWER; result from, be the necessary consequence of, be involved in, (*trade* ~*s the flag*); strive after, aim at; treat or take as guide or master, obey, espouse opinions or cause of; conform to (~ SUIT), act upon, take as rule; practise (profession etc.; ~ *the sea*, be sailor); keep up with mentally, grasp the meaning of, (argument, speaker); go or come after person or thing (~ *in his steps*; ~ *in the wake of*); come next in order, as *his arguments are as* ~*s* (not ~); happen after something else, ensue; result, be deducible, (*it must* ~ *as the night the day*). 2. ~ *after* (prep. & adv.), = ~ (in most senses, but with slightly formal effect); (Cricket, of side) ~ *on*, go in again out of turn after getting less than opponents by certain number (n., ~-*on*, doing this); ~ *out*, pursue to the end; ~ *through* (Golf), carry stroke through to fullest possible extent after striking ball (~-*through* n., this action); ~ *up*, pursue steadily, add another blow etc. to (previous blow etc.), (Footb. etc.) keep near (player with) ball to support; ~-*up*, the continuation of an action, (esp.) à second advertising circular sent referring to an earlier one. 3. n. (Billiards) stroke causing player's ball to roll on after object-ball, motion so given; (at restaurants) supplementary portion of half the quantity. [OE *folgian*, OS -*ōn*, OHG -*ēn*, ON *fylgia* f. Gmc *fulg*-]

fōll'ower (-ōer), n. In vbl senses; esp.: adherent, disciple; man courting maid-servant. [-ER¹]

fōll'owing[1] (-ō-), n. In vbl senses; also, body of adherents, followers. [-ING¹]

fōll'owing² (-ō-), a. In vbl senses; esp., now to be mentioned (also as pron. sing. or pl., *the* ~ *are noteworthy*). [-ING²]

fōll'ў, n. Being foolish, want of good sense, unwise conduct; foolish act, idea, or practice, ridiculous thing; costly structure (considered) useless (usu. with originator's name, —'*s F*~). [ME, f. OF *folie* f.·*fol* mad, FOOL¹, see -Y¹]

fomènt', v.t. Bathe with warm or medicated lotions, apply warmth to; foster, stimulate, or instigate (sentiment, conduct, sedition, etc.), whence ~ER¹ n. [f. F *fomenter* f. LL *fomentare* f. L *fomentum* (*fovēre* cherish, -MENT)]

fōmèntā'tion, n. In vbl senses; esp., (application of) warm flannels etc. for fomenting purposes. [f. LL *fomentatio* (prec., -ATION)]

fŏnd, a. Foolishly credulous or sanguine; over-affectionate, doting; tender, loving; ~ *of*, full of love for, much inclined to. Hence ~'LY² adv., ~'NESS n. [ME; p.p. of obs. *fon* be foolish]

fŏn'dant, n. Kind of sweetmeat. [F (*fondre* melt f. L *fundere* pour, -ANT)]

fŏn'dle, v.t. & i. Caress; toy amorously (*with, together*). [f. obs. *fond* vb (FOND), -LE(3)]

fŏns ĕt ŏrī'gō, phr. The source and origin (*of*). (L)

fŏnt, n. Receptacle for baptismal water; receptacle for holy water; oil-reservoir of lamp. [OE *font*, *fant*, ult. f. eccl. use of L *fons font*- spring]

fŏn'tal, a. Primary, original, of the fountain-head; baptismal. [f. OF, or LL *fontalis* (prec., -AL)]

fŏntanĕl(le)', n. Membranous space in infant's head at adjacent angles of parietal bones. [F (-*lle*), dim. of *fontaine* FOUNTAIN]

fōōd, n. Victuals, nourishment, provisions, (*be* ~ *for worms*, dead; *be* ~ *for fishes*, drowned; ~ *for powder*, soldiers); edibles (~ *& drink*); particular kind of ~; nutriment of plants; material for the mind (*mental, intellectual,* ~; ~ *for thought* or *meditation*); ~-*stuff*, thing used as ~. Hence ~'LESS a. [OE *fōda*, cogn. w. ON *fœtha*, Goth. *fōdeins* f. Gmc *fōdh*-,*fadh*-; cf. FEED¹]

fōōl¹, n., a., & v.i. & t. 1. Silly person, simpleton, person whose conduct one disapproves of, (*be a* ~ *to*, be nothing in comparison with; *play the* ~, blunder, trifle; *no* ~ *like an old* ~, esp. of aged lover; ~'*s bolt is soon shot*, his stock of argument is soon exhausted; *man is* ~ *or physician at thirty*, sensible man needs no doctor); jester, clown, in medieval great house (*play the* ~, indulge in buffoonery); dupe (*make a* ~ *of*; *be a* ~ *for one's pains*, take trouble to no end; *All Fools' day*, 1st April; *April*~, person taken in or sent on ~'s errand on that day; *send, go, on* ~'s *errand*, fruitless one; ~'s MATE¹; ~'s *paradise*, illusory happiness); ~'s-*cap*, ~'s'*cap*, cap with bells worn by medieval jester, dunce's conical paper cap, watermark of some old papermakers, writing paper 15-17×12-13½ in.; hence ~'ERY(4, 5),

~ŏc′racy, nn., ~′ish¹ a., ~′ishly² adv., ₒ~′ishness n., ~′proof² a. (of rules etc. so plain as to defy misinterpretation). 2. *adj. (colloq.). ~ish, silly. 3. vb. Play the ~, idle, trifle, (also *about* & *around*); cheat (person) *out of* money etc. or *into doing*, get (money etc.) by cajolery *out of* person; throw (time,.money) *away* ~ishly; make a ~ of, dupe, play tricks on. [ME, f. OF fol f. L follis bellows, later *empty- -headed person*]

fool², n. Creamy liquid of fruit stewed, crushed, & mixed with milk, cream, etc. (esp. *gooseberry* ~). [prob. f. prec.]

fool′hard|ў, a. Foolishly venturesome, delighting in needless risks. Hence ~i- ness n. [f. OF fol hardi (FOOL¹, HARDY¹)]

foot¹, n. (pl. *feet*). 1. Termination of leg beginning at ankle (FIND one's *feet; have feet of clay*, be liable to overthrow, see *Dan.* ii. 33). 2. Step, pace, tread, (*swift of* ~; *has a light* ~). 3. Infantry (*the 4th* ~ or *regiment of* ~; ~-*soldier*; *a captain of* ~; *horse,* ~, *& artillery*). 4. Lower end of bed, table, grave, couch, etc. (opp. *head*), part of stocking etc. covering~. 5. Metrical unit with varying number of syllables one of which is accented. 6. Lineal measure of 12 in. (*10 feet long; a ten-~ pole; six* ~ or *feet three*; see also SQUARE a., CUBIC). 7. Lower usu. projecting part, base. 8. (zool.). Kinds of loco- motive or adhesive organ in inverte- brates. 9. (bot.). Part by which petal is attached, root of hair. 10. Lowest part, bottom, of hill, ladder, wall, list, page, class, etc. 11. Dregs, oil refuse, coarse sugar, (pl. ~s). 12. Phrr.: *have one* ~ *in grave*, be near death; (*with* one's) *feet foremost*, being carried to burial; *find, know, length of* one's ~, learn his weak- nesses, be able to manage him; *measure another's* ~ *by* one's *own last*, judge others by oneself; *set, put, have,* one's ~ *on the neck of*, utterly subdue, hold in sub- jection; *on* one's *feet*, standing, in health, with a livelihood; *carry* one *off his feet*, make him enthusiastic, greatly excite; FALL¹ *on* one's *feet; keep* one's *feet*, not fall; *put* one's ~ *down*, take up firm position (fig.); *put* one's ~ *in it*, blunder; BEST¹ ~; CHANGE² ~ or *feet; at* one's *feet*, as his disciple, subject, or suppliant; *have* BALL¹ *at* one's *feet; with foal at* ~, of mare that has foaled; *on* ~, walking, not riding etc., also in motion (*set agitation, move- ment*, etc., *on* ~, start it), busy, projected, proceeding; *tread under* ~, oppress; *wet* etc. *under* ~, on the ground. 13. ~-*&- -mouth* (*disease*), kind of fever esp. in horned cattle; ~′*ball*, large round or elliptical inflated ball, game played with it, ~′*baller*, player at this; ~-*bath*, wash- ing of feet, small bath used for this; ~′*board*, ~man's platform at carriage- -back, board for getting in or out of carriage by, sloped board for driver's feet; ~′*boy*, page, boy servant in livery;

~-*bridge*, -*path*, -*road*, -*way*, etc., for ~-*passengers* only; ~-*drill*, -*pump*, etc., worked by or with help of ~; ~′*fall*, sound of ~*step*; ~-*fault* (Lawn Tennis), fault made by overstepping the base line while serving; ~-*gear*, boots, socks, etc.; || F~ Guards, Grenadier, Coldstream, Scots, Irish, Welsh, Guards; ~-*hill*, lying at base of mountain; ~′*hold*, support for feet, surface for standing on, also fig.; ~′*lights*, screened lights in front of stage (GET¹ *across the* ~*lights*); ~′*man*, infantry- man, liveried servant for carriage, door, & table, trivet to hang on grate bars; ~-*mark*, ~-*print*; ~-*muff*, for keeping feet warm; ~-*note*, inserted at ~ of page; ~-*pace*, walking pace, dais; ~′*pad*, un- mounted highwayman; ~-*page*, boy servant; ~-*pan*, for washing feet; ~- -*passenger*, one who walks, not rides or drives; ||~-*path* (for ~-passengers); ~- -*plate*, driver's and fireman's platform in locomotive; ~-*pound*, quantity of energy that will raise 1 lb. to height of 1 ft; ~′*print*, impression left by ~; ~-*race*, running-match between persons; ~-*rot*, disease of ~ in sheep & cattle; ~-*rule*, rigid measure 1 ft long; ||~-*slogger* (sl.), walker, infantryman, & so ~-*slogging* n. & a.; ~′*sore*, having sore feet, esp. with walking; ~′*stalk*, (Bot.) stalk of leaf or peduncle of flower. (Zool.) attachment of barnacle etc.; ~-*step*, tread, footprint, (*follow in* one's ~*steps*, do as he did); ~-*stone*, foundation stone, stone at ~ of grave; ~′*stool*, for resting feet on; ~′*sure*, sure-footed; ~′*warmer*, thing to warm feet, esp. flat hot-water tin formerly used in railway carriages; ~-*wear*, = ~-*gear*. Hence (-)~′ED², ~′LESS, aa. [OE, OS *fōt*, OHG *fuoz*, ON *fótr*, Goth. *fōtus* f. Gmc *fōt-* cogn. w. L *ped-*, Gk *pod-*]

foot², v.i. & t. ~ *it*, dance, (rare) pace, go; set foot on, traverse on foot (rare); put new foot to (stocking); add up or *up* (account); pay (bill); (of bill, items, etc.) mount *up to*. [f. prec.]

|| **foot′er**, n. (sl.). The game football. [-ER¹]

foot′ing, n. Placing of feet, foothold; surface for standing on, secure position, (lit. & fig.); conditions, relations, position, status, in which person is towards others, degree of intimacy etc.; entrance on new position, admittance to trade, society, etc., (only in *pay for* or *pay* one's ~, i.e. a customary fee for it); projecting course at foot of wall etc.; (reckoning of) sum total of column of figures etc. [FOOT² + -ING¹]

foo′tl|e, v.i., & n. (sl.). 1. Trifle, play the fool; hence ~ING² a. 2. n. Twaddle, folly. [orig. unkn.]

foo′zle, v.t., & n. (sl., esp. golf). 1. Do clumsily, bungle, make a mess of. 2. n. Clumsy failure. [f. G dial. *fuseln* work badly or slowly; cf. FUSEL OIL]

fŏp, n. Dandy, exquisite, vain man. Hence ~′LING¹(2), ~p′ERY(4, 5), nn.,

~p'ISH¹ a., ~p'ishLY² adv., ~p'ish-
NESS n. [in 15th c. 'fool', whence perh.
the 17th c. sense 'dandy']
for (fŏr, fŏr, fer, *according to position or
emphasis required*), prep. & conj. **1.** prep.
Representing, in place of, in exchange
against, as price or penalty of, in requital
of, (*sits* ~, *member* ~, *Liverpool*; *once* ~
all, instead of many repetitions, finally;
substituted ~; *agent* ~; *got it* ~ *6d.*;
thrashed ~ *his pains*; *do you take me* ~ *a
fool?*); in defence or support or favour of,
on side of, (*take my word* ~ *it*, be assured;
hurrah ~ *person or thing*; *am* ~ *tariff-
-reform*); with a view to, in order to be,
conducive(ly) to, (*go* ~ *a walk*; *went* ~ *a
soldier*; *is, did it*, ~ *her good*; ~ *sale*, to be
sold); to get, win, or save (*send, go*, ~ *a
cab*; *would not do it* ~ *the world*; *not paid
~*; *play* ~ *penny points*; *was tried* ~ *his
life*; *cannot do it* ~ *the life of me*; *run* ~
IT); to reach, arrive at, be received by, or
belong to (*left, sailed*, ~ *India*; *made* ~
shelter; *go* ~ (sl.), attack; *getting on* ~ *two
o'clock*; *bought shoes* ~ *the maids*; *won a
name* ~ *himself*); (after vbs, adjj., nn.,
& interjections, of emotion, faculty, or
fitness; after adjj. & advv. with *too,
enough*; after expressions implying fitness etc.) as regards, in the direction of,
(*don't care* ~ *games*; *a longing* ~ *praise*; *fit
~ nothing*; *ready* ~ *dinner*; *oh* ~ *wings!*;
now ~ *it!*; *too beautiful* ~ *words*; *good
enough* ~ *me*; *time* ~ *school*; *is not long* ~
this world, will soon die; *nothing* ~ *it but
to submit*, submission the only course
open; *is the man* ~ *the job*; *it is* ~ *you to
make the move*; *the motive* ~ *retreating*);
with the result, at the cost, to the amount,
of (*all out* ~ *44*; *150* ~ *6 wickets*; *drew on
him* ~ *£100*); to affect, as affecting, bene-
ficially or the reverse (*they live* ~ *each
other*; *can shift* ~ *myself*; *things look bad
~ you*; *it is bad* ~ *him to smoke*; & hence
~ with noun or pron. & infin. as neutral
noun-phrase = Latin acc. & inf., *it is
wicked* ~ *him to smoke, it is usual* ~ *hats
to be worn* = that hats should be worn);
in the character of, as, as being, (*hold it* ~
certain; *mistaken* ~ *him*; *be hanged* ~ *a
pirate*; *take* ~ *granted*; *I* ~ *one do not
believe it*; *did it* ~ *the second time*; ~
GOOD); by reason, under influence, because, on account, of (*did it* ~ *pure
wantonness*; *avoid it* ~ *fear of accidents*;
I tremble ~ *him*; *notorious* ~ *parsimony*;
do it ~ *my sake*; *fie* ~ *shame!*; *alas* ~ *him!*);
in spite of (~ *all that*, ~ *all you say*, ~ *all
he seems to dislike me, I still like him*); on
account of the hindrance of (*were it not,
but, except*, ~ *one thing I might be happy*);
corresponding to, in contrast with, (~
one enemy he has a hundred friends; *bulk
~ bulk*, taking equal bulk of each; *word
~ word*, literally, verbatim); so far as concerns, regarding, (~ *the rest*; ~ *my part*;
~ *all, aught, I know*; *hard up* ~ *money*;
wants ~ *nothing*); considering, making

the allowance required by, the usual
nature of (*a humane man* ~ *an executioner*;
very bright ~ *a winter day*); during, over,
to the extent of, (*has been so* ~ *months*;
walk ~ *two miles*; *made comfortable* ~ *life*,
~ *the present*; *left him alone* ~ *once*); ~ *all
the world*, exactly (*looked* ~ *all the world
like a porpoise*); *be for it* (sl.), be destined
for punishment. **2.** conj. (Introducing
new sentence or series of sentences containing proof of or reason for believing
what has been previously stated) seeing
that, since, in order to be convinced of
this observe or remember that . . . [OE,
OS *for*, Goth. *faur*, prob. shortened f.
Gmc *fora* FORE²]
for-, pref. formerly very common, but remaining only in some dozen common
words. Meanings: (1) away, off, apart,
(~*by*, ~*get*, ~*give*); (2) prohibition (~*bid*,
~*fend*); (3) abstention, neglect, (~*bear*,
~*go*, ~*sake*, ~*swear*); (4) bad effect (~*do*);
(5) excess, intensity (~*lorn*, ~*worn*).
[OE *for-*, *fær-*, OS *for-*, OHG *fir-*, *far-*,
Goth. *fair-*, *faur-*, cogn. w. Gk *peri*, *pro*,
para, & L *per*, *pro*]
fŏr'age, n., & v.t. & i. **1.** Food for horses
& cattle, esp. for horses in army; foraging
(*on the* ~ etc.); ||~*-cap*, infantry undress
cap. **2.** vb. Collect ~ from, ravage;
search for ~ or (fig.) *for* anything, rummage, supply with ~; get by foraging; so
fŏr'ager (-ĭj-) [-IER] n. [ME, f. OF
fourrage(r) f. *fuerre* f. WG *fōder* FODDER]
forăm'ĕn, n. (pl. *-mĭna*). Orifice, hole,
passage, (esp. in Anat., Zool., Bot.).
Hence **forăm'inATE²**, **-ātĕd**, aa. [L
(*forare* bore, -MEN)]
fŏrasmŭch' as (-az-; -az), conj. Seeing
that, since. [= *for as much as*]
fŏr'ray, n., & v.i. (Go on, make) incursion,
raid, inroad. [prob. n. f. vb f. ME *forayer*
f. OF *fourrier* f. *fuerre* FODDER + -ier -ER¹]
forbear¹ (fŏrb'ār, forbār'), n. (usu. pl.).
Ancestor(s). [FORE- + obs. *beer* (BE, -ER¹)]
forbear'² (-bār), v.t. & i. (-*bore*, -*borne*).
Abstain or refrain from or *from*; not use
or mention; be patient. Hence ~ANCE n.,
~ingLY² adv., (-bār'-'). [OE *forberan*
(FOR-(3), BEAR²)]
forbĭd', v.t. (-*băd* or -*băde*; -*bĭdden*). Command (person etc.) not *to* do, (person etc.)
not to go to (place), not allow (person etc.
something; person or thing to exist or
happen), (~ *him to go, him the court, him
wine*; ~ *gladiators, bullfights*; *was* ~*den
wine*); (of circumstances, hindrance, etc.)
exclude, prevent, make undesirable, (*God
~!*, may it not happen!); ~*den* or *prohibited* DEGREES; ~*den fruit*, thing desired
because not allowed. [OE *forbēodan*, see
FOR-(2), BID]
forbĭdd'ing, a. Repellent, of uninviting
appearance. Hence ~LY² adv., ~NESS n.
[-ING²]
forby̆(e)', prep. & adv. (Sc. & arch.).
Besides; not to mention; in addition.
[FOR-(1) + BY; cf. G *vorbei*]

force[1], n. **1.** Strength, power, impetus, violence, intense effort; military strength; body of armed men, army, (pl.) troops; body of police (*the* ~, *the police*); strength exerted on an object, coercion, (*by* ~, *per* ~, *by* compulsion). **2.** Mental or moral strength; influence, controlling power, efficacy, power to convince, vividness of effect, (*the* ~ *of circumstances brought it about; there is* ~ *in what you say; described with much* ~); (loose use) desirability, good sense, (*can't see the* ~ *of doing what one dislikes*). **3.** Binding power, validity, (*law remains in, comes into,* ~; *put in* ~, enforce); real import, precise meaning. **4.** (phys.). Measurable and determinable influence inclining body to motion, intensity of this, (formerly) kinetic energy (CONSERVATION *of* ~ or *energy*), (formerly) cause of any class of physical phenomena, e.g. of heat or motion, conceived as inherent in matter; (fig.) agency likened to these (*considers himself a* ~ *in the world*). **5.** *By* ~ *of*, by means of; (Mil.) *in* ~, in large numbers; *in great* ~, vigorous, fit, lively; ~-*pump*, that forces water beyond range of atmospheric pressure. Hence ~'LESS (-sl-) a. [ME, f. OF f. Rom. **fortia*(L *fortis* strong)]

force[2], v.t. **1.** Use violence to, ravish. **2.** Constrain, compel, (~ *one's hand*, compel him to act prematurely or adopt policy unwillingly), put strained sense upon (words), (Cards) compel (player) to trump or reveal his strength, compel player to play (certain card); ~*d landing*, compulsory landing of aircraft owing to damage, engine failure, etc.; so ~-*land* v.t. & i.; compel (person) *to do, into doing*, or *into* specified action. **3.** Strain to the utmost, urge, (~ *the pace* or *running*, adopt high speed in race to tire adversary out quickly; so ~ *the bidding* at auction; ~ *one's voice*, strain to get notes beyond usual compass or degree of loudness beyond what is easy or natural; ~*d march*, requiring special effort; ~*d* DRAUGHT[1]; ~ *the game*, run risks to score quickly; ~ *an analogy, simile,* etc., overstrain it). **4.** Overpower, capture, make way through, break open, (stronghold, defences, pass, lock, door) by force. **5.** Drive, propel. **6.** Impose, press, (thing) *upon* person (~ *a card*, in conjuring, make one choose a particular card unconsciously). **7.** Effect, produce, by effort (~ *a smile*, make oneself smile; ~ *one's way, a passage*); take by force, extort, wring, (~ *it out of his hands*; ~*d loan*; ~ *tears from his eyes, the facts out of him*). **8.** Artificially hasten the maturity of (plant, scholar). Hence fŏr'cĕDLY[2] adv. [ME, f. OF *forcer* (prec.)]

‖ **force**[3], n. (northern). Waterfall. [f. ON *fors*]

force'ful (-sf-), a. (Arch. or literary or affected for) forcible. Hence ~LY[2] adv., ~NESS n. [-FUL]

force majeure (mahzhĕr'), n. Irresistible compulsion, coercion diplomatically recognized as irresistible; war, strike, act of God, etc., excusing fulfilment of contract. [F]

force'meat (-sm-), ·n. Meat chopped, spiced, & seasoned for stuffing. [f. obs. *force* alt. f. FARCE[2]]

fŏr'cĕps, n. sing. & pl. Surgical pincers; (Anat., Entom., Zool.) organ resembling ~, whence fŏr'cipATE[2] a. [L (genit. -*ipis*)]

fŏr'cible, a. Done by, involving, force; telling, vivid, convincing, (of acts, words, style, artist, etc.); ~-*feeble*, disguising feebleness under show of force. Hence ~NESS n., fŏr'cibLY[2] adv. [AF, OF (FORCE, -IBLE)]

fŏrd, n., & v.t. & i. **1.** Shallow place where river etc. may be crossed by wading. **2.** vb. Cross (water), cross water, by wading. Hence ~'ABLE, ~'LESS, aa. [OE, OS *ford*, OHG *furt* f. WG **furd*-; cf. FARE]

fordo' (-ŏŏ), v.t. (arch.; -*did, -done* pr. dŭn). Kill, destroy, spoil; (p.p.) exhausted, tired out. [OE *fordōn* see FOR- (4), DO[1]]

fōre[1], a. & n. **1.** Situated in front (opp. HIND, BACK, AFT). **2.** n. ~ part, bow of ship; (Naut.) *at the* ~, on the ~-royal mast-head; *to the* ~, on the spot, ready to hand, available, alive, (recently) conspicuous (*come to the* ~, take leading part). [developed f. compounds w. FORE-]

fōre[2], adv. & prep. **1.** adv. In front (still in ~ *& aft*, at bow & stern, all over ship, backwards & forwards or lengthwise in ship; ~-*&-aft rigged*, having ~-*&*-aft sails, i.e. sails set lengthwise, not to yards, as chief sails; ~-*&-aft cap*, with peak at each end). **2.** prep. In presence of (in adjurations), as ~ *George* = by George. [OE, ME *fore*, OS, OHG *fora*, Goth. *faura*; in mod. naut. use perh. f. LG; prep. often mistakenly '*fore* as if short for *before*]

fōre[3], int. (golf), warning people in front of stroke. [prob. for BEFORE]

fore-, FORE[2] freely used as a pref. with vbs, their participial adjectives, vbl nouns, & nouns of action; also with other nouns. Meanings with vbs etc.: (1) in front (~-*runner*); (2) beforehand, in advance, (~*ordain*). Meanings with nouns other than verbal or of action: (3) in front, front-, (~*quarter*); (4) front part of (~-*arm*); (5) of, near, or towards stem of ship or connected w. foremast (~*castle*, ~-*hold*); (6) anticipatory, precedent, (~-*knowledge*).

fore'arm[1] (fŏr'ărm), n. Arm from elbow to wrist or finger-tips; corresponding part in foreleg or wing. [FORE-(4)]

forearm'[2] (fŏrărm'), v.t. Arm beforehand. [FORE-(2)]

forebear (fŏr'bâr), n. = FORBEAR[1].

forebōd|e' (forb-), v.t. Predict (rare); betoken, portend; have presentiment of (usu. evil) or *that*. Hence ~'ingLY[2] adv. [FORE-(2)]

forebŏd′ing (forb-), n. Prediction (rare), presage or omen, presentiment, (esp. of evil). [-ING¹]

fore-′căbin (fōr′k-), n. Cabin in fore part of ship, usu. for second-class passengers. [FORE-(5)]

forecast′¹ (fōr̄kahst′), v.t. (*forecast* or ~*ed*, see in etym.). Estimate, conjecture, beforehand. [ME; FORE-(2)+CAST¹; ~*ed* depends on mistaken assumption that the vb is derived f. foll.]

fore′cast² (fōr′kahst), n. Foresight, prudence, (rare); conjectural estimate of something future, esp. of coming weather. [f. prec.]

forecastle, fo′c′s′le, (fōk′sl), n. (Hist.) short raised deck at bow, (in warship, later but now obs.) part of upper deck forward of aftermost fore-shroud; (in modern ship) forward part under deck where sailors live. [FORE-(5)]

foreclos|e′ (fōr̄klōz′), v.t. & i. Bar, preclude, prevent, shut out from enjoyment *of*; (Mortgage Law) bar (person entitled to redeem) upon nonpayment of money due, bar (right of redemption), take away power of redeeming (mortgage), whence ~URE (fōr̄klōzh′er) n.; settle (arguable point etc.) by anticipation. [ME, f. OF *forclore*, p.p. *-clos* (OF *for* out f. L *foris*, CLOSE³)]

fore′court (fōr′kōrt), n. Enclosed space before building, outer court. [FORE-(3)]

fore′edge (fōr′ĕj), n. Front or outer edge (esp. of book); ~ *painting*, decoration of the front (occas. the top) edge of book with coloured design. [FORE-(3)]

fore′father (fōr′fahdher), n. (Pl.) the persons, esp. in earlier generations, from whom one's father or mother is descended, (loosely) the past generations of a family or race; (sing., rare) man from whom one is descended. [FORE-(6)]

fore′finger (fōr′fǐngger), n. Finger next thumb (also called *first* or *index finger*). [FORE-(3)]

fore′fŏŏt (fōr′f-), n. One of beast's front feet; (Naut.) foremost piece of keel, course in front of this (*crossing our* ~). [FORE-(3, 5)]

fore′front (fōr′frŭnt), n. Very front, foremost part, van, (*in the* ~ *of the battle*). [FORE-(3)]

foregather. See FORGATHER.

‖ **fore′gĭft** (fōr′g-), n. (law). Premium for lease. [FORE-(6)]

forego′¹ (fōr̄gō), v.t. & i. (-*went*, -*gone* pr. -*gawn*). Precede in place or time (~*ing*, previously mentioned); ~*ne conclusion*, decision or opinion come to in advance of the evidence or necessary facts, prejudice, result that can be or could have been foreseen. [ME; FORE-(2)]

forego². See FORGO.

foregŏ′er (fōrg-), n. Predecessor. [FORE-(1)]

fore′ground (fōr′g-), n. Part of view, esp. in picture, nearest observer; most conspicuous position. [FORE-(3)]

fore′hănd (fōr′h-), n. & a. 1. Part of horse in front of rider. 2. adj. (Of stroke at tennis etc.) not backhanded. [FORE-(3)]

forehead (fŏ′rĕd), n. Part of face above eyebrows & between temples. [OE *for-hēafod* see FORE-(4), HEAD¹]

fŏ′reign (-rǐn), a. Belonging to, proceeding from, other persons or things; alien *from* or *to*, irrelevant, dissimilar, or inappropriate, *to*; introduced from outside (esp. ~ *body* or *substance* in the tissues etc.); situated outside, coming from another district, parish, society, etc.; outside the country, not in one's own land; of, in, characteristic of, coming from, dealing with, some country not in the United Kingdom or English-speaking countries (~ & *home trade*; ~ *parts*, countries; *F~ Office*, department for ~ affairs or its building; ~ *letter-paper*, thin to reduce postage). Hence ~ISM(2, 4) n., ~IZE(3) v.t. & i., (-rǐn-). [ME *foren(e)* f. OF *forain* f. LL *foranus* (L *foras*, *-is* outside, -AN)]

fŏ′reigner (-rǐn-), n. Person born in foreign country or speaking foreign language; foreign ship, imported animal or article. [-ER¹]

forejŭdge′ (fōrj-), v.t. Judge or determine before hearing the evidence. [FORE-(2)]

foreknow (fōrnō′), v.t. (-*knew*, -*known*). Know beforehand, have prescience of. So **foreKNOWLEDGE** (fōrnŏl′ĭj) n. [FORE-(2)]

fŏ′rel, fŏ′rrel, n. Vellum-like parchment for covering account-books. [ME, f. OF *forrel* f. *fuerre* sheath; see FUR]

fore′land (fōr′l-), n. Cape, promontory; strip of land in front of something. [FORE-(3)]

fore′lĕg (fōr′l-), n. Beast's front leg. [FORE-(3)]

fore′lŏck¹ (fōr′l-), n. Lock of hair growing just above forehead (*take time, occasion*, etc., *by the* ~, not let chance slip). [FORE-(3)]

fore′lŏck² (fōr′l-), n., & v.t. Wedge put through hole in bolt to keep it in place; (vb) secure thus. [FORE-(3), LOCK²]

fore′man (fōr′m-), n. President & spokesman of jury; principal workman superintending others (*working* ~, one who both works & supervises). [FORE-(3)]

fore′mast (fōr′m-), n. Forward lower mast of ship (~ *man, seaman, hand*, sailor below rank of petty officer). [FORE-(5)]

fore′most (fōr′mōst, -ost), a. & adv. superl. 1. Most advanced in position, front, (*head, end*, etc., ~, with head etc. in front); most notable, best, chief. 2. adv. Before anything else in position, in the first place, (usu. *first & ~*). [OE *formest* (= Goth. *frumists*) f. *forma* (FORE-³

+superl. *-m*, = OS *formo*. Goth. *fruma*) + -EST; assim. to *fore* & *most*]

fore′name (fōrn-), n. First or Christian name. [FORE-(3)]

fore′noon (fōrn-), n. The day till noon, morning. [FORE² + NOON]

foren′s|ic, a. Of, used in, courts of law (~*ic medicine*, medical jurisprudence). Hence ~ICALLY adv. [f. L *forensis* (FORUM) + -IC]

foreordain′ (fōrōr-), v.t. Predestinate, appoint beforehand. So **foreORDINA′TION** (fōrōr-) n. [FORE-(2)]

fore′peak (fōrp-), n. (naut.). End of forehold in angle of bows. [FORE-(5)]

fore′plane (fōrp-), n. First plane used after saw or axe. [FORE-(6)]

fore-reach′ (fōr-r-), v.i. & t. Shoot ahead; gain upon, pass. [FORE-(1)]

fore-run′ (fōr-r-), v.t. (-nn-; *-ran*, *-run*). Be precursor of, foreshadow. Hence ~n′ER¹ (1, 2) n. [FORE-(1)]

fore′sail (fōr′sl, -sāl), n. Principal sail on foremast (lowest square sail, or fore-&- -aft bent on mast, or triangular before mast). [FORE-(5)]

foresee′ (fōrsē′), v.t. (*-saw*, *-seen*). See beforehand, have prescience, of, (noun, or *that*); exercise foresight (obs. exc. in ~ING² a., ~ingLY² adv.). [FORE-(2)]

foreshadow (fōrshăd′ō), v.t. Prefigure, serve as type or presage of. [FORE-(2)]

fore′sheets (fōrsh-), n. pl. Inner part of bows of boat with gratings for bowman. [FORE-(5)]

fore′shore (fōrsh-), n. Part of shore between high- & low-water marks, or between water & land cultivated or built on. [FORE-(4)]

foreshort′en (fōrsh-), v.t. Show, portray, (object) with the apparent shortening due to visual perspective. [FORE-(1)]

foreshow′ (fōrshō′), v.t. (p.p. ~*n*). Foretell; foreshadow, portend, prefigure. [OE *forescēawian* see FORE-(1), SHOW]

fore′sight (fōr′sīt), n. Foreseeing, prevision; care for the future; front sight of gun. [FORE-(2, 3)]

fore′skin (fōrs-), n. Prepuce. [FORE-(3)]

fo′rest, n., & v.t. 1. Large tract covered with trees & undergrowth sometimes mixed with pasture, trees growing in it (lit., & fig. as a ~ *of masts*); DEER-~; (with proper name prefixed) district formerly ~ but now cultivated, as *Sherwood F~*; ‖ (Law) unenclosed woodland district kept for hunting usu. owned by sovereign; ~*-tree*, of large growth fitted for ~. **2.** v.t. Plant with trees, convert into ~. [ME, f. OF f. med. L *forestis* (*silva* wood) outside (walls of park) f. L *foris* outside]

forestall′ (fōrstawl′), v.t. (Hist.) buy up (goods) in order to profit by enhanced price; be beforehand with in action, anticipate and so baffle; deal with before the regular time, anticipate. [f. OF *foresteall* n. ambush, see FORE-(6), STALL¹]

fore′stay (fōrs-), n. Stay from foremast-

head to ship's stem to support the foremast. [FORE-(5)]

fo′rester, n. Officer in charge of forest, or of growing timber; dweller in forest; (*F*~) member of the Ancient Order of F~s (friendly society); bird or beast of forest, e.g. New-Forest pony; kinds of moth. [ME, f. OF *forestier* (FOREST, -IER)]

fo′restry, n. Wooded country, forests; science & art of managing forests. [f. OF *foresterie* (FOREST, -ERY)]

fore′taste¹ (fōr′t-), n. Partial enjoyment or suffering (*of*) in advance, anticipation. [FORE-(2)]

foretaste′² (fōrt-), v.t. Taste beforehand, anticipate enjoyment etc. of. [FORE-(2)]

foretell′ (fōlt-), v.t. (*-tōld*). Predict, prophesy; presage, be precursor of. [FORE-(2)]

fore′thought (fōr′thawt), n. Previous contriving, deliberate intention; provident care. [FORE-(6)]

fore′time (fōrt-), n. The past, early days, old times. [FORE-(6)]

fore′token¹ (fōr′t-), n. Sign of something to come, prognostic. [FORE-(6)]

foretok′en² (fōrt-), v.t. Portend, point to. [FORE-(2)]

fore′top (fōrt-), n. TOP of foremast; *foretop-gall′ant mast*, mast above *fore-top²-mast*, i.e. mast above foremast; *foretopgall′ant-sail*, sail above *fore-top′sail*, i.e. sail above foresail. [FORE-(5)]

forewarn′ (fōrwōrn′), v.t. Warn beforehand (esp. in ~*ed is forearmed*). [FORE-(2)]

fore′woman (fōr′wŏŏman), n. President & spokeswoman of jury of matrons; chief workwoman supervising others. [FORE-(3)]

fore′word (fōr′wĕrd), n. Preface; introductory remarks, esp. by another than the author of the book etc. [from 1842; mod. formation of the anti-Latinists, after G *vorwort*; FORE-(3)]

fore′yard (fōr′yärd), n. Lowest yard on FOREMAST.

fôrf′eit (-fĭt), n. & a., & v.t. **1.** (Thing) lost owing to crime or fault (*his life was the* ~ or *was* ~, *his* ~ *life*); penalty for breach of contract or neglect, fine; trivial fine for breach of rules in clubs etc. or in games (*play* ~*s*), article surrendered by player in game of ~s to be redeemed by performing ludicrous task; forfeiture. **2.** v.t. Lose right to, be deprived of, have to pay, as penalty of crime, neglect, etc., or as necessary consequence of something; hence ~ABLE a., ~URE n., (-fĭt-). [ME, f. OF *forfait* p.p. of *forfaire* f. med. L *foris facere* transgress (L *foris* outside, *facere* do)]

fôrfĕnd′, v.t. Avert, keep off, (usu. in *God* ~ *!*). [FOR-(2)]

fôrf′icate, a. (zool.). Scissor-shaped. [f. L *forfex -icis* scissors + -ATE²]

fôrgăth′er (-dh-), v.i. Assemble, meet together, associate, converse. [16th c. Sc., f. Du. *vergaderen*, w. assim. to FOR-(5), GATHER]

forgave. See FORGIVE.

fŏrge¹, n. Smithy; blacksmith's hearth or fireplace with bellows; furnace or hearth for melting or refining metal, workshop containing it. [ME, f. OF f. L *fabrica* FABRIC]

fŏrge², v.t. & i. Shape by heating in fire and hammering; fabricate. invent, (tale, lie); make in fraudulent imitation, esp. write (document, signature) in order to pass off as written by another, whence **fŏr′gER¹** n. Hence **fŏr′geABLE** (-ja-) a. [ME, f. OF *forgier* f. L *fabricare* FABRICATE]

fŏrge³, v.i. Make way, advance, gradually or with difficulty, esp. ~ *ahead*, take lead in race, get start. [orig. unkn.]

fŏr′gery, n. Forging, counterfeiting, or falsifying, of document; spurious thing esp. document or signature. [FORGE², -ERY]

forgĕt′ (-g-), v.t. & i. (-*gŏt*,-*gotten* & poet. -*got*; -tt-). Lose remembrance of or *about* (noun, *that*, *how to*, or abs.); neglect (usu. *to* do), inadvertently omit to bring or mention or attend to; put out of mind, cease to think of, (esp. *forgive & ~*); disregard, slight; ~ *oneself*, neglect one's own interests, act unbecomingly or unworthily, lose consciousness; ~-*me-not*, kinds of myosotis, esp. one with small yellow-eyed blue flowers (~-*me-not blue* as name of colour). Hence ~FUL a. (*of*), ~fulLY² adv., ~fulNESS n., ~t′ABLE a. [OE *forgietan*, OS *fargetan*, OHG *fargezzan* see FOR-(1), GET]

forgĭv|e′ (-g-), v.t. & i. (-*gāve*, -*gĭven*). Remit, let off, (debt, person debt); pardon (offence, offender, offender offence, or abs.). Hence ~′ABLE a., ~e′nĕss (-gĭvn-) [~*en* + -NESS] n., ~′ING² a., ~′ingLY² adv., ~′ingNESS n., (-g-). [OE *forgiefan* see FOR-(1), GIVE]

forgŏ′, v.t. (-*wĕnt*, -*gone* pr. -gawn). Abstain from, go without, let go, omit to take or use, relinquish. [OE *forgān* see FOR-(3), GO]

fŏ′rĭnt, n. Principal monetary unit of Hungary. [Hung.]

fŏrk, n., & v.i. & t. 1. Pronged agricultural implement for digging, lifting, carrying, or throwing; two, three, or four, -pronged instrument used in eating at table or cooking; (also *tuning*-~) steel instrument giving when struck a fixed musical note; stake with ~ed end used as prop for vines etc.; ~ing, bifurcation, e.g. that of human legs, of diverging roads, or of branches; flash of ~ed lightning; hence ~′y² a. (poet.). 2. vb. Form ~, have or develop branches; lift, carry, dig, or throw with ~; (sl.) ~ *out* or *over* or *up*, hand over, pay. [OE *forca*, OS *furka*, OHG *furcha*, ON *forkr* f. L *furca*]

fŏrked (-kt), a. With fork or fork-like end, branching, divergent, cleft, (*three*-~ etc., with three etc. prongs); two-legged. [-ED²]

forlŏrn′, a. Desperate, hopeless, (cf. foll.) abandoned, forsaken, (poet.) deprived *of*, in pitiful condition, of wretched appearance. [p.p. of obs. *forlese*, OE *forlēosan* see FOR-(1), LOSE]

forlŏrn′ hōpe, n. Storming-party; desperate enterprise. [16th c., f. Du. *verloren hoop* lost troop (*hoop* = HEAP)]

fŏrm¹, n. 1. Shape, arrangement of parts, visible aspect (esp. apart from colour), shape of body (*face & ~*). 2. Person or animal as visible or tangible (*saw a ~*, *the ~ of —, before me*). 3. (philos.). That which makes anything (*matter*) a determinate species (Scholastic), conditions of thing's existence by knowing which we can produce it (Baconian), formative principle holding together the elements of thing (Kantian). 4. Mode in which thing exists or manifests itself (*in, under, take, the ~ of*), species, kind, variety. 5. (gram.). One of the shapes taken by a word in spelling, pronunciation, or inflexion, external characteristics of words apart from meaning. 6. ‖ Class in most (esp. the Public) schools (usu. numbered from *sixth* down to *first*). 7. Arrangement & style in literary or musical composition. 8. Customary method (*in due ~*; *that is common ~*, is of no special significance), set order of words, formula, regularly drawn document, ‖ document with blanks to be filled up. 9. Formality, mere piece of ceremony. 10. Behaviour according to rule or custom (*good, bad, ~*, satisfying or offending current ideals); correct procedure (*he knows the ~*). 11. Condition of health & training (*in, out of, ~*, fit or not for racing etc., of horses or athletes; *lose one's ~*), good spirits (*was in great ~*). 12. Long seat without back, bench. 13. (Print.; ‖ also ~*e*) body of type secured in chase for printing at one impression. 14. Hare's lair. [ME, f. OF *forme* f. L *forma*]

fŏrm², v.t. & i. 1. Fashion, mould, (*into* certain shape; *after, by, from, upon*, pattern; or abs.); assume shape, become solid. 2. Mould by discipline, train, instruct, (person, or faculty etc.); embody, organize, *into* a company etc. 3. Frame, make, produce; articulate (word); conceive, (idea, judgement); develop (habit); contract (alliance); be material of, make up, make *one* or *part of*. 4. (gram.). Construct (new word) by derivation, inflexion, etc. 5. (mil. etc.). Draw up (t. & i.; often *up*) in order, assume specified formation (~ *line, column*), ~ in a formation (*right, left, ~*). [ME, f. OF *fourmer* f. L *formare* (prec.)]

fŏrm-, comb. form of FORMIC or FORMYL, as *formAL′DEHYDE*, a disinfectant & antiseptic, *form′alIN* a solution of this.

-fŏrm, suf. (in actual use -*iform*, see -I-) f. F -*forme* f. L -*formis* (FORM¹) giving adjj. (1) w. sense *having the form of* (*cruciform, cuneiform*), (2) referring to number of forms (*uniform, multiform, diversiform*). *Chloroform* does not contain this suf.

fôrm′al, a. **1.** (Metaphys.) of the essence of a thing (~ CAUSE[1]), essential not material; of the outward form, shape, appearance, arrangement, or external qualities, (Log.) concerned with the form, not the matter, of reasoning. **2.** Valid in virtue .of its form, explicit and definite, not merely tacit. **3.** Ceremonial, required by convention (a ~ call), perfunctory, having the form without the spirit; observant of forms, precise, prim, excessively regular or symmetrical, stiff, methodical, whence ~ISM(2), ~IST(2), nn., ~is′TIC a. Hence ~LY[2] adv. [ME, f. L *formalis* (FORM[1], -AL)]

fôrmãl′itў, n. Conformity to rules, propriety; ceremony, elaborate procedure; formal or ceremonial act, requirement of etiquette or custom; being formal, precision of manners, stiffness of design. [f. F *formalité* (prec., -TY)]

fôrm′aliz|e, -is|e (-īz), v.t. Give definite shape or legal formality to; make ceremonious, precise, or rigid, imbue with formalism. Hence ~A′TION n. [-IZE]

fôrm′āt (or -ah), n. Shape & size of book. [F]

fôrmā′tion, n. Forming, being formed; thing formed; arrangement of parts, structure, (Mil.) disposition of troops; a number of aircraft flying in company, whence *fôrm′āte[1] v.i., (of aircraft) fly in(to) ~; (Geol.) assemblage of rocks of series of strata having some common characteristic. [late ME, f. OF or f. L *formatio* (FORM[2], -ATION)]

fôrm′ative, a. & n. Serving to fashion, of formation; (Gram., of flexional & derivative suffixes and prefixes) used in forming words, (n.) ~ element. [OF (-*if*, -*ive*) see FORM[2], -ATIVE]

‖ **fôrme,** n. (print.). See FORM[1].

fôrm′er, a. & pron. Of the past or an earlier period (*in* ~ *times*; *more like her* ~ *self*; *our* ~ *haunts*), whence ~LY[2] adv.; *the* ~ (with noun, or oftener as pron. with possessive *the* ~'s), the first or first mentioned of two (opp. LATTER). [ME, f. *forme* + -ER[3], after FOREMOST]

fôrm′|ic, a. (chem.). ~*ic acid*, colourless irritant volatile acid contained in fluid emitted by ants. Hence **fôrm′ate[2]** [-ATE[1](3)], ~ENE, ~YL, nn. [irreg. f. L *formica* ant + -IC]

fôrmicā′tion, n. Sensation as of ants crawling over the skin. [f. L *formicatio* -*onis* tingling, f. *formica* ant]

fôrm′idab|le, a. To be dreaded; likely to be hard to overcome, resist, or deal with. Hence ~leNESS n., ~LY[2] adv. [f. F, or L *formidabilis* (*formidare* fear, -ABLE)]

fôrm′less, a. Shapeless, without determinate or regular form. Hence ~LY[2] adv., ~NESS n. [-LESS]

fôrm′ūl|a, n. (pl. -*ae*, -*as*). Set form of words, definition, enunciation of principle in form of words, statement prescribed for use on some occasion; rule unintelligently followed, conventional usage or belief, whence ~ISM(3), ~IST(2), nn., ~is′TIC a.; recipe; principle serving to accommodate differences of aim or opinion (*diplomatists seeking a* ~*a*); (Math.) rule or statement in algebraic symbols; (Chem.) expression by symbols of substance's constituents; tabulation of certain facts by symbols & figures. Hence ~**arIZE**(3) [through obs. ~*ar* a.], ~IZE(3), vv.t.=FORMULATE, ~arĬZA′TION, ~ĬZA′TION, nn. [L, dim. of *forma* FORM[1]]

fôrm′ūlarў, n. & a. Collection of formulas; document or book of set forms esp. for belief or ritual; (adj.) in or of formulas. [f. F *formulaire* f. neut. of L *formularius* (prec., -ARY[1])]

fôrm′ūl|āte, v.t. Reduce to, express in, a formula; set forth systematically. Hence ~A′TION n. [FORMULA + -ATE[3]]

fôrn′icāt|e, v.i. Commit fornication. So ~OR n. [f. LL *fornicari* (*fornix -icis* brothel), -ATE[3]]

fôrnicā′tion, n. Voluntary sexual intercourse between man (occas. restricted to unmarried man) & unmarried woman (cf. *adultery*). [ME, f. OF f. LL *fornicationem* (prec., -ION)]

‖ **forpīned′** (-nd), a. (arch.). Wasted by hunger, torture, etc. [p.p. of obs. *forpine* see FOR-(5)]

forrader. See FORWARD[2].

forrel. See FOREL.

forsāke′, v.t. (-*sŏŏk*, -*sāken*). Give up, break off from, renounce; withdraw one's help, friendship, or companionship from, desert, abandon. [OE *forsacan* (= OS *forsakan*, OHG *firsahhan*) deny, renounce, refuse, f. FOR-(3) + *sacan* contend; see SAKE]

forsŏŏth′, adv. Truly, in truth, no doubt, (used parenthet. always in irony). [OE *forsōth* (FOR, SOOTH)]

‖ **forspĕnt′,** a. (arch.). Tired out. [p.p. of obs. *forspend* see FOR-(5), SPEND]

forswear′ (-wãr), v.t. (-*swōre*, -*swōrn*). Abjure, renounce on oath; ~ one*self*, swear falsely, perjure oneself; (p.p.) perjured. [OE *forswerian*, see FOR-(3, 1), SWEAR]

forsȳth′ia, n. (Kinds of) spring-flowering ornamental shrub bearing bright-yellow flowers. [f. W. *Forsyth* (d. 1804), English botanist, + -IA[1]]

fort, n. Fortified place (usu. single building or set of connected military buildings, cf. FORTRESS); trading-station, orig. fortified (hist.). [F, abs. use of *fort* strong f. L *fortis*]

fort′alice, n. (Arch. & poet.) fortress; (mod.) small outwork of fortification, small fort. [f. med. L *fortalitia* (L *fortis* strong)]

fôrte[1], n. Person's strong point; (Fenc.) sword-blade from hilt to middle (cf. FOIBLE). [f. F *fort* abs. use of adj.= strong; for substitution of fem. form cf. *morale, locale*]

fort'é², mus. direction (abbr. *f.*). Loud; ~ ~ (abbr. *ff.*), very loud ; ~ *piano* (abbr. *fp.*), loud & then immediately soft. [It.]

forth, adv. & prep. **1.** Forwards (now only in *back & ~*, to & fro) ; onwards in time (now only in *from this time ~*, & in comb. as *hence~*) ; forward, into view, (*bring, come, show*, etc., ~) ; out from home etc. (*sail, issue*, ~) ; out of doors (*cast ~*) ; & *so ~*, & so on, & the like ; *so far ~*, to that extent ; *so far ~ as*, to whatever extent. **2.** prep. (arch.). From out of. [OE, OS *forth*, MHG *vort* f. WG **fortha*]

forthcom'ing (-kŭ-), a. About or likely to come forth ; approaching ; ready to be produced when wanted. [prec., COME, -ING²]

forthright' (-rīt), adv., **forth'right** (-rīt), a. & n. **1.** adv. Straight forward ; straightway. **2.** adj. Going straight ; outspoken, unswerving ; decisive, dextrous. **3.** n. (arch.). Straight course (*~s & meanders*). [OE ; FORTH+RIGHT a. & adv.]

forthwith' (-th, -dh), adv. Immediately, without delay. [for *forth with* used abs.]

fortifica'tion, n. Fortifying ; strengthening of wine with alcohol ; (Mil.) providing, art or science of providing, with defensive works, (usu. pl.) defensive work(s), wall(s), earthwork(s), tower(s), etc. [F, f. LL *fortificationem* act of strengthening (foll., -ATION)]

fort'if‖ȳ, v.t. & i. Strengthen structure of ; impart vigour or physical strength or endurance to, strengthen mentally or morally, encourage ; increase nutritive value of (food) ; strengthen (liquors) with alcohol ; corroborate, confirm, (statement) ; provide (town, army, one*self*) with defensive works ; erect fortifications. Hence ~IABLE a. [late ME, f. OF *fortifier* f. LL *fortificare* (*fortis* strong, -FY)]

fortiss'ĭmō, mus. direction (abbr. *ff.*, *ffor.*, *forss.*). Very loud. [It.]

fortiter. See SUAVITER.

fort'itūde, n. Courage in pain or adversity. [F, f. L *fortitudo* (*fortis* strong, -TUDE)]

fort'night (-nīt), n. Period of two weeks (*today, this day, Monday*, etc., ~, a ~ from today etc. ; *would rather keep him* etc. a *week than a ~*, he etc. is a large eater). [OE *fēorwertȳne niht* fourteen nights]

fort'nightlȳ (-it-), a. & adv. (Happening, appearing) once every fortnight. [-LY¹, ²]

fort'ress, n., & v.t. Military stronghold, esp. strongly fortified town fit for large garrison ; (vb, poet.) serve as ~ to, protect. [ME, f. OF *forteresse* f. Rom. **fortaritia* (cf. FORTALICE), f. L *fortis* strong]

fortu'itism, fortu'itist, nn. Belief, believer, in chance & natural causes, not design, as causing adaptations in nature (cf. *teleology*, *-ist*). [foll. -ISM, -IST]

fortu'itous, a. Due to or characterized by chance, accidental, casual. Hence ~LY² adv., ~NESS n. [f. L *fortuitus* (*fors -tis* chance) +-OUS]

fortu'itȳ, n. Fortuitousness ; a chance occurrence ; accident ; unstudied or unintended character. [irreg. f. on prec. (-ITY)]

fort'ūnate, a. Favoured by fortune, lucky, prosperous ; auspicious, favourable. [ME, f. L *fortunatus* (FORTUNE, -ATE²)]

fort'ūnatelȳ (-tl-), adv. Luckily, successfully, (esp. as parenthesis qualifying whole sentence = it is a fortunate thing that). [-LY²]

fort'ūne¹ (-chŏŏn, -tūn), n. Chance, hap, luck, as a power in men's affairs (*F~*, this power personified as goddess ; *try the ~ of war*, see what it will bring, risk it ; SOLDIER *of ~*) ; luck good or bad that falls to anyone· or to an enterprise etc. (in sing. or pl. ; *try* one's ~, take some risky step), coming lot (*tell* person his ~, *tell ~s*, of gipsies etc., whence ~-tĕllER¹ n.) ; good luck ; prosperity, prosperous condition, wealth, (*make* one's ~, prosper ; *make a ~*, become rich ; *spent a small ~ on it*, large sum ; *marry a ~*, heiress), whence ~LESS (-nl-) a. ; *~-hunter*, man seeking rich wife. [ME, f. OF f. L *fortuna*]

fort'ūne² (-chŏŏn, -tūn), v.i. (arch. & poet.). Chance, occur, (esp. impers., *it ~d that*) ; come by chance *upon*. [ME, f. OF *fortuner* f. L *fortunare* make fortunate (prec.)]

fort'ȳ, a. & n. **1.** Four times ten, 40, xl, XL, (*~-one*, *~-first*, etc. ; ~ *winks*, short nap esp. after dinner) ; hence **fort'ieTH** a. & n. **2.** n. Age of ~ years (*after ~*, *over ~* ; *the forties*, years of life or century between 39 & 50 ; HUNGRY *Forties*) ; *roaring forties*, stormy ocean tracts between lat. 30° & 50° S. ; ‖ *the Forties*, sea area between N.E. coast of Scotland and S.W. coast of Norway (so named from its depth of ~ fathoms or more) ; ‖*~-PENNY nail*; *the F~-five*, Jacobite rebellion of 1745. [OE *fēowertig* (FOUR, -TY²)]

for'um, n. (Rom. Ant.) public place, market-place, place of assembly for judicial & other business, esp. at Rome ; place of public discussion ; periodical etc. giving opportunity for debate etc. ; court, the law courts, (fig. *the ~ of conscience* etc.). [L]

for'ward¹, a. & n. **1.** (Naut.) belonging to fore part of ship ; lying in one's line of motion (*the ~ horizon*), onward or towards the front (*the ~ path*; ~ *play* in cricket, see foll. ; ~ *movement*, special effort at political etc. progress ; ~ *school, party, opinions*, advanced or extreme). **2.** (commerce). Relating to future produce (*~ contract*). **3.** Advanced, progressing to maturity or completion, (of plant, crop, season) well advanced or early ; ready, prompt, eager, (often *to* do) ; precocious ; presumptuous, pert, whence ~LY² adv. ; hence ~NESS n. **4.** n. One of the first-line players in football, hockey, etc. [OE *foreweard* (FORE², -WARD), a.]

fŏr'ward²(s), adv. (-d is added below to senses in which the -s form is rare or not used). Towards the future, continuously onwards, (-d; *from this time* ~; *look* ~, ahead; CARRIAGE ~; *date* ~, of commercial orders, post-date). **2.** Towards the front in the direction one is facing, (Cricket; -d) *play* ~, reach ~ to play short-pitched ball; with continuous ~ motion (*rushing* ~), (Mil., as word of command, -d, = go ~, advance). **3.** In advance, ahead, (-d; *send him* ~; ~-*looking*, progressive); *backward(s) & *~, to & fro; to the front, into prominence, (-d; *bring* ~, draw attention to; *come* ~, offer oneself for task, post, etc.; *put* or *set* ~, allege, make one*self* too conspicuous). **4.** (naut.; -d). To, at, in, fore part of ship. **5.** Onward so as to make progress (-d; *go* ~, be going on, progress; *can't get any forwarder*, or usu. colloq. *forrader*, make no progress). [OE *foreweard*, prob. neut. acc. of prec.]

fŏr'ward³, v.t. Help forward, promote; accelerate growth of; send (letter etc.) on to further destination, (loosely) dispatch (goods etc.). [f. prec.]

‖ **forwear'ied** (-ĭd), **forwŏrn'**, aa. (arch.). Tired out. [FOR-(5), WEARY, WEAR², vv.]

fŏsse, n. Long narrow excavation, canal, ditch, trench, esp. in fortification; (Anat.), groove, depression, also **fŏssette'** n. [ME, f. OF, f. L *fossa* orig. fem. p.p. of *fodere* dig]

fŏss'ick, v.i. (sl.). Rummage, search about. [dial. wd current in Austral. gold-mining = search in crevices or abandoned workings]

fŏss'il, a. & n. Found buried, dug up, (~ *fuel* etc.; now rare); (thing) preserved in strata of earth with more or less chemical or other change of texture & recognizable as remains or impressions of plant or animal of past (usu. prehistoric) ages (~ *bones, shells, ivory*; *hunting for* ~*s*; also fig., as *words are* ~ *thoughts*); (person or thing) belonging to the past, antiquated, incapable of further development. Hence ~ATE³ v.t., ~A'TION n., ~ĬF'EROUS a., ~IZE(3) v.t. & i., ~IZA'TION n. [f. F *fossile* f. L *fossilis* (*fodere* fossdig, -IL)]

fŏssōr'ial, a. (zool.). Burrowing; used in burrowing. [f. LL *fossorius* (*fossor* digger f. *fodere* see prec., -OR) + -AL]

fŏs'ter¹, n. Food (obs. exc. in comb., as ~-*child, -father, -mother, -parent, -son, -daughter, -brother, -sister*, = having the specified relationship not by blood, but in virtue of nursing or bringing up); acting or treated as —; ~-*mother*, (also) = IN-CUBATOR. [OE *fōstor* (FOOD, suf. -*tro*-)]

fŏs'ter², v.t. (Arch.) tend affectionately, cherish, keep warm (in bosom), promote growth of; encourage or harbour (feeling); (of circumstances) be favourable to. Hence ~ER¹, **fŏs'trĔSS¹**, nn. [OE *fōstrian*, f. prec.]

fŏs'terage, n. Fostering; custom of employing foster-mothers. [-AGE]

fŏs'terling, n. Foster-child, nursling, protégé. [OE *fōstorling* (FOSTER¹, -LING¹)]

fougasse (foogahs'), n. Improvised mortar excavated in the ground, charged with stones, bits of iron, etc., and fired by gunpowder. [F]

fought. See FIGHT¹.

foul, a., n., adv., & v.i. & t. **1.** Offensive to the senses, loathsome, stinking, (~ *brood*, a disease of larval bees); dirty, soiled (~ *linen*), filthy; (sl.) revolting, disgusting; defaced with corrections (~ *copy*); charged with noxious matter (~ *air, water*); clogged, choked, (~ *gun--barrel*); (of ship's bottom) overgrown with weed, barnacles, etc.; morally polluted, obscene, disgustingly abusive, (*the* ~ *fiend*, the devil; ~ *deed, motive, talk*; ~-*mouthed, -tongued*); (of fish at or after spawning) in bad condition; ugly (now dial. exc. in *fair or* ~); unfair, against rules of game etc., (~ *blow, stroke, riding*; ~ *play*, in games, & fig. treachery, murder or violence); (of weather) wet, rough, stormy; (of wind) contrary; in collision (FALL¹ ~ *of*); entangled (*rope is* ~). **2.** n. Something ~ (*through* ~ *& fair*, through everything); collision, entanglement, esp. in riding, rowing, or running, irregular stroke or piece of play. **3.** adv. In irregular way (*hit him* ~; *play* one ~, deal treacherously with him). **4.** vb. Become ~, get clogged; make ~ or dirty (~ *one's own* NEST); pollute with guilt, dishonour; cause (anchor, cable) to become entangled, jam or block (crossing, railway line, traffic); become entangled; run ~ of, collide with. [OE, OS, OHG *fūl*, ON *fúll*, Goth. *fūls* f. Gmc **fūlaz*]

foul'ard (fool'ahr), n. Thin flexible material of silk or silk & cotton; handkerchief of it. [F]

foulé (foolā'), n. Light woollen dress material with glossy surface. [F, = pressed (cloth), p.p. of *fouler* FULL²]

foul'ly (-l-lĭ), adv. Abominably, cruelly, wickedly (*was* ~ *murdered*); with unmerited insult (~ *slandered*). [-LY²]

foul'nĔss, n. Foul condition; foul matter; disgusting wickedness. [-NESS]

foum'ărt (foo-), n. Polecat. [ME *fulmard* (FOUL, *mearth* marten)]

found¹, v.t. & i. Lay base of (building etc.); be original builder, begin building, of (town, edifice); set up, establish (esp. with endowment), originate, initiate, (institution); construct, base, (tale, one's fortunes, classification, rule, etc.) (*up*)*on* some ground, support, principle, etc. (also *is* ~*ed in justice* etc.; *well, ill,* etc., ~*ed*, reasonable, justified, baseless, etc.); rely, base oneself, (of argument etc.) be based, (*up*)*on*. [ME, f. OF *fonder* f. L *fundare* (*fundus* bottom)]

found², v.t. Melt & mould (metal), fuse (materials for glass); make (thing of molten metal, glass) by melting. So

foun'dry(3) n. [ME, f. OF *fondre* f. L *fundere fus-* pour]

found[3]. See FIND.

founda'tion, n. Establishing, constituting on permanent basis, esp. of an endowed institution; such institution, e.g. monastery, college, or hospital (*on the ~*, entitled to benefit by its funds, whence ‖ ~-ER[1] (-shon-) n.), or its revenues; solid ground or base, natural or artificial, on which building rests, lowest part of building usu. below ground-level; basis, groundwork, underlying principle, (*report has no ~*; *base religion on a moral ~*); body or ground on which other parts are overlaid, e.g. underskirt, first set of stitches in crochet or knitting; ~ *garment*, woman's supporting undergarment, e.g. corset, corslet, girdle; ~-*muslin*, *-net*, gummed fabrics for stiffening dresses & bonnets; ~-*school*, endowed; ~-*stone*, esp. one laid with ceremony to celebrate founding of edifice. [ME, f. OF *fondation* or L *fundatio* (FOUND[1], -ATION)]

foun'der[1], n. In vbl senses of FOUND[1]; esp., one who founds institutions (~-*member*; ‖ ~'s *kin*, relatives of ~ entitled to election or preference); ~'s *shares*, shares issued to ~s of public company as part-consideration for business taken over, & separate from ordinary capital. Hence ~SHIP, **foun'dress**[1], nn. [-ER[1]]

foun'der[2], n. In vbl senses of FOUND[3]. [-ER[2]]

foun'der[3], v.i. & t., & n. 1. (Of earth, building, etc.) fall down or in, give way; (of horse; or with rider substituted as subject) fall from overwork, collapse, fall lame, stick fast in bog etc.; cause (horse) to break down by overwork; (of ship) fill with water & sink, cause (ship) to do this; (Golf) hit (ball) into ground. 2. n. Inflammation of horse's foot from overwork; (also *chest, body*, ~) rheumatism of chest-muscles in horses. [ME, f. OF *fondrer* submerge, collapse, (L *fundus* bottom)]

found'ling, n. Deserted infant of unknown parents. [ME; p.p. of FIND + -LING[1]]

fount[1], n. (poet. or rhet.). Spring, source, fountain; (shop) reservoir of oil in lamp or of ink in pen. [f. L *fons -tis* on anal. of *mount*; from late 16th c.]

‖**fount**[2] (*or* fŏnt), n. (print.). Set of type of same face & size. [f. F *fonte* (*fondre* FOUND[2])]

foun'tain (-tǐn), n. Water-spring; source of river etc. (also fig., *Crown is the ~ of honour*; *poison the ~s of trust*); jet of water made to spout, structure provided for it, (also *drinking-~*) public erection with constant supply of drinking-water; reservoir in lamp, printing-press, etc., for oil, ink, etc. (~-*pen*, having this); ~-*head*, original source. Hence (-)~ED[2] (-ĭnd) a. [ME, f. OF *fontaine* f. LL *fontana* orig. fem. of L *fontanus* adj. (FOUNT[1], -AN)]

four (fōr), a. & n. 1. One more than three, 4, iv, IV, (~ *corners of earth* etc., remotest parts; ~ *corners of document* etc., its scope; *within the ~ seas*, in Gt Britain; ~ *figures*, some number from 1000 to 9999; *twenty* etc. -~ or ~-*&-twenty* etc.; ~-*&--twentieth* etc.); (ellipt.) ~ *hours* (~*o'clock*), ~ *horses* (*carriage* etc. *&~*); ‖ ~-*ale* (hist.), sold at 4*d.* a quart; ~ *by two*, rifle pull--through cloth; ~-*coupled*, with ~ coupled wheels; ~-*course*, with fourfold rotation (of crops); ~-DIMENSIONAL; *~-flusher* (sl.), bluffer, humbug [orig. Poker term]; ~-*footed*, quadruped (adj.); ‖ ~-*foot way*, space (4 ft. 8½ in.) between pair of rails; ~ FREEDOMS; ~-*handed*, (of monkeys) quadrumanous, (of games) for ~ persons, (of piece of music) for two players; ~-*horse*(d), drawn by ~ horses; ~-*in-hand*, vehicle with ~ horses driven by one person on the box (also adv., *drive* etc. ~-*in-hand*); ~-*oar*, (boat) with ~ oars; ~ *o'clock*, the plant marvel of Peru; ~-*part*, arranged for ~ voices to sing; ~'*pence*, sum or coin = 4*d.*; ~'*penny*, costing 4*d.*, (obs.) silver coin = 4*d.*; ~-*post* (of bed), having ~ posts to support canopy, ~-*poster*, such bed, (also) 4-masted ship; ~-*pounder*, gun throwing 4-lb. shot; ~-*rowed barley*, with ~ rows of awns; ~'*score*, eighty, age of 80 years; ~-*square*, square-shaped, solidly based or steady; ~-*stroke* (attrib., of internal-combustion engines), having a cycle of ~ strokes (intake, compression, combustion, and exhaust); *the ~ hundred*, the exclusive social set of any place; ~-*wheel*, ~-wheeled carriage; ~-*wheeler*, ~-wheeled hackney carriage; hence ~-FOLD a. & adv., ~-TEEN' a., ~-teenTH' a. & n., (fōr-). 2. n. The number ~; set of ~ persons or things, esp. ~-pipped card, domino, or side of die, ~-oared boat & crew (~*s*, races for these), hit etc. at cricket for ~ runs; *on all* ~*s* (earlier ~ = ~ limbs), crawling on hands & knees, (also, fig.) completely analogous or corresponding (*the cases are not on all* ~*s*; *is the simile on all* ~*s with the thing illustrated?*); ~-*pennyworth of* spirits (hist.); (pl.) ~-*per-cent.* stock. [OE *fēower*, OS *fiwar*, OHG *fior*, ON *fjórir*, Goth. *fidwōr*, cogn. w. Gk *tessares*, L *quatuor*]

fourgon (foor'gawn), n. Luggage-van. [F]

Four'ierism (fŏŏ-), n. Fourier's system for reorganization of society (PHALANSTERY). [Charles *Fourier*, French socialist, 1772–1837]

four'some (fōr-), n. Game of golf between two pairs, partners playing the same ball; (colloq.) a company or party of four persons. [FOUR, -SOME; orig. adj.]

fourth (fōr-), a. & n. 1. Next after third (*the, a*, ~, ellipt. as n., esp. = 4th day of month; ~ *part*, quarter); ~ ESTATE; *F~ Republic* (in France 1947–58). 2. n. Quarter, ~ part; (Mus.) interval of which the span involves four alphabetical notes, harmonic combination of notes thus separated; *F~ of June*, principal annual celebration at Eton College, speech-day and procession of boats; *F~ of July*, U.S. anniversary of declaration of Independence; ~ *party* (hist.), Lord R. Churchill, Sir H. D. Wolff, Sir J. Gorst, Mr Balfour, and a few other Conservatives who (1880- -5) attacked impartially the Liberal Government & the Conservative front bench; (pl.) articles of ~ quality. [OE *féortha*, OS *fiortho*, OHG *fiordo*, ON *fjórthi*, cogn. w. Gk *tetartos* L *quartus*]

fourth'ly (fōr-), adv. In the fourth place (in enumerations). [-LY²]

fōv'é|a, n. (anat. etc.; pl. ~ae pr. -ē). A small depression or pit. Hence ~AL, ~ATE², aa., pitted. [L]

fove'ola, n. (pl. -ae pr. -ē). A small fovea. Hence **fōv'éol**ATE², -ātéd, aa., pitted. [L, dim. of prec.]

fowl, n., & v.i. 1. Bird (rare), birds (rare exc. in *wild-~*), their flesh as food (only in *fish, flesh, & ~*); domestic cock or hen (often qualified, as *barn-door ~, game, guinea, -~*; ~*-pest*, infectious disease of ~s resembling chicken cholera; || ~*-run*, place where ~s may run, breeding establishment for ~s), its flesh as food. 2. v.i. Catch, hunt, shoot, or snare, wild-~, whence ~'ER¹, ~'ING¹, nn.; ~*ing-piece*, light gun used in~ing. [OE *fugol*, OS *-al*, OHG *fogal*, ON *fugl*, Goth. *fugls* f. Gmc **foglaz* perh. by dissim. f. **flugla-* (*flug-FLY²*)]

fōx¹, n. (fem. VIXEN, also *bitch-~*). Red- -furred sharp-snouted bushy-tailed quad- ruped preserved in England as beast of chase & proverbial for cunning; crafty person; northern constellation; FLYING ~; ~ *& geese*, game played on board; ~*-brush*, tail of ~; ~*-chase*, ~*-hunt*; ~*-*EARTH¹; ~*'glove*, tall plant with purple or white flowers like glove fingers; ~*'hole* (Mil.), hole in ground used as shelter against missiles or as firing-point; ~*'hound*, kind bred & trained to hunt ~es; ~*-hunt* n. & v.i., chasing of, chase, ~ with hounds, whence ~'**hunt**ER¹ n.; ~*-hunting* a. & n., (given to) this sport; ~*'tail*, ~'s tail, kinds of grass; ~*-terrier*, short-haired for unearthing ~, but kept chiefly as pet; ~*'trot*, an American dance. [OE *fox*, OS *vuhs*, OHG *fuhs* f. WG **fuhs*]

fōx², v.i. & t. Act craftily, dissemble; discolour (leaves of book, engraving, etc.) with brownish spots (esp. in p.p.); (sl.) deceive, trick. [f. prec.]

fōx'|ў̄, a. Fox-like, crafty(-looking); red- dish-brown, (Paint.) over-hot in colour; damaged with mildew etc. Hence ~i**NESS** n. [-Y²]

*|| **foyer** (fwah'yā), n. Large room in theatre etc. for audience's use during interval. [F]

fra (-ah), n. = FRATE as prefixed title. [It.]

frăc'as (-ah), n. (pl. same). Noisy quarrel, row. [F, f. It. *fracasso* uproar]

frăc'tion, n. 1. Dividing of Eucharistic bread. 2. (arith.). Numerical quantity that is not an integer, one or more aliquot parts, (*vulgar ~*, expressed by numerator above & denominator below a line; DECI-MAL~; *proper, improper, ~*, with numerator less, greater, than denominator). 3. Small piece or amount, scrap, (esp. *not a ~*). Hence ~AL ·(~*al distillation*, partial separation of liquids having different boiling-points by gradual heating), ~ARY¹, aa., (-shon-). [ME, f. OF *fraction* f. LL *fractionem* (L *frangere fract-* break, -ION)]

frăc'tionāte (-shon-), v.t. Separate (mixture) into portions of different properties by distillation etc. [prec. + -ATE³]

frăc'tionīze (-shon-), -ise (-īz), v.t. Break up into fractions (Math.), or portions. [-IZE]

frăc'tious (-shus), a. Unruly, cross, peevish. Hence ~LY² adv., ~NESS n., (-shus-). [f. FRACTION in obs. sense brawling + -OUS, after *captious* etc.]

frăc'ture, n., & v.t. & i. 1. Breaking, breakage, esp. of bone or cartilage (COM-POUND² ~); surface shown by mineral when broken with hammer; substitution of diphthong, diphthong substituted, for simple vowel owing to influence of following consonant. 2. vb. Cause ~ in, break continuity of, crack (t. & i.). [f. F, or L *fractura* (FRACTION, -URE)]

fraen'um, frē-, n. (pl. -*na*). Small ligament checking motion of organ. [L, = bridle]

frǎ'gile, a. Easily snapped or shattered, weak, perishable, of delicate frame or constitution. So **fragil'**ITY n. [f. F, or L *fragilis* (*frag-* root of *frangere* break)]

frăg'ment, n. Part broken off, detached piece; isolated or incomplete part, remainder of lost or destroyed whole, esp. extant remains or unfinished portion of a writing or work of art. Hence ~ARY¹ a., ~A'TION n. (~*ation bomb*, one breaking up into small ~s when exploded). [f. F, or L *fragmentum* (as prec., -MENT)]

frăg'rant, a. Sweet-smelling. So **frăg'**rANCE n. [f. obs. F, or L *fragrare* smell sweet, -ANT]

frail¹, n. Rush basket for packing figs, raisins, etc. [ME, f. OF *fraiel*, of unkn. orig.]

frail², a. Fragile; transient (~ *life, bliss*, etc.); in weak health; morally weak, unable to resist temptation, (euphem., of women) unchaste. [ME, f. OF *fraile* FRAGILE]

frail'tў̄, n. Liability to err or yield to temptation; fault, weakness, foible. [ME, f. OF *frailete* f. L *fragilitatem* (FRAGILE, -TY)]

fraise¹ (-z), n. (fortif.). Horizontal or down-sloping palisade round berm. [F, orig. = mesentery of calf]

fraise² (-z), n. Tool for enlarging circular hole or cutting teeth in watch wheels. [F (*fraiser* enlarge hole f. *fraise* as prec.)]

frămboes'ïa (-bēz-), n. Contagious tropical disease with raspberry-like swellings, the yaws. [mod. L, f. F *framboise* raspberry +-IA¹]

frăm|e¹, v.t. & i. Shape, direct, dispose, (thoughts, acts, another person) to a purpose (*for, to, to* do, or with adv.); give promise of being skilful etc. (usu. *well*); adapt, fit, *to* or *into*; construct by combination of parts or adaptation to design, contrive, devise, invent, compose, express, (complex article, plot, rule, story, theory); articulate (words); conceive, imagine; [f. foll.] set in a frame, serve as frame for (*landscape ~ed in an archway*), whence ~'ING¹(3) n.; (orig. U.S. sl.) concoct false charge against, devise plot with regard to; ~e *up* (orig. U.S. sl.), prearrange (event) with sinister intent, fake result of (race, election, etc.). Hence ~'ABLE a., ~'ER¹ n. [OE *framian* be helpful (*fram* forward, see FROM)]

frăme², n. Construction, constitution, build; established order, plan, system, (*the ~ of society* or *government*); temporary state (*of* mind); framed work or structure (*the ~ of heaven* or *earth*), human or animal body (*sobs shook her ~, man of gigantic ~*); skeleton of building, underlying support or essential substructure of anything; case or border enclosing picture, pane of glass, etc., whence ~'LESS (-ml-) a.; single complete image or picture transmitted in series of lines by television; (Gardening) glazed portable box-like structure protecting plants from cold; ‖ (Mining) inclined board for washing ore; (Snooker) triangular ~ for setting up balls, balls so set up, round of play during which balls are pocketed; ~ *aerial*, revolving aerial composed of rectangles or loops of wire, adapted for directional reception; ~*-house*, of wooden skeleton covered with boards; ~*-saw*, stretched in ~ to make it rigid; *~*-up*, conspiracy; ~*'work*, ~, structure, upon or into which casing or contents can be put (lit., fig.). [f. prec.]

frănc, n. French, Belgian, & Swiss monetary unit. [ME, f. OF, f. *Francorum Rex* king of the FRANKS, legend on earliest gold coin so called (14th c.)]

frăn'chïse (-z), n. (Chiefly hist. & U.S.) legal immunity or exemption from some burden or jurisdiction, privilege or exceptional right, granted to person, corporation, etc.; full membership of corporation or State, citizenship; right of voting at public elections esp. for member of Parliament, principle of qualification for this (FANCY¹~). [ME, f. OF (*franc* FRANK², -ISE)]

Frăncis'can, a. & n. (Friar) of the order founded 1209 by St Francis of Assisi; of the ~s. [f. F *franciscain* f. med. L *Franciscus* Francis +-AN]

frăn'cïum, n. Radio-active metallic element. [f. *France* +-IUM]

Frănc'o-, comb. form of med. L *Franci* the Franks, now used = French-&-, as ~*-German*. Hence ~PHIL(E), ~PHOBE, nn. & aa. [FRANK¹, -O-]

frănc'olin, n. Kind of partridge resembling pheasant. [F, f. It. *francolino*]

franc tireur (see Ap.), n. (pl. *-cs -rs*). Man of irregular light-infantry corps; a guerrilla fighter. [F]

frăn'gible (-j-), a. Breakable, fragile. [OF, f. L *frangere* to break +-IBLE]

frăn'gïpāne, -ăni, (-j-), n. (Perfume of) red jasmine; kind of almond cream or paste. [F, prob. f. *Frangipani*, maker]

Frănk¹, n. One of the Germanic nation or coalition that conquered France in 6th c.; (in Levantine use) person of Western nationality. Hence~'ISH¹ a. [OE *Franca*, OFrank. *Franko*, (whence med. L *Francus*, OF *Franc*), perh. f. weapon (cf. OE *franca* javelin)]

frănk², a. Ingenuous, open, candid, outspoken; undisguised, avowed. Hence ~'LY² adv., ~'NESS n. [f. OF *franc* f. med. L *francus* free f. prec. (full freedom being confined to the Franks)]

frănk³, v.t., & n. 1. (Hist.) superscribe (letter etc.) with signature ensuring gratis conveyance; facilitate coming & going of (person), give social passport to; convey (person) gratuitously; exempt from future payment etc. (*a ~ing duty, imposition*); ~*ing machine* (for stamping letters etc. and recording cost of postage incurred). 2. n. (hist.). ~ing signature, ~ed cover. [f. prec. in obs. sense *free of charge*]

Frănk'enstein (-tīn), n. ~*'s monster*, thing that becomes formidable to the person who has created it. [M. W. Shelley (d. 1851), *Frankenstein*]

Frănk'fort blăck, n. Fine black pigment used in copperplate engraving. [German town]

*frănk'furt(er) (-fer-), n. Highly seasoned German sausage. [f. *Frankfurt* German town]

frănk'incĕnse, n. Aromatic gum resin (prop. from trees of genus *Boswellia*) used for burning as incense. [ME, f. OF *franc encens* (FRANK² in obs. sense *luxuriant*, INCENSE¹)]

frănk'lin, n. (hist.). Land-owner of free but not noble birth in 14th & 15th cc. [ME *francoleyn* etc., as FRANK², w. second element of obsc. orig.]

frănk'-plĕdge, n. (hist.). System by which each member of tithing was responsible for every other (also rarely fig., e.g. of relation between members of a Government). [AF *franc plege* (FRANK², PLEDGE), mistransl. of OE *frithborh* peace-pledge (not free-pledge)]

frăn'tļic, a. Wildly excited, beside oneself with rage, pain, grief, etc.; showing frenzy, uncontrolled. Hence ~ICALLY,

~**ĭcLY²**, advv. [ME *frentik, frantik* f. OF *frenetic* PHRENETIC]

frăp, v.t. (naut.). (-pp-). Bind tightly. [f. F *frapper* bind, strike]

frăppé (-ăp'ā), a. (Esp. of wines) iced, cooled. [p.p. of F *frapper* strike]

frăss, n. Excrement of larvae; refuse left by boring insects. [f. G *frass* (*fressen* devour)]

frat'e (-ahtă), n. (pl. *-ti* pr. -tē). Friar. [It.]

frăt'er, n. (hist.). = REFECTORY. [ME, f. OF *fraitur* for *refreitor* f. med. L *refectorium* REFECTORY]

fratĕrn'al, a. (As) of brother(s), brotherly; *~ order*, FRIENDLY Society. [f. med. L *fraternalis* f. L *fraternus* (*frater* brother, -AL)]

fratĕrn'ĭtў, n. Being fraternal, brotherliness; religious body; guild, company with common interests, set of men of same class etc.; *students' society in university or college. [ME, f. OF *fraternite* f. L *fraternitatem* (prec., -TY)]

frăt'ernĭz|e, -is|e (-īz), v.i. Associate, make friends, behave as intimates, (*with, together*, or abs.). So ~A'TION n. [f. F *fraterniser* (L *fraternus* FRATERNAL, -IZE)]

frăt'rĭcĭd|e, n. Killing of one's, one who kills his, brother or sister. Hence ~AL a. [f. F, or L *fratricida*, LL -*cidium*, (*frater -tris* brother, -CIDE)]

Frau (frow), n. (Of German wife or widow) Mrs; German woman. [G]

fraud, n. Deceitfulness (rare); criminal deception, use of false representations, (in Law, *in ~, to the ~, of*, so as to defraud); dishonest artifice or trick (*pious ~*, deception intended to benefit deceived, & esp. to strengthen religious belief); person or thing not fulfilling expectation or description. [ME, f. OF *fraude* f. L *fraudem* nom. *fraus*]

fraud'ŭl|ent, a. Guilty of, of the nature of, characterized or effected by, fraud. Hence or cogn. ~ENCE n., ~entLY² adv. [ME, f. OF, or L *fraudulentus* (prec., -ULENT)]

fraught (frawt), a. Stored, equipped, *with* (poet.); (fig.) *~ with*, involving, attended with, full of, threatening or promising, destined to produce, woe, danger, meaning, etc. [ME, p.p. of obs. *fraught* vb load with cargo, f. MDu. *vrachten*; so obs. *fraught* n. f. *vracht* FREIGHT]

Fräul'ein (froil'īn), n. (Of German spinster) Miss (with surname; also alone as voc.); German spinster; German governess. [G]

Fraun'höfer (frown-) **lines**, n. pl. The dark lines in the solar spectrum. [J. von *Fraunhofer*, Bavarian optician (d. 1826)]

frăxĭnĕll'a, n. Kinds of garden dittany. [mod. L, dim. of L *fraxinus* ash]

fray¹, n. Noisy quarrel, brawl; fight, conflict, (lit. or fig.; *eager for the ~*). [for AFFRAY]

fray², v.t. & i. (Of deer) *~ head*, or *~*, rub velvet off new horns; wear through by rubbing, ravel *out* edge or end of, (usu. woven material); become ragged at edge. [f. F *frayer* f. L *fricare* rub]

frăzĭl', n. (Canad. & U.S.). Anchor-ice, ice crystals in a stream. [f. Can. F *frasil* snow floating in the water; cf. F *fraisil* cinders]

*****frăz'zle**, n. Worn or exhausted state (esp. *worn, beaten, to a ~*). [perh. as FRAY²]

freak, n. Caprice, vagary; capriciousness (*out of mere~*); product of sportive fancy; (also *~ of nature*) monstrosity, abnormally developed specimen. Hence ~'ISH¹ a., ~'ishLY² adv., ~'ishNESS n. [16th c., orig. unkn.]

freaked (-kt), ɑ. Oddly flecked or streaked. [-ED²]

frĕc'kle, n., & v.t. & i. 1. Light brown spot on skin, (pl.) sporadic sunburn. 2. vb. Spot, be spotted, with ~s. [alt. f. ME *frecken* f. ON *freknur* pl.]

free¹, a. (*freer, freest*, pr. -ēer, -ēĭst), & adv. 1. Not in bondage to another, having personal rights & social & political liberty, (*~ labour, of ~* men not slaves, & see 2); (of State, its citizens or institutions) subject neither to foreign domination nor to despotic government, having national & civil liberty; *~-born*, inheriting citizen rights & liberty; *~'hold*, (estate held by) tenure in fee simple or fee-tail or for term of life (also of corresponding tenure of office), (adj.) held by ~hold; *~'holder*, possessor of ~hold estate; *~'man*, person not slave or serf, citizen of ~ State (& see 4); *~'mason*, member of fraternity for mutual help & brotherly feeling called *F~ & Accepted Masons* having elaborate ritual & system of secret signs (the orig. ~ masons were prob. skilled masons emancipated & allowed to move from place to place in & after 14th c., & the *accepted* may have been honorary members of the ~ masons' societies); *~'masonry*, system & institutions of the ~masons, secret understanding between like characters, instinctive sympathy. 2. Loose (*~ wheel* in bicycle, driving-wheel able to revolve while pedals are at rest), unrestricted (*~ love*, sexual relations irrespective of marriage), at liberty, not confined, released from ties or duties, unimpeded (*~ trade*, left to its natural course without customs duties to restrict imports or protect home industries, this principle; *~-trader*, believer in it), unfettered in action (*have* or *give a ~ hand*, right of acting at discretion), permitted to do, independent (*F~ Church*, unconnected with State; *the F~ Churches*, nonconformists; *F~ Church of Scotland* (hist.), seceders of 1843 from Presbyterian establishment; *~ house*, public house not tied to a particular brewery; *~ lance*, medieval mercenary, modern politician or controversialist with no party allegiance, unattached journalist; *~ labour*, of workmen not belonging to trade unions, & see 1; ∼-*thinker*, -*thinking* n. & a., -*thought*, rejector etc. of authority in religious belief, rationalist etc.), unconstrained (∼ *step*, *gestures*); (of literary style) not observing strict laws of form (∼ *verse*, = VERS LIBRE), (of translation) not literal; allowable (*it is* ∼ *for* or *to him to do so*); open to all comers (∼ *fight*, in which anyone present joins); clear of obstructions, clear of or *from* something undesirable, (of wind) not adverse; not fixed, not in contact, (Chem.) not combined, (of power or energy) disengaged or available; ∼-*board*, part of ship's side between line of flotation & deck--level; ∼-*hand*, (of drawing) done without artificial aid to the hand; ∼-*stone*, kind of peach of which when ripe the stone is loose (& see 3); ∼ *will*, power of directing our own actions without constraint by necessity or fate (& see 3). **3.** Spontaneous, unforced, unearned, gratuitous, willing, (∼ *grace*, unmerited favour of God; ∼ *gift*, not in requital; *did it of my own* ∼ *will*, & so ∼-*will* adj., voluntary; ∼ *quarters*, gratuitous entertainment; *am* ∼ *to confess*, not unwilling); lavish, profuse, unstinted, copious, (∼ *of his money*, open-handed; so ∼-*handed*, liberal; ∼ *flow of water*; ∼ *liver*, *living*, indulger, indulgence, in pleasures esp. of the table); frank, unreserved, (∼-*spoken*, not concealing one's opinions, blunt; ∼ *& easy*, unceremonious, also as n., smoking--concert etc.), forward, familiar, impudent, (*make* or *be* ∼, take liberties *with*); (of talk, stories, etc.) broad, not quite decent; ∼'*stone*, fine-grained easily sawn sandstone or limestone (& see 2). **4.** Released or exempt *from* (∼ *from the ordinary rules*, *disease*, *difficulty*, etc.); having burgess rights (*made* ∼ *of the city*), having the entrée & use of (∼ *of the house*); not subject to tax, toll, duty, trade-restrictions, or fees (∼ *port*, open to all traders alike; ∼-*list*, of persons to be admitted ∼, duty-∼ articles, etc.; ∼ *school*, with no fees charged; ∼ *pass*, not paid for; also adv., *as the gallery is open* ∼, & in comb. as *carriage*-∼, without charge for conveyance); ∼'*man*, one who has the freedom of a city, company, etc. (& see 1). **5.** adv. ∼ly, without cost or payment, (Naut.) not close-hauled. Hence ∼'LY² adv. [OE *frēo*, OS, OHG *frī*, ON **frir*, Goth. *freis* f. Gmc **frijaz*, cogn. w. FRIEND]

free², v.t. (∼*d*). Make free, set at liberty, (∼*d'man*, emancipated slave, esp. in Rom. Hist.); relieve *from*, rid or ease *of*; clear, disengage, disentangle. [OE *frēon* (prec.)]

free'boot|er, n. Pirate, piratical adventurer. Hence by back formation **free'boot** v.i., ∼ING¹,² n. & a. [f. Du. *vrijbuiter* (FREE¹, BOOTY, -ER¹); cf. FILIBUSTER]

free'dom, n. Personal liberty, non--slavery; civil liberty, independence; liberty of action, right *to* do; power of self-determination, independence of fate

or necessity; frankness, outspokenness, undue familiarity (*take* ∼*s with*); facility, ease, in action; boldness of conception; (Physics) capability of motion; exemption *from* defect, disadvantage, burden, duty, etc.; privilege possessed by city or corporation; participation in privileges of membership of company etc. or citizenship *of* city (often given *honoris causa* to distinguished persons); unrestricted use *of* (*has the* ∼ *of the library*); *the four* ∼*s*, ∼ of speech and religion, ∼ from fear and want. [OE *frēodōm* (FREE¹, -DOM)]

free'martin, n. Hermaphrodite or imperfect female of ox kind. [orig. unkn.]

frees'ia (-z-), n. Kinds of iridaceous bulbous plant from Cape of Good Hope. [f. E. M. *Fries*, Sw. botanist (d. 1878) + -IA¹]

freeze, v.i. & t. (*frōze*, *frōzen*), & n. **1.** (Impers.) *it* ∼*s* etc., there is etc. frost; be converted into or covered with ice; become rigid as result of cold; become fastened *to* or *together* by frost, (sl.) ∼ *on to*, take or keep tight hold of; feel very cold (∼ *to death*, die by frost); be chilled by fear; cause to congeal, form ice upon, (fluid or moist thing; often *in*, *over*, *up*), preserve (meat etc.) by refrigeration; make (credits, assets, etc.) temporarily or permanently unrealizable; peg or stabilize (prices, wages, etc.); (by exagg.) ∼ one's *blood*, terrify him; chill (feelings), paralyse (powers); stiffen, harden, injure, kill, by chilling (*frozen to death*); (sl.) ∼ *out*, exclude from business, society, etc., by competition or boycotting etc.; ∼-*out*, variety of poker in which each player drops out as soon as he loses his capital; *freezing-mixture*, salt & snow or other mixture used to ∼ liquids; *freezing-point*, temperature at which liquid, esp. water, ∼s; *frozen limit* (colloq.), the extreme of the objectionable or unendurable. **2.** n. State, coming, period, of frost; stabilization of prices, wages, etc. [OE *frēosan*, OHG *friosan*, ON *frjósa* f. Gmc **freusan*]

freez'ing, a. In vbl senses; esp.: (by exagg.) very cold; (of manners) chilling, distant. Hence ∼LY² adv. [-ING²]

freight (frāt), n., & v.t. **1.** Hire of ship for transporting goods; transport of goods by water (in U.S. by land also), charge for this, cargo, shipload; load, burden. **2.** v.t. Load (ship) with cargo; hire or let out (ship) for carriage of goods & passengers. [f. MDu. *vrecht* var. of *vracht* see FRAUGHT]

freight'age (-āt-), n. Hire of ship for, cost of, conveyance of goods; freighting or hiring of ship; cargo. [-AGE]

freight'er (-āt-), n. One who (charters &) loads ship; one who consigns goods for carriage inland; one whose business is to receive & forward freight; cargo ship, freight-carrying aircraft. [-ER¹]

French, a. & n. **1.** Of France or its people; having the qualities attributed to ∼

people; || ~ *bean*, kidney or haricot bean used as vegetable both in unripe sliced pods & in ripe seeds; ~ *bread*, kind of fancy bread; ~ *chalk*, kind of steatite used for marking cloth & removing grease & as dry lubricant; ~ *drain* (of rubble, letting water soak away); ~ *grey*, tint composed of white with ivory black, Indian red, & Chinese blue; ~ HORN[1]; *take* ~ *leave*, depart, act, without asking leave or giving notice; || ~ *letter*, a contraceptive sheath; ~'*man*, man of ~ birth or nationality, (*good* etc.)~-spéaker, ~ *ship*, the red-legged partridge; ~ *polish*, kind of polish for wood; ~-*polish* v.t., polish with this, whence ~-**pŏl'ishER**[1] n.; ~ *roof*, mansard; ~ *toast*, fried bread; ~ *window*, glazed folding-door serving as window & door; ~'*woman*, woman of France. 2. n. The ~ language (~ *lesson*, *master*, etc., concerned with this); *the* ~ (pl.), the ~ people. Hence ~'NESS n., **Frĕn'chy** [2,3] a. & n. [OE *frencisc*, OHG *frenḳisc* (FRANK[1], -ISH[1])]

Frĕnch'i|fў, f-, v.t. Make French in form, character, or manners (usu. in p.p.). Hence ~FICA'TION n. [-FY]

Frĕnch'lĕss, a. Knowing no French. [-LESS]

frenetic. See PHRENETIC.

frenum. See FRAENUM.

frĕn'z|ў, n., & v.t. **1.** Mental dcrangement, temporary insanity, paroxysm of mania, (rare) delirious fury or agitation, wild folly. **2.** v.t. (usu. in p.p.). Drive to ~y, infuriate, (~*ied rage*, that of a ~*ied* person). [ME, f. OF *frenesie* f. med. L *phrenesia* for L f. Gk -*ēsis* f. *phrēn* mind; cf. FRANTIC]

frē'quencў n. Frequent occurrence, commonness of occurrence (*word* ~), being repeated at short intervals, (of pulse) number of beats per minute; (Phys.) rate of recurrence (of vibration etc.), number of repetitions in given time esp. per second (*high, medium, low,* ~, abbr. H.F., M.F., L.F., w. ref. to sound-waves, electro-magnetic waves, etc.); (Statistics) the ratio of the actual to the number of possible occurrences of an event; ~ *modulation* (Radio), varying the ~ of the carrier wave in accordance with speech or music, system of broadcasting using this method of modulation. [f. L *frequentia* (foll., -ENCY)]

frē'quent[1], a. Found near together, numerous, abundant; often occurring, common, happening in close succession, (of pulse) rapid, (*it is a* ~ *practice to*), whence ~LY[2] adv.; (with agent-noun) habitual, constant, (*a* ~ *caller*). [f. F, or L *frequens -entis* crowded]

frĕquĕnt' [2], v.t. Go often or habitually to (place, meetings, company, house). Hence or cogn. **frĕquĕnt**A'TION, ~ER[1], nn. [f. F *fréquenter* or L *frequentare* (prec.)]

frĕquĕn'tative, a. & n. (gram.). (Verb or verbal form or conjugation) expressing frequent repetition or intensity of action. [f. L *frequentativus* (prec., -ATIVE)]

frĕs'cō̄, n. (pl. -ōs, -oes), & v.t. Method of painting (esp. *in* ~), picture, in watercolour laid on wall or ceiling before plaster is dry; (vb) paint (wall etc., picture or subject) thus. [It., orig. adj.= foll.]

frĕsh, a., adv., & n. 1. New, novel, not previously known, used, met with, or introduced, (*brĕak* ~ *ground*, try something unhackneyed); additional, other, different, further, (*begin a* ~ *chapter*); recent, lately made or arrived, just come *from*; raw, inexperienced, (~'*man*, first-year man at University); not preserved by salting, pickling, smoking, tinning, etc. (~ *herrings, meat, fruit,* & see below; ~ *butter,* & see next sense); not salt (~ *water*; ~'*water* a., of ~ water, not of the sea, as ~*water fish, fishing, sailor*; ~ *butter,* not flavoured with salt, & see prec. sense), not salt or bitter, drinkable, (~ *water*); pure, untainted, invigorating, refreshing, cool, (of air, wind, water); not stale, musty, or vapid (~ *fish, meat, fruit,* & see above; ~ *egg*); not faded (~ *flowers, memories*); unsullied, bright & pure in colour (*a* ~ *complexion*), looking healthy or young; not weary, brisk, vigorous, fit, (*never felt* ~*er; as* ~ *as paint*, quite brisk, prob. a pun on the warning '~ paint'; *a* ~ *wind,* of some strength); excited with drink; *presumptuous, forward, cheeky, amorously impudent. **2.** adv. Newly, esp. in comb. as ~-*caught, -coined*; ~-*run,* (of salmon) lately come up from the sea. **3.** n. ~ part of day, year, etc. (*in the* ~ *of the morning*); rush of water in river, flood. Hence ~'EN[1] v.t. & i., ~'NESS n. [ME *fersse* f. OE *fersc* f. Gmc *friskaz*; ME *fresch* f. OF *freis*, fem. *fresche*, f. same Gmc orig.]

|| **frĕsh'er, n.** (sl.). = FRESHman. [-ER[1]]

frĕsh'ĕt, n. Rush of fresh water flowing into sea; flood of river from heavy rain or melted snow. [FRESH n. +-ET½ or f. OF *freschete* f. *frais* FRESH]

frĕsh'lў, adv. Recently (only with participles, = *fresh* adv.); afresh (rare); with unabated vigour; with fresh appearance, odour, etc. [-LY[2]]

frĕt[1], n., & v.t. (-tt-). **1.** Ornamental pattern made of continuous combinations of straight lines joined usu. at right angles (also *Greek* ~). **2.** v.t. Variegate, chequer; adorn (esp. ceiling) with carved or embossed work; ~-*saw,* very narrow saw stretched on frame for cutting thin wood in ornamental patterns; ~'*work,* carved work in decorative patterns esp. of straight lines, also wood cut with ~-saw. [ME, f. OF *frete* trellis-work & *freter* vb]

frĕt[2], v.t. & i. (-tt-), & n. **1.** Gnaw, wear or consume or torment by gnawing, (of moths etc., horses champing bit, action of frost, rust, corrosives, friction, etc., or the passions); make (passage etc.) by wearing away; chafe, irritate, annoy, worry, distress; distress oneself with regret or discontent (*at*; ~ *away* or *out* one's *life* etc.); ~ *& fume*, show angry impatience; (of stream etc.) flow or rise in little waves, chafe; ruffle (water). 2. n. Irritation, vexation, querulousness, (*in a* ~; ~ *& fume*; *on the* ~); hence ~'FUL a., ~'fulLY² adv., ~'fulNESS n., ~t'Y² a. [OE *fretan*, OHG *frezzan*, Goth. *fra-itan* f. Gmc **fra-* FOR-(5) + *etan EAT]

frĕt³, n. Bar or ridge on fingerboard of some stringed instruments fixing positions of fingers to produce required notes. Hence ~t'ED² a. [orig. unkn.]

Freud'ian (froid-), a. & n. (Disciple) of Freud or his doctrines of PSYCHO-*analysis*. [Sigmund *Freud* (d. 1939) + -IAN]

fri'able, a. Easily crumbled. Hence or cogn. **friABIL'ITY**, ~NESS, nn. [f. F, or L *friabilis* (*friare* crumble)]

fri'ar, n. Member of certain religious orders esp. the four mendicant orders of Franciscans (*Grey F~s*), Augustinians (*Austin F~s*), Dominicans (*Black F~s*), & Carmelites (*White F~s*); ~'*s balsam*, tincture of benzoin. Hence ~LY¹ a. [ME & OF *frere* f. L *fratrem* nom. *-ter* brother; for *friar* cf. CHOIR]

fri'arў, n. Convent of friars. [14/15th c. *frary*, *freyry*, f. OF *frairie*, *frerie* (*frere* (prec.) + -Y¹) w. assim. to prec.]

frib'ble, v.i., & n. Trifle, be frivolous; (n.) trifler. [imit.; earlier senses *stammer*, *totter*]

fric'andeau (-dō), n. (pl. *-x* pr. *-z*), & v.t. (Slice of) fried or stewed meat, esp. veal, served with sauce; (vb) make into ~x. [F]

fricassee', n., & v.t. Meat cut up, fried or stewed, & served with sauce, esp., ragout of birds or small animals cut up; (vb) make ~ of. [F, p.p. of *fricasser*]

fric'ative, a. & n. (Consonant) made by friction of breath in narrow opening, as *f*, *th*, Scotch *ch*. [f. L *fricare* rub + -ATIVE]

fric'tion, n. Medical chafing; rubbing of two bodies, attrition; (Phys., Mech.) resistance body meets with in moving over another (*angle of* ~, maximum angle at which one will remain on another without sliding); (fig.) clash of wills, temperaments, opinions, etc. (usu. between two persons); ~-*ball*, used in bearings to lessen ~; ~-*clutch*, *-cone*, *-coupling*, *-disc*, *-gear*(*ing*), contrivances for transmitting motion by ~. Hence ~AL, ~LESS, aa., (-shon-). [F, f. L *frictionem* (*fricare* rub, -ION)]

Frid'ay (-dĭ), n. Sixth day of week (*Good* ~, ~ before Easter-day, commemorating Crucifixion; *Black* ~, used as name for various disasters that fell on ~). [OE *frïgedæg*, OHG *frïatag*, ON *frjádagr* day of *Frigg*, wife of Odin, com.-WG transl. of LL *Veneris dies* day of planet Venus]

friend (frĕnd), n., & v.t. 1. One joined to another in intimacy & mutual benevo-

lence independently of sexual or family love; person who acts for one, e.g. as second in duel; (loosely) acquaintance, stranger that one comes across or has occasion to mention anew, (*my* ~ *in the brown hat now left me*; used in voc. as polite form or in irony, & by Quakers as ordinary address; preceding a name, as ~ *Jones*, *Dick*; || *my* honourable ~, of another M.P. in House of Commons; *my learned* ~, of another lawyer in court); (pl.) one's near relations, those responsible for one; sympathizer, helper, patron, (*no* ~ *of* or *to* *order*, *virtue*, etc.; *a* ~ *at court*, one whose influence may be made use of); helpful thing (*my shyness was here my best* ~); one who is not an enemy, who is on the same side; *be*, *keep*, *make*, ~*s*, be or get on good terms; (*F*~) Quaker (*Society of F~s*, the Quakers as a communion); hence ~'LESS a., ~'lèssNESS n., (frě-). 2. v.t. (poet.). Befriend, help. [OE *frēond*, OS *friund*, OHG *friunt*, ON *frǣndi*, Goth. *frijonds*, part. of Gmc *frijōjan f. *frijaz FREE; cf. FIEND, -ND²]

friend'lу (frĕ-), a., n., & adv. 1. Acting, disposed to act, as friend; characteristic of friends, expressing, showing, or prompted by, kindness (|| ~ *lead* among London poor, entertainment to raise funds for distressed person); not hostile, on amicable terms, (*a* ~ *nation*; ~ *action* at law, brought merely to get a point decided; ~ *match*, played for honour merely, not in competition for cup etc.); favourably disposed, ready to approve or help, (of things) serviceable, convenient, opportune; || *F*~ *Society*, for mutual insurance against distress in sickness or old age; hence **friend'liLY²** (rare) adv., **friend'liNESS** n., (frě-). 2. n. (w. pl.). Native of ~ tribe. 3. adv. (rare). In ~ manner (*used*, *received*, *us* ~). [-LY²]

friend'ship (frě-), n. Being friends, relation between friends; friendly disposition felt or shown. [-SHIP]

Friesian (frē'zhan), a. & n. (Of, one of) a breed of Friesland cattle. [var. of FRISIAN]

frieze¹, n. Coarse woollen cloth with nap usu. on one side only. [ME, f. OF (*drap de*) *frise* Frisian cloth]

frieze², n. Member of entablature coming between architrave & cornice; horizontal broad band of sculpture filling this; band of decoration elsewhere. [f. F *frise* f. med. L *frisium* f. L *Phrygium* (*opus* work) of Phrygia]

frig (-j), **fri(d)ge**, n. (colloq.). Refrigerator. [abbr.]

frig'ate, n. (Hist.) warship next in size & equipment to ships of the line, with 28–60 guns on main deck & raised quarter-deck & forecastle; corvette, sloop, small destroyer; (also ~-*bird*) large swift tropical bird of prey. [f. F *frégate* f. It. *fregata* of unkn. orig.]

fright (frīt), n., & v.t. 1. Sudden fear, violent terror, alarm; grotesque-looking or badly dressed person. **2. v.t.** (poet.). Frighten. [OE *fryhto* metathetic form of *fyrhto* = Goth. *faurhtei*, also OS, OHG *forhta*, f. Gmc *furht-* of unkn. orig.]

fright'en (-it-), v.t. Throw into a fright, terrify, (often *out of, into, doing*); drive *away, out of* (place etc.), *into* (submission etc.), by fright; ~*ed at* or *of* (*at* w. ref. to an occasion, *of* to habitual fear). [prec. (n.)+-EN¹]

fright'ful (-it-), a. Frightening (arch.); dreadful, shocking, revolting; ugly, hideous, whence ~NESS n. (esp., as mistransl. of G *Schrecklichkeit* terrorizing of civilian population as military resource); (sl.) very great, awful. Hence ~LY² adv. [-FUL]

fri'gid, a. Cold (esp. of climate or air; ~ *zone*, region enclosed by either polar circle);without ardour, apathetic, formal, forced; sexually irresponsive; chilling, depressing; dull, flat, insipid. Hence or cogn. **frigid'ITY**, ~NESS, nn., ~LY² adv. [f. L *frigidus* (*frigere* be cold f. *frigus* n. cold)]

frill, n., & v.t. & i. **1.** Ornamental edging of woven material, one side of strip being gathered & the other left loose with fluted appearance; similar paper ornament on ham-knuckle etc.; natural fringe of feathers, hair, etc., on bird, animal, or plant; (pl.) airs, affectation, (*puts on* ~s), useless embellishments or accomplishments; mesentery of animal; (Photog.) puckered gelatine film at edge of plate. **2. vb.** Decorate with a ~; (esp. Photog., of gelatine film) pucker at edges of plate etc. Hence ~ED² (-ld) a., ~'ERY(5), ~'ING¹ (3, 6), nn. [16th c., orig. unkn.]

frill'ies (-liz), n. pl. (colloq.). Frilled petticoats etc. [-Y² or -Y³]

fringe (-j), n., & v.t. **1.** Ornamental bordering of threads left loose or formed into tassels or twists; such bordering made separately; border, edging, (*Newgate* ~, beard allowed to grow below shaven chin); front hair cut short & allowed to hang over forehead; natural border of hair etc. in animal or plant; hence ~'LESS (-jl-), **frin'gy²**, aa. **2. v.t.** Adorn or encircle with ~, serve as ~ to; hence **frin'gING¹**(3) n. [ME & OF *frenge* f. Rom. *frimbia* f. L *fimbria*]

fripp'ery, n. Finery, needless or tawdry adornment esp. in dress; empty display esp. in literary style; knick-knacks, trifles. [f. OF *freperie* (*frepe* rag, -ERY)]

***Fris'co**, n. San Francisco. [abbr.]

frisette' (-z-), n. Band of small artificial curls on forehead. [F (*friser* FRIZZ)]

friseur (frēzer'), n. Hair-dresser. [as prec.]

Fris'ian (-z-), a. & n. (Native, language) of Friesland. [f. L *Frisii* pl. f. OFris. *Frise*+-AN]

frisk, v.i. & t., & n. **1.** Move sportively, gambol; *feel over*, search, (person) for weapon etc. (sl.). **2. n.** Gambol. Hence

fris'ky² a., **fris'kiLY²** adv., **fris'kiNESS** n. [f. obs. *frisk* a. f. OF *frisque* lively of unkn. orig.]

fris'ket, n. (print.). Thin iron frame keeping sheet in position while printing. [f. F *frisquette*]

frit, n., & v.t. (-tt-). **1.** Calcined mixture of sand & fluxes as material for glassmaking; vitreous composition from which soft porcelain is made. **2. v.t.** Make into ~, partially fuse, calcine. [f. It. *fritta* fem. p.p. of *friggere* FRY²]

frit'fly, n. Small fly destructive to wheat. [orig. unkn.]

frith. See FIRTH.

fritill'ary (or frit'-), n. Kinds of liliaceous plant, esp. snakeshead; kinds of butterfly. [f. L *fritillus* dice-box+-ARY¹]

fritt'er¹, n. Piece of fried batter often containing slices of fruit etc. (*apple, oyster*, etc., ~); (pl.) = FENKS. [ME, f. OF *friture* (L *frigere frict-* FRY², -URE), see -ER²(3)]

fritt'er², v.t. Subdivide minutely; throw (time, money, energy, etc.) *away* on divided aims. [f. obs. n. *fritter(s)* = obs. *fitters* n. pl. f. obs. *fitter* v. of unkn. orig.]

Fritz, nickname for the Germans or a German [G, abbr. of *Friedrich* Frederick]

friv'ol, v.i. & t. (-ll-). Be a trifler, trifle; throw (money, time) *away* foolishly. [back formation f. foll.]

friv'olous, a. Paltry, trumpery, trifling, futile; given to trifling, not serious, silly. Hence or cogn. **frivöl'ITY**, ~NESS, nn., ~LY² adv. [f. L *frivolus* +-OUS]

friz(z)¹, v.t., & n. **1.** Curl, crisp, form into mass of small curls, (hair, or person etc. in regard to it); dress (wash-leather etc.) with pumice or scraping-knife. **2. n.** Frizzed state, frizzed hair, row of curls; hence **frizz'y²** a. [f. F *friser*]

frizz², v.i. Make sputtering noise in frying. [f. FRY² w. imit. termin.]

friz'zle¹, v.t. & i., & n. **1.** Curl (t., & i. esp. with *up*, of hair etc.) in small crisp curls. **2. n.** ~d hair; hence **frizz'ly²** a. [orig. unkn.; earlier than FRIZZ¹]

friz'zle², v.i. & t. Fry, toast, or grill, with sputtering noise. [FRIZZ²+-LE(3)]

frō, adv. Away (only in *to & ~*, backwards & forwards, or of repeated journeys between two places). [f. ON *frá* prep. = OE FROM]

frŏck, n., & v.t. **1.** Monk's long gown with loose sleeves, (fig.) priestly character; = SMOCK-~; sailor's woollen jersey; child's skirt & bodice as outer dress for indoor use; woman's dress; || (also ~-*coat*) man's long-skirted coat not cut away in front; military coat of like shape. **2. v.t.** Invest with priestly office, cf. UN-FROCK. [14th c. f OF *froc*, perh. f. WG (OFris., OS, OHG) *hroc*]

***frōe, *frow** (frō), n. Cleaving tool with handle at right angles to blade. [subst. use of FROWARD ' turned away ']

Froe'belism (frer'-), n. Education of

young children on the kindergarten system. [F. W. A. *Froebel*, German educationalist (d. 1852), -ISM]

frŏg¹, n. Tailless amphibious animal developed from tadpole; (derog. for) Frenchman (as eating ~s), whence **Frŏgg′y²** (-g-) n.; ~-*eater*, Frenchman; ~-*fish*, kinds of fish esp. the angler; ~-*in--the-throat*, hoarseness; ~'*man*, person equipped for underwater operations orig. against enemy shipping; ~'s, ~, -*march*, carrying of prisoner face downwards by four men holding a limb each; ~-*spawn*, lit., & as names for kinds of freshwater algae. Hence ~g′y² (-g-) a. (esp. = cold as a ~). [OE *frogga*, pet name for *forsc*, *frosc*, *frox* = OHG *frosc*, ON *froskr* f. Gmc *froskaz*]

frŏg², n. Elastic horny substance in middle of sole of horse's foot. [perh. f. prec.]

frŏg³, n. Attachment to waistbelt to support sword, bayonet, etc.; military coat--fastening of spindle-shaped button & loop, whence~gED² (-gd) a. [orig. unkn.]

frŏg⁴, n. Grooved piece of iron at place in railway where tracks cross. [orig. unkn.]

frŏl′ĭc a. (arch.), v.i., & n. 1. Joyous, mirthful, sportive, full of pranks. 2. v.i. (-ck-). Play pranks, gambol. 3. n. Outburst of gaiety, prank, merriment, merry-making, gay party. Hence ~SOME a., ~SOMELY² adv., ~SOMENESS n. [f. Du. *vrolijk* adj. cf. G *fröhlich* (MDu. *vrō* glad, -LIKE)]

from (from, *emphatic or at end of clause* frŏm), prep. expressing separation & introducing:—**1.** Person, place, etc., whence motion takes place (*comes ~ the clouds*; *repeated ~ mouth to mouth*). **2.** Starting-point (~ *title to colophon*, throughout book; ~ *2nd July*; ~ *day to day*, daily; ~ *time to time*, occasionally; ~ *a child*, since childhood). **3.** Inferior limit (*saw ~ 10 to 20 boats*). **4.** Object etc. whence distance or remoteness is reckoned or stated (*ten miles ~ Rome*; *am far ~ saying*; ~ *home*, out, away; *absent, away, ~ home*; *apart ~ its moral aspect*). **5.** Thing or person got rid of, escaped, avoided, of which one is deprived etc., person or thing deprived, (*took his sword ~ him*; *released him ~ prison*; *cannot refrain ~ laughing*; *appeal ~ lower court, dissuade ~ folly*). **6.** State changed for another (~ *being attacked became the aggressor*; *raise penalty ~ banishment to death*). **7.** Thing distinguished (*doesn't know black ~ white*). **8.** Source (*dig gravel ~ pit*; *draw conclusion ~ premisses*; *quotations ~ the fathers*). **9.** Place of vantage etc. (*saw it ~ the roof*; ~ *his point of view*, as he sees things). **10.** Giver, sender, etc. (*gifts ~ Providence*; *frocks ~ Worth's*; *things not required ~ me*). **11.** Model (*painted ~ nature*). **12.** Reason, cause, motive, (*died ~ fatigue*; *suffering~ dementia*; ~ *his looks*

you might suppose). **13.** Advbs or advl phrr. of place or time (~ *long ago, of old*, *above*, etc.), or prepositions (~ *under her spectacles*; ~ *out the bed*). [OE *fram, from*, OS, OHG, Goth. *fram*, ON *frá* (FRO), f. Gmc *fra-* forward]

frŏnd, n. (Bot.) leaf-like organ formed by union of stem & foliage in certain flowerless plants, esp. ferns, & differing from leaf in usu. bearing fructification; (Zool.) leaf-like expansion in some animal organisms. Hence **frŏn′dAGE(1)** n., **frŏn′dOSE¹** a. [f. L *frons -dis* leaf]

Fronde (-awnd), n. Party that rebelled against Mazarin & Court during minority of Louis XIV; malcontent party; violent political opposition. [F, orig. = sling]

front (-ŭnt), n. & a., & v.i. & t. **1.** Forehead (poet.; *head & ~*, chief part or item); face (~ *to ~*; *have the ~*, be impudent enough usu. *to do*; *present, show, a bold ~*); (Mil.) foremost line or part of army etc., line of battle, part of ground towards real or imaginary enemy, scene of actual fighting (*go to the ~*, join troops on campaign), direction in which formed line faces (*change ~*); (fig.) organized body or department of activity (*home, kitchen, popular, ~*); (Archit.) any face of building, esp. that of main entrance; fore part of anything (opp. BACK); (Meteor.) boundary between cold & warm air masses (*cold, warm, ~*, forward boundary of a mass of advancing cold, warm, air); ‖ the promenade of a seaside resort; band of false hair, set of false curls, worn over woman's forehead; breast of man's shirt, also dicky; (with prep.) forward position (*in ~ of*, before, in advance of, confronting; *in ~*; *come to the ~*, become conspicuous); (ellipt.) = in ~ as adv. or adj. (*were beset ~ & rear*; *two-pair ~*, second-floor room in ~); hence ~′WARD a. & adv., ~′WARDS adv., (-ŭn-). **2.** adj. Of the, situated in, ~ (‖~ *bench*, reserved for ministers or ex-ministers in Parliament houses; ~ *door*, chief entrance of house); ~ *page*, first page of newspaper (usu. attrib., of news of striking journalistic importance). **3.** vb. Face, look, *to*, *towards*, (*up*)*on*; face, stand opposite to; have ~ on side of (street etc.); confront, meet, oppose; furnish with ~ (~*ed with stone*). [ME; n. OF, f. L *frons frŏntis*; vb f. OF *fronter*]

fron′tag|e (-ŭn-), n. Land abutting on street or water, land between front of building & road, whence ~ER¹(4) n.; extent of front; front of building; ground occupied by troops in camp or on parade; facing a certain way, exposure, outlook. [-AGE]

fron′tal¹ (-ŭn-), n. Covering for front of altar; façade. [ME, f. OF *frontel* f. L *frontale* (FRONT, -AL)]

fron′tal² (-ŭn-), a. Of forehead (~ *bone, artery*); of, on, front (~ *attack*, delivered direct, not on flank or rear). [-AL]

fron'tier (-ŭn-, -ŏn-), n. Part of a country that borders on another; the borders of civilization; (attrib.) of, on, the ~; ~*sman*, one living on or beyond the borders of civilization (*Legion of F~smen*, organization enrolling men with such experience). [ME, f. OF *frontier, -iere* f. *front* FRONT, see -ARY[1]]

Fron'tignac (-ĭnyăk), n. A muscat wine. [erron. for *-nan*, name of French town]

fron'tispiece (-ŭn-), n., & v.t. (Archit.) principal face of building, decorated entrance, pediment over door etc.; illustration facing title-page of book or one of its divisions (vb, supply *with* as ~). [f. F *frontispice* f. med. L *frontispicium* countenance (FRONT, *specere* look) w. assim. to *piece*]

front'less (-ŭn-), a. Unblushing (rare); without front. [-LESS]

front'let (-ŭn-), n. Band worn on forehead; = PHYLACTERY; animal's forehead; cloth hanging over upper part of altar frontal. [f. OF *frontelet* (FRONTAL[1], -LET)]

frŏn'to-, comb. form of L *frons -tis* = of the forehead & —, as ~*-nasal*. [for *fronti-* (-I-, -O-)]

fron'ton (frŭ-), n. Pediment. [F, f. It. *frontone* (FRONT, -OON)]

frōre, a. (poet.). Frozen, frosty. [arch. p.p. of FREEZE]

frost (-aw-, -ŏ-), n., & v.t. 1. Freezing, prevalence of temperature below freezing-point of water (‖ *ten degrees of* ~, 22° Fahrenheit; *hard, sharp,* ~; *white* or *hoar, black,* ~, with, without, rime; *Jack F~,* ~ personified), frozen state or consistence (*there is still* ~ *in the ground*), frozen dew or vapour (*windows covered with* ~); influence that chills, makes grey, etc.; (sl.) failure; ~*-bite,* inflammation or gangrene of & below skin from severe cold, ~*-bitten,* affected with this; ~*-work,* tracery made by ~ on glass etc.; hence ~'LESS a. 2. v.t. Nip, injure, (plants etc.) with ~; cover (as) with rime, powder with coating of sugar etc., whence ~ING(2) n.; give roughened or finely granulated surface to (glass, metal); turn (hair) white; arm (horse's shoes) against slipping by nails etc. [OE, OS, OHG, ON *frost* f. Gmc **frust-* f. **freusan* FREEZE]

fros'tǀy̆ (-aw-, -ŏ-), a. Cold with frost; cold, chilling, frigid, lacking in warmth of feeling; covered, seeming to be covered, with hoar-frost. Hence ~ILY[2] adv., ~I-NESS n. [-Y[2]]

froth (-ŏ-, -aw-), n., & v.i. & t. 1. Collection of small bubbles, foam; impure matter on liquid, scum; worthless matter, idle talk, etc.; ‖ ~*-blower* (joc.), beer-drinker (esp. as designation of member of a certain charitable Order); hence ~'Y[2] a., ~'ILY[2] adv., ~'INESS n. 2. vb. Emit, gather, ~; cause (beer etc.) to foam. [ME, f. ON *frotha, frauth,* cogn. w. OE *āfrēothan* to ~]

frou-frou (-ōō-, -ōō), n. Rustling, esp. of dresses. [F, imit.]

frow[1], n. Dutchwoman. [ME, f. Du. *vrouw* = G *frau* woman]

*frow[2]. See FROE.

frō'ward, a. (arch.). Perverse, refractory. Hence ~LY[2] adv., ~NESS n. [FRO, -WARD]

frown, v.i. & t., & n. 1. Knit brows esp. to express displeasure or concentrate attention; (of things) present gloomy aspect; express disapprobation (*at, on, upon*); put (interrupter, interruption, etc.) *down* with ~; express (defiance etc.) with ~; hence ~'ingLY[2] adv. 2. n. Vertically furrowed state of brow; look expressing severity, disapproval, or deep thought. [ME, f. OF *frongnier, froignier,* of obsc. orig.]

frowst, n., & v.i. (colloq.). Fusty heat in room (‖ vb, stay in, enjoy, this). Hence **frows'ty**[2] a. [cf. earlier *frowzy*]

frowz'ǀy̆, a. Ill-smelling, fusty, musty, close; slatternly, unkempt, dingy. Hence ~iNESS n. [17th c., of unkn. orig.; cf. 16th c. *frowy*]

froze(n). See FREEZE.

frŭctif'erous, a. Bearing fruit. [f. L *fructifer* (FRUIT, -FEROUS)]

frŭctifica'tion, n. (bot.). Fructifying; reproductive parts of plant, esp. of ferns & mosses. [f. LL *fructificatio* (foll., -FICATION)]

frŭc'tify, v.i. & t. Bear fruit (lit. & fig.); make fruitful, impregnate. [ME, f. OF *fructifier* f. L *fructificare* (FRUIT, -FY)]

frŭc'tōse, n. Fruit sugar. [f. L *fructus* FRUIT + -OSE[2]]

frŭc'tŭous, a. Full of, producing, fruit (lit. & fig.). [ME, f. OF, or L *fructuosus* (FRUIT, -OUS)]

frug'al (frōō-), a. Careful, sparing (*of*), economical, esp. as regards food; sparingly used or supplied, costing little. Hence or cogn. **frugăl'ITY** n., ~LY[2] adv., (frōō-). [f. L *frugalis,* see -AL]

frugiv'orous (frōō-), a. Feeding on fruit. [f. L *frux frugi-* fruit + -VOROUS]

fruit (frōōt), n., & v.i. & t. 1. (Usu. pl.) vegetable products fit for food (usu. ~*s of the earth*), so ~'AGE(1) (-ōōt-); n.; plant's or tree's edible product of seed with its envelope (also collect. in sing., as *feeds on* ~); vegetable seed with envelope as means of reproduction; (Bibl.) offspring (usu. ~ *of the body, loins, womb*); produce of action, (pl.) revenues produced (*the* ~*s of industry*); (sing. or pl.) result, issue, consequence; ~*-cake,* containing currants etc.; ~ *clipper,* fast ship carrying ~; ~*-knife,* with silver etc. blade against acid; ~*machine,* coin-operated gaming machine in which a player is successful who gets a certain combination of different coloured balls; ~*-piece,* picture of ~; ~ *salad,* of various ~s cut up & mixed in bowl often with cream etc.; ~ *sugar,* glucose, laevulose, or fructose; ~*-tree,* grown for its ~; hence (-)~'ED[2] a. 2. vb. Bear, make bear, ~. [ME, f. OF f. L *fructus -ūs* (*frui* enjoy)]

fruitār'ian (frōō-), n. Feeder on fruit. [-ARIAN]

fruit'er (frōōt-), n. Fruit-ship; tree producing fruit (*a sure ~*); ‖ fruit-grower. [15th c., f. OF *fruitier*; later f. FRUIT +-ER¹]

‖ **fruit'erer** (frōōt-), ʼn. Dealer in fruit. [15th c., f. prec. +-ER¹: cf. *poulterer*]

fruit'ful (frōōt-), a. Productive, fertile, causing fertility; productive of offspring, prolific, (lit. & fig.; *a session ~ in great measures*); beneficial, remunerative, whence ~LY² adv. Hence ~NESS n. [-FUL]

frui'tion (frōō-), n. Enjoyment, attainment of thing desired, realization of hopes etc. [ME, f. OF f. LL *fruitionem* (*frui fruit-*, enjoy, -ION)]

fruit'less (frōōt-), a. Not bearing fruit; yielding no profit, ineffectual, useless, empty, vain. Hence ~LY² adv., ~NESS n. [-LESS]

fruit'lĕt (frōōt-), n. (bot.). = DRUPEL. [-LET]

fruit'| y̆ (frōōt-), a. Of fruit; (of wine) tasting of the grape, whence ~INESS n.; (colloq.) suggestive, broad, full of rough humour or (usu. scandalous) interest. [-Y²]

frum'enty̆ (frōō-), **fŭrm'ĕty̆**, n. Hulled wheat boiled in milk & seasoned with cinnamon, sugar, etc. [ME, f. OF *frumentee* (*frument* f. L *frumentum* corn), -Y⁴]

frŭmp, n. Old-fashioned dowdily-dressed woman. Hence **frŭm'pish¹**, **frŭm'py²**, aa. [16th c., perh. f. (now dial.) *frumple* f. MDu. *verrompelen* RUMPLE]

frŭs'trāte¹, a. (arch.). Frustrated. [f. L *frustratus* (foll., -ATE²)]

frŭstr|āte'² (*also* frŭs⁴), v.t. Balk, baffle, neutralize, counteract, disappoint. So ~A'TION n. [f. L *frustrari* (*frustra* in vain), -ATE³]

frŭs'tūle, n. Two-valved shell of diatom. [F, f. L *frustulum* (foll., -ULE)]

frŭs'tum, n. (pl. -*ta*, -*tums*). Remainder of regular solid whose upper part has been cut off by plane parallel to base, or part intercepted between two planes. [L, = piece broken off]

frutĕs'cent (frōō-), a. (bot.). Of the nature of a frutex. [for *fruticescent* (foll., -ESCENT)]

frut'ĕx (frōō-), n. (bot.).(pl. -*tcēs*). Woody--stemmed plant smaller than tree, shrub. [L (genit. -*icis*)]

frut'icōse (frōō-), a. (Bot.) shrubby; (of minerals, zoophytes, etc.) looking like shrub. [prec., -OSE¹]

fry̆¹, n. Young fishes fresh from the spawn; young of salmon in second year; young of other creatures produced in large numbers, e.g. bees or frogs; *small ~*, young or insignificant beings, children etc. [ME, f. ON *frjó* = Goth. *fraiw* seed]

fry̆², v.t. & i., & n. 1. Cook (t. & i.) in boiling fat (*other* FISH¹ *to ~*; *~ing-pan*, shallow pan used; *out of ~ing-pan into* fire, from bad to worse). 2. n. Fried meat; ‖ various internal parts of animals usu. fried, esp. LAMB'*s ~*. [ME, f. OF *frire* f. L *frigere*]

fry̆'er, **frī'er**, n. Vessel for frying fish; one who fries (fish). [-ER¹]

‖ **fŭb'sy̆** (-z-), a. Fat or squat. [f. obs. *fubs* small fat person]

fuchsia (fūsh'*a*), n. Drooping-flowered shrub. [mod. L (*Fuchs* 16th-c. German botanist, -IA¹)]

fuch'sine (fōōk-), n. Salt of rosaniline forming deep red dye. [prec. (f. resemblance of colour to flower) +-INE⁴]

fūc'us, n. (pl. -*ci* pr. -si). Kinds of seaweed with flat leathery fronds. Hence **fūc'oID** a. [L, = rock-lichen, f. Gk *phukos*]

fŭd'dle, v.i. & t., & n. 1. Tipple, booze; intoxicate; stupefy, confuse. 2. n. Spell of drinking (*on the ~*), intoxication; confusion. [orig. unkn.]

fŭdd'y̆-dŭdd'y̆, a. & n. (colloq., joc.). Old-fashioned (person), ineffectual (old fogy). [orig. unkn.]

fŭdge¹, int. & n. Nonsense!; nonsense; piece of stop-press news inserted in newspaper page at the last minute by special means; soft-grained sweetmeat made with milk, sugar, chocolate, etc. [perh. f. foll.]

fŭdge², v.t. & i., & n. 1. Fit together, patch, make up, in a makeshift or dishonest way, cook, fake; practise such methods. 2. n. Piece of fudging. [perh. f. obs. *fadge* v.i., fit]

Fuehrer, **Füh—** (fūr⁴), n. Leader. [G]

fū'ĕl, n., & v.t. & i. (-ll-). 1. Material for fires, firing, coal, wood, etc.; something that feeds or inflames passion etc. 2. vb. Supply (fire) with ~; get ~. [ME, f. OF *fouaille* f. Rom. **focalia* f. FOCUS, -AL]

fŭg, n., & v.i., (colloq. : -gg-). 1. Fustiness of air in room; fluff and dust collected in corners etc. 2. v.i. Enjoy a frowsty atmosphere. Hence ~g'y² (-g-) a. [orig. unkn.]

fūgā'cious (-shus), a. Fleeting, evanescent, hard to capture or keep. So **fŭgā⁴city** (-ă⁴) n. [f. L *fugax* (*fugere* flee, -ACIOUS)]

fūg'al, a. Of the nature of a fugue. Hence ~LY² adv. [-AL]

-fūge, suf. in adjj. & nn. f. mod. L in *-fugus*. Acc. to L anal. the sense should be *fleeing from* (*fugere*) as in L *lucifugus*, *erifuga*; but in the mod. formations it is *putting to flight* (*fugare*) as in *febrifuge*, *vermifuge*.

fū'gitive, a. & n. 1. Fleeing, running away, that has taken flight; flitting, shifting; evanescent, of short duration, quickly fading; (of literature) of passing interest, ephemeral, occasional. 2. n. One who flees esp. from danger, enemy, justice, or owner: exile, refugee. [ME, f. OF (-*if*, -*ive*), f. L *fugitivus* (*fugere fugit-* flee, -IVE)]

fū'gleman (-gel-), n. (pl. -*men*). ‖ Soldier placed in front of regiment etc. while drilling to show the motions & time;

leader, organizer, spokesman, whence by back formation **fū′gle** v.i. [f. G *flügelmann* (*flügel* wing, *mann* man)]

fugue (fūg), n., & v.i. & t. **1.** Polyphonic composition in which a short melodic theme (' subject ') is introduced by one of the parts and successively taken up by the others, thereafter forming the main material of the texture (*double* ~, with two such themes), whence **fūg′uɪsт**(1) (-gi-) n.; loss of memory coupled with disappearance from one's usual haunts. **2.** vb. Compose or perform ~ (*fuguing* or ~*d*, in the form of a ~). [f. F, or It. f. L *fuga* flight]

-ful, suf. orig.=FULL a. **1.** Forming adjj. f. nn., w. sense *full of* (*beautiful*), & sometimes *having qualities of* (*masterful*); also adjj. f. adjj. or f. L adj. stems (*direful, grateful, tristful*), perh. on anal. of older synonyms in *-ful*; also f. vv. (*forgetful*), arising perh. f. cases in which first component might in form be either n. or v. (*helpful*, & esp. *thankful* where the sing. n. being disused *thank* would naturally be taken for verb); a pass. sense is seen in *bashful*=abashable. **2.** Forming nn., w. sense *amount required to fill* (*handful*). *Handful* is a differentiation f. *hand full*, which in the Teut. langg. had orig. besides its literal sense that of *quantity that fills a hand*. The differentiation is not carried out equally in all langg., G *handvoll* etc. taking their gender f. first component, though written as single wds. In mod. E *-ful* is a living suf. freely added to nn. (*boxful, houseful, churchful*); a reminiscence of its orig. is seen in *spoonsful, cupsful*, which are ambiguous & contrary to good mod. usage.

fŭl′crum, n. (pl. *-ra*). (Mech.) point against which lever is placed to get purchase or on which it turns or is supported; means by which influence etc. is brought to bear; (Bot.; usu. pl.) accessory organs, appendages, e.g. bracts, tendrils. [L, = post of couch (*fulcire* to prop)]

fulfil′ (fŏŏl-), v.t. (-ll-). Bring to consummation, carry out (prophecy, promise), satisfy (desire, prayer); perform, execute, do, (command, law); answer (purpose), comply with (conditions); bring to an end, finish, complete, (period, work). Hence ~MENT (fŏŏl-) n. [OE *fullfyllan* (FULL[1], FILL)]

fŭl′gent, a. (poet. & rhet.). Shining, brilliant. [f. L *fulgēre* shine, -ENT]

fŭl′gŭrite, n. (Geol.) rocky substance fused or vitrified by lightning, tube made by passage of lightning into sand; an explosive. [f. L *fulgur* lightning + -ITE[1](2)]

ful′ham (fŏŏl′am), n. (hist.). Loaded DIE[1]. [orig. unkn.]

Ful′ham Păl′ace (fŏŏl′am), n. Official residence of the Bishop of London.

fūli′ginous, a. Sooty, dusky. [f. LL *fuliginosus* (*fuligo -inis* soot, -OUS)]

full[1] (fŏŏl), a., v.t., & adv. **1.** Filled to utmost capacity, holding all (*of*, or abs.) its limits will allow, replete, (~ *to the brim, to overflowing*, & colloq. *up*); (of heart etc.) overcharged with emotion (~*-hearted*, stirred with deep feeling, also zealous, confident, courageous). **2.** Holding or having abundance *of*, crowded (*in a* ~ *house*, with a good proportion of members present), showing marked signs *of* (~ *of vitality*). **3.** Engrossed with the thought of (~ *of himself, of his subject*; ~ *of the news* etc., unable to keep from talking of it). **4.** Replete with food (arch. of persons; *a* ~ *stomach*); (chiefly Bibl.) having had one's fill of (~ *of years & honours*). **5.** Abundant, sufficient, copious, satisfactory, (*a* ~ *meal*; *turned it to* ~ *account*; *give* ~ *details*; *he is very* ~ *on this point*). **6.** Complete, entire, perfect, answering completely to its name, reaching the specified or usual limit, entirely visible, (~ *point* or *stop*, period in punctuation; ~ *daylight, membership*; ~ *brother, sister*, born of same father and mother; *of the* ~ *blood*, of pure descent, not hybrid, so ~*-blooded*, & see below; ~ *pay*, that allowed on active service; ~ *age*, after minority; ~ DRESS[2], & so ~*-dress rehearsal*; ~*-dress debate* in Parliament, prearranged on important question, not arising casually; ~ SWING n.; *at* ~ *length*, lying stretched out, also = *in* ~ below; ~*-length portrait* etc., of whole figure; ~ *moon*, with whole disc illuminated, also the time when this comes; ~ *face*, turned straight to spectator; *waited a* ~ *hour*; *it was* ~ *summer*). **7.** (Of light) intense, (of colour) deep, (of motion etc.) vigorous (*a* ~ *pulse*; ~ *gallop, speed*, etc., used adv. with *come* etc.; ~ *speed ahead!*, order to pursue course with energy. **8.** Swelling, plump, protuberant, (of dress) containing superfluous material arranged in folds etc. (vb, make ~, gather, pleat). **9.** ~*-back*, football player stationed behind; ~*-blooded*, vigorous, hearty, sensual, & see above; ~*-bodied*, esp. of wine with much BODY; ~*-bottomed*, (of wig) long behind, opp. BOB[1]; ~ *house*, *hand*, Poker hand with three of a kind and a pair; ~*-mouthed*, (of cattle) with ~ complement of teeth, (of dogs) baying loudly, (of oratory, style, etc.) sonorous, vigorous; ~ *pitch* (Cricket), a bowled ball pitched right up to the wicket without first touching the ground (also ~ *toss*); ~ *score* (Mus.), complete score comprising music for all performers; || ~*-timer*, child who attends during all school-hours (opp. *half-timer*). **10.** (used abs. as n.). Whole (*cannot tell you the* ~ *of it*; *in* ~, without abridgement; *to the* ~, to the utmost extent, quite); height, acme, (*season, moon, is past the* ~); hence ~′ISH[1](2) a. **11.** adv. Very (chiefly poet.; ~ *fain*; ~ *many a*; *know it* ~ *well*); quite, fully, (~ *six miles*; ~ *as useful as*); often in comb., as ~-*blown*, of flowers, quite open, also fig. as ~-*blown dignity*; ~-*grown*, having reached maturity); exactly (*hit him ~ on the nose*); more than sufficiently (*this chair is ~ high*. [OE *full*, OS *ful*, OHG *foll*, ON *fullr*, Goth. *fulls* f. Gmc **fullaz* cogn. w. Gk *polus*]

full[2] (fŏŏl), v.t. Cleanse & thicken (cloth). [ME, back form. f. foll.; cf. OF *fouler* FOIL[2]]

full'er[1] (fŏŏ-), n. One who fulls cloth; ~'*s· earth*, hydrous silicate of alumina. [OE *fullere*, f. L *fullo*+-ER[1]]

full'er[2] (fŏŏ-), n., & v.t. Grooved tool on which iron is shaped; groove made by this esp. in horse-shoes; (vb) stamp with ~. [orig.-unkn.]

ful(l)'ness (fŏŏl-), n. Being FULL[1]; esp.: (Bibl.) the ~ *of the heart*, emotion, genuine feelings, *the ~ of time*, the destined time, *the ~ of the world* etc., all that fills it; (of sound, colour, etc.) richness, volume, body. [-NESS]

full'y (fŏŏ-), adv. Completely, without deficiency; quite (esp. with numbers); ~ *fashioned*, (of women's stockings) seamed & shaped. [-LY[2]]

ful'mar (fŏŏ-) n. Sea-bird of petrel kind & gull's size. [perh. f. ON *fúll* FOUL[1]+ *már* MEW[1]]

fül'minant, a. Fulminating; (Path., of diseases) developing suddenly. [f. L as foll., -ANT]

fül'minat|e[1], v.i. & t. Flash like lightning, explode, detonate, (~*ing gold, mercury*, etc., various fulminates, see FULMINIC); thunder forth, utter or publish, (censure); issue (usu. official) censures *against* (esp. of Pope). Hence or cogn. **fülminA'TION** n., ~ORY a. [f. L *fulminare* (*fulmen* lightning), -ATE[3]]

fül'mine, v.t. & i. (poet.). Send forth (lightning, thunder); thunder (lit. & fig.). [as prec.]

fülmin'ic, a. (chem.), ~ *acid*, the hypothetical parent of the fulminates, many of which are explosive. Hence **fül'minate**[2] [-ATE[1](3)] n. [f. L *fulmen -inis* lightning +-IC]

ful'ness. See FULLNESS.

ful'some (fŭ-, fŏŏ-), a. Cloying, excessive, disgusting by excess, (of flattery, servility, exaggerated affection). Hence ~LY[2] (-ml-) adv., ~NESS (-mn-) n. [FULL[1], -SOME]

fül'vous, a. (nat. hist.). Reddish-yellow, tawny. So **fülves'CENT** a. [f. L *fulvus*+ -OUS]

fümäde', n. Smoked pilchard. [f. Sp. *fumado* smoked, f. L *fumare* FUME, -ADO(1)]

füm'aröle, n. Crevice in cone of volcano through which vapour issues. [f. F *fumarolle* f. LL *fumariolum* dim. of L *fumarium* smoke-chamber (*fumus* smoke, -ARY[1])]

füm'bl|e, v.i. & t., & n. 1. Use the hands awkwardly, grope about (*at*, *with*, fastening etc.; *for*, *after*, thing sought);

handle or deal with awkwardly or nervously (~*e the ball*, not stop it cleanly), hence ~ER[1] n. 2. n. Bungling attempt. [16th c., f. LG *fummeln*, Du. *fommelen*|

füme, n., & v.t. & i. 1. Odorous smoke, vapour, or exhalation; watery vapour; noxious vapour supposed to rise from stomach to brain (*the ~s of wine* etc.; also fig. of excitement, enthusiasm, etc.); fit of anger (*in a ~*); hence **füm'y**[2] a. 2. vb Perfume with incense; subject to chemical ~s esp. those of ammonia (photographic film, oak, to darken tints); emit ~s; (of vapour etc.) rise, be emitted; be pettish, chafe (*at*). [ME; n. f. OF *fum*, vb f. *fumer*, f. L *fumus*, *fumare*, smoke]

füm'ig|äte, v.t. Apply fumes to; disinfect or purify with fumes; perfume. Hence ~A'TION, ~ätOR, nn. [f. L *fumigare* (*fumus* smoke), -ATE[3]]

füm'itory, n. Herb formerly used in medicine. [ME, f. OF *fumeterre* f. med. L *fumus terrae* earth-smoke, w. assim. to -ORY]

fün, n., & v.i. (-nn-). 1. Sport, amusement, jocularity, drollery, (*make ~ of*, *poke ~ at*, ridicule; *for* or *in ~*, as a joke, not seriously; *is good, great*, ~, very amusing; *like ~*, vigorously, quickly, much; *what ~!*, how amusing!). 2. v.i. (rare). Indulge in ~, joke. [f. obs. *fun* vb, var. of *fon* befool; see FOND]

fünäm'bülist, n. Rope-walker. [ult. f. L *funambulus* (*funis* rope, *ambulare* walk), -IST]

fünc'tion, n., & v.i. 1: Activity proper to anything, mode of action by which it fulfils its purpose; office-holder's duty, employment, profession, calling; religious or other public ceremony or occasion, social meeting of formal or important kind; (Math.) variable quantity in relation to other(s) in terms of which it may be expressed or on which its value depends; hence ~LESS (-shon-) a. 2. v.i. Fulfil a ~, operate, act. [F, f. L *functionem* (*fungi funct-* perform, -ION)]

fünc'tional (-shon-), a. Official, merely formal, (rare); (Physiol.) of, affecting, the functions of an organ etc. only, not structural or organic (esp. of diseases), (of organ) having a function, not functionless or rudimentary; (Math.) of a FUNCTION; (of building etc.) shaped or constructed with regard only to its function, not to traditional or other theories of design. Hence ~LY[2] adv. [-AL]

fünc'tionary (-shon-), n. & a. 1. n. Official. 2. adj. = prec. (not in math. sense). [-ARY[1]; n. f. F *fonctionnaire*]

fünc'tionäte (-shon-), v.i. = FUNCTION v. [-ATE[3]]

fünd, n., & v.t. 1. Permanent stock of something ready to be drawn upon (*a ~ of common sense, tenderness, labour, knowledge*); stock of money, esp. one set apart for a purpose (SINK[1]*ing*~); (pl.) pecuniary resources (*in ~s*, having money, flush);

‖ the ~s, stock of national debt as mode of investment (has £10,000 in the ~s; ‖ ~-holder, such investor). 2. v.t. Convert (floating debt) into more or less permanent debt at fixed interest; put into a ~, collect, store, (rare); ‖ invest (money) in the ~s. [f. L fundus bottom]

fŭn′dament, n. The buttocks. [ME, f. OF fondement f. L fundamentum (FOUND[1], -MENT)]

fŭndamĕn′tal, a. & n. 1. Of the groundwork, going to the root of the matter, serving as base or foundation, essential, primary, original, from which others are derived, (a ~ change; the ~ rules; the ~ form); (Mus.) ~ note, lowest note of chord in its original (uninverted) form, ~ tone, produced by vibration of whole sonorous body (opp. harmonics produced by that of its parts); hence ~ITY (-ăl[4]) n., ~LY[2] adv. 2. n. Principle, rule, article, serving as groundwork of system (usu. pl.); (Mus.) ~ note or tone. [ME, f. LL fundamentalis (prec., -AL)]

*fŭndamĕn′tal‖ism, n. Maintenance, in opposition to modernism, of traditional orthodox beliefs such as the inerrancy of Scripture & literal acceptance of the creeds as fundamentals of protestant Christianity. So ~IST n. & a. [prec. + -ISM]

fūnĕb′rial, a. (rare). Of funeral (custom is ~ in origin). [f. L funebris (funus see foll.) + -AL]

fūn′eral, a. & n. 1. Of, used etc. at, burial or cremation of the dead (~ pile, pyre, pile of wood etc. on which corpse is burnt; ~ urn, holding ashes of cremated dead; ~ oration). 2. n. Burial of the dead with its observances, obsequies; burial procession; (colloq.) unpleasant concern; lookout (that's your ~). [ME; adj. OF, f. LL funeralis (L funus -eris funeral + -AL); n. f. OF funeraille f. med. L funeralia neut. pl. of funeralis, -AL(2)]

fūn′erarў, a. = FUNEBRIAL. [f. LL funerarius (prec., -ARY[1])]

fūnēr′eal, a. Appropriate to funeral, gloomy, dismal, dark. Hence ~LY[2] adv. [f. L funereus (FUNERAL) + -AL]

fŭn′gible (-j-), a. (legal). That can serve for, or be replaced by, another answering to the same definition (of goods etc. contracted for, when an individual specimen is not meant). [f. med. L fungibilis f. fungi (vice) serve (turn), -IBLE]

fŭn′gicide (-j-), n. Fungus-destroying substance. [FUNGUS, -I-, -CIDE]

fŭng′ous (-ngg-), a. Of fungi, having nature of a fungus; springing up like a mushroom, transitory. [f. L fungosus (foll., -OSE[1])]

fŭng′‖us (-ngg-), n. (pl. ~i pr. -jī, ~uses). Mushroom, toadstool, or allied plant including moulds; (Bot.) cryptogamous plant without chlorophyll feeding on organic matter; thing of sudden growth; (Path.) spongy morbid growth or ex-

crescence; skin-disease of fish. Hence ~AL (-ngg-), ~IFORM (-j-), ~IV′OROUS (-j-), ~OID, ~USY[2], (-ngg-), aa. [L, perh. cogn. w. Gk sphoggos SPONGE]

fūnic′ular, a. Of a rope or its tension (~ railway, worked by cable & stationary engine). [f. L funiculus (funis cord, -CULE) + -AR[1]]

fŭnk, n., & v.i. & t., (sl.). 1. Fear, panic, (blue ~, terror); coward; hence ~′Y[2] a.; ‖ ~-hole, trench dug-out, employment used as pretext for evading military service. 2. vb. Flinch, shrink, show cowardice; (try to) evade (undertaking), shirk; be afraid of; inspire fear in. [18th c. Oxford sl.; cf. contemporary Du. fonck, in de fonck sijn]

fŭnn′el, n. Diminishing tube, or truncated cone & tube, for conducting liquid, powder, etc., into small opening; ventilating or lighting shaft; metal chimney of steam engine or ship; ~-shaped lower part of chimney. Hence (-)~lED[2] (-ld) a. [ME fonel f. Pr. fonilh, (Sp. fonil) f. L infundibulum f. IN(fundere pour)]

fŭnn′iment, n. Joke, drollery. [foll., -MENT]

fŭnn′‖ў[1], a. Affording fun, comical; curious, queer, perplexing, hard to account for; ~y bone, part of elbow over which ulnar nerve passes; ~y-man, professional jester. Hence ~ILY[2] adv., ~INESS n. [-Y[2]]

‖ fŭnn′ў[2], n. Narrow clinker-built boat for one sculler. [perh. f. prec.]

fŭr, n., & v.t. & i. (-rr-). 1. Trimming or lining made of dressed coat of certain animals, e.g. ermine, beaver; coat of such animals, as material for trimming etc.; (usu. pl.) garment(s) of or having ~; short fine soft hair of certain animals distinguished from the longer hair, (pl.) skins of such animals with the ~; make the ~ fly, make a disturbance, stir up trouble, raise Cain; (collect.) furred animals (esp. ~ & feather; hunt ~, hares); crust adhering to surface, e.g. deposit of wine; coating formed on tongue in sickness; crust of carbonate of lime in kettle etc.; hence ~r′Y[2] a. 2. vb. Provide (garment, animal), clothe (person), coat (tongue, inside of kettle; also intr., become coated), with ~; clean ~ from (boiler); (Carpent.) level (floor-timbers) by inserting strips of wood. [ME; n. f. vb, OF forrer f. forre, fuerre sheath f. WG *fōder (= OE fōddor, OHG fuotar, Goth. fodr f. Gmc *fothrom)]

fŭrb′elow (-ō), n., & v.t. 1. Flounce, pleated border of skirt or petticoat; (pl., contempt.) showy ornaments; ‖ kind of wrinkled seaweed. 2. v.t. Adorn with ~ (s). [18th c. var. of FALBALA]

fŭrb′ish, v.t. Remove rust from, polish up, burnish; give new look to, renovate, revive, (something antiquated; usu. up). [ME, f. OF forbir (-ISH[2]) f. WG, OS furbian; cf. MHG vürben, OHG furben] úrc′ate¹ (-āt, -at), a. Forked, branched. Hence fúrcāt′o- comb. form. [f. LL furcatus (L furca fork, -ATE²)]

fúrc|āte′², v.i. Form a fork, divide. So ~A′TION n. [f. L furca fork + -ATE³]

fúrfurā′ceous (-ferāshŭs), a. Scurfy; (Bot.) covered with bran-like scales. [f. LL furfuraceus (L furfur bran, -ACEOUS)]

fū′rious, a. Full of fury, raging, frantic, violent; fast & ~, (of mirth etc.) eager, uproarious. Hence ~LY² adv. [ME, f. OF furieus f. L furiosus (FURY, -OUS)]

fúrl, v.t. & i. Roll up & bind (sail) on yard or boom; close, fold up, draw away, relinquish (fan, umbrella, wings, curtain, hopes); become ~ed, roll away like clouds. [16th c., f. F ferler f. OF fer(m) FIRM² + lier bind]

fúrl′ŏng, n. Eighth of mile. [OE furlang (furh furrow, LONG adj.); orig. = length of furrow in common field, regarded as square containing ten acres]

fúrl′ough (-lō), n., & v.t. Leave of absence, esp. to soldier; (vb) grant ~ to. [f. Du. verlof (after G verlaub) cogn. w. FOR-, LEAVE¹]

fúrm′ĕtў. See FRUMENTY.

fúrn′ace (-ĭs), n., & v.t. 1. Apparatus including chamber for combustibles in which minerals, metals, etc., may be subjected to continuous intense heat; hot plate; severe test (esp. tried in the ~); closed fireplace for heating building by hot pipes. 2. v.t. Heat in ~. [ME, f. OF fornais f. L fornacem nom. -ax (fornus oven)]

fúrn′ish, v.t. Provide with (~ed with, having); fit up (house, room) with all necessary appliances, esp. movable furniture (~ed house, rooms, etc., esp. let with furniture); provide, afford, yield. [f. OF furnir (-ISH²) f. Rom. *fornire ult. f. WG *frumjan (OS frummian) promote, f. root of FROM]

fúrn′iture, n. Contents of receptacle (~ of his pocket, money; ~ of my shelves, books; ~ of one's mind, knowledge & intelligence;; harness etc. of horse etc. (arch.); movable contents of house or room, tables, chairs, etc.; (Print.) pieces of wood or metal placed round or between type to make blank spaces and fasten the matter in the chase. [f. F fourniture (fournir FURNISH)]

fúrōr′e, n. Enthusiastic admiration, rage, craze. [It., f. L furorem (furere be mad, -OR¹)]

fü′rrier, n. Dealer in, dresser of, furs. [-IER]

fúrr′ing, n. In vbl senses; also (Shipbuild.), doubling of planks on ship's side. [-ING¹]

fü′rrow (-ō), n., & v.t. 1. Narrow trench made by plough; ship's track; rut, track, groove, long indentation, deep wrinkle, hollow between ridges; ‖ ~-slice, slice of earth turned up by mould-board of plough; hence ~LESS (-ōl-), ~Y² (-ōi), aa.

2. v.t. Plough; make ~s, grooves etc., in; mark with wrinkles. [OE furh, OHG furuh, ON for f. Gmc *furh-]

fúrth′er (-dh-), adv. & a. (for usage of fur-, far-, see FARTHER etym.), & v.t. 1. To or at more advanced point in space or time (unsafe to proceed ~; & then to lapse unless ~ continued); to greater extent, more, (inquire ~); (also ~more) in addition, moreover, also (esp. introducing fresh consideration in argument); at greater distance (I'll see you ~ first, euphem. for in hell, as strong refusal of request). 2. adj. Going beyond what exists or has been dealt with, additional, (threats of ~ punishment; till ~ notice, in announcing arrangement to continue during pleasure); more distant (on the ~ side), whence ~MOST a. 3. vb. Help on, promote, favour, (undertaking, movement, cause); hence ~ANCE n., ~SOME a. (-dh-). [OE furthor adv., furthra adj., (FORE², -THER), fyrthrian vb]

fúrth′est (-dh-), a. & adv. = FARTHEST. [superl. formed f. prec.]

fúrt′ive, a. Done by stealth, clandestine, meant to escape notice; sly, stealthy, stolen, taken secretly; thievish, pilfering. Hence ~LY² (-vl-) adv., ~NESS (-vn-) n. [f. F (-if, -ive) or L furtivus (furtum theft, -IVE)]

fū′runc|le (-ŭngkl), n. Boil, tumour. Hence ~ūlAR, ~ūlOUS, aa., (-ŭnk²). [f. L furunculus (fur thief, -UNCLE)]

fū′rў, n. Fierce passion, wild anger, rage, (in a ~, fit of rage); impetuosity in battle etc. (the Spanish F~, massacre by Spaniards at Antwerp in 1576); violence of weather, disease, etc. (like ~, furiously, hard); (usu. pl.) snake-haired goddess(es) of Gk myth (Alēc′tō, Tĭsĭph′onē, Megaer′a) sent from Tartarus to punish crime, (fig.) avenging spirits, remorseful pangs, (haunted by the furies of her father's blood); virago, angry or malignant woman. [ME, f. OF furie f. L furia (furere be mad)]

fúrze, n. Spiny yellow-flowered evergreen shrub growing on European waste lands, gorse, whin. Hence fúrz′ў² a. [OE fyrs of unkn. orig.]

fŭs′cous, a. (nat. hist.). Sombre, dark, in colour. So fŭs′co- comb. form. [L fuscus, -OUS]

fūse¹ (-z), v.t. & i., & n. 1. Melt (t. & i. with intense heat; blend, amalgamate, (t. & i.) into one whole (as by melting (of metals, living bones, institutions, motives, etc.); hence fūs′IBLE a., fūsiBIL′ITY n., (-z-). 2. n. (electr.). Piece of easily-fusible wire, placed in main or branch circuit, designed to melt when overloaded and thus interrupt the current and prevent the section being loaded above the safety limit. [f. L fundere fus- pour]

fūse² (-z), n., & v.t. 1. Tube, casing, cord, etc., filled or saturated with combustible matter for igniting bomb, blasting-charge, etc., component screwed into shell, mine, etc. designed to detonate explosive charge after an interval (*time*-~) or on impact or when subjected to magnetic or vibratory stimulation. **2.** v.t. Fit ~ to [f. It. *fuso* f. L *fusus* spindle]

fusee' (-z-), n. Conical pulley or wheel esp. in watch or clock; exostosis or bony tumour on horse's cannon-bone; large--headed match for lighting cigar or pipe in wind. [f. F *fusée* spindle, -EE)]

fus'elage (-z-), n. Framework of aeroplane. [F, f. *fuseler* cut in spindle form (*fuseau* dim. f. L *fusus*), -AGE]

fus'el oil (-z-), n. Mixture of several alcohols, chiefly amyl, produced, usu. in small amounts, during alcoholic fermentation·and making alcoholic liquors harmful or poisonous. [f. G *fusel* bad spirit, cf. *fuseln* FOOZLE]

fus'iform (-z-), a. (nat. hist.). Shaped like spindle or cigar, tapering at both ends. [f. L *fusus* spindle, -I-, -FORM]

fus'il (-z-), n. Obsolete light musket. [F, = It. *focile* (L *focus* hearth, fire, -IL)]

fusilier' (-z-), n. (usu. pl.). (Man of) certain British regiments formerly armed with fusils. [F, (prec., -IER)]

fusillade' (-z-), n., & v.t. **1.** (Wholesale execution by) continuous discharge of fire-arms. **2.** v.t. Assault (place), shoot down (persons), by ~. [F *fusiller* shoot f. FUSIL, -ADE)]

fu'sion (-zhn), n. Fusing; fused mass; blending of different things into one; coalition, whence ~IST(2) (-zhon-) n.; ~ *bomb*, hydrogen bomb. [f. F, or L *fusio* (FUSE[1], -ION); cf. FOISON]

fuss, n., & v.i. & t. **1.** Bustle, excessive commotion, ostentatious or nervous activity; treatment of trifles as important; abundance of petty detail; ~-*pot* (colloq.), person who is always making a ~; hence ~'Y² a., ~'iLY² adv., ~'iNESS n. **2.** vb. Make ~; busy oneself restlessly with trifles; move fussily *about*, *up & down*, etc.; agitate, worry, (person). [perh. imit. of sputtering or bubbling]

fustanell'a, n. Man's white kilt in modern Greece. [It., dim. of mod. Gk *phoustani* prob. f. It. *fustagno* FUSTIAN]

fus'tian, n. & a. **1.** Thick twilled short--napped cotton cloth usu. dyed dark; turgid speech or writing, bombast. **2.** adj. Made of ~, (fig.) bombastic, worthless, sorry, pretentious. [ME, f. OF *fustaigne* (med. L *fustaneus* adj. perh. = from *Fostat* suburb of Cairo)]

fus'tic, n. Two kinds of wood yielding yellow dye (*young* ~, Venetian sumach; ~ or *old* ~, Amer. & W. Ind.); dye from these. [f. F f. Sp. *fustoc* f. Arab. *fustuq* f. Gk as PISTACHIO]

fus'tig|āte, v.t. (joc.). Cudgel. So ~A⁴ TION n. [LL *fustigare* (*fustis* cudgel), -ATE³]

fus't|y, a. Stale-smelling, musty, mouldy; close, stuffy; antiquated, old-fashioned.

Hence ~iNESS n. [14th c., f. OF *fuste* smelling of the cask (*fust*, f. L *fustis* cudgel)]

fut. See PHUT.

fütch'el(l), n. One of timbers supporting shafts, pole, or axle-bar, of carriage. [orig. unkn.]

futh'orc (foo-), n. Runic alphabet. [its first six letters (*th* being one)]

füt'ile (-i-, -i-), a. Useless, ineffectual, vain, frivolous. Hence or cogn. **fütil'ity** n., (rare) ~LY² adv. [f. L *futilis* leaky, futile, f. *fud-* st. of *fundere* pour]

futt'ock, n. One of ship's middle timbers between floor & top timbers; ~ *plates*, iron plates in a ship's top to which the ~ *shrouds* (lower ends of which are fastened to ring on mast below) are fixed, as well as the dead-eyes of the topmast rigging. [ME *fot(t)ekes*, *fot(t)eken*, etc., f. MLG f. *fót* FOOT + -*ken* -KIN]

fu'ture, a. & n. **1.** About to happen, that will be hereafter (~ *life*, *state*, existence after death), that will be something specified (*my* ~ *wife*); of time to come, (Gram., of tense) describing event yet to happen. **2.** n. Time to come (*for the* ~, *in* ~, from now onwards; *past*, *present*, & ~); what will happen in the ~; person's, country's, etc., prospective condition; (Gram.) ~ tense; one's betrothed; (Commerc.; pl.) goods & stocks sold for ~ delivery, contracts for these; hence ~LESS (-cherl-) a. [OF (-*ur*, -*ure*), f. L *futurus* fut. part. of *esse* be f. st. *fu-* BE]

fu'turist (-che-), n. & a. **1.** (theol.). (One) believing that the prophecies of the Apocalypse etc. are still to be fulfilled. **2.** (art). Adherent of **fü'turism** (-che-) n., an early 20th-c. movement in (esp. Italian) art, literature, etc., marked by violent departure from traditional methods and by the use of arbitrary symbols in the expression of emotion. [-IST]

fütūr'itý, n. Future time; (sing. or pl.) future events; future condition, existence after death; ~ *stakes*, stakes raced for long after entries or nominations are made. [-ITY]

füzz, n. Loose volatile matter, fluff; fluffy or frizzed hair; ~-*ball*, a fungus, the puff-ball. [17th c., goes w. foll.]

füzz'|ý, a. Frayed, fluffy; blurred, indistinct; frizzed. Hence ~iLY² adv., ~iNESS n. [17th c., prob. f. Du. *voos*, LG *fussig* spongy]

fy, fye. = FIE.

-fy, suf. forming vbs. In the older E vbs -*fy* represented F -*fier*, L -*ficare*. L formed vbs in -*ficare* (with or without intervention of adjj. in -*ficus*) f. nn., w. sense *make*, *produce*, (*pacificare*, orig. intr., make peace) or *make into* (*deificare* deify); f. adjj. w. sense *bring into a state* (*sanctificare*); & f. vb stems w. causative sense (*horrificare* horrify). In med. L -*ficare* was often substituted for -*facere*;

hence F & E vbs in *-fier*, *-fy*, occas. repr.
L vbs in *-facere* (F *stupéfier*, but p.p.
stupéfait as well as *stupéfié*, stupefy;
OF *satisfier*, but mod. F *satisfaire*; F
liquéfier liquefy, *rubéfier* rubefy). Apart
f. these in *-efy* E has always *-ify* (-I-),
which is freely added to E adjj. & nn. to
form vbs chiefly joc. or colloq. (*speechify*, Frenchify; also, on vb, the irreg.
argufy). Vbs formed on adjj. have often
intr. as well as trans. sense (*solidify* make
or become solid). Vbs in *-ify* have nn. in
-ification, those representing L vbs in
-facere have nn. in *-FACTION*; but E has
petrifaction where F has the correct
pétrification.

fȳl′fot, n. Swastika, equal-armed cross of
which each arm is continued rectangularly, all clockwise or counterclockwise.
[name based on ancient direction for
design of painted window, in which ~
may mean either the particular pattern
or something to *fill the foot* of the window.]

fytte. See FIT[1].

G

G (jē), letter (pl. *Gs*, G's). (Mus.) fifth note
of diatonic scale of C major; corresponding scale or key; *G* CLEF.

găb, n. (colloq.). Talk, prattle, twaddle,
(*stop your* ~, hold your tongue; *gift of the*
~, talent for speaking, also loquacity).
[18th c. *gab* to talk, mouth = 17th c. *gob*
conversation, 16th c. *gob* mouth, perh. f.
Ir. *gob* beak, mouth]

găb′ardine (-ēn), n. Dress material of
cotton or silk with wool lining; material
for raincoats. [var. of GABERDINE]

găb′ble, v.i. & t., & n. 1. Talk volubly or
inarticulately, read aloud (t., often *over*,
& i.) too fast; utter too fast. 2. n. Voluble
confused unintelligible talk. [16th c., f.
MDu. *gabbelen*]

găb′bro, n. A basic igneous rock of
crystalline texture resembling dolerite
and granite. [It.]

gabĕlle′, n. Tax (usu. foreign tax), esp.
the French pre-Revolution salt-tax. [F,
f. It. *gabella* ult. f. Arab. *qabála* tribute]

găb′erdine (-ēn), n. Loose long upper
garment esp. of Jews & almsmen; a fine
hard-laid cloth. [f. OF *gauvardine* perh.
f. MHG *wallevart* pilgrimage]

găb′ion, n. Cylinder of wicker or woven
metal bands to be filled with earth for
use in fortification or engineering. [F,
f. It. *gabbione* (*gabbia* CAGE, -OON)]

gābionāde′, n. Line of gabions. [-ADE(1)]

gā′ble, n. Triangular upper part of wall
at end of ridged roof; (also ~*-end*)
~-topped wall; ~-shaped canopy over
window or door, whence **gā′blĒT**[1] n.
Hence (-)**gā′blED**[2] (-ld) a. [ME *gavel* f.
ON *gafl*; ME *gable* f. OF f. ON; cogn. w.
OE *geafol*, OHG *gabala* fork, OHG *gibil*
gable]

găb′ȳ, n. Simpleton. [orig. unkn.]

găd[1], int. of surprise, asseveration, etc.
(also *by* ~, *begad*). [= GOD]

găd[2], v.i. (-dd-), & n. Go about idly, rove,
wander, (usu. *about*, *abroad*, *out*); (of
plants, esp. in part.) straggle; (*up*)*on the*
~, going about, on the move; ~'*about*,
(person) given to ~ding. [perh. back
formation f. obs. *gadling* companion,
OE *gædeling* (*gæd* fellowship, -LING[1])]

gad(d)i (gŭd′ī), n. Cushioned throne of
Indian ruler; (transf.) the regal position.
[Hind. *gaddī* cushion]

găd′-flȳ, n. Breeze, cattle-biting fly;
irritating or worrying person; violent
impulse, oestrum. [f. obs. *gad* spike f.
ON *gaddr* cogn. w. YARD[1]]

gădg′ĕt, n. (colloq.). Small fitting or
contrivance in machinery etc.; (transf.)
dodge, device. [first in naut. use; orig.
unkn.]

Gadhĕl′ic (-dĕ-), a. & n. = GAELIC in its
wider sense. [literary f. Ir. *Gaedheal*
Gael + -IC]

găd′oid, a. & n. (Fish) of the cod family.
[f. Gk *gados* cod + -OID]

gadrōōn′, n. (usu. pl. or attrib.). Convex
curve(s) in series forming ornamental
edge like inverted fluting. [f. F *godron*;
cf. *goder* pucker]

găd′wall (-awl), n. A freshwater duck of
the north of Europe & America. [orig.
uncert.]

Gael (gāl), n. Scottish Celt; (rarely) Irish
Celt. [f. Sc.-Gael. *Gaidheal*]

Gael′ic (gāl-, găl-), a. & n. (Language) of
Scottish Celts, of Scottish & Irish &
Manx Celts. [-IC]

găff[1], n., & v.t. 1. Barbed fishing-spear;
stick with iron hook for landing large
fish; spar extending top of fore-&-aft
sail not set on stays. 2. v.t. Seize (fish)
with ~. [f. F *gaffe* boat-hook]

găff[2], n. (sl.). *Blow the* ~, let out plot.
[orig. unkn.]

‖ **găff**[3], n. (sl.). Public place of amusement, esp. (usu. *penny* ~) low theatre or
music-hall. [orig. unkn.]

gaffe, n. Blunder, indiscreet act or remark, *faux pas*. [F]

găff′er, n. Elderly rustic, old fellow, (also
as prefix to name); ‖ foreman of gang.
[contr. of *godfather*, *ga-* by assoc. w.
grandfather; cf. GAMMER, GOSSIP]

găg, n., & v.t. & i. (-gg-). 1. Thing thrust
into mouth to prevent speech or outcry
or (Surg.) hold it open for operation,
(Parl.) closure or GUILLOTINE, (vb, apply
~ to, silence, deprive of free speech). 2.
Actor's interpolations in dramatic dialogue (vb, make these); (Theatr.) carefully
prepared comic effect or business introduced into music-hall sketch, stage-play,
etc., (vb, make these); ~*-man*, professional deviser of ~s. 3. ~*-bit*, specially
powerful for horse-breaking, ~*-rein*,
arranged to make bit more powerful,
(*gag*, v.t.) apply ~*-bit* to (horse). 4. Joke,

hoax; (sl.) imposture, lie, (v.t., deceive; v.i., practise deceit). **5.** Retch, choke. [vb 15th c., perh. imit. of choking sound]

găg′a (or gah-), a. (sl.). Fatuous, senile; dotty. [F.]

găge¹, n., & v.t. **1.** Pledge, thing deposited as security; (glove thrown down as, any symbol of) challenge to fight. **2.** v.t. Stake, pledge, offer as guarantee. [ME; n. f. OF gage (f. Frank. *waddi, = OHG wetti, Goth wadi; see WED); vb f. F gager of same orig., or for ENGAGE]

găge². See GAUGE¹.

găge³, n. Greengage. [abbr.]

găg′gle, n., & v.i. **1.** Flock (of geese); (derog.) company (of women). **2.** v.i. (Of geese) cackle. [14th c. imit.; cf. Du. gaggelen]

gai′ety, n. Being gay, mirth; (usu. pl.) merrymaking, festive occasion(s), amusements; bright appearance. [f. F gaieté (GAY, -TY)]

Gaik′war, Gaek-, (gīk-), n. Ruler of Baroda. [Marathi, = cowherd]

gail′ÿ. See GAY.

gain¹, n. Increase of possessions etc., profit, advance, improvement; acquisition of wealth, lucre; (pl.) sums acquired by trade etc., emoluments, winnings; increase in amount. [OF (gaaignier GAIN²)]

gain², v.t. & i. Obtain, secure, (desired or desirable thing; ~ time, obtain delay by pretexts or slow methods; ~ the ear of, get favourable hearing from); win (sum) as profits or as result of changed conditions, earn, whence ~′ings (-z) [-ING¹ (2)] n. pl.; make a profit, be benefited, improve or advance in some respect, be enhanced by comparison or contrast; win (land from sea, battle, victory; ~ the upper hand, be victorious); bring over to one's interest or views, win over, persuade, prevail upon; reach, arrive at, (desired place); ~ ground, progress, advance, encroach (up)on; ~ (ground) (up)on, get closer to (person or thing pursued); (of sea) encroach (up)on land; ~ (up)on, win the favour of. Hence ~′ABLE a., ~′ER¹ n. [f. OF gaaignier to till, acquire, f. Rom. *guadaniare f. WG *waithanjan (OHG weidenen graze, hunt) f. *waitha pasture (OE wāth hunting)]

gain′ful, a. Lucrative, remunerative; bent on gain. [-FUL]

gainsay′, v.t. (arch., literary; past -said, pr. -ād or -ĕd). Deny, contradict. Hence ~ER¹ n. [f. obs. gáin- pref. against f. ON gegn (see AGAIN) +SAY]

gainst, 'gainst. (Poet. for) AGAINST.

gait, n. Manner of walking, bearing or carriage as one walks. [var. of GATE²]

gait′er, n. Covering of cloth, leather, etc., for leg below knee or for ankle. Hence ~ED² (-erd) a. [f. F guêtre]

găl′a (or gah¹), n.. Festive occasion, fête, (often attrib., as ~ day, dress, etc.). [F f. It.]

galăc′tĭc, a. (astron.). Of the galaxy. [f. Gk galaktikos (foll., -IC)]

galăc′to-, comb. form of Gk gala -aktos milk, used in scientific terms as ~gogue, (substance) inducing a flow of milk.

găl′antine ·(-ēn); n. White meat boned, spiced, tied, boiled, & served cold. [ME, f. OF, altered f. galatine jellied meat]

galăn′tÿ show (-ō), n. Pantomime on screen made by shadows of puppets. [perh. f. It. galanti pl. of galante GALLANT]

gălatē′a n. Superior striped cotton dress material (orig. used for children's sailor suits). [f. H.M.S. G~.]

găl′axÿ, n. Irregular luminous band of stars indistinguishable to naked eye encircling the heavens, Milky Way; brilliant company (of beauties, talent, etc.). [earlier also -ias, -ia f. OF galaxie & LL -ias, med. L -ia f. Gk galaxias (gala -aktos milk)]

găl′banum, n. Gum resin from some Persian species of ferula. [ME, f. L f. Gk khalbanē prob. f. Oriental wd]

gāle¹, n. (Also sweet~) bog-myrtle. [OE (also Du. & G) gagel]

gāle², n. Very strong wind, (naut.) storm, (poet.) gentle breeze. [orig. obsc.; cf. Norw. galen bad (of weather)]

‖ **gāle³**, n. Periodical payment of rent (hanging~, arrears of rent). [contr. f. obs. gavel in GAVELKIND]

gāl′e|a, n. (bot., zool.). Structure like helmet in shape, function, or position. So ~ATE², ~āted, aa. [L, = helmet]

‖ **galeen′ÿ**, n. Guinea-fowl. [f. Sp. gallina (morisca Moorish) hen]

Gāl′en, n. (joc.). Physician. [f. L f. Gk Galēnos, Pergamene 2nd-c. A.D. physician]

galēn′a, n. Common lead ore, lead sulphide, lead glance. [L, = lead ore (in partly purified state)]

galēn′ĭc, a., **galēn′ical**, a. & n. Of, according to, Galen; esp. (remedy) made of vegetable, not synthetic, components. [Galen +-IC(AL)]

Gălilē′an, a. Of the astronomer Galileo; ~ telescope (with bi-convex objective and bi-concave eyepiece). [-AN]

Găl′ilee, g-, n. Porch or chapel at entrance of church. [OF, = med. L galilaea, perh. as less sacred than church w. ref. to Galilee as opp. Judaea, or esp. to Matt. iv. 15 (~ of the Gentiles)]

gălima′tias (-ăsĭah), n. Confused or meaningless talk, rigmarole. [F, of unkn. orig.]

găl′ingăle (-ngg-), n. Aromatic root of E.-Ind. plants used in cookery & medicine; (also English~) kind of sedge. [ME, f. OF galingal f. Arab. khalanjan perh. f. Chin. ko-liang-kiang mild ginger from Ko]

găliot. = GALLIOT.

găl′ipŏt, n. Kind of hardened turpentine. [F, of unkn. orig.]

gall¹ (gawl), n. Secretion of liver, bile, (now only of lower animals); typical bitter substance, bitterness, (~ & wormwood); ~-bladder & its contents; asperity, rancour, (dip one's pen in ~, write violently), whence ~'-LESS (gawl⁴-l-) a.; *impudence (sl.); ~-bladder vessel containing the ~; ~-stone, calculous formation in ~-bladder. [OE gealla, ON gal, OS, OHG galla f. Gmc *gall- cogn. w. Gk kholē & YELLOW]

gall² (gawl), n. Painful swelling, pustule, blister, esp. in horse; sore produced by chafing; mental soreness or its cause; place rubbed bare, flaw; bare spot in field or coppice. [ME, f. MLG, MDu. galle (= OE gealla)]

gall³ (gawl), v.t. & i. Rub sore, injure by rubbing; vex, annoy, harass, humiliate, whence ~'ING² a. [f. prec., orig. as back formation f. gallED²]

gall⁴ (gawl), n. Excrescence produced by insect on trees, esp. on oak (also oak-~, used in making ink & tannin, & in dyeing & medicine); ~-fly, insect producing ~s; ~-nut, = ~. So (in ~ic acid) gall'ic¹ a. [ME, f. OF galle f. L galla]

gall'ant (also, in senses indicated below, occas. galănt'), a., n., & v.t. & i. 1. Showy, finely dressed, (arch.); grand, fine, stately, (of ship, horse, etc.); brave, chivalrous, ‖ (also Parl., as conventional epithet of a member of the services, as the honourable & ~ member); markedly attentive to women (galănt'); concerned with love, amatory, (galant'); hence ~LY² (or as above galănt'-) adv. 2. n. Man of fashion, fine gentleman; ladies' man, lover, paramour, (galănt'). 3. vb (galănt'). Play the ~, flirt with, flirt with; escort, act as cavalier to, (lady). [ME, f. OF galant part. of galer make merry]

gall'antry, n. Bravery, dashing courage; courtliness, devotion to women; a polite or amorous act or speech; conduct of a gallant, amorous intercourse or intrigue, sexual immorality. [f. F galanterie (prec., -ERY)]

gall'eon, n. (hist.). Vessel shorter & higher than galley; ship of war (usu. Spanish); large Spanish ship used in American trade. [f. F galion (galie GALLEY), or Sp. galeon; see -OON]

gall'ery, n., & v.t. 1. Covered space for walking in partly open at side, portico, colonnade; balcony long narrow passage in thickness of wall or supported on corbels, open towards interior of building; platform projecting from inner wall of church, hall, etc., providing extra room for audience or reserved for musicians (freq. minstrels' ~), reporters, strangers, etc.; (Theatr.) highest such balcony, persons there seated, least refined part of audience (play to the ~, appeal to lower taste, use claptrap); long narrow room (e.g. shooting-~, for indoor target practice or matches), passage, corridor; room or building used for showing works of art; chimney-holder of lamp; (Mil., Mining) horizontal underground passage; ~ hit (Cricket, & fig.,

from theatre) piece of showy play, so ~ shot, stroke; hence ~FUL(2) n. 2. v.t. Provide, pierce, etc., with ~ or galleries. [f. F galerie f. It. f. med. L galeria]

gall'ey, n. (pl. ~s). 1. (Chiefly hist.) low flat single-decked vessel using sails & oars, & usu. rowed by slaves or criminals; ancient Greek or Roman warship with one or more banks of oars; large open row-boat, e.g. that used by captain of man-of-war. 2. Ship's kitchen. 3. (print.). Oblong tray to which type is transferred from composing stick (~ proof, in slip form, not in sheets or pages). 4. ~-slave, person condemned to row in ~, (fig.) drudge; ~worm, kind of many-footed insect (from likeness of its legs to oars). [ME, f. OF galie, -ee f. med. L galea, med. Gk galaia]

galliăm'bic, a. & n. In the metre of e.g. Catullus's Attis; (n., usu. pl.) such verse(s). [f. L galliAMBUS song of Galli or priests of Cybele +-IC]

gall'iard, n. (hist.). Quick & lively dance in triple time for two persons. [ME, f. OF gaillard]

Gall'ic² (for gallic¹ see GALL⁴), a. Of the Gauls, Gaulish; (usu. joc.) French, whence gall'icISM(4) n., gall'icIZE(2, 3) v.t. & i. [f. L Gallicus (Gallus Gaul, -IC)]

Gall'ican, a. & n. Of the ancient church of Gaul or France; (adherent) of the school of French Roman Catholics following Bossuet & claiming partial autonomy (opp. ULTRAMONTANE), whence gall'ican-ISM(3), gall'icanIST(2), nn. [f. F, or L Gallicanus (prec., -AN)]

gall'icē (-sē), adv. In French (used in giving F for English phrase etc.). [L, =in Gaulish]

galligas'kins (-z), n. pl. (joc.). Breeches, trousers. [orig. wide hose of 16th & 17th cc., f. F garguesque for greguesque f. It. grechesca fem. of grechesco Greek (-ESQUE)]

gallimau'fry, n. Heterogeneous mixture, jumble, medley. [f. F galimafrée]

gallin|ā'ceous (-shus), a. Of the order Gallinae including domestic poultry, pheasants, partridges, etc. So ~A'CEAN (-āshan) a. & n. [f. L gallinaceus (gallina hen, -ACEOUS)]

gallina'zō (-ah-), n. (pl. ~s). An American vulture, the turkey buzzard. [f. Sp. gallinaza (L gallina hen, -aza augment.)]

Gall'iō, n. Person, esp. official, refusing to meddle outside his province. [Acts xviii]

gall'iot (-y-), n. Dutch cargo-boat or fishing-vessel; small (usu. Mediterranean) galley. [ME, f. OF galiote f. It. galeotta f. med. L galea GALLEY]

gall'ipŏt, n. Small earthen glazed pot used for ointments etc. [prob. f. GALLEY, as brought in galleys from the Mediterranean]

gall'ium, n. Soft bluish-white metal. [f. L gallus cock, transl. of Lecoq de Boisbaudran the discoverer 1875, +-IUM] gắllĭvănt', v.ĭ. Gad about (usu. ĭn part. or vbl n.). [perh. corruption of *gallant* v.]

Găllo-, comb. form=*French-*, as ∼-*Briton*, ∼-*German*, ∼-*Roman*. Hence ∼MAN'ĬA n., ∼MAN'ĬAC a. & n., Găll'OPHIL, Găll'O-PHOBE, nn. & aa., ∼PHOB'ĬA n. [*Gallus* GAUL, -O-]

gắll'on, n. A measure of capacity (|| *imperial* ∼, 277¼ cubic inches; *wine* ∼, 231) for liquids or corn etc. [ME, f. ONF *galon*, OF *jalon*, f. Rom. *gallone, cf. med. L *galeta*, OF *jaloie*]

gắllōōn', n. Narrow close-woven braid for binding dresses etc., of gold, silver, silk, or cotton. [f. F *galon* f. *galonner* trim with braid, of unkn. orig.]

gắll'op, n., & v.ĭ. & t. 1. Horse's or other quadruped's fastest pace, with all feet off ground together in each stride (*full* ∼, *at a* ∼, going thus); a ride at this pace. 2. vb. Go at a ∼ (of horse, or with its rider as subj., or of other quadruped); make (horse etc.) ∼; read, recite, or talk, fast (often *through*, *over*); move or progress rapidly (*in a* ∼*ing consumption*). [f. F *galop(er)* f. WG, see WALLOP]

gắllopāde', n. Lively, orig. Hungarian, dance. [F, see GALOP, -ADE(1)]

gắll'oper, n. In vbl senses; esp., || (Mil.) aide-de-camp, light field gun. [-ER¹]

Gallophil etc. See GALLO-.

Găllovĭd'ĭan, a. & n. (Native) of Gallo-way. [f. med. L *Gallovidia* +-AN]

gắll'oway (-o-), n. Horse of small strong breed from Galloway, SW. Scotland; small-sized horse; one of a breed of cattle peculiar to Galloway. [district]

gắll'ows (-ōz), n. pl. (usu. treated as sing.). Structure, usu. of two uprights & cross-piece, on which criminals are hanged; punishment of hanging (*a* ∼ *look*, *have the* ∼ *in* one's *face*, of sinister appearance); similar structure used for cookery, gymnastics, etc.; ∼-*bird*, person fit to be hanged; ∼-*ripe*, fit to be hanged; ∼-*tree*, = ∼. [ME, f. ON *galgi* = OE *gealga*, OS, OHG *galgo*, Goth. *galga* f. Gmc *galgon]

*Găll'up pŏll, n. Test of how representative sample of public is to vote, esp. as basis of forecasts. [G. H. *Gallup* (b. 1901)]

galōōt', n. (colloq.). Clumsy lout. [orig. unkn.]

gắll'op, n., & v.ĭ. 1. Lively dance in 2–4 time. 2. Dance a ∼. [vb f. n., F, see GALLOP]

galōre', adv. & n. (In) abundance (*with beef & ale* ∼; ∼ *of alcohol*; also *in* ∼). [f. Ir. *go leór* to sufficiency]

galŏsh', gol-, n. Overshoe usu. of rubber to keep shoes clean or dry; piece of leather etc. round lower part of boot or shoe uppers, whence ∼ED² (-sht) a. [ME, f. OF *galoche*, f. LL *gallicula* small Gallic shoe]

galŭmph', v.ĭ. Go prancing in triumph. [made by L. Carroll perh. on *gallop*, *triumph*]

găl'văn'|ĭc, a. 1. (hist.). Of, produced by, as of, electricity (∼*ic battery*, *pile*, former names for types of primary battery; ∼*ic electricity*, electricity from a primary battery). 2. (fig.). (Of smile, movement, etc.) sudden & forced. Hence ∼ICALLY adv. [foll., -IC]

găl'văn|ĭsm, n. (hist.). Electricity from a primary battery; the use of this or other direct-current electricity for medical purposes. Hence ∼IST(3) n. [f. F *galvanisme* (L. *Galvani* discoverer 1792, -ISM)]

găl'vanĭz|e, -is|e (-ĭz), v.t. Stimulate by or as by electricity (also fig., ∼*e into life*, rouse by shock or excitement); coat with metal by electrolysis; coat (iron) with zinc (usu. without the use of electricity) to protect it from rust. Hence ∼A'TION, ∼ER¹, nn. [f. F *galvaniser* (prec., -IZE)]

găl'vano-, comb. form of GALVANIC, GALVANISM, as ∼*graphy* (-ŏg⁴), method of producing copperplate engravings by ∼*plasty*, metal-coating by galvanism; ∼*meter* (-ŏm⁴), instrument for measuring electric currents; ∼SCOPE.

Gălwē'gĭan (-jn), a. & n. = GALLOVIDIAN. [f. *Galloway* on anal. of *Norwegian*]

găm'ba, n. (Also ∼ *stop*) organ stop with string tone. [earlier =, & short for, VIOLA¹ *da gamba*]

gămbāde', -ād'ō (pl. -*os*, -*oes*), n. Horse's leap or bound; fantastic movement, freak, escapade. [-*ade* F (Scott); -*ado* f. Sp. *gambada* (*gamba* leg, -ADO)]

găm'bier, n. Astringent extract of oriental plant used in tanning etc. [f. Malay *gambir* the plant]

găm'bĭt, n. Kinds of opening in chess in which player sacrifices pawn or piece to secure certain ends, many ∼s having special names as *King's*, *Queen's*, *Cunningham's*, ∼; (fig.) opening move in some action etc. [17th c. *gambett* f. It. *gambetto* tripping up (*gamba* leg); -*it* = F *gambit*, Sp. -*ito*]

găm'bl|e, v.ĭ. & t., & n. 1. Play games of chance for money, esp. for high stakes (∼*e away*, lose thus); take great risks to secure great results in war, finance, etc.; hence ∼ER¹ n., ∼ESOME (-ls-) a. 2. n. ∼*ing* (esp. *on the* ∼*e*); risky undertaking or attempt. [f. obs. (16th c.) *gamel*, var. of ME *gamen* GAME¹]

gămbōge' (-ōōzh), n. Gum resin from Cambodian & Siamese trees used as yellow pigment. [f. mod. L *gambogium* f. *Cambodia*]

găm'bol, n., & v.ĭ. (-ll-). Caper, frisk. [f. F GAMBADE]

gāme¹, n. 1. Jest (*make* ∼ *of*, ridicule); diversion, spell of play (*a* ∼ *of ball*); amusing incident (*what a* ∼*!*). 2. Contest played according to rules & decided by skill, strength, or luck (ROUND, SQUARE, ∼; *be on*, *off*, one's ∼, be in, out of, form; *have the* ∼ *in* one's *hands*, be sure to win or able to direct it; *play the* ∼ lit. & fig., observe the rules, behave honourably;

play a good, poor, ~, be skilful or not); (Gk & Rom. Ant.; pl.) athletic, dramatic, & musical contests, gladiatorial etc. shows; scheme, undertaking, etc., followed up like a ~ *(was playing a deep, double, winning, losing*, etc., ~; *the ~ is up,* success now impossible; *so that's your little ~*; *spoilt my ~*; *play one's ~*, advance his schemes unintentionally; ~ *not worth* CANDLE). **3.** pl. Dodges, tricks, *(none of your~s!)*. **4.** Single round in some contests, e.g. whist or tennis (~ *& ~*, one ~ scored to each side); (Commerc.) apparatus for a ~; winning score in ~ (~ *and*, short for ~ *& set* in tennis); state of ~ *(the ~ is four all, love three*, etc.). **5.** Hunted animal, quarry, object of pursuit, *(fair ~*, legitimately to be pursued or attacked; *so forbidden ~*); (collect.) wild animals, birds, etc., hunted for sport or food, flesh of these. **6.** Kept flock *of swans*. **7.** *~-act, -law* (usu. pl.), regulating the killing & preservation of ~; *~-bag*, for holding ~ killed by sportsman; ~ *ball*, state of ~ in tennis etc. at which one point may win; *~-chicken, -cock, -egg, -fowl*, of kind bred for c:ck-fighting; *~'keeper*, man employed to breed ~, prevent poaching, etc.; *~-licence*, to kill or deal in ~; *~-preserver*, landowner etc. who breeds ~ & applies *~-laws* strictly; *~s'manship*, art of winning *~s* by distracting one's opponent; *~-tenant*, lessee of shooting or fishing. [OE *gamen*, OS, OHG, ON *gaman*]

găme², a. Like a game-cock, spirited, (DIE² ~); having the spirit *to* do, *for* Hence *~'*LY² (-ml-) adv., *~'*NESS (-mn-) n. [f. GAME¹-*cock*]

găme³, v.i. & t. Play at games of chance for money, gamble; throw *away* in gambling; *gaming-house, -table*, frequented for gambling. Hence *~'*STER (-ms-) n. [(1) ME *gamen* f. OE *gam(e)nian*; (2) ME *game* f. GAME¹]

găme⁴, a. (Of leg, arm, etc.) lame, crippled. [18th c. dial., of unkn. orig.]

găme'some (-ms-), a. Sportive. Hence *~'*LY² adv., *~'*NESS n. [-SOME]

gămēte', n. (biol.). Sexual protoplasmic body, which unites with another for reproduction. [f. Gk *gametē* wife, *gametēs* husband, (*gameō* marry)]

gamin (see Ap.), n. (Street) urchin, neglected boy. [F]

gămm'a, n. Third letter (Γ, γ, = G) of Greek alphabet, used sometimes in enumerations to supplement 3 & c (~ *plus, minus*, rather better, worse, than third-class); kind of moth; *~ rays*, X-rays of very short wave-length emitted by radio-active substances. [Gk]

gămmăd'ion, n. = FYLFOT. [late Gk, dim. of prec., fylfot consisting of four gammas (Γ)]

gămm'er, n. (Rustic name for) old woman. [contr. of *godmother*, *ga*- by assoc. w. *grandmother*; cf. GAFFER, GOSSIP]

gămm'on¹, n., & v.t. **1.** Bottom piece of flitch of bacon including hind leg (usu. ~ *of bacon*); smoked or cured ham; ~ *& spinach* (as dish, &, with pun on *gammon³*, = humbug). **2.** v.t. Cure (bacon). [f. ONF *gambon* (*gambe* leg, -OON)]

gămm'on², n., & v.t. **1.** Kind of victory scoring two games at backgammon. **2.** v.t. Defeat (adversary) thus. [app. = ME *gamen* GAME¹]

gămm'on³, n., int., & v.i. & t. **1.** Humbug, deception; (int.) nonsense! **2.** vb. Talk plausibly; feign (intr.); hoax, deceive. [perh. as prec.]

gămm'on⁴, v.t., & n., (naut.). Lash (bowsprit) to stem; (n., also *~ing*) the lashing. [orig. unkn.]

gămm'y̆, a. (sl.). = GAME⁴. [orig. unkn.]

gămo-, comb. form of Gk *gamos* marriage, used esp. in Bot. describing plants with specified parts united, as *gamopet'alous* with petals united; also *gamogen'esis* sexual reproduction.

gămp, n. (colloq.). Umbrella, esp. large untidy one. [f. Mrs *G~* in Dickens' *Martin Chuzzlewit*]

găm'ut, n. **1.** (hist.). Lowest note in medieval scale = modern G on lowest line of bass stave; the Great Scale consisting of all notes used in medieval music (G as above to E in highest space of treble). **2.** (mod.). Whole series of recognized notes; major diatonic scale; people's or period's recognized scale; voice's or instrument's compass; whole range or scope of anything (*the whole ~ of crime*; *run up & down the ~*). [f. med. L *gamma ut* (GAMMA taken as name for note one tone lower than A of classical scale + *ut* first of six arbitrary names of notes forming hexachord, being the italicized syllables of a Sapphic stanza, *Ut* queant laxis *resonare* fibris *Mira* gestorum *famuli tuorum, Solve* polluti *labii* reatum, *Sancte Johannes*)]

găm'y̆, a. Abounding in game; = GAME² (rare); having flavour or scent of game kept till it is high. [-Y²]

găn'der, n. Male goose (*sauce for the goose is sauce for the ~*, use in retorting an argument etc. on its first user); fool, simpleton. [OE *gan(d)ra*, MLG *ganre*, LG, Du. *gander*; cogn. w. GANNET]

găng, n., & v.i. & t. **1.** Company of workmen, or of slaves or prisoners; band of persons acting or going about together esp. for criminal purpose or one disapproved by speaker (*v.i.*, join *up*, act in concert, *with*); set of tools etc. arranged to work simultaneously (v.t.), arrange (tools etc.) to work in co-ordination); *~-board*, plank usu. with cleats nailed on it for walking into or out of boat. **2.** v.i. (Sc.). Go; ~ *agley* (aglǎ'), (of plan etc.) go awry; ~ one's *ain gait*, take one's own course. [OE, OS, OHG *gang*, ON *gangr*, Goth. *gaggs*, Gmc f. *gangan* GO]

gänge (-j), v.t. Protect (fish-hook, part of fishing-line) with fine wire. Hence **gän′gḯng**¹ (-j-) n. [orig. unkn.]

gäng′er, n. Foreman of gang. [-ER¹]

Gängĕt′ic, a. Of the Ganges. [f. L *Gangeticus* (L f. Gk *Gangēs*, -IC)]

gäng′ling (-ngg-), a. Loosely built, straggling. [f. *gangle* frequent. of GANG]

gäng′li|on (-ngg-), n. (pl. -*lia*). Enlargement or knot on nerve, from which nerve--fibres radiate; mass of grey matter in central nervous system forming a nerve--nucleus (~*on-cell*, -*corpuscule*, -*globule*, nerve-cell in this); (fig.) centre of force, activity, or interest. Hence ~**ātĕd**, ~**onātĕd**, [-ATE³, -ED¹], ~**FORM**, ~**ŏn′IC**, aa. [f. Gk *gagglion*]

gäng′rēne (-ngg-), n., & v.i. & t. **1.** Necrosis, usu. with decomposition, of part of the body (often fig.); hence **gäng′rĕnous** a. **2.** vb. Become affected, affect, with mortification. [f. L f. Gk *gaggraina*]

gäng′ster, n. Member of a gang of violent criminals or roughs. [-STER]

gangue (gäng), n. Earth etc., matrix, in which ore is found. [F, f. G *gang* lode = GANG]

gäng′way, n. & int. Passage esp. between rows of seats (∥ in House of Commons, cross-passage half-way down giving access to back benches; members *above*, *below*, ~ are more, less, closely associated with official policy of their party); passage etc. on ship, esp. platform connecting quarterdeck & forecastle; opening in bulwarks by which ship is entered or left, bridge laid across from this to shore etc.; (int.) make way, please! [18th c., f. GANG + WAY]

gän′ister, n. Close-grained siliceous stone found, mixed with clay, in the lower coal--measures of Yorkshire, and used for furnace-linings. [orig. unkn.]

gänn′ĕt, n. A sea-bird, the solan (-goose). [OE *ganot*, OHG *ganazzo*, MHG *ganze*; cogn. w. GANDER]

gän′oid, a. & n. (Of fish-scale) enamelled, smooth & bright; (fish) having ~ scales. [f. F *ganoïde* f. Gk *ganos* brightness + -OID]

gän′try, gaun′, n. Four-footed wooden stand for barrels; structure supporting travelling crane, railway signals, etc. [prob. f. obs. contr. of GALLON + *tree*]

Gän′ymēde, n. (Joc.) waiter, potboy; (Astron.) largest satellite of Jupiter. [f. L f. Gk *Ganumēdēs* cupbearer of Zeus]

gaol (jāl), **jail,** n., & v.t. (*g-* in official, *g-* & *j-* indifferently in literary use, *j-* in U.S.). **1.** Public prison for detention of persons committed by process of law, (without article) confinement in this; ~-*bird*, prisoner, habitual criminal, rogue; ~-*delivery*, clearing of ~ esp. at assizes by trying all prisoners awaiting trial; ~-*fever*, virulent typhus formerly endemic in ~s. **2.** v.t. Put in ~. [ME, f. ONF

gaiole, OF *jaiole* (now *geôle*) f. Rom. dim. of L *cavea* CAGE]

gaol′er (jāl-), **jail′er, jail′or,** n. (see prec.). Man in charge of gaol or prisoners in it. Hence ~ESS¹ n. [as prec. + -ER²(2)]

gặp, n. Breach in hedge or wall; gorge, pass; unfilled space or interval, blank, break in continuity, (*stop, fill, supply, a ~*, make up deficiency; wide divergence in views, sympathies, etc. Hence ~**PED**² (-pt), ~**p′Y**², aa. [ME, f. ON, = chasm, cogn. w. foll.]

gặpe, v.i., & n. **1.** Open mouth wide, (of mouth, oysters, wounds, chasm, etc.) open or be open wide, split, part asunder; stare, gaze curiously, *at*; yawn. **2.** n. Yawn; open-mouthed stare; the ~*s*, poultry disease with gaping as symptom, (joc.) fit of yawning; expanse of open mouth or beak, part of beak that opens; rent, opening; ~-*seed* (joc.), staring, occasion for staring, thing stared at. [ME, f. ON *gapa* cogn. w. MHG *gaffen*]

gặp′er, n. In vbl senses; esp. kinds of bird, kind of mollusc. [-ER¹]

gặ′rage (*or* garahzh′), n., & v.t. **1.** Building or shed for storing or repair of motor--vehicles. **2.** v.t. Put (motor-car) in ~. [F]

gặrb, n., & v.t. **1.** Dress, costume, esp. of distinctive kind, way one is dressed. **2.** v.t. Attire, put (esp. distinctive) clothes upon (person; usu. pass. or refl.). [f. obs. F *garbe* f. It. *garbo* f. Gmc, cogn. w. GEAR]

gặrb′age, n. Offal used for food; refuse, filth; foul or worthless reading. [ME, orig. unkn.]

gặr′ble, v.t. Select best in, take pick of, (rare); make (usu. unfair or malicious) selections from (facts, statements, etc.), mutilate in order to misrepresent; (erron.) unintentionally distort or confuse (facts, statements). [f. It. *garbellare* f. Arab. *gharbala* sift cf. *kirbal* sieve]

gặrb′oard (-berd), n. (Also ~ *strake*) first range of planks laid on ship's bottom next keel; corresponding plates in iron ship. [f. Du. *gaarboord* (GATHER, BOARD)]

gắrçon (see Ap.), n. Waiter in French hotel etc. [F]

gặrd′en, n., & v.i. **1.** Piece of ground devoted to growing flowers, fruit, or vegetables (KITCHEN, ∥ MARKET, ~); (pl.) ornamental grounds for public resort (usu. *botanical, zoological*, etc., ~s); specially fertile region (*the ~ of England*, Kent, Worcestershire, etc.); ∥ (pl. with name prefixed as *Onslow, Spring, G~s*) set of houses in street, square, etc.; *the G~*, philosophy or school of Epicurus (cf. PORCH, ACADEMY); (attrib.; with or without hyphen) cultivated, not wild, (~ *plants*, ~-*cress*; *common or ~*, sl., ordinary), living in ~s (~-*spider*; ~-*white*, kind of butterfly; ~-*warbler*, kind of bird); ~ *city*, industrial or other town laid out systematically with a view to spacious and attractive surroundings; ∥ so ~ *suburb*;

~~-*frame*, forcing-frame for plants; ~~-*glass*, bell-glass for covering plant; ~~-*party*, social meeting on lawn or in ~; ~~-*plot*, piece of ground used as ~; ~ *seat*, bench etc. for use in ~; ‖ ~~-*stuff*, vegetables & fruit; (sl.) *lead up the* ~ (*path*), entice, mislead; hence ~ED² (-nd), ~~ESQUE', aa., ~ING¹(1) n. 2. v.i. Cultivate a ~. [ME, f. ONF *gardin* (OF *jardin*) f. Rom. *gardinus f. WG *gardo + -*inus* -INE¹; see YARD]

gárd'ener, n. Person who gardens, esp. servant employed to tend a garden, also, esp. *jobbing* ~, employee working at intervals. [ME, f. ONF *gardinier (OF *jard*-) as prec. + -ER²(2)]

gárdēn'ia, n. Kinds of trees & shrubs with large white or yellow flowers & usu. fragrant scent. [mod. L (Dr. A. *Garden* d. 1791, -IA¹)]

gāre'fowl (-rf-), n. The great auk. [f. ON *geirfugl* (*geir* of doubtful meaning)]

gār'fish, n. Fish with long spearlike snout & green bones. [app. f. OE *gār* spear]

gār'ganey, n. Kind of teal. [f. It. dial. var. of *garganello*]

gārgăn'tūan, a. Enormous, gigantic. [*Gargantua* giant in Rabelais + -AN]

gárg'ét (-g-), n. Inflamed state of head or throat in cattle, pigs, or poultry; inflammation of cow's or ewe's udder. [perh. f. obs. *garget* throat f. OF *gargate*, -*guette*]

gár'gle, v.t. & i., & n. 1. Wash (throat), wash throat, with liquid kept in motion by breath. 2. n. Liquid used thus. [f. F *gargouiller* (foll.)]

gárg'oyle, gúr-, n. Grotesque spout usu. with human or animal mouth, head, or body, projecting from gutter of (esp. Gothic) building to carry water clear of wall. [f. OF *gargouille* throat, gargoyle]

gáribăl'di, n. Kind of woman's or child's blouse, orig. of bright red; ‖ biscuit containing currants. [f. red shirts of *G*~ (Italian patriot 1807–82) & his followers]

gár'ish, a. Obtrusively bright, showy, gaudy, over-decorated. Hence~LY²adv., ~NESS n. [16th c. *gaurish* app. irreg. f. obs. *gaure* stare + -ISH¹]

gárl'and, n., & v.t. 1. Wreath of flowers, leaves, etc., worn on head or hung on something as decoration; distinction, palm, prize, for victory etc.; (arch.) anthology, miscellany; metal etc. imitation of ~. 2. v.t. Crown with ~, deck with ~s, serve as ~ to. [ME, f. OF *ger*-, *garlande* of unkn. orig.]

gárl'ic, n. Plant with bulbous strong-smelling pungent-tasting root used as flavouring in cookery. Hence (esp. of smell) ~KY² a. [OE *gárlēac* (*gár* spear, LEEK)]

gárm'eht, n., & v.t. Article of dress, esp. gown or cloak, (pl.) clothes; outward and visible covering of anything; (vb; poet., usu. in p.p.) attire. [ME & OF *garni*-, *garnement* (GARNISH, -MENT)]

gárn'er, n., & v.t. (poet. & rhet.). 1. Storehouse for corn, granary, (also fig.). 2. v.t. Store, deposit, collect. [ME, f. OF *gernier* f. L *granarium* GRANARY]

gárn'ét, n. Vitreous mineral, of which a deep transparent red kind is used as gem. [ME, f. OF *grenat*, -*ate* f. med. L *granatum* POMEGRANATE]

gárn'ish, v.t., & n. 1. Decorate, embellish, (esp. dish for table); (Law) serve notice on (person, called ~EE' n.) for purpose of attaching money belonging to debtor, summon (person) as party to litigation started between others; hence ~ER¹, ~MENT, nn. 2. n. (Also ~ING¹ n.) things used to decorate dish for table (also fig. of literary embellishments). [ME, f. OF *garnir* (-ISH²) f. WG *warnjan WARN]

gárn'iture, n. Appurtenances, accessories; adornment, trimming esp. of dish; costume. [F (GARNISH, -URE)]

garotte. See GARROTTE.

gá'rrét¹, n. Room (usu. squalid) on top floor or partly or entirely in roof, attic. [ME, f. OF *garite* watch-tower (*garir* defend, f. WG *warjan; see WEIR)]

gá'rrét², v.t. (archit.). Insert small pieces of stone in joints of (coarse masonry). [orig. unkn.]

gárrēteer', n. Dweller in garret, esp. poor literary hack. [-EER]

gá'rrison, n., & v.t. 1. Troops stationed in fortress, town, etc., to defend it (~ *town*, having ~). 2. v.t. Furnish with, occupy as, ~; place (troops, soldier) on ~ duty. [ME, f. OF *garison* (*garir* see GARRET¹), defence, w. sense of F & obs. E *garnison* (GARNISH)]

gá'rron, n. Small inferior horse bred in Scotland & Ireland. [f. Gael. *gearran*]

gá'rrot, n. Kind of sea duck. [F]

gar(r)ŏtt|e', n., & v.t. 1. Spanish method of capital punishment by strangulation, apparatus used in it; highway robbery performed by throttling victim. 2. v.t. Execute by strangulation; throttle in order to rob, whence ~ER¹ n. [f. F *garrotter* or Sp. *garrotear* f. *garrote* a stick (used in twisting cord tight), of unkn. orig.]

gá'rrulous (-rōō-), a. Given to talk, loquacious, wordy, (of bird, stream, etc.) chattering, babbling. Hence or cogn. **garrul'ITY** (-rōō-), ~NESS, nn., ~LY² adv. [f. L *garrulus* (*garrire* chatter) + -OUS]

gárt'er, n., & v.t. 1. Band worn above or below knee to keep stocking up; ‖ *the G*~, (badge of) highest order of English knighthood, membership of this; (*G*~)= *G*~ King of Arms. 2. v.t. Fasten (stocking), encircle (leg), with ~. [ME, f. OF *gartier* (*garet*, now *jarret*, bend of knee, perh. f. Celt., cf. Breton *gar*, W *gâr*, leg-bone)]

‖ gárth, n. (arch. & dial). Close, yard, garden, paddock, open space within cloisters. [ME f. ON *garthr* = OE *geard* YARD²]

găs, n. (pl. *găses*), & v.t. & i. (-ss-). **1.** Any aeriform or completely elastic fluid (used chiefly of those that do not become liquid or solid at ordinary temperatures, other ~es being usu. called *vapours*); such fluid, esp. COAL-~ or various mixtures with carburetted hydrogen, used for lighting or heating; *(colloq.)* petrol, gasoline, *(step on the* ~, accelerate motor engine by pressing down accelerator pedal with foot, also fig.); (Mining) explosive mixture of firedamp with air; hydrogen etc. used to fill balloon; nitrous oxide ~ as anaesthetic (often *laughing-*~); (also *poison*-~) kinds used to asphyxiate enemy in war; jet of ~ used for lighting; empty talk, boasting, humbug, windbag eloquence. **2.** ~-*bag*, bag for holding ~, (derog.) empty talker, airship's ~-container, airship or balloon (opp. aeroplane); ~ *bracket*, pipe with burner(s) projecting from wall; ~-*coal*, bituminous from which ~ can be made; ~-*coke*, residuum of coal when ~ has been made from it; ~-*engine*, -*motor*, with power obtained by production of ~ or rhythmical combustion and explosion of ~ in closed cylinder; ~-*fitter*, tradesman or workman providing house with ~-*fittings*, apparatus for heating or lighting with ~; ~-*helmet*, ~-*mask*, kinds of appliance including respirator worn as defence against poison-~; ~'*holder*, large receptacle for storing ~, gasometer; ~-*light*, light given by esp. coal-~, jet of burning ~ (~-*light paper, plates*, photographic materials that can be developed in weak artificial light); ~-*main*, main pipe supplying ~; ~-*man*, manufacturer of ~, collector of sums due for ~-supply; ~-*mask* (as ~-*helmet*); ~-*meter*, apparatus registering amount of ~ consumed; ~-*oven* (heated by ~); ~-*ring*, perforated with small holes & fed with ~ for cooking etc.; ~-*shell* (charged with poison-~, usu. in liquid form); ~-*tar*, COAL-tar produced in making ~; ~-*works*, manufactory of ~; hence găs-ÈOUS a., găsÈ'ITY n., ~'i-FORM, ~'LESS, aa., ~'IFY v.t., ~'IFiABLE a., ~IFICA'TION n. (also, underground production of ~ from unmined coal). **3.** vb. Supply (room, railway-carriage, etc.) with ~; project poison-~ upon (enemy, place), (pass.) be poisoned with ~; pass (thread, lace) through ~-flame to remove loose fibres; talk emptily or boastfully, whence ~s'ER[1] n. [wd invented by Van Helmont on Gk *khaos* CHAOS]

Găs'con, n. Native of Gascony; braggart. [F]

găsconāde', n., & v.i. Boast(ing). [f. F *gasconnade* (prec., -ADE)]

găsèlier', n. Gas-lamp, usu. suspended from ceiling, with several burners often on branches. [f. GAS after CHANDELIER]

găsh[1], n., & v.t. **1.** Long & deep slash, cut, or wound; cleft such as might be made by slashing cut; act of making such cut. **2.** v.t. Make ~ in, cut. [16th c., var. of

ME *garse* vb & n. f. OF **garse, garser* perh. f. LL c(h)*araxare* f. Gk *kharassō* incise]

‖ **găsh**[2], a. (naut. sl.). Spare, extra.

găs'kėt, n. Small cord for securing furled sail to yard; strip of tow etc. for packing piston or caulking joint. [orig. unkn.]

gasogene. See GAZOGENE.

găs'olēne, -ine (-ēn), n. Volatile inflammable liquid got in distilling petroleum & used for heating & lighting; *petrol. [GAS, -OL, -ENE, -INE[1]]

gasŏm'ėter, n. (Chem.) vessel for holding gas; large reservoir in which gas is stored for distribution by pipes. [f. F *gazomètre* (*gaz* GAS, *mètre* f. Gk *metron* measure)]

gasp (gahsp), v.i. & t., & n. **1.** Catch breath, strain *for* air or breath, with open mouth as in exhaustion or astonishment; ~ *life* etc. *away* or *out*, expire; ~ *out*, utter with ~s; hence ~'ingLY[2] adv., ~'ER[1] n., (esp., sl.) ‖ cheap cigarette. **2.** n. Convulsive catching of breath (*at* one's *last* ~, at point of death). [ME, f. ON *geispa* to yawn cf. *geip* idle talk]

găss'|y̆, a. Of, full of, like, gas; (of talk etc.) empty, verbose. Hence ~INESS n. [-Y[2]]

găs't(e)ropŏd, n. Mollusc (e.g. snail) with locomotive organ placed ventrally. So **găsterŏp'odous** a. [f. F *gastéropode* (GASTRO-, Gk *pous podos* foot)]

găstrae'a, n. (Assumed) primitive sac-like animal consisting of two layers (ectoderm & endoderm) of cells. [mod. L (GASTRO-)]

găs'tric, a. Of the stomach (~ *fever*, enteric; ~ *juice*, thin clear acid nearly colourless fluid secreted by stomach glands & effecting digestion). [f. Gk as foll. + -IC]

găstr(o)-, comb. form of Gk *gastēr* -(*e)ros* stomach, as *gastro-ente'ric*, of stomach & intestines, *găs'tro*CELE, *gastrŏT'OMY*, *gastr*IT'IS.

găstr|ŏl'ogy̆, n. Science of cookery. So ~OL'OGER, ~OL'OGIST, nn. [f. Gk *gastro-logia* (prec., -LOGY)]

găs'tronōme, n. Judge of cookery. [F, back formati on f. *gastronomie* see foll.]

găstrŏn'om|y̆, n. Art & science of good eating. So ~ER[1] n., **găstronŏm'ic**(AL) aa., **găstronŏm'icalLY[2]** adv., ~IST(3) n. [f. F *gastronomie* (GASTRO-, after *astronomie* etc.)]

*găt, n. (sl.). Gun, revolver. [abbr. of GATLING]

gāte[1], n., & v.t. **1.** Opening in wall of city or enclosure made for entrance & exit & capable of being closed with barrier; (Bibl.) place of judicial assembly in city; mountain pass; means of entrance or exit (~ *of ivory, horn*, by which false, true, dreams come; *Bosphorus & Hellespont are the two* ~s *of Constantinople*); barrier closing the opening of a wall, wooden or iron framework, solid or of bars or gratings, hung on hinges, turning on pivots, or sliding, single or double; contrivance regulating passage of water; number entering by payment at ~s to see football match etc., amount of money thus taken (also ~-*money*). **2.** ‖~-*bill* (Oxf. & Camb.), record of undergraduate's returns to college after hours, fines imposed for these; ~-*crasher* sl. (also *crasher*), uninvited intruder at party etc., so ~-*crash* v.i. & t.; ~'*house*, lodge of park etc., room over city ~ often used as prison; ~-*keeper*, attendant at~, ‖kind of butterfly; ~-*legged table* (with legs in ~--like frame swinging back to allow top to fold down); ~-*meeting*, at which money is taken for admission; ~-*post*, on which ~ is hung or against which it abuts (*between you & me & the* ~-*post*, or *bed--post*, in close confidence); ~'*way*, = ~ (first sense), frame of or structure built over ~, means of entrance or exit; hence ~'LESS (-tl-) a. **3.** v.t. (Oxf. & Camb.). ‖Confine to college entirely or after certain hours. [OE *gæt, geat*, OS, ON *gat* f. Gmc **gatom*]

gāte², n. (With prefixed name in North etc.) street. [ME, f. ON *gata*, OHG *gazza*, Goth. *gatwō* f. Gmc **gatwōn-*]

gãth'er (-dh-), v.t. & i. Bring together, cause to assemble, (*be ~ed to* one's *fathers*, die); acquire by collecting, amass; cull, pluck; collect (grain etc.) as harvest; receive addition of (*rolling stone ~s no moss*, change of calling does not pay; *complexion ~s colour; invalid ~s strength*; ~ *head*, acquire strength, swell as a festering sore; ~ *way*, begin to move, of ship); summon up (energies), gain or recover (breath); infer, deduce (*that*); draw (garment, brow) together in folds or wrinkles, esp. pucker (part of dress) by running thread through; pick *up* from ground; draw *up* (limbs, person) into smaller compass; sum *up* (scattered facts); summon *up* (thoughts, strength, etc.) for an effort; come together, congregate, form a mass; receive additions (*the tale ~ed, like a snowball*); come to a head, develop purulent swelling. [OE *gaderian*, cf. Du. *gaderen* gather & OE *geador* together]

gãth'ering (-dh-), n. In vbl senses; esp.: purulent swelling; assembly, meeting; ~-*coal*, large piece to keep fire in. [-ING²]

gãth'ers (-dherz), n. pl. Part of dress that is gathered or drawn in. [f. GATHER]

Găt'ling, n. (Also ~ *gun*) machine gun with clustered barrels. [R.J. ~, inventor (d. 1903)]

gauche (gōsh), a. Tactless, without ease or grace, socially awkward. [F]

gaucherie (gōsherē'), n. Gauche manners, a gauche action. [F]

gauch'ō (gow-, gaw-), n. (pl. -*os*). One of a mixed European & Amer.-Ind. people of mounted herdsmen. [Sp., prob. f. native S.-Amer. lang.]

gaud, n. Something gaudy, showy orna-

ment, gewgaw; (pl.) showy ceremonies, gaieties. [ME, f. OF *gaudir* make merry f. L *gaudēre* rejoice]

‖**gaud'y̆¹**, n. Grand entertainment, esp. annual college dinner to old members etc.; ~-*day*, day of rejoicing, day on which college ~ is held. [f. L *gaudium*, partly f. OF *gaudie* joy, wantonness]

gaud'⟨y̆²⟩, a. Tastelessly or inappropriately fine, showy, or brilliant (of dress, decoration, literary style, etc.). Hence ~ILY² adv., ~INESS n. [most prob. f. GAUD+-Y²]

gauffer. See GOFFER.

*gaufre. See GOFER.

gauge¹ (gāj), **gāge²** (in naut. sense), n. **1.** Standard measure to which things must conform, esp. measure of capacity or contents of barrel, diameter of bullet, or thickness of sheet iron; capacity, extent, scope, (*take the ~ of*. estimate); distance between pair of rails (*broad, narrow, ~*, of more, less, than 4 ft. 8½ in., *standard ~*). **2.** (naut.; *gage*). Relative position in respect to wind (*have the weather ~ of*, be to windward of, fig. have advantage of; also rarely *lee, southerly*, etc., ~). **3.** Graduated instrument measuring force or quantity of rainfall, stream, tide, wind, etc.; contrivance attached to vessel to show height of its contents; instrument for testing and verifying dimensions of tools, wire, etc.; adjustable carpenter's tool for marking parallel lines; (Print.) strip regulating depth of margin etc.; means of estimating, criterion, test. [f. ONF *gauge* (OF *jauge*) of unkn. orig.]

gauge² (gāj), v.t. Measure exactly (esp. objects of standard size, as wire, bolts; fluctuating quantities or forces, as rainfall, wind; depth of liquid content); find capacity or content of (cask etc.) by measurement & calculation (*gauging-rod*, exciseman's instrument for this); estimate, take measure of, (person, character); make uniform, bring to standard size or shape. Hence ~'ABLE a., **gau'gER¹** (1, 2) n., (gāj-). [f. ONF *gauger* (prec.)]

Gaul, n. Inhabitant of ancient Gaul; (joc.) Frenchman. [f. *Gaul* the country f. F *Gaule* f. Frank. **walha* foreigners; cf. WELSH]

Gaul'ish, a. & n. (Language) of ancient Gauls; (joc.) French (adj.). [prec.+-ISH¹]

Gauleiter (gow'līter), n. Nazi district political leader. [G]

gault, n. (geol.). Series of clay and marl beds between upper & lower greensand. [orig. unkn.]

gaunt, a. Lean, haggard; grim or desolate looking. Hence ~'NESS n. [15th c., of unkn. orig.]

gaunt'lĕt¹, n. (Hist.) armoured glove (*fling, throw, down the* ~, issue challenge; *pick, take, up the* ~, accept challenge); stout glove with long wrist for driving, fencing, wicket-keeping, etc. Hence ~ED² a. [late ME, f. OF *gantelet* (*gant* glove f. WG **want-*, med. L *wantus*).

gaunt'let,[2] *gänt-,** n. *Run the ~,* pass between rows of men who strike one with sticks, cords, etc., as military, naval, or school punishment (also fig. of being subjected to criticism). [earlier *gantlope* f. Sw. *gatlopp* (GATE[2], *lopp* course, cf. G *gassenlaufen*) w. assim. to prec.]

gauntry, -tree, See GANTRY.

gaur (gowr), n. The Indian wild ox. [Hind.]

gauss (gows), n. Unit of magnetic induction. Hence ~'AGE n. [after Karl *G~*, German mathematician (d. 1855)]

gauz|e, n. Thin transparent fabric of silk, cotton, wire, etc.; slight haze. Hence ~'Y[2] a., ~'INESS n. [f. F *gaze* f. *Gaza* in Palestine]

gave. See GIVE[1].

*gav'el,** n. Auctioneer's or chairman's or judge's hammer. [orig. unkn.]

∥ **gav'elkind,** n. (legal). Land-tenure, especially in Kent, involving equal division of intestate's property among all his sons. [f. obs. *gavel*, OE *gafol*, tribute, cogn. w. GIVE[1], +KIND[1]]

gavötte', n. Slow dance of 18th c.; music for it; piece of music in common time, each phrase beginning on third beat of bar. [F, f. Pr. *gavoto* (*Gavot* native of Alps)]

gawk, n. Awkward or bashful person. [rel. to obs. (12th c.) *gaw* gaze (f. ON *gá* heed), & 18th c. *gawk* vb stare]

gawk'|y̆, a. & n. Awkward, ungainly, bashful, (person). Hence ~INESS n. [f. prec., or *gawk* vb]

gay, a. (~*er*, ~*est*). Full of or disposed to or indicating mirth, light-hearted, sportive; airy, offhand; *(sl.) cheeky, impertinent; (euphem.) dissolute, immoral, living by prostitution; showy, brilliant, bright-coloured, finely dressed, (*with*). Hence **gai'LY**[2] adv. [ME, f. OF *gai*, of unkn. orig.]

gaze, v.i., & n. 1. Look fixedly (*at, on, upon*); hence **gāz'ER**[1] n. 2. n. Intent look (*stand at ~*, looking thus). [ME, orig. unkn., but cf. obs *gaw* (GAWK)]

gaze'bō, n. (pl. ~*s*, ~*es*, pr. -ōz). Structure whence a view may be had, belvedere, lantern, turret, balcony, etc. [perh. joc. formation f. prec. on L future (cf. LAVABO) or f. some Oriental word]

gazelle', n. Small graceful soft-eyed kinds of antelope. [F, f. Arab. *ghazal*]

gazette', n., & v.t. 1. (Hist.) news-sheet, periodical publication giving current events; ∥ one of three official journals (*London, Edinburgh, Belfast, G~*) issued by authority twice a week with lists of government appointments & bankrupts & other public matters; (in newspaper titles as *Birmingham, Shields, G~*) newspaper. 2. v.t. ∥ Publish in official ~ (esp. in pass. of officials as announced). [F, f. It. *gazzetta* f. *gazeta*, a Venetian small coin]

gazetteer', n. Geographical dictionary.

[so called as first provided for gazette-writers, earlier sense of ~]

gäz'ogëne, gäs-, n. Apparatus for making aerated waters. [f. F *gazogène* (GAS -GEN)]

gean (gēn), n. (Fruit of) wild cherry. [f. F *guigne*, of unkn. orig.]

gear (gēr), n., & v.t. & i. 1. Equipment, apparel, etc. (arch.); harness of draught animals; apparatus, appliances, tackle, tools; combination of wheels, levers, etc.; wheels working on one another by teeth etc.; arrangements connecting motor with its work (*in, out of, ~*, connected or working, with connexion interrupted or not working; *high, low, ~*, by which driven part of bicycle, motor-car, etc., revolves faster, slower, relatively to driving part; similarly *top, bottom, ~* of the available extremes), whence ~'ING[1](6) (gēr-) n.; rigging; goods, household utensils; ~-*box*, -*case*, enclosing ~ing of bicycle etc.; ~-*wheel*, cog-wheel, esp. that in bicycle which transmits motion of pedals to axle; hence ~'LESS (gēr-) a. 2. vb. Harness (draught animal; often *up*); put (machinery) in ~, provide with ~ (~ *up, down,* provide with high, low, ~); make (an industry or factory) subservient or ancillary *to* another, or *to* a programme; (of cog-wheel) fit exactly *into*, be in ~ *with*. [ME, f. ON *gervi*, OS *gerwi*, OHG *garawi* f. Gmc *garwjan* prepare]

gĕck'ō (g-), n. (pl. ~*s*, ~*es*). House lizard found in warm climates. [f. Malay *gekoq*, imit. of its cry]

∥ **gee**[1], **gee²gee,** n. (colloq.). Horse. [orig. child's wd, f. foll.]

gee², **gee-hō', gee²(h)ŭp', gee²wō',** intt. (Words of command to horse etc.) go on, go faster, (occas.) turn to right.

*gee³,** int. of asseveration, discovery, etc. [abbr. of *Jesus*]

geese. See GOOSE.

geez'er (g-), n. (sl.). Old person, old creature. [dial. pronunc. of *guiser* mummer (as GUISE +-ER[1])]

Gĕhĕnn'a (g-), n. Hell; place of burning, torment, or misery. [eccl. L, f. Hellenistic Gk *geenna* f. Heb. *gehinnom* hell, orig. valley of Hinnom where children were sacrificed]

Geig'er coun'ter (gīg-), n. Cylindrical device for detecting and recording radio-activity. [f. *Geiger*, German physicist (1882-)]

gei'sha (gā-), n. Japanese dancing-girl. [Jap.]

Geiss'ler (gī-) **tūbe,** n. Sealed tube filled with rarefied gas that becomes incandescent when an electric current is passed through it. [H. *Geissler*, German physicist (d. 1879)]

geist (gī-), n. Intellectuality & sensibility, capacity for or tendency to mental fervour. [G, as GHOST]

gĕl, n., & v.i. (-ll-). (Form) a semi-solid

colloidal solution. [first syllable of *gelatin*]

gĕl'atin(e) (*also* -ēn), n. Amorphous brittle transparent tasteless slightly yellow substance, basis of the jellies resulting from stewing skin, tendons, ligaments, bone-matrix, etc. (*vegetable* ∼, constituent of gluten identical with animal ∼; *blasting* ∼, an explosive nitro--glycerine compound; ∼ *paper*, coated with sensitized ∼ for photography). Hence gĕlatin'iFORM a., gĕlăt'ino- comb. form. [f. F *gélatine* f. It. *gelatina* (*gelata* JELLY, -IN)]

gĕlăt'in|ous, a. Jelly-like in consistence etc.; of gelatin. So ∼IZE(3) v.t. & i., ∼OID a. & n. [f. F *gélatineux* (prec., -OUS)]

gĕlā'tion, n. Solidification by freezing. [f. L *gelatio* (*gelare* freeze, -ATION)]

gĕld (g-), v.t. Deprive (usu. male animal) of generative power, castrate, excise testicles or ovaries of. Hence (-)∼'ER[1] n. [ME, f. ON *gelda*]

gĕl'ding (g-), n. Gelded horse or other animal. [ME, f. ON *geldingr* (prec., -ING[3])]

gĕl'id, a. Icy, ice-cold; chilly, cool. [f. L *gelidus* (*gelu* frost) cogn. w. COLD]

gĕl'ignite, n. A nitro-glycerine explosive. [f. GELATINE, L *ignis* fire, -ITE[1](2)]

gĕm, n., & v.t. (-mm-). 1. Precious stone, esp. when cut and polished; object of great beauty or worth, choicest part *of*, prized thing; precious or semi-precious stone with engraved design; hence ∼m'Y[2] a. 2. v.t. Adorn (as) with ∼s. [ME, f. L *gemma* bud, jewel]

Gĕmăr'a (g-), n. Later part of Talmud, commentary on MISHNA. [Aram., = completion]

gĕm'inate[1], a. (nat. hist.). Combined in pairs. [f. L *geminare* (*geminus* twin), -ATE[2]]

gĕm'in|āte[2], v.t. Double, repeat, arrange in pairs. So ∼A'TION n. [as prec., -ATE[3]]

Gĕm'inī, n. & (-ī) int. Constellation Castor and Pollux or the Twins, third sign of Zodiac, (also as arch. or vulg. int. of surprise, pr. jĭmīnī). [L, = twins]

gĕm'm'a, n. (bot., zool.; pl. -ae). Leaf--bud; (in mosses etc.) small cellular body that separates from mother-plant & starts fresh one; (Zool.) bud-like growth on animal of low organization becoming detached & developing into individual. [L, see GEM]

gĕm'm'ate[1], a. Having buds, reproducing by gemmation. [f. L *gemmatus* (prec., -ATE[2])]

gĕm'm'āte[2], v.i. Put forth buds, propagate by gemmation. [f. L *gemmare* (GEMMA), -ATE[3]]

gĕm'mā'tion, n. Act, manner, of budding, arrangement of buds, reproduction by gemmae, formation of new individual by protrusion & separation of part of the parent. So gĕm'm'ATIVE a. [F, f. L *gemmare* (as prec., -ATION)]

gĕmmif'erous, a. Producing precious stones; bearing buds = foll. [f. L *gemmifer* (GEMMA, -I-, -FEROUS)]

gĕmmip'arous, a. Of, propagating by, gemmation. Hence ∼LY[2] adv. [GEMMA, L -₋ *rus* (*parere* bring forth)]

gĕminŏ|l'ogў, n. Science of gems. Hence ∼L'OGIST n. [f. L *gemma* GEM, -O-, -LOGY]

gĕmm'ūle, n. (biol.). Small gemma; one of the hypothetical units in Darwin's theory of pangenesis. [F, f. L *gemmula* (GEMMA, -ULE)]

gems'bŏk (gĕmz-), n. Large S.-African antelope with long slender straight horns. [Du.]

‖ **gĕn,** n. (sl.). Information etc. published for all ranks. [first syllable of *general information*]

-gĕn, suf. forming nn. in scientific use f. F *-gène* f. Gk *-genēs* -born, of such a kind, (*gen-, gn-,* seen in *gi-gn-omai* be born, become). (1) in *oxygen* & later chem. formations *-gen* has the sense *that which produces* (*hydrogen, nitrogen, cyanogen*); (2) in *endogen, exogen,* etc. (bot.) *-gen*= growth (*acrogen, thallogen*).

gĕnăppe', n. Smooth kind of worsted. [f. *Genappe* in Belgium]

gendarme (see Ap.), n. (pl. ∼s). 1. Soldier, mounted or on foot, employed in police duties esp. in France. 2. (On a mountain) rock-tower occupying & blocking arête. [F]

gendarmerie (see Ap.), n. Force of gendarmes. [F]

gĕn'der[1], n. Grammatical classification (or one of the two, or three, classes) of objects roughly corresponding to the two sexes & sexlessness (MASCULINE, FEMININE, & NEUTER; see also COMMON[1], EPICENE), (of nouns & pronouns) property of belonging to such class, (of adjj.) appropriate form for accompanying a noun of any such class; (joc.) sex. Hence ∼LESS a. [ME, f. OF *gen(d)re* f. L GENUS]

gĕn'der[2], v.t.(poet.). = ENGENDER. [ME, f. OF *gen(d)rer* f. L *generare* (prec.)]

gĕne, n. (biol.). One of the factors or elements of which a germ-cell contains a pair transmitted each from one parent. [mod. formation, cf. -GEN]

gĕnĕalŏ'gical, a. Of genealogy; tracing family descent; ∼ *tree*, table showing descent of family or of animal species in shape of tree with branches. Hence ∼LY[2] adv. [f. F *généalogique* f. med. L f. Gk *genealogikos* (GENEALOGY, -IC) + -AL]

gĕnĕăl'og|ize, -ise (-ĭz), v.t. & i. Trace genealogy of; draw up genealogies. Hence ∼IST(1) n. [-IZE, -IZE]

gĕnĕăl'ogў, n. Account of descent from ancestor by enumeration of intermediate persons, pedigree; investigation of pedigrees; plant's or animal's line of development from earlier forms. [ME, f. OF (-*gie*) f. LL f. Gk *genealogia* (*genea* race, -LOGY)]

genera. See GENUS.

gĕn′eral, a. & n. 1. Completely or approximately universal, including or affecting all or nearly all parts, not partial, particular, local, or sectional, (~ *confession*, to be made by whole congregation; ~ ELECTION; *G*~ *Post Office*, ‖ head office in London; ~ *post*, first morning delivery, also name of indoor game); prevalent, widespread, usual, (*in a* ~ *way*, ordinarily); not limited in application, relating to whole class of objects, occasions, etc., true of all or (opp. *universal*) nearly all cases (*as a* ~ *rule*, in most cases), including points common to individuals of a class & neglecting differences (~ *word*, *term*, *notion*); not restricted to one department, not specialized, (‖ ~ *dealer*, trader in many articles; ~ *hospital*, large military hospital receiving sick and wounded from the field hospitals, one not specializing in any particular disease; ~ *practitioner*, doctor treating cases of all kinds; ‖~ *servant*, maid-of-all-work; ~ *reader*, of miscellaneous literature); roughly corresponding or‵adequate, sufficient for practical purposes, (~ *resemblance*, *idea*); vague, indefinite, (*spoke only in* ~ *terms*); (Mil., of officer) above rank of colonel; (appended to titles, as ADJUTANT~, ATTORNEY ~, POST²-*master* ~) chief, head, with unrestricted authority or sphere, (also joc. with other nn., as *lover* ~, one who makes love to all women); *in*~, generally, in all ordinary cases, barring special exceptions, for the most part. **2.** n. *The* ~ (arch.), the public; (pl.; now rare) ~ principles, notions, or rules; chief of religious order, e.g. of Jesuits, Dominicans; (Mil.) officer next below Field Marshal (also by courtesy of *lieutenant-*~ & *major-*~); commander of army; tactician, strategist, of specified merit (*a good*, *bad*, *great*, ~; *no* ~); ‖ = ~ servant above (colloq.). [ME, f. OF, f. L *generalis* (GENUS, -AL)]

gĕneraliss′imō, n. (pl. ~s). Commander of combined military & naval & air force, or of several armies. [It., superl. of *generale* GENERAL]

gĕnerăl′ĭty, n. Being general, applicability to whole class of instances; vagueness; general point, principle, law, or statement; main body, bulk, majority, *of*. [f. F *généralité* f. LL *generalitatem* (GENERAL, -TY)]

gĕneralĭzā′tion, n. (Forming of) general notion or proposition obtained by induction (often used disparagingly, esp. *hasty* ~, one based on too few instances). [foll., -ATION]

gĕn′eraliz|e, -is|e (-īz), v.t. & i. Reduce to general laws, form into a general notion, give a general character to, call by a general name; infer (law, conclusion) by induction; base general statement upon (facts etc.); (Math., Philos.) throw into general form, extend application of;

form general notions by abstraction; (Paint.) render only the typical characteristics of; make vague, use generalities, speak vaguely; bring into general use. Hence ~ER¹ n. [-IZE]

gĕn′erally, adv. For the most part, extensively; in a general sense, without regard to particulars, not specially, (~ *speaking*, in general); as a general rule, commonly. [-LY²]

gĕn′eralship, n. Office of a general; strategy, military skill; skilful management, tact, diplomacy. [-SHIP]

gĕn′erāte, v.t. Bring into existence, produce, evolve, (plants, animals, etc., usu. in pass.; heat, force, light, friction, electricity, etc.; result, state of things, state of mind, etc.); (Math.; of point, line, surface, conceived as moving) make (line, surface, solid). [f. L *generare* beget (GENUS), -ATE³]

gĕnerā′tion, n. Procreation, propagation of species, begetting or being begotten, (*equivocal* or SPONTANEOUS ~); production by natural or artificial process; single step in descent or pedigree (*have known them for three* ~s; *his descendant in the tenth* ~); whole body of persons born about same time (*my*, *the rising*, ~), average time in which children are ready to replace parents (reckoned at ⅓ of a century or at 30 years as a time-measure). [ME, f. OF, or L *generatio* (prec., -ATION)]

gĕn′erative (-āt-, -at-), a. Of procreation; able to produce, productive. [ME, f. LL *generativus* (prec., -ATIVE)]

gĕn′erātor, n. Begetter; apparatus for producing gases, steam, electricity, etc. [L (GENERATE, -OR)]

gĕnĕ′r|ĭc, a. Characteristic of a genus or class; applied to (any individual of) a large group or class; general, not specific or special. Hence ~ICALLY adv. [f. F *générique* or med. L *genericus* (GENUS, -IC)]

gĕn′erous, a. Magnanimous, noble-minded, not mean or prejudiced, free in giving, munificent, so gĕneros′ITY n.; (of soil) fertile; ample, abundant, copious; (of diet, colour, wine) rich & full. Hence ~LY² adv. [f. F *généreux* or L *generosus* (GENUS, -OUS) well-born, generous]

gĕn′esis, n. First book of O.T., with account of the Creation (*G*~); origin, mode of formation or generation, (also in comb. as *abio*~. *partheno*~). [L f. Gk *gen-* become]

gĕn′et, n. (Fur of) kind of civet-cat. [ME, f. OF *genete* f. Arab. *jarnait*]

gĕnĕt′|ĭc, a. Of, in, concerning, origin; of ~ics. Hence ~ICALLY adv., ~ICS n. pl., the study of heredity & variation, including loosely the physiology of reproduction & the art of breeding. [f. GENESIS on anal. of *antithesis* -*etic*]

gĕnĕv′a¹, n. Spirit distilled from grain & flavoured with juniper berries, Hollands. [f. Du. *genever* f. OF *genevre* f. L *juniperus* JUNIPER w. assim. to foll.]

Gĕnêv'a², a. (attrib.), & n. Of, from, Geneva (~ *bands*, clerical BAND¹s like those of Swiss Calvinists; ~ *Conventions*, of 1864–5 neutralizing ambulances etc. in war; ~ *cross*, red Greek cross on white ground distinguishing ambulances etc. in war; ~ *gown*, black, worn by Calvinists & low-churchmen in pulpit); (as n., used for) the ~ Conventions, the League of Nations or its proceedings. Hence **Gĕnêv'an, Gĕnêvese'**, aa. & nn.

gĕn'ial¹, a. Nuptial, generative, (~ *bed, instinct*; rare); conducive to growth, mild, warm, (of air, climate, etc.); cheering, enlivening; jovial, kindly, sociable, whence **gĕniăl'ITY** n., ~IZE(3) v.t.; of genius (rare). Hence ~LY² adv. [f. L *genialis* (GENIUS, -AL)]

gĕnĭ'al², a. (anat.). Of the chin. [f. Gk *geneion* chin (*genus* jaw cf. L *gena*)+ -AL]

gĕnĭc'ūlate, -ātĕd, aa. (nat. hist.). Having knee-like joints. [f. L *geniculatus* (*geniculum* f. *genu* knee, -CULE, -ATE²)]

gĕn'ie, n. (pl. usu. *gĕnĭi*, see GENIUS). Jinnee, sprite or goblin of Arabian tales. [f. F *génie* f. L GENIUS]

gĕnĭ'o-, comb. form of Gk *geneion* chin, as ~*hy'oid* of chin & hyoid bone.

gĕnĭs'ta, n. Kinds of yellow-flowered shrubs (including in some classifications the common broom). [L]

gĕn'ĭtal, a., & n. (pl.). 1. Of animal generation. 2. n. pl. External organs of generation. [f. OF *genital, -ailles*, or L *genitalis, -alia* (*gignere. genit-* beget, -AL)]

gĕn'ĭtive, a. & n. ~ *case* or ~, grammatical form of nouns, pronouns, adjectives, & participles, corresponding in inflected languages to *of, from*, & other prepositions with the noun representing, the source, possessor, etc. (~ ABSOLUTE, Gk construction corresponding to Latin ablative absolute). Hence **gĕnĭtīv'AL** a. [ME, f. OF -*if* or L *genitivus* (*casus* case) rendering Gk *genikē* (*ptōsis* case); as prec. +-IVE]

gĕn'ĭto-, comb. form of GENITAL, as ~- -*urinary* of the genital & urinary organs.

gĕn'ius, n. (pl. -*iuses, -ii*). Tutelary spirit of person, place, or institution (*good, evil*, ~, two opposed spirits or angels working for person's salvation or damnation, also person who powerfully influences one for good or ill); (usu. pl., *genii*, w. sing. GENIE) demon(s), supernatural being(s); nation's, age's, etc., prevalent feeling, opinions, or taste; character, spirit, drift, method, of a language, law, etc.; associations or inspirations *of* a place; natural ability, special mental endowments; (no pl.) exalted intellectual power, instinctive & extraordinary imaginative, creative, or inventive capacity, (pl. -*iuses*) person having this; ~ *loci* (L; lōs'ĭ), presiding deity, associations, etc., of the place. [L, in first sense, f. root of *gignere* beget]

Gĕn'ōa, n. Italian city '(~ *cake*, rich with almonds on top). Hence **GĕnōESE'** (-ēz) a. & n.

gĕn'ocide, n. Extermination of a race. [f. Gk *genos* race, -CIDE(2)]

genre (see Ap.), n. Kind, style; (also ~-*painting*) portrayal of scenes etc. from ordinary life. [F]

Gĕn'rō, ĝ-, n. pl. = Elder Statesmen (see STATESMAN). [Jap., = old men]

gēns (-z), n. (Rom. Ant.; pl. *gentēs*). Clan, sept, among Greeks or Romans. [L, genit. *gentis* (*gignere* beget)]

gĕnt, n. Gentleman (vulg.); person pretending to status of gentleman (joc.). [short for GENTLEMAN]

gĕnteel', a. (usu. iron.; vulg. in serious use). Appropriate to, characteristic of, belonging to, the upper classes, stylish, fashionable, well-dressed, elegant. Hence ~ISM(4) n., word used instead of the ordinary natural word because it is thought to be more ~ (e.g. *lady-dog* for *bitch, perspire* for *sweat*), ~LY² (-l-lǐ) adv. [16th c. *-ile*, re-adoption of F *gentil* GENTLE]

gĕn'tian (-shn, -tǐan), n. Kinds of usu. blue-flowered plant found esp. in mountain regions; ~-*bitter*, tonic extracted from its root; ~-*violet*, dye, used as antiseptic, esp. in treatment of burns. [ME, f. L *gentiana* (*Gentius* king of Illyria, -AN)]

Gĕn'tile, a. & n. (Person) not of Jewish race, (in Mormon use) non-Mormon, whence ~DOM (-ld-) n.; of a nation or tribe, (a. & n. in Gram.) (word) indicating nationality; heathen, pagan. [ME, f. L *gentilis* (GENS, -IL)]

gĕntili'tial (-shl), a. Of a nation, gens, or family (~ *noun, name, insignia*). [f. L *gentilitius* (*gentilis* GENTILE) +-AL]

gĕntil'itў, n. Gentle birth, status of gentleman or lady, (now rare); (usu. iron.) being genteel, social superiority, good manners, upper-class habits, (*shabby* ~, endeavour to keep up genteel appearances). [ME, f. OF *gentilite* (foll., -ITY)]

gĕn'tle, a. (-*er, -est*), n., & v.t. 1. Well-born, (Her.) having right to bear arms, (now only in ~ & *simple*, & in comb. as ~*folks*, GENTLEMAN); (of birth, blood, family, pursuits, etc.) honourable, belonging to or fit for the class of gentlemen; || (arch.) generous, noble, courteous (still playfully in ~ *reader*, author's apostrophe); tame, quiet, (*the* ~ *craft*, angling), easily managed; not stormy, rough, or violent; (of medicine) mild, not drastic; (of rule etc.) not severe; moderate (*a* ~ *heat*), gradual (*a* ~ *slope*); kind, mild, tender, (*the* ~ *sex*, women); ~*folk*(s), people of good position & family. 2. n. Maggot, larva of flesh-fly or bluebottle, used as fishing-bait (f. obs. sense *soft* of adj.); (pl., vulg.) ~folk. 3. v.t. Break in (horse), handle (horse) firmly but gently. [ME, f. OF *gentil* f. L *gentilis* GENTILE; cf. JAUNTY]

gĕn'tlehŏŏd (-telh-), n. Position or character attaching to gentle birth. [from 1860; -HOOD]

gĕn'tleman (-telm-), n. Man entitled to bear arms but not included in the nobility (chiefly hist.); member of certain professions etc. (arch.); ‖ man of gentle birth attached to household of sovereign or great person (~ *in waiting* etc.; ~*-at--arms*, one of sovereign's bodyguard); man of chivalrous instincts, fine feelings, & good breeding (*the* ~*'s psalm*, Ps. xv); man of good social position, man of wealth & leisure (~ *at* LARGE); (courteous synonym for) man, (pl., in voc.) male members of audience, also in letters = Sirs; ‖ (pl. as sing. n.) men's public lavatory; (Law) man who has no occupation; (joc.) *old* ~, the devil, *my* ~, the fellow I was speaking of, ~*'s* ~, valet; ‖ ~ *commoner* (hist.), privileged undergraduate at Oxf. & Camb.; ~ *farmer*, country ~ who farms; ‖ ~ RANKER; ~ *usher*, ~ acting as usher to great person; ~*'s agreement* (binding in honour, but not enforceable at law). Hence ~HOOD, ~SHIP(1), nn. [GENTLE + MAN after OF *gentilz hom*]

gĕn'tlemanlīke (-telm-), a. Appropriate to, resembling, a gentleman. [-LIKE]

gĕn'tlemanlｌy̆ (-telm-), a. Feeling, behaving, or looking, like a gentleman; befitting a gentleman. Hence ~ĪNESS n. [-LY¹]

gĕn'tleness (-tel-), n. Kindliness, mildness; freedom from severity, suddenness, violence, steepness, etc. [-NESS]

gĕn'tlewoman (-telwŏŏman), n. (pl. *-en*). Woman of good birth or breeding, lady. Hence ~HOOD n., ~LIKE, ~LY¹, aa., ~līNESS n. [GENTLE + WOMAN after OF *gentil-femme*]

gĕn'tly̆, adv. As gentleman or gentlewoman (only in ~ *born*, of gentle birth); quietly, moderately, softly, slowly,. (as remonstrance) not so fast etc.; mildly, tenderly, kindly. [-LY²]

gĕn'try̆, n. People next below the nobility in position & birth; (derog., esp. *these* ~) people. [prob. f. obs. *gentrice* f. OF *genterise* var. of *gentelise* (*gentil* GENTLE)]

gĕn'ūal, a. Of the knee. [L *genu* knee, -AL]

gĕn'ūflĕct, v.i. Bend the knee, esp. in worship. Hence or cogn. ~OR, gĕnū-flĕ'xION, nn., ~ORY a. [f. LL *genuflectere* *-flex-* (prec., *flectere* bend)]

gĕn'ūine, a. Of the original stock, pure--bred; really proceeding from its reputed source or author; having the supposed character, not counterfeit, properly so called. Hence ~LY² (-nl-) adv., ~NESS (-n-n-) n. [f. L *genuinus* innate, post-cl. authentic]

gĕn'us, n. (pl. *gĕn'era*). (Logic) kind of things including subordinate kinds or SPECIES (*highest* ~, not itself subordinate as species to higher ~; *subaltern* ~,

so subordinated); (Zool., Bot.) group of animals or plants having common structural characteristics distinct from those of all other groups,, & usu. containing several species (see CLASS; the generic & specific names, the former with capital initial, form the proper name; *the* ~ *Homo*, mankind); (loosely) kind, class, order, tribe. [f. L *genus -eris* cogn. w. KIN]

-gĕny̆, suf. forming nn. indicating mode of production f. F *-génie* (-GEN), as *anthropo'geny* history of human evolution, often with corresp. nn. in *-genesis* & adjj. in *-genetic*.

gĕo-, comb. form of Gk *gĕ* earth (Gk *geō-*), as ~*dynăm'ic* of the latent forces of the earth, ~*selĕn'ic* of earth & moon.

gĕocĕn'tric, a. Considered as viewed from the earth's centre (~ *latitude of planet*, in which it would appear to observer at earth's centre); having or representing the earth as centre, not HELIOcentric. [prec., *centric* (CENTRE¹, -IC)]

gĕ'ōde, n. (Concretionary stone containing) cavity lined with crystals or other mineral matter. Hence gĕŏd'IC a. [f. F *géode* or L f. Gk *geōdēs* earthy (*gĕ* earth, -ODE)]

gĕŏd'|ĕsy̆, n. Branch of mathematics dealing with figure & area of the earth or large portions of it. So gĕōdēs'IC, gĕodĕt'IC, aa. (~*esic*, ~*etic, line*, shortest possible on surface between two points), gĕodĕt'ICAL a., gĕodĕt'icalLY² adv., ~čSIST(3) n. [f. F *géodésie* or mod. L f. Gk GEO(*daisia* f. *daiō* divide)]

gĕŏg'nosy̆, n. = GEOLOGY; geology of a district; knowledge of the mineral character, grouping, & distribution, of particular rocks. So gĕognōs'TIC(AL) aa. [f. F *géognosie* (GEO-, Gk *gnōsis* knowledge, *gnōstos* known]

gĕogrăph'ic, -ic|al, aa. Of geography (~ *latitude*, angle made with plane of equator by perpendicular to earth's surface at any point; ~*al mile*, = 1′ of longitude on equator or about 2,000 yds). Hence ~alLY² adv. [f. F (-*ique*) or LL f. Gk GEO(*graphikos* GRAPHIC) + -AL]

gĕŏg'raphy̆, n. Science of the earth's surface, form, physical features, natural & political divisions, climate, productions, population, etc. (*mathematical, physical, & political*, ~, the science in these aspects); subject-matter of ~; features, arrangement, *of* place; treatise or manual of ~. So gĕŏG'RAPHER n. [f. F *géographie* or L f. Gk GEO(*graphia* -GRAPHY)]

gĕŏl'ogīze, -ise (-īz), v.i. & t. Devote time to examining places geologically, collecting specimens, etc.; examine (place) thus. [foll. + -IZE]

gĕŏl'ogy̆, n. Science of the earth's crust, its strata, & their relations & changes; geological features *of* district. Hence gĕolō'gIC(AL) aa. (*-ic* now only of things forming part of subject-matter of ~), ǵeŏlŏ′ǵicaLLY² adv., ǵeŏL′OGIST n. [f. mod. L f. GEO- + -LOGY]

ǵe′ŏmănc|ў, n. Divination from figure given by handful of earth thrown down, & hence from figures given by dots made at random. Hence or cogn. ~ER¹ n., ǵeomăn′tic a. [ME, f. OF geomancie f. med. L f. Gk GEO(manteia -MANCY)]

ǵeŏm′eter, n. Person skilled in geometry; kinds of caterpillar & corresp. moth (from caterpillar's seeming to measure ground by its mode of walking). [f. L f. Gk GEO(metrēs measurer)]

ǵeomĕt′ric, -ic|al, aa. Of, according to, geometry (~al tracery, with openings of ~ form, as circles, trefoils, etc.; ~al proportion, involving equal ratios in its two parts, as 1 : 3 :: 4 : 12; ~al progression, with constant ratio between successive quantities, as 1 : 3 : 9 : 27 : 81; ~ spider, constructing web of ~ pattern). Hence ~aLLY² adv. [f. L f. Gk geōmetrikos (prec. -IC) + -AL]

ǵeŏm′etrize, -ise (-īz), v.i. & t. Work, form, by geometrical methods. [f. LL geometrizare (as foll., -IZE)]

ǵeŏm′etrў, n. Science of properties & relations of magnitudes (as lines, surfaces, solids) in space. So ǵeomĕtri′cian (-ishn) n. [ME, f. OF geometrie f. L f. Gk GEO(metria measuring)]

ǵeomŏr′phŏl′ogў, n. Study of the physical features of the (crust of the) earth & its geological structures. [GEO-, MORPHOLOGY]

ǵeŏph′ag|ў, n. = DIRT-eating. So ~IST(1) n. [GEO-, Gk -phagia -eating]

ǵeophўs′ic|s (-z-), n. The physics of the earth. Hence ~AL a., ~IST n. [GEO-]

ǵeopŏl′itics, n. The politics of a country as determined by its geographical features. [GEO-]

ǵeopŏn′ic, a. (pedantic or joc.). Agricultural. [f. Gk GEO(ponikos f. ponos toil + -IC)]

‖ Geor′die (jôr-), n. (Sc. & north.). = COLLIER (all senses); native of Tyneside. [George, -Y³]

George (jôrj), n. 1. St ~, patron saint of England from time of Edw. III who chose him as patron of Order of the Garter (St ~'s day, 23rd April; St ~'s cross, vertical & horizontal red bars crossing in centre). 2. Jewel forming part of Garter insignia. 3. ‖ Automatic pilot of aircraft (sl.). 4. Brown ~, vessel of brown earthenware; by ~, oath .or exclamation; ‖ ~ Cross, Medal, (abbr. G.C., G.M.), decorations for gallantry instituted 1940. [f. L f. Gk Geōrgios supposed prince of Cappadocia martyred under Diocletian]

georgĕtte′ (jôr-), n. A thin silk dress-material. [f. dressmaker's name]

Geor′gian¹ (jôr-), a. Of the time of the first four Kings George of England; of the time of George V and VI. [-IAN]

Geor′gian² (jôr-), a. & n. (Inhabitant, language) of Georgia in the Caucasus; (inhabitant) of Georgia in U.S. [-AN]

Geor′ǵic (jôr-), n. One book (first, fourth, ~) of the ~s, Virgil's poem on husbandry. [f. L f. Gk geōrgika pl. neut. adj. (geōrgos husbandman f. GEO-, erg- work, -IC)]

ǵeostrŏph′ic, a. (meteorol.). Depending on the rotation of the earth. [GEO- + Gk strophikos f. strephō turn]

ǵeŏt′ropism, n. Plant-growth in relation to gravity (positive ~, tendency of roots to grow towards, negative ~, of stems to grow away from, centre of earth). So ǵeotrŏp′ic a., ǵeotrŏp′ICALLY adv. [GEO-, Gk tropikos (tropē a turning f. trepō turn + -IC, -ISM)]

ǵerăn′ium, n. Kinds of wild herbaceous plant bearing fruit like crane's bill, crane's-bill; kinds of cultivated pelargonium; colour of the scarlet ~. [L, f. Gk geranion (geranos crane)]

ǵer′falcon (-awkn, -awl-), n. Any large northern falcon, esp. the Icelandic. [ME, f. OF gerfaucon f. WG *gerfalco (= G gerfalke) f. ON geirfalki (for geir- cf. GAREFOWL), see FALCON]

ǵeriät′r|ic, a. Relating to ~ics n. pl., branch of medical science dealing with old age & its diseases. So ǵeriatri′cian (-ishn), ~IST(3), ~Y¹, (jĕri′a-), nn. [f. Gk gēras old age, iatros physician, -IC]

ǵerm, n., & v.i. 1. Portion of organism capable of developing into a new one (~-, usu. of female reproductive element, opp. sperm²), rudiment of animal or plant; micro-organism or microbe, esp. one of those supposed to cause disease (~- -CARRIER); (fig.) that from which something may spring, elementary principle (in ~, not yet developed); ~-cell, cell in body of an organism which is specialized for reproductive purposes, and which, when united to one of the opposite sex, forms a new individual, gamete; ~-plasm, nuclear part of ~-cell by which, according to Weismann's theory, hereditary characteristics are transmitted. 2. v.i. Germinate, sprout, (fig. only). [f. F germe f. L germen]

ǵerm′an¹, a. (Now only as appended to BROTHER, SISTER, COUSIN) in the fullest sense of relationship; = GERMANE. [ME, f. OF germain f. L germanus of same parents]

ǵerm′an², a. & n. 1. Of, characterizing, Germany or its inhabitants or language (~ measles, contagious disease like mild measles; ~ Ocean, North Sea; ~ sausage, large kind stuffed with spiced partly cooked meat; ~ text, black letter; ~ silver, white alloy of nickel, zinc, & copper). 2. n. Native, language, of Germany (High ~, form of ~ orig. spoken in South, but now in literary use throughout Germany; Low ~, dialects of Germany that are not High ~, also, all forms of WG, including English & Dutch, except High ~). Hence ~ISH¹ a., ~ISM(2,

3, 4), ~IST(1, 3), nn., ~IZE(2, 3, 4) v.t. & i., ~IZA'TION, ~IZER[1], nn., Gĕrmăn'o-comb. form., GĕrmănoMAN'IA n., Gĕrmăn-OPHIL, Gĕrmăn'OPHOEE, aa. & nn., ~ŏph'ilIST, GĕrmănOPHOB'IA, nn. [f. L Germanus a. & n. of related peoples of central & N. Europe, name perh. given by Celts to their neighbours (of. OIr. gair neighbour)]

gĕrmăn'der, n. Kinds of plant esp. the blue-flowered ~ speedwell. [f. med. L germandra ult. f. late Gk khamaidruon f. khamai on the ground +drus oak]

gĕrmāne', a. Relevant, pertinent, to the matter or subject. [var. of GERMAN[1]]

Gĕrmăn'ic, a. & n. Of the Germans (chiefly hist. in ~ Confederation, ~ Empire); of the Teutonic race or any Teutonic people (of language, = primitive Teutonic; also with limiting word: East ~, Gothic & some almost lost languages as Burgundian & Vandal; North ~, Scandinavian; West ~, High & Low German, English. Frisian, Dutch, etc.; see also INDO-~). [f. L Germanicus (GERMAN[2], -IC)]

gĕrmăn'ium, n. Brittle white metallic element. [mod. L, f. Germanus GERMAN[2] +-IUM]

gĕrm'icide, n. & a. (Substance) having power to destroy (esp. disease-)germs. Hence gĕrmicid'AL a. [-I-, -CIDE]

gĕrm'inal, a. Of germs, in the nature of a germ; in the earliest stage of development. Hence ~LY[2] adv. [as GERM, -AL]

gĕrm'in|āte, v.i. & t. Sprout, bud, put forth shoots, (lit. & fig.); cause to shoot, develop (trans.), produce. Hence or cogn. ~ANT a. (intr. usu. fig.), ~A'TION, ~ātoR, nn., ~ATIVE a. [f. L germinare (GERM), -ATE[3]]

gĕrm'on, n. Long-finned tunny. [F]

gĕrŏntŏc'racy̆ (g-, j-), n. Government by, governing body of, old men. [f. Gk gerōn -ontos old man, -CRACY]

gĕrŏntŏl'ogy̆ (g-, j-), n. Scientific study of old age & its diseases. [f. Gk gerōn (prec.), -LOGY]

-gerous, suf. (in use -igerous, see -I-) f. L -ger bearing (gerere bear) +-OUS; in some words taken f. L, & freely added to L stems, as in frondigerous leaf-bearing.

gĕrrymăn'der (g-), (erron.) ‖ jĕrry̆-, v.t. & n. 1. Manipulate (constituency etc.) unfairly so as to secure disproportionate influence at election for some party or class; hence ~ER[1] n. 2. n. Such manipulation. [vb f. n., orig. U.S.; anecdotic; substitution of name of governor Gerry of Massachusetts for sala- in salamander]

gĕ'rund, n. Forms of Latin verb -ndum, -ndi, -ndo) serving as cases of the infinitive in its noun use, constructed as nouns but able to govern like their verb; English verbal noun in -ING[1] when used distinctly as part of verb (his doing this is doubtful); ~-grinder, teacher of Latin. So gĕrun'dIAL a. [f. LL gerundium f.

gerundum, var. of gerendum gerund of gerere do = thing to be done, doing]

gĕrun'dive, a. & n. Of, like, the gerund; (n.; in L Gram.) verbal adjective from gerund stem having sense that should be done etc. Hence gĕrundiv'AL a., ~LY[2] adv. [f. LL gerundivus (prec., -IVE)]

gĕss'ō, n. Plaster of Paris, gypsum, prepared for use in painting & in sculpture. [It., f. L GYPSUM]

gestalt' (geshtahlt), n. (psych.). An organized whole in which each individual part affects every other, the whole being more than a sum of its parts; chiefly attrib., as ~ psychology, theory. [G, = form, shape]

Gesta'pō (gestah-), n. German secret state police of Nazi régime. [f. initial letters of Geheime Staats-Polizei]

gĕsta'tion, n. Carrying or being carried in the womb between conception & birth, this period. [f. L gestatio (gestare frequent. of gerere carry, -ATION)]

gĕstatōr'ial, a. ~ chair, for carrying the Pope on certain occasions. [f. L gestatorius (gestator carrier as prec. +-OR, -ORY)]

gĕstic'ul|āte, v.i. & t. Use expressive motion of limbs or body with or instead of speech; express thus. So ~A'TION, ~ātoR, nn., ~ATIVE, ~ātory, aa. [f. L gesticulari (gesticulus dim. of gestus GESTURE), -ATE[3]]

gĕs'ture, n., & v.i. & t. 1. Significant movement of limb or body; use of such movements as expression of feeling or rhetorical device; (transf.) step or move calculated to evoke response from another or to convey (esp. friendly) intention. 2. vb. = GESTICULATE. [ME, f. med. L gestura (L gerere gest- wield, -URE)]

gĕt[1] (g-), v.t. & i. (past gŏt; p.p. gŏt, & in comb. & arch. & U.S. gŏt'en). 1. trans. Obtain, procure, by effort or contrivance (~ coal, extract it from mine), earn (cannot ~ a living), gain (got little by it), win (~ the upper hand, start, advantage, sun, wind, better, of a person; ~ the best of it, be victorious; ~ fame, credit, glory, etc.; ~ knowledge or wind of, learn, hear rumours of); learn by heart or rote; obtain as result of calculation (we ~ 9·5 as the average); receive as gift, wages, etc.; extract by prayer, demand, inquiry, etc. (from, out of; could not ~ leave, any supper); come to have (desired thing, as rest, one's way, speech of someone, a sight of, possession of; ~ religion, be converted)- contract (idea etc.;; also ~ it into one's head, be convinced that; ~ measles; ~ person or thing on the brain, think of him exclusively, on one's nerves, be irritably affected by him); (of story etc.) ~ wind, become known; have inflicted on one, suffer, receive as one's lot or penalty, (fall, blow, the worst of it, six months; ~ it, be punished, scolded, etc.; ~ the BOOT[1], SACK[1], MITTEN); (with for or ind. obj.) procure, provide, (got him a place;

we can ~ it for you); catch (fish etc.); bring in, carry home, (crop); (colloq.) corner, puzzle, catch in argument, (esp. in perf. & past); (colloq.) understand (person or thing); (colloq.) take, eat, (dinner etc.); (colloq., in perf.) have (*have not got a penny*; *it has got to be done*, must); (now usu. only of animals) beget; (with compl.) succeed in bringing, placing, etc. (*got it over or across* see below, *through door, into room*, etc.), bring into some state (*~ with child*, make pregnant; *~ them ready*; *~ person upon* a subject, make him talk of it; *~ ship under way*, start her; esp. with p.p. as *~ it done, got the laws obeyed*) suffer injury etc. to some part of one (*got my wrist dislocated*; *shall ~ my feet wet*); induce, prevail upon, (person) *to do*. 2. intr. Succeed in coming or going *to, from, into, out of, through, over, here, there, as far as*, etc. (*where has it got to?*, what has become of it?; *~ across or over* (sc. the footlights), sl., reach audience, be effective; *~ there*, sl., succeed); (sl.) be off, clear out; (with infin.) acquire habit (one *soon ~s to like it*); come to be do*ing* (*they got talking*); become (*~ tired, hot, excited, drunk*; *~ well, better*, recover from illness; *~ clear, rid*, or *quit, of*; *•~ wise to*, become aware of; *~ under way*, begin to sail; *~ done with*, bring to an end; *~ married, used to it, shelved*). 3. (With prepp.): *~ at*, reach (whence *~-åt'-ABLE a.*), ~ hold of, ascertain, (sl.) tamper with, bribe, etc., (sl.) attack, banter, (*who are you ~ting at?*, often = trying to impose upon— expressing incredulity); *~ into*, (colloq.) put on (boots, clothes), (of liquor) affect, confuse, (one's *head*); *~ off*, dismount from, obtain release from (engagement etc.), not remain on (the grass etc.); *~ on*, mount (horse etc.), rise on one's *feet* or *legs* to speak in public; *~ over*, surmount (difficulty), show (evidence, argument) to be unconvincing, recover from (illness) or from surprise at, accomplish (distance, task, etc.), (sl.) circumvent; *~ round*, cajole, evade; *~ through*, bring to an end, (of Bill etc.) be passed by (Lords, Commons, etc.), while away (time etc.); *~ to*, begin (business etc.); *~ upon*, = ~ on. 4. (With advv.); *~ about*, go from place to place, begin walking after illness etc., (of rumours) be circulated; *~ abroad*, (of rumours) = *~ about*; *~ along*, advance, meet with success, fare *ill* or *well* etc., manage *without* something, live harmoniously *together* or *with*, (colloq.) *~ along with you!*, be off!, nonsense; *~ away*, escape, start, (imperat.) be off!; *~ away with it*, succeed in what one tries to do, escape retribution, act with impunity; *~ back*, come home etc., recover (lost thing; *~ back* one's or *some of* one's *own*, sl., have revenge); *~ down*, dismount; *~ in*, be elected as M.P., enter carriage, bring home (crop), collect (debts etc.), fit (work etc.) into given time, suc-

ceed in placing (blow), *~ one's hand in*, become at home with some operation, *can't ~ in a word* EDGEWAYS; *~ off*, escape (t. & i.), start, go to sleep, be acquitted or pardoned, be let off *with* or *for* specified penalty, procure acquittal or slight penalty for (person); *~ off with*, become on friendly or amorous terms with member of opposite sex; *~ on*, display (pace; *~ a move on*, sl., make a start), advance, make progress (*~ on or ~ out*, work or go), prosper, fare, manage *without* something, agree or live sociably *with*, *be ~ting on for*, approaching (an age etc.); *•~ on to*, succeed in understanding; *~ out*, (imperat.) be off!, nonsense!, transpire, elicit, succeed in uttering, publishing, etc., dismiss, be dismissed, in cricket; *~ out of*, issue or escape from (*got out of bed on wrong side*, is in bad temper; *~ out of sight*, one's *depth*, disappear, be in too deep water to stand; *~ out of hand*, break from control, also finish *work* etc.), abandon (habit) gradually, evade do*ing*, elicit (information) or obtain (money) from (person); *~ over*, bring (troublesome task) to an end; *~ through*, bring to or reach destination, (of Bill) be passed in Parliament, succeed in an examination; *~ through with*, succeed in doing or enduring; *~ together*, collect (t. & i.), unite in discussion, promotion of plan, etc.; *~-together n.*, (social) assembly; *~ under*, subdue (fire); *~ up*, rise esp. from bed, mount esp. on horseback, (of fire, wind, sea) begin to be violent, (of game) rise from cover, (of cricket-ball) rise sharply from pitch, organize, set on foot, (of laundress) dress (linen), make presentable, arrange the appearance of, (hair, the person, mounting of play, binding & print of book), make rise (*I got my, his, back up*, became, made him, angry or stubborn), produce (*~ up steam*, enough to work engine, also fig. of working oneself into anger or energy; ‖*~ the wind up*, sl., feel afraid), work up (factitious emotion, subject for examination etc.). Hence *~t'ABLE a.* [ME, f. ON *geta* = OE -gietan (cf. *beget, forget*), OS -getan, OHG -gezzän, Goth. *bigitan* f. Gmc *•getan*]

gĕt², n. Begetting, offspring, (of animals, esp. in sporting talk). [f. prec.]

gĕt'away (-a-w-), n. (Esp. of thieves etc.) escape, as *make* one's ~. [GET¹]

gĕt-ŭp', n. Style of equipment or costume, style of production of book etc. [GET¹]

gē'um, n. Kinds of rosaceous plant, avens, as HERB-bennet. [L, prob. = herb-bennet]

gew'gaw (g-), n. Gaudy plaything or ornament, bauble; paltry showy trifle. [ME, of unkn. orig.]

gey (gā), adv. (Sc.). Very, considerably, (also adj. *~ & —*, in same sense). [var. of GAY]

gey'ser (gāz-, gīz-), n. Intermittent hot spring throwing up column of water;

ü (gĕz- apparatus for heating water. [f. Icel. *Geysir* name of a particular specimen in Iceland (*geysa* to gush)]

Ghanai'an (gahnä'*an*), a. & n. (Native) of Ghana (formerly Gold Coast colony). [-IAN]

gharry (gă'rĭ), n. (Anglo-Ind.). Indian carriage (usu. horse-drawn and plying for hire). [Hind, *gāṛī*]

ghast'l|ȳ (gah-, gă-), a. & adv. Horrible, frightful, shocking; (colloq.) objectionable, deathlike, pale, wan, lurid; (of smile etc.) painfully forced; (adv., chiefly with adj. as ~ *pale*) ghastlily. Hence ~ĭLY² adv., ~ĭNESS n. [ME *gastliche* f. obs. *gast* terrify (cf. OE *gǣstan* torment) +-LY¹; *gh*- after GHOST]

gha(u)t (gawt), n. (Anglo-Ind.). *Eastern, Western, G*~*s*, two mountain chains along E & W. sides of Southern Hindostan; mountain pass, defile; flight of steps leading to river landing-place; *burning*-~, level spot at the top of river ~ on which Hindus burn their dead. [Hind. *ghaṭ*]

Gha'zi (gah-), n. Mohammedan anti-infidel. [Arab. p.p. of *ghaza* fight]

ghee (gē), n. Indian buffalo-milk butter clarified to resemble oil. [f. Hind. *ghī*]

gherk'in (gẽr-), n. Young green, or small kind of, cucumber used for pickling. [f. Du. *gurkkijn (now *gurkje*) f. Slavonic, ult. f. late Gk *aggourion*]

ghett'o (gĕ-), n. (hist.; pl. ~s). Jews' quarter in city. [It.; orig. much conjectured, but unkn.]

Ghib'ellin|e (gĭ-), n. & a. 1. One of emperor's faction (opp. GUELPH) in medieval Italian States; hence ~ISM(3) n. 2. adj. Adhering to ~es. [f. It. *Ghibellino* supposed to be f. G *Waiblingen* estate belonging to Hohenstaufen emperors]

ghōst (gō-), n., & v.t. & i. 1. Principle of life (now only in *give up the* ~, die); Spirit of God (now only in *Holy G*~, Third Person of Trinity). 2. Soul of dead person in Hades etc.; dead person appearing to the living (*raise, lay,* ~, cause it to appear or cease appearing), apparition, spectre; emaciated person; shadowy outline or semblance (*not the* ~ *of a chance,* none at all). 3. (opt.). Bright spot or secondary image in field of telescope due to defect of lens. 4. Artistic or literary hack doing the work for which his employer takes credit. 5. ~*-word,* one of which the existence is imaginary or based on a delusion, as CELT², FYLFOT; *the* ~ *walks* (Theatr. sl.), salaries are, or will be, paid; hence ~'HOOD n., ~'LIKE a. 6. vb. Haunt, prowl, act, as a ~; act as a ~ writer etc. (for). [OE *gāst*, OS *gēst*, OHG *geist* f. WG *gaist; sp. *gh*- first in Caxton, prob. due to Flem. *gheest*]

ghōst'l|ȳ (gō-), a. (Arch.) spiritual, incorporeal, concerned with sacred or ecclesiastical matters, (*our* ~*y enemy,* the Devil; ~*y father, adviser, director,* etc., confessor;

~*y comfort, counsel,* etc., administered by priest; ~*y weapons,* religious arguments, ecclesiastical penalties, etc.); (as) of a ghost, spectral. Hence ~ĭNESS n. [OE *gāstlic* (prec., -LY¹)]

ghoul (gōōl), n. Spirit preying on corpses in Eastern tales. Hence ~'ISH¹ a., ~'ishLY² adv., (gōō-). [f. Arab. *ghul* f. vb = seize]

|| **ghyll,** var. of GILL².

gial'lo anti'co (jahl-, ahntē-), n. Rich yellow marble found in Italian ruins. [It.]

gi'ant, n. & a. 1. Being of human form but superhuman stature, (Gk Myth.) one of the sons of Gaea (Earth) & Uranus (Heaven) or Tartarus (Hell) who warred against the Gods; agency of enormous power; abnormally tall person, animal, or plant; person of extraordinary ability, courage, strength, etc. (*there were* ~*s in those days,* our fathers were superior to us); ~ *cement,* specially tenacious kind; ~*-powder,* kind of dynamite; ||~(*'s*)-*stride,* gymnastic apparatus of pole with revolving head & hanging ropes enabling user to take huge strides round pole; hence ~ESS¹ n., ~ISM n., pathological condition characterized by abnormal growth, esp. of the bones, ~LIKE a. 2. adj. Of extraordinary size or force, gigantic, monstrous, (often in plant-names). [ME *geant* (afterwards affected by L) f. OF *geant* f. L f. Gk *gigant-* nom. -*gas*]

giaour (jowr), n. (Turkish contemptuous name for) infidel, esp. Christian. [f. Pers. *gaur*]

gib (g-, j-), n. Piece of wood or metal used to keep some part of a machine etc. in place; pin or wedge. [orig. unkn.]

gibb'er (j-, g-), v.i., & n. 1. Speak fast & inarticulately, chatter like an ape. 2. n. Such speed or sound. [imit.]

gibb'erish (g-, j-), n. Unintelligible speech, meaningless sounds, jargon, blundering or ungrammatical talk. [perh. f. prec. (but found earlier) +-ISH¹ as used in names of langg.]

gibb'ět, n., & v.t. 1. (Orig.) gallows; (later) upright post with arm on which bodies of executed criminals were hung up; death by hanging. 2. v.t. Put to death by hanging; expose on ~; hang up as on ~; hold up to infamy or contempt. [ME, f. OF *gibet* gallows dim. of *gibe* club]

gibb'on (g-), n. Kinds of long-armed ape esp. of Indian archipelago. [F (Buffon), alleged to be a native wd]

gibb'ous (g-), a. Convex, protuberant; (of moon or planet) having bright part greater than semicircle & less than circle; humped, hunchbacked. Hence or cogn. **gibbos'ITY** (-ŏs⁴) n., **gibbos'o-** comb. form, ~LY² adv., (g-). [f. L *gibbosus* f. *gibbus* hump, see -OUS]

gibe, jïbe, v.i. & t., & n. Flout, jeer, mock, (as vb, with *at,* or trans., or abs.).

Hence **gĭb′ER¹** n., **gĭb′ĭngLY²** adv. [orig. unkn.]

gĭb′lĕts, n. pl. Parts of goose taken out or cut off before cooking, as liver, gizzard, pinions, feet; *giblet soup*, made with these. [f. OF *gibelet* ragout of game]

gĭb′us, n. Opera or crush hat. [*G*~, maker]

gĭdd′ў (g-), a., & v.t. & i. **1.** Dizzy, disposed to fall, stagger, or spin round (*with sickness, success*, etc.); making dizzy (*a ~ precipice, maze, success*); circling with bewildering speed; mentally intoxicated, incapable of attention, excitable, frivolous (*play the ~ goat*, fool), inconstant, flighty; ||~-*go-round*, MERRY²-go-round; hence **gĭdd′ĭLY²** adv., **gĭdd′ĭNESS** n., (g-). **2.** vb. Make or become ~. [OE *gĭdig* insane (GOD, -Y²) lit. 'possessed by a god', as Gk *entheos*]

gĭft (g-), n., & v.t. **1.** Giving (*would not have it as a ~*, even gratis; *the living is in the ~ of —*, is his to bestow; *came to me by free ~*); (Law) voluntary transference of property without consideration; thing given, present, donation; faculty miraculously bestowed, virtue looked upon as emanation from heaven etc., (~ *of* TONGUES); natural endowment (~ *of the* GAB), talent, whence **gĭf′tED²** a.; ~-*book*, one given or suitable for giving as present; ~ *coupon*, voucher issued with certain commodities, a specified number of which entitles holder to a ~; ~-HORSE, one given; hence **gĭf′tĭe** [-Y³] (g-) n. (Sc.; *the ~ie gie us to see oursels as others see us*). **2.** v.t. Endow with ~s, present *with* as ~; bestow as ~ (*to* person; *away*). [ME, f. ON *gipt* = OE, OS, OHG *gift*, Goth. ·*gifts* f. Gmc *·geftiz* f. *·gebh-* GIVE]

gĭg¹ (g-), n. **1.** Light two-wheeled one-·horsed carriage (~-*lamps*, sl., spectacles; ~′*man*, person who keeps ~, member of GIGMANITY). **2.** Light narrow clinker-built ship's-boat for oars or sails; rowing-boat chiefly used for racing. [f. 13th c. in var. senses; orig. unkn.]

gĭg² (g-), n. Kind of fish-spear. [short for *fizgig, fishgig* f. Sp. *fisga* harpoon]

gĭgăn′t|ĭc, a. Giant-like in size, stature, etc., abnormally large, huge. Hence or cogn. ~ESQUE′ (-ĕsk) a., ~ĭCALLY adv. [f. L *gigas -antis* GIANT, -IC]

gĭg′gle (g-), v.i., & n. **1.** Laugh like an affected, ill-bred, or undisciplined girl, titter, have small bursts of half-suppressed laughter. **2.** n. Such laugh, freq. (*fit of*) *the ~s.* [imit.; cf. Du. *giggelen*, G *gickeln*]

gĭg′lĕt, -ot, (g-), n. Giggling girl. [14th c., f. obs. *gig* flighty girl (GIG¹), now associated with prec.]

gĭgmăn′ĭtỹ (g-), n. The respectable unimaginative middle classes, Philistines. [*gigman* (GIG¹) + -ITY (Carlylese wds)]

gĭg-mill (g-), n. Machine for raising nap on cloth; building in which these stand. [f. GIG¹]

gĭg′olō, n. (pl. ~s). Professional male dancing-partner. [F, formed as masc. of *gigole* dance-hall woman]

gĭg′ot, n. Leg of mutton; ~ *sleeve* = LEG-·*of-mutton* sleeve. [F]

gila (hē′la) mŏn′ster, n. Large venomous lizard of Arizona, New Mexico, etc. [*Gila*, river of Southern U.S.]

Gilbĕrt′ian (g-), a. Of the humorously topsy-turvy kind characteristic of Gilbert & Sullivan opera (*a ~ situation*). [W. S. *Gilbert*, librettist, d. 1911, -IAN]

gĭld¹ (g-), v.t. (p.p. usu. ~*ed* in the fully verbal use & in fig. use as adj., *gilt* as adj. in lit. sense). Cover with thin layer of gold laid on as gold leaf or otherwise (~ *pill*, soften down unpleasant necessity), whence **gĭl′dER¹**, **gĭl′dĭNG¹** (2, 4), nn.; make (condition etc.) tolerable or reputable by money (or with *money* etc. as subj.); tinge, adorn, with golden colour or light; give specious brilliance to by fair words; || *Gilded Chamber*, House of Lords; ~*ed* or *gilt spurs*, emblem of knighthood; ~*ed youth*, the young men of fashion & wealth; *gilt-cup*, buttercup. [OE *gyldan*, ON *gylla* f. Gmc *·gulthjan* (GOLD)]

gĭld². See GUILD.

gĭll¹ (g-), n. (usu. pl.), & v.t. **1.** Respiratory organ(s) in fishes & other water-·breathing animals; wattles or dewlap of fowls; vertical radiating plates on under side of mushrooms etc.; flesh below person's jaws & ears (*rosy about the ~s*, healthy-looking); ~-*cover*, bony case protecting fish's ~s; ~-*net*, for entangling fishes by the ~s; hence (-)~ED² (-ld) a. **2.** v.t. Gut (fish); cut off ~s of (mush-room); take in ~-net. [ME f. ON, whence Sw. *gäl*, Da. *gjælle*]

|| **gĭll²** (g-), n. Deep usu. wooded ravine; narrow mountain torrent. [ME, f. ON *gil* glen]

gĭll³, n. Quarter-pint liquid measure (||in some parts half-pint). [ME, f. OF *gille*, med. L *gillo*]

Gill⁴, n. Female name; *Jack & ~* (or *Jill*), lad & lass. [ME, abbr. of *Gillian* pop. form f. OF *Juliane* f. L *Juliana* (*Julius*)]

gillaroō′ (g-), n. Irish trout. [f. Ir. *giolla fellow, ruadh* red]

gĭll′ie (g-), n. **1.** (hist.). Highland chief's attendant. **2.** Man or boy attending sportsman in Scotland. [f. Gael. *gille* lad, servant]

gill′ўflower, n. (now rare). Clove-scented pink; other similarly scented flowers, as wallflower, white stock. [ME *gilofre* f. OF *gil-, girofle* f. med. L f. Gk *karuophullon* (*karuon* nut, *phullon* leaf) w. assim. to *flower*]

gĭlt¹ (g-). See GILD¹ (*cloth ~*, book-binding of cloth with ~ letters or tooling).

gĭlt² (g-), n. Gilding (*take the ~ off the gingerbread*, strip thing of adventitious attractions); ~-*edged paper, securities, stocks*, etc., such investments as trustees prefer or are restricted to. [f. prec.]

gilt³ (g-), n. Young sow. [ME, f. ON *gyltr*]

gim'bal, n. (pl. exc. in comb. as ~-*ring* etc.). Contrivance (usu. of rings & pivots) for keeping articles (esp. compass & chronometer) horizontal at sea. [16th c. var. of *gimel* f. ME f. OF *gemel* double finger-ring, f. L *gemellus* dim. of *geminus* twin]

gim'crăck, n. & a. **1.** Trumpery article, knick-knack, useless ornament; hence ~ERY(5) n.,~Y² a. **2.** adj. Showy & flimsy, worthless, trumpery. [ME *gibecrake* (? inlaid work), of unkn. orig.]

gim'lĕt (g-), n. Kind of boring-tool (usu. semi-cylindrical with wooden crosspiece as handle & worm at pointed end). [ME, f. OF *guimbelet*, dim. f. WG *wem-*, whence LG *wemel* boring-tool & obs. *wimble*]

‖ **gimm'er** (g-), n. (dial.). Young ewe; (derog.) woman. [ME, f. ON *gymbr*]

*•**gimm'ick** (g-), n. (sl.). Tricky device, device adopted for the purpose of attracting attention or publicity. [orig. unkn.]

gimp, **gўmp**, (g-), n. Silk, worsted, or cotton twist with cord or wire running through it; fishing-line of silk etc. bound with wire; (Lacemaking) coarser thread outlining design. [f. Du. *gimp* of unkn. orig.]

gin¹, n., & v.t. (-nn-). **1.** Snare, net, trap, (n. & v.t.). **2.** Hoisting apparatus, kinds of crane & windlass. **3.** Machine for separating cotton from its seeds (vb, remove seeds of with this). [ME; aphetic f. OF *engin* ENGINE]

gin², n. Spirit distilled from grain or malt, GENEVA¹; ~ & IT²; *pink* ~, ~ flavoured with angostura bitters; ‖~-*palace*, gaudily decorated public-house; ~ *sling*, American cold drink of ~ flavoured & sweetened. [short for GENEVA¹]

gin'gall (-gawl), **j-**, n. Musket fired from a rest, or light swivel gun, in China & India. [f. Hind. *janjal*]

gin'ger (-j-), n., a., & v.t. **1.** (Plant with) hot spicy root used in cooking & medicine & preserved in syrup or candy as sweet (*black* ~, unscraped, from E. Indies; *white* ~, scraped, from Jamaica; ~ *shall be hot in the mouth*, the love of pleasure is immortal). **2.** Mettle, spirit; stimulation (see vb; ‖~ *group* in Parliament, that urges Government to more decided action). **3.** (Of) light reddish-yellow colour (n. & a.). **4.** ~ *ale, beer, pop*, kinds of aerated ~-flavoured drink; ~ *brandy*, a cordial; ~*bread*, a cake made with treacle & flavoured with ~ (~*bread nut*, small button-like cake of it; *take the* GILT² *off the* ~*bread*), also (as adj., with allusion to fancy and often gilded shapes in which it was made) gaudy, showy, tawdry, (esp. ~*bread Gothic*); ~-*nut*, ~bread nut; ~-*race*, a root of ~, ~ *wine*, a British wine of fermented sugar, water, & bruised~ hence~Y² a. **5.** v.t. Flavour with ~ put ~ up fundament of (horse) to

produce liveliness, (fig.) rouse *up* (person). [OE & LL *gingiber* f. L *zingiber* f. Gk *ziggiberis* f. Skr. *çṛngavera* (*çṛnga* horn, *vera* body)]

gingeräde' (-j-), n. = GINGER *beer*. [f prec. after LEMONADE]

gin'gerlў (-j-), adv. & a. With, showing, extreme caution so as to avoid making a noise or injuring oneself or what is touched or trodden on. [perh. f. OF *gensor* compar. of *gent* graceful f. L *genitus* (well-)born]

gingham (gĭng'am), n. Kind of cotton or linen cloth of dyed yarn often in stripes or checks; (colloq.) umbrella. [f. Du. *gingang* or F *guingan* ult. f. Malay *ginggang* (orig. adj. = striped)]

gin'gili, n. (E.-Ind. plant yielding) a sweet oil. [f. Hind. *jinjali* f. Arab. *juljulan*]

gingiv'al, a. Of the gums. [L *gingiva* gum + -AL]

gingko. Var. of GINKGO.

gin'glўmus (g-, j-), n. (anat.). Hinge-like joint in body with motion only in two directions (e.g. elbow). [f. Gk *gigglumos* hinge]

*•**gink** (g-), n. (sl.). (Queer) fellow, chap.

gink'go (gĭngk'gō), n. (pl. ~*es*). Chinese & Japanese tree with fan-shaped leaves. [f. Jap. *gingko* f. Chin. *yinhing* silver apricot]

gin'sĕng, n. (Root of) medicinal plant found in China, Nepal, Canada, & Eastern U.S. [f. Chin. *jên shên* (*jên* man) perh. = image of man, w. allusion to forked root]

‖ **gipp'ō**, n. (army sl.). Soup, gravy, stew.

‖ **gipp'ў**, n. (army sl.). Egyptian soldier. [abbr.]

gip'sў, **gў-**, n. Member of a wandering race (called by themselves *Romany*) of Hindu origin with dark skin and hair, living by basket-making, horse-dealing, fortune-telling etc., & speaking a much corrupted Hindi; (playful) mischievous or dark-complexioned woman; ~ *bonnet*, with large side flaps; ~ *moth*, European moth very destructive to foliage; ~ *rose*, scabious; ~ *table*, light round one on tripod. Hence~DOM,~HOOD,~ISM(2), nn., ~ISH¹ a., ~FY (usu. in p.p. ~*fied*) v.t. [16th c. *gipcyan* for *Egyptian*, f. supposed orig. of the race when it appeared in England in early 16th c.]

giraffe' (-ahf, -åf), n. African ruminant quadruped with spotted skin & long neck & legs, camelopard. [ult. f. Arab. *zarafah*]

gi'randŏle, n. Revolving firework, discharge of rockets from revolving wheel; revolving jet of water; branched candle bracket or candlestick; ear-ring or pendant with large central stone surrounded by small ones. [F, f. It. *girandola* (*girare* see GYRATE)]

gi'rasŏl(e), n. Kind of opal reflecting reddish glow, fire-opal. [It. (-*e*), f. *girare* see prec. + *sole* sun, orig. = sunflower]

gĭrd¹ (g-), v.t. (poet. or rhet.; ~ed or girt). Encircle (waist, person as to waist) with belt etc. esp. to confine clothes (~ oneself, one's loins, prepare for action, often with up); invest with strength, power, etc.; equip with sword in belt; fasten (sword etc.) on with belt (on adv. or prep., upon, to); secure (clothes) on body with girdle or belt; put (cord etc.) round; encircle (town etc.) with besiegers or siege-works; (of belt, fence, etc.) encircle. [OE gyrdan, OS gurdian, OHG gurten, ON gyrtha f. Gmc *gurthjan (GIRTH)]

gĭrd² (g-), v.i., & n. Jeer, gibe, at. [ME strike etc., orig. unkn.]

gĭrd'er (g-), n. Beam supporting joists of floor; iron or steel beam for like use; latticed or other compound structure of steel etc. forming span of bridge, roof, etc. [GIRD¹ + -ER¹]

gĭr'dle¹ (g-), n., & v.t. **1.** Belt or (now usu.) cord used to gird waist; (orig. U.S.) corset; something that surrounds like a ~; part of cut gem dividing crown from base & embraced by the setting; (Anat.) bony supports for upper & lower limbs (shoulder or pectoral, pelvic or hip, ~); ring round tree made by removal of bark. **2.** v.t. Surround with ~ (often about, in, round); kill (tree) or make it more fruitful by girdling. [OE gyrdel, OHG gurtil, ON gyrthill (GIRD¹, -LE(1))]

‖ gĭr'dle² (g-), n. (Sc. & north.). Circular iron plate placed over fire for toasting cakes; ~-cake, so made. [var. of GRIDDLE]

gĭrl (g-), n. Female child, unmarried woman, (old ~), affectionate or disrespectful address or description for woman, mare, etc.; the ~s, daughters of family, married or not); maidservant; man's sweetheart (often best ~); female (~ friend); ~ guides, organization parallel to boy SCOUT. Hence ~'HOOD, ~'ie [-Y³], nn., ~'ISH¹ a., ~'ishLY² adv., ~'ishNESS n., (g-). [ME gurle, girle, gerle, perh. cogn. w. LG gör child]

Girŏn'dist, n. & a. (Member) of moderate republican party in French assembly 1791–3; (person) of such views. [f. F Girondiste (Gironde French department from which leaders of party came)]

gĭrt¹ (g-), n., & v.t. **1.** Measurement across or round surface that is not flat, with account taken of elevations & depressions. **2.** v.t. Measure ~ of; (of trees etc.) measure (so much) in ~. [var. of GIRTH]

gĭrt². See GIRD¹.

gĭrth (g-), n., & v.t. & i. **1.** Leather or cloth band tightened round body of horse etc. to secure saddle etc.; measurement round any more or less cylindrical thing; ~-web, woven material for ~s. **2.** vb. Surround; encircle (horse etc.), secure (saddle etc.), with ~; measure (so much) in ~. [ME, f. ON gjorth, Goth. gairda f. Gmc *gerda, cogn. w. GARTH, GIRD¹]

gist (j-), n. Real ground or point, substance or pith of a matter. [OF, 3rd sing. pres. of gesir lie f. L jacēre]

gitt'ern (g-), n. Gut-stringed instrument, kind of early guitar. [ME, f. OF guiterne; cf. CITHERN, GUITAR]

give¹ (g-), v.t. & i. (gāve, gĭv'en). (General sense) make another the recipient of something in subject's possession or at subject's disposal (with obj. of thing given, & ind. obj. usu. preceding obj. if without to & following it if with to; in pass., either obj. may become subj., the other being retained without to if direct, with or without to if indirect. Thus : I gave him a book; I gave £50 to the R.S.P.C.A.; I gave it him; he was ~n a book; a book was ~n him; the R.S.P.C.A. was ~n £50; £50 was ~n to, or ~n, the R.S.P.C.A. Corresponding constructions are to be assumed with the various senses unless they are inapplicable or exceptions are mentioned). **1.** Bestow gratuitously, hand over as present, confer ownership of with or without actual delivery, render (benefit etc.) without payment, (abs.) bestow alms or donations (to); confer, grant, (favour, honour, etc.); accord (one's heart, affection, confidence); (of God etc.) grant (faculty etc., or to be or do; ~ me, in imperat., I prefer or admire, as ~ me the good old times); bequeath; sanction marriage of (daughter etc.; usu. in marriage). **2.** Deliver, hand over, without reference to ownership, put (food etc.) before one, (~ MITTEN, SACK¹, BOOT¹, cf. GET), administer (medicine); deliver (message, love, compliments, etc.); commit, consign, entrust, (~ into custody or in CHARGE¹); pledge, assign as guarantee, (one's word, honour, etc.). **3.** Make over in exchange for payment, pay, sell for price, (~ as good as one gets, retort adequately in words or blows; so ~ a ROLAND for an Oliver; ~ one his due, admit any merits he may have; would ~ the world, one's ears, make any sacrifice to secure or for something, or if). **4.** Devote, dedicate, addict, (gave his life to it; much ~n to these pursuits). **5.** Put forth (some action or effort) to affect another or simply (~ him a kick; ~ a jump, cry, etc.; ~ orders; ~ person one's blessing; ~ you joy, prob. orig. with ellipse of God, now taken as = wish with I expressed or omitted; ~ the time of day, say good morning, evening, etc.); deliver (judgement etc.) authoritatively (~ the case, or it, for or against person; in cricket, ~ batsman out or not out); (p.p., of document) dated; provide (ball, party, dinner) as host. **6.** Present, offer, expose, hold out, show, (~ person one's hand; ~ a back, stand to be leapfrogged over; The Times ~s the facts; ~s no sign of life; thermometer ~s 80° in the shade); read, recite, sing, act, perform, (piece etc.). **7.** Make partaker of, impart, be source of, (gave me his sore throat; gave its name to the battle; ~ *a piece of* one's *mind*, scold, reproach; ~ *to the world*, publish; ~ person *to understand, know*, etc., inform, assure). **8.** Allot, assign, ascribe, grant, assume, (*he was* ~*n the contract, the name of John, quarters*; *under the* ~*n conditions*; ~*n health, the thing can be done*). **9.** Yield as product or result (*lamps* ~ *a bad light*; *analysis* ~*s the following figures*). **10.** Cause or allow to have (*solitude* ~*s it its only charm*; *gave me much pain*; *this* ~*s him a right to complain*; ~ one*self trouble*, take pains; ~ one*self airs*, be pretentious; *gave myself an hour to get there*; *was* ~*n a 'rest*). **11.** Collapse, lose firmness, yield to pressure, become relaxed, make room, shrink. **12.** (Of window, passage, etc.) look, lead, (*up*)*on*, *into*. **13.** (In phrr. with obj.): ‖~ one *best* (colloq.), admit his superiority; ~ *birth to*, bring forth (lit. & fig.); ~ *chase*, start in pursuit; ~ *ear*, listen; ~ *ground*, retreat; ~ *it him* etc., administer punishment (often *hot*); ~ *child* etc. *something to cry for*, chastise for causeless crying; ~ one *what for*, sl., punish or scold; ~ *place* (*to*), make room (for), yield precedence (to), be superseded (by); ~ *rise to*, occasion; ~ TONGUE; ~ *way*, retire, fail to resist, be superseded by (*to*), be dislodged, break down, make concessions, abandon oneself *to* grief etc., fall in price, begin to row or row harder. **14.** (With advv.); ~ *away*, alienate by gift, hand over (bride) to bridegroom, betray or expose to ridicule or detection (esp. sl. ~ *away the* SHOW[2]), distribute (prizes); ~ *back*, restore; ~ *forth*, emit, publish, report; ~ *in*, yield, cease fighting or arguing, hand in (document) to proper official, (p.p.) added as supplement; ~ *off*, emit (vapour etc.); ~ *out*, announce, emit, distribute, cease or break down from exhaustion etc., run short; ~ *over*, cease from do*ing*, abandon (habit etc.), desist, hand over (~*n over*, abandoned *to* evil courses etc.); ~ *up*, resign, surrender, part with (~ *up the* GHOST), deliver (fugitive etc.) into hands of pursuers etc., abandon one*self to* a feeling etc., cease to have to do with, cease from effort, (refl. & p.p.) devote or addict *to*, divulge (names of accomplices etc.), pronounce incurable or insoluble, renounce hope of. Hence **gĭv′ER**[1] (g-) n. [OE *giefan*, OS, OHG *geban*, ON *gefa*, Goth. *giban* f. Gmc **gebhan*; initial *g*- due to Scand., as in GET]

give[2] (g-), n. Yielding to pressure, elasticity, (*there is no* ~ *in a stone floor*); ~ *& take*, mutual concession, compromise, exchange of talk. [f. prec.]

gĭv′en (g-), a. In vbl senses; **~ name*, CHRISTIAN name. [p.p. of GIVE[1]]

gĭzz′ard (g-), n. Bird's second stomach for grinding the food mixed in the first with gastric juice; specially muscular stomach of some fish, insects, & molluscs;

fret one's ~, worry; *sticks in* one's ~, is unpalatable (fig.). [ME *giser* f. OF *g(u)iser* f. L *gigeria* cooked entrails of fowl]

glāb′rous, a. (anat. etc.). Free from hair or down, smooth-skinned. [f. L *glaber* + -OUS]

gla′cé (-ah-sā), a. (Of cloth, leather, etc.) smooth, polished; (of fruits) iced, sugared. [F]

gla′cial (-āsĭal, -āshĭal, -āshl), a. Of ice, icy; (Chem.) crystallized; (Geol.) characterized, produced, by the presence or agency of ice (~ *epoch, era, period*, when northern hemisphere was mostly covered with ice-sheet). Hence ~LY[2] adv. [f. F, or L *glacialis* (*glacies* ice, -AL)]

gla′ciātĕd (-sĭ-, -shĭ-), a. Marked or polished by ice-action; covered with glaciers or ice-sheet. So **glāciA′TION** n. [p.p. of *glaciate* f. L *glaciare* freeze, -ATE[3]]

glā′cier, n. Slowly moving river or mass of ice formed by accumulation of snow on high ground. Hence ~ED[2] (-erd) a. [F (*glace* ice)]

gla′cis (*or* glahsē′), n. Bank sloping down from fort, on which attackers are exposed to fire. [F, orig. = slippery place (OF *glacier* to slip)]

glăd, a., & v.t. (-dd-). **1.** Pleased (pred. only; *I am* ~, ~ *of it*, ~ *to hear it*, ~ *that it is so*, ~ *it is so, shall be* ~ *to come* etc.; iron., *should be* ~ *to know*); (of looks, feelings, etc.) marked by, filled with, expressing, joy; (of news or events) giving joy; (of nature etc.) bright, beautiful; *the* ~ *eye* (sl.), amorous or festive glance; ~ *hand* (orig. U.S.), the hand of welcome; ~ *rags* (sl.), Sunday or dress clothes; hence ~d′EN[6] v.t., ~′LY[2] adv., ~′NESS n., (poet.) ~′SOME a., ~′someLY[2] adv., ~′someNESS n. **2.** v.t. (arch.). Make ~. [OE *glæd*, OS *glad*, ON *glathr*, OHG *glat* smooth (the orig. sense), cogn. w. L *glaber*]

glāde, n. Clear open space or passage between forest trees. [orig. unkn.]

glăd′iātor, n. Man trained to fight with sword or other weapon at ancient Roman shows; political etc. champion in argument, controversialist. So **glădiatō′rIAL** a. [L (*gladius* sword)]

glădiōl′us (*or* gladi′o-), n. (pl. -*li*, -*luses*). Iridaceous plant with sword-shaped leaves & bright flower-spikes. [L, dim. of *gladius* sword]

Glăd′stone, n. & a. ~ (*bag*), kind of light portmanteau; ~ *claret*, cheap kinds that became common by Gladstone's reduction of duty 1860. [W.E. ~, statesman d. 1898]

glair, n., & v.t. **1.** White of egg; kinds of adhesive preparation made from it; any similar viscid substance; hence ~′EOUS, ~′Y[2], aa. **2.** v.t. Smear with ~. [ME, f. OF *glaire*, ult. f. L *clara* fem. of *clarus* CLEAR]

glaive, n. (arch. & poet.). Broadsword, sword. [ME, OF, app. f. L *gladius* sword]

glăm'our (-er), n., & v.t. 1. Magic, enchantment, (cast a ~ over, enchant); delusive or alluring beauty or charm; hence glăm'orous a. 2. v.t. Affect with ~, bewitch, enchant. [18th c. var. of GRAMMAR in sense GRAMARYE]

glance¹ (-ah-), v.i. & t., & n. 1. (Of weapon) glide off object instead of striking it full (often aside, off); (of talk or talker) pass quickly over, glide off or from, subject; ~ at, make passing & usu. sarcastic allusion to; (of bright object or light) flash, dart, gleam; (of eye) cast momentary look, flash, (~ at, give brief look at); ~ over, read cursorily; ~ down, up, etc.; ~ one's eye, direct it at, over, etc.; hence glan'cingLY² (-ah-) adv. 2. n. Swift oblique movement or impact, (Cricket) stroke with bat's face turned slantwise to ball; (sudden movement producing) flash or gleam; brief look (at, into, over, etc.). [15 c. glence etc. prob. a nasalized form of obs. glace in same sense, f. OF glacier slip]

glance² (-ah-), n. Lustrous ore (copper ~, native copper sulphide; lead ~, GALENA). [f. G glanz lustre]

glănd¹, n. (Physiol.) simple or complex organ composed of nucleated cells secreting constituents of the blood for use or ejection; (Bot.) secreting cell or group of cells on surface of plant-structure. So (see -UL-) glän'dULE n., glän'dÜLAR¹, ~ülif'EROUS, glän'dÜLOSE¹ (Bot.), glän'dÜLOUS, ~'LESS, aa. [f. F glande f. OF glandre f. L glandula (glans -dis acorn, -ULE)]

glănd², n. (mech.). Sleeve used to press a packing tight on a piston. [orig. unkn.]

glăn'der|s (-z), n. pl. Contagious horse-disease with swellings below jaw & mucous discharge from nostrils; the same communicated to man. Hence ~ĒD² (-erd), ~OUS, aa. [f. OF glandre see GLAND¹]

glăndif'erous, a. Bearing acorns. [f. L glandifer (GLAND¹, -FEROUS)]

glän'diform, a. Acorn-shaped; like gland. [GLAND¹, -FORM]

glār|e, v.i. & t., & n. 1. Shine dazzlingly or disagreeably; be over-conspicuous or obtrusive, whence ~'ingLY² adv., ~'ingNESS n.; look fixedly or fiercely (at, upon); express (hate, defiance) by look. 2. n. Strong fierce light, oppressive unrelieved sunshine; tawdry brilliance; fierce or fixed look; hence ~'Y² a. [ME, = MDu. & MLG glaren]

glass¹ (-ah-), n. 1. Substance, usu. transparent, lustrous, hard, & brittle, made by fusing sand with soda or potash or both & other ingredients (CROWN¹, FLINT, PLATE, WATER¹, ~); substances of similar properties or composition, as ~ of antimony, vitreous oxy-sulphide fused. 2. ~ utensils, ornaments, windows, greenhouses; ~ vessel esp. for drinking, amount of liquid contained in this, drink (a friendly ~, fond of his ~; has had a ~ too much,

is rather drunk); sand-~, hour-~; carriage window; plate of ~ covering picture; glazed frame for plants; looking-~; eye-~, (pl.) pair of spectacles; lens; ~ disc covering watch-face; telescope, spy-~, field-~, opera-~, microscope; barometer, weather-~. 3. ~-blower, one who blows & shapes ~; ~ case, chiefly of ~ for exhibiting or protecting objects; ~-cloth, linen cloth for drying ~es, cloth covered with powdered ~ like ~-paper; ~ cloth, woven fabric of fine-spun ~; ~-cutter, workman, tool, cutting ~; ~-culture, of plants under ~; ~-dust, powdered ~ for polishing; ~ eye, false eye of ~, kind of blindness in horses; ~'house, building where ~ is made, greenhouse, ~-roofed photographing-room, || (sl.) military prison; ~-paper, covered with ~-dust; ~ snake, snake-like lizard of Southern U.S., with very brittle tail; ~'ware, articles made of ~; ~ wool, ~ in form of fine fibres for packing & insulation; ~'wort, kinds of plant formerly used in ~-making. Hence ~'FUL(2) n., ~'LESS a. [OE glæs, OS, OHG glas f. WG *glas]

glass² (-ah-), v.t. Fit with glass, glaze, (rare); enclose in glass (rare); make (the eye) glassy (rare); mirror, occasion reflection of (often refl., as trees ~ themselves in the lake); ~-ing-jack, machine used in dressing leather. [f. prec., cf. earlier GLAZE]

glass'|y (-ah-), a. Having properties of, resembling, glass; (of eye etc.) lacking fire, dull, fixed; (of water) lustrous & transparent, or smooth, as glass (so ~y calm, surface, etc.). Hence ~ILY² adv., ~INESS n. [-Y²]

Gläswē'gian (-z-), a. & n. (Inhabitant) of Glasgow. [perh. on GALWEGIAN]

Glaub'er's salt(s) (glaw-, glow-), n. Crystalline (hydrated) sodium sulphate. [J. R. Glauber, German chemist (d. 1668)]

glaucōm'a, n. An eye-disease with tension of the globe & gradual loss of sight. Hence ~tOUS a. [f. L f. Gk glaukōma f. glaukos (foll.)]

glauc'ous, a. (esp. nat. hist.). Of dull greyish green or blue; (Bot.) covered with bloom as of grapes. [f. L f. Gk glaukos -OUS]

glāze, v.t. & i., & n. 1. Fit (window, picture) with glass, furnish (building) with glass windows (~ in, enclose thus). 2. Cover (pottery etc.) with vitreous substance fixed by fusion (n., this substance, smooth surface resulting); fix (paint) on pottery thus; overlay (cloth, leather, pastry, etc.) with smooth lustrous coating (n., this coating, surface produced). 3. Cover (eye) with a film (n., filmy look). 4. Cover (painted surface) with thin coat of different transparent colour to modify tone (n., this coat). 5. Give glassy surface to, e.g. by rubbing (n., polished look); become glassy (esp. of eyes); ~d frost,

= SILVER[1] *thaw*. Hence **glāz′ER**[1](1, 2) n., **glāz′Y**[2] a. [ME *glasen* (GLASS[1])]

glā′zier (-zher, -zĭer), n. One whose trade is to glaze windows etc. Hence **glā′ziERY** (2) n. [GLASS[1]; see -IER]

glāz′ing, n. In vbl senses also : windows; material used to produce glaze. [-ING[1]]

gleam, n., & v.i. **1.** Subdued or transient light; faint, temporary, or intermittent show of some quality etc. (*an occasional* ~ *of humour*; *not a* ~ *of hope*); hence ~′Y[2] a. **2.** v.i. Emit ~s, shine with subdued or interrupted brightness. [OE *glǣm*, cogn. w. OS *glīmo*, MHG *glīmen* shine, OHG *gleimo* glow-worm, WG *glaim-*]

glean, v.i. & t. Gather ears of corn left by reapers, gather (such remains); strip (field etc.) thus; collect in small quantities, scrape together, (news, facts, etc.). Hence ~′ER[1], ~′ING[1](1, 2), nn. [ME, f. OF *glener* f. LL *glennare*, of Celt. orig.]

glēbe, n. (Poet.) earth, land, a field; portion of land going with clergyman's benefice. [ME, f. L *gleba* clod, soil]

glee, n. **1.** Musical composition for three or more (prop. adult male) voices, one to each part, set to words grave or gay, often with contrasted movements & prop. without accompaniment. **2.** Mirth, lively & manifest delight, whence ~′FUL, ~′SOME, aa., ~′fuLLY[2] adv. [OE *glīw*, *glēo*, ON *glý*]

gleet, n. Thin morbid discharge from wound, ulcer, etc. (rare), or from the urethra. Hence ~′Y[2] a. [ME *glet* f. OF *glette* slime]

glēn, n. Narrow valley. [f. Gael. *gleann*]

glēn′doveer, n. Beautiful sprite of kind represented by Southey as occurring in Hindu myths. [altered f. *grandouver* in F travel-book perh. f. Skr. *gandharva* semi-divine spirit]

glĕngă′rrў (-n-g-), n. Kind of Highland cap. [place]

glēn′oid, a. (anat.). ~ *cavity*, *fossa*, *surface*, shallow cavity on bone (esp. scapula & temporal bone) receiving projection of other bone to form joint. [f. Gk *glēnoeidēs* (*glēnē* socket, -OID)]

glib, a. & adv. (-bb-). **1.** (Of surface etc.) smooth, offering no resistance, (of movement) unimpeded, easy, (rare); (of speaker, speech, etc.) fluent, ready, more voluble than sincere or thoughtful; hence ~′LY[2] adv., ~′NESS n. **2.** adv. Volubly (now rare). [rel. to obs. *glibbery* = MLG *glibberich*, Du. -*ig*, perh. of imit. orig.]

glĭd|e, v.i. & t., & n. **1.** Pass, change place, by smooth continuous movement (of liquid, ship, bird, carriage, snake, person skating, etc.); fly without engine (~′ER[1](2) n., engineless aeroplane); go quietly or stealthily; (of time etc.) pass gently & imperceptibly; pass gradually, shade off insensibly, *into*; cause to ~e (*light airs* ~*ed her on her course*); hence ~′ingLY[2] adv. **2.** n. Act of ~ing; (Mus.)

succession of sounds made in passing from one note to another without silencing voice or instrument; (Phon.) gradually changing sound made in passing from one position of speech organs to another. [OE, OS *glidan*, OHG *glītan*]

glim, n. (sl.). Light, candle, lantern, (DOUSE *the*~). [in 17th c. cant perh. short. f. GLIMMER or GLIMPSE, but cf. MDu., MHG *glimmen*]

glimm′er, v.i., & n. **1.** Shine faintly or intermittently. **2.** n. (Also ~ING[1] n.) feeble or wavering light, faint gleam of hope etc., glimpse, half view. [ME, cogn. w. MHG, Du. *glimmern*, (cf. Sw. *glimra*) f. WG *glim-*, *glaim-* (GLEAM)]

glimpse, n., & v.t. & i. **1.** Faint & transient appearance, momentary or imperfect view of, (*the* ~*s of the moon*, the earth by night, sublunary affairs). **2.** vb. Catch ~ of, see faintly or partly; (poet.) appear faintly, dawn. [ME *glimse*, corresp. to MHG *glimsen* f. WG *glimisōjan* (prec.)]

glint, v.i. & t., & n. Flash, glitter, sparkle, (v. & n.); make flash, reflect, (light). [n. f. vb, alt. of ME *glent* of Scand. orig., cf. Sw. *glänta*, *glinta*]

glissade′ (-ahd, -ād), n., & v.i. (mountaineering). Slide (n. & v.) down steep slope esp. of ice or snow usu. on the feet with support of ice-axe etc. [vb f. n., F (*glisser* slip, -ADE)]

glissé (glĭsā′), n. A sliding step in ballet in which the flat of the foot is freq. used (also *pas* ~). [F]

glis′ten (-Isn), v.i., & n. Shine fitfully; glitter, sparkle, (v. & n.). [n. f. vb, OE *glisnian* (*glisian* shine, -EN[6])]

glis′ter, v.i., & n., (arch.). Sparkle, glitter. [ME, f. MLG *glistern*, MDu. -*eren*, cogn. w. prec.]

glitt′er, v.i., & n. (Shine with) brilliant tremulous light, gleam, sparkle; be showy or splendid (*with* jewels etc.). [ME, f. ON *glitra* f. Gmc *glit-*]

gloam′ing, n. Evening twilight. [OE *glōmung* (*glōm* twilight cogn. w. GLOW, -ING[1])]

gloat, v.i. Feast eyes or mind lustfully, avariciously, malignantly, etc., (*up*)*on* or *over*. Hence ~′ingLY[2] adv. [orig. unkn., but perh. cogn. w. ON *glotta* grin, MHG *glotzen* stare]

glōbe, n., & v.t. & i. **1.** Spherical body; *the* earth; planet, star, sun; spherical chart of (*terrestrial* ~) the earth or (*celestial* ~) the constellations (*use of the* ~*s*, arch., teaching of geography & astronomy by these); golden orb as emblem of sovereignty; (Anat.) eyeball; approximately spherical glass vessel, esp. lampshade or fishbowl; ~-*fish*, able to inflate itself into globular form; ~-*flower*, ranunculaceous plant with round yellow flowers; ~ *lightning*, = FIRE[1]-*ball*; ~-*trotter*, -*trotting*, hurried traveller, travelling, through foreign countries for sightseeing; so **glōb′AL** (1) a. world-wide, embracing the totality of a group of items, categories, etc., **glob'oid** a. & n., **globose'** [1] a., **globos'ity** n. 2. vb. Make (usu. in pass.), or become, globular. [F, f. L *globus*]

glob'ular, a. Globe-shaped, spherical; composed of globules. Hence ~**ity** (-å'r-) n., ~**ly²** adv. [foll., -AR¹, & see -UL-]

glob'ule, n. Small globe or round particle, drop, pill. [f. F, or L *globulus* (GLOBE, -ULE)]

glob'ulin, n. Protein found usu. associated with albumen in animal tissues. [prec., -IN]

glochid'iate (-k-), a. (bot.). Barbed at tip. [f. Gk *glōkhidion* (*glōkhis* arrowhead), -ATE²]

glock'enspiel (-pēl), n. Musical instrument consisting of a series of metal bars struck by a hammer (earlier, a kind of CARILLON). [G, = bell-play]

glom'erate, a. (bot., anat.). Compactly clustered. [L *glomerare* (*glomus -eris* ball), -ATE²]

glom'erule (-ōōl), n. Clustered flower-head; cluster of small organisms, tissues, blood-vessels, etc. [f. mod. L *glomerulus* (L *glomus* see prec., -ULE)]

gloom¹, n. Darkness, obscurity; melancholy, despondency. [orig. f. foll.; sense 'darkness' perh. back form. f. GLOOMY]

gloom², v.i. & t. Look sullen, frown, be melancholy; (of sky etc.) lour, be dull or threatening; appear darkly or obscurely; cover with gloom, make dark or dismal. [ME *gloume* of unkn. orig.; cf. GLUM]

gloom'|y, a. Dark, unlighted; depressed, sullen; dismal, depressing. Hence ~**ily²** adv., ~**iness** n. [perh. f. prec. +-Y²]

glor'ia, n. (Short for) G~ *Patri*, doxology *Glory be to the Father* etc., G~ *tibi*, response *Glory be to thee* etc., or G~ *in excelsis*, hymn *Glory be to God on high*; aureole. [L, = glory]

glor'i|fy, v.t. Make glorious, exalt to the glory of heaven; invest with radiance; transform into something more splendid, invest (common or inferior thing) with charm or beauty (*nothing more than a* ~*fied*, or ~*fication of a, cottage*); extol, laud. Hence ~**fica'tion** n. [ME, f. OF *glorifier* f. LL *glorificare* (*glorificus* f. L *gloria* glory, -FIC)]

glor'iole, n. Aureole, halo. [F, f. L *gloriola* dim. of *gloria* glory]

glor'ious, a. Possessing glory, illustrious; conferring glory, honourable; splendid, magnificent, intensely delightful, (*a* ~ *view, day*; also joc., as ~ *fun*; & iron., as *the* ~ *uncertainty of cricket, a* ~ *muddle*); (colloq.) ecstatically happy with drink. Hence~**ly²** adv. [ME, f. AF f. L *gloriosus* (foll., -OSE¹)]

glor'y|¹, n. Exalted renown, honourable fame; subject for boasting, special distinction, ornament, pride; adoring praise & thanksgiving (~ *be!* or ~ *!*, vulgar excl. of surprise or delight); resplendent majesty, beauty, or magnificence, effulgence of heavenly light, imagined unearthly beauty; bliss & splendour of heaven (*go to* ~, die; *send to* ~, joc., kill); state of exaltation, prosperity, etc. (*is in his* ~); circle of light round head or figure of deity or saint, aureole, halo; ~*hole* (sl.), untidy room, drawer, or receptacle. [ME, f. L *gloria*]

glor'y², v.i. Exult, pride oneself, *in* thing or doing, *to* do. Hence ~**ingly²** adv. [ME, f. L *gloriari* boast (*gloria* glory)]

gloss¹, n., & v.t. & i. 1. Word inserted between lines or in margin to explain word in text; comment, explanation, interpretation, paraphrase; misrepresentation of another's words; glossary, interlinear translation, or set of notes. 2. vb. Insert~es in (text etc.); write~es; make comments esp. of unfavourable sort; read different sense into, explain away. [16th c. alt. of GLOZE after L *glossa*]

gloss², n., & v.t. 1. Superficial lustre; deceptive appearance, fair outside; hence ~**'y²** a., ~**'ily²** adv., ~**'iness** n. 2. v.t. Make ~y; give specious appearance to (often *over*). [vb f. n.; 16th c. of unkn. orig.; cf. obs. Du. *gloos*, Icel. *glossi*, nn., glow, blaze]

gloss'al, a. (anat.). Of the tongue, lingual. [f. Gk *glōssa* tongue +-AL]

gloss'ar|y, n. Collection of glosses; list & explanations of abstruse, obsolete, dialectal, or technical terms, partial dictionary. Hence **glōssār'ial** a., ~**ist**(1) n. [f. L *glossarium* (*glossa* GLOSS¹, -ARY¹)]

glóssāt'or, n. Commentator, esp. mediéval commentator on Civil & Canon Law. [med. L (*glossare* f. *glossa* GLOSS¹, -OR)]

glôss(o)-, comb. form of Gk *glōssa* tongue, as *gloss'*(o)-*epiglŏtt'ic* of tongue & epiglottis, *glossit'is*; also of GLOSS¹, as *glossōg'rapher* commentator, *glossōl'ogy* terminology.

glŏtt'|is, n. Opening at upper part of windpipe & between vocal chords, affecting modulation of voice by contracting or dilating. Hence ~**al** (~*al stop*, sound produced by the sudden explosive release of breath from behind the closed ~is), ~**ic**, aa. [Gk *glōttis* (*glōtta* var. of *glōssa* tongue)]

glove (-ŭv), n., & v.t. 1. Covering of leather, cotton, silk, wool, or formerly steel, for the hand, usu. with separated fingers (*throw down, take up, the* ~, make, accept, challenge; *fit like a* ~, exactly; HAND¹ *in* or *& ~*); (also boxing-~) padded ~ for boxing (*take off, without*, etc., *the* ~s, of arguing or contending in earnest, mercilessly, etc.); ~*fight*, fight with boxing-~s; ~*-sponge*, in shape of ~; ~*-stretcher*, instrument for enlarging ~-*fingers*; hence ~**LESS** (-ŭvl-) a., **glo'ver**[1] (3) (-ŭv-) n. 2. v.t. Provide with~s. [OE *glōf*, ON *glōfi*, perh. f. Gmo *galōfō* (*ga-* = ȳ-, cf. Goth. *lōfa* hand)]

glow (-ō), v.i., & n. 1. Be heated to

incandescence, throw out light & heat without flame; shine like thing intensely heated; show warm colour; burn with bodily heat or emotional fervour (*with*); ~-*worm*, coleopterous insect with winged male & wingless female, the latter emitting green light at tail; hence ~'ingLY² adv. **2.** n. ~ing state (*in a* ~, *all of a* ~, hot or flushed); brightness & warmth of colour, e.g. red of cheeks; ardour, passion; ~-*lamp*, with carbon etc. incandescent under electric current. [OE *glōwan*, OS *glōjan*, OHG *gluoen*, ON *glóa*]

glower (-owr), v.i. Stare, scowl, (usu. *at*). Hence ~'ingLY² adv. [orig. uncert.; perh. var. of 14th c. *glore* (Sc. dial.), or f. obs. (ME) *glow* stare + -ER⁵]

glŏxin'ia, n. American tropical plant with large bell flowers of various colours. [B. P. *Gloxin* botanist *c.* 1785 + -IA¹]

glōze, v.i. & t. ‖ Comment (*up*)*on* (arch.); palliate, explain away, extenuate, (usu. *over*); talk speciously, use fair words, fawn. Hence **glōz'ing**LY² adv. [ME, f. OF *gloser* f. *glose* f. L f. Gk *glōssa* (foreign) tongue or word; cf. GLOSS¹]

glucin'um (-ōōs-), n. White metal obtained from beryl, beryllium. [f. Gk *glukus* sweet (some compds of it being sweet)]

glu'cŏse (glōō-), n. (chem.). Grape-sugar or dextrose, commercially prepared from starch and other carbohydrates by hydrolysis. Hence **glucŏs'ic** a., **glu'cosIDE** n., (glōō-). [F, f. Gk *gleukos*, see -OSE²]

glue (-ōō), n., & v.t. **1.** Hard brittle brownish gelatin made by boiling hides & bones & used warm for uniting substances; adhesive or viscous substance got from other sources (*fish, vegetable, casein, resin,* ~); ~-*pot*, with outer coat holding water to heat ~; hence ~'Y² (glōō'ĭ) a. **2.** v.t. (part. *gluing*). Fasten or join (as) with ~; attach tightly or closely (*eye, ear,* ~*d to the keyhole*). [ME, f. OF *glu* f. LL *glus glutis*]

glŭm, a. Sullen, looking dejected or displeased. Hence ~'LY² adv., ~'NESS n. [rel. to dial. *glum* vb frown, var. of *gloume* GLOOM²]

glume (-ōōm), n. (bot.). Chafflike bract in inflorescence of grasses & sedges; husk of grain. Hence **gluma'ceous**, **glumose'**¹, aa., (-ōōm-). [f. L *gluma*]

glŭt, v.t. (-tt-), & n. **1.** Feed (person, stomach) or indulge (appetite, desire) to the full, overload with food (lit. or fig.), satiate, cloy; choke up, fill to excess; overstock (market) with goods. **2.** n. Full indulgence, one's fill, surfeit; supply exceeding demand (*a* ~ *in the market*). [n. f. vb ME f. OF *gloutir* swallow f. L *gluttire*]

glu't|ĕn (glōō-), n. Sticky substance, whence ~in**IZE**(3) v.t., ~**inous** a., ~**inousLY**² adv.,~**inos'ITY** n., (-ōō-); viscid animal secretion; nitrogenous part of

flour remaining as viscid substance when starch is washed out. [F, or f. L, genit. -*inis*, glue]

glütt'on, n. Excessive eater, gormandizer; greedy reader *of books*, person with great appetite *for work*; voracious animal of weasel kind but larger, wolverene. Hence or cogn. ~**IZE**(2) v.i., ~**ous** a., ~**ousLY**² adv.,~**Y**¹ n. [ME, f. OF *gluton*, -*un* f. L *gluttonem* nom. -*o* (*glutire* swallow)]

glÿ'cerināte, v.t. Treat with glycerine (esp. vaccine lymph). [-ATE³]

glÿ'cer|ine (-ēn), -**in**, n. Colourless sweet liquid got from any fatty substance, liquid or solid, by saponification, used as ointment, as vehicle for drugs, in explosives, etc. Hence **glÿcĕ'ric** a. (chem.), ~**ATE**¹ (3), ~**IDE**, ~**YL**, nn., ~**o**- comb. form. [f. F -*ine* f. Gk *glukeros* sweet, -IN]

glÿ'cerŏl, n. (chem.). (Name preferred in scientific use for) glycerine. [prec., -OL(1)]

glÿco-, comb. form, irreg. for *glycy*-, of Gk *glukus* sweet, also used in names of chem. compounds containing glycerol or other substance in *glyc*-.

glÿc'ogĕn, n., **glÿcogĕn'ic**, a., (chem.). (Substance) producing glucose in animal tissues. So **glÿcoGEN'ESIS** n. [prec., -GEN(1)]

glÿc'ŏl, n. Any aliphatic dihydric alcohol, esp. ethylene glycol. Hence **glÿcŏl(l)'ic** a. [GLYCO-, -OL(1)]

glÿcŏn'ic, a. & n. (Gk & L pros.). (Line, metre) normally of the form (‾ × ‾ × × ‾ × × ‾ ×). [*Glukōn* Gk poet, -IC]

glÿcosūr'|ia, n. (path.). Diseased condition with sugar in the urine. Hence ~**ic** a. [F *glycose* GLUCOSE, Gk *ouron* urine, -IA¹]

glÿph'ograph (-ahf), **glÿphŏg'raphÿ**, nn. (Plate or copy, -*ph*, made by) electrotype process giving raised copy of engraved plate for use in letterpress printing (-*y*). So **glÿph'ograph** (-ahf) v.t. & i., **glÿphŏg'rapher** n., **glÿpho-GRAPH'IC** a. [f. Gk *gluphē* carving (*gluphō* carve), -GRAPHY]

glÿp'tic, a. Of carving esp. on precious stones. [Gk *gluptikos* (*gluphō* carve, -IC)]

glÿp'todŏn, n. Extinct S.-Amer. quadruped allied to armadillos with fluted teeth. [f. Gk *gluptos* carved (as prec.) + *odous -ontos* tooth]

glÿptŏg'raphÿ, n. Art & science of gem-engraving. [as prec., -GRAPHY]

*****G-man**, n. (sl.). Federal criminal investigation officer. [Government]

gnarled (nārld), **gnārl'ÿ** (n-), aa. (Of tree; & fig.) covered with protuberances, twisted, rugged. [var. of obs. *knurled*, f. *knurl* knob (=MLG, MDu., MHG *knorre*); -ED², -Y²]

gnăsh (n-), v.i. & t. (Of teeth) strike together; grind the teeth, grind (the teeth). [var. of (north.) ME *gnast*, rel. to ON *gnastan* (imit.)]

gnăt (n-), n. Small two-winged fly of

which female has blood-sucking proboscis; (as type) insignificant annoyance, tiny thing, (strain at ~, be scrupulous about trifles). [OE gnætt, cogn. w. LG gnatte, G dial. gnatze]

gnǎth'ic (n-), a. Of jaws. [Gk gnathos jaw, -IC]

gnaw (n-), v.t. & i. (p.p. ~ed, ~n). Bite persistently, wear away thus (often away, off, in two, etc.; also intr. with at, into); (of destructive agents, pain, etc.) corrode, waste away, consume, torture. Hence ~'ingLY² adv. [OE, OS, OHG gnagan, ON gnaga]

gneiss (gnīs, nīs), n. (geol.). Laminated rock of quartz, feldspar, & mica. Hence ~'IC, ~'OID, ~'OSE¹, ~'Y², aa. [G]

gnōm'ē¹ (n-; also nōm), n. Maxim, aphorism. [f. Gk gnōmē (gignōskō know)]

gnome² (nōm), n. Diminutive spirit of subterranean race guarding treasures of earth (cf. SYLPH, SALAMANDER, NYMPH), goblin, dwarf. Hence gnōm'ISH¹ (n-) a. [F, f. mod. L gnomus (Paracelsus), perh. irreg. or erron. for genomos (Gk gē earth, -nomos dwelling)]

gnōm'ic (n-), a. Of, consisting of, using, GNOME¹s, sententious; (Gram.) ~ aorist, used without past* sense to express a general truth, e.g. men were deceivers ever. [also 17th c. -ical f. LL f. Gk gnōmikos (GNOME¹, -IC)]

gnōm'on (n-), n. Pillar, rod, pin or plate of sundial, showing time by its shadow on marked surface; column etc. used in observing sun's meridian altitude; (Geom.) part of parallelogram left when similar one has been taken from its corner. Hence gnōmŏn'IC (n-) a. [F, or L f. Gk gnōmōn indicator etc. (gignōskō know)]

gnōs'is (n-), n. Knowledge of spiritual mysteries; Gnosticism. [Gk (-ō-), = knowledge, as prec.]

gnŏs'tic (n-), a. & n. 1. Relating to knowledge, cognitive; having esoteric spiritual knowledge; of the Gnostics, occult, mystic. 2. n. (usu. pl.; G~) early Christian heretic(s) claiming GNOSIS, whence ~ISM(3) n., ~IZE(2, 3, 4) v.i. & t., (n-). [f. LL f. Gk gnōstikos (as prec., -IC)]

gnu (nū), n. Oxlike antelope. [Hottentot]

gō¹, v.i. & t. (went, gone pr. gawn, gŏn; 2nd sing. gŏest, 3rd goes pr. gŏz & arch. gŏeth). 1. Start, depart, move, continue moving, with self-originated or imparted motion, from some place, position, time, etc. (often not specified because obvious, whereas the goal etc. is always specified if it matters; cf. COME). 2. Journey, travel, proceed, progress, (going strong, with vigour; he will go far, reach distinction; go easy, straight; go west, sl., be killed or die; go the PACE; went miles round; go a walk, journey, voyage; go the same, the shortest, way). 3. (Of line etc.) lie, point, in certain direction. 4. Be guided by, act in harmony with, judge or

act upon, (a good rule to go by; have nothing to go upon; always goes with his party; promotion goes by favour; go with tide or times, do as others do). 5. Be habitually in specified state (go hungry, armed, in rags, in fear of one's life; six months etc. gone with child, having spent that time in gestation). 6. Be moving, acting, working, etc. (Who goes there?, sentry's challenge; a going concern, business in working order; clock does not go, goes well; tongue goes nineteen to the DOZEN). 7. Make specified motion (go like this with your left foot). 8. (Of bell, striking clock or hour, gun, etc.; also with interjections of sound as go bang, crack) sound (go phut, sl., collapse). 9. (Of time) pass, elapse. 10. Be current (the sovereign went anywhere; the story goes, it is said); be known by, or under, the name of; be on the average (is a good actor as actors go nowadays). 11. (Of document etc.) run, have specified tenor. 12. (Of verse, song) be rhythmical, be adaptable to a tune. 13. (Of events) turn out well, ill, HARD, etc., (of election etc.) issue for or against, (of constituency, politician, voter) take certain course or views (Liverpool went Labour; America went dry, adopted prohibition of intoxicants; case goes by default, takes its course against absent party; dinner, play, went well, succeeded; peace without SAYing). 14. Begin motion (Go!, starter's word in race; HERE goes!). 15. Get away free, unpunished, etc. 16. Be sold (go cheap, for 2/6, etc.; going!, gone!, auctioneer's announcement that bidding is almost, quite, closed). 17. (Of money) be spent (often in books etc.) 18. Be relinquished, abolished, or lost (Greek, the carriage, must go; my sight, our trade, is going; next wicket went for nothing). 19. Die (esp. in p.p.; & in many phrr., as go the way of all the earth or pop. of all flesh, to a better world, to one's account or own place, aloft, off the hooks, etc.). 20. Fail, give way, succumb, break down, crack. 21. Make way to, towards, into, etc. (go to Jericho, || Bath, blazes, hell, etc., be off out of speaker's presence; go to Canossa, humble oneself after recalcitrance, w. ref. to Emperor Henry IV in 1077; go to the DEVIL¹; which way goes to Bristol; go to a ball, to church, market, etc., attend it; go to school, get instruction; go to the bar, to sea, become barrister, sailor; go on the stage, the streets, become actor, prostitute; go to STOOL). 22. Proceed to do (went to find him), and do (esp. colloq. = be so foolish as to do; also vulg. have been & gone & done it, made a blunder etc.), (a-)doing, on pilgrimage, an errand, the spree, etc. 23. Act as bail (for person; also abs. in parenthesis I'll go bail, I assure you). 24. Have recourse, refer, appeal, to (|| go to the COUNTRY, test opinion by general election; go to war, work, etc.; vulg., would not go to or for to *do it*, be so inconsiderate etc. as to). **25.** Carry action to certain point (*went all lengths*; *will go so far as to say*; *will go as high as £100*, in bidding or offering price; *go halves* or *shares*, share equally *with*, or abs.; *went to great expense*, *trouble*, etc.; *go the whole* HOG; *go better* or *one better*, outbid or outdo adversary). **26.** Penetrate, sink, (*ship went to the bottom*; *goes to one's heart*, grieves him); find room, (of number) be capable of being contained in another either without remainder or simply, (*will not go into* or *in the basket*; *6 into 12 goes twice*, *into 5 will not go*, *into 13 goes twice and one over*; *thread too thick to go through needle*). **27.** Belong *in* receptacle, *on* shelf etc. **28.** Pass, be allotted, etc., *to* person (of prize, victory, inheritance, office, etc.), be applied *to* purpose, contribute *to* or *towards* result, amount together to (*12 inches go to the foot*, tend to show etc. **29.** Reach, extend, (*the difference goes deep*; *as*, *so*, *far as it goes*, caution against taking statement too widely; *goes a long* etc. *way*, has great etc. effect *towards*, also of food, money, etc., lasts long etc., buys much etc.). **30.** Pass into certain condition (*go brown*, *blind*, *mad*, *to seed*; *go hot & cold*, have accesses of fever or shame: *go to pieces*, break up). **31.** v.t. Bid, declare, as ~ NAP [3], *two spades*. **32.** Phrr.: ~ *native*, (of a white man) adopt the uncivilized mode of life of the natives among whom he lives; *go sick* (Mil.), enter oneself on the sick list; (sl.) *go it*, act vigorously, furiously, etc., indulge in dissipation; *go it alone*, act by oneself or without support; *going fifteen* etc., in one's fifteenth etc. year; *going to*, about to, intending to (used as fut. part.); *be gone*, take oneself off; *gone*, dead (often *dead & gone*); *gone on* (sl.), infatuated with; *far gone*, very ill, deeply entangled; *go fetch!* (order to dog). **33.** With prepp.: *go about*, set to work at; *go at*, attack, take in hand energetically; *go behind* (decision etc.), re-examine grounds of; *go for*, go to fetch, pass or be accounted as *nothing*, *little*, etc., be applicable to, strive to attain, (sl.) attack; *go into*, enter (profession, Parliament), frequent (society), take part in, allow oneself to pass into (hysterics etc.), dress oneself in (mourning etc.), investigate; *go off* one's HEAD [1]; *go on*, become chargeable to (parish, relief fund, etc.); *go over*, inspect details of, rehearse, retouch; *go through*, discuss in detail, scrutinize, perform, (ceremony, recitation, etc.), undergo, (of book) be sold out in (so many editions); *go up the line* (Mil.), leave the base for the front; *go with*, be concomitant of, take same view as, match, follow the drift of; *go without*, not have, put up with want of. **34.** With advv.: *go about*, move from place to place, endeavour *to* do; *go ahead*, proceed without hesitation; *go along with*, = go with;

go back from or *upon* one's *word* etc., fail to keep it; *go by*, pass; *go down*, sink (of ship), be continued *to* specified point, fall *before* conqueror, be recorded in writing, be swallowed, find acceptance *with*, || leave university; *go in*, enter as competitor (*go in & win!*, form of encouragement), (Cricket) take or begin innings, (of sun etc.) be obscured; *go in for*, take as one's object, pursuit, style, principle, etc.; *go off*, leave the stage, begin, explode, die, gradually cease to be felt, deteriorate, become unconscious in sleep, faint, etc., be got rid of by sale, succeed *well*, *badly*, etc.; *go on*, continue, persevere, (doing, *with*, *in*, or abs.), proceed as next step to do, conduct oneself *shamefully* etc., rail *at* (colloq.), appear on stage, begin bowling, take one's turn to do something, (colloq. in imperat.) don't talk nonsense; *going on for*, approaching (a time, age, etc.); *go out*, leave room or house, fight duel, be extinguished, leave office (of Government), cease to be fashionable, depart *to* colony etc., (esp. of girls) leave home for employment usu. *as* governess etc., mix in society, (of workmen) strike, (of heart etc.) expand with love etc. *to* person, play first 9 holes in round of golf; *go over*, change one's party or religion; *go round*, pay informal visit to, be long enough to encompass, (of food etc.) suffice for whole party; *go through with*, complete, not leave unfinished; *go to* (imperat.: arch.), interjection of remonstrance, incredulity, impatience, etc.; *go together*, be concomitant, match; *go under*, sink, fail, succumb. **35.** Comb.: *go-ahead*, enterprising; *go-as-you-please*, unfettered by regulations; *go-between*, intermediary, negotiator; *go-by*, passing (usu. in *give the go-by to*, outstrip, leave behind, elude, disregard, cut, slight); *go-cart*, wheeled frame for teaching child to walk, kind of perambulator, litter, palankeen, hand-cart; *go-off*, start (usu. *at the first go-off*); *go-to-meeting*, (of hat, clothes, etc.) fit or kept for going to church in. [OE, OS *gān*, OHG *gān*, *gēn* f. Gmc **gai-*, **gǣ-*]

gō², n. (pl. *goes*). Act of going (*come-&-go*, traffic, movement to & fro); mettle, spirit, dash, animation; (colloq.) embarrassing turn of affairs (*here's*, *what*, *a go!*; *a rum go*); (colloq.) success (*make a go of it*); turn at doing something (*have a go at*); portion of liquor or food served; (Cribbage) player's inability to play, counting one to opponent; (colloq.) *it's no go*, nothing can be done; (colloq.) *all* or *quite the go*, in fashion; (colloq.) *near go*, close shave; (colloq.) *on the go*, in motion, also in a state of decline; || LITTLE--*go*. [f. prec.]

goad, n., & v.t. **1.** Spiked stick used for urging cattle; thing that torments, incites, or stimulates. **2.** v.t. Urge with ~; irritate; instigate, drive, by annoyance (often *on*; also *to* do, *into* doing, *to* or *into* fury etc.). [OE *gād*, cogn. w. Lombard *gaida* arrowhead f. Gmc **gaidō*]

goal, n. Point marking end of race; object of effort or ambition; destination; posts between which ball is to be driven in football etc., points so won (DROP², *make, score, a ~*); (Rom. Ant.) pillar at turning-point in chariot race; *~'keeper*, player stationed to protect ~; *~-line*, line between each pair of *~*-posts produced as end-boundary of field of play (cf. TOUCH-*-line*). Hence *~'ie* [-Y³] n. (colloq.), *~*keeper. [ME *gol* (once) limit, common from 16th c., of unkn. orig.]

goat, n. Hardy lively wanton usu. horned & bearded ruminant quadruped (*sheep &* *~s*, the good & the wicked, see *Matt.* xxv. 32, 33); (pl.) sub-family to which *~* belongs; zodiacal sign Capricorn (*G~*); licentious person; *get* one's *~* (sl.), irritate one; *play the* GIDDY*~*; *~-god*, Pan; *~'herd*, one who tends *~*s; *~'beard*, meadowsweet, also salsify; *~'skin*, (garment, bottle, made of) skin of *~*; *~'sucker*, nocturnal bird resembling swift; *~'s wool*, non-existent thing. Hence *~'*ISH¹, *~'*Y², aa., *~'*ishLY² adv., *~'*ishNESS n. [OE *gāt*, OS *gēt*, OHG *geiz*, ON *geit*, Goth. *gaits* f. Gmc **gaitaz* cogn. w. L *haedus* kid]

goatee', n. Chin-tuft like goat's beard. [-EE]

goat'ling, n. Goat 1–2 years old. [-LING¹]

gŏb¹, n., & v.i. (vulg.). 1. Clot of slimy substance, e.g. spittle; mouth. 2. v.i. (-bb-). Spit. [f. OF *gob* mouthful]

*gŏb², n. (sl.). Sailor.

gŏbǎng', n. Game played on chequer-board. [f. Jap. *goban* f. Chin. *k'i pan* chessboard]

gŏbb'ĕt, n. (arch.). Piece, lump, esp. of raw flesh or food; extract from a text set for translation or comment. [ME, f. OF *gobet* (GOB¹, -ET¹)]

gŏb'ble¹, v.t. & i. Eat hurriedly & noisily; ||*~-stitch*, one made too long from hurry. Hence **gŏbb'ler¹** [-ER¹] n. [perh. f. GOB¹ +-LE(3)]

gŏb'ble², n. (golf). Rapid straight putt into the hole. [perh. f. prec.]

gŏb'ble³, v.i. (Of turkey-cock) make characteristic sound in throat; make such sound when speaking, from rage etc. Hence **gŏbb'ler²** n., turkey-cock. [imit.]

*gŏb'bledegook' (-beldi-), -dў-, n. (sl.). Pompous official jargon. [imit. of turkey-cock]

gŏb'elin, a. *G~ tapestry*, made, or imitated from that made, at the State factory in Paris called *Gobelins* after its founders.

gobe'mouche (gŏb'mōosh), n. (pl. *~s* pr. like sing.). Credulous newsmonger. [f. F *gobe-mouches* lit. fly-catcher (*gober* swallow, *mouches* flies)]

gŏb'lĕt, n. (Arch.) metal or glass drinking-cup, bowl-shaped & without handles, sometimes with foot & cover; (poet.) drinking-cup; (commerc.) glass with foot

& stem. [ME, f. OF *gobelet*, dim. of *gobel* of unkn. orig.]

gŏb'lin, n. Mischievous ugly demon. [ME, f. OF *gobelin*, med. L *gobelinus*, of obsc. orig.]

gŏb'ў, n. Small fish with ventral fins joined into a disc or sucker. [f. L *gobius*, co-, f. Gk *kōbios* GUDGEON]

gŏd¹, n. 1. Superhuman being worshipped as having power over nature & human fortunes, deity, (*~ of heaven*, Zeus, Jupiter; *~ of hell*, Dis, Pluto; *~ of the sea*, Poseidon, Neptune; *~ of day*, sun, Apollo, Phoebus; *~ of fire*, Hephaestus, Vulcan; *~ of war*, Ares, Mars; *~ of love, blind ~*, Eros, Cupid; *~ of wine*, Bacchus; *~ of this world*, the Devil; *Ye ~s!*, *Ye ~s & little fishes!*, mock-heroic exclamations; *feast, sight, for the ~s*, something exquisite etc.). 2. Image, animal, or other object, worshipped as symbolizing, being the visible habitation of, or itself possessing, divine power; an idol. 3. Adored, admired, or influential person. 4. (theatr., pl.). Occupants of gallery. 5. (*God*). Supreme being, Creator & Ruler of universe, (*God*, often *the Lord God, Almighty God, God Almighty*; *God the Father, Son, Holy Ghost*, Persons of Trinity; ACT¹ *of God*; *with God*, dead & in heaven; *God's truth*, the absolute truth; *God's earth*, the whole earth; *God's (own) country*, alleged description of the U.S. by Americans; *oh, my, good,* etc., *God!*, exclamations of pain, grief, or anger; *God bless, damn, help, you!, him!,* etc., *God forbid!, grant ~!*, prayers or imprecations; *God bless me!, my life!, my soul!, you!,* etc., exclamations of surprise; *God willing*, if circumstances allow; *under God*, used to qualify attribution of full agency to man; *thank God!*, parenthetic expression of pleasure at turn of events etc.; *God knows*, it is beyond mortal or my knowledge, I do not know, (also) I call God to witness that; *for God's sake*, with urgent petitions; *by God*, confirmatory oath; *so* HELP¹ *me God!*). 6. *~'father, ~'mother, ~'parent, ~'papa, ~'mamma*, sponsor at baptism, & so of the converse relation *~'child, ~'son, ~'daughter; ~'father* (fig.), person after whom person or thing is named, (vb) be responsible for, give one's name to; *~'fearing*, sincerely religious; *~'forsaken*, devoid of all merit, dismal (*what a ~forsaken hole!*); *God'man'*, Christ; *God's-acre* (imit. of German), churchyard; *God's book*, Bible; *~'send*, unexpected welcome event or acquisition; *God's image*, human body; *~'speed', ~'speed'*, utterance of words *God speed you!*, usu. in *bid* person *~speed*, wish him success in undertaking, journey, etc. Hence *~'*HOOD, *~'*SHIP, nn., *~'*WARD adv. & a., *~'*WARDS adv. [OE, OS, ON *god*, OHG *got*, Goth. *guth* f. Gmc **gutham*]

gŏd², v.t. (rare; -dd-). Deify; *~ it*, play the god. [f. prec.]

gŏdd'ĕss, n. Female deity in polytheism (esp., in Latin mythol.: ~ *of heaven, hell, love, wisdom, moon, corn, war,* Juno, Proserpine, Venus, Minerva, Diana, Ceres, Bellona); woman one adores. [-ESS[1]]

gŏ'det (-dā), n. Triangular piece of stuff inserted in a dress, glove, etc. (also attrib., as ~ *skirt*). [F]

godĕ'tia (-shа), n. Free-flowering hardy annual plant. [*Godet* Swiss botanist, -IA[1]]

gŏd'head (-ĕd), n. Being God or a god, divine nature, deity; *the G*~, God. [-HEAD]

gŏd'lĕss, a. Without a god; not recognizing God; impious, wicked. Hence ~NESS n. [-LESS]

gŏd'like, a. Resembling God or a god in some quality; fit for, like that of, a god. [-LIKE]

gŏd'l|y̆, a. Religious, pious, devout. Hence ~ĭNESS n. [-LY[1]]

godown', n. (Anglo-Ind.). Warehouse in parts of Asia, esp. India. [f. Malay *godong*]

gŏd'wit, n. Wading bird like curlew but with slightly upcurved bill. [orig. unkn.]

gŏ'er, n. Person, thing, that goes (*good, slow*, etc., ~; *comers & ~s*). [-ER[1]]

goes, goest, goeth. See GO[1].

Goethian (gĕrt'ĭan), a. & n. (Follower) of Goethe, like Goethe, his writings, views, etc. [J. W. von *Goethe*, German poet 1749–1832, -IAN]

gŏf'er, ***gau'fre** (gŏf'er), n. Thin batter-cake stamped with honeycomb pattern by the irons it is baked in. [f. F *gaufre* honeycomb, gofer, see WAFER, WAFFLE]

gof(f)'er, gŏph'er, gauff'er, (gō-, gŏ-), v.t., & n. 1. Make wavy, flute, crimp, (lace edge, trimming, etc.) with heated irons; ~ed *edges* of book, embossed. 2. n. Iron used for ~ing; ornamental plaiting used for frills etc. [f. F *gaufrer* stamp with patterned tool, f. *gaufre* (prec.)]

***gŏ'gĕtt'er,** n. (colloq.). One who secures what he sets out to get; pushing person, thruster. [GO[1], GET[1], -ER[1] (1)]

gŏg'gle, v.i. & t., a., & n. 1. Squint, roll eyes about (or with *eyes* as subj.), (of eyes) project; turn (eyes) sideways or from side to side. 2. adj. (Of eyes) protuberant, full & rolling; so ~-eyED[2] (-gel-ĭd) a. 3. n. pl. Kind of spectacles for protecting eyes from glare, dust, etc., often with coloured glasses, wire gauze, etc.; (sl.) round-lensed spectacles; sheep disease, staggers. [a. & n. f. vb, 14th c. prob. f. imit. base *gog (cf. *jog*) + -LE(3)]

gŏg'lĕt, gŭgg'lĕt, n. (Anglo-Ind.). Long-necked vessel usu. of porous ware for keeping water cool. [f. Port. *gorgoleta*]

Goid'ĕl, n. Member of GADHELIC races. Hence (= GADHELIC) **Goidĕl'ic** a. & n. [f. OIr. *Góidel*]

gŏ'ing, n. In vbl senses; esp.: condition of ground for walking, riding, etc.; (for *a-going*, & now regarded as part.) in action (*set the clock* ~), existing, to be had, (*one of the best fellows* ~; *there is cold*

beef ~); ~*s-on*, (usu. *strange, such*, etc.) behaviour. [-ING[1]]

goi'tre (-ter), n. Morbid enlargement of thyroid gland, often showing as large pendulous swelling in neck, bronchocele, dewlap. Hence **goi'trED[2]** (-terd) a. [F, back formation f. *goitreux* ult. f. L *guttur* throat, -OUS]

goit'rous, a. Affected with, like, of, (of places) characterized by prevalence of, goitre. [f. F *goitreux* see prec.]

Gŏlcŏn'da, n. Mine of wealth (lit. or fig.). [old name of Hyderabad]

gŏld, n. & a. 1. Precious yellow non-rusting malleable ductile metal of high specific gravity (*as* GOOD *as* ~; *go off* ~, abandon the ~ STANDARD); coins made of this, money in large sums, wealth; (fig.) brilliant, beautiful, or precious things, stuff, etc. (*a heart, voice, of* ~; *age of* ~, = GOLDEN *age*; *she is pure* ~; *all that glisters* or *glitters is not* ~); the metal used for coating surface or as pigment, gilding; the colour of the metal (*old* ~ n., dull brownish-golden yellow; *old* ~ adj., thus coloured); bull's eye of archery target (usu. gilt). 2. ~ *amalgam,* ~ combined with mercury in plastic state; ~*-beater,* one who beats ~ out into ~-leaf; ~*-beater's skin,* membrane used to separate leaves of ~ during beating, also as covering for slight wounds; ~ *bloc* (of countries with currencies tied to ~); ~ *brick* (orig. U.S. sl.), thing with only a surface appearance of value, sham, fraud; ~*crest,* very small bird with golden crest; ~*-digger,* one who digs for ~, *(sl.) coquette who wheedles money out of men; ~*-dust,* ~ in fine particles as often found; ~*-fever,* rage for going in search of ~; ~*-field,* district in which ~ is found; ~*'finch,* bright-coloured song-bird with patch of yellow on wings; ~*'fish,* small red Chinese carp kept for ornament; ~*-foil,* ~*-leaf,* ~ beaten into thin sheet, *-foil* being the thicker; ~*-mine,* lit. & fig. source of wealth; ~ *plate,* vessels made of ~; ~*-rush,* a rush to some new ~-field; ~*'smith,* worker in ~ (~*smith beetle,* with ~-coloured wing-covers); ‖ *Gold Stick,* (bearer of) gilt rod borne on State occasions by colonel of Lifeguards or captain of Gentlemen-at-arms. 3. adj. Wholly or chiefly of, coloured like, ~; (of sums in depreciated currencies) reckoned at par (~ *francs* etc., the stated amount at the nominal undepreciated value of the franc etc.). [OE, OS, OHG *gold,* ON *gull,* Goth. *gulth* f. Gmc *gullham; cogn. w. YELLOW]

gŏl'den, a. Made, consisting, of gold (*G*~ FLEECE; ~ *key,* money used to remove obstacle); abounding in, yielding, gold; coloured, shining, like gold; precious, excellent, important, (~ *opinions,* high respect; ~*-mouthed,* eloquent; *a* ~ *remedy, opportunity, saying; the* ~ *rule,* that in *Matt.* vii. 12; ~ *mean,* neither too much nor too little, principle of moderation; ~ *number*, named as important in fixing Easter, year's number in Metonic lunar cycle of 19 years; ~ *age*, first of four ages, see BRAZEN[1], when men were happy & innocent, also most prosperous period of nation's condition or literature); ~ *balls*, = *three* BALL[1]s; ~*-eye*, kind of sea-duck; *G*~ *Horn*, curved inlet of Bosporus, the harbour of Istanbul; ‖~*-knop*, ladybird; ~ *rain*, kind of firework; ~*-rod*, plant with rod-like stem & spike of bright yellow flowers; *G*~ *State*, California; ‖~ SYRUP; ~ *wedding*, fiftieth anniversary. [-EN[5], replacing *gülden* f. OE *gylden*]

gŏl'dĭlŏcks, n. Kinds of plant, esp. a species of buttercup. [f. obs. *goldy*[2], LOCK[1]]

gŏlf (*also* gŏf), n., & v.i. 1. Game for two persons or couples in which a small hard ball is struck with clubs having wooden or metal heads into each of a series of (18 or 9) holes on smooth greens at varying distances apart and separated by fairways, rough ground, hazards, etc., the object being to hole the ball in the fewest possible strokes; ~*-club*, implement used in striking ball, (premises occupied by) association for playing ~. 2. v.i. Play ~, whence **gŏl'fer**[1] (*also* gŏf[2]) n. [15th c. Sc., of unkn. orig.]

Goli'ath, n. Giant; ~ *beetle*, large African black white-striped beetle; ~ (*crane*), powerful travelling crane. [1 Sam. xvii]

gŏl'iwŏg, n. Grotesque usu. black doll; bugbear. [orig. unkn.]

gŏll'y̆, int. (Used, esp. by Negroes, for) God, *by* God. [deformation of GOD]

‖ **golosh**. See GALOSH.

gŏlŭp'tious (-shŭs), **golŏp′**, a. (joc.). Luscious, delightful. [joc. for *voluptuous*]

‖ **gŏmbeen'**, n. (Anglo-Ir.). Usury (~*-man*, money-lender). [f. Ir. *gaimbín* perh. f. same OCelt. as med. L *cambium* CHANGE]

gŏm(b)rōōn', n. Persian pottery, imitated in Chelsea ware. [town on Persian gulf]

Gomŏ'rrah, n. (Type of) wicked town. [*Gen*. xviii, xix]

-gon, suf. f. Gk *-gōnos* -angled, forming nn. as *hexagon*, *polygon*, *n-gon*, figure with six, several, *n*, angles.

gŏn'ăd, n. (biol.). Undifferentiated germ-gland, serving both as ovary & spermary. [f. Gk *gonē*, *gonos*, generation, seed, +-AD]

gŏn'dola, n. Light flat-bottomed boat with cabin amidships & high point at each end worked by one oar at stern, used on Venetian canals; car suspended from airship. [It.]

gŏndolier', n. Sculler of gondola. [F, f. It. *gondoliere* (prec., -IER)]

gone (gŏn, gawn), a. In vbl senses: esp.: lost, hopeless, (a ~ *man*, also **gon'er**[1], n., sl.; *a* ~ *case*, COON); past, bygone, (usu. *past & ~*); ~ *on* (sl.), enamoured of. [p.p. of GO]

---

gŏn'falon, n. Banner, often with streamers, hung from cross-bar, esp. as standard of some Italian republics. [f. It. *gonfalone* f. WG **gundfano* (**gund-* war, *fano* banner)]

gŏnfalonier', n. Standard-bearer; (hist.) chief magistrate in some Italian republies. [F, or f. It. *-iere* (prec., -IER)]

gŏng, n., & v.t. 1. Metal disc with turned rim giving resonant note when struck; saucer-shaped bell; (sl.) medal. 2. v.t. (Of motoring-traffic police) direct (motorist) to stop by striking ~. [f. Malay *gong*]

gŏn'gorism (-ngg-), n. A Spanish literary style marked by inversion, antithesis, & classical allusion, corresponding to EUPHUISM in England. [*Gongora y* Argote, Sp. poet, 1561–1627, +-ISM]

gŏnĭŏm'ĕter, n. Instrument for measuring angles. So **gŏnĭŏm'ETRY** n., **gŏnĭomĕt'rĭc**(AL) aa. [F (*-mètre*), f. Gk *gōnia* angle, -METER]

gŏnorrhoe'|a (-orĕa), n. Inflammatory discharge of mucus from urethra or vagina. Hence ~AL (-rō'al) a. [LL, f. Gk *gonorrhoia* (*gonos* seed, *rhoia* flux)]

gŏŏd, ă. (BETTER, BEST), & n. 1. Having the right qualities, satisfactory, adequate, (*a* ~ *fire*, not too small or dull; *meat keeps* ~, untainted; ~ *soil*, fertile; *not* ~ *enough*, colloq., not worth doing, accepting, etc.; ~ *money*, genuine; as conventional epithet in *the* ~ *ship* —, *the* ~ *town of* —; *a* ~ *law*, valid, sound; *is* ~ *eating* etc., attractive to eat etc.). 2. Commendable (esp. in ~ *men & true*; ~ *old* —*!*, colloq. form of approval; *that's a* ~ *un!*, sl., a lie worth telling; also in courteous, patronizing, ironically polite, or indignant address, as *my* ~ *friend, man, sir*, or in polite or indulgently contemptuous description, as *your* ~ *lady*, *the* ~ *man*; *the* ~ *people*, fairies; *a* ~ *family*, well-born; *in* ~ *spirits*, not depressed; *a* ~ *leg*, well shaped). 3. Right, proper, expedient, (*it is* ~ *to be here*; *I thought, it seemed*, ~ *to do* something; also abs. as excl. of approval or consent). 4. Morally excellent, virtuous. 5. Kind, benevolent, (so of God etc., esp. in prayers & exclamations, as ~ *God!*, ~ *heavens!*, ~ *gracious!*; *be so* ~ *as*, ~ *enough*, to, = please to; *how* ~ *of you!*; *did me a* ~ *turn* or *office*; *has always been* ~ *to me*; *say a* ~ *word for*, commend, defend). 6. (Esp. of child) well behaved, not giving trouble, (often *as* ~ *as gold*). 7. Gratifying, agreeable, favourable, advantageous, beneficial, wholesome, (~ *news*; *things are in* ~ *train*, going well; so in forms of greeting or parting, as ~ *morning*, ‖~ *day*, ~ *night*; *have a* ~ *time*, enjoy oneself; *have a* ~ *night*, sleep well; *a* ~ *saying* or *story* or *thing*, as ~ *as a play*, amusing; *oil is* ~ *for burns*; *beer is not* ~ *for him* or *his health*; *are acorns* ~ *to eat?*; *take in* ~ *part*, not be annoyed at). 8. Adapted to an end, efficient, suitable, competent, (esp. with agent-nouns, as a ~ driver; ~ at describing etc.; has been a ~ wife to him). 9. Reliable, safe, sure, (a ~ man, financially sound, able to meet liabilities; ~ debts, sure to be paid; a ~ life, likely to last long, such as insurance office will accept; ~ for an amount, safely to be trusted to pay it, also of draft etc., drawn for so much; ~ for, inclined for, up to, as ~ for a ten-mile walk). 10. Valid, sound, thorough, ample, considerable, (gave her a ~ beating; did it for ~ reasons; rule holds ~; a ~ excuse; a ~ DEAL¹, FEW, MANY; have a ~ mind, be much inclined to do; often as intensive before adj., as went a ~ round pace, will take a ~ long time). 11. Not less than (played for a ~ hour; it is three miles ~ from the station). 12. As ~ as, practically (he as ~ as told me so; as ~ as dead; it is as ~ as done); make ~, compensate for, pay (expense), fulfil (promise), effect (purpose), demonstrate (statement), substantiate (charge), gain & hold (position), replace or restore (thing lost or damaged), (without obj.) accomplish what one has attempted. 13. ~ breeding, correct or courteous manners; ~ fellow, virtuous man, sociable person, agreeable companion; ~-fellowship, conviviality, sociability; ~-for-nothing, ~-for-nought, aa. & nn., worthless (person); G~ FRIDAY; ~ humour, cheerful mood or disposition, amiability, whence ~-hum⌐ourED² a., ~-hum'ouredLY² (-merdli) adv.; ~-look'ing, handsome; ~-looking, of virtuous appearance; ~ looks, personal beauty; ~ luck, being fortunate, happy chance, (often ~ luck to you!, as wish); ‖ ~'man (arch.), head of household, husband, father, etc.; ~ money (colloq.), high wages; ‖ ~ morrow (arch.), = ~ morning; ~ nature, kindly disposition, willingness to propose one's own interests, whence ~-na'turED² a., ~-na'turedLY² adv.; ~-neighbourhood, -neighbourliness, -neighbourship, friendly conduct; ~ sense, soundness of judgement, practical wisdom; ~ temper, freedom from irritability, whence ~-tem'perED² a., ~-tem'peredLY² adv.; ~ thing, anything one approves of, advantageous bargain or speculation, witty saying, (pl.) dainties; ‖ ~'wife, mistress of house (esp. Sc.). 14. n. Virtuous persons (the ~; ~ & bad alike respect him). 15. What is ~ or beneficial, well-being, profit, benefit, advantage, (is a power for ~; deceive him for his ~; what ~ will it do?; much ~ may it do you!, often iron.; do ~, show kindness to, act philanthropically, be beneficial to or benefit; to the ~, as balance on right side, net profit, something extra, etc.; come to ~, yield ~ result; for ~, for ~ & all, permanently, finally, definitively; be any, some, no, much, ~, be of any etc. use; what is the ~ of it?; what ~ is it?). 16. Desirable end or object, thing worth attaining; no ~, some mischief (is up to,

after, no ~). 17. pl. Movable property; merchandise, wares, (piece of ~s, joc., person); ‖ things for transmission by rail etc. (opp. passengers; so ~s agent, station, train, etc.; by ~s, by ~s train). Hence ~'ISH¹(2) a. [OE, OS gōd, OHG guot, ON gōthr, Goth. gōths f. Gmc *gōdhaz cogn. w. gadh- in GATHER]

good-bye', int. & n. (Saying of) farewell. [contr. of God be with you!, with good substituted on anal. of good-night etc.]

good'l‖y, a. Comely, handsome; of considerable size etc.; (iron.) fine, grand. Hence ~INESS n. [OE gōdlic (GOOD, -LY¹)]

good'ness, n. Virtue; positive or comparative excellence; benevolence, kindness, generosity, (have the ~, be kind enough to); what is good in thing, its essence or strength; (in exclamations, substituted for) God (~ gracious!, excl. of surprise or indignation; ~ knows, I do not know, I appeal to Heaven to witness; I wish to ~; thank ~!; for ~' sake). [OE gōdnes (GOOD, -NESS)]

goodwill', n. Kindly feeling to person, favour; cheerful acquiescence, heartiness, zeal; established custom or popularity of business etc.; privilege granted by seller of business, of trading as recognized successor.

Good'wins, n. pl. The ~, the Goodwin sands. [place]

Good'wood, n. (Used for) race-meeting on course near ~ Park, Sussex (~ cup, chief prize at this). [place]

good'y¹, n. (arch.). Elderly woman of lower class (often as prefix to surname). [for GOODwife, cf. HUSSY]

good'y², n. A sweet, bonbon. [-Y³]

good'y³, good'y-good'y, a. Primly, pretentiously, inopportunely, obtrusively, weakly, or sentimentally virtuous (talk ~, in~ manner). Hence good'iNESS n. [-Y³]

goof, n. (sl.). Silly or stupid person. Hence ~'Y² a. (sl.), silly. [var. of dial. goff (16th c.) f. F goffe]

goog'ly, n. (cricket). Off-break ball bowled with leg-break action. [orig. unkn.]

*goon, n. Person hired by racketeers to terrorize workers; stupid person. [orig. unkn.]

goosän'der, n. Duck with sharp serrated bill. [app. f. GOOSE after bersander]

goose, n. (pl. geese pr. gēs). 1. Kinds of web-footed bird between duck & swan in size, female of this (opp. GANDER), its flesh, (all his geese are swans, he over-estimates; kill the ~ that lays the golden eggs, sacrifice future profit to present necessities; COOK² person's ~; say BO to ~; sauce for ~ is sauce for GANDER). 2. Simpleton, whence goos'eY³ n. 3. Tailor's smoothing iron (with handle like ~'s neck; pl. ~s). 4. FOX¹ & geese; ‖ ~-club, for providing poor people with Christmas ~ paid for by small instalments; ~-flesh, rough bristling state of skin produced by cold or fright; ~-foot, kinds of plant named from shape of leaves:~-*grass*, cleavers; ~'*herd*, one who tends geese; ~-*quill*, quill--feather of ~ esp. used as pen; ~-*skin*, = ~-flesh; ~-*step*, balancing-drill taught to army recruits & much used in German army. [OE *gōs*, OHG *gans*, ON *gās* f. Gmc *gans*- cogn. w. L *anser*, Gk *khēn*]

goose'berr|ÿ (-zb-), n. (Edible berry of) any thorny species of *Ribes*; wine made of ~ies; *play* ~*y*, act as chaperon, play propriety, for pair of lovers; ~*y*-FOOL². [16th c., perh. f. prec., but cf. contemporary *groser* (F *groseille*)]

∥ **goose'gŏg** (-zg-), n. (colloq.). Gooseberry. [joc.]

gopher¹. See GOFFER.

gŏph'er², n. American burrowing rodent; N.-American ground-squirrel; nocturnal burrowing land-tortoise of Southern U.S. [orig. unkn.]

gŏph'er³, n. Tree from wood of which Noah's ark was made; (*~-wood*) tree yielding yellowish timber. [Heb.]

gor'al, n. An Indian antelope. [native name]

gŏr'cŏck, n. Male of the red grouse. [*gor*- of unkn. orig.]

Gŏrd'ian, a. ~ *knot*, intricate knot, difficult problem or task, (*cut the ~ knot*, solve problem by force or by evading the conditions). [f. *Gordius*, who tied the knot cut by Alexander the Great, +-AN]

gŏre¹, n. Blood shed & thickened or clotted. Hence **gōr'ÿ²** a., **gōr'ĭLÿ²** adv. [OE *gor* dung, dirt, = OHG, ON *gor*, Du. *goor*]

gŏre², n., & v.t. 1. Wedge-shaped piece of cloth adjusting width of a garment; triangular or lune-shaped piece in umbrella, balloon, dome, globe, etc. 2. v.t. Shape, narrow, with ~. [OE *gāra* triangular piece of land, = OHG *gēro*, ON *geire*, cogn. w. OE *gār* spear, w. ref. to shape of spearhead]

gŏre³, v.t. Pierce with the horn or (rarely) tusk (also transf. of rocks piercing ship). [15th c. Sc. & north. *gorre*, of unkn. orig.]

gŏrge¹, n. (Rhet.) internal throat; what has been swallowed, contents of stomach, (*cast the ~ at*, reject with loathing; one's ~ *rises at*, one is sickened or disgusted by); (Fortif.) neck of bastion or other outwork, rear entrance to a work; narrow opening, usu. with stream, between hills; solid object meant to be swallowed as bait for fish. [ME, f. OF f. LL *gurga*, -*es* gullet, belly, f. L *gurges* abyss]

gŏrge², v.i. & t., & n. 1. Feed greedily; satiate, glut; swallow, devour greedily; fill full, distend, choke up. 2. n. Act of gorging, surfeit. [ME, f. OF *gorger* (prec.)]

gŏr'geous (-*jus*), a. Richly coloured, sumptuous, magnificent; (of diction) ornate, dazzling. Hence~LY² adv.,~NESS n., (-*jus*-). [earlier *gorgayse*, -*yas* f. OF *gorgias* of unkn. orig.]

gŏr'gĕt¹, n. (Hist.) piece of armour for

throat, woman's wimple; necklace; patch of colour on throat of bird etc.; ~ *patch*, distinguishing mark on collar of military uniform. [f. OF *gorgete* (GORGE¹, -ET¹)]

gŏr'gĕt², n. (surg.). Channel-shaped steel instrument used in operations for stone etc. [f. F *gorgeret* (GORGE¹, as tubular)]

Gŏr'gĭŏ, n. (pl. -*os*). (Gipsy for) non-gipsy. [Romany]

Gŏrg'on, n. (Gk Myth.) one of three snake-haired women (esp. MEDUSA) whose looks turned any beholder to stone; terrible or ugly person, repellent woman. Hence **gŏrgŏn'IAN** a. [f. L *Gorgo* -*onis* f. Gk *Gorgō* (*gorgos* terrible)]

gŏrgŏn'ia, n. (pl. -*iae*, -*ias*). Sea-fan, kind of polyp. [prec., as hardening in air, +-IA¹]

gŏrg'onize, -ise (-īz), v.t. Stare at like gorgon. [-IZE]

Gŏrgonzōl'a, n. A rich veined cheese. [~ in Italy]

gorill'a, n. Large powerful ferocious arboreal anthropoid ape. [Afr. for wild man in Gk account of Hanno's voyage 5th or 6th c. B.C.]

gŏrm'andize, -ise (-īz), n., & v.i. & t., *gourmandise* (see Ap.), n. 1. Habits of a GOURMAND, indulgence in good eating, gluttony. 2. vb. Eat, devour, voraciously, whence **gŏrm'andizER¹** n. [vb f. n., f. F *gourmandise* (GOURMAND, -ISE)]

gŏrm'lĕss, a. (colloq.). Foolish, lacking sense. [orig. *gaumless* f. dial. *gaum* understanding, +-LESS]

∥ **gŏrse,** n. Prickly yellow-flowered shrub, whin, furze. Hence **gŏrs'ÿ²** a. [OE *gorst* cogn. w. OHG *gersta*, L *hordeum*, barley]

Gŏrs'edd (-ĕdh), n. Meeting of Welsh bards & druids (esp. as daily preliminary to the eisteddfod). [W, = session]

∥ **gŏsh,** int. (Also *by* ~) by God. [for *God*]

gŏs'hawk (-s-h-), n. Kinds of large short--winged hawk. [OE *gōs-hafoc* (GOOSE, HAWK)]

Gōsh'en, n. Place of light or plenty. [*Gen.* xlv. 10 etc., *Exod.* viii. 22, ix. 26]

gŏs'ling (-z-) n. Young goose. [-LING¹]

gŏs'pel, n. 1. Glad tidings preached by Christ; religious doctrine of Christ & his apostles, Christian revelation; protestant or evangelical doctrine (opp. *mass*); record of Christ's life in books of four evangelists; any of those books; portion from one of them read at Communion service. 2. Thing that may safely be believed (*takes his dreams for* ~); principle that one acts upon, believes in, or preaches (*the ~ of efficiency, laissez faire, soap & water*). 3. ~-*book*, containing ~s read at Communion; ~ *oath*, sworn on the ~s; ∥~-*shop*, Methodist chapel; ~ *side*, N. side of altar, at which ~ is read; ~ *truth*, truths contained in ~, something as true as ~. [OE *godspel*, orig. *gōdspell* (GOOD tidings; SPELL¹), rendering LL *bona annuntiatio, bonus nuntius* = *evangelium* EVANGEL; early assoc. w. *god* GOD]

gŏs'peller, n. Reader of gospel in Communion service; *hot ~*, zealous puritan, rabid propagandist. [-ER¹]

gŏss'amer, n. & a. **1.** Light filmy substance, the webs of small spiders, floating in calm air or spread over grass; *a* thread of this; something flimsy; delicate gauze; hence ~ED² (*-erd*), ~Y², aa. **2.** adj. Light & flimsy as *~*. [ME *gossamer* app. = goose-summer or St Martin's summer, i.e. early November when geese were eaten, *~* being most seen then]

gŏss'ip, n., & v.i. **1.** ‖ (Arch.) familiar acquaintance, friend, (esp. of women); idle talker, newsmonger, tattler; idle talk, groundless rumours, tittle-tattle; easy unconstrained talk or writing esp. about persons or social incidents; hence ~RY(4, 5) n., ~Y² a. **2.** v.i. Talk idly or lightly, tattle; write‾in gossipy style; hence ~ER¹ n. [earlier senses, *sponsor, fellow--sponsor, one's child's sponsor, at baptism*; OE *godsibb* person related to one in God; see SIB]

gossōon', n. (Anglo-Ir.). Lad. [f. F *garçon*]

gŏt, past & p.p. of GET. *~-up*, factitious, artificially produced, adorned, etc., with a view to effect or deception.

Gŏth, n. One of a German tribe who invaded Eastern & Western Empires in 3rd–5th cc. & founded kingdoms in Italy, France, & Spain; rude, uncivilized, or ignorant person, one who destroys works of art (cf. VANDAL), whence ~'ISH¹ a. [OE *Gotan* (pl.), ON *Gotar*, Goth. *Gutos* or *Gutans*; ME *Gothe* f. LL *Gothi*, Gk *Gotthoi*]

Gŏt'ham (-tam), n. Typical foolish town (*wise man of ~*, fool); ⁎(colloq.) New York City (*usu. pr.* gŏ'tham). Hence ~ITE¹(1) n. [perh. f. the village in Notts.]

Gŏth'ic, a. & n. **1.** Of the Goths or their language. **2.** (archit.). In the pointed--arch style prevalent in Western Europe in 12th–16th cc., including in England the Early English, Decorated, & Perpendicular (*orig.* sense *not classical*). **3.** Barbarous, rude, uncouth. **4.** (Print., a. & n.) German, also black-letter, (type); hence Gŏth'ICALLY adv., ~ISM(2, 3, 4) n., ~IZE(2, 3) v.i. & t. **5.** n. *~* language; *~* architecture; *~* type. [f. F *gothique* or LL *gothicus* (GOTH, -IC)]

gŏtt'en, p.p.h. (arch., & U.S.) of GET¹.

gouache (gōō'ahsh), n. Way of painting in opaque colours ground in water & thickened with gum & honey. [F, f. It. *guazzo*]

Goud'a, n. Flat round cheese made at *~* in Holland. [place]

gouge (gowj, gōōj), n., & v.t. **1.** Concave--bladed chisel used in carpentry & surgery. **2.** v.t. Cut with *~*; cut *out* (a cork, a channel) (as) with *~*; force (*out*, esp. person's eye with thumb) (as) with *~*; force out eye of. [F, f. LL *gubia*]

goulash (gōō'lahsh), n. **1.** Highly seasoned stew of steak and vegetables. **2.** (Contract Bridge) re-deal of the four hands (unshuffled, but with each hand arranged in suits and order of value). [f. Magyar *gulyás-hús* f. *gulyás* herdsman + *hús* meat]

gourd (gōrd, goord), n. (Large fleshy fruit of) kinds of trailing or climbing plant; rind of the fruit emptied, dried, & used as bottle etc., whence ~'FUL(2) n. [ME, f. F *gourde* f. L *cucurbita*]

gourmand (goorm'and, & see Ap.), a. & n. **1.** Gluttonous, fond of eating. **2.** n. (Usu. as F) lover of delicate fare, judge of good eating; greedy feeder, glutton. Hence ~ISM(2) (goor-) n. [15th c. f. OF, alt. f. *gormet* GOURMET]

gourmandise, See GORMANDIZE.

gourmet (goorm'ā), n. Connoisseur of table delicacies, esp. of wine. [F, see GOURMAND]

gout, n. **1.** Paroxysmal disease with inflammation of smaller joints, esp. that of great toe, & chalk-stones (*rich, poor, man's ~*, ascribed to over, under, -feeding & drinking). **2.** Wheat-disease caused by ~*-fly*. **3.** Drop, splash, or spot. Hence ~'Y² a. (*~ies* as n. pl., overshoes), ~'ILY² adv., ~'iNESS n. [ME, f. OF *goute* f. L *gutta* drop w. ref. to medieval theory of flowing down of humours]

go'vern (gŭ-), v.t. & i. **1.** Rule with authority, conduct the policy, actions, & affairs, of (State, subject) despotically or constitutionally; regulate proceedings of (corporation etc.; *~ing body*, managers of hospital, school, etc.); be in military command of (fort, town). **2.** Exercise function of government in person (*king reigns but does not ~*, merely selects those who are to *~*). **3.** Sway, rule, influence, regulate, determine, (person, his acts, course or issue of events); be the predominating influence. **4.** Conduct one*self* in some way; curb, bridle, (one's passions, one*self*). **5.** Constitute a law, rule, standard, or principle, for; serve to decide (case). **6.** (Gram., esp. of vb or prep.) have (noun, case) depending on it, require (a certain case). Hence ~ABLE a., ~ABIL'ITY n. [ME, f. OF *governer* f. L *gubernare* steer, govern, f. Gk *kubernaō* steer]

go'vernance (gŭ-), n. Act, manner, fact, or function, of governing, sway, control. [ME, f. OF *governance* (prec., -ANCE)]

go'vernĕss (gŭ-), n. Female teacher, instructress, esp. of children in private household; ‖ *~-car*(*t*), light two-wheeled vehicle with side- seats face to face. [earlier *governeress* f. OF (GOVERNOR, -ESS¹)]

go'vernment (gŭ-), n. (More modern word for) GOVERNANCE; portion of country ruled by a governor, province; system of governing, form of polity; body or successive bodies of persons governing a State, the State as an agent, an administration or ministry (‖ *form a G~*, of

Prime Minister selecting colleagues); (Gram.) relation between GOVERNing & other word; || *G~ house*, official residence of governor; *G~ paper, securities*, bonds, exchequer bills, etc., issued by ~. Hence **governmĕn'tAL** a., **governmĕn'taLIY²** adv., (gŭ-). [OF (-*ement*), see GOVERN, -MENT]

go'vernor (gŭ-), n. 1. One who governs, ruler; official appointed to govern province, town, etc., representative of Crown in dominion (*G~ General*) or colony; executive head of each of U.S.; officer commanding fortress or garrison; head, or one of governing body, of institution; official in charge of prison. 2. One's employer, one's father, sir, (sl., freq. *guv'nor*). 3. (mech.). Automatic regulator of supply of gas, steam, water, etc., to machine, ensuring even motion. 4. Kind of fishing-fly. 5. ~ *general*, ~ with deputy ~s under him, whence ~-gĕn'eralSHIP n. Hence ~SHIP(1, 2) n. [ME, f. OF *governeor* f. L *gubernatorem* (GOVERN, -OR)]

|| **gow'an**, n. (Sc.). Daisy. [prob. var. of dial. *golland* & connected w. dial. *gold*, OE *golde*, marigold, perh. f. GOLD]

gowk, n. (Dial.) cuckoo; awkward or half-witted person, fool. [ME *goke* f. ON *gaukr* = OE *gēac*, OHG *gouh* f. Gmc **gaukaz*]

gown, n., & v.t. Loose flowing upper garment, esp. woman's dress (usu. of dress with pretensions to elegance, or in comb. as *tea, dinner, -~*), frock; ancient Roman toga (*arms, gown*, war & peace); official or uniform robe of various shapes worn by alderman, judge, lawyer, clergyman, member of university, college, or school, etc. (*town & ~*, non-members & members of university at Oxf. & Camb.); ~*s'man*, civilian, member of university; (vb, chiefly in p.p.) attire in ~. [ME, f. OF *goune* f. med. L *gunna* fur garment (cf. Byz. Gk *gouna* fur)]

goy, n. (Yiddish for) Gentile. [Heb., = nation]

Graaf'ian (-rahf-), a. ~ *follicle, vesicle*, one of small sacs in mammal ovary in which ova are matured. [R. de *Graaf*, Dutch anatomist d. 1673, -IAN]

grăb, v.t. & i. (-bb-), & n. 1. Seize suddenly; appropriate rapaciously; capture, arrest; make snatch *at*; hence (-)~b'ER¹ n. 2. n. Sudden clutch, grasp, seizure, or attempt to seize; practice of ~bing, rapacious proceedings esp. in politics or commerce; (mech.) device or implement for clutching; children's card game. [n. f. vb; f. MLG, MDu. *grabben*; cf. GRIP², GRIPE, GROPE]

grăb'ble, v.i. Grope about, feel for something; sprawl on all fours (often *for* something). [f. Du. *grabbeln* (prec., -LE(2))]

grāce, n., & v.t. 1. Pleasing quality, attractiveness, charm, esp. that belonging to elegant proportions or ease & refinement of movement, action, expression, or

manner, whence ~'FUL a., ~'fuLIY² adv., ~'fulNESS n., (-sf-). 2. Becomingness, air with which something is done, (*cannot with any ~ ask him*; *have the~ to*, do something that decency requires; *with a good ~*, as if willing; *with a bad ~*, reluctantly, ungraciously). 3. Attractive feature, accomplishment, ornament, (*airs & ~s*, behaviour put on with a view to effect or attraction). 4. (Mus.; also ~*-note, -notes*) embellishment of extra note(s) not essential to harmony or melody. 5. (Gk Myth.) *the G~s*, three beautiful goddess sisters (Aglaia, Euphrosyne, Thalia), the bestowers of beauty & charm. 6. Favour, benignant regard or its manifestation, on part of superior (*be in* one's *good ~s*, enjoy his favour or liking). 7. Unconstrained goodwill as ground of concession (*act of ~*, privilege, concession, that cannot be claimed as right, & see below; *by the ~ of God*, appended to royal titles); boon. 8. || (Univv.) permission of Congregation, also of College or Hall, to take degree, dispensation from statutes. 9. (theol.). Unmerited favour of God, divine regenerating, inspiring, & strengthening influence, condition (also *state of ~*) of being so influenced, divinely given talent etc., (*the —th year of ~*, with date = A.D.; *in this year of ~*, usu. iron., when Christianity has been so long established). 10. Favour shown by granting delay (*give a day's, year's*, etc., ~; *days of ~*, time allowed by law for payment of bill of exchange—in Britain three days—or insurance premium after it falls due). 11. Mercy, clemency, (*Act of ~*, formal, esp. general, pardon by Act of Parliament; & see above). 12. Short thanksgiving before or after meal (~*-cup*, cup of wine etc. passed round after ~, parting draught). 13. || *His, Her, Your, G~*, forms of address or description for duke, duchess, or archbishop. 14. v.t. Add ~ to, adorn, set off *with*; confer honour or dignity on, honour *with* title etc.; do credit to. [ME, f. OF *grace* f. L *gratia* (*gratus* pleasing, GRATEFUL)]

grāce'lĕss, (-sl-), a. Unregenerate, depraved, (arch. or joc.); wanting sense of decency, unabashed; without charm or elegance (rare); ~ *florin* (of 1849, on which the letters *D.G.* were omitted). Hence ~LY² adv., ~NESS n. [-LESS]

grā'cile, a. Slender; (erron.) gracefully slight. Hence **gracil'ITY** n., slenderness, (of literary style) unornamented simplicity. [f. L *gracilis* slender]

grā'cious (-shus), a. & int. 1. Agreeable, pleasing, (arch.); kindly, benevolent, courteous, (chiefly poet.); condescending, indulgent & beneficent to inferiors, (of exalted persons, or sarcastic or joc.; esp. as polite epithet of royal persons or their acts; *the ~ speech from the throne*); (of God) dispensing grace, merciful, benignant; hence ~LY² adv., ~NESS n.,

(-shus-). **2.** int. (Ellipt. for ~ *God*, as *good*)
~ *l*, *my* ~ *l*, excll. of surprise (also in ~
me l, ~ *goodness l*). [ME, f. OF, f. L
gratiosus (GRACE, -OUS)]

grac′kle, n. Kinds of bird allied to jack-daw. [ult. f. L *graculus* jackdaw]

gradāte′, v.i. & t. (Cause to) pass by
imperceptible degrees from one shade of
colour to another; arrange in steps or
grades. [back formation f. foll.]

gradā′tion, n. (Usu. pl.) stage(s) of
transition or advance; series of degrees
in rank, merit, intensity, divergence, etc.,
(pl.) such degrees; arrangement in such
degrees; (Fine arts) insensible passing
from one shade, tone, etc., to another;
(Philol.) ablaut. Hence ~AL a., ~aLlY
adv., (-shon-). [f. L *gradatio* (*gradus* step,
-ATION)]

grāde, n., & v.t. **1.** Degree in rank,
proficiency, quality, value, etc., class
of persons or things alike in these; *class,
form, in school. **2.** (Cattle-breeding)
variety produced by crossing native stock
with superior breed. **3.** (Zool.) group
supposed to have branched from parent
stock at same stage of development. **4.**
(Philol.) relative position in ablaut-series.
5. Gradient, slope, rate of ascent or
descent, (*on the up, down,* ~, rising or
falling, lit. & fig.; *make the* ~, succeed).
6. v.t. Arrange in~s, class, sort; blend so
as to affect~ of; colour with tints passing
into each other. **7.** Reduce (road, canal,
etc.) to easy gradients. **8.** (Cattle-breed-ing) cross with better breed (~ *up*, im-prove thus). **9.** (Philol., in pass.) be
changed by ablaut. [vb f. n., F, f. L
gradus step]

∥ **grāde′ly** (-dlĭ), a. (obs. exc. dial.).
Excellent, thorough; handsome, comely;
real, true, proper. [ME *greithlic* f. ON
greithligr (*greithr* = OE *gerǣde* READY,
-LY¹)]

grād′ient, n. ∥ Amount of slope, inclina-tion to the horizontal, in road, railway,
etc.; proportional rise or fall of thermo-meter or barometer in passing from one
region to another. [perh. formed on
GRADE after *salient*]

grād′in(e) (*also* -adēn′), n. One of series
of low steps or tier of seats; ledge at back
of altar. [f. It. *gradino* (*grado* GRADE)]

grăd′ūal¹, n. Respond sung between
Epistle & Gospel in the service of the
Mass. [so called as sung at steps of altar
or while deacon mounted ambo; f. med.
L *graduale* neut. adj. as n., see foll. &
GRAIL¹]

grăd′ūal², a. Taking place by degrees,
slowly progressive, not rapid, steep, or
abrupt; ~ *psalm*, = *song of* DEGREES.
Hence ~LY² adv., ~NESS n. [f. med. L
gradualis (L *gradus* -*ūs* step, -AL)]

grăd′ūănd, n. (Sc.), One about to receive
an academic degree. [f, med. L *gradu-andus* gerundive of *graduare* GRADU-ATE²]

grăd′ūate¹, n. One who holds academic
degree; chemist's graduated measuring-glass. [f. med. L *graduatus* (foll., -ATE²)]

grăd′ū∣āte², v.i. & t. Take, admit to
(chiefly U.S.), academic degree, (transf.)
qualify or perfect oneself *as*; mark out
in degrees or portions; arrange in grada-tions, apportion incidence of (tax) accord-ing to a scale; pass *away* by degrees,
change (intr.) gradually *into*; concentrate
(solution) by evaporation. Hence~A′TION,
~ātor, nn. [f. med. L *graduare* (*gradus*
-*ūs* step), -ATE³]

grăd′us, n. Dictionary of Latin prosody
used in schools to help in writing Latin
verse. [for ~ *ad Parnassum* step to
Parnassus]

Gr(a)e′cism (grē-), n. A Greek idiom, esp.
as imitated in another language; Greek
spirit, style, mode of expression, etc.,
imitation of these. [f. F *grécisme* or med.
L *graecismus* (*Graecus* GREEK, -ISM)]

Gr(a)e′cize (grē-), -**ise** (-īz), v.t. & i. Give
a Greek cast, character, or form, to;
favour, imitate, the Greeks. [f. L *graeci-zare* (prec., -IZE)]

Gr(a)e′co- (grē-), comb. form of L *Graecus*
GREEK, as ~-*Roman*. Hence ~MAN′IA(C)
nn., ~PHIL a. & n.

graffi′tō (-fē-), n. (pl. -*ti*, pr. -tē). Drawing
or writing scratched on wall etc., esp. on
ancient wall as at Pompeii; decoration
by scratches through plaster showing
different-coloured under-surface. [It.]

graft¹ (-ah-), n., & v.t. **1.** Shoot or scion
inserted in slit of another stock, from
which it receives sap; (Surg.) piece of
transplanted living tissue; process of
~ing; place where ~ is inserted. **2.** v.t.
Insert (scion) as ~ (*in, into, on, upon,
together*); (fig.) insert or fix *in* or *upon* so
as to produce vital or indissoluble union;
insert ~(s); insert ~(s) upon (stock);
(Surg.) transplant (living tissue); (Naut.)
cover (ring-bolt etc.) with weaving of
small cord; ~*ing-clay, -wax*, composition
for covering united parts of ~ & stock.
[15th c. for earlier *graff* n. & v. f. OF *grafe*
f. L f. Gk *graphion* stilus (*graphō* write)]

∥ **graft²** (-ah-), n. Depth of earth that may
be thrown up at once with spade;
crescent-bladed spade. [cogn. w. GRAVE²]

***graft³** (-ah-, -ă-), n., & v.i. (colloq.).
Illicit spoils in connexion with politics or
business, practices intended to secure
these; (vb) seek, make, ~, whence ~′ER¹
n. [orig. unkn.]

grail¹, n. = GRADUAL¹. [ME, f. OF *grael*
f. eccl. L *gradale* var. of *graduale* GRA-DUAL¹]

grail², n. (Also *holy* or *saint* ~, or
sangreal) platter used by Christ at Last
Supper, & in which Joseph of Arimathea
received his blood at the Cross. [ME, f.
OF *graal* etc. f. med. L *gradalis* dish, of
unkn. orig.; cf. SANGRAIL, -GREAL]

grail³, n. Comb-maker's file. [f. F *grêle*
(*grêler* make thin f. *grêle* adj. f. L *gracilis*)]

grain, n., & v.t. & i. **1.** A fruit or corn of a cereal; (collect. sing.) wheat or the allied food-grasses or their fruit, corn, a particular species of corn; ~ ELEVATOR; (pl.; also ~s of *Paradise* or *Guinea* ~s) capsules of W.-Afr. plant used as spice & drug; (pl.) refuse malt after brewing or distilling. **2.** Small hard particle of sand, gold, SALT, gunpowder (*large, small,* ~ *powder*), incense, etc. **3.** Smallest unit of weight, 1/480 of oz. Troy, 1/437.5 of oz. av., smallest possible quantity (*without a* ~ *of vanity, love*, etc.). **4.** (Hist.) kermes, cochineal, or dye made from either of these (*dye in* ~, dye in kermes, dye in any fast colour, dye in the fibre or thoroughly; *in* ~, thorough, genuine, by nature, downright, indelible); (poet.) dye, colour. **5.** Granular texture, roughness of surface, mottling; texture, arrangement & size of constituent particles, in flesh, skin, wood, stone, etc.; lines of fibre in wood giving a pattern, lamination or planes of cleavage in coal, stone, etc.; (fig.) nature, temper, tendency, (*against the*~, contrary to inclination). **6.** ~*-leather*, dressed with the ~-*side* (on which the hair was) out; ~*-sick* n., cattle-disease, distension of rumen; hence ~'LESS, ~'Y², (-)~ED² (-nd), aa. **7.** vb. Form (t. & i.) into ~s; dye in ~; give granular surface to; remove hair from (hides); paint in imitation of ~ of wood or marble; hence ~'ER¹(1, 2) n. [ME, f. OF f. L *gronum,* & f. OF *graine* f. Rom. **grana* collect. fem., orig. neut. pl. of L *granum*]

grains (-z), n. Forked fish-spear or harpoon. [orig. pl. of obs. *grain* fork, prong, f. ON *grein* division; now used as sing.]

graip, n. (Sc.). A three- or four-pronged fork used for lifting dung or digging potatoes etc. [f. ON *greip* corresp. to OE *grāp* grasp]

grǎllatŏr'ial, a. (zool.). Of the *Grallatores* or long-legged wading birds. [f. L *grallator* stilt-walker (*grallae* stilts)]

grǎll'och (-*ox*, see Ap.), n., & v.t. Dead deer's viscera; (vb) disembowel (deer etc.). [f. Gael. *grealach* intestines]

grǎm¹, n. Chick-pea; any pulse used as horse-fodder. [f. Port. *grão* f. L *granum* grain]

grǎm², grǎmme, n. Unit of mass in metric system, the thousandth part of the international prototype 'kilogram' held in the custody of the *Bureau International des Poids et Mesures* at Sèvres near Paris; *gram-force,* unit of force, that force which when applied to a body of mass one ~ imparts thereto the standard acceleration of exactly 980·665 centimetres per second squared. [F (-*me*), f. LL f. Gk *gramma* small weight, see -GRAM]

-**grǎm,** suf. (chiefly) f. Gk *gramma -atos* (*graphō* write, -M) thing written, letter of alphabet, forming nn. (1) prepositional compds f. Gk (*anagram, diagram, epigram*), (2) n. compds (*chronogram, logo-*

gram), (3) compds of Gk numeral with *gramma* or with *grammē* line, where Gk would have -*grammon* neut. adj., (4) *telegram* (1857), violating Gk anal., suggested *cablegram.*

grǎm'a, grǎmm'a, n. (Also ~ *grass*) kinds of low pasture grass in W. & S.W. parts of U.S. [f. Sp. *grama*]

‖ **grǎm'arȳe,** n. (arch.). Magic, necromancy. [ME, f. AF *gramarie* learning, GRAMMAR]

‖ **gramer'cȳ,** int. (arch.). Thank you. [ME, f. OF *grant merci* (God give you) great reward (GRAND, MERCY)]

grǎminā'ceous (-shus), **grǎmin'ĕous,** aa. Of, like, grass, grassy. So **grǎmin'ivorous** a. [f. L *gramen -inis* grass, -ACEOUS, & L *gramineus* (-EOUS)]

grǎmm'alogue (-ŏg), n. (shorthand). Word represented by single sign; letter or character standing for word, logogram. [irreg. f. Gk *gramma* (-GRAM), *logos* word]

grǎmm'ar, n. Art & science dealing with a language's inflexions or other means of showing relation between words as used in speech or writing, & its phonetic system (usu. divided into phonology, accidence, & syntax; *general, philosophical,* or *universal* ~, science of the distinctions of thought recognized & variously expressed in the grammatical systems of actual languages; *historical* ~, study of the development of a language's inflexions & syntax; *comparative* ~, study of the relation between two or more ~s); treatise or book on ~; person's manner of using grammatical forms, speech or writing regarded as good or bad by the rules of ~, what is correct according to those rules; body of forms & usages in a language (*Latin* ~); elements, rudiments, of an art or science; ~*-school,* ‖ school founded about 16th c. for teaching Latin, of which many are now of the public-school type. Hence~LESS a. [ME, f. OF *gramaire* irreg. f. L f. Gk *grammatikē* (*tekhnē* art) of letters (*gramma* see -GRAM)]

grammār'ian, n. One versed in grammar, philologist. [ME, f. OF *gramarien* (prec., -IAN)]

grammǎt'ĭc|al, a. Of grammar (~*al gender,* determined by form not sex; ~*al sense,* literal, irrespective of other considerations than the rules of grammar); conforming to the rules of grammar, or to the formal principles of an art, so (f. earlier *grammatic*)~IZE(3) v.t. Hence~alLY² adv. [f. F, or LL *grammaticalis* (GRAMMAR, -AL)]

grǎmme. See GRAM².

grǎm'ophōne, n. Phonograph of the kind using flat discs for its reproduction of sound. [irreg. form made by inverting PHONOGRAM]

grǎm'pus, n. Kinds of blowing spouting blunt-headed dolphin-like cetacean; person who breathes loud. [16th c. *graundepose* f. 14th c. *grapeys* f. OF *grapois* f. L *crassus piscis* fat fish]

grănadill'a, grĕ-, n. Kinds of passion-flower. [Sp., dim. of *granada* pomegranate]

grăn'ary̆, n. Storehouse for threshed grain; region producing, & esp. exporting, much corn. [f. L *granarium* (*granum* grain, -ARY[1]); cf. GARNER]

gránd, a. & n. **1.** (In official titles) chief over others, of highest rank, (G~ *Almoner, Falconer,* etc., holders of old offices still existing; G~ CROSS[1]; G~ *Duke, Duchess,* hist., ruler of some European States called G~ *Duchy,* also child of Tsar, whence G~dūc'AL a.; ~ *duke,* also, great horned owl; G~ *Master,* head of military order of knighthood, head of Freemasons or of one of their provinces, & of Oddfellows etc.; G~ *Vizier,* chief minister of a Moslem country, esp. formerly of Turkish Empire). **2.** (Law) great, principal, (opp. *petty, common; ~ assize, inquest, jury*). **3.** Of most or great importance (*that is the ~ question; made a ~ mistake*), final, summing up minor constituents, (~ *total; ~ finale; the ~ sum* or *result of his achievements*). **4.** (Distinguishing parts of large building) main (*the ~ staircase, entrance,* etc.). **5.** (In F phrases or imitations) great (~ *army,* G~ *Canal,* G~ *Hotel;* G~ *Fleet,* main British fleet in the war of 1914–18). **6.** Conducted with solemnity, splendour, etc.; fine, splendid, gorgeous. **7.** Belonging to high society, distinguished, (*do the ~,* put on airs); imposing, impressive, great & handsome. **8.** Dignified, lofty, in conception, treatment, or expression (~ *style,* fitted for great subjects); morally imposing, noble, admirable, (*the G~ Old Man* or *G.O.M.,* W. E. Gladstone). **9.** Very satisfactory (colloq.; *had a ~ run; ground was in ~ condition*). **10.** (In names of relationships) in the second degree of ascent or descent (~'*son,* one's child's son; ~*-nephew,* one's nephew's or niece's son; ~'*mother,* ~*-aunt,* one's parent's mother or aunt; so ~'*child; ~'daughter;* ~'*father,* ~*father's clock,* worked by weights in tall wooden case; ~'*mamma;* ~'*mother,* whence ~'*motherLY*[1] a., esp. of legislation etc. = excessively PATERNAL; *teach your~mother to suck EGGS;* ~*mother* v.t., coddle etc.' ~*niece* ~'*papa;* ~'*parent;* ~'*sire,* esp. of animal's sire, also = ancestor, old man, & a method of ringing changes on bells; ~*-uncle*). **11.** ~ *air,* distinguished appearance; || ~ *committee,* one of two standing committees of House of Commons sessionally appointed to consider Law & Trade Bills; ~ LODGE; G~ *Monarch,* Louis XIV of France; || G~ *National,* annual steeplechase at Liverpool; ~ *piano*(*forte*), large horizontal piano; ~ *stand,* principal stand for spectators at races etc.; ~ *tour* (arch.), tour of chief towns etc. of Europe completing education. **12.** n. ~ piano (*upright ~,* usu. a large upright piano with all improvements). **13.** *A

thousand dollars (sl.). Hence ~'LY[2] adv., ~'NESS n. [OF, f. L *grandis* full-grown]

grăn'dăm(e), n. (arch.). Grandmother; (*-m* only) animal's dam's dam; ancestress; old woman. [ME, f. AF *graund dame* (prec., DAM[2])]

grăn(d)'dăd, n. (Childish or affectionate for) grandfather. [GRAND, DAD]

grande (see Ap.), fem. of GRAND (~ *toilette* pr. twahlĕt', ceremonial costume; ~ *passion* pr. păs'yawn, engrossing love affair). [F]

grăndee', n. Spanish or Portuguese nobleman of highest rank: person of high rank or eminence. [f. Sp. & Port. *grande* GRAND]

grăn'deur (-dyer), n. Great power, rank, or eminence; great nobility of character; sublimity, majesty, of appearance or effect; conscious dignity, splendour of living, surroundings, etc. [F (GRAND)]

Grand Guignol (grahn gēnyŏl'), n. Dramatic entertainment in which short pieces often of strongly sensational type are played successively. [name (= Great Punch) of theatre in Paris; F *Guignol* name of a town character of Lyons (1795)]

grăndil'oqu|ent, a. Pompous in language; given to tall talk. Hence ~ENCE n., ~entLY[2] adv. [after *eloquent* f. L *grandiloquus* (GRAND, *-loquus* -speaking f. *loqui* speak)]

grăn'diōse, a. Producing, intended or trying to produce, an impression of greatness, planned on a magnificent scale, pompous. Hence **grăndiōs'ITY** (-ŏs[2]) n., ~LY[2] (-sl-) adv. [F, f. It. *grandioso* (GRAND, -OSE[1])]

Grăndisōn'ian, a. Marked by stately courtesy & chivalric magnanimity. [Sir C. *Grandison* in Richardson's novel, -IAN]

grănge (-j), n. || Barn (arch.); country house with farm-buildings attached. [ME, f. AF *graunge* f. med. L *granica* (*granum* grain)]

grăn'ger|ize (-j-), **-ise** (-īz), v.t. Extra-illustrate (book) by inserting prints etc. often cut from other books. Hence ~īzA[2]TION, ~īZER[1], ~ISM(1), ~ITE(1), nn. [J. *Granger* published 1769 a Hist. of England with blank pages for illustrations]

granif'erous, a. Producing grain or grain-like seed. So **grăn'iFORM, graniv'OROUS,** aa. [f. L *granifer* (GRAIN, -FEROUS)]

grăn'ite, n. Granular crystalline rock of quartz, orthoclase feldspar, & mica, used for building (*bite on ~,* waste pains, persist in vain); ~*ware,* speckled pottery imitating ~, kind of enamelled ironware; *the ~ city,* Aberdeen. Hence **granit'IC a., grăn'ĭtoID a. & n., granit'iFORM a.** [f. It. *granito* orig. grained (*grano* f. L *granum*)]

grănn'om, grăn'am, n. Kind of water-fly; imitation of it for fly-fishing. [orig. unkn.]

grănn'y̆, n. (Fam., affectionate, or derog. for) grandmother; (also ~'s *bend* or *knot*) reef-knot crossed the wrong way. [f. obs. *grannam* for GRANDAM +-Y³]

gränolith'ic, a. Of a kind of concrete. [L *granum* grain, Gk *lithos* stone, -IC]

grant (-ah-), v.t., & n. **1.** Consent to fulfil (request etc.; in p.p. formerly common, now rare, as answer to *I beg your pardon*); concede as indulgence, allow (person) to have (thing; noun, *that*, or *to* do); bestow (possession, right) formally, transfer (property) legally, whence **grant**EE', **grant**OR', (-ah-) nn.; concede (proposition) as basis for argument (noun, *this* etc., *that*-clause, or something *to be* something; *I* ~ *you*, I admit; *take for* ~*ed*, assume); hence ~'ABLE a. **2.** n. ~ing (*the* ~ *or refusal of*); formal conferment, legal assignment; thing, esp. sum. ~ed (often *capitation* ~, ~-*in-aid*); conveyance by written instrument; ~-*aided school*, one receiving some financial assistance from public funds. [ME, f. OF *greanter* f. Rom. **credentare* f. part. of *credere* entrust]

Granth (grŭnt), n. Sacred scriptures of the Sikhs. [Hindi, = book, code (f. Skr. *grantha* tying, literary composition)]

grăn'ül|ar, a. Of, like, grains; with granulated surface or structure. Hence ~ă'RITY n., ~arLY² adv., ~o- comb. form, ~OUS a. [f. LL *granulum* small grain (*granum*, -ULE), -UL-, -AR¹]

grăn'ül|āte, v.t. & i. Form (t. & i.) into grains; roughen surface of; (of wound etc.) form small prominences as beginning of healing or junction, heal, join. Hence or cogn. ~ATE² (-at) a., ~A'TION, ~ātOR, nn. [as prec., -ATE³]

grăn'üle, n. Small grain. [as prec.]

grāpe, n. Green or purple berry growing in clusters on vine, eaten as fruit or used in making wine (*the* ~, *the juice of the* ~, wine; *the* ~*s are sour, sour* ~*s*, said when person disparages what he vainly desires); ~-*shot*; diseased growth like bunch of ~s on pastern of horse etc., or on plants in cattle; ~-*brandy*, distilled from ~s, or wine, alone; ~-*CURE*¹; ~-*fruit*, large round yellow citrus fruit with rather acid juicy pulp; ~-*house*, vinery; ~-*scissors*, for thinning ~-bunches at early stage of growth, also for dividing bunches at table; ~-*shot* (hist.), small balls put several together in bag etc. to make scattering charge for cannon; ~-*stone*, one of seeds inside ~; ~-*sugar*, dextrose or glucose; ~-*vine*, vine, skating figure in which both feet are on ice together & form interlacing lines, rumour, (false) report. Hence **grāp'ERY**(3) n., **grāp'Y**² a. [ME, f. OF, bunch of ~s, prob. f. *graper* gather with vine-hook (f. *grape*, f. WG **krāppo* (= OHG *krāpfo* hook))]

grăph¹ (or -ahf), n., & v.t. Symbolic diagram expressing system of mathematical or chemical connexion; curve (in statistical statements); (v.t.) plot or trace on a ~. [abbr. of *graphic formula*]

graph² (-ahf), n., & v.t. Gelatine copying apparatus; (v.t.) copy; copy, multiply, with this. [colloq. abbr. of *chromograph, hectograph*, etc.]

-graph (-ahf), suf. repr. F *-graphe*, L f. Gk *-graphos*, -written, -writing, -writer, denoting (1) thing written in such a way (f. Gk, as *auto*~, *chiro*~, *holo*~; on Gk st., as *litho*~, *photo*~; & in hybrids, as *picto*~); (2) instrument that records something or by some means (*helio*~, *seismo*~, *tele*~); (3) write in such a way (*calli*~, *hecto*~).

-grapher, suf. repr. Gk *-graphos* (prec.) & forming nn. denoting one versed in -GRAPHY. [-ER¹]

grăph'ic(al rare), aa. Of drawing, painting, engraving, etching, etc.; vividly descriptive, lifelike; of writing; (of minerals) showing marks like writing on surface or in fracture; of diagrams or symbolic curves. [f. L f. Gk *graphikos* (*graphē* writing, -IC)]

-grăph'ic(al), suf. = of or by -GRAPHY.

grăph'ically, adv. As in a picture, vividly; by writing; by diagrams or GRAPH¹s. [-LY²]

grăph'īte, n. PLUMBAGO. Hence **graphit'**IC, **grăph'it**OID, aa. [f. G *graphit* (Gk *graphō* write, -ITE¹)]

grăph'iūre, n. S.-Afr. rodent with tail ending in pencil of hairs. [f. Gk *grapheion* pencil, *oura* tail]

graphöl'ogy, n. Study of, art of inferring character from, handwriting; system of graphic formulae, notation for GRAPH¹s. [f. Gk *graphē* writing, -LOGY]

grăph'otype, n. (Process for making) relief block for surface-printing. [as prec. +TYPE]

-graphy, suf. = F, G *-graphie*, L-*graphia*, repr. Gk *-graphia* forming nn. denoting (1) styles of writing, drawing, etc. (*litho*~, *brachy*~, *steno*~, *calli*~); (2) descriptive science (*geo*~, *biblio*~, *seleno*~).

grăp'nel, n. Iron-clawed instrument thrown with rope to seize object, esp. enemy's ship; small anchor with several flukes used for boats & balloons. [ME, f. AF **grapenel* f. OF *grapon* (mod. *grappin*) f. WG **krāppo* see GRAPE]

grăp'ple, n., & v.t. & i. **1.** Clutching-instrument, grapnel. **2.** Hold or grip (as) of wrestlers, close contest. **3.** vb. Seize, fasten, (as) with grapnel; take hold of, grip, with the hands, come to close quarters with; contend *with, together,* or abs., in close fight, battle *with*; ~ *with*, try to overcome, accomplish, or deal with. [(1) f. OF *grapil* dim. of *grappe*, see GRAPE, GRAPNEL]

grăp'pling, n. In vbl senses; also, ~-iron, grapnel. [-ING¹]

grasp (-ah-), v.t. & i., & n. **1.** ~ *at*, try to seize, accept with avidity; clutch at, seize greedily, (part.) avaricious, whence ~'ingLY² adv., ~'ingNESS n.; hold firmly (~ *nettle*, tackle difficulty or danger boldly), grip; get mental hold of, comprehend; hence ~'ABLE a. **2. n.** Fast hold, grip, (*within, beyond,* one's ~, close, not close, enough to be ~ed); control, mastery; mental hold, comprehensiveness of mind. [14th c. *grasp, grapse* perh. f. OE **grǣpsan* f. Gmc **graip-* GROPE, but cf. LG (G), EFris. *grapsen*]

grass (-ah-), n., & v.t. **1.** Herbage of which blades or leaves & stalks are eaten by cattle, horses, sheep, etc. (*not let ~ grow, ~ does not grow, under* one's *feet,* of person who wastes no time in doing something; *hear the ~ grow,* be of preternatural acuteness); any species of this (including in bot. use, excluding in pop. use, the cereals, reeds, & bamboos; usu. with defining words, as *bunch, spear, -~, ~ of Parnassus*); (sl.) asparagus; grazing, pasture, (*be at, go, put, send, turn out, to ~; at ~,* fig., out of work, making holiday, etc.; so perh. *~ widow,* wife whose husband is absent); pasture land; ~--covered ground (*keep off the ~*); (Mining) earth's surface, pit-head; *send, go, to ~,* knock (person), be knocked or fall, down; ~'*hopper,* kinds of jumping & chirping insect (*~-hopper-beam,* working-beam in engine pivoted at end instead of in middle); ~-*snake,* ‖ common ringed snake; ~-*tree,* kinds of Australasian tree; hence ~'LESS, ~'Y[2], aa. **2. v.t.** Cover with turf; lay (flax etc.) on ~ to bleach; knock down, fell, (opponent); bring (fish) to bank, (bird by shot) to ground. [OE *grǽs,* OS, OHG, ON, Goth. *gras* f. Gmc **grasom,* cogn. w. GREEN, GROW]

grāte[1], n. = GRATING (rare), whence **grăt'ED[2]** a.; (frame of metal bars for confining fuel in) fireplace or furnace. Hence ~'LESS (-tl-) a. [15th c., f. OF *grate* f. Rom. **grata, *crata* f. L *cratis* hurdle; cf. GRIDDLE]

grāte|e[2], v.t. & i. Reduce to small particles by rubbing on rough surface, whence (-)~'ER[1](2) n.; have irritating effect (*up*)*on;* grind (teeth); rub (i. & t.) with harsh scraping noise *against* or (*up*)*on* something else; sound harshly or discordantly (*a ~ing laugh, voice*); (of hinge etc.) creak. Hence ~'ingLY[2] adv. [15th c., f. OF *grater* f. Rom. **grattare* f. WG **krattōn* (= OHG *krazzōn*) SCRATCH]

grāte'ful (-tf-), a. Acceptable, comforting, refreshing; thankful, feeling or showing gratitude (*to* person, *for* thing). Hence ~LY[2] adv., ~NESS n. [f. obs. *grate* adj. f. L *gratus* +-FUL]

grăt'icūle, n. Fine lines or fibres incorporated in telescope or other optical instrument as measuring scale or as aid in locating objects; (Surveying) network or lines on paper representing meridians & parallels. [F, f. med. L *graticula* for *craticula* gridiron (L *cratis* hurdle, -ULE)]

grăt'ifȳ, v.t. Remunerate, fee, make present usu. of money to; bribe; please, satisfy, oblige, delight, whence ~ING[2] a.

(*to*), ~ingLY[2] adv.; please by compliance, assent to wish of, give free course to or indulge (desire, feeling, impulse). So **grătiFICA'TION** n. [f. F *gratifier* or L *gratificari* (*gratus* pleasing, -FY)]

gratin (see Ap.), n. Way of cooking, dish cooked, by crumbing bread or grating cheese & cooking between two fires to produce light crust; *au* (ō) *~,* so prepared. [F]

grāt'ing, n. Framework of parallel or crossed wooden or metal bars; (Opt.) set of parallel wires, or surface of glass etc. ruled with parallel lines, for producing spectra by diffraction. [GRATE[1]+-ING[1]]

grāt'is, adv. & a. Gratuitous(ly), (given, done) for nothing, without charge, free. [L, contracted abl. pl. of *gratia* favour]

grăt'itūde, n. Being thankful, appreciation of & inclination to return kindness. [f. F, or LL *gratitudo* (*gratus* thankful, -TUDE)]

gratū'itous, a. Got or given free, not earned or paid for; uncalled for, unwarranted, motiveless, done or acting without good or assignable reason (*a ~ lie* or *liar*). Hence ~LY[2] adv., ~NESS n. [f. L *gratuitus* spontaneous, cogn. w. *gratia* favour, +-OUS]

gratū'itȳ, n. Money present of amount fixed by giver in recognition of an inferior's good offices, tip; bounty to soldiers etc. on demobilization or retirement or some other occasions. [f. F *gratuité* or med. L *gratuitas* gift (*gratus* grateful, -TY)]

‖ **grăt'ūlāte, -ā'tion.** (Arch. for) congr-.
‖ **grăt'ūlātorȳ,** a. Expressing joy at another's success etc., complimentary, congratulatory. [f. LL *gratulatorius* (L *gratulari* congratulate +-ORY)]

gravăm'ĕn, n. (pl. *-mina,* rare). Grievance; ‖ memorial from Lower House of Convocation to Upper on disorders or grievances of Church; essence, worst part, *of* accusation. [LL, inconvenience (*gravare* to load f. *gravis* heavy, -MEN)]

grāve[1], n. Excavation to receive corpse, mound or monument over it, (*secret as the ~,* quite; *make one turn in his ~,* of act etc. that he would have been pained by while alive; *someone walking on my ~,* said when one shivers unaccountably; *one* FOOT[1] *in the ~*), whence ~'LESS (-vl-) a.; being dead, death, Hades, whence ~ WARD (-vw-) adv. & a.; receptacle of or for what is dead (*~ of reputations,* where many reputations have been lost); trench for earthing up potatoes etc.; ~--*clothes,* wrappings in which corpse is buried; ~-*digger,* lit., also kinds of insect that bury bodies of insects etc. as food for their larvae; ~'*stone,* stone over ~, inscribed stone at head or foot of ~; ~'*yard,* burial ground. [OE *grœf,* OS *graf,* OHG *grap* f. WG **grabhom*]

grāve[2], v.t. (p.p. ~n, ~d, as stated). (Arch.) bury (~d); (arch.) carve, sculpture, engrave, (material, representation; ~*n*, ~*d*; ~*n image*, idol); (fig.) fix indelibly (*on, in*, mind etc.; ~*n*, ~*d*). [OE *grafan*, OHG *graban*, ON *grafa*, Goth. *graban* f. Gmc **grabhan* (prec.; see GROOVE)]

grāve[3], a. & n. **1.** Important, weighty, needing serious thought; (of faults, difficulties, responsibilities, symptoms) formidable, threatening, serious; dignified, solemn, slow-moving, not gay; sombre, plain, not showy; hence ~'LY[2] (-vl-) adv. **2.** (Of accent) low-pitched, not acute; ~ ACCENT[1]. **3.** n. ~ accent. [f. F, or L *gravis* heavy, serious]

grāve[4], v.t. Clean (ship's bottom) by burning off accretions & tarring while aground or in *graving*-DOCK[4]. [perh. f. OF *grave = grève* shore]

grăv'el, n., & v.t. (-ll-). **1.** Coarse sand & small water-worn or pounded stones, much used for laying paths & roads; (Geol., Mining) stratum of this, esp. one containing gold (*pay* ~, containing enough gold to yield profit); (Path.) (disease with) aggregations of visible urinary crystals; ~*-blind*, more than SAND-BLIND (Shaks., *M. of V.*, ii. ii. 38); hence ~lY[2] a. **2.** v.t. Lay, strew, with ~; perplex, puzzle, nonplus, (f. obs. sense *run aground*). [ME, f. OF *gravele* f. *grave* (prec.)]

grăv'er, n. In vbl senses; esp., burin. [-ER[1]]

Graves (grahv), n. Light white wine produced in the ~ district of France. [place]

grăv'id, a. (literary). Pregnant. [f. L *gravidus* (GRAVE[3])]

grăv'it|āte, v.i. & t. Move or tend by force of gravity *towards* a body; sink (as) by gravity, tend to low level, settle down; (Diamond-digging) manipulate (gravel) so that heavy stones sink to bottom; (transf.) be strongly attracted *to(wards)* some centre of influence. Hence ~A'TION n., ~ā'tionAL (-shon-), ~ATIVE, aa. [f. mod. L *gravitare* (after GRAVITY), -ATE[3]]

grăv'itÿ, n. **1.** Being grave, solemnity; importance, seriousness; staidness, sobriety, serious demeanour. **2.** Weight (CENTRE[1] *of* ~; *specific* ~, relative weight of any kind of matter, expressed by ratio of given volume to same volume of a standard—usu. water for liquid or solid, & air for gas). **3.** Attractive force by which bodies tend to centre of earth, degree of intensity of this measured by acceleration, degree of intensity with which one body is affected by the attraction of gravitation exercised by another body. [f. F *gravité* or L *gravitas* (GRAVE[3], -TY)]

gravūre', n. (Short for) PHOTOGRAVURE.

grăv'ÿ, n. Juices that exude from flesh during & after cooking; dressing for food made from these with other materials; ~*-boat*, boat-shaped vessel for ~; ~ *beef*, part of leg of beef cooked for its~. [perh.

a misreading as *grave* of *grane* in OF cookery books; OF *grane, grenon* = stew]

gray. See GREY.

gray'ling, n. Silver-grey freshwater fish with long high dorsal fin; butterfly with grey under-side to wings. [GREY + -LING[1]]

grāz|e[1], v.i. & t. Feed (esp. cattle, or intr. of cattle) on growing grass etc. or ~'ING[1](3) n.; feed on (grass etc., often *down*); tend ~ing cattle; pasture cattle. [OE *grasian* (GRASS n.)]

grāz|e[2], v.t. & i., & n. **1.** Touch lightly in passing; abrade (skin etc.) in rubbing past; suffer slight abrasion of (part of body); go with passing contact *against*, *along*, *through*, *by*, *past*, etc. **2.** n. ~ing abrasion. [orig. obsc.; perh. by transf. f. prec. 'take off the grass close to the ground' (of a bullet etc.]

grā'zier (-zh*e*r), n. One who feeds cattle for market. Hence **grā'ziERY**(2) (-zherī) n. [GRASS + -IER]

grease[1] (-ēs), n. Fat of deer or other game (*in* ~, *in pride* or *prime of* ~, fit for killing, fat); melted fat of dead animals, esp. when soft; oily or fatty matter, esp. as lubricant; oily matter in wool, uncleansed wool, (*wool in the* ~, in fleeces); disease in horses' heels; ~*-box*, attached to train-wheel for lubrication; ~*-paint*, composition for painting actors' faces; ~*-trap*, appliance for catching ~ in drains. [ME, f. OF *graisse* f. Rom. **crassia* (L *crassus* a. fat)]

grease[2] (or -ēz), v.t. Anoint, soil, or lubricate, with grease (~ *the wheels*, make affairs go smoothly, esp. by money; ~ *palm of*, bribe; *like* ~*d lightning*, sl., very fast); affect (horse) with grease. [f. prec.]

greas'er (or -z-), n. In vbl senses, esp.: head fireman on steamer; *(sl.) native Mexican or Spanish-American. [-ER[1]]

greas'lÿ (or -z-), a. Smeared or covered with, containing, made of, like, with too much, grease; (of wool) uncleansed; (of horse) affected with the grease; slimy with mud or moisture; (of manners or expression) disagreeably unctuous; ~*y fritillary*, kind of butterfly; ~*y pole*, greased for climbing or working on in sports. Hence ~iLY[2] adv., ~iNESS n., (-z-). [-Y[2]]

great (grāt), a. & n. **1.** Large, big, (usu. with implied surprise, admiration, contempt, indignation, etc., as *made a* ~ *blot, look at that* ~ *wasp*; often colloq. preceding other adj., *a* ~ *big loaf* or *thick stick*; as distinctive epithet of the larger species or individual, as ~ *A, Z*, the capital letters, ~ *St John's wort*, also ~*er celandine* etc., ~ *titmouse, G*~ BEAR[1], *G*~ *Malvern* etc., *G*~ *Portland Street*; also in a few phrases, as *a* ~ DEAL[1], MANY; *the* ~ *majority*, much the larger part; ~*est common* MEASURE, *lived to a* ~ *age, a* ~ *while ago*; || ~ *with child*, arch., pregnant). **2.** Beyond the ordinary (*take* ~ *care*; *of* ~ *popularity*; *shows* ~ *ignorance*). **3.** Important, elevated, distinguished, critical, *the* chief, pre-eminent, (*it is a ~ thing to have —*; *a ~ occasion*; *the ~ attraction*; *the G~ Powers of Europe*, chief States; *the ~ world*, high society; in excll., as *G~ God!, Caesar!, Scott!*; *the G~*, appended in sense *the best known of the name*, as *Alexander the G~*, or prefixed in titles, as *the G~ King*, of ancient Persia, *the G~ Mogul*, etc., & burlesqued in *the G~* UNPAID, UNWASHED). **4.** Of remarkable ability, genius, intellectual or practical qualities, loftiness or integrity of character, (*a ~ judge, painter*, etc.; *the truly ~ man*; *~ thoughts*), whence *~-heart*ED[2] a. **5.** pred. Having much skill *at* or information *on*; highly satisfactory (*wouldn't it be~ if—?*). **6.** Fully deserving the name of, (with agent-nouns) doing the act much or on a large scale, (*a ~ scoundrel, flasco*; *~ friends*; *is a ~ dancer, landowner*). **7.** (Prefixed once or more to *uncle, aunt, nephew, niece*, & kinship words compounded with GRAND) one degree further removed upwards or downwards. **8.** *G~ Assize, Day*, or *Inquest*, Day of Judgement; *G~ Bible*, Coverdale's Version 1539; *G~* BRITAIN, CHARTER, CIRCLE[1]; ‖*~'*COAT[1], whence *~*coat*'*ED[2], *~*coat*'*LESS, aa.; *the ~* COMMONER; *G~er* BRITAIN; *~est happiness of the ~est number*, test principle of Benthamism; ‖ *~ go*, final examination for B.A. at Cambridge, cf. *greats* below; *~ gross*, twelve gross; *~ house*, chief house in village etc.; *~ organ*, chief manual with its related pipes and mechanism in an organ having two or more manuals; *~* PRIMER; *~ toe*, now usu. BIG *toe*; *G~ War* (of 1914–18). Hence *~'*EN[6] v.t. & i. (arch.), *~'*NESS n., (-ăt-). **9.** n. (Abs. use of adj.) *the~*, (pl.) *~* persons (also without *the* in *~ & small*); (sing.) what is *~*. **10.** ‖*~s*, Oxford B.A. final examination, esp. that for honours in Lit. Hum. [OE *grēat*, OS *grōt*, OHG *grōz* f. WG *grautaz*]

great'lў (-răt-), adv. Much, by much, (usu. with vbs, participles, or comparatives; *~ esteemed, superior*; *should ~ prefer*); nobly, loftily. [-LY[2]]

greave, n. (usu. pl.). Piece(s) of armour for shin(s). [ME, f. OF *greve* shin, greave, of unkn. orig.]

greaves (-vz), n. pl. Fibrous tallow refuse, used as food of dog etc. or fish-bait. [f. LG *greven* pl.]

grēbe, n. Kinds of short-bodied lobe-footed almost tailless diving bird; its plumage as trimming. [f. F *grèbe* of unkn. orig.]

Grē'cian (-shn), a. & n. **1.** Greek (rare except of architecture & facial outline; also in ‖ *~ bend*, affected attitude in walking prevalent c. 1870, *~ gift*, = GREEK *gift*, ‖ *~ knot*, way of dressing woman's hair at back of head, *~ nose*, straight & continuing forehead line without dip, *~ profile*, with *~ nose*, ‖ *~ slippers*, trade name

for oriental shape). **2.** n. Greek scholar; ‖ boy of highest class at Christ's Hospital. [f. L *Graecia* Greece + -AN]

Grecism, Grecize, Greco-. See **Grae-**.

greed, n. Insatiate longing esp. for wealth. [back formation f. foll.]

greed'|ў, a. Ravenous, voracious, gluttonous, avaricious, covetous, rapacious, (often *of*); eager, keen, intensely desirous (*to do*). Hence *~*ĬLY[2] adv., *~*ĬNESS n. [OE *grǣdig*, OS *grādag*, OHG *grātac*, ON *grāthugr*, Goth. *grēdags* f. Gmc **grǣdhuz* hunger]

Greek, n. & a. **1.** Native of Greece, member of *~* race, (*when ~ meets ~, then comes the tug of war*, orig. *~s joined ~s*, then *was*, said of equal encounter); member of *~* Church; cunning person, sharper; the *~* language (*~ to me*, beyond my comprehension), whence *~'*LESS a. **2.** adj. Of Greece or its people, Hellenic; of, according to, written or spoken in, *~* (*~ Fathers*, FATHER[1]s of the Church who wrote in *~*); *~ Church*, also *Orthodox* or *Eastern*, Church acknowledging Patriarch of Constantinople, divided from Rome in 9th c., & including esp. Christians of Greece, Russia, & Turkish Empire; *~* CALENDS, FIRE[1], FRET[1] or *key*; *~* CROSS[1]; *~ gift*, one given with intent to harm (Virg. *Aen.* ii. 49). [adj. f. n.; OE *Crēcas* (pl.), OHG *Chrēch*, Goth. *Krēks* f. Gmc **Krekaz* f. L *Graecus* f. Gk *Graikoi* prehistoric name of Hellenes; sp. *G-* already in OE *Grecas* after L]

green[1], a. & n. **1.** Of the colour between blue & yellow in the spectrum, coloured like grass, sea-water, emerald, olive, etc. **2.** Covered with herbage, verdant, in leaf, (*a ~ Christmas, season, Yule*, mild, without snow). **3.** (Of complexion) pale, sickly-hued, (*~ eye*, jealousy, whence *~'*eyED[2] (-īd) a.; *~ jaundice*, kind in which patient's skin is *~*); (fig.) jealous, envious. **4.** Vegetable (*~ food*, MEAT). **5.** (Of fruit etc.) unripe, young & tender, flourishing, not dried. **6.** Full of vitality, not withered or worn out, (*in the ~*, dry, tree, under good, bad, conditions; *a ~ old age*). **7.** Immature, undeveloped, inexperienced, gullible. **8.** Not dried, seasoned, or tanned. **9.** Fresh, not healed, (*a ~ wound*). **10.** **~'back*, U.S. legal-tender note, note issued by any U.S. national bank; *~-blind*, having retina insensitive to *~* rays; *~ cheese*, unripened cheese, whey cheese, cheese coloured *~* with sage; (*Board of*) *G~ Cloth*, Lord Steward's department of Royal Household; *~ crop*, used for food in *~* state (opp. *hay* etc.); ‖ *~ drake*, mayfly; *~ earth*, hydrous silicate of potassium, iron, & other bases; *~ fat*, of turtle, esteemed by epicures; *~'finch* or *~ linnet*, bird with yellow & *~* plumage; ‖ *~ fingers* (colloq.), skill in gardening; ‖ *~'fly*, kind of aphis; *~'gage*, roundish *~* fine-flavoured plum (Sir W. Gage c. 1725); *~ goose*, killed under four months old and eaten without stuffing; ~'*grocer(y)*, (business of, things sold by) retail dealer in fruit & vegetables; ~'*heart*, a British Guiana timber tree; ~'*horn*, ignoramus, raw hand, simpleton; ~'*house*, of glass for rearing delicate plants; ‖ ~ *light* (colloq.), permission to go ahead with some project; ~-*man*, golf-course keeper; ~ *manure*, growing plants ploughed into soil; ‖ ~-*peak*, ~ woodpecker (transl. of It. *picchio verde*); ~-*room*, accommodating actors & actresses when off stage; ~'*sand*, = ~ earth, kind of sandstone largely of this earth, stratum largely of this sandstone; ~'*shank*, large kind of sandpiper; ~'*sick(ness)*, (affected with) CHLOROSIS; ~-*stick*, bone-fracture, esp. in children, in which one side of bone is broken & one only bent; ~'*stone*, kinds of ~ eruptive rock containing feldspar & hornblende, also kind of jade; ~-*stuff*, vegetation, ~ vegetables; ~'*sward*, turf; ~ *table*, gaming table; ~'*tail*, grannom; ~ *tea*, made from steam-dried leaves; ~'*weed*, kind of genista used for dyeing; ~'*wood*, woodlands in summer, esp. as scene of outlaw life; ‖ ~'*yard*, enclosure for stray beasts, pound; hence ~'ISH[1](2), & (in comb. as ~*y-yellow*)~'Y[2], aa., ~'LY[2] adv., ~'NESS n. **11.** n. What is ~, ~ part of anything, ~ colour, (*do you see any* ~, i.e. sign of gullibility, *in my eye?*); ~ dye (usu. with epithet, as *mineral*, *Paris*, ~). **12.** Vigour, youth, virility, (usu. *in the* ~). **13.** Verdure, vegetation, also ~'ERY n. **14.** ‖ (pl.). ~ vegetables before or after cooking. **15.** Piece of public or common grassy land; grass-plot used for special purpose (esp. in comb. as *bleaching*, *bowling*, *putting*, ~~). [OE *grēne*, OS *grōni*, OHG *gruoni*, ON *grœnn* f. Gmc **grōnjaz* f. **gro-* (GROW)]

green[2], v.i. & t. Become green, esp. with verdure, dye green, soil etc. with green; (sl.) hoax, take in. [OE *grēnian* (prec.)]

green'er, n. (sl.). Raw hand, esp. newly arrived foreigner seeking work. [-ER[1]]

green'ing, n. Kind of apple, green when ripe. [-ING[3]]

green'lĕt, n. = VIREO. [GREEN[1], -LET]

greenth, n. (rare). Verdure. [-TH[1]]

Greenwich (grĭn'ĭj), n. Town in Kent formerly with State observatory now moved to Herstmonceux in Sussex (~ *time*, mean time for meridian of ~, standard time in Britain & some other countries); ~ *Hospital*, formerly used to accommodate old and disabled navy seamen (who are now out-pensioners), later occupied by the Royal Naval College for officer students.

greet[1], v.t. Accost with salutation; salute *with* words or gestures, receive on meeting or arrival *with* speech or action (friendly or not); (of cheers etc.) hail; (of sight etc.) meet (eye, ear). Hence ~'ING[1] n. [OE *grētan*, OS *grōtian*, OHG *gruozzen* f. WG **grōtjan* cry out etc.]

greet[2], v.i. (Sc.). Weep. [OE *grētan* (*grēotan*), OS (*griotan*), ON *grāta*, Goth. *grētan* f. Gmc **grētan*]

grĕff'ier, n. Registrar, notary, (esp. in foreign countries & Channel Islands). [F, f. med. L *graphiarius* f. L *graphium* stilus; see GRAFT[1]]

grĕgār'ious, a. Living in flocks or communities; fond of company; (Bot.) growing in clusters; of flocks, of crowds. Hence ~LY[2] adv., ~NESS n. [f. L *gregarius* (*grex -egis* flock, -ARY[1]) +-OUS]

Grĕgōr'ian, a. & n. **1.** Of, according to, the plain-chant or plain-song ritual music named after Pope Gregory I (n., a ~ chant); ~ *tones*, eight plain-song melodies prescribed for psalms in R.C. Ch. **2.** Established by Pope Gregory XIII (~ CALENDAR, correction 1582 of the Julian; ~ *style*=*new* STYLE[1]; ~ *epoch*, from 1582). [f. LL f. Gk *Grēgorios* Gregory +-AN]

grĕg'orỹ-powd'er, n. Compound powder of rhubarb, used as aperient. [J. *Gregory*, Scottish physician d. 1822]

grĕm'ial, n. Silk apron placed on bishop's lap at some ceremonies. [f. LL *gremialis* (L *gremium* lap, -AL)]

‖ grĕm'lin, n. (R.A.F. sl.). Mischievous sprite alleged to cause mishaps. [orig. unkn.]

grĕnāde', n. Small explosive shell thrown by hand or (*rifle-*~) shot from rifle-barrel; glass receptacle thrown to disperse chemicals for testing drains, extinguishing fires, etc. [F, f. Sp. *granada* POMEGRANATE]

grĕnadier', n. **1.** (Orig.) soldier who threw grenades; (now) ‖ *G~s* or *G~ Guards*, first regiment of household infantry. **2.** S.-Afr. weaver-bird with red & black plumage. [F (prec., -IER)]

grĕn'adine[1], n. Dish of veal or poultry fillets, trimmed, larded, & glazed. [F -*in*]

grĕn'adine[2], n. Dress-fabric of open silk or silk & wool. [F]

grĕn'adine[3] (-ēn), n. French cordial syrup of pomegranate. [see POMEGRANATE]

Gresham's law. See LAW[1].

grĕssōr'ial, a. (zool.). Walking, adapted for walking. [f. L *gradi gress-* walk, -OR, -IAL]

grew. See GROW.

grey (grā), (esp. U.S.) **gray**, a. & n., & v.i. & t. **1.** Intermediate between black & white, coloured like ashes or lead, (~ *monk*, Cistercian; ~ *friar*, Franciscan; ~ *sister*, of third order of St Francis; ~ *mare is better horse*, wife rules husband); between light & dark, dull, clouded, depressing, dismal; (of person or his or her hair) turning white with age etc.; ancient, immemorial; belonging to old age, experienced, mature; ~ *crow* or ~-*back*, hooded crow; ~'*beard*, old man, large stoneware jug for spirit, ‖ kind of lichen; ‖ ~-*coat*, Cumberland yeoman; ‖ ~ *drake*, kind of ephemera; ~ *eminence*, = *éminence grise* (see EMINENCE); ~ *goose*,

GREYLAG; ~-*headed*, old, of long service *in*, ancient, time-worn; ~-*hen*, female of black grouse (cf. BLACK[1]-*cock*); ~ *matter*, material of active part of brain; ~'*stone*, ~ volcanic rock; hence~'ISH[1](2) a., ~'LY[2] adv., ~'NESS n., (grā-). 2. n. ~ clothes; cold sunless light; ~ colour; ~ pigment; ~ horse (*the Greys* or *Scots Greys*, 2nd Dragoons). 3. vb. Become, make, ~; (Photog.) dull surface of (glass), give mezzotint effect to (photograph) by covering negative with such glass. [OE *grǣg*, OHG *grāo*, ON *grár* f. Gmc *grǣwaz*]

‖ grey'cing (grā-), n. (colloq.). Grey-hound-racing. [abbr.]

grey'hound (grā-), n. Slender long-legged keen-sighted swift dog used in coursing hares etc. (*ocean* ~, swift ship); ~-*racing*, modern sport in which mechanical hare is coursed by ~s as opportunity for betting. [OE *grīghund* corresp. to ON *greyhundr* f. *grey* bitch (not rel. to GREY)]

grey'lag (gōōse) (grā-), n. Common European wild goose. [*lag* said to refer to its staying long in England for a migrant]

grey'wacke (grā'wăke, *or* -āk), n. A conglomerate rock consisting of rounded pebbles and sand cemented together. [anglicized f. G *grauwacke* (*grau* grey + WACKE)]

grid, n. Frame of spaced parallel bars, grating, (Electr.) wire network between filament and anode of valve; system of numbered squares printed on military etc. map and forming basis of map references; network of lines, electric-power connexions, etc.; gridiron (for cooking, & docking). [back formation f. GRIDIRON]

grid'dle, n., & v.t. Circular iron plate for baking cakes on; miner's wire-bottomed screen (vb, screen with ~). [ME *gredil* f. OF *gredil* (later *grail*, *greil*) f. Rom. *graticulum* (*-ula*) f. L *craticula* dim. of *cratis* hurdle; cf. GRATE[1], GRILL[2]]

gride, v.i., & n. Cut, scrape, *along*, *through*, etc., with strident or grating sound (also ~s *its way*); (n.) grating sound. [orig. sense *pierce*, by metath. f. GIRD[2]]

grid'iron (-īrn), n. Barred metal cooking utensil for broiling; (Naut.) frame of parallel beams for supporting ship in dock; *football field (from the parallel lines marking out field of play); (Theatr.) plank structure over stage supporting mechanism for drop-scenes etc.; a naval evolution; (also ~-*pendulum*) compensation pendulum with parallel rods of different metals. [13th c. *gredire*, var. of *gredil* GRIDDLE, later assoc. w. *iron*; cf. ANDIRON]

grief, n. Deep or violent sorrow, keen regret, (*come to* ~, meet with disaster, fail, fall). [ME, f. OF (*grever* GRIEVE)]

griev'ance, n. Real or fancied ground of complaint. [f. OF *grevance* (prec., -ANCE)]

grieve[1], v.t. & i. Give deep sorrow to; feel grief (*at*, *for*, *about*, *over*). [ME, f. OF *grever* f. Rom. *gravare* f. L *gravare* (*gravis* heavy)]

‖ grieve[2], n. (Sc.). Farm-bailiff, overseer. [f. OE *gerēfa*; see REEVE[1]]

griev'ous, a. Bringing serious trouble, injurious; (of pain etc.) severe; flagrant, heinous; exciting grief. Hence ~LY[2] adv. [ME, f. OF *grevos* (GRIEVE[1], -OUS)]

griff'in[1], n. (Anglo-Ind.). (Also griff) newly arrived European, novice, greenhorn. Hence ~AGE(2), ~HOOD, ~SHIP, nn., ~ISH[1] a. [orig. unkn.]

griff'in[2], griff'on[1], grȳph'on, n. Fabulous creature with eagle's head & wings & lion's body; ‖ *the Griffin*, monument on site of Temple Bar, London; (-*fon*) kind of vulture (also ~-*vulture*). [ME, f. OF *grifoun* (L *gryphus* f. Gk *grups*, -OON)]

griff'on[2], n. Kind of foreign coarse-haired terrier-like dog. [F, = prec.]

grig, n. ‖ Small eel; grasshopper or cricket (*merry*, *lively*, *as a* ~; sense *cricket* doubtful, perh. invented to account for phrase). [orig. unkn.]

grill[1], v.t. & i., & n. 1. Broil (t. & i.) on gridiron (also fig. of torture or great heat), whence ~'ER[1] (1, 2) n.; *subject to severe questioning (esp. by police); scallop (oysters etc.). 2. n. ~ed food; (also ~-*room*) room where steaks etc. are ~ed & served. [f. F *griller* (foll.)]

grill[2], n. Gridiron. [F *gril* = OF *grail*, *greil* f. Rom. *graticulum* (*-ula*); see GRIDDLE]

grill'age, n. Heavy framework of cross-timbering as foundation for building in treacherous soil. [F (foll., -AGE)]

grille, grill[3], n. Grating, latticed screen, esp. in door for observing callers, in convent separating nuns from visitors, formerly in front of ladies' gallery in House of Commons, etc.; (Tennis) square opening in wall; spawn-hatching frame. Hence grillED[2] (-ld) a. [F, = OF *graille*, *greille* f. Rom. *graticula* (*-ulum*); see GRIDDLE]

grilse, n. Young salmon that has been only once to the sea. [orig. unkn.]

grim, a. (-mm-). Stern, unrelenting, merciless, severe; of forbidding or harsh aspect (often of death; *hold on like* ~ *death*, tight); sinister, ghastly, unmirthful, (*has a* ~ *truth in it*; *a* ~ *smile*; ~ *laughter*, *pastime*, etc.). Hence ~'LY[2] adv., ~'NESS n. [OE, OS, OHG *grim*, ON *grimmr* f. Gmc *grimmaz*]

grimace', n., & v.i. 1. Wry face expressing annoyance etc. or meant to raise a laugh; affected look; use of such looks, affectation. 2. v.i. Make wry face. Hence or cogn. grimā'CER[1], grimā'CIER, nn. [F, f. Sp. *grimazo* f. *grima* fright, f. Goth. *grimms* (GRIM)]

grimal'kin (-awl-, -ăl-), n. Old she-cat; spiteful old woman. [f. *grey* + *Malkin* (*Matilda*, -KIN)]

grime, n., & v.t. **1.** Soot, dirt, ingrained in some surface, esp. the skin; hence **grim′y²** a., **grim′iness** n. **2.** v.t. Blacken, befoul. [cf. Flem. *grijm(en)*]

Grimm's law. See LAW¹.

grin, v.i. & t. (-nn-), & n. **1.** Show teeth in sign of amusement or pain or in forced or unrestrained or stupid smile (often *at*; ~ *& bear it*, take pain etc. stoically; ~ *like Cheshire cat*, constantly & meaninglessly; ~ *through horse-collar*, in grimacing-match at rustic sports); express (contempt, satisfaction) by ~ning. **2.** n. Act of ~ning (often *on the* ~ or *broad* ~). [OE *grennian* (cf. OHG *grennan*, ON *grenja*) f. Gmc *gran-*; cogn. w. GROAN]

grind, v.t. & i. (*ground*), & n. **1.** Reduce to small particles or powder by crushing between mill-stones, teeth, etc. (often *down*, *small*, *to pieces*, *into dust*, etc.); (quasi-pass.) admit of being ground (*will not* ~ *fine*); oppress, harass with exactions, (often *down*; a ~*ing tyranny*; also ~ *the faces of the poor* etc.); produce (flour) by ~ing; sharpen or smooth by friction (*has an* AXE *to* ~; ~ *lenses*, *diamonds*, etc.); work (hand-mill); turn handle of (hurdy-gurdy; also abs.); produce, bring *out*, (music) from hurdy--gurdy; toil monotonously, study hard; teach (subject, pupil *in* it) laboriously; rub (t. & i.) gratingly *on*, *into*, or *against* (*ground his heel into it*; *ship was* ~*ing on rocks*), rub (teeth) hard together (~ *out an oath*, utter while ~ing teeth); ~*stone*, thick revolving stone disc for ~ing, sharpening, & polishing (*hold*, *keep*, one's *nose to the* ~*stone*, make him work incessantly), kind of stone used for these. **2.** n. ~ing; hard monotonous work or task (*the daily* ~ colloq., one's usual day's work); ‖ walk for exercise; steeplechase; ‖ (at Cambridge) a ferry. [ME, f. isolated OE *grindan*]

grin′der, n. Molar tooth; grinding--machine; upper mill-stone; person who grinds (esp. in comb. as *organ*, *knife*, ~); ‖ crammer. [-ER¹.]

grin′dery̌, n. ‖ Cobblers' material of all kinds. [GRIND, -ERY; perh. extended f. the cobbler's whetstone]

grin′gō (-ngg-), n. (Spanish-America; pl. -os). . Foreigner (esp. an Anglo--American). [Mex. Sp.]

grip¹, n. Firm hold, tight grasp or clasp (*at*, *come to*, ~*s*, close combat), grasping power; way of clasping hands; way of grasping or holding (*overlapping* ~); control, mastery, intellectual hold; power of arresting attention; part in machinery etc. that clips, part of weapon etc. that is held; = *GRIP²sack*; ~*brake*, worked by gripping with hand. [f. OE *gripe* grasp & *gripa* handful, both f. root of GRIPE]

grip², v.t. & i. (-pp-). Seize, grasp, or hold, tightly; take firm hold; compel attention of; *~'sack*, handbag. Hence

~**p′ER¹**(2) n. [late OE *grippa*, = MHG *gripfen*, f. root of GRIPE]

‖ **grip³**, n. Small open ditch. [OE *grype* cogn. w. *grēop* burrow]

gripe, v.t. & i., & n. **1.** Clutch, grip; oppress, pinch; affect with colic pains; (Naut.) secure with ~s, (of ship) come up into wind in spite of helm. **2.** n. Act of griping, clutch; hold, control, (*in the* ~ *of*); (pl.) colic pains; handle of implement or weapon; (Naut., pl.) lashings securing boat in its place; ~*water*, horse--medicine for colic. [OE, OS *gripan*, ᐧOHG *grifan*, ON *gripa*, Goth. *greipan*, cogn. w. GROPE]

grippe, n. Influenza. [F]

grisaille′ (-zăl, & see App.), n. Method of decorative painting, stained-glass window etc., in grey monochrome representing objects in relief. [F (*gris* grey)]

gris′eous (-z-), a. (bot., zool.). Bluish or pearl grey. [f. med. L *griseus* (prec.), -OUS]

grisette′ (-z-), n. French working-class girl (formerly dressed in grey). [F (*gris* see GRISAILLE, -ETTE)]

‖ **gris′kin**, n. Lean part of loin of bacon pig. [app. f. obs. *gris*, dial. *grice* f. ON *griss* young pig + -KIN]

gris′ly̌ (-z-), a. Causing horror, terror, or superstitious dread. [late OE *grislic*, f. *grisan*, obs. *grise* to shudder]

grist¹, n. Corn for grinding (*brings* ~ *to the mill*, is profitable; *all is* ~ *that comes to his mill*, he utilizes everything); malt crushed for brewing. [OE *grist* f. WG *grinst-* f. *grindan* GRIND]

grist², n. Size or thickness of yarn or rope. [perh. cogn. w. GIRD¹]

gri′stle (-sl), n. Whitish tough flexible tissue in vertebrates, cartilage, (*in the* ~, immature—infants having ~ for bone). Hence **gri′stly̌²** (-sli), a. [OE, = OFris. & MLG *gristel*, of unkn. orig.]

grit¹, n. Small particles of stone or sand, esp. as causing discomfort or clogging machinery etc., whence ~**t′y̌²** a., ~**t′iNESS** n.; (also ~*stone*) coarse sandstone; grain or texture of stone; (colloq.) strength of character, pluck, endurance. [OE *grēot*, OS *griot*, OHG *grioz*, ON *grjöt* f. Gmc *greut-*; cf. GRITS, GROATS]

grit², v.i. & t. (-tt-). Produce, move with, grating sound; grind (teeth). [f. prec.]

grits, n. pl. Husked but unground oats; coarse oatmeal. [OE *grytt(e)*, = OHG *gruzzi* f. WG *grut-*, cf. GRIT¹, GROATS]

‖ **griz′zle**, v.i. (colloq.). (Esp. of children) whimper, cry fretfully. [orig. unkn.]

griz′zled (-zeld), a. Grey(-haired). [f. *grizzle* grey f. OF *grisel* f. *gris* grey (-LE(2)) + -ED²]

griz′zly̌, a. & n. **1.** Grey, greyish, grey--haired, (~ *bear*, large fierce N.-Amer. kind); ~ *king*, *queen*, fishing-flies. **2.** n. ~ bear. [prec., -Y²]

groan, v.i. & t., & n. (Make) deep inarticulate sound expressing pain, grief, or disapproval (~ *inwardly*, be distressed);

utter with ~s (often *out*); be oppressed or loaded *under, beneath, with,* (~ *under injustice; shelf~s with books; ~ing board,* well-loaded table); long *for;* ~ *down,* silence (speaker) with ~s. Hence ~'ing-LY² adv. [OE *grānian* (cogn. w. OHG *grīnan* grin) f. Gmc *grain- cogn. w. GRIN]

groat, n. (hist.). Silver coin = 4*d.* issued 1351–1662 (occasionally used of the fourpenny piece 1836–56); small sum (*don't care a* ~). [f. MDu. *groot* orig. great, in sense *thick (penny),* cf. GROSCHEN]

groats, n. pl. Hulled (sometimes also crushed) grain, esp. oats. [rel. to OE *grotan* pl., *grot* fragment, f. WG *grut-*; cf. GRIT, GRITS]

Grōb'ian, n. Clownish slovenly person. [G, f. med. L *Grobianus,* joc. f. G *grob* coarse]

grō'cer, n. Dealer in spices, dried fruits, sugar, tinned foods, & miscellaneous domestic stores (~'s *itch,* eczema caused by handling sugar). Hence **grō'cer**Y(2, &, usu. pl., 1) n. [late ME; orig. one who sells in the gross, f. OF *grossier* f. med. L *grossarius* (GROSS, -ARY¹)]

grŏg, n., & v.i. & t. 1. Drink of spirit & water; social meeting with ~; ~-*blossom,* pimple or redness on nose from intemperance. 2. vb. Drink ~; extract spirit from (empty cask) by pouring in hot water. [reputedly f. GROGRAM, nickname (from his cloak) of Adm. Vernon, who in 1740 first had ~ served out instead of neat rum]

grŏgg'lў̆ (-g-), a. Drunk(en); bibulous; (of horse) weak in forelegs, tottering; unsteady, shaky. Hence ~INESS n. [-Y²]

grŏg'ram, n. Coarse fabric of silk, mohair & wool, or these mixed, often stiffened with gum. [f. F *gros grain* coarse grain]

groin¹, n., & v.t. 1. Depression between belly & thigh. 2. (archit.). Edge formed by intersecting vaults, arch supporting vault, (vb, build with ~s), whence ~'ING¹(6) n. [ME (f. OE) *grynde,* later *gryne, groin;* perh. f. Gmc *grundjo- GROUND]

***groin².** Var. of GROYNE.

Grōl'ier, n. ~ *binding* (in the highly ornate style introduced by Jean ~ de Servin, Vicomte d'Aiguisy (d. 1565), French book-collector).

***grŏm(m)'ĕt.** See GRUMMET.

grŏm'well, n. Kinds of plant with stony seeds formerly used in medicine. [ME, f. OF *gromil,* prob. f. med. L *gruinum milium* crane's millet (*grus* crane, MILLET)]

grōōm, n., & v.t. 1. ‖ One of certain officers of Royal Household (*G~ of the stole, in waiting,* etc.). 2. Servant having care of horses (vb, curry, tend, etc.; also in p.p. of persons, as *well~ed,* neatly got up, esp. with well-trimmed hair, beard, etc.). 3. Bridegroom; ~'s*man,* unmarried friend officially attending bridegroom at wedding. [ME *grom,* orig. male child, of unkn. orig.]

grōōve, n., & v.t. 1. Channel or hollow, esp. one made to direct motion or receive corresponding ridge (vb, make ~ or ~s in). 2. Piece of routine, undeviating course, rut, whence **grōōv'Y²** a., **grōōv'i**-NESS n. [f. Du. *groeve,* OHG *gruoba,* ON *gróf,* Goth. *grōba* cogn. w. GRAVE¹]

grōpe, v.i. Feel about as in dark (*for, after,* or abs.), search blindly (lit. & fig.); ~ one's *way,* find it by feeling, proceed tentatively. Hence **grōp'ing**LY² adv. [OE *grāpian* f. WG *graip-,* cogn. w. GRIP², GRIPE]

grōp'er, n. Var. of GROUPER.

grŏs'beak, n. Kinds of small bird with large strong beak. [f. F *grosbec* (GROSS², BEAK¹)]

grŏ'schen (-ōshn), n. Small bronze Austrian coin. [G]

gros de Naples (grō'denah'pl), n. Heavy silk fabric. [F (*gros* GROSS², *Naples*)]

grŏss¹, n. (pl. *gross*). Twelve dozen. [f. F *grosse* (*douzaine*) fem. of *gros* GROSS²]

grŏss², a. Luxuriant, rank; overfed, bloated, repulsively fat; flagrant, glaring; total, without deductions, not net; dense, thick, solid; not ethereal, transparent, or impalpable; (of food) coarse, greasy, uncleanly, repulsive, (~ *feeder,* one who likes such food, also, plant avid of manure); (of senses etc.) not delicate, dull; coarse in manners or morals, unrefined, indecent; (abs.) *in* (*the*) ~, in a general way, apart from detail, on the whole. Hence ~'LY² adv., ~'NESS n. [ME, f. OF *gros grosse* big f. LL *grossus*]

grŏt, n. (poet.). Grotto. [f. F *grotte* f. It. *grotta* GROTTO]

grotĕsque' (-sk), n. & a. 1. Decorative painting or sculpture with fantastic interweaving of human & animal forms with foliage; (pop.) comically distorted figure or design. 2. adj. (Archit.) in the above style; distorted, bizarre; ludicrous from incongruity, absurd; hence ~LY² (-skl-) adv., ~NESS (-skn-), **grotĕs'querie** (-skeri) [-ERY(5)], nn. [16th c. *crot-* f. F *crotesque* f. (w. assim. to OF *crote* GROTTO) It. *grottesca* (GROTTO, -ESQUE)]

grŏtt'ō, n. (pl. ~*es,* ~*s*). Picturesque cave; artificial ornamental cave, room etc. adorned with shells etc. in imitation of cave, as cool retreat. Hence ~ED²(-ōd) a. [f. It. *grotta* f. L f. Gk *kruptē* CRYPT]

***grouch,** v.i., & n. (colloq.). 1. Grumble. 2. n. Discontented person; fit of the sulks. [var. of *grutch,* see GRUDGE]

ground¹, n. 1. Bottom of sea (now chiefly fig., as *touch* ~, come to something solid after vague talk etc.; of ship, *take* ~, strand); (pl.) dregs, esp. of coffee, whence ~'Y² a. 2. (electr.). = EARTH¹. 3. Base, foundation, motive, valid reason, (*on the* ~ *of,* by reason or under pretext of; *on public* etc. ~s), whence ~'LESS a., ~'lĕssLY² adv., ~'lĕssNESS n. 4. Substratum, underlying part, surface worked upon in embroidery, painting, etc.

undecorated part, prevailing colour or tone; (Etching) composition spread on metal & cut through with needle where acid is to act. **5.** Surface of earth (*fall, be dashed, to the* ~, be abandoned, fail, of scheme, hope; BREAK¹ ~; *down to the* ~, colloq., in all respects, thoroughly; *above* ~, alive; *cut the* ~ *from under* one's *feet*, anticipate & stultify his arguments or plans). **6.** pl. Enclosed land for ornament or recreation attached to house. **7.** Position, area, or distance, on earth's surface (*cover much* ~, of inquiry, report, etc., be far-reaching; *stand, shift,* one's ~, maintain, change, one's argument or intention; *gain* ~, advance; *lose, give,* ~, retreat, decline). **8.** Area of special kind or use (*fishing-*~*s; forbidden* ~, subject that must be avoided; *classic*~, historic place; *cricket* etc. *-*~). **9.** Person's property in land. **10.** (cricket). *His* etc. ~, behind popping-crease (*in, out of, his* ~); ‖ paid staff of players attached to club. **11.** (In names of birds) terrestrial, (of beasts) burrowing or lying on ~, (of plants) dwarfish or trailing. **12.** ~*-ash,* ash sapling, walking-stick of this; ~*-bait* n. & v.t., (prepare with) bait thrown to bottom of intended fishing-~ to attract fish; ~ *bass,* short passage in bass of composition, repeated many times with upper part of music varied; ~*-box,* small BOX¹ used to edge garden beds; ~*-colour,* first coat of paint, prevailing colour on which design is done; ~*-fish,* living at bottom; ~*-fishing,* with bait near bottom; ‖~ *floor,* rooms etc. on or near level of outside~ (*get in on the* ~ *floor,* be admitted to company etc. on same terms as promoters); ‖~ *game,* hares, rabbits, etc.; ~*-gudgeon,* loach; ~*-hog,* Amer. marmot; ~*-ice,* formed at bottom of water, anchor-ice; ~ *ivy,* ale-hoof, creeping herb with bluish-purple flower & kidney-shaped leaf; ‖~ *landlord,* owner of ~ leased for building; ~*-man* (in charge of cricket etc. ~); ~*-note,* on which a common chord is built, fundamental bass; ~*-nut,* (edible tuber of) N.-Amer. wild bean, also W.-Ind. & Afr. pea with pod ripening under ~, PEAnut; ~*-pine,* herb with resinous smell, also clubmoss; ~*-plan,* plane drawing of divisions of building at ~ level, also outline or general design of anything; ~*-rent,* that paid to ~-landlord; ~ *sea,* heavy sea without apparent cause; ~*s'man,* = ~*-man;* ~ *speed* (Aviation), aircraft's speed relative to ~ (cf. AIR¹ *speed*); ~ *staff,* non-flying members of aerodrome staff; ~ *swell,* heavy sea caused by distant or past storm or earthquake; ~ *torpedo,* fixed to bottom of sea; ~*'work,* foundation or basis (usu. fig.), chief ingredient, general surface of thing showing where not overlaid with embroidery or other ornament. [OE, OS *grund,* OHG *grunt,* Goth. *°grundus* f. Gmc *°grunduz*]

ground², v.t. & i. Base, establish, (institution, principle, belief) *on* some fact or authority (in pass. also *in;* p.p., *well, ill,* etc., founded, also abs.=well founded, whence~'ĔDLY² adv.); instruct thoroughly (*in* elements), whence **groun'**DING¹ n.; prepare ground of (embroidery etc.); lay (esp. arms) on ground; (Electr.) connect with earth as conductor; alight on ground; run (t. & i.) ashore, strand; prevent (aircraft, airman) from flying. [f. prec.]

ground³, p.p. of GRIND. ~ *glass,* made non-transparent by grinding.

‖ **groun'dage,** n. Duty on ship lying on beach or entering port. [-AGE]

ground'ling, n. Kinds of GROUND¹*-fish;* creeping or dwarf plant; spectator or reader of inferior taste (ref. to *Hamlet* III. ii. 12). [-LING¹]

ground'sel¹, n. Kinds of weed, of which the commonest is used as food for cage-birds. [OE *gundæswelgiæ* perh. f. *gund* pus, SWALLOW¹, = pus-absorber, as being used for poultices, later assimilated to *ground*]

ground'sel², n. (arch.). Timber serving as foundation, lowest part of wooden framework; threshold. [SILL]

group (-ōōp), n., & v.t. & i. **1.** (Fine arts) two or more figures or objects forming complete design or distinct part of one; number of persons or things standing near together, knot, cluster; number of persons or things belonging or classed together (in Pol., used of smaller unit than the party, & esp. in assemblies where the two-party system does not prevail; in scientific classification, used vaguely of cross-divisions outside the regular hierarchy of class-terms); *Oxford G*~, see BUCHMANISM; ~ *captain,* officer of AIR¹ *Force.* **2.** vb. Form (t. & rarely i.) into a ~, place in a ~ *with;* form (t. & i. of colours, figures, etc.) into well-arranged & harmonious whole; classify. Hence ~'AGE(3) n. [f. F *groupe* f. It. *gruppo* f. Gmc *°krupp-* cogn. w. CROP¹]

group'er (-ōō-), n. Kinds of W.-Ind. & Austral. fish. [f. Port. *garupa* (prob. S.-Amer.)]

grouse¹, n. (pl. *grouse*). (Prop.) any wild gallinaceous bird with feathered feet; (pop.) moor fowl or game or red ~, reddish game-bird of British Isles (*black* ~, BLACK¹ *game; wood* or *great* ~, capercaillie; *white* ~, ptarmigan), its flesh. [orig. unkn.]

‖ **grouse²,** v.i., & n. (sl.). Grumble. [orig. unkn.]

grout¹, n., & v.t. **1.** Thin fluid mortar for filling interstices. **2.** v.t. Fill up or finish with this. [cf. F *grouter*]

‖ **grout²,** v.i. & t. (Of pigs) turn up earth, turn up (earth etc.), with snout. [18th c., var. of *groot* vb f. ME *groot* mud, rel. to OE *grēot* GRIT]

grōv|e, n. Small wood, group of trees, (in

Bible, mistransl. of Hebrew word=pillar used as idol, or name of goddess). Hence ~ED² (-vd), ~e'LESS (-vl-), ~'Y², aa. [excl. E, OE *grāf*]

grŏv'el (or -ŭv-), v.i. (-ll-). Lie prone, humble oneself, (often *in the dirt* or *dust*); (part.) abject, low, base, whence ~ling LY² adv. Hence ~IER¹ n. [back formation f. obs. *grovelling* adv. (obs. *on grufe* f. ON d *grúfu* on one's face, -LING²) taken as part. in lay ~*ling* etc.]

grow (-ō), v.i. & t. (*grew* pr. grōō, ~*n* p.p. often as act. intr. with *is*, cf. -ED¹ (2), & as adj.). **1.** Develop or exist as living plant (also joc. of lifeless things etc., be found in some place; ~ *into one, together,* etc., coalesce), germinate, sprout, spring up, be produced, come naturally into existence, arise. **2.** Increase in (freq. *in*) size, height (~ING¹ *pains*, neuralgic pains in limbs of the young), quantity, degree, power, etc. (~ *downwards*, diminish; *habit, person, picture,* etc., ~*s on* one, becomes more influential with or admired by him), whence ~'ing LY² (-ō'ĭ-) adv. **3.** Become gradually (~ *rich*); ~ *up*, advance to maturity (~*n-up* a. & n., adult); emerge from soil, reach full size; (of custom) arise, become common. **4.** Produce by cultivation, bring forth, let (beard etc.) ~, whence ~'ABLE (-ō'a-) a. **5.** pass. Be covered (often *up* or *over*) with some growth. [OE *grōwan*, OHG *gruoen*, ON *gróa* f. Gmc *grō-* cogn. w. GRASS, GREEN]

grow'er (-ō'er), n. Plant that grows in specified way (*fast, free,* etc., ~); person growing produce (often in comb., as *fruit-~*). [-ER¹]

growl, v.i. & t., & n. (Make) guttural sound of anger (*at*); rumble; murmur angrily, angry murmur, complain(t); utter with a ~ (*out*). Hence ~'ing LY² adv. [prob. imit.]

growl'er, n. In vbl senses; also: ‖ four-wheeled cab; kinds of fish; small iceberg. [-ER¹]

growl'erỹ, n. Growling; place to growl in, private room, den. [-ERY; cf. BOUDOIR]

grown, p.p. of GROW. ~ *man* etc., mature.

growth (-ōth), n. Growing, development, increase, (*of foreign* etc. ~, grown abroad etc.; *full* ~, size ultimately attained); cultivation *of* produce; what has grown or is growing, (Path.) morbid formation. [-TH¹]

groyne, *****groin**, n., & v.t. **1.** Timber framework or low broad wall run out to check drifting of beach & so stop encroachment of sea. **2.** v.t. Supply (beach) with ~s. [f. (dial.) *groin* snout f. OF *groin* f. LL *grunnium* pig's snout f. L *grunnire* grunt]

grŭb¹, n. Larva of insect, caterpillar, maggot; dull drudge, literary hack, sloven, smug; ball bowled along ground at cricket; (sl.) food, a feed; *~*-*stake* (Mining sl.), supply (prospector) with

outfit, provisions, etc., in return for part of profits, (n.) outfit etc. so supplied. [ME; perh. f. foll.]

grŭb², v.i. & t. (-bb-). Dig (t. & i.) superficially; clear (ground) of roots & stumps, clear away (roots etc.), (often *up*); fetch *up* or *out* by digging (fig., discover in books etc.); search, rummage, (intr.); plod, toil, *on, along, away*; (sl.) feed, provide (boarder etc.) with food, [prob. f. prec.]; ~-*axe, -hoe, -hook,* for ~*bing up* stumps. Hence (-)~b'ER¹(1, 2) n. [ME; perh. repr. OE *grybba* f. Gmc *grubh-, *grabh-* GRAVE²]

grŭbb'|ȳ, a. Of, infested with, grubs; dirty, grimy, slovenly, whence ~iNESS n. [-Y²]

Grŭb'street, n. & a. (Region inhabited by) the tribe of needy authors & literary hacks; (adj.) of these. [a London street (now Milton St) so inhabited in 17th c.]

grŭdge, v.t., & n. **1.** Be unwilling to give, grant, or allow (thing, person thing, thing *to* person), or *to* do; (part.) reluctant, whence **grŭdg'ing**LY² adv. **2.** n. Feeling of resentment or ill will (*have a ~ against*; *bear, owe, one a ~*). [f. ME *grutch* f. OF *grouchier* of unkn. orig.]

grŭel (-ōōil), n., & v.t. (-ll-). Liquid food chiefly for invalids of oatmeal etc. boiled in milk or water (*have, get,* one's ~, be punished, severely defeated, or killed; so *give* one *his* ~, & ~ vb sl. in same sense, whence ~ING¹ (-ōōil-) n.). [ME, f. OF, f. Rom. *grutellum*, f. Gmc *grŭt-* (GROATS)]

grue'some (-ōōs-), a. Grisly, disgusting. Hence ~LY² adv., ~NESS n. [f. Sc. & north. *grew* to shudder; cf. O Sw. *grua* + -SOME]

grŭff, a. Surly, laconic, rough-mannered, rough-voiced. Hence ~LY² adv., ~'NESS n., ~'ISH¹(2) a. [f. MDu., MLG *grof* coarse, = OHG *grob*]

grŭm'bl|e, v.i. & t., & n. (Utter) dull inarticulate sound, murmur, growl faintly; rumble; complain(t) (*at, about, over*); utter complainingly (often *out*). Hence ~ER¹ n., ~ing LY² adv. [f. obs. *grumme* +-LE(3); cf. MDu. *grommen*, MLG *grommelen*]

grume (-ōōm), n. (med.). Clot of blood, viscous fluid. So **grum'ous** (-ōō-) a. [f. L *grumus* small heap]

grŭmm'et, *****grŏm(m)'et**, n. (naut.). Ring usu. of twisted rope as fastening, rowlock, wad, etc. [f. obs. F *grommette* f. *gourmer* to curb, of unkn. orig.]

grŭm'p|ȳ, **grŭm'p|ish**, aa. Ill-tempered, surly. Hence ~iLY² adv., ~iNESS n. [f. *grumps* ill-humour +-Y²]

Grŭn'dỹism, n. Conventional propriety, prudery. [f. 'What will Mrs Grundy (a neighbour) say?' in Morton's *Speed the Plough* 1798]

grŭnt, v.i. & t., & n. (Utter) low gruff sound characteristic of pigs; express discontent, dissent, fatigue, etc., by this; utter with ~ (often *out*). Hence ~'ing LY²

adv. [OE *grunnettan*= OHG, G *grunzen*, frequent. of *grunian* imit.]

grün'ter, n. In vbl senses; esp.: pig; kinds of fish. [-ER¹]

gru'yère (grōō'yār), n. Swiss pale cows'-milk cheese with many cavities. [G~, Swiss town]

grȳs'bŏk, n. Small grey S.-Afr. antelope. [f. Du. *grijsbok* (*grijs* grey, BUCK¹)]

guacharo (gwahchah'rō), n. The oil-bird of S. America. [S.-Amer. Sp.]

guacho, incorrect for GAUCHO.

guai'ăc, -acum, (gwī-), n. Kinds of W.-Ind. trees & shrubs (-*um* only); brownish--green wood of two kinds of these used in medicine, lignum vitae; resin from these, drug made from it. [-*um* mod. L f. Sp. *guayaco* of Haytian orig.]

guan (gwahn), n. Kinds of S.-Amer. gallinaceous bird allied to curassow. [prob. native]

gua'na (gwah-), n. Iguana; any large lizard. [var. of IGUANA]

guana'cō (gwanah-), n. (pl. -*os*). Wild llama with reddish-brown wool. [native S.-Amer. *huanaco*]

gua'nō (gwah-), n. (pl. -*os*), & v.t. Excrement of sea-fowl found esp. in islands off Peru used as manure; artificial manure esp. that made from fish; (vb) fertilize with ~. [Sp., f. native *huanu*]

guarantee' (gă-), n., & v.t. **1.** Person making guaranty or giving security; guaranty; thing given or existing as security for fulfilment of conditions or permanence etc. of something; person to whom guaranty is given [correl. to *guarantor*; prop. a separate formation with -EE]; ~ *fund*, sum pledged as contingent indemnity for loss. **2.** v.t. Be ~ for, answer for due fulfilment of (contract etc.) or genuineness etc. of (article), assure permanence etc. of; engage *that* something has happened or will happen; secure possession of *to* person; secure *against* or *from* (risk etc.), or *in* (possession etc.); hence **gua'rant**OR (gă-; also -ôr') n. [in first sense, orig. *guaranté*, prob. f. Sp. *garante* = F *garant* WARRANT¹; other senses of n. by confusion w. foll. or misuse of -EE]

gua'rantў (gă-), n., & v.t. Undertaking written or other to answer for payment of debt or performance of obligation by another person liable in first instance; ground or basis of security; (vb) guarantee (now rare). [f. AF *guarantie*, var. of *warantie*, WARRANTY]

guard¹ (gărd), n. **1.** Defensive posture or motion in fencing, boxing, etc. (in cricket, position of bat to defend wicket; *take*, *give*, ~, of batsman, umpire, ascertaining correct spot on ground for this). **2.** Watch, vigilant state, (*keep* ~, *be on* ~, act as sentry etc.; *on*, *off*, one's ~, prepared, unprepared, against attack, surprise, or one's own impulses etc.). **3.** Protector, defender, sentry; || official in general charge of stage-coach (hist.) or train; || (pl.) household troops (including *Foot-*~*s*, *Horse-*~*s*,. *Life-*~*s*, & by extension some (orig. seven) regiments of *Dragoon G*~*s*). **4.** Body of soldiers etc. serving as protectors of place or person, escort, separate portion of army, etc; (*advance*, *rear*, -~; ~ *of honour*; HOME¹ *G*~; *mount*, *relieve*, ~, earlier *the* ~, take up, take others' place in, sentry duty). **5.** Contrivance to prevent injury or accident (often in comb., as *fire*, *trigger*, -~). **6.** ~-*boat*, boat going rounds of fleet in harbour to see that good watch is kept, also official harbour boat enforcing quarantine or customs regulations; ~-*book'* (arranged for the reception of additional leaves, letters, etc.); ~-*chain*, securing watch, brooch, etc.; ~'*house*, accommodating military ~ or securing prisoners; ~-*rail*, hand or other rail to prevent falling etc.; ~-*ring*, preventing other ring from slipping off finger, keeper; ~'*room*, as ~*house* above; ~-*ship*, warship protecting harbour & receiving seamen till they can join their ships; ~'*s'man*, || soldier, esp. officer, of *G*~*s*; ~-*tent*, as ~*house* above. Hence ~'LESS a. [ME, f. OF *garde* f. *garder* f. Rom. **wardare* WARD]

guard² (gărd), v.t. & i. Keep safe, stand guard over, keep (door etc.) so as to control passage, protect, defend (*from*, *against*); secure by explanations or stipulations etc. from misunderstanding or abuse, (Med.) administer correctives with (drug); keep (thoughts, speech) in check (~*ed language* etc., cautious, measured), whence ~'ĕDLY² adv., ~'ĕDNESS n.; use a fencing guard; take precautions *against*; (Curling, Bowling) protect (stone, bowl) by placing one's own between it & later player, (Chess) protect (piece, pawn) with another. Hence ~'ANT (her.), depicted full-face. [f. prec., or OF *garder*]

guard'ian (gär-), n. Keeper, defender, protector, (|| *G*~ *of the poor*, or *G*~, member of Board formerly elected to administer poor-laws in parish or district); (*G*~) title of newspaper; (Law) one having custody of person or property or both of infant, idiot, etc. (cf. WARD); superior of Franciscan convent; ~ *angel*, spirit watching over person or place. [late ME, f. AF *gardein*, OF *-en*, f. *garde* GUARD¹; see WARDEN]

guard'ianship (gär-), n. Office of guardian, legal tutelage; keeping, guard, (*under the* ~ *of the laws*). [-SHIP]

gua'va (gwah-), n. (Tropical myrtaceous tree yielding) acid fruit used for making jelly. [f. Sp. *guayaba* prob. f. S.-Amer. or W.-Ind. name]

guayule' (gwahyōōl'), n. Aster-like Mexican plant the sap of which furnishes a rubber substitute. [native name]

gŭbernatŏr'ial, a. Of a governor. [f. L *gubernator* GOVERNOR + -IAL]

guddle, v.t. & i. (Sc.). Catch (fish) with the hands, by groping under the stones or banks of a stream, grope for fish thus. [orig. unkn.]

gudg′eon[1] (-jon), n. Small freshwater fish used as bait; credulous person. [ME, f. F *goujon* f. L *gobionem* nom. -o GOBY]

gudg′eon[2] (-jon), n. Pivot at end of beam, axle, etc., on which bell, wheel, etc., works; ring of gate fitting on hook of post; socket in which rudder works; pin holding two blocks of stone etc. together; ~-*pin*, (esp.) that holding piston-rod & connecting-rod together. [ME, f. OF *gojon* dim. of *gouge* GOUGE]

Guebre (gē′ber, gä⁻), n. Zoroastrian, fire-worshipper, Parsee. [f. F *guèbre* f. Pers. *gabr*].

guel′der rōse (gĕ-; -z), n. Shrub with round bunches of creamy-white flowers, snowball tree. [*Guelders* in Netherlands]

Guelph, -lf, (gwĕ-), n. Member of medieval Italian party supporting Pope against Emperor (cf. GHIBELLINE). Hence ~′IC a. [f. It. *Guelfo* f. MHG *Welf* name (of founder of princely family of Guelphs, ancestors of British Royal Family) used as war-cry at battle of Weinsberg 1140 against Conrad III]

guerd′on (gĕr-), n., & v.t. (poet.). Reward, recompense. Hence ~LESS a. [ME, f. OF f. med. L *widerdonum* f. OHG *widarlōn* (*wider* again, LOAN) w. assim. to L *donum* gift]

Guern′sey (gĕrn′zĭ), n. One of Channel Islands; (*g*~; also ~ *shirt*, *coat*, *frock*) thick knitted woollen usu. blue outer tunic or jersey; ~ *cow*; ~ *lily*, kind of amaryllis orig. from S. Africa.

guer(r)ill′a (ger-), n. (Usu. now ~ *war*) irregular war waged by small bodies acting independently; man engaged in this. [Sp. (-*rr*-) dim. of *guerra* WAR]

guess (gĕs), v.t. & i., & n. 1. Estimate without measurement or detailed calculation; think likely, think one divines nature of, form hypothesis as to, conjecture, hazard opinion about, (noun, *that, how, when, whether*, etc., thing *to be*; also intr. with *at*; often abs. in parenthesis; *I* ~, chiefly U.S., I feel sure or know well); conjecture (answer to riddle, solution of problem) rightly, divine. 2. n. Rough estimate, conjecture, hypothesis, (*by* ~, at haphazard; *by* ~ *and by* God; *anybody's* ~, a matter of individual conjecture); ~-*work*, (procedure based on) ~*ing*; OTHER~. [n. f. vb, ME *gesse*, of uncert. orig.; cf. OSw. *gissa*, MLG, MDu. *gissen*; f. root of GET]

guest (gĕst), n. Person entertained at another's house or table (*paying* ~, boarder); person lodging at hotel, boarding-house, etc.; animal or vegetable parasite (cf. HOST[2]); ~-*chamber*, kept for ~s; ~-*house*, superior boarding-house; ~-*night*, on which ~s are entertained at club, college, mess, etc. Hence ~′SHIP n.

[OE *giest*, OS, OHG *gast*, ON *gestr*, Goth. *gasts* f. Gmc **gastiz* cogn. w. L *hostis*]

guest′-rōpe, guess′, (gĕs-), n. Second rope fastened to boat in tow to steady it; rope slung outside ship to give hold for boats coming alongside. [orig. uncert.; perh. f. GUEST]

guffaw′, n., & v.i. & t. 1. Coarse or boisterous laugh. 2. vb. Make, say with, ~. [orig. Sc.; imit.]

guggle. = GURGLE.

guichet (gēsh′ā), n. Grating, hatch, ticket-office window. [F]

guide[1] (gīd), n. 1. One who shows the way; hired conductor of traveller or tourist; (esp. in Switzerland etc.) professional mountain-climber. 2. (Mil.) one of company formed for reconnoitring etc.; (Naut.) ship on which rest of fleet regulate their movements. 3. Adviser; directing principle or standard (*the feelings are a bad* ~; *Scripture is our* ~). 4. = GIRL ~. 5. Book of rudiments, manual, (also ~-*book*) book of information on a city, cathedral, museum, etc., (*to*). 6. (mech.). Bar, rod, etc., directing motion of something, gauge etc. controlling tool. 7. Thing marking a position or guiding the eye. 8. ~-*post*, FINGER-*post*; ~-*rope*, GUY[1], small rope attached to load of crane to guide it, rope trailed along ground by balloon or small airship to assist in preserving altitude, one of several ropes steadying an airship before flight; ~′*way*, groove, track. Hence ~LESS (gīdl-) a. [ME, f. OF f. *guider* (foll.)]

guide[2] (gīd), v.t. Act as guide to, go before, lead, direct course of; arrange course of (events); be the principle, motive, or ground, of (action, judgement, etc.); conduct affairs of (State etc.); ~*d missile* (under remote control); *guiding-stick*, maulstick. Hence **guid′**ABLE a., **guid′**ANCE n., (gī-). [ME, f. OF *guaider*, older *guier* (whence ME *guy* vb) f. Rom. **widare* f. Gmc **witan* (cf. Goth. *fairweitjan* gaze intently) cogn. w. *witan* (WIT[1])]

guid′on (gī-, gē-), n. Pennant narrowing to point at free end (used as standard of dragoons). [F, f. It. *guidone* f. *guida* GUIDE][1]

g(u)ild (gī-), n. Society for mutual aid or prosecution of common object; *G*~-*hall*, in which a medieval ~ met, (freq., from being used as meeting-place of Corporation) town-hall; (*the*) *Guildhall*, hall of the Corporation of the City of London, used for State banquets, municipal meetings, etc.; ~ *socialism*, system by which the resources, methods, & profits, of each industry should be controlled by a council of its members. [f. OE *gield*, *gild* & ON *gildi* guild, payment, rel. to OS *geld*, OHG *gelt*, ON *gjald*, Goth. *gild* f. Gmc **geldh*-; see YIELD]

guil′der (gī-), n. Obsolete gold coin of Netherlands etc.; Dutch silver coin. [alt. of Du. *gulden* (GOLDEN)]

guile (gīl), n. Treachery, deceit, cunning devices. Hence ~'FUL a., ~'fulLY² adv., ~'fulNESS n., (gĭlf-), ~'LESS a., ~'lèssLY² adv., ~'lèssNESS n. (gīl-l-). [ME, f. OF of unkn. (presumably Gmc) orig.; cf. WILE]

guill'émot (gĭ-), n. Kinds of sea-bird. [F, f. *Guillaume* William]

guilloche (gĭlōsh', & see Ap.), n. Architectural ornament imitating braided ribbons. [f. F *guillochis*, or f. F *guilloche* the tool used]

guillotine (gĭl'ŏtēn, *or* -tēn'), n., & v.t. 1. Machine with knife-blade sliding in grooves for beheading; surgical instrument for excising uvula etc., kinds of machine for cutting paper etc.; || (Parl.) method of preventing obstruction by fixing times at which parts of Bill must be voted on. 2. v.t. Use the ~ upon. [F (Dr *Guillotin*, its proposer in 1789)]

guilt (gĭ-), n. The having committed a specified or implied offence; criminality, culpability. [OE *gylt*, of unkn. orig.]

guilt'lèss (gĭ-), a. Innocent (often *of* offence); not having knowledge or possession *of* (~ *of Greek, soap, moustache*, etc.). Hence ~LY² adv., ~NESS n. [-LESS]

guil't|ў (gĭ-), a. Criminal, culpable; conscious of, prompted by, guilt (~y *conscience, behaviour, look*); having committed a particular offence (*of*; ~y, *not* ~y, verdicts in criminal trials). Hence ~ILY² adv., ~INESS n. [-Y²]

guimp. = GIMP.

Guinea, ĝ-, (gĭn'ĭ), n. 1. (*G*~). Part of W. coast of Africa. 2. (*g*~). Former gold coin named as first coined for the African trade (1663-1717 nominally 20/- but of fluctuating value; from 1717 fixed at 21/-; last coined 1813), & now money of account 21/- used in stating professional fees, amount of subscriptions, & prices of pictures, horses, estates, etc. 3. *g*~-*fowl*, *-hen*, gallinaceous bird with slate-coloured white-spotted plumage domesticated in Europe; *G*~ GRAINS; *g*~-*pig*, S.-Amer. rodent now half-domesticated in Europe etc. as pet (origin of name doubtful), person receiving ~ fees, esp. company director or deputy clergyman, person used as subject for medical experiment; *G*~ *worm*, tropical parasite in human skin. [f. Port. *Guiné*]

guipure (gēp'oor, & see Ap.), n. Kind of lace; kind of gimp. [F]

guise (gīz), n. Style of attire, garb, (arch.); external appearance; semblance, assumed appearance, pretence, (*under, in, the ~ of*). [ME f. OF, f. Gmc (WISE²)]

guitar' (gĭ-), n., & v.i. (-rr-). 1. Six-stringed lute played with hand with fretted finger-board; hence ~IST(3) n. 2. v.i. Play ~. [f. Sp. *guitarra* f. Gk *kithara*; cf. CITHER, GITTERN]

*****gŭlch**, n. Ravine, esp. one with gold deposit. [perh. f. dial. *gulch* to swallow]

gul'den (gŏŏ-), n. Dutch silver coin. [Du.

& G, = golden (orig. name of various gold coins)]

gŭles (-lz), n., & a. (usu. after noun), (her.). Red. [ME, f. OF *goules* pl. ermine dyed red]

gŭlf, n., & v.t. 1. (Geog.) portion of sea, proportionally narrower at mouth than bay, partly surrounded by coast; deep hollow, chasm, abyss, (poet.) profound depth or the sea; whirlpool, what swallows up anything; impassable dividing line (*Luke* xvi. 26); || (Univ. sl.) degree allowed to honour-candidate who fails but deserves pass; *G*~-*stream*, oceanic warm current issuing from G~ of Mexico; ~-*weed*, seaweed of tropical waters with berry-like air vessels. 2. v.t. Engulf, swallow up; || (Univ.) give ~ to. [ME, f. OF *golfe* f. It. *golfo* f. late Gk *kolphos* (Gk *kolpos*)]

gŭll[1], n. Kinds of long-winged web-footed mostly marine bird, usu. white with mantle varying from pearl-grey to black, & bright bill. Hence ~'ERY(3) n. [ME; perh. f. W *gŵylan*]

gŭll[2], n., & v.t. Dupe, fool. So ~'IBLE a., ~IBIL'ITY n., ~'ISH¹ a. [uncert. which is source of other; for the n., cf. dial. *gull* young bird (ON *gulr* yellow); for the vb, cf. obs. *gull* vb 'stuff' or 'cram']

gŭll'èt, n. Food-passage from mouth to stomach, oesophagus; throat; water-channel, strait, defile, (arch. & dial.). [ME, f. OF dim. of *gole* (now *gueule*) f. L *gula*]

gŭll'ў[1], n., & v.t. 1. Water-worn ravine; deep artificial channel, gutter, drain, sink; (Cricket) fielding position between point & the slips; ~-*drain*, to sewer from ~-*hole*, opening in street for drainage; ~-*trap*, anti-gas TRAP¹ in ~-drains. 2. v.t. Make gullies in, form (channels) by water action. [f. F *goulet* (prec.)]

gŭll'ў[2], n. Large knife. [orig. unkn.]

gŭlōs'itў, n. (rare). Gluttony. [f. LL *gulositas* (L *gulosus* gluttonous f. *gula* GULLET)]

gŭlp, v.t. & i., & n. 1. Swallow (usu. *down*) hastily, greedily, or with effort (~ *down sobs, tears*, suppress them); perform act of swallowing with difficulty, gasp, choke; hence ~'ingLY² adv. 2. n. Act of ~ing (*drained it at one ~*); effort to swallow; large mouthful; hence ~'Y² a. [f. MDu. *gulpen* (imit.)]

gŭm[1], n. (usu. pl.). Firm flesh in which the teeth stand; ~*boil*, small abscess on ~s. [OE *gōma*, OHG *guomo*, ON *gómr*]

gŭm[2], n., & v.t. & i. (-mm-). 1. Viscid secretion of some trees & shrubs that hardens in drying but is soluble in water (cf. RESIN), used to stick paper etc. together & stiffen linen etc.; secretion collecting in inner corner of eye; hard transparent sweet made of gelatine etc.; (also ~-*tree*) any tree exuding ~, esp. kinds of eucalyptus (*up a*~-*tree*, in a fix, at end of one's resources); morbid secretion of ~ as disease of fruit-trees; *(pl.) rubber boots;

~ ARABIC; ~ *bichromate*, method of controlled photographic printing based on the CARBON process; ~ *boot*, rubber boot; ~ *dragon*, tragacanth; ~ *juniper*, sandarac; ~ *resin*, vegetable secretion of resin mixed with ~, as gamboge; ~ *senegal*, kind of ~ arabic from Senegal. **2.** vb. Stiffen, smear, with ~; fasten *down*, *together*, *up*, *in*, etc., with ~; exude ~. [ME, f. OF *gomme* f. L *gummi* f. Gk *kommi*]

‖ **gŭm**[3], n. (vulg.). God (in oaths, as *my*, *by*, ~ *!*). [deformation of *God*]

*gŭm′bō, n. = OKRA; soup thickened with okra pods. [of Negro orig.]

gŭm′lah, n. Large Indian earthenware water-jar. [Hind. *gamla*]

gŭmm′a, n.(path.; pl.~*s*,~*ta*). Syphilitic tumour. Hence ~TOUS a. [mod. L, f. L *gummi* GUM[2], from nature of contents]

gŭmm′|y̆, a. Viscid, sticky; abounding in, exuding, gum; (of ankles & legs) puffy, swollen. Hence ~ĬNESS n. [-Y[2]]

gŭmp′tion, n. (colloq.). Resource, enterprising spirit, go, ready practical sense; (Painting) vehicle for colour. [Sc., of unkn. orig.]

gŭn, n., & v.t. & i. **1.** Metal tube for throwing missiles with gunpowder or some explosive force, piece of ordnance, cannon, musket, fowling-piece, rifle, carbine, (*sure as a* ~, certainly, beyond question; *stand*, *stick*, *to* one's ~*s*, maintain position; *big* ~, eminent person; *blow great*~*s*, violently, a gale); *revolver (~ *moll*, gangster's mistress); starting-pistol (*beat*, *jump*, *the* ~, start before the signal is given, also fig.); insecticide spray. **2.** Member of shooting-party. **3.** ~-BARREL[1]; ~'*boat*, small vessel of shallow draught & with relatively heavy ~ armament; ~-CARRIAGE; ~-*cotton*, explosive made by steeping cotton in nitric & sulphuric acids used for blasting; ~ *crew*, team manning ~; ~ *dog*, one trained to follow ~s; ~-*fire*, firing of ~, esp. (Mil., Naut.) of morning or evening ~ to show time, independent firing by each ~ of a battery; ~-*harpoon*, propelled from ~, not by hand; ~-*lock*, mechanism by which charge of ~ is exploded; ~'*man*, (esp., U.-S. sl.) armed robber; ~-*metal*, alloy of copper & tin or zinc (formerly used for ~s); ~-*pit*, to protect ~ crews & ~s from enemy's fire; ~'*powder*, explosive of saltpetre, sulphur, & charcoal, for use in ~s & blasting (~*powder plot*, 5th Nov. 1605 to blow up Parliament), fine green tea of granular appearance, *white* ~-*powder*, kinds of modern explosive; ‖~'*room*, compartment in warship fitted up for junior officers or as lieutenants' mess-room (orig. for gunner & his mates); ~-*runner*, -*running*, (person engaged in) illegal introduction of fire-arms into country; ~'*shot*, range of ~ ~ (*out of*, *within*, ~*shot*); ~-*shy*, frightened at report of ~ (esp. of sporting dog);

~'*smith*, maker and repairer of small fire-arms; ~-*stock*, wooden mounting of ~-barrel. Hence (*heavily* etc.)~NED[2] (-nd), ~'LESS, aa. **4.** vb. (-nn-). Shoot (at), go shooting. [ME; perh. f. *Gunna* pet-form of ON *Gunnhildr* woman's name used as personal name (as with ships, & cf. *Mons Meg* cannon kept at Edinburgh) for ballistae & cannon (*una magna balista de cornu quae vocatur Domina Gunilda*, 1330)]

gŭnn′el[1], n. A small eel-shaped sea-fish, the butter-fish. [orig. unkn.]

gŭnn′el[2]. See GUNWALE.

gŭnn′er, n. ‖ Officer or man of artillery (as official term, private); *Master G*~, R.A. warrant officer in charge of equipment etc. in a fort, or similarly employed; (Naut.) warrant officer in charge of battery, magazine, etc. (~*'s daughter*, gun to which sailors were lashed for flogging; *kiss*, *marry*, *the*~*'s daughter*, be flogged); game-shooter. [-ER[2] (2)]

gŭnn′era, n. The prickly rhubarb, an ornamental foliage plant with large leaves. [f. J. E. *Gunnerus*, naturalist; see -A(1)]

gŭnn′ery̆, n. Construction & management of large guns (~-*lieutenant*, ‖ (sl.) ~ *jack*, with warrant of competence to supervise ~ from ~-*ship*, for training in ~); firing of guns. [-ERY]

gŭnn′ing, n. Shooting, esp. of game (usu. *go* ~); wildfowling in shooting-punt. [-ING[1]]

gŭnn′y̆, n. Coarse sacking, sack, usu. of jute fibre. [f. Hind. *goni* f. Skr. *goni* sack]

gŭn′ter, n. (Also *G*~'*s scale*) flat 2-ft rule with scales, logarithmic lines, etc., used for solving mechanically problems in surveying & navigation; topmast, or its sail, sliding up & down lower mast on rings (from resemblance to sliding G~'s scale); *G*~'*s chain*, 66-ft surveying CHAIN. [E. *G*~, mathematician d. 1626]

gŭn′wale (-nal), **gŭnn′el**, n. Upper edge of ship's or boat's side (~ *to*, *under*, level with, below, water). [GUN + WALE (formerly used to support guns); cf. CHANNEL[2]]

*gŭn′yah, n. Native Australian hut. [native]

gŭp, n. (Anglo-Ind.). Gossip. [Hind.]

gŭrgita′tion, n. Surging, bubbling motion or sound. [f. LL *gurgitare* to surge (*gurges* -*itis* whirlpool) + -ATION]

gŭr′gle, v.i. & t., & n. (Make) bubbling sound as of water from bottle or among stones; utter with such sounds. [imit.; or f. Du. *gorgelen*, G *gurgeln*, or It. *gorgogliare*, f. L (*gurgulio* gullet); cf. GARGLE, GUGGLE]

gŭr′jun, n. E.-Ind. tree yielding ~ balsam or oil, used medicinally. [native]

Gurkha (goork′a), n. Member of ruling Hindu race in Nepal (~ *regiments*, of ~s in British army). [native]

gŭrn′ard, gŭrn′ĕt, n. Kinds of sea-fish with large head, mailed cheeks, & three free pectoral rays. [ME, f. OF *gornart*, *gournart* ult. f. *gron(d)ir* (GRUNT)]

gŭ'rrah, n. Common Indian earthen jar. [native]

gŭ'rrў, n. Small Indian fort. [Hind. *ğarhĭ*]

guru (gōō'rōō), n. Hindu spiritual teacher. [Skr., = grave, dignified]

gŭsh, v.i. & t., & n. (Issue in, send forth) sudden or copious stream (often fig. of speech, tenderness, etc.); emit (water) copiously; (speak, behave, with) effusiveness, sentimental affectation, whence ~'ER[1] n., (also) oil-well from which the oil flows without pumping, ~'ingLY[2] adv., ~'Y[2] a. [ME *gosshe* perh. imit.]

gŭss'ĕt, n. Triangular piece let into garment to strengthen or enlarge some part; iron bracket strengthening angle of structure. Hence ~ED[2] a. [ME, f. OF *goussel (gousse* pod, shell) flexible piece filling up joint in mail-coat]

gŭst[1], n., & v.i. Sudden violent rush of wind; burst of rain, fire, smoke, sound, or passion; (v.i.) blow in ~s. Hence gŭs'tY[2] a., gŭs'tĭLY[2] adv. [f. ON *gustr*]

gŭst[2], n. (arch. & poet.). Sense of taste; keen relish (*have a ~ of*, appreciate); flavour. [ME, f. L *gustus* taste]

gŭstā'tion, n. Tasting. So gŭs'tATIVE, gŭs'tatorY, aa. [f. L *gustatio* (*gustare* f. *gustus* taste, -ATION)]

gŭs'tō, n. Special flavour (arch.; *enjoy the full ~ of*); zest, enjoyment with which something is done. [It., as GUST[2]]

gŭt, n., & v.t. & i. (-tt-). 1. (Pl.) bowels or entrails (esp. of animals), contents of anything (*has no ~s in it*, is of no real value or force); particular part of lower alimentary canal, intestine, (*blind ~*, caecum). 2. (Usu. pl.) belly as seat of appetite (vulg.); (pl., sl.) pluck, force of character, staying power. 3. Material for violin strings made from intestines of animals; *surgical ~* (for suture); material for fishing-lines made from intestines of silkworm. 4. Narrow water-passage, sound, straits, || (Oxf. & Camb.) bend of river in racing-course; defile, narrow lane or part of street. 5. vb. Take out ~s of, clean, (fish); remove or destroy internal fittings of (house etc.); extract essence of (book etc.); eat greedily (vulg.). [OE *guttas* pl., prob. cogn. w. *gēotan* pour]

gŭtt'ae, n. pl. Drops in a row as ornament esp. in Doric architecture. [pl. of L *gutta* drop]

gŭtta-pĕ̄rch'a, n. Tough greyish-black substance flexible when thin, of inspissated juice of various Malayan trees. [f. Malay *getah* gum, *percha* name of tree]

gŭtt'āte, a. (nat. hist.). Speckled. [f. L *guttatus* (*gutta* drop, -ATE[2])]

gŭtt'er, n., & v.t. & i. 1. Track made by running water (rare); shallow trough below eaves, or channel at side of street, carrying off rain-water (~*-child*, street arab; *take child* etc. *out of* ~, remove from

poor surroundings); open conduit for outflow of fluid (groove; ~*-man*, cheap street-vendor of trifles; ~ *press, journalism* (catering for depraved or vulgar tastes); ~*-snipe*, street arab. 2. vb. Furrow, channel; flow in streams; (of candle) melt away by becoming channelled so that wax etc. runs down. [ME, f. AF *gotere* f. Rom. **guttaria* (L *gutta*, -ER[2])]

gŭt'tle, v.i. & t. Eat gluttonously. Hence gŭtt'lER[1] n. [prob. f. GUT after GUZZLE]

gŭtt'ural, a. & n. Of the throat; (of sounds) produced in throat or by back of tongue & palate (n., ~ sound or letter, as k, g). Hence ~IZE(3) v.t., ~ISM(1) n., ~LY[2] adv. [F, f. L *guttur* throat+-AL]

gŭtt'uro-, comb. form of L *guttur* throat (see -o-), as ~*maxill'ary* of throat & jaws.

guy[1] (gī), n., & v.t. 1. Rope, chain, etc., to steady load of crane etc. or hold tent etc. in place. 2. v.t. Secure with ~(s). [of LG or Du. orig.; cf. LG, Du. *gei* brail etc.]

guy[2] (gī), n., & v.t. & i. 1. Effigy of Guy Fawkes burnt on 5th Nov.; || grotesquely dressed person, fright; *(sl.) man, fellow; || (sl.) act of decamping (*give the ~ to*, escape from; *do a ~*, disappear). 2. vb. Exhibit in effigy; ridicule; (sl.) run away. [person]

Guy's (gīz), n. (Used for) Guy's Hospital in London. [person]

gŭz'zle, v.i. & t. Drink, eat, greedily (i. & t.); consume (money etc.) in guzzling (often *away*). Hence gŭzz'lER[1] n. [imit.]

gwўn'iăd, n. White-fleshed lake fish of salmon kind. [W (*gwyn* white)]

gӯbe, *jibe, v.i. & t., & n. (Of fore-&-aft -sail or boom) swing across, make (sail) do this, in wearing or running before wind; (of ship, crew, etc.) change course so that this happens. [f. Du. *gijben*]

gӯle (g-), n. Quantity of beer brewed at once; fermenting wort; fermenting-tun. [f. MDu. *ghijl* (*gijlen* to ferment)]

gӯm, n. (colloq.). Gymnasium, gymnastics. [abbr.]

gӯmkha'na (-kah-), n. (orig. Anglo-Ind.). Public place with facilities for athletics; athletic-sports display. [mixture of *gym-* (*nastics*) & Hind. (*gend-*)*khana* ball-house, racquet court]

gӯmnā'sium (-z-), n. (pl. *-ums, -a*). 1. Place, room, or building, with appliances for practice in gymnastics. 2. Continental, esp. German, school of highest grade preparing for universities (*often pr.* gimnah'ziōōm; pl. occas. *-ien*), whence gӯmnā'siAL n. [L, f. Gk *gumnasion* (*gumnazō* exercise f. *gumnos* naked)]

gӯm'năst, n. Expert in gymnastics. [f. Gk *gumnastēs* (*gumnazō* see prec.)]

gӯmnăs't|ic, a. & n. 1. Of gymnastics, involving bodily or (rarely) mental exercise, discipline, effort, or activity; hence ~ICALLY adv. 2. n. Course of instruction regarded as discipline (*grammar is a good ~ic*); (pl.) exercises developing the muscles, esp. such as are performed in gymnasium (also in same sense as sing.). [f. L f. Gk *gumnastikos* (prec., -IC)]

gy̆mno-, comb. form of Gk *gumnos* naked, bare, used in many bot., zool., & biol. terms, as ~*sperm'ous* having seeds unprotected by seed-vessels.

gy̆mnŏs'oph|ist, n. One of ancient Hindu philosophic sect going nearly naked & given up to contemplation; mystic, ascetic. So ~Y[1] n. [F, or f. L f. Gk *gumnosophistai* pl. (prec., SOPHIST)]

gy̆mnŏt'us, n. The electric eel. [f. Gk *gumnos* naked + *nōton* back (from absence of dorsal fins)]

gy̆naecē'um (g-, j-), n. (Gk & Rom. Ant.) women's apartments in house; (Bot.; freq. incorrectly -*oe'cium*) female organs of flower. [L, f. Gk *gunaikeion* (*gunē* -*aikos* woman); -*oecium* from confusion with Gk *oikion* house]

gy̆naeco- (g-, j-), comb. form of Gk *gunē* -*aikos* woman, as ~*logy* (-ŏl[4]), science of diseases of women. Hence ~O'RACY (-ŏk[2]) n.

gy̆năn'drous (g-, j-), a. (bot.). With stamens & pistil united in one column as in orchids. [f. Gk *gunandros* (*gunē* woman, *anēr andros* man) of doubtful sex + -OUS]

gy̆n(o)- (g-, j-), shortened form of GYNAECO-, esp. in Bot.=pistil-, ovary-, as *gyn'obāse*, enlargement of receptacle supporting gynaeceum, *gyn'ophŏre*, pedicel supporting ovary, also (Zool.) bud-bearing branch in hydrozoa; also = woman-, whence **gy̆nŏc'RACY** n.

-gy̆nous (g-, j-), suf. f. mod. L f. Gk -*gunos* (*gunē* woman) + -OUS, forming adjj. = having specified female organs or pistils, as *mono*~, *tetra*~, *andro*~.

‖ **gy̆p¹**, n. College servant at Cambridge & Durham (cf. SCOUT¹); ~*room*, ~'s pantry. [perh. for obs. *gippo* scullion, orig. man's short tunic, f. obs. F *jupeau*]

‖ **gy̆p²**, n. (sl.). *Give* one ~, scold or punish or defeat him unmercifully, pain one. [orig. unkn.]

•**gy̆p³**, v.t. (sl.; -pp-). Cheat, swindle. [orig. unkn.]

gy̆ps. = GYPSUM.

gy̆psŏph'ila, n. Kinds of garden plant with profusion of small white composite flowers. [foll., -PHIL]

gy̆p's|um, n. Hydrated calcium sulphate, mineral from which plaster of Paris is made, whence ~ŏG'RAPHY n.; this used as manure, whence ~**um** v.t. Hence ~EOUS, ~ĬF'EROUS, ~OUS, aa. [L, f. Gk *gupsos*]

gy̆psy. See GIPSY.

gȳr'ate¹, a. (bot.). Arranged in rings or convolutions. [f. L *gyratus* (GYRE, -ATE²)]

gȳrate'², v.i. Go in circle or spiral, revolve, whirl. Hence **gȳrA'TION** n., **gȳr'atORY** a. [f. (LL *gyrare* (foll.), -ATE³]

gȳr'e, v.i., & n. (poet.). = prec.; (n.) gyration. [vb as prec.; n. f. L f. Gk *guros* ring]

gȳr'ō, n. (pl. -*os*). Gyroscope (see foll.); ~-*compass*, compass giving true north & bearings from it by means of a gyroscope. [abbr. of foll.]

gȳr'o-, comb. form of Gk *guros* ring, as ~*graph* (-ahf), instrument recording revolutions; ~-*magnetic* a., of the magnetic properties of a rotating electrical particle; ~*plane*, form of aircraft deriving its lift mainly from freely rotating overhead vanes; ~*scōpe*, ~*stăt*, instruments illustrating dynamics of rotating bodies, also (~*scope*) rapidly spinning wheel fixed in something, e.g. car on single rail, to keep it in equilibrium, & having, by the independent stability of its axis, great value in mechanics; ~-*tiller*, cultivator in which tines rotate round axis.

gȳrōse', a. (bot.). Folded & waved, marked with wavy lines. [GYRE, -OSE¹]

gyttja (gĭt'yă), n. (geol.). Late or post-glacial deposit, usu. covered over by peat of a later date, in Sweden. [Sw., = mud, ooze]

gȳve, n. (usu. pl.), & v.t. (poet.). Shackle, fetter. [ME *give* (*pr.* g-), of unkn. orig.]

H

H, h, (āch), letter (pl. *H*s, H's). DROP² one's *h*s; *H-iron*, girder of H-shaped section.

ha¹ (hah), int. expr. surprise, joy, suspicion, triumph, etc. [ME]

ha² (hah). See HUM v.

haaf (hahf), n. (In Shetland & Orkney) deep-sea fishing ground. [f. ON *haf* high sea]

hăb'ĕăs cŏrp'us, n. Writ requiring body of person to be brought before judge or into court, esp. to investigate lawfulness of his restraint; *Habeas Corpus Act* (of Charles II, 1679, facilitating use of this). [L, = you must have the body]

hăb'erdăsh|er, n. Dealer in small articles of dress etc. Hence ~ERY(1) n. [conn. w. obs. *haberdash* small wares, prob. f. AF *hapertas*, of unkn. orig.]

hăb'ergeon (-jon), n. (hist.). Sleeveless coat of mail. [ME, f. OF *haubergeon* (HAUBERK, -OON)]

hăb'ile, a. (literary). Skilful, dextrous. [15th c. var. of ABLE]

habil'iment, n. (Pl.) dress suited to any office or occasion (joc. of ordinary clothes); (sing.) equipment, attire, (rare). [ME, f. OF (*h*)*abillement* (*habiller* fit out f. *habile* ABLE, see -MENT)]

habil'it|āte, v.t. & i. Furnish (mine) with working capital; (intr.) qualify for office (esp. in German Univ.). So ~A'TION n. [f. med. L *habilitare* (as ABILITY), see -ATE³]

hăb'it¹, n. Settled tendency or practice, as *he is in*, *has* (*fallen into*), *the* or *a* ~ *of contradiction*; mental constitution, esp. ~ *of mind*; bodily constitution, as *a man of corpulent* ~; (Bot., Zool.) mode of growth; (arch.) dress, esp. of religious order; (also *riding-*~) lady's riding-dress. [ME, f. OF f. L *habitus -ūs* f. *habēre habit-have*, (refl.) be]

hăb′it², v.t. Clothe; ‖ (arch.) inhabit. [f. OF *habiter* f. L *habitare* inhabit, as prec.]

hăb′it|able, a. That can be inhabited. Hence ~aBIL′ITY, ~ableNESS, nn., ~abLY² adv. [ME, f. OF f. L *habitabilis* (as prec., see -ABLE)]

hăb′itant, n. Inhabitant; (pr. ahbĕtahń′) Canadian of French descent. [F (HABIT², -ANT)]

hăb′ĭtăt, n. Natural home of plant or animal; habitation, [L, 3rd sing pres. as HABIT²]

hăbĭtā′tion, n. Inhabiting, as *fit for human* ~; place of abode; branch of Primrose League. [ME, f. OF f. L *habitationem* (as HABIT², -ATION)]

habĭt′ŭal, a. Customary; constant, continual; given to (specified) habit, as *a* ~ *drunkard*. Hence ~LY² adv., ~NESS n. [f. med. L *habitualis* (as HABIT¹, -AL)]

habĭt′ū|āte, v.t. Accustom *to* thing, *to* doing. So ~A′TION n. [f. LL *habituare* (as HABIT¹), see -ATE³]

hăb′itūde, n. Mental or bodily constitution; custom, tendency. [ME, f. OF f. L *habitudinem* (*habēre* have, see -TUDE)]

habĭt′ŭé (-ā), n. Habitual visitor or resident. [F, p.p. of *habituer* (as HABITU-ATE)]

hachures (hăshūr′), n. pl. Lines used in hill-shading on maps to indicate slope. [F]

hacĭĕn′da (ă-, ah-), n. (Sp.-Amer.). Estate, plantation; factory, works. [Sp.]

hăck¹, n. Mattock; miner's pick; gash, wound, esp. from kick with toe of boot. [f. MLG *hakke*, & f. foll.]

hăck², v.t. & i. Cut, notch, mangle; kick shin of (opponent at football); deal cutting blows (*at*); emit short dry coughs; *a* ~*ing* (short dry frequent) *cough*; ~*-saw* (for metal-cutting). [OE *haccian*, MLG, MDu., MHG *hacken* f. WG *hakkôn]

hăck³, n. Board on which hawk's meat is laid; (of eyas hawk) *be at* ~ (not allowed to prey for itself); frame for drying bricks. [var. of HATCH¹, perh. assoc. w. HECK]

hăck⁴, n. Horse let out for hire; jade; horse for ordinary riding; common drudge (also attrib., as ~*writer*); *~*′stand*, cabstand. [abbr. of HACKNEY]

hăck⁵, v.t. & i. Make common, hackney; ride (horse), ride on horseback, on road at ordinary pace; use hired horses. [f. prec.]

hăck′erў, n. Indian bullock-cart. [perh. f. Hindi *chhakrā*]

hăc′kle¹, n., & v.t. 1. Steel flax-comb; long feathers on neck of domestic cock & other birds; *with his* ~*s up*, (of cock, dog, man) angry, ready to fight; artificial fly dressed with ~. 2. v.t. Dress (flax, fly) with ~. [ME *hechele, hek-, hakele*, f. OE *hacule, *hecile f. Gmc **hak-* prick,

pierce; cf. HOOK; cogn. w. MHG *hachele*, MLG, MDu. *hekele*]

hăc′kle², v.t. Hack, mangle. [HACK²+ -LE(3)]

hăck′lў, a. Rough, jagged. [f. prec. + -Y²]

hăck′matăck, n. Amer. larch. [native]

hăck′ney, n., & v.t. 1. Horse of middle size & quality for ordinary riding; drudge, hireling; ~*-carriage*, *-coach* (kept for hire). 2. v.t. (Esp. in p.p. ~*ed*) make common or trite. [orig. much disputed; Skeat conjectures ME f. *Hackenei* in Middlesex, whence OF *haquenee* & other Rom. forms]

had. See HAVE.

hădd′ock, n. Fish allied to cod. [ME, of unkn. orig.; OF *hadot* prob. f. E]

hāde, v.i. (geol., mining). Incline from the vertical. [orig. unkn.]

Hād′ēs (-z), n. (Gk Myth.). Lower world, abode of departed spirits. [Gk, orig. a name of Pluto]

Hădj′ĭ, Hăjj′ĭ, n. (Title of) Mohammedan pilgrim who has been to MECCA. [f. Arab. *ḥaji*]

hadn′t. See HAVE.

haeccē′itў (hĕks-), n. (philos.). Thisness; individuality. [f. med. L *haecceitas* (*haec* fem. of *hic* this, see -TY)]

haem′al, a. (anat.). Of the blood; situated on same side of body as the heart & great blood-vessels. [f. Gk *haima* blood + -AL]

haemăt′ic, a. & n. Of or containing blood; (n.) medicine acting on the blood. [f. Gk *haimatikos* (as foll., see -IC)]

haem′atin, n. (chem.). Bluish-black amorphous substance, constituent of haemoglobin. [f. Gk *haima -matos* blood + -IN]

haem′atite, hĕm′-, n. A red, brown, or blackish, iron oxide ore. [f. L f. Gk *haimatītēs* (*lithos*) blood-like stone (as prec., see -ITE)]

haem′ato-, (chiefly U.S.) **hĕm′ato-**, in comb. = Gk *haima -matos* blood, as ~*cele*, tumour containing extravasated blood.

haematūr′ia, n. (path.). Presence of blood in the urine. [f. prec. + Gk *ouron* urine]

haem′o-, hĕm′o-, in comb. short for H(A)EMATO-.

haemoglŏb′in, n. Oxygen-carrying pigment contained in red blood-cells of vertebrates. [f. HAEMO- + GLOBULIN]

haemophil′ia, hĕm-, n. (med.). (Hereditary) tendency to bleeding from even a slight injury. [f. Gk *haima* blood, -o-, *philia* affection]

haem′orrhage, hĕm′-, (hĕm′orĭj), n. Escape of blood from blood-vessels, bleeding. [17th c. f. L f. Gk *haimorrhagia* (*haima* blood + st. of *rhēgnumi* burst); 16th c. also *-agy* f. OF *-agie*]

haem′orrhoids, hĕm′-, (hĕm′oroidz), n. pl. Piles. [14th c. *emeraudes* (Bibl. *emerods*) f. OF *emeroyde*; later dir. f. L f. Gk *haimorrhoides* (*phlebes*) bleeding (veins) (*haima* blood + -*rhoos* -flowing)]

ha′fiz (hah-), n. Mohammedan who knows Koran by heart (used as title). [Arab.]

häf′nium, n. (chem.). Metallic element discovered in 1923. [Da. (*Kjöben*)*havn* Copenhagen + -IUM]

haft (hah-), n., & v.t. Wooden shaft of pick-axe, mattock, felling-axe, etc.; handle (of dagger, knife, etc.); (v.t.) furnish (knife etc.) with ~. [OE *hæfl(e)*, OHG *hefti*, ON *hepti* f. Gmc *haftjom* f. *haf-* HEAVE]

häg¹, n. Ugly old woman; witch; (formerly) evil spirit in female form; (also ~′*fish*) a parasite fish allied to lamprey; ~′*ridden*, afflicted by nightmare. Hence ~g′ISH¹ (-g-) a. [ME *hegge*, *hagge* perh. f. OE *hægtesse* (= OHG *hagazissa*, G *hexe*) of unkn. orig.]

‖ **häg²,** n. Soft place in moor; firm place in bog. [cf. ON *högg* ravine]

hagga′dah (-gah-), n. Legendary part of the Talmud; book recited at SEDER. [Heb., = tale, f. *higgid* tell]

häg′gard, a. & n. 1. Wild-looking (esp. as a result of fatigue, privation, worry, etc.). 2. (Of hawk) caught in her adult plumage, untamed; (n.) such a hawk. Hence ~NESS n. [f. F *hagard*, of unkn. orig.]

‖ **häg′gis** (-g-), n. Minced heart, lungs, & liver, of sheep etc., boiled in maw with suet, oatmeal, etc. [ME; orig. unkn.]

häg′gle, v.i., & n. Dispute, wrangle, (*about, over*); (v.i.) bargain. [f. dial. *hag* chop f. ON *höggva* (HEW) + -LE(3)]

häg′iarchy (-gī-; -kī), n. Rule, order, of saints. [f. foll. + Gk *arkhē* rule]

hägio- (-g-), comb. form of Gk *hagios* saint(ly), as: ~*cracy* (-ŏk²), government of holy persons; ~*grapha* (-ŏg²), books of the Hebrew Scriptures not included under Law & Prophets; ~*grapher* (-ŏg²), ~*graph′ic*, (writer) of any of these, or of saints′ lives; ~*graphy* (-ŏg²), writing of saints′ lives; ~*latry* (-ŏl²), worship of saints; ~*logy* (-ŏl²), literature treating of lives & legends of saints; ~*scope* (häg²), (modern term for) squint (eccl.).

hah, int. & v.i. = HA¹,².

ha ha (hah hah), int. repr. laughter.

ha-ha (hah′hah), n. Sunk fence bounding park or garden. [F]

hai(c)k (hah′ĭk, hāk), n. Arabian outer wrapper for head & body. [Arab. *ḥayk* f. *ḥak* weave]

hail¹, n. Pellets of frozen rain falling in shower, as ~′*storm*; shower of missiles, curses, questions, etc.; ~′*stone*, pellet of ~. Hence ~′Y² a. [OE *hægl*, OS, OHG *hagel*, ON *hagl* f. Gmc *hag(a)laz, -am*]

hail², v.i. & t. *It* ~*s*, hail falls; (fig.) pour down (blows, words, etc.), come down, violently. [OE *hagalian* (prec.)]

hail³, int. of greeting; ~*fellow*, ~*-fellow--well-met*, intimate, too intimate, *with*. [ellipt. use of obs. adj. *hail* f. ON *heill* sound, HALE, WHOLE]

hail⁴, v.t. & i., & n. 1. Salute; greet (person etc. *as* king etc., also ~ *him king*);

call to (ship, person) to attract attention; (of ship, person) be come *from* (place). 2. n. Salutation, esp. *within*~, near enough to be ~ed. [ME, f. prec.]

hair, n. 1. One or (collect. sing.) all of the fine filaments growing from skin of animals, esp. from human head (pl. ~*s* in collect. sense is arch.); (of plants) elongated cell growing from epidermis; ~*-like* thing; jot, tittle; *against the* ~, against the grain; *to a* ~, exactly; *a* ~ *of the* DOG *that bit you*; (sl.) *keep your* ~ *on*, keep cool; *get person by the short* ~*s* (sl.), have complete control over, have at one′s mercy; (of girl) *put up, turn up, her* ~, dress it in woman′s fashion; *do* or *put up, let down her* ~; *let* one′s (*back*) ~ *down* (colloq.), drop ceremony, behave in an unconventional way; *not turn a* ~, show no sign of exhaustion or discomposure; ~ *stands on end* (with fright or horror). 2. ~′*breadth* or ~′*s breadth*, minute distance (~*breadth escape*, very narrow); ~′*brush*, toilet brush for~; ~′*cloth* (made of ~, for various purposes); ~′*cut*, cutting of the ~; ~*-do* (colloq.), style or process of woman′s ~*dressing*; ~′*dresser*, one whose business is to dress and cut ~; ~*-line*, line, rope, made of ~, (also) up-stroke in writing; ~*-net*, *-oil* (used for the ~); ~′*pin* (for fastening the ~; ~*pin bend*, doubling back of road); ~*powder*, scented powder for ~, now used by men-servants; ~ *shirt* (of ~cloth, for ascetics); ~′*slide*, horn or tortoise-shell clip for keeping ~ in position; ~*-space* (Typ.), very thin space; ~*-splitting* a. & n., over-subtle(ty); ~′*spring*, fine spring in watch, regulating balance-wheel; ~*-stroke*, fine up-stroke in writing; ~ *trigger*, secondary trigger releasing main one by slight pressure. Hence ~′INESS n., (-)~ED² (-rd), ~′LESS, ~′LIKE, ~′Y², aa. (~*y-heeled*, sl., deficient in breeding or manners). [OE *hær, hēr*, OS, OHG, ON *hār*, f. Gmc *hǣram*]

häke¹, n. Fish like cod. [15th c., of unkn. orig.]

häke², haik, n. Wooden framework for drying bricks & other purposes. [prob. var. of HACK³, HECK]

hakeem′, -kim′¹ (-ēm), n. (In India & Mohammedan countries) physician. [Arab. *ḥakīm* wise, physician]

ha′kim² (hah-), n. (As prec.) judge, ruler, governor. [Arab. *ḥākim*]

hala′tion, n. (photog.). Spreading of light beyond its proper boundary in a negative (and consequent fogging) caused by internal reflection in the support of the emulsion. [irreg. f. HALO + -ATION]

häl′berd, -rt, n. (hist.). Combined spear & battle-axe. [f. OF *halebarde*, ult. f. MHG *helmbarte* (*helm* handle + *barte* axe)]

hälberdier′ (-ēr), n. Man armed with halberd. [f. OF *hallebardier* (as prec., see -IER)]

häl′cyon, n. & a. 1. Bird fabled by the ancients to breed in floating nest on sea at winter solstice, & to charm wind &

waves into calm for the purpose; (Zool.) Australasian kingfisher. 2. adj. Calm, esp. ~ *days* (orig. 14 days about winter solstice). [ME, f. L *halcyon* f. Gk *alkuŏn* kingfisher]

hāle[1], a. Robust, vigorous, (esp. of old persons). Hence ~'NESS (-ln-) n. [north. repr. of OE *hāl* WHOLE]

hāle[2], v.t. Drag, draw, forcibly (lit. & fig.). [ME, f. OF *haler* f. ON *hala* = OS, OHG *halôn*; cf. OE *geholian* obtain; see HAUL]

half (hahf), n. (pl. *halves* pr. hahvz), a., & adv. **1.** One of two equal or corresponding parts into which a thing is divided, as *the ~ of 10 is 5, cut it in ~* (into halves), *your ~ is bigger than mine, two ounces & a ~* (ounce) or *two & a ~ ounces, ~ of it is* (but *of them are*) *rotten*; (colloq.)=~-pint, -mile, -back, -holiday; ‖ school term (the school year being formerly divided into two portions); *better ~*, wife; *do a thing by halves* (imperfectly); *too clever by ~* (far); *go halves*, share equally (*with* person *in* thing); *cry halves*, claim equal share. **2.** adj. Forming a ~, as *a ~ length, a ~ share*; (adj. now viewed as=*the ~ of*) *~ the men, ~ your time, ~ a crown* (2/6), *~ a pint, ~ a pound* (*is ~ the battle, goes a long way towards success). **3.** adv. To the extent of ~, (loosely) to a considerable extent, as *it is ~ cooked, a ~-cooked potato, ~ dead, I ~ wish, not ~* (nearly) *long enough,* (colloq.) *not ~* (not at all) *bad, not ~ a bad fellow*; ‖ *not ~* (sl.), to the greatest possible extent, as *he didn't ~ swear* (swore violently); (adv., prob. orig. adj.) *~* (an hour) *past two* (o'clock); (Naut.) *~ three, 3½* (fathoms), *east ~-south* (5⅝° south of east). **4.** *~-&-~*, (what is) ~ one thing & ~ another, esp. mixture of ale & porter; *~ as much* or *many again*, 1½ times the amount; *~-back*, (Footb.) position, player, immediately behind forwards; *~-baked*, (fig.) not thorough, not earnest, *~-witted*; *~-ball* (Billiards etc.), with moving ball directed at edge of object ball; *~ binding* (book, leather back & corners, cloth or paper sides (similarly *~-bound, ~-calf, ~-morocco*, etc.); *~-blood*, person having one parent in common with another, this relationship, (also) person of mixed nationality; *~-blooded*, born of different races; *~-blue*, badge or colours (see BLUE[2]) awarded to second string or to representative in minor sports; *~-boot* (reaching up to the calf); *~-bred*, of mixed breed, mongrel; *~-breed*, *~-blooded* person; *~-brother, -sister* (by one parent only); *~ butt*, cue of length between ordinary cue & long butt; *~-caste* a. & n., *~-bre(e)d*, esp. (child) of European father & Indian mother; *~* COCK[1](2); ‖ *~-crown*, (n.) silver coin of 2/6, (usu. *~ a crown*, see above) amount of 2/6, (adj.) priced at or worth 2/6; *~-deck*, (esp.) quarters of cadets & apprentices on a merchant vessel; *~-fifteen, -thirty, -forty*

(Lawn Tennis), handicap (in strokes allowed in certain games of each set) given to a weaker player; *~-hearted*, lacking courage or zeal, so *~-heartedly, -ness*; *~* HITCH; *~ holiday*, day of which (the latter) is taken as holiday; *~-length*, portrait of upper ~ of person; *~-life* (Phys.), time during which radio-activity of substance falls to ~ of its original value; *~-mast high*, (of flag) lowered to ~ height of mast as mark of respect for the dead; *~ measures*, compromise, *~-&-~* policy etc.; *~ moon*, moon of which only ~ is illuminated, semicircular object; *~ mourning*, black relieved by grey etc.; *~(-)nelson*, a hold in wrestling (*get a ~ nelson on*, hold in a crippling position, gain complete mastery over); *~ pay*, reduced allowance to army etc. officer when neither retired nor in actual service; *~-seas-over*, drunk; *~-time*, time showing that ~ of a game or contest is completed; ‖ *~-timer*, (formerly) child attending school for ~ usual time, earning money in other ~; *~-title*, title or short title of a book, printed on recto of leaf preceding the title-leaf; also title of section of a book printed on recto of leaf preceding it; *~-tone*, illustration printed from a block (produced by photographic agency) in which the lights & shades of the original are represented by small or large dots (*~-tone block, process*); *~-truth*, statement that conveys only part of the truth; *~* VOLLEY; *~-way house*, inn midway between two towns etc., (fig.) compromise; *~-witted*, imbecile, so *~-wit* n.; *~-yearly* a. & adv., (occurring) every ~ year. [OE *h(e)alf*, OS *half*, OHG *halb* ON *halfr*, Goth. *halbs* f. Gmc *halbhaz*]

‖ **halfpenny** (hāp'nĭ), n. (pl. as PENNY). Bronze coin worth half a penny (*turn up again like a bad ~*, persistently, unfailingly); *three halfpence* (hāp'ens), (usu. for) a penny ~, 1½d.; *~-worth* (usu. pron. hāp'ath), *ha'p'orth*, as much as a ~ will buy.

hāl'ĭbut, hŏl', n. Large flat fish used for food. [ME, f. *haly* HOLY + *butt* flat fish]

hăl'ĭdom, n. (arch.). Holy thing, esp. (as oath) *by my~*. [OE *hāligdōm* (HOLY, -DOM)]

hălieut'ĭc, a. & n. Of fishing; (n. pl.) art of fishing. [f. L f. Gk *halieutikos* (*halieuŏ* fish f. *hals* sea, see -IC)]

hălitos'ĭs, n. (med.). Abnormally foul breath. [f. L *halitus* breath + -OSIS]

hall (hawl), n. Large public room in palace etc.; *servants' ~*, room in which servants dine; ‖ mansion, large residence esp. of landed proprietor; ‖ (Univv.) building set apart for residence or instruction of students; ‖ (in Eng. colleges etc.) common dining-room, dinner in this; building of guild, as *Saddlers' H~*; large room for public business; entrance-passage of house; *Liberty H~*, place where one may do as one likes; ~'*mark*, mark used at Goldsmiths' H~ (& by Government assay offices) for marking standard of gold & silver, (v.t.) stamp with this (often fig.). [OE *h(e)all*, OS, OHG *halla*, ON *hǫll* f. Gmc **hal-* cogn. w. HELL]

hallelujah, -luiah. See ALLELUIA.

halliard. See HALYARD.

hallō′, -loa′ (-lō), int., n., & v.i. Int. calling attention or expr. surprise; informal greeting; (n., & v.i.) (the) cry ~. [var. of earlier HOLLO]

hallōō′¹, int. inciting dogs to the chase, calling attention, or expressing surprise (also as n., the cry~). [perh. var. of HOLLO]

hallōō′², v.i. & t. Cry 'halloo!', esp. to dogs; urge on (dogs etc.) with shouts; shout (t. & i.) to attract attention; (prov.) *do not ~ until you are out of the* WOOD. [f. prec.; or = HALLOW³]

hăll′ow¹ (-ō), n. Holy person, saint, (now only in *all~s, ~mas*, feast of All-hallows, = ALL *Saints' Day*; *Hall'owe'en*, Sc., U.S., eve of this). [OE *hālga*, form of *hālig* HOLY]

hăll′ow² (-ō), v.t. Make holy; honour as holy. [OE *hālgian*, OS *hē*-, OHG *heilagōn*, ON *helga* f. Gmc **hailag-* HOLY]

hăll′ow³ (-ō), v.t. & i. Chase with shouts; incite with shouts; shout to incite dogs etc. [ME *halowen* prob. f. OF *halloer*]

Hallstatt (hahl'shtaht), a. (Used attrib.) relating to the civilization of a phase of the early iron age. [~, village in Upper Austria, where remains of this period were discovered]

hallu′cināte (-lōō-), v.t. Produce false impressions in the mind of (person). [f. L *(h)al(l)ucinari* wander in mind, see -ATE⁵]

hallucinā′tion (-lōō-), n. Illusion; apparent perception of external object not actually present. So **hallu′cinatory** (-lōō-) a. [f. L *alucinatio* (as prec., see -ATION)]

halm. See HAULM.

hăl′ma, n. Game played on board of 256 squares. [Gk, = leap, f. *hallomai* leap, see -M]

hāl′ō, n. (pl. ~*es*), & v.t. **1.** Circle of light round luminous body, esp. sun or moon; circle, ring; disc of light surrounding head of saint, nimbus; (fig.) ideal glory investing person etc. **2.** v.t. Surround with ~. [f. med. L *halo* f. L f. Gk *halōs* threshing-floor, disc of sun or moon]

hăl′ogĕn, n. (chem.). Any of the group of elements fluorine, chlorine, bromine, & iodine, which form haloids by simple union with a metal (e.g. sodium chloride or common salt). [f. Gk *hals* salt + -GEN]

hăl′oid, a. & n. (chem.). (Salt) having a composition like that of common salt. [f. Gk *hals* salt + -OID]

halt¹ (hawlt), n., & v.i. & t. **1.** Temporary stoppage on march or journey; ‖ railway stopping-place used for local services only and without regular station buildings etc.

2. v.i. Make a ~. **3.** v.t. Cause (troops etc.) to ~. [(vb f. n.) orig. in phr. *make halt* f. G *halt machen* (*halt* hold)]

halt² (hawlt), a. (arch.). Lame; crippled. [OE *h(e)alt*, OS *halt*, OHG *halz*, ON *haltr*, Goth. *halts* f. Gmc **haltaz*]

halt³ (hawlt), v.i., & n. Walk hesitatingly; hesitate, as ~ *between two opinions*; (of argument, verse, etc.) be defective; (arch.) be lame; (n., arch.) ~ing, limp. Hence ~*ing*LY² adv. [OE *h(e)altian*, f. prec.]

hal′ter (hawl-), n., & v.t. **1.** Rope, strap, with noose or headstall for horses or cattle; rope with noose for hanging person; death by hanging; ~-*break* v.t., accustom (horse) to ~. **2.** v.t. Fasten (often *up*) with ~, hang (person) with ~. [OE *hælftre*, OLG *heliftra*, OHG *halftra*, WG f. root *halbh*, whence HELVE]

halve (hahv), v.t. Divide into halves; share equally; reduce to half; (Golf) ~ *a hole with*, reach it in same number of strokes as (other player), ~ *a match*, win same number of holes; fit (crossing timbers) together by cutting out half thickness of each. [ME HALF*en*]

hăl′yard, hăll′iard, haul′yard, n. (naut.). Rope, tackle, for raising or lowering sail, yard, etc. [14th c. *halier* (HALE², -YER)]

hăm¹, n. Back of thigh, thigh & buttock; (formerly) bend of the knee; thigh of hog salted & dried in smoke or otherwise for food; (sl.) an amateur (*radio* ~, operator of an amateur radio station), an inexpert performer, (also ~ *actor*) an inexperienced or ineffective actor, one who rants & overacts; (sl.) ~-*fisted*, -*handed*, heavy-handed, clumsy. [OE *ham(m)*, *hom(m)*, OHG *ham(m)a*, ON *höm* f. Gmc **ham(m)*- be crooked]

hăm², n. (hist.). Town, village. [OE *ham* HOME; seen in *Oakham* etc.]

hămadrȳ′ăd, n. (Gk Myth.) nymph living & dying with the tree she inhabited; venomous Indian serpent; Abyssinian baboon. [f. L f. Gk *hamadruas* (*hama* with + *drus* tree)]

Hăm′burgh (-bĕrg, -buru), n. Black variety of grape; small variety of domestic fowl. [*Hamburg* in Germany]

*hăm′bŭrger (-ger), n. (Also *Hamburg steak*) chopped steak usu. cooked or eaten with onions; kind of sausage. [prec., -ER¹]

hāmes, n. pl. Two curved pieces of iron or wood forming (part of) collar of draught horse. [MDu., f. MDu. *hame*]

Hăm′ite¹, n. (Supposed) descendant of Ham, member of Egyptian or other African people. Hence **Hămit′ic** a. [-ITE]

hăm′ite², n. Fossil cephalopod with hook-shaped shell. [f. L *hamus* hook, see -ITE]

hăm′lĕt, n. Small village, esp. one without church. [f. OF *hamelet* dim. of *hamel* dim. f. OFrank. *haim* HOME]

hammam (hŭmahm', hŭm'ŭm), n. Turkish bath or bathing establishment. [Arab.]

hämm′er[1], n. Instrument for beating, breaking, driving nails, etc., with solid (usu. steel) head at right angles to handle; machine with metal block serving same purpose; similar contrivance, as for exploding charge in gun (whence ~LESS a.), striking string of piano, etc.; auctioneer's mallet indicating by rap that article is sold; *come under the*~, be sold by auction; *knight of the* ~, blacksmith; *throwing the* ~, athletic contest with heavy ~; ~ *and sickle,* symbol of worker and peasant, emblem on national flag of U.S.S.R.; ~ *and tongs,* with might & main; ~*-beam* (projecting from wall at foot of principal rafter); ~*-cloth* (covering driver's seat in coach; hist. unexpl.); ~*-head,* head of ~, kind of shark, African bird; ~*-lock,* hold in which a wrestler's arm is bent behind his back; ~*man,* ~*-smith,* smith who works with ~; ~*-toe* (permanently bent upwards). [OE *hamor,* OS -*ur,* OHG -*ar,* ON -*arr*]

hämm′er[2], v.t. & i. Strike, beat, drive, (as) with hammer; (colloq.) inflict heavy defeat(s) on in war or games; ~ *out,* devise; ~ (force) *idea into* person's *head*; work hard *at*; || (St. Exch.) declare (person) a defaulter with three taps of hammer. [f. prec.]

hämm′ock, n. Hanging bed of canvas or netting suspended by cords at ends, used esp. on board ship; ~ *chair* (made of canvas suspended on adjustable framework). [f. Sp. *hamaca* of Carib. orig.]

häm′per[1], n. Basketwork packing-case; consignment of eatables, wines, etc., however packed (usu. as a present; *Christmas* ~). [ME, f. obs. *hanaper* f. OF *hanapier* case for goblet (*hanap* f. WG (OFrank., OS) *hnap*)]

häm′per[2], v.t. & n. 1. Obstruct movement of (person etc.) with material obstacles; (fig.) impede, hinder. 2. n. (naut.). Necessary but cumbrous part of equipment of vessel. [ME, of unkn. orig.; perh. rel. to MHG *hemmen,* Icel. *hemja* restrain]

Hämp′ton Court (kört), n. (Used for) ~ Palace, now partly occupied by persons of rank in reduced circumstances, partly open to the public. [place]

häm′shäckle, v.t. Shackle (horse etc.) with rope connecting head and foreleg. [Sc. & north. dial., of unkn. orig.]

häm′ster, n. Rodent like large rat, with cheek-pouches for carrying grain to its winter store. [G]

häm′string, n., & v.t. (-inged or -ung). 1. (In man) one of five tendons at back of knee; (in quadrupeds) great tendon at back of knee in hind leg. 2. v.t. Cripple (person, animal) by cutting the ~s. [HAM[1]]

häm′ulus, n., (anat., zool., bot.; pl. -*li*). Hook-like process. [L, dim. of *hamus* hook]

händ[1], n. 1. Terminal part of human arm beyond wrist; similar member of all four

limbs of monkey; forefoot of quadruped. 2. Authority, disposal, as *in the* ~*s of*; agency, as *by the* ~*s of, pass through many* ~*s*; share in action, as *have a* ~ *in it.* 3. Pledge of marriage, as *give* one's ~ *to.* 4. (Usu. pl.) manual worker(s) of factory etc. 5. Person who does something, as *a picture by the same* ~; *all* ~*s,* the whole crew; *a good* ~ (skilful) *at singlestick* or *acrostics, an old parliamentary* ~; person, source, from which thing comes, as *first,* SECOND, ~ (*at 1st* etc. ~, directly, more or less indirectly; *first* etc. ~~, of hearsay); COOL ~. 6. Skill, as *a* ~ *for pastry*; style of workmanship; turn, innings, at cricket, billiards, etc. 7. Style of writing, as *a legible* ~; signature, as *witness the* ~ *of A.B.* 8. ~-like thing, esp. pointer of clock or watch (~ *of* BANANAs). 9. Fixed quantity of various commodities, e.g., bundle of tobacco leaves. 10. A lineal measure of horse's height, ~ = 4 in. 11. (Cards) cards dealt to a player, player holding these, as *first, third,* ~. 12. (Theatr. sl.) applause. 13. *At* ~, close by, about to happen soon; *by* ~, by manual labour (*brought up by* ~, of child fed from bottle); *for* one's *own* ~, on one's own account; (*live*) *from* ~ *to mouth,* improvidently; *in* ~, held in the ~, at one's disposal, under control, receiving attention; *off* ~, without preparation, then & there; *on* ~, in one's possession; on one's ~*s,* resting on one as a responsibility; *on all* ~*s,* to, from, all quarters; *on the one* ~, *on the other*~, (of contrasted points of view etc.); *out of* ~, at once, extempore, (also) out of control; *to* ~, within reach; *to* one's ~, ready for one without exertion on one's own part; *bear a* ~, take part *in*; *come to* ~, turn up, be received; *do a* ~'*s turn,* make the slightest effort (usu. w. neg.); *lay* ~*s on,* touch, seize; *take in* ~, undertake; *change* ~*s,* (of property) pass from one person to another; *clean* ~*s,* (fig.) innocence; *with a heavy* ~, oppressively; *with a high* ~, boldly, arrogantly; *have, keep,* one's ~ *in,* be in practice; *his* ~ *is out,* he is out of practice; (*win*) ~*s down,* easily; ~*s off !,* do not touch; ~*s up !* (direction to persons to hold up their ~s as a sign of assent etc., or to preclude resistance); ~ *in* ~, with ~s mutually clasped; *go* ~ *in* ~ *with,* keep step with, lit. & fig.; ~ *over* ~ or *fist,* with each ~ successively passing over the other, as in climbing rope, (fig.) with steady or rapid progress (in overtaking etc.); ~ *to* ~, (of conflict etc.) at close quarters; *bind* one ~ *& foot* (completely), *serve* (person) ~ *& foot* (assiduously); *be* ~ *in* (or *&*) *glove* (intimate) *with*; ~- (opp. *machine-,* as ~*-knitted,* -*sewn,* -*painted*). 14. ~'*bag* (small, carried by women in lieu of pocket); ~'*ball,* ball for throwing with ~, game played with this between two goals; ~*-barrow* (carried by ~); ~'*bell,* bell rung by ~, esp one of a set for musical performance; ~'bill, printed notice circulated by ~; ~'book, short treatise, manual, guide-book; ~-canter, gentle canter; ~'cart (pushed or drawn by ~); ~'cuff v.t., secure with ~cuffs (pair of metal rings joined by short chain, for securing prisoner's ~s); ‖ ~'fast(ing) (Sc.), betrothal; ~-gallop, easy gallop; ~'glass, magnifying glass held in ~, small mirror with handle; ~'grip, grasp, seizure with the ~ (friendly or hostile); ~'hold, something for the ~s to grip on (in climbing etc.); ~'line, fishing-line worked without rod; ~'made, made by ~ (esp. opp. to machine-made); ‖ ~'maid(en), female servant (arch., exc. fig.); ~ of glory, charm made from mandrake root or dried ~ of executed felon [transl. of F main de gloire, corrupted f. mandragore mandrake]; ~-organ, barrel-organ with crank turned by ~; ~-picked, (of supporters etc.) carefully chosen; ~'rail, railing along edge of stairs etc.; ~'shake, shake of person's ~ with one's own, as greeting; ~'spike, wooden lever shod with iron, used on shipboard & by artillery; ~'writing, writing with the ~ with pen or pencil, esp. of particular person. Hence (~)-~'ED², ~'LESS, aa. [OE hand, hond, OS hand, OHG hant, ON hönd, Goth. handus]

händ², v.t. Help (person) with the hand (into, out of, carriage etc.); (Naut.) take in (sail); deliver, transfer, by hand or otherwise (over to person, down or on to succeeding generations, in at office, on, up, etc.); ~-off (Rugby football), push off opponent with hand (also as v.t. and n.); ~-out, information ~ed out to the press etc., *food or money given to beggar at the door. [f. prec.]

händ'ful (-ŏŏl), n. (pl. ~s). Quantity that fills the hand; small number (of men etc.); (colloq.) troublesome person or task. [OE handfull (HAND¹, see -FUL)]

hän'dicăp, n., & v.t. (-pp-). 1. Race, competition, in which chances of competitors are equalized by start, difference in weight to be carried (in horse-races), etc.; extra weight or other condition imposed or advantage conferred on competitor; (fig.) hindrance. 2. v.t. Impose ~ on (competitor); (fig., of circumstances) place (person) at disadvantage. Hence ~PER¹ n. [in 17th c. app. f. phr. hand i' (= in) cap describing a kind of sporting lottery]

hän'dicraft (-ahft), n. Manual skill; manual art or trade or occupation; ~sman, man skilled in a ~. [alt. of older (f. OE) handcraft, after foll.]

hän'diwork (-wĕrk), n. Work done, thing made, by the hands or by anyone's personal agency. [OE handgeweorc (HAND¹ +collect. form of weorc WORK)]

handkerchief (hăng'kerchĭf), n. Square of linen, silk, etc., carried in pocket (pocket-~) for wiping nose etc. or worn

about neck (also neck ~, neckerchief); throw the ~ to (person, in certain games, to invite him to pursue), also, express condescending preference for (person). [HAND¹ +KERCHIEF]

hän'dle¹, n. That part of a thing which is made to hold it by; ~-bar of bicycle etc., steering-bar with ~ at each end; ~ to one's name, title; fact that may be taken advantage of (gave a ~ to his critics); fly off the ~ (colloq.), lose control of oneself. [OE handle f. HAND¹ +-LE]

hän'dle², v.t. Touch, feel, with the hands; manipulate; manage (thing, person); treat (person roughly, kindly, etc.); treat of (subject); deal in (goods). [OE handlian (prec.)]

hän(d)'sel (-ns-), n., & v.t. (-ll-). 1. Gift at beginning of New Year, or on entering on new circumstances; earnest-money; foretaste. 2. v.t. Give ~ to, inaugurate, be the first to try. [ME, corresp. to OE handselen giving into a person's hands, ON handsal giving of the hand (esp. in a promise); f. HAND¹ +OE sellan; see SELL]

händ'some (-ns-), a. Of fine form or figure; (of conduct etc.) generous, as a ~ present, ~ treatment; (prov.) ~ is that ~ does; (of price, fortune, etc.) considerable. Hence ~LY² (-ml-) adv., ~NESS (-mn-) n. [HAND¹, -SOME]

hän'dlў, a. Ready to hand; convenient to handle; clever with the hands; ~y-dandy, child's game in which one player guesses which of other player's hands conceals some object; ~y man (useful for odd jobs, often of sailors). Hence ~ILY² adv., ~INESS n. [-Y²]

häng¹, v.t. & i. (hŭng, exc. as below). 1. Suspend, attach loosely, (from, to, hook or other object above); suspend (meat, game) to dry (hung beef, so cured) or become tender or high. 2. Place (pictures) on wall (hung on the line, at best height for seeing; HANGING committee of Royal Academy etc.). 3. Attach (wall-paper); fit up (bells in belfry). 4. Rest (door on hinges, coach on springs) in free swinging position. 5. (past & p.p. ~ed). Suspend on gibbet as capital punishment; (as imprecation) ~!, ~ it, ~ you, I'll be ~ed if —. 6. Let droop, as ~ the head (from shame etc.). 7. Remain, be, suspended, lit. & fig., as sword, punishment, ~s over his head, rogue shall ~ for it; ~s in the balance, is undecided; curtain ~s loose, in folds, etc. 8. Decorate with (things suspended). 9. ~ (loiter) about; ~ back, show reluctance to act or move; ~ (lag) behind; ~ fire, (of fire-arm) be slow in going off (also fig.); ~ heavy, (of time) pass slowly; ~ off, ~ back; ~ on, depend or rely on, attend carefully to, stick closely (to), remain in office, stick to duty etc., (colloq., in telephoning) not ring off; ~ out, suspend from window etc., (intr.) protrude downwards, (sl.) reside; ~ together, be coherent, be associated; ~ up,

suspend, (fig.) put aside, postpone indefinitely; ~'*dog* n. & a., base & sneaking (fellow), ashamed; ~'*man*, executioner; ~'*nail*, = AGNAIL; ~'*over* n. (sl.), unpleasant after-effects of (esp. alcoholic) dissipation. [(1) OE *hōn* trans. (Goth. *hāhan*); (2) OE *hangian* intr. (OS *hangōn*); (3) ON *hengja* causal; f. Gmc **hang-*, **hanh-*]

‖ **hăng²**, n. Downward droop or bend; the way a thing hangs; *get the ~ of*, get the knack of, understand; (colloq.) *not a ~*, not at all. [f. prec.]

hăng'ar (*or* -ngg-), n. Shed for housing aircraft etc. [F]

‖ **hăng'er¹**, n. Wood on side of steep hill. [OE *hangra* f. *hangian* HANG¹]

hăng'er², n. In vbl senses, esp.: *bell*, *paper*, ~~; loop etc. by which thing is hung; chain, rod, to which pot is hung in fireplace by pot-hook; stroke with double curve in writing (⟨), cf. POT-*hook*; short sword, orig. hung from belt; ~*-on*, follower, dependent. [-ER¹]

hăng'ĭng, n. In vbl senses, esp.: drapery with which walls etc. are hung (usu. pl.); ‖ ~ *committee* (deciding on ~ of pictures in exhibition); *a ~ matter* (resulting in capital punishment). [-ING¹]

hănk, n. Circular loop or coil, esp. as definite length of cotton yarn (840 yds), worsted (560 yds), etc.; (Naut.) ring of rope, iron, etc., for securing staysails to stays. [f. ON *hǫnk* hank, cf. Swed. *hank* string, Da. *hank* handle]

hänk'er, v.i. Crave, long, *after*. Hence ~ING¹ n. [rel. to syn. obs. *hank* (-ER⁵); cf. Du. *hunkeren*, *hank*-]

hănk'ў, n. (colloq.). Handkerchief. [abbr.; see -Y³]

hănk'ў-pănk'ў, n. Jugglery; underhand dealing. [arbitrary, perh. on *hocus-pocus*]

Hăn'over, n. *House of ~*, British sovereigns from George I. Hence **Hănovēr'ĬAN** a. & n. [place]

Hăns (-z), n. (Nickname for) German or Dutchman. [G & Du. f. L *Johannes* John]

Hăn'sard, n. Official report of proceedings in British Parliament. Hence ‖ ~IZE v.t., confront (M.P.) with his former utterances recorded in ~. [Luke ~ (d. 1828), original compiler]

Hänse, n. (hist.). Guild of merchants; political and commercial league of Germanic towns, whence **HănsĕAT'Ic** a.; entrance-fee of guild. [f. MLG (=MHG) *Hanse*, =OHG, Goth. *hansa* (= OE *hōs*) company; in med. L (AL) *hansa*]

hăn'som (*căb*), n. Two-wheeled cabriolet for two inside, with driver mounted behind and reins going over roof. [*Hansom*, patentee, 1834]

hăp¹, n. (arch.). Chance, luck, lot; (w. pl.) chance occurrence. [ME, f. ON *happ*]

hăp², v.t. (arch.; -pp-). Come about by chance; happen (*to* do). [ME *happe(n)*, f. prec.]

hăp'dăx lĕgŏm'ĕnon, n. (pl. *-ena*). Word of which only one use is recorded. [Gk, = once said]

hăphăz'ard (-p-h-), n., a., & adv. Mere chance, esp. *at, by, ~*; casual(ly). [HAP¹ + HAZARD]

hăp'lĕss, a. Unlucky. Hence ~LY² adv. [-LESS]

hăplŏg'raphў, n. The mistake of writing once what should be written twice (e.g. *philogy* for *philology*), cf. DITTOGRAPHY. [f. Gk *haplous* single + -GRAPHY]

hăp'lў, adv. (arch.). By chance; perhaps. [HAP¹ + -LY²]

‖ **ha'p'orth**. See HALFPENNY.

hăpp'en, v.i. Come to pass (by chance or otherwise), whence ~ING¹ n. (usu. pl.); chance, have the fortune, *to* (do); come *upon* (person, thing) by chance; (euphem., of death) *if anything should ~ to me, if I die*. [ME (HAP¹ + -EN⁶)]

hăpp'ў, a. (Of person or circumstance) lucky, fortunate; contented with one's lot; *I shall be ~* (pleased) *to assist*; ~ FAMILY; apt, felicitous (of language or conduct); (sl.) dazed (*bomb*, *shell*, ~~); ~*-go-lucky*, haphazard (adj.). Hence **hăpp'ĬLY²** adv., **hăpp'ĬNESS** n. [f. HAP¹ + -Y²]

hăra-ki'ri, n. Suicide by disembowelment, as practised by higher classes in Japan when in disgrace or sentenced to death. [Jap. (vulg.), f. *hara* belly + *kiri* cut]

harăngue' (-ng), n., & v.i. & t. Speech to an assembly; loud or vehement address; (v.i.) make ~; (v.t.) make ~ to. [ME *arang* f. OF *arenge* f. Pr. *arenga*, It. *aringa* f. Goth. **haririggs* 'army-ring' as legal court]

hă'ras (*or* ahrah'), n. Breeding station for horses. [ME, f. OF *haras* of unkn. orig.]

hă'rass, v.t. Vex by repeated attacks; trouble, worry. Hence ~MENT n. [f. F *harasser*, f. OF *harer* set a dog on]

harb'inger (-j-), n., & v.t. One who announces another's approach, forerunner; (formerly) one sent to purvey lodgings for army, royal train, etc.; (v.t.) announce approach of. [ME, f. OF *herbergere* f. *herberge* lodging f. WG **heriberga* (*heri* army + *bergan* protect); *-n-* as in *messenger*]

harb'our (-ber), n., & v.t. & i. 1. Place of shelter for ships; shelter; ~*-master*, officer in charge of ~. 2. v.t. Give shelter to (esp. vermin, criminal, evil thoughts); (v.i.) come to anchor in ~. Hence ~LESS (-berl-) a. [(vb f. n.) ME *hereberge* f. OE **hereborg* f. WG **heriberga* (prec.)]

harb'ourage (-ber-), n. (Place of) shelter. [-AGE]

hard, a., n., & adv. 1. Firm, unyielding to touch, solid; ~ *cash*, specie, as opp. to paper currency; ~ *facts* (not disputable like opinions etc.); difficult (*to* do; ~ *nut to crack*, ~ *problem*, *person ~ to make out or influence*); ~ *of hearing*, somewhat deaf; difficult to understand or explain, as ~ *words, question*; (of person or conduct) unfeeling, harsh (~ *as nails*); involving undue or unfair suffering (~ *cases make bad law*); stingy; difficult to bear, as ~ *life, times*, LINE²s; ~ (severe) *winter; a~ bargain* (without concession); harsh, unpleasant,. to eye or ear; *(of liquor) spirituous; ~ *water* (unfit for washing owing to its mineral salts); (of markets and prices) high, unyielding; (Phonetics) *k, t, and p, are~ as opposed to g, d, & b, c is~ in cat, g is~ in go*; strenuous, as ~ *fight*, ~ *labour* (imposed on some criminals, abolished in U.K. in 1948), ~ *row to hoe* (difficult task), ~ *worker;* ~ *swearing*, (euphem. for) unabashed perjury. **2.** n. ‖ Sloping roadway across foreshore; (sl.) = ~ labour *(got 2 years*~). **3.** adv. Strenuously, severely, as *try* ~, *raining* ~, *freezing* ~, ~ *pressed* (closely pursued); with difficulty, as ~*-earned*, ~*-baked, -boiled* (so as to be~); ~*-boiled*, (also, orig. U.S. colloq.) callous, ~*-headed*, tough; *be* ~ *put to it*, be in difficulties; *die* ~ (only after~ struggle), & cf. DIE²*·*~; *it will go* ~ *with him* (prove to his disadvantage); *it shall go* ~ *but* (short of overpowering difficulties) *I will find them;* ~ *by*, close by; ~ *(up)on*, too severe in criticism or treatment (*don't be too* ~ *on him*), (of circumstances) bearing with undue severity on; ~ *upon*, close to; *run* (person) ~, pursue him closely. **4.** ~ *& fast*, (of rules) strict; ‖~*'bake*, almond toffee; ~*'bitten*, tough in fight etc.; ~*'board*, sheet (usu. 8 ft by 4 ft) of compressed and processed wood-pulp fibre used for panels of doors, cupboards, partitions, etc.; ‖~ *core*, heavy material forming foundation of road; ~ *court*, lawn tennis court made of asphalt, concrete, etc. (opp. *grass court*); ~ *currency*, one not likely to depreciate suddenly or fluctuate greatly in value; ~*-favoured, -featured*, of harsh or ugly features; ~*-fisted*, stingy; ~*-headed*, practical, not sentimental; ~*-hearted*, unfeeling, so ~*-heartedly, -ness;* ~ *hit*, severely troubled; ~*-laid*, (of string, fabric, etc.) tightly twisted or woven; ‖~*-lying money*, extra pay granted to officers & men while serving in torpedo boats & other small craft; ~*-mouthed*, (of horse) not easily controlled by bit (also fig.); ~ *set*, set so as to be~, (of egg) that has been subjected to incubation, (of person) hungry; ~*'shell*, having a~ shell, (fig.) rigid, uncompromising, esp. *Hardshell Baptists*; ~ *tack*, ship-biscuit; ~ *up*, in want (esp. of money), at a loss *for*, (Naut., adv., of tiller) as far as possible to windward; ~*'ware*, ironmongery; ~²*wareman*, dealer in this; ~*'wood*, wood of deciduous trees as opposed to pines and firs. Hence ~*'NESS* n. [OE *h(e)ard*, OS *hard*, OHG *hart*, ON *harthr*, Goth. *hardus* cogn. w. Gk *kratus* strong]

hărd'en, v.t. & i. Make or become hard, callous (esp. in p.p.), or robust. [-EN⁶]

hărd'ihŏŏd, n. Boldness, audacity. [f. HARDY a.+-HOOD]

hărd'lў, adv. In a hard manner; with difficulty; harshly; scarcely. [-LY²]

hărd'shĭp, n. Hardness of fate or circumstance; severe suffering or privation. [-SHIP]

hărd'lў¹, a. Bold, audacious, whence ~ILY² adv.; robust, capable of endurance; (Hort., of plants) able to grow in the open air all the year; *half* ~*y*, requiring shelter in winter only; ~*y annual*, one that may be sown, or sows itself, in the open, (fig., joc.) subject that comes up yearly. Hence ~INESS n. [ME, f. OF *hardi* p.p. of *hardir* f. WG **hardjan* make HARD]

hărd'ў², n. Blacksmith's bar of hard iron for cutting metal on etc. [prob. f. prec. or HARD]

hāre, n. ‖ Kinds of rodent of medium size with tawny fur, long ears, short tail, and hind legs longer than fore ones, inhabiting fields, hills, etc.; BELGIAN ~; *mad as a March* ~ (~ in breeding season); (prov.) *first catch your* ~ (*then cook him*); *hold* (or *run*) *with the* ~ *& run* (or *hunt*) *with the hounds*, keep in with both sides; ~ *& hounds*, paper-chase; ~*'bell* (-ãrb-), *hairbell*, round-leaved bell-flower, also (see BLUE¹-*bell*) wild hyacinth; ~*-brained*, rash, wild; ~*'lip* (-ãrl-), fissure of upper lip; ~*'s-foot*, species of clover with soft hair about flowers, (also) corkwood tree, (also) ~*'s* foot used for applying rouge etc. to face. [OE *hara*, OHG *haso*, ON *heri*]

hār'em, -am, hareem', -im (-ēm), n. Women's part of Mohammedan dwelling-house; its occupants; (usu. *-am*) Mohammedan sacred place. [f. Arab. *haram, -im*, prohibited f. *harama* prohibit]

hă'ricot(-kō), n. Ragout (usu. of mutton); ~ (*bean*), French bean. [F]

hărk, v.i. & t. Listen (usu. *to*, rarely trans.; also abs. in imper.); (as call to hounds) go *forward, away, off*, etc.; ~ *back*, (of hounds) retrace course to find scent, (fig.) revert (*to* subject), (trans.) recall (hounds). [ME *herkien*, OE **heorcian*, = MLG, MDu. *horken*, OHG *hŏrechen;* cf. HEARKEN]

hārl¹, v.t. & i. (Sc.). Drag along the ground; drag oneself along; rough-cast with lime and small gravel. [ME, of unkn. orig.]

hārl(e)², n. Barb, fibre, of feather. [f. MLG *herle. harle*, fibre of flax or hemp]

Hārlei'an (-lē-), a. Of (the library of) Robert Harley, Earl of Oxford, d. 1724. [-EAN]

hărl'equĭn, n. **1.** Character in Italian comedy; mute character in English pantomime, invisible to clown & pantaloon, usu. wearing particoloured tights; buffoon. **2.** (Also ~ *duck*) northern duck with variegated plumage. [F, f. It. *arlecchino*]

hàrléquināde', n. Part of pantomime in which harlequin plays chief part. [f. F *arlequinade* (as prec., see -ADE)]

Hàrl'ey Street, n. London street associated with fashionable physicians.

hàrl'ot, n., & v.i. Prostitute; (v.i.) play the ~. Hence ~RY(4) n. [ME, f. OF *har-, herlot* lad, knave, vagabond, of unkn. orig.]

hàrm, n., & v.t. Damage, hurt, (*out of* ~'s *way*, in safety). Hence ~'FUL, ~'LESS (doing no ~), aa., ~'fulLY², ~'lèssLY², advv., ~'fulNESS, ~'lèssNESS, nn. [OE *hearm*, OS, OHG *harm*, ON *harmr* f. Gmc *harmaz*]

hàrmätt'an, n. Parching land-wind on coast of Upper Guinea in Dec., Jan., & Feb. [f. W.-Afr. *haramata*]

hàrmŏn'ĭc, a. & n. 1. Harmonious, concordant; relating to harmony; ~ *tones* (produced by vibration of aliquot parts of strings etc.); ~ *quantities* (whose reciprocals are in arithmetical progression, as ¼, ⅓, ½, or as 12, 15, 20), ~ *progression*, series of these. 2. n. ~ tone. Hence **hàrmŏn'ĭcALLY** adv. [f. L f. Gk *harmonikos* (as HARMONY, see -IC)]

hàrmŏn'ica, n. Name of several musical instruments; *mouth organ. [L fem. adj. as prec.]

hàrmŏn'ious, a. Concordant, forming a consistent or agreeable whole; free from dissent; sweet-sounding; singing, playing, tunefully. Hence ~LY² adv. [f. F *harmonieux* (as HARMONY)]

hàrm'on|ĭst, n. Person skilled in harmony; musician; collator of parallel narratives, whence ~ĭs'tĭc a.; harmonizer. [f. HARMONIZE, see -IST]

hàrmŏn'ium, n. Keyboard instrument in which notes are produced by air blown through reeds. [F, as HARMONY]

hàrm'oniz|e, -is|e (-ĭz), v.t. & i. Bring into, be in, harmony (*with*); make, be, agreeable in artistic effect; add notes to (melody) to form chords. Hence ~A'TION n. [f. F *harmoniser* (as HARMONY, see -IZE)]

hàrmonŏm'ēter, n. Instrument measuring harmonic relations of notes. [f. F *harmonomètre* (as foll., see -METER)]

hàrm'onÿ, n. Agreement; *pre-established* ~ (between body & soul before their creation); agreeable effect of apt arrangement of parts; combination of simultaneous notes to form chords (cf. MELODY); sweet or melodious sound; collation of parallel narratives etc., esp. of the four Gospels. [ME, f. OF *harmonie* f. L f. Gk *harmonia* (*harmo-* join)]

hàrn'ess, n., & v.t. 1. Gear of draught horse or other animal; (fig.) working equipment; *in* ~, in the routine of daily work; apparatus in loom for shifting warp-threads; (hist.) defensive armour; ~-*cask* (with rimmed cover, for keeping salt meat on board ship). 2. v.t. Put ~ on

(horse etc.); (fig.) utilize (river, waterfall, natural forces) for motive power. [ME; (vb f. OF *harneschier*) f. OF *harneis*, of obsc. orig.]

hàrp¹, n. Stringed musical instrument, roughly triangular, played with the fingers. [OE *hearpe*, OS, ON *harpa*, OHG *harfa*, f. Gmc *harpôn*]

hàrp², v.i. Play on harp, whence ~'ER¹, ~'IST, nn.; dwell tediously *on* (subject). [OE *hearpian* (as prec.)]

hàrpoŏn', n., & v.t. 1. Spear-like missile with rope attached, for catching whales etc.; ~-*gun* (for firing this). 2. v.t. Strike, spear, with ~. [(vb f. n.) f. F *harpon* (*harpe* clamp f. L f. Gk *harpē* sickle)]

hàrp'sichŏrd (-k-), n. Keyboard instrument with strings plucked by quill or leather points, used 16th–18th c. [f. obs. F *harpechorde* (LL *harpa* harp + *chorda* string)]

hàrp'ÿ, n. (Gk & L Myth.) rapacious monster with woman's face & body & bird's wings & claws; rapacious person; ~-*eagle*, S.-Amer. bird of prey. [f. L f. Gk *harpuiai* pl. (cf. *harpazō* snatch)]

hàr'quèbus, ār-, n. (hist.). Early type of portable gun, supported on tripod by hook or on forked rest. So ~IER' n. [f. F (h)*arquebuse*, ult. f. MLG *hakebusse* or MHG *hakenbühse* (*haken* hook + *bühse* gun)]

hä'rridan, n. Haggard old woman, vixen. [17th c. cant; perh. f. F *haridelle* old jade]

hä'rrier¹, n. One who harries. [-ER¹]

hä'rrier², n. Hound used for hunting hare; (pl.) pack of these with huntsmen (also as name of hare-&-hounds club); kinds of raptorial bird. [f. HARE +-IER, prob. assoc. w. prec.]

Hä'rris tweed, n. Kind made in Harris in the Hebrides.

Harrōv'ian, a. & n. (Member) of Harrow school; (inhabitant) of Harrow. [-IAN]

hä'rrow¹ (-ō), n. Heavy frame with iron teeth for breaking clods on ploughed land, covering seed, etc.; *under the* ~, in distress. [ME *harwe*, obsc. rel. to MLG, MDu. *harke* rake, ON *hervi* harrow]

hä'rrow² (-ō), v.t. Draw harrow over (land); lacerate, wound, (lit., & fig. the feelings etc.), whence ~ING² (-ōī-) a. [f. prec.]

hä'rrow³ (-ō), v.t. Harry, spoil, (chiefly in phr. ~ *hell*, of Christ). [var. of foll.]

hä'rrÿ, v.t. Ravage, waste, spoil, (land, or abs.); despoil (person); harass, worry. [OE *hergian*, OS, OHG *heriōn*, ON *herja* f. Gmc *harjaz* army]

hàrsh, a. Rough to the touch, taste, eye, or ear; repugnant to feelings or judgement; cruel, unfeeling. Hence ~'LY² adv., ~'NESS n. [(l) ME *harsk* corresp. in form to OSw., Da. *harsk* rank, rancid; (2) 16th c. *harsh* f. syn. MLG *harsch* (HAIR, -ISH)]

hàrt, n. Male of (esp. red) deer, esp. after fifth year; ~ *of ten* (branches on horns);

~'s-tongue, fern with slender undivided fronds. [OE *heor(o)t*, OS *herut*, OHG *hir(u)z*, ON *hjǫrtr* f. Gmc *herutlaz*]

hart'al, n. Closing of Indian shops as political gesture or mark of sorrow. [Hindi]

hart'(e)beest, n. S.-African kind of antelope. [S.-Afr. Du.]

harts'horn (-s-h-), n. Substance got from horns of hart, formerly chief source of ammonia; (*spirit of*)~, aqueous solution of ammonia; *salt of* ~, smelling-salts.

har'um-scar'um, a. & n. Reckless (person, conduct). [arbitrary]

harv'est, n., & v.t. **1.** (Season for) reaping & gathering in of grain or other products; corn-crop; season's yield of any natural product; (fig.) product of any action; ~-*bug*, mite troublesome during ~; ~ *festival*, thanksgiving service for ~; ~ *home*, close of ~ing, festival of this; ~ *moon* (full within fortnight of Sep. 22 or 23); ~ *mouse*, small species, nesting in stalks of growing grain. **2.** v.t. Reap & gather in (crop, or abs.), lay up, husband. [OE *hærfest*, OS *hervist*, OHG *herbist*, ON *haust* f. Gmc *harbhistaz*]

harv'ester, n. Reaper; reaping-machine (esp. sheaf-binding); harvest-bug; ~-*thresher*, COMBINE. [-ER¹]

has. See HAVE¹.

has'been (-z-), n. (colloq.). Person who, thing which, has lost a quality or proficiency formerly possessed, a back number. [HAVE¹]

hash¹, v.t. (Also ~ *up*) cut (meat, also fig.) in small pieces. [f. F *hacher* (*hache* HATCHET)]

hash², n. Dish of hashed meat; old matter served up in new form; medley; *make a* ~ *of*, spoil in dealing with; *settle* person's ~, make an end of, do for, him.

Hash'emite, a. ~ *Kingdom of the Jordan*, country bounded by Syria, Israel, Saudi Arabia, and Iraq.

hash'ish, -eesh, n. Top leaves & tender parts of hemp, dried for smoking or chewing as a drug, in Arabia, Egypt, Turkey, etc. (cf. BHANG). [Arab. *hashish* dry herb]

has'let, hars'-, n. Piece of meat to be roasted, esp. pig's fry. [ME *hastelet* f. OF dim. of *haste* roast meat, spit, f. OLG *harst* roast]

hasn't (-z-). See HAVE¹.

hasp (bah-), n., & v.t. Fastening contrivance, esp. clasp passing over staple & secured by padlock; hank, skein, of yarn; (v.t.) fasten with ~. [OE *hæpse, hæsp*; corresp. to MLG *haspe*, OHG *haspa*, ON *hespa*]

hass'ock, n. Hard cushion for kneeling on esp. in church; tuft of matted grass etc.; ǁ(in Kent) soft calcareous sandstone. [OE *hassuc*, of unkn. orig.]

hast. See HAVE¹.

has'tate, a. (chiefly bot.). Spear-shaped. [f. L *hastatus* (*hasta* spear, see -ATE²)]

haste, n., & v.i. **1.** Urgency of movement; hurry, precipitancy, as *more* ~, *less speed*; *make* ~, be quick (*to do, and do*). **2.** v.i. Make ~ (*to do*, or abs.). [ME; (vb f. OF *haster*) f. OF *haste* f. WG *haisti-violence*, cogn. w. ON *heifst*, Goth. *haifsts*]

ha'sten (-sn), v.t. & i. Cause (person) to make haste; accelerate (work etc.); make haste; come or go in haste (*to* etc.). [ME; -EN⁶]

has'ty, a. Hurried; speedy; rash, inconsiderate; quick-tempered; ǁ~*y pudding* (of flour stirred to thick batter in boiling milk or water). Hence ~ILY², ~INESS n. [f. OF *hastif* (as HASTE¹, see -IVE)]

hat, n., & v.t. (-tt-). **1.** Man's, woman's, outdoor head-covering, usu. with brim (cf. BONNET, CAP); *top, high, chimney-pot,* ~, cylindrical silk ~; *opera* ~ (cylindrical compressible); *cardinal's or red* ~, (fig.) office of cardinal; ~ *in hand*, servile(ly); *send round the* ~, solicit contributions; *talk through* one's ~ (sl.), boast or bluff or exaggerate; *as black as my* ~, quite black; ~'*band* (put round ~); ~-*block* (for moulding ~ on); ~ *trick*, (Cricket) taking 3 wickets by successive balls, (transf.) scoring of 3 goals by same player, winning of 3 races, etc.; ǁ *bad* ~ (sl.), immoral or dishonourable person. **2.** v.t. Cover, furnish, with ~. Hence ~'FUL, ~'t'ER (3; *as mad as a* ~*ter*), nn., ~'LESS a. [OE *hætt*, ON *höttr* f. Gmc *hattuz*; cf. HOOD]

hatch¹, n. Lower half of divided door; aperture in door, wall, floor or deck; (Naut.) ~way, trap-door covering this; *under* ~*es*, below deck, (fig.) down out of sight, brought low, dead; floodgate; ~'*way*, opening in ship's deck for lowering cargo. [OE *hæcc*, MLG *heck*, f. WG *hak-*; cf. HACK³, HAKE², HECK]

hatch², v.t. & i., & n. **1.** Bring forth (young birds etc., or abs.) from egg; incubate (egg); emerge from egg; (of egg) produce young; contrive & develop (plot etc.). **2.** n. ~ing, brood ~ed, (~*es*, *catches*, *matches, & dispatches*, newspaper list of births, engagements, marriages, & deaths). [ME *hacche*, rel. to MHG *heckcn*, Sw. *häcka*, Da. *hække*, of unkn. orig.]

hatch³, v.t., & n. **1.** Engrave (usu. parallel) lines on (surface); (Archit.) ~*ed moulding* (with two crossing sets of parallel lines). **2.** n. Engraved line. [(n. f. vb) f. F *hacher* (as HATCHET)]

hatch'ery, n. Place for hatching eggs esp. of fish & poultry. [-ERY]

hatch'et, n. Light short-handled axe; ~ (narrow, sharp) *face*; BURY *the* ~; throw *the helve after the* ~, add new loss to that already incurred. [ME, f. OF *hachette* dim. of *hache* f. WG *hapja* (= OHG *happa, heppa* sickle-shaped knife)]

hatch'ment, n. Large (usu. diamond-shaped) tablet with deceased person's armorial bearings, formerly affixed to house, now only on wall of church. [contr. of ACHIEVEMENT]

K

hāte[1], n. (chiefly poet.). Hatred. [ME *hate* (replacing OE *hete*) partly f. vb, partly f. ON *hatr*; see foll.]

hāte[2], v.t. Have strong dislike of; bear malice to. Hence hāt′ABLE a. [OE *hatian*, OS *hatōn*, OHG *hazzōn*, ON *hata*, Goth. *hatan* f. Gmc *hatōjan*]

hāte′ful (-tf-), a. Exciting hatred. Hence ~LY[2] adv., ~NESS n. [-FUL]

hāth. Arch. 3rd sing. pres. of HAVE[1].

hāt′rĕd, n. Active dislike; enmity, ill will. [ME (HATE[1] + -red = OE *rǣden* condition)]

hătt′ĭ, n. Turkish edict made irrevocable by Sultan's mark. [abbr. of Pers. *khaṭ-ṭisherif, -humayun*, sacred writing]

haub′erk, n. Coat of mail. [ME, f. OF *hau(s)berc* f. WG *halsberg* (*hals* neck + *bergan* protect)]

‖ haugh (haw, *Sc.* hahx), n. Piece of flat alluvial land by river. [ME, prob. f. OE *healh* corner]

haught′|ў̆ (-awt-), a. Proud, arrogant; dignified. Hence ~iLY[2] adv., ~īNESS n. [extension of *haught* a., (earlier *haut*) f. OF *haut* f. L *altus* high, -Y[2]]

haul, v.t. & i., & n. 1. Pull, drag, forcibly; transport by cart or other conveyance; pull *at, upon*, (rope etc.); (Naut.) turn ship's course; ~ *upon the wind*, bring ship round to sail closer to wind; (of wind) shift. 2. n. Act of ~ing, (fig.) amount gained, acquisition. Hence ~′AGE(3) n. [17th c. var. of HALE[2]]

‖ haul′ier, n. One who hauls (esp. tubs in coal-mine to bottom of shaft); jobbing carter. [f. prec., see -YER]

‖ ha(u)lm (hawm, hahm), n. Stalk, stem; (collect. sing.) stems, stalks, of peas, beans, potatoes, etc., without the pods etc. [OE *h(e)alm*, OS, OHG *halm*, ON *halmr* f. Gmc *halmaz*]

haunch (haw-, hah-), n. Part of body (esp. of sheep, deer) on side of spine between last ribs & hip-bone; leg & loin of deer etc. as food; side of arch between crown & piers. [ME, f. OF *hanche*, f. WG *hanka*; cf. LG, G *hanke* hind leg of a horse]

haunt, v.t. & i., & n. 1. Frequent (place); frequent company of (person); (of thoughts etc.) visit (person) frequently; (p.p.) visited, frequented, by ghosts; stay habitually (*in, about*, place, *with* person). 2. n. Place of frequent resort, usual feeding-place of animals, den frequented by criminals. [ME, f. OF *hanter*, of unkn. orig.]

haut′boy (hōb-), hō′boy, ōb′oe (-bō), n. Wood-wind double-reed instrument of treble pitch; reed-stop on organ imitating this; tall species of strawberry. [f. F *hautbois* (*haut* high + *bois* wood)]

haute école (ōt′ākŏl), n. The more difficult feats of horsemanship. [F, = high school]

hauteur (ōtŏ̄r′, & see Ap.), n. Haughtiness of manner. [F]

haut goût (hōgoō′), n. Taint, high flavour. [F, = seasoning, lit. high flavour]

Havăn′a, n. Cigar made at Havana or in Cuba. [place]

hāve[1] (or hav), v.t. & i. & auxil. (Pres.: *I* have, arch. *thou hast, he has*, pr. hăz, haz, arch. *he hath, we, you, they, have*; past *had*, pr. hăd, had, arch. 2nd sing. *hădst*; p.p. *had*; abbr. *I've, we've*, etc., *I'd, we'd* etc., *'s* = *has*; colloq. neg. *haven't, hasn't, hadn't*). Hold in possession; experience the existence of (persons etc. in various relations), as *I ~ two sons, no uncle, no equals*; possess, contain, as appendage, part, quality, etc., as *June has 30 days, trees ~ leaves, it has its advantages*; enjoy, suffer, as *I had that pleasure, a toothache, no fear*; permit (person) to, as *I will not ~ you say such things*; know, as *he has no Greek*; be burdened with, as *I had my work to do*; be obliged, as *I had to do my work*; retain, as ~ *this in mind*; entertain, as ~ *no doubt*; show by action etc. that one possesses, as ~ *the impudence to say*; engage in, carry on, as *had some conversation, ~ a game, ~ a try* (make an attempt); *he will ~ it* (maintains) *that*; as *Plato has* (expresses) *it*; obtain, receive, take (food), as *we had news, ~ an egg*; *the Ayes ~ it* (~ the advantage); *let him ~ it*, punish or reprimand him; *I had him there* (gained advantage over him); ‖ (sl.) *you were had* (cheated); ~ *her make* (cause her to make) *a copy*; ~ *him* (cause him to be) *shot*; ~ *him up*, cause him to be brought before court of justice; *I had my leg broken* (experienced such breakage); ~ *it your own way* (form of refusal to argue further); *he has had it* (sl.), he is a fatal casualty, he is now a back number, there's no longer any chance of his getting it, his fate is sealed; ~ *at*, make attack upon; ~ *done*, stop; ~ *on*, be wearing (clothes); ~ *it out*, settle dispute (*with* person) by discussion etc., (also) get tooth extracted; *~ nothing on* (person), ~ no advantage over, ~ no incriminating evidence against; (in past subj., = would ~) *had rather* (would prefer to) *go, had better go*, would act more wisely in going; (auxiliary) *I ~, had, shall ~, packed*, my packing is, was, will be, complete, *had I* (if I had) *known* etc. [OE *habban*, OS *hebbian*, OHG *habēn*, ON *hafa*, Goth. *haban* f. Gmc *habbēn* of uncert. orig.]

hāve[2], n. ~*s & ~-nots*, rich & poor; ‖ (sl.) a swindle, take-in. [f. prec.]

hāv′en, n. Harbour, port; (fig., often ~ *of rest*) refuge. [OE *hæfen* f. ON *höfn* corresp. to MLG *havene*, MDu. *haven*]

haven't (hăvnt). See HAVE[1].

‖ hāv′er, v.i., & n. (Sc.). 1. Talk foolishly; babble. 2. n. (usu. pl.). Foolish talk, nonsense. [orig. unkn.]

hăv′ersăck, n. Stout canvas bag for provisions. [f. F *havresac* f. G *habersack* (*haber* oats + SACK[1])]

hăv′ildar, n. Sepoy officer corresponding

to sergeant. [f. Pers. *ħawāldār* (Arab. *ħawalah* charge + Pers. *dār* holder)]

hāv'ing, n. In vbl senses; also, property, belongings, (often pl.). [-ING¹]

hāv'oc, n., & v.t. (~*king*, ~*ked*). Devastation, destruction, as *make* ~ *of*, *play* ~ *among*; *cry* ~, give signal to army to seize spoil (now fig.); (v.t.) devastate (often abs.). [f. AF *havok* f. OF *havot* of unkn. orig.]

haw¹, n. (Fruit of) hawthorn; (hist.) hedge, enclosure; ~*'buck,* country bumpkin; ~*'finch,* common grosbeak. [OE *haga,* MLG, MDu. *hage,* OHG *hac,* ON *hagi* f. Gmc **hagon-,* see HEDGE]

haw², n. Third eyelid of horse, dog, etc., cartilage within inner corner of eye. [orig. unkn.]

haw³. See HUM¹.

haw‑haw¹, int. & n. Boisterous laugh. Hence **haw‑haw** v.i. [imit.]

haw‑haw². = HA-HA.

hawk¹, n., & v.i. & t. **1.** Bird of prey used in falconry, with rounded wings shorter than falcon's; *know a* ~ *from a handsaw* (perh. corrupt of HERNSHAW), have ordinary discernment (see *Haml.* II. ii. 397); rapacious person; ~*-eyed,* keen-sighted; ~*-moth,* fast-flying moth, mostly large and crepuscular; ~*-nosed,* with aquiline nose; ~*'s-bill,* kind of turtle. **2.** v.i. Hunt game with ~; (v.t. & t.) ~ *(at)*, attack as ~ does, (of swallows etc.) hunt insects. Hence ~'ISH¹, ~'LIKE, aa. [OE *heafoc,* OS *habuc,* OHG *habuh,* ON *haukr* f. Gmc **habhukaz*]

hawk², v.t. Carry (goods) about for sale (often fig.). [back form. f. HAWKER]

hawk³, v.i. & t. Clear the throat noisily; bring (phlegm etc.) *up* from throat. [imit.]

hawk⁴, n. Plasterer's square board with handle. [orig. unkn.]

hawk'er, n. One who hawks goods about. [16th c., prob. f. LG; cf. MLG *hoker,* LG *höker,* Du. *heuker*; see HUCKSTER]

hawse (-z), n. Part of ship's bows in which ~*-holes* are cut for cables; space between head of anchored vessel & anchors; situation of cables before ship's stem when moored with two anchors out from forward, one on starboard, other on port bow. [15th c. *halse,* prob. f. ON *hals* neck]

haws'er (-s-, -z-), n. (naut.). Large rope, small cable, now often of steel. [ME, f. AF *haucer,* -*eour* f. OF *haucier* hoist f. Rom. **altiare (altus* high); cf. LL *altare* exalt]

haw'thorn, n. Thorny shrub, with white, red, or pink blossom & small dark red berry, the HAW¹. [OE *hagathorn* as HAW¹, see THORN)]

hay¹, n., & v.t. & i. **1.** Grass mown & dried for fodder; *Burgundian* ~, lucerne; *look for a needle in a* BOTTLE³ (or *bundle*) *of* ~; *make* ~, turn it over for exposure to sun; *make* ~ *of,* throw into confusion;

make ~ *while the sun shines,* seize opportunities. **2.** ~*'box* (stuffed with ~, in which heated food is left to continue cooking); ~*'cock,* conical heap of ~; ~ *fever,* summer disorder usu. with asthmatic symptoms, caused by pollen or dust; ~*-fork* (for turning over or loading ~); ~*'maker,* one who lifts, tosses, & spreads ~ after mowing, apparatus for shaking & drying ~, (sl.) swinging blow; ~*'rick,* ~*'stack,* regular pile of ~ with pointed or ridged top; *~*'seed* (colloq.), a rustic, hick; *~*'wire,* anything tangled (*go* ~*wire,* become excited or distracted). **3.** v.t. Put (land) under ~, make into ~; (v.i.) make ~. [OE *hēg, hīeg,* OS *hōi,* OHG *hewi,* ON *hey,* Goth. *hawi* f. Gmc **hauwan* HEW]

hay², hey² (hā), n. (Figure in) country dance. [orig. unkn.]

hay'ward (-ord), n. Officer of parish etc. in charge of fences & enclosures. [ME, f. obs. *hay* hedge (as HAW¹) + WARD]

hāz'ard, n., & v.t. **1.** Game at dice, with complicated chances; chance; danger; *at all* ~*s* (risks); each of winning openings in tennis-court; ‖ (Billiards) *winning* ~, striking object ball into pocket, *losing* ~, pocketing own ball off another; (Golf) obstruction in playing a shot, e.g. bunker, water, road, etc.; ‖ (in Ireland) cab-stand. **2.** v.t. Expose to ~, run the ~ of; venture on (action, statement, guess). [(vb f. F *hasarder*) ME, f. OF *hasard,* of Arab. orig.]

hāz'ardous, a. Risky; dependent on chance. Hence ~LY² adv., ~NESS n. [-OUS]

hāze¹, n., & v.t. **1.** Obscuration of atmosphere near earth, mainly due to heat, smoke, or fine dust; (fig.) mental obscurity or confusion. **2.** v.t. Make hazy. [prob. back form. f. earlier HAZY]

hāze², v.t. (naut.). Harass with overwork, *bully. [cf. OF *haser* harass, worry]

hāz'el, n. Bush whose fruit is the ~*-nut*; (stick of) its wood; reddish-brown or greenish-brown colour (esp. of eyes). Hence ~LY² a. [OE *hæsel,* OHG *hasal,* ON *hasl* f. Gmc **hasalaz*]

hāz'|ȳ, a. Misty; vague, indistinct; slightly drunk. Hence ~ILY² adv., ~iNESS n. [17th c., naut., also *hawsey, heysey,* of unkn. orig.]

H-bomb (āch'bŏm), n. Hydrogen bomb. [*H* for HYDROGEN]

hē¹, pron. (obj. *him,* poss. *his,* pl. *they,* obj. *them,* poss. *their*), & n. (pl. *hes*). **1.** pron. The male person in question. **2.** n. Male; (attrib. esp. of animals) *he-goat* etc.; **he-man,* masterful or virile man. [OE, f. Gmc st. (3rd pers. sing.) *hi-,* as in OFris., OS *he, hi* (cf. Goth. *hi(ta)* etc.); var. st. *i-*repr. by OHG *ir, er,* Goth. *is*]

hē², int. expr. amusement or derision (often repeated, *he he*). [in many langg.]

head (hĕd), n. **1.** Anterior part of body of animal, upper part of man's body, containing mouth, sense-organs, and brain;

(as measure) *taller by a* ~, (Horse-racing)
won by a ~; *cannot make* ~ *or tail of*
(understand). 2. Seat of intellect or imagination; natural aptitude or talent (*a
good* ~ *for business*). 3. ~ache, esp. as
result of overnight intoxication (colloq.).
4. Life, as *it cost him his* ~. 5. Image of
~, esp. on one side of coin (opp. to *tail*),
as ~*s I win, tails you lose*. 6. Antlers of
deer, as *deer of the first* ~ (when antlers
are first developed). 7. Person, as *crowned*
~*s, some hot*~ (hasty person); individual,
as *twopence a* or *per* ~, esp. of cattle, as
every ~ *of cattle, twenty* ~; *large* ~ (number) *of game*; *good* ~ (stock) *of shell*. 8.
Thing like ~ in form or position, e.g.
cutting or striking part of tool, knobbed
end of nail etc.; (of plants) compact mass
of leaves or flowers at top of stem.
9. Foam on top of liquor; ‖ cream on top
of milk. 10. Top (of mast, staircase,
page, etc.). 11. Maturated part of boil
etc. 12. Upper end; end of table occupied
by host; end of lake at which river enters
it; end of bed at which one's ~ rests;
FOUNTAIN-~. 13. Body of water kept at
height for mill etc.; pressure (per unit of
area) of confined body of steam etc. 14.
Front (of procession, army, etc.); front
part of plough, holding the share; bows
of ship, as *by the* ~, with ~ lower in water
than stern, (fig.) slightly drunk. 15. Promontory, as *BeachyH*~. 16. Underground
passage for working coal mine. 17. Ruler,
chief, (often attrib.); master etc. of
college; ~ master of school. 18. Position
of command, as *at the* ~ *of*. 19. Main
division in discourse; category. 20.
Culmination, crisis, as *come to a* ~. 21.
(naut.). Seamen's latrine in ship's bows.
22. Phrases: *beat* person's ~ *off*, outdo
him thoroughly; *by* (*the*) ~ *and ears*,
forcibly (esp. of dragging in a story); *by*
(*the*) ~ *and shoulders*, = by ~ and ears,
(also) considerably (*taller*, & fig. of mental
or moral stature); *from* ~ *to foot*, all over
the person; *give* (horse) *his* ~, let him go
freely; ~ *first* or *foremost*, with the ~
foremost (of plunge etc.), (fig.) precipitately; ~ *of hair*, the hair on the ~,
esp. when copious; ~ *over heels*, topsy-
-turvy; *keep* one's ~, keep calm; *keep*
one's ~ *above water*, (fig.) keep out of
debt; *lay* (our etc.) ~*s together*, consult
together; *lose* one's ~, be beheaded,
(also) become confused; *make* ~, press
forward; *make* ~ *against*, resist successfully; *off* one's ~, crazy; *old* ~ *on young
shoulders*, wisdom in the young; *on* one's
~ (of vengeance falling, guilt resting, on
person); (*stand* etc.) *on* one's ~, with feet
in air (*could do it on my* ~, sl., find it quite
easy); *out of* one's ~, from one's own
invention; *over* ~ & EARS; *over* one's ~,
above one, esp. fig. of danger impending
etc., (also) beyond one's comprehension,
as he talks over our ~*s*, (also) *person is
promoted over another's* ~ (who has prior

claim); *put* (thing) *into* person's~, suggest
it to him; *put* (thing) *out of* one's~, cease
to think of it, give up the idea of it; *put*
(thing) *out of* person's~, make him forget
it (*something put it out of my* ~); *talk*
person's ~ *off*, weary him with talk;
(prov.) *two* ~*s* (minds) *are better than one.*
23. Comb.: ~*'ache*, continuous pain in ~,
(colloq.) troublesome problem; ~*'achy*
(-kĭ), suffering from, producing, this; ~
& front, essence (of offence etc.; but cf.
Oth. I. iii. 80), (pop.) leader, ringleader;
~*'band*, band worn round ~; ~*'borough*
(hist.), petty constable; ~*-dress*, covering
(esp. woman's ornamental attire) for the
~; ~*'fast*, rope at ~ of vessel to make her
fast to wharf etc.; ~*'gear*, hat, cap, ~-
-dress; ~*-hunter*, savage who collects ~*s*
of his enemies as trophies; ~*'land*, promontory, (also) strip left unploughed at
end of field; ~*'light*, powerful light carried
on front of locomotive, car, or aeroplane,
or at mast-head of ship; ~*'line*, line at
top of page containing title etc., title or
sub-title in newspaper, (pl., also) ‖ summary at beginning of BBC news bulle-
tin; ~*'man*, chief man, chief of tribe etc.;
‖~ *master, mistress*, principal master,
mistress, of school; ~*-money* (paid for or
by each person); ~*'on* (adj.), involving
the meeting ~ to ~ of two vehicles (*a* ~-
-*on collision*), or of the ~ of a vehicle with
stationary object; ~*-on'* (adv.), with the
~ pointed directly towards some object;
~*'phone*, (in wireless and other telephony)
telephone receiver fitting over~; ~*'piece*,
helmet, (also) intellect, man of intellect,
(also) ornamental engraving at ~ of
chapter etc. in book, cf. TAIL[1]-*piece*; ~*-
quarters*, (Mil.) quarters of officer commanding army, corps, division, etc.,
(gen.) centre of operations; ~*'spring*,
main source of stream (also fig.); ~*'stall*,
part of bridle or halter that fits round ~;
~*'stock*, bearings of revolving parts in
machine; ~*'stone*, gravestone; ~ *stone*,
chief stone in foundation (also fig.); ~*-
-voice*, one of higher registers of voice in
singing or speaking; ~*'way*, progress, (of
ship) rate of progress, (Archit.) height of
arch etc.; ~ *wind* (meeting one directly
in front); ~*-word*, word forming a heading;~*-work*, mental work. Hence (-)~*'ED*,
~*'LESS*, aa., (hĕd-). [OE *hēafod*, OS
hōbid, OHG *houbit*, ON *haufuth*, Goth.
haubith f. Gmc **haubhudh-*]

head[2] (hĕd), v.t. & i. Furnish with head;
(also~ *down*) lop off head of (plant, tree);
be, form, the head of; place name etc.,
(of name etc.) be placed, at the head of
(chapter, list, etc.); come to a head,
develop; be, put oneself, at the head
of (a company etc.); lead; excel; oppose;
go round the head of (lake etc.); (Footb.)
strike (ball) with head; ~ *back, off*, get
ahead of so as to turn back, aside; (intr.)
front (in named direction); (of ship) make
for (place, point). [f. prec.]

-head, suf. = -HOOD, f. ME -hĕd(e) repr. OE -*hǣdu), a phonetic var. of -hŏd, see -HOOD. Orig. an independent noun, it became a suf. in early ME & survives in godhead, maidenhead (distinct in meaning f. godhood, maidenhood); now repl. by -HOOD.

head′er (hĕd-), n. One who puts heads on casks etc.; brick, stone, laid at right angle to face of wall (cf. STRETCHER); plunge head first. [-ER¹]

head′ing (hĕd-), n. In vbl senses; also or esp.: (Footb.) striking ball with head; title etc. at head of page etc.; horizontal passage in preparation for tunnel. [-ING¹]

head′long (hĕd-), adv. & a. Head foremost (in falling etc.);˙ precipitate(ly); impetuous(ly). [ME headling (HEAD¹+ -LING²), assim. to -LONG]

head′most (hĕd-), a. Foremost.

heads′man (hĕd-), n. One who beheads; man in command of whaling boat. [HEAD¹ + -ES + MAN]

head′strong (hĕd-), a. Violently self--willed. Hence ~NESS n. [= strong in head]

head′y (hĕd-), a. (Of person, thing, action) impetuous, violent; (of liquor etc.) apt to intoxicate. Hence ~ILY² adv., ~INESS n. [-Y²]

heal, v.t. & i. Restore (person, wound) to health (lit. & fig.); cure (person of disease); (of wound) become sound or whole; ~-all, universal remedy (pop. name of various plants). Hence ~′ER¹ n. (time is a great ~er). [OE hǣlan, OS hēlian, OHG heilan, ON heila, Goth. hailjan f. Gmc *hailas WHOLE]

health (hĕl-), n. Soundness of body (also fig.); condition of body, as good, bad, ~; ~-officer, officer of ~, (charged with administering ~ laws etc.); toast drunk in person's honour; BILL⁴ of ~. [OE hǣlth, OHG heilida f. WG *hailitha (WHOLE, -TH¹)]

health′ful (hĕl-), a. Health-giving; conducive to moral or spiritual welfare. Hence ~LY² adv., ~NESS n. [-FUL]

health′y (hĕl-), a. Having good health (lit. & fig.); conducive to good health. Hence ~ILY² adv., ~INESS n. [HEALTH + -Y²]

heap¹, n. Group of things lying one on another; (colloq.) large number, as a ~ of people, ~s of times, (adv.) he is ~s better; (colloq.) struck all of a ~, mentally prostrated. [OE hēap, OS hōp, OHG houf, hūfo, f. Gmc *haupaz, *hŭpon-]

heap², v.t. Pile (things up, together, etc.) in a heap; load (cart, person, etc. with goods, benefits, etc.); accumulate (insults etc. upon). [OE hēapian, as prec.]

hear, v.t. & i. (heard pr. hĕrd). Perceive (sound etc. or intr.) with the ear, as I ~d a groan, I ~ him groaning, I ~d him groan (but he was ~d to groan); listen, give audience, to, as ~ him out (to the end), ~ him, his lesson, ~ a sermon; listen judicially to (case, plaintiff, etc.); grant (prayer); he will not ~ (entertain the notion) of it; you will ~ of this (be reprimanded for it); be informed (that, of, about); ~ from, receive letter or message from; ~ tell of (arch.), be told about; || (as form of cheering, often iron.) ~! ~!. Hence ~′ABLE a., ~′ER¹ n.. [OE hieran, OS hōrian, OHG hōrren, ON heyra, Goth. hausjan f. Gmc *hauzjan]

hear′ing, n. In vbl senses, esp.: perception by ear, as hard of ~, deaf; within, out of, ~, near enough, too far off, to be heard; give him a fair ~, listen impartially to him; ~ aid, small sound amplifier worn by deaf people. [-ING¹]

heark′en (här-), härk-, v.i. Listen ˙(to). [OE he(o)rcnian (as HARK, -EN⁶)]

hear′say, n. What one hears (but does not know to be true), gossip, (often attrib.; as ~ evidence).

hearse (hĕrs), n. Vehicle for carrying coffin at funeral; (formerly) framework supporting pall at funeral, often adapted for carrying tapers. [ME, f. OF herse, f. L hirpicem (nom. -ex) rake, harrow]

heart (härt), n. 1. Hollow organ keeping up circulation of blood by contracting & dilating; right, left, ~ (side of ~); smoker's ~ (~ disorder due to smoking). 2. Breast; mind; soul (~ to ~, with candour; so ~-to-~ talks) after one's (own) ~ (desire). 3. Seat of the emotions, esp. of love, as give, lose, one's ~ to, win the ~ of, (person); union of ~s (depending on affection, not constraint). 4. Sensibility, as he has no ~; courage, as pluck up or take, lose, ~. 5. (As term of endearment to person) dear, sweet, ~; (Naut.) my ~s (brave fellows). 6. Central part, esp. of tree, as (fig.) ~ of oak, courageous man; vital part, essence, (the ~ of the matter). 7. (Of land) fertility, as out of ~, in poor condition. 8. ~-shaped thing; (Cards, pl.) suit marked with ~s, (sing.) one of these. 9. At ~, in one's inmost feelings; by ~, in, from, memory, as have, learn, say, by ~; from one's ~, sincerely; in one's ~, secretly, in one's essential feelings; in ~, in good spirits; near(est) one's ~, dear(est) to one; out of ~, in low spirits; with all one's ~, sincerely, with the utmost goodwill; find in one's ~, (esp. w. neg.) prevail on oneself (to do); have thing at ~, be deeply interested in it; lay thing to ~, think it over seriously; searchings of ~, misgivings; take thing to ~, be much affected by it; break person's ~, overwhelm him with sorrow; cry one's ~ out, cry violently; eat one's ~ out, pine away from vexation. etc.; have a ~ (sl.), be merciful; have the ~, (esp. w. neg.) be hard-hearted enough (to do); ~ & hand, enthusiastically; in one's ~ of ~s (inmost feelings); ~ & soul, with all one's energy; have one's ~ in one's mouth, be violently alarmed or startled; his ~ is in the right place, he means well; take ~ of grace, pluck up courage; *wear* one's~ *upon* one's *sleeve*, lack proper reserve; *it does my ~ good*, it rejoices me. **10.** ~'*ache*, mental anguish; ~'*beat*, pulsation of ~, (fig.) emotion; ~('s)-*blood*, life-blood, life; ~-*break*, overwhelming distress;~-*breaking*, -*broken*, causing, crushed by, this;~'*burn*, burning sensation in lower part of chest; ~-*burning*, jealousy, grudge; ~-*disease* (of ~); ~'*felt*, sincere (*emotion* etc.); ~-*rending*, distressing; ~'s²*ease*, pansy; ~'*sick*, despondent; ~'*sore*, grieved at~; ~-*strings*, (fig.) ~, deepest affections; ~-*whole*, undismayed, with the ~ unengaged, not in love. Hence ~~'ED² (här-) a. [OE *heorte*, OS *herta*, OHG *herza*, ON *hjarta*, Goth. *hairtō* cogn. w. L *cor -dis*, Gk *kardia*]

heart'en (här-), v.t. & i. Inspirit, cheer (often *up*, also *on*); (intr.) cheer *up*. [f. arch. vb *heart* (OE *hiertan*, as prec.) + -EN⁶]

hearth (här-), n. Floor of fireplace; ~-*rug* (laid before fireplace); ~'*stone*, flat stone forming ~, (also) stone etc. for whitening~s. [OE *heorth*, OS *herth*, OHG *hert* f. WG *herth-*]

heart'ily (här-), adv. With goodwill, courage, or appetite; very, as ~ *sick of it*. [HEARTY, -LY²]

heart'less (här-), a. Unfeeling, pitiless, cruel. Hence~LY² adv.,~NESS n. [-LESS]

heart'|y (här-), a. & n. **1.** Cordial, genial; (of feelings) sincere; vigorous; (of meals) abundant. **2.** n. (As address to sailors) *my ~ies*; ‖ (in English university use) outdoor man, athlete (opp. AESTHETE). Hence ~ĪNESS n. [-Y²]

heat¹, n. **1.** Hotness; sensation, perception, of this; *red*, *white*, etc., ~, at which metals etc. are red, white, etc. **2.** (phys.). Kinetic & potential energy of the invisible molecules of bodies, capable of transmission by conduction or radiation (formerly held an elastic material fluid); *latent ~*, ~ required to convert a solid into liquid or vapour, or a liquid into vapour; *specific ~*, ~ required to raise temperature of a given substance to given extent (usu. one degree), usu. calculated relatively to water. **3.** Hot weather. **4.** Inflamed state of body. **5.** Pungency of flavour. **6.** *Prickly ~*, skin disease common in hot climates. **7.** Single effort, esp. *at a ~*; (*trial*) ~*s*, races, contests, the winners of which compete in *final* (~). **8.** Warmth of feeling, anger; violent stage (of debate etc.). **9.** Sexual excitement of animals during breeding season (*on*, *in*, *at*, ~, of females). **10.** ~-*spot*, freckle, (also) point of the skin at which ~ can be felt; ~-*stroke*, prostration by excessive ~; ~-*wave*, wave of radiant ~, (also) access of great ~ in atmosphere regarded as passing from place to place. [OE *hǣtu*, OFris. *hēte*, cogn. w. OS *hittia*, OHG *hizza*, Goth. *heitō*; f. Gmc *hail-*, *hit-*, *hǐt-* (see HOT)]

heat², v.t. & i. Make hot; inflame (blood etc.); inflame with passion, whence ~'ĕDLY² adv.; (intr.) become hot (lit. & fig.). Hence ~'ER¹(2) n. [OE *hǣtan*, OHG *heizan*, ON *heita* f. Gmc *haitjan* f. *hailaz* HOT]

heath, n. ‖ Bare flat waste tract of land, esp. if covered with shrubs; name of such shrubs, esp. of genus *Erica*; ~-*bell*, flower of ~ & other plants; ~-*berry*, bilberry, crowberry, & other berries; ~-*cock*, blackcock. Hence ~'Y² a. [OE *hæth*, cogn. w. OHG *heida*, ON *heithr*, Goth. *haithi* f. Gmc *haith-*]

heath'en (-dh-), a. & n. (One who is) neither Christian, Jewish, nor Mohammedan; (n. pl. collect.) *the ~*; unenlightened person; *the ~* CHINEE. Hence ~DOM, ~ISM(2), ~ishNESS, ~RY, nn., ~ISH¹ a., ~ishLY² adv., ~IZE(3) v.t. & i., (-dh-). [OE *hǣthen*, OS *hēthin*, OHG *heidan*, ON *heithinn*, Goth. *haithnō* gentile, f. Gmc *haith-* HEATH, rendering LL *paganus* PAGAN]

hea'ther (hĕdh-), n. Various species of genus *Calluna vulgaris* (called in the North *Ling*); ‖ *take to the ~* (Sc.), become an outlaw; ~-*bell*, (flower of) species of *Erica*; ~ *mixture*, (fabric) of mixed hues supposed to resemble ~. Hence ~Y² a. [14th c. Sc. & north. *hathir*, *haddir*, of unkn. orig.; since 18th c. assim. to *heath*]

heave¹, v.t. & i. (past & p.p. ~*d* or, esp. naut., *hōve*). Lift (heavy thing); (of vein or stratum) displace (another); utter (groan, sigh) with effort; (Naut. & colloq.) throw; (Naut.) haul up, haul, by rope; rise, swell up; rise with alternate falls, as waves; pant; retch; pull (*at* rope etc.); ~ *down*, turn (ship) over on one side for cleaning etc.; ~ *to*, bring (vessel, or abs.) to standstill with head to wind; ~ *in sight*, become visible; ~ *ho* (cry of sailors in heaving anchor up). [OE *hebban*, OS -*ian*, OHG *heffen*, ON *hefja*, Goth. *hafjan* f. Gmc *hafjan* cogn. w. L *capere*]

heave², n. Heaving; ~ *of the sea*, force exerted by swell of sea on ship's course; a recognized trip or throw in wrestling (*Cornwall* ~); horizontal displacement of vein or stratum; (pl.) disease of horses, broken wind. [f. prec.]

hea'ven (hĕ-), n. Sky, firmament, (in prose now usu. pl.); region of the atmosphere in which clouds float, winds blow, & birds fly; (formerly) each of the heavenly SPHERES; habitation of God & his angels, usually placed beyond sky (cf. HELL); *seventh ~*, ~ *of ~s*, highest of seven ~s recognized by Jews, abode of God; *in the seventh ~*, in a state of extreme delight or exaltation; God, Providence, as *it is H~'s will*; (in asseverations & exclamations) *by ~ !*, *good ~s !*; place, state, of supreme bliss; ~-*born*, of divine origin; ~-*sent*. Hence ~WARD a., ~WARD(S) adv. [OE *heofon*, OS *heban*, MLG *heven*, of unkn. orig.]

hea'venlÿ (hŏ-), a. Of heaven, divine, (*the H~ City*, Paradise); of the sky, as ~ *bodies; the H~ Twins*, = GEMINI; ~ HOST[1]; of superhuman excellence; (colloq.) *what ~ (excellent) figs !*; ~*-minded*, holy, devout. Hence hea'venliNESS (hŏ-) n. [ME, f. OF *heofonlic* (as prec., see -LY[1])]

Hea'viside (hē-) lay'er, n. Layer of the atmosphere that reflects wireless waves back & causes them to follow the contour of the earth. [Oliver *Heaviside*, English physicist (d. 1925)]

hea'vÿ (hĕ-), a., n., & adv. 1. Of great weight; of great specific gravity; weighty because abundant, as *a ~ crop*; laden *with*; (of ordnance of the larger kind) ~ *guns, metal, artillery*; (fig.) ~ *metal*, formidable opponent(s); (Mil.) carrying ~ arms. 2. Striking, falling, with force, as ~ *storm, sea*. 3. (Of ground) clinging, difficult to travel over. 4. (Of bread etc.) dense from not having risen; (of food) hard to digest. 5. (Of horse) ~ *in* or *on hand*, bearing or hanging on bit, (fig.) dull, hard to entertain. 6. (Of sky) overcast, gloomy. 7. Clumsy in appearance or effect; (of persons) intellectually slow; unwieldy; (of artistic or literary productions) dull, tedious; (Theatr.) serious, sombre, as ~ *father*. 8. Oppressive, grievous, as *a ~ fate*; sad, as ~ *news*; despondent; doleful; drowsy; *it lies ~* (makes its weight felt); *time hangs ~* (passes slowly). 9. n. pl. || *The Heavies*, Dragoon Guards, (also) ~ artillery. 10. adv. Heavily (now chiefly in compounds; as ~*-buying*, *-laden*, *-pulling*). 11. ~*-armed*, bearing ~ arms or armour; ~ CHEMICALS; ~*-hearted*, melancholy, doleful; ~ *oil*, a heavier-than-water oil obtained from coal-tar by distillation; ~ *spar*, barytes; ~ *swell* (colloq.), man who emphasizes his real or imagined importance by overdressing etc.; ~*water*, water with a density about 10 per cent. greater than that of ordinary water, the oxide of DEUTERIUM or ~ *hydrogen*; ~*-weight*, jockey etc. of more than average weight, boxer over 12st. 7. Hence hea'viLY[2] adv., hea'viNESS n., ~ISH[1] a., (hŏ-). [OE *hefig*, OS *hebig*, OHG *hebig*, ON *höfugr*, f. Gmc *hafjan* HEAVE]

hĕb'domăd, n. Week (esp. in reference to *Dan*. ix. 27). [f. L f. Gk *hebdomas -ados* (*hepta* seven, see -AD)]

hĕbdŏm'adal, a. Weekly; || (Oxf. Univ.) *H~ Council*, board meeting weekly. [f. LL *hebdomadalis* (as prec., see -AL)]

Hēb'ê, n. (Gk Myth.) goddess of youth, cupbearer of Olympus; (joc.) waitress, barmaid. [Gk]

hĕb'ĕtāte, v.t. & i. Make, become, dull. [f. L *hebetare* (*hebes -etis* blunt), see -ATE[3]]

hĕb'ĕtūde, n. Stupidity. [f. LL *hebetudo* (*hebes*, see prec., -TUDE)]

Hēbrā'|ic, a. Of Hebrew or the Hebrews. Hence ~ICALLY adv. [f. LL f. Gk *Hebraïkos* (as HEBREW, see -IC)]

Hēb'rā|ism, n. Attribute of the Hebrews; Hebrew system of thought or religion; Hebrew idiom or expression esp. in the Greek of the Bible. So ~IZE(3) v.t. & i., ~is'tic a., ~is'tICALLY adv. [f. late Gk *Hebraïsmos*, or as prec. +-ISM, after *Hellenism* etc.]

Hēb'rāist, n. Hebrew scholar; adherent of Hebrew thought or religion. [as prec. -IST]

Hēb'rew (-ōō), n. & a. 1. Israelite, Jew; *Epistle to the ~s*, book in N.T.; language of the ancient ~s; *modern ~*, as now used by Jews; (colloq.) unintelligible speech (cf. GREEK). 2. adj. Of ~, of the Jews. [ME, f. OF *Ebreu* f. med. L *Ebreus* f. L f. Gk *Hebraios* f. Aram. *'ebrai* = Heb. *'ibri* one from the other side ('*abar* cross over)]

hĕc'atomb (-ŏm, -ōōm), n. (Gk Ant.). Great public sacrifice (prop. 100 oxen). [f. L f. Gk *hekatombē* (*hekaton* hundred + *bous* ox)]

hĕck¹, n. Frame obstructing passage of fish in river. [ME, northern form of HATCH¹]

hĕck², n. & int. (sl.). Euphem. for HELL esp. in imprecations.

hĕc'kle, v.t., & n. (Dress *flax, hemp*, with) HACKLE¹; catechize (esp. election candidate) severely. [15th c. *hekele* etc.; see HACKLE¹]

hĕc'tāre, n. (In metric system) superficial measure of 100 ares (2.471 acres). [f. HECTO- + ARE¹]

hĕc'tic, a. & n. 1. ~ *fever*, that which accompanies consumption and similar diseases, attended with flushed cheeks and hot skin; consumptive; morbidly flushed (lit. & fig.); (sl.) exciting, wild, impassioned, (*for a ~ moment*). 2. n. ~ fever, patient, flush. [14th c. etik. f. OF *etique* (mod. *hectique*) f. LL f. Gk *hektikos*; hec- after F & LL]

hĕc'to-, irreg. contr. of Gk *hekaton* hundred, used as comb. form, as: ~*graph*, apparatus for multiplying copies, (v.t.) multiply with this; (metric system) (~*gram*), weight of 100 grams (3.52 oz); (~*litre*, *-liter*, (-lēter), 100 litres (3.531 cub. ft), ~*metre* (-ter), *-meter*, 100 metres (328·089 ft); cf. CENTI-.

hĕc'tor, n., & v.t. & i. Bluster(er), bully. [(vb f. n.) f. Gk *Hektōr*, son of Priam and Hecuba, Trojan hero in *Iliad*]

hĕd'dles, n. pl. Small cords or wires through which warp is passed in loom before going through the reed. [16th c. var. of syn. *heald* f. OE *hefeld* f. *hef-* raise (HEAVE)]

hedge¹, n. Fence of bushes or low trees, living (*quickset ~*) or dead (*dead ~*), or of turf, stone, etc. (*doesn't grow on every ~*, is rare); line of things or persons forming barrier; (fig.) barrier; (Betting) act, means, of hedging; || ~*-priest*, illiterate priest of low status; ~*row*, row of bushes forming ~; || ~*-school*, low-class school, (formerly) open-air school esp. in Ireland;

~-**sparrow**, common British and European bird, allied to the warblers. [OE *hecg, hegg*, ME *hegge, heg*, = MDu. *hegghe*, OHG *hegga, hecka* f. Gmc *hagjō-see HAW[1]]

hĕdge[2], v.t. & i. Surround with hedge (lit. & fig.); fence *off*; hem *in*; make, trim, hedges, whence **hĕdg′ER**[1] n.; secure oneself against loss on (bet, speculation, or abs.) by compensating transactions on the other side; (intr.) avoid committing oneself. [f. prec.]

hĕdge′hŏg (-jh-), n. Small spiny, nocturnal, almost omnivorous mammal, rolling itself up into ball for defence; name of various animals armed with spines; (Mil.) small self-contained defensive position bristling with fortifications on all sides; prickly seed-vessel of some plants; person hard to get on with, whence ~**gy**[2] (-g-) a. [HEDGE (from its habits) + HOG (from its snout)]

hĕdŏn′ic, a. & n. Of pleasure; (n. pl.) doctrine of pleasure. [f. Gk *hēdonikos* (foll., -IC)]

hĕd′on|ism, n. Doctrine that pleasure is the chief good. So ~**IST** n., ~**is′tic** a. [f. Gk *hēdonē* pleasure + -ISM]

heed, v.t. (Sc. & literary), & n. **1.** Concern oneself about, take notice of. **2.** n. Careful attention, as *take* ~, *pay* or *give* ~ *to*. Hence ~**′FUL**, ~**′LESS**, aa., ~**′fulLY**[2], ~**′lessLY**[2], advv., ~**′fulNESS**, ~**′lessNESS**, nn. [OE *hēdan*, OS *hōdian*, OHG *huotan* f. WG *hōdjan*; n. f. vb]

hee′haw′, n. Ass's bray; loud laugh. [imit.]

heel[1], n. **1.** Hinder part of human foot below ankle (~ *of Achilles*, only vulnerable spot, weak point); (Anat.) corresponding part of hind limb in quadruped, often raised above ground; (pop., of quadruped) hinder part of hoof, (pl.) hind feet. **2.** Part of stocking that covers ~; part of boot that supports ~. **3.** Thing like ~ in shape or position, as handle end of violin bow, crook in head of golf club, after end of ship's keel; (hort.) irregularly shaped piece of plant attached to a cutting. **4.** *Cad, low-down person (sl.). **5.** *At* ~, *al, on, upon*, one's ~*s*, close behind one; *down at* ~, (of shoes) with ~ part crushed down, (of person) wearing such shoes, slovenly; *to* ~, (of dog) close behind, under control; ~-&-*toe* WALK[1]*ing*; ~*s over head*, (usu.) *head over* ~*s*, upside down, in a somersault; *kick* one's ~*s*, stand waiting; COOL[2] one's ~*s*; *lay, clap, by the* ~*s*, imprison; *show a clean pair of* ~*s*, *take to* one's ~*s*, run away; *have the* ~*s of*, out-run; *turn on* one's ~, turn sharply round; *be carried with the* ~*s foremost* (as a corpse); (Cribbage) *his* ~*s*, knave if turned up by dealer, scoring two (cf. NOB); ~′*ball*, shoemaker's polishing mixture of hard wax and .lamp-black; ~′*tap*, a thickness of leather in ~, liquor left at bottom of glass. [OE *hēla, hæla*,

OFris. *hēla*, MDu. *hiele*, ON *hœll* f. Gmc *hāhil* cogn. w. HOUGH]

heel[2], v.i. & t. Touch ground with heel, e.g. in dancing; furnish (boot etc.) with heel; chase or follow closely; (Football) pass ball *out* at back of scrummage with the heels; (Golf) strike (ball) with heel of club. Hence *~ED*[2] (-ld) a. (colloq.), armed with revolver, supplied with money. [f. prec.]

heel[3], v.i. & t. (Of ship etc.) lean over owing to pressure of wind or uneven load; cause (ship) to do this. [alt. f. 14th c. *heeld, hield* f. OE *hieldan*, OS *heldian*, OHG *heldan* f. Gmc *halthjan* incline, lean]

heel[4], n. (naut.). Inclination of heeling ship (cf. LIST[3]). [f. prec.]

hĕft, n., & v.t. (dial., U.S.). Weight; (dial.) lift, push, (v.t.) lift, esp. to judge weight. [(vb prob. f. n.) 16th c., f. HEAVE vb, cf. *weave weft*]

hĕf′tУ, a. Sturdy, stalwart, (a *battalion of* ~ *fellows*). [prec., -Y[2]]

Hēgēl′ian (hā-, hĕ-), a. & n. Relating to G. W. F. *Hegel* (d. 1831) or his philosophy; (n.) a follower of Hegel. [-IAN]

hegemŏn′ic (hĕgi-, hĕgī-), a. Ruling, supreme. [f. Gk *hēgemonikos* (as foll., see -IC)]

hēgĕm′onУ (-g-, -j-; *also* hĕg[2]), n. Leadership, esp. of one State of a confederacy [f. Gk *hēgemonia* (*hēgemōn* leader)]

hĕ′gira, -jira, n. Mohammed's flight from Mecca to Medina; Mohammedan era reckoned from this (622 A.D.). [med. L, f. Arab. *hijrah* departure from one's country (*hajara* separate)]

hei′fer (hĕf-), n. Young cow esp. one that has not had calf, female calf. [OE *heahfore*, of unkn. orig.]

heigh (hā), int. expr. encouragement or inquiry; ~-*ho*, int. expr. boredom, disappointment, etc.

height (hīt), n. Measurement from base to top; elevation above ground or recognized (esp. sea) level; considerable elevation, as *situated at a* ~; high point; top; *the* ~ (utmost degree) *of folly* etc.; rising ground; *at its* ~ (highest degree). [OE *hiehth(o)*, OHG *hōhida*, Goth. *hauhitha*; see HIGH, -TH[1]]

height′en (hīt-), v.t. & i. Make high(er); intensify; inflate (description, story); (intr.) rise (usu. fig.). [prec. + -EN[6]]

hei′nous (hān-), a. (Of crime or criminal) odious, atrocious. Hence ~**LY**[2] adv., ~**NESS** n. [ME, f. OF *hainos, -eus* (*haine* hatred f. *hair*); see -OUS]

heir (ār), n. Person receiving or entitled to receive property or rank as legal representative of former owner; (fig.) one to whom something (joy, punishment, etc.) is morally due; ~ APPARENT; ~-*at-law* (by right of blood); ~ *in tail* (to entailed estate); ~ *male*, male ~ tracing descent wholly through males; ~ PRESUMPTIVE. Hence ~**′DOM**, ~**′ESS**[1], ~**′SHIP**, nn., ~**′LESS**

a., (āī-). [ME, f. OF, f. LL *herem* = L *heredem* (nom. *heres*)]

heir′loom (āī-), n. Chattel that follows devolution of real estate ; piece of personal property that has been in family for generations (also fig. of qualities). [prec. + LOOM[1]]

hejira. See HEGIRA.

held. See HOLD[1].

hēle, heal, v.t. Cover, hide, (now dial.) ; set (plant) in the ground and cover it *in*. [OE *hęlian* f. st. *hal-* of *helan* ; cf. HELL]

hel′i-, comb. form of HELICOPTER, as in ~*drōme*, ~*pŏrt*, station for helicopters.

hēli′acal, a. (astron.). Relating to, near, the sun ; ~ *rising, setting*, first rising of a star after, last setting before, a period of invisibility due to conjunction with the sun. [f. LL f. Gk *hēliakos* (*hēlios* sun, see-AC) + -AL]

Hēliăn′thus, n. Genus including common sunflower. [f. Gk *hēlios* sun + *anthos* flower]

hĕl′iclal, a. Spiral. Hence or cogn.~alLY[2] adv., ~OID, ~oid′AL, aa. [as HELIX + -AL]

Hĕl′icon, n. Boeotian mountain, sacred to Muses ; source of poetic inspiration. So **Hēlicōn′IAN** a. [L, f. Gk *Helikōn*]

hĕl′icŏpter, n. Flying-machine deriving both its lift and its propulsive power from horizontally revolving blades or rotors, and capable of ascending and descending vertically. [f. Gk *helix -ikos* screw, *pteron* wing]

hĕl′iō, n. (colloq.). Abbr. of HELIOgram, *-graph.*

hĕl′io-, comb. form of Gk *hēlios* sun, as : ~*cĕn′tric*, as viewed from centre of sun, taking sun as centre ; ~*chrōmy*, photographic representation in natural colours ; ~*gram*, message by ~graph (3) ; ~*graph*, n., (1) engraving obtained by exposure to light, (2) apparatus for photographing sun, (3) signalling apparatus reflecting flashes of sunlight ; ~*graph*, v.t., send (message) by ~graph, photograph by ~graphy ; ~*graph′ic*, of ~graphy ; ~*graphy* (-ŏg²), description of the sun, engraving process, signalling by ~graph ; ~*gravūre′*, photogravure ; ~*mcter* (-ŏm²), instrument for finding angular distance between two stars (orig. for measuring diameter of sun) ; ~*scope*, apparatus for observing sun without injury to eye ; ~*thĕ′rapy*, use of sun-baths in treating disease ; ~*trop′ic*, ~*tropism* (-ŏt²), (of plants) turning, property of turning, in particular way under influence of light ; ~*type*, picture obtained from gelatine film exposed to light.

hēliolith′ic, a. Of the civilization characterized by megaliths & sun-worship. [f. HELIO-, after *eolithic* etc.]

hēliōs′is, n. (Bot.) spots on leaves caused by concentration of sun's rays through glass etc. ; sunstroke. [Gk *hēliōsis* (*hēlios* sun, see -OSIS)]

hĕl′iotrōpe, n. Plant with fragrant purple flowers ; colour, scent, of these ; bloodstone. [f. L f. Gk *hēliotropion* plant turning flowers to the sun (*hēlios* sun + -*tropos* f. *trepō* turn)]

hĕl′ium, n. A colourless inodorous inert gaseous element, inferred as existing in sun's atmosphere in 1868, first obtained in 1895. [f. Gk *hēlios* sun, -IUM]

hĕl′ix, n. (pl. *-īcēs*). Spiral (like corkscrew, or in one plane like watch-spring) ; (Archit.) spiral ornament ; rim of external ear ; genus including common snail. [L f. Gk *helix*]

hĕll, n. Abode of the dead ; abode of condemned spirits ; place, state, of wickedness or misery ; *a* ~ *of a* (considerable) *noise* ; den for captives in Prisoner's Base & other games ; gaming-house ; (in imprecations) ~ *!, what the* ~ *do you want?* ; *give* (a person) ~, make things hot for him ; *like* ~, desperately, extremely (often as mere intensive) ; ~-*box* (printer's sl.), receptacle for refuse type ; ~-*cat*, spiteful or furious woman ; ~ *for leather*, at top riding-speed (usu. *ride* ~ *for leather*) ; ~-*hound*, fiend ; ~-*weed*, name of various plants. Hence ~′ISH[1] a., ~′ishLY[2] adv., ~′ishNESS n., ~′WARD adv. & a. [OE *hel(l)*, OS *hellja*, OHG *hella*, ON *hel*, Goth. *halja* f. Gmc **hel-, *hal-* to hide, HELE]

hĕll′ebōre, n. Ancient name of various plants supposed to cure madness ; (Bot.) species including Christmas rose. [ME, f. OF, ult. f. L f. Gk *helleboros*]

Hĕll′ēne, n. Ancient Greek of genuine Greek race ; subject of modern kingdom of Greece. So **Hēllĕn′IC** a. [f. Gk *Hellēn*]

Hĕll′en|ism, n. Greek idiom or construction ; imitation of the Greeks ; Grecian culture ; Greek nationality. So ~-IZE(3) v.t. & i. [f. Gk *Hellēnismos* (as prec., see -ISM)]

Hĕll′en|ist, n. One who used the Greek language but was not a Greek ; Greek scholar. Hence ~-**is′t**IC a. [f. Gk *Hellēn- istēs* (as prec., see -IST)]

hĕllō′, n. & v. = HALLO.

hĕlm[1], n. (Arch.) helmet ; (also ~-*cloud*) cloud forming over mountain before or during storm. Hence ~ED[2] (-md) a. [OE, OS, OHG, ON *hjalmr*, Goth. *hilms* f. Gmc **helmaz* f. **hel-* (HELL)]

hĕlm[2], n., & v.t. 1. Tiller, wheel, by which rudder is used ; space through which ~ is turned, as *more, little,* ~ ; *down (with the)* ~, *up (with the)* ~, place ~ so as to bring rudder to leeward, to windward ; *weather, lee,* ~, ~ put up, down ; (fig.) government, guidance, (*take the* ~, assume control) ; ~*s′man*, steersman. 2. v.t. Steer (usu. fig.). [OE *helma* corr. to ON *hjalm* ; cf. MHG *helm* handle]

hĕl′mĕt, n. Defensive head-cover of soldiers, firemen, etc. ; felt or pith hat for hot climates ; upper part of retort ; (Bot.) arched upper part of corolla in some flowers ; shell of a genus of molluscs.

Hence ~ED² a. [ME, f. OF dim. of *helme*
f. WG (HELM¹)]

hĕl′minth, n. Worm (usu. intestinal).
Hence ~i′ASIS n., disease characterized by
presence of ~s in the body, **hĕlmin′thIC**,
hĕlmin′thoID, aa., ~ŏL′OGY n. [f. Gk
helmins -inthos maw-worm]

hĕl′ot, n. (*H*~) one of a class of serfs in
ancient Sparta; *drunken H*~ (made drunk
as warning to Spartan youth); serf.
Hence ~ISM(2), ~RY(1, 2), nn., ~IZE(3) v.t.
[f. L *Helotes* f. Gk *Heilōtes* (pl. of *Heilōs*)
taken as=inhabitant of *Helos*, Laconian
town]

hĕlp¹, v.t. (~*ed*; arch. past *hōlp* & p.p. *hōl-
pen*). Aid, assist, as ~ *me*, ~ *me to lift it*,
~ *me to an answer*, ~ *the work on* or
forward, ~ *me over the stile*, ~ *me out* (*of
a difficulty*); ~ *person on, off, with coat*
etc., ~ *him to put it on, take it off*; ~
(*person*) *to*, serve him with (*food*); distribute (*food at meal*); remedy, prevent,
as *it can't be* ~*ed*, *I can't* ~ *that, don't
be longer than you can* ~ (*cannot*); (w.
neg.) refrain from or avoid doing (*cannot
~ hoping that* —); (in invocation or oath)
so ~ *me God* (as I keep my word, as I
speak the truth, etc.). [OE, OS *helpan*,
OHG *helfan*, ON *hjalpa*, Goth. *hilpan* f.
Gmc *help-*, *halp-*, *hulp-*]

hĕlp², n. Assistance, as *we need your* ~,
she, it, is a great ~, *by* ~ *of*; *domestic
servant*, employees; ‖ *lady* ~, assistant &
companion to mistress of house; *mother's*
~, superior nursemaid; remedy or escape,
as *there is no* ~ *for it*; helping (of food).
[OE *help*, f. prec.]

hĕlp′ful, a. (Of person or thing) useful,
serviceable. Hence ~LY² adv., ~NESS n.
[-FUL]

hĕl′ping, n. In vbl senses, esp. portion
of food served. [-ING¹]

hĕlp′lèss, a. Lacking help; unable to help
oneself. Hence ~LY² adv., ~NESS n.
[-LESS]

hĕlp′māte, n. Helpful companion or
partner (usu. husband or wife). [HELP +
MATE, prob. infl. by foll.]

hĕlp′meet, n. = prec. [formed by misunderstanding of *Gen.* ii. 18, 20, *help meet*
(i.e. suitable) being taken as one
word]

hĕl′ter-skĕl′ter, adv., a., & n.. (In) disordered haste. [imit.]

hĕlve, n. Handle of weapon or tool; *throw
the* ~ *after the* HATCHET. [OE *hielfe* (WG
halbhjo-) f. Gmc *hal-* as in HALTER, with
MLG, MDu. *helf*, OHG *halp*]

Hĕlvē′tian (-shn), a. & n. Swiss. [f. L
Helvetius + -AN]

hĕm¹, n. Border, edge, of cloth etc., esp.
border made by turning in edge & sewing
it down. [OE *hem(m)* (once), perh. rel. to
dial. *ham* enclosed pasture; cf. NFris.
heam hem]

hĕm², v.t. (-mm-). Turn down & sew in
edge of (cloth etc., or abs.); ~ *in, about,
round*, enclose, confine. [f. prec.]

hĕm³, int., n., & v.i. **1.** (Also *h'm*) int.
calling attention or expressing hesitation.
2. n. Utterance of this. **3.** v.t. (-mm-).
Utter sound ~, clear throat, hesitate in
speech. [imit.]

hemato- etc. See **haemato-**.

hĕmi-, pref. in wds f. Gk or on Gk elements, = half-, affecting one half, etc., as
~*anŏp′sia*, half-blindness, *hem′icycle*, half-
-moon figure, ‖ ~*dĕmĭsĕmĭquāv′er*, half a
demisemiquaver, ~*hĕd′ral* (Cryst.), having
half proper number of planes, ~*metăb′ola*,
insects undergoing incomplete metamorphosis, ~*plē′gia*, paralysis of one side.
[Gk *hēmi-* = L *semi-*]

hĕm′isphēre, n. Half sphere; half the
celestial sphere, esp. as divided by the
equinoctial or by the ecliptic; half
the earth, containing (*Eastern* ~) Europe,
Asia, & Africa, or (*Western* ~) America;
Northern, Southern, ~*s*, halves of the
earth as divided by equator; *Magdeburg*
~*s*, pair of brass ~*s* exhausted of air to
show atmospheric pressure by their cohesion. Hence **hĕmisphĕ′rIC(AL)** aa.
[ME forms f. OF *emisp(h)ere* & LL *hemis-
phaerium* f. Gk HEMI(*sphaira* SPHERE)]

hĕm′istich (-k), n. Half of line of verse.
[f. L f. Gk HEMI(*stikhion* f. *stikhos* verse)]

hĕm′lŏck, n. Poisonous umbelliferous
plant, used as powerful sedative; poisonous potion got from this. [OE *hymlic(e)*,
of unkn. orig.]

hemorrhage etc. See **haem-**.

hĕmp, n. Herbaceous plant, native
of India; its cortical fibre used for rope
& stout fabrics; (joc.) rope for hanging;
name of various other plants yielding
fibre (*European, Manilla*, ~, with soft,
hard, fibre); ~ *agrimony*, perennial plant
of the daisy family with pale-purple
flowers and hairy leaves. Hence **hĕm′-
pEN**⁵ a. [OE *henep*, OHG *hanaf*, ON
hampr f. Gmc *hanapiz* cogn. w. Gk
kannabis]

hĕm′stitch, v.t., & n. (Hem *cloth* etc.
with) kind of ornamental stitch.

hĕn, n. Female of common domestic fowl,
pheasant, partridge, woodcock, etc. (~
blackbird, ~ *thrush*, etc., cf. COCK¹); occas.
second element in name of female birds,
as *guinea-*~, *pea-*~, *moor-*~ etc.; *like a
*~ *with one chicken*, absurdly fussy; ~
& chickens, name of a compound daisy
& other plants; ~′*bane*, narcotic &
poisonous plant, drug got from this;
~-*coop* (for keeping poultry in); ~ *crab,
lobster*, female; ~-*harrier*, blue hawk, a
bird of prey; ~-*hearted*, pusillanimous;
~-*party* (of women only, colloq.; cf.
STAG-*party*); ~′*pecked*, domineered over
by one's wife; ~-*roost*, place where fowls
roost at night; ~-*run*, enclosure for fowls.
[OE *henn*, OHG *henna* f. WG *hannja*
dim. of *hano* (OE *hana* cock)]

hence, adv. (Arch.) from here, from this,
(often pleonast. *from* ~); (poet., rhet.)
~ *!*, go away, ~ *with*, away with, take

away, go ~, die; ~forth', ~for'ward, from this time forward; *five years* ~, in five years' time from now; as a result from this; from this origin; as an inference from this (~ *it appears that*), therefore. [ME *hennes* f. *henne* adv. (OE *hionan* f. root of HE) +-ES]

hĕnch′man, n. 1. (hist.). Squire, page of honour. 2. Chief attendant of Highland chief; trusty follower; political supporter. [14th c., f. OE *hengest* male horse (Du. & G *hengst*) +MAN]

hĕn′dĕca- in comb. = Gk *hendeka* eleven, as *hendĕc'agon*, plane rectilineal figure of eleven sides; ~*sўllăb′ĭc* a. & n., (verse) of eleven syllables, ~*syll'able*, such a verse (esp., in Gk & Latin: ⌣ – (or –⌣) –⌣⌣–⌣–⌣⌣̸).

hĕndī′adўs, n. Expression of a complex idea by two words connected with *&* (e.g. *in goblets & gold* for *in golden goblets*). [med. L, f. Gk *hen dia duoin* one thing by two]

Hĕn′ley, n. (Used for) annual regatta at ~-on-Thames. [place]

hĕnn′a, n. Egyptian privet; its shoots & leaves used as a dye for esp. the hair. [Arab. *henna'*]

hĕnn′ў, a. & n. Hen-like; (n.) hen-like cock. [HEN +-Y²]

hĕn′othĕism, n. Belief in one God without asserting that he is the only God (cf. MONOTHEISM). [f. Gk *heis henos* one +*theos* god +-ISM]

hĕpăt′ĭc, a. Of, good for, the liver; liver-hued. [f. LL f. Gk *hĕpatikos* (HEPATO-, -IC)]

hĕpăt′ĭca, n. Anemone with lobed leaves resembling the liver. [med. L, fem. of *hepaticus* (prec.)]

hĕpatī′tis, n. Inflammation of the liver. [HEPATO-, -ITIS]

hĕp′ătĭz|e, -is|e (-ĭz), v.t. Convert (lungs) into liver-substance.. Hence ~A′TION n. [as foll. +-IZE]

hĕpato-, comb. form of Gk *hĕpar -atos* liver, as ~*genous* (-ŏjˁ), originating in the liver.

Hĕp′plewhite (-elwīt), n. A delicate style of furniture. [G. ~, d. 1786]

hĕp′ta- in comb. = Gk *hepta* seven, as: ~*chord*, 7-stringed instrument, 7-note scale; ~*glot* a. & n., (book) in seven languages; ~*gon*, plane rectilineal figure of seven sides, so ~*gonal* (-ăgˁ) a.; ~*hĕd′ron* (-a-h-), solid of seven faces; ~*sўllăb′ĭc*, of seven syllables; ~*teuch* (-k), first seven books of Bible.

hĕp′tad, n. Set, group, of seven. [f. LL f. Gk *heptas -ados* set of seven (*hepta*)]

hĕp′tärchў (-k-) n. Government by seven rulers; seven kingdoms of Angles & Saxons in Britain. So **hĕptärch′ic(al)** (-k-) aa. [f. HEPTA- + Gk -*arkhia* government]

her¹, pron. Objective case of SHE; colloq. also subjective, as *Was that* ~? [OE *hire*, dat. of *hio, heo*, SHE]

her², pron. & a. Possessive case of, & adj. corresp. to, SHE, with absolute form ~*s*, as *it is* ~ *hat, it is* ~*s*, ~*s is best, my father & ~*s suffer(s) for it*, ~ (vulg. ~*s*) *& my* (common) *father*, ~ (vulg. ~*s*) *& my* (respective) *father(s)*. [OE *hi(e)re*, genitive as prec.]

hĕ′rald¹, n. 1. Officer who made State proclamations, bore messages between princes, officiated in the tourney, arranged various State ceremonials, regulated use of armorial bearings, settled questions of precedence, & recorded names & pedigrees of those entitled to armorial bearings; ‖*H*~*s' College*, corporation (now) recording pedigrees & granting bearings. 2. Messenger (often as title of newspaper); forerunner. [ME, f. OF *heraut*, f. WG *heriwald* 'army-wielder']

hĕ′rald², v.t. Proclaim the approach of; usher in. [ME, f. OF *herauder* (as prec.)]

hĕräl′dĭc, a. Of heraldry. [-IC]

hĕ′raldrў, n. Science of a herald; CANT³-*ing* ~; armorial bearings; heraldic pomp. [-RY]

hĕrb, n. Plant whose stem is not woody or persistent; plant of which leaves etc. are used for food, medicine, scent, flavour, etc.; ~ *beer*, drink made from ~*s*; ~ *bennet*, yellow-flowered species of Avens [prob. f. OF *herbe beneite* = L *herba benedicta* blessed herb]; ~ *Robert*, kind of geranium; ~-*tea*, -*water*, medicinal infusion of herbs. So ~A′CEOUS (-āshŭs; ~*aceous border* in gardens, one devoted to perennial flowering plants), ~ĬF′EROUS, ĬV′OROUS, ~′LESS, aa. [ME, f. OF *erbe* f. L *herba* grass]

hĕrb′age, n. Herbs collectively; succulent parts of herbs; (Law) right of pasture on another's ground. [ME, f. OF (prec., -AGE)]

hĕrb′al, a. & n. (Book with descriptions) of herbs. [f. med. L *herbalis* (as prec., see -AL)]

hĕrb′alĭst, n. One skilled in herbs (now of early botanical writers); dealer in medicinal herbs. [prec. +-IST]

hĕrbār′ium, n. (Book, case, room, for) collection of dried plants. [LL HERB, -ARIUM)]

hĕrb′or|ĭze, -ise (-ĭz), v.i. Gather herbs, botanize. So ~ĬZA′TION, ~ĬST, nn. [f. F *herboriser*, irreg. f. *herbe* HERB, after *arboriser*]

hĕrb′ў, a. Abounding in herbs; of the nature of a herb. [-Y²]

Hĕrcū′lēan (*also* -ŏ'an), a. Of Hercules; strong as Hercules; difficult as his labours. [f. L *Herculeus* (as foll.) +-AN]

Hĕrc′ūlēs (-z), n. (Gk & Rom. Myth.) hero of prodigious strength, who performed 12 immense labours; *Pillars of* ~, rocks on either side of Strait of Gibraltar, (fig.) ultimate limit; strong man; ~ *beetle* (S.-Amer., 5 in. long); a northern constellation. [L, f. Gk *Hēraklēs*]

hẽrd[1], n. Company of animals, esp. cattle, feeding or travelling together; large number of people (derog.), esp. *the, the common, the vulgar, ~*; *the ~ instinct*, gregariousness & mutual influence as a psychological factor; **~book**, pedigree--book of cattle or pigs; **~s'man**, keeper of ~s. [OE *heord*, OHG *herta*, ON *hjorth*, Goth. *hairda* f. Gmc *herdō*]

hẽrd[2], n. Keeper of herds, herdsman, esp. w. word prefixed, as *cow~, swine~*. [OE *hirde*, OS *hirdi*, OHG *hirti*, ON *hirthir*, Goth. *hairdeis* f. Gmc *herdjaz*]

hẽrd[3], v.i. & t. Go in a herd (*together, with* others; esp. fig. of persons); tend (sheep, cattle). [f. HERD[1,2]]

hēre, adv. & n. **1.** In this place; in this country; (answering roll-call) *~ l,* I am present; (calling attention to person's presence) *my son ~ will show you*; (in drinking healths) *~'s* (a health) *to*; in this life (esp. *~ below*); at this point (in discourse etc.); in this matter; to this place; *look ~* (in this direction; esp. in bespeaking attention or making protest); *I don't belong ~* (to this place); *~ & there*, in various places; *~, there, & everywhere*, everywhere, all about; *neither ~ nor there*, not to the point, of no importance; (colloq., to announce commencement of bold act) *~ goes l* **2.** n. This place or point, as *from, to, near, ~.* **3.** *~'about(s)'*, somewhere near *~*; *~af'ter*, in future, later on, in the world to come, (n.) the future, the world to come; *~at'* (arch.), at this; *~by'*, by this means, as a result; *~in'*, in this point, book, etc.; *~inaf'ter*, below (in document etc.); *~inbefore'*, in a preceding part (of this document etc.); *~of'* (arch.), of this; *~to'* (arch.), to this matter; *~tofore'*, formerly; *~un'der*, below (in book etc.); *~upon'*, after this, in consequence of this; *~with'*, with this (esp. of enclosure in letter etc.). [OE, OS, ON, Goth. *hēr*, OHG *hiar*, app. f. Gmc *hi-* (HE[1])]

hēred'ita|ble, a. That may be inherited. So *~BIL'ITY* n. [obs. F, f. *héréditer*, f. LL *hereditare* (*heres -edis* heir), see **-ABLE**]

hēredit'ament (or hīrĕd[4]), n. Property that can be inherited; real property; inheritance. [f. med. L *hereditamentum* (as prec., see **-MENT**)]

hēredĭtār'ian, n. One who holds the doctrine of heredity. [f. HEREDITY, see **-ARIAN**]

hēred'itar|y̆, a. Descending by inheritance; (of diseases, instincts, etc.) transmitted from one generation to another; like, the same as, that one's parents had, as *~y creed, hatred*; of, holding position by, inheritance. Hence *~ILY*[2] adv., *~INESS* n. [f. L *hereditarius* (as HEREDITY, see **-ARY**[1])]

hēred'it|y̆, n. Tendency of like to beget like. Hence *~ISM*(3) n. [f. F *hérédité* or L *hereditas* heirship (as HEIR, see **-TY**)]

Hē'rĕford, n. (Used for) a breed of cattle originating in Herefordshire, England.

Hērer'o (-ār'ō), n. Name of negroid people and their language in S.W. Africa.

hērēs'iãrch (-k), n. Leader, founder, of a heresy. [f. LL (-*cha*) f. Gk *hairesiarkhēs* (as foll. +*-arkhēs* ruler)]

hē'rĕsy̆, n. Opinion contrary to the orthodox doctrine of the Christian Church, or to the accepted doctrine on any subject. Hence **hĕrēsiŏl'OGIST**, **hĕrēsiŏl'OGY**, nn. [ME, f. OF (*h*)*eresie* f. Rom. *heresia* f. L & LL *haeresis* f. Gk *hairesis* choice, sect (*haireomai* choose)]

hē'rĕtic, n. Holder of an unorthodox opinion (orig. in the matter of religion). So **hĕrĕt'ICAL** a. [ME, f. OF *heretique* f. LL f. Gk *hairetikos* (as prec., see -IC)]

‖ **hē'riot**, n. (law). Render of best live beast or dead chattel, or money payment, to lord on decease of tenant (now only of manorial tenures). [OE *heregeatwa* (*here* army +*geatwa* trappings)]

hē'ritab|le, a. That passes to heirs-at-law (opp. to movable property); transmissible from parent to child; capable of inheriting. Hence *~LY*[2] adv. [ME, f. OF, f. *heriter* f. LL *hereditare* (see HEREDITABLE)]

hē'ritage, n. What is or may be inherited; (fig.) portion allotted to any one; (Bibl.) the ancient Israelites, the Church; inherited lot. [ME, f. OF (as prec., see -AGE)]

hē'ritor, n. One who inherits. [f. AF *heriter*, OF -*ier* (as HEREDITARY), assim. to wds in -OR]

hẽrl, n. Var. of HARL(E)[2].

hẽrmăph'rod|īte, n. & a. **1.** Human being, animal, combining characteristics of both sexes; (Zool.) animal having normally both male & female sexual organs, e.g. earth-worm; (Bot.) plant in which same flower has stamens & pistils; person, thing, combining opposite qualities; ship having characters of two kinds of craft. **2.** adj. Combining both sexes or opposite characteristics. Hence *~it'IC*(AL) aa., *~ĪTISM* n. [f. L f. Gk *Hermaphroditos*, who became one with the nymph Salmacis]

hẽrmĕneut'ic, a. & n. Of interpretation; (n. pl.) interpretation, esp. of Scripture. So *~AL* a. [f. Gk *hermēneutikos* (*hermēneuō* interpret, see -IC)]

Hẽrm'ēs (-z), n. (Gk Myth.) son of Zeus & Maia, messenger of the gods, god of science, eloquence, etc.; *~ Trismegistus* (Thrice-Great), Neo-platonist name of Egyptian god Thoth, as author of mysterious doctrines, secrets of alchemy, etc. [L f. Gk *Hermēs*]

hẽrmĕt'|ic, a. Of alchemy, as *~ic art*; *~ic seal*, air-tight closure by fusion etc. (also fig.), whence *~ICALLY* adv. [f. mod. L *hermeticus* irreg. f. HERMES *Trismegistus*]

hẽrm'it, n. Early Christian recluse; person living in solitude; *~-crab*, kind that lives in mollusc's cast-off shell to protect its shell-less hinder parts. [ME, f. OF (*h*)*ermite* f. LL (-*ta*) f. Gk *erēmitēs* (*erēmia* desert, see -ITE[1]); cf. EREMITE] hĕrm'itage, n. Hermit's abode; solitary abode; French wine from hill near Valence (with ruined ~ on top). [ME, f. OF (as prec., see -AGE)]

hern. See HERON.

hĕrn'i|a, n. (path.). Rupture. Hence ~AL, ~ARY¹, aa., ~ŏt'omy n. [L]

hĕrn'shaw. [ME, f. OF heronceau, dim. of HERON]

hēr'ō, n. (pl. ~es). (Gk Ant.) man of superhuman qualities favoured by the gods, demigod; illustrious warrior, (rhet.) one who has fought for his country (homes for ~es, housing for ex-service men); man admired for achievements & noble qualities; chief man in poem, play, or story; ~-worship(per), worship(per) of the ancient ~es or of some great man or men. [f. L f. Gk hērōs]

hērō'ĭc, a. & n. 1. (Of acts or qualities) of, fit for, a hero; (of persons) having the qualities of a hero; the ~ age (of Greece, before return from Troy); (of poetry) dealing with heroes; ~ verse, that used in ~ poetry (Gk & L hexameter, E five-foot iambic, F Alexandrine); (of language) grand, high-flown; bold, attempting great things. 2. n. ~ verse; (n. pl.) high-flown language or sentiments. Hence hērō'ic-ALLY adv. [f. F -ique or L f. Gk hērōikos (as prec., see -IC)]

hērōĭ-cŏm'ĭc, a. Combining the heroic with the comic. [HERO + -I- + COMIC]

hērō'ĭfy, v.t. Make a hero of. [as prec. + -FY]

hĕr'oïn (or hĭrō'ĭn), n. A sedative drug prepared from morphine. [P]

hĕr'oïne, n. Demigoddess; heroic woman; chief woman in poem, novel, etc. [f. L f. Gk hērōïnē, fem. of hērōs HERO]

hĕr'oïsm, n. Heroic conduct or qualities. [f. F héroïsme (heros HERO, see -ISM)]

hĕr'oïze, -ise (-īz), v.t. & i. Make a hero of; make heroic; play the hero. [-IZE]

hĕr'on, hĕrn (poet. etc.), n. Long-legged wading bird. [ME, f. OF hai(g)ron f. WG (Frank.) *haigiro = OHG heigaro (G reiher), OE hrāgra heron]

hĕr'onry, n. Place where herons breed. [-RY]

hĕrp'ēs (-z), n. Skin disease, with patches of distinct vesicles. Hence hĕrpĕt'ic a. [L, f. Gk herpēs, -ētos shingles (herpō creep)]

hĕrpĕt|ŏl'ogy, n. Study of reptiles. So ~ŏl'ogist n. [f. Gk herpeton reptile (herpō creep) + -LOGY]

Herr (hār), n. (pl. Herren). German equivalent of Mr; German gentleman.

hĕr'ring, n. North Atlantic fish, much used for food, coming near coast in large shoals to spawn; kippered ~, = KIPPER; RED ~; ~-bone, stitch resembling bones of ~, (Archit.) zigzag arrangement of stones or tiles, (v.t.) work with ~-bone stitch, mark with ~-bone pattern; ~-pond, (joc.) North Atlantic. [OE hǣring, hēring, MLG hēr-, hārink, OHG hārinc]

Herrn'huter (hārn'hōō-), n. One of the sect of Moravians. [f. Herrnhut, their first German settlement]

hers. See HER.

hĕrsĕlf', pron. Emphatic & reflexive form corr. to SHE, as she ~ told me, she said it ~, she has hurt ~, ask the woman ~; she is not ~ (in her normal state of body or mind). [OE hire self]

Hĕrt'zian, a. ~ waves, electric waves (so called from the discoveries of H. R. Hertz, German physicist, d. 1894); ~ telegraphy, wireless. [-IAN]

hĕs'it|ant (-z-), a. Hesitating; irresolute. So ~ANCE, ~ANCY, nn. [as foll., see -ANT]

hĕs'ităt|e (-z-), v.i. Show, speak with, indecision; scruple, be reluctant, to (do). Hence or cogn. ~ingLY² adv., hĕsĭtA²-TION n., ~IVE a., (-z-). [f. L haesitare frequent. of haerēre haes- stick fast, see -ATE³]

Hĕspēr'ian, a. (poet.). Western. [f. L f. Gk Hesperios (as HESPERUS) + -AN]

Hĕs'peris, n. Genus of plants including ROCKET¹ & dame's violet. [L, f. Gk Hesperis of evening, of the West (as foll.)]

Hĕspērŏrn'is, n. American genus of fossil birds. [as foll + Gk ornis bird]

Hĕs'perus, n. Evening star. [L, f. Gk hesperos a. & n., western evening (star)]

Hē'ssian (-shn), a. & n. 1. Of Hesse in Germany; ~ (boot), high boot first worn by ~ troops; ~ fly, fly whose larva destroys wheat. 2. n. Strong coarse cloth of hemp or jute. [-IAN]

hĕst, n. (arch.). Behest. [OE hǣs (hātan, see HIGHT), assim. to OE nn. in -t]

hĕt, p.p. (now dial. & U.S.). Heated; ~ up (sl.), excited. [p.p. of HEAT²]

hĕtaer'a (-tēr̄a), -air'a (-īr̄a), n. (pl. -rae). Courtesan, mistress. [Gk hetaira, fem. of hetairos companion]

hĕtaer'ism (-ēr̄-), -air'ism (-īr̄-), n. Open concubinage; communal marriage in a tribe. [f. Gk hetairismos (as prec., see -ISM)]

hĕt'ero- (before vowel heter-), comb. form of Gk heteros other, different; freq. opp. to homo-, occas. to auto-, homoeo-, iso-, ortho-, syn-: ~chrōm'ous, of different colours; ~cȳc'lic, (of chem. compounds) with molecule of a ring composed of atoms of different kinds; ~gamous (-ŏg²), irregular as regards stamens & pistils; ~graphy (-ŏg²), incorrect or inconsistent spelling; ~morph'ic, of dissimilar forms; ~morph'ism, diversity of form; ~nomous (-ŏn²), subject to different laws (of growth etc.), subject to an external law (cf. AUTONOMOUS); ~nomy (-ŏn²), presence of a different law, subjection to external law; ~pāth'ic, = ALLOPATHIC, (also) differing in effect; ~phyll'ous, bearing leaves of different forms on same plant; ~sexual a., relating to or characterized by the normal relation of the sexes (also as n.; opp. HOMOSEXUAL); ~taxy, abnormal disposition of organs or parts.

hĕt′eroclite, a. & n. (gram.). Irregularly declined; (n.) ~ noun. [16th c. f. F *hétéroclite* or LL f. Gk HETERO(*klitos* f. *klinō* inflect)]

hĕt′erodŏx, a. (Of person or opinion) not orthodox. So ~Y [1] n. [17th c. f. LL f. Gk HETERO(*doxos* f. *doxa* opinion)]

hĕt′erodyne, n. & a. (Relating to) production of a lower (audible) frequency from the combination of two high frequencies (in radio). [HETERO-, Gk *dunamis* force]

hĕterogĕn′eous, a. Diverse in character; composed of diverse elements; (Math.) incommensurable because of different kinds. Hence or cogn. hĕterogĕnĕ′ITY, ~NESS, nn., ~LY [2] adv. [f. scholastic L *heterogeneus* f. Gk HETERO(*genēs* f. *genos* kind) + -OUS]

hĕterogĕn′esis, n. Birth of a living being otherwise than from parent of same kind, esp. spontaneous generation from inorganic matter. So hĕterogĕnET′IC a. [HETERO-]

hĕterozyg′|ōte, n. (Mendelism). Zygote resulting from fusion of unlike gametes. So ~OUS a. [HETERO-].

hĕt′man, n. Polish military commander (retained as title among Cossacks). [Polish]

heuris′tic (hūr-), a. & n. Serving to discover; ~ *method*, system of education under which the pupil is trained to find out things for himself, so ~s n. pl. [irreg. f. Gk·*heuriskō* find, see -IC]

hew, v.t. & i. (p.p. ~n or ~ed). Chop, cut, (thing *down, away, off, asunder, to pieces,* etc.) with axe, sword, etc.; cut into shape; ~ one's *way*, make a way for oneself by ~ing; deal cutting blows *at, among,* etc. [OE *hēawan,* OS *hauwan,* OHG *houwan,* ON *höggva* f. Gmc *hauw-*]

hew′er, n. One who hews; man who cuts coal from seam; ~s *of wood & drawers of water,* drudges (*Joshua* ix. 21). [-ER [1]]

hĕx′a- in comb. (before vowel, & in some mod. words before consonant, *hex*-) = Gk *hex* six, as: ~*chord* (-k-), diatonic series of six notes with semitone between third & fourth; ~*gon,* ~*gonal* (-ăg[L]), (figure) h'aving six sides; ~*gram,* figure formed by two intersecting equilateral triangles (the angular points coinciding with those of a ~gon), figure of six lines; ~*hĕd′ral* (-a-h-) a., ~*hĕd′ron* (-a-h-) n., (figure) having six faces; ~*pod* n. & a., (insect) with six feet; ~*pody* (-ăp[L]), line of verse of six feet; ~*style* a. & n., (portico) of six columns; ~*syllăb′ic;* ~*teuch* (-k), first six books of Bible.

hĕx′ad, n. A six (uses as PENTAD). [f. Gk *hexas -ados* (*hex* six, -AD)]

hĕxăm′eter, n. Line of six metrical feet, esp. *dactylic* ~ (five dactyls & trochee or spondee, any of first four feet, & rarely the fifth, being replaced by spondee). Hence hĕxamĕt′ric a., hĕxăm′etrist n. [L, f. Gk HEXA(*metros* f. *metron* measure)]

hĕx′apla, n. Six-fold text in parallel

columns, esp. of Old or New Testament. [Gk, neut. pl. of HEXA(*ploos* -fold)]

hey (hā), int. calling attention, or of joy, surprise, or interrogation; ~ *for* —! (expr. applause or exultant appreciation); ~ *presto* (conjuror's phrase of command, hence used to announce surprising transformation etc.). [ME, Du., G]

hey′day [1] (hā-), int. expr. joy, surprise, etc. [16th c., orig. obsc.; cf. LG (G) *heidi, heida,* excl. denoting gaiety]

hey′day [2] (hā-), n. Full bloom, flush, (of youth, vigour, prosperity, etc.). [16th c., perh. sb. use of prec.; later assoc. w. *day*]

·hey′duck (hī′dŏŏk), n. Hungarian of an ennobled military class; Polish liveried retainer. [f. Pol. *hajduk* brigand]

hī, int. calling attention. [parallel form to HEY]

hiāt′us, n. (pl. ~es). Break, gap, esp. in a series, account, or chain of proof; break between two vowels coming together not in the same syllable. [L, vbl n. f. *hiare* gape]

hib′ern|āte, v.i. Spend the winter (of animals) in torpid state, (of persons) in mild climate; (fig.) remain inactive. So ~ANT a., ~A′TION n. [f. L *hibernare* (*hibernus* wintry), see -ATE [3]]

Hibĕrn′ian, a. & n. (Native) of Ireland. [f. L *Hibernia* + -AN]

Hibĕrn′icism, n. Irish idiom, expression, or bull. [as prec., on *Anglicism* etc.]

hībis′cus, n. Cultivated malvaceous plant or shrub; rose-mallow. [L f. Gk *hibiskos* marsh mallow]

hicc′up, n., & v.i. & t. Involuntary spasm of respiratory organs, with sudden closure of glottis & characteristic sound; (v.i.) make ~; (v.t.) say, bring *out,* with ~(s). [(vb f. n.) earlier *hicket,* imit.; *hiccough* due to pop. etym.]

hīc jā′cĕt, n. Epitaph. [L, = here lies]

*hick, H-, n. (colloq.). Countryman, farmer, provincial. [by-form of *Richard;* cf. *Dick*]

hick′ory, n. N.-Amer. tree allied to walnut, with tough heavy wood; wood, stick, of this. [f. native Virginian *pohickery*]

hid, hidden. See HIDE [2].

hidăl′gō, n. (pl. ~s). Spanish gentleman. [Sp., f. *hijo dalgo* son of a 'somebody']

hide [1], n., & v.t. 1. Animal's skin, raw or ·dressed; (joc.) human skin, as *to save his own* ~; ~*bound,* (of cattle) with skin clinging close as result of bad feeding, (fig.) narrow-minded. 2. v.t. (colloq.). Flog. Hence (-)hid′ED [2] a. [OE *hȳd,* OS *hūd,* OHG *hūt,* ON *húth* f. Gmc *hudhiz* cogn. w. L *cutis*]

hide [2], v.t. & i. (past *hid,* p.p.·*hidden, hĭd*), & n. 1. Put, keep, out of sight (~ one's *light under a* BUSHEL); keep (fact) secret (*from*); keep (thing) from view without that intention; ~ one's *head,* keep out of sight from shame etc.; (intr.) conceal oneself; ~-*&-seek,* children's game (also fig. of dealings with evasive person or thing). **2.** n. Place of concealment used in observation of wild animals; ~-*out* (colloq.), hiding-place. [OE *hȳdan*, MLG, MDu. *hûden*, f. WG *hûdjan*]

hide[3], n. (hist.). Measure of land, as much as would support one free family & dependants (varied from 60 to 120 acres according to locality). [OE *hĭd, hĭgid,* f. *hĭw-, hĭg-* household]

hid′eous, a. Frightful, repulsive, revolting, to senses or mind, as ~ *crime, noise, pattern.* Hence~LY[2] adv.,~NESS n. [ME, f. AF *hidous* = OF *hidos, -eus,* earlier *hisdos* f. *hisde* horror, of unkn. orig.; see -EOUS]

hid′ing[1], n. Thrashing. [f. HIDE[1]+-ING[1]]

hid′ing[2], n. In vbl senses of HIDE[2], esp.: *be in ~,* remain hidden; ~*-place,* place of concealment. [-ING[1]]

hie, v.i. (poet.; part. *hying*). Go quickly (*to* etc.); (with pers. pron. used reflexively, orig. dat.) ~ *thee, he ~d him.* [OE *hĭgian* strive, pant, cf. MDu., MLG *hĭgen* pant]

hi′erärch (-k), n. Chief priest; archbishop. [f. med. L (*-cha*) f. Gk *hierarkhēs* (*hieros* sacred +-*arkhēs* ruler)]

hi′erärchў (-k-), n. Each of three divisions of angels; the angels; priestly government; organized priesthood in successive grades; any graded organization. Hence .hierärch′IC(AL) aa., hi′erärchISM(3) n., (-k-). [ME, f. OF *ierarchie* or LL (*ier-*) f. Gk *hierarkhia* (as prec.)]

hierät′ic, a. Of the priests (esp. of ancient Egyptian writing, & of Egyptian & Greek traditional styles of art); priestly. [f. L f. Gk *hieratikos* f. *hieraomai* be a priest (*hiereus*), -IC]

hiero- in comb. = Gk *hieros* sacred, holy, as: ~*cracy* (-ŏk²), priestly rule; ~*gram,* ~*graph,* (hĭ²), sacred inscription or symbol; ~*latry* (-ŏl²), worship of saints; ~*logў* (-ŏl²), sacred literature or lore.

hi′eroglўph, n. Figure of an object standing for a word, syllable, or sound, as used in ancient Egyptian & other writing; writing of this kind; secret symbol; writing difficult to make out. [f. foll.]

hieroglўph′ic, a. & n. **1.** Of, written in, hieroglyphs; symbolical. **2.** n. pl. Hieroglyphs. Hence~AL a.,~ALLY[2] adv. [f. F *-ique* or LL f. Gk HIERO(*gluphikos* f. *gluphē* carving, see -IC)]

hi′erophănt, n. (Gk Ant.) Initiating priest; expounder of sacred mysteries. Hence **hierophăn′tIC** a. [f. LL f. Gk HIERO(*phantēs* f. *phainō* show)]

hi′-fi′. See HIGH-*fidelity.*

hig′gle,v.i. Dispute about terms; chaffer. [app. modification of HAGGLE]

hig′gledy-pig′gledў (-geld-), adv., a., & n. (In) utter confusion. [symbolic]

high (hī), a., n., & adv. **1.** Of great or specified upward extent, as *a ~ hill, one inch ~;* situated far above ground, sea level, etc.; upper, inland, as *H~ Asia, H~ Dutch, German;* (of physical actions) extending to or from, performed at, a

height, as ~ *jump,* ~ *flying;* of exalted rank; *the Most H~,* God; of exalted quality, as ~ *art,* ~ *minds;* ~ *spirit* (courageous, enterprising); *a* ~ (very favourable) *opinion of;* ~ *life,* that of the upper classes; ~ (luxurious) *feeding;* (of meat or game) slightly tainted; great, intense, extreme, as *in* ~ *favour,* ~ *pressure,* ~ *temperature; how is that for* ~ *?* (sl. appeal to wonder); ~ *latitude* (far from equator); ~ *colour,* (esp.) red complexion, flush, blush; expensive, as *corn is* ~; (of time) far advanced, as ~ *noon, it is* ~ *time to go;* (of sounds) acute in pitch, shrill; ~ (angry) *words;* extreme in opinion, as *a* ~ *Tory;* ~ (elated, hilarious) *spirits;* ~ *& dry,* (of ship) out of the water, (fig.) out of the current of events, stranded; (of officers etc.) chief, as *H~ Admiral, Chancellor; with a* ~ HAND; *on the* ~ HORSE; ~ *& low,* (people) of all conditions, (adv.) everywhere (esp. *search* ~ *& low*); ~ *& mighty,* arrogant; *on the* ~ *ropes,* (colloq.) elated, disdainful, enraged. **2.** n. A ~ level or figure; the ~est card dealt or drawn; *from on* ~, from heaven or a ~ place; *on* ~, in or to heaven or a ~ place; *the H~* (colloq.), H~ Street, esp. at Oxford. **3.** adv. Far up, aloft; in, to, a ~ degree; at a ~ price; (of sounds) at, to, a ~ pitch; *play* ~, play for ~ stakes, play card of ~ value; *run* ~, (of sea) have strong current with ~ tide (also fig. of feelings). **4.** ~ (chief) *altar;* *~-′ball,* a whisky-and-soda served in a tall glass; ~-*blower,* horse that flaps nostrils noisily; ~-*born,* of noble birth; ~-′*brow,* a. & n. (colloq.), (person) of detached intellectual or cultural interests (~-*browed,* of~brow kind); *H~ Church* n. & a., (party, principles) giving a ~ place to authority of Episcopate and priesthood, saving grace of sacraments, etc.; *H~-Churchman,* holder of these principles; ~(*er*) *command,* the commander-in-chief of an army and his staff; ||*H~ Court* (*of Justice*), court below Court of Appeal, see JUDICATURE; ~ *day,* festal day; ~ EXPLOSIVE; ~ *falut′in(g)* (-lōo-) a. & n. [orig. unkn.], bombast(ic); ~ *farming,* extensive use of fertilizers in cultivation; ~-*fidelity* a., (of radio receiver etc.) reproducing sound faithfully (colloq. abbr. *hi-fi*); ~′*flown,* extravagant, bombastic; ~-*flyer, -flier,* (fig.) ambitious person, one who has ~-flown notions; ~′*flying,* (fig.) ambitious; ~ FREQUENCY; ~-*handed,* overbearing, arbitrary; *~-hat,* (n.) person affecting superiority, (v.t.) treat superciliously, (v.i.) assume a superior attitude; ~ JINKS; *High′lander,* inhabitant of (esp. the Scottish) Highlands; *Highland line,* imaginary line dividing Highlands of Scotland from Lowlands; ~′*lands,* mountainous or elevated country, esp. (*Highlands*) hilly parts of N. Scotland; ~′*light,* (of paintings etc.) any of the brightest parts of the subject or its representation (often pl.), moment or detail of vivid interest, outstanding feature; ~'*light* v.t., bring into prominence; ~*lows* (arch.), boots reaching over ankles; ~ MASS¹; ~*-mind'ed*, of morally lofty character, (arch.) proud (*Lord, I am not* ~*-minded*); ~*-mind'edness*, one of these qualities; ~*-pitched*, (of sound) acute in pitch, (of roof etc.) steep, (fig.) of lofty character; ~ *priest*, chief priest, esp. of the Jews; ~ *priori road* (joc.), resort to assumption (see A PRIORI) in preference to reasoning; ~*-ranking*, senior; ~ *road*, main road; ~ *school* (for secondary education); ~ SEAS; ~*spirited*, of lofty or courageous spirit; ~*stepp'er*, horse that lifts its feet ~ in walking & trotting (also fig.); ‖ *H*~ *Street* (often proper name of principal street in town, at Oxford usu. *the H*~); ~*strung*, in ~ state of vigour or sensitiveness; ‖ ~ *table* (for the fellows of college, colloq. *the* ~); ~ *tea*, tea at which meat is served; ~ TIDE; ~ TREASON; ~ *water*, state of tide when water is ~est, time when tide is at the full; ~*-wa'ter mark*, level reached at ~ water, (fig.) recorded maximum in any fluctuation; ~*way*, public road (often *the queen's, king's,* ~*way*), main route by land or water, (fig.) ordinary direct course (of action etc.); ‖ *Highway Code,* an official code of directions for road users (first issued 1930); ~*wayman*, man (usu. mounted, cf. FOOT-*pad*) who robs passengers on ~way; ~-WING. [OE *hēah*, OS, OHG *hōh*, ON *hár*, Goth. *hauhs* f. Gmc *hauhaz*]

high'lỹ (hīl-), adv. In a high degree, as ~ *amusing,* ~ *polished,* ~ *probable*; commend, esteem, ~; honourably, favourably, as *think, speak,* ~ *of*; ~ *descended* (of noble parentage). [OE *hēalice* (as prec., see -LY²)]

high'nèss (hīn-), n. Title of various British and other princes etc., as *His, Her, (Royal, Serene, Imperial) H*~; (used where *height* is not idiomatic) *the* ~ *of his character, of taxation, fell from sheer* ~ *of* (but *reached the height of his*) *ambition.* [OE *hēanes* (as HIGH, see -NESS)]

hight (hīt), p.p. (arch., poet., joc.). Called, named. [p.p. (from 14th c.) of OE *hātan*]

ˠhiˑjäcker, n. (sl.). Person who preys on bootleggers, appropriating & profiting by their illicit liquor. [orig. unkn.]

hijra. = HEGIRA.

hīke, n., & v.i. & t. (colloq.). 1. Long tramp in the country undertaken for pleasure or exercise, walking-tour. 2. vb. Walk vigorously or laboriously; go for long tramp; HITCH*-*; hoist, shove, force to move. Hence **hīk'ER¹** n. [orig. unkn.]

hilār'ious, a. Mirthful, joyous. Hence or cogn.~LY² adv.,~NESS, hilă'RITY, nn. [f. L *hilaris* +-OUS]

‖ **Hil'arỹ,** n. ~ *term*, legal or university term beginning in Jan. [*Hilarius,* d. 367, w. festival 13 Jan.]

hill, n., & v.t. Natural elevation of earth's surface, small mountain; *the* ~s (Anglo-Ind.), a ~-station as health-resort etc.; heap, mound, however raised, as *ant-. dung-, mole-,* ~; (v.t.) form into ~, bank up (plants) with soil. Hence ~'Y² a., ~'ÍNESS n. [OE *hyll*, MDu. *hil(le), hul,* LG *hull*; cogn. w. L *collis*]

hillō', -loa' (-lō), (or hǐ*-*), int. used to hail distant person or to express surprise at meeting. [cf. HALLO]

hill'ock, n. Small hill or mound. [-OCK]

hilt, n., & v.t. Handle of sword or dagger; *prove* etc. *up to the* ~, completely; (v.t.) furnish with ~. [OE, MDu. *hilt,* ON *hjalt*; also OS *hilta,* OHG *helza*]

hil'um, n. (bot.; pl. *-la*). Point of attachment of seed to seed-vessel. [L, = little thing, trifle]

him, pron. Objective case of HE; colloq. also subjective, esp. after *than,* as *that's* ~, *you are worse than* ~. [OE, dat. of HE & IT]

himsèlf', pron. Emphatic & reflexive form corr. to HE, as *he did it* ~, *he* ~ *told me, I saw the man* ~, *he hurt* ~; *he is not* ~ (not in his normal state of body or mind). [HIM + SELF]

hind¹, n. Female of (esp. red) deer, esp. in and after third year. [OE, ON *hind,* also OHG *hinta*; f. Gmc **hindō*]

‖ **hind²,** n. Farm servant, esp. (in Scotland & northern England) married & skilled farm-workman, formerly having charge of two horses, & provided with cottage on the farm; steward; rustic, boor. [ME *hine* f. OE *hīne* pl., app. f. *hīna, hīgna* gen. pl. of *hīgan, hīwan* 'members of a family'; cf. HIDE³]

hind³, a. Situated at the back, posterior, (less usu. than *hinder* exc. of things in pairs, front & back, as ~ *leg, quarters, wheel*). [ME (cf. OE *hindan* adv.), of uncert. orig.; perh. (1) shortened f. OE *behindan* BEHIND, or (2), less likely, f. HINDER adj.; ult. extended f. *hin-* (HENCE) f. *hi-* (HE)]

hind'er¹, a. See prec.

hin'der², v.t. Impede, obstruct, prevent, as *you will* ~ *him,* ~ *his work,* ~ *its completion,* ~ *him from working* (or abs.). [ME *hindre* f. OE *hindrian* (= ON *hindra,* OHG *hintarōn*) f. Gmc **hindar* HIND³]

Hin'di (-ē), a. & n. (Of) a major set of languages (*W. & E.* ~) of N. India. [Hindi (*Hind* India)]

hind'most, a. Furthest behind; most remote. [HIND³]

hin'drance, n. Obstruction, prevention; obstacle. [f. HINDER² + -ANCE]

hind'sight (-sīt), n. Back sight of gun; (joc.) wisdom after the event (opp. *fore-sight*). [HIND³, SIGHT¹]

Hindu' (-dōō), **-doo'**, (or hǐ*-*), n. & a. 1. Aryan of N. India who (also, any one who) professes Hinduism. 2. adj. Of the ~s, that is a ~; (loosely) Indian. [Pers., f. *hind* India = Skr. *Sindhu* river (esp. the Indus)]

Hin'duism (-ōō-), **-dōōïsm**, n. Polytheistic religion of the Hindus. [-ISM]

Hin'duïze (-ōō-), **-dōōïze**, **-ise** (-iz), v.t. Render Hindu in religion, customs, etc. [-IZE]

Hindusta'ni (-ahnē), a. & n. **1.** adj. Of Hindustan or its people; of Hindustani. **2.** n. An Indic language with large admixture of Arabic, Persian, etc., current as standard language & lingua franca in much of India & Pakistan. [Hindi, = of *Hindustan* (HINDU + -*stan* place)]

hinge (-j), n., & v.t. & i. **1.** Movable joint or mechanism like that by which door is hung on side post; natural joint doing similar work, as that of bivalve shell; small piece of gummed paper for fastening postage stamp to album or sheet; *off the* ~*s*, in disordered state of body or mind; (fig.) central principle, critical point, on which all turns. **2.** v.t. Attach (as) with ~. **3.** v.i. (Of door etc. or fig.) hang & turn *on* (post, principle, etc.). Hence **hing**ED[2] (-jd), ~'LESS (-jl-), aa. [ME *heng* rel. to HANG; cf. MLG *heng(e)*, Du. *henghe* hinge]

hinn'ȳ[1], n. Offspring of she-ass by stallion, cf. MULE[1]. [f. L *hinnus*]

‖ **hinn'ȳ**[2], **-nie.** See HONEY.

hint, n., & v.t. & i. **1.** Slight indication, covert or indirect suggestion. **2.** v.t. Suggest slightly (thing, *that*). **3.** v.i. ~ *at*, give a ~ of. [(vb f. n.) app. f. obs. *hent* (OE *hentan*) lay hold of, of uncert. orig.]

hin'terländ, n. District behind coast or river's banks, freq. with suggestion of sparse population or inferior civilization. [G]

hip[1], n. Projection of pelvis & upper part of thigh-bone, in men & quadrupeds; *have* (person) *on the* ~ (at a disadvantage); *smite* ~ *& thigh* (unsparingly); (Archit.) arris of roof from ridge to eaves; ~-*bath* (in which one sits immersed to the ~s); ~-*disease* (of ~-joint, with fungous growth); ~-*roof* (with ends as well as sides inclined). Hence (-)**hipp**ED[2] (-pt) a. [OE *hype*, OHG *huf*, Goth. *hups* f. Gmc *hupiz*]

hip[2], **hĕp**, n. Fruit of (esp. wild) rose. [OE *hēope*, OS *hiopo*, OHG *hiufo* f. Gmc *heup-*]

hip[3], **hȳp**, n. Morbid depression, the blues. [= *hyp*(*ochondria*)]

hip[4], v.t. (-pp-). Make low-spirited. [f. prec.]

hip[5], int. introducing united cheer, as ~, ~, *hurrah*.

hipe, v.t., & n. Throw (antagonist in wrestling) in a particular manner; (n.) such throw. [perh. f. HIP[1]]

hipp'ō, n. (colloq.; pl. ~*s*). Hippopotamus. [abbr.]

hippo- in comb. = Gk *hippos* horse, as: ~*cen'taur*, = CENTAUR; ~*phagy* (-ŏf-), practice of eating horse-flesh; ~PHIL (hǐ-); ~PHOB'IA.

hippocăm'pus, n. (pl. *-pī*). Kinds of small fishes, sea-horse; (Anat.) ~ *major*, *minor*, eminences on floor of each lateral ventricle of brain. [f. L f. Gk HIPPO- (*kampos* sea-monster)]

hipp'ocrăs, n. (hist.). Wine flavoured with spices. [ME, f. OF *ipocras* f. *Hippokratēs* Gk physician of 5th c. B.C., prob. because strained through filter called *Hippocrates's sleeve*]

Hipp'ocrēne, n. Fountain on Mount Helicon sacred to the Muses. [L f. Gk (*hippos* horse, *krēnē* fountain, as having been produced by stroke of Pegasus's hoof)]

hipp'odrōme, n. (Gk & Rom. Ant.) course for chariot races etc.; circus; (*H*~) theatre for various stage entertainments. [F, or f. L f. Gk HIPPO(*dromos* race, course)]

hipp'ogriph, **-grȳph**, n. Fabulous griffin-like creature with body of horse. [f. F *hippogriffe* f. It. *ippogrifo* (HIPPO- + *grifo* GRIFFIN)]

hippopŏt'amus, n. (pl. *-muses*, *-mī*). Large African pachydermatous quadruped inhabiting rivers etc. [ME, f. L f. Gk HIPPO(*potamos* river)]

hïr'cine, a. Goat-like. [f. L *hircinus* (*hircus* goat, see -INE[1])]

hïre[1], n. Payment by contract for use of thing or for personal service; engagement on these terms; (fig.) reward; ‖ ~-*purchase*, ~ *system* (by which hired thing becomes hirer's after certain number of payments); *on* ~, ready to be hired. [OE *hȳr*, OLG **hūria*, G *heuer* f. WG **hūrja*]

hïre[2], v.t. Employ (person) for wages; procure, grant (also ~ *out*), temporary use of (thing) for stipulated payment; **borrow* (money); **~d girl*, domestic servant. Hence **hïr'**ABLE a. [OE *hȳrian*, OLG **hurian* f. prec.]

hire'ling (hīr'l-), n. One who serves for hire (usu. derog.). [OE *hȳrling* (as HIRE[1], see -LING[1])]

hïrs'ūte, a. Hairy, shaggy; untrimmed. Hence ~NESS (-tn-) n. [f. L *hirsutus*]

his (hǐz), a. & pron. Possessive case of, & adj. corr. to, HE, also in absolute use, as ~ *hat, it is* ~. [OE, genit. of HE & IT]

his'pid, a. (bot., zool.). Shaggy; bristly. [f. L *hispidus*]

hiss, v.i. & t., & n. (Of person, snake, goose, liquid poured on fire, etc.) (make) sharp sibilant sound of *s*, esp. as sign of disapproval or derision; express disapproval of (person etc.) thus; ~ *off* (the stage), *away, down,* etc., drive off etc. by ~es; utter (quoted words) with angry ~. [ME; imit.]

hist, int. used to call attention, enjoin silence, or incite dog etc.

histo-, comb. form of Gk *histos* web, tissue, in biol. wds. as: ~*gen'esis*, ~*geny* (-oj-), production of organic tissues; ~*genĕt'ic*, concerned with this; ~*logy* (-ŏl-), science of organic tissues, whence

~*lo'gical*, ~*logist* (-ŏl²); ~*lysis* (-ŏl²), breaking down of organic tissues.

histōr'ian, n. Writer of history (esp. in higher sense, as opp. to mere annalist or compiler); *English, ancient,* ~, writer or student of English, ancient, history. [f. F *historien* f. L as HISTORY +-AN]

histōr'iātĕd, a. (Of ornamental letters etc.) decorated with figures of men or animals. [f. med. L *historiare* (as HISTORY), see -ATE²]

histō'ric, a. Noted in history; (Lat. & Gk Gram.) ~ *tenses*, those normally used of past events, imperfect, Gk aorist & Lat. perfect in same sense, pluperfect, (cf. PRIMARY), ~ *present* (used for past), ~ *infinitive* (used for indicative); = foll. [f. L f. Gk *historikos* (as HISTORY, see -IC)]

histō'rical, a. Of history, as ~ *evidence, principles*; belonging to history, not legend; ~ *method* (of investigation), that based on history; in connexion with history, from the historian's point of view (*of purely* ~ *interest*); belonging to the past, not of the present; (of novel, picture, etc.) dealing with ~ events; = prec. Hence ~LY² adv. [-AL]

histori'citў, n. Historical character, genuineness, of alleged event etc. [-ITY]

histōriŏg'rapher, n. Writer of history, esp. official historian of a court etc. [f. LL *historiographus* (as HISTORY, see -GRAPHER)]

histōriŏg'raphў, n. Writing of history. Hence **histōriŏgrăph'IC**(AL) aa. [f. Gk *historiographia* (as foll., see -GRAPHY)]

his'torў, n. Continuous methodical record of public events; (no pl.) study of growth of nations; whole train of events connected with nation, person, thing, etc.; eventful past career, as *this knife has a* ~; (no pl.) aggregate of past events, course of human affairs; *ancient* ~ (usu. to A.D. 476), (joc.) thing that is out of date; *medieval, modern,* ~ (to, from, 15th c.); systematic account of natural phenomena etc., esp. NATURAL¹ ~; historical play. [late ME, f. L *historia*]

his'trion, n. Stage-player (usu. derŏg.). [16th c. f. F, or L *histrio*]

histriŏn'|ic, a. & n. 1. Of actors or acting; stagy, hypocritical, whence **his'trion**ISM, ~ICISM, nn. 2. n. pl. Theatricals, theatrical art, pretence. Hence ~ICALLY adv. [17th c. (16th c. -*ical*) f. prec., or as prec., +-IC; cf. LL *histrionicus*, F -*ique*]

hit¹, v.t. & i. (*hit*). Strike with blow or missile; direct blow *at*; (of moving body) strike; (intr.) strike *against, upon*; deliver (blow, person etc. a blow); (fig.) affect sensibly, wound, as *hard* ~ (e.g. by money losses); (also ~ *upon*) light upón, get at, (thing aimed at); (also ~ *off*) imitate to a nicety; fall in with, suit; ~ *below the belt*, play foul in boxing & fig.; ~ *it*, ~ *the* (right) *nail on the head*, guess right, express the exact truth; ~ *it off*,

agree (*with, together*); ~ *out*, deal vigorous blows; ~ *up* (Cricket), score, make (runs). [late OE *hittan*, f. ON *hitta* meet with]

hit², n. Blow, stroke; stroke of sarcasm etc. (*at*); stroke of good luck; successful attempt. [f. prec.]

hitch¹, v.t. & i. Move (thing) with jerk; shift; ~ *up*, lift with jerk; contrive to bring (thing *into* story etc.); fasten with loop, hook, etc.; become so fastened (*in, on to,* etc.); ~ one's WAGGON *to a star*; *~-hike* v.i., & n., travel by begging lifts from passing motor vehicles. [15th c., of obsc. orig.; partly syn. w. Sc. *hotch* move by jerks]

hitch², n. Jerk, abrupt pull or push; (Naut.) noose, knot, of various kinds, as *half* ~ (formed by passing end of rope round its standing part & then through the bight); CLOVE~; temporary stoppage; impediment. [f. prec.]

hith'er (-dh-), adv. & a. 1. To, towards, this place (now usu. *here*); ~ *& thither*, in various directions, here & there. 2. adj. Situated on this side, *the* nearer (of two). 3. *~to'* (-tŏŏ), up to this time; *~ward* (arch.), in this direction. [OE *hider*, corresp. to ON *hethra*, Goth. *hidrē*, f. *hi-* (HE) +suf. cogn. w. L (*ci*)*tra*; -*th-* as in FATHER]

Hit'ler|ism, n. The political system, aims, or methods of the German Fuehrer, Adolf Hitler (1889–1945). So ~ITE¹(1) a. & n. [-ISM]

Hitt'ite, n. & a. 1. Member, language, of an ancient people of Turkey & Syria. 2. adj. Of the ~s or ~. [f. Heb. *Hittīm*]

hive, n., & v.t. & i. 1. (Also *bee*~) artificial habitation for bees; (fig.) busy swarming place; ~ful of bees; swarming multitude; ~-shaped thing. 2. v.t. Place (bees) in ~, house (persons etc.) snugly, hoard up; (v.i.) enter ~, live together like bees; ~ *off*, (of firm) assign production of some goods to subsidiary company. [OE *hŷf* (= Gmc type **hūfiz*), not repr. elsewhere in Gmc; whence ON *húfr* hull of ship]

hives (-vz), n. pl. Skin eruption; inflammation of bowels, larynx, etc. [Sc. & north. (f. c. 1500), of unkn. orig.]

h'm. = HEM³, HUM².

hō, int. expr. surprise, admiration, triumph, derision; calling attention; added to other intt. as *heigh-ho, what ho*, or (Naut.) to name of destination etc., as *westward ho*. [ME; imit.; cf. ON *hó*]

hoar (hōr), a. & n. 1. Grey-haired with age; greyish white; ~-*frost*, frozen water vapour deposited in clear still weather on lawns etc.; (of things) grey with age; ǁ~'*stone*, ancient boundary stone. 2. n. Hoariness, ~-frost. [OE *hār*, OHG *hēr*, ON *hárr* f. Gmc **hairaz*]

hoard (hōrd), n., & v.t. & i. 1. Stock, store, (esp. of money) laid by; amassed stock of facts etc.; (Archaeol.) ancient cache of treasure etc. 2. v.t. Amass (money etc. or abs.) & put away, store *up*; treasure up in the heart; (v.i.) overstock oneself with food etc. in time of scarcity. [OE, OS *hord*, OHG *hort*, ON *hodd*, Goth. *huzd* f. Gmc **huzdom*]

‖ **hoard′ing** (hōr-), n. Fence of boards round building during erection or repairs, often used for posting bills. [f. obs. *hoard* (-ING¹) f. AN *hurdis* f. OF *hourd*, *hourt* f. WG **hord* (= OHG *hurd*); see HURDLE]

hoarhound. See HOREHOUND.

hoarse (hōrs), a. (Of voice) rough, husky, croaking; having such a voice. Hence ~′LY² (-sl-) adv., **hoars′**EN⁶ v.t. & i., ~⁻ NESS (-sn-) n. [late ME *hors* f. ON **hārs* f. Gmc **hairsaz*; earlier ME *hōs*, OE *hās*, OS *hēs*, OHG *heis(i)* f. Gmc **haisaz*]

hoar′‖y (hōr-), a. (Of hair) grey, white, with age; having such air, venerable; (Bot., Entom.) covered with short white hairs. Hence ~iNESS n. [-Y²]

hoax, v.t., & n. **1.** Deceive, take in, (person) by way of joke. **2.** n. Humorous or mischievous deception. [*c.* 1800, app. contr. f. HOCUS]

hob, n. Side casing of fireplace, having surface level with top of grate; peg, pin, as mark in quoits etc.; ‖ shoe of sledge; = HOBNAIL. [orig. unkn.]

hŏb′ble¹, v.i. & t. Walk lamely, limp; (fig.) proceed haltingly in action or speech; (of verse) have halting rhythm; cause to ~; tie together legs of (horse etc.) to prevent it from straying etc.; tie (legs) thus. [(1) 14th c.; prob. LG; cf. Du. *hobbelen* rock from side to side, stammer; (2) see HOPPLE]

hŏb′ble², n. Uneven or infirm gait; awkward situation; rope, clog, etc., for hobbling horse etc.; ~ *skirt* (so narrow at foot as to impede wearer in walking). [f. prec.]

hŏb′blede|hoy′ (-beldĭ-), hŏbbad-, hŏbbĕd-, n. Awkward youth, between boyhood & manhood. Hence ~hoy′HOOD, ~hoy′ISM, nn., ~hoy′ISH¹ a. (-beldĭ-). [16th c.; of many forms, & much disputed orig.]

hŏbb′y̆, n. Favourite subject or occupation that is not one's main business; (arch.) small horse; (hist.) early type of velocipede. [ME *hobyn, hoby*, a by-name of *Robin*; cf. DOBBIN]

hŏbb′y̆², n. A small falcon. [f. OF *hobe*]

hŏbb′y̆-horse, n. Wicker horse used in morris-dance etc.; child's stick with horse's head; rocking-horse; horse on merry-go-round; (now rare) = HOBBY¹.

hŏb′gŏblin, n. Mischievous imp; bogy; bugbear. [f. *hob* for *Rob(in)*+GOBLIN]

hŏb′nail, n. Heavy-headed nail for boot-soles. [HOB]

hŏb′nailed (-ld), a. Furnished or set with hobnails; ~ *liver* (studded with projections like nail-heads). [-ED²]

hŏb′-nŏb, v.i. (-bb-). Drink together; hold familiar intercourse (*with*). [f. *hob*

or *nob* = give & take, earlier *hab nab*, = have or not have]

*hŏb′ō, n. (pl. ~s). Wandering workman or tramp. [orig. unkn.]

Hŏb′son's choice. See CHOICE¹. [person]

hŏck¹, n. Joint of quadruped's hindleg between true knee & fetlock. [southern by-form of HOUGH]

hŏck², n. German white wine (prop. that of Hochheim). [17th c., short f. G *Hoch-heimer*]

hŏck³, v.t., & n. (sl.). Pawn, pledge; *in* ~, in pawn, in prison, or in debt. [f. Du. *hok* in sl. sense of debt]

hŏck′ey, n. Game played with ball (or puck in *ice* ~) & curved clubs between goals. [16th c., orig. unkn.]

Hŏck′tide, n. (hist.). Old festival kept on second Monday and Tuesday after Easter. [f. *hoke*, of unkn. orig.]

hōc′us, v.t. (-ss-). Take in, hoax; stupefy (person) with drugs; drug (liquor). [f. obs. n. *hocus*=foll.]

hōc′us-pōc′us, n., & v.i. & t. (-ss-). Jugglery, deception; typical conjuring formula; (v.i.) juggle; (v.t.) play tricks on. [17th-c. sham L]

hŏd, n. Builder's light open trough on staff for carrying mortar etc.; ~′*man*, labourer who carries ~, (fig.) mechanical worker, literary hack. [prob. = dial. *hot* f. OF *hotte* pannier, of Gmc orig.]

‖ **hŏdd′en**, n. (Sc.). Coarse woollen cloth; ~ *grey*, grey ~, typical rustic garb. [orig. unkn.]

‖ **Hŏdge**, n. Typical English agricultural labourer. [pet form of *Roger*]

hŏdge′pŏdge, n. = HOTCHPOTCH. [assim. to prec.]

hŏdiẽrn′al, a. Of the present day. [f. L *hodiernus (hodie* today)+-AL]

hŏdŏm′eter, ŏd-, n. Instrument for measuring distance travelled by wheeled vehicle. [f. F *odomètre* f. Gk *hodos* way, see -METER]

hoe, n., & v.t. & i. (part. ~*ing*). **1.** Tool for loosening soil, scraping up weeds, etc.; *Dutch* ~, kind pushed forward by user. **2.** v.t. Weed (crops), loosen (ground), dig *up*, cut *down*, with ~; (v.i.) use ~. [ME, f. OF *houe* f. OFrank. *hauwa* f. Gmc **hauwan* HEW]

hŏg¹, n. Swine, esp. castrated male reared for slaughter; ‖ (dial.) young sheep before first shearing; (fig.) coarse, gluttonous, or filthy person; = ROAD¹·~; *go the whole* ~, do the thing thoroughly; ~′*back*, ~'*s-back*, crested hill-ridge; ~*-fish*, fish with bristles on head; ~ *in armour*, stiff clumsy person; ~ *mane*, horse's mane cut short; ~'*s pudding*, ~'s entrail variously stuffed; ~*-wash*, kitchen swill etc. for ~s. Hence ~g′ISH¹ (-g-), ~′LIKE, aa., ~g′ish-LY² adv., ~g′ishNESS, ~′LING¹, nn. [14th c.; deriv. *hoggaster* 12th c.; orig. unkn.]

hŏg², v.t. & i. (-gg-). Raise (back etc.), rise, archwise in the centre; cut (mane)

short; (colloq.) behave like a road-hog.
[f. prec.]

‖ **hŏgg′ĕt** (-g-), n. Yearling sheep. [HOG¹
+-ET¹]

hŏgg′in (-g-), n. Mixture of sand & gravel.
[19th c., of unkn. orig.]

hŏg′manay, n. (Sc.). Last day of year;
gift of cake etc. demanded by children
on that day. [17th c., corresp. in sense &
use to OF *aguillanneuf*, of unkn. orig.;
the Norman form *hoguinané* may have
been the immed. source]

hŏgs′head (-z-hĕd), n. Large cask; liquid
measure, 52½ imperial gallons (abbr. *hhd*).
[ME, f. HOG¹+HEAD; orig. unexpl.]

hoi(c)k, v.t. & i. Force (aeroplane) to
turn abruptly upwards; ~ aeroplane.
[orig. unkn.]

hoick(s), int. used to incite hounds (also
yoicks). [orig. unkn.]

hoi polloi. See POLLOI.

hoist¹, v.t., & n. **1.** Raise aloft (esp. flags);
raise by means of tackle etc. **2.** n. ~ing,
shove up; goods elevator, lift. [16th c.
alt. of *hoise* f. (15th c.) *hysse*, prob. of LG
orig.; cf. LG *hissen* (16th c.), Du. *hijschen*]

hoist², p.p. ~ *with his own petard*, blown
up by his own bomb, ruined by his own
devices against others. [p.p. of *hoise*, see
prec.]

hoit′y̆-toit′y̆, n., a., & int. **1.** n. (arch.).
Riotous or giddy conduct. **2.** adj. Frolicsome; haughty; petulant. **3.** int. expr.
surprised protest at undue assumption
etc. [17th c., f. obs. *hoit* indulge in riotous
mirth; orig. unkn.]

hŏk′ey-pōk′ey, n. = HOCUS-POCUS; cheap
ice-cream sold by street vendors. [f.
HOCUS-POCUS; second sense of unkn. orig.]

hŏk′um, n. (orig. U.S., sl.). Theatrical
plot or business, (now esp.) film scenario,
designed to appeal to the uncritical;
bunkum. [orig. unkn.]

hōld¹, v.t. & i. (*hĕld*; also arch. p.p. ~*en*
in formal reports of meetings etc.). **1.**
Keep fast, grasp (*held !* at Rugby football, claim that ball being held by opponent as well as runner must be put down);
keep (oneself, one's head, etc.) in particular attitude, esp. *up*; (of vessel) contain;
possess, be the owner or holder or tenant
of, (property, stocks, land); (Mil.) keep
possession of (place); occupy (place,
person's thoughts, etc.); engross (person,
his attention); keep (person etc.) in specified place, condition, etc., as ~ *him at bay,
in suspense*; *detain in custody; ~ *thing
over* one, threaten him constantly with it;
make (person) adhere *to* (terms, promise);
observe, celebrate, conduct, (festival,
meeting, conversation); use (insolent etc.
language); ~ *to* (bind by) *bail*; restrain,
as ~ *your noise, tongue*, (~ one's *hand*,
refrain from punishing or other action;
there is no ~ing him etc., he etc. is restive
or in high spirits or determined); think,
believe, (thing, *that*, person etc. *to* be; ~
it good, think it advisable *to* do); (of judge

or court) lay down, decide (*that*); entertain specified feeling towards, as ~ *him
in esteem, contempt*; ~ thing *cheap* (not
value it); ~ *dear* (regard with affection).
2. intr. Remain unbroken, not give way;
~ *by, to*, adhere to (choice, purpose, etc.);
~ *with* (sl., usu. neg.), approve of; (of
laws etc., also ~ *good, true*) be valid,
apply; keep going, esp. ~ *on* one's *way*;
(arch.) ~ *!*, stop, wait. **3.** ~ one's *head
high*, behave proudly; ~ *up* one's *head*,
not be downcast; ~ one's *ground*, or
one's *own*, not give way, (of sick person)
not get worse; ~ *the BABY*; ~ *water*, (fig.)
be sound, bear examination. **4.** ~ *aloof*,
avoid communication with persons etc.;
~ *back*, (trans.) restrain, (intr.) hesitate,
refrain *from*; *~ *down*, remain in (one's
situation), keep (one's job); ~ *forth*, speak
publicly (usu. derog.); ~ *hard*, stop (imperative); ~ *in*, confine, keep in check;
~ *off*, (intr.) delay; ~ *on*, keep one's grasp
on something, not ring off, (colloq. imper.)
stop; ~ *out*, (trans.) stretch forth, offer
(inducement etc.), (intr.) endure, persist,
(of besieged fortress etc.) keep from
yielding; ~ *over*, postpone; ~ *together* t.
& i., (cause to) cohere; ~ *up*, support,
sustain, (lit. & fig.), exhibit, display, (esp.
to derision etc.), arrest progress of, obstruct, stop & rob on highway, (of horse)
keep up, not fall; *~up*, detention by
force (of person, vehicle, train, etc.)
for purposes of robbery (also attrib.),
stoppage or delay by traffic, fog, etc.
5. *~all*, portable case for clothes etc.;
~back, hindrance; *~fast*, firm grasp,
staple or clamp securing object to wall
etc. [OE *h(e)aldan*, OS *haldan*, OHG
halten, ON *halda*, Goth. *haldan*]

hōld², n. Grasp (lit. & fig.), esp. *take, get,
keep, ~ of*; opportunity of holding, thing
to hold by; (fig.) ~ (*on*), influence (over).
[f. prec.]

hōld³, n. Cavity in ship below deck, where
cargo is stowed. [16th c. alt. of 15th c.
holl, hole, f. MDu. *hol* HOLE]

hōld′er, n. In vbl senses, esp.: occupant
of office etc.; contrivance for holding
something, as *cigar, pen*, ~. [-ER¹]

hōld′ing, n. In vbl senses, esp.: tenure of
land; land held; stocks etc. held; ~ *company*, one created to hold the shares of
other companies. [-ING¹]

hōle¹, n. Hollow place in solid body;
deep place in stream etc.; animal's
burrow; small mean abode; cavity into
which ball etc. must be got in various
games; (Golf) point scored by player who
gets ball from one ~ to another with
fewest strokes, distance from tee to ~;
perforation; (sl.) awkward situation (*am
in rather, a devil of, a hole*); FOX¹~;
FUNK-~; *pick ~s in*, find fault with; *make
a ~ in*, use large amount of; *round* (square)
peg in square (round) ~, person not fitted
for his place; *~-&-corner*, secret, underhand. Hence **hōl′ey²** a. [OE, OS, OHG,

ON *hol*, neut. of adj. *hol* f. Gmc **hulaz*; cogn. w. HELL, HELM[1], HOLLOW]

hōle[2], v.t. & i. Make holes in; (Naut.) pierce side of (ship); make (shaft, tunnel); (Mining, intr.) dig through from one working to another; put into hole; (also ~ *out*) put (golf-ball, or abs.) into hole. [OE *holian*, as prec.]

hŏl'iday (-dĭ *or* -dă), n. Day of cessation from work or of recreation; (usu. pl.) period of this, vacation; ‖ BANK[2] ~; BLIND[1] *man's* ~; *make* ~, *take a* ~, cease from work; ~ (gay) *clothes*; ‖ ~ *task* (to be done by schoolboy during ~s); = HOLY *day*. [OE *hāligdæg*, see HOLY & DAY]

hŏl'ily, adv. In a holy manner. [-LY[2]]

hŏl'iness, n. Sanctity; *H*~, *his H*~, title of Pope. [OE *hāligness* (HOLY, -NESS)]

hŏl'ism, n. (philos.). Tendency in nature to form wholes that are more than the sum of the parts by creative evolution. [as HOLO- +-ISM]

hŏll'a, int. See HOLLO. [f. F *holà*]

Hŏll'and, n. Province of northern Netherlands, kingdom of the Netherlands, whence ~ER[1](4) n.; a linen fabric; *brown* ~, this unbleached. [Du., f. *holt* wood +*-lant* land]

Hŏll'ands (-z), n. A grain spirit. [f. Du. *hollandsch genever*, Holland gin]

hŏll'ō[1], int. calling attention; (n.) the cry ~. [conn. w. HOLLA]

hŏll'ō[2], -low[1] (-ō), -la, -loa (-ō), v.i. & t. Shout (i. & t.); call to hounds. [as prec.]

hŏll'ow[2] (-ō), a., n., & adv. Having a hole, not solid; ~ SQUARE; empty, hungry; (of sound) not full-toned; (fig.) empty, insincere, false; (n.) ~ place, hole, valley, basin; (adv.) *beaten* ~ (completely); ~-*eyed*, with eyes deep sunk; ~-*hearted*, insincere; ~ *race* etc., feebly contested; ~ *ware*, ~ articles of metal, china, etc., as pots, kettles, jugs. Hence ~LY[2] (-ŏli) adv., ~NESS (-ŏn-) n. [ME *holg, holu*, adj. f. OE *holh* n., cogn. w. HOLE[1]]

hŏll'ow[3] (-ō), v.t. (Also ~ *out*) excavate; bend into hollow shape. [f. prec.]

‖ **Hŏll'oway** (-o-w-), n. (Used for) ~ prison (for women; formerly for debtors). [place]

hŏll'y, n. Evergreen shrub with prickly leaves, small white flowers, & red berries. [f. OE *holegn* (dial. *hollin*), cogn. w. OS, OHG *hulis* (G *hulst*)]

hŏll'yhŏck, n. Tall plant with large flowers of many varieties of colour. [f. HOLY + obs. *hock* mallow, OE *hoc*, of unkn. orig.]

Hŏll'ywŏŏd, n. (Used for) moving pictures of American type, chiefly made at ~ in California. [place]

holm[1], -me, (hōm), n. Islet, esp. in river or near mainland; ‖ flat ground by river, submerged in time of flood. [f. ON *holmr*]

holm[2] (hōm), n. (Usu. ~-*oak*) evergreen oak, ilex. [ME alt. of obs. *holin*; see HOLLY]

hŏl'o-, comb. form of Gk *holos*·whole, as: ~*graph* a. & n., (document) wholly in handwriting of person in whose name it

appears; ~*hĕd'ral*, (of crystal) having full number of planes for perfect symmetry; ~*metăb'ola* n. pl., insects undergoing complete metamorphosis; ~*phŏte*, apparatus for making available all the light of a lamp (in lighthouse etc.).

hŏl'ocaust, n. Whole burnt-offering; wholesale sacrifice (fig.) or destruction. [ME, f. OF *holocauste* f. LL f. Gk HOLO-*kauston* burnt f. *kaiō*)]

hŏlothūr'ian, a. & n. (Animal) of the genus *Holothuria*, sea-slug. [f. mod. L *Holothuria* n. pl. f. Gk *holothourion*, a zoophyte]

holpen. See HELP[1].

hŏl'ster, n. Leather case for pistol, fixed to saddle or worn on belt. [17th-c.; syn. w. Du. *holster*; rel. & orig. unkn.]

‖ **hŏlt**[1], n. (Poet.) wood, copse; wooded hill. [OE, OS, ON *holt*, OHG *holz* f. Gmc **hultaz*]

hŏlt[2], n. Animal's (esp. otter's) lair. [var. of HOLD[2]]

hŏl'us-bŏl'us, adv. All in a lump, altogether. [app. sham L]

hŏl'ў, a. & v. n. **1**. Consecrated, sacred; morally & spiritually perfect; belonging to, commissioned by, devoted to, God; of high moral excellence. **2**. n. ~ *of holies*, inner chamber of sanctuary in Jewish temple, separated by veil from ~ *place* or outer chamber, (fig.) innermost shrine. **3**. *H*~ *Alliance*, covenant formed in 1815–16 between the sovereigns of Russia, Prussia, and Austria, by which they bound themselves to be guided by Christian principles in domestic and foreign policy; *H*~ CITY; ~ *cross* (of Christ); *H*~ *Cross day*, festival of Exaltation of the Cross, Sep. 14: ~ *day*, religious festival; *H*~ FAMILY; *H*~ *Ghost*, *Spirit*, third person of the Godhead; *H*~ GRAIL; ~ *Joe* (naut. sl.), pious person; *H*~ *Land*, W. Palestine, esp. Judaea; *H*~ OFFICE; ~ ORDERS; *H*~ ROMAN *Empire*; ~ *terror* (sl.), formidable person, embarrassing child, bore; *H*~ *Thursday*, (prop.) Ascension Day, (pop.) Thursday in *H*~ Week; *H*~ *Saturday* (in *H*~ Week); ~ *water*, water dedicated to ~ uses, or blessed by a priest; *H*~ *Week* (before Easter Sunday); ~ *Willie*, a hypocritically pious person; *H*~ *Writ*, writings collectively, esp. the Bible. [OE *hālig*, OS *hēlag*, OHG *heilag*, ON *heilagr*, Goth. *hailags* f. Gmc **hailagaz* f. **hailaz* WHOLE]

hŏl'ўstōne, n., & v.t. (Scour with) soft sandstone used for scouring decks. [19th c.; cf. Du. *bijbel*, LG *bibel* in similar naut. use]

hŏm, n. Sacred plant of ancient Persians & Parsees; its juice. [Pers.]

hŏm'age, n. (Feud.) formal public acknowledgement of allegiance; acknowledgement of superiority, dutiful reverence, as *pay, do*, ~ *to* (person, his qualities). [ME, f. OF *omage* f. med. L *hominaticum* (*homo* -*minis* man, see -AGE)] *hombre* (ŏm'brā), n. Man. [Sp.]

Hŏm'bŭrg, n. (Used for) soft felt hat with narrow brim and dent in top of crown, trilby. [~ in Prussia, where first worn]

hōme[1], n., a., & adv. **1.** Dwelling-place; fixed residence of family or household; native land; ~ *of lost causes*, Oxford; *long* or *last* ~, the grave; place where thing is native or most common; institution of refuge or rest for destitute or infirm persons, as *convalescent, nursing,* ~ (for the sick); (in games) goal; *a ~ from* ~, place where one feels at ~; *at* ~, in one's own house or native land, at one's ease, familiar *with* or *on* or *in* (subject etc.), accessible to callers (esp. *not at* ~), (n.) see *ᴀᴛ*-ʜᴏᴍᴇ. **2.** adj. Of, connected with, ~; carried on at ~; proceeding from ~; in the neighbourhood of ~; ‖*H*~ *Counties,* those nearest to London (Middlesex, Surrey, Kent, Essex, & occas. Hertford & Sussex); carried on, produced, in one's own country, as ~ *industries, products; the* ~ *trade* or *market* (inland; opp. *foreign*); treating of domestic affairs; ‖*H*~ *Office,* department of Secretary of State for *H*~ Affairs, building used for this; that comes ~ to one, as ~ *question, truth, thrust.* **3.** adv. To one's ~ or country, as *come, go,* ~; arrived at ~, as *he is* ~; to the point aimed at, as *the thrust went* ~; as far as possible, as *drive a nail* ~; *bring charge* ~ *to* person, convict him of it; *come* ~ *to,* be realized by; *nothing to write* ~ *about* (colloq.), unexciting, trivial. **4.** ~-*born,* native; ~-*bred,* bred at ~; ~-*brewed* a. & n., (beer etc.) brewed at ~; ~-*cŏming,* arrival at home; ~-*felt,* felt intimately; *H*~ *Guard,* (member of) British citizen army formed in 1940 (orig. called *Local Defence Volunteers*); ~-*keeping* a., stay-at-home; ~-*made,* made át ~ or for ~ consumption; *H*~ *Rule,* government of a country by its own citizens; ~*'sick(ness),* depressed, depression, as result of absence from ~; ~*'work,* work (to be) done at ~, esp. lessons to be done by a school-child at ~. Hence ~*'ʟᴇss,* ~*'ʟɪᴋᴇ,* aa., (-ml-). [OE *hām,* OS *hēm,* OHG *heim,* ON *heimr,* Goth. *haims*]

hōme[2], v.i. & t. Go home (esp. of pigeons); send or guide homewards; furnish (person etc.) with a home. [f. prec.]

hōme'l|ў (-ml-), a. Simple, plain; primitive; unpretending; *(of persons or features) uncomely,·plain. Hence ~ɪɴᴇss ·n. [-ʟʏ[1]]

homeo-. See under *homoeo-.*

hōm'er, n. Homing pigeon. [-ᴇʀ[1]]

Home'ric, a. Of, in the style of, Homer or the poems ascribed to him; ~ *laughter* (like that of Homer's gods as they watched lame Hephaestus hobbling); ~ *question* (of authorship of *Iliad* & *Odyssey*). [f. L f. Gk *homērikos* (*Homēros;* traditional author of *Iliad* & *Odyssey,* see -ɪᴄ)]

hōme'spŭn (-ms-), a. & n. (Cloth made of yarn) spun at home; (anything) plain, homely.

hōme'stead (-mstĕd), n. House with outbuildings; farm. [OE *hāmstede* (ʜᴏᴍᴇ, sᴛᴇᴀᴅ)]

hōme'ward (-mw-), adv. & a., -**wards** (-z), adv. (Going, leading) towards home; ~-ʙᴏᴜɴᴅ[5], (esp. of ship) preparing to go, or on the way, home. [-ᴡᴀʀᴅ(s)]

hŏm'icide, n. **1.** One who kills a human being. **2.** Killing of a human being (*culpable, justifiable,*~). Hence **hŏmicid‿ᴀʟ** a. [ME, f. OF f. L (1) *homicida,* (2) *homicidium* (*homo* man, see -ᴄɪᴅᴇ)]

hŏmilĕt'ic, a. & n. Of homilies; (n. pl.) art of preaching. [f. LL f. Gk *homilētikos* (*homileō* hold converse, consort, as foll.; see -ᴇᴛɪᴄ)]

hŏm'il|ў, n. Sermon (*Books of H*~*ies,* for use in parish churches of the Ch. of England, published in 1547 & 1563); tedious moralizing discourse. [ME, f. OF *omelie* f. eccl. L f. Gk *homilia* f. *homilos* crowd (*homou* together + *ilē* crowd)]

hōm'ing, a. That goes home; (of pigeons) trained to fly home, bred for long-distance racing; ~ *device,* mechanism for automatic guiding of missiles. [part. of ʜᴏᴍᴇ[2]]

hŏm'inў, n. Coarsely ground maize boiled with water or milk. [of Amer.-Ind. orig.]

hŏm'ō, n. (zool.). Man; *H*~ *săp'iens* (L= wise), modern man regarded as a species. [L]

hŏm'o-, comb. form of Gk *homos* same, as: ~*cen'tric,* having same centre; ~*gamous* (-ŏg²), (Bot.) having all florets hermaphrodite or of same sex; ~*genĕt'ic,* having common descent or origin; ~*geny* (-ŏj'-), similarity due to common descent; ~*morph'ic,* ~*morph'ous,* of same or similar form; ~*nomous* (-ŏn²), having same law of growth; ~*phone,* word having same sound as another, but of different meaning or origin (e.g. *gait, gate*), (also) symbol denoting same sound as another; ~*phŏn'ic,* (Mus.) of same pitch, characterized by the predominance of one part or melody; ~*phonous* (ŏf²), (of music) ~*phonic,* (of symbols) denoting same sound; ~*phony* (-ŏf²), unison; ~*plăs'tic,* similar in structure; ~*type,* part, organ, like another in structure; ~*zўg'ōte* (Mendelism), zygote of like gametes (cf. ʜᴇᴛᴇʀᴏᴢʏɢᴏᴛᴇ), & so ~*zўg'ous* a.

hŏm'oeopăth (-mĭ-), ·n. One who practises homoeopathy. [f. foll.]

hōmoe|ŏp'athў (-mĭ-), n. Hahnemann's treatment of disease by drugs (usu. in minute doses) that in healthy person would produce symptoms like those of the disease. So ~*opăth'ɪᴄ* a. (often joc., = minute), ~*opăth'ɪᴄᴀʟʟʏ* adv., ~*ŏp'ath-ɪsᴛ* n., (-mĭ-). [f. Gk *homoios* like + -*patheia* f. *pathos* suffering; first used by Hahnemann (G *homöopathie*)]

hōmogēn'eous, a. Of the same kind;

consisting of parts all of the same kind, uniform. Hence or cogn. **hŏmŏgĕnē′ITY, ~NESS**, nn., **~LY**[2] adv., **homŏ′gĕnIZE** v.t., make~, make (milk) more digestible by breaking up the fat droplets into smaller particles. [f. schol. L *homogeneus* f. Gk HOMO(*genēs* f. *genos* kind) + -OUS]

hŏm′ograph (-ahf), n. Word spelt like another, but with different meaning. [HOMO- + -GRAPH]

hŏmoious′ian (-ows-), a. & n. (One who held that Father & Son in the Godhead were) of like substance (cf. HOMOOUSIAN). [f. LL f. Gk *homoiousios* (*homoios* like + *ousia* essence) + -AN]

‖**hŏmŏl′og|āte**, v.t. (Sc.). Acknowledge, admit; confirm. So ~A′TION n. [f. med. L *homologare* f. Gk HOMO(*logeō* f. *logos* word), see -ATE[3]]

homŏl′ogize, -ise (-īz), v.i. & t. Be homologous, correspond; make homologous. [as foll. + -IZE]

homŏl′ogous, a. Having the same relation, relative position, etc.; corresponding. [f. med. L f. Gk HOMO(*logos* ratio)]

hŏm′ologue (-ŏg), n. Homologous thing. [F, f. Gk (neut. adj.) as prec.]

homŏl′ogy̆, n. Correspondence, sameness of relation. Hence **hŏmolŏ′gICAL** a., **hŏmolŏ′gICALLY**[2] adv. [f. med. L f. Gk *homologia* (as prec.)]

hŏm′onȳm, n. Word of same form as another but different sense (e.g. POLE[1], POLE[2]); namesake. So **hŏmonȳm′IC**, **homŏn′ȳmOUS**, aa. [f. L f. Gk *homōnumon*, neut. adj. (HOMO- + *onoma* name)]

hŏmŏous′ian, hŏmous-, (-ow-), a. & n. (One who held the persons of the Trinity to be) of the same substance (cf. HOMOIOUSIAN). [f. LL *homousianus* f. LL f. Gk HOMO(*ousios* f. *ousia* essence) + -AN]

hŏmosĕx′ual, a. & n. Having a sexual propensity for persons of one's own sex; (n.) ~ person. [irreg. f. HOMO- + SEXUAL]

homūnc′ūle, -cle, n. Little man, manikin. [f. L *homunculus* (*homo -minis* man, see -CULE)]

hŏm′y̆, a. Suggesting home, home-like. [-Y[1]]

hōne, n., & v.t. 1. Whetstone, esp. for razors; various stones as material for this. 2. v.t. Sharpen on ~. [OE *hān*, = ON *hein*]

hŏn′ĕst (ŏ-), a. Fair & upright in speech & act, not lying, cheating, or stealing; sincere; (of act or feeling) showing uprightness; (of gain etc.) gained by fair means, as *turn, earn, an* ~ *penny*; (of things) unadulterated, unsophisticated; (arch., of woman) chaste, virtuous; *make an* ~ *woman of*, marry (seduced woman); (patronizing or joc.) good, worthy; ~ *Injun* (= Indian), sl. phr. questioning (~ *Injun?*) or confirming statement. Hence ~LY[2] adv. [ME, f. OF *honeste* f. L *honestus* (*honos* HONOUR)]

hŏn′ĕsty̆ (ŏ-), n. Uprightness; truthfulness; ~ *is the best policy* (maxim of self-

-interested morality); plant with purple flowers & translucent pods. [ME, f. OF *oneste* f. L *honestatem* (prec., -TY)]

ho′ney (hŭ-), n. (pl. ~*s*). Sweet viscid yellow fluid, the nectar of flowers collected by bees & other insects; (fig.) sweetness; (also Sc. & North. *hinnie*, -*ny*) sweetheart, darling; ~-*bee*, common hive-bee; ~-*buzzard*, bird of prey feeding on larvae of bees & wasps; ~ *dew*, sweet sticky substance found on leaves & stems, excreted by aphides, ideally sweet substance, tobacco sweetened with molasses; ~*suckle*, woodbine, climbing shrub with fragrant yellow and pink flowers; ~-*sweet*, sweet as ~. Hence ~ED[2], **honied**, (hŭn′id), a. [OE *hunig*, OS *honig*, OHG *hona(n)g*, ON *hunang* f. Gmc **huna(n)gam*]

ho′neycŏmb (hŭ-; -m), n., & v.t. 1. Bees' wax structure of hexagonal cells for honey & eggs; cavernous flaw in metal, esp. guns; ornamental or other work hexagonally arranged. 2. v.t. Make full of cavities, undermine, mark with ~ pattern. [OE *hunigcamb*, see prec. & COMB]

ho′neymōon (hŭ-), n., & v.t. 1. Holiday spent together by newly married couple. 2. v.i. Spend ~ (*in, at*, place). [16th c., HONEY + MOON, reference being orig. to waning affection, not to period of a month]

hŏng, n. (In China) set of buildings used as factory etc.; foreign trading establishment in China or Japan. [f. Chin. *hang* row, rank]

hŏnk, n., & v.i. 1. Wild goose's cry; sound of motor horn. 2. v.i. Emit or give ~. [imit.]

hŏnorār′ium (hŏ-, ŏ-), n. (pl. -*ums*, -*a*). (Voluntary) fee esp. for professional services nominally rendered without payment. [L as foll.]

hŏn′orary̆ (ŏ-), a. Conferred as an honour (without the usual requirements, functions, etc.); holding ~ title or position; ~ *secretary, treasurer*, etc., serving without pay (abbr. *hon.*); (of obligations) depending on honour, not legally enforceable. [f. L *honorarius* (as HONOUR[1], see -ARY[1])]

hŏnorif′ic (ŏ-), a. & n. (Expression) implying respect (esp. of Oriental forms of speech). [f. L *honorificus* (as HONOUR[1], see -FIC)]

hŏnōr′is caus′a, adv. phr. As a mark of esteem. [L, = for the sake of honour]

hŏn′our[1] (ŏ-), n. 1. High respect; glory; reputation, good name; nobleness of mind. 2. Allegiance to what is right or to conventional standard of conduct; (of woman) chastity, reputation for this. 3. Exalted position (*your, his, H*~, said to or of County-Court judge, & in rustic speech to or of any person of rank). 4. Thing conferred as distinction; (Golf) right of driving off first as having won last hole (*it is my* ~); (pl.) civilities rendered to guests etc., esp. *do the* ~*s of* (the table, a house, the town, etc.); *last, funeral*, ~s, observances of respect at funeral; *military* ~s, marks of respect paid by troops at burial of soldier, to royalty, etc.; ~s *of war*, privileges granted to capitulating force, as that of marching out with colours flying etc. **5.** (Univv., pl.) special distinction for proficiency beyond that required to pass examination. **6.** Person, thing, that reflects ~ on (*to*) another, *as he is an ~ to his profession*. **7.** (In whist) ace, king, queen, knave, of trumps (in bridge the ten also). **8.** (commerce.). *Acceptance* (of protested bill by third party) *for the* ~ *of* (to save the credit of) drawer or indorser. **9.** *In* ~ (celebration) *of*; *bound in* ~ (as a moral duty) *to* (do); *be on* one's ~ (under moral obligation) *to* (do); (forms of asseveration) *upon my* ~, (colloq.) *bright*; *code, law, of* ~, rules forming conventional standard of conduct; AFFAIR, DEBT, LEGION, MAID, POINT[1], WORD[1], *of* ~. [ME, f. OF (*h*)*onor* f. L *honorem* (nom. -*or*) repute, office, beauty]

hŏn′our[2] (ŏ-), v.t. Respect highly; confer dignity upon; (Commerc.) accept, pay, (bill) when due. [ME, f. OF *honorer* f. L *honorare* (as prec.)]

hŏn′ourable (ŏner-), a. Worthy of honour; bringing honour to its possessor; consistent with honour; upright; person's *intentions* (in courting woman) *are* ~, he has marriage in view; title (abbr. *Hon.*) ‖ of wives of younger sons of Earls and of all sons of Viscounts and Barons, Maids of Honour, Justices of High Court, Lords of Session, members of Government or Executive Councils in Dominions & Colonies; ‖ *Most H*~, title of Marquises, Order of Bath, & Privy Council; ‖ *Right H*~, title of peers below rank of Marquis, Privy Councillors, & others. Hence **hŏn′ourably**[2] (ŏner-) adv. [ME, f. OF *honorable* f. L *honorabilis* (as prec., see -BLE)]

*****hŏŏch**, n. (sl.). Alcoholic liquor. [abbr. of Alaskan *hoochinoo*]

hŏŏd, n., & v.t. **1.** Covering for head & neck, whether part of cloak etc. or separate; (Univv.) badge worn over gown etc. to indicate degree; leather covering for hawk's head; *bonnet of motor-car; thing like ~ in shape or use. **2.** v.t. Cover with ~. Hence ~′ED[2] a. [(vb f. n.) OE *hōd*, OHG *huot* f. WG *hōd*-, cogn. w. HAT]

-hŏŏd, suf. forming nn. of condition or quality on nn. & aa., ME -*hōd*. Orig. an independent noun, OE *hād* (person(ality), sex, condition, quality, rank) = OS *hēd*, OHG *heit*, ON *heithr*, Goth. *haidus* f. Gmc *haiduz*. It became a suf. in ME both in new formations on aa. & nn. & to replace -HEAD in similar wds.

hŏŏd′ie, -dў, n. (Also ~ *crow, grey, hooded, Royston*, ~) piebald grey and black crow. [HOOD + -Y[3]]

*****hŏŏd′lum**, n. Street rowdy, young ruffian. [orig. unkn.]

‖ **hŏŏd′man-blind**, n. Old name for BLIND-MAN'S-BUFF.

hŏŏ′dŏŏ, n., & v.t. (chiefly U.S.). Bad luck; (vb) render unlucky. [var. of VOODOO]

hŏŏd′wink, v.t. Deceive, humbug; blindfold. [HOOD n. + WINK v.]

*****hŏŏ′ey**, n. & int. (sl.). Nonsense, humbug. [orig. unkn.]

hŏŏf, n. (pl. *-fs, -ves*), & v.t. & i. **1.** Horny casing of foot of horse & other animals; CLOVEN ~; (joc.) human foot; ~*-pad*, pad to prevent one foot from striking the other; ~*-pick* (for removing stones from ~). **2.** v.t. Strike with ~ (sl., of person) kick (another) *out* etc.; (v.i.) go on foot. Hence (-)~ED[2] (-ft) a. [OE, OS *hōf*, OHG *huof*, ON *hófr* f. Gmc *hōfaz*]

hŏŏk[1], n. Piece of metal or other material bent back at an angle or with round bend, for catching hold or for hanging things upon; (sl.) anchor; (also *fish*-~) bent piece of wire, usu. barbed, for catching fish; ~, *line, & sinker*, (fig.) entire(ly); (fig.) trap, snare; stroke (see foll.) in cricket or golf; (Boxing) short swinging blow with elbow bent; curved cutting instrument, esp. *reaping*-~; ~ *& eye*, small metal ~ & loop as dress-fastening; sharp bend, e.g. in river; projecting point of land, esp. *H*~ *of Holland*; = POT-~; *by* ~ *or by crook*, by fair means or foul; (sl.) *on* one's *own* ~ (account); take one's ~ (sl.), = *hook it* (see foll.); ~-*nose*(d), (having) aquiline nose; ~*-worm*, kind of nematoid worm infesting men and animals, male of which has ~-like spines. [OE *hōc*, MLG *hōk*, Du. *hoek*]

hŏŏk[2], v.t. & i. Grasp with hook; secure with hook(s); ~ *on, in, up*, etc., attach with hook; ~ *on* intr., take person's arm; (sl.) steal; catch (fish) with hook (also fig., esp. husband); (Golf) drive (ball) slightly to left; (Cricket) play (ball) round from off to on side without hitting it at the pitch; (Rugby football) secure and pass (ball) backward with foot in scrummage; (Boxing) strike (opponent) with elbow bent; ~ *it* (sl.), make off, run away; ~*-up* (orig. U.S.), interconnexion of broadcasting stations for special transmissions. [f. prec.]

hŏŏk′ah (-ka), n. Smoking-pipe with long flexible tube, smoke being drawn through water in vase to which tube and bowl are attached. [f. Arab. *ḥuqqah*, casket, hookah-bottle]

hŏŏked (-kt), a. Hook-shaped; furnished with hook(s). [-ED[1,2]]

hŏŏk′er[1], n. In vbl senses, esp. (Rugby football) each of the two players in front row of scrummage who try to get the ball by hooking it. [-ER[1]]

hŏŏk′er[2], n. Kinds of small Dutch & Irish sailing ship (*the old* ~, said scornfully or fondly of any ship). [17th c., f. Du. *hoeker* fishing-boat f. *hoek* HOOK[1]]

hŏŏk'ey, -ÿ, n. *Play* ~ (sl.), play truant; *blind* ~, gambling game at cards. [f. HOOK[1,2]]

hŏŏ'lee, hō'li (-lē), n. Hindu festival in honour of Krishna & the milkmaids. [Hind. (-*i*)]

‖ **hŏŏl'ĭgan,** n. One of gang of young street roughs. Hence ~ISM(3) n. [name]

hŏŏp[1], n., & v.t. **1.** Circular band of metal, wood, etc., esp. for binding staves of casks etc.; wooden or iron circle trundled along by child; circle of elastic material for expanding woman's skirt; iron arch used in croquet; large ring with paper stretched over it through which circus--riders jump (*go through the* ~ or ~*s*, undergo an ordeal); kind of finger-ring; ~-*iron* (in long thin strips for binding purposes); ~ *petticoat* (expanded by ~s). **2.** v.t. Bind with ~s, surround as ~ does. [late OE *hōp*, MDu. *hoop*]

hŏŏp[2], v.i., & n. **1.** Utter the cry ~: ~*ing cough,* see WHOOP. **2.** n. The cry ~, sound heard in whooping cough. [ME, f. OF *houper* (imit.); cf. WHOOP]

hŏŏp-la (-ah), n. Game played at fairs etc., in which rings are thrown at objects that are won if encircled.

hŏŏp'oe (-ōō), n. S.-European bird with variegated plumage & large erectile crest. [17th c., alt. of 15th c. *hoop* f. OF *huppe* f. L *upupa*]

hŏŏsh, n. (sl.). Hotchpotch or stew in Arctic travel. [orig. unkn.]

*Hŏŏ'sier (-zher), n. (Nickname for) inhabitant of State of Indiana. [orig. unkn.]

hŏŏt, v.i. & t., & n. **1.** Make loud sounds, esp. of disapproval (*at* or abs.); assail (person etc.) with derisive shouts; drive (person) *out, away,* etc. by ~ing; (of owl) utter cry; (of steam whistle or motor car or driver) sound (intr.). **2.** n. Inarticulate shout, esp. of derision or disapprobation; owl's cry; *not care, not worth, a* ~ or *two* ~*s* (sl., = anything at all). [ME *huten,* imit.]

‖ **hŏŏt(s),** int. (Sc. & north.) expr. dissatisfaction or impatience. [cf. Sw. *hut* begone, W *hwt* away, Ir. *ut* out, all in similar sense]

hŏŏt'er, n. In vbl senses, esp. siren, steam whistle, etc, as signal for work to begin or cease. [·ER[1]]

hŏŏve, n. Disease of cattle, with inflation of stomach, usu. caused by green fodder. [19th c., perh. ult. rel. to *hove,* p.p. of HEAVE]

Hŏŏv'er, n., & v.t. Make of vacuum cleaner; (v.t.) clean (carpet etc.) with ~. [P]

hooves. See HOOF.

hŏp[1], n., & v.t. & i. (-pp-). **1.** Climbing perennial plant, cultivated for the cones borne by the female; (pl.) ripe cones of this, used for giving bitter flavour to malt liquor etc.; ~*-bind, -bine,* climbing stem of ~; ~*-fly,* aphis destructive to ~s;

‖ ~*-garden,* field for cultivation of ~s; ~--*picker,* labourer, machine, employed to pick ~s; ~*-pillow* (stuffed with ~s, to produce sleep); ~-POCKET; ~*-pole* (on which ~ plant is trained). **2.** v.t. Flavour with ~s; (v.i.) bear, gather, ~s. [ME *hoppe* f. MLG, MDu. *hoppe* = OS *hoppo,* OHG *hopfo*; orig. unkn.]

hŏp[2], v.i. & t. (-pp-). Spring (of person) on one foot, (of animals) with all feet at once; (trans.) ~ over (ditch etc.); (sl.) ~ (*the twig* or *stick*), depart suddenly, die, ~ (*it*), go away, ~ *off,* (of aircraft) start; *cloud-*~*ping,* (of aircraft) flying from cloud to cloud esp. to gain cover; *hedge, wave, -*~*ping,* flying very low over land, over water; ‖ ~-*ʟo'-my-thumb,* dwarf, pygmy; ~*'scotch,* child's game of ~ping on one foot & with it pushing flat stone etc., over *scotches* (lines) marked on ground. [OE *hoppian,* MHG *hopfen,* ON *hoppa* f. Gmc *hoppōjan]

hŏp[3], n. Hopping (*on the* ~, colloq., bustling about); spring; (colloq.) informal dance; (Aviation) one of the stages of a long-distance flight; ~, *skip* (or *step*), & *jump,* exercise consisting of these three movements in sequence. [f. prec.]

hŏpe[1], n. Expectation & desire combined (*of* thing, *of doing, that*); feeling of trust; ground of ~, probability, (*hoping against* ~, clinging to a mere possibility); person, thing, that ~ centres in; FORLORN HOPE. [OE *hopa, tōhopa,* OLG *tōhopa,* MLG, MDu. *hope,* MHG *hoffe*; OE-LG, of unkn. orig.]

hŏpe[2], v.i. & t. Look with expectation & desire (*for* thing or abs.); expect & desire (thing, *that, to* do.) [OE *hopian,* MLG, MDu: *hopen;* see prec.]

hŏpe'ful (-pf-), a. & n. Feeling hope; inspiring hope, promising, often iron. as (n.) *young* ~ (of boy or girl). Hence ~LY[2] adv., ~NESS n. [HOPE[1]+-FUL]

hŏpe'less (-pl-), a. Feeling no hope; admitting no hope, as *a* ~ *case.* Hence ~LY[2] adv., ~NESS n. [-LESS]

hŏp'lite, n. Heavy-armed foot-soldier of ancient Greece. [f. Gk *hoplitēs* (*hoplon* weapon, see -ITE[1])]

hŏpp'er[1], n. One who hops; hopping insect, esp. flea or cheese-maggot; inverted pyramid or cone (orig. with hopping motion) through which grain passes in mill; similar contrivance in various machines; barge carrying away mud etc. from dredging-machine & discharging it; ~*-light* or *-casement* (hinged below with opening at top for ventilation). [HOP[2]+-ER[1]]

hŏpp'er[2], n. Hop-picker. [HOP[1]+-ER[1]]

hŏp'ple, v.t., & n. Fasten together legs of (horse etc.); (n.) apparatus for this. [16th c., prob. LG; cf. early mod. Flem. *hoppelen* = MDu. *hobelen* jump, dance; *hobble,* in same sense, in 19th c. var. infl. by earlier senses of HOBBLE]

hŏr'arÿ, a. Of the hours; occurring every

hour. [f. LL *horarius* (*hora* hour, see -ARY[1])]

Horā′tian (-shn), a. Of, like, (the poems of) Horace (Q. Horatius Flaccus, d. B.C. 8). [f. L *Horatianus* (*Horatius*, see -AN)]

horde, n. Troop of Tartar or other nomads; gang, troop, (usu. in contempt). [ult. f. Turki *orda*, see URDU]

hore′hound, hoar-, (hōr-), n. Herb with bitter aromatic juice used for coughs etc. (also *common, white,~*); other allied herbs. [OE *hāre hūne* (*hār* hoar+*hūne*, a plant)]

hori′zon, n. Line at which earth & sky appear to meet; *apparent, sensible, visible, ~*, circle of contact with earth's surface of a cone whose vertex is at observer's eye; *celestial, rational, true, ~*, great circle of the celestial sphere, plane of which passes through centre of earth & is parallel to that of sensible ~ of a place; (fig.) limit of mental perception, experience, interest, etc.; *on the ~* (fig., of events just imminent or becoming apparent). [ME, f. OF *orizonte* f. LL *horizontem* (nom. *-on*) f. Gk *horizōn* (*kuklos*) bounding (circle)]

hŏrizŏn′tal, a. & n. 1. Of, at, the horizon; parallel to the plane of this, at right angles to the vertical; level, flat; (of machinery etc.) having its parts working in ~ direction. 2. n. ~ line, bar, etc. Hence ~ITY (-ăl⁴) n., ~LY² adv. [16th c., f. F, or mod. L (as prec. +-AL)]

hŏr′mŏne, n. (physiol.). Kinds of internal secretion that pass into the blood & stimulate organs to action. [f Gk *hormōn* part. of *hormaō* impel]

hŏrn¹, n. 1. Non-deciduous excrescence, often curved & pointed, on head of cattle, sheep, goats, & other mammals, found in pairs, single, or one in front of another; *take* the BULL¹ *by the ~s*; each of two deciduous branched appendages on head of deer; projection on head of other animals, as snail's tentacles, insect's antennae, crest of horned owl; emblem of cuckold; *draw in* one's *~s*, restrain one's ardour, draw back; substance of which *~s* consist; *~-shavings* (used as manure); thing made of *~*, as SHOE-*~*; drinking-vessel, powder-flask, made of ~; GATE¹ of ~; ~ *of plenty*, = CORNUCOPIA; wind instrument (not now made of ~, but of brass), as *hunting-~, French~* (of trumpet class, used in orchestra), *English ~* (kind of oboe); *~-shaped* projection; extremity of moon or other crescent; arm, branch, of bay, river, etc.; either alternative of a dilemma; *the H~*, Cape H~. 2. *~-bar*, cross-bar of carriage; *~beam*, tree of beech kind with hard tough wood; *~ bill*, bird with ~-like excrescence on bill; *~book* (hist.), paper containing alphabet, Lord's Prayer, etc., mounted on wooden tablet with handle, & protected by thin plate of ~; *~-mad* (arch.), stark mad (orig. of horned beasts); *~-plate*, axle-guard of railway carriage; *~-rimmed* (of

spectacles or their wearers); *~-stone*, brittle siliceous rock; *~-work* (fortif.), outwork consisting of two demi-bastions joined by a curtain. Hence ~′FUL n., ~′LESS a. [OE, OS, OHG, ON *horn*, Goth. *haurn* f. Gmc **hornaz, -am*, cogn. w. L *cornu*]

hŏrn², v.t. & i. Furnish with horns (esp. in p.p.); shorten or cut off (horns of cattle); gore with the horns; adjust (frame of ship) at right angles to line of keel; **~ in*, intrude, interfere. [f. prec.]

hŏrn′blĕnde, n. Dark-brown, black, or green mineral, a constituent of granite & many rocks, composed chiefly of silicates of calcium, magnesium, & iron, [G (*horn*+BLENDE)]

hŏrn′er, n. Maker of horn spoons, combs, etc.: one who blows a horn. [HORN¹+-ER¹]

hŏrn′ĕt, n. Large insect of wasp family, inflicting serious sting; *bring ~s' nest about* one's *ears*, stir up host of enemies. [OE *hyrnet*(u) = OHG *hornuz*; ME *hernet*, *harnet*, *hornet* prob. f. MLG, MDu. *horn(e)te*; perh. rel. to HORN; cf. OS *hornobero*]

hŏrn′pïpe, n. Obsolete wind instrument (music for) lively dance, usu. of single person (esp. associated with merry-making of sailors).

hŏrn′|ȳ, a. Of, like, horn; abounding in horns; hard as horn, callous, as *~y handed*. Hence ~ĭNESS n. [-Y²]

hŏ′rolŏge, n. Time-piece, dial, clock. So horŏl′ogER¹(3), horŏl′ogIST(3), nn. [ME, f. OF *orloge* f. L f. Gk *hōrologion* (*hōra* time+*-logos* -telling)]

horŏl′ogȳ, n. Study of measuring time or making clocks, watches, etc. So hŏrolŏ′gIC(AL) aa. [f. Gk *hōra* time+-O-+-LOGY]

horŏp′ter, n. Aggregate of points seen single in any given position of eyes. [f. Gk *horos* limit+*optēr* one who looks]

hŏ′roscŏpe, n. (astrol.). Observation of sky & planets at certain moment, esp. at person's birth; scheme showing disposition of the heavens at particular moment; *cast a ~*, erect such scheme by calculating degree of ecliptic on eastern horizon at person's birth etc. So hŏroscŏp′IC(AL) aa., horŏs′copY¹ n. [ME, f. OF, or L f. Gk *hōroscopos* (*hōra* time+*skopos* observer)]

hŏ′rrent, a. (poet.). Bristling. [f. L *horrēre* bristle, shudder at, see -ENT]

hŏ′rrib|le, a. Exciting, fit to excite, horror; hideous, shocking; (colloq.) excessive, unpleasant, as *~le noise, bore, weather*. Hence ~leNESS (-beln-) n., ~LY² adv. [ME, f. OF f. L *horribilis* (as prec., see -BLE)]

hŏ′rrid, a. Terrible, frightful; (poet., arch.) rough, bristling; (colloq.) as prec. Hence ~LY² adv., ~NESS n. [f. L *horridus* (as prec., see -ID¹)]

hŏ′rrifȳ, v.t. Excite horror in; shock,

scandalize. So **horri**ғ'ıc a., **hŏrrı**ғıc-
a'тıон n. (joc.). [f. L *horrificare* (as
HORRENT, see -FY)]

hŏrripilā'tion, n. Goose-flesh; bristling
of the skin caused by chill, fright, etc.
[f. LL *horripilatio,* ult. f. L *horrēre* to
bristle +*pilus* hair]

hŏ'rror, n. Terrified shuddering; intense
dislike (*of*); (Med.) shuddering, as
symptom of disease; *the* ~s, fit of ~ or
depression, esp. as in delirium tremens;
~*-struck* or *-stricken*, shocked; horrifying
thing; *Chamber of H*~s, place full of ~s
(orig. room of criminals etc. in Tussaud's
waxwork exhibition). [ME, f. OF *orror* f.
L *horrorem* (as prec., see -OR]

hors (see Ap.), adv. & prep. Outside, as
~ *concours*, (of exhibit) not competing for
prize; ~ *de combat* pred. a., out of fight,
disabled; ~*-d'œuvre* (pl. usu. *-s*), extra
dish served as relish at beginning or in
interval of meal. [F wds]

hŏrse[1], n. 1. Solid-hoofed quadruped with
flowing mane & tail, used as beast of
burden & draught, & for riding on (*you
may take a* ~ *to the water, but you can't
make him drink*, prov.); (esp.) adult male
~, stallion or gelding, (cf. MARE, COLT);
(collect. sing.) cavalry; *high* ~, trained
for HAUTE ÉCOLE; *light* ~, lightly armed
mounted soldiers; SEA-~. 2. Vaulting-
-block in gymnasium; frame (often with
legs) on which something is supported, as
clothes- ~ ; (Naut.) rope, bar, in various
uses; (Mining) obstruction in vein. 3. *To*
~, (as command) mount your ~s; FLOG
a dead ~; *grin through a* ~*-collar*, practise
elementary humour; *look a gift*~ *in the
mouth*, find fault with a gift; *mount, ride,
the high* ~, put on airs; DARK, WILLING, ~;
put the CART *before the* ~; *eat, work, like a*
~ (much); *on* ~*back*, mounted on a ~.
4. ~ *artillery* (the light mobile type);
~*-block*, small platform of stone or wood
for mounting ~; ‖ ~*-box*, closed vehicle
for taking ~ by rail or for slinging ~ into
ship, (joc.) large pew; ~*-breaker*, one who
breaks in ~s; ~*-chestnut*, large tree with
conical clusters of white or pink or red
flower, fruit of this (like edible chestnut,
but of coarse bitter taste); ~*-cloth* (used
to cover ~, or as part of trappings);
~*-*COPER; ~*'flesh*, flesh of ~, esp. as food,
~s collectively; ~*-fly*, insect (of various
kinds) troublesome to ~s; ‖ *H*~ *Guards*,
cavalry brigade of English Household
troops, esp. (*Royal H.G.*) second regiment
of it, (also) headquarters of such cavalry,
esp. a building in Whitehall, (also) military authorities at head of army; ~ *hair*,
hair from mane or tail of ~ (often attrib.);
~ *latitudes*, belt of calms at northern edge
of N.E. trade-winds; ~*-laugh*, loud coarse
laugh; ~*'leech*, large kind of leech, in-
satiable person, (*daughters of the* ~*leech*,
Prov. xxx. 15); ~*-mackerel*, (kinds of) large
fish of the mackerel type, cavally, scad,
tunny, etc.; ~*'man*, (skilled) rider on

~*back*; ~*'manship*, art of riding, skill in
riding, on ~back; ~*-marines*, imaginary
corps of mounted marines, as type of non-
existent body, (prov.) *tell that* (nonsense)
to the ~*-marines*; ~*-mastership*, skill in
managing ~s; ~*-mushroom*, coarse but
edible variety with hollow stem; *~ opera
(sl.), western film; ~*'play*, boisterous
play; ~*-pond* (for watering & washing
~s, prov. as ducking-place for obnoxious
persons); ~*'power*, machine by which
work of ~ is made to drive other machinery, (Mech.) unit of rate of doing work,
=550 foot-pounds per second (abbr.
h.p.); ~*-race* (between ~s with riders);
~*-radish*, plant whose pungent root is
scraped or grated as condiment; ~ *sense*
(colloq.), plain rough sagacity; ~*'shoe*,
iron shoe for ~, thing of this shape (often
attrib., as ~*shoe table*); ~*-tail*, tail of ~
(used in Turkey as standard, or as ensign
denoting rank of pasha), genus of cryptogamous plants like ~'s tail; ~*'whip*, whip
for ~, (v.t.) chastise (person) with this;
~*'woman*, woman who rides on ~back.
Hence ~*'LESS* (-sl-) a. [OE *hors*, OS, OHG
hros, ON *hross* f. Gmc **horsam, -az*]

hŏrse[2], v.t. & i. Provide (person, vehicle)
with horse(s); carry (person) on one's
back; place (person) on man's back to be
flogged; (intr.) mount, go, on horseback.
[f. prec.]

hŏrs'|ỹ, a. Concerned with, addicted to,
horses or horse-racing; affecting dress
& language of groom or jockey. Hence
~*-*ıLY[2] adv., ~*-*ıNESS n. [f. HORSE[1]+-Y[2]]

hŏrt'at|ive, a. Tending, serving, to ex-
hort. So ~ORY a. [f. L *hortativus* (*hortari*
exhort, see -IVE)]

hŏrt'ıculture, n. Art of garden cultivation. Hence **hŏrtıcŭl'tur**AL a., **hŏrtıcŭl'tur**ısт n., (-cher-). [f. L *hortus* garden
+CULTURE]

hŏrt'us sĭcc'us, n. Arranged collection
of dried plants; (fig.) collection of uninteresting facts etc. [L, = dry garden]

hōsănn'a (-z-), n. Cry of ~, shout of
adoration (*Matt.* xxi. 9, 15, etc.). [ME, f.
LL f. Gk *hōsanna* f. Heb. *hosha'na* for
hoshi'ahnna save, pray!]

hose (hōz), n., & v.t. 1. (Collect. as pl.)
stockings, *half-*~, socks, (now chiefly
shop); (w. pl. ~s) flexible tube for watering plants etc., putting out fires, dispersing rioters, etc.; ‖ ~*-tops*, footless stockings. 2. v.t. Provide with ~, drench or
water with ~. [OE, OS, OHG, ON *hosa*
f. Gmc **husōn-*]

hō'sier (-zher), n. Dealer in hose &
frame-knitted or woven underclothing.
Hence **hō'si**ERY(1) (-zher-) n. [f. HOSE+
-IER]

hŏs'pice, n. House of rest for travellers,
esp. one kept by religious order; ‖ home
for the destitute or sick. [F, f. L *hospi-
tium* (as HOST[2]]

hŏs'pitab|le, a. Giving, disposed to give,
welcome & entertainment to strangers or

guests. Hence ~LY² adv. [F, f. med. L
hospitare entertain, as prec., -ABLE]

hŏs'pital, n. Institution for care of the
sick or wounded; charitable institution
(in proper names, as Christ's H~, public
school formerly in London); (hist.)
hospice, establishment of Knights Hos-
pitallers; ~ fever, kind of typhus formerly
prevalent in crowded ~s; H~ Saturday,
Sunday, days for collecting money
in streets etc. (Saturday), in churches
(Sunday), for the local ~s. Hence ~IZE
v.t., admit to, treat in, ~, ~ĪZA'TION n.
[ME, f. OF f. med. L hospitale neut. adj.
place for guests (as HOST², see -AL)]

hŏs'pitalism, n. (Hygienic imperfections
of) the hospital system. [-ISM]

hŏspităl'ĭtў, n. Friendly & liberal reception of guests or strangers; afford me the
~ of your columns, print my letter. [ME,
f. OF hospitalite f. L hospitalitatem (as
HOSPITAL, see -TY)]

hŏs'pital(l)er, n. Member of charitable
religious order; ‖ (in some London hospitals) chaplain; Knights H~s, order of
military monks founded c. 1048. [ME, f.
OF hospitalier f. med. L hospitalarius (as
prec., see -ARY¹)]

host¹, n. Large number (of; person is a
~ in himself, can do as much as a number
of ordinary persons); (arch.) army;
(Bibl.) Lord (God) of ~s (armies), ~(s) of
heaven, sun, moon, & stars, (also) angels.
[ME, f. OF f. L hostis stranger, enemy]

host², n. One who lodges or entertains
another; landlord of inn; reckon without
one's ~, overlook difficulty, opposition,
etc.; (Biol.) animal, plant, having parasite
or commensal. [ME, f. OF oste f. L
hospitem (nom. -pes) host, guest]

host³, n. Bread consecrated in the
Eucharist. [ME, f. OF oiste f. L hostia
victim]

hŏs'tage, n. Person given to another as
pledge; pledge, security; ~ to fortune,
person, thing, that one may lose. Hence
~SHIP (-ĭjsh-) n. [ME, f. OF (h)ostage f.
Rom. *obsidaticum f. LL obsidiatus f. L
obses -idis hostage, see -AGE]

‖ hŏs'tel, n. Inn; house of residence for
students or other special class; YOUTH ~.
[ME, f. OF (as HOSPITAL)]

‖ hŏs'telrў, n. Inn. [ME, f. OF ostelerie
(ostelier innkeeper, f. med. L as HOSPITAL-
LER, see -ERY)]

hŏs'tĕss, n. Woman who entertains
guests; mistress of inn; AIR¹ ~. [ME, f.
OF ostesse (HOST², -ESS¹)]

hŏs'tile, a. Of an enemy; unfriendly;
opposed. Hence ~LY² (-l-lĭ) adv. [f. F, or
L hostilis (as HOST¹, see -IL)]

hŏstĭl'ĭtў, n. Enmity; state of warfare;
(pl.) acts of warfare; opposition (in
thought etc.). [f. F hostilité or LL hosti-
litas (as prec., see -TY)]

hostler (ŏs'ler), n. = OSTLER.

hŏt¹, a. & adv. (-tt-). 1. Of a high temperature; very warm; communicating or

feeling heat; producing the sensation of
heat, as ~ fever, blush; (of pepper etc.)
pungent, biting; ardent, passionate;
angry; excited; exciting; (Hunt., of
scent) strong; (fig., of news etc.) fresh,
recent; ‖ (colloq., of Treasury bills)
newly issued; (of a hit, return, etc., in
ball-games) difficult for opponent to deal
with; (of competitor in race or other
sporting event) strongly fancied to win
(a ~ favourite); (of dance music) highly
elaborated & florid, fast & with great
emphasis on rhythm; (sl., of stolen
jewellery, bank-notes, etc.) easily identi-
fiable & so difficult to dispose of; BLOW¹
~ & cold; ~ & ~, (of food) served as soon
as cooked; give it him ~, chastise, reprimand, him severely; make it, the place,
too ~ (uncomfortable, by persecution) for,
to hold, him. 2. adv. Hotly, eagerly,
angrily. 3. ~ air (sl.), excited or boastful
talk; ~ & strong, vehement(ly); ~'bed,
bed of earth heated by fermenting manure, (fig.) place favourable to growth of
(vice. etc.); ~ blast (of heated air forced
into furnace); ~-blooded, ardent, passionate; ~-brained, ~-headed, excitable; ~
cockles (hist.), rustic game in which blind-
folded person guessed who struck him;
*~ dog (colloq.), ~ sausage sandwiched in
roll of bread; ~'foot, in ~ haste; ~'head,
impetuous person; ~'house, heated building with glass roof & sides for growing
plants out of season or from warmer
climate; ~-pot, mutton, beef, with
potatoes etc. cooked in oven in tight-
-lidded pot; ~-press, press of glazed
boards & ~ metal plates for smoothing
paper or cloth, (v.t.) press (paper etc.)
in this; ~-short, (of iron) brittle in its
~ state; ~'spur, rash person (sobriquet
of Sir H. Percy, d. 1403); ~ stuff (sl.),
person of high spirit, vigour, skill, or
strong will or passions; ~ water, (fig.)
trouble, disgrace, scrape; ~ well, spring
of naturally ~ water, reservoir in condensing steam-engine. Hence ~LY²
adv., ~'NESS n. [OE hāt, OS hēt, OHG
heiz, ON heitr f. Gmc *haitaz; see
HEAT¹]

hŏt², v.t. (colloq.; -tt-). Heat, warm up.
[f. prec.]

hŏtch'pŏtch, -pŏt, n. Dish of many
mixed ingredients, esp. mutton broth
with vegetables; (Law) blending of properties for purpose of securing equal
division (esp. of property of intestate
parent); mixture, medley. [ME hochepot
f. OF (hocher shake + POT); -potch (15th c.)
by assim.]

hotěl' (also hō-, ō-, o-), n. House for entertainment of travellers etc., (usu. large)
inn. [F hôtel, later form of HOSTEL]

hotěl'ier, n. Hotel-keeper. [F hôtelier]

Hŏtt'entŏt, n. Member of S.-Afr. people
formerly occupying region near the
Cape; (fig.) person of inferior intellect or
culture. [Du., perh. = stammerer]

‖ **hough** (hŏk), n., & v.t. **1.** Joint of quadruped's hind leg between true knee & fetlock. **2.** v.t. Hamstring, whence ~ ′ER¹ (hŏk′er) n. [ME ho(u)gh = OE hōh (heel) in hōhsinu hamstring; cf. HOCK¹]

hound¹, n. Dog for chase, esp. one hunting by scent; the ~s, pack of fox-~s; MASTER of ~s; despicable man; player who follows scent in HARE & ~s; dogfish (short for ~′fish); nurse′~, smooth~, kinds of dogfish; ~′s-tongue, kinds of plants of the borage family. Hence ~′ISH¹ a. [OE, OS hund, OHG hunt, ON hundr, Goth. hunds f. Gmc *hundaz cogn. w. L canis, Gk kuŏn]

hound², v.t. Chase (as) with hound; set (hound, or fig. person) at (quarry etc.); urge (person) on. [f. prec.]

hour (owr), n. Twenty-fourth part of day, 60 minutes; short indefinite period of time; the time o'clock; (pl.) fixed time for daily work etc., as office ~s are 10 to 3; at the eleventh~, at a late stage (Matt: xx); small~s, 1, 2, etc., a.m.; good or early, bad or late, regular, ~s, (time for getting up & going to bed); the question of the~ (present time); in a good, evil, ~, (un)luckily; (prayers to be said at) seven stated times of day appointed for prayer; (Astron.) 15° of longitude; ~-circle, meridian (24 of which are usu. marked on globe); ~-glass, sand-glass running for an ~; ~-hand (showing ~ on clock etc.). [ME-ure etc. f. OF (h)ure f. L f. Gk hōra season, hour]

houri (hoor′ĭ, howr′ĭ), n. Nymph of Mohammedan Paradise; voluptuously beautiful woman. [F, f. Pers. hurī f. Arab. ḥaura (ḥawira have eyes like gazelle's)]

hour′ly (owr-), a. & adv. (Occurring, done, reckoned) every hour; continual(ly), frequent(ly). [HOUR + -LY¹,²]

house¹ (hows), n. (pl. pron. -zĭz). **1.** Building for human habitation or (usu. w. defining prefix) occupation, as ALMS~, BAKE~, LIGHT¹~, SUMMER~; ~ of God, church, place of worship; inn (a drink on the ~, at innkeeper's expense); bow down in the ~ of Rimmon, sacrifice one's principles for the sake of conformity (2 Kings v. 18); ALE, COFFEE, EATING, -~; PUBLIC, TIEd, ~. **2.** Building for keeping animals or goods, as hen-~, STORE~, WARE¹~. **3.** (Place of abode of) religious fraternity. **4.** ‖ (Oxf. Univ.) the H~, Christ Church. **5.** = (boys in) BOARDING--~. **6.** (Building used by) an assembly, public offices, firms, & institutions, as H~ of COMMONS, LORDS, H~s of PARLIAMENT; make a H~, secure presence of 40 members in H~ of Commons; ‖ the H~, (colloq.) Stock Exchange, (euphem.) work~, (Pol.) H~ of Commons or Lords (a question was asked in the H~); CLEARING, CUSTOM, -~; ‖ COUNTING-HOUSE. **7.** (Audience in) theatre (full ~, with all seats engaged); performance in theatre etc.

(second ~ starts at 9 o'clock). **8.** Household, family, dynasty (the H~ of Windsor, British Royal family); mercantile firm. **9.** (astrol.). Twelfth part of heavens. **10.** A game of chance playable by large numbers with no apparatus but pencil & paper; (Army sl.) gambling form of lotto. **11.** attrib. (Of animals) kept in, frequenting, infesting, the ~, as ~-cat, -fly, etc. **12.** ~ of call, ~ where carriers call for commissions, where person may be heard of, etc.; ~ of cards (built by child out of playing-cards; often fig. of insecure scheme etc.); ~ of ill fame, brothel; ‖ H~ of Keys, branch of Manx legislature; ~ & home, (emphatic) home; ~-to~, carried on from ~ to ~; BRING down the ~; keep ~, maintain, provide for, à household; keep open ~, provide general hospitality; keep the ~, not go outdoors; like a ~ on fire, vigorously, fast. **13.** ‖ ~-agent (for sale & letting of ~s); ~′boat, boat fitted up for living in; ~′breaker, person entering another's ~ by day (cf. BURGLAR) with felonious intent, man employed in demolishing old ~s; ~ dinner, (at clubs) specially appointed dinner for members & guests; ~-dog (kept to guard~); ~-flag, that flown by a firm's ship; ~-flannel (coarse, for cleaning floor etc.); ~′keeper, woman managing affairs of household, (also) person in charge of ~, office, etc.; ~′keeping, (good, bad, liberal, etc.) domestic economy; ~′leek, plant with pink flowers growing on walls & roofs; ~′maid, female servant in charge of reception & bed rooms; ~maid's knee, inflammation of knee-cap due to kneeling; ~′master (of school boarding-~); ~ party (of guests staying at country ~ etc.); ‖ ~-place, living-room in farm-~ etc.; ~-proud, preoccupied with the care & beautification of the home; ~-room, accommodation in ~ (would not give it ~-room, take it as a gift); ~-surgeon, -physician, residing in hospital; ~-to~ collection etc., performed or conducted by calling at~ after~; ~-top, esp. proclaim from the ~-tops, publicly; ~-trained, (of domestic animals) trained to be clean in the ~; ~-warming, celebration of entrance into new~; ~′work, cleaning, cooking, etc. Hence ~′FUL(2) (-sf-) n., ~′LESS (-sl-) a. [OE hūs, OS, OHG, ON hūs, Goth. -hūs f. Gmc *hūsam]

house² (-z), v.t. & i. Receive (person etc.), store (goods), in house or as house does; (Naut.) place (gun etc.) in secure position, lower (upper masts); take shelter (as) in house; provide houses for (population; esp. the housing problem); (Carpentry) fix in a socket, mortise, etc. [OE husian (as prec.)]

house′hōld (-s-h-), n. Inmates of house; domestic establishment; (pl.) second quality of flour; ‖ ~ troops (employed nominally to guard sovereign's person); ~ gods, (Rom. Ant.) Lares & Penates, (fig.) essentials of home life; ~ *word*, familiar saying or name. [HOUSE[1] + HOLD[2]]

house′hōlder (-s-b-), n. One who occupies house as his own dwelling (esp. formerly as entitled to franchise); head of household. [HOUSE[1] + HOLDER]

housewife, n. 1. (hows′wif). Mistress of family; (*good, bad*) domestic economist. 2. (hŭz′if). Case for needles, thread, etc. Hence **house′wifeLY**[1] (-flī) a. [ME *hus(e)wif* (HOUSE[1], WIFE)]

house′wifery (-swifrï), n. Domestic economy, housekeeping. [prec. + -RY]

hous′ing (-z-), n. Horse's cloth covering, for protection or ornament. [f. obs. *house* f. OF *houce* f. OFrank. **hulfti* (cf. MHG *hulft, hulst* covering)]

Houyhnhnm (hwī′nïm), n. Horse with human characteristics (*Gulliver's Travels*). [imit. of horse's neigh; made by Swift]

Hōv′a, n. One of ruling tribe in Madagascar. [native]

hove. See HEAVE.

hŏv′el (*or* hŭ-), n. Open shed, out-house; miserable dwelling; conical building enclosing kiln. [15th c., of unkn. orig.]

hŏv′eller (*or* hŭ-), n. Unlicensed pilot or boatman, esp. one who goes out to wrecks. [18th c., of unkn. orig.]

hŏv′er (*or* hŭ-), v.i. & n. (Of bird etc., esp. of hawk) hang in the air (*over, about,* spot); loiter *about* (person, place); (n.) ~ing, state of suspense. [frequent. of & replacing ME *hove*, of unkn. orig.; -ER[5]]

how, adv. & n. 1. (In direct or indirect question) in what way, as ~ *does he do it?*, *ask him* ~ *he does it, tell him* ~ *to do it*, (with intensive addition) ~ *the deuce, devil, dickens,* ~ *ever,* ~ *on earth;* ~ *are you?,* ~ *do you do?*, what is your state of health? ; ~ *is that for high, queer,* etc.? (colloq. invitation to wonder); (colloq.) ~ *-d'ye-do,* embarrassing situation ; (Crick.) ~'s *that?,* is he out or not? ; ~ *now?,* what is the meaning of this? ; ~ (can you show that to be) *so?* ; ~ (at what price) *is corn?* ; (in indirect statement, rhet. for) that (*told us* ~ *God was almighty*); (in question or exclamation) to what extent, as ~ *far is it?,* ~ *far it is!,* ~ *many are there?,* ~ *many there are!,* ~ *would you like it?,* ~ *he snores!*; (in relative clause) in whatever way, as, (*do it* ~ *you can*); **& ~!* (sl.), = & a good deal more (chiefly used ironically or intensively); *here's* ~ *!* = here's your good health (drinking formula). 2. n. *The* way a thing is done (*the* ~ *of it*). 3. ~*bē′it* (arch.), nevertheless; ~*ev′er,* in whatever way, to whatever extent, nevertheless, (arch.) in any case; ~ EVER; ~*soev′er, how* — *soever,* in whatsoever manner, to what extent soever; ~ *much?,* (sl.) what? (as request to person to repeat his remark or a particular word; *he plays the saxtuba. Plays the* ~ *much?*). [OE *hū*, OS *hwō*, OHG *wuo*, f. Gmc **hwō* f. stem **hwa-* WHO]

howd′ah (-*a*), n. Seat for two or more, usu. with canopy, on elephant's back. [f. Pers. *haudah* f. Arab. *haudaj* litter]

how′itzer, n. Short piece of ordnance for high-angle firing of shells at lower velocities than a gun. [17/18th c. *howitts, haubitz, hauwitzer,. haubitzer,* combining the forms of Du. *houwitser,* (f.) G *haubitze* f. Czech *houfnice* catapult]

howl[1], v.i. & t. (Of animals) utter long loud doleful cry; (of persons) utter long cry of pain, derision, etc., freq. of (esp. child's) loud weeping; utter (words) with ~ing. [ME *houle,* = MLG, MDu. *hūlen,* MHG *hūlen, hiulen* (imit.)]

howl[2], n. Long doleful cry of dog, wolf, etc.; loud cry of pain; yell of derision; (Wireless) whining noise in receiver during tuning-in, often affecting other listeners. [f. prec.]

howl′er, n. In vbl senses; esp. : S.-Amer. monkey; (sl.) glaring blunder. [-ER[1]]

‖ **howl′ét,** n. (dial.). Owl. [late ME, f. OF *hulotte* f. OFrank. *hūwila* OWL]

howl′ing, a. That howls; ~ DERVISH; (Bibl.) ~ (dreary) *wilderness*; (sl.) extreme, glaring, as *a* ~ *shame.* [-ING[2]]

hoy[1], n. Small vessel, usu. rigged as sloop, carrying passengers & goods esp. for short distances. [f. MDu. *hoei,* of unkn. orig.]

hoy[2], int. used to call attention, drive beasts, & (Naut.) hail or call aloft. [natural cry]

hoy′a, n. Kinds of climbing plants with pink, white, or yellow flowers, known as *wax-flowers.* [T. *Hoy,* gardener, d. 1821]

hoyd′en, n. Boisterous girl. Hence ~HOOD, ~ISM, nn., ~ISH[1] a. [prob. f. MDu. *heyden* (= HEATHEN) rude fellow]

hŭb[1], n. Central part of wheel, rotating on or with axle, & from which spokes radiate; nave; (fig.) central point of interest etc. (esp. ~ *of the universe*). [orig. unkn.]

hŭb[2], **hŭbb′ў,** n. (colloq.) Husband. [abbr.]

hŭb′ble-bŭbble, n. Form of hookah; bubbling noise; confused talk. [imit.]

hŭbb′ŭb, n. Confused din; disturbance, riot; confused yelling of war-cry. [of Ir. orig.; cf. Gael. *ubub* int. of contempt, Ir. *abu,* a war-cry]

***hŭb′rĭs,** n. Insolent pride or security; (Gk tragedy) overweening pride leading to NEMESIS. So **hūbris′tic** a. [Gk; prop. *hy-*]

hŭck′abăck, n. Stout linen fabric with rough surface, for towels etc. [orig. unkn.]

hŭc′kle, n. Hip; haunch; ~-*back*(ed), hump-back(ed); ~-*bone,* hip, haunch, -bone, (also) knuckle-bone of quadruped. [f. obs. *huck* hip (cf. earlier *huck(le)bone*), of unkn. orig.]

hŭc′kleberrў (-kelb-), n. (Fruit of) low berry-bearing shrub common in N. Amer. [prob. alt. of *hurtleberry* WHORTLEBERRY]

hŭck'st|er¹, n. Pedlar, hawker; mercenary person. Hence ~ERY(2) n. [c. 1200, of uncert. orig.; cf. dial. *huck* vb, *hucker* n. & vb, *huckle* vb (all later); MDu. *hoekster*, *hoeker*; MHG *hucker* etc.; cf. HAWKER]

hŭck'ster², v.i. & t. Bargain, haggle; carry on petty traffic in (lit. & fig.); adulterate. Hence ~ER¹, ~ESS¹, nn. [f. prec.]

hŭd'dle, v.t. & i., & n. **1.** Heap together confusedly; crowd (things etc.) promiscuously *together, up, into, out of,* etc.; coil one*self up*; hurry *over, through,* botch *up,* (work etc.); (intr.) nestle closely *together.* **2.** n. Confused mass; confusion, bustle; *(secret) conference, esp. *go into* a ~ (*with*) (sl.). [16th c., of obsc. orig.; perh. ult. rel. to root *hŭd-* HIDE²]

Hūdibrăs'tic, a. In the metre or manner of Butler's *Hudibras,* mock-heroic poem 1663–78, esp. of comical compound rhymes. [after *fantastic* etc.]

hūe¹, n. Colour, tint; variety of colour caused by admixture of another. Hence **-hued²** (hūd) a. [OE *hīew, hīw* form etc., Goth. *hiwi* f. Gmc *hewja-*]

hūe², n. ~ *& cry*: loud cry raised for pursuit of wrongdoer; outcry (*against*); proclamation for capture of criminal. [f. OF *hu, heu,* outcry, f. *huer* (imit.)]

hŭff¹, v.t. & i. Bully, storm at; bully (person *into, out of,* thing or do*ing*); offend; take offence; (Draughts) remove (opponent's man) from board as forfeit (orig. after blowing on the piece). [imit. f. sound of blowing; v. & n. f. 16th c.]

hŭff, n. Fit of petulance, esp. *in a ~, take ~*; (Draughts) act of huffing. Hence ~'ISH¹, ~'Y², aa., ~'ILY², ~'ISHLY², advv., ~'INESS, ~'ISHNESS, nn. [see prec.]

hŭg, v.t. (-gg-), & n. **1.** Squeeze tightly in one's arms, usu. with affection; (of bear) squeeze (man etc.) between its foreleg*s*; delight in, cling to, (prejudices etc.); exhibit fondness for (person); congratulate one*self* (*on, for*); keep close to (shore, kerb, etc.); ~*-me-tight*, woollen wrap. **2.** n. Strong clasp; grip in wrestling, esp. *Cornish ~.* [late 16th c., of unkn. orig.]

hūge, a. Very large; enormous; (of immaterial things) great. Hence ~'NESS (-jn-) n. [ME *huge, hoge* f. OF *ahuge, ahoge* of unkn. orig.]

hūge'ly (-jli), adv. Enormously, very much. [prec.+-LY²]

hū'geous (-jus), ⋅a. (usu. joc.). Huge. Hence ~LY² adv., ~NESS n., (-jus-). [-OUS]

hŭgg'er-mŭgg'er (-g-), n., a., adv., & v.t. & i. Secrecy; secret(ly); confusion; confused(ly); (v.t.) conceal, hush *up*; (v.i.) proceed in secret or muddled fashion. [prob. rel. to ME *hoder* huddle, *moker* conceal; cf. syn. 15th c. *hoder moder,* 16th c. *hucker mucker*]

‖**hŭgg'ery** (-g-), n. Practice (on part of barrister etc.) of courting attorney etc. for employment. [f. HUG¹+-ERY]

Hŭg'uenŏt (-ge-; *or* -nō), n.(hist.). French Protestant. [F, assim. of G *eidgenoss* confederate to F pers. name *Hugues*]

*•**huh** (hŭ), int. expr. interrogation, contempt, etc.

hul'a (-ōō-), n. Hawaiian woman's dance (also *hula-hula).* [native word]

hŭlk, n. Body of dismantled ship, used as store vessel etc. or (pl., hist.) as prison; unwieldy vessel; (fig.) big person or mass. [ME, f. OE *hulc* (= OHG *holcho,* G *hulk*) & MLG, MDu. *hulk*(e), ult. f. med. L *hulcus* f. Gk *holkas* ship of burden]

hŭl'king, a. Bulky; clumsy. [prec.+ -ING²]

hŭll¹, n., & v.t. **1.** Outer covering of fruit, esp. pod of peas & beans; (fig.) covering. **2.** v.t. Remove ~ of. [OE *hulu* f. st. *hul-* rel. to *helan* cover; see HELL]

hŭll², n., & v.t. **1.** Frame of ship, airship, flying-boat, etc.; ~ *down,* far away, so that ~ is invisible. **2.** v.t. Strike (ship) in ~ with shot, torpedo, etc. [15th c., of obsc. orig.; perh. spec. use of prec.]

hŭllabalōō', n. Uproar. [18th c, redupl. of *hallo, hullo,* etc.]

hŭllō', -loa (-lō), int. used to call attention, express surprise, or answer⋅call, esp. on telephone. [cf. HALLO]

hŭm¹, v.i. & t. (-mm-). Make continuous murmuring sound, as of bee, spinning top, etc.; make low inarticulate vocal sound, esp. (usu. ~ *& haw* or *ha*) of hesitation; sing with closed lips; (colloq.) be in state of activity, as *make things ~*; (sl.) smell unpleasantly; (v.t.) utter, sing, with closed lips. [ME, imit.; so MHG *hummen*]

hŭm², n. Humming sound esp. of hesitation (usu. ~*s & ha's*), applause, surprise, etc.; (sl.) bad smell. [imit.]

hum³ (hem), int. expr. hesitation, dissent, etc.

hŭm⁴, n. (sl.). Sham, hoax. [= HUMBUG]

hūm'an, a. & n. Of, belonging to, man, as ~ *nature;* that is a man or consists of men, as ~ *race, creature;* of man as opp. to God, as *to err is ~, to forgive divine*; having, showing, the qualities distinctive of man, as *more, less, than ~;* (n.) ~ being. Hence ~NESS (-n -n-) n. [ME *humain*(e) f. OF, f. L *humanus* (*homo* man, see -AN)]

hūmāne', a. Benevolent, compassionate; ‖*H~ Society* (for rescue of drowning persons); ~ *killer,* instrument for painless slaughter of cattle; (of branches of study) tending to refinement, elegant, cf. LITERAE HUMANIORES. Hence ~LY² (-nl-) adv., ~NESS (-n-n-) n. [differentiated f. prec. after 1700]

hūm'anism, n. Devotion to human interests; system concerned with human (not divine) interests, or with the human race (not the individual); Religion of HUMANITY; literary culture, esp. that of the humanists. [f. after foll.; -ISM]

hūm'anist, n. Student of human nature or human affairs; student (esp. in 14th– 16th cc.) of Roman & Greek literature &

antiquities, whence **hūmanis'tīc** a. [16th c. f. F -*iste* f. It. *umanista* (as HUMAN, see -IST)]

hūmănĭtār'ian, n. & a. 1. One who professes humanism (Religion of Humanity), visionary philanthropist. 2. adj. Holding, concerned with, the views of ∼s. Hence ∼ISM n. [f. foll. + -ARIAN]

hūmăn'ĭt|ў̆, n. Human nature; (pl.) human attributes; the human race; humaneness, benevolence; (pl.) benevolent acts; *Religion of H∼y* (rejecting the supernatural & concerned chiefly or wholly with the advancement of man's welfare); *the ∼ies*, polite scholarship, esp. of Latin & Greek classics; ‖ (Sc. Univv.; *H∼y*) study of Latin. [ME, f. OF -*ite* f. L *humanitatem* (as HUMAN, -TY)]

hŭm'anĭz|e, -**is|e** (-īz), v.t. & i. Make human, give human character to (∼*ed milk*, cow's milk prepared to resemble human milk); make, become, humane. Hence ∼A'TION n. [f. F *humaniser* (as HUMAN, see -IZE)]

hŭm'ankĭnd', n. Mankind.

hŭm'anlў̆, adv. In a human manner; by human means; from human point of view; with human feeling. [-LY²]

hŭm'ble, a. (*comp. & sup. pron.* -bler, -blĭst), & v.t. 1. Having, showing, low estimate of one's own importance; (formerly, esp. in subscribing letter) *your ∼ servant*; of lowly condition; (of things) of modest pretensions, dimensions, etc.; *eat ∼ pie*, make ∼ apology, submit to humiliation; ∼ *plant*, common SENSITIVE plant. 2. v.t. Make ∼, bring low, abase (one*self* etc.). Hence ∼NESS (-bel-) n., **hŭm'blY²** adv. [ME (*h*)*umble* f. OF f. L *humilis* lowly (*humus* ground, -IL)]

hŭm'ble-bee (-bel-), n. Bumble-bee. [15th c., prob. f. obs. (14th c.) *humble* hum, as BUMBLE-BEE f. *bumble*; but cf. MLG *hummelbē*, MDu. *hommel*, OHG *humbal*]

hŭm'bŭg, n., & v.t. & i. (-gg-). 1. Fraud, sham; deception; (as int.) nonsense!; impostor; kind of hard boiled sweet usu. flavoured with peppermint. 2. v.t. Delude (person *into*, *out of*, thing or do*ing*); (v.i.) be, behave like, a ∼. Hence **hŭmbŭg'ERY** (-g-) n. [f. c. 1750, sl., of unkn. orig.]

*•**hŭmdĭng'er**, n. (sl.). Excellent person or thing. [orig. unkn.]

hŭm'drŭm, a. & n., & v.i. (-mm-). Commonplace(ness), dull(ness); (v.i.) proceed in ∼ way. Hence ∼NESS n. [f. 1550; prob. redupl. f. HUM v.]

hŭm'er|us, n. (anat.). Bone of the upper arm in man; corresponding bone in other vertebrates. Hence ∼AL a., (also n., ∼al veil, oblong silk scarf worn round priest's shoulders during parts of the Mass etc.). [L, = shoulder]

hŭm'ĭd, a. Moist, damp. So **hūmĭd'ĭFY** v.t., **hūmĭd'ĭTY** n. (*relative ∼ity*, amount

of moisture in atmosphere as compared with that of complete saturation at the given temperature). [f. F *humide* or L *humidus* (*umēre* be moist, see -ID¹)]

hūmĭl'ĭ|āte, v.t. Lower the dignity or self-respect of; mortify. Hence or cogn. ∼āting² a., ∼A'TION n. [f. LL *humiliare* (as HUMBLE, see -ATE²)]

hūmĭl'ĭtў̆, n. Humbleness, meekness; humble condition. [ME, f. OF *humilite* f. L *humilitatem* (as HUMBLE, see -TY)]

‖ **hŭmm'el**, a. (Sc.). (Of cattle and stags) hornless. [cf. LG *hommel* hornless beast]

hŭmm'ĭng, a. In vbl senses; ∼-*bird* (of several species that make ∼ sound by vibration of wings); ∼-*top* (∼ when it spins). [f. HUM v. + -ING¹]

hŭmm'ock, n. Hillock, knoll; rising ground, esp. in marsh; hump or ridge in icefield. Hence ∼Y² a. [orig. naut.; 16th c. *ham-*, *hom-*; orig. unkn.]

hūm'oral, a. (med.). Of the bodily humours; ∼ *pathology*, doctrine referring all disease to state of the humours, whence ∼ISM, ∼IST, nn., ∼ĭs'tIC a. [f. F, or med. L **humoralis* as HUMOUR, see -AL]

hūm'orist, n. Facetious person; humorous talker, actor, or writer. Hence **hūmorĭs'tIC** a. [16th c., f. F *humoriste* (as prec., see -IST)]

hūm'orous, a. Full of humour; facetious, funny. Hence ∼LY² adv., ∼NESS n. [-OUS]

hūm'our¹ (-mer; *also* ū-), n. State of mind, mood; inclination, as *in the ∼ for fighting*; facetiousness, comicality; faculty of perceiving this; jocose imagination (less intellectual & more sympathetic than wit), whence ∼LESS a.; *out of ∼*, displeased; *good, ill, ∼* (temper), whence ∼ED² (-erd) a.; *cardinal ∼s* (hist.), four chief fluids of the body (blood, phlegm, choler, melancholy), determining person's physical & mental qualities; *aqueous, vitreous, ∼*, transparent fluid parts of the eye. [ME, f. AF f. L (*h*)*umorem* moisture (as HUMID, see -OR)]

hūm'our² (-mer; *also* ū-), v.t. Gratify, indulge, (person, taste, temper, etc.); adapt oneself to, make concessions to. [f. prec.]

hūm'oursome (-mer-), a. Capricious; peevish. Hence ∼NESS n. [-SOME]

hŭmp, n., & v.t. 1. Protuberance, esp. on the back, as deformity or (in camel etc.) as normal feature; rounded boss of earth etc.; (fig.) critical point (of undertaking, ordeal, etc.), esp. in phr. *over the ∼*, over the worst, well begun; ‖ (sl.) fit of depression or vexation, as *it gives me the ∼*; ∼*'back*, (person having) back with a ∼; ∼*'backed*, having such a back. 2. v.t. Make ∼-shaped; annoy, depress; (Austral.) hoist up, shoulder, (one's pack, swag, or *bluey*). Hence ∼ED² (-pt), ∼'LESS, ∼'Y², aa. [f. 1680, ∼-*backed* replacing *crump-backed*; perh. rel. to LG *humpel* hump, LG *humpe*, Du. *homp* lump, hunk (of bread)]

humph (hmf), int., & v.i. Int. expr. doubt or dissatisfaction; (v.i.) utter this.

hŭmp'tў-dŭmp'tў, n. Short dumpy person; (from nursery rhyme in which H~ is taken to mean an egg) person, thing, that once thrown down cannot be restored; person who makes words mean what he chooses. [app. f. *hump*(y) & *dump*(y); -*ty* unexpl.]

hŭm'pў, n. Australian hut. [native *oompi*]

hŭm'us, n. Vegetable mould. [L, =ground]

Hŭn, n. One of an Asiatic nomad race who invaded & ravaged Europe in 4th & 5th cc.; (derog.) German (esp. Prussian). Hence ~n'ISH[1] a. [OE *Hūne* f. med. L *Hunni*]

hŭnch[1], v.t. Bend, arch, convexly; thrust *out*, *up*, to form a hump. [orig. unkn.]

hŭnch[2], n. Hump; thick piece; ~'*back*(ed), hump-back(ed); *presentiment, intuition. Hence ~'Y[2] a. [orig. unkn.]

hŭn'dred, n. & a. (Cardinal number) ten times ten (100, C), as *a, one, six, several,* ~ *men, a, one, six* ~ *of them* or *of my friends,* ~s *of men,* ~s *of them, some, several,* ~s *of* etc.; (ordinal, in compds) *the* ~-*&*--*first, six*-~-*&*-*ninth*; (also ~ *& one*) large number; *not a* ~ *miles from* (joc.), at or close to; *a* ~ *per cent efficient*, doing the utmost in practice that it theoretically should; ~ pounds (of money); || (chiefly hist.) subdivision of county or shire, having its own court; CHILTERN HUNDREDS; *great, long,* ~, 120; ~ *of* BRICK[1]*s*; ~*weight*, 112lb. avoirdupois (abbr. *cwt*), *100lb.; ~s *& thousands*, sweets like small shot used chiefly for decorating cakes etc. Hence ~FOLD n., ~TH[2] a. & n. (*Old Hundredth*, hymn 'All people that . . .', version of Ps. C, or its tune). [OE, f. *hund* (cogn. w. L *centum*) + Gmc *rath*- number (cf. Goth. *rathjō* number]

hŭng. See HANG v.

Hŭngār'ian (-ngg-), a. & n. **1.** Of Hungary or its inhabitants. **2.** n. Native, language, of Hungary. [f. med. L *Hungaria* + -AN]

hŭng'er[1] (-ngg-), n. Uneasy sensation, exhausted condition, caused by want of food; (fig.) strong desire (*for, after*, etc.); ~-*march* (undertaken by body of unemployed to call attention to their condition; so ~-*marcher*); ~-*strike*, prisoner's refusal to take food in order to procure release. [OE *hungor*, OS, OHG -*ar*, ON *hungr*, (Goth. *huggrjan* vb), f. Gmc *hungruz*]

hŭng'er[2] (-ngg-), v.i. & t. Feel hunger; have craving (*for, after*); (p.p., arch.) hungry; (trans.) starve (*into* submission, *out of* place etc.). [OE *hyngran*, assim. to prec.]

hŭn'grў (-ngg-), a. Feeling hunger (~ *as a* ~ *hunter*); showing hunger, as *a* ~ *look*; inducing hunger, as *a* ~ *air*; ~ *rice*, W.--African grain allied to millet; (fig.) eager, greedy; (of soil) poor, barren; || *H~ Forties* (hist.), the decade 1840-9 in England, a period of great distress among

the poor. Hence **hŭn'grILY**[2] adv., **hŭn'grINESS** n. [OE *hungrig* (as HUNGER[1], see -Y[2])]

hŭnk, n. Large piece cut off; clumsy piece; hunch. [19th c.; cf. WFlem. *hunke*]

|| **hŭnk'ers**, n. pl. The hams (esp. in phr. *on* one's ~, in a squatting position). [Sc., f. *hunker* to squat]

hŭnks, n. Close-fisted man, miser. [orig. unkn.]

*hŭnkў-dōr'ў, a. (sl.). Excellent, top--hole.

Hŭnnish. See HUN.

hŭnt[1], v.i. & t. Pursue wild animals, go fox-~ing; (trans.) chase (these) for food or sport; seek *after, for*; drive *away, out*; scour (district) in pursuit of game; use (horse, hounds) in ~ing; *shoot (game); ~ *down*, bring to bay; ~ *out*, track out, find by search; ~ *up*, search for; ~ *in* COUPLES; ~ *the hare, slipper, squirrel,* games. [OE *huntian* f. *hunta* hunter, cogn. w. OE *hentan*, Goth. *hinthan* seize]

hŭnt[2], n. Hunting (lit. & fig.); persons hunting with a pack; hunting district; ~ *ball* (given by members of ~, men wearing pink). [f. prec.]

hŭn'ter, n. One who hunts; (fig.) *fortune, place*, etc., ~; horse for hunting; watch with hinged cover protecting glass or (*half*-~) outer part of it; ~'*s moon*, next full moon after harvest moon. Hence **hŭn'trESS**[1] n. [-ER[1]]

hŭn'ting, n. In vbl senses; ~-*box*, small house for use during ~-season; ~ COG[1]; ~-*crop*; ~-*ground*, place where one hunts (often fig.); *happy* ~-*ground*(s), the future state (prop. as expected by Amer. Indians), good place for ~ (fig.); ~-*horn*, horn used in ~, second pommel on near side of side-saddle. [-ING[1]]

hŭnts'man, n. Hunter; man in charge of (esp. fox-) hounds.

hŭr'dle, n., & v.t. Portable rectangular frame strengthened with withes or wooden bars, for temporary fence etc.; wooden frame to be jumped over in ~--*race*; (hist.) frame on which traitors were dragged to execution; (v.t.) fence *off* etc. with ~s. [OE *hyrdel* (-LE), f. Gmc *hurdiz* (= Goth. *haurds*, ON *hurth* door, OHG *hurt* hurdle), cogn. w. L *cratis*]

hŭrd'ler, n. One who makes hurdles, or runs in hurdle-races. [-ER[1]]

hŭrd'ў-gŭrdў, n. Musical instrument with droning sound, played by turning handle, orig. one with rosined wheel turned by right hand & played by left; (colloq.) barrel organ & street piano. [prob. imit.]

hŭrl, v.t., & n. **1.** Throw violently from some position (lit. & fig.); throw (missile etc., also fig.); || (Sc.) convey in a wheeled vehicle. **2.** n. ~ing, violent throw; || (Sc.) a ride in a wheeled vehicle. [ME, prob. imit., but corresp. in form & partly sense w. LG *hurreln*]

hŭrl'ey, n. (Ir.). Kind of hockey. [as prec.]

Hŭrl'ingham (-ngam), n. (Used for) ~ Park, Fulham, headquarters of ~ Polo Club.

hŭrl'y̆, n. (arch.). Commotion. [as HURL]

hŭrl'y̆-bŭrl'y̆, n. Commotion, tumult. [f. 1540; redupl. f. HURL v.]

hurrah' (hu-, hoo-), -ray', int., n., & v.i. Int. expr. exultation or approbation; (n.) this cry; (v.i.) shout ~. [replaces huzza; cf. Swed. & Da. hurra, Du. hoera]

hŭ'rricane, n. Storm with violent wind with velocity of 75 miles an hour or over, esp. W.-Indian cyclone (also fig.); ~-bird, frigate-bird; ~ deck, light upper deck; ~ lamp (designed to resist wind). [f. Sp. huracan, of Carib orig.]

hŭ'rry[1], n. Undue haste; eagerness to get a thing done quickly; eagerness (to do, for thing); (w. neg. or interrog.) need for haste; (colloq.) you will not beat that in a ~ (easily), shall not ask again in a ~ (willingly); ~-scurry adv., adj., & n., (in) disorderly haste, (v.i.) proceed thus. [16th c., rel. to HURL, HURLY, HURLY-BURLY, etc.]

hŭ'rry[2], v.t. & i. Carry, drive, (person etc. away, along, into, into doing, etc.) with undue haste; move, act, with great or undue haste; ~y up, make haste. Hence ~iedLY[2] adv., ~iedNESS n., (-id-). [as prec.]

hŭrst, n. Hillock; sandbank in sea or river; wooded eminence; wood. [OE hyrst, rel. to OS, OHG hurst]

hŭrt[1], n. Wound, material injury; harm, wrong. Hence ~FUL, ~'LESS, aa., ~'fulLY[2] adv., ~'fulNESS n. [ME, f. OF hurte f. hurter (foll.)]

hŭrt[2], v.t. & i. (hurt). Cause bodily injury or pain to; damage; inflict injury upon; distress, wound, (person, his feelings etc.); (colloq.) suffer injury or pain (does your hand ~?). [ME, f. OF hurter (mod. heurter) f. Gallo-rom. *hurtare]

hŭr'tle, v.t. & i., & n. Strike against; hurl swiftly; strike against; move with clattering sound; come with a crash; (n.) hurtling, clashing sound. [f. HURT[2] + -LE(3)]

hŭs'band[1] (-z-), n. Man joined to woman by marriage; || (arch.) good, bad, ~ (economist). Hence ~HOOD, ~SHIP, nn., ~LIKE a. [late OE husbonda f. ON husbondi; see HOUSE & BOND[4]]

hŭs'band[2] (-z-), v.t. Manage thriftily, economize; || (arch.) till (ground), cultivate (plants); (poet., joc.) provide with husband; (rare) marry (woman). [f. prec.]

hŭs'bandman (-z-), n. Farmer.

hŭs'bandry̆ (-z-), n. Farming; (good, bad) economy; careful management. [-RY]

hŭsh[1], n. Stillness; silence; ~-money, paid to prevent exposure. [f. foll.]

hŭsh[2], v.t. & i. Silence, quiet; ~ up, suppress (affair); be silent, stop. (as int.) ~!; ~'aby̆, int. used to lull child; ~!~ adj. phr., to be kept specially secret; ~-ship (of great length, speed, & gun-power,

secretly built; cf. Q-ship). [back formation f. obs. adj. husht f. husht, hust, intt. (imit.)]

hŭsk, n., & v.t. 1. Dry outer covering of some fruits or seeds; (fig.) worthless outside part of anything; disease of cattle. 2. v.t. Remove ~ from. [late ME, of unkn. orig.]

hŭs'k|y̆[1], a. & n. Of, full of, husks; dry as a husk; (of voice or person) dry, hoarse, whence ~iLY[2] adv., ~iNESS n.; (colloq.) tough, strong, hefty (& as n., ~y person). [-Y[2]]

hŭs'ky̆[2], n. Eskimo dog; (H~) Eskimo person or language. [? contr. f. ESKIMO]

|| **hussar'** (-z-), n. Soldier of light cavalry regiment (orig. Hungarian light horseman of 15th c.). [f. Hung. huszár f. OSerb. husar f. It. corsaro CORSAIR]

Hŭss'ite, n. Follower of John Huss, Bohemian religious reformer of 15th c. [-ITE[1]]

hŭss'y̆, -zzy̆, n. Woman of light or worthless character; pert girl. [f. HOUSEWIFE]

hŭs'tings (-z), n. Platform from which (before 1872) candidates for Parliament were nominated; election proceedings; court (now rarely) held in Guildhall of London. [OE husting f. ON husthing house-assembly]

hŭs'tl|e (-sl), v.t. & i., & n. 1. Push roughly, jostle; thrust (person etc. into, out of, etc.); impel unceremoniously (into thing or doing); (v.i.) push roughly against; push one's way; hurry, bustle. 2. n. ~ing. [17th c., f. MDu. husselen shake, toss]

hŭt, n., & v.t. & i. (-tt-). 1. Small mean house of rude construction; (Mil.) temporary wooden house for troops; ~-circle (Archaeol.), ring of stones or earth indicating site of prehistoric ~. 2. v.t. Place (troops etc.) in ~s; (v.i.) lodge in ~. Hence ~'MENT n., ~ encampment. [17th c., f. F hutte f. MHG hütte]

hŭtch, n. Box-like pen for rabbits etc.; hut, cabin, small house; truck used in mining etc. [ME, f. OF huche f. med. L hutica of unkn. orig.]

Huzoor', n. Title of respect used by Indians in addressing superiors. [Arab. hadŭr the presence]

huzza' (-ah), int., n., & v.i. & t. (arch.). Int. of exultation, encouragement, or applause; (make, greet with) the cry ~. [16th c., imit.]

hy̆'acinth, n. Kinds of bulbous plants with bell-shaped flowers of various colours, esp. purplish blue, so (esp. as Homeric epithet of doubtful sense for locks, hair) ~iNE[2] (-in[L]) a.; this colour; precious stone, orange variety of zircon. [in 16th c. replacing JACINTH; f. F hyacinthe f. L f. Gk huakinthos, flower & gem, also name of youth loved by Apollo]

Hy̆'adēs (-z), n. pl. Group of stars near Pleiades. [f. Gk Huades (acc. to pop. etym., f. huō rain, but perh. f. hus swine)]

hyaena. See HYENA.

hy′aline, a. & n. Glass-like, vitreous (chiefly techn.); (n., poet.) smooth sea, clear sky, etc. [f. LL f. Gk *hualinos* (*hualos* glass, see -INE²)]

hy′alite, n. Colourless variety of opal. [f. Gk *hualos* glass, see -ITE]

hy′aloid, a. & n. (anat.). Glassy; ~ (*membrane*), thin transparent membrane enveloping vitreous humour of eye. [f. F *hyaloïde* f. LL f. Gk *hualoeidēs* (as prec., see -OID)]

hyb′rid, n. & a. 1. Offspring of two animals or plants of different species or varieties; person of mixed nationality; (fig.) thing, word, composed of incongruous elements, esp. of different languages. 2. adj. Cross-bred, mongrel; heterogeneous; ‖~ *bill* in Parliament, one combining characteristics of public & private bill, & referred to a~ *committee*. Hence~ITY (-Id²) n. [f. L *hybrida, hibrida* offspring of tame sow & wild boar]

hyb′ridism, n. Fact, condition, of being hybrid; cross-breeding. [prec. +-ISM]

hyb′ridiz|e, -is|e (-īz), v.t. & i. Subject (species etc.) to cross-breeding; produce hybrids; (of animal or plant) interbreed. Hence ~ABLE a., ~A′TION n. [HYBRID + -IZE]

hyd′atid, n. (path.). Cyst containing watery fluid, morbid formation (esp. one formed by, & containing, a tape-worm larva). [f. Gk *hudatis -idos* watery vesicle (*hudōr -atos* water, -ID²)]

Hyde Park, n. A London park, a fashionable resort, & the scene of many political and other demonstrations.

hyd′ra, n. (Gk Myth.) snake whose many heads grew again when cut off; (fig.) thing hard to extirpate; water-snake; a fresh-water polyp. [L, f. Gk *hudra* water--snake]

hydrăn′gea (-ja), n. Kinds of shrubs with globular clusters of white, blue, or pink flowers. [f. Gk *hudōr* water +*aggos* vessel]

hyd′rant, n. Pipe (esp. in street) with nozzle to which hose can be attached, for drawing water from main. [U.S., f. Gk *hudōr* water +-ANT]

hyd′rate¹, n. (chem.). Compound of water with another compound or an element. [f. F *hydrate* f. Gk *hudōr* water, see -ATE¹]

hyd′r|āte², v.t. (chem.). Combine with water. Hence ~A′TION n. [f. prec.]

hydraul′ic, a. & n. 1. Of water conveyed through pipes or channels; operated by water-power, as ~ *lift*; ~ *ram*, automatic pump in which kinetic energy of descending column of water raises some of the water above its original level; hardening under water, as ~ *cement*; ~ *press*, hydrostatic press. 2. n. pl. Science of conveyance of liquids through pipes etc., esp. as motive power. Hence or cogn. **hydraul′ICALLY** adv., **hydrauli′-**

cian (-ĭshn) n. [f. L f. Gk *hudraulikos* (*hudōr* water +*aulos* pipe, see -IC)]

hyd′r|ic, a. (chem.). Of, containing, hydrogen. So ~IDE n. [f. HYDROGEN + -IC]

hyd′rō, n. (pl. ~s). = HYDROPATHIC. [colloq. abbr.]

hydro-, comb. form of Gk *hudōr* water, (1) in miscell. terms, w. sense ‘having to do with water ’, (2) in names of diseases, w. sense ‘dropsical ’ or ‘affected with accumulation of serous fluid ’, (3) in chem. terms, usu. w. sense ‘combined with hydrogen’; as: ~*carb′on*, compound of hydrogen & carbon; ~*cĕph′alus*, water on the brain; ~*cephăl′ic*, ~*cĕph′alous*, affected with this; ~*chlor′ic*, containing hydrogen & chlorine; ~*cyăn′ic*, containing hydrogen & cyanogen, esp. ~*cyanic acid*, prussic acid; ~*dўnăm′ic(al)*, of the forces acting on or· exerted by liquids; ~*dў-năm′ics*, science of these forces; ~*elĕc′tric*, developing electricity by utilization of water power, (of electricity) produced by utilization of water-power; ~*grapher* (-ŏg²), person skilled in, ~*graph′ic(al)* having to do with, ~*graphy*; ~*graphy* (-ŏg²), scientific description of the waters of the earth; ~*kinĕt′ic(s)*, (science) of the motion of liquids; ~*logy* (-ŏl²), science of the properties, laws, etc., of water; ~*lysis* (-ŏl²), decomposition of a compound by reaction with water, the water also being decomposed ; ~*măn′ia*, craving for water; ~*mechăn′ics* (of liquids); ~*meter* (-ŏm²), instrument for finding specific gravity of liquids (occas. also of solids); ~*mĕt′ric*, ~*metry* (-ŏm²), concerned with, determination of, specific gravity of liquids; *hўd′rophane*, opal that absorbs water & becomes transparent on immersion; *hўd′rophone*, instrument for detection of sound-waves in water; *hўd′rophўte*, aquatic plant; *hўd′roplane*, fin-like device enabling submarine to rise or fall, light fast motor-boat designed to skim over surface, seaplane; ~*pneumăt′ic*, involving combined action of water & air; ~*quin′one*, preparation from quinone, used (Phot.) as developer; *hўd′rosphere*, waters of the earth’s surface; *hўd′rostat*, electrical device for detecting presence of water; ~*therapeut′ic*, ~*thĕ′rapy*, hydropathic, hydropathy; ~*therm′al*, of the action of heated water on earth’s crust; ~*thor′ax*, dropsy of the chest; ~*tropism* (-ŏt²), (of plants) tendency to turn to or from moisture; ~*zō′a* n. pl., class of coelenterate animals chiefly marine, including jelly-fish & fresh-water hydra.

hyd′rogĕn, n. Colourless invisible odourless gas, an element, the lightest substance known, combining with oxygen to form water; ~ *bomb*, (also *fusion* or *thermo-nuclear bomb*) immensely powerful bomb utilizing fusion of ~ atomic nuclei. Hence **hydrŏ′gĕn**OUS a. [f. F HYDRO(*gène* -GEN)]

hȳdrŏ'gĕn|āte, v.t. Charge, cause to combine, with hydrogen. So ~IZE v.t. [prec. +-ATE³]

hȳd'roid, a. & n. (zool.). (Animal) like, allied to, the hydra (polyp). [-OID]

hȳd'romĕl, n. Mixture of honey & water; *vinous* ~ (also *mead*), this fermented. [L, f. Gk *hudromeli* (*meli* honey, see HYDRO-)]

hȳdropăth'ic, a. & n. 1. Of, concerned with, hydropathy. **2. n.** Hotel where ~ treatment may be had. [f. foll. +-IC]

hȳdrŏp'ath|ȳ, n. Medical treatment by external & internal application of water. So ~IST n. [f. G *hydropathie* (HYDRO-, -PATHY)]

hȳdrophōb'|ĭa, n. Aversion to water, esp. as symptom of rabies in man; rabies, esp. in man; (joc.) dread of water. So ~IC a. [16th c., f. LL f. Gk *hudro*PHOBIA, see HYDRO-]

hȳdrŏp'ic, a. Dropsical. [ME, f. OF *ydropique* f. L f. Gk *hudrōpikos* (as HYDROPSY, see -IC)]

hȳdropŏn'ics, n. Soilless culture, art of growing plants without soil, in water impregnated with chemicals. [HYDRO-, Gk *ponos* labour]

hȳd'rŏpsȳ, n. (arch. or med.). Dropsy. [ME, f. OF *ydropisie* f. med. L *hydropisia* (for L -*sis*) f. Gk *hudrōps* (*hudōr* water)]

hȳdrostăt'ic, a. & n. 1. Of the equilibrium of liquids & the pressure exerted by liquids at rest; ~ *paradox*, principle that any quantity of a perfect liquid, however small, may be made to balance any other quantity; ~ *press* (also *hydraulic, Bramah's, press*), machine in which pressure of a body of water is multiplied by transmission from small to larger cylinder. **2. n. pl.** Branch of mechanics concerned with the pressure & equilibrium of liquids at rest. Hence ~AL a., ~alLY² adv. [17th c., f. Gk *hudrostatēs* ~ balance (HYDRO-, STATIC)]

hȳd'rous, a. (chem., mineral.). Containing water. [f. Gk *hudōr* water +-OUS]

hȳdrŏx'ide, n. (chem.). Compound of element or radical with hydrogen & oxygen, not with water. [HYDRO- +OXIDE]

hȳēn'a, hȳaen'a, n. Carnivorous quadruped allied to dog tribe; *striped* ~, variety whose howl is compared to fiendish laughter; cruel, treacherous, or rapacious person; Tasmanian tiger; ~-*dog*, S.-African canine quadruped like~. [L (-*ae*-) f. Gk *huaina* fem. f. *hus* pig]

hȳeto-, comb. form of Gk *huetos* rain, as ~*graphy* (-ŏg⁴), mapping of rainfall, ~*meter* (-ŏm⁴), rain-gauge.

Hȳgei'a (-jē'a), **n.** Goddess of health; health personified. Hence **hȳgēi'AN** (-jē'an) a. [f. Gk *Hugeia* late for *Hugieia* (*hugiēs* healthy)]

hȳ'gĭ|ēne (or -jēn), **n.** Principles of health; sanitary science. Hence ~**ĕn'**IC(AL) (na.), ~**ĕn'ical**LY² adv., ~**ĕn'**ICS, ~**en**IST, nn., (or -jēn⁴). [f. F *hygiène* f. Gk *hugieinē* (*tekhnē* art) of health, f. *hugiēs* healthy]

hȳgro-, comb. form of Gk *hugros* wet, fluid, as: *hȳg'rodeik* (-dĭk), form of ~*meter*; ~*logy* (-ŏl⁴), study of the humidity of atmosphere etc.; ~*meter* (-ŏm⁴), instrument for measuring humidity of air or gas; ~*mĕt'ric*, ~*metry* (-ŏm⁴), concerned with, measurement of, humidity; *hȳg'roscōpe*, instrument indicating but not measuring humidity of air; ~*scop'ic*, of the ~scope, (of bodies) tending to absorb moisture.

Hȳk'sōs (-z), **n. pl.** The shepherd kings of Egypt (about 2000 B.C.). [Gk *Huksōs*]

hȳl'ic, a. Of matter, material. [f. LL f. Gk *hulikos* (*hulē* matter, see -IC)]

hȳlo-, comb. form of Gk *hulē* matter, as: ~*morph'ism*, doctrine that primordial matter is first cause of the universe; *hȳl'otheism*, doctrine that God & matter are identical; *hȳl'otheist*, ~*thĕts'tic*, holder of, concerned with, this doctrine; ~*zō'ism*, ~*zoist*(ic), ~*zō'ic*, materialism, -ist(ic).

Hȳm'ĕn¹, n. (Gk & Rom. Myth.). God of marriage. So **hȳmĕnē'AL**a., **hȳmĕnē'al**LY² adv. [L, f. Gk *Humĕn*]

hȳm'ĕn², n. (anat.). Virginal membrane, stretched across external orifice of vagina. [f. LL f. Gk *humēn* membrane]

hȳmĕn|o-, comb. form of Gk *humēn* membrane, as ~*ŏp'tera* n. pl., large order of insects with four membranous wings, so ~*ŏp'teral*, ~*ŏp'terous*, aa.

hymn (hĭm), **n., & v.t. & i. 1.** Song of praise to God, esp. metrical composition sung in religious service; song of praise in honour of a god or other exalted being; ~-*book* (of ~s). **2. v.t.** Praise (God etc.) in ~s, express (praise etc.) in ~; (v.i.) sing ~s. Hence **hȳm'n**IC a., **hȳm'n**IST n. [ME *ymne* etc. f. OF *ymne* f. L f. Gk *humnos*; OE dir. f. L]

hȳm'n|al, a. & n. Of hymns; (n.) hymn-book, so ~ARY¹ n. [n. 15th c. f. med. L *hymnale* (prec. +-AL)]

hȳm'nod|ȳ, n. Singing of hymns; composition of hymns, whence ~IST n.; hymns collectively. [f. med. L f. Gk *humnōdia* (*humnos* hymn +*ōdē* song, ODE)]

hȳmnŏg'rapher, n. Composer of hymns. [f. LL f. Gk *humnographos* (as prec., see -GRAPHER)]

hȳmnŏl'og|ȳ, n. Composition, study of, hymns; hymns collectively. So **hȳmno-lŏ'g**IC a., ~IST n. [HYMN +-O- +-LOGY]

hȳ'oid a. & n. (anat.). **1.** ~ *bone*, tongue-bone between chin & thyroid cartilage; pertaining to this. **2. n.** ~ bone. [f. F *hyoïde* f. Gk *huoeidēs* shaped like letter U]

hȳoscy'amine, hȳ'oscine, nn. Alkaloids contained in henbane & used in medicine. [L, f. Gk *huoskuamos* henbane (*hus huos* pig, *kuamos* bean), -INE⁵]

hyp. See HIP³.

hȳpaeth'ral, -pēth'ral, a. Open to the sky, roofless (orig. of Gk temples); open-air. [f. L f. Gk *hupaithros* (*aithēr* air, see HYPO-)]

hўpăll′agĕ, n. (gram.). Reversal of natural relations of two elements in a proposition (e.g. *apply the wound to water* for *apply water to the wound*). [LL, f. Gk *hupallagē* (*allassō* exchange, see HYPO-)]

hўper-, pref. = Gk *huper* in senses 'over', 'above', 'exceeding', 'excessive'.

hўperaesth|ēs′ĭa, n. (Path.) morbid sensitiveness of nerves; excessive sensibility. So ~ET′IC (-ĕt̆-) a. [HYPER-+Gk -*aisthēsia* f. *aisthanomai* perceive]

hўpĕrb′atŏn, n. Inversion of normal order of words, esp. for sake of emphasis. [L, f. Gk *huperbaton* (*bainō* step, see HYPER-)]

hўpĕrb′ola, n. (geom.). Curve produced when cone is cut by plane making larger angle with base than side of cone makes (cf. ELLIPSE). Hence **hўperbŏl′IC** a. [mod. L, f. Gk *huperbolē* f. *huperballō* exceed (*ballō* throw, see HYPER-)]

hўpĕrb′ol|ē, n. (rhet.). Exaggerated statement not meant to be taken literally. Hence **hўperbŏl′ICAL** a., **hўperbŏl′ical-LY**[2] adv., ~ISM, ~IST, nn. [L, as prec.]

hўperbŏr′ean, a. & n. (Inhabitant) of the extreme north of the earth or (colloq.) of a country; (Gk Myth.) one of a race living in land of sunshine & plenty beyond north wind. [f. LL *hyperboreanus* (L -*boreus*) f. Gk *huperboreos* (*Boreas* north wind, see HYPER-)]

hўpercătalĕc′tic, a. (pros.). (Of verse) having extra syllable after last complete dipody. [f. LL HYPER(*catalecticus* CATALECTIC)]

hўpercrit′ĭc|al, a. Too critical, esp. of small faults. Hence ~alLY[2] adv., ~ISM n., ~IZE v.t. & i. [f. mod. L *hypercriticus* (HYPER-, CRITICAL)]

hўpermĕt′rĭc(al), aa. (Of verse) having a redundant syllable; (of syllable) redundant. [f. Gk *hypermetros* (*metron* metre, HYPER-)]

hўpermĕtr|ōp′ĭa, n. Morbidly long sight. Hence ~ŏp′IC a. [as prec.+Gk *ōps* eye +-*ia* -Y[1]]

hўperphўs′ĭcal (-z-), a. Supernatural. [HYPER-]

hўp′ersthēne, n. Orthorhombic rock-forming mineral of the pyroxene group. [f. F HYPER(*stène* f. Gk *sthenos* strength, from its hardness)]

hўpertĕn′s|ion (-shn), n. Abnormally high blood pressure. So ~IVE a. [HYPER-+TENSION]

hўpĕrt′roph|ў, n. Enlargement (*of* organ etc.) due to excessive nutrition. Hence or cogn. **hўpertrŏph′IC**, ~iED[2] (-ĭd), aa. [HYPER- + Gk -*trophia* nourishment f. *trephō*]

hypethral. See HYPAETHRAL.

hўph′en, n., & v.t. 1. Sign (-) used to join two words together, to join separated syllables of word broken at end of line, or to divide word into parts; short pause between syllables in speaking. 2. v.t. Join (words) with ~, write (compound word)

with ~. [LL, f. Gk *huphen* together (*hupo* under+*hen* one)] <

hўph′enāte, v.t. = prec. vb (~*d* Americans*, German-Americans, Irish-Americans, etc.). [prec., -ATE[3]]

hўpno- (bef. vowel *hypn*-), comb. form of Gk *hupnos* sleep, as : ~*gen′esis*, ~*genĕt′ic*, induction of, inducing, the hypnotic state; ~*logy* (-ŏl̆-), science of the phenomena of sleep.

hўpnōs′ĭs, n. (pl. -*ōsēs*). Artificially produced sleep; hypnotic state. [f. Gk *hupnoō* make sleep, -OSIS]

hўpnŏt′ĭc, a. & n. 1. Of, producing, hypnotism. 2. n. Thing that produces sleep; person under influence of hypnotism. [f. F *hypnotique* f. LL f. Gk *hupnōtikos* (as prec., see -OTIC)]

hўp′not|ism, n. (Artificial production of) a state resembling deep sleep, in which the subject acts only on external suggestion. So ~IST n., ~IZE v.t. [f. prec. +-ISM]

hўp′ō, n. (photog.). The salt formerly called hyposulphite, now thiosulphate, of soda, used in fixing. [abbr.]

hўpo-, pref. (bef. vowel *hyp*-) = Gk *hupo* under, below, slightly; (Chem.) forming names of oxygen compounds lower in the series than those with the simple name. Exx.: *hўp′oblast*, inner layer of cells in blastoderm; ~*brăn′chial* (-ngk-), situated under the gills; ~*cўc′loid*, curve traced by point in circumference of circle rolling round interior circumference of another circle; ~*gās′trium*, lowest region of abdomen; ~*gē′al*, ~*gē′an*, aa., underground; *hўp′ogĕne*, (of rocks) formed under the surface; ~*ge′um*, pl. ~*gea*, underground chamber; ~*gloss′al* (*nerve*), motor nerve of tongue; ~*gynous* (-ŏj̆-) (Bot.), situated below pistils or ovary; *hўp′onăsty* (Bot.), tendency in plant-organs to grow more rapidly on under side; ~*phŏs′phite*, salt of hypophosphorous acid; *hўp′ostȳle*, (hall etc.) with roof supported on pillars; ~*trachel′ium* (-kĕ-), lower part of capital of column.

hўp′ocaust, n. (Rom. Ant.). Hollow space under floor in which heat from furnace was accumulated for heating house or bath. [f. L f. Gk *hupokauston* place heated from below (*kaiō*, *kau*-, burn, see prec.)]

hўpochŏn′dr|ĭa (-k-), n. Morbid depression either apparently causeless or due to (unnecessary) anxiety about health. So ~ĭ′ASIS n. [f. LL f. Gk (*ta*) *hupokhondria* soft parts of body below costal cartilages (*khondros* cartilage, see HYPO-)]

hўpochŏn′dr|ĭăc (-k-), a. & n. 1. Of, affected by, hypochondria. 2. n. ~iac person. Hence ~ĭ′acAL a., ~ĭ′acalLY[2] adv. [f. F *hypochondriaque* f. med. L f. Gk *hupokhondriakos* (as prec., see -AC)]

hўpocoris′tic, a. (gram.). Of the nature of a pet-name. [f. Gk *hupokoristikos* (*hupokorizomai* play the child)]

hỹpŏc'rĭsỹ, n. Simulation of virtue or goodness; dissimulation, pretence. [ME, f. OF *ypocrisie* f. eccl. L f. Gk *hupokrisis* lit. acting of a part f. *hupokrinomai* (*hupo*-HYPO- +*krinō* decide, judge)]

hỹp'ocrite, n. Person guilty of hypocrisy; dissembler, pretender. So **hỹpocrit'ICAL** a., **hỹpocrit'icalLY**[2] adv. [ME, f. OF *ypocrite* f. eccl. L (-*ta*) f. Gk *hupokritēs* actor (as prec.)]

hỹpodĕrm'|ic, a. & n. **1.** (Med., of drugs etc.) introduced beneath the skin, as ~*ic injection*; ~*ic needle, syringe*, for ~*ic* injection; (Anat.) lying under the skin. **2.** n. ~*ic* injection, syringe. Hence ~*ICALLY* adv. [f. HYPO- +Gk *derma* skin +-IC]

hỹpŏs'tas|ĭs, n. (pl. ~*es*, pr. -ēz). **1.** (med.). Excess of blood in organs of body. **2.** (metaphys.). Underlying substance, opp. to attributes or to what is unsubstantial. **3.** (theol.). Personality (of Christ), person (of the Godhead). So **hỹpostăt'IC(AL) aa.**, **hỹpostăt'icalLY**[2] adv., ~*IZE(3)*, **hỹpŏs'tatIZE(3)**, vv.t. (metaphys.). [f. LL f. Gk *hupostasis* (*hupo*- HYPO- + *stasis* standing, state)]

hỹpotĕn's|ion (-shn), n. Low blood pressure. So ~*IVE* a. [HYPO- +TENSION]

hỹpŏt'ĕnūse, n. Side opposite right angle of triangle. [f. L f. Gk *hupoteinousa* (*grammē*) subtending line (*hupo*- HYPO- + *teinō* stretch); also (improp.) -*thenuse*]

hỹp'othĕc, n. (Rom. & Sc. Law). Security established by law over thing belonging to debtor. So **hỹpŏth'ĕcARY**[1] a. [f. F *hypothèque* or LL f. Gk *hupothēkē*]

hỹpŏth'ĕc|āte, v.t. Pledge, mortgage. Hence ~*A'TION* n. [f. med. L *hypothecare* (as prec.), see -ATE[3]]

hỹpŏth'ĕsĭs, n. (pl. -*thesēs*). Supposition made as basis for reasoning, without assumption of its truth, or as starting-point for investigation; groundless assumption. So **hỹpothĕt'IC(AL) aa.**, **hỹpothĕt'icalLY**[2] adv. [f. LL f. Gk *hupothesis* foundation]

hỹpŏth'ĕsize, -ise (-īz), v.i. & t. Frame a hypothesis; (trans.) assume. [f. prec. +-IZE]

hỹpso-, comb. form of Gk *hupsos* height, as: ~*graphy* (-ŏg²), department of geography dealing with altitudes; ~*meter* (-ŏm²), ~*mĕt'ric(al)*, ~*metry* (-ŏm²), instrument for, concerned with, science of, measuring altitudes.

Hȳr'ăx, n. Genus of small rabbit-like mammals, including Syrian rock-rabbit and S.-Afr. rock-badger. [f. Gk *hurax* shrew-mouse]

hỹs'on, n. Kind of green tea from China. [f. Chin. *hsi-ch'un* lit. bright spring]

‖ **hȳ²spỹ, I spỹ**, n. Kind of hide-&-seek.

hỹss'op, n. Small bushy aromatic herb, formerly used medicinally; (Bibl.) plant whose twigs were used for sprinkling in Jewish rites, bunch of this used in purification. [ME *ysope* f. OF f. L f. Gk

hyssōpos, of Semitic orig.; *h*- f. 16th c.; OE dir. f. L]

hỹsterēs'ĭs, n. (phys.). Lagging of magnetic induction behind the magnetizing force. [f. Gk *husterēsis* (*husteros* coming after)]

hỹstĕr'ia, n. Functional disturbance of nervous system (esp. of women), characterized by anaesthesia, convulsions, etc., & usu. attended with disturbance of moral & intellectual faculties (formerly thought to be due to disturbance of womb); morbid excitement. [mod. medical L, on foll.]

hỹstĕ'rĭc, a. & n. **1.** = foll. **2.** n. pl. Hysterical fits or convulsions. [f. L f. Gk *husterikos* of the womb (*hustera*, see -IC)]

hỹstĕ'rical, a. Of, affected with, hysteria; morbidly emotional. Hence ~*LY*[2] adv. [as prec. +-AL]

hỹstero-, comb. form of Gk *hustera* womb, as: ~*gĕn'ic*, ~*geny* (-ŏj²), productive, production, of HYSTERIA; ~*logy* (-ŏl²), treatise on the uterus; ~*tomy* (-ŏt²), operation of cutting into the uterus.

hỹs'terŏn prŏt'erŏn, n. (Gram.) figure of speech in which what should come last is put first; inversion of natural order. [LL, f. Gk *husteron proteron* latter (put in place of) former]

I

I[1], **i**, (ī), letter (pl. *Is*, I's). As Roman numeral I or i = 1, as i 1, ii 2, iii 3, iv (rarely iiii) 4, vi 6, viii 8, ix (rarely viiii) 9, xi 11, xiv 14, li 51, cii 102, miv 1,004.

I[2] (ī), pron. & n. Subjective case of 1st pers. pron. (objective *me*, poss. *my*; pl. *we*, obj. *us*, poss. *our*); (n., metaphys.) *the I*, the ego, subject or object of self-consciousness. [OE *ic*, OS *ik*, OHG *ih*, ON *ek*, Goth. *ik*, cogn. w. L, Gk *egō*]

-i, suf. forming pl. of L nn. in -*us* & -*er* of 2nd decl. & of Ital. wds in -*o*, -*e*; retained in E in wds of scientific or learned use, as *cirri, foci, dilettanti, literati*; also freq. in mod. L names of groups or orders in Nat. Hist., as *acanthopterygii, acrocarpi*.

-i-, connecting vowel in L, being stem--vowel, as in *omnivorus*, weakened representative of this, as in *herbivorus* (*herba*-), *granivorus* (*grano*-), or merely connective, as in *graminivorus* (*gramin-*); so in E wds f. L or thr. F, & in mod. wds formed on L models, as *hydriform, setiform*. Cf. -O-.

-ia[1], suf., f. L & Gk -*ia*, forming abstract nn. etc., as *hydrophobia, mania, militia*; freq. in mod. L terms of pathology (*cephalalgia, hysteria*); of bot. (classes, as *Cryptogamia*, & personal names, as *dahlia, fuchsia*); in name of countries, as *Australia*; & in names of alkaloids, as *morphia, strychnia*, (in more recent nomenclature -*ine*). F -*ie* f. -*ia* gives -Y¹.

-ia², suf. forming pl. of Gk nn. in -ion & L nn. in -ium, as *paraphernalia, regalia*; freq. in mod. L names of classes etc. in zool., as *mammalia, reptilia*.

-ial, suf. repr. L -*ialis*, in adjj. f. n. -stems in -*io*-, -*ia*-, as *curialis, tibialis*; much used in med. L, F, & E, to form adjj. f. L adjj. in -*is* & -*ius*, as *celestial, dictatorial* (L -*tis*, -*rius*). Cf. -AL.

i'amb, n. = IAMBUS. [Anglicized f. IAMBUS]

iam'bic, a. & n. (pros.). Of, containing, based on, iambuses; (n.) ~ verse. [f. F *iambique* or LL f. Gk *iambikos* (as foll., see -IC)]

iam'bus, n. (pl. -*buses*, -*bī*). The metrical foot ⌣‾. [L, f. Gk *iambos* iambus, lampoon (*iaptō* assail)]

-ian, suf. of aa. & nn. = L -*anus* -AN added to stems in -*i*-, as *Italian, Virgilian*, or w. connective -*i*-, as *Christian*; esp. forming aa. on proper names, as *Addisonian, Bostonian*, (varying in place-names with -*er*, as *Londoner*, & often added to Latinized stems, as *Mancunian, Glaswegian, Oxonian, Liverpudlian*).

Iber'ian (ī-), a. & n. **1.** Of ancient Iberia; of Spain & Portugal as one country. **2.** n. Inhabitant, language, of ancient Iberia. [f. L *Iberia* f. Gk *Ibērēs* Spaniards + -AN]

ib'ex, n. (pl. ~*es*). Wild goat of Alps & Apennines, with large recurved horns. [L]

ibid'ĕm, adv. In the same book, chapter, passage, etc. (abbr. *ib., ibid.*). [L]

ib'is, n. (pl. ~*es*). Stork-like bird with long curved bill found in lakes & swamps of warm climates; *Sacred I*~, kind venerated by ancient Egyptians. [L f. Gk]

-ible, suf. f. L -*ibilis*, i.e. -*bilis* -BLE as appended to p.p. stems, 3rd conj. vbs, & some 2nd conj. (*terrible*), or f. L -*ībilis* (-*bilis* with 4th conj.); also in mod. formations, as *avertible*. Displaced by -*able* in many wds taken thr. F or formed really or apparently on E vbs. Meaning: ' that can be —d '.

-ic, suf. **1.** In adjj., immed. repr. F -*ique*, f. L -*icus* (= Gk -*ikos*) in wds of L formation as *classicus, publicus*, or in L adoptives f. Gk, as *grammaticus, poeticus*. Later E adjj. in -*ic* are direct f. Gk, or on Gk elements, or (esp. scientific terms) on wds f, L or other langg., as *carbonic, Byronic*. (Chem.) -*ic* in names of oxygen acids etc. indicates higher degree of oxidation than -*ous*, as in *chloric, sulphuric*. **2.** Gk adjj. in -*ikos* were used as nn. in 3 ways: in masc. sing., as *kritikos* man able to discern, critic; in fem. sing., as *mousikē* (*tekhnē*) art of the muses, music; in neut. pl., as *ta oikonomika* things pertaining to management, economics. In L the last two both became -*ica*, whence much fluctuation in med. L as to grammatical treatment. The Rom. langg. usu. had fem. sing. for names of arts & sciences, but F occas. had pl., as *les mathématiques*. E wds before 1500 were sing., as still *arithmetic, music, magic, logic, rhetoric*; later, -*ics* became usu. form for names of sciences, as *acoustics, conics, dynamics*, (treated as sing.), & of practical matters, as *athletics, politics, tactics*, (pl.). Besides this spec. use, other adjj. in -*ic* become nn., as *epic, emetic, cosmetic, rustic, mechanic*.

-ical, suf. (-*ic* + -*al*) forming adjj. f. nn., as *musical*, or more commonly secondary adjj. f. adjj. as *comical, historical*. Many adjj. have both the -*ic* & -*ical* form, often with distinction in meaning (see -AL).

-ically, suf. (-*ical* + -LY²) forming advv. corr. to adjj. in -*ic*, -*ical*, advv. in -*icly*, as *publicly, politicly*, being rare.

ice¹, n. **1.** Frozen water; *dry* ~, frozen carbon dioxide; *break the* ~, (fig.) make a beginning, break through reserve or stiffness; CUT² *no* ~; *on thin* ~ (fig.), on dangerous ground; (w. pl.) frozen confection, ~-cream, water-~. **2.** ~*-age*, glacial period; ~*-axe* (used by Alpine climbers for cutting steps); ~'*blink*, luminous appearance on horizon, caused by reflexion from ~; ~*-boat*, boat mounted on runners for travelling on ~, (also ~*-breaker*) boat used for breaking ~ on river etc.; *~'*box*, refrigerator; ~--*cream*, flavoured cream or custard congealed in freezing-mixture; *coconut* etc. ~, slabs of sugar flavoured with coconut etc.; ~*-fall*, steep part of glacier like frozen waterfall; ~*-field*, expanse of ~, esp. in Polar regions; ~*-foot*, belt of ~ along coast in Arctic regions; ~*-hockey* (played on skates); ~*-house*, building often partly or wholly underground for storing ~; ~'*man*, man skilled in traversing ~, (also) maker of ~s; (~-)PACK¹; ~*-pick*, stiletto for splitting up table ~; ~*-plant* (with leaves covered with watery vesicles looking like ~-specks); ~ *pudding*, a frozen confection; ~*-run*, artificial tobogganing track of ~; ~*-wool* (glossy kind used in crochet etc.). [OE *īs*, OLG, OHG *īs*, ON *īss* f. Gmc *isa-]

ice², v.t. & i. Freeze; cover (as) with ice; cool (wine) in ice; cover (cake etc.) with concretion of sugar; become covered with ice, freeze *up*. [f. prec.]

-ice, suf., OF, f. L -*itia* in abstract nn. (*justice, avarice, malice, notice*, & F formations *cowardice, jaundice*) & f. L -*itius*, -*itium*, (*novice, precipice, service*). But E -*ice* has freq. diff. orig., as in *apprentice, bodice, practice*, where -*ice* is partly due to assim. See -ISE².

ice'berg (ĭs'b-), n. Huge floating mass of ice, detached portion of glacier carried out to sea; (fig.) unemotional or cold-blooded person. [prob. f. Du. *ijsberg* (*ijs* ice + *berg* hill)]

Ice'land (īs'l-), n. Large island between Norway and Greenland; ~ *lichen, moss*, edible species; ~ *poppy*, yellow Arctic poppy; ~ *spar*, transparent variety of calcite. Hence ~ER¹(4) n. [ME, f. ON *Island* (*īss* ice + LAND¹)]

Icelăn'dic (īsl-), a. & n. (Language) of Iceland. [-IC]

Ich'abŏd (ik-), n. (As exclamation of regret =) the glory has departed. [Heb., see 1 *Sam.* iv. 21]

ichneum'on (-k-), n. **1.** Small brown weasel-like quadruped allied to mongoose, noted for destroying crocodiles' eggs. **2.** (Also ~*fly*) small parasitic hymenopterous insect depositing eggs in or on larva of another insect. [L, f. Gk *ikhneumōn* spider-hunting wasp f. *ikhneuō* track (*ikhnos*)]

ichno- (ik-) in comb. = Gk *ikhnos* track, trace, as: ~*graph'ic*(*al*), ~*graphy* (-ŏg²), (of) the drawing of ground-plans; ~*lite* (ik²), fossil footprint (also *ichnite*, pr. ĭk'nīt); ~*logy* (-ŏl²), study of fossil footprints.

ich'ōr (īk-), n. (Gk Myth.) fluid flowing like blood in veins of gods; (Path.) watery acrid discharge from wounds etc. Hence ~OUS (īk'or-) a. [Gk *ikhōr*]

ichthӯo- (ik-) in comb. (bef. vowel *ichthy-*) = Gk *ikhthus* fish, as: ~*grapher*, ~*graphy*, (-ŏg²), writer on, description of, fishes; ~*latry* (-ŏl²), worship of a fish-god; ~*lite* (ik²), fossil fish; ~*logy* (-ŏl²), study of fishes, whence ~*lo'gical*, ~*logist* (-ŏl²); ~*phagi*, ~*phagist*, (-ŏl²), fish-eater(s); ~*phagous* (-ŏl²), fish-eating; *ichthyōr'nis*, extinct genus of toothed birds.

ich'thӯoid (-k-), a. & n. Fish-like; (n.) vertebrate of fish type. [as prec. +-OID]

ichthӯosaur'us (-k-), n. Extinct marine animal with large head, tapering body, four paddles, & long tail. [ICHTHYO- + Gk *sauros* lizard]

ichthӯ|ōs'is (-k-), n. Disease in which epidermis becomes dry & horny. So ~OT'IC (-ŏt²) a. [f. Gk *ikhthus* fish +-OSIS]

-ician (-ĭshn), suf. (= F -*icien*), spec. form of -IAN (ME & F -*ien*) added to names of arts or sciences in -*ic*(*s*) to form personal designations (= one skilled in or concerned with), as *arithmetician*, *logician*, *optician*, *politician*; occas. used when there is no corresp. n. (& even no adj.) in -*ic*, as *algebrician, mortician.*

i'cicle, n. Tapering ice-formation, produced by freezing of successive drops trickling from the point of attachment. [ME (f. Scand., cf. MSw. *isikil*) f. ICE + (dial.) *ickle* (= OE *gicel*, ON *jǫkull* ~); repl. OE **īsgicel* (cf. MLG *isjokel*)]

i'cing, n. In vbl senses of ICE², esp.: sugar etc. coating of cake etc.; formation of ice on aircraft. [-ING¹]

ic'kle, a. (nursery). Little.

ic'ŏn, n. Image, statue; (Eastern Church) painting, mosaic, etc., of sacred personage, itself regarded as sacred. [L, f. Gk *eikōn* image]

ĭcŏn'ic, a. Of (the nature of) an image or portrait; (of statues) following a conventional type. [f. L f. Gk *eikonikos* (as prec., see -IC)]

icono- in comb. = Gk *eikōn* image, as:

~*graphy* (-ŏg²), illustration of subject by drawings or figures, book whose essence is pictures, treatise on pictures or statuary, study of portraits esp. of an individual; so ~*grapher* (-ŏg²), ~*graph'ic*; ~*later*, ~*latry*, (-ŏl²), worshipper, worship, of images; ~*logy* (-ŏl²), study of icons (in any sense); ~*machy* (-ŏm²akĭ), war against use of images in connexion with worship; ~*stasis* (-ŏs²), (Eastern Church) screen separating sanctuary from main body of church, & on which icons are placed.

ĭcŏn'oclăsm, n. Breaking of images (lit. & fig.). [prec. + Gk *klasma* (*klaō* break, -M)]

ĭcŏn'oclăst, n. Breaker of images, esp. one who took part in movement in 8th & 9th cc. against use of images in religious worship in churches of the East; (fig.) one who assails cherished beliefs. Hence ~IC (-ăs²) a. [f. med. L f. Gk *eikonoklastēs* (*eikōn* ICON + *klastēs* f. *klaō* break)]

iconŏm'ēter, n. (Photog.) direct-vision view-finder (either fixed to camera, or detached & adjustable for various lenses & sizes of plate); (Surv.) optical instrument for ascertaining size or distance of an object. [ICONO- + -METER]

ic'osahĕd'ron (-a-h-), n. Solid contained by twenty plane faces. [f. Gk *eikosaedron* (*eikosi* twenty + *hedra* base)]

-ics. See -IC(2).

ic'tus, n. (pros.). Rhythmical or metrical stress. [L, = blow, f. *icere* strike]

i'cӯ, a. Abounding in, covered with, ice; very cold (lit., & fig. as ~ *manners*). Hence **i'ciLY²** adv., **i'ciNESS** n. [-Y²]

ĭd, n. (Biol.) a unit of germ-plasm or idioplasm; (Psycho-anal.) *the* instinctive impulses of the individual. [first sense, abbr. IDIOPLASM; second, f. L *id* that]

-id¹, suf. repr. F -*ide* f. L -*idus*, which forms adjj. chiefly f. vbs w. -*ē*- stems, as *timidus* timid f. *timēre*, but also f. vbs w. -*i*- or consonant stem, as *rapidus* rapid f. *rapēre*, & f. nn:, as *morbidus* morbid f. *morbus*. Earlier E wds come thr. F, others f. L direct.

-id², suf. of nn. (= F -*ide*) f. L f. Gk -*id*-(nom. -*is*), as *chrysalid, pyramid*. In bot., *amaryllid, orchid*, etc., should denote plants amaryllis, orchis, etc., but in fact denote members of the family of which these are typical genera (*Amaryllideae, Orchidaceae*).

-id³, suf. of nn. & aa. (zool.). **1.** f. L names of families in -*idae* pl. of -*ides* f. Gk -*idēs* son of, as *Seleucid*, member of the dynasty founded by Seleucus. **2.** f. L names of classes in -*ida* taken as neut. pl. of -*ides* (= Gk -*idēs*), as *Arachnid*, member of the class *Arachnida*. **3.** (Astron.) applied to groups or showers of meteors radiating from a constellation, after which they are named, as *Leonid*.

-id⁴, suf. Early spelling of -IDE, now chiefly U.S.

ide, n. Fish allied to carp. [f. Swed. *id*]

-ide, suf. (chem.) forming names of simple compounds of an element with another element or radical, the suf. *-ide* being added to the name (usu. abbrev.) of the more electro-negative element, as *sodium chloride, carbon sulphide, calcium carbide*; first used in *oxide* from *oxygen*.

īdē'a (or *-īa*), n. **1.** Archetype, pattern, as distinguished from its realization in individuals; (Platonic) eternally existing pattern of which individual things in any class are imperfect copies. **2.** Conception, plan, of thing to be aimed at, created, etc.; plan of action. **3.** Notion conceived by the mind; way of thinking (*the young* ~, the child's mind); vague belief, fancy, as *the* ~ *of his doing such a thing, I had no* ~ *you were there*. **4.** (Descartes, Locke) immediate object of thought or mental perception; (Kant) conception of reason transcending all experience. **5.** *Man of* ~*s*, resourceful person; **the big* ~, scheme, proposal (usu. ironical: *what's the big* ~*?*, what folly have you in mind?). Hence ~'d, ~ED², (-I'ad), ~LESS (-I'al-), aa. [L f. Gk, = form, kind, f. *id-* see]

īdē'al, a. & n. **1.** Answering to one's highest conception; embodying an idea; existing only in idea; visionary; relating to, consisting of, (Platonic) ideas. **2.** n. Perfect type; actual thing as standard for imitation. Hence ~LY² adv. [f. F *idéal* f. LL *idealis* (as prec., see -AL)]

īdē'al|ism, n. Representation of things in ideal form, imaginative treatment, practice of forming or following after ideals, (cf. REALISM), so ~īZA'TION n., ~IZE v.t. & i.; (Philos.) system of thought in which the object of external perception is held to consist of ideas (cf. REALISM). So ~IST n., ~īs'tIC a. [-ISM]

īdēǎl'itȳ, n. Quality of being ideal; (Phrenol.) imaginative faculty. [-ITY]

īdē'āte, v.t. & i. Imagine, conceive; form ideas. Hence īdēA'TION n., īdēā⁻ tionAL (-shon-) a. [f. IDEA + -ATE³]

īdée fixe (ēdāfēks'), n. Idea that dominates the mind, monomania. [F, lit. fixed idea]

id'ĕm, n. or adv. (abbr. *id*.). (In) the same author (ī-); the same word (ī-); *idem quod* (abbr. *i.q.*), the same as. [L]

īdĕn'tic, a. (Diplom.) ~ *note*, simultaneous & uniformly worded expression of opinion from several powers to another; = foll. [f. med. L *identicus* (cf. IDENTITY)]

īdĕn'tical, a. (Of one thing viewed at different times) the very same; (of different things) agreeing in every detail (*with*); (of twins) developed from a single fertilized ovum; (Logic, Math.) expressing an identity (~ *proposition*, of the type *Man is man*). Hence ~LY² adv. [-AL]

īdĕn'tifȳ, v.t. Treat (thing) as identical (*with*); associate oneself inseparably *with* (party, policy, etc.); establish identity of. Hence ~fIABLE a., ~fICA'TION n. (~*fication* or ~*ty disc*, of rubber or metal worn by

soldier etc. on active service & bearing his name etc.). [f. med. L *identificare* (as foll., see -FY)]

īdĕn'titȳ, n. Absolute sameness; individuality, personality, (~ *disc*, see prec.); (Alg.) equality of two expressions for all values of the literal quantities, expression of this, e.g. $(x+1)^2 = x^2 + 2x + 1$. [f. LL *identitas*, irreg. f. *idem* same (see -TY)]

id'ĕo-, comb. form of Gk *idea* IDEA, as: ~*gram*, ~*graph*, character symbolizing the idea of a thing without expressing its name (e.g. Chinese characters), whence ~*graph'ic*(*al*), ~*graphy* (-ŏg⁴).

īdĕŏl'ogȳ, n. Science of ideas; visionary speculation; manner of thinking characteristic of a class or individual, ideas at the basis of some economic or political theory or system, as *Fascist, Nazi*, ~. So **īdēolō'gICAL** a., **īdĕŏl'ogIST** n., **īd'ēo-LOGUE** (-lŏg) n., theorist, visionary. [f. F *idéologie* (prec., -LOGY)]

īdes (īdz), n. pl. (Rom. Ant.). Eighth day after nones (15th of March, May, July, October, 13th of other months). [OF, f. L *Idūs*]

īd ĕst (abbr. *i.e.*). That is to say. [L]

id'iocȳ, n. Extreme mental imbecility. [16th c., irreg. f. IDIOT + -CY, after *hypocrite, -isy* etc.]

id'iom, n. Language of a people or country; specific character of this; form of expression peculiar to a language, peculiarity. [f. F *idiome* or LL f. Gk *idiōma -matos* (*idioomai* make one's own f. *idios*, see -M)]

idiomăt'|ic, a. Characteristic of a particular language; relating to or conforming to idiom. Hence ~ICALLY adv. [f. F (prec., -IC)]

idiŏp'athȳ, n. (path.). Disease not preceded or occasioned by another. Hence **idiopăth'IC** a., **idiopăth'ICALLY** adv. [f. Gk *idiopatheia* (*idios* own, see -PATHY)]

id'ioplăsm, n. (biol.). Portion of PLASM that determines an organism's nature. [Gk *idios* own, PLASM]

idiosync'rasȳ, n. Mental constitution, view, feeling, peculiar to a person; mode of expression peculiar to an author; (Med.) physical constitution peculiar to a person. So **idiosyncrăt'IC** a. [f. Gk *idiosugkrasia* (*idios* own + *sun* together + *krasis* mixture f. *kerannumi* mix)]

id'iot, n. Person so deficient in mind as to be permanently incapable of rational conduct; utter fool; ~-*stitch*, TRICOT-stitch (the easiest in crochet work). So **īdiŏt'IC** a., **īdiŏt'ICALLY** adv. [ME, f. OF f. L (-*ta*) f. Gk *idiōtēs* private person, 'layman', ignorant person, f. *idios* own, private]

ī'dle, a. (-er, -est), & v.i. & t. **1.** (Of action, thought, word) ineffective, worthless, vain; groundless; useless; unoccupied; lazy, indolent; ~ *wheel* or ~*r*, safety wheel coming into operation in case of breakdown, (also) intermediate wheel between two geared wheels. **2.** v.i. Be ~; (of motor-car, aero, etc., engine) revolve slowly with throttle nearly closed; (v.t.) pass (time etc.) *away* in ~ness. Hence ~NESS (ī'dln-), **īd'lER**[1], nn., **īd'LY**[2] adv. [OE *īdel*, OS *īdal*, OHG *ītal*]

īd'lèsse, n. Idleness. [pseudo-arch.. -ESS[2]]

Ido (ēd'ō), n. An artificial universal language based on Esperanto. [= offspring (in Ido)]

īd'ol, n. Image of deity used as object of worship; false god; person, thing, that is the object of excessive devotion; phantom; (Logic) false mental conception, ~s *of the tribe, cave, market, theatre,* (L *idola tribus, specus, fori, theatri*), four classes of fallacies (Bacon, *Nov. Org.* I. xxxix) referable respectively to limitations of human mind, prejudices of idiosyncrasy, influence of words, philosophical & logical prepossessions. [ME *ydele, ydole* f. OF f. L f. Gk *eidōlon* phantom (*eidos* form)]

īdŏl'at|er, n. Worshipper of idols; devoted admirer (*of*). So ~rESS[1], ~rY[2] (*honour* one *on this side* ~*ry*, short of making a god of him), nn., ~rOUS a., ~rOUSLY[2] adv. [(1) ME *idolatrer* f. OF+ -ER[1], or f. IDOLATRY+-ER[1]; (2) 16th c. *idolater* alt. f. (1), or f. OF *idolatre (-astre)* f. Rom. **idolatra* f. LL f. Gk *eidōlolatrēs* (IDOL, -LATRY)]

īd'oliz|e, -**is|e** (-īz), v.t. & i. Make an idol of; venerate, love, to excess; practise idolatry. Hence ~A'TION n. [-IZE]

īdŏl'um, n. (pl. -*la*). Mental image, idea; (Logic) fallacy (see IDOL). [L, as IDOL]

īd'ўll, -ўl, n. Description in verse or (*prose* ~) in prose of picturesque scene or incident, esp. in rustic life; episode suitable for such treatment, freq. a love-story. Hence **īdўll'IC** a., **īdўll'ICALLY** adv., ~IST n., ~IZE(1) v.t. [f. L f. Gk *eidullion* (*eidos* form)]

-ie, earlier form of -Y[3], & usu. in Sc.; also in E·use, cf. *birdie, doggie*.

-ier, suf. forming personal nn. denoting occupation etc. (1) in wds of ME age, in wh. the suf., of obsc. & app. diverse orig., is unstressed, & varies, or has varied, w. -*yer*, as *collier, grazier, hosier, bowyer, lawyer*; (2) in later wds f. 16th c. the suf., normally accented, is F -*ier* f. L -*arius* (-ARY[1]), as *bombardier, cavalier*; many of these occur w. anglicized sp., as *muleteer*; see -EER.

if, conj. & n. **1.** On the condition or supposition that, as *if you are* (now) *tired we will sit down, if you* (hereafter) *see him give him the message, if he has found it he will send it, if he had fair warning he has nothing to complain of, if he had been warned he has* (or *had*) *nothing to complain of*, (w. past tense implying that condition is not fulfilled) *if I knew what to do I should do it, if he had been warned he would have* (or *would .have had*) *nothing to complain of*;

whenever, as *if I feel any doubt I inquire, if I felt any doubt I inquired, if I had been badly treated I complained*; whether, as *ask, see, try, if you can turn the handle*; (when *if* is omitted, order of verb & subject is inverted, as) *were I* (if I were) *in your place, would, could, should, might, had, he* (if he would, could, etc.), (poet.) *loved I not honour more*; (without apodosis) *if I only knew!*, I wish I knew, *if I haven't lost my watch!* (I have, to' my surprise or disgust); *as if*, as the case would be if, as *it seems as if he meant* (vulg. *means*) *to compromise, he talks as* (he would) *if he were drunk; as if you didn't know*, you know quite well. **2.** n. Condition, supposition, as *if ifs & ans were pots & pans*. [OE *gif*, OS *ef* (*of*), OHG *ibu, oba*, ON *ef*, Goth. *ibai*]

ig'loo, n. Eskimo dome-shaped hut, esp. one built of snow. [native, = house]

ig'nèous, a. Of fire, fiery; produced by volcanic agency. [f. L *igneus* (*ignis* fire) +-ous]

īg'nīs făt'ūus, n. Will-o'-the-wisp, phosphorescent light (now rarely) seen on marshy ground, supposed due to spontaneous combustion of gas from decaying organic matter; delusive hope or gain. [med. or mod. L, = foolish fire]

ignīt|e', v.t. & i. Make intensely hot; (Chem.) heat to the point of combustion or chemical change; set fire to; take fire. Hence or cogn. ~'ABLE a., **ignī'TION** n., (also) mechanism for, act of, starting combustion of the mixture in cylinder of internal-combustion engine. [f. L *ignire* -*t-* (*ignis* fire)]

ignō'b|le, a. (-er, -est). Of low birth, position, or reputation; mean, base, dishonourable. Hence ~leNESS (-ln-) n., ~LY[2] adv. [F, or f. L *ignobilis* (*in-* not +(*g*)*nobilis* NOBLE)]

ig'nominў, n. Dishonour, infamy; infamous conduct. So **ignomin'ious** a. (now usu. in less damnatory sense, = humiliating), **ignomin'iousLY**[2] adv. [f. F *ignominie* or L *ignominia* (*in-* not + (*g*)*nomen* name)]

ignōrām'us, n.(pl.~*es*). Ignorant person. [L, = we do not know, (legal) we take no notice of (bill); mod. sense perh. f. Ruggle's *Ignoramus* (1615) exposing lawyers' ignorance]

ig'norance, n. Want of knowledge (*of* thing, or in general; *where* ~ *is bliss, 'tis folly to be wise*). [ME, f. OF f. L *ignorantia* (as foll., see -ANCE)]

ig'norant, a. Lacking knowledge; uninformed (*of, in*, subject, *of* fact). Hence ~LY[2] adv. [ME, f. OF f. L, as IGNORE, see -ANT]

īgnōrā'tio (-shīō) **ēlěn'chi** (-kī), n. (logic). Argument that appears to refute opponent while actually disproving something not advanced by him. [L]

ignōre', v.t. Refuse to take notice of; (of Grand Jury) reject (bill) as unfounded. [f.

F *ignorer* or L *ignorare* not know, ignore (*in-* not +*gno-* know)]

ĭgnŏt'ŭm pēr ĭgnŏt'ĭus, n. Explanation obscurer than the thing it is meant to explain. [L, = the unknown by the still less known]

ĭgua'na (-gwah-), n. Large W.-Ind. & S.-Amer. arboreal lizard. [Sp., f. Carib *iwana*]

ĭguăn'odŏn (-gw-), n. Large herbivorous lizard, found fossil. [f. prec. + Gk *odous odontos* tooth, after *mastodon* etc.]

IHS, abbr. repr. Gk *Iēsous* Jesus (Gk cap. *ē* being like H); often taken to mean *Jesus Hominum Salvator* (Saviour of men), *In Hoc Signo* (*vinces*) in this sign (thou shalt conquer), *In Hac* (*cruce*) *Salus* in this (cross) is salvation.

ĭl-, pref. = IN [1, 2] before *l*.

ĭk'on, n. Var. of ICON.

-ĭl, -ĭle, suf. of adjj. & sometimes nn., repr. L *-ĭlis* or when added to *-i-* stems *-ĭlis* (*civilis*). In OF *-ĭlis* appeared as *-il*, but *-ĭlis* lost *i*, tonic accent falling on prec. syllable (*humble* L *humilem*, *frêle* L *fragilem*). L wds adopted early in OF took *-il* masc., *-ile* fem. (*civil*, *-ile*); later wds have *-ile* for both genders (*agile*, *facile*). Few E wds have *-il* (*civil*, *fossil*, *utensil*); & the tendency (not in U.S.) is to pronounce *-ile* of either origin with *ī*.

ĭl'ĕx, n. (pl. ~*es*). Holm-oak; (Bot.) genus including common holly. [L]

ĭl'ĭăc, a. Of the flank(-bone), as ~ *artery*; ~ *passion*, painful affection due to intestinal obstruction. [f. LL *iliacus*, in form f. L *ilia* flanks (see -AC); in sense f. L *ileus* f. Gk *eileos* colic]

ĭl'ĭad (ĭ-), n. Epic poem attributed to Homer & describing siege of Troy; (fig.) ~ (long series) *of woes*. [f. L f. Gk *Ilias -ados* (*poiēsis*) (poem) of Ilium or Troy]

ĭl'ĭum, n. (pl. *-ia*). Hip-bone. [L, see ILIAC]

∥ **ĭlk**, a. (Sc.). *Of that* ~, of the same, as *Guthrie of that* ~, Guthrie of Guthrie; (vulg.) *that* ~, that family, class, or set. [OE *ilca* same, f. ĭ-, ī- (st. of HE, cf. Goth. *is*) +*lik-* (LIKE [1], -LY [1])]

ĭll, a., n., & adv. **1.** Out of health, sick, as *he is* ~, *was taken* ~, (*of* or *with* disease, *with* anxiety etc.); (of health) unsound, disordered; morally bad, as ~ *fame*, disrepute, ~ *blood*, ~ *will*, animosity, strife, ~ *nature*, churlishness, ~ (morose) *humour*, *temper*; harmful, as (prov.) ~ *weeds grow apace*; *do an* ~ *turn to person*, harm him or his interests; wretched, disastrous, as (prov.) *it's an* ~ *wind that blows nobody good*; (arch.) difficult, as ~ *to please*; faulty, unskilful, as ~ *management*; (of manners or conduct) improper; ~ (imperfect) *success*. **2.** n. Evil, the opposite of good; harm, injury; *speak* ~ (something unfavourable) *of*; (pl.) misfortunes. **3.** adv. Badly, as *behaved* ~; *take* (thing) ~, take offence at it; unfavourably, as *it would have gone* ~ *with him*; imperfectly,

scarcely, as ~ *provided*, *it* ~ *became him to speak*; ~ *at ease*, embarrassed, uneasy. **4.** ~*-advised'*, *-advis'ĕdly*, imprudent(ly); ~*-affec'ted*, not well disposed; ~*-bred*, badly brought up, rude; ~ *breed'ing*, bad manners; ~*-condi'tioned*, of evil disposition, (also) in bad condition; ~*-disposed'*, disposed to evil, malevolent, (also) unfavourably disposed (*towards*); ~*-fat'ed*, destined to, bringing, bad fortune; ~*-fav'oured*, uncomely, (also) displeasing, objectionable; ~*-gott'en*, gained by evil means; ~*-hum'oured*, bad-tempered; ~*-judged'*, unwise; ~*-mann'ered*, unmannerly, rude; ~*-na'tured*(*ly*), churlish(ly); ~*-om'ened*, attended by bad omens; ~*-starred'*, born under an evil star, unlucky; ~*-tem'pered*, morose, peevish; ~*-timed'*, unseasonable; ~*-treat'*, *-use'*, treat badly. [ME *ill* f. ON *illr* of unkn. orig.]

ĭllā'tion, n. Deduction, conclusion; thing deduced. [f. L *illatio* (as INFER, see -ION)]

ĭllăt'ĭve, a. (Of words) stating, introducing, an inference, as ~ *particles*; inferential. Hence ~LY [2] (-vl-) adv. [f. L *illativus* (as prec., see -IVE)]

ĭllĕg'al, a. Not legal; contrary to law. Hence or cogn. **ĭllĕgăl'ĭTY** n., ~LY [2] adv. [f. F, or med. L IL(*legalis* LEGAL)]

ĭllĕg'ĭble, a. Not legible. Hence ~ĬBIL [4] ITY n., ~ĭBLY [2] adv. [IL-]

ĭllĕgĭt'im|āte [1], a. & n. Not authorized by law; improper; not born in lawful wedlock, bastard; wrongly inferred; abnormal; (n.) one whose position is ~ate, esp. bastard. Hence ~ACY n., ~ateLY [2] adv. [f. LL *illegitimus*, after LEGITIMATE]

ĭllĕgĭt'im|āte [2], v.t. Declare illegitimate. Hence ~A'TION n. [f. prec.]

ĭllĭb'eral, a. Not befitting a free man; without liberal culture; vulgar, sordid; narrow-minded; stingy. Hence or cogn. ~ITY (-ăl[2]) n., ~LY [2] adv. [f. F, or L IL(*liberalis* LIBERAL)]

ĭllĭc'it, a. Unlawful, forbidden, esp. ~ *still*. Hence ~LY [2] adv. [f. L *illicitus* (IL-, LICIT)]

ĭllĭm'it|able, a. Boundless. Hence ~ABIL'ITY, ~ableNESS, nn., ~abLY [2] adv. [IL-]

ĭllĭt'er|āte, a. & n. Ignorant of letters; unlearned; unable to read; (n.) ~ate person. Hence ~ACY, ~ateNESS, nn. [f. L IL(*litteratus* LITERATE)]

ĭll'nĕss, n. Unhealthy condition of body, sickness. [-NESS]

ĭllŏ'gĭcal, a. Devoid of, contrary to, logic. Hence ~ITY (-ăl[2]) n., ~LY [2] adv. [IL-]

ĭllume' (-lōō-, -lū-), v.t. (poet.). Light up, make bright, (lit. & fig.). [poet. shortening of ILLUMINE]

ĭllum'in|āte (-ōō-, -ū-), v.t. Light up, whence ~ANT a. & n.; give spiritual or intellectual light to; throw light upon (subject); shed lustre upon; decorate (buildings etc.) profusely with lights as sign of festivity; decorate (initial letter in manuscript etc.) with gold, silver, &

brilliant colours. So ~A'TION, ~ātor, nn., ~ātive a., (-ōō-, -ŭ-). [f. L IL(*luminare* f. *lumen -minis* light), see -ATE[3]]

illumināt'i (-ōō-, -ŭ-; *also* -ah'tē), n. pl. Secret society founded by Weishaupt in 1776, holding deistic & republican principles, & organized like freemasons; persons claiming to possess special enlightenment. So illum'inISM(3), illum'inIST(2), nn., (-ōō-, -ŭ-). [L (as prec., see -ATE[2]) or It., whence occasional sing. -*ato*]

illum'ine (-ōō-, -ŭ-), v.t. Light up; enlighten spiritually; brighten. [ME, f. OF *illuminer* (as ILLUMINATE)]

illu'sion (-lōōzhn), n. Deception, delusion; sensuous perception of an external object involving a false belief; a transparent tulle. [ME, f. F f. L *illusionem* f. IL(*ludere lus-* play), see -ION]

illu'sion|ist (-lōōzhon-), n. One who disbelieves in objective existence, so ~ISM n.; one who produces illusions, esp. conjurer. [-IST]

illus'|ive (-lōō-), a. Deceptive. Hence or cogn. ~ively[2], ~orily[2], advv., ~iveNESS, ~oriNESS, nn., ~ory a. [as ILLUSION, see -IVE]

ill'ustrāt|e, v.t. Make clear, explain; make clear by examples; elucidate (description etc.) by drawings; ornament (book, newspaper, etc.) with designs. Hence ~OR n. [f. L IL(*lustrare* light up, f. st. of *lumen* light)]

illustrā'tion, n. Illustrating; example; drawing etc. illustrating book or article in paper. [ME, f. OF, f. L *illustrationem* (prec., -ATION)]

illus'trative, a. Serving as explanation or example (*of*). Hence ~LY[2] (-vl-) adv. [as ILLUSTRATE, see -IVE]

illus'trious, a. Distinguished, renowned. Hence ~LY[2] adv., ~NESS n. [f. L IL(*lustris* see ILLUSTRATE) +-OUS]

im-[1, 2], pref. = IN-[1, 2] before *b, m, p*.

im'age[1], n. Artificial imitation of the external form of an object, e.g. statue (esp. of saint etc. as object of veneration); optical counterpart produced by rays of light reflected from mirror, refracted through lens, etc.; form, semblance; counterpart, as *he is the very ~ of his father*; type; simile, metaphor; idea, conception. Hence ~LESS (-ijl-) a. [ME, f. OF f. L *imaginem* (nom. -*go*)]

im'age[2], v.t. Make an image of, portray; reflect, mirror; picture (thing *to* one*self*); describe vividly; typify. Hence ~ABLE (-ija-) a. [f. prec.]

im'agery (-ij-), n. Images; statuary, carving, figurative illustration. [ME, f. OF *imagerie* (as IMAGE[1], see -ERY)]

imā'ginab|le, a. That can be imagined, as *the greatest difficulty ~le, took all the trouble ~le*. Hence ~LY[2] adv. [ME, f. LL *imaginabilis* (as IMAGINE, see -BLE)]

imā'ginal, a. (entom.). Of an insect imago. [f. L as IMAGE[1] +-AL]

imā'ginar|y̆, a. Existing only in imagina-

tion; (Math.) having no real existence, but assumed to exist for a special purpose (e.g. square root of negative quantity). Hence ~iLY[2] adv. [ME, f. L *imaginarius* (as prec., see -ARY[1])]

imāginā'tion, n. Imagining; mental faculty forming images of external objects not present to the senses; fancy; creative faculty of the mind. [ME, f. OF f. L *imaginationem* (as IMAGINE, see -ATION)]

imā'ginative (*or* -ātiv), a. Of, given to using, having or showing in a high degree, the faculty of imagination. Hence ~LY[2] (-vl-) adv., ~NESS (-vn-) n. [OF (-*if, -ive*), as prec., see -ATIVE]

imā'gine, v.t. Form mental image of; conceive (thing, thing *to* be or do, *that* it is, *how, what*, etc.); guess, as *cannot ~ what he is doing*; suppose, be of opinion, (*that*); take into one's head (idea, *that*). [ME, f. OF *imaginer* f. L *imaginari* (as IMAGE[1])]

im'agist, n. One of a group of early 20th--c. poets who, in revolt against romanticism, seek clarity of expression through the use of precise images. [IMAGE[1] +-IST(2)]

imāg'ō, n. (pl. -*gines* pr. -jĭnēz, -*gos*). Final & perfect stage of insect after all metamorphoses, e.g. butterfly. [mod. L sense of *imago* IMAGE[1]]

imam', imaum', (-ahm), n. Officiating priest of mosque; title of various Mohammedan leaders. Hence imam'ATE[1] (-ahm-) n. [Arab. (*am*) f. *amma* go before]

imbāl'ance, n. Lack of balance. [IM-[2]]

im'bécile (-ēl, -īl), a. & n. 1. Mentally weak, stupid, idiotic; physically weak. 2. n. Person of weak intellect. Hence or cogn. ~LY[2] (-l-l-) adv., imbēcil'ity n. [f. F *imbécille* (now -*ile*) f. L *imbecillus*]

imbibe', v.t. Drink in, assimilate, (ideas etc.); drink (liquid); inhale (air etc.); absorb (moisture etc.). So imbibi'tion n. [(1) f. OF *imbiber*; (2) f. L IM[1](*bibere* drink)]

im'bric|āte, v.t. & i. Arrange (leaves, scales of fish, etc.), be arranged, so as to overlap like tiles. So ~ATE[2] (-at), ~ātiVE, aa., ~A'TION n. [f. L *imbricare* form like a tile (*imbrex -icis* f. *imber* shower), -ATE[3]]

imbro'glio (-ōlyō), n. (pl. ~*s*). Confused heap; complicated (esp. political or dramatic) situation. [It., f. *broglio*, cf. BROIL[1]]

imbrue' (-ōō), v.t. Stain (one's hand, sword, etc., *in, with*, blood, slaughter, etc.). [f. OF *embrouer* bedabble f. *en* IM-+*breu* f. Rom. **brodum*; see BROTH]

imbrute' (ĕm-, -ōōt), v.t. Brutalize. [IM-[1]]

imbue' (-ōō), v.t. Saturate (*with*); dye (*with*); permeate, inspire, (*with* feelings etc.); = IMBRUE. [16th c., f. F *imbu* or its source L *imbuere* moisten]

im'it|āte, v.t. Follow example of; mimic; be (consciously or not) like. So ~ABIL-

ITY, ~ātoR, nn., ~ABLE a. [f. L *imitari*, see -ATE[3]]

imitā'tion, n. Imitating (~ *is the sincerest flattery*); copy; counterfeit (often attrib., as ~ *leather*); (Mus.) repetition of melody etc., usu. at different pitch, in another part or voice. [f. F, or L *imitatio* (prec., -ATION)]

im'itātive, a. Following model or example (*of*); ~ *arts*, painting & sculpture; ~ *word*, one that reproduces a natural sound (e.g. *fizz*) or whose sound is thought to correspond to appearances etc. of object described; counterfeit. Hence ~LY[2] adv., ~NESS n. [f. LL *imitativus* (as IMITATE, see -ATIVE)]

immac'ūlate, a. Pure, spotless; faultless (often iron.); *I*~ *Conception* (of Virgin Mary, as conceived free from taint of original sin); (Nat. Hist.) not spotted. Hence immāc'ūlACY, ~NESS, nn., ~LY[2] adv. [f. L IM[2](*maculatus* f. *macula* spot)]

imm'anjent, a. Indwelling, inherent, (*in*); (of God) permanently pervading the universe. Hence ~ENCE, ~ENCY, nn. [f. LL IM[1](*manēre* remain), see -ENT]

immatēr'ial, a. Not material, incorporeal; unimportant. Hence ~ITY (-ăl[z]) n., ~IZE(3) v.t. [f. LL IM[2](*materialis* MATERIAL)]

immatēr'ial|ism, n. Doctrine that matter does not exist in itself apart from perception. So ~IST n. [-ISM]

immatūr|e', a. Not mature. So ~'ITY n. [f. L IM[2](*maturus* MATURE)]

immea'sur|able (-mĕzher-), a. Not measurable, immense. Hence ~ABIL'ITY, ~ableNESS, nn., ~abLY[2] adv. [IM-[2]]

immēd'iate, a. (Of person or thing in its relation to another) not separated by any intervening medium; (of relation or action) direct, without intervening medium; (Logic) ~ *inference* (from single premiss, without intervention of middle term); nearest, next, as *my* ~ *neighbour*, *predecessor*; occurring at once, without delay, as *an* ~ *reply*. Hence immēd'iACY, ~NESS (-tn-), nn., ~LY[2] (-tl-) adv. [f. F *-at*, or LL IM[2](*mediatus* MEDIATE)]

immēmōr'ial, a. Ancient beyond memory; very old. Hence ~LY[2] adv. [f. med. L IM[2](*memorialis* MEMORIAL)]

immēnse', a. Vast, huge; (sl.) very good. Hence or cogn. ~NESS (-sn-), immĕns'ITY, nn. [F, f. L IM[2](*mensus* p.p. of *metiri* measure) immeasurable]

immĕnse'ly (-sll), adv. In an immense degree; (colloq.) very much. [-LY[2]]

immĕrse', v.t. Dip, plunge, (*in* liquid); put overhead in water, esp. baptize thus; bury, imbed, (*in*); involve deeply, absorb, (*in* debt, difficulties, thought, etc.). [f. L IM[1](*mergere mers-* dip)]

immĕr'sion (-shn), n. Immersing; baptism by plunging whole person in water (cf. AFFUSION); (fig.) absorption (*in* thought etc.); (Astron.) disappearance of celestial body behind another or in its shadow; ~ *heater*, electric heater designed for direct ~ in a liquid. [f. LL *immersio* (prec., -ION)]

imm'igr|āte, v.i. & t. Come as settler (*into* foreign country); bring in (person) as settler. So ~ANT a. & n., ~A'TION n. [f. L IM[1](*migrare* MIGRATE)]

imm'in|ent, a. (Of events, esp. dangers) impending, soon to happen. Hence or cogn. ~ENCE n., ~entLY[2] adv. [f. L IM[1](*minēre*, see EMINENT) overhang, see -ENT]

immis'c|ible, a. That cannot be mixed. Hence ~iBIL'ITY n., ~ibLY[2] adv. [f. LL *immiscibilis* f. IM-[2]+L *miscēre* mix, see -BLE]

immit'igab|le, a. That cannot be softened or toned down. Hence ~LY[2] adv. [f. LL IM[2](*mitigabilis*, see MITIGATE)]

immix'ture, n. Mixing up; being involved (*in*). [f. L IM[1](*miscēre mixt-* mix) +-URE]

immōb'īle, a. Immovable; not mobile; motionless. So immoBIL'ITY n. [OF, f. L IM[2](*mobilis* MOBILE)]

immōb'iliz|e, -is|e (-īz), v.t. Fix immovably; make (troops, vehicle) incapable of being shifted; withdraw (specie) from circulation. Hence ~A'TION n. [f. F *immobiliser* (as prec., see -IZE)]

immŏd'erate, a. Excessive, wanting in moderation. Hence ~LY[2] (-tl-) adv. [ME, f. L IM[2](*moderatus* MODERATE)]

immŏd'est, a. Indecent, indelicate; forward, impudent. Hence ~LY[2] adv., ~Y[1] n. [f. L IM[2](*modestus* MODEST)]

imm'ol|āte, v.t. Kill (victim) as sacrifice; (fig.) sacrifice (thing etc. *to* another). So ~A'TION, ~ātoR, nn. [f. L IM[1](*molare* sprinkle with meal (*mola*), sacrifice, -ATE[3]]

immō'ral, a. Opposed to morality; morally evil; vicious, dissolute. Hence immorăl'ITY n., ~LY[2] adv. [IM-[2]]

immŏrt'al, a. & n. 1. Undying; divine; unfading, incorruptible; famous for all time; (colloq.) constant, long-lasting. 2. n. ~ being, esp. (pl.) gods of antiquity; person esp. author of enduring fame, member of French Academy; (pl.) royal bodyguard of ancient Persia. So ~ITY (-ăl[z]) n. [f. L IM[2](*mortalis* MORTAL)]

immŏrt'aliz|e, -is|e (-īz), v.t. Confer enduring fame upon; endow with endless life; perpetuate. Hence ~A'TION n. [-IZE]

immŏrt'allÿ, adv. Eternally; (colloq.) infinitely, very. [-LY[2]]

immŏrtĕlle', n. Composite flower of papery texture retaining colour after being dried, often used to adorn graves. [F, fem. of *immortel* IMMORTAL]

immo'v|able (-moo-), a. & n. That cannot be moved; motionless; not subject to change; ~*able* FEAST; steadfast, unyielding; emotionless; (Law, of property) consisting of land, houses, etc. (also as n. pl.). Hence ~ABIL'ITY, ~ableNESS, nn., ~abLY[2] adv. [IM-[2]]

immūne', a. & n. Having immunity (*from, against, to*, poison, contagion, etc.);

(n.)~ person. [f. L ɪᴍ²*munis* exempt from public burden (*munus*); med. use f. F]

immūn'ĭtў, n. (Law) exemption (*from* taxation, jurisdiction, etc.); freedom (*from*); being proof against contagion etc. (*from*). [f. L *immunitas* (as prec., see -ᴛʏ); med. use f. F]

imm'ūnīz|e, -is|e (-īz), v.t. Render immune (*against* contagion). Hence ~ᴀ'ᴛɪᴏɴ n. [-ɪᴢᴇ]

immūre', v.t. Imprison; shut one*self* up. Hence ~ᴍᴇɴᴛ (-ūᵊrm-) n. [f. F *emmurer* or med. L ɪᴍ¹(*murare* f. *murus* wall)]

immūt'|able, a. Unchangeable; not subject to variation in different cases. Hence ~ᴀʙɪʟ'ɪᴛʏ n., ~**abLʏ²** adv. [f. L ɪᴍ²(*mutabilis* ᴍᴜᴛᴀʙʟᴇ)]

imp¹, n. Child of the devil; little devil; mischievous child; ‖ (arch.) child. [OE *impa* young shoot, scion, conn. w. foll.]

imp², v.t. Mend broken pinion feather of falcon by inserting new feather in stump of broken one and binding with silk; (rare) enlarge, eke *out*. [OE *impian* = OHG *impfôn, impitôn* f. Rom. *impotare f. med. L *impotus* graft f. Gk *emphuein* implant]

im'păct¹, n. Striking (*on, against*), collision; effect, influence. [f. L *impingere* -*pact-* ɪᴍᴘɪɴɢᴇ]

impăct'², v.t. Press, fix, firmly (*into, in*). So **impăc'tɪᴏɴ** n. [back formation f. *impacted* f. L p.p. as prec. + -ᴇᴅ¹]

impair', v.t. Damage; weaken. So ~ᴍᴇɴᴛ n. [ME *empeir* f. OF *empeirer* f. Rom. *impejorare (*pejor* worse)]

impa'la (-ah-), n. Small African antelope. [Zulu]

impāle', v.t. Transfix (body etc. *upon, with*, stake etc., esp. as form of capital punishment); (Her.) combine (two coats of arms) by placing side by side on one shield separated by vertical line down middle; ‖ (rare) fence in with stakes. So ~ᴍᴇɴᴛ (-lm-) n. [f. F *empaler* or med. L ɪᴍ¹(*palare* f. *palus* stake)]

impăl'p|able, a. Imperceptible to the touch; not easily grasped by the mind, intangible. Hence ~ᴀʙɪʟ'ɪᴛʏ n., ~**abLʏ²** adv. [f. F, or LL ɪᴍ²(*palpabilis* ᴘᴀʟᴘᴀʙʟᴇ)]

impăl'ūdĭsm, n. Morbid state, with tendency to intermittent fevers & enlargement of spleen, found in dwellers in marshes. [f. ɪᴍ-¹ + L *palus -udis* marsh + -ɪsᴍ]

impān'ate (*or* ĭm'pa-), a. (Of the body of Christ) contained in the bread after consecration. So **impanᴀ'ᴛɪᴏɴ** n. [f. med. L ɪᴍ¹(*panare* f. *panis* bread), see -ᴀᴛᴇ²]

impanel. See ᴇᴍᴘᴀɴᴇʟ.

impă'radise, êm-, v.t. Bring into state of supreme happiness; ravish; make a paradise of (place, state). [16th c.; cf. contemporary *paradise* vb, It. *imparadisare*, F *emparadiser*]

impărisўllăb'ĭc, a. & n. (Gk & Lat. Gram.). (Noun) that has fewer syllables

in nominative than in other cases. [f. L ɪᴍ²(*par* equal) + ꜱʏʟʟᴀʙɪᴄ]

impȧrk', v.t. Enclose (beasts) in park; enclose (land) for park. Hence ~ᴀ'ᴛɪᴏɴ n. [f. OF ᴇᴍ(*parquer* f. *parc* ᴘᴀʀᴋ)]

impȧrt', v.t. Give share of (thing *to* person etc.); communicate (news etc. *to*). Hence ~ᴀ'ᴛɪᴏɴ, ~ᴍᴇɴᴛ, nn. [15c., f. OF *impartir* f. L ɪᴍ¹(*partire* ᴘᴀʀᴛ²)]

impȧr'tial (-shal), a. Not partial, unprejudiced, fair. Hence ~ɪᴛʏ (-shĭăl²) n., ~ʟʏ² (-shal-) adv. [ɪᴍ-²]

impȧrt'ible, a. (Of estate) not divisible. [f. LL ɪᴍ²(*partibilis* ᴘᴀʀᴛɪʙʟᴇ)]

impass'|able (-pah-), a. That cannot be traversed. Hence ~ᴀʙɪʟ'ɪᴛʏ, ~**able**ɴᴇss, nn. [ɪᴍ-²]

impasse' (-ahs; *or* ăṅpahs'), n. Blind alley; position from which there is no escape. [F (ɪᴍ-² + *passer* ᴘᴀss¹)]

impăss'|ible, a. Incapable of feeling or emotion; incapable of suffering injury; not subject to suffering. Hence ~ɪʙɪʟ'ɪᴛʏ, ~**ible**ɴᴇss, nn., ~**ibLʏ²** adv. [ME, f. OF, or LL ɪᴍ²(*passibilis* ᴘᴀssɪʙʟᴇ)]

impă'ssion (-shn), v.t. Stir the passions of, excite strongly, (chiefly in p.p.). [f. It. ɪᴍ¹(*passionare* f. *passione* ᴘᴀssɪᴏɴ)]

impăss'ive, a. Deficient in feeling or emotion; serene; without sensation; not subject to suffering. Hence ~ʟʏ² adv., ~ɴᴇss, **impăssiv'**ɪᴛʏ, nn. [ɪᴍ-²]

impāste', v.t. Enclose (as) with paste; make a paste; paint by laying on colours thickly. [f. It. ɪᴍ¹(*pastare* f. *pasta* ᴘᴀsᴛᴇ)]

impăs'tō, n. (paint.). Laying on of paint thickly. [It., as prec.]

impā'ti|ent (-shent), a. Not enduring with composure; intolerant *of*; restlessly desirous (*for* thing, *to* do). Hence or cogn. ~ᴇɴᴄᴇ (-shens) n., ~**entLʏ²** (-shent-) adv. [ME, f. OF f. L ɪᴍ²(*patientem* part. of *pati* suffer)]

impawn', v.t. Put in pawn; (fig.) pledge, plight. [ɪᴍ-¹]

ĭmpay'able (*or* ăṅpāyah'bl), a. Beyond price; (colloq.) going beyond ordinary limits. [F (ɪᴍ-²)]

impeach', v.t. Call in question, disparage, (character etc.); accuse (person) *of*, charge (*with*); find fault with (thing); accuse of treason or other high crime before competent tribunal. Hence ~ᴀʙʟᴇ a. [ME, f. OF *empechier* impede f. LL ɪᴍ¹-(*pedicare* f. *pedica* fetter, f. *pes pedis* foot) entangle]

impeach'ment, n. Calling in question; accusation, esp. (joc.) *the soft* ~ (Sheridan, *Rivals* v. iii); accusation & prosecution for treason etc. [f. OF *empechement* (as prec., see -ᴍᴇɴᴛ)]

impĕcc'|able, a. Not liable to sin; (of things) faultless. Hence or cogn. ~ᴀʙɪʟ'ɪᴛʏ n., ~**abLʏ²** adv., ~ᴀɴᴛ a. [f. L ɪᴍ²(*peccabilis* f. *peccare* sin, see -ʙʟᴇ)]

impĕcūn'i|ous, a. Having little or no money. Hence ~ᴏs'ɪᴛʏ n. [f. ɪᴍ-² + obs.

pecunious f. L *pecuniosus* (*pecunia* money f. *pecu* cattle, see -OUS)]

imped'ance, n. (electr.). Total virtual resistance of electric circuit to alternating current, arising from the resistance & the reactance of the circuit. [f. foll. +-ANCE]

impēde', v.t. Retard, hinder. [f. L IM¹-(*pedire* f. *pes* foot) lit. shackle the feet of]

impěd'iment, n. Hindrance, obstruction, esp. *just cause or* ~; ~ (*in* one's *speech*), stammer; (pl., also L *impedimen'ta*) baggage, esp. of army. Hence ~AL (-ĕn⁴) a. [f. L *impedimentum* (as prec., see -MENT)]

impěl', v.t. (-ll-). Drive, force, (person etc. *to* action, *to* do); drive forward, propel. So ~l'ENT a. & n. [f. L IM¹(*pellere puls-* drive)]

impend', v.i. Hang, be suspended, (*over*); (fig., of danger) hang threateningly (*over*); be imminent. So **impěn'd**ENCE, -ENCY, nn., **impěn'd**ENT a. [f. L IM¹(*pendēre* hang)]

impěn'ětr|able, a. That cannot be penetrated; inscrutable, unfathomable; impervious (*to*, *by* ideas etc.); (Nat. Phil.) having that property in virtue of which two bodies cannot occupy same place at same time. So ~ABIL'ITY, ~ableNESS, nn., ~ablY² adv. [f. F *impénétrable* f. L IM²(*penetrabilis* PENETRABLE)]

impěn'ětrāte, v.t. Penetrate deeply. [IM-¹]

impěn'it|ent, a. Not penitent. Hence or cogn. ~ENCE, ~ENCY, nn., ~entLY² adv. [f. LL IM²(*paenitens* PENITENT)]

impě'rative, a. & n. 1. (Gram.) expressing command; commanding, peremptory; urgent; obligatory. 2. n.~ mood, whence **impěrativ'AL** a.; CATEGORICAL ~. Hence ~LY² (-vl-) adv., ~NESS (-vn-) n. [f. LL *imperativus* f. IM¹(*perare* = *parare* make ready) command, -IVE]

imperāt'or, n. (Rom. Hist.). Commander (title conferred by salutation of soldiers on victorious general, under the Republic); emperor. So **imperātōr'IAL** a. [L (as prec., see -OR)]

impercěp'tib|le, a. That cannot be perceived; very slight, gradual, or subtle. Hence ~LY² adv. [f. F, or med. L IM²(*perceptibilis* PERCEPTIBLE)]

impercip'ient, a. Lacking perception. [IM-²]

im'perence, n. (Form, ascribed to illiterate speakers, of) impudence.

imperf'ěct, a. & n. 1. Not fully formed or done; incomplete; faulty; (Gram.) ~ *tenses*, those that denote action going on but not completed (e.g. *he is*, *he will be*, *singing*, but usu. of past time, as *he was singing*). 2. n.~ tense. Hence ~LY² adv. [ME *imparfit* etc., f. OF; see IM-², PERFECT]

imperfěc'tion, n. Incompleteness; faultiness; fault, blemish. [ME, f. OF f. LL *imperfectionem* (as prec., see -ION)]

imperf'orate, a. Not perforated, esp. (Anat.) lacking the normal opening (also of sheet of postage-stamps or single stamp). [IM-²]

impēr'ial, a. & n. 1. Of an empire or sovereign state ranking with an empire. 2. *I*~ *Institute*, former name of COMMONWEALTH *Institute*; ~ *preference*, taxing of imports from parts of the Empire at lower rates than those from foreign countries. 3. Of an emperor; supreme in authority; majestic, august; magnificent. 4. (Of weights & measures used by statute in U.K.) ~ *gallon*, *acre*, etc.; (of paper) 22×32 in. 5. n. Small part of beard left growing beneath lower lip (from Napoleon III); trunk for luggage, adapted for roof of coach; Russian tsarist gold coin= 15 silver roubles. Hence ~LY² adv. [ME, f. OF, f. L *imperialis* (IMPERIUM, see -AL)]

impēr'ial|ism, n. Rule of an emperor; (hist.) extension of British Empire where trade required protection of the flag; (hist.) union of different parts of British Empire for purposes of warlike defence, internal commerce, etc.; belief in value of colonies & dependencies (cf. LITTLE *Englandism*). So~**īs'**TIC a., ~IZE(3) v.t. [-ISM]

impēr'ialist, n. Adherent of an emperor, esp. (1600–1800) of German Emperor; advocate of imperial rule, esp. adherent of Bonaparte family; advocate of (British) imperialism. [17th c., f. F *impérialiste* (as prec., -IST)]

impě'ril, v.t. (-ll-). Bring into danger. [IM-¹]

impēr'ious, a. Overbearing, domineering; urgent, imperative. Hence ~LY² adv., ~NESS n. [f. L *imperiosus* (as IMPERIUM, see -OUS)]

impě'rish|able, a. That cannot perish. Hence~ABIL'ITY, ~ableNESS, nn., ~ablY² adv. [IM-²]

impēr'ium, n. Absolute power; empire;~ *in imperio*, supreme authority within jurisdiction of another authority. [L, = command, dominion]

impěrm'an|ent, a. Not permanent. Hence ~ENCE, ~ENCY, nn. [IM-²]

impěrm'ě|able, a. That cannot be passed through; (Phys.) that does not permit passage of fluids. Hence ~ABIL'ITY n. [f. LL IM²(*permeabilis* PERMEABLE)]

impermiss'ible, a. Not permissible. [IM-²]

imperscrip'tible, a. Not backed by written authority. [f. IM-²+L PER-(*scribere script*- write) register, see -BLE]

impers'onal, a. (Gram.) ~ *verb*, verb when used only in 3rd sing. (e.g. *it rains*, *methinks*); having no personality or personal reference or tone. Hence ~ITY (-ăl⁴) n., ~LY² adv. [f. LL IM²(*personalis* PERSONAL)]

impers'on|āte, v.t. Represent in bodily form, personify; play the part of; PERSONATE²; act (character). Hence ~A'TION, ~ātor, nn., ~ātive a. [f. IM-¹+L *persona* PERSON +-ATE³]

imperson'ify, v.t. Personify. [IM-¹]

impert'in|ent, a. Not to the point; intrusive; out of place, absurd; insolent, saucy. Hence or cogn. ~ENCE n., ~ently² adv. [f. F, or LL IM²(*pertinens* PERTINENT)]

imperturb'|able, a. Not excitable, calm. Hence ~ABIL'ITY, ~ableNESS, nn., ~ably² adv. [late ME, f. LL IM² (*perturbabilis* PERTURBABLE)]

imperv'ious, a. Not affording passage (*to*); (fig.) ~ (deaf) *to argument* etc. Hence ~LY² adv., ~NESS n. [f. L IM²(*pervius* PERVIOUS)]

impetig'o, n. Contagious pustular disease of skin. So **impeti'gin**ous a. [L, gen. -*ginis*, f. IM¹(*petere* seek) assail]

im'petr|ate, v.t. (Theol.) obtain by request; (rare) ask for. So ~A'TION n., ~atory a. [f. L IM¹(*petrare* = *patrare* bring to pass), see -ATE³]

impet'uous, a. Moving violently or rapidly; acting with rash or sudden energy. Hence or cogn. **impetu**os'ITY, ~NESS, nn., ~LY² adv. [ME, f. OF *impetuous* f. L *impetuosus* (as foll., see -OUS)]

im'petus, n. (pl. ~*es*). Force with which a body moves; (fig.) moving force, impulse. [L, = assault, force, f. IM¹(*petere* seek) assail]

im'peyan (-pī'an), a. ~ *pheasant*, E.-Indian pheasant, with crested head & brilliant plumage. [Sir Elijah *Impey*, 1787]

im'pi, n. Body of Kaffir warriors. [Zulu]

impi'ety, n. Ungodliness; want of dutifulness or reverence. [ME, f. OF *impiete* or L IM²(*pietas* PIETY)]

impinge' (-j), v.i. & t. Make impact (*on*, *upon*); (trans.; arch.) make (thing) do this. Hence ~MENT (-jm-) n. [f. L IM¹(*pingere* = *pangere* fix, drive) drive (thing) at]

im'pious, a. Not pious, wicked, profane. Hence ~LY² adv. [f. L IM²(*pius* PIOUS)]

im'pish, a. Of, like, an imp. Hence ~LY² adv., ~NESS n. [-ISH¹]

impit'eous, a. (poet.). Pitiless. [IM-²]

implac'|able (*or* -lāk²-), a. That cannot be appeased. Hence or cogn. ~ABIL'ITY n., ~ably² adv. [f. F, or L IM²(*placabilis* PLACABLE)]

implacen'tal, a. With no placenta. [IM-²]

implant' (-ahnt), v.t. Insert, infix, (*in*); instil (principle, idea, etc., *in* mind etc.); plant. Hence ~A'TION (-ahn-) n. [f. F *implanter* or LL IM¹(*plantare* PLANT)]

implaus'|ible (-z-), a. Not plausible. Hence or cogn. ~iBIL'ITY n., ~ibLY adv. [IM-²]

implead', v.t. (law). Prosecute or take proceedings against (person). [IM-¹]

impledge', v.t. Put in pledge, pawn. [IM-¹]

im'plement¹, n. Article of furniture, dress, etc., (pl.) equipment of these; tool, instrument, (esp. in pl.); [] (Sc. Law) full performance. [ult. f. LL *implementum* f. L IM¹(*plēre* fill), see -MENT]

im'plemēnt² (*or* -mĕnt'), v.t. Complete

(contract etc.); fulfil (engagement); fill up, supplement. [f. prec.]

imple'tion, n. Filling; fullness. [f. LL *impletio* f. IM¹(*plēre plet*- fill), see -ION]

im'plicate¹, n. Thing implied. [f. L IM¹(*plicare plicat*- or *plicit*- fold), see -ATE²]

im'plic|āte², v.t. Entwine, entangle; involve, imply, as inference, so ~ātive a.; involve (person *in* charge, crime, etc.); (pass.) be affected *in* (a thing's operation). So ~A'TION n. [as prec., see -ATE³]

impli'cit, a. Implied though not plainly expressed; virtually contained (*in*); ~ *faith* (not independently reached by the individual, but involved in general belief of Church, absolute, unreserved, cf. EXPLICIT). Hence ~LY² adv., ~NESS n. [f. F -*ite*, or L *implicit*- as IMPLICATE¹]

implor|e', v.t. Beg earnestly for; entreat (person *to* do). Hence ~'inGLY² adv., ~'ingNESS n. [f. F *implorer* or L IM¹-(*plorare* weep)]

impluv'ium (-plōō-), n. (Rom. Ant.). Square basin in middle of atrium receiving rain-water from open space in roof. [L, f. IM¹(*pluere* rain)]

imply', v.t. Involve the truth of (thing not expressly asserted, *that*); mean; insinuate, hint. Hence **impli'éd**LY² adv. [ME *en*-, *em*-, *im*- f. OF *emplier* f. L *implicare* (IMPLICATE¹); cf. doublet EMPLOY]

[] **impōld'er**, v.t. Make a POLDER of; reclaim from sea. [f. Du. *inpolderen*, see IM-¹, POLDER]

impōl'icy, n. Bad policy; inexpediency. [IM-²]

impolite', a. (-est). Uncivil, rude. Hence ~LY² (-tl-) adv., ~NESS (-tn-) n. [f. L IM²(*politus* POLITE)]

impōl'itic, a. Not politic; inexpedient. Hence ~LY² adv. [IM-²]

imponderabil'ia, n. pl. Imponderables. [L]

impon'derable, a. & n. **1.** (Phys.) having no weight; very light; (fig.) that cannot be estimated. **2.** n. ~ thing (esp. fig., pl., of qualities, emotions, etc.). [IM-²]

impon'ent, a. & n. (Person) that imposes a duty etc. [f. L IM¹(*ponere* place) lay on, see -ENT]

import'¹, v.t. Bring, introduce, (thing, esp. goods from foreign country, *into*), whence ~ABLE a., ~ABIL'ITY, ~A'TION, ~ER¹, nn.; imply, indicate, mean, (thing, (*that*); express, make known, (*that*); be of consequence to, as *questions that* ~ *us nearly, it* ~*s us to know*. [f. L IM¹(*portare* carry) bring in, in med. L = be of consequence]

im'port², n. What is implied, meaning; importance; (usu. pl.) commodity imported; importation. [f. prec.]

import'ance, n. Being important; weight, significance; personal consequence, dignity; pompousness (usu. *self*-~). [F, f. med. L *importantia* (as IMPORT¹, see -ANCE)]

impôrt'ant, a. Carrying with it great consequence (*to* person concerned or purpose etc.), weighty, momentous; consequential, pompous. Hence ~LY² adv. [F, f. med. L as IMPORT¹, see -ANT]

impôrt'ûnate, a. Persistent, pressing, in solicitation; (of affairs) urgent.· Hence or cogn. ~LY² adv., impôrtûn'ITY n. [f. L IM²(*portunus* f. *portus* port) inconvenient, -ATE²]

impôrtûne' (*or* impôr¹-), v.t. Solicit pressingly (person or abs.). [f. F *importuner* f. med. L *importunari* (as prec.)]

impôs|e' (-z), v.t. & i. (Arch.) place (thing) *upon*; (Print.) lay (pages of type) in proper order & secure them in a chase; lay (tax, duty, charge, obligation, *upon*); palm off (thing *upon* person); exert influence (*on* person) by striking character or appearance, whence ~'ingLY² adv., ~'ingNESS n., (-z-); ~e *upon*, take advantage of (person); practise deception (*upon*). [f. F IM¹(*poser*, cf. COMPOSE)]

imposi'tion (-z-), n. In vbl senses of IMPOSE; also or esp.: laying on *of hands* (in ordination etc.); impost, tax, duty; piece of deception or overcharge; ‖ work set as punishment at school (colloq. abbr. *impo, impot*). [ME, f. OF, or L *impositio* f. IM¹(*ponere posit-* place), -ION]

impôss'|ible, a. Not possible (often w. *it* as subj., as *it is ~ible to alter them*); (loosely) not easy, not convenient; (colloq.) outrageous, intolerable, as *an ~ible hat, person*. Hence or cogn. ~ibIL'ITY n., ~ibLY² adv. [ME, f. OF f. L IM²(*possibilis* POSSIBLE)]

im'pôst¹, n. (Hist.) tax, duty, tribute; (Racing sl.) weight horse carries in handicap. [f. F *impost* f. med. L *impostus, -um* (as IMPOSITION)]

im'pôst², n. Upper course of pillar, bearing arch. [f. F *imposte* or It. *imposta* (as prec.)]

impôs't|or, n. One who assumes a false character or passes himself off for someone else; swindler. Hence ~rous a. [f. F *imposteur* f. LL *impostor* (as IMPOST¹, see -OR)]

impôs'tûme, -thume (-tûm), n. (arch.). Purulent swelling, abscess, (lit. & fig.). [ME, f. OF *empostume* f. L f. Gk APO(*stēma* f. *sta-* stand, -M)]

impôs'ture, n. Fraudulent deception. [F, f. LL *impostura* (IMPOST¹, -URE)]

‖ im'pôt. See IMPOSITION.

im'pot|ent, a. Powerless; helpless, decrepit; (of males) wholly lacking in sexual power. Hence or cogn. ~ENCE, ~ENCY, nn., ~entLY² adv. [ME, f. OF, f. L IM²(*potens* POTENT)]

impound', v.t. Shut up (cattle) in pound; shut up (person, thing) as in pound; take legal possession of; confiscate. [IM-¹]

impôv'erish, v.t. Make poor; exhaust strength of. So ~MENT n. [ME, f. OF EM(*poverir* f. *povre* POOR), see -ISH²]

impràc'tic|able, a. Impossible in prac-

tice; (of persons or things) unmanageable; (of roads etc.) impassable. Hence ~ABIL²ITY, ~ableNESS, nn., ~abLY² adv. [IM-²]

im'prèc|āte, v.t. Invoke, call down, (evil *upon* person etc.). So ~A'TION n. (esp., spoken curse), ~ātORY a. [f. L IM¹(*precari* pray)]

imprég'n|able, a. (Of fortress etc.) that cannot be taken by arms; (fig.) proof against attack. Hence ~abIL'ITY n., ~abLY² adv. [late ME & OF *imprenable* (IM-², *prendre* take); -g- f. 16th c.]

imprég'nate¹, a. Pregnant (lit. & fig.); permeated (*with*). [f. LL IM¹(*praegnare* be pregnant), see -ATE²]

imprég'n|āte², v.t. Make (female) pregnant; (Biol.) fecundate (female reproductive cell or ovum); fill, saturate, (*with*); imbue, fill, (*with* feelings, moral qualities, etc.). Hence ~A'TION n. [as prec., see ATE³]

impresâr'iō, n. (pl. ~s). Organizer of public entertainments, esp. manager of operatic or concert company. [It. (*impresa* undertaking, as EMPRISE, see -ARY¹)]

imprescrip'tible, a. Not subject to prescription, that cannot be legally taken away, esp. ~ *right*. [F (IM-²)]

im'prèss¹, n. Stamping; mark made by seal, stamp, etc.; (fig.) characteristic mark. [f. foll.]

imprèss'², v.t. Apply (mark etc.) with pressure, imprint, stamp, (*on*); imprint, enforce, (idea etc., *that, what*, etc., *on* person, his mind); mark (thing *with* stamp etc. lit. & fig.); affect, influence, deeply, whence ~ibLE a., ~ibIL'ITY n.; affect (person) strongly (*with* idea etc.). [ME, f. OF *empresser* & L IM¹(*primere=premere* PRESS²)]

imprèss'³, v.t. Force (men) to serve in army or navy (hist.); seize (goods etc.) for public service; enlist, make use of, (thing) in argument etc. Hence ~MENT n. [IM-¹ +PRESS³]

imprè'ssion (-shn), n. Impressing (of mark); mark impressed; print taken from type or engraving; (printing of) number of copies forming one issue of book, edition, (also, unaltered reprint from standing type or plates, as opp. to *edition*); effect produced (esp. on mind or feelings); notion, (vague) belief, impressed on the mind, as *that is my ~, I was under the ~ that*. [ME, f. OF f. L *impressio* (as IMPRESS², see -ION)]

imprè'ssion|able (-shon-), a. Susceptible of impressions, easily influenced. Hence ~abIL'ITY n. [F (*impressionner*, as prec., see -ABLE)]

imprè'ssion|ism (-shon-), n. Method of painting or writing so as to give general tone & effect without elaborate detail, or (in painting, opp. *pre-Raphaelitism*) with details so treated as to be apprehended simultaneously, & not successively with changes of focus, cf. POST-~*ism*. So ~ARY¹, ~is'tic, aa., ~IST n. [-ISM]

impress'ive, a. (Of language, scenes, etc.) able to excite deep feeling. Hence ~LY² (-vl-) adv., ~NESS (-vn-) n. [-IVE]

im'prest, n. Money advanced to person to be used in State business. [f. phr. *in prest* (15th c., f. OF *prest* loan) on account, in advance]

imprīmāt'ŭr, n. Official licence to print (now usu. of works sanctioned by R.-C. Church); (fig.) sanction. [mod. L. = let it be printed]

imprīm'īs, adv. In the first place. [assim. f. L *in primis* among the first things]

im'print¹, n. Impression, stamp, (lit. & fig.); *publisher's, printer's,* ~ (name, place etc., on title-page or at end of book). [f. F *empreinte* stamp (as foll.)]

imprint'², v.t. Stamp (figure etc. *on*); impress (idea etc. *on, in,* mind etc.); impress (quality etc. *on, in*); stamp (thing *with* figure). [ME, f. OF *empreinter* f. *empreindre, -preint* f. L IM¹(*primere = premere* press)]

impris'on (-z-), v.t. Put into prison; (fig.) confine, shut up. So ~MENT (-z-) n. [ME, f. OF EM(*prisoner* f. PRISON)]

improb'|able, a. Not likely to be true or to happen. Hence ~ABIL'ITY n., ~ablY² adv. [f. F, or L IM²(*probabilis* PROBABLE)]

improb'ity, n. Wickedness; dishonesty. [f. L *improbitas* f. IM²(*probus* honest), see -TY]

imprŏmp'tū, adv., n., & a. Extempore (performance, composition, speech); musical composition having character of improvisation. [17th c., f. F, = L *in promptu* in readiness (*promere,* see PROMPT)]

imprŏp'er, a. Inaccurate, wrong; ~ *fraction* (greater than 1, with numerator greater than denominator); unseemly, indecent. Hence ~LY² adv. [f. F *impropre* or L *improprius* (IM-², PROPER)]

‖**imprŏp'ri|āte**, v.t. Annex (ecclesiastical benefice) to corporation or person as property; place (tithes, ecclesiastical property) in lay hands. So ~ATE² (-at) a., ~A'TION n. [f. med. L IM¹(*propriare* f. *proprius* own), see -ATE³]

‖**imprŏp'riātor**, n. One to whom benefice is impropriated. [as prec., see -OR]

impropri'ĕtȳ, n. Incorrectness; unfitness; indecency. [f. F *-été* or L IM²(*proprietas* PROPRIETY)]

improv'|able (-ōōv-), a. That can be improved; adapted for cultivation. Hence ~ABIL'ITY, ~ableNESS, nn. [-ABLE]

improve' (-ōōv), v.t. & i. Make, become, better; ~ *away,* get rid of by improvements; make good use of (*the occasion, the opportunity*); ~ *upon,* produce something better than; preach on (*the occasion*) with a view to edification. So ~MENT (-ōōvm-) n., (also) addition, alteration, etc., that adds to the value (of lands, houses, etc.). [16th c. *em-, improw(e)* f. AF f. OF *em-* EM-+*prou* profit]

improv'er (-ōōv-), n. In vbl senses; also

or esp.: one who works at trade for low wage or none to improve his skill; = DRESS-~. [-ER¹]

imprŏv'id|ent, a. Unforeseeing; heedless; thriftless. Hence or cogn. ~ENCE n., ~entLY² adv. [IM-²]

imprŏv'isātor (-z-), **imprŏvisātōr'e** (-vēzahtōrĕ), n. (It. pl. *-ori,* pron. -ōrĕ). One who improvises or composes extempore. So **imprŏv(v)isatric'e** (-vēzahtrēch'ā) [-TRIX] n. [It. (-*e,*) as IMPROVISE, see -OR]

improvise' (-z; *also* ĭm²), v.t. Compose, utter, (verse, music, etc., or abs.) extempore; provide, get up, extempore. Hence **imprŏvisa'TION** n., **improvisatōr'IAL, improvis'atorY**, aa., (-z-). [f. F *improviser* (f. It. *improv(v)isare*) f. L IM-² (*provisus* p.p. as PROVIDE) or on the earlier E *improvisation*]

imprud'|ent (-rōō-), a. Rash, indiscreet. Hence or cogn. ~ENCE n., ~entLY² adv. [f. L IM²(*prudens* PRUDENT)]

im'pŭd|ent, a. Shamelessly forward; unblushing; insolently disrespectful. Hence or cogn. ~ENCE n., ~entLY² adv. [ME, f. L IM²*pudens* (*pudēre* be ashamed, -ENT)]

impŭdi'citȳ, n. Shamelessness, immodesty. [f. F *impudicité* f. L IM²(*pudicus* as prec), -TY]

impŭgn' (-ūn), v.t. Assail by word, call in question, (statement, action). Hence ~ABLE a., ~MENT n., (-ūn-). [f. L IM-¹ (*pugnare* fight) assail]

impū'iss|ant, a. Impotent, weak. So ~ANCE n. [F (IM-²+PUISSANT)]

im'pŭlse, n. Impelling, push; (Dynam.) indefinitely large force enduring inappreciably short time but producing finite momentum, e.g. blow of hammer, (also) product of average value of force multiplied by time during which it acts; mental incitement; sudden tendency to act without reflection; impetus. [f. L *impulsus -ūs* (as IMPEL)]

impŭl'sion (-shn), n. Impelling push; mental impulse; impetus. [ME, f. OF, f. L *impulsionem* (as IMPEL, see -ION)]

impŭl'sive, a. Tending to impel; (of persons, conduct, etc.) apt to be moved, prompted, by sudden impulse. Hence ~LY² (-vl-) adv.; ~NESS (-vn-) n. [f. F (-*if, -ive*) or LL *impulsivus* (as prec., see -IVE)]

impūn'itȳ, n. Exemption from punishment, esp. *with* ~; exemption from injury as consequence of act. [f. L *impunitas* f. IM²(*punis* f. *poena* penalty), see -TY]

impūre', a. Dirty; unchaste; mixed with foreign matter, adulterated, (lit. & fig.); (of colour) mixed with another colour. Hence or cogn. ~LY² (-rl-) adv., **impūr'-** ITY n. [f. L IM²(*purus* PURE)]

impūt|e', v.t. Attribute, ascribe, (fault etc., rarely good quality etc., *to* person etc.); (Theol.) ascribe (righteousness, guilt, *to* person) by vicarious substitution. So ~ABIL'ITY, ~A'TION, nn., ~'ABLE,

~'ative, aa., ~'atively² adv. [ME, f. OF *imputer* f. L IM¹(*putare* reckon) enter in the account]

in¹, prep. expr. inclusion or position within limits of space, time, circumstance, etc., as: *in Europe, England, London* (so of any large city or of town etc. *in which* speaker lives, cf. AT), *in the house, a box, a car, a pond, a crowd*; (of dress etc.) *in muslin, mourning, white, brown boots*; *in* (the works of) *Thackeray*; (of part affected) *blind in one eye*; (of ratio) *not one in a hundred*; (of body etc. to which one belongs etc.) *in the army, shares in a company*; (of non-physical regions) *in politics, fancy, my opinion*; (of situation, often idiomatic) *in* CLOVER, HOT *water, fetters, leading-strings, the* DARK², *health, hope (of), sorrow,* CALF, *in* (supplied with) *cash, in* (under influence of) *liquor*; (of occupation) *in search of, in pursuance of, in* (while) *crossing the river*; (of form or arrangement) *packed in dozens, sold in building-plots, falling in folds, in* ORDER¹ (2) *to or that*; (of instrument or material) *drank his health in a glass of whisky, the coat was in green velvet*; (of purpose) *in reply to, in quest of, in honour of*; (of time) *in* (during) *the day, in* (within the space of) *three months, in* (at the end of) *five minutes*; *in itself*, apart from all else, absolutely; (colloq.) *the latest thing in* (within the sphere of) *radios*; (of person's capacity etc.) *as far as in me lies, did not think he had it in him* (was capable of it); *not in it*, not in the running, not a serious competitor; *nothing, little, not much, in it*, (Racing) no decided advantage as yet gained by any competitor, no guessing who will win; (with vbs of motion or change) *put it in your pocket, cut it in half, throw it in the fire*; (expr. relation of vb to indirect object), *believe in, trust in, share in, engage in, rejoice in*; (so with adjj. & nn.) *weak in* (as regards) *algebra, wanting in courage, your trust in him, a change in the constitution*; (of number or dimension) *seven in number, four feet in width*; (forming adv. phr.) *in fact, in truth, in honour, in any case; in so* (or *as*) *far as*, in such measure as; *in that*, since, because. [OE, OS, OHG, Goth. *in*, QN *i*, cogn. w. L *in*, Gk *en*]

in², adv. expr. position bounded by certain limits or motion to a point enclosed by them, as: *come in, send him in, walk in*, (into house, enclosed ground, etc.), *put a notice in* (into a paper), *lock him in, he is in* (the house etc., esp. = at home); *in with it*, put, take, it in; *throw in the harness* (to the bargain, in addition); *a coat with the woolly side in* (nearest the body); *the Liberals were in* (office); *short skirts, oysters, are in* (in fashion or season); (Crick.) *before he had been in* (batting) *five minutes*; *keep the fire in* (burning); *train, boat, summer, is in* (arrived); (with trans. vbs) *burn, cut, rub*, (thing) *in* (so as to

penetrate into another), *hem, cover, wall*, (thing) *in* (so as to enclose it); *in for*, involved in, committed to, (usu. something unpleasant, esp. *it*), also, engaged in competition for (race, prize, etc.); *be, keep, in* (on friendly terms) *with*; *breed in & in* (repeatedly within same stock); *in & out*, now in, now out, to & fro, with alternation or oscillation; *in on it* (colloq.), in the know. [OE *in(n)*, OS, OHG *in* (G *ein*), ON, Goth. *inn*, also OE *inne*, OS, OHG, Goth. *inna*, ON *inni*, derivatives f. prec.]

in³, a. Internal, living etc. inside, as *in patient, in-patient*, one who remains in hospital while under treatment. [prec. used attrib.]

in⁴, n. (Pl.) political party in office; *ins & outs*, turnings to & fro (usu. fig.), details (*of* procedure etc.). [f. IN²]

in⁵, prep. (L). *In ăbsĕn'tĭa*, in (his or her) absence; *in ărtĭc'ŭlō mŏr'tĭs*, in the instant of death; *in* CAMERA; *in căp'ĭtĕ*, in chief, holding or held immediately of the crown; *in commĕn'dam*, as a charge or trust (of benefice pending appointment of regular incumbent, or of its revenue enjoyed by layman etc.); *in cŏntŭmā'ciam* (-shĭ-), in contempt of court; *in ĕss'ĕ*, in actual existence, cf. *in posse*; *in extĕn'sō*, at full length; *in extrēm'ĭs*, at the point of death; *in flagrăn'tĕ dĕlĭc'tō*, in the very act of committing an offence; *in fŏrm'a paup'erĭs*, as poor person not liable to costs; *in lŏc'ō parĕn'tĭs*, in place of a parent; *in mĕd'ĭās rēs*, into the thick of it; *in mĕmōr'ĭăm*, in memory of; *in nŭb'ĭbus*, in the clouds, vague, speculative; *in pārt'ĭbus* (*infĭdēl'ĭum*), (of Rom. Cath. titular bishop) in a heretical country; *in pŏss'ĕ*, potentially, opp. to *in esse*; *in prŏp'rĭa pĕrsōn'a*, in his (her) own person; *in pur'ĭs nătŭrāl'ĭbus*, stark naked; *in* RE²; *in sĭt'ū*, in its (original) place; *in stāt'ū pūpillār'ī*,under guardianship; *in stāt'ū quō*, in the same state (as formerly); *in tĕrrōr'ĕm*, as a warning; *in tōt'ō*, completely; *in vĭt'rō*, (in laboratory use) in a test-tube etc. (lit. in glass).

in-¹, pref. = L *in* in, on, into, towards, against (becoming *il-* before *l*, *im-* before *b, m, p, ir-* before *r*). In OF *in-, im-*, became *en-, em-*; E has usu. *in-, im-*, in wds obviously of L orig., to which the wds adopted from OF were, from the 14th c., made to conform (see EN-¹). Words that still retain both forms are given in this dictionary under the more usual form.

in-², pref. = L *in-* (*il-* etc. as prec.), cogn. w. Gk *a, an-*, Gmc **un-*, prefixed to adjj. & their derivatives to express negation. As living E pref., *in-* often interchanges with *un-*, which is preferred in wds not obviously answering to L types (*unavailing, uncertain, undevout*).

-in, n. a modification of the chem. suf. -INE⁵ forming names of neutral substances such as glycerides, glucosides, proteins, etc.

(*albumin, casein, fibrin, gelatin*) to distinguish them from names of alkaloids & basic substances. Some wds of this class were formerly spelt *-ine*, & are still so spelt in pop. use (*margarine, gelatine*).

-ina¹, L fem. suf. found in *regina*, extended in It. or Sp. & used in E to form fem. titles (*czarina*) & proper names (*Georgina*); occurring also in names of musical instruments (*concertina, seraphina*). Cf. -INE⁴.

-ina², suf., neut. pl. of (often mod.) L adjj., used, in agreement with *animalia* animals understood, to form names of groups of animals related to some typical genus, as *Bombycina* (genus *Bombyx*).

ĭnabil'ĭtў, n. Being unable; lack of power or means. [IN-²]

ĭnăccĕss'|ĭble (-ks-), **a.** That cannot be reached; (of persons) not open to advances, unapproachable. Hence ~ĭBIL'ITУ n., ~ĭBLY² adv. [F, or f. LL IN²(*accessibilis* ACCESSIBLE)]

ĭnăcc'ūr|ate, a. Not accurate. Hence ~ACУ n., ~ateLУ² adv. [IN-²]

ĭnăc't|ion, n. Absence of action; sluggishness, inertness. So ~IVE a., ~ĭveLУ² adv., ~ĭv'ITУ n. [IN-²]

ĭnadăptabil'ĭtў, n. Want of adaptability. [IN-²]

ĭnăd'ĕqu|ate, a. Not adequate (*to* purpose, *to* do); insufficient. Hence ~ACУ n., ~ateLУ² adv. [IN-²]

ĭnadhēs'ĭve (-h-), **a.** Not adhesive. [IN-²]

ĭnadmiss'|ĭble, a. That cannot be admitted or allowed. Hence ~ĭBIL'ITУ n. [IN-²]

ĭnadvĕrt'|ent, a. Not properly attentive; negligent; (of actions) unintentional. Hence or cogn. ~ENCE, ~ENCУ, nn., ~entLУ² adv. [f. earlier *inadvertence, -ency* (IN-², ADVERT, -ENT)]

ĭnadvĭs'able (-z-), **a.** Not advisable. [IN-²]

ĭnăl'ĭen|able, a. Not alienable. Hence ~ABIL'ITУ n., ~abLУ² adv. [IN-²]

ĭnal'ter|able (-awl-), **a.** Unalterable. Hence ~ABIL'ITУ n., ~abLУ² adv. [IN-²]

ĭnămora'tō (-rah-), **n.** (fem. *-ta*). Lover. [It. (now *inn-*) f. IN ¹(*amorare* f. amore f. L *amor* love) enamour]

ĭnāne', a. & n. Empty, void, silly; senseless; (n.) *the* ~, vacuity, infinite space. Hence or cogn. ~LУ² (-nl-) adv., ĭnăn'ITУ n. [f. L *inanis* empty, vain]

ĭnăn'imate, a. Destitute of life; not endowed with animal life, as ~ *nature* (outside the animal world); spiritless, dull. Hence or cogn.~LУ² adv., ĭnănimА²TION n. [f. LL IN²(*animatus* ANIMATE¹)]

ĭnani'tion, n. Emptiness, esp. from want of nourishment. [f. LL *inanitio* f. *inanire* make empty (as INANE), see -ION]

ĭnappeas'able (-z-), **a.** Not appeasable. [IN-²]

ĭnappĕll'able, n. Not to be appealed against. [f. IN-²+L *appellare* APPEAL+ -BLE]

ĭnăpp'ĕtence, n. Want of appetence. [F (IN-², APPETENCE)]

ĭnăpp'lic|able, a. Not applicable, unsuitable, (*to* case, purpose). Hence ~ABIL'ITУ n., ~abLУ² adv. [IN-²]

ĭnăpp'osite, a. Not apposite, out of place. Hence ~LУ² adv. [IN-²]

ĭnapprē'ciab|le (-sha-), **a.** Imperceptible, not worth reckoning; that cannot be appreciated. Hence ~LУ² adv. [IN-²]

ĭnapprēcia'tion, n. Failure to appreciate. So ĭnapprē'ciative (-sha-) a. [IN-²]

ĭnăpprĕhĕn'sĭble, a. That cannot be grasped by senses or intellect. [f. LL *-ibilis* (IN-², APPREHENSIBLE)]

ĭnapproach'able, a. Unapproachable. [IN-²]

ĭnapprōp'rĭate, a. Not appropriate. Hence~LУ² adv.,~NESS n. [IN-²]

ĭnăpt', a. Unfit, unskilful. Hence ĭnăp'tITUDE, ~NESS, nn., ~LУ² adv. [IN-²]

ĭnărch', v.t. Graft by connecting growing branch without separation from parent stock. [IN-¹+ARCH v.]

ĭnărm', v.t. (poet.). Embrace. [IN¹+ ARM¹]

ĭnărtic'ūlate, a. Not jointed; (of speech) not articulate; unable to speak distinctly; dumb. Hence ~LУ² adv., ~NESS n. [f. LL IN²(*articulatus* ARTICULATE)]

ĭnărtifi'cial (-shal), **a.** Lacking in art, inartistic; artless, natural. Hence ~LУ² adv. [f. L IN²(*artificialis* ARTIFICIAL)]

ĭnărtis't|ic, a. Not following the principles of art; unskilled in art. Hence ~ICALLY adv. [IN-²]

ĭnasmŭch' (-az-), **adv.** ~ *as*, since, because; (arch.) in so far *as*. [ME; orig. three wds]

ĭnattĕn't|ion, n. Want of attention, heedlessness; neglect to show courtesy. So ~IVE a., ~ĭveLУ² adv., ~ĭveNESS n. [IN-², or f. F]

ĭnaud'|ĭble, a. That cannot be heard. Hence ~ĭBIL'ITУ n., ~ĭbLУ² adv. [f. LL IN²(*audibilis* AUDIBLE)]

ĭnaug'ūral, a. & n. Of inauguration; *(n.)* ~ speech or address. [F, f. *inaugurer* (as foll.)]

ĭnaug'ūr|āte, v.t. Admit (person) to office etc. with ceremony; enter with ceremony upon (undertaking etc.); initiate public use of (building etc.). Hence or cogn. ~A'TION, ~ātOR, nn., ~ātORУ a. [f. L IN¹(*augurare* take omens, f. *augur*), see -ATE³]

ĭnauspi'cious (-shus), **a.** Not of good omen; unlucky. Hence ~LУ² adv., ~NESS n. [IN-²]

in'board (-ōrd), **adv. & a.** (naut.). (Situated) within sides of or towards centre of ship. [IN¹]

in'bŏrn, a. Implanted by nature. [IN²]

inbreathe' (-dh), **v.t.** Breathe (thing) in (lit. & fig.). [IN²]

in'brĕd, a. Innate, inherent by nature; bred in and in. [IN²]

in'breeding, n. Breeding in & in, breeding from animals closely related. [IN²]

Inc'a (I-), n. Emperor or king of Peru before Spanish conquest; one of royal race of Peru. [Peruv.]

incăl'cŭl|able, a. Too great for calculation; that cannot be reckoned beforehand; (of person, character, etc.) uncertain. Hence ~aBIL'ITY n., ~abLY² adv. [IN-²]

incăndĕsce', v.i. & t. Glow, cause to glow, with heat. [f. after foll.]

incăndĕs'c|ent, a. Glowing with heat; shining brightly; (of electric & other light) produced by glowing of filament etc. Hence ~ENCE n. [F, f. L IN¹(candescere incept. of candēre be white), see -ENT]

incăntā'tion, n. (Use of) magical formula; spell, charm. [ME, f. OF f. LL incantationem f. IN¹(cantare chant) bewitch, see -ION]

incăp'|able, a. Not capable (of conduct etc., of doing; often in good sense, = too honest etc. to do); not susceptible (of improvement etc.); lacking in ordinary powers, as drunk & ~able. Hence ~aBIL'ITY n., ~abLY² adv. [f. F, or LL IN²(capabilis CAPABLE)]

incapā'cit|āte, v.t. Render incapable or unfit (for work etc., for, from, doing). Hence ~A'TION n. [f. foll.+-ATE³]

incapā'citў, n. Inability (for doing, for work etc., to do, or abs.); legal disqualification. [f. F IN²(capacité CAPACITY)]

incăr'cer|āte, v.t. Imprison (lit. & fig.). Hence or cogn. ~A'TION, ~ātOR, nn. [f. med. L IN¹(carcerare f. carcer prison), see -ATE³]

incărn'adĭne, a., & v.t. (poet.). (Dye) flesh-coloured, crimson. [(vb f. a.) IN¹(-ine) f. It. incarnadino (for -tino) f. incarnato INCARNATE¹]

incărn'ate¹, a. (Of person, spirit, quality, etc.) embodied in flesh, esp. in human form, as he is an ~ fiend, Liberty ~; (as p.p., of Christ) was ~ by the Holy Ghost. [ME, f. LL IN¹(carnare f. caro carnis flesh), see -ATE²]

incărn'āte² (or ĭn'k-), v.t. Embody in flesh; put (idea etc.) into concrete form, realize; (of person etc.) be living embodiment of (quality). [as prec., see -ATE³]

incărnā'tion, n. Embodiment in (esp. human) flesh, esp. the I~ (of Christ); impersonation, living type, (of quality etc.). [ME, f. OF f. LL incarnationem (as prec. see -ION)]

incau'tious (-shus), a. Rash. Hence~LY² adv., ~NESS n. [IN-²]

incĕn'diar|ў, a. & n. 1. Of, guilty of, the malicious setting on fire of property (~y bomb, filled with inflammatory substance(s) for causing fires); (fig.) tending to stir up strife, inflammatory. 2. n. ~y person (lit. & fig.); ~y bomb. Hence

~ISM n. [f. L incendiarius f. incendium conflagration f. IN(cendere cens- set fire to), see -ARY¹]

in'cense¹, n. Gum, spice, producing sweet smell when burned; smoke of this, esp. in religious ceremonial; (fig.) praise, flattery. [ME, f. OF encens f. LL incensum thing burnt, incense, neut. p.p. as prec.]

in'cens|e², v.t. Fumigate (person, thing) with incense; burn incense to (deity etc.); suffuse with fragrance. Hence ~A'TION n. [ME, f. OF encenser (as prec.)]

incĕnse'³, v.t. Enrage, make angry (~d against, with, at, by). [ME, f. OF incenser f. L incendere (see INCENDIARY)]

in'cĕnsorў, n. Vessel for burning incense, censer. [f. med. L incensorium (INCENSE¹, -ORY)]

incĕn'tive, a. & n. 1. Tending to incite. 2. n. Incitement (to action, to do, to doing), provocation, motive. [f. L incentivus setting the tune f. IN¹(cinere cent- = canere sing) sing to; -IVE]

incĕpt', v.i. & t. ‖ (Formerly at Camb. Univ.) commence the taking of Master's or Doctor's degree, so **incĕp'toR** n.; (Biol.) take in. [f. L IN¹(cipere cept- = capere take) begin]

incĕp'tion, n. Beginning; ‖ (Camb. Univ.) incepting. [ME, f. OF, or L inceptio (as prec., see -ION)]

incĕp'tive, a. & n. Beginning; initial; (Gram.) ~ verb, one that denotes the beginning of an action; (n.) ~ verb. [f. LL inceptivus (as INCEPT, see -IVE)]

incĕrt'itŭde, n. Uncertainty. [f. F, or LL incertitudo (IN-², CERTITUDE)]

incĕss'ant, a. Unceasing, continual, repeated. Hence **incĕss'ANCY, ~NESS,** nn., ~LY² adv. [f. F, or LL IN²(cessans -ant part. of cessare CEASE)]

in'cĕst, n. Sexual commerce of near kindred. [ME, f. L incestus -ūs or IN²(cestum neut. adj. = castum chaste)]

incĕs'tŭous, a. Involving, guilty of, incest. Hence~LY² adv. [f. LL incestuosus (as prec., see -OUS)]

inch¹, n., & v.t. & i. 1. Twelfth part of (linear) foot; square, cubic, ~, area equal to square, content equal to cube, whose side is an ~; (as unit of rainfall) quantity that would cover surface to depth of an ~; (of atmospheric or other pressure) amount that balances weight of column of mercury 1 in. high in mercurial barometer; small amount; by ~es, bit by bit; every ~, entirely; (pl.) stature (a man of your ~es); give him an ~ & he'll take an ELL; flog person within an ~ of his life, almost to death; an ~ of cold iron, stab with a dagger etc. 2. v.t. & i. Move by ~es, edge in, forward, etc. [OE ynce = OHG unza, Goth. unkja f. L uncia twelfth part, see OUNCE¹]

‖ **inch²,** n. Small (esp. Scottish) island (freq. in place names). [f. Gael. innis]

In wds from incalculable to incautious pronounce ĭn-k-, not ĭngk-.

in′choate¹ (ĭn-kō-), a. Just begun; un-developed. [f. L IN¹(*cohare, choare*), see -ATE²]

in′cho|āte² (ĭn-kō-), v.t. Begin; originate. So ~A′TION n., ~ātive (or -kō′a-) a. [prec., -ATE³]

in′cidence, n. Falling on, contact with, a thing; *what is the ~ of the tax?*, on whom will it fall? ; (Phys.) falling of line, or of thing, moving in a line, upon a surface; *angle of ~*, that which the incident line, ray, etc., makes with the perpendicular to the surface at point of ~ ; range, scope, extent, of influence. [ME, f. OF (as INCIDENT², see -ENCE)]

in′cident¹, n. Subordinate or accessory event; event, occurrence; hostile clash of e.g. troops of countries not at war, as *frontier ~* ; detached event attracting general attention; distinct piece of action in play or poem; (Law) privilege, burden, etc., attaching to estate etc. [ME, f. OF (as foll.)]

in′cident², a. Apt to occur, naturally at-taching, (*to*); (Law) attaching *to* (cf. prec.); (of light etc.) falling, striking, (*upon*). [ME, f. OF, or L IN¹(*cīdere* = *cadere* fall), see -ENT]

inciden′tal, a. Casual, not essential; liable to happen *to*; ~ *images, colours* (perceived as consequence of impressions no longer present); ~ *music* (introduced during the action of a play). Hence ~LY² adv. (also, loosely, by the way, parenthet-ically).

incin′er|āte, v.t. Reduce to ashes; con-sume (body etc.) by fire. Hence or cogn. ~A′TION, ~ātoR, nn. [INCIDENT¹+-AL] [f. med. L IN¹(*cinerare* f. *cinis -eris* ashes), see -ATE³]

incip′i|ent, a. Beginning; in an initial stage. Hence ~ENCE, ~ENCY, nn., ~ent-LY² adv. [f. L as INCEPT, see -ENT]

in′cipit, sent. n. (Here) begins (book etc.), cf. EXPLICIT¹. [L]

incise′ (-z), v.t. Make a cut in; engrave. [f. F *inciser* f. L IN¹(*cīdere cis-* = *caedere* cut)]

inci′sion (-zhn), n. Cutting into a thing; cut, division produced by cutting, notch. [ME, f. OF f. L *incisionem* (prec., -ɪON)]

incis′ive, a. Cutting, penetrating; (fig.) mentally sharp; acute, trenchant. Hence ~LY² (-vl-) adv., ~NESS (-vn-) n. [F (-*if*, -*ive*), or f. med. L *incisivus* (as INCISE, see -IVE)]

incis′or (-z-), n. Any tooth between the canine teeth in either jaw. [med. L, = cutter (as INCISE, see -OR)]

incite′, v.t. Urge, stir up, (person etc. *to* action, *to* do). Hence or cogn. incitA′TION, ~MENT (-tm-), nn. [late ME, f. F *inciter* f. L IN¹(*citare* rouse frequent. of *ciēre cit-*)]

incivil′ity, n. Rudeness, discourtesy. [f. F *incivilité* or LL IN²(*civilitas* CIVILITY)]

in′civism, n. Want of good citizenship,

esp. of loyalty to French Revolution principles. [f. F IN²(*civisme* f. L *civis* citizen)]

‖ **in-clearing,** n. The cheques etc. collec-tively payable by a bank & received through clearing-house for settlement. [IN adv.]

inclĕm′|ent, a. (Of weather or climate) severe, esp. cold or stormy. So ~ENCY n. [f. F, or L IN²(*clemens* CLEMENT)]

inclin′able, a. Inclined, disposed; (*to* thing, *to* do); favourable (*to*). [ME, f. OF *enclinable* (as INCLINE¹, see -ABLE)]

inclinā′tion, n. Leaning, slope, slant; difference of direction of two lines, esp. as measured by angle between them; dis-position, propensity, (*to, for, towards,* thing, *to* do); liking, affection, (*for*). [ME, f. OF, or f. L *inclinatio* (foll., -ATION)]

incline′¹, v.t. & i. Bend (head, body, one-*self*) forward or downward; ~ *one's ear,* listen favourably (*to* person, prayer, etc.); dispose (mind, heart, person, *to* do), as ~ *our hearts to keep this law, I am ~d to think*; be disposed, as *I ~ to think*; lean, cause to lean, from the vertical etc.; ~*d* (sloping) *plane,* one of the MECHANICAL *powers*; tend (*to* corpulence etc.). [ME en- f. OF *encliner* f. L IN¹(*clinare* bend)]

in′cline² (or -īn′), n. Inclined plane; slope. [f. prec.]

inclinŏm′eter, n. Instrument measuring vertical intensity of earth's magnetic force as shown by dip of magnetic needle, or for measuring slope. [INCLINE+-0-+ -METER]

includ′e′ (-lōō-), v.t. Comprise, embrace, (thing etc.) as part of a whole; (part. in abs. constr.) if we ~e, as *seven were killed,* ~*ing the guard*; treat, regard, as so comprised; *~e out,* (specifically) exclude; (p.p.) shut in. [ME, f. L IN¹(*cludere clus-* = *claudere* shut)]

inclus′ive (-lōō-), a. Including, compris-ing, (*of,* or abs.); (abbr. *incl.*) *pages 7 to 26 ~* (including pages 7 & 26); including much or all, as ~ *terms* (at hotel etc.). Hence or cogn. **inclu′sion** (-lōōzhn) n., ~LY² adv., ~NESS n. [f. med. L *inclusivus* (as prec., see -IVE)]

incŏg′, a., n., & adv. Colloq. abbr. of foll.

incŏg′nitō, a. & n. (pl. -*ti* pron. -tē; fem. -*ta* pron. -ta, pl. -*te* pron. -tä), & adv. (Person) concealed under disguised character; (adv.) with one's name, character, etc., concealed, as *travel, do good, ~*. [It., =unknown, f. L IN²(*cognitus* p.p. of *cognoscere* get to know)]

incŏg′nizable (-kŏgn-, -kŏn-), a. That cannot be apprehended by senses or in-tellect. [IN-²]

incŏg′niz|ant (as prec.), a. Unaware, un-conscious *of*. So ~ANCE n. [IN-²]

incohēr′|ent, a. Not coherent (lit. & fig.). So ~ENCE n., ~entLY² adv. [IN-²]

incohēs′ive, a. Not cohesive. [IN-²]

In wds from *in-clearing* to *incurve,* pronounce in-k-, not ingk-.

incombŭs′t|ible, a. That cannot be consumed by fire. Hence ~ĬBIL′ITY n. [f. med. L IN²(*combustibilis* COMBUSTIBLE).

in′come, n. Periodical (usu. annual) receipts from one's business, lands, work, investments, etc.; ~ *tax* (levied on this). [IN adv.]

in′com′er (-kŭ-), n. One who comes in; immigrant; intruder; successor. [IN adv.]

in′com′ing¹ (-kŭ-), n. Entrance, arrival; (usu. pl.) revenue, income. [IN adv.]

in′coming² (-kŭ-), a. Succeeding; immigrant; (of profit) accruing. [IN adv.]

incommĕn′sur|able (-sher-), a. (Of magnitudes) having no common measure integral or fractional (*with* another); irrational, surd; not comparable in respect of magnitude; not worthy to be measured *with*. Hence ~ABIL′ITY n., ~abLY² adv. [f. LL IN²(*commensurabilis* COMMENSURABLE)]

incommĕn′surate (-sher-), a. Out of proportion, inadequate, (*with, to*); = prec. Hence ~NESS n. [IN-²]

incommŏde′, v.t. Trouble, annoy; hinder. [f. F *incommoder* or L IN²(*commodare* f. *commodus* COMMODIOUS)]

incommŏd′ious, a. Not affording good accommodation, uncomfortable. Hence ~NESS n. [IN-²]

incommūn′ic|able, a. That cannot be shared; that cannot be told. Hence ~ABIL′ITY, ~ableNESS, nn., ~abLY² adv. [f. F, or LL IN² (*communicabilis* COMMUNICABLE)]

incommūnica′dō (-ah-), a. Without means of communication, (of prisoner) in solitary confinement. [Sp. (-omu-)]

incommūn′icātive, a. Not communicative. Hence ~LY² adv., ~NESS n. [IN-²]

incommūt′ab|le, a. Unchangeable; not commutable. Hence ~LY² adv. [ME, f. OF, or L IN²(*commutabilis* COMMUTABLE)]

incompăct′, a. Not compact (esp. fig.). [IN-²]

incŏm′parab|le, a. Matchless; not to be compared (*with, to*). Hence ~leNESS n., ~LY² adv. [ME, f. OF f. L IN²(*comparabilis* COMPARABLE)]

incompăt′|ible, a. Opposed in character, discordant; inconsistent (*with*). So ~ĭBIL′ITY n. [f. OF, or med. L IN²(*compatibilis* COMPATIBLE)]

incŏm′pĕt|ent, a. Not qualified or able (*to* do); not legally qualified. Hence or cogn. ~ENCE, ~ENCY, nn., ~entLY² adv. [f. F, or LL IN²(*competens* COMPETENT)]

incomplēte′, a. Not complete. Hence ~LY² (-tl-) adv., ~NESS (-tn-) n. [ME, f. OF, or LL IN²(*completus* COMPLETE)]

incŏmprĕhĕn′s|ible, a. That cannot be understood (Athanas. Creed) boundless (also as n., *three* ~*ibles*). Hence ~ĭBIL′ITY, ~ibleNESS, nn., ~ĭbLY² adv. [ME, f. L IN²(*comprehensibilis* COMPREHENSIBLE)]

incŏmprĕhĕn′sion (-shn), n. Failure to understand. [IN-²]

incomprĕss′|ible, a. That cannot be compressed. Hence ~ĬBIL′ITY n. [IN-²]

incompūt′able, a. That cannot be computed. [IN-²]

inconceiv′|able (-sēv-), a. That cannot be imagined; (pop.) very remarkable. Hence ~ABIL′ITY n., ~abLY² adv. [IN-²]

inconclus′īve (-klōō-), a. (Of argument, evidence, action) not decisive or convincing. Hence ~LY² adv., ~NESS n. [IN-²]

incondĕn′sable, a. That cannot be condensed, esp. that cannot be reduced to liquid or solid condition. [IN-²]

incŏn′dite, a. (Of literary composition etc.) ill constructed; crude, unpolished. [f. L IN²(*conditus* p.p. of *condere* put together)]

inconfŏrm′ĭtў, n. Dissimilarity, want of conformity, (*to, with*); = NONCONFORMITY. [IN-²]

incŏng′ruous (-kŏnggrōŏ-), a. Disagreeing, out of keeping, (*with*); out of place, absurd. Hence or cogn. **incongru′ITY** (-grōō-), ~NESS, nn., ~LY² adv. [f. L IN²(*congruus* CONGRUOUS)]

inconsĕc′ūtive, a. Wanting in sequence, inconsequent. Hence ~LY² adv., ~NESS n. [IN-²]

incŏn′sĕqu|ent, a. Not following naturally, irrelevant; wanting in logical sequence; disconnected. Hence or cogn. ~ENCE n., ~ĕn′tIAL (-shal) a., ~ĕn′tialLY² (-shal-), ~entLY², advv. [f. L IN²(*consequens* CONSEQUENT)]

inconsid′erable, a. Not worth considering; of small size, value, etc. [f. F, or IN-²+CONSIDERABLE]

inconsid′er|ate, a. (Of person or action) thoughtless, rash; lacking in regard for feelings etc. of others. Hence or cogn. ~ateLY² adv., ~ateNESS, ~A′TION, nn. [f. L IN²(*consideratus* CONSIDERATE)]

inconsis′t|ent, a. Not in keeping, discordant, incompatible, (*with*); (of single thing) having ~ent parts; acting at variance with one's own principles or former conduct. Hence ~ENCY n., ~entLY² adv. [IN-²]

inconsŏl′ab|le, a. (Of person, his grief, etc.) that cannot be consoled. Hence ~LY² adv. [f. F, or L IN²(*consolabilis* CONSOLABLE)]

incŏn′son|ant, a. Not harmonizing (*with, to*). Hence ~ANCE n. [IN-²]

inconspic′ūous, a. Not conspicuous; (Bot., of flowers) small, pale, or green. Hence ~NESS n. [f. LL IN²(*conspicuus* CONSPICUOUS)]

incŏn′st|ant, a. (Of person) fickle, changeable; variable, irregular. Hence or cogn. ~ancy n., ~antLY² adv. [ME, f. OF f. L IN²(*constantem* CONSTANT)]

inconsūm′able, a. That cannot be consumed by fire etc.; (Pol. Econ.) not meant to be consumed in use. [IN-²]

incontĕs′tab|le, a. That cannot be disputed. Hence ~LY² adv. [F (IN-²)]

incŏn'tin|ent, a. Wanting in self-restraint (esp. in regard to sexual appetite); unable to hold in something (*of* secrets, tongue, urine, etc.). So ~ENCE n. [ME, f. OF, or L IN²(*continens* CONTINENT)]

incŏn'tinentlў, adv. (literary). At once, immediately. [arch. *incontinent* adv. (thr. F) f. LL *in continenti* (*tempore*) in continuous time, +-LY²]

incŏntrovert'ib|le, a. Not to be disputed. Hence ~LY² adv. [IN-²]

inconvēn'ience, n., & v.t. Want of adaptation to personal requirement or ease; instance of this; (v.t.) put (person etc.) to ~, incommode. [ME, f. OF, f. LL *inconvenientia* (as foll., see -ENCE)]

inconvēn'ient, a. Unfavourable to ease or comfort, awkward, troublesome. Hence ~LY² adv. [ME, f. OF *inconvenient* f. L IN²(*convenientem* CONVENIENT)]

inconvert'|ible, a. Not convertible (esp. of currency). Hence ~ĪBIL'ITY n., ~ĭBLY² adv. [f. LL IN²(*convertibilis* CONVERTIBLE)]

inconvin'cible, a. Not to be convinced. [IN-²]

incŏordinā'tion, n. Want of coordination. [IN-²]

incŏrp'orate¹, a. (Of company etc.) formed into a corporation; (of persons) united in a corporation. [as foll., see -ATE²]

incŏrp'or|āte², v.t. & i. Unite (*in* one body, *with* another thing); combine (ingredients) into one substance; constitute as a legal corporation; become ~ated (*with*); ~ated, abbr. *inc.* (esp. U.S.), forming a legal corporation. Hence or cogn. ~A'TION, ~ātor, nn. [ME, f. LL IN¹-(*corporare* f. *corpus -oris* body), -ATE³]

incŏrpŏr'eal, a. Not composed of matter; of immaterial beings; (Law) having no material existence, esp. ~ *hereditament*. Hence ~LY² adv., incŏrporē'ity n. [f. L IN²(*corporeus* f. *corpus -oris* body) + -AL]

incorrĕct', a. Not in accordance with fact; (of style etc.) improper, faulty; (of book) not properly corrected for press. Hence ~LY² adv., ~NESS n. [ME, f. OF, or L IN²(*correctus* CORRECT)]

incŏ'rrig|ible, a. (Of person or habit) incurably bad or depraved. Hence ~ĪBIL'ITY n., ~ĭBLY² adv. [ME, f. OF, or L IN²(*corrigibilis* CORRIGIBLE)]

incorrŭp't|ible, a. That cannot decay, so ~ION n. (bibl.); eternal; that cannot be corrupted, esp. bribed. Hence or cogn. ~ĪBIL'ITY n., ~ĭBLY² adv. [ME, f. LL IN²(*corruptibilis* CORRUPTIBLE)]

incrăss'ate, a. (bot., zool.). Of thick or swollen form. [f. LL IN¹(*crassare* f. *crassus* thick), see -ATE²]

increas|e'¹, v.i. & t. Become greater; grow in numbers, esp. by propagation; advance (*in* quality, attainment, etc.); make greater or more numerous; intensify (quality). Hence ~'ingLY² adv. [ME, f. OF *encreistre* (st. *-eiss-*) f. L IN¹(*crescere* grow)]

in'crease², n. Growth, enlargement; growth in numbers, multiplication (of men, animals, or plants); *on the* ~, increasing; increased amount; (arch.) crops. [f. prec.]

incrĕd'|ible, a. That cannot be believed; (colloq.) hard to believe, surprising. So ~ĪBIL'ITY n., ~ĭBLY² adv. [ME, f. L IN²(*credibilis* CREDIBLE)]

incrĕd'ūlous, a. Unbelieving (*of* or abs.). Hence or cogn. incrĕdūl'ITY n., ~LY² adv. [f. L IN²(*credulus* CREDULOUS)]

in'crèment, n. Increase; amount of this; profit; UNEARNED ~, see UN-²(1); (Math.) small amount by which variable quantity increases. [ME, f. L *incrementum* (as INCREASE, see -MENT)]

incrim'in|āte, v.t. Charge with crime; involve in accusation. Hence ~atORY a. [f. LL IN¹(*criminare* CRIMINATE)]

incrŭstā'tion, n. Encrusting; crust, hard coating; facing of marble etc. on building; (fig.) accretion of habit; scab. [f. F, or LL *incrustatio* (as ENCRUST, see -ATION)]

in'cūbāte, v.t. & i. Hatch (eggs) by sitting on them or otherwise; sit on eggs, brood. [f. L IN¹(*cubare cubit-* or *cubat-* lie), see -ATE³]

incūbā'tion, n. Hatching; *artificial* ~ (by artificial heat); (of the Holy Ghost) brooding; (Path.) phase through which germs of disease pass before development of first symptoms. So **in'cūbātīve, in'cūbātory, aa.** [f. L *incubatio* (as prec., see -ATION)]

in'cūbātor, n. Apparatus for hatching birds, rearing children born prematurely, or developing bacteria. [f. INCUBATE +-OR]

in'cūbus, n. (pl. *-bī*, *-buses*). Evil spirit supposed to descend on sleeping persons; nightmare; person, thing, that oppresses like nightmare. [ME; LL, = L *incubo* nightmare (as INCUBATE)]

in'culc|āte, v.t. Urge, impress, (fact, habit, idea) persistently (*upon* or *in* person, mind). So ~A'TION, ~ātor, nn. [f. L IN¹(*culcare* = *calcare* tread f. *calx -lcis* heel), -ATE³]

in'culpāte, v.t. Accuse, blame; involve in charge. Hence incŭlpA'TION n., incŭl'patory a. [f. LL IN¹(*culpare* f. *culpa* fault), -ATE³]

incŭlt', a. (rare). Untilled; unpolished, rude; (of person or manners) coarse. [f. L IN²(*cultus* p.p. of *colere* till)]

incŭm'bency, n. Office, tenure, sphere, of an incumbent. [f. foll., see -ENCY]

incŭm'bent¹, n. Holder of ecclesiastical benefice or (rare, exc. U.S.) of any office. [as foll.]

incŭm'bent², a. Lying, pressing, (*on*); resting (*up*)*on* (person) as duty, as *it is* ~

In wds from *in-clearing* to *incurve*, pronounce in-k-, not ingk-.

on you to warn them. [f. L IN¹(*cumbere* lie), -ENT]

incŭnăb'ŭla, n. pl. Early stages of thing; (w. sing. *-um*) books printed early, esp. before 1501. [L, = swaddling-clothes, f. *cunae* cradle]

incŭr', v.t. (-rr-). Fall into, bring on one-self, (danger, blame, punishment, etc.). [f. L IN¹(*currere curs-* run)]

incŭr'|able, a. & n. (Person) that cannot be cured. Hence ~ABIL'ITY, ~ableNESS, nn., ~abLY² adv. [ME, f. OF f. LL IN²(*curabilis* CURABLE)]

incŭr'ious, a. Devoid of curiosity; heed-less, careless, uninteresting (usu. *not* ~). Hence incūriōs'ITY n., ~LY² adv. [f. L IN²(*curiosus* CURIOUS)]

incŭr's|ion (-shn), n. Hostile invasion; sudden attack. So ~IVE a. [ME, f. L *incursio* (as INCUR, see -ION)]

incŭrv|e', v.t. Bend into a curve; curve inwards (esp. in p.p.). So ~A'TION n. [f. L IN¹(*curvare* CURVE)]

in'cus, n. Bone of ear receiving vibra-tions from MALLEUS. [L, = anvil (as foll.)]

incūse'¹ (ĭnkūz'), a. & n. (Of impression on coin etc.) hammered or stamped in; (n.) such impression. [f. L IN¹(*cudere cus-*forge)]

incūse'² (ĭnkūz'), v.t. (esp. in p.p.). Im-press (figure etc.) by stamping; mark (coin etc.) with such figure. [as prec.]

Ind (I-), n. (arch. or poet.). India. [ME, f. OF *Inde*]

inda'ba (-ah-), n. A conference between or with S.-African natives. [Zulu, = business]

indĕbt'ĕd (-dĕt-), a. Owing money (*to*); owing gratitude (*to* person, or fig. *to* thing, *for* benefit etc.). Hence ~NESS n. [ME, f. OF *endette* p.p. of EN(*detter* f. *dette* DEBT)]

indĕ'cent, a. Unbecoming; immodest, obscene. Hence or cogn. **indĕ'cENCY** n., ~LY² adv. [f. F, or L IN²(*decens* DECENT)]

indĕcĭd'ūous, a. Not deciduous. [IN-²]

indĕcĭph'erable, a. That cannot be de-ciphered. [IN-²]

indĕcī'sion (-zhn), n. Want of decision, hesitation. [f. F IN²(*décision* DECISION)]

indĕcī'sive, a. Not decisive; undecided, irresolute. Hence ~LY² adv., ~NESS n. [IN-²]

indĕclīn'able, a. That cannot be de-clined; having no inflexions. [ME, f. OF & L (LL) IN²(*declinabilis* DECLINABLE)]

·indĕcompōs'able (-z-), a. That cannot be decomposed or resolved into constituents. [IN-²]

indĕcōr'ous (*or* -dĕk'o-), a. Improper; in bad taste. Hence ~LY² adv., ~NESS n. [f. L IN²(*decorus* DECOROUS)]

indĕcōr'um, n. Lack of decorum; im-proper proceeding. [L, neut. adj. as prec.]

indeed', adv. In truth, really, as *he was*, ~, *a remarkable man*; (intensifying) *I shall be very glad* ~, *this is quick work* ~, *yes,*

~ *!, no,* ~ *!*; (echoing last speaker's words with approval or iron.) *who is this Mr Smith?—who is he,* ~ *!* (= you may well ask, or, can you ask?); (concessive) *there are* ~ *exceptions*; (interrog.) really? is it so?; as int., expr. irony, contempt, in-credulity, etc. [ME; IN prep. +DEED]

indĕfăt'ig|able, a. (Of persons, qualities, etc.) that cannot be tired out, unremit-ting. Hence ~ABIL'ITY n., ~abLY² adv. [f. obs. F *indéfatigable* or L IN²(*defatigabilis* f. DE*fatigare* wear out, see -BLE)]

indĕfeas'|ible (-z-), a. That cannot be forfeited or done away with, esp. ~*ible right*. Hence ~ĭBIL'ITY n., ~ĭbLY² adv. [IN-²]

indĕfĕc'tible, a. Unfailing, not liable to defect or decay; faultless. [f. F, or LL IN²(*defectibilis* DEFECTIBLE)]

indĕfĕn's|ible, a. Admitting of no defence (by force of arms or by argument). Hence ~ĭBIL'ITY n., ~ĭbLY² adv. [IN-²]

indĕfin'ab|le, a. That cannot be defined. Hence ~LY² adv. [IN-²]

indĕf'inite, a. Vague, undefined; un-limited; (Gram., of adjj., pronouns, etc.) not determining the person, thing, time, etc., to which they refer, esp. ~ *article* (a, an); (of tenses) denoting an action with-out specifying whether it is continuous or complete (e.g. Greek aorist, English past). Hence ~LY² (-tl-) adv., ~NESS (-tn-), **indĕfin'ĭTUDE**, nn. [f. L IN²(*definitus* DEFINITE)]

indĕhis'cent, a. (bot.). Not dehiscent. [IN-²]

indĕl'|ible, a. (Of mark, stain, ink, etc., & fig. of disgrace etc.) that cannot be blotted out. Hence ~ĭBIL'ITY n., ~ĭbLY² adv. [f. F *indélébile* or L IN²(*delebilis* f. *delēre* DELETE, see -BLE)]

indĕl'ic|ate, a. Coarse, unrefined; im-modest; tactless. Hence ~ACY n., ~atELY² adv. [IN-²]

indĕm'ni|fў, v.t. Protect, secure, (person *from, against*, harm or loss); secure (per-son) against legal responsibility (*for* actions); compensate (person *for* loss, ex-penses incurred, etc.). Hence ~FICA'TION n. [f. L IN²(*demnis* f. *damnum* loss), see -FY]

indĕm'nitў, n. Security against damage or loss; legal exemption from penalties etc. incurred; compensation for loss in-curred; sum paid for this, esp. sum ex-acted by victorious belligerent as one condition of peace. [f. F *indemnité* f. LL *indemnitas* (as prec., see -TY)]

indĕmōn'strable, a. That cannot be proved (esp. of primary truths). [f. F, or L IN² (*demonstrabilis* DEMONSTRABLE)]

indĕnt'¹, v.t. & i. 1. Make tooth-like notches in; form deep recesses in (coast-line etc.). 2. Divide (document drawn up in duplicate) into two halves with zig-zag line, draw up (document) in exact duplicate. 3. (print.). Set back (beginning of line) farther from margin to mark new paragraph etc. **4.** Make requisition (prop. written order with duplicate) *upon* (person *for* thing); order (goods) by an indent. [ME, f. AF *endenter* f. med. L IN¹⁻ (*dentare* f. *dens -ntis* tooth)]

Indĕnt'² (or ĭn⁴), n. Indentation; indenture; ‖ official requisition for stores; order (esp. from abroad) for goods. [f. prec.]

Indĕnt'³, v.t. Make a dent in; impress (mark etc.). [IN⁻¹]

In'dĕnt⁴, n. Dent, depression. [f. prec.]

In'dĕntā'tion, n. Indenting; cut, notch; zigzag; deep recess in coastline etc. [IN-DENT¹,³ +-ATION]

Indĕn'tion, n. Indenting of line in printing; = prec. [irreg. f. INDENT¹ +-ION]

Indĕn'ture, n., & v.t. **1.** Indented document (see INDENT¹); any sealed agreement or contract, esp. that which binds apprentice to master; *take up* one's *~s*, receive them back on completion of service; formal list, certificate, etc.; indentation. **2.** v.t. Bind (person) by *~s* esp. as apprentice. [ME, f. AF *endenture* (as INDENT¹, see -URE)]

Indĕpĕn'den|ce, -en|cy̆, nn. 1. (*~ce*). Being independent (*on, of,* or abs.); independent income; **I~ce Day,* July 4 (on which, in 1776, the DECLARATION of I~ce was made). **2.** (*~cy*). = CONGREGA-TIONALISM (hist.); independent State. [f. foll., see -ENCE, -ENCY]

Indĕpĕn'dent, a. & n. 1. Not depending on authority (*of,* or abs.); (*I~*)=CONGREGA-TIONAL (hist.); not depending on something else for its validity, efficiency, etc., as *~ proof, research, observer*; not needing to earn one's livelihood; *~ income* (dispensing one from earning livelihood); unwilling to be under obligation to others. **2.** n. Person who acts (in politics etc.) *~ly* of any party; Congregationalist (hist.). [IN⁻²; partly f. F]

Indĕscrīb'|able, a. Vague, indefinite; too great, beautiful, bad, etc., to be described. Hence *~*ABIL'ITY n., *~*abLY² adv. [IN⁻²]

Indĕstrŭc't|ible, a. That cannot be destroyed. Hence *~*ĭBIL'ITY n., *~* ĭbLY² adv. [IN⁻²]

Indĕtĕrm'inable, a. That cannot be ascertained; (of disputes etc.) that cannot be settled. [ME, f. LL IN²(*determinabilis* DETERMINABLE)]

Indĕtĕrm'inate, a. Not fixed in extent, character, etc.; vague; left doubtful; *~ sentence,* one that leaves prisoner's release dependent on his conduct & on probability of amendment; *~ vowel,* sound in *ago,* moment, cousin, opine, support, certain; (Math., of quantity) not limited to fixed value(s). Hence *~*LY² (-tl-) adv., *~*NESS (-tn-) n. [ME, f. LL IN²(*determinatus* DETERMINATE)]

Indĕtĕrminā'tion, n. Want of determination; being indeterminate. [IN⁻²]

Indĕtĕrm'in|ism, n. Theory that human

action is not wholly determined by motives. So *~*IST n. [IN⁻²]

In'dĕx, n. (pl. *~es, in'dicēs*), & v.t. **1.** Forefinger; (on instruments) pointer showing measurements etc.; *~ number* (indicating the relative level of prices or wages at a particular date compared with the figure (100) ruling at a period taken as standard); guiding principle; alphabetical list, usu. at end of book, of names, subjects, etc. with references; (R.C.) *the I~,* list of books forbidden to Roman Catholics, or to be read only in expurgated editions (in full, *I~ librōr'um prohĭbĭtōr'um*); *~ ~ ĕxpurgatōr'ius,* list of passages to be expunged in books otherwise permitted (in fig. use often confused with last); (Alg.) exponent (pl. *indices*). **2.** v.t. Furnish (book) with *~* (esp. in p.p.), enter (word etc.) in *~*. Hence *~*LESS a. [L (gen. *-icis*), = forefinger, informer, sign, f. IN⁻¹+*dic-* INDICATE]

In'dia (I-), n. Country of S. Asia east of river Indus & south of Himalayas; *Republic of ~,* (since 1947) this country excluding Pakistan; *~man,* ship engaged in Indian trade; *~ Office,* former department of British Government dealing with Indian affairs; *~ paper,* soft absorbent kind imported from China, used for proofs of engravings (*Oxford ~ paper,* thin tough opaque printing-paper); *~ proof* (on *~ paper*); *~rubber, india-rubber,* coagulated juice of certain plants, used for rubbing out pencil marks etc. [L, f. Gk (*Indos* Indus, f. Pers. *hind* = Skr. *sindhu* river, *-IA¹*)]

In'dian (I-), a. & n. (Native) of India; (one) of the original inhabitants of America & W. Indies; European, esp. Englishman, formerly resident in India; *Red ~,* one of aboriginal race of N. America; ‖*~ civilian,* member of former *~* Civil Service; *~ club* (bottle-shaped, for use in gymnastics); ‖*~ corn,* maize, N. American graminaceous plant; *~ cress,* TROPA-EOLUM; *~ file,* single file; *India(n) ink,* black pigment made in China & Japan; *~ meal* (made from *~* corn); *~ summer,* period of calm dry hazy weather in late autumn in North. U.S., also transf. in other countries; *~ weed,* tobacco. Hence *~*IZE(3) v.t., *~*ĭZA'TION n., process or policy of making *~* in character or composition. [-AN]

In'dic|āte, v.t. Point out, make known, show; suggest, call for; state briefly; be a sign of, betoken, (thing, *that,* etc.); *~ated horse-power* (shown by *~*ator; abbr. *i.h.p.*). So *~*A'TION n. [f. L IN¹(*dicare* make known), see -ATE³]

Indic'ative, a. & n. 1. (Gram.) stating a thing as a fact, not as conception, wish, etc., of speaker; (*also* In'dĭkătĭv) suggestive, giving indications, *of.* **2.** n. *~* mood. Hence *~*LY² (-vl-). [f. F (*-if, -ive*) or LL *indicativus* (prec., -IVE)]

in'dicāt|or, n. Person, thing, that points

out, esp. recording instrument attached to apparatus etc. Hence ～ORY a. [LL (as prec., see -OR)]

ĭndĭ'cĭum (-shĭ-), n. (pl. -*ĭa*). Indication, sign, (now rare). [L (as INDEX)]

indĭct' (-ĭt), v.t. Accuse (person *for* riot etc., *as* a rioter, *on* charge), esp. by legal process. [ME, f. AF *enditer* indict f. OF *enditer* make known f. Rom. *IN¹(*dictare* DICTATE); see INDITE]

indĭct'able (-ĭt-), a. Liable, (of action) rendering one liable, to be indicted. [-ABLE]

indĭc'tion, n. Fiscal period of 15 years instituted by Constantine & reckoned from Sep. 1st, 312; assessment of property-tax by Roman Emperors at beginning of each 15 years; this tax; proclamation. [ME, f. L *indictio* f. IN¹(*dicere dict-* say), see -ION]

indĭct'ment (-ĭt-), n. Formal accusation; legal process in which this is preferred to & presented by Grand Jury; document containing charge; *bill of* ～, written accusation as preferred to Grand Jury. [ME, f. AF *enditement* (as INDICT, see -MENT)]

indĭff'er|ence, n. Absence of interest or attention (*to, towards,* or abs.); neutrality; unimportance, esp. *a matter of* ～*ence,* so ～ENCY n. [f. L *indifferentia* (as foll., see -ENCE)]

indĭff'erent, a. Having no inclination for or against (*to*); neither good nor bad; rather bad, esp. *very* ～; neutral in chemical, electrical, or magnetic quality. Hence ～LY² adv. [ME, f. OF f. L IN²-(*differens* DIFFERENT)]

indĭff'erent|ism, n. Spirit of indifference, professed or practised, esp. in religious matters. So ～IST n. [-ISM]

in'dĭgēne, n. Native. [f. F *indigène* f. L *indigena* (indi- = IN-¹ +*gen-* be born)]

indĭ'gěnous, a. Native (esp. of flora & fauna), belonging naturally, (*to* soil etc., also fig.). Hence ～LY² adv. [f. L *indigenus* (as prec.) +-OUS]

in'dĭg|ent, a. Needy, poor. So ～ENCE n. [ME, f. OF f. L *indigēre* (indi- = IN-¹ +*egēre* want), see -ENT]

indĭgěs'tĕd, a. Shapeless; not thought out; not digested in stomach. [f. obs. *indigest* a. f. L IN²(*digestus* p.p. as DIGEST²) +-ED¹; or f. IN-² + DIGESTED]

indĭgěs't|ible, a. Not digestible (lit. & fig.). Hence ～ĪBIL'ITY n. [f. LL IN²-(*digestibilis* DIGESTIBLE)]

indĭgěs'tion (-schon), n. Difficulty in digesting food, dyspepsia; undigested condition (lit. & fig.). [ME, f. OF f. LL IN²(*digestionem* DIGESTION)]

indĭgěs'tive, a. Suffering from, tending to, indigestion. [IN-²]

‖**indĭgn'** (-ĭn), a.(arch.). Unworthy. [ME, f. OF *indigne* or f. L IN²(*dignus* worthy)]

indĭg'nant, a. Moved by mingled anger & scorn or feeling of injured innocence (*at* thing, *with* person, or abs.). Hence ～LY² adv. [f. L *indignari* (as prec.), see -ANT]

indĭgnā'tion, n. Anger excited by supposed meanness, injustice, wickedness, or misconduct (*at* thing, *against, with,* person), freq. *righteous* ～; ～*-meeting* (to express public ～). [ME, f. OF, or L *indignatio* (prec., -ATION)]

indĭg'nĭtў, n. Unworthy treatment; slight, insult. [f. F, or L *indignitas* (as INDIGN, see -TY)]

in'dĭgō, n. (pl. ～*s*). (Orig.) blue powder from plants of genus *Indigofera*, used as dye, now chiefly synthetic; ～ *blue,* blue-violet (often attrib.); ～*-bird,* N.-Amer. species of painted finch; ～ *white,* reduced ～, a white crystalline powder. Hence **indĭgŏt'ĬC** [-*t*- euphon.] a. [16th c. *indico* (f. Sp.), *indigo* (f. Pg.) f. L f. Gk *indikon* Indian (dye)]

indĭrěct', a. **1.** (Of road etc.) not straight; not going straight to the point. **2.** (Pol. Econ., of taxes) not direct, paid by consumer in the form of increased price for the taxed goods. **3.** (gram.). ～ *speech,* reported speech, with necessary changes of pronouns, tenses, etc. (e.g. *I will help you,* he said *he would help me*); ～ *object,* person, thing, affected by verbal action but not primarily acted on (e.g. *him* in *give him the book*); ～ *passive,* passive having for subject the ～ object of the active (e.g. *I* in *I was told it*). **4.** Not directly aimed at, as an ～ *result.* Hence ～LY² adv., ～NESS n. [ME, f. OF, or LL IN²(*directus* DIRECT²)]

indĭrěc'tion, n. Roundabout means, esp. *by* ～ (after Shak. *Ham.* II. i. 66); deceit, trickery. [prec. +-ION]

indiscěrn'ib|le, a. & n. (Thing) that cannot be discerned or distinguished from another; *identity of* ～*les,* doctrine that things cannot exist together as separate entities unless they have different attributes. Hence ～LY² adv. [f. LL IN²(*discernibilis* DISCERNIBLE)]

indiscěrp't|ible, a. Incapable of, not destructible by, dissolution of parts. Hence ～ĪBIL'ITY n. [IN-²]

indis'ciplin|e, n. Want of discipline. So ～ABLE a. [f. F, or IN-²]

indiscreet', a. Injudicious, unwary. Hence ～LY² adv. [ME, f. LL IN²(*discretus* DISCREET)]

indis'crēte, a. Not divided into distinct parts. [IN-², or f. L; see DISCRETE]

indiscrē'tion, n. Injudicious conduct; accidental or (*calculated* ～) supposed accidental revelation of official secret etc.; imprudence; transgression of social morality. [ME, f. OF, or LL IN²(*discretio* DISCRETION)]

indiscrim'in|ate, a. Confused, promiscuous; making no distinctions. Hence ～ateLY² adv., ～ateNESS, ～A'TION, nn., ～ativE a. [IN-²]

indispěn's|able, a. That cannot be dispensed with, necessary; (of law, duty, etc.) that cannot be set aside. Hence ～aBIL'ITY, ～ableNESS, nn., ～abLY² adv. [f. med. L IN²(*dispensabilis* DISPENSABLE)]

indispose' (-z), v.t. Render unfit or unable (*for* thing, *to* do); make averse (*towards, from*, thing, *to* do); (esp. in p.p.) put out of health. [back form. f. *indisposed*, f. F -*sé* or L *indispositus*, partly f. IN-² + DISPOSED]

indisposi'tion (-zĭ-), n. Ill health, ailment, (esp. of passing kind); disinclination (*to* thing, *to* do); aversion (*to, towards*). [f. F, or IN-² + DISPOSITION]

indis'put|able, a. That cannot be disputed. Hence ~aBIL'ITY, ~ableNESS, nn., ~abLY² adv. [f. LL IN²(*disputabilis* DISPUTABLE)]

indiss'ol|uble (-lŏŏ-; or ĭndĭsŏl'-), a. Lasting, stable, as *an* ~*uble bond*; that cannot be dissolved or decomposed. Hence ~uBIL'ITY n., ~ubLY² adv. [f. L IN²(*dissolubilis* DISSOLUBLE)]

indistinct', a. Not distinct; confused, obscure. Hence ~LY² adv., ~NESS n. [f. L IN²(*distinctus* DISTINCT)]

indistinc'tive, a. Not distinctive. Hence ~LY² adv. [IN-²]

indisting'uishab|le (-nggw-), a. Not distinguishable. Hence ~LY² adv. [IN-²]

indistrib'utable, a. That cannot be distributed. [IN-²]

indite', v.t. Put into words, compose, (poem, speech, etc.); (usu. joc.) write (letter etc.). [ME, f. OF EN(*diter* f. L *dictare* DICTATE); see INDICT]

indivert'ib|le, a. That cannot be turned aside. Hence ~LY² adv. [IN-² + DIVERT + -IBLE]

individ'ual, a. & n. 1. Single; particular, special, opp. to *general*; having distinct character; characteristic of particular person. 2. n. Single member of class; single human being, opp. to *society, family*, etc.; (vulg.) person, as *an* ~ of *unassuming prepossessing appearance*. [f. med. L *individualis* f. IN²(*dividuus* f. *dividere* DIVIDE), see -AL]

individ'ual|ism, n. Self-centred feeling or conduct, egoism; social theory favouring free action of individuals (cf. SOCIALISM). So ~IST n. (freq., U.S., or of U.S., *rugged* ~*ist*), ~is'tIC a. [f. F -*isme* (as prec., -ISM)]

individŭal'itў, n. Separate existence; individual character, esp. when strongly marked; (pl.) individual tastes etc. [-ITY]

individ'ualĭz|e, -is|e (-īz), v.t. Give individual character to; specify. Hence ~A'TION n. [-IZE]

individ'uallў, adv. Personally, in an individual capacity; in a distinctive manner; one by one, not collectively; ~ *different*, different as individuals though perhaps identical in species. [-LY²]

individ'ū|āte, v.t. Individualize, form into an individual. So ~A'TION n. [f. obs. F -*er*, or med. L *individuare* (as INDIVIDUAL), see -ATE³]

indivis'|ible (-z-), a. & n. Not divisible; (n.) infinitely small particle or quantity.

Hence ~IBIL'ITY n., ~ibLY² adv. [f. LL IN²(*divisibilis* DIVISIBLE)]

In'dō- (I-) in comb. = Indian, as: ~-*Ar'yan*, Aryan of or in India; ~-*Chinese'*, of the region between India & China; ~-*Europe'an*, ~-*German'ic*, of the family of languages spoken over greater part of Europe & Asia as far as N. India; ~-*Irān'ian*, of the subfamily of ~-European languages spoken chiefly in India & Persia; ~*nēs'ian*, of the East Indian Islands. [f. L f. Gk *Indos*]

indō'cile (or -dŏsĭl), a. Not docile. Hence **indocil'ITY** n. [f. F, or L IN²(*docilis* DOCILE)]

indŏc'trin|āte, v.t. Teach, instruct; imbue with a doctrine, idea, or opinion. Hence ~A'TION n. [IN-¹, DOCTRINE, -ATE³]

in'dol|ent, a. Slothful, lazy; (Med.) causing no pain, as ~*ent tumour*. Hence or cogn. ~ENCE n., ~entLY² adv. [f. LL *indolens* (IN-² + *dolēre* grieve, see -ENT)]

indŏm'itab|le, a. Unyielding; stubbornly persistent. Hence ~LY² adv. [f. LL IN²(*domitabilis* f. *domitare* tame, see -BLE)]

in'door (-dōr), a. Situated, carried on, within doors or under cover, as ~ *games*; within workhouse, as ~ *relief* (hist.). [IN prep.]

indoors' (-ōrz), adv. Within a house; under cover. [earlier *within doors*]

indōrsā'tion, n. Endorsement. [f. *indorse* var. of ENDORSE + -ATION]

indōrsee', n. One in whose favour note or bill is endorsed. [as prec., see -EE]

in'draught (-ahft), **-draft** (-ah-), n. Drawing in; inward flow or current. [IN adv.]

in'dri, n. Babacoote, lemurine animal of Madagascar. [f. Malagasy *indry* behold, mistaken for its name]

indūb'itab|le, a. That cannot be doubted. Hence ~LY² adv. [f. F, or L IN²(*dubitabilis* f. *dubitare* doubt, see -BLE)]

indūce', v.t. Prevail on, persuade, (*to* do, now rarely *to* action etc.; *nothing shall* ~ *me to*, I will never); bring about, give rise to; (Electr.) produce (current) by induction; infer, derive as an induction. [ME, f. L IN¹(*ducere duct-* lead)]

indūce'ment (-sm-), n. What induces; attraction that leads one on (*to*). [-MENT]

indŭct', v.t. Introduce formally into possession (*to* benefice); install (*into* seat, room, etc.); introduce, initiate, (*to, into*). [ME; as INDUCE]

indŭc'tile, a. Not ductile. [IN-²]

indŭc'tion, n. Inducting; ‖ (arch.) preamble, prologue, introduction; production (*of* facts) to prove general statement; inferring of general law from particular instances (cf. DEDUCTION); *mathematical*~, proving universal truth of theorem by showing (1) that if true of any particular case it is true of the next case in a series, (2) that it is .true of a particular case; (Electr., Magnet.) bringing about of electric or magnetic state in a body by proximity (without contact) of electrified or magnetized body; ~-*coil* (for converting direct current to alternating by ~). So **indŭc'tANCE** n., capacity for magnetic ~, coefficient of self-~ in magnetic circuits. [ME, f. OF, or L *inductio* (as INDUCE, see -ION)]

indŭc'tive, a. (Of reasoning etc.) of, based on, induction; of electric or magnetic induction. Hence ~LY² (-vl-) adv., ~NESS (-vn-) n. [f. LL *inductivus* (as INDUCE, see -IVE)]

indŭc'tor, n. One who inducts clergyman; any part of electric induction apparatus. [L, as INDUCE, see -OR]

indŭlge' (-j), v.t. & i. Gratify (person, one-*self, in* wish, matter, etc.); gratify (person *with* thing given); give free course to, entertain, (desire etc.); (intr.) take one's pleasure freely *in* (strong language, cycling, a cigar); (colloq.) partake (too freely) of intoxicants. Hence **indŭl'gENT** a., **indŭl'gentLY²** adv. [f. L *indulgēre*, -*dult*-]

indŭl'gence, n. Indulging (*in*, t. & i.); (also *self*-~) habitual indulging of one's desires; privilege granted; *Declaration of I~*, proclamation of religious liberties, esp. those of Charles II in 1672 & of James II in 1687; (R.-C. Ch.) remission of punishment still due to sin after sacramental absolution. [ME, f. OF, or L *indulgentia* (as prec., see -ENCE)]

indŭl'genced (-nst), a. (R.-C. Ch.). (Of prayers, material objects, etc.) procuring indulgence to the user. [-ED²]

indŭlt', n. Pope's licence for thing not sanctioned by common law of Church. [F, f. LL *indultum*, neut. p.p. as INDULGE]

indun'a (-ōō-), n. (S. Afr.). Native headman. [Zulu]

in'dūr|āte, v.t. & i. Make, become, hard; make callous or unfeeling; become inveterate. Hence or cogn. ~A'TION n., ~ātive a. [f. L IN¹(*durare* f. *durus* hard), see -ATE³]

indūs'ĭum (-z-), n. (pl. -ia). Membranous shield covering fruit-cluster of fern; collection of hairs enclosing stigma of some flowers; case of larva. [L, = tunic, f. in-*duere* ENDUE]

indŭs'trĭal, a. & n. **1.** Of industries (~ *maintenance*, system by which each industry should provide for its own unemployed; *the* ~ *revolution*, changes in the relation between employers & employed brought about in the late 18th & early 19th cc. esp. by mechanical inventions); designed, or only fit, for ~ use (~ *alcohol*); ~ *school* (hist.), one where neglected children were taught a trade besides ordinary subjects. **2.** n. One engaged in ~ pursuits; (pl.) shares in joint-stock ~ enterprise. Hence ~ISM(3), ~IST(3), nn., ~IZE(3) v.t., ~LY² adv. [as INDUSTRY, see -AL; in 19th c. partly f. F -*el*]

indŭs'trĭous, a. Diligent, hard-working. Hence ~LY² adv. [f. F -*ieux* or LL *industriosus* (as foll., see -OUS)]

in'dustrў, n. Diligence; habitual employment in useful work; branch of trade or manufacture. [f. F (-*ie*) or L *industria*]

indwĕll', v.t. & i. (*indwell*). (Usu. fig., of spirit, principle, etc.) inhabit, occupy; (intr.) be permanently present *in*. Hence ~ER¹ n. [IN prep.]

-ine¹, suf. of adj., repr. L -*īnus*, w. sense ' pertaining to, of the nature of '; appearing in F as -*in* masc., -*ine* fem., in E formerly as -*in*, now usu. as -*ine* (*asinine, divine, marine, supine*). On model of proper names f. L, adjj. like *Florentine', Caroline*, are formed in E. Nat. Hist. forms adjj. on names of genera (*equine, caprine, feline*); these have (-īn) unstressed; others have (-īn) stressed or not (*divine', Al'pine*), (-īn) unstressed (*fem'-inine*), or (-ēn) stressed (*marine*).

-ine², suf. of adjj., repr. L -*īnus* f. Gk -*īnos* in names of minerals, plants, etc. (*adamantine, hyacinthine*); also repr. orig. L -*īnus* (*pristine*). Norman pronunc. (-īn) is giving place to (-īn).

-ine³, suf. forming fem. nn., repr. F -*ine* f. L -*īna* f. Gk -*īnē* (*heroine*). E represents in same way -*in* in G *markgräfin* etc. (*margravine*).

-ine⁴, suf. of nn., repr. F -*ine* f. L -*īna* (-*inus*), orig. = -INE¹ used in L to form abstract nn. f. vbs (*rapina* rapine, *ruina* ruin), f. agent nouns (*disciplina, doctrina, medicina*), & f. other sources (*resina, urina*). L adjj. in -*inus*, -*ina*, were also used as nn. (*concubina, lupinus*), esp. in prop. names (*Antoninus, Agrippina*). For -*ina*, E has -*ine*, sometimes -*in* (*resin*); for -*inus*, E has -*in* (*Crispin, Justin*) or -*ine* (*lupine, Constantine*). E further forms names of derivative products (*dentine, brilliantine, nectarine*). Fem. names of Rom. orig. also often take -*ine* (-īn), as *Caroline, Catharine*.

-ine⁵, suf. (chem.), offshoot of prec. in names of derived substances, orig. used unsystematically, & interchangeable with -IN; now confined to alkaloids & basic substances (*aconitine, cocaine, nicotine*) & (less freq.) Hofmann's names of hydrocarbons; also retained in the four elements *chlorine, fluorine, iodine, bromine*; formerly denoting mineral species now ending in -ITE¹ (*erythrine, -ite*).

inĕb'riate¹, a. & n. **1.** Drunken. **2.** n. ~ person, esp. habitual drunkard. [f. L IN¹(*ebriare* f. *ebrius* drunk), see -ATE²]

inĕb'ri|āte², v.t. Make drunk, intoxicate (lit. & fig.). So ~A'TION n. [as prec., -ATE³]

inĕbri'etў, n. (Habit of) drunkenness. [f. INEBRIATE, after EBRIETY]

inĕd'|ible, a. Not edible. Hence ~IBIL'ITY n. [IN-²]

inĕd'itĕd, a. Not published; published without editorial alterations or additions. [IN-²]

ĭnĕff'ab|le, a. Unutterable, too great for words. Hence ~LY² adv. [ME, f. OF, or L IN²(*effabilis* f. EF*fari* speak, utter, see -BLE)]

ĭnĕffāce'|able (-sabl), a. That cannot be effaced. Hence ~ABIL'ITY n., ~abLY² adv. [IN-²]

ĭnĕffĕc'tĭve, a. Not producing the desired effect; (of person) inefficient; lacking artistic effect. Hence ~LY² adv., ~NESS n. [IN-²]

ĭnĕffĕc'tŭal, a. Without effect, fruitless. Hence ~LY² adv., ~NESS n. [IN-²]

ĭnĕfficā'cious (-shŭs), a. (Of remedy etc.) not efficacious. [IN-²]

ĭnĕffi'ci|ent (-shent), a. (Of person) not fully capable, not well qualified; ineffective. Hence ~ENCY n., ~entLY² adv., (-shen-). [IN-²]

ĭnĕlăs'tĭc, a. Not elastic; unadaptable, unyielding. Hence **ĭnĕlăsti'ciTY** n. [IN-²]

ĭnĕl'ĕg|ant, a. Ungraceful; unrefined; (of style) unpolished. Hence ~ANCE n., ~antLY² adv. [f. F IN²(*élégant* ELEGANT)]

ĭnĕl'ĭg|ible, a. Not eligible (esp. of men unfit for military service). Hence ~i-BIL'ITY n., ~ĭbLY² adv. [IN-²]

ĭnĕlŭc'table, a. That cannot be escaped from. [f. L IN²(*eluctabilis* f. E*luctari* struggle out, see -BLE)]

ĭnĕpt', a. Out of place; absurd, silly. Hence or cogn. **ĭnĕp'tĭTUDE,** ~NESS, nn., ~LY² adv. [f. L IN²(*eptus* = *aptus* APT)]

ĭnĕ'quable, a. Not uniform; of unequal incidence. [f. L *inaequabilis* uneven]

ĭnĕqual'ĭtў (-ŏl-), n. Want of equality in magnitude, quality, rank, circumstances, etc.; variableness; (of surface) irregularity; (Astron.) deviation from uniformity in motion of heavenly body. [f. obs. F *inéqualité* or L IN²(*aequalitas* EQUALITY)]

ĭnĕquilăt'eral, a. Of unequal sides. [IN-²]

ĭnĕ'quitab|le, a. Unfair, unjust. Hence ~LY² adv. [IN-²]

ĭnĕ'quitў, n. Unfairness. [IN-²]

ĭnĕrăd'icab|le, a. That cannot be rooted out. Hence ~LY² adv. [IN-²]

ĭnĕr'rab|le, a. Not liable to err. Hence or cogn. ~ABIL'ITY, ~ANCY, nn., ~abLY² adv., ~ANT a. [f. L IN²(*errabilis* f. *errare* ERR, see -BLE)]

ĭnĕrt', a. Without inherent power of action, motion, or resistance; without active chemical or other properties; sluggish, slow. Hence ~LY² adv., ~NESS n. [f. L IN²(*ers -ertis* f. *ars* ART)]

ĭnĕr'tia (-shĭa), n. (Phys.) property of matter by which it continues in its existing state of rest or uniform motion in straight line, unless that state is changed by external force (also *vis inertiae* force of ~); inertness, sloth. [L, as prec.]

ĭnĕscāp'able, a. Not to be escaped. [IN-²]

ĭnĕssĕn'tial (-shal), a. Not indispensable. [IN-²]

ĭnĕs'tĭmab|le, a. Too great, intense, precious, etc., to be estimated. Hence ~LY² adv. [ME, f. OF f. L IN²(*aestimabilis* ESTIMABLE)]

ĭnĕv'ĭt|able, a. Unavoidable, sure to happen, esp. *the ~able*; (colloq.) tiresomely familiar (*the ~able Derby dog*); (of character-drawing, development of plot, etc.) so true to nature etc. as to preclude alternative treatment or solution, convincing. Hence ~ABIL'ITY, ~ableNESS, nn., ~abLY² adv. [f. L IN-² (*evitabilis* E*vitare* avoid, see -BLE)]

ĭnĕxăct' (-gz-), a. Not exact. Hence **ĭnĕxăc'tĭTUDE,** ~NESS, nn., ~LY² adv. [IN-²]

ĭnĕxcūs'ab|le (-za-), a. (Of person, action, etc.) that cannot be justified. Hence ~LY² adv. [f. F, or L IN²(*excusabilis* EX-CUSABLE)]

ĭnĕxĕc'ūtable (-gz-), a. That cannot be carried out. [IN-²]

ĭnĕxhaus't|ĭble (-ĭgzaw-), a. That cannot be exhausted. Hence ~ĭBIL'ITY n., ~ĭbLY² adv. [IN-²]

ĭnĕx'or|able, a. Relentless. Hence ~a-BIL'ITY n., ~abLY² adv. [f. F, or L IN²(*exorabilis* f. EX*orare* entreat, -ABLE)]

ĭnĕxpĕc'tant, a. Not expectant. [IN-²]

ĭnĕxpē'di|ent, a. Not expedient. Hence ~ENCY n. [IN-²]

ĭnĕxpĕn'sĭve, a. Cheap. Hence ~LY² adv., ~NESS n. [IN-²]

ĭnĕxpēr'ienc|e, n. Want of experience. So ~ED² (-st) a. [f. F, or LL IN²(*experientia* EXPERIENCE)]

ĭnĕxpĕrt', a. Unskilled. Hence ~LY² adv. [f. OF, or L IN²(*expertus* EXPERT)]

ĭnĕx'piab|le, a. (Of offence) that cannot be expiated; (of resentment etc.) implacable. Hence ~LY² adv. [f. L IN²(*expiabilis* EXPIABLE)]

ĭnĕx'plic|able, a. That cannot be explained or accounted for. Hence ~ABIL'ITY n., ~abLY² adv. [f. F, or L IN²(*explicabilis* EXPLICABLE)]

ĭnĕxpli'cĭt, a. Not definitely or clearly expressed. Hence ~LY² adv., ~NESS n. [IN-²]

ĭnĕxplōs'ĭve, a. Not explosive. [IN-²]

ĭnĕxprĕss'ib|le, a. & n. That cannot be expressed in words; (n. pl., joc. & arch.) trousers. Hence ~LY² adv. [IN-²]

ĭnĕxprĕss'ĭve, a. Not expressive; (arch.) inexpressible. Hence ~LY² adv., ~NESS n. [IN-²]

ĭnĕxpŭg'nable, a. Impregnable, invincible, (lit. & fig.). [f. F, or L IN²(*expugnabilis* f. EX*pugnare* storm, see -BLE)]

ĭnĕxtĕn'sible, a. Not extensible. [IN-²]

ĭnĕxting'uĭshable (-nggw-), a. Unquenchable (lit. & fig.). [IN-²]

ĭnĕx'tricab|le, a. (Of place, state, etc.) that cannot be escaped from; (of knot, problem, etc.) that cannot be unravelled or solved. Hence ~LY² adv. [f. F, or L IN²(*extricabilis* EXTRICABLE)]

ĭnfăll'ĭbil|ism, n. Principle of the Pope's infallibility. So ~IST n. [-ISM]

ĭnfăll'|ible, a. Incapable of erring; (of method, test, proof, etc.) unfailing. Hence

~ĭBIL'ITY n. (esp. as attribute of the Pope speaking *ex cathedrâ*, defined 1870 by the Vatican Council), ~ĭBLY² adv. [f. med. L IN²(*fallibilis* FALLIBLE)]

ĭn'famize, -ise (-īz), v.t. Render infamous. [f. L IN²(*famis* f. *fama* fame) infamous, see -IZE]

ĭn'famous, a. Of ill fame, notoriously vile; abominable; (Law) deprived of all or some rights of citizen on account of ~ crime. Hence or cogn. ~LY² adv., **ĭn'famỹ**¹ n. [ME, f. med. L *infamosus* = L *infamis* (see prec.)]

ĭn'fancỹ, n. Early childhood, babyhood; (Law) minority (to end of one's 21st year); early state of development. [f. L *infantia* (foll., -ANCY)]

ĭn'fant, n. Babe; child under 7 years of age; minor (under 21); ~-*school* (for children, usu. under 7). [ME, f. OF *enfant* f. L IN²(*fans -ntis* part. of *fari* speak)]

ĭnfăn'ta, n. (hist.). Daughter of king & queen of Spain or Portugal (usu. eldest daughter who is not heir to throne). So **ĭnfăn'te** (-tā) n. (second son). [Sp., Port., f. L as prec.]

ĭnfăn'ti|cĭde, n. Murder of infant after birth, esp. with mother's consent; custom of killing new-born infants. Hence or cogn. ~CIDE(1) n., ~cĭd'AL a. [f. LL *infanticidium* (as INFANT, see -CIDE(2))]

ĭn'fant|ile, a. Of, as of, infants (~*ile paralysis*, POLIOMYELITIS); in its infancy. So ~INE¹ a. [f. LL *infantilis* (INFANT, -IL)]

ĭnfăn'tilism, n. (med.). State of being mentally or physically undeveloped. [prec., -ISM]

ĭn'fantrỹ, n. Foot-soldiers; ~*man* (-ăn), soldier of ~ regiment. [f. F *infanterie* f. It. *infanteria* (*infante* youth, foot-soldier, as INFANT, see -ERY)]

ĭnfăt'ū|āte, v.t. Affect (person) with extreme folly; inspire with extravagant passion. Hence ~ātĕdLY² adv., ~A'TION n. [f. L IN¹(*fatuare* f. *fatuus* foolish), see -ATE³]

ĭnfĕct', v.t. Fill (air etc.) with noxious corruption or germs; affect (person, body, mind, *with* disease etc. lit. & fig.); imbue (person *with* opinion etc.). So **ĭnfĕc'tive** a., **ĭnfĕc'tiveNESS**, **ĭnfĕctiv'ITY**, nn. [ME, f. L IN¹(*ficere fect-* = *facere* make) taint]

ĭnfĕc'tion, n. Communication of disease, esp. by agency of atmosphere or water etc. (cf. CONTAGION); moral contamination; diffusive influence of example, sympathy, etc. [ME, f. OF, or LL *infectio* (as INFECT, see -ION)]

ĭnfĕc'tious (-shŭs), a. Infecting with disease, pestilential; (of disease) liable to be transmitted by air or water (cf. CONTAGIOUS); (of emotions etc.) apt to spread, catching. Hence ~LY² adv., ~NESS n. [prec., -IOUS]

ĭnfēlicif'ic, a. Producing unhappiness. [IN-²]

ĭnfēli'citous, a. Not felicitous. [IN-²]

ĭnfēli'citỹ, n. Unhappiness; misfortune;

inaptness of expression etc. [ME, f. L IN²(*felicitas* FELICITY)]

ĭnfēr', v.t. (-rr-). Deduce, conclude, (thing, *that, when*, etc.; *from* fact etc.); (of fact or statement) imply. Hence **ĭn'ferABLE** a. [f. L IN¹(*ferre* bring)]

ĭn'ference, n. Inferring; thing inferred. Hence **ĭnferĕn'tIAL** (-shal) a., **ĭnferĕn'tiaLLY²** adv. [f. med. L *inferentia* (as prec., see -ENCE)]

ĭnfēr'ior, a. & n. 1. Situated below (~ LIMIT¹); lower in rank, quality, etc. (*to*, or abs.); of poor quality; (of planets) whose orbit lies within that of the earth; (Bot., of calyx) below ovary, (of ovary) below calyx; (Print.) placed at bottom of ordinary letters (e.g. H₂, C_n). 2. n. Person ~ to another esp. in rank (*kind to* ~*s*). Hence **ĭnfēriŏ'rITY** n. (~*ity complex*, abnormal reactions, such as assertiveness or megalomania, from suppressed sense of ~ity, (pop.) sense of ~ity), ~LY² adv. [L, comp. of *inferus* low]

ĭnfĕrn'al, a. Of hell; hellish, fiendish; (colloq.) abominable, confounded; ~ *machine* (now usu. joc.), apparatus (usu. disguised) for producing explosion destructive of life or property. Hence ~ITY (-ăl²) n., ~LY² adv. [ME, f. OF, f. LL *infernalis* (*infernus* situated below, see -AL)]

ĭnfĕrn'o, n. (pl. ~*s*). Hell (esp. w. reference to Dante's *Divine Comedy*); scene of horror. [It., f. L *infernus*, see prec.]

ĭnfĕr'rable, a. = INFERABLE.

ĭnfĕrt'ile, a. Not fertile. So **ĭnfĕrtil'ITY** n. [F, f. LL IN²(*fertilis* FERTILE)]

ĭnfĕst', v.t. (Of vermin, pirates, diseases, etc.) haunt, swarm in or about, (place). So ~A'TION n. [f. F *infester* or L *infestare* assail (*infestus* hostile)]

‖ **ĭnfeŭda'tion**, n. Enfeoffment; ~ *of tithes*, granting of tithes to laymen. [f. med. L *infeudatio* f. IN¹(*feudare* f. *feudum* fee), see -ATION]

ĭn'fidel, n. & a. 1. Disbeliever in religion; (hist.) adherent of religion opposed to Christianity; (from Jewish or Mohammedan point of view) disbeliever in the true religion; (gen.) disbeliever. 2. adj. Unbelieving, of unbelievers. Hence ~IZE(3) v.t. & i. [late ME, f. OF *infidele* or L IN²(*fidelis* faithful f. *fides* faith)]

ĭnfidĕl'itỹ, n. Disbelief in Christianity; disloyalty, esp. (also *conjugal* ~) to husband or wife. [f. F *-té* or L *infidelitas* (as prec., see -TY)]

ĭn'field, n. Farm land around or near homestead; arable land; land regularly manured & cropped; (Cricket) part of the ground near the wicket, or fieldsmen stationed there (opp. OUTFIELD). [IN³]

ĭn'fight'ing (-fīt-), n. Boxing at closer quarters than arm's length. [IN²]

ĭnfil'tr|āte (*or* ĭn'fĭl-), v.t. & i. Introduce (fluid) by filtration (*into, through*); permeate (t. & i.) by filtration. Hence ~A'TION n. (esp. Mil. & Pol.), gradual unobserved occupation of ground or territory by detached parties or settlers). [IN-¹, after F *infiltrer*]

in'finite, a. & n. Boundless, endless; very great; (w. pl. noun) innumerable, very many; (Gram., of verb parts) not limited by person or number, e.g. infinitive, gerund, supine (cf. FINITE); (n.) *the I~*, God; *the ~*, *~* space. Hence ~LY² (-tl-) adv. [ME, f. L IN²(*finitus* FINITE)]

infinitĕs'imal, a. & n. Infinitely or very small (amount); *~ calculus*, the differential & integral calculuses conceived as one. Hence ~LY² adv. [as prec. on CENTESIMAL etc.]

infin'itive, a. & n. (gram.). (Verb-form) that expresses the verbal notion without predicating it of any subject (e.g. *ask, to ask*). Hence **infinitiv'**AL a. [f. L IN-² (*finitivus* f. *finire -it-* define, see -IVE)]

infin'itūde, n. Boundlessness; boundless number or extent (*of*). [as INFINITE, -TUDE]

infin'itў̆, n. = prec.; (Math.) infinite quantity (symbol: ∞). [ME, f. OF *infinite* f. L *infinitas* (as INFINITE, see -TY)]

infĭrm', a. Physically weak, esp. through age; (of person, mind, judgement, etc.) weak, irresolute (often *~ of purpose*). Hence or cogn. ~ITY n., ~LY² adv. [ME, f. L IN²(*firmus* FIRM²)]

infĭrm'arў̆, n. Hospital; sick-quarters in school, workhouse, etc. [f. med. L *infirmaria* (as prec., see -ARY¹)]

infix'¹, v.t. Fix (thing in another); impress (fact etc. *in* mind); (Gram.) insert (formative element) in body of word. [IN adv.]

in'fix², n. (gram.). Modifying element infixed in word, esp. *nasal ~*, as *n* in Latin *fingo* from stem *fig-*. [IN-¹, after *prefix*, *suffix*]

inflāme', v.t. & i. Set ablaze; light up (as) with flame; excite passionately (*~d with*, *by*); raise (body, blood, etc.) to morbid heat; aggravate; catch fire; become excited; become morbidly ~d. [ME, f. OF *enflammer* f. L IN¹(*flammare* f. *flamma* flame)]

inflămm'|able, a. & n. Easily set on fire; easily excited; (n.) ~able substance. Hence~ABIL'ITY, ~ableNESS, nn. [f. prec., see -BLE; cf. F *inflammable*]

inflammā'tion, n. Inflaming (lit. & fig.); morbid process affecting a part of the body with heat, swelling, pain, & redness. [f. L *inflammatio* (as prec., see -ATION)]

inflămm'atorў̆, a. Tending to inflame with desire or passion (usu. in bad sense); of, tending to, inflammation of the body. [f. L as INFLAME, see -ORY]

inflāte', v.t. Distend with air or gas; puff up (person *with* pride etc.); (Finance) resort to inflation of (the currency, or abs.); raise (price) artificially; (p.p., of language) bombastic. So **inflā'**TION n. (in vbl senses, & esp.) undue increase in the quantity of money in relation to goods

available for purchase (cf. DEFLATION). **inflāt'**OR n. [f. L IN¹(*flare* blow), see -ATE³]

inflĕct', v.t. Bend inwards, curve; (Gram.) vary form of (word) to express grammatical relation; (Mus.) flatten, sharpen, (note). [ME, f. L IN¹(*flectere flex-* bend)]

inflĕc'tion, = INFLEXION.

inflĕc'tive, a. (gram.). Of inflexion. [-IVE]

inflĕx'|ible, a. Unbendable; (fig.) unbending, rigid. Hence ~iBIL'ITY n., ~iBLY² adv. [f. L IN²(*flexibilis* FLEXIBLE)]

inflē'xion (-kshon), n. Inflecting; inflected form of word; suffix etc. used to inflect; modulation of voice; (Geom.) change of curve from convex to concave. Hence ~AL, ~LESS, aa., (-kshon-). [f. F, or L *inflexio* (as INFLECT, see -ION)]

inflict', v.t. Lay on (stroke, wound, *upon*); impose (suffering, penalty, *oneself*, one's company, etc., *upon*). Hence or cogn. ~ABLE a., **inflic'**TION n. (esp., troublesome or boring experience), ~OR n. [f. L IN¹(*fligere flict-* dash)]

inflorĕs'cence, n. (bot.). Arrangement of flowers of plant in relation to axis & to each other; collective flower of plant; flowering (also fig.). [f. LL IN¹(*florescere* come into flower f. *flos floris*), see -ESCENT, -ENCE]

in'flow (-ō), n. Flowing in. So ~ING¹ ² (-ōīng) n. & a. [IN adv.]

in'fluence (-lŏŏ-), n., & v.t. 1. (Astrol.) flowing from stars of ethereal fluid affecting character & destiny of man (also fig. of personal power); action insensibly exercised (*upon*); UNDUE ~; ascendancy, moral power, (*over*, *with*, person etc.); thing, person, exercising (usu. non-material) power; (colloq., ellipt.) *under the ~* (sc. *of alcohol, of drink*); (Electr.) = INDUCTION. 2. v.t. Exert ~ upon, have effect upon. [ME, f. OF, or LL *influentia* f. L IN¹(*fluere* flow), see -ENCE]

in'fluent (-lŏŏ-), a. & n. Flowing in (lit. & fig.); (n.) tributary stream. [ME, f. L as prec., see -ENT]

influĕn'tial (-lŏŏĕnshal), a. Having great influence. Hence ~LY² adv. [f. med. L *influentialis* (INFLUENCE, -AL)]

influĕn'za (-lŏŏ-), n. Infectious febrile disorder, usu. with rapid prostration & severe catarrh; (also ~ *cold*) severe catarrh; (fig.) mental or commercial epidemic. [It., as INFLUENCE]

in'flŭx, n. Flowing in, esp. of stream etc. (*into* river etc.), or of persons or things (*into* place etc.). [f. F, or LL IN¹(*fluxus* FLUX)]

infōrm', v.t. & i. Inspire, imbue, (person, heart, thing, *with* feeling, principle, quality, etc.), tell (person *of* thing, *that*, *how*, etc.), so ~ANT n.; bring charge (*against* person). [ME, f. OF *enformer* f. L IN¹(*formare* f. *forma* form) give shape to, fashion]

infōrm'al, a. Not according to due form; without formality. Hence ~ITY (-ăl²) n., ~LY² adv. [IN-²]

informā'tion, n. Informing, telling; thing told, knowledge, items of knowledge, news, (*on*, *about*); (Law) charge, complaint, lodged with court or magistrate (*against*). Hence ~AL a. [ME, f. OF *enformacion* f. L *informationem* (as INFORM, see -ATION)]

inform'at|ive, a. Giving information, instructive. So ~ORY a. [-ATIVE]

informed' (-md), a. Instructed, knowing the facts, educated, intelligent, esp. *well, ill, ~*. [-ED¹]

inform'er, n. One who informs against another, esp. (also *common ~*) one who makes it his business to detect offenders & lay information against them. [-ER¹]

ĭn'fra, adv. (abbr. *inf.*). Below, lower down, further on, (in book), as *vide ~*, see below. [L, = below]

ĭnfra- in comb.= L *infra* below; used esp. in anat. terms in sense 'below, under, some part', as *~ren'al, ~scap'ular, ~stern'al,* beneath the kidneys, shoulder-blade, breast-bone; *~red',* of invisible rays beyond red end of spectrum; *~structure,* system of airfields, telecommunications, and public services forming a basis for defence.

infrăc'tion, n. Violation, infringement. [f. L *infractio* (as INFRINGE, see -ION)]

ĭn'fra dĭg., pred. a. Beneath one's dignity, unbecoming. [abbr. L *infra dignitatem*]

in'fralăpsār'ian, n. & a. Calvinist who held that God's election of some was consequent to his prescience of the Fall, or that it contemplated man as already fallen (cf. SUBLAPSARIAN, SUPRALAPSARIAN); (adj.) of these views. [f. INFRA- +L *lapsus* fall +-ARIAN]

infre'qu|ent, a. Not frequent. Hence or cogn. ~ENCY n., ~entLY² adv. [f. L IN²(*frequens* FREQUENT¹)]

infringe' (-j), v.t. Transgress, violate, (law, oath, etc.). Hence ~MENT (-jm-) n. [f. L IN¹(*fringere fract-=frangere* break)]

infrŭc'tŭous, a. Unfruitful; (fig.) fruitless. [f. L IN²(*fructuosus* FRUCTUOUS), see -OUS]

infundib'ūlar, a. Funnel-shaped. [f. L *infundibulum* funnel (used in E of parts of body) f. IN¹(*fundere* pour)]

infūr'iāte, v.t. Fill with fury, enrage. [f. med. L IN¹(*furiare* f. *furia* FURY), see -ATE³]

infūs|e' (-z), v.t. & i. Pour (thing *into*); (fig.) instil (grace, spirit, life, etc., *into*); steep (herb. tea, etc.) in liquid to extract its soluble constituents, whence ~'ER¹(2) (-z-) n.; (v.i.) undergo infusion (*let it ~e for five minutes*). [f. L IN¹(*fundere fus-* pour)]

infūs'|ible (-z-), a. That cannot be fused or melted. Hence ~iBIL'ITY n. [IN-²]

infū'sion (-zhn), n. Infusing (lit. & fig.); liquid extract thus obtained; infused element, admixture. [f. F, or L *infusio* (as INFUSE, see -ION)]

infūsōr'|ia, n. pl. Class of protozoa

found in infusions of decaying animal or vegetable matter. Hence ~IAL a., ~IAN, infūs'ORY, aa. & nn. [mod. L (INFUSE, -ORY, -IA²)]

-ing¹, suf. forming vbl nn., OE *-ung, -ing,* f. Gmc *-ungō, -ingō. -ing* orig. formed mere nn. of action (*asking*), but came in ME to acquire partly vbl (gerundial) character, being qualified by adv. (*the habit of speaking loosely*) or governing an object (*the idea of building him a house*). This use, peculiar to E, led to introduction of perf., fut., & pass. forms (*having killed, being killed*). The substantival nature of *-ing* is marked by the possess. case or adj. that often precedes it (*after John's behaving so badly, upon my granting the request*); but mod. tendency is to drop the possess. sign exc. with pronn. or single nn. Meanings: (1) vbl action (*bicycling, forebodings*), esp. as occupation (*banking*) or as inflicted (*thrashing*), or formed f. nn. (*soldiering*); (2) thing produced by vbl action (*carving, filings, building*); (3) material for (*sacking*), whether f. n. or vb (*fencing*=what fences or serves as fence); (4) what is used to do vbl action (*binding, dentist's filling*); (5) what is to be operated on (*washing, darning*); (6) set or arrangement of (*colouring, feathering*).

-ing², suf. of pres. part. (often used as adj., as *charming,* occas. as prep. or adv., as *during*). OE *-ende* (= OHG *-anti,* L *-ent-,* Gk *-ont-,* Skr. *-ant-*) was weakened to *-inde* & thus confused with *-inge* -ING¹, which became the regular form in 14th c. As result of the confusion, some constructions gerundial in orig. now appear participial, as *he went hunting* (i.e. on hunting, vbl n.), *the ark was building* (on building). On the other hand, some wds in *-ing* that might be explained as attrib. nouns in -ING¹ are perh. better regarded as quasi-pass. participles (*washing tie, cooking apple, breech-loading gun*). Compds are formed with advv. & adjj. (*well-meaning, fair-seeming*; for stress cf. *-ED²*), & with objective nn. (*cheese-paring, heart-breaking*; stressed on first component).

-ing³, suf. (OE *-ing,* Gmc *-inga*; cf. *-LING¹*) forming nn. w. sense ' one belonging to ', ' one having the quality of '; also used as patronymic & dim. Exx.: *Atheling, king, shilling, farthing, Riding, gelding, herring, whiting.*

in'gathering (in-gădh-), n. Gathering in, harvest.

ingĕm'ināte (-j-), v.t. Repeat, reiterate, (esp. *~ peace,* constantly urge it). [f. L IN¹(*geminare* GEMINATE)]

ingĕn'ious (-j-), a. Clever at contriving; cleverly contrived (*~ machine, explanation, theory*). Hence ~LY² adv. [f. F *ingénieux* or L *ingeniosus* (*ingenium* cleverness, see -OUS)]

ingénue (see Ap.), n. Artless girl, esp. a stage type. [F]

L

ingĕnū′itў (-j-), n. Skill in contriving. [f. L *ingenuitas* ingenuousness (as foll., see -TY); E meaning by confusion of IN- GENIOUS w. foll.]

ingĕn′ūous (-j-), a. Open, frank; inno- cent, artless. Hence ~LY² adv., ~NESS n. [f. L IN¹(*genuus* f. *gen-* beget) free-born, frank]

ingĕst′ (-j-), v.t. Take in (food) to the stomach. So **ingĕs′tION** (-schon) n., **ingĕs′tIVE** a. [f. L IN¹(*gerere gest-* carry)]

ingle (ing′gl), n. Fire burning on hearth; ~-*nook*, chimney-corner. [Sc., perh. f. Gael. *aingeal* fire, light]

inglŏr′ious (in-g-), a. Shameful, ignomi- nious; obscure. Hence ~LY² adv. [f. F *-eux* or L IN²(*gloriosus* GLORIOUS)]

in′gōing (in-g-), a. & n. Going in; sum paid for fixtures, improvements, etc., by incoming tenant of business or other premises.

ing′ot (-ngg-), n. Mass (usu. oblong) of cast metal, esp. of gold, silver, or steel. [ME; perh. f. IN adv.+*goten* p.p. of OE *geōtan* cast]

ingrain (in²grān *before noun*, in-grān′ *after n. or in pred.*), a. Dyed in grain; inherent, inveterate, ingrained. [orig. two wds]

ingrained (in′-grānd *before noun*, -ānd′ *elsewhere*), a. Deeply rooted, inveterate; thorough. Hence **ingrain′edLY²** (in-g-) adv. [var. of ENGRAINED]

‖ **ingrāte′** (in-g-, *or* in²), a. & n. (arch.). Ungrateful; (n.) ungrateful person. [f. OF, or L IN²(*gratus* grateful)]

ingrā′tiāt|e (in-grāshi-), v.t. Bring one- *self* into favour *with*. Hence ~**ingLY²** adv. [f. It. *ingratiare* f. L *in gratiam* into favour, see -ATE³]

ingrăt′itūde (in-g-), n. Want of gratitude. [ME, f. OF, f. LL *ingratitudo* (as INGRATE, see -TUDE)]

ingravĕs′c|ent (in-g-), a. (med.). (Of disease etc.) growing worse. So ~ENCE n. [f. L IN¹(*gravescere* f. *gravis* heavy), see -ENT]

ingrēd′ient (in-g-), n. Component part, element, in a mixture. [f. L IN¹(*gredi gress-* = *gradi* step) enter, see -ENT]

in′grĕss (in-g-), n. Going in; right of entrance. [f. L *ingressus -ūs* (as prec.)]

in²group′ (-ōōp), n. (sociol.). Group of people sharing common interests. [IN a.]

in′growing (-n-grōī-), a. Growing in- wards, esp. (of nail) growing into the flesh, also of branches of tree. So **in²growth** (in-grōth) n. [IN adv.]

ing′uinal (-nggw-), a. Of the groin. [f. L *inguinalis* (*inguen -inis* groin, see -AL)]

ingūr′git|āte (-n-g-), v.t. Swallow greedi- ly; (fig.) engulf. So ~A′TION n. [f. L IN¹(*gurgitare* f. *gurges -itis* whirlpool), see -ATE³]

inhăb′it, v.t. (Of men or animals) dwell in, occupy, (region, town, house; also fig.). Hence or cogn. ~ABLE a., ~ANT, ~A′TION, nn. [ME *en-, in-*, f. OF *enhabiter* or L IN¹(*habitare* dwell, see HABIT)]

inhăb′itancў, n. Residence as inhabitant, esp. during specified period, so as to ac- quire rights etc. [-ANCY]

inhāle′, v.t. Breathe in (air, gas, etc., or abs.), take (esp. tobacco-smoke or abs. of this) into the lungs (also fig.). So **inhalā′TION**, **inhăl′ER¹**(2), nn. [f. L IN¹(*halare* breathe)]

inharmŏn′ic, a. Not harmonic. [IN-²]

inharmŏn′ious, a. Not harmonious. Hence ~LY² adv. [IN-²]

inhēr|e′, v.i. (Of qualities etc.) exist, abide, *in*; (of rights etc.) be vested *in* (person etc.). So ~′ENCE n., ~′ENT a., ~′entLY² adv. [f. L IN¹(*haerēre haes-* stick)]

inhĕ′rit, v.t. Receive (property, rank, title).by legal descent or succession; de- rive (quality, character) from one's pro- genitors; (abs.) succeed as heir. Hence ~OR, ~RESS¹, **inhĕ′rITRIX**, nn. [ME, f. OF *enheriter* f. LL *inhereditare* f. *heres hered-* HEIR]

inhĕ′rit|able- Capable of inheriting or of being inherited (lit. & fig.). Hence ~ABIL′ITY n. [AF (as prec., see -ABLE)]

inhĕ′ritance, n. Inheriting; what is in- herited (lit. & fig.). [f. AF *enheritance* (as prec., see -ANCE)]

inhē′sion (-zhn), n. Inhering. [f. LL *in- haesio* (as INHERE, see -ION)]

inhib′it, v.t. Forbid, prohibit, (person etc. *from* doing; esp. in Eccl. Law); for- bid (ecclesiastic) to exercise clerical func- tions; hinder, restrain, (action, process). So **inhibi′tION** n., (in vbl senses, & esp. Psych.) instinctive or induced habitual shrinking from some impulse or action as a thing forbidden, ~ORY a. [f. L IN¹(*hibēre hibit-* = *habere* hold)]

inhomŏgĕn′eous, a. Not homogeneous. Hence **inhomŏgĕnē′ITY** n. [IN-²]

inhŏs′pitab|le, a. Not hospitable; (of re- gion, coast, etc.) not affording shelter etc. Hence ~leNESS n., ~LY² adv. [f. F, or med. L -*abilis*]

inhŏspităl′itў, n. Being inhospitable. [f. F -*lé*, or L -*ilas* (IN-², HOSPITALITY)]

inhūm′an, a. (Of person or conduct) brutal, unfeeling, barbarous, so ~ITY (-ăn²) n., ~LY² adv.; not of the ordinary human type. [f. F (*-ain*), or L IN²(*humanus* HUMAN)]

inhūm|e′, v.t. Bury. Hence ~A′TION n. [f. L IN¹(*humare* f. *humus* ground)]

inim′ical, a. Hostile (*to*); harmful (*to*). Hence ~LY² adv. [f. LL *inimicalis* f. IN²(*imicus* = *amicus* friend), see -AL]

inim′itab|le, a. That defies imitation. Hence ~leNESS n., ~LY² adv. [f. F, or L IN²(*imitabilis* IMITABLE)]

ini′quit|ў, n. Unrighteousness, wicked- ness; gross injustice. Hence ~OUS a., ~OUSLY² adv. [ME, f. OF *iniquite* f. L *iniquitatem* f. IN²(*iquus* = *aequus* just), see -TY]

ini′tial (-shal), a. & n., & v.t. (-ll-, -l-). **1.** Of, existing or occurring at, the beginning, as ~ *stage, expenses, difficulties*; ~ *letter* (standing at beginning of word). **2.** n. ~ letter, esp. (pl.) first letters of person's name & surname. **3.** v.t. Mark, sign, with ~s. Hence ~LY² adv. [f. L *initialis* f. *initium* f. IN¹(*ire it-* go), see -AL]

Ini'ti|āte¹ (-shI-), v.t. Begin, set going, originate; admit (person), esp. with introductory rites or forms, (*into* society, office, secret, *in* mysteries, science, etc.). So ~A'TION, ~ātOR, ~ātRIX, nn., ~atORY (-shya-) a. [f. L *initiare* (as INITIAL), see -ATE³]

Ini'tiate² (-shI-), a. & n. (Person) who has been initiated. [as prec., see -ATE²]

Ini'tiative (-shya-), n. & a. **1.** First step, origination; *take the* ~, take the lead (*in* doing); *have the* (power, right, to take the) ~, (Mil.) be able to make enemy conform to one's movements; ability to initiate things, enterprise (esp. with negative or virtual negative as *he lacks, has little or no*, ~); right of citizen(s) outside legislature to originate legislation (as in Switzerland). **2.** adj. Beginning, originating. [f. F (as prec., see -ive)]

Ini'tio (-shiō), adv. At the beginning (in reference to passage in book etc.; abbr. *init*.); AB~. [L]

Injĕct', v.t. Drive, force, (fluid, medicine, *into* cavity etc.) as by syringe; fill (cavity etc. *with*) by ~ing. Hence **injĕc'tOR** n. [f. L IN¹(*jicĕre ject-* = *jacĕre* throw)]

Injĕc'tion, n. Injecting; liquid or solution injected. [f. F, or L *injectio* (as prec., see -ION)]

injudi'cious (-jōōdIshus), a. Unwise, ill-judged. Hence ~LY² adv., ~NESS n. [IN-⁴]

In'jun (I-), n. (colloq. & dial.). American Indian, esp. in HONEST ~.

injŭnc'tion, n. Authoritative admonition or order; judicial process restraining person from wrongful act or compelling restitution etc. to injured party, whence **injŭnct'** v.t. (colloq.). [f. LL *injunctio* f. *injungere* ENJOIN, see -ION]

In'jure (-jer), v.t. Do wrong to; hurt, harm, impair. [back formation f. INJURY]

In'jured (-jerd), a. Wronged; showing sense of wrong, offended, as *in an* ~ *voice*. [p.p. of prec.]

Injur'ious (-oor-), a. Wrongful; (of language) insulting, calumnious; hurtful. Hence ~LY² adv., ~NESS n. [f. F *injurieux* or L *injuriosus* (as foll., see -OUS)]

In'jury, n. Wrongful action or treatment; harm, damage. [ME, f. L IN²(*juria* f. *jus juris* right) wrong]

Injŭs'tice, n. Want of equity, unfairness; unjust act; *you do him an* ~ (judge him unfairly). [ME, f. OF f. L IN²(*justitia* JUSTICE)]

Ink, n., & v.t. **1.** Fluid (black, red, etc.) for writing with pen; MARKING~; (*printer's* ~) viscous paste similarly used in printing; black liquid ejected by cuttle-fish etc. from bladder (~*bag*) to assist its escape; ~*bottle*, *-pot* (for holding ~);

~*-horn*, small vessel of horn formerly used for holding ~; ~*-pad* (for ~ing rubber stamp etc.); ~*stand*, stand for one or more ~-bottles, often with pen-tray etc.; ~*-well* (pot fitted into hole in desk). **2.** v.t. Mark (*in*, *over*, etc.) with ~; cover (types etc.) with ~ so as to print from them. Hence ~'iNESS n., ~'LESS, ~'Y², aa. [ME *enke, inke* f. OF *enque* f. LL *encau(s)tum* f. Gk *egkauston* (as ENCAUSTIC) purple ~ used by Roman emperors for signature]

ink'er, n. Telegraph instrument recording message in ink; (Print. etc.) inking-roller. [-ER¹]

ink'ling, n. Hint, slight knowledge or suspicion, (*of*). [f. ME *inkle* utter in an undertone; orig. unkn.]

in'land (-and, -ănd), n., a., & adv. **1.** Interior of country. **2.** adj. Placed in this, remote from sea or border; carried on within limits of a country, as ~ *trade*, ~ *duty* (on ~ trade), ‖ ~ *revenue* (consisting of taxes & ~ duties). **3.** adv. In, towards, the interior. Hence ~ER¹(4) n., ~ISH¹ a. [IN³]

in'law, n. (colloq.). (Usu. pl.) relative by marriage. [IN prep.]

inlay'¹, v.t. (*inlaid*). Embed (thing *in* another) so that their surfaces are even; ornament (thing with another inlaid); insert (page, plate, cut) in space cut in larger stouter page. [IN²]

in'lay² (or Inlā'), n. Inlaid work. [f. prec.]

in'lĕt, n. Small arm of sea, creek; piece inserted. [IN adv.+LET² v.]

in'lier, n. (geol.). Space occupied by one formation & completely surrounded by later formation. [IN adv.]

in'lў, adv. (poet.). Inwardly, in the heart; intimately. [OE *innlice* (IN¹, see -LY²)]

in'lўing, a. Lying inside. [IN adv.]

in'māte, n. Occupant (*of* house etc.), esp. one of several; now usu. occupant of institution, asylum, etc. [IN adv.]

in'mŏst (or -ost), a. Most inward; (fig.) deepest, most intimate. [OE *innemest* (IN adv., see -MOST)]

inn, n. Public house for lodging etc. of travellers, smaller & less pretentious than hotel & usu. in country or small town; ~*'keeper*, one who keeps an ~; ‖ *Inns of Court*, (buildings in London belonging to) four legal societies having exclusive right of admitting persons to practise at bar (*Inner Temple, Middle Temple, Lincoln's Inn, Gray's Inn*); ‖ *Inns of Chancery* (hist.), buildings in London formerly used as hostels for law students. [OE, f. IN adv.]

inn'ards (-dz), n. pl. (colloq.). Entrails. [INWARD n.]

innāte (or In²), a. Inborn, natural. Hence ~LY² (-tl-) adv., ~NESS (-tn-) n. [f. L IN¹(*natus* p.p. of *nasci* be born)]

innăv'igable, a. Not navigable. [f. F, or L IN²(*navigabilis* NAVIGABLE)]

inn'er, a. & n. **1.** Interior, internal; ~ *tube*, separate inflatable tube inside cover of pneumatic tire; *the ~ man*, man's soul or mind, (joc.) stomach, as *refreshed his ~ man*. 2. n. Division of target next outside bull's-eye, shot that strikes this. Hence ~MOST a. [OE *innera* a., compar. of IN²]

innerv′|āte, v.t. Supply (organ etc.) with nerve-force or nerves. Hence ~A′TION n. [f. IN-¹+NERVE+-ATE³]

inn′ings (-z), n. (pl. same, colloq. ~*es*). 1. (crick. etc.). Portion of game played by either side while in or batting, play of one batsman during his turn. 2. (fig.). Tenure of office, dominance, of political party, cause, etc. [orig. pl.; in sense 1 sing. *inning* is usu. in U.S.; f. IN adv.+ -ING¹]

inn′ocent, a. & n. 1. Free from moral wrong, sinless; ignorant of evil (without implication of virtue); not guilty (*of* crime etc.); (colloq.) *windows ~ of* (without) *glass*; simple, guileless; harmless. 2. n. ~ person, esp. young child; *I ~s' Day*, Dec. 28, festival of the slaughter of children by Herod (*Matt*. ii. 16); ‖ (Parl. sl.) *massacre* or *slaughter of the ~ s*, sacrifice of measures at end of session for want of time; simple person; idiot. Hence or cogn. **inn′ocence**, -ENCY (rare), nn., ~LY² adv. [ME, f. OF, or L IN²(*nocens -ent-* part. of *nocēre* hurt)]

innŏc′ūous, a. Not injurious, harmless (esp. of snakes). Hence **innocū′ITY**, ~NESS, nn., ~LY² adv. [f. L IN²(*nocuus* as prec.)+-OUS]

innŏm′ināte, a. Unnamed; (Anat.) ~ *bone*, hip-bone (made up of three original bones). [f. LL IN²(*nominatus*, as NOMIN-ATE)]

inn′ov|āte, v.i. Bring in novelties; make changes *in*. Hence or cogn. ~A′TION, ~ātoR, nn., ~ātoRY a. [f. L IN¹(*novare* make new f. *novus*), see -ATE³]

innŏ′xious (-kshus), a. Harmless. Hence ~LY² adv., ~NESS n. [f. L IN²(*noxius* NOXIOUS)]

innuĕn′dō, n. (pl. ~*es*), & v.i. Oblique hint, allusive remark (usu. depreciatory); (v.i.) make ~es. [L, gerund of IN¹(*nuere* nod), = by nodding, i.e. by way of explanation, as ‘he, innuendo the plaintiff ’, i.e., to wit]

innūm′erable, a. Countless. [ME f. L IN²(*numerabilis* NUMERABLE)]

innūtri′tion, n. Lack of nutrition. [IN-²]

innūtri′tious (-shus), a. Not nourishing. [IN-²]

inobsĕrv′ance (-z-), n. Inattention; non-observance (*of* law etc.). [f. F, or L IN²(*ob-servantia* OBSERVANCE)]

inŏccupā′tion, n. Want of occupation. [IN-²]

inŏc′ul|āte, v.t. Impregnate (person, animal, *with* virus or germs of disease) to induce milder form of it & so safeguard person against its attacks (cf. VACCINATE); implant (disease etc.) thus (*on, into,* person etc.); insert (bud, scion) in plant,

treat (plant) thus. Hence or cogn. ~Aᴸ TION, ~ātoR, nn., ~ātīve a. [f. L IN¹(*ocu-lare* f. *oculus* eye, bud) engraft, see -ATE³]

inŏd′orous, a. Having no odour. [f. L IN²(*odorus* ODOROUS)]

inoffĕn′sive, a. Unoffending; not objectionable. Hence ~LY² adv., ~NESS n. [IN-²]

inoffi′cious (-shus), a. Without office or function; (Law) not in accordance with moral duty. [f. L IN²(*officiosus* dutiful, see OFFICIOUS)]

inŏp′erable, a. (Of tumours etc.) that cannot be operated on. [IN-²]

inŏp′erative, a. Not working or taking effect. [IN-²]

inŏpp′ortūne, a. Unseasonable. Hence ~LY² adv., ~NESS n. [f. LL IN²(*opportunus* OPPORTUNE)]

inŏrd′ināte, a. Immoderate, excessive; intemperate; disorderly. Hence ~LY² adv. [ME, f. L IN²(*ordinatus* p.p. of *ordinare* f. *ordo -dinis* order)]

inŏrgăn′ic, a. Having no organized physical structure; (Chem., of compounds etc.) of mineral origin, not ORGANIC; ~ *chemistry*, that of ~ substances; not arising by natural growth, extraneous. [IN-²]

inŏrganizā′tion, n. Lack of organization. [IN-²]

inŏrnāte′, a. Not ornate. [IN-²]

inŏs′cūl|āte, v.i. & t. (Of blood-vessels etc.) join, have terminal connexion, (*with*); (of fibres etc.) unite closely, be interwoven; (trans.) unite (fibres etc.) closely. Hence ~A′TION n. [f. IN-¹+LL *osculare* furnish with mouth (*osculum* dim. of *os* mouth), -ATE³]

in′pouring (-pōr-), a. & n. Pouring in.

in′quĕst (in-kw-), n. Legal or judicial inquiry to ascertain matter of fact; inquisition; = CORONER'S ~; *great, last*, ~, last Judgement; coroner's jury; *grand ~* (hist.), grand jury (*grand ~ of the nation*, House of Commons). [ME, f. OF *en-queste* f. Rom.* *inquesta* as INQUIRE]

inqui′etūde (in-kw-), n. Uneasiness of mind or body. [ME, f. OF, or LL (-*do*) f. IN²(*quietus* QUIET), -TUDE]

in′quilīne (in-kw-), n. Animal living in the home of another, commensal. [f. L *inquilinus* IN-¹, *colere* dwell)]

inquīr|e′, en-, (in-kw-), v.i. & t. Make search (*into* matter); seek information (*of* person, *about, after*, thing etc.); ~*e after, for, him* (how he is); ask *for* (goods in shop etc.); ask to be told (person's name, business, etc., *whether, how*, etc.). Hence ~′ingLY² adv. [ME *enquere* f. OF *enquerre* f. Rom.* *inquaerere* f. L IN¹-(*quirere quisit-* = *quaerere* seek)]

inquīr′|ÿ, en-, (in-kw-), n. Asking; question; investigation; *make ~ies*, ask (*about* etc.); *court of ~y* (investigating circumstances of mishap etc.). [f. prec. +-Y⁴]

inquisi′tion (in-kwiz-), n. Search, investigation; judicial or official inquiry; (Rom. Cath.) *the I~* (hist.), ecclesiastical tribunal for suppression of heresy, the Holy Office. Hence ~AL (in-kwĭzĭsh-) a. [ME, f. OF f. L *inquisitionem* (as INQUIRE, see -ION)]

Inqui'sitive (ĭn-kwĭz-), a. Inquiring, curious; prying. Hence ~LY² adv., ~NESS n. [ME, f. OF (-*if*, -*ive*), f. LL *inquisitivus* (as prec., see -IVE)]

Inquis'itor (ĭn-kwĭz-), n. Official investigator; officer of the Inquisition (hist.); *Grand I~*, director of court of Inquisition in some countries; *I~ General*, head of this in Spain. [f. OF *inquisiteur* f. L *inquisitorem* (as INQUIRE, see -OR)]

Inquisitŏr'ial (ĭn-kwĭz-), a. Of, like, an inquisitor; offensively prying. Hence ~LY² adv. [f. med. L *inquisitorius* (as prec., see -ORY) + -AL]

In'road, n. Hostile incursion, raid; (fig.) forcible encroachment. [IN adv. + ROAD¹ n. in sense ' riding ']

In'rush, n. Rushing in. [IN adv.]

Insăl'iv|ate, v.t. Mix (food) with saliva. Hence ~A'TION n. [f. IN-¹ + SALIVA + -ATE³]

Insalub'r|ious (-lōō-), a. (Of climate or place) unhealthy. So ~ITY n. [f. L IN²(*salubris* SALUBRIOUS)]

Insane', a. Mad; senseless; ~ *asylum* (for ~ persons). Hence or cogn. ~LY² (-nl-) adv., **insăn'ITY** n. [f. L IN²(*sanus* SANE)]

Insăn'itary, a. Not sanitary. [IN-²]

Insa'ti|able (-sha-), a. That cannot be satisfied; inordinately greedy (*of*). Hence ~ABIL'ITY n., ~abLY² adv., (-sha-). [ME, f. OF, or L IN²(*satiabilis*, as SATIATE, see -BLE)]

Insa'tiate (-shyat), a. Never satisfied. [f. L IN²(*satiatus*, as prec.)]

Inscrĭb|e', v.t. Write (words etc. *in*, *on*, stone, metal, paper, etc.); enter name of (person) on list, in book (esp. for presentation); || (esp. in p.p.) issue (loan) in form of shares with registered holders, as ~*ed stock*; mark (sheet, tablet, etc., *with* characters); (Geom.) trace (figure) within another so that some particular points (or all angular points) of it lie in the boundary of that other (cf. CIRCUMSCRIBE), whence ~'ABLE a. [f. L IN¹(*scribere script*-write)]

Inscrip'tion, n. Words inscribed, esp. on monument, coin, stone, etc., so ~AL (-shon-), **inscrip'tIVE**, aa.; inscribing (*of* loan). [ME, f. L *inscriptio* (as prec., see -ION)]

Inscrut'|able (-rōō-), a. That cannot be penetrated (fig.), wholly mysterious. Hence ~ABIL'ITY, ~ableNESS, nn., ~abLY² adv. [ME, f. LL IN²(*scrutabilis* f. *scrutari* search, see -BLE)]

In'sĕct, n. Small invertebrate segmented animal having head, thorax, abdomen, and three pairs of thoracic legs, usu. with one or two pairs of thoracic wings; (fig.) insignificant person or creature; ~-*powder* (for killing or driving away ~). Hence ~ĭv'ORA n. pl., **insĕc'tivORE** n., ~ĭv'OROUS

a. [f. L *insectum* (*animal*) notched animal, f. IN¹(*secare sect*- cut)]

Insĕctār'ium, n. Place for keeping insects. [-ARIUM]

Insĕc'ti|cĭde, n. Insect-killer, esp. preparation used for killing insects. Hence ~cĭd'AL a. [-CIDE]

Insĕctŏl'ogy, n. Science of insects, esp. in their economic relations to man. [f. F *insectologie* (as INSECT, see -O- & -LOGY)]

Insĕcūr|e', a. Unsafe; (of ice, ground, etc.) liable to give way. Hence or cogn. ~e'LY² (-rl-) adv., ~'ITY n. [f. med. L IN²(*securus* SECURE)]

Insĕm'in|ate, v.t. Sow (seed etc., lit. & fig., *in*). Hence ~A'TION n., esp. artificial ~ation of animals. [f. L IN¹(*seminare* f. *semen -minis* seed), see -ATE³]

Insĕn'sate, a. Without sensibility, unfeeling; stupid; mad; without physical sensation. Hence ~LY² (-tl-) adv. [f. LL IN²(*sensatus* f. *sensus* SENSE, see -ATE²)]

Insensibil'ity, n. Lack of mental feeling or emotion; indifference (*to*); unconsciousness, swoon. [f. LL *insensibilitas* (as foll., see -TY)]

Insĕn'sib|le, a. Too small or gradual to be perceived, inappreciable, whence ~LY² adv.; unconscious, as *he fell down & was long* ~*le*; unaware (*of*, *to*, *how*, etc.); emotionless, callous. [ME, f. OF, or L IN²(*sensibilis* SENSIBLE)]

Insĕn'sitive, a. Not sensitive (*to* touch, sight, light, mental or moral impressions). Hence ~NESS n. [IN-²]

Insĕn'tient (-shĭ-), a. Inanimate. [IN-²]

Insĕp'ar|able, a. & n. That cannot be separated; (Gram.) ~*able prefix*, one that cannot be used as separate word (e.g. *dis-*, *mis-*, *un-*); (n., usu. pl.) ~able person or thing, esp. friend. Hence ~ABIL'ITY n., ~abLY² adv. [ME, f. L IN²(*separabilis* SEPARABLE)]

Insĕrt', v.t. Place, fit, thrust, (thing *in*, *into*, another, *between* edges etc.); introduce (letter, word, article, *in*, *into*, written matter, newspaper, etc.). [f. L IN¹(*serere sert*- join)]

Insĕr'tion, n. Inserting; thing inserted, esp. in writing or print; each appearance of an advertisement in newspaper etc.; ornamental needlework etc. inserted into plain material, as *lace*~; (Anat.) mode of attachment of muscle, organ, etc. [f. F, or LL *insertio* (as prec., see -ION)]

In'sĕt¹, n. Extra page(s) inserted in sheet or book; small map etc. inserted within border of larger; piece let into dress; pair of white slips worn as edging to waistcoat opening. [IN adv. + SET n.]

Insĕt'², v.t. (~ or ~*ted*). Put in as an inset. [IN adv. + SET v. or f. prec.]

In'shŏre', adv. & a. Close to shore; ~ *of*, nearer to shore than. [IN¹]

Inside, n., a., adv., & prep. **1.** n. (In'sīd'). Inner side or surface, (of path) side next to wall or away from road; inner part, interior; (insĭd'), stomach & bowels (colloq.); ‖ *the* in*'side*' (middle part) *of a week*; (insid') passenger travelling ~ coach etc. (hist.); *turned in'side out*, so that inner side becomes outer. **2. adj.** (in'sid). Situated on or in, derived from, the ~ (~ *information*, not accessible to outsiders; *an* ~ *job*, burglary by a resident). **3. adv.** (insid'). On or in the ~; (colloq.) ~ *of* (in less than) *a week*. **4. prep.** (insid'). On the inner side of, within. [IN a. +SIDE]

insid'er, n. One who is in some society, organization, etc. (cf. OUTSIDER); one who is in the secret. [f. prec. +-ER¹]

insid'ious, a. Treacherous, crafty; proceeding secretly or subtly, as ~ *disease*. Hence ~LY² adv., ~NESS n. [f. L *insidiosus* cunning f. IN¹(*sidiae* f. *sedēre* sit) ambush, see -OUS]

in'sight (-īt), n. Penetration (*into* character, circumstances, etc.) with the understanding. [IN adv. +SIGHT]

insig'nia, n. pl. Badges, distinguishing marks, (*of* office, honour, etc.). [L, neut. pl. of IN¹(*signis* f. *signum* SIGN¹) distinguished]

insignif'ic|ant, a. Unimportant, trifling; contemptible; meaningless. Hence ~ANCE, ~ANCY, nn., ~antLY² adv. [IN-²]

insincēre', a. Not sincere, disingenuous. Hence ~LY² (-rl-) adv. **insincē'rity** n. [f. L IN²(*sincerus* SINCERE)]

insin'u|āte, v.t. Introduce (thing, one*self, into* place; oneself, person, *into* favour, office, etc.) gradually or subtly; convey indirectly, hint obliquely, (idea, *that*). Hence ~ātingLY² adv., ~A'TION, ~ātor, nn., ~ātive a. [f. L IN¹(*sinuare* f. *sinus* -*ūs* curve), see -ATE³]

insip'id, a. Tasteless; wanting in flavour; lifeless, dull, uninteresting. Hence ~ITY (-id²), ~NESS, nn., ~LY² adv. [f. LL IN²(*sipidus*=*sapidus* well-tasting, f. *sapere* taste, be wise, see -ID¹)]

insist', v.i. & t. Dwell long or emphatically (*on*), as ~ *on this point, on his un-punctuality*; maintain positively, as ~ *on his innocence*, ~ (*on it) that he is innocent*; make a stand *on* as essential (*I* ~ *on being present, on your being present, on your presence, on it that you shall be present*). Hence ~ENCE, ~ENCY, nn., ~ENT a., ~entLY² adv. [f. F *insister*, or L IN¹(*sistere* stand)]

insobri'ĕtў, n. Intemperance, esp. in drinking. [IN-²]

insolā'tion, n. Exposure to sun's rays, for purposes of bleaching etc., as medical treatment, or as cause of disease. [f. L *insolatio* f. IN¹(*solare* f. *sol* sun), see -ATION]

in'sol|ent, a. Offensively contemptuous, insulting. Hence or cogn. ~ENCE n., ~entLY² adv. [f. L IN²(*solens* part. of *solēre* be accustomed), see -ENT]

insŏl'|ūble, a. That cannot be solved; that cannot be dissolved. Hence ~ŪBIL-ITY, ~ūbleNESS, nn., ~ūblY² adv. [ME, f. L IN²(*solubilis* SOLUBLE)]

insŏl'vent, a. & n. (Debtor) unable to pay debts; relating to ~s, as ~ *laws*. Hence **insŏl'vENCY** n. [IN-²]

insŏm'nia, n. Habitual sleeplessness. [L, f. IN²(*somnis* f. *somnus* sleep) sleepless]

insomŭch', adv. To such an extent *that*.

insouci|ant, a. Careless, unconcerned. So ~ANCE n. [F (*soucier* care)]

inspăn', v.t. (S.-Afr.; -nn-). Yoke (oxen etc.) in team to vehicle; harness (wagon). [f. Du. IN¹(*spannen* SPAN²)]

inspĕct', v.t. Look closely into; examine officially. So **inspĕc'tION**, **inspĕc'tOR** (esp., police officer below superintendent & above sergeant, also official appointed to ~ & send in reports, e.g. ~*or of schools, of mines, of weights & measures*), **inspĕc'torSHIP**, nn., **inspĕc'torAL**, ~ōr'IAL, aa. [f. L IN¹(*spicere spect-* look), & *inspectare*]

inspĕc'torate, n. Office of inspector; body of inspectors; district under inspector. [-ATE¹]

inspirā'tion, n. Drawing in of breath; inspiring; divine influence, esp. that which is thought to visit poets etc. & that under which books of Scripture are held to have been written, whether *verbal* ~ (dictating every word), *plenary* ~ (covering all subjects treated), or *moral* ~ (confined to moral & religious teaching), whence ~ISM(3), ~IST(2), nn.; thought etc. inspired, prompting; sudden happy idea; inspiring principle. Hence ~AL a. [ME, f. OF f. LL *inspirationem* (as INSPIRE, see -ATION)]

in'spirātor, n. Apparatus for drawing in air or vapour. [L (as foll., see -OR)]

inspīr'|e', v.t. Breathe in, inhale, (air etc. or abs.), whence ~'atORY a.; infuse thought or feeling into (person; esp. of divine or supernatural agency; often in p.p.); animate (person etc. *with* feeling); infuse (feeling *into* person etc.), create (feeling *in* person); *an* ~*ed article* (in journal), one secretly suggested by or emanating from influential person etc. [ME, f. OF *enspirer* f. L IN¹(*spirāre* breathe)]

inspi'rit, v.t. Put life into, animate; encourage (person *to* action, *to* do). Hence ~ING² a. [IN-¹ +SPIRIT n.]

inspiss'|āte (or IN²), v.t. Thicken, condense. So ~A'TION n. [f. LL IN¹(*spissare* f. *spissus* thick), see -ATE³]

instabil'itў, n. Lack of stability (usu. fig. of moral qualities etc.). [ME, f. OF *instabilite* f. L *instabilitatem* f. IN²(*stabilis* STABLE¹), see -TY]

install' (-awl), v.t. Place (person *in* office or dignity) with ceremonies, whence ~ANT (-awl-) a. & n.; establish (person, one*self, in* place, condition, etc.); place (heating or lighting apparatus etc.) in position for use. So ~A'TION n. (also, usu. pl., buildings etc. for technical operation). [f. med. L IN¹(*stallare* f. *stallum* STALL¹)]

instal'ment (-awl-). n. Each of several parts. successively falling due, of a sum payable; each of several parts supplied etc. at different times. [f. obs. IN¹(*stall* v. arrange, fix)+-MENT]

in'stance¹, n. Fact illustrating a general truth, example; particular case (*in your, this, ~*); *for~*, as an example; *at the ~* (request, suggestion) *of*; (Law) process, suit, as *court of first ~* (primary jurisdiction); *in the first ~*, in the first place, at the first stage of a proceeding. [ME, f. OF f. L *instantia* (as INSTANT¹, see -ANCE)]

in'stance², v.t. Cite (fact, case) as an instance; (usu. pass.) exemplify. [f. prec.]

in'stancy̆, n. Urgency. [as prec., -ANCY]

in'stant¹, a. Urgent, pressing; (abbr. *inst.*) of the current month, as *the 6th inst.* (cf. PROXIMO, ULTIMO); immediate. [F, f. L IN¹(*stare* stand) be present, press upon, see -ANT]

in'stant², n. Precise (esp. the present) point of time, moment, as *come this ~, I went that ~* or *on the ~*; *I told you the ~* (as soon as) *I knew*; short space of time, moment. [after med. L *instans* (prec.)]

instantané (see Ap.), n. Snapshot, (fig.) short sketch in a few sentences. [F]

instantăn'éous, a. Occurring, done, in an instant; (Dynam.) existing at a particular instant. Hence ~LY² adv., ~NESS n. [f. med. L -*eus* (INSTANT², -ANEOUS), after LL *momentaneus*]

instăn'ter, adv. Immediately, at once, (now usu. joc.). [L, f. *instans* INSTANT¹]

in'stantly̆, adv. At once. [INSTANT¹ + -LY²]

in'star, n. Form assumed by insect at particular stage of development. [L]

instaura'tion, n. Restoration, renewal. So in'staurātor n. [f. L *instauratio* f. IN¹(*staurare*, see RESTORE & -ATION)]

instead' (-ĕd), adv. As a substitute or alternative; in place *of*, as *~ of this, ~ of going, you should be out ~ of (sitting) in on this fine day*, (also *in his, my, our*, STEAD). [ME; IN prep.+STEAD n.]

in'stĕp, n. Upper surface of foot between toes & ankle; part of shoe etc. fitting this; *~-shaped thing*. [16th c., ult. f. IN+STEP, but immed. orig. obsc.]

in'stig|āte, v.t. Urge on, incite, (person *to* action, *to* do freq. something evil); bring about (revolt, murder, etc.) by persuasion. So ~A'TION, ~ātor, nn. [f. L *instigare* urge, incite; see -ATE³]

instil(l)', v.t. (-ll-). Put in (liquid *into* thing) by drops; infuse (feeling, ideas, etc. *into* person, mind, etc.) gradually. Hence or cogn. instillA'TION, instil'MENT, nn. [f. L IN¹(*stillare* drop); cf. DISTIL]

in'stinct¹, n. Innate propensity, esp. in lower animals, to certain seemingly rational acts performed without conscious design; HERD¹ *~*; innate impulse; intuition, unconscious skill. Hence instinc'TIVE a., instinc'tiveLY² (-vl-) adv. [f. L *instinctus -ūs* f. IN¹(*stinguere stinct-* prick) incite]

instinct'², pred. a. Imbued, charged,

(*with* life, beauty, force, etc.). [f. L p.p. as prec.]

in'stitūte¹, n. 1. Society, organization, for promotion of scientific or other object; building used by this. 2. pl. Digest of elements of a subject, esp. of jurisprudence, as *I~s of Justinian*. [f. L neut. p.p. as foll.]

in'stitūte², v.t. Establish, found; set on foot (inquiry etc.); appoint (person *to, into*, benefice). [ME, f. L IN¹(*stituere -tut-* = *statuere* set up)]

institū'tion, n. Instituting; establishment (*of* person) in cure of souls; established law, custom, or practice; (colloq.) of person etc.) familiar object; organization for promotion of some public object; building used by this. Hence ~AL (-shon-) a., (also, of religion) organized into or finding expression through ~s (churches, priests, ritual, etc.). [ME, f. OF f. L *institutionem* (as prec., see -ION)]

instrŭct', v.t. Teach (person etc. *in* subject); inform (person *that, when*, etc.); (of client, solicitor) give information to (solicitor, counsel); direct, command, (person *to* do). Hence or cogn. instrŭc'toR, instrŭc'tRESS¹, nn. [ME, f. L IN¹(*struere struct-* pile up) build, teach]

instrŭc'tion, n. Teaching; (pl.) directions, orders; (pl.) directions to solicitor or counsel. Hence ~AL (-shon-) a. [ME, f. OF, f. L (in sense LL) *instructionem* (as prec., see -ION)]

instrŭc'tive, a. Tending to instruct, conveying a lesson. Hence ~LY² adv., ~NESS n. [-IVE]

in'strument (-rŏŏ-), n., & v.t. 1. Thing used in performing an action; person so made use of; tool, implement, esp. for delicate or scientific work; (also *musical ~*) contrivance for producing musical sounds by vibration of strings etc. (*stringed* etc. *~s*) or of body of air in pipe etc. (*wind ~s*); formal, esp. legal, document. 2. v.t. Arrange (music) for *~s*. [ME, f. OF, or L *instrumentum* (as IN-*struct*, see -MENT)]

instrumĕn'tal (-rŏŏ-), a. Serving as instrument or means (*to* purpose, *in* work, *in* doing); of, arising from, an instrument, as *~ errors*; (of music) performed on instruments (cf. VOCAL), whence ~IST(3) n.; (Gram.) *~ case* (denoting the instrument). Hence ~LY² adv. [f. F, or med. L *instrumentalis* (as INSTRUMENT, see -AL)]

instrumĕntăl'ity̆ (-rŏŏ-), n. Agency, means, esp. *by the~ of*. [-ITY]

instrumĕnta'tion (-rŏŏ-), n. Arrangement of music for instruments; study of character, power, pitch, etc., of musical instruments; operation with surgical or other instrument; instrumentality. [F, (as INSTRUMENT, see -ATION)]

insubŏrd'in|ate, a. Disobedient, rebellious. Hence~A'TION n. [IN-²]

insubstăn'tial (-shl), a. Not real; lacking solidity or substance. Hence ~ITY

(-shĭăl²) n. [f. LL IN²(*substantialis* SUB-STANTIAL)]

insŭff´erab|le, a. Unbearable, unbearably arrogant, corceited, etc. Hence ~LY² adv. [IN-²]

insuffi´ci|ent (-shent), a. Not sufficient, inadequate. Hence or cogn. ~ENCY n., ~ently² adv., (-shen-). [f. OF, or LL IN²(*sufficiens* SUFFICIENT)]

in´sŭfflāt|e, v.t. Blow, breathe, (air, gas, etc.) into cavity of the body etc.; treat (nose etc.) thus. Hence ~OR n., (also) device for blowing powder on to surface of object in order to make latent finger--prints visible. [f. LL IN¹(SUF*flare* blow upon), see -ATE³]

insŭfflā´tion, n. Blowing on or into; breathing on person as rite of exorcism. [f. LL *insufflatio* (as prec., see -ION)]

in´sŭlar, a. Of (the nature of) an island; applied to a development of Latin handwriting current in the British Isles in the early Middle Ages; of, like, islanders, esp. ignorant of or indifferent to other countries & their culture, narrow-minded, whence ~ISM n. Hence **insŭlā´rITY** n., ~LY² adv. [f. LL *insularis* (as foll., see -AR¹)]

in´sŭl|āte, v.t. Make (land) into an island; detach (person, thing) from surroundings, isolate; isolate (thing) by interposition of non-conductors, to prevent passage of electricity or heat. Hence ~A´TION, ~ā-toR, nn. [f. L *insula* island +-ATE³]

in´sŭlin, n. A specific for diabetes extracted from the islets of Langerhans in the pancreas of animals. [f. L *insula* island +-IN]

in´sŭlt¹, n. Insulting speech or action, affront. [f. F, or LL IN¹(*sultus* = *saltus* leap, as foll.)]

insŭlt´², v.t. Treat with scornful abuse, offer indignity to; (of person or thing) affront. Hence ~ingLY² adv. [f. F *insulter*, or L IN¹(*sultare* = *saltare*, frequent. of *salire salt*- leap)]

insŭp´er|able, a. (Of barriers etc. & fig. of difficulties etc.) that cannot be surmounted or overcome; ‖ (rare) unsurpassable. Hence ~ABIL´ITY n., ~abLY² adv. [ME, f. OF, or L IN²(*superabilis* f. *superare* overcome, -BLE)]

insuppŏrt´ab|le, a. Unbearable. Hence ~LY² adv. [f. F, or LL IN²(*supportabilis* SUPPORT, -ABLE)]

insur´ance (-shoor-), n. Insuring; sum paid for this, premium; *National I~ Act*, one requiring wage-earners to make weekly payments supplemented by their employers in return for which they receive State assistance in sickness, unemployment, etc. [earlier *en-*, f. OF *enseurance* (as ENSURE, see -ANCE)]

insur´ant (-shoor-), n. Person to whom insurance policy is issued. [f. foll. +-ANT]

insur|e´ (-shoor), v.t. Secure payment of sum of money in event of loss of or damage to (property, life; cf. ASSURANCE)

by payment of premium; secure payment of (sum of money) thus (said of owner of the property or of insurance company); *the ~ed*, the person to whom such payment is secured; make certain. Hence ~´ABLE (-shoor-) a. [ME, earlier ENSURE]

insur´er (-shoor-), n. One who insures property in consideration of premium, underwriter. [-ER¹]

insŭr´g|ent, a. & n. **1.** Rising in active revolt; (of sea etc.) rushing in. **2.** n. Rebel. Hence ~ENCY n. [f. L IN¹(*surgere surrect*- rise), see -ENT]

insurmoun´tab|le (-ser-), a. Not to be surmounted. Hence ~LY² adv. [IN-²]

insurrec´tion (-su-), n. Rising in open resistance to established authority; incipient rebellion. Hence ~AL, ~ARY¹, aa., ~IST(3) n., (-urĕksho-). [ME, f. OF f. LL *insurrectionem* (as INSURGENT, see -ION)]

insuscĕp´t|ible, a. Not susceptible (*of* treatment, *to* agency etc.). Hence ~IBIL´ITY n. [IN-²]

intäct´, a. Untouched; entire; unimpaired. [ME, f. L IN²(*tactus* p.p. of *tangere* touch)]

inta´glĭātĕd (-tăl-), a. Carved on the surface. [f. It. *intagliato* p.p. of IN¹(*tagliare* cut), as ENTAIL²]

inta´gliŏ (-tăl-), n. (pl. ~s), & v.t. Engraved design; carving in hard material; gem with incised design (cf. CAMEO); (v.t.) engrave (material, design) thus. [(vb f. n.) It. (as prec.)]

in´tāke, n. Place where water is taken into channel or pipe from river etc.; airway in mine; abrupt narrowing in pipe, stocking, etc.; person(s) or thing(s) taken in or received; land reclaimed from moor. [IN adv. +TAKE v.]

intăn´g|ible (-j-), a. & n. **1.** That cannot be touched; impalpable; that cannot be grasped mentally. **2.** n. ~ible thing. Hence ~IBIL´ITY n., ~IbLY² adv. [f. med. L IN²(*tangibilis* TANGIBLE)]

in´tĕger, n. Whole number, undivided quantity, (cf. FRACTION); thing complete in itself. [L, adj. = untouched, whole; see ENTIRE]

in´tĕgral, a. & n. **1.** Of, necessary to the completeness of, a whole; whole, complete; (Math.) of, denoted by, an integer, involving only integers; ~ *calculus* (dealing with finding & properties of ~s of functions, cf. DIFFERENTIAL). **2.** n. Quantity of which a given function is the differential coefficient. Hence or cogn. ~ITY (-ăl-) n., ~LY² adv. [f. LL *integralis* (as prec., see -AL)]

in´tĕgrant, a. (Of parts) component, making up a whole. [as foll., see -ANT]

in´tĕgrate¹, a. Made up of parts; whole, complete. [as foll., see -ATE³]

in´tĕgr|āte², v.t. Complete (imperfect thing) by addition of parts; combine (parts) into a whole; (Math.) find the integral of; indicate mean value or total sum of (area, temperature, etc.), whence

~**ātor** n. Hence or cogn. ~**A'TION** n.,
~**ātive** a. [f. L *integrare* make whole
(INTEGER), see -ATE³]
intĕg′rity, n. Wholeness; soundness; uprightness, honesty. [ME, f. OF *-te*, or L
integritas (INTEGER, see -TY)]
intĕg′ūment, n. Skin, husk, rind, or
other (usu. natural) covering. Hence
~**ARY**¹ (-ĕn⁴) a. [f. L *integumentum* f.
IN¹(*tegere* cover), see -MENT]
in′tĕllĕct, n. Faculty of knowing &
reasoning; understanding; person, persons collectively, of good understanding.
[ME, f. L *intellectus -ūs* (as INTELLIGENT)]
intĕllĕc′t|ion, n. Action, process, of
understanding, esp. as opp. to *imagination*. So ~**IVE** a. [f. med. L *intellectio* (as
INTELLIGENT, see -ION)]
intĕllĕc′tūal, a. & n. **1.** Of, appealing to,
requiring the exercise of, intellect. **2.**
(Person) possessing a good understanding, enlightened person, esp. *the ~s* (*of* a
country etc.). Hence or cogn. ~**ITY** (-ăl⁴),
~**īzA′TION**, nn., ~**IZE**(3) v.t. & i., ~**LY**² adv.
[ME, f. L *intellectualis* (as INTELLECT, see
-AL)]
intĕllĕc′tūal|ism, n. Doctrine that know-
ledge is wholly or mainly derived from
pure reason. So ~**IST**(2) n. [-ISM]
intĕll′igence, n. Intellect, understanding,
whence **intĕllĭgĕn′tIAL** (-shăl) a.; quickness of understanding, sagacity, (of
person or animal; ~ *test*; ~ *quotient*, abbr.
I.Q., a number denoting the ratio of a
given person's ~ to the normal or average); rational being; information, news,
(*I~ Department*, engaged in collecting
information esp. for mil. purposes). [ME,
f. OF, f. L *intelligentia* (as INTELLIGENT)]
intĕll′igencer, n. Bringer of news, informant; secret agent, spy. [f. prec. +
-ER¹]
intĕll′igent, a. Having or showing (usu.
a high degree of) understanding; clever,
quick of mind. Hence ~**LY**² adv. [f.
L *intelligere* understand (INTER- + *legere*
gather, pick out, read), -ENT]
intĕllĭgĕn′sia, -zia, n. The part of a
nation that aspires to independent thinking. [Russ. *intelligentsiya*]
intĕll′ig|ible, a. That can be understood,
comprehensible *to*; (Philos.) that can be
apprehended only by the intellect, not by
the senses. Hence ~**ĭBIL′ITY** n., ~**ĭbLY**²
adv. [f. L *intelligibilis* (as prec., see
-BLE)]
intĕm′per|ate, a. (Of person or conduct
or speech) immoderate, unbridled, violent; excessive in the indulgence of an
appetite; addicted to drinking. Hence or
cogn. ~**ANCE** n., ~**ately**² adv. [f. L IN²-
(*temperatus*, as TEMPER v.)]
intĕnd′, v.t. Purpose, design, as *we ~ to
go*, *we ~ no harm*, *we ~ that it shall be done
today*, *was this ~ed* (done on purpose)?;
design, destine, (person, thing) for a purpose, as *we ~ our son for the bar*, *~ him to
go*, *~ it as a stopgap*, *this bun is ~ed for*

you (to eat), *this daub is ~ed for* (meant
to represent) *me*; mean, as *what exactly do
you ~ by the word?*. [ME *en-, in-* f. OF
entendre & IN¹(*tendere tent-* or *tens-* stretch,
tend) strain, direct, purpose]
intĕn′dan|t, n. Superintendent, manager,
of public business etc. (chiefly as foreign
title). Hence ~**CY** n. [F, f. L as prec.,
-ANT]
intĕn′dĕd, n. (colloq.). Affianced lover, as
your his, her, ~. [p.p. of INTEND as n.]
intĕnd′ment, n. True meaning as fixed
by law. [ME *en-* f. OF *entendement* meaning (as INTEND, see -MENT)]
intĕnse′, a. (-er, -est). (Of quality etc.)
existing in a high degree, violent, vehement; having some quality in high
degree; (of feeling or action) eager,
ardent; feeling, apt to feel, ~ emotion.
Hence ~**LY**² (-sl-) adv., ~**NESS** (-sn-),
intĕnsīFICA′TION, **intĕn′sITY**, nn., **intĕn**⁴
siFY v.t. & i., (also, Photog.) increase the
opacity of the deposit in a negative by
chemical or other means. [ME, f. OF as
INTENT²]
intĕn′sion (-shn), n. Intensity, high
degree, of a quality; strenuous exertion of
mind or will. [f. L *intensio* (INTEND, -ION)]
intĕn′sive, a. Of, relating to, intensity
as opp. to extent; producing intensity;
(Gram.) expressing intensity, giving
force; concentrated, directed to a single
point or area or subject, (~ *bombardment,
study*); (Econ.) serving to increase production of given area, as ~ *methods,
agriculture*; (Med.) ~ *inoculation* (in
which intensity of matter introduced is
increased in successive operations).
Hence ~**LY**² (-vl-) adv. [F (*-if, -ive*), f.
med. L as INTEND, see -IVE]
intĕnt′¹, n. Intention, purpose, esp. *with
~ to* (defraud etc.), *with malicious, good,
etc., ~*; (pl.) *to all ~s & purposes*, practically, virtually. [ME & OF (1) *entent* f.
L *intentus -ūs*, (2) *entente* f. Rom. **intenta*
fem. p.p., both as INTEND]
intĕnt′², a. Resolved, bent, (*on doing, on*
object); sedulously occupied (*on*); (of
faculties, looks, etc.) earnest, eager.
Hence ~**LY**² adv., ~**NESS** n. [f. L as
INTEND]
intĕn′tion, n. Intending; thing intended,
purpose, whence (-)~**ED**² (-shond) a.;
ultimate aim; (pl., colloq.) purposes in
respect of proposal of marriage; (Med.)
second ~, healing of wound by granula-
tion, *first ~*, healing without this by
immediate re-union of parts; (Logic) conception, as *first ~s*, primary conceptions
of things (e.g. a tree, an oak), *second ~s*,
secondary conceptions (e.g. difference,
identity, species); (Theol.) *special, particular, ~*, special object for which mass
is celebrated etc. [ME, f. OF, f. L *inten-
tionem* (as INTEND, see -ION)]
intĕn′tional (-shon-), a. Done on purpose.
Hence ~**LY**² adv. [f. med. L *intentionalis*
(as prec., see -AL)]

inter'[1], v.t. (-rr-). Deposit (corpse etc.) in earth, tomb, etc.; bury. [ME en- f. OF enterrer f. Rom. *IN[1](terrare f. terra earth)]

in'ter[2], prep. (L). Between, among, as ~ āl'ia, amongst other things; ~ nōs, sē, between ourselves, themselves; ~ viv'ōs, between the living (esp. of gift as opp. legacy).

inter-, pref. = prec. Inter- is used freely to form (1) vbs, nn., & aa., expr. mutual or reciprocal action or relation, or with sense ' among ', ' between ', as: ~bed', embed (thing) between others; ~cen'sal, between two censuses; ~collē'giate, carried on etc. between colleges; ~colum'nar, placed, existing, between two columns; ~columnia'tion, placing of columns at intervals, such interval; ~connect', connect by reciprocal links; ~convert'ible, interchangeable; ~cross', t. & i., lay, lie, across each other, (cause to) propagate with each other; ~flow, n. & v.i., flow into each other; ~grada'tion, gradual approximation; ~grade, (v.i.) pass into another form by intervening grades, (n.) such grade; ~growth', growing of things into each other; ~jac'ulatory, expressed in parenthetical ejaculations; ~knit', intertwine; ~lap', overlap; ~link', link together (things, one with another); ~ocean'ic, between, connecting, two oceans; ~plait', plait together; ~plan'etary a., between planets; ~provin'cial, situated, carried on, between provinces; ~punc'tion, punctuation; ~punc'tuate, punctuate; ~ra'cial, existing between different races; ~shoot', shoot or glance (t. & i.) at intervals, variegate (thing with colours etc., esp. in p.p. ~shot); in'terspace, interval of space or time; ~tan'gle, tangle together, whence ~tan'glement n.; ~tex'ture, interweaving; ~trib'al, existing between different tribes; ~twist', twist together; ~vein', intersect (às) with veins; ~work', (trans.) interweave lit. & fig., (intr.) work upon each other; ~wreathe', wreathe together. (2) Scientific, esp. anat., wds w. sense ' between ', chiefly adjj., as: ~artic'ular, between contiguous surfaces of a joint; ~cos'tal, between the ribs (of body or ship), (n. pl.) ~costal parts; ~di'gital, between fingers or toes; ~di'gitate, interlock like fingers of clasped hands, so ~digita'tion n.; ~fa'cial, included between two faces of crystal or other solid; ~fem'oral, between the thighs; ~folia'ceous, placed alternately between a pair of opposite leaves; ~gla'cial, between glacial periods; ~lob'ular, between lobes; in'ternode, (Bot.) part of stem between two of the knots from which leaves arise, (Anat.) slender part between two joints, esp. bone of finger or toe; ~oss'eous between bones; ~pari'etal, between right & left parietal bones of skull; ~sep'tal, between partitions; ~spin'al, ~spin'ous,

between spines or spinous processes; ~stell'ar, between stars; ~stratifica'tion, ~strat'ified, interspersion, interspersed, (with strata).

in'teract[1], n. Interval between two acts of play; interlude. [INTER-, after ENTR'ACTE]

interăct'[2], v.t. Act reciprocally, act on each other. Hence interăc'TION n., interăc'TIVE a. [INTER-]

interblĕnd', v.t. & i. Mingle (things, one with another); (intr.) blend with each other. [INTER-]

interbreed', v.t. & i. Cross-breed; (intr., of animals of different race or species) breed with each other. [INTER-]

intĕrc'alary, a. (Of day or month) inserted in calendar to harmonize calendar with solar year, e.g. Feb. 29 in leap years; (of year) having such additions; interpolated, intervening. [f. L intercalarius (as foll., see -ARY[1])]

intĕrc'al|āte, v.t. Insert (intercalary day etc., or abs.); interpose (anything out of ordinary course, esp. in p.p. of strata). So ~A'TION n. [f. L INTER(calare proclaim), see -ATE[3]]

intercēde', v.i. Interpose on behalf of another, plead (with one person for another). [f. L INTER(cedere cess- go) intervene]

inter|cĕpt', v.t. Seize, catch, (person etc.) on the way from place to place; cut off (light etc. from); check, stop; (Math.) mark off (space) between two points etc. Hence or cogn. ~cĕp'TION, ~cĕp'TOR, nn., ~cĕp'TIVE a. [f. L INTER(cipere cept- = capere take)]

inter|cĕ'ssion (-shn), n. Interceding, esp. by prayer. So ~cĕss'OR n., ~cĕssor'IAL, ~cĕss'ORY, aa. [f. L intercessio (as INTERCEDE, see -ION)]

in'terchānge[1] (-j), n. Reciprocal exchange (of things) between two persons etc.; alternation. [f. OF entrechange (as foll.)]

interchānge'[2] (-j), v.t. (Of two persons) exchange (things) with each other; put each of (two things) in the other's place; alternate. Hence or cogn. ~ABIL'ITY, ~ableNESS, nn., ~ABLE a., ~ablY[2] adv. (-jab-). [ME, f. OF entrechangier (entre-INTER- f. changier CHANGE)]

intercolōn'ial, a. Existing, carried on, between different colonies. [INTER-]

in'tercŏm, n. System of intercommunication esp. in aircraft. [abbr.]

intercommūn'ic|āte, v.i. Have mutual intercourse; have free passage to each other. So ~A'TION n. [INTER-]

intercommūn'ion (-yon), n. Intimate intercourse; mutual action or relation. [INTER-]

intercommūn'itȳ, n. Being common to various parties; having things in common. [INTER-]

in'tercourse (-ōrs), n. Social communication, dealings, between individuals; communion between man & God; communication for trade purposes etc. between different countries etc.; sexual connexion. [ME, f. OF *entrecours* f. *entrecorre* run between f. L INTER(*currere curs-* run)]

intercŭ'rr|ent, a. (Of time or event) intervening; (of disease) occurring during progress of another, (also) recurring at intervals. Hence ~ENCE n. [f. L as prec., -ENT]

interdĕ|pĕnd', v.i. Depend on each other. So ~pĕn'dENCE, -ENCY, nn., ~pĕn'dENT a., ~pĕn'dentLY² adv. [INTER-]

in'terdict¹, n. Authoritative prohibition; (Sc. Law)=INJUNCTION; (R.-C. Ch.) sentence debarring person or place from ecclesiastical functions etc. [ME & OF *entredit* f. L *interdictum* p.p. of INTER(*dicere dict-* say)]

interdict'², v.t. Prohibit (action); forbid use of; restrain (person *from doing*); forbid (thing *to* person). So interdic'tION n., interdic'tory a. [ME, as prec.]

in'terèst¹, n. 1. Legal concern, title, right, (*in* property); pecuniary stake (*in* commercial undertaking etc.); VESTED ~s. 2. Advantage, profit, as *it is* (*to*) *your ~ to go, I do it in your ~, in the ~* (or ~s) *of truth*. 3. Thing in which one is concerned; principle in which a party is concerned; party having a common ~, as *the brewing ~*. 4. Selfish pursuit of one's own welfare; *make ~*, bring personal ~ to bear (*with* person). 5. Concern, curiosity, or quality exciting them (*take an ~, no ~, in; this has no ~ for me*). 6. Money paid for use of money lent or for forbearance of debt (*with* ~, transf., with increased force etc., as *returned the blow, his kindness, with ~*); *simple ~* (reckoned on principal only, & paid at fixed intervals); *compound ~* (reckoned on principal & on accumulations of ~). [ME *interesse*, f. AF, alt. app. after OF *interest*; f. L INTER(*esse* be), & *interest*, 3rd sing. pres. = it matters]

in'terèst², v.t. Cause (person) to take personal interest or share (*in*); (p.p.) having a private interest, not impartial or disinterested, as ~*ed parties, motives*; excite curiosity or attention of, whence ~ING² a. (‖ *in an~ing condition*, pregnant), ~ĭngLY² adv. Hence ~ĕdLY² adv. [alt. f. earlier *interess* vb after prec.]

interfēre', v.t. (Of things) come into collision or opposition (*with*): (of person) meddle (*with* or abs.), whence ~fēr'ING² a.; intervene, take part, (*in*); (Physics, of waves of light etc.) strike against each other; (of horse) knock one leg against another. Hence ~fēr'ENCE n. [f. obs. F *s'entreférir* strike each other (*entre-* INTER- + *férir* f. L *ferire* strike)]

interfērŏm'ēter, n. Instrument for measuring the length of light-waves by means of interference phenomena. [prec. + -METER]

intĕrf'luent (-ōō-), a. Flowing into each other. [f. L INTER(*fluere* flow), see -ENT]

interfūse' (-z), v.t. & i. Intersperse, mix, (thing *with*); blend (things) together; (of two things) blend with each other. So interfū'sion (-zhn) n. [f. L INTER(*fundere fus-* pour)]

in'terim, adv., n., & a. 1. adv. (arch.). Meanwhile. 2. n. Intervening time; *the I~* (Eccl.), truce pending a General Council between German Protestants & the Papacy in 16th c. 3. adj. Intervening; provisional, temporary; ~ *dividend* (paid between two annual etc. balances & not in pursuance of a published balance-sheet). [L (INTER + adv. suf. -*im*)]

intēr'ior, a. & n. 1. Situated within; inland, remote from coast or frontier; internal, domestic, opp. to *foreign*; existing in mind or soul, inward. 2. n. ~ part, inside; inland region; inside of building or room (also attrib., as ~ *decorator, decoration*), picture of this; inner nature, soul; (department dealing with) home affairs of a country, as *Minister of the I~*. Hence ~LY² adv. [L, compar. adj. f. INTER²]

interjā'cent, a. Lying between, intermediate. [f . L INTER(*jacēre* lie), see -ENT]

interjĕct', v.t. Throw in, interpose, (remark etc.) abruptly; remark parenthetically. [f. L INTER(*jicēre ject-* = *jacēre* throw)]

interjĕc'tion, n. Ejaculation, exclamation; natural ejaculation viewed as part of speech (e.g. *ah!, whew!*). Hence or cogn. ~AL (-shon-), interjĕc'tory, aa., ~alLY² adv. [ME, f. OF f. L *interjectionem* (prec., -ION)]

interlāce', v.t. & i. Bind together intricately, entangle; interweave (often fig.); mingle (two things, one *with* another); (intr.) cross each other intricately. Hence ~MENT (-sm-) n. [ME *entre-*, f. OF *entre-lacier* (*entre-* INTER- + *lacier* LACE²)]

interlārd', v.t. Mix (writing, speech, *with* foreign words etc.). [f. F *entrelarder* (*entre-* INTER- + *larder* LARD²)]

in'terleaf, n. (pl. -*ves*). Extra leaf (usu. blank) between leaves of book. [INTER-]

interleave', v.t. Insert (usu. blank) leaves between leaves of (book), (also fig.). [f. as prec.]

interline', v.t. Insert words between lines of (document etc.); insert (words) thus. So interlinĕa'tion n. [ME, f. med. L INTER(*lineare* f. *linea* LINE³)]

interlin'ear, a. Written, printed, between the lines. [ME, f. med. L INTER(*linearis* LINEAR)]

interlŏck', v.i. & t. (Intr.) engage with each other by overlapping etc.; (trans., usu. pass.) lock, clasp, within each other; (Railways) connect (levers for signals etc.) by bolts etc. to ensure uniformity of movement. [INTER-]

interlŏc'ū|tor, n. One who takes part in dialogue or conversation; compère of nigger minstrel troupe; *my ~tor.* the person in conversation with me. Hence or cogn. **interlocū′**tion, ~tress¹, ~trix, nn., ~tory a., (also) pronounced during course of a legal action (*an ~tory decree*). [f. L INTER(*loqui locut-* talk), see -OR]

in′terlōper, n. Intruder, one who (esp. for profit) thrusts himself into others' affairs; (hist.) unauthorized trader. So **interlōpe′** v.i. [INTER- +*loper* f. *lope* dial. form of LEAP]

in′terlude (-lōōd), n. Pause between acts of play; what fills this up; (Mus.) instrumental piece played between verses of psalm or hymn etc.; intervening time or space of different character; event, amusing incident, etc., interposed; (hist.) dramatic or mimic representation between acts of mystery-plays or moralities. [f. med. L INTER(*ludium* f. *ludus* play)]

intermă′rriage (-rĭj), n. Marriage between members of different families, castes, tribes, etc., or (loosely) between near relations. [INTER-]

intermă′rrў, v.i. (Of tribes, nations, families, etc.) become connected by marriage (*with* other tribes etc.). [INTER-]

interměd′dle, v.i. Concern oneself (*with, in,* esp. what is not one's business). [ME, f. AF *entremedler* (*entre-* INTER- +*medler* MEDDLE)]

interměd′iarў, a. & n. **1.** Acting between parties, mediatory; intermediate. **2.** n. ~ person, thing, esp. mediator. [f. INTER-MEDIUM + -ARY¹, or f. F *intermédiare*]

interměd′iate¹, a. & n. Coming *between* two things, as regards time, place, or order; (n.) ~ thing. Hence ~LY² (-tl-) adv. [f. med. L *intermediatus* (as INTER-MEDIUM, see -ATE²)]

interměd′i|āte², v.i. Act between others, mediate, (*between*). Hence ~A′TION, ~ā-tor, nn. [f. prec., after MEDIATE]

interměd′ium, n. (pl. *-ia, -iums*). Intermediate thing, medium, esp. one serving to transmit energy through space. [LL, neut. of L adj. INTER(*medius* middle)]

intĕrm′ent, n. Burial. [ME; INTER¹ + -MENT]

intermě′zzo (-dzō), n. (pl. *-zi, -zos*).. Short light dramatic or other performance between acts of drama or opera, short movement connecting main divisions of large musical work. [It., pop. form of *intermedio* (as INTERMEDIATE¹)]

intermīgrā′tion, n. Reciprocal migration. [INTER-]

intĕrm′inab|le, a. Endless; tediously long. Hence ~leness n., ~LY² adv. [ME, f. LL IN²(*terminabilis* f. *terminare* TERMIN-ATE, see -BLE)]

intermingle (-mĭng′gl), v.t. & i. Mix together (two things, one *with* another); (intr.) mingle (*with*). [INTER-]

intermi′ssion (-shn), n. Pause, cessation, esp. *without* ~; (musical selection during)

interval in theatre etc. [f. F, or L *inter-missio* (as foll., see -ION)]

intermit′, v.t. & i. (-tt-). Suspend, discontinue; stop for a time (esp. of fever, pain, etc., or of pulse). Hence or cogn. ~t′ence n., ~t′ent a., ~t′entLY² adv. [f. L INTER(*mittere miss-* send)]

intermix′, v.t. & i. Mix together. So ~tURE n. [first in p.p., see MIX]

intĕrn′¹, v.t. Oblige to reside within limits of country etc. Hence ~EE′ n., ~MENT n. (*~ment camp,* for prisoners of war & aliens). [f. F *interner* f. L *internus* internal (*in* +suf. *-ternus*)]

•in′tĕrn², n. Advanced student or recent graduate residing in hospital & acting as assistant physician or surgeon. [after F *interne*]

intĕrn′al, a. & n. **1.** Of, situated in, the inside of a thing; of the inner nature of a thing, intrinsic; ~ *evidence*, derived from what is contained in the thing itself (cf. EXTERNAL); ~*combustion engine* (in which motive power is derived from explosion of mixture of gas, or vaporized oil or petrol, & air in the cylinder); of the domestic affairs of a country; *•~* (inland) *revenue;* of the mind or soul, inward, subjective. **2.** n. pl. Intrinsic qualities. Hence ~ITY (-ăl⁴) n., ~LY² adv. [f. late med. L *internalis* (as INTERN¹, see -AL)]

interna′tional (-shon-), a. & n. **1.** Existing, carried on, between different nations; of the I~ Working Men's Associations (for promoting joint political action of working classes in all countries). **2.** n. One who takes part in ~ (usu. athletic) contests; ~ *contest; first, second, third,* I~, three Associations as above (1st, Marxist, 1862–73; 2nd, French socialist, 1889 —; 3rd, Russian communist, abbr. *Comintern,* 1919–43); member of any of these. Hence ~ITY (-shonăl⁴) n., ~LY² adv. [INTER-]

internationale′ (-shonahl), n. *The ~,* (orig. French) communist song sung at demonstrations; = *International Association* (see prec.). [F]

interna′tional|ist (-shon-), n. One who advocates community of interests between nations, esp. supporter of Association named in prec., so ~ISM n.; one versed in international law. [-IST]

interna′tionaliz|e (-shon-), -is|e (-īz), v.t. Make international, esp. bring (territory etc.) under combined protection etc. of different nations. Hence~A′TION n. [-IZE]

internē′cine, a. Mutually destructive; (orig.) deadly, as~ *war.* [f. L *internecinus* f. INTER(*necare* kill) destroy, see -INE¹]

internŭn′cial (-shal), a. (Of nerves) communicating between different parts of the system. [f. foll. + -AL]

internŭn′cio (-shĭō), n. Ambassador of Pope when or where no nuncio is employed; (hist.) minister representing (esp.

Austrian) government at Ottoman Porte. [**f**. It. *internunzio* **f**. L INTER(*nuntius* messenger)]

interŏs′cŭl|āte, v.i. Intermingle with each other; form connecting link. Hence ∼A′TION n. [INTER-]

interpāge′, v.t. Print, insert, on intermediate pages. [INTER-]

intĕrp′ĕll|āte, v.t. (In foreign, esp. French, Chamber) interrupt order of day by demanding explanation from (Minister concerned). So ∼A′TION, ∼āt′OR, nn. [f. L INTER(*pellare* var. of *pellere* drive), see -ATE³]

interpĕn′ĕtr|āte, v.t. & i. Penetrate thoroughly, pervade; penetrate reciprocally; (intr., of two) penetrate each other. So ∼A′TION n., ∼ātIVE a. [INTER-]

in′terplay, n. Reciprocal play; operation of two things on each other. [INTER-]

interplead′, v.i. Litigate with each other in order to settle a point in which a third party is concerned. [INTER-]

intĕrp′ol|āte, v.t. Make insertions in (book etc.), esp. so as to give false impressions as to date etc.; insert (intermediate term) in series. So ∼A′TION, ∼ātOR, nn. [f. L INTER(*polare* cogn. w. *polire* POLISH¹) furbish up, -ATE³]

interpōs|e′ (-z), v.t. & i. Insert, make intervene, (*between*); put forth, introduce, (veto, objection, authority, etc.) by way of interference; intervene (*between* disputants etc.); say (quoted words) as an interruption; **make an interruption**. Hence ∼′AL (-z-) n. [f. F INTER(*poser*, see COMPOSE)]

intĕrposi′tion (-z-), n. Interposing; thing interposed; interference. [ME, f. OF, f. L *interpositionem* f.(*ponere posit-*place)]

intĕrp′rĕt, v.t. & i. Expound the meaning of (abstruse words, writings, dreams, etc.); make out the meaning of; bring out the meaning of, render, by artistic representation or performance; explain, understand, in specified manner, as *this we ∼ as a threat*; act as interpreter. Hence or cogn. ∼ABLE, ∼ATIVE (-ātIv), aa., ∼A′TION n. [ME, f. OF *interpreter* or L *interpretari* f. *interpres-pretis* explainer]

intĕrp′rĕt|er, n. One who interprets; one whose office it is to translate orally in their presence the words of persons speaking different languages. Hence ∼ership, ∼ress¹, nn. [ME, f. OF *interpreteur* f. LL *interpretatorem* (as prec., see -OR)]

interrĕg′num, n. (pl. *-na, -nums*). Period during which State has no normal ruler, esp. between end of king's reign & accession of successor; interval, pause. [L INTER(*regnum* REIGN)]

interrĕlā′tion, n. Mutual relation. [INTER-]

interrĕlā′tionship (-shon-), n. Mutual relationship. [INTER-]

intĕ′rrogāt|e, v.t. Ask questions of (per-

son etc.), esp. closely or formally. So ∼OR n. [f. L INTER(*rogare* ask), see -ATE³]

intĕrrogā′tion, n. Asking questions; question; *point, mark, note, of* (used to express) ∼ (?), in Greek (;). [f. F, or L *interrogatio* (as prec., see -ATION)]

interrŏg′ative, a. & n. 1. Of, having the form or force of, a question; of inquiry, as *an ∼ tone*; (Gram., of words) used in asking question, as ∼ *pronouns* (*who?*, *which?*, etc.). 2. n. ∼ word, esp. pronoun. Hence ∼LY² (-vl-) adv. [f. LL *interrogativus* (as prec., see -IVE)]

interrŏg′atory, a. & n. 1. Of inquiry, as *an ∼ tone*. 2. n. Question, set of questions, esp. (Law) one formally put to accused person etc. [f. LL *interrogatorius* (as prec., see -ORY)]

inter|rŭpt′, v.t. Break in upon (action, process, speech, person speaking, etc., or abs.); obstruct (view etc.); break the continuity of. Hence or cogn. ∼rŭp′tĕdLY² adv., ∼rŭp′tER¹, ∼rŭp′tION, nn., ∼rŭp′tORY a. [ME, f. L INTER(*rumpere rupt-* break)]

intersĕct′, v.t. & i. Divide (thing) by passing or lying across it; (of lines etc.) cross, cut, each other. [f. L INTER-(*secare sect-* cut)]

intersĕc′tion, n. Intersecting; point, line, common to intersecting lines, planes; place where two roads intersect. Hence ∼AL (-shon-) a. [f. L *intersectio* (as prec., see -ION)]

interspĕrse′, v.t. Scatter, place here & there (*between, among*); diversify (thing) *with* (others so scattered). So **interspĕr′sion** (-shn) n. [f. L INTER(*spergere spers-* = *spargere* scatter)]

*in′terstāte, a. Existing, carried on, between States. [INTER-]

intĕr′stice (or In′ter-), n. Intervening space; chink, crevice. [f. LL *interstitium* f. INTER(*sistere stit-* stand)]

interstĭ′tial (-shl), a. Of, forming, occupying, interstice(s). [as prec. + -AL]

intertwine′, v.t. & i. Entwine (things, one *with* another); become entwined. Hence ∼MENT (-nm-) n. [INTER-]

in′terval, n. Intervening time or space; pause; break, gap, esp. in theatre etc.; *at ∼s*, here & there, now & then; (Mus.) difference of pitch between two sounds, in melody or harmony; distance between persons or things in respect of qualities. Hence **intervăll′IC** a. [ME, f. OF *-valle* & L INTER(*vallum* rampart) space between ramparts, interval]

intervēn|e′, v.i. Come in as something extraneous; occur in the meantime; (of person or thing) come between, interfere, so as to prevent or modify result etc. (*between* persons, *in* affair); (Law) interpose in lawsuit to which one was not an original party (|| esp. of Queen's Proctor in divorce cases), whence ∼′ER¹ n.; lie, be situated, *between*. So ∼′īENT a., intervĕn′tion n. [f. L INTER(*venire vent-* come)]

in'terview (-vū); n., & v.t. **1.** Meeting of persons face to face, esp. for purpose of conference; oral examination of candidate; meeting between person employed by newspaper & someone from whom he seeks to get statements for publication. **2.** v.t. Have an ∼ with (person), esp. with a view to publication of his statements. Hence ∼ER¹ (-vūer) n. [(vb f. n.) f. F *entrevue* f. *s'entrevoir* (*entre*- INTER- +*voir* f. L *vidēre* see)]

intervŏlve', v.t. Wind, roll up, (things) within each other. [f. INTER- +L *volvere* roll]

interweave', v.t. Weave together, interlace, (things, one *with* another); blend (things) intimately. [INTER-]

interwind', v.t. & i. Wind together. [INTER-]

intĕs'tate, a. & n. **1.** (Of person) not having made a will, as *he died* ∼. **2.** n. ∼ person. Hence **intĕs'tACY** n. [f. L IN²(*testatus* p.p. of *testari* make will f. *testis* witness)]

intĕs'tin|e¹, n. (Usu. pl.) lower part of alimentary canal from pyloric end of stomach to anus; *small, large,* ∼*e,* parts of this. So ∼AL (*or* -in²) a. [f. L neut. adj. as foll.]

intĕs'tine², a. (Of wars etc.) internal, domestic, civil; ∼ *motion* (entirely within a body). [f. L *intestīnus* internal (*intus* within)]

in'timate¹, a. & n. **1.** Close in acquaintance, familiar, as ∼ *friend*(*ship*); ∼ (close) *connexion;* ∼ *knowledge* (resulting from familiarity); essential, intrinsic; (of diary) recording emotions etc. **2.** n. ∼ friend. Hence **in'timACY** n., (also, euphem.) illicit sexual relations, ∼LY² (-tl-) adv. [foll., -ATE²]

in'tim|āte², v.t. Make known, state, announce, (fact, wish, *that*); imply, hint. So ∼A'TION n. [f. LL *intimare* (*intimus* inmost), -ATE³]

intim'id|āte, v.t. Inspire with fear, cow, esp. in order to influence conduct. Hence ∼A'TION, ∼ātOR, nn. [f. med. L IN¹(*timidare* f. *timidus* TIMID), see -ATE³]

intim'itў, n. Inwardness; privacy. [f. F *intimité* (as INTIMATE¹, -ITY)]

intinc'tion, n. Dipping of the Eucharistic bread in the wine, to enable the communicant to receive both kinds. [f. LL *intinctio* f. IN¹(*tingere tinct*- TINGE)]

intit'ūle, v.t. Entitle (Act of Parliament, usu. p.p.). [f. OF *intituler* f. LL IN¹(*titulare* f. *titulus* TITLE)]

in'to (-tŏŏ), prep. **1.** Expr. motion or direction to a point within a thing, lit. & fig., as *come ∼ the garden, throw it ∼ the fire, look ∼ the box, the matter, inquire ∼ it, get ∼ trouble, come ∼* (acquire) *property, watching far on ∼ the night.* **2.** Expr. change, condition, result, as *turn stones ∼ gold, collect them ∼ heaps, divide them ∼*

three classes, flogged ∼ submission. [OE; IN +TO]

in'-toed (-ōd), a. Having the toes turned inwards. [IN adv. +TOE +-ED²]

intŏl'erab|le, a. That cannot be endured. Hence ∼leNESS n., ∼LY² adv. [ME, f. L IN²(*tolerabilis* TOLERABLE)]

intŏl'er|ant, a. Not tolerant (*of,* esp. religious opinions differing from one's own). Hence or cogn. ∼ANCE n., ∼antLY² adv. [f. L IN²(*tolerans* TOLERANT)]

in'tonāte, v.t. = INTONE. [-ATE³]

intonā'tion, n. Reciting in singing voice; (Church Mus.) opening phrase of plainsong melody; utterance, production, of musical tones; modulation of voice, accent. [as foll., see -ATION]

intōne', v.t. Recite (psalm, prayer, etc., or abs.) in singing voice; utter with particular tone. [f. OF *entoner* & med. L IN¹(*tonare* f. *tonus* TONE)]

intŏx'icant, a. & n. Intoxicating (liquor). [as foll., see -ANT]

intŏx'ic|āte, v.t. Make drunk; excite, exhilarate, beyond self-control (∼*ated with, by*). Hence ∼ātING²a., ∼A'TION n. [f. med. L IN¹(*toxicare* poison f. L f. Gk *toxikon*), see -ATE³]

intra- in comb. = L *intra* on the inside, within, as: ∼*crān'ial,* within the skull; ∼*mŭr'al,* existing, done, within walls; ∼*na'tional,* (not inter)national; ∼*vēn'ous,* in(to) a vein or veins.

intrāc't|able, a. Not docile, refractory; (of things) not easily dealt with. Hence ∼aBIL'ITY, ∼ableNESS, nn., ∼abLY² adv. [f. F, or L IN²(*tractabilis* TRACTABLE)]

intrād'ōs, n. (archit.). Lower or interior curve of arch (cf. EXTRADOS). [F (INTRA- +*dos* back)]

intran'sig|ent (-z-), a. & n. **1.** Uncompromising in politics. **2.** n. An irreconcilable (in politics). So ∼ENCE n. [f. F *intransigeant* f. Sp. *los intransigentes* extreme republicans f. IN-² +L TRANS- (*igere*=*agere* act) come to an understanding, see -ENT]

intran'sitive (-ahns-), a. & n. (Verb) that does not take a direct object (cf. TRANSITIVE). Hence ∼LY² adv. [f. LL IN²(*transitivus* TRANSITIVE)]

in'trant, n. One who enters a college, association, etc. [f. L *intrare* enter, see -ANT]

intrĕp'id, a. Fearless, brave. Hence **intrĕpid'ITY** n., ∼LY² adv. [f. L IN²(*trepidus* alarmed)]

in'tric|ate, a. Perplexingly entangled; involved; obscure. Hence ∼ACY n., ∼ateLY² adv. [f. L IN¹(*tricare* f. *tricae* tricks), see -ATE²]

in'trĭg(u)ant (-gant; *or* ăṅtrēgahṅ') n. (fem., ∼*e,* pr. ăṅtrēgahṅt'). Intriguer. [F (-*guant*), part. as foll.]

intrigue'¹ (-ēg), v.i. & t. Carry on underhand plot; employ secret influence (*with*);

have a liaison (*with*); (as gallicism, v.t.) rouse the interest or curiosity of. [f. F *intriguer* f. It. *intrigare* (as INTRICATE)]

intrigue'[2] (-ēg), n. Underhand plotting or plot; secret amour, liaison. [F, f. It. *intrigo* f. *intrigare* (as INTRICATE)]

intrin's|ic, a. Belonging naturally, inherent, essential, esp. ~*ic value* (cf. EXTRINSIC). Hence ~ICALLY adv. [f. F *intrinsèque* f. LL *intrinsecus* (adj. f. L adv.); cf. EXTRINSIC]

intro- in comb. = L *intro* to the inside, as: ~*fle'xion*, inward bending; ~*gre'ssion*, going or coming in; ~*suscep'tion*, (Physiol., Biol.) = INTUSSUSCEPTION.

introduce', v.t. Bring in; place in, insert, bring into use (custom, idea, improvement, etc., *into* place, system, etc.); usher in, bring forward, (matter etc.); (of conjunctions etc.) open (sentence); make known, esp. in formal manner (person *to* another); bring (young lady) out, into society; draw attention of (person *to* subject etc.); bring (bill etc.) before Parliament. So **introduc'tory** a. [f. L INTRO(*ducere duct-* lead)]

introduc'tion, n. Introducing; preliminary matter prefixed to book (usu. longer & less personal than a PREFACE, which it freq. follows); (as title) introductory treatise; formal presentation of one person to another; *letter of* ~ (given by one person to another & introducing him to a third). [ME, f. OF, or L *introductio* (as prec., see -ION)]

intro'it, n. (eccl.). Psalm, antiphon, sung while priest approaches altar to celebrate Mass or Holy Communion. [ME, f. OF or f. L *introitus -ūs* f. INTRO(*ire it-* go)]

intromit', v.t. (arch.; -tt-). Let in, admit, (*into*); insert. So **intromi'ssion** (-shn) n., esp., in Sc. Law, intermeddling with the effects of another, ~*t*'ENT a. [f. L INTRO(*mittere miss-* send)]

intro|spect', v.t. Examine one's own thoughts & feelings. Hence ~**spec'tion** n., examination or observation of one's own mental processes, ~**spec'tionist**, ~**spec'tiveness**, nn., ~-**spec'tive** a., ~**spec'tively**[2] adv. [f. L INTRO(*spicere spect-* look)]

intro|vert', v.t. Turn (mind, thought) inwards upon itself; (esp. Zool.) withdraw (organ etc.) within its own tube or base, as finger of glove, whence ~**vers'ible** a. Hence ~**ver'sion** (-shn) n., **in'trovert** n., person given to ~version (opp. EXTROVERT), ~**vers'ive**, ~**vert'ive**, aa. [17th c., f. INTRO- +L *vertere vers-* turn]

intrud|e' (-rōod), v.t. & i. Thrust, force, (thing *into*); force (thing *upon* person); come uninvited, thrust oneself in, (*into* place, company, etc., *upon* person, his privacy, etc.). Hence ~'ER[1] (-ōō-) n. (also, raiding aircraft). [f. L IN[1](*trudere trus-* thrust)]

intru'sion (-rōozhn), n. Intruding; forcing in; forcing oneself in (*into, upon*);

(Geol.) influx of rock in state of fusion between strata etc.; settlement of minister of Church of Scotland without consent of congregation (hist.), whence ~IST(2) n. So **intrus'ive** a., **intrus'ively**[2] adv., **trus'iveness** n., (-rōōs-). [ME, f. OF or f. med. L *intrusio* (as prec., see -ION)]

in'tub|āte, v.t. (med.). Insert tube into (larynx etc.) to keep it open. Hence ~A'TION n. [f. IN-[1] +L *tuba* tube +-ATE[3]]

in'tuit, v.t. & i. Know by intuition; receive knowledge by direct perception. [f. L IN[1](*tuēri tuit-* look)]

intui'tion, n. Immediate apprehension by the mind without reasoning; immediate apprehension by sense; immediate insight. Hence ~AL (-shon-) a. [f. F, or LL *intuitio* (as prec., see -ION)]

intui'tional|ism (-shon-), n. Doctrine that the perception of truth is by intuition. So ~IST n. [-ISM]

intui'tion|ism (-shon-), n. Doctrine that in perception external objects are known immediately by intuition; = prec. So ~IST n. [-ISM]

intu'itive, a. Of, possessing, perceived by, intuition. Hence ~LY[2] (-vl-) adv., ~NESS (-vn-) n. [f. med. L *intuitivus* (INTUIT, -IVE)]

intu'itiv|ism, n. Doctrine that ethical principles are matters of intuition. So ~IST n. [-ISM]

intumes'c|ent, a. Swelling up. So ~ENCE n. [f. L IN[1](*tumescere* incept. of *tumēre* swell), see -ENT]

in'tussuscep'tion, n. (Physiol.) taking in of foreign matter by living organism, & its conversion into organic tissue; taking in (*of* ideas etc.); withdrawal of one portion of intestine within another. [f. F, or L *intus* within +*susceptio* f. SUS(*cipere=capere* take) take up, see -ION]

inunc'tion, n. Smearing, rubbing, with oil. [ME, ·f. OF *en-* or L IN[1](*unctio* UNCTION)]

in'und|āte, v.t. Overflow, flood, (land etc. *with* water, also fig.). So ~A'TION n. [f. L IN[1](*undare* flow f. *unda* wave), see -ATE[3]]

inurbāne', a. Not urbane, discourteous. Hence **inurbān'ity** n. [f. L IN[2](*urbanus* URBANE)]

inūre', **en-**, v.t. & i. Accustom, habituate, (person etc. *to* thing, *to* do), whence ~MENT (-ūrm-) n.; (intr., chiefly Law; often *en-*) come into operation, take effect. [IN-[1] +obs. *ure* work (cf. MANURE), f. OF *uevre* f. L *opera*]

inūrn', v.t. Put (ashes of cremated body) in an urn. [IN-[1]]

inūt'ile, a. Useless. So **inūtil'ity** n. [F, f. L IN[2](*utilis* useful)]

invād|e', v.t. Make hostile inroad into (country etc.); swarm into; (fig. of sounds, diseases, feelings, etc.) assail; encroach upon (rights etc.). Hence ~'ER[1] n. [f. L IN[1](*vadere vas-* go)]

invā'gin|āte, v.t. Put in a sheath; introvert (tubular sheath). Hence ~A'TION n. [f. IN-[1] +L *vagina* sheath +-ATE[3]]

in'valid[1] (-ĕd), a. & n. (Person) enfeebled or disabled by illness or injury. Hence ~HOOD, ~ISM(3), nn., (-ĕd-). [f. L IN[2](*validus* VALID), pronunc. after F *invalide*]

invalid'[2] (-ēd ; *also* In[2]), v.t. & i. Lay up, disable, (person) by illness (usu. pass.); treat as an invalid; remove from active service, send *home* etc., as an invalid; (intr.) become an invalid, go on the sick-list. [f. prec.]

invăl'id[3], a. Not valid, esp. having no legal force. Hence ~LY[2] adv. [as IN-VALID[1]]

invăl'id|āte, v.t. Make (esp. argument etc.) INVALID[3]. Hence ~A'TION n. [prec. + -ATE[3]]

invalid'ity, n. Want of validity; bodily infirmity. [INVALID[3],[1] + -ITY]

invăl'ūable, a. Above price, priceless. [IN-[2]]

in'vär, n. An iron-nickel alloy with negligible coefficient of expansion, used in manufacture of clocks and scientific instruments. [abbr. of foll.; P]

invār'i|able, a. Unchangeable; always the same; (Math.) constant, fixed. Hence ~ABIL'ITY, ~ableNESS, nn., ~abLY[2] adv. [f. F, or LL IN[2](*variabilis* VARIABLE)]

invā'sion (-zhn), n. Invading; encroachment. So **invās'IVE** a. [f. F, or LL *invasio* (as INVADE, see -ION)]

invĕc'tive, n. Violent attack in words; abusive oratory. [ME, f. OF, & LL *invectivus* adj., *-iva* n. (as foll., see -IVE)]

inveigh' (-vā), v.i. Speak violently, rail loudly, *against*. [f. L IN[1](*vehi* pass. of *vehere*-carry) go into, assail]

invei'gle (-vĕ-, -vā-), v.t. Entice, seduce, (*into* place, conduct, etc., *into* do*ing*). Hence ~MENT·(-vĕgelm-, -vā-) n. [c. 1500 *en-*, *in-* f. F *aveugler* f. *aveugle* blind]

in vĕn'it, invĕnēr'unt (abbr. *inv.*), v. sing. & pl. 3rd pers. (So-&-so) designed this work (used with artist's signature). [L, perf. of *invenio*, see foll.]

invĕnt', v.t. Devise, originate, (new method, instrument, etc.); fabricate (false story etc.). Hence or cogn. **invĕn'tIVE** a., **invĕn'tiveLY**[2] adv., **invĕn'tiveNESS, invĕn'tOR**(esp. in Law, patentee of INVENTION), **invĕn'trESS**[1], nn. [f. L IN[1](*venire vent-* come) find, contrive]

invĕn'tion, n. Inventing; thing invented, contrivance, (Law) any new manufacture the subject of letters patent; fictitious story; inventiveness; *I~ of the Cross*, (festival, May 3, commemorating) finding of the Cross by Helena mother of Constantine, A.D. 326. [ME, f. OF, f. L *inventionem* (as prec., see -ION)]

in'ventory, n., & v.t. **1.** Detailed list (of goods, furniture, etc.); stock of goods in this; *trader's stock. **2.** v.t. Enter goods etc.) in ~, make ~ of. [f. med. L *inventorium* f. LL *-arium* (whence obs. *-ary*); as INVENT, see -ORY]

inverā'cĭty, n. Untruthfulness. [IN-[2]]

Invernĕss' (I-), n. Town in Scotland; ~

cloak, coat, or *i~* as n., man's sleeveless cloak with removable cape.

invẽrse' (*or* In[2]), a. & n. **1.** Inverted in position, order, or relations; ~ *ratio, proportion* (between two quantities one of which increases in proportion as the other decreases). **2.** n. Inverted state, thing that is the direct opposite (*of* another). Hence **invẽrse'LY**[2] (-sl-) adv. [f. L as INVERT]

invẽr'sion (-shn), n. Turning upside down; reversal of normal position, order, or relation, esp. (Gram.) of order of words; reversal of a ratio; (Mus.) process or result of inverting (see foll.). So **invẽrs'IVE** a. [f. L *inversio* (as foll., see -ION)]

invẽrt'[1], v.t. Turn upside down (~*ed commas*, those above the line before & after quotations, the first single or double comma being ~ed, as *what is a 'German peace'* or *"German peace"?*); reverse position, order, or relation, of; (Mus.) change relative position of notes of (chord, interval) by placing lowest note higher. [f. L IN[1](*vertere vers-* turn)]

in'vẽrt[2], n. Inverted arch, as at bottom of sewer; (Psych.) person whose sex instincts are inverted; ~ *sugar*, mixture of dextrose & laevulose. [f. prec.]

invẽrt'ĕbrate, a. & n. **1.** Not having backbone or spinal column; (fig.) wanting in firmness. **2.** n. ~animal or (fig.) person. [f. IN-[2]+L *vertebra* joint of spine+-ATE[2]]

invĕst', v.t. & i. **1.** Clothe (person etc. *in, with*); cover as garment; clothe, endue, (person etc. *with* qualities, insignia of office, rank, etc.). **2.** Lay siege to. **3.** Employ (money *in* stocks etc.); (intr.) ~ *in*, put money into (stocks), lay out money on, as ~ *in a car*. Hence **invẽs'tor** n. [f. F *investir* or L IN[1](*vestire* clothe); sense 3 f. It. *investire*]

invĕs'tig|āte, v.t. Examine, inquire into. Hence or cogn. ~A'TION, ~ātor, nn., ~ātive, ~ātory, aa. [f. L IN[1](*vestigare* track), see -ATE[3]]

invĕs'titure, n. Formal investing of person(*with* office); enduing (*with* attributes). [f. med. L *investitura* (as INVEST, see -URE)]

invĕst'ment, n. Investing of money; money invested; property in which money is invested; investiture; clothing; (Mil.) act of besieging, blockade. [-MENT]

invĕt'er|ate, a. Long-established; (of disease, habit, prejudice, etc.) deep-rooted, obstinate. Hence ~ACY n., ~ateLY[2] (-tl-) adv. [f. L IN[1](*veterare* make old f. *vetus -eris* old), see -ATE[2]]

invid'ious, a. (Of conduct etc.) giving offence, esp. by real or seeming injustice etc.; (of thing) likely to excite ill feeling against the possessor. Hence ~LY[2] adv., ~NESS n. [f. L *invidiosus* (*invidia* ENVY, see -OUS)]

invi'gil|āte, v.i. ‖ Watch over students at examination. Hence ~A'TION, ~ātor, nn. [f. L IN[1](*vigilare* watch), -ATE[3]]

invig'or|āte, v.t. Make vigorous; animate. Hence ~**átive** a., ~**átor** n. [f. IN-[1]+L *vigor* VIGOUR+-ATE[3]]

invin'c|ible, a. Unconquerable (lit. & fig.). Hence ~IBIL'ITY n., ~IBLY[2] adv. [ME, f. OF, f. L IN[2](*vincibilis* f. *vincere* conquer, -BLE)]

invi'ol|able, a. Not to be violated; (of laws, persons, places, etc.) to be kept sacred from infraction, profanation, etc. Hence ~ABIL'ITY n., ~ABLY[2] adv. [f. F, or L IN[2](*violabilis*, as foll., see -BLE)]

invi'olate, a. (Of laws, places, etc.) not violated; unbroken; unprofaned. Hence **invi'olACY,**~NESS, nn.,~LY[2] adv. [ME, f. L IN[2](*violatus* p.p. as VIOLATE)]

invis'ib|le (-z-), a. & n. That cannot be seen; not to be seen at particular time, as *when I called she was* ~*le*; too small to be seen; ~*le exports,* shipping services, insurance, & similar items that account for the apparent excess of a. country's imports over exports; (n.) *the* ~*le*, the unseen world, God. Hence or cogn. **invisibil'ity,** ~**leness,** nn., ~LY[2] adv., (-z-). [ME, f. OF, f. L IN[2](*visibilis* VISIBLE)]

invit|e', v.t., & n. **1.** Request courteously to come (*to* dinner, *to* one's house, *in*, etc.); request courteously (*to* do what is presumably agreeable); solicit courteously (suggestions, opinion, confidences); bring on, tend to bring on, (thing) unintentionally; (of thing) present inducements, attract, whence ~'**ingLY**[2] adv., ~'**ingNESS** n. **2.** n. (colloq. or vulg.). Invitation. So **invit'TION** n., ~'**atORY** a. [f. F *inviter* or L *invitare*]

invocā'tion, n. Invoking, calling upon God etc. in prayer; *the* ~, (esp.) the words ' In the name of the Father ' etc. as used by preacher before sermon (cf. ASCRIPTION); appeal to Muse for inspiration or assistance in poem. So **invŏc'atORY** (*or* In'vokā-) a. [ME, f. OF, f. L *invocationem* (as INVOKE, see -ATION)]

in'voice, n., & v.t. **1.** List of goods shipped or sent, with prices & charges. **2.** v.t. Make an~ of (goods). [app. orig. *invoyes* pl. of *invoy* as ENVOY[1]; -*ce* as in TRUCE]

invōke', v.t. Call on (God etc.) in prayer or as witness; appeal to (person's authority etc.); summon (spirit) by charms; ask earnestly for (vengeance, help, etc.). [f. F *invoquer* f. L IN[1](*vocare* call)]

in'volucre (-lōōker), n. Covering, envelope, (esp. Anat.); (Bot.) whorl of bracts surrounding inflorescence. [f. F, or L *involucrum* (as INVOLVE)]

invŏl'untar|ȳ, a. Done without exercise of the will, unintentional. Hence ~**iLY**[2] adv., ~**iNESS** n. [f. LL IN[2](*voluntarius* VOLUNTARY)]

in'volute (-lōōt), a. & n. **1.** Involved, intricate; curled spirally; (Bot.) rolled inwards at edges. **2.** n. (geom.). Locus of point in a straight line that rolls without sliding on a curve in the plane of that curve (cf. EVOLUTE). [as INVOLVE]

involu'tion (-lōō-), n. Involving; entanglement; intricacy; curling inwards; part so curled; (Math.) raising of quantity to any power. [f. L *involutio* (as foll., see -ION)]

involve', v.t. Wrap (thing *in* another); wind spirally; entangle (person, thing, *in* difficulties, mystery, etc.); implicate (person *in* charge, crime); include (*in*); imply, entail; (p.p.) complicated in thought or form (*an* ~*d sentence*). [ME, f. L IN[1](*volvere volut-* roll)]

involve'ment (-vm-), n. Involving; financial embarrassment; complicated affair. [-MENT]

invŭl'ner|able, a. That cannot be wounded or hurt (esp. fig.). Hence ~ABIL'ITY n., ~ABLY[2] adv. [f. L IN[2](*vulnerabilis* VULNERABLE)]

in'ward, a. & n. **1.** Situated within; mental, spiritual; directed towards the inside. **2.** n. pl. Entrails (freq. colloq. *innards*). [OE *innanweard* (*innan* in adv., see -WARD)]

in'wardlȳ, adv. On the inside; (of speaking) not aloud; in mind or spirit. [-LY[2]]

in'wardness, n. Inner nature, essence; quality of being inward; spirituality. [-NESS]

in'ward(s) (-z), adv. (Of motion or position) towards the inside; within mind or soul. [prec.]

inweave', èn-, v.t. Weave in (thing *with* another, lit. & fig.). [IN-[1]]

inwrought (ïnrawt', *before noun* In[1]), a. (Of fabric) decorated (*with* pattern); (of pattern) wrought (*in*, *on*, fabric); (fig.) intimately blended (*with*). [IN+*wrought* p.p. of WORK]

inya'la (-ah-), n. S. Afr. antelope. [native]

i'od|ine (-ēn), n. Non-metallic element resembling chlorine & bromine in chemical properties, used in medicine & photography. Hence **iŏd'ic** a., ~**IDE** n., compound of ~ine with another element or radical, ~**ISM**(5) n., ~**IZE**(5) v.t. [f. F *iode* f. Gk *iōdēs* violet-like (*ion* violet, see -OID) from colour of its vapour, +-INE[5]]

iŏ'dofŏrm (*or* i'o-), n. Compound of iodine chemically analogous to chloroform, a pale yellow solid with antiseptic properties. [f. prec.+-o-, after CHLOROFORM]

i'olite, n. Silicate of aluminium, iron, & magnesium, of blue or violet colour. [f. Gk *ion* violet, see -LITE]

i'on, n. One of the electrically charged particles into which the atoms or molecules of certain chemicals (esp. salts, acids, & bases) are dissociated by solution in water, and which make such a solution a conductor of electricity; a similarly charged molecule of gas occurring e.g. in air. Hence ~**IZE** v.t., convert into ~, ~**izA'TION** n. [Gk *ion* neut. part. of *eimi* go]

-ion, suf., mainly thr. F -*ion* (also direct) f. L -*ionem* (nom. -*io*) forming nouns of condition or action, rarely f. adjj. & f. (*communio*), occas. f. vb stems (*legio*), but chiefly f. p.p. stems in *t, s, x*, producing the compd suff. -TION, -SION (-*xioņ*), -ITION, -ATION.

Iŏn'ian (ī-), a. & n. 1. Of Ionia; (Mus.) ~ *mode*: ancient Greek MODE; eleventh of eccl. modes, with C as final & G as dominant, corresp. to modern major key of C. 2. n. Member of part of the Hellenic race which occupied Attica, western Asia Minor, ~ Islands, etc. [f. L f. Gk *Iōnios* +-AN]

Iŏn'ic (ī-), a. Of Ionia, as ~ *dialect*, that of which Attic was a development; ~ ORDER (characterized by two lateral volutes of the capital); (Pros.) *i*~ *ā majŏr'ē*, metrical foot — — ∪ ∪, *i*~ *ā minŏr'ē*, ∪ ∪ — —. [f. L f. Gk *Iōnikos*]

Iŏn'ium, n. Radio-active element obtained from uranium. [f. ION +-IUM]

Iŏn'osphēre, n. = HEAVISIDE LAYER. [f. ION, -O-, SPHERE]

-ior[1], suf., later spelling of -IOUR, as in *warrior*.

-ior[2], suf. = L -*ior* of comparatives, as in *senior, ulterior*. See also -OR.

Iŏt'a, n. Greek letter (*I, ι,* = I); atom, jot, (after *Matt.* v. 18). [Gk *iōta*]

Iŏt'acism, n. Excessive use of iota; pronunciation of other Greek vowels like iota (ē), cf. ITACISM. [f. LL f. Gk *iōtakismos*]

I O U (ī ō ū'), n. Signed document bearing these letters followed by specified sum, constituting formal acknowledgement of debt. [= I owe you]

-iour, suf. =-*i*- representing some formative or stem element +-*our* -OR, as *saviour*, ME & AF *sauveor* f. LL *salvatorem*.

-ious, suf. repr. L -*iosus*, F -*ieux*, = -*i*- (part of another suf.) +-OUS, w. sense ' characterized by, full of '. L has -*iosus* (1) in adjj. f. derivative nn. in -*ia, -ies, -ius, -ium, (invidiosus, perniciosus, odiosus*, & by false anal. *curiosus* f. *cura*), (2) in adjj. f. nn. in -*ion*- (nom. -*io*), as *ambitiosus, captiosus, religiosus*. E tends to use -*ious* for any noun in -*ion* (*rebellious, cautious, contradictious*). E also forms adjj. in -*ious* by adding -OUS to stem of L adjj. in -*ius* (*various*); see also -ITIOUS & -OUS.

Ipĕcăcūăn'ha (-na), n. Root of a S.-Amer. shrub, used as emetic & purgative. [Port., f. native *ipekaaguene*]

Ip'sĕ dix'ĭt, n. Dogmatic statement resting on bare authority. [L, = he himself (the master) said it]

Ipsīss'ĭma vĕrb'a, n. pl. The precise words [L]

Ip'sŏ făc'tŏ, adv. By that very fact. [L]

ir-[1,2] (I-r), preff. = IN-[1,2] before *r*.

irā'dè (-ah-), n. (hist.). Written decree of Sultan of Turkey. [Turk., f. Arab. *iradah* will]

Irak', Iraq' (Irahk'). n. Arab kingdom including Mesopotamia, formerly administered by British Empire as mandatary. So Ira'ki, -qi, (-ahki) a.

Irān'ian (īr-), a. & n. 1. Persian ; (of languages) of the Asiatic family comprising Zend, Old Persian, & their modern descendants. 2. n. Member of ~ race. [Pers. *iran* Persia, -IAN]

irăs'c|ible (*or* īr-), a. Irritable, hot-tempered. Hence ~iBIL'ITY n. [f. F, or LL *irascibilis* (*irasci* grow angry, see -BLE)]

irāte', a. Angry. [f. L *iratus* p.p. as prec.]

īre, n. (poet.). Anger. [f. OF, f L *ira*] ~'fuLLY[2] adv., (īrf-). [ME, f. OF, f L *ira*]

īrĕn'ic(al), aa. Aiming or aimed at peace. [f. Gk *eirēnikos* (*eirēnē* peace) +-AL]

irenicon. See EIRENICON.

īridā'ceous (-shus), a. Of the iris kind. [-ACEOUS]

īridĕs'c|ent, a. Showing colours like those of rainbow; changing colour with position. Hence ~ENCE n. [as IRIS +-ESCENT]

īrid'ium, n. White metallic element of the platinum group. [as IRIS +-IUM]

īridos'mine (*or* īr-), n. Native alloy or mixture of osmium & iridium, used in pointing gold pens. [IRID(IUM) + OSM-(IUM) + -INE[2]]

īr'is, n. 1. Flat circular coloured membrane behind cornea of eye, with circular opening (PUPIL) in centre. 2. Kinds of plants, chiefly with tuberous roots, sword-shaped leaves, & showy flowers; FLORENTINE ~. 3. Kind of rock-crystal reflecting prismatic colours. 4. ~ *diaphragm* (Opt.), contractile diaphragm of thin overlapping plates for regulating the admission of light to a lens or lens system. [ME, f. L, f. Gk *iris -idos* (goddess of) rainbow, iris]

Ir'ish (īr-), a. & n. 1. Of Ireland; ‖ ~ *bridge*, open stone drain carrying water across road; ~ BULL[4]; ~ STEW. 2. n. ~ language; (as pl.) *the* ~ (people); ~*man*, ~*woman*, native of Ireland. Hence ~ISM(4) n., ~IZE(3) v.t. [f. *Ir*- st. of OE *Iras* n. pl. +-ISH[1]]

īrit'is, n. Inflammation of the iris. [-ITIS]

îrk, v.t. (arch.). Disgust, tire, bore, esp. *it* ~s (*me, him*, etc.). [ME *irken*, of unkn. orig.]

îrk'some, a. Tedious, tiresome. Hence ~LY[2] (-ml-) adv., ~NESS (-mn-) n. [-SOME]

iron[1] (ī'ern), n. & a. 1. Metal largely used for tools etc. (*wrought* ~, *cast* ~, STEEL), often fig. as type of hardness, as *a man of* ~, *rod of* ~; preparation of ~ as tonic; tool made of ~, as *curling, grappling,* ~; branding tool; golf-club with ~ head; ~ tool for smoothing out linen etc.; (usu. pl.) fetters (esp. *in* ~*s*, handcuffed); (esp. in pl.) stirrup; (pl.) leg-supports to correct malformations etc.; *the* ~ *entered into his soul* (Ps. cv. 18, L mistranslation of Heb. ' his person entered into the iron ', i.e. fetters); (Provv.) *strike while the* ~ *is hot* (at a good opportunity), *have* (*too*) *many*

~s *in the fire* (many undertakings, also, many expedients). **2.** adj. Of ~, very robust, firm, unyielding, merciless. **3.** ~ *age,* age of cruelty, oppression, etc. (cf. BRAZEN[1]), (also, cf. BRONZE, STONE, *age*) era of ~ implements; ~-*bark,* species of eucalyptus with solid bark; ~-*bound,* bound with ~, (of coast) rock-bound, (fig.) rigorous, hard & fast; ~*clad,* clad in, protected with, ~, (n., hist.) ship cased with plates of ~; *I*~ *Cross,* Prussian war decoration; ~ *curtain* (fig.), barrier to passage of information at (esp. Western) limit of Soviet sphere of influence; *I*~ *Duke,* Duke of Wellington; ~-*grey* a. & n., (of) the colour of freshly broken ~; ~ *horse,* locomotive steam-engine, also, bicycle or tricycle; ~ *lung,* case fitted over patient's body, used for administering artificial respiration by means of mechanical pumps; ~*master,* manufacturer of ~; ~-*mould,* spot caused by ~-rust or ink-stain, (v.t. & i.) stain, with this; ~ *rations,* soldier's modicum of food to be touched only in emergency; *I*~*sides,* man of great bravery, esp. (pl.) Cromwell's troopers; ~-*stone,* name of various hard ~-ores; ~*work,* work in ~, things made of ~; ~*works* (sing. or pl.), place where ~ is smelted or ~ goods are made. [(1) OE *īsern, īsen* = OS, OHG, ON *īsarn,* Goth. *eisarn* f. Gmc **īsarnam*; (2) OE *īren,* whence mod. E form, not paralleled in other langg.]

iron²(ī'ern), v.t. Furnish, cover, with iron; shackle with irons; smooth (linen etc.) with flat-iron etc.; smooth *out* (difficulties etc.). [f. prec.]

īrŏn'ic|(al), aa. Of, using, said in, addicted to, irony. Hence ~alLY² adv. [f. LL f. Gk *eirōnikos* (as IRONY¹, see -IC)]

ī'ronist, n. One who uses irony. [f. Gk *eirōn* dissembler + -IST]

‖ **ir'onmong|er** (i'ernmŭngg-), n. Dealer in hardware etc. Hence ~ERY(1, 2, 3) n.

ī'ronȳ¹, n. Expression of one's meaning by language of opposite or different tendency, esp. simulated adoption of another's point of view for purpose of ridicule; ill-timed or perverse arrival of event or circumstance in itself desirable, due to the feigned good will & actual malice *of* (Fate, circumstance, etc.); use of language that has an inner meaning for a privileged audience & an outer meaning for the persons addressed or concerned (occas.. including speaker, cf. TRAGIC ~); *Socratic* ~, simulation of ignorance as means of confuting adversary. [f. L f. Gk *eirōneia* simulated ignorance]

irony² (īrn'I), a. Of like, iron. [-Y²]

irrā'di|ant, a. Shining brightly. So ~ANCE n. [as foll., see -ANT]

irrād'iāt|e, v.t. Shine upon; (fig.) throw light on (subject); light up (face etc. *with* joy etc.); subject to sunlight or ultra-violet rays Hence~IVE a. [f. L IR¹(*radiare* f. *radius* RAY¹), see -ATE³]

irrādiā'tion, n. Shining, illumination, (lit. & fig.); apparent extension of edges of illuminated object seen against dark ground. [F, or f. prec., see -ATION]

irrā'tional (-shon-), a. & n. **1.** Unreasonable, illogical, absurd; not endowed with reason; (Math., of roots etc.) not rational, not commensurable with the natural numbers (e.g. non-terminating decimal). **2.** n. ~ number, surd. Hence ~ITY (-shonălⁱ-) n., ~IZE(3) v.t., ~LY² adv. [f. L IR²(*rationalis* RATIONAL)]

irrēclaim'ab|le, a. Not to be reclaimed or reformed. Hence ~LY² adv. [IR-²]

irrěc'ognizable,a. Unrecognizable. [IR-²]

irrěc'oncil|able, a. & n. **1.** Implacably hostile; (of ideas etc.) incompatible. **2.** n. Implacable opponent of political measure etc. Hence ~aBIL'ITY, ~ableNESS, nn., ~abLY² adv. [IR-²]

irrēco'verab|le (-kŭ-), a. That cannot be recovered or remedied. Hence ~LY² adv. [IR-²]

irrēcūs'able (-z-), a. That must be accepted. [f. LL IR²(*recusabilis* f. *recusare* refuse, see -BLE)]

irrēdeem'ab|le, a. (Of government annuities) not terminable by repayment; (of paper currency) for which issuing authority does not undertake to ·pay coin; irreclaimable, hopeless, whence ~LY² adv. [IR-²]

irrēděn't|ist, n. (It. politics) advocate of recovery to Italy of all Italian-speaking districts; Greek, Pole, etc., of similar views. So ~ISM n. [f. It. *irredentista* f. (*Italia*) *irredenta* unredeemed (Italy)]

irrēdū'c|ible, a. That cannot be brought (*to* desired condition); that cannot be reduced, as ~*ible minimum*; that cannot be simplified. Hence ~iBIL'ITY n. [IR-²]

irrěf'ragab|le, a. (Of statement, argument, person)indisputable, unanswerable. Hence ~LY² adv. [f. LL IR²(*refragabilis* f. EF*fragari,* see -BLE)]

irrēfrăn'gible, a. Inviolable; (Opt.) incapable of being refracted. [IR-²]

irrěf'ūt|able (*or* -ūtⁱ), a. Not to be refuted. Hence ~aBIL'ITY n., ~abLY² adv. [f. LL IR²(*refutabilis* REFUTABLE)]

irrěg'ular, a. & n. **1.** Not regular, contrary to rule; abnormal; not of symmetrical form; (of surface) uneven; disorderly; uneven in duration, order, etc.; (Gram., of part of speech) not normally inflected; (of troops) not in regular service. **2.** n. pl. ~ troops. Hence or cogn. ~ITY (-ă'r-) n., ~LY² adv. [ME, f. OF *irreguler* f. LL IR²(*regularis* REGULAR)]

irrěl'ative, a. Unconnected, unrelated, (*to*); having no relations, absolute. Hence ~LY² adv. [IR-²]

irrěl'ev|ant, a. Not to the point; that does not apply (*to* matter in hand). Hence ~ANCE, ~ANCY, nn., ~antLY² adv. [IR-²]

irrěli'g|ion (-jn), n. Hostility to, disregard of, religion. Hence or cogn. ~ionIST(2) (-jon-) n., ~ioUS (-jus) a., ~iousLY² adv. [f. F, or L IR²(*religio* RELIGION)]

irrěmēd'iab|le, a. That cannot be remedied. Hence ~LY² adv. [f. L IR²- (*remediabilis* REMEDIABLE)]

irrěmiss'ib|le, a. Unpardonable; unalterably binding. Hence~LY²adv. [ME, f. OF *irremissible* f. LL IR²(*remissibilis*, as REMIT, see -BLE)]

irrěmo'v|able (-mōō-), a. That cannot be removed, esp. from office. Hence ~abIL'ITY n., ~abLY² adv. [IR-²]

irrěp'arab|le, a. (Of injury, loss, etc.) that cannot be rectified or made good. Hence ~leNESS n., ~LY² adv. [ME, f. OF *irreparable* f. L IR²(*reparabilis* REPARABLE)]

irrěplāce'able (-sa-), a. Of which the loss cannot be made good. [IR-²]

irrěprěss'ib|le, a. & n. Not to be repressed or restrained; (n., colloq.) ~le person. Hence ~LY² adv. [IR-², REPRESS, -IBLE]

irrěproach'|able, a. Free from blame, faultless. Hence ~abIL'ITY n., ~abLY² adv. [f. F IR²(*réprochable*, as REPROACH v., see -ABLE)]

irrěsis't|ible (-zĭs-), a. Too strong, convincing, charming, etc., to be resisted. Hence ~ĭBIL'ITY n., ~ibLY² adv. [f. LL IR²(*resistibilis*, as RESIST, see -BLE)]

irrěs'olute (-zolŏōt), a. Undecided, hesitating; wanting in resolution. Hence or cogn. ~LY² adv., ~NESS, **irrěsolu'tion** (-zolŏō-), nn. [IR-²]

irrěsol'vable (-zŏl-), a. That cannot be resolved into parts; (of problem) that cannot be solved. [IR-²]

irrěspěc'tive, a. ~ *of*, not taking into account, without reference to, (often quasi-adv., as *the posts were filled* ~ *of nationality*). Hence ~LY² adv. [IR-²]

irrěspŏn's|ible, a. Not responsible for conduct; acting, done, without due sense of responsibility. Hence ~ĭBIL'ITY n., ~ibLY² adv. [IR-²]

irrěspŏn'sive, a. Not responsive (*to*). Hence ~NESS n. [IR-²]

irrětěn'tion, n. Failure to retain (esp. the urine). [IR-²]

irrětěn'tive, a. Not retentive. Hence ~NESS n. [IR-²]

irrětriev'|able, a. That cannot be retrieved. Hence ~abIL'ITY n., ~abLY² adv. [IR-²]

irrěv'er|ent, a. Wanting in reverence. Hence or cogn. ~ENCE n., ~ěn'tIAL (-shl) a., ~entLY² adv. [f. L IR²(*reverens* REVERENT)]

irrěvěrs'|ible, a. Unalterable; not reversible. Hence~ĭBIL'ITY n.,~ibLY² adv. [IR-²]

irrěv'oc|able, a. Unalterable; gone beyond recall. Hence ~abIL'ITY n., ~abLY² adv. [f. L IR²(*revocabilis* REVOCABLE)]

I'rrig|āte, v.t. (Of streams etc.) supply (land) with water; water (land) with

channels etc.; (Med.) supply (wound etc.) with constant flow of liquid; (fig.) refresh as with moisture. Hence or cogn. ~ABLE, ~ātIVE, aa., ~A'TION, ~ātoR, nn. [f. L IR¹(*rigare* moisten), see -ATE³]

i'rrit|able, a. Quick to anger, touchy, whence~abLY² adv.; (of organ etc.) very sensitive to contact etc.; (Physiol., of muscles & nerves) capable of being excited to vital action by physical stimulus. So ~abIL'ITY n. [f. L *irritabilis* (as IRRITATE¹, see -BLE)]

i'rritancy¹, n. Irritation, annoyance. [as IRRITANT, see -ANCY]

i'rritancy², n. (law). Making, being, null & void. [as IRRITATE², see -ANCY]

i'rritant, a. & n. **1.** Causing (usu. physical) irritation. **2.** n. ~ substance or agency (also fig.). [as foll., see -ANT]

i'rritāt|e¹, v.t. Excite to anger, annoy, vex, (~*ed at, by, with, against*), whence ~ingLY² adv.; excite, produce uneasy sensation in, (bodily organ etc.); (Physiol.) stimulate (organ) to vital action. Hence or cogn. irrita'tION n., ~IVE a. [f. L *irritare*, see -ATE³]

i'rritāte², v.t. (law). Make null & void. [f. L *irritare* f. IR²(*ritus* = *ratus* established) invalid, see -ATE³]

irrŭp'tion, n. Invasion; violent entry. [f. L *irruptio* f. IR¹(*rumpere rupt-* break), see -ION]

Irv'ingīte (ẽrv-), n. Member of a religious body called by its members the Catholic Apostolic Church. [E. *Irving*, minister of Ch. of Scotland, d. 1834]

is. See BE.

Isaběll'a, **Is'aběl**, (Iz-), a. & n. Greyish yellow. Hence **isaběll'ine** (-z-) a. [Sp. *Isabella*, F *Isabelle*, = *Elisabeth*]

ĭsagŏ'gic, a. & n. Introductory; (n. pl.) study of literary & external history of Bible. [f. L f. Gk *eisagōgikos* f. *eisagōgē* introduction (*eis* into +*agōgē* leading f. *agō*), see -IC]

is'atin, n. (chem.). Crystalline reddish substance got from indigo by oxidation. [f. L f. Gk *isatis* woad +-IN] .

ischiăt'ic, -dic, (-k-), a. Of the hip, sciatic. [f. LL *ischiaticus*, alt. f. L f. Gk *iskhiadikos* f. *iskhias -ados* pain in hip (*iskhion*), see -IC]

-ise¹. See -IZE.

-ise², suf. of nn., = OF *-ise*, prop. f. L *-itia*, but also (in learned formations) f. L *-icia, -itia, -icium, -itium* (OF *justise, juise, servise*, f. L *justitia, judicium, servitium*). In wds f. L, later F changed *-ise* to *-ice*, which E adopted; but in native wds F & E retain *-ise* (*franchise, merchandise*; E also has *exercise*, F *-ice*). See -ICE.

-ish¹, suf. of adjj., = OE, OS, OHG *-isc*, Goth. *-isks*, ON *-iskr*, cogn. w. Gk *-iskos* dim. suf. of nn. In old formations, prec. vowel was modified, as still in *English, French, Welsh*. **1.** OE chiefly formed aa. f. national names (*British, Danish*), with a few in sense ' belonging to, of the nature of ' (*heathenish, outlandish*); later aa. have usu. not the neutral sense (*boyish, girlish*), but that of ' having the bad qualities of ' (*foppish, monkish, swinish*; f. names of things *bookish, hellish*; f. vbs & advv. *snappish, stand-offish, uppish*). **2**. Sense peculiar to E is ' somewhat ' (*stiffish*). **3**. Colloq. added to names of hours of the day or numbers of years to denote ' round about, somewhere near ' (*eightish, fortyish*).

-ish², suf. of vbs repr. F *-iss-* seen in some parts of vbs in *-ir* (*périssant, finissais*), f. L inceptive suf. *-isc-*, used in It. & F to form vbs without incept. sense to correspond to L vbs in *-ire, -ere*. In a few wds F *-iss-* became in E *-ise* (*chastise, advertise*); on the other hand, other F endings have become *-ish* (ADMONISH, LAVISH, RELISH).

Ish'mäel (I-), n. Outcast, one at war with society. Hence ∼ITE¹ n. [*Gen.* xvi. 12]

is'inglass (izĭngglahs), n. Whitish semi-transparent substance, a form of gelatin, got from some freshwater fish, esp. sturgeon, & used in making jellies, glue, etc. [corrupt. of obs. Du. *huisenblas* sturgeon's bladder]

Is'lam (Iz-; *or* -ahm′), n. Mohammedan-ism; the Mohammedan world. Hence **Islăm'ĭc**, ∼it'ĭc, aa., ∼ISM(3), ∼ITE¹(1), nn., (Iz-). [Arab., = surrender, f. *aslama* he surrendered f. *salama* he became safe, whence also *salaam*, *Moslem*, *Mussulman*]

isl'and (il-), n., & v.t. **1**. Piece of land surrounded by water; (fig.) anything detached or isolated; esp. woodland surrounded by prairie, street REFUGE; (Naut.) ship's superstructure, bridge, etc.; (Physiol.) detached portion of tissue or group of cells. **2**. v.t. Make into an ∼, isolate; dot as with ∼s. Hence ∼ER¹(4) n. [ME *iland* f. OE *igland* (f. *ieg* = ON, OFris. *ey* isle + LAND); *-s-* by assoc. w. *isle*]

isle (il), n. Island (in prose usu. only with proper name, as *Isle of Wight, British Isles,* & usu. of small islands); *Isles of the* BLEST. [ME, f. OF *ile* f. L *insula*; later ME & OF *isle* after L]

isl'ĕt (il-), n. Little island; isolated tract or spot. [f. F *islette* (as prec., see -ET¹)]

ism (I'zm), n. Any distinctive doctrine or practice (∼s & ologies). [foll. used as n.]

-ism, suf. forming abstract nn.: (1) of action on vbs in -IZE, as *baptism*; (2) of typical conduct or condition on class nouns, as *heroism, barbarism*; (3) of system or principle on name of subject or founder or connected catchword, as *conservatism, Arianism, jingoism*; (4) of peculiarity in language, as *gallicism, archaism*; (5) of morbid condition induced by excessive use of drug, as *alcoholism*. [= F *-isme* f. L f. Gk *-ismos* or *-isma* f. *-izō* -IZE]

isn't. See BE.

iso- in comb. = Gk *isos* equal, as: *is'obăr*

n., ∼bă'ric a., (line on map) connecting places at which atmospheric pressure is the same (at given time or on the average); *is'ocheim* (-kim) n., ∼*cheim'al,* ∼*chĭm'enal,* (-k-), aa. & nn., (line on map) connecting places of same mean winter temperature; ∼*chromăt'ic,* of same colour; ∼*chronous* (-ŏk²), occupying equal time, vibrating uniformly, as pendulum; ∼*clin'al,* ∼*clin'ic,* showing equal magnetic inclination (∼*clinic lines*, lines joining, on a map or chart, points at which the magnetic dip is the same); ∼*cracy* (-ŏk²) n., ∼*crăt'ic a.,* (polity) in which all have equal political power; ∼*dynăm'ic,* indicating equal magnetic force; ∼*gē'otherm,* line connecting points in interior of earth having same temperature; ∼*gŏn'ic,* indicating equal angles (of magnetic variation); ∼*mĕ'ric,* composed of same elements in same proportions, & having same molecular weight, but with atoms differently grouped; ∼*mĕt'ric(al)*, of equal measure; ∼*mŏrph'ism,* ∼*mŏrph'ous,* (property of) crystallizing in same or closely related geometric forms; ∼*nomy* (-ŏn²), equality of political rights; ∼*perimĕt'rical,* having equal perimeters; ∼*seis'mal* (-sīz-), connecting points at which earthquake-shock is of same intensity; ∼*theral* (-ŏth²) a. & n., (line) connecting places of same mean summer temperature; *is'othĕrm* n., ∼*thĕrm'al* a. & n., (line) connecting places of same mean annual temperature.

is'olăt|e, v.t. Place apart or alone; (Chem.) free (substance) from its combinations; (Electr.) = INSULATE; subject (person etc.) to quarantine. Hence ∼OR n. [orig. in p.p., f. F *isolé* f. It. *isolato* (as INSULATE)]

isolā'tion, n. Isolating or being isolated; ∼ *hospital* or *ward* (for patients with infectious diseases). Hence ∼ISM(3) n., policy of holding aloof from affairs of other countries, ∼IST n., advocate of this policy (also attrib.). [prec., -ATION]

-ison, suf. of nn., f. OF *-aison, -eison, -ison,* f. L *-ationem, -etionem, -itionem*; later formations took -ATION, -ITION.

is'opŏd, n. Kinds of crustacea comprising wood-lice and allied marine and fresh-water species. [f. F *isopode* (ISO-, Gk *pous podos* foot]

isŏs'celēs (-selēz), a. (Of triangle) having two sides equal. [LL, f. Gk ISO(*skelēs* f. *skelos* leg)]

is'otōpe, n. One of two or more forms of an element differing from each other in weight of atoms. Hence **īsotŏp'īo a.,** **īsŏt'opy** n. [f. ISO- + Gk *topos* place]

Is'raël (Iz-), n. The Jewish people, whence ∼ITE¹(1) n., ∼ĪtISH¹ a.; (fig.) God's elect; the Jewish State established in Palestine in 1948, also attrib. Hence ∼i (Izrāl'I) a. & n., (inhabitant) of this State. [LL (earlier *istrahel, israhel*), f. Gk *Israēl* f. Heb. *yisrael* striver with God (*Gen.* xxxii. 28)]

iss'ūe¹, n. 1. Outgoing, outflow; termination (*of* matter etc.); discharge of blood etc., incision to procure this. **2.** Way out, outlet; mouth of river. **3.** Progeny, children, as *without male* ~. **4.** Result, outcome; *in the* ~, as things turn out. **5.** Point in question, esp. (Law) between contending parties in action, as ~ *of fact* (when fact is denied), ~ *of law* (when application of the law is contested). **6.** *At* ~, (of persons) at variance, (of things) in dispute; *join* ~, proceed to argue (*with* person *on* point agreed upon as basis of dispute), (Law) submit an ~ jointly for decision, (of one party) accept the ~ tendered by the other. **7.** Giving out, issuing, (*of* bills of exchange, notes, stamps, etc.); number of coins, notes, copies of newspaper, etc., issued at one time; (of book) part of EDITION with special features issued at certain period. Hence ~LESS (-ŭl-) a. [ME, f. OF *issue* fem. of *issu*, p.p. of OF *issir* f. L *exire*]

iss'ūe², v.i. & t. Go or come out (often *out*, *forth*); emerge from a condition; be derived, spring, (*from*); result (*from*); end, result, (*in*); come out, be published; send forth; publish, put into circulation, (notes, newspaper), whence **iss'ū**ABLE a., **iss'ū**ANCE n.; (Mil.) supply (soldier) *with* article of equipment. [f. prec.]

-ist, suf. forming personal nn.: (1) of agent, corresp. to GR vbs in *-izō* or possible E vbs in -IZE, as *antagonist*, *plagiarist*; (2) of adherent of creed etc. in -ISM, as *atheist*, *ventriloquist*, *Darwinist*, *fatalist*; (3) of one concerned with any subject (apart from *-ism*, *-ize*), as *dentist*, *tobacconist*, *balloonist*, esp. as player of musical instrument (*violinist*). [= F *-iste*, It. & Sp. *-ista*, f. L *-ista* f. Gk *-istēs* (*-izō* -IZE + *-tēs* agent-suf.); *tobacconist*, *accompanist* are formed irreg.]

-ister, suf. of nn., f. OF *-istre*, by-form of *-iste* -IST, perh. by false anal. f. *ministre* (L *minister*) etc.; in E prob. associated with -ER¹. Exx.: *chorister*, *palmister*, *sophister*.

isth'm|us (or **is'mus**), (pl. ~*uses*). Neck of land; (Anat., Bot.) narrow part connecting two larger parts. Hence ~IAN a. [L, f. Gk *isthmos*]

is'tle (-tlĭ), n. Fibre used for cord, nets, etc., got from species of agave etc. [f. Mex. *ixtli*]

it¹, pron. (poss. *its*; pl. *they*, obj. *them*, poss. *their*). **1.** The thing in question; the person in question, as *who is it* (that knocks)?, *it* (the person that knocks) *is I*, (arch. poet.) *it* (what occupies my mind) *is the miller's daughter, & she is grown so dear,* (nursery sympathetic) *has it lost its rattle then?* (have you, your). **2.** (As subjects of impers. vb) *it rains, it is cold; it* (the season) *is winter, it* (the day) *is Ash Wednesday, it is Ash Wednesday today, it* (the distance) *is 6 miles to Oxford; it says in the Bible* (the Bible says) *that all men*

are liars; I would go if it were not (would go but) *for the expense.* **3.** (As subject, anticipating deferred virtual subject in more or less conscious apposition) *it is absurd talking* (or *to talk*) *like that, it is incredible that he should refuse, it is a dirty business, this meat-canning.* **4.** (Anticipating deferred subject introduced by *that* conj., separated from *it* by adv. predicate) *it is seldom that he fails, it is in vain that you quibble, it is to him that you must apply.* **5.** (As antecedent to relative of either number & any gender, separated by predicate) *it was a purse that he dropped, it was the Russians that began it.* **6.** (As indef. obj. w. trans. or intr. vb) *face it out, carry it with a high hand, deuce take it, run for it, lord it over him, cab it* (go habitually or on the particular occasion in cab), *give it him* (*hot*), *have done it* (blundered). **7.** The ne plus ultra (colloq.; *for barefaced lying you really are* it). **8.** Sex appeal (colloq.). [OE *hit* (neut. nom. & acc.) f. (orig. demonstr.) stem *hi-* (see HE), = (in form & sense) OFris., OLFrank. *hit*, (in form) Goth. *hita* (demonstr.); the neut. pronn. OS *it*, OHG *iz*, Goth *ita* are from the parallel stem *i-* (see HE)]

‖ **it²,** n. (colloq.). Short for *Italian vermouth* (in *gin &* ~). [abbr.]

it'acism (ē-), n. Pronunciation of Greek ē like English ē, cf. ETACISM; substitution in MS. of Greek iota for other vowels. [f. Gk *ēta* the letter ē, spelt *ita* to indicate the pronunc. (ēta)]

Ital'ian (ităl'yan), a. & n. **1.** Of Italy; ~ *cloth*, satin-faced linen cloth for linings; ~ *handwriting*, that now current in Britain, Italy, France, etc., opp. to Gothic; ~ *iron* (cylindrical, with rounded end, for crimping lace etc.); ‖ ~ *warehouse*(*man*), for supply of ~ groceries, fruits, olive oil, etc. **2.** n. Language, native, of Italy. Hence ~ATE² a., having ~ style or appearance, ~ISM (2, 4) n., ~IZE(3) v.t. & i. [15th c., f. It. *Italiano* f. Rom. **Italianus* f. L *Italia* Italy, see -AN]

itǎl'ic, a. & n. **1.** (*I*~) of ancient Italy, esp. as apart from Rome; ~ *type*, sloping type introduced by Aldus Manutius of Venice (c. 1500). **2.** n. pl. Letters thus sloping, now used for emphasis or distinction, e.g. to indicate foreign word (cf. ROMAN). [f. L f. Gk *Italikos* (*Italia* Italy, see -IC)]

itǎl'icize, -ise (-īz), v.t. Print (words) in italics, usu. for emphasis or distinction. [-IZE]

Itǎl'iot (I-), **-ōte,** n. & a. (Inhabitant) of ancient-Greek colonies in S. Italy. [f. Gk *Italiōtēs* (*Italia* Italy, see -OT²)]

itch¹, n. Irritation in the skin; contagious disease accompanied by this & caused by the ~*-mite*, which burrows in the skin; restless desire, hankering, (*for* thing, *to* do). Hence ~'NESS n., ~'Y² a. [OE *gicce*, as foll.]

itch², v.i. Feel irritation in skin; *scratch where it ~es* (where there is an ~ing); (of person or his *fingers*) crave uneasily (*for* thing, *to* do). [OE *gicc(e)an*, OS *jukkian*, OHG *jucchen* f. WG *jukkjan*]

-ite¹, suf. of adjj. & nn., = F *-ite* f. L *-ita* f. Gk *-ĭtēs* (also used in E, as *pyrites*), w. sense '(one) belonging to or connected with'; (1) in names of persons, in mod. formation often derog. (*Stagirite,Sybarite, Parnellite, Shelleyite, Israelite, Preraphaelite*); (2) in names of fossil organisms (*ammonite, belemnite*); of mineral species, often superseding *-ane, -in, -ine,* etc. (*anthracite, haematite, graphite, darwinite*); of constituent parts of body or organ (*somite, cerite,* segment of body, of horn); of some saccharine substances, glucoses, etc. (*dulcite,pinite*); of explosives (*cordite, dynamite*); of commercial products (*ebonite, vulcanite*); of salts of acids denominated by aa. in *-ous* (*nitrite, sulphite*).

-ite², suf. formed in adjj. f. L p.p. in *-ītus* (*erudite, composite*) & similar. vbl nn. (*appetite*), & in vbs formed on L p:p. stem in *-it-* (*expedite, unite*); but vbs f. L p.p. st. *-it-* end in *-it* (*deposit, merit*).

ĭt'ĕm, n. & adv. **1.** Article, unit, included in enumeration (properly not the first); entry of this in account etc.; detail of news etc. in newspaper etc.; hence *•~IZE(3)* v.t., state by *~s.* **2.** adv. Likewise, also, (introducing mention of *~*). [L, adv., = in like manner, also]

ĭt'er|āte, v.t. Repeat (quoted words etc.); make (charge, assertion, objection, etc.) repeatedly. Hence or cogn. *~ANCE, ~ANCY, ~A'TION,* nn., *~atIVE* a. [f. L *iterare* (*iterum* again), see *-ATE³*]

-ites. See *-ITE¹*.

Ithūr'iel's spear (I-), n. Infallible test of genuineness. [Milt. *Par. Lost,* iv. 810]

ĭthўphăll'ĭc, a. & n. Of the phallus carried in Bacchic festivals; lewd; in the metre used for Bacchic hymns; (n.) poem in this metre, licentious poem. [f. LL f. Gk *ithuphallikos* (*ithus* straight +*phallos* PHALLUS, see *-IC*)]

ĭtin'er|ant, a. Travelling from place to place; (of justices) travelling on circuit; (of Methodist ministry) removing from circuit to circuit. Hence *~ACY, ~ANCY,* nn. [as ITINERATE, see *-ANT*]

ĭtin'erarў, n. & a. Route; record of travel; guide-book; (adj.) of travelling, of roads. [f. LL *itinerarius* a., *-um* n. (also used in E), f. *iter itineris* journey, see *-ARY¹*]

ĭtin'er|āte, v.i. Travel from place to place; (of Methodist minister) remove from circuit to circuit. Hence *~A'TION* n. [f. L *itinerari* (as prec.), see *-ATE³*]

-ition, suf., thr. F *-ition* (or dir.) f. L *-itionem* (nom. *-itio*) = *-ION* appended to L 2nd or 3rd or 4th conj. p.p. stems in *-it-, -it-* (*admonition, perdition, sortition*).

-itious¹, suf. of adjj., f. L *-icius* + *-ous* (*-t-*

by confus. of *c* & *t* in LL MSS.), formed usu. on L p.p. stems (*factitious*).

-itious², suf. in which *-ious* is appended to L stems in *-it-* chiefly nn. in *-itio* (*ambitious, nutritious,* cf. *supposit-*ITIOUS¹).

-itis, suf. forming esp. names of inflammatory diseases (*appendicitis, bronchitis*), f. Gk *-itis,* forming the fem. of adjj. in *-ĭtēs,* w. *nusos* disease understood.

-itous, suf. of adjj., = *-IT*(Y) + *-OUS,* corresp. to F *-iteux,* L *-itosus* for *-italosus* (*calamitosus* calamitous).

its, poss. a. See IT. [replaces HIS *c.* 1600]

ĭtsĕlf', pron. Emphatic & reflexive form corresp. to IT; *by ~,* automatically, apart from its surroundings; *in ~,* apart from its surroundings, viewed in its essential qualities etc. [IT + SELF, but often treated as ITS + *self,* cf. *its own self*]

-ity [ME & OF *-ite* (mod. F *-ité*) f. L *-itatem*], the usu. form in wh. the suf. (L *-tas, -tatem,* expr. state or condition) appears in E, either f. learned F adoptives or dir. f. L. In L the *-i-* is usu. either the stem-vowel (*suavitas* suavity) or its weakened repr. (*puritas* (*puro-*) purity), rarely a mere connective, as in *majoritas* majority. The phonetic resultant in OF of L *-itatem* was *-te* (*-ete*): see *-TY¹*.

-ium, suf. forming names of metallic elements, but some (esp. later) metals have names in *-um,* the L termination for metals.

-ive, suf. forming adjj. w. sense 'tending to, having the nature of', f. F *-if* (fem. *-ive*) f. L *-ivus* added to p.p. stem (*activus, passivus*), pres. stem (*cadivus*), or noun (*tempestivus*). Most E wds are of mod. formation, chiefly in *-sive, -tive,* & esp. *-ative,* which tends to become living suf. (*talkative*). Some are formed immed. on vb stems (esp. in *-s, -c, -t*), as *amusive, coercive.* As in L these adjj. are freely used as nn., e.g. *adjective, captive.*

ĭv'orў, n. Hard white substance composing main part of tusks of elephant, hippopotamus, walrus, narwhal, & (*fossil ~*) mammoth; *vegetable ~,* hard albumen of seed of S.-Amer. palm (*~-nut*); *black~* (hist.), African Negro slaves; colour of *~*; (sl., pl.) dice, billiard-balls, piano-keys; (sl., sing. or pl.) teeth; (pl.) articles made of *~*; *~ black,* black pigment from calcined *~*; *~* TOWER. [ME, f. OF *yvoire* f. L *eboreus* a. (*ebur -oris*)]

ĭv'ў, n. Climbing evergreen shrub, with dark-green shining leaves, usu. five-angled; *~ geranium, ~*-leaved pelargonium. Hence *ĭv'ĭED²* (*-ĭd*) a. [OE *ĭfig,* rel. to MLG *if(lōf),* OHG *ebah, ebahewi* (G *epheu, efeu*)]

ĭx'ĭa, n. Kinds of S.-Afr. iridaceous plants, with large showy flowers. [Gk]

Ixi'on's wheel (I-), n. (Gk Myth.). Wheel on which Ixion was condemned to revolve eternally in Hades.

ĭz'ard, n. Capriform antelope of Pyrenees, allied to chamois. [f. F *isard,* orig. unkn.]

-ize, -ise, suf. of vbs, = F *-iser* f. LL *-izare* f. Gk *-izō*; in Gk either intr., ' act like ', as *hellenizō* speak, act as a, Greek, or trans., as *katharizō* clean; Christian Gk vbs, as *euaggelizō* evangelize, were first Latinized, & *-izare* so established as L for Gk vbs (cf. G *-iren* for Rom. vbs); F extended *-iser* to form vbs from nouns etc., whence the mod. use. *-ize* is the better spelling for all wds, mod. or f. Gk, that contain the Gk suf. & is here uniformly so written (*advertise, surprise*, etc., do not). Meanings: (1) trans., treat in such a way (*catechize*); (2) intr., follow, have, such a practice or feeling (*apostatize, sympathize*); (3) t. & i., bring, come into such a state (*pulverize, anglicize, cicatrize*); (4) t. & i., act like, treat on system of, (*Calvinize, Bowdlerize*); (5) trans., impregnate etc. with (*oxidize*). Nn. are formed in *-izer, -ization*, as well as *-IST, -ISM*.

izz'ard, n. (arch.). The letter z (*from A to I~*). [var. of ZED]

izz'at, n. (Anglo-Ind. and Eastern). Honour, reputation, self-respect (occas. self-importance). [Arab.]

J

J, j, (jā), letter (pl. *Js, J's*).

jā'al-goat (*or* yah-), n. Wild goat of Sinai, Upper Egypt, etc. [f. Heb. *ya'ēl* wild goat]

jăb, v.t. (-bb-), & n. **1.** Poke roughly; stab; thrust (thing) abruptly (*into*). **2.** n. Abrupt blow with pointed thing or fist. [var., orig. Sc., of JOB[3]]

jăbb'er, v.i. & t., & n. **1.** Speak volubly & with little sense; utter (words) rapidly & indistinctly; chatter, as monkeys etc. **2.** n. ~ing, gabble, gibberish. [imit., see -ER[5]]

jăb'iru (-ōō), n. Tropical American bird of stork family. [native]

jăborăn'di, n. Dried leaflets of Brazilian plant with diuretic & sudorific properties. [f. native *jaburandi*]

jabot (zhăbō'), n. Ornamental frill on woman's bodice; (hist.) frill on man's shirt-front. [F, orig. unkn.]

jăc'ana (-ah), n. Small tropical wading bird with disproportionately large straight claws (enabling it to walk on floating leaves). [native *jasaná*]

jăcarăn'da, n. Kinds of tropical American hardwood tree with scented wood & trumpet-shaped blue flowers. [Braz.]

jā'cinth, n. Reddish-orange gem, variety of zircon. [ME *iacynt* f. OF *iacinte* or med. L *iacint(h)us* f. L *hyacinthus* HYACINTH]

jăck[1], n. (*J~*) familiar form of name *John*, esp. as type of the common people, as *J~ & Jill*, lad & lass; *every man ~*, every individual; = ~ tar; ‖ labourer, man who does odd jobs, etc.; CHEAP *J~*; STEEPLE-*~*;

(Cards) knave; machine for turning spit in roasting meat; machine for lifting heavy weights; (also *carriage-~*) machine for lifting axle off ground while cleaning wheel; BOOT[1]*-~*; parts of various machines etc.; pike, esp. young or small one; (Bowls) ball for players to aim at; *J~ Frost*, frost personified; *before you could say J~ Robinson*, very quickly or suddenly; *J~-a-dandy*, dandy; *~'ass*, male ass, dolt, blockhead; *laughing ~ass*, giant kingfisher of Australia; *~'boot*, large boot coming above knee; *~'daw*, thievish small crow haunting church towers; *J~ in office*, self-important official; *~-in-the-box*, toy figure that springs out of box when opened, (also) kind of firework; *J~-in-the-green*, man or boy enclosed in framework covered with leaves in May-day sports; *J~ Ketch*, common hangman; *~-knife*, large clasp-knife for the pocket; *J~ of all trades*, one who can turn his hand to anything; *~-o'-lantern*, will-o'-the-wisp (often fig.); *~-plane* (for coarse work); *~'pot* (Poker), accumulating pool that can only be opened by player holding two *~s* or better, (transf.) prize in lottery etc.; *~ pudding*, buffoon, clown; *~-rafter*, short rafter in hip-roof; *~-snipe* (small species); *~ tar*, common sailor; *~-towel* (endless, hung from roller). [ME *Jakke*, by-name for *John* (erron. assoc. w. F *Jaques*)]

jăck[2], v.t. Hoist with jack; ~ *up*, abandon (attempt etc., or abs.). [first sense f. prec.; second prob. imit.; cf. *chuck*]

jăck[3], n. Ship's flag, smaller than ensign, esp. one flown from *~-staff* at bow, indicating nationality, as *British, French, ~*; single flag flown on foremast as signal for pilot (Brit. pilot's *~*, union *~* with white border); UNION *J~*; *~-staff*, (also) stick on which flag is bent that is to show above mast-head. [prob. = JACK[1]]

jăck[4], n. (arch.). Foot-soldier's sleeveless tunic; (also *black ~*) vessel for liquor, usu. of waxed leather coated with tar etc. [ME, f. OF *jaque* (whence G *jacke*), of unkn. orig.]

jăck[5], n. E.-Ind. fruit, like bread-fruit but coarser. [f. Port. *jaca* f. Malayalam *chakka*]

jăck'al (-awl), n., & v.i. (-ll-). Animal of dog kind, of size of fox, formerly supposed to hunt up lion's prey for him; (fig.) person who does preparatory drudgery etc.; (vb) act as *~ (for)*. [f. Turk. *chakal* f. Pers. *shagal*, cogn. w. Skr. *s'rgala*]

jăck'anāpes (-ps), n. ‖ (Arch.) monkey; pert fellow; coxcomb; pert child. [earliest form *Jack Napes* (1450), supposed to refer to Duke of Suffolk, whose badge was an ape's clog & chain]

jăck'arōō, n. (Austral. sl.). New chum, novice. [perh. portmanteau of *Jack* and *kangaroo*]

jăck'ĕt, n., & v.t. **1.** Sleeved outer garment for man or woman; NORFOLK, ETON, ‖ DINNER, ~; *dust his* ~, beat him; outer covering round boiler etc. for protection, keeping in heat, etc.; paper wrapper, freq. coloured & artistically designed, in which a bound book is issued; animal's coat; *potatoes boiled in their* ~*s* (skins). **2.** v.t. Cover with~. [15 c., f. OF *jaquet*, dim. as JACK[4]]

Jăc'ob, n. ~'*s ladder*, plant with corymbs of blue or white flowers, & leaves suggesting ladder, (Naut.) rope ladder with wooden rungs, esp. one slung from a boom to the water; ~'*s staff*, surveyor's iron-shod rod used instead of tripod, (also) instrument for measuring distances & heights. [f. LL f. Gk *Iakōbos* f. Heb. *ya'aqob*]

Jăcobē'an, a. Of the reign of James I; of St James the Less; (in furniture trade) of the colour of dark oak. [f. mod. L *Jacobaeus*, as prec. +-EAN]

Jăc'obin[1], n. Dominican friar [from convent near to church of S. Jacques]; member of extreme democratic club established in Paris in old ~ convent (1789), sympathizer with its principles, extreme radical, whence **Jăcobin'IC**(AL) aa:, ~ISM(3) n., ~IZE(3) v.t. [F, f. med. L *Jacobinus* (JACOB, -INE[1])]

jăc'obin[2], n. Pigeon with reversed feathers on back of neck, suggesting cowl. [f. F *jacobine*, fem. as prec.]

Jăc'ob|ite, n. Adherent of James II after his abdication, or of his descendants. Hence ~ĭt'ICAL a., ~ĭtISM(3) n. [f. L *Jacobus* James +-ITE[1]]

jacōb'ŭs, n. (pl. ~*es*). English gold coin struck in reign of James I, worth 20–24*s*. [as prec.]

jăc'onèt, n. Cotton cloth of medium thickness, esp. dyed waterproofed kind for poulticing etc. [f. Hind. *Jagannathi* f. place-name; see JUGGERNAUT]

Jacquard (jăk'ård) **lōom**, n. Loom fitted with apparatus invented by J. M. Jacquard of Lyons (d. 1834) to facilitate the weaving of figured fabrics.

jacquerie (zhăkerē'), n. Rising of peasantry, esp. that of 1357–8 in France. [F (*Jacques* James, peasant, see -ERY)]

jăctitā'tion, n. ‖ (Law) ~ *of marriage*, offence of falsely claiming to be a person's wife or husband; (Med.) restless tossing of body in illness; twitching of limb or muscle. [f. med. L *jactitatio* f. L *jactitare* toss, boast, (*jacēre jact-* throw), see -ATION]

jāde[1], n., & v.t. Inferior, wearied, or worn-out horse; (in reprobation, usu. playful) woman; (v.t., esp. in p.p.) wear out with hard work. [ME; orig. unkn.]

jāde[2], A silicate of lime & magnesia, a hard green, blue, or white stone, a variant of hornblende; (also ~'**ite**, pr. -dīt) silicate of sodium & aluminium like this in appearance. [f. F *le jade* for *l'ejade* f. Sp. (*piedra de*) *ijada* (stone of) the colic, f. L *ilia* pl. flank]

j'adoube (zhahdōōb'), phr. Expression used by a chess-player touching a piece he does not propose to move (= I adjust). [F]

Jaeg'er (yăg-), n. Kind of woollen clothing-material from which vegetable fibres are excluded as unwholesome. [person; P]

‖ **Jăff'a**, n. (Used for) kind of dessert orange. [~ in Israel, the bibl. *Joppa*]

jăg[1], n. Sharp projection, e.g. point of rock. Hence ~g'Y[2] (-g-) a. [c. 1400, prob. imit.]

jăg[2], v.t. (-gg-). Cut, tear, in uneven manner; make indentations in, whence ~g'ER[1](2) n. Hence ~g'ĕdLY[2] adv., ~g'ĕdNESS n., (-g-). [f. prec.]

jăg[3], n. (sl.). Drinking bout. [16th c. (dial.), = load for one horse; orig. unkn.]

jäger = YAGER.

jăgg'erY (-g-), n. Coarse brown Indian sugar made from palm-sap; other crude sugar. [f. Indo-Port. *jágara* SUGAR]

jaghir|(e)' (jagēr'), n. (India). Assignment by the State of a district & its revenue to an individual or body, with power to administer; tract so assigned. Hence ~'dår (-ård-) n., holder of a ~e [Pers. *dår* holder]. [f. Pers. *jå* place +*gīr* holding]

jăg'uar (-war, -ūar), n. Large carnivorous spotted mammal of cat kind, in some wooded parts of America. [f. native *yaguara*]

Jah, n. Jehovah. [repr. Heb. *Yah* shortened form of *Yahweh* JEHOVAH]

jail etc. See GAOL etc.

Jain (jīn), n. & a. (Member) of a non-Brahminical E.-Ind. sect, with doctrines like those of Buddhism. Hence ~'ISM n. [f. Hind. f. Skr. *jaina* of a Buddha (*jina* f. root *ji* conquer)]

jăl'ap, n. Purgative drug got esp. from tuberous roots of a Mexican climbing plant. [F, f. Sp. *jalapa* f. *Xalapa*, *Ja-*, Mexican city, f. Aztec *Xalapan* (*xalli* sand +*all* water +*pan* upon)]

*jalŏp(p)'ў, n. Dilapidated motor-car. [orig. unkn.]

jalousie (zhăl'ōozē), n. Slatted shutter on outside of window, Venetian blind. [F, as JEALOUSY]

jăm[1], v.t. & i. (-mm-), & n. **1.** Squeeze (thing) between two surfaces; cause (part of machine) to be fixed so that it cannot work; squeeze (things) together in compact mass; thrust (thing) violently (*into* space); block, fill up, (passage etc.) by crowding into it; become tightly wedged; (Radio) make (message, instrument) unintelligible by operating elsewhere. **2.** n. Crush, squeeze, stoppage (of machine etc.) due to this; crowded mass; (colloq.) fix, awkward position; ~-*stroke*, = PENDULUM *stroke*. [imit.]

jăm[2], n. Conserve of fruit, made by boiling it with sugar to a thick consistency; (sl.) *real* ~, a real treat. [f. prec.]

Jamaic′a, n. ~ (*rum*), rum made in ~.

jamb (jăm), n. Side post of doorway, window, etc., esp. (pl.) stone sides or cheeks of fireplace. [ME, f. OF *jambe* f. LL *gamba* leg]

jămboree′, n. Celebration, merry-making; large rally of boy scouts. [U.-S. sl.]

‖ **Jān(e)′ite** (-nī-), n. Admirer of Jane Austen's novels. [-ITE¹(1)]

jangle (jăng′gl), v.i. & t., & n. (Make) harsh noise; cause (bell etc.) to do this; speak, utter, in discordant or noisy way; (arch.) dispute, wrangle, (n. & vb). [ME, f. OF *jangler*, of unkn. orig.]

jăn′itor, n. Doorkeeper, caretaker. [L, f. *janua* door]

jăn′izarў, -nīssarў, (jă-, yă-), n. (Hist.) one of body of Turkish infantry forming Sultan's guard (abolished in 1826); Turkish soldier; (fig.) personal instrument of tyranny. [ult. f. Turk. *yeñitsheri* (*yeñi* new + *tsheri* soldiery)]

jănn′ock, a. (dial., esp. Lancs. & Yorks.). Straightforward, honest, genuine. [orig. unkn.]

Jăn′sen|ĭst, n. Member of party in Rom. Cath. Church esp. in France holding with Cornelius Jansen (d. 1638) the perverseness & inability for good of the natural human will. So ~ISM n., ~ĭs′tIC a. [-IST]

Jăn′uarў, n. (abbr. *Jan.*). First month of year. [ME & ONF *Jenever*, f. L *Januarius* (*mensis* month) of JANUS, see -ARY¹]

Jān′us, n. Ancient Italian god, whose temple was closed in time of peace, guardian of doors & gates, represented with faces on front & back of head. [L]

Jăp, a. & n. (colloq.). Japanese. [abbr.]

Japăn′¹, n. 1. (*J*~) island group on east of Asia, whence **JăpanESE′** (-ēz) a. & n., **JăpanESQUE′** (-ĕsk) a. 2. Hard varnish, esp. kind brought orig. from J~; work in Japanese style. [app. f. Malay *Japung* f. Chin. *Jih-pun* sunrise (*jih* (Jap. *ni*, see NIPPON) sun + *pun* origin)]

japăn′², v.t. (-nn-). Lacquer with japan; make black & glossy as with japan. [f. prec.]

jāpe, v.i., & n. (literary). Jest. [f. 14th c., of unkn. orig.]

Japhĕt′ic, a. Of, descended from, Japheth son of Noah; Indo-European. [-IC]

Japŏn′ic, a. Japanese. [f. *japon* = JAPAN +-IC]

Japŏn′ica, n. Kinds of Japanese plant, esp. ornamental variety of pear or quince. [mod. L fem. adj. as prec.]

jăr¹, n. Sound, vibration, esp. harsh one; thrill of nerves or feelings, shock; want of harmony, disagreement; quarrel. [as foll.]

jăr², v.i. & t. (-rr-). Sound discordantly, make grating impression (*upon* person, his ear, nerves, etc.); strike with grating sound (*upon, against,* object); (of body affected) vibrate, resound, discordantly; (of opinion, statement, action) be at variance, disagree, (*with*); dispute,

wrangle; cause (thing) to ~; send shock through (nerves). Hence ~r′ingLY² adv. [prob. imit.]

jăr³, n. Earthenware, stoneware, or glass vessel with or without handle(s), usu. cylindrical; LEYDEN ~. Hence ~′FUL(2) n. [f. F *jarre* f. Arab. *jarrah*]

jăr⁴, n. (colloq.). *On the, on a, on,* ~, ajar. [later form of obs. *char*; see AJAR¹]

jardiniére (zhầrdīnyầr′), n. Ornamental pot or stand for display of growing flowers in room, on window-sill, etc. [F]

jằrg′on¹, n. Unintelligible words, gibberish; barbarous or debased language; mode of speech full of unfamiliar terms, as *critics'* ~, *metaphysical* ~; twittering of birds. Hence ~IZE(2, 3) v.t. & i. [ME, f. OF, of unkn. orig.]

jằrg′on², jằrgŏōn′, n. Translucent, colourless, or smoky variety of zircon found in Ceylon. [F, perh. ult. f. ZIRCON]

jằrgonĕlle′, n. Kind of pear that ripens early. [F, dim. of prec.]

jằrl (y-), n. (hist.). Old Norse or Danish chief. [ON, orig. man of noble birth; = EARL]

jằ′rrah, n. (Durable timber of) W.--Austral. mahogany gum-tree. [f. native *jerrhyl*]

‖ **jằrv′ey,** n. (pl.~*s*). Hackney-coachman; driver of Irish car. [by-form of surname *Jarvis*]

‖ **jãs′ey,** n. (old sl.). Wig, esp. of worsted. [said to be = Jersey]

jăs′min(e), jĕss′amin(e), n. Kinds of shrubs with white or yellow flowers, esp. *common* or *white* ~, climbing shrub with fragrant flowers; *winter* ~, with yellow flowers. [16th c., with F *jasmin, jessemin* f. Arab. f. Pers. *yasmin*]

jas′per (-ah-), n. Opaque variety of quartz, usu. red, yellow, or brown. [ME, f. OF *jaspre* f. L f. Gk *iaspis*, of oriental orig., = any bright chalcedony except carnelian; cf. Heb. *yashpeh*]

Jat (jaht), n. Member of a people widely distributed in N.W. India & varying in religion & occupation.

jaun′dice, n., & v.t. 1. Morbid state caused by obstruction of bile, & marked by yellowness of skin, fluids, & tissues, constipation, & loss of appetite; disordered vision (usu. fig.), as characteristic of this. 2. v.t. Affect with ~; (fig. esp. in p.p.) affect (person, his judgement etc.) with envy or jealousy. [ME *iaunes, iaund-*, f. OF *jaunice* f. *jaune* yellow, -ICE]

jaunt, v.i., & n. (Take) excursion, journey, esp. for pleasure; ~*ing-car,* light two--wheeled vehicle popular in Ireland. [16th c., orig. unkn.]

jaun′t|ў, a. & n. 1. Having or affecting easy sprightliness, airy self-satisfaction. 2. n. (naut. sl.). ‖ Head of ship's police. Hence ~ĭLY² adv., ~ĭNESS n. [17th c. *jentee* repr. F pron. of F *gentil*; cf. GENTEEL]

Ja′van, Javanese′ (-ēz), (jah-), aa. & nn.

(Native) of Java; (-ese) language of central Java. [-AN; later -ESE after *Japanese*]

jăv′elin (-vl-), n. Light spear, dart. [f. F *javeline*, prob. of Celt. orig.]

jaw, n., & v.i. & t. **1.** Lower, upper, ~, two bones or sets of bones forming framework of mouth & masticating apparatus in vertebrates : ~-*bone*, each of the two bones forming lower ~ in most mammals, these two combined into one in others; (pl.) bones of mouth including teeth, mouth; (pl.) narrow mouth of valley, channel, etc.; (pl.) seizing members of machine, e.g. vice; (colloq.) loquacity, as *hold your* ~, stop talking, (also) sermonizing talk, lecture (esp. PI ²~); ~-*breaker* (colloq.), word hard to pronounce. **2.** vb. (sl.). Speak esp. at tedious length : lecture (person). [ME *jow(e)*, later *jaw(e)*, w. collateral *chaw(e)* (1530–1675); orig. unexpl.]

jay, n. Noisy chattering European bird of brilliant plumage; genus to which this belongs; (fig.) impertinent chatterer, simpleton; *~-walker*, pedestrian who crosses, or walks in, a street or road without due care or regard for traffic regulations. [ME, f. OF (mod. F *geai*), f. LL *gaius, gaia*]

jăzz, n., a., & v.i. & t. **1.** Music & dance of U.-S. Negro origin with characteristic harmony & ragtime rhythm; noisy or grotesque proceedings. **2.** adj. Discordant, loud in colour etc., rude, burlesque; ~ *band* (of such combinations as piano, trumpet, saxophone, banjo, & drums). **3.** vb. Play, dance, indulge in, ~; transform into, arrange as, ~. [orig. unkn.]

jea′lous (jĕl-), a. Solicitous for preservation *of* (rights etc.); resentful towards another on account of known or suspected rivalry; envious (*of* person, his advantages, etc.); (Bibl., of God) intolerant of unfaithfulness; (of inquiry, supervision, etc.) suspiciously vigilant. Hence ~LY² adv. [ME, f. OF *gelos* f. med. L *zelosus* (as ZEAL, see -OUS)]

jea′lousy (jĕlu-), n. Quality, state, of being jealous. [ME, f. OF *gelosie* (as prec., see -Y¹)]

jean (jān *or* jēn), n. Twilled cotton cloth; (pl.) garment of this, tight-fitting rather short slacks. [16th c., attrib. use of ME *Gene, Jane*, &c., = OF *Janne(s)*, mod. F *Gênes*, Genoa]

*jeep, n. Small utility motor vehicle. [f. *g p*, pr. jē pē, initials of *general purposes*]

jeer¹, n. (naut.). (Usu. pl.) tackle for hoisting & lowering lower yards. [orig. unkn.]

jeer², v.i. & t., & n. **1.** Scoff derisively (*at*); deride. **2.** n. Gibe, taunt. [orig. unkn.]

jehad. See JIHAD.

Jĕhŏv′ah (-*a*), n. Principal name of God in O.T. [repr. Heb. *Yahwe(h)*]

Jĕhŏv′ist, n. Author(s) of those parts of the Hexateuch in which God is called

Jehovah (cf. ELOHIST). Hence **Jĕhŏvĭs′tic** a. [-IST]

Jē′hū, n. (joc.). Furious driver; driver. [2 *Kings* ix. 20]

jĕjune′ (-ōōn), a. Meagre, scanty; (of land) barren; unsatisfying to the mind. Hence ~LY² adv., ~NESS n. [f. L *jejunus* fasting]

Jĕk′ўll and Hȳde, n. Single person in whom two personalities alternate. [*Dr J. & Mr H.*, by Stevenson]

*jĕll, n. & v.i. (colloq.). Jelly. [f. foll.]

jĕll′ў, n., & v.t. & i. **1.** Soft stiff semitransparent food, consisting chiefly of gelatin, got from skin, bones, etc., by boiling & cooling; similar preparation of juice of fruit etc.; ~-*bag* (for straining ~); ~-*fish*, pop. name of medusa or sea-nettle; ‖ ~-*graph*, copying apparatus employing sheet of ~ in tray. **2.** vb. (Cause to) set as ~, congeal. [ME, f. OF *gelee* frost, jelly, f. Rom. *gelata* (L *gelare* freeze, see -Y⁴)]

jĕm′adār, n. Junior native officer of Indian army; Indian police-officer; head servant; (Anglo-Ind. colloq.) sweeper (domestic scavenger). [Urdu, f. Pers. (Arab.) *jama'* collection (of men)+Pers. *dār* holder]

‖ jĕmĭm′as (-z), n. pl. (colloq.). Elastic-sided boots; goloshed cloth over-boots. [f. female personal name]

jĕmm′ў, n. Crowbar used by burglars, usu. made in sections; ‖ sheep's head as a dish. [fam. form of *James*]

je ne sais quoi (zhenesăkwah′), n. An indescribable something. [F, = I know not what]

jĕnn′ĕt, n. Small Spanish horse. [f. F *genet* f. Sp. *jinete* light horseman]

jĕnn′ĕtĭng, n. Kind of early apple. [f. F name *Jeannet*+-ING³]

jĕnn′ў, n. Locomotive crane; = SPINNING-~~; a stroke at billiards; she-ass; ~ *wren*, (pop. & nursery name for) wren. [fam. form of *Janet*]

jeo′pardize (jĕp-), -**ise** (-īz), v.t. Endanger. [foll., -IZE]

jeo′pardy (jĕp-), n. Danger. [ME *iuparti* f. OF *iu (ieu) parti* divided (i.e. even) game, f. L *jocus* game+*partitus* p.p. of *partiri* divide f. *pars -rtis* part]

jĕqui′ritў, n. Indian twining shrub with parti-coloured seeds used for ornament & in medicine. [f. F *jéqwirity* f. Tupi--Guarani *jekiritî*]

jĕrbŏ′a (*or* jĕrb²), n. Small rodent of African deserts, with long hind legs & great jumping powers. [f. Arab. *yarbu'* flesh of loins, jerboa]

jĕrĕmī′ad, n. Lamentation, doleful complaint. [f. F *jérémiade* f. *Jérémie* f. LL *Jeremias* Jeremiah, see -AD]

Jĕrĕmī′ah, n. Doleful prophet or denouncer of the times. [*Lamentations* of ~, O.-T. bk]

Jĕ′richo (-kō), n. Town in Palestine; *go to* ~ (to the devil).

jerid' (-ēd), **-eed**, n. Javelin used by Persian, Turkish, & Arabian horsemen; game in which this is used. [f. Arab. *jarid*]

jerk¹, n. Sharp sudden pull, twist, etc.; involuntary spasmodic contraction of muscle; (pl.) spasmodic movements of limbs or face, esp. in religious excitement; PHYSICAL ~s. Hence ~'ILY² adv., ~'INESS n., ~'Y² a. [16th c., imit.]

jerk², v.t. & i. Pull, thrust, twist, etc., with a jerk; throw with suddenly arrested motion; (intr.) move with a jerk. [as prec.]

jerk³, v.t. Cure (esp. beef) by cutting in long slices & drying in sun. [f. Amer. Sp. *charquear* (*charque* f. Peruv. *ccharqui* dried flesh)]

jerk'in, n. (hist.). Man's close-fitting jacket, often of leather. [c. 1500, of unkn. orig.]

Jeroboʹam, n. Wine-bottle of 8–12 times ordinary size. ['A mighty man of valour' ' who made Israel to sin '—1 *Kings* xi. 28, xiv. 16]

jeʹrry̆, n. ~-*builder*, -*building*, builder, building, of unsubstantial houses with bad materials; ~-*built*, so built; ‖ (also ~--*shop*) low beer-shop; ‖ (sl.) chamber-pot; (army sl., *j*~) German soldier, the Germans; *je'rrican*, ~*can*, kind of (orig. German) petrol-can. [variously derived]

jerrymander. Erron. var. of GERRY-MANDER.

jerʹsey (-zĭ), n. (pl. ~s). 1. (*J*~). One of the Channel Islands (often attrib.); J~ cow. 2. Close-fitting woollen knitted tunic, esp. as worn in athletic exercises; similar garment worn as undervest; woman's close-fitting knitted jacket.

Jerusʹalem (-rōō-), n. City in Israel; ~ (*pony*), donkey; ~ ARTICHOKE.

jess, n., & v.t. 1. Short strap of leather, silk, etc., round legs of hawk used in falconry. 2. v.t. Put ~es on (hawk). [ME *ges* f. OF *ges* nom. of *get* (mod. F *jet*) f. L *jactus -ūs* throw f. *jacĕre jact-*]

jessamine. See JASMINE.

Jessʹe̬, n. ~ *window* (with Christ's descent from ~ represented). [*Is.* xi. 1, *Matt.* i. 6, 16]

jest¹, n. Piece of raillery or banter; taunt, ·jeer; joke; fun, esp. *in* ~, not seriously; object of derision, as *a standing* ~; ~--*book*, book of ~s. [orig. = exploit, f. OF *geste* f. L *gesta*, neut. pl. p.p. of *gerere* do]

jest², v.i. Joke; jeer; speak, act, in trifling manner, whence ~'INGLY² adv. [f. prec.]

jesʹter, n. One who jests, esp. professed maker of amusement maintained in court or.noble household. [-ER¹]

Jesʹuit (-z-), n. Member of Society of Jesus, R.-C. order founded by Ignatius Loyola (1533); (derog., hist.) dissembling person, equivocator; ~*s'* (Peruvian) *bark*. Hence **Jĕsuit'ICAL** a., **Jĕsuit'icalLY²** adv., ~ISM(2), ~RY(4), nn., ~IZE(3) v.t. & i., (-z-). [f. mod. L *Jesuita* (*Jesus*, see -ITE¹)]

jet¹, n. & a. Hard black lignite taking brilliant polish; (of) colour of this, deep glossy black, (also ~-*black*). [ME *gete*, *ieet*, f. OF *jaiet* f. L f. Gk *gagatēs*]

jet², n. Stream of water, steam, gas, etc., shot forward or upwards esp. from small opening; spout, nozzle, for emitting water etc. thus; (colloq.) ~-propelled plane; ~-*propelled*, (esp. of aircraft) plane; ~-*propelled*, (esp. of aircraft) deriving propulsive power from the backward thrust of high-velocity ~s of gas discharged through nozzles in the rear of the wings, fuselage, etc.; so *jet* attrib., as ~ *engine*, *plane*. [f. foll. & f. F *jet* as foll.]

jet³, v.t. & i. (-tt-). Spurt forth in jets. [f. F *jeter* throw f. LL *jectare* = L *jactare* frequent. of *jacĕre jact*- throw]

jetʹsam, n. Goods thrown overboard from ship to lighten it, & (in mod. use) washed ashore (cf. FLOTSAM). [contr. of foll.]

jettʹison, n., & v.t. 1. Throwing of goods overboard, esp. to lighten ship in distress. 2. Throw (goods) overboard thus. [f. AF *getteson* (OF *getaison*) f. L *jactationem* (*jactare* throw, see JET³ & -ATION)]

jettʹon, n. Counter with stamped or engraved device. [F *jeton* (*jeter*, see JET³)]

jettʹy̆¹, n. Mole running out to defend harbour or coast; landing-pier. [f. OF *jetee* (mole) thrown out, fem. p.p. as JET³]

jettʹy̆², a. Jet-black. [JET¹, -Y²]

jeu (see Ap.), n. (pl. ~*x*, pr. zhēr). ~ *de mots* (demō), play on words, pun; ~ *d'esprit* (dēsprē'), witty or humorous (usu. literary) trifle. [F]

jeune fille (zhĕrn fē'ye), n. Young girl, miss. [F]

jeune premier (zhĕrn premyā'), n. (theatr.). Juvenile lead. [F]

jeunesse dorée (see Ap.), n. The gilded youth, young swells. [F]

Jew (jōō), n. One of the Hebrew or Jewish people, or one who professes Judaism; (transf., derog., vulg.) usurer, trader who drives hard bargains; ~-*baiting*, persecution of ~s; ~*'s-ear*, edible cup-shaped fungus; ~*'s-harp*, small lyre-shaped musical instrument, played by holding frame between teeth & striking metal tongue. Hence ~'ESS¹ n., ~'ISH¹ a., (jōō-). [ME, f. OF *giu* f. L f. Gk *Ioudaios* f. Aramaic *y'hudai*=Heb. *y'hudi* f. *y'hudah* Judah]

jew'el (jōō-), n., & v.t. (-ll-). 1. Ornament containing precious stone(s), worn for personal adornment; precious stone; highly prized person or thing; *the* ~--*house*, room in Tower of London in which crown ~s are kept; hence or cogn. ~'IER¹, ~IERY(1), ~RY, nn., ~IY² a. 2. v.t. Adorn, furnish, with ~s; fit (watch) with ~s for the pivot-holes. [ME, f. AF *juel* = OF *joel*, *jouel*, *joiel*, of disputed orig.]

jew'ing (jōō-), n. Wattles at base of beak in some domestic pigeons. [*Jew* (from resemblance to hooked nose)+-ING¹]

Jewry (joor'Ĭ), n. The Jews; (hist.) Jews' quarter in town etc. [ME, f. AF *juerie* (JEW, -ERY)]

jezail' (-zīl), n. Long Afghan musket. [Pers. *jazā'īl*]

Jěz'ébel, n. Impudent or abandoned woman; woman who paints her face. [~, wife of Ahab]

jib[1], n. Triangular stay-sail from outer end of ~-boom to fore-topmast head in large ships, from bowsprit to masthead in smaller ones; *cut of his* ~, his personal appearance; ~-*boom*, spar run out from end of bowsprit; projecting arm of crane. [17th c., goes w. foll.]

jib[2], v.t. & i. (naut.; -bb-). Pull (sail, yard) round from one side of ship to the other; (intr., of sail etc.) swing round thus. [17th c., shortened f. *jibe*, GYBE]

jib[3], v.i. (-bb-). (Of horse etc.) stop & refuse to go on, move backwards or sideways instead of going on, whence ~b'ER[1] n.; (fig.) refuse to proceed in some action; ~ *at*, show repugnance to (course, person). [19th c., of unkn. orig.]

jibb'a(h) (-ba), **jŭ-** (*or* jŏŏ-), **dj-**, n. Mohammedan's long cloth coat. [var. of Arab. *jubbah*]

jib door (dōr), n. Door flush with wall in which it stands, usu. painted etc. so as to be indistinguishable. [orig. unkn.]

jibe. See GIBE.

jiff' (ў), n. (colloq.). Very short time, as *in a* ~, (*wait*) *half a* ~. [18th c., of unkn. orig.]

jig[1], n. Lively dance; music for this, usu. in three-four or six-eight time; appliance that holds a piece of work & guides the tools operating upon it. [16th c., orig. unkn.; perh. ult. imit.]

jig[2], v.i. & t. (-gg-). Dance a jig; move (t. & i.) up & down rapidly & jerkily; separate coarser & finer portions of (ore) by shaking it under water in box with perforated bottom; work upon with a ~, equip with ~s; ~'*saw*, machine fretsaw (~*saw puzzle*, picture pasted on board & cut in irregular pieces with ~saw). [goes w. prec.]

jigg'er[1] (-g-), n. (Naut.) small tackle consisting of a double & single block with rope; small sail, small smack with this; (Billiards) rest for cue (sl.); (Golf) iron club with narrow face; one who jigs ore; ~-*mast*, aftermost mast in four-master. [partly f. prec. +-ER[1]]

jigg'er[2] (-g-), n. = CHIGOE. [corrupt.]

jigg'ered (-gerd), a. (colloq.). (As mild oath) confounded (*I'm* ~). [euphem.]

‖ **jigg'erў-pōk'erў** (-g-), n. (colloq.). Underhand scheming; hocus-pocus, humbug. [cf. Sc. *joukery-pawkery*]

jig'gle, v.t. Rock or jerk lightly. [f. JIG[2] +-LE(3)]

jihad', **jė-**, (-ahd), n. Religious war of Mohammedans against unbelievers; (fig.) crusade for or against a doctrine etc. [Arab. *jihad*]

Jill. Var. of GILL[4], as in JACK *&·* ~.

jilt, n., & v.t. 1. One esp. a woman who capriciously casts off lover after encouragement. 2. v.t. Play the ~ towards, be faithless to. [' a new canting word ' in 1674, of unkn. orig.]

***Jim Crow** (-ō), n. Negro (~ *car*, to which Negroes in some southern States of U.S. are restricted on railroads); implement for straightening iron bars or rails by screw pressure. [nickname]

jim'-jăms', n. pl. (sl.). Delirium tremens; fit of the creeps. [whimsical reduplication]

‖ **jimp**] a. (Sc.). Slender, graceful; scanty. [c. 1500, of unkn. orig.]

jingl|**e** (jĭng'gl), n., & v.i. & t. 1. Mingled noise like that of small bells, links of chain, etc.; repetition of same or similar sounds in words, esp. if designed to catch the attention; ~*ing* verse; Irish & Australian covered two-wheeled car. 2. vb. Make, cause (keys etc.) to make, a ~e; (of writing) be full of alliterations, rhymes, etc. [ME; imit.]

jing'ō (-ngg-), int., n. (pl. ~*es*), & a. 1. (In asseverations) *by* (*the living*) ~ !; supporter of bellicose policy, blustering patriot (orig. supporter of Disraeli's policy in 1878, f. use of *by* ~ in popular song). 2. adj. Vulgarly dashing. Hence ~ISM(2), ~IST(2), nn., ~IS'TIC a. [17th c.; orig. conjurer's gibberish]

jink, v.i. & t., & n. 1. Move elusively, dodge, elude by dodging; (sl.) manœuvre aircraft, be manœuvred, jerkily to avoid anti-aircraft fire etc. 2. n. Act of ~ing; *high* ~s, boisterous sport, merrymaking. [orig. So.; prob. imit. of nimble motion]

jinnee', n. (pl. *jinn*, often used as sing.; fem. ~*yeh* pr. -yā). (In Mohammedan demonology) spirit, lower than angels, able to appear in human & animal forms, & having supernatural power over men (also GENIE). [f. Arab. *jinni*; cf. GENIE]

jinrick'sha, **-rik'isha**, n. Light two-wheeled hooded vehicle drawn by man or men, first used in Japan c. 1870. [Jap. (*-kisha*), f. *jin* man + *riki* power + *sha* vehicle]

***jinx**, n. (sl.). Person or thing that brings bad luck. [orig. unkn.]

jīrg'a, n. Assembly of Afghan headmen. [Pushtu]

***jit'ney**, n. (sl.). Five cents; motor-bus carrying passengers at low rates. [orig. unkn.]

jitt'er, v.i., & n. (sl., orig. U.S.). 1. Be nervous, act nervously; ~*bug* n., person addicted to dancing to ' hot ' music, nervous person. 2. n. pl. Extreme nervousness, ' nerves ', (*have the* ~s, be in a blue funk). Hence ~Y[2] a. (sl.), nervy, jumpy. [imit.; cf. dial. *chitter*]

jiu-jitsu. See JU-JUTSU.

jive, n., & v.i. 1. Kind of jazz music. 2. v.i. Play ~, dance to ~. [orig. unkn.]

jŏb¹, n. Piece of work, esp. one done for hire or profit; (colloq.) employment, post; transaction in which duty is sacrificed to private advantage; anything one has to do (*on the ~*, sl., in action, alert); *do person's ~*, ruin him; *bad ~*, thing on which labour is wasted, failure; *good, bad, ~* (state of affairs); *~ lot*, lot of goods bought as speculation; ‖*~'master*, one who lets out horses & carriages by the ~; *~-work*, done & paid for by the ~. [16th c., of unkn. orig.]

jŏb², v.i. & t. (-bb-). Do jobs; ‖ hire (horse, carriage) for definite time or job, let out on hire thus; buy & sell (stock, goods) as broker; deal in stocks; turn position of trust to private advantage; deal corruptly with (matter), whence ~b'ERY(4) n. Hence ~b'ER¹ n. [f. prec.]

jŏb³, v.t. & i. (-bb-), & n. **1**. Prod, stab slightly; hurt (horse) with bit; (intr.) thrust *at* (thing). **2**. n. Prod, thrust, jerk at bit. [15th c., app. imit.; cf. JAB]

Jŏb⁴, n. Patriarch whose story forms *Book of Job* in O.T. (*would try the patience of ~*, is vexatious); *~'s comforter*, one who under guise of comforter aggravates distress; *~'s tears*, seeds of a grass used as beads.

jŏbā'tion, n. (colloq.). Reprimand, esp. lengthy one. [17th c., f. obs. *jobe* reprove f. prec. +-ATION)]

‖ **jŏbb'ernowl** (-ōl), n. (colloq.). Stupid head; stupid person. [f. obs. *jobard* fool (f. F, f. *jobe* silly) +NOLL]

‖ **Jŏck**, n. (army sl.). Scottish esp. Highland soldier. [= Jack]

jŏck'ey¹, n. (pl. ~s). Professional rider in horse-races (also colloq. *jock*); *J~ Club*, club established at Newmarket, the body controlling horse-racing; ‖ lad, understrapper. Hence ~DOM, ~SHIP(3), nn. [f. Sc. *Jock* Jack +-Y³]

jŏck'ey², v.t. & i. Outwit, cheat; get (person etc.) *away, out, in*, etc., by trickery; cheat (person *into, out of, doing*); (intr.) cheat; *~ for position*, try to gain an advantageous position esp. by skilful manœuvring in yacht-racing, try to gain an unfair advantage. [f. prec.]

jŏck'ō, n. (pl. ~s). Chimpanzee. [F, made by Buffon f. Gaboon *engeco* (prop. *ncheko*)]

jocōse', a. Playful; waggish. Hence ~LY² adv., ~NESS, jocŏs'ITY, nn. [f. L *jocosus* (*jocus* jest, see -OSE¹)]

jŏc'ūlar, a. Mirthful; humorous. Hence or cogn. ~ITY (-ă'r-) n., ~LY² adv. [f. L *jocularis* (*joculus* dim. of *jocus* jest, -AR¹)]

jŏc'und, a. Merry, sprightly; pleasant. Hence or cogn. **jocŭn'dITY** n., ~LY² adv. [ME, f. OF, f. LL *jucundus* f. L *jucundus*, influenced by assoc. w. *jocus* jest]

Jodhpurs' (jŏdpoorz], n. pl. Long breeches for riding etc., tight from knee to ankle. [*Jodhpur* in India]

‖ **Jōe**, n. *Not for ~* (i.e. me)*!*, sl. refusal.

Jōe Mill'er, n. Stale joke, chestnut. [f. *Joseph Miller*, comedian, d. 1738]

jō'ey¹, n. (pl. ~s). Young kangaroo; young animal. [f. native Austral. *joe*]

‖ **jō'ey²**, n. (sl.). A threepenny (orig. in 1836 a fourpenny) bit. [f. *Joseph* Hume]

jŏg, v.t. & i. (-gg-), & n. **1**. Shake with push or jerk; nudge (person), esp. to arouse attention; stimulate (person's, one's own, memory); move up & down with unsteady motion; proceed laboriously, trudge, (often *on, along*); go on one's way, depart, as *we must be ~ging*; proceed, get through the time, as *we must ~ on somehow, matters ~ along*; *~'trot*, slow regular trot, (fig.) monotonous progression (often attrib.). **2**. n. Shake, push, nudge, slow walk or trot. [16th c., app. imit.]

jŏg'gle¹, v.t. & i., & n. **1**. Shake, move, (as) by repeated jerks. **2**. n. Slight shake. [f. prec. +-LE(3)]

jŏg'gle², n., & v.t. **1**. Joint of two pieces of stone or timber, contrived to prevent their sliding on one another; notch in one of two pieces, projection in the other, or small piece let in between both, for this purpose. **2**. v.t. Join by means of a ~. [(vb f.n.) perh. f. *jog* = JAG¹]

Jŏhänn'ine, a. Of the apostle John. [f. L as JOHN, see -INE¹]

Jŏhänn'isbérger (-g-), n. Fine white wine from Johannisberg in the Rheingau. [G]

John (jŏn), n. Masculine Christian name; *~ BARLEYcorn*; *~ Bull*, English nation, typical Englishman; *~ Chinaman*, typical Chinese; *~ COMPANY*; *~ Doe*, fictitious character in law (cf. RICHARD *Roe*); *~ DORY¹*; *~-o'-Groat's (House)*, north of Scotland (*from ~-'o-Groat's to Land's End*, through Gt Britain). [f. LL *Jo(h)annes* f. Gk *Iōannēs* f. Heb. *Yokhanan*]

John'ian (jŏn-), a. & n. (Member) of St John's College, Cambridge. [-IAN]

johnn'y (jŏn-), n. ‖ Fellow, esp. fashionable idler; ‖ *J~ Armstrong* (naut. sl.), hand-power; *J~ Raw*, novice; *~-cake*, cake of (U.S.) maize-meal or (Austral.) wheat-meal. [f. JOHN, -Y³]

Johnsōn'ian (jŏn-), a. Of, like, Samuel Johnson, man of letters & lexicographer (d. 1784), esp., abounding in Latin-derived polysyllables. So **JohnsonESE'** (jŏnsŏnēz') n. [-IAN]

joie de vivre (zhwah de vē'vr), n. Feeling of healthy enjoyment of life. [F, = joy of living]

join, v.t. & i., & n. **1**. Put together, fasten, unite, (things, one *to* another); connect (two points) by straight line; unite (persons, one *with* or *to* another) in marriage, friendship, alliance, etc.; (intr.) come together, be united, (*with, to*, or abs.); take part with others (*in doing*); come into the company of (person); become member of (club etc.); take, resume, one's place in (regiment, ship, company, etc.); come into connexion with, as *the Cherwell ~s the Thames below Oxford*; *~ battle*, begin fighting; *~ hands*, clasp one's hands together, clasp each other's hands, (fig.) combine in action or enterprise; ~ ISSUE¹; ~ up (intr.), enlist in the army etc. 2. n. Point, line, of junction. [ME, f. OF *joindre* (st. *joign-*) f. L *jungere junct-* join]

join'der, n. (rare exc. law). Joining, union. [f. F *joindre* JOIN taken as noun, cf. -ER⁴]

join'|er, n. In vbl senses, esp. one who makes furniture, house fittings, & other woodwork lighter than carpenter's, whence~ERY(1, 2) n. [ME, f. AF *joignour* (JOIN, -ER¹, -OR)]

joint¹, n. Place at which two things are joined together; structure in animal body by which two bones are fitted together; *out of* ~, (of bone) dislocated, (fig.) out of order; *put* (person's) NOSE *out of* ~; part of stem from which leaf or branch grows; point at which, contrivance by which, two parts of artificial structure are joined, rigidly or so as to allow of movement; (Geol.) fissure in mass of rock; one of the parts of which a body is made up; ‖ one of the parts into which butcher divides carcass, esp. as served at table; (sl., esp. U.S.) a place of meeting or resort; ~-*stool* (orig. *joined*), one made of parts fitted by a joiner, night-stool, commode. Hence ~'LESS a. [ME, f. OF, p.p. as JOIN]

joint², a. Held or done by, belonging to, two or more persons etc. in conjunction, as ~ *action, opinion, estate*; (of persons) sharing (*with* others in possession, action, state, etc.), as ~ *owners*; *during their* ~ *lives*, while they are all alive; ~ *stock*, capital held ~ly, common fund, (attrib.) holding, formed on basis of, a ~ stock, as ~-*stock bank, company.* Hence ~'LY² adv. [ME, f. OF, as prec.]

joint³, v.t. Connect by joints; fill up joints (of masonry etc.) with mortar etc., point; prepare (board etc.) for being joined to another by planing its edge; divide (body, member) at a joint or into joints. [f. JOINT¹]

join'ter, n. In vbl senses, esp.: plane for jointing; mason's tool for pointing; workman employed in jointing esp. electric wire. [-ER¹]

join'tress, n. Widow who holds a jointure. [f. obs. *jointer* joint possessor + -ESS¹]

join'ture, n., & v.t. 1. Estate settled on a wife, to be enjoyed by her after her husband's death. 2. v.t. Provide (wife) with ~. [ME, f. OF, f. L *junctura* (as JOIN, see -URE)]

joist, n. One of parallel timbers stretched on edge from wall to wall for ceiling laths or floor boards to be nailed to. Hence jois'tED² a. [ME *giste* f. OF *giste* (*gesir* lie f. L *jacēre*)]

jōke¹, n. Thing said or done to excite laughter; witticism, jest; ridiculous circumstance; *practical* ~, trick played on person in order to have laugh at his

expense; *it is no* ~ (a serious matter). Hence jōk'Y² a. [f. 17th c., prob. f. L *jocus* jest]

jōke², v.i. & t. Make jokes; poke fun at, banter. Hence jōk'ingLY² adv. [f. prec. or f. L *jocari* as prec.]

jōk'er, n. One who jokes; (sl.) fellow, chap; (Cards) odd (often blank) card in some games, counting as (highest) trump; *a clause unobtrusively inserted in a bill or document & affecting its operation in a way not immediately apparent. [-ER¹]

jokul, jökull (yŏ'kŏŏl, yĕr-), n. Snow-mountain in Iceland. [Icel. *jökull;* see ICICLE]

jŏll'i|fý, v.i. & t. Make merry, esp. tipple; make jolly. Hence ~FICA'TION n. [-FY]

jŏll'itY, n. Merrymaking, festivity. [ME, f. OF *jolivete* (as JOLLY, see -TY)]

jŏll'ÿ, a., adv., n., & v.t. 1. Joyful; slightly drunk; festive, jovial; *the* ~ *god*, Bacchus; (colloq., of person or thing) very pleasant, delightful, (often iron., as *he must be a* ~ *fool to do it*), whence jŏll'iLY² adv. 2. adv. (colloq.). Very, as *he will be* ~ *savage, you will* ~ *well have to.* 3. n. (sl.). ‖ Royal Marine. 4. v.t. (colloq.). Flatter, cajole (usu. ~ *along*); chaff, banter. [ME & OF *joli(f)* gay, pretty; ult. orig. unkn.]

jŏll'ÿ-boat, n. (Also *jolly*) clinker-built ship's boat, smaller than cutter. [18th c., of unkn. orig.; cf. 16-17th c. *jolywat, gellywatie;* cf. YAWL²]

jŏlt, v.t. & i., & n. 1. Shake (person etc.) with jerk from seat etc., esp. in locomotion; (of vehicle) move along with jerks, as on rough road. 2. n. Such jerk. Hence jŏl'tУ² a. [c. 1600, of unkn. orig.]

jŏl'terhead (-hĕd), n. Clumsy head; stupid person. [extension of obs. *joli-head*, of unkn. orig.]

Jōn'ah (-*a*), n. Person who brings, or is sacrificed lest he bring, ill luck. [see *Jonah*, O.T. book]

Jŏn'athan, n. 1. (*Brother*) ~, personified people of, typical citizen of, United States. 2. Kind of dessert apple. [perh. f. ~ Trumbull, governor of Connecticut]

jongleur (see Ap.), n. (hist.). Itinerant minstrel. [F, var. of *jougleur* JUGGLER]

jŏn'quil (or jŭ-), n. Species of narcissus, daffodil with rushlike leaves; ~ *colour*, pale yellow. [f. mod. L *jonquilla* = F *jonquille*, Sp. *junquillo*, f. L dim. of *juncus* reed]

jŏrd'an, n. (not in polite use). Chamber-pot. [ME also *jurdan(e)* vessel used by alchemists; orig. unascert.]

Jŏrd'an alm'ond (ahm-), n. Fine almond esp. from Malaga. [ME *jardyne*, app. f. OF or Sp. *jardin* garden]

jŏr'um, n. Large drinking-bowl; its contents, esp. punch. [orig. unkn.; conject. = *Joram* (2 Sam. viii. 10); cf. JEROBOAM]

jōs'éph (-z-), n. (*J~*) chaste man; woman's long riding-cloak of 18th c. [see *Gen.* xxxix, xxxvii. 3]

*jŏsh, n., & v.t. & i. (sl.). **1.** Good-natured joke, leg-pull. **2.** vb. Hoax, banter; indulge in ridicule. Hence ∼'ER¹ n. [U.S.]

jŏs'kĭn, n. (sl.). Country bumpkin, dolt. [cf. *bumpkin*, & *joss* dial. to bump]

jŏss, n. Chinese idol; ∼*-house*, Chinese temple; ∼*-stick* (of fragrant tinder mixed with clay, as incense). [app. f. Port. *deos* f. L *deus* god]

‖ **jŏss'er**, n. (sl.). Fool; fellow. [-ER¹]

jŏ'stle (-sl), v.i. & t., & n. **1.** Knock, push, *against*; struggle *with* (person *for* thing); push against, elbow; push (person *away*, *from*, etc.). **2.** n. Jostling, encounter. [earlier *justle*, f. *just* JOUST + -LE(3)]

jŏt¹, n. (Usu. w. negative expressed or implied) small amount, whit; ∼ *or* TITTLE. [f. L f. Gk *iōta* letter *i*]

jŏt², v.t. (-tt-). Write (usu. *down*) briefly or hastily. [prob. f. prec.]

joule (jōōl), n. (electr.). Unit of work or energy, amount of work done or heat generated by a current of one ampere acting for one second against a resistance of one ohm. [Dr. J. P. *Joule*, Eng. physicist (d. 1889)]

jounce, v.t. & i. Bump, bounce, jolt. [15th c., of unkn. orig.]

journ'al (jĕr-), n. **1.** (In bookkeeping by double entry) book in which each transaction is entered, with statement of accounts to which it is to be debited & credited. **2.** Daily record of events; (Parl.) the *J*∼*s*, record of daily proceedings; (Naut.) log-book; daily newspaper, other periodical. **3.** Part of shaft or axle that rests on bearings (hist. unexpl.); ∼*-box* (enclosing ∼ & bearings). [ME, f. OF f. LL *diurnalis* DIURNAL]

journ'al|ist (jĕr-), n. One whose business it is to edit or write for a public journal. Hence or cogn. ∼ESE' (-ēz) n., style of language characteristic of (hasty or inferior) newspaper writing, ∼ISM n., ∼is'tic a. [-IST]

journ'alize (jĕr-), -ise (-īz), v.t. & i. (Bookk.) enter in journal; record in, keep, private journal. [-IZE]

journ'ey (jĕr-), n. (pl. ∼s), & v.i. **1.** Distance travelled in specified time, as *a day's*, *4 days'*, ∼; expedition to some distance, round of travel (usu. by land, cf. VOYAGE), as *take*, *undertake*, *perform*, *a* ∼; ∼*man*, qualified (dist. *apprentice*) mechanic or artisan who works for another, (fig.) mere hireling; (Astron.)∼*man* (*clock*), secondary clock in observatory; ∼*-work*, work of a ∼man (esp. fig.). **2.** v.i. Make a ∼. [ME; (vb f. AF *journeyer*) f. OF *jornee* day, day's work or journey, f. Rom. *diurnata day (LL *diurnum* day f. L *-us* daily); see -Y⁴]

joust (jōōst), **jŭst**, v.i., & n. (Engage in) combat between two knights etc. on horseback with lances. [(n. f. OF *juste*) ME *just*(*e*) f. OF *juster* f. Rom. *juxtare approach (*juxta* near)]

Jŏve, n. Jupiter, esp. ‖ *by* ∼ *!* [f. L *Jovem* (nom. *Jupiter*)]

jŏv'ial, a. Merry; convivial. Hence or cogn. ∼ITY (-ăl²) n., ∼LY² adv. [f. F f. It. *gioviale* f. LL *jovialis* of Jupiter (*Jupiter Jovis*, see -AL)]

Jŏv'ian, a. Of, like, Jove; of the planet Jupiter. [f. F *jovien* or LL *Jovianus* (as prec., -AN)]

jowl, n. Jawbone, jaw; cheek, esp. *cheek by* ∼; external throat or neck when prominent, dewlap of cattle, crop of bird; head & shoulders of salmon & other fish. [(1) ME *chaul* jaw (f. OE *ceafl*); (2) ME *cholle* neck (cf. OE *ceolur*); (3) ME *cholle* head of man, beast, fish; f. 16th c. all levelled out into unexplained *joule*, *jowl*]

joy¹, n. Vivid emotion of pleasure, gladness; thing that causes delight; ∼*-bells* (rung on festive occasions); ∼*-ride* (sl.), stolen or other pleasure-ride in motor etc.; ∼*'stick* (sl.), control lever of aeroplane. Hence or cogn. ∼'FUL, ∼'LESS, ∼'OUS, aa., ∼'fulLY², ∼'lessLY², ∼'ousLY², advv., ∼'fulNESS, ∼'lessNESS, ∼'ousNESS, nn. [ME, f. OF *joie* f. Rom. *gaudia fem. f. L *gaudia* pl. of *gaudium*]

joy², v.i. & t. (chiefly poet.). Rejoice; gladden. [ME, f. OF *joir* rejoice ult. f. L *gaudēre* rejoice]

jub'il|āte¹ (jōō-), v.i. Exult, make demonstrations of joy. Hence or cogn. ∼ANCE, ∼A'TION, nn., ∼ANT a., ∼antLY² adv. [f. L *jubilare* (*jubilum* shout), see -ATE³]

Jŭbīlāt'e² (jōō-; *or* yōōbīlaht'ĭ), n. Hundredth psalm as canticle in Anglican service; outburst of triumph. [L, = shout ye (its first word)]

jub'ilee (jōō-), n. **1.** (Jewish hist.) year of emancipation & restoration, kept every 50 years, acc. to *Lev.* xxv; (R.-C. Ch.) year of remission from penal consequences of sin, granted formerly at various intervals, now at any time. **2.** Fiftieth anniversary; *silver* ∼, twenty-fifth anniversary; *Diamond J*∼, 1897, sixtieth year of reign of Queen Victoria. **3.** Season of rejoicing; exultant joy. [ME, f. OF *jubile* f. LL *jubilaeus* (*annus year*) of jubilee f. Gk *iōbēlaios* (*iōbēlos* f. Heb. *yobel* ram, ram's-horn trumpet, jubilee) by assoc. w. L *jubilare* shout]

Judā'ic (jōō-), a. Jewish. [f. L f. Gk . *Ioudaïkos* (*Ioudaios* JEW¹, see -IC)]

Jud'ā|ize (jōō-), -**ise** (-īz), v.i. & t. Follow Jewish customs or rites; make Jewish. So ∼ISM, ∼IST, nn. [f. LL *judaizare* f. Gk *ioudaïzō* (as prec., see -IZE)]

jud'as (jōō-), n. (*J*∼) disciple who betrayed Christ, infamous traitor; peephole in door; (of beard etc.) *J*∼*-colour*(*ed*), red; *J*∼ *kiss* (see *Matt.* xxvi. 48); *J*∼*-tree* (with purple flowers appearing before the leaves).

jŭdd'er, v.i. & n. **1.** Shake, wobble. **2.** n. Shaking, wobbling. [imit.]

Jud'enhetze (yōōdenhĕtze), n. Systematic persecution of Jews. [G]

judge¹, n. Public officer appointed to hear & try causes in court of justice; (of God) supreme arbiter; (Heb. hist.) officer having temporary authority in Israel in period between Joshua & the kings; (pl., abbr. *Judg.*) book of O.T.; person appointed to decide dispute or contest; person who decides a question; person who is qualified to decide on merits of thing or question, as *am no ~ of that, good~ of claret*; *J~ Advocate General,* civil officer in supreme control of courts martial in army and R.A.F.; *~-made law,* principles based on *~s'* decisions. Hence *~'ship*(1, 2) n. [ME, f. OF *juge* f. L *judicem* (nom. *-dex*) f. *jus* right *+ -dicus* speaking]

judge², v.t. & i. Pronounce sentence on (person) in court of justice; try (cause); decide (question); decide, decree, (*that* etc.); form opinion about, estimate, (person etc. *by* his deeds etc.); (arch.) criticize, censure (*~ not that ye be not ~d*); conclude, consider, suppose, (thing *to be, that,* etc., *from* or *by* data); act as judge; form a judgement (*of* thing etc.). [ME, f. OF *jugier* f. L *judicare* (as prec.)]

judgemat'ic|(al) (-jm-), aa. (colloq.). Judicious, discerning. Hence *~alLY²* adv. [f. JUDGE, on *dogmatic* etc.]

judge'ment (-jm-), **-gment** (-jm-), n. Sentence of court of justice; *the last ~* (by God at end of world); misfortune viewed as sign of divine displeasure, as *it is a ~ on you for getting up late*; criticism; opinion, estimate, as *in my~*; critical faculty, discernment; good sense; *~-day* (of God's final *~*); *~ debt* (for payment of which a *~* has been given); *~ creditor, debtor* (for, against, whom *~* has been given); ‖*~ summons* (for failure to pay *~* debt); *~-seat,* judge's seat, tribunal. [ME, f. OF *jugement* (as prec., see -MENT)]

jud'icature (jōō-; *also* -kā-), n. Administration of justice; *Supreme Court of J~ in England* (consisting of the Court of Appeal & the High Court of Justice; the latter is composed of the Queen's Bench, the Chancery, & the Probate, Divorce, & Admiralty divisions, & the Court of Criminal Appeal); judge's (term of) office; body of judges; court of justice. [f. F, or med. L *judicatura* (as JUDGE, -URE)]

judicial (jōōdĭsh'al), a. Of, done by, proper to, a court of law; *~ murder,* legal but unjust death sentence; inflicted as a divine judgement (esp. *~ blindness,* punitive infatuation); having the function of judgement, as *a ~ assembly*; of, proper to, a judge; expressing a judgement, critical; impartial. Hence *~LY²* adv. [ME, f. OF, or L *judicialis* (as foll., -AL)]

judiciary (jōōdĭsh'arĭ), n. The judges of a State collectively. [f. L *judiciarius* (*judicium,* see foll.)]

judicious (jōōdĭsh'us), a. Sensible, prudent; sound in discernment and judgement. Hence *~LY²* adv., *~NESS* n. [f. F *judicieux* f. L *judicium* judgement (as JUDGE¹), see -OUS]

ju'dō (jōō-), n. (Now usu. name for) JU-JUTSU.

jug¹, n. Deep vessel for holding liquids, with handle & often with spout, whence *~'FUL*(2) n.; (sl., also *stone-~*) prison. [perh. f. *Jug,* pet form of *Joan* &c.]

jug², v.t. (-gg-). Stew, boil, (hare, rabbit) in jug or jar (usu. in p.p.); (sl.) imprison. [f. prec.]

jug³, v.i. (-gg-). (Of nightingale or other bird) utter sound *jug.* So *~, ~-~,* nn. [imit.]

jug'ate (jōō-), a. (bot.). Having leaflets in pairs. [f. L *jugare* join (*jugum* yoke), see -ATE²]

Jugg'ernaut (-g-), n. (Hind. myth.) Krishna, eighth avatar of Vishnu, his idol at Puri, annually dragged in procession on huge car, under wheels of which devotees are said to have formerly thrown themselves; (fig., also *~ car*) institution, notion, to which persons blindly sacrifice themselves or others. [f. Hind. *Jagannath* f. Skr. *-natha* (*jagat* world *+ natha* lord)]

jugg'ins (-gĭnz), n. (sl.). Simpleton. [perh. f. proper name *Juggins* (as JUG¹); cf. MUGGINS]

jug'gle, v.i. & t., & n. **1.** Play conjuring tricks; *~ with,* deceive (person), misrepresent (facts); cheat (person etc. *out of* thing); bring, get, change, (*away, into,* etc.) by trickery. **2.** n. Piece of juggling, fraud. [ME, f. OF *jogler* f. L *joculari* jest (*joculus* dim. of *jocus* jest)]

jugg'l|er, n. Conjurer; trickster, impostor. So *~ERY*(2, 4) n. [ME, f. OF *jo(u)glære,* acc. *-eor,* f. L *joculator, -orem* (as prec., see -OR)]

Jugoslav (ūg'oslahv), a. & n. (Inhabitant) of the State, including Serbia, Montenegro, & parts of the former Austrian Empire, called *Jugoslavia.* [Serb., = south Slav]

jug'ular (*or* jōō-), a. & n. **1.** Of the neck or throat; *~ veins,* great veins of neck, conveying blood (*external ~*) from superficial parts of head, (*internal ~*) from inside of skull; (of fish) having the ventral fins in front of the pectoral. **2.** n. *~* vein. [f. LL *jugularis* f. L *jugulum* collar-bone, throat]

jug'ulate (*or* jōō-), v.t. Kill, esp. (fig.) arrest course of (disease etc.) by powerful remedy etc. [f. L *jugulare* (as prec.), see -ATE²]

juice (jōōs), n. Liquid part of vegetables or fruits; fluid part of animal body or substance, esp. *the ~s,* the bodily humours, *gastric ~*; (fig.) essence, spirit, of anything; (sl.) petrol or electricity used in engine etc. Hence *~'LESS* (-sl-) a. [ME, f. OF *jus* f. L *jus* broth, juice]

jui'c|y (jōō-), a. Full of juice, succulent;

(of weather) wet; (colloq.) of rich intellectual quality, interesting; (art sl.) of rich colouring suggestive of moisture. Hence ~ĭNESS n. [-Y²]

ju-ju (jōō'jōō), n. (W.-Afr.). Charm or fetish; ban effected by this. [perh. f. F *jou-jou* toy]

ju'jube (jōō'jōōb), n. Edible berry-like drupe of certain plants; lozenge of gelatin etc. flavoured with or imitating this. [F, or med. L *jujuba* f. Gk *zizuphon*]

ju-jutsu, jiu-jitsu, (jōōjutsōō'), n. Japanese art of wrestling etc. (now usu. *judo*). [Jap. *(ju-)*]

*juke-box** (jōōk-), n. Machine that automatically plays selected gramophone records when coin is inserted. [*juke* app. of W.-Afr. orig.]

jul'ĕp (jōō-), n. Sweet drink, esp. as vehicle for medicine; medicated drink as stimulant etc.; *iced & spiced spirit & water, esp. *mint* ~. [ME, f. OF, f. Arab. *julab* f. Pers. *gulab* (*gul* rose +*ab* water)]

Jul'ĭan (jōō-), a. Of Julius Caesar; ~ *calendar* (introduced by him, in which the year consisted of 365 days, every fourth year having 366,. cf. GREGORIAN. [f. L *Julianus (Julius,* see -AN)]

julienne (see Ap.), n. Soup of vegetables cooked in meat broth. [F]

July' (jōō-), n. Seventh month of year, called after Julius Caesar. [ME & OF *Jule, Juil* f. L *Julius;* also *Julie* f. AF f. L; 18th-c. pron. jōō'lĭ, mod. pron. irreg. & unexpl.]

jŭm'bal, -ble¹, n. Kinds of crisp thin sweet cake. [perh. orig. a use of GIMBAL]

jŭm'ble², v.i. & t. Move (t. & i.) about in disorder; mix *up*, confuse. [prob. imit.]

jŭm'ble³, n. Confused assemblage; muddle; jolting; ‖~-sale (of miscellaneous cheap articles at bazaar etc.); ~-shop (where miscellaneous goods are sold). Hence **jŭmb'lͷ²** a. [f. prec.]

jŭm'bō, n. (pl. ~s). Big clumsy person, animal, or thing, esp. (*J~*) famous elephant in London Zool. Gardens; notably successful person. [perh. = second element in MUMBO-JUMBO]

jŭmp¹, n. Leap, bound, spring from ground; *long, high,* ~, athletic competitions; start caused by shock or excitement, esp. (sl.) *the* ~s, delirium tremens; abrupt rise in amount, price, value, etc.; sudden transition, gap in series, argument,etc. Hence **jŭm'pĭNESS** n., **jŭm'pͷ²** a. [f. foll.]

jŭmp², v.i. & t. **1.** Spring from ground etc. by flexion & sudden muscular extension of legs or (of fish) tail; move suddenly with leap or bound (*up* from seat etc., *out,* etc.); ~ *in,* get quickly into carriage etc.; start with sudden jerk from excitement, shock, etc., esp. ~ *for joy.* **2.** Rise suddenly in price etc. **3.** Come *to,* arrive *at,* (conclusion) hastily. **4.** ~ *at,* (fig.) accept (offer, bargain) eagerly; ~ *(up)on,* attack (offender etc.) crushingly

with word or act. **5.** Agree, coincide, *(together,* one *with* another). **6.** Pass over (gate etc.) by leap; (of railway carriage) leave (line). **7.** Help (child etc.) to ~ *down* etc.; cause (thing) to ~; startle (person, nerves). **8.** Cook (potatoes etc.) in frying-pan, occasionally shaking them (usu. in p.p.). **9.** Pounce upon (thing); steal a march upon (~ *the queue*); take summary possession of (claim abandoned or forfeited by former occupant. **10.** Skip over (subject, part of book, etc.). **11.** Drill (rock, hole in rock) with jumper. **12.** ~ *down* person's *throat,* answer, interrupt, him violently; ~ *out of* one's *skin,* ~ with surprise; ~ *over the* BROOMstick. Hence ~'ABLE a. [f. 1500; prob. imit.]

jŭm'per¹, n. In vbl senses, esp.: member of Welsh Methodist body (or later sects) who jump(ed) as part of worship; jumping insect, e.g. flea; rope made fast to keep yard, mast, etc., from jumping; heavy chisel-ended iron bar for drilling blasting-holes. [-ER¹]

jŭm'per², n. Loose outer jacket of canvas etc. worn by sailors etc.; woman's loose outer garment of any material slipped on over head & reaching hips. [prob. f. (17th c., now dial.) *jump* short coat perh. f. F *juppe*]

jŭm'ping, a. In vbl senses, esp. in names of ~ animals, as ~*-deer,* N.-Amer. black-tailed deer; ~*-bean,* seed of Mexican plant ~ owing to movements of enclosed larva; ~ CAT¹. [-ING²]

jŭnc'tion, n. Joining; joint, meeting-place; station where railway lines meet & unite (often in proper names, as *Clapham J~*). [f. L *junctio* (as JOIN, see -ION)]

jŭnc'ture, n. Joining; place where things join; concurrence of events, state of affairs, as *at this* ~. [ME, f. L *junctura* (JOIN, -URE)]

June (jōōn), n. Sixth month of year. [ME *Juyn* f. OF *Juin* f. L *Junius;* also ME *June,* after L]

jungle (jŭng'gl), n. Land overgrown with underwood or tangled vegetation, esp. in India (often attrib. of animals inhabiting ~, as ~*-bear,* -*cat,* -*fowl*); wild tangled mass; ~ *fever,* kind of severe malaria. Hence **jŭng'lͷ**LED², **jŭng'lͷ²,** (-ngg-), aa. [f. Hind. *jangal* desert, forest]

jun'ior (jōō-), a. & n. **1.** The younger (esp. of son having same name as father, as *John Smith~,* or of younger of two boys of same surname in school; abbr. *jun., jr*); of less standing, of lower position, as ~ *partner.* **2.** n.: ~ person, as *the* ~*s, is my* ~. Cf. SENIOR. Hence ~ITY (-ŏ'r-) n. [L, compar. of *juvenis* young]

jun'iorate (jōō-), n. (In Society of Jesus) two-years' course attended by junior members before entering priesthood. [-ATE¹]

jun'iper (jōō-), n. Kinds of coniferous evergreen shrubs, esp. *common* ~, shrub with prickly leaves & dark berries yielding *oil of* ~ used in medicine & in making gin. [ME, f. L *juniperus*]

junk[1], n., & v.t. Old cable cut up for oakum etc.; discarded material, rubbish; lump, chunk; (naut.) salt meat; lump of tissue in sperm-whale, containing spermaceti; ~-*shop*, marine store, (derog.) antique dealer's shop; (v.t.) divide into ~s. [f. 1485, of unkn. orig.]

junk[2], n. Flat-bottomed sailing vessel used in Chinese seas. [16th c., app. ult. f. Javanese *djong*]

junker (yŏŏng'ker), n. Young German noble; member of exclusive aristocratic party in Prussia. [G, earlier *junkher* (YOUNG, HERR); see YOUNKER]

junk'ét, n., & v.i. 1. Dish of sweetened curds & whey, usu. with scalded cream on top; feast. 2. v.i. Feast, picnic. Hence ~ING[1] n. [ME *jonket*, app. f. ONF *jonquette* rush-basket (for making ~) f. *jonc* rush f. L *juncus*]

Jun'ō (jōō-), n. (pl. ~s). Wife of Jupiter; woman of stately beauty; third of the asteroids. [L]

jun'ta, n. Deliberative or administrative council in Spain or Italy; = foll. [Sp., f. L *juncta*, fem. p.p. as JOIN]

jun'tō, n. (pl. ~s). Clique, faction, political or other combination of persons. [erroneous f. prec.]

jupe (jōōp), n. Woman's skirt. [F]

Ju'piter (jōō-), n. (Rom. myth.) king of gods; ~ *Plu'vius* (plōō-), god of rain (joc.); largest planet of solar system. [L]

jur'al (joor-), a. Of law, of (moral) rights & obligations. [f. L *jus juris* right + -AL]

Jurass'ic (joor-), a. Of the Jura mountains between France & Switzerland; marked like these by prevalence of oolitic limestone. [f. F *jurassique* after *liassic, triassic*]

‖**jur'at** (joor-), n. Municipal officer like alderman; life magistrate in Channel Is. [f. med. L *juratus* (*jurare* swear)]

jurid'ical (joor-), a. Of judicial proceedings; legal. [f. L *juridicus* (*jus juris* right + -*dicus* f. *dicere* say) + -AL]

jur'isconsult' (joor-), n. One learned in law, jurist. [f. L *jurisconsultus* (*jus juris* law + p.p. as CONSULT)]

jurisdic'tion (joor-), n. Administration of justice; legal or other authority; extent of this, territory it extends over. Hence ~AL (joorĭsdĭk'shon-) a. [ME *jure-, juri-, juris-* f. OF *jure-, juridiction* & L *jurisdictio* (as prec., see DICTION)]

jurisprud'|ence (joorĭsprōō-), n. Science, philosophy, of human law, whence ~en-TIAL (joorĭsprōōděn'shal) a.; skill in law, so ~ENT (joorĭsprōō-)'a. & n. [f. LL *jurisprudentia* (as prec., see PRUDENCE)]

jur'ist (joor-), n. One versed in law; legal writer; student of, graduate in, law. Hence **juris'tic**(AL) aa., **juris'tical**LY[2] adv., (joor-). [f. F *juriste* or med. L *jurista* (*jus juris* law, see -IST)]

jur'or (joor-), n. Member of jury; one who takes an oath (cf. NON-*juror*). [ME, f. AF *jurour* (OF *jureor*) f. L *juratorem* (*jurare* swear, see -OR)]

jur'y (joor-), n. Body of persons sworn to render verdict on question submitted to them in court of justice; *grand* ~ (of persons formerly appointed to inquire into indictments before they were submitted to trial ~); *trial, common, petty,* ~ (of 12 persons who try final issue of fact in civil or criminal cases & pronounce verdict); *special* ~ (of persons of certain station in society); CORONER's ~; ~ *of matrons* (in case where pregnancy is pleaded in stay of execution); body of persons selected to award prizes in competition; ~-*box*, enclosure for ~ in court; ~-*man*, ~ *woman*, member of ~. [ME, f. AF (OF) *juree* oath, inquiry, f. med. L *jurata* (*jurare* swear, cf. -Y[4])]

jur'y-mast (joor'Imahst), n. Temporary mast in place of broken or lost one. [orig. unkn.]

jüss'ive, a. (gram.). Expressing a command. [f. L *jubēre juss-* command]

just[1], a. (Of person or conduct) equitable, fair, (*to* person etc.); (of treatment etc.) deserved, as *a* ~ *reward*; (of feelings, opinions, etc.) well-grounded, as ~ *resentment, fear*; right in amount etc., proper. Hence ~'LY[2] adv., ~'NESS n. [ME, f. OF *juste* or L *justus* (*jus* right)]

just[2], adv. Exactly, as ~ *at that spot,* ~ *there,* ~ *then,* ~ *three o'clock,* ~ *as you say,* ~ *so, that is* ~ *it* (precisely the point in question), ~ *how many there are remains to be seen*; barely, as *I* ~ *managed it*; exactly at that moment, (loosely) not long before, as *I have* ~ (a moment, or not long, ago) *seen him pass*; ~ *now*, at this moment, (also) a little time ago; (colloq.) positively, quite, as *it is* ~ *splendid, not* ~ *yet*; (as sl. emphasizer) *Won't I* ~ *give it him!, 'Did he swear? Didn't he,* ~*!'* [ME, f. prec.]

just[3]. See JOUST.

jüs'tice, n. Just conduct; fairness; exercise of authority in maintenance of right; *poetic*(*al*) ~, reward of virtue & punishment of vice; judicial proceedings, as *Court of J*~; magistrate; judge, esp. (in England) of Supreme Court of Judicature, whence ~SHIP n.; *J*~ *of the Peace*, lay magistrate appointed to preserve peace in county, town, etc.; *do* ~ *to*, treat fairly, show due appreciation of; *do* one*self* ~, perform worthily of one's abilities. [ME, f. OF (-*ice, -ise*), f. L *justitia* (as JUST[1], see -ICE)]

jüsti'ciable (-shya-), a. Subject to jurisdiction; (n.) person subject to jurisdiction (*of* another). [OF, f. *justicier* bring to trial f. med. L *justitiare* (as prec.), see -ABLE]

jüsti'ciar (-shyar), n. Chief political & judicial officer under Norman & early Plantagenet kings. [as foll., see -AR[2]]

justi′ciary̆ (-shy̆a-), n. & a. **1.** Administrator of justice; = prec. **2.** adj. Of the administration of justice. [f. med. L *justiliarius* (JUSTICE, -ARY¹)]

jŭs′ti|fy̆, v.t. Show the justice or rightness of (person, act, etc.); vindicate, (of circumstances) be such as to ~fy; (theol.) declare (person) free from penalty of sin on ground of Christ's righteousness or (Rom. Cath.) of the infusion of grace; (print.) adjust (line of type) to fill a space neatly; make good (statement etc.); adduce adequate grounds for (conduct, claim, etc.); ~*fy bail*, show by oath of person furnishing bail that he is pecuniarily qualified. Hence or cogn. ~fiaBIL-ITY, ~FICA′TION, nn., ~fiABLE, ~ficătIVE, ~ficătoRY, aa., ~fiabLY² adv. [f. F *justifier* f. LL *justificare* (as JUST¹, see -FY)]

jŭt, n., & v.i. (-tt-). **1.** Projection; protruding point. **2.** v.i. Project (often *out, forth*). [var. of JET², ³]

jute¹ (jōot), n. Fibre from certain plants, chiefly imported from Bengal, used for sacking, mats, etc. [f. Bengali *jhoṭo* f. Skr. *juṭa = jaṭa* braid of hair]

Jute² (jōot), n. One of Low German tribe invading Britain in 5th & 6th cc. [rendering Baeda's *Jutae*, *Juti*, in OE *Eotas*, *Iōtas* = Icel. *Iōtar* people of Jutland]

juvenĕs′c|ence (jōo-), n. (Transition from infancy to) youth. So ~ENT a. [f. L *juvenescere* reach age of youth (*juvenis* young), see -ENCE]

juv′ĕnile (jōo-), a. & n. **1.** Young, youthful; suited to, characteristic of, youth. **2.** n. Young person; (pl., trade term for) books meant for children. Hence or cogn. ~LY² (-l-lĭ) adv., **juvenil′ITY** (jōo-) n. [f. L *juvenilis* (as prec., -IL)]

juvenil′ia (jōo-), n. pl. Works produced in author's youth (often as title of collection of such writings). [L, neut. pl. of *juvenilis* JUVENILE]

jŭxtapōse′ (-z), v.t. Place (things) side by side. [f. F *juxtaposer* (L *juxta* next + *poser*, see COMPOSE)]

jŭxtaposi′tion (-zĭ-), n. Placing, being placed, side by side. [F (L *juxta* next, POSITION)]

K

K, k, (kā), letter (pl. Ks, K's).

kaama (kah′ma), n. Hartebeest. [S. Afr.]

Kaba′ka (-bah′-), n. (Title of) ruler of Buganda. [native]

kabbalah. = CABBALA.

Kabȳle′, n. A Berber of Algeria or Tunis; Berber dialect spoken by the ~s. [f. Arab. *qabā′ĭl* tribes]

kădd′ĭsh, n. Jewish mourner's prayer; the *Magnificat* in the synagogue service. [f. Aram. *qaddish* holy]

kadi. See CADI.

Kăff′ir (-fer), (obs.) **Căf′fre** (-fer), n. Member of a S.-Afr. people of Bantu family; (pl.) S.-Afr. mine shares. [as foll.]

Kăf′ir (-er), n. Native of Kafiristan in Asia. [Arab. *kāfir* infidel]

ka′gō (kah-), n. Japanese basket-work palanquin slung on pole. [f. Jap. *kango* of Chin. orig.]

kail(yard). See KALE.

kain′it(e) (kīn-), n. Hydrated double salt of magnesium chloride & sulphate & potassium sulphate, used as fertilizer. [G (-*it*), f. Gk *kainos* new, see -ITE¹]

kai′ser (kīz-), n. (hist.). Emperor; German Emperor; Emperor of Austria; head of Holy Roman Empire. Hence ~SHIP n. [in mod. E f. G *kaiser* & Du. *keizer*; in ME f. OE *cāsere* f. Gmc adoption (thr. Gk whence Goth.) *kaisar*) of L CAESAR]

kajă′wah (-jahwa), n. Camel-litter for women. [Hind. & Pers.]

ka′ka (kah-), n. New Zealand parrot. So ~pō n., New Zealand owl-like nocturnal parrot. [Maori (*po* = night)]

kăkemōn′ō, n. Japanese wall-picture (usu. painted on silk & mounted on rollers). [f. Jap. *kake-* hang +*mono* thing]

kala-azar (kahlah-ahzăr′), n. Virulent infectious malarial disease of oriental tropics. [Assamese, = black disease]

kāle, kail, n. Kinds of cole or cabbage, esp. borecole, kind with wrinkled leaves; *Scotch* ~, kind with purplish leaves; broth made of this or other vegetables; SEA ~; ~′*yard*, kitchen-garden; ~*yard school*, writers of fiction describing, with much use of the vernacular, common life in Scotland. [ME; northern form of COLE]

kaleid′o|scōpe (-lĭd-), n. Tube through which are seen symmetrical figures, produced by reflections of pieces of coloured glass, & varied by rotation of the tube; (fig.) constantly changing group of bright objects. Hence ~scōp′IC(AL) aa., ~scōp-icalLY² adv. [f. Gk *kalos* beautiful + *eidos* form + -SCOPE]

kalends. See CALENDS.

kăl′ĭ, n. Prickly saltwort, from which soda--ash was obtained. [f. Arab. *qali* ALKALI]

kalian, -lioun, (kahlyahn′, -yōon), n. Persian form of hookah. [Pers. (-*an*), f. Arab. *qalyan, -un*]

Kăl′mŭck, -mȳk, a. & n. (Member, language) of a Mongolian people living on the Caspian.

ka′lŏng (kah-), n. Malay frugivorous fox--bat, largest known bat. [Malay]

kăl′pa, n. Great age of the world, day of Brahma, (4,320,000,000 years). [Skr.]

kămerad′ (-ahd), int. of German soldier offering to surrender. [G, f. F as COMRADE]

ka′mĭ (kah-), n. Japanese title of governors etc.; divinity, god, in Japanese native religion.

kămpŏng′, n. Enclosed space, village. [Malay; see COMPOUND³]

kăn′aka, n. South Sea Islander, esp. one formerly employed in Queensland on sugar plantations. [Polynesian, = man]

Kănarēse' (-z), n. (Member of) Dravidian people living in western India; language of the ~. [f. N. & S. *Kanara* in India]

kăngaroō' (-ngg-), n. Marsupial mammal with strongly developed hindquarters & great leaping-power, native of Australia, Tasmania, etc.; ~ *rat*, small Australian marsupial; (sl., pl.) W.-Australian mining shares, dealers in these; ~ *bicycle*, one with sloping back, early form of safety; ‖ ~ *closure* (when chairman in committee selects some amendments for discussion and excludes others). [perh. native Austral.]

kanoōn', n. Kind of harp with fifty to sixty strings. [f. Pers. or Arab. *qanun*]

Kăn't|ian, a. Of Immanuel Kant, German philosopher, d. 1804. So ~ISM n. [-IAN]

ka'olin (kah-, kā-), n. Fine white clay produced by decomposition of feldspar, used in making porcelain. Hence ~IZE(3) v.t. [F, f. Chin. *kao-ling*, name of mountain (*kao* high + *ling* hill)]

kăpĕll'meister (-mī-), n. Conductor of orchestra, opera, choir, etc.; ~ *music*, uninspired music in routine style. [G]

kăp'ŏk, n. Fine cotton wool surrounding seeds of certain tree, used for stuffing cushions etc. [f. Malay *kapoq*]

kăpp'a, n. Greek letter k (*K*, κ).

kăput' (-ŏŏt), a. (sl.). Done for, smashed (in pred. use only). [G]

Kär'aïte, n. Member of Jewish sect that rejects Rabbinical tradition & interprets scriptures literally, found chiefly in Crimea. [f. Heb. *q'raim* (*qara* read) + -ITE[1]]

kărm'a, n. (Buddh.). Sum of person's actions in one of his successive states of existence, viewed as deciding his fate in the next; destiny. [Skr., = action, fate]

kar(r)oō', n. Elevated plateau of clayey soil in S. Africa, waterless in dry season; *the Great K~* (in Cape Province). [of Hottentot orig.]

karŏss', n. Mantle of animals' skins with the hair on, used by S.-African natives. [f. Afrikaans *karos*, of unkn. orig.]

kărt'el, n. Wooden bed in S.-African ox-wagon. [Afrikaans, prob. f. Port. *catel* f. Tamil *kaṭṭil* bedstead]

kartĕll'. See CARTEL.

kătabăt'ic, a. (meteorol.). (Of winds) caused by air flowing downward (cf. ANABATIC). [f. Gk *katabatikos* f. *katabainō* go down]

katăb'olism, cata-, n. (biol.). Breaking down of animal tissues (cf. METABOLISM). [f. Gk *katabolē* throwing down (*kataballō* throw down) + -ISM]

kathode. Var. of CATHODE.

kation. Var. of CATION.

kăt'ўdid, n. Large green orthopterous insect abounding in America. [imit. of the sound the insect produces]

kauri (kowr'ĭ), n. Coniferous tree of New Zealand, furnishing valuable timber & a resin, ~-*gum*. [Maori]

ka'va (kah-), n. (Diuretic beverage from roots of) a Polynesian shrub. [native]

kavăss', n. Armed constable, servant, or courier, in Turkey. [f. Turk. *qawwas* bow-maker (*qaws* bow)]

kay'ak (kī-), n. Eskimo canoe of light wooden framework covered with seal-skins. [Eskimo]

kea (kā'a), n. Green alpine parrot of New Zealand which destroys sheep for their kidney-fat. [Maori, imit.]

kĕck, v.i. Make sound as if about to vomit; ~ *at*, reject (food etc.) with loathing. [imit.]

keddah. See KHEDA.

kĕdge, v.i. & t., & n. **1.** Warp ship by means of hawser attached to small anchor; (of ship) move thus; move (ship) thus. **2.** n. (Also ~-*anchor*) small anchor for this purpose. [perh. spec. use of obs. *cagge*, dial. *cadge* bind, tie]

kĕdg'eree, n. Indian dish of rice, split pulse, onions, eggs, etc.; European dish of fish, rice, eggs, etc. [f. Hind. *khichri*, Skr. *k'ŗsara*]

‖ **keek**, v.i., & n. (Sc.). Peep. [ME *kike*] cf. MDu., MLG *kīken*]

keel[1], n., & v.t. **1.** Lowest longitudinal timber of vessel, on which framework of the whole is built up; combination of iron plates serving same purpose in iron vessel; (poet.) ship; *false* ~ (attached to bottom of true ~ to protect it); ~-*blocks* (on which ~ rests in building etc.); ~-*haul*, haul (person) under ~ as punishment. **2.** v.t. Turn (ship) ~ upwards; ~ *over*, upset, capsize, (person etc.). Hence ~'LESS (-l-l-) a. [ME *kele*, f. ON *kjölr* f. Gmc *keluz*]

keel[2], n. Flat-bottomed vessel, esp. of kind used on Tyne etc. for loading colliers; amount carried by this. [ME *kele* f. Angl. *kēl, kĭl*, MDu. *kiel*, ship, boat, = OE *cēol* &c. f. Gmc *keulaz*]

keelson. See KELSON.

keen[1], n. Irish funeral song accompanied with wailing. [f. Ir. *caoine*, as foll.]

keen[2], v.i. & t. Utter the keen; bewail (person) thus; utter in wailing tone. [f. Ir. *caoinim* wail]

keen[3], a. Having sharp edge or point; (of edge etc.) sharp; (of sound, light, etc.) penetrating, vivid, strong; (of frost) moderately hard; (of pain etc.) acute, bitter; (of person, desire, interest) eager, ardent, (colloq. *on* thing, *on doing*; ~ *as mustard*, enthusiastic, w. pun on *Keen's* mustard); (of eyes, sight, smell) sharp, highly sensitive; intellectually acute; ~-*set*, hungry, eager, (*for*). Hence ~'LY[2] adv., ~'NESS n. [OE *cēne*, OHG *kuoni*, ON *kœnn* f. Gmc *kōnjaz*]

keep[1], v.t. & i. (*kĕpt*). **1.** Pay due regard to, observe, stand by, (law, promise, faith, treaty, appointment; ~ *the* PEACE). **2.** Celebrate (feast, ceremony, etc.). **3.** Guard, protect, (person, as *God* ~ *you!*

fortress, town, etc., goal at football etc.).
4. Have charge of; retain possession of,
not lose or destroy. **5.** Maintain (house
etc.) in proper order (~ *open house*, entertain all comers), carry on (shop etc.);
maintain (diary, accounts, books) by
making requisite entries. **6.** Provide for
sustenance of (family, one*self*, etc.); own
& manage (cows, bees, etc.); maintain
(woman) as mistress. **7.** Have (commodity) habitually on sale. **8.** ~ COM-
PANY[1], PACE, STEP, LOOK[1] *out*, TIME, WATCH[1],
WICKET (also abs., act as wicket-keeper).
9. Maintain in proper or specified condition (often in spec. senses, as ~ *the* BALL[1]
rolling, POT *boiling*, one's HAIR *on*, one's
HEAD[1]; ~ one's *balance*, not lose it, lit. &
fig.). **10.** Detain (person *in prison*, *in
custody*, etc.); restrain (person, thing,
one*self*, *from doing*, *from* thing); refrain
from. **11.** Reserve (thing *for* future time
etc.). **12.** Conceal, as ~ one's COUNSEL[1],
a secret. **13.** Continue to follow (way,
course; ~ *track of*, follow the course or
development of). **14.** Remain in (one's
bed, room, house); retain one's place in
(the saddle, the field, the stage, one's
ground, etc.) against opposition; ~ one's
feet, not fall; ~ HOUSE; remain (indoors
etc.); ǁ (colloq., esp. Camb. Univ.) reside,
as *where do you* ~ *?* **15.** Remain in specified condition, as ~ *in good health*, ~ *in*
TOUCH *with*, ~ *cool*, (colloq.) ~ *friends*.
16. Continue in specified direction, course,
or action, as ~ *straight on for two miles, she
~s giggling*. **17.** (Of food etc.) remain
in good condition; (fig., of news etc.)
admit of being reserved for later occasion.
18. ~ (work, cause to work, persistently)
at; ~ (abstain) *from*; ~ *to*, adhere to
(course, promise), confine oneself to; ~
(thing etc.) *to* one*self*, refuse to share it
with others; ~ one*self to* one*self*, avoid
society. **19.** ~ *away*, avoid coming,
prevent from coming; ~ *back*, hold back,
retard progress of, conceal; ~ *down*, hold
in subjection, ~ low in amount, (mil.)
lie low in skirmishing; ~ *in*, confine,
restrain, (feelings etc.), confine (schoolboy) after hours, ~ (fire) burning, (intr.)
remain indoors, remain on good terms
with; ~ one's HAND *in*; ~ *off*, ward off,
avert, (intr.) stay at a distance; ~ *on*,
continue to hold, use, show, etc., (intr.)
continue (do*ing*); ~ *out*, not let enter; ~
together, remain, cause to remain, together; ~ *under*, hold in subjection; ~
up, prevent (one's spirits, prices, etc.)
from sinking, maintain (~ one's END[1] *up*;
~ *it up*, not slacken), ~ in repair, in
efficient or proper state, etc., (~ *up
appearances*; ~ *up your Greek*), carry on
(correspondence etc.), cause (person) to
sit up at night, (intr.) bear up, not break
down, proceed at equal pace *with* (~ *up
with the Joneses*, ~ on terms of equality
with one's neighbours). [late OE *cēpan* of
unkn. orig.]

keep², n. (Hist.) tower, stronghold; maintenance, food required for this, as *you
don't earn your* ~; *for* ~s (colloq.), in permanence. [f. prec.]

keep'er, n. In vbl senses, esp. : ǁ=GAME[1]-
-~; custodian of museum, art gallery,
etc.; lunatic's attendant; ring that keeps
another, esp. wedding-ring, on the finger.
[-ER[1]]

keep'ing, n. In vbl senses, also or esp.:
custody, charge, as *in safe* ~, *in his* ~;
agreement, harmony, (orig. esp. of painting) as *in, out of*, ~ (*with*); (attrib., or
intr. part.) fit for ~, as ~ *apples*; *~-
-room*, sitting-room usually occupied.
[-ING[1]]

keep'sāke, n. Thing kept for sake, or in
remembrance, of giver; (attrib.) namby-
-pamby, like certain literary annuals of
19th c. called ~s. [KEEP[1]+SAKE]

keeshond (kās'hŏnd), n. Breed of Dutch
dogs resembling the chow. [Du.]

kĕf, keif (kif), **kief** n. Drowsy state
produced by bhang etc.; enjoyment of
idleness; Indian hemp etc. smoked to
produce ~. [f. Arab. *kaif*, colloq. *kef*,
well-being]

kĕffi'yeh (-fēyă), n. Bedouin Arab's kerchief worn as head-dress. [f. Arab.
kaffiyah, kuffiyeh, perh. f. LL *cofea* COIF]

kĕf'ir (-er), n. Effervescent liquor like
koumiss, used for invalids. [Caucas.]

kĕg, n. Small barrel, usu. of less than 10
gals. [f. 15th c. *cag*, f. ON *kaggi*, of unkn.
orig.]

kĕlp, n. Large kinds of seaweed; calcined
ashes of seaweed used for the sake of carbonate of soda, iodine, etc. contained,
formerly used in making soap & glass.
[ME *cŭlp(e)*, of unkn. orig.]

kĕl'pīe, -pў, n. (Sc.). Water-spirit, usu.
in form of horse, reputed to delight in
the drowning of travellers etc. [orig.
unkn.]

kĕl'son, keel'son, n. Line of timber
fastening ship's floor-timbers to keel.
[ME *kelswayn, -sweyn, -swyn(e), -syng* f.
MDu. **kelswijn*, MLG **kelswin* (as KEEL,
SWINE); *kelson* as *bosun* f. *boatswain*]

kelt¹ etc. See CELT etc.

kĕlt², n. Salmon or sea trout after
spawning. [ME; orig. unkn.]

kĕmp, n. Coarse hair in wool. Hence
kĕm'pY²a. [f. ON *kampr* beard, whisker]

kĕn¹, n. Range of sight or knowledge, esp.
in, out of, beyond, one's ~. [f. foll.]

ǁ **kĕn²**, v.t. (now Sc. or north.; *kĕnt*).
Recognize at sight; know (person, thing,
fact, *that* etc.). [OE *cennan*, OS *kennian*,
OHG *chennan*, ON *kenna*, Goth. *kannjan*
f. Gmc **kann- kann²*]

kĕnn'el¹, n., & v.i. & t. (-ll-). **1.** House for
shelter of house-dog or hounds; mean
dwelling. **2.** v.i. Live in, go to, ~; (v.t.)
put into, keep in,~ [ME, f. ONF **kenil* (F
chenil) f. med. L *canile* (*canis* dog)]

kĕnn'el², n. Gutter. [earlier *cannel* f. OF
canel CHANNEL]

kĕnōs′ĭs, n. (theol.). Renunciation of divine nature, at least in part, by Christ in the incarnation. So **kĕnOT′IC** (-ŏt²) a., **kĕnŏt′ĭcĭsM**(3) n. [Gk *kenōsis (kenoō* vb empty f. *kenos*, see -OSIS)]

Kĕn′tĭsh, a. Of Kent; ‖ ~ *fire*, prolonged volley of applause or demonstration of dissent; ~ *man* (born W. of Medway, opp. *man of Kent* born E.); ~ *rag*, hard limestone found in Kent. [OE *Centisc (Cent* f. L *Cantium*, see -ISH¹)]

kĕnt′lĕdġe,′ n. (naut.). Pig-iron used as permanent ballast. [f. F *quintelage* ballast, w. assim. to *kentle* QUINTAL; see -AGE]

kĕp′ĭ, n. French military cap with horizontal peak. [f. F *képi* f. G-Swiss *käppi* dim. of *kappe* cap]

Kepler′s laws. See LAW¹.

kept. See KEEP¹.

kĕ′ratĭn, n. Nitrogenous substance forming the basis of horns, claws, nails, etc. [as foll. + -IN]

kĕ′ratōse, a. & n. 1. Of horny substance. 2. n. Horn-like substance forming part of some sponges. [f. Gk *keras -atos* horn + -OSE¹]

‖ **kĕrb**, *curb, n. 1. Stone edging to pavement or raised path; ~*stone*, one of stones forming this. 2. (St. Exch. sl.). The STREET; ~*stone broker* (not a member of the Stock Exchange); ~*market*, (place for) sale of securities after hours or of shares not dealt with on the Stock Exchange). [var. of CURB n.]

kĕrch′ief (-ĭf), n. Cloth used to cover head; (poet.) handkerchief. Hence ~ED² (-ĭft) a. [ME *curchef, ker-*, f. OF *couvrechief, cuevre-, (covrir* COVER + *chief* head f. L *caput*)]

kĕrf, n. Slit made by cutting, esp. with saw; cut end of felled tree. [OE *cyrf*, st. of CARVE]

kĕrm′es (-ĭz), n. Pregnant female of an insect, formerly taken for a berry, feeding on ~ *oak*, an evergreen oak of S. Europe & N. Africa; red dye-stuff consisting of dried bodies of these; amorphous trisulphide of antimony, of brilliant red. [also 16th c. *chermez*, f. F *kermes* & It. *chermes* f. Arab. & Pers. *qirmiz*]

kĕrm′ĭs n. Periodical·fair in Holland etc., with much noisy merrymaking. [Du., orig.=mass on anniversary of dedication of church, when yearly fair was held. (*kerk* KIRK + *miss* MASS¹)]

kĕrn(e), n. (hist.). Light-armed Irish foot-soldier; peasant, boor. [f. Ir. *ceithern*]

kĕrn′el, n. Softer (usu. edible) part within hard shell of nut or stone-fruit; body of seed within husk etc., e.g. grain of wheat; nucleus, centre of formation (often fig.). [OE *cyrnel*, dim. of CORN]

kĕ′rosēne, -ine (-ēn), n. Lamp-oil obtained by distillation of petroleum & from coal & bituminous shale, paraffin. [irreg. f. Gk *kēros* wax + -ENE]

Kĕ′rrў, n. attrib. ~ *blue*, a breed of terrier. [place]

kĕrs′ey (-zĭ), n. Kind of coarse narrow cloth woven from long wool, usu. ribbed. [ME, prob. f. K~ in Suffolk]

kĕrs′eymēre (-zĭ-), n. Twilled fine woollen cloth; (pl.) trousers of this. [alt. of *cassimere*, var. of CASHMERE, assim. to prec.]

kĕs′trel, n. Species of small hawk. [16th c. *cast-, kist-, kest-*, perh. f. OF *cresserelle* of unkn. orig.]

kĕtch, n. Two-masted vessel with mizzen-mast stepped forward of rudder. [in 15th c. *cache, catch*, f. CATCH¹·²]

kĕtch′up, n. Sauce made from juice of mushrooms, tomatoes, etc. [prob. f. Chin. *kôe-chiap* brine of pickled fish]

kĕt′ōne, n. One of a class of organic compounds allied to the aldehydes of which acetone is the simplest. [f. G *keton* alt. of *acetone*]

kĕt′tle, n. Vessel, usu. of metal with spout & handle, for boiling water; FISH¹-~; *a pretty ~ of fish*, awkward state of affairs; ~-*drum(mer)*, (player of) hollow brass or copper hemisphere, over edge of which parchment is stretched & tuned to definite note; ~-*drum*, (also) large afternoon tea-party; ~-*holder*, piece of cloth etc. to protect hand from heat of ~ handle. Hence ~FUL(2) n. [f. ON *ketill* = OE *cetel*, *cietel* (ME *chetel*), OS *ketel*, OHG *kezzil*, Goth. **katils** f. L *catillus, catinus*]

kĕv′el, n. (naut.). Peg, cleat, usu. fixed in pairs, to which certain ropes are belayed. [ME, f. ONF *keville* (F *cheville*) f. L *clavicula* dim. of *clavis* key]

Kew Gárdens, n. pl. National botanical gardens at Kew, London.

key¹ (kē), n. 1. Instrument, usu. of iron, for moving bolt of lock forwards or backwards; *get, have, the ~ of the street*, be shut out for the night, homeless; MASTER¹ ~. 2. *House of Keys*, elective branch of legislature of I. of Man; *St Peter′s ~s*, cross ~s borne in Papal arms. 3. What gives or precludes opportunity for or access to something; *golden, silver, ~, money* used as bribe. 4.(pl.). Ecclesiastical authority as transmitted to the Pope, esp. *power of the ~s*. 5. Place that from its position gives control of sea, territory, etc. 6. Solution, explanation, literal translation of foreign book; book of solutions of mathematical problems etc.; word or system for solving cipher or code (also ~′*word*). 7. (Mus.) system of notes definitely related to each other & based on particular note; (fig.) tone, style, of thought or expression; ~′*note*, note on which a ~ is based, (fig.) prevailing tone or idea. 8. Piece of wood or metal inserted between others to secure them. 9. Part of first coat of wall plaster passing between laths & so securing the rest. 10. Lever pressed by finger in playing organ, piano, flute, concertina, etc.; similar lever in typewriter etc. 11. Instrument for grasping screws, pegs, nuts, etc., esp. one for winding. **12.** ~*'board*, set of ~s on piano etc.; ~*-bugle* (fitted with ~s to increase number of sounds); ~*'hole* (by which ~ is put into lock); ~ *industry*, one essential to the carrying on of others, e.g. coal-mining, dyeing; ~ *map* (in bare outline, to simplify use of full map); ~ *(move)*, (chess) first move in solution of a problem; ~*-ring* (for keeping ~s on); ~*-stone*, voussoir at summit of arch locking the whole together, (fig.) central principle etc. on which all depends. Hence ~'LESS (kē-) a. [OE *cǣg(e)*, OFris *kei, kay*, of unkn. orig.]

key² (kē), v.t. Fasten (often *in, on*, etc.) with pin, wedge, bolt, etc.; regulate pitch of strings of (piano etc.); word (an advertisement in a particular periodical) so that answers to it can be identified (usu. by varying the form of address given); (fig.) ~ *up*, stimulate (person *to do, to condition* etc.), raise the tone or standard of, brace up, raise (offer, demand, endeavour). [f. prec.]

key³ (kē), n. Low island or reef. [f. Sp. *cayo*, see CAY, QUAY]

khadd'ar (kă-), n. Indian homespun cloth. [Hindi]

khakan (kahkahn'), n. = KHAN¹. [f. Turk. *khaqan* king, emperor]

kha'ki (kah-), a. & n. **1.** Dust-coloured, dull-yellow. **2.** n. ~ fabric of twilled cotton or wool, used in Brit. army since S.-African war. [Hind., = dusty (*khak* dust)]

khal'ifa, khal'ifāt, (kă-), nn. = CALIPH- (ATE).

kham'sin (kă-), n. Hot S. or S.E. wind in Egypt for about 50 days in March, April, & May. [Arab. (*khamsun* fifty)]

khan¹ (kăn, kahn), n. Title of rulers & officials in Central Asia, Afghanistan, etc.; (hist.) supreme ruler of Turkish, Tartar, & Mongol tribes, & emperor of China, in Middle Ages. Hence ~'ATE¹(1) n. [Turk., alt. f. KHAKAN]

khan² (kăn, kahn), n. Caravanserai. [Arab., = inn]

khe'da (kā-), *kĕdd'ah*, n. Enclosure used in Bengal etc. to catch elephants. [Hind. (*-da*)]

Khedive' (kĭdēv'), n. (hist.). Title of viceroy of Egypt, accorded to Ismail Pasha by Turkish Government in 1867; abolished in 1914. Hence Khedi'v(I)AL (kĭdē-) aa. [f. F *khédive* ult. f. Pers.]

khi (kī), n. Greek letter (*X, χ*)=ch. [Gk] *khid'mutgar* (kĭ-), n. Male servant who waits at table (in India). [f. Urdu *khid-malgar* (*khidmat* service + *-gar* suf.)]

khil'afāt, n. = KHALIFAT; (hist.) ~ *agitation*, anti-British movement in India based on Moslem resentment of the loss of power by Islam in & after the 1914–18 war, & contemporary Hindu discontents.

‖ **kib'ble¹,** n. Iron hoisting-bucket used in mines. [17th c., f. G *kübel*]

‖ **kib'ble²,** v.t. Grind coarsely. [orig. unkn.]

kibbutz' (-ōōts), n. (pl. ~*zĭm*). Communal farming centre in Israel. [mod. Heb.]

kībe, n. Ulcerated chilblain, esp. on heel; *tread on* one's ~s, hurt his feelings. [ME; prob. f. W *cibi* (also *cibwst*)]

kĭbĭt'ka, n. Tartar's circular tent covered with felt; Tartar household; Russian hooded sledge. [Russ.]

*****kib'itzer,** n. (colloq.). Meddlesome person, one who gives advice gratuitously, one who watches a game of cards from behind the players. [Yiddish, f. G *kiebitz* looker-on]

kib'lah, n. Point to which Mohammedans turn at prayer, i.e. temple at Mecca. [f. Arab. *qiblah* (*qabala* be opposite)]

kib'ōsh (*or* kĭbŏsh'), n. (sl.). Nonsense, humbug; *put the* ~ *on*, do for, knock on the head. [orig. unkn.]

kick¹, n. Act of kicking; (colloq.) reacting-power, resilience, (*has no* ~ *left*); (colloq.) sharp stimulant effect, pleasurable thrill (*has some* ~ *in it*); DROP¹-, PLACE-, ~; *more* ~s (harshness) *than halfpence* (kindness); recoil of gun when discharged; (footb.) *good, bad,* etc., ~ (kicker), ~*-off*, ~ with which game is started; ~*-starter*, lever on motor-cycle by kicking which it can be started. [f. foll.]

kick², v.i. & t. **1.** Strike out with the foot; ~ *against the pricks*, resist to one's own hurt. **2.** Show annoyance, dislike, etc. (*against, at*, proposal, treatment). **3.** Strike with foot; (sl.) ~ *the bucket*, die; ~ one's HEELS. **4.** Drive, move, (thing) by ~ing. **5.** (footb.). Score (goal) by a kick. **6.** Drive forcibly & contemptuously (*out, downstairs*, etc.; ~ one *upstairs*, fig., shelve him by giving him peerage or titular promotion). **7.** ~ *off*, throw off (shoes) by ~ing, (footb.) begin game; ~ *up*, raise (dust), create (fuss, noise), ~ *up* its *heels* (of horse in play); ~*ing-strap* (arranged to prevent carriage-horse from ~ing). [ME *kike*, of unkn. orig.]

kick³, n. Indentation in bottom of glass bottle. [orig. unkn.]

kick'er, n. In vbl senses, esp. horse given to kicking. [-ER¹]

kick'shaw, n. Fancy dish in cookery (usu. derog.); toy, trifle. [f. F *quelque chose* something]

kid¹, n., & v.t. & i. (-dd-). **1.** Young of goat; leather from skin of this, used for gloves & boots; *the Kids or Kid*, three small stars in Auriga; (sl.) child, whence ~d'y³ n.; ~*-glove* (adj.), over-dainty, avoiding everyday work etc. **2.** v.t. Give birth to (~); (v.i.) give birth to ~. [ME *kide* f. ON *kith* f. Gmc **kithjam*, rel. to OHG *chizzî, -în*]

kid², v.t. (-dd-). & n. (sl.). Hoax, humbug, (vb often abs.). [perh. f. prec.]

kid³, n. Small wooden tub, esp. (formerly) sailor's mess-tub. [perh. var. of KIT¹]

Kidd'erminster, n. Town in Worcestershire; ~ *carpet* (with pattern formed by intersection of two cloths of different colours).

kid'dle, n. Barrier in river with opening fitted with nets etc. to catch fish; arrangement of stake-nets on sea-beach. [ME, f. AF *kidel*, = OF *quidel, guidel*, mod. *-eau*]

kid'nap, v.t. (-pp-). Steal (child); carry off (person) by illegal force. Hence~pER[1] n. [KID[1]+*nap* = NAB]

kid'ney, n. (pl.~s). One of pair of glandular organs in abdominal cavity of mammals, birds, & reptiles, serving to excrete urine & so remove effete nitrogenous matter from blood; ~ of sheep, cattle, & pigs, as food; temperament, nature, as *a man of that* ~, *of the right* ~; (also ~ *potato*) oval kind of potato; || ~ *bean*, (1) dwarf French bean, (2) scarlet-runner. [ME *kidnei*, pl. *kidneiren*, of obsc. formation]

kief, See KEF.

kie-kie (kē'kē), **n.** New Zealand climbing plant with leaves used for baskets etc. [Maori]

kier, n. Vat in which cloth is boiled for bleaching etc. [f. ON *ker*, = OHG *char*, Goth. *kas*]

kieselguhr (kē'zlgoor), **n.** Diatomaceous earth used for polishing & as absorbent of nitro-glycerine in manufacture of dynamite. [G *kiesel* gravel+dial. *guhr* earthy deposit]

Kikuyu' (-ōōyōō), **n.** (Member, language, of) a Bantu-speaking people of E. Africa; (used for) the controversy in the Anglican Church on the admissibility to Holy Communion of members of other Christian Churches. [~ in Brit. E. Africa (now Kenya), a conference at which in 1913 gave rise to the controversy]

kil'derkin, n. Cask for liquids etc., containing 16 or 18 gal.; this as measure. [alt. of ME *kinderkin* f. MDu. *kinde(r)kin, kinneken*, dim. of *kintal* QUINTAL; see -KIN]

kill[1] v.t. & i. 1. Put to death, slay (~ *two birds with one stone*, effect two purposes at once); (of disease, grief, shock, drink, poison, etc.) cause the death of; ~ *off*, get rid of (number of persons etc.) by ~ ing. **2.** (Abs., esp. sport.) perform act of ~ing, do execution. **3.** (Intr., quasi-pass.) yield good or much meat when ~ed, as *pigs do not ~ well at that age.* **4.** Represent in fiction etc. as dead, as ~ *your villain in the last chapter.* **5.** Destroy vitality of (plant, disease, etc.); destroy, put an end to, (feelings etc.). **6.** Neutralize (colour etc.) by contrast. **7.** Consume (time) for the sake of doing so. **8.** Overwhelm (person) with admiration, amusement, etc. (*got up to* ~, fascinatingly dressed), whence ~'ING[2] a., ~'ingLY[2] adv. **9.** (lawn tennis) strike (ball) so that it cannot be returned; (footb.) stop (ball) dead. **10.** Contrive defeat of (bill in Parliament). **11.** ~ (fatally harm) *with* (mistaken) *kindness*; ~*-devil*, artificial bait made to spin in water; ~'*joy*, one who throws gloom over social enjoyment; ~*-time* n. & a., (occupation) intended to ~ time. [ME *cülle, kille*, of unkn. orig.]

kill[2], n. Act of killing; animal killed, esp. by sportsman. [f. prec.]

kill'er, n. One who, that which, kills; murderous ruffian; HUMANE ~; ~ *whale*, voracious cetacean (esp. the grampus). [-ER[1]]

kill'ick, -ock, n. Heavy stone used by small craft as anchor; small anchor; || (nav. sl.) leading rating. [17th c., of unkn. orig.]

kiln (or kil), **n.** Furnace, oven, for burning, baking, or drying, esp. (*lime-*~) for calcining lime, or (*brick-*~) baking bricks; ~*-dry* v.t.; dry in ~. [OE *cylene* f. L *culina* kitchen]

kil'o (or kē-), **n.** (pl.~s). Abbr. for KILOGRAM(ME), KILOMETRE. [F]

kil'o- in comb., arbitrary representative (f. F) of Gk *khilioi* 1,000, as; ~*cycle*, unit of frequency of vibration (1,000 oscillations per second) used esp. of wireless waves; ~*gram(me)*, weight of 1,000 grammes (2·205 lb. avoird.); ~*gramme'tre* (*-ter*), energy that will raise one kilogram to the height of one metre; ~*litre*, ~*liter*, (*-lēter*), measure of 1,000 litres (35·31 cub. ft); ~*mètre*, ~*mēter*, measure of 1,000 metres (3280.89 ft), whence ~*mēt'ric(al)* aa.; ~*ton*, unit of explosive power equivalent to 1,000 tons of T.N.T.; ~*watt*, 1,000 watts.

kilt[1], v.t. Tuck up (skirts) round body; gather in vertical pleats (esp. in p.p.). [of Scand. orig.; cf. Da. *kilte* (*op*) tuck (up), Sw. dial. *kilta* swathe, ON *killing*, *kjalta* skirt, lap]

kilt[2], n. Skirt, usu. of tartan cloth, reaching from waist to knee, part of Highland male dress; similar garment worn by children & young women. Hence **kil'tie** [-Y[3]] n., wearer of a ~, esp. kilted Highland soldier. [f. prec.]

***kil'ter, kĕ-, n.** Good working order (*out of* ~, not working properly). [Eng. dial.]

kimōn'ō, n. (pl.~s). Long loose Japanese robe with wide short sleeves, held together by a sash; European dressing-gown or wrap modelled on this. [Jap.]

kin, n. & a. Ancestral stock, family, as *comes of good* ~; one's relatives; KITH & ~; (pred. adj.) related, as *we are* ~, *he is* ~ *to me; of* ~, akin, related by blood ties or (fig.) in character; *near of* ~, closely related; NEXT *of* ~. Hence ~'LESS a. [OE *cynn*, OS *kunni*, OHG *chunni*, ON *kyn*, Goth. *kuni* f. Gmc *kunjam* f. root *kin, *kan, *kun* cogn. w. L *genus*]

-kin, suf. form. dimm., corresp. to MDu. *-kijn, -ken*, MLG *-kin* = OHG *-chin*, G *-chen*; chiefly in wds f. Du., incl. early proper names, as *Malkin, Perkin, Simkin*; some wds in *-kin* are of doubtful orig.

Lambkin is the only E formation of real currency.

kin′chin, n. (cant). Child; ~ *lay*, practice of stealing money from children sent on errands. [16th c. cant, prob. f. G *kindchen* (*kind* child, see prec.)]

kin′cŏb (-ngk-), n. Rich Indian stuff embroidered with gold or silver. [f. Urdu *kimkhab*]

kind[1], n. **1.** Race, natural group, of animals, plants, etc., as *human* ~, *the rabbit* ~. **2.** Class, sort, variety, as *of what* ~ *is it?*, *of a different* ~; *something of the* ~, something like the thing in question; *nothing of the* ~, not at all like it; (derog.) *we had coffee of a* ~ (that scarcely deserved the name). **3.** (eccl.). Each of the two elements in the Eucharist. **4.** (In transposed constr.) *what* ~ *of tree is this?*, of what ~ is this tree?, *this is the* ~ *of thing I meant* (a thing of the ~ I meant); (colloq.) *these* ~ *of men* (men of this ~) *annoy me.* **5.** (Implying looseness, vagueness, exaggeration, etc., in the term used) *he is a* ~ *of stockbroker, of millionaire, felt a* ~ *of compunction*; (colloq.) *I* ~ *of* (to some extent) *expected it.* ‖ **6.** (arch.). Nature in general, as *the law of* ~; way, fashion, natural to person etc., as *they act after their* ~. **7.** Character, quality, as *they differ in* ~ (not merely in degree). **8.** *In* ~, (of payment) in goods or natural produce, not in money, (of repayment, esp. fig.) *repay his insolence in* ~ (with insolence). [OE *gecynde* (*ge-* Y- + **cynde* f. root *kun-* see KIN)]

kind[2], a. Of gentle or benevolent nature; friendly in one's conduct *to* (person etc.); affectionate; ~*-hearted*, having a ~ heart. Hence ~′lȳ[1] [-LY[2]] adv. (often politely in requests, or ironically in commands), ~′NESS n. [OE *gecynde* (as prec.); orig. = natural, native]

kin′dergärten, n. School for developing minds of children by object-lessons, toys, games, etc. Hence ~ISM n. [G, = children's garden]

kin′dle, v.t. & i. Set on fire, light, (flame, fire, substance); (fig.) inflame, inspire, (passion etc.), stir up (person *to* emotion etc., *to* do); (intr.) catch fire, burst into flame; (fig.) become animated, glow with passion etc.; make, become, bright, (cause to) glow (often *up*); hence **kind′-** LING[1] n., (esp., sing. or pl.) small wood for lighting fires. [ME, f. ON *kynda* kindle +-LE(3); cf. ON *kyndill* candle, torch]

kind′l|ȳ[2] (for ~*y*[1] see KIND[2]), a. Kind; (of climate etc.) pleasant, genial; ‖ (arch.) native-born, as *a* ~*y Scot.* Hence ~ĭLY[2] adv., ~ĭNESS n. [OE *gecyndelic* (as KIND[2], see -LY[1])]

kin′drĕd, n. & a. **1.** Blood relationship; (fig.) resemblance in character; one's relatives. **2.** adj. Related by blood; (fig.) allied, connected, similar, as *frost & ~ phenomena*, ~ *spirit*. [ME, f. KIN + -*red*, OE *ræden* condition, reckoning]

kine. See COW[1].

kinēm′a, orig. form of CINEMA.

kinĕmăt′ic, a. & n. **1.** Of motion considered abstractly without reference to force or mass. **2.** n. pl. Science of this. Hence ~AL a. [f. Gk *kinēma -matos* motion (*kineō* move, see -M) + -IC]

kinematograph, -ic, -y. = CINEMATO-GRAPH etc.

kinĕt′ic, a. & n. **1.** Of, due to, motion; ~ ENERGY; ~ *theory of heat, of gases* (that heat, the gaseous state, is due to motion of particles). **2.** n. pl. Science of the relations between the motions of bodies & the forces acting on them. [f. Gk *kinēti-kos* (*kineō* move, see -ETIC)]

king[1], n. **1.** Male sovereign (esp. hereditary) ruler of independent state. **2.** (Hist.) *K*~ *Emperor* (of U.K. & India; also of Austria-Hungary); *K*~ *Log*, *K*~ *Stork*, rulers going to extremes of laissez-faire, oppression (w. ref. to fable of the frogs); *K*~ *of* ~*s*, God, (also) title assumed by many Eastern ~s; *K*~ *of Terrors*, Death; *K*~ *Charles's* SPANIEL; ‖ *K*~*'s* BENCH, BOUNTY, COLOUR[1], COUNSEL[1], ENGLISH, EVIDENCE, HEAD[1], HIGHWAY, PIPE[1], SHIL-LING, WEATHER; *K*~ *of the Castle*, child's game. **3.** Great merchant etc., as *fur, railway*, ~. **4.** ~ *of beasts, birds*, lion, eagle. **5.** Best kind (*of* fruits, plants, etc.). **6.** (Chess) piece that has to be protected from checkmate, ~*'s bishop, knight, rook, pawn* (placed on ~'s side of board at beginning); (draughts) piece that, having traversed the board & reached opponent's base-line, is crowned; (cards) card bearing representation of ~, & usu. ranking next below ace. **7.** ~*'bird*, kind of bird of paradise, (also) American tyrant fly-catcher; ~ *'bolt*, main or large bolt; ~*-crab*, kinds of marine arachnid with crustacean affinities having horseshoe--shaped carapace; ~*'craft*, skilful exercise of royalty; ~*'cup*, buttercup, ‖ (also) marsh marigold; ~*'fisher*, small bird with dagger-shaped bill & brilliant plumage, feeding on fish it captures by diving; ~*'maker*, one who sets up ~s, esp. Earl of Warwick in reign of Henry VI; ‖ *K*~ *of Arms*, any of five chief heralds of College of Arms, *Garter*, *Clarenc*(*i*)*eux*, *Norroy*, (Scotland) *Lyon*, (Ireland, formerly) *Ulster*; ~*'pin*, = ~*bolt*, also fig.; ~*'post*, upright post from tie-beam to rafter-top; ~*'s evil*, scrofula, formerly held to be curable by ~'s touch; ~*'s peg*, drink of champagne & brandy; ‖ *K*~*'s Roll* (of employers pledged to employ at least a fixed proportion of ex-service men). Hence ~′LESS, ~′LIKE, ~′LY[1], aa., ~′liNESS, ~′SHIP(1), nn. [OE *cyning*, OS, OHG *kuning*, ON *kuningr* f. Gmc **kuningaz* (KIN, -ING[3])]

king[2], v.i. & t. Act the king, govern, esp. ~ *it*; make (person) a king. [f. prec.]

king′dom, n. Monarchical State; *United K*~, Great Britain & Northern Ireland;

territory subject to king; spiritual reign of God, sphere of this, esp. *the ~ of heaven*; domain; province of nature, esp. *animal, vegetable, mineral, ~*; (sl.) *~-come*, the next world (echo of *thy ~ come* in Lord's Prayer). Hence ~ED² (-omd) a. [OE *cyningdōm* (as KING¹, see -DOM)]

king′|let, n. Petty king (usu. derog.), so ~LING¹ n.; golden-crested wren. [-LET]

kink, n., & v.i. & t. 1. Back twist in wire or chain or rope such as may cause obstruction or a break; (fig.) mental twist, crotchet. 2. v.i. (Of rope etc.) form a ~; (v.t.) cause (rope) to do this. Hence ~′Y² a. [f. MLG *kinke*, Du. *kink* f. root **kink*, **kik* twist; cf. Icel. *kikna* bend at the knees; vb f. Du. *kinken*]

kink′ajou (-ōō), n. Arboreal animal with prehensile tail allied to racoon. [f. F *quincajou* f. N. Amer. Ind.]

kinn′ikinic′, n. Mixture of dried sumach-leaves, bark of willow, etc., as substitute for tobacco, or mixed with it; any plant used for this. [Algonquin]

ki′no (kē-), n. Gum of various trees, resembling catechu, & used in medicine & tanning as astringent. [W.-Afr.]

kins′|folk (-ōk), n. pl. Relations by blood. So ~MAN, ~WOMAN, nn. [f. KIN + FOLK]

kin′ship, n. Blood relationship; similarity, alliance, in character. [-SHIP]

kin′tal, early form of QUINTAL.

kiōsk′, n. Light open pavilion in Turkey & Persia; *Yildiz K~*, Turkish Sultan's palace; light out-of-door structure for sale of newspapers, bandstand, etc.; structure for public telephone. [f. F *kiosque* f. Turk. *kiushk*]

kip¹, n. Hide of young or small beast as used for leather. [in E sense 'set or bundle of hides' f. MDu. *kip, kijp*]

kip², n., & v.i. (-pp-; sl.). Common lodging-house; lodging; bed; (v.i.) sleep. [cf. Da. *kippe* mean hut or alehouse]

kipp′er¹, n. Male salmon in spawning season; kippered fish, esp. herring. [of obsc. orig.; formally = OE *cypera* (once)]

kipp′er², v.t. Cure (salmon, herring, etc.) by splitting open, cleaning, rubbing with salt, pepper, etc., & drying in open air or smoke. [f. prec.]

Kirghiz (kērgēz′), a. & n. (Member, language) of a Mongolian people living on the Caspian, N.E. of the Kalmucks.

|| kirk, n. (Sc. & north.) church; (in E use) *K~ of Scotland*, Church of Scotland as opp. to Church of England or to Episcopal Church in Scotland; *~′man*, member of *K~ of Scotland*; *~ session*, lowest court in *K~ of Scotland* & (hist.) other Presbyterian Churches, composed of ministers & elders. [ME, f. ON *kirkja*, itself f. OE *circe* CHURCH]

kirsch(wasser) (kērsh′vahsẽr), n. Spirit distilled from fermented liquor of wild cherries. [G (*kirsche* cherry + *wasser* water)]

|| kir′tle, n. (arch.). Woman's gown or

outer petticoat; man's tunic or coat. [OE *cyrtel*, = ON *kyrtill*, ult. perh. f. L *curtus* short]

kis′mĕt, n. Destiny. [Turk., f. Arab. *qisma(t)* f. *qasama* divide]

kiss¹, n. Caress given with lips; (billiards) impact between moving balls; kind of sugar-plum. [OE *coss* (ME *cos(s), cus(s), kisse*) f. Gmc. **kussaz* (foll.); form *kiss* f. the vb]

kiss², v.t. Touch with the lips, esp. as sign of love, affection, greeting, or reverence; (abs., of two persons) *~ & be friends*, become reconciled; (billiards, of ball) touch (ball) with KISS¹ (also abs. of two balls); *~ away*, remove (tears etc.) with kisses; *~ the book* (Bible, in taking oath); *~ the dust*, yield abject submission, (also) be slain; *~ the ground*, prostrate oneself in token of homage, (fig.) be brought low; *~ one's hand to*, wave a kiss to; *~ hands* or *the hand* (of sovereign etc. as ceremonial salutation or on appointment to office); *~ the rod*, accept chastisement submissively; *~-in-the-ring*, game for young people in which one pursues & *~es* another of opposite sex; *~-me-quick*, small bonnet standing far back on head, curl worn on forehead. Hence ~′ABLE a., ~′ablY² adv. [OE *cyssan*, OS *cussian*, OHG *chussen*, ON *kyssa* (Goth. *kukjan*) f. Gmc **kussjan* f. **kussaz*]

kiss′ing¹, a. In vbl senses; *~-crust*, soft crust where loaf has touched another in baking. [-ING²]

kiss′ing², n. In vbl senses; || *~-gate* (hung in U or V shaped enclosure); *~ kind*, on affectionate terms. [-ING¹]

kit¹, n., & v.t. & i. (-tt-). 1. || Wooden tub for various purposes; (articles carried in) soldier's etc. pack etc.; personal equipment, esp. as packed for travelling; workman's outfit; *~-bag* (for carrying soldier's or traveller's *~*). 2. vb. Fit out, be fitted out, with *~* (freq. *up*). [f. MDu. *kitte* wooden vessel; orig. unkn.]

kit², n. Abbr. of KITTEN.

kit³, n. (now rare). Small fiddle used by dancing-master. [perh. ult. as CITHERN]

kit′-căt, n. *K~ Club*, club of Whig politicians founded under James II; member of this; *~ (portrait)*, portrait of less than half-length, but including hands. [f. *Christopher* (or *Kit*) *Cat*, keeper of pie-house where club met]

kitch′en, n. Part of house where food is cooked; *~ garden* (for fruit & vegetables); *~-maid*, servant employed in *~*, usu. under cook; *~ MIDDEN*; *~ physic*, good & plentiful food; *~-stuff*, *~ requisites*, esp. vegetables. [OE *cycene*, OS **kukina*, OHG *chuhhina* f. **cocina* var. of LL *coquina* (*coquere* cook)]

kitch′ener, n. || Cooking-range; person in charge of monastery kitchen. [-ER¹]

kitchĕnĕtte′, n. Small room, alcove, etc., fitted up as miniature kitchen & scullery (esp. in modern flat). [-ETTE] kīte, n., v.i. & t. **1.** Bird of prey of same family as falcon, with long wings, usu. forked tail, & no tooth in bill; rapacious person, sharper; toy consisting of light wooden frame, usu. in form of isosceles triangle with circular arc as base, with paper stretched over it, flown in strong wind by string; BOX²-~; *fly a* ~, (fig.) make experiment to gauge public opinion etc.; (commerc. sl.) accommodation bill (*fly a*~, raise money by this); (pl.) highest sails of ship, set only in light wind; ~ *balloon*, sausage-shaped captive balloon for military observation; *K*~'*mark*, trade mark (representing a ~) on goods approved by the British Standards Institution. **2.** v.i. Soar like ~; (v.t.) cause to do this, (commerc.) convert into ~. [OE *cŷta*, of unkn. orig.]

kith, n. ~ *& kin*, friends & relations. [OE *cŷthth* f. Gmc **kunthitha* f. **kunth-* known (see UNCOUTH, -TH¹)]

kitsch n. Worthless pretentiousness in (esp. dramatic) art. [G]

kitt'en, n., & v.t. **1.** Young of cat; skittish young girl. **2.** v.t. Bring forth (~s, or abs.). Hence ~ISH¹ a. [ME *kito(u)n*, *ketoun* f. AF **kitoun*, **ket-* = OF *chitoun*, *chetoun* dim. of *chat* CAT]

kitt'iwāke, n. Kind of sea-gull. [imit.]

kit'tle, a. Ticklish, difficult to deal with, esp. ~ *cattle* (usu. fig. of persons or things). [f. ME (now Sc. & dial.) *kittle*, prob. f. ON *kitla* = OS *kitilōn*, OHG *chizzilōn*]

kittul' (-ōōl), kītōōl', n. Kind of palm; strong black fibre from leaf-stalks of this. [f. Sinhalese *kitul*]

kitt'y¹, n. Pet name for kitten. [f. KIT² + -Y³]

kitt'y², n. Pool in some card games; joint fund; (bowls) jack. [orig. unkn.]

ki'wi (kē'wē), n. = APTERYX; || (sl.) non-flying member of Air Force; (colloq., *K*~) a New Zealander. [Maori]

Klăx'on, n. Powerful electric motor-horn. [P; f. Gk *klazō* shriek]

klĕpht, n. One of the Greeks who after Turkish conquest of Greece in 15th c. maintained independence in mountains; brigand. [f. mod. Gk *klephtēs* f. Gk *kleptēs* thief]

klĕpt|omān'ia, n. Irresistible tendency to theft in persons not tempted to it by needy circumstances. Hence ~MAN'IAC n. [f. Gk *kleptēs* thief + -O- + -MANIA]

klip'sprĭnger, n. Small S.-Afr. antelope. [Afrikaans (*klip* rock + *springer* springer)]

klōōf, n. Ravine, valley, in S. Africa. [Du., = cleft]

kn-. In all words beginning thus k is silent.

knăck, n. Acquired faculty of doing a thing adroitly; ingenious device; trick, habit, of action, speech, etc. Hence ~'Y² a. [prob. = ME *knack* sharp blow or sound, of LG orig.: cf. Du., LG *knak* &c.; ult. imit.]

knăck'|er, n. || One who buys & slaughters useless horses, whence ~ERY(3) n.; one who buys old houses, ships, etc., for the materials. [orig. unkn.]

knăg, n. Knot in wood, base of a branch. Hence ~g'Y² (-g-) a. [ME, perh. f. LG *knagge*]

knăp¹, n. (dial.). Crest of hill, rising ground. [OE *cnæp(p)*, cogn. w. ON *knappr* knob]

knăp², v.t. (-pp-). Break (flints for roads or building) with hammer, whence ~p'ER¹(1, 2) n.; (Bibl., dial.) knock, rap, snap asunder. [goes w. 15th c. *knap* smart blow, of imit. orig.; cf. KNACK]

knăp'săck, n. Soldier's or traveller's canvas or leather bag, strapped to back & used for carrying necessaries, cf. RUCK-SACK. [LG, prob. f. *knappen* bite + SACK¹]

knăp'weed, n. Common weed with hard stem & light purple flowers on dark globular head. [earlier *knopweed* (KNOP + WEED)]

knâr, n. Knot in wood, esp. protuberance covered with bark on trunk or at root of tree. [ME *knarre*, rel. to LG *knarre(n)*, Du. *knar* stump of tree, knot, knob; cf. KNUR(R)]

knăv|e, n. Unprincipled man, rogue, whence ~'ERY(4), ~'ishNESS, nn., ~'ISH¹ a., ~'ishLY² adv.; (cards) lowest court-card of each suit. [OE *cnafa* boy, servant, = OHG *knabo* f. WG **knabhon-*]

knead, v.t. Work up (moist flour or clay) into dough or paste; make (bread, pottery) thus; (fig.) blend, weld together; operate on (muscles etc.) as if ~ing, massage. Hence ~'ABLE a., ~'ER¹(1, 2) n. [OE *cnedan*, OS *knedan*, OHG *knetan*, ON *knotha* f. Gmc **kned-*, **knud-*]

knead'ing, n. In vbl senses; ~-*trough*, wooden trough in which dough is kneaded. [-ING¹]

knee¹, n. **1.** Joint between thigh & lower leg in man, corresponding joint in animals; *give a* ~ *to*, support (pugilist) on one's ~ between rounds, act as second to; *on* one's~*s*, kneeling, esp. in supplication, worship, or submission; *bring* (person) *to his* ~*s*, reduce him to submission; *is on the* ~*s of the gods*, is yet uncertain (after Homer). **2.** Part of garment covering the ~. **3.** Thing like ~ in shape or position, esp. piece of wood or iron with angular bend. **4.** ~-*breeches* (reaching down to or just below ~); ~-*cap*, convex bone in front of ~-joint, (also) protective covering for~; ~-*deep*, so deep as to reach the~s; ~-*hole* (*table*), (writing-table with) hole between drawer pedestals to admit ~s: ~ *holly*, butcher's broom; ~-*joint*, joint of ~, joint of two pieces hinged together; ~-*pan*, ~-cap; ~-*swell*, (in Amer. organ etc.) lever worked by ~, for producing crescendo & diminuendo effects. [OE *cnēo(w)*, OS *knio*, OHG *kneo*, ON *knē*, Goth. *kniu* f. Gmc **knewam*, cogn. w. L *genu*]

knee[2], v.t. Touch with the knee; fasten (framework etc.) with knees; (colloq.) cause (trousers) to bulge at knees. [f. prec.]

kneel, v.i. (*knĕlt*). Fall, rest, on the knee(s) esp. in prayer or reverence (*to* person). [ME *cneolen* f. OE *cnēowlian* (as KNEE[1])]

knell[1], n. Sound of bell, esp. of one rung solemnly after death or at funeral; (fig.) announcement, event, etc., regarded as an omen of death or extinction. [OE *cnyll* (as foll.)]

knell[2], v.i. & t. (arch.). (Of bell) ring, esp. at death or funeral; give forth doleful sound; (fig.) sound ominously; (v.t.) proclaim as by a knell. [ME *knylle* f. OE *cnyllan*; ME *knell* prob. imit. alt. (cf. *bell*)]

knelt. See KNEEL.

Knĕss'ĕt, n. Israeli parliament. [Heb.]

knew. See KNOW[1].

knick'erbŏcker, n. (*K~*) New Yorker; (pl.) loose-fitting breeches gathered in at knee. [*K~*, pretended author of W. Irving's *History of New York*]

knick'ers, n. pl. Knickerbockers (colloq.); woman's drawers of knickerbocker shape. [abbr. of prec.]

knick'-knăck, nick'-năck, n. Light dainty article of furniture, dress, or food; trinket, gimcrack. Hence ~ERY(2, 5) n., ~ISH[1] a. [redupl. of KNACK in obs. sense 'trinket']

knife, n. (pl. *knives* pr. nīvz), & v.t. (-*fed*). 1. Blade with sharpened longitudinal edge fixed in handle either rigidly, as in *table, carving, ~*, or with hinge, as in *pocket-~* or PEN[3]*~*, used as cutting instrument or as weapon; (of malicious or vindictive person) *get a ~ into* (person); *war to the~*, relentless war; blade forming part of machine, as in turnip-cutter etc.; *the ~*, surgical operations, as *have a horror of the ~*; *before you can say ~*, very quickly or suddenly; *play a good ~ & fork*, eat heartily. 2. *~-board* (on which knives are cleaned), (transf.) ‖ double bench placed lengthways on the top of omnibus; *~-boy* (formerly employed to clean table-knives); *~-edge*, edge of ~, steel wedge on which pendulum etc. oscillates, = ARÊTE; *~-grinder*, itinerant sharpener of knives etc., one who grinds knives etc. in process of making; *~-machine* (for cleaning knives); *~-rest*, metal or glass support for carving ~ or fork at table. 3. v.t. Cut, stab, with ~. [late OE *cnif* f. ON *knifr*, = MLG *knif*, MDu. *cnijf*, f. Gmc *knibhaz*]

knight (nīt), n., & v.t. 1. Military follower, esp. one devoted to service of (lady) as attendant or champion in war or tournament. 2. Person, usu. one of noble birth who had served as page & squire, raised to honourable military rank by king or qualified person. 3. One on whom corresponding rank is conferred as reward for personal merit or services to crown or country. 4. (hist.). (Also, ~ *of the shire*) person representing shire or county in parliament. 5. (Rom. Ant.) one of the class of equites, orig. the cavalry of Roman army; (Gk Ant.) citizen of second class at Athens. 6. Piece in game of chess, usu. with horse's head. 7. ~ BACHELOR, COMMANDER, COMPANION[1], HOSPITALLER, TEMPLAR; ~ *errant*, medieval ~ wandering in search of chivalrous adventures, (fig.) person of chivalrous or of quixotic spirit; *~-errantry*, practice, conduct, of a ~ errant (lit. & fig.); *~-heads*, two vertical timbers supporting bowsprit; ~ *of the post*, one who got his living by giving false evidence; *~-service* (hist.), tenure of land by military service. 8. v.t. Confer *~hood* on. Hence ~'HOOD n., ~'LIKE, ~'LY[1], aa., ~'LY[2] adv. (poet.), (nit-). [OE *cniht*, OS, OHG *kneht* f. WG **knehta*]

knight'age (nīt-), n. Whole body of knights; list & account of knights. [-AGE]

knit, v.t. & i. (*~ted* or *knit*). Form (close texture, garments etc. of this) of interlooping yarn or thread; contract (brow) in wrinkles; make, become, close or compact (esp. in p.p., as *a well-~frame*); (fig.) unite (t. & i.) intimately by means of common interests, marriage, etc., (often *together*); ~ *up*, repair by ~ting, (fig.) close up, conclude, (argument etc.). [OE *cnyttan*, MDu., MLG *knutten* (G dial. *knütten*) f. WG **knuttjan* f. **knutt-* KNOT[1]]

knitt'ing, n. In vbl senses, esp. work in process of ~; *~-needle*, slender rod of steel, wood, ivory, etc., two or more of which are used together in ~. [f. prec. + -ING[1]]

knit'tle, n. (naut.). Small line made of yarn. [f. KNIT + -LE]

knŏb, n., & v.t. & i. (-bb-). 1. Rounded protuberance, esp. at end or on surface of thing; handle of door (often *door-~*) or drawer; small lump (of sugar, coal, etc.); (sl.) head (usu. *nob*); *~'kerrie* [after Afrikaans *knopkierie*], short stick with ~bed head as weapon of S.-Afr. tribes; *~'stick*, ~bed stick, esp. as weapon, ‖ (also) workman who works during strike; *with ~s on* (sl.), = that, & more (phr. indicating ironic or emphatic agreement). 2. v.t. Furnish with ~s; (v.i.) bulge *out*. Hence ~b'Y[2] a., ~b'iNESS n. [ME *knobbe* f. MLG *knobbe*; cf. Flem. *knobbe(n)* lump of bread]

knŏb'bl|e, n. Small knob. Hence ~Y[2] a. [15th c., f. Du. & LG *knobbel* dim. of prec.]

knŏck[1], v.t. & i. 1. Strike with hard blow; strike door, strike *at the door*, to gain admittance; (of motor or other engine) make thumping or rattling noise as result of loose bearing or other mechanical defect; *(sl.) criticize; ‖ (sl.) make strong impression on, as *what ~s me is his impudence*; ~ (person etc.) *on the head*, stun, kill, him by blow on head, (fig.) put an end to (scheme etc.); ~ *one's head against*, (fig.) come into unpleasant collision with

(unfavourable facts or conditions); ~ *head*
vb, kotow; drive (thing) *in, out, off*, etc.,
by striking (see also below); ~ *into a*
COCK²*ed hat*; ~ one *into the middle of next*
week, send him flying; ~ *the bottom out of*,
render (argument etc.) invalid. **2.**~ *about*,
strike repeatedly, treat roughly, (intr.)
wander, lead irregular life; ~ *against*,
collide with, come across casually; ~ *back*
(sl.), drink; ~ *down*, strike (person etc.)
to ground with blow, (fig.) cause to
succumb, (at auction) dispose of (article
to bidder) by knock with hammer, (colloq.)
call upon (person *for* a song etc.), (colloq.)
lower (prices), (commerc.) take (machinery etc.) to pieces to save space in transport; ~ *off*, strike off with blow, leave off
work, leave off (work), (colloq.) dispatch
(business) or rapidly compose (verses etc.),
deduct (sum from price, bill, etc.), ~
person's *head off*, (fig.) surpass him easily;
~ *out*, empty (one's pipe) by tapping,
disable (pugilist) so that he cannot respond to call of ' Time ', (fig.) vanquish,
(colloq.) make (plan etc.) hastily; ~
together, put hastily together; ~ *under*,
submit, knuckle under; ~ *up*, drive upwards with blow, make or arrange hastily,
score (runs) rapidly at cricket, arouse
(person) by ~ing at door, exhaust, become
exhausted, *(sl.) make pregnant. **3.** ~*
about n. & a., boisterous, noisy (performance in music-hall etc.), wandering irregularly, (of clothes) suitable for rough use;
~*-down* a. & n., (of blow, lit. & fig.) overwhelming, (of price at auction) reserve,
minimum, (n.) free fight; ~*-knees* (that ~
together in walking); ~*-kneed*, having
~*-knees; ~*-out*, (blow) that~s boxer out,
(n.) ‖ one of gang who join at auction to
buy goods at low price, afterwards re-
selling among themselves, this practice,
such sale, (sl.) outstanding person or thing.
[late OE *cnocian*,=ON *knoka*, prob. imit.]
knock², n. Blow; rap esp. at door; sound
of knocking in motor etc. engine (see
prec.); (sl.) innings at cricket; ~*-up*,
practice or casual game at cricket, fives,
etc.; *take the*~ (sl.), be hard hit financially.
[f. prec.]
knock'er, n. In vbl senses, esp.: appendage, usu. of iron or brass, so hinged
to door that it may be struck against
metal plate to call attention (*up to the* ~,
sl., to perfection); goblin held to dwell
in mines & indicate presence of ore by
knocking. [-ER¹]
knoll¹, n. Small hill, mound. [OE *cnoll*
hill-top, rel. to MDu., MHG *knolle* clod,
ON *knollr* hill-top]
‖ **knoll²**, v.t. & i. (arch.). Ring (bell); (of
bell) sound; toll out (hours); summon by
sound of bell. [var. of KNELL]
knop, n. (arch.). Knob; bud of flower.
[ME, f. MLG, MDu. *knoppe*, = OHG
chnopf]

knopkierie, n. Afrikaans sp. of KNOB*kerrie*.
knot¹, n. **1.** Intertwining of parts of one or
more ropes, strings, etc., to fasten them together; GRANNY'S, REEF¹-, SLIP-, WEAVER'S,
~; ribbon etc. so tied as ornament or
adjunct to dress, as SHOULDER, SWORD,
TOP, TRUE-*love*, -~. **2.** (naut.). Division
marked by ~s on log-line, as measure of
speed; unit of speed equivalent to a
nautical mile per hour; (loosely) nautical
mile (6,080 ft). **3.** Difficulty, problem;
GORDIAN ~; central point in problem or
plot of story etc., cf. DENOUEMENT;
marriage, wedding, ~ (bond). **4.** Hard
lump in animal body; excrescence in
stem, branch, or root, of plant; (hard
mass formed in trunk at insertion of
branch, causing) round cross-grained
piece in board; node on stem of plant.
5. Group, cluster, of persons or things.
6. ‖ (Usu. *porter's* ~) double shoulder-pad
used for carrying loads. **7.** ~-*grass*,
common weed with intricate creeping
stems & pale pink flowers; ~'*work*, ornamental work representing or consisting
of intertwined cords, (also) kind of fancy
needlework. Hence ~'LESS a. [OE *cnotta*,
= Du. *knot*, LG *knütte*, MHG *knotze* f.
WG **knutton*-; cogn. w. OHG *chnodo*,
chnoto (G *knoten*)]
knot², v.t. & i. (-tt-). Tie (string etc.) in
knot; make knots for fringes, (trans.)
make (fringe) thus, whence ~t'ING¹ n.;
knit (one's brows); unite closely or
intricately; entangle. [f. prec.]
knot³, n. Small wading bird of sandpiper
family. [orig. unkn.]
knott'|ў, a. Full of knots; (fig.) puzzling,
hard to explain, as ~*y subject, question,*
point. Hence ~iNESS n. [f. KNOT¹ + -Y²]
knout (or nŏŏt), n., & v.t. (Flog with)
scourge formerly used in Russia, often
fatal in its effects. [F, f. Russ. *knut*]
know¹ (nŏ), v.t. & i. (*knew* pron. nū,
~*n*). **1.** Recognize, identify, as *I knew*
him at once, knew him for an American,
shall you ~ *him again?*; be able to distinguish (*don't* ~ *him from Adam;* ~ *one*
from another, a HAWK¹ *from a handsaw*).
2. Be acquainted with (thing, place,
person) *by sight, to speak to,* etc. (~ *by*
name, have heard the name of, be able to
give the name of); have personal experience of (fear, pain, etc.); be on intimate
terms with; (bibl.) have sexual intercourse with. **3.** Be aware of (fact), be
aware (*that, how, what,* etc.); ~ (person
etc.) *to be* (that he is). **4.** Be versed in
(language etc.). **5.** *He would do it if he*
knew how (knew the way); *all one* ~*s*, all
one can, (adv.) to the utmost of one's
power; ~ *about,* have information about;
I ~ *better* (*than that*), I am too well informed of the facts to believe that; ~
better than, be too well-mannered *to* do;
~ *of,* be aware of; *not that I* ~ *of,* not so

far as I ~; ~ one's *own mind*, not vacillate; ~ *what's what*, have proper knowledge of the world & of things in general; *don't you* ~ (esp. as parenthetic expletive in various contexts; *it's such a bore, don't you* ~); ~ *the* ROPES. 6. ~*-all*, one who ~s or professes to ~ everything; ~*-how*, faculty of~ing how, technical expertness; ~*-nothing*, ignorant person, (also) agnostic, whence ~*-nothingism*. Hence ~ABIL'ITY, ~'ableNESS, nn., ~'ABLE a., (nŏa-). [OE (*ge*)*cnāwan*, OHG -*cnāhan*, ON *knā*, cogn. w. L (*g*)*nosco*, Gk *gignōskō*]

know² (nō), n. (colloq.). *In the* ~, knowing (about) the thing in question or what is not generally known. [f. prec.]

know'ing (nōī-), a. In vbl senses, esp.: cunning, wide-awake (freq. rather derog.); (colloq.) stylish, smart, as *a* ~ *hat*. Hence ~NESS n. [-ING²]

know'inglỹ (nōī-), adv. In a knowing manner; consciously, intentionally, as *I have never* ~ *injured him*. [-LY²]

knowl'edge (nŏl-), n. Knowing, familiarity gained by experience, (*of* person, thing, fact); person's range of information, as *it came to my* ~ (became known to me), *not to my* ~, not so far as I know, *he had to my* (*certain*) ~ *been bribed* (I know he had); theoretical or practical understanding (*of* subject, language, etc.); the sum of what is known, as *every branch of* ~; (philos.) certain understanding, dist. from opinion. Hence ~ABLE (nŏllja-) a. (colloq.), well-informed, intelligent. [ME *knaulege*, w. earlier vb *knawlechen*, f. ᴋɴᴏᴡ; second element obsc., perh. f. OE -*læcan* f. *lāc*, as in *wedlock*]

knŭc'kle, n., & v.t. & i. 1. Bone at finger--joint, esp. at root of finger; projection of carpal or tarsal joint of quadruped; joint of meat consisting of this with parts above & below it; *a* ʀᴀᴘ¹ *on the* ~*s*; *near the* ~ (colloq.), verging on the indecent; ~*bone*, bone forming ~, esp. of sheep or the like, (pl.) game played with such bones; ||~*duster*, metal instrument protecting ~s from injury in striking. 2. v.t. Strike, press, rub, with ~s; (v.i.) place ~s on ground in playing at marbles; ~ *down, under*, give in, submit (*to*). [ME *knokel* f. MLG, MDu. *knōkel*, dim. of *knoke* bone; cf. G *knöchel*, *knochen*]

knŭr(r), n. Hard excrescence on trunk of tree; hard concretion; wooden ball in north-country game like trap-ball. [ME *knorre*, rel. to MLG, MDu., MHG *knorre*; cf. ᴋɴᴀʀ.]

knŭrl, n. Knot, knob (esp., that by which typewriter platen is turned); bead or ridge in metal work, whence ~ᴇᴅ² (-ld) a. [prob. f. prec.]

knŭt, joc. spelling of ɴᴜᴛ used of youths.

kō'a, n. An acacia in Sandwich Is. [native]

koa'la (-ah-), n. Native bear of Australia, a tailless arboreal marsupial. [native]

kōb'ŏld, n. (Germ. myth.). Familiar spirit, brownie; underground spirit in mines etc. [G, of obsc. orig.]

kŏd'äk, n. Kind of photographic camera with continuous roll of sensitized film. [P]

koedoe, n. Afrikaans sp. of ᴋᴏᴏᴅᴏᴏ.

kō'ĕl, n. Indian & Australian kinds of cuckoo. [f. Hind. *kóïl* f. Skr. *kokila*]

koh'i-noor (kōī-), n. Famous Indian diamond, property of British Crown since 1849; anything superb (*of* its class). [f. Pers. *kohi nur* (*koh* mountain + *nur* light)]

kohl (kōl), n. Powder, usu. antimony, used in East to darken eyelids etc. [f. Arab. *koh'l*, see ᴀʟᴄᴏʜᴏʟ]

kohlra'bi (kōlrah-), n. Cabbage with turnip-shaped stem. [G, f. It. *cavoli rape* pl. (see ᴄᴏʟᴇ & ʀᴀᴘᴇ³)]

Koin'ē, n. The common literary language of the Greeks from the close of classical Attic to the Byzantine era. [f. Gk *koinē* (*dialektos*) common (language)]

kola. See ᴄᴏʟᴀ.

Kōlār'ian, a. & n. Of various primitive non-Aryan tribes in the forests & hill districts of Bengal; (n.) ~ native. [f. *Kolar* = Canarese *kallar* thieves +-ɪᴀɴ]

kolin'skỹ, n. Fur of the Siberian mink. [Russ. (-*ski*) f. *Kola*, district in N.-W. Russia]

kŏlkhoz' (-kōz), n. Collective farm in U.S.S.R. [Russ. *kol(lektivnoe) khoz-(yaistvo)* collective farm]

komita(d)ji. Var. of ᴄᴏᴍɪᴛᴀᴅᴊɪ.

kōō'dŏō, kudu (kōō'dōō), n. Large white--striped spiral-horned S.-Afr. antelope. [native]

kōōkabūr'a, n.(Austral.). Laughing jackass. [native]

koolah. Obs. form of ᴋᴏᴀʟᴀ.

kopec(k), -peek, -pek, = ᴄᴏᴘᴇᴄᴋ.

kŏp'je (-pī), n. (S.-Afr.). Small hill. [Du., dim. of *kop* head]

koppie, n. S.Afr. sp. of ᴋᴏᴘᴊᴇ.

Kōr'an (*or* Korahn'), n. Sacred book of the Mohammedans, collection of Mohammed's oral revelations, written in Arabic. Hence korän'ɪᴄ a. [f. Arab. *quran* recitation (*qara'a* read)]

kōsh'er, a. & n. 1. (Of food or shop where food is sold or used) fulfilling requirements of Jewish law. 2. n. ~ food or shop. [f. Heb. *kasher* right]

kōtow', n., & v.i. 1. Chinese custom of touching ground with forehead as sign of worship or absolute submission. 2. v.i. Perform the ~, act obsequiously (*to* person etc.). [(vb f. n.) f. Chin. *k'o-t'ou* (*k'o* knock+*t'ou* head)]

kŏt'wal (-ahl), n. Chief constable of Indian town; magistrate. [Hind.]

koum'iss (kōō-), n. Fermented liquor prepared from mare's milk. [f. Tartar *kumiz*]

kourb'äsh (koor-), koorb-, n. Hide whip as instrument of punishment in Turkey & Egypt. [f. Arab. *qurbash* f. Turk. *qirbach*]

kowtow. Var. of KOTOW.

kraal (krahl), n. S.-African village of huts enclosed by fence; enclosure for cattle or sheep. [Afrikaans, f. Port. CORRAL]

krait (krīt), n. Peculiarly venomous snake common in Bengal. [Hind. *karait*]

kra'ken (-ah-, -ă-), n. Mythical sea--monster appearing off coast of Norway. [Norw.]

krans (-ah-), n. (S.-Afr.). Precipitous or overhanging wall of rocks. [Du. *krans* coronet]

krěm'lin, n. Citadel within Russian town, esp. that of Moscow; *the K~,* (used for) the Russian Government. [F, f. Russ. *kreml*]

kreu'tzer (kroit-), n. Small silver & copper coins formerly current in Germany & Austria. [f. G *kreuzer* (*kreuz* cross)]

krieg'spiel, n. War-game in which blocks representing troops etc. are moved about on maps. [G]

kris. See CREESE.

Krish'naïsm, n. Worship of Krishnâ, great deity of later Hinduism, worshipped as incarnation of Vishnu. [-ISM]

kroměs'ký, n. Minced chicken etc. rolled in bacon & fried. [f. Russ.]

krōn'e (-e), n. Silver coin of Denmark, Norway, & Sweden; former Austrian silver coin; former German 10-mark gold piece. [G & Da. *krone,* Sw. *krona,* crown]

Krōō, Krou, Kru (-ōō), n. & a. (Member) of Negro race on coast of Liberia, skilful as seamen (often, for the n., *~-boy, ~--man*). [W.-Afr.]

krȳp'tŏn, n. (chem.). A rare inert gaseous element discovered by Ramsay in 1898. [f. Gk *krupton* hidden, neut. adj. f. *kruptō* hide]

Ksha'trïya (-ah-), n. Member of the second or military caste of the Hindus. [Skr., f. *kshatra* rule]

kūd'ōs (sl.). Glory, renown. [Gk]

Kufic. See CUFIC.

•KūᴸKlŭx(-Klǎn'), n. Secret society hostile to Negroes & R. Catholics formed in southern States after civil war; similar organization in U.S. to combat alien influences after 1914–18 war. [arbitrary]

kuk'rī (kŏŏ-), n. Curved knife broadening towards point, used by Gurkhas of Nepal. [Hind.]

kul'ǎk (kŏŏ-), n. (Russ. pl. *~i*). Well-to-do Russian peasant (-proprietor). [Russ., = tight-fisted person]

kultur (kŏŏltoor'), n. Civilization as conceived by the Germans. [G, = culture]

kultur'kampf (kŏŏltoor'kahmpf), n. Conflict between German imperial government and Pope for control of schools and church appointments (1872–87). [G]

kümm'el (see Ap.), n. Cumin-flavoured liqueur. [G]

Kuomintǎng' (kŏŏō-), n. Nationalist party in China (founded in 1012). [Chin., lit. ' people's national party ']

Kurd (koord), n. Native of Kurdistan.

kursaal (koor'zahl), n. Building for use of visitors esp. at German health resort. [G, = cure-room]

kvǎss, n. Russian rye-beer. [f. Russ. *kvas*]

kȳ'anīze, -ise (-īz), v.t. Treat (wood) with solution of corrosive sublimate to prevent decay. [f. J. H. *Kyan,* inventor, +-IZE]

kyl'in (kē-), n. Fabulous composite animal figured on Chinese & Japanese pottery. [f. Chin. *ch'i-lin* (*ch'i* male +*lin* female)]

‖ **kȳl'ōe,** n. One of small breed of long--horned Scotch cattle. [K~, place-name]

kȳm'ograph(-ahf),n. Instrument recording variations in pressure, e.g. in sound--waxes. [Gk *kuma* wave +-o-+-GRAPH(2)]

kyrie eleison (kēr'iĭ llā'ison, ki'riĕ), n. Words of short petition used in Eastern & Roman Churches, esp. at beginning of Mass, musical setting of these; response to commandments in Communion Service in Anglican Church. [f. Gk *Kurie eleēson* Lord, have mercy]

L

L (ĕl), letter (pl. *Ls,* L's). Thing shaped like L (*L-iron,* = ANGLE[1]-*iron*); rectangular joint of pipes etc.; Roman numeral = 50, as CL 150, XL 40, lx 60, lv 55, (LXX, the Septuagint).

la (lah), **lah,** n. (mus.). Sixth note of octave. [first syl. of L *labii,* see GAMUT]

laag'er (lahg-), n., & v.t. & i. 1. Camp, encampment, esp. in circle of wagons; (mil.) park for armoured vehicles. 2. vb. Form (vehicles) into ~; encamp (persons) in ~; encamp. [S.-Afr. Du., & G, *lager,* Du. *leger,* see LEAGUER[1]]

lăb, n. (colloq.). Laboratory. [abbr.]

lăb'arum, n. Constantine the Great's imperial standard with Christian added to Roman-military symbols; symbolic banner. [LL *labarum,* of unkn. orig.]

labdacism. See LAMBDACISM.

lăběfǎc'tion, n. Shaking, weakening, downfall. [f. L *labefacere* (*labare* totter, *facere* make), see -FACTION]

lăb'el, n., & v.t. (-ll-). 1. Slip of paper, card, linen, metal, etc., for attaching to object & indicating its nature, owner, name, destination, etc.; (fig.) short classifying phrase or name applied to persons etc. (freq. derog. in literary or artistic criticism); adhesive stamp; (archit.) dripstone. 2. v.t. Attach ~ to; assign to a category (*as,* obj. & compl., or abs.). [ME, f. OF, prob. f. OFrank. *labba* (= OHG *lappa* LAP[1]) +dim. *-el*]

lăb'ial, a. & n. Of the lips; (anat., zool.) of, like, serving as, a lip, lip-like part, or labium; (mus.) ~ *pipe,* in organ, one furnished with lips, flue-pipe; (phonet.) (sound) requiring closure or approximation of lips (*p, b, f, v,* also *m, w,* & vowels in which lips are rounded, as *o*), whence

~ISM(1), ~ĭZA'TION, nn., ~IZE(3) v.t. [f. med. L labialis (LABIUM, -AL)]

lăb'iate, a. & n. (Bot.) with corolla or calyx divided into two parts suggesting lips (n., such plant); (bot., zool.) like lip or labium. [LABIUM + -ATE²]

lăb'ile, a. (phys., chem.). Unstable, liable to displacement or change. [f. LL labilis (labi to LAPSE², -IL)]

lăb'io-, comb. form of foll. = of the lip(s) & —, as ~dental, made with lip & teeth.

lăb'ĭum, n. (pl. -ia). (Anat.; usu. pl.) lip(s) of female pudendum; floor of mouth of insects, crustaceans, etc.; inner lip of univalve shell; lip, esp. the lower, of labiate corolla. [L, = lip]

lăb'oratory̆ (or labŏ²-), n. Room or building used for experiments in natural science, esp. chemistry, or for research (also fig., ~ of the mind, of ideas, etc.). Hence lăboratōr'ial a. [f. med. L laboratorium (laborare LABOUR², -ORY)]

labōr'ious, a. Hard-working; toilsome; (of style etc.) showing signs of toil, not facile or fluent. Hence ~LY² adv., ~NESS n. [ME, f. OF laborieus f. L laboriosus (foll., -IOUS)]

lăb'our¹ (-ber), n. 1. Bodily or mental toil, exertion, (HARD ~; lost ~, fruitless efforts; ~ of love, task one delights in); toil tending to supply wants of community; body of those who contribute by toil to production, labourers; (opp. CAPITAL², usu. L~) the working classes as a political force. 2. Task (~ of Hercules, Herculean ~, one needing enormous strength etc.). 3. Pains of childbirth, travail, (in ~). 4. ‖ L~ Exchange, local office under State for finding employment for those seeking it; ~-market, supply of ~ with reference to demand on it; L~ Party, that claiming to represent wage-earners, M.P.s elected by it. [ME, f. OF labor f. L laborem nom. -or]

lăb'our² (-ber), v.i. & t. Use labour, exert oneself, work hard; strive for end or to do; advance with difficulty (wheels ~ in the sand); be troubled (her ~ing heart) or impeded, suffer under mistake etc.; (of ship) roll or pitch heavily; (arch. or poet.) till (ground); elaborate, work out in detail, treat at length, (I will not ~ the point; ~ed, much elaborated, showing signs of labour, not spontaneous); ~ing man, labourer. [ME, f. OF labourer f. L laborare (labor LABOUR¹)]

lăb'ourer (-ber-), n. In vbl senses; esp., man doing for wages work that requires strength or patience rather than skill or training. [ME, f. OF laboureur (as prec., -ER¹)]

lăb'ourite (-ber-), n. Member, adherent, of Labour Party. [-ITE¹(1)]

Lăb'radōr, n. attrib. ~ dog, retriever, breed of retriever. [place]

lăb'rĕt, n. Piece of shell, bone, etc., inserted in lip as ornament. [L labrum lip, -ET¹]

labŭrn'um, n. Small tree with racemes of bright yellow flowers. [L]

lăb'yrinth, n. Complicated irregular structure with many passages hard to find way through or about without guidance, maze; intricate or tortuous arrangement; (anat.) complex cavity of internal ear; entangled state of affairs. Hence ~INE² (-ĭn'thĭn) a. [f. F labyrinthe or L f. Gk laburinthos]

lăbyrin'thodŏn, n., -dŏnt, n. & a. (Kinds of large fossil amphibian) with labyrinthine teeth. [-dont f. -don mod. L, f. Gk as prec. + odous -ontos tooth]

lăc¹, n. A resinous substance secreted by the lac insect as a protective covering. [f. Hind. lakh f. Skr. laksha]

lăc², lăkh(-k), n. (Anglo-Ind.). A hundred thousand (usu. ~ of rupees). [Hind. -kh) f. Skr. laksha]

lāce¹, n. Cord or leather strip for fastening or tightening opposite edges of shoes, corsets, etc., by help of eyelets or hooks; braid for trimming men's coats etc. (usu. gold or silver ~); fine open fabric of linen, cotton, silk, woollen, or metal threads usu. with inwrought or applied patterns; ~-glass, Venetian with ~-like designs; ~-pillow, laid on lap of woman making ~. Hence lā'CY² a. [ME, f. OF laz, las, f. Rom. *lacium f. L laqueus noose]

lāce², v.t. & i. Fasten or tighten (shoe, corsets, etc.) with lace(s) (freq. ~ up); compress waist of by drawing stay-laces tight, (intr.) compress one's waist; interlace or embroider (fabric) with thread etc.; pass (cord etc.) through; trim with lace; diversify (flower with streaks of colour); lash, beat, (also intr. as ~ into person); flavour, fortify, (milk, beer, etc.) with spirit. Hence lā'CING¹(1, 3, 6) n. [ME, f. OF lacier f. Rom. *laciare as prec.]

lă'cer|āte, v.t. Mangle, tear, (esp. flesh or tissues); afflict, distress, (heart, feelings). Hence or cogn.~ABLE,~ATE²(-at),~ATIVE, aa.,~A'TION n. [f. L lacerare (lacer torn), -ATE³]

lacĕrt'ian, -tĭne, aa. Of lizards; lizard-like. [f. L lacerta lizard + -IAN, -INE¹]

lācĕt', n. Work made of braid or tape shaped into a design with lace stitches. [-ET¹]

lăch'es (-ĭz), n. (Law) negligence in performing a legal duty, delay in asserting right, claiming privilege, etc.; culpable negligence. [ME, f. OF laschesse (lasche f. Rom. *lascus f. L laxus LAX)]

lach'ry̆ma Chris'ti (lăk-; krĭ-), n. Strong sweet red S.-Ital. wine. [L, = Christ's tear]

lăch'ry̆mal (-k-), a. & n. Of, for, tears (~ vase, or ~ as n., to hold tears; ~ canal, duct, gland, sac, in anat.; also ~s as n., these organs). [med. L (-alis), f. L lacrima tear]

lăchry̆mā'tion (-k-), n. Flow of tears. [f. L lacrimatio (lacrimare as prec., -ATION)]

lăch'ry̆matory̆ (-k-), a. & n. 1. Of, causing, tears (~ bomb, emitting gas that disables by making eyes water). **2. n.** Phial of kind found in anc.-Roman tombs & conjectured to be tear-bottles. [f. *lacrimare* see prec. +-ORY]

lăch'rўmōse (-k-), a. Tearful, given to weeping. Hence ~LY² adv. [f. L *lacrimosus* (*lacrima* tear, -OSE¹)]

lacin'iate, -ātéd, aa. (bot., zool.). Cut into deep irregular segments, slashed, jagged, fringed. [f. L *lacinia* lappet, -ATE²]

lăck, n., & v.i. & t. **1.** Deficiency, want, need, *of* (*no* ~, plenty *of*; *for* ~, owing to want or absence *of*). **2.** vb. Be wanting (only in part. forms, as *money was* ~*ing*, *is* ~*ing in courage*); be without, not have, be deficient in; ~'*land,* (person) having no land; ~'*lustre,* (of eye etc.) dull. [early ME *lac, lacen,* corresp. to MLG *lak,* MDu. *lac* deficiency, MDu. *laken* to lack]

lăckadais'ical (-z-), a. Languishing, affected, given to airs & graces, feebly sentimental; listless. Hence ~LY² adv., ~NESS n. [f. arch. *lackaday,* -*daisy,* int. (ALACK) +-ICAL]

lacker. See LACQUER.

lăck'ey, lăc'quey (-kĭ), n. (pl. ~s), & v.t. **1.** Footman, man-servant (usu. liveried); obsequious person, parasite. **2.** v.t. Dance attendance on, behave servilely to. [f. F *laquais* (obs. *alaquais*) f. Sp. *lacayo*]

Lacōn'ian, a. & n. (Inhabitant) of Laconia, Spartan. [f. L *Laconia* +-AN]

lacŏn'ĭc, a. Brief, concise, sententious; given to such speech or style. Hence ~ICALLY adv., ~ĬCISM(2) n. [f. L f. Gk *lakōnikos* (*Lakōn* Spartan, -IC)]

lăc'onism, n. Brevity of speech; short pithy saying. [f. Gk *lakōnismos* (*lakōnizō* behave like Spartan or *Lakōn,* -ISM)]

lăc'quer (-ker), **lăck'er,** n.,& v.t. **1.** Gold-coloured varnish of shellac dissolved in alcohol used esp. as coating for brass; kinds of resinous varnish (esp. *Japanese* ~) taking hard polish & used for wood etc., articles so coated. **2.** v.t. Coat with ~. [f. obs. F *lacre* sealing-wax, f. unexpl. var. of Port. *lacca* LAC¹]

lacquey. See LACKEY.

lacrim-, lacrym-. See lachrym-.

lacrosse (lahkraws', -ŏs), n. Game like hockey, but with ball driven by & carried in CROSSE, orig. N.-Amer. [F *la* the + CROSSE]

lăctā'tion, n. Suckling; secreting of milk. [f. L *lactare* suckle (*lac -tis* milk) +-ATION]

lăc'tèal, a. & n. **1.** Of milk; conveying chyle or other milky fluid. **2.** n. pl. Vessels of mesentery doing this. [f. L *lacteus* (*lac* see prec.) +-AL]

lăctĕs'cence, n., **lăctĕs'cent,** a. Milky (appearance); (yielding) milky juice. [f. L *lactescere* (*lactēre* be milky, see prec.), -ENCE, -ENT]

lăc't|ĭc, a. (chem.). Of milk; ~*ic acid,* formed in sour milk, whence ~ATE¹(3)) n. [f. L *lac -tis* milk +-IC]

lăctif'erous, a. Yielding milk or milky fluid. [f. LL *lactifer* (prec., -FEROUS)]

lăc'to-, comb. form (-ĭ-, -o-) of L as prec.; ~*prot'ein,* albuminous constituent of milk; ~METER (-ŏm²),~SCOPE, instruments for testing purity of milk.

lăctōse', n. Milk sugar, less sweet than cane sugar. [as prec. +-OSE²]

lacūn'|a, n. (pl. ~*ae,* ~*as*). Hiatus, blank, missing portion (esp. in ancient MS, book, etc.), empty part; cavity in bone, tissue etc. Hence ~AL, ~AR, ~ARY, ~OSE¹, aa. [L (*lacus* LAKE¹)]

lacūs'trine, a. Of, dwelling or growing in, lake(s); ~ *age,* of LAKE¹-dwellings. [f. L *lacus* LAKE¹ (after *paluster* marshy) +-INE¹]

lacy. See LACE¹.

lăd, n. Boy, youth, young fellow; fellow; stable-man (of any age). Hence ~d'ie [-y³] n. [ME *ladde,* of unkn. orig.]

lădd'er, n., & v.i. Set of steps (called *rungs*) inserted usu. in two uprights of wood or metal or in two cords to serve as (usu. portable) means of ascending building etc.; STEP²-~; ‖ (transf.) vertical flaw in stocking caused by stitch(es) becoming undone through several rows (v.i., develop~), whence~PROOF² a.; (fig.) means of rising in the world or attaining object (*kick down* ~, abandon friends or occupation that have helped one to rise), & see RUNG¹; ~*-dredge,* with buckets carried round on ~-like chain; ~*-stitch,* crossbar stitch in embroidery. [OE *hlǣd(d)er* = MDu. *lēdere,* OHG *leitara* f. Gmc **hli-, *hlai-* (LEAN²)]

lāde, v.t. (p.p. ~n). Put cargo on board (ship); ship (goods) as cargo (BILL⁴ *of lading),* whence **lād'ING¹**(3) n.; (p.p., of vehicle, beast of burden, person, tree, branch, table, etc.) loaded (*with*); (p.p.) painfully burdened *with* sin, sorrow, etc. [OE, OS, OHG *hladan,* ON *hlatha,* Goth. *-hlathan;* cf. LAST²]

la-di-da' (lah-, -ah), a. & n. (Person given to) swagger or pretension in manners & pronunciation; pretentious in this way. [imit. of pronunciation used]

Ladin' (-ēn), n. RHAETO-ROMANIC of the Engadine. [f. It *Ladino* f. L LATINus]

lā'dle, n., & v.t. **1.** Large spoon with cup bowl & long handle for transferring liquids; hence ~FUL(2) (-dlfŏŏl) n. **2.** v.t. Transfer (liquid) with ~ from one receptacle to another. [OE *hlædel* f. *hladan* LADE +-LE(1)]

lād'ў, n. **1.** Ruling woman (poet. exc. in ~ *of the manor, our sovereign* ~). **2.** Woman to whom man is devoted, mistress, love. **3.** *Our L*~, Virgin Mary. **4.** Woman belonging to, or fitted by manners, habits, & sentiments, for the upper classes (corresp. to GENTLEMAN; ‖ ~ *of bedchamber,* ~*-in-waiting,* ~ attending sovereign; FINE³ ~). **5.** (Courteously for) woman (as voc., only poet. or vulg. in sing., but usu. form of address in pl.). **6.**‖ (Title used as less formal prefix for) Marchioness (of), Countess (of), Viscountess, Baroness, (also prefixed to Christian name of) daughter of duke, marquis, or earl, (or to husband's Christian name of) wife of holder of courtesy title *lord* William etc., (or to surname of) wife of baronet or knight, (also in the compound title) *L~ Mayoress*, wife of Lord Mayor. **7.** *My ~*, form of address used chiefly by servants etc. to holders of title ~; *my dear* or *good ~* (address in ord. use). **8.** Wife (arch. or vulg., exc. of those who hold the title ~); *your good ~*, your wife, **9.** *Ladies & gentlemen* (voc. in addressing company of both sexes). **10.** (With *clerk, doctor, president, dog*, etc.) female; || (with *cook, parlourmaid, help*, etc.) claiming to be treated as ~. **11.** *Ladies* (as sing. n.), women's public lavatory etc.; *Ladies' chain*, figure in quadrille; *Ladies' gallery*, in House of Commons reserved for ladies. **12.** ~ *of EASY virtue*; *painted ~*, kind of butterfly. **13.** *L~-altar* (in L~-chapel); ~*bird*, coleopterous insect, usu. reddish--brown with black spots; *L~ Bountiful*, ~ playing the part of Providence in a village etc. (character in Farquhar's *Beaux's Stratagem*); ~*-chair*, made by two persons' interlaced hands to carry wounded man etc.; *L~-chapel*, in large church usu. east of high altar, dedicated to Virgin; ~*-clock*, *-cow*, ~*bird*; *L~ Day*, Feast of the Annunciation, 25th March, || one of the quarter-days; ~*-fern*, tall slender kind; || ~ *help*, ~ employed as domestic; ~*-killer*, man devoting himself to making conquests of ladies; ~*-love*, sweetheart; *L~'s BED¹-straw*; ~*'s companion*, roll containing cottons etc.; || *L~'s cushion*, mossy saxifrage; || *L~'s finger*, kidney vetch; *L~'s laces*, kind of striped grass; ~*'s-maid*, in charge of ~'s toilet; ~*'s man*, *ladies' man*, (fond of female society); *L~'s mantle*, rosaceous plant with yellowish--green flowers; *L~-smock*, cuckoo-flower; *L~'s slipper*, orchidaceous wild & garden plant with usu. yellow bag- or slipper--shaped flowers, calceolaria; *L~'s tresses*, kind of orchis. Hence ~HOOD n. [OE *hlǽfdīge* (*hláf* LOAF, *dig-* knead cf. DOUGH); in ~*-altar*, *-bird*, *-chapel*, *-clock*, *-cow*, *-day*, *-smock*, ~ is old genit. = (Our) Lady's]

lad'yfy, -ify, v.t. Make lady of; call lady; (p.p.) having the airs of a fine lady. [-FY]

lad'ylike, a. With manners etc. of a lady; (of man) effeminate; befitting a lady. [-LIKE]

lad'yship, n. Being a lady; *her, your, ~, their ~s*, she, you, they (in respectful mention of or address to titular lady). [-SHIP]

laer, n. Afrikaans sp. of LAAGER.

l(a)evo- (lēv'o), comb. form of L *laevus* left, esp. in terms concerned with chem. property of causing plane of polarized light ray to rotate to left (opp. DEXTRO-); so ~*gȳr'ous*, ~*rot'atory*, of substances having this; ~*-com'pound*, chemical compound having it.

l(a)ev'ūlōse (lēv-), n. (chem.). Laevo-rotatory sugar of fruit & honey, fruit--sugar. [prec., -UL-, -OSE²]

lăg¹, v.i. (-gg-), & n. **1.** Go too slow, not keep pace, fall behind (often *behind* adv. & prep.). **2.** n. (phys.). (Amount of) retardation in current or movement (~ *of tide*, interval by which it falls behind mean time in 1st & 3rd quarters of moon, cf. PRIMING²; TIME¹ ~. Hence ~g'ARD n. & a., ~g'ER¹ n., ~g'ING² a., (-g-). [16th c. 'hindmost person', 'hang back'; perh. f. a fanciful distortion of *last* in children's games (*fog, seg, ~*, = 1st, 2nd, last, in diall.)]

lăg², v.t. (-gg-), & n. (sl.). **1.** Send to penal servitude; apprehend, arrest. **2.** n. Convict, esp. *old ~*. [orig. unkn.]

lăg³, n., & v.t. (-gg-). **1.** (Piece of the) non-conducting cover of boiler etc. **2.** Case with ~s, whence ~g'ING¹(3) (-g-) n. [f. ON *logg* barrel-rim]

lăg'an, lig'an, n. (legal). Goods or wreckage lying on bed of sea. [OF, perh. of Scand. orig. f. root of LIE³, LAY³]

la'ger (laher-), n. Light kind of (orig. German or Bohemian) beer. [f. G *lager-bier* (*lager* store)]

lagōōn', -une (-ōōn), n. Stretch of salt water parted from sea by low sandbank; enclosed water of atoll. [f. F *lagune*, f. It. & Sp. *laguna* f. L LACUNA]

lah. See LA.

la'ic, a. & n. Non-cleric(al), lay(man), secular, temporal. So ~AL a., ~alLY² adv. [f. LL f. Gk *laikos* (*laos* people, -IC)]

la'iciz|e, -is|e (-īz), v.t. Make lay; commit (school etc.), throw open (office), to laymen. Hence ~A'TION n. [prec., -IZE]

laid. See LAY³.

lain. See LIE³.

lair, n., & v.i. & t. **1.** Place where animals lie down; || shed or enclosure for cattle on way to market, whence ~'AGE(1, 3) n.; wild beast's lying-place. **2.** vb. Go to, rest or place in, ~. [OE *leger*, OS *-ar*, OHG *-er*, ON *legr*, Goth. *ligrs* bed f. Gmc *leg-* LIE³]

|| laird, n. (Sc.). Landed proprietor in Scotland. Hence ~'SHIP n. [Sc. form of LORD w. changed sense]

La'is, n. Accomplished or beautiful courtesan. [name of two celebrated Greek hetaerae]

laissez-aller (lās'ā āl'ā), n. Unconstrained freedom, absence of constraint. [F, = let go]

laiss'ez-faire (-sā-), n. Government abstention from interference with individual action esp. in commerce. [F, = let act]

la'ity, n. Being a layman; laymen. [f. LAY² + -ITY]

lāke¹, n. Large body of water entirely surrounded by land; *the Great L~*, Atlantic ocean; *the Great L~s*, Superior, Huron, Michigan, Erie, & Ontario, forming boundary of U.S. & Canada; ~*-country*, ~*land*, *the L~s*, region of

English ~s in Westmorland, Cumberland, & Lancs.; ~-*dweller*, prehistoric inhabitant of ~ *dwelling*, built on piles driven into bed of ~; ~ *poets*, Coleridge, Southey, & Wordsworth, who lived in ~land. Hence ~'LESS a., ~'LET n., (-kl-). [ME, f. OF *lac* f. L *lacus*]

lake², n. Pigment, orig. made from lac, now formed by dye & mordant. [var. of LAC¹]

lakh. See LAC².

Lall'an, a. & n. (Sc.). 1. Of the Lowlands of Scotland. 2. n. (Also ~s) Lowland Scots dialect. [var. of LOW¹*land*]

lalla'tion, n. LAMBDACISM. [f. L *lallare* sing lullaby +-ATION]

lam, v.t. & i. (sl.; -mm-). Thrash, hit (t., & i. with *into*) hard with cane etc. [perh. f. Scand.; cf. ON *lemja* beat so as to LAME]

la'ma¹ (lah-), n. Tibetan or Mongolian Buddhist monk; (*Dalai* (pr. dăl'ĭ) L~, (obs.) *Grand* L~, head of ~ist church & ruler of Tibet. Hence ~ISM n., ~IST n. & a. [Tibetan *blama* (silent *b*)]

lama². See LLAMA.

Lamarck'ian, a. & n. (Follower) of Lamarck or his theory of organic evolution by the inheritance of acquired characters. [*Lamarck*, F botanist & zoologist, d. 1829, +-IAN]

lama'sery̆ (-mah-), n. Monastery of lamas. [f. F *lamaserie* irreg. f. LAMA¹]

lamb (-m), n., & v.t. & i. 1. Young of sheep (*as well be hanged for a sheep as for a* ~, sin boldly, go the whole hog; *like a* ~, unresistingly; *wolf, fox, in* ~'s *skin*, hypocrite); its flesh as food; young member of church flock; innocent, weak, or dear person; *The* L~ (*of God*), Christ; ~'s-*fry*, product of ~'s castration; ~'s *-skin*, with wool on, or as leather; ~'s-*tails*, || hazel catkins; ~'s-*wool*, used in hosiery; hence ~'HOOD (-mh-), ~'KIN (-mk-), nn., ~'LIKE (-ml-) a. 2. vb. (Pass.; of ~s) be brought forth; bring forth ~, yean; tend (~ing ewes), whence ~'ER¹ (-mer) n. [OE (= OS, OHG, ON, Goth.) *lamb* f. Gmc *lambaz*]

lambaste', v.t. (dial.). Thrash, beat. [perh. = LAM +BASTE³]

lamb'da, n. Greek letter L (*Λ λ*); ~ *moth*, with ~ on wings. [Gk, also *labda*]

la(m)b'dacism, n. Pronunciation of *r* as *l*. [prec., -ISM]

lamb'doid, lambdoid'al, aa. *Λ* -shaped (~ *suture*, connecting two parietal bones with occipital). [f. F *lambdoïde* f. Gk *lambdoeidēs* (LAMBDA, -OID) +-AL]

lamb'b|ent, a. (Of flame or light) playing on surface without burning it, with soft radiance; (of eyes, sky, etc.) softly radiant; (of wit etc.) gently brilliant. Hence ~ENCY n., ~entLY² adv. [f. L *lambere* lick, -ENT]

Lam'beth, n. (Used for) Archbishop of Canterbury's palace at ~, the Archbishop as representing the Church, etc.;

~ *degree*, honorary degree conferred by the Archbishop of Canterbury.

lam'brequin (-kĭn), n. Short piece of drapery over top of door or window, or hung from mantelpiece. [F, f. Du. *lamperkin*, dim. of *lamper* veil; see -KIN]

lame, a., & v.t. 1. Crippled by injury or defect in a limb, esp. foot or leg, limping or unable to walk, (of person, limb, steps, etc.; ~ *of* or *in a leg* etc.); (of argument, story, excuse) imperfect, unsatisfactory; (of metre) halting; ~ DUCK¹; hence **lam'ISH**¹(2) a., ~'LY² (-ml-) adv., ~'NESS (-mn-) n. 2. v.t. Make ~, cripple, (lit. & fig.). [OE *lama*, OS *lamo*, OHG *lam*, ON *lami* f. Gmc *lamon*]

lamé (lahmā'), a. & n. (Material) with gold or silver thread inwoven. [F]

lamell'|a, n. (pl. ~ae). Thin plate, scale, layer, or film, esp. of bone or tissue. Hence ~AR¹, **lam'ellATE²**, -ātěd, ~OSE¹, aa., ~-I- comb. form. [L, dim. of LAMINA]

lament', n., & v.t. & i. 1. Passionate expression of grief; elegy, dirge. 2. vb. Express or feel grief for or about, be distressed at, regret, (also intr. with *for* or *over*, or abs.); (p.p.) mourned for (esp. conventionally of the dead, as *the late* ~*ed* ―). [vb f. F *lamenter* or L -*ari*; n. f. vb, or L *lamentum*]

lam'entab|le, a. Mournful (arch.); (of events, fate, condition, character, etc.) deplorable, regrettable. Hence ~LY² adv. [ME, f. OF, or L *lamentabilis* (prec., -ABLE)]

lamenta'tion, n. Lamenting, lament; L~s (of *Jeremiah*), O.-T. book (abbr. *Lam.*). [ME, f. OF, or L *lamentatio* (LAMENT, -ATION)]

lam'ia, n. Monster in woman's shape preying on human beings & sucking children's blood. [L f. Gk]

lam'in|a, n. (pl. ~ae). Thin plate, scale, layer, or flake, of metal, bone, membrane, stratified rock, vegetable tissue, etc. Hence ~AR¹, ~OSE¹, aa., ~-I- comb. form. [L]

lam'in|āte, v.t. & i. Beat or roll (metal) into thin plates; split (t. & i.) into layers or leaves; overlay with metal plates; manufacture by placing layer on layer. Hence or cogn. ~ATE² (-at) a., ~A'TION n. [prec. +-ATE³]

Lamm'as, n. First of August, formerly observed as harvest festival (*later* ~, non-existent date, day that will never come, cf. *Greek* CALENDS). [OE *hlāfmæsse* (LOAF¹, MASS¹)]

lamm'ergeyer (-gī-), n. Bearded vulture, largest European bird of prey. [f. G *lämmergeier* (*lämmer* lambs, *geier* vulture)]

lamp, n., & v.i. & t. 1. Vessel with oil & wick for giving light; glass vessel enclosing candle, gas-jet, incandescent wire, or other illuminant (*smell of the* ~, betray nocturnal study, be laborious in style etc.); SAFETY ~; SPIRIT¹~; (fig.) sun, moon, star; source of spiritual or intellectual light, hope, etc.; ~'*black*, pigment made from soot; ~-*chimney*, glass cylinder making draught for ~-flame; ~'*light*, given by ~ or ~s; ~'*lighter*, man who formerly lighted street ~s (*like a ~lighter*, with speed); ~'*post*, usu. of iron supporting street ~; hence ~'LESS a. 2. vb. Shine; supply with ~s; illuminate; *(sl.) look at. [ME, f. OF *lampe* f. LL *lampada* = L f. Gk *lampas*]

lăm'pas[1], n. Horse-disease with swelling in roof of mouth. [F, of obsc. orig.; cf. F dial. *lampas* throat]

lăm'pas[2], n. Kind of flowered silk orig. from China. [F]

lăm'pion, n. Pot of usu. coloured glass with oil & wick used in illuminations. [F, f. It. *lampione* (*lampa* LAMP, -OON)]

lămpōōn', n., & v.t. 1. Virulent or scurrilous piece of satire; hence ~IST (1) n. 2. v.t. Write ~ or ~s against, whence ~ER[1] n. [f. F *lampon* conjectured to be f. *lampons* let us drink]

lăm'prey, n. (pl.~s). Eel-like pseudo-fish with sucker mouth, pouch gills, & seven spiracles on each side, & fistula on top, of head. [ME, f. OF *lampreie* f. med. L *lampreda*, (whence OE *lampreda*, OHG *lampreta*) ; cf. *lampetra* (as f. L *lambere* lick + *petra* stone); see LIMPET]

Lăncăs'trian, a. & n. (Inhabitant) of Lancashire or Lancaster; (adherent) of family descended from John of Gaunt Duke of Lancaster, or of the Red-rose party fighting for it in Wars of the Roses. [*Lancaster*, -IAN]

lance[1] (-ah-), n. Weapon with long wooden shaft & pointed steel head used by horseman in charging; similar implement for spearing fish or killing harpooned whale; FREE'~; (pl., w. numbers) = lancers; ~-*corporal* (&, sl., ~*jack*) N.C.O. below corporal; ~-*sergeant*, corporal acting as sergeant; ~-*fish*, launce; ~-*snake*, venomous Amer. kind; ~'*wood*, tough elastic W.-Ind. kind used for carriage-shafts, fishing-rods, etc. [ME, f. OF, f. L *lancea*; ~-*corporal* on anal. of obs. *lancepesade* lowest grade of N.C.O.]

lance[2] (-ah-), v.t. Fling, launch, (poet.); (surg.) prick or cut open with lancet; pierce with lance. [ME; poet. sense f. OF *lancier* f. LL *lanceare* (*lancea* LANCE[1]); other senses f. prec.]

lance'lĕt (-ahnsl-), n. Small fish-like animal. [LANCE[1], -LET]

lăn'cĕolate, a. Shaped like spear-head, tapering to each end. [f..LL *lanceolatus* (*lanceola* dim. of *lancea* lance, -ATE[2])]

la'ncer (-ah-), n. Soldier of cavalry regiment orig. armed with lances; (pl.) kind of quadrille, music for it. [f. F *lancier* (LANCE[1], -IER)]

la'ncĕt (-ah-), n. 1. Surgical instrument usu. with two edges & point for bleeding or lancing. 2. (Also ~ *arch, light, window*, etc.) narrow arch or window with pointed

head, whence ~ED[2] a. [ME, f. OF *lancette* (LANCE[1], -ETTE)]

la'ncināting (lah-), a. (Of pain) acute, shooting. [part. of rare *lancinate* f. L *lancinare* rend]

lănd[1], n. 1. Solid part of earth's surface (opp. *sea*, *water*; *travel by* ~; *how the* ~ *lies*, what is the state of affairs); ground, soil, expanse of country; country, nation, State, (~ *of promise*, Canaan; ~ *of hope & glory*; ~ *of* CAKE[1]*s*; ~ *of the leal*, heaven; ~ *of the living*, present life); landed property, (pl.) estates; (S. Afr.) ground fenced off for tillage; strip of plough or pasture ~ parted from others by water furrows. 2. Any of the divisions between the rifling-grooves in guns. 3. ~-*agent*, -*agency*, || steward(ship) of estate, agent, agency, for sale etc. of estates; ~'*bank*, || issuing notes on security of landed property; ~-*breeze*, blowing seaward from ~; ~-*carriage*, transport by ~; ~-*crab*, kinds that live on ~ but breed in sea; ~'*fall* (naut.), approach to ~ esp. for first time on voyage (*good, bad*, ~*fall*, according, not according, to calculation); ~ *force(s)*, military, not naval; ||~'*girl* (doing farmwork, esp. in wartime); ~-*grabber*, (esp.) man who took Irish farm after eviction of tenant; ~-*holder*, proprietor or (usu.) tenant of ~; ~-*hunger*, -*hungry*, eager(ness) to acquire ~; || ~-*jobber*, speculator in ~; ~'*lady*, woman keeping inn, boarding-house, or lodgings, also woman having tenants; ~-*law* (usu. pl.), law(s) of landed property; *L~ League*, Irish association 1879–81 for reducing rents, introducing peasant--proprietorship, etc.; ~-*locked*, almost or quite enclosed by ~; ~'*lord*, person of whom another holds any tenement (opp. *tenant*), keeper of inn, lodgings, etc.; ~'*lubber* (naut.), person ignorant of the sea & ships; ~'*mark*, object marking boundary of country, estate, etc., conspicuous object in district etc., object or event or change marking stage in process or turning-point in history; ~'*mine*, explosive mine laid in or on ground, parachute mine; ~'*owner*, owner of ~; ~'*rail*, corncrake; *L~'s End*, western point of Cornwall (see JOHN-*o'-Groat's*); ~-*service*, military; ~-*shark*, one who lives by preying on seamen ashore; ~-*sick* (naut.; of ship), impeded in movement by nearness of ~; ~'*slide* (orig. U.S.), overwhelming majority of votes for one side, esp. in an election; ||~'*slip*, sliding down of mass of ~ on cliff or mountain; ~*s'man*, non-sailor; ~-*swell*, roll of water near shore; ~-*tax*, assessed on landed property; ~-*tie*, rod, beam, or piece of masonry, securing or supporting wall etc. by connecting some part of it with the ground; ~-*wind*, = ~-*breeze*. Hence ~'LESS a., ~'WARD a. & adv., ~-WARDS adv. [OE, OS *land*, OHG *lant*, ON, Goth. *land* f. Gmc *landam*]

lănd², v.t. & i. Set or go ashore (p.p. = having come ashore, see -ED¹(2), esp. in comb. as *newly-~ed*), disembark (*at*); (of aircraft) come down to ground or surface of water; set down from vehicle; bring to, reach or find oneself in, a certain place, stage, or position; deal (person blow etc.; *~ed him one in the eye*); bring (fish) to land, (fig.) win (prize etc.); (trans. of jockey, intr. of horse) bring or come in (*first* etc., or abs. = first); alight after jump etc. [f. prec.]

Land³ (lahnt), n. (pl. *Länder*, pr. lĕn⁻). Land, country. [G]

lăn´dau, n. Four-wheeled carriage with top of which front & back halves can be independently raised & lowered. [*L~* in Germany]

lăndaulĕt(te)´, n. Coupé with landau top. [-LET]

lănd´dröst n. (hist.). Magistrate in S. Africa. [Du., = sheriff]

lăn´dĕd, a. Possessed of land (*the ~ interest*, owners & holders of land); consisting of land (*~ estate, property*). [LAND¹ +-ED²]

lănd´grāve, n. (fem. *-gravine*, pr. -avēn). (Former) German title of nobility. [f. MHG *lantgrāve* (LAND¹, G *graf* count)]

lăn´ding, n. In ˎvbl senses; also: (also *~-place*) place for disembarking; platform between two flights of stairs; *~-craft*, any of numerous types of naval craft esp. designed for putting ashore troops and equipment; *~-net*, for landing large fish when hooked; *~-stage*, platform, often floating, on which passengers & goods are disembarked. [-ING¹]

lănd´lôrdism, n. System by which land is owned by landlords receiving fixed rents from tenants (esp. derog. of former Irish system); advocacy of this. [-ISM]

lăndŏc´racy, n. (joc.). The landed class. So **lănd´ocrat** n. [-CRACY]

lănd´scāpe (*or* -ns-; earlier **-skǐp**), n. (Picture representing, art reproducing, or actual piece of) inland scenery; ||*~-gardening, -gardener*, laying, layer, out of grounds in imitation of natural scenery; *~-marble*, kind with treelike markings; *~-painter*, who paints~s, also **lănd´scāp-ist**(1) n. [*c.* 1600 f. MDu. *landscap* (LAND¹, -SHIP)]

lănd´sturm (lah-, -oorm), n. (Hist., in Germany etc.) general levy in war, of men outside army, navy, & Landwehr. [G]

lănd´tag (lah-, -ahx), n. Legislative body, diet, of a German State. [G]

lănd´wehr (lah-, -vär), n. (In Germany etc.) militia serving continuously only during war. [G]

lāne, n. Narrow road usu. between hedges (*it is a long ~ that has no turning*, change is sure to come), narrow street; passage made or left between rows of persons; strip of road for single line of traffic; course prescribed for ocean steamers; *red ~*, throat; ||*the ˎL~*, Drury L~

(theatre). [OE *lane*, = OFris. *lana, laen*, Du. *laan*, of unkn. orig.]

lăng´rage, -idge, (-ngg-), n. Case-shot with irregular pieces of iron formerly used to damage rigging. [orig. unkn.]

||**lăng sȳne**, adv. & n. (In) the old days. [Sc., = long since]

lăng´uage (-nggw-), n. A vocabulary & way of using it prevalent in one or more countries (DEAD ~); (transf.) method of expression (*finger ~*, talk by conventional signs with fingers; *~ of flowers*, symbolic meanings attached to various kinds); words & their use; faculty of speech; person's style of expressing himself (*bad ~*, or ||vulg. ~, oaths & abusive talk; *strong ~*, expressing vehement feelings); professional or sectional vocabulary; literary style, wording; *~-master*, teacher of (usu. mod. foreign) ~ or ~s. [ME, f. OF *langage* (L *lingua* tongue, -AGE)]

langue d'oc, langue d'oïl, nn. (see Ap.). Medieval French as spoken south, north, of the Loire, the latter the staple of modern French. [OF *langue* LANGUAGE, & *oc* (= L *hoc*), *oïl* (= L *hoc ille*), these being the respective forms for *yes*]

lăng´uid (-nggw-), a. Inert, lacking vigour, indisposed to exertion, spiritless, apathetic, not vivid, dull, uninteresting, sluggish, slow-moving, faint, weak. Hence ~LY² adv., ~NESS n. [f. F *languide*, or L *languidus* (foll., -ID¹)]

lăng´uish (-nggw-), v.i. Grow or be feeble, lose or lack vitality; live *under* enfeebling or depressing conditions; grow slack, lose intensity; droop, pine (*for*); put on languid look, affect sentimental tenderness, whence ~**inGLY²** adv. Hence ~MENT n. [ME, f. OF *languir* (-ISH²) f. L *languēre*]

lăng´uor (-ngger), n. Faintness, fatigue; lassitude, inertia, want of alertness; soft or tender mood or effect; slackness, dullness, drooping state; (of sky etc.) oppressive stillness. So ~OUS a., ~OUSLY² adv., (-nggo-). [ME, f. OF f. L *languorem* nom. *-or* (prec., -OR)]

langur (lŭnggoor), n. (Kinds of) common Indian long-tailed monkey. [Hind.]

lăn´iary, a. & n. (Tooth) adapted for tearing, canine. [f. L *laniarius* (*lanius* butcher f. *laniare* tear, -ARY¹)]

lănif´erous, -i´gerous, aa. Wool-bearing. [f. L (*-fer, -ger*) f. *lana* wool, -FEROUS, -GEROUS]

lănk, a. Shrunken, spare; tall & lean; (of grass etc.) long & flaccid; (of hair) straight & limp, not wavy. [OE *hlanc* f..Gmc *hlank-* (cf. MHG *lenken* bend); cf. FLANK, LINK¹]

lănk´|y̆, a. Ungracefully lean & long or tall (of limbs, person). Hence ~**iNESS** n. [-Y²]

lănn´er, lănn´erĕt, nn. Kind of falcon, female of it, (-*er*); (-*et*) male of it. [ME, f. OF *lanier* prob. f. OF *lanier* cowardly]

lăn´olin, n. Fat which permeates sheep's

wool as basis of ointments. [G, f. L *lana* wool + -OL(2) + -IN]

läns'quenĕt (-kĭ-), n. Card-game of German origin. [F, f. G *landsknecht* 17th-c. mercenary]

län'tern, n. Transparent case protecting flame of candle etc. (BULL[1]'s-*eye*, CHINESE, DARK[1], HURRICANE, MAGIC, ~); ‖ *parish* ~, the moon; = magic~, whence ~IST(3) n.; light-chamber of lighthouse; erection on top of dome or room with glazed sides to admit light; luminous proboscis of ~-*fly*; ~ *jaws*, long & thin, giving hollow look to face, whence ~-jawED[2] a. [ME, f. OF *lanterne* f. L *lanterna*]

län'thanum, n. (chem.). Rare element belonging to aluminium group, discovered 1839–41. [f. Gk *lanthanō* escape notice, + -UM]

‖ **län'thorn** (-tern), n. Lantern. [pop. assim. of *lantern* to *horn*, common former material]

län'yard, n. (Naut.) short rope or line attached to something to secure it; cord attached to breech mechanism for firing gun; cord hanging round the neck or looped round the shoulder, to which may be attached a knife, whistle, or the like. [15th c. *lanyer*, earlier *layner*, f. OF *laniere* (-*yard* f. 17th c.)]

Lāodīcē'an, a. & n. (Person) lukewarm esp. in religion or politics. [*Rev.* iii. 15, 16]

läp[1], n. Hanging part or flap of garment, saddle, etc.; lobe of ear; front part of skirt held up to contain something; waist to knees of one sitting, with dress, as place on which child is nursed or object held (*in Fortune's* ~, *in the* ~ *of luxury*, etc.), whence ~FUL(2) n.; hollow among hills; ~-*dog*, small pet dog; ~-*stone*, shoemaker's stone held in ~ to beat leather on. [OE *lappa, læppa*, OS *lappo*, OHG *lappa*; cf. ON *leppr* rag]

läp[2], v.t. & i. (-pp-). Coil, fold, wrap, (garment etc. *about, round*, advv. or prepp.); enfold, swathe, *in* wraps etc.; (of influences etc.) surround, encircle, (often *round*), enfold caressingly (esp. pass., ~*ped in luxury*); make (valve, roof--slate, etc.) overlap; project *over* something (also ~ *over* adv. = *overlap* intr.); (racing) pass (competitor) by one or more laps. [ME, prob. f. prec.]

läp[3], n. Amount of overlapping, overlapping part (*half*-~, joining of rails, shafts, etc., by halving thickness of each at end); layer or sheet (of cotton etc. being made) wound on roller; single turn of rope, silk, thread, etc., round drum or reel; one circuit of race-track; ~-*joint*, = *half*-~ above; ~-*streak*, clinker-built boat. [f. prec.]

läp[4], n., & v.t. (-pp-). 1. Rotating disc for polishing gem or metal. 2. v.t. Polish with ~. [perh. f. prec.]

läp[5], v.i. & t. (-pp-), & n. 1. Take up liquid, drink (*up* liquid), by scooping with tongue; consume (liquid) greedily (usu.

up or *down*), also fig.; (of water) move, beat upon (shore), with sound of ~ping. 2. n. Liquid food for dogs; single act of ~ping, amount taken up by it; sound of ~ping, amount taken up by it; sound of wavelets on beach etc. [ME *lape*. OE *lapian* = MLG, MDu. *lapen*, OHG *laffan* f. Gmc **lap-*; ME *lap* prob. f. OF *laper*]

läpar‖(o)-, comb. form of Gk *lapara* flank, in anat. & surg. terms; *lap'arocele*, lumbar hernia; ~*ĕc'tomy*, excision of part of intestine at side; ~*ŏt'omy*, cutting of abdominal walls.

lapĕl', n. Part of coat-breast folded back. Hence ~lED[2] (-ld') a. [LAP[1], -EL]

läp'icīde, n. Cutter of stones or inscriptions on stone. [f. L *lapicida* irreg. f. *lapis* -*idis* stone; see -CIDE]

läp'idary̆, a. & n. 1. Concerned with stones (esp. ~ *bee*, building in stone walls etc.); engraved on stone, (of style) suitable for inscriptions, monumental. 2. n. Cutter, polisher, or engraver, of gems. [f. L *lapidarius* (*lapis* -*idis* stone, -ARY[1])]

läp'id‖āte, v.t. Stone, stone to death. So ~A'TION n. [f. L *lapidare* (prec.), -ATE[3]]

lapid'i‖fy̆, v.t. Make into stone. Hence ~FICA'TION n. [f. F *lapidifier* f. med. L *lapidificare* (prec., -FY)]

läp'is läz'ŭlī, n. A sodium aluminium silicate containing combined sulphur, bright blue pigment from it; its colour. [L *lapis* + med. L *lazuli* gen. of *lazulum*; see AZURE]

Läpp, n. & a. 1. One of dwarfish race of northern Scandinavia; (also ~'ISH[1] n.) their language; *Läp'land*, their country, whence Läp'landER[1](4)n. 2. adj. (Also ~[1] ISH[1] a.) of the ~s or their language. [f. Sw. *Lapp*, perh. term of contempt, cf. MHG *lappe* simpleton]

läp'ĕt, n. Flap, fold, loose or overlapping piece of garment, flesh, membrane, etc.; lobe of ear etc.; = lapel; streamer of lady's head-dress; (also ~-*moth*) kind of large moth. Hence ~ED[2] a. [LAP[1] + -ET[1]]

Lappōn'ian, a. & n. = LAPP. [f. med. L *Lappo* -*onis* + -IAN]

läpse[1], n. Slip of memory, tongue, or pen, slight mistake; weak or careless deviation from right, moral slip; falling away *from* faith or *into* heresy; decline to lower state; termination of right or privilege through disuse; (of water) gentle flow; passage or interval *of* time; ~ *rate* (meteor.), rate of fall of temperature with height. [f. L *lapsus* -*ūs* (*labi laps-* glide)]

läpse[2], v.i. Fail to maintain position or state for want of effort or vigour; fall *back* or *away* (often *into* inferior or previous state); (of benefice, estate, right, etc.) fall in, pass away, become void, revert *to* someone, by failure of conditions, heirs, etc.; glide, flow, subside, pass *away*; (p.p.) that has lapsed, see -ED[2](2). [f. L *lapsare* (prec.); partly f. the n.]

läp'sus, n. (pl. -*ūs*). Slip (usu. in ~

ling'uae, pr. -gwē, of the tongue,~ *căl'ami* of the pen). [L]

Laput'an, a. & n. (Inhabitant) of Laputa; chimerical, visionary, absurd. [*Laputa* in *Gulliver's Travels* + -AN]

lăp'wing, n. Bird of plover family, peewit. [OE *hlēapewince* (*hlēapan* LEAP¹, WINK, w. ref. to manner of flight) assim. to LAP², WING]

lăr, n. 1. (pl. *lăr'es*, pr. -ēz). Ancient-Roman household deity (usu. pl.: *Lares, Lares & Penates*, the home). 2. (pl. ~*s*, pr. -z). White-handed Burmese gibbon. [L]

∥ **lărb'oard** (-berd), n. & a. (naut.). (Older term now replaced, to save confusion with *starboard*, by) PORT⁵. [ME *lad(d)c-, lathe-* (perh. = LADE), in 16th c. alt. after *starboard*]

lăr'cĕn|y̆, n. (Law) felonious taking away of another's personal goods with intent to convert them to one's own use (*grand, petty*, ~*y*, formerly, of property above, below, value of 12*d*.); theft. Hence ~ER¹, ~IST(1), nn.,~OUS a.,~OUSLY² adv. [f. AF *larcin* f. L *latrocinium* (*latro* robber) + -Y¹]

lărch, n. Bright-foliaged & deciduous coniferous tree yielding Venice turpentine, tough timber, & bark used in tanning; its wood. [f. G *lärche* f. L *larix-icis*]

lărd¹, n. Internal fat of abdomen of pigs esp. when rendered & clarified for use in cooking & pharmacy. Hence ~'Y² a. [ME, f. OF, = bacon, f. L *lar(i)dum* cogn. w. Gk *larinos* fat]

lărd², v.t. Insert strips of bacon in (meat etc.) before cooking (~*ing-needle, -pin*, instrument for doing this); garnish (talk, writing) *with* metaphors, technical terms, foreign words, etc. [ME, f. OF *larder* (prec.)]

lărdā'ceous (-shŭs), a. (med.). Lardlike (esp. of degeneration of tissue or of patient suffering from it). [-ACEOUS]

lărd'er, n. Room or closet for meat etc. [ME, f. OF *lardier* f. med. L *lardarium* (LARD¹, -ARY¹)]

lărd'on, lărdŏŏn', n. Strip of bacon or pork used to lard meat. [F (-*on*); LARD¹, -OON]

lărd'y̆-dăr̆d'y̆, a. (sl.). Affected, languidly foppish. [cf. LA-DI-DA]

lares. See LAR.

lăr̄ge, a., n., & adv. 1. (Arch.) liberal, generous, kindly, munificent, unprejudiced, (still in ~ *views, charity, tolerance*, ~-*minded*, whence ~-**mind'ed**NESS n., ~-*hearted*, whence ~-**heart'ed**NESS (-har-) n., etc.); of wide range, comprehensive, (~ *powers, discretion*); (of artistic treatment) free, sweeping, broad; of considerable or relatively great magnitude (less colloq. than *big*, & without emotional implications of *great*; seldom used of persons except as in ~ *of limb* =with ~ limbs etc.); (with agent nouns) on a ~ *scale* (~ *& small farmers*); hence lăr̄'gᴵsʜ¹(2) a.,~ᴸ NESS (-jn-) n., lăr̄'gᴇɴ⁶ v.i. & t. (poet.).

2. n. (now only with *at, in*). *At* ~: at liberty, free; (of narration etc.) at full length, with details; as a body or whole (*popular with the people at* ~); *representing a whole State etc. & not merely a part of it; without particularizing, without definite aim, (*scatters imputations at* ~; *gentleman at* ~, gentleman attached to the court without special duties, person who has no occupation); *in* ~, on ~ scale (opp. *in little*). 3. adv. BY¹ *& ~*. [ME, f. OF f. fem. of L *largus* copious]

lăr̄ge'ly̆ (-jl-), adv. In adj. senses: also, to a great or preponderating extent (*is* ~ *due to*). [-LY²]

lăr̄'gĕss(e), n. (arch.). Money or gifts freely bestowed esp. by great person on occasion of rejoicing; generous or plentiful bestowal. [ME, f. OF (-*e*), f. L *largus* copious, -ESS²]

lăr̄g'5, adv. & n. (mus.). (Movement) in slow time with broad dignified treatment. [It., = broad]

lă'riat, n. Rope for picketing horses etc.; lasso. [f. Sp. *la reata* f. *reatar* tie again (RE-, L *aptare* fit)]

lărk¹, lăv'erock (-vr-; poet.), n. Kinds of small bird with sandy-brown plumage & long hind-claws, esp. the SKYlark (*crested, horned, red, shore,* ~, other kinds); *rise with the* ~, get up early; *if the sky fall, we shall catch* ~*s* (comfort for alarmists); ~-*heel*, ~-spur, also Indian cress or garden nasturtium; ~'*spur*, plant of genus Delphinium with spur-shaped calyx. [OE *lāferce*, = MLG, MDu. *lēwer(i)ke*, OHG *lērahha*, ON *lǣvirki*]

lărk², n., & v.t. 1. Frolic, spree, amusing incident (*what a* ~ *!*, how amusing!); hence ~'Y² a. 2. v.i. Play tricks, frolic. [orig. unkn.]

lărn, v.t. & i. (Joc. & vulg. for) LEARN.

lă'rrikin, n. (Usu. young) street rowdy, hooligan. [c. 1870, Australian; perh. f. name *Larry*]

lă'rrup, v.t. (colloq.). Thrash. [dial.]

lă'rum, n. (Now rare for) ALARUM.

lărv'|a, n. (pl. ~*ae*). Insect from time of leaving egg till transformation into pupa, grub; immature form of other animals that undergo some metamorphosis. Hence ~AL a., ~I- comb. form. [L, = ghost, mask]

laryn'goscŏpe (-ngg-), n. Mirror apparatus for examining larynx. [LARYNX, -SCOPE]

lărȳngŏt'omy̆ (-ngg-), n. Cutting into larynx from without, esp. to provide breathing-channel. [foll., -TOMY]

lă'ry̆nx, n. Cavity in throat holding vocal cords. Hence **larȳn'gē**AL a. (also n., hypothetical phonetic element of a laryngeal quality supposed to have existed in Proto-Indo-European), **larȳn'gic**, a., **lărȳngᴵᴛ'ɪs** n., (-j-), **larȳn'go**comb. form, **lărȳngŏl'ogy** n., (-ngg-). [f. Gk *larugx -ggos*]

Lăs'car, n. (E.·) Indian sailor. [erron. f.

Hind. LASHKAR army, or f. *lashkari* military]

lasciv'ious, a. Lustful, wanton; inciting to lust. Hence ~LY² adv., ~NESS n. [ME, f. LL *lasciviosus* (L *lascivia* f. *lascivus* sportive, -OSE¹)]

lash¹, v.i. & t. **1.** Make sudden movement of limb, tail, etc.; pour, rush, vehemently, whence ~'ings [-ING¹(2)] n. pl. (sl.), plenty (*of*); strike violently *at*; hit or (of horse) kick *out*; break *out* into excess, strong language, etc. **2.** Beat with lash, flog; (of waves) beat upon; castigate in words, rebuke, satirize; urge as with lashes (~ one*self into a fury*, work up a rage); hence ~'ING¹(1) n. **3.** Fasten (*down*, *on*, *together*, *to* something) with cord, twine, etc., whence ~'ING¹(4) n.; ~-*up* a. & n., makeshift. [sense 1 perh. imit.; sense 2 f. foll.; sense 3 prob. separate wd, of unkn. orig.]

lash², n. Stroke with thong, whip, etc.; flexible part of whip (*the* ~, punishment of flogging); = EYE-~, whence ~'LESS a.; goading influence. [f. prec. in sense 1]

lash'er, n. In vbl senses; ‖ esp. (water rushing over) weir, pool below weir. [-ER¹]

lash'kar, n. Body of armed Indian tribesmen. [Hind., = army]

‖ **läs'pring**, n. Young salmon. [perh. alt. of obs. *lax-pink* (LAX², PINK⁵)]

lasque (lahsk), n. Flat, ill-formed, or veiny diamond. [perh. f. Pers. *lashk* piece]

lass, n. Girl (north., poet., etc.); sweetheart. Hence ~'ie [-Y³] n. [ME *lasce*, cf. MSw. *lösk* (*kona*) unmarried (woman)]

lass'itüde, n. Weariness, languor, disinclination to exert or interest oneself. [f. F, or L *lassitudo* (*lassus* tired, -TUDE)]

lass'o (or lasōō'), n. (pl. ~s), & v.t. **1.** Sp.-Amer. noosed rope of untanned hide for catching cattle etc. **2.** v.t. Catch with ~. [f. Sp. *lazo* LACE¹]

last¹ (-ah-), n. Shoemaker's wooden model for shaping shoe etc. on (*stick to* one*'s* ~, not meddle with things one does not understand, w. ref. to L prov. *ne sutor supra crepidam*). [OE *læste* last; cf. OHG *leist* last, Goth. *laists* track, OHG *-leisa* track, f. Gmc **lais-*; cf. LAST⁴]

last² (-ah-), n. Commercial measure of weight, capacity, or quantity, varying with place & goods (~ *of wool*, 12 sacks or 4,368 lb.; ~ *of malt*, 10 qrs or 80 bushels). [OE *hlæst*, MLG, MDu. *last*, OHG (*h*)*last*, f. Gmc **hlath-* LADE + n. suff. *-sti-*]

last³ (-ah-), a., n., & adv. **1.** After all others, coming at the end, (*the* ~ *two* etc. = the ~ & ~ but one etc., *the two* etc. ~ being now usu. held incorrect in this sense; ~ *but not least*, ~ in order of mention or occurrence but not of importance); belonging to the end, esp. of life or the world (*the four* ~ *things*, death, judgement, heaven, hell; ~ *day*, Day of Judgement; *on* one's ~ LEGS); next before expressed or implied point of time, latest

up to date, most recent, (*in the* ~ *fortnight*, ~ *Christmas*, ~ *Tuesday* or *Tuesday* ~; ~ *evening* or *night* or *week* or *month* or *year* used as adverbs, but not ~ *morning*, *day*, or *afternoon*; also ellipt, as n. for ~ *letter, joke, baby*, etc., *as I said in my* ~, *have you heard* —*'s* ~*?*, *Mrs* —*'s* ~); lowest, of least rank or estimation; only remaining (~ *crust, resource*); latest *to be* (*was the* ~ *to be consulted*); least likely, willing, suitable, etc. *to* or *to be* (*should be the* ~ *to do it*; *is the* ~ *thing to try*); conclusive, definitive, (*has said the* ~ *word on the matter*); most up-to-date (*the* ~ *thing in hats*); utmost, extreme, (*is of the* ~ *importance*). **2.** n. ~-mentioned person or thing (*the, this, which*, ~); ~ day or moments, death, (*the* or *his* etc. ~); ~ performance of certain acts (*breathe, look*, one's ~); ~ mention (*shall never hear the* ~ *of it*); *at* ~, (also) *at long* ~, in the end, after much delay; *to, till, the* ~, to the end, esp. till death. **3.** adv. After all others (~ *came &* ~ *did go*; freq. in comb., as ~-*made, -mentioned*); on the ~ occasion before the present (*when did you see him* ~*?*); (in enumerations) in the ~ place, finally, also ~'LY² adv. [OE *latost* superl. of *læt* a., *late* adv.; see LATE¹, -EST; loss of *-t-* as in BEST]

last⁴ (-ah-), v.i. & t., & n. **1.** Go on, remain unexhausted or adequate or alive; suffice (*will* ~ *me eight months*; *will* ~ *my time*); ~ *out*, continue esp. in vigour or use at least as long as. **2.** Staying power, stamina. [OE *læstan*, OS *lēstian*, OHG *leisten*, Goth. *laistjan* f. Gmc **laist-* LAST¹]

last'ing (-ah-), a. & n. **1.** Enduring, permanent (*no* ~ *benefit*); durable; hence ~LY² adv., ~NESS n. **2.** n. Kind of durable cloth. [-ING²]

Lätaki'a (-ēa), n. Kind of Turkish tobacco chiefly used in mixtures. [~ (anc. *Laodicea*), a Syrian port]

latch, n., & v.t. **1.** Door or gate fastening, made of small bar falling into catch & lifted by lever etc. from outside; small spring-lock of outer door catching when door is closed & worked by ~key; ~'key, any outer-door key, (fig.) symbol of emancipation; *on the* ~, fastened by ~ only. **2.** v.t. Fasten with ~. [(1) prob. f. obs. (exc. dial.) *latch* vb f. OE *læccan* grasp; (2) f. sense 1]

‖ **latch'êt**, n. (arch.). Thong for fastening shoe. [f. OF *lachet*, var. of *lacet* dim. of *laz, las* LACE¹]

läte¹, a. (comp. ~*r*, LATTER; superl. ~*st*, LAST³), & n. After the due or usual time (*was* ~ *for dinner*; *it is too* ~ *to go*; with agent nouns, as ~-*comer* = one who comes ~); backward in flowering, ripening, etc.; far on in day or night (~ *dinner*, in evening; ~ *hours*, after usual time for rising or going to bed), or in time (*on Wednesday at* ~*st*, then if not before); far on in a period, development, etc. (~ *stained glass*, ~ LATIN); no longer alive, no longer having specified status etc., that was recently so-&-so, (the ~ prime minister, dead or resigned; my ~ husband, residence); of recent date (the ~ floods, war; of ~ years, in the last few; also as n. in of ~, recently); || ~ fee, on letter posted after ordinary collection time. Hence lāt′EN⁶ v.t. & i., ~′NESS (-tn-) n., lāt′ISH¹ (2) a. & adv. [OE læt, OS lat, OHG laz, ON latr, Goth. lats f. Gmc *lataz slow, cogn. w. L lassus]

lāte², adv. (~r, ~st, LAST³). After proper time (better ~ than never), far on in time (this happened ~r on; sooner or ~r, early or ~, soon or ~, some time or other); at or till late hour (we sat ~); (poet.) recently, lately, (I sent thee~ a rosy wreath); formerly but not now (his own room, ~ the chaplain's); at late stage of development etc. (traces remained as ~ as the Stuart times); ~ in the day, (colloq.) at a late stage, esp. unreasonably ~ in the proceedings etc. [OE late, adv. form of prec.]

lateen′, a. ~ sail, triangular on long yard at angle of 45° to mast; (of ship etc.) so rigged. [f. F (voile) latine Latin (sail), named as common in Mediterranean]

lāte′lÿ (-tl-), adv. Not long ago, recently, in recent times. [OE lætlīce (LATE¹, -LIKE)]

lāt′ent, a. Hidden, concealed; existing but not developed or manifest; dormant; ~ HEAT. Hence lāt′ENCY n., ~LY² adv. [f. L latēre be hidden, -ENT]

-later, suf. See -LATRY.

lāt′eral, a. & n. 1. Of, at, towards, from, the side, side-, (~ branch of family, descended from brother or sister of person in direct line). 2. n. Side part, member, or object, esp. ~ shoot or branch. Hence ~LY² adv. [f. L lateralis (latus -eris side, -AL)]

Lăt′eran, n. & a. The ~, St John ~, cathedral church of St John ~ (Sancti Joannis in ~o) in Rome; ~ Council, one of five general councils of Western Church there held. [f. L ~a, ~um, named f. ancient-Roman family of Plautii ~i]

lăt′erite, n. Red friable ferruginous surface clay much used for roadmaking in tropics. [f. L later brick + -ITE¹(2)]

lăt′ex, n. (bot.). Milky fluid of (esp. rubber) plant. [L, = liquid]

lath (-ah-), n. (pl. pr. -dhz), & v.t. 1. Piece of sawn or riven timber 4/16 in. to 3/8 in. thick & 1 in. to 1½ in. wide esp. for use as support for slates or plaster or as material for trellis or Venetian blind (as thin as a ~, of persons, when la′thy² (-ah-) a.; ~ & plaster, material for interior wall-faces, ceilings, partitions, etc.). 2. v.t. Provide (wall, ceiling) with ~s, whence la′thing¹(3) (-ah-) n. [ME laththe, repr. OE *læthth-, = OS, OHG latta; ult. rel. obsc.]

|| lāthe¹ (-dh), n. One of the administrative districts of Kent. [OE læth estate]

lāthe² (-dh), n. (Also turning-~) machine for turning wood, metal, ivory, etc., by rotating article against tools used; (also potter's ~) machine with horizontal revolving disc for throwing & turning pottery; ~-bearer, -carrier, -dog, appliance connecting object with ~ centres or holders; ~-bed, lower framework of ~ with slot from end to end for adjustment. [prob. rel. to Da. -lad structure, frame, as in drejelad turning-lathe, f. ON hlath, rel. to hlatha LADE]

lăth′er (-dh-), n., & v.t. & i. 1. Froth of soap & water; frothy sweat esp. of horse; (fig.) state of agitation; hence ~Y² a. 2. vb. Cover (esp. chin etc. for shaving) with ~; (of horse) become covered with ~; (of soap) form ~; beat, thrash, whence ~ING¹(1) n. [OE lēathor = ON lauthr washing-soda, f. Gmc *lauthram cogn. w. L lavare wash]

lathi (laht′ï), n. Long heavy iron-bound stick used as weapon by Indian natives & police. [Hind.]

lătifŭn′dia, n. pl. Large estates, esp. as characterizing a country's social system. [L (sing. -um), f. latus broad, fundus farm]

Lăt′in, a. & n. 1. Of Latium or ancient ~s or Romans; of, like, in, the language of the ancient Romans, whence ~ISM(4) n.; of the Roman Catholic Church; ~ (see WESTERN) Church; (of peoples) inheriting Roman customs etc., speaking one of the languages descended from ~, Romance, (the ~ peoples, France, Spain, Portugal, Italy, etc.); ~ Quarter (F Quartier Latin), educational centre of Paris, where ~ was spoken in the Middle Ages, noted for its unconventional mode of life. Hence ~ATE² a., having a ~ character. 2. n. The ~ language (old ~, before about 75 B.C., preclassical; classical ~, that of great writers of late republican & early imperial Rome, about 75 B.C. to A.D. 175; late ~, about A.D. 175 to 600; medieval ~, about A.D. 600 to 1500; modern ~, since A.D. 1500; low ~, = medieval, or late & medieval; SILVER¹ ~; thieves' ~, secret language of thieves etc.; DOG ~), whence ~LESS a., ~IST(3) n.; inhabitant of Latium, (Rom. ant.) Italian with special franchise. [ME, f. OF, or L Latinus (Latium Roman district, -INE¹)]

Latin′ē, adv. In Latin (giving Latin equivalent of word etc.). [L]

Latin′itÿ, n. Way person writes Latin, quality of Latin style or grammar. [f. L Latinitas (prec., -TY)]

lăt′iniz|e, -is|e (-īz), v.t. & i. Give Latin form to (word), put into Latin; make conformable to ideas, customs, etc., of the ancient Romans, Latin peoples, or Latin Church; use Latin forms, idioms, etc. Hence ~A′TION, ~ER¹, nn. [f. LL latinizare (LATIN, -IZE)]

lăt′itūd|e, n. 1. (Joc.) breadth (hat with great ~e of brim); (rare) scope, full extent, (understood, taken, in its proper ~e). 2. Freedom from narrowness, liberality of interpretation, tolerated variety of action or opinion, whence (esp. of religious matters) ~inAR'IAN a. & n., ~inAR'ianISM(3) n. **3.** (geog.). Angular distance on a meridian (*degree, minute*, etc., *of ~e*); place's angular distance on its meridian N. or S. of equator (*in ~e 40° N.* etc.); (usu. pl.) regions, climes, esp. w. ref. to temperature (*high ~es*, far N. or S.; *low ~es*, near equator). **4.** (astron.). Angular distance of heavenly body from ecliptic. So ~inAL (-ūd²) a. (geog.). [ME, f. L *latitudo -inis* (*latus* broad, -TUDE)]

latrine' (-ēn), n. Place for evacuation of bowels or bladder, esp. in camp, barracks, hospital, etc. [F, f. L *latrina* for *lavatrina* (*lavare* wash, -INE)¹]

-latry, suf. f. Gk *latreia* worship, in wds f. an existing Gk original (*idolatry*), & mod. formations on same model (*angelolatry, Mariolatry*). In (humorous) hybrid formations -o- is added to the initial component as *lordolatry, babyolatry*. Corresponding personal nn. (-worshipper) are formed in -(o)*later* f. Gk *-latrēs*.

lätt'en, n. Alloy of copper, zinc, lead, & tin, formerly used for monumental brasses; sheet tin; metal in thin plates. [ME *latoun* f. OF *laton, leiton*]

lätt'er, a. (Arch.) later, second, (*~ grass*, aftermath); belonging to end of period, world, etc. (*in these ~ days*, at this late period of the world's history; *~ end, death*); second-mentioned (opp. *former*; also *the ~* ellipt. = second-mentioned thing or person); *~-day*, modern (*~-day saints*, Mormons). [OE *lætra* comp. of *læt* LATE¹, *later* being a new formation]

lätt'erly̆, adv. Towards the end of life or some period; nowadays, of late. [f. prec.]

lätt'ice, n. Structure of cross laths with interstices serving as screen, door, etc.; (also *~-work*) laths so arranged; *~ bridge*, made with *~* girders; *~ frame* or *girder*, girder made of two flanges connected by iron *~-work*; *~ window*, one having *~*, also one with small panes set in diagonal lead-work. Hence **lätt'iceD**² (-st) a., **lätt'icing**¹(6) n. [ME, f. OF *lattis* f. *latte* (f. WG **latta* LATH), +-*is* -ICE]

Lät'vian, a. & n. (Inhabitant) of the Socialist Soviet Republic of Latvia, the country of the Letts, on the Gulf of Riga in the Baltic. [f. *Latvi* see LETTISH +-AN]

laud, n., & v.t. **1.** Praise (rare exc. in hymns); (pl.) first of day-hours of church; hymn of praise. **2.** v.t. Praise, celebrate; so ~A'TION, ~āt'OR,nn., ~'ATIVE, ~'ATORY, aa. [ME; n. f. OF *laude*, vb f. L *laudare*, f. L *laudem* nom. *laus* praise]

laud'|able, a. Commendable, praiseworthy; (med., of secretions) healthy, sound. Hence or cogn. ~ABIL'ITY n., ~abLY² adv. [f. L *laudabilis* (prec., -ABLE)]

laudanum (lŏd'num), n. Tincture of opium. [name given by Paracelsus to a

costly panacea or elixir, later transferred to preparations containing opium; perh. var. of L f d. Gk *lādanon, lē-*, a gum-resin, f. *lēdon* mastic]

laudāt'or tĕm'porĭs ăc'tī (sē pŭ'erō), phr. One who prefers the good old days (when he was a boy). [L, = praiser of time past]

laugh (-ahf, -äf), v.i. & t., & n. **1.** Make the sounds & movements of face & sides by which lively amusement, sense of the ludicrous, exultation, & scorn, are instinctively expressed, have these emotions, (*~ in* one's *sleeve*, be secretly amused; *~ing* HYENA, JACKASS; *~ on wrong side of mouth*, have revulsion from joy or amusement to tears or vexation; *he ~s best who ~s last*, warning against premature exultation); (of water, landscape, corn, etc.) be lively with play of movement or light; utter *~ingly*; hold up *to scorn*; *~ at*, make fun of, ridicule, also look pleasantly or smile at; get (person) *out of* habit, belief, etc., by ridicule (*~ person, opinion*, etc., *out of court*, deprive of a hearing by ridicule); *~ away*, dismiss (subject) with a *~*, while away (time) with jests; *~ down*, silence with laughter; *~ off* (embarrassment etc.), get rid of with a jest; *~ over*, discuss with laughter; hence *~'ER*¹ n., *~'ING*² a., *~'ingLY*² adv., (-ahf-, -äf-). **2.** n. Sound made in, act of, *~ing* (*join in the ~*, esp. of person taking banter good-humouredly; *have, get, the ~ of*, turn the tables on assailant, also *have the ~ on* one's *side*); person's manner of *~ing*. [OE *hliehhan*, OS **hlahhian*, OHG *hlahhan*, ON *hlæja*, Goth. *hlahjan* f. Gmc **hlah-*]

laugh'ab|le (-ahf-, -äf-), a. Exciting laughter, amusing. Hence ~LY² adv. [prec. n. or v. +-ABLE]

laugh'ing (-ahf-, -äf-), n. In vbl senses: esp.: *no ~ matter*, serious thing, not a fit subject for *~*; *~-gas*, nitrous oxide, with intoxicating effect when inhaled, used as anaesthetic; *~-stock*, person or thing generally ridiculed. [-ING¹]

laugh'ter (-ahf-, -äf-), n. Laughing; HOMERIC *~*. [OE *hleahtor*, OHG *hlahtar*, ON *hlátr* f. Gmc **hlahtraz*]

launce (lahns, läns), n. Sand-eel. [perh. f. LANCE¹, cf. *garfish*]

launch¹ (law-, lah-), v.t. & i., & n. **1.** Hurl, discharge, send forth, (missile, blow, censure, threat, decree); burst (usu. *out*) *into* expense, strong language, etc. (also *~ out*, abs., spend money freely, expatiate in words); set (vessel) afloat; send off, start, (person, enterprise) on a course; go *forth, out*, on an enterprise; *~ing pad, site*, etc., pad etc. from which rockets are *~ed*. **2.** n. Process of *~ing* ship. [ME, f. AF *launcher* = OF *lancier* LANCE²]

launch² (law-, lah-), n. Man-of-war's largest boat, used for shore-going, visiting other ships, etc. (*admiral's ~*, canopied or cabined *~* for use of admiral); engined pleasure-boat on rivers etc. [f. Sp. *lancha* pinnace perh. f. Malay *lancharan* (*lanchar* swift)]

laun′der (lawn-, lahn-), v.t. & i. (Chiefly as p.p.) wash & get up (linen); (of fabric, with adv.) admit of being ~ed. Hence ~ETTE′ (-ĕt) n., establishment with automatic washing machines available for public use. [f. ME *launder* n., washer of linen, contr. of *lavander* f. OF *-ier* f. Rom. *lavandarius* (*lavanda* neut. pl. gerundive of L *lavare* wash, -ARY[1])]

laun′dress (lawn-, lahn-), n. Woman who washes & gets up linen; ‖ caretaker of chambers in Inns of Court. [f. *launder* n. (prec.) +-ESS[1]]

laun′dry (lawn-, lahn-), n. Establishment for washing linen; batch of clothes sent to or from ~. [contr. f. *lavendry* (f. OF *lavanderie*) after *launder*; see -RY]

laur′eate (or lŏ-), a. & n. Wreathed with, (of wreath) consisting of, laurel; worthy of laurels as poet (*poet* ~, or ~ as n., poet receiving stipend as writer of Court odes, whence ~SHIP (-t-sh-) n.), or for eloquence etc. [f. L *laureatus* (*laurea* laurel-wreath f. *laurus* laurel, -ATE[2])]

lau′rel (lŏ-), n., & v.t. (-ll-). 1. Kinds of garden shrub (*Portugal* ~, with large glossy leaves); foliage of bay-tree as emblem of victory or distinction in poetry (collect. sing. or pl.; *reap*, *win*, ~*s*; *rest on* one's ~*s*, cease to strive for further glory; *look to* one's ~*s*, beware of losing pre-eminence); ~-*bottle*, filled with ~-leaves for killing insects. 2. v.t. Wreathe with ~. [ME *lorer* f. OF *lorier* f. *lor* f. L *laurus*; -*l* by dissim.]

laurustin′us, -res-, (lŏ-), n. Evergreen flowering shrub. [mod. L f. L *laurus* laurel +*tinus* a plant]

la′va (lah-), n. Matter flowing from volcano, solid substance it cools into; (w. pl.) kind, bed, of ~. [It. (*lavare* It. & L wash)]

lavāb′o, n. (pl. ~s). Ritual washing of celebrant's hands at offertory, towel or basin used for this; monastery washing-trough; wash-basin, (pl.) lavatory, (after F). [L, = I will wash, first wd of *Ps.* xxv. 6]

lavā′tion, n. Washing. [f. L *lavatio* (*lavare* wash, -ATION)]

lăv′atory, n. Vessel for washing (arch.); room etc. for washing hands & face; (euphem.) water-closet(s) and urinal. [f. LL *lavatorium* f. *lavare* wash, -ORY(2)]

lāve, v.t. (poet.). Wash, bathe; (of stream etc.) wash against, flow along. [ME *lave* f. OF *laver* f. L *lavare* wash; coalescing w. OE *lafian* wash by affusion, rel. to MDu. *laven*, OHG *labōn* refresh]

lāve′ment (-vm-), n. (med.). Injection, enema. [F (prec., -MENT)]

lăv′ender, n., & v.t. 1. Small lilac-flowered narrow-leaved shrub cultivated for perfume; its flowers & stalks laid among linen etc. (*lay up in* ~, often fig., preserve piously for future use); pale blue

colour with trace of red; ~-*water*, perfume of distilled ~, alcohol, & ambergris. 2. v.t. Put ~ among (linen). [ME, f. AF *lavendre*, ult. dissimilated f. med. L *lavandula* etc.; further history obsc.]

lāv′er[1], n. Kinds of marine algae, esp. the edible species. [L]

lāv′er[2], n. (Bibl.) large brazen vessel for Jewish priests' ablutions; (arch.) washing or fountain basin, font. [ME *lavo*(u)*r* f. OF *lavcor*, *-eoir* LAVATORY] f. OF *lavcor*, *-eoir* LAVATORY]

laverock. See LARK[1].

lăv′ish, a., & v.t. 1. Giving or producing without stint, profuse, prodigal, (*of* money etc., *in* giving); very or over abundant; hence ~LY[2] adv., ~NESS n. 2. v.t. Bestow or spend (money, effort, blood, admiration, etc.) profusely; hence ~MENT n. [15th c. *lavas*, f. obs. n. *lavas* (later *-ish*) profusion, f. OF *lavasse* (-*ache*) deluge of rain; see -ISH[2]]

law[1], n. 1. Body of enacted or customary rules recognized by a community as binding, this personified, (*the* ~ *forbids*, *allows*; often *the* ~ *of the land*; *the* ~ *of the Medes & Persians*, unalterable ~, see *Dan.* vi. 12; *lay down the* ~, talk authoritatively, hector). 2. One of these rules. 3. Their controlling influence, ~-abiding state of society, (often ~ *& order*; *necessity knows no* ~, over-rides its sanctity; *be a* ~ *unto* oneself, take one's own line, disregard convention); the ~s as a system (COURT *of* ~; so SON-*in*-~ etc.) or science (*learned in the* ~; *read* ~, study the ~s), jurisprudence. 4. Binding injunctions (*give the* ~ *to*, impose one's will upon; *his word is* ~). 5. (With defining word) one of the branches of the study of ~, the ~s concerning specified department, (*commercial* ~; *the* ~ *of evidence*; CANON, CIVIL, COMMON[1], MARTIAL, ~; *international* ~, ~ *of nations*, regulating relations between States). 6. The statute & common ~ (opp. EQUITY). 7. (In pred. use, of decisions, opinions, etc.; also *good*, *bad*, etc., ~) borne out, or not, by the relevant ~s (*it may be common sense, but it is not* ~). 8. The legal profession (usu. *the* ~; *bred to the* ~); legal knowledge. 9. Judicial remedy, ~ courts as providing it, litigation, (*go to* ~; *have*, *take*, *the* ~ *of* person; *take the* ~ *into* one's *own hands*, redress one's wrong by force); *the Law Courts*, ‖ (esp.) the ROYAL *Courts of Justice*. 10. (Also ~ *of Moses*) precepts of Pentateuch, Mosaic dispensation. 11. Rule of action or procedure, esp. in an art, department of life, or game. 12. (Also ~ *of nature* or *natural* ~) correct statement of invariable sequence between specified conditions & specified phenomenon (~*s of motion*, three propositions formulated by Newton; *Gresham's* ~, that bad money drives out good; *Kepler's* ~*s*, three propositions on planetary motions; *Grimm's*, *Verner's*, ~, on consonant changes in Germanic languages; *Parkinson's* ~, that work expands so as to fill the time available for its completion, and that subordinates multiply at a fixed rate regardless of the amount of work produced). **13.** ~s of nature, regularity in nature (*where they saw chance, we see* ~); *Law of Nature* (see also above) or *Reason*, principles of conduct recognized as pleasing to God or as intrinsically reasonable. **14.** (Sport) allowance, start, given to hunted animal or competitor in race, (whence gen.) time of grace, respite. **15.** ~*-abiding*(*ness*), obedient, obedience, to ~; ~ *calf*, unstained used for binding ~-books; ~ COURT[1]; ~ *French*, the Anglo-Norman terms used in ~-books & ~; ~*'giver*, one who makes (esp. code of) ~s; || ~-*hand*, handwriting used in legal documents; ~ *Latin*, barbarous Latin of early English statutes; || *Law Lord*, Lord of Appeal in Ordinary, member of House of Lords qualified to perform its legal work; ~*'maker*, legislator; ~ *merchant*, mercantile ~, ~s regulating trade & commerce, differing in some respects from Common Law; ~ *officer*, legal functionary, || esp. Attorney-General or Solicitor-General or Lord Advocate; ~*-stationer*, selling stationery needed by lawyers || & taking in documents to be engrossed; ~*'suit*, prosecution of claim in ~court; ~*-term*, word or expression used in ~, also period appointed for sitting of ~ courts; ~*-writer*, writer on ~, || also engrosser of legal documents. [late OE *lagu* f. ON **lagu* pl. of *lag* something 'laid down' or fixed, cogn. w. LAY[3]]

|| **law[2], laws,** int. (vulg.) expressing astonishment. [var. of LO, or earlier *la*, or *lor'* for *Lord*]

law'ful, a. Permitted, appointed, qualified, or recognized, by law, not illegal or (of child) illegitimate. Hence ~LY[2] adv., ~NESS n. [-FUL]

lawk(s), int. (vulg.) expressing astonishment; *lawk-a-mussy* (vulg.), = Lord have mercy. [for ALACK or *Lord*]

law'less, a. (Of country etc.) where law is non-existent or inoperative; regardless of, disobedient to, uncontrolled by, law, unbridled, licentious. Hence ~NESS n. [-LESS]

lawn[1], n. Kind of fine linen used esp. for bishop's sleeves; ~ *sieve*, fine sieve of ~ or silk. Hence ~'Y[2] a. [prob. f. *Laon* in France]

lawn[2], n. || Glade (arch.); (extent of) grass-covered land; close-mown turf-covered piece of pleasure-ground or garden, whence ~'Y[2] a.; ~*-mower*, machine with revolving spiral knives for mowing ~s; ~*-sprinkler*, machine for watering ~s etc.; ~ *tennis*, modification of tennis played by two persons (*single*) or four (*double*) on a level court ('grass' or 'hard') without walls. [16th c., f. ME *laund*(*e*) f. OF *launde* (mod. *lande*) f. Gaulish **landa* LAND[1]]

law'yer (*or* loi'er), n. Member of legal profession, esp. attorney, solicitor; person versed in law (*good, no,* etc., ~); *Penang* ~, walking-stick of Penang palm (perh. f. native tree name); SEA~. [-YER]

lax[1], a. Loose, relaxed, not compact, porous, (rare); negligent, careless, not strict, vague. Hence or cogn. ~'ITY n., ~'LY[2] adv. [ME, f. L *laxus* cogn. w. *languēre* LANGUISH]

lax[2], n. Swedish or Norwegian salmon. [OE *leax*, OS, OHG *lahs*, ON (Sw., Da.) *lax* f. Gmc **lahs-*]

lax'ative, a. & n. (Medicine) tending to loosen the bowels. [F (*-if, -ive*), f. LL *laxativus* (*laxare*, see LAX[1], -ATIVE)]

lay[1], n. Short lyric or narrative poem meant to be sung; (poet.) song, poem, song of birds. [ME, f. OF *lai*, of unkn. orig.]

lay[2], a. Non-clerical, not in orders; of, done by, ~man or laity; non-professional, not expert, (esp. w. ref. to law or medicine); ~ *brother, sister,* person who has taken habit & vows of religious order but is employed in manual labour & excused other duties; ~ *clerk,* singing man in cathedral or collegiate church, parish clerk; ~ *communion,* membership of church as ~man, also communicating of laity in eucharist; ~ *deacon,* man in deacon's order but also following secular employment; || ~ *lord,* peer who is not LAW[1] lord; ~*'man,* one of the laity, non-expert in regard to some profession, art, or science (esp. law or medicine); ~ *reader,* ~man licensed to conduct religious services. [ME, f. OF *lai* f. LL f. Gk *laikos* LAIC]

lay[3], v.t. & i. (*laid*), & n. **1.** Prostrate (~ *low,* bring down, humble); (of wind or rain) beat down (crops); cause (sea, wind, dust, misgivings, ghost) to subside. **2.** Deposit; place in recumbent posture (~ *to sleep* or *rest,* lit., & fig. = bury; ~ one's *bones,* be buried *in* specified place); (of hen) produce (egg, or abs.); put down (amount, one's head or life, etc.) as wager, stake, (abs.) announce readiness to bet (*that* ——). **3.** Place, set, apply, (~ *to* HEART; ~ *heads together,* confer; *laid a spark to the train*; ~ *hounds on scent*; ~ *hold on* or *of,* seize, grasp, & fig. make capital *of* opponent's weak point etc.; ~ one's *hopes on*; ~ *great store upon,* value highly; ~ *snare, trap, ambush*; ~ WAIT[2]; ~ *siege to,* besiege, importune); locate (scene; *scene of tale is laid in London*); put (limb etc.) in certain position (*horse laid his ears back*; ~ *hands on,* seize, appropriate, also do violence to, esp. one*self* = commit suicide, also find, as *cannot* ~ *my hands upon it,* also confirm or ordain by imposition of hands); aim (big gun) for direction; (with compl.) put into specified state (~ *land fallow, under water*; ~ person *under obligation,* oblige him, *under necessity,* compel him, *under contribution,* make him contribute; ~

bare, denude, reveal; ~ *waste*, ravage; ~ *open*, reveal, explain, also break skin of; ~ *fast, by the heels*, confine or imprison; ~ ABOARD). 4. Present, put forward, (esp. *claim to* something; ~ *an information*, bring indictment in legal form); place (facts, question) for consideration *before* person; (Parl.) *Foreign Secretary* etc. *will ~ papers* (i.e. on the table, to give information to the House of Commons); (of suitor) fix (damages) *at* certain sum; (arch.) impute (fault) *to* person or (mod.) *to* his *charge, at* or *to* his *door*; represent (evil) as consequent *on* some cause. 5. Impose (penalty, command, obligation, burden, tax), cast (blame), (*up*)*on* (~ *stress, weight, emphasis, on*, emphasize, treat as important); bring (stick etc.) down *on* (also ~ *blows* or *it on* adv.; & abs. ~ *into*, sl., belabour, ~ *about* one, hit out on all sides). 6. Dispose, arrange, esp. horizontally (foundation, floor, bricks, submarine cable; ~ *table, cloth,* or *breakfast* etc., prepare table for meal; ~ *the fire*, put fuel ready for lighting); make (strand, rope) by twisting yarn or strands; fix outlines of, devise (plan, plot; ~ one's ACCOUNT[2]); put (colour etc.) on a surface in layers; cover, coat, strew, (surface) *with* carpet, metal, straw, etc.; *laid paper* (having ribbed surface owing to wires used in making). 7. v.i. (vulg., also naut.). = LIE[3]; ~ *on your oars*, stop rowing but keep oars out; ~*about* n., habitual loafer or tramp. 8. ~ *aside* or *by*, put away, cease to use or practise or think of, abandon, save (money etc.) for future needs; ~ *down*, put on the ground etc. (~ *down* one's *arms*, surrender), relinquish (office, hopes), pay or wager (money), sacrifice (one's life), (begin to) construct (ship, railway), formulate (rule, principle, course; ~ *down the* LAW[1]), set down (chart etc.) on paper, convert (land) into pasture (*in, to, under, with*, grass, clover, etc.), store (wine) in cellar; ~ *in*, provide oneself with stock of, (also, colloq.) shower blows; ~ *off*, discharge (temporarily) for lack of work, (colloq.) desist; ~ *on*, impose (tax, command, penalty), deal blows, inflict (blows), ply (lash etc.), apply coat of (paint etc.; ~ *it on thick* or *with a trowel*, use obvious flattery), provide pipes etc. supplying (gas, water, electricity), provide (entertainment, means of transport, etc.); ~ *out*, spread, expose to view etc., prepare (body) for burial, (sl.) kill, (colloq.) put (person) out of action temporarily at football etc., expend (money), (refl.) take pains *to* do, dispose (grounds, garden) according to a plan; ~ *up*, store, put by, put (ship) out of commission, save (money, or abs.), (pass.) be confined to bed or house. 9. n. Line of business, job, pursuit, (sl.); direction or amount of twist in rope-strands; way, position, or direction, in which something (esp. country) lies, lie;

~*by*, portion of road widened to permit a vehicle to stop there without interfering with traffic; ~*out*, disposing or arrangement of ground etc., (of plans etc.) drawing showing arrangement, make-up of book, newspaper, advertisement, etc.; ~ *shaft*, secondary shaft of a machine, not forming part of main system of power-transmission. [OE *lecgan*, OS *leggian*, OHG *legen, lecken*, ON *leggja*, Goth. *lagjan* f. Gmc **leg-*, **lag-* LIE[3]]

lay[4]. See LIE[3].

lay′er, n., & v.t. & i. In vbl senses; also: stratum, thickness of matter (esp. one of several) spread over surface; (gardening) shoot fastened into earth to strike root while attached to parent plant (v.t., propagate thus); (pl.) patches of laid corn (v.i., of corn, be laid flat by weakness of growth); oyster-bed; *good, bad*, etc., ~ (of fowls); ~*s & backers*, persons betting against, on, individual horse etc.; ~*stool*, root from which ~s are produced. Hence~ED[2] (-erd) a. [LAY[3], -ER[1]]

layĕtte′, n. Clothes, toilet articles, & bedding, needed for newborn child. [F]

lay fig′ure (-ger), n. Jointed wooden figure of human body used by artists for arranging drapery on etc.; unimportant person, nonentity; unreal character in novel etc. [*lay* f. obs. *layman* lay figure f. Du. *leeman* (*led* joint)]

lay′lock, n. (Dial. for) LILAC.

lay⸰off (-awf), n. Period during which a workman is temporarily discharged; slack season. [LAY[3]]

|| **lay′stall** (-awl), n. Refuse heap. [LAY[3], STALL]

lăz′ar, n. (arch.). Poor & diseased person, esp. leper; ~*house*, = foll. [ME, f. med. L *lazarus* f. proper name (*Luke* xvi. 20)]

lăzarĕt′, -ĕtt′ō (pl. *-os*), n. Hospital (chiefly in foreign countries) for diseased poor, esp. lepers; building or ship for performing quarantine in; after part of ship's hold used for stores. [F (*-et*), f. It. *lazzaretto* (*lazzaro* LAZAR)]

Lăz′arus, n. Beggar, poor man, (esp. in contrasts, ~ *& Dives* etc.). [see LAZAR]

lāze, v.i. & t., & n. (colloq.). 1. Be lazy; pass (time) *away* in laziness. 2. n. Lazy time. [back formation f. LAZY]

lăz′ūlī, n. = LAPIS LAZULI.

lāz′ў, a., & v.i. & t. 1. Averse to labour, indolent, slothful; appropriate to or inducing indolence; ~*bed*, bed for potato-growing about 6 ft wide with trench on each side; ~*bones*, ~ person; ~ *pinion*, serving as transmitter of motion between other pinions or wheels; ~*tongs*, arrangement of zigzag levers for picking up distant objects; hence **lāz′iLY**[2] adv., **lāz′i**NESS n. 2. vb. = LAZE. [16th c. *laysie, lasie, laesy*, of LG orig.; cf. LG *lasich, läsig*, lazy]

lăzzarōn′e, n. (pl. *-ni*, pr. *-nĕ*). Neapolitan street-lounger living by odd jobs & begging. [It. (LAZAR, -OON)] 'ld, abbr. of *would* (now rare, cf. 'D).

-le, -el, suf. **1.** f. ME *-el, -le,* f. OE *-el, -ela, -(e)le* in nn. (Gmc *-ila-), *-ol, -ul, -el,* in adjj.; after *ch,* soft *g, n, r, sh, th, v, -el* is retained, & after *m* the suf. becomes *-ble.* Nn. formed on n. stems have dim. sense (*bramble*), or that of tool, appliance, (*thimble, handle*); nn. formed on vb stems express agent (*beadle*), instrument (*bridle, girdle*), or less definite relations (*bundle*); adjj. formed on vb stems have the sense *apt or liable to the vbl action* (*brittle, nimble*). **2.** Occas. repr. ME *-el, -elle,* in nn. f. OF *-el* (mod. F usu. *-eau*) f. L *-ellus, -ellum* (*bowel, tunnel, castle, mantle*), OF *-ele* (mod. *-elle*) f. L *-ella* (*chapel, novel*); also f. other sources, as L *-ale* (*cattle*); f. F *-aille* f. L *-alia* see *-AL* (*battle*), or F *-eille* f. L *-icula* (*bottle*); f. L *-ulus, -ula, -ulum,* (*angle*); *-el* in some mod. scientific wds on L anal. (*carpel*). **3.** Verbal, f. ME *-(e)len* f. OE *-lian* f. Gmc *-ilōjan,* w. frequent. or dim. sense (*nestle, twinkle, wrestle, crumple, dazzle*).

lea¹, n. (poet.). Tract of open ground, esp. grass land. [OE *lēa(h),* cogn. w. OHG *lōh* grove, f. Gmc *lauh-,* cogn. w. L *lucus*]

lea², n. Measure of yarn (300, 200, 120, & 80 yds in different districts etc.). [ME *lee,* perh. rel. to F *lier* f. L *ligare* to bind]

leach, v.t. Make (liquid) percolate through some material; subject (bark, ore) to action of percolating fluid; purge (soluble matter) *away* etc. by such means. [prob. repr. OE *leccan* to water]

lead¹ (lĕd), n., & v.t. & i. **1.** Heavy easily fusible soft malleable base metal of dull pale bluish-grey colour (*red ~,* red oxide of ~ used as pigment, minium; *white ~,* mixture of ~ carbonate & hydrated ~ oxide used as pigment, ceruse; = BLACK¹-~, whence ~ is used, w. pl., for the small stick of graphite in pencil or pencil-case; *ounce of ~,* bullet). **2.** Lump of ~ used in sounding water (*cast, heave, the ~; arm the ~,* fill hollow in it with tallow, to learn nature of bottom; ‖ *swing the ~,* sl., malinger or scrimshank). **3.** ‖ pl. Strips of ~ used to cover roof, piece of (esp. horizontal) ~-covered roof; ~ frames or cames holding glass of lattice or painted window. **4.** (print.). Metal strip to give space between lines. **5.** ~ *comb,* made of ~ & used to darken hair; ~ *pencil,* of graphite usu. enclosed in cedar; ~-*poisoning,* acute or chronic poisoning by taking of ~ into system; ~*s'man,* sailor who heaves the ~; ~ *wool,* ~ in a fibrous state, used for jointing water-pipes; ~-*work,* plumber's or glazier's work; ~-*works,* place where ~-ore is smelted; ~*'wort,* plumbago; hence ~*'LESS a.* **6.** vb. Cover, weight, frame, (panes) with ~, (print.) separate lines of (printed matter) with ~s: (of gun-barrel) become foul with coating of ~. [OE *lēad,* MLG *lōd,* MHG *lōt*]

lead² (lēd), v.t. & i. (*lĕd*). **1.** Force to go with one (~ *captive,* take away as prison-

er). **2.** Conduct, guide, esp. by going in front (of person, also of motive, circumstance, etc.; *curiosity, chance, led him to Rome; ~* one *a* DANCE²; *~* one *a life,* worry him constantly; *~ the way,* go first, take the lead in course lit. or fig.). **3.** (Of commander) direct movements of. **4.** Conduct (person) by the hand or contact, (animal) by halter etc., (*led horse,* spare horse led by groom etc.; *led captain,* hanger-on, toady, parasite; ~ woman *to altar,* marry); (Sc.) cart (corn etc.); guide by persuasion (*is easier led than driven; ~ astray,* esp. tempt to sin etc.; *~ by the nose,* induce to do unconsciously all one wishes). **5.** Guide actions or opinions of, bring by argument etc. *to* conclusion, induce to do (~ one *to suppose* etc., deceive him into thinking); ply (witness) with leading questions. **6.** (Of road etc.) conduct (person, or usu. abs.) *to* place (*all roads ~ to Rome;* also fig. = have as result, *this led to confusion*). **7.** Make (rope, water, etc.) go through pulley, channel, etc. **8.** Pass, go through, spend, (life etc., esp. w. epithet as *~ a miserable existence, a double life*). **9.** Have first place in (~ *the dance, van*); (abs.) go first (~ *off,* begin intr.), be first at some point in race, be ahead in game (*Kent led on the first innings*). **10.** Direct by example (~ *orchestra, band, chórus,* etc.), set (fashion); be official director or spokesman of (party), ‖ act as leading counsel in (case, or usu. abs.). **11.** (cards). Play as first card, be first-player, in trick (~ *up to,* play so as to elicit higher card in later player's hand), play one of (suit) when ~ing. **12.** ~ *away,* (usu. in pass.) induce to follow unthinkingly; ~ *off,* begin (dance, conversation, or abs.); ~ *on,* entice into going farther than was intended; ~ *up the* GARDEN (*path*); ~ *up to,* form preparation for, serve to introduce, direct conversation towards, (subject). Hence ~'ABLE a. [OE *lædan,* OS *lēdian,* OHG *leiten,* ON *leitha,* f. Gmc *laidhjan* f. *laidhō* LOAD¹]

lead³ (lēd), n. Direction given by going in front, example, (*follow the ~ of; give one a ~,* encourage him by doing thing, esp. leaping fence in hunting, first); leading place, leadership, (*take the ~*); artificial water-course, esp. leading to mill; (electr.) conductor conveying current from source to place of use, (~-*in,* conducting wire joining wireless receiver with external aerial); channel in ice-field; string etc. for leading dog; (cards) act or right of playing first (*return ~,* lead from suit already led by partner); (theatr.) (player of) chief part; ~-*off,* commencement. [f. prec.]

lea'den (lĕd-), a. (As) of lead (*sleep's ~ sceptre,* stupefying power; ~ *sword,* useless); heavy, slow, burdensome, (~ *limbs*) inert, deadening, (~ *rule*); lead-coloured. [-EN¹]

Leadenhall (lĕd′enhawl′), n. (Used for) ~ meat and poultry market in London.

lead′er (lēd²-), n. In vbl senses of LEAD² (FOLLOW *my* ~); also or esp.: ~ *of House of Commons & House of Lords*, member of Government with official initiative in business; ‖ counsel who leads in case, also Q.C., also senior counsel of circuit; front horse(s) in team or tandem (opp. WHEEL-ER); leading performer in orchestra; shoot growing at apex of stem or principal branch; tendon; ‖ = LEADING² *article*; (print.) line of dots or dashes to guide eye. Hence ~LESS a., ~SHIP(1, 3) n. [-ER¹]

‖ **leaderĕtte′** (lĕd-), n. Short editorial paragraph after leading article. [prec., -ETTE]

lead′ing¹ (lēd²-), n. In vbl senses; esp.: *men of light & ~*, of deserved influence; ~*-business*, parts usu. taken by ~ actor; ~*-rein*, to lead horse with; ~*-staff*, attached to ring in bull's nose; ~*-strings*, with which children were formerly taught to walk (*in* ~*-strings*, in state of pupilage). [-ING¹]

lead′ing² (lēd²-), a. In vbl senses; ‖ ~ *article*, editorial expression of opinion at full length in newspaper, (commerc). article of trade sold at low price to attract custom for other things; ~ *case* (law), serving as precedent for deciding others; ~ *edge*, foremost edge of aircraft's wing, opp. *trailing edge*; ~ *lady, man*, taking chief part in play; ~ *motive*, transl. of LEITMOTIV; ~ *note*, seventh of diatonic scale, semitone below keynote; ~ *question*, prompting desired answer. [-ING²]

leaf, n. (pl. *leaves*), & v.i. & t. **1.** Expanded organ (usu. green) of plant springing from side of stem or branch or direct from root; (pop.) petal (esp. *rose-*~); foliage (*fall of the* ~, autumn; *in* ~, with leaves out), leaves of tobacco or tea. **2.** Single thickness of folded paper, esp. (= 2 pages) in book (*take a* ~ *out of* person's BOOK¹; *turn over a new* ~, mend one's ways). **3.** Very thin sheet of metal, esp. gold or silver, or horn, marble, talc, etc. **4.** Hinged part or flap of door, shutter, table (also used of extra section inserted in expansible table), bridge (= bascule), or rifle-sight. **5.** Tooth of pinion. **6.** ~ *brass*, brass foil; ~ *insect* (having wings resembling ~ of plant); ~*-lard* (made from layers of fat round pig's kidneys); ~*-mould*, soil composed chiefly of decaying leaves; hence ~′AGE(1) n., (-)~ED² (-ft), ~′LESS, aa., ~′lĕssNESS n., ~′Y² a., ~′iNESS n. **7.** vb. Put forth leaves; turn over leaves or pages of (book etc.). [OE *lēaf*, OS *lōf*, OHG *loup*, ON *lauf*, Goth. *laufs* f. Gmc *laubhaz, -am*]

leaf′lĕt, n. (Bot.) one division of compound leaf; young leaf; small leaf of paper, or sheet or leaves folded but not stitched, with printed matter, esp. for gratuitous distribution. [-LET]

league¹ (-g), n. Varying measure of road-distance, usu. about three miles. [ME; ult. f. LL *leuga, leuca*, of Gaulish orig.]

league² (-g), n., & v.t. & i. **1.** Compact for mutual protection & assistance or prosecution of common interests, parties (whether States or individuals) to such compact, (*Solemn L~ & COVENANT*; PRIMROSE *L~*; *in* ~ *with*, allied with); ‖ *L~ football* (in which clubs forming a ~ play each other for championship); *L~ of Nations* (established by the treaty of peace 1919 to try to prevent war), now replaced by UNITED *Nations*. **2.** vb. Join (t. & i.) in ~ (esp. in p.p. ~*d together* or *with*). [f. F *ligue* f. It. *liga*, var. of *lega* f. *legare* (L *ligare* bind)]

‖ **leag′uer¹** (-ger), n., & v.t. & i.=LAAGER. [f. Du. *leger* camp, cogn. w. LAIR]

leag′uer² (-ger), n. Member of LEAGUE². [-ER¹]

leak, n., & v.i. & t. **1.** Hole caused by injury, wear, etc., through which fluid makes way into or out of vessel that is immersed in or contains it or through a DIKE (*spring a* ~, develop one). **2.** vb. Let fluid, (of fluid) pass, out or in through ~; (of secrets etc.) transpire, come *out* gradually; hence ~′AGE(3) n., what ~s out or in, transpiring of secrets, unexplained disappearance of money pointing to embezzlement etc.; divulge (secret etc.). [of LG orig.; M Du. *lek, lēk-* n. (cogn. w. ON *lcki*), *lekan* vb (ON *leka*, cf. OHG *zelechen*, (G *leck*) leaky), f. Gmc **lek-*, **lak-*]

leak′|ÿ, a. Having leak(s); incontinent of urine; given to letting out secrets. Hence ~iNESS n. [-Y²]

‖ **leal**, a. (Sc. & literary). Loyal, honest, (LAND¹ *of the* ~). [ME, f. OF *leel, leal, loial* LOYAL]

lean¹, a. & n. **1.** (Of persons) thin, not plump; meagre, of poor quality, innutritious, (~ *crops, diet*; ~ *years*, of scarcity); unremunerative; (of meat) consisting chiefly of muscular tissue, not of fat. **2.** n. ~ part of meat. Hence ~′NESS n. [OE *hlæne*, f. Gmc *hlainjaz]

lean², v.i. & t. (past & p.p. ~ed, or ~t pr. lĕnt), & n. **1.** Incline one's body against something for support, support oneself (of thing, be supported in sloping position) *against* or *on* (mil., ~ *upon*, have as protection on flank); rely or depend (*up*)*on*; incline body *back, forward, over, towards*, etc. (~ *over backwards*, go to the other extreme, go to the limit of eagerness to agree); stand obliquely, out of the perpendicular (~*ing tower*); have tendency *to* mercy etc., be partial *to* cause, opinion, or person, whence ~′ING¹(1) n.; place (thing) in ~ing position; ~*to′*, building with rafters resting against side of another, pent-house. **2.** n. Inclination, slope, (*has a decided* ~ *to the right*). [OE *hleonian, hlinian*, OS *hlinōn*, OHG *(h)linēn*, f. Gmc **hli-*, **hlai-*; cogn. w. LADDER, CLIMAX]

leap[1], v.i. & t. (past & p.p. ~t pr. lĕpt, or ~ed). = JUMP (LOOK[1] before you ~); ~-frog, (n.) game in which players vault with parted legs over others bending down, (vb) perform such vault (over). Hence ~'ER[1] n. [OE hléapan, OS -hlōpan, OHG hlauffan, ON hlaupa, Goth. -hlaupan f. Gmc *hlaupan]

leap[2], n. Jump (~ in the dark, hazardous attempt of doubtful issue; by ~s & bounds, with startlingly rapid progress); thing to be jumped; ~-day, 29th Feb.; ~-year, with intercalary day (perh. because fixed festivals after February in ~-year fall two weekdays, instead of as usual one, later than in the preceding year), ~-year proposal (joc., of woman to man, allowable only in ~-year). [OE hlȳp f. root of prec.]

learn (lĕrn), v.t. & i. (past & p.p. ~t, ~ed pr. -nd). Get knowledge of (subject) or skill in (art etc.) by study, experience, or being taught (from, of); commit to memory (esp. ~ by heart or rote); become aware by information or from observation that, how, etc. (I am or have yet to ~, do not know, usu. with implication of disbelief), be informed of, ascertain; receive instruction; (arch., joc., or vulg.) teach. Hence ~'ABLE a., ~'ER[1] n., (lĕr-). [OE leornian, OS linōn, OHG lirnēn, lernēn f. Gmc *lis-, *lais-; see LORE[1]]

learn'èd (lĕr-), a. Deeply read, erudite; showing profound knowledge; || (in conventionally courteous mention of lawyer in House of Commons, law courts, etc.) ~ in the law (esp. my ~ friend or brother); (of language, profession, etc.) pursued or studied by, (of words in a language) introduced by, ~ men. Hence ~LY[2] adv. [f. prec. in obs. sense (still in vulg. use) teach, +-ED[1]]

learn'ing (lĕr-), n. In vbl senses; esp. (possession of) knowledge got by study, esp. of language or literary or historical science (the new ~, studies, esp. of Greek, introduced into England in 16th c., renaissance). [-ING[1]]

lease[1], n., & v.t. 1. Contract by which lessor, usu. in consideration of rent, conveys land or tenement to lessee for specified time (put out to ~; by or on ~; a new ~ of life, prospect of living due to recovered health or removal of anxiety etc.); ~'hold(er), (person having) tenure, real property held, by ~; L~-Lend (later Lend-L~), applied orig. in 1941 to an arrangement whereby sites in British oversea possessions were ~d to the United States as bases in exchange for the loan of destroyers, later extended to the pooling of the resources & output of the United Nations, also attrib. & as v.t. 2. v.t. Grant or take ~ of. [f. AF les = OF lais, leis, f. lesser, laissier f. L laxare (LAX) to loose]

lease[2], n. Crossing of warp-threads in loom;. = foll. (weaving). [app. var. of

LEASH, perh. by confusion w. F lisse, lice]

leash, n., & v.t. 1. Thong in which hounds or coursing-dogs are held (hold in ~, control); set of three hounds, hares, etc.; (weaving) cord with eye to receive warp-thread extending between parallel laths of loom-heddle. 2. v.t. Connect, hold in, with ~. [ME, f. OF lesse f. spec. use of lesser, laissier; see LEASE[1]]

leas'ing (-z-), n. (bibl.). Lying, lie. [OE léasung f. léasian f. léas false, f. Gmc *laus-; see LOOSE[1], -LESS]

least, a., n., & adv. 1. Smallest, slightest, (the ~, esp. after neg., any however small; ~ common MULTIPLE; line of ~ RESISTANCE). 2. n. ~ amount (to say the ~ of it, to put the case moderately; ~ said soonest mended, discussion will only make things worse); at ~, at all events, even if a wider statement is disputable, (also at the ~) at the lowest computation; (in) the ~, in the smallest degree, at all. 3. adv. In the ~ degree. [OE lǽst, lǽsest f. Gmc *laisistaz, superl. of *laisiz (LESS, -EST)]

least'wäys (-z-; vulg.), **least'wïse** (-z-; rare), advv. Or at least, or rather, [-WAYS, -WISE]

|| **leat**, n. Open water-course conducting water to mill etc. [OE -gelǽt (Y-+root of LET[2])]

lea'ther (lĕdh-), n., & v.t. 1. Skin prepared for use by tanning or similar process (patent ~, with fine black varnished surface; || American ~, kind of oilcloth; ~ & (prop. or) prunella, a difference in clothes only, see Pope, Essay, iv. 204; nothing like ~, one's own goods will serve all purposes; vb, cover or arm with ~). 2. Article, or part of one, made of ~, piece of ~ for polishing; thong (esp. stirrup-~; vb, beat with strap, whence ~ING[1](1) n.); (sl.) cricket-ball (~-hunting, fielding) or football; (pl.) leggings or breeches. 3. ~-back, kind of turtle; ~-head, blockhead; ~-jacket, kinds of fish, || crane-fly grub; ~-neck, (sailor's name, w. ref. to ~ stock formerly worn, for) soldier; ~-wood, kinds of tough-barked tree. Hence ~ETTE'(2) n., ~n [-EN[5]], ~Y[2] (esp. of meat etc., tough), aa. [OE lether, OS -ar, OHG ledar, ON lethr f. Gmc *lethram]

lea'theroid (lĕdh-), n. Cotton paper chemically treated & resembling raw hide. [-OID]

leave[1], n. Permission (to do; by your ~, apology, often iron., for taking liberty, making unwelcome statement, etc., esp. as porter's formula for asking person to make way for him & his load; without a ' with your ~ ' or ' by your ~ ', colloq., without even asking ~); (in Services, offices, schools) ~ (of absence), permission to be absent from duty, period for which this lasts (on ~, absent thus; ~-breaker, person remaining away beyond the period; || TICKET of ~); take (one's) ~ (of), bid farewell (to; *take ~ of* one's *senses*, go mad), whence ~*taking*[1](1) n.; FRENCH~; WAY ~. [OE *lēaf*, OHG *louba* (cf. *irlouben*, Goth. *uslaubjan* to permit), f. WG *laubhā*; cogn. w. BELIEF, LIEF, LOVE]

leave[2], v.t. (*left*), & n. 1. Cause to or let remain, depart without taking, (~*s a wife & three sons; six from seven ~s one*; ~*s much* etc. *to be desired*, is unsatisfactory; *left his gloves*); bequeath. 2. Abstain from consuming or dealing with; (pass.) remain over. 3. Let remain in specified state (*this ~s me cool, cold*, does not excite me; ~ *it at that*, colloq., abstain from comment or further action; *be well* etc. *left*, provided for by legacy etc.; ~ *undone, unsaid*, etc.). 4. Commit, refer, *to* another agent etc. than oneself (~ *it to you, sir*, fix my pay yourself; *nothing was left to accident*; ~ *him to himself*, do not try to control). 5. Allow (person, thing) *to* do something without interference. 6. Deposit, entrust, (thing, instructions, message), station (person), to be seen to, delivered, etc., or to discharge function, in one's absence (~ *card on* person, as equivalent of formal call). 7. Quit, go away from, (*left him quite well an hour ago*; ~ *this* or *here*; ~ *the track, room*); (abs.) depart (*we ~ tomorrow*, often *for* destination). 8. Pass (object) so as to put it in specified relative direction (~ *the church on the left*). 9. Cease to reside at (place), belong to (school, society), or serve (employer), (also abs., as *I am leaving at Christmas*). 10. Abandon, forsake (esp. ~ *in the lurch*; *get left*, colloq., be deserted or worsted). 11. ~ *alone*, not interfere with; ~ *behind*, go away without, ~ *as* consequence or trace, pass; ~ *go* (vulg.), relax one's hold; ~ *hold of*, cease holding; ~ *off*, cease to wear, discontinue (habit, doing, *work*), (intr.) come to or make an end; ~ *out*, omit; ~ *over*, let stand over for the time. 12. n. (billiards). Position in which player ~s the balls. Hence (usu. pl.) leav*ING*[1](2) n. [OE *lǣfan*, OS *-lēbian*, OHG *leiben*, ON *leifa*, Goth. *-laibjan* f. Gmc *laibhjan* f. *libh-*, *laibh-* (LIFE, LIVE)]

(-)leaved (-vd), a. Having leaves (rare); having — leaves (*one-~ table; red-~*). [f. LEAF+-ED[2]]

lea'ven (lĕ-), n., & v.t. 1. Substance added to dough to produce fermentation, esp. fermenting dough reserved for purpose; (fig.) spreading & transforming influence (*Matt.* xiii. 33), tinge or admixture of some quality; *the old ~*, traces of unregenerate state (1 *Cor.* v. 6, 7). 2. v.t. Ferment (dough) with ~; permeate & transform, modify *with* tempering element. [ME *levain(e)* f. OF *levain* f. Rom. spec. use of L *levamen* (*levare* lift, -MEN)]

leaves. See LEAF.

lebensraum (lāb'ensrowm), n. Territory which the Germans believed was needed for their natural development. [G, = living-space]

lĕch'er, n. (arch.). Fornicator, debauchee. So ~OUS a., ~OUSLY[2] adv., lĕch'ERY(4) n. [ME, f. OF *lecheor* etc., f. *lechier* to live in debauchery or gluttony, f. Frank. *likkōn* LICK]

lĕc'tern, n. Reading or singing desk in church, esp. that for the lessons. [ME *lettorne* f. OF *lettrun, leitrun* f. LL *lectrum* (*legere lect-* read)]

lĕc'tionary (-sho-), n. Book containing, list of, portions of Scripture appointed to be read at divine service. [f. med. L *lectionarium* (*lectio* reading, see prec., -ARY[1])]

lĕc'tur|e, n., & v.i. & t. 1. Discourse before audience or class on given subject, usu. by way of instruction; admonition, reproof, (*read one a ~e*, reprove him). 2. vb. Deliver ~e or ~es (*on* subject); instruct or entertain (class etc.) by ~e; admonish, reprimand; hence ~ER[1] (-kche)- n. [ME, f. OF, or med. L *lectura* (*legere lect-* read, -URE)]

lĕc'tureship (-kcher-), (rare) -urership, n. Office of lecturer. [prec.+-SHIP (unusual formation)]

led. See LEAD[2].

lĕdge, n. Narrow horizontal surface projecting from wall etc.; shelf-like projection on side of rock or mountain; ridge of rocks, esp. below water; (mining) stratum of metal-bearing rock. Hence lĕdg'Y[2], lĕdgED[2] (-jd), aa. [poss. f. ME *legge* LAY[3]]

lĕdg'er, n. & a. 1. Principal book of the set used for recording trade transactions, containing debtor-&-creditor accounts; horizontal timber in scaffolding, parallel to face of building; flat grave-stone; ~-blade, stationary blade in cloth-shearing machine acting with revolving spiral blade; ~-tackle, kind of fishing-tackle in which lead bullet keeps bait on bottom. 2. adj. (mus.). ~ (or *leger*) *line*, short line added above or below stave for. outside notes (perh. attrib. use of n. in scaffolding sense). [f. the senses of Du. *ligger & legger*, the forms being conformed to the dial. (ME) *ligge, legge* of LIE[3], LAY[3] (cf. LEDGE)]

lee, n. Shelter given by neighbouring object (*under the ~ of*); (also ~ *side*) sheltered side, side away from wind, (opp. *windward, weather side*; often attrib., ~ or ~-, = belonging to ship's ~ side, or to leeward of other object, whence ~'MOST a.); ~-board, plank frame fixed to side of flat-bottomed vessel & let down into water to diminish ~way; ~ *shore*, shore to leeward of ship; ~'*way*, lateral drift of ship to leeward of course (*make up ~way*, fig., struggle out of bad position, often *much ~way to make up*). [OE *hlēo*, OS *hleo*, ON *hlé* f. Gmc *hlew-*]

‖ leech[1], n. (arch., poet., or joc.). Physician, healer; ~'*craft*, art of healing. [OE *lǣce*, OS *lāki*, OHG *lāhhi*, Goth. *lēkeis* f. Gmc *lǣkjaz*]

leech², n. Kinds of aquatic bloodsucking worm, esp. that used medicinally for bleeding (*stick like a ~*, persistently); person who sucks profit out of others. [OE *læce*, cf. MDu. *lake*]

‖ **leech³**, n. Perpendicular or sloping side of sail. [15th c., orig. unkn.; rel. to ON *lik* (cf. Sw. *lik*, Da. *lig* bolt-rope), Du. *lijk*, G *liek* leech-line]

leek, n. Culinary herb like onion, but with cylindrical bulb; this as Welsh national emblem (cf. ROSE ; *eat the~*, pocket affront, see Shak. *Hen. V*, v. i.). [OE *lēac*, OHG *louh*, ON *laukr* f. Gmc **laukaz*]

leer¹, v.i., & n. Glance (esp. sideways) with sly, lascivious, or malign expression. Hence ~'in**G**LY² adv. [16th c., perh. f. obs. *leer* cheek, as though ' to glance over one's cheek ']

leer², n. Annealing-furnace for glass. [orig. unkn.]

leer'ȳ, a. (sl.). Knowing, sly. [perh. f. LEER¹ n. + -Y²]

lees (-z), n. pl. Sediment of wine etc. (*drink, drain, to the ~*, lit. & fig.); basest part, refuse. [ME *lic*, pl. *lies*, f. OF *lie*, f. med. L *lia* (pl. *liae*) f. Gaulish *liga*]

leet¹, n. (hist.). Yearly or half-yearly court of record (also *court ~*) holdable by lords of certain manors; its jurisdiction, its district. [ME, f. AF *lete* (= AL *leta*) of unkn. orig.]

‖ **leet²**, n. (Sc.). Selected list of candidates for some office; *short ~*, select list for final choice. [15th c. *lite*, prob. f. AF, OF *lit(t)e*, var. of *liste* LIST¹]

lee'ward (or, esp. *naut.*, lū'ard), a., adv., & n. On, towards, the sheltered side (opp. *windward*); (n.) this direction (*to ~*, *on the ~ of*). Hence ~MOST a. [LEE + -WARD]

lee'wardlȳ (see prec.), a. (Of ship) apt to fall to leeward (opp. *weatherly*). [-LY¹]

left¹, a., adv., & n. **1.** Belonging to the side of a person's body that is westward when he faces N. or that has normally the less-used hand, having corresponding relation to front of any object (*~ wing* or *flank* of army; *~ bank* of river, assuming it to face the way it flows); situated nearer to or more directly in front of observer's or speaker's *~* hand than his right; *~ hand*, lit., &=region or direction nearer the *~* hand, (*on the ~ hand of*, in that direction relatively to; *marry with the ~ hand*, morganatically; *~-hand blow*, delivered with it; *~-hand man*, standing next one on *~*; *~-hand rope*, twisted counter-clockwise); *over the ~* (*shoulder* now rare), sl. phr. denoting that what is said is to be interpreted by contraries; *~ turn*, that brings one's front to face as one's *~* side did before; hence ~'MOST a., ~'WARD a. & adv., ~'WARDS adv. **2.** adv. On or to the *~* side. **3.** n. *~* hand (lit. in pugilism, as *got in one with his ~*; *cannon to ~ of them*); *~ wing* of army; (pol., *L~*, orig. of continental legislatures) more radical section of legislative chamber seated on president's *~*, political radicals collectively; advanced or innovating section of philosophical school, religious sect, etc. Hence (colloq.) ~'ISM(3) n., principles or policy of the political *~*, ~'IST(2) n. & a. [ME *lüft, lift, left*; orig. sense ' weak, worthless ' in OE *lyft-ādl* paralysis, also EFris. *luf*, Du. *loof*; sense ' left ' in MDu., LG *luchter, lucht, luft*, NFris. *leeft, leefter*]

left². See LEAVE².

left'-hånd'ed, a. Having left hand more serviceable than right, using it by preference; awkward, clumsy; ambiguous, double-edged, of doubtful sincerity or validity, (esp. *~ compliment*; also occas. of marriage = fictitious, cf. correct sense below); (arch.) ill-omened, sinister; (of marriage) morganatic (from German custom by which bridegroom gave left hand in such marriages); adapted for use of, (of blow) delivered with, left hand. Hence ~LY² adv., ~NESS n. [-ED²]

left'-hånd'er, n. Left-handed person (esp. in games) or blow. [-ER¹]

lěg, n., & v.i. & t. (-gg-). **1.** Organ of support & locomotion in animal, esp. human, body, part of this from hip to ankle, (*all ~s*, overgrown; BOOT² *is on other ~*; *pull one's ~*, colloq., befool him; *give one a ~ up*, help him to mount or get over obstacle material or other; BONE *in* one's *~*; *have the ~s of*, be able to go faster than; *put one's* BEST¹ *~ foremost*; *shake a ~*, dance; *show a ~*, get out of bed; *stretch* one's *~s*, take walking exercise; *take to* one's *~s*, run away; *on* one's *~s*, also joc. *hind ~s*, standing esp. to make speech, also well enough to go about, also in prosperous or established state, esp. *set* one *on his ~s*; *stand on* one's *own ~s*, be self-reliant or independent; FALL¹ *on* one's *~s*; *has not a ~ to stand on*, cannot support thesis by any facts or sound reasons; *on* one's *last ~s*, near death or end; *walk* etc. one *off* his *~s*, tire him out in walking etc.; *feel, find*, one's *~s*, get power of standing or walking; *keep* one's *~s*, not fall; *~ before wicket*, abbr. *l.b.w.*, illegal stopping of cricket ball by batsman's *~*, SEA-*~s*). **2.** *~* of animal as food (*~ of mutton*; *~-of--mutton sail, sleeve*, so shaped). **3.** Obeisance made by drawing back one *~* (usu. *make a ~*; arch.). **4.** ‖ Swindler (for BLACK¹-*~*). **5.** (crick.). Part of field to left rear of batsman in position (*~ stump*, stump nearest this; *long, short, square, ~*, fielders variously posted in it; *hit to ~*, ~). **6.** Artificial *~* (*cork, wooden*, etc., ~). **7.** Part of garment covering *~*. **8.** Support, pole, prop. of machine etc.; support of chair, table, bed, etc.; one branch of forked object; side of triangle other than base. **9.** (naut.). Run made on single tack (usu. *long, short*, ~). **10.** (colloq.). One of two games constituting a round; hop or stage of long-distance flight or journey. **11.** *Give ~-bail*, decamp; ~-BYE; ~-*guard*, pad for ankle, shin, & knee, in cricket; ~-*pull* (colloq.), an attempt to befool a person; ~-*rest*, support for seated invalid's ~; ~ *theory* (cricket), bowling to ~ with fieldsmen massed on that side. Hence (-)~ǥED² (-gd), ~'LESS, aa. **12.** v.*i.* ~ *it*, walk or run hard; (v.t.) propel (boat) through canal-tunnel by pushing with ~s against tunnel-sides, whence ~ǥ'ER¹(-g-)n. [ME, f. ON *leggr*, f.'*lagjaz*]

lěg'acў, n. Sum of money or article given by will; material or immaterial thing handed down by predecessor; ~-*hunter*, person who pays court to another to secure ~. [ME, f. OF *legacie* legateship, f. med. L *legatia* (LEGATE, -ACY)]

lěg'al, a. Of, based on, falling within province of, occupied with, law (~ *aid*, official assistance allowed under certain conditions towards the expense of litigation); required or appointed by law (~ *tender*, money that creditor is bound to accept in payment); *~(bank) holiday*; recognized by law as distinguished from equity; lawful, whence ~IZE(3) v.t., ~IZA'TION n.; (theol.) of the Mosaic law, of salvation by works not faith. Hence ~LY² adv. [f. F, or L *legalis* (*lex legis* law, -AL), cf. LEAL, LOYAL]

lěg'al|ism, n. (Theol.) preference of the Law to the Gospel, doctrine of justification by works; exaltation of law or formula, red tape. So ~IST(2) n. [-ISM]

lěgăl'itў, n. Legalism; lawfulness. [f. F *légalité* or med. L -*itas* (LEGAL, -ITY)]

lěg'ate¹, n. Ecclesiastic deputed to represent Pope (~ ā lāt'ěrĕ, one of highest class & full powers), whence lěg'atINE¹ (-In) a.; (arch.) ambassador, delegate. Hence ~SHIP (-tship)·n. [ME, f. OF *legat* f. L *legatus* p.p. of *legare* commission)]

lěgāt|e'², v.t. Bequeath (often *give & ~e*). So ~OR n. [f. L *legare* (prec.), -ATE³]

lěgatee', n. Recipient of legacy. [prec., -EE]

lěgā'tion, n. Sending of legate or deputy; body of deputies; diplomatic minister & his suite (esp. when he does not rank as ambassador), his official residence; legateship. [ME, f. L *legatio* (LEGATE¹, -ION)]

lěga'tō (-ah-), mus. direction. Smoothly, without breaks. [It., = bound (L *ligare* bind)]

lě'gend, n. Collection of lives of saints or similar stories, esp. *the (Golden) L~*, particular 13th-c. collection (hist.); traditional story popularly regarded as historical, myth, such literature or tradition (so *in* ~), whence ~ARY¹ a.; inscription or motto, esp. on coin or medal; (print.) title on illustration. Hence ~RY(5) n. [ME, f. OF *legende* f. med. L *legenda* what is read (L *legere* read)]

lě'ger. Var. of LEDGER a.

lě'gerdĕmain', n. Sleight of hand, conjuring tricks, juggling; trickery, sophistry. [f. F *léger de main* light of hand]

lěgg'ĭng (-g-), n. (usu. pl.). Outer covering of leather etc. for leg from knee to ankle. [-ING¹]

lěgg'lў (-g-), a. Lanky-legged (esp. of boy, colt, puppy). Hence ~ĭNESS n. [-Y²]

lěghorn' (-gŏrn), n. Kind of straw plaiting for hats etc.; kind of domestic fowl. [imported f. L~ (now *Livorno*) in Italy]

lě'g|ible, a. (Of handwriting or print) clear, capable of being read. Hence ~ĭBIL'ITY n., ~ĭBLY² adv. [f. LL *legibilis* (*legere* read, -IBLE)]

lě'ġion (-jn), n. Division of 3,000–6,000 men, including complement of cavalry, in ancient Roman army; || *British L~*, national association of ex-service men formed 1921 & incorporated 1925 by Royal Charter; *foreign*~, body of foreign volunteers in modern, esp. French, army; vast host, multitude, or number (*their name is L~*, they are numberless, see *Mark* v. 9); *L~ of Honour*, French order of distinction. [ME, f. OF f. L *legionem* nom. -*o* (*legere* choose)]

lě'ġionarў (-jo-), a. & n. (Soldier) of (a) legion(s). [f. L *legionarius* (prec., -ARY¹)]

lě'ġioned (-jond), a. (poet.). In legions. [-ED¹]

lěġĭslā'tion, n. (Enacting of) laws. Hence lě'ġĭslATIVE a., lě'ġĭslātĭvelY² adv. [f. LL *legislatio* (*lex legis* law, *latio* proposing f. *lat-* part. st. of *ferre* bring, -ION)]

lě'ġĭsl|ātor, n. Lawgiver, member of legislative body. Hence ~āte (by back formation) v.i., ~atŏr'IAL a. (rare), ~ātress¹ n. [L (as prec., -OR)]

lě'ġĭslāture, n. Legislative body of a State. [after prec., -URE]

lě'ġĭst, n. Person versed in law. [f. F *légiste* f. med. L *legista* (L *lex legis* law, -IST)]

lěġĭt'ĭm|ate¹, a. Born in lawful wedlock (also said of parent, birth, descent, etc.); lawful, proper, regular, conforming to standard type (*the ~ate drama*, body of plays, Shakespearian or other, of recognized merit, normal comedy & tragedy as dist. from musical comedy, farce, revue, etc., also ellipt., sl., *the ~ate*); (of sovereign's title) based on strict hereditary right; logically admissible. Hence ~ACY n., ~atelY² (-tl-) adv., ~atIZE(3) v.t. [as foll., -ATE²]

lěġĭt'ĭm|āte², v.t. Make legitimate by decree, enactment, or proof; justify, serve as justification for. Hence ~A'TION n. [f. med. L *legitimare* (L *legitimus* lawful f. *lex legis* law), -ATE³]

lěġĭt'ĭm|ism, n. Adherence to sovereign or pretender whose claim is based on direct descent (esp. in Spanish & French politics). So ~IST(2) n. & a. [f. F *légitimisme* (*légitime* f. L see prec., -ISM)]

lěġĭt'ĭmĭz|e, -ĭs|e (-ĭz), v.t. Legitimatize (see LEGITIMATE¹). Hence ~A'TION n. [as LEGITIMATE², -IZE]

lěg'um, n. genit. pl. (*abbr.* LL.). Of laws

(in titles of academic degrees). [L (*lex law*)]

lég′ūme, légūm′en, n. Fruit, edible part, pod, of leguminous plant; vegetable used for food. [F (*légume*), f. L (*-en*) f. *legere* pick]

légūm′inous, a. Of, like, of the botanical family of, pulse. [LEGUMEN *-inis*, -OUS]

lei (lāi′, lā), n. Garland of flowers. [Hawaiian]

Leibnit′zian (līb-), a. & n. (Follower) of G. W. Leibnitz (d. 1716) or his philosophy. [-IAN]

leis′ter (lēs-), n., & v.t. Pronged salmon-spear; (vb) spear with this. [f. ON *lióstr* (*liósta* to strike)]

leisur|e (lĕzh′er), n. (Opportunity *to do, for,* afforded by) free time, time at one's own disposal (*wait* etc. one's ~*e*, wait till he has ~*e; at* ~*e*, not occupied, also deliberately, without hurry; *at* one's ~*e*, when one has time). Hence ~ED² (lezh⁴erd), ~eLESS (-erl-), aa. [ME, f. OF *leisir* n. use of infin. f. L *licēre* be allowed; see -URE]

lei′surel|y (lĕzh′er-), a. & adv. Having, acting or done at, leisure, deliberate; hence ~iNESS n.; (adv.) deliberately, without haste. [-LY¹, ³]

leit-motiv, -if (līt′mōtēf′), n. (mus.). Theme associated throughout piece with some person, situation, or sentiment. [G (LEAD², MOTIVE)]

‖ **lĕm′an,** n. (arch.). Lover, sweetheart; unlawful lover or (usu., in mod. archaistic use) mistress. [ME *leofmon* (LIEF, MAN)]

lĕmm′a, n. (pl. ~*ta*, ~*s*). Assumed or demonstrated proposition used in argument or proof; argument or subject of literary composition, dictionary article, annotation, etc., prefixed as heading; motto appended to picture etc. [L, f. Gk (-ē-) f. root of *lambanō* take]

lĕmm′ing, n. Small arctic rodent resembling vole. [Norw.]

lĕm′on¹, n. Pale-yellow oval acid-juiced fruit used for flavouring & for making the beverage ~ADE(1) (-ād′) n.; SALT *of* ~, an oxalate used in removing ink-stains; tree bearing ~s; pale-yellow colour; (sl.) unattractive girl (cf. PEACH¹); ~*-drop,* sugar-plum flavoured with ~; ~ *kāli,* effervescing drink of tartaric acid, soda bicarbonate, & water; ~*-plant,* ~-scented verbena; ~ *pudding* (flavoured with ~); ‖~ *squash,* drink of ~-juice & soda-water; ~*-squeezer,* instrument for pressing juice out. Hence ~Y² a. [ME, f. OF *limon* f. Oriental source (Arab. *laimun,* Pers. *limun*), cf. LIME²]

lĕm′on², n. (Usu. ~ *dab,* ~ *sole*) kind of plaice resembling sole. [f. F *limande*]

lĕm′ūr, n. Kinds of nocturnal mammal esp. of Madagascar, allied to monkeys but with pointed muzzle. Hence **lĕm′ūr**INE¹ a., **lĕm′ūr**OID-a. & n. [f. L *lemures* pl. spirits of the dead]

lĕnd, v.t. (*lĕnt*). Grant (person) use of (thing) on understanding that it or its equivalent shall be returned; let out (money) at interest, (books etc.; so ~*ing-library*) for hire; bestow, contribute, (something of temporary service or effect, as *enchantment, aid, dignity;* ~ *ear, an ear,* one's *ears,* listen; ~ *a hand* or *helping hand,* help;· arch., ~ person *a box on the ear*); accommodate one*self to* some policy or purpose (thing ~*s itself to,* is serviceable for); *Lend-Lease,* (later form of) LEASE¹-*Lend.* Hence ~′ABLE a., lĕn′dER¹, lĕn′dING¹(1, 4), nn. [ME *lend,* for *len* f. OE *lǣnan* f. (past & p.p.) *lǣn* LOAN; cf. Du. *leenen,* OHG *lēhanōn*]

lĕngth, n. **1.** Thing's measurement from end to end, greatest of body's three dimensions (*know* ~ *of* person's FOOT). **2.** Extent in, of, or with regard to, time (*a stay of some* ~; *the* ~ *of a speech*). **3.** Distance thing extends (*at arm's* ~, as far away as an arm can reach; *keep* one *at arm's* ~, avoid intimacy with him; *ships a cable's* ~ *apart; horse, boat, wins by three* etc. ~*s,* i.e. of itself). **4.** (With *go*) degree of thoroughness in action (*prepared to go all* ~*s, went to great* ~*s, will not go the* ~ *of asserting*). **5.** (pros.). Vowel's or syllable's quantity. **6.** (crick.). Distance from wicket at which ball pitches (*bowler keeps a good* ~; ~ or *good-*~ *ball,* that pitches at right ~). **7.** Long stretch or extent; piece of cloth etc. of certain ~. **8.** *At* ~, in detail or without curtailment (also *at full, great, some,* ~), at last or after a long time; *at full* ~ (see above; also) lying with body fully extended. Hence ~′WAYS (-āz) adv., ~′WISE (-īz) adv. & a. [OE *lengthu* = Du. *lengte,* ON *lengd* f. Gmc **langithō* (LONG, -TH¹)]

lĕng′then, v.t. & i. Make or become longer; (pros.) make (vowel) long. [-EN⁶]

lĕng′th|y, a. (Of speech, writing, style, speaker, etc.) of unusual length, prolix, tedious. Hence ~iLY² adv., ~iNESS n. [-Y²; orig. an Americanism]

lēn′i|ent (-nye-), a. Emollient (arch.); tolerant, gentle, indisposed to severity; (of punishment etc.) mild. Hence ~ENCE, ~ENCY, nn., ~entLY² adv., (-nye-). [f. L *lenire* soothe (*lenis* gentle), -ENT]

Lĕn′in|ism, n. Policy & economic principles of Lenin (assumed name of V. I. Ulianov (d. 1924), leader of the Russian Revolution of 1917). So ~IST n. & a., ~ITE¹ n. & a. [-ISM]

lēn′itive, a. & n. Soothing (drug, appliance), palliative. [f. med. L *lenitivus* LENIENT, -IVE)]

lĕn′ity, n. Mercifulness; mercy shown. f. L *lenitas* (*lenis* gentle, -TY)]

lĕns (-z), n. (pl. ~*es*). Piece of glass or other transparent surface with both sides (or one only) curved for concentrating or dispersing light-rays; combination of ~es in photography; (anat.) = CRYSTALLINE ~, one facet of compound eye. Hence ~ED² (-zd), ~′LESS (-z-), aa. [L *lens lentis* lentil]

Lent[1], n. Period from Ash Wednesday to Easter Eve of which the 40 week-days are devoted to fasting & penitence in commemoration of Christ in the wilderness; ‖ (pl., at Cambridge) ~-term boat--races; ‖ ~ *lily*, daffodil; ‖~ *term*, university term in which ~ falls (called HILARY in some univv.). [f. LENTEN]

lent[2]. See LEND.

-lent, suf. in adjj. f. L-*lentus*, approx. = -FUL; the L suf. is normally preceded by -*u*- (*turbulentus*); but *pestilentus, violentus.*

Len'ten, l-, a. Of, in, or appropriate to, Lent (~ *fare*, without meat; ~ *face*, dismal look). [prop. n., of which the attrib. use is now regarded as adj. = LENT[1] + -EN[5]; orig. sense *spring*, now obs. in E, but the only sense in cogn. Gmc wds; OE *lencten*, = MDu, *lentin*, OHG *lengizin, lenzin*, f. WG *lang*- LONG, perh. w. ref. to lengthening of day in spring]

lentic'ular, a. Shaped like lentil or lens, double-convex; of the lens of the eye. [f. LL *lenticularis* (foll., -AR[1])]

len'til, n. (Double-convex seed of) leguminous plant grown for food. [F (-*lle*), f. Rom. *lenticula* f. L -*icula* (LENS, -CULE)]

len'tisk, n. The mastic tree. [f. L *lentiscus*]

len'titude, n. Sluggishness. [f. L *lentitudo* (*lentus* slow, -TUDE)]

len'tŏ, mus. direction. Slow(ly). [It.]

len'toid, a. Lens-shaped. [LENS, -OID]

Lē'ŏ, n. Zodiacal constellation the Lion; fifth sign of the zodiac. [L, = LION]

Lē'onid, n. One of the meteors that seem to radiate from Leo. [f. L *leo -onis*, -ID[3]]

le'onine[1], a. Lionlike, of lions. [ME, f. OF *leonin* or L *leoninus* (prec., -INE[1])]

Lē'onine[2], a. & n. Of, made or invented by, person (esp. one of the Popes) called Leo; ~ *City*, part of Rome round Vatican fortified by Leo IV; ~ *verse*, line (also ~ as n.) or lines of medieval Latin verse in hexameter or elegiac metre with internal rhyme (e.g. *Daemon languebat, monachus tunc esse volebat*). [as prec.; inventor of ~ verse unknown]

leo'pard (lĕp-), n. Large African & S.--Asian carnivorous quadruped with dark--spotted yellowish-fawn coat, panther, (*black* ~, black-coated kind; *American* ~, jaguar; *hunting* ~, cheetah; *snow* ~, ounce; *can the* ~ *change his spots?*, character persists; (her.) lion passant guardant as in arms of England; (in names of animals etc.) ~-, spotted like ~; ~'s *bane*, kinds of composite plant of thistle family. Hence ~ESS[1] n. [ME, f. OF f. LL f. late Gk *leopardos* (LION, PARD)]

le'otard, n. Short close-fitting garment worn with tights by acrobats, ballet--dancers, etc. [J. *Léotard*, 19th-c. French trapeze performer]

Lĕp'cha, n. One of a race of people inhabiting Sikkim & parts of Tibet.

lĕp'er, n. Person with leprosy. [14th c. attrib. use of ME *leper* leprosy f. OF *lepre*

f. L f. Gk *lepra* fem. of *lepros* scaly (*lepos* scale)]

lĕpidŏp'ter|ous, a. Of the *Lepidoptera*, order of insects with four membranous scale-covered wings including butterflies & moths. So ~IST(3) n. [f. Gk *lepis -idos* scale, *pteron* wing, -OUS]

lĕp'orine, a. Of the hare kind. [f. L *leporinus* (*lepus -oris* hare, -INE[1])]

lĕprechaun' (-χ-; see Ap.), n. (Irish). Sprite. [f. OIr. *luchorpán* (*lu* small, *corp* body)]

lĕp'rosy̆, n. Chronic infectious disease affecting skin and nerves, resulting in mutilations and deformities; (arch.) any loathsome disease; (fig.) moral corruption or contagion. [foll., -Y[1]]

lĕp'rous, a. Having, like, (as) of, leprosy. [ME, f. OF, f. LL *leprosus* (*lepra* see LEPER, -OSE[1])]

lĕpto-, comb. form of Gk *leptos* fine, small, thin, delicate, in zool. & bot. terms, as ~*cephăl'ic* narrow-skulled, ~*dac'tyl* n. & a., (bird) with long slender toes.

Lĕs'bian (-z-), a. & n. Of Lesbos (~ *vice*, SAPPHISM); (n.) female homosexual. Hence ~ISM n. [L f. Gk *Lesbios* (*Lesbos*), -AN]

lèse-majesté (lāz măzh'ĕstă), n. = foll. (in frequent use about foreign States, & joc. of presumptuous conduct on the part of inferiors etc.). [F]

lese-măj'ĕstў (lēz-), n. (civil law). Treason. [f. F *lèse-majesté* f. L *laesa majestas* injured majesty (of the sovereign people)]

lē'sion (-zhn), n. Damage, injury, esp. (path.) morbid change in functioning or texture of organs. [f. OF f. L *laesionem* nom. -o (*laedere laes-* injure, -ION)]

lĕss, a., prep., n., & adv. **1.** adj. (Of abstracts expressing measurement, as *size, degree, duration, number*) smaller (opp. *greater*; *in a* ~ *degree, of* ~ *magnitude* or *importance*); of smaller quantity, not so much, not so much of, (opp. *more*; *find* ~ *difficulty*; *eat* ~ *meat*; *of two evils choose the* ~; *may your shadow never be* ~, may you not grow thin); of lower rank etc. (rare; *no* ~ *a person than*; *James, Ajax, the L*~). **2.** prep. Minus, deducting, (*a year* ~ *three days*). **3.** n. Smaller amount, quantity, or number (*cannot take* ~; *in* ~ *than no time*, joc., very quickly or soon; (colloq.) ~ *of your lip!*; often *far, little, much, nothing, something,* ~; *expected nothing* ~ *than an attack*, expected an attack & nothing ~ *than an attack*, but see under the adv.). **4.** adv. To smaller extent, in lower degree, (often *none the, no, not the,* ~; ~ *known* etc. or ~-*known* etc.; *do not suspect him of equivocation, still* ~ or *much* ~ *of lying*; *nothing* ~, anything rather; *expected nothing* ~ *than an attack*, did not expect attack at all, but see the now usu. sense under n.). [OE. *lǣs* adv. = OFris. *lēs* f. Gmc **laisiz* f. **laisa*-; OE *lǣssa* adj. = OFris. *lēssa* f. Gmc **laisizon*-]

-less, suf. f. OE *lēas* (used both as separate adj. in sense *free from, devoid of*, & as suf.) forming adjj. (*guileless, homeless*) & advv. (*doubtless*) f. nn. On anal. of compds in which the component n. was of same form as the corr. vb (*countless, dauntless, numberless*) & the sense was *unable, -less* has been appended to vbs (*resistless, describeless, tireless*).

lĕssee', n. Holder of, tenant (*of* house, theatre, etc.) under, lease. Hence ~SHIP n. [AF, = OF *laissee* (LEASE[1], -EE)]

lĕss'en, v.i. & t. Decrease, diminish. [-EN[6]]

lĕss'er, a. (attrib. only). Not so great as the other or the rest, minor, (*the L~ Bear; the ~ evils of life*). [double comparat.; LESS + -ER[3]]

lĕss'on, n., & v.t. 1. One of two readings from O.T. (*first ~*) & N.T. (*second ~*) at morning & evening prayer (PROPER ~); thing to be learnt by pupil; amount of teaching given at one time, time assigned to it, (pl.) systematic instruction *in* subject (*give, take, ~s in*); occurrence, example, rebuke, or punishment, that serves as encouragement or warning. 2. v.t. Admonish, rebuke, discipline. [ME, f. OF *lecon* f. L *lectionem* (*legere lect-* read, -ION)]

lĕss'ŏr, n. Person who lets on lease. [AF (LEASE[1], -OR)]

lĕst, conj. In order that — not, for fear that; (after *fear* vb or n., & similar words) that. [OE *thȳ lǣs the* whereby less; *thȳ* was dropped in ME, & *les the* became *leste* by normal change]

lĕt,[1] v.t. (arch.; *letted* or *let*), & n. 1. Hinder, obstruct. 2. n. Stoppage, hindrance, (arch.); (rackets, lawn tennis, etc.) obstruction of ball or player in certain ways, requiring round to be played again. [OE *lettan*, OS *-ian*, OHG *lezzan*, ON *letja*, Goth. *latjan* hinder f. Gmc *lata-* LATE]

lĕt[2], v.t. & aux. (*let*), & n. 1. v.t. Allow or cause (liquid, air) to escape (~ BLOOD); grant use of for rent or hire (also intr. in pass. sense, as *the rooms ~ well; to ~*, offered for rent; || n., ~ting, as *cannot get a ~ for the rooms*); allow to, suffer to, (*we ~ them go; I was ~ see him*; pass. now rare, & occas. followed by *to*); cause to (only in ~ one *know* etc., inform him). 2. ~ *alone*, not interfere with, attend to, or do (~ WELL[3] *alone*; ~ one *alone to* do, he may be trusted to; ~ *alone* imperat., not to mention, far less or more); ~ *be*, not interfere with, attend to, or do; ~ *down*, lower, fail (friend) at need, disappoint (~ *him down gently*, avoid humiliating abruptly), (n., ~-*down*) disappointment; ~ DRIVE[1]; ~ *fall*, drop (lit., & fig. hint, significant word) intentionally or by accident, (geom.) draw (perpendicular) from outside point (*up*)*on* line; ~ FLY[2]; ~ *go*, release, set at liberty, lose hold of, lose or relinquish hold *of*, dismiss from

thought, cease to restrain (~ one*self go*, give way to enthusiasm, impulse, etc.); ~ *in*, admit or open door to (~ *in a flood of light; this would ~ in all sorts of evils*; ~ one*self in*, with latchkey etc.), insert into surface of something, involve in loss or difficulty (often *for*); ~ (trans.) *into*, admit to, insert into surface of, make acquainted with (secret etc.); ~ (intr. or abs.) *into*, assail with blows or words; ~ *loose*, release or unchain (dog, fury, maniac, etc.); ~ *off* adv., discharge (gun, & fig. joke etc.), not punish or compel, punish *with* light penalty, allow or cause (fluid, steam, etc.) to pass away, (n., ~-*off*) being allowed to escape something (esp. in cricket, not being caught etc. when there is a chance); ~ *off* prep., excuse (person penalty); ~ *on*, sl., peach, reveal secret, betray fact; ~ (trans.) *out*, open door for exit to, exculpate, allow (person etc., secret) to escape (~ *the cat out of the* BAG[1]), make (garment) looser, put out to hire esp. to several tenants, divulge (often *that*); ~ (intr. or abs.) *out*, strike out with fist, lash out with heels, use strong language; ~ *slip*, loose from leash, miss (opportunity); ~ *up* (colloq.), become less severe, diminish; ~-*up* n., cessation, diminution. 3. v. aux. supplying 1st & 3rd persons of imperat. in exhortations (~ *us pray*; ~ *you & me try now*), commands (~ *it be done*, ~ *him do it, at once*), assumptions (~ *AB be equal to CD*), & permissions (~ *him do his worst*). [OE *lǣtan*, OS *lātan*, OHG *lāzan*, ON *lāta*, Goth. *lētan* f. Gmc *lǣt-* rel. to *lat-* LATE]

-let, suf. forming nn. usu. dim. (*ringlet, streamlet*), but occas. denoting articles of attire or ornament (*armlet, frontlet*); *-let* appears to come f. wrong division of wds taken f. OF diminutives in which *-el(e)* (see -ET[1]) is added to nn. in *-el* (f. L *-ellus, -ella, -ellum*, dim. suff., or L *-ale* neut. adj. used as n.), as *chaplet, hamlet*, f. OF *chapelet, hamelet*, dimm. of *chapel, hamel*, mod. F *chapeau, hameau*.

lēth'al, a. Causing, sufficient or designed to cause, death (~ *chamber*, for killing animals painlessly). Hence **lēthăl'ITY** n. [f. L *let(h)alis* (*letum* death, -AL)]

lĕth'arg||**ȳ**, n. Morbid drowsiness, prolonged & unnatural sleep; torpid, inert, or apathetic state, want of interest & energy. So **lĕthăr'gic** a., **lĕthăr'gically** adv., **~IZE**(3) v.t. [f. LL f. Gk *lēthargia* (*lēthargos* forgetful f. *lēth-, lanthanō* forget), -Y[1]]

Lēth'ē, n. (River in Hades producing) forgetfulness of the past. So **Lēthē'AN** a. [L, use of Gk *lēthē* forgetfulness, see prec.]

Lĕtt, n. Member of a people living about the Baltic; = LETTISH n. [see LETTISH]

lĕtt'er, n., & v.t. 1. Character representing one or more of the simple or compound sounds used in speech, one of the alphabetic symbols, (*capital ~, of the* large form A, B, etc., opp. *small*, a, b, etc. ; ROMAN, ITALIC, ~); (print. type,) fount of type (now chiefly in *return of* ~ for DIS-TRIBUTION; (pl.) ~ing, inscription, (now only in PROOF[1] *before* ~s). **2.** Missive, epistle, (~ *of advice*, notifying dispatch of goods, drawing of bill, etc. ; ~ *of attorney*, = POWER *of attorney*); (pl.) epistle of legal or formal kind for various purposes (~s PATENT, *of* ADMINISTRATION, etc. ; ‖ ~s *of business*, royal authority to Convocation to deal with a matter). **3.** Precise terms of statement (*to the* ~, with adherence to every detail), strict verbal interpretation (opp. SPIRIT; esp. *in* ~ *& in spirit*, in form & substance). **4.** pl. Literature, acquaintance with books, erudition, (*man of* ~s, scholar, author; *commonwealth* or *republic of* ~s, authors as a body; *the profession of* ~s, authorship), whence ~ED[2] (-erd) n. **5.** ~*-balance*, for ascertaining postage of ~s; ~*-book*, in which copies of correspondence are kept; ‖ ~*-box*, into which ~s are delivered; ‖ ~*-card*, folded card with gummed edge for use as postal missive; ~*-case*, pocket-book for holding ~s; ~*-lock*, kind of padlock opened by making out of certain ~s on it a word known to owner; ~*-paper*, paper for ~s; ~*-perfect* (theatr.), knowing one's part perfectly; ~*press*, contents of illustrated book other than the illustrations, printed matter relating to illustration; ~*-weight*, = ~*-balance*, occas. = paper-weight; ~*-worship*, undue devotion to the ~; ~*-writer*, lit., also as title for manuals of ~*-writing*; hence ~LESS a. **6.** v.t. Impress title etc. on (book-cover); classify with ~s of the alphabet. Hence ~ING[1](1, 6) n. [ME, f. OF *lettre* f. L *littera* ~ of alphabet, (pl.) epistle]

Lĕtt′ic, a. & n. = foll.; (of) the group of languages comprising Lettish, Lithuanian, & Old Prussian; of these peoples. [as foll., -IC]

Lĕtt′ish, a. & n. (Language) of the Letts. [*Lett* f. G *Lette* f. native *Latvi* + -ISH[1]]

lĕtt′uce (-tǐs), n. Garden herb with crisp leaves much used as salad (*cabbage*, COS, ~, kinds of it). [ME *letuse*, rel. to OF *laitue* (f. L *lactuca*) poss. thr. a var. **letuse* f. Rom. **lactucea*, **lattucea*]

leuc′o-, comb. form of Gk *leukos* white, as ~*cyte*, colourless corpuscle of blood or found in lymph etc.; ~*pathy* (-ŏp[2]-), albinism; ~*rrhoe′a*, mucous discharge from female genitals, the whites; ~*tomy* (-ŏt[2]-), incision by kind of needle (~*tome*) into frontal lobe of brain to relieve some cases of mental disorder.

leukaem′ia, n. (med.). Disease in which there is an excess of white corpuscles in the blood. [f. Gk *leukos* white, *haima* blood; see -IA[1]]

lĕv, n. (pl. ~*a*). Bulgarian monetary unit. [Bulg., = lion]

Lèvănt′[1], n. Eastern part of Mediterranean with its islands & neighbouring

countries; ~ MOROCCO. [F, part. of *lever* rise, used as n. = east, f. L *levare* lift]

‖ **lèvănt′**[2], v.i. Abscond, bolt, esp. with betting or gaming losses unpaid. Hence **lèvăn′ter**[1] [-ER[1]] n. [perh. f. Sp. *levantar el campo* break up camp (*levar* f. L *levare* lift)]

lèvăn′ter[2], n. (*L*~) inhabitant of Levant; strong Mediterranean easterly wind. [LEVANT[1], -ER[1]]

Lèvăn′tine (or lĕv′an-), a. & n. Of, trading to, inhabitant of, the Levant. [-INE[1]]

lèvāt′or, n. (Also ~*-muscle*) muscle that raises structure or organ. [mod. L, agent- n. f. L *levare* raise]

lĕv′ee (-vǐ), n. (Formerly) reception of visitors on rising from bed; assembly held by sovereign or his representative at which men only are received; assembly of visitors. [f. F *levé* var. of *lever*, see LEVY, -EE]

levee[2] (lǐvē′, lĕv′ǐ), n. Embankment against river floods. [f. F *levée* fem. p.p. of *lever* [L *levare* raise)]

lĕv′el, n., a., & v.t. (-ll-). **1.** Instrument giving line parallel to plane of horizon for testing whether things are horizontal; horizontal line or plane (*on a* ~ *with*, in same horizontal plane as; *find* one's ~, reach right place with regard to others; *water finds its* ~, its surface in communicating receptacles will be at same ~ unless they have no common ~); plane or standard in social, moral, or intellectual matters; more or less ~ surface; flat country; *on the* ~ (colloq.), truthful(ly), honest(ly). **2.** adj. Horizontal, perpendicular to the plumb-line; on a ~ or equality (*with*, or abs.; ~ *race*, in which leading competitors are close together; ‖ ~ CROSSING); even, equable, uniform, well-balanced, in quality, style, temper, judgement, etc. (~*-headed*; *do* one's ~ *best*, not be remiss, take all possible pains); hence ~LY[2] adv. (rare), ~NESS n. **3.** v.t. Make ~, even, or uniform; place on same ~, bring *up* or *down* to a standard; raze, lay low, (*to* or *with the ground*, *in the dust*, or abs.); (rarely) knock (person) down; abolish (distinctions); aim (missile, or abs.), lay (gun), direct (satire, accusation, or abs.), (*at* or *against*); ~*ling*-*screw*, for adjusting parts of machine etc. to exact ~. [ME, f. OF *livel* (mod. *niveau*) f. Rom. **libellum* f. L *libella* dim. of *libra* balance]

lĕv′eller, n. In vbl senses; esp., person who would abolish social distinctions, advocate of equality. [-ER[1]]

lĕv′er, n., & v.i. & t. **1.** Bar used to prize up heavy or fixed object; (mech.) straight bar or other rigid structure of which one point (*fulcrum*) is fixed, another is connected with the force (*weight*) to be resisted or acted upon, & a third is connected with the force (*power*) applied (~ *of first order* with fulcrum, *of second order* with weight, *of third order* with power, between the other two); piece by which barrel of breechloader is opened; = ~ watch; ~-, acting as or worked by ~; ~ escapement, with connexion between pallet & balance made by two ~s; ~ watch, with ~ escapement. **2.** vb. Use ~; lift, move, act on, with ~ (often *along, away, out, over, up*, etc.). [ME, f. OF *leveour* f. lever (L *levare*), see -OR]

lĕv'erage, n. Action of, way of applying, lever; set or system of levers; power, mechanical advantage gained by use of lever; means of accomplishing a purpose, power, influence. [-AGE]

lĕv'erĕt, n. Young (esp. first-year) hare. [f. AF *leveret* (= OF *levreteau*), dim. of OF *lievre* f. L *leporem* nom. *-us* hare, -ET[1]]

lévī'athan, n. Sea monster (bibl.); huge ship; anything very large of its kind; person of formidable ability, power, or wealth; (in allusion to Hobbes) auto-cratic monarch or state. [LL, l. Heb. *livyathan*]

lĕv'igāte, v.t. Reduce to fine smooth powder; make smooth paste of. Hence ~A'TION n. [f. L *levigare* (*lēvis* smooth), -ATE[3]]

lĕv'in, n. (poet.). (Flash of) lightning. [ME *leven(e)*, of unkn. orig.]

lĕv'ir|āte, n. Jewish etc. custom by which dead man's brother or next of kin had to marry his widow. Hence ~ăt'IC(AL) aa. [f. LL *levir* brother-in-law + -ATE[1]]

lĕv'it|āte, v.i. & t. (Make) rise & float in air (w. ref. to spiritualism). Hence ~A'-TION n. [f. L *lĕvis* light, after GRAVITATION]

Lēv'ite, n. One of tribe of Levi, esp. of that part of it which provided assistants to priests in worship of Jewish temple. [ME, f. LL f. Gk *leuitēs* (Leui f. Heb. Levi)]

Lēvit'ic|al, a. Of Levites or the tribe of Levi; of Levites' ritual; of Leviticus. So ~ISM(3) n. [f. LL f. Gk *leuitikos* (prec., -IC) + -AL]

Lēvit'icus, n. (abb. *Lev.*). Third book of Pentateuch with Levitical law & ritual. [prec.]

lĕv'itȳ, n. Lightness of weight (rare); want of thought, frivolity, unseasonable jocularity, inconstancy; light behaviour. [f. F *levité* or L *levitas* (*lēvis* light, -TY)]

levulose. See LAEVULOSE.

lĕv'ȳ, n., & v.t. **1.** Collecting of assess-ment, tax, etc. (*capital* ~, appropriation by the State of a fixed proportion of all or some of the wealth in the country); enrolling of men for war etc. (~ *in mass*, of all able-bodied men); amount or num-ber levied, body of men enrolled (also pl.). **2.** v.t. Raise (contribution, taxes), impose (rate, toll), whence lĕv'IABLE a.; raise (sum) by legal execution or process on person's goods; extort (~ *blackmail*); enlist, enrol, (soldiers, army); collect men & munitions for, proceed to make, (war; usu. *upon, against*). [ME, f. OF *levee* (*lever* f. L *levare* raise), see -Y[4]]

lewd, a. Base, worthless, (bibl.); lascivi-ous, unchaste, indecent, whence ~'LY[2] adv., ~'NESS n. [OE *lǣwede* lay, not clerical; orig. unkn.]

lew'is (lōō-), n. Iron contrivance for gripping heavy blocks of stone for lifting; son of a freemason. [orig. unkn.]

Lew'is gŭn (lōō-), n. Kind of light machine-gun. [I. N. *Lewis*, inventor]

lew'isite (lōō-), n. A blister gas used in chemical warfare. [W. L. *Lewis*, -ITE[1](2)]

lĕx'ical, a. Of the words of a language (opp. *grammatical*); (as) of a lexicon. Hence ~LY[2] adv. [f. Gk *lexikos*, & LEXI-CON, + -AL]

lĕxĭcŏg'raphȳ, n. Dictionary-making. So lĕxĭcŏg'RAPHER n., lĕxĭcoGRAPH'ICAL a. [foll., -GRAPHY]

lĕx'icon, n. Dictionary, esp. of Greek, Hebrew, Syriac, or Arabic. [Gk·(-*kon*), neut. of *lexikos* (*lexis* word f. *legō* speak, -IC)]

lĕxig'raphȳ, n. System of writing in which each character represents a word. [*lexis*, see prec., -GRAPHY]

lĕx tălïōn'ĭs, n. The law of retaliation, an eye for an eye. [L]

ley (lā), n. Land temporarily under grass. [var. of LEA[1]]

Ley'den (lī-), n. Dutch city (~ *jar*, kind of electrical condenser invented 1745 at ~; ~ *battery*, of several ~ jars).

li (lē), n. Chinese mile (about 633 yds); Chinese weight (about ⅓ gr.). [Chin.]

liabĭl'itȳ, n. Being liable ‖ (*limited* ~, being responsible only to limited amount for debts of trading company; so *limited--~ company*, or ellipt. *limited company*); what one is liable for, (pl.) debts or pecu-niary obligations. [foll. -BILITY]

lī'able, a. Legally bound, answerable *for*, subject or amenable *to* tax or penalty, under obligation *to* do; exposed or open *to*, apt *to* do or suffer, something undesir-able (*difficulties are* ~ *to occur*). [of obsc. orig.; conjectured to be AF *liable* that may be bound, f. *lier* f. L *ligare* bind]

liais'on (-zn), n. **1.** Illicit intimacy be-tween a man & a woman. **2.** Sounding of ordinarily silent final consonant before vowel or mute *h* in French. **3.** (mil. etc.). Connexion, touch, (~ *officer*, acting as go--between for allied forces or units of the same force). So **liaise'** (-āz) v.i., estab-lish or maintain ~ *with*. [F, f. *lier* (L *ligare* bind, -ATION)]

lia'na (-ah-), **liane'** (-ahn), n. Kinds of climbing & twining tropical-forest plant. [f. F *liane*, of obsc. orig.]

li'ar, n. Teller (esp. habitual) of lie(s). [OE *lēogere* (LIE[2], -AR[3])]

li'as, n. Blue limestone rock of some S.-W. counties; (geol.) lower strata of Jurassic series, blue argillaceous lime-stone rich in fossils. Hence **liăss'IC** a. [c. 1400, f. OF *liois* (mod. *liais*)]

libā'tion, n. (Pouring of) drink-offering

to god; (joc.) potation. [f. L *libatio* (*libare* pour a little of, -ATION)]

lib'el, n., & v.t. (-ll-). **1.** (Civil & eccl. law) plaintiff's written declaration; (law) published statement damaging to person's reputation, act of publishing it (*the greater the truth, the greater the ~*); (pop.) false & defamatory statement, (transf.) thing that brings discredit *on* by unsuccessful portrayal etc. (*the portrait is a ~ on him*; *the book, play, is a ~ on human nature*); hence ~LIST(1) n., ~LOUS a., ~LOUSLY² adv. **2.** v.t. Defame by ~lous statements, accuse falsely & maliciously, (law) publish ~ against, whence ~IER¹ n.; (eccl. & Admiralty law) bring suit against, whence ~IANT(1), ~IEE', nn. [ME, f. OF, or L *libellus* dim. of *liber* book]

lib'eral, a. & n. **1.** Fit for a gentleman (now rare exc. in ~ *education*, i.e. directed to general enlargement of mind, not professional or technical); *~ arts (dist. from science & technology); generous, open-handed, not sparing of; ample, abundant;not rigorous or literal;open-minded, candid, unprejudiced; (pol.) favourable to democratic reforms & abolition of privilege (esp. *L~ party*; cf. CONSERVATIVE; *L~ Conservative*, member of Conservative party not ill disposed to reforms; *L~ Unionist*, member of section that seceded from L~ party in 1886 on Home Rule), whence ~ISM(3) n., ~IST(2) n. & a., ~ĭs'tIC a., ~IZE(3) v.t. & (rarely) i., ~IZA'TION n.; hence ~LY² adv. **2.** n. (*L~*) member of (esp. the British) L~ party. [ME, f. OF f. L *liberalis* (*liber* free (man), -AL)]

liberăl'itỹ, n. Free giving, munificence; freedom from prejudice, breadth of mind. [ME, f. OF *liberalite* f. L *liberalitatem* (prec., -TY)]

lib'erăt|e, v.t. Set at liberty, release *from* (in chem., from combination). Hence ~OR n. [f. L *liberare* (*liber* free), -ATE³]

libera'tion, n. Releasing, release; ∥ *L~ Society*, advocating church disestablishment, whence ~ISM(3) n., ~IST(2) n. & a., (-sho-). [ME, f. OF, or L *liberatio* (prec., -ATION)]

libertar'ĭan, n. & a. Believer, believing, in free will (opp. *necessitarian*); advocate of liberty. Hence ~ISM(3) n. [-ARIAN]

libert'ĭcide, n. & a. Destroyer, destructive, of liberty. [F (LIBERTY, -CIDE)]

lib'ertĭn|e, n. & a. Free-thinker on religion; licentious (man); free-thinking, antinomian; *chartered ~e*, person allowed to do as he pleases (Shak. *Hen. V*, I. i. 48). Hence ~ISM(2) & (in same sense) ~AGE, nn. [f. L *libertinus* freedman (*libertus* made free, cogn. w. *liber* free)]

lib'ertỹ, n. **1.** Being free from captivity, imprisonment, slavery, or despotic control (CAP¹ of ~; *natural ~*, state in which there are no laws; *civil ~*, natural ~ limited only by laws established on behalf of community; ~ *of conscience*,

system allowing all members of State to follow what form of religion seems good to them; ~ *of the press*, system by which anyone may print & publish what he pleases without previous permission, but not without liability to penalties for publishing libellous or criminal matter). **2.** Right or power to do as one pleases or *to* do something; (philos.) freedom from control of fate or necessity. **3.** A setting aside of rules, licence, (*take the ~ to do*, *of doing*, presume or venture to; *take liberties*, be unduly familiar *with* person or abs., deal freely *with* rules or facts). **4.** Freedom from despotic rule personified. **5.** pl. Privileges, immunities, or rights, enjoyed by prescription or grant. **6.** *At ~*, free (*set at ~*, liberate), having the right *to* do, disengaged; ~ HALL; ~ *man*, sailor with leave to go ashore. [ME, f. OF *liberte* f. L *libertatem* (*liber* free, -TY¹)]

libĭd'inous, a. Lustful. Hence ~LY² adv. [ME, f. L *libidinosus* (*libīdo -inis* lust, -OUS)]

libĭd'ō, n. (psych.). Emotional craving prompting any specific human (esp. sexual) activity. [L, = lust]

lib'ra, n. (pl. -ae). **1.** Pound weight (used only in abbr. *lb*., as 1 lb., 10 lb.); pound sterling (used only in abbr. *£. s. d.*, or *l.* placed after figure as 50*l.*). **2.** (astron.; *L~*) zodiacal constellation the Scales, seventh sign of zodiac. [L]

librar'ĭan, n. Custodian of library. Hence ~SHIP(1) n. [f. L as foll. + -AN]

lib'rarỹ, n. Room or building containing books for reading or reference; room in large house devoted to books; collection of books for use by the public, some part of it, or members of some society, public institution charged with care of such collection, (*lending ~*, from which books may be taken away with or without payment; *reference ~*, in which books may be consulted; *free ~*, *public ~*, used by public without payment & usu. supported by rates; *circulating ~*, letting out use of books for profit); person's book-collection; series of books issued by publisher in similar bindings as connected in some way; *walking ~*, person of erudition; ~ *edition*, of good size & print. [ME, f. OF *librairie* f. *libraire* f. L *librarius*, -*a* (a. & n.) f. *liber* book; see -ARY¹, -Y¹]

librāte', v.i. Oscillate, be poised, balance, sway, quiver. Hence **lib'ratory** a. [f. L *librare* (*libra* balance), -ATE³]

librā'tion, n. Librating (~ *of moon*, apparent oscillation by which parts near edge of disc are alternately visible & invisible). [f. L *libratio* (prec., -ATION)]

librĕtt'|ō, n. (pl. -*ti*, pr. -tē). Book or words of an opera or long musical work. Hence ~IST(1) n. [It., dim. of *libro* book f. L *liber -bri*]

Lib'ỹan, a. & n. (Inhabitant) of ancient Libya; (poet.) N. African; (of) the Berber language or the group of mod. Hamitic languages to which it belongs. [f. L f. Gk *Libuē*+-AN]

lice. See LOUSE.

li'cence¹, n. **1.** Leave, permission, *(have I your ~ to remove the fence?)*; permit from government etc. to marry, print something, preach, carry on some trade (esp. that in alcoholic liquor), etc. **2.** University certificate of competence in some faculty. **3.** Liberty of action esp. when excessive, abuse of freedom, disregard of law or propriety; licentiousness. **4.** Writer's or artist's irregularity in grammar, metre, perspective, etc. (usu. *poetic ~*). [ME, f. OF, f. L *licentia (licēre* be lawful, -ENCE)]

li'cense, -ce², v.t. Allow (person *to* do, thing to be done; rare); (in p.p.) allow complete freedom to (*a~d satirist*); grant permit (see prec.) to (person; ǁ*~d* VICTU-ALLER); authorize use of (premises) for certain purpose; authorize publication of (book etc.) or performance of (play). Hence **licenSEE'** n. [ME, f. prec.; *-se* on anal. of *practise, prophesy,* vv., cf. *practice, prophecy,* nn.; the distinction perh. comes by imit. of spelling in pairs like *advise, advice,* where the sound differs]

li'censer, n. In vbl senses; esp. *~ of the press* (hist.), *~ of plays,* officials licensing publication or performance when satisfied that law, morals, & decency are not outraged. [-ER¹]

licēn'tiate (-shǐat), n. Holder of university licence or attestation of competence from collegiate or examining body (chiefly in abbr. L. as part of title); licensed preacher not yet having appointment esp. in Presbyterian Church. [f. med. L *licentiare* (LICENCE¹), -ATE²]

licēn'tious (-shŭs), a. Disregarding accepted rules esp. of grammar or style (rare); lascivious, libertine, lewd. Hence ~LY² adv., ~NESS n. [f. L *licentiosus* (LICENCE¹, -OSE¹)]

lich, lych, lyke, n. (obs.). ǁ Corpse; *-ch-gate,* roofed gateway of churchyard where coffin awaits clergyman's arrival; *-ch-house,* mortuary; ǁ *-ch-owl,* screech-owl (boding death); *-ch-stone,* to place coffin on at *~-gate;* ǁ *lyke-wake,* watch kept at night over corpse. [OE, OS *lik,* OHG *lih,* ON *lik,* Goth. *leik* f. Gmc **likam* body; cf. LIKE]

li'chen (-k-), n. Kinds of cellular cryptogamic plant (prob. fungus parasitic on alga) usu. of green, grey, or yellow tint growing on & colouring rocks, tree-trunks, roofs, walls, etc., whence ~ED² (-kend) a., ~ŏL'OGY n.; skin-disease with reddish eruption. Hence ~OUS a. [f. L f. Gk *leikhēn*]

li'cit, a. Not illicit. Hence ~LY² adv. [f. L *licitus (licēre* be lawful)]

lick, v.t. & i., & n. **1.** Pass tongue over to taste, moisten, clean, etc. (*~ one's chops*

or *lips,* in relish or anticipation of food; *~ into shape,* mould, make presentable or efficient; *~ one's shoes,* show servility to him; *~ the dust,* fall, be vanquished); take *up* or *off,* make *clean,* by *~*ing; (of waves, flame, etc.) play lightly over, (of flame) swallow *up* in passing; (sl.) thrash (person, fault *out of* person), beat in fight or competition, excel, (*~s creation,* is beyond everything), whence *~'*ING¹(1) n.; (sl.) surpass comprehension of (*this ~s me*); (sl.) go, hasten, (*as hard as he could ~*); *~'spittle,* toady. **2.** n. Act of *~*ing with tongue; (also *salt-~*) spot to which animals resort for salt; smart blow with stick etc.; (sl.) pace (*at a great ~; full* or *at full ~*). [OE *liccian,* OS *liccōn,* OHG *leckōn* f. WG **likkōn*]

lick'erish, li'quorish (-ker-), a. Fond of dainty fare; greedy, longing; lecherous [alt. f. ME *lickerous* f. AF var. of OF *lecheros;* see LECHER]

licorice. See LIQUORICE.

licorŏus. Var. of *lickerous,* LICKERISH.

lic'tor, n. Officer attending ancient--Roman consul (12 *~*s) & dictator (24 *~*s), bearing fasces, & executing sentence on offenders. [L, perh. f. st. of *ligare* bind]

lid, n. Hinged or detached cover for aperture, esp. for opening at top of vessel; *with the ~ off,* with all horrors etc. exposed to view; ǁ *put the ~ on* (sl.), be the culmination (of), surpass all; = EYE¹-*lid;* (bot., conch.) operculum. Hence (-)~d'ED², ~'LESS, aa. [OE *hlid,* OHG *hlit* (G *lid*), ON *hlith* f. Gmc **hlidham*]

ǁ **Lid'ŏ** (lē-), n. Public open-air swimming pool. [bathing beach in Venice]

lie¹, n. Intentional false statement (*tell a ~,* make this; *act a ~,* deceive without verbal lying; *while ~,* excused or justified by its motive; *give one the ~,* accuse him of lying; *give the ~ to* supposition etc., serve to show its falsity, belie it); imposture, false belief, mistaken convention, (*worship, maintain, a ~*). [OE *lyge* (cf. OHG *lugi,* ON *lygi*) f. Gmc **lug-,* see foll.]

lie², v.i. & t. (*lỹ'ing*). Speak falsely, tell lie(s), (*you ~ in your teeth, throat,* arch. or joc. forms of accusation); take *away* (reputation etc.), get (oneself, person) *into, out of,* by lying; (of things) deceive (part., deceptive). [OE *lēogan,* OS, OHG *liogan,* ON *ljúga,* Goth. *liugan* f. Gmc **leug-, *lug-*]

lie³, v.i. (*lỹ'ing;* past *lay;* p.p. *lain* & bibl. *lĭ'en*). **1.** Of persons or animals: Have one's body in more or less horizontal position along ground or surface (often *asleep, sick,* etc.; *~* DOGGO; *let sleeping dogs ~,* avoid mooting debatable questions; *~ on the bed* one *has made,* endure consequences of past acts); have sexual intercourse *with;* (of the dead) be in the grave *at* or *in, ~ in* STATE; assume lying position (usu. *down, back,* etc.); be kept or remain in specified state (*~ in prison,* *at the mercy of, helpless, idle,* CLOSE[1], LOW[1], PERDU, *in ambush, in* WAIT[2]; ~ *out of* one's *money,* remain unpaid); (of game-birds) not rise; (of troops) be encamped *at, in, near,* a place. **2.** Of things: Be at rest, usu. more or less horizontally, on surface (~ *in ruins* or *the dust,* be fallen; ~ *heavy,* be a weight on one's *stomach* or *conscience*); be stored up in specified place (*money lying at the bank*); remain in specified state esp. *idle, hid, barren*; be situated (*land lying high, to the east, round*; *find out how the land* ~s, fig., how affairs stand); be spread out to view (~s *on the surface, before us, open*); (of road) lead *through, by, along, among,* etc.; (of ship) float in berth or at anchor; (of abstracts) exist, be to be found, reside, be arranged or related, in some position or manner (*the choice* ~s *between* —; *his acquaintance lay among* —; *knows where his interest* ~s; *how do they* ~ *to each other?*; *as far as in me* ~s, to best of my power; ~s *with you to* do, is your business or right; *the remedy* ~s *in education*; *her strength lay in* her *weakness*; ~s *in a* NUT*shell*); (law) be admissible or sustainable (*action, appeal, objection, will not* ~). **3.** With advv.: ~ *by,* be unused, keep quiet or retired; ~ *down* in part., behaving in abject manner, not standing up to opponent etc., (*take* defeat, chastisement, & esp. *it, lying down*); ~ *in,* be brought to bed in childbirth (*lying-in hospital*); ~ *off* (naut.), stand some distance from shore or other ship; ~ *over,* be deferred; ~ *to* (naut.), come almost to a stop with head near wind by backing or shortening sail; ~ *up,* go into or be in retirement, take to one's bed or room, (of ship) go into dock or be out of commission. **4.** ~'-*abed,* late riser. [OE *licgan,* OS *liggian,* OHG *liggen,* ON *liggja,* (Goth. *ligan*), f. Gmc **ligjan* f. **leg-, *lag-, *læg-,* cogn. w. L *lectus* bed]

lie[4], n. Way, direction, or position, in which thing lies; ~ *of the land,* (fig.) posture of affairs; place where beast, bird, or fish, is accustomed to lie. [f. prec.]

Lie'big('s extract of beef) (lē-), n. Concentrated preparation of beef without albumen, gelatin, or fat. [Baron von *Liebig,* d. 1873, inventor]

lied (lēd), n. (pl. ~er). German song or poem of ballad kind. [G]

lief, adv. (comp. ~er, rare). Gladly, willingly, (usu. *I would as* ~ do something out of the question *as*). [OE *lēof* dear (cogn. w. LOVE); ME *I had as* ~ (adj.) i.e. should find it as pleasant, early altered to *I would as* ~ (adv.)]

liege, a. & n. **1.** (Of superior) entitled to receive, (of vassal) bound to give, feudal service or allegiance (~ *lord,* feudal superior, sovereign; ~'*man,* sworn vassal, faithful follower). **2.** n. ~ lord (esp. *my* ~ voc.); vassal, subject, (usu. *the* ~s).

[ME, f. OF *lige, liege* f. med. L *laeticus* f. *laetus,* of WG orig.]

li'en[1] (lē'en), n. Right to keep possession of property till debt due in respect of it is discharged (usu. *a* ~ *on* or *upon*). [F, f. L *ligamen* (*ligare* bind, -MEN)]

lien[2]. See LIE[3].

lierne', n. Short rib connecting bosses & intersections of vaulting-ribs. [15th c. *leyrn,* f. F *lierne*]

lieu (lū), n. *In* ~, in the place, instead, *of.* [F, f. L *locus* place]

lieuten'ant (lĕft-, left-, *in navy* let-; ***lōō-), n. (*abbr.* Lieut. *& in comb.* Lt-). Deputy, substitute, vicegerent, acting for a superior (still as formal title in *L*~ *of the Tower,* acting commandant of Tower of London; & see LORD *L*~, DEPUTY *L*~); ~, ~*-colonel,* ~*-commander,* ~*-general,* OFFICERS of navy & army; ~*-governor-* (ship), (position of) actual governor of district etc. in subordination to governor general. Hence **lieutĕn'ANCY** n. [ME, f. OF (prec., TENANT)]

life, n. (pl. *lives*). **1.** State of functional activity peculiar to organized matter, & esp. to the portion of it constituting an animal or plant before death, animate existence, being alive, (*a matter of* ~ *& death,* something on which it depends whether one shall live or die; NECESSARY, STAFF, *of* ~; *come, bring, to* ~, recover (i. & t.) from swoon; *lose, save, lay down,* one's ~; *safe in, escape with,* ~ *& limb*; SELL one's ~ *dear(ly)*; *great sacrifice of* ~, many killed; *have no regard for human* ~, kill men or let them die recklessly; *for* one's, *for dear,* ~, to'escape death; *cannot for the* ~ *of me* etc. by exag., could not if my ~ depended on it; '*pon my* ~, asseveration). **2.** Energy, liveliness, vivacity, animation; vivifying influence (*was the* ~, or ~ *& soul, of the party*; *my* ~, voc. of affection). **3.** Living things & their motions (*very little* ~ *to be seen*); the living form or model, ~*-size* figure etc., (*taken from the* ~; *as large as* ~, ~*-size,* also joc. as *here he is as large as* ~, i.e. in person; *portray* etc. *to the* ~, with fidelity to the original), whence ~LIKE (-fī-) a. **4.** Period from birth to death, birth to present time, or present time to death (*have done it all my* ~; *have the time of* one's ~, sl., enjoy oneself as never before; ~ *sentence, rent, annuity,* to continue for rest of person's ~; ‖ *lease for three* etc. *lives,* to terminate with last of three etc. named persons' lives; ~ ASSURANCE; INSURE one's ~; *expectation of* ~, average period that person at specified age may expect to live; *a good, bad,* ~, person likely to pass, fall short of, this average; *new* LEASE[1] *of* ~). **5.** Fresh start after narrowly escaped lit. or metaph. death (*cat has nine lives,* is hard to kill; *batsman was given a* ~, not put out on giving a chance; *pool-player has three lives,* successive chances). **6.** Individual's actions & fortunes, manner of existence, (*with all the pleasure in* ~, greatest possible; *nothing in* ~, at all; *this* ~, that on earth; *the other, future, eternal, everlasting,* ~, state of existence after death; *the* SIMPLE ~; *has led a good* etc. ~); written story of these, biography. **7.** Active part of existence, business & pleasures of the world, (*see* ~, mix freely with others; *high, low,* ~, social customs of upper, lower, classes). **8.** (theol.). Salvation, regenerate condition, (also *eternal, everlasting,* ~, see above also). **9.** ~*'belt*, of buoyant material to support body in water; ~*-blood*, blood necessary to ~, vitalizing influence, involuntary twitching of lip or eyelid; ~*'boat*, of special construction for saving ~ in storms; ~*-breath*, inspiring influence, sustaining principle; ~*'*BUOY[1]; ~ *estate*, property that one holds for ~ but cannot dispose of further; ~*-giving*, that gives, sustains, or restores, physical or spiritual ~; ~*-guard*, body-guard of soldiers; || *L*~ *Guards*, regiment of household cavalry; || *L*~*-Guardsman*, soldier of L~ Guards; ~ *interest*, right to ~ estate; ~*-jacket*, as ~*belt*; ~*'line*, rope used for ~-saving, e.g. that attached to ~buoy, diver's signalling line, (palmistry) = line of ~; ~*'long*, continued for a ~time; ~*-office*, for ~-assurance; ~ *peer(age)*, with title lapsing at death; ~*-preserver*, short stick with heavily loaded end; ~*-spring*, source of ~; ~*-strings*, hold on ~ (~*-strings are cut* or *broken*, person dies); ~*-table*, statistics of expectation of ~; ~*'time*, duration of person's ~; ~*-work*, task pursued through ~. Hence ~*'*LESS a., ~*'*lèssLY[2] adv., ~*'*lèssNESS n., (-fl-), (-)lïvED[2] (-vd)'a. (esp. *long-, short-*). [OE, OS *lif*, ON *líf*, OHG *lib* life, body, f. Gmc *libham* f. *libh-* (LIVE[2]), *laibh-* (LEAVE[2])]

lif'er, n. (sl.). One sentenced to, sentence of, imprisonment for life. [-ER[1]]

lift, v.t. & i., & n. **1.** Raise to higher position, take up, hoist, (often *up, off, out*), elevate to higher plane of thought or feeling, give upward direction to (eyes, face), (~ *up* or ~ one's *hands* or *heart*, in prayer etc.; ~ one's *hand*, to take oath; ~ *a hand*, make the slightest effort, usu. *to* do; *never* ~*ed a hand against* one, struck him; ~ *up* one's *head*, recover vigour after prostration, ~ *up* another's *head*, bibl., restore to liberty or dignity; ~ *up* one's *heel*, kick; ~ *up* one's *horn*, be ambitious or proud; ~ *up a cry*, one's *voice*, cry out; hold or have on high (*church* ~*s its spire*); steal (esp. cattle), take (passage, information) in the way of plagiarism; remove (tents etc.); dig up (potatoes); hit (cricket-ball) into air; (of ship afloat) rise on wave; yield to a ~ (*window will not* ~); (of cloud, fog, darkness) rise, disperse; (of floor) swell upwards, bulge. **2.** n. ~ing (DEAD ~); *give* one *a* ~, take him up into vehicle for part of way; also fig. give him helping hand);

AIR[1]-~; one layer of leather in boot-heel; apparatus for raising & lowering people or things to other floor of house, elevator, hoist; rise in the ground; upward pressure which the air exerts on an aircraft, counteracting the force of gravity. [ME, f. ON *lypta* f. Gmc *luftjan* f. *luftuz* air (whence OE *lyft* (obs. E *lift*), ON *loft* LOFT)]

lig'ament, n. Tie, bond of union, (rare); (anat.) short band of tough flexible fibrous tissue binding bones together, (loosely) any membranous fold keeping organ in position, similar part in lower organisms. Hence ~AL, ~ARY[1], ~OUS, aa., (-mĕn^t-). [ME, f. L *ligamentum* (*ligare* bind, -MENT)]

lig|āte', v.t. (surg.). Tie up (bleeding artery etc.). Hence ~A'TION n. [f. L *ligare*, -ATE[3]]

lig'ature, n., & v.t. Thing used in tying, esp. band or cord used to tie up bleeding artery, strangulate tumour, etc. (vb, bind with ~); thing that unites, bond; tying, ligation; (mus.) slur, tie; (print.) two or more letters joined (fi etc.). [ME, f. LL *ligatura* (prec., -URE)]

lig'er (-g-), n. Offspring of lion and tigress. [portmanteau wd]

light[1] (lit), n. **1.** The natural agent that stimulates the sense of sight. **2.** Medium or condition of space in which sight is possible (opp. *darkness*). **3.** Appearance of brightness (NORTHERN ~*s*; ZODIACAL ~; *saw a distant* ~). **4.** Sensation peculiar to optic nerve. **5.** Amount of illumination in place (*in a good* ~, easily visible); one's fair or ordinary share of this (*stand in* one's ~, deprive him of this, (fig.) prejudice his chances). **6.** Vivacity in person's eyes. **7.** Favouring aspect (~ *of* one's *countenance*, his favour, approving presence, or sanction, often iron.). **8.** Sun's direct or diffused or reflected rays, daylight, (*see the* ~, be born). **9.** Being visible or exposed (*come, bring, to* ~, be revealed, reveal). **10.** (Poet.) eyesight; (sl., pl.) eyes. **11.** Object from which brightness emanates (~ *of* one's *eyes*, beloved person), sun or other heavenly body, ignited candle or lamp or the like (*see the* RED ~); (collect.) lamps etc. illuminating place; beacon lamp esp. of ship or ~house. ~house; (fig.) eminent person or luminary (often *shining* ~). **12.** Mental illumination, elucidation (*throw, shed,* ~ *upon*, help to explain), enlightenment (*by the* ~ *of nature*, without aid of revelation or teaching; *men of* ~ *&* LEADING[1]); (pl.) facts or discoveries serving to explain subject (*we have many new* ~*s upon it since then*); (pl.) one's natural or acquired mental powers (usu. *do* one's *best* etc. *according to* one's ~*s*); (sing.) aspect in which thing is viewed (*in the* ~ *of these facts*, with the help given by them; *appeared in the* ~ *of a scoundrel*, seemed to be one; *place thing in a good* ~, represent it favourably); (in acrostic puzzles) one of the words whose initial & final letters make up the answer. **13.** (theol.). Brightness of heaven, illumination of soul by divine truth. **14.** Window or opening in wall for admission of ~, perpendicular division of mullioned window, glazed compartment of side or roof in greenhouse. **15.** (paint.). Illuminated surface, part of picture represented as lighted up. **16.** (law). ~ falling on windows, the obstruction of which by neighbour is illegal (*Ancient L~s*, inscription giving notice of this). **17.** Flame or spark serving to ignite (*strike a ~*, produce this with match etc.); thing used for igniting, spill, taper, match. **18.** ~ *due*, *duty*, toll on ships for maintenance of ~'*houses* (tower or other structure) & ~'*ships* (moored or anchored) containing beacon ~s for warning or guiding ships at sea. Hence ~'LESS a. [OE *léoht*, OS, OHG *lioht*, f. Gmc **leuhtam*, cogn. w. Goth. *liuhath*, L *lux*]

light² (lit), a. Well provided with light, not dark; pale-coloured (often prefixed to adjj. & nn. of colour, as *a ~-blue ribbon, I prefer ~ blue; the ~ BLUE²s*). [as prec.]

light³ (lit), v.t. & i. (*lit* or *~ed*; as attrib. adj., *~ed* is usu.). Set (lamp etc.), fire, combustible) burning (often *up*; *~ up*, abs., begin to smoke pipe etc., also kindle the lights in street or room at dusk), (of fuel, lamp, etc.) take fire, begin to burn; give light to (room, street, etc.; *~ up*, ~ brightly or make conspicuous by light); brighten (t. & i., with *eyes, face*, etc., as obj. or subj.) with animation; show (person his) way or surroundings with a light. Hence (-)~'er¹ (lit-), see -ER¹(1, 2), n., (esp.) automatic device for ~ing cigarette etc. [OE *lihtan*, OS *liuhtian*, OHG *-en*, Goth. *liuhtjan* f. Gmc **leuht-LIGHT¹*]

light⁴ (lit), a. & adv. **1.** Of little weight, not heavy, (*~-armed*, with ~ equipment & weapons); deficient in weight (~ *coin*, *gold*, etc.). **2.** Of small specific gravity. **3.** Having or intended for a small load (~ *ship*, unladen; ~ *waterline* etc., that of ship when ~; ~ *engine*, with no train attached; ~ *railway*, for ~ traffic; ~ *porter*; ~ *horse*, ~-*armed cavalry*, & so ~ *horseman*, ~ *infantry*; ~ *marching order*, in which only arms & ammunition are taken); (of ship, cart, etc.) made ~ly for small loads & quick movement. **4.** (Of building) not looking heavy, graceful, elegant. **5.** Acting gently, applied delicately, not violent, (~ *hand*, lit., & fig. = tactful management, whence ~'-hand'ED² a., ~'hand'edLY² adv., ~'-hand'edNESS n.; ~ *touch, blow, wind, step*, etc.). **6.** Not dense or tenacious; porous, friable, (~ *soil, pastry*). **7.** Easy of digestion; (of wine or beer) not strong. **8.** (Of syllable) unemphatic. **9.** Not important (*make ~ of*, treat as of no

consequence), slight, trivial, venial, not grave, jesting, thoughtless, frivolous (whence ~'mind'ED² a., ~'mind'edNESS n.). **10.** Wanton, unchaste, (esp. of women or their conduct). **11.** Nimble, quick-moving, (~ *of foot*; ~ *heels*, whence ~'heelED'² a.; ~ *movements*; ~ *rhythm*; ~ *fingers*, good at stealing, whence ~'-fing'erED² a.). **12.** Fickle, inconstant. **13.** Easily borne (~ *punishment, taxation, rule, expense*) or done (~ *work, task*). **14.** Aimed or aiming at entertainment merely (~ *literature, writer, comedy, comedian, programme*). **15.** (Of sleep) easily disturbed, not profound, (so ~ *sleeper*). **16.** Free from sorrow, cheerful, sanguine, (~ *heart*; *did it with a ~ heart*, sanguinely, rashly; so ~'heart'ED² a., ~'heart'edLY² adv., ~'heart'edNESS n.). **17.** Delirious (now only in ~'head'ED² a., ~'head'ed-NESS n.). **18.** || ~-BOB⁵; ~'foot, springy, nimble; ~ *heavy* (BOX⁵); ~-o'-love, fickle woman, harlot; ~-weight a., ~ weight n., (man or animal) below average weight, esp. in boxing 9 st. 9 to 9 st., (person) of little importance; hence ~'LY² adv., ~'NESS n., (lit-). **19.** adv. In ~ manner (esp. *tread, sleep, ~*; ~ *come ~ go*, what is easily gained is soon lost). [OE *léoht*, OS *liht*, OHG *liht(i)*, ON *léttr*, Goth. *leihts* f. Gmc **linh-, *lung-*, cogn. w. LUNG]

light⁵ (lit), v.t. & i. (*lit* or *~ed*). (Naut.) lift (rope etc.) along, lend a hand in hauling ropes etc.; (arch.) alight, descend, come down; chance, come by chance, (*up)on*. [OE *lihtan*, OHG *(gi)-lihten*, ON *létta* fr. Gmc **lihtjan* f. **linht-*LIGHT⁴; sense ' alight ' f. idea of relieving horse etc. of weight]

light'en¹ (lit-), v.t. & i. Reduce load of (ship etc.), (of ship) have her load reduced; relieve (heart etc.), (of heart etc.) feel relief; reduce weight of, (fig.) mitigate; grow lighter. [LIGHT⁴+-EN⁶]

light'en² (lit-), v.t. & i. Shed light upon, make bright, (also fig., as ~ *our darkness*); (of face, eyes, sky, etc.) grow bright, shine, flash; (of sky, clouds, or *it*) emit lightning (also fig. of scorn etc.). [LIGHT²+-EN⁶]

light'er² (lit-; for *lighter³* see LIGHT³), n. & v.t. **1.** Boat, usu. flat-bottomed, for unloading & loading ships not brought to wharf & for transporting goods in harbour. **2.** v.t. Remove (goods) in ~. Hence ~AGE (4) n. [15th c., f. MDu. *lichter* (as LIGHT⁵, -ER¹]

light'ish¹, ² (lit-), aa. Somewhat LIGHT²; somewhat LIGHT⁴. [-ISH¹(2)]

light'ning (lit-), n. Visible electric discharge between clouds or cloud & ground (*forked, chain*, or *chained ~*, ~-*flash* in form of zigzag or divided line; *sheet ~*, ~ flash of diffused brightness; *summer, heat, ~, sheet~* without audible thunder, result of distant storm; *like ~*, with greatest conceivable speed; *with ~ speed*); ~-*rod* or -*conductor*, metal rod or wire fixed to exposed part of building or to mast to divert~ into earth or sea;~ *strike*, labour strike at short notice by way of surprise. [14th c., differentiated form of *lightening* vbl n. of LIGHTEN[2]]

lights (līts), n. pl. Lungs of sheep, pigs, bullocks, etc., used as a food esp. for cats & dogs. [n. use of LIGHT[4], cf. LUNG]

light′some[1] (līt-), a. (rare & poet.). Light, graceful, elegant, in appearance; light-hearted, merry; nimble. Hence ~LY[2] adv., ~NESS n. [ME, f. LIGHT[4], -SOME]

light′some[2] (līt-), a. (rare). Light-giving, luminous; well lighted, bright. [ME, f. LIGHT[1], -SOME]

light′wŏŏd (līt-), n. Kinds of tree with light wood; kinds of tree with wood that burns with bright flame. [LIGHT[4], [1]]

lign-aloes (līnăl′ōz), n. The drug aloes; aloes-wood, an aromatic Mexican wood. [ME, f. LL *lignum aloes* wood of the ALOE]

lig′nēous, a. (Of plants) woody (opp. *herbaceous*). [f. L *ligneus* (foll.)+-OUS]

lig′ni-, comb. form of L *lignum* wood. Hence ~F′EROUS, ~FORM, aa., ~FY v.t. & i., ~FICA′TION n.

lig′nite, n. Brown coal showing traces of ligneous structure. [F, see prec., -ITE[1](2)]

lig′num vīt′ae, n. Guaiacum. [L, = wood of life]

lig′ūlate, a. (bot.). With strap-shaped fillet(s). [L *ligula* strap+-ATE[2]]

like[1], a. (often governing noun like trans. part.; *more, most*, rarely or poet. ~*r*, ~*st*), prep., adv. (arch.), conj. (colloq.), & n. **1.** adj. Similar, resembling something or each other or the original, (*in ~ manner* or *wise*; *on this & the ~ subjects*; *the two letters are very ~*; *as ~ as two peas*; ~ *father ~ son*, ~ *master ~ man*, as the one is so will the other be; *the picture is not~*; in alg., ~ *signs*, both positive or both negative, ~ *quantities*, expressed by same letters; occas. with *with*, as *beings of ~ passions with us*; now rarely, & chiefly in comp. ~*r*, with *to*, as ~*r to God than man*); resembling, such as, (*nothing ~* LEATHER, as good as; *what is he, it*, ~ *?*, what sort of person or thing is he or it?; *look* ~, have appearance of; ~ *that*, of the kind just seen or referred to; *a critic ~ you*, of the class that you exemplify; *something ~ £1,000*, nearly, about; *something ~ a day*, with stress on ~, remarkably fine or otherwise satisfactory; so abs., *this is something ~*; *nothing ~ as good*, not nearly); characteristic of (*that is ~ your impudence*; *it was~ him to think of himself last*); in promising state or right mood for *doing* (*looks ~ lasting*; *feel ~ working* or *stopping work*; also *looks ~* with n. = promises the finding or suggests the agency of, as *looks ~ rabbits*): (arch.) likely, (arch. & colloq.) likely *to* (*had*, = *was*, ~ *to have* done, narrowly escaped doing); ~*-minded*, having same tastes, views, etc. **2.** prep. In the manner of, to the same degree as, (*cannot do it ~*

you; *do not talk ~ that*; ~ *a shot*, without demur, willingly, regardless of consequences; ~ *fun*, *blazes*, *one o'clock*, *anything*, MAD, etc., vigorously); (in proverbial or joc. pseudo-proverbial phrr.; emphasizing vbs) *blush ~ a peony*, *drink ~ a fish*, *fit ~ a glove*, *get on ~ a house on fire*, *smoke* i.e. tobacco ~ *a chimney*, *spread ~ wildfire*, *swear ~ a trooper*, *swim ~ a duck*; less usu. w. noun in objective relation, *hate* person etc. ~ *poison*, *scatter them ~ chaff*. **3.** adv. In the same manner *as* (arch.); probably (now only in *very ~*, ~ *enough*, usu. parenthetic); (illit.) so to speak (*by way of argument ~*). **4.** conj. (for arch. ~ *as*; colloq.). As (*cannot do it ~ you do*; *snow is falling ~ in January*). **5.** n. Counterpart, equal, ~ thing or person, (*mix with your~s*; *shall not see his ~ again*; *did you ever see the ~ of it?*; ~ *cures~*; *the~s of me*, colloq., persons so humble as I; *the~s of you*, colloq., persons so distinguished as you); (golf) stroke that equalizes number of strokes played by each side; (ellipt. use of adj. with pl. ~) thing(s) of the same kind (*will never do the ~ again*; *& the ~* often as pl. = etcetera, as *music, painting, & the ~*; *or the ~*, or other thing(s) of the kind). [ME *līch*, *līk*, shortened form (= ON *līkr*) of OE *gelic* = OS *gilik*, OHG *gilih*, ON *glikr*, Goth. *galeiks* f. Gmc **galik-*, see Y-, LICH]

like[2], v.t. & i., & n. **1.** Be pleasing to (arch. or joc.; chiefly impers., *it ~s me not*, *well*, etc.); thrive (obs. exc. in *well--liking*); find agreeable, congenial, or satisfactory, feel attracted by, wish for, (*I ~ you*, the *offer*, his *visits*, (iron.) his *impudence*, her *to be within reach*, *to see them now & then*; *do not ~ such subjects discussed*; *should much~ to come*; *should~ to know* or *see* (iron.), think you will find it hard to tell me, am not likely to see; *should ~ time to consider it*; *how do you ~ it?*, do you ~ it much or little or dislike it?, whence lik′ABLE a., lik′ableNESS n.; *if you ~* (expr. consent to request, as *you will come if you ~*, or limited assent, as *I am shy if you~*, i.e. but not misanthropic, or emphatic selection, as I *am shy if you ~*, i.e. but someone else is not); suit (only in *I ~ it*, i.e. kind of food, *but it does not ~ me*). **2.** n. (Usu. pl.) liking(s), predilection(s) (esp. ~*s & dislikes*). [OE *lician*, OS *likōn*, OHG *lihhēn*, ON *lika*, Goth. *leikan* f. Gmc **likam* (prec., LICH)]

-like, suf. (i.e. LIKE a. & adv. in comp.). **1.** Appended to nn. ~ forms adjj. (*god~*, *woman~*, *plumbago-~*); advv of similar form are perh. arch., & in mod. use possible advv. can usu. be explained as adjj. (*he, coward~, refuscd*). **2.** Appended to adjj. it forms adjj. chiefly Sc. (*human-~*, *auld~*) & Sc. advv.

like′lihŏŏd (-kl-), n. Being likely, probability, (esp. *in all~*, probably). [-HOOD]

like′lĭy̆ (-kl-), a. & adv. (*more, most, -ier,*

-iest). **1.** Probable, such as might well happen, or be or prove true, or turn out to be the thing specified, (*a ~ story*, often iron.; *it is not ~ he will come*; *his most ~ halting-place is* —); to be expected *to* (*he, this, is* or *was not ~ to come, happen*); promising, apparently suitable *for* purpose or *to* do or be, capable-looking, (*called at every ~ house; six ~ young fellows; the likeliest place for smugglers* or *to find him in*). **2.** adv. Probably (usu. *most* or *very ~*). [f. ON *likligr* (LIKE[1], -LY[1])]

lik'en, v.t. Find or point out resemblance in (thing) *to*; (rare) make like *to* (*its arbitrary character ~s it to a despotism*). [-EN[6]]

like'ness (-kn-), n. Being like, resemblance (*between, to*); semblance (*enemy in ~ of friend*); representation, copy, portrait (*take* one's ~, portray him); person or thing having the exact appearance of another. [-NESS]

like'wise (-kwīz), adv. & conj. Similarly (bibl.); also, moreover, too. [for *in like wise*]

likin (lē'kēn'), n. Provincial transit duty in China. [Chin.]

lik'ing, n. What one likes, one's taste (*is it to your ~?*); regard, fondness, taste, fancy, *for* (*have a ~ for him, for precise statement; no ~ for flattery*). [OE *līcung* (LIKE[2], -ING[1])]

***lil.** Dial. var. of LITTLE.

lil'ac, n. & a. Shrub with fragrant pale pinkish-violet, or white, blossoms; (of) pale pinkish-violet colour. [17th c., f. F *lilac* (mod. *lilas*) f. Sp. f. Arab. f. Pers. *lilak*]

liliā'ceous (-shus), a. Of the lily kind. [f. LL *liliaceus* (LILY, -ACEOUS)]

Lillibullēr'ō, n. Song popular at end of 17th c., often referred to by writers. [part of refrain]

Lillipū'tian (-shn), a. & n. Native of Lilliput, diminutive (person or thing). [*Lilliput* in *Gulliver's Travels*, -IAN]

lilt, v.t. & i., & n. **1.** Sing melodiously or rhythmically. **2.** n. (Song with) marked rhythmical cadence or swing. [ME *lulte* (cf. 1450 *lilt-pipe*), of unkn. orig.]

lil'y̆, n. (Flower of) kinds of bulbous plant bearing large showy white or reddish or purplish flowers on tall slender stem, esp. the white or madonna ~ (*orange, tiger, turk's cap, etc., ~*); kinds of plant allied to these (*belladonna, calla, Guernsey, Lent, water, etc., ~*); ~ *of the valley*, spring herb with two large leaves & racemes of white bell-shaped fragrant flowers; person or thing of special whiteness or purity (*lilies & roses, fair complexion*); heraldic fleur-de-lis (*the lilies*, arms of old French monarchy, Bourbon dynasty); (attrib.) delicately white (~ *maid, hand*, etc.), pallid; ~*-iron*, harpoon with detachable head for killing swordfish; ~*-liv'ered*, cowardly; ~*-white*, as a ~.

Hence **lil'iED**[2] (-lĭd) a. [OE *lilie* f. L *lilium*]

limb[1] (-m), n., & v.t. **1.** Leg, arm, or wing (*escape with life & ~*, without grave injury); (orig. ~ *of the devil* or *Satan*) mischievous child, so ~ *of the law*, lawyer, policeman, etc.; main branch of tree (*out on a ~*, isolated, stranded), one of four branches of cross, clause of sentence, spur of mountain; hence (-)~ED[2] (-md), ~'LESS (-ml-), aa. **2.** v.t. Disable ~ of (person or animal), dismember (body). [OE *lim*, = ON *limr*, f. Gmc **li-* as in dial. *lith*]

limb[2] (-m), n. (scient.). Edge of surface; graduated edge of quadrant etc.; edge (*eastern, lower*, etc., ~) of sun, moon, etc.; expanded part of petal, sepal, or leaf. [f. F *limbe* or L *limbus* hem; see LIMBO]

lim'bate, a. (biol., bot.). Having distinct or different-coloured border. [f. LL *limbatus* (prec., -ATE[2])]

lim'bĕc, n. (arch.). = ALEMBIC.

lim'ber[1], n., & v.t. **1.** Detachable front of gun-carriage (two wheels, axle, pole, & ammunition-box). **2.** v.t. Attach ~ to (gun), fasten together two parts of (gun-carriage; also abs.), (usu. *up*). [15th c. *limo(u)r*, 16th c. *lymnar*, app. rel. to med. L *limonarius* (F -*ier*), f. *limo* shaft (F *limon*)]

lim'ber[2], n. (naut.). One of the holes cut in floor-timbers for drainage to pump-well. [perh. f. F *lumière* light, so used]

lim'ber[3], a., & v.t. **1.** Flexible; lithe, nimble. **2.** v.t. Make ~; also abs. [16th c., of unkn. orig.]

lim'bō, n. (pl. ~*s*). Region on border of hell where pre-Christian just men & unbaptized infants are confined; prison, durance; condition of neglect or oblivion. [ME, f. med. L phr. *in limbo* (LIMB[2])]

lime[1], n., & v.t. **1.** Sticky substance made from holly bark for catching small birds (usu. *bird~*). **2.** White caustic alkaline earth (calcium oxide) got by burning ~*-stone*, kinds of rock chiefly carbonate of calcium, & used for making mortar, as fertilizer, etc. (also *quick-~*; *slaked ~*, this after combination with water, hydrate of calcium), whence ~'LESS (-ml-), lim'Y[2], aa. **3.** ~*-burner*, maker of ~; ~*-cast*, outer layer of ~ on building; ~*'kiln*, for burning ~*stone*; ~*'light*, intense white light got by heating cylinder of ~ in oxyhydrogen flame (*the ~light*, fig., w. ref. to use in theatre, full glare of publicity); ~*-pit*, for steeping hides to remove hair; ~*-twig*, smeared with bird~. **4.** v.t. Smear (twigs), catch (bird), with bird~ (also fig.); treat, dress (land), with ~; steep (skins) in ~ & water. [OE *lim*, = MDu., OHG *lim*, ON *lim* f. Gmc **lim-* cogn. w. L *limus* mud, & LOAM]

lime[2], n. Round fruit smaller & more acid than lemon; ~*-juice*, used as drink & esp. as antiscorbutic; **~-juicer* (naut. sl.), British sailor (also **lim'ey*) or ship (because use of ~-juice was enforced on board); *limey, (also, sl.) any British person. [F, f. Arab, limah; cf. LEMON]

lime³, n. Ornamental tree with heart--shaped leaves & small fragrant yellowish blossom (often ~-tree). [alt. of line = lind; see LINDEN]

lim′ĕn, n. (psych.). Limit below which given stimulus ceases to be perceptible, minimum of nerve-excitation required to produce sensation. Hence lim′inAL a. [L (genit. -inis), = threshold, representing G schwelle]

lim′erick, n. Kind of nonsense verse (now usu. applied to the five-line form based on Lear's nursery rhymes; [said to be f. chorus ' Will you come up to ~? ' sung after extempore verses contributed each by member of party]

‖ lime′-wort (-êrt), limp′, n. = BROOK¹-lime. [f. *lime, *lempe, OE hleomece]

lim′it¹, n. Bounding line, terminal point (superior, inferior, ~, earliest & latest possible date, largest & smallest possible or permissible amount), bound that may not or cannot be passed, (without ~, un-limited; is the ~, sl., is the last straw, intolerable etc.; ~ man, receiving longest start allowed in handicap, opp. scratch). Hence ~LESS a. [ME, f. OF limite f. L limitem nom. -mes]

lim′it², v.t. Confine within limits, set (usu. immaterial) bounds to, restrict to; serve as limit to; (p.p.) scanty; ‖ ~ed company, see LIABILITY; ~ed mail, taking only ~ed number of passengers; ~ed monarchy etc., subject to constitutional restrictions (opp. absolute). So ~ATIVE a. [ME, f. OF limiter, or f. L limitare (prec.)]

limitār′ian, n. & a. (Holder) of doctrine that only a limited part of mankind is to be saved. [LIMIT¹, -ARIAN]

lim′itary, a. Subject to restriction; of, on, serving as, limit. [f. L limitaris (LIMIT¹, -ARY²)]

limitā′tion, n. Limiting; limited condi-tion, disability or inability, (has his ~s, is not talented in all directions); limiting rule or circumstance; legally specified period beyond which action cannot be brought, estate or law is not to continue, etc. (statute of ~s, any that fixes such period). [f. L limitatio (LIMIT², -ATION)]

lim′itrophe (-ŏf), a. (Of district etc.) on frontier, adjacent to. [F, f. LL -us (L limes LIMIT¹, Gk -trophos -feeding), orig. of lands set apart for support of frontier troops]

‖ limn (-m), v.t. (arch.). Paint (picture); depict, portray. Hence lim′nER¹ n. [f. obs. lumine illuminate (MSS.) f. OF luminer f. med. L luminare (L lumen -inis light)]

limnŏl′ogў, n. Study of physical pheno-mena of lakes; study of pond-life. [Gk limnē lake, -o-, -LOGY]

lim′ousine (-ōŏzēn), n. Motor-car with permanently enclosed body (cf. cabriolet). [F, fem. adj. = of Limoges]

limp¹, v.i., & n. 1. Walk lamely, (of verse) halt; (of damaged ship, aircraft, etc.) proceed slowly or with difficulty. 2. n. Lame walk. Hence ~′ingLY² adv. [cogn. w. OE lemp-healt lame, MHG limpfen limp, f. WG *limp-, *lamp-]

limp², a. Not stiff, flexible, (of book-bindings) not stiffened with mill-board; (fig.) wanting in energy. Hence ~′LY² adv., ~′NESS n. [18th c., of unkn. orig.; cf. MHG lampen hang limp]

lim′pĕt, n. Gasteropod mollusc with tent-shaped shell sticking tightly to rocks; (fig.) person, esp. State employee, who clings to office; ~ mine (attached to ·ship's bottom). [late OE lempedu f. med. L lampreda limpet, LAMPREY]

lim′pid, a. Pellucid, clear, not turbid, (of liquids, atmosphere, eyes, literary style). Hence or cogn. ~LY² adv., ~ITY (-id²), ~NESS, nn. [f. F -ide or L limpidus]

limp′kin, n. Kinds of bird between cranes & rails. [LIMP¹, -KIN, from their movements]

‖ limp-wort. See LIME-WORT.

lin′age, n. Number of lines in printed matter; payment according to this. [-AGE]

linch′pin, n. Pin passed through axle-end to keep wheel on. [OE lynis, OS lunisa (G lünse) +PIN]

Lin′coln green (-ngkon), n. Bright green stuff made at Lincoln.

linc′tus (-ngk-), n. Medicine to be licked up; soothing cough mixture. [L, f. lingere lick]

lin′den, n. Lime-tree. [sb. use of obs. adj. linden f. OE lind lime-tree (= OHG linda, ON lind) +-EN⁵; cf. LIME³]

line¹, n. Fine long flax separated from the tow. [OE lin, = OS, OHG, ON lin, Goth. lein f. Gmc *linam, cogn. w. or f. L linum]

line², n. (Order of main senses) 1. Cord; 2. Long narrow mark; 3. Row; 4. Series; 5. Direction. 1. Piece of rope (esp. naut., e.g. for sounding; so prob. hard ~s, bad luck, hardship; also=stitches-~); wire or cable for telegraph or telephone (hold the ~; the ~ is bad; ~′man, charged with keeping wire etc. in repair), route tra-versed by this; cord bearing fish-hook(s) (~-fishing, opp. net-fishing; HOOK¹, ~, & sinker; give one ~ enough, let him go his own way for a time in order to secure or detect him later); cord for measuring, levelling, etc. (PLUMB-~; by rule &-~, with precision); (pl.) one's lot in life (Ps. xvi. 6, w. ref. to marking out land); rule or canon (obs. exc. in ~ upon ~, see Is. xxviii. 10, with slow & regular progress). 2. Long narrow mark traced on surface; use of these in draughtsmanship (boldness, purity, of ~; translate life etc. into ~ & colour; ~-drawing, done with pen or pencil; ~-engraving, done with incised ~s, as opp. etching & mezzotint; ~-work, with pen or pencil not wash etc.; ~ of beauty, ~ with two opposite curves like elongated S); one of the very narrow vertical sections in which televised scenes are photographed and reproduced; (games) mark limiting court or ground or special parts of them; thing resembling traced mark, band of colour, seam, furrow, wrinkle (~ *of life, fortune*, etc., folds in palm of hand significant in palmistry); (math.) straight or curved continuous extent ·of length without breadth, track of moving point, (with defining word, as *isothermal*~) curve connecting all points having specified common property; *the L*~, equator; straight ~ (~ *of* FIRE[1], *force*, etc.; *picture hung on the*~, exhibited with its centre about level of spectator's eye; *go as straight as a*~); contour, outline, lineament (*the savage*~s *of his mouth*), (pl.) plan or draft (esp. of ship in horizontal, vertical, & oblique sections) or manner of procedure (*on conservative, political, the same*, etc., ~s; *on the* ~s *laid down by* someone); (as measure) 1/12 inch; limit, boundary, (DRAW[1] *the* ~; so *dividing* ~; *on the* ~, not clearly one thing or the other). **3.** Row of persons or ·things (*come, bring, into* ~, agree or co-operate, induce to do so; *toe the*~, fig., accept party programme etc.); (mil.) connected series of field--works (GO[1] *up the* ~); ‖ also row of tents or huts in camp; (naut.) ~ *abreast*, number of parallel ships ranged on ~ crossing keels at right angles, ~ *ahead*, ships following in a string, ~ *of* BATTLE[1], *ship of the* ~ or ~*-of*-BATTLE[1] *ship*; (mil.) double row (front & rear ranks) of men ranged side by side, also arrangement of companies side by side (opp. COLUMN; *drawn up in, form, wheel into*, ~; *all along the* ~, at every point, often fig. of success etc.); (army) *the* ~*,* regular & numbered regiments (not Guards, Engineers, or Artillery, & occas. understood to exclude Cavalry); row of words in page or newspaper column (*read between the* ~s, detect hidden meaning in document, speech, etc.; ~*-filling*, flourish or ornament in blank space at end of~ in MS.); (by exag.) short letter (*just a* ~ *to tell you that* —); single verse of poetry; (pl.) piece of poetry (often *upon* subject or *to* person); ‖ (pl.) specified amount (*100* etc. ~s) of usu. Latin verse to be written out as school punishment; (pl., also *marriage* ~s) certificate of marriage; (pl.) words of actor's part. **4.** Series or regular succession of steamers, buses, aircraft, etc., plying between certain places; connected series of persons or things following one another in time (*can show a long* ~ *of heroes*), esp. several generations of family (*male, female, direct*, etc., ~), family, lineage, stock (*comes of a good*~). **5.** Direction, course, track, (~ *of march, communication, ·*etc.); (Railways) single track of rails (*up, down,* ~, *to, from*, chief terminus esp. London), one branch of system (*main, branch, loop,*

~) or whole system under one management (*Southern* etc. ~); course followed in riding to hounds (*take, keep to*, one's *own*, ~, often also fig.); course of procedure, conduct, thought, etc.; department of activity, province, branch of business, (*something in, out of*, one's~, that interests or concerns one, or not; *in the banking, oil-&-colour*, etc., ~); (commerc.) class of goods, order for or stock of this. [(1) ME *li(g)ne* f. OF *ligne* f. L *linea* f. *linum* LINE[1]; (2) OE *line* = OHG, ON *lina*, f. Gmc **linam* (prec.)]

line[3], v.t. & i. Mark *in, off, out*, with lines on paper etc.; cover with lines (*a face* ~*d with pain*); ~ *through*, cross out; draw (men or objects) *up* in line; come *up* or spread (t. & i.) *out* in line; post troops etc; along (road, hedge, etc.) (of troops) form open or close line along (pass etc.), (of things) stand at intervals along (wall etc.). [f. prec.]

line[4], v.t. Apply layer of (usu. different) material to inside of (garment, box, vessel, bag, etc.); fill (purse, pocket, stomach, etc.); serve as lining for. Hence **lin′er**[1] [-ER[1]] n., (esp.) removable metal lining saving wear & tear (in heavy guns & machinery), **lin′**ING[1](4) n. (*every cloud has a silver lining*, there is good in every evil). [f. LINE[1], w. ref. to use of linen for linings]

line[5], v.t. Copulate with, cover, (bitch). [ME, f. OF *lignier*]

lin′eage, n. Lineal descent, ancestry, pedigree. [ME, f. OF *lignage* (L *linea* LINE[2], -AGE)]

lin′eal, a. In the direct line of descent or ancestry (opp. *collateral*); (rare) of, in, line(s), linear. Hence ~LY[2] adv. [ME, f. OF *lineal* f. LL *linealis* (LINE[2], -AL)]

lin′eament, n. (Usu. pl.) distinctive feature(s), or characteristic(s) esp. feature(s) of face, (sing. chiefly in *every* ~). [ME, f. L *lineamentum* f. *lineare* (f. *linea* LINE[2]), -MENT]

lin′ear, a. Of, in, line(s) (~ PERSPECTIVE); (math., physics) involving measurement in one dimension only (~ *equation*, of first degree); long, narrow, & of uniform breadth. Hence ~LY[2] adv. [f. L *linearis* (LINE[2], -AR[1])]

lineā′tion, n. Drawing of, marking with, arrangement of, lines. [ME, f. L *lineatio* (LINEAMENT, -ATION)]

lin′en, a. & n. **1.** Made of flax (~ *cloth*). **2.** n. Cloth woven from flax, (with pl.) particular kind of this; (collect.) shirts, sheets, cloths, etc., of~, calico, etc. (*wash* one's *dirty* ~ *at home, in public*, keep, not keep, quiet about domestic quarrels etc.); ‖ ~*-draper*, dealer in ~, calico, etc.; ~*-fold*, carved or moulded ornament representing a fold or scroll of ~; hence ~ETTE′(2) n. [OE *linen*, OS, OHG *linīn* f. WG (LINE[1], -EN[5])]

lin′er[2] (for *liner*[1] see LINE[4]), n. Ship, usu. steamer, belonging to line of passenger ships; aircraft belonging to a regular line, used esp. for passenger transport. [-ER¹]

lines'man (-nz-), n. ‖ Soldier of line regiment; (lawn tennis, football) official assisting umpire or referee by deciding whether or where ball touches or crosses line. [*line's* (LINE²)]

ling¹, n. Long slender N.-Europ. sea-fish used (usu. cured) for food. [ME *lenge*, *linge*, f. MDu.; cf. early mod. Du. *lenghe*, *linghe*, = ON *langa*; perh. cogn. w. LONG¹]

ling², n. Kinds of heather. Hence **lin'gy²** (-ngi) a. [ME *lyng* f. ON *lyng*]

-ling¹, suf. forming nn.; OE, OS, OHG *-ling*, ON *-lingr*, Goth. *-liggs* f. Gmc *-ingaz* -ING³ appended to *-ila-* -LE(1). **1.** In OE, ME, & mod. E, ~ is added to nn. to form nn. denoting person or thing connected w. primary n. (*hire~*, *nurs~*, *sap~*), & to adjj. to form nn. (*gray~*, *dar~*, *young~*); so also, f. adv., *under~*. On anal. of *nurs~* etc., where first component is ambiguous, *shave~*, *starve~*, are formed on vv. **2.** In ON ~ had dim. force; instances of this appear in E in 14th & 15th cc. (*cod~*, *duck~*); in this use alone (esp. in formation of contemptuous dimm., as *lord~*, *prince~*) the suf. is a living one.

-ling², **-lings**, suf. forming advv.; Gmc *-ling*, *-lang*, *-lung*, (+-ES) used in OE added to nn. to form advv. of direction, as *bæcling* back, *andlang* ALONG, *grundlunga* to ground; in other wds the suf. forms advv. of condition or situation (*darkling*), usu. now dial. only; see -LONG.

ling'a(m) (-ngg-), n. The phallus (esp. as symbol of Siva). [Skr. *linga*]

ling'er (-ngg-), v.i. & t. Put off departure esp. from reluctance to go; stay about, not depart or arrive at expected or right time; dally *round* place or *over* or (*up*)*on* subject; drag *on* a feeble existence (of invalids & moribund customs); be protracted (*~ing disease, agonies*); be tardy, delay; throw (time) *away* in delays. Hence ~ER¹ n., ~ingLY² adv. [f. obs. *leng* (OE *lengan* (f. LONG¹), = OHG *langēn*, lengthen)+-ER⁵]

lingerie (see Ap.), n. (Stock of) linen articles, women's underwear. [F]

ling'o (-ngg-), n. (pl. ~es). (Derog. for) foreign language, vocabulary of special subject or class of people. [alt. f. *lingua* (It., Pg., LINGUA FRANCA), *-o* being a common ending of ' foreign ' wds]

-lings. See -LING².

ling'ua frănc'a (-nggwa), n. Mixture of Italian, French, Greek, & Spanish, used in the Levant; any language serving as medium between different peoples (also fig. of common ideas etc.). [It., =Frankish tongue]

ling'ual (-nggw-), a. & n. (Anat.) of the tongue; (phonet.) formed by the tongue (n., ~ sound; both a. & n. now rare),

whence ~IZE(3) v.t.: of speech or languages (~ *studies*). [f. med. L *lingualis* (L *lingua* tongue, -AL)]

ling'uiform (-nggw-), a. (bot., anat., zool.). Tongue-shaped. [prec., -I-, -FORM]

ling'uist (-nggw-), n. Person skilled in foreign languages (*good, bad, no,* ~). [f. L *lingua* language +-IST] ⸱

linguis't|ic (-nggw-), a. & n. **1.** Of the study of languages; of language, lingual. **2.** n. pl. ~ic science. Hence ~ICALLY adv. [prec. +-IC; sense 2 f. F *-ique*, G *-ik*]

ling'ulate (-ngg-), a. Tongue-shaped. [f. L *lingula* dim. of *lingua* tongue, -ATE²]

ling'uo- (-nggw-), comb. form of L *lingua* tongue (-o-), as ~*den'tal* made with tongue & teeth (of sounds).

‖ **lin'hay, linn'(e)y**, (lĭn'ĭ), n. (S.-W. Eng. dial.). Farm-shed or outbuilding open along front. [orig. unkn.; first element perh. f. LEAN²]

lin'iment, n. Liquid usu. made with oil used in rubbing body for rheumatism etc., embrocation. [f. LL *linimentum* (*linire* smear, -MENT)]

lin'ing. See LINE³.

link¹, n., & v.t. & i. **1.** One ring or loop of chain (as measure, 1/100 of surveying chain or 7·92 in.); = SLEEVE-~; loop in knitting etc.; connecting part, thing or person that unites others, filler of gap, member of series (MISSING ~). **2.** vb. Connect, join, (things, persons) *together* or (thing, person) *to*; clasp (hands); hook (arm *in* or *through* another's, or arms); attach oneself *on* or *in* to system, company, etc. Hence ~'AGE(1, 3) n. [ME, f. ON **hlenkr*, cogn. w. OE *hlanc* LANK, OHG *hlanca* FLANK, f. Gmc **hlank-*]

link², n. Torch of pitch & tow formerly used for lighting people along streets; ~*'boy*, ~*'man*, employed to carry ~s. [16th c., orig. unkn.]

links, n. pl Level or undulating sandy ground near sea-shore, with turf & coarse grass (Sc.); ground on which golf is played, often resembling that of prec. sense (also *a* ~ as sing.). [OE *hlinc* perh. cogn. w. LEAN²]

‖ **linn**, n. (chiefly Sc.). Waterfall; pool below this; precipice, ravine. [perh. mixture of OE *hlynn* torrent & Gael. *linne*]

Linn(a)e'an (-nēan), a. & n. (Follower) of Linnaeus or his system of classifying plants & animals. [*Linnaeus* latinized name of C. Linné, Swedish naturalist (d. 1778), +-AN]

linn'et, n. Common brown or warm-grey song-bird. [f. OF *linette* (*lin* flax, f. its food)]

linn(e)y. See LINHAY.

lin'ocŭt, n. Design cut in relief on block of linoleum; print obtained from this. [LINO]

linol'eum, n. (also **lin'o** abbr.). Floor-cloth of canvas with thick coat of oxidized linseed oil etc. Hence ~ED² (-md) a. [L *linum* flax, *oleum* oil]

lin'otȳpe, n. Machine for producing

lines of words as substitute for type-
-setting by hand, much used in printing
newspapers. [= *line o' type*]

lin'sǎng, n. Civet cat of Borneo & Java.
[Javanese]

lin'seed, n. Seed of flax; ~ *cake*, ~ (with
the ~ *oil* pressed out) as cattle-food; ~
meal, ground ~ ; ~ *poultice*, of ~ or ~
meal. [late OE *linsǣd* (LINE[1], SEED)]

lin'sey-woōl'sey (-z-, -z-), n. Dress
material of coarse inferior wool woven on
cotton warp (orig. of wool & flax); (fig.)
strange medley, nonsense. [15th c., f.
linsey (poss. f. LINE[1]+obs. *say* silk)+
WOOL, w. jingling termination]

lin'stǒck, n. (hist.). Match-holder used in
old gunnery. [16th c. *lint-*, *lineslocke*, f.
Du. *lontstok* (*lont* match, *stok* stick), w.
assim. to LINT & LINE[1]]

lint, n. Soft material for dressing wounds
made by scraping linen cloth on one side.
[14th c. northern *lint*, obsc. rel. to LINE[1];
ult. orig. unkn.]

lin'tel, n. Horizontal timber or stone
over door or window. Hence ~lED[2] (-ld)
a. [ME, f. OF *lintel* threshold, f. Rom.
limitale (cf. var. OF *lintier* f. *limitare*)
by conf. w. LL *liminare* (L *limen* threshold); see LIMIT[1], -LE(2)]

lin'ў, a. Marked with lines; wrinkled;
(art) using line too much. Hence **lin'i-**
NESS. [-Y[2]]

li'on, n. 1. Large powerful tawny African
& S.-Asian (formerly also European)
carnivorous mammal with tufted tail &
(in the male) flowing shaggy mane (~ *in
the way* or *path*, obstacle, esp. imaginary;
~'s *mouth*, perilous position; ~'s *share*,
largest or best part; ~ *& unicorn*, supporters of royal arms; ~'s *skin*, false
assumption of courage; *twist* ~'s *tail*, of
foreign, esp. U.-S., journalists or orators
defying or insulting Great Britain). 2.
Courageous person, so ~heartED[2] a.
3. pl. ‖ Sights worth seeing in town etc.
(from custom of showing country visitors
the ~s formerly kept in Tower of London;
see, show, the ~s). 4. Person of literary or
other celebrity sought after to be shown
off at social gatherings (~-*hunter*, host or
hostess depending much on ~s), whence
~HOOD, ~SHIP, nn. 5. National emblem of
Great Britain (*the British L*~, the nation
personified). 6. (*L*~) constellation &
zodiacal sign LEO. Hence~LIKE a.,~ESS[1],
~ET[1], nn. [ME, f. AF *liun* f. L *leonem*
nom. *leo* f. Gk *leōn leontos*]

li'on|ize, -**ise** (-īz), v.t. & i. See or show
the sights (see prec.) of (place); show these
to (visitor); see the sights; treat (person)
as celebrity, make a lion (see prec.) of,
whence~ISM(1) n. [-IZE]

lip, n., & v.t. (-pp-). 1. One of the fleshy
edges of the opening of the mouth (*upper*,
lower or *under*, ~ ; *bite* one's ~, in vexation or to repress emotion, stifle laugh,
etc.; *stiff upper*~, fortitude or obstinacy;
curl one's ~, in scorn; *hang* one's ~, in

humiliation; *lick*, *smack*, one's ~s, in
enjoyment or anticipation of food or fig.;
hang on one's~s, listen to his every word
in reverence; *word* etc. *escapes* one's ~s,
is uttered thoughtlessly). 2. Saucy talk,
impudence, (sl., esp. *none of your* ~ !).
3. Edge of cup, vessel, cavity, wound,
etc. 4. ~-, from the ~s only, professed,
not heartfelt or sincere, (~-*homage*,
-*religion*, -*Christian*, -*service*, -*worship*)
~-*deep*, superficial, insincere; ~-*language*,
-*reading*, -*speaking*, use & interpretation
of motions of ~s to & by the deaf or
dumb; ~'*salve*, ointment for sore ~s,
(fig.) flattery; ~'*stick*, stick of cosmetic
for colouring ~s; hence (-)~pED[2] (-pt).
~'LESS, aa. 5. v.t. Touch with ~s, apply
~s to; (of water) just touch, lap; (golf)
hit ball just to edge of (hole), (of ball)
reach edge of (hole) but fail to drop in;
murmur, utter softly. [OE *lippa*, MLG,
MDu., (G) *lippe*, MSw. *lippe* f. Gmc
lipjon- cogn. w. L *labrum*]

lipǒg'raphў, n. Omission of letter(s) or
word(s) in writing. [f. Gk *lip-* st. of *leipō*
omit, -GRAPHY]

lipp'er, n. (naut.). Rippling or ruffled
motion, surface roughness, of sea. [16th
c. n. & vb, prob. frequent. f. LAP[5]]

li'quate', v.t. Separate or purify (metals)
by liquefying. Hence **liqua'TION** n. [f. L
liquare melt, cogn. w. LIQUOR, -ATE[3]]

li'que|fý, v.t. & i. Bring (solid or gas) or
come into liquid condition. Hence or
cogn. ~FA'CIENT (-āshent) a. & n., ~FAC-
TION n., ~fǎctive, ~fiABLE, aa., ~fiER[1](1,
2) n. [f. F *liquéfier* f. L *liquefacere* (*liquēre*
be LIQUID, -FY)]

liques'cent, a. Becoming, apt to become,
liquid. [f. L *liquescere* (prec., -ESCENT)]

liqueur' (-kūr), n. Strong alcoholic liquor
sweetened & flavoured with aromatic
substances & usu. drunk in small quantities; mixture of sugar & alcohol or
wines used to flavour champagne, whence
~ v.t.; ~ *brandy*, of special quality for
drinking as ~ ; ~-*glass*, very small for ~s;
~-*frame*, -*stand*, for holding ~-bottles.
[F, = LIQUOR]

li'quid, a. & n. 1. (Substance that is) in-
compressible but offering no resistance
to change of shape, neither solid nor
gaseous, resembling water or oil in
normal state, in fluid but not gaseous
condition (~ *air*, reduced to ~ state by
intense cold; ~ *fire*, projected from flame-
-thrower); watery. 2. Having the transparence, translucence, or brightness, of
water or wine (~ *lustre*, *eyes*, *sky*, *air*,
blue). 3. (Of sounds) flowing clear, fluent,
pure, not grating or discordant, not
guttural, vowel-like, (*blackbird's* ~ *notes*;
in his ~ *Italian*; n., one of the letters *l*, *r*,
& occas. *m*, *n*). 4. Not fixed, unstable,
(*has very* ~ *convictions* or *principles*).
5. (Of assets, securities, etc.) easily convertible into cash. Hence or cogn. ~ITY
(-ĭḋ), ~NESS, nn., ~IZE(3) v.t., ~LY[2] adv.

[ME, f. L *liquidus* (*liquēre* be liquid cf. LIQUATE, LIQUOR)]

li′quid|āte, v.t. & i. Pay, clear off, (debt); put an end to, suppress, get rid of, (often by violent means); wind up, ascertain liabilities & apportion assets of, (company, firm), whence ~ātoʀ n.; (intr., of company) have this done. Hence~A′TION n. (*go into ~ation*, of company, have its affairs wound up, become bankrupt). [f. med. L *liquidare* make clear (LIQUID, -ATE³)]

li′quor (-ker), n., & v.t. & i. 1. Liquid part of secretion or product of operation; liquid used as wash etc.; water used in brewing; liquid (usu. fermented or distilled) for drinking. (*malt ~*, ale, beer, porter, etc.; *spirituous ~*, spirits; DISGUISEd *with~*; *in ~*, *the worse for ~*, more or less drunk; *a ~* or *~-up*, sl., taking of *~* as refreshment); water in which food has been boiled; (pharmacy, pr. lik′wōr) solution of specified drug in water (*~ ammoniae* etc.). 2. vb. Dress (leather, shoes) with grease or oil; steep (malt etc.) in water; (sl.) *~ up* or *~*, have a drink of alcoholic *~*. [ME *licour(e)* f. OF *licour* f. L *liquorem* (*liquēre* see LIQUID, -OR)]

li′quorice (-ko-), **lic′orice**, n. (Black substance used in medicine & as sweetmeat made from) root of *Glycyrrhiza glabra*; the plant. [ME, f. AF *lycorys* f. LL *liquiritia* f. Gk *glukurrhiza* (*glukus* sweet, *rhiza* root)]

li′quorish (-ko-), a. Fond of, indicating fondness for, liquor. Hence ~LY² adv., ~NESS n. [misuse of LICKERISH]

lira (lēr′a), n. (pl. *lire* pr. -ā, ~s; abbr. *L.*). Italian & Turkish monetary unit. [It., f. L LIBRA]

lisle thread (līl thrĕd), n. Fine hard-twisted thread made orig. at Lisle (now Lille) in France.

lisp, v.i. & t., & n. 1. Substitute one of the sounds of *th* for sibilants in speaking; (of child) speak with imperfect pronunciation; say with a *~* (often *out*); hence ~′ingLY² adv. 2. n. ~ing pronunciation; rippling of waters, rustling of leaves. [OE *-wlispian* (f. *wlisp* adj., = OHG *lisp*), = MLG *wlispen*, LG, Du., OHG *lispen*]

liss′om(e), a. Lithe, supple, agile. Hence ~NESS n. [contr. of LITHE*some*]

list¹, n., & v.t. & i. 1. Selvage or edge of cloth, usu. of different material, whence ~′ING¹(3) n.; such edges torn off & used as a material (*~ slippers*; *line edges of door with ~*, to keep out draughts; vb, fasten *~* round edges of, as *have ~ed my doors*). 2. pl. Palisades enclosing tilting-ground; (fig.) scene of contest (*enter the ~s against*, challenge or accept challenge of, usu. to controversy). 3. Roll or catalogue of names, of persons or things belonging to a class, of articles with prices, of things to be done, etc. (*active ~*, of officers in army or navy or air force

liable to be called on for service; *free ~*, of persons to be admitted free to theatre etc., also of duty-free articles; ARMY, CIVIL, SICK, *~~*); (vb) enter in a *~*, (now rare or vulg.) go as soldier, enlist. [senses 1 & 2: OE *liste*, = MDu. *lijste*, OHG *lista* (sense 2 infl. by OF *lisse*, of obsc. orig.); sense 3 f. F *liste* f. Gmc as in 1]

‖ **list²**, v.t. (arch.; 3 sing. pres. *~* or *~eth*, past *~* or *~ed*). Be pleasing to (*shall do what him ~eth*; *did as him ~*); desire, choose, (*to* do or abs.; *ye who ~ to hear*; *wind bloweth where it ~eth*). [OE *lystan*, OS *lustian*, OHG *lusten*, ON *lysta* f. Gmc **lustjan* f. **lustuz* LUST]

list³, n., & v.i. Lean(ing) over to one side (of ship, owing to leak, shifting cargo, subsidence, etc., cf. HEEL³; also of building, fence, etc.). [17th–18th c. also *lust*, of obsc. orig.; perh. transf. use of obs. *list* pleasure, inclination, f. prec.]

‖ **list⁴**, v.i. & t. (arch.). Listen, listen to. [OE *hlystan*, f. *hlyst* sense of hearing, = OS, ON *hlust* f. Gmc **hlustiz* f. **hlus-*; cogn. w. LOUD]

li′sten (-sn), v.i. & t. Make effort to hear something, hear person speaking with attention; give ear to or now usu. *to* (person or sound or story); yield *to* temptation or request; *~ in*, tap telephonic communication, use wireless receiving set; *~ing-post*, point near enemy's lines for detecting his movements by sound. Hence ~ER¹ (-sn-) n. (*good ~er*, one who habitually *~s* with interest or sympathy), (also) person· receiving broadcast wireless programmes. [O Northumb. *lysna*, **hlysna*, MHG *lüsenen* f. Gmc **hlus-* (prec.)]

lis′terine, n. An antiseptic solution. [Lord *Lister* (d. 1912), -INE⁴; P]

lis′terīze, **-ise** (-īz), v.t. Treat (wound) on the antiseptic methods introduced by Lord Lister. So **listēr′IAN** a. [-IZE]

list′lèss, a. Languid, indifferent, uninterested, disinclined for exertion. Hence ~LY² adv., ~NESS n. [ME, f. obs. *list* inclination (LIST²)+-LESS]

lit. See LIGHT³·⁵; *~ up* (sl.), drunk.

lit′anў, n. Series of petitions for use in church services or processions recited by clergy & responded to usu. in repeated formula(s) by people (*the L~*, that contained in the Book of Common Prayer); *~-desk*, *-stool*, at which reciter of *~* kneels. [ME, f. OF f. LL f. Gk *litaneia* prayer]

litchi (lēchē′), n. Fruit(-tree) orig. from China grown in Bengal. [f. Chin. *li-chī*]

-lite, suf. forming names of minerals; F, f. Gk *lithos* stone; usu. preceded by -o-.

lit′eracў, n. Ability to read & write. [LITERATE, -CY, after *illiteracy*]

‖ **lit′erae hūmānĭō′rĕs** (-z), n. (abbr. *Lit. Hūm.*). Polite letters, esp. as name of classical school or examination for B.A. degree at Oxford. [L]

lit′eral, a. & n. 1. Of, in, expressed by, letter(s) of alphabet (*~ error*, also *~* as n., misprint). **2.** Following the letter, text, or exact or original words (~ *translation, transcript,* etc.), whence ~-ism(4) n. **3.** Taking words in their usual or primary sense & applying the ordinary rules of grammar, without mysticism or allegory or metaphor, (~ *interpretation*; *I hear nothing in the ~ sense of the word,* with the ears as opp. other means of getting news), whence ~ism(3), ~ist (2), nn.; (of persons) prosaic, matter-of-fact. **4.** So called without exaggeration (~ *decimation*; often incorrectly used, as *a ~ flood of pamphlets*). Hence ~ITY (-ăl²), ~NESS, nn., ~LY² adv. [ME, f. OF, or LL *litteralis* (LETTER, -AL)]

lit'eralize, -ise (-īz), v.t. Take (metaphor etc.) in literal sense. [-IZE]

literā′um doc′tor, n. Doctor of literature (as University degree). [L]

lit'erar|y, a. Of, constituting, occupied with, literature, polite learning, or books & written composition esp. of the kind valued for form (~*y history of a thing,* of its treatment in literature; ~*y property,* exclusive right of publication, books etc. subject to this; ~*y man,* man of LETTERS); (of word or idiom) uncolloquial, affected by writers. Hence ~ILY² adv., ~INESS n. [f. L *litterarius* (LETTER, -ARY¹)]

lit'erate, a. & n. (Person) having some acquaintance with literature or (now usu.) able to read & write; ‖ man admitted to Anglican orders without university degree. [ME, f. L *litteratus* (LETTER, -ATE²)]

literā′ti, n. pl. Men of letters, the learned class. [L, as prec.]

literā′tim, adv. Letter for letter, textually, literally. [med. L]

lit'erātor, n. Literary man. [L (LITERATE, -OR) elementary teacher, grammarian, sciolist]

lit'erature, n. Literary culture (arch.); literary production (*engaged in* ~), the literary profession (~ *was represented by* ~); realm of letters, writings of country or period; writings whose value lies in beauty of form or emotional effect (LIGHT⁴ ~); *the* books treating *of* a subject; (colloq.)ˊprinted matter. [ME, f. OF, or L *litteratura* (LITERATE, -URE)]

-lith, suf. repr. Gk *lithos* stone (*aerolith, monolith*); cf. -LITE.

lith'ārge (-j), n. Lead monoxide. [ME, f. OF *litarge* f. L f. Gk *litharguros* (*lithos* stone, *arguros* silver)]

lithe (-dh), a. Flexible, supple. Hence ~′NESS (-dhn-) n., ~′SOME (-dhs-) a. [OE *lithe,* OS *lithi,* OHG *lindi* f. Gmc *lin-,* cogn. w. L *lentus*]

lith'ia, n. Oxide of lithium; ~*-water,* used for gout. [changed f. earlier *lithion* f. Gk neut. of *litheios* (*lithos* stone) after *soda* etc.]

lith'ic, a. Of the stone or calculus; of stone. [f. Gk *lithikos* (prec., -IC)]

lith'ium, n. Metallic element resembling sodium. [LITHIA, -IUM]

lith(o)-, comb. form of Gk *lithos* stone, esp. in wds having ref. either to the treatment of stone in the bladder or kidneys, or to the use of stone in printing.

lith'ograph (-ahf), n., & v.t. **1.** Lithographic print. **2.** v.t. Print by lithography; write or engrave on stone. [prec., -GRAPH]

lithŏg′raphy, n. Drawing or writing on kind of yellow slaty limestone (*lithographic stone*) so that impressions in ink can be taken. So **lithŏg′rapher** n., **lithograph′ic** a. [LITHO-, -GRAPHY]

lithŏl′ogy̆, n. Science of the nature & composition of stones & rocks, whence **litholō′gical** a.; department of medical science dealing with calculus. [LITHO-, -LOGY]

lithŏntrip′tic, a. & n. (Medicine) that breaks up stone in bladder. [f. F *lithontriptique* f. Gk *lithŏn thruptika* (drugs) comminutive of stones]

lith'ophyte (Zool.) polyp whose substance is calcareous, as some corals; (bot.) plant that grows on stone. [LITHO-, Gk *phuton* plant (*phuō* grow)]

lithŏt′om|y̆, n. Operation of cutting for stone in bladder. Hence or cogn. **lithotŏm′ic**(AL) aa., ~IST(1) n., ~IZE(1) v.t. [f. LL f. Gk *lithotomia* (LITHO-, -TOMY)]

lithŏt′rit|y̆, n. Operation of crushing stone in bladder into small particles that can be passed through urethra. Hence ~IST(1) n., ~IZE(1) v.t. [f. LITHO- + L *terere trit-* rub, replacing LITHONTRIPTIC etc.]

Lithuā′nian, a. & n. (Language or native) of Lithuania. [-AN]

lit'ig|āte, v.i. & t. Go to law, be party to lawsuit; contest (point) at law, whence ~ABLE a. Hence ~ANT(1) n. & a., ~A′TION n. [f. L *litigare* (*lis litis* lawsuit), -ATE³]

liti'gious (-jus), a. Given to litigation, fond of going to law; disputable at law, offering matter for lawsuit; of lawsuits. Hence ~LY² adv., ~NESS n. [ME, f. OF *litigieux* or L *litigiosus* (*litigium* litigation, cf. prec.)]

lit'mus, n. Blue colouring-matter got from lichens that is turned red by acid & restored to blue by alkali; ~*-paper,* unsized & stained with ~ as test for acids. [ME, f. ONorw. *litmosi* f. ON *litr* (whence E dial. *lit*) dye +*mosi* moss]

lit'otēs (-z), n. Understatement often ironical (as ' *scoundrel* ' *is* rather *a rude word*), esp. the expressing of an affirmative by the negative of its contrary, as *no small* for *great.* [Gk (-ēs) f. *litos* plain, meagre]

litre (lēt′er), n. Unit of capacity in metric system, = cube of 1/10 metre, about 1¾ pints. [F, from 1793, f. *litron,* an obs. measure of capacity, f. med. L f. Gk *litra* pound]

litt'er, n., & v.t. & i. **1.** Vehicle containing couch shut in by curtains & carried on men's shoulders or by beasts; framework with couch for transporting sick &

wounded; straw, rushes, etc., as bedding esp. for animals; straw & dung of farm-yard; odds & ends, leavings, state of untidiness, disorderly accumulation of papers etc., whence ~Y² a.; the young brought forth at a birth. 2. vb. Provide (horse etc.) with ~ as bed (usu. *down*); spread ~ or straw on (floor, stable; usu. *down*); make (place) untidy (of objects lying about, or of person *with* these or simply); scatter & leave lying; bring forth (whelps etc., or abs.). [ME, f. AF *litere* (OF *-iere*) f. Rom. *lectaria* (L *lectus* bed, -ARY¹)]

litterae, -rarum. See **lite-**.

littérateur (see Ap.), n. Literary man. [F]

lit'tle, a. (LESS, LESSER, LEAST; also *smaller, smallest*), n., & adv. (LESS, LEAST). **1.** Small (often with emotional implications not given by *small*, cf. GREAT), not great or big (the idiomatic antitheses are *great & ~, big & ~, great & small, large & small*, not *large & ~* nor *big & small*); (as distinctive epithet) of smaller or smallest size etc. (*the L~ Auk, L~ Malvern, the L~* BEAR¹, *the ~ finger* or *toe*). **2.** Young (*the ~ Joneses*, Jones's children; *~ man* or *woman*, boy or girl, esp. as voc.; *his, her, its, our, ~ ones*, children or cubs etc.). **3.** As of a child, evoking tenderness, patronage, amusement, etc., (*her poor ~ efforts to please; we know his ~ ways; so that is your ~ game*, what you are hoping to do undetected). **4.** Short in stature, distance, or time (*a ~ man; the ~ people*, fairies; *will go a ~ way with you; wait a ~ while*). **5.** Trivial, unimportant, (*every ~ difficulty*); mean, paltry, contemptible, (*with the ~ cunning of ~ minds*). **6.** Not much (*gained ~ advantage from it*; often *but* or *very ~*). **7.** *A ~*, some though not much, even a small amount of, (prob. f. the n. use with ellipse of *of; give me a ~ butter; a ~ care would have prevented it*); (abs.) *the ~*, persons of ~ power or importance, what is ~; *in ~*, on a small scale; ~-*ease* (hist.), prison-cell too small to stand or lie full-length in; ~-*Englander, -dism*, (hist.; holder of) principle that Great Britain should contract her responsibilities for colonies & dependencies (opp. IMPERIALIST, -ISM); ‖ ~-*go* (rare), first examination for B.A. degree at Cambridge; ‖ ~ *Mary* (colloq.), the stomach; *L~ Masters*, group of 16th-c. German engravers, followers of Dürer, named from size of their prints. Hence ~NESS (-ln-) n. **8.** n. Not much, only a small amount, a mere trifle, (~ *or nothing*, hardly anything; *did not a ~ for the cause*, much; *got but, very, rather, ~ out of it*; *a ~ makes us laugh; gives me ~ of his company; did what ~ he could; the ~ of his work that remains*); a certain but no great amount (*knows a ~ of everything; a ~*, rather, somewhat; *not a ~*, extremely); (for a) short time or distance (*after, for*,

a ~; leave me here a ~; ~ by ~, by ~ & ~, by degrees). **9.** adv. To a small extent only (*I like him ~; ~ -known authors; is ~ more than a cento*); not at all (*he ~ knows, dreams*, etc.). [OE *lȳtel*, = OS *luttil*, OHG *luzzil* f. WG *luttil* f. Gmc *lut-*]

litt'oral, a. & n. **1.** Of, on, the shore. **2.** n. Region lying along the shore. [(1) f. L *litoralis* (*litus -oris* shore, -AL); (2) f. It. *-ale*, F *-al*]

lit'urgy (-ter-), n. Communion office of Eastern Church; form of public worship, set of formularies for this; *the* Book of Common Prayer; (Gk ant.) public office or duty performed gratuitously by rich Athenian. Hence **litūr'gICAL** a., **litūr'giGALLY²** adv. [f. LL f. Gk *leitourgia* public worship]

liv'able, a. (Of house, room, climate, etc.) fit to live in; (of life) worth living; companionable, easy to live with. Hence ~NESS n. [LIVE², -ABLE; cf. RELIABLE]

live¹, a. (attrib.). That is alive, living; (joc.) actual, not pretended or pictured or toy (*a real ~ burglar, steam-engine, mountain*); (of broadcast) heard or seen during the occurrence of an event, not a recording; full of power, energy, or importance, not obsolete or exhausted, (*make the question a ~ issue*); glowing (~ *embers*); (of shell, match, wire) unexploded, unkindled, charged with electricity; (of rock) not detached, seeming to form part of the earth's frame; (of wheels etc. in machinery) moving or imparting motion; ~-*bait*, living fish or worm as fishing-bait; ~ *load*, stress resulting from transverse motion of weights (as of locomotive crossing bridge); ~-*oak*, Amer. evergreen tree; ~*stock*, animals kept or dealt in for use or profit; ~ *wire* (fig.), highly energetic forceful person. [aphetic f. ALIVE]

live², v.i. & t. **1.** Be alive, have animal or vegetable life. **2.** Subsist (*up*)*on* (~ *on fruit*), depend (*up*)*on* for subsistence (~*s upon his wife, wife's earnings*, etc.; *living* WAGE¹); (fig.) sustain one's position or repute (*up*)*on* (~*s on his name*), get livelihood *by* one's wits etc. or *by doing*, (~ *& let ~*, condone others' failings to secure the same treatment for oneself; *~ from* HAND¹ *to mouth*). **3.** Conduct oneself *honestly, viciously, like a saint*, etc. (~ *up to* one's *principles, faith*, etc., put them in practice). **4.** Arrange one's habits, expenditure, feeding, etc. (~ FAST⁴, *in* CLOVER; ~ *well*, on dainty food; ~ *on air*, (appear to) take no food; ~ *in a small way*, cheaply & quietly; ~ *a double life*, (esp.) sustain two different characters, act two different parts, in life; ~ *to oneself*, in isolation). **5.** (With cogn. obj.) spend, pass, experience, (~ *a virtuous life; he ~d what he narrated*). **6.** Wear *down* (scandal, prejudice, effect of past guilt) by blameless course of life. **7.** Express in one's life (~ *a lie*). **8.** Enjoy life intensely. **9.** Continue alive, have one's life prolonged, (*patient cannot* ~; ~*d to see his children's children*; ~ *& learn!*, way of greeting new fact; ~ *out the night*, remain alive through it); (of things) survive (*his memory* ~*s*), (of ship) escape destruction (*nothing could* ~ *afloat*); dwell (‖ ~ *in, out*, of shop-assistants or domestic servants residing on premises or not), spend daytime *in* room (*room does not seem to be* ~*d in*). [OE *libban, lifian*, OS *libbian*, OHG *lebēn*, ON *lifa*, Goth. *liban* f. Gmc **libhǣ-* f. **libh-* LIFE]

live′lihōōd (-vl-), n. Means of living, sustenance. [OE *liflād* (LIFE, *lād* course) assim. to obs. *livelihood* liveliness]

live′lŏng (-vl-), a. (poet., rhet.). Whole length of (*the* ~ *day, night, summer*), with implication of weariness or delight. [c. 1400 *lefe* (= LIEF) *longe*; in 16th c. assim. to LIVE[2]]

live′l|ў (-vl-), a. Lifelike, realistic, (*a* ~*y description*; *give a* ~*y idea of*); full of life, vigorous, energetic, brisk, vivid, interesting; (joc.) exciting, dangerous, difficult, (*police had a* ~*y time*; *press is making it* or *things* ~*y for* —); (of colour) bright; gay, vivacious; (of boat etc.) rising lightly to waves. Hence ~ĭLY[2] adv., ~ĭNESS n. (*a certain* ~*iness*, sl., some heavy gunfire). [OE *liflic* (LIFE, -LY[1])]

liv′en, v.t. & i. Brighten, cheer, (usu. *up*). [LIFE, -EN[6]]

liv′er[1], n. Large glandular organ in vertebrates secreting bile & purifying venous blood; (also ~*-complaint*) diseased state of ~, whence ~ISH[1] a.; (also ~*-colour*) dark reddish brown; flesh of some animals' ~ used as food; (arch.) ~ as seat of emotion (*hot* ~, passionate or amorous temperament; *white* or *lily* ~, cowardice, whence -~ED[2] a.); ~*-line*, one of lines of palm significant in palmistry; ~ *wing*, right wing of cooked fowl, under which ~ is tucked; ~*wort*, kinds of plant with ~*-shaped* parts or used in ~ disease. Hence ~LESS a. [OE *lifer* MDu. *lever*, OHG *lebara*, ON *lifr* f. Gmc **libh-*]

liv′er[2], n. One who lives in specified way (*clean, loose*, ~; *good* ~, virtuous person, also one given to *good* LIVING[1]). [-ER[1]]

Liverpŭd′lian, a. & n. (Inhabitant) of Liverpool. [joc. formation]

liv′erỹ[1], n. **1.** Provision of food or clothing served out to retainers etc. (hist.); allowance of provender for horses (*at* ~, of horse, kept for owner & fed & groomed for fixed charge). **2.** Distinctive clothes worn by member of city company or person's servant (*in, out of*, ~, of servant, so attired or in plain clothes; also fig., *birds in their winter* ~, *the* ~ *of grief, of other men's opinions*, etc.), whence **liv′eri**ED[2] (-rĭd) a. **3.** Membership of city company (*take up* one's ~, become ~*man*). **4.** (law). Legal delivery of property (‖ *sue* one's ~, bring suit as heir in court of wards to get possession), writ allowing

this. **5.** ‖ ~ *company*, one of London City companies that had formerly distinctive costume; ‖ ~ *fine*, payment for becoming member of ~ company; ~*man*, member of ~ company, keeper of or attendant in ~ stable; ~ *servant*, wearing ~; ~ *stable*, where horses are kept at ~ or let out for hire. [ME, f. AF *livere*, OF *livree* (*livrer* see DELIVER, -Y[4])]

liv′ery[2], a. Of the consistence or colour of liver; ‖ (of soil) tenacious; having a disordered liver, feeling out of sorts, irritable. [-Y[2]]

liv′id, a. Of bluish leaden colour; discoloured as by bruise; ‖ (colloq.) furiously angry. Hence or cogn. **livid′**ITY n., ~LY[2] adv. [f. F *livide* or L *lividus*]

liv′ing[1], n. In vbl senses; also or esp.: livelihood, maintenance, (*make* one's ~); ‖ (eccl.) benefice; *good* ~, luxurious feeding; *plain* ~ *& high thinking*, frugal & philosophic life; ~*-room* (for general day use); ~*-space*, transl. of LEBENSRAUM; ~ *wage*, on which it is possible for worker to live in more comfort than on *subsistence wage*. [-ING[1]]

liv′ing[2], a. In vbl senses; esp.: contemporary, now existent, (*no man* ~ *could do better*; *the greatest* ~ *master of irony*; *the first of* ~ *artists*; *the* ~, those now alive; *in the land of the* ~, alive); (of likeness) exact, whence ~LY[2] adv.; ~ *water*, perennially flowing; ~ *rock, coal*, = LIVE[1]; ~ *language*, still in vernacular use; ~ *death*, state of hopeless misery; *within* ~ *memory*, that of persons still ~. [-ING[2]]

livre (lē′vr), n. Old French money of account (20 sous). [F, f. L LIBRA]

lixiv′i|āte, v.t. Separate (substance) into soluble & insoluble constituents by percolation of water. Hence ~A′TION n. [f. L *lixivius* made into lye (*lix*), -ATE[3]]

liz′ard, n. Kinds of reptile having usu. long body & tail, four legs, & scaly or granulated hide; fancy variety of canary. [ME, f. OF *lesard* f. L *lacertus* w. assim. to -ARD]

′ll, contr. of WILL in *I'll, he'll, that'll*, etc.

lla′ma (lah-, lyah-), n. S.-Amer. ruminant allied to camel but smaller, humpless, & woolly-haired, used as beast of burden; (material made of) its wool. [Sp., prob. f. Peruvian]

lla′nō (lah-, lyah-), n. S.-Amer. treeless plain or steppe. Hence **llanero** (lyahnār′ō) n., inhabitant of the ~s. [Sp., f. L *planus -num* PLAIN[1]]

Lloyd′s (loidz), n. Incorporated society of underwriters in London; ~ *list*, newspaper devoted to maritime intelligence; ~ *register*, annual alphabetic list of ships assigned to various classes. [orig. 17th-c. coffee-house established by Edward *Lloyd*]

lō, int. (arch.). Look!, see!, behold! (freq. *lo and behold!*, as joc. introduction of surprising fact). [combining OE *lā* int. & ME *lo* = *loke*, LOOK[1]]

loach, n. Small edible freshwater fish. [ME, f. OF *loche*, of unkn. orig.]

load[1], n. What is (to be) carried, burden; amount usu. carried (*cart*-~ etc.) recognized unit in measure or weight of certain substances; material object or force acting as weight or clog, resistance of machinery worked to motive power, pressure of superstructure on arch etc.; (electr.) amount of current supplied by a dynamo or generating station at any given time (see PEAK[1]); burden of responsibility, care, grief, etc. (*take a ~ off* one's *mind*, relieve him of anxiety); (pl., colloq.) plenty, superabundance, heaps, lots, *of*; ~-*displacement, -draught*, of ship when laden; ~-*shedding*, temporary curtailment of supply of electricity to a specific area to prevent excessive ~ on generating plant; ~'*stone, lodestone*, magnetic oxide of iron, piece of it used as magnet, thing that attracts, (= way stone, see etym.); ~-(*water*)*line*, ship's flotation line when laden, Plimsoll's mark. [OE *lād* way, journey, conveyance, corresp. to OHG *leita*, ON *leith* way, course, f. Gmc *laidhō* (LEAD[2]); cf. LODE]

load[2], v.t. & i. Put load on or aboard (person, vehicle, ship, etc.), (of ship, vehicle, person responsible for these, or person) take load aboard etc. (often *up*); place (load, cargo) aboard ship, on vehicle, etc.; add weight to, be burden upon, oppress *with* (*stomach* ~*ed with food*), weight with lead (*a* ~*ed cane* ; ~*ed dice*, so weighted as to fall with a certain face up), strain bearing-capacity of (*table* ~*ed with food*); adulterate with something to increase weight or (of wines) strength; supply or assail overwhelmingly *with* (~*ed her with gifts, praise, abuse* ; *air* ~*ed with carbon*); charge (fire-arms; *am* ~*ed*, have my gun etc. charged); insert film in (camera); charge with some hidden implication (esp. in p.p., as *a* ~*ed question*); (Stock-Exch.) buy heavily of stock (~*ed up with*, having large amounts of in hand as security); (life-insurance) add extra charge or ~'ING[1] n. to (premium) for special reasons. [f. prec.]

load'er, n. In vbl senses; esp.: attendant loading sportsman's guns; loading--machine ; ~, gun loaded in specified way (*breech, muzzle, single,* -~), so -load'ING[2] a. [-ER[1]]

loaf[1], n. (pl. *loaves* pr. lōvz). Piece of bread baked alone or as separate or separable part of batch, usu. of some standard weight as 1lb., 2lb., or 4lb. (COTTAGE, *household, tinned,* ~, various shapes; QUARTERN ~ ; *brown* ~, of BROWN bread; *white* ~, of FIRSTS; *loaves & fishes*, personal profit as inducement to religious profession or public service, see *John* vi. 26; *half a* ~ *is better than no bread*, motto of compromise, opp. *all or nothing*); (sl.) head (*use* one's ~, use one's common sense); (also *sugar*-~) conical moulded mass of sugar (~ *sugar*, this as whole or cut into lumps); ‖ solid roundish head of cabbage or lettuce, whence **loaveD**[2] (-vd) a. [OE *hlāf*, OHG *leip* (G *laib*), ON *hleifr*, Goth. *hlaifs* f. Gmc *hlaibhaz*]

‖ **loaf**[2], **loave,** v.t. (Of cabbage etc.) form a loaf or head. [f. prec.]

loaf[3], v.i. & t., & n. **1.** Spend time idly; saunter; ~ (time) *away*, spend in ~ing; hence ~'ER[1] n. **2.** n. ~ing (*going to have a, on the,* ~). [orig. unkn.]

loam, n. Paste of clay & water, composition of moistened clay & sand with chopped straw etc. used in making bricks, plastering, etc.; fertile soil chiefly of clay & sand with admixture of decayed vegetable matter, whence ~'Y[2] a. [OE *lām*, MDu. *leem*, OHG *leimo* f. Gmc *laim*-, f. *lai*-, *lī*- (LIME[1])]

loan[1], n., & v.t. **1.** Thing, esp. sum of money, lent to be returned with or without interest; word, custom, etc., adopted by one people from another (so ~-*god, -myth, -word*); lending or being lent (*on* ~ ; *may I have the* ~ *of* — ?, may I borrow it?); money contribution from individuals or public bodies to State expenses acknowledged as debt; arrangement or contract by which a government receives advances of money usu. for stipulated interest. **2.** ~ *collection*, of pictures etc. lent by owners for exhibition; ~-*holder*, person holding debentures or other acknowledgements of ~, mortgagee; ~-*office*, for lending money to private borrowers, also for receiving subscriptions to government ~; ~-*society*, of periodical subscribers to fund from which members may have ~s; ~-*translation*, expression adopted by one language from another in more or less literally translated form (e.g. *reason of State* f. F *raison d'état, marriage of convenience* f. F *mariage de convenance*). **3.** v.t. (now chiefly U.S.). Grant ~ of, whence ~'ABLE a., ~EE[1], ~'ER[1], nn. [ME *lan*(*e*) f. ON *lān*, = OE *lǣn* (see LEND), M.Du. *lēne*, OHG *lēhan*, f. Gmc *laihwn*-, cogn. w. Goth. *leihwan* lend]

loan[2], **loan'ing,** nn. (Sc.). Lane; open place where cows are milked. [ME by--form of LANE; -ING[1]]

loath, lōth, a. (pred. only). Disinclined, reluctant, unwilling, (usu. *to* do or abs.; also *for* person *to* do, or *that*; *nothing* ~, quite willing or willingly); ~-*to-depart*, tune played as farewell. [OE *lāth*, OS *lēth*, OHG *leid*, ON *leithr* f. Gmc *laithaz*]

loath|e (-dh), v.t. Regard with disgust, abominate, detest. Hence ~'ING[1](1) n., ~'ing LY[2] adv, (-dh-). [OE *lāthian* f. Gmc *laithjan* (prec.)]

loath'l|ỹ (-dh-), a. (Arch. & literary for) loathsome. Hence ~iNESS n. [OE *lāthlic* (LOATH, -LY[1])]

loath'some (-th-, -dh-), a. Exciting nausea or disgust, offensive to the senses, sickening, repulsive, odious. Hence ~LY[2] adv., ~NESS n. [ME, f. LOATH, -SOME]

loaves. See LOAF¹.

lob, v.i. & t. (-bb-), & n. **1.** Walk, run, or move, heavily or clumsily or slowly (often *along*); toss, bowl, or send, (ball) with slow or high-pitched motion. **2.** n. Ball bowled underhand at cricket or sent high in air at lawn tennis. [earlier: pendulous object; bumpkin; prob. of LG, Du. orig. (MLG *lobbe, lubbe,* Du. *lob, lobbe* seed-lobe, Du. *lobbes* bumpkin); cf. LUBBER]

lŏb′|āte, a. (nat. hist.). Having lobe(s). Hence ~A′TION n. [LOBE, -ATE²]

lŏbb′y̆, n., & v.t. & i. **1.** Porch, anteroom, entrance-hall, corridor; (in House of Commons etc.) large hall open to public used esp. for interviews between members & outsiders, (also *division* ~) one of two corridors to which members retire to vote; *body of~ists. **2.** vb (chiefly U.S.). Influence (members of legislature), get (bill etc.) *through,* by ~ interviews etc.; frequent ~ of legislature, solicit members' votes, whence ~IST(1) n. [f. med. L *lobia, lobium,* LODGE¹]

lŏbe, n. Roundish & flattish projecting or pendulous part, often one of two or more such parts divided by fissure (so ~ *of liver* or *lungs*; ~*s of brain*; ~ *of ear,* lower soft pendulous external part). Hence **lŏb′AR¹** a. (esp. of the lungs, as *lobar pneumonia*).

lŏbED² (-bd), ~′LESS (-bl-), aa. [f. LL f. Gk *lobos* lobe, pod]

lŏbĕc′tomy̆, n. (med.). Excision of lobe of an organ, as of a lung, thyroid gland, etc. [-ECTOMY]

lobēl′ĭa, n. Kinds of herbaceous plant with blue, scarlet, or purple flowers having deeply cleft corolla without spur. [M. de *Lobel* (d. 1616), -IA¹]

lŏblŏll′y̆ măn, boy, nn. (naut.). Surgeon's mate, attendant. [perh. f. dial. *lob* eat, up noisily + dial. *lolly* soup]

lŏbŏt′omy̆, n. (med.). = LEUCO*tomy*. [f. LOBE, -O-, -TOMY]

lŏb′scouse (-ows), n. Sailor's dish of meat stewed with vegetables & ship's biscuit. [cf. LOBLOLLY; LG(G) *labskaus* said to be f. E]

lŏb′ster, n. Large marine stalk-eyed ten--footed long-tailed edible crustacean with large claws formed by first pair of feet, bluish black before & scarlet after boiling; its flesh as food; ~-*eyed,* with protruding eyes; ~ *joint* (adaptable kind in pipe or tube); ~-*pot,* basket in which ~s are trapped. [OE *lopustre* corrupt. of L *locusta* crustacean, LOCUST]

lŏb′ŭl|e, n. Small lobe. Hence ~AR¹ a. [LOBE, -ULE]

lŏb′worm (-wĕrm), n. Large earthworm used as fishing-bait; marine worm (also *lug*) similarly used. [f. obs. *lob* n., see LOB]

lōcal′¹, lōcale′, (-ahl), n. Scene or locality of operations or events. [F (-*l*), abs. use of adj. = foll.; -*e* is E respelling to indicate stress, cf. MORALE]

lōc′al², a. & n. **1.** In regard to place (~ *habitation,* position in space as test of thing's material existence; *London is a* ~ *name;* ~ *adverb*). **2.** Belonging to, existing in, or peculiar to certain place(s) (~ *time,* reckoned from sun's transit over place's meridian; *the* ~ *lawyer;* *globe-flower is very* ~, not generally distributed; ~ *government,* administration of town etc. by inhabitants' representatives, ‖ *L~ Government Board,* State department later absorbed by MINISTRY *of Health;* ‖~ *examination,* held in various places under university board & giving certificates to boys & girls; ~ *preacher,* Methodist layman authorized to preach in his own circuit; ~ *option, veto,* system by which inhabitants of district may prohibit sale of liquor in it; ~ *colour,* details characteristic of the scene or time represented in novel or other literary work inserted to give actuality, & see below). **3.** Affecting, of, a part & not the whole (~ *disease, pain, remedy;* ~ *colour* in picture, that of separate objects apart from general colour-scheme, & see above). **4.** (math.). Of a locus. **5.** ‖ (Post.; written on cover of letter as warning to P.O. officials) for delivery in this town or district. Hence ~LY² adv. **6.** n. Inhabitant of, professional man practising in, particular district; ~ preacher; (item of) ~ news in newspaper; postage-stamp current in limited district; train serving stations of district; ‖ (colloq.) the ~ public house; ‖ (pl.) ~ examination(s). [ME, f. OF, f. LL *localis* (*locus* place, -AL)]

lōc′alism, n. Attachment to a place; limitation of ideas etc. resulting; favouring of what is local; a local idiom, custom, etc. [-ISM]

lōcăl′ĭty̆, n. Thing's position, place where it is; site or scene of something; faculty of remembering & recognizing places, finding one's way, etc. [f. F *localité* or LL *localitas* (LOCAL², -TY)]

lōc′aliz|e, -is|e (-īz), v.t. Invest with the characteristics of a particular place; restrict to particular place; attach to districts, decentralize; concentrate (attention) *upon;* (rare) = LOCATE. Hence ~ABLE a., ~A′TION n. [-IZE]

locāte′, v.t. *Establish in a place, (pass.) *be situated; state locality of; discover exact place of (~ *the enemy's camp*). Hence locA′TION n., (also, cinemat.) place outside studio where (part of) picture is filmed (esp. *on location*). [f. L *locare* (*locus* place), -ATE³]

lōc′ative, a. & n. (gram.). (Case) denoting place where. [prec., -IVE, after *vocative*]

‖ **loch** (lŏχ), n. Scottish lake; an arm of the sea, esp. when narrow or partially landlocked. [Gael.]

lŏck¹, n. Portion of fairly long hair that hangs together, tress, (pl.) hair of head; tuft of wool or cotton. Hence ~~ED² (kt)

lock a. [OE *loc*, OS *lok*, OHG *loc*, ON *lokkr*, f. Gmc *lokkaz*]

lock², n. **1.** Appliance for fastening door, lid, etc., with bolt that requires key of particular shape to work it (*under ~ & key*, locked up); appliance to keep wheel from revolving or slewing. **2.** Mechanism for exploding charge of gun (*~, stock, & barrel*, whole of thing, completely). **3.** Confined section of canal at point where level changes for raising & lowering boats by use of sluiced gates. **4.** Ante-chamber to chamber in which engineering work is done in compressed air. **5.** Interlocking, e.g. block or jam of vehicles in street. **6.** Extent to which fore-wheel's can be made to cross hind-wheel's plane. **7.** (Also *L~ Hospital*) hospital for venereal disease. **8.** *~'fast*, secured with *~*; *~-keeper*, *= ~sman*; *~'man*, coroner's summoner in I. of Man; *~s'man*, keeper of canal *~*; *~'smith*, maker & mender of *~s*. Hence *~'LESS* a. [OE *loc*, corresp. to OS *lok*, OHG *loh* hole, ON *lok* lid, f. Gmc *lokam*]

lock³, v.t. & i. **1.** Fasten (door, box, etc.) with lock, shut *up* (house etc.) by fastening doors thus, (of door etc.) admit of being so fastened, have a lock; shut (person, thing) *up*, *in*, or *into*; *~ the stable door after the horse has been stolen*, take precautions too late. **2.** (Of land, hills, etc.) hem in (usu. in pass.). **3.** (fig.). Store (*up* or *away*) inaccessibly (*facts ~ed up in hieroglyphics*; *capital ~ed up in land*); imprison (*senses ~ed in sleep*). **4.** Keep (person) *out* by *~ing* door (esp. of employer coercing workmen by refusing them work; *~-out* n., this procedure, cf. STRIKE). **5.** Bring or come into rigidly fixed position, engage, (make) catch, fasten by interlacing or fitting of corresponding parts, entangle; (p.p.) joined in hostile or other embrace. **6.** (mil.). (Of rear rank) march so close to front rank that feet overlap. **7.** (Of vehicle or wheels) (have fore-wheels that) admit of being slewed into different planes from those of hind-wheels. **8.** Provide (canal etc.) with locks; convey (boat) *up* or *down* through lock; go through lock. **9.** *~-chain*, for *~ing* wheels of vehicle; *~-jaw*, *~ed-jaw*, (pop. name for) trismus, variety of tetanus, tonic spasm of muscles of mastication causing jaws to remain rigidly closed; *~-nut*, extra nut screwed over another to prevent its starting; *~-spring*, closing watch-case; *~-stitch*, sewing-machine stitch by which two threads are firmly *~ed* together; *~-up*, (time of) *~ing* up school etc. for night, unrealizable state of invested capital or amount of capital *~ed* up, house or room for temporary detention of prisoners, (attrib.) that can be *~ed* up (*~-up garage*). [ME, f. prec.]

lock'age, n. Amount of rise or fall effected by canal locks; toll for use of lock; use or number of locks. [-AGE]

lock'er, n. In vbl senses; also: small cup-board, esp. one of many reserved each for individual's use in public room, e.g. cricket pavilion or schoolroom; (naut.) chest or compartment for clothes, stores, ammunition, etc. (*not a shot in the ~*, no money in one's pocket; DAVY JONES'S LOCKER). [-ER¹]

lock'et, n. Metal plate or band on scabbard; small gold or silver case holding portrait, lock of hair, etc., & usu. hung from neck. [f. OF *loquet* dim. of *loc* latch f. WG *lok* LOCK², -ET¹]

Lock'|ian, a. Of John Locke (d. 1704) or his philosophy or followers. So *~IST*(2) n. [-IAN]

loc'ō¹, n. Locomotive engine. [abbr.]

loc'ō², n. Poisonous leguminous plant found in U.S. (*~-disease*, brain disease affecting cattle eating *~*). Hence *~*, *~ED²*(-ōd), aa. (sl.), crazy. [Sp., = insane]

loc'ō citāt'ō, adv. (abbr. *loc. cit.* or *l.c.*). In the passage already quoted. [L]

locomō'tion, n. (Power of) motion from place to place; travel, way (esp. artificial) of travelling. [17th c., f. L *loco* abl. of *locus* place + *motio* MOTION; suggested by the scholastic phr. *in loco moveri* move in space]

loc'omōtive, a. & n. **1.** Of locomotion (*~ faculty, power*), (joc.) of travel (*in these ~ days*); having power of or given to locomotion, not stationary, (*the ~ bivalves*; *a ~ person*, joc., constantly travelling; *~ engine*, that goes from place to place by its own power, esp. steam-engine for drawing train along rails); effecting locomotion (*the ~ organs*). **2.** n. *~* engine; *~* animal. [(1) 17th c. as prec.; see -IVE; (2) n.f. adj., short for *~ engine*]

loc'omōtor, n. & a. **1.** Locomotive person or thing. **2.** adj. Of locomotion (*~ ATAXY*). [as prec., MOTOR]

loc'omōtory, a. Of, having, locomotion. [as prec., MOTORY]

loc'ūl|us, n. (zool., anat., bot.; pl. *~ī*). One of a number of small separate cavities. Hence *~AR¹* a. [L, dim. of LOCUS]

loc'um tēn'ēns (-z; also colloq. **loc'um**), n. Deputy acting esp. for clergyman or doctor. Hence **loc'um-tēn'ency** n. [med. L, (one) holding place TENANT, (foll.)]

loc'us, n. (pl. *-ci* pr. *-sī*). Locality or exact place of something; (math.) curve etc. made by all points satisfying particular equation of relation between co-ordinates, or by point, line, or surface, moving according to mathematically defined conditions; *~ class'icus*, best known or most authoritative passage on a subject; *~ in quō*, scene of event; *~ pocnilēn'tiae* (-shiē), opportunity allowed for receding until decisive step has been taken; *~ stān'dī*, recognized position, right to intervene, appear in court, etc. [L, = place]

loc'ust, n. Kinds of African & Asian winged edible insect migrating in swarms

& consuming vegetation of districts; person of devouring or destructive propensities; fruit of carob-tree; cassia pod; (also ∼-*tree*) kinds of tree, esp. carob & false acacia; ∼-*bird*, -*eater*, kinds of bird feeding on ∼s. [ME, f. L *locusta* lobster, locust]

locū′tion, n. Style of speech; word or phrase considered in regard to style, idiom, (*a barbarous* ∼; *to use the Greek* ∼). [ME, f. L *locutio* (*loqui locut*- speak, -ION)]

lŏc′ūtorў̆, n. Parlour or conversation--room in monastery; grille for interviews between inmates of monastery & outsiders. [f. LL *locutorium* (prec., -ORY)]

lōde, n. ‖ Watercourse, open drain in fens; vein of metal ore; ∼′*star*, loadstar, star that is steered by, esp. the pole-star, (fig.) guiding principle, object of pursuit; ∼′*stone* see LOAD[1] *stone*. [var. of LOAD[1]]

lŏdge[1], n. 1. Small house (arch.). 2. Cottage at gates of park or grounds of large house, occupied by gardener or other servant; house (e.g. in Scottish Highlands) occupied in the hunting or shooting season. 3. Porter's room at gate of college, factory, or house of chambers or flats. 4. (Freemasonry etc.) (place of meeting for) members of branch; *grand* ∼, governing body of freemasons & societies imitating them. 5. Residence of head of college at Cambridge, cf. LODGINGS. 6. Beaver's or otter's lair. 7. N.-Amer. Indian's tent or wigwam. [ME *log(g)e* f. OF *loge* f. Rom. *lobia*, med. L *laubia*, *lobia* (LOBBY), f. Gmc *laubja* f. *laubam* LEAF]

lŏdge[2], v.t. & i. 1. Provide with sleeping--quarters; receive as guest or inmate; establish as resident *in* house or room(s), (pass.) be *well, ill*, etc., accommodated in regard to house-room. 2. Serve as habitation for, contain, (pass.) be contained *in*. 3. Leave *in* place or *with* person for security. 4. Deposit in court or with official a formal statement of (complaint, information); (pop.) allege (objection etc.). 5. Place (power etc.) *in, with, in the hands of*, (person). 6. (Of wind) lay (crops) flat. 7. (Make, let) stick or remain in place without falling or going further (∼*d bullet, bullet* ∼*d, in his brain; tide* ∼*s mud in the cavities*). 8. Reside, be situated; ‖ be inmate paying for accommodation in another's house, whence **lŏdg′ER**[1] n. (∼*r franchise*, right to vote at election of M.P. enjoyed by a class of ∼rs before the 1918 extension). [ME, f. OF *logier* (prec.)]

lŏdg′ing, n. In vbl senses; esp.: accommodation in hired rooms; dwelling-place, abode, (pl.) room(s) hired elsewhere than in hotel for residing in, residence of head of college at Oxford (cf. LODGE[1]); ∼-*house*, in which ∼s are let (‖ *common* ∼ -*house*, usu. one with dormitory in which bed can be had for the night); ∼ *turn*, spell of

duty in railway service during which a train crew sleeps away from home for a night. [ME, -ING[1]]

lŏdge′ment, -gment, (-jm-), n. (Mil.) temporary defensive work on captured part of enemy's works; stable position gained, foothold, (*make, effect, a* ∼); (law) deposit(ing) of money; accumulation of matter intercepted in fall or transit. [f. F *logement* (prec., -MENT)]

lö′ĕss, n. Deposit of fine yellowish-grey loam in Rhine & other river valleys. [G *löss*]

loft (law-, lŏ-), n., & v.t. 1. Attic; room over stable; pigeon-house; flock of pigeons; gallery in church or hall; (golf) backward slope in club-head, ∼ing stroke. 2. v.t. Hit (golf-ball) high up, clear (obstacle) thus; keep (pigeons) in ∼. [late OE *loft* f. ON *loft* air, sky, upper room, cogn. w. OE *lyft*; see LIFT]

lof′ter (law-, lŏ-), n. Golf-club for lofting. [-ER[1]]

lof′t|ў̆ (law-, lŏ-), a. Of imposing height, towering, soaring, (∼*y mountain, flight, stature*; not of persons); haughty, consciously superior or dignified, (∼*y contempt, good humour*); exalted, distinguished, high-flying, high-flown, elevated, sublime, grandiose. Hence ∼ILЎ[2] adv., ∼INESS n. [-Y[2]]

lŏg[1], n., & v.t. (-gg-). 1. Unhewn piece of felled tree or similar rough mass of wood (*in the* ∼, unhewn; *float, lie, fall, like a* ∼, in helpless or stunned state; *roll my* ∼ *& I'll roll yours*, applied to mutual help, esp. to unprincipled political combinations & puffing of each other's works by author--reviewers, whence ∼′*roll* v.i., ∼′*roll*-ING[1, 2] n. & a.; *King Log*. fainéant ruler, w. ref. to fable of Jupiter & the frogs, cf. STORK). 2. Float attached to line wound on reel for gauging speed of ship, other apparatus for same purpose, (*heave, throw, the* ∼, use this; *sail by the* ∼, calculate ship's position by it); = ∼-*book*. 3. ‖ Table by which journeyman-tailor's work-time is assessed. 4. ∼-*board*, on which entries are made for transcription into ∼-*book*, book with permanent record daily made of all events occurring in ship's voyage including rate of progress shown by ∼, (also) traveller's diary etc.; ∼ *cabin*, hut built of ∼s; ∼-*line*, to which float of ship's ∼ is attached; ∼′*wood*, (wood of) Amer. tree used in dyeing. 5. v.t. Cut into ∼s; enter (distance made etc.) in ship's ∼-*book*, (of ship) make (distance); enter (seaman's name with offence committed) in ∼-*book*, fine (offender). [ME *logge*, of obsc. orig.; cf. contemporary CLOG]

lŏg[2], = LOGARITHM of (prefixed to number or algebraic symbol).

lŏg′anbĕrrў̆, n. Fruit got by cross between raspberry & blackberry. [J. H. *Logan*, of California]

lŏg′an(-stōne), n. Poised heavy stone

rocking at a touch. [= *logging* (dial. *log* to rock)]

lŏgaoed′ic (-aē-), a. & n. (Line) in metre composed of dactyls & trochees. [f. LL f. Gk *logaoidikos* combining prose & poetry (*logos* speech, *aoidē* song, -IC)]

lŏg′arithm, n. One of a class of arithmetical functions tabulated for use in abridging calculation & enabling computer to substitute addition & subtraction for multiplication & division, & the latter two for involution & evolution; index of power to which fixed number (the *base*) must be raised to produce given number (*the ~ of 1,000 is 3; common ~s*, whose base is 10). Hence **lŏgarith′mic** a., **lŏgarith′mically** adv. [f. Gk *logos* reckoning, ratio, *arithmos* number]

loge (lōzh), n. Box in theatre etc. [F]

-loger, suf. repr. L -*logus* or Gk -*logos*. *Astrologer*, the oldest wd of the type, may be either f. L *astrologus* + -ER[1] (afterwards a common type of formation) or f. *astrology* + -ER[1] (cf. -GRAPHER). As living suf., ~ was used to form personal nn. corresp. to wds in -LOGY, but is now superseded by -LOGIST.

lŏgg′erhead (-gerhĕd), n. **1.** Blockhead, fool, (arch.; *We three ~s be*, inscription under two wooden heads on inn-sign). **2.** Iron instrument with ball at end heated for melting pitch etc.; post built into boat for catching turn of rope to; kinds of large-headed turtle & bird. **3.** *At ~s* (*with*), disagreeing or disputing (with), (prob. f. notion of trying whose head is harder). [prob. f. dial. *logger* block of wood for hobbling horse]

lŏgg′ia (-jya), n. (pl. ~s or *loggie* pr. -ā). Open-sided gallery or arcade. [It., = LODGE]

lo′gic, n. Science of reasoning, proof, thinking, or inference; particular scheme of or treatise on this; chain of reasoning, correct or incorrect use of argument, ability in argument, arguments (CHOP[4] ~; *argues with great learning & ~*; *is not governed by ~*); (with purposely perverted sense) converting-power, compulsion, (*the ~ of events, facts, necessity, war*, etc.). So **logi′cian** (-Ishn) n. [ME, f. OF *logique* f. LL *logica*, -e sing. (also L (Cic.) *logica* pl. = Gk *ta logika*) f. Gk *logikē* (*tekhnē* art) of reason f. LOGOS, -IC(2)]

-logic, -logical, suff. orig. repr. Gk adjj. in -*logikos* (thr. F & L), derived f. adjj. & nn. in -*logos, -logon*, wh. have derivative nn. in -*logia* -LOGY. Such adjj. are commonly apprehended as if f. -*logy* + -IC. Hence mod. formations in -*logy* may always have correl. adjj. in -*logical* (rarely -*logic*) & nn. in -*logist* (occas. -LOGER).

lo′gical, a. Of logic or formal argument; not contravening the laws of thought, correctly reasoned; deducible, defensible on ground of consistency, reasonably to be believed or done; capable of correct

reasoning. Hence ~ITY (-ăl[2]) n., ~LY[2] adv. [f. obs. F, or med. L *logicalis* (prec., -AL)]

lo′gie (-gī), n. Zinc ornament looking like jewel used in theatres. [D. *Logie*, inventor]

lŏg′iŏn (-g-), n. (pl. -*ia*). Saying of Christ, not recorded in Gospels but preserved elsewhere. [Gk, = oracle (LOGOS)]

-logist, suf. forming nn. meaning *one versed in -logy*, f. -LOGY, -IST.

logis′tics, n. pl. Art of moving & quartering troops (cf. STRATEGY, TACTICS), & supplying & maintaining a fleet. So **logis′tic** a. [f. F *logistique* (*loger* LODGE[2], -IC)]

lŏg′ogram, n. Sign or character representing a word in shorthand. [LOGOS, -GRAM]

lŏg′ograph (-ahf), n. = prec.; = LOGOTYPE. [LOGOS, -GRAPH]

logog′rapher, n. (Gk ant.). One of the Greek prose historians before Herodotus; ancient-Greek professional speech-writer for law courts. [f. LL f. Gk *logographos* (LOGOS, -GRAPHER)]

lŏg′ogriph, n. Kind of anagrammatic word-puzzle. [f. F *logogriphe* (LOGOS, Gk *griphos* riddle)]

logŏm′achy (-k-), n. (literary). Dispute about words, controversy turning on merely verbal points. [f. Gk *logomakhia* (LOGOS, -*makhia* -fighting)]

lŏg′os, n. (no pl.). The Word or Second Person of the Trinity; [Gk, = word, reason, f. *legō* speak, used in mystic sense by Hellenistic & Neo-Platonist philosophers & in St John]

lŏg′otype, n. Word, or more letters than one, cast in one piece but not as ligature, for use in printing. [prec., TYPE]

-logue (lŏg), suf. repr. Gk -*logos, -logon*, chiefly in wds f. F (*cata~, dia~*). Personal nn. = *one skilled in* -LOGY (*ideo~*) are now rare, -LOGER or -LOGIST being usu. preferred.

-logy, suf. f. Gk -*logia* (in early instances, thr. F -*logie* f. med. L -*logia*). **1.** In most wds -*log*- is the *o* form of Gk *leg*- speak, -*logia* indicating the character, action, or branch of knowledge, of a person (Gk -*logos* n. or a.) who speaks in a certain way (*brachy~, tauto~, eu~*) or treats of a certain subject (*theo~, astro~*). E compounds of the latter kind, in which first component is alw. n., take -o- with some exceptions (*genea~, minera~*). *Socio~, termino~*, are hybrids. **2.** In a few wds -*log*- is the Gk *logos* discourse (*tri~, tetra~*).

loin, n. (Pl.) part of body on both sides of spine between false ribs & hip-bones (*gird up* one's ~s, prepare for journey or effort; *fruit, child*, etc., *of, sprung from*, etc., one's ~s, one's begotten offspring); joint of meat that includes the ~ vertebrae; ~*-cloth*, worn for decency & fastened round ~s. Hence ~ED[2] (-nd) a. [ME, f. OF *loigne* f. Rom. *lumbea* (fem. of *-eus* adj.) f. L *lumbus*]

loir (loi′er), n. The fat dormouse. [F, f. pop. L *lere, f. L glirem nom. glis]

loit′er, v.i. & t. Linger on the way, hang about; travel indolently & with frequent pauses; pass (time etc.) away in ~ing. Hence ~ER¹ n., ~ingLY² adv. [ME, f. MDu. loteren wag about]

loll, v.t. & i. Hang (one's tongue) out, (of tongue) hang (usu. out); stand, sit, or recline, in lazy attitude; let (one's head or limbs) rest lazily on something. Hence ~ingLY² adv. [14th c.; prob. imit.]

Lŏll′ard, n. One of the 14th-c. heretics who followed Wyclif or held opinions like his. Hence ~ISM(3) n. [f. MDu. lollaerd (lollen mumble, -ARD)]

lŏllipŏp, n. (usu. pl.). Sweetmeat(s), sugar-plum(s). [orig. unkn.; cf. lolly (north. dial.) tongue]

lŏll′op, v.i. (colloq.). Flop about; move or proceed in a lounging or ungainly way. [extension of LOLL]

lŏll′y̆, n. (Colloq.) lollipop; (sl.) money. [abbr.]

Lom′bard (lŭ-, lŏ-), n. & a. 1. One of the Germanic 6th-c. conquerors of Italy; native of Lombardy. 2. adj. Of the ~s or Lombardy, Lombardic; ~ street, a London street formerly occupied by ~ bankers, & still containing many of chief London banks, (transf.) the money market, financiers as a body (~ Street to a china orange, virtual certainty, long odds). [ME, f. OF lombard or MDu. -baert, f. It. Lombardo f. LL Longobardus, L Lango-, f. Gmc *Langobardhaz (LONG¹, L Bardi name of the people)]

Lŏmbărd′ic, a. Of the Lombards or Lombardy (esp. of N.-Ital. 7th–13th-c. architecture & 15th–16th-c. painting). [f: med. L Lombardicus (prec., -IC)]

lŏm′ent, n. (bot.). Kind of pod that breaks up when mature into one-seeded joints. Hence ~A′CEOUS (-āshǔs) a. [f. L lomentum bean-meal (orig. cosmetic) f. lo-, lavare, wash, -MENT]

Lo′ndon (lŭ-), attrib. a. ~ clay, geological formation in lower division of eocene tertiary in S.-E. England; ~ ivy, fog or smoke of ~; ~ particular, colloq., kind of fog peculiar to ~; ~ pride, kind of saxifrage; ~ smoke, dull grey colour. So ~ER¹(4), ~ISM(4), nn., ~IZE(3) v.t.

lŏne, attrib. a. Solitary, companionless, unfrequented, uninhabited, lonely, (poet. or rhet., exc. in ~ hand, hand played or player playing against the rest at quadrille & euchre, also fig.); feeling or making feel lonely, whence ~′SOME (-ns-) a., ~′someLY² adv., ~′someNESS n.; (of woman) single or widowed. [ME; aphetic f. ALONE]

lŏne′l|y̆ (-nl-), a. Solitary, companionless, isolated; unfrequented. Hence ~iNESS n. [-LY¹]

lŏng¹, a. & n. 1. Measuring much from end to end in space or time (~ line, distance; journey; ~ life, whence ~′lIvED²

(-vd′) a.; make a ~ arm, reach out for something esp. at table; has a ~ arm, can make his power felt far; ~ face, dismal; ~ head, of more than average length, (fig.) shrewdness or foresight, whence ~′-head′ED² a., ~′head′edNESS n., (-hĕd-), lit. & fig.; make a ~ nose, cock a SNOOK; ~ tongue, loquacity; two etc. ~ miles etc., more than that; by a ~ CHALK¹; grievance etc. of ~ standing, not recent); (prefixed to name; colloq.) tall (L~ Tom, gun of great length & range). 2. Far-reaching, acting at a distance, involving great interval or difference, (~ sight, that sees distant but not near objects, (fig.) penetration, whence ~′sight′ED² a., ~′sight′edNESS n., (-sit-), lit. & fig.; little PITCHERS have ~ ears; take ~ views, consider remote effects; ~ odds in betting, very uneven; ~ bowls, fighting at ~ range, opp. close quarters; ~ date, distant date for maturing of bill etc.; ~ waist in dress, made far down). 3. (Usu. appended to measurement) having specified length or duration (tail 6 in. ~; vacation is two months ~; as BROAD as it is ~). 4. Of elongated shape; remarkable for or distinguished by or concerned with length or duration (~ clay, churchwarden pipe; ~ DIVISION; ~ drink, one served in tall glass; ~ ears, stupidity as of ass, whence ~′earED² (-ērd′) a.; ~ finger, the second; ~ jump, measured along ground, opp. high jump; ~ measure, miles, yards, inches, etc.; ~ metre, hymn--stanza of four eight-syllable lines; L~ Parliament, that elected 1640 & dissolved 1660; ~ PRIMER; ~ robe, legal attire, esp. gentlemen of the ~ robe, lawyers; in the ~ run, in the end after vicissitudes; ‖ ~ service, system of military etc. enlistment for many e.g. 12 years; ‖ ~ vacation, summer vacation of law-courts & universities; ~ wind, capacity for running far without rest, or fig. for talking or writing at tedious length, whence ~′wind′ED² a., ~′wind′edNESS n.). 5. Expressed by many ciphers or consisting of many individuals (~ figure or price, heavy cost; ~ family, of many children; ~ bill, of many items; ~ suit, many cards of one suit in a hand, also, colloq., thing at which one excels). 6. Lengthy, prolix, tedious. 7. Of more than the usual numerical amount (~ DOZEN, HUNDRED). 8. Lasting, going far back or forward, (a ~ custom, memory, farewell). 9. (phonet., pros.). (Of vowel or syllable) having the greater of the two recognized durations, (also, of vowel) having the pronunciation shown in its name (e.g., pate & lucre have ~, pat & put or but short a & u). 10. ~-bill, kinds of bird, esp. snipe; ~′boat, sailing-ship's largest boat (cf. LAUNCH²); ~-bow, drawn by hand & discharging ~ feathered arrow (cf. CROSS-BOW), draw the ~-bow, tell exaggerated or invented stories; ~ butt, cue for reaching billiard-ball beyond range of half-butt; ~ *cloth*, kind of calico made in ~ pieces; ~*-clothes*, & arch. *-coats*, clothes of baby in arms; ~*-distance*, (of weather forecast) made several days in advance; ~ *field*, ~ off or on (see below), also part of ground behind bowler; ‖~ FIRM[1]; ~'*hand*, ordinary writing (opp. SHORT*hand*); ~ *hop*, short-pitched ball in cricket; (*daddy-*) ~*-legs*, crane-fly; ~ *off*, *on*, man fielding at bowler's left, right, rear; ~ *pig*, sailors' transl. of cannibals' name for human flesh; ‖~ *pull*, over-measure given by public-houses to attract custom; ~'*shanks*, stilt or ~*-legged* plover; ~'*stop*, man fielding straight behind wicket--keeper, (vb) field there; ~ *wave* (radio), having a wave-length of (about) 800 metres or more; hence ~'ISH[1](2) a., ~'WAYS, ~'WISE, (-z), advv. **11.** n. ~ interval or period (*shall see you before* ~; *shall not be away for* ~; *will not take* ~; *it is* ~ *since I saw him*; *so at* ~*est*, to mention the most distant date possible); recital at length (*the* ~ *& the short of it*, all that can or need be said, the total upshot); ~ syllable (~*s & shorts*, verse esp. classical); (archit.) ~*s & shorts*, ~ & short blocks placed alternately; ‖ = ~ vacation. [OE, OS, OHG *lang*, ON *langr*, Goth. *laggs* f. Gmc *langaz* cogn. w. L *longus*]

long[2], adv. (~*er*, ~*est*, pr. -ngg-). For a long time (*have* ~ *thought so*; *nor wants that little* ~; *so or as* ~ *as*, transf., provided that, if only; *be* ~ *doing*, &, prob. by confusion of the adv. w. the adj., *in doing*, take a long time, be slow, to do, *as he was* ~ *finding it out, the chance was* ~ *in coming*; *not be* ~ *for this world*, have short time to live; ~*-liver*, one who lives ~); by a long time (~ *before, after, since, ago*); (appended to nn. of duration) throughout specified time (*all day* ~, *his life* ~); (comp., with *no, any, much*, etc.) after implied point of time (*shall not wait any* ~*er*; *no* ~*er*, not henceforth as formerly); ~*-ago* a. & n., (belonging to the distant past; ~*-drawn*(-*out*), unduly prolonged; ~*-standing*, that has ~ existed; ~*-suffering* n. & a., bearing provocation patiently. [OE *lange* (prec.)]

long[3], v.i. Yearn, wish vehemently, *for* thing or *to* do. Hence ~'ING[1](1)n., ~'ING**LY**[2] adv. [OE *langian* seem LONG[1] to]

-long, suf., f. LONG[1], has ousted -LING[2] in *side~*, *head~*. *End~* f. ON *endlangr* adj. orig. meaning *extending from end to end* was used in E as adv. meaning *endwise*, & ~ thus came to be regarded as var. of *-ling*.

longanim'itӯ (-ngg-), n. (rare). Long--suffering, forbearance. [ME, f. LL *longanimitas* (LL *longanimus*, *-is* f. L *longus* long, *animus* spirit, -TY)]

lŏn'geron (-j-), n. (usu. in pl.). Longitudinal member of aeroplane's fuselage or nacelle. [F, = girder]

lŏngĕv'al, **-gae-**, (-j-), a. Long-lived. [f. L *longaevus* (*longus* long, *aevum* age, -AL)]

lŏngĕv'itӯ (-j-), n. Long life. [f. LL *longaevitas* (prec., -TY)]

lŏn'gi- (-jĭ-), comb. form of L *longus* long in scientific terms, as ~*caud'ate* long--tailed, ~*corn* kinds of beetle with long threadlike antennae.

lŏn'gitūde (-j-), n. Length (now joc.); (geog.) angular distance east or west from a standard meridian, as that of Greenwich, to the meridian of any place, reckoned to 180° E. or W. (*abbr.* long.); (astron.) angular distance eastward on ecliptic from vernal equinoctial point to foot of body's or point's circle of latitude. [ME, f. L *longitudo* *-inis* (prec., -TUDE)]

lŏngitūd'inal (-jĭ-), a. Of or in length; running lengthwise; of longitude. Hence ~LY[2] adv. [-AL]

Lŏng'obărd, n. = LOMBARD (1st sense).

lŏng'-shore, a. Existing or found or employed on, frequenting, the shore; ~*man*, landsman employed in loading ships, shore-fishing, etc. [for *along shore*]

longue haleine (lawṅggahlān), n. *Work* etc. *of* (or *de*) ~ (requiring long persistent effort; esp. of books). [F, = long-winded]

longueur (lawṅgḗr), n. Tedious passage in book, film, or play (usu. pl.). [F]

loo, n., & v.t. Round card-game with penalties paid to the pool; (having to pay) this penalty; *unlimited* ~, in which penalty is=amount already in pool; (vb) subject to the penalty. [abbr. of obs. *lanterloo* f. F *lanturelu* refrain of a song]

loob'ӯ, n. Silly fellow. [cf. LOB, LUBBER]

loof'ah (-*a*), n. Pod of *Luffa aegyptiaca* used as flesh-brush. [f. Arab. *lufah* the plant]

look, v.i. & t., & n. **1.** Use one's sight, turn eyes in some direction, direct eyes *at*, (*fair* etc. *to* ~ *at*, in outward appearance; ~ *before you leap*, avoid precipitate action; *to* ~ *at him* etc., judging by his etc. ~*s*; *will not* ~ *at*, refuses to take, rejects, scorns). **2.** Contemplate, examine, (~*ed me through & through*; ~ *a gift* HORSE[1] *in the mouth*; ~ one, *death*, etc., *in the face*, face him etc. boldly or at close quarters). **3.** Express, threaten, show, by one's ~s (~ *compassion, death, daggers*, etc.). **4.** Ascertain or observe by sight *who, how, whether*, etc. **5.** (fig.). Make mental search (*let him* ~ *at home*), inquire (*when one* ~*s deeper*), aim one's attention *at* & consider (*way of* ~*ing at things*; *what I* ~ *at is the comfort of it*), take care or make sure *that*, expect to do; (~ *you!*, observe, mind; ~ *here!*, formula for demanding attention or expostulating; ~ *sharp*, orig., keep strict watch, now, lose no time, bestir oneself). **6.** (Of things) face, be turned, have or afford outlook, in some direction (*towards, on to, into, down*, etc.). **7.** Have certain appearance, seem, (~ *grave* etc., whence ~'ING[2] a.; ~ *a fool*, *every inch a king*, BLACK[1], BLUE[1]; ~ *small*, be exposed as mean etc.; ~ *alive !*, make haste; ~ *well* or *ill*, in good or bad health, also of things, seem to be going so; ~*s to be*, seems; ~ *as if*, suggest by appearance the belief that; ~ *like*, seem to be, also threaten or promise, as *it ~s like rain*, *he ~s like biting* or *winning*); seem to be (~*s his age*, seems as old as he really is; ~ one*self again*, seem recovered). 8. ~- -*in'*, informal call or visit, (sport) *will have a ~-in*, come near winning & perhaps win; ~*ing-glass*, mirror, quicksilvered glass for mirrors; ~*-out'*, watch, ~ing out, (*keep a good ~-out*; *on the ~-out for* or *to* do), post of observation, man or party or boat stationed to ~ out, view over landscape, prospect of luck (*it's a bad ~- -out for him*), person's own concern (*that is his ~-out*, he must see to that himself); ∥ ~-*see* (sl.), a survey, inspection. 9. (With prepp.); ~ *about* one, examine one's surroundings, take time to form plans; ~ *after*, follow with the eye, seek for, attend to, take care of; ~ *down* one's *nose at* (colloq.), regard with covert displeasure; ~ *for*, expect, hope or be on the watch for, search for (~ *for* TROUBLE); ~ *into*, examine the inside of (box etc.), dip into (book), investigate; ~ *on*, regard *as*, regard *with* distrust etc.; ~ *over*, inspect, overlook or pardon; ~ *through*, direct eyes through (window etc.), penetrate (veil etc.) with sight or (pretence or pre- tender) with insight, be visible through (*his greed ~s through his eyes*), glance through (book etc.); ~ *to*, consider, take care of, be careful about (~ *to your man- ners*; ~ *to it that*), keep watch over, rely on (person or thing) *for*, expect, count upon, aim at; ~ *towards* (colloq.), drink health of; ~ *upon*, regard *with* specified feeling (also with adv., as *favourably*), regard *as*. 10. (With advv.): ~ *about*, be on the watch, be in search *for*, let one's eyes rove; ~ *ahead*, (of rower) turn round to see where he is going (esp. imperat.); ~ *back*, be half-hearted about enterprise one has begun (usu. w. neg.), turn one's thoughts *upon* or *to* something past, cease to progress (usu. w. neg.), ~ in again, call back; ~ *down*, subdue with a ~, (com- merc.) sink in price, ~ *down* (up)on, consider oneself superior to; ~ *forward to*, anticipate (usu. with pleasure, also *with apprehension* etc.); ~ *in*, make short visit or call; ~ *on*, be mere spectator, whence ~ER¹-ŏn' n.; ~ *on with*, read from book etc. at same time as (another person); ~ *out*, direct eyes or put head out of window etc., be vigilant, keep one's eyes open *for* expected person, be prepared *for* squalls etc., have or afford outlook *on*, *over*, etc., select by inspection; ~ *over*, inspect one by one or part by part; ~ *round*, pass. examine the possibilities etc, with a view to deciding on a course; ~ *through*, survey with searching glance (~*ed him through*), inspect exhaustively or successively; ~

up, (esp. commerc.) improve in price or prosperity, search for (esp. word in dictionary or facts in book of reference), call on (person), raise eyes (~ *up to*, re- spect, venerate), ~ one *up & down*, scrutinize him keenly or contemptuously; hence ~'ER¹ n., (esp.) *handsome person (colloq.; also *good-~er*). 11. n. Act of ~ing, direction of eyes, glance (*a kind*, *scornful*, ~); (sing. or pl.) appearance of face, expression, personal aspect, (*good ~s*, beauty); (of things) appearance (*the place has a European ~*). [OE lōcian, OS lōcon, f. WG *lōk-, *lōg- (OHG luogēn)]

loom¹, n. Machine for weaving yarn or thread into fabric; (inboard part of) shaft of oar. [ME *lome* f. OE *gelōma* tool, of unkn. orig.]

loom², v.i., & n. 1. Appear indistinctly, be seen in vague & often magnified or threatening shape, (lit. & fig.; often ~ *large* etc.). 2. n. Vague first appearance of land at sea etc. [cf. EFris. *lōmen* move slowly, MHG *lüemen* be weary]

loom³, n. Kinds of guillemot & diver. Hence ~'ERY(3) n. [f. ON *lómr*]

loon¹, n. (Sc. & arch.). Scamp, idler, boor; lad. [15th c. *loun*, of obsc. orig.]

loon², n. Kinds of water-bird, esp. of diver & grebe. [app. = LOOM³ w. assim. to prec.]

loon'y̆, lu-, n. & a. (sl.). Lunatic, esp. ~-*bin*, mental home. [-Y³]

loop¹, n., & v.t. & i. 1. Figure produced by a curve, or bent string or withe, that crosses itself; attachment or ornament formed of cord, thread, etc., so crossed & fastened at crossing; ring or curved piece of metal as handle etc.; (also ~-*line*) railway or telegraph line that diverges from main line & joins it again; circuit in centrifugal railway along top of which passenger travels head downwards (~*ing the* ~, bicyclist's or airman's similar feat); (skating) curve crossing itself made on single edge; hence ∥ ~'Y² a. (sl.), crazy. 2. vb. Form (string etc.) into ~(s); form ~ (esp. of LOOPER larvae) en- close (as) with ~; fasten (*up*, *back*) or join (*together*) with ~(s). [c. 1400, of unkn. orig.]

loop², n. (rare). = LOOP-HOLE. [ME, prob. conn. w. MDu. *lūpen* to peer]

loop'er, n. Caterpillar of geometer moths, progressing by arching itself into loops; contrivance in sewing-machine etc. for making loops. [-ER¹]

loop'-hŏle, n., & v.t. 1. Narrow vertical slit in wall for shooting or looking through or to admit light or air; outlet, means of evading rule etc. 2. v.t. Make ~s in (wall etc.). [LOOP²]

loose¹, a. 1. Released from bonds or re- straint. 2. Detached or detachable from its place (*come*, *get*, ~; *play* FAST² *& ~*); (chem.) free, uncombined; hanging partly free (esp. ~ *end*; *at a ~ end*, with- out definite occupation); not rigidly

fixed, apt to shift, (*have a* SCREW ~).
3. Slack, relaxed, not tense or tight, (*with
a ~ rein*, lit. of riding, & fig. indulgently;
~ *'tongue*, given to blabbing; ~ *bowels*,·
tending to diarrhoea; ~ *clothes*; ~ *build
or make*, ungainly figure). **4.** Not compact, dense, or serried (~ *soil, fabric*; ~
order, military arrangement with wide
intervals; ~ *handwriting*, straggling; || ~
play or game in football, in which players
do not lock together). **5.** (Of statements,
ideas, etc.) inexact, indefinite, vague,
incorrect; (of translation) not close or
faithful; (of style) ungrammatical; (of
agent) doing the act ~ly (~ *thinker*).
6.(crick.).~ *bowling*, inaccurately pitched,
~ *fielding*, careless or bungling. **7.** Morally
lax, dissolute, wanton in speech or act,
(~ *fish*, dissolute person; *on the* ~, having
a spree). **8.** ~ BOX²; ~*-leaf* (of ledgers,
notebooks, etc.) with each leaf separate
& detachable;· ~-, ~ly, as ~*-flowing,
-fitting*. Hence. ~'LY² (-sl-) adv., ~'NESS
(-sn-) n., lōōs'ISH¹(2) a. [ME lōs f. ON
louss, lauss (= OE *lēas*, OS, OHG *lōs*,
Goth. *laus*), f. Gmc **laus-*; cf. LOSE]
lōōse², v.t., & n. **1.** Release, set free,
free from constraint (*wine* ~*d his tongue*);
untie, undo, (knot, fetters, seal, hair of
head); detach from moorings; discharge
(arrow), (abs.) discharge gun (*at*); relax
(now only in ~ *hold*). **2.** n. Vent, free expression, (give ~ or *a* ~ *to* one's *feelings*
etc.); || loose play (see prec.). [ME; f.
prec.]
lōōs'en, v.t. & i. Loose (person's tongue);
make or become less tight or compact or
firm; relieve (bowels) from costiveness or
(cough) from dryness; relax (discipline
etc.). [-EN⁶]
lōōse'strife (-s-s-), n. Two kinds of
herbaceous plant (*golden or yellow*, & *red
or purple or spiked*, ~). [mistransl. of
LL f. Gk *lusimakhion* (Gk pers. name
Lusimakhos) as if directly f. *luō* undo,
makhē battle]
lōōt, n., & v.t. & i. **1.** Goods taken from
enemy, spoil; booty, illicit gains made by
official; **2.** vb. Plunder, sack, (city etc., or
abs.); carry off as booty. Hence ~'ER¹
n. [f. Hind. *luṭ*]
lŏp¹, n., & v.t. & i. (-pp-). **1.** Smaller
branches & twigs of trees (~ *& top*, ~ *&
crop*, trimmings of tree). **2.** vb. Cut off
branches & twigs & rarely top of (tree);
strip tree of (branches etc.; often *off,
away*), whence ~p'ings [-ING¹(2)] n. pl.;
cut off (person's limb or head); make
~ping strokes *at*. [(1) 15th c., orig. unkn.;
(2) prob. f. (1)]
lŏp², v.i. & t. (-pp-), & n. **1.** Hang limply;
let (ears) hang; slouch, dawdle, hang
about; = LOPE; ~-ears, drooping ears,
whence ~*'-*earED² (-ērd) a.; ~*-ear*, kind of
rabbit; hence ~p'Y² a. **2.** n. ~*-eared*
rabbit. [(1) imit., cf. LOB; (2) short for
~*-rabbit*]
lŏp³, v.i. (-pp-), & n. **1.** (Of water) break

in short lumpy waves. **2.** n. Such motion
of water. [imit.]
lōpe, v.i., & n. (Run with) long bounding
stride (esp. of animals). [ME, var. of Sc.
loup f. ON *hloupa* LEAP¹]
lŏph'o-, comb. form of Gk *lophos* crest, in
scientific wds as : ~*dŏnt*, (animal) with
transverse ridges on crowns of molars;
~*brăn'chiate*, (fish) with gills disposed in
tufts.
lŏp-sid'ĕd, a. With one side lower or
smaller than the other, unevenly
balanced. Hence ~LY² adv., ~NESS n.
[f. LOP²]
loquā'cious (-shŭs), a. Talkative; (of
birds, water) chattering, babbling. Hence
or cogn. ~LY² adv., ~NESS, loquA'CITY
(-ăs-), nn. [L *loquax* (*loqui* talk), -ACIOUS]
lō'quat (-ŏt), n. Chinese & Japanese fruit
(-tree) naturalized in S. Europe, Australia,
etc. [f. Chin. *luh kwat* rush orange]
lŏ'quĭtŭr, v.i. 3 sing. pres. (abbr. *loq.*).
Speaks (with speaker's name added, as
stage-direction or notice to reader). [L]
|| **lōr, lŏr'**, form of LORD used (vulg.) as int.
lōr'al, a. Of the LORE². [-AL]
lŏr'cha, n. Ship with hull of European
shape but Chinese rig. [Port.]
lŏrd, n. & int., & v.i. & t. **1.** Master, ruler,
chief, prince, sovereign, (*our sovereign* ~
the King; ~*s of creation*, mankind, also
joc. men as opp. women); (poet.) owner
(~ *of few acres*; cf. *landlord*); magnate in
some trade (*the cotton* ~*s*; cf. *king*). **2.**
Feudal superior (MESNE ~; ~ *of the* MANOR;
~ PARAMOUNT). **3.** (poet. & joc.). Husband
(also ~ *& master*). **4.** (astrol.). Dominant
planet. **5.** (Usu. *the L*~ exc. in voc. ; also
with *God*) God (*L*~ *knows who, how*, etc.,
I cannot guess who etc., some one etc. or
other; *L*~ *have mercy, L*~ *bless me* or *us* or
my soul or *you*, excll. of surprise etc.;
also *L*~! alone as excl.); Christ (*the* or
more usu. *our L*~; *in the year of our L*~,
anno domini; *L*~*'s day*, Sunday); *L*~*'s
prayer*, the *Our Father*; *L*~*'s supper*,
Eucharist; *L*~*'s table*, Christian altar,
Eucharist. **6.** Nobleman, peer of the
realm or person entitled by courtesy to
the prefix *L*~ (see below) as part of his
ordinary style (*live, treat, like a* ~, fare,
entertain, sumptuously; *drunk as, swear
like, a* ~, excessively; *L*~ *in waiting,
of the Bedchamber*, nobleman attending
sovereign, called by former title if queen
is reigning, by latter if king); (pl., *the
L*~*s*) temporal & spiritual peers of Parliament (*House of L*~*s*, upper legislative
chamber of United Kingdom, also committee of specially qualified members of
this appointed as ultimate judicial appeal
court). **7.** pl. (Also in full *L*~*s Commissioners*) members of board performing
duties of high State office put in commission (*L*~*s of the Admiralty, Treasury*,
etc.; *First L*~, president of such board;
Civil L~, civilian member of Admiralty
board, opp. *Sea L*~*s*); *L*~*s of Session*,

judges of Scottish *Court of* SESSION. **8.** First word of many official titles (*L*~ CHAMBERLAIN, CHANCELLOR, *Chief Justice, High Commissioner*; *L*~ *Justice General, L*~ *Justice Clerk*, president, vice-president, of Scottish Court of Justiciary; *L*~ *Lieutenant*, viceroy of Ireland till 1922, chief executive authority & head of magistracy in each county; *L*~ *Rector*, triennially elected honorary head of a Scottish university court; *L*~ MAYOR; *L*~ *Bishop*, any bishop in ceremonious mention). **9.** (Prefixed as part of personal designation) marquis, earl, viscount, or baron (whether peer, or peer's eldest son holding his second title by courtesy; with suppression of *of*, e.g. *Earl of*, or *L*~, *Derby*; ~ is invariable instead of *baron*, which is used as prefix only in foreign titles); (followed by Christian & family name) younger son of duke or marquis. **10.** *My* ~ (voc.), respectful or polite formula for addressing nobleman below duke, bishop, ~ mayor, or judge of supreme court; ~*s & ladies*, wild arum; hence ~'LESS a., ~'LING[1](2), ~ŌL'ATRY, nn. **11.** vb. Play the ~ *over* (usu. in pass., *will not be* ~*ed over*; or with *it*, as ~*ing it over his household*); ennoble, confer title of ~ upon. [OE *hláford* f. *hláfweard* = bread--keeper (LOAF[1], WARD)]

lōrd'l|ȳ, a. Haughty, imperious, lofty, disdainful; grand, magnificent, fit for or belonging to a lord. Hence ~iNESS n. [OE *hláfordlic* (prec., -LY[1])]

lōrdōs'is, n. (med.). Forward curvature of spine. [Gk, f. *lordos* bent back, -OSIS]

Lōrd's (-z), n. (Used for) ~ cricket ground in London, headquarters of the M.C.C. and English cricket. [Thomas *Lord* (d. 1832), maker of successive grounds named after him]

lōrd'ship, n. Dominion, rule, ownership *of* or *over*; domain, estate, manor; lord's personality (*your* ~, *his* ~, you, he, in speaking deferentially to or of a lord, also joc. to or of other persons or animals). [-SHIP]

lōre[1], n. **1.** (arch.). Doctrine; erudition; scholarship. **2.** Body of traditions & facts on a subject (*ghost, bird, animal, fairy*, etc., ~). [OE *lár*, OS, OHG *lēra* f. Gmc **laizō* f. **lais-* LEARN]

lōre[2], n. (nat. hist.). Strap-like surface, in birds between eye & upper mandible, in snakes between eye & nostril. [f. L *lorum* strap]

lorgnette (lōrnyĕt'), n. Pair of eye-glasses usu. held by long handle; opera-glass. [F]

lō'ricate, a. (zool.). Having defensive armour of bone, plates, scales, etc. [f. L *loricatus* (*lorica* cuirass f. *lorum* strap, -ATE[2])]

lō'rikeet (*or* -eet'), n. Small brightly--coloured Polynesian parrot allied to the lory. [dim. of LORY, after *parakeet*]

lō'rimer, -iner, n. (hist.). Bit-maker,

spurrier, (now only in title of a livery company). [ME, f. OF *loremier, -nier* (*lorain* harness-strap f. L *lorum* thong)]

lōr'is, n. Small slender tailless nocturnal climbing quadrumanous Sinhalese mammal; kinds of lemur. [F]

lōrn, a. (poet. & joc.). Desolate, forlorn, (often *lone* ~). [p.p. of obs. *leese* OE *lēosan* LOSE]

‖ **lŏ'rrȳ,** n. Long low flat wagon; truck used on railways & tramways; motor truck for transporting goods, troops etc. [orig. unkn.; cf. RULLEY]

lōr'ȳ, n. Kinds of bright-plumaged parrot--like bird. [f. Malay *luri*]

lose (lōoz), v.t. & i. (*lost* pr. law- *or* lŏ-). **1.** Be deprived of, cease by negligence, misadventure, separation, death, etc., to possess or have (property, life, quality, limb, father, friend, etc.; *doctor*~*s patient*, fails to keep him alive, also is left by him for another doctor; ~ *patience*, one's *temper*, become impatient, angry; ~ one's HEAD[1]; ~ one's HEART; ~ HEART; ~ *ground*, fail to keep position, recede, decline; *have lost my cold*, got rid of it; ~ *interest*, of person, cease to be interested, of thing, cease to interest); (pass.) disappear, perish, die or be dead, (*letter--writing is a lost art*; *the ship & all hands were lost*; *lost to sense of duty, shame*, etc., no longer affected by them; *lost soul, damned*). **2.** Suffer loss or detriment, incur disadvantage, be the worse off in money or otherwise by transaction etc., (*the publisher lost by it*; *the army lost heavily*; *story does not* ~ *in the telling*, is if anything exaggerated). **3.** Become unable to find, fail to keep in sight or follow or mentally grasp, (~ *a document*, one's *way, the thread of a discourse, a person* etc. under observation). **4.** Spend (time, opportunities, pains) to no purpose, waste, (pass., *be lost upon*, fail to influence or draw the attention of). **5.** Fail to obtain, catch, see, or hear (~ one's *train*, *a legacy, a word or remark, a fox*). **6.** Forfeit (stake), be defeated in (*game, battle, lawsuit*, or abs.; *losing battle, game*, in which defeat seems inevitable; *cannot play a losing game*, ~s heart or temper in it); fail to carry (motion). **7.** Cause person the loss of, cost, (*will* ~ *you your place*); (refl. & pass.) go astray, become merged or engrossed (*in*), be obscured (*in*); ‖ *losing* HAZARD. Hence los'ABLE (-ōoz-) a. [OE *losian* perish, destroy (*los* LOSS); later sense-development infl. by obs. (cogn.) *leese*, wh. it superseded]

‖ **lŏs'el** (-z-), n. (arch.). Profligate, rake, ne'er-do-well. [ME, app. f. *los-*, stem of LOSE]

los'er (-ōoz-), n. In vbl senses; esp.: *be a* ~ *by*, suffer loss by; *good* ~, person not dejected or angered by losing game etc.; person, horse, etc., that loses race etc.; ‖ (billiards) losing HAZARD. [-ER[1]]

loss (laws, lŏs), n. Losing or being lost

(see LOSE); person, thing, or amount lost (CUT² *a* or *the*~); detriment, disadvantage, resulting from ~ (person etc. *is a great, no little*, etc., ~, the ~ of him is a serious etc. blow); PROFIT¹ & ~; *at a* ~ (*for, to discover*, etc.), puzzled, at fault; *~ *leader*, article sold at a ~ to attract custom. [ME *los*, *loss(e)* poss. back form. f. *lost*, p.p. of LOSE; not continuous w. OE & ME *los* in phr. *to lose* (= ON *los* dispersion, rout) f.Gmc *lus-* cogn. w. LOOSE¹]

löss (G), n. = LOESS.

lost. See LOSE.

löt, n., & v.t. (-tt-). **1.** One of a set of objects used to secure a chance decision in dividing goods, selecting officials, etc. (now only in *draw, cast, ~s*, usu. *between, for, who*, etc., & in *throw* or *cast in* one's *~ with*, share fortunes of); this method of deciding (*the ~*; *by ~*); choice resulting from it (*the ~ fell upon me*). **2.** What falls to person by ~, share (*have no part nor ~ in*); person's destiny, fortune, condition, (*the ~ falls to me, it falls to my ~, it falls to me as my ~, to do*). **3.** ‖ Tax, due, (SCOT¹ & ~). **4.** Plot or allotment of land. **5.** Article or set of articles offered separately at sale, item at auction, (*bad ~*, disreputable or vicious person). **6.** Number or quantity of persons or things of same kind or somehow associated (*the ~*, the whole number or quantity); (colloq.) considerable number or amount, *a good or great deal* (also in pl., as *has ~s of friends*). **7.** v.t. Divide (land, usu. *out*, or goods for sale) into ~s. [OE *hlot*, w. var. cognates in Gmc, f. Gmc *hleut-*, *hlaut-*, *hlut-*]

loth. See LOATH.

Lŏthār′ĭō, n. (pl. ~s). Libertine, rake. (character in Rowe's *Fair Penitent*)

lō′tion, n. Liquid preparation used externally to heal wound, cure skin-disease, clear complexion, etc. [f. L *lotio* (*lavare lot-* wash, -ION)]

lŏtt′erӯ, n. Arrangement for distributing prizes by chance among purchasers of tickets; *~-wheel*, wheel with box used for shuffling numbers corresponding to those on tickets; (fig.) thing that defies calculation (*life, marriage, is a ~*). [f. It. *lotteria* (LOT, LOTTO)]

lŏtt′ō, n. Game of chance with drawing of numbers as in lottery. [It.]

lō′tus, n. Plant represented in ancient Greek legend as inducing luxurious dreaminess & distaste for active life (*~-eater*, person given to indolent enjoyment; so *~-eating* a. & n.); Egyptian & Asian water-lily; kinds of plant, esp. bird's-foot trefoil; *~-land*, place of indolent enjoyment. [L, f. Gk *lōtos*]

loud, a. & adv. **1.** Strongly audible, sonorous (*~ speaker*, naut. *~ hailer*, apparatus that converts electrical impulses into sounds ~ enough to be heard at some distance); clamorous, noisy; (of colour, dress, pattern, manners) obtrusive, conspicuous, flashy; hence *~'EN*⁶

v.i., *~'ISH*(2) a., *~'LY*² adv., *~'NESS* **2.** adv. *~ly* (*don't talk so ~*; *laughed ~*, *long*); *~-SPOKEN*. [OE, OS *hlūd*, OHG *hlūt*, f. WG *hlūth-*, cogn. w. Gk *klutos* renowned]

lough (see Ap.), n. (Anglo-Ir.). Lake, arm of sea. [ME, perh. repr. O Northumb. *luh* (= *fretum*, *stagnum*), f. Ir. *loch* LOCH]

Louis (lōō′ĭ), n. (pl. *Louis* pr. -z). Name of many French kings; *louis* or *louis-d'or* (-dôr′), French gold coin of about 20 fr. from ~ XIII to ~ XVI; ~ *Treize* (trāz), *Quatorze* (kătôrz′), *Quinze* (kănz), *Seize* (sāz), used adj. of furniture etc. in styles prevalent in those reigns.

loung|e (-j), v.i. & t., & n. **1.** Go lazily, saunter; loll, recline; idle (intr., & *~e away* time etc.); hence *~'ER*¹ n., *~'ingLY*² adv., (-j-). **2.** n. Spell of *~ing*, saunter, stroll; place where one can *~e*, esp. entrance-hall or gallery furnished for the purpose (*~e-lizard*, sl., professional dancer at hotel *~e-dances*); sitting-room in house; sofa or deep chair; ‖ *~e suit*, man's suit for day wear, with tailless jacket. [c. 1500, of unkn. orig.]

lour, lower, (lowr), v.i., & n. **1.** Frown, scowl, look sullen, (*on, upon, at*); (of clouds, sky, storm) look dark & threatening; hence *~'ingLY*² adv. **2.** n. Scowl, gloominess of sky etc., whence *~'Y*² a. [ME *loure*, of obsc. orig.; cf. Du. *loeren* frown, MHG *lūren*; see LURK]

louse, n. (pl. *lice*). Parasitic insect infesting human hair & skin; kinds of parasite of mammals, birds, fish, & plants; *~wort*, kind of plant with purple-pink flowers found in marshes and wet fields. Hence **lous′y**² (-z-) a., (also, sl.), disgusting, abundantly supplied *with* money etc., **lous′iNESS** (-z-) n. [OE *lūs*, MLG, OHG *lūs*, ON *lús*]

lout¹, n. Awkward fellow, bumpkin, clown. Hence *~'ISH*¹ a., *~'ishLY*² adv., *~'ishNESS* n. [16th c., perh. of dial. orig., conn. w. foll.]

lout², v.i. (arch.). Bow, make obeisance. [OE *lūtan*, = ON *lúta*]

louver, -vre, (lōō′er), n. Domed turret-like erection on hall-roof etc. with side openings to let smoke out or air in; (pl., also *~-boards*) arrangement of overlapping boards or slips of glass to admit air but exclude rain. Hence **louv′erED**² (-erd) a. [ME, f. OF *lover*, repr. by med. L *lodium*; orig. unkn.]

Louvre (lōōvr), n. *The ~*, former royal palace, now art museum, in Paris. [F]

lo′vab|le (lŭ-), a. Deserving love, amiable. Hence *~LY*² adv., *~leNESS* n. [LOVE², -ABLE]

lo′vage (lŭ-), n. Kinds of herb. [ME *loveache* alt. f. OF *levesche* f. LL *levisticum* f. L *ligusticum*]

love (lŭv), n. **1.** Warm affection, attachment, liking, or fondness, paternal benevolence, affectionate devotion, (*of, for, to*, or *towards* person, *for* or *to* thing;

give ~ *to*, convey affectionate message to, *send* one's ~ *to*, get this done; *for the* ~ *of*, for sake or in name of, esp. in adjurations; *for* ~ *or money*, by any means, esp. *cannot get it* etc. *for* ~ *or money*; *labour of* ~, that one delights in, or that one does for ~ of someone; *there's no* ~ *lost between them*, they dislike each other; *play for* ~, for the pleasure of it, not for stakes). **2.** Sexual affection or passion or desire, relation between sweethearts, this feeling as a literary subject, a personified influence, or a god (also representation of Cupid, or of naked winged child, or in pl. children, symbolizing ~), (*in* ~, possessed by this; *in* ~ *with*, enamoured of, also transf. fond of a pursuit, thing, etc.; *fall in* ~, become enamoured; *all's* FAIR[2] *in* ~ *& war*; ~ *in a cottage*, marriage on insufficient means; *make* ~, pay amorous attentions *to* or abs., whence ~-MAKING[1] n.). **3.** Beloved one, sweetheart, (esp. of woman, cf. LOVER; hence ~'Y[3] n.; *my* ~, common form of address between husband & wife); (colloq.) delightful person or pretty thing (*he is an old* ~; *what* ~*s of teacups !*). **4.** (In games) no score, nothing, nil, (~ *all*, neither side has yet scored; ~ *game*, in which loser has not scored). **5.** ~-*affair*, affair between lovers, amour; ~-*apple*, (old name for) tomato; ~-*begotten*, illegitimate; ~-*bird*, small bird of parrot kind said to pine away at death of its mate; ~-*child*, illegitimate; ~-*feast*, meal in token of brotherly ~ among early Christians, religious service among Methodists etc. imitating this; ~-*in-a--mist*, fennel-flower; ~-*in-idleness*, heart's--ease; ~-*knot*, peculiarly interlaced bow of ribbon; ~-*letter*, between sweethearts & concerned with ~ ; ~-*lies-bleeding*, garden plant with long drooping spike of purple--red bloom; ~-*lock*, tress or curl worn on temple or forehead; ~-*lorn*, pining with ~, deserted by one's love(r); ~-*match*, marriage made for ~'s sake only; ~-*philtre*, philtre; ~-*seat*, armchair or sofa for two persons; ~-*sick*, languishing with ~ ; ~-*song*, about or expressing ~; ~-*story*, novel etc. of which main theme is ~, facts of a wooing etc.; ~-*token*, thing given in sign of ~. Hence ~'WORTHY a., ~'worthiNESS n. [OE *lufu*, OHG *luba*, cogn. w. Goth. *lubains* f. Gmc **leubh-*, **laubh-*, **lubh-*; see LIEF, LEAVE[1], BELIEVE]

love[2] (lŭv), v.t. & i. Hold dear, bear love to, be in love with, be fond of, (~ *me*, ~ *my* DOG[1]; *Lord* ~ *you !*, excl. of surprise at person's mistake etc.; ~ *one's love with an A, a B*, etc., formula in game of forfeits); be in love; cling to, delight in, enjoy having, be addicted to, admire or be glad of the existence of, (life, honour, comfort, golf, do*ing*, virtue, man who knows his own mind, etc.); (w. inf.) be (habitually) inclined (*children* ~ *to ape their elders*); (colloq.) like, be delighted,

(*he simply* ~*s to find mistakes*; *Will you come ?* — *I should* ~ *to*). [OE *lufian* (prec.)]

Love'lace (lŭvl-), n. Libertine, accomplished rake. [character in Richardson's *Clarissa Harlowe* (1747–48)]

love'less (lŭvl-), a. Unloving; unloved, Hence ~LY[2] adv., ~NESS n. [-LESS]

love'l|y̆ (lŭvl-), a. & n. Attractively or admirably beautiful; *beautiful in moral quality; (colloq.) delightful, very pleasing, intensely amusing; (n., sl.) a ~ young woman. Hence ~iLY[2] adv. (rare), ~iNESS n. [OE *luflic* (LOVE[1], -LY[1])]

lo'ver (lŭ-), n. Woman's sweetheart or suitor (*it was a* ~ *and his lass*), (pl.) pair in love; paramour, gallant; admirer, devotee, of thing, action, or idea; ~*s' knot*, LOVE[1]-knot. Hence ~LESS a., ~LIKE, ~LY[1,2], aa. & advv. [-ER[1]]

lo'ving (lŭ-), a. That loves, affectionate, (*our* ~ *subjects*, formula in royal proclamation; *your* ~ *friend* etc., formula in concluding letter); manifesting or proceeding from love (~-*cup*, large drinking-vessel passed round at banquet; ~-*kindness*, tender consideration). Hence ~LY[2] adv., ~NESS n. [-ING[2]]

low[1] (lō), a. & adv. (~*er*, ~*est*, as aa. & advv.), & n. **1.** Not reaching far up, not high or tall, (~ *house*, *forehead*, *stature*; not used of persons; ~ *dress*, leaving neck & part of shoulders & breast exposed, so ~ *neck*; ~ *relief*, bas-relief). **2.** Not elevated in geographical etc. position (*Low Countries*, Netherlands; *Low* GER-MAN[2], DUTCH; *Lower Egypt* etc.; ~ *moon* etc., near horizon; ~ *tide* or *water*, level of ebbed sea, time of extreme ebb; ~-*water mark*, ~est point reached by ebb--tide, & fig.; *in* ~ *water*, out of funds etc.). **3.** Of or in humble rank or position (the ~*er orders* or *classes*; ~ *birth*; *high & ~*, every one). **4.** Not exalted or sublime, commonplace, undignified, little civilized, not highly organized; abject, mean, degraded, coarse, vulgar, (~ *cunning*). **5.** Ill-nourished, not nourishing, indicative of ill nutrition, wanting in vigour, depressed, not intense, (~ *condition*, *diet*, *fever*; ~ *spirits*, whence ~-spi'ritED[2] a.). **6.** Of small amount as measured by a scale or degrees (~ *price*, *wages*, *rates*, *temperature*; *have* ~ *opinion of*, do not estimate highly; *at* ~*est*, to mention the least possible amount etc.; ~ *latitudes*, near equator). **7.** (Of sounds) not shrill or high up, produced by slow vibrations, (also) not loud. **8.** (Of liquid, receptacle, supply of anything, esp. fig. of purse or money) nearly exhausted or empty (often *run* ~). **9.** Recent (chiefly in compar. & superl.; *belongs to a* ~*er date*). **10.** (Also ~-*church*) giving ~ place to authority of bishops & priests, inherent grace of sacraments, ecclesiastical organization, & ritual, not sacerdotal, approximating to protestant nonconformity, (*Low Church*, party in Church of England thus minded; *Low Churchman*, member of it). **11.** *Bring* ~, depress, reduce, in health, wealth, or position; *lay* ~, overthrow; *lie* ~, crouch, be prostrate or dead or abased, keep quiet or out of the way, say nothing, bide one's time; BURN² ~. **12.** ~'*brow* (colloq.), (one who is) not highly intellectual or cultured (opp. HIGH*brow*); ~'*browed*, lit., also (of rocks) beetling, (of building etc.) with ~ entrance, gloomy; ~ *celebration* of Eucharist, without choir or assistant ministers; ~ *comedian*, actor in ~ *comedy*, in which subject & treatment border on farce; ~*-down*, abject, mean, dishonourable; **~-down* n. (sl.), true facts, inside information; ‖ ~*er boy*, in ~*er* school at public schools; ~*er* CASE²; ~*er chamber*, ~*er House*; ~*er critic(ism)*, of the verbal or textual kind; ~*er deck*, immediately over hold (‖ *the* ~*er deck*, petty officers & men of the Navy or of a ship); ~*er Empire*, later Roman Empire, usu. from Constantine; ~*er House*, ~*er* branch of legislative assembly, e.g. House of Commons; ~*er school* in public schools, usu. forms below fifth; ~*er world*, the earth, (also) hell; ~'*land*, (usu. pl.) ~*lying country*, (adj.) of or in this; *Low'lands* (-andz), part of Scotland lying S. & E. of Highlands, whence **Low'land**ER¹(4) n.; *Low⸺land* (adj.), of or in this; ~ *life*, that of the ~*er* classes, whence ~'**l**'**ived**² (-vd'), a.; ~ MASS¹; ~ *pitch*, ~ key or note, also slight angular elevation of roof, whence ~*-pitch*ED² a.; ~ PRESSURE; *Low Sunday, Week*, after Easter Day & Week; ~'WING; hence ~'**er**MOST (~*lō'er*-), ~'ISH¹(2) (lō'ĭ-), aa., ~'NESS (lō'n-) n. **13.** adv. in or to ~ or mean position (*hangs* ~; *aim* or *shoot* ~ or ~*er*; *tackle* ~ in football, catch at or below waist; *bowed* ~; *never fell so* ~ *as that*); on poor diet (*live* ~ *for a time*); for small stakes (*play* ~); in ~ tone, on or to ~ note, (*talk* ~; *cannot get so* ~); (of date) late (*find it as* ~ *as the 18th century*); ~*-born*, of humble birth; ~*-bred*, of vulgar manners; ~ *down*, far down, also in mean or ungenerous way (esp. *play it* ~ *down*, or ~, *upon*, treat scurvily). **14.** n. What is ~; an area of ~ barometric pressure; **a* ~ level or figure. [ME *lāh* (*lāg*-) f. ON *lágr*, = MDu. *lage*, MHG *læge* f. Gmc **lǣg-* (LIE³)]

low² (lō), v.i. & t., & n. **1.** Utter cry (as) of cow, moo; say, utter *forth*, with ~*ing* sound. **2.** n. Cow's cry. [OE *hlōwan*, = OHG *hluojen*, f. Gmc **hlō-* cogn. w. L *clamare*]

low'er¹ (lō'er), v.t. & i. Let or haul down; (naut., abs.) let down boat, haul down sail, etc. (freq. ~ *away*); diminish height of; sink, descend, slope downwards; diminish (price etc.), (of price etc.) come down; diminish (t. & i.) in intensity or pitch; degrade, disgrace; reduce bodily condition of (*a* ~*ing diet*). [f. *lower* comp. of LOW¹]

lower². See LOUR.

low'l‖**ÿ** (lō-), a. & adv. **1.** Humb[le] behaviour, or condition, mo[dest], tending. **2.** adv. In ~*y* ma[nner], ~**ĭLY**² adv., ~**ĭNESS** n. [LOW...]

lŏxodrŏm'|ĭc, a. & n. Of c[rossing] or sailing by the RHUMB; (n.) ~[, ‖ ~*al*] ⸱ table. Hence ~ICS n. [f. Gk *loxos* oblique, *dromos* course, -IC]

loy'al, a. & n. **1.** True, faithful, to duty, love, or obligation (*to*); faithful in allegiance to sovereign, government, or mother-country; enthusiastically devoted to sovereign's person & family; exhibiting loyalty; hence ~ISM(3), ~IST(2), nn., ~IZE(3) v.t., ~LY² adv. **2.** n. Person who remains ~ in time of disaffection. [16th c., f. F *loyal*, OF *loial* etc. (see LEAL) f. L *legalis* LEGAL]

loy'alty, n. Loyal temper or conduct. [c. 1400, f. OF *loialte* (prec., -TY)]

lŏz'enge (-j), n. RHOMB, diamond figure, esp. as bearing in heraldry; ~*-shaped* shield for spinster's or widow's arms; ~*-shaped* facet of cut gem; small tablet (orig. ~*-shaped*) of flavoured sugar, medicine, meat essence, etc., to be dissolved in mouth; ~*-shaped* pane in casement. [ME, f. OF *losenge*, perh. deriv. of Iber.-Rom. **lausa*, cf. Pr. *lausa* tombstone]

lŏz'enged (-jd), a. With lozenges of alternate colours; with lozenge panes. [-ED²]

£.s.d. (ĕl'ĕsdē'), n. Pounds, shillings, & pence; money, riches; *L. S.Dē'ism* (joc.), money-worship. [L *librae, solidi, denarii*, pounds, shillings, pence]

'lt. See WILL¹.

lŭbb'er, n. Big clumsy stupid fellow, lout; clumsy seaman; ~'*s hole* (naut.), hole in platform of ship's top (saving climbing by FUTTOCK shrouds); ~'*s line* (naut.), line marked on compass showing direction of ship's head. Hence ~LIKE a., ~LY¹, ² a. & adv., ~**lĭ**NESS n. [14th c., of obsc. orig.; cf. 16th c. (now dial.) *lob* bumpkin; dial. Sw. *lubber*; Da. *lobbes* clown; see LOB]

lub'ric|āte (lōō-, lū-), v.t. Make slippery or smooth by applying fluid or unguent; minimize friction of (machinery) with grease etc. (also fig.). Hence ~ANT (2) a. & n., ~ātOR, ~A'TION, nn. [f. L *lubricare* (*lubricus* slippery), -ATE³]

lubri'ci|ty (lōō-, lū-), n. Slipperiness, smoothness, oiliness, (lit. & fig.); lewdness, wantonness. So- ~OUS (-shŭs), **lub'ric**OUS, aa. [f. F *lubricité* or LL *lubricitas* (prec., -TY)]

Luc'an (lōō-, lū-), a. Of St Luke. [f. LL *Lucas* L*r*ke, -AN]

Lucca (lŏŏk'a, lŭk'a), n. ~ *oil*, superior quality of olive oil. [~, in N. Italy]

luce (lōōs, lūs), n. Pike fish, esp. when full-grown. [ME, f. OF *lus* f. LL *lucius*]

lu'cent (lōō-, lū-), a. Shining, luminous; translucent. Hence **lu'cency** n. [f. L *lucēre* shine (*lux lucis* light), -ENT]

‖ lucĕrn(e)' (lōō-, lū-), n. Cloverlike plant

for fodder. [f. F *luzerne*, f. Prov. *erno* glow-worm, w. ref. to the shiny *eeds*]

Lucian'ic (loōsǐ-), a. After the manner of Lucian, witty & scoffing. [f. Gk *Loukianos* +-IC]

lu'cid (loō-, lū-), a. Bright (poet.); (entom., bot.) with smooth shining surface; clear, pellucid, (usu. fig. of reasoning, literary style, etc.); ~ *interval*, period of sanity between attacks of madness. or of quiet between disturbances. Hence or cogn. **lucid'ITY** n., ~**LY**[2] adv. [f. F *lucide*, or L *lucidus* (LUCENT)]

Lu'cifer (loō-, lū-), n. **1.** (Planet Venus as) morning star. **2.** (Supposed name, see A.V. & R.V. of *Isa.* xiv. 12, of) the chief. rebel angel, Satan, the devil, (as *proud as* ~). **3.** *l~* (*match*), friction match (now rare). [L, light-bringing, morning star, (*lux lucis* light, *-fer* f. *ferre* bring)]

lucif'ūgous (loō-, lū-), a. (nat. hist.). Shunning daylight. [f. L *lucifugus* (prec., *fugere* flee), -OUS]

lŭck, n. **1.** (Chance as bestower of) good or ill fortune, fortuitous events affecting one's interests, person's apparent tendency to be (un)fortunate, supposed tendency of chance to bring a succession of (un)favourable events, (*bad* ~ *to him* etc.!, form of imprecation; *as* ~ *would have it*, fortunately or unfortunately; *down on* one's~, dispirited by misfortune, temporarily unfortunate; *try* one's ~, make a venture at gaming-table or in anything; *just my* ~, usu. = I am unlucky as usual; *worse* ~, parenth., more's the pity, unfortunately for me or us). **2.** Good fortune, success due to chance, (*have the* ~, be fortunate enough to; *for* ~, to bring good ~; *in, out of,* ~; *have no* ~), whence ~**'LESS** a., ~**'lèssNESS** n. **3.** ~*-money*, *-penny*, piece of money kept for ~, also sum returned by seller to buyer esp. in livestock sale. [ME, f. LG *luk*, f. MLG *geluke*, = MDu. *ghelucke*, MHG *gelücke*]

lŭck'ily, adv. (As ordinary adv.) by luck (rare); (as qualification of sentence or clause) which is etc. a fortunate thing, thank goodness, (~ *for me I was wrong*; *on a snow-slope which was* ~ *in good order*). [foll., -LY[2]]

lŭck'y̆[1], a. Constantly attended by good luck, enjoying it on a particular occasion, having as much success or happiness as one deserves & more, (*you're a* ~ *dog*, form of congratulation esp. to accepted lover; ~ *beggar!,* ~ *bargee!,* of or to person in luck); right by luck, of the nature of a fluke, (~ *guess,·hit, shot*); coming in the nick of time; presaging bringing, worn etc. for, good luck, well-omened, (~ *penny, stone, ɖay*); ~*-bag, -tub,* at bazaars etc. containing articles of more or less value for one of which payer of small sum may dip. Hence **lŭck'iNESS** n. [-Y[2]]

lŭck'y̆[2], n. (sl.). *Cut* one's ~, decamp, make off. [orig. unkn.]

luc'rative (loō-, lū-), a. Yielding gain, profitable. 'Hence ~**LY**[2] adv., ~**NESS** n. [ME, f. L *lucrativus* (*lucrari* to gain, see foll., -ATIVE)]

lucre (loōk'er, lū-), n. Pecuniary profit or gain (derog.); FILTHy ~. [ME, f. OF, or L *lucrum*]

Lucretia (loōkrēsh'a), n. Model of chastity, woman preferring honour to life. [see Livy i. 57–8]

luc'ūbrāt|e (loō-, lū-), v.i. Express one's meditations in writing; produce lucubrations. Hence ~**OR** n. [f. L *lucubrare* work by lamplight (*lux lucis* light), -ATE[3]]

lucūbrā'tion (loō-, lū-), n. Nocturnal study or meditation; literary work esp. of pedantic or elaborate character. [f. L *lucubratio* (prec., -ATION)]

luc'ūlent (loō-, lū-), a. (rare). Clear, convincing, lucid, (~ *proof, instance, explanation*). Hence ~**LY**[2] adv. [f. L *luculentus* (*lux lucis* light, -LENT)]

luc'us ā nŏn lucēn'dō (loō-, lū-), n. Paradoxical derivation; (transf.) reference of effect to paradoxical cause, explanation by contraries. [L, = *lucus* (grove) is derived from *lucēre* (shine) because it does not shine there]

‖ **lŭd.** *My* ~, = my lord in representations of counsel's pronunciation in addressing judge.

Lŭdd'ite, n. & a. (Member) of band of mechanics (1811–16) who raised riots for destruction of machinery. [orig. doubtful; leaders were called *Captain Ludd*]

lud'icrous (loō-, lū-), a. Absurd, ridiculous, exciting or deserving derision. Hence ~**LY**[2] adv., ~**NESS** n., **lud'icro**comb. form. [f. L *ludicrus* prob. f. *ludicrum* stage-play (*ludere* play)]

lŭd'ō (or loō-), n. Simple game played with dice & counters on special board. [L, = I play]

lues (loō'ēz), n. Plague, contagious disease, contagion, (~ *Boswellian'a*, biographer's tendency to magnify his subject, see BOSWELL); (also ~ *venēr'ea*) syphilis, whence (irreg.) **luET'IC** (loōĕt[4]) a. [L, genit. *luis*]

lŭff, n., & v.i. & t. (naut.). **1.** Side of fore-&-aft sail next mast or stay; ‖ broadest part of ship's bow where sides begin to curve in. **2.** vb. Bring ship's head, bring head of (ship), nearer wind; turn (helm) so as to secure this; (yacht-racing) get windward side of (opponent; *-ing-match*, struggle for this). [ME *lof(e)*, *loof*, = MLG *lōf*, LG, Da. *luv*, Du. *loef*; in ME app. a contrivance (e.g. an auxiliary rudder) for altering ship's course; poss. rel. to ON *lófi*, Goth. *lōfa* flat hand]

Luftwaffe (loōft'vahfe), n. German Air Force. [G]

lŭg[1], n. Large marine worm used as bait. [orig. unkn.]

lŭg[2], n. = LUG-SAIL.

lŭg[3], v.t. & i. (-gg-), & n. **1.** Drag or tug (heavy object) with effort or violence;

(intr.) pull hard *at*; bring (subject etc.) irrelevantly *in* or *into*; force (person) *along*. **2.** n. Hard or rough pull. [ME; cf. Sw. *lugga* pull person's hair (*lugg* forelock)]

lŭg⁴, n. ‖ (Sc.) ear; (mech.) projection from a casting etc. by which it may be fixed in place. [prob. of Scand. orig.; cf. prec.]

luge (loozh), .n., & v.i. **1.** Short raised toboggan used in Switzerland. **2.** v.i. Toboggan in this. [Swiss dial. wd]

lŭgg'age, n. ‖ Traveller's baggage, portmanteaus, boxes, etc. [LUG³, -AGE]

lŭgg'er (-g-), n. Small ship with four--cornered sails set fore & aft. [18th c., f. foll.]

lŭg'sail (-sl), n. Four-cornered sail bent on yard slung at a third or quarter of its length from one end. [17th c., of unkn. orig.]

lugŭb'rious (loo-, lū-), a. Doleful, dismal, mournful. Hence ~LY² adv., ~NESS n. [f. L *lugubris* (*lugēre* mourn), -OUS]

lukewarm (look'worm, lū-), a. & n. Moderately warm, tepid; not zealous, indifferent, (n., ~ person). Hence ~LY² adv., ~NESS n. [ME, f. (dial.) *luke*, rel. to (dial.) *lew* (OE *hleow, OHG *lāo*, ON *hlýr*)]

lŭll, v.t. & i., & n. **1.** Soothe or send to sleep by sounds or caresses, quiet (suspicion etc.) usu. by deception (usu. pass.) quiet (sea, storm); (of storm or noise) lessen, fall quiet; hence ~'ingLY² adv. **2.** n. Intermission in storm lit. or fig. [ME, imit.; cf. Sw. *lulla*, Du. *lullen*]

lŭll'abÿ, n., & v.t. Soothing refrain or song to put child to sleep; (vb) sing to sleep. [prec., -*by* as in BYE-BYE]

lŭmbāg'ō, n. (pl. ~s). Rheumatic affection in loins. Hence **lŭmbā'ginous** a. [LL; f. L *lumbus* loin]

lŭm'bar, a. & n. (Artery, vein, nerve, or vertebra) of or in loin. [prec., -AR¹]

lŭm'ber¹, v.i. Move in clumsy blundering noisy way (*along, past, by,* etc.). Hence ~ING² a., ~ingLY² adv., ~SOME a. [ME *lomere*, perh. f. *lome* LAME]

lŭm'ber², .n., & v.t. & i. **1.** Disused articles of furniture etc. taking up room (~-*room*, in which such things are kept), useless or cumbrous material; superfluous fat; roughly prepared timber (~-*carrier*, boat in ~-*trade*; ~*jack*, ~man; ~-*mill*, for sawing ~; ~*man*, feller, dresser, or conveyer of ~; ~-*scaler*, one who measures ~). **2.** vb. Fill up inconveniently, obstruct, (room, place; often *up, over*); heap together, treat, as ~; cut & prepare forest timber, whence ~ER¹ n. [poss. f. prec.; later assoc. w. obs. *lumber* pawnbroker's shop]

lŭm'bo-, comb. form of L *lumbus* loin, as ~-*abdom'inal* of loins & abdomen.

lŭm'brical, a. & n. ~ *muscle* or ~, one of the muscles flexing fingers or toes. [f. L *lumbricus* earthworm, w. ref. to the shape]

lum'inarÿ (loo-, lū-), n; Natural light--giving body, esp. sun or moon; person of intellectual, moral, or spiritual eminence, person of light & leading. [ME, f. OF *luminaire* or LL *luminarium*, -*are* (L *lumen* -*inis* light, -ARY¹)]

luminif'erous (loo-, lū-), a. Producing or transmitting light. [prec., -FEROUS]

lum'inous (loo-, lū-), a. Emitting or full of light, bright, shining, (~ *paint*, phosphorescent kind making thing conspicuous at night), whence **luminŏs'ITY** n.; (of writers etc.) throwing light upon subject. Hence ~NESS n., ~LY² adv. [ME, f. L *luminosus* (*lumen* -*inis* light, -OUS)]

lŭmm'é, int. (vulg.) of surprise or emphasis. [= (Lord) love me]

lŭmp¹, n., & v.t. & i. **1.** Compact shapeless or unshapely mass (~ *in throat*, feeling of pressure caused by emotion; *is a* ~ *of selfishness*, is selfish through & through); great quantity, lot, heap; mass of clay or dough ready for moulding or baking; protuberance, excrescence, swelling, bruise; heavy dull person; *in the* ~, taking things as a whole, in gross, wholesale; ~ *sugar*, loaf sugar broken or cut into ~s or cubes; ~ *sum*, covering number of items, also paid down at once (opp. *instalments*). **2.** vb. Put together in one ~, mass together, treat as all alike, disregard differences between or among, (*together, with, in with, under* title etc.); lay whole of (sum) *on* horse, event, etc.; rise or collect (intr.) into ~s; go heavily *along*, sit heavily *down*. [ME *lump*, of Scand. orig.; cf. Norw. & Sw. dial. *lump* block, stump, log, Da. *lump*(*e*) lump]

lŭmp², n. Uncouth spiny-finned leaden--blue fish clinging tightly to objects by sucking-disc on belly. [16th c. f. MDu. *lompe*, MLG *lumpen* (G *lumpfisch*); cf. Du. *lomp* heavy, clumsy]

lŭmp³, v.t. Be displeased at, put up with ungraciously, (now only · in *if you don't like it you may* ~ *it*). [imit.; cf. *dump, grump*, etc.]

lŭm'per, n. Labourer employed in (un)--loading cargoes; ‖ small contractor taking work in the lump & giving it out in the piece; classifier who avoids minute subdivision. [LUMP¹, -ER¹]

lŭm'ping, a. (colloq.). Big, plentiful, (~ *weight*, good weight). [LUMP¹, -ING²]

lŭm'pish, a. Heavy & clumsy; stupid, lethargic. Hence ~LY² adv., ~NESS n. [LUMP¹, -ISH¹]

lŭm'p|ÿ, a. Full of or covered with lumps; (of water) cut up by wind into small waves. Hence ~iLY² adv., ~iNESS n. [-Y²]

lun'acÿ (loo-, lū-), n. Being a lunatic, insanity (formerly of the intermittent kind attributed to changes of moon), (law) such mental unsoundness as interferes with civil rights or transactions ‖ (*Commission of* ~, authorization of inquiry into person's sanity; *Commissioner in* ~, member of board of ten for inspecting asylums etc.; *Master in* ~, officer investigating cases of alleged ~); great folly. [LUNATIC, -ACY]

lun′ar (lōō-, lū-), a. & n. **1.** Of, in, as of, the moon (~ CYCLE; ~ *distance*, of moon from sun, planet, or star, used in finding longitude at sea; ~ *month*, interval between new moons, about 29¼ days, (pop.) period of four weeks; ~ *nodes*, at which moon's orbit cuts ecliptic; ~ *observation*, finding of longitude by ~ distance ; ~ *politics*, unpractical questions ; ~ *rainbow*, made by moon's rays); (of light, glory, etc.) pale, feeble; crescent-shaped, lunate, (esp. ~ *bone* in wrist); of or containing silver (from alchemists' use of *luna* moon for silver; ~ *caustic*, nitrate of silver fused). **2.** n. ~ distance or observation; ~ bone. [f. L *lunaris* (luna moon, -AR¹)]

lunār′ian (lōō-, lū-), n. Inhabitant of moon; astronomer or navigator with special knowledge of the moon. [prec., -IAN]

lun′āte (lōō-, lū-), a. (nat. hist.). Crescent-shaped. [f. L *lunatus* (luna moon, -ATE²)]

lun′atic (lōō-, lū-), a. & n. Insane (person; see LUNACY), mad(man); (of actions etc.) outrageously foolish, frantic, mad; eccentric, foolish, (person); ~ *asylum*, hospital for reception & treatment of ~s (now *mental home* or *hospital*); ~ *fringe*, the more eccentric or visionary adherents of a political or other movement. [ME, f. LL *lunaticus* (luna moon, -ATIC)]

·lunā′tion (lōō-, lū-), n. Time from one new moon to next. [ME, f. med. L *lunatio* (prec., -ATION)]

lŭnch, n., & v.i. & t., **lŭn′cheon** (-chn), n., (-*ch* now usu. exc. in formal or ceremonious use). **1.** (With late diners) midday meal; (with midday diners) light refreshment taken between breakfast & dinner. **2.** vb (-*ch*). Take ~; provide ~ for. [(1) *lunch*, *luncheon* (in 16th c., a thick piece or hunk), app. f. LUMP, after *hump*, *hunch*, etc., w. *luncheon* as an extension (cf. *punch*, *puncheon*, etc.); (2) *luncheon* (17th c.) slight repast between meals; (3) *lunch* (19th c.) abbr. f. *luncheon*]

lune (lōōn, lūn), n. (geom.). Figure formed on sphere or plane by two arcs enclosing space. [F, f. L *luna* moon]

lunĕtte′ (lōō-, lū-), n. Arched aperture in concave ceiling to admit light; crescent-shaped or semicircular space in dome or ceiling decorated with painting etc.; (fortif.) work larger than redan, with two faces & two flanks; watch-glass of flattened shape; hole for neck in guillotine. [F (prec., -ETTE)]

lŭng, n. Either of the pair of breathing-organs in man & most vertebrates (*good* ~s, strong voice); IRON¹~; ~*s of London* etc., open spaces in or close to great city; ~*s of oak*, ~*wort*; ~*-fish*, having ~s as well as gills; ~*-power*, power of voice; ~*'wort*, plant of borage kind with white--spotted leaves likened to diseased ~,

(‖ also ~*s of oak*) kind of lichen supposed to be good for ~-disease. Hence -~ED² (-gd), ~′LESS, aa. [OE *lungen*, MLG *lunge*, OHG *lungun*, ON *lunga* f. Gmc *lung-, cogn. w. LIGHT⁴]

lŭnge¹ (-j), **longe** (-ŭnj), n., & v.t. **1.** Long rope with which horse-breaker holds horse while he makes it canter in circle; circular exercise-ground for training horses. **2.** v.t. Exercise (horse) with or in ~. [f. F *longe*, ult. f. L *longus* long]

lŭnge² (-j), n., & v.i. & t. **1.** Thrust with sword etc. esp. in fencing; sudden forward movement, plunge, rush. **2.** vb. Make ~ in fencing, deliver blow from shoulder in boxing, (*at*, *out*); (of horse) kick *out*; drive (weapon, sting, etc.) violently in some direction; rush, make sudden start in some direction. [18th c. *longe*, aphetic f. earlier *allonge*, F, f. *allonger* lunge (à *long* LONG¹)]

lunisōl′ar (lōō-, lū-), a. Of sun & moon (~ *period*, of 532 years between agreements of solar & lunar cycles; ~ *year*, with divisions regulated by changes of moon, & average length made to agree with sun's revolution). [f. L *luna* moon, -I-, L *sol* sun, -AR¹]

lŭnk′ah (-a), n. Kind of strong Indian cheroot. [f. Hind. *lanka* islands (of delta, where the tobacco is grown)]

luny. See LOONY.

lup′in(e¹ (lōō-, lū-), n. Kinds of garden & fodder plant with long tapering spikes of blue, purple, white, or yellow flowers; (usu. pl.) seed of these. [ME, f. L *lupinus*]

lup′ine² (lōō-, lū-), a. Of wolf or wolves, wolf-like. [f. L *lupinus* (*lupus* wolf, -INE¹)]

lup′|us (lōō-, lū-), n. Ulcerous disease of skin. Hence ~OID, ~OUS, aa. [L, = wolf]

lŭrch¹, n. *Leave in the* ~, desert (friend, ally) in difficulties. [16th c. = state of score in some games in which winner was far ahead of loser, f. F *lourche* game like backgammon, also bad defeat in this]

lŭrch², n., & v.i. **1.** Sudden lean to one side, stagger. **2.** v.i. Make ~(es), stagger. [18th c., naut., of unkn. orig.]

lŭrch′er, n. Petty thief, swindler; spy; ‖ cross-bred dog between collie or sheep-dog & greyhound, used esp. by poachers. [f. obs. *lurch* vb var. of LURK]

lūre, n., & v.t. **1.** Falconer's apparatus for recalling hawk (bunch of feathers, within which it finds its food while being trained, attached to thong); something used to entice, decoy; enticing quality *of a* pursuit etc. **2.** v.t. Recall (hawk) with ~; entice (person, animal; usu. *away* or *into*). [ME, f. OF *luerre*, f. WG *löder* = MHG *luoder* bait]

lūr′id, a. Ghastly, wan, glaring, unnatural, stormy, terrible, in colour or combination of colours or lights (of complexion, landscape, sky, lightning, thunder-clouds, smoky flame, glance, etc.; *casts a* ~ *light on* facts or character, explains or reveals them in a tragic or terrible way); (bot. etc.) of dingy yellowish brown. Hence ~LY² adv., ~NESS n. [f. L *luridus* pale- -yellow]

lŭrk, v.i., & n. Be hidden *in, under, about,* etc.; escape notice, exist unobserved, be latent; (n.) *on the* ~, spying; ~*ing-place,* hiding-place. [northern ME, f. LOUR w. frequent. *-k* as in *talk*; cf. Norw. *lurka* sneak forth]

lŭ'scious (-shŭs), a. Richly sweet in taste or smell; sickly sweet, cloying; (of language or literary style) over-rich in sound, imagery, or voluptuous suggestion. Hence ~LY² adv., ~NESS n. [orig. obsc.; perh. alt. of obs. *licious,* aphetic f. DELICIOUS]

lŭsh¹, a. Luxuriant & succulent (of plants, esp. grass). [var. of obs. *lash* (15th c.), f. OF *lasche* LAX]

lŭsh², n., & v.t. & i. (sl.). 1. Liquor, drink. 2. vb. Ply with liquor; drink. [18th c. cant, of unkn. orig.]

lŭsh'y̆, a. (sl.). Drunk. [-Y²]

lŭst, n., & v.i. 1. (Bibl., theol.) sensuous appetite regarded as sinful; animal desire for sexual indulgence, lascivious passion, whence ~'FUL a., ~'fulNESS n.; passionate enjoyment or desire of (~ *of battle, conquest, accumulation, applause*). 2. v.i. Have strong or excessive desire (usu. *after* or *for*). [OE, OS, OHG *lust,* Goth. *lustus* f. Gmc **lustuz*]

lŭs'tral, a. Of, used in, ceremonial purification. [f. L *lustralis* (LUSTRUM, -AL)]

lŭs'tr|āte, v.t. Purify by expiatory sacrifice, ceremonial washing, or other such rite. So ~A'TION n. [f. L *lustrare* (LUSTRUM), -ATE³]

lŭs'tre¹ (-ter), n., & v.t. 1. Gloss, refulgence, shining surface, brilliance, bright light, radiant beauty, whence ~LESS (-terl-), lŭs'trOUS, aa., lŭs'trousLY² adv.; splendour, glory, distinction, (*add* ~ *to, throw* or *shed* ~ *on*). 2. (Prismatic glass pendant of) chandelier. 3. Thin dress--material with cotton warp, woollen woof, & lustrous surface; kind of wool with lustrous surface. 4. v.t. Put ~ on (cloth, pottery, etc.). [F (L *lustrare* illumine)]

lŭs'tre² (-ter), n. = LUSTRUM.

lŭs'trine, **lŭs'tring**, nn. Glossy silk fabric. [LUSTRE¹]

lŭs'trum, n. (pl. *-a, -ums*). Period of five years. [L, orig. purificatory sacrifice after quinquennial census]

lŭs't|y̆, a. Healthy & strong; vigorous, lively. Hence ~iHOOD, ~iNESS, nn., ~iLY² adv. [-Y²]

lu'sus natūr'æ (lōō-, lŭ-), n. Sport or freak of nature, strikingly abnormal natural production. [L]

lu'tanist (lōō-, lŭ-), n. Lute-player. [f. med. L *lutanista* (*lutana* LUTE¹, -IST)]

lute¹ (lōōt, lūt), n. Guitar-like instrument used in 14th–17th centuries (RIFT *within the* ~). [ME, f. OF *luth* f. Arab. *al'ud*]

lute² (lōōt, lūt), n., & v.t. 1. Clay or

cement used to stop hole, make joint airtight, coat crucible, protect graft, etc. 2. v.t. Apply ~ to. Hence lu'tING¹(3) n. [ME, f. OF *lut* n., *luter* vb, or L *lutum* mud, clay, *lutare*]

lu'tĕo- (lōō-, lŭ-), comb. form of L *luteus* orange-coloured (*lutum* weld), as~*ful'vous* orange-tawny.

lu'tĕous (lōō-, lŭ-), a. (nat. hist.). Of deep orange yellow. [prec., -OUS]

lute'string (lōōts-, lŭ-), n. Glossy silk fabric. [app. assim. of *lustring* var. of LUSTRINE to *lute, string*]

Lutetian (lōōtē'shn, lŭ-), a. Parisian. [f. L *Lutetia* ancient name of Paris, -AN]

Lu'theran (lōō-, lŭ-), a. & n. (Follower) of Martin Luther (d. 1546), (member) of Church accepting the Augsburg confession. Hence ~ISM(3) n., ~IZE(2) v.i., (3) v.t. [-AN]

lŭx'|āte, v.t. Dislocate (joint etc.). So ~A'TION n. [f. L *luxare* (*luxus* dislocated, -ATE³]

lŭxūr'i|ant, a. Prolific (lit., & of imagination etc.); profuse of growth, exuberant, rank; (of literary or artistic style) florid, richly ornamented. Hence ~ANCE n., ~antLY² adv. [f. L *luxuriare* grow rank (*luxuria* LUXURY, -ANT]

lŭxūr'iāte, v.i. Revel, enjoy oneself, *in* or *on*; take one's ease, be luxurious. [prec., -ATE³]

lŭxūr'ious, a. Given, contributing, to luxury, self-indulgent, voluptuous, very comfortable. Hence ~LY² adv., ~NESS n. [ME, f. OF f. L *luxuriosus* (foll., -OUS)]

lŭx'ury (-ksherī), n. (Habitual use of) choice or costly food, dress, furniture, etc.; thing that one enjoys; thing desirable but not indispensable; luxuriousness. [ME, f. OF *luxurie* f. L *luxuria* (*luxus* abundance)]

-ly¹, suf. f. OE *-lic,* = OS *-lik,* OHG *-lich,* ON *-ligr,* Goth. *-leiks* f. Gmc **-liko-* (*likam* form). The suf. forms adjj. f. nn. w. sense *having the qualities of* (*kingly, scholarly, soldierly*), or w. sense of recurrence (*daily, hourly*).

-ly², suf. forming advv., f. OE *-lice,* = OS *-liko,* OHG *-licho,* ON *-liga,* Goth. *-leiko* f. Gmc **-liko-* (prec.) + adv. suf. *-ō.* In Gmc an adv. in *-ly* implies the existence of an adj. in *-ly¹*; but even in OE the suf. (in the form *-lice*) was added to other adjj., & later became the usu. ending for advv. Down to 17th c. adv. *-ly* was added even to adjj. in *-ly,* the orig. *-likō* being thus doubly represented; these advv. in *-lily* are now avoided as awkward, & as the adv. use of the adj. (*to live godly*) is also avoided, adjj. in *-ly* have in ordinary use no corr. adv. *Partly* is a solitary formation on n. Wds in *-le* have *-ly* for *-lely* (*feebly, supply,* not *feeblely, supplely*).

ly̆căn'thropy̆, n. Transformation of witch into a wolf; form of madness in which patient imagines himself some beast &

exhibits depraved appetites, change of voice, etc. [f. Gk *lukanthrōpia* (*lukos* wolf, *anthrōpos* man, -Y¹)]

lycée (lēs'ā), n. State secondary school in France. [F; see foll.]

Lȳcē'um, n. Garden at Athens in which Aristotle taught, his philosophy & followers (cf. ACADEMY, GARDEN, PORCH); literary institution, lecture-hall, teaching--place. [L, f. Gk *Lukeion* neut. of *Lukeios* epithet of Apollo (from whose neighbouring temple the ~ was named)]

lych. See LICH.

Lȳch'nis (-k-), n. Genus of plants including campion & ragged robin. [L, f. Gk *lukhnis* red flower (*lukhnos* lamp)]

lȳc'opŏd, -pōd'ium, n. Clubmoss; (-*ium* only) fine powder from kind of ~ used as absorbent in surgery, & in making stage--lightning. [-*d* anglicized f. -*ium* mod. L (Gk *lukos* wolf, *pous podos* foot)]

lȳdd'ĭte, n. High explosive chiefly of picric acid used in shells. [*Lydd* in Kent, -ITE¹]

Lȳd'ian, a. & n. (Language, inhabitant) of Lydia, ancient division of Asia Minor; ~ *mode*: ancient Greek MODE, reputedly effeminate in character; fifth of eccl. modes, with F as final & C as dominant. [f. L f. Gk *Ludios*, -AN]

lȳe, n. Water alkalized by lixiviation of vegetable ashes, any strong alkaline solution esp. for washing, any detergent. [OE *lēag*, MDu. *loghe*, OHG *louga*, ON *laug* f. Gmc *laugō* f. *lau-* (cf. LATHER)]

lȳ'ing¹, n. In vbl senses of LIE²,³; also: place to lie (*soft, dry,* ~); ~ *in*, being in childbirth (also attrib., as ~-*in hospital*). [-ING¹]

lȳ'ing², a. In vbl senses of LIE²,³; esp.: deceitful, false, whence ~LY² adv.; -~, placed, as *low*-~ *land*. [-ING²]

‖ **lȳke-wāke**, n. Watch kept at night over dead body. [LICH, WAKE²]

lȳme-grass (-ahs), n. Kind of grass planted on sand to keep it from shifting. [perh. f. LIME¹ w. ref. to its binding effect]

lȳmph, n. Pure water (poet.); (physiol.) colourless alkaline fluid from tissues or organs of body, like blood but without red corpuscles; exudation from sore etc., (also *vaccine* ~) matter taken from cowpox vesicles & used in vaccination, other morbid matter used for similar purposes. Hence ~'OUS a. [f. L *lympha* water]

lȳmphăt'ĭc, a. & n. 1. Of, secreting, conveying, lymph, (~ *gland, vessel;* ~ *system*, these glands & vessels); (of persons or temperament) flabby-muscled, pale-skinned, sluggish, (qualities formerly attributed to excess of lymph). 2. n. Veinlike vessel conveying lymph. [in 17th c. also 'frenzied', f. L *lymphaticus* mad (*lympha*, see prec.); now assoc. w. *lymph* (on anal. of *spermatic* etc.)]

lȳncē'an a. Lynx-eyed, keen-sighted. [f. L f. Gk *lugkeios* (*lugx* lynx), -AN; often

also w. ref. to *Lynceus* the keen-sighted Argonaut]

lȳnch, n., & v.t. **1.** ~ (or *L*~) *law*, procedure of self-constituted illegal court that summarily executes person charged with flagrant offence; *Judge L*~, imaginary authority to whom sentences are attributed. **2.** v.t. Execute (person) thus. [orig. U.S., earlier *Lynch's law*, named after Captain William *L*~ of Virginia, indemnified 1782 for illegally punishing persons]

lynchpin. Var. of LINCHPIN.

lȳnx, n. Kinds of animal of the cat tribe with tufted ear-tips, short tail, spotted fur, & proverbially keen sight; ~ *fur;* ~*-eyed*, sharp-sighted. [L, f. Gk *lugx*]

Lȳ'on, n. (Also ~ *King of Arms*) chief herald of Scotland. [arch. for *lion;* named f. lion on royal shield]

Lȳr'a, n. Northern constellation. [L, f. Gk *lura* LYRE]

Lȳr'aid, Lȳr'id, n. (usu. pl.). Meteor(s) radiating from Lyra about 20 Apr. [-ID²]

lȳr'ate, a. (nat. hist.). Lyre-shaped. [-ATE²].

lyre (līr), n. Obsolete instrument of harp kind but of size fit for holding up in left hand, & with strings supported by two symmetrically curved horns, chiefly used for accompanying voice; ~*-bird*, Australian bird with ~-shaped tail. So **lȳr'**IST(3) n., player on ~, (*pr.* lī'r-) lyric poet. [ME, f. L f. Gk *lura*]

lȳ'ric, a. & n. **1.** Of or for the lyre, meant to be sung; of the nature of, expressed or fit to be expressed in, song (~ *drama*, opera); (of poem) expressing writer's own thoughts & sentiments usu. at no great length & in stanzas or strophes, (of poet), writing in this manner. **2.** n. ~ poem, (pl.) ~ verses. Hence ~o- comb. form. [f. L f. Gk. *lurikos* (prec., -IC)]

lȳ'rical, a. = prec.; resembling, couched in or using language appropriate to, lyric poetry. Hence ~LY² adv. [-AL]

lȳ'ricism, n. Lyric character or (w. pl.) expression; high-flown sentiments. [-ISM]

lȳs'ol, n. Saponified mixture of cresol (see CREOSOTE) & oil, soluble in water, used as disinfectant. [P; f. Gk *lusis* (*luō* loosen) + -OL]

M

M, m, (ĕm), letter (pl. *M*s, M's). (As numeral) 1,000, as MMCI 2,101, MCMLI 1,951; (Print., m), = EM.

-m, -ma, -me, suf. in nn. taken f. Gk (-*ma -matos*), usu. expr. result of verbal action; as *phlegm, poem, comma, coma, scheme, theme.* Adjj. formed on these show the -*at*- of the Gk stem (*phlegmatic, comatose*).

ma (mah), n. (vulg.). = MAMMA¹.

ma'am (mahm, măm, m'm), n. Madam (esp. used at Court in addressing Queen or royal princess, *pr.* **măm**, or by servants, *pr.* **m'm**).

maca'bre (-ahbr), a. *Danse* ~, dance of death; grim, gruesome. [15th c. -*bree* f. F *macabré* (mod. F, erron., *macabre*), conject. referred to *Macabé* Maccabee]

macăc'ō[1], n. Monkey of genus Macacus. [Port., = monkey]

macăc'ō[2], n. Kinds of lemur. [f. F (Buffon) *mococo*, of unkn. orig.]

macăd'am, a. & n. **1.** (Of roads) made in the manner & with the materials advocated by J. L. McAdam (d. 1836), i.e. with successive layers of broken stone of nearly uniform size, each subjected to pressure before next is laid. **2.** n. Such material; TAR~; TARMAC. Hence~IZE v.t., ~ĪZA'TION n.

măcarŏn'|ĭ, n. **1.** Wheaten paste formed into long tubes, used as food; ~*i cheese*, savoury pudding of ~i & cheese baked. **2.** (hist.). 18th-c. exquisite affecting continental tastes, whence ~ISM n. [f. It. *maccaroni*, f. late Gk *makaria* barley food]

măcarŏn'ic, a. & n. pl. (Verses) of burlesque form containing Latin (or other foreign) words & vernacular words with Latin etc. terminations; medley. [f. prec.+-IC]

măcaroōn', n. Small cake or biscuit of ground almonds, white of egg, sugar, etc. [f. F *macaron* (as MACARONI)]

macăss'ar, a. & n. ~ (*oil*), kind of hair oil. [f. *Mangkasara*, in island of Celebes]

macaw'[1], n. Kinds of parrot. [f. Port. *macao*; cf. Tupi *macavuana*]

macaw'[2], n. Kinds of palm. [prob. Carib]

Măccabē'an, a. Of the *Maccabees*, Jewish princes who freed Judaea from tyranny of Antiochus Epiphanes, *c.* 166 B.C. [f. LL f. Gk *Makkabaios*+-AN]

măcc'aboy, -baw, n. Kind of snuff, usu. scented with attar of roses. [f. *Macouba*, district in Martinique]

māce[1], n. (Hist.) heavy usu. metal-headed & spiked club; staff of office resembling this; ~-*bearer*, official carrying this staff; stick used in bagatelle. [ME, f. OF *masse* f. Rom. *mattea*]

māce[2], n. Dried outer covering of nutmeg, as spice. [ME *macis* (taken as pl., whence *mace*), f. OF *macis*, f. L *macir*]

mă'cēdoine (-ĕdwahn), n. Fruit or vegetables in jelly as a dish or as cook's material. [F]

mă'cer|āte, v.t. & i. Soften by soaking; waste away by fasting. So ~A'TION n. [f. L *macerare*, see -ATE[3]]

mach. See MACH (NUMBER).

machan' (-ahn), n. (Anglo-Ind.). Elevated platform used in tiger-shooting etc. [Hind.]

machete (-ăt'ā), n. See MATCHET.

Măchiavĕll'|ĭ (-kǐ-), n. Unscrupulous schemer; one who practises duplicity in statecraft, whence ~IAN a., ~ISM n. [f. Niccolò *Machiavelli* (d. 1527), Florentine statesman, author of work *del Principe*, in

---

which unscrupulous statecraft is thought to be advocated]

machic'ol|āte, v.t. Furnish (parapet etc.) with openings between supporting corbels for dropping stones etc. on assailants. Hence ~A'TION n. [18th c., f. OF *mache-*, *machicoler*]

machicoulis (mahshĭkōōl'ĭ), n. Machicolation. [f. F *măchicoulis*]

măch'in|āte (-k-), v.i. Lay plots, intrigue. So ~A'TION, ~ātOR,' nn. [f. F *machiner* or L *machinari* contrive (foll., -ATE[3])]

machine' (-shēn), n., & v.t. & i. **1.** Apparatus for applying mechanical power, having several parts each with definite function (the kind often being specified, as *sewing, printing*, ~); bicycle, tricycle; *bathing-*~ (see BATHE[1]); person who acts mechanically & without intelligence, or with unfailing regularity; (mech.) instrument that transmits force or directs its application, as *simple* ~, one without parts, e.g. lever; controlling political organization; ~-*gun*, mounted gun mechanically loaded & fired, delivering continuous fire, (v.t.) shoot at with ~-gun; ~-*made*, made by~ (occas. derog.); ~ *tool*, mechanically operated tool for working on metal, wood, and plastics. **2.** vb. Make or operate on with ~ (esp. of sewing & printing); use ~. [F, f. L *machina* f. Gk *mēkhanē* f. *mēkhos* contrivance, cogn. w. MAY[1]]

machi'nerȳ (-shē-), n. Machines; work of a machine, mechanism; contrivances, esp. supernatural persons & incidents, used in literary work. [f. prec.+-ERY]

machi'nist (-shē-), n. One who makes or controls machinery; one who works (esp. sewing-) machine. [f. as prec.+-IST]

mach (nŭm'ber) (mahχ), n. Ratio of the speed of a body to the speed of sound in the surrounding atmosphere. [E. *Mach,* Austrian physicist (d. 1916)]

măc(k), n. (colloq.). Mackintosh. [abbr.]

măck'erel, n. Sea-fish used as food & approaching shore in shoals in summer to spawn; ~ *breeze, gale* (strong, & so favourable to ~-catching); ~ *sky* (dappled with small white fleecy clouds). [ME, f. AF *nakerel*, OF *maquerel*]

măc(k)'intōsh, n. Waterproof material of rubber & cloth for garments, esp. that patented by C. Macintosh (d. 1843); cloak, coat, of this.

mă'cle, n. Twin crystal; dark spot in mineral. [F, f. MACULA]

Mâcon (mahkawn'), n. Wine produced in the neighbourhood of~ in France. [place]

mácra'mé (-rahmǐ), n. Fringe, trimming, of knotted thread or cord. [prob. f. Turk. *maqrama* towel]

măc'ro-, comb. form of Gk *makros* long, large, as; ~*cephal'ic*, long, large, -Headed; ~*cosm*, the great world, the universe, (cf. MICROCOSM), any great whole; ~*meter* (-ŏm[t]), instrument for measuring distant objects; ~*scop'ic*, visible to naked eye.

măc′rŏn, n. Mark placed over vowel (ā) to show that it is long. [Gk, neut. adj. as prec.]

măc′ŭl|a, n. (pl. ~ae). Dark spot in sun; spot in mineral; spot, esp. permanent one, in skin, whence ~AR¹ a., ~A′TION n. [L]

măd¹, a. (-dd-). Out of one's mind, insane; (of person or conduct) wildly foolish; like ~, furiously, violently, as I ran like ~; wildly excited, infatuated, (after, about, for, on, thing, subject, etc.); (colloq.) annoyed, as I was rather ~ at missing my train; (of animals) rabid; (prov.) ~ as a March HARE, as a hatter; extravagant, wild, in gaiety; ~′cap, wildly impulsive person; ~-doctor (treating the ~); ~′house, lunatic asylum; ~′man, ~′woman, ~ person. Hence ~′LY² adv., ~′NESS n. [f. OE gemǣd(e)d p.p. of *gemǣden f. gemād mad, corresp. to OS gimēd, OHG gameit, Goth. gamaiths (crippled) f. Gmc *maidh-]

măd², v.t. & i. (-dd-; rare). Make mad; be mad, act madly, as the ~ding crowd (as quot. from Gray's Elegy, now often taken as = distracting). [f. prec.]

măd′am, n. Polite formal address to woman; (euphem.) brothel-keeper. [ME, f. OF ma DAME my lady]

madame (madahm′, madd′am; pl. mesdames pr. mādahm′). F form of prec. as title or form of address; M~ Tussaud's (tōōsōz′), show in London of waxwork figures of celebrated & notorious persons (often w. ref. to the chamber of HORRORS in it). [as prec.]

mădd′en, v.t. & i. Make, become, mad; irritate. Hence ~ingLY²‚adv. [f. MAD¹ + -EN⁶]

mădd′er, n. Herbaceous climbing plant with yellowish flowers; dye got from this. [OE mædere, rel. to ON mathra (Sw. madra, Norw. modra), MLG, MDu. mēde]

māde, a. P.p. of MAKE. Special uses: ~ dish (of several ingredients); ~ gravy (artificially compounded); a ~ man, one whose success in life is assured; (of person etc.) well, stoutly, loosely, powerfully, ~ (built, formed).

Madeir′a (-ēra), n. Island in Atlantic Ocean; white wine there produced; ~ cake, kind of sponge-cake. [Port., f. L materia MATTER, timber from its thick woods]

mademoiselle (mădamazĕl′, & see Ap.), n. (pl. mesdemoiselles, pr. mādmwazĕl′). Unmarried Frenchwoman; French gover-. ness. [F]

măd′ia, n. Plant allied to sunflower; ~ oil (got from its seed, & made into cake for cattle). [f. Chil. madi]

madŏnn′a, n. (Picture, statue, of) Virgin Mary; ~ lily (white, as in pictures of M~). [It. (ma = mia my+donna lady f. L domina)]

madrăs′ah (-a), **mĕdrĕss′eh** (-ā), n.

Mohammedan college. [Arab. (-sah) f. darasa v. study]

măd′rē|pōre, n. Kinds of perforate corals; animal producing these. Hence ~pŏ′ric,~pōr′iform, aa. [F, f. It. madrepora (madre mother+poro, coral-like but porous substance)]

măd′rig|al, n. Short amatory poem; part-song for several voices, prop. with elaborate contrapuntal imitation & without instrumental accompaniment. Hence ~ăl′ian a. [f. It. -gale, of unkn. orig.]

maduro (mahdoor′ō), a. (Of cigars) full-flavoured. [Sp., = matured]

Maecēn′ăs, n. Generous patron of literature or art. [~, patron of Horace & Virgil]

mael′strom (māl-), n. Whirlpool on W. coast of Norway; great whirlpool (lit. & fig.). Large mod. Du., f. malen grind, whirl, +stroom STREAM]

maen′ad, n. Bacchante. [f. L f. Gk mainas -ados f. mainomai rave]

maěstōs′ō (mah-), adv. (mus.). Majestically. [It.]

maěs′trō (mah-), n. (pl. -ri, pr. -ē). Great musical composer, teacher, or conductor. [It.]

Mae′ Wĕst (mā), n. (sl.). Airman's life-jacket. [person]

măff′ick, v.i. Exult riotously. [back formation f. Mafeking (relief of which in 1900‚was celebrated extravagantly in London etc.), treated as gerund]

mafia (mah′fia), n. Hostility to law & its miniters among Sicilian population, often shown in crimes; those who share in this. [Sicil.]

‖ **măg¹,** n. (sl.). Halfpenny. [orig. unkn.]

măg², n. (Short for) MAGNETO (esp. in comb., as ~-generator).

măgazine′ (-zēn), n. **1.** Store for arms, ammunition, & provisions, in time of war; store for gunpowder or other explosives; ~ gun (with chamber containing supply of cartridges fed automatically to the breech). **2.** Periodical publication (now usu. illustrated) containing articles by various writers. [f. F magasin f. Arab. makhazin pl. of makhzan storehouse (khazana store up)]

Măg′dalĕn, -lēne, n. Reformed prostitute. [Mary Magdalene of Magdala (Luke viii. 2) identified with the sinner of Luke vii. 37. ·Magdalen College, Oxford, & Magdalene College, Cambridge, are pr. mawd′lin]

Măgdalēn′ian, a. (archaeol.). Of the (latest) palaeolithic period represented by remains found at La·Madeleine, Dordogne, France. [-IAN]

māge, n. (arch.). Magician; learned person. [F f. mage MAGUS]

magĕn′ta, n. & a. **1.** Brilliant crimson aniline dye, discovered soon after battle at M~ in N. Italy (1859). **2.** adj. Coloured with or like ~.

măgg′ot, n. Larva, esp. of cheese-fly & bluebottle; red ~, larva of wheat-midge;

whimsical fancy, esp. ~ *in* one's *head*.
Hence ~Y[2] a. [ME; app. alt. form of
maddock, early ME *mathek* f. ON *mathkr*,
see MAWKISH]

Mā'gi. See MAGUS.

Mā'gian, a. & n. (One) of the Magi;
magician. Hence~ISM(3) n. [-IAN]

mă'gic, a. & n. (Of) the pretended art
of influencing course of events by occult
control of nature or of spirits, witchcraft;
black, white, natural, ~ (involving invocation of devils, angels, no personal
spirit); inexplicable or remarkable influence producing surprising results; ~
square, one divided into smaller squares
containing each a number, so arranged
that sum of a row, vertical, horizontal, or
diagonal, is always same; ~ *lantern,*
optical instrument throwing magnified
image of glass picture on white screen in
dark room; ~ *mirror* (in which future or
distant scenes are presented to spectator).
Hence ~AL a., ~alLY[2] adv. [ME, f. OF
magique a. & n. f. L *magicus* a., LL
magica n. f. Gk *magikos* (as MAGUS, see
-IC)]

magi'cian (-shn), n. One skilled in magic,
wizard, conjuror. [ME, f. OF *magicien*
(as prec., see -ICIAN)]

magilp'. See MEGILP.

Maginot line (mah'zhěnō), n. French
fortified line on Franco-German frontier
before the 1939–45 war. [person]

măgisteŕ'ial, a. Of, conducted by, a
magistrate; invested with authority;
dictatorial; (of opinions) authoritative.
Hence ~LY[2] adv. [f. LL *magisterialis* f.
LL*magisterius* (as MASTER)]

magis'tral, a. Of a master or masters,
as *the* ~ *staff* (of a school); (pharm., of
remedy etc.) devised by physician for
particular case, not included in the pharmacopoeia (cf. OFFICINAL). [F, or f. L
magistralis (as MASTER, see -AL)]

mă'gistr|ate, n. Civil officer administer-
ing law, JUSTICE of the peace. Hence or
cogn. ~ACY, ~ateSHIP, ~atURE, nn. [ME,
f. L *magistratus* -*ūs* (orig. office of) magistrate (as prec., see -ATE[1])]

Măglemōs'ian (-z-), a.. Of the early
European culture illustrated by articles
found at Maglemose in Denmark. [-IAN]

măg'ma, n. (pl. ~*ta,* ~*s*). Crude pasty
mixture of mineral or organic matters;
one of supposed fluid strata under solid
crust of earth. [L f. Gk (*massō* knead,
root *mag*-, see -M)]

Măg'na C(h)aŕt'a (k-), n. Great charter
of English personal & political liberty obtained from John in 1215. [med. L]

măgnāl'ium, n. Light tough alloy of
aluminium & magnesium. [MAGN(ESIUM)
+AL(UMINIUM)+-IUM]

măgnăn'imous, a. High-souled, above
petty feelings. Hence or cogn. mă°na-
nim'ITY n., ~LY[2] adv. [f. L *magnanimus*
(*magnus* great+*animus* soul)+-OUS]

măg'nāte, n. Great man; wealthy or

eminent man. [f. LL *magnas -atis* (*magnus* great)]

măgnē'si|a (-sha), n. Oxide of magne-
sium; (pop.) hydrated magnesium carbonate, white powder used as antacid &
cathartic. Hence ~AN (-shn) a. [ME, f.
med. L, f. Gk *magnēsia* (*lithos* stone) of
Magnesia, (1) loadstone, (2) perh. talc]

măgnēs'ium (*or* -shyum), n. Metallic
element, present in magnesia; ~ *flare,*
light, blinding light got by burning~ wire.
[f. prec., see -IUM]

măg'nět, n. Piece of iron or ore having
the properties of attracting iron & of
pointing north & south when suspended,
natural (as in loadstone) or induced by
contact with a ~, by induction, or by
electric current; *horse-shoe* ~ (in shape
of bar bent till ends nearly meet); =
LOAD[1]*stone*; (fig.) thing that attracts.
[ME, f. OF *magnete* or L f. Gk *Magnēs
-ētos* (*lithos* stone) of Magnesia]

măgnět'ic, a. & n. **1.** Having properties
of magnet; producing, produced by, acting by, magnetism; ~ *equator,* ACLINIC
line; ~ *mine,* submarine mine detonated
by approach of large mass of ~ material,
e.g. ship; ~ NEEDLE, NORTH; capable of
receiving properties of, or being attracted
by, loadstone; (fig.) very attractive;
mesmeric. **2.** n. pl. Science of magnetism. Hence **măg'nět'**ICALLY adv. [f. F
-*ique* or LL *magneticus* (prec., -IC)]

măg'nětism, n. Magnetic phenomena;
natural agency producing these; *terrestrial* ~, magnetic properties of the
earth as a whole; *animal*~, = MESMERISM;
(fig.) attraction, personal charm. So
măg'nětIST(3) n. [-ISM]

măg'nětite, n. Magnetic iron oxide.
[-ITE]

măg'nětiz|e,-is|e (-iz), v.t. Give magnetic
properties to; attract (lit. & fig.) as magnet
does; mesmerize. Hence ~A'TION n. [-IZE]

măgnět'ō, n. (pl. ~*s*). An electric generator using magnets which are independent
of the current produced (esp. type of
igniting-apparatus of internal-combustion engines producing the required
intermittent high-tension current independently of a battery). [abbr. of
magneto-electric].

măgnět'o-, comb. form of Gk *magnēs
magnēt-* MAGNET, as: ~-*elec'tric,* (of
electric generators) using magnets which
are independent of the current produced,
so ~-*electri'city*; ~*graph,* instrument
recording movements of ~*meter* (-ŏm'-)
(instrument measuring magnetic forces;
esp. terrestrial magnetism).

măg'nětrŏn, n. (phys.). Thermionic tube
for generating very high frequency oscillations. [f. MAGNET+(ELEC)TRON]

măgnif'ic(al), aa. (arch.). Magnificent,
sublime. [f. F *magnifique* or L *magnificus*
(*magnus* great, see -FIC)+-AL]

mă$gnif'icăt, n. Hymn of Virgin Mary
in *Luke* i. 46–55, used as canticle, &

beginning thus. [L, 3rd sing. of *magnifi-care* MAGNIFY]

măgnif'ic|ent, a. Splendid, stately; sumptuously constructed or adorned; splendidly lavish; (colloq.) fine, excellent. Hence or cogn. ~ENCE n., ~entLY² adv. [OF, f. L *magnificent-* stem seen in comp. & sup. of *magnificus* MAGNIFIC]

măgnif'icō, n. (pl. ~es). Venetian magnate; grandee. [It., as MAGNIFIC]

măg'ni|fy, v.t. Increase apparent size of (thing), as with lens or microscope; exaggerate; (rare) increase; (arch.) extol. Hence or cogn. ~FICA'TION, ~fīER¹(2), nn. [ME, f. L *magnificare* (*magnus* great, see -FY), partly thr. OF]

măgnil'oqu|ent, a. Lofty in expression; boastful. Hence ~ENCE n., ~entLY² adv. [f. L *magniloquus* (*magnus* great + -*loquus* -speaking) + -ENT]

măg'nitūde, n. Largeness; size; importance; *first, seventh*, etc., ~, classes of fixed stars arranged according to degree of brilliancy, (fig.) *of the first* ~ (importance). [ME, f. L *magnitudo* (*magnus* great, see -TUDE)]

Măgnōl'ia, n. Genus of trees or shrubs cultivated for foliage & flower. [f. P. *Magnol*, botanist (d. 1715), -IA¹]

măg'num, n. (Bottle containing) two quarts (of wine or spirits). [L, neut. of *magnus* great]

măg'num·bōn'um, n. Large yellow cooking plum; kind of potato. [L wds = large good]

magnum opus. See OPUS.

măg'pīe, n. 1. European bird with long pointed tail & black-&-white plumage; idle chatterer; variety of pigeon. 2. (Rifle shot that strikes) outermost division but one of target. [f. *mag* abbr. of *Margaret* + PIE¹]

măg'us, n. (pl. -*gi*, pr. -jī). Member of ancient Persian priestly caste; sorcerer; *the* (*three*) *Magi*, the 'wise men' from the East who brought offerings to the infant Christ. [L, f. Gk *magos* f. OPers. *magus*]

Magyar, n. & a. 1. (mŏd'yar). (Member, language) of the people now predominant in Hungary. 2. (măg'yar). ~ (*blouse*), blouse with sleeves cut in one piece with main part of garment. [native]

Mahabharata (mahhahbah'rata), n. An ancient Hindu epic. [Skr.]

Maharaja(h) (mah-harahj'a), n. Title of some Indian princes. [Hind. (*maha* great + RAJAH)]

Maharanee (mah-harahn'ī), n. Maharajah's wife. [Hind. (*maha* great, *rani* queen)]

Mahăt'ma (ma-h-), n., (esoteric Buddhism). One of a class of persons with preternatural powers, supposed to exist in India & Tibet; pop. prefixed as title in India to names of exalted personages, esp. Gandhi. [f. Skr. *mahatman* (*maha* great + *atman* soul)]

Mahd'ī, n. Spiritual & temporal leader expected by Mohammedans (often applied to leaders of insurrection in Sudan), whence **Mahd'(ī)ISM**(3) n. [f. Arab. *mahdiy* he who is guided right, p.p. of *hada* guide]

mah-jŏng(g)', n. A Chinese game for four played with 144 pieces called tiles, adopted in Europe & America c. 1923. [Chin., = sparrows]

mahlstick. See MAULSTICK.

mahŏg'any (ma-h-), n. Wood of a tropical American tree, much used for furniture, & taking high polish; the tree; dining-table (*have* one's *knees under* person's ~, be dining with him); the colour of ~, reddish-brown, (often attrib.). [orig. unkn.]

Mahŏm'ĕtan (ma-h-). See MOHAMMEDAN.

Mahound' (ma-hoond), n. (arch., joc.). Mohammed. [f. OF *Mahun* short for *Mahomet*]

mahout' (ma-howt), n. Elephant-driver. [f. Hind. *mahaut*]

Mahrătt'a (mară-), n. Member of a warlike Indian race. [Hind. *Marhaṭṭa*]

mah'seer, n. Large Indian freshwater game fish. [Hind. *mahāsir*]

maid, n. Girl; young unmarried woman; spinster; *old* ~, elderly spinster, (also) round game at cards; (also ~'*servant*) female servant, as *house-, nurse-, lady's-*, ~, ~ *of all work*; ~ *of honour*, unmarried lady attending on queen or princess, (also) kind of cheesecake. Hence ~'ISH¹ a., ~'Y³ n. [early ME, shortened f. MAIDEN]

maidan (mīdahn'), n. (Anglo-Ind.). Open space in town; parade-ground. [Pers.]

maid'en, n. & a. 1. Girl; spinster; (hist.) kind of·guillotine·used at Edinburgh; = ~ *over.* 2. adj. Unmarried; ~ *name* (before marriage); (of female animals) uncoupled; (of horse) that has never won prize, (of race) open to such horses; (of plant) grown from seed; (of soldier, sword, etc.) untried; ‖~ *assize*, one at which there are no cases for trial; (crick.) ~ *over* (in which no runs are scored); ~ *speech*, M.P.'s first speech in the House; ~*hair*, kinds of fern with fine hairlike stalks & delicate fronds; ~*head* (-hĕd), virginity. Hence ~HOOD n., ~ISH¹, ~LIKE, ~LY¹, aa. [OE *mægden*, dim. (-EN²) f. *mægeth* = OS *magath*, OHG *magad*, Goth. *magaths*, Gmc **magathiz*]

maieut'ic (maū-), a. (Of Socratic mode of inquiry) obstetric, serving to bring out a person's latent ideas into clear consciousness, pertaining to intellectual midwifery. [f. Gk *maieutikos* f. *maieuomai* act as midwife (*maia*), see -IC]

mail¹, n. Armour composed of rings or chain-work, defensive armour for the body, as *chain, plate, ring*, -~. [ME, f. OF *maille* f. L *macula* spot, mesh]

mail², v.t. Clothe (as) with mail; *the* ~*ed fist*, (fig.) physical force. [f. prec.]

mail³, n., & v.t. 1. Bag of letters for conveyance by post; this system of conveyance, the post, (esp. for foreign letters); *the ~*, all that is so conveyed on one occasion; ~ *(train)*, train carrying this; ‖ ~*-cart*, cart for carrying ~ by road, (also) light vehicle for carrying children; ~*-coach*, (now) = ~*-cart*, (formerly) stage--coach for entire conveyance of ~; ~ *order*, order for goods sent by post (~*--order firm*, firm doing business on this system); FAN[3]~. 2. v.t. Send (letters etc.) by post. [ME & OF *male* wallet f. WG (= OHG) *malha*]

maim, v.t. Mutilate, cripple, (lit. & fig.). [ME *maynhe* &c. f. OF *mahaignier* &c., of unkn. orig.]

main[1], n. (In game of hazard) number (5, 6, 7, 8, or 9) called by caster before dice are thrown; match between cocks. [16th c., app. spec. application of MAIN[3]]

main[2], n. Physical force (only in *with might & ~*); SPANISH ~; (poet.) high sea; *in the ~*, for the most part; principal channel, duct, etc., for water, sewage, etc. [OE *mægen*, OS *megin*, OHG *magan*, ON *magn, megin* f. Gmc **mag-* MAY v.]

main[3], a. 1. Exerted to the full, as *by ~ force*; chief in size or extent, as *the ~ body* (of army etc.); principal, most important, as *the ~ point* (in argument), ‖ *~ line* (of railway), whence ~'LY[2] adv.; *have an eye to the ~ chance* (one's own interests). 2. (naut.) ~ *brace* (attached to ~ yard, esp. *splice the ~ brace*, serve extra rum ration); ~ *deck*, (in man-of--war) deck next below spar deck, (in merchantman) upper deck between poop & forecastle; ~'*mast*, principal mast; ~'*sail* (-sāl, -sl), (in square-rigged vessel) sail that is bent to the ~ yard, (in fore-&--aft rigged vessel) sail set on after part of ~mast; ~'*stay*, stay from ~top to foot of foremast, (fig.) chief support; ~'*top*, 'platform above head of lower ~ mast; ~ *yard*, yard on which ~sail is extended. 3. ~'*land*, extent of land excluding the neighbouring islands; ~'*spring*, principal spring of watch, clock, etc., (fig.) chief motive power or incentive; **M~ Street*, principal street of a town (esp. allus., as *M~-street ideals*). [ME, f. ON *meginn*, *megn* adj.; partly f. OE *mægen-* (prec.) in compp.]

maintain' (or mĕn-), v.t. Carry on, keep up, (war, contest, action at law, condition, position, attitude, relations, correspondence); cause (person etc.) to continue *in* (condition, possession of thing, etc.); support (life, one's state in life) by nourishment, expenditure, etc.; furnish (one-*self*, children) with means of subsistence; keep (road etc.) in repair; back up (cause, party); assert as true (opinion, statement, *that*). Hence ~ABLE a. [ME, f. OF *maintenir* f. Rom. **manutenere* f. L *manu tenēre* hold in the hand]

main'tenance, n. Maintaining; enough to support life; *cap of ~*, cap, hat, worn

as symbol of official dignity or carried before sovereign etc.; (law) offence of aiding a party in litigation without lawful cause. [ME, f. OF (as prec., see -ANCE)]

maison(n)ĕtte' (-z-), n. Small house; part of a house let separately (not necessarily all on one floor). [F (-*nn*-), dim. of *maison* house]

maître d'hôtel (mātr dōtĕl'), n. Major--domo; hotel manager. [F, = house-master]

‖ **maize**, n. Indian corn, its grain. [f. Sp. *maiz*, of Cuban orig.]

majĕs't|ic, a. Possessing grandeur, imposing. Hence ~ICALLY adv. [f. foll. + -IC]

măj'ĕstў, n. Impressive stateliness of aspect, bearing, language, etc.; sovereign power; (in speaking to or of sovereign) *(Your, His, Her, M~*, you, he, she, as *Your M~ forgets that with the best of intentions it is scarcely in your M~'s* (or *your) power to miss your train)*; representation of God (the Father or Son) enthroned within aureole. [ME, f. OF *majeste* f. L *majestatem* (as MAJOR[2], see -TY)]

Mäjlis', n. Persian parliament. [Pers.]

majŏl'ica, maio- (-yŏ-), n. Kinds of glazed & ornamented Italian ware; modern imitation of these. [f. It. *maiolica*, f. former name of *Majorca*]

măj'or[1], n. Officer next below lieutenant--colonel & above captain (also in army sl. for *sergeant-~*). Hence ~SHIP n. [F, short for *sergent-major*]

măj'or[2], a. & n., & v.i. 1. Greater (not foll. by *than*) of two things, classes, etc.; ~ PROPHETS; ~ *epilepsy*, epilepsy proper; ~ *suit* (bridge), spades or hearts; (log.) ~ *term* (that enters into predicate of conclusion of syllogism), ~ *premiss* (containing ~ term); ~ *axis* of conic section (passing through the foci); (mus., of intervals) greater by chromatic semitone than minor intervals, as ~ *third*, (of keys) in which scale has a ~ third; ~ *part*, majority (*of*); (mil.) ~*-general* (see OFFICER), SERGEANT-~; *bugle, drum, pipe, trumpet,* ~ (head bugler etc. of unit); ‖ (in schools) *Brown, Smith,* ~ (the elder or first to enter school); of full age. 2. n. Person of full age; (log., ellipt. for) ~ term or premiss (*I deny your ~*); **stu*dent's special subject or course (v.i., take, or qualify, *in* a ~); ~*-dōm'ō* (pl. *-os*), chief official of Italian or Spanish princely household, house-steward. [L, compar. of *magnus* great]

majŏ'rĭtў, n. 1. Greater number or part (*of); the (great) ~*, the dead, esp. *join the (great) ~*, die; *absolute* ~ of votes, more than half number of electors or actual voters; number by which votes cast on one side exceed those on other. 2. Full age, as *attained his~*. 3. Office of MAJOR[1]. [f. F *majorité* f. med. L *majoritatem* (as prec., see -TY)]

majŭs'cūl|e, a. & n. (palaeogr.). Large (letter), whether capital or uncial. Hence

~AR¹ a. [F, f. L *majuscula* (*littera* letter, dim. of MAJOR)]

māke¹, v.t. & i. (*māde*).. **1.** Construct, frame, as *God made man* (*a rational creature*), *bees ~ cells of wax, you were made for this work*; *pipes are made* (consist) *of clay*. **2.** ~ GOOD, SURE. **3.** Compose, draw up, (book, will). **4.** Prepare (tea, coffee, beds); ~ HAY; ~ (arrange & light materials for) *a fire*. **5.** Cause to exist, bring about, (disturbance, sport, noise, one's mark in the world, a corner in wheat); ~ *no* BONES; ~ *fun, game, of*, trifle with, treat with ridicule; ~ (conclude treaty of) *peace*; ~ (give) *place, room, way* (*for* others); ~ one's *way*, progress. **6.** Result in, as *it ~s a difference*; '*find*' ~*s* (becomes) *in the past tense* '*found*'. **7.** Establish, enact, (distinctions, rules, laws); ~ FRIENDS. **8.** Get together (a HOUSE¹, quorum); ~ *a bag*, kill number of game; ~ *a book*, arrange series of bets on some event; ~ WATER¹. **9.** ~ *a habit of it*, cause it to become one, so ~ *an* EXAMPLE¹, *exhibition, fool, beast* (*of* oneself, person); ~ *a night of it*, carry it (festivity etc.) on through the night. **10.** ~ *of*, conclude to be the meaning or character of (*can you ~ anything of it?*; *what am I to ~ of your behaviour?*); ~ *much, little, the best*, etc., *of*, derive much etc. advantage from, (also) attach much etc. importance to, so ~ LIGHT⁴ *of*; ~ *a* HASH² *of*. **11.** Entertain, feel, (doubt, scruple, *of, about*); ~ HEAD *or tail of*. **12.** (Naut.) discern, come in sight of, (also) arrive at; (sl.) catch (a train etc.); *~ it*, succeed in traversing a certain distance, (fig.) be successful. **13.** Amount to, as *2 & 2 ~ 4*; constitute, as *one swallow does not ~ a summer*; form, be counted as, (*this ~s the tenth time*; *will you ~ one of the party?*); serve for, as *this ~s pleasant reading*. **14.** Become, turn out to be, 'as *she will ~ a good wife*. **15.** Gain, acquire, (money, a living, one's fortune); (cards) win (trick), play (card) to advantage, (also) shuffle (cards, or abs.). **16.** Proceed (*towards* etc.), also w. *for* (~ *for home*). **17.** ~ *sail*, set sail, (also) spread additional sail. **18.** Secure the advancement of, cf. MADE; ~ *or mar*, cause success or ruin of. **19.** Cause to be, as ~ *it* HOT, ~ *oneself a martyr*, ~ *oneself* SCARCE, ~ *him a duke*; convert *into*. **20.** Consider to be, (*what do you ~ the time?*; *I ~ it 5 miles*). **21.** Cause, compel, (without *to* in act.), as ~ *him repeat it*, but *he was made to repeat it*. **22.** ~ *believe*, pretend (*to* do, *that*); ~ *do*, manage *with* (something) as an inferior or temporary substitute; *what bird do you ~* (consider) *that to be?*; *he ~s Richard die* (represents him as having died) *in 1026*. **23.** Wage (war). **24.** Execute (bodily movement, bow, FACE¹, LEG). **25.** Perform (journey etc., & with many nn. expr. vbl action, as *acquisition, attempt, blunder, start, venture*); ~ (eat) *a good breakfast*; ~ HEAD¹,

LOVE. **26.** Accomplish (distance, knots, etc.). **27.** ~ *as if one had*, pretend one has; ~ BOLD, FREE¹, MERRY. **28.** (Of flood or ebb tide) begin to flow or ebb. **29.** ~ *after*, pursue; ~ *against*, be unfavourable to; ~ (hasten) *away*; ~ *away with*, get rid of, kill, squander; ~ *for*, conduce to (happiness etc.), confirm (view), proceed towards, assail; ~ *off*, run away, decamp, (often *with* stolen goods etc.); ~ *out*, draw up, write out, (list, document, cheque), get together with difficulty, as *articles put in to ~ out a volume*, (try to) prove, as *how do you ~ that out?*, *you ~ me out* (*to* be) *a hypocrite*, understand, as *I can't ~ him out*, *can't ~ out what he wants*, decipher (handwriting etc.), distinguish by sight, as *I made out a figure in the distance*; ~ *over*, transfer possession of (thing *to* person), esp. by assignment; ~ *up*, supply (deficiency), complete (amount, party), compensate, as ~ *up lost ground*, ~ *up for lost time, we must ~ it up to* (compensate) *him somehow*, compound, put together, (medicine, hay *into* bundles, butter, etc.), sew together (coat etc.), get together (company, sum of money), arrange (type) in pages, compile (list, account, document), concoct (story), (of parts) compose (whole), prepare (actor) for his part by dressing, false hair, etc., apply cosmetics (to), arrange (marriage etc.), settle (dispute), ~ *it up*, be reconciled, ~ *up* one's *mind to*, decide *to* (do), resolve upon (course); ~ *up to*, court, curry favour with. **30.** ‖ ~'*bate* (arch.), breeder of strife; ~--*believe*, pretence; ~'*peace*, peacemaker; ~'*shift*, temporary substitute or device; ~-*up*, disguise of actor, cosmetics etc. used for this, making up of type, type made up; (cosmetics for) woman's facial decoration; person's character & temperament; ~'*weight*, small quantity added to ~ up weight, (also fig. of persons), (fig.) unimportant point added to ~ case seem stronger. [OE *macian*, OS *makon*, OHG *mahhōn* f. WG *makōjan* f. *mak-* fit, suitable, cogn. w. MATCH¹]

māke², n. (Of natural or manufactured thing) style of structure or composition; mental or moral disposition; *American* ~, made in America; *is this your own ~* (made by you)?; *on the ~* (sl.), intent on gain; (electr.) making of contact, position in which this is made, esp. *at* ~; ‖ ~ *& mend* (naut.), a period of leisure or no fixed duties for the hands (orig. for work on their clothes). [f. prec.]

māk'er, n. In vbl senses, esp. *the, our*, etc., *M*~, the Creator; (arch.) poet. [-ER¹]

māk'ing, n. In vbl senses, esp.: *be the ~ of*, ensure success or favourable development of; (pl.) earnings, profits; (pl.) essential qualities, as *he has the ~s of a general*; **(pl.) paper & tobacco for rolling a cigarette. [-ING¹]

māl- pref. = F *mal* f. L *male* badly, in

sense (1) bad(ly), as *maltreat*, (2) un-, as *maladroit*.

Malăcc'a, n. Town & district on Malay peninsula; ~ *cane*, rich-brown walking-cane, from stem of a palm.

măl'achite (-kit), n. Hydrous carbonate of copper, green mineral taking high polish. [f. OF *melochite* (Gk *malakhē* mallow, see -ITE[1])]

măl'aco-, comb. form of Gk *malakos* soft, as: ~*derm*, soft-skinned animal (esp. of sea-anemones & of one division of reptiles); ~*logist*, ~*logy*, (-ŏl[2]), student, science, of molluscs; ~*ptery'gian* a. & n., soft-finned (fish).

măladjŭst'ment, n. Faulty adjustment. [MAL-]

măladmĭnĭstrā'tion, n. Faulty administration. [MAL-]

măl'adroit, a. Clumsy, bungling. Hence ~LY[2] adv., ~NESS n. [F (MAL- + ADROIT)]

măl'adў, n. Ailment, disease, (lit. & fig.). [ME, f. OF *maladie* f. *malade* sick f. pop. L *male habitus* (*male* ill + *habitus* p.p. of *habēre* have)]

măl'a fīd'ē, adv. & a. (Acting, done) in bad faith. [L]

Măl'aga, n. Seaport in S. Spain; white wine from this.

Mălagăs'ў, a. & n. (Language, inhabitant) of Madagascar. [used in native lang., but prob. of foreign orig.]

măl'aise (-z), n. Bodily discomfort, esp. without development of specific disease; also fig. [F (OF *mal* bad + *aise* EASE)]

mal'amŭte, **măl'e-**, n. An Eskimo dog. [name of Alaskan Eskimo tribe]

măl'anders, **măll'en-**, n. pl. Scabby eruption behind knee in horses. [ME, f. OF *malandre* f. L *malandria*]

măl'apĕrt, a. & n. (arch.). Impudent, saucy, (person). [ME, f. OF (MAL- + *apert* = *espert* EXPERT)]

măl'aprŏp(ism), n. Ludicrous misuse of word, esp. in mistake for one resembling it (e.g. *a nice derangement of epitaphs* for *arrangement of epitaphs*). Hence **măla-prŏp'IAN** a. [f. Mrs *Malaprop* in Sheridan's *Rivals*]

măl̆ăpropos' (-pō), adv., a., & n. (Thing) inopportunely (said, done, or happening). [f. F *mal à propos* (*mal* ill, see APROPOS)]

măl'ar, a. & n. (Bone) of the cheek. [f. L *mala* jaw, see -AR[1]]

mălār'|ia, n. Kinds of intermittent & remittent fever caused by bite of mosquito, which conveys the germs; unwholesome atmosphere caused by exhalations of marshes, to which these fevers were formerly referred. Hence ~IAL, ~ĭAN, ~ĭous, aa. [f. It. *mal' aria* bad air]

Malay', a. & n. (Language, member) of a people predominating in Malaya & Eastern Archipelago; ~ *fowl*, large domestic variety. Hence ~AN a. & n. [f. native *malayu*]

Mălaya'lam (-yah-), n. Language of Malabar. [native]

măl'contĕnt, a. & n. Discontented (person), (one) inclined to rebellion. [F (MAL-)]

măl de mer' (mār), n. Seasickness. [F]

māle, a. & n. 1. Of the sex that begets offspring or performs the fecundating function (used of persons or animals, & of plants whose flowers contain only fecundating organs, also of plants to which sex was once attributed on account of colour etc., as ~ *fern*, commonest lowland fern); (of men or ~ animals; (of parts of machinery etc.) designed to enter or fill the corresponding FEMALE part, as ~ *screw*; ~ (MASCULINE) *rhyme*. 2. n. ~ person or animal. [ME, f. OF, f. L *masculus* (*mas* male, see -CULE)]

māle- in comb. = L *male* ill.

mālĕdic't|ion, n. Curse. So ~ORY a. [ME, f. L *maledictio* f. MALE(*dicere dict-* speak), see -ION, MALISON]

măl'ĕfăctor, n. Criminal: evil-doer. So **mālĕfăc'tION** n. [ME, f. L, f. MALE(*facere fact-* do), see -OR]

malĕf'ic, a. (Of magical arts etc.) harmful, baleful. [f. L MALE(*ficus* -FIC)]

malĕf'ic|ent, a. Hurtful (*to*); criminal. So ~ENCE n. [f. L altered stem of *maleficus* MALEFIC; cf. MAGNIFICENT]

malĕv'ol|ent, a. Desirous of evil to others. Hence or cogn. ~ENCE n., ~entLY[2] adv. [16th c. *mali-* f. (obs.) F *mali-* f. L *mali-*, MALE(*volens* part. of *velle* wish)]

mālfeas'|ance (-ēz-), n. (law). Evil-doing, esp. official misconduct. So ~ANT a. & n. [AF, f. OF MAL(*faisant* part. of *faire* do f. L *facere*), see -ANCE]

mălfŏrm|a'tion, n. Faulty formation. So ~ED[1] (-md') a. [MAL-]

māl'ic, a. (chem.), ~ *acid* (derived from apple & other fruits). [f. F *malique* f. L *malum* apple, see -IC]

măl'ice, n. Active ill-will; desire to tease; *bear* ~ (*to*), cherish vindictive feelings (against); (law) wrongful intention, esp. as increasing guilt of certain offences, esp. murder; ~ PREPENSE. So **mali'cious** (-shŭs) a., **mali'cious**LY[2] (-shŭs-) adv. [ME, f. OF, f. L *malitia* (*malus* bad, see -ICE)]

malĭgn'[1] (-īn), a. (Of things) injurious; (of diseases) = MALIGNANT; malevolent. Hence ~LY[2] adv. [ME, f. OF *maligne* or L *malignus* (*malus* bad, cf. BENIGN)]

malĭgn'[2] (-īn), v.t. Speak ill of, slander. [ME, f. OF *malignier* or LL *malignare* contrive maliciously, as prec.]

malĭg'n|ant, a. & n. 1. (Of disease) very virulent or infectious (now usu. denoting definite variety of disease, as ~*ant cholera*); harmful; feeling or showing intense ill-will. 2. (hist.). Supporter of, supporting, Charles I against Parliament. Hence ~ANCY n., ~antLY[2] adv. [f. LL part. as prec.]

malĭg'nitў, n. Deep-rooted ill-will; (of diseases) malignant character. [ME, f. OF *malignite* or L *malignitas* (as MALIGN[1], see -TY)]

maling'er (-ngg-), v.i. Pretend, produce, or protract, illness in order to escape duty (esp. of soldiers, sailors, etc.). Hence ~**ER**[1] n. [f. F *malingre* sickly, of obsc. orig.]

māl'ism, n. Doctrine that it is a bad world. [f. L *malus* bad + -ISM]

māl'ison (-sn, -zn), n. (arch.). Curse. [ME, f. OF *maleison* MALEDICTION]

mall (mawl, măl), n. Sheltered walk as promenade, ‖ esp. *the M~* (măl) in St James's Park, London, orig. alley for game of PALL-MALL; (hist.) this game, alley for it, mallet for it. [special use of MAUL[1]]

măll'ard, n. Wild drake or duck; its flesh. [ME, f. OF *mal(l)art*, of obsc. orig.]

măll'éable, a. (Of metals etc.) that can be hammered or pressed out of form without tendency to return to it or to fracture; (fig.) adaptable, pliable. Hence **mălléa**BIL'ITY n. [ME, f. OF, f. L *malleare* hammer (*malleus*), see -BLE]

măll'émŭck, mŏll'ymawk, n. Fulmar, petrel, or similar bird. [f. Du. *mallemok* (*mal* foolish + *mok* gull)]

măll'ét, n. Hammer, usu. of wood; implement for striking croquet or polo ball. [ME, f. OF *maillet*, dim. as MAUL[1]]

măll'éus, n. Bone of ear transmitting vibrations of tympanum to incus. [L, = hammer]

măll'ow (-ō), n. Wild plant with hairy stems & leaves & purple flowers; garden varieties of this. [OE *mealuwe* f. L *malva*]

malm (mahm), n. Soft chalky rock; loamy soil from disintegration of this; fine-quality brick made originally from ~, marl, or similar chalky clay. [OE *mealm*, cogn. w. OS, OHG *melm* dust, ON *malmr* ore, Goth. *malma* sand f. *mel-* grind (MEAL[1])]

mălmais'on (-z-), n. Kind of carnation. [*M~*, palace of empress Josephine]

malmsey (mahm'zĭ), n. Strong sweet wine from Greece, Spain, etc. [ME, f. med. L *malmasia* (in MDu., MLG *malmesie, -eye*, MHG *malmasier*), f. later var. of Gk *Monemvasia* in the Morea; see MALVOISIE]

mălnŭtri'tion, n. Insufficient nutrition. [MAL-]

mălŏd'orous, a. Evil-smelling. [MAL-]

mălprăc'tice, n. Wrongdoing; (law) physician's improper or negligent treatment of patient; (law) illegal action for one's own benefit while in position of trust. [MAL-]

malt[1] (mawlt), n. Barley or other grain prepared for brewing or distilling; *extract of* ~ (as food for invalids); ~ *liquor* (made from ~ by fermentation, not distillation, e.g. beer, stout); ~*-house* (for preparing & storing ~); ~*-worm*, (fig.) toper. [OE *mealt*, OS *malt*, OHG *malz*, ON *malt* f. Gmc **malt-* cogn. w. MELT]

malt[2] (mawlt), v.t. & i. Convert (grain)

into malt; (of seeds) come to condition of malt from germination's being checked by drought. [f. prec.]

Mal'ta (maw-), n. Island in Mediterranean; ~ *fever*, complicated fever common in ~.

Maltese' (mawltēz), a. & n. (pl. same). (Language, native) of Malta; ~ *cat, dog*, fancy kinds; ~ CROSS[1]. [-ESE]

măl'tha, n. Cement of pitch & wax or other ingredients. [L f. Gk]

Mălthūs'ian (-z-), a. & n. (Follower) of T. R. Malthus (d. 1835) who advocated moral restraint (pop. understood as abstention from marriage) as means of checking increase of population. Hence ~ISM (-zhan-) n. [-IAN]

mal'ting (maw-), n. In vbl senses; also, malt-house. [-ING[1]]

mal'tōse (maw-), n. (chem.), Sugar produced from starch-paste by action of malt. [F (MALT + -OSE[2])]

măltreat', v.t. Ill-treat. So ~MENT n. [f. F MAL(*traiter* TREAT)]

maltster (mawl(t)'ster), n. One who makes malt. [-STER]

mălvā'ceous (-shus), a. Of the genus Mallow. [f. L *malvaceus* (as MALLOW, -ACEOUS)]

mălversa'tion, n. Corrupt behaviour in position of trust; corrupt administration (*of* public money etc.). [F, f. *malverser* f. L *male* badly + *versari* behave frequent. of *vertere* vers- turn, see -ATION]

mălvoisie' (-vwazē'), n. = MALMSEY. [ME, f. OF *malvesie* (mod. *-voi-*) f. med. L *malvasia*, var. of *malmasia*; see MALMSEY]

măm'ba, n. (Kinds of) venomous African snake. [f. Kaffir *m'namba*]

măm'elon, n. Rounded eminence. [F, = nipple f. *mamelle* breast f. MAMILLA]

Măm'éluke (-ōōk), n. (hist.). Member of military body (orig. Caucasian slaves) that seized throne of Egypt in 1254; (in Mohammedan countries) slave. [ult. f. Arab. *mamluk* slave (*malaka* possess)]

mamill'|a, n. Nipple of female breast; nipple-shaped organ etc. So **măm'il**-**l**ARY[1], **măm'ill**ATE[2](2), **măm'ill**ATED[1], ~**ī**FORM, aa. [L, dim. of MAMMA[2]]

mam(m)a'[1] (-ah), n. Mother (used esp. by children). [instinctive]

mămm'|a[2], n. (pl. ~**ae**). Milk-secreting organ of female in mammals; corresponding structure in males. Hence ~ARY[1], **mamm**ĪF'EROUS, ~**ī**FORM, aa. [L]

măm'mal, n. One of foll. class. [f. foll.]

Mammăl'ĭa, n. pl. Class of animals having mammae for nourishment of young. Hence **mammăl'**IAN a. & n., **mam**-**măl'**OGIST, **mammăl'**OGY, nn. [neut. pl. of LL *mammalis* (as MAMMA[2], see -AL)]

mămmalif'erous, a. (geol.). Containing mammalian remains. [f. prec. + -FEROUS]

mămmee', n. Tropical American tree with large yellow-pulped fruit. [f. Sp. *mamey* f. Haytian]

mămm'on, n. Wealth regarded as idol or evil influence; the worldly rich; *the ~*

of unrighteousness, wealth ill used or ill gotten. Hence ~ISH¹ a., ~ISM, ~JST, ~ITE, nn. [f. LL *mam*(*m*)*ona* f. Gk *mamōnas* f. Aram. *mamon* riches; see *Matt.* vi. 24, *Luke* xvi. 9–13]

mămm'oth, n. & a. **1.** Large extinct elephant. **2.** adj. Huge. [f. Russ. *mammot*]

mămm'y̆, n. Child's word for mother; *coloured woman in charge of white children. [f. *mam* (instinctive) + -Y³]

măn¹, n. (pl. *měn*). **1.** Human being (*a* ~ *& a* brother, fellow ~); (in indefinite or general application) person, as *any*, *no*, ~, *some*, *few*, *men*; (*all*) *to a* ~, all without exception. **2.** The human race (~ *is born unto trouble*; ~ *is a political animal*). **3.** *Inner, outer,* ~, spiritual, material, parts of ~, (joc.) interior, esp. stomach, exterior, of ~; NEW, OLD, ~. **4.** Adult male, opp. to *woman, boy,* or both; ~ *& boy* (adv.), from boyhood upwards. **5.** (As impatient or lively vocative) *nonsense,* ~ *! hurry up,* ~ (*alive*) *!*; (joc. or endearing) *little* ~, young boy. **6.** One, as *what can a* ~ *do in such a case?* **7.** Individual (male) person, as ~ *for* ~, *between* ~ *&* ~, *5/- per* ~; *as a* ~, viewed simply in regard to his personal character; *if you want noise, he is your* ~ (can supply you); *I'm your* ~ (accept your offer etc.); *be* one's *own* ~, be free to act, (also) be in full possession of one's faculties, senses, etc.; *every* ~ JACK¹. **8.** (In comb., denoting one who follows profession, uses implement, trades in article, etc.) *clergy*~, *post*~, *brake*~, *pen*~, *rag-&-bone-* ~; BEST¹, HANDY, ~. **9.** ~ eminently endowed with manly qualities, as *be a, play the,* ~. **10.** Husband, in ~ *& wife.* **11.** (Hist.) vassal; ~servant, valet; workman, as *the employers locked out the men.* **12.** (Usu. pl.) soldiers, esp. common soldiers. **13.** Piece in game of chess, draughts, etc. **14.** ~ *of* STRAW. **15.** (In comb.) ship, as ~-*of-war,* armed ship belonging to a country's navy, INDIA~, MERCHANT~. **16.** ~ *of the* WORLD; ~ *Friday,* servile follower, factotum, (name given by Robinson Crusoe to his servant); ~ *about town,* ‖ London society idler; ~-*at-arms,* soldier, esp. heavy-armed & mounted; ~-(male) *child*; ~-*eater,* cannibal, biting horse, ~-*eating* shark or tiger; ~-*handle,* move by force of ~ alone, (sl.) handle roughly; ~-*hole,* opening in floor, sewer, etc., for ~ to pass through; ~-*hour,* work done by one ~ in one hour; ~ *in the moon,* semblance of ~ in moon, esp. as type of imaginary person; *the* ~ *in* (*or on*) *the street,* the ordinary ~ (esp. as opp. experts on the matter in question); ~-MILLINER; ~ *of Kent* (see KENTISH); ~-*of LETTERS*; ~-'*power,* amount of men available for military or other service; ~-'*servant,* male servant; ~-'*slaughter,* slaughter of human beings, (Law) criminal homicide without malice aforethought; ~-'*trap* (for catching men, esp. trespassers). Hence ~'LESS a. [O E

man(*n*), OS, OHG *man,* ON *mathr,* Goth. *manna,* f. Gmc **mann-, *mannon-*]

măn², v.t. (-nn-). Furnish (fort, ship, etc.) with men for service or defence; (naut.) place men at (part of ship); fill (post); fortify spirits or courage of (esp. one*self*). [OE *mannian,* as prec.]

măn'acle, n. (usu. pl.), & v.t. **1.** Fetter (prop. for the hand; also fig.). **2.** v.t. Fetter with ~s. [ME, f. OF *manicle* handcuff f. L *manicula* dim. of *manus* hand]

măn'age¹, n. (arch.). Training of horse; trained movements of horse; riding--school. [f. It. *maneggio,* as foll.]

măn'age², v.t. & i. Handle, wield, (tool etc.); conduct (undertaking etc.); control (household, institution, State); take charge of (cattle etc.); subject (person, animal) to one's control; gain one's ends with (person etc.) by flattery, dictation, etc., whence **măn'ag**ING² (-nĭj-) a.; contrive (*to do,* often iron., as *he* ~*d to muddle it*); succeed in one's aim (often *with* inadequate material etc.); (with *can* or *be able to*) cope with, make proper use of, as *can you* ~ *another slice?* Hence ~ABIL'ITY, ~ableNESS, nn., ~ABLE a., ~ablY² adv., (-ĭja-). [f. It. *maneggiare* f. Rom. **manidiare* (*manus* hand)]

măn'agement (-ĭjm-), n. In vbl senses; also or esp.: trickery, deceitful contrivance; *the* ~, governing body, board of directors, etc. [-MENT]

măn'ager (-nĭj-), n. Person conducting a business, institution, etc. (esp. *general* ~); ‖ member of either House of Parliament appointed with others for some duty in which both Houses are concerned; *good, bad,* etc., ~ (of money, household affairs, etc.); ‖ (law) person appointed, usu. by Court of Chancery, to manage a business for benefit of creditors etc. Hence ~ESS¹, ~SHIP, nn., **mănagēr'IAL** a. [-ER¹]

măn'akin, n. (Kinds of) brightly-coloured small tropical American bird. [var. of MANIKIN]

mănatee', n. Large aquatic herbivorous mammal, sea-cow. [f. Sp. *manati* f. Carib *manattoui*]

Măn'chester, n. ‖ ~ *goods,* cotton textiles (sold in ~ *department* of a shop); ~ *School,* adherents of the doctrines of free trade & *laissez-faire* (name given by Disraeli to Cobden & Bright & their followers). [place]

mănchineel', n. W.-Ind. tree with poisonous milky sap & acrid fruit. [f. F *mancenille* f. Sp. *manzan*(*ill*)*a* f. L *matiana* kind of apple f. Roman gens *Matia*]

măn'ciple, n. Officer who buys provisions for college, inn of court, etc. [ME. f. OF, f. L *mancipium* = (in med. L) office of *manceps* buyer (*manus* hand + *capere* take)]

Măncūn'ian, a. & n. (Inhabitant) of Manchester. [f. L *Mancunium* Manchester, -AN]

-**mancy**, suf. f. OF -*mancie* f. LL f. Gk *manteia* divination, = divination by —; see -CY.

Mandae'an, a. & n. (Member, language) of a Gnostic sect surviving in Iraq. [f. Aram. *mandā* knowledge]

mandam'us, n. ‖ Judicial writ issued from Queen's Bench Division as command to inferior court. [L, = we command]

man'darin[1], n. Chinese official in any of 9 grades (hist.); standard spoken Chinese; party leader who lags behind the times; nodding toy figure in Chinese costume; ~ *duck*, small Chinese duck noted for its bright plumage. [f. Port. *mandarim* f. Malay f. Hind. *mantri* f. Skr. *mantrin* counsellor]

man'darin[2], -**ine** (-ēn), n. Small flat deep-coloured orange; colour of this (got from coal-tar); a liqueur. [F (-*ine*); perh. f. prec. w. ref. to his yellow robes]

man'dataṛy, n. (law). One to whom a mandate is given (for spec. sense see foll.). [f. LL *mandatarius* (foll., -ARY[1])]

man'date[1], n. Judicial or legal command from superior; commission to act for another, esp. one from League of Nations to a State (the *mandatary*) to govern a people not qualified for independence; (poet.) command; papal rescript; (law) contract by which mandatary undertakes to perform gratuitously some service in respect of thing committed to him; (after F *mandat*) political authority supposed to be given by electors to (party in) parliament. [f. L *mandatum*, neut. p.p. of *mandare* command (*manus* hand +*dare* give)]

mandāte'[2], v.t. Commit (territory etc. *to* mandatary). [f. prec.]

man'dataṛy, a. & n. 1. Of, conveying, a command, compulsory. 2. n. = MANDATARY. [f. LL *mandatorius* (as prec., see -ORY)]

man'dible, n. Jaw, esp. lower jaw in mammals & fishes; upper or lower part of bird's beak; (in insects) either half of upper pair of jaws. So **mandib'ūlar**[1], **mandib'ūlate**[2](2), aa. [f. F or LL *mandibula* (*mandere* masticate)]

mandōl'a, -**ōr'a**, n. Kind of mandolin or lute. [It., var. of PANDORA]

man'dolin(e), n. Musical instrument of lute kind with paired metal strings, played with plectrum. [F (-*ine*), f. It. *mandolino* dim. of prec.]

mandrăg'ora, n. = foll., esp. as type of narcotic (Shak. *Othello* III. iii. 330). [ME also -*oras*, f. L (LL -*ora*) f. Gk *mandragoras*]

man'drāke, n. Poisonous plant with emetic & narcotic properties, with root thought to resemble human form & to shriek when plucked. [ME *mandrag(g)e*, shortened f. prec., assoc. w. *drake* dragon]

man'drel, -**il**, n. (In lathe) axis to which work is fixed while turned; cylindrical rod round which metal or other material is forged or shaped; (dial.) miner's pick. [orig. unkn., cf. F *mandrin*]

man'drill, n. Large, hideous, & ferocious baboon. [prob. MAN[1]+DRILL[3]]

man'dūc|āte, v.t. Chew, eat. So ~A'TION n., ~**ātory** a. [f. L *manducare* (*mandere* chew), see -ATE[3]]

māne, n. Long hair on neck of horse, lion, etc. (also fig. of person). Hence (-)**mānED**[2] (-nd), ~'**LESS** (-nl-), aa. [OE *manu*, OHG *mana*, ON *mǫn* f. Gmc **manō*]

manège (-ēge, (manāzh'), n. Riding--school; movements of trained horse; horsemanship. [F (-*ège*), as MANAGE[1]]

mān'ēs (-z), n. pl. Deified souls of departed ancestors; shade of departed person, as object of reverence. [L]

man'ful, a. Brave, resolute. Hence ~LY[2] adv., ~NESS n. [MAN[1]+-FUL]

man'gabey (-ā), n. African species of monkey. [*M*~, region of Madagascar]

mang'anese (-ngganēz), n. Black mineral used in glass-making etc.; metallic element of which this is the oxide. Hence **mangane'sIAN** ·(-nggganēz-), **mangăn'IC** (-ngg-), aa. ʻ[f. F *manganèse*, f. It. -*ese*, alt. f. MAGNESIA]

mānge (-j), n. Skin disease in hairy & woolly animals, caused by an arachnidan parasite; (loosely) dirty condition of skin. [ME *manjewe* f. OF *manjue* itch f. *mangier* (mod. *manger*) eat (as MANDUCATE)]

‖ **mang'el** (-wŭrz'el), **mang'old** (-wŭrz'el), (-ngg-), n. Large kind of beet, used as cattle food. [G -*gold*- (-*gel*-), f. *mangold* beet +*wurzel* root]

man'ger (-j-), n. Box, trough, in stable etc. for horses or cattle to eat from; DOG *in the* ~. [ME, f. OF *mangeoire* f. Rom. *manducatoria (as MANDUCATE, see -ORY)]

mangle[1] (măng'gl), n., & v.t. 1. Machine of two or more cylinders for rolling & pressing washed clothes. 2. v.t. Press (clothes) in ~. [f. Du. *mangel* (-*eln* vb), ult. f. Gk as MANGONEL]

mangle[2] (măng'gl), v.t. Hack, lacerate, by blows; cut roughly so as to disfigure; spoil (quotation, text, etc.) by gross blunders, disguise (words) by mispronouncing. [f. AF *ma(ha)ngler*, app. frequent. of *mahaignier* MAIM]

mang'o (-nggō), n. (pl. ~*es*). (Indian tree bearing) fleshy fruit yellowish-red in colour, eaten ripe or used green for pickles etc.; ~-*fish*, golden-coloured Indian fish; ~ *trick* (in which ~-tree appears to spring up & bear fruit in few hours). [f. Port. *manga* f. Tamil *mankay* (*man* ~-tree +*kay* fruit)]

mangold (-wurzel). See MANGEL.

mang'onel (-ngg-), n. (hist.). Military engine for casting stones etc. [ME, f. OF *mangonel(le)*, dim. f. LL *manganum*, -*gonum*, -*gona* f. Gk *magganon*]

mang'osteen (-ngg-), n. (E.-Indian tree bearing) fruit with thick red rind & white juicy pulp. [f. Malay *mangustan*]

mång'rōve (-rgg-), n. Tropical tree or

shrub, bark of which is used in medicine & tanning. [17th c., of unkn. orig.]

măn'g|y (-ji), a. Having the mange; squalid, shabby. Hence ~**ILY**[2] adv., ~**INESS** n. [f. MANGE +-Y[2]]

mănhătt'an, n. Cocktail made of vermouth, whisky, etc. [M~, in N. York]

măn'hōŏd, n. State of being a man (in any sense); ~ *suffrage* (granted to all male citizens of lawful age not disqualified by crime, insanity, etc.); manliness, courage; the men of a country. [MAN[1] +-HOOD]

măn'ia, n. Mental derangement marked by excitement, hallucination, & violence; great enthusiasm (*for* thing, do*ing*). Hence **măn'IC** a., of or affected by ~ (*manic-depressive psychosis*, kind of mental disorder alternating between periods of elation and depression, occas. with intermediate periods of sanity). [LL f. Gk, = madness]

-mănia, suf. denoting scientifically a special type of madness (*klepto*~, *megalo*~, *nympho*~); also (pop.) eager pursuit (*biblio*~) or admiration (*Anglo*~). Hence personal suf. *-maniac* (cf. -PHOBE, -PHOBIA). [as prec.]

măn'iăc, a. & n. (Person) affected with mania, raving mad(man). Hence **mani‿acAL** a., **mani'acalLY**[2] adv. [f. LL *maniacus* (as MANIA, see -AC)]

-măniac, suf. See -MANIA.

Mănichee' (-k-), n. Adherent of religious system (3rd to 5th c.) that represented Satan as coeternal with God. Hence **Mănich(a)e'AN** a. & n., **Măn'ich(a)eISM** n., (-kē-). [f. LL f. Gk *Manikhaios*, founder of sect, living in Persia]

măn'icŭr|e, n., & v.t. **1.** (One who undertakes) treatment of hands & finger-nails as profession. **2.** v.t. Apply ~e treatment to (hands, person). Hence ~**IST** n. [(vb f. n.) F (L *manus* hand +*cura* care)]

măn'ifèst[1], n. List of cargo for use. of Customs officers. [f. F *manifeste* (as MANIFEST[3])]

măn'ifèst[2], a. Clear, obvious, to eye or mind. Hence ~**LY**[2] adv. [ME, f. L *manifestus*]

măn'ifèst[3], v.t. & i. Show plainly to eye or mind; be evidence of, prove; display, evince, (quality, feeling) by one's acts etc.; (of thing) reveal *itself*; record in ship's manifest; (of ghost) appear. So ~**A'TION** n., ~**atIVE** (-ĕs‿) a. [ME, f. OF *manifester* or L *manifestare* (as prec.)]

mănifès'tō, n. (pl.~s). Public declaration of policy by sovereign, State, or body of individuals. [It., as MANIFEST[2]]

măn'ifōld[1], a. & n. **1.** Having various forms, applications, etc.; performing several functions at once; many & various, as ~*vexations*; ~*writer*, carbon copying-apparatus. **2.** n. (mech.). Pipe or chamber with several openings. Hence ~**LY**[2] adv., ~**NESS** n. [OE *manigfeald*, repr. in OS, OHG, ON, Goth.; f. MANY + -FOLD]

măn'ifōld[2], v.t. Multiply copies of (letters etc.) as by MANIFOLD[1] writer. [OE & ME (obs.) f. prec.; in mod. use formed anew]

măn'ikin, n. Little man, dwarf; artist's lay figure; anatomical model of the body; small tropical American bird. [f. Du. *manneken,* dim. of MAN[1]]

manill'a[1], n. Metal bracelet used by African tribes as medium of exchange. [Sp.; prob. dim. of L *manus* hand]

Manill'a[2], **-il'a,** n. (*-ila*) capital of Philippine islands; (also ~ *hemp*) fibrous material for ropes, matting, etc.; cheroot made in ~; ~ *paper,* brown wrapping-paper made from ~ hemp etc. [native (-*ila*)]

manille', n. Second best trump or honour in quadrille & ombre. [corrupt. of Sp. *malilla* dim. *mala* bad f L *malus*]

măn'iŏc, n. Cassava; meal made from it. [f. Tupi *mandioca*]

măn'iple, n. **1.** (Rom. ant.) subdivision of legion, containing 120 or 60 men. **2.** Eucharistic vestment, strip hanging from left arm. [OF, f. L *manipulus* (*manus* hand)]

manip'ŭl|āte, v.t. Handle, treat, esp. with skill (material thing, question); manage (person) by dextrous (esp. unfair) use of influence etc. Hence or cogn. ~**A'TION**, ~**ātOR** nn., ~**ātIVE**, ~**ātORY**, aa. [back formation f. *manipulation*, after F *manipuler* (f. L as prec.)]

măn'itou (-ōō), n. (Amer. Ind.). Good or evil spirit; thing having supernatural power. [f. Algonquin *manitu*, -*tu*]

mănkind, n. **1.** (-kīnd'). Human species. **2.** (măn‿). Male sex. [MAN[1] +KIND n.]

măn'like, a. Having good or bad qualities of a man; (of woman) mannish. [-LIKE]

măn'l|y, a. Having a man's virtues, courage, frankness, etc.; (of woman) having a man's qualities; (of things, qualities, etc.) befitting a man. Hence ~**INESS** n. [-LY[1]]

mănn'a, n. Substance supplied as food to Israelites (*Exod.* xvi); spiritual nourishment, esp. the Eucharistic; sweet juice from ~-*ash* & other plants, used as gentle laxative (~ *in tears, in sorts,* superior, inferior, kinds of this); ~-*croup*, coarse granular wheat meal [Russ. *krupa* groats]. [ME f. LL f. Gk, f. Heb. *man*, explained as=*man hu?* what is it?, but perh.=Arab. *mann* exudation of *Tamarix gallica*]

mănn'équin (*or* -kin), n. Person, usu. woman, employed by dressmakers etc. to wear & show off costumes. [F, = lay figure, f. Du. as MANIKIN]

mănn'er, n. Way a thing is done or happens, as *in, after, this* ~; (arch.) *in* a ~ *of speaking*, so to speak; (gram.) *adverb of* ~, one that asks or tells how; *to the* ~ *born,* (Shak. *Ham.* I. iv. 15) destined by birth to be subject to the custom, (pop.) naturally fitted for the position etc.; (pl.) modes of life, conditions of society; outward bearing; *the grand ~ʹ*, old-fashioned dignity; (pl.) *good, bad*, etc. behaviour in social intercourse, habits indicating good breeding, as *he has no ~s*, whence ~LESS a.; style in literature or art; mannerism; (arch.) kind, sort, as *what ~ of man is he?*; *all ~ of*, every kind of; *no ~ of right*, no right at all; *in a ~*, in some sense, to some extent. [ME, f. AF *manere* = OF *maniere* f. Rom. **manuaria* mode of handling, fem. of L *manuarius* of the hand (*manus*), -ARY[1]]

mann′ered (-erd), a. *Ill, well, rough, -~*, having bad etc. manners; (of style, artist writer) showing mannerism. [-ED[2]]

mann′er|ism, n. Excessive addiction to a distinctive manner in art or literature; trick of style; trick of gesture or speech (esp. of an actor). Hence ~IST n., ~ɪsʹTIC(AL) aa. [-ISM]

mann′erl|y̆, a. Well-mannered, polite. Hence ~INESS n. [-LY[1]]

mann′ish, a. (Of woman) masculine; characteristic of man as opp. to woman, as *what a ~ way to thread a needle!* Hence ~NESS n. [-ISH[1]]

mann′īte, n. (Also *~-sugar*) substance obtained from manna. Hence **mann′i-** tōSE[2] n. [f. MANNA +-ITE[1]]

manœu′vre[1], ***-euver**, (-nōōver, -nū-), n. Planned movement of troops or ships of war; deceptive or elusive movement; skilful plan; MASS[2] *of ~*. [F, f. med. L *man(u)opera*, as foll.; cf. MANURE[1]]

manœu′vr|e|[2], *-euver, (as prec.), v.i. & t. Perform, cause (troops) to perform, manœuvres; employ artifice; force, drive, (person, thing, *into, out, away*, etc.) by contrivance; manipulate adroitly. Hence ~ER[1] n. [f. F *manoeuvrer* f. med. L *man(u)- operare* (*manus* hand, *operari* to work); cf. MANURE[2]]

manŏm′ĕter, n. Pressure gauge for gases & vapours. Hence **mănŏmĕt′rĭc** a. [f. F *manomètre* (Gk *manos* thin, see -METER)]

ma nŏn trŏp′pō, mus. direction appended to another. But not to excess. [It.]

măn′or, n. English territorial unit, orig. of nature of feudal lordship, now consisting of lord's demesne & of lands from whose holders he can exact certain fees etc.; *lord of the ~*, person, corporation, having rights of this; *~-house*, his mansion. Hence **manōr′ɪAL** a. [ME, f. AF *maner*, OF *manoir*, f. L *manēre* remain]

manqué (see Ap.), a. (after its n.). That might have been but is not, that has missed being, (*a Napoleon, comic actor, ~*). [F]

măn′sard, n. (Usu. *~ roof*) curb roof in which each face has two slopes, lower one steeper than upper. [f. F *mansarde* (F. *M~*, architect, d. 1666)]

mănse, n. Ecclesiastical residence, esp. Scottish Presbyterian minister's house. [ME, f. med. L *mansus, -sa, -sum*, house (*manēre mans-* remain)]

măn′sion (-shn), n. Large residence (‖ in pl. often of large buildings divided into flats); ‖ *~-house*, house of lord of manor or landed proprietor, official residence, esp. (*the M~-house*) of Lord Mayor of London. [ME, f. OF, f. L *mansionem* (as prec., see -ION)]

măn′suetŭde (-swĭ-), n. (rare). Meekness, docility. [ME, f. L *mansuetudo* (*mansuetus* tame f. *manus* hand, *suesco* be used)]

măn′tel, n. (Now usu. *~-piece*) structure of wood, marble, etc., above & around fireplace; (usu. *~-shelf*) shelf projecting from wall above fireplace; *~-board*, wooden shelf (usu. draped) fixed upon this; *~-tree*, beam across opening of fireplace. [var. of MANTLE[1]]

mănt(e)′lĕt, n. Kinds of short mantle; bullet-proof screen for gunners. [ME, f. OF (-*el*-), dim. of *mantel* MANTLE[1]]

măn′tic, a. Of divination. [f. Gk *mantikos* (*mantis* prophet, see -IC)]

măntĭll′a, n. Large veil covering woman's hair & shoulders; small cape. [Sp., dim. of *manta* MANTLE[1]]

măn′tis, n. Orthopterous insect; *praying ~*, kind that holds forelegs in position suggesting hands folded in prayer. [Gk, = prophet]

măntĭss′a, n. Decimal part of logarithm. [L, = makeweight]

măn′tle[1], n. Woman's loose sleeveless cloak; (fig.) covering; fragile lace-like tube fixed round gas-jet to give incandescent light; outer fold of skin enclosing mollusc's viscera. [(1) OE *mentel*, (2) f. OF *mantel*, both f. L *mantellum* cloak]

măn′tle[2], v.t. & i. Clothe (as) in mantle; cover, conceal, envelop; (of liquids) become covered with coating or scum; (of blood) suffuse cheeks, (of face) glow, with blush. [f. prec.]

mantlet. See MANTELET.

măn′tŭa, n. Woman's loose gown in 17th– –18th cc.; *~-maker*, dressmaker. [corrupt. of *manteau* (F, as MANTLE[1])]

măn′ūal, a. & n. **1.** Of, done with, the hands, as *~ labour*; (mil.) *~ (exercise)*, drill in handling rifle; *~ fire-engine* (worked by hand, not steam); *~* (finger) *alphabet*; SIGN[1] *~*. **2.** n. Small book for handy use, handbook; organ keyboard played with hands; (hist.) book of the forms to be used by priests in the administration of the Sacraments. Hence ~LY[2] adv. [ME, f. OF *manuel*, later assim. to L *manualis* (*manus* hand, see -AL)]

mănŭfăc′torў, n. Factory, workshop. [f. L as foll., see -ORY]

mănŭfăc′ture[1], n. Making of articles by physical labour or machinery, esp. on large scale; branch of such industry, as *woollen ~*; *of home, English*, etc., *~*, made at home etc.; (derog.) mechanical production (of literature etc.). [c. 1600 f. F, f. L *manu* by hand +*facture* (whence E *facture* 15th c.) f. L *factura* (*facere fact-* make, see -URE)]

mănŭfăc'tur|e², v.t. Work up (material) for use; produce (articles) by labour, esp. on large scale (derog. of literary work etc.); invent, fabricate, (story). Hence ~**ER¹** n. [f. prec.]

mănŭmit', v.t. (hist.; -tt-). Set (slave) free. So **mănŭmi'ssion** n. [f. L manu-mittere (manus hand + mittere miss-send)]

manūre'¹, n. Any substance, esp. dung and compost, spread over or mixed with soil to fertilize it. Hence **manūr'ial** a. [f. foll.]

manūre'², v.t. Apply manure to (land, or abs., also fig.). [ME, f. AF maynoverer, = OF manouvrer MANŒUVRE²]

măn'ūscript, a. & n. (abbr. MS. pr. ĕmĕs', pl. MSS. pr. ĕmĕs'ĭz). (Book, document) written by hand, not printed; author's copy for printer. [f. med. L manuscriptus (manu by hand + scriptus p.p. of scribere write)]

măn'ward, a. Tending, directed, towards man. [-WARD]

Mănx, a. & n. **1.** Of the Isle of Man, as ~ cat, tailless variety; ~'man, inhabitant of I. of Man. **2.** n. ~ cat, language; (as pl., Manx) ~ people. [f. ON *manskr f. Man- (OIr. Manu)]

ma'nỹ (mĕ-), a. & n. Numerous, as ~ times, (poet., rhet.) ~ a time (& oft), ~ & ~ a time, ~ people wish, ~ wish, ~ of us wish, how ~ (of them) can I have?, as ~ as you like, (pred., rare) his reasons were ~ and good, six mistakes in as ~ (six) lines; ~ 's the, there are ~ that (~ 's the tale he has told us); ~ 's the time, often (~ 's the time I have seen you do it); the ~, the multitude; the one & the ~ (philos.), unity & plurality; one too ~, not wanted, in the way; he was (one) too ~ for us (out-witted, baffled, us); a good, great, ~, fair, large, number; ~-headed beast, monster, the populace; ~plies (mĕn'ĭplĭz), (dial. for) third STOMACH; ~-sided, having ~ sides, aspects, capabilities, etc., so ~-sidedness. [OE manig, OS, OHG manag, Goth. manags f. Gmc *managaz]

Maori (mowr'ĭ), n. Member, language, of brown race in New Zealand. [native]

măp¹, n. Representation (usu. on plane surface, cf. GLOBE) of (part of) earth's surface, showing physical & political features etc., or of the heavens; off the ~ (colloq.), of no account, obsolete; on the ~ (colloq.), to be reckoned with, of importance. Hence ~'less a. [f. L mappa napkin; in med. L mappa mundi map of world]

măp², v.t. (-pp-). Represent on map; ~ out, plan out, arrange in detail (course of conduct, one's time, etc.). [f. prec.]

mā'ple, n. Kinds of trees & shrubs grown for shade, ornament, wood, or sugar; wood of these; ~-leaf, emblem of Canada. [ME mapul etc., OE mapeltrēow; cf. OE, OS mapulder, MLG mapeldorn]

Maquis (mahkē'), n. Secret force of patriots in France in 1939–45 war. [F, = brushwood, f. Corsican It. macchia]

măr, v.t. (-rr-). Impair fatally, ruin, esp. make (or mend) or ~; spoil, disfigure; ~'plot, one who hinders undertaking by officiousness. [OE merran, OS merrian, OHG merren, ON merja, Goth. marzjan f. Gmc *marz-]

mă'rabou (-bōō), n. Large W.-Afr. stork; tuft of down from its wings or tail as trimming for hat etc. [F, prob. f. vulg. Arab. use of foll.]

mă'rabout (-bōōt), n. Mohammedan hermit or monk, esp. in N. Africa; shrine marking ~'s burial-place. [F, f. Arab. murabit]

măraschi'nō (-kē-), n. (pl. ~s). Liqueur from a small black cherry. [It. (marasca small black cherry, for amarasca f. amaro bitter f. L amarus)]

mărăs'm|us (-z-), n. Wasting away of body. Hence ~**ic** a. [f. Gk marasmos (maraino wither)] .

Mă'rathon, n. ~ (race), a race of abnormal length (w. ref. to Phidippides, who ran 150 miles to secure Spartan aid for the Athenians in the battle of ~ in 490 B.C.); (attrib.) requiring extreme endurance (applied to competitions of various kinds).

maraud', v.i. & t. Make plundering raid (on); go about pilfering: (trans.) plunder. Hence ~**ER¹** n. [f. F marauder (maraud rogue)]

mărave'dī (-vā-), n. (hist.). Gold & silver Spanish coins. [Sp. f. Arab. Murabiṭin MARABOUTS, Moorish dynasty at Cordova]

mar'ble, n., & v.t. **1.** Limestone in crystalline (also, in granular) state & capable of taking polish, used in sculpture & architecture; this as type of hardness or durability or smoothness (often attrib.); (pl.) collection of sculptures, as Elgin ~s; small ball of ~, clay, glass, etc., as toy. **2.** v.t. Stain, colour, (paper, edges of book, soap) to look like variegated ~ (esp. in p.p.). Hence **marb'lly²** a. [ME, f. OF marbre, marble, f. L marmor]

marc, n. Refuse from pressed fruit. [F, f. marcher tread, MARCH⁵]

Marc'an, a. Of St Mark. [f. L Marcus Mark, -AN]

mar'casite, n. (Usu. white iron) pyrites. [15th c., f. med. L marcasita, f. Arab. marqashita]

marcĕl', n., & v.t. (-ll-). **1.** ~ (wave), kind of artificial wave in hair. **2.** v.t. Wave (hair) thus. [M~, inventor of method]

marcĕs'c|ent, a. (Of parts of plant) withering but not falling. Hence ~**ENCE** n. [f. L marcescere incept. of marcēre wither, see -ESCENT]

March¹, n. (abbr. Mar.). Third month of year; ~ brown, fly used in angling; ~ HARE. [ME, f. OF march(e), dial. var. of marz, mars, f. L Martius (mensis month) of Mars]

march², n. (hist.). Boundary, frontiers,

(often pl., esp. of borderland between England & Scotland or Wales); tract of (often debatable) land between two countries. [ME, f. OF *marche* f. Gmc *marko* MARK[1]]

mārch[3], v.i. (Of countries, estates, etc.) border *upon*, have common frontier *with*. [ME, f. OF *marchir* (as prec.)]

mārch[4], n. (Mil.) marching of troops; *line* (route) *of* ~; long toilsome walk; progress (*of events, time, intellect, mind*); distance covered by troops in a day; FORCE*d* ~; uniform step of troops etc., as QUICK, SLOW, ~; ~ *past*, ~ of troops in line past saluting-point at review; (mus.) composition meant to accompany ~, as DEAD ~. [f. F *marche* (as foll.)]

mārch[5], v.i. & t. Walk *away, forth, past* (reviewing officer or sovereign), *out*, etc., in military manner with regular and measured tread; walk, proceed, steadily; ~*ing orders*, direction for troops to depart for war etc.; (as gallicism) make progress; (trans.) cause to go *on, off*, etc. [f. F *marcher*, f. Gallo-Rom. **marcare* f. LL *marcus* hammer]

mār'chioness (-sho-), n. Wife, widow, of marquis; lady holding in her own right position equal to that of marquis. [f. med. L *marchionissa* f. *marchio -onis* (MARCH[2]) captain of the marches]

mārch'pāne, mārz'ipăn, n. Paste of pounded almonds, sugar, etc., made up into small cakes etc.; such cake. [c. 1500 *marchpayne*, later *marzepaine* (cf. F *marcepain*, It. *marzapane*), *mazapane* (cf. F *massepain*), *marzipan* (f. G); orig. unkn.]

mārcōn'i, n., & v.i. & t. (hist.). 1. = foll. 2. vb. Send ~, send (message) thus. [see foll.]

mārcōn'igrăm, n. (hist.). Message sent by Marconi's system of wireless telegraphy. [*Marconi* (d. 1937) inventor, -GRAM]

Mardi gras (mård'ēgrah), n. Shrove Tuesday; last day of carnival. [F, = fat Tuesday]

mār'e[1], n. ~ *claus'um*, sea under jurisdiction of particular country; ~ *lib'erum*, sea open to all nations. [L]

māre[2], n. Female of equine animal, esp. horse; GREY[1] ~; SHANKS'*s* ~; ~'*s-nest*, illusory discovery; ~'*s-tail*, kinds of aquatic plant, long straight streaks of cirrus. [OE *mere*, MDu., MLG *mer(r)ie*, OHG *mar(i)ha*, ON *merr* f. Gmc **marhjōn*, f. **marhaz* horse; see MARSHAL]

Maréchal Niel (*usu. pr.* mårsh'al nēl), n. Kind of climbing rose. [after Adolphe *Niel*, Marshal of France (d. 1869)]

marēmm'a, n. Low marshy unhealthy country by seashore. [It.]

mārg'arine (-g-, -j-; *also* -ēn), n. Substance made from edible oils and meat fats with water or skimmed milk, used as a spread on bread etc. and as a cooking fat. [F, misapplication of a chem. term, f. Gk *margaron* pearl, see -IN]

mārg'ay, n. S.-Amer. tiger-cat. [F, f. native *mbaracaia*]

mārge[1], n. (poet.). Margin. [F, as MARGIN]

mārge[2], n. (colloq.). Margarine. [abbr.]

mār'gin, n., & v.t. 1. Edge, border, of surface, whence ~ATE[2](2), ~ātèd, aa.; condition near the limit below or beyond which a thing ceases to be possible etc.; extra amount (of time, money, etc.) over & above the necessary; (commerc.) sum deposited with stockbroker to cover risk of loss on transaction of account; space round main body of matter on page. 2. v.t. Furnish with ~ or marginal notes; deposit ~ on (stock). [ME, f. L *margo -ginis*]

mār'ginal, a. Of, written in, the margin; having ~ notes; of, at, the edge; (of land) difficult & expensive to cultivate; close to the limit. Hence ~LY[2] adv. [-AL]

margināl'ia, n. pl. Marginal notes. [mod. L neut. pl., as MARGIN, see -AL]

mārg'rāve, n. (hist.). German title of some princes of Holy Roman Empire, orig. of military governor of border province. [f. MDu. *markgrave* border count (MARK[1] + *grave* count)]

mārg'ravine, n. Margrave's wife. [f. Du. *markgravin* (as prec., see -INE[3])]

mārg'uerite (-gerēt), n. Ox-eye daisy. [F, f. L (-*la*) f. Gk *margarītēs* (*margaron* pearl, see -ITE[1])]

mariage de convenance (see Ap.), n. Marriage contracted from prudential motives. [F]

Mār'ian, a. & n. 1. Of the Virgin Mary, Mary Queen of England (orig. of Mary Tudor), or Mary Queen of Scots. 2. n. Adherent of the last. [f. LL *Maria* Mary + -AN]

mā'rĭd, n. Jinn of most powerful class. [Arab., part. of *marada* rebel]

mā'rigōld, n. Kinds of plant with golden or yellow flowers; CORN ~ ; MARSH ~. [ME, f. *Mary* (prob. the Virgin) + *gold*]

marijuana, -huana, (mahrīhwah'nah), n. Dried leaves of Indian hemp, used to make narcotic cigarettes (called *reefers*). [Sp. -*hu*-]

marim'ba, n. Primitive African xylophone; modern orchestral instrument evolved from this. [native name]

mărināde', n., & (*also -te*) v.t. Pickle of wine, vinegar, & spices; fish, meat, thus pickled; (v.t.) pickle with ~. [F, f. Sp. *marinada* (*marinar* pickle in brine, as foll., -ADE)]

marine' (-ēn), a. & n. 1. Of, found in, produced by, the sea; of shipping or naval matters, as ~ *insurance*; || ~ *stores*, old ships' materials & similar odds & ends as merchandise; for use at sea; (of soldiers) serving on board ship. 2. n. Country's shipping, fleet, or navy, esp. *mercantile, merchant*, ~ ; soldier on warship (*blue, red*, ~s, hist., artillery, light infantry); specialist in Commando &

amphibious warfare; *tell that to the* (HORSE[1])~*s*. [ME, f. OF *marin* (fem. *-ine*) f. L *marinus* (*mare* sea, -INE[1])]

ma'riner, n. Sailor, seaman; *master* ~, captain of merchant ship. [ME, f. AF (OF *-ier*), f. Rom. *marinarius (as prec., see -ARY[1])]

Marin'|ism (-ēn-), n. Affected style of It. poet Marini (d. 1625). So ~IST n. [-ISM]

Mariöl'atry̆, n. (derog.). Worship of the Virgin Mary. [f. Gk *Maria* Mary + -LATRY]

mărionĕtte', n. Puppet worked by strings, representing person etc. [f. F *marionnette* (*Marion* dim. of *Marie* Mary, -ETTE)]

ma'rish, n. & a. (poet.). Marsh(y). [ME & OF *mareis* f. WG *marisk MARSH]

Mar'ist, n. Member of Rom. Cath. Society of Mary. [f. F *Mariste* (*Marie* Mary, see -IST)]

ma'rital (*or* marĭt²), a. Of a husband; of marriage. Hence ~LY² adv. [f. L *maritalis* (*maritus* husband, see -AL)]

ma'ritime, a. Living, found, near the sea; connected with the sea, as ~ *insurance*. [f. L *maritimus* (*mare* sea)]

marj'oram, n. Aromatic herb used in cookery. [ME, f. OF *majorane* f. Rom. *majorana, of unkn. orig.]

mark¹, n. 1. Target or other object to be aimed at; *beside, wide of, the* ~, not hitting it, (fig.) not to the point. 2. (boxing). Pit of stomach. 3. Desired object, as *hit, miss, the* ~. 4. Sign indication, (*of* quality, character, etc.), esp. ~ *of mouth*, depression in horse's tooth indicating age. 5. Affixed or impressed sign, seal, etc.; EAR¹, HALL, TRADE, -~. 6. Cross etc. made in place of signature by illiterate person. 7. Written symbol; this as sign of *good* or *bad* conduct. 8. Unit of numerical award of merit in examination, as *he gained 46* ~*s*. 9. Line etc. serving to indicate position; *Plimsoll's* ~, line showing how far ship may legally be submerged when loaded; *below, up to*, etc., *the* ~ (standard). 10. (footb.). Heel-~ on ground made by player who has caught the ball direct from kick or knock on or throw forward by opponent. 11. Stain, scar, etc., esp. BIRTH-~. 12. *Make* one's ~, attain distinction; *of* ~, noteworthy. 13. (As apology for mentioning anything horrible etc.) (*God*) *save the* ~ (freq. sarcastic). 14. (hist.). Tract of land held by Teutonic village community. 15. (athletics). Line indicating the starting-point (*get off the* ~, start). 16. *Easy* ~ (orig. U.S., sl.), person easily gulled. [OE *mearc*, OS *marka*, OHG *marcha*, ON *mǫrk*, Goth. *marka* f. Gmc *markō boundary]

mark², v.t. 1. Make a mark on (thing) by stamping, cutting, writing, etc.; put identifying mark or name on (linen); attach figures indicating prices to (goods); (pass.) have natural marks, as ~*ed with silver spots*. 2. ~ *out*, trace out boundaries

for (ground), plan (course), destine, as ~*ed out for slaughter*; ~ *off*, separate (thing *from* another, lit. & fig.) by boundary. 3. Name or indicate (place on map, length of syllable) by signs or marks. 4. Record (points gained in games). 5. Manifest (one's displeasure etc. *by*); (pass.) *a* ~*ed difference*, whence ~'ĕdLY² adv., ~'ĕdNESS n. 6. Accompany, be a feature of, as *no triumph* ~*s her manner*. 7. ~ *time*, move feet as in marching, but without advancing (often fig.). 8. See, notice; observe mentally, as ~ *my words*; *a* ~*ed man*, one whose conduct is watched with suspicion or hostility, (also) one expected to reach eminence. 9. (Also ~ *down*) note & remember spot to which (grouse etc.) has retired. 10. ‖ (footb.). Keep close to (opponent) so as to hamper him if he receives ball. 11. ~ *down*, (also) ~ at a lower price; ~ *up*, ~ at a higher price; ~*²up* n., amount added by shopkeepers to cost price of goods to cover overhead charges & profit. [OE *mearcian*, OS *markōn*, OHG *marchōn*, ON *marka* f. Gmc *markōjan (as prec.)]

mark³, n. Denomination of weight for gold & silver, usu. 8 oz (now only for continental weights); German coin (formerly about 1/-); (hist.) English money of account. [late OE *marc*, MDu. *marc*, MHG *mark*, ON *mǫrk*, obsc. rel. to med. L *marca, marcus*]

mark'er, n. In vbl senses, esp.: one who marks down game; one who records score, esp. in billiards; flare etc. to assist bombers in air-raid; = BOOK¹-~. [MARK² + -ER¹]

mark'ĕt¹, n. Gathering of people for purchase & sale of provisions, livestock, etc.; time of this; *bring* one's *eggs or hogs to a bad* ~, fail in one's schemes; open space or covered building in which cattle etc. are exposed for sale; *make a* ~ *of*, (fig.) barter away; demand (*for* commodity); *the corn* ~, the trade in corn; *come into the* ~, be offered for sale; *put on the* ~, offer for sale; BLACK¹ ~; (*European*) *Common M*~, economic and political association of certain (European) countries as a unit with internal free trade and common external tariffs; MONEY-~; STOCK-~; rate of purchase & sale, ~ *value*, as *the* ~ *fell*; seat of trade; ~ *cross* (erected in ~-place); ~-*day* (on which ~ is held); ‖ ~ *garden* (in which vegetables are grown for ~); ~-*place*, square, open space, where ~ is held; ‖ ~-*town* (where ~ is held); ~ *value*, saleable value (dist. from cost & from BOOK¹ *value*). [late OE *market* = OS *-at*, OHG *-āt*, f. pop. L *marcatus* f. L *mercatus*; see MERCHANT]

mark'ĕt², v.i. & t. Buy or sell in market; sell (goods) in market or elsewhere; whence ~ABLE a., ~abLY² adv. [f. prec.]

mar'khor (-kōr), n. Large spiral-horned

wild goat of N. India. [Pers., = snake-
-eater]

mȧrk'ing, n. In vbl senses, esp. colouring
of feathers, skin. etc.; ~-*ink* (indelible,
for marking linen). [MARK²+-ING¹]

mȧrks'man, n. (pl. *-men*). One skilled or
practised in aiming at mark, esp. one who
attains certain standard of proficiency
in rifle practice. Hence ~SHIP (1, 3) n.
[MARK¹+-ES+MAN]

Mȧrk Tăp'ley, n. Invincibly cheery person. [character in Dickens's *Martin
Chuzzlewit*]

mȧrl, n., & v.t. **1.** Soil consisting of clay
and carbonate of lime, a valuable fertilizer. **2.** v.t. Apply~ to (ground). Hence
~'Y² a. [ME, f. OF *marle* f. med. L
margila f. L *marga*]

Marl'borough House (mawl'bro), n.
Royal Palace used as a London residence.

mȧrl'ine (naut.). Small line of two
strands; ~-*spike, marlinspike*, pointed
hard-wood or iron tool for separating
strands of rope in splicing. [(a) 15th c., f.
Du. *marlijn, -ing* (*marren, marlen* bind,
+LINE², -ING¹); (b) *marlin-spike* f. *marling-*
f. (15th c.) *marl* f. LG, Du. *marlen*, frequent. of *marren*; so LG *marl-spieker*]

mȧrl'ite, n. Kind of marl that resists
action of air. [-ITE¹]

mȧrm'alãde, n. Preserve of oranges or
specified fruit. [f. F *marmelade* f. Port.
-lada f. *marmelo* quince f. L f. Gk *meli-
mēlon* (*meli* honey +*mēlon* apple) see -ADE]

mȧrm'ite, n. Extract made from fresh
brewer's yeast. [**P**; F, = cooking-pot]

mȧrm'olite, n. Laminated serpentine of
pale green colour. [irreg. f. Gk *marmairō*
shine, see -LITE]

mȧrmȯr'eal, a. (poet.). Of, like, marble.
[f. L *marmoreus* (as MARBLE) +-AL]

mȧrm'osĕt (-z-), n. Small tropical
American monkey with bushy tail. [f.
OF *marmouset* grotesque image]

mȧrm'ot, n. Rodent of squirrel family.
[f. F *marmotte* prob. f. Roumansch *mur-
mont* f. L *murem* (nom. *mus*) *montis* mountain mouse]

mȧ'rocain, n. A dress-fabric made in silk
(or other materials). [F, = Moroccan]

Mȧ'ronïte, n. One of a sect of Syrian
Christians dwelling in Lebanon. [f. med.
L *Maronita* (*Maron* founder, see -ITE¹)]

maroon'¹, n. & a. **1.** (Of) brownish-
-crimson colour. **2.** Firework exploding
with loud report. [f. F *marron* chestnut f.
It. *marrone*]

maroon'², n. One of class of Negroes,
orig. fugitive slaves, in mountains &
forests of Dutch Guiana & W. Indies;
marooned person. [f. F *marron*, f. Sp.
cimarron wild]

maroon'³, v.t. & i. Put (person) ashore &
leave him on desolate island or coast as
punishment; idle, hang about. [f. prec.]

mȧrque (-k), n. (hist.). *Letter(s) of ~ (&
reprisal)*, licence to fit out armed vessel &
employ it in capture of enemy's merchant

shipping; (sing.) ship carrying such
licence. [f. AF, OF *marque* f. Prov. *marca*
f. *marcar* seize as a pledge]

mȧrquee' (-kē), n. Large tent. [f. MAR-
QUISE taken as pl. n.]

mȧr'quetry̆, -terie, (-kĭ-), n. Inlaid work.
[F (*-erie*), f. *marqueter* variegate (MARK¹)]

mȧr'quis, -quĕss, n. Noble ranking between duke & earl or (in foreign countries)
count. Hence **mȧr'quis**ATE¹(1) n. [ME,
f. OF *marchis* f. Rom. *marchensis*
(MARCH², -ESE)]

mȧrquise' (-kēz), n. **1.** (Of foreign nobility) marchioness. **2.** Finger-ring set with
oval pointed cluster of gems. **3.** (arch.).
Tent. [F, fem. of *marquis*]

mȧr'quois (-kwoiz), n. ~ *scale*, apparatus for drawing equidistant parallel lines.
[app. blunder for F *marquoir* marker
(MARK¹)]

mȧ'rram, n. A shore grass that binds
sand. [f. ON *maráilmr* (*marr* sea, HAULM)]

mȧ'rriäge (-rĭj), n. Relation between
married persons, wedlock; *give, take, in
~* (as husband or wife); *communal ~*,
system by which all the men in small
community are married to all the women;
companionate ~, see COMPANION¹; *act,
ceremony, of marrying; civil~* (performed
by civil official without religious ceremony); (fig.) intimate union (*the ~ of true
minds*); (cards) union of king & queen of
same suit; ~ *articles*, antenuptial agreement respecting rights of property &
succession; ~-*bed*, (fig.) marital inter-
course; ~ LICENCE¹; ||~ *lines*, certificate
of marriage; ~ *market*, supply & demand
of eligible partners for ~; ~ *settlement,
arrangement securing property to wife
& sometimes to children. [ME, f. OF
mariage f. *marier* MARRY¹; see -AGE]

mȧ'rriägeable (-rĭja-), a. Of an age to
marry; (of age) fit for marriage. [-ABLE]

mȧ'rried (-ĭd), a. United in wedlock; of
person(s) so united, as ~ *life*. [p.p. of
MARRY¹]

marron glacé (see Ap.), n. Chestnut iced
with sugar as sweetmeat. [F]

mȧ'rrow¹ (-ō), n. Soft fatty substance in
cavities of bones, often a type of rich
food or of vitality (*chilled to the ~*, right
through); *spinal ~*, substance forming
spinal cord; essential part, as *pith & ~*;
vegetable~, kind of pumpkin; ~*bone*, bone
containing edible ~, (pl., joc.) knees;
~(*fat*), kind of large pea; ~-*spoon* (for
getting ~ from bones). Hence ~LESS
(-ōl-), ~Y² (-ōi), aa. [OE *mearg*, OS, OHG
marg, ON *mergr* f. Gmc **mazg-*]

|| **mȧ'rrow²** (-ō), n. (dial.). Mate, consort,
match, very image *of*. [15th c., prob. f.
ON *margr* friendly, communicative]

mȧ'rry̆, v.t. & i. (Of priest etc.) join
(persons, one *to* another) in wedlock; (of
parent or guardian) give (son, daughter,
etc.) in marriage (also ~ *off*, implying
activity on parents' part); (of either contracting party) take in marriage; (fig.)

marry unite intimately; (naut.) splice (rope-ends) together without increasing girth; (intr.) take husband or wife. [ME, f. OF *marier* f. L *maritare* f. *maritus* husband]

mǎ'rry², int. (arch.) expr. surprise, asseveration, indignation, etc.; ~ *come up* (expr. indignant or contemptuous surprise). [ME, = (the Virgin) *Mary*]

Mǎrs (-z), Roman god of war; warfare; planet fourth in order of distance from sun. [L]

Marsa'la (-sah-), n. White wine like light sherry, from ~ in Sicily.

Mǎrseillaise' (-selāz, & see Ap.), n. National song of French Republic, first sung by Marseilles patriots. [F, fem. adj. f. *Marseille*, -ESE]

Mǎrseilles' (-sālz), n. Seaport in S. France; stiff cotton fabric like piqué. [E name for *Marseille*]

mǎrsh, n. Low land flooded in winter & usu. watery at all times; ~ *gas*, light carburetted hydrogen; ~ *mallow*, (confection made from root of) shrubby herb growing near salt~es; ~ *marigold*, golden-flowered ranunculaceous plant growing in moist meadows. Hence ~'INESS n., ~'Y² a. [OE *mersc*, *merisc*, MLG, MDu. *mersch*, f. WG **marisk* (MARISH), f. Gmc **mari-* sea, MERE¹]

mǎrsh'al¹, n. || EARL ~; officer of highest rank in some foreign armies; PROVOST ~; FIELD ~, ~ *of the Royal* AIR¹ *Force*, AIR¹~; (hist.) *knight* ~, officer of royal household with judicial functions; || (*judge's*) ~, official accompanying judge on circuit, with secretarial duties; officer arranging ceremonies etc. Hence ~SHIP n. [ME, f. OF *mareschal*, *-cal* f. LL *mariscalcus* (Lex Salica) f. OFrank. *marhskalk* f. *marh* horse (cf. MARE) + *skalk* servant]

mǎrsh'al², v.t. & i. (-ll-). Arrange in due order (persons at feast etc., soldiers, facts, etc.); (her.) combine (coat of arms); conduct (person) ceremoniously (*into* etc.); ~*ling yard*, railway yard in which goods trains etc. are assembled. [f. prec.]

mǎrsh'alsea, n. (hist.). Court held, prison in Southwark controlled, by knight marshal. [alt. f. *marshalcy* (MARSHAL¹ + -CY)]

mǎrsūp'ial, a. & n. (anat., zool.). 1. Of, like, a pouch, as ~ *muscle*. 2. (Animal) of the class of mammals characterized by having a pouch in which to carry their young, born imperfect. [f. L f. Gk *marsupion* pouch dim. of *marsipos* purse + -AL]

mǎrt, n. Market-place; auction room; trade centre. [ME, f. Du. (obs.) *mart*, *markt*, f. L as MARKET]

mǎrtěll'ō, n. (hist.; pl. ~s). ~ (*tower*), small circular fort, usu. on coast to prevent hostile landing. [alt. f. Cape *Mortella* in Corsica]

mǎrt'en, n. Animal like weasel, with valuable fur. [ME, f. Du. *martren* f. OF (*peau* skin) *martrine*, adj. f. *martre* (whence obs. E *marter*) + -*ine* —INE¹]

mǎr'tial (-shl), a. Of, suitable for, appropriate to, warfare, whence ~IZE (-sha-) v.t.; ~ *law*, military government, by which ordinary law is suspended; brave; fond of fighting; (*M*~) of the planet Mars. Hence ~LY² adv. [ME, f. OF, or L *martialis* of MARS, see -AL]

Mǎr'tian (-shn), a. & n. (Inhabitant) of Mars. [f. L *Martius* of MARS + -AN]

mǎrt'in, n. 1. *St M*~, bishop of Tours in 4th c.; *M*~*mas*, *St M*~*'s day*, Nov. 11; || *St M*~*'s summer*, fine season about this time. 2. Birds of swallow family esp. *house-*~, which builds mud nest on house walls etc.; SAND-~. [F, f. L *Martinus*]

mǎrtinět', n. Strict (esp. military or naval) disciplinarian. Hence ~t'ISM n., ~t'ISH¹ a. [*M*~, French drill-master in reign of Louis XIV]

mǎrt'ingāle (-ngg-), n. 1. Strap, set of straps, fastened at one end to nose-band, at other end to girth, of horse to prevent rearing etc.; (naut.) rope for guying down jibboom. 2. Gambling system of doubling stakes in hope of eventual turn of luck. [F, of unkn. orig.]

mǎrti'ni¹ (-ēnī), n. The *M*~-Henry rifle. [*M*~, inventor of its breech action]

mǎrti'ni² (-ēnī), n. Cocktail made of gin, vermouth, orange bitters, etc. [*M*~, inventor]

mǎrt'lět, n. Swift; (her.) footless bird. [f. F *martelet* alt. f. *martinet* dim. f. MARTIN]

mǎrtyr (-er), n., & v.t. 1. One who undergoes penalty of death for persistence in Christian faith or obedience to law of Church, or undergoes death or suffering for any great cause; ~ *to* (constant sufferer from) *gout* etc.; *make a* ~ *of* oneself, (pretend to) sacrifice one's inclinations, for sake of credit thus gained. 2. v.t. Put to death as ~, torment. [OE, f. LL f. late Gk *martur* = Gk *martus -uros* witness]

mǎrt'yrdom (-ter-), n. Sufferings & death of martyr; torment. [-DOM]

mǎrt'yrize, -ise (-īz), v.t. Make a martyr of (one*self*, person). [ME, f. OF, or LL *martyrizare* (MARTYR, -IZE)]

mǎrtyr|o-, comb. form of Gk *martur -uros*, as: ~*ol'atry*, worship of martyrs; ~*ol'ogy*, list, register, history, of martyrs, whence ~*olō'gical*.

mǎrt'yrȳ, n. Shrine, church, erected in honour of martyr. [ME, f. OF *-ie* or LL f. Gk *marturion* (as MARTYR)]

mǎrv'el¹, n. Wonderful thing; wonderful example of (quality); (arch.) astonishment; ~ *of Peru*, showy garden plant with flowers opening in afternoon. [ME, f. OF *merveille* f. LL *mirabilia* neut. pl. of L *mirabilis* (*mirari* wonder at, see -BLE)]

mǎrv'el², v.i. (-ll-). Be surprised (*at*, *that*); wonder (*how*, *why*, etc.). [ME, f. OF *merveillier* (as prec.)]

mǎrv'ellous, a. Astonishing; extravagantly improbable, esp. *the* ~. Hence

~LY² adv.,~NESS n. [ME, f. OF *merveillos* (as prec., -OUS)]

Mārx′|ian, a. & n. (Adherent) of the doctrines of the German socialist Karl Marx (1818–83). So ~ISM(3) n., ~IST(2) n. & à. [-IAN] -

marzipan. See MARCHPANE.

mascār′a, n. Preparation for darkening eyelashes etc.[It. *mascara,maschera* MASK¹]

mäs′cot, n. Person, thing, that brings luck. [f. F *mascotte*, f. Prov. *mascotto* dim. of *masco* witch]

ma′sculine (mah-, mä-), a. & n. **1.** Of the gender to which names of males normally belong; ~ *rhyme* (in French verse, between words ending in stressed syllables, not *e* mute), ~ *ending*, ending of line with stressed syllable; of the male sex; manly, vigorous; (of woman) having qualities appropriate to man. **2.** n. ~ gender, word. Hence ~NESS, **masculin′ITY**, nn., (mah-, mä-). [ME, f. OF *masculin* (fem. *-ine)* f. L *masculinus* (as MALE, see -INE¹)]

mäsh¹, n.. Malt mixed with hot water to form wort; (also *bran* ~) mixture of boiled grain, bran, etc., given warm to horses etc.; soft pulp made by crushing, mixing with water, etc.; (sl.) mashed potatoes (*sausage & ~*); confused mixture; ~*-tub* (in which malt is mashed). [OE *māsc, māx-*, = MLG *mēsch*, MHG *meisch* f. WG **maisk-*, perh. cogn. w. MIX]

mäsh², v.t. Mix (malt) with hot water; crush, pound, to pulp; reduce (potatoes etc.) to uniform mass by crushing. [ME, f. prec.]

mäsh³, v.t., & n. (obsolesc. sl.). **1.** Excite sentimental admiration in (one of opposite sex); *be* ~*ed on*, have such admiration for. **2.** n. Person on whom one of opposite sex is ~ed. [orig. unkn.]

mäsh′er, n. (obsolesc. sl.). Fop posing as lady-killer. [prec.]

mäsh′ie, -ȳ, n. Iron golf club used for lofting or for medium distances; ~ *niblick*, club intermediate between ~ & niblick. [orig. unkn.]

ma′sjid (mŭ-), n. Mosque. [Arab.]

mask¹ (mah-), n. Covering, usu. of velvet or silk, for concealing face at balls etc., or of wire, gauze, etc., for protection; hollow figure of human head worn by ancient Greek & Roman actors; clay or wax likeness of person's face, esp. (also *death*~) one made by taking mould from face; (fig.) disguise, as *throw off the* ~; masked person; face, head, of fox. [f. F *masque*, f. It. *maschera* f. Arab. *maskhara*⁴]

mask² (mah-), v.t. Cover (face) with mask; (pass.) be disguised with mask; (mil.) conceal (battery etc.) from enemy's view, hinder (army etc.) from action by watching with adequate force, hinder (friendly force) by standing in line of its fire; disguise (feelings etc.); ~*ed ball* (at which masks are worn). [f. prec.]

ma′sker, -quer, (mah-), n. One who

takes part in masquerade or masque. [prec. +-ER¹]

mäskinön′ge (-j, -jĭ), n. Large pike in great lakes of N. America. [Odjibwa]

masochism (măz′okĭzm), n. Form of (esp. sexual) perversion in which a sufferer derives pleasure from pain or humiliation (opp. SADISM). [f. L. von Sacher-*Masoch* (d. 1895), Austrian novelist who described a case of ~]

mäs′on, n., & v.t. **1.** Worker in stone; (~'s *mark*, device carved on stone by ~); freemason, whence **masön′IC** a. **2.** v.t. Build, strengthen, with masonry. [ME, f. OF *masson*, mod. *maçon*, f. Rom. **mation-*, **macion-*; ult. orig. obsc.]

mäs′onrȳ, n. Mason's work, stonework. [ME, f. OF *maçonnerie* (as MASON, see -ERY)]

Mäs(s)ōr′a(h) (-ra), n. Body of traditional information on text of Hebrew Bible. [f. Heb. *masoreth* perh. = bond]

Mäs(s)′orēte, -īte, n. Jewish scholar contributing to the Masora. Hence **mäs(s)orēt′IC** a. [(-ete) corrupt. of Heb. as prec.; (-ite) prec. +-ITE¹]

masque (mahsk), n. Amateur histrionic & musical entertainment, orig. in dumb show, later with metrical dialogue; dramatic composition for this. [as MASK¹]

masquerāde′¹ (mahske-), n. Masked ball; false show, pretence. [f. Sp. *mascarada* (*máscara* mask, see -ADE)]

masquerāde′² (mahske-), v.i. Appear in disguise; assume false appearance. [f. prec.]

mäss¹ (*or* mahs), n. (A) celebration (usu. Rom. or Anglo-Cath.) of the Eucharist, as ~ *was said, we attend, go to, hear,* ~, ~*es were said for his soul*; liturgy used in this; musical setting of parts of this; *high* ~ (with incense, music, & assistance of deacon & subdeacon); *low* ~ (with no music & minimum of ceremony). [OE *mæsse* f. Rom. **messa* f. eccl. L *missa*, app. f. *mittere miss-* dismiss]

mäss², n., & v.t. & i. **1.** Coherent body of matter of indefinite shape; dense aggregation of objects, as a ~ *of fibres*; large number (*of*); *he is a* ~ *of* (covered with) *bruises*; unbroken expanse (*of* light etc.); *the* (*great*)~, the majority (*of*); *the* ~*es*, the lower orders, cf. CLASSes; *in the* ~, in the aggregate; (phys.) quantity of matter a body contains; ~ ENERGY; ~ *meeting*, large (usu. political) assembly of people; ~ *observation*, study & reporting of social customs etc. of ordinary people; ~ *of manœuvre*, body of troops kept free for strategic needs; ~ *production* (of large quantities of a standardized article by standardized mechanical processes); ~ *spectrograph*, apparatus separating isotopes by atomic discharge through electric & magnetic fields. **2.** vb. Gather (t. & i.) into ~; (mil.) concentrate (troops). [ME; (vb f. OF *masser*) f. OF *masse* f. L *massa* prob. f. Gk *maza* barley-cake (*massō* knead)]

mass'acre (-ker), n., & v.t. **1.** General slaughter, carnage, (of persons, occas. of animals). **2.** v.t. Make a ~ of, murder cruelly or violently (a number of persons). [F; in OF *maçacre, macecle,* &c. shambles, whence *maceclier* butcher, executioner, ult. orig. unkn.; vb f. F *massacrer*]

massage' (-ahzh; *or* mäs²), n., & v.t. **1.** Rubbing, kneading, etc., of muscles & joints of the body with the hands, to stimulate their action, etc. **2.** v.t. Treat (part, person) thus. [F, f. *masser* treat with massage, perh. f. Port. *amassar* knead, f. *massa* dough (MASS²), see -AGE]

massé (mäs'ā), n. (billiards). Stroke made with cue held perpendicular. [F, p.p. of *masser* make such stroke (as MACE¹)]

masseur', masseuse', (-ḗr, -ḗrz, & see Ap.), nn. Man, woman, who practises massage. So **mäss'ER¹, mäss'OR**, nn. [F (as MASSAGE, see -OR)]

mäss'if (*or* mahsēf'), n. Mountain heights forming a compact group. [F (see MASSIVE) in n. use]

mäss'ive, a. Large & heavy or solid; (of features, head, etc.) largely moulded; (fig.) solid, substantial; impressive, imposing; (psych.; of sensation etc.) having large volume or magnitude. Hence ~LY² adv., ~NESS n. [ME, f. OF (-*if*, -*ive*), as MASS², see -IVE]

mäss'|ÿ, a. Solid; weighty. Hence~ÏNESS n. [MASS² + -Y²]

mast¹ (-ah-), n. **1.** Long pole of timber, iron, etc., set up on ship's keel to support sails; BEFORE *the*~; HALF~; *high*; hence (of ship) -~'ED² a., -~'ER¹ n.; ~-*head*, highest part of ~, esp. of lower ~ as place of observation or punishment, (v.t.) send (sailor) to this, raise (sail) to its position. **2.** Post, or lattice-work upright, for supporting a wireless aerial; (also *mooring*-~) strong steel tower to top of which an airship can be moored. [OE *mæst*, OHG *mast,* ON *mastr* f. Gmc **mastaz*]

mast² (-ah-), n. Fruit of beech, oak, & other forest-trees, esp. as food for swine. [OE *mæst*, MDu., OHG *mast,* WG corresp. to Gmc **mast-*]

mäs'taba, n. (archaeol.). Ancient Egyptian tomb with sloping sides & flat roof. [Arab. *maṣṭaba* bench]

ma'ster¹ (mah-), n. **1.** Person having control; (naut.) captain of merchant vessel; employer; owner of dog, horse, etc.; male head of household, as ~ *of the house; be* ~ *of*, have at one's disposal; *be* one's *own* ~, be independent or free to do as one will; *make* one*self* ~ *of*, acquire thorough knowledge of or facility in using; one who has or gets the upper hand, as *we will see which of us is* ~. **2.** Teacher, tutor, esp. (also *school*~) in school; HOUSE¹~; teacher in philosophy etc. **3.** *The M*~, Christ; *M*~ *of Arts* (abbr. *M.A.*), holder of university degree

orig. giving authority to teach in university. **4.** Skilled workman, or one in business on his own account, as ~ *carpenter*. **5.** Great artist, esp. *old* ~ (esp. of painters of 13th-17th cc.), picture etc. by a ~. **6.** Head of some colleges. **7.** ‖ (As title of legal functionaries) *M*~ *in Chancery* etc.; *M*~ *of Ceremonies* (see CEREMONY), MISRULE, *the* ROLLS; *M*~ (organizer, leader, esp. in Royal Household & Inns of Court) *of the revels; M*~ *of the Horse*, official in English royal household; *M*~ (one who has control) *of foxhounds* (abbr. *M.F.H.*), *beagles*, etc. **8.** (Prefixed, esp. by servants & in address of letter, to name of young gentleman) *M*~ *Tom, M*~ *Jones*. **9.** attrib. Commanding, superior, (*a* ~ *mind*). **10.** ~-*at-arms*, police officer on man-of-war; ~-*key* (opening many locks, each also opened by separate key); ~ *mason*, (as above, also) freemason who has passed third degree; ~-*piece*, consummate piece of workmanship; ~-*stroke*, surpassingly skilful act (of policy etc.). Hence ~DOM, ~HOOD, nn., ~LESS a. [OE *mægcester* (later also f. OF *maistre*) f. L *magister* cogn. w. *magis* more]

ma'ster² (mah-), v.t. Overcome, defeat; reduce to subjection; acquire complete knowledge of (subject) or facility in using (instrument etc.); rule as a master. [ME, f. prec.]

ma'sterful (mah-), a. Self-willed, imperious. Hence ~LY² adv., ~NESS n. [-FUL]

ma'sterl|ÿ (mah-), a. Worthy of a master, very skilful. Hence~ÏNESS n. [-LY¹]

ma'stership (mah-), n. Dominion, control; office, function, of master, esp. in school. [-SHIP]

ma'sterÿ (mah-), n. Sway, dominion; *the* upper hand; masterly skill; masterly use or knowledge (*of* instrument, subject). [ME, f. OF *maistrie* (as MASTER¹, see -Y¹)]

mäs'tic, n. Gum or resin exuding from bark of certain trees, used in making varnish; trees yielding this; kinds of cement; liquor flavoured with ~, used in Turkey & Greece; ~ colour, pale yellow. Hence **mästi'cIC** a. (chem.). [ME, f. OF, f. LL *mastichum* f. L f. Gk *mastikhē*]

mäs'tic|āte, v.t. Grind (food) with teeth, chew. Hence or cogn. ~ABIL'ITY, ~A'TION, ~ātor, nn., ~ātorY a. [f. LL *masticare*, -ATE³]

ma'stiff (mah-), n. Large strong dog with drooping ears & pendulous lips. [ME; obsc. f. OF *mastin* f. Rom. **mansuetinus* f. *mansuetus* tame, see -INE¹]

mästit'is, n. Inflammation of female breast. [f. Gk *mastos* breast, see -ITIS]

mäs'todōn, n. Large extinct mammal like elephant, with nipple-shaped tubercles on crowns of molar teeth. Hence **mästodōn'tIC** a. [f. Gk *mastos* breast + *odous odontos* tooth]

mäs'toid, a. & n. (anat.). **1.** Shaped like

female breast; ~ *operation*, surgical procedure for relief of disease of tympanum or ear-drum; ~ *process*, conical prominence in the temporal bone to which muscles are attached. **2.** n. ~ process; (colloq.) abscess on ~ process. [f. Gk *mastos* breast, see -OID]

mãs'turb|āte (-*ter*-), v.i. Produce an orgasm by exciting one's own genitals. Hence ~A'TION n. [f. L *masturbari*, see -ATE³]

mãt¹, n. Coarse fabric of plaited rushes, straw, etc., for lying upon, packing furniture, etc.; piece of this for wiping shoes upon, esp. *door-*~ ; *on the* ~ (army sl.), in trouble (i.e. on the orderly room ~ before the C.O.). [OE *matt(e)*, OHG *matta* f. LL *matta*]

mãt², v.t. & i. (-tt-). Cover, furnish with mats; entangle (often *together*) in thick mass (esp. in p.p., as ~*ted hair*); become ~ted. [f. prec.]

mãt³, **mãtt**, a., n., & v.t. (-tt-). **1.** (Of colours, surfaces, etc.) dull, without lustre. **2.** n. Border of dead gold round framed picture; appearance of unburnished gold; roughened or frosted groundwork. **3.** v.t. Make (gilding etc.) dull; frost (glass). [(vb f. F *mater*) F, identical w. *mat* MATE¹; see CHECKMATE]

mãt'adŏr, n. Man appointed to kill bull in bull-fight; principal card in some games. [Sp., f. *matar* kill f. Arab. *mat* (prec.)+ -OR]

mãtch¹, n. **1.** Person able to contend with another as an equal, as *find, meet*, one's ~, *be* (*more than*) *a* ~ *for*; person equal to another in some quality, as *we shall never see his* ~ ; person, thing, exactly like or corresponding to another. **2.** Contest of skill etc. in which persons are matched against each other, as *cricket-*~. **3.** Matrimonial alliance; *make a* ~, bring this about; person viewed in regard to his or her eligibility for marriage, esp. as to rank or fortune, as *he is an excellent* ~. **4.** ~*-board*, one with tongue cut along one edge & groove along another, so as to fit into similar boards; ~*'maker*, one fond of scheming to bring about marriages; ~ *play* (golf), in which the score is reckoned by counting the holes won by each side; ~ *point*(s), state of a game when one side needs only one more point to win the ~ (occas. ~ *ball*). [OE *gemæcca* mate, companion, f. Gmc **mako-* fit, suitable; see MAKE¹; later senses infl. by foll.]

mãtch², v.t. & i. Join (person *with* another) in marriage; prove a match for; place (person etc.) in conflict *against* another; *well* ~*ed*, fit to contend with each other, live together, etc., on equal terms; place (person, thing) in competition *with*; be equal, correspond in quantity, quality, colour, etc., to (thing etc.; also intr. *with*) as *the carpets* ~ *the wall-paper, these ribbons do not* ~, *do not* ~ *with your hat, trimmed with velvet to* ~ ;

find material etc. that ~es with (another), as *can you* ~ *me this silk?* [ME, f. prec.]

mãtch³, n. Short piece of wood, wax taper, etc., tipped with composition that bursts into flame when rubbed on rough or (*safety* ~) specially prepared surface; piece of wick, cord, etc., designed to burn at uniform rate, for firing cannon etc.; ~*-box* (for holding ~es); ~*'lock*, (gun with) lock in which ~ is placed for igniting powder; ~*'wood*, wood suitable for ~es, minute splinters, (*make* ~*wood of*, utterly smash). [ME, f. OF *mesche*, of obsc. orig.]

mãtch'ét (*or* -ĕt'), n. Broad heavy knife used in America etc. as tool & weapon. [f. Sp. *machete*]

mãtch'lèss, a. Without an equal, peerless. Hence ~LY² adv. [MATCH¹+-LESS]

mãte¹, n., & v.t. (chess). = CHECKMATE; *fool's* ~ (in which first player is ~d at opponent's second move); STALE¹~. [see CHECKMATE]

mãte², n. **1.** (In working-classes) companion, fellow worker, (also as general form of address). **2.** One of a pair, esp. of birds; fitting partner in marriage. **3.** (naut.). Officer on merchant ship who sees to execution of master's commands & takes command in his absence, (also) assistant to some functionary, as *cook's, gunner's, surgeon's,* ~. Hence ~'LESS (-tl-) a., *mãt'*(*e*)Y² a., sociable, familiar (*with*). [ME, f. MLG *mate* f. *gemate* (cf. OHG *gimazzo*) f. WG **gimato* messmate (*ga-* Y- +*mat* MEAT)]

mãte³, v.t. & i. Join (two persons, one *with* another) in marriage; marry (*with*, or abs.); pair (birds), (of birds) pair; keep company (*with*). [f. prec.]

mã'té (-ā), n. (Vessel for) infusion of leaves of a shrub, Paraguay tea; the shrub. [f. Sp. *mate* f. native *mati*]

matelot, ‖ **mãt'lō(w)**, (mãt'lō), n. (naut. sl.). Sailor. [F (-*elot*)]

mãt'elote (-ot), n. Dish of fish etc. with sauce of wine, onions, etc. [F, f. *matelot* sailor]

mãt'er, n. ‖ Mother (sl.); DURA MATER, PIA MATER; ~*famil'ias*, mother of household. [L]

matēr'ial, a. & n. **1.** Concerned with the matter, not the form, of reasoning; of matter, corporeal; ~ *theory* of heat (that it is a ~ substance); (of conduct, point of view, etc.) unspiritual; concerned with bodily comfort etc., as ~ *well-being*; important, essential, (*to*, or abs.; *at the* ~ *dates*). **2.** n. Matter from which thing is made, as *raw* (unmanufactured) ~; elements, constituent parts, (*of* substance, *for* historical composition etc.); stuff, fabric; *writing-*~*s* (requisites). Hence ~ITY (-ăl⁻) n., ~LY² adv. [ME, f. OF *materiel, -al,* f. LL *materialis* (as MATTER, see-AL)]

matēr'ial|ism, n. Opinion that nothing exists but matter & its movements & modifications, also, that consciousness &

will are wholly due to material agency; (Art) tendency to lay stress on material aspect of objects. So ~IST n., ~ĬS'TIC a., ~ĬS'TICALLY adv. [-ISM]

matēr'ializ|e, -is|e (-ĭz), v.t. & i. Make, represent as, material; cause (spirit) to appear, (of spirit) appear, in bodily form; become actual fact; make materialistic. Hence ~A'TION n. [-IZE]

matēr'ĭa mĕd'ĭca, n. Remedial substances used in practice of medicine. [med. L]

matériel (matārĭĕl'), n. Stock-in-trade, available means (opp. *personnel*). [F, as MATERIAL]

matĕrn'al, a. Of mothers; motherly; related on the mother's side, as ~ *uncle*, mother's brother; (joc.) one's mother's. Hence ~LY² adv. [ME, f. OF *maternel* or L *maternus* (*mater* mother), see -AL]

matĕrn'itỹ, n. Motherhood; motherliness; ~ *hospital*, *nurse*, *ward*, (for women during confinement); ~ *robe*, *skirt*, (suitable for wear by pregnant woman). [f. F *maternité* or med. L *maternitas* (prec., -TY)]

măthĕmăt'ical, a. Of mathematics; (of proofs etc.) rigorously precise. Hence ~LY² adv. [f. F *-ique* or L f. Gk *mathēmatikos* (*mathēma* science f. *manthanō*, root *math-*, learn, see -IC)]

măthĕmăt'ics, n. pl. (usu. treated as sing.). (Also *pure* ~) abstract science of space & quantity; (also *mixed*, *applied*, ~) this applied to branches of physical research, e.g. astronomy. So **măthĕmati'CIAN** (-ĭshn) n. [as prec., see -ICS]

mati'cō (-tē-), n. Peruvian shrub; its leaves used as styptic. [Sp., dim of *Mateo* Matthew]

măt'in, n. (Pl.) one of canonical hours of breviary, prop. a midnight office, but also recited at daybreak; (pl.) morning prayer in Church of England (often *mattins*); (poet., sing. or pl.) morning song of birds. [ME, f. OF *matines* f. eccl. L *matutinas*, acc. fem. pl. adj. as n. f. L *matutinus* of the morning, see -INE¹]

matinée (măt'ĭnā), n. Afternoon theatrical or musical performance (*the* ~ *hat*, lady's hat obstructing, also hat designed not to obstruct, view of stage). [F, = what occupies a morning (*matin* morning)]

măt'lō, -low (-lō). See MATELOT.

măt'răss, n. Long-necked glass vessel with round or oval body, used for distilling etc. [f. F *matras*, of unkn. orig.]

măt'rĭärch (-k), n. Woman corresponding in status to patriarch (usu. joc.). [f. L *mater* mother on false anal. of *patriarch*]

măt'rĭärchỹ (-k-), n. Social organization in which mother is head of family. So **mătrĭärch'AL** (-k-) a. [prec. + -Y¹]

măt'rĭcĭd|e, n. One who kills his, killing of one's, own mother. So ~AL a. [f. L *matricida* (MATER, see -CIDE)]

matric'ŭl|āte, v.t. & i. Admit (student) to privileges of university; (intr.) be thus

admitted. Hence ~A'TION n., ~ātORY a. [f. med. L *matriculare* f. LL *matricula* register, dim. of MATRIX, +-ATE³]

măt'rimonỹ, n. 1. Rite of marriage; state of being married. 2. A card game; combination of king & queen of trumps in some card games. So **mătrimōn'iAL** a., **mătrimōn'iALLY²** adv. [ME, f. OF *matremoine* f. L *matrimonium* (*mater* -tris mother, see -MONY)]

măt'rix, n. (pl. *-ices* pr. -ĭsēz, *-ixes*). Womb; place in which thing is developed; formative part of animal organ; mass of rock etc. enclosing gems etc.; (biol.) substance between cells; mould in which type etc. is cast or shaped. [L, f. *mater* mother]

măt'ron, n. Married woman; woman managing domestic affairs of hospital, school, etc. Hence ~AGE(1, 2), ~HOOD, ~SHIP, nn., ~AL, ~LY¹, aa. [ME, f. OF *matrone* f. L *matrona* (*mater* mother)]

mătt. Var. of MAT³ (esp. photogr.).

mătt'amōre, n. Subterranean dwelling or storehouse. [f. F *matamore* f. Arab *maṭmūrah* (*ṭamara* store up)]

mătt'er¹, n. 1. Substance(s) of which a physical thing is made. 2. Purulent discharge, whence ~Y² a., purulent, festering. 3. Physical substance in general, as opp. to spirit, mind, etc. 4. (log.). Particular content of proposition, distinguished from its form. 5. Material for thought or expression; substance of book, speech, etc. (often opp. to *manner* or *form*). 6. Occasion (*of*, *for*, complaint, regret, etc.). 7. Thing(s), as *printed* ~; *postal* ~, all that may be sent by post; *no* ~, it is of no importance (*when*, *how*, etc., or abs.); *what* ~?, that need not disquiet us. 8. Affair; thing (of a kind specified esp. by vbl n.), as a *hanging* ~, no *laughing* ~, *money* ~s; *that is a* ~ (case, question) *of habit* etc.; *for that* ~, so far as that is concerned; *a* ~ *of* (about) *40 years*; *what is the* ~?, what is amiss (*with*)? (*what is the* ~ *with* —?, sl., surely — will do); *in the* ~ *of*, as regards. 9. ~ *of course* (also as adj., w. hyphens), thing to be expected in natural course; ~ *of fact*, what pertains to the sphere of fact (opp. to *opinion* etc.), esp. *as a* ~ *of fact*, (law) part of judicial inquiry concerned with truth of alleged facts (opp. to ~ *of law*), (adj., with hyphens) unimaginative, prosaic. [ME, f. AF *materie*, *-ere*, OF *-iere* f. L *materia* timber, stuff]

mătt'er², v.i. 1. Be of importance, signify, (*to* person etc. *how*, *when*, etc.,; esp. w. neg.). 2. Secrete or discharge pus. [f. prec.]

mătt'ing, n. In vbl senses (MAT²), esp. fabric of hemp, bast, grass, etc. as covering etc., as *coco-nut* ~. [-ING¹]

mattins. See MATIN.

mătt'ock, n. Tool of PICK¹ shape, with an adze & a chisel edge as ends of head. [OE *mattuc*, of unkn. orig.]

mätt'oid, n. Person of erratic mind, compound of genius & fool. [f. It. *mattoide* (*matto* mad)]

mätt'ress, n. Canvas case stuffed with hair, straw, feathers, etc., as bed or support for bed; (usu. *spring* ~) similar appliance of springs stretched in frame. [ME, f. OF *materas* f. It. *materasso* prob. f. Arab. *almaṭraḥ* place, cushion (*ṭaraḥa* throw)]

mät'ūrāte, v.i. (med.). (Of pustule etc.) come to maturation. [as MATURE², -ATE³]

mätūrā'tion, n. Ripening of morbific matter esp. of cataract; causing of this, whence **matūr'ative** a.; ripening of fruit; maturing, development. [f. F, or L *maturatio* (as MATURE², see -ATION)]

matūre'¹, a. Complete in natural development; with fully developed powers of body & mind; ~ (careful) *deliberation*, ~ *plans* (formed after this); (of bill) due. So ~LY² (-rl-) adv., ~NESS (-rn-), **matūr'ity**, nn. [ME, f. L *maturus* ripe]

matūre'², v.t. & i. Develop fully; ripen; perfect (plan etc.); come to maturity; (of bill) become due. [f. obs. F *maturer* or L *maturare* (as prec.); & f. prec.]

matūtin'al (*or* matūt'inal), a. Of, occurring in, the morning; early. So **mät'ūtine** a. [f. LL *matutinalis* (*matutinus* f. *Matuta* goddess of dawn)]

maud, n. Scots shepherd's grey striped plaid; travelling-rug like this. [orig. unkn.]

maud'lin, a. & n. Mawkishly sentimental, esp. of tearful stage of drunkenness; (n.) mawkish sentiment. [(adj. f. n.) f. OF *Madelaine* MAGDALEN]

|| **mau'gre** (-ger), prep. (arch.). In spite of. [ME, f. OF *maugre* (*mal* bad f. L *malus* + *gré* f. L *gratus* pleasing)]

maul'¹, mall (mawl), n. Kinds of special hammer, commonly of wood. [ME, f. OF *mail* f. L *malleus* hammer]

maul'², v.t. Beat & bruise; handle (material thing, subject, quotation) roughly or carelessly; damage by criticism. [f. prec.]

maul'stick, mahl-, n. Light stick held by painter in left hand as support for right, with padded leather ball at one end. [f. Du. *maalstok* (*malen* paint + *stok* stick)]

maund, n. Asian measure of weight of varying value (Indian standard ~ = 82⅔ lb.). [Hind. & Pers. *man*]

maun'der, v.i. Move, act, listlessly; talk in dreamy or rambling manner. [perh. imit.; cf. dial. *daunder*]

maun'dy̆, n. (In R.-C. countries) ceremony of washing the feet of poor people (*John* xiii. 14); (in English use) distribution of ~ *money* (specially minted silver coins) by royal almoner to the poor on *M~ Thursday* (next before Easter). [ME, f. OF *mande* f. L *mandatum* (*novum*) MANDATE]

Mau'ser (mowz-), n. Kind of magazine rifle or pistol. [W. ~, inventor (d. 1882)]

mausolē'um, n. Magnificent tomb, orig. that of Mausolus king of Caria erected by his queen Artemisia in 4th c. B.C. [L, f. Gk *Mausōleion* (*Mausōlos*)]

mauvais (mō'vā, & see Ap.), a. ~ *sujet* (see Ap.), black sheep, rogue; ~ *quart d'heure* (kȧrdēr', & see Ap.), short but unpleasant experience, interview, etc. [F]

mauvaise honte (mōvāz'awnt, & see Ap.), n. False shame; painful diffidence. [F, = ill shame]

mauve (mōv), n. & a. **1.** Bright but delicate purple dye from coal-tar aniline. **2.** adj. Of the colour of this. [F, f. L *malva* MALLOW]

*****mäv'erick**, n., & v.i. Unbranded calf or yearling; (transf.) masterless person, rover; (v.i.) stray. [f. S. A. *M~*, Texas engineer who owned unbranded cattle c. 1850]

māv'is, n. (poet.). Song-thrush. [ME, f. OF *mauvis*, of unkn. orig.]

mavour'neen (-oor-), n. & int. My darling. [Ir. *mo mhuirnin*]

maw, ·n. Stomach (only joc. of men), esp. last of ruminant's four stomachs; ~'*worm*, intestinal worm. [OE *maga*, MDu. *maghe*, OHG *mago*, ON *magi* f. Gmc **magon*-]

mawk'ish, a. Of faint sickly flavour; feebly sentimental. Hence ~LY² adv., ~NESS n. [f. obs. *mawk* maggot f. ON *mathkr* + -ISH¹]

maw'seed, n. Seed of opium poppy. [f. G (dial.) *mohsamen* (G *mohn* poppy)]

mäxill'|a, n. (pl. ~*ae*). Jaw(bone), esp. upper jaw in animals & most vertebrates. Hence ~ARY¹, ~ìFORM, aa. [L]

mäx'im'¹, n. A general truth drawn from science or experience; principle, rule of conduct. [ME, f. OF *maxime* or med. L *maxima* (*propositio*), fem. adj., greatest]

Mäx'im², n. Single-barrelled quick-firing machine gun, with water-casing to keep parts cool. [H. ~, inventor (d. 1916)]

mäx'imalist, n. Person who holds out for the maximum of his demands & rejects compromises. [MAXIMUM, -AL, -IST]

mäx'imiz|e, -is|e (-iz), v.t. Increase, magnify, to the utmost; interpret (doctrine etc.) vigorously. Hence ~A'TION n. [f. L *maximus* greatest + -IZE]

mäx'imum, n. (pl. usu. *-ima*), & a. Highest possible magnitude or quantity (often attrib.); ~ *price* (that may not be exceeded); ~ *thermometer* (recording highest temperature within given period); (adj.) largest or largest possible. [L, neut. as prec.]

|| **mäx'imus**, a. (In schools) eldest of the name, as *Jones* ~. [see MAXIMIZE]

may'¹, v. aux. (3rd sing. *may*; past *might*, pr. mīt; no infin. or part. or gerund). **1.** Expr. possibility, as *it* ~ *be true* (neg. *it cannot be*), *it* ~ *not be* (perhaps is not) *true*, *you* ~ *walk miles without seeing one*, *he* ~ or *might* (perhaps will) *lose his way*, *I was afraid he might* (perhaps would) *lose his way, I ~ have been* (perhaps was) *wrong, afraid he might have* (perhaps had) *lost it.* **2.** Expr. permission, as *you ~* (neg. MUST[4] *not* or *cannot*) *go, I wish I might; you might* (I request you to) *call at the baker's; you might* (ought to, yet do not) *offer to help, you might* (ought to) *have offered.* **3.** (In final clauses, & after *wish, fear,* etc.) *take, took, such a course as ~, might, avert the danger; I hope he ~, hoped he might, succeed.* **4.** (Expr. wish) *~ you live to repent it!* **5.** (In questions, emphasizing uncertainty) *who ~ you be?* **6.** *~'be* (also arch. *~hăp'*), perhaps; *might-have-been,* a past possibility. [OE *mæg* (1st sing.) = OS, OHG, Goth. *mag,* ON *må,* f. Gmc **mag-* be strong; cf. MAIN[2], MIGHT]

may[2], n. (poet.). Maiden. [ME, perh. f. ON *møy, mey* = Goth. *mawi*]

May[3], n. **1.** Fifth month of year; (fig.) bloom, prime; *Queen of (the) ~,* girl chosen to be queen of games on *~* Day. **2.** (may). Hawthorn (blossom). [||(Camb. Univ., pl.) *~* examination, *~* boat-races held during *~ Week* (late in *~* or early in June). **4.** *~ Day,* May 1 (*may*ING[1], keeping this, picking may); || *May'fair,* district in West End of London (named from fair formerly held in*~*); *may'fly,* an ephemeral insect; *~ games,* on *~* Day; *may'pole,* pole painted & decked with flowers, for dancing round on *~* Day; || *~ meetings* (of religious & philanthropic societies held during *~* in London). [ME, f. OF *mai* f. L *Maius*]

ma'ya (mah-), n. (Hind. philos.). Illusion. [Skr.]

Ma'yan (mah-), a. Of the ancient culture of the Mayas before their conquest by the TOLTECS.

may'day, n. International radio-telephonic distress signal used by ships & aircraft. [pron. of F *m'aider* help me]

may'hĕm, n. (hist.). Crime of maiming a person so as to render him partly or wholly defenceless. [f. AF *mahaym* MAIM]

mayonnaise' (-āz), n. (*Salmon, chicken,* etc., *~,* dish with) dressing of eggs, oil, cream, vinegar, etc. [F]

mayor (mār), n. Head of municipal corporation of city or borough (in London & some other cities *Lord M~*); *~ of the palace,* nominal subordinate to whom the power of his titular superior has passed (see ROI *fainéant*). Hence **may'or**AL a. [ME, f. OF *maire,* as MAJOR[2]]

may'oralty, n. Mayor's (period of) office. [f. OF *mairalte* (as prec., see -AL & -TY)]

may'orĕss, n. Mayor's wife; female mayor; lady fulfilling ceremonial duties of *~.* [-ESS[1]]

măz'ard, -zz-, n. (Arch.) head; face; wild sweet cherry of Europe. [alt. of MAZER]

măzarine' (-ēn), n. & a. Deep rich blue. [perh. f. name of Cardinal *Mazarin* (d. 1661), or Duchesse de *Mazarin* (d. 1699)]

Măz'daïsm, n. Zoroastrianism. [f. Avestic *mazda,* good principle in Persian theology]

māze, n., & v.t.* **1.** Complex network of paths, labyrinth; confused mass etc. **2.** v.t. Bewilder, confuse, (esp. in p.p.). Hence **māz'i**LY[2] adv., **māz'i**NESS n., **māz'**Y[2] a. [ME; cf. AMAZE, rel. to which is uncert.]

māz'er, n. (hist.). Hard-wood drinking-bowl, usu. silver-mounted. [ME, f. OF *masere, masdre* maple-wood, f. WG **maser;* cf. OS *masur,* OHG *masar* excrescence on tree, maple (cf. *māsa* spot), ON *mǫsurr,* see MEASLES]

mazŭrk'a, n. Lively Polish dance; music for this in triple time. [Polish, = woman of province Mazovia]

măzz'ard, n. Var. of MAZARD.

*McCär'thy|ism (makär-), n. Policy of hunting out (suspected) Communists & removing them esp. from Government departments. Hence *~*ITE[1] a. & n. [f. Joseph *McCarthy,* U.S. senator (d. 1957), -ISM]

me[1] (mē, mĭ), pron., objective case of I (& colloq. subjective, as *it's only me*); (arch. & poet., reflexive) myself, *I laid me down;* (arch.) corresp. to ETHIC dative (*but me no buts*); (in intt.) *ah me!, dear me!* [repr. OE acc. (1) *mē,* (2) *mec,* & dat. (3) *mē;* (1) = OS *mĭ, mē* f. Aryan **me, *eme,* cf. L *mē,* Gk (e)*me:* (2) = OS, ON, Goth. *mik,* OHG *mih* f. Aryan **me-gé,* cf. Gk *emege;* (3) = OS *mī,* OHG *mir,* ON *mér,* Goth. *miz* f. Aryan **mes*]

mē[2]. See MI.

mead[1], n. Alcoholic liquor of fermented honey & water. [OE *meodu,* MLG *mede,* OHG *metu,* ON *mjǫthr* f.* Gmc **meduz,* cogn. w. Gk *methu* wine]

mead[2], n. (poet.). = foll. [see foll.]

meadow (mĕd'ō), n. Piece of grass land, esp. one used for hay; low well-watered ground, esp. near river; *~ brown,* common brown butterfly; *~ pipit,* titlark; *~ saffron,* perennial plant abundant in *~*s, with lilac flowers; *~-sweet,* rosaceous plant common in moist *~*s, with creamy-white fragrant flowers. Hence *~*Y[2] (mĕd'ŏĭ) a. [OE *mǣdwe* obl. case of *mǣd* (whence prec.) f. Gmc **mǣdwō* f. **mǣ-*MOW[3]]

mea'gre (-ger), a. (Of persons etc.) lean, thin; poor, scanty, (esp. of meals, as *~ fare*); (of literary composition, ideas, art) wanting in fullness. Hence *~*LY[2] adv., *~*NESS n., (-ger-). [ME, f. OF *megre* f. L *macer*]

meal[1], n. Edible part of any grain or pulse (usu. exc. FLOUR) ground to powder; WHOLE *~.* [OE *melu,* OS, OHG *melo,* ON *mjǫl* f. Gmc **mel-,* cogn. w. L *molere* grind]

meal[2], n., & v.i. Customary (also, any) occasion of taking food; food so taken (*make a ~ of,* consume); || quantity of milk given by cow at a milking; *~'time,* usual time of eating; (v.i.) eat a ~. [OE *mǣl* mark, fixed time, meal, = OS, OHG, ON *māl*, Goth *mēl* f. Gmc **mǣlam*]

meal'ie, n. (S.-Afr.). Maize (usu. pl.). [f. Afrikaans *milje* f. Port. *milho* MILLET]

meal'ў, a. Of, like, containing, meal; (of boiled potatoes) dry & powdery; ~--*bug*, insect infesting vines etc.; ~ *prim-rose* (mauve-flowered with powdery stem); (of horses) spotty; (of complexion) pale; (usu. ~-*mouthed*) apt to mince matters, soft-spoken. Hence meal'INESS n. [MEAL¹+-Y²]

mean¹, n. 1. Condition, quality, virtue, course, equally removed from two opposite (usu. blamable) extremes, esp. *the golden, happy, ~*. 2. (math.). Term between first & last terms of arithmetical, geometrical, etc., progression. 3. pl. (Often treated as sing., as *a ~s*) that by which a result is brought about, as *it has been the ~s of extending our trade, by fair ~s*, WAYS *& ~s*, ~*s of grace* (sacraments etc.). 4. Pecuniary resources, as *he lives beyond his, on his own*, ~*s* (also attrib., as ~*s test*, principle of requiring some proof of need as condition of assistance); wealth, as *a man of ~s*. 5. *By all* (*manner of*)~*s*, in every possible way, at any cost, certainly; *by no* (*manner of*)~*s*, not at all, certainly not; *by* ~*s* (the instrumentality) *of* (person, thing, doing). [f. foll., partly thr. F]

mean², a. (Math.) equally far from two extremes, as *5 is the ~ quantity between 2 & 8*; ~ *sea level* (half-way between those of high and low water); ~ *sun*, fictitious sun moving in celestial equator at ~ rate of real sun; ~ *proportional*, second of three quantities of which first is to it as it is to third; *in the* ~ (inter-, vening) *time, while*; ~*'time*, ~*'while*, advv., in the ~ time. [ME, f. OF *men, meien*, f. L *medianus* MEDIAN]

mean³, a. (Of capacity, understanding, etc.) inferior, poor; (hist.) ~ *white*, landless white man in S. United States; not imposing in appearance, shabby; *he is no* ~ (a good) *scholar*; ignoble, small-minded; stingy; uncomfortable, malicious, ill tempered; *(colloq.) secretly ashamed (*feel* ~). Hence ~'LY² advv., ~'NESS n. [ME, repr. OE *gemǣne*, OS *gimēni*, OHG *gimeini*, Goth. *gamains*, cogn. w. L *communis*]

mean⁴, v.t. (~*t*, pr. mĕnt). Purpose, have in mind, (*mischief, business, to do*); design, destine, for an object etc., as ~ *it to be used*, ~ *it for a stopgap, he was~t* (by parents etc., also, by Providence) *for a soldier*; *I ~ you to* (am determined that you shall) *go*; ~ *well to, by*, be kindly disposed towards; intend to convey (specified sense) or indicate (object), as *I ~ that he is stingy, I ~ his father*; (of a person) be of (specified) importance *to* (another); (of words or person) signify, import, (thing, *that*); *what do you* ~ *by*

(how do you justify) *it?* [OE *mǣnan*, OS *mēnian*, OHG *meinen* f. WG **mainjan*]

měăn'der, n., & v.i. 1. (Pl.) sinuous windings of river; (pl.) winding paths; (usu. pl.) circuitous journey; ornamental pattern of lines winding in & out. 2. v.i. Wander at random, (of stream) wind about. [(vb f. n.) L, f. Gk *Maiandros*, river in Phrygia]

měăn'drine, a. Full of windings (esp. of genus of corals with surface like human brain). [MEANDER + -INE¹]

mean'ing¹, n. What is meant; *with ~*, significantly. Hence ~LESS a. [-ING¹]

mean'ing², a. Expressive, significant, whence ~LY² adv.; *well-~*, having good intention. [-ING²]

mea'sles (-zlz), n. pl. Infectious disease of man, marked by red spots on skin; such spots; disease in swine; GERMAN² ~. [ME *masele*(s) (pl.), f. MLG *masele*, = M.Du. *masel*, Du. *mazelen*; cf. OHG *masala* pustule, cogn. w. *masar* MAZER]

meas'lу (-z-), a. Of, affected with, measles; (sl.) contemptible, worthless. [f. prec. + -Y²]

measure¹ (mĕzh'er), n. 1. Size, quantity, found by measuring, whence ~LESS a., beyond ~, infinite; *short, full*, ~, less, not less, than professed amount; ‖ *clothes made to* ~ (in accordance with measurements taken); *take* (person's) ~, measure him for clothes etc., (fig.) gauge his character, abilities, etc. 2. Degree or extent or amount (esp. *in a* or *some* ~, partly). 3. Vessel of standard capacity for dealing out liquids etc., as *pint* ~. 4. Rod, tape, etc., for measuring, as *tape-* ~, *yard-*~. 5. Unit of capacity, e.g. bushel, as *20* ~*s of wheat*. 6. System of measuring, as *liquid, linear*, ~, dist. *weight*. 7. That by which a thing is computed, as *a chain's weakest link is the* ~ *of its strength*. 8. Quantity contained in another an exact number of times; *greatest common* ~ (greatest that divides each of given quantities). 9. Prescribed extent or quantity, as *set* ~*s to*, limit, *beyond* ~, excessively. 10. Poetical rhythm, metre; time of piece of music; (mus.) bar; (arch.) dance, as *tread a* ~. 11. Suitable action, as *take* ~*s*. 12. Legislative enactment. [ME, f. OF *mesure* f. L *mensura* (*metiri mens-* measure, -URE)]

measur|e² (mĕzh'er), v.t. & i. 1. Ascertain extent or quantity of (thing) by comparison with fixed unit or with object of known size; ascertain size & proportions of (person) for clothes. 2. Look (person) up & down *with* one's *eye*. 3. Mark off or *off* (line etc. of given length). 4. ~*e* one's *length*, fall prostrate; ~*e swords*, (of duellists) see that swords are of equal length, (fig.) try one's strength *with* (person). 5. Estimate (immaterial thing, person's character, etc.) by some standard or rule. 6. Deal *out* (thing *to* person). 7. Bring (one's strength etc.) into competition *with* (another's). **8.** (poet.). Traverse (distance). **9.** v.i. Take measurements; be of specified size (*it ~es six inches*); *~e up to*, have necessary qualifications for. Hence ~**ABLE** (mězh′*er*-) a. (*within ~able distance of* ruin etc.), getting near it), ~**abLY²** adv., ~e**MENT** (mězh′*erm*-) n. (esp., pl., detailed dimensions). [ME, f. OF *mesurer* (as prec.)]

mea′sured (mězh′erd),.a. In vbl senses, also: rhythmical, regular in movement, as ~ *tread*; (of language) carefully weighed. [p.p. of prec.]

meat, n. Animal flesh as food, ŭsu. (also *butcher's* ~) excluding fish & poultry; *green* ~, grass, green vegetables, as food; (arch.) food of any kind (*as full as an egg is of* ~, quite full; *one man's* ~ *is another man's poison*); *this was* ~ *& drink* (a great pleasure) *to him*; (arch.) meal, as *before, after,* ~; ~*-safe*, cupboard for storing ~, usu. of wire gauze etc.; (bibl.) ~*-offering* (R.V. *meal-*), sacrifice of flour & oil. Hence~′**LESS** a. [OE *mete* food, OS *meti, mat,* OHG *maz,* ON *matr,* Goth. *mats*]

meāt′us, n. (anat.; pl. *-ūs, -uses*). Channel, passage, in the body, as *auditory* ~, channel of the ear. [L, f. *meare* flow, run]

meat′ÿ, a. Full of meat, fleshy; (fig.) full of substance; of or like meat. [-Y²]

Mĕcc′a, n. Mohammed's birthplace; (fig.) place óne aspires to visit, (also) birthplace of a faith, policy, pursuit, etc. [f. Arab. *makkah*]

mĕcca′nō (-ah-), n. Set of miniature parts from which engineering models can be constructed. [P]

mĕchăn′ĭc (-k-), n. **1.** Handicraftsman; skilled workman, esp. one who makes or uses machinery. **2.** pl. Branch of applied mathematics treating of motion & tendencies to motion, (also) science of machinery. [ME, f. OF *-ique* or L f. Gk *mēkhanikos* adj. (as MACHINE, see -IC)]

mĕchăn′ical (-k-), a. Of machines or mechanism; *the ~ powers*, lever, wheel & axle, pulley, inclined plane, wedge, screw; of the nature of handicraft; working, produced, by machinery; ~ *drawing* (done with compasses etc.); ~ *transport* (abbr. M.T.), motor branch of R.A.S.C.; (of persons or actions)'like machines, automatic, lacking originality; (of agencies, principles, etc.) belonging to mechanics; (of theories etc.) explaining phenomena by assumption of ~ action, whence~ ISM n.; of mechanics as a science. Hence~LY² adv., ~NESS a. [ME, as prec., see -AL]

mĕchani′cian (-kanĭshn), n. One skilled in constructing machinery. [MECHANIC+-IAN]

mĕch′anĭsm (-k-), n. Structure, adaptation of parts, of machine (lit. & fig.); system of mutually adapted parts working together (as) in machine; (art) mechanical execution, technique. [f. mod. L *mechanismus* (as MACHINE, -ISM)]

mĕch′an|ĭst (-k-), n. Machinist (now rare); mechanician, expert in mechanics; (philos.) one who holds that all natural phenomena admit of mechanical explanation (opp. VITALIST), whence ~**ĭs′tĭc** a. [f. MECHANIC+-IST]

mĕch′anĭz|e (-k-), -**ĭs|e** (-ĭz), v.t. Give mechanical character to. Hence ~**A′TION** n., (esp.) substitution of motor transport for horse-drawn vehicles, replacement of cavalry by tanks & armóured cars, etc. [-IZE]

Mĕch′lin (-k-), n. (Also ~ *lace*) lace made at ~ (now *Mechelen* or *Malines*) in Belgium.

mĕd′al, n. Piece of metal, usu. in form of coin, struck or cast with inscription & device to commemorate event etc., also awarded as distinction to soldier, scholar, etc., for services rendered, proficiency, etc.; *the reverse of the* ~, other side of question; ~ *play* (golf), play in which the score is reckoned by counting the number of strokes taken for the round, opp. *match play*. Hence~**IED²** (-ld), **mĕdăll′ĭc** aa. [f. F *médaille* f. It. *medaglia* f. Rom. *medallia* f. *metallea* f. *metallum* METAL]

mĕdăll′ion (-yon), n. Large medal; thing so shaped, e.g. decorative panel or tablet, portrait, etc. [f. F *médaillon* (as prec., see -OON)]

mĕd′allist, n. Engraver, designer, of medals; recipient of medal, as *gold* ~. [-IST]

mĕd′dl|e, v.i. Busy oneself unduly *with*, interfere *in*. Hence ~**ER¹**, ~**esome**NESS, nn., ~**esome** (-dls-) a. [ME, f. OF *medler*, var. of *mesler* f. Rom. *miscŭlare* f. L *miscēre* mix]

mēd′ĭa n. (pl. *-ae*). Voiced or soft mute (*b, d, g*), cf. TENUIS; middle membrane of artery or vessel. [L, fem. of *medius* middle]

mĕdiaev′al, -dĭēv′al, a. Of, imitating, the Middle Ages. Hence ~ISM(2), ~IST(3), nn., ~IZE(2, 3) v.t. & i., ~LY² adv. [f. L *medius* middle+*aevum* age +-AL]

mĕd′ial, a. Situated in the middle; of average dimensions. Hence ~LY² adv. [f. LL *medialis* (as prec., see -AL)]

mĕd′ian, a. & n. **1.** Situated in the middle. **2.** n. (Anat.) ~ artery, vein, nerve, etc.; (math.) straight line drawn from angular point of triangle to middle of opposite side. [f. F *médian* or L *medianus* (as prec., see -AN)]

mĕd′iant, n. (mus.). Third of any scale. [f. It. *mediante* (as MEDIATE², see -ANT)]

mĕdiästin′|um, n. (anat.). Membranous middle septum, esp. between lungs. Hence ~AL a. [med. L, neut. adj., = middle, f. L *medius*]

mĕd′iate¹, a. Connected not directly but through some other person or thing; involving intermediate agency. Hence ~LY² adv. [as foll., see -ATE²]

mĕd′i|āte², v.i. & t. Form connecting link between; intervene (*between two* persons) for purpose of reconciling them; be the medium for bringing about (result) or conveying (gift etc.). So ~A'TION n. [f. LL *mediare* (*medius* middle), see -ATE[3]]

měd'iatiz|e, -is|e (-īz), v.t. Annex (principality) to another State, leaving former sovereign his title & some rights of government. Hence ~A'TION n. [f. F *médiatiser* (*médiat*, as MEDIATE[1], see -IZE)]

měd'iātor, n. One who mediates, esp. Christ. Hence or cogn. ~MEDIATŌR'IAL, **měd'iātory, aa., měd'iātrix** n. [ME, f. OF *mediatour* f. LL *mediatorem* (as MEDIATE[2], see -OR)]

měd'icable, a. Admitting of remedial treatment. [f. L *medicabilis* (as MEDICATE, see -BLE)]

měd'ical, a. & n. 1. Of the healing art; ~ *man*, physician or surgeon; of medicine as opp. to surgery, obstetrics, etc.; requiring ~, not surgical, treatment; ~ *jurisprudence*, the legal knowledge required of a doctor. **2.** n. (colloq.). ~ student. Hence ~LY[2] adv. [f. F *médical* or LL *medicalis* (*medicus* physician, see -AL)]

mědic'ament (*or* měd²), n. Substance used in curative treatment. [F, or f. L *medicamentum* (as MEDICATE, see -MENT)]

měd'icăster, n. Quack. [f. L *medicus* physician, see -ASTER]

měd'ic|āte, v.t. Treat medically; impregnate with medicinal substance. Hence or cogn. ~A'TION n., ~ātive a. [f. L *medicari* (as prec.), see -ATE[3]]

Mědicě'an, a. Of the Medici family, rulers of Florence in 15th c. [f. mod. L *Mediceus* +-AN]

mědi'cinal, a. Of medicine; having healing properties. Hence ~LY[2] adv. [ME, f. OF f. L *medicinalis* (as foll., see -AL)]

medicine (měd'sn, měd'isin), n., & v.t. **1.** Art of restoring & preserving health, esp. by means of remedial substances & regulation of diet etc., as opp. to surgery & obstetrics; substance, esp. one taken internally, used in this; (among savages) spell, charm, fetish, as ~*man*, magician; *take* one's ~, submit to the disagreeable; ~ *ball*, stuffed leather ball thrown & caught as means of exercise. **2.** v.t. (arch.). Give ~ to, cure with ~. [ME; (vb f. OF *medeciner*) f. OF *medecine* f. L *medicina* (*medicus* physician)]

měd'icō, n. (colloq.; pl. ~s). Doctor. [It.]

měd'ico-, irreg. comb. form of L *medicus* physician, medical-, as ~*botan'ical*, ~*galvan'ic*, ~*judi'cial*.

medieval. See MEDIAEVAL.

měd'iōcre (-ker), a. Of middling quality, indifferent, neither good nor bad. So **mědiŏc'rity** n. (in adj. senses, & esp. ~ person). [f. F *médiocre* or L *mediocris* of middle degree (*medius* middle)]

měd'itāt|e, v.t. & i. Plan mentally, design; (intr.) exercise the mind in (esp. religious) contemplation (*on, upon*, subject). Hence or cogn. **mědita'tion, ~or**,

~**iveness, nn., ~ive a., ~ively**[2] adv. [f. L *meditari*, see -ATE[3]]

měditerrăn'ēan, a. & n. (Of land) remote from coast (rare); (of water surfaces) land-locked; *M*~ (*Sea*), that which separates Europe from Africa. [f. L *mediterraneus* (*medius* middle+*terra* land)+-AN]

měd'ium, n. & a. (pl. *-a, -ums*). **1.** Middle quality, degree, etc. (*between* extremes, or abs.); intervening substance through which impressions are conveyed to senses etc., e.g. air; (fig.) environment, conditions of life; agency, means, as *by, through, the ~ of*; ~ *of circulation*, what serves as instrument of commercial transactions, e.g. coin; liquid vehicle with which pigments are mixed, e.g. oil, water; person claiming ultraphysical perception and revealing its results to others, whence ~ISM n., ~is'tic a., ~IZE(3) v.t. **2.** adj. Intermediate between two degrees or amounts, average, moderate; ~ *bowler* (neither fast nor slow); ~ *wave* (radio), having a wave-length between 100 & 800 metres. [L, neut. of *medius* middle]

měd'lar, n. (Tree with) fruit like small brown apple, eaten when decayed. [ME, f. OF *medler* f. *medle (whence obs. E *medle*) f. *mesle* f. L f. Gk *mespilē, -on*]

měd'ley, n. (pl. ~s), a., & v.t. Heterogeneous mixture; mixed company; literary miscellany; (adj.) mixed, motley; (v.t.) make a ~ of, intermix. [ME, f. OF *medlee* var. of *meslee* (as MEDDLE)]

Mědŏc' (mā-), n. Red wine from ~, district in S.W. France.

mědŭll'a, n. Marrow of bones; spinal marrow; ~ (*oblongā'ta* prolonged) hindmost segment of brain; central parts of some organs, esp. kidney; pith of mammalian hair; soft internal tissue of plants. So **mědŭll'ARY**[2] a. [L, = pith, marrow, prob. cogn. w. *medius* middle]

mědūs'|a, n. (pl. ~*ae,~as*). **1.** (Gk myth.; *M*~a) one of the three GORGONS, with snakes for hair. **2.** (zool.). Jelly-fish, whence ~AL, ~AN, aa., ~OID a. & n. [L, f. Gk *Medousa*]

meed, n. (poet.). Reward; merited portion (*of* praise etc.). [OE *mēd*, OS *mēda*, OHG *mēta* f. WG *mēda cogn. w. Goth. *mizdō*, Gk *misthos* reward]

meek, a. Piously humble & submissive; submitting tamely to injury etc.; (provv.) *as ~ as a lamb, as Moses.* Hence ~'LY[2] adv., ~'NESS n. [ME *meoc* f. ON *miukr* soft, gentle]

meer'kăt, n. Small S.-Afr. mammal like an ichneumon. [Du., = sea-cat]

meer'schaum (-shm), n. Hydrous silicate of magnesium, found in soft white masses; tobacco-pipe with ~ bowl. [G, = sea-foam (*meer* sea+*schaum* foam)]

meet[1], n. Meeting of hounds & men for hunt or of cyclists etc. [f. foll.]

meet[2], v.t. & i. (*mět*). **1.** Come face to face with (person coming from opposite direction); go to place to receive (person, train, etc.) on arrival; make the acquaintance of (imperat., U.-S. form of introduction, as ~ *Dr Smith*); ~ (person) *half-way*, respond to friendly advances of, come to compromise with. **2.** (Of line, road, etc.) reach point of contact with (another line etc.). **3.** ~ *the eye, ear*, be visible, audible; ~ person's *eye*, see he is looking at one, (also) return his gaze. **4.** Oppose in battle or duel; grapple with (evils etc.). **5.** Come by accident or design into the company of. **6.** Come into conformity with (person, his wishes). **7.** Satisfy (demand; ~ *the case*, be adequate); pay (bill) at maturity. **8.** (Of two or more persons) come face to face; come *together*, as *they had* or *were met together*; assemble for purpose of conference, business, etc. **9.** Come into contact (*waistcoat won't* ~, is too small); (of qualities) unite in same person. **10.** ~ *with*, come across (person, obstacle, etc.), experience (treatment etc.). [OE *mētan*, OS *mōtian*, ON *mǽta*, Goth. *gamōtjan* f. Gmc **mōt-* MOOT]

meet[3], a. (arch.). Suitable, fit, proper, (*for* thing, *to* do, *to* be done); *it is* ~ (proper) *that*. Hence ~'LY[2] adv., ~'NESS n. [ME *mēte* repr. OE *gemǽte* f. Gmc **gamǣtja-* (*ga- Y- + **mǣt-* METE[2])]

meet'ing, n. In vbl senses, esp.: duel; race-~; assembly of people for entertainment etc.; assembly for worship; persons assembled, as *address the* ~; ~-*house*, place of worship (usu. disparaging· exc. of Quakers); ~-*place* (appointed for ~). [MEET[2] + -ING[1]]

mĕg'a-, comb. form of Gk *megas* great, as: ~*cephăl'ic*, large-headed; ~*lith*, large stone, esp. as monument; ~*lith'ic*, made of, marked by use of, large stones; ~*phŏne*, instrument for carrying sound a long distance, large speaking-trumpet (v.t., announce with ~phone); ~*pŏde*, ~*pŏd*, kinds of mound-building birds (lit. large-footed); ~*scope*, kind of magic lantern; ~*scŏp'ic*, visible to naked eye; ~*thēr'ium*, extinct kind of huge herbivorous sloth-like animals; ~*ton* 1,000,000 tons; ~*watt*, 1,000 kilowatts.

mĕg'alo-, comb. form of Gk *megas megal*-great, as: ~*măn'ĭa*, insanity of self--exaltation, passion for big things; ~*saur'us*, extinct kind of huge carnivorous lizards.

mĕgăss(e)', n. Fibrous residue after expression of sugar from cane. [orig. unkn.; cf. BAGASSE]

mĕgg'er (-g-), n. (electr.). Apparatus for measuring insulation resistance. [P; cf. MEGOHM]

mĕgilp' (-g-), n. Vehicle (usu. linseed oil & turpentine) for oil colours. [orig. unkn.]

mĕg'ohm (-ōm), n. (electr.). Unit of resistance (one million ohms). [MEGA- + OHM]

mĕg'rĭm[1], n. Severe headache usu. on one side only; whim, fancy; (pl.) low spirits, vapours; (pl.) staggers, vertigo,

in horses etc. [ME *mygrane* f. OF *migraine* f. LL f. Gk HEMI(*krania* CRANIUM)]

mĕg'rĭm[2], n. (Local name for) the smooth sole or similar flat fish. [orig. unkn.]

meios'is (mīŏ-), n. = LITOTES; (biol.) phase of nuclear change in germ cells. [Gk *meiōsis* (*meioō* lessen, f. *meiōn* less, see -OSIS)]

meis'tersĭnger (mīs-), n. pl. & sing. German lyric poets & musicians of 14th--16th cc. organized in guilds & having elaborate technique; (sing.) member of such guild. [G (*master*)]

mĕkŏm'ēter, n. Portable military range--finder. [f. Gk *mēkos* length + -METER]

mĕlanchŏl'ĭa (-k-), n. Emotional mental disease marked by depression & ill--grounded fears. [LL, see MELANCHOLY]

mĕlanchŏl'ic (-k-), a. Melancholy; liable to melancholy. [f. L f. Gk *melagkholikos* (as foll., see -IC)]

mĕl'ancholy (-k-), n. & a. **1.** (Habitual or constitutional tendency to) sadness & depression; pensive sadness. **2.** adj. (Of persons) sad, gloomy; (of things) saddening, depressing. [ME; (adj. f. n.) f. OF (-*lie*), f. LL f. Gk *melagkholia* (*melas* black + *kholē* bile)]

Mĕlănē's|ĭa (-sha), n. Group of islands N.E. of Australia, in which the dominant race is dark-skinned & frizzly-haired. Hence ~ĬAN a. & n., (native, language) of these islands. [f. Gk *melas* black + *nēsos* island + -IA[1]]

mélange (see Ap.), n. Mixture, medley. [F (*méler* mix, as MEDDLE)]

mĕl'anism, n. Darkness of colour resulting from abnormal development of black pigment in epidermis, hair, etc. [f. Gk *melas -anos* black + -ISM]

mĕlanŏch'rōī (-k-), n. pl. (anthrop.). Smooth-haired class of men with dark hair & pale complexion. [f. Gk *melanokhroos* (*melas* black + *khroa* skin)]

mĕlan|ōs'is, n. Morbid deposit, abnormal development, of black pigment in tissue; black cancer. Hence ~OT'IC (-ŏt[2]) a. [Gk *melanōsis* f. *melanoō* blacken (*melas* black), see -OSIS]

Mĕl'ba, n. ~ *toast* (also *toast* ~), thin crisp toast; PÊCHE ~. [Dame Nellie ~, Australian prima donna (d. 1931)]

*mĕld[1], v.t. & i. Merge. [perh. f. *melt* + *weld*]

mĕld[2], v.t. & i., & n. (In some card games) declare for a score; (n.) act of ~ing, group of cards (to be) ~ed. [f. G *melden* announce]

mêlée (mĕl'ā), n. Mixed fight, skirmish; lively debate. [F, as MEDLEY]

mĕl'ic, a. (Of poem, esp. Gk lyric) meant to be sung. [f. Gk *melikos* (*melos* song, -IC)]

mĕl'inite, n. An explosive of French invention. [f. F *mélinite* f. Gk *mēlinos* (*mēlon* apple), see -ITE[1]]

mĕl'ior|āte, v.t. & i. Improve. Hence ~A'TION n. [f. LL *meliorare* (as foll.), -ATE[3]] mel'ior|ism, n. Doctrine that the world may be made better by human effort. So ~IST n. [L *melior* better + -ISM]

mell'ay, n. (arch.). = MÊLÉE.

mellif'erous, a. Yielding, producing, honey. [f. L *mellifer* (*mel* honey, see -FEROUS)]

mellif'lu|ous (-lōō-), a. (Of voice, words) sweet as honey. So ~ENCE n., ~ENT a., (-lōō-). [f. LL *melliffuus* (*mel* honey, *fluere* flow) + -OUS]

mell'ow (-ō), a. (~er, ~est), & v.t. & i. 1. (Of fruit) soft, sweet, & juicy; (of wine) well-matured; (of earth) rich, loamy; (of character) softened by age or experience; (of sound, colour, light) full & pure without harshness; genial, jovial; partly intoxicated. 2. vb. Make, become, ~. Hence ~LY² (-ōlī) adv., ~NESS (-ōn-) n. [15th c., formally corresp. to OE *melu melw-* MEAL¹, of wh. *mellow* may be an attrib. use]

melōd'ēon, -dion, -dium, n. Small organ with suction-operated reeds; kind of accordion. [f. MELODY]

melōd'ic, a. Of or relating to melody. [f. F *mélodique* (as MELODY, see -IC)]

melōd'ious, a. Of, producing, melody; sweet-sounding. Hence ~LY² adv., ~NESS n. [ME, f. OF -*ieus* (as MELODY, see -OUS)]

mel'odist, n. Singer; composer of melodies. [f. MELODY + -IST]

mel'odize, -ise (-īz), v.i. & t. Make melody; make melodious. [f. MELODY + -IZE]

mel'odrama (-rah-), n. Sensational dramatic piece with violent appeals to emotions & happy ending; language, behaviour, suggestive of this; (formerly) play with songs interspersed & with orchestral music accompanying the action. Hence melodramăt'ic a., melodramăt'ically adv., melodrăm'atist n., melodrăm'atize v.t. [earlier -*drame* f. F *mélodrame* (Gk *melos* music + F *drame* DRAMA)]

mel'ody, n. Sweet music; musical arrangement of words; arrangement of single notes in musically expressive succession; principal part in harmonized music, air. [ME, f. OF *melodie* f. LL f. Gk *melōidia* (*melos* song, see ODE)]

mel'on, n. Kinds of gourd, esp. WATER~; ~-*cutting* (sl.), sharing of spoils or profits. [ME, f. OF, f. LL *melonem* (nom. -*lo*), shortened f. L (-*po*) f. Gk *mēlopepōn* (*mēlon* apple + *pepōn* gourd)]

Melpŏm'ēnē, n. The MUSE¹ of tragedy. [Gk]

melt¹, n. Melted metal; amount melted at a time. [f. foll.]

melt², v.i. & t. (p.p. ~ed &, as adj. of metal, *mŏllen*). Become liquefied by heat; ~ *away*, disappear thus; (colloq., of person) suffer extreme heat; (of tender food) *it* ~s (is easily dissolved) *in the mouth*; (of clouds) break *into rain*; (of person, heart, feelings) be softened by or

with pity or love, dissolve *into tears*, esp. *the* ~*ing mood*, whence mel'tinGly² adv.; dwindle *away*; (of sound) be soft & liquid; pass imperceptibly *into* (another form); reduce (metal etc.) to liquid condition by heat; ~ *down* (plate etc., to use the metal as raw material); *go into the* ~*ing-pot* (fig.), be revolutionized; soften (person, feelings). [OE *meltan*, *mieltan*, corresp. to ON *melta* digest, Goth. *maltjan* dissolve, f. Gmc **melt-*; cogn. w. MALT]

mel'ton, n. Kind of cloth for men's clothes;·|| *M*~ *Mowbray* (mōb-) *pie*, kind of pasty. [*M*~ *Mowbray*, in Leics.]

měm'ber, n. Part, organ, of body, esp. limb; *unruly* ~, tongue; (fig.) ~ *of Christ*, Christian; constituent portion of complex structure; person belonging to a society etc.; *M*~ (one formally elected to take part in proceedings) *of Parliament* (abbr. *M.P.*, pl. *M.M.P.* or *M.P.s*); person admitted to Order of the British Empire, 5th class (M.B.E.), or to Royal Victorian Order, 4th or 5th class (M.V.O.); part, branch, of political body; division, clause, of sentence; group of figures, part of numerical expression. Hence (-)~ED² (-*erd*), ~LESS, aa. [ME, f. OF *membre* f. L *membrum* limb]

měm'bership, n. Being a member; number of members. [-SHIP]

měm'brāne, n. Pliable sheet-like connective tissue or lining in animal or vegetable body; morbid formation in some diseases; skin of parchment, forming part of a roll. So membranA'CEOUS (-āshus), membrān'EOUS, měm'brANOUS, aa. [f. L *membrana*~, parchment, as MEMBER]

měm'brum virīl'ē, n. = PENIS. [L,=male member]

měmen'tō, n. (pl. ~*es*, ~*s*). Object serving as reminder or warning, or kept as memorial of person or event; ~ *mō'rī* (= remember you must die), warning or reminder of death (e.g. of skull). [L, imperat. of *meminisse* remember]

měm'oir (-wăr), n. Record of events, history written from personal knowledge or special sources of information; (auto)-biography; essay on learned subject specially studied by the writer. [f. F *mémoire* masc., spec. use of *mémoire* fem. MEMORY]

měm'orabil'ĭa, n. pl. Memorable things. [L, neut. pl. as foll.]

měm'or|able, a. Worth remembering, not to be forgotten, easily remembered. Hence ~ABIL'ITY n., ~abLY² adv. [ME, f. OF, or L *memorabilis* (*memorare* bring to mind f. *memor* mindful, -BLE)]

měmorăn'dum, n. (pl. -*da*, -*dums*; abbr. *mem.*, *memo.*). Note to help the memory; record of events etc. for future use; (law) document recording terms of contract etc.; informal letter without signature etc., usu. on paper headed *M*~. [ME, f. L, neut. sing. gerundive as prec.]

memŏr′ial, a. & n. **1.** (Of statue, festival, etc.) serving to commemorate; of memory. **2.** n. ~ object, custom, etc.; record, chronicle, (usu. pl.); informal State paper of various kinds; statement of facts as basis of petition etc. Hence ~IST n. [ME, f. OF, f. L *memorialis* (as MEMORY, see -AL)]

memŏr′ialize, **-ise** (-īz), v.t. Commemorate; address memorial to (person). [prec. +-IZE]

memŏr′ia tech′nĭca (těk-), n. System, contrivance, used to assist memory. [L, = artificial memory]

mĕm′orize, **-ise** (-īz), v.t. Put on record; commit to memory. [f. foll. +-IZE]

mĕm′ory̆, n. Faculty of remembering; this in an individual, as *a good, bad,* ~ (*convenient* or *accommodating* ~, that retains only what it is to one's interest to remember); recollection; information storage device in electronic computer; *in* ~ *of*, as a record of, to keep alive the ~ of; posthumous repute, as *his* ~ *has been censured, of blessed, happy,* etc., ~ (used esp. of deceased princes etc.); length of time over which ~ extends, as *beyond, within, the* ~ *of men, within living* ~. [ME, f. OF *memorie, memoire* f. L *memoria* f. *memor* mindful]

mĕm′sah′ĭb, n. (In India) European married lady. [f. MA'AM + SAHIB]

-men, suf. in L wds, often side by side with L *-mentum* -MENT & w. same meaning, as *fundamen-tum.* Many wds of slightly technical or learned use, as *acumen, stamen, gravamen, albumen, cognomen, regimen, specimen.*

mĕn′ace¹, n. (literary). Threat. [ME, f. OF f. Rom. *minacia* = L *-iae* (L *minax* f. *minari* threaten)]

mĕn′ac|e², v.t. Threaten. Hence ~INGLY² adv. [ME, f. OF *menacer* f. Rom. *minaciare* (as prec.)]

ménage (mănazh′), n. Household management; domestic establishment; ~ *à trois* (trwah), household consisting of husband, wife, & lover of one of these. [f. OF *manaige* f. Rom. *mansionaticum* (as MANSION, see -AGE)]

mĕnä′gerie, n. Collection of wild animals in cages etc. [f. F *ménagerie* (as prec., see -ERY)]

mĕnd¹, n. Repaired hole in material etc.; *on the* ~, improving in health or (of affairs etc.) condition. [f. foll.]

mĕnd², v.t. & i. Restore to sound condition, repair, (broken articles, clothes, roads, etc.); ~ (correct) one's *ways*; *least said soonest* ~*ed* (rectified); ~ (add fuel to) *fire*; cut to required shape (quill pen); (intr.) regain health; ~ (improve state of) *matters*; ~ (quicken) one's *pace*; ~ *or end*, improve or abolish. Hence ~′ABLE a. [ME, aphetic f. AMEND]

mĕndā′cious (-shus), a. Lying, untruthful. Hence or cogn. ~LY² adv., mĕndă′CITY n. [f. L *mendax* f. root of *mentiri* lie, see -ACIOUS]

Mĕn′delĭsm, n. A proven theory of heredity which reduces to numerical law the recurrence of inherited characters. So **Mĕndēl′ian** a. & n. [G. J. *Mendel,* 1822–84]

mĕn′dic|ant, a. & n. **1.** Begging; ~*ant friars* (living solely on alms). **2.** n. Beggar. Hence or cogn. ~ANCY, mĕndĭ′CITY, nn. [f. L *mendicare* (*mendicus* beggar), see -ANT]

mĕnhād′en, n. Fish of herring family, used for manure, & yielding valuable oil. [Amer. Ind. *munnawhatteaug*]

mĕn′hir (-ēr), n. (archaeol.). Tall upright monumental stone found in Europe, Africa, & Asia. [f. Breton *men hir* long stone]

mĕn′ial, a. & n. **1.** (Of service) servile; (of servant, usu. derog.) domestic. **2.** n. ~ servant. Hence ~LY² adv. [AF, f. OF *mesnie* household (obs. E *meinie*) f. Rom. *mansionata* (as MANSION, see -ADE)]

mĕn′inx, n. (usu. in pl. *menĭn′gēs*). Any of three membranes enveloping brain & spinal cord (*dura mater, arachnoid, pia mater*). Hence mĕnĭn′gĕAL a., mĕnĭn-gĭT′IS (-jīt-), mĕnĭn′gŏCELE, nn. [Gk *mēninx*]

menĭs′cus, n. (pl. *-cī*). Lens convex on one side, concave on the other; (math.) figure of crescent form; (phys.) curved upper surface of liquid in tube. [f. Gk *mēniskos* crescent (*mēnē* moon)]

Mĕnn′onīte, n. Member of a Protestant sect that arose in Friesland in 16th c. with tenets resembling those of Quakers & Baptists. [f. *Menno* Simons, founder]

mĕn′o-, comb. form of Gk *mēn mēno-* month, as: ~*pause*, final cessation, ~*rrhă′gia* excessive flow, ~*rrhoe′a*, ordinary flow, of the menses.

mĕnŏl′ogy̆, n. Calendar, esp. that of Greek Church, with biographies of saints. [f. late Gk *mēnologion* (*mēn* month + *logos* account)]

mĕns (-nz) *cŏn′scia* (-shĭa) *rĕc′tī,* L phr. = a clear conscience.

mĕn′sēs (-z), n. pl. Flow of blood from mucous coat of uterus of female, occurring on the average at intervals of lunar month. [L, pl. of *mensis* month]

Mĕn′shĕvĭk, n. Russian socialist of the more moderate party (cf. BOLSHEVIK). [Russ., = minority within the party, cf. BOLSHEVIK]

mĕns (-nz) *sān′a ĭn cŏrp′orĕ sān′ō,* L phr. = sound mind in sound body, used esp. as expressing the ideal of education. [Juvenal X. 356]

mĕn′stru|al (-ōŏ-), a. Of the menses, so ~OUS a.; (astron.) monthly. [f. L *menstrualis* (as MENSTRUUM, see -AL)]

mĕn′stru|āte (-ōŏ-), v.i. Discharge the menses. Hence ~A′TION n. [f. LL *menstruare* (as foll.), see -ATE)]

mĕn′struum (-ōŏ-), n. (pl. *-rua*). Solvent (lit. & fig.). [neut. of L *menstruus* monthly (*mensis* month)]

měn'surable, a. Measurable, having fixed limits; (mus.) having fixed rhythm. [F, or LL *mensurabilis* (LL *mensurare* f. L *mensura* MEASURE, see -BLE)]

měn'sūral, a. Of measure; (mus.)=prec. [f. LL *mensuralis* (as MEASURE, see -AL)]

měnsūrā'tion, n. Measuring; (math.) rules for finding lengths, areas, & volumes. [f. LL *mensuratio* (as MENSURABLE, see -ATION)]

-ment, suf., f. F -*ment* (or direct) f. L -*mentum*, forming nn. expr. result or means of vbl action, as *fragmentum*, *alimentum*, *ornamentum*; f. F are *habili~*, *abridge~*; E formations, freq. *hybrid*, are *amaze~*, *better~*, *embank~*, *bereave~*; a few are on adjj., as *odd~*, *funni~*.

měn'tal¹, a. & n. Of the mind; done by the mind, as ~ *arithmetic* (performed without use of written figures); (colloq.) affected with ~ disorder; ~ *patient* (under care for disordered mind); ~ RESERVATION; ~ *home*, *hospital*, ASYLUM; (n., colloq.) ~ case or patient. Hence~LY² adv. [ME, f. OF, or LL *mentalis* (*mens -ntis* mind, see -AL)]

měn'tal², a.· Of the chin. [F, f. L *mentum* chin, see -AL]

měntǎl'itў, n. The being mental or in or of the mind; (degree of) intellectual power; (loosely) mind, disposition, character. [f. MENTAL¹+-ITY]

měntā'tion, n. Mental action; state of mind. [f. L *mens -ntis* mind, see -ATION]

měn'thŏl, n. Camphor-like substance got from oil of peppermint etc., used to relieve neuralgia etc. [G, f. L *mentha* mint, see -OL(2)]

měn'tion¹, n. Mentioning, naming, (of thing); = ~ in dispatches; *honourable ~*, award of merit to candidate in examination, work of art, etc., not entitled to prize. [ME, f. OF, f. L *mentionem* (*menroot* of *mens* mind, see -ION)]

měn'tion², v.t. Refer to, remark upon, specify by name (esp. thing not obviously essential to context, as *this was expressly ~ed*; *that*); (in deprecation of apology or thanks) *don't ~ it*; (introducing fact or thing of secondary or, as rhet. artifice, of primary importance) *not to ~*. [f. F *mentionner* (as prec.)]

měn'tŏr, n. Experienced & trusted adviser. [F, f. Gk *Mentōr* adviser of Telemachus (root *men-* think)]

měn'ū (& see Ap.), n. Bill of fare. [F adj. = small, n. = detailed list]

měp'acrine (-ēn), n. Odourless yellow anti-malarial chemical. [f. *methoxyacridine* w. inorganic -p-]

Měphist|ŏph'elēs (-z), n. Evil Spirit to whom Faust, in German legend, sold his soul; fiendish person. Hence ~**ŏphělE'AN**, ~**ophěl'IAN**, aa. [G, of unkn. orig.]

měphit'is, n. Noxious emanation, esp. from the earth; noisome or poisonous stench. So **měphit'IC** a. [L]

měrc'antil|e, a. Of trade, commercial;

~*e theory* (that money is the only wealth); ~*e marine*, shipping employed in commerce; mercenary, ·fond of bargaining. Hence ~ISM, ~IST, nn. [F, f. It. *mercantil* (as MERCHANT)]

Měrcāt'or. See PROJECTION.

měr'cēnar|ỹ, a. & n. **1.** Working merely for money or other reward; hired. **2.** n. Hired soldier in foreign service. Hence ~INESS n. [ME, f. L *mercenarius* (*merces -edis* reward, see -ARY¹)]

|| **měr'c|er**, n. Dealer in textile fabrics, esp. silks & other costly materials. Hence ~ERY(1) n. [ME, f. AF *mercer* (OF -*ier*) f. Rom. **merciarius* (*merx mercis* goods, -ARY¹)]

měr'cerize, -ise (-īz), v.t. Treat (cotton fabrics & thread) with caustic alkali under tension to give greater strength and impart lustre. [J. *Mercer* (d. 1866), patentee, +-IZE]

měrch'andise (-z), n. Commodities of commerce, goods for sale. [ME, f. OF *marchandise* (as foll., see -ISE)]

měrch'ant, n. & a. Wholesale trader, esp. with foreign countries; ~ *prince*, wealthy ~; LAW¹ ~; ~ *ship*, ~*man*, (ship conveying merchandise); ~ (mercantile marine) *service*; ~ (sl.), one given to — (*speed-~*, speed-loving motorist; *lob-~*, slow bowler). [ME, f. OF *marchant* f. Rom. **mercatare* frequent. of *mercari* trade (*merx mercis* merchandise), see -ANT]

měrch'antable, a. Salable, marketable. [ME, f. *merchant* v. (now rare) f. OF *marcheander* (as prec.) +-ABLE]

měr'ciful, a. Having, showing, or feeling mercy. Hence~LY² adv.,~NESS n. [-FUL]

měr'cilĕss, a. Pitiless, showing no mercy. Hence ~LY² adv.,~NESS n. [-LESS]

mercūr'ial, a. & n. **1.** Sprightly, ready-witted, & volatile, whence ~ITY (-ǎlⁱ) n.; of, containing, mercury; (*M~*) of the planet Mercury. **2.** n. ~ drug, whence ~ISM(5) n., ~IZE(5) v.t. Hence ~LY² adv. [ME, f. OF *mercuriel* or L *mercurialis* (MERCURY, -AL)]

měrc'ūrў, n. **1.** (*M~*) Roman god of eloquence, skill, thieving, etc., & messenger of gods, messenger (joc., & often in newspaper titles). **2.** (*M~*) planet nearest to sun. **3.** A white normally liquid metal usu. got from cinnabar & used in barometers, thermometers, amalgams, & mirrors (*the ~ is rising*, weather or temper is improving); quicksilver, whence **mercūr'IC**, **měrc'ūroUS**, aa. (chem.); (fig.) liveliness (*has no ~ in him*). [ME, f. L *Mercurius*, prob. f.*merx -rcis* merchandise]

měr'cў, n. Compassion shown by one to another who is in his power & has no claim to kindness (*have ~ on* or *upon*, *show ~ to*; ~!, ~ *on* or *upon us!*), appeals, or excll. usu. playful of terror or surprise); compassionateness; *at the ~ of*, wholly in the power of, liable to danger or harm from; *that is a ~* (blessing, thing to be thankful for); (joc.) *left to the* *tender mercies of*, exposed to probable rough handling by; ~-*seat*, golden covering of Ark of Covenant, throne of God; (attrib., passing into adj.) administered or performed out of~ or pity for suffering person (~ *killing*). [ME, f. OF *merci* f. L *mercedem* (nom. -*ces*) reward, (Christian L) pity]

mēre¹, n. Lake, pond, (poet., exc. in place names). [OE *mere*, OS, OHG *meri*, ON *marr*, Goth. *mari* cogn. w. L *mare* sea]

mēre², a. That is solely what the noun implies, as *a*~ *swindler, the*~*st buffoonery* (law) ~ *right* (without possession). Hence ~LY² (mēr'lĭ) adv. [f. L *merus* unmixed]

mere³ (mĕ'rĭ), n. Maori war-club, esp. one made of greenstone. [Maori]

mĕrĕtrī'cious (-shŭs), a. Of, befitting, a harlot; (of ornament, literary style, etc.) showily attractive. Hence ~LY² adv., ~NESS n. [f. L *meretricius* f. *meretrix* harlot (*mereri* earn, see -TRIX)+-OUS]

mĕrgăn'ser, n. Diving fish-eating duck. [f. L *mergus* diver + *anser* goose]

mĕrge, v.t. & i. Lose, cause (thing) to lose, character or identity *in* (another), esp. sink (title, estate, *in* greater one). Hence mēr'GENCE n. [f. law F *merger* f. L *mergere mers-* dip]

mēr'ger, n. Merging; combination. [-ER⁴]

mĕrĭd'ian, n. & a. 1. Circle passing through celestial poles & zenith of any place on earth's surface; circle lying in the plane of this & passing through the place & the poles, as ~ *of Greenwich* (of longitude 0° in British maps); point at which sun or star attains highest altitude; prime, full splendour; *calculated for the* ~ (to suit the tastes etc.) *of* (place, people). 2. adj. Of noon; (fig.) of the period of greatest splendour, vigour,· etc. [ME; (n. f. adj.) f. OF *meridien* or L *meridianus* (*meridies* midday f. *medius* middle + *dies* day, see -AN)]

mĕrĭd'ional, a. & n. Of (the inhabitants of) the south of Europe; of a meridian; (n.) inhabitant of the south (esp. of France). [f. OF *meridional* f. LL *meridionalis* (irreg. as prec., -AL)]

meringue' (-ăng), n. Confection of sugar, white of eggs, etc., small cake of this. [F]

meri'nō (-rē-), n. (pl. ~*s*). (Also ~ *sheep*) kind of sheep with fine wool; soft woollen or wool-&-cotton material like French cashmere, orig. of ~ wool; fine woollen yarn. [Sp., prob. f. L *majorinus* of a larger kind (*major* greater, see -INE¹)]

mĕ'rit, n., & v.t. 1. Quality of deserving well; excellence, worth; (usu. pl.) thing that entitles to reward or gratitude; *make a* ~ *of*, view, represent, (one's own conduct) as meritorious; *the* ~*s*, intrinsic rights & wrongs (of case etc., esp. law); *judge* (proposal etc.) *on its* ~*s* (with only its intrinsic excellences etc. in view). 2. v.t. Deserve (reward, punishment). [ME; (vb f. F *mériter*) f. OF *merite* f. L *meritum* neut. p.p. of *mereri* earn, deserve]

mĕrĭtôr'ious, a. (Of person or act) deserving reward, praise, or gratitude (often as term of limited praise, = well-meant, well-meaning). Hence ~LY² adv., ~NESS n. [ME, f. L *meritorius* (*mereri merit-* earn, see -ORY)+-OUS]

mĕrle, n. (arch., Sc.). Blackbird. [F, f. L *merulus, -la*]

mĕrl'in, n. Kind of falcon. [ME, f. AF *merilun* f. OF *esmerillon* augm. (-*oon*) f. *esmeril* f. Rom. *smerillo f. WG *smiril; cf. OHG *smiril* (G *schmerl*)]

mĕrl'on, n. Part of embattled parapet between two embrasures. [F, f. It. *merlone* (*merlo* battlement, perh. f. *mergola* dim. f. L *mergae* pitchfork; see -OON)]

mĕrm'aid, n. Half-human being, with head & trunk of woman & tail of fish. So mĕrm'AN n. [ME, f. MERE¹ + MAID]

mē'ro-, comb. form of Gk *meros* part, in senses ' partly ', ' partial ', as: ~*blast*, ovum that is only partly germinal; ~*hēd'ral*, (of crystal) having less than full number of faces admissible.

-merous, suf. (bot.) = having so many parts, as *dimerous, 5-merous*. [f. Gk as prec. +-OUS]

Mĕrovin'gian (-j-), a. & n. (King) of the Frankish line founded by Clovis & reigning in Gaul & Germany *c.* 500–750. [f. F *Mérovingien* f. med. L *Merovingi* of Germanic orig.]

mē'rriment, n. Hilarious enjoyment, mirth, fun. [f. obs. vb *merry* be merry + -MENT]

mē'rry¹, n. Kind of black cherry. [f. F *merise* taken as pl. (cf. CHERRY)]

mĕ'rry², a. Joyous, mirthful; ~ (pleasant) *England*; *the* ~ *monarch*, Charles II; slightly tipsy; *make* ~, be festive; *make* ~ *over*, make fun of; ~ *andrew*, mountebank's assistant, clown, buffoon, (also fig.); ~ DANCERS; ~-*go-round*, revolving machine with wooden horses or cars; ~-*making*, festivity; ~*thought*, forked bone between neck & breast of bird. Hence mē'rrILY² adv., mē'rrINESS n. (rare). [OE *myr(i)ge*, corresp. to MDu. *merch (whence *merchte* mirth, *mergen* obs. vb *merry*); f. Gmc **murgi-*, whence OHG *murgi* short, Goth. *gamaurgjan* shorten]

*me'sa (mā-), n. High rocky tableland with precipitous sides. [Sp., = table, f. L *mensa*]

mésalliance (see Ap.), n. Marriage with person of inferior social position. [F]

mesdames, mesdemoiselles, See MA-DAME, MADEMOISELLE.

mèseems' (-z), v.i. (arch.). It seems to me. [*me* dat. + SEEMS]

mèsēmbrian'thĕmum, -brў-, n. Kinds of succulent plant with bright flowers. [f. Gk *mesēmbria* noon + *anthemon* flower]

mĕs'enterў, n. Fold of peritoneum attaching some part of intestinal canal to posterior wall of abdomen. Hence mĕs-èntĕ'rIC a., mĕsènterIT'IS n. [f. med. L

f. Gk *mesenterion* (MESO-+*enteron* intestine)]

mesh[1], n. Open space, interstice, of net; (pl.) network, (fig.) snare; (physiol., pl.) interlaced structure; (of teeth of wheels) *in* ~, engaged. [16th c. *meash, mash* f. MDu. *maesche, masche* = OHG *mâsca*; cogn. w. OE *max*, ON *mǫskvi* net]

mesh[2], v.t. & i. Catch in net (lit. & fig.); (of teeth of wheel) be engaged (*with* others). [f. prec.]

mes'ial (mēz-, mĕs-), a. Of; in, directed towards, middle line of a body. Hence ~LY[2] adv. [irreg. f. Gk *mesos* middle +-IAL]

mes'mer|ism (mĕz-), n. Hypnotic state, usu. involving insensibility to pain & muscular rigidity, produced on patient by operator's influence over will & nervous system; doctrine concerning, influence producing, this. Hence **mĕs-mĕ'ric** a., ~IST, ~IZA'TION, nn., ~IZE(4) v.t., (mĕz-). [F. A. *Mesmer*, Austrian physician, d. 1815, +-ISM]

mesne (mēn), a. Intermediate, as ~ *profits* (received from estate by wrongful tenant between two dates); ~ *process*, proceedings in suit intervening between primary & final process; (feud.) ~ *lord* (holding of superior lord). [ME, altered sp. of AF *meen* MEAN[2]]

mĕs'o-, comb. form of Gk *mesos* middle, intermediate, as; ~*cephăl'ic*, (of skull) intermediate between BRACHYCEPHALIC and DOLICHOCEPHALIC; ~*gas'ter*, membrane attaching stomach to dorsal wall of abdomen; ~*lith'ic*, of stone age between palaeolithic & neolithic; ~*phyll*, inner tissue of leaf; ~*tron*, sub-atomic positive or negative particle having a mass about 200 times that of an electron; *M*~*zō'ic,*of second geological period (cf. CAINOZOIC, PALAEOZOIC).

mĕs'ŏn, n. (phys.). Fundamental particle intermediate in mass between proton & electron, found in cosmic rays & atomic nuclei. [f. Gk *mesos* middle]

Mĕs'pot, n. (sl.). Mesopotamia. [abbr.]

mĕs'quit(e) (-kēt), n. N.-Amer. leguminous tree; (also ~*-grass*) kinds of grass growing near this. [f. Mex. Sp. *mezquite*]

mĕss[1], n. 1. Portion of liquid or pulpy food (freq. *savoury* ~); ~ *of pottage*, material comfort etc. for which something higher is sacrificed (*Gen.* xxv. 29–34); liquid or mixed food for hounds etc.; concoction, medley. 2. Dirty or untidy state of things; *make a* ~ *of*, bungle (undertaking). 3. Company of persons who take meals together, esp. in the fighting services; meal so taken, as *at* ~, *go to* ~ (often attrib., as ~*-jacket*, coat worn at ~); ~*'mate*, one of the same (usu. ship's) ~. Hence ~'Y[2] a. (~*y floor, food, job*), ~'ILY[2] adv., ~'INESS n. [ME, f. OF *mes* f. LL *missus* course at dinner p.p. of *mittere* send]

mĕss[2], v.t. & i. Make a mess of, dirty,

(thing), freq. ~ *up*; muddle (business); potter *about*; take one's meals (*with* or abs.). [f. prec.]

mĕss'age[1], n. Oral or written communication sent by one person to another; prophet's, writer's, preacher's, inspired communication. [ME, f. OF, f. Rom. *missaticum* (*mittere* miss- send, see -AGE)]

mĕss'age[2], v.t. Send as a message; transmit (plan etc.) by signalling etc. [f. prec.]

mĕss'enger, n. One who carries a message; paper sent up string from flier to kite; endless rope passing from capstan to cable to haul it in. [ME & OF *messagier* (prec., -ER[1]); -*n*- as in *passenger*]

Mĕssi'ah (-*a*), n. Promised deliverer of Jews; Christ as this; liberator of oppressed people or country. Hence ~SHIP n. [ME *Messie* f. OF, *Messias* f. LL f. Gk *Messias* f. Heb. *mashiaḥ* anointed; *Messiah* alt. sp. to give the wd a more Hebraic aspect]

Mĕssiăn'ic, a. Of the, inspired by hope or belief in a, Messiah. [prec., -AN, -IC]

messieurs' (mĕsyĕr'), n. pl. Pl. of MONSIEUR or (in abbr. form *Messrs*, pron. mĕs'erz) of Mr, used esp. as prefix to name of firm, or introducing list of gentlemen.

mĕss'uage (-swǐj), n. (law). Dwelling-house with outbuildings & land assigned to its use. [ME, f. AF *messuage*, perh. alt. sp. f. OF *mesnage* dwelling f. Rom. *mansionaticum* (MANSION, -AGE)]

mĕsti'zō (-tē-), n. (pl. ~*s*). Spanish or Portuguese half-caste, esp. child of Spaniard & Amer.-Indian. [Sp.]

mĕt[1]. See MEET[2].

mĕt[2], a. (colloq.). Meteorological etc. [abbr.]

mĕta- in comb. (before vowel *met-*, before aspirate *meth-*) = Gk *meta* with, after; occas. w. sense ' change '.

mĕtăb'olism, n. Process, in organism or single cell, by which nutritive material is built up into living matter (*constructive* ~) or protoplasm is broken down into simpler substances (*destructive* ~). So **mĕtabŏl'ic** a., **mĕtăb'olize**(3) v.t. [f. Gk *metabolē* change f. META(*ballō* throw) change+-ISM]

mĕtacărp'us, n. Part of hand between wrist & fingers. [f. META-+Gk *karpos* wrist]

mĕt'age, n. Official measuring of load of coal etc.; duty paid for this. [f. METE[2] +-AGE]

mĕtagĕn'esǐs, n. Alternation between sexual & asexual reproduction. So **mĕta-gĕnĕt'ic** a. [META-+GENESIS]

mĕt'al, n., & v.t. (-ll-). 1. Any of a class of substances represented by gold, silver, copper, iron, lead, tin, etc., all of which are crystalline when solid and many of which are opaque, ductile, malleable, of high specific gravity, good conductors of heat & electricity, and characterized by a peculiar lustre; BELL[1], BRITANNIA, GUN,

WHITE, YELLOW, ~; HEAVY ~; (mil.) tanks, armoured vehicles, etc.; material used for making glass, in molten state; (also *road*-~) broken stone for macadam roads or railway; || (pl.) rails of a railway line (*train leaves the* ~*s*, is derailed). 2. v.t. Furnish, fit, with ~; mend (road) with ~. [ME, f. OF, or L f. Gk *metallon* mine]

mĕtăll′ic, a. Of metal(s); ~ *currency*, gold, silver, copper, etc., cf. PAPER; characteristic of metals as ~ *lustre* (peculiar sheen of metals), ~ *sound*. So **mĕt′allĭNE**[1] a. [f. F (-*ique*), or L f. Gk *metallikos* (as METAL, see -IC)]

mĕt′allĭz|e, -is|e (-īz), v.t. Render metallic; coat with thin layer of metal; vulcanize (rubber). Hence ~A′TION n. [-IZE]

mĕtallŏg′raphў, n. Descriptive science of internal structure of metals. [f. METAL +-GRAPHY)]

mĕt′alloid, a. & n. 1. Having form or appearance of metal. 2. n. Element with characteristics both of metals and non--metals. [-OID]

mĕtăll′urgў (-ler-; or mĕt′al-), n. Art of working metals, esp. of extracting metals from their ores. Hence **mĕtallūr′gĭc(AL)** aa., **mĕtăll′urgĭST** (-ler-) n. [f. Gk *metallourgos* metal-worker (*metallon* METAL + -*ergos* -worker), see -Y[1]]

mĕt′amēre, n. (zool.). One of several similar segments of a body. [f. META- + Gk *meros* part]

mĕtamĕ′ric, a. (Chem.) having same composition & molecular weight, but different chemical properties; (zool.) of metameres. So **mĕtăm′erISM** n. (chem., zool.). [as prec. + -IC]

mĕtamŏrph′|ic, a. Of, marked by, metamorphosis; (geol., of rock) that has undergone transformation by natural agencies, whence ~ISM n. [f. META- + Gk *morphē* form + -IC]

mĕtamŏrph′ōse (-z), v.t. Change in form, turn (*to, into*, new form); change nature of. [f. foll.; cf. *anchylose, diagnose*]

mĕtamŏrph′osis, n. (pl. -*oses*, pr. -ēz). Change of form (by magic or by natural development etc.); changed form; change of character, conditions, etc. [L, f. Gk *metamorphōsis* f. META(*morphoō* f. *morphē* form)]

mĕt′aphor, n. Application of name or descriptive term to an object to which it is not literally applicable (e.g. *a glaring error*); instance of this; *mixed* ~, combination of inconsistent ~. Hence **mĕtaphŏ′rĭcAL** a., **mĕtaphŏ′rĭcALLY**[2] adv. [f. F *métaphore* or L f. Gk *metaphora* f. META(*pherō* bear) transfer]

mĕt′aphrāse (-z), n., & v.t. Translation, esp. word-for-word; (v.t.) put into other words. So **mĕtaphrăs′tIC** a. [f. Gk *metaphrasis* f. META*phrazō* translate]

mĕtaphўs′ical (-z-), a. & n. 1. Of metaphysics; based on abstract general

reasoning; over-subtle; incorporeal; supernatural; visionary; (of some 17th c. poets, esp. Donne) addicted to fanciful conceits and far-fetched imagery. 2. n. (esp. pl.). *The M*~*s*, ~ poets. Hence ~LY[2] adv. [-AL]

mĕtaphўs′|ics (-z-), n. pl. (often treated as sing.). Theoretical philosophy of being & knowing; philosophy of mind; (pop.) abstract or subtle talk, mere theory. So ~I′CIAN (-ĭshn) n., ~ĭCIZE(2) v.i. [ME -*ic*, later -*ics* (see -IC 2) f. med. L *metaphysica* fem. sing. & neut. pl., f. med. Gk *phusika* f. Gk *ta meta ta phusika* the works *meta*-(of Aristotle) placed after thePHYSICS]

mĕt′aplăsm (-z-), n. (biol.). Part of protoplasm that contains formative material. [META- + -*plasm* as in PROTOPLASM]

mĕtapŏl′itics, n. pl. Abstract political science (often derog.). Hence **mĕtapŏlit′icAL** a., **mĕtapŏliti′CIAN** (-ĭshn) n. [META-, after METAPHYSICS]

mĕtapsych′ics (-sīk-), n. pl. Psychical research. [META- + PSYCHICS, after *metaphysics*]

mĕtăs′tasis, n. (pl. -*ses*, pr. -sēz). Transference of bodily function, disease, etc., from one part or organ to another; transformation of chemical compounds into others in process of assimilation by an organism. So **mĕtastăt′ic** a. [LL f. Gk, f. *methistēmi* change]

mĕtatărs′|us, n. (anat.).. Group of five long bones of foot between tarsus & toes. Hence ~AL a. [META-]

mĕtăth′esis, n. (pl. -*ses*, pr. -sēz). (Gram.) transposition of sounds or letters in word; (chem.) interchange of atoms between two molecules. [LL f. Gk, f. META(*tithēmi* place) transpose]

métayage (mĕt′āyahzh), n. Land tenure in which farmer pays part (usu. half) of produce as rent to owner, who furnishes stock & seed. [F, see foll., -AGE]

mĕtayer (mĕt′āyā), n. Holder of land on prec. system. [F, f. med. L *medietarius* (*medietas* MOIETY, see -ARY[1])]

mēte[1], n. Boundary, boundary stone, esp. (law) ~*s & bounds*. [ME, f. OF, f. L *meta* goal]

mēte[2], v.t. (literary). (Poet.) measure; portion *out*, allŏt, (punishment, reward); || ~-*wand, -yard*, (fig.) standard of estimation. [OE, OS *metan*, OHG *mezzan*, ON *meta*, Goth. *mitan* f. Gmc **met-, *mæt-* MEET[3]]

mĕtĕmpī′ric, n. (Also ~*s*) philosophy of things outside the sphere of experience; believer in this. Hence ~AL a., ~IST n. [f. META- + EMPIRIC, after *metaphysics*]

mĕtĕmpsŷchōs′|is (-k-), n. (pl. ~*es*, pr. -ēz). Transmigration of soul of human being or animal at death into new body of same or different species. Hence ~IST(2) n. [LL f. Gk (META- + *en* in + *psukhē* soul + -OSIS)]

mĕt′ĕor, n. (Any atmospheric phenomenon, esp.) shooting star, small mass of matter from celestial space rendered luminous by collision with earth's atmosphere. [ME, f. med. L *meteorum* f. Gk *meteõros* lofty, (neut. pl.) atmospheric phenomena (META- +*aeirō* raise)]

metĕŏ′ric, a. Of the atmosphere; dependent on atmospheric conditions; of meteors; (fig.) dazzling, rapid. [prec. + -IC, partly f. med. L *-icus*]

mĕt′eor|ite, n. Fallen meteor, meteoric stone. So ~OLITE n. [METEOR+-ITE[1]]

mĕt′eorograph (-ahf), n. Apparatus recording meteorological phenomena. [METEOR, -GRAPH]

mĕt′eor|oid, n. Body moving through space, of same nature as' those which by passing through atmosphere become visible as meteors. Hence ~oid′AL a. [-OID]

metĕor|ŏl′ogў, n. Study of motions & phenomena of atmosphere, esp. for weather forecast; atmospheric character (*of region*). Hence or cogn. ~olŏ′gic(AL) aa., ~olŏ′gicaLLY[2] adv., ~ŏl′ogist n. [f. Gk *meteōrologia* (as METEOR, -LOGY)]

mĕt′er, n. Person, thing, that measures, esp. *gas, water, etc.*, ~~, instruments for recording volume of gas etc. supplied. [(1) person: 14th c. f. METE[2]+-ER[1]; (2) instrument: 19th c., prob. application of (1) suggested by *gasometer* & other wds w. foll. suf.]

-meter, suf. in names of measuring instruments on Gk nn. (but not on Gk anal.), as *barometer*, L nn., as *calorimeter*, mod. wds as if Gk or L, as *gasometer*, or without assim. to Gk or L, as *ammeter*. [f. Gk *metron* measure]

mĕth′āne, n. (chem.). Odourless colourless inflammable gaseous hydrocarbon, marsh gas, fire-damp. [f. METH(YL)+-ANE]

methĕg′lin, n. (hist., dial.). Spiced kind of mead. [f. W *meddyglyn* (*meddyg* healing f. L *medicus* + *llyn* liquor)]

methinks′, v.i. (arch.; past *methought* pr. -awt). It seems to me. [ME dat. + THINKS]

mĕth′od, n. Special form of procedure esp. in any branch of mental activity, whence ~ŏl′OGY n.; orderly arrangement of ideas; orderliness, regular habits; *there's ~ in his etc. madness*, (joc.) his conduct or proposal is not so mad as it seems; (nat. hist.) scheme of classification. Hence or cogn. **mĕthŏd′ICAL** a., **mĕthŏd′icaLLY[2]** adv. [f. F (*-ode*), or L f. Gk *methodos* (META-+*hodos* way)]

mĕth′odist, n. 1. (*M~*) member of any of several religious bodies (now united) originating in the evangelistic movement of Charles & John Wesley & George Whitefield, whence **mĕthodis′tic**(AL) aa., **mĕthodis′ticaLLY[2]** adv. 2. (derog.). Person of strict religious views. 3. One who follows a method, esp. in nat. hist. Hence **Mĕth′odISM** n. [-IST]

mĕth′odize, -ise (-īz), v.t. Reduce to order, arrange in orderly manner. [-IZE]

methought. See METHINKS.

Mĕthus′elah (-ōōzela), n. A pre-Noachian patriarch who is stated to have lived 969 years (hence as type of longevity). [Heb.]

mĕth′ўl, n. Radical of ~ alcohol (wood spirit) present in many organic compounds. Hence **mĕthўl′ic** a. [F (& G) *mēthyl*, back form. f. F *mēthylene* (Gk *methu* wine + *hulē* wood)]

mĕth′ўlāte, v.t. Mix, impregnate, (esp. spirit of wine, to make it unfit for drinking, so as to exempt it from duties) with methyl alcohol, as ~*d spirit*. [-ATE[3]]

mĕtic′ūlous, a. Over-scrupulous about minute details; (pop.) very careful, accurate. Hence ~LY[2] adv. [f. L *meticulosus*, (or F *-eux*), f. *metus* fear, see -CULE, -OUS]

mētier (mĕt′yā), n. One's trade, profession, or line. [F]

mĕt′is, n. Offspring of white & American Indian, esp. in Canada. [f. F *métis* f. LL *misticius* (*miscēre* mix), whence MESTIZO]

Mĕton′ic, a. ~ *cycle*, period of 19 years (235 lunar months) covering all the changes of the moon. [*Meton*, Athenian astronomer of 5th c. B.C.]

mĕton′ўmў, n. Substitution of the name of an attribute for that of the thing meant (e.g. *crown* for *king*). Hence **mĕtonўm′ICAL** a., **mĕtonўm′icaLLY[2]** adv. [f. LL f. Gk *metōnumia* (META-+*onoma* name)]

mĕt′ope (-opĭ, -ōp), n. (archit.). Square space between triglyphs in Doric frieze. [f. L f. Gk *metopē* (META-+*opē* hole for beam)]

mē′tre[2] (-ter), n. Any form of poetic rhythm, determined by character & number of feet. Hence **mĕtri′CIAN** (-ĭshn), **mĕt′rICS, mĕt′rIST**, nn. [ME, f. OF, f. L f. Gk *metron* measure; OE *meter* dir. f. L]

mē′tre[2] (-ter), n. Unit of length in metric system (39·37 in.). [f. F *metre* (as prec.)]

mĕt′ric, a. Of the METRE[2]; ~ *system*, decimal measuring-system with the metre, & the litre & gram determined by it, as units of length, capacity, & weight (the prefixing to *metre* etc. of the Greek-derived *deca-, hecto-, kilo-*, denotes multiplication by 10, 100, 1,000, as *kilo-metre* 1,000 metres; that of the Latin-derived *deci-, centi-, milli-*, division by 10, 100, 1,000, as *decilitre* tenth of a litre). [f. F *mētrique* (prec., -IC)]

mĕt′rical, a. Of, composed in, metre, esp. ~ *psalms*; of, involving, measurement, as ~ *geometry*. Hence ~LY[2] adv. [ME, f. OF, or L f. Gk *metrikos* (METRE[1], -ICAL)]

mĕtrŏl′ogў, n. Science, system, of weights & measures. Hence **mĕtrolŏ′gic**AL a. [as METRE[1]+-LOGY]

mĕt′ronōme, n. (mus.). Instrument marking time by means of pendulum, beating rod, etc. Hence **mĕtronŏm′ic** a. [as METRE[1]+Gk *nomos* law]

mĕtrŏp′olis, n. Chief city of a country; capital; ‖ *the ~*, London; metropolitan bishop's see; centre of activity. [LL, f. Gk *metropolis* parent State (*mētĕr -tros* mother+*polis* city)]

metropol'itan, a. & n. Of a or the metropolis; belonging to, forming (part of), mother country as dist. from its colonies etc.; of an ecclesiastical metropolis; ∼ (*bishop*), bishop having authority over bishops of a province, in the West equivalent to archbishop, in Greek church ranking above archbishop & below patriarch, whence ∼ATE[1] (-*at*) n.; ∼ *magistrate*, paid London magistrate, cf. STIPENDIARY; inhabitant of a metropolis. [f. LL *metropolitanus* f. Gk *mētropolĭtēs* (as prec., -ITE[1]), see -AN]

•**metry**, suf. in names of systems corresp. to instruments in -METER on anal. of Gk *geōmetria* GEOMETRY, but also in hybrids, as *alkalimetry*. [f. Gk -*metria* (-*metrēs* measurer, as METRE[1])]

met'tl|e, n. Quality of disposition; natural ardour; spirit, courage; *be on one's* ∼*e* (incited to do one's best). Hence (-)∼ED[2] (-ld), ∼ESOME (-tls-), aa. [var. of METAL n.]

mē'um, n. ∼ *& tū'um*, mine & thine (used to express rights of property). [L, neut. of *meus*]

mew[1], n. (Also *sea*-∼) gull, esp. common gull. [OE *mǣw*, OS *mēu*, MDu., MLG *mēwe* (whence G *möwe*)]

mew[2], n., & v.t. 1. Cage for hawks, esp. while moulting. 2. v.t. Put (hawk) in ∼; (fig.) shut *up*, confine. [ME, f. OF *mue*, f. *muer* (foll.)]

mew[3], v.t.(arch.). (Of hawk) moult, shed, (feathers). [ME, f. OF *muer* f. L *mutare* change]

mew[4], v.i., & n. 1. (Of cat, sea-birds) utter sound *mew*. 2. n. This sound, esp. of cat. [ME; imit.]

mewl, **mūle**, v.i. Cry feebly, whimper; mew like cat. [imit., cf. MIAUL]

‖ **mews**, n. Set of stabling round open yard. [pl. (now used as sing.) of MEW[2]; orig. of royal stables on site of hawks' mews]

me'zzanine (-ēn), n. Low storey between two others (usu. between ground & first floors); (theatr.) floor beneath stage. [F, f. It. *mezzanino* dim. of *mezzano* f. L *medianus* MEDIAN]

mè'zzo (-dzō), adv. (Mus.) half, moderately, as ∼ FORTE[2], PIANO[1]; ∼-*rĭlie'vo* (-lyāvō), half-relief, in which figures project half their true proportions; ∼-*sopra'no*, (person with, part for) voice between soprano & contralto. [It., f. L *medius* middle]

me'zzotint (-dz-), n., & v.t. 1. Method of engraving in which plate is roughened uniformly, lights & half-lights being given by scraping away the roughness thus produced, deep shadows by leaving it; print produced by this. 2. v.t. Engrave in ∼. [f. It. *mezzotinto* (also used in E) f. *mezzo* half+*tinto* TINT]

mi (mē), **mē**, n. (mus.). Third note of octave. [first syllable of L *mira*, see GAMUT]

miaow (mǐow'), n., & v.i. (Make) cry of cat. [imit.]

miãs'm|a (-z-), n. (pl. ∼*ata*, ∼*as*). Infectious or noxious emanation. Hence ∼AL, ∼ãt'ic, aa., (-z-). [Gk, f. *miainō* pollute, see -M)]

miaul', v.i. Cry like cat. [f. F *miauler*, imit.]

mic'a, n. Any of several minerals composed of silicate of aluminium with other silicates, found in small glittering scales in granite etc., or in crystals, used as an (electrical) insulator; ∼-*schist*, -*slate*, slaty rock of quartz & ∼. Hence **micA'CEOUS** (-āshus) a. [L, = crumb]

Micaw'ber, n. ∼, *Mr* ∼, *Wilkins* ∼, sanguine idler trusting that something good will turn up. Hence ∼ISM(3) n. [person in Dickens's *David Copperfield*].

mice. See MOUSE[1].

Mich'ael (-kel), n. An archangel; *Order of St* ∼ *& St George*, English civil & military order of knighthood, now esp. awarded for distinguished services abroad; ∼*mas* (mǐk'el-), feast of St ∼, Sep. 29, ‖ a quarter-day. [f. Heb. *mikhael* who is like God?]

‖ **mic'kle**, mŭc', a. & n. (arch., Sc.). Much, great; (n.) a large amount (in prov. *many a little*, or *pickle*, *makes a* ∼). [OE *micel*, OS *mikil*, OHG *mihhil*, ON *mikell*, Goth. *mikils* f. Gmc **mikilaz*, cogn. w. Gk *megalo*-]

mic'ro-[1], comb. form of Gk *mikros* small, as: ∼*cĕphăl'ic* a. & n., (person) with abnormally small head, so ∼*cĕph'alous* a.; ∼*film* n. P, (photographic reproduction on) a very small film; (v.t. & i.) photograph on ∼film; ∼*lith'ic*, constructed of small stones, marked by monuments so constructed; ∼*logy* (-ŏl'-), hair-splitting; ∼*meter* (-ŏm'-), instrument for measuring small objects or (astron.) distances, so ∼*met'rical*, ∼*metry* (-ŏm'-); ∼-*organism*, organism of (ultra) microscopic size; ∼*phŏt'ograph* (of microscopic object on magnified scale); ∼*phyte*, microscopic plant, esp. bacterium; ∼*seism* (-sizm), faint earthquake tremor, whence ∼*seismic*, ∼*seis'mograph*, ∼*seismol'ogy*; ∼*spore*, parasitic fungus with small spores, small spore; ∼*tōme*, instrument for cutting thin sections for microscope; ∼*tōne*, mus. interval smaller than semitone; ∼*wave*, Hertzian wave of length between 50 cms & 1 cm; ∼*zȳme*, zymotic microbe.

mic'ro-[2] (etym. as prec.) prefixed in physics to unit-names = the millionth part of the unit; ∼*ampere*, ∼*coulomb*, ∼*farad*, ∼*gram*, ∼*litre*, ∼*metre*, ∼*milli-metre*, *mic'rŏhm*, ∼*volt*.

mic'rōbe, n. Minute living being, plant or animal (esp. of bacteria causing diseases & fermentation). Hence **microb'iAL** a.,

microbiŏl′ogy n. [F (MICRO-¹ + Gk *bios* life)]

mic′rocŏsm (-zm), n. Man viewed as epitome of the universe; any community or complex unity so viewed; miniature representation (*of*). Hence **microcŏs′mic** (-z-) a. [ME, f. med. L MICRO¹(*cosmus* f. Gk *kosmos* world); partly thr. F *microcosme*]

mic′rŏn, n. The millionth of a metre. [f. Gk neut. of *mikros* small]

mic′rophōne, n. Instrument for intensifying small sounds or converting sound waves into electrical energy which may be reconverted into sound after transmission by wire or wireless, as the transmitter of a telephone or (colloq. abbr. *mike*) the mouthpiece for broadcasting. [f. MICRO-¹ + Gk *phōnē* sound]

mic′roscōpe, n. Instrument magnifying objects by means of lens(es) so as to reveal details invisible to naked eye. [MICRO-¹ + -SCOPE]

microscŏp′ic, a. Of the microscope, whence ~AL a.;. too small to be visible (in detail) without microscope. Hence ~alLY² adv. [-IC]

micrŏs′cop|y̆, n. Use of the microscope. So ~IST n. [-Y¹]

mictūri′tion, n. ·Morbidly frequent desire to make water; (improp.) making water. [f. L *micturire* -*it*-, desiderative f. *mingere mict*- make water, see -ION]

mid¹, a. (sup. ~′*most*). The middle of (usu. after *in*, as *in ~ air*, *career*, *Channel*, *course*, *stream*, *winter*; also with *from*, *to*, etc., as *from ~ June to ~ August*; also in attrib. compounds, as *a ~winter day*); that is in the middle, medium, half, (~ *iron*, golf iron with medium loft; ~ *off*, ~ *on*, = ~wicket off, on; ~′*rib*, central rib of leaf; ~*way′* adv., in middle of distance between places; ~*wicket off* or *on*, fielder near bowler on off, on, side); ~-WING. [OE *midd*, OS *middi*, OHG *mitti*, ON *mithr*, Goth. *midjis* f. Gmc *midhja*- cogn. w. L *medius*]

mid², prep. (poet.). = AMID.

mid′day, n. Noon (often attrib.). [OE *middæg*, see MID¹ & DAY]

midd′en, n. Dunghill; *kitchen ~*, prehistoric refuse-heap, chiefly of shells & bones. [ME *myddyng*, of Scand. orig.; cf. Da. *mødding*]

mid′dle¹, a. (not pred.; rare sup. ~*most*) & n. 1. (Of member of group) so placed as to have same number of members on each side; equidistant from extremities; intermediate in rank, quality, etc.; ~ *course*, *way*, compromise between two extremes; (gram.) applied to a voice in (esp. Greek) verbs that developed passive senses but retained active or quasi-reflexive senses; *M~* ENGLISH; ~ *age*, between youth & old age; ~*-aged*, of such age; *the M~ Ages* (about 1000–1400, or in a wider sense 600–1500); ∥ ~ *article*, brief essay of literary kind in weekly or other

journal often placed between political articles & book-reviews; ~ *class*, class of society between upper & lower (often attrib., ~*-class*); *M~* EAST; ~ (second) *finger*; *M~ Kingdom*, China (orig. of Honan as central & sovereign State); ~ *life*, the ~ part of life, ~ age; *in the ~ of*, while (doi*ng*), during (progress); (log.) ~ (*term*), term common to both premisses, *principle of excluded ~* (that anything must be included either under a given term or under its negative); ~*man*, any of the traders through whose hands commodity passes from producer to consumer; ~ *passage*, sea journey between W. Africa & W. Indies (with ref. to the slave trade); ~ *watch* (from midnight to 4 a.m.); ~*-weight* (boxing), from 11 st. 11 to 11st. 2. 2. n. ~ point or position or part′ (*of*), waist; ~ voice; ∥ ~ article. [OE *middel*, OS -*il*, OHG *mittil* f. WG *middil*- f. Gmc *midhja*- MID]

mid′dle², v.t. (Footb.) return (ball or abs.) from wing to mid field in front of goal; (crick.) strike (ball) with middle of bat; (techn.) place in the middle; (naut.) fold in the middle. [f. prec.]

midd′ling, a. & adv. 1. (Commerc., of goods) of the second of three grades, so ~s n. pl. (also in spec. senses, flour of medium fineness, & comminuted bran); moderately good; second-rate; (colloq.) fairly well (in health), as *I am only ~*. 2. adv. Fairly or moderately, as ~ *good*, *fast*. Hence ~LY² adv. [of Sc. orig., f. MID¹ + -LING¹ & ² (confused)]

midd′y̆, n. See MIDSHIP.

midge, n. Kinds of gnat-like insect; small person. [OE *mycg(e)*, OS *muggia*, OHG *mucca*, f. Gmc *mugi*-]

midg′et, n. Extremely small person, esp. when exhibited as curiosity; very small thing (also attrib.). [f. prec. + -ET¹]

midinĕtte′ (mēdē-), n. Parisian shop-girl (esp. milliner's assistant). [F]

mid′land, n. & a. 1. Middle part of country; (pl.) *the* middle inland counties ·of England). 2. adj. Of, in, the ~ or ~s. [MID + LAND]

mid′night (-nīt), n. The middle of the night, 12 o'clock; intense darkness (often attrib.). [OE *midniht* (MID + NIGHT)]

mid′răsh n. (pl. ~*im*, pr. -ăsh′ĕm). Ancient Jewish commentary on part of Hebrew Scriptures. [Heb.]

mid′riff, n. Diaphragm. [OE *midhrif* (*midd* MID + *hrif* belly)]

mid′ship, n. Middle part of ship or boat; ~*man* (abbr. *middy*—not used by Royal ·Navy), rank between naval cadet & sub-lieutenant; ~*s*, = AMIDSHIPS. [MID + SHIP]

midst, n., adv., & prep. *In the ~ of*, among, during the continuance of; *in our*, *your*, ~, among us, you; (adv., only in phr.) *first*, ~, *& last*; (prep., poet.) in the ~ of. [prob. comb. (1) MID + -*st*, see -ES, & (2) sup. of MID]

mid'summer, n. Period of summer solstice, about June 21; *M~ day*, June 24, ‖ a quarter-day; *~* (the height of) *madness*. [MID]

mid'wife, n. (pl. *-wives*). Woman who assists other women in childbirth. Hence **mid'wifᴇʀʏ(2)** (-wĭfrĭ, *°-wī-*) **n.,** obstetrics. [ME, f. MID¹, or obs prep. *mid* with (cf. G *mit*), +WIFE]

mien (mēn), n. (literary). Air, bearing, of person, as showing character or mood. [prob. aphetic f. obs. *demean* n., assim. to F *mine* expression]

miff, n., & **v.i.** & **t.** (colloq.). Petty quarrel; huff; (v.i.) take offence *with* or *at*; (v.t.) put out of humour. [perh. imit.; cf. G *muff*, exclamation of disgust]

might¹ (mīt), n. Great (bodily or mental) strength; power to enforce one's will (opp. *right*); *with ~ & MAIN²*. [OE *miht*, OS, OHG *maht*, Goth. *mahts* f. Gmc *°mahtiz* f. *°mag- MAY¹*]

might². See MAY¹.

might'|ȳ (-ĭt-), a. & adv. **1.** Powerful, strong, in body or mind; (bibl.)*~y works*, miracles; massive, bulky; (colloq.) great, considerable; HIGH *& ~y*. **2.** adv. (colloq.). Very, as *that is ~y easy*. Hence **~ɪLʏ²** adv., **~ɪɴᴇss** n. (esp. in *your* etc. *high ~iness* as burlesque title). [OE *mihtig* (MIGHT¹) f.-Y²)]

mignon (see Ap.), a. Small & delicately formed. [F]

mignonette' (mĭnyo-), n. **1.** Plant with fragrant flowers; colour of these, greyish green. **2.** Kinds of lace & fine net. [f. F (*-onn*-), dim. of prec.]

migraine' (mē-), n. = MEGRIM (first sense). [as MEGRIM]

migrāte' (or mī'ᴛ), v.i. Move from one place (country, town, college, house) to another; (of birds & fishes) come & go with the seasons. Hence or cogn. **mĭg'ʀᴀɴᴛ** a. & n., **mĭgʀᴀ'ᴛɪᴏɴ, mĭgʀāt́ OR, nn., mĭg'ʀᴀᴛOʀʏ** a. [f. L *migrare*, see -ᴀᴛᴇ³]

mĭka'dŏ, (-kah-), n. (pl. *~s*). Emperor of Japan. [Jap. *mi* august+*kado* door]

‖ mike¹, v.i., & **n.** (sl.). Shirk work, idle; (n.) idling (*on the~*). [orig. unkn.]

mike², n. (colloq.). Microphone. [abbr.]

mil, n. A thousand (*per ~, as per cent*); (pharm., short for) MILLILITRE; unit measure for diameter of wire etc., = ¹⁄₁₀₀₀ in. [f. L *mille* thousand, *millesimum* thousandth]

mil'age, n. Var. of MILEAGE.

Milanese' (-z), a. & n. (pl. same). (Native) of Milan, chief city of Lombardy; *the ~*, territory of old duchy of Milan. [It. (*Milano* Milan), -ᴇsᴇ]

milch, a. (Of domestic mammals) giving, kept for, milk; *~ cow*, (fig.) source of profit, esp. person from whom money is easily drawn. [ME *mielch*, rel. to OE *meolc*, OHG *melch* (G *melk*), ON *mjolkr*; see MILK]

mild, a. Gentle & conciliatory; (of rule, punishment, etc.) not severe; (of weather) moderately warm; (of medicine) operating gently; (of food, tobacco, etc.) not sharp or strong in taste etc.; (of beer) not strongly flavoured with hops, opp. to *bitter*; tame, feeble, lacking in energy or vivacity; *~ steel*, containing small percentage of carbon, strong & tough, but not readily tempered. Hence *~'ᴇɴ⁶* v.t. & i., *~'Lʏ²* adv., *~'ɴᴇss* n. [OE *milde*, OS *mildi*, OHG *milti*, ON *mildr*, Goth. *milds* f. Gmc *°mildh-*]

mil'dew, n., & **v.t.** & **i.** **1.** Destructive growth of minute fungi on plants; similar growth on paper, leather, etc., exposed to damp. **2.** vb. Taint, be tainted, with *~*. Hence *~ʏ²* a. [OE *meledēaw* (= OHG *militou*) f. Gmc *°melith* honey + *°dawwa-* DEW]

mile, n. Unit of lineal measure, in Britain now 1,760 yards (orig. Roman measure of 1,000 paces, about 1,618 yards); *geographical, nautical, ~,* one minute of great circle of earth, fixed by British Admiralty at 6,080 feet; *race* extending over a *~*; *not 100 ~s from*, in or at or close to (as sham-mysterious indication); *~'stone*, pillar set up on road to mark*~s*, (fig.) stage, event, in life. Hence *~'ᴀɢᴇ* (-lĭj) n., *~s* travelled, used, etc.; expenses per *~*. [OE *mīl*, OHG *mīla*, f. WG *°milja* f. L *mīl(l)ia* pl. of *mīlle* thousand]

mil'er, n. (colloq.). Man, horse, qualified or trained specially to run a mile; also in comb., as *three-~*. [-ᴇʀ¹]

Milē'sian (-shn), a. & n. (joc.). Irish(man). [f. *Milesius* fabulous Spanish king whose sons are said to have conquered Ireland *c.* 1300 B.C., +-ᴀɴ]

mil'foil, n. Common yarrow & other plants. [ME & OF f. L *millefolium* (*mille* thousand +*folium* leaf)]

mil'iarȳ, a. (path.). Like millet-seed in size or form, as *~ gland, tubercle*; *~ fever* (marked by rash like measles, with vesicles of form of millet-seed). [f. L *miliarius* (as MILLET, -ᴀʀʏ¹)]

milieu (see Ap.), n. Environment, state of life, social surroundings. [F]

mil'itant, a. Engaged in warfare, as *the Church~*; combative. Hence **mil'iᴛᴀɴᴄʏ** n., *~Lʏ²* adv. [ME, f. OF f. L, as MILITATE, see -ᴀɴᴛ]

mil'itar|ism, n. Spirit, tendencies, of the professional soldier; undue prevalence of military spirit or ideals. So *~ɪᴢᴀ'ᴛɪᴏɴ* n., *~ɪᴢᴇ(3)* v.t. [f. F *militarisme* (as MILITARY, see -ɪsᴍ)]

mil'itarist, n. Student of military science; one dominated by military ideas. [-ɪsᴛ]

mil'itarȳ, a. & n. **1.** Of, done by, befitting, soldiers; *~ band*, wood-wind, brass, & percussion combination; *~ chest*, treasury of army; *~ fever*, enteric; *~ testament*, soldier's nuncupative will.

2. n. (Usu. *the* ~) soldiery, troops, the army. Hence **mil'itari**LY adv. [f. F *militaire* or L *militaris* (*miles -itis* soldier, see -ARY²)]

mil'itāte, v.i. Take part in warfare (usu. fig.); (of facts, evidence) have force, tell, (*against*, rarely *in favour of*, conclusion etc.). [f. L *militare* (*miles -itis* soldier) see -ATE³]

mili'tia (-sha), n. Military force, esp. citizen army; branch of British military service formerly raised by the several counties, usu. by voluntary enlistment; ‖ British conscript army formed 1939; ~*man*, member of the ~. [L (prec., -IA¹)]

milk¹, n. **1.** Opaque white fluid secreted by female mammals for nourishment of their young; (fig.) ~ *for babes*, simple forms of literature, doctrine, etc., opp. to *strong meat*; CONDENSEd ~; ~ *& honey*, abundant means of enjoyment; ~ *of human kindness*, kindness natural to humanity; *no use crying over spilt* ~ (irremediable loss or error); ~-like juice of plants; ~-like preparation of herbs, drugs, etc., as ~ *of almonds*. **2.** ~ *& water*, feeble or mawkish discourse or sentiment (attrib. ~-*&-water*); ~-*bar* (for sale of beverages made from ~, other non--alcoholic drinks, ice cream, etc.); ~-*crust*, skin-eruption in infants; ~-*fever* (occurring to women shortly after childbirth); ~-*leg*, swelling, esp. of legs, after childbirth; ‖ ~-*float*, light low vehicle used in delivering ~; ~'*maid*, woman who milks or works in dairy; ~'*man*, man who sells or delivers ~; ~-*powder*, ~ dehydrated by evaporation; ~ *pudding* (of rice, sago, tapioca, etc., baked with ~ in dish); ~ *punch*, drink made of spirits & ~; ~--SHAKE²; ~'*sop*, spiritless man or youth; ~-*tooth*, temporary tooth in young mammals; ~-*walk*, ~man's round; ~'*weed*, kinds of wild plant with milky juice; ~-*white* (as ~); ~'*wort*, kinds of heath or pasture plant formerly supposed to increase production of ~. [OE *meoluc*, OS *miluk*, OHG *-uh*, ON *mjolk*, Goth. *miluks* f. Gmc **melk-* to milk, cogn. w. L *mulgēre*]

milk², v.t. Draw milk from (cow, ewe, goat); ~ *the ram* or *bull*, engage in hopeless enterprise; get money out of, exploit, (person); (sl.) steal message from (telegraph or telephone wire); extract juice, virus, etc., from (snake etc.). [OE *milcian, meolcian* (as prec.)]

mil'k|y̆, a. Of, like, mixed with, milk; (of liquid) cloudy, not clear; effeminate, weakly amiable; *M*~*y Way*, luminous band of countless stars encircling the heavens. Hence ~ĭNESS n. [-Y²]

mill¹, n. **1.** Building fitted with machinery for grinding corn (often *water*~, *wind*~; *put, go, through the* ~, subject to, undergo, training or experience; *the* ~*s of God grind slowly*, retribution is often delayed).

2. Any mechanical apparatus for grinding corn; apparatus for grinding any solid substance to powder or pulp, as *coffee, pepper, paper,* ~. **3.** Any machine, or building fitted with machinery, for manufacturing processes etc., as *saw, cotton, silk,* ~ (~-*hand*, factory worker). **4.** Pugilistic encounter. **5.** ~'*board*, stout pasteboard for bookbinding etc.; ~-*dam*, dam put across stream to make it available for ~; ~-*pond*, water retained by this (*like a* ~-*pond*, said of calm sea), (joc.) = HERRING-*pond*; ~-*race*, current of water that drives ~-wheel; ~'*stone*, one of pair of circular stones for grinding corn, as NETHER ~*stone, see far into a* ~*stone*, (usu. iron.) be extraordinarily acuté, *between upper & nether* ~*stone*, subject to irresistible pressure; ~*stone grit*, a hard siliceous rock; ~-*wheel*, one (esp. water-wheel) used to drive ~; ~'*wright*, one who designs or erects ~s. [OE *mylen*, OS *mulin*, OHG *muli*(n), f. LL *molinum, -na* (*mola* mill f. *molere* grind)]

mill², v.t. & i. Thicken (cloth etc.) by fulling; grind (corn), produce (flour), in mill; produce regular markings on edge of (coin, esp. in p.p.); beat (chocolate) to froth; beat, strike, fight, (person); (of cattle or persons) move round & round in a mass; ~*ing machine*, machine tool for cutting grooves or slots in metal sheets. [f. prec.]

*mill³, n. One-thousandth of a dollar, money of account. [f. L *millesimum* thousandth part, on anal. of CENT]

millēnār'ian, a. & n. Of the millennium; (person) believing in this. Hence ~ISM n. [as foll. + -AN]

mill'ĕnary̆, a. & n. (Period) of 1,000 years; of, (person) believing in, the millennium. [f. LL *millenarius* consisting of a thousand (*milleni* a thousand each f. *mille* thousand, -ARY¹)]

millĕnn'i|um, n. Period of a thousand years, esp. that of Christ's reign in person on earth (*Rev.* xx. 1–5); (fig.) period of good government, great happiness, & prosperity. Hence ~AL a. [f. L *mille* thousand + *annus* year, on anal. of *biennium* two years' space]

mill'épēde, mill'ī-, n. Kinds of myriapods, with numerous legs usu. placed on each segment in double pairs; kinds of terrestrial crustacean, esp. common woodlouse & armadillo. [f. L *millepeda* woodlouse (*mille* thousand + *pes pedis* foot)]

mill'er, n. Proprietor, tenant, of corn--mill; one who works any mill; kinds of white or white-powdered insect; cock-chafer; ~'s *thumb*, bull-head & other fishes. [MILL¹ + -ER¹]

millĕs'imal, a. & n. Thousandth (part); consisting of thousandths. [f. L *millesimus* (*mille* thousand + -AL)]

mill'ĕt, n. Gramineous plant, native of India, bearing large crop of small nutritious seeds; its seed; ~-*grass*, a tall hand-some grass. [F, dim. of *mil* f. L *milium*]

mill'i-, comb. form of L *mille* thousand, = one thousandth of a — (in metric system), as: ~*gram* ('0154 of English grain); ~*litre* (-ēter; ·061 cub. in.); ~*mētre* (-*ter*; ·0394 in.).

‖ **mill'iard** (-*yard*), n. A thousand millions. [F (*mille* thousand)]

mill'in|er, n. Person (usu. woman) who makes up hats & other female head-gear; *man*~*er*, (fig.) man busied in trifling occupations. Hence~ERY(1) n. [f. *Milan* +-ER[1]; orig.=vendor of Milan goods]

mill'ion (-yon), n. & a. A thousand thousand (things, *of* things, or abs.); a ~ pounds or *dollars*; *the* ~, bulk of the population. Hence ~FOLD a. & adv., ~TH[2] a. & n., (-yon-). [ME, f. OF f. It. *millione* (*mille* thousand +-*one* -OON)]

millionaire' (-yon-), n. Person possessing a million pounds, dollars, francs, etc.; person of great wealth. [f. F *millionnaire* (prec., -ARY[1])]

millipede. See MILLEPEDE.

Mills bŏmb (-z; -m), n. Oval hand-grenade. [inventor (d. 1932)]

milŏr(d)', n. French word for English lord or wealthy Englishman. [f. E *my lord*]

mil'reis (-āis), n. Former Portuguese gold coin. [Port. (*mil* thousand +REIS)]

milt, n., & v.t. 1. Spleen in mammals; analogous organ in other vertebrates; roe of male fish. 2. v.t. Impregnate (roe of female). [OE *milte*, corresp. to MDu. *milte*, OHG *milzi*, ON *milti*, f. Gmc *milt*-prob. cogn. w. MELT]

mil'ter, n. Male fish in spawning time. [-ER[1]]

Miltŏn'ic, a. Of, in the style of, Milton. So **Miltōn'IAN** a. [-IC]

mime, n., & v.i. 1. (Gk or Rom. ant.) simple farcical drama marked by mimi-cry; performer in this; pantomimist, buffoon. 2. v.i. Act with mimic gesture, usu. without words. [f. L f. Gk *mimos*]

mim'eograph (-ahf), n., & v.t. Apparatus for holding stencils of written pages, from which many copies may be taken; (v.t.) reproduce by means of ~. [irreg. f. Gk *mimeomai* imitate, see -GRAPH]

mimēs'is, n. (biol.). Close external re-semblance between animal & another animal or inanimate object. [Gk, = imitation (as prec.)]

mimĕt'|ic, a. Of, addicted to, imitation, mimicry, or mimesis. Hence ~ICALLY adv. [f. Gk *mimētikos* (as prec., see -ETIC)]

mim'ic[1], a. & n. 1. Apt to imitate; imita-tive as opp. to *real*. 2. n. Person skilled in ludicrous imitation. [f. F -*ique*, or L f. Gk *mimikos* (as MIME, see -IC)]

mim'ic[2], v.t. (~*ked*, ~*king*). Ridicule by imitating (person, manner, etc.); copy minutely or servilely; (of things) resemble closely. [f. prec.]

mim'icr|y, n. Mimicking; thing that mimics another; (zool.) = MIMESIS. [MIMIC[1] +-RY]

mim'iny-pim'iny, a. Over-refined, fin-icking. [imit.]

mimōs'a (*or* -z-), n. Kinds of leguminous shrubs, including common sensitive plant. [f. L as MIME +-*osa* fem. suf., see -OSE[1]]

mim'ūlus, n. Kinds of flowering plants, incl. monkey-flower. [app. dim. as prec.]

min'a[1], n. (pl. -*ae*). Ancient-Greek denomination of money; ancient unit of weight in Greece, Egypt, etc., about 1 lb. [L, f. Gk *mna*]

min'a[2], n. Kinds of eastern passerine bird. [f. Hind. *maina*]

minā'cious (-shus), a. Threatening. Hence ~LY[2] adv., minA'CITY n. [f. L *minax* (*minari* threaten), see -ACIOUS]

‖ **minā̄r'**, n. Lighthouse; turret. [f. Arab. *manar* f. root of *nar* fire]

min'arĕt, n. Slender turret connected with mosque, from which muezzin calls people to prayer. [f. Arab. *manarat* (as prec.)]

min'atory, a. Threatening. [f. LL *mina-torius* (*minari* threaten, -ORY)]

mince[1], n. Minced meat; ~'*meal*, mix-ture of currants, raisins, sugar, apples, candied-peel, etc., for ~ *pie* (small round pie containing this); *make* ~*meat of*, de-stroy (person, argument, etc.). [f. foll.]

mince[2], v.t. & i. Cut (meat etc.) small; (usu. w. negative) ~ *matters*, express oneself politely in condemnation; re-strain (one's words) within bounds of politeness; utter (words), walk, with affected delicacy, whence **min'cingLY[2]** adv. [ME, f. OF *mincier* f. Rom. *min-utiare*, as MINUTIA; cf. MINISH]

‖ **Min'cing Lāne**, n. (Used for) the wholesale trade in tea & similar imports. [London street]

mind[1], n. 1. Remembrance, as *have* or *keep in* ~, *bring* or *call to* ~, remember, *go* or *pass out of* ~, be forgotten; TIME[1] *out of* ~. 2. Candid opinion, as *speak* one's ~, *tell* (person) one's ~, *give* him *a piece of* one's ~. 3. *Be of* (person's) ~, agree in opinion with him; *to my* ~, as I think; *be of a* or *one* ~, agree; *know* one's *own* ~, form & adhere to decision; *make up* one's ~, resolve (*to do, to* a course etc., or abs.), reconcile oneself to fact as inevitable (*the crop is ruined, we must make up our* ~*s to that*); *change* one's ~, alter one's pur-pose; *have a good* or *great* ~, *half a* ~, be strongly, somewhat, disposed (to do); *be in two* ~*s*, vacillate, be irresolute; MONTH'*s* ~. 4. Direction of thoughts or desires, as *set* one's ~ *on*, desire to attain, *give* one's ~ (attention) *to*; *to* one's ~, as one would have it. 5. Way of thinking & feeling, as *frame, state, of* ~. 6. Seat of consciousness, thought, volition, & feel-ing. 7. Soul, opp. to *body*; ~'*s eye*, mental view. 8. Person, as embodying mental qualities. 9. Intellectual powers, opp. to will & emotions, whence ~'LESS a. 10. ABSENCE, PRESENCE, of ~; ~-stuff (philos.), supposed rudimentary form of psychical existence regarded as the reality of which matter is an aspect. [ME mynd f. OE gemynd,.~ OHG gimunt, Goth. gamunds f. Gmc *gamundhiz f. root *men-, *man-, *mun-, cogn. w. L mens]

mind², v.t. & i. 1. Bear in mind (chiefly in imperat.); give heed to, as never ~ the expense. 2. Concern oneself (never ~ imperat., take comfort, also as refusal to answer question). 3. Apply oneself to (business etc.; ~ your own business, leave other people's alone). 4. (Chiefly in neg. or quasi-neg. sentences) object to, as would you ~ ringing?, I should not ~ (should like) a cup of tea, if you don't ~ (have no objection). 5. Remember & take care (that thing is done, or omit that). 6. ~ you or ~ (parenth. imperat.), please to observe (but I have no objection, ~ you; now ~, not a word till I give the signal); (sl.)~ your eye, be on the lookout; ~ one's P's & Q's, be careful as to one's words or behaviour. 7. Be on one's guard against or about, as ~ the step (remember there is one). 8. Have charge of. Hence ~'ER¹ n., one whose business it is to attend to something, (now esp.) machine-~er. [f. prec.]

mind′ed, a. Disposed (to do); having (specified) mind, as high, small,-~. [-ED²]

mind′ful, a. Taking thought or care (of, or abs.). Hence ~LY² adv., ~NESS n. [MIND¹+-FUL]

mine¹, n. 1. Excavation in earth for metal, coal, salt, etc.; (fig.) abundant source (of information etc.); iron ore. 2. (Mil. etc.) subterranean gallery in which explosive is placed to blow up fortifications, (formerly) subterranean passage under wall of besieged fortress; receptacle filled with explosive placed in or on ground for destroying enemy personnel or material, or moored beneath or floating on or near surface of water for destroying or impeding enemy ships; ACOUSTIC, MAGNETIC, ~; ~'field, area of land or sea beset with ~s; ~'layer, ship or aircraft for laying ~s; ~'sweeper, ship for clearing away floating or submarine ~s; ~'thrower [tr. of G minenwerfer], trench mortar. [ME, f. OF mine, f. Gallo-Rom. *mina, of Celt. orig.]

mine², v.t. & i. Burrow in (earth); make (hole) underground; make subterranean passages under; (fig.) undermine; (mil. etc.) lay mines under or in; obtain (metal etc.) from mine; dig in (earth etc.) for ore etc. Hence min′ING¹(1) n. (freq. in comb., as coal, gold, -mining; also attrib., as mining engineer). [ME, f. OF miner, rel. to prec.; cf. MINERAL]

mine³, poss. pron. & a. corresponding in pred. & elliptical uses to MY, as it is ~, I have lost ~, me & ~ (my relations), is a friend of ~; also used (arch., poet.) before

noun beginning with vowel or h, as ~ eyes. [OE min, OS, OHG min, ON minn, Goth. meins f. Gmc *mīn- f. *me- ME]

min′er, n. One who works in a mine; soldier whose duty it is to lay mines; SAPPERS & ~s. [ME, f. OF minour (as MINE², see -OR)]

min′eral, a. & n. (Substance) obtained by mining; (belonging to) any of the species into which inorganic substances are classified; ~ KINGDOM; ~ water, water found in nature impregnated with ~ substance, artificial imitation of this, esp. soda-water, also, other effervescent drink, e.g. ginger-beer; || (esp. in pl.) artificial ~ water; ~ WOOL. Hence ~īZA′TION n., ~IZE(3) v.t. & i. [ME, f. OF mineral f. med. L mineralis f. minera f. OF miniere f. *mina MINE¹]

miner|ăl′ogў, n. Science of minerals. Hence ~alŏ′gICAL a.,~alŏ′gICALLY² adv., ~ăl′ogIST n. [f. prec. +-LOGY]

Minĕrv′a, n. Roman goddess of wisdom; ~ press, printing-press in London, ultra-sentimental novels issued from it c. 1800. [L]

min′ĕver, -ĭver, n. Kind of fur used in ceremonial costume. [ME, f. OF menu vair (menu small, as MINUTE³; VAIR)]

mingle (ming′gl), v.t. & i. Mix, blend; ~ their etc. tears, weep together; ~ with, go about among. [late ME mengel f. obs. meng (OE mengan, cogn. w. AMONG) +-LE(3); cf. MDu. mengelen]

|| min′gỳ (-ji), a. (colloq.). Mean, stingy. [prob. portmanteau of MEAN³ and STINGY]

min′iāte, v.t. Paint with vermilion; illuminate (manuscript). [f. L miniare f. MINIUM, see -ATE³]

min′iature, n. & a., & v.t. 1. Picture in illuminated manuscript; small-scale minutely finished portrait, usu. on ivory or vellum; this branch of painting, as portrait in ~; reduced image; in ~, on a small scale. 2. adj. Represented on small scale, small-scale. 3. v.t. Represent in ~. Hence min′iatŭRIST (-ya-) n. [f. It. f. L miniare (as prec., -URE)]

min′icăb, n. Small taxi. [MINI(ATURE) CAB]

min′ifў, v.t. Represent as smaller or less important than it is; lessen in size or importance. [irreg. f. L minor less, see -FY]

min′ikin, n. & a. Diminutive (creature); affected, mincing. [f. Du. minneken (minne love +-kijn -KIN)]

min′im, n. (Mus.) note half the value of SEMIbreve; single down-stroke of pen; creature of the smallest size or importance; sixtieth part of fluid drachm. [f. L minimus smallest]

min′imal a. Very minute; the least possible, of minimum. [as prec., see -AL]

min′imalist, n. Person ready to accept a minimum provisionally (opp. MAXIMAL-IST). [prec., -IST]

min′imīz|e, -is|e (-īz), v.t. Reduce to, estimate at, smallest possible amount or degree. Hence ~A'TION n. [as prec., see -IZE]

min'imum, n. (pl. -ima), & a. Least amount attainable, usual, etc.; ~ thermometer (automatically recording lowest temperature within period); ~ wage (than which, by law or agreement, less is not to be offered); (adj.) smallest (possible). [L, neut. as foll.]

|| min'imus, a. (In schools) youngest of the name, as Jones ~. [L, = least]

min'ion (-yon), n. Favourite child, servant, animal, etc. (derog.); royal favourite; slave; ~s of the law, gaolers, police, etc.; (print.) size of TYPE. [f. F mignon, of Gaulish orig.]

min'ish, v.t. & i. (arch.). Diminish (t. & i.); reduce in power etc. [ME, f. OF menusier, var. of mincier: see MINCE²]

min'ister¹, n. Person employed in execution of (purpose, will, etc.); person administering department of State; PRIME ~; political agent accredited by one State to another, cf. AMBASSADOR; clergyman esp. in Presbyterian and Nonconformist Churches; (also ~ general) superior of some religious orders; || M~ of State, departmental senior ~ intermediate between head of department and junior ~. [ME, f. OF ministre f. L minister servant (minus less)]

min'ister², v.i. & t. Render aid or service (to person, cause, etc.; ~ing angel, w. ref. to Mark i. 13, esp. of sick-nurse etc.); be helpful, contribute, (to result); (arch.) furnish, supply, (help etc.). [ME, f. OF ministrer f. L ministrare (prec.)]

minister'ial, a. Concerned with the execution of law; subsidiary, instrumental; of a minister of religion or his office; of a minister of State; siding with the Ministry against Opposition, whence ~IST(2) n. Hence ~LY² adv. [f. obs. F -ial (now -iel), or LL ministerialis (as MINISTRY, see -AL)]

ministrā'tion, n. Ministering, esp. in religious matters; supplying (of). So min'istrANT a. & n., min'istrative a. [ME, f. L ministratio (as MINISTER², see -ATION)]

min'istry, n. Ministering; the body of ministers of the government or of religion; the clerical profession; State department, as M~ of Agriculture, Fisheries, and Food, of Aviation, of Defence, of Education, of Health, of Housing and Local Government, of Labour, of Pensions and National Insurance, of Power, of Public Building and Works, of Transport. [ME, f. L ministerium (as MINISTER¹)]

min'ium, n. Red lead; cinnabar. [L]

min'iver. See MINEVER.

mink, n. Small semi-aquatic stoat-like animal; its fur. [cf. Sw. mänk, menk]

minn'esinger, n. German lyrical poet & singer in 12–14th cc. [G (minne love)]

Minn'ie, n. (army sl.). Trench mortar. [abbr. of G minenwerfer minethrower]

minn'ow (-ō), n. Small freshwater fish (loosely used of several kinds, esp. stickleback); Triton among the ~s, one who seems great from insignificance of others. [late ME menow, repr. OE *mynwe, myne, = OHG mun(i)wa (G münne)]

Minō'an, a. (archaeol.). Of the Cretan civilization (3000–1500 B.C.) named from king Minos. [f. Gk Minōs + -AN]

min'or, a. & n. 1. Lesser (not followed by than), as ~ PROPHETS; ~ canon, clergyman assisting in daily cathedral service, not member of chapter; comparatively unimportant, as ~ poet; (log.) ~ term, subject of conclusion of categorical syllogism, ~ premiss (containing this); (mus.) ~ interval, see MAJOR², ~ key (in which scale has ~ third), (fig.) conversation in a ~ key (doleful); ~ sixt (bridge), diamonds or clubs; (in schools) Jones ~ (the younger). 2. n. Franciscan friar; ~ term or premiss; person under age. [L, = less]

Minōrc'a, n. One of the Balearic Isles; ~ (fowl), black variety brought from Spain. [f. Sp. Menorca]

minō'rity, n. State of being under age, period of this; smaller number or part, esp. smaller party voting together against majority; number of votes cast for this. [f. F minorité or med. L minoritas (as MINOR, see -TY)]

Min'otaur (-tȯr), n. The ~, fabulous monster, half bull half man, fed with human flesh. [f. Gk Minōtauros (Minōs, king of Crete, husband of ~'s mother, + tauros bull)]

min'ster, n. Church of a monastery; name given to some large or important churches. [OE mynster= OHG munist(i)rt f. Rom. monisterium f. LL f. Gk monastērion MONASTERY]

min'strel, n. Mediaeval singer or musician, who sang or recited (often his own) poetry; (hist.) person who entertained his patrons with singing, buffoonery, etc.; (pl.) band of public entertainers, with blacked faces etc., performing songs & music ostensibly of Negro origin. [ME, f. OF menestral (as MINISTERIAL)]

min'strelsy, n. Minstrel's art; minstrels; minstrel poetry. [ME, f. OF menestralsie, as prec.]

mint¹, n. Place where money is coined, usu. under State authority; (fig.) source of invention etc.; (transf.) ~ state, condition, (of books, prints, postage-stamps, etc.) fresh, unsoiled, perfect; vast sum of money; ~-mark, mark placed on coin to show at what ~ it was struck (also fig.); ~-master, superintendent of coinage at ~. [OE mynet, OS munita, OHG munizza f. WG *munita f. L moneta MONEY]

mint², v.t. Make (coin) by stamping metal; invent, coin, (word, phrase, etc.). Hence min'tAGE(3, 4) n. [f. prec.]

mint³, n. Aromatic plant, much used in cookery; ~ sauce (of finely chopped

~ with vinegar & sugar, eaten with roast lamb), || also, with pun on *mint*[1], money. [OE *minte*, OHG *minza* f. WG *minta* f. L *ment(h)a* f. Gk *minthē*]

minuĕt', n. Slow stately dance for two in triple measure; music for this, music in same rhythm & style. [f. F *menuet*, dim. of *menu* (as MINUTE a.)]

min'us, quasi-prep. & a. With the deduction of (symbol −), as *7 ~ 4 is equal to 3*; (colloq.) deprived of, as *he came back ~ an arm*; *a ~* (negative) *quantity*. [L, neut. of MINOR]

minŭs'cūle, a. & n. (Of kind of cursive script developed in 7th c.) small; (n.) small letter. [F, f. L *minuscula* (*littera* letter, dim. of MINOR): cf. MAJUSCULE]

min'ute[1] (-ĭt), n. 1. Sixtieth part of hour; short time, instant; exact point of time, as *the~* (*that*), as soon as. 2. Sixtieth part of degree (in angles). 3. Rough draft, memorandum; (pl.) brief summary of proceedings of assembly, committee, etc.; official memorandum authorizing or recommending a course, as *a Treasury ~*. 4. *~-book* (for writing ~s in); *~-gun* (fired at intervals of a ~); *~-hand* (indicating ~s on watch or clock); *~-man* (hist.), American militiaman of revolutionary period (because ready to march at a ~'s notice); *~-mark* (', cf. SECOND-*mark*). [ME, f. OF, f. L *minuta* fem. as MINUTE[3]; *~ of time* etc., f. med. L (*pars*) *minuta* (*prima*); see SECOND]

min'ute[2] (-ĭt), v.t. Find the exact tin.e of; draft (document, scheme); record in minutes; *~ down*, make a note of. [f. prec.]

minūte'[3], a. Very small; trifling, petty; (of inquiry, inquirer, etc.) accurate, precise. Hence ~ly[1] (-ūt'lĭ) [-LY[2]] adv., ~NESS (-ūt'n-) n. [ME, f. L *minutus*, p.p. of *minuere* lessen]

min'ute|ly[2] (-nĭtlĭ), a. Occurring every minute. So ~LY[2] (-nĭtlĭ) adv. [MINUTE[1] +-LY[1]]

minū'tia (-shĭa), n. (usu. in pl. *-ae*). Precise or trivial detail. [L (as MINUTE[3])]

minx, n. Pert girl, hussy, flirt. [16th c., poss. orig. f. MINIKIN +-ES]

Mī'ocēne, a. & n. (geol.). (Of) a division of the Tertiary preceding the Pliocene. [irreg. f. Gk *meiōn* less +*kainos* new]

mir (mēr), n. Russian village community. [Russ.]

mi'racle, n. Marvellous event due to some supernatural agency; remarkable occurrence; remarkable specimen (*of* ingenuity, impudence, etc.); *to a ~*, surprisingly well; (also *~ play*) dramatic representation in Middle Ages, based on life of Christ or saints. [ME, f. OF f. L *miraculum* (*mirari* wonder f. *mirus* wonderful)]

mirac'ulous, a. Supernatural; surprising. Hence ~LY[2] adv., ~NESS n. [f. F *miraculeux* f. med. L *miraculosus* (as prec., see -OUS)]

mirage' (-ahzh), n. Optical illusion, esp. illusive appearance of sheet of water in desert etc. (also fig.). [F, f. *se mirer* be reflected; see MIRROR]

mīre[1], n. Swampy ground, bog; *stick, find oneself, in the ~* (in difficulties); mud, dirt. [ME, f. ON *myrr* f. Gmc *meus-*, *mus-*: see MOSS]

mīre[2], v.t. Plunge in mire; (fig.) involve in difficulties; defile, bespatter. [f. prec.]

mi'rror, n., & v.t. 1. Polished usu. glass surface reflecting image, looking-glass; (fig.) what gives faithful reflection or true description of thing. 2. v.t. Reflect as in ~. [ME, f. OF *mirour* f. Rom. *miratorium* (*mirare* look at, f. L *mirari* wonder at, see -ORY)]

mĭrth, n. Merriment, laughter. Hence ~'FUL, ~'LESS, aa., ~'fulLY[2] adv., ~'fulNESS n. [OE *myrgth* (MERRY[2], -TH[1])]

mĭr'y̆, a. Muddy; vile. [f. MIRE[1] +-Y[2]]

mir'za (mēr'zah), n. (In Persia) title added to name of prince or prefixed to that of official or man of learning. [Pers.]

mis-[1], pref. added freely to vbs & vbl nn. w. sense 'amiss', 'badly', 'wrongly', 'unfavourably', or intensifying unfavourable meaning contained in vb (*misdoubt*). [OE, OS, ON *mis-*, OHG, Goth. *missa-*, f. Gmc *missa-* (1) divergent (2) mutual]

mis-[2], pref. to vbs, adjj., & nn., derived f. F, in same sense as prec. [f. OF *mes-* f. MINUS, used in com.-Rom. as pref.]

misadvĕn'ture, n. (Piece of) bad luck; (law) *homicide by ~* (accident). [ME, f. OF *mesaventure* (see MIS-[2] & ADVENTURE)]

misalli'ance, n. Unsuitable alliance, esp. marriage. [MIS-[1], after MÉSALLIANCE]

mis'anthrōpe, n. Hater of mankind; one who avoids human society. Hence or cogn. **misanthrŏp'IC**(AL) aa., **misăn'thropIST**, **misăn'thropY**[1], nn., **misăn'thropIZE**(2)v.i. [f. Gk *misanthrōpos* (*miseō* hate +*anthrōpos* man)]

misapplicā'tion, n. Wrong application, wrong use (esp. of funds). [MIS-[1]]

misapplȳ', v.t. Apply wrongly. [MIS-[1]]

misăpprĕh|ĕnd', v.t. Misunderstand (words, person). So ~ĕn'sion (-shn) n., ~ĕn'sive a. [MIS-[1]]

misapprōp'rĭ|āte, v.t. Apply (usu. another's money) to wrong (esp. one's own) use. So ~A'TION n. [MIS-[1]]

misbĕcome' (-ŭm), v.t. Suit ill, be unbecoming to. [MIS-[1]]

misbĕgŏtt'en, a. Illegitimate, bastard; (often as general term of opprobrium). [MIS-[1] +*begotten* p.p. of BEGET]

misbĕhāve', v.t. Behave (oneself, or abs.) improperly. So **misbĕhāv'iour** (-yer) n. [ME; MIS-[1]]

misbĕl|ief', n. Wrong religious belief;

false opinion. So ~iev'er n., ~iev'ing a. [ME; MIS-¹]

misbéseem', v.t. Misbecome. [MIS-¹]

miscăl'cŭl|āte, v.t. & i. Calculate (amount, results, etc., or abs.) wrongly. So ~A'TION n. [MIS-¹]

miscall' (-awl), v.t. Call by a wrong name; ‖ (dial.) call (person) names. [ME; MIS-¹]

miscă'rriage (-rĭj), n. Failure (of letter) to reach destination; ~ (failure of court to attain the ends) of justice; untimely delivery (of woman), abortion; failure (of scheme etc.). [MIS-¹]

miscă'rrȳ, v.i. (Of person or business) fail, be unsuccessful; (of woman) be delivered prematurely (of child); (of letter) fail to reach destination. [ME; MIS-¹]

miscas'ting (-ah-), n. Wrong addition (of accounts); unsuitable casting (of actors). [MIS-¹]

miscégénā'tion, n. Mixture of races, esp. sexual union of whites with Negroes. [irreg. f. L miscére mix+genus race + -ATION]

miscellán'éa, n. Literary miscellany. [L, neut. pl. as foll.]

miscellán'éous, a. Of mixed composition or character; (w. pl. noun) of various kinds; (of persons) many-sided. Hence ~LY² adv., ~NESS n. [f. L miscellaneus (miscellus mixed f. miscére mix, see -ANEOUS)]

mis'cellanȳ (or mĭsĕl²), n. Mixture, medley; collection of treatises etc, in one volume; such volume. Hence mĭscĕll²anIST(3) n. [app. f. F miscellanées fem. pl. or MISCELLANEA]

mischance' (-ahns), n. (Piece of) bad luck, esp. by ~. [ME, f. OF mesch(e)ance (MIS-², CHANCE n.)]

mischief (-chĭf), n. Harm, injury, wrought by person or other agent (do one a ~, vulg., wound or kill him); make ~, create discord, so ~-maker, -making; the ~ (annoying part) of it is that etc.; worker, source, of harm or annoyance; vexatious conduct, esp. of children; pranks, scrapes, (get into, keep out of, ~); playful malice, archness, satire, (eyes full of ~); where the ~ (devil) have you been? [ME, f. OF meschief (MIS-², chief end, CHIEF)]

mis'chievous (-chĭv-), a. (Of things) having harmful effects; (of persons, conduct, etc.) disposed to acts of playful malice or annoyance. Hence ~LY² adv., ~NESS n. [ME, f. AF meschevous (prec., -OUS)]

mis'ci|ble (-sĭ-), a. That can be mixed (with). Hence ~BIL'ITY n. [f. med. L miscibilis, f. L miscére mix, -IBLE]

misconceive' (-sēv), v.i. & t. Have a wrong conception (of, or abs.); misunderstand (word, person). So misconcĕp²tion n. [ME; MIS-¹]

miscŏn'duct, n. Improper conduct, esp. adultery; bad management. So miscondŭct' v.t. & refl. [MIS-¹]

miscŏn'strue (-ōō; or -konstrōō'), v.t. Put wrong construction on (word, action); mistake meaning of (person). So misconstrŭc'tion n. [ME; MIS-¹]

miscount', n., & v.t. & i. (Make) wrong count, esp. of votes; count (things) wrongly. [MIS-¹]

mis'créant, a. & n. 1. (Arch.) heretical; depraved. 2. n. (arch.). Heretic; vile wretch. [ME, f. OF mescreant (MIS-² + creant f. L credere believe, see -ANT)]

miscré|āt'éd, a. Ill-formed (often as abusive epithet). So ~A'TION n. [MIS-¹]

mis-cŭe', n., & v.i. (billiards). 1. Failure to strike ball properly with cue. 2. v.i. Make a ~. [MIS-¹ or MISS v.)]

misdāte', v.t. Date wrong. [MIS-¹]

misdeal', v.t. & i., & n. 1. Make mistake in dealing (cards, but usu. abs.). 2. n. Such mistake. [MIS-¹]

misdeed', n. Evil deed; crime. [OE misdǣd (see MIS-¹ & DEED)]

misdeem', v.t. & i. (arch., poet.). Have wrong opinion of; mistake (person, thing for another); form wrong judgement (of). [ME, f. ON misdœma (MIS-¹, DEEM)]

misdémean'ant, n. Person convicted of misdemeanour or guilty of misconduct; first, second, -class ~ (to be treated with more, less, indulgence). [f. arch. misdemean, f. foll. (-ANT)]

misdémean'our (-nor), n. (Law) indictable offence less heinous than felony; offence, misdeed. [ME; MIS-¹]

misdirĕct', v.t. Direct (person, blow, etc.) wrongly. So misdirĕc'tion n. [MIS-¹]

misdo'ing (-dōō-), n. Misdeed. [MIS-¹]

misdoubt' (-owt), v.t. (arch.). Have doubts as to the truth or existence of; have misgivings, be suspicious, about; suspect (that). [MIS-¹]

mise (mēz, mīz), n. (Hist.) settlement by agreement, as M~ of Lewes (between Henry III & barons, 1264); ~ en scène (F, see Ap.), scenery & properties of acted play, (fig.) surroundings of an event. [ME, f. OF fem. p.p. of mettre put f. L mittere miss- send, used as n.]

mis'er¹ (-z-), n. One who hoards wealth & lives miserably; avaricious person. [L, = wretched]

mis'er² (-z-), n. Boring instrument for well-sinking. [orig. unkn.]

mis'erab|le (-z-), a. Wretchedly unhappy; (of events etc.) causing wretchedness; contemptible, mean, as a ~le hovel. Hence ~LY² adv. [f. F misérable or L miserabilis (miserari pity f. miser wretched, -BLE)]

mĭserēr'é (-z-), n. Fifty-first psalm (M~ mei Deus); cry for mercy; (improp.) = foll. (last sense). [ME, f. L, = have mercy (miserēri as MISER¹)]

misé'ricŏrd (-z-), n. 1. Apartment in monastery in which some indulgences were permitted. 2. Dagger for giving the *coup de grâce.* **3.** Shelving projection on under side of hinged seat in choir stall, serving when seat was turned up to support person standing. [ME, f. OF *misericorde* f. L *misericordia* f. *misericors* compassionate (stem of *misereri* pity + *cors -rdis* heart)]

mis′erl|ў (-z-), a. Like a miser, stingy. Hence ~**iness** a. [-ly¹]

mis′erў (-z-), n. Wretched state of mind or of outward circumstances; (cards, colloq. for F *misère*) declaration by which caller undertakes not to take any tricks. [ME, f. AF *miserie f. L *miseria* (as MISER¹)]

misfeas′ance (-z-), n. (Law) transgression, esp. wrongful exercise of lawful authority (also gen., esp. joc.). [ME, f. OF *mesfaisance* f. *mesfaire* misdo (MIS-², *faire* do f. L *facere*), -ANCE; cf. MALFEASANCE]

misfīre′, v.i., & n. (Of gun, motor engine, etc.) fail(ing) to go off or start action. [for phr. *to miss fire*]

misfit′, n. Garment etc. that does not fit the person it is meant for; badly adjusted person. [MIS-¹]

misfŏrt′une (-chn, -tyŏŏn), n. Bad luck (*more his ~ than his fault*). [MIS-¹]

misgīve′, v.t. (Person's) *mind ~s him*, fills him with suspicion or foreboding (*about* thing, *that*). [MIS-¹]

misgiv′ing, n. Feeling of mistrust or apprehension. [f. prec. + -ING¹]

misgo′vern (-gŭ-), v.t. Govern (State etc.) badly. So ~MENT n. [ME; MIS-¹]

misguid|e′ (-gīd), v.t. (chiefly in p.p.). Mislead, cause to err in thought or action. Hence ~**′ĕdly²** adv. [MIS-¹]

mishăn′dle (-s-h-), v.t. Handle (person, thing) roughly or rudely, ill-treat. [MIS-¹]

mishăp′ (-s-h-), n. Unlucky accident. [ME; MIS-¹]

mishear′ (-s-h-), v.t. Hear amiss or imperfectly. [OE *misheran*; MIS-¹]

mis′hit, n., & v.t. **1.** Faulty or bad hit. **2.** v.t. (*pr.* mis-hit′). Hit (a ball) faultily. [MIS-¹]

mish′măsh, n. Confused mixture. [ME; redupl. f. MASH n.]

mish′n|a(h) (-na), n. Collection of precepts forming basis of Talmud. Hence ~**ic** a. [post-bibl. Heb., = repetition, instruction, (*shanah* repeat)]

misin|fŏrm′, v.t. Give wrong information to, mislead. So ~**formā′tion** n. [ME; MIS-¹]

misintĕrp′rĕt, v.t. Give wrong interpretation to, make wrong inference from. So ~**A′TION** n. [MIS-¹]

misjŭdge′, v.t. & i. Judge wrongly (person etc., or abs.); have wrong opinion of. [MIS-¹]

mislay′, v.t. Put (thing) by accident where it cannot readily be found. [MIS-¹]

mislead′ (-lēd), v.t. Lead astray, cause to

go wrong, in conduct; give wrong impression to. [OE *mislædan*; MIS-¹]

mislike′, v.t. (arch.). Dislike. [OE; MIS-¹]

mismăn′age, v.t. Manage badly or wrongly. So ~MENT (-ĭjm-) n. [MIS-¹]

misnāme′, v.t. Call by wrong name. [MIS-¹]

misnŏm′er, n. Use of wrong name, wrong use of term. [ME, f. AF, f. OF *mesnommer* (*mes-* MIS-² + *nommer* name f. L *nominare*)]

mĭso-, comb. form (irreg.) of Gk *miseō* hate, = 'hater, hatred, of ', as: ~*logist*, ~*logy*, (-ŏl-), hater, hatred, of reason or of learning; ~*nē′ism*, ~*nē′ist*, hatred, hater, of novelty.

mĭsŏg′am|ў, n. Hatred of marriage. So ~**ist** n. [MISO-, Gk *gamos* marriage, -Y¹]

mĭsŏg′ўnist (-j-, -g-), n. Hater of women. So **mĭsogўn′ic** a. [f. Gk MISO(*gunēs* f. *gunē* woman) + -IST]

mis′pickel, n. (min.). Arsenical pyrites. [G]

misplāce′, v.t. Put in wrong place or hands; set (affections) on wrong object; place (confidence) amiss; time (words, action) badly. So ~MENT (-sm-) n. [MIS-¹]

misprint′, n., & v.t. **1.** Mistake in printing. **2.** v.t. Print wrongly. [MIS-¹]

mispri′sion¹ (-zhn), n. (law). Wrong action or omission, esp. ~ *of treason* or *felony*, (now restricted to) concealment of one's knowledge of treasonable designs etc. [ME, f. AF, f. OF *mesprision* f. *mesprendre* mistake (MIS-², PRISON)]

‖ **mispri′sion²** (-zhn), n. (arch.). Contempt; failure to appreciate the value (*of*). [f. foll., after prec.]

misprīze′, v.t. Despise; fail to appreciate. [ME, f. OF *mespriser* (see MIS-² & PRIZE¹)]

mispro|nounce′, v.t. Pronounce wrongly. So ~**nŭnciā′tion** n. [MIS-¹]

misquōte′, v.t. Quote wrongly. So **misquotā′tion** n. [MIS-¹]

misread′, v.t. (-*read*, pr. -rĕd). Read or interpret wrongly. [MIS-¹]

misrĕprĕsĕnt′ (-z-), v.t. Represent wrongly, give false account of. So ~**ā′tion** n. [MIS-¹]

misrule′ (-ōōl), n. Bad government; *Lord, Abbot, Master, of M~* (hist.), person presiding over Christmas revels. [ME; MIS-¹]

miss¹, n. Failure to hit or attain; *a ~ is as good as a mile*, failure or escape is what it is, however narrow the margin; miscarriage; NEAR²~; (billiards) *give a* ~, avoid hitting object ball so as to leave one's own in safe position; *give* (something) *a* ~, (also, transf.) avoid, leave alone (*I shall give the party, the prunes, a* ~). [f. foll.]

miss², v.t. & i. (Of person or missile) fail to hit (mark etc., or abs.); fail to find, get, or meet; let slip (opportunity); fail to catch (train); ~ *the* BUS; fail to hear or understand (remark etc.); (also ~ *out*) leave out (words etc. in reading, writing, etc.); fail to keep (appointment) or perform; notice esp. with regret the absence of, feel the want of; (ellipt., of internal--combustion engines) misfire; ~ *fire*, (of gun) fail to go off, (fig.) fail in one's object; *~ *out* (*on*), fail to get (something), be unsuccessful; (naut.) ~ *stays*, fail in attempt to go about from one tack to another. ·[OE, OHG *missan*, MLG, MDu. *missen*, ON *missa* f. Gmc *missjan* f. *missa-* MIS-[1]]

miss[3], n. (As title of unmarried woman or girl) *M~ Smith*, (pl. *the M~ Smiths*, *the Misses Smith*; *M~* 1963 or current year, the modern girl, also, chosen beauty of that year, so *M~ Great Britain* etc.); (usu. derog. or playful) girl, esp. school-girl, as *a pert* ~, whence ~'ISH[1], a., ~'ish-NESS n.; (voc., in servants' or trade use) young lady. [abbr. of MISTRESS]

miss'al, n. Book containing service of Mass for whole year; (loosely) Rom. Cath. service-book, esp. illuminated one. [ME, f. med. L *missale* (MASS[1], -AL)]

miss'el, n. (Usu. ~-*thrush*) kind of thrush that feeds on mistletoe etc. berries. [OE *mistel* basil, mistletoe, = OHG, ON *mistil*; orig. unkn.]

mis-shāp'en, a. Ill-shaped, deformed. [ME, f. MIS-[1] + *shapen* p.p. of SHAPE]

miss'ile, a. & n. (Object, weapon) suit-able for throwing or for discharge from machine or engine (or, rarely, gun); = GUIDE[2]*d* ~. [f. L *missilis* (*mittere miss-* send, see -IL)]

miss'ing, a. In vbl senses; also: wanting, not in its place, as *there is a page* ~, *a page is* ~; *the* ~, soldiers neither present after battle etc. nor known to have been killed or wounded; ~ *link*, thing lacking to complete series, (zool.) hypothetical intermediate type, esp. between man & anthropoid apes. [MISS[2] + -ING[2]]

mi'ssion (-shn), n. 1. Body of persons sent to foreign country to conduct negotiations etc. 2. Body sent by re-ligious community to convert heathen; field of missionary activity; missionary post; organization in a district for con-version of the people; course of religious services etc. for this purpose. 3. Errand of political or other ~; operational sortie. 4. Person's vocation or divinely appointed work in life. [F, or f. L *missio* (*mittere miss-* send, -ION)]

mi'ssionarў (-sho-), a. & n. 1. Of, con-cerned with, religious missions; ~-*box* (for contributions to ~ work). 2. n. Person who goes on ~ work; || person attached to magistrates' court to influ-ence or help offenders or applicants. [-ARY[1]]

mi'ssioner (-sho-), n. Missionary; person in charge of parochial mission. [-ER[1]]

miss'ĭs, -us, n. (As used by servants) the mistress; (vulg., joc.) *the* ~, one's own or another's wife; see also MRS. [corrupt. of MISTRESS]

miss'ive, a. & n. 1. *Letter*(*s*) ~, letter from sovereign to dean & chapter nominating person to be elected bishop. 2. n. Letter, esp. official one. [ME, f. OF or f. med. L *missivus* (as MISSION, -IVE)]

mis-spĕll', v.t. (-spĕlt). Spell wrongly. [MIS-[1]]

mis-spĕnd', v.t. (-spĕnt). Spend amiss or wastefully (esp. in p.p.). [ME; MIS-[1]]

mis-stāte', v.t. State wrongly. Hence ~MENT (-tm-) n. [MIS-[1]]

miss'ў, n. (Affectionate, playful, or de-rog.) = MISS[3] (not followed by name). [-Y[3]]

mist, n., & v.i. & t. 1. Water vapour de-scending in fine drops smaller than rain-drops & causing obscuration of the atmosphere; *Scotch* ~, ~ like fine rain frequent on Scottish hills; filmy appear-ance before eyes caused by disorders of body or by tears; ~-*net*, fine-threaded net used to catch birds. 2. vb. Cover, be covered, as with ~. Hence ~'FUL a., ~'LIKE a. & adv. [OE (= MLG, MDu.) *mist*, Icel. *mistur*]

mistāke'[1], n. Misunderstanding of a thing's meaning; error, fault, in thought or action; (emphasizing preceding state-ment) *and*, or *make*, *no* ~, undoubtedly. [f. foll.]

mistăk|e'[2], v.t. & i. Misunderstand meaning or intention of (person, state-ment, purpose); err in opinion; (p.p.) wrong in opinion, (of action etc.) ill--judged, as *you are* ~*en*, ~*en kindness*, whence ~'enLY[2] adv., ~'enNESS(-n-n-)n.; ~*e A for* (think he is) *B*; *there is no* ~*ing*, no one can help recognizing (person, fact). Hence ~'ABLE a. [ME, f. ON *mistaka* (MIS-[1] + *taka* TAKE)]

mis'ter, n. (pl. *Messrs*, pr. mĕs'erz), & v.t. 1. Title prefixed to man's name or ·to designation of office etc. (written *Mr*), as *Mr Jones*, *Mr Secretary*, *Mr Speaker*; *Mr Right* (joc.), destined husband; (alone as voc., vulg.) = *sir*; the word ~ as title, as *please don't call me* ~; untitled person, as *be he prince or mere* ~. 2. v.t. Address as Mr, as *don't* ~ *me*. [weakened form of MASTER]

mis'tĭgris, n. (cards). (Blank card in) a variety of poker. [f. F *mistigri* knave of clubs]

mistime', v.t. Say, do, (thing) out of season (esp. in p.p.). [ME; MIS-[1]]

mis'tletoe (-zltō, -sltō), n. Parasitic plant growing on apple & other trees, & bearing glutinous fruit used in making birdlime; *kiss under the* ~ (w. ref. to the custom permitting a girl standing below ~ used as Christmas decoration to be kissed by the finder). [OE *mistiltān*, = ON *mistil-teinn* (as MISSEL + *tān* twig)]

mis'tral (or -trahl'), n. Cold NW. wind

in Mediterranean provinces of France etc. [F & Pr., f. L as MAGISTRAL]

misträns|lāte' (-z-), v.t. Translate incorrectly. So ~lā'TION n. [MIS-¹]

mistreat', v.t. Treat badly. Hence ~'MENT n. [ME; MIS-¹]

mis'trèss, n. Woman in authority over servants; female head of household. **2.** Woman who has power to control or dispose *of*, as *you are ~ of the situation, you are your own ~*, (fig. of countries) *~ of the world* etc. **3.** Woman who has thorough knowledge (*of* subject). **4.** Woman loved & courted by a man; woman illicitly occupying place of wife or having habitual illicit intercourse with man. **5.** Female teacher in school or of special subject, as *music-~*. **6.** ‖ *M~ of the Robes*, lady charged with care of Queen's wardrobe. **7.** (As title) see MRS. Hence ~-SHIP n. [ME, f. OF *maistresse* (*maistre* MASTER¹, see -ESS¹)]

mistri'al, n. Trial vitiated by error. [MIS-¹]

mistrŭst', v.t., & n. **1.** Feel no confidence in (person, one*self*, one's powers etc.). **2.** n. Lack of confidence, whence ~FUL a., ~fulLY² adv., ~fulNESS n. [ME; MIS-¹]

mis'tỹ, a. Of, covered with, mist; indistinct in form; (fig.) obscure, vague, as *a ~y idea*. Hence ~ĭLY² adv., ~ĭNESS n. [OE *mistig* (as MIST, see -Y²)]

misŭnderständ', v.t. (-*stŏŏd*). Take (words etc., or abs.) in wrong sense; misinterpret words or actions of (person, esp. in p.p.). So ~ĭng n. [ME; MIS-¹]

misūse' (-z), v.t. Use wrongly, apply to wrong purpose; ill-treat. So **misūse'** (-s) n. [ME; MIS-¹]

mite, n. Kinds of arachnid, esp. *cheese-~* (found in cheese), whence **mit'Y²** a.; (orig.) Flemish copper coin of small value, (pop.) half-farthing (as in *Mark* xii. 42); modest contribution, the best one can do, as *let me offer my ~ of comfort*; (colloq.) *not a ~*, not at all; small object, esp. child; *a ~ of a* (a tiny) child etc. [(1) OE *mite*, MLG, MDu. *mite*, OHG *miza* gnat f. Gmc *mitōn-*; (2) ME, f. MLG, MDu. *mite* (prob. same as (1)]

Mith'|räs, -ra, n. Persian god identified with sun. Hence ~rā'ĭc a., ~raĭsM, ~raĭsT(2), nn. [L f. Gk (-*as*) f. OPers. (-*a*)]

mithrid'at|ĭze, -|ĭse (-ĭz), v.t. Render proof against poison by gradually increasing doses of it. So **mithridăt'ĭc** a., ~ĭsM n. [f. *Mithridates VI*, king of Pontus, +-IZE]

mit'ĭg|āte, v.t. Appease (anger etc.); alleviate (pain, grief); reduce severity of (punishment); moderate (heat, cold, severity, etc.). So ~A'TION n., ~ătORY a. [ME, f. L *mitigare* (*mitis* mild), see -ATE³]

mitŏs'ĭs, n. (biol.; pl. -*oses* pr. -ŏs'ēz). Process of division of a cell into minute threads. Hence **mitŏt'ĭc** a. [f. Gk *mitos* thread +-OSIS]

mitrailleuse' (-trahyẽrz, & see Ap.), n. Many-barrelled breech-loading machine gun discharging small missiles simultaneously or in rapid succession. [F, fem. agent-n. f. *mitrailler* (*mitraille* small missiles, OF small money, f. *mite* MITE)]

mit'ral, a. & n. Of, like, a mitre;~ (*valve*), a valve of the heart. [f. mod. L *mitralis* (as foll., see -AL)]

mī'tre¹ (-ter), n. Bishop's & abbot's tall cap, deeply cleft at top, esp. as symbol of episcopal office, whence **mī'trED²** (-terd) a.; [perh. different wd] joint of two pieces of wood etc. at angle of 90°, such that line of junction bisects this angle; *~-block, -board, -box*, guide for saw in cutting *~-joints; ~-wheels*, pair of bevelled cog-wheels with teeth set at 45° & axes at right angles. [ME, f. OF, f. L f. Gk *mitra* girdle, turban]

mī'tre² (-ter), v.t. Bestow mitre on; join with mitre; shape off (end of wood etc.) to a mitre; *mitring-machine* (for doing this). [ME, f. prec.]

mitt'en, mitt, n. (*Mitten*) kind of glove with thumb but no fingers, for warmth or protection in hedgers' work etc.; (pl., sl.) boxing-gloves; (now usu. *mitt*) woman's lace or knitted glove covering forearm & part of hand, but not fingers; *frozen ~* (sl.), chilly reception; *give, get, the mitten* (sl.), dismiss (lover), be dismissed, (gen.) be dismissed from office etc. Hence **mitt'enED²** (-nd) a. [ME, f. OF *mitaine*, f. Rom. **medietana* (sc. *muffula* MUFFLE²)]

mitt'imus, n. Warrant committing person to prison; (colloq.) dismissal from office, as *get* one's *~*. [L, = we send]

mix, v.t. & i. Put together (two or more substances or groups, one *with* another) so that the particles or members of each are diffused among those of the others (also of immaterial things); prepare (compound) by ~ing ingredients; (intr.) join, be ~ed, as *oil will not ~ with water, they* (persons) *do not ~ well* (get on together); have intercourse *with*; ~ *up, ~* thoroughly, also, confuse esp. in thought, so *~-up* n.; *be ~ed up*, be involved (*in, with*, shady dealings etc.). Hence ~'ER¹ n.: one who, that which, ~es (esp. apparatus controlling the combination of various sounds in preparation of talking films & in dramatic broadcasting); (orig. U.S., colloq.) *good, bad, ~er*, one who gets on well, badly, with other people (esp. those of a different social class). [back formation f. foll., taken as E p.p.]

mixed (-kst), a. In vbl senses, esp.: of diverse qualities or elements; (of company) not select, containing persons of doubtful status; (colloq.) mentally confused, muddled; ill-adjusted, so *~-up* adj.; for persons of both sexes, as *~*

school, bathing; ~ MATHEMATICS. Hence **mix′ĕdNESS** n. [15th c. *mixt* f. OF *mixte* f. L *mixtus* p.p. of *miscēre* mix]

‖ **mix′en**, n. (dial.). Dung-hill. [OE, f. *meox* dung +-EN³; cogn. w. OS *mehs*, OHG *mist*, Goth. *maihstus*]

mix′ture, n. Mixing; what is mixed, esp, medical preparation (*the* ~ *as before*, also transf.); HEATHER ~; mechanical mixing of two substances, involving no change in their character, opp. to *chemical combination*; gas or vaporized oil mixed with air, forming explosive charge in internal-combustion engine. [F, or f. L *mixtura* (as MIXED, see -URE)]

Miz′pah, n. ~ *ring*, one inscribed ~ w. ref. to *Gen.* xxxi. 49 & given as love-token.

miz(z)′en, n. (naut.). (Also ~-*sail*) lowest fore-&-aft sail (rarely set, SPANKER being usual) of full-rigged ship's ~-*mast* (aftermost mast of three-masted ship); ~ *yard* (on which ~ is extended). [15th c., f. OF *misaine* f. It. *mezzana* ~-sail, fem. of *mezzano*; see MEZZANINE]

‖ **miz′zle**¹, v. impers., & n. Drizzle. Hence **miz′zlY**² a. [15th c., of LG orig.; cf. MDu. *miezelen*, LG *miseln*, & *misig* drizzly]

miz′zle², v.i. (sl.). Go, decamp. [orig. unkn.]

mnĕmŏn′ic (n-), a. & n. **1.** Of, designed to aid, the memory. **2.** n. pl. Art of, system for, improving memory. Hence **mnĕm′onIST** (n-) n. [f. LL f. Gk *mnēmonikos* (*mnēmōn* mindful f. *mna* -remember, see -IC)]

mnĕmotech′n|y̆ (n-, -tĕk-), n. = prec. (n. pl.). Hence ~IC a. [f. Gk *mnēmē* memory +*tekhnē* art]

mō, abbr. (colloq.) for *moment* (esp. *wait, in, half a mo*).

mō′a, n. = DINORNIS. [Maori]

moan¹, n. Long low murmur of physical or mental suffering; (arch.) *make* (one's) ~, complain. Hence ~′FUL a. [ME, f. OE *mān*, whence *mǣnan*, obs. *mean*, vb, replaced by foll.]

moan², v.i. & t. Make moan(s); utter (specified words) with moans; lament (misfortune etc.); lament for (dead person etc.). [f. prec.]

moat, n., & v.t. Deep wide ditch surrounding house, castle, etc., usu. filled with water; (v.t.) surround (as) with ~. [ME *mot(e)* f. OF *mot(t)e* mound]

mŏb¹, n. The lower orders; rabble, tumultuous crowd; promiscuous assemblage of persons; ~ *law* (imposed, enforced, by ~); ~'*s′man*, swell pickpocket; *swell* ~, class of stylishly dressed pickpockets. Hence ~b′ISH¹ a., ~ŏc′RACY n. [abbr. of *mobile*, n. (17th c.), short for *mobile vulgus*, L, = excitable crowd (MOBILE)]

mŏb², v.t. & i. (-bb-). (Of mob) attack, molest; assemble in a mob. [f. prec.]

mŏb-′căp, n. Woman's indoor cap cover-

ing whole head, worn in 18th & early 19th cc. [f. obs. (18th c.) *mob*; cf. obs. vb (17th c.) *mob* muffle the head]

mŏb′ile, a. Movable, not fixed, free to move; (of person or mind) easily, too easily, changing; (of troops) that may be easily moved from place to place. So **mobil′ITY** n. [f. F, or L *mobilis* (*movēre* move, see -BLE)]

mŏb′ilĭz|e, -is|e (-īz), v.t. Render movable, bring into circulation; prepare (forces) for active service (also quasi-pass. of forces). So ~ABLE a., ~A′TION n. [f. F *mobiliser*, as prec.]

mŏcc′asĭn, n. Foot-gear of deerskin etc. worn by N.-Amer. Indians, trappers, etc. [f. native *mockasin*]

mō′cha¹ (-k-), n. Kind of chalcedony. [perh. same as foll.]

mō′cha² (-k-), n. (Also *M*~ *coffee*) fine quality of coffee, orig. from *M*~, Arabian port at entrance of Red Sea.

mŏck¹, n. (arch.). Derision; thing deserving scorn; imitation, counterfeit. [ME, f. MOCK³]

mŏck², a. (not pred.). Sham; ~ *sun, moon*, = PARHELION, PARASELENE; ~ *duck, goose*, pork with duck stuffing; ~-*turtle soup* (usu. of calf's head, to imitate turtle); ~-*heroic* a. & n., burlesquely imitating, burlesque imitation of, heroic style. [prec. & foll.]

mŏck³, v.t. & i. Hold up to ridicule; defy contemptuously; impose upon; ridicule by imitation; mimic, counterfeit; scoff *at*; ~*ing-bird*, American song-bird that mimics notes of other birds, other birds that do this; ~-*up* n., special model showing appearance of (part of) proposed machine. Hence ~′ingLY² adv. [ME *mokke, mocque,* f. OF *mocquer*]

mŏck′erY̆, n. Derision; subject, occasion, of this; counterfeit representation (*of*); ludicrously or insultingly futile action etc. [ME, f. OF *moquerie* (as prec., see -ERY)]

mōd′al, a. Of mode or form as opp. to substance; ~ *legacy* (with directions as to mode in which it is to be applied); (gram.) of the mood of a verb, (of particle) denoting manner; (log.) ~ *proposition*, one in which predicate is affirmed of subject under some qualification, (also) one that involves affirmation of possibility, impossibility, necessity, or contingency. Hence or cogn. **modāl′ITY** n. (esp. in pl. = method laid down for discharge of obligation etc.), ~LY² adv. [f. med. L *modalis* (as foll., see -AL)]

mōde, n. **1.** Way, manner, in which thing is done; prevailing fashion or custom; (arch.) *the* ~, the fashion in dress etc. **2.** (mus.). Ancient Greek scale system, as DORIAN, LYDIAN, PHRYGIAN, ~; used similarly in mediaeval music; in modern music, each of the two chief scale systems (MAJOR², MINOR, ~). **3.** (log.). Character of modal proposition. [(1) F; (2) & (3) f. L *modus* measure, manner]

mŏd´el¹, n. Representation in three dimensions of proposed structure etc.; *working* ~ (imitating movements of machine it represents); figure in clay, wax, etc., to be reproduced in other material; design, style of structure; person, thing, proposed for imitation; person who poses for artists; woman in draper's shop wearing clothes etc. to show their effect to customers; *The New M~*, plan for reorganization of Parliamentary army 1644–5; (attrib.) exemplary, ideally perfect. [f. F *modèle* (earlier *-elle*) f. It. *modello* dim. of *modo* (as MODE)]

mŏd´el², v.t. & i. (-ll-). Fashion, shape, (figure) in clay, wax, etc.; give shape to (document, argument, etc.); form (thing) *after, on, upon,* a model; (of mannequin) display (garment) by wearing it; (v.i.) act or pose as artist's model or mannequin. [f. prec.]

mŏd´ēna, n. Deep purple. [*M~*, Italian city]

mŏd´erat|e¹, a. & n. **1.** Avoiding extremes, temperate in conduct or expression; (of wind) of medium strength; fairly large or good; ~*e prices*, low (in advertisements etc., as *prices strictly ~e*). **2.** n. One who holds ~e opinions in politics etc., whence ~ISM n. Hence ~ELY² adv., ~eNESS n. [ME, f. L *moderare* (*modus* MODE) +-ATE²]

mŏd´erāte², v.t. & i. Render less violent, intense, vigorous, etc.; (of fury, storm, etc.) become less vehement; act as moderator. [as prec., see -ATE³]

mŏderā´tion, n. Moderating; moderateness; *in ~*, in a moderate manner or degree; || (Oxf. Univ., pl.) *M~s* first public examination for degree of B.A. (abbr. *Mods*). [ME, f. OF *moderation* or L *moderatio* (as MODERATE², see -ATION)]

mŏd´erātor, n. Arbitrator; mediator; presiding officer; || one of two officers presiding over mathematical tripos at Cambridge; || examiner for moderations; Presbyterian minister presiding over any ecclesiastical body; ~ *lamp* (with contrivance for regulating flow of oil). Hence ~SHIP n. [ME, f. OF *moderateur* or f. L *moderator* (as prec., see -OR)]

mŏd´ern, a. & n. **1.** Of the present & recent times; ~ *English* (from 1500 onwards); ~ *history* (subsequent to Middle Ages); || ~ *school*, ~ *side*, in school (in which ~ subjects are chiefly or exclusively taught); new-fashioned, not antiquated. **2.** n. Person living in ~ times. Hence or cogn. **modern´ITY**, ~NESS, ~IZA´TION, nn., ~IZE(3) v.t. & i., ~LY² adv. [f. LL *modernus* (*modo* just now)]

mŏd´ern|ism, n. Modern view(s) or method(s), esp. tendency in matters of religious belief to subordinate tradition to harmony with modern thought; so ~IST(2) n.; modern term or expression. [-ISM]

mŏd´est, a. Having a humble estimate of one's own merits; retiring, bashful; (esp. of women) decorous in manner & conduct, scrupulously chaste; (of demands, statements, etc.) not excessive (freq. iron.); (of things) unpretentious in appearance, amount, etc. Hence or cogn. ~LY² adv., ~Y¹ n. (~*y* or ~*y vest*, lace slip worn above point of corsage). [f. F *modeste* or L *modestus* (*modus* MODE)]

mŏd´icum, n. Small quantity (*of* food etc.). [L, neut. of *modicus* moderate (*modus* measure)]

mŏd´i|fy, v.t. Make less severe or decided, tone down; make partial changes in; (gram.) qualify sense of (word etc.); change (vowel) by umlaut. Hence or cogn. ~fiaBIL´ITY, ~FICA´TION, nn., ~fiABLE, ~ficāTORY, aa. [ME, f. OF *modifier* f. L *modificare* (as MODE, see -FY)]

modill´ion (-yon), n. (archit.). Projecting bracket under corona of cornice in Corinthian & other orders. [f. It. *modiglione*]

mŏd´ish, a. Fashionable. Hence ~LY² adv., ~NESS n. [f. MODE +-ISH¹]

mŏdiste´ (-ēst), n. Milliner, dressmaker. [F (as MODE, see -IST)]

mŏd´ŭl|āte, v.t. & i. Regulate, adjust; vary (thing) conformably *to*; adjust or vary tone or pitch of (speaking voice); (mus.) pass (*from* one key *to* another). So ~A´TION n. (also, radio) alteration in amplitude or frequency of a wave by a frequency of a different order, ~ātOR n., chart used in tonic sol-fa system for exercise in sight-singing. [f. L *modulari* measure, adjust, (as foll.), see -ATE³]

mŏd´ūle, n. Standard, unit, for measuring; (archit.) unit of length for expressing proportions, usu. semidiameter of column at base. [F, or f. L (as foll.)]

mŏd´ūlus, n. (pl. *-lī*). Constant multiplier or coefficient; constant indicating relation between amount of physical effect & that of force producing it. [L,=measure, dim. of foll.]

mŏd´us, n. ~ *ŏperăn´dī*, way a person goes to work, way a thing operates; ~ *vīvěn´dī*, mode of living, i.e. arrangement between disputants pending settlement of debate, arrangement between people(s) who agree to differ; money payment in lieu of tithe (orig. ~ *decimăn´dī*). [L, = MODE]

mofětte´, n. (Fissure in earth from which issues) exhalation of mephitic gas. [F, or f. It. (Naples) *mofetta*]

mofŭss´il, n. (Anglo-Ind.). Rural localities as opp. to chief station. [f. Hind. *mufaççil* f. Arab. *mufaççal*]

Mogŭl´, n. & a. Mongolian; *the* (*Great* or *Grand*) ~, emperor of Delhi; (*m~*) tycoon. [f. Pers. *mugul* f. MONGOL]

mō´hair, n. (Fine camlet, yarn, from) hair of Angora goat. [ult. f. Arab. *mukhayyar* lit. = choice, select, (*khayyara* choose)]

Mohămm´ĕdan, n. & a. (Follower) of Mohammed, founder of the Moslem religion. Hence ~ISM(3) n., ~IZE(3) v.t. [*Mohammed* f. Arab. *Muḥammad*+-AN]

Moha'rram (-hŭr-), **Mu-**, n. First month of Mohammedan year; great Shiite fast during first ten days of this month. [Arab. (*Mu-*), = sacred]

Mō'hawk, n. One of a tribe of N.-Amer. Indians; their language; (skating) step from either edge in one direction to same edge on other foot in opposite direction (cf. CHOCTAW). [native]

Mō'hŏck, n. (hist.). One of a class of aristocratic ruffians infesting London streets at night in 18th c. [f. prec.]

mō'hŭr, n. (Also *gold* ~) former gold coin of India, worth 15 rupees. [f. Pers. *muhr* seal]

∥ **moid'er**, v.t. (dial.). To perplex, confuse, worry (esp. in p.p.). [orig. unkn.]

moid'ōre, n. Former Portuguese gold coin. [f. Port. *moeda d'ouro* (*moeda* MONEY +*ouro* gold)]

moi'ĕtý, n. Half, esp. in legal use; (loosely) one of two parts into which thing is divided. [ME, f. OF *moit(i)e* f. L *medietatem* middle point (as MEDIUM, see -TY)]

moil, v.i. Drudge, esp. *toil & ~*. [ME, f. OF *moillier* moisten, paddle in mud, f. Rom. *molliare* f. L *mollis* soft]

moire (mwahr), n. (Also ~ *antique*, see Ap.) watered fabric, usu. silk, orig. mohair. [F, earlier *mouaire*, f. MOHAIR]

moiré(mwah'rā), a. & n. (Of silk) watered; (of metals) having clouded appearance like watered silk; (n.) this appearance. [F, p.p. of *moirer* f. prec.]

moist, a. Slightly wet, damp; (of season etc.) rainy; (of disease) marked by discharge of matter etc. Hence ~'NESS n. [ME, f. OF *moiste*]

moi'sten (-sn), v.t. & i. Make moist; become moist. [-EN⁶]

mois'ture, n. Water or other liquid diffused in small quantity as vapour, condensed on surface, etc. Hence ~LESS a. [ME, f. OF *moistour* (as MOIST, see -OR)]

mōke, n. (sl.). Donkey. [orig. unkn.]

mōk'ō, n. Maori system of tattooing. [Maori]

mōl'ar¹, a. & n. 1. (Usu. of mammal's back teeth) serving to grind. 2. n. ~ tooth. [f. L *molaris* (*mola* millstone, see -AR¹)]

mōl'ar², a. Of mass; acting on or by means of large masses; freq. opp. MOLECULAR. [f. L *moles* mass, see -AR¹]

molăss'ĕs (-z), n. pl. (treated as sing.). Uncrystallized syrup drained from raw sugar; syrup got from sugar in process of refining, treacle. [f. Port. *melaço* f. LL *mellaceum* must (*mel* honey, see -ACEOUS)]

mōle¹, n. Spot, blemish, small lump on human skin. [OE *māl*, corresp. to OHG *meil*, Goth. *mail*]

mōle², n. Small burrowing animal with (usu. blackish) velvety fur & very small eyes; other mammals of same family;

blind as a ~ (quite); ~*-cricket*, nocturnal burrowing insect; ~'*hill*, small mound thrown up by ~ in burrowing (*make mountains out of* ~*hills*, exaggerate obstacles etc.); ~'*skin*, skin of ~ as fur, kind of cotton fustian with surface shaved before dyeing, (pl.) clothes, esp. trousers, of this. [ME *molle* f. MDu. *moll(e)*, *mol*, MLG *mol*, *mul*]

mōle³, n. Massive structure, usu. of stone, as pier, breakwater, or junction between places separated by water; artificial harbour. [f. F *môle* f. med. Gk *mōlos* f. L *moles* mass]

molĕc'ūlar, a. Of, relating to, consisting of, molecules; ~ *weight* of substance (of one of its molecules relatively to the weight of one atom of hydrogen). Hence ~ITY (-ă'r-) n., ~LY² adv. [-AR¹]

mŏl'ĕcūle, n. (Physics, chem.) one of the minute groups of atoms (in some elements, esp. the inert gases, one of the single atoms) of which material substances consist, the smallest portion to which a substance can be reduced by subdivision without losing its chemical identity; (loosely) small particle. [f. F *molécule* f. L *moles* mass; see -CULE]

molĕst', v.t. Meddle hostilely or injuriously with (person). So **mōlĕsta'**TION n. [f. OF *molester* f. L *molestare* (*molestus* troublesome)]

Mŏl'in∣ism, n. Doctrine of Luis Molina (d. 1600), that efficacy of grace depends on the will that freely accepts it; doctrine of Miguel de Molinos (d. 1696), quietism. Hence ~IST n. [f. *Molina, Molinos,* +-ISM]

mŏll, n. Prostitute; gangster's mistress. [pet form of *Mary*]

mŏll'i∣fý, v.t. Appease, soften. So ~-FICA'TION n. [ME, f. OF *mollifier* or L *mollificare* (*mollis* soft, see -FY)]

mŏll'usc, n. Animal belonging to the *Mollusca*, sub-kingdom of soft-bodied & usu. hard-shelled animals, including limpets, snails, cuttle-fish, oyster, mussel, etc. Hence **mollŭs'cAN**, **mollŭs'cous**, aa., **mollŭs'coID** a. & n. [f. F *mollusque* f. L *molluscus* (*mollis* soft)]

mŏll'ý, n. Effeminate man or boy, milksop; ~*-coddle*, (n.) milksop, (v.t.) coddle, cocker up. [pet form of *Mary*]

Mŏl'ŏch (-k), n. Canaanite idol to whom children were sacrificed (often fig.); thorn-lizard, a hideous Australian reptile. [LL f. Gk, f. Heb. *molek*]

molŏss'us, n. Metrical foot – – –. [Gk]

Mŏl'otŏv. Name of Soviet commissar used attrib.; ~ *cocktail* (sl.), anti-tank inflammatory fire-grenade used in 1939–45 war.

mōl'ten. See MELT.

mŏl'tō, adv. Very (preceding mus. direction, as ~ *espressivo*). [It., f. L *multus* much]

mōl'ý, n. Fabulous herb with white flower & black root, endowed with magic properties; wild garlic & other plants. [L, f. Gk *mōlu*]

molyb'denum, n. Silvery-white brittle metallic element with which steel is alloyed for making high-speed tools. [earlier *-dena*, f. L f. Gk *molubdaina* f. *molubdos* lead]

mōm'ent, n. 1. Minute point of time, instant; *one* ~, *half a* ~, (colloq.) *half a mŏ*, (ellipt.) wait a ~; *come here this* ~ (at once); *came the very* ~ (as soon as) *I heard of it*; *timed to the* ~ (with absolute accuracy); *the* ~ (time that affords an opportunity); *am, was, busy at the* ~ (just now, then), so *men of* (important at) *the* ~; PSYCHOLOGICAL ~. 2. (mech.). ~ *of a force about a point*, measure of its power in causing rotation. 3. Importance, as *of great, little, no,* ~, whence **momĕn'tous** a., **momĕn'tousLY²** adv., **momĕn'tous-NESS** n. [ME, f. OF, or L *momentum*]

mōm'entar|ȳ, a. Lasting only a moment; short-lived, transitory. Hence ~ILY² adv., ~INESS n. [f. L *momentarius* (as prec., see -ARY¹)]

mōm'entlȳ, adv. From moment to moment; every moment; for a moment. [-LY²]

momĕn'tum, n. (pl. *-ta*). (Mech.) quantity of motion of moving body, product of its mass by its velocity; (pop.) impetus gained by movement (lit. & fig.). [L (as MOVE, see -MENT)]

Mōm'us, n. Greek god of ridicule; fault-finder. [f. Gk *Mōmos*]

mŏn'ac(h)al (-k-), a. Monastic. So **mŏn'achISM** (-k-) n. '[f. LL *monachalis* (MONK, -AL)]

mŏn'ad, n. The number one, unit; ultimate unit of being (e.g. a soul, an atom, a person, God), esp. in philosophy of Leibnitz, whence ~ISM(3), ~ŏl'ogy, nn.; (biol.) simple organism assumed as first term in genealogy of living beings; (chem.) element, radical, with combining power of one atom of hydrogen. Hence **monăd'ic** a. [f. LL f. Gk *monas -ados* unit]

mōnadĕlph'ous, a. (bot.). (Of stamens) having filaments united into one bundle; (of plants) with ~ stamens. [f. Gk *monos* one + *adelphos*, brother + -OUS]

monăn'drous, a. (bot.). Having a single stamen. [f. Gk *monandros* (*monos* one + *anĕr andros* male) + -OUS]

monăn'drȳ, n. Custom of having only one husband at a time. [as prec. + -Y¹]

mŏn'arch (-k), n. 1. Sovereign with title of king, queen, emperor, empress, or equivalent; supreme ruler (often fig.). 2. Large orange & black butterfly. Hence **monärch'AL,** **monärch'IC**(AL), aa., **monärch'aLLY²,** **monärch'ICALLY,** advv., (-k-). [f. F (*-arque*) or L (*-cha*) f. Gk *monarkhēs* (*monos* alone + *arkhō* rule)]

mŏn'arch|ism (-k-), n. Principles of, attachment to, monarchy. So ~IST (-k-) n. [-ISM]

mŏn'archȳ (-k-), n. (State under)

monarchical government; *constitutional, limited,* ~ (subject to constitutional restrictions). [ME, f. OF *monarchie* or L f. Gk *monarkhia* (MONARCH, -Y¹)]

mŏn'asterȳ, n. Residence of community (usu. of monks) living secluded under religious vows. [ME, f. eccl. L f. late Gk *monastērion* (*monazō* live alone f. *monos*)]

monăs't|ic, a. Of monks or monasteries; (bookbind.) finished by tooling without gold (also *antique*). So ~ICALLY adv., ~ICISM(3) n., ~ICIZE(3) v.t. [f. F (*-ique*) or LL f. Gk *monastikos* (as prec., see -IC)]

mondaine (mawńdān'), n. Woman of the fashionable world; worldly woman. [F]

Mon'day (mŭn'dĭ), n. Second day of week; *Black* ~ (school sl.), first day of term; || *St* ~, ~ as day of little work (w. ref. to saint's-day holidays). [OE *Mōnan dæg* (= moon's day), rendering LL *lunae dies*]

Mon'dayish (mŭn'dĭ-), a. (Of clergy) indisposed as result of Sunday work; (of others) slack as result of Sunday holiday. [-ISH¹]

monde (mawńd), n. The fashionable world, society; the set in which one moves. [F]

mŏn'dial, a. World-wide. [F, f. LL *mundialis* f. L *mundus* world]

mo'nĕtarȳ (mŭ-, mŏ-), a. Of the coinage; of money. [f. F *monétaire* or LL *monetarius* (as MONEY, see -ARY¹)]

mo'nĕtiz|e (mŭ-, mŏ-), -is|e (-īz), v.t. Put (metal) into circulation as money. Hence ~A'TION n. [f. L *moneta* MONEY + -IZE]

mo'ney (mŭ-), n. (pl. ~s). 1. Current coin; coin & promissory documents representing it (*paper* ~), esp. government & bank notes; (w. pl.) particular coin; (pl.) sums of ~; ~ *of* ACCOUNT²; CONSCIENCE ~; property viewed as convertible into ~; coin in reference to its purchasing power, as (prov.) ~ *makes the mare to go, time is* ~, *for* LOVE¹ *or* ~; *make* ~, acquire wealth, *coin* ~, do this rapidly; || ~ *for jam* or *for old rope* (sl.), a profitable return for little or no trouble; *not every man's* ~, not worth its price to every one. 2. ~*-bag,* bag for ~, (pl.) wealth; ~*-bags,* wealthy or avaricious person; ~*-box,* closed box into which savings or contributions are dropped through slit; ~*-changer,* one whose business it is to change ~ at fixed rate; ~*-grubber,* person sordidly intent on amassing ~, ~*-grubbing* a. & n., (given to) this practice; ~*-lender* (derog.), one whose business it is to lend ~ at interest; ~*-market,* sphere of operation of dealers in stocks etc.; ~ ORDER¹(3); ~*-spinner,* small spider thought to bring good luck, something that brings in much ~, e.g. book, film, play, etc.; ~*-wort,* plant with round glossy leaves; ~*'s-worth,* anything recognized as equivalent to ~. Hence ~LESS (mŭn'ĭl-) a. [ME, f. OF *moneie* f. L *moneta* mint, money, orig. goddess in whose temple at Rome ~ was coined]

moneyed (mŭn'ĭd), a. Rich; consisting of money, as ~ *resources, assistance*; ~ *interest*, the class concerned in money as a possession. [-ED²]

mo'nger (mŭngg-), n. Dealer, trader, (chiefly in comb., as *cheese*~, *fish*~, *iron*~, *coster*~, & fig. *scandal*~ etc.). [OE *mangere* (*mangian* to traffic f. L *mango* dealer)]

Mŏng'ol (-ngg-), n. & a. (Member) of Asian people now inhabiting Mongolia, between China & Siberia. Hence ~OID a., of Mongolian type (also, n. = MONGO-LIAN). [native, perh. f. *mong* brave]

Mŏngōl'ian (-ngg-), a. & n. = prec.; (anthrop.) of the yellow-skinned straight-haired type of mankind; of a class of idiots like ~s. [-IAN]

mŏng'ōōse, mŭng'ōōse, (-ngg-), n. (pl. ~s). An ichneumon, common in India, & able to kill venomous snakes unharmed; kind of lemur. [f. native *mangus*]

mo'ngrel (mŭngg-), n. & a. 1. Dog of no definable breed; animal, plant, resulting from crossing of different breeds or kinds; person not of pure race. 2. adj. Of mixed origin, nature, or character. Hence ~ISM(2) n., ~IZE(3) v.t., ~LY¹ a. [app. f. root *mang-, mong-*, mix, +-REL]

‖ **mŏn'ial,** n. Mullion. [ME, f. OF *moinel* middle f. *moien* MEAN² (-AL)]

mŏnil'ifŏrm, a. Suggesting necklace or string of beads. [F, or mod. L *moniliformis* (*monile* necklace, -FORM)]

mŏn'|ism, n. Doctrine that only one being exists; any of the theories that deny the duality of matter & mind. Hence ~IST n., **monis'tic** a. [f. Gk *monos* one, -ISM]

moni'tion, n. Warning (*of* danger); formal notice from bishop or ecclesiastical court admonishing person to refrain from some offence; (in courts that use civil law process) summons. [ME, f. OF, or L *monitio* (*monēre monit-* warn, -ION)]

mŏn'itor, n., & v.t. & i. 1. (arch.). One who admonishes. 2. Senior pupil in school with duties of keeping order etc., whence **mŏnitōr'ial** a., ~SHIP n. 3. Lizard supposed to give warning of approach of crocodiles. 4. Shallow-draught warship of heavy gunpower. 5. One who listens to & reports on foreign broadcasts, misuse of official telephones, etc. 6. Detector of induced radio-activity, esp. in workers in an atomic plant. 7. vb. Act as ~ (sense 5), act as ~ of. Hence **mŏn'itress¹** n. [L (as prec., -OR)]

mŏn'itory, a. & n. 1. Warning, admonitory. 2. n. Bishop's or pope's letter of admonition. [f. L *monitorius* (as prec., see -ORY)]

monk (mŭ-), n. Member of community of men living apart under vows of poverty, chastity, & obedience; ~'s-*hood*, plant with hood-shaped flowers. Hence ~ᴸ HOOD, ~'SHIP, nn. [OE *munuc*, = OS *munik*, OHG *munih*, ON *munkr*, f.

*monicus var. of LL f. Gk *monachos* solitary (*monos* alone)]

monk'|erў (mŭ-), n. (colloq.). Monastic life; monastery; monks; monkish practices. So ~DOM n. [-ERY]

mo'nkey (mŭ-), n. (pl. ~s), & v.t. & i. 1. Mammal of a group closely allied to & resembling man, ranging from anthropoid apes to marmosets; (as term of playful contempt, to or of person) *young* ~ etc. 2. Machine hammer for pile-driving etc.; globular earthenware water-vessel with straight upright neck. 3. (sl.). ‖ *Put his* ~ *up*, enrage him; *get* one's ~ *up*, become angry. 4. ‖ £500 (sl.). 5. ~-*bread*, fruit of baobab tree; ~-*cup*, pitcher-plant; ~-*flower*, kind of mimulus with bright yellow flowers; ~-*jacket*, short close-fitting one worn by sailors etc.; ‖ ~-*nut*, peanut; ~-*puzzle*, puzzle-~, Chile pine, prickly tree of genus *Araucaria*; ~-*wrench*, one with adjustable jaws. 6. v.t. Mimic, mock; (v.i.) play mischievous tricks (*with*), fool *about*. Hence ~ISH¹ a., ~ishNESS n., (mŭng'kĭ-). [16th c., of unkn. (poss. LG) orig.]

monk'ish (mŭ-), a. Of monks, monastic; characteristic of monks (usu. in bad sense). [-ISH¹]

mŏn'o-, comb. form (bef. vowels *mon-*) of Gk *monos* alone, sole, single; as: (1) ~-*bās'ic* (chem.), having one base or atom of a base; ~-*carp'ic*, ~-*carp'ous*, bearing fruit only once; ~-*cěph'alous* (bot.), having only one head; ~-*clin'al*, (of strata) dipping in one & the same direction; ~-*cŏtў-lēd'on*(*ous*), (plant with) single cotyledon; *monŏc'racy*, government by single person; *monŏc'ūlar*, with, adapted to, one eye; ~-*cycle*, velocipede with one wheel; ~-*dac⁰tylous*, having one finger, toe, or claw; ~-*drama*, piece for one performer; *mo-noe'cious* (-nēshus), (bot.) with male & female organs on same plant, (zool.) hermaphrodite; ~-*gen'esis*, development of all beings from single cell, so ~-*genět'ic* a.; *monŏg'eny*, descent of mankind from one pair of ancestors; ~-*glot* a. & n., (one) who uses only one language; *monŏ'gўnous*, with only one pistil or stigma; *monŏ'gўny*, usage of mating with only one female; ~-*idě'ism*, concentration on single idea, esp. as form of monomania; *monŏl⁰atry*, worship of one god without denying that others may exist; ~-*măn'ia*, insanity on one subject only, so ~-*măn'iăc* n., ~-*mani'acal* a.; ~-*mer*, one of the units forming a polymer molecule, (also) a compound which can undergo polymerization; ~-*mět'allism*, standard of currency based on one metal, so ~-*metăll'ic* a.; ~-*morph'ic*, ~-*morph'ous*, not changing form during development; ~-*pět'alous*, having corolla in one piece, or petals united into tube; ~-*phthong*, single vowel sound; ~-*plane*, aeroplane with one plane; ~-*psy'chism* (-sĭk-), theory that all souls are one; ~-*rail*, railway on one rail;

~*rhyme*, poem in which all lines have same rhyme; ~*sperm'ous* (bot.), having one seed; *monŏs'tichous* (-k-) (bot., zool.), arranged in, consisting of, one layer or row; ~*strŏph'ic*, consisting of repetitions of one strophic arrangement; ~*tint*, representation, picture, in only one colour; ~*trēme*, member of lowest order of mammals with one vent for urinary, genital, & digestive organs; ~*type*, composing-machine that casts & sets up single types P; ~*tỹp'ic*, represented by only one type. (2) chem. wds denoting presence of a single atom or combining equivalent, as ~*brŏm'ide*, ~*carb'on*, ~*chlor'ide*, *monŏv̄-alent*, *monŏx'ide*.

mŏn'ochŏrd (-k-), n. Instrument for determination of musical intervals. [ME, f. OF *monocorde* or LL f. Gk MONO(*khordon* f. *chordē* CHORD)]

mŏnochromăt'ic (-k-), a. (Of light) presenting one colour only; executed in monochrome. [MONO- +CHROMATIC]

mŏn'ochrōme (-k-), n. & a. 1. Painting executed in different tints of one colour; representation in one colour. 2. adj. Having only one colour. [ult. f. Gk MONO-(*khrōmatos* f. *khrōma* colour)]

mŏn'ocle, n. Single eye-glass. [F, f. LL *monoculus* one-eyed (MONO- +*oculus* eye)]

mŏn'od|ỹ, n. Ode sung by single actor in Greek tragedy; poem in which mourner bewails someone's death. Hence or cogn. **monŏd'ic** a., ~IST n. [f. LL f. Gk *mon-ōidia* f. *monōidos* singing alone (MONO- +*ōid-*, *aoid-*, f. *aeidō* sing)]

monŏg'am|ỹ, n. Practice, circumstance, of being married to one at a time; (rare) practice of marrying only once; (zool.) habit of having only one mate. Hence or cogn. ~IST n., ~OUS a. [f. F *monogamie* f. LL f. Gk MONO(*gamia* f. *gamos* marriage)]

mŏn'ogrăm, n. Two or more letters, esp. person's initials, interwoven. So **mŏno-grammăt'ic** a. [f. LL *monogramma* f. Gk MONO(*grammon*, neut. adj. as -GRAM)]

mŏn'ograph (-ahf), n., & v.t. Separate treatise on single object or class of objects; (v.t.) write a ~ on. Hence **monŏg'raph-ER**[1], **monŏg'raphIST**, nn., **mŏnogrăph'-ic** a., **mŏnogrăph'ICALLY** adv. [MONO- + -GRAPH]

mŏn'olith, n. Single block of stone, esp. shaped into pillar or monument. Hence **mŏnolith'ic** a., (also) solidly uniform throughout, showing or allowing no variation. [f. F -*lithe*, or L f. Gk MONO-(*lithos* stone)]

mŏn'ologue (-ŏg), n. Scene in drama in which one person speaks by himself; dramatic composition for single performer; long speech by one person in a company; soliloquy. Hence **mŏnolŏ'gi-CAL** a., **monŏl'ogIST**, **mŏn'olŏguIST** (-gIst), nn., **monŏl'ogIZE**(2) v.i. [F,=one who loves to hear himself talk, f. Gk MONO(*logos* -LOGUE)]

‖ **mŏn'omărk**, n. Combination of letters

and/or figures registered as identification mark for goods, articles, addresses, etc. [MONO-]

monōm'ial, n. & a. (alg.). (Expression) consisting of one term. [MONO-, on *bino-mial*]

Monŏph'ỹsīte, n. One who holds there is only one nature in the person of Christ. [f. eccl. L (-*ta*) f. eccl. Gk MONO(*phusilēs* f. *phusis* nature, see -ITE[1])]

monŏp'olist, n. One who favours monopoly; one who assumes monopoly (*of*). [-IST]

monŏp'olīz|e, -is|e (-īz), v.t. Obtain exclusive possession or control of (trade, commodity, the conversation, person's attention, etc.). Hence ~A'TION n. [f. foll. +-IZE]

monŏp'olỹ, n. Exclusive possession of the trade in some commodity; this conferred as privilege by State; exclusive possession, control, or exercise (*of*); thing that is monopolized. [f. L f. Gk MONO-(*pōlion* f. *pōleō* sell)]

mŏnosỹll'|able, n. Word of one syllable; *speak in* ~*ables*, answer little but Yes or No, with intentional curtness. Hence or cogn. ~**ăb'ic** a., ~**ăb'ICALLY** adv., ~abISM(2) n., ~abIZE(3) v.t. [f. L MONO-(*syllabus* SYLLABLE)]

mŏn'othe|ism, n. Doctrine that there is only one God. Hence ~IST n., ~**is'tic** a. [f. MONO- + Gk *theos* god +-ISM]

mŏn'otŏne, a. & n., & v.t. 1. (Utterance of successive syllables) without change of pitch, whence **mŏnotŏn'ic** a. (mus.); sameness of style in writing. 2. v.t. Recite, speak, sing, in unvaried tone. [f. late Gk MONO(*tonos* TONE)]

monŏt'on|ous, a. (Of sound or utterance) without variation in tone or cadence; lacking in variety, wearisome through sameness. Hence or cogn. ~IZE(3) v.t., ~**ousLY**[2] adv., ~**ousNESS**, ~**Y**[1], nn. [as prec. +-OUS]

Monrōe'|ism (-ōī-), n. Monroe DOCTRINE. So ~IST n. [-ISM]

monseigneur (see Ap.), n. (pl. *nosseigneurs* pr. nosănyēr'). French title given to eminent persons, esp. princes, cardinals, archbishops, & bishops. [F]

monsieur (musyēr', & see Ap.), n. (pl. *messieurs* pr. mĕsyēr'). French equivalent of MR, but also used by itself as substitute for name, as *did M~ ring?*; Frenchman; (hist.) title of second son or next younger brother of French king. [F]

monsignor(e) (mŏnsēnyōr', -ĭ; pl. -*ori*), n. Title of some R.-C. prelates, officers of Papal court, & others. [It., after MON-SEIGNEUR]

monsōōn', n. Wind in S. Asia, esp. in Indian Ocean, blowing from SW. in summer (*wet* ~) & NE. in winter (*dry* ~); rainy season; other winds with periodic alternations. [f. Du. *monssoen* f. Port. *monção* perh. f. Arab. *mausim*, lit. season, (*wasama* mark)]

mŏn'ster, n. & a. **1.** Mis-shapen animal or plant, abortion; imaginary animal compounded of incongruous elements, e.g. centaur, sphinx, griffin; inhumanly wicked person, inhuman example of (cruelty etc.); animal, thing, of huge size. **2.** adj. Huge. . [ME, f. OF *monstre* f. L *monstrum* portent, monster (*monēre* warn)]

mŏn'strance, n. (R.-C. Ch.). Open or transparent vessel of gold or silver in which the host is exposed. [f. OF, f. med. L *monstrantia* (*monstrare* show, see -ANCE)]

mŏnstrŏs'itў, n. Monstrousness; abortion, imaginary monster, outrageous thing. [f. LL *monstrositas* (as foll., see -TY)]

mŏn'strous, a. & adv. **1.** Abnormally formed, of the nature of a monster; huge; outrageously wrong or absurd; atrocious. **2.** adv. (arch.). Extremely, as ~ *good friends*. Hence~LY[2] adv.,~NESS n. [ME, f. OF *monstreux* f. LL *monstrosus* (MONSTER, -OUS)]

mŏn'tage (-ahzh), n. (cinemat.). Selection, cutting, & piecing together as a consecutive whole of the separate shots taken in the making of a film.· [F, f. *monter* to mount]

mŏn'tāne, a. Of, inhabiting, mountainous country. [f. L *montanus* (as MOUNT, see -ANE)]

mŏntbrē'tia (-sha), n. Iridaceous plant with bright orange-coloured flowers. [after A. F. E. D. de *Montbret*, French botanist (d. 1801), -IA[1]]

mŏn'tè, n. Spanish game of chance, played with 45 cards; *three-card* ~, game of Mexican origin. [Sp., = mountain, heap of cards]

Mŏntenēg'rin, n. & a. (Inhabitant) of Montenegro (now in Jugoslavia). [-INE[1]]

Montessŏr'i sўs'tèm, n. Method of educating very young children, both normal & defective, initiated c. 1900 by Dr Maria Montessori of Rome (by direction of natural activities rather than strict control).

month (mŭ-), n. Any of the twelve portions into which the year is divided (also *calendar* ~); *lunar* ~, period in which moon makes complete revolution; space of time from a day in one ~ to corresponding day in next; space of 28 days; ~ *of Sundays*, indefinite period; *this day* ~, a ~ from today; ~*'s mind*, mass etc. in commemoration of deceased person a ~ after death, ‖ (also) inclination, liking: [OE *mōnath*, OS *mānoth*, OHG *mānōd*, ON *mánathr*, Goth. *mēnōths* f. Gmc **mænōth-* cogn. w. MOON]

mo'nthlў (mŭn-), a. & n. **1.** Done, recurring, payable, etc., once a month; ~ *nurse* (attending woman during first month after childbirth); ~ *rose*, a rose, supposed to flower monthly. **2.** n. Magazine etc. published each month; (pl.) menses. So **mo'nthLY[2]** (mŭn-) adv. [-LY[1]]

mŏn'tĭcūle, n. Small hill; small mound caused by volcanic eruption; minute eminence on surface of animal etc. [F, f. LL *monticulus* (mons MOUNT, see -CULE)]

mŏn'ūment, n. Written record; anything that serves to commemorate, esp. structure, building; ‖ *the M*~, column in London commemorating fire of London in 1666; stone or other structure placed over grave or in church etc. in memory of the dead. [ME, f. L *monu-, monimentum* (*monēre* remind, see -MENT)]

mŏnūmĕn'tal, a. Of, serving as, a monument; ~ *mason*, tombstone maker; (of literary works) massive & permanent; stupendous, as ~ *ignorance*. Hence ~LY[2] adv. [f. LL *monumentalis* (as prec., see -AL)]

mŏnūmĕn'talĭze, -ise (-īz), v.t. Record, commemorate, as by monument. [prec. +-IZE]

-mony, suf. repr. L *-monia, -monium* (occas. thr. F *-moine, -monie,* as *matri*~, *patri*~, *cere*~), wh. formed nn. f. aa. (*acrimony*), nn. (*patrimonium*), & vbs (*alimonium*).

mōō, v.i., & n. (Of cow or ox) low, make the sound *moo*; (n.) this sound. [imit.]

mōōch, mouch (mōō-), v.i. & ˙t. (sl.). Loiter *about*, slouch *along*; (trans.) steal. [15th c. *mouche*, identified w. ME (now dial.) *miche*, app. f. OF *muchier* hide, skulk]

mōōd[1], n. State of mind or feeling; *in the* ~, *in no* ~, inclined, disinclined, (for thing, *to* do). [OE, OS *mōd*, OHG *muot*, ON *móthr*, Goth. *mōths* f. Gmc **mōda-*]

mōōd[2], n. (Gram.) any of the groups of forms in conjugation of verb that serve to indicate its function, as *indicative, imperative, subjunctive,* ~; (mus.) = MODE (log.) any of the classes into which each of the figures of valid categorical syllogism is subdivided. [var. of MODE, by assoc. w. prec.]

mōōd'ў, a. Gloomy, sullen. Hence ~ĬLY[2] adv., ~ĬNESS n. [OE *mōdig* (see MOOD[1] & -Y[2]]

moollah. See MULLAH.

mōōl'vĭ(e), mou-, n. Mohammedan doctor of the law; learned person, teacher (esp. as term of respect among Indian Moslems). [Hind. *mulvi* f. Arab. *maulawiyy* = judicial]

mōōn[1], n. **1.** Satellite of the earth, revolving round it monthly, & deriving light from sun & reflecting it to earth; this in particular month, regarded as a distinct object from that visible in other months, as *age of the* ~, *new* ~ (at beginning of revolution), *full* ~ (with disc entirely illuminated); HARVEST, HUNTER'S, ~; (poet.) month (*where summer is but three* ~*s long*); *once in a* BLUE[1]~; *old* ~ *in new* ~*'s arms*, ~ during first quarter, when dark part of orb is made faintly luminous by earth-light. **2.** ~*'beam*, ray of ~*light*; ~*'calf*, born fool; ~*'flower,* oxeye daisy; ~'*light*, light of ~ (often attrib.); ~*light flitting*, removal of household goods by night to avoid paying rent; ~'*lighter* (hist.), one who in Ireland perpetrated outrages by night on tenants who incurred hostility of Land League; ~'*lit*, lit up by ~; ~'*raker*, ‖ native of Wiltshire, sail above the horizon; ~*raking* (fig.), daydreaming, woolgathering; ~'*shine*, visionary talk or ideas, (also) smuggled spirits; *~'*shiner* (sl.), illicit distiller, spirit-smuggler; ~'*shiny*, lighted by ~, (also) visionary; ~'*stone*, feldspar of pearly appearance; ~'*struck*, deranged in mind. Hence ~*LESS* a. [OE *mōna*, OS, OHG *māno*, ON *māni*, Goth *mēna* f. Gmc *mænon-*; cogn. w. L *mensis* month]

mōōn², v.i. & t. Move, look, listlessly (*about, around*, etc.); pass *away* (time) in listless manner. [f. prec.]

mōōn'shee, munshi (mōōn'shē), n. Secretary or language-teacher in India. [f. Hind. *munshi* f. Arab. *munshi'* (*ansha'a* compose)]

mōōn'y, a. Of, like, the moon; listless, stupidly dreamy. [MOON¹'²+-Y²]

moor¹, n. Tract of open waste ground, esp. if covered with heather; (in Cornwall) waste land where tin is found; ~ *game*, red (rarely, black) grouse; ~'*cock*, male of this; ~'*hen*, female of this, (also) water-hen; ~'*land*, country abounding in heather; ~'*stone*, kind of granite. Hence ~'ISH¹, ~'Y², aa. [OE, OS *mōr*, OHG *muor*, f. Gmc *mōr-*]

Moor², n. One of a Mohammedan people, mixed Berber & Arab, inhabiting NW. Africa. Hence ~'ISH¹ a. [ME, f. OF *More* f. L f. Gk *Mauros* inhabitant of Mauretania, region of N. Africa]

moor³, v.t. Attach (boat or other floating thing) to moorings; ~*ing*-MAST¹. Hence ~'AGE(3, 4) n. [15th c. *more*, prob. f. (M)LG *mōren*, rel. to MDu. *māren*]

moor'ing, n. (Usu. pl.) permanent anchors & chains laid down for ships to be moored to, what a floating object is moored to; (pl.) place where vessel is moored. [-ING¹]

mōōse, n. (pl.~). N.-Amer. animal closely allied to or same as European elk. [f. native *moos*]

mōōt, n., a., & v.t. **1.** (Hist.) assembly; (law) students' discussion of hypothetical case for practice. **2.** adj. Debatable (freq. ~ *point*). **3.** v.t. Raise (question) for discussion. [(1) OE (*ge*)*mōt* f. Gmc *mōt-*, whence MEET¹; (2) f. (1); (3) OE *mōtian* f. (1)]

mŏp¹, n. Bundle of coarse yarn or cloth fastened at end of stick, for cleaning floors etc.; similar instruments for various purposes; ~'*head*, (fig.) thick head of hair like ~, person with this. Hence ~p'y² a. [15th c. *mappe* perh. ult. conn. w. L *mappa* napkin]

mŏp², v.t. (-pp-). Wipe, clean, (as) with mop; wipe tears, sweat, etc., from (brow etc.); (sl.) ~ *the floor with*, have & use over-

whelming advantage of (combatant); ~ *up*, wipe up (as) with mop, (sl.) absorb (profits etc.), dispatch, make an end of, (mil.) complete the occupation of (district etc.) by capturing or killing troops left there, capture or kill (stragglers). [f. prec.]

mŏp³, v.i. (-pp-), & n. ~ & *mow*, make grimaces; ~*s & mows*, grimaces. [perh. imit.; cf. Du. *moppen* pout]

‖ **mŏp⁴**, n. A fair or gathering in the autumn at which farm hands & servants were hired. [perh. = *mop-fair* (MOP¹)]

mōpe, v.i. & t., & n. **1.** Abandon oneself to listless condition; (refl. or pass.) make one*self*, be, the victim of ennui. **2.** n. One who ~s; *the* ~s, depression of spirits. Hence mōp'ISH¹ a., mōp'ishLY² adv., mōp'ishNESS n. [orig. unkn.]

mōp'ĕd, n. Motorized pedal cycle. [f. *mo*(*torized*) *ped*(*al*)]

mō'pōke, more'pōrk (mōrp-), n. In New Zealand, an owl; in Tasmania, nightjar; in Australia, various birds. [imit. of bird's note]

moquette' (-kĕt), n. Material of wool & hemp or linen, used for carpets & upholstery. [F]

mŏ'ra, -rra, n. Italian game in which player guesses number of fingers held up simultaneously by another. [It. *mora*]

moraine', n. Debris carried down & deposited by glacier. [F]

mŏ'ral, a. & n. **1.** Concerned with character or disposition, or with the distinction between right & wrong; ~ *sense*, power of distinguishing right & wrong; (of literary work etc.) dealing with regulation of conduct, as ~ *science*; ~ *philosophy*, ethics; ~ *law*, the requirements to which right action must conform; (of rights etc.) founded on ~ law; capable of ~ action; ~ *victory*, defeat, indecisive result, that eventually produces the ~ effects of victory; ~ *courage*, courage to encounter odium, contempt, etc., rather than abandon right course; ~ly good, conforming to rules of morality; virtuous as regards general conduct; ~ *certainly*, probability so great as to admit of no reasonable doubt. **2.** n. The ~ teaching of a fable, story, event, etc. (*draw the* ~, show what it is); ~ maxim or principle (*point a* ~, illustrate or apply it); (pl.) ~ habits, esp. sexual conduct; =foll. Hence ~LY² adv. [ME, f. L *moralis* (*mos* custom, pl. *mores* morals, -AL)]

morale' (-ahl), n. Moral condition, esp. (of troops) as regards discipline & confidence. [f. F *moral* respelt to preserve pronunciation, cf. LOCAL(E), CHORAL(E)]

mŏ'ralism, n. Natural system of morality, religion reduced to moral practice. [-ISM]

mŏ'ral|ist, n. One who practises or teaches morality; man who is merely moral. Hence ~is'tIC a. [MORAL+-IST]

morăl'ity, n. Moral science; (pl.) moral

principles, points of ethics; particular system of morals, as *commercial* ~; moral conduct (esp. good); moralizing; (hist.) kind of drama inculcating moral lesson, popular in 16th c. [ME, f. OF *moralite* or LL *moralitas* (MORAL, -TY)]

mŏ′raliz|e, -is|e (-īz), v.i. & t. Indulge in moral reflection or talk (*on* subject); interpret morally, point the moral of; improve the morals of. So ~A′TION n. [f. F *moraliser* or med. L *moralizare* (as MORAL, see -IZE)]

morass′, n. (literary). Bog, marsh. [f. Du. *moeras* f. MDu. *marasch* f. OF as MARISH]

mŏr′ăt, n. (hist.). Drink made of honey flavoured with mulberries. [f. med. L *moratum* (*morus* mulberry, see -ATE[1])]

mŏratŏr′ium, n. (Period of) legal authorization to debtors to postpone payment. [neut. of LL *moratorius* (L *morari* delay, -TORY)]

Morāv′ian, a. & n. (Inhabitant) of Moravia; (one) of Protestant sect holding Hussite doctrines, founded in Saxony by ~ emigrants. [f. *Moravia*, now part of Czechoslovakia, -AN]

mŏrb′id, a. (Of mind, ideas, etc.) unwholesome, sickly; given to ~ feelings; (med.) of the nature, or indicative, of disease; ~ *anatomy* (of diseased organs etc.). Hence ~LY[2] adv., ~NESS n. [f. L *morbidus* f. *morbus* disease (*mori* die)]

mŏrbĭde′zza (-ĕtsa), n. (painting). Lifelike delicacy in flesh-tints. [It. (as prec.)]

mŏrbid′itў, n. Morbidness; prevalence of disease (in a district). [-ITY]

mŏrbif′ic, a. Causing disease. [f. F *morbifique* (L *morbus* disease, see -FIC)]

mŏrceau′ (-sō), n. Short literary or musical composition. [F (as MORSEL)]

mŏrd′|ant, a. & n. **1.** (Of sarcasm etc.) caustic, biting, so ~A′CIOUS (-āshus) a., ~A′CITY, ~ANCY, nn.; pungent, smarting. **2.** (Of acids) corrosive or cleansing (n., such acid). **3.** (Substance) serving to fix colouring-matter or gold-leaf. [F, part. of *mordre* bite f. L *mordēre*]

mŏrd′ent, n. (mus.). Grace consisting in rapid alternation of written note with one immediately below it. [G, f. It. *mordente* part. of *mordere* bite, as prec.]

mōre, a. & adv. **1.** Existing in greater quantity, amount, or degree, as *there is* ~ *truth in it than you think, 10 is 2* ~ *than 8, bring some* ~ *water*; (abs.) greater quantity, as ~ *is meant than meets the ear, hope to see* ~ *of you*; *what is* ~ (~ important); ~ *than one person has* (not *have*) *found it so*. **2.** adv. In greater degree, as *you must attend* ~ *to details*, ~ *in sorrow than in anger*, ~ *frightened than hurt*; (forming compar. of most adjj. of more than one syllable & most advv.) ~ *absurd(ly)*, ~ *curious*, ~ *easily*, ~ *truly*; ~ *&* ~, in an increasing degree; ~ *or less*, in greater or less degree, or thereabouts; THE ~; *be no* ~, be dead; again, as *once, twice, never,*

~; *neither* ~ *nor less than* (simply, literally) absurd etc. [OE *māra*, OS, OHG *mēro*, ON *meire*, Goth. *maiza* f. Gmc **maizon-* f. *mais adv.]

moreen′, n. Stout woollen or woollen & cotton material for curtains etc. [perh. fanciful f. MOIRE]

morĕl′[1], n. Kinds of nightshade, esp. black nightshade. [ME, f. OF *morele*, fem. of adj. (-el) as n., f. med. L *maur-*, *morellus* f. *maurus* MOOR[2]]

morĕl′[2], n. An edible fungus. [f. F *morille*, f. Du. *morilje*; cf. OHG *morhila* (G *morchel*)]

morĕll′ō, n. Bitter kind of cherry. [f. It. *morello* (as MOREL[1])]

moreov′er (-mōrŏv-), adv. Further, besides, (introducing new statement). [MORE + OVER]

morepork. See MOPOKE.

mōr′es (-ēz), n. pl. Customs or conventions regarded as essential or vital to a social group. [L]

Morĕsque′ (-k), a. Moorish in style or design. [F, f. It. *moresco* (*Moro* Moor, see -ESQUE)]

mŏrganăt′|ic, a. ~*ic marriage*, one between man of exalted rank & woman of lower rank, who remains in her former station, the issue having no claim to succeed to possessions or title of father; ~*ic wife* (so married). Hence~ICALLY adv. [f. med. L phr. *matrimonium ad morganaticam*, prob. f. *morganaticum* f. OHG *morgangeba morning gift from husband to wife the morning after consummation of marriage (the ~ic wife's only claim on husband's possessions)]

mŏr′gue[1] (-g), n. Building (esp. one formerly in Paris) in which bodies of persons found dead are exposed for identification; (journalism) repository where miscellaneous material for reference is kept. [F, app. same wd as foll.]

mŏr′gue[2] (-g), n. Haughty demeanour. esp. (~ *anglaise*, see Ap.) as English characteristic. [16th c., F, of unkn. orig.]

mŏ′ribŭnd, a. At the point of death (lit. & fig.). [f. L *moribundus* (*mori* die)]

mŏ′rion, n. (hist.). Helmet without beaver or visor. [F, f. Sp. *morrion* f. *morra* skull]

Moris′cō, a. & n. **1.** Moorish. **2.** n. Moor, esp. in Spain; morris dance. [Sp. (*Moro* MOOR[2])]

Mŏrm′on, n. Member of religious body founded in 1830 by Joseph Smith in New York on basis of supposed Divine revelations in *Book of* ~ (imaginary author); (loosely) person who practises polygamy (once regarded as chief feature of the sect). Hence ~ISM r.

mŏrn, n. (poet.). Morning. [OE *morgen*, *myrgen*, *margen*, OS, OHG *morgan*, ON *myrginn*, *merginn*, Goth *maurgins* f. Gmc **murgan-*, **murgin-*, **margan-*]

mŏrn′ing, n. Early part of day-time, ending at noon, or at hour of midday

meal; *good* ~, form of salutation; (poet.)
dawn; (attrib. of clothes) meant to be
worn in the ~, as ~ *coat*, tail-coat with
front sloped away; ~ *draught*, liquor
taken before breakfast; ~ *gift* (see MOR-
GANATIC, etym.); ~ *glory*, kind of convolvulus; ~ *performance*, matinée; ~
prayer, Anglican service of matins; ~-
-room, sitting-room for the ~; ~ *star*,
Venus (or other planet or bright star)
seen in E. before sunrise; ~ *watch* (naut.),
4–8 A.M. [ME *mor(we)ning* f. *morwen* MORN
+-ING[1], after *evening*]

morocc'o, n. (pl. ~s). Leather made (orig.
in Morocco, now also in Europe) from
goatskins tanned with sumac; *French* ~,
inferior small-grained kind; *Levant* ~,
high-grade large-grained kind. [f. It.
Marocco f. name of chief city *Marrakesh*]

mōr'on, n. Adult whose mental development is arrested at the stage normal in
a child of 9–12 years; (pop.) degenerate
brute, fool. Hence **morŏn'**IC a. [neut. of
Gk *mōros* dull]

morōse', a. Sullen, gloomy, & unsocial.
Hence ~LY[2] adv., ~NESS n. [f. L *morosus*
(*mos moris* manner, see -OSE[1])]

morph'ēme, n. (philol.). A morphological
element considered in respect of its
functional relations in a linguistic system.
[F (*-ème*), f. Gk *morphē* form]

Morph'eus, n. God of dreams or sleep;
in the arms of ~, asleep. [L]

morph'ine, morph'ia, nn. Alkaloid narcotic principle of opium, largely used to
alleviate pain. Hence **morph'in**ISM(5) n.
[f. G *morphin* (prec., -INE[5] (-IA[1]))]

morphŏl'og|ỹ, n. (Biol.) study of the
form of animals & plants; (philol.) study
of the form of words. Hence **morpholŏ'gICAL** a., **morpholŏ'gICAL**LY[2] adv.,
~IST n. (biol.). [f. Gk *morphē* form +-LOGY]

mŏ'rris, a. & n. ~ (*dance*), grotesque
dance by persons in fancy costume, usu.
as characters in Robin Hood legend
(medieval, & as modern revival); ~-*pike*
(hist.), form of pike supposed to be of
Moorish origin. [f. *morys*, var. of MOORISH]

mŏ'rris tūbe, n. Small-bore rifle barrel
insertable in rifle for practice on miniature
range. [R. *Morris* (d. 1891), inventor]

mŏ'rrow (-ō), n. (literary). *The* ~, the
following day; (fig.) *on the* ~ *of* (time
following on) *a long war* etc. [ME *morwe*,
moru, shortened var. of *morwen* MORN]

mŏrse[1], n. Walrus. [f. Lapp *morsa*]

Mŏrse[2], n. & a. (Of) the recording telegraph invented by S. F. B. Morse (d.
1872), as ~ *alphabet*, *code* (in which letters
are represented by variations on two signs,
e.g. dot & dash, long & short flash, etc.).

mŏrse[3], n. Clasp, often jewelled etc., of
cope. [ME, f. OF *mors* f. L *morsus* bite,
catch]

mŏrs'el, n. Mouthful, small piece, (*of* food
etc.); fragment. [ME, f. OF, dim. of
mors a bite f. L *mordēre mors-* bite]

mŏrt[1], n. Note sounded on horn at death

of deer, wild boar, etc. [16th c., alt. f. ME
mote f. OF *mot* note of horn]

mŏrt[2], n. Salmon in third year. [orig.
unkn.]

mŏrt[3], n. (dial.). A great amount or
number of (*a* ~ *of*). [orig. unkn.]

mŏrt'al, a. & n. **1.** Subject to death;
causing death, fatal, (*to*, often fig.); (of
battle) fought to the death; (of enemy)
implacable; (of pain, fear, etc.) deadly;
(of sin) entailing spiritual death, deadly;
accompanying death, as ~ *agony*; (sl.)
very great, as *in a* ~ *hurry*; (sl.) long
& tedious, as *for two* ~ *hours*. **2.** n. ~,
esp. human, being; (joc.) person, as *a*
thirsty ~. Hence ~LY[2] adv. [ME. f. OF
mortel or L *mortalis* (*mors -tis* death, see
-AL)]

mŏrtăl'itỹ, n. Mortal nature; loss of life
on large scale; number of deaths in given
period etc.; death-rate; BILL[4]s *of* ~; ~
tables (showing expectation of life at
various ages etc.). [ME, f. OF *mortalite* f. L
mortalitatem (as prec., see -TY)]

mŏrt'ar, n., & v.t. **1.** Vessel of hard material, e.g. marble, in which ingredients are
pounded with pestle. **2.** Short piece of
ordnance for throwing shells at high
angles; contrivance for firing shells in
pyrotechnic displays. **3.** Mixture of lime,
sand, & water, for joining stones or bricks.
whence ~LESS, ~Y[2], aa.; ~-*board*, board
for holding ~, (pop.) square college cap.
4. v.t. Plaster, join, with ~; attack,
bombard, with ~s. [ME, f. OF *mortier* f.
L *mortarium*]

mortgage[1] (mŏrg'ij), n. Conveyance of
property by debtor (*mortgager*, -*or*) to
creditor (*mortgagee*) as security for debt,
with proviso that it shall be reconveyed
on payment of debt · within certain
period; deed effecting this. [ME, f. OF,
= dead pledge (*mort* f. L *mortuus* dead +
GAGE[1])]

mortgage[2] (mŏrg'ij), v.t. Make over
(property) by mortgage; pledge (one*self*,
one's powers etc., *to* object etc.). Hence
mortgageEE' (mŏrg-), **mortgag**ER[1]
(mŏrg[2]), **mortgag**OR' (mŏrgaj**ŏr'**), nn.
(see prec.). [f. obs. F *mor(t)gager*, or prec.]

*****mŏrti'cian** (-shn), n. Undertaker. [f. L
mors -tis death +-ICIAN]

mŏrt'i|fỹ, v.t. & i. Bring (body, passions,
etc.) into subjection by self-denial or discipline; cause (person) to feel humiliated,
wound (feelings), whence ~**fỹ**ING[2] a.;
(intr., of flesh) be affected by gangrene or
necrosis. So ~FICA'TION n. [ME, f. OF
mortifier f. LL *mortificare* (*mors -tis* death,
see -FY)]

mŏrt'ise, -ice, n., & v.t. **1.** Hole in a
framework designed to receive the end of
some other part esp. a TENON; ~ *chisel*
(with stout blade, for cutting ~s); ~ *lock*
(recessed in frame of door etc.). **2.** v.t.
Join (things *together*, one *to* or *into* another) securely, esp. by tenon & ~. [ME,
f. OF *morteise*, f. Arab. *murtazz* fixed in]

mort'main, n. (law). (Condition of) lands or tenements held inalienably by ecclesiastical or other corporation; (fig.) *in* ~, under posthumous control. [ME, f. OF *mortemain* f. med. L *mortua manus* dead hand, prob. in allusion to impersonal ownership]

mort'ūarў, a. & n. **1.** Of death or burial. **2.** n. Building in which dead bodies are kept for a time. [ME, f. AF *mortuarie* f. L *mortuarius* (*mortuus* dead, see -ARY[1])]

mosā'ic[1] (-z-), a., n., & v.t. (~*king*, ~*ked*). **1.** (Form or work of art) in which pictures etc. are produced by joining together minute pieces of glass, stone, etc., of different colours (also fig. of any diversified whole); ~ *disease* (in plants, esp. tobacco, maize, & sugar-cane); ~ *woolwork* (producing effect like that of ~); ~ *gold*, a disulphide of tin, also alloy of copper & zinc used in cheap jewellery etc. **2.** v.t. Adorn with ~s; combine (as) into ~. Hence ~IST(3) n. [f. F *mosaïque* f. It. *mosaico* f. med. L *mo-*, *musaicus* f. Gk *mouseion* mosaic work, f. *mousa* MUSE[1]]

Mosā'ic[2] (-z-), a. Of Moses, esp. ~ *Law* (in Pentateuch). [f. LL *Moses*+-IC]

mōsasaur'us (-ōr-), n. (pl. -*rī*). Large extinct marine reptile, first found near Maestricht on Meuse. [L *Mosa* Meuse + Gk *sauros* lizard]

mŏschatĕl' (-k-), n. Small plant with pale-green flowers & musky smell. [f. F *moscatelle* f. It. *moscatella* (*moscato* MUSK)]

mŏselle' (-z-), n. Dry white wine produced near the river M~ in Germany.

Mŏs'lĕm, Mŭs'lim, (or -z-), a. & n. (pl. -*ms*, -*min*). Mohammedan. Hence **Mŏs'lĕm**ISM n. [Arab. (-*im*), part. of *aslama*; see ISLAM]

mŏsque (-k), n. Mohammedan place of worship. [f. F *mosquée* f. It. *moschea* f. Arab. *masgid* (*sagada* vb worship)]

mosqui'tō (-kē-), n. (pl. ~*es*). Kinds of gnat, female of which punctures skins of animals with long proboscis & sucks their blood; ~*-net*, -*curtain* (to keep off ~es); ~*-craft*, small light vessels for rapid manœuvring. [Sp. dim. of *mosca* f. L *musca* fly]

mŏss, n., & v.t. **1.** Wet spongy soil; peat-bog; kinds of small herbaceous cryptogamous plant, some growing in bogs, others on surface of ground, trees, stones etc., in crowded masses, whence ~'INESS n., ~'Y[2] a.; *rolling stone gathers no* ~, one who constantly changes his place or employment will not grow rich. **2.** ~'*bunker*, = MENHADEN; ~*-grown*, overgrown with ~; ‖ ~*-hag*, broken ground from which peat has been taken; ~*-rose*, garden variety of cabbage rose, with ~*-like* growth on calyx & stalk; ~'*trooper*, border freebooter of 17th c. **3.** v.t. Cover with ~. [OE (MDu., OHG) *mos* bog, (cf. ON *mosi*), f. Gmc **mos*-; cogn. w. OE *mēos*, OHG *mios* moss, ON *myrr* MIRE]

mōst, a. & adv. **1.** Existing in greatest quantity or degree, as *you have made* ~ *mistakes, see who can make* ~ *noise,* (abs., quasi-noun) *this is the* ~ *I can do*; *make the* ~ *of it,* employ it to the best advantage, (also) represent it at the best or worst; the majority, as ~ *people think so,* (quasi-n.) ~ *of them are broken*; *for the* ~ *part,* in the main, usually, whence ~'LY[2] adv. **2.** adv. In the highest degree, as *what* ~ *annoys me,* (forming superl. of most adjj. of more than one syllable & most advv.) ~ *ludicrous*(*ly*), ~ *certain*(*ly*), ~ *callous*(*ly*); *ten at* ~, not more than ten; *this is at* ~ (is no more than) *a makeshift.* [OE *mǣst*, OS *mēst*, OHG *meist*, ON *mestr*, Goth. *maists* f. Gmc **maist-* (**mais* MORE, -EST)]

-most, suf. forming superl. adjj, formed not on adjj. but on prep. stems (*after*~, *fore*~, *in*~, *ut*~) & later on wds indicating position in place, time, or order, (*back*~, *top*~, *centre*~, & the compar. *upper*~, *utter*~, *further*~, etc.); also in *better*~; altered form of OE *-mest,* combining two superl. suff., *-mo-* & *-isto-* -EST, cf. L *optimus,* Gk *beltistos*; in late OE *-mest* was confused with MOST (see prec.), whence usu. mod. pronunc. (mōst) for the unstressed (most).

mot (mō), n. (pl. ~*s,* pr. mōz) Witty saying; BON MOT; ~ *juste* (see Ap.), expression that conveys a desired shade of meaning with more precision than any other. [F, = word, f. Rom. **mottum* = L *muttum* (*muttire* murmur)]

mōte, n. Particle of dust; ~ *in* (another's) *eye,* trifling fault if compared to one's own (see *Matt.* vii. 3). [OE *mot,* corresp. to Du. *mot* dust, sawdust]

mot'ĕl, n. Hotel or group of furnished cabins by the roadside where motorists may stay for the night. [f. *motorists'* hotel]

motĕt', n. (mus.). Anthem (usu. unaccompanied) in R.C. or Lutheran Church; non-ecclesiastical work on similar lines. [ME, f. OF, dim. of MOT]

mŏth, n. (Also *clothes-*~) small nocturnal lepidopterous insect breeding in cloth etc., on which its larva feeds (~, *the* ~, collect., ~s), whence ~'Y[2] a.; insect of the order *Lepidoptera* excluding butterflies, apt to scorch itself by fluttering about light; (fig.) person hovering around temptation; ~*-ball* (of chemical preventive for keeping ~s from clothes), (also) airtight plastic cover sprayed on & enclosing working parts of gun-mountings, machinery, etc. of ship, (v.t.) enclose thus; ~*-eaten,* destroyed by ~s, (fig.) antiquated, time-worn. [OE *moththe,* corresp. to MDu., MLG, MHG, ON *motte*]

mo'ther[1] (mŭdh-), n. **1.** Female parent. **2.** Quality, condition, etc., that gives rise to another, as *necessity is the* ~ *of invention.* **3.** Head of female religious community (often *M*~ *Superior*). **4.** (Term of address for) elderly woman of lower class. **5.** (Also *artificial* ~) apparatus for rearing chickens. **6.** (Arch., f. obs. sense *womb*) hysteria. **7.** *M*~ *Carey's* CHICKEN; *M*~ *Church* (as of maternal authority); *M*~-*Church* (whence others have sprung); ~ *country*, country in relation to its colonies; ~-*craft*, skill in treatment of offspring; ~ *earth*, earth as ~ of its inhabitants etc., (joc.) the ground; *M*~ *Hubbard*, person in nursery rhyme, kind of cloak or overall; ~-*in-law*, one's wife's or husband's ~; ~*land*, one's native land; ~ *lodge* (freemasonry), masonic lodge in which one was initiated; ~ *of pearl*, smooth shining iridescent substance forming inner layer of some shells (often attrib., w. hyphens); ~ *of thousands* or *millions*, ivy-leaved toadflax; ‖ ~ *ship* (in charge of torpedo-boats, submarines, etc.); ~'s *son*, man, esp. *every* ~'s *son of* (*you* etc.); ~ *tongue*, one's native tongue, (also) tongue from which others spring; ~ *wit*, native wit, common sense. Hence~HOOD n., ~LESS, ~LIKE, aa. [OE *mōdor*, OS *mōdar*, OHG *muotar*, ON *mōthir* f. Gmc **mōthar-* cōgn. w. L *mater*]

mo'ther[2] (mŭdh-), v.t. Give birth to (usu. fig.); protect as a mother; acknowledge or profess oneself the mother of (child, lit. & fig.); ‖ ~*ing Sunday*, 4th Sunday in Lent, with old custom of visiting parents with gifts. [f. prec.]

mo'ther[3] (mŭdh-), n. (Also ~ *of vinegar*) mucilaginous substance produced in vinegar during fermentation by mould-fungus. Hence~Y[2] a. [prob.=MOTHER[1]; cf. MDu. *moeder*, G *mutter* in same sense]

mo'therl|ŷ (mŭdh-), a. Having, showing, the good qualities of a mother. Hence ~ĪNESS n. [OE *mōdorlic* (MOTHER[1], -LY[1])]

mōtif' (-ēf), n. Constituent feature, dominant idea, in artistic composition; ornament of lace etc. sewn separately on dress. [F, as MOTIVE a.]

mōt'ile, a. (zool., bot.). Capable of motion. Hence motil'ITY n. [as MOVE, see -IL]

mō'tion[1], n. **1.** Moving, change of place; manner of moving the body in walking etc.; change of posture; gesture; *in* ~, moving, not at rest; *put in* ~, set going or working; **~ picture*, cinematographic film. **2.** Formal proposal in deliberative assembly; (law) application by party etc. for rule or order of court. **3.** Evacuation of bowels. **4.** Piece of moving mechanism. Hence ~AL, ~LESS, aa., (-shon-). [ME, f. OF, f. L *motionem* (as MOVE, -ION)]

mō'tion[2], v.t. & i. Direct (person *to*, *towards*, *away*, etc., *to* do) by sign or gesture; make gesture (*to* person) directing him (*to* do). [f. prec.]

mōt'ive[1], a. & n. **1.** Tending to initiate movement, whence **mōtiv'ITY** n.; ~ *power*, moving or impelling power, esp. form of mechanical energy used to drive machinery, e.g. steam, electricity; con-

cerned with movement. **2.** n. What induces a person to act, e.g. desire, fear, circumstance, whence ~LESS a.; = MOTIF. [ME, f. OF *motif* f. LL *motivus* (MOVE, -IVE)]

mōt'ive[2], **mōt'ivāte**, vv.t. Supply a motive to, be the motive or motif of. Hence **mōtivā'TION** n. [f. prec. n.]

mōt'ley, a. & n. **1.** Diversified in colour; of varied character, as ~ *assembly*. **2.** n. Incongruous mixture; (hist.) fool's particoloured dress, esp. *wear* ~, play the fool. [ME; orig. obsc.; poss. f. AF **motelé*, f. MOTE +-LE]

mōt'or, n., a., & v.i. & t. **1.** What imparts motion; machine supplying motive power for carriage or vessel, esp. internal-combustion engine, as (attrib.) ~ (*bi*)*cycle*, *cab*, (*omni*)*bus*, *boat*, *mower*, *ship*; ‖ ~-*car*; ~, *bandit*, thief who uses a ~-car in his depredations; ‖ ~-*car*, car propelled by ~ for use on ordinary roads, whence ~IST(3) n.; ~ *cycle*, bicycle etc. worked by ~ engine; ~*way*, arterial road specially made for fast-moving ~ traffic. **2.** (anat.). Muscle designed to move a part of the body; (nerve) designed to excite muscular activity, whence **motōr'IAL**, **mōt'ORY**, aa. **3.** vb. Go or convey in ~-car. [L (MOVE, -OR)]

***mōt'orcāde**, n. Procession or parade of motor-cars. [f. MOTOR(-*car*)+(CAVAL-)CADE]

mōt'orīz|e, -is|e (-īz), v.t. Equip (troops etc.) with motor transport. Hence ~A'TION n. [-IZE]

mōt'tle, n., & v.t. **1.** Arrangement of spots or confluent blotches of colour; such spot; variegated woollen yarn. **2.** v.t. Mark (esp. soap) with ~s (esp. in p.p.). [prob. f. MOTLEY]

mōtt'ō, n. (pl. ~*es*). Sentence inscribed on some object & expressing appropriate sentiment; word or sentence accompanying coat of arms or crest; maxim adopted as rule of conduct; verses etc. in paper cracker; quotation prefixed to book or chapter; (mus.) recurrent phrase having some symbolical significance. [It., as MOT]

moue (mōō), n. POUT[2]. [F; see MOW[2]]

mouff'lon (mōō-), n. Wild mountain sheep of S. Europe. [f. F *mouflon* f. LL *mufronem*]

moujik, muzhik, (mōō'zhĭk), n. Russian peasant; lady's loose fur cape. [f. Russ. *muzhik* peasant]

mould[1] (mōld), n. Loose earth; upper soil of cultivated land; *man of* ~, mere mortal; ~-*board*, board in plough that turns over the furrow-slice. [OE *molde*, MDu. *moude*, OHG *molta*, ON *mold*, Goth. *mulda* f. Gmc **moldō* f. **mul-*, **mel-* (MEAL[1])]

mould[2] (mōld), n. Pattern, templet, used by masons, bricklayers, etc., as guide in shaping mouldings; hollow form into which molten metal etc. is cast to cool into required shape; metal or earthenware vessel used to give shape to puddings etc., pudding etc. so shaped; (fig.) *cast in heroic* etc. ~, of such character; form, shape, esp. of animal body; (archit.) group of mouldings; ~ *candle* (made in a ~); ~*-loft*, room on floor of which plans of ship are drawn full size. [ME *mold*(*e*) app. f. OF *modle* f. MODULUS]

mould[3] (mōld), v.t. Produce (object) in certain shape, *out of* (elements), or *upon* (pattern), lit. & fig.; bring into certain shape; shape (bread) into loaves. [f. prec.]

mould[4] (mōld), n. Woolly or furry growth of minute fungi on things that lie for some time in moist warm air. [prob. f. obs *mould* a., p.p. of *moul* grow mouldy]

moul'der[1] (mōl-), n. One who moulds, esp. workman making moulds for casting. [-ER[1]]

moul'der[2] (mōl-), v.i. Decay to dust, rot *away*, (often fig.). [perh. MOULD[1] + -ER[5]: but cf. Norw. dial. *muldra* crumble]

moul'ding (mōl-), n. In vbl senses, esp. moulded object, esp. ornamental variety of outline in cornices etc. of building, woodwork, etc.; ~*-board* (on which dough is kneaded); *picture*~ (for framing pictures). [MOULD[3] + -ING[1]]

moul'd|y̆[1] (mōl-), a. Overgrown with mould; (fig.) stale, out-of-date; (sl.) dull, tiresome, boring. Hence ~**iNESS** n. [MOULD[4] + -Y[2]]

moul'dy̆[2] (mōl-), n. (nav. sl.). Torpedo.

moulin (mōōlăn'), n. Nearly vertical shaft in glacier, formed by surface water falling through crack in ice. [F, lit. = mill]

moult (mōlt), v.t. & i., & n. **1.** (Of birds) shed (feathers), shed feathers, in changing plumage (also fig.); (loosely, of animals) shed hair etc. **2.** n. ~ing. [ME *mouten* f. OE *mūtian*, = OLG *-mūtōn*, OHG *mūzzōn*, WG f. L *mutare* change; *-l-* after *fault* &c.]

mound[1], n. Ball of gold etc. representing earth, surmounting crown etc., & used in heraldry. [ME, f. OF *monde* f. L *mundus* world]

mound[2], n., & v.t. Elevation of earth or stones, esp. of earth heaped on grave; hillock; ~*-builder*, one of prehistoric Indian race in N. America who erected ~s, (also) kinds of bird depositing eggs in a ~; (v.t.) enclose with, heap up in, ~s. [in 16th c. (1) hedge or fence: orig. unkn.; (2) embankment &c., perh. after MOUNT[1]]

mount[1], n. Mountain, hill, (abbr. *Mt*, preceding name, as *Mt Ephraim*); (palmistry) fleshy prominence on palm of hand. [OE *munt* f. L *mons -ntis*; in ME reinforced by OF *mont*]

mount[2], v.i. & t. **1.** Ascend (hill etc. or abs.); proceed upwards; (of blood) rise into cheeks. **2.** Rise to higher level of rank, power, intensity, etc.; (also ~ *up*) rise in amount. **3.** Get *on* horse etc. for purpose of riding; get on (horse etc. or abs.); put (person) on horse etc.; furnish (person) with horse. **4.** Raise (guns) into position on a fixed ~ING[1]; put (loom etc.) in working order; put picture etc.) in a MOUNT[3]; fit (gems etc.) in gold etc.; fix (object) on microscope slide. **5.** Put (play) on stage; display (article of costume). **6.** ~ *an offensive* (mil.), act on, take, the offensive; ~ (go on duty as) *guard* (over thing or abs.). [ME, f. OF *munter* f. Rom. *:montare* f. *mons* (prec.)]

mount[3], n. Margin surrounding picture, card on which drawing is mounted; ornamental metal parts of thing; horse for person's riding; chance of riding, esp. as jockey. [f. prec.]

moun'tain (-tĭn), n. Natural elevation of earth's surface, large or high & steep hill; *waves ran* ~s (very) *high*, ~*-high*; large heap or pile; (also ~ *wine*) Malaga wine from ~ grapes; *the M*~, extreme party in first French Revolution, occupying elevated position in chamber of assembly; ~ *ash*, tree with delicate pinnate leaves & scarlet berries, rowan; ~ *chain*, series of ~s; ~ *dew* (colloq.), Scotch whisky; ~ *sickness*, malady caused by rarefied ~ air; ~ *tobacco*, species of arnica. [ME, f. OF *montaigne* f. Rom. **montania*, = LL *montana* mountain (MOUNT[1], -AN)]

mountaineer' (-tĭn-), n. Dweller amongst mountains; one skilled in mountain climbing, whence ~ING[1] n. [-EER]

moun'tainous (-tĭn-), a. Abounding in mountains; huge. [ME, f. OF *montagnous* f. LL *montaniosus* MOUNTAIN, -OUS]

moun'tĕbănk, n. Itinerant quack who held forth to audience from platform; charlatan. Hence ~ERY(4) n. [f. It. *montambanco = monta in banco* mount on bench]

mourn (mŏrn), v.i. & t. Feel sorrow or regret (*for, over*, dead person, lost thing, loss, misfortune, etc.); show conventional signs of grief for period after person's death; sorrow for (dead person, thing). [OE *murnan*, OS *mornon*, OHG *mornĕn*, ON *morna*, Goth. *maurnan* be anxious]

mourn'er (mŏr-), n. One who mourns, esp. who attends funeral of friend or relation; person hired to attend funeral. [-ER[1]]

mourn'ful (mŏr-), a. Doleful, sad, sorrowful. Hence ~LY[2] adv., ~NESS n. [MOURN + -FUL]

mourn'ing (mŏr-), n. In vbl senses, also or esp.: (wearing of) black clothes as sign of ~; DEEP[1], HALF, ~; *complimentary* ~ (worn as tribute to unrelated dead); *in* ~, wearing such garments, (sl., of the eye) blacked in fighting etc., (sl., of finger-nails) dirty; ~*-coach* (attending funeral); ~*-paper*, notepaper with black edge; ~*-ring* (worn as memorial of deceased person). [-ING[1]]

mouse[1] (mows), n. (pl. *mīce*). Animal of any of the smaller species of a genus of

rodents, esp. *house*, *field-*, *harvest-*, ~;
timid, shy, retiring person; weight & cord
for passing sash-lines over pulleys etc.;
(sl.) black eye; ~*-colour*, dark grey with
yellow tinge; ~*-ear*, hawkweed & other
plants; ~*'trap* (for catching mice; ~*trap
cheese*, of poor quality). Hence **mous'**Y² ²
a. [OE *mūs* (= OS, OHG, ON *mús*), f.
Gmc *mūs-* cogn. w. L *mus*]
mouse² (-z), v.i. & t. (Of cat or owl) hunt
for or catch mice, whence **mous'**ER¹ (-z-)
n.; search industriously, prowl *about* in
search of something; (naut.) put some
turns of spunyarn round (point & shank
of a hook). [ME, f. prec.]
mousse (mōōs), n. Dish of flavoured
cream whipped & frozen (*chestnut, chocolate*, etc.,~). [F, = froth]
mousseline(mōōslēn'),n. French muslin;
~*-de-laine*, dress material of wool & cotton; ~*-de-soie* (swah), thin silk fabric of
muslin-like texture. [F, see MUSLIN]
moustache, *mus-*,(mustahsh'),n. Hair
on either side (usu. in pl.) or both sides of
a man's upper lip; similar hair round
mouths of some animals; ~*-cup* (with
partial cover to protect~ when drinking).
[F, f. It. *mostaccio* f. Gk *mustax -akos*]
Moustēr'ian (mōō-), a. (archaeol.). Of
the palaeolithic epoch represented by
remains found in the Moustier cave in
France. [-IAN]
mouth¹ (mowth), n. (*pl. pr.* -dhz). **1.**
External orifice in head, with cavity behind it containing apparatus of mastication & organs of vocal utterance; (sl.)
impudent talk, cheek; (of horse, with
reference to his readiness to feel & obey
pressure of bit) *good, bad, hard*, ~; ~
waters at (food; referring to flow of saliva
caused by anticipation); *useless* ~, one
who does no work but must be fed; *this
sounds strange in your* ~ (when said by
you); *put words into his* ~, tell him what
to say; *put* (speech) *into* person's ~,
represent him as having made it; *take the
words out of* person's ~, say what he was
about to say; (of dog) *give* ~, bark, bay;
down in the ~, dejected; *laugh on wrong
side of* one's ~, show chagrin; *make a
wry* ~, grimace in sign of disapproval etc.
2. Opening of bag, sack, cave, furnace,
etc.; outfall of river. **3.** ~*-filling*, bombastic, inflated; ~*-organ*, thin rectangular
box containing metal reeds, each tuned
to a note, moved before ~ to play tunes;
~*'piece*, part of pipe, musical instrument,
etc., placed between lips, (also) one who
speaks for another or others. Hence
(-)~ED² (-dhd), ~'LESS, aa., ~'FUL n.
[OE, OS *mūth*, mund, OHG *mund*, ON
munnr, muthr, Goth *munths* f. Gmc
munthaz cogn. w. L *mentum* chin]
mouth² (mowdh), v.t. & i. Utter (words
or abs.) pompously or very distinctly,
rant, declaim; take (food) in, touch with,
the mouth; train mouth of (horse); grimace. [f. prec.]

mouth'y (-dhĭ), a. Railing, ranting; bombastic. [MOUTH¹ + -Y²]
mo'vable (mōō-), a. & n. **1.** That can be
moved; (of property) that can be removed, personal as opp. to *real*; ~ *feast*,
one that varies its date, (joc.) meal taken
at no regular time. **2.** n. Article of furniture that may be removed from the
house, opp. to *fixture*; (pl.) personal property. Hence **movabil'ITY, ~NESS, nn.**
(mōō-). [ME, f. OF (as MOVE², see -ABLE)]
move¹ (mōōv), n. Moving of a piece in
chess & other games; player's turn to
do this; change of residence, business
premises, etc.; device, step taken to
secure object; *on the* ~, moving about;
make a ~, go, esp. rise & go from dinner-
-table etc.; *get a* ~ *on* (sl.), hurry up,
bestir oneself. [f. foll.]
move²(mōōv),v.t. & i. **1.** Change position
of; change position of (piece) in chess etc.;
put, keep, in motion, shake, stir; ~
heaven & earth, make every effort (*to* do);
change posture of (one's body, limbs,
etc.). **2.** Cause (bowels) to act. **3.** Provoke
(laughter, anger, etc., *in* person, person
to these); affect (person) with (usu. tender
or sympathetic) emotion, whence **mo'-**
VING² a., **mo'vingLY² adv., (mōō-).**
4. Prompt, incline, (person *to* action, *to*
do); *the spirit* (orig. in Quaker use,
= Holy Spirit) ~*s me*, I feel inclined (*to*
do). **5.** Make formal application to court
etc. *for*); propose (question, resolution,
that thing be done) in deliberative
assembly. **6.** Go, pass, (*about, away*,
etc.) from place to place; make progress,
as *the work* ~*s slowly*; make a move at
chess etc. **7.** Change one's abode; ~
about, do this often; ~ *in*, take possession
of new abode. **8.** ~ *on* (policeman's order
to person who stands too long in one
place), (trans.) cause person to ~ on by
giving this order. **9.** (Of person or part
of body) change posture; (of inanimate
things) suffer change of position; *moving
staircase*, one made on principle of endless
chain, with steps moving up or down
continuously, escalator. **10.** (Of bowels)
be ~d. **11.** Make request or application
(*for*); take action, proceed, (*in* matter).
Hence ~'LESS a. (rare). [ME, f. AF *mover*,
OF *movoir* f. L *movēre mot-*]
move'ment (mōōvm-), n. Moving; military evolution; moving parts of mechanism (esp. of clock or watch), particular
group of these; mental impulse; development of poem, story, etc.; (mus.) principal
division of a musical work (e.g. suite,
sonata, symphony), having a distinctive
structure of its own; series of actions &
endeavours of a body of persons for
special object, as *the* OXFORD ~, *the* Labour
~; activity in' market for some commodity. [ME, f. OF f. med. L *movi-
mentum* (as prec., see -MENT)]
mo'ver (mōō-), n. In vbl senses, esp.: one
who moves proposal; *prime* ~, initial

source (natural or mechanical) of motive power, (also) author of fruitful idea. [-ER¹]

mo'vies (mōōvĭz), n. pl. (sl.). Cinema pictures. [= *moving pictures*]

mow¹ (mō), n. Stack of hay, corn, peas, etc.; place in barn where hay etc. is heaped; ~'*burnt*, spoilt by becoming overheated in the ~. [OE *mūga*, = ON *múgi* swath, crowd]

mow² (mō, mow), n., & v.i. See MOP³. [ME, f. OF *moue* mouth, lip, pout, or f. MDu. *mouwe*, in same sense]

mow³ (mō), v.t. (~*ed* pr. mōd, ~*n*). Cut down (grass etc. or abs.) with scythe or machine; cut down produce of (field) thus; destroy sweepingly, cut *off* or *down* in great numbers. Hence ~'ER¹(1, 2) (mō'er) n. [OE *māwan*, OHG *māen*, f. Gmc **mǣ-* as in MEADOW]

mŏx'a, n. Down from dried leaves of a plant, used for burning on skin as counter--irritant for gout; anything so used. [f. Jap. *mokusa* (*moe kusa* burning herb)]

moy'a, n. Volcanic must. [S.-Amer. Sp.]

Mŏzä'rab, n. (hist.). Christian owning allegiance to Moorish king but allowed his own religion. Hence ~IC a. [f. Sp. *Mozárabe* f. Arab. *musta'rib* would-be Arab ('*arab*)]

Mprĕt, n. Albanian ruler. [f. L *imperator* emperor]

Mr (mĭs'ter). See MISTER.

Mrs (mĭs'ĭz), n. Title prefixed to surname of married woman who has no superior title; *Mrs Grundy* (see GRUNDYISM). [abbr. of MISTRESS]

mū, n. Greek letter M (*M, μ*). [Gk]

mŭch, a. & adv. **1.** Existing in great quantity, as ~ *trouble, too ~ noise, not ~ rain*, (abs., quasi-n.) *I have stood ~, ~ of what you say is true; too ~* (more than a match) *for*; THINK, MAKE, ~ *of*; *he is not ~ of a* (not a good) *scholar; how ~* (what price) *is it?; how ~* (what amount) *do I owe you?* **2.** adv. In a great degree (qualifying vb or p.p., cf. VERY), as *I ~ regret the mistake, was ~ annoyed*; (qualifying compar. or superl. adj.) ~ *better, ~ the most likely*; pretty nearly, as ~ *of a size*, about the same size. Hence ~'LY² adv. (joc.). [ME, f. *muchel* MICKLE]

mŭch'nĕss, n. Greatness in quantity or degree; *much of a ~*, very nearly the same or alike. [prec. + -NESS]

mū'cilage, n. Viscous substance from various plants; gum; viscous fluid in animal bodies, e.g. mucus. So **mūci-lā'ginous** a. [F, f. LL *mucilago -ginis* (MUCUS)]

mŭck¹, n. Farmyard manure; dirt; (colloq.) anything disgusting; (colloq.) untidy state; ~*rake* (for collecting ~, usu. fig.); ~'*worm*, worm that lives in ~, (fig.) money-grubber, street arab. Hence ~'Y² a. [ME *muk* f. ON *myki* dung]

mŭck², v.t. & i. Make dirty; remove muck from; manure with muck; (sl.)

bungle (job); (sl.) go aimlessly *about*. [ME, f. prec.; cf. ON *moka* shovel dung]

‖ **mŭck'er**, n. (sl.). Heavy fall (lit. & fig.); *come a ~*, experience this; *go a ~*, plunge into extravagance (*on, over*, purchase). [-ER¹]

mŭc'kle. See MICKLE.

mūc'ous, a. Of, covered with, mucus, as ~ *membrane*, internal prolongation of the skin so covered. So **mūcŏs'ITY** n. [f. L *mucosus* (as MUCUS, see -OUS)]

mūc'rō, n. (bot., zool.; pl. ~*nes* pr. -ōn'ēz). Pointed part or organ. Hence **mūc'ron-ATE²(2)** a. [L, = point]

mūc'us, n. Slimy substance secreted by mucous membrane; gummy substance found in all plants; slimy substance exuded by some animals, esp.. fishes. [L, cogn. w. *emungere* blow the nose]

mŭd, n. Wet soft earthy matter, mire; (fig.) what is worthless or polluting (*his name is ~*); *fling, throw, ~*, make disgraceful imputations; *here's ~ in your eye!*, sl. drinking toast; STICK *in the ~*; ~*bath* (in ~ of mineral springs, for rheumatism etc.); ~'*guard*, (metal) hood covering wheel of cycle etc. to protect rider from ~; ~'*lark*, one who dabbles, works, or lives, in ~, esp. street arab; ~ *pie*, ~ shaped like pie by child; ~ *volcano* (discharging ~). [ME *mode, mudde*, f. MLG *mudde*; cf. MHG *mot* bog]

mudär', **ma-**, n. E.-Ind. shrub, of which root-bark is used in medicine & inner bark yields silky fibre (yercum). [Hind. (*ma-*)]

mŭd'dle¹, n. Disorder; *make a ~ of*, bungle; ~*-headed*(*ness*), stupid(ity). [f. foll.]

mŭd'dle², v.t. & i. Bewilder, esp. with drink; mix (things *up, together*) blunderingly; bungle (affair); busy oneself in confused & ineffective way; ~ *on*, get on in haphazard way; ~ *through*, attain one's end by tenacity not skill. [f. MUD +-LE(3); cf. MDu. *moddelen*, f. *modden* dabble in mud]

mŭdd'|ỹ, a., & v.t. **1.** Like, abounding in, covered with, mud; (of liquid) turbid; (of light) dull; (of voice) thick; mentally confused; obscure. **2.** v.t. Make ~y. Hence ~ĭLY² adv., ~ĭNESS n. [(vb f. adj.) f. MUD +-Y²]

mudir (mōōdēr'), n. Governor of Turkish village or of Egyptian province. [Turk. f. Arab., part. of *adara* govern]

muĕzz'in (mōō-), n. Mohammedan crier who proclaims hours of prayer usu. from minaret. [f. Arab. *mu'adhdhin* (*adhana* proclaim)]

mŭff¹, n. Woman's fur or other covering (usu. cylindrical) into which both hands are thrust from opposite ends to keep them warm; *foot~*, contrivance serving same purpose for feet. [f. Du. *mof*, MDu. *moffel*, f. F *moufle*, as MUFFLE²]

mŭff², n., & v.t. **1.** Person who is awkward or stupid, orig. in some athletic sport;

failure, esp. to catch ball at cricket etc.
2. v.t. Bungle, miss (catch, ball, etc.).
Hence ~'ISH¹ a. [orig. unkn.]

‖ **müffetee'**, n. Worsted cuff worn on
wrist. [app. irreg. f. MUFF¹]

müff'in, n. ‖ Light flat round spongy
cake, eaten toasted & buttered; ‖ ~-*bell*
(rung by ~-*man*, seller of ~s). [orig.
unkn.; cf. OF *mouflet* soft (bread)]

müffineer', n. Small castor for sprinkling
salt or sugar on muffins. [-EER]

müf'fle¹, n. Thick part of upper lip &
nose of ruminants & rodents. [f. F *mufle*,
of unkn. orig.]

müf'fle², n. 1. Leather glove for lunatics
who tear clothes etc.; mitten. 2. Receptacle placed within furnace, in which substances may be heated without contact
with products of combustion; chamber
in kiln for baking pottery. [f. F *moufle*
mitten f. med. L *muffula*; cf. MDu. *moffel*
MUFF]

müf'fle³, v.t. Wrap, cover *up*, (one*self*,
one's throat etc., or abs.) for warmth;
wrap up head of (person) to prevent his
speaking; wrap up (oars, bell, drum,
horse's hoofs) to deaden sound; repress,
deaden, sound of (curse etc., usu. in p.p.).
[ME, perh. f. OF *enmoufler* f. *moufle*
MUFFLE²]

müff'ler, n. Wrap, scarf, worn for
warmth; boxing-glove; thick glove;
thing used to deaden sound, esp. felt
pad between hammer & string of piano.
[f. prec.+-ER¹]

müf'ti, n. 1. Mohammedan priest or expounder of law. 2. ‖ Plain clothes worn
by one who has right to wear uniform,
esp. *in* ~. [Arab., part. of *afta* decide
point of law]

müg¹, n. Drinking-vessel, usu. cylindrical, with or without handle; its contents;
a cooling drink; [perh. diff. wd] (sl.) face,
mouth. [perh. of Scand. orig.; cf. Norw.
mugga, mugge, Sw. *mugg*, LG *mukke*]

‖ **müg²**, n. (sl.). Simpleton, muff.

‖ **müg³**, v.i. & t. (-gg-), & n. (sl.). 1. Study
hard (*at* subject or abs.); (also ~ *up*) get
up (subject). 2. n. One who studies hard;
examination. [orig. unkn.]

mügg'er (-g-), n. Broad-nosed Indian
crocodile. [f. Hind. *magar*]

mügg'ins (-g-), n. Simpleton; children's
game of cards; game of dominoes. [perh.
the surname M~, w. allusion to MUG²]

Müggletōn'ian (-gel-), a. & n. (Member)
of sect founded by, & believing in personal
inspiration of, L. Muggleton & John
Reeve, c. 1650. [-IAN]

müg'gў |ў (-g-), a. (Of weather, day, etc.)
damp & warm. Hence ~iNESS n. [f. dial.
mug drizzle, cf. ON *mugga*, +-Y²]

***müg'wùmp**, n. Great man, boss;
one who holds aloof from party politics;
one who sits on the fence. [f. native
mugquomp great chief]

Muhammadan. See MOHAMMEDAN.

mūlätt'ō, n. (pl. ~s), & a. 1. Offspring of

European & Negro. 2. adj. Of ~ colour,
tawny. [f. Sp. *mulato* young mule,
mulatto, irreg. f. *mulo* MULE¹]

mŭl'berrў, n. 1. Kinds of tree, leaves of
which are much used for feeding silkworms: its fruit; ~ *bush*, children's game
with ditty *Here we go round the* ~ *bush*.
2. (M~) code name of prefabricated harbour used in the invasion on D-DAY and
subsequently. [ME *mol-, mool-, mulberry*,
by dissim. f. OE *mōr*, ME *moor*, f. L
morum mulberry; thus MHG *mûlber* (G
maulbeere) f. OHG *mûrberi*]

mŭlch, n., & v.t. 1. Mixture of wet
straw, leaves, etc., spread to protect roots
of newly planted trees etc. 2. v.t. Treat
with ~. [prob. subst. use of ME *molsh*
soft; cf. dial. *melsh, melch* (= OE *melsc*)]

mŭlct, n., & v.t. 1. Fine imposed for
offence. 2. v.t. Punish (person) by fine
(*in* amount, or with amount as second
object), deprive (person etc. *of*). [f. obs.
F *mul(c)te, mul(c)ter*, or L *mul(c)ta,
mul(c)tare*]

mūle¹, n. 1. Offspring of he-ass & mare, or
(pop.) of she-ass & stallion (prop. *hinny*),
used as beast of draught & burden &
noted for obstinacy; stupid or obstinate
person; hybrid plant or animal; ~
canary, cross between canary & other
finch. 2. Kind of spinning-machine.
Hence **mūl'ish¹** a., **mūl'ishLY²** adv.,
mūl'ishNESS n. [ME, f. OF *mul(e)*, f. L
mulus, -la; OE *mûl* f. L]

mūle², v.i. = MEWL.

mūle³, n. Heelless slipper. [F]

mūlēteer', n. Mule-driver. [f. F *muletier*
(*mulet* dim. of OF *mul* mule, see -EER)]

mūliĕb'ritў, n. Womanhood; the normal
characteristics of a woman (opp. VIRILITY);
softness, effeminacy. [f. LL *muliebritas*
(*mulier* woman)]

mŭll¹, n. Thin variety of plain muslin.
[shortened f. *mulmull* f. Hind. *malmal*]

‖ **mŭll²**, n. & v.t. 1. Muddle, mess,
esp. *make a* ~ *of*. 2. v.t. Make a ~ of
(catch etc.); ponder *over*. [n. perh. f.
ME *mul* dust, ashes, f. MDu. *mol, mul*
(MULLOCK)]

mŭll³, v.t. Make (wine, beer) into a hot
drink with sugar, spices, yolk of egg,
etc. [orig. unkn.]

‖ **mŭll⁴**, n. (Sc.). Promontory (*M~ of
Kintyre*). [Icelandic *múli*]

‖ **mŭll⁵**, n. (Sc.). Snuffbox. [var. of MILL¹,
box orig. having a grinder]

mŭll'ah, mōōll'ah, n. Mohammedan
learned in theology & sacred law. [f.
Pers., Turk., Hind., *mulla* f. Arab. *maula*]

mŭll'ein (-lin), n. Kinds of herbaceous
plant with woolly leaves & yellow flowers.
[ME, f. AF *moleine*, f. Gaulish *melena*]

mŭll'er, n. Tool used for grinding powders etc. on slab. [ME *mol-, mulour* f. *mul*
grind (MULL² v.)+-ER; cf. MULLOCK]

mŭll'ét, n. Two genera of fishes of which
red & grey ~ are the types. [ME, f. OF
mulet dim. f. L *mullus* red ~]

mŭllĭgatawn′y̆, n. (Also ~ *soup*) E.-Ind. highly seasoned soup; ~ *paste*, curry paste used for this. [f. Tamil *milagu-lannir* pepper-water]

mŭll′ĭgrŭbs (-z), n. pl. Depression of spirits; stomach-ache. [arbitrary]

mŭll′ion (-yon), n. Vertical bar dividing lights in window. Hence ~ED[2] (-yond) a. [prob. metathetic f. MONIAL]

mŭll′ock, n. .(Austral.) rock containing no gold, also, refuse from which gold has been extracted; (dial.) rubbish. [f. dial. *mull* dust, rubbish, rel. to OE *myl* dust, MDu. *mul, mol* f. Gmc root **mul-* grind, +-OCK]

mŭltăng′ūlar (-ngg-), a. Many-angled. [f. MULTI-+ANGULAR]

mŭlté′ĭty̆, n. Manifoldness. [f. L *multus* many; cf. *variety*]

mŭl′ti-, comb. form (bef. vowel occas. *mult-*) of L *multus* many, as : ~*colour(ed)*, of many colours; ~*fīd* (bot., zool.), cleft into many parts; ~*flŏr′ous*, (of stalk) bearing more than three flowers; ~*foil* (archit.), ornament consisting of more than 5 foils; ~*form*, having many forms, of many kinds, so ~*form′ity* n. ; ~*lăt′eral*, having many sides, (of an agreement, treaty, etc.) in which three or more parties participate; ~*lĭng′ual* (-nggw-), in many languages; ~*millionaire′* (-yon-), person with fortune of several millions; ~*nŏm′ial* a. & n. (alg.), (expression) of more than two terms; *multĭp′arous*, bringing forth many young at a birth, (of woman) who has borne more than one child; ~*pārt′ite*, divided into many parts; ~*ra′cial*, (composed) of many races; ~*valve* a. & n., (shell, animal with shell) of many valves; *multĭv′ocal* a. & n., (word) susceptible of many meanings; *multŏc′ular*, having many eyes; *multŭng′ūlate* a. & n., (animal) with more than two functional hoofs.

mŭltifār′ious, a. Having great variety; (w. pl. n.) many & various. Hence ~LY[2] adv., ~NESS n. [f. L MULTI(*farius* f. *-fariam* adv.)+-OUS]

mŭl′tiple, a. & n. **1.** Of many parts, elements, or individual components (~ *shop*, with branches in various places); (w. pl. n.) many & various; ~ PERSONALITY. **2.** n. Quantity that contains another some number of times without remainder, as *14 is à* ~ *of 7*; *least common*~, (abbr. L.C.M.) least quantity that contains two or more given quantities exactly; ~ *shop* or store. [F, f. LL *multiplus* = foll.]

mŭl′tiplĕx, a. Manifold, of many elements. [L (MULTI-+*-plex -plicis* -fold)]

mŭl′tiplicable, a. Multipliable. [f. L *multiplicabilis* (as MULTIPLY, see -ABLE)]

mŭltiplĭcănd′, n. Quantity to be multiplied, cf. MULTIPLIER. [f. L as MULTIPLY]

mŭltiplĭcā′tion, n. Multiplying, esp. the arithmetical process (*symbol of* ~, ×, as in 2 × 3); ~ *table*, table of products of factors taken in pairs. So **mŭl′tiplica-**

-tive a. [ME, f. OF, or f. L *multiplicatio* (as MULTIPLY, see -ATION)]

mŭltipli′cĭty̆, n. Manifold variety; *a, the,* ~ (great number) *of.* [f. F (*-ité*), or LL *multiplicitas* (as MULTIPLEX, see -TY)]

mŭl′tiplĭer, n. In vbl senses, esp. : quantity by which MULTIPLICAND is multiplied; (econ.) factor by which an increment of income exceeds the resulting increment of saving or investment; (electr., magn.) instrument for multiplying intensity of force, current, etc., so as to make it appreciable. [f. foll.+-ER[1]]

mŭl′tiply̆, v.t. & i. Produce large number of (instances etc.); breed (animals), propagate (plants); (intr.) increase in number by procreation; (math.) substitute for (given number, the ~*icand*) a number (the *product*) equal to a given number (the ~*ier*) of times its value, as ~*y 6 by 4 & the product is 24*, or *6* ~ *ied by 4 is 24*. Hence ~ĪABLE a. [ME, f, OF *multiplier* f. L *multiplicare* (MULTIPLEX)]

mŭl′tĭ|tūde, n. Numerousness; great number (*of*); large gathering of people, crowd; *the* ~*tude*, the common people. Hence ~**tūd′inous** a., ~**tūd′inousLY**[2] adv., ~**tūd′inousNESS** n. [ME, f. OF, or L *multitudo -dinis* (*multus* many, see -TUDE)]

mŭltitūd′in|ĭsm, n. Principle that prefers interests of multitudes to those of individuals. So ~IST n. [as prec.+-ISM]

mŭl′tum ĭn pārv′ō, n. Much in small compass; (attrib., w. hyphens) small but comprehensive. [L]

‖ **mŭl′ture**, n. Toll of grain or flour paid to miller. [ME, f. OF *molture* f. med. L *molitura* (*molere -it-* grind, see -URE)]

mŭm[1], int. & a. **1.** Silence!, esp. ~*'s the word*. **2.** adj. Silent. [ME *mom(me)* n. & v., imit.; cf. MLG *mummen,* Du. *mommen*]

mŭm[2], v.i. (-mm-). Act in dumb show. [16th c., f. OF *momer* f. *momon* mask]

mŭm[3], n. (hist.). Kind of beer orig. brewed in Brunswick. [f. G *mumme*]

‖ **mŭm**[4], n. (nursery). = MUMMY[2].

mŭm′ble, v.i. & t., & n. **1.** Speak indistinctly; utter indistinctly; bite, chew, (as) with toothless gums. **2.** n. Indistinct utterance. [ME *momele,* as MUM[1], -LE(3); cf. MDu. *mom-, mummelen*]

Mŭm′bō Jŭm′bō, n. (pl. ~*s*). Grotesque idol said to have been worshipped by some tribes; (fig.) object of senseless veneration: meaningless ritual. [orig. unkn.]

mŭmm′er, n. Play-actor; actor in folk-play. [ME, f. OF *momeur* (*momer* MUM[2])]

mŭmm′ery̆, n. Performance of mummers; ridiculous (esp. religious) ceremonial. [f. OF *momerie* (as prec., see -ERY), whence Du. *mommerij,* G *mummerei*]

mŭmm′ĭ|fy̆, v.t. Preserve (body) by embalming & drying; shrivel, dry up, (tissues etc., esp. in p.p.). Hence ~FICA-TION n. [f. F *momifier* (as foll., see -FY)]

mŭmm'ў¹, n. 1. Body of human being or animal embalmed for burial; dried-up body. 2. Pulpy substance or mass, esp. *beat* (thing) *to a* ~. 3. Rich brown pigment. [f. F *momie* f. med. L *mumia* f. Arab. *mumiya* (*mum* wax)]

|| **mŭmm'ў²**, n. Mother. [nursery form of MAMMA¹]

mŭmp¹, v.i. Be silent & sullen; assume demure expression, whence ~'ING² [17th c.; also 16th c. as n.= grimace, ' mouth '; imit.]

mŭmp², v.i. Beg, go about begging. [17th c., f. Du. *mompen* cheat]

mŭmps, n. pl. (treated as sing.). Contagious disease with swelling of parotid & salivary glands; sulks, whence **mŭm-PISH¹** a. [16th c., f. MUMP¹]

mŭnch, v.t. & i. Eat (food, or abs.) with much action of jaws, as cattle chew fodder. [ME, imit.; cf. *crunch*]

Munchaus'en (-zn), n. *Baron* ~, hero of extravagant book of adventures written in English by R. E. Raspe, a German (1785); extravagantly mendacious story.

mŭn'dāne, a. Of this world; of the universe. Hence ~LY² adv., ~NESS n. [ME, f. OF *mondain* f. L *mundanus* f. *mundus* world, see -AN]

mŭng'ō (-ngg-), n. Substance used in making cloth of poorer quality than SHODDY. [poss. f. dial. *mong* mixture; cf. *stingo*]

Mŭn'ich (-ĭk), n. An act of appeasement between nations. [f. the agreement to dismember Czechoslovakia made with Hitler in 1938 at ~ in S. Germany]

mŭni'cipal, a. Of, under, local self--government or corporate government of city or town, whence ~ISM(2), ~IST(2, 3), nn., ~IZE(3) v.t.; carried on etc. by a municipality (~ *debt, kitchen, trading, undertaking*); ~ *law,* that of particular State, opp. to law of nations. Hence ~LY² adv. [f. L *municipalis* f. *municeps -cipis* citizen of city that had privileges of Roman citizens (*munia* civic offices + root of *capere* take), see -AL]

mŭnicipăl'itў, n. Town, district, having local self-government; governing body of this. [f. F *municipalité* (as prec., see -TY)]

mŭnif'ic|ent, a. Splendidly generous, bountiful. Hence or cogn. ~ENCE n., ~entLY² adv. [f. L *munificent-,* var. stem of *munificus* (*munus* gift, see -FIC)]

mŭn'iment, n. (usu. pl.). Document kept as evidence of rights or privileges; archives (esp. in ~-*room*) [ME, f. OF, f. L *munimentum* defence (*munire* fortify, -MENT)]

mŭni'tion, n., & v.t. 1. (Pl. exc. in comb.) military weapons, ammunition, equipment, & stores (*Ministry* etc. *of* ~s; ~-*factory*); (arch.) ~, or ~s, *of war*; hence ~ER¹ (-sho-) n. (esp. worker in ~-factory).

2. v.t. Supply with ~s. [F, f. L *munitionem* fortification (as prec., see -ION)]

munnion. = MULLION.

munshi. See MOONSHEE.

mŭnt'jak, n. Small Asian deer. [f. native *minchek*]

Mŭntz, n. (Also ~ *metal*), alloy (60% copper, 40% zinc) used for sheathing ships etc. [G. F. ~, inventor]

mur'age, n. (hist.). Tax levied for building or repairing walls of town. [ME, f. OF, in med. L *muragium* (*murus* wall, see -AGE)]

mur'al, a. & n. 1. Of, like, on, a wall, as ~ *paintings*; (Rom. ant.) ~ *crown,* garland (given to soldiers who first scaled wall of besieged town). 2. n. ~ painting etc. [f. F, or L *muralis* (*murus* wall, see -AL)]

Mŭratōr'ian, a. Of Muratori, Italian scholar, d. 1750; ~ *fragment* or *canon,* earliest Western canon of N.T. [-AN]

mŭrd'er¹, n. Unlawful killing of human being with malice aforethought (freq. *wilful* ~); JUDICIAL ~; (prov.) ~ *will out* (cannot be hidden); *the* ~ *is out,* the secret is revealed or mystery explained; (as int. of alarm) ~!; *cry blue* ~, make extravagant outcry. [OE *morthor,* Goth *maurthr* f. Gmc **murthram,* cogn. w. L *mori* die]

mŭrd'er², v.t. Kill (human being) unlawfully with malice aforethought; kill wickedly or inhumanly; spoil by bad execution, mispronunciation, etc. Hence ~ER¹, ~ESS¹, nn. [OE *myrthrian,* OHG *murdran,* Goth. *maurthrjan* (prec.)]

mŭrd'erous, a. (Of person, weapon, action, etc.) capable of, bent on, involving, murder. Hence ~LY² adv. [-OUS]

mūre, v.t. Confine as in prison; shut *up.* [ME, f. OF *murer* f. LL *murare,* see IM-MURE]

mūr'ex, n. (pl. *-ĭcēs, -exes*). Shellfish yielding purple dye. [L]

mūr'iate, n. (now commerc.). Chloride. [F, f. *muriatique,* as foll.]

mūriăt'ic, a. (now commerc.). ~ (hydrochloric) *acid.* [f. L *muriaticus* (*muria* brine, see -ATIC)]

mŭrk, mĭrk, a. (Of night, day, place, etc.) dark; misty, gloomy. [OE *mirce,* OS *mirki,* ON *myrkr* f. Gmc **merkw-*]

·**mŭrk'|ў**, a. Dark, gloomy; (of darkness) thick. Hence ~ĭLY² adv., ~iNESS n. [f. *murk* n. darkness, rel. to prec., +-Y²]

mŭrm'ur¹ (-ẽr), n. Subdued continuous sound, as of waves, brook, etc.; subdued expression of discontent; softly spoken word or speech. Hence ~OUS a., ~OUSLY² adv. [ME, f. OF *murmure* or L *murmur*]

mŭrm'ur² (-er), v.i. & t. Make low continuous sound; complain in low tones, grumble, (*at, against*); utter (words) in low voice. [ME, f. OF *murmurer* f. L *murmurare* (*murmur*)]

mŭrph'ў, n. (sl.). Potato. [Irish surname]

mŭ'rrain (-rĭn), n. Infectious disease in .cattle; (arch.) *a* ~ (plague) *on you!* [ME,

f. OF *morine* f. Rom. *morire f. L *mori* die]

mŭ′rrey, a. & n. (arch.). (Of) the colour of a mulberry, purple-red. [ME, f. OF *more* f. med. L *moratum* (*morum* mulberry)]

mŭ′rrhine (-rĭn, -rīn), a. ~ *glass*, modern delicate ware from the East, made of fluor-spar. [f. L *murr(h)inus* (*murra*, substance of which precious vases etc. were made, see -INE[1])]

mŭs′cadine, n. Musk-flavoured kinds of grape. [prob. Engl. form. as MUSCAT]

mŭs′cardine, n. Disease of silkworms caused by vegetable parasite. [F]

mŭs′căt, mŭscatĕl′, -dĕl′, nn. Muscadine; strong sweet wine from muscadines; (-*tel*) raisin from muscadine. [(-*at*) F, f. Pr. *muscat* adj. f. LL *muscatus* (MUSK, -ATE); (-*tel*, -*del*) OF dim.]

mŭ′scle (-sl), n., & v.i. **1.** Any of the contractile fibrous bands or bundles that produce movement in animal body; *not move a* ~, be perfectly motionless; that part of the animal body which is composed of ~s, the chief constituent of flesh; ~*-bound*, with ~s stiff & inelastic through over-exercise or over-training; hence ~LESS a. **2.** v.i. *(sl.). ~ *in*, intrude by violent means (as of one racketeer poaching on another's preserves). [f. F, or L *musculus* dim. of *mus* mouse]

mŭsc|ŏl′ogў, n. Study of mosses. So ~ŏL′OGIST n. [f. L *muscus* moss, -LOGY]

mŭscova′dō (-vah-), n. Unrefined sugar got from juice of sugar-cane by evaporation & draining off molasses. [f. Sp. *mascabado* (sugar) of lowest quality]

mŭs′covite[1], n. Common mica (earlier *Muscovy glass*). [as foll.]

Mŭs′covite[2], n. & a. Russian; citizen of Moscow. [f. foll. + -ITE[1]]

Mŭs′covў, n. (Arch.) Russia; ~ *duck*, MUSK-duck. [f. F *Muscovie* f. Russ. *Moskova* Moscow]

mŭs′cūlar, a. Of, affecting, the muscles; having well-developed muscles; ~ *Christianity*, ideal of religious character exhibited in writings of C. Kingsley. Hence **mŭscŭlă′rITY** n. [as MUSCLE, see -AR[1]]

mŭs′cūlature n. Muscular system of body or organ. [F, as MUSCLE, see -URE]

mūse[1] (-z), n. The *Muses*, nine goddesses, daughters of Zeus & Mnemosyne, inspirers of poetry, music, etc. (*Calliope, Clio, Erato, Euterpe, Melpomene, Polyhymnia, Terpsichore, Thalia, Urania*, Muse of epic poetry, history, lyric poetry, music, tragedy, sacred song, dancing, comedy, astronomy); *the* ~, poet's inspiring goddess, poet's genius; (poet.) poet. [ME, f. OF, or f. L f. Gk *Mousa*]

mūse[2] (-z), v.i., & n. **1.** Ponder, reflect, (*on, upon*): gaze meditatively (*on* scene etc.). **2.** n. (arch.). Fit of abstraction. [ME, f. OF *muser* to waste time]

mūsĕtte′ (-z-), n. Kind of bagpipe; soft

pastoral air imitating bagpipe's sound; dance for which this served; reed stop on organ. [OF, dim. of *muse* bagpipe]

mūsē′um (-z-), n. Building used for storing & exhibition of objects illustrating antiquities, natural history, art, etc.; ~ *piece*, specimen of art, manufacture, etc., fit for a ~ (also derog. of old-fashioned person, machine, etc.). [L, f. Gk *mouseion* seat of the Muses (*Mousa*)]

mŭsh[1], n. Soft pulp; (N.-Amer.) kind of porridge. Hence ~′iNESS n., ~′Y[2] a. (also sl., weakly sentimental, soppy). [app. var. of MASH[1]]

mŭsh[2], v.i., & n. (U.S. & Canada). (Go on) journey across snow with dog-sledge. [prob. corrupt. f. F *marchons* imper. of *marcher* advance]

mŭsh′rōōm, n., & v.i. **1.** Edible kind of fungus, proverbial for rapid growth (~ *growth* etc., sudden development or thing suddenly developed); (fig.) upstart; (colloq.) lady's hat with down-curved brim. **2.** v.i. Gather ~s; spring up rapidly, expand like a ~ cap. [ME, f. OF *mousseron*, f. LL *mussirionem*]

mŭs′ic (-z-), n. Art of combining sounds with a view to beauty of form & expression of emotion; sounds so produced; pleasant sound, e.g. song of bird, murmur of brook, cry of hounds; *set* (poem etc.) *to* ~, provide it with ~ to which it may be sung; written or printed score of musical composition; *face the* ~, face one's critics etc., not shirk; *rough* ~, noisy uproar, esp. with vexatious intention; *~ *box*, = MUSICAL *box*; ~ *-hall* ‖ (used for singing, dancing, & other entertainments); ~ *-stool* (with adjustable seat, for piano-player). [ME, f. OF *musique* f. L f. Gk *mousikē* (*lekhnē* art) of the Muses (*Mousa* Muse, see -IC)]

mŭs′ical (-z-), a. & n. **1.** Of music; (of sounds, voice, etc.) melodious, harmonious; fond of, skilled in, music; set to, accompanied by, music; ~ *box*, mechanical ~ instrument played by causing toothed cylinder to work in comb-like metal plate; ~ *chairs*, drawing-room game in which *n* players circulate round *n* − 1 chairs till music ceases, when the one who finds no seat is eliminated, and a chair is removed before the next round; ~ *comedy*, light dramatic entertainment of songs, dialogue, & dancing connected by a slender plot; ~ *film* (in which music is an important feature); ~ *glasses*, kinds of ~ instrument in which notes are produced by graduated glass bowls or tubes; ~ *ride*, military equestrian dance-like exercise performed to ~ accompaniment. **2.** n. (colloq.). ~ film or comedy; *MUSICALE. Hence **mūsicăl′ITY**, ~NESS, nn., ~LY[2] adv., (-z-). [ME, f. OF f. med. L *musicalis* (*musica* MUSIC, see -AL)]

*mūsicale′ (-zikahl), n. Musical party. [F, for *soirée* or *matinée* ~]

mūsi′cian (-zĭshn), n. Person skilled in

science or practice of music. [ME, f. OF *musicien* (MUSIC, -ICIAN); cf. *physician*]

mūsicŏl′og|ў̆ (-z-), n. All study of music except that directed to proficiency in performance or composition. Hence ~IST n., **mūsicolŏ′gical** a., (-z-). [f. MUSIC + -OLOGY]

mŭsk, n. Odoriferous reddish-brown substance secreted in gland by male ~-deer, used for perfumes & as stimulant etc.; kinds of plant with ~y smell; ~-deer, small hornless ruminant of Central Asia; ~-duck (also Muscovy duck), tropical American variety, (also) Australian variety male of which has ~y smell; ~melon, common melon; ~-ox, ruminant with curved horns found in Arctic America; ~-rat (also musquash), large N.-Amer. aquatic rodent, its fur; ~-rose, rambling rose with large fragrant white flowers; ~-tree, -wood, trees with ~y smell. Hence **mŭs′kŷ²** a. [ME, f. OF musc f. LL muscus f. late Gk mosk(h)os f. Pers. mušk]

mŭs′kĕt, n. Infantry soldier's hand-gun (now usu. of obsolete kinds, cf. RIFLE); ~-shot, shot fired from ~, range of ~. [f. F mousquet f. It. moschetto sparrow-hawk]

mŭskĕteer′, n. (hist.). Soldier armed with musket. [-EER]

mŭs′kĕtrŷ, n. Muskets; art of using, troops armed with, muskets. [f. F mousqueterie (as MUSKET, see -ERY)]

Muslim. See MOSLEM.

mŭs′lĭn (-z-), n. Kinds of delicately woven cotton fabric for ladies' dresses, curtains, etc.; (sl.) bit of ~, woman, girl; ~-de-laine, see MOUSSELINE. Hence ~ED² (-nd) a. [f. F mousseline f. It. mussolina (Mussolo, = Mosul in Iraq whence ~ came, see -INE¹)]

mŭslĭnĕt′ (-z-), n. Thick kind of muslin. [-ET¹]

mŭs′mon, n. = MOUFFLON. [f. L mus(i)mo f. late Gk mousmōn]

mŭs′quash (-ŏsh), n. (Fur of) MUSK-rat. [f. Algonkin muskwessu]

***mŭss**, v.t., & n. (colloq.). 1. Disarrange, throw into disorder (up). 2. n. State of confusion, untidiness, mess. Hence ~′ў̆² a. [app. var. of MESS]

mŭssal′ (-ahl), n. (Anglo-Ind.). Torch; (also ~chee) torch-bearer. [f. Arab. mas'al]

mŭss′el, n. Kinds (sea, freshwater, ~) of bivalve mollusc; ~ plum, dark purple plum. [OE muscle = OS, OHG muscula, f. Rom. *muscula bivalve, fem. corresp. to L musculus (as MUSCLE); ME mussel f. MDu., MLG mussel]

mŭss′uck, n. (Anglo-Ind.). Leather water-bag. [Hind. masak]

Mŭss′ulman, n. & a. (pl. ~s). Mohammedan. [f. Pers. musulmān (as MOSLEM)]

mŭst¹, n. New wine; grape-juice before fermentation is complete. [OE, ME, f. L mustum neut. of mustus new]

mŭst², n. Mustiness, mould. [back formation f. MUSTY]

mŭst³, a. & n. 1. (Of male elephants & camels) in state of frenzy. 2. n. This state. [f. Hind. f. Pers. mast intoxicated]

mŭst⁴, v. auxil. (3rd sing. must; past must, only as below; no infin. or part. or gerund), & n. 1. Be obliged to (do), as you ~ (neg. need not, see below & cf. MAY¹) find it, it ~ be found, (w. necessity less emphasized) we ~ see what can be done, I ~ ask you to retract that, you ~ know (I now tell you); be certain to (do), as you ~ lose, whichever happens; you ~ be (surely are) aware of this; he ~ be (clearly is) mad; (as past tense, reporting reflection made at the time) it was too late now to retreat, he ~ make good his word or incur lasting disgrace; (past or historic present, w. reference to perverse destiny) just as I was getting better, what ~ I do but break my leg?, just as I was busiest, he ~ come worrying; ~ have done, (1) surely did, as you ~ have known quite well what I meant, (2) necessarily would have done, as you ~ have caught it if you had run; (w. negative belonging in sense to dependent vb, cf. MAY¹) you ~ not infer (~ avoid the inference), you ~ never contradict. 2. n. A ~, a thing that cannot or should not be missed. [OE mōste (= OHG muosa, G musste) f. pret. pres. mōt (= Goth. gamōt, OHG muoz, G muss), ME & arch. mote may, be permitted to]

***mustache.** See MOUSTACHE.

musta′chio (-ahshō), n. (arch.; pl. ~s). Moustache. [(partly f. Sp. mostacho) f. It. as MOUSTACHE]

mŭs′tăng, n. Wild horse of Mexico & California; ~ (small red Texas) grape. [f. Sp. mestengo (now mesteño), app. f. mesta company of graziers]

mŭs′tard, n. Kinds of plant, esp. black & white ~, seeds of which are ground, made into paste, & used as condiment or for poultice or ~ plaster; (fig.) *zestful thing or person (sl.); grain of ~ seed, small thing capable of vast development (Matt. xiii. 31); || ~ & cress (used in seed-leaf for salad); field ~, charlock; French ~ (mixed with vinegar); ~ gas, kind of liquid poison gas, a powerful irritant & vesicant; ~-pot (for table ~). [ME, f. OF mostarde, f. Rom. *mosto MUST¹; orig. of the condiment as prepared w. must]

mŭs′ter¹, n. Assembling of men for inspection etc. (pass ~, be accepted as adequate), assembly, collection; ~-book, (for registering military forces); ~-roll, official list of officers & men in army or ship's company (also fig.). [ME, f. OF mo(u)stre f. L monstrare show]

mŭs′ter², v.t. & i. Collect (orig. soldiers) for inspection, to check numbers, etc.; collect, get together, (t. & i.); summon (courage, strength, etc.; often up). [ME, f. OF mostrer f. L as prec.]

mŭs′t|ў̆, a. Mouldy; of mouldy or stale

smell or taste; (fig.) stale, antiquated. Hence ~iness n. [16th c., of obsc. orig.; perh. alt. f. *moisty* (MOIST)]

mūt'able, a. Liable to change; fickle. Hence **mūt**abil'ity n. [f. L *mutabilis* (*mutare* change, see -BLE)]

mūtā'tion, n. Change, alteration; (biol.) genetic change which when transmitted to offspring gives rise to heritable variation; (mus.) ~ *stop*, organ stop in which notes produced are not at normal pitch but at that of some harmonic (other than mere octaves). [ME, f. OF, or f. L *mutatio* (as prec., see -ATION)]

mūtāt'is mūtăn'dis, adv. With due alteration of details (in comparing cases). [L]

‖ **mūtch,** n. (Sc.). Woman's or child's linen cap. [ME, f. MDu. *mutse*, = G *mütze*]

mūte¹, a. & n. 1. Silent; not emitting articulate sound; (law) *stand ~ of malice*, refuse deliberately to plead; (of person or animal) dumb; (of hounds) not giving tongue; not expressed in speech, as ~ *appeal, adoration*; temporarily bereft of speech; (of consonant) produced by entire interruption of passage of breath or, complete closure of organs of mouth, stopped, (usu. applied to *b p f d t th k g*); (of letter) not pronounced, as *the* e in late or in French aime *is* ~. 2. n. ~ consonant; dumb person; actor whose part is in dumb show; dumb servant in Oriental countries; hired mourner; clip for deadening resonance of strings of violin etc.; pad for deadening sound of wind instrument. Hence ~'ly² adv., ~'ness n. [ME & OF *muet*, dim. of *mu* f. L *mutus*]

mūte², v.t. Deaden, muffle, the sound of (esp. musical instrument). [f. prec.]

mūte³, v.i. & t. (Of birds) void the faeces, discharge thus. [f. OF *muetir*]

mūt'ilāte, v.t. Deprive (person etc.) of limb or organ; cut off, destroy the use of, (limb etc.); render (book etc.) imperfect by excision etc. So ~A'TION, ~ātor, nn. [f. L *mutilare* (*mutilus* maimed), see -ATE³]

mūtineer', n. One who mutinies. [f. F *mutinier* (*mutin* rebellious, ult. f. L *movēre* mōt- MOVE)]

mūt'inous, a. Rebellious. Hence ~ly² adv. [f. obs. *mutine* rebellion f. F *mutin* (see prec.) +-OUS]

mūt'iny, n., & v.i. 1. Open revolt against constituted authority, esp. of soldiers etc. against officers; *Indian M~*, revolt of Bengal native troops, 1857–8; *M~ Act* (dealing with offences against military & naval discipline, now embodied in Army Act, 1881). 2. v.i. Revolt (*against* or abs.). [n. f. obs. *mutine* (vb or n.) as prec. +-Y¹; vb f. n.]

mūt'ism, n. Muteness; silence; dumbness. [f. F *mutisme* f. L as MUTE¹, see -ISM]

mūt'o-, comb. form (irreg.) of L *mutare* change, as: ~*graph*, apparatus for taking series of photographs of moving objects,

(v.t.) portray with this; ~*scope*, apparatus for exhibiting scene recorded by ~graph, so ~*scŏp'ic* a.

mŭtt,'n. (sl.). Ignorant blunderer, dunderhead; small dog (derog.). [perh. abbr. of *mutton-head*]

mŭtt'er, v.i. & t., & n. 1. Speak low in barely audible manner; murmur, grumble, (*against, at*): utter (words etc.) in low tone; (fig.) say in secret. 2. n. ~ing, ~ed words. [ME, imit., w. suf. -ER⁵]

mŭtt'on, n. Flesh of sheep as food; (joc.) sheep (*to our ~s*, gallicism = let us come back to our subject); *dead as ~*, quite dead; *eat one's ~*, dine *with*; ~ *chop*, piece of ~ (usu. rib & half vertebra to which it is attached) for frying etc., side whisker shaped like this; ~ *dressed like lamb* (colloq.), elderly woman got up to look young; ~-*head* (colloq.), dull, stupid person. Hence ~y² a. [ME, f. OF *moton* f. med. L *multonem* f. Gaul. *multo*, cf. OIr. *molt* ram]

mūt'ual, a. (Of feelings, actions, etc.) felt, done, by each to(wards) the other, as ~ *affection, benefit, suspicion*; standing in (specified) ~ relation, as ~ *well-wishers*; ~ *admiration society*, set of persons who overestimate each other's merits; ~ *insurance company* (in which some or all of the profits are divided among the policy-holders); (commerc.) ~ *terms* (by which exchange of services takes the place of money payments); (improp.) common to two or more persons, as *our* ~ *friend*. Hence **mūtūăl'ity** n., ~ly² adv. [ME, f. OF *mutuel* f. L *mutuus* borrowed (cf. *mutare* change), see -AL]

mūt'ual|ism, n. Doctrine that mutual dependence is necessary to well-being. So ~ist n. [-ISM]

mūt'ule, n. (archit.). Modillion proper to cornice in Doric order. [F, or L *mutulus*]

muzhik. See MOUJIK.

‖ **mŭzz,** v.t. (sl.). Make muzzy. [orig. obsc.]

mŭz'zle¹, n. Projecting part of animal's head including nose & mouth; open end of fire-arm; contrivance of strap or wire put over animal's head to prevent its biting, eating, etc.; ~-*loader*, gun that is loaded at the ~. [ME, f. OF *musel* f. med. L *musellum* dim. of *musum*]

mŭz'zle², v.t. Put muzzle on (animal, its mouth, &, fig., a person); impose silence upon; take in (sail). [f. prec.]

mŭzz'|ly, a. Dull, spiritless; stupid from drinking. Hence ~ily² adv., ~iness n. [cf. earlier *mussy, mosy*]

my (mī, mǐ), poss. adj. of 1st pers. sing. (with abs. form MINE); (prefixed to some terms of address) *my boy, friend, man, son, daughter*, (not colloq. w. other terms of relationship), *dear, darling, love*; *my* (vulg. *mine*) *& her* (common) *father, my* (vulg. *mine*) *& her* (respective) *father*(s); (in ejaculations) *my! my eye!*, etc. [ME *mī*, reduced f. OE *min* MINE³]

myăl'gia (-ja), n. (path.). Muscular rheumatism. [Gk *mus* muscle, *algos* pain, -IA[1]]

my'alism, n. Kind of sorcery practised esp. in W. Indies. [prob. of W.-Afr. orig.]

my'all, n. Austral. acacia, with scented wood used for pipes. [f. native *maial*]

mycěl'i|um, n. (bot.). Spawn of fungi. Hence ~AL a. [f. Gk *mukēs* mushroom + Latin ending]

Mycēnae'an, a. (archaeol.). Of the prehellenic or Achaean culture illustrated by remains at Mycenae in Greece, & by Homer. [f. L f. Gk *Mukēnaios* +-AN]

mycětōm'a, n. Fungoid disease of foot or hand. [f. Gk *mukēs mukēt-* mushroom, see -M]

mycŏl'og|ў, n. Study of fungi. So ~IST n. [irreg. f. Gk as prec., see -LOGY]

mycōs'is, n. Presence of, disease caused by, parasitic fungi. [as prec., see -OSIS]

myelīt'is, n. Inflammation of spinal cord. [f. Gk *muelos* marrow, see -ITIS]

Mўl'odŏn, n. Extinct genus of gigantic sloths with cylindrical teeth. [f. Gk *mulē* mill + *odous -ontos* tooth]

myna(h). = MINA[2].

mўnheer', n. Dutchman. [f. Du. *mijnheer* Mr, sir, (*mijn* my + *heer* master)]

myo-, comb. form of Gk *mus muos* muscle, as: ~*card'ium*, muscular substance of heart, whence ~*cardīt'is*; *mўŏl'ogy*, science of muscles.

my'ōpe, n. Short-sighted person. Hence or cogn. **mўŏp'IA**[1], **mў'opy**[1], nn., **mўŏp'IC** a. [F, f. LL f. Gk *muōps* (*muō* shut + *ōps* eye)]

mўōs'is, n. Contraction of pupil of eye. So **mўŏT'IC** a. [f. Gk *muō* shut, see -OSIS]

mў'osōte, n. Forget-me-not. [f. foll.]

Myosōt'is, n. Genus of small plants with blue, pink, or white flowers. [L, f. Gk *muosōtis* (*mus muos* mouse + *ous ōtos* ear)]

mў'riad, a. & n. (poet., rhet.). Ten thousand; (of) indefinitely great number. [f. LL f. Gk *murias -ados* (*murioi* 10,000)]

mў'riapŏd, a. & n. (Animal) with many legs, of the class comprising centipedes & millepedes. [as prec. + Gk *pous podos* foot]

mўriora'ma (-rah-, -rä-), n. Entertainment consisting of series of views. [f. Gk *murios* countless + *horama* view (*horaō* see)]

myrm'idon (mêr-), n. (M~) any of a warlike Thessalian people who followed Achilles; hired ruffian; base servant, as ~ of the law, policeman, bailiff, etc. [f. L f. Gk *Murmidones* pl.]

mўrŏb'alan, n. Astringent plum-like fruit used in dyeing, tanning, etc. [f. F (-bol-) or L *myrobalanum* f. Gk *myrobalanos* (*muron* unguent + *balanos* acorn)]

myrrh[1] (mêr), n. Gum resin used in perfumery & medicine, & in incense. Hence ~'IC, ~'Y[2], aa. [OE *myrra*, f. L *murra*, *myrr(h)a* f. Gk *murra*]

.myrrh[2] (mêr), n. Sweet cicely, an aromatic plant. [f. L *myrrhis*, f. Gk]

Myr'tle (mêr-), n. Genus of plants, esp. common ~, shrub with shiny evergreen leaves & white scented flowers, sacred to Venus. So **myrtA'CEOUS** (mêrtā'shus) a., of family *Myrtaceae* (~ etc.). [ME, f. med. L *myrtilla, -us*, dim. f. L f. Gk *murtos*]

mўsělf', pron. Emphatic & poetical & reflexive form corresp. to *I*, as *I saw it* ~, *I* ~ (for my part) *am doubtful, I have hurt* ~; *I am not* ~ (in my normal state of body or mind). [f. ME + SELF; *my*- partly on anal. of *herself*]

mўs'tagogue (-ŏg), n. Teacher of mystical doctrines, esp. (Gk ant.) to candidates for initiation in Eleusinian & other mysteries; freq. derog. So **mўstagŏ'gIC**(AL) aa. [F, or f. L f. Gk *mustagōgos* (*mustēs* one initiated into mysteries + -*agōgos* -leading)]

mўstēr'ious, a. Full of, wrapt in, mystery; (of persons) delighting in mystery. Hence ~LY[2] adv., ~NESS n. [f. foll. + -OUS]

mўs'terў[1], n. Hidden or inexplicable matter; *make a* ~ *of*, treat as a secret; secrecy, obscurity, as *is wrapped in* ~; (practice of) making a secret of (unimportant) things; religious truth divinely revealed, esp. one beyond human reason; religious rite, esp. (pl.) Eucharist; (pl.) secret religious rites of Greeks, Romans, etc.; miracle-play; ~*-ship*, warship disguised as tramp steamer etc. to decoy submarines in the 1914-18 war. [ME, f. AF *misterie*, = OF *mistere* f. or f. L Gk *mustērion* (*muo* close lips or eyes)]

‖ **mўs'terў**[2], n. (arch.). Handicraft, trade, esp. (in indentures) *art & *~. [ME, f. med. L *mi(ni)sterium* (MINISTER), confused w. prec.]

mўs'tic, a. & n. **1.** Spiritually allegorical; occult, esoteric; of hidden meaning, mysterious; mysterious & awe-inspiring. **2.** n. One who seeks by contemplation & self-surrender to obtain union with or absorption into the Deity, or who believes in spiritual apprehension of truths beyond the understanding, whence ~ISM n. (often derog.). Hence ~AL a., ~alIY[2] adv., ~IZE(3) v.t. [ME, f. OF *mystique* or L f. Gk *mustikos* (as MYSTERY[1], -IC)]

mўs'ti|fў, v.t. Hoax, play on credulity of; bewilder; wrap up in mystery. So ~FICA-TION n. [f. F *mystifier* (irreg. as prec., -FY)]

mўstique' (-têk), n. The atmosphere of mystery & veneration investing some creeds, doctrines, arts, professions, etc., or personages; any professional skill or technique which mystifies & impresses the layman. [F, as MYSTIC]

myth (or mĭ-), n. Purely fictitious narrative usu. involving supernatural persons etc. & embodying popular ideas on natural phenomena etc.; allegory, as *Platonic* ~; fictitious person or thing. So **myth'-IC**(AL) aa., **myth'icalLY**[2] adv. [f. Gk *muthos*]

mȳth′ic|ize, -|ise (-īz), v.t. Treat (story etc.) as a myth, interpret mythically. So **~ISM, ~IST,** nn. [MYTHIC + -IZE]

mȳtho-, comb. form of Gk *muthos* myth, as: *~grapher* (-ŏg̃ᴸ), writer of myths; *~graphy* (-ŏg̃ᴸ), representation of myths in plastic art; *~pœic* (-pē′ĭk), *~poёt′ic,* making, productive of, myths; *~pŏ′et, ~pŏ′etry,* poetical writer, writing, of myths.

mȳthŏl′og|ȳ (or mĭ-), n. Body of myths, esp. relating to particular person or subject; study of myths. Hence or cogn. **~ERᴵ, ~IST,** nn., **mȳtholŏ′gic(al)** aa., **mȳtholŏ′gically²** adv., **~IZE**(2, 3) v.t. & i. [ME, f. OF *mythologie* or LL f. Gk *muthologia* (see prec., & -LOGY)]

mȳth′us, n. Myth. [mod. L, as MYTH]

mȳxoedēm′a (-ēd-), n. A metabolic disease caused by sluggish working or atrophy of the thyroid gland, & characterized by thickening of the subcutaneous tissues & loss of physical & mental energy. [f. Gk *muxa* mucus + OEDEMA]

mȳxōm′a, n. (path.; pl. *~ta*). Tumour of mucous or gelatinous tissue. Hence **~TOS′IS** n., virus disease in rabbits. [mod. L, f. Gk *muxa* mucus; see -OMA]

N

N (ĕn), letter (pl. *Ns,* N's). (Print.) *n* (also *en*) unit of measurement; (math.) indefinite number *(to the nth,* to any required power, also fig. to any extent, to the utmost); *N-rays, N¹-rays,* forms of radiation.

năb, v.t. (sl.; -bb-). Apprehend, arrest; catch in wrong-doing. [17th c., also *nap,* as in KIDNAP; orig. unkn.]

năb′ŏb, n. (Hist.) Mohammedan official or governor under Mogul empire; (arch.) wealthy luxurious person, esp. one returned from India with fortune. [f. Port. or Sp. *nabab,* NAWAB]

Năb′ŏth's vine′yard (-ny-), n. Possession that one will stick at nothing to secure. [see 1 *Kings* xxi]

năc′arăt, n. Bright orange-red colour. [F, f. Sp. & Port. *nacarado* (NACRE)]

nacĕlle′, n. Outer casing of aeroplane's engine; car of airship. [F, f. LL *navicella* dim. of L *navis* ship]

nā′cre (-ker), n. (Shellfish yielding) mother of pearl. Hence **nāc′rĕous, nāc′rous,** aa. [F, = Sp. & Port. *nacar,* med. L *nac-(ch)ara*]

nād′ir, n. Point of heavens directly under observer (opp. ZENITH); (transf.) lowest point, place or time of greatest depression etc. [ME, f. OF, f. Arab. *naḍīr (es-semt)* opposite to (zenith)]

năg¹, n. Small riding horse or pony; horse (colloq.). [c. 1400, of unkn. orig.; cf. MDu. *negghe*]

năg², v.i. & t. (-gg-). Find fault or scold (intr.) persistently *(at* person); annoy

thus. Hence **~g′ING¹** (-g-) n. [of dial., prob. Scand., orig.; cf. Norw. & Sw. *nagga* gnaw, irritate]

naga′na (-ahna), n. (S. Africa). Disease of livestock transmitted by tsetse fly. [Zulu *nakane*]

năg′ŏr, n. Senegal antelope. [wd made by Buffon]

nai′ad (nī-), n. (pl. *~s, ~es* pr. -ēz). Water--nymph. [f. L f. Gk *naias -ados* (*naŏ* flow)]

naif (nah-ēf′), a. (rare, exc. of males). = NAÏVE. [F]

nail¹, n. 1. Horny covering of outer tip of finger & upper tip of toe (*~-brush, -scissors,* for cleaning & paring *~s;* TOOTH *&-~*), whence *~ED²* (-ld) a.; claw, talon; hard excrescence on some soft-billed birds' upper mandible. 2. Small metal spike usu. with point & broadened head driven in with hammer to hold things together or as peg or ornament *(hit ~,* or *right ~, on head,* give true explanation, propose or do right thing, hit the mark; *~ in* one's COFFIN; *on the ~;* without delay, esp. of payment; *hard as ~s,* in fine training, (also, of character) hard-boiled; *right as ~s,* quite right); *~-head,* architectural ornament. 3. An old measure of length (2¼ in.). Hence *~′LESS* a. [OE *nægel,* OS, OHG *nagal,* ON *nagl,* Goth. *nagls* f. Gmc *naglaz*]

nail², v.t. Fasten with nails (*on, to, together, down, in,* etc.; *~ colours to mast,* persist in course of action; *~* (usu. *lie) to counter, barndoor,* expose as spurious, vile; *~ up,* close, affix at height, with nails); fix or keep fixed (person, attention, etc.); secure, catch, engage, succeed in getting hold of, (person or thing). Hence *~′ING²* a. [OE *næglan* f. prec.]

nail′er, n. Nail-maker, whence **nail′ERY**(3) n. [-ER¹]

nain′sŏŏk, n. Fine cotton fabric, orig. Indian. [f. Hind. *nainsukh (nain* eye, *sukh* pleasure)]

naïve (nah-ēv′), **naive** (nāv), a. Artless, unaffected; amusingly simple. Hence **naïve′LY², naive′lȳ,** (-vl-), adv., **naïveté** (nah-ēv′tā), **naïveTY** (nah-ēv′tĭ), **naiv′étȳ,** n. [F, fem. of *naif* L *nativus* NATIVE]

nāk′ĕd, a. Unclothed, nude, (*as ~ as my mother bore me);* defenceless; unsheathed; plain, undisguised, (*the ~ truth; ~ facts; in its ~ absurdity),* exposed for examination (*his ~ heart);* devoid *of;* treeless, leafless, barren; (of rock) exposed, without vegetation; (of rooms) unfurnished; without ornament; (of candles etc.) exposed to air; without leaves, hairs, scales, shell, etc.; without addition, comment, support, evidence, etc. (*~ faith, quotations, word, assertion);* unassisted (*~ eye,* without telescope etc.); *~ lady, ~ boys,* meadow saffron. Hence *~LY²* adv., *~NESS* n. (*the ~ness of the land,* person's or institution's or State's lack of resources or openness to attack, see *Gen.* xlii. 9). [OE *nacod,* OHG *nakot,* ON

nǫkkvithr, Goth. *naqaδ-* f. Gmc **naq-,* cogn. w. L *nudus*]

nāk′er, n. (hist.). Kettledrum. [ME, f. OF *nacre,* f. Arab. & Pers. *naqāra(h)*]

năm′bȳ-păm′bȳ, a. & n. 1. Insipidly pretty, mildly sentimental. 2. n. Talk of this kind. [formed on name of Ambrose Philips, pastoral writer, d. 1749]

name¹, n. 1. Word by which individual person, animal, place, or thing, is spoken of or to (*mention* person *by* ~; *Tom by* ~, *by* ~ *Tom,* called; *know by* ~, individually, also by hearsay only; *of* or *by the* ~ *of,* called; *put* one's ~ *down for,* apply as candidate etc., promise to subscribe; *keep* one's ~ *on, take* one's ~ *off, the books,* remain, cease to be, member of college, club, etc.). 2. Word denoting any object of thought, esp. one applicable to many individuals (*call* person ~*s,* describe him by uncomplimentary ~*s; give it a* ~, colloq., mention the drink, present, etc., that you wish); PROPER ~. 3. Person as known, famed, or spoken of (*adore the* ~ *of God; Nelson himself & many great* ~*s were there*). 4. All who go under one ~, family, clan, people. 5. Reputation (*has an ill, a good,* ~; *has a* ~ *for honesty, the* ~ *of being honest; win* oneself *a* ~; *bequeath a great* ~; *persons of* ~; one's good ~). 6. Merely nominal existence, practically non-existent thing, (opp. *fact, reality, deed; virtuous in* ~; *honour had become a* ~). 7. *In* person's ~, *in the* ~ *of,* invoking, relying upon, calling to witness, (*in God's* ~; *in the* ~ *of goodness, fortune, common sense*), acting as deputy for or in the interest of (*in* one's *own* ~, independently, without authority); ~*-child,* one named after another (*my* etc. ~*-child*); ~*-day,* day of saint after whom person is named (esp. of continental sovereigns); ~*-part,* that after which play is named, title-role; ~′*sāke* (-ms-), person or thing with same ~ as another (*his* etc. ~*sake*) [probably for *the* ~*'s sake*]. [OE *nama,* OS, OHG *namo,* ON *nafn,* Goth. *namo* f. Gmc **namon,* cogn. w. L *nomen*]

name², v.t. Give name to (*after, from*), call so-&-so; call (person, thing) by right name; nominate, appoint (*to* office etc.); mention, specify, (*not to be* ~*d on* or *in same day with,* quite inferior to; ~ *your price*); ‖ (of Speaker) mention (M.P.) as disobedient to Chair (~!, vb or n., appeal to do this, or to give name of some person alluded to in speech); cite as instance; specify as something desired (~ *the day,* of woman fixing date for wedding). Hence **nām′ABLE** a. [OE (*ge*)*namian* as prec.]

name′less (-ml-), a. Obscure, inglorious, not mentioned by name, left unnamed on purpose (esp. *who shall be* ~); anonymous, unknown; having no name, bearing no name-inscription; inexpressible, indefinable; too bad to be named, abominable, loathsome, (esp. ~ *vices*). [-LESS]

name′lȳ (-ml-), adv. That is to say, viz. [NAME¹, -LY²]

‖ **nammet.** Var. of NUMMET.

năn′cȳ, n. & a. (sl.). Effeminate (man or boy); homosexual. [pet-form of female name *Ann*]

nănkeen′, n. Kind of cotton cloth orig. made of naturally yellow cotton; (pl.) trousers of this; yellow or pale buff colour. [f. *Nankin(g)* in China]

nănn′ȳ, n. ~ (*-goat*), she-goat (cf. BILLY); child's nurse. [f. the female name]

năp¹, v.i. (-pp-), & n. 1. Sleep lightly or briefly (*catch* ~*ping,* find asleep, take unawares, detect in negligence or error). 2. n. Short sleep, doze, esp. by day (often *take a* ~). [OE *hnappian,* app. rel. to OHG (*h*)*naffezan* (MHG *nafzen*) to slumber]

năp², n., & v.t. (-pp-). 1. Surface given to cloth by raising & then cutting & smoothing the short fibres, pile, whence ~′LESS a.; soft or downy surface. 2. v.t. Raise ~ on (cloth). [ME *noppe* f. MDu. or MLG *noppe(n)*]

năp³, n., & v.t. 1. A card-game (~ *hand,* fig., position that justifies confident expectation of winning if one takes a risk; *go* ~, risk attempting highest form of win in ~, also fig.); (betting) the putting of all one's money on one chance, a tipster's choice for this. 2. v.t. Name (horse) as probable winner. [abbr. of *Napoleon*]

năp′alm (-ahm), n. Product of naphthalene & coconut oil (~ *bomb,* one containing jellied petrol). [f. NA(PHTHALENE), PALM¹]

nāpe, n. Back of or usu. *of* neck. [ME, of unkn. orig.]

năp′erȳ, n. (Sc. & arch.). Household, esp. table, linen. [ME, f. OF *naperie* f. *nape* (as NAPKIN), see -ERY]

năph′tha, n. Kinds of inflammable oil got by dry distillation of organic substances, as coal, shale, or petroleum. [L, f. Gk, = inflammable volatile liquid issuing from earth]

năph′thal‖ēne, -ine, n. White crystalline substance got in distilling coal-tar & used in manufacture of dyes etc. Hence ~IZE(5) v.t. [prec. + -*l-* + -ENE, -INE⁸]

năp′kin, n. (Also *table-*~) square piece of linen for wiping lips or fingers with at meals, or serving fish etc. on; small towel esp. for nursery purposes, baby's diaper; *lay up* etc. *in a* ~, make no use of (*Luke* xix. 20); ~*-ring,* to distinguish person's table-~. [ME, f. OF *nappe* f. L *mappa* (MAP¹), +-KIN]

Nāp′les yĕll′ow (-lz; -ō), n. Bright yellow pigment used by artists. [f. *Naples* in Italy]

napōl′éon, n. French gold twenty-franc piece of Napoleon I (*double* ~, forty-franc piece); kind of top-boot; the game NAP³. [f. name of French emperor]

Napōlĕŏn′‖ic, a. Of, like, etc., Napoleon I or the Napoleon family. Hence or cogn. ~ICALLY² adv., Napōl′éonISM(3), Napōl′éonIST(2), nn., Napōl′éonIZE(4) v.t. & i. [as prec., -IC]

‖ **napōō'** (nah-), int. (obs. army sl.). Vanished!, lost!, done!, finished!, no go! [f. F dial. *n'a pu* (= *il n'y en a plus*) there isn't any more]

năpp' y̆[1], a. (arch.). (Of ale etc.) foaming, heady, strong. [app. f. NAP[2], -Y[2]]

‖ **năpp'y̆**[2], n. (colloq.). Baby's napkin. [abbr.; see -Y[3]]

napu (nah'pōō), n. Musk-deer of Java & Sumatra. [Malay]

năr'cĕīne, n. Alkaloid got from opium occas. used instead of morphine. [F, f. Gk *narkē* numbness + -INE[5]]

nărciss'|ism, n. (psycho-anal.). Tendency to self-worship, absorption in one's own personal perfections. Hence ~is'tIC a. [Gk *Narkissos* youth who fell in love with his reflection in water, -ISM]

nărciss'|us, n. (pl. ~uses, ~ī). Kinds of bulbous plant, esp. one bearing heavily scented single white flower with un-divided corona edged with crimson & yellow. [L, f. Gk *narkissos*]

nărc'olĕpsy̆, n. Disease with fits of somnolence. [f. Gk *narkē* numbness + (EPI)LEPSY]

nărcōs'is, n. Operation or effects of nar-cotics; state of insensibility. [f. Gk *nar-kōsis* (*narkoō* benumb); see -OSIS]

nărcŏt'|ic, a. & n. (Substance) inducing drowsiness, sleep, stupor, or insensibility; (fig.) soporific (a. & n.); of narcosis. Hence ~ICALLY adv., **nărc'otIZE**(3, 5) v.t., **nărcotizA'TION**, **nărc'otISM**(5), **nărc'ot-IST**(2), nn. [ME, f. OF *narcotique* or med. L f. Gk *narkōtikos* (prec., -IC)]

nărd, n. (Plant yielding) aromatic balsam of ancients. [ME, f. L f. Gk *nardos* f. Oriental wd]

nărg'hile (-gĭlē), n. Oriental tobacco--pipe with smoke passed through water, hookah. [f. Pers. *nargileh* (*nargil* coco-nut)]

nărk, n. (sl.). Police decoy or spy. [Romany *nak* nose]

narr|āte', v.t. Relate, recount, give con-tinuous account of, (abs.) utter or write narrative. Hence or cogn. ~A'TION, ~āt'OR, ~āt'rESS[1], nn. [f. L *narrare*, see -ATE[3]]

nă'rrative, n. & a. 1. Tale, story, recital of facts, esp., in fiction, story told in first person; kind of composition or talk that confines itself to these. 2. adj. In the form of, concerned with, narration, whence ~LY[2] adv. [f. F *narratif* (-*ive*) f. LL *narrativus* (prec., -IVE)]

nă'rrow (-ō), a. (~er, ~est) & n., & v.i. & t. 1. Of small width in proportion to length, wanting in breadth, constricted, (*the ~ way*, righteousness, see *Matt.* vii. 14; ~ *vowels*, made with tongue & uvula tense); of small size, confined or confin-ing, (*the ~ bed*, cell, *house*, grave; *within ~ bounds* etc.); of limited scope, restricted, (*in the ~est sense*; ~ *circumstances*, poverty); with little margin (*a ~ major-ity, escape*); lacking in breadth of view or

sympathy, illiberal, prejudiced, exclusive, self-centred, whence ~-mind'ED[2] a., ~-mind'ĕdLY[2] adv., ~-mind'ĕdNESS n.; searching, precise, exact, (*after a ~ examination*; ~ *cloth*, under 52 in., of single width usu. about a yard; ~ *goods*, ribbons, braid, etc.; ~ GAUGE on railway, any of less than 4 ft 8½ in. (formerly, the' gauge of 4ft 8½ in.); ‖ ~ *seas*, English & Irish channels; hence ~ISH[1] (-ŏĭ-) a., ~LY[2] (-ōl-) adv., ~NESS (-ŏn-) n. 2. n. (usu. pl.). ~ part of a sound, strait, river, pass, or street. 3. vb. Make or become ~er, diminish, lessen, contract. [OE *nearu*, OS *naru*; cf. MDu. *nare* dismal; ult. orig. unkn.]

năr'thĕx, n. Railed-off western portico or ante-nave in early Christian churches for women, penitents, & catechumens. [Gk (-*ēx*), orig. name of a plant = FERULA]

năr'whal (-wal), n. Arctic delphinoid ceta-cean with straight horn(s) developed from one or both of its two teeth. [f. Da. or Sw. *narhval* (*hval* WHALE); ON *ndhvalr* (perh. f. *nár* corpse)]

năs'al (-z-), a. & n. 1. Of the nose (~ *organ*, joc., nose). 2. (Of letters or sounds) re-quiring the nose passage to be open (n., such a letter etc., e.g. *m*, *n*, *ng*), of voice or speech) having the twang described as speaking through the nose, whence ~IZE(2, 3) v.i. & t., ~īzA'TION n., (-z-). Hence **nasăl'ITY** n., ~LY[2] adv., (-z-). [f. med. L **nasalis* (L *nasus* nose, -AL)]

năs'cent, a. In the act of being born, just beginning to be, not yet ·mature. So **năs'cENCY** n. [f. L *nasci* be born, -ENT]

năse'berry̆ (-zb-), n. Tree yielding Sapodilla plum. [f. Sp., Port., *néspera* medlar]

năs'o- (-z-), comb. form of L *nasus* nose, as ~*fron'tal* of nose & forehead.

nastŭr'tium (-shm), n. (Bot.) kinds of pungent-tasting cruciferous plants in-cluding watercress; (improp.) trailing garden plant with bright yellow or red flowers. [L]

nas't|y̆ (nah-), a. Disgustingly dirty, filthy; obscene, delighting in obscenity; disagreeable to smell or taste, unpalat-able lit. & fig., annoying, objectionable (also colloq. of a person, as *a ~y bit* or *piece of work*); (of weather etc.) foul, wet, stormy; hard to deal with or get rid of, serious, (*a ~y sea*, *fence*, *blow*, *illness*; *a ~y one*, rebuff, snub, disabling blow, etc.); ill-natured, spiteful *to*. Hence~ĭLY[2] adv., ~iNESS n. [ME, of unkn. orig.; cf. Du. *nestig* dirty]

năt'al, a. Of, from, one's birth. [ME, f. L *natalis* (NATION, -AL)]

natăl'ity̆, n. Birth-rate. [F (-*té*), as prec., -TY]

nată'tion, n. Swimming. [f. L *natatio* (*natare* swim, -ATION)]

natatŏr'ial, **năt'atory̆**, aa. Swimming, of swimming. [LL *natatorius* (prec.), -ORY, -AL]

nāt′ēs (-z), n. pl. (anat.). Buttocks; anterior pair of optic lobes in brain. [L]

nāth(e)′lēss (-thl-), adv. (arch.). Nevertheless. [f. OE *nā* (*ne* not, *ā* ever) +THE (2) +LESS]

nā′tion, n. Congeries of people, either of diverse races or of common descent, language, history, etc., inhabiting a territory bounded by defined limits (*most favoured~*, to which State accords lowest scale of import duties); || (in medieval & some Scots univv.) body of students from particular country or district; LAW of *~s*; LEAGUE[2] *of N~s*; UNITED *N~s*. Hence *~*HOOD n. [ME, f. OF f. L *nationem* nom. -*o* (*nasci nat-* be born, -ION)]

nā′tional (-sho-), a. & n. **1.** Of a or the nation, common to the whole nation; peculiar to or characteristic of a particular nation; *~ anthem,* ' God save the Queen ' & corresponding hymns of other peoples; *~* DEBT; ||*N~ Gallery,* ||*N~ Portrait Gallery,* buildings in London in which pictures, portraits, owned by the nation are permanently exhibited; *N~ Government,* coalition of parties; *N~* INSUR-ANCE; *~ newspapers* (circulating throughout the country); *N~ Socialist,* NAZI; ||*N~ Society,* founded 1811 to promote education of the poor; ||*Grand N~* (*Steeplechase*), chief steeplechase of year, at Aintree in March. **2.** n. pl. One's fellow countrymen (*consul's powers over his own ~s*); citizens of a specified country. Hence *~*LY[2] adv. [F (prec., -AL)]

nā′tional|ism (-sho-), n. Patriotic feeling, principles, or efforts; policy of national independence. So *~*IST(2) n. [-ISM]

nātional̆′it|y̆ (-sho-), n. Being national, national quality; patriotic sentiment; one's nation (*what is his ~y?*); a nation (*men of all ~ies*); existence as a nation; race forming part of one or more political nations. [-ITY]

nā′tionaliz|e (-sho-), -is|e (-ĭz), v.t. Make national; make into a nation; naturalize (foreigner); convert (land, railways, coal-mines, etc.) into national property or undertakings. Hence *~*A′TION n. [-IZE]

nāt′ive[1], n. **1.** One born, or whose parents are domiciled, in a place (*of*); local inhabitant; (Austral.) white born in Australia. **2.** Member of non-European or uncivilized people. **3.** Indigenous animal or plant; oyster reared wholly or partly in British waters, esp. in artificial beds. [ME, f. med.L *nativus* n. (L *nativus* a., see foll.)]

nāt′ive[2], a. **1.** Belonging to a person or thing by nature, innate, inherent, natural *to,* whence *~*LY[2] adv. **2.** Unadorned, simple, artless. **3.** Of one's birth, where one was born; belonging to one by right of birth. **4.** (Of metals etc.) found in pure or uncombined state (*~ rock,* in its original place). **5.** Born in a place (esp. of non-Europeans), indigenous, not exotic; of the natives of a place. [ME,

f. OF *natif* (-*ive*) or L *nativus* (NATION, -IVE)]

nāt′īv|ism, n. (philos.). Doctrine of innate ideas. So *~*IST(2) n. [-ISM]

nativ′ĭt̆y̆, n. Birth of Christ, the Virgin, or St John Baptist; picture of the N*~* of Christ; festival of Christ's N*~*, Christmas, or of birth of Virgin (8 Sept.) or St John (24 June); birth; (astrol.) horoscope. [ME, f. OF *nativite* f. LL *nativitatem* (NATIVE, -TY)]

nāt′ron, n. Native SESQUIcarbonate of soda. [F, f. Sp., f. Arab. *natrun* f. Gk *nitron* NITRE]

nătt′er, v.i. (colloq.). Chatter idly; grumble, talk fretfully. Hence *~*ed (-*erd*), *~*y̆, aa., peevish. [var. of dial. *gnatter* be peevish]

|| **nătt′erjăck**, n. British species of toad with yellow stripe down back. [perh. f. prec., from its loud croak]

nătt′ier blue (-*ō͞o*), n. Soft shade of blue, much used by the French painter J. M. Nattier (d. 1766).

nătt′|y̆, a. Spruce, trim, daintily tidy; deft-handed; showing deftness. Hence *~*ĭLY[2] adv.,*~*ĭNESS n. [of unkn. (sl.) orig.]

nătural (-cher-), a. & n. **1.** Based on the innate moral sense, instinctive, (*~ law, justice*). **2.** Constituted by nature (*~ DAY, year*). **3.** (mus.). *~ note* or *key,* not sharp or flat, so *B ~, F ~,* etc.; *~ scale,* having no sharps or flats, i.e. C major. **4.** (sci.). *~ classification,* (now obs.) *orders* with abbr. N.O., etc., esp. in bot. of Jussieu's arrangement of species according to likeness as opp. Linnaeus's sexual system. **5.** Normal, conformable to the ordinary course of nature, not exceptional or miraculous or irregular, (*~ MAGIC; ~ death,* by age or disease, not accident, poison, or violence). **6.** Not enlightened or communicated by revelation (*the ~ man; ~ religion, theology*). **7.** Physically existing, not spiritual or intellectual or fictitious, concerned with physical things, (*the ~ world;* one's *~ life,* duration of one's life on earth; *~ law*). **8.** Existing in or by nature, not artificial, innate, inherent, self-sown, uncultivated. **9.** Lifelike; unaffected, easy-mannered, not disfigured or disguised. **10.** Not surprising, to be expected. **11.** Consonant or easy *to* (*comes~to him*). **12.** Destined to be such by nature (*~ enemies, antithesis*). **13.** So related by nature only, illegitimate, (*~ son, child, brother,* etc.). **14.** Dealing with nature as a study (*~ history,* study of animal or vegetable life, esp. as set forth for popular use, also aggregate of facts about the *~* objects or the characteristics *of* a place or class; *~ historian,* writer on *~* history; *~ philosophy,* physics; *~ philosopher,* physicist; *~* SCIENCE). **15.** *~-born,* having the character or position by birth. Hence *~*NESS n. **16.** n. Person half-witted from birth; person who is naturally expert in some respect; thing that is by nature successful, a certainty. **17.** (mus.). ~ note, white key in piano. **18.** Hand making 21 as first dealt in vingt-et-un. [adj. (ME) f. OF -al or L naturalis (NATURE, -AL); n. (16th c.) f. adj. & F naturel]

nă′turalism (-cher-), n. Action based on natural instincts; moral or religious system on purely natural basis; (philos.) view of the world that excludes the supernatural or spiritual; realistic method, adherence to nature, in literature & art; indifference to conventions. [prec. +-ISM, partly thr. F naturalisme]

nă′turalist (-cher-), n. & a. **1.** One who believes in or practises naturalism; student of animals or plants; ‖ (shop) dealer in cage animals, dogs, etc.; ‖ (shop) taxidermist. **2.** adj. = foll. [f. F -iste (as prec., -IST)]

năturalis′t|ĭc (-cher-), a. Of, according to, naturalism; of natural history. Hence ~ICALLY adv. [-IC]

nă′turaliz|e (-cher-), -is|e (-īz), v.t. & i. Admit (alien) to citizenship; adopt (foreign word, custom, etc.); introduce (animal, plant) into another country; become ~ed; free from conventions, make natural; free from the miraculous, place on naturalistic basis; pursue natural history. Hence ~A′TION n. [f. F naturaliser (NATURAL, -IZE)]

nă′turally (-cher-), adv. In adj. senses; esp. as might be expected, of course. [-LY²]

nă′ture, n. **1.** Thing's essential qualities, (in or by or from the ~ of the case or of things, inevitably considering these qualities); person's or animal's innate character (whence -nă′turED² (-cherd) a.; by ~, innately; GOOD, ILL, SECOND, ~); general characteristics & feelings of mankind (often human~; TOUCH² of~); specified element of human character (the rational, animal, moral, ~); person of specified character (sanguine ~s do not feel this; there are ~s who can never—). **2.** Kind, sort, class, (things of this~; is in or of the ~ of a command). **3.** Inherent impulses determining character or action (against~, unnatural, immoral). **4.** Vital force or functions or needs (~ is exhausted; such a diet will not support ~; ease ~, evacuate bowels or bladder). **5.** Resin or sap in wood (esp. full of~, still resinous). **6.** Physical power causing phenomena of material world, these phenomena as a whole, (N~, these personified; N~'s engineering; all ~ looks gay; N~ is the best physician; LAW¹ of~; in the course of ~, in the ordinary course; debt of ~, death; in ~, actually existing, also anywhere, at all; against or contrary to~, miraculous, miraculously). **7.** Naturalness or fidelity in art. **8.** State of ~, unregenerate condition (opp. state of GRACE¹), condition of man before society is organized, uncultivated or undomesticated state of plants or animals, bodily nakedness. **9.**~-printing, method of producing print of leaves etc. by pressing them on prepared plate; ~ study (as school subject), practical study of plant & animal life, physical phenomena, etc. [ME, f. OF, f. L natura (nasci nat- be born, -URE)]

naught (nawt), n. & pred. a. (arch.). **1.** Nothing, nought, (set at~, or NOUGHT); (arith.) cipher, nought. **2.** adj. Worthless, useless. [OE nāwiht, -wuht (nā see NATHLESS, WIGHT)]

naught′|y̆ (nawt-), a. (used of, to, or by children, or in imit. of childish speech). Wayward, disobedient, badly behaved; wicked, blameworthy, indecent. Hence ~ILY² adv., ~INESS n. [prec., -Y²]

naus′ĕa, n. Feeling of sickness; sea-sickness; loathing. [L, f. Gk nausia (naus ship)]

naus′ĕāt|e, v.t. & i. Reject (food, or fig.) with loathing; affect with nausea, whence ~ING² a.; feel sick (at), loathe food, occupation, etc. [f. L nauseare (prec.), -ATE³]

naus′ĕous, a. Causing nausea; offensive to taste or smell, nasty; disgusting, loathsome. Hence ~LY² adv., ~NESS n. [f. NAUSEA +-OUS or f. L nauseosus]

nautch, n. E.-Indian exhibition of professional dancing-girls (~-girl, one of these). [f. Hind. nach]

naut′ical, a. Of sailors or navigation, naval, maritime; ~ almanac, year-book containing astronomical & tidal information for navigators etc. Hence ~LY² adv. [f. F nautique or L f. Gk nautikos (nautēs sailor f. naus ship), see -ICAL]

naut′ilus, n. (pl. -luses, -li). Paper ~, small cephalopod of which the female has very thin shell & webbed sail-like arms; pearly ~, cephalopod with chambered shell having nacreous septa. [f. L f. Gk nautilos sailor (prec.)]

năv′al, a. Of, in, for, etc., ships or (usu.) the or a navy (~ stores, all materials used in shipping; ~ officer, in navy); fought, won, etc., by or consisting of or based on ships of war. Hence ~LY² adv. [ME, f. L navalis (navis ship, -AL)]

năve¹, n. Central block of wheel holding axle & spokes, hub. [OE nafu, OS, OHG naba, ON nof, f. Gmc *nabhō, see NAVEL]

năve², n. Body of church from West door to chancel, usu. separated by pillars from aisles. [f. L navis (in med. L); cf. It. nave]

năv′el, n. Depression in front of belly left by abruption of umbilical cord; central point of anything; ~ orange, large orange with ~-like formation at top; ~-string, structure connecting foetus & placenta, umbilical cord; ~wort, pennywort. [OE nafela, OHG nabalo, ON nafli, f. Gmc *nabhalan- f. *nabh- NAVE¹; cogn. w. L UMBILICUS]

năv′icĕrt, n. Certificate that ship's cargo does not contravene war contraband regulations; commercial passport for a particular consignment. [f. L *navis* ship +CERT(IFICATE)]

navic′ūlar, a. & n. Boat-shaped (of shrines, & of parts of plants or body; esp. ~ *bone* in hand or usu. foot; ~ *disease*, or ~ as noun, disease in horse's ~ bone). [f. F -*aire* or LL *navicularis* (L *navicula* dim. of *navis* ship, -AR[1])]

năv′igă|ble, a. (Of river, sea, etc.) affording passage for ships; seaworthy (*in ~ble condition*); (of balloon) steerable, dirigible. Hence ~BIL′ITY n. [f. F, or L *navigabilis* (foll., -ABLE)]

năv′igăte, v.i. & t. Voyage, sail ship; sail over or up or down (sea, river); manage, direct course of, (ship or aircraft). [f. L *navigare* (*navis* ship, *agere* drive), -ATE[3]]

năvigā′tion, n. (*inland* ~, communication by canals & rivers; *aerial* ~, of airship or aeroplane); methods of determining ship's or aircraft's position & course by geometry & nautical astronomy, seamanship; voyage; ~*coal*, steam-coal. [f. F, or L *navigatio* (prec., -ATION)]

năv′igător, n. One charged with or skilled in navigation; sea explorer; || (now rare) navvy. [L (NAVIGATE, -OR)]

năvv′y̆, n. || Labourer employed in excavating for canals, railways, roads, etc.; (also *steam-~*) mechanical excavator. [c. 1830, abbr. of prec.]

năv′y̆, n. Fleet (poet.); whole of State's ships of war with their crews & all the organization for their maintenance; officers & men of ~; ||~ *bill*, issued by Admiralty in lieu of cash payment; ~ *blue* n., ~-*blue* a., (of) the dark blue used in naval uniform; ||~ *cut*, cake tobacco finely sliced; ~ *league*, association founded to rouse national interest in ~; ~ *list*, official book with all naval officers' names & other information. [ME, f. OF *navie* ship, fleet f. L *navia* ship, pop. var. of cl. L *navis*]

nawab′ (-wawb), n. Title of governor or nobleman in India; (rare) rich retired Anglo-Indian, nabob. [f. Hind. *nawwab*, pl. f. Arab. *nā′ib* deputy: cf. NABOB]

nay, particle equivalent to negative sentence, & n. **1.** = NO[4] (arch.); why, well, (vaguely introducing comment on another's statement etc.; arch.); or rather, & even, & more than that, (*weighty*, ~ *unanswerable*). **2.** n. The word ~ (*will not take* ~, disregards refusals; *yea & ~*, shilly-shally; *say* ~, utter denial or usu. refusal, = refuse or contradict, as *cannot say him ~*). [ME, f. ON *nei* (*ne* not, *ei* AYE]

Năzarēne′, n. & a. Native of Nazareth; (in Jewish, Moham., use) Christian; member of early Jewish-Christian sect (adj., of this sect). [ME, f. LL f. Gk *Nazarēnos* (*Nazaret* Nazareth)]

Năz′arīte[1], n. Native of Nazareth. [f. LL *Nazaraeus* f. Gk *Nazōraios* + -ITE[1](1)]

Năz′arīte[2], -zir-, n. Hebrew who had taken certain vows of abstinence (*Numb.* vi). [f. LL *Nazaraeus* f. Heb. *nazir* (*nazar* separate oneself) + -ITE[1](2)]

năze, n. Promontory, headland, ness. [= NESS]

Nazi (naht′sĭ, nah′zĭ), n. & a. (Member) of the German National Socialist party. Hence ~DOM, Na′z(ĭ)ISM, nn., ~FY v.t. [repr. pronunc. of *Nati*- in G *Nationalsozialist*]

Nĕăn′derthal (-tahl), a. Of or belonging to the primeval type of man widely distributed in palaeolithic Europe. [f. the ~ valley in the Rhine province where parts of a skeleton were found in 1857]

neap, a. & n., & v.t. & i. **1.** ~*-tide*' or ~, tide soon after moon's first & third quarters in which high-water level is at lowest, cf. SPRING[2]*tide*. **2.** vb. (Of tides) tend towards ~; (of tide) reach highest point of ~*-tide*; (pass., of ship) be prevented from getting off by ~ing of tides. [OE *nēpflōd*, of unkn. orig.]

Nĕapŏl′itan, a. & n. (Inhabitant) of Naples (~ *ice*, ice-cream made in strata of different colours & flavours, sweetmeat of similar appearance; ~ *violet*, double sweet-scented kind of viola). [f. L *Neapolitanus* (*Neapolites* f. L f. Gk *Neapolis* f. *neos* new, *polis* city, -AN)]

near[1], adv. & prep. (~*er*, ~*est*, also as advv. & prepp.). **1.** To, at, a short distance, in(to) proximity in space or time, (*far & ~*, everywhere; ~ *at hand*, within easy reach, not far in the future; ~ *by*, not far off; ~ *upon*, not far in time from); almost, nearly, *not* nearly or anything like, (now usu. *nearly*; *was* ~ *dead with fright*; *lasted* ~ *a century*; so ~ *upon*; *not* ~ *so numerous*); closely (*as* ~ *as one can guess*; *the* ~*er it resembles him the less I like it*); parsimoniously (*lives very* ~); *go* ~ *to do*, *come* or *go* ~ *doing*, nearly do etc. **2.** prep. ~ in space, time, condition, or resemblance, to (*comes no* ~*er the end*; *lies* ~ *his heart*, affects him deeply; *the time draws* ~ *Christmas*; *sun is* ~ *setting*; *hope came* ~ *fulfilment*; *who comes* ~*est him in wit?*); (in comb.) resembling, intended as a substitute for, as ~*-beer*. [ME, f. ON *nǣr* orig. comp. of *nā-* = OE *nēah* NIGH]

near[2], a. (often governing n. in pred. use; so also in comp. & superl.). Closely related (~ *relation*; *is* ~ *akin to*; *is* ~ *me in blood*; ~ *& dear*), intimate (*a* ~ *friend*); (of parts of animals or vehicles, or horses etc. in team) left (opp. *off*; *the* ~ *fore leg, wheel*; *the* ~ *wheeler*); close at hand, close to, in place or time (also, esp. U.S., ~*by*; *the* ~*est man*; *on a* ~ *day*; *the man* ~ or ~*est you*; *is* ~*er to*, or ~*er*, *us*; ~ *work*, that must be done with the eye close to it; *the* ~ *distance*, part of scene between background & foreground; *the* ~ *prospect of reward*); (of road or way) direct; close, narrow, (*a* ~ *guess, resemblance, transla-*

tion, race, escape); niggardly; ~ *miss*, not a hit, but ~ enough to damage target, esp. in bombing; ~-*sighted*, short-sighted. Hence ~'ISH¹(2) a., ~'NESS n. [ME, f. prec.]

near³, v.i. & t. Draw near (*to*), approach. [f. NEAR¹, ²]

Nēärc'tic, a. (zool.). Of arctic & temperate parts of N. America. [f. Gk *neos* new (w. ref. to the New World), ARCTIC]

near'lў, adv. Closely (*examine it* ~; ~ *related*; *concerns me* ~; *approached the place* ~; *correspond, resemble*, ~); almost; *not* ~, nothing like, far from. [NEAR², -LY²]

neat¹, n. (sing. & collect. as pl.). Any animal of ox kind; (collect.) cattle; ~-*herd*, cowherd; ~-*house*, cattle-shed; ~'*s-foot*, ~'*s-tongue*, used as food; ~'*s-leather*, ox-hide. [OE *nēat*, OS *nōt*, OHG *nōz*, ON *naut* f. Gmc *nautam*; cogn. w. OE *nēotan* possess]

neat², a. (Of liquor, esp. alcoholic) undiluted; of elegant simplicity in form or arrangement, nicely made or proportioned; (of language, style, sayings) brief, clear, & pointed, cleverly phrased, epigrammatic; deft, dextrous, cleverly done; tidy, methodical; ~-*handed*, dextrous. Hence ~'LY² adv., ~'NESS n. [f. F *net* f. L *nitidus* shining (*nitēre* shine)]

neath, prep. (poet.). Beneath. [f. BE-NEATH]

nĕb, n. (Sc.). Beak or bill; nose; snout; tip, spout, point. [OE *nebb* = ON *nef*, rcl. to MDu., MLG *nebbe*; cf. NIB]

nĕb'ŭla, n. (pl. -*lae*). Clouded speck on cornea causing defective sight; (astron.) luminous patch made by cluster of distant stars or by gaseous or stellar matter outside solar system. [L, =mist, rel. to Gk *nephelē* cloud]

nĕb'ūlar, a. Of nebula(e); ~ *theory* or *hypothesis*, that solar & stellar systems were developed from nebulae. [-AR¹]

nĕbūl'ium, n. Element formerly assumed to exist in gaseous nebulae as cause of bright lines in green part of spectrum. (These lines are now believed to be due to one of the known terrestrial elements in a more rarefied gaseous state than has yet been produced on earth.) [-IUM]

nĕb'ūlous, a. (Astron.) of, like, nebula(e); ~ *star*, small cluster of indistinct stars, or star in luminous haze; cloud-like; hazy, vague, indistinct, formless; clouded, turbid. So **nĕbŭlos'ITY** n. [f. F (-*eux*) or L *nebulosus* (NEBULA, -OUS)]

nĕcèssār'ian, n. & a. = NECESSITARIAN. Hence ~ISM(3) n. [NECESSARY, -ARIAN]

nĕ'cèssarılў, adv. As a necessary result, inevitably. [-LY²]

nĕ'cèssar|ў, a. & n. 1. Indispensable, requisite, (*to* or *for* person etc.; *it is* ~*y that, to* do); requiring to, that must, be done; determined by predestination or natural laws, not by free will, happening or existing by necessity; (of concept or mental process) inevitably resulting from nature of things or the mind, inevitably produced by previous state of things; (of agent) having no independent volition. 2. n. Thing without which life cannot be maintained (often *the* ~*ies of life*); (loosely) desirable thing not generally regarded as a luxury; (abs. use of adj.) *the* ~*y* (sl.), money or action needed for a purpose (*provide, find, do, the* ~*y*). [ME, f. AF **necessarie* (OF -*aire*) f. L *necessarius* (*necesse* needful, -ARY¹)]

nĕcèssitār'ian, n. & a. (Person) denying free will & maintaining that all action is determined by antecedent causes. Hence ~ISM(3) n. [NECESSITY, -ARIAN]

nĕcèss'itāte, v.t. Force, compel, (person) *to* do (now rare); render necessary, involve as condition or accompaniment or result. [f. med. L *necessitare* (NECESSITY), -ATE³]

nĕcèss'itous, a. Poor, needy. [foll., -OUS]

'nĕcèss'itў, n. Constraint or compulsion regarded as a law prevailing through the material universe & governing all human action (often *physical* ~; *logical* ~, compulsion to believe that of which the opposite is inconceivable; *absolute, moral, natural*, etc., ~); constraining power of circumstances, state of things compelling to certain course, (*of* ~, unavoidably; *make a virtue of* ~, claim credit for doing what one cannot help doing, do thing with a good grace; *am under the* ~ *of doing*; ~ *knows no law*, absolves from any offence); imperative need (*for*; ~ *is the mother of invention*); indispensability (*the* ~ *of protecting life & property*); indispensable thing, necessary; (usu. pl.) want, poverty, hardship, pressing need. [ME, f. OF *necessite* f. L *necessitatem* (*necesse* needful, -TY)]

nĕck¹, n., & v.i. & t. 1. Part of body that connects head with shoulders (*break* one's ~, dislocate vertebrae of this, be killed so; *break* ~ *of* task etc., get hardest part of it over; *save* one's ~, escape hanging; ~ *& crop*, headlong, bodily; *get it in the* ~, sl., suffer fatal or severe blow; *stick* or *shoot* one's ~ *out*, sl., invite attack; *talk through* (*the back of*) one's ~, sl., talk foolishly or wildly; ~ *or nothing*, desperately, staking all on success, *it is* a case for desperate attempts; ~ *& ~*, running even in race); (sl.) impudence; flesh of animal's ~ as food (esp. ~ *of mutton*); part of shirt etc. that touches ~. 2. Narrow part *of* vessel, esp. of bottle near mouth, or *of* passage, pass, or channel; pass, narrow channel, isthmus; narrow connecting part between two parts of thing; (archit.) lower part of capital. 3. ~'*band*, part of garment round ~; ~'*cloth*, cravat; ~'*erchief* (-chǐf), kerchief worn round ~; ~'*lace* (-lǐs), ornament of precious stones or metal, or beads etc., worn round ~; ~'*tie*, band of silk etc. securing or seeming to secure shirt-collar;

~-*verse*, Latin verse (usu. beginning of *Ps.* li) printed in black letter by reading which person claiming benefit of clergy might save his ~; ~'*wear* (shop), collars & ties; hence (-)~ED² (-kt) a. 4. vb. *(sl.). (Of couples) clasp one another round the ~; hug, embrace, (person); ~*ing* (petting) party. [OE *hnecca*, MDu., MLG *necke*, cogn. w. OHG *hnacch*, ON *hnakki*]

‖ **nĕck²**, n. Last sheaf of corn cut. [orig. unkn.]

nĕck′ing, n. (archit.). Part of column between shaft & capital. [NECK¹, -ING¹]

nĕck′lĕt, n. Ornament or fur protector for neck. [-LET]

nĕc′ro-, comb. form of Gk *nekros* corpse, dead body, as ~*gĕn′ic* produced by contact with dead bodies, ~PHIL(E), ~*phŏre* burying beetle, ~*biōs′is* decay in tissues of body, ~LATRY (-ŏl⁴), ~*logy* (-ŏl⁴) death--roll or obituary notice, ~*phagous* (-ŏf⁴) feeding on carrion, ~*polis*(-ŏp⁴) cemetery, *nĕc′ropsy* or ~*scopy* (-ŏs⁴), post-mortem examination.

nĕc′romănc‖y̆, n. Art of predicting by means of communication with the dead; magic, enchantment. So~ER¹ n., **nĕcromän′tic** a. [ME, f. OF *nigromancie* f. med. L *nigromantia* changed by assoc. w. L *niger* black f. LL f. Gk *nekromanteia* (prec., -MANCY)]

nĕcrōs′is, n. (path.; pl. *-ōsēs*). Death of circumscribed piece of tissue, esp. mortification of bones. Hence **nĕcrŏt′ic** a., **nĕc′rotize**(3) v.i. [f. Gk *nekrōsis* (*nekroŏ* kill, see NECRO-, -OSIS)]

nĕc′tar, n. (Gk myth.) drink of the gods (cf. AMBROSIA); any delicious drink; sweet fluid or honey produced by plants; kind of aerated water. Hence or cogn. **nĕctār′EAN, nĕctār′EOUS, ~ED²**(-*ard*), ~**ĭF′ER-OUS, ~OUS**, aa. [f. L f. Gk *nektar*]

nĕc′tarĭne, n. Kind of peach with thin downless skin & firm flesh. [n. use of obs. or rare adj. (NECTAR, -INE¹)]

nĕc′tary̆, n. Flower's or plant's honey--secreting organ. [irreg. f. NECTAR + -ARY¹]

Nĕdd′y̆, n. Donkey. [dim. of Edward; -Y³]

née (nā), a. Born (used in adding woman's maiden name as *Mrs Smith*, ~ *Jones*). [F]

need¹, n. Circumstances requiring some course (*if* ~ *be* or *were*, *there is no* etc. ~, *to do* or abs.; *have* ~, require *to*; *had* ~, ought to, as *had* ~ *remember*); necessity for presence or possession *of* (*the* ~ *of further securities*); *have* ~ *of*, require, want); emergency, crisis, time of difficulty, (*a friend in* ~ *is a friend indeed*; *good at* ~; *failed him in his* ~); destitution, lack of necessaries, poverty, whence ~'Y² a., ~'INESS n.; thing wanted, respect in which want is felt, requirement, (*my* ~*s are few*); (pl.) offices of nature (*do* one's ~*s*); ~'*fire*, fire got from dry wood by friction, beacon, bonfire. [OE *nīed*, OS·*nōd*, OHG *nōt*, ON *nauth*, Goth. *nauths* f. Gmc **naudhiz, *nauthiz*]

need², v.i. & t. (3 sing. pres. ~*s*, & ~

as specified below). Be necessary (arch.; *it* ~*s not*, it is needless; *there* ~*s*, so-&-so is required; *more than* ~*s*, than is necessary; *what* ~ or ~*s?*, why should one?); stand in need of, require, (intr.) be needy; be under necessity or obligation to (do etc.) or *to do* (3 sing. ~ , & *to* omitted, in neg. & interrog. forms; *he* ~ *not trouble himself*; *it* ~*s to be done with care*; *why* ~ *he have come tonight?*; ~ *not have done* etc., usu. form = did not ~ to do etc.; often ellipt., as *don't be longer away than you* ~). [OE *nēodian* (prec.)]

need′ful, a. Requisite, necessary, indispensable, (*to, for*, or abs.; *it is* ~ *to* do, or *that*; *the* ~, what is necessary, esp. sl., the money or action required, also *do the* ~ in football, convert try into goal). Hence ~NESS n. [-FUL]

nee′dle, n., & v.t. & i. 1. Thin round long piece of steel pointed at one end & with eye for thread at other used in sewing (*knitting, darning, packing, crochet*, etc., ~-, shapes or modifications of it for different purposes; *sharp as a* ~, lit., & fig. acute, observant; *look for* ~ *in* BOTTLE³ etc. *of hay*; PINS & ~*s*; ~'*s eye*, least possible aperture, esp. w. ref. to *Matt.* xix. 24). 2. Piece of magnetized steel used as indicator on dial of compass & magnetic & electric apparatus, esp. in telegraphy; strip of standard gold or silver used for comparison in assaying with touchstone. 3. Pointed etching instrument; pointed surgical instrument used in soft cataract; end of hypodermic syringe; thin pointed piece of metal, wood, or fibre, or long thorn, that receives & transmits the vibrations set up by a revolving gramophone record; steel pin exploding cartridge of breechloader. 4. Obelisk; sharp rock, peak. 5. Beam used as temporary support during under--pinning. 6. ~-shaped crystal. 7. Leaf of fir or pine. 8. ‖ *The* ~ (sl.), fit of nervousness. 9. ~-*bath*, shower-bath with fine spray discharged horizontally from vertical pipes surrounding bather; ~-*book*, book-shaped case for ~s; ~-*fish*, kinds of fish, esp. garfish; ~-*ful*, length of thread etc. put into ~ at once; ~ *game, match*, etc., one closely contested & arousing personal feeling or animosity; ~-*lace*, made with ~s not bobbins; ~-*point*, fine sharp point, also point-lace made with ~s; ~-*woman*, sempstress, also *good* or *bad* user of ~; ~-*work*, sewing or embroidery. 10. vb. Sew, pierce, or operate on, with ~; thread (one's way) between or through things; under-pin with ~-beams; form ~-shaped crystals; thread one's way; incite, irritate, prod into action. [OE *nǣdl*, OS *nādla*, OHG *nādala*, ON *nál*, Goth. *nēthla* f. Gmc **nē*- sew, cogn. w. L *nēre* spin]

need′lĕss, a. Unnecessary, uncalled for, (~ *to say* used parenth., as I need not tell you). Hence ~LY² adv., ~NESS n. [·LESS]

‖ **need′ments**, n. pl. Things needed, esp. personal necessaries carried on journey. [NEED n. or v., -MENT]

needs (-z), adv. Of necessity (now only after or before *must*; ~ *must* do, cannot help or avoid or get out of doing; *must* ~ do, occas. = ~ *must* do, usu. foolishly insists or insisted on doing). [OE *nēdes*, *nỹdes* (NEED[1], -ES)]

ne′er (nār), adv. (Poet.) never (not used ellipt for sentence like *never*); ~ *a*, not a single; ~*-do-well*, ~*-do-weel*, good-for-nothing (person). [contr. of NEVER]

nefār′ious, a. Wicked, iniquitous. Hence ~LY[2] adv., ~NESS n. [f. L *nefarius* (*nefas* wrong), -OUS]

negāte′, v.t. Nullify, deny existence of, imply or involve non-existence of, be the negation of. [f. L *negare* deny, -ATE[3]]

negā′tion, n. Denying; negative statement or doctrine; refusal, contradiction, denial *of*; (log.) affirmation of difference or exclusion; absence or opposite of something actual or positive; negative or unreal thing, nonentity. So **neg′atory** a. [f. F, or L *negatio* (prec., -ATION)]

negā′tionist (-sho-), n. One who denies accepted beliefs without proposing substitutes. [-IST]

neg′ative[1], a. **1.** Expressing or implying denial, prohibition, or refusal (~ *proposition* in logic, asserting difference or discrepancy; ~ *statute, vote, answer*; ~ *voice*, right of veto). **2.** Wanting, consisting in the want of, positive attributes (~ *virtue*, abstention from wrongdoing; ~ *instance, evidence*, of non-occurrence of something). **3.** (Alg.) denoting quantities to be subtracted from others or from zero (~ *sign*, —); (colloq., joc.) ~ *quantity*, nothing. **4.** (electr.). Of the kind produced by friction on resin etc. (opp. *positive*, on glass), containing or producing such electricity. **5.** Of opposite nature to thing regarded as positive (*debt is* ~ *capital, & capital* ~ *debt*). **6.** (photog.). Having lights & shadows of the actual object or scene reversed. Hence ~LY[2] adv., ~NESS, **nēgativ′ITY**, nn. [f. OF (*-if, -ive*), or LL *negativus* (NEGATE, -IVE)]

neg′ative[2], n. **1.** Negative statement, reply, or word (*it is hard to prove a* ~; *he returned a* ~, answered ' no ' etc.; *two* ~*s make an affirmative*; right of veto; *in the* ~, negative(ly) (esp. in ministerial answers in Parliament, *the answer is in the* ~, no; *it was decided in the* ~, proposal was rejected). **2.** Negative quality, want of something, (*his character is made up of* ~*s*). **3.** (alg.). Negative or minus quantity. **4.** (photog.). Image on glass etc. with reversed lights & shadows from which positive pictures are taken. **5.** Negative plate or metal in voltaic battery. [f. prec., or F *négative* or LL *negativa*]

neg′ative[3], v.t. Veto, reject, refuse to accept or countenance; disprove (infer-ence, hypothesis); contradict (statement); neutralize (effect). [f. prec. adj.]

neg′ativ|ism, n. Attitude of NEGATIONIST. So ~IST(2) n. [-ISM]

neglĕct′, v.t., & n. **1.** Slight, not pay attentions to; leave uncared-for; leave undone, be remiss about; omit *to* do or doing; hence ~ABLE a. (rare). **2.** n. ~ing or being ~ed; disregard *of*; negligence; hence ~FUL a., ~fulLY[2] adv., ~fulNESS n. [(n. f. L *neglectus -ūs*) f. L *neglegere -lect-* (*neg-* not, *legere* pick up)]

négligé (nĕg′lĭzhā), n. Free & easy or unceremonious attire. [F, p.p. of *négliger* (prec.)]

neg′ligeable, a. (rare). Negligible. [f. F *négligeable* (prec., -ABLE)]

neg′lig|ence, n. Want of proper care or attention, (piece of) carelessness; *contributory* ~*ence*, ~*ence* on a person's part that has helped to bring about the injury that he has suffered; freedom from restraint or artificiality in literature or art. So ~ENT a.' (*of* duty etc.), ~entLY[2] adv. [ME, f. OF, or L *neglegentia* (NEGLECT, -ENCE)]

neg′ligible, a. That need not be regarded (esp. ~ *quantity*). [as prec., -IBLE]

negō′ti|āte (-shǐ-), v.i. & t. **1.** Confer (*with* another) with view to compromise or agreement. **2.** Arrange (affair), bring about (desired object), by ~ating. **3.** Transfer (bill) to another for a consideration, convert into cash or notes, get or give value for (bill, cheque) in money. **4.** Clear, get over, dispose of, (fence, obstacle, difficulty). Hence or cogn. ~ABLE (-sha-) a., ~ANT(1) (-shǐ-) n., ~A′TION (-sǐ-, -shǐ-), ~ātōR (-shǐ-), ~atrESS[1] (-sha-), ~atrIX (-sha-), nn. [f. L *negotiari* (*negotium* business), -ATE[3]]

Něg′rĕss. See NEGRO.

nēgrill′ō, n. (pl. ~s). Small Negro; one of dwarf Negro people in Central & S. Africa. [Sp., dim. of NEGRO]

nēgri′tō (-rē-), n. (pl. ~s). One of small negroid people in the Malayo-Polynesian region. [as prec.]

Něg′rō, n. (pl. ~es; fem. *Negress*) & a. **1.** Member, esp. male, of black-skinned woolly-haired flat-nosed thick-lipped African people. **2.** adj. Of this race, black-skinned, (*n* ~ *minstrels*, troupe of real or sham ~es performing ~ songs & dances); occupied by, connected with, ~es; black or dark (*n*~ *ant, bat, monkey*, dark species). **3.** *n*~*-head*, strong black plug tobacco, also inferior indiarubber. Hence **nēg′rOID** a. & n., **nēgroid′**AL a., **nĕg′ro**PHIL a. & n., **nēgroph′il**ISM n., **nēgro**PHOB′IA n. [Sp., f. L *nigrum* nom. *niger* black]

Něg′us[1], n. Ruler of Abyssinia. [native]

něg′us[2], n. Hot sweetened wine & water. [Col. F. N~, d. 1732]

neigh (nā), v.i., & n. (Utter) cry (as) of horse. [OE *hnǣgan*, = MDu. *neyen*, MHG *nēgen* of imit. orig.]

neighbour (nāb'er), n., & v.t. & i. **1.** Dweller next door, near, in same street or village or district, or in adjacent country (*my ~ Jones*; *are next-door ~s*; *his nearest ~ is 12 miles off*; *our ~s across the Channel*), esp. regarded as one who should be friendly (*good, bad, ~s*; *~LY[1]* a., *~lINESS* n.) or as having claim on others' friendliness (*duty to* one's*~*, to any fellow man); person or thing near or next another (*my ~ at dinner*; *falling tree brought down its ~*); (attrib.) *~ing*; hence *~LESS* a., *~SHIP* n. **2.** vb. Adjoin, border upon, border *upon*, (chiefly now in *~ING[2]* a.). [OE *nēahgebūr* (NIGH, BOOR)]

neighboured (nāb'erd), a. Having neighbours or surroundings of specified kind (*ill ~*; *a beautifully ~ town*). [-ED[2],[1]]

neighbourhōod (nāb'er-), n. Neighbourly feeling or conduct (usu. *good~*); nearness, vicinity of (*in the ~ of £100*, about); neighbours, people of a district, district. [-HOOD]

neith'er (nīdh-, nēdh-), adv., conj., a., & pron. **1.** adv. (Introducing word, clause, etc., that is to be negatived equally with a following one attached to it by *nor*) not either, not on the one hand, (*~ knowing nor caring*; *~ you nor I know*, *~ he nor I know*, *~ I nor he knows*; also often vulg., *~ he nor she know*; *~ does cowardice ensure nor courage preclude defeat*; *~ HERE nor there*); (colloq.; placed at end to emphasize preceding negative) either, any more than something else, (*I don't know that ~*); (in apodosis after negative protasis) not either (*if you do not go, ~ shall I*); (bibl.) not even (*but ~ so did their witness agree*). **2.** conj. (arch.). Nor, nor yet, (*I know not, ~ can I guess*). **3.** adj. & pron. Not either, not the one nor the other, (*~ accusation, ~ of the accusations, is true*; *~ of them knows*, often also irreg. *know*); (loosely) none of any number of specified things. [ME *naither, neyther*, assim. of OE *nawther* contr. of *nāhwæther* (*nā* not, WHETHER) to EITHER]

něk, n. (S.-Afr.). = COL. [Du., = NECK[1]]

něk'ton, n. (biol.). The forms of free-swimming organic life found at various depths in the ocean & in lakes, taken collectively. [G, f. Gk *nēktos* swimming (*nēkhō* swim)]

něll'ў, n. Largest kind of petrel. [perh. the feminine name]

něm'at|o-, comb. form of Gk *nēma -atos* thread in scientific terms (= filamentous, having filament, thread-like), as *~ocўst*, cell in jelly-fish etc. containing coiled thread that can be projected as sting, *~ōde* & *~oid*, aa. & nn., (worm) of slender cylindrical shape.

Něm'ėsis, n. Goddess of retribution; retributive justice, downfall that satisfies this. [Gk (*nemō* give what is due)]

něm'ĭnė, abl. of L *nemo* no one; *~ contradicente* or *dissentiente* (pr. kŏntradīsěn'tī, dīsěntiěn'tī; abbr. *něm. con.* or *diss.*),

unanimously (or without a dissenting vote).

něm'ŏ mē ĭmpūn'ē lăcěss'ĭt, sent. No one attacks me with impunity. [L]

něn'uphăr, n. Water-lily. [med. L, f. Arab.-Pers. *ninufar*]

nē'o-, comb. form of Gk *neos* new, used as living pref. to adjj. & nn., & adding the notions *new, modern, later, recast, lately found* or *invented* (*~-Cath'olic*, *~-păg'anism*; *~-Căm'brian*, geol., of the later Cambrian period; *~-clăss'ic(ism)*; *~-Hěll'enism*, revival of Greek ideals; *~-Malthū'sianism* (-zha-), use of preventives against conception; *~-Plăt'onism*, 3rd-cent. mixture of Platonic ideas with Oriental mysticism; *nē'odoxy*, new doctrine or view; *nēŏnlŏl'ogy*, study of extant animals; *~zō'ic*, geol., of later period of geological history, post-palaeozoic).

nēolith'ĭc, a. Of the later stone age, when ground or polished stone weapons & implements prevailed. [prec., Gk *lithos* stone, -IC]

nēolō'gĭan, a. & n. **1.** Of, inclined to, marked by, neologism in theology. **2.** n. Neologist in theol. [NEOLOGY, -AN]

nēŏl'og|ism, nēŏl'og|ў, nn. Coining or using of new words, new-coined word; tendency to or adoption of novel or rationalistic religious views. So *~IST(1)* n., *~IZE(2)* v.i. [f. F *néologie, néologisme* (NEO-, -LOGY)]

nē'ŏn, n. (chem.). Inert gaseous element occurring in the atmosphere; used in illuminated signs (*~ lights*), giving a coloured glow when electricity is passed through it in a sealed low-pressure tube. [neut. of Gk *neos* new]

nē'ophrŏn, n. White Egyptian vulture & allied birds. [name of man turned to vulture in *Metamorphoses* of Antoninus Liberalis]

nē'ophўte, n. New convert esp. among primitive Christians or Roman Catholics; newly ordained R.-C. priest; novice of religious order; beginner, novice, tiro. [f. eccl. L f. Gk *neophutos* newly planted (NEO-, *phuō* plant)]

nēotě'rĭc, a. Recent, newfangled, modern. [f. LL f. Gk *neōterikos* (*neōteros* comp. of *neos* new, -IC)]

nēotrŏp'ĭcal, a. Of, found in, tropical & S. America. [NEO-, TROPICAL]

nēpěn'the(s) (-ī, -ēz), n. Drug producing forgetfulness of grief (poet.); (-*s*) kinds of plants with pitcher-shaped leaves, pitcher-plant. [(-*s*) L f. Gk, neut. of *nēpenthēs* griefless (*nē-* not, *penthos* grief)]

nē'phew (-v-), n. Brother's or sister's son. [ME, f. OF *neveu* f. L *nepotem* nom. -*pos* grandson, nephew]

nephŏl'ogў, n. Study of the clouds. [f. Gk *nephos* cloud, -LOGY]

nephrit'ĭc, a. Of or in the kidneys, renal. [f. LL f. Gk *nephritikos* (foll., -IC)]

nephrit'ĭs, n. Inflammation of the kidneys. [LL f. Gk (*nephros* kidney, -ITIS)]

něphr|(o)-, comb. form of Gk *nephros* kidney, as ~*ěc'tomy* excision of kidney, ~ŏL'OGY, ~ŏT'OMY.

nē plŭs ŭl'tra, n. Prohibition of advance, impassable obstacle; furthest point attained or attainable; highest pitch or form *of*, acme, culmination. [L, = not more beyond, supposed inscription on Pillars of Hercules]

něp'ot|ism, n. Undue favour from holder of patronage to relatives (orig. from Pope to illegitimate sons called nephews). So ~IST(1) n. [f. F -*isme*, or It. *nepotismo* (as NEPHEW, -ISM)]

Něp'tūne, n. 1. (God of) the sea (~'s *cup*, kinds of coral). 2. One of the farthest planets of solar system. [f. L *Neptunus*]

Něptūn'ian, a. & n. (Geol.) produced by water action; (person) maintaining aqueous origin of certain rocks, so **Něp'tūn-IST(2)** n. (opp. *Vulcanist*); of planet Neptune. [f. L *Neptunius* (prec.), -AN]

něptūn'ium n. Unstable element produced when uranium atoms absorb bombarding neutrons, & changing to plutonium. [as NEPTUNE, -IUM]

nēr'ěid, n. Sea-nymph; (zool.) long sea-worm or centipede. [f. L f. Gk *Nēreis -idos* daughter of sea-god Nereus]

ner'ō ănti'cō (nār-, -tē-), n. Kind of black marble found in Roman ruins. [It.]

nēr'oli, n. Essential oil from orange--flowers used in perfumery. [F (*né-*), f. It., f. name of Italian princess]

Nērōn'ian, a. Of, as of, the emperor Nero or his times, cruel, licentious, tyrannical. [f. L *Neronianus* (*Nero -onis*, -IAN)]

nēr'ate, a. (bot.). (Of leaves) having ribs. So **nērVA'TION** n. [foll., -ATE[2]]

nēr've, n., & v.t. 1. Sinew, tendon, (now poet.), exc. in *strain every* ~, make all possible efforts; also in pl. fig., as *good laws are the* ~*s of a State*). 2. Vigour, energy, well-strung state. 3. (bot.). Rib, esp. midrib, of leaf. 4. (anat.). Fibre or bundle of fibres connecting & conveying impulses of sensation & motion between brain or spinal cord or ganglionic organ & some part of body. 5. pl. Bodily state in regard to physical sensitiveness & interaction between brain & other parts, disordered state in these respects, exaggerated sensitiveness, nervousness, (*does not know what* ~*s are*, of equable temperament; *a fit of* ~*s*, nervous state; *get on* one's ~*s*, be a worry or annoyance to him; *has iron* ~*s*, ~*s of steel*, etc., is not easily upset or frightened; WAR[1] *of* ~*s*). 6. Nervous fibre. 7. Coolness in danger, boldness, assurance, (*lose* one's ~, become timid or irresolute); (colloq.) audacity, impudence. 8. ~-*centre*, group of closely connected ganglion-cells; ~-*knot*, ganglion; hence (-)**nērVED[2]** (-vd) a., **nērv'o-** comb. form. 9. v.t. Give strength, vigour, or courage, to; collect one*self* to face danger or suffering. [f. L *nervus*, rel. to Gk *neuron*]

nēr've'lěss (-vl-), a. Inert, wanting in vigour or spirit, listless; (of style) flabby, diffuse; (bot., entom.) without nervures; (anat., zool.) without nerves. Hence ~LY[2] adv., ~NESS n. [-LESS]

nērv'īne, a. & n. (med.). (Medicine) relieving nerve-disorders. [NERVE, -INE[1]]

nērv'ous, a. Sinewy, muscular, (arch.); (of literary style) vigorous, terse; full of nerves; of the nerves (~ *system*, nerves & nerve-centres as a whole); acting on the nerves; having disordered or delicate nerves, excitable, highly strung, easily agitated, timid. Hence ~LY[2] adv., ~NESS n. [f. L *nervosus* (NERVE, -OSE[1])]

nērv'ure (-yer), n. One of the tubes forming framework of insect's wing, vein; principal vein of leaf. [F (NERVE, -URE)]

nērv'ý, a. Sinewy, strong, (poet.); (sl.) cool, confident, impudent; jerky, nervous; (sl.) trying to the nerves. [-Y[2]]

nescience (něsh'yens), n. Not knowing, absence of knowledge *of*. [f. LL *nescientia* f. L *nescire* not know (*ne-* not, *scire* know), -ENCE]

nescient (něsh'yent), a. & n. Ignorant (*of*); agnostic (a. & n.). [prec., -ENT]

něss, n. Promontory, headland, cape. [OE *næs*, = ON *nes*, LG *nesse*, rel. to OE *nasu* NOSE]

-ness, suf. appended freely to adj. (*bitter*~), participles (*loving*~, *tired*~), compd adjj. (*tongue-tied*~), & adj. phrr. (*up-to--date*~) to form nn. expressing state or condition. [OE -*nes(s)* &c., OS -*nesse* &c., OHG -*nessi* &c., Goth. (-*in*)*assus*; the n is not orig. part of suf. but an accretion f. stem]

něst, n., & v.t. & i. 1. Structure or place made or chosen by bird for laying eggs & sheltering young (*it's an ill bird that fouls its own* ~, one should not speak ill of home etc.; FEATHER[2] one's ~); animal's or insect's abode or spawning or breeding place; snug or secluded retreat, lodging, shelter, bed, receptacle; haunt *of* robbers etc.; fostering-place *of* vice etc.; brood, swarm; collection, series, *of* similar objects; small chest *of* drawers; ~-*egg*, real or imitation egg left in ~ to induce hen to go on laying there, sum of money kept as reserve or nucleus; hence ~'FUL(2) n., ~'LIKE a. 2. vb. Make or have ~ in specified place, take to ~-building; (p.p.) established (as) in ~, (of boxes etc.) packed one inside another; take bird's ~s or eggs. [OE, OHG *nest* cogn. w. L *nidus*]

ně'stle (-sl), v.i. & t. = prec. vb (first sense; now rare); settle oneself, be settled, comfortably *down*, or *in*, *into*, *among*, etc., leaves, wraps, chair, etc.; press oneself affectionately *close to, to*, person; lie half--hidden or embedded; push (head, face, shoulder, etc.) affectionately or snugly *in*; hold embraced (usu. in p.p.). [OE *nestlian*, = MDu., MLG *nestelen*, see NEST, -LE(3)]

ně'stling (-sl-, -stl-), n. Bird too young to leave nest. [ME, f. NEST n. + -LING¹, or prec + -ING²]

Nĕs'tŏr, n. Wise old man, senior *of* company etc. [name of character in Homer's *Iliad*]

Nĕstŏr'ian, a. & n. (Adherent) of doctrine of Nestorius patriarch of Constantinople A.D. 428 asserting that Christ had distinct divine & human persons. Hence ~ISM(3) n. [f. LL *Nestorianus* (-AN)]

nĕt¹, n., & v.t. & i. (-tt-). 1. Meshed fabric of twine, cord, hair, etc.; piece of this used for catching fish etc. (*beach, casting, trawl, herring, lark, clap*, etc., ~~), or for covering, confining, protecting, carrying, etc. (*fruit, hair, tennis, cricket*, etc., ~~); moral or mental snare; spider's web; reticulation, ~*work*; ~*'ball*, girls' game in which a ball has to be thrown so as to fall through an elevated horizontal ring from which a ~ hangs; ~*'work*, arrangement with intersecting lines & interstices recalling those of ~, complex system *of* railways, rivers, canals, etc., ramification, number of broadcasting stations connected for simultaneous broadcast of same programme; hence ~*'FUL*(2) n. 2. vb. Cover, confine, catch, with ~(s); fish (river etc.) with ~s, set ~s in (river); make netting; make (purse, hammock, etc.) by ~ting; (usu. in p.p.) mark with ~like pattern, reticulate. [OE *net(t)*, OS *net(t)*, OHG *nezzi*, ON *net*, Goth. *nati* f. Gmc **natja-*]

nĕt², a., & v.t. (-tt-). 1. Free from deduction, remaining after necessary deductions, (~ *profit*, true profit, actual gain after working expenses have been paid, opp. GROSS; ~ *price*, real price off which discount is not allowed, opp. *nominal, publisher's, price*). 2. v.t. Gain or yield (sum) as ~ profit. [F, see NEAT²]

nē tĕm'erĕ. The papal decree of 1907 under which marriages between Roman Catholics and others are not valid unless solemnized by R.-C. bishop or his deputy. [initial L words, = lest rashly]

nĕth'er (-dh-), a. (arch. or joc.). Lower (~ *lip* or *jaw*; ~ *garments* etc., trousers; ~ *man* or *person*, legs etc.; ~ *millstone*, simile for hard heart etc.; ~ *world*, rarely the earth, usu. hell, also ~ *regions*). Hence ~MOST a. [OE *nithera* &c., f. OE (ME) advv. *nithor, nither* lower, downwards, f. Gmc **nithar*; see -THER]

Nĕth'erlander, n., **Nĕth'erlandish**, a., **Nĕth'erlands**, attrib., (-dh-). (Native) of the Netherlands. [f. Du. *Nederlander, -landsch, (Nederland, -ER¹, -ISH¹)*]

nĕt'suke (-sŏŏkă), n. Carved buttonlike ornament worn by Japanese. [Jap.]

nĕtt'ing, n. In vbl senses; also: netted string, thread, or wire; piece of this used for various purposes. [-ING¹]

nĕt'tle, n., & v.t. 1. Kinds of plants including *great* or *common* ~ & *small* ~, two species growing profusely on waste land & covered with stinging hairs; other plants resembling these, esp. DEAD- ~~; GRASP *the* ~; ~*-rash*, eruption on skin in patches like those made by ~ stings. 2. v.t. Beat with ~s; get one*self* stung with ~s; irritate, provoke, annoy. [OE *netele*, MDu. *netele*, MLG *net(t)ele*, OHG *nezzila*, f. Gmc **nat-* (OHG *nazza*) + dim. suf. -LE(1)]

neum(e) (nūm), n. (mus.). Sign in plainsong indicating note or group of notes to be sung to a syllable. [ME, f. OF *neume*, f. med. L *neuma* f. Gk *pneuma* breath]

neur'al (nūr-), a. Of the nerves, of the central nervous system. [f. Gk *neuron* nerve, -AL]

neurā'tion (nūr-), n. Distribution of nervures, venation. [irreg. f. foll., -ATION]

neur|(o)- (nūr-), comb. form of Gk *neuron* nerve; ~*ăl'gia* (-jᴀ), affection of nerve(s) usu. of head or face causing intense intermittent pain, so ~*ăl'gic* a.; ~*ăsthĕn'ia*, nervous debility, so ~*ăsthĕn'ic* a.; ~*ĕc'tomy*, excision of nerve; ~*'ine*, nerve-tissue; ~IT'IS n.; ~*ŏl'OGY*, ~*ŏl'OGIST*, ~*olŏ'GICAL*; ~*o-mŭs'cular*, of nerves & muscles; ~*'opăth*, person of abnormal nervous sensibility or affected by nervous disease, so ~*opăth'IC* a., ~*opathŏL'OGY*, ~*ŏp'athY¹*; ~*ŏp'athist*, specialist in ~opathy; ~*o-physiŏl'OGY*, physiology of nervous system; ~*o-psych'ic* (-sik-), of nervous & psychic functions; ~*ŏp'terous*, of the *Neuroptera*, order of insects having four naked membranous transparent wings with reticulate neuration; ~*ŏt'omy*, cutting of nerve to produce sensory paralysis; ~*ÿpnŏl'ogy*, science of hypnotism.

neurōm'a (nūr-), n. (pl. ~*ta*). Tumour on nerve or in nerve-tissue. [f. Gk *neuron* nerve, -OMA]

neurōs'is (nūr-), n. (pl. ~*ōsĕs*). Functional derangement due to disorders of nervous system; change in nerve-cells of brain prior to psychic activity. [as prec., -OSIS]

neurŏt'ic (nūr-), a. & n. (Drug) affecting nervous system; (person) affected with nervous disorder, of abnormal sensibility. [as prec., -OTIC]

neut'er, a. & n. 1. (Gram.) neither masculine nor feminine (cf. COMMON¹, EPICENE), (of verb) intransitive; neutral, not taking or assisting either side, in war, argument, opinion, etc. (esp. *stand* ~, remain neutral, declare neutrality); (bot.) without pistils & stamens, asexual; (entom.) sexually undeveloped, sterile. 2. n. ~ noun, adjective, verb, or gender; person standing ~; sexually undeveloped female insect, esp. bee or ant; castrated animal. [L, = neither (*ne-* not, *uter* either)]

neut'ral, a. & n.. 1. Not assisting either of two belligerent States, belonging to a State that thus stands aloof, exempted or excluded from active or passive hostilities, taking neither side in dispute or difference of opinion, indifferent, impartial. **2.** Not distinctly marked or coloured, indefinite, vague, indeterminate, (~ *tint*, grey or slate-colour, whence ~-*tint'*ED² a. lit. & fig.). **3.** (Chem.) neither acid nor alkaline; (electr.) neither positive nor negative; (entom., bot.) sexually undeveloped, asexual; hence or cogn. **neutrăl'**ITY n., ~LY² adv. **4.** n. ~ State or person; subject of ~ State. **5.** Position of the parts in a gear mechanism in which no power is transmitted. [f. obs. F, or L *neutralis* of neuter gender (prec., -AL)]

neut'raliz|e, -is|e (-īz), v.t. Counterbalance, render ineffective by opposite force or effect; exempt or exclude (place) from sphere of hostilities. Hence ~A'TION n. [f. F -*iser* or med. L *neutralisare* (prec., -IZE)]

neut'rŏn, n. Electrically neutral particle of about the same mass as a proton and probably consisting of an electron & a proton in close association. [f. NEUTRAL after *electron*]

névé (něv'ā), n. Expanse of granular snow not yet compressed into ice at head of glacier. [F (L *nix nivis* snow, -ATE²)]

něv'er, adv. At no time, on no occasion, not ever, (often ~ *before, since, after, yet*; also repeated for emphasis; NOW *or* ~; ~ *is a long word* or *day*, comment on rash renunciation or despair or negative prophecy; *it is* ~ *too late to mend*, reformation is always possible); (colloq. expressing surprise or incredulity in sentence or el-lipt.) surely not, you do not mean it, (*you* ~ *left the key in the lock!*; '*He ate the whole turkey.*'—'*Never!*'; *I* ~ *did!*, *Well, I* ~ *!*, i.e. heard of such a thing etc.); not at all (~ *fear*; ~ *mind*, do not be troubled); ~ *a*, not a, no — at all; ~ *a one*, none; (in condit. clauses) ~ *so*, to unlimited extent, ever so; (with compar.) ~ *the*, none the; (with particles etc.) ~-*enough-to-be-regretted*, ~-*to-be-forgotten*, ~-*ceasing, -dying, -ending, -fading, -failing*; ~*more'*, at no future time; *Never Never* (*Land*), north Queensland; (joc.) ~-~ (hire-purchase) *plan, system*; ~*the-less'* adv. & conj., for all that, but for all that, notwithstanding, all the same. [OE *næfre* (*ne* not, *æfre* EVER)]

new¹, a. **1.** Not existing before, now first made, brought into existence, invented, introduced, known or heard of, experienced, or discovered, (*New* TESTAMENT); unfamiliar *to*. **2.** Renewed, fresh, further, additional; different, changed, (*a* ~ *morality*; ~ *man*, theol., one converted to Christianity, *put on the* ~ *man*, show conversion by amendment; *a* ~ *fashion*, whence ~-**fă'shion**ED² (-shond) a.; *my* ~ *tailor*; *lead a* ~ *life*; ~ STYLE; *turn over a* ~ LEAF). **3.** (With *the*, as distinctive epithet implying difference of character) later, modern, ~*fangled*, (*the* ~ LEARNING, MODEL, COMEDY; *the* ~ *diplomacy, journalism, theology*, etc., advanced in method or

doctrine, usu. derog.; *the* ~ *poor, rich*, classes recently impoverished, enriched; *the* ~ *woman*, women who aspire to freedom & independence & reject convention; *the New World*, America). **4.** Of recent origin, growth, arrival, or manufacture, now first used, not worn or exhausted, (~ *red sandstone*; ~ *potatoes, wine, cheese*; ~ *furniture, clothes*; ~ *countries, soil*; *a heart, pleasures, ever* ~; ~ CHUM; ~ *members* of Parliament etc.; ~ *look*, recent (1947) fashion in women's dress marked esp. by longer & fuller skirt, (colloq.) up--to-date appearance; not yet accustomed *to*, fresh *from*. **5.** (Of family or person) lately risen in position. **6.** ~ *comer*, person lately arrived; ~ DEAL²; *New Englander*, inhabitant of *New England*, six NE. States of U.S.A.; ~**făng'led** [-nggled; f. obs. ~*fangle* a. in same sense (-*fangel* inclined to take f. OE st. *fang*-, infin. *fōn* take)], fond of novelty (now rare), different from the good old fashion, objectionably novel; ~ *moon*, moon when first seen as crescent after conjunction with sun, time of such appearance, (bibl.) Hebrew festival; ~ *year*, coming or lately begun year, first few days of year (~--*year's gift, wishes*, etc.; ~-*year's day*, 1 Jan.; ~-*year's eve*, 31 Dec.); *New Zealander*, Maori, also European inhabitant in New Zealand. Hence ~'ISH¹ a., ~'NESS n. [OE *nīwe*, OS *niwi*, OHG *niuwi*, ON *nȳr*, Goth. *niujis* f. Gmc **neujaz*, cogn. w. L *novus*]

new², adv. (preceding, & now usu. hy-phened with, qualified word). **1.** Newly, recently, just, (~-*blown*, having just come into bloom, lit. & fig.; ~-*born*, & see below; ~-*built*, & see below; ~--*coined*, esp. of words; ~-*come*, lately arrived; ~'-*comer*, one who has lately come; ~-*fallen snow*; ~-*fledged*; ~-*found*; ~-*laid eggs*; ~-*made*; ~-*mown hay* or *lawn*). **2.** Anew, afresh, re-, (~-*born*, regenerated, & see above; ~-*build*, rebuild, & see above; ~-*create*; ~-*front*, put new front to; ~-*furnish*; ~-*model*, recast). [f. prec.]

new'ĕl, n. Centre pillar of winding stair (*open* or *hollow* ~, central well of winding stair); post supporting stair-handrail at top or bottom. [ME, f. OF *nouel* f. Rom. **nucale* f. LL *nucalis* like a nut (L *nux nucis* nut, -AL)]

Newfound'land (*or* -fŭndlănd'), n. Island at mouth of St Lawrence (~ *dog* or ~, also ~*er*, large breed of spaniel kind noted for swimming powers). Hence ~ER¹(4) n.

Newg'ate, n. Celebrated London prison (~ *Calendar*, publication with accounts of ~ prisoners; ~ *fringe, frill*, beard grown below chin while face is shaven; || ~ *knocker*, curl worn by costermongers etc.). [place]

newl'y, adv. Recently (usu. with p.p. = NEW² in sense 1 & often now preferred;

hyphened w. attrib. part.; *the ~-discovered country*; *~-wed* a. & n.; *a guest ~ arrived*): in new manner. [-LY²]

Newm'árkèt, n. Town noted for horse--races (*~ coat* or *~*, close-fitting overcoat for men or women); a card-game.

news (-z), n. pl. (usu. followed by sing. vb). 1. Tidings, new information, fresh events reported, (*have you heard the, this*, or rarely *these, ~?*; *ill ~ flies apace*; *no ~ is good ~*; *that is no ~*, already well known; *is there any, what is the, ~?*); interesting information; (*N~*) part of newspaper title, as *Evening N~*. 2. ||*~agent*, dealer in *~papers* etc., *~-boy, -man*, selling *~* papers in streets; *~'cast(er)*, radio broadcast(er) of news reports; *~-letter*, letter sent out periodically with the *~* to country towns etc.; *~'monger*, gossip; *~'paper*, printed publication usu. daily or weekly containing the *~*, advertisements, & literary matter; *~'print*, paper for printing *~papers* on; *~-reel*, cinema film giving the *~* of the day; *~-room*, || reserved for *~paper-reading*; *~-sheet*, simple form of *~paper*; *~-stand*, stall for sale of *~papers*; *~-vendor*, *~paper-seller*. Hence *~'LESS*, *~'Y², aa., ~'INESS* n., (-z-). [ME, pl. of NEW¹ after OF *noveles* (F *nouvelles*) or med. L *nova* neut. pl. of L *novus* new]

newt, n. Small tailed amphibian allied to salamander, eft. [ME, for *ewt* (*a newt = an ewt*, cf. NICKNAME) var. of *ewet* EFT]

Newtōn'ian, a. & n. 1. Of Newton or his theory of the universe; devised etc. by Newton. 2. n. Follower of Newton; *~* telescope or reflector. [Sir Isaac *Newton* (1642–1727), -IAN]

nĕxt, a. (occas. governing noun), adv., prep., & n. 1. adj. Lying, living, being, nearest or nearest *to* or nearest to (*in the ~ house*; *my ~ neighbour*; *lives ~ door*, in the *~* house; *~-door neighbours*; *~-door to felony*, *to blasphemous*, almost; *~ to nothing, none, impossible*, almost; *the chair ~ the fire*; *the skin with the flesh ~ it*; *the shop ~ to the corner*); soonest come to, first ensuing, immediately following, coming nearest in order etc. *to*, immediately *before*, (*will ask the ~ man I see, the ~ policeman*; *shall return ~ year, ~ Friday*, on *Friday ~*; *what is the ~ article?*, shopman's formula; *the Sunday ~ before Easter*; *what is true one day may be false the ~*; *not till ~ time*, joc. addition to promise of abstention; *the ~ town to London in size*; *~-best*, second--best; *the person ~ him*, or *~ to him*, in rank). 2. adv. (Often indistinguishable f. pred. use of adj.) in the *~* place or degree, on the *~* occasion, (*in the week ~ ensuing*; *~ came a strange figure*; *what ~?*, can anything follow to beat this for absurdity etc.?; *placed his chair ~ to hers*; *New York was the largest city ~ to London*; *when I ~ saw him he was lame*). 3. prep. (Often indistinguishable f. pred. adj. governing noun) in or into the *~* place, on the *~*

occasion, in the *~* degree, to (*I was standing ~ him*; *placed his chair ~ hers*; *loves him ~ her own child*; *wear flannel ~ your skin*). 4. n. (or ellipt. use of adj.). *~* person or thing (*~ of kin*, person nearest of kin to someone; *will tell you in my ~*, i.e. letter; *to be continued in our ~*, i.e. issue of magazine etc.; *her~*, i.e. husband, *was a greengrocer*, i.e. child, *was a girl*; *~ please*, ask your *~* question, let the *~* man come, etc.). [OE *nēahst* (NIGH, -EST)]

nĕx'us, n. Bond, link, connexion, (fig.); *the cash ~* (consisting in money payments). [L (*nectere nex-* bind)]

Niăg'ara, n. Cataract, torrent, din, (*shoot ~*, run fearful risks). [N.-Amer. waterfall]

nib, n., & v.t. (-bb-). 1. Point of quill pen; metal or quill pen-point; point of tool etc. 2. pl. Fragments of crushed cocoa-beans. 3. v.t. Make, mend, insert *~* of, (pen). [f. M Du. *nib*, or MLG *nibbe*, var. f. *nebbe* NEB]

nib'ble, v.t. & i., & n. 1. Take small bites at; bite (t. & i.) gently or cautiously or playfully (esp. of fish with bait, or rabbits; often *~ at*, lit., & fig. of dallying with temptation, bargain, etc.); carp *at*, make trifling criticisms. 2. n. Act of nibbling, esp. of fish at bait; enough (grass etc.) to *~ at*. [f. LG *nibbelen*, also *gnibbelen, knabbelen*, whence obs. *knabble*]

nib'lick, n. Golf-club with large round heavy head, used esp. for playing out of bunkers. [orig. unkn.]

nibs (-z), n. (sl.). *His* etc. *~*, burlesque title after *His Grace* etc. [cf. earlier (cant) *nabs*]

nīce, a. & adv. 1. Fastidious, dainty, hard to please, of refined or critical tastes; precise, punctilious, scrupulous, particular, (*must not be too ~ about the means*). 2. Requiring precision, care, tact, or discrimination (*a ~ experiment, question, point, negotiation*). 3. Minute, subtle, (*a ~ distinction, shade of meaning*). 4. Attentive, close, (*a ~ inquiry, observer*). 5. Delicately sensitive, discriminative, or deft (*a ~ ear, judgement, hand*; *weighed in the ~st scales*, lit. or fig.). 6. (colloq.). Agreeable, attractive, delightful, well-flavoured, satisfactory, kind, friendly, considerate, generally commendable (often iron., as *here is a ~ mess*). 7. *~* (*and*), satisfactorily, as *the house stands ~ & high, car is going ~ & fast, this is a ~ long one*; *~-looking*, pretty or of engaging appearance. Hence *~'LY²* (-sl-) adv., *~'NESS* (-sn-) n., *nī'cISH¹*(2) a. [ME senses, *stupid, wanton*; OF, f. L *nescius* ignorant (NESCIENCE)]

Nīcēne' (or *nī²*), a. Of Nicaea (*first & second ~ councils*, held A.D. 325, 787, to settle the Arian controversy & the question of images; *~ Creed*, formal statement of Christian belief based on that adopted at first *~* council). [f. LL *Nicaenus, Nicenus* (L f. Gk *Nikaia*)]

nī'cĕtўy, n. Punctiliousness; precision,

accuracy, (to a ~, exactly); intricate or subtle quality (a point of great ~); minute distinction, subtle or unimportant detail, (pl.) minutiae. [ME, f. OF *nicete* (NICE, -TY)]

niche, n., & v.t. **1.** Vertical recess in wall to contain statue, vase, etc.; (fig.) place destined for person's occupation, esp. ~ *in the temple of fame*, right to be remembered for one's achievements. **2.** v.t. Place (statue etc.) in ~ (usu. in p.p.); ensconce, settle, (esp. one*self*, or in p.p.) in some hollow or corner. [F, f. *nicher* make a nest, f. Rom. **nidicare* f. *nidus* nest]

nick[1], n. Notch serving as catch, guide, mark, etc.; (print.) groove on side of type-letter; certain throws in hazard; *in the* ~ (*of time*), just at the right moment. [orig. unkn.]

nick[2], v.t. & i. Make nick(s) in, indent; make incision at root of (horse's tail; also with *horse* etc. as obj.) to make him carry it higher; hit upon, guess rightly, (~ *it, the truth*, etc.); just catch (the time, a train, etc.); catch, nab, (criminals etc.); make (certain winning throws) at hazard; cut *in* by short cut, at corner, etc., in hunting or racing; (of breeding stocks) mingle *well* etc. with others. [orig. unkn.]

nick'el, n., & v.t. (-ll-). **1.** Hard silvery-white lustrous ductile metallic element much used esp. in alloys; U.S. five-cent piece or kinds of Continental coin corresponding to English & French coppers; ~ *brass*, alloy of copper, ~, & zinc; ~ *silver*, alloy like German silver; ~ *steel*, alloy of iron with ~. **2.** v.t. Coat with ~. [abbr. of G *kupfernickel* copper-coloured ore f. which ~ was first got (*kupfer* copper, *nickel* demon, w. ref. to disappointing nature of ore, which yielded no copper); cf. COBALT]

nick'-nack. See KNICK-KNACK.

nick'name, n., & v.t. **1.** Name added to or substituted for person's, place's, or thing's proper name; abbreviation or familiar form of Christian name. **2.** v.t. Call (person or thing a ~), give~ to, (*some people are never ~d*; *they* ~ *patience cowardice*; *Cumberland*, *~d Butcher*). [15th c. *neke-*, orig. *an* EKE[1]-*name*, cf. NEWT]

nico'tian (-shǐ-), a. & n. Of tobacco; (n.) smoker. [foll., -IAN]

nic'otin|e (-tēn), n. Poisonous alkaloid extracted as oily liquid from tobacco. Hence ~ISM(5) n., ~IZE(5) v.t. [F (*Nicot*, introducer of tobacco into France, -INE[5])]

nic'tāte, nic'titāte, vv.i. Close & open the eyes, wink, chiefly in *nict(it)ating* membrane, third or inner eyelid of many animals. Hence nictA'TION, nictitA'TION, nn. [f. (med.) L *nictitare* frequent. of) L *nictare*, -ATE[3]]

ni'cy̆, n. (nursery). Sweet, lollipop. [NICE, -Y[3]]

nidamen'tal, a. Serving as receptacle for

ova in molluscs etc. (~ *gland, capsule, ribbon*). [f. L *nidamentum* (NIDUS, -MENT)]

nid(d)'ering, n. & a. (pseudo-arch.). Base or cowardly (person). [misreading of obs. *nithing* f. ON *nithingr*; given currency by Scott]

nid'dle-nŏd'dle, a., & v.i. & t. **1.** Nodding, quivering, unsteady. **2.** vb. Keep nodding (head, or intr.), totter, sway. [redupl. f. NOD, -LE(3)]

‖ **nide**, n. Brood of pheasants. [f. L NIDUS]

nid'ificāte, nid'ifȳ, vv.i. Build nest(s). So nidificA'TION n. [f. L *nidificare* (NIDUS, -FY), -ATE[3]]

nid'-nŏd, v.i. & t. (-dd-). Keep nodding. [reduplicated f. NOD]

nid'us, n. (pl. -*dī, -duses*). Place in which insects etc. deposit eggs; place in which spores or seeds develop; place of origin or development for disease, or for some quality, doctrine, etc.; natural receptacle; collection of eggs, tubercles, etc. [L, see NEST]

niece, n. One's brother's or sister's daughter. [ME & OF *nece, nice* f. LL *neptia* (also *nepta, neptis*) niece f. L *neptis* granddaughter]

niĕll'ō, n. (pl. -*li* pr. -lē, *-lōs*). Black composition for filling engraved lines in silver or other metal; (specimen of) such ornamental work. Hence ~ED[2] (-ōd) a. [It., f. neut. of L *nigellus* dim. of *niger* black]

Nier'steiner (nēr̄stī-), n. Rhenish wine from Nierstein. [G]

Nietzsch'ean (nēch[1]-), a. & n. (Admirer, follower) of the German philosopher F. Nietzsche (d. 1900); (supporter) of his principles (see OVERMAN). [-AN]

*nif'ty, a. (sl.). Spruce, smart, stylish; smelly.

nigg'ard, n. & a. Stingy person, grudging giver *of*; (adj., rhet. & poet.) = foll. [ME, alt., by suf. substitution, f. earlier (obs.) *nigon*, perh. of Scand. orig.; cf. NIGGLE]

nigg'ardl|y̆, a. & adv. Parsimonious, stingy, sparing, scanty, giving or given grudgingly or in small amounts; hence ~INESS n.; (adv.) in ~y manner. [-LY[1, 2]]

nigg'er (-g-), n. Negro (usu. derog.; ***~** *in the woodpile* or *fence*, sl., suspicious circumstance, something that spoils a good thing); *work like a* ~, toil very hard; (loosely) member of any dark-skinned people, e.g. E.-Indian, native Australian; ~(-*brown*), dark shade of brown; ~ *minstrel*, see NEGRO; ~ *melody, song*, etc., such as prevail among American Negroes; ~*head*, = NEGRO-*head*. Hence ~DOM n. [18th c. alt. f. *neger* (16th c.) f. F *nègre* f. Sp. *negro* NEGRO]

‖ **nig'gle**, v.i. Spend time, be over-elaborate, on petty details. [app. of Scand. orig.; cf. Norw. *nigla*]

nigg'ling, a. Trifling, petty, lacking in breadth, largeness, or boldness of effect; (of handwriting) cramped. [-ING[2]]

nigh (nī), adv., prep., & a., (comp. & sup. formerly *near*, *next*, now ~*er*, ~*est*, also as advv., prepp., & aa., cf. NEAR¹, ²). = NEAR¹, ² (arch., poet., or dial.). [OE *nēah*, OS, OHG *nāh*, ON *ná*-, Goth. *nēhwa*; the orig. comp. & superl. are repr. by NEAR, NEXT; the forms ~*er*, ~*est* date f. 16th c.]

night (nīt), n. **1.** Dark period between day & day, time from 6 p.m. to 6 a.m. or from sunset to sunrise, darkness then prevailing, the dark, (also ~'*fall*) end of daylight, weather or experiences or occupation of a ~, (*black*, *dark*, *as* ~; *went forth into the* ~; *the* ~ *of ignorance* or *barbarism*; *stayed three* ~*s with them*; *a dirty* ~, *stormy* or *rainy*; *have a good*, *bad*, ~, *sleep well* or *ill*, *be comfortable* or *in pain*, cf. GOOD-~; *make a* ~ *of it*, spend ~ in festivity; ~ *out*, festive evening, also evening on which servant is allowed out; ~ *& day*, always, without cessation; *all* ~, *all* ~ *long*, for the whole ~; *by* ~, during, under cover of, the ~; *at* ~, at ~*fall*, in the evening, also added to the hours from 6 p.m. to midnight, cf. *in the morning* of hours 1–6 a.m.; *cannot sleep o'* ~*s for thinking of*); ~-, by, like, during, appropriate to, employed for, active in, the ~ (-*veiled*, -*black*, -*walking*, -*haunted*, *brawl*, -*attire*, *lamp*, -*porter*, -*moth*). **2.** ~-*bird*, esp. owl or nightingale, also person esp. of disreputable character who goes about by ~; ~-*blindness*, nyctalopia; ~-*boat*, passenger-boat crossing by ~; ~'*cap*, worn in bed, also alcoholic drink taken before going to bed; ‖ ~-*cellar*, underground drinkshop of low class; ~-*chair*, = ~-*stool*; ~-*clothes*, worn in bed; ~-*club* (open to members for dancing, supper, etc.); ~-*dress*, ~-*gown* (also ~'*Y*³ n., pr. nīt'ĭ), woman's or child's ~ attire; ~-*flower*, that opens at ~ & closes in the day; ~-*glass*, short telescope for ~ use at sea; ~-*hag*, female demon riding the air at ~, ~*mare*; ~-*hawk*, thieving or other nocturnal prowler; ~-*jar*, the GOAT*sucker*; ~-*light*, short thick candle giving dim light through ~ for invalids etc.; ~-*line*, left with baited hooks to catch fish by ~; ~-*long*, lasting through the ~; ~'*man*, employed to remove ~-*soil*; ~'*mare*, female monster sitting upon & seeming to suffocate sleeper, incubus, oppressive or paralysing or terrifying or fantastically horrible dream (whence ~'*mārᴵsн*¹ a.), also haunting fear or thing vaguely dreaded; ~-*piece*, (painting of) ~ scene or landscape; ~-*school*, providing instruction for workmen after day's work; ~ *season*, = ~-*time* (poet., rhet.); ~-*shirt*, boy's or man's long shirt for sleeping in; ~-*soil*, contents of cesspools etc. removed at ~; ~-*stool*, close-**stool** or commode for use at ~; ~-*suit*, set of pyjamas; ~-*time*, ~ as a state of things or opportunity (*in the* ~-*time*, *by* ~); ~-*watch*, (person or party keeping) watch by

~, Hebrew or Roman division (one of three or four) of the ~ (*in the* ~-*watches*, during the anxious, wearisome, wakeful, etc., ~); ~-*work*, done, that must be done, by ~. Hence ~'LESS (nīt-) a. [OE *neaht*, *niht*, OS, OHG *naht*, ON *nátt*, Goth. *nahts* f. Gmc **naht*- cogn. w. L *nox -ctis*]

night'ingāle (nītingg-), n. Small reddish-brown migratory bird singing melodiously & powerfully both by night & in the day. [OE *nihtegale* (obs. *nightgale*), OS, OHG *nahta*-, *nahtigala* (NIGHT, *galan* sing); forms -*in*- f. 13th c.]

night'lўʸ¹ (nīt-), a. Happening, done, existing, etc., in the night; happening every night; (poet.) of or suiting night. [OE *nihtlīc* (NIGHT, -LY¹)]

night'lўʸ² (nīt-), adv. Every night. [-LYʸ²]

night'shāde (nīt-), n. Kinds of plants, esp. *black* ~ with white flowers & black poisonous berries, *woody* ~ with purple flowers & bright red berries (also *bitter*-*sweet*), & *deadly* ~ or BELLADONNA. [OE *nihtscada*, OHG *nahtscato*, app. f. NIGHT + SHADE]

nigrĕs'c|ent, a. Blackish. So ~ENCE n. [f. L *nigrescere* (*niger* black), -ENT]

nig'rĭtūde, n. Blackness (lit. & fig.). [f. L *nigritudo* (prec., -TUDE]

nī'hĭl ăd rěm, pred. a. Irrelevant. [L]

ni'hĭl|ism (nī'ĭl-, nī'hĭl-), n. Negative doctrines, total rejection of current beliefs, in religion or morals; (philos.) scepticism that denies all existence; doctrines of extreme revolutionary party in 19th-c. Russia finding nothing to approve of in the constituted order of things. Hence ~IST(2) n., ~is'TIC a. [f. L *nihil* nothing, -ISM]

nīhil'itў, n. Non-existence, nothingness; mere nothing, trifle, nullity. [f. med. L *nihilitas* (prec., -TY)]

nil, n. Nothing, no number or amount, (esp. in scoring at games etc., as *three goals to* ~); ~ *admirari* (ădmīrār'ī), attitude of being surprised at, or admiring, nothing, nonchalance. [L]

nil'gai (-gī), n. Var. of NYLGHAU.

‖ **nill**, v.i., 3rd sing. pres. condit. *Will he* ~ *he*, whether he likes it or not (now usu. *willy-nilly*). [OE; obs. *ne* not, WILL¹]

Nĭlŏm'ēter, n. Graduated pillar etc. showing height to which Nile rises. [f. Gk *Neilometrion* (-METER)]

Nilŏt'ic, a. Of the Nile or Nile region or its inhabitants. [f. Gk *Neilōtikos* (*Neilos* Nile, -OTʸ², -IC)]

nim'ble, a. Quick in movement, agile, swift, (*the* ~ *shilling*, or *ninepence* arch., circulating quickly); (of the mind etc.) versatile, clever, quick to apprehend, dextrous. Hence ~NESS n., nim'blўʸ² adv. [f. OE *numol* f. *niman* take, -LE (1)]

nim'bus, n. (pl. -*bī*, -*buses*). Bright cloud or halo investing deity or person or thing; bright disc or aureole round or over head of saint etc. in picture; (meteorol.) rain-cloud. Hence ~ED² (-st) a. [L, = cloud]

nimi′ĕtў, n. (rare). Excess, too much. [f. LL *nimietas* f. *nimis* too much, -TY]

nim′inў-pim′inў, a. Affected, mincing, prim. [imit.]

Nim′rŏd, n. Great hunter or sportsman. [see *Gen.* x. 8, 9]

ninc′ompōōp, n. Simpleton, person without sense or character, ninny. [17th c. *nicom-*, of unkn. orig.]

nine, a. & n. **1.** One more than eight, 9, ix, IX, (often agreeing with understood noun, as ~ *of the men,* ~ *of them,* ~ *o'clock* or ~, *cost* ~ *& six, will be* ~ *next birthday*; ~*-o'clock wind,* blowing from rifleman's left hand; *twenty-*~ etc. or, not beyond ~ *& ninety,* ~ *& twenty* etc.; *the N*~, the Muses; ~ *days' wonder,* novelty that attracts much attention but is soon forgotten; ~ *times out of ten,* generally; *possession is* ~ POINTS *of the law; cat has* ~ *lives,* see LIFE); ‖ ~*'pins,* kinds of skittles; ~ *tenths,* nearly the whole; hence ~*'*FOLD (-nf-) a. & adv. **2.** n. The number ~; card of ~ pips; *to the* ~*s,* to perfection (esp. *dressed up to the* ~*s,* elaborately). [OE, OS *nigon* &c., f. Gmc **nigun,* var.’ of **niwun* (whence OHG, Goth. *niun,* ON *niu*); cogn. w. L *novem*]

nine′teen′ (-nt-), a. & n. One more than eighteen, 19, xix, XIX, (*is nearly* ~, years old; *twice* ~ *is 38; a* ~*-&-sixpenny pair of shoes;* ~ *to the* DOZEN). Hence ~TH² a. (~*th hole,* joc., golf-club's bar) & n. [-TEEN]

nine′t|ў (-nt-), a. & n. **1.** Nine times ten, 90, xc, XC, (~*y-one* etc., or *one* etc. *& ~y;* ~*y-first* etc.; ~*y-nine out of a hundred,* nearly all); hence~ĭĕTH² a. & n. **2.** n. The number ~y; (pl.) *the* ~*ies,* degrees on thermometer etc., years of century or life, between 89 & 100. [-TY²]

Nin′ĕvīte, n. Inhabitant of Nineveh. [f. LL *Ninevita* (*Niniveh,* -ITE¹)]

ninn′ў, n. Simpleton, fool, person of weak character or mind. [perh. for INNOCENT]

ninon (nē′nawn), n. Light-weight silk dress fabric. [F]

ninth, a. & n. **1.** Next after eighth (*on the* ~, day of month; ~ *part,* one of nine equal parts into which thing may be divided; ~ *part of a man,* tailor). **2.** n. ~ part; (mus.) interval of octave & second. [NINE, -TH²]

ninth′lў, adv. In the ninth place (in enumerations). [-LY²]

Ni′obè, n. Inconsolable bereaved woman. Hence **Niobē′AN** a. [Gk (*-ē*), woman turned to stone while weeping for slain children]

niŏb′|ium, n. (chem.). A rare metallic element usu. found associated with tantalum. Hence ~IC (chem.), ~OUS (chem.), aa. [prec., -IUM; named 1845]

nip¹, v.t. & i. (-pp-), & n. **1.** Pinch, squeeze sharply, bite; pinch *off* (bud etc.); check growth of (esp. ~ *in the* BUD¹; lit. & fig.); (of cold) affect injuriously, pain, whence~p′ING² a., ~p′ingLY² adv.; take *up, out,* etc., hurriedly or unob-

served; (sl.) step etc. nimbly *in(to), out, up,* whence ~p′Y² a., ‖ (also as n., colloq. P, waitress in a restaurant of Messrs J. Lyons & Co., Ltd). **2.** n. Pinch, sharp squeeze, bite; sharp saying, sarcasm; (check to vegetation caused by) coldness of air. [14th c., rel. to obs. *nipe* f. MDu. *nipen* (Du. *nijpen*)]

nip², n., & v.i. & t. (-pp-). Small quantity of spirits etc. as pick-me-up; (vb) take ~s, take ~s of. [app. short f. 17th c. (obs.) *nipperkin* small measure, prob. of LG orig.; cf. LG, Du. *nippen* to sip]

ni′pa (nē-, ni-), n. Kind of E.-Indian palm. [f. Malay *nipah*]

nipp′er, n. In vbl senses of NIP¹, ²; also or esp.: kinds of fish; ‖ boy, lad, esp. costermonger's assistant or street arab; (pl.) implement with jaws for gripping or cutting, forceps, pincers, pliers, (often *pair of* ~*s*); (pl.) pince-nez; horse's incisor tooth; crustacean's claw. [-ER¹]

nip′ple, n. Small projection in which mammary ducts terminate in mammal of either sex, teat, esp. on woman's breast; cover for protecting woman's teat while child sucks; teat of nursing-bottle; ~ like protuberance on skin, glass, metal, etc.; small rounded elevation on mountain; perforated projection of musket-lock on which percussion-cap was placed; ‖ ~*wort,* yellow-flowered weed. [16th c. also *neble, nible,* perh. dim. f. NEB +-LE(1)]

Nipp′on, n. Japan. Hence **Nippōn′IAN** a. [f. Dai ~, native name of Japan (lit. 'Great land of the rising sun ')]

nīrva′na (-vah-), n. Buddhist beatitude, i.e. extinction of individuality & absorption into the supreme spirit. [Skr., f. *nirvā* (*nir, nis* out +*vā* to blow)]

nīs′i, conj. (legal). Unless (*decree, order, rule,* etc., ~, decree etc. valid unless cause is shown for rescinding it before appointed time at which it is 'made absolute '; ‖ ~ *pri′us,* hearing of civil causes by judges of assize, court-business of this kind). [L; ~ *prius,* unless previously, words from writ directing sheriff to provide jury on certain day unless judges come sooner]

Niss′en hŭt, n. Tunnel-shaped hut of corrugated iron with cement floor. [P. N. *Nissen* (d. 1930)]

nit, n. Egg of louse or other parasitic insect. [OE *hnitu,* = MDu., MLG *nēte,* OHG (*h*)*niz*]

nit′ŏn, n. (Orig. name of) RADON. [f. L *nitēre* to shine, after *argon* etc.]

nit′rate¹, n. Salt given by combination of nitric acid with base, or compound made by interaction of nitric acid & alcohol; (short for) *potassium* or *sodium* ~. [f. F, or NITRE +-ATE¹(3)]

nitr|āte′², v.t. Treat, combine, or impregnate, with nitric acid. Hence ~A′TION n. [foll., -ATE³]

ni′tre (-er), n. Saltpetre, potassium nitrate; *cubic* ~, sodium nitrate. [ME, f.

OF, f. L f. Gk *nitron* perh. of Oriental orig.]

nit'ric, a. Of, containing, nitrogen; ~ *acid*, clear colourless pungent highly corrosive & caustic liquid, aquafortis. [f. F *nitrique* (prec., -IC)]

nit'ri|fy, v.t. Impregnate with nitrogen, turn into nitrous or nitric acid. So ~FICA̱TION n. [f. F *nitrifier* (NITRE, -FY)]

nit'rite, n. Compound of base or alcohol with nitrous acid. [NITRE, -ITE¹(2)]

nitro-, comb. form of Gk *nitron* NITRE, = of, containing, made with or by use of, nitric acid or nitroxyl or nitre or nitrogen; ~-*a'cid*, compound of nitric with organic acid; ~-*com'pound* (made by action of nitric acid); ~-*explos'ive* (prepared by means of nitric acid); ~-*gly'cerin(e)*, yellowish oily violently explosive liquid made by adding glycerine to mixture of nitric & sulphuric acids; ~-*powd'er*, gunpowder made with nitric acid; ~-*sulphur'ic*, formed by mixture of nitric & sulphuric acids; *nitrŏx'yl*, chemical grouping of nitrogen & oxygen.

nit'rogen, n. Colourless tasteless scentless gas forming four-fifths of atmosphere. Hence **nitro'gĕn**ous a. [f. F *nitrogène*, see NITRE, -GEN(1)]

nit'rous, a. Of, like, impregnated with, nitre (~ *acid*, containing less oxygen than nitric acid; ~ *oxide*, gas used as anaesthetic, laughing-gas). [f. L *nitrosus* (NITRE, -OUS); later f. F *nitreux*]

nit'wit, n. A person of little intelligence. Hence ~TED² a. [cf. U.S. sl. *nit* none]

‖ **nix¹**, int. (sl.) giving warning to confederates etc. that master etc. is approaching. [orig. unkn.]

nix², n. (fem. ~'*ie*). Water-elf. [G (fem. *nixe*), cogn. w. obs. *nicker* (OE *nicor*)]

nix³, n. (sl.). Nothing. [f. colloq. Du. *niks*, G *nix*, (for *nichts*)]

Nizam' (-ahm), n. Former title of ruler of Hyderabad; (man, men, of) Turkish regular army. [Hind. & Turk., f. Arab. *niẓām* order, arrangement]

nō¹, a. 1. Not any (*no circumstances could justify it*; *no date*, abbr. *n.d.*, = undated, in library lists etc. (of books, letters, etc.); *no song no supper*, you must sing first; *no* END¹; *by no* MEAN¹*s*). 2. Not a, quite other than a, (*service of no honourable kind*; *is no part of my plan*; *is no genius*); hardly any (*is no distance*; *did it in no time*; *there is* etc. *no —ing*, none is etc. possible (*there's no accounting for tastes*; *there was no mistaking what he meant*). 3. Imperfect substitute for, absence of, (often *no-*; *these opinions or rather no opinions*; *his faith or no-faith*). 4. (In ellipt. sentences) we will not have any, let there not be any, there is not any, (*no Popery*, surrender, etc., whence *no--Popery riots*, a *no-confidence vote*, etc.; *now no mistake*, understand me clearly; *& no* MISTAKE¹; *no cards*, *no flowers*, invitations to funeral are not being sent

out, floral tributes are not desired; *no* DOUBT¹; *no* FEAR¹; *no* WONDER¹). 5. *No ball*, unlawfully delivered ball in cricket, umpire's announcement of this, (vb, *no-ball*) pronounce (bowler) to have bowled no ball; *no-being*, non-existence; *no'body*, no person (*everybody's* BUSINESS *is nobody's business*; *nobody ever did his*, or irreg. *their*, *work better*), (w. pl.) person of no importance, authority, or position; *no bon* (army sl.), no good; *no* GO² ; *no'how*, in no way, by no means, (now chiefly dial.), *be*, *feel*, *look*, etc., *nohow*, out of order, out of sorts; *no man*, no person (*no man's land*, piece of waste, unowned, or debatable ground, esp. mil. the space between opposed trenches); *no meaning*, nonsense; *no one*, no person, (also, as adj.) no single (*no one man could lift it*); *no side* (football), (referee's announcement of the) end of the game; *no thoroughfare*, notice that path, street, etc., is closed at other end, or that entrance is not permitted, (also) such path; *no trump(s)* (bridge), declaration, bid, involving playing without a trump suit; *no--trumper*, hand on which a no-trump bid can be, or has been, made; *no'way(s)*, *no'wise*, in no manner, not at all; *no̱--whence*, *no'whither*, from, to, no place; *no whit*, not at all (usu. w. compar.). [for NONE, orig. only before consonants]

nō², adv. (Alw. as alternative after *or*) not (usu. *whether or no*, in either case, also *tell me whether or no*; *pleasant or no*, *it is true*). [prob. f. prec. by extension of adj. use as in *whether there be any church or no* (*church*)]

nō³, adv. 1. (Alw. with compar.) by no amount, not at all, (*no better than before*; *is no better than she should be*, is not quite respectable; *no sooner had he said it than*, as soon as he had said it; *no sooner said than done*; *no* LONG¹*er*). 2. *No less* (*than*), as much (n., a., adv.) or many (as) (*gave me £50, no less*, *no less than £50*; *no less than ten people have told me*; *did it no less for my warning*; *is no less than a scandal*; *a no less fatal victory*). 3. *No more*, (n.) nothing further (*have no more to say*; *want no more of it*; often ellipt. for *say no more* or *let us have no more of it*); (adj.) not any more (*no more wine?*); (adv.) no longer (*is no more*, is dead or passed away), never again, to no greater extent (*is no more a lord than I am*; *could no more help laughing than I could fly*), just as little, neither, (*you did not come, no more did he*). [OE *nā*, see NATHLESS]

nō⁴, particle equivalent to negative sentence, & n. (pl. *noes*). 1. The answer to your question is negative, your request or command will not be complied with, the statement made or course intended or conclusion arrived at is not correct or satisfactory, (*no*, *nor*, form for substituting stronger phrase, as *a man could not lift it*, *no*, *nor half a dozen*). 2. n. The word *no*, a denial or refusal, (*two noes make a yes*; *will not take no for an answer*, persists in spite of refusals); (pl.) voters against a motion (*the noes have it*, are in a majority). [as prec.]

nō⁵, noh, n. Kind of (orig. religious) Japanese drama with dance & song. [Jap.]

Nōach′ian, Nōach′ic, (-k-), aa. Of Noah or his time. [*Noach* = Noah, -IAN]

Nō′ah (-*a*), n. Hebrew patriarch; ~*'s ark*, in which ~, his family, & animals were saved (*Gen.* vi), imitation of it as child's plaything, large or cumbrous or old--fashioned trunk or vehicle, small bivalve, detached fragment of flying cloud; ~*'s nightcap*, the plant eschscholtzia (w. ref. to conical bud-sheaths).

nōb¹, n., & v.t. (sl.; -bb-). Head; (cribbage) knave of same suit as turn-up (*one for his* ~, point scored by holder of this); (vb, boxing) hit on the head. [perh. var. of KNOB]

nōb², n. (sl.). Member of upper classes. [Sc. form (f. 18th c.) *knabb, nab*. orig. unkn.]

∥ **nōb′ble,** v.t. (sl.). Tamper with (racehorse) to prevent its winning; secure partiality of by underhand means; get hold of (money etc.) dishonestly; catch (criminal). [orig. unkn.]

nōbb′y̆, a. (sl.). Suitable for a NOB², smart, elegant. [-Y²]

Nōbĕl′ prize, n. One of the annual prizes (for physics, chemistry, medicine, literature, & the promotion of peace) awarded from the bequest of Alfred Nobel (d. 1896), Swedish inventor of dynamite.

nobil′iary̆ (-lya-), a. Of (the) nobility (~ *particle*, preposition, as French *de*, German *von*, prefixed to title; ~ *pride, rank*, etc.). [f. F *nobiliaire* (NOBLE, -ARY)]

nobil′ity̆, n. Noble character, mind, birth, or rank; *the* or *a* class of nobles. [ME, f. OF -*ite* or L *nobilitas* (foll., -TY)]

nō′ble, a. & n. 1. Illustrious by rank, title, or birth, belonging to the nobility; of lofty character or ideals (so ~-**mīnd′ED²** a., ~-**mīnd′ĕdNESS** n.); showing greatness of character, magnanimous, morally elevated; splendid, magnificent, stately, imposing, impressive, in appearance; excellent, admirable, (*a* ~ *horse, cellar,* etc.); (of metals such as gold, silver, platinum) resisting chemical action, not corroding or tarnishing in air or water, not˙ easily attacked by acids; ~*man*, peer; ~*woman*, woman of ~ birth or rank; hence ~NESS n., **nōb′LY²** adv. 2. n. ~*man*; obsolete coin, usu. 6/8. [ME, f. OF, f. L *nobilis* (*noscere* KNOW, -BLE)]

noblĕsse′, n. The class of nobles (esp. of a foreign country); ~ *oblige* (ōblēzh′), privilege entails responsibility. [F]

nŏck¹, n., & v.t. 1. Notch at ends of bow for holding string; notch(ed horn tip) of arrow for receiving bowstring. 2. v.t. Set

(arrow) on string. [14th c., prob. rel. to foll.]

nŏck², n. Forward upper corner of some sails. [f. MLG *nock*, MDu. *nocke*]

nŏct∣(i)-, comb. form of L *nox noctis* night = by night, as ~*ăm′bŭlant* night-walking, ~*ĭflōr′ous* night-flowering, ~*ĭlūc′a* phosphorescent animalcule, ~*ĭv′agant*, ~*ĭv′agous*, night-wandering.

nŏc′tŭle, n. Largest British species of bat. [F, f. It. *nottola* bat]

nŏctŭrn′al, a. Of, in, done by, active in, the night. [f. LL (-*alis*) f. L *nocturnus* (NOCT-), -AL]

nŏc′tŭrne, n. Dreamy musical piece; (paint.) night-scene. [F, cf. prec.]

nŏd, v.i. & t. (-dd-), & n. 1. Incline head slightly & quickly in salutation (~*ding acquaintance*, very slight one *with* person or subject), assent, or command; let head fall forward in drowsiness, be drowsy, make sleepy mistake (*Homer sometimes* ~*s*, the best of us may be dull or make a slip); (of buildings etc., also fig.) incline from perpendicular (esp. ~*s to its fall*); (of plumes) dance up & down; incline (head); signify (assent etc.) by ~. 2. n. ~ding of the head; this as sign of absolute power (*the empire was at* or *dependent on his* ~); *land of Nod*, sleep (with ref. to phr. in *Gen.* iv. 16). [ME *nodde*, orig. unkn.]

nŏd′dle¹, n. (colloq.). Head, pate. [15th c. *nodle*, orig. unkn.]

nŏd′dle², v.t. Nod or wag (head). [NOD, -LE(3)]

nŏdd′y̆, n. Simpleton; noodle; tropical sea-bird. [16th c., goes w. obs. *noddy* adj. silly, of unkn. orig.]

nōde, n. Knob on root or branch; point at which leaves spring; hard tumour esp. on gouty or rheumatic joint; intersecting point of planet's orbit & ecliptic or of two great circles of celestial sphere, whence **nōd′ICAL** a.; point or line of rest in vibrating body; central point in system; point at which curve crosses itself. Hence **nōd′AL** a. [f. L NODUS]

nōdōse′, a. Knotty, knobbed. [f. L *nodosus* (NODUS, -OSE¹)]

nōdŏs′ity̆, n. Knottiness; knot, protuberance. [f. LL *nodositas* (prec., -TY)]

nŏd′ŭl∣e, n. Small rounded lump of anything; small node in plant; small knotty tumour, ganglion. Hence ~AR¹, ~ātĕd [-ATE²], ~ōse¹, ~ōus, aa., ~A′TION n. [f. L *nodulus* (foll., -ULE)]

nōd′us, n. (pl. -*dī*). Knotty point, difficulty, complication in plot of story etc. [L, = knot]

Nŏĕl′. = NOWEL.

noĕt′ic, a. & n. 1. Of the intellect; purely intellectual or abstract; given to intellectual speculation. 2. n. (Sing. or pl.) science of the intellect. [f. Gk *noētikos* (*noētos* f. *noeō* apprehend, -IC)]

nŏg¹, n., & v.t. (-gg-). 1. Pin, peg, small block, of wood; snag or stump on tree. 2. v.t. Secure with ~s; build in form of

O

(brick-, concrete, stone-) ~g'ING¹ (-g-) n., i.e. brickwork etc. in timber frame. [orig. unkn.]

|| nŏg², n. Kind of strong beer brewed in E. Anglia. [orig. unkn.]

nŏgg'in (-g-), n. Small mug; small measure, usu. ¼ pint, of liquor. [orig. unkn.]

noil, n. (Sing. or pl.) short wool-combings. [orig. unkn.]

noise (-z), n., & v.t. & i. 1. Loud outcry, clamour, shouting, din of voices & movements; any sound, esp. loud or harsh or undesired one, whence ~'LESS a., ~'lĕss-LY² adv., ~'lĕssNESS n., (-zl-); big ~ (colloq., orig. U.S.), person of importance; make a ~, lit., also talk or complain much about, also be much talked of, attain notoriety in the world. 2. vb. Make public, spread abroad, (person's fame, fact; it was ~d abroad that—); (rare) make ~. [ME, f. OF noise, = Prov. nausa, f. L nausea]

noisette¹ (nwahzĕt'), n. Kind of rose, cross between China & musk. [N~, grower, 1817]

noisette² (as prec.), n. (Usu. pl.) small piece(s) of meat cooked in certain way. [F]

nois'ome, a. Harmful, noxious; ill--smelling; objectionable, offensive. Hence ~NESS n. [ME; obs. noy for ANNOY n., -SOME]

nois'|y̆ (-z-), a. Clamorous, turbulent; full of, making much, noise; (of colour, costume, literary style) loud, conspicuous, violent, glaring. Hence ~ILY² adv., ~iNESS n. [-Y²]

nŏl'ens·vŏl'ens (-z), adv. Willy-nilly, perforce. [L part. = unwilling, willing]

nŏl'i mē tăn'gerĕ(-j-), n. Erosive ulcer(s), lupus; warning against meddling or approach (carries a ~ in his face; a ~ manner); picture of Christ as he appeared to Magdalen at sepulchre (John xx. 17). [L, = touch me not]

|| nŏll, n. (now dial.). (Crown of) head. [OE knoll, corresp. to MDu. nolle, OHG (h)nol, nollo point, summit, hill, obsc. rel. to KNOLL]

nŏll'é prŏs'equī, n. (legal). Relinquishment by plaintiff or prosecutor of (part of) his suit, stay of proceedings, entry of it on record. [L, = to refuse to pursue]

nŏl'ō ĕpĭscopār'ī, n. (Formula expressing) avoidance of responsible office. [LL, = I do not wish to be a bishop]

nŏm'ad (also nō-), n. & a. (Member of tribe) roaming from place to place for pasture; wanderer, wandering. Hence or cogn. nomăd'IC a., nomăd'ICALLY adv., ~ISM(2) n., ~IZE(2) v.i. [f. L f. Gk nomas -ados (nemō to pasture)]

nŏm'āde. Var. (now rare) of prec.

nom de guerre (see Ap.), n. Pseudonym, sobriquet, assumed name under which person fights, plays, writes, etc. [F, = war-name]

nom de plume (see Ap.), n. Writer's pseudonym, title or initials or borrowed name under which he writes. [formed in E of F words = pen-name on anal. of prec.]

nŏm'enclātor, n. Slave or client in ancient Rome charged with naming persons met, usher assigning places at banquet, (also in mod. use with ref. to these senses); giver or inventor of names, esp. in nat.-hist. classification. [L (nomen name, calare call, -OR)]

nŏm'encl|āture, n. Catalogue, register, (now rare); person's or community's system of names for things; terminology of a science etc.; systematic naming. So ~ATIVE a. [f. L nomenclatura (prec., -URE)]

nŏm'inal, a. Of, as, like, a noun (~ & verbal roots); of, in, names (~ & essential distinctions; ~ definition, statement of all marks connoted in name of concept); existing in name only, not real or actual, (~ & real price, ruler; ~ sum, rent, etc., virtually nothing), whence ~LY² adv.; consisting of, giving, the names (~ list of officers etc.; ~ roll). [f. L nominalis f. nomen -inis name; see -AL]

nŏm'inal|ism, n. (philos.). Doctrine that universals or abstract concepts are mere names (opp. realism). So ~IST(2) n., ~is'-tIC a. [f. F nominalisme (prec., -ISM)]

nŏm'ināt|e, v.t. Call by the name of, mention by name, name or appoint (date, place), (now rare); appoint, propose for election, to office (a board of six~ed & six elected members; the candidates were ~ed today), whence or cogn. ~OR, nŏminEE', nn. [f. L nominare (NOMINAL), -ATE³]

nŏminā'tion, n. In vbl senses; also, right of nominating for appointment (have a ~ at your service). [ME, f. OF, or L nomin-atio (prec., -ATION)]

nŏm'inative, a. & n. 1. (Case) used as or in agreement with subject of verb, (~ absolute, construction like Latin ablative absolute, as this being so, I did nothing); of this case (~ ending, form); word in this case, (loosely) subject (of verb); hence nŏminativ'AL a. 2. (pr. -ātiv). Of, appointed by, nomination (the ~ & the elective principles, members). [ME, f. OF (-if, -ive) or L nominativus (NOMINATE, -IVE)]

nŏn, Latin adv. = not, forming part of phrases: ~ assump'sĭt (he did not undertake), plea that defendant made no promise; ~ cŏm'pŏs (mĕn'tĭs), (not master of his mind), lunatic, mad, (legal, & in gen. use); ~ ĕss'ĕ (not to be), non-existence; ~ ĕst ĭnven'tus (he has not been found), ~ ĕst, or ~ ĭnven'tus, sheriff's statement, in returning writ, that defendant is not to be found in his bailiwick (legal, & transf. in gen. use); ~ li'quĕt (it is not clear), jury's verdict in doubtful case deferring matter to another day; ~ nŏb'ĭs (not unto us; Ps. cxv), formula attributing victory etc. not to oneself but to God, song of rejoicing; ~ plă'cĕt (it does not please), negative vote in ecclesiastical or university assemblies (also as v.t., throw out); ~ *plus ul'tra*, = NE PLUS ULTRA ; ~ *pŏss'ŭmus* (we cannot), statement of inability, refusal to act or move ; ~ *sē'quitur* (it does not follow), illogical inference, paradoxical result.

nŏn-, pref. (AF *noun-* = OF *non-*, *nom-* (mod. F *non-*), f. prec.) now freely prefixed : **1.** Usu. to vbl n. giving neg. vbl n. corresp. to *not* w. parent vb, = failure to do, abstention from doing, or rarely to other n. giving neg. abstract n. corresp. to *not* w. connected adj. ; ~*-accep'tance*; ~*-ac'cess*, impossibility of access for sexual intercourse (in questions of paternity); ~*-acquain'tance*; ~*-appear'ance* (esp. in court as party or witness); ~*-atten'dance*; ~*-claim*, failure to make claim within legal time; ~*-committ'al*, avoidance of committing oneself to definite course or either side (usu. attrib., as ~*-committal answer*); ~*-compli'ance*; ~*-co-opera'tion* (Indian pol.), refusal or failure to co-operate (with the British); ~*-feas'ance* (-z-; legal), omission of act that ought to have been done; ~*-interfer'ence*, *-interven'tion*, principle or practice, esp. in politics & international affairs, of keeping aloof from others' disputes; ~*-intru'sion* (Church of Scotland), principle that patron shall not thrust unacceptable minister on congregation; ~*-join'der* (legal), omission of partner etc. to join another as party to suit; ~*-pay'ment*; ~*-percep'tion*; ~*-perform'ance*; ~*-resis'tance* (hist.), 17th-c. principle that authority must not be resisted even if unjustly exercised; ~*-success'*; ~*-us'age*; ~*-use'*; ~*-us'er* (legal), neglect to use a right, by which it may become void. **2.** To n. of designation, giving n. (occas. w. derivatives) = person, thing, or all, that is not the thing specified; ~*-abstain'er*, one who does not abstain (esp. from liquor); ~*-eg'o* (metaphys.), all that is not the conscious self, the object as opposed to the subject; ~*-mem'ber* (so ~*-mem'bership*); ~*-met'al* (esp. chem. = element that is not a metal; so ~*-metall'ic*). **3.** To attrib. n., giving adj. (occas. w. derivatives) that can only be used attributively, = unconnected with, not involving; ~*-jur'y*, tried without jury; ~*-part'y*, that may be dealt with ‡irrespective of political partisanship; ~*-skid'*, (of tires) safe against skidding; ~*-soci'ety*, *-ŭn'ion* (also ~*-ŭn'ionist*), not belonging to a workman's society or trade union; ~*-stop'*, (of trains, buses, etc.) not stopping at intermediate stations, halts, etc., (of journey) made without a stop, (n.) ~*-stop* train, bus, or run, (adv.) without a stop. **4.** To adj. (usu. participial in *-ant*, *-ent*, *-ing*, *-ate*, *-ed*) giving adj. (& occas. n. or derivatives) = not-; ~*-belli'gerent* a. & n., (country) taking no active part in war; ~*-colle'giate*, (student) not belonging to a college, (of universities)

without colleges; ~*-com'batant*, (person, esp. in the fighting services, e.g. surgeon, chaplain, ambulance man) who has not to fight, civilian; ~*-commi'ssioned*, not holding commission (esp. of army officers such as *sergeant*, *corporal*, abbr. N.C.O. or *non--com.*); ~*-commūn'icant*, (person) who does not attend the communion service; ~*-conduc'ting*, that will not conduct heat or electricity (so ~*-conduc'tor*, ~*-conducting medium* or substance; ~*-conductibil'ity*); ‖~*-content*, voter against motion in House of Lords; ~*-essen'tial* a. & n.; ~*-Euclid'ean*, denying or dispensing with any of the assumptions of Euclid's geometry; ~*-exis'tent*, *-exis'tence*; ~*-flammable*, (of flannelette etc.) not inflammable; ~*-jur'ing*, *-jur'or*, (joor-; hist.), (beneficed clergyman) who refused oath of allegiance to William & Mary; ~*-nuclear*, (of warfare, weapons, etc.) conventional; ~*-off'ice-holding* etc.; ‖~*-provid'ed*, (of schools) other than PROVIDED. **5.** To adj. requiring a neutral negative form free from some special sense, usu. of condemnation, attached to the compd in *in-*, *un-*, = not coming under the description of, not; ~*-effec'tive*, (soldier, sailor) not qualified for active service (cf. INEFFECTIVE); ~*-hūm'an*, not belonging to human race (cf. INHUMAN); ~*-lo'gical*, proceeding by other means than logic (cf. ILLOGICAL); ~*-mo'ral*, unconcerned with morality (cf. IMMORAL); ~*-na'tural*, deviating from the natural order (cf. UNNATURAL). **6.** To adv., as ~*-conten'tiously*.

nŏn'age, n. Being under age, minority; immaturity, early stage. [ME, f. OF (prec., AGE)]

nŏnagénār'ian, a. & n. (Person) between 89 & 100 years old. [f. L *nonagenarius* (*nonageni* 90 each, -ARY[1]), -IAN]

nŏn'arў, a. & n. (Arith., of SCALE[3] of notation) having nine as basis; (n.) group of nine. [f. L *nonarius* (*nonus* ninth, -ARY[1])]

nŏnce, n. Time being, present occasion, (only in *for the* ~); ~*-word*, coined for one occasion. [ME *to*, **for*, *then ances* = (for) the ONCE, cf. NEWT]

nŏn'chal|ant (-sh-), a. Unexcited, unmoved, cool, indifferent. Hence ~ANCE n., ~antLY[2] adv. [F, part. of *nonchaloir* (NON-, L *calēre* be warm)]

nŏnconfŏrm'ist, n. One who does not conform to doctrine or discipline of an established Church, esp. member of sect dissenting from Anglican Church (usu. not including Roman-Catholics), protestant dissenter (*the* ~ *conscience*, opinions as to right & wrong prevalent among ~s esp. as affecting their political attitude). [NON-(2)]

nŏnconfŏrm'itў, n. Principles, practice, the body, of nonconformists, protestant dissent; failure to conform (*to* rule etc.); want of correspondence between things. [NON-(2)]

nŏn'dĕscript, a. & n. (Person, thing) not easily classified, neither one thing nor another, hybrid. [NON-(4), L *descriptus* (DESCRIBE)]

none (nŭn), pron., a., & adv. **1.** Not any of (~ *of them came*; ~ *of them is*, or *are*, acc. to sense required; ~ *of this concerns me*; ~ *of your impudence !*); no person, no one, (now rare; ~ *can tell*); no persons (~ *but fools have ever believed it*). **2.** adj. (rarely with noun; usu. ellipt. = *no* with reference defined by noun previously used or shortly to follow). No, not any, not to be counted in specified class, (*make of* ~ *effect*, arch.; *you have money & I have* ~; *he is* ~ *of my friends*, ~ *of your canting hypocrites*; *his understanding is* ~ *of the clearest*; *this is* ~ *other but the house of God*; *seeking rest & finding* ~; *if a linguist is wanted, I am* ~; *would rather have a bad reputation than* ~ *at all*; *poetry we have almost* ~). **3.** adv. By no amount, not at all, (w. *the* & comparat., *so*, or *too*; *am* ~ *the better for it*; ~ *the less*, = NEVER*the-less*; *are* ~ *so fond of him*; *the pay is* ~ *too high*). [OE *nān* (ne not, ONE)]

nonĕn'titў, n. **1.** (nŏn-). Non-existence, non-existent thing, figment. **2.** (non-). Person or thing of no importance, cipher. [NON-(2)]

nōnes, n. pl. **1.** (Rom. ant.). Ninth day by inclusive reckoning before IDES, i.e. 7th of Mar., May, July, Oct., & 5th of other months. **2.** (eccl.). Daily office orig. said at ninth hour or 3 p.m. [sense 1 f. OF *nones* or L *nonae*, sense 2 pl. of rare *none* f. L *nona*, (*nonus* ninth); cf. NOON]

nonesuch. See NONSUCH.

nŏnĕt', n. (mus.). Composition for nine. instruments or voices. [f. It. *nonetto* (*nono* ninth f. L *nonus*)]

nonill'ion (-yon), n. ‖ Ninth power of million, 1 with 54 ciphers. [see NONARY, BILLION]

nŏn'ius, n. Contrivance for graduating mathematical instruments, of which the VERNIER is an improved form. [latinized from *Nuñes*, Portuguese inventor]

nŏnpareil' (-rĕl), a. & n. Unrivalled or unique (person, thing); (print.) size of TYPE; kinds of comfit, apple, bird, wheat, moth, etc. [F (NON-, *pareil* equal, f. L PAR]

nŏnplŭs', n., & v.t. (-ss-). **1.** State of perplexity, standstill, (usu. *at a* ~), perplexed, *reduce* etc. *to a* ~). **2.** v.t. Reduce to hopeless perplexity. [f. L *non plus* not more]

nŏn-rĕs'id|ent (-z-), a. & n. (Clergyman) not residing where his duties require him, absentee (incumbent); (person) sojourning in place only for short time or residing elsewhere. So ~ENCE n. [NON-(2)]

nŏn'sense, n. & int. **1.** Absurd or meaningless words or ideas, foolish or extravagant conduct; arrangement etc. that one disapproves of. **2.** int. You are talking or proposing ~, it surely cannot be true, etc. **3.** ~-*book*, meant to amuse by absurdity; ~ *verses*, having no sense or an

absurd one. Hence **nŏnsĕn'**SICAL a., **nŏnsĕn'sicallў**[2] adv. [NON-(2)]

nŏn'sŭch, none'sŭch (nŭns-), n. Person or thing that is unrivalled, paragon; kind of lucerne. [NONE, SUCH, usu. now assim. to NON-]

nŏn'suit (-ūt), n., & v.t. **1.** Stoppage of suit by judge when plaintiff fails to make out legal case or bring sufficient evidence. **2.** v.t. Subject (plaintiff) to ~. [ME, f. AF *no(u)nsuit* (NON-(1); SUIT)]

nŏn'us. See PRIMUS[1].

noo'dle[1], n. Simpleton. Hence ~DOM n. [orig. unkn.]

noo'dle[2], n. Strip of dough made of flour & eggs, dried & used in soups. [f. G *nudel*]

nŏŏk, n. Out-of-the-way corner, recess, secluded place. [ME, of unkn., prob. Scand., orig.]

noon, n. Twelve o'clock in the day, midday; ~'*day*, ~'*tide*, midday. [OE *nōn*, = ON *nón*; cf. OS, OHG, ON *nōna*, f. L *nona* (*hora*) ninth hour; orig. = 3 p.m.]

noose, n., & v.t. **1.** Loop with running knot, tightening as rope or wire is pulled, esp. in snare, lasso, or hangman's halter; the marriage tie; snare or bond. **2.** v.t. Capture with ~, ensnare; make ~ on (cord); arrange (cord) in ~ *round* neck etc. [late ME *nose*, perh. f. OF *nous* f. L *nodus* knot]

nŏp'al, n. American cactus grown in plantations for breeding cochineal. Hence ~RY(3) n. [Sp., f. Mex. *nopalli* cactus]

nor (nôr, nor), adv. & conj. **1.** (arch.). Neither (as the first *nor* in ~ *gold* ~ *silver*). **2.** conj. And not, & no more, neither, & not either, (*had neither arms* ~ *provisions*; *not a man* ~ *a child was to be seen*; *I said I had not seen it*, ~ *had I*; *all that is true*, ~ *must we forget*; also poet. & arch. w. omission of preceding *neither* or ~, as *thou* ~ *I have made the world*)." [contr. f. obs. *nother* (OE *nā* see NATHLESS, WHETHER)]

nor'-. Shortened form of NORTH.

Nŏrd'ĭc, a. (ethnol.). Of the tall blond dolichocephalic people found in northern Europe esp. in Scandinavia (of more limited application than *Teutonic*). [f. F *nordique*, f. *nord* NORTH, see -IC]

Nŏr'folk (-ok), n. English county (‖ ~ *capon*, red herring; ‖ ~ *dumpling, turkey*, inhabitant or native of ~; ~ *jacket*, man's loose jacket with waistband; ~ *plover*, stone-curlew).

‖ **nŏr'l'and**, n. Northern region. [for *northland*]

nŏrm, n. Standard, pattern, type. [f. L *norma* carpenter's square]

nŏrm'al, a. & n. **1.** (Geom.) standing at right angles, perpendicular; conforming to standard, regular, usual, typical; ~ *school*, for training teachers; hence **nŏrmā'lɪTY** (also irreg. ~CY) n., ~IZE(3) v.t., ~IZA'TION n., ~LY[2] adv. **2.** n. (Geom.) ~ line; (phys.) average or mean of observed quantities; usual state, level, etc.,

~ temperature (98·4° F.) of human body.
[f. L *normalis* (prec., -AL)]

Nŏrm′an, n. & a. **1.** Inhabitant or native of Normandy, descendant of mixed Scandinavian & Frankish race there established; = ~ *French* below; = ~ *style* below. **2.** adj. Of the ~s (~ *Conquest*, of England by ~s 1066; ~ *English*, English as spoken or influenced by ~s; ~ *French*, French as spoken by ~s or later in English law-courts; ~ STYLE in architecture, whence ~ESQUE′, pr. -ĕsk, a.); hence ~ISM(2, 4) n., ~IZE(3, 4) v.t. & i., ~IZA′TION n. [f. OF *Normans* pl. f. Gmc *NORTHman*]

Nŏrn, n. One of the female fates of Scandinavian mythology. [ON, orig. unkn.]

‖ **Nŏ′rroy**, n. Third KING *of Arms*, with jurisdiction north of the Trent. [ME, f. AF *nor-* NORTH + *rey*, *roy* king]

Nŏrse, n. & a. **1.** The Norwegian language (*Old* ~, language of Norway & its colonies down to 14th c.). **2.** adj. Norwegian, of Norway, so ~′*land*, ~′*man*. [f. Du. *noorsch* (*noord* NORTH, -ISH[1])]

Nŏrsk, n. & a. = prec. [Scand.]

nŏrth, adv., n., & a., (abbr. N.; in compp. & derivv. often shortened to *nor′-*). **1.** Towards or in the region lying to right of observer on equator at equinox who faces setting sun (~ BY *east* etc.; ~ *of*, further ~ than; DUE[1] ~; *lies* etc. ~ *& south*, lengthwise along line running between ~ & south); ~-*east′*, ~-*west′*, (abbr. NE., NW.), advv., nn., & aa., (regions) midway between ~ & east, west, ~-~-*east′*, ~-~-*west′*, (abbr. NNE., NNW.), advv., nn., & aa., (regions) midway between ~ & ~-*east*, ~-*west*, (with uses & derivatives corresponding to those of *north*; so esp. ~-*east′erly*, *-west′erly*, *-east′ern*, *-west′ern*, *-east′ward*, *-west′ward*, *-east′wardly*, *-west′wardly*, see NORTHERLY etc.; ~-*east*, ~-*west*, *passage*, passages for ships along northern coasts of Europe & Asia, northern coast of America, formerly thought of as possible routes to E., & from Atlantic to Pacific; the *N*~-*west*, = NW. territories of Canada); hence ~′WARD adv., n., & a., ~′WARDS adv. & n. **2.** n. Cardinal point lying ~ (*magnetic* ~, point indicated by ~ end of compass-needle); northern part of England (beyond Humber), Great Britain, Scotland, Ireland, or Europe; *northern States in which slavery did not exist; northern part *of* any country; ~ wind. **3.** adj. Situated, dwelling, in or more towards the ~ (*N*~ *Germany*, *Wales*, *America*; ~ *latitude*; ~ POLE[2], whence ~-*pōl′*AR a.; ~ *transept*); facing ~ (~ *window*, *aspect*); coming from the ~ (~ *wind*; ~ *light*, esp. as desired by painters & factory designers); *N*~ *Britain*, Scotland (abbr. N.B. in addresses); *N*~ *Briton*, Scot; ‖~ *country*, ~ part of England or Great Britain (~-*coun′tryman*, native of northern England); ~-*coun′try*, from or characteristic of ~ country); *N*~′*land* (poet.), northern lands, northern part of

a country; ~ *light*, Aurora Borealis; *N*~′*man*, native of Norway or Scandinavia; *N*~ *Sea*, between Britain, Netherlands, Germany, & Scandinavia; *N*~ *star*, POLE[2]-*star*. [OE, OS *north*, OHG *nort*, ON *northr*]

nŏrth-east′er, nŏr-, n. NE. wind. [-ER[1]]

***nŏrth′er**, n. Strong cold north wind blowing in autumn & winter over Texas, Florida, & Gulf of Mexico. [-ER[1]]

nŏrth′erlў (-dh-), a. & adv. = foll. (rare); (of direction) towards the north; (of wind) blowing from the north or thereabouts. [f. NORTH as EASTERLY]

nŏrth′ern (-dh-), a. & n. **1.** Living or situated in, coming from, the north esp. of England or Europe; *of the NORTH; (of wind) northerly (rare); characteristic of the north (*a pallid* ~ *day*); ~ *lights*, Aurora Borealis; hence ~ER[1](4) n., ~MOST a. **2.** n. ~er. [-ERN]

nŏrth′ing, n. Northward progress or deviation in sailing or travelling (*two miles* ~; *have made very little* ~). [-ING[1]]

Nŏrthŭm′brian, a. & n. (Native, dialect) of ancient Northumbria (England N. of Humber) or modern Northumberland. [obs. *Northumber*, person living beyond Humber, +-IAN]

nŏrth′wardlў, adv. & a. Northwards; (of wind) northerly. [-LY[2]]

nŏrth-wĕst′er, nŏr-, n. NW. wind. [-ER[1]]

nŏr′ward(s) (-z). = NORTH*ward(s)*.

Nŏrwē′gian (-jn), a. & n. (Native, language) of Norway. [f. med. L *Norvegia* + -AN, w. assim. to *Norway*]

nŏr′-wĕst′er, n. North-wester; glass of strong liquor; oilskin hat, sou′-wester. [NOR′-]

nōse (nōz), n., & v.t. & i. **1.** Member of face or head placed above mouth containing nostrils & serving as organ of smell (*as plain as the* ~ *in your face*, easily seen; *bite* or *snap* one's ~ *off*, answer him snappishly; *count* or *tell* ~s, count supporters etc., decide question by mere numbers; *cut off* one's ~ *to spite* one's *face*, indulge pique at one's own expense; *follow* one's ~, go straight forward, be guided by instinct; *keep* one's ~ *to the* GRINDSTONE; LEAD[1] *by the* ~; *look down* one's ~ (with disdain) *at*; *make a* LONG[1] ~; ~ *of wax*, person or thing easily influenced or moulded; *parson's or pope's* ~, rump of cooked fowl; *pay through the* ~, be overcharged, have to pay exorbitant prices; *poke*, *thrust*, etc., one's ~, pry or intrude *into* something; *put* one's ~ *out of joint*, supplant or disconcert or frustrate him; *speak through* one's ~, pronounce with nasal twang; *turn up* one's ~ *at*, show disdain for; *under* one's ~, straight before him, regardless of his displeasure). **2.** Sense of smell (*has a good* ~, esp. of dogs, & fig. of detectives etc.). **3.** ‖ Odour, perfume, of hay, tea, etc. **4.** Open end or nozzle of pipe, tube, bellows, retort, etc. **5.** Prow; projecting part. **6.** ~-*ape*, proboscis-monkey; ~'*bag*, containing fodder for hanging to horse's head; ~'*band*, lower band of bridle passing over ~ & attached to cheek-straps; ~'*dive*, aeroplane's downward plunge (v.i., make this); ~-*flute*, musical instrument blown with ~ among Siamese, Fijians, etc.; ~'*gay* [GAY in obs. n. use = toy], bunch of (esp. sweet-scented) flowers; ~-*monkey*, proboscis-monkey; ~-*piece*, = ~band, also part of microscope to which object--glass is attached; ~'*pipe*, piece of piping used as nozzle; ~'*rag* (sl.), pocket-handkerchief; ~'*ring*, fixed in ~ of bull etc. for leading, also ornament worn by savages; ~'*warmer* (sl.), short pipe; hence (-)nōsED² (-zd), ~'LESS (-zl-), aa. **7.** vb. Perceive smell of, discover by smell, (fig.) detect (~*s a job in everything*), smell *out*; rub with the ~, thrust ~ against or into; sniff (*at, about* adv. & prep.), pry or search (*after, for*); push one's way, push (one's *way*), with the ~ (esp. of ship); (of strata etc.) dip *in*, basset *out*. [OE *nosu*, MDu., MLG *nose*, obsc. rel. to OE *nasu*, MDu. *nase*, OHG *nasa* (G *nase*), ON *nǫs*; cogn. w. L *nasus*; see NAZE, NESS]

nōs′er (-z-), n. Strong head wind (esp. *dead*~). [prec., -ER¹]

nōs′ing (-z-), n. Rounded edge of step, moulding, etc., or metal shield for it. [NOSE, -ING¹]

noso-, comb. form of Gk *nosos* disease, as *nosŏG′RAPHY*, systematic description of diseases; *nosŏL′OGY*, (branch of medical science dealing with) classification of diseases (so *nŏsoLO′GICAL*, *nosŏL′OGIST*).

nŏstăl′g|ia, n. Home-sickness as a disease; sentimental yearning for (some period of) the past. Hence ~IC a. [f. Gk *nostos*-return home, Gk *algos* pain, -IA¹]

nŏs′tŏc, n. Kinds of gelatinous blue-green algae. [name invented by Paracelsus]

Nŏstradām′us, n. Prediction-monger, professed seer. [latinized f. M. de *Nostredame*, French physician who made prophecies 1555]

nŏs′tril, n. Either opening in nose admitting air to lungs & smells to olfactory nerves (*stink in* one's ~*s*, be offensive to him). Hence(-)~lED²(-ld)a. [OE *nosthyrl* (NOSE, obs. *thirl* f. OE *thȳrel* hole, cf. THRILL)]

nŏs′trum, n. Medicine prepared by person recommending it, quack remedy, patent medicine; pet scheme for political or social reform, special device. [L, neut. of *noster* our, my]

nōs′ȳ (-z-), a. & n. Large-nosed (person; esp. of Duke of Wellington); ill-smelling (esp. of heated corn, mouldy hay, etc.); fragrant (of tea); sensitive to bad smells; (sl.) inquisitive (‖ esp. *N*~ *Parker*, busy--body). [-Y²]

nŏt, n′t (see below), adv. **1.** Negativing & following ordinary verbs (arch. for usu. neg. form with *do*; *I know* ~; *I doubt* ~;

say ~ *so*; *fear* ~; *saidst thou*~?). **2.** (Often *n′t* joined to word) negativing auxiliaries & vb *be*, & following them or (in questions having *not* in full) their subjects (*I cannot* or *can't say*; *he will* ~ or *won't*, or arch. *he′ll* ~, *come*; *she is* ~, *isn't*, or vulg. *ain't*, *here*; *do* ~, or usu. *don′t, stir*; *didn′t you*, or formally *did you* ~, *tell me?*; *am I* ~, or *ain′t I*, *aren′t we, smart?*). **3.** Negativing & preceding particles & infinitives (~ *knowing*, *I cannot say*; *begged him* ~ *to move*). **4.** Used elliptically for negative sentence or verb or phrase (*Are you ill? Not at all. Not so. If it clears we will go out; if* ~, ~. *Popular or* ~, *it is right. I would as soon do it as* ~); preceding *that* with sense *it is* ~ *to be inferred, however, that*, or *but what* or (formal) *but that* or (arch.) *but* with sense *all the same* or *nevertheless* (*If he said so*—~ *that he ever did—he lied. I cannot do it*; ~ *but what* etc. *a stronger man might*). **5.** Preceding word etc. that is to be rejected for one that follows with *but* or to emphasize by contrast one already used (*He is* ~ *my son, but yours*, or *but my nephew. He is your son*, ~ or *& ~ mine*). **6.** Preceding emphatic appended pronoun (*they will* ~ *be ′had′*, ~ *they*). **7.** Preceding a with sense ~ *one* (~ *a hair of your head shall be touched*). **8.** Preceding in litotes or periphrasis a word of opposite sense to that required (~ *a few*, ~ *seldom*; ~ *once* or *or nor twice*, many times; ~ *too well*, rather ill, rather badly; ~ *unconnected with*; ~ *reluctant*, only too glad). **9.** ~ *at* HOME; ~-*being*, non-existence; ‖ ~ *half* (adv. sl.), very, very much, (‘*Was he annoyed?′ ′Not half′*, i.e. yes, exceedingly); ~ *out*; ~-*self*, = NON-*ego*; ~ *sufficient*, or usu. *N.S.*, banker's mark on dishonoured cheque. [ME; contr. of NOUGHT]

nŏt′a bēn′e, vb imperat. (abbr. N.B.). Observe what follows, take notice, (usu. drawing attention to a qualification of what has preceded). [L, = note well]

nŏtabil′itȳ, n. Prominent person, (rare) notable object or thing worth seeing; worthiness of notice (*names of no historical* ~); ‖ (arch.) housewifely skill. [ME, f. OF *notabilite* or LL (med. L) *notabilitas* (foll., -ITY)]

nŏt′able, a. & n. **1.** Worthy of note, remarkable, striking, eminent; (chem.) perceptible (*a* ~ *quantity of*); (of women; *occas. pr.* nŏt-) capable, bustling, housewifely; hence **nŏt′ablȳ²** adv. **2.** n. Eminent person (esp. *Assembly of N*~*s*, irregular council serving as temporary parliament in emergencies). [ME, f. OF, f. L *notabilis* (NOTE², -ABLE)]

nŏt′arȳ, n. Person publicly authorized to draw up or attest contracts etc., protest bills of exchange etc., & perform other formalities (also ~ *public*). Hence **notār′IAL** a., **notār′iaLLȳ²** adv. [ME, f. L *notarius* secretary (NOTE¹, ², -ARY¹)]

nota′tion, n. Representing of numbers,

quantities, pitch and duration of sound, etc., by symbols; any set of symbols used for this, esp. in arith., alg., & mus.; *note, annotation; SCALE³ *of* ~. [f. L *notatio* (NOTE², -ATION)]

nŏtch, n., & v.t. **1.** V-shaped indentation in edge or on convex surface; nick made on stick etc. by way of keeping count; *defile, pass; ~-*wing*, kinds of moth; hence ~′Y², ~ED² (-cht; bot., zool.), aa. **2.** v.t. Make ~es in; make *into* space by ~ing; score (items etc.; often *up, down*) by ~es; secure or insert (steps in staircase etc.) by ~es. [16th c., f. obs. F *oche* (mod. *hoche*) with (*a*)*n* prefixed, cf. NEWT]

nōte¹, & n. **1.** Written sign representing pitch & duration of a musical sound; key of pianoforte etc.; single tone of definite pitch made by musical instrument, voice, etc.; (single tone in) bird's song or call; significant sound or way of expressing oneself (*there is a ~ of self-complacency in his voice*; *sound the ~ of war*). **2.** Sign, token, characteristic, distinguishing feature, proof of genuineness, guarantee consisting *of*, (*these are the ~s of Neo-paganism*; *catholicity is one ~ of the true Church*; *has the ~ of catholicity*); stigma, mark of censure, (*on which the law has set a ~ of infamy*); mark *of exclamation* or *admiration, interrogation*. **3.** Brief record of facts, impressions, or topics for speech or article (usu. pl.; *make* or *take a ~ of,* ~*s*; COMPARE~*s*; *preaches from*~*s*; *spoke for an hour without a ~*); annotation appended to passage in book etc.; short or informal letter; formal diplomatic communication; (usu. ~ *of hand*) written promise to pay sum by certain time; ‖ BANK³-~; CIRCULAR ~. **4.** Eminence (*critic, philo-. sopher, person, of* ~, distinguished); notice, attention, (*worthy of* ~; *take* ~ *of*), whence ~′WORTHY (-twêrdhǐ) a. **5.** ~′*book*, for entering memoranda in; ~′*case*, pocket wallet for holding bank-~*s*; ~′*paper*, kinds used for (esp. private) correspondence. Hence ~′LESS a., ~′LET n., (-tl-). [ME, f. OF, f. L *nota* mark]

nōte², v.t. Observe, notice, give attention to; set down, set *down*, as thing to be remembered or observed; annotate (book etc.); (p.p.) celebrated, well known *for*. [ME, f. OF *noter* f. L *notare* (prec.)]

no′thing (nŭ-), n. & adv. **1.** No thing (with adj. following, as ~ *great is easy*). **2.** Not anything, nought, (*has ~ in him*, is insignificant or without individuality; *there is~ in it*, it is untrue or unimportant, & see IN¹; ~ *doing*, sl. announcement of failure or refusal of request; ~ *venture ~ have*, excuse for or encouragement to bold action; ~ *like* LEATHER; NECK *or* ~; *dance on* ~, be hanged; *fade away* etc. *to* ~, disappear gradually; *no* ~, colloq., conclusion of negative list, as *no bread, no butter, no cheese, no* ~; ~ *else than* or *but,* ~ *but, force* etc., merely force etc.,

force etc. alone, unmistakable force etc.; *there is ~ for it but to*, no alternative; ~ *if not critical* etc., critical as leading characteristic; *get thing for* ~, gratis; *have endured it for* ~, to no purpose; so *it was not for ~ that he read Plato*; *that is ~ to you*, not your concern; *make ~ of*, treat as trifle; *make ~ of doing*, do without hesitation or as ordinary matter; *can make ~ of*, cannot understand, find solution of, use, develop, or deal with; *come to* ~, turn out useless, fail, not amount to anything; *have ~ to do with*, not be concerned with, avoid dealing with or society of; *all to* ~, longest odds). **3.** Trifle, very inferior thing, (*that is*~, i.e. in comparison with what I am going to tell you; *he is ~ without his money*; *learning is ~ to*, i.e. compared with, *genius*). **4.** (arith.). No amount, nought, (*multiply 6 by* ~, *& the result is* ~). **5.** Non-existence, what does not exist. **6.** (With *a* & pl.) trifling thing, event, remark, or person (*the little ~s of life*; *whisper soft ~s*; *the new commander--in-chief was a* ~). **7.** (Of religious belief) *be* ~, belong to no denomination, be an atheist or agnostic. **8.** adv. Not at all, in no way, (*differs ~ from*; *is ~ less than monstrous*, positively; *helps us* ~; *avails ~*; *is ~ like as or so good* etc.; *is ~ near so extensive*; ~ LO(A)TH); *(as int., colloq.) not at all (Is it gold? Gold* ~; *it's pinch-beck*). [OE *nān thing*, NO¹, THING]

no′thingnèss (nŭ-), n. Non-existence, the non-existent; worthlessness, triviality, unimportance, insignificance, trifles. [-NESS]

nōt′ice, n., & v.t. **1.** Intimation, intelligence, warning, (*give, have,* ~; *at short, ten minutes'*, etc., ~, with such time for preparation); information or directions pasted on ~-board. **2.** Formal intimation of something or instructions *to do* something (~ *to* QUIT; *till* FURTHER¹ ~); announcement by party to agreement that it is to terminate at specified time (esp. between landlord & tenant or employer & employed; *give a week's* etc.~; *take my* ~). **3.** Heed, attention, cognizance, observation, (*come into* ~, attract attention; *takes no ~ of it*, does not observe it, or takes no action in consequence of it; *brought it to his* ~; *take ~ that*, I warn you that; *baby takes* ~, shows signs of intelligence). **4.** Paragraph or article upon something in newspaper, esp. review *of* book, play, etc. **5.** ~-*board*, bearing ~ or provided for ~s to be posted on. **6.** v.t. Remark upon, speak of. **7.** Perceive, take ~ of; treat with politeness or condescension. **8.** Serve with ~, give ~ to, (*was ~d to quit*); hence ~ABLE a., ~ABLY² adv. [ME, f. OF, f. L *notitia* (*notus* p.p. of *noscere* know, -ICE)]

nōt′ifiable, a. (Of diseases) that must be notified to public-health authorities. [-ABLE]

nōt′ify, v.t. Make known, announce, report; inform, give notice to, (person *of*, *that*, or abs.). So **nŏtĬfica'tion** n. [ME, f. OF *notifier* f. L *notificare* (NOTICE, -FY)]

nŏ'tion, n. **1.** General concept under which particular thing may be classed (in philos., *first, second*, ~, = first, second, INTENTION). **2.** Idea, conception, (*the ~ of my doing it is absurd*; *what he means I have not the haziest ~*); view, opinion, theory, vaguely held or insecurely based, (*has a ~ that*; *such is the common ~*). **3.** Faculty, capability, or intention *of* (*has no ~ of obeying, obedience, discipline, letting himself be made a fool of*). **4.** *Something in the way of miscellaneous wares, esp. cheap useful ingenious article. **5.** pl. || Traditional special vocabulary of Winchester College. [f. L *notio* (NOTICE, -ION)]

nŏ'tional (-sho-), a. (Of knowledge etc.) speculative, not based on experiment or demonstration, whence ~IST(2) n., ~LY² adv.; (of things, relations, etc.) existing only in thought, imaginary; (of persons) fanciful. [f. med. L *notionalis* (prec., -AL)]

nŏto-, comb. form of Gk *nōton* back, in scientific terms, as ~*branch'iate* (-ngk-), having dorsal gills; *nōt'ochord*, cartilaginous band forming basis of spinal column; ~*nec'ta* [Gk *nēktēs* swimmer], water-beetle swimming on back, the boat-fly.

Nŏtogae'a (-jëa), n. Zoological region comprising Australian, New-Zealand, & neotropical regions. [f. Gk *notos* south, *gaia* land]

notŏr'ious, a. (Of facts) well or commonly known (esp. *it is ~ that*); (with designations of persons, conduct, etc., that imply condemnation) undisguised, talked of, generally known to deserve the name, (~ *smuggler, offender, vice*); unfavourably known (*for* some quality or conduct, or abs.; *a ship ~ for ill-luck*; *the ~ Titus Oates*). Hence or cogn. **notŏri'ĕty** n., ~LY² adv. [f. med. L *notorius* (NOTICE, -ORY), -OUS]

Notŏr'nis, n. (zool.). Genus of rare flightless birds, chiefly of New Zealand. [f. Gk *notos* south, *ornis* bird]

Notre-Dame (nōtre dahm'), n. The Cathedral of Paris. [F, = Our Lady]

nŏtwithstănd'ing, prep., adv., & conj. **1.** In spite of, not the less for, (~ *his resistance*; *this ~*. The second order is the orig., the prep. having been developed f. a part. abs.). **2.** adv. Nevertheless, all the same. **3.** conj. (arch.). (Developed from prep. or part. abs. with *that*, still occas. retained) although, in spite of the fact (*that*). [ME, f. NOT, WITHSTAND, -ING²]

nougat (nōog'ah), n. Sweetmeat of sugar, nuts, etc. [F (L *nux nucis* nut, -ATE¹)]

nought (nawt), n. Nothing (poet., arch., & arith.; *come, bring to*, ~, be ruined or fail, ruin or baffle; *set at ~*, disregard, ridicule); figure 0, cipher, (~*s & crosses*, child's game). [OE *nōwiht* f. *ne* not +*ōwiht*, var. of *āwiht* AUGHT]

noum'ĕn|ŏn, n. (pl. ~*a*). Object of intellectual intuition devoid of all phenomenal attributes. Hence ~AL a., ~ally² adv. [f. Gk *nooumenon* neut. pres. part. pass. of *noeō* apprehend, taken by Kant as antithesis to *phenomenon*]

noun, n. (gram.). Word used as name of person or thing, substantive; (formerly) substantive or adjective. Hence ~'AL a. (rare). [ME, f. AF, = OF *nun, nom*, f. L *nomen* name]

nou'rish (nŭ-), v.t. Sustain with food (lit. & fig.), whence ~ING² a.; foster, cherish, nurse, (feeling, hope, etc.) in one's heart. [ME, f. OF *norir* (-ISH²) f. L *nutrire*]

nou'rishment (nŭ-), n. Sustenance, food; nourishing. [ME, f. OF *norissement* (prec., -MENT)]

nous, n. (Gk philos.) mind, intellect; (colloq.) common sense, gumption. [Gk]

nouveau riche (nōōv'ō rēsh'), n. Wealthy parvenu. [F, = new rich]

nouv'ĕlle (nōō-), n. Short novel. [F]

nŏv'el¹, n. **1.** One of the tales in such a collection as Boccaccio's *Decameron*. **2.** Fictitious prose narrative of volume length portraying characters & actions representative of real life in continuous plot; *the* ~, this type of literature; whence ~ESE' (-ēz) n. **3.** (Rom. law). New decree supplementary to the Codex. [f. It. *novella* f. L neut. pl. as foll.]

nŏv'el², a. Of new kind or nature, strange, hitherto unknown. [ME, f. OF, f. L *novellus* dim. of *novus* new]

nŏvelĕtte', n. Short novel, story of moderate length, (freq. derog.); (mus.) piano piece of free form with several themes. [-ETTE]

nŏv'el|ist, n. Novel-writer. Hence ~ist'ic a. [-IST]

nŏv'eliz|e, -is|e (-īz), v.t. Convert (drama, facts) into a novel. Hence ~A'TION n. [-IZE]

nŏv'eltȳ, n. New or unusual thing or occurrence; novel character *of* something. [ME, f. OF *novelte* (NOVEL², -TY)]

Novĕm'ber, n. Eleventh month. [ME; L *novem* nine); cf. DECEMBER]

novĕn'a, n. (R.-C. Church). Devotion consisting of special prayers or service on nine successive days. [med. L, f. L *novem* nine]

novĕrc'al, a. Stepmotherly. [f. L *novercalis* (*noverca* stepmother, -AL)]

nŏv'ice, n. Person received in religious house on probation before taking the vows; new convert; inexperienced person, beginner, tiro. [ME, f. OF, f. L *novicius* (*novus* new, -ITIOUS¹)]

novi'ciate, -tiate, (-shĬ-), n. Novice's probationary period or initiation or apprenticeship; novice; quarters assigned to novices. [f. F *noviciat* or med. L *novitiatus* (prec., -ATE¹)]

nŏv'ocaine, n. (pharm.). A regional anaesthetic. [P; f. L *novus* new + (CO)CAINE]

now, adv., conj., & n. **1.** adv. At the present time; by this time; under the present circumstances (*I cannot ~ ever* *believe you again*; ~ *that I know you, it is different*); immediately (*must go* ~); in the immediate past (*just* ~, & arch. *even, but,* ~); (in narrative) then, next, by that time, (*Caesar* ~ *marched east*; *it was* ~ *clear*); (*every*) ~ *& then* or *again*, from time to time, intermittently; ~ ... ~, ~ ... *then*, ~ ... *& again*, at one moment — at another; ~ *or never !*, this is the nick of time. **2.** (Without temporal force, giving various tones, soothing, reproving, explanatory, threatening, etc., to sentence) pray, I beg, I insist, I warn you, & yet, you must know, it must be admitted, surely, (*Now what do you mean by it ?. Oh, come* ~ *!. No nonsense* ~ *!. You have revealed the secret;* ~ *you were paid to keep it. Now Barabbas was a robber. Now this was bad enough, but* —. *Now then, what mischief are you at ?. You don't mean it,* ~). **3.** conj. (Orig., as often still, *now* adv. followed by *that*) consequently upon or simultaneously with the fact that (*Now I am a man I think otherwise. Now you mention it, I do remember*). **4.** n. This time, the present (chiefly after prepp.; *is there by, ere, till,* ~, *from* ~ *till,* etc.; *read the future in the* ~). [OE *nū*, also in all older Gmc langg., corresp. to L *nunc*, Gk *nun*, Skr. *nū*]

now′aday, a. Of nowadays. [f. foll.]

now′adays (-z), adv. & n. (At) the present day, (in) these advanced or newfangled times. [ME, f. NOW adv., A², DAY, -ES]

Nowel (nōēl′), int. expr. joy in Christmas carols. [ME, f. OF *noel* f. L NATAL*is*]

no′where (-hwār, -wār), adv. In, at, to, no place (~ *near*, not nearly; *be, come in,* ~, not be placed in race or competition). [OE *nā-,* later *nōhwǣr*; NO¹, WHERE]

no′xious (-kshus), a. Harmful, unwholesome. Hence ~LY² adv., ~NESS n. [f. L *noxius* (*noxa* harm), -OUS]

noyade (nwahyahd′), n. Execution by drowning, esp. wholesale as in France in 1794. [F]

noyau (nwahyō′), n. Liqueur of brandy flavoured with fruit-kernels. [F (L *nux nucis* nut, -AL)]

noz′zle, n. Spout, mouthpiece, end fitted to hose etc. [NOSE, -LE(1)]

n't. See NOT.

nū, n. Greek letter (*N, ν*) = n. [Gk]

nuance (see Ap.), n. Delicate difference in or shade of meaning, feeling, opinion, colour, etc. [F, f. *nuer* to shade, ult. f. L *nubes* cloud]

nub, nub′ble, nn. Small knob or lump, esp. of coal; (*nub*) point or gist (*of* matter or story). Hence **nubb′ly²** a. [app. var. of *knub,* f. MLG *knubbe, knobbe* KNOB]

nub′ile, a. Marriageable (esp. of women). Hence **nubil′ITY** n. [f. L *nubilis* (*nubere* become wife)]

nu′chal (-kl), a. Of nape of neck. [f. *nucha* nape, f. med. L *nucha* spinal cord]

nuci-, comb. form of L *nux nucis* nut, as *nucif′*EROUS, *nū′civ′*OROUS.

nuc′lear, a. Of, relating to, constituting, a nucleus; = ~-*powered*; ~ (= ATOMIC) *bomb*; ~ *energy* (released or absorbed during reactions taking place in atomic nuclei); ~ *fission,* splitting up of a heavy atom, e.g. of uranium, into two or more new atoms, with an enormous release of energy; ~ *fuel,* source of atomic energy; ~ *physics* (dealing with the atomic nucleus); ~ *power* (derived from ~ energy); ~-*powered* a., (of ship) using ~ power; ~ *reactor,* atomic PILE²; ~ (= ATOMIC) *war.* [f. NUCLEUS, -AR¹]

nuc′leôle, n. (biol.). Nucleus of or within a nucleus. Hence ~olAR¹, ~olāt′ed [-ATE²], aa., ~olo- comb. form. [f. L *nucleolus* dim. of foll.]

nuc′leôlus, n. (pl. ~ī). (Astron.) condensed part of comet's head; (phys.) positively charged central portion constituting main mass of atom; central part or thing round which others are collected, kernel of aggregate or mass, beginning meant to receive additions, central part of ovule, seed, plant-cell, animal cell, etc., portion of medullary matter from which nerves spring, (*the* ~*us of a sun-spot, community, library, story, empire,* etc.). Hence ~AL, ~ARY, aa., ~o- comb. form. [L, dim. of *nux nucis* nut]

nūde, a. & n. **1.** Naked, bare, unclothed, undraped, (~ *contract* in law, lacking a consideration & therefore void unless under seal); so **nūd′i-** comb. form (zool.), **nūd′**ITY n.; (as colour adj., esp. of stockings) flesh-coloured. **2.** n. ~ figure in painting or sculpture; *the* ~, the undraped figure, undraped state. Hence **nūd′**IST n., adherent of the cult of the ~ (also attrib., as *nudist colony*). [f. L *nudus*]

nūdge, v.t., & n. **1.** Push slightly with elbow to draw attention privately, (fig.) draw attention of. **2.** n. Such push. [orig. unkn.; cf. Norw. dial. *nugga, nyggja* to push, rub]

nu′gae (-gē, -jē), n. pl. Trifles, learned triflings, profitless minutiae. [L]

nūg′atory, a. Trifling, worthless, futile; inoperative, not valid. [f. L *nugatorius* (*nugari* trifle f. prec., -ORY)]

nugg′ar, n. Large broad-beamed boat used on upper Nile. [native]

nugg′et (-g-), n. Rough lump of native gold. [app. f. dial. *nug* lump &c.]

nuis′ance (nūs-), n. Anything injurious or obnoxious to the community or member of it for which legal remedy may be had (|| *commit no* ~, notice to public not to defile place); obnoxious person, offensive object, annoying action, anything disagreeable (also attrib., as ~ *value*). [ME, f. OF, f. *nuire nuis-* f. L *nocēre* hurt, -ANCE)]

null, a. & n. Not binding, invalid, (often ~ *& void*); without character or expression; non-existent, amounting to nothing, (rare); || (n.) dummy letter in a cipher. [f. F *nul* or L *nullus* (*ne* not, *ullus* any)]

nŭll'a bŏn'a, n. Sheriff's return stating that party has no goods to be distrained upon. [L, = no goods]

nŭll'ah (-*a*), n. (Anglo-Ind.). Stream, watercourse, ravine. [f. Hind. *nala*]

nŭll'i|fÿ, v.t. Cancel, neutralize. So ~FICA'TION n. [f. F *nullifier* (as NULL, -FY), or med. L *nullificare* annul]

nŭll'ipōre, n. Kind of marine vegetation. [f. L *nullus* no + PORE[1]]

nŭll'itÿ, n. Being null, invalidity, (esp. ·~ *of marriage*; ~ *suit*, for this); act, document, etc., that is null; nothingness; a mere nontity; a nonentity. [f. F *nullité* or med. L *nullitas* (NULL, -ITY)]

numb (-m), a., & v.t. **1.** Deprived of feeling or power of motion (~ *with cold* etc.); ~-*fish*, the electric ray or TORPEDO; ~'*skull*, NUMSKULL; hence ~'LY[2] (-mlĭ) adv., ~'NESS (-mn-) n. **2.** v.t. Make ~, (fig.) stupefy, paralyse. [15th c. *nome*, p.p. of obs. *nim* take (OE, OS, Goth. *niman*)]

nŭm'ber[1], n. (written Nº, for *numero* = in ~, with pl. Nºˢ, before distinguishing figure, as *bedroom Nº 15, Nºˢ 1–10*). **1.** Tale, count, sum, company, or aggregate, of persons (also *of*) or things (also *of*) or abstract units, symbol or figure representing such aggregate, ticket etc. bearing such figure, person or thing (esp. single issue of magazine, or part of opera etc.) whose place in series is indicated by such figure, (*the ~ of fools is infinite; N~s*, abbr. *Num.*, O.T. book containing census; *the greatest ~ on record is 59 persons*; *to the ~ of 80*, as many as; GOLDEN ~; *science of* ~*s*, arithmetic; *took the driver's ~*; *sleeps in Nº 5*; *Nº 9* (pill), army doctor's reputed panacea; *Nº 10 Downing Street, Nº 10*, (used for) Prime Minister's official residence (when he is also First Lord of the Treasury); one's ~ *goes up*, he dies; ~ *one*, oneself, esp. in *take care of* ~ *one*, also ‖ (nav. ·sl.) first lieutenant; *story issued in* ~*s*, in parts successively published bearing ~*s*; *back* ~, earlier issue of magazine, (fig.) anything out of date; *is not of our* ~, included among us; *is now added to the* ~ *of my enemies*); (sing. or pl.) *large, small*, etc., or large, collection or company of or abs. (*were present in great, only in small*, or *in*, ~*s*; *saw a great*, or *a*, ~ *of birds*; *a small* ~ *came*; *there are* ~*s who live by begging*). **2.** pl. Numerical preponderance (*won by* ~*s* or *force of* ~*s*). **3.** Numerical reckoning (*the laws of* ~ *& proportion pervade Nature*; *without* ~, innumerable, also ~LESS a.; *in* ~, when counted or estimated, numerically, as *one people exceeds another in* ~). **4.** (gram.). Class of word-forms including all singular, all plural, or all dual etc. words (*Greek has three* ~*s*; '*things*' *is of the plural* ~). **5.** Rhythm; (pl.) groups of musical notes, metrical feet, verses. [ME, f. OF *nombre* f. L *numerus*]

nŭm'ber[2], v.t. Count, ascertain number of; (pass.) be restricted in number (*his years are* ~*ed*, he has not long to live); include, regard as, *among*, *in*, or *with* some class; assign a number to, distinguish with a number; have lived, live, (so many years); be able to show (so many inhabitants etc.); amount to (specified number). [ME, f. OF *nombrer* f. L *numerare* (prec.)]

‖ **nŭm'bles** (-blz), n. pl. (arch.). Deer's entrails. [ME, f. OF *num-, nombles* loin &c., app. f. *lomble*(s) f. L *lumbulus* dim. of *lumbus* loin; later *umbles*, whence HUMBLE pie]

nŭm'erable, a. That can be numbered. [f. L *numerabilis* (NUMBER[2], -ABLE)]

nŭm'eral, a. & n. (Word, figure, group of figures) denoting a number; of number. [f. LL *numeralis* (NUMBER[1], -AL)]

nŭmerā'tion, n. Method or process of numbering or computing; calculation; assigning of numbers; (arith.) expression in words of number written in figures; ~ *table*, showing value of figures according to their place in system of notation. [ME, f. OF, or L *numeratio* (NUMBER[2], -ATION)]

nŭm'erātor, n. Number above line in vulgar fraction showing how many of the parts indicated by the denominator are taken; person who numbers. [LL (NUMBER[2], -OR)]

nŭmē'ric, a. What is either a number, a proper or improper fraction, or an incommensurable ratio. [f. L *numerus* number, -IC]

nŭmē'rical, a. Of, in, denoting etc. number. Hence ~LY[2] adv. [-AL]

nŭm'erous, a. Comprising many units (*a* ~ *acquaintance, library, family, army, class*); coming from many individuals (*the* ~ *voice of the people*; *a* ~ *hum*); (arch.) thronged (*a* ~ *country*); (with pl. noun) many (*received* ~ *gifts*); (of verse or prose) rhythmic, harmonious. Hence ~LY[2] adv. [f. L *numerosus* (NUMBER[1], -OUS)]

nŭm'inous, n. *The* ~, the combined feeling of attraction & awe characteristic of man's sense of communion with God & religion. [f. L *numen -inis* divine will, divinity + -OUS]

nūmismăt'|ic (-z-), a. Of coins or coinage. So ~ICALLY adv., ~ICS, **nūmis'mati**ST(3), **nūmismatŏL'OGY**, nn. [F (-*ique*), f. L (*num-*) f. Gk *nomisma -atos* coin (*nomizō* use currently f. *nomos* custom), -IC]

nŭmm'arÿ, nŭmm'ūlarÿ, aa. Of, in, coin. [f. L *nummarius* (*nummus* coin, -ARY[1]), & *nummulus* dim. + -ARY[1]]

‖ **nŭmm'ĕt**, n. (dial.). Lunch. [= *noon meat*]

nŭmm'ūlite, n. Disc-like fossil shell of Tertiary strata. [*nummulus* (see NUMMARY), -ITE[1](2)]

nŭm'nah (-*a*), n. Saddle-cloth, pad placed under saddle. [Anglo-Ind. *numdah* felt f. Hind. *namda* f. Pers. *namad* carpet]

nŭm'skŭll, n. Dolt or his head. [NUMB]

nŭn, ŋ. Woman living in convent usu.

under vow of poverty, chastity, & obedience; kinds of bird & moth; ~'s *cloth*, thin woollen stuff; ~'s *thread*, fine white sewing cotton; ~'s *veiling*, thin dress--stuff. Hence ~'HOOD, ~'SHIP, nn., ~'LIKE, ~n'ISH[1], aa. [OE *nunne*, OHG, ON *nunna*, f. LL *nonna* fem. of *nonnus* mònk, orig. title given to elderly persons; in ME reinforced f. OF *nonne*]

nun'atăk (-ōon-), n. Isolated peak of rock projecting above surface of land ice or snow e.g. in Greenland. [Eskimo]

nŭn'buoy (-boi), n. Buoy circular in middle & tapering to each end. [f. obs. *nun* spinning-top]

nŭnc dĭmĭtt'ĭs, n. The canticle *Lord, now lettest thou* (*sing* ~, be willing to depart from life etc.). [L, = now lettest thou go]

nŭn'ciature (-shatūr), n. (Tenure of) office of papal nuncio. [f. It. *nunziatura* (foll.)]

nŭn'cio (-shĭō), n. (pl. ~s). Pope's ambassador at foreign court. [It., f. L *nuncius* messenger]

nŭnc'ŭp|āte, v.t. Declare (will, testament) orally, not in writing. So ~A'TION n., ~ATIVE a. [f. L *nuncupare* name, (*nomen* name, *capere* take), -ATE[3]]

nŭnnā'tion, n. Addition of final *n* in declension of (orig. Arabic) nouns. [f. Arab. *nun* the letter *n* +-ATION]

nŭnn'erў, n. Religious house for nuns, convent. [ME, f. AF *nonnerie* (NUN, -ERY(3)]

nŭph'är, n. Yellow water-lily. [for NENUPHAR]

nŭp'tial (-shl), a. & n. **1.** Of marriage or wedding. **2.** n. (usu. pl.). Wedding. [f. F, or L *nuptialis* (*nuptiae* wedding f. *nubere nupt*- become wife)]

nûrse[1], n. **1.** Woman employed to suckle & take charge of infant (usu. *wet*-~), or having charge of young children (also *dry*-~). **2.** Country etc. that fosters some quality etc. (*the* ~ *of liberty*). **3.** Nursing or being nursed (*at* ~, *put out* or *put to* ~, of child, & fig. of estate). **4.** Person, usu. woman, charged with or trained for care of the sick or decrepit. **5.** (Forestry) tree planted as shelter to others; (entom.) sexually imperfect bee, ănt, etc., caring for the young brood, worker; (zool.) individual in asexual stage of metagenesis. **6.** ~*-child*, foster-child; ~*-frog*, kind of which male carries eggs till hatched; ~*-maid*, girl having charge of child(ren); ||~ *ship*, (nav.), = MOTHER[1] ship. Hence **nûrs'erў**[3] n. [reduced f. ME & OF *norice* f. LL *nutricia* fem. of *nutricius*, *-itius* f. L *nutrix -icis* (*nutrire* nourish)]

nûrse[2], v.t. & i. **1.** Suckle (child), give suck, act as wet-nurse; act as nursemaid to, have charge of; (pass.) be brought up (*in* luxury, certain place, etc.). **2.** Foster, tend, promote development of, (the arts, hatred, etc.); manage (plants, estate) with solicitude; cherish (grievance etc.). **3.** Wait upon (sick person), try to cure (sickness), be sick-nurse. **4.** Hold or clasp (baby, one's knees or foot) caressingly; sit close over (fire). **5.** || Keep (constituency) in good humour by attentions. **6.** (billiards). Keep (balls) together for series of cannons. **7.** ||*Nursing home*, private hospital, house for surgical operations, reception of invalids, etc.; *nursing father, mother,* foster-. [later form of ME *nursh* f. NOURISH, assim. to NURSE[1]]

nûrse[3], n. Kinds of dogfish or shark. [15th c. *nusse*, perh. f. obs. *huss* dogfish, of obsc. orig. w. adherent (*a*)*n*, cf. NEWT]

nûrs'erў, n. **1.** Room assigned to children & their nurses (~ *governess*, one combining duties of nurse & governess). **2.** Practice, institution, sphere, place, in or by which qualities or classes of people are fostered or bred. **3.** Plot of ground in which young plants are reared for transplantation (~*man*, owner of this); fish--rearing pond; place where animal life is developed. **4.** (billiards). Grouped balls (see NURSE[2]; esp. in ~ *cannon*). [14th c., prob. f. AF *noriccrie* (NURSE[1], -ERY)]

nûrs(e)'ling (-sl-), n. Infant, esp. in relation to its nurse; ~ *of*, person or thing bred in or fostered by. [NURSE[1], -LING[1]]

nûr'ture, n., & v.t. **1.** Bringing up, training, fostering care; nourishment. **2.** v.t. Nourish, rear, foster, train, educate. [ME, f. OF *nurture*, var. of *noureture*, f. Rom. **nutritura* (L *nutrire* nourish, -URE)]

nŭt, n., & v.i. (-tt-). **1.** Fruit consisting of hard or leathery shell enclosing edible kérnel (see also EARTH-~, PEA-~; DEAF~; *can't shoot* etc. *for* ~*s*, sl., do thing even tolerably well; *hard* ~ *to crack*, difficult problem, person or thing hard to deal with or get the better of; *be* ~*s* or *dead* ~*s on*, sl., delight in, be skilful at). **2.** (sl.). Showy young man (now rare); head (*off* one's ~, insane, mad); (pl.) crazy (also **nerts*). **3.** Small toothed projection on spindle engaging with cog-wheel, small spur-wheel. **4.** Small usu. hexagonal metal block pierced with screw-thread to accommodate screw on bolt etc. and operated by spanner. **5.** Holder that tightens or relaxes horse-hair of fiddle--bow etc. **6.** pl. Small lumps of coal. **7.** ~*-brown*, coloured like ripe hazel-~ (esp. of girl's complexion, & of ale); ~*-butter*, food like butter made from ~s; ~*-cracker*, (usu. pl.) instrument for cracking ~s, prominent chin & nose with points naturally, or by loss of teeth, near each other (also used attrib. in sing., as *a* ~*-cracker face*), (sing.) common European but rare British bird; ~*-gall*, gall found on dyer's oak used as dye-stuff; ~*-hatch*, small climbing bird feeding on ~s, insects, &c. [HATCH[3]]; ~*-oil*, got esp. from hazel-~s & walnuts, & used in paints & varnishes; ~*-palm*, Australian palm bearing ~s; ~*-shell*, hard exterior covering of ~, tiny receptacle or dwelling, briefest possible way of expressing, epitome, (*can give it you in a ~shell*); ~-*tree*, bearing ~s, esp. hazel; ~-*weevil*, beetle laying eggs in green hazel & filbert ~s. **8.** v.i. Seek or gather ~s (usu. in gerund, *went ~ting* etc.). [OE *hnutu*, MLG, MDu. *note*, OHG (*h*)*nuz*, ON *hnot* f. Gmc. **hnut-*]

nŭt′|āte, v.i. (bot.). Nod, droop. So ~ANT a. [f. L *nutare* frequent. of *nuere* nod, -ATE³]

nūtā′tion, n. Nodding; (astron.) oscillation of earth's axis making motion of pole of equator round pole of ecliptic wavy; oscillation of spinning top; curvature in stem of growing plant. [f. L *nutatio* (prec., -ION)]

nŭt′mĕg, n. Hard aromatic spheroidal seed got from fruit of evergreen E.-Indian tree (~-*tree*), used as spice & in medicine; ~-*apple*, fruit of ~-tree yielding mace & ~s; ~-*liver*, diseased state of liver, red atrophy. [ME; partial transl. of OF *nois mugede*, = med. L *nux muscata* musky nut]

nŭt′ria, n. Skin or fur of the S.-Amer. coypu, an aquatic rodent. [Sp., = otter f. L *lutra*]

nŭt′rient, a. Serving as or providing nourishment. [f. L *nutrire* nourish, -ENT]

nŭt′riment, n. Nourishing food (lit. & fig.). Hence **nūtrimĕn′tAL** a. (rare). [f. L *nutrimentum* (prec., -MENT)]

nūtri′tion, n. (Supplying or receiving of) nourishment, food. Hence ~AL (-shon-) a., of or relating to ~. [f. F, or LL *nutritio* (as NUTRIENT, -ION)]

nūtri′tious (-shŭs), a. Nourishing, efficient as food. Hence ~LY² adv., ~NESS n. [f. L *nutritius* (NURSE¹, -ITIOUS²)]

nŭt′ritive, a. & n. Serving as food; concerned in nutrition; (n.) article of food. [ME, f. OF (-*if*, -*ive*) f. med. L *nutritivus* (NUTRIENT, -IVE)]

nŭtt′ỹ, a. Abounding in nuts; tasting like nuts, of rich mellow flavour; (sl.) amorous or enthusiastic (*upon*); *(sl.) crazy. [-Y²]

nŭx vŏm′ica, n. Seed of E.-Ind. tree yielding the poison strychnine. [med. L (L *nux* nut, *vomere* vomit, -IC)]

nŭz′zle, v.i. & t. Nose, burrow or press or rub or sniff with the nose, press nose or press (nose) *into* or *against*; nestle, lie snug, (also refl.). [NOSE¹, -LE(3)]

nȳctalōp′ia, n. Night-blindness or recurrent loss of vision after sunset; inability to see clearly except at night. [LL (Gk *nuktalōps* f. *nukt-* night, *alaos* blind, *ōps* eye, -IA¹); incorrect second sense due to overlooking of -*al-*]

nȳctitrŏp′ic, a. (bot.). Turning in certain direction at night. [f. combining form of Gk *nux nuktos* night + *tropos* turn, -IC]

nȳl′ghau (-gaw), n. Short-horned Indian antelope. [f. Pers. *nilgaw* (*nil* blue, *gaw* ox)]

nȳl′ŏn, n. Synthetic plastic material of great toughness, tensile strength, & elas-

ticity, widely used in industry & as a dress fabric; (pl., colloq.) garments, esp. women's stockings, made of ~. [P]

nȳmph, n. **1.** One of class of mythological semi-divine maidens inhabiting sea, rivers, fountains, hills, woods, or trees, or attending superior deities, whence or cogn. ~ē′AN, ~′ISH¹, ~′LIKE, aa. **2.**(poet.). Young & beautiful woman. **3.** Immature form of insect which has incomplete metamorphosis. [ME, f. OF *nimphe* f. L f. Gk *numphē*]

nȳm′pholĕpsỹ, n. Ecstasy or frenzy caused by desire of the unattainable. [foll., after *epilepsy*]

nȳm′pholĕpt, n. Person inspired by violent enthusiasm esp. for an ideal. Hence ~ĕp′tIC a. [f. Gk *numpholēptos* nymph-caught (NYMPH, *lambanō* take)]

nȳmpho|mān′ia, n. (path.). Morbid & uncontrollable sexual desire in women. Hence ~MAN′IAC n. [f. Gk *numphē* bride, -O-, -MANIA]

nȳstăg′mus, n. Eye-disease common among miners, with continual oscillation of eyeballs. [f. Gk *nustagmos* nodding (*nustazō* nod)]

O

O¹ (ō), letter (pl. *Os*, *O*'s, *Oes*). O-shaped mark, circle, (esp. *round O*).

O², **oh**, (ō), int. prefixed to vocative name (O), or expressing various emotions (usu. *oh* if separated by punctuation, otherwise *O*. *O dear me!*; *O for a breathing-space!*; *Oh, what a lie!*; *Oh, is that so?*); *O yes!*, = OYES. [ME. prob. f. L]

O′¹ (o), pref. of Irish names, as *O'Connor*. [Ir. *ó*, *ua*, descendant]

o′² (o), prep. short for *of*, *on*, still in some phrases, as (= *of*) *o'clock*, *Jack-o'-lantern*, *Will-o'-the-wisp*, *man-o'-war*, (colloq.) *cup o' tea*, (= *on*) *cannot sleep o' nights*.

-o-, terminal vowel of combining forms of wds; prop. used in Gk compounds, (-*i-* being usu. in L), but now extended to many scientific & other terms made of non-Gk wds (*occipito-frontal*, *joco-serious*), &, in meaning, expressing not merely modification of second element by first (*Franco - German* = essentially German with some French characteristics), but equal or any other relations (*Franco--German war*); used also in forming true derivatives w. Gk endings as -*cracy*, -*logy*, & perh. taken for part of the suf., whence ' ologies ' etc.

oaf, n. (pl. ~s, oaves). Elf's child, changeling, (arch.); misbegotten, deformed, or idiot child; awkward lout. Hence ~′ISH¹ a. [var. of obs. *auf* f. ON *álfr* ELF]

oak, n. **1.** Kinds of tree & shrub, of which the best known is a forest tree yielding hard timber & acorns & having jagged leaves (*dyer's*, *holm*, *scarlet*, etc., ~, other species; *dwarf*, *ground*, etc., ~, plants

named from some resemblance to ~);
wood of the ~ (HEART of ~), (poet.)
wooden ships; ‖ (Univ.) outer door of set
of rooms (sport one's ~, shut this to exclude visitors); leaves of ~ (~ is still
worn on 29th May); colour of young ~
leaves; the Oaks, race at Epsom for three-
-year-old fillies [f. name of estate]; (attrib., =, but now more usual than) ~en.
2. ~-apple, -fig, -gall, -plum, -potato,
-spangle, -wart, kinds of excrescence produced on ~s by gall-flies; ‖ ~-apple day,
29th May (Charles II restored 1660) on
which ~-apples are worn in memory of
the ROYAL-~ incident; ~-beauty, -egger,
-hook-tip, kinds of moth bred on or
resembling leaf etc. of ~; ~-fern, smooth
three-branched polypody; ~-tree, ~;
~-wood, forest, copse, etc., of ~s, also ~
timber. Hence ~'EN⁵ a.,~'LET,~'LING¹(2),
nn. [OE āc, OHG eih, ON eik f. Gmc *aiks]
oak'um, n. Loose fibre got by picking old
rope to pieces & used esp. in caulking
(pick ~, make this, esp. as formerly
common task of convicts & paupers).
[OE ǣ-, ācumbe, OHG āchambi, f. ǣ-
away, off +camb- st. of COMB]
oar (ōr), n., & v.t. & i. 1. Pole with blade
used (usu. in even numbers) to propel
boat by leverage, esp. one worked by
single rower (cf. SWEEP) with both hands
(cf. SCULL), or to steer (chained to the ~,
constrained to work hard & long, with
allusion to galley-slaves; pair-~, four-~,
etc., boat with two, four, etc., ~s; pulls
a good ~, is good ~sman; put in one's ~,
interfere; have an ~ in every man's boat,
be a meddler; rest on one's ~s, cease work
for a time); good, bad, young, practised,
etc., ~sman; (fig.) wing, fin, arm used
in swimming, etc.; ~s'man, ~s'woman,
rower, whence ~s'manSHIP(3) n.; hence
~'AGE(1) n. (poet.), (-)ED² (ōrd), ~'LESS,
~'Y² (poet.), aa., (ōr-). 2. vb. Row (t. &
i.; poet.; ~ boat, water, air,' one's way;
~ one's arms or hands, move them as in
swimming). [OE ār, cogn. w. ON ár, ǫr,
f. Gmc *airō, perh. cogn. w. Gk eretmos
oar, eretēs rower]
ōā'sis, n. (pl. oasēs). Fertile spot in desert
(lit. & fig.). [LL f. Gk, app. of Egypt.
orig.]
oast, n. Hop-drying kiln; ~-house, building containing this. [OE āst, = MLG,
MDu. eist, f. Gmc. *aistaz, cogn. w. L
aestus heat]
oat, n. (Pl.) (grain yielded by) hardy
cereal grown in cool climates as food for
men & horses; (sing., rare exc. in comb.)
~-plant, variety of ~s; wild ~, tall
grass resembling ~s (sow one's wild ~s,
indulge in youthful follies before becoming steady); (poet.) ~-stem used as
musical pipe by shepherds etc., pastoral
or bucolic poetry; ~'cake, thin unleavened cake made of ~meal, esp. in Scot-

land & N.; ~'meal, meal from ~s used
esp. in ~cake & porridge; *feel one's ~s
(colloq.), feel important, display self-
-importance. Hence ~'EN⁵ a. [OE āte,
pl. ātan, excl. E, of unkn. orig.]
oath, n. (pl. ōthz). 1. Solemn appeal to
God or revered or dreaded person or object in witness that statement is true or
promise shall be kept (take an, make,
swear an, ~, bind oneself thus; on ~,
having thus sworn, made or stated or
given by sworn person; BIBLE, CORPORAL¹,
~); (form of words containing) statement
or promise so corroborated (~ of allegiance, office, supremacy, etc.). 2. Name
of God etc. used as expletive to give emphasis or express anger etc., piece of profanity in speech, curse. [OE āth, OS ēth,
OHG eid, ON eithr, Goth aiths f. Gmc
*aithaz]
ob-, (before c-) oc-, (before f-) of-, (before
p-) op-, pref. f. L ob in the way of, occurring chiefly in wds already compounded
in L, w. senses: 1. Exposure, openness,
(object, obnoxious, obtrude, obverse). 2.
Meeting (occasion, occur, offend), facing
(observe, obstetric, obviate, obvious, opportune), direction (oblation, oblique, oblong,
obsecrate, obtest, offer), spontaneity or
friendliness (obey, obsequious, office). 3.
Opposition or hostility (objurgate, obloquy,
obstreperous, oppose, oppress, opprobrium,
oppugn) or resistance (obdurate, obmules-
cent, obstinate, obtuse). 4. Hindrance,
blocking, veiling, (obbligato, obese, obfus-
cate, oblige, obliterate, obscure, obsess,
obstacle, obstruct, obturate, occlude, occult,
oppilate). 5. Finality or completeness
(obiit, oblivion, obsolete, obtain, obtruncate,
occident, occupy). 6. (In mod. sci. wds)
inversely, in direction or manner contrary to the usual (obconical, obcordate,
oblanceolate, obovate, shaped like cone,
heart, spike, egg, tapering downwards).
ŏbblīga'tō (-ah-), a. & n. (mus.). 1. (Of accompaniment or part) inseparable, forming integral part of the composition, (opp.
ad libitum). 2. n. (pl. ~s). Such part or accompaniment. [It., f. L obligatus (OBLIGE)]
ŏb'dūrate (or -ūr⁴), a. Hardened, impenitent, stubborn. Hence ŏb'dūrACY n.,
~LY² adv., (or -ūr⁴). [ME, f. L OB(durare
harden f. durus hard), -ATE²]
ŏb'ĕah (-a), ŏb'ĭ¹, n. Kind of sorcery
practised by Negroes. [W. Afr.]
obēd'ience, n. Obeying as act or practice
or quality, submission to another's rule,
compliance with law or command, (in ~
to, actuated by or in accordance with;
passive ~, surrender of one's will to
another's without co-operation, also
compliance with commands irrespective
of their nature); (eccl., esp. R.-C.) being
obeyed, (sphere of) authority, district or
body of persons bound to ~, (return to the
~ of the Pope; not belonging to either the

Roman or the Byzantine ~). [ME, f. OF *obedience* f. L *obedientia* (OBEY, -ENCE)]

obēd'ient, a. Submissive to or complying with superior's will, dutiful, (|| *your* ~ *servant*, phase spoken formerly in courtesy, now only ironically, in taking leave, & written as concluding formula in letters of official or public character). Hence ~LY[2] adv. [ME, f. OF *obedient* (OBEY, -ENT)]

obēdiĕn'tiarў (-sha-), n. Holder of any office under superior in monastery or convent. [ME, f. med. L *obedientiarius* (OBEDIENCE, -ARY[1])]

obeis'ance (-bās-), n. Gesture, esp. bow or curtsy, expressing submission, respect, or salutation (arch. ; *make an, do, pay,* ~) ; deference, homage, submission, (*do, make, pay,* ~). [ME, f. OF *obeisance* (OBEY, -ANCE)]

ŏb'élisk, n. 1. Tapering usu. monolithic shaft of stone square or rectangular in section with pyramidal apex; ~-shaped mountain, tree, etc. **2.** (Also *obelus*) mark used in ancient MSS. to indicate that word or passage is spurious etc. (—, ÷) ; (also *obelus*) mark of reference to note in margin etc. (†; *double* ~, ‡). [f. L f. Gk *obeliskos* dim. of *obelos* spit]

ŏb'élize, -ise (-īz), v.t. Mark with the obelisk as spurious etc. [f. Gk *obelizō* (*obelos* see prec., -IZE)]

ŏb'élus, n. (pl. *-li*). See OBELISK.

obēse', a. Corpulent. So **obēs'ITY** n. [f. L OB(*esus* p.p., = having eaten, of *ĕdere* eat)]

obey' (-bā), v.t. & i. Perform bidding of, be obedient to ; execute (command); be actuated by (force, impulse); do what one is bidden. [ME, f. OF *obeir* f. L OB(*edire* = *audire* hear)]

ŏb'fusc|āte, v.t. Darken, obscure, (mind etc.); stupefy, bewilder. So ~A'TION n. [f. LL OB(*fuscare* f. *fuscus* dark), -ATE[3]]

obi[1]. See OBEAH.

ŏb'i[2], n. Bright broad sash worn by Japanese women & children. [Jap.]

ŏb'ĭit, v.i. 3rd sing. past (abbr. *ob.*). Died (with date of death). [L, f. OB(*ire it-* go) die]

ŏb'it, n. (arch.). Memorial service esp. in institution on anniversary of founder's or benefactor's death. [ME, f. OF *obit,* f. L *obitus* death, as prec.]

ŏb'ĭter, adv. By the way, in passing, (usu. ~ *dic'tum*, pl. *-ta*, judge's expression of opinion uttered in arguing point or giving judgement but not essential to his decision & therefore without binding authority; also gen., incidental remark). [L, = *ob iter* by the way]

obit'ūar|ў, n. & a. 1. Notice of death(s) esp. in newspaper, brief biography of deceased person; hence ~IST(1) n. **2.** adj. Recording a death, concerning deceased person. [f. med. L *obituarius* (L *obitus* death, see OBIT, -ARY[1])]

ŏb'ject[1], n. 1. Thing placed before eyes or presented to sense, material thing, thing observed with optical instrument or represented in picture. **2.** Person or thing of pitiable or ridiculous aspect. **3.** Person or thing to which action or feeling is directed, subject *of* or *for,* (*the Bible had been the* ~ *of his study; he is a proper* ~ *of* or *for charity*). **4.** Thing aimed at, end, purpose; *no* ~, formula in advertisements etc. announcing that the other party may make his own terms in the specified respect (*money, time, distance,* etc., *no* ~). **5.** (philos.). Thing thought of or apprehended as correlative to the thinking mind or subject, external thing, *the* non- -ego. **6.** (gram.). Noun or noun-equivalent governed by active transitive verb or by preposition (*direct, indirect,* ~, that primarily, secondarily, affected by action, as *shilling, him,* in *I gave him a shilling*). **7.** ~-*ball,* at which player aims his in billiards etc.; ~-*finder,* contrivance for registering position of ~ on mounted microscopic slide so as to find it again; ~-*glass* or -*lens,* lens in telescope etc. nearest the ~ ; ~-*lesson,* instruction about a material ~ that is present for inspection, (fig.) striking practical illustration of some principle; ~-*plate,* on which ~ is placed for microscopic examination: ~-*staff,* surveyor's levelling staff. Hence ~LESS a. [ME, f. med. L *objectum* thing presented to the mind, p.p. of L OB(*jicere ject-* throw)]

objĕct'[2], v.t. & i. Adduce (quality, fact) as objection (*to* theory etc.); state (usu. *that-*clause) as damaging fact *to* or *against* person etc.; state objection, feel or express disapproval, have objection or dislike *to* (*I* ~ *to being,* & incorrectly *to be, treated like this*; || *I* ~, words used in House of Commons in announcing intention to oppose a motion etc. & so shelve it as not unopposed business). Hence **objĕc'toR** n. (*conscientious* ~*or,* excused compulsory service, vaccination, etc. on pleading conscience). [ME, f. L *object-* (prec.)]

objĕc'ti|fў, v.t. Present as object of sense, make objective, express in concrete form, embody. Hence ~FICA'TION n. [OBJECT[1], -I-, -FY]

objĕc'tion, n. Objecting, thing objected, adverse reason or statement; expression or feeling of disapproval or dislike. [ME, f. OF, or LL *objectio* (OBJECT[1], -ION)]

objĕc'tionab|le (-sho-), a. Open to objection; undesirable, unpleasant, offensive, disapproved of. Hence ~LY[2] adv. [prec., -ABLE]

objĕc'tive, a. & n. 1. (philos.). Belonging not to the consciousness or the perceiving or thinking SUBJECT[2], but to what is presented to this, external to the mind, real. **2.** (Of person, writing, picture, etc.) dealing with outward things, exhibiting actual facts uncoloured by exhibitor's feelings or opinions; (med., of symptoms) observed by another & not only felt by patient, whence ~NESS, **objéctiv'ITY**, nn. **3**. (gram.). Constructed as, appropriate to, the object (~ *case* in English, that governed by transitive verb or preposition, distinguished in form from the subjective only in some personal pronouns, as *him*, cf. *he*; ~ *genitive*, as in ' the fear *of God* ', cf. SUBJECTIVE *genitive*). **4**. (Mil.) ~ *point*, towards which advance of troops is directed, (transf.) point aimed at; hence ~LY[2] adv. **5**. n.=OBJECT[1]-*glass*; (gram.) ~ case; (mil. & transf.) ~ point. [f. med. L *objectivus* (OBJECT[1], -IVE)]

objéc'tivism, n. Tendency to lay stress on the objective; doctrine that knowledge of non-ego is prior & superior to that of ego. [-ISM]

ob'jūrg|āte, v.t. Chide, scold. So ~A'TION n., ~ātORY (*or* -ērg'a-) a. [f. L OB(*jurgare* quarrel), -ATE[3]]

ob'lāte[1], n. Person dedicated to monastic or religious life or work. [f. (med. L sense of) L OB(*latus* p.p. of *ferre* bring)]

oblāte'[2] (*or* ōb[4]), a. (geom.). (Of spheroid) flattened at poles (cf. PROLATE). [as prec.; sense of *ob-* doubtful]

oblā'tion, n. (Presenting of bread & wine to God in) Eucharist; thing offered to God, sacrifice, victim; donation for pious uses. Hence ~AL (-sho-), **ōb'latORY**, aa. [ME, f. OF or LL *oblatio* (OBLATE[1], -ION)]

ob'li̇̄gāte, v.t. Bind (person legally or morally) *to* do (chiefly in p.p.). [f. L (OBLIGE, -ATE[3])]

obli̇̄gā'tion, n. Binding agreement esp. one enforceable under legal penalty, written contract or bond; constraining power of a law, precept, duty, contract, etc. (*of* ~, obligatory); one's bounden duty, a duty, burdensome task; (indebtedness for) service or benefit (*be, put, under an* ~; *repay an* ~). [ME, f. OF f. L *obligationem* (OBLIGE, -ATION)]

obli̇̄g'atory (*or* ōb'li̇̄gā-), a. Legally or morally binding, imperative & not merely permissive; constituting an obligation. [ME, f. LL *obligatorius* (foll., -TORY)]

oblige', v.t. Bind (person, one*self*) by oath, promise, contract, etc., *to* person or *to* do (arch., legal; also with *oath* etc. as subj.); be binding on; make indebted by conferring favour, gratify *by doing* or *with*; (colloq.) make contribution to entertainment (*with* song etc., or abs.); (pass.) be bound (*to* person) by gratitude (*for* small service); constrain, compel, *to* do. [ME, f. OF *obliger* f. L OB(*ligare* bind)]

obligee', n. (Law) person to whom another is bound by contract or to whom bond is given (cf. OBLIGOR); (rare) person who has received a favour. [prec., -EE]

obli'ging, a. Courteous, accommodating, ready to do kindness, complaisant. Hence ~LY[2] adv., ~NESS n. [-ING[2]]

ōb'li̇̄gōr, n. (legal). One who binds him-

self to another or gives bond. [OBLIGE, -OR]

oblique' (-ēk), a., & v.i. **1**. Slanting, declining from the vertical or horizontal, diverging from straight line or course. **2**. (Geom.) (of line, plane figure, surface) inclined at other than right angle, (of angle) acute or obtuse, (of cone, cylinder, etc.) with axis not perpendicular to plane of base; (anat.) neither parallel nor perpendicular to body's or limb's long axis; (bot., of leaf) with unequal sides. **3**. Not going straight to the point, roundabout, indirect. **4**. (gram.). ~ *case*, other than nominative or vocative; ~ *oration* or *narration* or *speech*, speaker's words with the changes of person, tense, etc., usual in reports, indirect speech; hence or cogn. ~LY[2] (-ēkl-) adv., **obli'quITY** n. **5**. v.i. (esp. mil.). Advance ~ly. [f. L *obliquus*]

oblit'er|āte, v.t. Blot out, efface, erase, destroy, leave no clear traces of. So ~A'TION n. [f. L *oblitterare*, see -ATE[3]]

obliv'ion, n. Having or being forgotten, disregard, unregarded state, (*Act, Bill, of O*~, amnesty; *fall into* ~, be forgotten or disused). [ME, f. OF, f. L *oblivionem* f. *oblivisci* forget, -ION]

obliv'ious, a. Forgetful, unmindful, (*of*); (poet.) of, inducing, oblivion. Hence ~LY[2] adv., ~NESS n. [ME, f. L *obliviosus* (*oblivium* forgetfulness as prec., -OSE[1])]

ōb'lŏng, a. & n. **1**. Deviating from square or circular form by having one long axis, (of spheroid) prolate; (geom.) rectangular with adjacent sides unequal; (of paper, book, rectangular postage stamp or panel, etc.) greater in breadth than height; hence **oblŏng'o-** (-nggō) comb. form (bot.). **2**. n. ~ figure or object. [f. L OB(*longus* long)]

ōb'loquy̆, n. Abuse, detraction; being generally ill spoken of. [ME, f. LL *obloquium* f. L OB(*loqui* speak) gainsay]

ōbmūtĕs'c|ence, n. Obstinate silence. So ~ENT a. [f. L OB(*mutescere* f. *mutus* dumb, -ESCENT, -ENCE)]

obnō'xious (-kshus), a. Liable *to* harm or evil or attack (now rare); offensive, objectionable, disliked, whence ~LY[2] adv. Hence ~NESS n. [f. L *obnoxiosus*, or *obnoxius* +-OUS]

ōb'ŏe, n. Wood-wind double-reed instrument of treble pitch & plaintive incisive tone; organ reed-stop imitating this. Hence **ōb'ŏIST**(3) n. [It., f. F as HAUTBOY]

ōb'ol, n. Ancient-Greek silver coin. [f. L f. Gk *obolos*]

obscēne', a. Repulsive, filthy, loathsome, (arch.); grossly indecent, lewd. Hence or cogn. ~LY[2] adv., **obscēn'ITY** n. [f. F *obscène* or L *obscenus*]

obscūr'ant, n. Opponent of inquiry, enlightenment, & reform. Hence ~ISM(3) n., ~IST(2) n. & a. [= G *obscurant*, f. L (OBSCURE, -ANT)]

obscūre', a. & n., & v.t. **1**. Dark, dim, (~ *rays*, invisible heat-rays of solar spectrum); (of colour) dingy, dull, indefinite;

indistinct, not clear; hidden, remote
from observation; unnoticed; unknown
to fame, humble; unexplained, doubtful;
not perspicuous or clearly expressed;
hence or cogn. ~LY² adv., obscūr′ITY n.
2. n. Obscurity, indistinctness. 3. v.t.
Make ~, dark, indistinct, or unintelligible; dim glory of, outshine; conceal
from sight; so ŏbscūrA′TION n. [ME; adj.
f. OF *obscur* f. L *obscurus*; vb f. adj. or f.
L *obscurare*]

ŏbscūr′um pēr ŏbscūr′īus, n.=IGNOTUM
PER IGNOTIUS. [L, = the obscure by the
still more obscure]

ŏbsĕcrā′tion, n. Earnest entreaty; Litany petition beginning with *By.* [ME, f.
L *obsecratio* f. OB(*secrare* = *sacrare* f. *sacer*
sacred) entreat]

ŏb′sĕquies (-ĭz), n. pl. Funeral rites, a
funeral. Hence obsē′quiAL a. [ME; pl.
of obs. *obsequy* f. OF *obseque* f. med. L
obsequiae mixture of L *exsequiae* funeral
with *obsequium* see foll.]

obsē′quious, a. Obedient, dutiful, (arch.);
servile, fawning. Hence~LY² adv.,~NESS
n. [ME, f. L *obsequiosus* f. OB(*sequium* f.
sequi follow) compliance]

obsērv′|ance (-z-), n. Keeping or per-
formance of (also *of*) law, duty, custom,
ritual, etc.; act of religious or ceremonial
character, customary rite; the rule of a
religious order; ‖ paying of deference or
respect (arch.), also~ANCY n. [ME, f. OF,
f. L *observantia* (OBSERVE, -ANCE)]

obsērv′ant (-z-), a. & n. 1. Attentive in
observance; acute or diligent in taking
notice; hence ~LY² adv. 2. n. Member
of branch of Franciscan order that observes the strict rule. [F (OBSERVE,
-ANT)]

ŏbservā′tion (-z-), n. 1. Noticing or being
noticed, perception, faculty of taking
notice; *post, attitude, of* ~, favourable for
watching from or in; ~ *car*, in train esp.
in U.S., so built as to afford good views.
2. (mil.). Watching of fortress or hostile
position or movements (*army* etc. *of* ~, so
engaged; ~ *post*, abbr. *O. P.* or *O. Pip*,
esp. for watching effect of artillery fire).
3. Accurate watching & noting of phenomena as they occur in nature (cf. *experiment*) with regard to cause & effect or
mutual relations. 4. Taking of sun's or
other heavenly body's altitude to find
latitude or longitude. 5. Remark or
statement, esp. one of the nature of comment. Hence ~AL a., ~alLY² adv.,
(-zervāsho-). [ME, f. L *observatio* (OBSERVE,
-ATION)]

obsērv′atorў (-z-), n. Building etc. whence
natural, esp. astronomical, phenomena
may be observed. [f. F *observatoire*, f. L
observare see foll., -TORY]

obsērv|e′ (-z-), v.t. & i. 1. Keep, follow,
adhere to, perform duly, (law, command,
appointed time, method, principle, silence,

rite, anniversary, etc.). 2. Perceive, mark,
watch, take notice of, become conscious
of, (the ~*ed of all* ~*ers*, person etc. on
whom etc. attention is concentrated).
3. Examine & note (phenomena) without
aid of experiment. 4. Say, esp. by way of
comment; make remark(s) *on.* Hence
~′ABLE a., ~′ER¹ n. (esp., interested spectator, person carried in aeroplane to note
enemy's position etc., person trained to
watch for & identify aircraft; *O*~*er*, as
newspaper title), ~′inģLY² adv. [ME, f.
OF *observer* f. L OB(*servare* keep)]

obsĕss′, v.t. (Of evil spirit, delusion, or
fixed idea) haunt, harass, preoccupy, fill
mind of, (~*ed by, with*). So obsē′ssION
(-shn) n. [f. L OB(*sidēre sess-=sedēre* sit)
besiege]

obsid′ian, n. Dark vitreous lava or
volcanic rock like bottle-glass. [f. L
obsidianus, false reading for *Obsianus*
(*Obsius* personal name, -AN)]

ŏbsolĕs′c|ent, a. Becoming obsolete, go-
ing out of use or date; (biol., of organ
once developed more fully) gradually disappearing. So ~ENCE n. [f. L OB(*solescere*
f. *solēre* be accustomed, see -ESCENT), -ENT]

ŏb′solēte, a. & n. 1. Disused, discarded,
antiquated; (biol.) less developed than
formerly or in cognate species, rudimentary; hence ~NESS, ŏb′solētISM(3, 4), nn.
2. n. ~ person or thing. [f. L *obsoletus*
p.p. as prec.]

ŏb′stacle, n. Hindrance, impediment, (~-
race, in which artificial or natural ~s
have to be passed). [ME, f. OF, f. L
obstaculum f. OB(*stare* stand) impede]

obstĕt′ric(al), aa. Of midwifery, of childbirth & its antecedents & sequels, as
branch of medicine & surgery. Hence
obstĕt′rICS, ŏbstĕtrī′CIAN (-ĭshn), nn.
[irreg. f. L *obstetricius* f. *obstetrix* midwife
f. OB(*stare* or *sistere* stand), -TRIX]

ŏb′stin|ate, a. Stubborn, inflexible, self-
willed, refractory. Hence or cogn. ~ACY
n., ~ateLY² adv. [ME, f. L *obstinatus* p.p.
of OB(*stinare* deriv. form of *stare* stand)
persist]

obstrĕp′erous, a. Noisy, vociferous; turbulent, unruly, noisily resisting control.
Hence ~LY² adv., ~NESS n. [f. L *obstre-
perus* f. OB(*strepere* make noise), -OUS]

obstrŭct′, v.t. & i. Block up, fill with impediments, make impassable or difficult
of passage; prevent or retard progress of,
impede; practise (esp. Parliamentary)
obstruction. [f. L OB(*struere struct*- build)]

obstrŭc′tion, n. Blocking or being
blocked, making or becoming more or
less impassable; hindering, esp. of Parliamentary business by talking against time,
whence ~ISM(3), ~IST(2), (-sho-), nn.;
obstacle (~-*guard*, bar fixed before locomotive to remove ~s from rails). [f. L
obstructio (prec., -ION)]

obstrŭc′tive, a. & n. 1. Causing, intended

to produce, obstruction; hence ~LY[2] adv., ~NESS n. 2. n. ~ person, esp. in House of Commons. [as OBSTRUCT, -IVE]

obtain', v.t. & i. Acquire, have granted one, get, whence ~MENT n. (rare), ~ABLE a.; be prevalent or established or in vogue. [ME, f. OF obtenir f. L OB(tinēre = tenēre hold) keep]

obtĕct', a. (entom.). (Of the pupae of certain insects) enclosed in an outer chitinous case. [f. L OB(tegere tect- cover)]

obtĕst', v.t. & i. (arch.). Adjure, supplicate, call to witness; protest. So **ŏbtĕsta'TION** n. [f. L OB(testari f. testis witness)]

obtrude' (-ōōd), v.t. Thrust forward (upon or on person or his attention) importunately. So **obtru'sION** (-ōōzhn) n., **obtrus'IVE** a., **obtrus'iveLY**[2] adv., **obtrus'iveNESS** n., (-ōō-). [f. L OB(trudere trus- push)]

obtrŭnc'āte, v.t. Cut off head of, top. [f. L OB(truncare f. truncus maimed), -ATE[3]]

obtŭnd', v.t. (med.). Blunt, deaden, (sense or faculty). [ME, f. L OB(tundere tusbeat)]

ŏb'tūr|āte, v.t. Stop up, close, seal, (orifice in body, breech of gun, etc.). Hence or cogn. ~A'TION, ~ātoR, nn. [f. L obturare, -ATE[3]]

obtūse', a. Of blunt form, not sharp--pointed or sharp-edged; (geom., of angle) greater than one & less than two right angles; (of pain, the senses) dull, not acute; stupid, slow of perception. Hence ~LY[2] adv., ~NESS n., **obtūs'I**- comb. form. [f. L p.p. of OBTUNDere]

ŏb'vĕrse, a. & n. 1. Narrower at base or point of attachment than at apex (esp. in nat. hist., including as general term OBovate, OBlanceolate, etc.); answering as counterpart to something else; hence ~LY[2] adv. 2. n. Side of coin or medal bearing the head or principal design (cf. REVERSE); face of anything meant to be presented, front; counterpart of a fact or truth. [f. L obversus p.p. (foll.)]

obvĕrt', v.t. (log.). Infer another proposition with contradictory predicate by changing quality of (proposition). So **obvĕr'sION** (-shn) n. [f. L OB(vertere versturn)]

ŏb'viāte, v.t. Clear away, get rid of, get round, neutralize (danger, inconvenience, etc.). [f. LL OB(viare f. via way) withstand]

ŏb'vious, a. Open to eye or mind, clearly perceptible, palpable, indubitable. Hence ~LY[2] adv., ~NESS n. [f. L obvius (ob viam in the way), -OUS]

oc-, pref. See OB-.

ŏcari'na (-rē-), n. Small egg-shaped porcelain or metal musical wind-instrument. [It. (oca goose, -INA[1])]

occā'sion (-zhn), n., & v.t. 1. Juncture suitable for doing something, opportunity, (take ~, avail oneself of opportunity to do; take ~ by the FORELOCK[1]). 2. Reason,

ground, justification, incitement, need, (there is no ~ to be angry; avoid all ~s of quarrel; Queen has no ~ for services of officer, formula of dismissal; gave ~ to a burst of laughter). 3. Subsidiary, incidental, or immediate cause (the cause of a revolution may be obscure while its ~ is obvious). 4. pl. Affairs, business, (esp. go about one's lawful ~s). 5. (Particular time marked by) special occurrence (on this festive ~; on the ~ of his marriage; celebrate the ~; rise to the ~, show requisite energy etc.; this is a great ~); (up)on ~, whenever need arises, now & then. 6. v.t. Be the ~ or cause of, bring about esp. incidentally, cause (action etc., or person or thing to do). [ME, f. OF, or L occasio f. OC(cidere cas- = cadere fall), -ION]

occā'sional (-zho-), a. Arising out of, made or meant for, adapted for use on, acting on, special occasion(s); happening irregularly as occasion presents itself; coming now & then, not regular or frequent; ~ cause, secondary cause, occasion, also apparent cause (see foll.); || ~ licence (to sell liquor only at specified times & places). Hence ~ITY (-ăl²) n., ~LY² adv. [-AL]

occā'sional|ism (-zho-), n. Doctrine of some Cartesians that volition & sensation are connected with the following & preceding material phenomena not causally but as separate productions of God on the same occasion. So ~IST(2) n. [-ISM]

Oc'cident (ŏks-), n. The west; western Europe; Europe; Europe & America; America; European as opposed to Oriental civilization, whence **ŏcciden'talISM(3)** n., **ŏcciden'talIZE(3)** v.t., **ŏcciden'talIST** (2, 3) n., (-ks-). So **ŏcciden'tAL** a., **ŏcciden'talLY²** adv., (-ks-). [ME, f. OF, or f. L occident- setting (OCCASION, -ENT)]

ŏc'ciput (ŏks-), n. Back of head. So **ŏccip'itAL** a., **ŏccip'ito-** comb. form, (-ks-). [L OC(ciput -itis = caput head)]

occlude' (-lōō-), v.t. (sci.). Stop up, close, obstruct, (pores, orifice); (chem.) absorb & retain (gases). So **occlu'sION** (-lōōzhn) n., (also, meteor.) closing of the cold front on to the warm front in a depression, **occlus'OR** (-lōō-) n. [f. L OC(cludere -clus- = claudere shut)]

occŭlt'[1], a. Kept secret, esoteric; recondite, mysterious, beyond the range of ordinary knowledge; involving the supernatural, mystical, magical, whence ~ISM(3), ~IST(2, 3), nn.; the ~, that which is ~. Hence ~LY² adv., ~NESS n. [f. L OC(culere -cult- cf. celare hide)]

occŭlt'[2], v.t. & i. Conceal, cut off from view by passing in front, (usu. astron., & applied only when concealing body is of much greater apparent size than concealed); ~ing light in lighthouses, one that is cut off at regular intervals. So **ŏcculta'TION** n. [f. L occultare frequent. as prec.]

ŏcc'ŭp|ant, n. Person holding property,

esp. land, in actual possession; one who occupies, or resides or is in, a place; one who establishes title to unowned thing by taking possession. Hence ~ANCY n. [F, or f. L as OCCUPY, -ANT]

occupā′tion, n. Occupying or being occupied; taking or holding possession, esp. of country or district by military force (*army of* ~, left to hold occupied region till regular government is set up), tenure, occupancy; what occupies one, means of filling one's time, temporary or regular employment, business, calling, pursuit; || ~ *franchise*, right to vote as tenant; ~ *bridge*, *road*, etc., private for use of occupiers of land. Hence ~AL (-sho) a., (esp.) incident to or arising from a person's ~ (~*al disease*), based on or utilizing esp. light employment (~*al therapy*). [ME, f. OF, f. L *occupationem* (OCCUPY, -ATION)]

occ′upier, n. Person in (esp. temporary or subordinate) possession esp. of land or house, holder, occupant. [ME, f. foll., -ER¹]

occ′upy, v.t. Take possession of (country, region, town, strategic position) by military force or settlement; hold (office), reside in, tenant; take up or fill (space, time), reside or be in (place, position); busy, keep engaged, (esp. in pass. & refl.; *occupied*, ~ one*self*, *with* or *in*). [ME; irreg. f. OF *occuper* f. L OC(*cupare* cf. *capere* take) seize]

occur′, v.i. (-rr-). Be met with, be found, exist, in some place or conditions; come into one's mind (esp. *it* ~*s* or ~*red to me that* ~); take place, befall, happen. [f. L OC(*currere* run) go to meet]

occu′rrence, n. Happening (*is of frequent* ~, often occurs); incident, event. [F, = med. L *occurrentia* (prec., -ENT), -ENCE]

ocean (ō′shn), n. Great body of water surrounding the land of the globe; one of the main areas into which geographers divide this (usu. reckoned as five, the *Atlantic*, *Pacific*, *Indian*, *Arctic*, & *Antarctic*, *O*~*s*; *German* ~, = NORTH *Sea*); the sea (also poet, without *the*, as *the dark unfathomed caves of* ~); immense expanse or quantity of anything (often ~*s of*); ~ *greyhound*, swift ship, esp. passenger liner; ~ *lane*, track prescribed for steamers; ~ *tramp*, cargo-carrying steamer not engaged in single trade. Hence ~OG′RAPHY (ōsha-) n., ~OGRAPH′IC(AL) (osēa-, ōsha-) aa., ~WARD(S) adv. [ME, f. L f. Gk *ōkeanos* stream encircling earth's disc, Atlantic]

Ocean′ia (ōshǐ-, ōsǐ-), n. Islands of Pacific & adjacent seas. [f. F *Océanie* (prec., -IA¹)]

Ocean′ian (ōshǐăn′yan, ōsǐ-), a. & n. (Native) of Oceania. [-AN]

oceăn′ic, O-, (ōshǐ-, ōsǐ-) a. Of, like, etc., the ocean; of Oceania. [-IC]

Oce′anid (os-), n. (pl. ~*s*, ~*es* pr. -ăn′ĭdēz). Ocean nymph of Greek mythology. [f. Gk *Ōkeanis* -*idos* daughter of Ocean]

ocell′us, n. (pl. -*lī*). One of simple as

opposed to compound eyes of insects; facet of compound eye; spot of colour surrounded by ring of other colour, whence ō′cellATE², -ātěd, aa. [L, dim. of *oculus* eye]

ō′celot, n. Animal of cat tribe of S. & Central America, resembling leopard. [F, abridged by Buffon f. Mex. *tlal*(*ocelotl* jaguar) of the field, & applied to different animal]

|| **och** (see Ap.), int. = *oh*, *ah*, used in Scotland & Ireland.

ŏchlŏc′racў (-kl-), n. Mob-rule. Hence **ŏch′locRAT** n., **ŏchlocRAT′IC** a., (-kl-). [f. F *ochlocratie* f. Gk *okhlokratia* (*okhlos* mob, -CRACY)]

ochre (ōk′er), n. Kinds of native earth consisting of clay & hydrated oxide of iron used as pigments varying from light yellow to brown; pale brownish yellow. Hence ~ISH (ōk′er-), **ochrA′CEOUS** (-krāshus), ~OUS (ōk′rǐ-), **ŏch′rOUS**, **ŏch′rY²**, (-kr-), aa., ~O- (ōk′rǐ-) comb. form. [ME, f. OF *ocre* f. L f. Gk *ōkhra* yellow ochre f. *ōkhros* yellow]

-ock, suf. forming nn. orig. w. dim. sense (*hill*~, *bitt*~, *bull*~, *padd*~), which many of them have lost (*padd*~, *bull*~, *poll*~); *hass*~, *bann*~, *matt*~, are prob. of different orig.

o′clock. See CLOCK¹.

oct-. = OCTA-, OCTO-, before vowel.

ŏc′ta-, comb. form of Gk *oktō* eight. Hence **ŏctăm′EROUS** a.

ŏc′tachŏrd (-k-), a. & n. Eight-stringed (musical instrument); series of eight notes, e.g. the diatonic scale. Hence ~AL (-kŏrd²) a. [f. L f. Gk *oktakhordos* (prec., CHORD)]

ŏc′tad, n. Group of eight. [f. LL f. Gk *oktas* f. *oktō* eight, -AD(1)]

ŏc′tagon, n. & a. Plane figure with eight angles & sides, object or building of such section; so **ŏctăg′onAL** a., **ŏctăg′onALLY²** adv.; (adj.) ~al. [f. L f. Gk *oktagōnos* (OCTA-, *gōnia* angle)]

ŏctahē′dr|on, n. Solid figure contained by eight plane faces, & usu. by eight triangles (*regular* ~*on*, by equal & equilateral triangles); body, esp. crystal, of regular ~al form. So ~AL a. [f. Gk *oktaedron* (OCTA-, *hedra* seat)]

ŏc′tāne, n. Hydrocarbon of the paraffin series; *high*-~, (of fuels used in internal-combustion engines) having good anti-knock properties, not detonating readily during the power stroke. [OCT-, -ANE(2)]

ŏc′tant, n. **1.** Arc of circle=1/8 of circumference; 1/8 of circular area contained within two radii & arc; one of eight parts into which three planes intersecting (esp. at right angles) at point divide space round it. **2.** (astron.). Point in planet's apparent course 45° distant from given point, esp. point at which moon is 45° from conjunction or opposition with sun. **3.** Instrument in form of graduated eighth of circle used in astronomy &

navigation. [ṛ. L *octans* (L *octo* eight, cf. QUADRANT)]

ŏc'tarchy (-kĭ), n. Aggregate of eight petty kingdoms (substituted by some historians for HEPTARCHY). [OCTA-, cf. HEPTARCHY]

octaroon. See OCTOROON.

ŏc'tastyle, a. & n. (Portico or building) with eight columns at end or in front. [f. L f. Gk *oktastulos* (OCTA-, *stulos* pillar)]

ŏc'tateuch (-k), n. First 8 O.-T. books. [f. LL f. Gk OCTA*teukhos*, cf. PENTATEUCH]

ŏc'tave (-ĭv), n. **1.** The day week of a festival, eight days including festival & its day week. **2.** Group or stanza of eight lines, octet. **3.** (mus.). Note produced by twice or half the vibration rate of given note & eight diatonic degrees above·or below it (*second* ~, ~ *of the* ~ in same direction; so *third* etc. ~); interval between note & its ~; series of notes filling this; note & its ~ sounding together. **4.** Group of eight. **5.** A fencing position. **6.** ‖ Wine-cask holding 13½ gal. **7.** ~-*coupler*, device connecting organ-keys an ~ apart; ~-*flute*, piccolo, also organ flute-stop an ~ higher than the ordinary. [(1) ME, f. OF, f. L *octava dies* eighth day by inclusive reckoning (*octavus* f. *octo* eight); (2) repr. OTTAVA RIMA; (3) F, f. med. L *octava* (*vox*)]

octāv'ō, n. (abbr. *8vo*, *oct.*; pl. ~s). (Size of) book or page given by folding sheet three times to form quire of eight leaves. [f. L IN⁵ *octavo* (prec.)]

octāv'us, See PRIMUS¹.

octĕnn'ial, a. Lasting, recurring every, eight years. [f. LL OCT(*ennium* f. *annus* year) period of eight years, -AL]

octĕt(te)', n. (Composition for) eight singers or players; group of eight lines, esp. the first eight of sonnet. [f. L *octo* eight, after DUET, QUARTET(TE)]

octill'ion (-lyon), n. ‖ Eighth power of million (1 followed by 48 ciphers). Hence ~TH² a. & n. [F (now = ninth power of thousand) as prec. after MILLION]

‖ **octingĕntĕn'arў** (-j-), n. 800th anniversary. [f. L *octingenti* 800, after CENTENARY]

octo-, oct-, comb. form of L *octo*, & occas. (= OCTA-) of Gk *oktō*, eight.

Octŏb'er (ŏ-), n. Tenth month; beer brewed in ~ (arch.). [OE, f. L (prec.), cf. DECEMBER; ME *Octobre* f. OF]

Octŏb'rist (ŏ-), n. & a. (Member) of moderate party in Russian Duma. [*Oct.* 30, 1905, date of Imperial Constitutional Manifesto]

octōcĕntĕn'arў (*or* -sĕn'tĕn-), **octōcĕntĕnn'ial**, nn. (Irreg. for) OCTINGENTENARY.

octōdĕ'cimō, n. (abbr. *18mo*; pl.~s). (Size of) book or page given by folding sheets into eighteen leaves. [for IN⁵ ~ f. L OCTO-(*decimus* tenth) eighteenth, cf. OCTAVO]

octōgĕnār'ian, a. & n. (Person) between 79 & 90 years old. [f. L *octogenarius* (*octogeni* eighty each, -ARY¹), -AN¹]

ŏc'tonal, a. Proceeding by eights (of coinage, numeral system, etc.). [f. L *octoni*, see foll., -AL]

octōnār'ian, a. & n. (pros.). Eight-foot (line). [f. L *octonarius versus* eight-foot line (*octoni* eight each f. *octo* eight, -ARY¹), -AN]

ŏc'tonarў, a. & n. = OCTONAL; (n.) group of eight, eight-line stanza (esp. of divisions of *Ps.* 119). [see prec.]

ŏc'topus, n. (pl. ~es). (Kinds of) cephalopod mollusc with eight suckered arms round mouth; organized & usu. harmful ramified power or influence. [f. Gk *oktopous* eight-footed (OCTO-, *pous* foot)]

octorōōn', -ta-, n. Offspring of quadroon & white, person of one-eighth Negro blood. [irreg. f. OCTO- after QUADROON]

octosўllăb'ic, a. & n. Eight-syllable (verse). [f. LL OCTO(*syllabus* f. *syllaba* SYLLABLE), -IC]

octosўll'able, n. & a. = prec.; word of eight syllables. [see prec.]

ŏc'troi (-rwab), n. Duty levied in some continental countries on goods entering town; place where, officials by whom, it is levied. [F (*octroyer* grant, as AUTHORIZE)]

ŏc'tŭple, a., n., & v.t. Eightfold; (n.) product after multiplication by eight *of*; (vb) multiply by eight. [f. L *octuplus* a. (*octo* eight, cf. DOUBLE)]

ŏc'ūlar, a. & n. Of, for; by, with, etc., the eye(s) or sight, visual, (~ *demonstration*, proof appealing to the eyes); (n.) eye-piece of optical instrument. Hence ~LY² adv. [f. LL *ocularis* (*oculus* eye, -AR¹)]

ŏc'ūlarist, n. Maker of artificial eyes. [f. F *oculariste* (prec., -IST)]

ŏc'ūlate, -āted, aa. = OCELLATE. [f. L *oculus* eye, -ATE²]

ŏc'ūlist, n. Specialist in eye-diseases. Hence ~is'tic a. [f. F *oculiste* (L *oculus* eye, -IST)]

ŏc'ūlo-, comb. form of L *oculus* eye, (-o-), as ~*nās'al* of eye & nose.

ŏd, n. Power assumed to pervade nature & account for magnetism, crystallization, chemical action, mesmerism, etc. [arbitrary formation of Baron v. Reichenbach 1788–1869]

ŏd'alisque (-k), n. Eastern female slave or concubine, esp. in Turkish Sultan's seraglio. [F, f. Turk. *odaliq* (*odah* chamber, -*liq* function)]

ŏdd, a. & n.. **1.** Left over when the rest have been divided into two numerically equal sets (*the* ~ *man*, to whom casting-vote falls in uneven-numbered committee etc.; *the* ~ *trick* in whist, thirteenth when each side has won six; ~ *man out*, way of selecting one of three persons by tossing coins till only two agree). **2.** (Of number) not divisible by two (~ *& even*, a game of chance); (of things or persons numbered consecutively) bearing such number. **3.** (Appended to number, sum, weight, etc.) with something over of lower denomination etc. (*forty* ~, between 40 & 50; *sixty thousand* ~, with some extra hundreds, tens, or units; *sixty*~ *thousand*, between 60 & 70 thousand; *twelve pounds* ~, with some shillings or pence). **4.** By which round number, given sum, etc., is exceeded (*Here is a pound note; pay the bill & keep the* ~ *money. There are* 1006; *what shall we do with the*~ *six?*). **5.** Additional, casual, beside the reckoning, unconnected, unoccupied, incalculable, (*picks up* ~ *jobs; do it at* ~ *moments*; *in some* ~ *corner*; ~ *numbers, volumes,* belonging to incomplete sets of magazines etc.). **6.** Extraordinary, strange, queer, remarkable, eccentric, whence ~'ɪsʜ¹(2) a., ~'ʟʏ² adv. **7.** ~'*fellow*, member of friendly society of Oddfellows with rites imitative of freemasonry; hence ~'ɴᴇss n. **8.** n. (golf). *The* ~, the stroke which one player has played more than his opponent (opp. *the like*). [ME, f. ON *odda*- in *odda-mathr* third man, odd man, *odda-tala* odd number, f. *oddi* angle, triangle, cogn. w. OE *ord* tip]

ŏdd'ĭtў, n. Strangeness; peculiar trait; queer person; fantastic object, strange event. [-ɪᴛʏ]

ŏdd'ments, n. pl. Odds & ends. [-ᴍᴇɴᴛ]

ŏdds, n. pl. (formerly always, & still in phrases as below, treated as sing.). Inequalities (*make* ~ *even*, do away with these); difference (*what's the* ~?, what does it matter?); variance, strife, (*are at* ~ *with fate*); balance of advantage (*the* ~ *are in our favour; have fought against longer* ~); equalizing allowance to weaker competitor (*give, receive,* ~); ratio between amounts staked by parties to bet (*lay, give,* ~ *of three to one,* said of party offering the advantage; *take* ~, accept the advantage; ~*-on*, state of betting when ~ are laid); chances or balance of probability in favour of some result (*it is* ~ *or long* ~ *that* or *but, the* ~ *are that, he will do it*); ~ *& ends*, remnants, stray articles, (perh. alteration of earlier *odd ends*). [app. pl. of ODD used as n.; cf. *news*]

ōde, n. (Orig.) poem meant to be sung (*choral* ~, song of chorus in Greek play etc.); (mod.) rhymed or rarely unrhymed lyric often in form of address, usu. of exalted style and enthusiastic tone, often in varied or irregular metre, & usu. between 50 & 200 lines in length. [f. F, f. LL *oda* f. Gk *ōidē* contr. of *aoidē* (*aeidō* sing)]

-ode, suf. forming nn. w. sense *thing of the nature of* (*geode, phyllode*); *anode, cathode, electrode,* are not examples. [f. Gk -*ōdēs* adj. ending (-o-, -*eidēs* -like)]

ōdē'um, n. (pl. -*s*, -*ĕa*). Building for musical performances, esp. among ancient Greeks & Romans. [f. L f. Gk *ōideion*]

ŏd'ĭc, a. Of OD. [-ɪᴄ]

ŏd'ious, a. Hateful, repulsive. Hence ~ʟʏ² adv., ~ɴᴇss n. [ME, f. OF *odieus* f. L *odiosus* (ODIUM, -OSE¹)]

ōd'ium, n. General or widespread dislike or reprobation incurred by person or attaching to action (*exposed me to* ~; *the* ~ *of the transaction*); ~ *theolo'gĭcum,* bitterness notoriously characterizing theologians who disagree. [L, = hatred]

odometer. See hod-.

odŏn't|(o)-, comb. form of Gk *odous odontos* tooth, as ~*orhŷnc'ous,* having toothlike serrations in the bill; ~*oglŏss'um,* kinds of orchids with large beautifully coloured flowers with tongue-shaped lips; ~ᴏɪᴅ; *ŏdontŏl'ogʏ.*

ōdorif'erous, a. Diffusive (usu. agreeable) scent, fragrant. Hence ~ʟʏ² adv. [ME, f. L *odorifer* (ODOUR, -FEROUS)]

ōd'orous, a. (chiefly poet.).=prec. Hence ~ʟʏ² adv. [foll., -ous]

ōd'our (-der), n. Pleasant or unpleasant smell, whence ~ʟᴇss a.; fragrance; (arch., usu. pl.) substance(s) emitting sweet scent, perfume(s); (fig.) savour, trace, (*no* ~ *of intolerance attaches to it*); *good* or *bad* or *ill* repute or favour (*is in bad* ~ *with the nonconformists*); ~ *of sanctity,* reputation for holiness (orig. lit., sweet ~ exhaled by dying or exhumed saint). [ME, f. AF *odour,* OF *odor* f. L *odorem* -OR)]

ōd'ўl, n. = OD. [-ʏʟ]

Od'ўssey (ŏ-), n. (pl. ~*s*). One of two great ancient-Greek national epics (cf. ILIAD) describing adventures of Odysseus or Ulysses returning from siege of Troy; any of the 24 books of this (*in the fourth* etc. ~); series of wanderings, long adventurous journey. [f. L f. Gk *Odusseia* (*Odusseus,* -ɪA¹)]

oe'cist (ēs-), n. Founder of (esp. ancient- -Greek) colony. [f. Gk *oikistēs* (*oikizō* settle f. *oikos* house, -ɪsᴛ)]

oecŏl'ogў (ēk-), n. Var. of ECOLOGY.

oecūmĕn'ical (ēk-), a. Of or representing the whole Christian world or universal church, general, universal, catholic, (of general councils of early, & of mod. R.-C., Church) world-wide. So **oecūmĕni'cɪᴛʏ** (ēk-) n. [f. LL f. Gk *oikoumenikos* f. *hē oikoumenē* the inhabited (earth) f. *oikeō* inhabit, -ᴀʟ]

oedēm'a (ēd-), n. (path.; no pl.). Swollen state of tissue etc. with serous fluid, local dropsy. Hence ~ᴛᴏsᴇ¹, ~ᴛᴏᴜs, aa., ~-tousʟʏ² adv., (ĕdĕm⁴ or ēdĕm⁴). [f. Gk *oidēma -atos* (*oideō* swell)]

Oed'ipus (ēd-), n. Solver of riddles; ~ *complex,* a sexual complex held by psycho- -analysts of the Freudian school to influence the child in regard to the parent of opposite sex. [f. Gk *Oidipous,* who guessed the Sphinx's riddle, & in ignorance married his mother]

o'er (ōr), adv. & prep. = OVER (poet.).

oer'stĕd (ẽr-), n. Unit of magnetic force. [O~, Danish physicist (d. 1851)]

oesŏph'ag|us (ēs-), n. (pl.~*i* pr. -jī, ~*uses*). Canal from mouth to stomach, gullet. Hence **oesophă'gĕᴀʟ** (-j-) a., ~o- comb. form. [f. Gk *oisophagos*]

oes′trogen (ēs-), n. Female sex-hormone. [foll., -GEN]

oes′trum, -us, (ēs-), n. Gadfly; stimulus, vehement impulse, frenzy; sexual heat of animals, rut. [f. Gk *oistros*]

of (ŏv,˘ov), prep. connecting its noun with preceding n., adj., adv., or vb, & indicating the relations roughly classified as follows: **1.** Removal, separation, point of departure, privation, (*north, within a mile, upwards, have the advantage, of;* *back of,* behind; *wide of the mark; heal, rid, ease, brought to* BED[1], *of; destitute, empty, free, bare, of;* take LEAVE[1] *of; balk, cheat, defraud, deprive, disappoint, of; independently, guiltless, irrespective, of*). **2.** Origin, derivation, cause, agency, authorship, (*be, come, descend, spring, of; borrow, buy, win, receive, hire, of;* TAKE *it ill of; have comfort, wish* one *joy, of; ask, demand, learn, expect, of;* of one's own ACCORD[2]; *of* COURSE[1], *of* RIGHT, *of* NECESSITY; *of* oneself, spontaneously; *die of; smell, savour, smack, of; tired, ashamed, afraid, glad, proud, of; sick of measles,* laid up with, *sick of delays,* disgusted by; *warned of God, forsaken of God & man,* by; *it was kind, foolish, naughty, clever, cruel, well done, of you to say so; has the approval of his master; the works of Shakespeare, Iliad of Homer*). **3.** Material, substance, closer definition, identity, (*house of cards; built of brick; make a* FOOL[1], *the* BEST[1], *of;* MAKE[1] *much of; a family of eight; the name of Jones; the class of idiots; city of Rome, vice of drunkenness; a fool of a man, her scamp of a husband, the worst liar of any man I know; had a bad time, troublesome journey, of it*). **4.** Concern, reference, direction, respect, (*think well of him; never heard of it; was informed of the fact; is true of every case; repent, beware, of; cannot conceive, accept, approve,* THINK, *of;, does not admit or allow of; accuse, convict, suspect, of; avail, bethink, oneself of;* SHORT, *guilty, certain, sure, confident, fond, of; swift of foot, blind of an eye, hard of heart,* HARD *of hearing; at 30 years of age*). **5.** Objective relation (*the levying of taxes; love of virtue; in search of knowledge; great eaters of pork; redolent, productive, fruitful, lavish, prodigal, sparing, capable, sensible, careful, observant, desirous, impatient, characteristic, destructive, indicative, of*). **6.** Description, quality, condition, (*man of tact, person of consequence, farm of 100 acres, the hour of prayer, potatoes of our own growing; girl of ten years,* or, with mixed construction, *of ten years old*).. **7.** Partition, classification, inclusion, selection, (*no more of that; some, five, of us,* = (a) a portion, or five, of us who are more numerous, or by extention, (b) we, being several or five persons; so *any* part, or *the whole, of it; the most dangerous of enemies; he of all men,* he most or least of all; *is the one thing of all others that,* illog. for *of all that; song of*

songs, *holy of holies,* those best deserving the name; *is one of a, ten, thousand,* such as occurs only in one among 1,000, 10,000, cases; *a friend of mine, of the vicar's,* i.e. orig. in the number of my, the vicar's, friends, but extended to illog. contexts, as *that long nose of his, this only son of the vicar's; drink deep of flattery, partake of food; was sworn of the Council,* admitted as member; *his temper is of the quickest,* belongs to the quickest class; *a sort of thud; comes in of an evening,* at some time in the evenings; *of old, yore, late years, late,* somewhere in the specified periods). **8.** Belonging, connexion, possession, (*we of the middle class; companions of his exile; articles of clothing; the manners of today; a thing of the past; the master of the house; the widow of the man who was killed; a topic of conversation;* esp. with words that naturally require supplementing, as *the cause, result, counterpart, opposite, image, of*). **9.** BECAUSE, *by* MEAN'S, *for* FEAR[1], *for the* SAKE, *in* BEHALF, *in* CASE[1], *in* FACE[1], *in* RESPECT, *in* SPITE, INSTEAD, *on* ACCOUNT[2], *on* BEHALF, *on the* POINT, *of.* [OE *of,* unaccented form of *æf,* orig. *af,* = OS, ON, Goth *af,* OHG *ab*(a) f. Gmc *abh*(a), cogn. w. L *ab,* Gk *apo*]

of-, pref. See OB-.

off (awf, ŏf), adv., prep., a., n., & v.t. **1.** adv. Away, at or to a distance, (*rode ∼; beat ∼ the attack; keep assailant ∼; ward ∼ disaster; take oneself, be, make, ∼,* depart; *∼ with you !,* go; *∼ with his head !,* behead him; *fall, go, ∼,* deteriorate; of ship, *fall ∼,* become less close to wind; *the bullet glanced ∼; go ∼,* fall asleep; *is far, three miles, two years, ∼*); (so as to be) out of position, not on or touching or dependent or attached, loose, separate, gone, (*my hat is ∼; take his clothes ∼; cut, break, shake, etc., ∼; throw ∼ reserve,* become open or candid; *be ∼ with the old love,* have severed connexion; *get* one's *daughters, stock, ∼,* disposed of by marriage, sale; *the gilt is ∼,* disillusionment has come; *we are ∼ now,* just started, starting, or about to start); so as to break continuity or continuance, discontinued, stopped, not obtainable, (*broke ∼,* ceased to speak; *leave ∼ work; the engagement, bargain, negotiation, is ∼; declare ∼,* refuse or rescind engagement; *cut ∼ supplies; the gas, asparagus, is ∼,* no longer to be got); to the end, entirely, so as to be clear, (*clear, drink, pay, polish, work, ∼*); BUY, COME, DASH[1], GET, MARK[2], PALM, PASS, RATTLE, SHOW, TAKE, ∼; RIGHT, STRAIGHT, ∼; *well, badly, comfortably,* etc., *∼,* so circumstanced or supplied with money; *∼ & on,* intermittently, waveringly, now & again; *∼-load, ∼-saddle,* S.-Afr. for *un-.* **2.** prep. From, away or down or up from, disengaged or distant from, (so as to be) no longer on, (*drove them ∼ the seas; is ∼ the beaten track; fell ∼ a ladder; take cover ∼ dish; eats ∼ silver plate; take thing,* *matter,* ~ *one's hands,* relieve him of it; *had borrowed £20* ~ *plaintiff* vulg.; ~ one's HEAD [1], FEED [2]; ~*-beat,* unusual or unconventional; ~. *colour,* out of condition, indisposed; ~ one's *game,* not playing as well as usual; ~ *smoking,* not indulging in it, disinclined for it; *took something* ~ *the price*; *is* ~ *duty* or *work*; *cut a slice*~, *dine* ~, *the joint*; *was only a yard*~*me*; *keep ship two points*~ *the wind*; ~ *the point,* irrelevant(ly); ~ *the map,* sl., vanished, no longer existing; *in a street* ~ *the Strand,* turning out of it; *from* ~, arch., poet., or vulg., = ~; ~*-hand,* extempore, without premeditation, unceremoniously, whence ~hǎnd', ~-hǎnd'ED [2], aa., ~hǎnd'ĕdLY [2] adv., ~-hǎnd'ĕdNESS n.; ~ *shore,* a short way out to sea; so ~*-shore fisheries*; *~-shore purchases,* goods and services purchased by one country in another country; ~*-shore wind,* blowing seawards; *anchored* ~ *the point, cape,* etc., opposite & a short way from it; ~ *side* in football, between ball & opponents' goal, so ~*-side play, rule*; ~*-white,* not quite white); with a handicap of (*he plays*~ 5). 3. adj. Farther, far, (*on the* ~ *side of the wall*); (of horses etc. or vehicles) right (opp. NEAR [2], w. ref. to side at which rider usu. mounts; *the* ~ *leader, front wheel, hind leg, side*); (crick.) towards, in, or coming from, that half of the field as divided by line through two middle stumps in which playing batsman does not stand (opp. ON [2], LEG; *an* ~ *drive,* whence ~**drive'** v.t.; ~ *stump*; LONG [1] ~; *an* ~ *break*); subordinate, divergent, (*in an* ~ *street*; fig. of argument etc., *that is an* ~ *issue*); contingent, improbable, (*there is an* ~ *chance that*); disengaged (*will do it on my next* ~ *day*); ||~*-licence,* to sell beer etc. for consumption ~ the premises; ~*-print,* a separate, printed copy of article etc. that was orig. part of larger publication. 4. n. (crick.) The ~ side. 5. v.t.(colloq.). Announce intention of abandoning or annulling (negotiation, agreement, undertaking); withdraw from negotiation or engagement with (person). (different. sp. of OF, since 15/16th c.]

ǒff'al, n. Refuse, waste stuff, scraps, garbage; parts cut off as waste from carcass meant for food, esp. entrails, also head, tail, kidneys, heart, tongue, liver, etc.; carrion, putrid flesh; low-priced fish (e.g. plaice as opp. sole or other prime fish); bran or other by-product of grain (often pl.); offscourings, dregs; ~ *milk, wheat, wood,* etc., inferior. [ME, f. MDu. *afval* f. *af* OF+*vallen* FALL [1]]

offence', *offense', n. Stumbling-block, occasion of unbelief etc., (now rare); attacking, aggressive action, taking the offensive, (*the most effective defence is* ~); wounding of the feelings, wounded feeling, annoyance, umbrage, (*no* ~ *was meant; too quick to take* ~; *give* ~ *to*;

cannot be done without ~); transgression, misdemeanour, illegal act, (esp. *commit an* ~ *against*). Hence ~LESS (sl-) a. [ME & OF *offens* f. L *offensus, -ūs* annoyance, & ME & F *offense* f. L *offensa* a striking against, both f. OF(*fendere fens-* strike)]

offend', v.i. & t. Stumble morally, do amiss, transgress, (*against* law, decency, person, etc.), whence ~ER [1] n. (esp. FIRST ~*er*), ~ING [2] a.; wound feelings of, anger, cause resentment or disgust in, outrage, (*am sorry you are*~*cd*; ~*ed at* or *by* thing, *with* or *by* person; ~ *her delicacy, my sense of justice*), whence ~ĕdLY [2] adv. [ME, f. OF *offendre* f. L as prec.]

offĕn'sive, a. & n. 1. Aggressive, intended for or used in attack, (~ *arms, movement*; opp. DEFENSIVE); meant to give offence, insulting, (~ *language*); disgusting, ill--smelling, nauseous, repulsive; hence ~LY [2] adv., ~NESS n. 2. n. Attitude of assailant, aggressive action, (*take, act on, abandon, the* ~); an attack, ~ campaign or stroke, (*the long-expected German* ~); movement, as *peace* ~. [f. F (*-if, -ive*) or f. med. L *offensivus* (OFFENCE, -IVE)]

ǒff'er [1], v.t. & i. 1. Present (victim, first--fruits, prayer) to deity, revered person, etc., by way of sacrifice, give in worship or devotion, whence ~ING [1](4) n. 2. Hold out in hand, or tender in words or otherwise, for acceptance or refusal (~*ed me his hymn-book to look over*; TAKEN *& ~ed; was* ~*ed a free pardon*; ~ *an opinion, a few remarks,* etc.; ~ *no apology*). 3. Make proposal of marriage. 4. Show for sale. 5. Give opportunity to enemy for *battle.* 6. Express readiness to do if desired; essay, try to show, (violence, resistance, etc., often *to*); show an intention *to do* (~*ed to strike me*). 7. (Of things) present to sight or notice (*each age* ~*s its characteristic riddles*); present itself, occur, (*as opportunity* ~*s; the first path that* ~*ed*). [OE *offrian* in religious sense f. L OF(*ferre* bring); other senses f. OF *offrir* of same orig.]

ǒff'er [2], n. Expression of readiness to give or do if desired, or to sell on terms (*on* ~, for sale at certain price), proposal esp. of marriage; bid. [ME, f. OF *offre* (prec.)]

ǒff'ertorў, n. Part of mass or communion preceding canon, at which alms of congregation are usu. collected; (improp., by confusion of offertory & offerings) the alms collected; collection of money at religious service. [ME, f. eccl. L *offertorium* (LL *offert-* for L *oblat-* p.p. st. of *offerre* OFFER [1], -ORY) offering]

ǒff'ice, n. 1. Piece of kindness, attention, service, (*ill* ~) disservice, (*owing to, by, the good* or *ill* ~*s of*). 2. Duty attaching to one's position, task, function, (*it is my* ~, *the* ~ *of the arteries, to*). 3. Position with duties attached to it, place of authority or trust or service esp. of public kind (*was given an* ~ *under Government*), tenure of official position esp. that of minister of

State (*take, enter upon, hold, leave, resign,* ~; JACK[1] *in* ~). **4.** Ceremonial duty (esp. *perform the last* ~*s to,* rites due to the dead). **5.** (eccl.). Authorized form of worship, daily service of R.-C. breviary (also *divine* ~; *say* ~, recite this), Anglican morning & evening prayer, (introit at beginning of) mass or communion service, any occasional service such as the *O*~ *for the Dead.* **6.** Place for transacting business (*goes down to the* ~ *at 9 a.m.*); room etc. in which the clerks of an establishment work, counting-house; (with qualification) room etc. set apart for business of particular department of large concern (|| *booking, inquiry, goods, lost-property,* ~ in railway station) or local branch of dispersed organization (*our Manchester* ~; *a post, telegraph,* ~) or company for specified purpose (*insurance, fire* or *fire-insurance,* ~). **7.** (*O*~) quarters or staff or collective authority of a Government department (*the* FOREIGN, WAR[1], POST[2], *O*~). **8.** pl. Parts of house devoted to household work, storage, etc. **9.** || (sl.). Hint, signal, as *give, take, the* ~. **10.** *Holy O*~, the inquisition; ~-*bearer,* official or officer. [ME, f. OF f. L OF(*ficium* f. *facere* do) service]

off'icer, n., & v.t. **1.** Holder of public, civil, or ecclesiastical office, queen's servant or minister, appointed or elected functionary, (usu. with qualification, as ~ *of* HEALTH, *of the Household,* or *public, medical,* ~; || *relieving* ~, see RELIEVE). **2.** President, treasurer, secretary, etc., of society. **3.** Bailiff, constable. **4.** Person holding authority in navy, army, air force, or mercantile marine, esp. with commission in army or navy (GENERAL, STAFF, COMMISSION[1]*ed,* FIELD[1], COMPANY[1], BREVET, WARRANT[1], NON-*commissioned,* ~ in army; FLAG[4], COMMISSION[1]*ed,* WARRANT[1], PETTY, ~ in navy; *Naval* ~*s*: Admiral of the Fleet, Admiral, Vice-Adm., Rear-Adm., Commodore, Captain, Commander, Lieut.-Commander, Lieutenant, Sublieut., Midshipman; *Army* ~*s*: Field Marshal, General, Lieut.-Gen., Major-Gen., BRIGADIER (formerly *Brigadier-Gen.*), Colonel, Lieut.-Col., Major, Captain, Lieutenant, Second Lieut.; AIR[1] *Force* ~*s*); || *Officers' Training Corps* (abbr. O.T.C.; orig. for the Territorial Force, & multiplied for the 1914–18 war); member of 4th class of Order of the British Empire (O.B.E.). **5.** v.t. (usu. in p.p.). Provide with ~s, act as commander of. [ME, f. AF *officer,* = OF -*ier,* f. med. L *officiarius* (prec., -ARY[1])]

offi'cial (-shl), a. & n. **1.** Of an office, the discharge of duties, or the tenure of an office; holding office, employed in public capacity; derived from or vouched for by person(s) in office, properly authorized; (med.) according to the pharmacopoeia, officinal; usual with persons in office (~ *solemnity, red tape,* etc.); hence ~LY[2]

adv. ~IZE(3) v.t., (-sha-). **2.** n. Presiding officer or judge of archbishop's, bishop's, or esp. archdeacon's court (usu. ~ *principal*); person holding public office or engaged in ~ duties, whence ~DOM, ~ESE' (-ēz), ~ jargon, ~ISM(2), nn., (-sha-). [adj. 16th c. f. F f. LL *officialis* (OFFICE, -AL); n. ME f. AF, OF (as prec.)]

offi'ci|āte (-shī-), v.i. Discharge priestly office, perform divine service, so ~ANT(1) n.; act in some official capacity, esp. on particular occasion (usu. *as* host, best man, etc.). [f. med. L *officiare* perform divine service (OFFICE), -ATE[3]]

offi'cinal, a. (Of herb or drug) used in medicine or the arts; (of medical preparation) kept ready at druggists', made from pharmacopoeia recipe (now usu. OFFICIAL), (of name) adopted in pharmacopoeia. Hence ~LY[2] adv. [f. med. L *officinalis* f. L *officina,* -AL]

offi'cious (-shus), a. (Given to) offering service that is not wanted, doing or undertaking more than is required, intrusive, meddlesome, whence ~NESS n.; (diplom., opp. *official*) informal, unofficially friendly or candid, not binding. Hence ~LY[2] adv. [f. L *officiosus* obliging (OFFICE, -OUS)]

off'ing (or aw-), n. Part of visible sea distant from shore or beyond anchoring ground (*was seen in the* ~); position at distance from shore (*gain, keep,* etc., *an* ~; freq. fig., cf. *horizon.* [OFF, -ING[1]]

off'ish (aw-, ŏ-), a. (colloq.). Inclined to aloofness, distant or stiff in manner. Hence ~NESS n. [OFF, -ISH[1]; cf. UPPISH]

off'scourings (awfskowr-, ŏ-), n. pl. Refuse, filth, dregs, (usu. *of*; lit., & fig. of persons, as *the* ~ *of humanity*). [OFF, SCOUR, -ING[1](2)]

off'sĕt (aw-, ŏ-), n., & v.t. **1.** Start, set-off, outset, (rare); short side shoot from stem or root serving for propagation, (transf. & fig.) offshoot, scion, mountain-spur; compensation, set-off, consideration or amount diminishing or neutralizing effect of contrary one; (surv.) short distance measured perpendicularly from main line of measurement; (archit.) sloping ledge in wall etc. where thickness of part above is diminished; bend made in pipe to carry it past obstacle; (typ.) smudging of clean sheet through being laid on freshly-printed surface; ~ *process,* method of printing in which ink is first transferred from a plate to a uniform rubber surface and then to the paper etc. **2.** v.t. Counterbalance, compensate. [OFF, SET[1]]

off'shōot (aw-, ŏ-), n. Side shoot or branch (lit. & fig.), derivative. [OFF, SHOOT]

off'spring (or aw-), n. Progeny, issue, (fig.) result. [OE (OF, OFF, SPRING)]

Of'lăg (ŏ-), n. German prison camp for officers. [G, = *Offiziers lager*]

oft (aw-, ŏ-), adv. Often (arch. except in comb. with p.p. or part., as ~-*told,* ~-*recurring; many a time & ~,* often);

~*limes*, often (arch.). [OE *oft*, OS *oft*(*o*), OHG *ofto*, ON *oft*, Goth. *ufta*]

often (aw'fn, ŏ'fn; *occas.* -ten), adv. & a. (~*er*, ~*est*). Frequently, many times, at short intervals, (with singular generalized subject) in a considerable proportion of the instances (*the victim ~ dies of it*); ~ *& ~*, emphatic form; ~*times, ~* (arch.); (adj.; arch.) frequent (*by ~ study of it*). [ME, extended f. prec.]

ŏg'dŏăd, n. The number, a set of, eight. [f. LL f. Gk *ogdoas* (*oktō* eight, -AD)]

ŏgee', n. & a. (Moulding) showing in section a double continuous curve, concave below passing into convex above; S-shaped (line); ~ *arch, doorway, window,* with two ~ curves meeting at apex. Hence ~'d' [-ED²] a. [app. f. F OGIVE, being the usu. moulding in groin-ribs]

ŏg(h)am (ŏg'am), n. Ancient British and Irish alphabet of twenty characters; inscription in this; one of the characters. [OIr. *ogam*, referred to *Ogma* supposed inventor]

ogive (ŏj'īv, ojīv'), n. Diagonal groin or rib of vault; pointed or Gothic arch, whence **ogiv'al** a. [F, of unkn. orig.]

ō'gle, v.i. & t., & n. **1.** Cast amorous glances; eye amorously; hence **ōg'ler¹** n. **2.** n. Amorous glance. [late 17th c. cant, of LG orig.; cf. LG *oegeln* (= G *äugeln*) to eye or ogle]

Og'pu (ŏg'pōō), n. Former (1922–35) organization for combating counterrevolutionary activities in Soviet Russia. [initial letters of *Obedinennoe Gosudarstvennoe Policheskoe Upravlenie*, United State Political Administration]

ō'gre (-ger), n. Man-eating giant. Hence or cogn. ~ISH¹ (-ger-), **ōg'rish¹**, aa., **ōg'ress¹** n. [F, first used by Perrault 1697, of unkn. orig.]

Ogy'gian (o-), a. Of obscure antiquity, prehistoric. [f. L f. Gk *Ōgugios* of *Ōgugēs* mythical king of Attica or Boeotia]

oh (ō), int. See O².

ohm (ōm), n. Unit of electrical resistance; ~*-ammeter*, instrument measuring electrical current & resistance. Hence ~'AGE n., electrical resistance measured in ~s, ~'METER n. [G. S. *Ohm*, German physicist 1787–1854]

ohō', int. expressing surprise or exultation. [O², HO]

oh yes. See OYEZ.

-oid, suf. forming adjj. & nn. w. sense (*something*) *having the form of, resembling*; chiefly on Gk (*rhomboid*), rarely L (*fucoid*) or other (*alkaloid*) stems; adjj. as *thyroid, simioid*, nn. as *asteroid, amygdaloid*; from the nn. an adj. in *-oidal* is formed as *cycloidal*. [f. mod. L *-oīdes* f. Gk *-oeidēs* (-o-+*-eidēs* like) f. which also -ODE]

oil¹, n. **1.** (Kinds of) liquid viscid unctuous inflammable chemically neutral substance lighter than & insoluble in water & soluble in alcohol & ether (there are three classes: *fatty* or *fixed* ~s of animal

or vegetable origin, greasy & non-distillable, subdivided into *drying* ~s, which by exposure harden into varnish, & *non--drying* ~s, which by exposure ferment, the latter used as lubricants, illuminants, soap constituents, etc.; *essential* or *volatile* ~s chiefly of vegetable origin. acrid, limpid, & distillable, giving plants etc. their scent, used in medicine & perfumery; *mineral* ~s used as illuminants. Particular kinds are named from source with *of*, as ~ *of almonds*, or with source or use preceding, as *cod-liver, olive, salad, hair,* ~); *pour ~ on the flame* etc., aggravate passion etc.; *pour~ on the waters*, smooth matters over; *smell of ~*, bear marks of study; *burn the midnight ~*, read or work far into the night; *strike ~*, lit., find petroleum by sinking shaft, fig., attain prosperity or success; ~ *& vinegar*, type of dissimilar or irreconcilable things; *strap* etc. ~, flogging with strap etc. **2.** = ~-colour (often pl.). **3.** = ~skin (usu. pl.). **4.** ~*-bird, -nut, -palm, -plant, -seed, -tree,* kinds of bird etc. from which ~ is got; ~*-bush*, ~-filled socket for upright spindle [BUSH³]; ~'*cake*, mass of compressed linseed etc. left when~ has been expressed, used as cattle food or manure; ~'*can*, containing ~, esp. long-nozzled for oiling machinery; ~'*cloth*, fabric waterproofed with ~, ~-skin, canvas coated with drying~ & used to cover table or floor; ~*-coat*, of ~skin; ~*-colour*, paint made by grinding pigment in ~ (usu. pl.); ~(-)*engine* (driven by the explosion of vaporized ~ mixed with air); ~'*field*, district yielding mineral ~; ~*-gauge*, hydrometer measuring specific gravity of ~s; ~*-gilding, -gold*, goldleaf laid on linseed~ mixed with yellow pigment; ~*-gland*, secreting ~; ~*-hole*, in machinery to receive lubricating ~; ~'*man*, maker or seller of ~s; ~*-meal*, ground linseed cake; ~*-paint*, = ~-colour; ~*-painting*, art of painting, picture painted, in ~-colours; ~*-paper*, made transparent or waterproof by soaking in ~; ~*-press*, apparatus for pressing ~ from seeds etc.; ~'*skin*, cloth waterproofed with ~, garment or (pl.) suit of this; ~*-spring*, yielding mineral ~; ~*-stone*, (fine-grained stone used with ~ as) whetstone; ~-TANKER. Hence ~'LESS a. [ME *oile*, *oile* f. OF *olie* = OF *oile* &c. f. L *oleum* (*olea* olive); OE *ele* dir. f. L]

oil², v.t. & i. Apply oil to, lubricate, (~ *the wheels*, lit., & fig. make things go smoothly by courtesy, bribery, etc.; ~ one's *hand* or ~ one, bribe him; ~ one's *tongue*, say smooth things, flatter); (with *butter, grease*, etc., as subj. or obj.) turn (t. & i.) into oily liquid; impregnate or treat with oil (~*ed sardines*; ~*ed silk*, waterproofed with oil); ~*ed* (sl.), slightly drunk. [f. prec.]

oil'er, n. In vbl senses: esp. oilcan for oiling machinery. [-ER¹]

oil'| y̆, a. Of, like, covered or soaked with, oil; (of manner etc.) fawning, insinuating, unctuous. Hence ~ILY² adv., ~iNESS n. [-Y²]

oint'ment, n. Unctuous preparation applied to skin to heal or beautify, unguent. [ME oigne-, ointment f. OF oignement f. oindre (ANOINT, -MENT); forms oint- after obs. vb oint ANOINT]

Oireachtas (ŏr'axthăs), n. Legislature of Eire, the President & two Houses, Dail Eireann (Chamber of Deputies) & Seanad Eireann (Senate). [Ir.]

oka'pi (-ah-), n. Bright-coloured partially striped Central-Afr. ruminant discovered 1900 with likeness to giraffe, deer, & zebra. [native]

ŏk'ra, n. Tall malvaceous plant bearing mucilaginous seed-pods used as a vegetable & for thickening soups. [W.-Afr. native name]

-ol, chem. suf. 1. Termination of alcohol used in names of alcohols in the wider sense or analogous compounds (methol, phenol). 2. = L oleum oil (benzol).

ŏld, a. (ELDER¹, eldest, in particular uses; ordinarily ~er, ~est), & n. 1. Advanced in age, far on in natural period of existence, not young or near its beginning, (the ~, aged people; young & ~, every one; ~ age, later part of life; ~·age pensions, || weekly payments to ~ persons on account of their age; || Old Lady of Threadneedle Street, Bank of England; ~ man of the sea, person who cannot be shaken off; ~ man, woman, party, etc.; ~ man, also as name for southernwood, & naut. sl. for ship's captain; my etc. ~ man, colloq., husband; ~ man's beard, kind of moss, also wild clematis; my etc. ~ woman, colloq., wife; ~ woman, fussy or timid man, whence ~-wo'maniSH¹, ~-wo̱' manLY¹, aa., ~-wo'manishNESS, ~-wo̱' manliNESS, nn., (-woo-); my etc. ~ bones, I or me etc. who am ~; the century grows ~). 2. Having characteristics, experience, feebleness, etc., of age (~ head on young shoulders, wisdom beyond one's years; child has an ~ face; ~ buffer, fogy, etc.; a man is as ~ as he feels); worn, dilapidated, shabby, (~ clothes etc.). 3. (Appended to period of time) of age (is ten years ~, a ten-year-~ boy, a boy OF ten years ~, could read Greek at ten years ~; also ellipt. four etc. -year-~, person or animal, esp. racehorse, of that age, w. pl. -~s). 4. Practised or inveterate in action or quality or as agent etc. (~ in crime, folly, cunning, diplomacy; an ~ campaigner, offender; ~ bird, person on his guard against snares; ~ hand, practised workman, person of experience in something, at doing; ~ STAGER; '~ bachelor, man confirmed in bachelorhood; ~ maid, elderly spinster, whence ~-maid'ISH¹ a., also precise & tidy & fidgety man, also a round card game). 5. Dating from far back, made long ago, long established

or known or familiar or dear, ancient, not new or recent, primeval, (~ Ocean, Night, etc.; ~ red SANDstone; of ~ standing, long established; so ~-established; ~ as the hills; ~ countries, long inhabited or civilized; ~ friends; an ~ debt, grudge, ~ SCOREs; an ~ name, family; ~ wine, matured with keeping; ~ gold, colour of tarnished gold; ~ CATHOLIC; the ~, what is not new; ~ TESTAMENT; ~ boy, chap, fellow, man, esp. in voc., intimate or person treated as such, also in mod.·sl. ~ bean, egg, fruit, thing, top; Old England; Old Glory, the Stars & Stripes; the ~ one or gentleman, Old Harry, Nick, Scratch, etc., the devil; good ~ with name, sl. exclamation in real or ironical commendation of person's or thing's performance; have a fine, good, high, etc., ~ time etc., sl., be well amused or entertained; any ~ thing, sl., anything no matter what). 6. Belonging only or chiefly to the past, obsolete or obsolescent, out of date, antiquated, antique, concerned with antiquity, not modern, bygone, only lingering on, former, quondam, (the good ~ times, customs etc. of earlier generations; ~ annals; ~ fashions, that have gone or are going out, whence ~- -fā'shionED² a., ~-fā'shionedNESS n., (-shond-), opp. newfangled etc.; am ~- -fashioned enough to think, used in ironical self-depreciation; of the ~ school, ~- -fashioned; the ~ country, home, etc., used by colonists or colonials of mother- -country; call up ~ memories; the ~ order changeth; have lost my ~ beliefs; ~ boy, former member of school; so ~ Etonian etc.; ~ guard, original or past or right- -wing member(s) of party etc.; ~ SCHOOL¹ tie; the Old COMEDY, HUNDREDTH; ~ masters, great painters of earlier times, pictures by these; ~ London, Paris, England, etc., London etc. as it once was, or the extant relics of its former state; the ~ man, one's unregenerate self; the Old World, Eastern hemisphere; ~-world, not American, also belonging to ~ times, & so ~-time attrib.; Old STYLE, abbr. o.s.; the ~ year, just ended or about to end; ~ clothes, discarded; ~-clothesman, dealer in these); hence ~'ISH¹(2) a., ~'NESS n. (rare). 7. n. ~ time (only in of ~ adj. & adv., as the men of ~, of ~ there were giants; have heard it of ~, from long ago). [OE, OS ald, OHG alt, f. Gmc *aldhaz (cf. Goth. altheis) f. *al- grow, nourish, cogn. w. L alere feed]

|| ŏl'den¹, a. (arch. & literary). Old-time, of a former age, (esp. the ~ time). [-EN⁵]

|| ŏl'den², v.t. & i. Make or grow feeble etc. as with age. [-EN⁶]

ŏld'ster, n. One who is no longer a youngster (usu. antithetically to youngster). [-STER]

ōlĕa'ginous, a. Having properties of or producing oil, oily, fatty, greasy. [f. F oléagineux f. L oleaginus (olea olive)] ōlĕăn'der, n. Evergreen poisonous Levantine shrub with leathery lanceolate leaves & fine red & white flowers. [med. L]

ōlĕăs'ter, n. The wild olive; small yellow--flowered tree like it. [L (olea olive, -ASTER)]

ōl'ĕo-, comb. form of L oleum oil, (-O-), as ~graph, picture printed in oils, so ~GRAPHY (-ŏgᴸ); ~marg'arine, fatty substance extracted from beef fat & serving as constituent of margarine, •margarine made from vegetable oils; ~meter (-ŏmᴸ), instrument determining density & purity of oils; ~res'in, natural mixture of volatile oil & resin, balsam, also artificial mixture of fixed or volatile oil & resin etc.

ōlfăc't|ion, n. Smelling, sense of smell. So ~IVE a. [f. L olfacere v.t. (olēre v.i. smell, facere fact- make); see -TION]

ōlfăc'tory, a. & n. Concerned with smelling (~ organ, nose; ~ nerves); (n., usu. pl.) ~ organ. [prec., -ORY]

olib'anum, n. Aromatic gum resin used as incense. [ME, f. med. L, f. LL f. Gk libanos frankincense]

ōl'id, a. Rank-smelling, fetid. [f. L olidus (olēre smell, -ID¹)]

ōl'ĭgắrch (-k), n. Member of oligarchy. [f. Gk oligarkhēs (oligoi few, arkhō rule)]

ōl'ĭgắrchy (-kĭ), n. Government, State governed, by the few; members of such government. So ōlĭgắrch'IC(AL) aa., ōlĭgắrch'icalᴸʏ² adv., (-kĭ-). [f. Gk oligarkhia (prec., -ʏ¹)]

ōl'ĭg|(o)-, comb. form of Gk oligos small, oligoi few, as ~ocarp'ous, having few fruits; ~ocēne, geol., between MIOCENE & EOCENE.

ōl'ĭō, n. (pl. ~s). Mixed dish, hotchpotch, stew of various meats & vegetables; medley, farrago, miscellany. [f. Sp. olla stew f. L olla jar]

ōlivā'ceous (-shᴜs), a. (nat. hist.). Olive--green, of dusky yellowish green. [L oliva olive, -ACEOUS]

ōl'ivary̆, a. (anat.). Olive-shaped, oval. [f. L olivarius (foll., -ARY¹)]

ōl'ive, n. & a. 1. (Also ~-tree, evergreen tree with narrow leaves hoary below & axillary clusters of small white flowers, bearing) small oval drupe with hard stone & bitter pulp, of dusky yellowish green when unripe & bluish black when ripe, yielding oil, & pickled unripe for eating as relish; leaf, branch, or wreath of ~ as emblem of peace (also ~-branch, often fig.; hold out the ~-branch, make overtures, show disposition, for reconciliation); wood of the ~ (also ~-wood). 2. ~-shaped kinds of gasteropod mollusc. 3. pl. Slices of beef or veal rolled up with herbs & stewed (usu. beef, veal, ~s). 4. ~--shaped bar or button for fastening garment by insertion in corresponding loop, whence ōl'ivet¹ or ōlivette' n. 5. ~ colour. 6. ~ crown, garland of ~ as sign of victory; ~-branch, see above, also (usu.

pl., w. ref. to Ps. cxxviii. 3) child(ren); ~ oil, extracted from ~s. 7. adj. Coloured like the unripe ~ (also ~-green); (of complexion) yellowish-brown. [ME, f. OF, f. L oliva]

ōl'iver¹, n. Tilt-hammer attached to axle & worked by treadle for shaping nails etc. [orig. unkn.]

Ol'iver² (ŏ-), n. See ROLAND.

ōl'ivine, -ĭn, n. Kind of chrysolite, chiefly olive-green. [L oliva olive, -INE⁴]

ōll'a podri'da (-rē-), rarely ōll'a, n. = OLIO. [Sp., = lit. rotten pot (OLIO, L PUTRIDᴜs)]

(-)ŏl'ogy̆, suf. f. -O-+-LOGY; as quasi- n. used joc. = any science, w. pl. = the sciences, mere theory.

olym'piăd, n. Period of four years between celebrations of Olympic games, used by ancient Greeks in dating events (abb. Ol.), 776 B.C. being first year of first O~; celebration of modern Olympic games. [f. F·(-ade), or L f. Gk olumpias -ad- (Olumpios see foll., -AD)]

Olym'piăn, a. & n. 1. Of Olympus, celestial; (of manners etc.) magnificent, condescending, superior; = foll. 2. n. Dweller in Olympus, one of the greater ancient-Greek gods; person of superhuman calmness & detachment. [f. L f. Gk Olumpios +-AN]

Olym'pic, a. Of or at Olympia in Elis in the Peloponnese (~ games. held there every four years by ancient Greeks with athletic, literary, & musical competitions; also, modern quadrennial international athletic meeting at various places, the first at Athens 1896). [f. L f. Gk Olumpikos of Olympus (Olympia being named from the games in honour of Zeus of Olympus)]

Olym'pus, n. Thessalian mountain on which dwelt the chief Greek gods, divine abode, heaven. [L, f. Gk Olumpos]

-oma, -ome, suf. f. Gk -ōma, denoting result, f. vbs in -ousthai (as rhizōma f. rhizousthai take root); (1) nn. denoting some formation or member of the nature of that denoted by the radical part, in this use now superseded by -ome, as rhizome, trichome; (2) names of tumours or other abnormal growths, as carcinoma, sarcoma; cf. -MA, -ME.

ŏm'bre (-ber, & see Ap.), n. Card-game popular in 17th–18th cc. [f. Sp. hombre f. L hominem nom. homo man, perh. thr. F (h)ombre]

ŏmbro-, comb. form of Gk ombros rain, as ~LOGY (-ŏlᴸ), ~METER (-ŏmᴸ).

ōm'ĕga, n. Last letter (Ω, ω) of Greek alphabet, long o; last of series; final development etc. (ALPHA & ~). [Gk, = great o]

ŏm'ĕlĕt(te) (-ml-), n. Beaten eggs fried in melted butter & folded & often flavoured with or containing herbs, cheese, chopped ham, jam, etc.(savoury~, with herbs etc. , sweet ~, with sugar or jam; cannot make

omen, n., & v.t. Occurrence or object portending good or evil, prognostic, presage; prophetic signification (*is of good* etc. ~); (vb) foreshow, give presage of. [L]

omĕn'tǀum, n. (anat.; pl. ~*a*). Fold of peritoneum connecting stomach with other viscera, caul. Hence ~AL a. [L]

omic'ron, n. Greek letter (*O*, *o*) = ŏ. [Gk, = small o]

ŏm'inous, a. Giving or being an omen (*of good or evil, or abs.*), portentous, (rare); of evil omen, inauspicious, foreshowing disaster, threatening. Hence ~LY² adv. [f. L *ominosus* (OMEN -*inis*, -OUS)]

omǐ'ssion (-shn), n. Omitting, non-inclusion; non-performance, neglect, duty not done, (*sins of* ~ *& commission*, negative & positive). So **omiss'IVE** a. [ME, f. OF, or LL *omissio* (foll., -ION)]

omit', v.t. (-tt-). Leave out, not insert or include; leave undone, neglect doing, fail *to* do. So **omiss'IBLE** a. [f. L *omittere* -*iss*- (*o*- for OB-, *mittere* send)]

ŏmni-, comb. form of L *omnis* all, in compounds taken f. L or formed chiefly w. L elements, w. sense *all*-, *of all things*, *in all ways* or *places*, as ~*com'petent*, having jurisdiction in all cases; ~*far'ious*, of all sorts; **ŏmnǐf'ic**, all-creating; **ŏmnǐ'genous**, of all kinds; **ŏmnǐp'otence**, infinite power, also God, also great influence; so **ŏmnǐp'o-tent** a. (*the Omnǐpotent*, God), ~*p'otent*LY² adv.; ~*pres'ence*, ubiquity, also being widespread or constantly met with; so ~*pres'ent* a.; **ŏmnǐ'science** (-shens), infinite knowledge, also God, also wide information or the affectation of it; so **ŏmnǐ'scient** (-shyent) a. (*the Omniscient*, God), ~*'scient*LY² adv.; **ŏmnǐv'orous**, feeding on anything that offers (esp. fig. of reading); so ~*v'orous*LY² adv., ~*v'orous*NESS n.

ŏm'nibus, n. (pl. ~*es*) & a. **1.** (Now usu. *bŭs*) large wheeled public vehicle plying on fixed route & taking up & setting down passengers at fixed, or at any, points in this; (also *hotel* ~) vehicle conveying guests between hotel & railway station; (also *private* or *family* ~) vehicle provided by railway company for conveying party & luggage to or from station; ~ book. **2.** adj. Serving several objects at once, comprising several items, (*an* ~ *bill*, *resolution*, *clause*, etc.; ~ *book*, volume containing several stories, plays, etc. (freq. by a single author), published at a low price to be within the reach of all; ~ *box* in theatre, box on pit tier appropriated to number of subscribers; ‖~ *train*, stopping at all stations; ~ *bar*, *wire*, etc. in electricity, through which whole current passes). [f. F (1828), f. L dat. pl. of *omnis* = for all].

ŏm'nium găth'erum (-dh-), n. Miscel-laneous assemblage of persons or things, queer mixture, party to which everyone is invited. [mock L (L *omnium* of all, GATHER)]

ŏm'oplāte, n. Shoulder-blade, scapula. [in 16th c. f. F f. Gk *ōmoplatē* (*ōmos* shoulder, *platē* blade)]

ŏm'phalo-, comb. form of Gk *omphalos* NAVEL, chiefly in surg. & med. wds as ~CELE; ~TOMY (-ŏt⁴), dividing of umbilical cord.

ŏm'phalŏs, n. (Gk ant.) boss on shield, conical stone at Delphi supposed to be central point of earth; centre, hub, (*the centre & ~ of a world-wide empire*). [see prec.]

on¹ (ŏn, on), prep. (See UPON for idiomatic preference.) **1.** (So as to be) supported by or attached to or covering or enclosing (*sat on the table*; *floats on the water*; *is on the horns of a dilemma*; *lives on the continent*, *on an annuity*; *have you a match on you?*, about your person; *is*, *gets*, *falls*, *on his* LEGS, *knees*, etc.; *travels on foot*, *wheels*, *the wing*, *the wings of the wind*; *tread on air*, *one's toes*; *dropped it*, *threw him*, *on the floor*; *had*, *put*, *a ring*, *gloves on his finger*, *hands*; *put a notice on the board*; *hangs on the wall*; *walks on the ceiling*; *has a blister on the sole of his foot*; *a scholar on the foundation*; *a colonel on half-pay*; *went on board*; *is on the jury*, *committee*, *general staff*; *a writer on the press*; *dog is on the chain*; *on the* BENCH, BOARD¹s, CARD²s, FENCE¹, MARKET¹, NAIL¹, PARISH, RACK³, SHELF, SPOT¹, STREETS, STUMP, TURF, WAY; *on* CHANGE¹, HAND¹, *one's* HAND¹s, *one's own* HOOK¹, *one's* KNEE¹s, TENTER*hooks*; *on a* LEVEL¹, *an* EQUALITY, *a* PAR). **2.** With axis, pivot, basis, motive, standard, confirmation, or guarantee, consisting in (*turn on one's heel*; *works on a peg*; *based on fact*; *imprisonment on suspicion*; *on my conscience*; *swear on the Bible*; *had it on good authority*; *decided on no evidence*; *did it on purpose*, *deliberation*; *got it on good terms*; *on account of*; *on the average*, *whole*; *on penalty of death*; *charged him on his life to do it*; *a tax on paper*; *borrowed money on his jewels*; *interest on one's capital*; *profit on sales*). **3.** (So as to be) close to, in the direction of, touching, arrived at, against, just at, (*house is on the shore*, *road*; *on Fifth Avenue*; *on the right*, *North*, *far side*, *both sides*, *of*; *Clacton-on-Sea*; *marched on London*; *hit him on the head*; *a box on the ear*; *left a card on him*; *serve a notice*, *writ*, *on*; *lay hold*, *seize*, *on*; *bowling is on the wicket*, *straight*; *drew his knife on me*; *smile*, *frown*, *turn one's back*, *on*; *make an attack on*; *put one on inquiring or inquiry*, *induce him to inquire*; *curse*, *plague*, etc., *on him*, *it!*; *rose on their oppressors*; *on* HIGH; *on side* in football, not OFF *side*; *ship is driving on shore*; *an on-shore wind*). **4.** (Of time) during, exactly at, contemporaneously with, immediately after, as a result of, (*happened on the morning* etc. *of 29 Feb.*, *on Christmas eve*, *on the next day*; *on the instant*, immediately; *on time*, *the minute*, etc., punctually; *on arriving*, *my return*, *analysis*, *examination*, *I found*). **5.** In manner specified by adj. (*on the cheap*, *sly*, SQUARE) or state or action specified by noun (*on fire*, TAP, *loan*, *lease*, *sale*, *strike*, *guard*; *on the look-out*, *move*, *run*, *wane*, *watch*; *on one's best behaviour*). **6.** Concerning, about, while engaged with, so as to affect, (*keen*, *mad*, *bent*, *determined*, *set*, *on*; *gone on*, sl., enamoured of; *court martial was held on him*; *my opinion on free trade*; *writes*, *speaks*, *lectures*, *on finance*; *a book*, *an essay*, *on grammar*; *meditating on vanity*; *take vengeance on person*; *have something on* (against, to the disadvantage of) *person*; *the drinks are on* (to be paid for by) *me*; *did it on my way*; *was*, *went*, *on an errand*; *is not binding on us*; *work tells severely on him*; *title was conferred on him*; *draw cheque on bank*; *condoled with him on his loss*). **7.** Added to (*ruin on ruin*, *heaps on heaps*). [OE *an*, *on*, OS, OHG *an*, *ana*, ON *d*, Goth. *ana* f. Gmc, cogn. w. Gk *ana*; hence A[2]]

ŏn², adv., a., & n. **1.** (So as to be) supported by, attached to, covering, enclosing, or touching, something (*has*, *drew*, *his boots on*; *put the tablecloth on*; *keep your HAIR on*; *on with your coat*, put it on). **2.** In some direction, towards something, farther forward, towards point of contact, in advanced position or state, with continued movement or action, in operation or activity, (LOOK¹, LOOK¹*er-*, *on*; *getting on for two o'clock*; *broadside*, *stem*, *end*, *on*, with that part forward; ellipt. for imperat. of *go* or *come on*, as *on*, *Stanley*, *on!*; *send on*, in front of oneself; MOVE² *on*; *happened later on*; *from that day on*; *was well on in the day*; *is rather on*, sl., half-drunk; *speak*, *work*, *wait*, etc., *on*, continue to do; so *struggle on to the end*, cf. *on to* below; *slow bowler is*, *went*, *on*, is, began, bowling; *Macbeth is on*, being performed; *gas*, *water*, *is on*, lit. running, or procurable by turning tap; *get*, *be*, *on*, make, have made, bet; *drove Jones on for 4* in cricket, to the on). **3.** CARRY¹, CATCH¹, COME,¹ GET¹, GO¹, HOLD¹, KEEP¹, PUT¹, TAKE¹, TRY, *on*. **4.** *Be on* (colloq.), be in favour of, willing to be a party to, something (*There's a show tonight*; *are you on?*); *be on to* (person), be aware of his intentions etc., find fault with, nag (*he's always on to me*); *on & off*, = OFF *& on*; *on to*, compound prep. (corresponding to *on* as *into* to *in*, but usu. written as two words, & avoided in writing though common in speech; to be distinguished from the use in which each word has independent force as in *went on to the next*), to a position on (*jumped on to the landing-stage*). **5.** adj. Towards or in part of field to left front of playing batsman's wicket (cf. OFF, LEG;

MID¹ *on*; *an on drive*, whence **ŏn-drive'** v.t.); ‖ *on licence*, for selling beer etc. to be drunk on premises. **6.** n. The on side in cricket (*a fine drive to the on*). [f. prec.]

on-, pref. used with attrib. participles, gerunds, verbal nouns, agent-nouns in -ER¹, & other derivative nn., f. vv. followed idiomatically by ON² (occas. alternatively with the reverse order): *on'coming* n. & a., approach(ing); *on'fall* n., assault; *on'flow*, onward flow; *on'goings* or *goings-on'*, (usu. strange or improper) proceedings; *on'hanger*, HANGER²-*on*; *on'looker* or LOOK¹*er-on'*; *on'rush* n., *on'rushing* a.; ONSET.

ŏn'ager, n. (pl. -*s*, -*gri*). Kinds of wild ass. [ME, f. L, f. Gk *onagros* (*onos* ass, *agrios* wild)]

ŏn'anism, n. Interrupted coition; masturbation. [*Onan* (*Gen.* xxxviii. 9) -ISM]

once (wŭns), adv., conj., & n. **1.** For one time or on one occasion only, multiplied by one, by one degree, (*have read it more than~*; *shall die~*; *~ or twice*, *~ & again*, a few times; *~ more*, again, another time; *~ for all*, in final manner, definitively; *~ in a while or way*, very rarely; *~ & away*, = *~ for all*, *~ in a way*; *~ bit(ten) twice shy*, pain, loss, etc., teaches caution; *~ nought is nought*; *second cousin ~* REMOVED). **2.** (In negative or conditional or indefinite clause etc.) ever, at all, even for one or the first time, (*if we ~ lose sight of him*; *when ~ he understands*; *have not seen him ~*; *~ within call*, *we are safe*). **3.** On a certain but unspecified past occasion (also *~ upon a time*), at some period in the past, former(ly), (*~ there was a giant*; *a ~-famous doctrine*, *~-loved friend*; *my ~ master*, *ally*). **4.** *At ~*, immediately, without delay, at the same time, (*do it at ~*, *please*; *don't all speak at ~*, lit., & as iron. deprecation inviting offers etc. from reluctant party; *at ~ stern & tender*); *for this*, *or that*, *~*, on one occasion by way of exception; **~-over* n. (colloq.), preliminary inspection (often with additional sense of cursoriness). **5.** conj. As soon as, if *~*, when *~*. (*~ he hesitates*, *we have him*). **6.** n. One time, performance, etc. (*~ is enough for me*). [ME *ānes*, *ōnes*, (ONE, -ES)]

‖ **oncer** (wŭn'ser), n. (colloq.). One who attends church only once on a Sunday. [ONCE + -ER¹]

on dit (see Ap.), n. Piece of hearsay. [F]

one (wŭn), a., n., & pron. **1.** numeral adj. Single & integral, neither none nor fractional nor plural, numbered by the first or lowest integer, half of two, a, (*~ man~ vote*, opp. PLURAL *vote*; *~ vote ~ value*, principle of equal constituencies; *~-&- -twenty* etc., or usu. *twenty* etc. *~*; *~-&- -twentieth* etc., twenty etc. *-first*; *~ dozen*, *hundred*, etc., precise or formal for *a*; *~ man in ten*, *a thousand*, etc., relatively few; *some~ man must direct*; *for ~ thing*, *he drinks*; ∼ *or two people*, a few; *God is* ∼). **2. adj.** with secondary senses developed from the numeral. *The only*, single, forming a unity, united, identical, the same, unchanging, a particular but undefined, to be contrasted with another, (*the* ∼ *way to do it*; *no* ∼ *man is equal to it*; *is* ∼ *& undivided*; *cried out with* ∼ *voice*; *were made* ∼, married; *become* ∼, coalesce; *remains for ever* ∼, always the same; *all in* ∼ *direction*; *met him* ∼ *night*; *will take you there* ∼ *day*; ∼ *man's meat is another man's poison*). **3. numeral noun.** (With *a* & pl. often used as substitute for repetition of previously expressed or implied noun) the number ∼, thing numbered with it, written symbol for it, a unit, unity, a single thing or person or example, (∼ *is half of two*; *in the year* ∼, long ago; *Aeneid, book* ∼, first book of; *number* ∼, oneself. esp. as centre of selfish care; *write down a* ∼, *three* ∼*s*; *came by* ∼*s & twos*; *sell scores where they sold* ∼*s*; *never a* ∼, none; *will you make* ∼*?*, arch., join the party; *ten etc. to* ∼, long odds, high probability; *all in* ∼, combined; *the all & the* ∼, totality & unity; *at* ∼, reconciled, in agreement; *I lose a neighbour & you gain* ∼; *pick me out a good* ∼, some good ∼*s*; *which, what kind of*, ∼ *or* ∼*s do you like?*; *that* ∼, *the* ∼ *in the window, will do*). **4. adj.** used ellipt. for itself or *a* with noun elsewhere expressed or customarily omitted & to be supplied with more or less of certainty. Single person or thing of the kind implied (∼ *of them lost his or her hat*; ∼ *of the richest men in England*; *shall see you again* ∼ *of these fine days*; *at* ∼ *o'clock* or ∼, i.e. hour; ∼ *& sixpence*, i.e. shilling; *gave him* ∼ *in the eye*, *owe him* ∼, *that was a nasty* ∼, blow lit. or fig.; *at* ∼*-&-twenty*, years of age; *I for* ∼ *do not believe it*; *go* ∼ *better*, bid, offer, risk, more by ∼ point; *is* ∼ *too many for him*, too hard etc. for him to deal with by ∼ degree; *it is all* ∼ *to me*, the same thing, indifferent; ∼ *& all*, all jointly & severally; ∼ *by* ∼, ∼ *after another*, singly, successively; ∼ *with another*, on the average; ∼ *or the* ∼ —, *the other*, formula distinguishing members of pair, as ∼ *is immoral, the other non--moral*, also with pl. constr., as *sheep & goats, of which the* ∼ *are the good* etc.; ∼ *another*, formula of reciprocity with ∼ orig. subjective & *another* objective or possessive, as *struck* ∼ *another, write to* ∼ *another, buy* ∼ *another's goods*). **5. pron.** A particular but unspecified person (arch.; ∼ *came running*; ∼ *said it pleased him not*); a person of specified kind (ANY, EVERY, SOME, NO[1], SUCH *a*, ∼; *many a* ∼, rhet., many people; LITTLE, *dear, loved,* ∼*s*; *the Holy One, One above*, God; *the Evil One*, the devil; *behaves like* ∼ *frenzied*; *what a* ∼ *he is to make excuses!* colloq.; *bought it from* ∼ *Stephens*); any person, esp. the speaker, spoken of as representing people in general (possessive ∼*'s*,

objective ∼, reference-form ∼, refl. ∼*self*, formerly *his, him, he & him, himself*, or ungrammatically *their, them, they & them, themselves*; *if* ∼ *cuts off* ∼*'s nose*, ∼ *hurts only* ∼*self*; *it offends* ∼ *to be told* ∼ *is not wanted*; also incorrectly for *I*, as ∼ *let it pass, for* ∼ *did not want to seem mean*). **6.** ∼*-armed bandit* (sl.), FRUIT machine; ∼*-eyed*, having only, blind of, ∼ eye; ∼*-handed*, having, done etc. with, ∼ hand only; ∼*-horse*, drawn or worked by single horse, (fig., sl.) petty, poorly equipped; ∼*-idea'd, -ideaed*, possessed by single idea, narrow-minded; ∼*-legged*, having only ∼ leg, (fig.) ∼*-sided*, unequal; ∼*-man*, requiring, consisting of, done or managed by, ∼ man; ∼*-pair*, ‖ room or set of rooms on first floor (above ∼ pair or flight of stairs; ∼*-pair back, front*, ‖ such room in back or front of house); ∼*self'*, reflexive, & emphatic appositional, form of ∼ as generalizing pronoun (*to starve* ∼*self is suicide*; *to do right* ∼*self is the great thing*); ∼*-sided*, having, occurring on, ∼ side only (*a* ∼*-sided street*, with houses on ∼ side only; *a* ∼*-sided plant*, with leaves or flowers all on ∼ side of stem), larger etc. on ∼ side, partial, unfair, prejudiced; so ∼*-sid'edLY*[2] adv., ∼*-sid'edNESS* n.; ∼*'step*, vigorous kind of foxtrot in duple time; ∼*-way street* (in which traffic may pass in ∼ direction only). Hence ∼*'FOLD* a. [OE *ān*, OS *ēn*, OHG *ein*, ON *einn*, Goth. *ains* f. Gmc **ainaz*, cogn. w. L *unus*]

-ōne, chem. suf. (1) used unsystematically as in OZONE; (2) in names of hydrocarbons (see -ANE). [f. Gk -*ōnē* fem. patronymic]

oneir'o- (-nīr-), comb. form of Gk *oneiros* dream; ∼MANCY; ∼*crit'ic*, interpreter of dreams; so ∼*crit'icAL* a., ∼*crit'icISM* n.

one'nèss (wŭn-n-), n. Being one, singleness; singularity, uniqueness; wholeness, unity, union, agreement, concord; identity, sameness, changelessness. [-NESS]

on'er (wŭ-), n. Remarkable or pre--eminent person or thing (sl.; *a* ∼ *at*, expert in; *gave him a* ∼, severe blow); (colloq.) stroke etc. counting one, esp. one-run hit at cricket; ‖ (sl.) thumping lie. [-ER[1]]

ŏn'erous, a. Burdensome, causing or requiring trouble, (∼ *property* in law, accompanied with obligations). Hence ∼LY[2] adv., ∼NESS n. [ME, f. OF *onereus* f. L *onerosus* (*onus oneris* burden, -OUS)]

onion (ŭn'yon), n., & v.t. **1.** (Plant with) edible rounded bulb of many concentric coats & pungent smell & flavour, much used in cooking or eaten pickled; FLAMING ∼*s*; *know one's* ∼*s* (sl.), be good at one's job; *off* one's ∼ (sl.), off one's head; ∼*--couch* or *-grass* or *twitch*, kind of wild oat; ∼*-shell*, kinds of mollusc; hence ∼Y[2] (ŭn'yo·) a. **2.** v.t. Rub (eyes) with ∼ to make them water. [ME, f. OF *oignon* f. L *unionem* nom. -o large pearl, onion]

ŏn'ly[1], a. That is (or are) the one (or all the) specimen(s) of the class, sole, (*the* ∼

way is to die; the ~ child of his parents;
the ~ instances known; was an ~ son; one
~ object was visible; my one & ~ hope;
motley's the ~ wear, best or ~ one worth
considering). [OE *ānlīc* (ONE, -LY¹)]

ŏn'lў², adv. & conj. **1.** Solely, merely, exclusively, & no one or nothing more or
besides or else, & that is all, *(is right be-*
cause it is customary ~, is right ~ because
it is customary, is ~ right because it is
customary; ~ you or you ~ can guess, no
one else can; *you can ~ guess or guess ~,*
can do no more; *I ~ thought I would do it,*
formed the design & did not execute it,
or did it without external instigation;
I not ~ heard it, but saw it; if ~, assuming
merely that, also as wishing formula, as
if ~ someone would leave me a legacy!;
~ not, all but; *has ~ just come, came ~*
yesterday, no longer ago; *~ too glad, true,*
etc., glad etc. & not, as might be expected,
the opposite). **2.** conj. It must however
be added that, but then, *(he makes good*
resolutions, ~ he never keeps them); with
the exception, were it not, *that (he does*
well, ~ that he is nervous at the start; ~
that you would be bored, I should —). [ME
ōnliche, f. *ōnlich* (ONLY¹); see ONE, -LY²]

ŏn'omatŏp, -ōpe, adj. Onomatopoeic
word. [shortened f. foll.]

onŏmato|poe'ia (-pēa, -pēya), n. Forma-
tion of names or words from sounds that
resemble those associated with the object
or action to be named, or that seem naturally suggestive of its qualities; word so
formed (e.g. *cuckoo).* So **~poe'ıc** (-pē-),
~pŏĕt'ıc, aa., **~poe'ıcally** (-pē-), **~pŏĕt²-**
ıcally, advv. [f. LL f. Gk *onomatopoiia*
word-making *(onoma -atos* name, *poieō*
make)]

ŏn'sĕt, n. Attack, assault, impetuous beginning, (esp. *at the first ~).* [f. *to* SET on]

ŏn'slaught (-awt), n. Onset, fierce attack.
[early 17th c., f. Du. *aanslag (aan* on, *slag*
blow) w. assim. to obs. *slaught]*

ŏn'to, prep. See ON² *to.*

ŏnto-, comb. form of *on, ont-,* neut. part.
of Gk *eimi* am: **~gĕn'esis,** origin & development of the individual being (cf.
PHYLOGENESIS), whence **~genĕt'ıc** a.,
~genĕt'ıcally adv.; *ontŏ'geny,* = ~-
genesis, also embryology; *ontŏl'ogy,* department of metaphysics concerned with
the essence of things or being in the
abstract, so ~*lo'gical* a., ~*lo'gically* adv.,
ŏntŏl'ogist n.]

ŏn'us, n. (no pl.). Burden, duty, responsibility; *~ proban'di,* = BURDEN¹ *of proof.*
[L]

ŏn'ward, adv. & a., **ŏn'wards** (-z), adv.
Further on, towards the front, with
advancing motion; (adj.) directed ~.
[ON², -WARD(S)]

ŏn'ỹmous, a. Not anonymous. [f. Gk
onuma name + -ous after *anonymous]*

ŏn'ỹx, n. Kind of quartz allied to agate
with different colours in layers; (path.)
opacity of lower part of cornea; *~ marble,*

of banded ~-like structure. [ME *oniche*
f. OF *oniche, onix* f. L f. Gk *onux* finger-
-nail, onyx]

ōo-, ō-, comb. form of Gk *ōion* egg,
ovum, in scientific usu. biol. wds, as
ōogĕn'esis, production or development of
ovum; *ooe'cium* (ōē-), budlike sac for
receiving & fertilizing ova in polyzoa;
ōŏg'amous, reproducing by union of male
& female cells; *ōŏl'ogy,* study, collection,
of birds' eggs, so *ōolo'gical, ōŏl'ogist*
ō'osperm, fertilized ovum or female cell.

ōō'dle, n. (colloq.). (Always in pl.) superabundance *(~s of money).* [orig. unkn.]

ōof, n. (sl.). Money, pelf, cash; **~-bird,**
source of money, rich person. Hence
~'y² a. [for *oof-tish* Yiddish = G *auf*
dem tische on the table]

ō'olīte, n. Granular limestone, each grain
being a calcareous particle in carbonate
of lime, roe-stone; (geol.) series of fossili-
ferous rocks of this formation lying between Chalk, or Wealden, & Lias. Hence
ōolīt'ıc a. [f. F *oölithe* (OO-, -LITE)]

ōŏl'ŏng, n. A dark kind of cured Chinese
tea. [Chin. *wulung,* = black dragon]

ōŏm, n. (S.-Afr.). Uncle (esp. *Oom Paul* =
President Kruger). [Du.]

-ōōn, suf. formerly used in borrowing F
wds in *-on (drag~)* except when the final
syl. was not accented *(baron);* esp. for F
-on f. It. *-one* f. L *-onem* nom. *-o (ball~,*
buff~, cart~); rarely in native wds *(spit-*
t~); F wds now taken have *-on* in E
(chignon); the L expresses humorous or
contemptuous description *(Naso* Nosey),
the It. bigness or coarseness, the F (exc. in
It. borrowings) small size; in E the suf.
has no definite meaning.

ōōnt, n. (Anglo-Ind.). Camel. [Hind.]

ōōze¹, n. **1.** Wet mud, slime, esp. in river-
-bed or estuary or on ocean bottom. **2.**
Tanning liquor, infusion of oak-bark etc.;
~-calf, calf-skin through which dye has
been forced. **3.** Exudation, sluggish flow,
something that oozes. Hence **ōōz'y²** a.,
ōōz'ıLY² adv., **ōōz'ıness** n. [1 f. OE *wāse*
cogn. w. ON *veisa* puddle; 2 f. OE *wōs*
juice, sap; 3 f. foll.]

ōōze², v.i. & t. (Of moisture) pass slowly
through the pores of a body, exude, percolate; (of substance) exude moisture; (fig.)
leak *out or away (the secret ~d out; my*
courage is oozing away); emit (moisture,
information, encouragement). [ME *wōsen,*
f. prec. 2]

ōp, n. (colloq.). Operation. [abbr.]

op-. See OB-.

opā'cĭtў, n. Being opaque, quality of not
allowing passage to or (rarely) of not reflecting light, non-transparency, obscurity; obscurity of meaning, obtuseness of
understanding. [f. F *opacité* f. L *opacita-*
tem (OPAQUE, -TY)]

ōp'ah (-*a*), n. Rare brilliant-coloured large
N.-Atlantic fish of mackerel family,
king-fish, moon-fish. [W.-Afr. name]

ŏp'al, n. Amorphous quartz-like form of

hydrous silica some kinds of which show changing colours (e.g. *common* ~, milk-white or bluish with green, yellow, & red reflexions), whence ~ES'CENT, ~ESQUE' (-ĕsk), aa., ~ES'CENCE n.; (commerc.) semi--translucent white glass. [f. F *opale*, or L *opalus*]

ōp'al|ine, a. & n. **1.** Opal-like, opalescent, iridescent. **2.** n. Semi-translucent white glass. So ~IZE(3) v.t.

opāque' (-k), a. (~*r*, ~*st*), & n. Not reflecting (rare) or transmitting light, not shining (rare), impenetrable to sight; not lucid, obscure; obtuse, dull-witted; (n.) *the* ~, darkness. Hence ~LY² (-kl-) adv., ~NESS (-kn-) n. [15th c. *opak*, f. L *opacus*; sp. now assim. to F]

ōpe, v.t. & i. (Poet. for) OPEN². [ME, after obs. adj. *ope* reduced f. *open* on anal. of p.p. (cf. *awake*, *wove*, f. *awaken*, *woven*)]

ōp'en¹, a. (~*er*, ~*est*), & n. **1.** Not closed or blocked up, allowing of entrance or passage or access, having gate or door or lid or part of boundary withdrawn, unenclosed, unconfined, uncovered, bare, exposed, undisguised, public, manifest, not exclusive or limited, (~ *gate*, *passage*, *church*, *drawer*, *box*, *field*, *grave*, *carriage*, *hostilities*, *scandal*, *contempt*; ~ *air*, outdoors; *door flew* ~; ~ *boat*, undecked; *lay* ~, expose esp. by cutting skin etc. of; ~ *ears*, eagerly attentive, whence ~-earED² a.; ~ *mouth*, in voracity, frankness, etc., & esp. in gaping stupidity or surprise, whence ~-mouthED², pr. -dhd, a.; ~ *mind*, accessibility to new ideas, unprejudiced or undecided state, whence ~-mindED² a., ~-mind'edLY² adv., ~-mind'edNESS n.; *is* ~ *to conviction*, *offers*, etc.; *keep* ~ *doors* or *house*, entertain all comers, be hospitable; *the* ~ *door*, free admission of foreign nations to country for trade; *force an* ~ *door*, demand from willing giver; *the exhibition is now* ~, admitting visitors; *shop*, *show*, *court*, *is* ~ *at such hours*; ~ *heart*, frankness, unsuspiciousness, kindliness, cordiality, whence ~-heartED² a., ~-heart'edLY² adv., ~-heart'edNESS n.; ~ *champion*, ‖ *scholarship*, successful, won, after unrestricted competition; *race is* ~ *to all*; *position is* ~ *to attack*; O~ *Brethren*, less exclusive section of the Plymouth Brethren; ~*cast* (surface) *coal*; ~ *hearth process* (of steel-making in shallow reverberatory furnace); ~ *time*, what is not CLOSE¹ time; *river*, *harbour*, *is* ~, free of ice; ~ *weather*, *winter*, not frosty; *bowels are* ~, not constipated; ~ *country*, without houses, free of fences; *there are three courses* ~ *to us*; ~ *question*, matter on which differences of opinion are legitimate; ~ VERDICT). **2.** Expanded, unfolded, outspread, spread out, not close, with intervals, porous, communicative, frank, (~ *book*, *flower*; ~ *letter*, esp. protest etc. printed in newspaper etc. but addressing individual; ~ *country*,

affording wide views; ~ *order*, mil. & nav., formation with wide spaces between men or ships; ~ *harmony*, of chord with wide intervals; ~ *ice*, through which navigation is possible; *receive with* ~ *arms*, heartily, whence ~-armED a.; *with* ~ *eyes*, not unconsciously or under misapprehension, also in eager attention or surprise, whence ~-eyED² (-īd) a.; *has an* ~ *hand*, gives freely, whence ~-handED² a., ~-hand'edLY² adv., ~-hand'edNESS n.; ~ *face*, ingenuous-looking, whence ~-facED² a.; ~ *work* or ~*work*, pattern with interstices in metal, lace, etc.; *will be* ~ *with you*, speak frankly). **3.** (mus.). (Of note) produced from unstopped pipe or string or without slide, key, or piston. **4.** (phonet.). (Of vowel) produced with relatively wide opening or mouth (cf. CLOSE¹); (of syllable) ending in vowel; hence ~NESS n. **5.** n. *The* ~, ~ space or country or air, public view. [OE *open*, OS *opan*, OHG *offan*, ON *opinn*; f. root of UP]

ōp'en², v.t.&i. **1.** Make or become OPEN¹ or more open (~ SESAME; *shops* ~ *at 9 a.m.*; ~ *a business*, *shop*, *account*, *campaign*, etc., start or establish it or set it going; ~ *fire*, begin shooting; abs. for ~ *book*, as ~*ed at p. 12*; ~ *ground*, break up with plough etc.; ~ *bowels*, cause evacuation; ~*s a prospect* lit. or fig., brings it to view; ~ *the door to*, give opportunity for; ~ *one's designs*, reveal or communicate them; ~ *one's eyes*, show surprise; ~ *another's eyes*, undeceive or enlighten him; ~ *the mind*, *heart*, etc., expand or enlarge it; *not* ~ *lips*, remain silent; ~ *the* BALL²; ~ PARLIAMENT; ~ *the case*, (of counsel in lawcourt) make preliminary statement before calling witnesses; ~ *the debate*, begin it, be first speaker; *door*, *room*, ~*s into passage*, on to lawn, etc.; *the wonders of astronomy were* ~*ing to him*, becoming known; ~ *one's shoulders* in cricket, of batsman's attitude in driving). **2.** Commence speaking (~*ed upon the fiscal question*, *with a compliment*, etc.). **3.** Make a start (*lard* ~*ed active*, was in demand at once; *session* ~*ed yesterday*). **4.** (Of hounds, & derog. of men) begin to give tongue. **5.** (naut.). Get view of by change of position, come into full view, (*take care not to* ~ *the obelisk*; *the harbour light* ~*ed*). **6.** ~ *out*, unfold, develop, expand, (t. & i.), accelerate, become communicative; ~ *up*, make accessible, bring to notice, reveal. Hence ~ABLE a., (-)~ER¹ (1, 2) n. [OE *openian*, f. prec.]

ōp'ening¹ (-pn-), n. In vbl senses; also or esp.: gap, passage, aperture; commencement, initial part; counsel's preliminary statement of case; (chess) recognized sequence of moves for beginning game; opportunity, favourable conjuncture *for*. [ME; -ING¹]

ōp'ening² (-pn-), a. In vbl senses; esp., initial, first, (*his* ~ *remarks*). [ME; -ING²]

ŏp'enlў, adv. Without concealment, publicly, frankly. [ME; -LY²]

ŏp'era¹, n. Dramatic performance or composition of which music is an essential part, branch of art concerned with these, (grand ~, without spoken dialogue; comic ~, of humorous character; opéra comique F, with spoken dialogue, not necessarily humorous; ~ bouffe pr. bōof, of farcical character); ~-cloak, -hood, lady's for wearing at ~ or going to evening parties; ~-glass(es), small binocular for use at ~ or theatre; ~-hat, man's tall collapsible hat; ~-house, theatre for performance of ~. [It. f. L, = labour, work]

ŏp'era²; See OPUS.

ŏp'erāt|e, v.i. & t. **1.** Be in action, produce an effect, exercise influence, (the tax ~es to our disadvantage); play (up)on person's fears etc., try to act (up)on; (of medicines etc.) have desired effect, act. **2.** Perform surgical or other operation (whence, of cases, **ŏp'erable** a.); (try to) execute purpose; (mil.) carry on strategic movements; (of stockbroker etc.) buy & sell esp. with view of influencing prices. **3.** Bring about, accomplish, (energy ~es changes); manage, work, conduct, (chiefly U.S.). **4.** ~ing-room, -table, for use in surgery; ~ing-theatre, room for surgical operations done before students. So ~OR n. [f. L operari work (opus -eris work), -ATE³]

ŏperāt'|ĭc, a. Of, like, opera. Hence ~ICALLY adv. [irreg. f. OPERA, after dramatic]

ŏpera'tion, n. **1.** Working, action, way thing works, efficacy, validity, scope, (is in, comes into, ~; its ~ is easily explained; must extend its ~, make it valid for longer time or in wider sphere). **2.** Active process, activity, performance, discharge of function, (the ~ of breathing, thinking, pruning, etc.). **3.** Financial transaction. **4.** (surg.). Thing done with hand or instrument to some part of body to remedy deformity, injury, disease, pain, etc. (colloq. abbr. op.). **5.** Strategic movement of troops, ships, etc. (COMBINED ~). **6.** (math.). Subjection of number or quantity to process affecting its value or form, e.g. multiplication. Hence ~AL (-sho-) a., (esp.) engaged in or on, used for, (warlike) ~s. [ME, f. OF, f. L operationem (OPERATE, -ION)]

ŏp'erative, a. & n. **1.** Having effect, in operation, efficacious; practical, not theoretical or contemplative, (the ~ part of the work); of surgical operations; hence ~LY² adv. **2.** n. Worker, artisan, mechanic, workman, mill-hand. [f. F (-if, -ive), or LL operativus (OPERATE, -IVE)]

ŏp'eratize, -ise (-īz), v.t. Put into operatic form. [irreg. after dramatize, cf. OPERATIC]

opĕrc'ŭl|um, n. (pl. ~a). Fish's gill-cover; lid or valve closing aperture of shell when tenant is retracted; similar lidlike struc-

ture in plants, eggs of some insects, etc. Hence ~AR¹, ~ATE², ~ātĕd, aa., ~I-comb. form. [L (operire cover, -CULE)]

ŏperĕtt'a, n. One-act or short light opera. [It. (OPERA, -ETTE)]

ŏp'erōse, a. (pedant.). Requiring or showing or taking great pains, laborious. Hence ~LY² adv., ~NESS n. [f. L operosus (opus -eris work, -OSE¹)]

ŏph'icleide (-lid), n. Keyed wind-instrument consisting of tapering brass tube bent double serving as bass or alto to key-bugle; (also tuba) powerful organ reed-pipe. [f. F ophicléide (Gk ophis serpent, kleis -dos key)]

ophid'ian, a. & n. (Member) of the Ophidia or order of reptiles including snakes. [mod. L ophidia (-IA²), irreg. f. Gk ophis snake, -AN]

ŏphio-, comb. form of Gk ophis snake, as ~LATER, ~LATRY, (-ŏl²), serpent-worship(per), ~LOGY (-ŏl²).

ŏph'ite, n. Serpentine, serpentine marble. Hence ophit'IC a. [f. L f. Gk ophitēs f. ophis snake, -ITE²(2)]

ŏphthăl'mia, n. Inflammation of the eye. [LL f. Gk (ophthalmos eye)]

ŏphthăl'mic, a. & n. Of the eye; affected with ophthalmia; (remedy) good for eye--disease. [f. L f. Gk ophthalmikos (prec., -IC)]

ŏphthălm|(o)-, comb. form of Gk ophthalmos eye, as ~IT'IS, ~ŏL'OGY, ~ŏL'OGIST, ~ŏT'OMY; ŏphthăl'moSCOPE, instrument for inspecting retina.

ŏp'iate¹, a. (arch.), & n. **1.** Containing opium, narcotic, soporific. **2.** n. Drug containing opium & easing pain or inducing sleep. [f. med. L opiatus (OPIUM, -ATE²)]

ŏp'iāte², v.t. Mix with opium. [app. f. med. L *opiare (OPIUM), -ATE³]

opine', v.t. Express or hold the opinion (that, or abs. in parenthesis). [f. L opinari]

opin'ion (-yon), n. **1.** Judgement or belief based on grounds short of proof, provisional conviction, view held as probable, (in my ~, as it seems to me; am of ~ that, believe; a matter of ~, disputable point); (also public ~) views or sentiment, esp. on moral questions, prevalent among people in general. **2.** What one thinks on or on a particular question, a belief, a conviction, (the COURAGE of, act up to, one's ~s). **3.** Formal statement by expert when consulted of what he holds to be the fact or the right course, professional advice, (you had better have another ~). **4.** Estimate (have, formed, a very high, low, favourable, ~ of him); (with neg.) favourable estimate (have no ~ of Frenchmen). [ME, f. OF, f. L opinionem (OPINE, -ION)]

opin'ionātĕd (-nyo-), a. Obstinate in opinion, dogmatic; self-willed. Hence ~NESS n. [f. obs. opinionate in same sense, perh. latinized form of obs. opinionED²]

opin'ionātive (-nyo-), a. = prec. [OPINION +-ATIVE, cf. TALKATIVE]

O. Pip. See OBSERVATION, PIP⁵.

ŏpĭsŏm'ĕter, n. Instrument for measuring curved lines as on map, made of wheel running on screw. [f. Gk *opisō* backwards, -METER]

opis'thŏgraph (-ahf), n. (Gk & Rom. ant.). Parchment or slab with writing on both sides. [f. Gk *opisthographos* f. *opisthen* behind + -GRAPH]

ŏp'ium, n., & v.t. **1.** Reddish-brown heavy-scented bitter drug prepared from juice of kind of poppy, smoked or eaten as stimulant, intoxicant, or narcotic, & used as sedative (LAUDANUM) in medicine; ~ *den,* haunt of ~-smokers; ~ *habit,* that of taking ~; hence ~ISM(5) n., ~IZE(5) v.t. **2.** v.t. Drug or treat with ~. [ME, f. L f. Gk *opion* poppy-juice (*opos* juice)]

ŏpodĕl'dŏc, n. Kinds of soap liniment. [wd used & prob. made by Paracelsus for kinds of medical plaster]

opŏp'anăx, n. A fetid gum resin formerly used in medicine; a gum resin used in perfumery. [ME, f. L f. Gk, f. *opos* juice, *panax* (*pas pantos* all, *akos* cure) name of plant]

opŏss'um, n. Kinds of American small arboreal or aquatic nocturnal marsupial with thumbed hind-foot (see also POSSUM); (Austral.) = PHALANGER. [Amer.-Ind.]

∥ **ŏpp'idan,** a. & n. (Inhabitant) of a town (now rare); (at Eton) non-colleger, boy in boarding-house in town. [f. L *oppidanus* (*oppidum* town, -AN)]

ŏpp'il|āte, v.t. (med.). Block up, obstruct. So ~A'TION n. [f. L OP(*pilare* ram)]

oppŏn'ency, n. (rare). Antagonism, opposition. [foll., -ENCY]

oppŏn'ent, a. & n. **1.** Opposing, contrary, opposed, (now rare); ~ *muscle,* opposing thumb or lateral digit to other digit). **2.** n. Adversary, antagonist. [f. L OP(*ponere* place), -ENT]

ŏpp'ortūne (*also* -ūn'), a. (Of time) suitable, well-selected or as favourable as if chosen; (of action or event) well-timed, done or occurring by design or chance at favourable conjuncture. Hence ~LY² adv., ~NESS n., (*also* -ūn⁴). [ME, f. OF *opportun* f. L OP(*portunus* f. *portus* -ūs* harbour)]

ŏpportūn'|ism, n. Allowing of due or undue weight to circumstances of the moment in determining policy; preference of what can to what should be done, compromise, practical politics, adaptation to circumstances; putting of expediency before principle or place before power, political time-serving. So ~IST (2) n. [f. prec. after It. (-*ismo*) & F (-*isme*)]

ŏpportūn'ity, n. Opportuneness (rare); favourable juncture, good chance, opening, (*of doing, to* do, *for* action, or abs.; *find, make, get, seize, give, afford, an* ~; *take the* ~ *of*). [ME, f. OF *opportunite* f. L *opportunitatem* (OPPORTUNE, -TY)]

oppŏs|e' (-z), v.t. **1.** Place or produce or cite (thing, person) as obstacle, antagon-

ist, counterpoise, or contrast, *to,* represent (things) as antithetical, (*to fury let us* ~e *patience; you are* ~*ing things that are practically identical; to Plato I* ~e *Aristotle;* ~*ed himself to it with all his power; the thumb can be* ~*ed to any of the fingers,* placed against it front to front, whence ~'ABLE (-z-) a., ~aBIL'ITY n.). **2.** Set oneself against (person, thing); withstand, resist, obstruct, propose the rejection of (resolution, motion, etc.); (abs.) act as opponent or check (*it is the duty of an opposition to* ~e). **3.** p.p. Contrary, opposite, contrasted, (*characters strongly* ~*ed; black is* ~*ed to white*); (of persons) hostile, adverse, (*is firmly* ~*ed to protection*). [ME, f. OF OP(*poser* POSE¹)]

oppōse'lĕss (-zĭ-), a. (poet.). Irresistible. [-LESS]

ŏpp'osite (-z-), a. (often governing n. by ellipse of *to*), n., adv., & prep. **1.** Contrary in position (to), facing, front to front or back to back (with), (*on* ~ *sides of the square; came from, went in,* ~ *directions; the tree* ~ *to* or ~ *the house;* ~ *leaves* etc. in bot., placed at same height on ~ sides of stem, or placed straight in front of other organ, opp. *alternate;* ~ *number,* person or thing similarly placed in another set etc. to the given one); of contrary kind, diametrically different *to* or *from,* the other of a contrasted pair, (*of an* ~ *kind to, from, what I expected; much liked by the* ~ *sex*); hence ~LY² adv. (chiefly bot.), ~NESS n., (-z-). **2.** n. ~ thing or term (*you are cold-blooded, she is the* ~; *the most extreme* ~*s have some qualities in common*). **3.** adv. & prep. In ~ place, position, or direction (to) (*there was an explosion* ~, in the house across the street; ~ *prompter* in theatre, abbr. *o.p.,* usu. to actor's right; *happened* ~ *the Mansion House); play* ~, (of leads in stage-play or film) háve (specified actor or actress) as one's leading man, lady. [ME, f. OF, f. L OP(*positus* p.p. of *ponere* place)]

oppŏs'iti- (-z-), comb. form of L *oppositus* (prec.) in bot. wds, as ~*fol'ious,* opposite-leaved; ~*sep'alous,* (of stamen) placed straight in front of sepal.

ŏpposi'tion (-z-), n. **1.** Placing opposite (~ *of the thumb,* cf. OPPOSE); diametrically opposite position (esp. astron., of two heavenly bodies when their longitude differs by 180°, opp. CONJUNCTION; *planet is in* ~, opposite sun); contrast, antithesis. **2.** (log.). Relation between two propositions with same subject & predicate but differing in quantity or quality or both. **3.** Antagonism, resistance, being hostile, (*offer a determined* ~; *did it in* ~ *to public opinion; was in* ~ *at the time,* belonging to the ~ in next sense). **4.** ∥ *The* O~*, Her Majesty's* O~, chief parliamentary party opposed to that in office (*the leader of the* O~; *the* O~ *whips, benches,* etc.). **5.** Any party opposed to some proposal. Hence ~AL a. (rare), ~IST(2) n. & a. (rare), (-zĭsho-). [ME, f. OF, f. L OP(*positionem* POSITION)]

oppŏs'itive (-z-), a. (rare). Adversative, antithetic; fond of opposing. [prec., -IVE]

oppress', v.t. Overwhelm with superior weight or numbers or irresistible power; lie heavy on, weigh down, (spirits, imagination, etc.); govern tyrannically, keep under by coercion, subject to continual cruelty or injustice. So **oppre'ssion** (-shn), ~OR, nn., ~IVE a., ~ively² adv., ~iveness n. [ME, f. OF *oppresser* f. med. L OP(*pressare* frequent. of L *premere* press)]

opprŏb'rĭous, a. Conveying reproach, abusive, vituperative. Hence ~LY² adv. [ME, f. OF -*eux*, or LL *opprobriosus* (foll., -OUS)]

opprŏb'rĭum, n. Disgrace attaching to some act or conduct, infamy, crying of shame. [L, f. OP(*probrare* f. *probrum* disgraceful act)]

oppugn' (-ūn), v.t. Controvert, call in question, whence ~ER¹ (-ūn²) n.; (rare) attack, resist, be in conflict with, (so **oppŭg'nant** a. & n., **oppŭg'nance**, op-pŭg'nancy, ŏppŭgna'tion, nn., all rare). [ME, f. L OP(*pugnare* fight) attack, besiege]

ŏp'simăth, n. (rare). One who learns late in life. So **ŏpsim'athy¹** n. [f. Gk *opsi-mathēs* (*opse* late, *math-*learn)]

ŏpsŏn'ic, a. Having the effect on bacteria of making them easier of consumption by phagocytes (~ *action, power*; ~ *index*, numerical expression of the phagocytic power of the serum of a patient under anti-bacterial injections as below). So **ŏp'sonin** n., the substance produced in patient's blood by injection of dead cultures of the bacteria of his disease. [f. Gk *opson* cooked meat, +-IC]

ŏpt, v.i. Exercise an option, make choice, (*between* alternatives or *for* alternative or *out*). Hence ~'ANT n. [f. F *opter* f. L *optare* choose, wish]

ŏp'tative (or ŏptā²), a. & n. (gram.). 1. Expressing wish (~ *mood*, set of verbal forms of this kind, distinct chiefly in Sanskrit and Greek; ~ *use of subjunctive*); hence ~LY² adv. 2. n. ~ mood, verbal form belonging to it. [F (-*if*, -*ive*), f. LL *optativus* (prec., -ATIVE)]

ŏp'tic, a. & n. 1. (anat.). Of the eye or sense of sight (~ *nerve, neuritis*, etc.; ~ *angle*, between lines from extremities of object to eye, or from two eyes to one point). 2. n. Eye (now usu. joc.); || device fastened to neck of bottle for measuring out spirits; (pl., with sing. constr.) science of sight & esp. of the laws of its medium, light. [f. F *optique* or med. L f. Gk *optikos* (*optos* seen f. *op*- see); *optics* renders med. L *optica*; see -IC]

ŏp'tical, a. Visual, ocular, (~ *illusion*, produced by too implicit confidence in the evidence of sight); of sight or light

in relation to each other, belonging to optics, constructed to assist sight or on the principles of optics. Hence ~LY² adv. [as prec., see -ICAL]

ŏpti'cian (-shn), n. Maker or seller of optical instruments esp. spectacles. [f. F *opticien* (OPTIC, -ICIAN)]

|| **optime**. See WRANGLER.

ŏp'tim|ism, n. Doctrine, esp. as set forth by Leibnitz, that the actual world is the best of all possible worlds; view that good must ultimately prevail over evil in the universe; sanguine disposition, inclination to take bright views. So ~IST(2) n. & a., ~is'tic a., ~is'tically adv., ~-IZE(2) v.i. [f. F *optimisme* (L *optimus* best, -ISM)]

ŏp'timum, n. (chiefly biol.). Most favourable (natural) conditions (for growth, reproduction, etc.); (attrib.) best or most favourable (~ *temperature*). [L, neut. of *optimus* best]

ŏp'tion, n. Choice, choosing, thing that is or may be chosen, (*make one's* ~; *none of the* ~*s is satisfactory*); liberty of choosing, freedom of choice, (LOCAL² ~; *imprisonment without the* ~ *of a fine*; *have no* ~ *but to*, must); (St., Exch. etc.) purchased right to call for or make delivery within specified time of specified stocks etc. at specified rate. [F, or f. L *optio* (st. of *optare* choose, -TION)]

ŏp'tional (-sho-), a. Not obligatory. [prec., -AL]

ŏptŏ|m'eter, n. Instrument for testing the refractive power & visual range of the eye. Hence ~m'etrist n., sight-tester, ~m'etry n. [f. Gk *optos* seen +-METER]

ŏp'tophŏne, n. Instrument converting light into sound, & so enabling the blind to read print etc. by ear. [f. as prec., + Gk *phōnē* sound]

ŏp'ūlent, a. Rich, wealthy; abounding, abundant, well stored. Hence or cogn. **ŏp'ūlence** n., ~LY² adv. [f. L *opulentus* (*opes* wealth, -ULENT)]

ŏp'us, n. (pl. rare **ŏp'era**). Musician's separate composition of any kind (used esp. in citing it from among its works by number; abbr. *op.*; *Beethoven op. 15*); **măg'num** ~, ~ **măg'num**, or ~, great literary undertaking, writer's or other artist's chief production. [L, = work]

opŭs'cūle, **ŏpŭs'cūlum** (pl. -*la*), n. Minor musical or literary composition. [(-*ule* F) f. L (-*um*) dim. of prec. (-CULE)]

ōr¹, n. (her.). Gold or yellow in armorial bearings. [F, f. L *aurum* gold]

|| **ōr²**, prep. & conj. (arch.). Before, ere, (chiefly now in *or ever, or e'er*, poet.). [OE *ār* f. ON *ár* (= Goth. *air*) early, assim. in sense to OE *ær* ERE]

or³ (ŏr, or), conj. introducing second of two alternatives (*white or black*), all but the first (*white or grey or black*) or only the last (*white, grey, or black*) of any number, the second of each of several pairs (*white or black, red or yellow, blue or green*), or (poet.) each of two (*or in the heart or in the head*). An alternative introduced by *or* may be (1) on equal footing with preceding (*shall you be there or not?*; *any Tom, Dick, or Harry*); (2) as true as the preceding (*ripe tomatoes are red or yellow*); (3) mere synonym (*common or garden*); (4) indication that preceding is doubtfully accurate (*one or two, five or six*, etc., a few); (5) explanation of preceding (*saw a dug-out or hollowed-tree boat*); (6) statement of only remaining possibility 'or choice given (often after *either*; *a thing must surely be or not be*; *for goodness' sake either take it or leave it*); (7) statement of result of rejection etc. of preceding (often with *else*; *she must weep or she must die*; *make haste, or else you will be late*); (8) second etc. member of indirect question or conditional protasis after WHETHER (*ask him whether he was there or not*; *must do it whether I like or dislike it*). In syntax, a set of alternatives with or is sing. if each member is sing. (*man or woman, boy or girl, goes unmolested*; not *go*); if the members differ in number etc., the nearest prevails (*were you or he, was he or you, there?*; *either he or you were, either you or he was*), but some forms (e.g., *was I or you on duty?*) are avoided; forms in which difference of gender in the members causes difficulty with pronouns (*a landlord or landlady expects their, his or her, his, rent*) are usually avoided, *their rent* or *the rent due to them* being ungrammatical, *his or her rent* or *the rent due to him or her* clumsy, & *his rent* or *the rent due to him* slovenly. [reduced form of obs. *other* conj. which superseded OE *oththe* or]

-or, a term. of wds, & form of var. suff., of L orig. 1. (a) L *-or, -orem*, OF *-or, -ur* (F *-eur*), in ME first *-or, -ur*, later *-our*, which was subsequently largely refash. after L *-or*. In Gt. Britain many early spellings *-our* have survived, but Amer. usage favours *-or* in all. Generally, the sp. *-or* repr. either (i) older wds in *-our* refash. after L *-or*, or (ii) later adoptives taken f. F or direct f. L; (b) L nn. in *-ator, -ctor, -itor* developed regularly in OF as *-ëor, -ëur* (F *-eur*), in AF *-cour*, ME *-our*, which thus fell together w. wds f. simple L *-or, -orem* (see (a), above). 2. In E wds, this term. appears in the foll. suff.: (a) *-or* (formerly freq. *-our*), ult. repr. L *-or, -orem* in nn. of condition f. intr. vbs, as *error, horror*; (b) *-or* (formerly freq. *-our*), repr. L *-or, -orem* of agent- nn. f. p.p. or supine stems, as (i) *actor, confessor, doctor*; (ii) repr. L *-ator* etc. (see 1(b)), as *donor, emperor, vendor*, & anal. formations in OF or AF on the vb, as *tailor, warrior*; (iii) f. L wds in *-ator* &c. (see 1 (b)) in later adoptives (f. OF, or AF, or L) retaining the L *-t-*, as *administrator, creditor*; (c) *-or* is occas. an alt. of another suf., as in *bachelor, chancellor* (earlier *-er*), or of E *-er*, as in *sailor*

(earlier *-er*). When *-or* & *-er* coexist, *-or* has occas. a more legal or professional sense; conversely, *-or* has been altered to *-er*, as in *barber* (ME & AF *barbour*); (d) *-or (-our)* occas. repr. F *-oir (manor, mirror)*; (e) *-or* repr. ME, AF *-our* f. L *-or*, var. of *-ior* suf. of compar. degree: see *-IOR*[2].

ŏ'rach(e), n. Kinds of wild and kitchen-garden plants of goosefoot family. [15/16th c. *arage, arache* f. AF *arasche* (= F *arroche*), ult. f. L *atriplex* f. Gk *atraphaxus*]

ŏ'racle, n. **1.** Place at which ancient Greeks etc. were accustomed to consult their deities for advice or prophecy (*work the ~*, secure desired answer by tampering with priests etc., also fig. bring secret influence to bear in one's favour); response, often ambiguous or obscure, given at such place. **2.** Holy of holies or mercy-seat in Jewish temple. **3.** (Vehicle, personal or other, of) divine inspiration or revelation. **4.** Person or thing serving as infallible guide, test, or indicator (*I am Sir O~*); authoritative, profoundly wise, or mysterious adviser or advice, judge or judgement, prophet or prophecy. Hence (esp. w. ref. to obscurity) **orăc̱ūlAR**[1] a., **orăc'ūlarLY**[2] adv., **orăcŭlă'rITY** n. [ME, f. OF, f. L *oraculum* f. *orare* speak]

ŏr'al, a. & n. **1.** Spoken, verbal, by word of mouth; (anat.) of the mouth. **2.** n. (colloq.). ~ examination etc. Hence **~LY**[2] adv. [f. LL *oralis* (L *os oris* mouth, *-AL*)]

ŏ'range[1] (-inj), n. & a. **1.** (Evergreen tree bearing) large roundish many-celled juicy acid or sweet fruit enclosed in bright reddish-yellow tough rind (*squeeze the ~*, take all the good from anything; *squeezed ~*, thing from which no more good can be got; BLOOD[1] ~; *China ~*, former name of common ~; MANDARIN[2] ~; *mock ~*, the shrub syringa; TANGERINE ~; *~s & lemons*, nursery game, also kind of toad-flax; *Blenheim ~*, kind of apple); (also *~-colour*) reddish-yellow; *~-blossom*, flowers of ~, worn by brides at wedding; *~-fin*, kind of trout; ~ MARMALADE; *~ stick*, thin pointed stick for finger-nails; *~ -tip*, kind of butterfly. **2.** adj.~-coloured, reddish-yellow. Hence **ŏ'rangERY**(3) (-inj-) n. [ME. f. OF, ult. f. Arab. *nāranj*]

Orange[2] (ŏ'rĭnj), n. Town on Rhône from which *Princes of ~* took title (*William of ~* in Eng. hist., King William III); (attrib. & comb.) connected with Irish ultra-protestant party (prob. f. the *~men*, political society formed 1795 for protestant ascendancy in Ireland, prob. named after ~ lodge of freemasons in Belfast, prob. named after William), whence **ŏ'rangISM**(3) (-inj-) n. [F, = L *Arausio*]

ŏrangeade' (-injăd), n. Effervescent or still drink of orange juice etc. [-ADE]

orăng̱'outăng' (-ōŏt-), **ŏr'ang-ut'an** (-ōŏt-), n. Large long-armed arboreal

anthropoid ape of Borneo & Sumatra.
[Malay (-*utan*) = man of the woods]
ŏrāte′, v.i. (joc.). Make speech, hold forth,
play the orator. [back form. f. foll.]
ŏrā′tion, n. Formal address or harangue
or discourse esp. of ceremonial kind;
(gram.) language, way of speaking (*direct,
indirect* or *oblique*, ~, person's words as
actually spoken, or with the changes of
person, tense, etc., usual in reporting).
[ME, f. L *oratio* (*orare* speak, -ATION)]
ŏ′rator, n. Maker of a speech; eloquent
public speaker; ‖ *Public O~.* official at
Oxford & Cambridge speaking for university on State occasions. Hence
ŏ′ratRESS[1] n. [ME, f. OF *orateur* f. L
oratorem (prec., -OR)]
ŏratō̆r′iō, n. (pl. ~*s*). Semi-dramatic
musical composition usu. on sacred
theme performed by soloists, chorus, &
orchestra, without action, scenery, or
costume. [It., orig. of musical services at
oratory of St Philip Neri]
ŏ′ratorize, -ise (-īz), v.i. = ORATE. [-IZE]
ŏ′ratory̆[1], n. Small chapel, place for private worship; (*O~*) R.-C. religious society
of simple priests without vows founded
in Rome 1564 to give plain preaching &
popular services, also any branch of this
in England etc., whence **ŏratō̆r′IAN** a. &
n. [ME, f. LL *oratorium* neut. of L *ora-
torius* (*orare* pray, speak, -TORY)]
ŏ′ratory̆[2], n. (Art of making) speeches,
rhetoric; highly coloured presentment of
facts, eloquent or exaggerating language.
Hence **ŏratō̆′rICAL** a., **ŏratō̆′ricalLY**[2]
adv. [f. L *oratoria* (*ars* art) of speaking,
fem. as prec.]
ŏrb, n., & v.t. & i. 1. Circle, circular disc,
ring, (now rare); sphere, globe; heavenly
body; eyeball, eye, (poet.); globe surmounted by cross as part of regalia; organized or collective whole; hence ~′LESS
a. 2. vb. Enclose in, gather (t. & i.) into,
~. [f. L *orbis* ring]
ŏrbic′ŭl|ar, a. Circular, discoid, ring-
-shaped (~*ar muscle*, sphincter); spherical,
globular, rounded, (fig.) forming complete whole. Hence or cogn. ~ă′rITY n.,
~arLY[2] adv., ~ATE[2] a. (nat. hist.). [ME,
f. L *orbicularis* (*orbiculus* dim. as prec.,
-AR[1])]
ŏrb′it, n., & v.i. 1. Eye-socket, whence
~o- comb. form; border round eye of
bird or insect; curved course of planet,
comet, satellite, etc.; (fig.) range, sphere
of action. 2. v.i. (Of satellite etc.) move
in an ~. Hence ~AL a. [f. L *orbita* track
of wheel or moon (*orbis* ring)]
ŏrc, ŏrc′a, n. Kinds of cetacean; sea or
other monster. [f. F *orque*, or f. L *orca* kind
of whale]
Orcād′ian (ō̆r-), a. & n. (Native) of Orkney. [f. L *Orcades* Orkney Islands, -IAN]
ŏrch′ard, n. Enclosure with fruit-trees;
~*man*, fruit-grower, also ~IST(3) n. [OE
ortgeard f. L *hortus* garden, YARD[2]; cf.
Goth. *aurtigards*]

ŏrchĕs′t|ĭc (-k-), a. Of dancing. Hence
~ICS n. [f. Gk *orkhēstikos* (*orkhēstēs*
dancer, see foll.)]
ŏr′chĕstra (-k-), n. 1. Semicircular space
in front of ancient-Greek theatre-stage
where chorus danced & sang. 2. Part of
modern theatre or concert-room assigned
to band or chorus. 3. Body of instrumental performers, or combination of
bowed, wood-wind, brass, & percussion
instruments, in theatre or concert-room,
whence **ŏrchĕs′trAL** (-k-) a. [L, f. Gk
orkhēstra (*orkheomai* dance)]
ŏr′chĕstr|āte (-k-), v.t. & i. Compose (t. &
i.), arrange, or score, for orchestral performance. Hence ~A′TION n. [-ATE[3]]
ŏrchestri′na (-kĭstrē-), ***ŏrchĕs′trion**
(-k-), nn. Elaborate kind of barrel-organ
meant to give orchestra-like effect. [-INA[1]]
ŏr′chid, ŏr′chis (-k-), n. Member of
large family of monocotyledonous plants
(-*is* is usu. of wild English kinds, -*id* of
exotics or in bot. use), of which English
kinds are terrestrial with tuberous root &
erect fleshy stem with spike of usu. red or
purple flowers, & many exotic kinds have
flowers of fantastic shapes & brilliant
colours. Hence **ŏrchid**A′CEOUS (-kĭdāshus)
a., **ŏr′chid**IST(3) (-k-) n. [(-*id* made 1845
by Lindley, see -ID[2]) f. L f. Gk *orkhis -ios*
testicle, orchis, (w. ref. to shape of tuber)]
ŏr′chido- (-k-), assumed comb. form of Gk
orkhis (prec.), correctly *orchio-*, as
~MAN′IA, ~LOGY (-ŏl̆-).
ŏr′chil, n. Red or violet dye from lichen.
[ME, f. OF *orchel*, of unkn. orig.]
ŏrchīt′is (-k-), n. Inflammation of the
testicles. [f. Gk *orkhis* testicle +-ITIS]
ŏr′cin, n. (chem.). Colourless crystalline
substance extracted from lichens & yielding various dyes when compounded. [f.
mod. L *orcina* (ORCHIL, -IN)]
ŏrdain′, v.t. (Eccl.) appoint ceremonially
to Christian ministry, confer holy orders
(esp. those of deacon or priest) on (*was
~ed priest, elder*, etc., or abs.); (of God,
fate, etc.) destine, appoint, (*has ~ed the
time, death as our lot, us mortal, us to die,
that we should live*); appoint authoritatively, decree, enact, (*what the laws ~; ~
that —*). [ME, f. OF *ordener* f. L *ordinare*
(*ordo -inis* order)]
ŏrdain′ment, n. (rare). Decree(ing).
-[MENT]
ŏrdeal′ (*or* ō̆rd′ēl), n. Ancient Teutonic
mode of deciding suspected person's guilt
or innocence by subjecting him to physical test such as plunging of hand in boiling water, safe endurance of which was
taken as divine acquittal; experience that
tests character or endurance, severe trial.
[in 16th c. repr. med. L *ordalium* or OE
ordāl, -dēl (= OS *urdēli*, OHG *urteili*)
judgement, corresp. to vb *ādǣlan* deal
out (= OHG *irteilen*)]
ŏrd′er[1], n. (Main senses) 1. Rank, row,
class. 2. Sequence, arrangement. 3. Mandate. 1. Tier (now rare; ~ *on* ~ *of*

sculptured figures); social class or rank, separate & homogeneous set of persons, (*esp. the higher, lower, ~s; all ~s & degrees of men; the ~ of baronets; the clerical, military, ~*); kind, sort, (*talents of a high, considerations of quite another, ~*); any of the nine grades of angels (seraphim, cherubim, thrones, dominations, principalities, powers, virtues, archangels, angels); grade of Christian ministry (*holy ~s* in Anglican church, those of bishop, priest, & deacon, in R.-C., these & subdeacon; *minor ~s* in R.-C. Church, those of acolyte, exorcist, reader, & doorkeeper); (pl.) status of clergyman (*take ~s*, be ordained; *in ~s*, ordained; often in these phrr., & always elsewhere, *holy ~s*); fraternity of monks or friars, or formerly of knights, bound by common rule of life (*the Franciscan ~; the Teutonic ~; the ~ of Templars*); || company usu. instituted by sovereign to which distinguished persons are admitted by way of honour or reward (*~ of the Garter, the Bath, Merit*, etc.), insignia worn by members of this (*sent him, wears, the ~ of the Golden Fleece*); (archit.) mode of treatment with established proportions between parts, esp. one of the *five (classical) ~s*, Doric, Ionic, Corinthian, Tuscan, & Composite, of column and entablature, the first three being Greek in origin, the others Roman; (math.) degree of complexity (*line, equation, fluxion, of the first* etc. *~*), (also *~ of magnitude*) class in a system of classification determined by size (*measurements of the ~ of one in a million*); (nat. hist.) classification-group below CLASS[1] & above family (*natural ~* in bot., abbr. N.O., of plants allied in general structure, not merely agreeing in single characteristic as in Linnaean system). **2.** Sequence, succession, manner of following, (*in alphabetical, chronological*, etc., *~*; *out of ~*, not systematically arranged; *follow the ~ of events; inverts the natural ~; take them in ~*, one after another according to some principle); regular array, condition in which every part or unit is in its right place, tidiness, normal or healthy or efficient state, (*drew them up in ~; are scattered without any ~; love of ~; is in bad, out of, ~*, not working rightly; *is in ~ or good ~*, fit for use); || (arch.) suitable action, measures, (*take ~ to do; take ~ with*, arrange, dispose of); constitution of the world, way things normally happen, collective manifestations of natural forces or laws, natural or moral or spiritual system with definite tendencies, (esp. *the ~ of nature* or *things* or *the world*; *the old ~ changeth*; *whether there is a moral ~ or not*); stated form of divine service (*the ~ of confirmation*); principles of decorum & rules of procedure accepted by legislative assembly or public meeting, or enforced by its president (*Speaker called him to ~; O~! O~!*, protest against in-

fringement of it; *rise to ~* or *a point of ~*, interrupt debate etc. with inquiry whether something being said or done is *in* or *out of ~; ~ of the day*, programme, business set down for treatment, whence, in gen. use, prevailing state of things, as *industry, thunder, cricket, is the ~ of the day*; || *~-paper*, written or printed *~ of the day*; || *~-book*, in which motions to be submitted to the House of Commons must be entered); prevalence of constituted authority, law-abiding state, absence of riot, turbulence, & violent crime, (often *law & ~; ~ was restored; keep ~*, enforce it); *close, open, ~* (mil. etc.), formation with narrow, wide, spaces between men or ships; *marching, review*, etc., *~* (mil.), the regulation uniform & equipment carried by the soldier in marching, at review, etc. (cf. MARCH[5]*ing ~s*); (mil.) *the ~*, position of company etc. with arms ordered (see foll.); *in ~ to do*, with a view to, for the purpose of, doing; *in ~ that*, with the intention or to the end that. **3.** Mandate, injunction, authoritative direction or instruction, (often pl.; *gave ~s, an ~, the ~, for* something *to* be done, *that it should be* done, etc.; *is obedient to ~s*; || *O~ in Council*, sovereign *~ on* some administrative matter given by advice of Privy Council; *by ~*, according to direction of the proper authority; *judge gave, made, refused, an* or *the ~*); (banking etc.) instruction to pay money or deliver property signed by owner or responsible agent (*~ cheque, cheque to* person's *~*, one requiring payee's endorsement before being cashed; *postal, money* or pop. *post-office, ~*, kinds of Post-Office cheque for remitting money, the latter non-transferable); (commerc.) direction to manufacturer, tradesman, etc., to supply something (*made to ~*, according to special directions, to suit individual measurements, etc., opp. *ready-made*; *grocer has sent for ~s*; *is on ~*, has been ordered but not yet supplied; *a large ~*, colloq., difficult job; *~-book*, in which tradesman enters *~s*; *~-clerk*, with duty of entering *~s*; *~-form*, skeleton *~* to be filled in by customer); pass admitting bearer gratis, cheap, or as privilege, to theatre, museum, private house, etc. [ME, f. OF *ordre* f. L *ordinem* nom. *-o*]

ōrd′er², v.t. Put in order, array, regulate, (arch.; *~ed his troops; ~* one's *affairs; has ~ed his life well*); (mil.) *~ arms*, stand rifles butt on ground & hold them close to right side; (of God, fate, etc.) ordain (*so we hoped, but it was otherwise ~ed*); command, bid, prescribe, (*~ a retreat*, thing *to be* done, person *to do*, *that* person or thing *should*; *~ed him a mustard plaster*); command or direct (person etc.) to go *to, away, home*, etc. (*was ~ed to Egypt; ~ about*, send hither & thither, domineer over); direct tradesman, servant, etc., to supply (~ *dinner*, settle what it shall consist of). [ME, f. prec.]

órd'erl|ў, a. & n. **1.** Methodically arranged or inclined, regular, obedient to discipline, not unruly, well-behaved, whence ~INESS n.; (mil.) of, charged with conveyance or execution of, orders ‖ (~*y book*, regimental or company book for entry of orders; ~*y officer*, officer of the day; ~*y room*, in barracks for company's business); ‖ ~*y bin*, street box for refuse. **2.** n. Soldier in attendance on officer to carry orders etc.; attendant in (esp. military) hospital; street cleaner. [-LY¹]

órd'inal, a. & n. **1.** (Number) defining thing's position in series (*first, twentieth*, etc., *are* ~*s* or ~ *numbers*; cf. CARDINAL). **2.** Of a nat.-hist. order. **3.** n. Service--book used at ordinations. [ME, f. LL *ordinalis* (ORDER¹, -AL)]

órd'inance, n. Authoritative direction, decree (SELF-*denying* ~); religious rite; (rare) collocation of parts in literary work or architecture. [ME, f. OF *ordenance* f. med. L *ordinancia* (ORDAIN, -ANCE)]

órd'inánd, n. Candidate for ordination. [f. L *ordinandus* (*ordinare* ORDAIN)]

órd'inarў, a. & n. **1.** Regular, normal, customary, usual, not exceptional, not above the usual, commonplace, (‖ *in* ~ appended to *physician* etc., by permanent appointment, not temporary or extraordinary; *in the* ~ *way I should refuse*, if the circumstances were not exceptional; *something out of the* ~; ~ *seaman*, abbr. O.S., lower rating than *able*; *in* ~, of ships laid up, not in commission), whence **órd'inarILY²** adv., **órd'inariNESS** n. **2.** ‖ (Authority) having immediate or *ex officio* & not deputed jurisdiction (*the O*~, archbishop in province, bishop in diocese; *O*~ or *Lord O*~ in Scotland, one of five judges of Court of Session constituting Outer House). **3.** Rule or book laying down order of divine service. **4.** ‖ Public meal provided at fixed time & price in inn etc. **5.** (her.). Charge of earliest, simplest, & commonest kind (esp. chief, pale, bend, fesse, bar, chevron, cross, saltire). **6.** Early type of bicycle, with one large & one very small wheel (opp. *safety*). [f. L *ordinarius* (ORDER¹, -ARY¹); partly thr. OF -*arie*, F -*aire*]

órd'inate, n. (geom.). Any of series of parallel chords of conic section in relation to bisecting diameter (esp. used of half the chord, from curve to diameter); straight line from any point drawn parallel to one co-ordinate axis & meeting the other. [16th c., f. L (*linea*) *ordinate* (*applicata*) line applied parallel]

órdinā'tion, n. Arrangement in ranks, classification; conferring of holy orders, admission to church ministry; decreeing, ordainment. [ME, f. OF, or L *ordinatio* (ORDAIN, -ATION)]

órdinee', n. Newly ordained deacon. [ORDAIN, -EE]

órd'nance, n. Mounted guns, cannon, ‖ branch of public service dealing esp. with military stores & materials (*Royal Army O*~ *Corps*, formerly with wider powers *Board of O*~; ‖ ~ *survey*, Government survey of Great Britain & Ireland; ‖ ~ *datum*, mean sea level as defined for ~ survey). [var. of ORDINANCE]

órd'ūre (*or* -*dyer*), n. Excrement, dung; obscenity, foul language. [ME, f. OF (*ord* foul f. L HORRID*us*, -URE)]

ōre, n. Solid native mineral aggregate from which valuable constituent(s) not necessarily metal may be usefully extracted; (poet.) metal, esp. gold. [in form repr. OE *ār* brass (= OS, OHG *ēr*, ON *eir*, Goth. *aiz*, cogn. w. L *aes aeris*); in sense repr. OE *ōra* (= Du. *oer*, LG *ūr*, ore, of unkn. orig.]

ōr'ĕăd, n. (L & Gk myth.). Mountain nymph. [f. L *oreas* -*ados* f. Gk *oreias* f. *oros* mountain, -AD(1)]

ŏrĕc'tic, a. (philos., med.). Of desire or appetite, appetitive. [f. Gk *orektikos* (*oregō* stretch out, -IC)]

ōr'ĕide, n. Kind of brass resembling gold used in imitation jewellery. [f. F *oréide* (*or* f. L *aurum* gold); see -IDE, OROIDE]

ōrfe, n. Kind of goldfish. [G & F, f. L f. Gk *orphos* sea perch]

ōrg'an, n. **1.** Musical instrument of pipes supplied with wind by bellows, sounded by keys, & distributed into sets or stops having special tone, which in turn form groups or partial ~s (*great, choir, swell, solo, pedal*, ~) each with separate keyboard, whence ~IST(3) n.; = BARREL¹-~ (~-*grinder*, player of this); keyboard wind-instrument with metal reeds, harmonium; AMERICAN ~; *mouth* ~, child's toy reed-instrument. **2.** Part of animal or vegetable body adapted for special vital function (~*s of speech, perception, digestion, generation*, etc.; NASAL ~). **3.** Person's voice with reference to its quality or power (*has a magnificent* ~). **4.** Medium of communication, mouthpiece of opinion, esp. newspaper or magazine or review representing a party, cause, sect, pursuit, etc. **5.** ~-*blower*, person or mechanism working~ bellows; ~-*builder*, of musical ~s; ~-*loft*, gallery in church or concert-room for ~; ~ *piano*, with mechanism giving sustained tones as in ~; ~-*screen*, ornamental screen often between choir & nave on which ~ is placed in cathedral etc.; ~-*stop*, set of pipes of similar tone in ~, handle of mechanism that brings it into action. Hence ~LESS a. [ME, f. OF *organe*, f. L f. Gk *organon* tool (*erg*- WORK)]

ōrg'andie, n. Kind of very fine translucent muslin. [F (-*di*), of unkn. orig.]

ōrgăn'ic, a. **1.** (Physiol.) of the bodily organs, vital; (path., of disease) affecting structure of an organ (opp. *functional*). **2.** Having organs or organized physical structure, of animals or plants, (opp. *in-*

organic). **3.** (chem.). (Of compound substances etc.) existing as constituent of organized bodies or formed from bodies so existing, containing carbon in its molecule (~ *chemistry*, that of carbon compounds). **4.** Constitutional, inherent, fundamental, structural. **5.** Organized or systematic or co-ordinated (~ *unity*; *an* ~ *whole*). Hence **ōrgăn'**ICALLY adv. [f. F (*-ique*) or L f. Gk *organikos* (ORGAN, -IC)]

ōrg'anism, n. Organized body with connected interdependent parts sharing common life, (material structure of) individual animal or plant; whole with interdependent parts compared to living being. [f. F (*-isme*); see ORGANIZE, -ISM]

ōrganizā'tion, n. In vbl senses of foll.; also, organized body or system or society. [ME, f. med. L *organizatio* (foll., -ATION)]

ōrg'aniz|e, -is|e (-īz), v.t. & i. Furnish with organs, make organic, make into living being or tissue, (usu. in p.p.), (intr.) become organic; form into an organic whole (with constituents or resulting whole as obj.); give orderly structure to, frame & put into working order, make arrangements for or get up (undertaking involving co-operation). Hence ~ABLE a., ~ER[1] n. [ME, f. med. L *organizare* (ORGAN, -IZE)]

ōrg'anŏn, -anum, n. Instrument of thought, system of or treatise on logic. [Gk (*-on*), & L (*-um*), see ORGAN; *-on* was title of Aristotle's logical writings, & *novum* (new) *organum* that of Bacon's]

ōrg'anothĕ'rapў, n. Treatment of disease with organic extracts. [f. *organo-* comb. form of Gk *organon* ORGAN, +-THERAPY]

ōrg'anzine (-ēn), n. Silk thread in which the main twist is in contrary direction to that of the strands. [f. F *organsin* f. It. *organzino*, of unkn. orig.]

ōrg'ăsm, n. Violent excitement, rage, paroxysm; height of venereal excitement in coition. So **ōrgăs'**TIC a. [f. mod. L *orgasmus*, f. Gk *orgaō* swell]

ōr'geăt (*or* -zhah), n. Cooling drink made from barley or almonds & orange-flower water. [F, f. Pr. *orjat* (*orge* barley, -ADE)]

ōrgiăs'tic, a. Of the nature of an orgy. [f. Gk *orgiastikos* (*orgiastēs* agent n. f. *orgiazō* celebrate ORGY)]

ōr'gў, n. (Gk &. Rom. ant.; usu. pl.) secret rites in worship of various gods, esp. in that of Bacchus celebrated with wild dancing, drinking, and singing; drunken or licentious revel, (pl.) revelry or debauchery. [earlier pl. only, f. F *orgies* f. L f. Gk *orgia* pl.]

-orial. See -ORY.

ōr'iel, n. Large windowed polygonal recess projecting usu. from upper storey & supported from ground or on corbels; (also ~ *window*) window of ~, projecting window of upper storey. [ME, f. OF *oriol*, of undetermined orig.]

ōr'ient[1], n. & a. **1.** *The* eastward part of sky or earth (poet.); *the* East or countries E. of Mediterranean; ~ pearl; peculiar lustre of pearl of best quality. **.2.** adj. Oriental (poet.); (of precious stones and pearls, of finest kinds, as coming anciently from the East) lustrous, sparkling, precious; (of sun, daylight, etc., or fig.) rising, nascent. [ME, f. OF f. L *orientem* nom. *-ens* rising sun, east, (*oriri* rise, -ENT)]

ōrient'[2], **ō'rientāte**, (*or* ōr-), vv.t. & i. Place (building etc.) so as to face E., build (church) with chancel end due E., bury with feet eastward; place or exactly determine position of with regard to points of compass, settle or find bearings of, (fig.) bring into clearly understood relations (~ *oneself*, determine how one stands); (intr.) turn eastward or in specified direction. Hence **ōrienta'**TION n. [f. F *orienter* (prec.)]

ōrien'tal (*or* ōr-), a. & n. Easterly (arch.); (inhabitant) of the East or countries E. of Mediterranean, esp. Asian, occurring in or coming from or characteristic of the civilization etc. of the East, whence ~ISM(2, 4), ~IST(3), nn., ~IZE(2, 3) v.i. & t.; (of pearls etc.) orient; ~ *stitch*, close kind of herringbone stitch. Hence ~LY[2] adv. [ME, f. OF, or L *orientalis* (ORIENT[1], -AL)]

ō'rifice, n. Aperture, mouth of cavity, perforation, vent. [F, f. LL *orificium* (*os oris* mouth, *-ficere = facere* make)]

ō'riflămme, n. Sacred banner of St Denis, banderole of red silk on lance received by early French kings from abbot of St Denis on starting for war; (fig.) anything material or ideal serving as rallying-point in struggle; bright conspicuous object, blaze of colour, etc. [ME, f. OF (L *aurum* gold, *flamma* flame)]

ō'rigan, orig'anum, n. Wild marjoram, & kinds of allied plant. [ME, f. OF *origan* & L (*-um*), f. Gk *origanon*]

ō'rigin, n. Derivation, beginning or rising from something, person's extraction, source, starting-point, (*a word of Latin, a man of humble,* ~). [f. F *origine*, or L *origo -in-* (*oriri* rise)]

ori'ginal, a. & n. **1.** Existent from the first, primitive, innate, initial, earliest, (~ *sin*, innate depravity common to all human beings in consequence of the fall) that has served as pattern, of which copy or translation has been made, not derivative or dependent, first-hand, not imitative, novel in character or style, inventive, creative, thinking or acting for oneself, (*where is the* ~ *picture?*; *what does the* ~ *Greek say?*; *where whooping-cough is* ~; *is it an* ~ *drawing or a woodcut?*; *made a very* ~ *remark*; *has an* ~ *mind*; ~ *people do* ~ *things*); hence or cogn. **originăl'**ITY n., ~LY[2] adv. **2.** n. Pattern, archetype, thing from which another is copied or translated, (*several transcripts from the* same ~, *reads Don Quixote in the* ~); eccentric person. [ME, f. OF, f. L *originalis* (prec., -AL)]

ori'gin|āte, v.t. & i. Give origin to, initiate, cause to begin, whence ~ATIVE a.; have origin, take rise, (usu. *from* or *in* thing or place, *with* or *from* person). So ~A'TION, ~ātOR, nn. [f. med. L. *originari* (ORIGIN, -ATE³)]

ōrinās'al (-zl), a. & n. Of, sounded with, both mouth & nose (esp. of French nasalized vowels); (n.) ~ vowel. [L *os oris* mouth, -I-, L *nasus* nose, -AL]

ōr'iōle, n. (Also *golden* ~) bird with black & yellow plumage visiting British Isles in summer; other old-world birds of same genus; kinds of bird of similarly coloured American genus. [f. med. L *oriolus* f. L *aureolus* dim. of *aureus* golden (*aurum* gold)]

Ori'on, n. (astron.). Brilliant constellation S. of zodiac, figured as hunter with belt & sword (~'s *belt*, three bright stars in short line across ~; ~'s *hound*, Sirius). [L, f. Gk *Ōriōn*]

Ori'onid, n. (astron.). One of meteor-system with radiant point in Orion. [prec., see -ID³]

-orious. See -ORY.

ŏ'rison (-zn), n. A prayer (usu. in pl.). [ME, f. OF, f. L *orationem* speech (*orare* speak, pray, -ATION)]

Orl'éans (ôr-), n. Kind of plum; fabric of cotton warp & worsted weft. [name of French city]

ōrl'op, n. Lowest deck of ship with three or more decks. [ME, f. MDu. *overloop* covering (*overloopen* run over, see OVER, LEAP¹)]

ōrm'er, n. Edible univalve mollusc, the sea-ear. [Channel-I. F, f. F *ormier* contr. of *oreille de mer* ear of sea]

ōrm'olu (-lōō), n. Gilded bronze used in decorating furniture; gold-coloured alloy of copper, zinc, & tin; articles made of or decorated with these. [f. F *or moulu* ground gold (for use in gilding)]

ōrn'ament¹, n. (Eccl., usu. pl.) what is necessary for worship (e.g. altar, chalice, sacred vessels, service books); ~ *rubric*, that immediately before Order for Morning & Evening Prayer in prayer-book); thing used or serving to adorn, quality or person whose existence or presence confers grace or honour, (*mantelpiece crowded with* ~s; *the* ~ *of a quiet spirit*; *was an* ~ *to his country or age*); (pl., mus.) grace notes; (sing. only) adorning, being adorned, embellishment, features or work added for decorative purposes, (*a tower rich in* ~; *by way of* ~). Hence ~AL a., ~alLY² adv., ~alIST(3), ~alISM(3), nn., (*all* -ĕn⁴). [ME, f. OF *ornement* f. L *ornamentum* equipment (*ornare* equip,-MENT)]

ōrn'amĕnt² (*or* -ĕnt'), v.t. Adorn, beautify. Hence ~A'TION n. [f. prec.]

ōrnāte', a. Elaborately adorned; (of literary style) embellished with flowers of

rhetoric etc. Hence ~LY² adv., ~NESS n. [ME, f. L *ornatus* p.p. (prec.)]

ōrnith|(o)-, comb. form of Gk *ornis* -*ithos* bird, in many scientific wds, as *orn'ithoID*, approaching birds in structure (of some reptiles); ~ŏL'OGY, ~ŏLO'GICAL, ~ŏL'OGIST; *ornith'oMANCY*; ~*orhync'us* (-rĭ-), Australian duck-billed platypus, an aquatic mammal with dark-brown fur, webbed feet, & duck's bill, & laying eggs; ~*ŏs'copy*, augury.

ŏrogĕn'esis, n. (geol.). Process of making mountains. So **ŏrogĕn**ET'IC a. [f. Gk *oros* mountain, GENESIS]

ŏrŏg'raphȳ, **ŏrĕŏ-**, n. Branch of physical geography dealing with mountains; hence **ŏrOGRAPH'IC**(AL) aa. So **ŏr(ĕ)ŏL** OGY n., **ŏr(ĕ)OLO'GICAL** a., **ŏr(ĕ)ŏL'OGIST** n. [Gk *oros -eos* mountain, -GRAPHY]

ŏrohipp'us, n. Fossil quadruped held to be ancestral form of horse. [Gk *oros* mountain, *hippos* horse]

ōr'oide, n. Gold-coloured alloy of copper & zinc. [F *or* gold f. L *aurum*, Gk *eidos* form; cf. -OID, OREIDE]

ōr'otŭnd, a. (Of utterance or phrasing) swelling, mouth-filling, imposing, dignified, pompous, magniloquent, pretentious. [f. L *ore rotundo* (Hor. *A.P.* 323) with round mouth]

ōrph'an, n. & a., & v.t. **1.** (Child) bereaved of parent(s); hence ~HOOD n., ~IZE(3) v.t. **2.** v.t. Bereave of parent(s). [ME, f. LL f. Gk *orphanos* bereaved]

ōrph'anage, n. Orphanhood; institution for orphans' education etc. [-AGE]

Orph'ic, Orphē'an, (ōr-), aa. Of Orpheus or the mysteries or doctrines associated with his name, oracular, mysterious, (usu. -*ic*); like Orpheus's music, melodious, entrancing, (usu. -*ean*). [f. Gk *Orphikos* (*Orpheus*, -IC)]

ōrph'rey, ōrf'ray, n. Ornamental often richly embroidered stripes and borders of ecclesiastical vestment. [ME *orfreis* (gold) embroidery, f. OF f. med. L *auri-frisium* etc. f. L *aurum* gold + *Phrygius* Phrygian, also 'embroidered'; loss of -*s* as in PEA]

ōrp'iment, n. A mineral, trisulphide of arsenic, formerly used as yellow dye and as artists' pigment. [ME, f. OF f. L *auripigmentum* (*aurum* gold, PIGMENT)]

ōrp'in(e), n. Succulent herbaceous fleshy-leaved purple-flowered plant. [ME, f. OF (-*n*), prob. alt. of prec., orig. of yellow-flowered species of same genus]

Orp'ington (ōr-), n. A breed of poultry. [town in Kent]

ŏ'rra, a. (Sc.). Odd, not matched, occasional, extra. [orig. unkn.]

ŏ'rrerȳ, n. Clockwork model of the planetary system. [named after Earl of O~ *c.* 1700]

ŏ'rris¹, n. Kind of iris, flower-de-luce, (now rare); ~-*root*, fragrant root of three species of iris used in perfumery & medi-

cine; ~-*powder*, powdered ~-*root*. [16th
c., app. an unexpl. alt. of IRIS]

ŏ′rris², n. Kinds of gold or silver lace or
embroidery. [*c.* 1700, app. alt. of *orfreis*
ORPHREY]

ŏrt, n. (dial. & arch.; usu. pl.). Refuse
scrap(s), leavings. [15th-c. *ortys* pl., f.
MLG *orte*, cf. Du. *oor-aete* remains of food]

ŏrth|(o)-, comb. form of Gk *orthos* straight,
in many scientific wds w. senses *straight,
rectangular, upright, right, correct*: ~*o-
cephăl′ic*, with breadth of skull from ⅗ to
⅘ of length, between brachycephalic &
dolichocephalic; ~*ochromăt′ic*, giving correct relative intensity to colours in photography; *orth′oclăse*, common feldspar in
crystals with two cleavages at right
angles; ~*odŏn′tia* (-shia), ~*odŏn′tics*, nn.,
correction of irregularities in teeth,
~*dŏn′tic* a., ~*odŏn′list*; ~*ō′epy*, science of
correct pronunciation, whence ~*ŏĕp′ic*,
~*ō′epist*(3); ~*ogĕn′esis*, a view of evolution according to which variations
follow a defined direction & are not merely
sporadic & fortuitous; ~*ŏg′nathous*, up-
right-jawed, not prognathous; ~*ŏg′onal*,
of or involving right angles; ~*ŏp′terous*,
of the insect order *Orthoptera* with straight
narrow forewings including cockroaches,
crickets, grasshoppers, etc.; ~*ŏp′tic*, of
straight or correct seeing, esp. used as n.
or a. of opaque perforated eyeglass assisting aim in rifle-shooting; ~*orhŏm′bic* a.
(cryst.), having three unequal axes at
right angles to each other; *orth′otone*,
(word) having independent accent, not
enclitic or proclitic.

ŏrth′odŏx, a. Holding correct or the currently accepted opinions esp. on religious
doctrine, not heretical or independent-
-minded or original; generally accepted as
right or true esp. in theology, in harmony
with what is authoritatively established,
approved, conventional; *the O~ Church*,
the Eastern or Greek recognizing Patriarch of Constantinople as head & the
national Churches of Russia, Romania,
etc., in communion with it. Hence ~LY²
adv. [f. F -*doxe* or LL -*doxus*, ult. f. Gk
ORTHO(*doxos* f. *doxa* opinion)]

ŏrth′odŏxў, n. Being orthodox. [f. LL f.
Gk *orthodoxia* (prec., -Y¹)]

ŏrthŏg′raphў, n. 1. Correct or conventional spelling; spelling with reference
to its correctness (*his ~ is shocking*).
2. Perspective projection used in maps &
elevations in which the point of sight is
supposed infinitely distant so that the
rays are parallel, map etc. so projected.
So **ŏrthogrăph′ic(AL)** aa., **ŏrthogrăph′i-
calLY²** adv. [ME, f. OF *ortografie* f. L f.
Gk ORTHO(*graphia* -GRAPHY)]

ŏrth′opaedў, n. The curing of deformities
in children or others, surgery directed to
this. So **ŏrthopaed′ic** a. [f. F ORTHO-
(*pédie* f. Gk *paideia* rearing of children)]

ŏrt′olan, n. The garden bunting, small
bird esteemed as table delicacy. [F, f. Pr.

ortolan orig. gardener f. L *hortulanus*
(*hortulus* dim. of *hortus* garden, -AN)]

-ory, suf. (1) of nn., originating in ONF &
AF -*orie* = OF -*oire* (*glorie, gloire*),
whence ME -*orie*, later -*ory*, wh. came
to be the normal E repr. of L -*oria*,
-*orium*, F -*oire*, most numerous being
adaptations of L wds in -*orium* (*dormit~,
laborat~*). In some tech. wds L -*orium* is
preserved, as *auditorium, crematorium.*
(2) of adjj., (whence also nn.), originating
in AF -*ori*, -*orie*, & repr. (occas. thr. OF
-*oir*, -*oire*) L -*orius*, -*a*, -*um*. As every L
vb could form agent n. in -*or*, E has
adjj. in -*ory* corresp. to L vbs even when
L has neither adj. in -*orius* nor agent n.
in -*or* (*compuls~, dispensal~, illus~*), or
when the L vb is not itself repr. in E
(*annal~, perfunct~*). As alternatives to
-*ory*, E has often -*orial* (~ + -AL), less
often -*orious* (~ + -OUS).

O′rỹx (ŏ-), n. (Genus of) large straight-
-horned African antelope. [ME, f. L, f.
Gk *orux*]

Ŏs′can (ŏ-), a. & n. (Of, in) the language,
allied to Latin, of the Osci, Opsci, or
Opici, a primitive people of Campania.
[L *Osci*, -AN]

*****Ŏs′car** (ŏs-), n. One of the statuettes
awarded by the Motion Picture Academy
for excellence in acting, directing, etc.
[man's name]

ŏs′cill|āte, v.i. & t. Swing (i., rarely
t.) like pendulum, move to & fro between
two points; vacillate, vary between extremes of opinion, action, condition,
etc.; (electr., of current) undergo high-
-frequency alternations as across spark-
-gap or in valve-transmitter circuit; (of
radio receivers) radiate electromagnetic
waves owing to faulty operation. Hence
or cogn. ~A′TION, ~ātoR, nn., ~ātoRY a.
[f. L *oscillare*, -ATE³]

oscitā′tion (ŏsĭ-), n. (rare). Yawning,
inattention, negligence. [f. L *oscitatio*
(*oscitare* gape f. *os* mouth, *citare* move,
-ATION)]

ŏs′cŭlar, a. Of the mouth, of kissing
(joc.); (math.) that osculates. [f. L
osculum mouth, kiss, (*os* mouth, -CULE),
-AR¹]

ŏs′cŭl|āte, v.i. & t. 1. Kiss (i. & t., rare,
usu. joc.). 2. (Nat. hist., of species etc.)
.have contact through intermediate species etc., have common characters *with*
another or with each other; (math., of
curve or surface) have contact of higher
order with, coincide in three or more
points. Hence or cogn. ~ANT a. (esp. nat.
hist.), ~A′TION n., ~ātoRY a. (esp. math.).
[f. L *osculari* kiss (prec.), -ATE³]

-ose¹, suf. f. L -*osus* abounding in; chiefly
in adjj. of a technical kind, adjj. in ordinary use forming -OUS; but there are *bellicose, jocose, grandiose*, & a few others.
Nn. are formed from them usu. in -*osity*,
also in -*oseness*.

-ose², suf. in chem. wds formed on *glucose*

(mod. F adoption of Gk *gleukos* must) giving names for the related carbo--hydrates *saccharose* & *cellulose* & isomeric substances, as *dextrose, laevulose*.

ō'sier (-zher), n. (Shoot of) species of willow used in basket-work; ~-BED[1]; (attrib.) of ~s. [ME, f. OF, cf. med. L *auseria, os-*, willow-bed]

-ōsis, suf. forming nn. of process or condition on Gk & occas. L stems; names of diseases or pathological states (*amaur~, trichin~*); a few rhetorical terms (*mei~*); & some in gen. use (*metamorph~, apothe~*). [f. Gk *-ōsis* n. suf. usu. f. vbs in *-oō*]

-ōsity, suf. See -OSE[1], -OUS.

Osmän'lï (ŏs-), a. & n. = OTTOMAN[1]. [Turk., native wd for which *Ottoman* is the use. E form]

ŏs'mium (ŏs-, ŏz-), n. A metal of the platinum group, having the greatest density of any known substance. [f. Gk *osmē* smell, -IUM]

ŏs'mōse, ŏsmōs'ïs, (ŏs-, ŏz-), n. (phys.). (Tendency to) percolation & intermixture of fluids separated by porous septa. Hence ōsmŏt'ıc a., ŏsmŏt'ıcALLY adv. [irreg. f. Gk *ōsmos* push (*ōtheō* push) +-OSIS]

ŏs'mund (ŏz-, ŏs-), n. The flowering or royal fern; any fern of genus *Osmunda*. [ME, f. AF *osmunde*, OF *osmonde*, of unkn. orig.]

ŏs'prey (-ā, -I), n. (pl. ~s). 1. Large bird preying on fish, the fishing-eagle, or sea--hawk. 2. (Milliner's name for) egret--plume on hat or bonnet. [ME, app. ult. repr. L *ossifraga* sea-eagle, osprey, whence also F *orfraie*]

ŏss'éous, a. Consisting of bone, ossified; having bony skeleton (~ *& cartilaginous fishes*); abounding in fossil bones. [f. L *osseus* (*os ossis* bone) +-OUS]

ŏss'icle, n. (anat.). Small bone, small piece of bony or chitinous or calcareous substance in animal framework. [f. L *ossiculum* (prec., -CULE)]

ŏss'ifrage, n. = OSPREY. [OSPREY]

ŏss'ifȳ, v.i. & t. Turn (i. & t.) into bone, harden, make or become rigid or callous or unprogressive. So ŏssıF'ıc a., ŏssï-FICA'TION n. [L *os ossis* bone, -FY]

ŏss'üarȳ, n. Receptacle for bones of dead, charnel-house, bone-urn; cave in which ancient bones are found. [f. LL *ossu-arium* (irreg. f. *os* see prec., -ARY[1])]

ŏstĕn'sib|le, a. Professed, for show, put forward to conceal the real, (*his~le errand was to* —). Hence ~LY[2] adv. [F, f. med. L *ostensibilis* (L *ostendere -ens-*, -IBLE)]

ŏstĕn'sorȳ, n. Receptacle for displaying Host to congregation, monstrance. [f. med. L *ostensorium* as prec., +-ORY(2)]

ŏstentä't|ion, n. Pretentious display esp. of wealth or luxury, showing off, attempt or intention to attract notice. Hence ~IOUS (-shus) a., ~iousLY[2] adv. [ME, f. OF, f. L *ostentationem* (*ostentare* frequent. of *ostendere -ent-* show, -ATION)]

ŏstĕ|(o)-, comb. form of Gk *osteon* bone in many med. & anat. terms, as ~IT'IS; ~*ogen'esis*, formation of bone; ~*ŏg'raphy*, scientific description of the bones; ŏs'te-OID a.; ~*ŏl'ogy*, anatomy dealing with bones, animal's bony structure; ~*oma-lā'cia*, softening of bone by loss of earthy salts; ~*omÿelit'is*, inflammation of the marrow of a bone; ~*ŏp'athy*, manipulative surgery as a profession, ŏs'teopath, practitioner of it.

ŏs'tler (-sl-), n. Stableman at inn. [earlier *hostler* (HOSTEL, -ER[1])]

ŏs'trac|īze, -|ise (-īz), v.t. 1. (Gk ant.; at Athens) banish (dangerously powerful or unpopular citizen) for ten or five years by peculiar voting-system, name of person to be ~ized being written on potsherd. 2. Exclude from society, favour or common privileges, send to Coventry, etc. So ~ISM(1) n. [f. Gk *ostrakizō* (*ostrakon* potsherd)]

ŏs'trei-, ŏs'trĕo-, comb. forms of L *ostrea, ostreum*, & Gk *ostreon*, oyster, as *os'treiculture*, oyster-breeding; *ostreŏph'a-gous*, eating oysters.

ŏs'trich, n. Large swift-running African & Arabian bird with wing & tail feathers valued as ornaments, swallowing hard substances to assist working of gizzard, & reputed to bury its head in sand when pursued in the belief that it cannot be seen (*has the digestion of an* ~; ~ *policy, belief*, etc., depending on self-delusion); ~*-farm*, breeding ~es for feathers; ~*-plume*, feather, or bunched feathers, of ~; ~*-tip*, tip of ~*-feather*. [ME, f. OF *ostrice, -iche* (mod. *autruche*) f. Rom. **avis struthio* (*avis* bird, LL f. Gk *strouthiōn* ostrich f. *strouthos* sparrow, ostrich)]

-ot[1], suf. = F *-ot*, orig. dim., but often not so now; *ballot, chariot, parrot*.

-ot[2], -ote, suf. expressing nativity in ancient Gk names, as *Epirot*, & in mod. names from places near Greece, as *Cypriot*; also in a few Gk derivatives of other meanings (*idiot, helot, patriot, zealot*). [repr. F *-ote*, L *-ota*, Gk *-ōtēs*]

o'ther (ŭdh-), a., n. or pron., & adv. 1. Not the same as one or more or some already mentioned or implied, separate in identity, distinct in kind, alternative or further or additional, *the* etc. only remaining, *every* second, different *than* or *from*, (for sing. use with *an*, see ANOTHER; *we have* ~ *evidence*; ~ *people think otherwise*; *it must be decided by quite* ~ *considerations*; *have no* ~ *place to go to*; ~ *things being equal*, if the conditions are or were, in everything but the point in question, alike, *as* ~ *things being equal, I should prefer you to him, but he is rich & you are poor*; *a few* ~ *examples would be useful*; *give me some* ~ *ones*; *now open the, your,* ~ *eye*; *happens every* ~ *day*, on alternate days, as often as not; *any person* ~ *than your-self, do not wish him, them,* ~ *than he is, they are*; *a world far* ~ *from ours*; *on the*

~ *hand,* used to introduce fact or argument making against or contrasted with previous one; *the ~ day* adv., *a few days ago*; *some time or ~* adv., one day etc.; *someone or ~,* a person unknown; *some idiots or ~ have been shouting all night*; *it was none ~ than Jones,* = no ~ one or person; *the ~ world,* future life, *~- -world,* concerned with or thinking of this only, whence ~-**wor'ld**LY[1] (-wēr-) a., ~-**wor'ld**INESS n.; often ellipt. with numerals, as *another, the~ two,* i.e. person or persons, thing or things, of kind not needing specification); ~*guess* a. [corrupt. of ~*gates* adv. (GATE[2], -ES) in another way], of very different kind (arch. & colloq.); ~*whence,* from elsewhere; ~*where(s),* elsewhere (poet.); ~*while(s),*. at ~ times. **2.** n. or pron. (orig. elliptic use of adj., & often indistinguishable from this in sing., but now distinguished in pl. by *-s,* cf. *the ~ six, the six* ~*s*). ~ person, thing, specimen, etc. (*give me another, some* ~*s*; *do good to* ~*s*; *if this soap is, these candles are, too soft, have you any* ~, ~*s ?*; *one or* ~ *of us will be there*; *let* ~*s talk, I act*; *I can do no* ~, arch., nothing else; *you are the man of all* ~*s for the work*; *one neutralizes the* ~; *they neutralize* EACH ~ or ONE *another*; *in* ~*s of his sermons*). **3.** adv. Otherwise (~ *than cursorily*). [OE *ōther,* OS *ōdar, andar,* OHG *ander,* ON *annarr,* Goth. *anthar,* cogn. w. Skr. *antaras*; see -THER]

o'therness (ŭdh-), n. (rare). Being other, diversity, difference; thing or existence that is not the thing mentioned or the thinking subject. [-NESS]

o'therwise (ŭdh'*erwiz*), adv. In a different way (*could not have acted* ~; *Judas,* ~ *called, or* ~, *Iscariot*; occas. preceded by *any, no,* with reminiscence of its etym., as *could do it no* ~, *does not influence him any* ~ *than by example*); if circumstances are or were different, else, or '(*seize the chance,* ~ *you will regret it*); in other respects (*he is unruly, but not* ~ *blameworthy*; also qualifying the adj. sense in n., as *his* ~ *dullness*); in different state (*how can it be* ~ *than fatal ?*; *should not wish it* ~); *& ~, or* ~, ungrammatical substitute for *&* or *or* followed by the negation or opposite of a noun or adj. or by *other* (*the merits or* ~ *of the Bill,* i.e. *or demerits* usu. omissible; *additions automatic & ~,* i.e. *& other*); ~*-minded,* having different, or jarring, inclinations or views, averse to current opinions. [OE *on olhre wīsan* (OTHER, WISE[2])]

ōt'ic (or ŏ-), a. Of or relating to the ear. [f. Gk *ous ōtos* ear, -IC]

-ōtic, suf. forming aa. corresp. to nn. in -OSIS, in sense *affected with* or *producing* or *resembling -osis,* so *neur~, hypn~, narc~*; *Quix~, ex~, er~,* are not exx. [f. Gk *-ōtikos* f. nn. in *-ōtēs* formed on same stems as -OSIS]

otiose (ōshiōs', *also* ō²-), a. At leisure, lazy,

unoccupied, (rare); sterile, futile, (rare); not required, serving no practical purpose, functionless. Hence ~LY[2] adv., ~NESS n. [f. L *otiosus* (*otium* leisure, -OSE[1])]

o'tium cŭm dĭgnĭtāt'e (ōshl-), n. Dignified ease. [L]

ōt(o)-, comb. form of Gk *ous ōtos* ear, as *ōtōL'OGY,* science of ear diseases, anatomy, etc.; *ōt'oSCOPE,* instrument for examining cavity of ear, or for auscultation of sounds in it.

otta'va ri'ma (-tah-, rē-), n. Stanza of eight lines, 11-syllabled in Italian, 10- -syllabled in English, with rhymes *ab ababacc* (as in Byron's *Don Juan*). [It.]

ŏtt'er, n. Furred aquatic fish-eating mammal with short legs, round feet, and webbed toes; its fur; kinds of fishing- -tackle (also as name for the paravane when used on non-naval craft); ~*-dog, -hound,* breed used in ~-hunting; ~- *-spear,* used in ~-hunting. [OE *otr,* MDu., MLG *otter,* OHG *ottar,* ON *otr* f. Gmc **otraz,* cogn. w. Skr. *udras* otter, & WATER]

ŏtt'ō, n. ~ *of roses,* = ATTAR. [f. ATTAR]

Ott'oman[1] (ŏ-), a. & n. **1.** Of the dynasty of Othman I, his branch of the Turks, or the empire ruled by his descendants, Turkish. **2.** n. (pl. ~*s*). ~ person, Turk. [F, f. Arab. name of *Othman* (pronounced in Turk. *osman,* whence OSMANLI)]

ŏtt'oman[2], n. Cushioned seat like sofa or chair without back or arms, often a box with cushioned top. [f. prec. (cf. DIVAN)]

ou'bit (ōō-), n. = WOOBUT.

oubliëtte' (ōō-), n. Secret dungeon with entrance only by trapdoor. [F *oublier* forget)]

‖ **ouch,** n. (arch.). Clasp or buckle often jewelled; setting of precious stone. [ME *ouche* f. *nouche,* OF *nouche, nosche,* etc. f. WG **nuskja* clasp; loss of *n-* as in *adder*]

ought[1] (awt), n. (vulg.). Figure denoting nothing, nought. [perh. f. *an ought* for *a nought,* cf. ADDER]

ought[2] (awt), v. aux. (the only form in use, except arch. ~*est* or ~*st,* is ~ serving as present or past finite) expressing duty, rightness, shortcoming, advisability, or strong probability; the past sense (except when merely due to sequence of tenses in reporting etc.) is indicated by a following perf. infin. Exx.: *we ~ to love our neighbours*; *it ~ not to be allowed*; *you ~ to know better*; *you ~ to go to Pinafore*; *Eclipse ~ to win*; *it ~ to be done at once, have been done long ago*; *I told you it ~ to be, have been, done*; *I said it, & still think I ~ to have said it.* [OE *āhte* past of *āgan* OWE; the mod. uses represent the imperf. subj. = would owe]

ought[3], var. of AUGHT.

ouija (wē'jah, -yah), n. (Also ~*-board*) board lettered with alphabet & other signs, used with movable pointer to obtain messages in spiritualistic séances. [f. F *oui* and G *ja,* = yes]

ounce[1], n. (abbr. *oz*). Unit of weight, 1/12 lb. in Troy weight, 1/16 lb. in avoirdupois (also fig., as *an ~ of practice* etc. *is worth a pound of theory* etc.); (pharm.) 1/20 pint, *1/16 pint. [ME, f. OF *unce* f. L *uncia* twelfth of pound or foot (cf. INCH[1])]

ounce[2], n. (Poet. etc.) lynx or other vaguely identified medium-sized feline beast; (zool.) the mountain panther or snow leopard smaller than leopard but marked like it. [ME, f. OF *once* for earlier *lonce* (*l* mistaken for def. art.), = It. *lonza* f. Rom. **luncea* f. L *lynx* LYNX]

our (owr), a. Of or belonging to us (see WE), that we are concerned with or speaking or thinking of, (*is in ~ midst*; *acting on ~ behalf*; *have done ~ share*; *Our Father*, the creator of us men; *Our Saviour, Lady*, of us Christians, Christ, the Virgin; *given under Our seal*, of Us the king or queen, emperor or empress; *a worthless book in ~ opinion*, of us the present spokesman of a newspaper etc.). [OE *ūre* orig. genit. pl. of first pers. pron. = of us (thus OS *ūser*, OHG *unsĕr*, ON *vár*, Goth *unsara*); then inflected as adj. to form poss. adj. (= OS *ūsa*, OHG *unser-*, ON *várr*, Goth. *unsar*)]

-our, suf. in *colour* etc.; see -OR.

ours (owrz), pron. & pred. a. **1.** The one(s) belonging to us (*~ is a large family*; *I like ~ better*; *let me give you one of ~*; *look at this garden of ~*, this our garden); ‖ our regiment or corps (*Jones of ~*). **2.** pred. adj. Belonging to us (*became ~ by purchase*). [OUR, -ES; double possessive for the emphatic abs. use]

oursĕl|f′ (owr-), pron. (pl. *~ves*, which is the usu. form, the sing. being used similarly when *We* represents a sovereign, & alternatively with the pl. when *we* represents a newspaper writer or the average man). **1.** (emphat.; usu. pl.). We or us in person, in particular, or in our normal condition, & not others, or alone, (usu. in apposition with *we*, & either next after it or later, rarely substituted for it; usu. substituted for *us*, rarely after it in apposition; *we ~ves will see to it*; *we will see to it ~ves*; *~ves are first to be thought of*; *it was good for the others, if not for ~ves*; *let us do it ~ves*; *we were not ~ves for some time*; *what touches us ~f shall be last served*; *can we imagine a world in which ~f does not exist?*). **2.** (refl.; usu. pl., always in objective case). The person(s) previously described as *we* (*we shall only harm, do harm to, ~ves*; *we cannot persuade ~f or ~ves that the Government is in earnest*; *we shall give ~ves the pleasure of calling*. [OUR, SELF]

-ous, suf. forming adjj. meaning 'abounding in, characterized by ', ult. f. L *-osus* (see -OSE[1]). AF, OF, & early ME *-os, -us*, later ME *-ous*, which form has been retained, & has now become the established anglicizer for many L adjj., esp. in *-eus, -ius, -er, -ax, -acis, -ox -cis, -endus -ulus*, & *-vorus* (*igne~, dubi~, adulter~, capaci~, feroci~, tremend~, bibul~, herbivor~*); for *righte~, courte~, gorge~*, etc., see -EOUS; (chem. of acids etc.) with larger proportion of the element indicated by the stem than those in -IC (*chlor~ acid*). Nn. f. adjj. in -ous have usu. *-ousness*, sometimes *-osity* (*curiosity*), cf. -OSE[1].

ousel. See OUZEL.

oust, v.t. Put out of possession, eject, deprive *of*, expel *from*, drive out, force oneself or be put into the place of. Hence **oust**′TER[4] n. (legal), ejection. [f. AF *ouster*, OF *oster* (now *ôter*) take away, f. L OB(*stare* stand) oppose, hinder]

out, adv., prep., n., a., int., & v.t., (for spec. uses of the adv. in comb. with vbs see the vbs). **1. adv.** Away from or not in or at a place, the right or normal state, the fashion, etc., (*is ~*, not at home; *keep him ~*; *go ~ for a walk*; *has her Sundays ~*; *arm is ~*, dislocated; *Tories are ~*, not in office; *her son is ~ in Canada*; *anchored some way ~*; *on the voyage ~*; *batsman is ~*, no longer in possession of wicket; *all ~*, side's innings over; *~, not ~*, umpire's decision against, for, batsman in answer to claim of opponents; *miners are ~*, not at work, on strike; *candle, fire, is ~*, not burning; *crinolines are ~*, not in fashion; *was ~ in my calculations*, incorrect; *~ with*, no longer on friendly terms with; also as interj., *~ with him* etc., turn him *~*); in(to) the open, publicity, existence, notice, hearing, sight, clearness, etc. (*book, rose, chicken, secret, girl, is ~*, published, open, hatched, revealed, introduced to society; *is the best game ~*; *tell him right ~*; *the eruption is ~ all over him*; *~ for, ~ to do*, colloq., engaged in seeking, as *is ~ for kudos, to capture the market*; *all ~*, sl., showing one's utmost pace or effort; *~ at* ELBOW[1]s; *~ & about*, able to leave bed or house & appear; also ellipt. for *come ~*, as *murder will ~*); to or at an end, completely, (*she had her cry ~*; *tired ~*; *before the week is ~*; *~ & away*, by far; *~ & ~*[1] thorough, -ly, surpassing, -ly, whence **out-&-out**′ER[1] n. sl.); *~ of* compd prep., from within, not within, from among, beyond range of, (so as to be) without, from, owing to, by use of (material), at specified distance from (town etc.), beyond, transgressing rules of, (*come ~ of the house*; *happened ~ of England*; *~ of doors*, in or into the open air, so *~-of-door* as adj.; *must choose ~ of these*; *is ~ of sight*; *was swindled ~ of his money*; *is ~ of breath, his mind, work, brown sugar*, etc.; *get money ~ of him*; *a filly got by Persimmon ~ of Lutetia*; *asked ~ of curiosity*; *what did you make it ~ of?*; *is seven miles ~ of Liverpool*; *~ of wedlock*, without marriage; *times ~ of number*, beyond counting; *~ of doubt*, undoubtedly; *is ~ of drawing*, incorrectly drawn; *~ of it*, not included, forlorn, at a loss, wrongly informed or mistaken; ~ *of* DATE[2], CHARACTER[1], HAND[1], one's *own* HEAD[1], KEEPING, TEMPER, *the* WOOD, SORTS, *the* WAY). **2.** prep. = ~ of (only now in *from* ~, as *from* ~ *the dungeon came a groan*). **3.** n. *The* ~s, the party ~ of office; *the* IN[1]s *&* ~s. **4.** adj. *An* ~ *match*, played away from home ground; ~ *size*, beyond the ordinary; ~*'size* n. & a., (of) exceptionally large size (in garments etc.). **5.** int. (arch.). Expr. abhorrence, reproach, etc. (*Out upon you!*). **6.** v.t. (sl. or colloq.). Eject forcibly; (boxing) knock ~. [OE (= OS, ON, Goth.) *ūt*, OHG *uz*, cogn. w. Skr. *ud-*]

out-, pref. = prec. prefixed adverbially or adjectivally or prepositionally to vbs or nn. **1.** To any vb, making equivalent of same vb followed by *out*; chiefly in poet. & rhet. use. So ~*blaze'*, ~*branch'*, ~*speak'*, ~*spread'*.

2. Vbs that are followed in other parts by *out* often form partt. & gerunds with prefixed *out*; the meaning is often a specialized one. So ~*'cast* a. & n., (person) cast out from home & friends, homeless & friendless (vagabond); || ~*ᷓclearing* n., sending out of bills & cheques to Clearing-house for settlement; ~*'fighting*, boxing at arm's length, opp. *infighting*; ~*'lying* a., situated far from a centre, remote; ~*mōd'ed*, a., out of fashion; ~*'spoken* (*or* -ōk[ᷓ]) a., frank, given to plain speaking, whence ~*spok'en*LY[2] adv., ~*spok'en*NESS n.; ~*'spread*; ~*'standing* a., prominent, still unsettled; ~*'stretched*; ~*'worn'*, worn out (poet.), (fig.) out of date, obsolete; exhausted.

3. Nn. are formed f. vbs that can be followed by *out*, either with the simple vb form or with a derivative n.; the meaning, which is often specialized, may be:—
a. the verbal action or its occurrence. So ~*'break*, a breaking out of emotion esp. anger, hostilities, disease, volcanic energy, etc., ~crop, an insurrection; ~*'burst*, explosion of feeling esp. expressed by vehement· words, volcanic eruption; ~crop; ~*'crop*, emergence of stratum, vein, or rock, at surface (also b.); ~*'cry* (also c.); ~*'flow*; ~*'going* (also b.); ~*'look* (also c.); ~*'rush* (also b.); ~*'sight*, perception of external things (only as antithesis to *insight*); ~*ᷓthrust*, outward pressure of some part in architecture.
b. that which does the action. So ~*ᷓcome*, issue, result; ~*'crop* (also a.); ~*'fit*, complete equipment material or mental, (colloq.) group of persons regarded as a unit, gang, (v.t.; -tt-) provide (person) *with*; ~*'fitter*, supplier of equipment; ~*ᷓflow* (also a.); ~*'go*, ~*'goings* (also a. in sing.), expenditure, ~lay; ~*'growth*, offshoot, natural product; ~*'lier*, ~lying part or member, (geol.) minor part of

formation separated from main body by denudation; ~*'pour*; ~*'rush* (also a.).
c. that which is made or done by or suffers the action. So ~*'cry* (also a.), clamour, uproar; ~*'lay*, what one spends, expenses; ~*'look*, what one sees on looking out, view, prospect, esp. fig. of what seems likely to happen, mental attitude; ~*'pouring*, effusion, verbal or literary expression of emotion; ~*'put*, ~*ᷓturn*, amount produced by manufacture, mining, labour, etc.; ~*ᷓthrow*, amount ejected.
d. the place or time of occurrence. So ~*'fall*, ~let of river etc.; ~*'let*, means of exit or escape, vent, way out; ~*'set*, start, commencement, (usu. *at or from the* ~ *set*).

4. *out-* is prefixed w. adj. force to nn., meaning: —
a. external. So ~*'back* a. & n. (Austral.), (of) the more remote settlements; OUTLINE, OUTSIDE.
b. connected but separate, subordinate & detached, not at the centre, some way off. So ~*'building*, ~house; ~*'field*, ~lying land of farm, ~lying region of thought etc., (crick.) part remote from wickets; ~*'house*, house or building or shed belonging to & near or built against main house; ~*land'ish* a. [f. obs. ~*'land* foreign countries], foreign looking or sounding, unfamiliar, bizarre, uncouth; ~*ᷓpatient*, *-pensioner*, receiving aid from institution etc. without being lodged in it; ~*'post*, detachment on guard at some distance from army to prevent surprise; || ~*ᷓrelief*, ~door relief (5); ~*'rider*, mounted attendant riding before, behind, or with carriage, also commercial traveller; OUTRIGGER; ~*'runner*, running attendant on carriage, horse in traces outside shafts, dog acting as guide to sledge--team; ~*'sentry*, man stationed as ~-post; ~*'skirts*, outer border, fringe, of city, district, etc., or subject; ~*'station*, at distance from headquarters; || ~*'voter*, non-resident parliamentary elector; ~*ᷓwork*, advanced or detached part of fortification, also work done outside shop or house; ~*'worker*, one who does ~work.

5. *out-* is prefixed to & governs nn. with the force of *out of*, forming adjj. or advv.
f. which vbs or nn. may be secondary formations. So ~*'board* a. & adv., (naut.) on or towards or nearer than something else to ship's outside, (of a motor-boat) having the engine & driving apparatus attached outside the boat; ~*'caste* a. & n., (person) having lost or been expelled from his or not belonging to a caste; ~*'caste* v.t., expel from caste; || ~*'college* a., not residing in or not belonging to a or the college; ~*'door* a., done or existing or used ~doors || (~*door relief*, given to person not resident in workhouse or institution; ~*door agitation* etc., conducted outside

For words in out- not given see OUT-.

Parliament); ~*doors'* adv., in the open air; ~*'law* n. & v.t. [OE *ūtlaga* n. f. *ūtlag* a. outlawed], person deprived of the protection of the law, banished or exiled person, (vb) proscribe, declare ~law, whence ~*'law*RY, condition of or condemnation a⸝ ~law.

6. *out-* with general sense of excess is prefixed

a. to simple vbs capable of taking the same object, adding the idea of more than, or successfully, doing the action. So ~*bal'ance*, weigh down; ~*brave'*, defy; ~*face'*, look out of countenance; ~*fight'*; ~*-hec'tor*; ~*last'* (*will not*~ *last six months*); also b.); ~*match'*; ~*meas'ure*; ~*riv'al*; ~*scold'*; ~*'trump'*, at cards.

b. to any vb, or n. such as *general* used for the nonce as vb, enabling it to take as obj. a person or thing that the subj. surpasses or defeats by doing the action more, better, or longer. So ~*-act'*, *-arg'ue*, *-bell'ow*; ~*bid'*, bid higher than at auction, promise more than, surpass in exaggeration or anecdote; ~*-blaze'*, *-brag'*, *-dance'*, *-dare'*; ~*do'*, surpass; ~*-eat'*; ~*fight'*, fight better than (also a.); ~*fly'*; ~*gen'eral*, defeat by superior generalship; ~*go'*, go faster than, (fig.) surpass; ~*grow'*, grow faster or get taller than (also c.); ~*-hec'tor*, be more formidable at hectoring than (also a.); ~*-jock'ey*, overreach; ~*-jug'gle*; ~*-jump'*; ~*lab'our*; ~*last'*, last longer than (another; also a.); ~*live'* (also c.); ~*manœu'vre*, *-march'*, *-paint'*, *-preach'*, *-reach'*, *-reas'on*, *-ride'*, *-row'* (-ō); ~*run'* (~*run the* CONSTABLE; also c.); ~*sail'*; ~*scold'* (also a.); ~*shine'* lit. & fig.; ~*shoot'*; ~*sing'*; ~*sit'*, stay longer than (other guests); ~*spar'kle*, *-spend'*, *-stare'*; ~*stay'* (also c.); ~*stink'*, *-swim'*, *-talk'*, *-think'*, *-thun'der*, *-toil'*, *-trade'*, *-trav'el*; ~*vie'*, surpass in competition; ~*vote'*, ~*walk'*; ~*watch'*, keep awake longer than (also c.); ~*weep'*; ~*weigh'*, exceed in weight, value, importance, or influence; ~*work'*; ~*yell'*.

c. to vb, enabling it to take as obj. something in the nature of a limit or amount that is exceeded. So ~*grow'*, get too big for (clothes), get rid of (childish habit or ailment or taste) with advancing age, (also b.); ~*live'*, live beyond (a century, the ordinary span, etc.), come safely through (accident etc.), get over effect of (disrepute etc.), (also b.); ~*ride'*, (of ship) keep afloat through (storm; also b.); ~*run'*, pass the limit of (*his imagination* ~*runs the facts*; also b.); ~*stay'* (*never*~*stay your welcome*; also b.); ~*step'*, pass limit of (~*steps the truth*); ~*watch'*, keep awake beyond the end of (the night etc.; also b.); ~*wear'*, pass away (time) by endurance.

d. to n. or rarely adj., forming vb expressing that subj. surpasses obj. in this respect. ~*class'*, belong to higher class than; ~*-dis'tance*, get far ahead of; ~*flank'*, have flank overlapping that of (enemy); ~*num'ber*; ~*pace'*, go faster than; ~*-range'*, (of gun or its user) have longer range than; *~*smart'* v.t. (colloq.), be too clever for, ~wit; ~*speed'*; ~*val'ue*; ~*voice'*, speak louder or more effectively or persuasively than; ~*wit'*, prove too clever for, overreach, take in.

e. to name of person noted for some quality, forming vb (w. the name usu. repeated as obj.) indicating that subj. surpasses even him in it. So ~*-he'rod* Herod, ~*-zol'a* Zola, be more blustering, realistic, than Herod or Zola.

out'back, a. & n., see OUT- 4 a; **outbal'ance** v.t., OUT- 6 a; **outbid'** v.t. (-dd-), OUT- 6 b; **out'board** a. & adv., OUT- 5; **outbrave'** v.t., OUT- 6 a; **out'break** n., OUT- 3 a; **out'building** n., OUT- 4 b; **out'burst** n., OUT- 3 a; **out'cast** a. & n., OUT- 2; **out'caste** a. & n., **outcaste'** v.t., OUT- 5; **outclass'** v.t., OUT- 6 d; || **out'clearing** n., OUT- 2; || **out'college** a., OUT- 5; **out'come** n., OUT- 3 b; **out'crop** n., OUT- 3 a b; **out'cry** n., OUT- 3 a c; **outdis'tance** v.t., OUT- 6 d; **outdo'** v.t., OUT- 6 b; **out'door** a., **outdoors'** adv., OUT- 5.

out'er, a. & n. **1.** Farther from centre or inside, relatively far out, external, of the outside; objective, physical, not subjective or psychical; ~ *space*, immense expanse beyond the earth; *the* ~ *man*, personal appearance, dress; *the* ~ *world*, people outside one's own circle; hence ~MOST a. **2.** n. Circle of rifle-target farthest from the bull's-eye, hit on this. [14th-c. formation substituted for & differentiated f. UTTER as compar. of OUT]

outface', v.t., see OUT- 6 a; **out'fall** n., OUT- 3 d; **out'field** n., OUT- 4 b; **out'fighting**, OUT- 2; **out'fit**, **out'fitter**, nn., OUT- 3 b; **outflank'** v.t., OUT- 6 d; **out'flow** n., OUT- 3 a; **outgen'eral** v.t., OUT- 6 b; **outgo'** n., OUT- 3 b, vb, OUT- 6 b; **out'going(s)** n., OUT- 3 a b; **outgrow'** v.t., OUT- 6 b c; **out'growth** n., OUT- 3 b; **out-he'rod** v.t., OUT- 6 e; **out'house** n., OUT- 4 b.

out'ing, n. Pleasure-trip, holiday away from home. [f. obs. *out* vb put or go out, -ING¹]

out-jock'ey, v.t., see OUT- 6 b; **outland'ish** a., OUT- 4 b; **outlast'** v.t., OUT- 6 a b; **out'law** n. & v.t., **out'lawry** n., OUT- 5; **out'lay** n., OUT- 3 c; **out'let** n., OUT- 3 d; **out'lier** n., OUT- 3 b.

out'line, n., & v.t. **1.** (Sing. or pl.) lines enclosing the apparently plane figure presented by any object to sight, contour, external boundary; sketch containing only contour lines & no shading (*in* ~, so sketched); rough draught, verbal description of essential parts only, summary, (pl.) main features, general prin-

ciples. **2. v.t.** Draw or describe in ~;
mark ~ of in decorating etc. [OUT- 4 a]
outlive', v.t., see OUT- 6 b c; **out'look** n.,
OUT- 3 c; **out'lying** a., OUT- 2; **outmanœu'vre** v.t., OUT- 6 b; **outmarch'**
v.t., OUT- 6 b; **outmatch'** v.t., OUT- 6 a;
outmod'ed a., OUT- 2.
out'most, a. = OUTERMOST.
out'ness, n. Externality, objectivity.
[-NESS]
outnum'ber, v.t., see OUT- 6 d; **outpace'**
v.t., OUT- 6 d; **out'patient** n., OUT- 4 b;
out'post n., OUT- 4 b; **out'pouring** n.,
OUT- 3 c; **out'put** n., OUT- 3 c.
out'rage, n. (-ĭj), & v.t. (-āj). **1.** Forcible
violation of others' rights, sentiments,
etc. (*never safe from* ~); deed of violence,
gross or wanton offence or indignity (*an
~ upon decency, justice,* etc.). **2. v.t:** Do
violence to, subject to ~, injure, insult,
violate, ravish; infringe (law, morality,
etc.) flagrantly. [ME, f. OF *ultrage outrage*, f. *outrer* exceed (L *ultra* beyond,
-AGE)]
outra'geous (-jŭs), a. Immoderate, extravagant, extraordinary; violent, furious;
grossly cruel, immoral, offensive, or abusive. Hence ~LY² adv., ~NESS n. [ME, f.
OF *outrageus* (prec., -OUS)]
outrange', v.t. See OUT- 6 d.
outré (oō'trā), a. Outside the bounds of
propriety, eccentric, outraging decorum.
[F]
|| **out'-relief**, n., see OUT- 4 b; **outride'** v.t.,
OUT- 6 b c; **out'rider** n., OUT- 4 b.
out'rigged (-gd), a. (Of boat etc.) having
outriggers. [f. OUT-, RIG, -ED¹, after foll.]
out'rigger (-g-), n. Beam, spar, framework, rigged out & projecting from or
over ship's side for various purposes;
similar projecting beam etc. in building;
extension of splinter-bar enabling extra
horse to be harnessed outside shafts, such
horse; iron bracket bearing rowlock attached horizontally to boat's side to
increase leverage of oar, boat with these.
[OUT-, RIG, -ER¹; perh. partly after obs.
(naut.) *outrigger*]
outright' (-rīt), adv. & a. **1.** Altogether,
entirely, once for all, not by degrees or
instalments or half & half, (*kill, buy,* ~);
without reservation, openly. **2.** adj.
Downright, direct, thorough, whence ~-
NESS (-rīt-) n. [OUT, RIGHT]
outriv'al, v.t. (-ll-), see OUT- 6 a; **outrun'**
v.t., OUT- 6 b c; **out'runner** n., OUT- 4 b;
out'set n., OUT- 3 d; **outshine'** v.t. OUT-
6 b.
outside', n., adj., adv., & prep. **1.** External surface, outer parts, (*knows only
the ~s of books; ride on the ~ of an
omnibus*); external appearance, outward
aspect; all that is without, *the* world as
distinguished from the thinking subject,
(*impressions from the* ~); position without
(*open the door from* ~); highest computation (*there were a hundred, it is a mile, at
the* ~); (pl.) outer sheets of ream of paper;

|| ~ passenger on coach etc.; ~ *in*, = INSIDE *out*. **2.** adj. Of, on, nearer, the ~,
outer, (~ *edge* in skating, progression on
outer edge of one skate; ~ *seat*, nearer the
end; ~ *work*, done off the premises; || ~
porter, conveying luggage from station);
(of a chance) remote, very unlikely; not
belonging to some circle or institution (~
opinion, esp. of people not in Parliament;
~ *broker*, not member of Stock Exchange); greatest existent or possible or
probable (*quote the* ~ *prices*). **3.** adv. On
or to the ~, the open air, open sea, etc.,
not within or enclosed or included, (*come*
~, out from room or house, esp. as
challenge to fight; *is black* ~ *& in*;
~ *of*, = ~ prep.; *get* ~ *of*, sl., eat or drink;
~ *of his own family no one will speak to
him*). **4.** prep. External to, not included
in, beyond the limits of, not in, to the
~ of, at or to the exterior of, (*natural
forces are* ~ *morality; cannot go* ~ *the
evidence*). [OUT- 4 a, SIDE¹]
outsid'er, n. Non-member of some circle,
party, profession, etc., uninitiated person,
layman; person without special knowledge, breeding, etc., or not fit to mix with
good society (freq. *rank* ~); competitor
not known to have a chance in race or
competition. [-ER¹]
out'sight, n., see OUT- 3 a; **outsit'** v.t.,
OUT- 6 b; **out'skirts** n. pl., OUT- 4 b;
outsmart' v.t., OUT- 6d.
out'span, v.i. & t. (-nn-), & n. (S. Afr.).
1. Unyoke, unharness. **2.** n. Act, time, or
place of ~ning. [f. Du. *uitspannen* (OUT,
SPAN²); cf. INSPAN]
out'spoken, a., see OUT- 2; **out'spread** a.,
OUT- 2; **out'standing** a., OUT- 2; **outstay'**
v.t., OUT- 6 b c; **outstep'** v.t., OUT- 6 c;
out'stretched a., OUT- 2.
outstrip', v.t. (-pp-). Pass in running etc.;
surpass in competition or relative progress or ability. [OUT- 6 b, obs. *strip* run
fast]
out'thrust, n., see OUT- 3 a; **out'turn** n.,
OUT- 3 c; **outval'ue** v.t., OUT- 6 d;
outvie' v.t., OUT- 6b; **outvoice'** v.t., OUT-
6 d; **outvote'** v.t., OUT- 6 b; **out'voter** n.,
OUT- 4 b.
out'ward, a., adv., & n. **1.** Outer (arch.);
directed towards the outside; bodily, external, material, visible, apparent, superficial, (*the* ~ *eye*, ~ opp. *mind's eye*; ~
form, appearance; ~ *man* in theol., body,
opp. *soul*, also joc. = clothing etc.; *to* ~
seeming, apparently; ~ *things*, the world
around us); hence ~LY² adv. **2.** adv.
= OUTWARDS (~-*bound*, of ship or passenger, going away from home). **3.** n. ~
appearance; (pl.) ~ things, externals.
[OE *ūtweard* (OUT, -WARD)]
out'wardness, n. External existence, objectivity; interest or belief in outward
things, objective-mindedness. [-NESS]
out'wards (-z), adv. In an outward
direction, towards what is outside.
[-WARDS]

outwatch', v.t., see OUT- 6 b c; **outwear'** v.t., OUT- 6 c; **outweigh'** v.t., OUT- 6 b; **outwit'** v.t. (-tt-), OUT- 6 d.

‖ **out'with** (-dh), prep. (Sc.). Outside of. [f. OUT adv. +WITH]

out'work, n., see OUT- 4 b; **outwork'** v.t., OUT- 6 b; **out'worker** n., OUT- 4 b; **out'worn** a., OUT- 2.

ouzel, -sel, (ōō'zl), n. Kinds of small bird (*ring, water, brook,* ~). [OE *ōsle,* = OHG *amsala*; orig. unkn.]

ova. See OVUM.

ōv'al, a. & n. **1.** Egg-shaped or ellipsoidal; having the outline of an egg or elliptical; hence ~LY² adv., ~NESS n. **2.** n. Closed curve with one axis considerably longer than the other, like ellipse or outline of egg; thing with ~ outline; ‖ *the O~,* the Surrey County cricket ground, Kennington O~ in S. London. [ME, f. med. L *ovalis* (OVUM, -AL)]

ōv'arÿ, n. Either of two reproductive organs in which ova are produced in female animals, whence **ōvāriŏt'OMY**, **ōvarIT'IS**, nn.; lower part of pistil, consisting of one or more carpels, seed-vessel, germen. Hence **ōvār'IAN** a., **ovārio**-comb. form. [f. mod. L *ovarium* (OVUM, -ARY¹)]

ōv'āte, a. (nat. hist.). Egg-shaped as solid or in outline, oval. Hence **ovāt'o**- comb. form. [f. L *ovatus* (OVUM, -ATE²)]

ovā'tion, n. (Rom. ant.) lesser TRIUMPH; enthusiastic reception, spontaneous applause. [f. L *ovatio* (*ovare* exult, -ATION)]

o'ven (ŭ-), n. Brick or stone or iron receptacle for baking bread or other food in (*Dutch* ~, metal box of which open side is turned towards ordinary fire); small furnace or kiln used in chemistry, metallurgy, etc.; ~*-bird,* kinds making domed or ~-shaped nests. [OE *ofen,* OHG *ovan,* ON *ofn,* Goth. *auhns*]

ōv'er, adv., n., a., & prep., **o'er** (ōr), adv. & prep. (poet.). **1.** Outward & downward from brink or from erect position (*lean, fall, jump, knock,* etc., ~). **2.** So as to cover or touch whole surface (*brush, paint, it* ~). **3.** With motion above something, so as to pass across something, (*climb, look, boil,* ~). **4.** So as to produce fold or reverse position, upside down, (*bend it* ~; *turn* ~, turn other side of leaf up; *turn him* ~ *on his face; roll* ~ *& ~,* so that same point comes uppermost repeatedly); (crick., as umpire's direction) change ends for bowling etc. **5.** Across a street or other space or distance (*take this* ~ *to the post-office; asked him* ~, to come as visitor from some place not far off; *is* ~ *in, am going* ~ *to, America;* ~ *against,* in opposite situation to, in contrast with). **6.** With transference or change from one hand, party, etc., to another (*malcontents went* ~ *to the enemy; handed* ~ *the seals; made* ~ *the balance to a charity;* GIVE¹~). **7.** Too, in excess, in addition, besides, more, apart, (~ *anxious*

etc. more than is right, see OVER-; *not* ~ *well* etc., rather badly etc.; *shall have something* ~; *20 lb. & ~; that can stand* ~, not be dealt with now; ~ *& above,* moreover, into the bargain). **8.** From beginning to end, with repetition, with detailed consideration, (*read, count,* ~; *did it six times* ~, ~ *& ~,* ~ *again,* ~ *& ~ again; talk, think, the matter* ~). **9.** At an end, done with, settled, (*the struggle is* ~). **10.** *All* ~, in characteristic attitude, behaviour, etc. (*that is Jones all* ~, that is what one would expect of Jones). **11.** n. (crick.). Number of balls (orig. 4 or 5, later 6 or 8) allowed between two calls of ~ (sense 4); the play that results; MAIDEN ~. **12.** adj. Upper, outer, superior, excessive, (usu. written as one word with n., see OVER-). **13.** prep. Above, on, at all or various points upon, to & fro upon, all through, round about, concerning, engaged with, (*a* ~ *b,* i.e. *a/b,* = *c; an umbrella* ~ *his head; projects* ~ *the street; doubt hangs* ~ *the question;* ~ *our heads,* beyond our comprehension, also without consulting us; HAND¹ ~ *hand; writing* ~ *the signature X.;* ~ *head & ears,* completely immersed lit. & fig.; ~ *shoes* ~ *boots,* no half measures; *with his hat* ~ *his eyes; draw a veil* ~ *it; a change came* ~ *him; blush spread* ~ *his face; rice is grown all* ~ *India; you may travel* ~ *Europe* or *Europe* ~; *all the world* ~, in all countries etc.; *went* ~ *his notes; sitting* ~ *the fire, a cheerful glass,* etc.; *pause* ~ *the details; laugh* ~ *the absurdity of it; go to sleep* ~ *one's work); all* ~ (sl.), infatuated with (a person); ~ *all,* from end to end (in attrib. use ~-*all; an* ~-*all length of 200 ft*); see also OVERALL. **14.** With or so as to get or give superiority to, beyond, more than, (*is king, reigns, has jurisdiction,* ~ *twenty millions; was victor, won the victory, was victorious,* ~; *set him* ~ *the rest; has no command* ~ *herself; give me the preference* ~ *him; cost* ~ *£50;* ~ *& above,* besides, not to mention). **15.** Out & down from, down from edge of, so as to clear, across, on or to the other side of, throughout, through duration of, till end of, (*fell* ~ *the edge, precipice: stumble* ~, be tripped up by; *jumped* ~ *the brook;* ~ *the bags* or *top,* of troops emerging from trench to attack; *looking* ~ *the hedge; spoke* ~ *her shoulder; coursing* ~ *the plain; a pass* ~ *the company's line; the house* ~ *the way,* opposite; *the King* ~ *the water,* Jacobite phr. for exiled king; *if we can tide* ~ *the next month; payments spread* ~ *a series of years; will not live* ~ *today; can you stay* ~ *Wednesday?*). Hence ~LY² adv. (chiefly U.S. & Sc.), excessively, too. [OE *ofer,* OS *obar,* OHG *ubar,* ON *yfir,* Goth. *ufar,* cogn. w. Gk *huper,* Skr. *upari* f. *up-* (whence Gmc **uf-* in ABOVE) with compar. term.]

ōv'er-, pref. = prec. Unless otherwise shown stress is on first part of compound.

1. Used as adj. in agreement with second part of compound, = upper, outer, of higher kind, upside down, extra, to or in higher position. So ~*arm* a. & adv., = ~-*hand*; ~*coat*, worn outside another; ~*dress*, outer part of gown made to resemble one dress worn over & showing parts of another of different colour etc.; ~*fault* (geol.), reverse fault with inclination towards upthrow side; ~*fold* (geol.), fold of strata so complete that middle part is upside down; ~*hand* a. & adv., with hand above object held, with hand above shoulder (~*hand bowling*; *bowls* ~-*hand*), out of water (~*hand stroke* in swimming), etc.; ~*lord*, supreme lord, suzerain, whence ~*lord'*SHIP n.; ~*man*, mining ~*seer*, an underground foreman, (philos., also *superman*) the ideal man, beyond good & evil, or superior to moral restrictions, of Nietzsche's philosophy; ~*plus*, surplus, superabundance; ‖ ~*shoe*, of rubber or felt worn outside another; ~-*sleeve*, *for* pulling on over sleeve to protect it; ~*soul*, God as animating the universe & including all human souls; ~*thrust* (geol.), thrust of strata on one side over those of other side of fault; ~*time*, during which workman works beyond regular hours; ~*tone* n. (mus.), upper PARTIALS; ~*weight*, preponderance, excessive weight.

2. As prep. governing second component & making with it n., a., or adv. So ~*all* n., woman's loose work-garment, (pl.) outer trousers or leggings or combination suit for dirty work, ‖ (mil., pl.) officer's full-dress tight trousers; ~*board* adv., from within ship into water (usu. *fall*, *throw*, ~*board*; *throw* ~*board*, fig., abandon, discard); ~*door* n., ornamental woodwork above door; ~*front* n., armflap of Inverness cape etc.; ~*ground* a., raised above ground, not underground; ~*head'* adv., on high, in the sky, in the storey above; ~*head* a., placed ~head (esp. ~-*head wires*; ~*head charges* etc., commerc., those due to office expenses, management, interest on capital, & other general needs of a business); ~*house* a., (of wires) supported on housetops instead of poles; ~*knee* a., reaching above knee; ~*land'* adv., by land & not sea; ~*land* a., entirely or partly by land (esp. of route by Mediterranean to India, or from Atlantic to Pacific across continent); ~*leaf'* adv., on other side of leaf (of book); ~*mantel* n., ornamental shelves etc. over mantelpiece; ~*night'* adv., on the preceding evening with a view to, or as regarded from, the next day; ~*night* a., done etc. ~night; ~*proof* a., containing more alcohol than proof spirit; ~*sea(s)'* adv., ~*sea(s)* a., across or beyond sea; ~*side'* adv., ~*side* a., (of loading & unloading ship) over the side into or out of lighters; ~*time'* adv., beyond regular hours of work; ~*weight* a., beyond weight allowed (esp. ~*weight luggage*).

3. As prep. prefixed to vbs, but itself governing case independently, often with specialized sense; also in abs. uses of, or in derivatives from, such vbs. So ~*brim'* v.t. & i. (*water* ~*brimmed the cup*; also said of the vessel); ~*come'* v.t. & i., prevail over, master, get the better of, be victorious, (p.p.) exhausted, made helpless, deprived of self-possession, (*with* or *by* emotion etc.; ~*come with liquor*, drunk); ~*crow'* v.t., exult or triumph over (rival), outswagger; ~*flow* n., what ~flows or is superfluous (~*flow meeting*, of those who have not found room at a demonstration etc. & ·meet elsewhere); ~*flow'* v.t. & i., flow over (brim etc.), flood (surface), (fig., of crowd etc.) extend beyond limits of (room etc.), (of receptacle etc.) be so full that contents ~flow, (of kindness, harvest, etc.) be very abundant, whence ~*flow*-ING[1,2] a. & n. (esp. *full to* ~*flowing*), ~*flow'ing*LY[2] adv.; ~*grow'* v.t. (of creeping plants); ~*growth* n., plants that have grown over anything, (fig.) accretion; ~*hang'* v.t. & i. (-*hung*), jut out over, jut out, (fig.) impend over, impend; so ~*hang* n., fact or amount of ~hanging; ~*lap'* v.t., partly cover, cover & extend beyond, (reciprocally of pl. subj.) partly coincide (*the great difficulty in classification is the* ~*lapping of species*); ~*lap* n., fact or process of ~lapping, ~lapping part; ~*leap'* v.t., leap over, surmount, omit, ignore; ~*lie'* v.t., lie on top of, smother (child) thus; ~*look'* v.t., have prospect of or over from above, be higher than, fail to observe, take no notice of, condone, superintend, ~see, bewitch with the evil eye; ~*pass'* v.t. & i., pass over, across, beyond, etc., get to the end of, surmount, surpass; ~*ride'* v.t., ride over (enemy's country) with armed force, trample (person) under one's horse's hoofs, (fig.) trample under foot, set aside, refuse to comply with, have or claim superior authority to (~*riding clause, authority*), (surg., of fractured bone) ~lap; ~*run*, v.t., flood, harry & spoil (enemy's country), (of vermin, weeds, etc.) swarm or spread over, exceed (limit); ~*sail'ing*, (of masonry course etc.) projecting beyond the one below; ~*see'* v.t. look at from above (rare), superintend or look after (workmen, execution of work, etc.), whence ~*seer* (-sēr) n. (‖ ~*seer of the poor*, hist., parish officer charged with poor-relief & other duties); ~*shoot'* v.t., send missile, go, beyond (mark etc. lit. & fig.; ~*shoot the mark*, also ~*shoot* one*self*, go too far, exaggerate, ~do something; ~*shot wheel*, turned by water flowing above it); ~*sight* n., supervision, omission to notice, mistake of inadvertence; ~-*spread'* v.t., become diffused over, cover or occupy surface of; ~*step'* v.t., pass beyond (boundary lit. or fig.).

4. As adverb in local senses (*above, by way of cover, down from above or from*

erectness, past, beyond, in addition)
modifying vb or derived n. without itself
governing object. So ~arch' v.t. & i.;
~bal'ance v.i. & t., lose balance & fall,
cause to do this; ~bear' v.t., bear down
or upset by weight or force, put down or
repress by power or authority, surpass in
importance etc., outweigh; ~bear'ing a.,
domineering, masterful, whence ~bear‑
ingLY² adv., ~bear'ingNESS n.; ~blown'
p.p., (of storm etc.) passed; ~can'opy
v.t.; ~cloud' v.t.; ~crust' v.t.; ~fall n.,
turbulent stretch of sea etc. caused by
set of tide or current over submarine
ledge or meeting of currents, ~flow opening to keep water of lock or canal up or
down to required level; ~film' v.t.;
~gild' v.t.; ~haul' v.t., pull to pieces for
purposes of examining, examine condition of, (esp. naut.) catch up, come up
with; ~haul n., thorough examination,
esp. with a view to repairs; ~hear' v.t.,
hear as an eavesdropper or as an unperceived or unintentional listener; ~lay'
v.t., cover surface of with coating etc., (incorrectly) ~lie; ~lay n., thing laid over
something, coverlet, small tablecloth,
etc.; ~passed', -past', a., gone by, past;
~sew v.t., sew (two edges) with every
stitch passing in same direction through
both, the inter-stitch parts of thread lying
across & outside united edge; ~shad'ow
v.t., shelter from sun, protect from attack
(rare), cast into the shade, diminish con-
spicuousness of by outshining; ~spill
n., what is spilt, surplus population etc.;
~spread' v.t., cover with (chiefly pass.;
heaven was ~spread with clouds); ~strung
a., (of piano) with strings in sets crossing
each other obliquely; ~take' v.t., come
up with, catch up, catch up and pass,
(person etc. who has start, or arrears of
work), (of storm, misfortune, etc.) come
suddenly upon (~taken in drink, drunk);
~throw' v.t., upset, knock down, cast out
from power, vanquish, subvert, put an
end to (institution etc.); ~throw n.,
defeat, subversion, (crick.) fielder's
return not stopped near wicket & so
allowing further run(s); ~turn' v.t. & i.,
upset, (cause to) fall down or over, ~-
throw, subvert, abolish; ~turn n., upsetting, revolution; ~whelm' v.t., bury
beneath superincumbent mass, submerge
utterly, crush, bring to sudden ruin, overpower with emotion etc., deluge with inquiries etc.; ~whel'ming a., irresistible by
numbers, amount, etc., whence ~whel'm-
ingLY² adv.

5. As adv. with trans. vb, adding sense
of effectually, completely, into submission.
So ~awe' v.t.; ~cloy' v.t.; ~joyed' p.p.,
transported with joy (at); ~mas'ter v.t.;
~persuade' v.t., persuade in spite of
reluctance or better judgement.

6. As adv. or adj. prefixed to vb, adj.,
adv., or n., adding notion of excess over
the desirable, the truth, or a definite

limit. So ~-abound' v.i.; ~-abun'dant a.;
~-abun'dantly adv.; ~-abun'dance n.;
~act' v.t. & i., act (part, emotion, etc.),
act part, with exaggeration; ~-ac'tive a.;
~-activ'ity n.; ~-anx'ious a.; ~-anx'iously
adv.; ~-anxi'ety n.; ~bid' v.t. (bridge),
make a higher bid than (one's partner),
bid more on (one's hand) than it is worth,
so ~bid n.; ~blow' v.t. (mus.), blow (pipe
etc.) with such force as to produce
harmonic instead of fundamental note;
~blown' a., (of flowers) too fully open,
past prime, also fig. of female beauty;
~bold' a.; ~burd'en v.t., & n.; ~burd'ensome a.; ~bu'sy a., too much occupied,
officious; ~buy' v.i., buy more than
enough to meet demand; ~call' v.t.
(bridge), = ~bid; ~call n.; ~-cap'italize
v.t., fix or estimate capital of (company
etc.) too high; ~-care' n.; ~-care'ful a.;
~-cau'tion n.; ~-cau'tious a.; ~-cau'tiously
adv.; ~charge' v.t., put too much explosive or electricity or the like into, put
exaggerated details or too much detail
into (description, picture, etc.), charge too
high a price for (thing) or to (person),
charge (specified sum) beyond right
price; ~charge n., excessive charge (of
explosive, or in money, see prec.); ~-
col'our v.t., exaggerate (details of description etc.); ~-con'fident a.; ~-con'fidently
adv.; ~-con'fidence n.; ~-cred'ulous a.;
~-credul'ity n.; ~crop' v.t., exhaust
(land) by continuous cropping; ~crowd'
v.t.; ~-cunn'ing n., cunning that ~-
reaches itself; ~-cur'ious a., too inquisitive, too careful or precise or fastidious;
~-cur'iously adv.; ~-curios'ity n.; ~-
-del'icacy n.; ~-del'icate a.; ~-devel'op v.t.
(photog.); ~do' v.t., carry to excess, go
too far in, cook too much (esp. in p.p.),
overtax strength of; ~dose' v.t.; ~dose
n.; ~draft n., ~drawing of bank account,
amount by which draft exceeds balance;
~draw' v.t. & i., draw cheque in excess
of (one's account) or in excess of one's
account, exaggerate in describing;
~dress' v.t. & i.; ~drive' v.t., drive (horse
etc.), work (person), to exhaustion; ~-
-eag'er a.; ~-eag'erly adv.; ~-eag'erness
n.; ~-earn'est a.; ~-es'timate v.t., put
value or amount of too high; ~-es'timate
(-at) n.; ~-excite' v.t.; ~-exer'tion n.;
~-expose' v.t., ~-expo'sure n., (photog.);
~-fatigue' v.t., & n.; ~fish', v.t., fish
(stream etc.) to depletion; ~fond' a.;
~-fulfil'ment n., completion of a Soviet
five-year plan before the appointed time;
~-go'vern v.t., subject to needless restrictions &°regulations; ~-go'vernment
n.; ~growth' n., growth too great for
health etc., ~-haste' n., ~-has'ty a.;
~-has'tily adv.; ~-heal' v.t.; ~-housed'
(-zd) a., living in too large a house, ~
-indulge' v.t. & i., ~-indul'gence n.,
~-iss'ue v.t., issue (notes, shares, etc.)
beyond authorized amount or ability to
pay, ~-iss'ue n. things or amount so

issued; ~-*lab'our* v.t., elaborate to excess; ~-*lad'en* a.; ~*large'* a.; ~*load'* v.t.; ~*load* n.; ~*long'* a.; ~-*ma'ny* a.; ~*mast'ed* a., with too tall or heavy masts; ~-*mea'sure* n., amount beyond the due or sufficient; ~-*mod'est* a.; ~*much'* a., n., & adv. (*be not righteous* ~*much*); ~-*nice'* a., too fastidious; ~-*nice'ness*, ~-*ni'cety*, nn.; ~*pay'* v.t., recompense (person, service) too highly; ~-*peo'pled* a., ~stocked with people; ~*pitch'* v.t., bowl (cricket ball) so that it pitches too near wicket; ~-*pop'ulated* a., too thickly populated; ~-*popula'tion* n., ~-populated condition; ~*pot'* v.t., plant in too large a pot; ~*praise'* v.t., & n.; ~*pre'ssure* n., pressing or being pressed too hard, esp. ~work; ~*print'* v.t. (photog.), also, print additional matter on (an already printed surface, esp. of postage stamps); ~-*:produce'* v.i. & t., produce too much of (commodity, or usu. abs.) for the demand; ~-*produc'tion* n.; ~-*pun'ish* v.t.; ~*rate'* v.t., have too high an opinion of, assess too high for rating purposes; ~-*read'* v.i., do too much reading; ~-*refine'* v.i., make too subtle distinctions; ~*ride'* v.t., exhaust (horse) by riding; ~*ripe* a.; ~-*scrup'ulous* a.; ~*sell'* v.t. & i., sell more of (commodity, stock, or abs.) than one can deliver; ~-*sen'sitive* a.; ~-*sen'sitiveness* n.; ~-*soli'citous* a.; ~-*soli'citude* n.; ~*state'* v.t., state too strongly, exaggerate; ~-*state'ment* n.; ~*stock'* v.t.; ~*stock* n.; ~*strain'* v.t., damage by exertion, make too much of (scruples etc.; esp. in p.p.); ~*strain* n., ~straining or being ~strained; ~*strung'* a., (of person, his nerves, etc.) intensely strained or wound up; ~*stud'y* v.i., & n.; ~-*su'btle* a.; ~-*supply'* n.; ~-*swoll'en* a.; ~*task'* v.t., give or be too heavy a task to or for; ~*tax'* v.t., make excessive demand on (person's strength etc.), burden with excessive taxes; ~*tire'* v.t.; ~*toil'* n.; ~*tone'* v.t. (photog.); ~*train'* v.t. & i., subject to or undergo too much athletic training, with injury to condition; ~-*use'* v.t.; ~-*use* n.; ~*val'ue* v.t.; ~*ween'ing* a., arrogant, presumptuous, conceited, self-confident; ~*weight'ed* a., unduly loaded *with*; ~*wind'* v.t., wind (watch etc.) beyond proper stopping-point; ~*work'* v.t. & i., (cause to) work too hard, weary or exhaust with work; ~*work'* n., excessive work; ~*wrought'* a., ~-excited, suffering reaction from excitement, too elaborate; ~-*zeal'* n.; ~-*zea'lous* a.; ~-*:zea'lously* adv.

7. Prefixed to vb & enabling it to take *self* as obj., or be used in p.p., with sense *damage oneself by doing action to excess*; many of these compounds can also be used abs. in same sense. So ~*drink'*, ~*eat'*, ~*feed'* (also trans.), ~*grow'* (in p.p., that has ~grown himself etc.); ~*jump'* one*self*, strain sinew etc. in jumping; ~*preach'*; ~*reach'* one*self*, strain oneself by reaching too far, defeat one's object by going too far, (of horse) injure forefoot by striking it with hind-hoof; ~*run'*; ~*sleep'* one*self*, miss intended hour of rising by sleeping too long, also v.i.; ~*smoke'*; ~*spend'* (one*self* or abs.), spend money beyond one's means; ~*toiled'* p.p.; ~*walk'*; ~*watched'* p.p., exhausted by keeping awake; ~*write'* one*self*, damage one's work by writing too much.

8. Prefixed to vb or deriv., or adj., with added sense of *more than*. So ~*bal'ance* v.t., outweigh lit. & fig.; ~*balance* n., (amount of) excess; ~*due'* a.; ~*fill'* v.t.; ~*full'* a.; ~*match'* v.t., be too strong etc. for, defeat; ~*match* n.; ~*poise'* v.t., outweigh; ~*subscribe'* v.t., subscribe more than amount of (loan etc.; usu. in p.p.).

9. As prefix making trans. vb out of intr. vb, or vb not taking same obj., or n, usu. with sense of *exceeding*. So ~*build'*, build too closely on (land); ~*cast'*, cover (sky etc.) with clouds or darkness (usu. p.p.), stitch over (edge) to prevent unravelling, esp. with blanket or button-hole stitch; ~*live'*, live beyond (other person, specified age, etc.); ~*pow'er*, reduce to submission, subdue, master, make (thing) ineffective or imperceptible by greater intensity, (of heat, emotion, etc.) be too intense for, ~whelm; ~*pow'ering*, a., irresistible; ~*pow'eringly* adv.; ~*reach'*, circumvent, outwit, get the better of by cunning or artifice; ~-*rent'*, charge too high a rent for (land etc.) or to (farmer etc.); ~*rule'*, set aside (decision, argument, proposed course) by superior authority, annul decision or reject proposal of (person); ~*stay'*, stay beyond (one's welcome etc.); ~*top'*, be or become higher than; ~*trump'*, play higher trump than.

overact, v.t. & i., see OVER- 6; **overall** n., OVER- 2; **overarch** v.t. & i., OVER- 4; **overarm** a. & adv., OVER- 1; **overawe** v.t., OVER- 5; **overbalance** v.i. & t., & n., OVER- 4, 8; **overbear** v.t., **overbearing** a., OVER- 4; **overbid** v.t., & n., **overblow** v.t., OVER- 6; **overblown** a., OVER- 4, 6; **overboard** adv., OVER- 2; **overbrim** v.t. & i., OVER- 3; **overbuild** v.t., OVER- 9; **overburden** v.t., **overbusy** a., **overbuy** v.i., **overcall** v.t., & n., OVER- 6; **overcanopy** v.t., OVER- 4; **over-capitalize** v.t., **overcare** n., OVER- 6; **overcast** v.t., OVER- 9; **over-caution** n., **overcharge** v.t., & n., OVER- 6; **overcloud** v.t., OVER- 4; **overcloy** v.t., OVER- 5; **overcoat** n., OVER- 1; **over-colour** v.t., OVER-'6; **overcome** v.t., OVER- 3; **over-confidence** n., **over-credulity** n., **overcrop** v.t., OVER- 6; **overcrow** v.t., OVER- 3; **overcrowd** v.t., OVER- 6; **overcrust** v.t., OVER- 4; **overcunning** n., **over-curious** a., **over-delicacy** n., **over-develop** v.t., **overdo** v.t., OVER- 6; **overdoor** n., OVER- 2; **overdose** v.t. & n., **overdraft** n.,

overdraw v.t. & i., OVER- 6; **overdress** n. OVER- 1, v.i. OVER- 6; **overdrink** v. refl. & i., OVER- 7; **overdrive** v.t., OVER- 6; **overdue** a., OVER- 8; **overeat** v. refl. & i., OVER- 7; **over-estimate** v.t., & n., **over--expose** v.t., **over-exposure** n., OVER- 6; **overfall** n., OVER- 4; **over-fatigue** v.t., & n., OVER- 6; **overfault** n., OVER- 1; **overfeed** v.t. & i., OVER- 7; **overfill** v.t., OVER- 8; **overfilm** v.t., OVER- 4; **overfish** v.t., OVER- 6; **overflow** v.t. & i., & n., **overflowing** n. & a., OVER- 3; **overfold** n., OVER- 1; **overfront** n., OVER- 2; **over--fulfilment** n., OVER- 6; **overfull** a., OVER- 8; **overgild** v.t., OVER- 4; **over-govern** v.t., **over-government** n., OVER- 6; **overground** a., OVER- 2; **overgrow** v.t. OVER- 3, v. refl. & i. OVER- 7; **overgrowth** n., OVER- 3, 6; **overhand** adv. & a., OVER- 1; **overhang** v.t. & i., & n., OVER- 3; **overhaul** v.t., & n., OVER- 4; **overhead** adv. & a., OVER- 2; **overhear** v.t., OVER- 4; **overhouse** a., OVER- 2; **overhoused** a., **over-indulgence** n., **over-issue** v.t., & n., OVER- 6; **overjoyed** a., OVER- 5; **overjump** v. refl., OVER- 7; **overknee** a., OVER- 2; **overlabour** v.t., **overladen** a., OVER- 6; **overland** adv. & a., OVER- 2; **overlap** v.t. & i., & n., OVER- 3; **overlay** v.t., & n., OVER- 4; **overleaf** adv., OVER- 2; **overleap** v.t., **overlie** v.t., OVER- 3; **overlive** v.t., OVER- 9; **overload** v.t., & n., OVER- 6; **overlook** v.t., OVER- 3; **overlord, overlordship, overman,** nn., OVER- 1; **overmantel** n., OVER- 2; **overmany,** **overmasted,** aa., OVER- 6; **overmaster** v.t., OVER- 5; **over-match** v.t., & n., OVER- 8; **over-measure** n., **overmuch** a., adv., & n., **over-nice** a., **over-niceness, over-nicety,** nn., OVER- 6; **overnight** adv. & a., OVER- 2; **overpass** v.t., OVER- 3; **overpassed, -past,** a., OVER- 4; **overpay** v.t., **overpeopled** a., OVER- 6; **over-persuade** v.t., OVER- 5; **overpitch** v.t., OVER- 6; **overplus** n., OVER- 1; **overpoise** v.t., OVER- 8; **over-population** n., **overpot** v.t., OVER- 6; **overpower** v.t., **overpowering** a., OVER- 9; **overpraise** v.t., & n., OVER- 6; **over-preach** v. refl. & i., OVER- 7; **overpressure** n., **overprint** v.t., **over-produce** v.t. & i., **over-production** n., OVER- 6; **overproof** a., OVER- 2; **overrate** v.t., OVER- 6; **overreach** v. refl. & i. OVER- 7, v.t. OVER- 9; **over-read** v.i., **over-refine** v.i., OVER- 6; **over-rent** v.t., OVER- 9; **override** v.t., OVER- 3, 6; **overripe** a., OVER- 6; **overrule** v.t., OVER- 9; **overrun** v.t., OVER- 3, 7; **oversailing** a., OVER- 3; **oversea** a., & adv., **overseas** a. & adv., OVER- 2; **oversee** v.t., **overseer** n., OVER- 3; **oversell** v.i. & t., OVER- 6; **oversew** v.t., OVER- 4; **overshadow** v.t., OVER- 4; **overshoe** n., OVER- 1; **overshoot** v.t., **overshot** a., OVER- 2; **oversight** n., OVER- 3.

‖ **ōv′erslaugh** (-aw), n. (mil.). Passing over of one's turn of duty in consideration of another duty that takes precedence of it. [f. Du. *overslag* (*overslaan* omit f. OVER, *slaan* strike)]

oversleep, v. refl. & i., see OVER- 7; **over-sleeve** n., OVER- 1; **oversmoke** v. refl. & i., OVER- 7; **oversoul** n., OVER- 1; **over-spend** v. refl. & i., OVER- 7; **overspill** n., OVER- 4; **overspread** v.t., OVER- 3, 4; **overstate** v.t., **overstatement** n., OVER- 6; **overstay** v.t., OVER- 9; **overstep** v.t., OVER- 3; **overstock** v.t., & n., **overstrain** v.t., & n., OVER- 6; **overstrung** a., OVER- 4, 6; **overstudy** v. i., & n., OVER- 6; **oversubscribe** v.t., OVER- 8; **over-supply** n., **overswollen** a., OVER- 6.

ōv′ert, a. Openly done, unconcealed, patent; *market* ∼, open displaying of goods for sale to all comers. Hence ∼LY² adv. [ME, f. OF, p.p. of *ovrir* (now *ouvrir*)]

overtake, v.t., see OVER- 4; **overtask** v.t., **overtax** v.t., OVER- 6; **overthrow** v.t., & n., OVER- 4; **overthrust** n., OVER- 1; **overtime** adv. OVER- 2, n. OVER- 1; **overtire** v.t., OVER- 6; **overtoil** n., OVER- 6; **overtoiled** a., OVER- 7; **overtone** v.t., OVER- 6; **overtone** n., OVER- 1; **overtop** v.t., OVER- 9; **overtrain** v.t. & i., OVER- 6; **overtrump** v.t., OVER- 9.

ōv′erture, n. Opening of negotiations with another, formal proposal or offer, (usu. pl., esp. *make* ∼*s to*); (mus.) orchestral piece opening opera, oratorio, etc. (*concert* ∼, one-movement composition in same style); beginning of poem etc. [ME, f. OF, f. L *apertura* APERTURE]

overturn, v.t. & i., & n., see OVER- 4; **over-use** v.t., & n., **overvalue** v.t., OVER- 6; **overwalk** v. refl. & i., **overwatched** a., OVER- 7; **overweening** a., OVER- 6; **overweight** n. OVER- 1, adj. OVER- 2; **overweighted** a., OVER- 6; **overwhelm** v.t., **overwhelming** a., OVER- 4; **overwind** v.t., **overwork** v.t. & i., & n., OVER- 6; **overwrite** v. refl. & i., OVER- 7; **overwrought** a., OVER- 6.

ōvi-¹, comb. form of OVUM; *ov′iduct* n., canal through which ova pass from ovary esp. in oviparous animals; *ov′iform* a., egg-shaped; *ovip′arous* a., producing young by means of eggs expelled from body before being hatched (opp. VIVIPAROUS); *ovipōs′it* (-z-) v.i., lay egg(s), esp. with *ovipōs′itor* n., pointed tubular organ with which female insect deposits eggs; *ovorhomboid′al* etc., between rhomboid etc. & oval; *ovŏl′ogy* n., science of the formation of animals' ova; *ovovivĭp′arous* a., producing young by eggs hatched within body.

ŏvĭ-², comb. form of L *ovis* sheep; ∼·*bŏv′ine* a & n., (animal) having characters intermediate between sheep & ox, musk-ox; *ov′icide* n. (joc.), sheep-killing.

Ovid′ian, a. (As) of Ovid or his poetry. [L *Ovidius* Ovid, -IAN]

ōv′ine, a. Of, like, sheep. [f. LL *ovinus* (*ovis* sheep, -INE¹)]

ōvo-, irreg. f. OVI-[1] (see -O-).

ōv'oid, a. & n. **1.** Solidly or superficially egg-shaped, oval with one end more pointed. **2.** n. ~ body or surface. [f. F *ovoïde* (OVUM, -OID)]

ōv'olō, n. (pl. -*li* pr. -lē). Convex moulding of quarter-circle or quarter-ellipse section, receding downwards. [It. (now *uovolo*), dim. of *uovo* egg f. L OVUM]

ōv'ūle, n. Rudimentary seed, female germ-cell, unfertilized ovum. Hence **ōv'ūl**AR[1] a. [F (foll., -ULE)]

ōv'um, n. (pl. *ova*). Female germ in animals, capable of developing into new individual when fertilized by male sperm, egg esp. of mammals, fish, or insects. [L, = egg]

ow, int. expr. sudden pain.

owe (ō), v.t. & i. (*owing*). Be under obligation to (re)pay (person money, money *to* person, money) or render (person honour etc., gratitude etc. *to* person), be in debt (*for* thing, with creditor in dat.; *he* ~*s not any man*; *I* ~ *you for your services*, ~*d for all my clothes*); ~ one *a grudge*, cherish resentment against him; be indebted for *to* person (or with dat.; *we* ~ *to Newton the principle of gravitation*; *I* ~ *him much*). [a preterite-present vb like CAN, DARE, MAY: OE *āgan* (see OUGHT[2]), OS *ēgan*, OHG *eigan*, ON *eiga*, Goth. *aigan* f. Gmc *aig-*]

Ow'énism (ō-), n. Communistic co-operation advocated by Robert Owen (d. 1858). [-ISM]

ow'ing (ōī-), pred. a. Yet to be paid, owed, due, (*paid all that was* ~); ~ *to*, attributable to, caused by, (*all this was* ~ *merely to ill luck*), (as prep.) on account of (~ *to the drought, crops are short*). [OWE, -ING[2]]

owl, n. Kinds of large-headed hook-beaked large-eyed soft-plumaged nocturnal bird of prey (esp. *barn* ~, *tawny* ~, & *long-eared* or *horned* ~, each with other names, as *church*, *screech*, *hooting*, etc., ~; *fly with the* ~, have nocturnal habits; ~*s to Athens*, = COAL[1]*s to Newcastle*); solemn person, wise-looking dullard, whence ~'ISH[1] a., ~'ISHL Y[2] adv.; (also ~ *pigeon*) fancy variety of pigeon; ~-*light*, dusk, twilight. Hence ~'ERY(3) n. [OE *ūle*, OLG *ūla*, ON *ugla*, f. Gmc *ūwwalōn*, cf. OHG *ūwila*; ult. imit., cf. L *ululula*]

owl'ét, n. Owl, young owl. [earlier HOWLET]

own[1] (ōn), a. **1.** (Appended to possessive adj. or case) in full ownership, proper, peculiar, individual, & not another's, (*saw it with my* ~ *eyes*; *has a value all its* ~; *let them* STEW[2] *in their* ~ *juice*; *loves truth for its* ~ *sake*; *be one's* ~ *man*, independent, free; *God's* ~ *heaven*; *may I have it for my* ~ or *my very* ~?; *my* ~ *sweetheart* etc., or abs. *my* ~, esp. in voc. expressing affection; often also used to emphasize not the ownership; but the personality of the subject etc., as *cooks*

her ~ *meals, every man his* ~ *lawyer, am my* ~ *master*; also used abs.=private property, kindred, etc., as *may I not do what I will with my* ~?, *the* DEVIL[1]'s ~; *of* one's ~, belonging to one, as *I have nothing of my* ~, *will give you one of my* ~; *get* one's ~ *back*, colloq., get even with, revenge oneself (*on*); *hold* one's ~, maintain position, not be defeated; *on* one's ~, independently, on one's ~ *account or* responsibility or resources). **2.** (Without preceding possessive) ~ *brother, sister*, with both parents the same; ~ *cousin*, first. [OE *ǣgen, āgen*, OS *ēgan*, OHG *eigan*, ON *eiginn* f. Gmc **aiganaz* f. p.p. of *aigan* possess; see OWE]

own[2] (ōn), v.t. & i. Have as property, possess, whence **ow'**NER[1], **ow'ner**SHIP(1), nn., **ow'ner**LESS a., (ōn-); acknowledge authorship, paternity, or possession, of (*child, pamphlet, hat, that nobody will* ~); admit as existent, valid, true, etc. (~*s his deficiencies, himself indebted, he or that he did not know*); confess to (~*s to a sense of shame, to having done*); ~ *up*, colloq., make frank confession; submit to (person's sway etc.) without protest; *the* ~*er* (nav. sl.), captain of the ship. [OE *āgnian* f. *ǣgen* OWN[1])]

ōx, n. (pl. *oxen*). **1.** Any bovine animal, individual of kinds of large usu. horned cloven-footed ruminant used when domesticated for draught, for supplying milk, and for eating as meat, (esp.) castrated male of domestic species, (*the black ox has trod on one's foot*, misfortune or old age has come upon him); *ox-bird*, kinds of small bird, esp. the dunlin. **2.** *Ox-eye*, large human eye, whence **ōx-eyED**[2] (-īd) a., kinds of plant esp. (*yellow ox-eye*) corn marigold, (*white ox-eye*) ox-eyed daisy; *ox-fence* or ox'ER[1] n., strong cattle-fence of railing & hedge & occas. ditch; *ox-gall* (used for cleansing, & in painting & pharmacy); *ox'herd*, cowherd; *ox'hide*; *ox'lip*, primula, (pop.) hybrid of primrose & cowslip; *ox'tail*, tail of ox, much used for soup-making. [OE *oxa*, OS, OHG *ohso*, ON *uxi, oxi*, Goth. *auhsa* f. Gmc **ohsan-*, cogn. w. Skr. *ukshan*]

ōx-, comb. form (chem.) = OXY-, as *oxacet'ic* or *oxyacet'ic*, or = OXAL-, as *oxam'ic*.

ōxal(o)-, comb. form of *oxalic acid*, whence **ōx'al**ATE[1](3) n.; *oxalo-nit'rate* etc.

ōxäl'ic, a. (chem.). Derived from wood-sorrel (~ *acid*, a highly poisonous & sour acid found in wood-sorrel & other plants). [f. F *oxalique* (L f. Gk *oxalis* kinds of plant including wood-sorrel, -IC)]

Ox'bridge (ō-), n. Name for a university of ancient foundation. [*Ox(ford)*, (*Cam*)-*bridge*]

Ox'ford (ō-), n. University town in England; ‖~ *bags*, very wide trousers; ~ *blue* (dark with purple tinge); ~ *clay*, deposit of stiff blue clay underlying coral rag in midland counties; ‖~ *frame*, picture-frame of which sides cross each other at corners & project ; ~ *Group* (*Movement*), see BUCHMANISM; ~ *movement*, for revival of Catholic doctrine & observance in Church of England begun *c.* 1833 ; ~ *shirting*, kind of shirt or dress material; ~ *shoes*, low shoes lacing over instep ; ~ *Tracts*, the ' TRACT²s for the Times '.

ŏx'ĭdāte, v.t. & i. Oxidize. Hence **ŏxĭdᴀ'TION** n., oxidizing or being oxidized. [f. F *oxider*, -ᴀTE³]

ŏx'ĭde, n. Compound of oxygen with another element or with organic radical. [F, f. *oxygène* + -*ide*, after *acide*; see OXY-, -IDE]

ŏx'ĭdiz|e, -is|e (-ĭz), v.t. & i. Cause to combine with oxygen ; cover (metal) with coating of oxide, make rusty ; take up or enter into combination with oxygen, rust ; ~*ed silver*, (incorrect name for) silver with dark coat of silver sulphide. Hence ~ABLE a., ~ᴀ'TION, ~ER¹(2), nn. [prec., -IZE]

Oxōn'ĭan (ŏ-), a. & n. (Member) of University of Oxford ; (citizen) of Oxford. [*Oxonia* latinized name of *Ox*(*en*)*ford*,-AN]

‖ **ŏx'ter**, n., & v.t. (Sc.). **1.** Armpit; inner side of upper arm. **2.** v.t. Support with or by taking the arm, put under the arm ; hug. [f. OE *ōhsta*, *ōxta*]

ŏxў-, comb. form of Gk *oxus* sharp : (1) in gen. senses, as ~*carp'ous*, with pointed fruit; ~*ōp'ia*, abnormal keenness of vision; OXYGEN; OXYMORON; OXYTONE; (2) in chem. wds as comb. form of *oxygen*, (a) denoting presence or admixture of oxygen; ~*acet'ylene*, consisting of, involving use of, a mixture of oxygen & acetylene (~*acetylene blowpipe*, for producing intensely hot flame for welding etc.); ~*house²gas*, ~*pa'raffin*, etc., used attrib. of flame produced by mixing the vapour of the gas etc. with oxygen; ~*cal'cium light*, limelight; ~*hyd'rogen blowpipe, flame, light*, etc.; ~*a'cid* (& see b.); *ox'ysalt*, containing oxygen; (b)loosely used for *hydroxy-*, denoting compound of organic substance having atom of hydroxyl substituted for one of hydrogen, as ~*a'cid* (& see a.).

ŏx'ўgĕn, n. Colourless tasteless scentless gas, one of the non-metallic elements, existing in air & combined in water & most minerals & organic substances, & being essential to animal & vegetable life. Hence **ŏxў'gĕnOUS** a. [f. F *oxygène* acidifying principle, see OXY-(2), -GEN; it was at first held to be the essential principle in formation of acids]

ŏx'ўgĕn|āte (*or* ŏksĭ²-), v.t. Supply, treat, or mix, with oxygen, oxidize ; charge (blood) with oxygen by respiration. So ~ANT(2), ~ᴀ'TION, nn. [f. F *oxygéner* (prec.), -ᴀTE³]

ŏx'ўgĕnīze (*or* ŏksĭ²-), **-ise** (-ĭz), v.t. = prec. [-IZE]

ŏx'ўmĕl, n. Syrup of honey & vinegar. [L f. Gk *oxumeli* (OXY-, *meli* honey)]

ŏxўmōr'on, n. (rhet.). Figure of speech

with pointed conjunction of seeming contradictories (e.g. *faith unfaithful kept him falsely true*). [Gk (-*mō*-) f. OXY-(1), *mōros* foolish]

ŏx'ўtone, a. & n. (Gk gram.). (Word) with acute accent on last syllable. [f. Gk *oxutonos* f. OXY-(1), *tonos* TONE]

oy'er, n. Criminal trial under the writ of ~ *& terminer* or commission to judges on circuit to hold courts. [ME, f. AF *oyer et terminer* (L *audire* hear, *terminare* determine), -ER⁴]

oyez, oyes, o yes, (ōyĕs'), int. uttered, usu. thrice, by public crier or court officer to bespeak silence & attention. [ME, f. AF, OF (-*z*), imperat. pl. of *oïr* hear = L *audiatis* (*audire* hear)]

oys'ter, n. Kinds of edible bivalve mollusc usu. eaten alive; ~-shaped morsel of meat in fowl's back; ~-*bank, -bed*, part of sea-bottom where ~s breed or are bred; ~-*bar*, counter in restaurant etc. where ~s are served; ~-*catcher*, coastal wading bird; ~-*farm*, sea bottom used for breeding ~s; ~-*knife*, of shape adapted for opening ~s; ~ *patty*, piece of pastry containing cooked ~s. [ME, f. OF *oistre* (now *huître*) f. L *ostrea* (-*eum*) f. Gk *ostreon*]

ozō'cerite, ozŏk'erit, n. Wax-like fossil resin used for candles, insulating, etc. [G (-*kerit*), f. Gk *ozō* smell, *kēros* wax, -ITE¹]

ōz'ōn|e, n. Condensed form of oxygen with three atoms to molecule having pungent refreshing odour. (fig.) exhilarating influence. Hence **ozōn'IC**, ~**iF'ER**OUS, aa., ~IZE(3, 5) v.t., ~**īzER**¹(2), ~**ōn'ETER**, nn. [f. G *ozon* (Gk *ozō* smell, -ONE)]

P

P, p, (pē), letter (pl. *P*s, P's). *Mind one's P's & Q's*, be careful of propriety.

pa¹ (pah), n. (colloq.). = PAPA. [abbr.]

pa² (pah), **pah**, n. (hist.). Native fort in New Zealand; (now) Maori village. [Maori]

păb'ūlum, n. Food (often fig., as *mental* ~). [L (*pascere* feed)]

p̆ăc'a, n. Kinds of large rodents in Central & South America. [native]

pāce¹, n. Single step in walking or running; space traversed in this (about 30 in.); space between successive stationary positions of same foot in walking (about 60 in.); mode of walking or running, gait; any of various gaits of (esp. trained) horse, mule, etc.; = AMBLE; (fig.) *put* person *through his* ~*s*, test his qualities in action etc.; speed in walking or running; rate of progression (often fig.); *keep* ~, advance at equal rate *with*; *go the* ~, at great speed, (fig.) indulge in dissipation; ~*-maker*, rider, runner, etc., who sets ~ for another in race etc.; ‖ ~-*stĭck*, drill-sergeant's adjustable two-legged appliance for measuring length of ~.

Hence -**pācED**[2] (-st) a. [ME, f. OF pas f. L passus (pandere pass- stretch)]

pāce[2], v.t. & t. Walk with slow or regular pace; traverse thus; measure (distance) by pacing; (of horse) amble; set pace for (rider, runner, etc.). [f. prec.]

pā'cĕ[3], prep. ~ tū'ă, ~ Smith, (in announcing contrary opinion) with all deference to you, to Smith. [L, abl. of PAX]

pā'cer, n. In vbl senses, esp. horse that paces. [-ER[1]]

pacha etc. See PASHA etc.

pachi'sĭ (-chē[2]), n. Four-handed Indian game with cowries for dice. [Hind., = of 25]

păch'ўdĕrm (-k-), n. Thick-skinned quadruped. one of Cuvier's (now discarded) group Pachydermata (hoofed quadrupeds that do not chew cud, e.g. elephant, horse, etc.); (fig.) thick-skinned person. So **păchўdĕrm'atous** (-k-) a. [f. F pachyderme f. Gk pakhudermos (pakhus thick +derma -matos skin)]

pacif'ic, a. & n. Tending to peace; of peaceful disposition; the P~ (Ocean), that between America & Asia. Hence **pacif'I-CALLY** adv. [f. F -ique, or L pacificus (pax pacis peace, see -FIC)]

pācifica'tion, n. Pacifying; treaty of peace. So **pacif'icātORY** a. [F, f. L pacificationem (as PACIFY, see -FICATION)]

pacif'icism, pā'cifĭsm, n. The doctrine that the abolition of war is both desirable & possible. Hence **pacif'ICIST, pā'cifIST**, n. [f. F pacifisme, -iste; shorter forms earlier & preferred to pedantically correct longer forms]

pā'cifў, v.t. Appease (person, anger, excitement, etc.); reduce (country etc.) to state of peace. [ME, f. OF pacifier f. L pacificare (as PACIFIC, see -FY)]

păck[1], n. 1. Bundle of things wrapped up or tied together for carrying; parcel, esp. pedlar's bundle or soldier's knapsack. 2. A measure of various goods. 3. Lot, set, (~ of fools, lies, nonsense, etc.). 4. Number of hounds kept together for hunting, or of beasts (esp. wolves) or birds (esp. grouse) naturally associating; organized group of U-boats. 5. (In rugby footb.) a side's forwards. 6. Set of playing-cards. 7. Large area of large pieces of floating ice in sea. 8. Quantity of fish, fruit, etc., packed in a season etc.; (commerc.) method of packing for the market. 9. ~-drill, military punishment of walking up and down in full marching ORDER[1](2); ~-horse (for carrying ~s); ~'man, pedlar; ~-saddle (adapted for supporting~s); ~'thread, stout thread for sewing or tying up ~s. [ME, f. MDu. pak, MLG pak, packe, of unkn. orig.]

păck[2], v.t. & i. 1. Put (things) together into bundle, box, bag, etc., for transport or storing (often ~ up, esp. abs.); (of things) admit of being ~ed well, easily, etc. 2. Prepare & put up (meat, fruit, etc.) in tins etc. for preservation. 3. Put

closely together; (naut.) ~ (put) on all sail; form (hounds) into pack; place (cards) together in pack; (intr.) crowd together, (of animals) form into pack. 4. Cover (thing) with something pressed tightly round; (med.) wrap (body etc.) in wet cloth. 5. (boxing sl.). Be capable of delivering (a punch) with skill or force. 6. Fill (bag, box, etc.) with clothes etc.; cram (space etc. with); load (beast) with pack. 7. Depart with one's belongings; send (person) ~ing, dismiss him summarily; ~ (person) off, send him away. 8. [prob. diff. wd]. Select (jury etc.) so as to secure partial decision. 9. (sl.). ~ it in, end it, finish; ~ it up, desist; ~ up, (of an engine) peter out, go out of action. [ME, f. prec.]

păck'age, n., & v.t. 1. Bundle of things packed, parcel; box etc. in which goods are packed; ~ deal, transaction agreed to as a whole, the less favourable items as well as the more favourable. 2. v.t. Make up into, enclose in, a ~. [-AGE]

păck'er, n. In vbl senses, esp.: one who packs meat, fruit, etc., for market; machine for packing. [-ER[1]]

păck'ĕt, n. Small package; || (sl.) considerable sum won or lost in betting, speculation, etc.; || catch, stop, a ~ (sl.), be (severely) wounded by bullet etc.; ~(-boat), mail-boat. [PACK[1]+-ET[1]]

păck'ing, n. In vbl senses; also (oil-absorbing) material closing a joint or assisting in lubrication of a journal; ~-box, = STUFFING-box; ~-needle, large needle for sewing up packages; ~-sheet, (1) sheet for packing goods in, (2) wet sheet used in hydropathy. [-ING[1]]

pāct, n. Compact; PEACE P~. [ME, f. OF, f. L pactum, neut. p.p. of paciscere agree]

păd[1], n. 1. (sl.). Road, esp. gentleman, knight, squire, of the ~, highwayman; FOOT'~. 2. (Also ~-nag) easy-paced horse. [16th c. cant, f. Du., LG pad PATH]

păd[2], v.t. & i. (-dd-). Tramp along (road etc.) on foot; travel on foot; ~ it, ~ the hoof, (sl.), go on foot. [f. prec., or LG padden, pedden tread]

păd[3], n. 1. Soft stuffed saddle without tree; part of double harness to which girths are attached. 2. Cushion, stuffing, used to diminish jarring, fill out hollows, etc.; guard for parts of body in cricket etc. 3. Number of sheets of blotting-, writing-, or drawing-paper fastened together at edge. 4. Fleshy cushion forming sole of foot in some quadrupeds; paw of fox, hare, etc. 5. Socket of brace, tool-handle. [16th c., of unkn. orig.]

păd[4], v.t, (-dd-). Furnish with a pad, stuff; fill out (sentence etc.) with superfluous words; ~ded cell, room in lunatic asylum with ~ded walls. Hence ~d'ING[1] (4) n. [19th c., f. prec.]

păd[5], n. Open pannier used as measure of fruit etc. [16th c., var. of ped (14th c.), of unkn. orig.]

păd'dle¹, n. Small spade-like implement with long handle; short broad-bladed oar used without rowlock; *double* ~ (with blade at each end); one of the boards fitted round circumference of ~-wheel; ~-shaped instrument; (zool.) fin or flipper; ~-*wheel*, wheel for propelling ship, with boards round circumference so as to press backward against water; ~-*box*, casing over upper part of this. [c. 1400, of unkn. orig.; cf. syn. (Sc. & north.) *pattle*]

păd'dle², v.i. & t., & n. **1.** Move on water, propel canoe, by means of paddles; ~ one's *own canoe*, (fig.) depend on oneself alone; row gently. **2.** n. Action, spell, of paddling. [f. prec.]

păd'dle³, v.i. Dabble with the feet in shallow water; toy with the fingers (*in, on, about,* thing); (of child) toddle. [cf. PUDDLE² & LG *pudeln* (POODLE)]

păd'dock¹, n. Small field, esp. as part of stud farm; turf enclosure near racecourse, where horses are assembled before race; (Austral.) field, plot of land. [app. var. of (now dial.) *parrock* (OE *pearroc*): see PARK]

‖ **păd'dock²,** n. (arch., dial.). Frog or toad. [f. ME *padde* (= ON *padda*, MDu., MLG *padde*) toad, +-OCK]

Păd'dy¹, n. (Nickname for) Irishman. [pet-form of *Padraig, Patrick*]

păd'dy², n. Rice in the straw or in the husk. [f. Malay *padi*]

‖ **păd'dy³, păd'dywhăck,** nn. (colloq.). A rage, fit of temper. [PADDY¹]

Pa'dishah, Pa'dshah, (pah-), n. Title in Persia of Shah, in Europe formerly of Sultan of Turkey, and in India of British sovereign. [Pers. (*pati* master + *shah* SHAH)]

păd'lŏck, n., & v.t. **1.** Detachable lock hanging by pivoted hook on object fastened; ~ *law*, one providing for closing & locking up premises. **2.** v.t. Secure with ~. [ME; first elem. unexpl.]

padouk (pahdowk'), n. Burmese timber-tree; its wood, resembling rosewood. [native name]

padre (pahd'rā), n. (colloq.). Chaplain. [f. It., Sp., Pg. *padre* father, priest]

padrŏn'e, n. Master of Mediterranean trading-vessel; Italian employer of street musicians, begging-children, etc.; proprietor of Italian inn. [It.]

păd'ūasoy, n. Strong corded silk fabric much worn in 18th c. (cf. POULT-DE-SOIE). [18th c. *poudesoy* f. F *pou-de-soie*, of unkn. orig.; assoc. w. *Padua*]

pae'an, n. Chant of thanksgiving for deliverance (orig.) addressed to Apollo or Artemis; song of praise or triumph. [L, f. Gk *paian* hymn to Apollo under name of Paian]

paed'er|ăsty, pēd'-, n. Sodomy with a boy. So ~**ăst** a., sodomite. [f. Gk *paiderastia* (*pais paidos* boy +*erastēs* lover)]

paed|(o)-, pēd|(o)-, comb. form of Gk

pais paidos; ~*o-băp'tism,* infant baptism, ~*o-băp'tist,* adherent of this; ~*o-gĕn'esis,* reproduction by immature insect; ~*i-ăt'ric* a., relating to ~*iăt'rics* n. pl., branch of medical science dealing with the study of childhood & the diseases of children, so ~*iatri'cian* (-shn), ~*iăt'rist,* nn. [Gk *iatros* physician]

pae'on, n. Metrical foot of one long syllable placed first, second, third, or fourth (*first* etc. ~) & three short. Hence **paeŏn'ic** a. [L, f. Gk *paiōn,* Attic form of *paian* PAEAN]

păg'an, n. & a. Heathen; unenlightened (person). Hence ~**DOM,** ~**ISM**(2), nn., ~**ISH¹** a., ~**IZE**(3) v.t. & i. [ME, f. L *paganus* (*pagus* country district, -AN); sense 'heathen' in Christian L]

păge¹, n., & v.t. **1.** Boy, usu. in livery, employed to attend to door, go on errands, etc.; ‖ ~ *of honour, of the presence,* etc., titles of various officers of royal household; boy employed as personal attendant of person of rank; boy in training for knighthood & attached to knight's service (hist.); hence ~'**HOOD,** ~'**SHIP,** nn. **2.** v.t. *Summon by means of a ~ (who calls out the name of person wanted until found). [ME, f. OF, f. It. *paggio* f. Gk *paidion,* dim. of *pais* boy (PAEDO-)]

păge², n. One side of leaf of book etc.; (fig.) episode fit to fill a ~ in history etc. [F, f. L *pagina* (*pangere* fasten)]

păge³, v.t. Put consecutive numbers on pages of (book etc.). [f. prec.]

pă'geant (-jnt; *also* pā-), n. Brilliant spectacle, esp. procession, arranged for effect; spectacular procession, or play performed in the open, illustrating the history of a place; tableau, allegorical device, etc., on fixed stage or moving car; (fig.) empty or specious show. [14th c. *pagyn* (in contemporary AL *pagina*), of unkn. orig.; later -*t* as in *ancient*]

pă'geantry (-jn-), n. Splendid display; empty show. [prec.+-RY]

‖**Pă'gĕtt, M.P.,** n. Traveller who expects to know all there is to know of a country in a few months. [character in Kipling]

pă'gin|al, a. Of pages; page for page. So ~**ARY¹** a. [f. LL *paginalis* (PAGE², -AL)]

pă'gin|āte, v.t. Page (book etc.). Hence ~**A'TION** n. [f. L *pagina* PAGE² +-ATE³]

pagŏd'a, n. **1.** Sacred building, esp. tower usu. of pyramidal form, in India, China, etc.; ornamental imitation of this. **2.** Gold coin once current in S. India; ~-*tree,* kinds of Indian & Chinese tree, (fig.) tree fabled to produce ~s (coin), esp. *shake the* ~-*tree,* make rapid fortune in India. [f. Port. *pagode* of Ind. orig.]

pagūr'ian, a. & n. (Of) the hermit-crab. [f. L f. Gk *pagouros,* kind of crab, +-IAN]

pah¹, int. expr. disgust. [natural]

pah², n. Var. of PA².

paid. See PAY².

pail, n. Vessel, usu. round, of wood or metal for carrying liquids etc.; amount

contained in this, as *half a ~ of milk*.
Hence ~'FUL n. [ME *payle*, of uncert.
orig.; cf. OE *pægel* gill, OF *paelle* frying-
-pan, wine-measure, etc. f. L *patella* dim.
of *patina* dish]

paillasse, palliasse, (pălyăs' *or* păl'yas),
n. Straw mattress. [F (*pai-*), f. *paille*
straw f. L *palea*]

paillette (pălyĕt'), n. Piece of bright
metal used in enamel painting; spangle.
[F (dim. as prec.)]

pain[1], n. Suffering, distress, of body or
mind, whence~'FUL,~'LESS, aa.,~'fulLY[2],
~'lèssLY[2], advv.,~'fulNESS, ~'lèssNESS,
nn.; (pl.) throes of childbirth;(pl.) trouble
taken, esp. *take~s, be at the~s of* (doing),
get (a thrashing etc.) *for* one's~s; punishment, now only in *~s & penalties, on* or
under ~ of (death or other punishment
to be incurred); *~-killer*, medicine for
alleviating ~; *~s'taking*, careful, industrious. [ME, f. OF *peine* f. L *poena*
penalty]

pain[2], v.t. & i. Inflict pain upon; give
rise to pain, ache (*my arm is~ing*). [ME,
f. OF *pener* f. LL *poenare* (as prec.)]

paint[1], n. Colouring-matter, suspended in
liquid vehicle so as to impart colour to a
'surface; LUMINOUS ~; colouring-matter
'for face etc., rouge etc.; *~'brush*, house-
-painter's, artist's brush. [f. foll.]

paint[2], v.t. Portray, represent, (object, or
abs.) in colours; adorn (wall etc.) with
~ing; (fig.) represent (incident etc.) in
words vividly as by ~ing; *not so black
as he is ~ed* (represented); cover surface
of (object) with paint; apply paint of
specified colour to, as ~ *the door green*;
(sl.) ~ *the town red*, cause commotion by
riotous spree etc.; apply rouge to (face,
often abs.); ~ *out*, efface with paint;
~ed lady, butterfly of orange-red colour
with black & white spots. Hence ~'ING[1]
(1, 2) n. [ME, f. *peint*, p.p. of OF *peindre*
f. L *pingere pict-* paint]

paint'er[1], n. One who paints pictures;
workman who colours woodwork etc.
with paint; *~'s colic*, form of colic to
which ~s who work with lead are liable.
So **paint'ress**[1] n. [ME, f. AF, OF *pein-
tour* f. Rom. *pinctorem f. L *pictor* (as
prec., see -OR)]

paint'er[2], n. Rope attached to bow of
boat for making it fast to ship, stake,
etc.; *cut the ~*, (fig.).effect a separation.
[c. 1400 *paynter* (also obs. vb *paynt*) rope
or chain to secure anchor when carried at
cathead; orig. obsc.; cf. OF *penteur* rope
passing over mast-head]

paint'y̆, a. Of paint; (of picture) overcharged with paint. [-Y[2]]

pair[1], n. Set of two, couple, (esp. *of* things
that usu. exist or are used in couples, as
gloves, shoes, sculls, heels, eyes); *~
royal*, set of three cards of same denomination or of three dice turning up same
number; article consisting of two corresponding parts not used separately, as

~ of scissors, tongs, trousers; engaged or
married couple; mated couple of animals;
~ (*of horses*), two horses harnessed together; (Parl.) two voters on opposite
sides absenting themselves from division
by mutual agreement, person willing to
act thus (*cannot find a~*); the other member of a ~ (*where is the ~ to this sock?*);
~ (flight) *of stairs, of steps* (*one, two, three,
-~ front* or *back*, room on the first etc.
floor or its occupant; *another ~ of* SHOES;
~-horse a., for a ~ of horses; *~-oar*, boat
rowed by ~ of oars. [ME, f. OF *paire* f. L
paria neut. pl. of *par* equal]

pair[2], v.t. & i. Arrange (persons, things),
be arranged, in couples; unite (t. & i.) in
love or marriage; (of animals) mate;
unite (*with* one of opposite sex); ~ *off*,
put two by two, (intr.) go off in pairs,
(Parl.) make a pair, (colloq.) marry (*with*).
[f. prec.]

pajamas. See PYJAMAS.

Pakistan' (pah-, -ahn), n. Moslem autonomy; proposed separate Moslem State
(established as a separate Dominion in
1947); since 1956 an independent republic
in Asia. [f. Punjab, Afghan Frontier,
Kashmir, Baluchi*stan*, lands where
Moslems predominated]

păl, n., & v.i. (sl.; -ll-). 1. Comrade, mate.
2. v.i. (Usu. ~ *up*) associate (*with*). [E
Gipsy]

păl'ace, n. Official residence of sovereign, archbishop, or bishop; stately mansion; spacious building for entertainment,
refreshment, etc.; || GIN[2]-~; || ~ *car*,
luxurious railway-carriage. [ME, f. OF
palais f. L *Palatium*, hill in Rome,
house of Augustus built on this]

păl'adin, n. Any of the Twelve Peers of
Charlemagne's court, of whom the Count
Palatine was the chief; knight errant,
champion. [F, as PALATINE[1]]

pălae(o), **pălē**(o)-, comb. form of Gk
palaios ancient (cf. NEO-), as: *~ocrys'tic*, of
ancient ice, frozen from remote ages;
~ŏg'raphy, study of ancient writing, so
~ŏg'rapher,~ograph'ic;~olith'ic, marked
by use of primitive stone implements;
~ŏntŏl'ogy, study of extinct organized
beings, so *~ŏntolo'gical, ~ŏntŏl'ogist*;
păl'aeothēre, extinct genus of tapir-like
mammal; *~ozō'ic*, of, containing, ancient
forms of life, of the first geological period
(cf. CAINOZOIC, MESOZOIC).

palaes'tra, palĕs', n. Wrestling-school,
gymnasium. [L, f. Gk *palaistra* (*palaiō*
wrestle)]

păl'afitte, n. Prehistoric hut on piles
over lake in Switzerland or N. Italy. [F,
f. It. *palafitta* pile-fence (*palo* stake + *fitto*
fixed)]

pălanquin', -nkeen', (-kēn), n. Covered
litter for one, in India & the East, carried
usu. by four or six men; (loosely) closed
carriage in the East. [f. Port. *palanquim*,
cf. Malay *palangki*, Hind. *palki*]

păl'atab|le, a. Pleasant to the taste; (fig.)

agreeable to the mind. Hence ~LY² adv. [f. PALATE+-ABLE]

păl'atal, a. & n. Of the palate; (sound) made by placing tongue against (usu. hard) palate, whence~IZE(3) v.t. [F (foll., -AL)]

păl'ate, n. 1. Roof of the mouth in vertebrates; *bony* or *hard*, *soft*, ~, its front, back part; *cleft* ~ (see CLEAVE¹). 2. Sense of taste; mental taste, liking. [f. L *palatum*]

palā'tial (-shl), a. Like a palace; splendid. [f. L as PALACE+-AL]

palāt'inate, n. 1. Territory under a count palatine; *the* (*Rhine*) *P~*, State of old German Empire, under rule of the Count Palatine of the Rhine. 2. ‖ (In Durham Univ.) light shade of purple or lavender, blazer of this colour as sports distinction. [f. foll.+-ATE¹]

păl'atīne¹, a. & n. 1. (*Count*) *P~*, count having within the territory jurisdiction such as elsewhere belongs only to sovereign (in Eng. Hist. also *Earl P~*); *County P~*, his territory (still in England of Lancashire and Durham). 2. n. Woman's fur tippet. [F (-*in*, -*ine*), f. L *palatinus* of the PALACE, see -INE¹]

păl'atīne², a. & n. Of the palate; (n. pl., also ~ *boncs*) two bones forming hard palate. [F (-*in*, -*ine*), as PALATE, see -INE¹]

păl'atŏgrăm, n. Record of the use made of the palate in producing a sound. [f. L *palatum* palate+-GRAM]

pala'ver (-lah-), n., & v.i. & t. 1. Conference, (prolonged) discussion, esp. between African or other natives & traders etc.; profuse or idle talk; cajolery; (sl.) affair, business. 2. vb. Talk profusely; flatter, wheedle. [vb f. n. f. Port. *palavra* word f. L as PARABLE]

pāle¹, n. Pointed piece of wood for fence etc., stake; boundary, esp. (fig.) *within*, *beyond*, etc., *the* ~; (hist.) *the* (*English*) *P~*, part of Ireland under English rule; (her.) vertical stripe in middle of shield. [ME, f. OF *pal* f. L *pālŭs* stake; cf. PEEL¹]

pāle², a. (Of person or complexion) of whitish or ashen appearance; (of colours) faint; faintly coloured; of faint lustre, dim; ~*-face*, supposed N.-Amer.-Ind. name for white man. Hence ~'LY² adv., ~'NESS n. [ME, f. OF *pal*(*l*)*e* f. L *pallidus* (*pallĕre* be pale)]

pāle³, v.i. & t. Grow pale; (fig.) become pale in comparison (usu. *before* or *beside*); make pale. [ME, f. OF *palir* (as prec.)]

pāled (-ld), a. Having palings. [PALE¹, -ED²]

palěs'tra. See PALAESTRA.

păl'etot (-etō), n. Loose cloak for man or woman. [F]

păl'ětte, n. Artist's thin wooden slab carried in hand and used for holding and mixing colours when painting; colours used by particular artist or on particular occasion; ~*-knife*, thin steel blade with handle for mixing colours. [F, dim. of *pale* shovel; cf. PEEL²]

pa'lfrey (paw-, pǎ-), n. (arch., poet.). Saddle-horse for ordinary riding, esp. for ladies. [ME, f. OF *palefrey* f. med. L *palafredus*, LL *paraveredus* (Gk *para* beside, extra, + *veredus* light horse, whence G *pferd*]

Pa'li (pah-), n. Language used in canonical books of Buddhists. [for *pali-bhasa* (*pali* canon+*bhasa* language)]

păl'ĭkā̆r, n. Member of band of Greek or Albanian military chief, esp. during War of Independence. [f. mod. Gk *palikari* lad (Gk *pallax -akos* youth)]

păl'impsĕst, n. & a. Writing-material, manuscript, the original writing on which has been effaced to make room for a second; (improp.) monumental brass turned & re-engraved on reverse side; (adj.) so treated. [f. L f. Gk *palimpsestos* (*palin* again+*psaō* rub smooth)]

păl'indrōme, n. & a. (Word, verse, etc.) that reads the same backwards as forwards (e.g. *madam*, *radar*). Hence **pălindrŏm'ic** a. [f. Gk *palindromos* running back again (*palin* again+*drom-* run)]

păl'ing, n. (Fence of) pales. [PALE¹, -ING¹]

pălin|gĕn'esĭs (-nj-), n. Regeneration (lit. & fig.); revival; (biol.) exact reproduction of ancestral character, whence ~**gĕnĕt'ic** a. [f. Gk *palin* again+GENESIS]

păl'inōde, n. Poem in which author retracts thing said in former poem; recantation. [F, or f. LL f. Gk *palinōidia* (*palin* again+*ōidē* song)]

pălisāde', n., & v.t. 1. Fence of pales or of iron railings; (mil.) strong wooden stake. 2. v.t. Furnish, enclose, with ~. [f. F *palissade* f. Prov. -*ada*, as PALE¹, see -ADE]

păl'ish, a. Somewhat pale. [-ISH¹]

pall¹ (pawl), n. Cloth, usu. of black or purple or white velvet, spread over coffin, hearse, or tomb; woollen vestment worn by Pope & some metropolitans or archbishops; (fig.) mantle, cloak; ~'*bearer*, person holding up corner of ~ at funeral. [OE *pæll*, f. L *pallium* cloak]

pall² (pawl), v.i. & t. Become insipid (now only fig.), esp. ~ *on* (person, mind, taste); satiate, cloy. [ME, aphetic f. APPAL]

Pallād'ian, a. (archit.). In the neoclassical style of the 16th-c. Italian Palladio. [-AN]

pallād'ium¹, n. (pl. -*ia*). Image of Pallas on which safety of Troy was held to depend; safeguard. [ME, f. L f. Gk *palladion*]

pallād'ium², n. Rare hard white metallic element of platinum group. [f. *Pallas*, an asteroid+-IUM]

păll'ět¹, n. Straw bed; mattress. [ME *paillet* f. AF *paillette* straw, f. OF *paille* f. L *palea*]

păll'ět², n. Flat wooden blade with handle, used by potters etc.; artist's PALETTE; projection on a part of a machine, serving to change mode of motion of wheel; valve under each pipe in wind-chest of organ. [f. F *palette* PALETTE]

palliasse. See PAILLASSE.

păll'i|āte, v.t. Alleviate (disease) without curing; extenuate, excuse. So ~A'TION n. [f. LL *palliare* cloak (PALLIUM), see -ATE³]

păll'iative, a. & n. (Thing) that serves to palliate. [F (-*if*, -*ive*), as prec., see -IVE]

păll'id, a. Pale. Hence ~LY² adv., ~NESS n. [f. L *pallidus*, as PALE²]

păll'i|um, n. Man's large rectangular cloak, esp. among the Greeks; archbishop's PALL¹; integumental fold of mollusc, whence~AL a. [L]

pall-mall (pĕl'mĕl'), n. Game in which ball was driven through iron ring suspended in long alley; ‖ *Pall-Mall*, street in London developed from such an alley, & noted for clubs. [f. obs. F *pallemaille* f. It. *pallamaglio*(*palla* ball +*maglio* MALLET)]

păll'or, n. Paleness. [L (*pallēre* be pale, see -OR)]

păll'y, a. (colloq.). Friendly. [PAL, -Y²]

palm¹ (pahm), n. Large family of trees, chiefly tropical, usu. with upright unbranched stem & head of large pinnate or fan-shaped leaves; branch of ~-tree as symbol of victory; supreme excellence, prize for this, esp. *bear*, *yield*, *the* ~; branch of various trees substituted for ~ in northern countries, esp. in celebrating *P*~ *Sunday*; ~-*honey*, refined sap of coquito ~; ~-*oil* (got from various ~s; also, with pun on *palm²*, bribe-money); *P*~ *Sunday*, Sunday before Easter, on which Christ's entry into Jerusalem is celebrated by processions, in which branches of ~ are carried. Hence **palmA'CEOUS** (-āshus) a. [OE *palm(a)* f. L *palma* (foll.); ME *palme* reinforced by OF *palme*]

palm² (pahm), n. Part of hand between wrist & fingers, esp. its inner surface; part of glove that covers this; breadth (about 4 in.), length (about 8 in.), of hand as measure; *grease* person's ~, bribe him; *sailmaker's* ~, lead boss mounted in leather straps fastened round ~, used as thimble. Hence (-)~ED² (pahmd) a., ~'FUL n. [ME, f. OF *paume* f. L *palma*; later assim. to L]

palm³ (pahm), v.t. Impose fraudulently, pass *off* (thing *on* person); conceal (cards, dice, etc.) in hand; touch with palm; bribe. [prec.]

Păl'ma Chris'ti (k-), n. Castor-oil plant. [med. L, = palm of Christ, from handlike shape of leaves]

păl'mar, a. Of, in, the palm of the hand. [f. L *palmaris* (as PALM², see -AR¹)]

păl'marỹ, a. Bearing the palm, pre-eminent, esp. ~ *emendation*, a certain textual correction. [f. L *palmarius* (as PALM¹, see -ARY¹)]

păl'mate, -ātĕd, aa. PALM²-shaped. [f. L *palmatus* (as PALM¹, see -ATE²)]

pa'lmer (pahm-), n. **1.** Pilgrim returning

from Holy Land with palm branch or leaf; itinerant monk under vow of poverty. **2.** (Also ~-*worm*) destructive hairy caterpillar. **3.** Hairy artificial fly in angling. [ME, f. AF, = OF *palmier* f. med. L *palmarius* pilgrim (PALMARY)]

pălmett'ō, n. (pl. ~s). Kinds of small palm, esp. dwarf fan-palm. [f. Sp. *palmito* dim. of *palma* PALM¹, refash. on It. wds in -*etto*]

păl'miped, -pēde, a. & a. Web-footed (bird). [f. L *palmipes* -*pedis* (as PALM² + *pes pedis* foot)]

pa'lmistrỹ (pahm-), n. Divination from palm of hand. So **pa'lmIST**(3) (pahm-) n. [15th c., f. PALM²+(orig. -*estry*) second element unexpl.; -*ist* is a 19th c. back form.]

pa'lmỹ (pahm-), a. Of, like, abounding in, palms; triumphant, flourishing, esp. ~ *days*. [PALM¹+-Y²]

pălmỹr'a, n. Kind of palm grown in India & Ceylon, with fan-shaped leaves used for matting etc. [f. Port. *palmeira*]

pălp, păl'pus (pl. -*pī*), nn. Jointed sense-organ in insects etc., feeler. Hence **pāl:PAL** a. [L (-*pus*)]

păl'p|able, a. That can be touched or felt; readily perceived by senses or mind. Hence ~ABIL'ITY n., ~abLY² adv. [ME, f. LL *palpabilis* (as foll., see -BLE)]

păl'p|āte, v.t. Handle, esp. in medical examination. So ~A'TION n. [f. L *palpare*, -ATE³]

păl'pĕbral, a. Of the eyelids. [f. LL *palpebralis* (*palpebra* eyelid, see -AL)]

păl'pitāte, v.i. Pulsate, throb; tremble (*with* fear, pleasure, etc.). [f. L *palpitare* frequent. as PALPATE, see -ATE³]

pălpitā'tion, n. Throbbing; increased activity of heart due to exertion, agitation, or disease. [f. L *palpitatio* (as prec., see -ATION)]

pa'lsgrāve (pawl-), n. Count palatine. [16th c. *paltsgrave* f. Du., (= G *pfalzgraf*) f. *palts* PALATINATE +*grave* count]

pa'lstāve (pawl-), n. Celt of bronze etc. shaped to fit into split handle. [f. Da. *paalstav* f. Icel. *pálstafr* (*páll* hoe)].

palsy (pawl'zĭ), n., & v.t. Paralysis; (fig.) cause, condition, of utter helplessness. **2.** v.t. Paralyse (usu. fig.). [ME *pa(r)lesie* f. OF *paralisie* as PARALYSIS]

pa'lter (pawl-), v.i. Shuffle, equivocate, (*with* person); haggle (*with* person *about* thing); trifle (*with* subject). [orig. unkn.]

pa'ltrỹ (pàwl-), a. Worthless, petty, contemptible. Hence ~INESS n. [16th c., app. attrib. use of (now dial.) *palt*, *pelt* rubbish +-RY (cf. *trumpery*); cf. EFris., LG *palte* rag, MDu. *palt*; LG *paltrig* ragged]

palūd'al (or păl:), a. Of a marsh; malarial. [f. L *palūs* -*udis* marsh +-AL]

pāl'ỹ, a. (poet.). Somewhat pale. [-Y²]

păm, n. Knave of clubs, esp. in five-card loo. [F *Pamphile*, cf. Sc. *Pamphie*, prob. f. Gk name *Pamphilos*]

păm'pa, n. (usu. pl., pr. -az, -as). Large treeless plain in S. America south of the Amazon; ~(s)-grass, large ornamental grass introduced into Europe from S. America. [Sp., f. Peruv. pampa steppe, flat]

păm'per, v.t. Over-indulge (person, tastes, etc.); ~ed menial, flunkey. [ME, in form f. obs. pamp cram+-ER[3]; cf. WFlem. pamperen, G dial. pampen in same sense]

pămper'o (-āī'ō), n. (pl. ~s). Strong cold S.W. wind blowing from Andes to Atlantic. [Sp., as PAMPA]

pămph'lĕt, n. Small usu. unbound treatise, esp. in prose on subject of current interest. [ME, f. Pamphilet, familiar name of 12th-c. Latin amatory poem Pamphilus seu de Amore, see -ET[1]]

pămphlĕteer', n., & v.i. **1.** Writer of pamphlets. **2.** v.i. Write pamphlets. [-EER]

păn[1], n. Metal or earthenware vessel, usu. shallow, for domestic purposes; STEW, WARM[2]ing, ~; ~like vessel in which substances are heated etc.; part of lock that held the priming in obsolete types of gun; hollow in ground, as SALT-~; (also hard-~) substratum of soil; BRAIN-~; ~'cake, thin flat batter-cake fried in ~, esp. flat as a ~cake, quite flat (v.i., sl., of aeroplane, descend vertically in level position). Hence ~'FUL n. [OE panne, OS panna, OHG pfanna, of uncert. orig.]

păn[2], v.t. & i. (-nn-). Criticize severely (colloq.); ~ off, out, wash (gold-bearing gravel) in pan; (intr.) ~ out, yield gold, (fig.) succeed, work, (well etc.). [f. prec.]

Păn[3], n. Greek rural god; the spirit of nature, paganism, the pre-Christian or the non-moral world. [Gk]

pan[4] (pahn), n. Leaf of the BETEL; (used for) the mixture of ~, lime, & areca-nut parings chewed by Asians as a masticatory. [Hind.]

păn-, comb. form of Gk pas, neut. pan all, as ~-Af'rican, of, for, all Africans; ~-Ang'lican, of the Anglican Church & its branches (~-Anglican conference); ~-cos'mism, doctrine that material universe is all that exists; ~-gen'esis, theory that each unit of an organism reproduces itself; ~-Germ'an, of all the Germans in political union; ~-Hell'enism, political union of all Greeks, so ~-Hellēn'ic a.; ~-Is'lam, union of Mohammedan world, so ~-Islām'ic a.; ~-logis'tic, (of Hegel's philosophy) treating only the rational as real, so ~'logism; ~-Sla'vism (-lah-), movement for political union of all Slavs; ~-sperm'atism, ~-sperm'y, theory that the atmosphere is full of minute germs that develop in favourable environment.

pănacĕ'a, n. Universal remedy. [L, f. Gk panakeia f. PAN(akēs remedy)]

panache' (-ahsh, -ăsh), n. Tuft, plume, of feathers esp. as head-dress or on helmet;

(fig.) display, swagger. [F, f. It. pennachio (penna feather)]

pana'da (-nah-), n. Bread boiled to pulp & flavoured. [Sp. (pan bread f. L panis, see -ADE)]

Panama' (-ah), n. ~ (hat), hat of fine pliant strawlike material made (orig. in Ecuador) from leaves of the screw-pine. [place]

panchayat (pŭnchī'at), n. (India). Village council. [Tamil panchāyattu f. Skr. pancha five]

pănchromăt'ic(-k-),a.(photog.). Equally sensitive to all spectrum colours. [PAN-]

păncrăt'ic, a. Of the pancratium; (opt., of eyepiece) extensively adjustable. [f. foll. +-IC]

păncrā'ti|um (-shĭ-), n. (Gk ant.). Athletic contest combining wrestling & boxing. So ~AST, **pănc'ratIST**, n. [L, f. Gk pagkration (PAN-+kratos strength)]

pănc'rĕ|ăs, n. Gland near stomach discharging a digestive secretion (~atic juice) into duodenum, sweetbread. So ~ăt'ic a., ~atIN n., one of the active principles of ~atic juice, digestive extract prepared from the ~ases of animals. [f. Gk pagkreas (PAN-+kreas -atos flesh)]

păn'da, n. Indian racoon-like animal, red bear-cat; giant ~, Tibetan black-and-white bear-like mammal. [native]

Păndē'an, -aean, a. Of PAN[3]; ~ pipe, = PAN-PIPE. [irreg. f. Gk Pan]

păn'dĕct, n. (usu. pl.). Compendium in 50 books of Roman civil law made by order of Justinian in 6th c.;·complete body of laws. [f. F pandecte, or L f. Gk PAN(dektēs f. dekhomai receive) all-receiver]

păndĕm'ic, a. & n. (Disease) prevalent over the whole of a country or over the world; ~, or păndēm'ian, VENUS. [f. Gk PAN(dēmos people)+-IC]

păndĕmōn'ium, n. Abode of all demons; place of lawless violence or uproar; utter confusion. [mod. L (Milton) f. PAN-+DEMON]

păn'der, n., & v.i. & t. **1.** Go-between in clandestine amours, procurer; one who ministers to evil designs.. **2.** v.i. Minister (to base passions, evil designs); (v.t.) act as ~ to (person's lust). [vb f. n. f. Pandare, character in Chaucer's Troilus & Criseyde & in Boccaccio, f. L f. Gk Pandaros]

pandit. See PUNDIT.

păndŏr'a, -dōre', n. Stringed instrument of cither type. [It., f. LL f. Gk pandoura]

Păndŏr'a's bŏx, n. The box in which Hope alone remained when by its rash opening all objects of desire were dispersed to play havoc among mankind. [Gk myth., see Hesiod, Op. 50-105]

păn'dour (-oor), -oor, n. (Pl.) force of rapacious & brutal soldiers raised by Baron Trenck in 1741 & afterwards enrolled in Austrian army. [f. Serbo-

-Croatian *pàndur* f. med. L *banderius* follower of a BANNER]

pāne¹, n. Single sheet of glass in compartment of window; rectangular division of chequered pattern etc. Hence ~'LESS (-nl-) a. [ME, f. OF *pan* f. L *pannus* piece of cloth]

pāne², v.t. Make up (garment etc.) of strips of different colours (chiefly in p.p.). [f. prec.]

pănĕġŷ'ric, n. & a. Laudatory discourse (*upon*); (adj.) laudatory. Hence ~AL a. [f. F *panégyrique* f. L f. Gk *panēgurikos* f. PAN(*ēguris* = agora assembly), see -IC]

păn'ĕġŷrize, -ise (-ĭz), v.t. Speak, write, in praise of, eulogize. So **pănĕġŷ'rIST** n. [f. Gk *panēgurizō* (as prec., see -IZE)]

păn'el¹, n. 1. Stuffed lining of saddle; kind of saddle. 2. Slip of parchment; list of jury; jury; ‖ (Sc. law) person(s) on trial, the accused; ‖ list of the doctors registered in a district as accepting Insurance-Act patients (*on the* ~, so registered); team in some radio quiz programmes, whence ~lIST n., member of this. 3. Distinct compartment of surface, esp. of wainscot, door, etc., often sunk below or raised above general level. 4. Piece of stuff of different kind or colour inserted in woman's dress. 5. Large size of photograph, with height much greater than width. [ME & OF, f. Rom. **pannellus* dim. as PANE¹]

păn'el², v.t. (-ll-). Saddle (beast) with panel; fit (wall, door, etc.) with panels; ornament (dress etc.) with panel(s). Hence ~lING¹(2) n. [f. prec.]

păng, n. Shooting pain; sudden sharp mental pain. [orig. unkn.]

păn'ga (-ngg-), n. African MATCHET. [native]

păngōl'in (-ngg-), n. Scaly ant-eater. [f. Malay *peng-goling* roller (from habit of rolling itself up)]

*păn'hăndle, n., & v.t. & i. 1. Narrow strip of one political division of a country extending between two others. 2. v.t. & i. (sl.). Beg (from). [PAN¹]

păn'ĭc¹, n. Kinds of grasses including Italian millet. [f. L *panicum*]

păn'ĭc², a., n., & v.t. & i. 1. (Of terror) unreasoning, excessive. 2. n. Infectious fright, sudden alarm (e.g., in commerce) leading to hasty measures; ~*-monger*, one who fosters a ~. 3. vb. Affect, be affected, with ~. Hence ~ky² a. (colloq.). [f. F *panique* f. Gk *panikos* of god Pan, reputed to cause ~]

păn'ĭcle, n.(bot.). Loose irregular type of compound inflorescence, as in oats. [f. L *panicula*, dim. of *panus* ear of millet]

pănĭfĭcā'tion, n. Bread-making. [F, f. L *panis* bread, see -FICATION]

pănjăn'drum, n. Mock title of exalted personage; pompous official or pretender. [arbitrary]

‖ pănn'age, n. (Right of, payment for) pasturage of swine; acorns, beech-mast,

etc., as food for swine. [ME, f. OF *pasnage*, *panage* f. med. L *pastionaticum* (L *pastio* pasture f. *pascere past-*, -AGE)]

pănne, n. A soft long-napped cloth used as dress-material. [F]

pănn'ier¹ (-nyer), n. 1. Basket, esp. one of those carried, usu. in pairs, by beast of burden or on the shoulders; covered basket for surgical instruments & medicines for ambulance. 2. Part of skirt looped up round hips. [ME, f. OF *panier* f. L *panarium* bread-basket (*panis* bread, see -ARY¹)]

‖ pănn'ier² (-nyer), n. (colloq.). Robed waiter in Inner Temple. [orig. unkn.]

pănn'ikin, n. Small metal drinking-vessel; its contents. [f. PAN¹ + -KIN]

pănn'opl|ŷ, n. Complete suit of armour (often fig.). Hence ~iED² (-lĭd) a. [f. Gk PAN(*oplia* f. *hopla* arms)]

pănŏp'tĭcon, n. Bentham's proposed circular prison with cells round warders' well in centre. [f. PAN- + Gk *optikos* of sight (*op-* see)]

pănora'ma (-rah-, -ră-), n. Picture of landscape etc. arranged on inside of cylindrical surface or successively rolled out before spectator; continuous passing scene; unbroken view of surrounding region (often fig.). Hence **pănorăm'ic** a., **pănorăm'ICALLY** adv. [f. PAN- + Gk *horama* view (*horaō* see)]

păn'-pīpe(s), n. Musical instrument made of series of reeds. [*Pan*, Greek rural god, + PIPE]

păn'sy (-zĭ), n. 1. Wild & garden plant with flowers of various colours, hearts-ease. 2. (colloq.). (Also ~ *boy*) effeminate youth, homosexual. [f. F *pensée* thought, pansy, f. *penser* think f. L *pensare* frequent. of *pendere* pens- weigh]

pănt, v.i. & t., & n. 1. Gasp for breath; (fig.) yearn (*for, after,* thing, *to* do); throb violently; utter gaspingly. 2. n. Gasp, throb. [ME, shortened f. OF *pantaisier* pant, f. Rom. **pantasiare* for **ph-* be oppressed with nightmare (as PHANTASY)]

pant- in comb. = PANTO- before vowels.

păntagru'el|ism (-ōōĭ-), n. Extravagant coarse humour like that of Pantagruel, a character in Rabelais. So **păntagruěl'IAN** (-ōō-) a., ~IST n. [-ISM]

păntalĕt(te)s' (-ts), n. pl. Woman's drawers, cycling knickerbockers, etc. [f. foll., see -ETTE]

păntalōōn', n. 1. (*P*~). Character in Italian comedy wearing ~s ; (now) clown's butt & abettor in pantomime. 2. (hist.; pl. or sing.). Garment of breeches & stockings in one piece, close-fitting breeches down to ankle as transition from knee-breeches to trousers. 3. (pl.; chiefly U.S., & now usu. *pants*). Trousers. [f. F *pantalon* f. It. *pantalone*, Venetian character in Italian comedy, perh. f. *San Pantaleone*, favourite Venetian saint]

‖ păntěch'nicon (-kn-), n. Furniture warehouse (orig. name of a bazaar); ~ *van* (for removing furniture). [f. PAN- + Gk *tekhnikon* of art (*tekhnē*, see -IC)]

păn'thĕ|ĭsm, n. Doctrine that God is everything & everything God; heathen worship of all gods. So ~IST n., ~is'tĭC(AL) aa. [f. PAN- + Gk *theos* god + -ISM]

păn'thĕon (*or* -ē'on), n. Temple dedicated to all the gods, esp. circular one at Rome; deities of a people collectively; building in which illustrious dead are buried or have memorials; building in London opened for public entertainment in 1772. [ME, f. L f. Gk PAN(*theion* holy f. *theos* god)]

păn'ther, n. Leopard; *American* ~, puma or cougar. Hence ~ESS[1] n. [ME, f. OF *pantere* f. L *panthera* f. Gk *panthēr*]

păn'ties (-tĕz), n. pl. (colloq.). Pants worn by children; close-fitting knickers worn by women. [dim. of PANTS; see -Y[3]]

păn'tile, n. Roof tile transversely curved to ogee shape, one curve being much larger than the other. [PAN[1] + TILE]

păntisŏc'racy̆, n. Community in which all are equal & all rule. [PANT- + Gk *isocratia* isocracy]

panto-, comb. form of Gk *pas pantos* all, as: ~*lo'gic*, *pantŏl'ogy*, (of) universal knowledge; ~*morph'ic*, taking all shapes; ~*pragmat'ic* a. & n., (person) meddling in everything; ~*scŏp'ic*, with wide range of vision.

păn'to|graph (-ahf), n. Instrument for copying plan etc. on any scale. Hence ~**grăph'ĭc** a. [f. F (-*graphe*), f. PANTO- + Gk -*graphos* writing]

păn'tomim|e, n., & v.t. & i. **1.** (hist.). Roman actor performing in dumb show, mimic actor. **2.** ‖ Dramatic entertainment usu. produced about Christmas & based on a fairy tale, with singing, dancing, clowning, topical jokes, a TRANSFORMATION scene, & certain stock roles. **3.** Dumb show. **4.** vb. Express (thing), express oneself, by dumb show. Hence or cogn. **păntomim'ĭc** a., ~IST(3) n. [f. F, or L f. Gk PANTO(*mimos* MIME)]

păn'try̆, n. Room in which bread & other provisions. or (*butler's*, *housemaid's*, ~) plate, table-linen, etc., are kept; ~*man*, butler or his assistant. [ME, f. OF *paneterie* f. *panetier* baker f. med. L *panetarius* (*panis* bread, -ER[1]); see -ERY]

pănts, n. pl. (colloq.). (Chiefly U.S.). trousers; ‖ (shop) long tight drawers. [abbr. of PANTALOON]

păn'zer (-tser), a. & n. Armoured (~ *division*, *troops*); (n. pl., colloq.) ~ troops. [G, = armour]

păp[1], n. (arch.). Nipple of woman's breast; corresponding part of man; (pl.) conical hilltops side by side. [ME, of Scand. orig.; cf. Sw. dial. *pappe*, *papp*; ult. imit.]

păp[2], n. Soft or semi-liquid food for infants br invalids; mash, pulp. Hence

~**p'y̆[2]** a. [ME, prob. f. MLG, MDu. *pappe*]

papa' (-ah), n. Father (used chiefly by children). [F f. L; imit.]

păp'acy̆, n. Pope's (tenure of) office; papal system. [ME, f. med. L *papatia* (*papa* pope, -ACY)]

păp'al, a. Of the pope or his office. Hence ~ISM(3), ~IST(2), nn., ~IZE(3) v.t. & i., ~LY[2] adv. [ME, f. OF *papal* f. med. L *papalis* (as prec., see -AL)]

papāv'erous, a. Like, allied to, the poppy. So **papāverA'ceous** (-āshus) a. [f. L *papaver* poppy + -OUS]

papaw', **pawpaw'**, n. (Fruit of) palmlike S.-Amer. tree of which stem, leaves, & fruit contain a milky juice that makes meat 'tender; *N.-Amer. tree with purple flowers & oblong edible fruit. [16th c. *papayo* &c., f. Sp., Port. *papaya*, of Carib. orig.]

păp'er[1], n. **1.** Substance used for writing, printing, drawing, wrapping up parcels, etc., made of interlaced fibres of rags, straw, wood, etc.; *commit to* ~, write down; *put pen to* ~, begin writing; negotiable documents, e.g. bills of exchange; (also ~ *money*) bank-notes etc. used as currency, opp. to coin, so ~ *currency* (cf. METALLIC); (sl.) free passes to theatre etc.; (pl.) documents proving person's or ship's identity, standing, etc.; *send in* one's ~s, resign; set of questions in examination; = NEWS~; essay, dissertation, esp. one read to learned society; ~ *war(fare)* (carried on in books or news-~s); *on* ~, hypothetically, to judge from statistics, etc., as *on* ~ *he is the better man*, so (attrib.) ~ *profits* (hypothetical). **2.** ~-*bag cookery*, method of cooking food of various kinds by enclosing it in buttered ~-bag before putting it in moderately hot oven; ~-*chase*, cross-country run in which a trail of torn-up ~ is laid by one or more runners to set a course for the rest; ~-*hangings*, *wall*-~, ~ for covering walls of room etc.; ~-*hanger*, one who covers walls with these; ~-*knife* (of ivory, wood, etc., for cutting open leaves of book etc.); ~-*mill* (in which ~ is made); ~-*stainer*, one who stains ~ or makes ~-hangings; ~-*weight*, small heavy object for securing loose ~s from being displaced. Hence ~Y[2] a. [ME, f. AF *papir*, = OF *papier* f. PAPYRUS]

păp'er[2], v.t. Enclose in paper; decorate (wall etc.) with paper; furnish with paper; (sl.) fill (theatre etc.) by means of free passes. [f. prec.]

papier mâché (păp'yă măsh'ā), n. Moulded paper pulp used for boxes, trays, etc. [F, = chewed paper]

papiliona'ceous (-yonāshus), a. (bot.). With corolla like a butterfly. [f. L *papilio* -*onis* butterfly, see -ACEOUS]

papill'a, n. (pl. -ae). Small nipple-like

protuberance in a part or organ of the body; (bot.) small fleshy projection on plant. Hence or cogn. **păp′il**lARY[1], **păp′il**lATE[2](2), **păp′il**lOSE[1], aa. [L, = nipple, dim. of PAPULA]

păp′ist, n. Advocate of papal supremacy; Roman Catholic (usu. in hostile or joc. sense). Hence **papis′tic**(AL) aa., **papis′tical**lY[2] adv., **~ry** n. [f. F *papiste*, or 16th-c. I, *papista* (*papa* POPE, see -IST)]

papoose′, n. N.-Amer.-Indian young child. [native]

papoōsh′, -ouche′ (-ōōsh). n.=BABOUCHE. [f. Pers. *paposh* (*pa* foot +*posh* covering)]

păpp′us, n. (bot.). Downy appendage on fruit of thistles, dandelions, etc. So **păppOSE′**[1] a. [mod. L, f. Gk *pappos*]

păp′rika (-ē-), n. Hungarian red pepper. [Hungarian]

păp′ūl|a, -ūl|e, nn. (pl. *~ae,~es*). Pimple; small fleshy projection on plant. Hence **~ar**[1], **~ose′**[1], **~ous**, aa. [L (*-la*)]

păpyrā′ceous (-shŭs), a. (nat. hist.). Of the nature of, thin as, paper. [f. PAPYRUS, see -ACEOUS]

papy̆ro-, comb. form of Gk *papuros* usu. in sense ‘ paper ’, as : *~graph*, apparatus for copying documents by means of paper-stencil; *~graphy* (-ŏg⁻), *~type*, copying processes in which picture etc. is transferred from paper to zinc plate etc.) *~logist*, *~logy*, (-ŏl⁻), student, study, of ancient papyri.

papy̆r′us, n. (pl. *-rī*). Aquatic plant of sedge family, paper reed; ancient writing-material prepared by Egyptians etc. from stem of this; (with pl.) MS. written on this. [ME, f. L, f. Gk *papuros*]

pär[1], n. Equality, equal footing, esp. *on a ~ (with)*; *~ of exchange*, recognized value of one country's currency in terms of another's; (of stocks, shares, etc.) *at ~*, at face value, *above ~*, at a premium, *below ~*, at a discount; average·or normal amount, degree, or condition, as *on a ~*, on an average, *above, below, up to,~*; (golf) the number of strokes a scratch player should require for a hole or course (calculated according to a formula & usu. less than the BOGEY figures). [L, a. & n., = equal(ity)]

pär[2], n. (colloq.). Paragraph (also *pä′ra*).

para-[1] (bef. vowel or *h* usu. *par-*), comb. form of Gk *para*, used in wds adopted from Gk or formed on Gk models, in senses ‘ beside ’, ‘ beyond ’, ‘ wrong, irregular ’, esp. in scientific terms; *~mil′itary* a., having a status or function ancillary to that of military forces; (chem., before a vowel *par-*) denoting modification of substance to whose name prefix is attached (*parăl′dehyde*, polymer of ALDEHYDE, used as narcotic & remedy against insomnia).

para-[2],[f]. F f. It. *para-* imperat. of *parare* ward off, shelter, as *parachute, parasol.*

parăb′asis, n. (pl. *-basēs*). Part sung by chorus in Greek comedy, addressed to audience usu. in the poet's name. [Gk, f. PARA[1](*bainō* go) go aside, step forward]

pä′rable, n. Fictitious narrative used to typify moral or spiritual relations (*the ~s of Christ in the Gospels*); allegory; (arch.) enigmatical saying, proverb; (arch.) *take up* one's *~*, begin to discourse. [ME, f. OF *parabole*, f. LL sense ‘ parable ’ of L *parabola* comparison (foll.)]

parăb′ola, n.- Plane curve formed by intersection of cone with plane parallel to its side. [f. mod. L f. Gk PARA[1] (*bolē* throw, f. *ballō*) placing side by side, comparison]

parabŏl′ic(al), aa. 1. (Usu. *~ical*) of, expressed in, a parable, whence *~ICALLY* adv. 2. (Usu. *~ic*) of, like, a parabola. [f. LL f. late Gk *parabolikos* (as prec., -IC)]

parăb′oloid, n. Solid some of whose plane sections are parabolas, esp. (also *~ of revolution*) that generated by revolution of parabola about its axis. [-OID]

parăch′ronism (-k-), n. Error in chronology. [f. PARA-[1] + Gk *khronos* time +-ISM]

pä′rachute (-shōōt), n., & v.t. & i. 1. Umbrella-like apparatus for descending. safely from a height, esp. from aircraft, (*~ flare*, one dropped by *~* to illuminate target area; *~ mine*, large case containing explosive dropped from aircraft by *~*; *~ troops*, (airborne troops landing by *~*); natural or artificial contrivance serving this purpose. 2. vb. Convey, descend, (as if) by means of *~*. Hence **pä′rachut**IST (-shōōt-) n., user of *~*, (pl.) *~* troops. [F (PARA-[2] +*chute* fall)]

pä′raclēte, n. Advocate (as title of the Holy Spirit, see *John* xiv. 16, 26, etc.). [ME, f. LL f. Gk PARA[1](*klētos* f. *kaleō* call)]

parāde′[1], n. 1. Display, ostentation, esp. *make a ~ of* (one's virtue etc.); *programme ~* (radio), list of items to be seen or heard. 2. Muster of troops for inspection, esp. one held regularly at set hours; ground used for this. 3. Public square or promenade (often as name of street). [F, = show, f. Sp. *parada* & It. *parata* f. L *parare* prepare, furnish, see -ADE]

parāde′[2], v.t. & i. Assemble (troops) for review or other purpose; display ostentatiously; march through (streets etc.) with display; (intr.) march in procession with display. [f. prec.]

pä′radigm (-īm), n. Example, pattern, esp. of inflexion of noun, verb, etc. So **paradigmăt′IC** (-ig-) a. [f. LL f. Gk *paradeigma* f. PARA[1](*deiknumi* show)]

pä′radise, n. (Also *earthly ~*) garden of Eden; heaven; region, state, of supreme bliss; FOOL's *~*; park in which animals are kept; BIRD *of ~*. Hence or cogn. **paradisă′ic**(AL) [irreg. on *Mosaic* etc.], **părádis′eAN**, **părádis′ic**(AL), **părádis′iAL**, **părádis′iAN**, **părádis′ic**(AL), aa. [ME, f. OF *paradis* f. LL f. Gk *paradeisos* f. OPers. *pairidaeza* park (*pairi* around +*diz* mould); cf. PARVIS]

păr′adŏs (*or* -dō), n. Elevation of earth

behind fortified place to secure from reverse attack or fire, esp. the mound along back of trench. [F (PARA-² + *dos* back f. L *dorsum*)]

pa'radŏx, n. Statement contrary to received opinion; seemingly absurd though perhaps really well-founded statement; self-contradictory, essentially absurd, statement; person, thing, conflicting with preconceived notions of what is reasonable or possible; HYDROSTATIC ~. Hence or cogn. ~ER¹(3), ~IST(3), ~ICÁL⫶ ITY, ~Y¹, nn., **păradŏx'ICAL** a., **păradŏx⫶ ICAL**LY² adv. [f. LL f. Gk *paradoxon* neut. adj. (PARA-¹ + *doxa* opinion)]

păradŏx'ūre, n. Palm-cat, animal with remarkable long curving tail. [f. Gk *paradoxos* (see prec.) + *oura* tail]

pă'raffĭn, n., & v.t. Colourless tasteless inodorous oily & waxy substance got by distillation from petroleum & shale & used for making candles etc. (~ *wax*, solid ~ obtained by distillation from petroleum; *liquid* ~, odourless tasteless mild laxative); ‖ (also ~ *oil*) oil so obtained & used as illuminant or lubricant; (v.t.) treat with ~. [G (1830), f. L *parum* little + *affinis*, from small AFFINITY it has for other bodies]

păragŏ'ge (-jĭ), n. (gram.). Addition of letter or syllable to a word. Hence **păragŏ'gĭc** a. [LL, f. Gk *paragōgē* leading past (PARA-¹ + *agōgē* f. *agō* lead)]

pă'ragon, n., & v.t. Model of excellence; supremely excellent person or thing, model (*of* virtue etc.); perfect diamond of more than 100 carats; (v.t., poet.) compare (thing *with*). [obs. F (mod. *paran-gone*) f. It. *paragone*, f. med. Gk *parakone* whetstone]

pă'ragraph (-ahf, -ăf), n., & v.t. **1.** Distinct passage or section in book etc., marked by indentation of first line; symbol (usu. ¶) formerly used to mark new ~, now as REFERENCE mark; detached item of news etc. in newspaper, freq. without heading, whence ~ER¹(3), ~IST(3), ~Y¹, nn. **2.** v.t. Write ~ about (person, thing), arrange (article etc.) in ~s. Hence **păragrăph'IC** a., **păragrăph'ICALLY** adv. [f. F *paragraphe* f. med. L f. Gk PARA¹- (*graphos* f. *graphō* write) short stroke marking break in sense]

pă'raguay (-gwā, -gwĭ), n.=MATÉ. [name of S.-Amer. river & republic]

părahēli|ŏt'ropism, n. Tendency in plants to turn leaves parallel to incidence of light-rays. So ~**otrŏp'ic** a. [PARA-¹ + HELIOTROPISM]

pă'rakeet, pă'roquet (-kĕt), n. Small (esp. long-tailed) kinds of parrot. [f. obs. F *paroquet* (mod. *perro-*), = It. *parro-*, *perrochetto*; perh. ult. f. *Pierrot* dim. of *Pierre* Peter; see PARROT]

pă'rakite, n. **1.** Kite acting like parachute. **2.** Tailless kite for scientific purposes. [1. f. PARACHUTE + KITE. 2. PARA-¹]

păralip'sis, -leip'sis (-lĭ-), n. Trick of

securing emphasis by professing to omit all mention of subject, e.g. *I say nothing of his antecedents, how from youth upwards etc.* [f. LL f. Gk PARA¹(*leipsis* f. *leipō* leave) passing over]

pă'rall|ăx, n. (Angular amount of) apparent displacement of object, caused by actual change of point of observation. So ~**ăc'tic** a. [f. F *parallaxe* f. Gk *parallaxis* change f. *parallassō* (PARA-¹ + *allassō*)]

pă'rallel¹, a. & n. **1.** (Of lines etc.) continuously equidistant, (of line) having this relation *to*; ~ *bars*, pair of ~ bars supported on posts for gymnastic exercises; ~ *ruler*, two rulers connected by pivoted cross-pieces, for drawing ~ lines; (fig.) precisely similar, analogous, or corresponding. **2.** n. ~ (*of latitude*), each of the ~ circles marking degrees of latitude on earth's surface in map, as *the 49th* ~; (mil.) trench ~ to general face of works attacked; person, thing, precisely analogous to another; ~ position; comparison, as *draw a ~ between* (two things); two ~ lines (‖) as REFERENCE mark. [f. F *parallèle* f. L f. Gk *parallēlos* (PARA-¹ + *allēlous* one another)]

pă'rallel², v.t. (-l-). Represent as similar, compare, (things, one *with* another); find, mention, something parallel or corresponding to; be parallel, correspond, to. [f. prec.]

părallelĕp'ipĕd (*or* -epĭp'ĭd), n. Solid contained by parallelograms. [f. Gk *parallēlepipedon*, as PARALLEL¹ + EPI(*pedon* ground) plane surface]

pă'rallelism, n. Being parallel (lit. or fig.); comparison or correspondence of successive passages, esp. in Hebrew poetry. [f. Gk *parallēlismos* f. *parallēlizō*]

părallĕl'ogrăm, n. Four-sided rectilineal figure whose opposite sides are parallel; ~ *of forces*, (~ illustrating) theorem that if two forces acting at a point be represented in magnitude & direction by two sides of a ~, their resultant is represented by a diagonal drawn from that point. [f. F *parallélogramme* f. LL f. Gk *parallēlogrammon* (as PARALLEL¹ + *grammē* line)]

părăl'og|ism, n. Illogical reasoning (esp. of which reasoner is unconscious, cf. SOPHISM); fallacy. So ~**IZE**(2) v.i. [f. F *paralogisme* f. LL f. Gk *paralogismos* f. *paralogizomai* f. PARA¹(*logos* reason) contrary to reason]

pă'ralȳs|e (-z), v.t. Affect with paralysis; (fig.) render powerless, cripple. Hence ~**A'TION** n. [app. f. F *paralyser*, as foll.; cf. ANALYSE]

parăl'ysis, n. Nervous affection marked by impairment or loss of motor or sensory function of nerves; (fig.) state of utter powerlessness. [L, f. Gk *paralusis* f. PARA¹(*luŏ* loose) disable]

părălȳt'|ic, a. & n. (Person) affected with paralysis (lit. or fig.); (sl.) very drunk. Hence ~**ICALLY** adv. [ME, f. OF *para-*

lytique f. L f. Gk *paralutikos* (as prec., see -IC)]

păra|mǎgnĕt'ĭc, a. Capable of being attracted by poles of magnet (cf. DIAMAG-NETIC). So ~mǎg'nétISM n. [PARA-¹ + MAGNETIC]

păramǎtt'a, n. Light dress fabric of merino wool & silk or cotton. [f. *Par(r)a-matta*, town in New S. Wales]

parǎm'éter, n. (math.). Quantity constant in case considered, but varying in different cases. [f. PARA-¹ + Gk *metron* measure]

pǎ'ramō, n. (pl.~*s*). High treeless plateau in tropical parts of S. America. [f. Sp. & Pg. *páramo* f. L *paramus*]

pǎ'ramount, a. Supreme; *lord, lady,* ~ (in supreme authority); pre-eminent, as *of* ~ *importance*; superior (*to*). Hence ~CY n., ~LY² adv. [f. AF *paramont* f. OF *par* by + *amont* above f. L *ad montem* to the hill]

pǎ'ramour (-oor), n. (rhet.). Illicit partner of married man or woman. [ME, f. OF *par amour* by love]

par'ǎng (pahr-), n. Malay heavy sheath-knife. [Malay]

pǎranoi'a, -noe'a (-nēa), n. Mental derangement, esp. when marked by delusions of grandeur, persecution, etc. Hence **pǎranoi'AC a. & n.** [Gk (-*noia*) f. PARA¹(*noos* mind) distracted]

pǎ'rapĕt, n. Low wall at edge of balcony, roof, etc., or along sides of bridge etc.; (mil.) defence of earth or stone to conceal & protect troops, esp. mound along front of trench (cf. *parados*). Hence ~ED² a. [f. F, or It. PARA²(*petto* breast f. L *pectus*)]

pǎ'rǎph, n. Flourish after a signature, orig. as precaution against forgery. [f. OF *paraphe* f. med. L *paraphus* for *para-graphus* PARAGRAPH]

pǎraphĕrnāl'ia, n. pl. Personal belongings; mechanical accessories, appointments, etc.; (formerly) articles of personal property that law allowed married woman to keep & treat as her own. [med. L, neut. pl. adj. f. LL f. Gk PARA¹(*pherna* f. *phernē* dower), see -AL]

pǎ'raphrāse (-z), n., & v.t. 1. Free rendering or amplification of a passage, expression of its sense in other words; any of a collection of metrical ~s of passages of Scripture used in Church of Scotland etc. 2. v.t. Express meaning of (passage) in other words. So **pǎraphrǎs'tIC a., pǎraphrǎs'tICALLY adv.** [(n.) F, or f. L f. Gk *paraphrasis* f. PARA¹(*phrazō* tell); (vb) f. F *paraphraser*]

pǎraplē'g|ia, n. Paralysis of lower limbs & part or whole of trunk. So ~IC a. [Gk (-ē-) f. PARA¹(*plēg-* strike)]

pǎ'rasǎng, n. Ancient-Persian measure of length, about 3½ miles. [f. L (-*ga*) f. Gk *parasaggēs*, of Pers. orig.]

pǎraselēn'ē, n. (pl. -ae). Bright spot on lunar halo, mock-moon. [PARA-¹ + Gk *selēnē* moon]

pǎ'rasĭt|e, n. Interested hanger-on, toady; animal, plant, living in or upon another & drawing nutriment directly from it (cf. COMMENSAL, SYMbiosis); (loosely) plant that climbs about another plant, wall, etc. Hence or cogn. **pǎrasit'IC(AL) aa., ~ISM(2), ~ÖL'OGY, nn.** [f. L f. Gk PARA¹(*sitos* food)]

pǎrasit'icĭde, n. Agent that destroys parasites. [as prec. +-CIDE]

pǎ'rasĭtize, -ise (-īz), v.t. Infest as a parasite (chiefly in p.p.). [as prec. +-IZE]

pǎrasŏl' (*or* pǎ'r-), n. Sunshade. [F, f. It. PARA²(*sole* sun f. L *sol*)]

pǎrasўn'thĕsis, n. (philol.). Derivation from a compound. So **pǎrasўnthĕt'IC a.** [PARA-¹ + SYNTHESIS]

pǎratǎx'ĭs, n. (gram.). Placing of clauses etc. one after another, without words to indicate co-ordination or subordination. So **pǎratǎc'tIC a., pǎratǎc'tICALLY adv.** [f. Gk PARA¹(*taxis* arrangement f. *tassō*)]

pǎ'ratroōp|s,' n. pl. Airborne troops landing by parachute (~*er*, one of these). [PARA(CHUTE) TROOP]

pǎratȳph'oid, n. Kinds of fever resembling typhoid, but caused by different bacteria. [PARA-¹]

pǎ'ravāne, n. Torpedo-shaped device towed at a depth regulated by its vanes or planes to cut the moorings of submerged mines. [PARA-²]

pǎr avion (ǎvyawn'), phr. By airmail. [F, = by aeroplane]

parb'oil, v.t. Boil partially; (fig.) overheat. [ME, f. OF *parboillir* f. LL PER-(*bullire* boil) boil thoroughly, by confus. w. *part*]

parb'ŭckle, n., & v.t. 1. Rope for raising or lowering casks & cylindrical objects, the middle being secured at the upper level, & both ends passed under & round the object & then hauled or let slowly out. **2.** v.t. Raise (*up*) or lower (*down*) thus. [17th c. *unkle*, orig. unkn.]

pǎr'cel¹, n. & adv. 1. (Arch.) part, esp. PART¹ *&* ~; piece of land, esp. as part of estate; goods etc. wrapped up in single package; ~ *post*, branch of postal service concerned with ~s; (commerc.) quantity dealt with in one transaction. **2.** adv. (arch.). Partly, as ~ *blind, drunk*; ~ *gilt*, partly gilded, esp. (of cup etc.) with inner surface gilt. [ME, f. OF *parcelle* f. Rom. *particella*, dim. as PARTICLE]

pǎr'cel², v.t. (-ll-). Divide (usu. *out*) into portions; (naut.) cover (caulked seam) with canvas strips & pitch, wrap (rope) with canvas strips. [f. prec.]

pǎr'celling, n. In vbl senses, esp. (naut.) strip of canvas, usu. tarred, for binding round rope. [-ING¹]

pǎr'cėnary, n. Joint heirship. [f. AF *parcenarie* = OF *parçonerie* (as foll., see -ERY)]

pǎr'cėner, n. Coheir. [ME, f. AF, = OF *parconier* f. med. L *parti(ti)onarius* (PARTI-TION, -ER²)]

P

parch, v.t. & i. Roast (pease etc.) slightly; (of sun, thirst, etc.) make (earth, person, etc.) hot & dry; become hot & dry. [ME *perch, parche*, of unkn. orig.]

parch'ment, n. Skin, esp. of sheep or goat, prepared for writing, painting, etc.; manuscript on this; ~-like skin, esp. husk of coffee-bean. Hence ~Y² a. [ME, f. OF *parchemin* f. Rom. *particaminum, blending LL *pergamina* of Pergamum w. *Parthica pelles* Parthian skin]

‖ **pard¹**, n. (arch.). Leopard. [ME, f. OF, f. L f. Gk *pardos*]

***pard²**, n. (sl.). Partner. [abbr.]

pard'on¹, n. Forgiveness; (eccl.) = IN-DULGENCE, festival at which this is granted; (law) remission of legal consequences of crime; *general* ~ (for offences generally, or to number of persons not named individually); courteous forbearance, esp. *I beg your* ~ (apology for thing done, for dissent or contradiction, or for not hearing or understanding what was said). [ME & OF *perdun, pardon* f. *perduner*, see foll.]

pard'on², v.t. Forgive (person, offence, person his offence); make allowance for, excuse, (person, fault, person *for doing*). So ~ABLE a., ~ableNESS n., ~ablY² adv. [ME, f. OF *pardoner* f. med. L PER(*donare* give) concede, remit]

pard'oner, n. (hist.). Person licensed to sell papal pardons or indulgences. [PARDON¹ + -ER²]

pare, v.t. Trim (thing) by cutting away irregular parts etc.; cut away skin, rind, etc. of (fruit etc.); ~ (nails etc.) *to the quick* (so deep as to reach sensitive parts); (fig.) diminish little by little (often *away, down*); shave, cut, *off, away*, (edges etc.). Hence **par'ER¹**(2), **par'ING¹**(1, 2), nn. [ME, f. OF *parer* f. L *parare* prepare]

parego'ric, a. & n. ~ (*elixir*), camphorated tincture of opium flavoured with aniseed & benzoic acid. [f. LL f. Gk *paregorikos* soothing (PARA-¹ + -*agoros* speaking f. *agora* assembly)]

pareir'a (-āra), n. Drug from root of Brazilian shrub, used in urinary disorders. [f. Port. *parreira* vine trained against wall]

paren'chym|**a** (-ngk-), n. (Anat.) proper substance of gland, organ, etc., as distinguished from flesh & connective tissue; (bot.) tissue of cells of about equal length & breadth placed side by side (cf. PROS-ENCHYMA), usu. soft & succulent, found esp. in softer parts of leaves, pulp of fruits, etc. Hence ~AL, **parenchym'a-tous**, aa., (-ngk-). [f. Gk *paregkhuma* something poured in beside (PARA-¹ + *egkhuma* f. *egkheō* pour in f. *en* in + *kheō* pour)]

par'ent, n. Father or mother; forefather, esp. *our first* ~s, Adam & Eve; animal, plant, from which others are derived, (often attrib., as the ~ *bird, tree*); (fig.) source, origin, (*of* evils etc.). So **paren'tAL** a., **paren'talLY²** adv., ~HOOD (-t-h-)

n. [ME, f. OF f. L *parens* (*parĕre* beget, see -ENT)]

par'entage, n. Descent from parents, lineage, as *his* ~ *is unknown*. [F, as prec., see -AGE]

paren'thesis, n. (pl. -*theses*). Word, clause, sentence, inserted into a passage to which it is not grammatically essential, and usu. marked off by brackets, dashes, or commas; (sing. or pl.) round brackets ( ) used for this; (fig.) interlude, interval. [LL, f. Gk *parenthesis* f. *paren-tithēmi* put in beside (PARA-¹ + EN-(2) + *tithēmi* place)]

paren'thesize, -ise (-īz), v.t. Insert (words etc., or abs.) as parenthesis; put between marks of parenthesis. [f. prec., see -IZE]

parenthĕt'ic, a. Of, inserted as a, parenthesis; (fig.) interposed. So ~AL a., ~alLY² adv. [f. med. L *parentheticus* (as PARENTHESIS, see -ETIC)]

parer'gon, n. (pl. -*erga*). By-work, work apart from one's main employment. [L, f. Gk *parergon* (PARA-¹ + *ergon* work)]

pă'resis, n. (med.). Partial paralysis, affecting muscular motion but not sensation. So **parET'IC** a. [f. Gk *paresis* f. *pariēmi* let go (PARA-¹ + *hiēmi* let go)]

par excellence (see Ap.), adv. By virtue of special excellence, above all others that may be so called, as *Mayfair was the fashionable quarter* ~. [F]

par'get (-j-), v.t., & n. **1.** Plaster (wall etc.). **2.** n. Plaster. [ME, f. OF, f. (w. confus. of pref.) OF *porgeter* (*porget*) in same sense, f. *pour*- PRO- + *jeter* throw]

parhel'ion (-lyon), n. (pl. -*ia*). Spot on solar halo at which light is intensified, mock sun. Hence ~I'ACAL, ~IC, aa. [f. L f. Gk *parēlion* (PARA-¹ + *hēlios* sun)]

par'iah (or pă²), n. Member of a low caste in S. India; member of low or no caste; (fig.) social outcast; ~-*dog*, vagabond dog of low breed in India etc. [f. Tamil *paṛaiyar* pl. of *paṛaiyan* drummer (*paṛai* drum)]

Par'ian, a. & n. **1.** Of the island of Paros, famed for white marble. **2.** n. Fine white kind of porcelain. [f. L *Parius* of Paros + -AN]

pari'etal, a. Of the wall of the body or of any of its cavities; ~ *bones*, pair forming part of sides & top of skull; (bot.) of the wall of a hollow structure etc. [f. F, or LL *parietalis* (*paries -etis* wall, see -AL)]

pari mŭt'üĕl (pahrē), n. Form of betting in which winners divide losers' stakes (less a percentage for management). [F, = mutual stake]

pār'ĭ păss'ŭ, adv. With equal pace; simultaneously & equally. [L]

Pā'ris, n. Capital of France; ~ *blue*, kinds of pigment; ~ *doll*, dressmaker's lay figure; ~ *green*, poisonous chemical used as pigment & insecticide; ~ *white*, fine whiting used in polishing.

pă'rish, n. Subdivision of county, having its own church & clergyman; ‖ (also *civil*

~) district constituted for administration of Poor law etc., as *go on the* ~, receive parochial relief; the inhabitants of a ~; ~ *clerk*, official performing various duties connected with the church, esp. (formerly) leading responses; ‖~ *council*, local administrative body in rural civil ~; ~ LANTERN; ~ *register*, book recording christenings, marriages, & burials, at ~ church. [ME *paroche, -osse,* f. OF *paroche, -oisse* f. LL *parochia, -ocia,* f. Gk *paroikia* district round (a church) f. *paroikos* (PARA-[1] + *-oikos* -dwelling f. *oikeō* dwell)]

parish'ioner (-sho-), n. Inhabitant of parish. [f. ME (obs.) *parishen* (f. OF *paroissien,* as prec. + *-ien* = -IAN) + -ER[1]]

Pari'sian (-zhyan), a. & n. (Native, inhabitant) of Paris. [f. F *parisien* f. med. L *parisianus* (*Parisii* Paris, see -AN)]

părisўllăb'ic, a. (Of Gk & L nouns) having same number of syllables in nominative as in oblique cases of singular. [f. L *par* equal + SYLLABIC]

pă'rity, n. Equality, esp. among members or ministers of church; parallelism, analogy, as ~ *of reasoning;* (commerc.) equivalence in another currency, being *at* PAR[1]. [f. F *parité* or LL *paritas* (PAR[1], -TY)]

park[1], n. **1.** Large enclosed piece of ground, usu. with woodland & pasture, attached to country house etc.; enclosure in town ornamentally laid out for public recreation; large tract of land kept in natural state for public benefit. **2.** (Space occupied by) artillery, stores, etc., in encampment; area assigned for motor--cars etc. to wait in. **3.** *Oyster-*~, enclosed area for oyster-breeding, overflowed by sea at high tide. Hence ~'ISH[1] a. [ME, f. OF *parc* f. Rom. **parricus,* whence OHG *pferrih,* OE *pearroc* (see PADDOCK[1])]

park[2], v.t. Enclose (ground) in or as park; (mil.) arrange (artillery etc.) compactly in a park; leave (car etc.) in park; (colloq.) deposit and leave; ~*ing-meter,* coin--operated meter that charges for car ~ed at side of street. [f. prec.]

park'a, n. Skin jacket with hood attached, worn by Eskimos. [Aleutian]

‖ **Park'hŭrst,** n. ~ (*prison*), a convict prison. [place]

‖ **park'in,** n. (dial.). Cake of oatmeal & treacle. [perh. f. name P~]

Parkinson's law. See LAW[1].

‖ **park'ў,** a. (sl.). Chilly (of air, morning, etc.). [orig. unkn.]

pārl'ance, n. Way of speaking, as *in common, legal,* etc., ~. [f. AF & OF, f. *parler* speak f. Rom. **paraulare* f. **parabolare* f. L PARABOLA (in LL speech, whence Rom. **paraula* word, F PAROLE); see -ANCE]

Pārl'ement (-mahṅ), n. (hist.). French judicial court (abolished 1792). [F]

Pārlementaire' (-mahṅtār), n. Bearer of a flag of truce. [F]

pārl'ey[1], n. (pl. ~s). Conference for debating of points in dispute, esp. (mil.) discussion of terms, as *beat, sound, a* ~, call for it by drum or trumpet. [f. foll., or obs. F *parlée* (p.p.), or F *parler;* see PARLANCE]

pārl'ey[2], v.i. & t. Discuss terms (*with* enemy etc.); speak (esp. foreign language). [f. prec., or F *parler* (prec.)]

pārleyvoo' (-līv-), n., & v.i. (joc.). **1.** French; Frenchman. **2.** v.i. Speak French. [f. F *parlez-vous* (*français*)? do you speak (French)?]

pārl'iament (-lam-), n. **1.** Council forming with the Sovereign the supreme legislature of United Kingdom, consisting of House of Lords (Spiritual & Temporal) & House of Commons (representatives of counties, cities, etc.); (of Sovereign) *open P*~, declare it open with ceremonial; corresponding legislative assembly in other countries; *the P~ Act,* that of 1911 depriving the Lords of their veto on money bills & making their veto on other bills merely suspensory; LONG[1] P~ (met Nov. 3rd, 1640, dissolved March 1660); *Short P*~ (sat from Apr. 13 to May 5, 1640). **2.** (Also ~*-cake*) thin crisp cake of gingerbread. [ME, f. OF *parlement* speaking (as PARLANCE, see -MENT)]

pārliamentār'ian (-lam-), n. & a. **1.** Skilled debater in parliament; adherent of Parliament in Civil War of 17th c. **2.** adj. = foll. [foll., -AN]

pārliamēn'tarў (-lam-), a. Of parliament (*old* ~ HAND[1]); ‖~ *agent* (charged with interests of party concerned in private legislation of Parliament); enacted, established, by Parliament; ‖~ *train* (formerly carrying passengers at rate not above 1*d.* per mile); (of language) admissible in Parliament, (colloq.) civil. [-ARY[1]]

pārl'our (-ler), n. Ordinary sitting-room of family in private house; room in inn for private conversation; ~ *boarder,* boarding-school pupil living in principal's family; **~ car,* luxuriously fitted railway coach; ‖~*maid,* maid who waits at table. [ME & AF *parlur,* OF *parleor,* f. *parler* (see PARLANCE, -ORY)]

pārl'ous, a. & adv. (arch., joc.). Perilous; hard to deal with; surprisingly clever etc.; (adv.) extremely. [ME, = PERILOUS]

Pārmèsàn' (-z-), a. & n. ~ (*cheese*), kind of cheese made at Parma & elsewhere. [F, f. It. *parmegiano* of Parma]

Pārnăss'|us, n. Mountain in central Greece, anciently sacred to Muses; *grass of* ~, white-flowered plant found in bogs. So ~IAN a. & n., (esp., member) of a later 19th-c. school of French poets. [L, f. Gk *Parna(s)sos*]

Pārn'ell|ism, n. Policy of Irish Home--Rule party led by C. S. Parnell from 1880 to 1891. So ~ITE[1] n. [-ISM]

parŏch'ial (-k-), a. Of a parish; (fig., of affairs etc.) confined to narrow area. Hence ~ISM, **parŏchiăl'**ITY, nn., ~IZE(3) v.t., ~LY² adv., (-k-). [ME, f. AF & OF, f. LL *parochialis* (as PARISH, see -AL)]

pă′rod|ў̆, n., & v.t. **1.** Composition in which an author's characteristics are ridiculed by imitation; feeble imitation, travesty. **2.** v.t. Make (literary work, manner, etc.) ridiculous by imitation. So ~IST(3) n. [f. F *parodie* or L f. Gk *parōidia* (PARA-¹ + *ōidē* ODE)]

parōle′, n., & v.t. **1.** (Also ~ *of honour*, F ~ *d'honneur* pr. dǒnĕr′) word of honour, esp. (mil.) prisoner's promise that he will not attempt escape, or will refrain to custody if liberated, or will refrain from taking up arms against captors for stated period; *on* ~, (liberated) on this understanding; (mil.) password used only by officers or inspectors of guard (cf. COUNTERSIGN). **2.** v.t. Put (prisoner) on ~. [F, = word; see PARLANCE]

păronomās′ia (-zya, -sīa), n. Word-play, pun. [L, f. Gk *paronomasia* (PARA-¹ + *onomasia* f. *onomazō* f. *onoma* name)]

paroquet. See PARAKEET.

parŏt′id, a. & n. **1.** Situated near the ear, esp., ~ *gland* (in front of ear, with ~ *duct*, opening into mouth). **2.** n. ~ gland. [f. F *parotide* or L f. Gk *parōtis*, *-idos* (PARA-¹ + *ous ōtos* ear)]

părotit′is, n. Mumps. [f. prec. + -ITIS]

pă′roxỹsm, n. Fit of disease; fit (*of* rage, laughter, etc.). Hence **păroxỹs′-mAL** (-zm-) a. [f. F *paroxysme* or med. L f. Gk *paroxusmos* f. *paroxunō* exasperate (PARA-¹ + *oxunō* sharpen f. *oxus* sharp)]

parŏx′ỹtone, a. & n. (Gk gram.). (Word) with acute accent on last syllable but one. [f. Gk *paroxutonos* (PARA-¹ + OXY-TONE)]

pā́rp′en, n. Stone passing through wall from side to side, with two smooth vertical faces. [ME, f. OF *parpain* of unkn. orig.]

păr′quet (-kĭt), n., & v.t. **1.** Wooden flooring of pieces of wood, often of different kinds, arranged in pattern. **2.** v.t. Floor (room) thus. So ~RY(1) n. [F, = small compartment, floor, dim. of *parc* PARK]

părr, pă̄r, n. Young salmon. [Sc., orig. unkn.]

pă′rri|cīde, n. **1.** One who murders his father or near relative or one whose person is held sacred; person guilty of treason against his country. **2.** Any of these crimes. So ~cid′AL a. [F, or f. L (1) *parricida* (2) *-cidium*; see -CIDE]

pă′rrot, n., & v.t. Kinds of birds, of which many species have beautiful plumage, & some can be taught to repeat words; person who repeats another's words or imitates his actions unintelligently; (v.t.) repeat (words, or abs.) mechanically, drill (person etc.) to do this, whence ~RY(4) n.; ~-*fish*, kinds with brilliant colouring or mouth like ~'s bill. [prob. f. obs. & dial. F *perrot* parrot, dim. of *Pierre* Peter; cf. PARAKEET]

pă′rrỹ, v.t., & n. **1.** Ward off, avert, (weapon, blow, awkward question). **2.** n. Warding off. [repr. F *parez*, imper. of *parer* f. It. *parare* ward off]

pā̄rse (-z, -s), v.t. Describe (word) grammatically, stating inflexion, relation to sentence, etc.; resolve (sentence) into its component parts & describe them. [f. ME (obs.) f. OF *pars*, pl. of *part* PART¹, or f. L *pars*]

pā̄rs′ĕc, n. Unit of stellar distances, the distance at which a star would have a parallax of one second of arc, i.e. at which the mean radius of the earth's orbit subtends this angle. [f. PAR(ALLAX) + SEC(OND)]

Pā̄rsee′, n. **1.** Adherent of ZOROASTRIAN-ism, descendant of Persians who fled to India from Mohammedan persecution in 7th & 8th cc., whence ~ISM(3) n. **2.** Language of Persia under Sassanian kings. [f. Pers. *Parsi* Persian (*Pars* Persia)]

pā̄rs′im|onỹ, n. Carefulness in employment of money etc. or (fig.) of immaterial things; stinginess; *law of* ~*ony* (that no more causes or forces should be assumed than are necessary to account for the facts). So ~ōn′ious a., ~ōn′iousLY² adv. ~ōn′iousNESS n. [f. L *parsimonia*, *parci-* (*parcere pars-* spare, see -MONY)]

pā̄rs′ley, n. Biennial umbelliferous plant with white flowers & aromatic leaves, used for seasoning & garnishing dishes; ~ *fern* (with leaves like ~). [ME *persil* etc. f. OF *peresil* f. Rom. *petrosilium f. L f. Gk *petroselinon* (*petra* rock + *selinon* parsley); OE *petersilie*, ME *petrosilye* dir. f. Rom.]

pā̄rs′nip, n. (Plant with yellow flowers &) pale yellow root used as culinary vegetable; *fine words* BUTTER² *no* ~*s.* [ME *passenep* (w. assim. to *nep* turnip) f. OF *pasnaie* f. L *pastinaca*]

pā̄rs′on, n. Rector; vicar or any beneficed clergyman; (colloq.) any clergyman; ~*-bird*, New Zealand bird with dark plumage & white neck; ~'s *nose*, rump of fowl etc. Hence **pā̄rson′Ic** a. [ME *person*(*e*), *parson* f. OF *persone* f. L *persona* PERSON, (med. L) rector]

pā̄rs′onage, n. Rector's or other incumbent's house. [ME *personage*, *parsonage*, f. OF (prec. + -AGE)]

pā̄rt¹, n. & adv. **1.** Some but not all of a thing or number of things, (*a*) ~ *of it was spoilt*, (*a*) ~ *of them have arrived*, (*a*) *great part of this is true*, *most* ~ (the majority) *of them failed*. **2.** Division of books etc., esp. as much as is issued at one time. **3.** Portion of animal body; *the* (privy) ~*s*. **4.** Each of several equal portions of a whole, as *three* ~*s* (quarters), *19* ~*s* (twentieths), *take 3* ~*s of sugar, 5 of flour, 2 of ground, rice*, etc. **5.** Portion allotted, share, esp. *have neither* ~ *nor lot* (no concern) *in*; ART² *&* ~; person's share in action, his duty, as *I have done my* ~, *it was not my* ~ *to interfere.* **6.** Character assigned to actor on stage; words spoken by actor on stage; copy of these; (fig.) *play a noble, an unworthy,* ~, behave nobly etc.; *play a* ~, act deceitfully. **7.** (mus.). Melody assigned to particular voice or instrument. **8.** pl. (arch.). Abilities, as *a man of (good)* ~*s.* **9.** pl. Region (*a stranger in these* ~*s*). **10.** Side in dispute. **11.** ~ *& parcel,* essential ~; ~ *of speech,* each of the grammatical classes of words (noun, adjective, pronoun, verb, adverb, preposition, conjunction, interjection); *for the most* ~, in most cases, mostly; *take* ~, assist (*in doing, in* discussion etc.); *take the* ~ *of,* support, back up; *for my* ~, as far as I am concerned; *in* ~, partly; *take* (words, action) *in good* ~, not be offended at; *on the* ~ *of,* proceeding from, done etc. by, as *there was no objection on my* ~; ~*-owner,* one who owns in common with others; ~*-song,* song with three or more voice-~*s,* freq. without accompaniment, & harmonic rather than contrapuntal in character; ~ *time,* less than full time; ~*-timer* (colloq.), ~*-time* worker. **12.** adv. In ~, partly (*made* ~ *of iron & ~ of wood*; *a lie that is* ~ *truth*). [ME, f. OF *part* f. L *pars partis*; in OE dir. f. L]

pārt², v.t. & i. **1.** Divide (t. & i.) into parts, as *the crowd* ~*ed & let him through, an islet* ~*s the stream, the cord* ~*ed* (broke). **2.** Separate (hair of head) with comb; separate (combatants, friends, etc.); ~ *company,* dissolve companionship (*with*); ~ BRASS *rags with.* **3.** Quit one another's company, as *let us* ~ *friends, the best of friends must* ~; ~ *from* or *with,* say goodbye to; ~ *with,* give up, surrender, (property etc.). **4.** (colloq.). ~ with one's money, pay, (*if I know him, he won't* ~). **5.** (arch.). Distribute (thing) in shares. [ME, f. OF *partir* f. L *partiri* (prec.)]

pārtāke', v.t. & i. (*-took, -taken*). Take a share in; take a share (*in* or *of* thing, *with* person); take, esp. eat or drink some or (colloq.) all *of,* as *he partook of our lowly fare, partook of a bun*; have some (of quality etc.), as *his manner* ~*s of insolence.* [16th c., back form. f. *partaker, partaking* = part-taker etc.]

‖ **pārt'an,** n. (Sc.). Crab. [Celt.]

pārterre' (-târ), n. Level space in garden occupied by flower-beds; part of ground--floor of auditorium of theatre, behind orchestra. [F, = *par terre* on the ground]

pārtheno|gĕn'ĕsis, n. (biol.). Reproduction without sexual union. So ~**gĕnET'IC** a. [f. Gk *parthenos* virgin]

Pārth'ian, a. Of Parthia, ancient kingdom of W. Asia; ~ *shaft, glance,* etc., remark, glance, etc., reserved for the moment of departure, like missile shot backwards by flying ~ horseman. [-AN]

pārti (pärtē'), n. Person regarded as eligible etc. in the marriage market (*is quite a, a desirable, an unsuitable,* ~); ~ *pris* (prē), preconceived view, bias. [F]

pār'tial (-shl), a. & n. **1.** Biased, unfair; ~ *to,* having a liking for (person, thing); forming only a part, not complete, as *a* ~ *success*; ~ *eclipse* (in which part only of the luminary is covered or darkened). **2.** n. (mus.). A ~ note; *upper* ~*s,* higher notes more faintly heard than main note produced from string, pipe, etc. Hence ~LY² (-sha-) adv. [ME, f. OF *parcial* f. LL *partialis* (as PART¹, see -AL)]

pārtiăl'ity (-shǐ-), n. Bias, favouritism; fondness (*for*). [ME, f. OF *parcialite* f. med. L *partialitas* (as prec., see -TY)]

pārt'ible, a. That can or must be divided (*among*; esp. of heritable property). [f. LL *partibilis* f. L as PART², -IBLE]

parti'cip|āte, v.t. & i. Have share in (thing *with* person); have share (*in* thing *with* person); have something *of,* as *his poems* ~*ate of the nature of satire.* So ~ANT, **pārticipA'TION,** ~**ātoR,** nn. [f. L *participare* (as PART¹ + *cip-* = *cap-* st. of *capere* take)]

pārt'iciple, n. Verbal adjective qualifying noun but retaining some properties of verb, e.g. tense & government of object. So ~**d** (-ld), **pārticip'iAL,** aa., **particip'iaL**LY² adv. [ME, f. OF, by-form of *participe* f. L *participium* (as prec.)]

pārt'icle, n. Minute portion of matter; smallest possible amount, as *has not a* ~ *of sense*; minor part of speech, esp. short indeclinable one; common prefix or suffix such as *un-, out-, -ness, -ship.* [ME, f. L *particula* (PART¹, -CULE)]

pārt'icoloured, pārt'y̆-, (-ŭlerd), a. Partly of one colour, partly of another. [f. PARTY²]

partic'ular, a. & n. **1.** Relating to one as distinguished from others, special; *P*~ *Baptists,* body holding doctrines of ~ *election & ~ redemption* (i.e. of only some of the human race); (log., of a proposition) in which something is predicated of some, not all, of a class (opp. *universal*); one considered apart from others, individual, as *this* ~ *tax is no worse than others*; worth notice, special, as *took* ~ *trouble, for no* ~ *reason*; minute, as *full & ~ account*; scrupulously exact; fastidious (*about, what* or *as to what* one eats etc.); *in* ~, especially, as *mentioned one case in* ~. **2.** n. Detail, item; (pl.) detailed account. Hence or cogn. ~ITY (-ǎ'r-) n., ~LY² adv. [ME, f. OF *particuler* f. L *particularis* (as PARTICLE, see -AR¹)]

partic'ular|ism, n. Doctrine of PARTICULAR election or redemption; exclusive devotion to a party, sect, etc.; principle of leaving political independence to each State in an empire etc. So ~IST n. [f. F *-isme* or G *-ismus*: see -ISM]

partic'ulariz|e, -is|e (-īz), v.t. Name specially or one by one, specify, (often abs.). Hence ~A'TION n. [f. F *particulariser* (as PARTICULAR, see -IZE)]

pārt'ing, n. In vbl senses, esp.: leave--taking (often attrib., as ~ *injunctions*);

dividing line of combed hair; ~ *of the ways*, point at which road divides into two or more (often fig. of choice between courses). [-ING[1]]

părtisăn'[1] (-z-), **-zăn**, (*or* părt[2]), n. **1.** Adherent of party, cause, etc., esp. unreasoning one (often attrib., as *in a ~ spirit*). **2.** (mil.). Member of light irregular troops employed in special enterprises (hist.); (in recent use) a guerrilla (applied orig. to Russians resisting in parts of their country occupied by the enemy). Hence ~SHIP n. [F, f. It. *partigiano* (*parte* PART[1], see -AN)]

părt'isan[2] (-zn), **-zan**, n. (hist.). Long-handled spear like halberd. [f. 16th c. F *partizane* f. It. *partesana, partigiana*]

părt'ite, a. (bot., entom.). Divided (nearly) to the base. [f. L *partiri* -*it*-PART[2]]

părti'tion, n., & v.t. **1.** Division into parts; such part; structure separating two such parts, esp. slight wall, whence ~ED[2] (-shond) a.; division of a country; (law) division of real property between joint tenants etc. **2.** v.t. Divide into parts; ~ *off*, separate (part of room etc.) by a ~. [ME, f. OF, f. L *partitionem* (as prec., see -ION)]

părt'itive, a. & n. (Word) denoting part of a collective whole (e.g. *some, any*); ~ *genitive*, that used to indicate a whole divided into parts, expressed in English by *of*, as in *most of us*. Hence ~LY[2] adv. [f. F, or med. L *partitivus* (PARTITE, -IVE)]

Părt'lèt, n. (arch.). Used as proper name for a hen, esp. *Dame ~*, also applied to women. [f. OF *Pertelote*, proper name]

părt'lў, adv. With respect to a part; in some degree. [-LY[2]]

părt'ner, n., & v.t. **1.** Sharer (*with* person, *in* or *of* thing); person associated with others in business of which he shares risks & profits; || SLEEP[2]*ing* ~; · || *predominant* ~, England (among constituents of United Kingdom); wife, husband; companion in dance, esp. *dancing ~*; player associated with another in many games; (naut., pl.) timber framework round hole in deck through which mast, pump, etc., passes. **2.** v.t. Associate (persons, one *with* another) as ~s, (also) be ~ of. Hence ~LESS a., ~SHIP n. (1) ME alt. of PARCENER, after PART[1]; (2) (naut.) ME *pauteneres* pl. f. OF *pautonier* servant (= F *valet*); cf. similar use of *carlings* f. ON *karl* CARL, CHURL]

părt'ridge, n. Kinds of game-bird, esp. *common* or *grey* ~; ~*wood*, hard red wood used for cabinet work etc., (also) speckled effect produced on wood by certain fungus. [ME *pertrich* etc. f. OF *perdriz* etc. f. L f. Gk *perdix* -*dikos*; -*rich* for -*riz* unexpl.]

părtur'ient, a. About to give birth (often fig. of the mind etc.). [f. L *parturire* be in labour (*parĕre part*- bear), see -ENT]

părtūri'tion, n. Act of bringing forth young, childbirth (also fig.). [f. LL *parturitio*, as prec., see -ION]

pārtūr'iunt mŏn'tēs (-z), (, *născĕt'ŭr rĭdĭc'ŭlŭs mŭs*), sent. (As comment on fiasco) the mountains are in labour (, the product a poor mouse). [Hor., *A.P.* 139]

pārt'ў[1], n. Body of persons united in a cause, opinion, etc.; system of taking sides on public questions; ~ *spirit*, zeal for a ~ (freq. derog.); body of persons travelling or engaged together, as *fishing, reading, -~*; social gathering, esp. of invited guests at private house, as *dinner, tea, ~*. **2.** Each of the two or more persons making the two sides in legal action, contract, marriage, etc.; accessory (*to* action); (now vulg. or joc.) person, as *an old ~ with spectacles*. **3.** ~*-coloured*, see PARTI-COLOURED; ~*-wall*, wall shared by each of the occupiers of the two buildings etc. thàt it separates. [ME, f. OF *partie*, p.p. of *partir* f. L as PART[2]]

pārt'ў[2], a. (her.). Divided into parts of different tinctures. [f. OF *parti*, as prec.]

pärv'enu (-ōō, & see Ap.), n. Person of obscure origin who has gained wealth or position, upstart, (often attrib.). [F, p.p. of *parvenir* arrive f. L PER(*venire* come)]

pärv'is, n. Enclosed area in front of cathedral, church, etc. [ME, f. OF *pare(v)is*, f. *pareīs*, f. Rom. *paravisus f. LL *paradisus* PARADISE, court in front of St Peter's, Rome]

pas (pah), n. Precedence, esp. *dispute, give, take, the ~*; step in dancing, as ~ *seul* (sŭl, & see Ap.), ~ *de deux* (dedŭr', & see Ap.), dance for one, two. [F, = step]

păsch'al (-k-), a. Of the Jewish Passover; of Easter. [ME, f. OF *pascal* f. LL *paschalis* (*pascha* f. Gk *paskha* f. Heb. *pesakh* Passover f. *pasakh* pass over, see -AL)]

păsh, n. (sl.). Passion. [abbr.]

pasha, -cha, (pah'sha, pä'sha, pashah'), n. (hist.). Turkish officer of high rank, e.g. military commander, governor of province, etc.; ~ *of three, two, tails, of one tail*, (of first, second, third, grade; from number of horse-tails displayed'as symbol in war). [Turk. *pasha*; cf. BASHAW]

pa'shalic, -ch-, (pah-; *also* pashah[2]), n. (hist.). Jurisdiction of pasha. [f. Turk. *pashalik*]

pä'shm, n. Under-fur of hairy quadrupeds in Tibet etc., esp. that of goats as used for Cashmere shawls. [Pers., = wool]

păsque'-flower (-skf-), n. Anemone with bell-shaped purple flowers. [16th c. *passe-flower*, f. F *passe-fleur*; assim. to *pasque* = obs. *pasch* (as PASCHAL), Easter]

pāsquināde', n. Lampoon, satire, orig. one affixed to public place. [f. It. *pasquinata* (*Pasquino*, statue at Rome on which Latin verses were annually posted, see -ADE)]

pass[1] (-ah-), v.i. & t. (p.p. ~*ed* or as adj. *past*). **1.** intr. Move onward, proceed, (*along, down, over, on,* etc.); circulate, be current; ~ *for,* be accepted as; ~ (be currently known) *by the name of*; be transported from place to place; change (*into* something, *from* one state *to* another); die (now usu. ~ *hence,* ~ *from among us,* etc.); go by, as *saw the procession* ~, *time* ~*es rapidly, remarks* ~ *unnoticed*; come to an end, as *kingdoms & nations* ~; get through, effect a passage; go uncensured, be accepted as adequate; (of bill in Parliament, proposal, etc.) be sanctioned; (of candidate) satisfy examiner; happen, be done or said, as *I saw* or *heard what was* ~*ing*; adjudicate (*upon*); (of judgement) be given (*for* plaintiff etc.); (cards) forgo one's opportunity, e.g. of making a bid, (also) throw up one's hand; ~*ed pawn* (chess), pawn with no opposing pawn on its own or adjoining files. **2.** trans. Leave (thing etc.) on one side or behind as one goes (*has* ~*ed the chair,* been chairman, president, mayor, etc.); ~ *a dividend,* not declare it; go across (sea, frontier, mountain range); (of bill) be examined & approved by (House of Commons etc.); reach standard required by (examiner, examination); ~ MUSTER[1], outstrip; surpass; be too great for, as *it* ~*es my comprehension*; transport (usu. w. prep. or adv.); move, cause to go, as ~*ed his hand across his forehead,* ~ *your eye* (glance) *over this letter,* ~ *a rope round it,* ~ (= *hand*) *in* one's CHECK[1]*s*; (football, hockey, etc.) kick or hand or hit (ball) to player of one's own side (also abs.); cause to go by, as ~ (troops) *in review*; cause, allow, (measure in Parliament, candidate for examination, etc.) to proceed after scrutiny; spend (*time, the winter,* etc.); hand round, transfer, as *read this & ~ it on*; give currency to (coin, esp. base coin); pledge (one's word, oath, etc.); utter (criticism, judicial sentence, *upon*); ~ *the* TIME[1] *of day*; ~ *water,* void urine. **3.** Spec. senses w. advv. & prepp.: ~ *away,* die, come to an end; ~ *by* (adv. or prep.), omit, disregard, walk etc. past; ~ *off,* (of sensations etc.) fade away, (of proceedings) be carried through (*without a hitch* etc.), (trans.) palm off (thing *upon* person *for* or *as* what it is not), distract attention from (awkward situation or allusion); ~ *out* (colloq.), die, become insensible as a result of drinking; ~ *over* (adv. or prep.), omit, make no remark upon, as ~ *over his subsequent conduct,* ~ *it over in silence*; ~ *through,* experience; *~ *up,* refuse to have further dealings with, renounce. [ME, f. OF *passer* f. Rom. *passare f. L *passus* PACE[1]]

pass[2] (-ah-), n. **1.** Passing, esp. of examination; ||(Univ.) attainment of standard that satisfies examiners but does not entitle to honours. **2.** *Bring to* ~, accomplish, carry out; *come to* ~, happen. **3.** Critical position, as *things have come to a*

(*strange*) ~. **4.** Written permission to pass into or out of a place, or to be absent from quarters (*on* ~, away thus); disc etc. given to person leaving a place of entertainment temporarily so that on presenting this he will be re-admitted without payment; (usu. *free* ~) ticket authorizing holder to travel free on railway etc. **5.** Thrust in fencing; juggling trick; passing of hands over anything, esp. in mesmerism; *make a* ~ *at* (sl.), make amatory advances to. **6.** (football etc.). Transference of ball to another player of one's own side. **7.** ~'*book,* book supplied by bank to person having current or deposit account, showing all sums deposited & drawn; ~'*key,* private key to gate etc. for special purposes, (also) master-key; ||~'*man,* one who takes ~ degree at university; ~'*word,* selected word or phrase distinguishing friend from enemy. [partly f. prec., partly f. F *passe,* f. *passer* as prec.]

pass[3] (-ah-), n. Narrow passage through mountains; (mil.) such passage viewed as key to a country (*sell the* ~, fig., betray a cause); navigable channel, esp. at river's mouth; passage for fish over weir. [ME, f. OF *pas* f. L *passus* PACE[1]]

pa'ssab|le (-ah-), a. In vbl senses, esp. that can pass muster, fairly good, whence ~**LY**[2] adv. [ME, f. OF as PASS[1], see -ABLE]

päss'age[1], n. Passing, transit (BIRD *of* ~); transition from one state to another; liberty, right, to pass through; voyage, crossing, from port to port; right of conveyance as passenger by sea; passing of a measure into law; way by which one passes; corridor etc. giving communication between different rooms in house; (pl.) what passes between two persons mutually, interchange of confidences etc.; ~ (*of* or *at arms*), fight (often fig.); short part of book etc., as *famous, difficult, corrupt,* ~; particular phrase in a piece of music. [ME, f. OF (as PASS[1], see -AGE)]

päss'age[2], v.i. & t. (Of horse or rider) move sideways, by pressure of rein on horse's neck & of rider's leg on opposite side; make (horse) do this. [f. F *passager,* earlier *passéger* f. It. *passeggiare* (*passeggio* walk f. L *passus* PACE[1])]

päss'ant, a. (her.). Walking, & looking to dexter side, with three paws on ground & dexter fore-paw raised. [ME, f. OF, part. as PASS[1]]

passé (päs'ā, & see Ap.), a. (fem. ~*e*). Past the prime, esp. (of woman) past the period of greatest beauty; behind the times. [F, p.p. as PASS[1]]

pässe'menterie (-smentrǐ, & see Ap.), n. Trimming of gold or silver lace, braid, beads, etc. [F (*passement* gold lace etc. as PASS[1], see -MENT & -ERY)]

päss'enger (-j-), n. Traveller in public conveyance by land or water or air; (colloq.) member of team, crew, etc., who does, or can do, no effective work; *foot-*~, traveller on foot; ~*-pigeon,* wild pigeon of N. America, capable of long flight (now rare or extinct). [ME *passager* f. OF -*ier* (PASSAGE, see -ER²(2)); -*n*- as in *messenger* etc.]

passe-partout (pahspártŏŏ'), n. Master--key; mount for photograph etc.; picture--frame (esp. for mounted photographs) consisting of two pieces of glass fastened together at edges with adhesive tape. [F, = pass everywhere]

pa′sser (-ah-), n. In vbl senses; ~-*by*, one who passes, esp. casually. [-ER¹]

păss′erine, a. & n. (Bird) of the order of *Passeres* or perchers; of the size of a sparrow. [f. L *passer* sparrow + -INE¹]

păss′|ible, a. (theol.). Capable of feeling or suffering. So ~iBIL′ITY n. [ME, f. LL *passibilis* (*pati pass*- suffer, see -BLE)]

pắss′im, adv. (Of allusions, phrases, etc., to be found in specified author or book) in every part, as *this occurs in Milton* ~. [L, = scatteredly (*pandere pass*- spread)]

pa′ssing¹ (-ah-), n. In vbl senses; ~-*bell* (rung in moment of person's death); ~--*note* (not belonging to the harmony but interposed to secure smooth transition). [-ING¹]

pa′ssing² (-ah-), a. & adv. In vbl senses, esp.: transient, fleeting; cursory, incidental; (adv., arch.) very (~ *strange*, *rich*). [-ING²]

pă′ssion¹ (-shn), n. **1.** Strong emotion; outburst of anger; sexual love; strong enthusiasm (*for* thing, *for* doing). **2.** (*The P*~) sufferings of Christ on cross, (musical setting of) narrative of this from Gospels; ~-*play*, mystery-play representing Christ's P~; ~-*flower*, kinds of (chiefly climbing) plants, flower of which was supposed to suggest instruments of Christ's P~; *P*~ *Sunday*, fifth Sunday in Lent; *P*~ *Week*, week between P~ *Sunday* and PALM *Sunday*, (also)=HOLY *Week*. Hence ~LESS a., ~lèssLY² adv., ~lèss-NESS n., (-sho-). [ME, f. OF f. L *passionem* (*pati pass*- suffer, see -ION)]

pă′ssion² (-shn), v.i. (poet.). Feel or express passion. [f. OF *passionner*, as prec.]

pă′ssional¹ (-sho-), n. Book of the sufferings of saints & martyrs. [f. med. L *passionale* neut. adj. as n. (as foll.)]

pă′ssional² (-sho-), a. Of, marked by, passion. [f. LL *passionalis* (as PASSION¹, see -AL)]

pă′ssionate (-sho-), a. Dominated by, easily moved to, strong feeling, esp. love or anger; due to, (of language etc.) showing, passion. Hence ~LY² adv., ~NESS n. [ME, f. med. L *passionatus* (as PASSION¹, see -ATE²)]

Pă′ssionist (-sho-), n. Member of an R.-C. order pledged to do their utmost to keep alive the memory of Christ's Passion. [-IST]

păss′ive, a. & n. **1.** Suffering action, acted upon; (gram.) ~ *voice* (comprising those forms of transitive verbs that attribute the verbal action to the person etc. to whom it is directed, cf. ACTIVE); offering

no opposition, submissive; ~ RESISTANCE; not active, inert; ~ *debt* (on which no interest is paid). **2.** n. (gram.). ~ voice or form of verb. Hence ~LY² adv., ~NESS, **passiv′ITY**, nn. [ME, f. OF, or L *passivus* (*pati pass*- suffer, see -IVE)]

pa′ssŏver (-ah-), n. (*P*~) Jewish festival commemorating liberation of Israelites from Egyptian bondage (*Exod.* xii), held from 14th to 21st day of month Nisan; Paschal lamb, (fig.) Christ (1 *Cor.* v. 7). [f. *pass over*]

pa′sspŏrt (-ah-), n. Document issued by competent authority permitting person specified in it to travel in the country & entitling bearer to protection; (fig.) thing that ensures admission, as *flattery is the sole* ~ *to his favour*. [f. F *passeport* (*passer* PASS¹ + PORT¹)]

past¹ (-ah-), a. & n. **1.** As p.p. or adj. in vbl senses of PASS¹, esp.: gone by in time, as *his prime is* ~, *our* ~ *years*; just gone by, as *the* ~ *month*, *for some time* ~; (gram.) expressing ~ action or state, as ~ *tense*, ~ *participle*; ~ *master*, one who has been master in guild, freemasons' lodge, etc., (also) thorough master (*in*, *of*, a subject). **2.** n. ~ time, esp. *the* ~; what has happened in ~ time, as *cannot undo the* ~; person's ~ life or career, esp. one that will not bear inquiry, as *a woman with a* ~.

past² (-ah-), prep. & adv. **1.** Beyond in time or place, as *stayed till* ~ *two o'clock*, *half* ~ *three*, *old man* ~ *seventy*, *ran* ~ *the house*; beyond the range or compass of, as ~ *endurance*, *bearing*, *praying for*. **2.** adv. So as to pass by, as *hastens* ~. [prob. f. misuse of *am past* with object, *past* being then mistaken for prep., e.g. *I was now* ~ *the house*]

păste¹, n. Flour moistened & kneaded, with butter, suet, etc., as cooking material; kinds of sweet confection; relish of pounded fish, as *anchovy* ~; cement of flour & water; any soft plastic mixture; hard vitreous composition used in making imitation gems; ~-*board*, stiff substance made by pasting together sheets of paper, (attrib., fig.) unsubstantial, flimsy, (sl.) visiting-card, railway-ticket. [ME, f. OF f. LL *pasta*, perh. f. Gk *pastē* (*pastos* sprinkled)]

păste², v.t. Fasten with paste; stick *up* (playbill etc.) on wall with paste; cover (thing *with* paper etc.) by pasting; (sl.) beat, thrash. [f. prec.]

păs′tel, n. Woad; blue dye from this; artists' crayon made of dried paste compounded of pigments with gum-water; drawing in ~, whence ~(l)IST n. [F, f. It. *pastello*, dim. of *pasta* PASTE¹]

păs′tern, n. Part of horse's foot between fetlock & hoof. [ME *pastron* f. OF *pasturon* f. *pasture* hobble]

păs′teurism (-ter-), n. Prevention or cure of diseases esp. hydrophobia by successive inoculations. [f. L. *Pasteur*, French scientist (1822–1895) + -ISM]

pắs'teurĭz|e (-ter-), **-is|e** (-ĭz), v.t. Subject (milk etc.) to Pasteur's method of partial sterilization ; treat by pasteurism. Hence ~A'TION n. [-IZE]

păsti'ccio (-ĭchō), **păstiche'** (-ēsh), nn. Medley, esp. musical composition, picture, made up from various sources ; (usu. -iche) literary or other work of art composed in the style of a known author. [F (-iche) f. It. (-iccio), f. pasta PASTE[1]]

păs'til, păstille' (-tĕl), n. Small roll of aromatic paste burnt as fumigator etc. ; lozenge. [F (-le), f. L pastillus]

pa'stĭme (-ah-), n. Recreation ; game, sport. [f. PASS[1] + TIME]

pa'stor (-ah-), n. **1.** Minister in charge of church or congregation, whence ~SHIP n. ; person exercising spiritual guidance. **2.** Kind of starling. [ME & AF -our, OF -or, f. L pastorem shepherd (pascere past-feed, see -OR)]

pa'storal (-ah-), a. & n. **1.** Of shepherds ; (of land) used for pasture ; (of poems etc.) portraying country life, whence ~ISM n. ; of a pastor, as ~ epistles (of Paul to Timothy & Titus, dealing with pastor's work). **2.** n. ~ play, poem, poetry, or picture ; letter from pastor, esp. bishop, to clergy or people. Hence ~ITY (-ăl²) n., ~LY² adv. [f. L pastoralis (as prec., see -AL)]

pastora'lě (pahstorah-), n. (pl. -ali pr. -lě, or -ales). Simple opera etc. with rural subject ; slow quiet instrumental composition with notes flowing in groups of three & usu. with drone notes in bass suggesting bagpipes. [It., as prec.]

pa'storate (-ah-), n. Pastor's (tenure of) office ; body of pastors. [f. med. L pastoratus (as PASTOR, see -ATE[1])]

păs'trў, n. Baked flour-paste; articles of food made wholly or partly of this ; ‖ ~-cook, one who makes ~, esp. for public sale. [app. f. PASTE[1] + -RY]

pa'sturaġe (-ahscher-), n. Pasturing; herbage for cattle etc. ; pasture-land. [f. OF, f. pasturer (as foll., see -AGE)]

pa'sture (-ah-), n., & v.t. & i. **1.** Herbage for cattle ; (piece of) land covered with this. **2.** v.t. Lead, put, (cattle) to ~; (of sheep etc.) eat down (grass-land) ; (of person) put sheep etc. on (land) to graze, whence **pa'sturABLE** (-ahscher-) a. **3.** v.i. Graze. [ME, f. OF f. LL pastura (as PASTOR, see -URE)]

pa'stў¹ (pah-, pǎ-), n. Pie of meat, fruit, jam, etc. enclosed in paste & baked without dish. [ME & OF pastee f. LL pasta PASTE[1] + p.p. ending -ee, see -Y[4]]

pās'tў², a. Of, like, paste ; (also ~-faced) of pale complexion. [-Y²]

păt¹, n. Stroke, tap, esp. with hand as caress etc. ; small mass (esp. of butter) formed by patting ; sound made by striking lightly with something flat. [ME, prob. imit.]

păt², v.t. & i. (-tt-). Strike (thing) gently with flat surface (~'ball, ‖ poor or feeble

lawn tennis) ; flatten thus ; ~-a-cake, first words of nursery rhyme, connected child's game ; strike gently with inner surface of fingers, esp. to mark sympathy, approbation, etc. ; (fig.) ~ (person, oneself) on the back, express approbation of ; beat lightly upon. [16th c., goes w. prec.]

păt³, adv. & a. Apposite(ly), opportune-(ly), as story came ~ to his purpose ; ready for any occasion, as has the story ~; stand ~, (poker) abide by hand dealt to one, not draw other cards, (fig.) refuse to change, stick to one's decision etc. [16th c., goes w. PAT[1, 2]]

Pǎt⁴, n. (Nickname for) Irishman. [abbr. of Patrick]

pǎtagĭ'um, n. (zool. ; pl. -ia). Wing-membrane of bat or similar animal ; scale covering wing-joint in Lepidoptera. [L, f. Gk patageion gold edging on gown]

pǎtavin'itў, n. Dialectal characteristics of Patavium (Padua) as seen in Livy's Latin ; provincialism. [f. L patavinitas (Patavinus of Padua, see -INE[1] & -ITY)]

pǎtch¹, n. **1.** Piece of cloth, metal, etc. put on to mend hole or rent ; piece of plaster etc. put over wound ; pad worn to protect injured eye ; not a ~ on, not comparable to, nothing to. **2.** Small disc etc. of black silk stuck on either side of face, worn in 17th & 18th cc. for adornment. **3.** Large or irregular spot on surface. **4.** Piece of ground ; number of plants growing on this, as brier-~. **5.** Scrap, remnant. **6.** Strike a bad ~, go through a period of bad luck ; ~-pocket (consisting of a piece of cloth sewn on garment) ; ~-work, work made up of fragments of different kinds & colours (often fig. & attrib.). Hence ~'ERY(1), ~'INESS, nn., ~'ILY² adv., ~'Y² a. [ME pacche, perh. var. of peche ; see PIECE]

pǎtch², v.t. Put patch(es) on ; ~ up, repair with patches ; (of material) serve as patch to ; (fig., usu. ~ up) repair, set to rights (matter, trouble, quarrel), freq. temporarily or imperfectly ; (usu. ~ up) put together hastily ; piece (things) together (lit. or fig.) ; appear as patches on (surface). [f. prec.]

pǎtch'oulĭ (-ōol- ; also pachōō²), n. Odoriferous Indian plant ; perfume got from ~. [native]

pāte, n. (now colloq.). Head, often as seat of intellect. Hence **-pāt'ED²** a. [ME, of unkn. orig.]

pâté (pǎt'ā, & see Ap.), n. Pie, patty ; ~ de foie gras (de fwah grah), pie etc. of fatted goose liver. [F, f. OF paste, cf. PASTY]

patĕll'a, n. (pl. -ae). Knee-cap, whence **patĕll'AR¹, patĕll'ATE²**(2), aa. ; (Rom. ant.) small pan. [L, dim. as foll.]

păt'en, n. Shallow dish used for bread at eucharist ; thin circular plate of metal. [ME, f. OF patene or L patena, -ina]

păt'ent¹ (or pǎ-), a. ‖ Letters ~ (OF lettres patentes, L litterae patentes), open letter from sovereign etc. conferring right, title, etc., esp. sole right for a term to make, use, or sell, some invention; conferred, protected, by this; ~ LEATHER; ~ *log*, elaborated rotary form of ship's log, recording speed on dial fixed on taffrail; (fig.) to which one has proprietary claim; (colloq.) such as might be patented, ingenious, well-contrived; (of door etc.) open, (fig.) plain, obvious, whence **pāt′-** ENCY n., ~LY² adv. [ME, f. OF, & L *patēre* lie open, see -ENT]

pāt′ent² (*or* pă-), n. ‖ = *letters* PATENT¹; government grant of exclusive privilege of making or selling new invention; invention, process, so protected; (fig.) sign that one is entitled to something, possesses a quality, etc., as *a ~ of gentility*; ~ *office* (from which ~s are issued); ‖~-*roll* (containing ~s issued in Great Britain in a year). [short for *letters patent*]

pāt′ent³ (*or* pă-), v.t. Obtain patent for (invention). [f. prec.]

pătentee′, n. Taker-out or holder of a patent, person for the time being entitled to the benefit of a patent. [-EE]

pāt′er, n. Father (sl.). [L, = father]

păterfamil′iăs, n. (Rom. law & joc.) head of family. [L]

patern′al, a. Of a father; fatherly; related through the father, as ~ *grandmother*, father's mother; ~ *government*, *legislation*, etc. (that limits the freedom of the subject by well-meant regulations). Hence ~LY² adv. [f. LL *paternalis* (*paternus* f. *pater* father), see -AL]

patern′itў, n. Fatherhood; one's paternal origin; (fig.) authorship, source. [ME, f. OF *paternite* or LL *paternitas* (as prec., see -TY)]

pāt′ernŏs′ter, n. The Lord's Prayer, esp. in Latin; *black*, *white*, ~, forms of words said as charms etc.; *devil's* ~, muttered imprecation; bead in rosary indicating that ~ is to be said; ~ *line*, weighted fishing-tackle with hooks at intervals. [OE, ME, f. L *pater noster* our father]

path, n. (pahth, *pl. pr.* pahdhz). Footway, esp. one merely beaten by feet, not specially constructed (also ~'*way*); track laid for foot or cycle racing, esp. *cinder* ~; line along which person or thing moves; ~'*finder*, explorer, aircraft (or its pilot) sent ahead of bombers to guide them to their objective & mark out their targets. Hence ~'LESS (-ah-) a. [OE *pæth*, OLG *pad*, OHG *pfad* f. WG **patha*]

Pathan′ (-tahn), n. Member of a people inhabiting N.W. Pakistan and S.E. Afghanistan. [f. PUSHTOO]

pathĕt′ⁱic, a. & n. Exciting pity or sadness; of the emotions (~*ic fallacy*, crediting nature with human emotion); (n. pl.) study of, indulgence in, demonstration of, these. Hence ~ICALLY adv. [f. F *pathétique*, f. LL f. Gk *pathētikos* (*path*-, root of *paskhō* suffer, see -ETIC)]

păth′ic, n. = CATAMITE. [f. L f. Gk *pathikos* passive (PATHOS, -IC)]

pătho-, comb. form of Gk *pathos* suffering, disease, passion, as: ~*gen′esis*, ~*genў* (-ŏj⁴), production of disease, so ~*genĕt′ic*, ~*gĕn′ic*, ~*genous* (-ŏj⁴), aa.; ~*gnomŏn′ic*, characteristic of particular disease; ~*gnomy* (-ŏg⁴), study of the emotions, so ~*gnŏm′ic* a.; *pathŏl′ogy*, science of (usu. bodily) diseases, so ~*lo′gical* a., ~*lo′gically* adv., *pathŏl′ogist* n.

păth′ŏs, n. Quality in speech, writing, events, etc., that excites pity or sadness. [f. Gk *pathos* suffering, see PATHETIC]

-pathў, suf. repr. Gk *-patheia* suffering, feeling, the second element of the word HOMOEOPATHY, extended to ALLOPATHY & (w. sense curative treatment) to other compds, as *hydro~*, *kinesi~*, *electro~*.

pā′tience (-shns), n. 1. Calm endurance of pain or any provocation; perseverance; *have no ~ with*, be irritated by, be unable to endure, (person, his conduct, etc.); *out of ~ with*, no longer able to endure; *the ~ of Job*, the utmost limits of ~ (*would try the ~ of Job*). 2. Game of cards, usu. for one. 3. ~-*dock*, kinds of plant. [ME, f. OF, f. L *patientia* (as foll., see -ENCE)]

pā′tient (-shnt), a. & n. 1. Having, showing, patience; ~ *of*, enduring with patience, (also) admitting of or compatible with (*the facts are ~ of two interpretations*). 2. n. Person under medical treatment. Hence ~LY² adv. [ME, f. OF, f. L *pati* suffer, see -ENT]

păt′in|a, n. Incrustation, usu. green, on surface of old bronze, esteemed as ornament; gloss produced by age on woodwork. Hence ~ātĕd [-ATE²], ~ous, aa. ~A′TION n. [f. It. *patina*, whence F *patine*, f. L *patina* dish]

pa′tiŏ (pah-), n. (pl. ~s). Inner court open to sky in Spanish or Span.-Amer. house. [Sp.]

păt′ois (-twah, & see Ap.), n. Dialect of common people in a district, differing materially from the literary language. [F, of unkn. orig.]

pāt′riărch (-k), n. 1. Father & ruler of family or tribe; (pl.) sons of Jacob, (also) Abraham, Isaac, & Jacob, & their forefathers. 2. (In early & Eastern Churches) bishop, esp. of Antioch, Alexandria, Constantinople, Jerusalem, or Rome; (in R.-C. Church) bishop ranking next above primates & metropolitans. 3. Founder of an order, science, etc.; venerable old man; *the* oldest living representative (*of* a class etc.). Hence **pātriărch′al** (-k-) a. [ME, f. OF *patriarche* f. LL (-cha) f. Gk *patriarkhēs* (*patria* family f. *pater* father & *arkhēs* ruler)]

pāt′riărchate (-k-), n. Office, see, residence, of ecclesiastical patriarch; rank of tribal patriarch. [f. med. L PATRIARCH-*atus* (-ATE¹)]

pāt′riărch|ў (-k-), n. Patriarchal system of society, government, etc. So ~ISM n. [f. med. L f. Gk *patriarkhia* (as PATRIARCH, see -Y¹)]

patri'cian (-shn), n. & a. **1.** Ancient Roman noble (cf. PLEBEIAN); member of a noble order in later Roman Empire; officer representing Roman Emperor in provinces of Italy & Africa; nobleman (cf. PLEBEIAN), esp. (hist.) in some Italian republics. **2.** adj. Noble, aristocratic, esp. of the ancient Roman nobility. Hence ~SHIP n. [f. L *patricius* (*pater -tris* father, pl. senators, nobles) + -AN]

patri'ciate (-shǐ-), n. Patrician order, aristocracy; rank of patrician. [f. L *patriciatus* (as prec., see -ATE[1])]

păt'ricīde, n. Parricide (less correct & less usual than *parricide*, but occas. preferred in the narrower sense of murder(er) of one's father). Hence **pătricīd'al** n. [PATER, -CIDE]

păt'rimonǐ, n. Property inherited from one's father or ancestors, heritage (often fig.); endowment of church etc. So **pătrimōn'iAL** a. [ME *-moigne* f. OF *patrimoine* f. L *patrimonium* (*pater -tris* father, see -MONY)]

păt'riot, n. One who defends or is zealous for his country's freedom or rights. Hence or cogn. **pătriŏt'IC** a., **pătriŏt'ICALLY** adv., ~ISM n. [f. F *patriote* f. LL (*-ta*) f. Gk *patriōtēs* (*patrios* of one's fathers f. *pater -tros* father, see -OT[2])]

patris'tic, a. Of (the study of the writings of) the Fathers of the Church. [f. G *patristisch* f. L *pater -tris* father + -IST + -IC]

patrōl', n., & v.i. & t. (-ll-). **1.** Going the rounds of garrison, camp, etc.; perambulation of town etc. by police (*~man*, policeman; *~ wagon*, prison van); detachment of guard, police constable(s), told off for this; detachment of troops sent out to reconnoitre; routine operational flight of aircraft. **2.** vb. Act as ~; go round (camp, town, etc.) as ~. [n. (thr. F *patrouille*) & vb. f. F *patrouiller*, orig. = paddle in mud, earlier *patouiller*, cf. OF *patoueil* puddle, mire]

păt'ron, n. One who countenances, protects, or gives influential support to (person, cause, art, etc.); (shop) regular customer; (also ~ *saint*) tutelary saint; (Rom. ant.) former owner of manumitted slave, (also) protector of a CLIENT; ‖ one who has right of presentation to benefice. So **păt'roNESS**[1] n. [ME, f. OF, = patron PATTERN, f. L *patronus* (*pater -tris* father)]

păt'ronage, n. Support, encouragement, given by patron; ‖ right of presentation to benefice or office, as *has a great deal of ~ in his hands*; patronizing airs; customer's support. [ME, f. OF (as prec., see -AGE)]

păt'ronal, a. Of a patron saint (*the ~ festival* etc.). [F, or f. LL *patronalis* (as prec., -AL)]

păt'ronize, -is|e (-ïz), v.t. Act as patron towards, support, encourage, (person, practice, etc.); treat condescendingly, whence ~ingLY[2] adv. [f. F, or med. L; see -IZE]

pătronym'ĭc, a. & n. (Name) derived from that of a father or ancestor. [f. LL f. Gk *patrōnumikos* f. *patrōnumos* (*pater -tros* father + *onoma* name), see -IC]

***patrōōn'**, n. (hist.). Possessor of landed estate with manorial privileges (abolished *c.* 1850) under Dutch governments of New York & New Jersey. [Du. *patroon* PATRON]

pătt'en, n. Overshoe with wooden sole on iron ring etc., for raising wearer's shoes out of mud etc. [ME, f. OF *patin*, f. *patte* paw + -*in* -INE[1]]

pătt'er[1], n. Lingo of a profession or class; speechifying; rapid speech introduced into song; words of song, comedy, etc. [18th c. cant, f. foll.]

pătt'er[2], v.t. & i. Repeat (prayers etc.) in rapid mechanical way; talk glibly. [14th c., f. *pater* = PATERNOSTER]

pătt'er[3], v.i. & t., & n. **1.** Make rapid succession of taps, as rain on window-pane; run with short quick steps; cause (water etc.) to ~. **2.** n. Succession of taps. [f. PAT[2] + -ER[5]]

pătt'ern, n., & v.t. **1.** Excellent example, as *she is a ~ of domestic virtues*; (attrib.) perfect, ideal, model, (esp. of persons, as ~ *wife, father*); model from which thing is to be made; sample (of tailor's cloth etc.); decorative design as executed on carpet, wallpaper, cloth, etc.; marks made by shot from gun on target; ~*-room*, *-shop*, part of foundry etc. in which ~s are prepared. **2.** v.t. Model (thing *after, upon*, design etc.), decorate with ~. [ME *patron* (see PATRON); different. in sense & sp. since 16/17th c.]

pătt'ǐ, n. Little pie or pasty; ~*pan* (for baking~ in). [f. F *pâté* PASTY[1]]

păt'ulous, a. Open, expanded; (of boughs etc.) spreading. Hence ~LY[2] adv., ~NESS n. [f. L *patulus* (*patēre* be open) + -OUS]

pau'citǐ, n. Smallness of number or quantity. [ME, f. OF *paucite* or L *paucitas* (*paucus* few, see -TY)]

Paul, n. *Rob* PETER[1] *to pay* ~; ~ *Pry*, inquisitive person (character in comedy by J. Poole 1825).

Paul'ine, a. & n. **1.** Of St Paul, as *the ~ epistles*. **2.** n. ‖ Member of St Paul's School in London. [-INE[1]]

paulo-pŏst-fū'ture, n. (Gk gram.) tense expressing state resulting from future act, future-perfect; (joc.) immediate future. [f. med. L, = future a little after]

paunch, n., & v.t. **1.** Belly, stomach; ruminant's first stomach; (naut.) thick strong mat, (*rubbing ~*) wooden shield on mast, to prevent chafing. **2.** v.t. Disembowel. [ME, f. ONF *panche* f. Rom. ***pantica** f. L *pantex -icis*]

paup'er, n. Person without means of livelihood, beggar; recipient of poor-law relief; person who may sue IN[5] *forma pauperis*. Hence ~DOM, ~ISM(2). ~ĭzA‑TION, nn., ~IZE(3) v.t. [L, = poor]

pause (-z), n., & v.i. **1.** Interval of inaction or silence, esp. from hesitation; temporary stop; *give ~ to*, cause (person) to hesitate; break made in speaking or reading; (mus.) mark (⌢ or ⌣) over or under note or rest that is to be lengthened indefinitely. **2.** v.i. Make a ~, wait; linger *upon* (word etc.). [ME, f. OF, f. L *pausa* f. Gk *pausis* (*pauō* stop)]

pav'age, n. Paving; tax, toll, towards paving of streets. [AF, OF (PAVE, -AGE)]

pav'an, n. Stately dance in which dancers were elaborately dressed. [f. F *pavane* f. Sp. *pavana*,⸴poss. f. *pavo* PEACOCK]

pave, v.t. Cover (street, floor, etc.) with or as with pavement (often fig., as *~d with flowers, with good intentions*); (fig.) ~ (prepare) *the way* (*for*, *to*, reform etc.). Hence **pāv'ER**[1], **pāv'IOUR** (-vyer), nn. [ME, f. OF *paver* f. L *pavire* beat, ram, or back form. f. *pavement*]

pavé (păv'ā), n. Pavement; setting of jewels placed close together. [F, p.p. as prec.]

pāve'ment (-vm-), n. Covering of street, floor, etc., made of stones, tiles, wooden blocks, asphalt, etc., ‖ esp. paved footway at side of road (*crazy ~*, of irregular flat stones for garden paths etc.); ‖ *~-artist*, one who draws coloured figures on ~ to get money from passers-by; (zool.) *~-like* formation of close-set teeth etc. [ME, f. OF f. L *pavimentum* (as PAVE, see -MENT)]

pavil'ion (-lyon), n., & v.t. **1.** Tent, esp. large peaked one; light ornamental building, esp. one attached to cricket or other ground for players and distinguished spectators; projecting (usu. highly decorated) sub-division of building; part of cut gem-stone below girdle. **2.** v.t. Enclose in, furnish with, ~. [ME, f. OF *paveillon* f. L *papilionem* (nom. *-io*) butterfly, in LL, tent]

pavona'zzo (pah-, -ätsō), a. & n. (Marble) with peacock-coloured markings. [It.]

păv'onine, a. Of, like, a peacock. [f. L *pavoninus* (*pavo -onis* peacock, see -INE[1])]

paw[1], n. Foot of beast having claws or nails, opp. to HOOF; (colloq.) hand, person's handwriting. [ME *pawe*, *powe* f. OF *poue* f. WG (Frank.) **pauta* = MDu., MLG *pōte*]

paw[2], v.t. & i. Strike with paw; (of horse) strike (ground), strike ground, with hoofs; (colloq.) handle awkwardly or rudely. [f. prec.]

‖ **pawk'**/ȳ, a. (Sc., dial.). Drily humorous. Hence ~ILY[2] adv., ~INESS n. [f. Sc. & north. dial. *pawk* trick, of unkn. orig., +-Y[2]]

pawl, n., & v.t. **1.** Lever with catch for teeth of wheel or bar; (naut.) short bar used to prevent capstan, windlass, etc., from recoiling. **2.** v.t. Secure (capstan etc.) with ~. [f. LG, Du. *pal*]

pawn[1], n. Piece of smallest size & value in chess (often fig. of persons). [ME, f. AF *poun*, OF *peon* f. L *pedonem* (nom. *-o*), in med. L foot-soldier (*pes pedis* foot)]

pawn[2], n. Thing, person, left in another's keeping as security, pledge, (now chiefly fig.); state of being pledged, esp. *in*, *at*, *~*; *~'broker*, one who lends money upon interest on security of personal property pawned; *~'broking*, his occupation; *~'shop*, his place of business. [ME, f. OF *pan*, obsc. rel. to OFris., OS *pand*, OHG *pfant*]

pawn[3], v.t. Deposit (thing) as security for payment of money or performance of action; (fig.) pledge (one's life, honour, word). [f. prec.]

pawnee', n. Person with whom pawn is deposited. [-EE]

pawpaw'. Var. of PAPAW.

păx, n. **1.** Tablet with representation of Crucifixion etc. kissed at Mass by priests & congregation, osculatory; the kiss of peace as liturgical feature at High Mass. **2.** *~ Rōmān'a, Brĭtănn'ĭca*, peace imposed by Roman, British, rule; *~ vōb'īs, vōbīs'cum*, peace be to, with, you (esp. as priestly blessing). **3.** ‖ (school sl., as int.). Peace!, truce! [ME, f. L, = peace]

păx'wăx, n. (dial., colloq.). Stout tendon extending from dorsal vertebrae to occiput in man & other mammals. [ME *faxwax*, app. f. OE *feax* hair + **weax* growth (WAX[2])]

pay[1], n. Payment: *in the ~* (employment) *of*; wages; *~-day*, day on which payment is (to be) made, ‖ (Stock Exch.) day on which transfer of stock has to be paid for; *~ load*, part of aircraft's load which produces revenue; *~'master*, official who pays troops, workmen, etc. (often fig.); *~master general*, ‖ minister at head of a department of Treasury. [ME, f. OF *paie*, f. *payer* (foll.)]

pay[2], v.t. & i. (paid). **1.** Give (person) what is due in discharge of debt or *for* services done or goods received; *~ off*, *~* in full & discharge or be quit of (ship's crew, creditor, etc.); (fig.) reward, recompense; *~* (person) *out*, punish him; *~ him in his own* COIN; (colloq.) *that has put paid to* (settled) *him*. **2.** Recompense (work). **3.** Hand over (money owed *to* person, or w. double object); hand over the amount of (debt, wages, ransom, tithes). **4.** *~ in*, *~* to one's own or another's banking account; *~* one's *way*, not get into debt; *~ through the* NOSE, *~ the* PIPER; *~ up*, *~* full amount of (arrears, or abs.). **5.** Render, bestow, (attention, respect, court, compliment, *to*). **6.** (Of business etc.) yield adequate return, yield adequate return to (person). **7.** *~ for*, hand over the price of, bear the cost of (*~ for* one's WHISTLE), (fig.) be punished for (fault etc.); *~ off*, yield results, succeed, (of ship) fall off to leeward when helm is put up; (naut.) *~ out*, *away*, let out (rope) by slackening it. **8.** ‖ *~-as-you-earn* (abbr. *P.A.Y.E.*), method of collecting income-tax by deducting at source as income is earned. Hence *~EE'*, *~'ER*[1], nn. [ME, f.

OF *paier* f. L *pacare* appease (*pax pacis* peace)]

|| **pay**[3], v.t. (naut.). Smear with pitch, tar, etc., as defence against wet. [f. OF *peier* f. L *picare* (*pix picis* pitch)]

pay'able, a. That must be paid, due; that may be paid; (of mine etc.) profitable. [-ABLE]

pay'ment, n. Paying; amount paid; (fig.) recompense. [ME, f. OF *paiement* (PAY[2])]

payn'im, n. (arch.). Pagan, esp. Mohammedan (often attrib.). [ME, f. OF *paienime* f. LL *paganismus* (PAGAN, see -ISM)]

paysage' (-zazh), n. Rural scene, landscape; landscape painting, so **pays'agist** n. [F]

pea, n. 1. Leguminous plant whose seeds are used for food; its seed, as *green ~s* (gathered unripe for food); SPLIT ~*s*; SWEET ~; *as like as two ~s*, undistinguishable. 2. ~*nut*, (plant whose fruit is a pod containing) seed used as food & yielding oil; ~*shooter*, tube from which dried ~s are shot; ~ *soup* (made from esp. dried ~s); ~*souper* (colloq.), thick yellow fog; ~*soupy*, (of fog) thick & yellow. [back formation f. PEASE taken as pl.]

peace, n. 1. Freedom from, cessation of, war, as ~ *with honour*, ~ *at any price*, *make* (bring about) ~; *a treaty of* ~ between two powers at war. 2. Freedom from civil disorder; BREACH[1] *of the* ~; *the* (*queen's*) ~, general ~ of the realm as secured by law, as *commission*, JUSTICE, *of the* ~, *be sworn of the* ~ (made a magistrate). 3. Quiet, tranquillity; (in & after bibl. use) ~ *be with you*, ~ *to his ashes!*; mental calm, as ~ *of mind, conscience.* 4. *At* ~, in state of friendliness, not at strife (*with*); *hold* one's ~, keep silence; *keep the* ~, prevent, refrain from, strife; *make* (person's, one's) ~, bring person, oneself, back into friendly relations (*with*); ~*maker*, one who brings about ~; ~ OFFERING; ~*offering*, propitiatory gift, (bibl.) offering presented as thanksgiving to God; ~ *pipe*, CALUMET, tobacco-pipe as token of ~ among N.-Amer. Indians. [ME & OF *pais* f. L *pacem* (nom. *pax*)]

peace'ab|le, a. Disposed, tending, to peace; free from disturbance, peaceful. Hence ~leNESS n., ~LY[2] adv. [ME & OF *peisible* &c. (as prec., see -BLE)]

peace'ful (-sf-), a. Characterized by, belonging to a state of, peace; ~ CO-EXISTENCE. Hence ~LY[2] adv., ~NESS n. [ME; -FUL]

peach[1], n. Large fruit, usu. round, with downy white or yellow skin flushed with red, highly flavoured sweet pulp, & rough stone; (also ~*tree*) tree bearing this; (sl.) person or thing of superlative merit, specially attractive girl; ~*blow*, (glaze of) delicate purplish-pink colour; ~ *brandy*, spirituous liquor from ~ juice; ~

-*colour(ed)*, (of) soft pale red; ~ *Melba*, = PÊCHE MELBA. [ME, f. OF *pesche* f. Rom. **persica* f. L *persicum* (*malum*), lit. Persian apple]

peach[2], v.i. (now sl.). Turn informer; inform (*against, upon*, accomplice). [ME, aphetic f. *appeach* f. OF *empechier* IM-PEACH]

pea'chick, n. Young pea-fowl.

peach'|y̆, a. Like a peach, esp. (of cheeks) in colour & softness. Hence ~iNESS n. [-Y[2]]

pea'cŏck, n., & v.t. & i. 1. Bird with splendid plumage & tail that can be expanded erect like fan (often as type of ostentatious display; *proud as a* ~); ~ *blue*, lustrous blue of ~'s neck; ~ *butterfly*, maroon butterfly with ocellated wings; || ~ *coal* (iridescent); ~*fish*, fish with brilliant green, blue, red, & white colouring. 2. vb. Plume one*self*, make display; strut about ostentatiously, whence ~ERY (4) n. Hence ~ISH[1], ~LIKE, aa. [ME *pecock* f. OE *pēa* (also *pāwa* whence ME *pocock*) f. L *pavo*, +COCK[1]]

pea'fowl, n. Peacock or peahen. [see prec.]

pea'hĕn, n. Female of the peacock. [ME, see PEACOCK]

pea'jăcket, n. Sailor's short overcoat of coarse woollen cloth. [f. obs. *pee* f. MDu. *pie* (now *pij*) pea-jacket+JACKET, or dir. f. Du. *pij-jekker*]

peak[1], n. 1. Projecting part of brim of cap. 2. (naut.). Narrow part of ship's hold esp. (also *fore~, after~*) at bow or stern; upper outer corner of sail extended by gaff. 3. Pointed top, esp. of mountain; point e.g. of beard. 4. Highest point in curve or record of fluctuations (~*load*, maximum of electric power, traffic, etc.). Hence ~ED[2] (-kt), ~'Y[2], aa. [16th c. equivalent of PIKE[1] (as 15th c. *peaked* for ME *piked*), of obsc. form.; w. sense 2 cf. LG *piek*]

peak[2], v.i. Waste away, esp. (Shakespeare) ~ *& pine*; (p.p.) sharp-featured, pinched. So ~'Y[2] a., sickly, puny. [16th c., of obsc. orig.]

peak[3], v.t. & i. (naut.). Tilt (yard) vertically; place (oars) APEAK; (of whale) raise (tail, flukes), raise tail or flukes, straight up in diving vertically. [f. APEAK]

peaky. See PEAK[1], PEAK[2].

peal[1], n., & v.i. & t. 1. Loud ringing of bell(s), esp. series of changes on set of bells; set of bells; loud volley of sound, esp. of thunder or laughter. 2. v.i. Sound forth in a ~. 3. v.t. Utter sonorously; ~ *bells*, ring them in ~s. [ME *pele*, aphetic f. *apele* APPEAL]

peal[2], peel, n. (In Ireland) salmon grilse; (in England) sea-trout. [orig. unkn.]

pear (pâr), n. A fleshy fruit, tapering towards stalk; ~*shaped*; ~*tree*; PRICKLY ~. [OE *pere*, MDu., MLG *pere* f. WG **pera* f. Rom. **pira* f. L *pirum*]

pearl[1] (pĕrl), 1. n. Concretion, usu. white

or bluish-grey, formed within shell of ~-*oyster* & other bivalve mollusc, having beautiful lustre & highly prized as gem; MOTHER ¹-*of*-~; SEED ~. 2. Precious thing, finest example (*of* its kind); *cast*~*s before swine*, offer good thing to one incapable of appreciating it. 3. ~-like thing, e.g. dewdrop, tear, tooth. 4. Size of TYPE. 5. Small fragment of various substances. 6. ~-*ash*, potassium carbonate; ~-*barley*, -*sago*, etc. (reduced by attrition to small rounded grains); ~--*diver*, one who dives for ~-oysters; ~--*fisher*, one who fishes for~s; ~-*fishery*, his occupation, place of this; ~-*powder*, -*white*, cosmetic used to whiten skin; ~-*shell*, mother-of-~ as naturally found. Hence ~ED² (-ld), ~'Y², aa., ~'INESS n., (pẽr-). [ME, f. OF *perle* f. Rom. *perla, of obsc. orig.]

pearl² (pẽrl), v.t. & i. Sprinkle with pearly drops; make pearly in colour etc.; reduce (barley etc.) to small pearls; form pearl--like drops; fish for pearls. [f. prec.]

pearl³ (pẽrl), n. One of a row of fine loops forming decorative edging on pillow-lace etc. [app. var. of PURL¹]

|| **pear'lies** (pẽr'liz), n. pl. Costermongers' dress with mother-of-pearl buttons.

pear'main (pār-), n. Kind of apple. [f. OF *permain* prob. f. Rom. *parmanus of Parma]

pea'sant (pĕz-), n. Countryman, rustic, worker on the land. [ME, f. AF *paisant*, OF *paisent* f. *pais* country f. LL *pagensis* (*pagus* canton)]

pea'santrỹ (pĕz-), n. (Body of) peasants. [-RY]

pease (-z), n. Peas, esp. in ~-*pudding*; (arch.) ~'*cod*, pea-pod. [OE *pise* pea, pl. *pisan*, f. LL *pisa* f. L *pisum* f. Gk *pison*; cf. PEA]

peat¹, n. (Cut piece of) vegetable matter decomposed by water & partly carbonized, used for fuel; ~'*bog*, ~'*moss*, bog composed of ~; ~'*reek*, smoke of, whisky distilled over, ~-fire. Hence ~'ERY(3) n., ~'Y² a. [ME *pete* f. Celt. *pett-; see PIECE]

peat², n. (arch.). Girl, belle, (esp. *proud* ~). [16th c., of unkn. orig.]

pĕb'ble, n. Small stone worn & rounded by action of water; colourless transparent rock-crystal used for spectacles, lens of this; kinds of agate or other gem. Hence **pĕbb'lỹ²** a. [OE *papol-stān*; ME *pobble*, *puble*; 16th c. *pebble*; orig. unkn.]

pĕbrine (pābrēn'), n. Epidemic disease of silkworms characterized by black spots. [F, f. Pr. *pebrino* (*pebre* PEPPER)]

pecăn', n. Kind of hickory of the Mississippi region; its nut. [Algonkin *pakan*]

pĕcc'|able, a. Liable to sin. Hence ~ABIL'ITY n. [f. F, or med. L *peccabilis* (*peccare* sin, see -ABLE)]

pĕccadill'ō, n. (pl. ~es). Trifling offence. [f. Sp. *pecadillo*, dim. of *pecado* sin, as foll., or It. *peccadiglio*]

pĕcc'|ant, a. Sinning; (med.) morbid, inducing disease. So ~ANCY n. [f. L *peccare* sin, see -ANT]

pĕcc'arỹ, n. American gregarious quadruped allied to swine. [f. native *pakira*]

pĕccāv'ī, sent. & n. I have sinned, esp. *cry* ~; (n.) this confession. [L]

pêche Mĕl'ba (pāsh), n. (Also *peach Melba*) confection of ice-cream & peaches flavoured with liqueurs etc. [F, after Dame Nellie *Melba*, Australian prima donna (d. 1931)]

pĕck¹, n. Measure of capacity for dry goods, = 2 gallons; vessel used for this; *a* ~ (large number, amount) *of troubles*, *of dirt*. [ME, AF *pek*, of unkn. orig.; cf. OF *pek* (once), *picote*, *picotin* peck]

pĕck², v.t. & i., & n. 1. Strike (thing) with beak; ~ *out*, pluck out thus; make (hole etc.) thus; kiss (person's cheek etc.) perfunctorily; aim *at* (thing) with beak, (fig.) carp *at*; (colloq.) eat (food, or abs.), esp. in nibbling fashion; mark with short strokes; break (ground, wall, etc. *up*, *down*, etc.) with pointed tool. 2. n. Stroke with beak, mark made with this; hasty kiss; (sl.) victuals. [prob. f. MLG *pekken*, of unkn. orig.]

pĕck³, v.t. & i. (sl.). Throw (stone), throw stones (*at*). [dial. var. of PITCH²]

pĕck'er, n. Bird that pecks (chiefly in comb., esp. WOOD~); kind of hoe; || (sl.) *keep your* ~ (spirits, perh. orig. = beak) *up*. [-ER¹]

pĕck'ish, a. (colloq.). Hungry. [-ISH¹]

Pĕck'sniff, n. Unctuous hypocrite prating of benevolence etc. [in Dickens' *Martin Chuzzlewit*]

pĕc't|ĕn, n. (zool.). pl. ~*ines* pr. -ēz). Comb-like structure of various kinds in animal bodies, so ~inATE², ~inātĕd, aa., ~inA'TION n.; scallop. [L, gen. -*tinis*, comb]

pĕc't|in, n. (chem.). Soluble gum-like carbohydrate, the setting agent in jams & jellies, formed in fruits from pectose by ripening or (in fruits & fruit-juice) by heating. So ~IC a. [f. Gk *pēktos* congealed (*pēgnumi* make solid)+-IN]

pĕc'toral, n. & a. 1. Ornamental breast-plate, esp. that of Jewish high priest; ~ fin, muscle, etc. 2. adj. Of, for, good for diseases of, the breast or chest; worn on the breast (~ *cross*, by bishops). [ME, f. OF, or L *pectoralis* a., -*le* n. (*pectus* -*oris* breast, see -AL)]

pĕc'tōse, n. (chem.). Insoluble substance related to cellulose & found with it in unripe fruits etc. [as PECTIN, see -OSE²]

pĕc'ūl|āte, v.t. & i. Embezzle (money, or abs.). So ~A'TION, ~ātOR, nn. [f. L *peculari* (as foll.), see -ATE³]

pĕcūl'iar, a. & n. 1. Belonging exclusively *to*; belonging to the individual, esp. one's *own* ~ (character etc.); particular, special, as *a point of* ~ *interest*; strange, odd, as *a* ~ *flavour*, *he has always been a little* ~; ~ *people*, the Jews, (in wider sense) God's elect, (*P~ People*) evangelical Christian denomination founded 1838 relying on divine healing for cure of disease. **2.** n. ~ property, privilege, etc.; parish, church, exempt from jurisdiction of diocese in which it lies; (*P~*) one of the P~ People. [ME, f. OF *peculier*, or L *peculiaris* of private property (*peculium* f. *pecu* cattle, see -AR[1])]

pěcūliǎ'rǐtў, n. Being peculiar; characteristic; oddity. [-ITY]

pěcūl'iarlў, adv. As regards oneself alone, individually, as *does not affect him ~*; especially, more than usually, as ~ *annoying*; oddly, as *they dress ~*. [-LY[2]]

pěcūn'iar|ў, a. (Consisting of) money, as ~*y aid, considerations*; (of offence) having ~*y* penalty. Hence ~**ĭLY[2]** adv. [f. L *pecuniarius* (*pecunia* money f. *pecu* cattle, see -ARY[1])]

pěd'agōgue (-g), n. Schoolmaster, teacher, (usu. derog. implying pedantry). Hence or cogn. **pědagōg'IC**(AL) (-ŏg-, -ōj-) aa., **pědagōg'icaLLY[2]** adv., **pěd'agōg(u)-ISM**(1) (-gĭzm) n. [ME, f. OF f. L f. Gk *paidagōgos* (*pais paidos* boy +-*agōgos* f. *agō* lead)]

pěd'agōg|y (-gǐ, -jǐ), n. Science of teaching. So ~**ICS** (-gŏg²-, -gōj²-) n. [f. F *pédagogie* f. Gk *paidagōgia*, as prec.]

pěd'al[1], n., & v.i. & t. (-ll-). **1.** (In organ) each of the wooden keys played upon by the feet, (also) foot-lever for drawing out several stops at once or other purposes; (in piano) foot-lever for making the tone fuller (*loud ~*) or softer (*soft ~*); foot-lever in various machines, esp. bicycle (~ *cycle*) or tricycle; (mus.) note sustained in one part, usu. bass, through successive harmonies some of which are independent of it. **2.** vb. Play on organ ~s, work bicycle ~s; work (bicycle) thus. [f. F *pédale* f. It. *pedale* f. L as foll.]

pěd'al[2], a. (zool.). Of the feet or foot (esp. of mollusc). [f. L *pedalis* (*pes pedis* foot, see -AL)]

pěd'ant, n. One who overrates or parades book-learning or technical knowledge or insists on strict adherence to formal rules; one who is possessed by a theory, doctrinaire. Hence or cogn. **pědăn'TIC** a., **pědăn'TICALLY** adv., ~**IZE**(2, 3) v.t. & i., ~**ŏc'RACY,** ~**RY**(1, 4, 5), nn. [ME, f. F, f. It. *pedante*; app. f. *pedagogue* +-*ant* -ANT]

pěd'ate, a. (Zool.) footed; (bot., of leaf) having divisions like toes or bird's claws. [f. L *pedatus* (*pes pedis* foot, see -ATE[2])]

pěd'dle, v.i. & t. Follow occupation of pedlar; busy oneself with trifles; deal out in small quantities, retail, (usu. fig.). [(1)16th c., app. back form. f. PEDLAR; (2)16th c., var. of PIDDLE]

pederasty. See PAEDERASTY.

pěd'ěstal, n., & v.t. (-ll-). Base supporting column or pillar; base of statue etc.; each of two supports of knee-hole table; foundation (lit. & fig.); movable cupboard for chamber-pots; (v.t.) set, support, on

~. [f. F *piédestal* f. It. *piedestallo* (*piè* foot f. L *pes pedis*+*di* of + *stallo* STALL[1])]

pěděs'trian, a. & n. **1.** Going, performed, on foot; of walking; prosaic, dull, uninspired. **2.** n. One who walks, esp. as athletic performance, whence ~**ISM**(2) n., ~**IZE**(2) v.i. [f. F (-*tre*) or L *pedester -tris* +-IAN]

pěd'icel, pěd'icle, nn. (bot., zool.). Small (esp. subordinate, cf. PEDUNCLE) stalk-like structure in plant or animal. Hence **pěd'icellATE[2], pědic'ūlATE[2],** aa. [f. mod. L *pedicellus* dim. of L *pediculus* dim. of *pes pedis* foot, see -CULE]

pědic'ūlar, -lous, aa. Lousy. So **pědic-ūlos'IS** n. [f. L *pedicularis, -losus* (*pediculus* louse, see -AR[1], -OUS)]

pěd'icure, n., & v.t. **1.** Chiropody; chiropodist. **2.** v.t. Cure or treat (feet) by removing corns etc. [f. F *pédicure* f. L *pes pedis* foot +*cura* care]

pěd'igree, n. Genealogical table; ancestral line (of man or animal); derivation (of word); ancient descent; (attrib.) having known line of descent, as ~ *cattle*. Hence **pěd'igreED[2]** a. [15th c. *pedegru* etc., f. AF = OF *pie de grue* crane's foot, mark denoting succession in ~s]

pěd'iment, n. Triangular part crowning front of building in Grecian style, esp. over portico; similarly placed member of same or other form in Roman & Renaissance styles. Hence **pědiměn'TAL,** ~**ED[2],** aa. [c. 1600 *periment*, perh. corrupt. of PYRAMID]

pěd'lar, n. Travelling vendor of small wares usu. carried in pack; (fig.) retailer (*of gossip* etc.); ~*'s French*, thieves' cant. Hence **pěd'laRY** n. [14th c. *pedlere*, alt. of *pedder* (13th c.), f. *ped* pannier (14th c.), of unkn. orig.]

pedo-. See PAEDO-.

pědŏl'|ogў, n. Science of soils. Hence ~**L'OGIST** n. [f. Gk *pedon* ground, -LOGY]

pědomět'er, n. Instrument for estimating distance travelled on foot by recording number of steps taken. [f. F *pédomètre* f. L *pes pedis* foot +-o- + -METER]

pěd'rail, n. Device for facilitating progress of heavy vehicles over rough ground by attachment of broad footlike supporting surfaces to wheel-rims. [f. L *pes pedis* foot +RAIL[1]]

pědunc'|le (-ŭng'kl), n. (Bot.) stalk of flower, fruit, or cluster, esp. main stalk bearing solitary flower or subordinate stalks (*pedicels*); (zool.) stalklike process in animal body. Hence ~**ūlAR[1],** ~**ūlATE[2]** (-at), aa. [f. mod. L *pedunculus* f. L *pes pedis* foot +-UNCLE]

pee, v.i., & n. (colloq.). Urinate; urination. [f. PISS, cf. F *pipi*]

peek, v.i. Peep, peer, (*in, out*, etc.); ~-*a-boo* (now U.S.), = BO-PEEP. [ME *pike, pyke,* of unkn. orig.]

peel[1], n. (hist.). Small square tower built in 16th c. in border counties of England

& Scotland. [ME *pel* stake, palisade, f. AF *pel*, = OF *piel* f. L *palus* stake; cf. PALE[1]]

peel[2], n. Shovel, esp. baker's for thrusting loaves etc. into oven. [ME & OF *pele* f. L *pala*; cf. PALETTE]

peel[3], v.t. & i., & n. **1.** Strip the ~, rind, bark, etc., from (orange, potato, tree, etc.); take *off* (skin, ~, etc.); (arch., from *Isa.* xviii. 2, perh. mistransl.) *scattered & ~ed* (pillaged); (intr., of tree, animal body, etc.) become bare of bark, skin, etc., (of bark, surface, etc.) come off or *off* like ~, (of person, now sl.) strip for exercise etc. **2.** n. Rind, outer coating, of fruit; *candied* ~ (usu. of citron). Hence ~'er[1] [-ER[1](1, 2)] n., ~'ING[1](2) n. (esp. *potato ~ings*). [in 17th c. different. f. PILL[2]]

peel[4], n. See PEAL[2].

peel'er[2], n. ‖ Policeman (sl.); member of Irish constabulary, founded under Peel's secretaryship (hist.). [Robert *Peel* (d. 1850), cf. BOBBY, +-ER[1]]

Peel'ite, n. Conservative siding with Sir R. Peel when he introduced measure for repeal of Corn-laws in 1846. [-ITE[1]]

peen, n. Wedge-shaped or thin end of a hammer-head (opp. *face*). [also *pane*, of uncert. orig.; cf. Norw. *pen*, *pænn* in same sense]

peep[1], v.i., & n. (Make) feeble shrill sound of young birds, mice, etc., chirp, squeak. [late ME var. of PIPE[2]]

peep[2], v.i. Look through narrow aperture (*at*, *into*, etc.); look furtively (*~ing Tom*, type of prurient curiosity, in tale of Godiva); (of daylight, flower, distant object) come cautiously or partly into view, emerge, (often *out*); (fig., of qualities etc.) show itself unconsciously. [late 15th c.; cf. earlier *pike* (= PEEK), *kike*, *keke*]

peep[3], n. Furtive or peering glance; first appearance, esp. *of dawn*, *of day*; ~*-of--day boys*, Protestant organization in Ireland (1784–95) searching opponents' houses at daybreak for arms; ~*-hole*, small hole to peep through; ~*-show*, small exhibition of pictures etc. viewed through lens in small orifice (also fig.); ~ *sight*, aperture sight of some rifles. [f. prec.]

peep'er, n. One who peeps; (sl.) eye. [PEEP[2] + -ER[1]]

peep'ul, **pi'pal** (pē-), n. Large Indian fig-tree allied to banyan, bo-tree. [Hind. *pīpal*]

peer[1], n. **1.** An equal in civil standing or rank; equal in any respect, as *you will not easily find his* ~, whence ~'LESS a., ~'lessLY[2] adv., ~'lessNESS n. **2.** Member of one of the degrees (duke, marquis, earl, viscount, baron) of nobility in United Kingdom, whence ~'ESS[1] n.; ~*s of the realm* or *United Kingdom* (all of whom may sit in House of Lords), ~*s of Scotland*, *of Ireland*, (represented in H. of Lords by 16 elected to each parliament,

by 28 elected for life); noble (of any country). [ME & OF *per* f. L *par* equal]

peer[2], v.t. & i. Rank with, equal; rank as equal *with*; make (man) a peer. [ME, f. OF *perer* f. LL *pariare* (*par* equal)]

peer[3], v.i. Look narrowly (*into*, *at*, etc.); appear, peep out; come in sight. [16th c., of obsc. orig.; cf. syn. (14th c., now dial.) *pire*, of LG orig.]

peer'age, n. The peers; nobility, aristocracy; rank of peer; book containing list of peers with genealogy etc. [-AGE]

peeved (-vd), a. (sl.). Irritated. [PEEV(ISH), -ED[1]]

peev'ish, a. Querulous, irritable. Hence ~LY[2] adv., ~NESS n. [ME, of unkn. orig.]

peewit. See PEWIT.

pĕg[1], n. Pin, bolt, of wood, metal, etc., usu. round & slightly tapering, for holding together parts of framework etc., stopping up vent of cask, hanging hats etc. on, holding ropes of tent, tightening or loosening strings of violin etc., marking cribbage score, etc.; *round* ~ *in square* HOLE[1]; CLOTHES-~; (fig.) *a* ~ *to hang* (discourse etc.) *on*, (occasion, pretext, theme); ‖ a drink, esp. of spirits; *off the* ~, (of clothes) ready-made; ‖ *put* (a man) *on the* ~ (army sl.), bring before the C.O. for an offence; *take* (person) *down a* ~ *or two*, humble him; ~'*top*, pear-shaped spinning-top with métal ~, ~*top trousers* (wide at hips, narrow at ankles). [ME, of LG orig., cf. MDu. *pegge*, dial. Du. *peg*, LG *pigge*]

pĕg[2], v.t. & i. (-gg-). Fix (thing *down*, *in*, *out*, etc.) with peg; ~ *down*, restrict (*to* rules etc.); (Stock Exch.) prevent price of (stock etc.) from falling (rising) by freely buying (selling) at given price; stabilize (prices, wages, etc.); strike, pierce, aim *at*, with peg; (sl.) throw (stone), throw stones etc., (*at*); mark (score) with pegs on cribbage-board; mark *out* boundaries of (mining claim etc.); ~ (*away*), work persistently (*at*); drive pegs into (cricket--bat); ~ *out*, (croquet) hit peg with ball as final stroke in game, (sl.) die, be ruined. [f. prec.]

Pĕg'asus, n. Winged horse that with stroke of hoof caused fountain Hippocrene to flow on Mt Helicon, (fig.) poetic genius. [L, f. Gk *Pēgasos* (*pēgē* fount)]

peignoir (pän'wahr, & see Ap.), n. Woman's loose dressing-gown. [F (*peigner* comb)]

peine forte et dure (pän fŏrtā dūr'), n. Severe & hard punishment, i.e. pressing to death, inflicted on person charged with felony who refused to plead. [F]

pěj'orative (*or* pijŏ'r-), a. & n. Depreciatory (word), as *the* ~ *suffix* *-aster*. [f. LL *pejorare* make worse (*pejor*), see -ATIVE]

pěk'an, n. N.-Amer. carnivorous beast of weasel family, valued for fur. [f. native *pékané*]

pēke, n. PEKIN(G)ESE dog. [abbr.]

pěk'in' (*or* -ing'), n. Kind of silk stuff; [f. F *pékin* as used by Napoleon I's soldiers] civilian. [f. F *pékin* f. Chin. *Pe-king* northern capital]

Pēkin(g)ēse' (-z), n. & a. (Inhabitant) of Peking(g); small short-legged snub-nosed dog with long silky hair. [-ESE]

Pĕk'ing măn, n. Prehistoric type of man represented by remains first found in 1929 at Peking.

pĕk'ŏe, n. Superior kind of black tea. [f. Chin. *pek-ho* (*pek* white + *ho* down), leaves being picked young with down on them]

pĕl'age, n. Fur, hair, wool, etc., of quadruped. [F *poil* hair + -AGE]

Pēlă'gian[1], a. & n. (Follower) of the monk Pelagius (4th–5th c.), who denied doctrine of original sin. Hence ~ISM n. [-AN]

pēlă'gian[2], a. & n. Of, inhabiting, inhabitant of, the open sea. [f. L *pelagius* (*pelagus* sea f. Gk *pelagos*) + -AN]

pēlă'gic, a. Of, performed on, the open sea, esp. ~ *sealing, whaling.* [f. L *pelagicus* (as prec., -IC)]

Pĕlărgŏn'ium, n. Genus of plants with showy flowers & fragrant leaves (pop. called *geranium*). [f. Gk *pelargos* stork]

Pēlăs'gic (-zj- *or* -zg-), a. Of the Pelasgians, an ancient people, on coasts & islands of Eastern Mediterranean & Aegean; ~ *architecture*, oldest form of masonry found in Greece. [f. L *Pelasgus* (*Pelasgi* f. Gk *Pelasgoi*, see -IC)]

pĕl'erine (*or* -ēn'), n. Woman's long narrow cape or tippet. [f. F *pèlerine*, fem. of *pèlerin* PILGRIM]

pĕlf, n. Money, wealth, (usu. derog. or joc.). [ME, f. ONF **pelfe*, var. of OF *pelfre*, of unkn. orig.; see PILFER]

pĕl'ican, n. Large water-fowl with pouch for storing fish, fabled to feed its young with its own blood. [OE, in ME reinforced by OF *pelican* f. LL *pelicanus* f. Gk *pelekan*]

pĕlisse' (-ēs), n. Woman's mantle with armholes or sleeves, reaching to ankles; child's outdoor garment worn over other clothes; hussar officer's fur-trimmed undress jacket. [F, f. med. L *pellicia* (*vestis* garment) of fur (*pellis* skin)]

pĕllăg'r|a, n. Deficiency disease characterized by cracking of skin & often ending in insanity. So ~OUS a. [It., f. *pelle agra* rough skin]

pĕll'ĕt, n., & v.t. Small ball of paper, bread, etc.; pill; small shot; circular boss . in coins etc.; (vb) hit with (esp. paper) ~s. [ME, f. OF *pelote* f. Rom. **pelota* f. L *pila* ball]

pĕll'icle, n. Thin skin; membrane; film. Hence *pellic'ūlAR*[1] a. [f. L *pellicula*, dim. of *pellis* skin]

pĕll'itory, n. **1.** (~ *of Spain*) plant with pungent-flavoured root, used as local irritant etc. **2.** (~ *of the wall*) low bushy plant with greenish flowers growing on or at foot of walls. [**1.** alt. f. ME *pelletre* f. OF, f. L f. Gk *purethron* PYRETHRUM; **2.** f. LL *parietaria* (*paries* -*etis* wall)]

pĕll'-mĕll', adv., a., & n. **1.** In disorder, promiscuously; headlong, recklessly. **2.** adj. Confused, tumultuous. **3.** n. Confusion, medley, mêlée. [f. F *pêle-mêle* (*pêle* orig. uncert. + *mêle* f. *mêler* mix)]

pĕllū'cid, a. Transparent, clear; clear in style or expression; mentally clear. Hence or cogn. **pĕllūcid'ITY** n., ~LY[2] adv. [f. L *pellucidus* f. PER(*lucēre* shine), see -ID[1]]

Pĕl'manism, n. A 20th-c. mind-training system. [P]

pĕl'mĕt, n. Valance or narrow pendant border (esp. over window or door to conceal curtain rods). [prob. f. F *palmette* conventional palm-leaf design used on cornices]

pēlŏr'us, n. Sighting device on ship's compass for taking bearings. [f. P~, reputed name of Hannibal's pilot]

pĕlŏt'a, n. Basque game played with ball & wicker racket. [Sp., = ball, see PELLET]

pĕlt[1], n. Skin of sheep or goat with short wool on; undressed skin of fur-bearing animal; raw skin of sheep etc. stripped of wool or fur, so **pĕl'tRY**(1) n. [ME, obsc. rel. to obs. *pell* or *pellet* skin, or back form. f. *peltry*; ult. f. L *pellis* skin]

pĕlt[2], v.t. & i., & n. **1.** Assail with missiles (also fig.); (intr., of rain etc.) beat with violence; strike repeatedly with missiles, go on firing *at.* **2.** n. ~ing; (*at*) *full* ~ (speed). [c. 1500, of unkn. orig.]

pĕl't|a, n. (pl. ~ae). Small light shield of ancient Greeks, Romans, etc.; (bot.) shield-like structure, so ~ATE[2](2) a. [L, f. Gk *peltē*]

pĕl'v|is, n. (anat.). Basin-shaped cavity formed in most vertebrates by haunch--bones with sacrum & other vertebrae, whence ~IC a.; basin-like cavity of kidney. [L, = basin]

Pĕm'broke, n. Town in Wales; ~ *table, p*~, table on four fixed legs with hinged flaps that can be spread out & supported.

pĕmm'ican, n. N.-Amer.-Ind. cake of dried & pounded meat mixed with melted fat; beef so treated & flavoured with currants etc. for travellers; (fig.) condensed literary matter. [f. native *pimecan* (*pime* fat)]

pĕm'phig|us, n. (path.). Formation of watery vesicles or eruptions on skin of body. Hence ~OID, ~OUS, aa. [f. Gk *pemphix -igos* bubble]

pĕn[1], n. Small enclosure for cows, sheep, poultry, etc., or for other purposes; (W.--Ind.) farm, plantation; *submarine* ~, enclosure (often with concrete roof) for sheltering submarines. [OE *penn*, of unkn. orig.]

pĕn[2], v.t. (-nn-). Enclose, shut *up*, shut *in*; shut up (cattle etc.) in pen. [ME *pennen*, app. f. prec.]

pĕn[3], n., & v.t. (-nn-). **1.** Quill-feather with quill pointed & split into two sections, for writing with ink; similar instrument of steel, gold, etc., fitted into rod of wood etc. (~'*holder*); writing, style of this, as *made a living with his* ~, *wields a formidable* ~; FOUNTAIN-~. **2.** ~ *& ink*, instruments of writing, writing; ~-*&-ink* a., drawn, written, with these; ~-*feather*, quill-feather of bird's wing; ~'*knife*, small knife usu. carried in pocket; ~'*man* (-*an*), one who writes a (*good, bad*, etc.) hand, author; ~'*manship*, skill in writing, style of handwriting, action or style of literary composition; ~-*name*, literary pseudonym; ~'*wiper*, appliance usu. of small pieces of cloth for wiping ~ after use. **3.** v.t. Write, compose & write, (letter etc.). Hence ~FUL n. [ME, f. OF *penne* f. L *penna* feather]

pen[4], n. Female swan. [orig. unkn.]

pēn'al, a. Of punishment; concerned with inflicting this, as ~ *laws*; (of offence) punishable, esp. by law; inflicted as punishment, as ~ *servitude*, imprisonment with hard labour (abolished 1948); used as place of punishment, as a ~ *colony*. Hence ~LY[2] adv. [ME, f. OF, or L *poenalis* f. *poena* (PAIN[1]), see -AL]

pēn'alize, -ise (-īz), v.t. Make, declare, (action) penal; (sport.) subject (competitor, also fig.) to penalty or comparative disadvantage. [-IZE]

pěn'alty, n. Punishment, esp. (payment of) sum of money, for breach of law, rule, or contract; *the* ~ *of*, disadvantage resulting from (quality etc.); (sport.) disadvantage imposed on competitor for breaking rule or winning previous contest; (bridge) points added to player's score under the laws of the game; (football) ~ *area*, part of ground in front of goal in which a breach of the rules by defenders involves award of a ~ *kick* (at goal). [ult. f. med. L *poenalitas* (as PENAL, see -TY)]

pěn'ance, n., & v.t. (In theological use) a sacrament including contrition, confession, satisfaction, & absolution; act of self-mortification as expression of penitence, esp. one imposed by priest; *do* ~, perform such act; (v.t.) impose ~ on. [ME, f. OF *pēneance* f. L *paenitentia* (as PENITENT, see -ANCE)]

pēnănn'ūlar, a. Almost ring-like. [f. L *paene* almost, ANNULAR]

Pěnāt'ēs (-z), n. pl. (Rom. myth.). Household gods. [L]

pence. See PENNY.

penchant (see Ap.), n. Inclination, liking, (*for*). [F, part. of *pencher* incline]

pěn'cil[1], n. (Arch.) artist's paint-brush (still tech. of small brushes, esp. in comb., as *sable*-, *camelhair*, ~); (fig.) draughtsman's art or style; instrument for drawing or writing, esp. of graphite enclosed in cylinder of wood or in metal case with tapering end; (optics) set of rays meeting at a point; (geom.) figure formed by set of straight lines meeting at a point; ~-*shaped object*; ~-*case*, holder, usu. of metal, for ~ or ~-lead. [ME, f. OF *pincel* ult. f. L *penicillum* paint-brush]

pěn'cil[2], v.t. (-ll-). Tint or mark (as) with lead pencil; jot down with pencil; enter (horse's name) in betting-book, whence ~IER[1] n. (racing sl.), bookmaker or his clerk; (esp. in p.p.) mark delicately with thin concentric lines of colour or shading. [f. prec.]

pěn'dant[1], -ent[1], n. **1.** Hanging ornament, esp. one attached to necklace, bracelet, etc. **2.** (naut.). (Also *pennant*) short rope hanging from head of mast etc. with eye at lower end for receiving hooks of tackles, (also) tapering flag, esp. that flown at mast-head of vessel in commission; *broad* ~, short swallow-tailed ~ distinguishing commodore's ship in squadron; shank & ring of watch by which it is suspended. **3.** (*Also pr.* pahn'dahn) match, parallel, companion, complement, (*to*). [ME, f. OF (-*ant*), f. *pendre* hang f. L *pendēre*, see -ANT]

pěn'dent[2], -ant[2], a. Hanging; overhanging; undecided, pending, whence ~D-ENCY n.; (gram.) of which the construction is incomplete, esp. ~ *nominative* (with no verb). [ME, as prec.]

pěnděn'tě lit'ě, adv. Pending the suit. [L]

pěnděn'tive, n. (archit.). Each of spherical triangles formed by intersection of dome ·by two pairs of opposite arches springing from the four supporting columns. [F (-*if*, -*ive*), adj., as PENDANT[1] +-IVE]

pěnd'ing, a. & prep. **1.** Undecided, awaiting decision or settlement, as *a suit, a treaty, was then* ~. **2.** prep. During, as ~ *these negotiations* (orig. = while these negotiations are ~); until, as ~ *his return*. [after F PENDANT[2], -ING]

pěndrăg'on, n. Ancient British or Welsh prince. [W, = chief leader (*pen* head + DRAGON standard)]

pěn'dūlāte, v.i. Swing like a pendulum; (fig.) be undecided. [as foll. +-ATE[3]]

pěn'dūline, a. (Of nest) suspended; (of bird) building such nest. [F (as foll. + -INE[1])]

pěn'dūlous, a. Suspended, hanging down, (esp. of bird's nest, flower, etc.); oscillating. Hence ~LY[2] adv. [f. L *pendulus* (*pendēre* hang) +-OUS]

pěn'dūlum, n. Body suspended so as to be free to swing, esp. rod with weighted end regulating movement of clock's works; *swing of the* ~, alternation of power between political parties; COMPENSATION ~; person, thing, that oscillates (lit. & fig.). [f. L neut. adj. as prec.]

Pénél'opē, n. Chaste wife. [f. Gk *Penelopē*, wife of Odysseus]

pěn'ěplain, n. (geol.). A region that is almost a plain. [f. L *paene* almost, PLAIN[1]]

pěnětrāl'ia, n. pl. Innermost shrine or recesses. [L, neut. pl. of *penetralis* interior, as foll., -IA(2)]

pěn'ětr|āte, v.t. & i. Find access into or through, pass through; (of sight) pierce through (darkness, thicket, etc.); permeate; imbue (person, thing, *with*); (fig.) see into, find out, discern, (person's mind, meaning, design, the truth); (intr.) make a way (*into*, *through*, *to*); (part.) gifted with or suggestive of insight, (of voice etc.) easily heard through or above other sounds. Hence or cogn. ~aBIL′ITY, ~A′TION, ~ātoR, nn., ~aBLE, ~ātIVE, aa., ~ātinGLY², ~ātiveLY², advv. [f. L *penetrare* f. root of *penitus* interior, see -ATE³]

pĕng′uĭn (-nggw-), n. Sea-fowl of southern hemisphere with wings represented by scaly paddles with which it swims under water. [orig. obsc.]

pĕn′ĭal, a. Of the penis. [-AL]

pĕn′ĭcĭllate, a. (nat. hist.). Furnished with, forming, small tuft(s); marked with streaks as of pencil or brush. [as PENCIL, -ATE²]

pĕnĭcĭll′ĭn, n. Therapeutic drug (first discovered in mould) for preventing the growth of certain disease bacteria. [f. mod. L *penicillium* mould (L *penicillum* PENCIL¹) +-IN]

pĕnin′sŭla, n. Piece of land almost surrounded by water or projecting far into the sea; the *P~*, (in the Peninsular war) Spain & Portugal, (in 1914–18 war) Gallipoli. [f. L *paeninsula* (*paene* almost + *insula* island)]

pĕnin′sŭlar, a. & n. 1. Of (the nature of) a peninsula; of the Peninsula or of the war there carried on between French & English etc. (1808–14). 2. n. Inhabitant of a peninsula; (*P~*) soldier of the P~ war. [-AR¹]

pĕnin′sŭlāte, v.t. Make (land) into a peninsula. [-ATE³]

pĕn′ĭs, n. (pl. *-nēs*). Copulatory organ of male animal. [L, = tail, penis]

pĕn′ĭt|ent, a. & n. 1. That repents, contrite. 2. n. Repentant sinner, person doing penance under direction of confessor; (pl.) various R.-C. orders associated for mutual discipline etc. Hence or cogn. ~ENCE n., ~entLY² adv. [ME, f. OF *penitent* f. L *paenitēre* repent, -ENT]

pĕnĭtĕn′tĭal (-nshl), a. Of penitence or penance; the ~ psalms (vi, xxxii, xxxviii, li, cii, cxxx, cxliii). Hence ~LY² adv. [f. LL *paenitentialis* (*paenitentia* penitence, as prec., see -ENCE & -AL)]

pĕnĭtĕn′tĭarў (-sha-), n. & a. 1. Office in papal court deciding questions of penance, dispensations, etc.; *Grand P~*, cardinal presiding over this; ‖ asylum for prostitutes resolving on amendment; reformatory prison. 2. adj. Of penance, of reformatory treatment. [ult. f. med. L *penitentiarius* adj. & n. (PENITENCE, -ARY)]

pĕnn′ant, n. = PENDANT¹ (naut.); = PEN-NON. [compromise between *pendant* & *pennon*]

pĕnn′ĭfŏrm, a. (nat. hist.). Having the form or appearance of a feather. So pĕnnĭF′EROUS a. [f. L *penna* feather, see -FORM]

pĕnn′ĭlĕss, a. Having no money; poor, destitute. [f. PENNY +-LESS]

pĕnn′ĭll, n. (pl. ~*ion* pr. -il′yon). (Stanza of) improvised verse sung to harp at Eisteddfod etc. [Welsh, f. *penn* head]

pĕnn′on, n. Long narrow flag, triangular or swallow-tailed, esp. as military ensign of lancer regiments; long pointed streamer of ship; flag. Hence ~ED² (-nd) a. [ME, f. OF *penon* f. L *penna* feather, see -OON]

pĕnn′ў, n. (pl. *pĕnce* exc. as below). 1. English bronze coin worth 1/12 of shilling (in pl. *pence* combined with numbers from 2 to 11 & 20, pr. without stress, as *six′pence* but *eight′een pence′*; after numeral written *d*. = DENARIUS, as 6*d*.; pl. *pennies* of individual coins as such, as *gave me my change in pennies, doled it out in single pennies*; *(colloq.) a cent; (bibl.) = DENARIUS. 2. A pretty ~, a good sum of money; PETER′s ~, *pence*; a ~ *for your thoughts* (said to person absorbed in thought); *in for a ~, in for a pound*, thing once begun must be concluded at all costs; *take care of the pence*, be sparing in small outlays; *turn an honest ~*, make something by an odd job; *a ~ plain & twopence coloured* (jeer at cheap showiness). 3. ~*-a-line*, a, (of writing) cheap, superficial, ~*-a-liner*, hack writer; ‖ ~ *blood* (sl.), = ~ DREADFUL; ‖ ~ *farthing* (colloq.), old type of high bicycle; ~*-in-the*-SLOT; ‖ ~ *post* (for conveyance of letters at former ordinary charge of 1*d*. irrespective of distance); ~*-weight* (abbr. *dwt*), measure of weight, 24 grains, 1/20 of an ounce Troy; ~ *wise*, (over-)careful in small expenditures, esp. ~ *wise & pound foolish*, careful in small, wasteful in large matters; ~*wort* (-wẽrt), (also *wall ~wort*) plant with rounded concave leaves growing in crevices of rocks & walls, (*marsh* or *water ~wort*) small herb with rounded leaves growing in marshy places; ~*worth*, *penn′orth*, (pĕn′īwẽrth, pĕn′erth), as much as can be bought for a ~, *not a ~worth*, not the least bit, *a good, bad, ~worth* (bargain); ‖ *five~, ten~*, etc., *nail*, sizes of nail orig. costing 5*d*. etc. per 100. [OE, OS *penning*, OHG *pfenning*, ON *penningr*, of unkn. orig.]

pĕnn′ўroy′al, n. Kind of mint cultivated for supposed medicinal virtues. [app. f. earlier *pulyole ryale* f. OF *poliol* thyme (dim. f. L *pulegium*) +ROYAL]

pēnŏl′og|ў, n. Study of punishment & of prison management. Hence pēnolŏ′gĭCAL a., ~IST n. [f. L *poena* penalty +-o- + -LOGY]

pĕn′sĭle, a. Hanging down, pendulous; (of bird etc.) that constructs ~ nest. [f. L *pensilis* (*pendēre pens-* hang, see -IL)]

pĕn′sĭon (-shn), n., & v.t. 1. Periodical payment made esp. by government, company, or employer, in consideration of past services or of relinquishment of rights etc.(‖ *Ministry of P~s*, department instituted in 1914–18 war); such payment to person who is not a professed servant for good will, secret service, etc., or to artists, scientists, etc., to enable them to carry on work of public interest; *old-age* ~, weekly payment by government to poor persons, or every one, after specified age. **2.** ‖ Consultative assembly of members of Gray's Inn. **3.** (*pr.* pahǹ'sǐ-awǹ). Boarding-house at fixed rate; *live en* ~ (as boarder). **4.** *v.t.* Grant ~ to, buy over with ~; ~ *off*, dismiss with ~. Hence ~LESS (-sho-) a. [ME, f. OF f. L *pensionem* payment (*penděre* pens-pay, -ION)]

pěn'sionable (-sho-), **a.** Entitled, (of services etc.) entitling person, to pension. [-ABLE]

pěn'sionarў (-sho-), **a.** & **n.** (Recipient) of a pension; creature, hireling; *Grand P*~ (hist.), first minister of Holland & Zealand (1619–1794). [f. med. L *pensionarius* (as PENSION, see -ARY¹)]

pěn'sioner (-sho-), **n.** Recipient of pension; hireling, creature (obs.); ‖ (Camb. Univ.) undergraduate who is not a scholar on the foundation or a sizar but pays for his own commons etc. (= COM-MONER at Oxf. Univ.). [ME, f. AF *pensionner* (OF *-ier*) (as prec.)]

pěn'sive, a. Plunged in thought; melancholy. Hence ~LY² adv., ~NESS n. [ME, f. OF (*-if*, *-ive*), f. *penser* think f. L *pensare* frequent. of *penděre* pens- weigh]

pěn'stŏck, n. Sluice, flood-gate. [PEN¹ in sense ' mill-dam ' + STOCK]

pěnt, a. Closely confined, shut *in* or *up*. [p.p. of *pend* var. of PEN²]

pěnt|a- (bef. vowel *pent-*), comb. form of Gk *pente* five, as : *pen'tachord* (-k-), musical instrument of 5 strings, series of 5 notes; ~*adac'tyl* a. & n., (person, animal) with 5 toes or fingers on each limb, so ~*adactyl'ic* a., ~*adac'tylism* n.; ~*ā'gynous*, with 5 pistils; ~*ahěd'ron* (-a-h-), solid figure of 5 faces, so ~*ahěd'ral* a.; ~*ăm'erous*, (bot., also written 5-*merous*) having parts of flower-whorl 5 in number, (zool.) consisting of 5 joints; ~*ăn'drous*, with 5 free stamens; ~*apet'alous*, with 5 petals; ~*ăp'ody*, verse, sequence in verse, of 5 feet; *pen'tastich* (-k), group of 5 lines in verse; ~*atŏm'ic*, having 5 atoms of some substance in the molecule; ~*atŏn'ic*, of 5 notes; ~*ăv'alent*, with combining power of 5 atoms of hydrogen etc.

pěn'tacle, n. Figure used as symbol, esp. in magic, prob. = PENTAGRAM. [F, or f. med. L*pentaculum*, app. f. PENTA-+-CULE]

pěn'tăd, ņ. The number, group of, five; five-day period; (chem.) element, radical, with combining power of five. [f. LL f. Gk *pentas -ados* (*pente* five, -AD)]

pěn'tagon, n. Five-sided (usu. plane rectilineal) figure; *the P*~, headquarters of U.S. defence forces. Hence pěntăg'ọNAL a. [f. F (-*gone*) or LL f. Gk PENTA(*gōnon* f. *gōnia* angle)]

pěn'tagrăm, n. Five-pointed star formed by producing sides of pentagon both ways till they intersect, formerly used as mystic symbol. [f. Gk PENTA(*grammon* f. *grammē* line)]

pěntăm'ēter, n. (Gk & Lat. pros.) form of dactylic verse composed of two halves each of two feet (dactyls in second half, dactyls or spondees in first) & long syllable, chiefly used alternately with hexameters to form elegiac verse; English iambic verse of ten syllables. [L, f. Gk PENTA(*metros* f. *metron* measure)]

pěn'tāne, n. Paraffin hydrocarbon having five carbon atoms in the molecule occurring as a colourless fluid in petroleum etc. [f. Gk *pente* five + -ANE(2)]

Pěn'tateuch (-k), n. First five books of O.T., traditionally ascribed to Moses. Hence pěntateuch'AL (-kl) a. [f. LL f. Gk PENTA(*teukhos* implement, in late Gk, book) of five books]

pěntăth'lŏn, n. (Gk ant.) athletic contest of five events in each of which all competitors took part; similar contest (in riding, fencing, pistol-shooting, swimming, cross-country running) in modern Olympic Games. [Gk, f. PENTA- + *athlon* contest]

Pěn'těcŏst, n. Jewish harvest festival, on fiftieth day after the second day of Passover (*Levit.* xxiii. 15, 16), (later) synagogue anniversary of giving of Law on Sinai; (arch.) Whit Sunday. Hence pěntěcŏs'tAL a. [OE, ME, f. LL f. Gk *pentēcostē* (*hēmera*) fiftieth (day)]

pěn'thouse (-t-h-), (arch.) **pěn'tǐce, n.** Sloping roof, esp. as subsidiary structure attached to wall of main building; *apartment or flat built on roof; awning, canopy, or the like. [ME *pentis*, aphetic f. OF *apentis*, *-dis*, = med. L *appendicium*, in LL = appendage]

pěn'tŏde, a. (Of wireless valves) having five electrodes. [f. Gk *pente* five + *hodos* way]

Pěn'tonville, n. Prison in Islington, London.

pěntstēm'on (*or* pěnt'-), **n.** Genus of American herbaceous plants allied to foxglove with showy flowers, usu. tubular & two-lipped. [irreg. f. PENTA- + Gk *stēmōn* warp (cf. STAMEN)]

pěnŭlt' (*or* pē⁴), **pěnŭl'timate**, **aa.** & **nn.** Last but one; (n.) last syllable but one. [(-*ult* abbr.) f. L *paene* almost + ULTIMATE after L *paenultimus*]

pěnŭm'br|a, n. Partly shaded region around shadow of opaque body, esp. round total shadow of moon or earth in eclipse; lighter outer part of sun-spot; partial shadow. Hence ~AL a. [f. L *paene* almost + *umbra* shadow]

pěnūr'ious, a. Poor, scanty; stingy, grudging, whence ~LY² adv., ~NESS n. [f. med. L *penuriosus* (foll., -OUS)]

pěn'urў, n. Destitution, poverty; lack, scarcity, (*of*). [ME, f. L *penuria*]

pē'on (*or* pŭn), n. (In India) office-
-messenger, attendant, orderly; (Span.
Amer.) day-labourer; (Mex.) enslaved
debtor (hist.). [(1) f. Port. *peão*, F *pion*;
(2) f. Sp. *peon*; f. L as PAWN¹]

pē'onage, n. Employment, service, of
peons. [-AGE]

pē'onў, n. Plant with large globular red
or white flowers, in cultivation often
double. [ME & ONF *pione* f. L f. Gk
paiōnia (*Paiōn*, physician of the gods);
later *peony* assim. to L, whence dir. OE
peonie]

people (pē'pl), n., & v.t. **1.** Persons composing community, race, or nation, as *the
English ~, English-speaking ~s, a warlike
~*, (treated as sing.); the persons belonging to a place or forming a company or
class etc. (*the ~ of the western counties
were in revolt, the ~ here are furious*),
subjects of king etc., congregation of
parish priest etc., (as pl.); armed followers,
retinue, workpeople, etc., (as pl.); CHOSEN,
PECULIAR, ~; one's parents or other
relatives, as *his ~ are sure to hear of it*;
the commonalty (as pl.); *the* body of
enfranchised or qualified citizens (as sing.
or pl.); persons in general, as ~ *don't like
to be kept waiting*. **2.** v.t. Fill with ~,
populate, fill (place *with* animals etc.); (of
persons, animals, etc.) inhabit, occupy,
fill, esp. in p.p., as *a thickly ~d country*.
[ME, f. OF *pople, poeple, peuple*, etc., f. L
populus]

*****pĕp**, n. (sl.). Vigour, go, spirit; ~ *pill* (for
inducing ~); ~ *talk*, exhortation to
activity. Hence *~p'ў² a. (sl.), full of ~.
[abbr. *pepper*]

pĕperi'nō (-rē-), n. Light porous (usu.
brown) volcanic rock formed of sand,
cinders, etc. [It., f. *pepere* PEPPER, see
-INE¹]

pĕpp'er¹, n. **1.** Pungent aromatic condiment got from dried berries of certain
plants used whole (~*corns*) or ground into
powder; *black ~*, plant chiefly used for
this; *black, white*, ~ (from unripe, ripe,
berries); CAYENNE ~; (fig.) anything pungent. **2.** ~*-&-salt*, cloth of dark & light
wools woven together, showing small dots
of dark & light intermingled; ~*box*,
small usu. round box with perforated lid
for sprinkling ~, ‖ irregular buttress in
Eton fives-court; ~*-castor, -er*, = ~*box*
(1st sense); ~*corn*, dried berry of black
~, esp. as nominal rent; ~*mint*, kind
of mint grown for its essential oil, this
oil, lozenge flavoured with ~*mint*; ~*-pot*,
= ~*-castor,·* (also) W.-Ind. dish of meat
etc. stewed with red ~ etc., (also, as nickname) Jamaican. [OE *pipor*, OHG
pfeffar, ON *piparr* f. L *piper* = Gk *peperi*
of oriental orig.]

pĕpp'er², v.t. Sprinkle, treat, with pepper; besprinkle as with pepper; pelt
with missiles (lit. or fig.); punish severely.
[f. prec.]

pĕpp'erў, a. Of, like, abounding in,

pepper; (fig.) pungent, stinging, hot-
-tempered. [-Y²]

pĕp'sin, n. A ferment contained in gastric
juice, converting proteins into peptones
in presence of weak acid. [f. Gk *pepsis*
digestion (*pep-* cook)+-IN]

pĕp'tic, a. & n. Digestive; ~ *glands*
(secreting gastric juice); (n. pl., joc.)
digestive organs. [f. Gk *peptikos* (as
prec., see -IC)]

pĕp't|ōne, n. Class of albuminoid sub-
stances soluble in water & non-coagulable
by heat into which proteins are converted
by the action of pepsin in the process of
digestion. Hence ~**ONIZE**(3) v.t. [f. G
pepton f. Gk *pepton* cooked]

pĕr, prep. Through, by, by means of.
1. In L phrr. (usu. ital.); ~ *ann'um*, (so
much) by the year, yearly; ~ *căp'ut* (&
erron. ~ *căp'ita*), a head, each; ~ *cŏn'tra*
adv. & n., (on) the opposite side (of an
account etc.); ~ *dĭ'ĕm, mĕn'sĕm*, (so much)
by the day, month; ~ *mĭll'e*, in or to the
thousand; ~ *prŏcūrātiōn'ĕm* (abbrr. ~
proc., ~ *pro.*, p.p.), by proxy, by the
action of (person signing document); ~
săl'tum, without intermediate steps, all
at once; ~ *sē*, by or in itself, intrinsically.
2. As E prep.; by, by means or instrumentality of, as ~ *post, rail, steamer,
bearer*; (joc.) as ~ *usual*, as usual; for
each, as *a shilling ~ man, 5 ~ cent*; ~
second ~ second, ~ second every second
(of rate of acceleration over indefinite
period). [L]

per-, pref. = L prep. *per* (prec.). **1.** In L
senses; through, all over, (~*forate,~vade*);
completely, very (~*turb*); to destruction,
to the bad, (~*vert*, ~*dition*). **2.** Chem.
denoting maximum of some element in
combination; in names of binary compounds in *-ide* (formerly *-uret*), as
~*chloride, ~iodide, ~oxide, ~sulphide*; in
adjj. in *-ic* naming oxides, acids, etc., as
~*chloric, ~iodic,~manganic*; in names of
salts of these etc., as ~*chlorate, ~iodate,
~manganate, ~sulphate*.

pĕradvĕn'ture, adv. & n. (arch. or joc.).
1. Perhaps; *if, lest*, ~, if, lest, it chance
that. **2.** n. Uncertainty, chance, conjecture; *beyond, without, (all)* ~ (doubt).
[ME, f. OF *per* or *par aventure* by chance
(PER+*aventure* ADVENTURE)]

pĕrai' (-rahĭ, -rī), **pira'ya** (-rahya), n.
Voracious Amer. freshwater fish. [native
(-*ya*)]

perăm'būl|āte, v.t. Walk through, over,
or about; travel through & inspect (territory); formally establish boundaries of
(parish etc.) by walking round them.
Hence or cogn. ~**A'TION** n., ~**ātORУ** a.
[f. L PER(*ambulare* walk), see -ATE³]

‖ **perăm'būlātor**, n. Hand carriage for
one or two children, with three or four
wheels, pushed from behind (colloq.
abbr. *prăm*). [f. prec.+-OR]

percāle' (*or* -ahl), n. A closely woven
cotton fabric. [F, of unkn. orig.]

perceive' (-sĕv), v.t. Apprehend with the mind, observe, understand, (circumstance, *that, how,* etc.); apprehend through one of the senses, esp. sight. [ME, f. *perceivre,* north. form of OF *percoivre,* f. L`PER(*cipere cept-* = *capere* take)]

percĕn'tage, n. Rate, proportion, per cent; (loosely) proportion, as *only a small* ~ *of books are worth reading.* [-AGE]

pĕr'cĕpt, n. (philos.). Object of perception; mental product, as opp. to action, of perceiving. [as PERCEIVE]

percĕp'tible, a. That can be perceived by senses or intellect. Hence ~iBIL'ITY n., ~iBLY² adv. [f. LL *perceptibilis* (as prec., see -BLE)]

percĕp't|ion, n. Act, faculty, of perceiving; intuitive recognition (*of* truth, aesthetic quality, etc.); (philos.) action by which the mind refers its sensations to external object as cause; (law) collection (of rents etc.). Hence or cogn. ~ionAL (-sho-), ~IVE, aa., ~ively² adv., ~iveNESS, **percĕptiv'ITY,** nn. [ME, f. OF, or L *perceptio* (as PERCEIVE, see -ION)]

pĕrch¹, n. European spiny-finned freshwater fish, used as food. [ME, f. OF *perche* f. L f. Gk *perkē*]

pĕrch², n. 1. Horizontal bar for bird to rest upon; anything serving for this, as *bird takes its* ~ (alights); (fig.) elevated or secure position; *hop the* ~, die, *knock* (person) *off* his ~, vanquish, destroy, him; centre pole of some four-wheeled vehicles. 2. (Also *pole, rod*) measure of length esp. for land, 5½ yds; *square* ~, 30¼ sq. yds. [ME, f. OF *perche* f. L *pertica* pole]

pĕrch³, v.i. & t. Alight, rest, as bird (*upon* bough etc.); (of person etc.) settle, alight, (*upon*); place (as) upon perch (esp. in p.p., as *town* ~*ed on a hill*). Hence ~'ER¹ n., (one of) a large class of passerine birds with feet adapted for ~ing. [ME, f. OF *percher,* as prec.]

perchance' (-ah-), adv. (arch.). By chance; possibly, maybe. [ME, f. AF *par chance* (*par* by +CHANCE)]

percheron (pär'sherawň), n. Strong & swift horse bred in le Perche, district of France. [F]

percip'i|ent, a. & n. 1. Perceiving, conscious. 2. n. One who perceives esp. (telepathy) something outside range of senses. Hence ~ENCE n. [f. L as PERCEIVE, see -ENT]

pĕrc'ol|āte, v.i. & t. (Of liquid) filter, ooze, through (also fig.); (trans.) ooze through, permeate; (of person or strainer) strain (liquid, powder) through pores etc. Hence or cogn. ~A'TION, ~ātOR, nn. [f. L PER(*colare* strain f. *colum* strainer), -ATE³]

percŭss', v.t. (med.). Tap gently with finger or instrument for purposes of diagnosis etc. [f. L PER(*cutere cuss-* = *quatere* shake) strike]

percŭ'ssion (-shn), n. Forcible striking of one (usu. solid) body against another;

(med.) percussing; (mus.) *instrument of* (played by) ~; ~ *cap,* small copper cap or cylinder in fire-arm, containing fulminating powder and exploded by ~ of a hammer. So **percŭss'IVE** a. [f. F, or L *percussio* (as prec., see -ION)]

percūtān'ēous, a. Made, done, through the skin. [PER-+CUTANEOUS]

perdi'tion, n. Eternal death, damnation. [ME, f. OF *perdiciun* f. LL *perditionem* f. PER(*dere dit-* = *dare* give) destroy, see -ION]

pĕrdū(e)', a. (Mil.) placed as an outpost in hiding, esp. *lie* ~; (often as F, with fem. *-due*) hidden. [F, p.p. of *perdre* lose, as prec.]

perdūr'|able, a. Permanent; eternal; durable. Hence or cogn. ~ABIL'ITY n., ~abLY² adv. [ME, f. OF f. LL PER(*durabilis* DURABLE)]

père (pâr, & see Ap.), n. Father (appended to surname to distinguish father from son, cf. FILS). [F]

pĕ'rĕgrin|āte, v.i. (now joc.). Travel, journey. So ~A'TION, ~ātOR, nn. [f. L *peregrinari* (as foll.), see -ATE³]

pĕ'rĕgrin(e), a. & n. 1. (arch.). Foreign, imported from abroad, outlandish. 2. ~ (*falcon*), kind esteemed for hawking. [f. L *peregrinus* (*peregre* abroad, f. PER + *ager* field, see -INE¹)]

pĕ'rĕmptor|y̆ (or *perĕmp²*), a. Final, esp. (law) ~*y mandamus* (in which the command is absolute), ~*y writ* (enforcing defendant's appearance without option); (of statement or command) admitting no denial or refusal; absolutely fixed, essential; (of person etc.) dogmatic, imperious, dictatorial. Hence ~iLY² adv., ~iNESS n. [f. L *peremptorius* destructive f. PER(*imere empt-* = *emere* take, buy) destroy, cut off, see -ORY: in legal use f. LL]

perĕnn'ial (-nyal), a. & n. 1. Lasting through, (of stream) flowing through all seasons of the year; lasting long or for ever; (of plant) living several years (cf. ANNUAL). 2. n. ~ plant. Hence **perĕnniăl'ITY** n., ~LY² adv. [f. L PER(*ennis* f. *annus* year)+-AL]

pĕrf'ĕct¹, a. & n. 1. Complete, not deficient; faultless; (of lesson) thoroughly learned; thoroughly trained or skilled (*in* duties etc.); exact, precise, as *a* ~ *square, circle*; entire, unqualified, as *a* ~ *stranger,* ~ *nonsense*; (gram., of tense) denoting completed event or action viewed in relation to the present (*future* ~, giving sense *will have done*); (bot.) having all four whorls of the flower; (mus.) ~ *interval*, fourth & fifth as they would occur in the major or minor scale starting upon the lower note of the interval, also the octave. 2. n. ~ tense. Hence ~LY² adv., (esp.) quite, quite well, completely, ~NESS n. [ME & OF *parfit, -fet* f. L PER(*ficere fect-* = *facere* do) complete]

perfect'² (or pĕrf'ĭkt), v.t. Complete, carry through; make perfect, improve,

Hence ~ĪBIL'ITY n., **perfĕc'tĬBLE** a. [f. prec.]

perfĕc'tion, n. Completion; making perfect; full development; faultlessness; (loosely) comparative excellence; perfect person or thing; highest pitch, extreme, perfect specimen or manifestation, (*of* quality etc.); (w. pl.) accomplishment. [ME, f. OF, f. L *perfectionem* (as PERFECT[1], see -ION)]

perfĕc'tion|ĭst (-sho-), n. One who holds that religious or moral perfection may be attained; one who aims at perfection in his work (freq. derog.); (*P~ist*) member of communistic community of Oneida Creek, N.Y. So ~ISM n. [-IST]

perfĕrv'id, a. Very fervid. [PER-]

pĕrf'idy, n. Breach of faith, treachery. Hence or cogn. **perfid'ĬOUS** a., **perfid'i-**OUSLY[2] adv., **perfid'iousNESS** n. [f. L *perfidia* f. PER(*fidus* f. *fides* faith) treacherous]

perfŏl'iate, a. (bot.). Having the stalk apparently passing through the leaf. [f. PER-+L *folium* leaf +-ATE[2]]

pĕrf'or|āte, v.t. & i. Make hole(s) through, pierce, esp. make rows of holes in (sheet) to separate stamps, coupons, etc., make an opening into; pass, extend, through; (intr.) penetrate (*into, through,* etc.). Hence or cogn. ~A'TION, ~ātOR, nn., ~ātIVE a. [f. L PER(*forare* bore), see -ATE[3]]

perfŏrce', adv. & n. Of necessity; (n., rare) necessity, as *of, by,* ~. [ME, f. OF *par force* by FORCE]

perfŏrm', v.t. & i. Carry into effect (command, promise, task, operation, etc.); go through, execute, (public function, play, piece of music, etc.); (intr.) act in play, play, sing, etc.; (of trained animals) execute tricks etc. at public show etc., whence ~ING[2] a. Hence ~ABLE a., ~ER[1] n. [ME *perforne* (alt., thr. AF, to -*forme* (FORM)) f. OF *parfo(u)rnir* (whence 14th c. (obs.) *perFURNISH* perform, furnish)]

perfŏrm'ance, n. Execution (*of* command etc.); carrying out, doing; notable feat; performing of play or public exhibition, as *there are two ~s a day, the afternoon ~.* [-ANCE, perh. thr. AF]

pĕrf'ume[1], n. Odorous fumes of burning substance; sweet smell; smell; fluid containing essence of flowers etc., scent. Hence ~LESS a. [f. F *parfum,* as foll.]

perfume'[2], v.t. Impart sweet scent to, impregnate with sweet smell, (esp. in p.p.). [f. F *parfumer* (PER- +L *fumare* smoke)]

perfŭm'|er, n. Maker, seller, of perfumes. Hence ~ERY(1, 2, 3) n. [-ER[1]]

perfŭnc'tor|ў, a. Done merely for sake of getting through a duty, acting thus, superficial, mechanical, as *a ~y inspection, inquirer, in a ~y manner.* Hence ~iLY[2] adv., ~iNESS n. [f. LL *perfunctorius* f. PER(*fungi funct-* perform), see -ORY]

perfūse' (-z), v.t. Besprinkle (*with* water etc.); cover, suffuse, (*with* radiance etc.); pour (water etc.) through or over. Hence or cogn. **perfū'SION** (-zhn) n., **perfūs'IVE** a. [f. L PER(*fundere fus-* pour)]

pergamĕn'ĕous, a. Of or like parchment. [f. L *pergamena* PARCHMENT +-EOUS]

pĕrg'ola, n. Arbour, covered walk, formed of growing plants trained over trellis-work. [It., f. L *pergula* projecting roof (*pergere* proceed)]

pergŭnn'ah (-*a*), -**ga'na** (-gŭ-), n. Division of territory in India, group of villages. [f. Pers. & Hind. *parganah* district]

perhăps' (*colloq.* prăps), adv. It may be, possibly, as ~ *he has lost it, he has ~ lost it, ~ you would like to see it?* [PER +HAPS (pl.)]

pĕr'i, n. (Pers. myth.) fairy, good (orig. evil) genius; beautiful or graceful being. [Pers.]

pĕri-, pref. = Gk *peri* round, about, as: *pĕ'rianth,* floral envelope; ~*cardīt'is* n., inflammation of the ~cardium; ~*card'ium,* membranous sac enclosing the heart, so ~*card'iac,* ~*card'ial,* aa.; *pĕ'ricarp,* seed-vessel, wall of ripened ovary of plant; ~*chon'drium* (-k-), membrane enveloping cartilages (except at joints); ~*clīn'al* (geol.), sloping in all directions from central point; ~*gўnous* (perĭj[2]-), (of stamen) situated around pistil or.ovary; ~*ŏs'tĕum,* membrane enveloping the bones, so ~*ŏs'tĕal,* ~*ostIT'IS* n.; ~*pteral* (perĭp[2]-), (of temple) surrounded by single row of pillars; *pĕ'risperm,* mass of albumen outside embryo-sac in some seeds; *pĕ'ristōme,* (bot.) fringe of small teeth around mouth of capsule in mosses, (zool.) parts around mouth in various invertebrates; ~*tўphlīt'is,* inflammation of some part around the caecum, e.g. appendicitis.

pĕ'riăpt, n. Thing worn about the person as charm, amulet. [f. F *périapte* f. Gk PERI(*apton* f. *haptō* fasten)]

pĕ'riclāse, n. Mineral consisting of magnesia & protoxide of iron, found esp. on Vesuvius. [f. PERI- (= ' very ') +Gk *klasis* breaking, from its perfect cleavage]

peric'opē, n. Short passage, paragraph; portion of Scripture read in public worship. [f. LL f. Gk PERI(*kopē* cutting f. *koptō* cut)]

pĕricrān'ium, n. Membrane enveloping skull; (joc.) skull, brain, intellect. [f. Gk PERI(*kranion* CRANIUM)]

pĕ'ridŏt, n. (Jeweller's name for) olivine, kind of chrysolite. [ME *peritot(e)* f. OF *peritot* (mod. *péridot*), of unkn. orig.]

pĕ'rigee, n. That point in planet's (esp. moon's) orbit at which it is nearest to earth (cf. APOGEE). Hence **pĕrigē'AN** a. [16th c. *perige(e), perigeum,* f. F *périgée* & ' mod. L f. late Gk PERI(*geion* f. *gē* earth)]

For other words in *peri-* see PERI-.

pĕrĭhēl'ion (-lyon), n. That point in planet's orbit at which it is nearest to sun (cf. APHELION). [Graecized f. mod. L *perihelium* (PERI- + Gk *hēlios* sun), after *perigeum* (prec.)]

pĕ'ril, n., & v.t. (-ll-). **1.** Danger; *in ~ of* (in danger of losing) one's *life* etc.; *you do it at your ~*, you take the risk; *keep off at your ~* (take the risk if you do not). **2.** v.t. Expose to danger, imperil. Hence or cogn. ~OUS a., ~OUSLY² adv., ~OUSNESS n. [ME, f. OF *peril* f. L *periculum*]

perim'ēter, n. Circumference, outline, of closed figure; length of this; outer boundary of camp or fortification; instrument for measuring the field of vision. [f. L f. Gk PERI(*metros* f. *metron* measure)]

pĕrĭnē'|um, n. (anat.). Region of the body between anus & scrotum or vulva. Hence ~AL a. [LL, f. Gk *pĕrinaios*, cf. *pĕris -inos* scrotum]

pēr'iod, n. & a. **1.** Round of time marked by recurrence of astronomical coincidences; time of planet's revolution. **2.** Time during which disease runs its course; (usu. pl.) menses. **3.** Indefinite portion of history, life, etc.; any portion of time; *the ~*, the present day (*the girl, costume, catchwords*, etc., *of the ~*). **4.** Complete sentence, esp. one of several clauses; (pl.) rhetorical language. **5.** Full pause at end of sentence, full stop (.) marking this, (*put a ~ to*, bring to an end). **6.** Set of figures marked off in large number, as in numeration, recurring decimals, etc. **7.** adj. Belonging to, characteristic of, a particular (past) ~ (esp. of furniture, dress, & architecture). [ME, f. OF *periode* f. L f. Gk PERI(ODOS = *hodos* way)]

pērĭŏd'ĭc, a. Of revolution of heavenly body, as ~ *motion*; recurring at regular intervals, so **pērĭodi'ciTY** n.; recurring at intervals; ~ *table* (chem.), arrangement of elements in order of atomic numbers & in which elements of similar chemical properties appear periodically & fall into definite groups; expressed in periods. [f. F *périodique* or L f. Gk *periodikos* (as prec., see -IC)]

pērĭŏd'ĭcal, a. & n. **1.** = prec. (not in last sense). **2.** (Magazine, miscellany) published at regular intervals, e.g. monthly. Hence ~LY² adv. [-AL]

pĕrĭpatĕt'|ĭc, a. & n. **1.** (P~*ic*). Aristotelian (a. & n.; so called from Aristotle's custom of walking in Lyceum while teaching). **2.** Walking from place to place on one's business, itinerant, whence ~ICALLY adv. **3.** n. (chiefly joc.). Itinerant dealer. Hence ~ĭCISM(2, 3) n. [f. F *péripatétique* or L f. Gk *peripatētikos* f. PERI(*pateō* walk), see -IC]

pĕrĭpetei'a (-īa), -tia, n. Sudden change of fortune in drama or in life. [Gk PERI(*peteia* f. *pet-* fall)]

pĕrĭph'er|ў, n. Bounding line esp. of round surface; external boundary or surface. Hence ~AL a., ~alLY² adv. [f. LL f. Gk PERI(*phereia* f. *pherō* bear) circumference]

pĕrĭph'ras|ĭs, n. (pl. ~ēs). Roundabout way of speaking, circumlocution; roundabout phrase. Hence or cogn. **pĕrĭphrăs'tĭc** a. (~*tic conjugation, genitive*, one formed ANALYTICALLY w. aux. vb, as preposition, instead of by inflexion, as *did go*=went, *of Caesar*=Caesar's), **pĕrĭphrăs'tĭcalLY** adv. [L f. Gk, f. PERI(*phrazō* declare, vbl adj. *-phrastos*)]

perique' (-ēk), n. Dark Louisiana tobacco of a choice kind. [Louisiana F]

pĕ'rĭscōpe, n. Kinds of tube-&-mirror apparatus by which an observer in a trench or in a submarine submerged to a small depth can see things above the parapet or water; kind of photographic object-glass. Hence **pĕrĭscŏp'ĭc** a., enabling one to see distinctly for some distance round axis of vision. [PERI-, -SCOPE]

pĕ'rĭsh, v.i. & t. Suffer destruction, lose life, come to untimely end (by the sword etc.); (of cold or exposure) reduce to distress or inefficiency (usu. in pass.; *we were ~ed with cold; in ~ing cold*; *the heat had ~ed all vegetation*, whence ~ingLY² adv.; *we were ~ed* (much incommoded) *with cold, hunger*, etc. Hence ||~ER¹ n. (sl.), blighter, ||~ING² a. (sl.), beastly, bloody. [ME, f. OF *perir* (see -ISH²) f. L PER(*ire* go)]

pĕ'rĭshable, a. & n. **1.** Liable to perish; subject to speedy decay. **2.** n. pl. Things (esp. foodstuffs in transit) subject to this. Hence ~NESS n. [-ABLE]

pĕrĭspŏm'ĕnon (pl. *-ena*), a. & n. (Gk gram.). (Word) with circumflex accent on last syllable. [Gk neut. part. of PERI(*spaō* draw) draw round, mark with circumflex]

perĭss'o- in comb. = Gk *perissos*, uneven, odd, redundant, as ~*dac'tўlate* (zool.), having an odd number of toes on each foot.

perĭs'talĭth, n. (archaeol.). Ring of standing stones round burial-mound etc. [irreg. f. Gk PERI(*statos* standing) + -LITH]

pĕrĭstăl'|tĭc, a. (physiol.). Applied to the automatic muscular movement consisting of wave-like contractions in successive circles, by which contents of alimentary canal etc. are propelled along it. So ~sĭs n., ~tic movement, ~tĭcALLY adv. [f. Gk *peristaltikos* (PERI-, *stellō* send)]

pĕ'rĭstўle, n. Row of columns surrounding temple, court, cloister, etc.; space so surrounded. [f. F *péristyle* f. L f. Gk PERI(*stulon* f. *stulos* pillar)]

pĕrĭton|ē'um, -n|ae'um, n. (anat.). Double serous membrane lining cavity of abdomen. Hence ~ē'AL a., ~IT'IS n. [LL, f. Gk PERI(*tonaion* f. *ton-* stem of *teinō* stretch)]

For other words in *peri-* see PERI-.

pĕ'riwig, n. Wig. Hence ~ĝED² (-gd) a. [16th c. *perwyke* etc., f. F *perruque* PERUKE]

pĕ'riwinkle¹, n. Kinds of plants, esp. *lesser & greater*~, evergreen trailing plants with light-blue flowers; ~ (*blue*), colour of ~s. [ME, f. AF *pervenke* = OF *pervenche* f. LL *pervinca*, w. assim. to foll.]

pĕ'riwinkle², n. Edible gastropod mollusc, winkle. [f. 1530, of unkn. orig.; cf. syn. OE *pinewinclan* (? *wine-*)]

pĕrj'ur|e (-jer), v. refl. ~e one*self*, forswear oneself; (p.p.) guilty of perjury. So ~ER¹ (-er-) n. [ME, f. AF = OF *parjurer* f. L PER(*jurare* swear)]

pĕrj'ury (-eri), n. Swearing to statement known to be false; wilful utterance of false evidence while on oath; breach of oath. So **perjur'ious** (-joor-) a., **perjur'iously²** adv. [ME, f. AF *perjurie* f. L *perjurium* as prec.]

pĕrk¹, v.i. & t., & a. (Also ~ *up*) lift one's head, thrust oneself forward, briskly or impudently; (trans.) smarten *up*; hold *up* (head, tail) self-assertively; (adj., rare) perky. [ME, of unkn. orig.]

pĕrk², n. (sl.). (Usu. pl.) perquisite. [abbr.]

pĕrk'|y̆, a. Self-assertive, saucy, pert. Hence~ILY²adv.,~iNESS n. [PERK¹+-Y²]

pĕrl'ite, n. Obsidian or other vitreous rock in form of enamel-like globules. [= F -*ite*, G -*it*, as PEARL, see -ITE¹]

pĕrm, n. (colloq.). Permanent wave; permutation. [abbr.]

pĕrm'alloy, n. Alloy of nickel & iron of great sensitiveness to magnetic forces, used for cores of telegraphic cables. [f. PERM(EABLE)+ALLOY]

pĕrm'anent, a. Lasting, intended to last, indefinitely (cf. TEMPORARY); ~ *set*, condition of metal after being subjected to the strain of use; ~ *wave*, artificial wave in the hair intended to last for some time produced by one of several processes (colloq. abbr. *perm*); ‖~ *way*, finished road-bed of railway. Hence or cogn. **pĕrm'anENCE**, **pĕrm'anENCY** (esp. = ~ thing or arrangement), nn., ~LY² adv. [ME, f. OF, or L PER(*manēre* remain), -ENT]

permăng'anate (-ngg-), n. (chem.). Salt of permanganic acid, esp. *potassium* ~ or ~ *of potash*, used as disinfectant & oxidizer when dissolved in water. [f. foll., -ATE¹(3)]

pĕrmăngăn'ic (-ngg-), a. (chem.). ~ *acid*, acid obtained from manganese. [PER-, MANGANIC]

pĕrm'e|āte, v.t. & i. Penetrate, pervade, saturate; diffuse itself *through*, *among*, etc. Hence or cogn. ~ABIL'ITY, ~ANCE, ~A'TION, nn., ~ABLE, ~ANT, aa. [f. L PER(*meare* pass, go), see -ATE³]

Pĕrm'ian, a. Of the uppermost division of the Palaeozoic series of strata, consisting chiefly of red sandstone & magnesian limestone. [*Perm*, E.-Russian province, +-IAN]

permiss'ib|le, a. Allowable. Hence ~LY² adv. [ME, f. OF, f. med. L *permissibilis* (as PERMIT¹, see -BLE)]

permi'ssion (-shn), n. Leave, licence, (*to do*). [ME, f. OF, or L *permissio* (as PERMIT¹, see -ION)]

permiss'ive, a. Giving permission; ~ *legislation* (giving powers, but not enjoining their use). Hence ~LY² adv., ~NESS n. [ME, f. OF (-*if*, -*ive*), as foll., see -IVE]

permit'¹, v.t. & i. (-tt-). Allow, as ~ *me to remark*, *appeals are* ~*ted*, ~ *it to be altered*, *weather* ~*ting*; (intr.) admit *of* (alteration etc.). [f. L PER(*mittere miss*- let go)]

pĕrm'it², n. Written order giving permission esp. for landing or removal of dutiable goods etc.; (*also* permit') permission. [f. prec.]

pĕrmūtā'tion, n. (Math.) variation of the order of a set of things lineally arranged, any one such arrangement, colloq. abbr. *perm*; (rare) alteration. [ME, f. OF *permutacion* or L *permutatio* (foll., -ION)]

permūte', v.t. Alter the order of. [ME, f. OF *permuter* or L PER(*mutare* change)]

pĕrn, n. HONEY-buzzard. [irreg. f. Gk *pternis*, kind of hawk]

perni'cious (-shus), a. Destructive, ruinous, fatal; ~ *anaemia*, severe freq. fatal kind. Hence ~LY² adv., ~NESS n. [f. L *perniciosus* (*pernicies* ruin f. *nex necis* death, see -OUS)]

pernick'et̆y̆, a. (colloq.). Fastidious; ticklish, requiring careful handling. [orig. Sc., of unkn. orig.]

pĕrnŏctā'tion, n. Passing the night; (eccl.) all-night vigil. [f. LL *pernoctatio* f. PER(*noctare* f. *nox noctis* night), see -ATION]

pĕ'ror|āte, v.i. Sum up & conclude speech, so ~A'TION n.; speak at length. [f. L PER(*orare* speak)]

perŏx'ide, n., & v.t. 1. (Chem.) compound of oxygen with another element containing the greatest possible proportion of oxygen; (pop.) = ~ *of hydrogen*, a colourless viscid liquid used as an antiseptic, and (esp.) to bleach hair. 2. v.t. Bleach (hair) with this. [PER-2+OXIDE]

perpĕnd'¹, v.t. (arch.). Ponder, consider, (matter, or abs.). [f. L PER(*pendĕre* weigh)]

pĕrp'end², n. Var. of PARPEN.

pĕrpendic'ular, a. & n. 1. At right angles to plane of horizon; (loosely, of ascent etc.) very steep; erect, upright; (joc.) in standing position; (geom.) at right angles (*to* given line, plane, or surface); ~ STYLE. 2. n. Plumb-rule or other instrument for showing ~ line; (pl.) two datum--lines used in designing ship & fixing its nominal length (*between* ~s); ~ *line*; *the* ~, ~ *line* or direction (*is out of* ~ *or the* ~, not straight up and down); ‖ (sl.) meal etc. at which guests stand. Hence ~ITY (-ă'r-) n., ~LY² adv. [16th c., f. L *perpendicularis* (*perpendiculum* plumb--line, see -AR¹); in 14th c. f. OF -*er*]

pĕrp'ĕtr|āte, v.t. Perform, commit,

(crime, blunder, pun or other thing viewed as outrageous). So ~A'TION, ~āTOR, nn. [f. L PER(petrare = patrare effect), -ATE³]

perpĕt'ūal, a. Eternal; permanent during life; applicable, valid, for ever or for indefinite time; ~ motion (of machine that should go on for ever unless stopped by external force or worn out); continuous; (colloq.) frequent, repeated, as this ~ nagging; ~ calendar, that can be used ~ly or over a long period of time; ~ curate (hist.), clergyman appointed at instance of lay rector of benefice to execute spiritual duties of benefice (now known as VICAR). Hence ~LY² adv. [ME -el f. OF perpetuel f. L perpetualis f. perpetuus, see -AL]

perpĕt'ū|āte, v.t. Make perpetual; preserve from oblivion. Hence or cogn. ~ANCE, ~A'TION, ~āTOR, nn. [f. L perpetuare (as prec.), see -ATE³]

pĕrpĕtū'itў, n. Quality of being perpetual; in, to, for, ~, for ever; perpetual possession or position; perpetual annuity. [ME, f. OF perpetuite f. L perpetuitatem (as PERPETUAL, see -TY)]

perplĕx', v.t. Bewilder, puzzle, (person, his mind); complicate, confuse, (matter); entangle, intertwine, (esp. in p.p.). Hence ~ĕdLY², ~ĭngLY², advv. [f. obs. perplex a. f. L PER(plexus p.p. of plectere plait)]

perplĕx'itў, n. Bewilderment; what causes this; entangled state. [ME, f. OF -ite, or LL perplexitas (as prec., see -TY)]

pĕr'quisite (-z-), n. (sl. abbr. perk). Casual profit, esp. ‖ (law) that coming to lord of manor beyond regular revenue; thing that has served its primary use and to which subordinate or servant has then a customary right, as remains of the daily commons are among the ~s of college scouts; customary gratuity. [ME, f. L PER(quirere quisit-, = quaerere seek) search for]

pĕ'rron, n. Platform in front of door of church or other large building, ascended by steps. [F, f. L petra stone, see -OON]

pĕ'rrў, n. Drink from juice of pears fermented. [ME pereye f. OF pere f. Rom. *piratum f. L pirum PEAR, see -Y⁴]

pĕrse, a. & n. (arch.). Bluish-grey, bluish grey. [ME, f. OF pers, -e f. med. L persus, perh. f. Persia; cf. obs. inde INDIGO]

pĕrs'ĕc|ūte, v.t. Pursue with enmity and injury (esp. holder of opinion held to be heretical); harass, worry; importune (person with questions etc.). So ~ū'TION n. (~ution mania, insane delusion that one is ~uted), ~ūToR n. [ME, f. OF persecuter f. L PER(sequi secut- follow) pursue]

pĕrsĕvēr'|ance, n. Steadfast pursuit of an aim, constant persistence, so ~ANT a. (rare); (theol.) continuance in state of grace. [ME, f. OF f. L perseverantia (foll., -ANCE)]

pĕrsĕvēr|e', v.i. Continue steadfastly, persist, (in course, in doing, with task, or abs.). Hence ~'ĭngLY² adv. [ME, f. OF

persĕver'er f. L perseverare f. PER(severus SEVERE)]

Pĕr'sian (-shn), a. & n. (Inhabitant, language) of Persia, as ~ carpet, cat (with long silky hair & thick tail). [-AN]

pĕrsiĕnnes' (-nz), n. pl. Outside window blinds of light horizontal laths. [F, = Persian (fem. pl. adj.)]

pĕrs'iflage (-ahzh), n. Light raillery, banter. [F, f. persifler banter, see -AGE]

persimm'on, n. American date-plum, yellow fruit becoming sweet when softened by frost. [corrupt. of native name]

persist', v.i. Continue firmly or obstinately (in opinion, course, doing) esp. against remonstrance etc.; (of institutions, customs, etc.) continue in existence, survive. Hence or cogn. ~ENCE, ~ENCY, nn., ~ENT a. (esp., in zool. & bot., of horns, hair, leaves, etc.) permanent (opp. DECIDUOUS), ~entLY² adv. [f. L PER(sistere stand)]

pĕrs'on, n. 1. Individual human being; (derog.) who is this ~?; young ~, young man or (usu.) woman; living body of human being, as he had a fine ~, attracted by her fortune not her ~; acting, appearing, in his own (proper) ~ or in ~ (himself, personally); found a friend in (the ~ of) his landlord; (law) human being (natural ~) or body corporate (artificial ~) with recognized rights & duties; character in play or story. 2. The three ~s (modes of being) of the Godhead, Father, Son, Holy Spirit. 3. (gram.). Each of the three classes of personal pronouns etc. denoting respectively the ~ etc. speaking (first ~), spoken to (second ~), & spoken of (third ~). 4. (zool.). Individual of a compound or colonial organism. [ME, f. OF persone f. L persona player's mask, character in play, (LL) human being]

persōn'a, n. Person, as: ~ grāt'a, nŏn grāt'a, acceptable, unacceptable, person; IN⁵ prŏp'ria~. [L]

pĕrs'onable, a. Handsome, comely. [ME, f. OF, see PERSON, -ABLE]

pĕrs'onage, n. Person of rank or importance; person; character in play etc. [ME, f. OF, see PERSON, -AGE]

pĕrs'onal, a. & n. 1. One's own, individual, private, as to suit his ~ convenience, this is ~ to myself; done, made, etc., in person, as ~ service, acquaintance, interview; directed, referring, (esp. hostilely) to an individual, as ~ abuse, remarks; ~ (also AGONY) column, part of a newspaper devoted to short advertisements for a ~ or semi-~ nature; making, given to making, ~ remarks, as do not let us become~; (law) ~ property, estate, chattels or chattel interests in land, all property except land and those interests in land that pass to one's heir, (cf. REAL); (gram.) of, denoting, one of the three persons, esp. ~ pronouns. 2. n. (usu. pl.). *Newspaper paragraph relating to individual person(s). [ME, f. OF f. L personalis (PERSON, -AL)]

pḗrsonál′it|y̆, n. Being a person; personal existence or identity; distinctive personal character; person; (of remarks) fact of being aimed at an individual, (usu. pl.) such remark(s); (rare) = PERSONALTY; *multiple ~y* (psych.), the apparent existence of two or more distinct and alternating *~ies* in a single individual; *~y cult*, extreme adulation of the individual. [ME, f. OF *personalte* f. LL *personalitatem* (as prec., see -TY)]

pḗrs′onaliz|e, -is|e (-īz), v.t. Personify. Hence ~A′TION n. [PERSONAL + -IZE]

pḗrs′onall̆y̆, adv. In person, in one's own person, as *he conducted them ~, a ~- -conducted tour* (conducted by guide), *writ was served on them ~*; *a God existing ~* (as a person); for one's own part, as *~ I see no objection.* [-LY²]

pḗrs′onalt̆y̆, n. Personal estate. [f. AF *personalte* PERSONALITY]

pḗrs′onate¹, a. (bot.). Having the opening of the lips closed by upward projection of the lower, as in snapdragon. [f. L *personatus* masked (as foll., see -ATE²)]

pḗrs′on|āte², v.t. Play the part of (character in drama, also fig.); pretend to be (person) esp. for fraudulent purpose. Hence ~A′TION, ~āto̅R, nn. [f. LL *personare* (as PERSON), see -ATE³]

persŏnifĭcā′tion, n. Personifying; person, thing, viewed as striking example or embodiment *of* (quality etc.). [f. foll., see -FICATION]

persŏn′ify̆, v.t. Attribute personal nature to (abstraction); symbolize (quality) by figure in human form; embody (quality) in one's own person, exemplify typically, (esp. in p.p.). [f. F *personnifier*, see PERSON & -FY]

pḗrsonnĕl′, n. Body of persons engaged in some public service or in a factory, office, etc. (opp. MATÉRIEL). [F, = PERSON-AL, adj. as n.]

perspĕc′tive, n. & a. **1.** Art of delineating solid objects on plane surface so as to give same impression of relative positions, magnitudes, etc., as the actual objects do when viewed from particular point; picture so drawn; apparent relation between visible objects as to position, distance, etc.; *linear ~* (concerned with apparent form, magnitude, & position, of objects); (fig.) relation in which parts of subject are viewed by the mind; view, prospect, (lit. & fig.); *in* (drawn according to rules of) *~.* **2.** adj. Of, in, *~*, whence *~*LY² adv. [ME, f. med. L *perspectiva* (ars art) f. PER(*spicere spect-* look), see -IVE]

pḗrs′pĕx, n. Tough unsplinterable plastic material, much lighter than glass, used for transparent parts of aircraft etc. [P; f. L PER(*spicere spect-* look)]

perspĭcā′cious (-shus), a. Having mental penetration or discernment. Hence or cogn. *~*LY² adv., **perspĭcā′city** n. [f. L *perspicax* (as prec., see -ACIOUS)]

perspĭc′ŭous, a. Easily understood, clearly expressed; (of person) clear in expression. Hence or cogn. **pḗrspĭcū′ity**, *~*NESS, nn., *~*LY² adv. [f. L *perspicuus* (as prec.), +-OUS]

perspīr′able, a. Allowing the passage of perspiration; that can be thrown off in perspiration. [c. 1600, F (as foll., -ABLE)]

pḗrspīrā′tion, n. Sweating; sweat. So **perspīr′atoRy** a. [F (as foll., -ATION)]

perspīre′, v.i. & t. Sweat; (trans.) give off (liquid) through pores in form of vapour or moisture. [f. L PER(*spirare* breathe) breathe, (of wind) blow]

persuād|e′ (-sw-), v.t. Convince (person, one*self*, *of* fact, *that* thing is so); induce (person *to* do, *into* action); (p.p.) convinced (*of* thing, *that*). Hence or cogn. *~*′ABLE a., *~*′ER¹ n., **persuās′IBLE** a., **persuāsiBIL′ITY** n., (-sw-). [f. L PER-(*suadere suas-* advise)]

persua′sion (-swāzhn), n. Persuading; persuasiveness; conviction, as *it is my private ~ that he is mad*; religious belief; sect holding this, as *he is of the Roman Catholic ~*; (joc.) race, kind, sort, as *a man of the Jewish ~* (Jew), *no one of the male ~ was there.* [ME, f. OF, or L *persuasio* (as prec. see -ION)]

persuās′ive (-sw-), a. & n. Able to persuade, winning; (n.) motive, inducement. Hence *~*LY² adv., *~*NESS n. [f. med. L *persuasivus* (as PERSUADE, see -IVE)]

pḗrt, a. Forward, saucy, in speech or conduct. Hence *~*LY² adv., *~*′NESS n. [ME, aphetic f. *apert* f. OF f. L (1) *apertus* p.p. of *aperire* open (2) *expertus* EXPERT]

pertain′, v.i. Belong as part, appendage, or accessory, *to*; be appropriate *to*; have reference, relate, *to*. [ME, f. OF *partenir* f. L PER(*tinēre* = *tenēre* hold)]

pḗrtinā′cious (-shus), a. Stubborn, persistent, obstinate. Hence or cogn. *~*LY² adv., *~*NESS, **pḗrtinā′city**, nn. [f. L PER(*tinax* = *tenax* TENACIOUS)]

pḗrt′in|ent, a. & n. Pertaining, relevant, apposite, (*to* matter in hand etc.); to the point; ‖ (n., usu. pl.) appurtenance(s). Hence or cogn. *~*ENCE, *~*ENCY, nn., *~*entLY² adv. [ME, f. OF, or L as PER-TAIN, see -ENT]

perturb′, v.t. Throw into (physical) confusion; disturb mentally, agitate. So **pḗrturbā′TION** (-ter-) n., *~*atIVE (*or* pḗrt′erbāt-) a. [ME, f. OF, or L PER-(*turbare* disturb)]

peruke′ (-o̅o̅k), n. Wig. [f. F *perruque* f. It. *perruca, parrucca*, of unkn. orig.]

peruse′ (-o̅o̅z), v.t. Read thoroughly or carefully; read; (fig.) examine (person's face etc.) carefully. Hence **peru′sAL** (-o̅o̅zl) n. [late 15th c. (1) ‘ use up ’, f. PER- + USE; (2) ‘ go through ’, of obsc. hist.]

Peru′vian (-o̅o̅-), a. & n. **1.** Of Peru; *~ bark* (of CINCHONA tree). **2.** n. Native of Peru. [f. mod. L *Peruvia* Peru + -AN]

pervāde′, v.t. Spread through, permeate, saturate, (often fig. of influences etc.).

Hence or cogn. **pervā′sion** (-zhn), **per-vās′iveness**, nn., **pervās′ive** a., **per-vās′ively**[2] adv. [f. L PER(*vadere vas-* go)]

pervèrse′, a. Persistent in error; different from what is reasonable or required; wayward; peevish; perverted, wicked; (of verdict) against weight of evidence or judge's direction. Hence or cogn. ~LY[2] adv., ~NESS, **pervèrs′ity**, nn. [ME, f. OF *pervers, -e*, f. L *perversus* as foll.]

pervèrt′[1], v.t. Turn aside (thing) from its proper use; misconstrue, misapply, (words etc.); lead astray (person, mind) from right opinion or conduct or esp. religious belief. Hence or cogn. **pervèr′sion** (-shn) n., **pervèr′sive** a. [ME, f. OF *pervertir* or L PER(*vertere vers-* turn)]

pervèrt′[2], n. Perverted person, apostate; (psych.) person showing sexual perversion. [f. prec., cf. CONVERT[2]]

pervi′ous, a. Affording passage (*to*); permeable; (fig.) accessible (*to* reason etc.). Hence ~NESS n. [f. L PER(*vius* f. *via* way) +-OUS]

pese′ta (-sā-), n. Spanish silver coin and monetary unit. [Sp.]

Peshi′tō, -tta, (-shē-), n. Principal ancient Syriac version of O. & N.T. [f. Syriac *p'shīṭ(t)ā, -ô*, simple]

peshwa (pāsh′wah), n. (hist.). Hereditary sovereign (earlier, chief minister) of the Mahratta State. [Pers., = chief]

*****pes′ky**, a. (colloq.). Troublesome, confounded, annoying, plaguy. [orig. unkn.]

pe′sō (pā-), n. Silver coin used in most S.-Amer. republics. [Sp.]

pess′ary, n. (med.). Instrument worn in the vagina to prevent uterine displacements; vaginal suppository. [ME, f. LL *pessarium* f. LL *pessum, -us* f. Gk *pessos* oval stone]

pess′im|ism, n. Tendency to look at the worst aspect of things (cf. OPTIMISM); doctrine that this world is the worst possible, or that all things tend to evil. So ~IST n., ~is′tic a., ~is′tically adv. [f. L *pessimus* worst +-ISM]

pest, n. Troublesome or destructive person, animal, or thing; (now rare) pestilence; ~*-house*, hospital for plague etc. [f. F *peste* or L *pestis* plague]

pes′ter, v.t. Trouble, plague. [hist. obsc.; 16th c. 'entangle', 'crowd'; cf. later *em-, impester* f. F *empester*; mod. sense infl. by *pest*]

pestif′erous, a. Noxious, pestilential; (fig.) bearing moral contagion, pernicious. [f. L *pestifer, -ferus* (PEST, -FEROUS)]

pes′tilence, n. Any fatal epidemic disease, esp. bubonic plague. So **pěsti-lěn′tial** (-shl) a. [ME, f. OF, f. L *pestilentia* (as foll., see -ENCE)]

pes′tilent, a. Destructive to life, deadly; (fig.) injurious to morals etc.; (colloq.) troublesome, plaguy. Hence ~LY[2] adv. [f. L *pestilens* (also *-lentus*) f. *pestis* plague]

pě′stle (-sl), n., & v.t. & i. Club-shaped instrument for pounding substances in a mortar; kinds of appliance for pounding etc.; (v.t.) pound (as) with ~; (v.i.) use ~. [ME, f. OF *pestel* f. L *pistillum* (*pinsere pist-* pound)]

pěstŏl′ogy̆, n. Scientific study of pests (esp. harmful insects) & the methods of dealing with them. [f. L *pestis* PEST + -O- +-LOGY]

pet[1], n., & v.t. (-tt-). 1. Animal tamed & kept as favourite or treated with fondness; darling, favourite, (often attrib.); one's ~ *aversion*, what one specially dislikes; ~*-cock*, small stop-cock for draining, letting out steam, etc.; ~ *name*, one expressing fondness or familiarity. 2. v.t. Treat as a ~, fondle; *~ting party* (colloq.), social gathering of young people at which hugging, kissing, etc., are indulged in. [16th c. Sc. & north., orig. unkn.]

pet[2], n. Offence at being slighted, ill-humour, esp. *take* (usu. *the*) ~, *be in a* ~. [c. 1600, of unkn. orig.]

pet′al, n. Each of the divisions of the corolla of a flower. Hence ~INE (-ĭn), (-)~(l)ED[2] (-ld), ~OID, aa. [f. mod. L *petalum*; LL in sense thin plate, leaf, f. Gk (*pet-* spread)]

pet′alŏn, n. Gold plate on mitre of Jewish high priest. [as PETAL]

pétărd′, n. Small engine of war formerly used to blow in door etc.; kind of firework, cracker; HOIST[2] *with his own* ~. [f. F *pétard* (*péter* break wind ult. f. L *pedere*, see -ARD)]

pet′asus, n. Ancient Greek low-crowned broad-brimmed hat, esp. as worn by Hermes; winged hat of Hermes. [L, f. Gk *petasos*]

pétaur′ist (-tŏr-), n. Marsupial of the genus *Petaurista* with a patagium enabling it to take flying leaps. [f. L (*-ta*) f. Gk *petauristēs* performer on spring-board (*petauron*)]

Pet′er[1], n. A male Christian name; *St* ~, one of Christ's disciples; *rob* ~ *to pay Paul*, take away from one to give to another, discharge one debt by incurring another; BLUE ~; ~'*s fish*, haddock or other fish with marks supposed to have been made by St ~'s thumb & finger; ~*-penny*, ~'*s-penny* or *pence*, (hist.) annual tax of penny paid to papal see; (since 1860) voluntary payments to papal treasury. [f. L f. Gk *Petros* stone]

pet′er[2], v.i. (sl.). (Of stream, vein of ore, & fig.) ~ *out*, give out, come to an end. [orig. unkn.]

pet′ersham, n. Thick ribbed or corded silk ribbon; heavy overcoat or breeches formerly worn; cloth for these. [Viscount P~, *c.* 1812]

pet′iŏl|e, n. (bot.). Leaf-stalk. Hence ~AR[1], ~ATE[2](-āt), aa. [f. L *petiolus* little foot, stalk]

petit (petē′), a. (pl. ~*s* pr. petē′). ~ *four* (foor), small fancy biscuit; ~*s-chevaux* (shevō′), a gambling game; ~*-maître* (mā'tr), dandy, coxcomb; ~ *mal* (măl), mild form of epilepsy; ~ *souper* (sōōp'ā), informal supper for a few intimates; ~*s soins* (see Ap.), small attentions; ~ *verre* (vār), glass of liqueur. [F, = little]

petite (petēt'), a. (Of woman) of small dainty make. [F, fem. of prec.]

pěti'tio (-tīshĭō, -tĭtĭō), n. ~ *prĭncĭp'ĭi*, begging the question. [L, as foll.]

pěti'tion, n., & v.t. & i. **1.** Asking, supplication, request; formal written supplication from one or more persons to sovereign etc.; *P*~ *& Advice* (hist.), Parliament's remonstrance to Cromwell 1657; *P*~ *of Right* (hist.), parliamentary declaration of rights & liberties of the people assented to by Charles I in 1628; (law) kinds of formal written application to a court. **2.** v.t. Make ~ to (sovereign etc. *for* thing, *to* do). **3.** v.i. Ask humbly (*for* thing, *to* be allowed to do etc.). So ~ARY[1] (-sho-) a., ~ER[1] (-sho-) n. (esp., plaintiff in divorce suit). [ME, f. OF *petition* f. L *petitionem* (*petere* -*tit*- seek, see -ION)]

pět'rel, n. Kinds of oceanic bird spending nearly all their lives at sea; (also *storm*-~, *stormy* ~) small sea-bird with black & white plumage & long wings. [17th c. also *pitteral*, of uncert. orig.; later assoc. w. St *Peter* (-REL)]

pětrifăc'tion, n. Petrifying; petrified substance or mass. [irreg. f. foll., see -FACTION; reg. *petrification* is now rare]

pět'rif| y̆, v.t. & i. Convert into stone; (fig.) paralyse, stupefy, with astonishment, terror, etc. (~*ied with fear* etc.); deprive (mind, doctrine, etc.) of vitality, stiffen; (intr.) turn into stone (lit. & fig.). [f. F *pétrifier* f. L f. Gk *petra* rock, see -FY]

pět'ro-, comb. form of Gk *petra* rock, as: ~*glyph*, rock-carving; ~*graph*, rock-inscription; ~*graphy* (pĭtrŏg'-), scientific description of formation & composition of rocks, so ~*grapher* (pĭtrŏg'-) n., ~*graph*-*ic(al)* aa.; ~*logy* (pĭtrŏl'-), study of origin, structure, etc., of rocks, so ~*lo'gic(al)* aa., ~*lo'gically* adv., ~*logist* (pĭtrŏl'-) n.

‖ pět'rol, n. Refined petroleum as used in motor-cars, aircraft, etc. [f. F *pétrole* f. foll.]

pětrŏl'eum, n. Mineral oil found in upper strata of earth, used as fuel for heating & in internal-combustion engines. [med. L (L & Gk *petra* rock +L *oleum* oil)]

pétroleur (pātrŏlěr'), n. (fem. -*euse* pr. -ěrz). Incendiary who uses petroleum. [F]

pětrŏl'ic, a. Of petrol or petroleum. [-IC]

pět'ronel, n. (hist.). Large pistol used esp. by horse-soldiers in 16–17th cc. [f. F *petrinal*, dial. form of *poitrinal* (*poitrine* chest, ult. f. L *pectus* -*oris*, see -AL); the butt end rested against chest in firing]

pět'rous, a. Of, like, rock, esp. (anat.) applied to hard part of the temporal bone. [f. L *petrosus* (L & Gk *petra* rock, see -OUS)]

pětt'icoat, n. Woman's (under-)garment fastened round waist & hanging loose usu. inside a skirt (*have known him since he was in* ~*s*, a small child); *she is a Cromwell in* ~*s* (in all but sex); woman, girl, (pl.) female sex; (attrib.) feminine, esp. ~ *government*, predominance of woman in the home or in politics. Hence ~ED[2], ~LESS, aa. [orig. (15th c.) *petty coat*]

pětt'ifŏg, v.i. (-gg-). Practise legal chicanery; quibble, wrangle, about petty points. [app. back formation f. foll.]

pětt'ifŏgg|er (-g-), n. Inferior legal practitioner; rascally attorney; petty practitioner in any department. Hence ~ERY(4) n., ~ING[2] a., (-g-). [f. PETTY; -*fogger* unexpl.]

pětt'ish, a. Peevish, petulant, easily put out. Hence ~LY[2] adv., ~NESS n. [f. PET[2] + -ISH[1]]

pětt'itoes (-ōz), n. pl. Pig's trotters. [orig. giblets, f. F *petite oie* giblets of a goose, w. assim. to *petty*, *toes*]

pětt'ō, n. *In* ~, in one's own breast, in secret. [It., f. L *pectus*]

pětt'|y̆, a. Unimportant, trivial; little--minded; minor, inferior, on a small scale, as ~*y princes, farmers*; ~*y cash*, small cash items of receipt or expenditure; ~*y officer*, in navy corresponding in rank to N.C.O.; ~*y* JURY, LARCENY, ‖ SESSION. Hence ~ĬLY[2] adv., ~ĬNESS n. [late ME phonetic sp., after F pronunc., of orig. *petit* (f. OF)]

pět'ŭl|ant, a. Peevishly impatient or irritable. Hence or cogn. ~ANCE n., ~antLY[2] adv. [f. F *pétulant* f. L *petulantem* ult. f. *petere* seek, see -ANT]

pětŭn'ia, n. Plant with white, purple, or violet flowers of funnel shape; dark violet, purple, (esp. attrib.). [f. F *petun* f. S.-Amer. Guarani *pety* tobacco]

pětŭn'tsě (-ōōn-, -ŭn-), n. White earth used in China for making porcelain. [f. Chin. *pai-tun-ize* (*pai* white + *tun* stone + suf. -*ize*)]

pew, n., & v.t. Enclosed compartment or fixed bench with back in church; (colloq.) seat, as *find, take, a* ~; ~-*rent* (for ~ or seats in church); (v.t.) furnish with ~s, enclose in ~. Hence ~'AGE(4) n., ~'LESS a. [ME *puwe* f. OF *puye* balcony f. L *podia* pl. of *podium* f. Gk *podion* pedestal]

pewit, peewit, (pē'wĭt, pū'ĭt), n. Lapwing; its cry; ~ (*gull*), black-headed gull. [imit.]

pewt'er, n. Grey alloy of tin & lead or other metal; utensils of this; ~ pot; ‖ (sl.) prize-money. [ME & OF *peutre*, = It. *peltro*; orig. unkn.]

pfĕnn'ig, -ing, n. Small German copper coin 1/100 of a mark. [G, cogn. w. PENNY]

phā'éton (*or* fā'tn), n. Light four-wheeled open carriage usu. drawn by pair of horses. [F, f. Gk *Phaethōn*, son of Helios (Sun-god) and famous for bad driving of sun chariot]

phăgěd|aen'a, -d|ēn'a (-j-, -g-), n.

Spreading ulcer. So ~aen'IC, ~ĕn'IC, a. [L, f. Gk phagedaina (phag- eat)]

phăg'ocyte, n. Leucocyte capable of guarding the system against infection by absorbing microbes. [f. Gk phag- eat + -o- + -CYTE]

-phagous in comb. = Gk -phagos -eating + -OUS. So -phagy (Gk -phagia).

phăl'ănge (-j), n. See PHALANX.

phalăn'ğeal (-j-), a. (anat.). Of a phalanx. [-AL]

phalăn'ğer (-j-), n. Kinds of Australian marsupial of arboreal habits, e.g. flying squirrel or opossum. [mod. L (Buffon), f. Gk phalaggion spider's web (PHALANX), from webbed toes of hind feet]

phăl'anst|erȳ, n. (Buildings of) socialistic PHALANX. Hence ~ēr'IAN a. & n. [f. F phalanstère f. foll. after monastère]

phăl'ăn|x, n. (pl. ~xes, ~ges pr. -jĕz). 1. (Gk ant.) line of battle, esp. body of Macedonian infantry drawn up in close order. 2. Set of persons banded together for common purpose; socialistic community of about 1800 persons as proposed by Fourier. 3. (Anat., also ~ge) each bone of finger or toe; (bot.) bundle of stamens united by filaments. [L, f. Gk phalagx -ggos]

phăl'arope, n. Kinds of small wading and swimming bird noted for their tameness. [F, irreg. f. Gk phalaris coot + pous foot]

phăll'|us, n. (pl. ~i). Image of the penis, venerated in religious systems as symbolizing generative power in nature. Hence or cogn. ~IC a., ~(ĭc)ISM(3) nn. [LL, f. Gk phallos]

phană'riŏt, n. Resident in the Phanar quarter of Constantinople; member of the Greek official class under the Turks. [f. mod. Gk phanariōtēs (phanari lighthouse f. Gk phanarion, see -OT²)]

phăn'er|ogăm, n. (bot.). Plant that has stamens & pistils, flowering plant, (cf. CRYPTOGAM). So ~ogăm'IC, ~ŏg'amOUS, aa. [f. F phanérogame f. Gk phaneros visible + gamos marriage]

phăn'si̱gār, n. Thug. [Hind. (phansi noose)]

phăn'tăsm, n. Illusion, phantom; illusive likeness (of); (psychics) supposed vision of absent (living or dead) person. Hence **phăntăs'mAL**, **phăntăs'mIC**, aa., **phăntăs'malLY²** adv., (-z-). [ME fan- f. OF fantasme f. L f. Gk phantasma (phantazō make visible f. phainō show)]

phăntăsmağ|ŏr'ia (-z-), n. Exhibition of optical illusions in London in 1802; shifting scene of real or imagined figures. Hence ~ŏr'IC a. [f. prec. + (?) Gk agora assembly]

phăn'tasȳ. See FANTASY (the ph- form is used esp. for the first sense there given).

phăn'tom, n. Apparition, spectre; image (of); vain show, form without substance or reality; mental illusion; (attrib.) apparent, illusive, as ~ tumour, temporary swelling. [ME & OF fantosme PHANTASM]

Phār'aoh (-rō), n. Generic name of ancient Egyptian kings; ~'s serpent, chemical toy fusing in serpentine form. [f. LL f. Gk Pharaō ult. f. Egypt. pr'o great house]

Phă'risee, n. One of ancient Jewish sect distinguished by strict observance of traditional & written law & pretensions to sanctity; self-righteous person, formalist, hypocrite. Hence or cogn. **Phărisā'IC(AL)** aa., **Phărisā'icalLY²** adv., **Phă'risāism** n. [(a) OE fari-, phariscus, ME -sew; (b) ME, f. OF pharise; f. LL f. Gk Pharisaios ult. f. Heb. parush separated]

phărmaceut'|ical (-sū-, -kū-), a. Of, engaged in, pharmacy; of the use or sale of medicinal drugs. Hence or cogn. ~icalLY² adv., ~ICS n. [f. LL f. Gk pharmakeutikos (pharmakeutēs druggist f. pharmakon drug) + -AL]

phărmacŏl'og|ȳ, n. Science of action of drugs on body. Hence ~IST n. [f. Gk pharmakon drug + -LOGY]

phărmacopoe'|ia (-pēa), n. Book (esp. one officially published) containing list of drugs with directions for use; stock of drugs. Hence ~iAL (-pēal) a. [f. Gk pharmakopoiia (as prec. + -poiia making f. poieō make)]

phărm'acȳ, n. Preparation & (esp. medicinal) dispensing of drugs; drug-store, dispensary. [ME, f. OF farmacie f. med. L f. Gk pharmakeia practice of the druggist (pharmakeus f. pharmakon drug)]

phār'ŏs, n. Lighthouse or beacon to guide mariners. [L f. Gk Pharos, island off Alexandria, lighthouse on this]

pharȳng'o- (-ngg-) in comb. = foll., as: ~cēle, abnormal enlargement at base of pharynx; ~tomy (-ŏt-), incision into pharynx.

phă'rȳnx, n. Cavity, with enclosing muscles & mucous membrane, behind & communicating with nose, mouth, & larynx. Hence **pharȳng'AL** (-ngg-), **pharȳn'ğēAL** (-j-), aa., **phărȳnğIT'IS** (-j-) n. [f. Gk pharugx -ggos]

phāse (-z), n., & v.t. 1. Aspect of moon or planet, according to amount of illumination (esp. applied to new moon, first quarter, full moon, last quarter); stage of change or development; aspect (of situation or question); (phys.) particular stage in recurring sequence of movements or changes (esp. of alternating electric currents), usu. expressed in degrees, the complete sequence or period being 360°; three-~, (of electric generators, motors, etc.) designed to supply or use simultaneously three separate alternating currents of the same voltage, but having their periods 120° apart. 2. v.t. Carry out (programme etc.) in ~s or stages. Hence **phās'IC** (-z-) a. [f. Gk phasis appearance (phan- show), also in E w. pl. pron. -sĕz]

phea'sant (fĕz-), n. A game-bird naturalized in Britain & other parts of Europe;

~-*eyed*, (of flowers) marked like ~'s eye. [ME, f. AF *fesant* f. OF *fesan* f. L f. Gk *phasianus* (bird) of the river *Phasis* in Asia Minor]

phen(o)-, formative element f. Gk *phainein* to shine, in chem. names of substances derived from coal-tar (orig. in manufacture of illuminating gas), as: *phenǎ'cetin*, an antipyretic; *phēn'ol*, carbolic acid; *phěn'ȳl*, radical found in benzene, phenol, etc.

phěnŏl'ogȳ, n. Study of the times of recurring natural phenomena esp. in relation to climatic conditions. So **phěnolŏ'ģĭcal** a. [f. PHENOMENON +-LOGY]

phěnŏm'ěnal, a. Of the nature of a phenomenon; cognizable by, evidenced only by, the senses; concerned with phenomena; remarkable, prodigious. Hence ~LY[2] adv., ~IZE v.t., make, or represent as, ~. [-AL]

phěnŏm'ěn(al)|ism, n. Doctrine that phenomena are the only objects of knowledge. So ~IST n., ~**is'tic** a. [prec. +-ISM]

phěnŏm'ěnon, n. (pl. *-ena*). Thing that appears or is perceived, esp. thing the cause of which is in question; (philos.) that of which a sense or the mind directly takes note, immediate object of perception; remarkable person, thing, occurrence, etc. [f. LL f. Gk *phainomenon* neut. part. of *phainomai* appear]

phew, int. expr. impatience or disgust.

phī, n. Greek letter (Φ, ϕ) = ph. [Gk]

phī'al, n. Small glass bottle, esp. for liquid medicine. [ME, f. OF *fiole* f. LL *fiola* f. L f. Gk *phialē* broad flat vessel]

phil- in comb. = PHILO- before vowel or *h*. **-phil, -phile**, suf. forming nn. w. sense ' lover of ' & adjj. = ' -loving ', as *bibliophil(e)*, *Russophil(e)*, *gastrophil(e)*; repr. Gk *philos* dear, in Gk found as suf. only in personal names w. sense ' dear to ' (*Diphilos* dear to Zeus), the sense ' loving ' being given in Gk by PHILO-. Hence **-philous** adj. suf.

philan'der, v.i. Make love esp. in trifling manner, dangle after woman. Hence ~ER[1] n. [f. *philander* n. f. Gk PHIL(*andros* f. *anēr* man) prop.=fond of men, taken in sense ' lover ']

phil'anthrōpe, n. = PHILANTHROPIST. [f. Gk PHIL(*anthrōpos* man)]

philanthrŏp'|ic, a. Loving one's fellow men, benevolent, humane. Hence ~ICALLY adv. [f. F *philanthropique* (as prec., see -IC)]

philǎn'throp|ist, n. Lover of mankind; one who exerts himself for the well-being of his fellow men. So ~ISM n. [f. PHILANTHROPY +-IST]

philǎn'thropize, -ise (-īz), v.i. & t. Practise philanthropy; make (persons) objects of this; make philanthropic. [-IZE]

philǎn'thropȳ, n. Love, practical benevolence, towards mankind. [f. LL f. Gk *philanthrōpia* (as PHILANTHROPE)]

philǎt'el|ȳ, n. Stamp-collecting. Hence **philatěl'ic** a., ~IST n. [f. F PHIL(*atélie* f. Gk *ateleia* exemption from payment f. *a-* not +*telos* toll, tax)]

philharmŏn'ic (-lär-), a. & n. (Person) fond of music. [f. F PHIL(*harmonique* HARMONIC)]

phil'hellēne (-lel-), a. & n. (Person) loving or friendly to the Greeks or supporting the cause of Greek independence. So **philhellěn'ic** (-lel-) a., **philhěll'ěnism**, **philhěll'ěnist**, nn. [f. Gk PHIL(*ellēn* = *Hellēn* Greek)]

Philipp'ī. *Thou shalt see me at* ~, *meet at* ~, phrases threatening retribution (w. ref. to Shakesp., *J.C.*, IV. iii. 283). [battle at ~, 42 B.C.]

philipp'ic, n. (Pl.) orations of Demosthenes against Philip of Macedon, Cicero's orations against Antony; bitter invective. [f. L f. Gk *philippikos* (*Philippos* Philip, see -IC)]

philippi'na (-pē-), **-pine'** (-ēn), **philopoen'a** (-pē-), *-open'a, n. Almond or other nut with double kernel, the finding of which at dessert etc. & sharing it with another person involves the giving or receiving of a present at next meeting; the present; the custom. [perh. f. G *vielliebchen* darling (*viel* much +*liebchen* dim. of *lieb* dear)]

Phil'istīne, n. & a. 1. One of an alien warlike people in S. Palestine who harassed the Israelites; (joc.) enemy into whose hands one may fall, e.g. bailiff, critic, etc.; (in German univv., after G *philister*) non-student, outsider; uncultured person, one whose interests are material & commonplace, whence **phil'istinism** n. 2. adj. Uncultured, commonplace, prosaic. [f. F *Philistin* or LL f. Gk *Philistinos* =*Palaistinos* f. Assyr. *Palastu, Pilistu*]

phillum'ěnist (-lōō-, -lū-), n. Student or collector of match-box labels. [f. PHIL-, L *lumen* light, -IST]

philo-, comb. form (bef. vowel or *h, phil-*) of root phil- in Gk *philein* to love, *philos* friend, in wds f. Gk & mod. formations, as : ~*bib'lic*, fond of books ; ~*gȳnist* (-ŏj-), lover of women; *phil'omath*, lover of learning, esp. of mathematics ; ~*progen*_itive_, prolific, (phrenol.) loving one's offspring, whence ~*progen'itiveness* ; ~*tech'nic* (-těk-), fond of (esp. the industrial) arts.

philŏl'og|ȳ, n. Science of language; (now rare) love of learning & literature. Hence ~ER[1], **philolŏ'ģian**, ~IST, nn., **philolŏ'ģical** a., **philolŏ'ģicalLY**[2] adv., ~IZE(2) v.i. [f. F (*-ie*), & L f. Gk PHILO-(*logia* = -LOGY) love of learning]

Phil'omël, Philomēl'a, nn. (poet.). The nightingale. [f. F *philomèle* or L f. Gk PHILO(*mēla* f. *melos* song or *mēlon* apple), cap. *P* in reference to myth of ~ transformed into nightingale]

philop(o)en'a. See PHILIPPINA.

philos'opher, n. Lover of wisdom; *natural, moral,* ~, student of natural, moral, philosophy; one who regulates his life by the light of philosophy; one who shows philosophic calmness in trying circumstances; ~*s'* (not ~*'s*) *stone*, supreme object of alchemy, substance supposed to change other metals into gold or silver. [ME, f. AF var. of OF *philo-*, *filosofe* f. L f. Gk *philosophos* (as PHILOSOPHY)]

philosŏph'ic|(al), aa. Of, consonant with, philosophy; skilled in, devoted to, philosophy (often in titles of societies); wise; calm; temperate. Hence ~**aLLY²** adv. [f. LL *philosophicus* f. Gk as prec., see -IC]

philŏs'oph|ism, n. Philosophizing system (usu. derog., esp. of the French Encyclopaedists). So ~**IST** n. [f. F *philosophisme* (as PHILOSOPHER, see -ISM)]

philŏs'ophīze, -ise (-īz), v.i. & t. Play the philosopher; speculate, theorize; moralize; render philosophic. [as PHILOSOPHER + -IZE]

philŏs'ophў, n. Love of wisdom or knowledge, esp. that which deals with ultimate reality, or with the most general causes & principles of things; *natural* ~, study of natural objects & phenomena; *moral* ~, study of principles of human action or conduct; (w. pl.) philosophical system; system for conduct of life; serenity, resignation. [ME, f. OF *filosofie* f. L f. Gk PHILO(*sophia* wisdom f. *sophos* wise)]

phil'tre (-*ter*), **-ter**, n. Love-potion. [F (-*tre*), f. L f. Gk *philtron* f. *phileō* love]

phiz, n. (colloq.). Face; expression of face. [abbr. of PHYSIOGNOMY]

phleb|it'is, n. Inflammation of walls of vein. Hence ~**it'IC** a. [f. Gk as foll. + -ITIS]

phlĕb'o-, comb. form of Gk *phleps phlebos* vein, as: ~*lite*, ~*lith*, morbid calcareous concretion in vein, so ~*lit(h)'iç* a.

phlĕbŏt'om|īze, -ise (-īz), v.i. & t. Practise phlebotomy; bleed (person, part of body). So ~**IST** n. [f. F *phlébotomiser* (foll., -IZE)]

phlĕbŏt'omў, n. Blood-letting as medical operation. [ME, f. OF *flebotomie* f. LL f. Gk *phlebotomia* f. PHLEBO(*tomos* -cutter f. *temnō* cut)]

phlegm (flĕm), n. **1.** Thick viscid (semi-) fluid substance secreted by mucous membranes (formerly regarded as one of the four HUMOURS) esp. when morbid or excessive & discharged by cough etc., whence ~**Y²** (flĕm'ĭ) a. **2.** Coolness, sluggishness, apathy, (supposed to result from predominance of ~ in constitution), so **phlĕgmăt'IC** a., **phlĕgmăt'ICALLY** adv. [ME & OF *fleume*, *fleme* f. LL f. Gk *phlegma* -*atos* heat, phlegm (*phlegō* burn)]

phlĕg'mon, n. Inflammatory tumour, boil. Hence **phlĕgmŏn'IC**, ~**OUS**, aa. [f. L, f. Gk *phlegmonē* (*phlegō* burn)]

phlŏ'ĕm, n. (bot.). Bast with associated tissues. [f. Gk *phloos* bark + -*ēma*]

phlogĭs'tic (-j-, -g-), a. Of phlogiston; (med.) inflammatory. [-IC]

phlogĭs'ton (-j-, -g-), n. Principle of inflammability formerly supposed to exist in combustible bodies. [Gk, f. *phlogizō* set on fire (*phlox phlogos* flame, see -IZE)]

phloriz'in (*or* flō'rĭ-), n. (chem.). Bitter substance got from bark of root of apple & other trees. [f. Gk *phloos* bark + *rhiza* root + -IN]

Phlŏx, n. Genus of plants with clusters of flowers of various colours. [L f. Gk *phlox* (lit. flame), a plant]

-phōbe, suf. forming aa. & nn., = -fearing, -fearer, f. F -*phobe* f. L f. Gk -*phobos*, adj. suf. f. *phobos* fear, as in *hydro*~, *Anglo*~, *Russo*~.

phŏb'ia, n. (Morbid) fear or aversion. [foll. used as a separate wd]

-phōb'ia, suf. f. L f. Gk -*phobia*, forming abstract nn. f. adjj. in -PHOBE, as *hydro*~, *Anglo*~, *xeno*~.

Phoeb'us (fēb-), n. The Greek sun-god; (poet.) the sun. [L, f. Gk *Phoibos*]

Phoenician (fēnĭsh'n), a. & n. (Inhabitant) of Phoenicia (ancient name for part of coast of Syria) or its colonies; Carthaginian. [ME, f. OF *phenicien* f. LL *Phoenicia* f. L f. Gk *Phoinikē* + -AN]

phoen'ix (fē-), **phē-**, n. (Myth.) bird, the only one of its kind, that after living five or six centuries in Arabian desert burnt itself on funeral pile & rose from the ashes with renewed youth to live through another cycle; paragon. [ME & OF *fenix* f. L f. Gk *phoinix* Phoenician, purple, phoenix; OE dir. f. L]

phŏn, n. (phys.). Unit of loudness used in measuring intensity of sounds. [f. Gk *phōnē* voice]

phōn'|āte, v.i. Utter vocal sound (usu. opp. to *articulate*). Hence **phonA'TION** n., ~**atORY** a. [f. Gk *phōnē* voice + -ATE³]

phonaut'ŏgraph (-ahf), n. Apparatus for automatically recording vibrations of sound. [as prec. + AUTO- + -GRAPH]

phōne¹, n., & v.i. & t. (colloq.). Telephone.

phōne², n. Simple vowel or consonant sound. [f. Gk *phōnē* voice]

phōn'ēme, n. (philol.). A unit of significant sound in a given language. Hence **phōnēm'IC** a. [f. F -*ème* f. Gk *phōnēma* sound]

phonĕn'doscōpe, n. Apparatus for making small sounds (esp. in human body) distinctly audible. [as PHONE² + Gk *endon* within + -SCOPE]

phonĕt'ic, a. & n. **1.** Representing vocal sounds, esp. (of systems of spelling) using always same symbol for same sound, whence ~**ISM**, ~**IST**, nn., ~**IZE**(3) v.t.; of vocal sounds. **2.** n. pl. (Study of) ~ phenomena of a language. Hence **phonĕt'ICALLY** adv., **phōnĕti'CIAN** (-ĭshn) n. [f. Gk *phōnētikos* (*phōneō* speak, see -ETIC)]

phŏn'ĕtist, n. Person versed in phonetics; advocate of phonetic spelling. [-IST]

***phŏn'ey, -ў**, a. (sl.). Sham, counterfeit, fictitious. [orig. unkn.]

phŏn′ĭc, a. Of sound, acoustic; of vocal sounds. [f. Gk *phōnē* voice + -IC]

phōn′o-, comb. form of Gk *phōnē* sound, used in many modern technical terms, as: ~*lite*, kinds of volcanic rock ringing when struck; *phonŏl′ogy*, science of vocal sounds, system of sounds in a language, so ~*lo′gic(al)* aa., ~*lo′gically* adv., *phonŏl′ogist* n.; *phonŏm′eter*, instrument recording number or force of sound-waves; ~*pŏre*, apparatus for transmitting telephone messages along telegraph wire without interfering with the current transmitting telegraph messages [Gk *poros* passage], so ~*pŏ′ric* a.; ~*scope*, apparatus for testing musical strings, (also) instrument for representing sound-vibrations in visible form; ~*type*, phonetic print, character used in this, so ~*tȳp′ic(al)* aa., ~*tȳpist*, ~*tȳpy*, nn.

phōn′ŏgram, n. Symbol representing spoken sound, esp. in Pitman's phonography; sound-record made by phonograph. [PHONO- + -GRAM]

phōn′ŏgraph (-ahf), n., & v.t. ‖ Earlier form of gramophone using cylinders; *gramophone*; (v.t.) record, reproduce, by ~. [PHONO- + -GRAPH]

phonŏg′raph|ȳ, n. Pitman's phonetic shorthand, whence ~ER[1], ~IST, nn.; automatic recording of sounds, as by phonograph. Hence **phōnŏgráph′IC** a., **phōnŏgráph′ICALLY** adv. [PHONO- + -GRAPHY]

-phŏre, suf. = bearer, f. Gk *-phoros* (*pherō* bear), used to form technical wds, as *carpophore*, *semaphore*. Hence **-phorous**, adj. suf., = *-phore* + -OUS, synonymous w. -FEROUS, but prop. used only in wds f. Gk as *carpophorous*.

phŏrm′ium, n. (Kinds of) liliaceous plant whose fibre is used commercially; New Zealand flax. [f. Gk *phormion* a species of plant]

phŏs′gēne, n. A poison gas, carbon oxychloride, used in the 1914–18 war. [f. Gk *phŏs* light + -GEN(1), w. ref. to its orig. production by action of sunlight on chlorine & carbonic oxide]

phŏs′phate, n. A salt of phosphoric acid, esp. (pl.) of lime or iron & alumina as constituents of cereals etc. Hence **phŏsphăt′IC** a. [F (PHOSPHO- + -ATE[1])]

phŏs′phēne, n. Appearance of rings of light produced by pressure on eyeball, due to irritation of retina. [irreg. f. Gk *phŏs* light + *phainō* show]

phŏs′phide, n. (chem.). Combination of phosphorus with other element or radical. [f. PHOSPHO- + -IDE]

phŏs′phine (-ēn), n. A colourless ill-smelling gas, a hydride of phosphorus, a compound having the structure of an amine, with phosphorus in place of nitrogen. Hence **phŏsphin′IC** a. [f. PHOSPHO- + -INE[5]]

phŏs′phite, n. (chem.). A salt of phosphorous acid. [F (PHOSPHO- + -ITE[1])]

phosph(o)- in comb. = PHOSPHORUS.

phŏs′phorāte, v.t. Combine, impregnate, with phosphorus. [-ATE[3]]

phŏs′phor-brŏnze, n. Tough hard bronze alloy containing a small proportion of phosphorus, used (esp.) for bearings. [PHOSPHORUS]

phŏsphor|ĕsce′, v.i. Emit luminosity without combustion, or by gentle combustion without sensible heat. So ~ĕs′CENCE n., ~ĕs′CENT a. [f. PHOSPHORUS + L *-escere* of inceptive vbs]

phŏs′phorīte, n. A non-crystallized variety of phosphate of lime. [f. PHOSPHORUS + -ITE[1]]

phŏs′phor|o- in comb. = phosphorus, as: ~*ogĕn′ic*, causing ~escence; ~*ograph*, evanescent picture on ~escent surface, so ~*ograph′ic* a., ~*ŏg′raphy* n.; ~*oscŏpe*, apparatus for measuring duration of ~escence, (also) toy containing various ~escent substances glowing with different coloured lights.

phŏs′phor|us, n. A non-metallic element, a yellowish wax-like substance undergoing slow combustion at ordinary temperatures & hence appearing luminous in the dark; ~*us necrŏs′is* (colloq. *phossy jaw*), gangrene of jawbone due to ~*us* fumes esp. in match-making. Hence or cogn. **phŏsphŏ′rIC**, ~OUS, aa., ~ISM(5) n. (path.). [L, = morning star, f. Gk *phŏs-phoros* (*phŏs* light + *-phoros* -bringing)]

phŏss′ȳ. See PHOSPHORUS.

phŏt′ism, n. Hallucinatory sensation or vision of light. [f. Gk *phŏtismos* (*phŏtizō* shine f. *phŏs phŏtos* light, see -ISM)]

phŏt′ō, n. (pl. ~*s*), & v.t. = PHOTOGRAPH; ~ *finish*, close finish of horse-race photographed to enable judge to decide winner or placed horses.

phŏt′o-, comb. form of Gk *phŏs phŏtos* light (occas. = photographic), as: ~*chromy* (-krō-), colour-photography; ~*-electric* a., marked by or utilizing emission of electrons from solid, liquid, or gaseous bodies when exposed to light of suitable wave-lengths; ~*-electric cell*, cell or vacuum-tube that uses the ~-electric effect to produce an electric current; ~*-electricity* n.; ~*gen*, kind of paraffin oil; ~*gĕn′ic*, producing or emitting light, (also) suitable for being photographed; ~*glyph*, ~*glyphy*, engraved plate produced by action of light, art of producing such plates; *photŏm′eter*, instrument for measuring intensity of light, so ~*met′ric*, ~*photŏm′etry*; ~*mic′rograph*, photograph of object as enlarged under the microscope; ~*phŏb′ia* (path.), dread of light; ~*phone*, apparatus in which sounds are transmitted by light; ~*sphere*, luminous envelope of sun or star from which its light & heat radiate, so ~*sphĕ′ric* a.; ~*stăt* (P), apparatus for making direct facsimile reproductions of documents, drawings, etc., a reproduction so made; ~SYN′THESIS, process by which the energy of sunlight is trapped by the chlorophyll of green plants and used to build up complex materials from carbon dioxide and water; ~*teleg'raphy*, electric reproduction of pictures, writing, etc., at a distance (cf. TELEPHOTOGRAPHY); ~*type*, plate for printing from produced by photographic process, picture etc. printed from this; ~*zincog'raphy*, photographic production of design on zinc plate.

phot'ograph (-ahf), n., & v.t. **1.** Picture, likeness, taken by means of chemical action of light on sensitive film on basis of glass, paper, metal, etc. **2.** v.t. Take~ of (person etc., or abs.); (quasi-pass.) *I always ~ badly* (come out badly in ~). Hence **photog'raph**ER[1], **photog'raph**Y[1], nn., **photograph'ic** a., **photograph'ic**-ALLY adv. [PHOTO-+-GRAPH]

photogravure', n., & v.t. **1.** Picture produced from photographic negative transferred to metal plate & etched in; this process. **2.** v.t. Reproduce thus. [F (PHOTO-+*gravure* engraving)]

phrase (-z), n., & v.t. **1.** Mode of expression, diction, as *in simple ~, felicity of~*; an idiomatic expression; small group of words usu. without predicate, esp. preposition with the word(s) it governs, equivalent to adjective, adverb, or noun (e.g. the house *on the hill*, I refuse *to do it*); short pithy expression; (pl.) mere words, as *we have had enough of ~s*; (mus.) short & more or less independent passage forming part of longer passage or of whole piece; ~*-monger*, person addicted to fine-sounding~s. **2.** v.t. Express in words, as *thus he ~d it*. [f. L f. Gk *phrasis* (*phrazo* declare, tell)]

phras'eogram, n. Written symbol representing a phrase esp. in shorthand. [as prec.+-o-+-GRAM]

phras'eograph (-ahf), n. Phrase for which there is a phraseogram. [as PHRASE+-o-+-GRAPH].

phrase|ol'ogy, n. Choice or arrangement of words; mode of expression. Hence ~olo'gICAL a., ~olo'gicalLY[2] adv. [as PHRASE+-o-+-LOGY]

phrat'ry, n. (Gk hist.) a kinship unit, esp. (in Athens) each of three sub-divisions of the (*phyle* or) tribe; tribal division among primitive races. [ME, f. Gk *phratria* (*phrater*, *-tor*, clansman, cogn. w. BROTHER)]

phrenet'ic, a. Frantic; fanatic. [ME, f. OF *frenetike* f. L f. Gk *phrenitikos* (*phrenitis* delirium, as foll., see -ITIS & -IC)]

phren'ic, a. (anat.). Of the diaphragm. [f. mod. L *phrenicus* or F *phrénique* f. Gk *phren phrenos* diaphragm, mind, see -IC]

phrenol'og|y, n. Study of external conformation of cranium as index to development & position of organs belonging to the various mental faculties. Hence **phrenolo'g**ICAL a., **phrenolo'g**icalLY[2] adv., ~IST n. [as prec.+-LOGY]

phron'tistery, n. (joc.). Place for thinking in, thinkery. [f. Gk *phrontisterion* (*phrontizo* think f. *phrontis* thought)]

Phry'gian, a. Of Phrygia, ancient country in Asia Minor; (mus.) ~ *mode*, ancient Greek MODE reputedly warlike in character, third of eccl. modes with E as final & C as dominant; ~ *cap*, ancient conical peaked cap now identified with cap of liberty. [f. L *Phrygianus* (*Phrygia*, see -AN)]

phthis'is (th-, fth-), n. Progressive wasting disease, esp. pulmonary consumption. So (through OF *tisike*) **phthis'ical** (tiz-, fthiz-) a., of, having, ~. [L f. Gk (*phthino* decay)]

phut, 'n. & adv. The sound of a bladder collapsing, a bullet passing, etc.; (adv., esp.) *go ~*, collapse (also fig. of scheme etc.). [f. Hind. *phatna* to burst]

phylac'ter|y, n. Small leather box containing Hebrew texts on vellum, worn by Jews to remind them to keep the law (*make broad* one's ~*y* or ~*ies*, make a display of righteousness); (usu. ostentatious) religious observance; amulet, charm. [ME, f. LL f. Gk *phulakterion* amulet (*phulasso* guard)]

phylet'ic, a. (biol.). Of a phylum, racial. [f. Gk *phuletikos* (*phuletes* tribesman f. *phule* tribe, see -IC)]

phyll|o-, comb. form of Gk *phullon* leaf, as: ~*oph'agan*, animal that feeds on leaves, so ~*oph'agous* a.; ~*opod* a. & n., leaf-footed (crustacean); ~*ostome*, leaf-nosed bat; ~*otax'is*, arrangement of leaves on axis or stem; ~*oxer'a* [f. Gk *xeros* dry], kinds of plant-lice, vine-pest.

phylo-, comb. form of Gk *phulon* race, tribe, in biol. wds, as: ~*gen'esis*, ~*geny* (oj-), racial evolution of animal or plant type, history of this, so ~*genet'ic*, ~*gen'ic*, aa., ~*genet'ically* adv.

phyl'um, n. (biol.; pl. *-la*). Division of animal kingdom containing classes of animals. [mod. L f. Gk *phulon* race]

phys'ic (-z-), n., & v.t. (-ck-). **1.** Art of healing; medical profession; (colloq.) medicine, as *a dose of ~.* **2.** pl. (usu. treated as sing.). Sciences treating of properties of matter & energy or of action of different forms of energy on matter in general (excluding chemistry & biology). **3.** v.t. Dose with ~ (lit. & fig.). [ME, f. OF *fisique* f. L f. Gk *phusike* (*episteme* knowledge) of nature (*phusis*, see -IC)]

phys'ical (-z-), a. Of matter, material, as ~ *force* (opp. to *moral*); of, according to laws of, natural philosophy, as ~ *explanations of miracles, a ~ impossibility*; belonging to physics; bodily, as ~ *exercise, strength, beauty, training* (also sl. ~ *jerks*); ~ *geography* (dealing with natural features). Hence ~LY[2] adv., **phys'ico**-comb. form. [f. med. L *physicalis* (as prec., see -AL)]

physi'cian (-zishn), n. One who practises

the healing art including medicine & surgery; one legally qualified in medicine as well as in surgery; (fig.) healer. [ME & OF *fisicien* (as PHYSIC, see -ICIAN)]

phys'ic|ist (-z-), n. Person skilled in physics or natural science in general; believer in the material origin of vital phenomena (cf. VITALIST), so ~ISM n. [PHYSIC + -IST]

phys'icky (-z-), a. Suggestive of physic. [-Y²]

physi|o- (-z-), comb. form of Gk *phusis* nature, as: ~ŏc'racy, government according to natural order; *phys'iocrat*, advocate of this, esp. member of Quesnay's school in France in 18th c.; ~ŏ'geny, genesis of vital functions; ~ŏl'atry, nature-worship; ~othĕ'rapy, treatment of disease by physical agencies, not by drugs; ~othĕ'rapist, person skilled in this.

physiogn'om|y (-zĭŏn-, -zĭŏgn-), n. Art of judging character from features of face or form of body, whence ~IST(3) n.; cast of features, type of face; (vulg.) face; external features of country etc.; characteristic (moral or other) aspect. Hence or cogn. **physiognŏm'ic(AL)** aa., **physiognŏm'icalLY²** adv., (-zĭŏn-, -zĭŏgn-). [ME *fisnomie* etc. f. OF *fiz-*, *phisnomie* f. med. L *phisionomia* f. Gk *phusiognōmonia* judging of a man's nature (by his features) f. *phusis* nature + *gnōmōn* judge f. *gnō-* know]

physiŏg'raph|y (-z-), n. Description of nature, of natural phenomena, or of a class of objects; physical geography. Hence ~ER¹ n., **physiŏgrăph'ic(AL)** aa. [PHYSIO- + -GRAPHY]

physiŏl'og|y (-z-), n. Science of normal functions & phenomena of living things (comprising *animal* & *vegetable* ~y). Hence or cogn. **physiolŏ'gic(AL)** aa., **physiolŏ'gicalLY²** adv., ~IST n. [f. F (-*ie*), or L f. Gk *phusiologia*, see PHYSIO- & -LOGY]

physique' (-zēk), n. Bodily structure, organization, & development. [F, n. f. adj. (as PHYSIC)]

-phyte, suf. repr. Gk *phuton* plant, denoting a vegetable organism, as *proto~*, *sapro~*. See also ZOOPHYTE.

phyt|o-, comb. form of Gk *phuton* plant, as: ~ogen'esis, ~ŏ'geny, generation or evolution of plants; ~ŏg'raphy, descriptive botany; *phyt'omer*, plant unit; ~ŏph'agous, feeding on plants; ~ŏt'omy, dissection of plants; ~ozŏ'on (pl. *-zo'a*), plant-like animal or zoophyte.

pi¹, n. Greek letter p (*Π*, *π*), esp. (math., *π*) as symbol of ratio of circumference to diameter (approx. 3·14159). [f. Gk *p(eriphereia)* PERIPHERY]

|| **pi²**, a. (school sl.). = PIOUS; *pi jaw*, sermonizing, moral lecture. [abbr.]

piăc'ular, a. Expiatory. [f. L *piacularis* (*piaculum* expiation f. *piare* appease, see -AR¹)]

piăffe', v.i. (Of horse etc.) move as in trot, but slower. [f. F *piaffer*, to strut]

piăff'er, n. Movement of piaffing. [as prec.]

pi'a măt'er, n. (anat.). Innermost MENINX. [med. L transl. of Arab. *umm raqiqah* tender mother]

pianĕtte' (pĕa-), n. Low pianino. [PIANO², -ETTE]

piani'nō (pĕanē-), n. (pl. ~s). Small upright piano. [It., dim. of PIANO²]

pianĭss'imō, adv. & n. (mus.). (Passage to be played) very softly. [It., superl. of PIANO¹]

pi'anist (pĕa-), n. Player on piano. [f. F *pianiste* (also in E, usu. as fem.), see -IST]

pia'nō¹ (-ah-), adv. & n. (mus.). (Passage to be played) softly; (fig.)· subdued(ly). [It., f. L *planus* flat]

piăn'ō², n. (pl. ~s). Musical instrument with metal strings struck by hammers worked by levers from a keyboard (vibration being stopped by dampers), & with pedals regulating character of tone; *grand* ~, large horizontal ~ of full tone; *upright* ~, vertical ~; *cottage* ~, small upright ~; ~ *organ*, mechanical ~ constructed like barrel-organ; ~-*player*, contrivance for playing~ mechanically. [It., earlier *piano e forte* soft & strong]

piănofŏrt'è (or piăn'ofŏrt), n. (Full name, now in formal use only, for) PIANO².

pianŏl'a (pĕa-), n. Kind of mechanical piano-player. [P]

piăs'tre (-ter), -ter, n. Spanish silver coin; small Turkish & Egyptian coin. [F (-*tre*), f. It. *piastra*, ult. as PLASTER]

piăzz'a (-tza), n. Public square or market-place esp. in Italian town; *veranda of house. [It., ult. f. L *platea* f. Gk *plateia* (*h..los*) broad (street)]

pibroch (pē'brŏχ), n. Series of variations on a theme for bagpipe, chiefly martial. [f. Gael. *piobaireachd* (*piobair* piper f. *piob* f. E PIPE)]

pic'a, n. Size of TYPE¹. [hist. obsc.; in late 15th c., a collection of rules about Easter & other movable feasts, in med. (Anglo-) L *pica*, in ME *pie*, *pye*, then identified w. L *pica* PIE¹]

pic'adŏr, n. Mounted man with lance in bull-fight. [Sp. (*picar* prick)]

pic'amăr, n. Bitter oil got from wood-tar. [f. L *pix picis* pitch + *amarus* bitter]

picarĕsque' (-k), a. (Of a style of fiction) dealing with adventures of rogues. [F, f. Sp. *picaresco* (*picaro* rogue, -ESQUE)]

picarōŏn', n., & v.i. Rogue; thief; pirate; pirate ship; (v.i.) play the pirate or brigand. [f. Sp. *picaron* (as prec., see -OON)]

***picayune'** (-yōōn), n. & a. 1. Small coin, esp. 5-cent piece; (colloq.) insignificant person or thing. 2. adj. Mean, contemptible. [in Louisiana, f..F *picaillon* f. Pr. *picaioun*]

picc'alilli, n. Pickle of chopped vegetables & hot spices. [18th c., orig. unkn.]

picc'aninný, **pick'-**, n. & a. Child, esp. of Negroes or S.-African or Australian

,natives; (adj.) very small, baby. [f. Sp. *pequeño* or Port. *pequeno*, dim. *-nino*, small]

picc'olō, n. (pl. ~s). Small flute, octave higher than the ordinary. [It., = small (flute)]

pice, n. Pakistani coin. [f. Hind. *paisa*]

pichiciāg'ō, n. Small burrowing animal of Chili, allied to armadillos. [f. Sp. *pichiciego* perh. f. native *pichey* + Sp. *ciego* blind f. L *caecus*]

pick¹, n. Tool consisting of iron bar usu. curved with point at one end & point or chisel-edge at other, with wooden handle passing through middle perpendicularly, used for breaking up hard ground etc., and for getting coal; instrument for picking; TOOTH~. [ME *pic, pykk,* app. collateral form of PIKE¹]

pick², v.t. & i. **1.** Break surface of (ground etc.) with or as with pick; make (hole etc.) thus; (fig.) ~ HOLES *in.* **2.** Probe (teeth etc.) with pointed instrument to remove extraneous matter. **3.** Clear (bone, carcass) of adherent flesh; pluck, gather, (flower, fruit, etc.) from stalk etc. **4.** (Of birds) take up (grains etc.) in bill; (of persons) eat (food, or meal, or abs.) in small bits, (colloq.) eat (t. & i.). **5.** Select carefully, as ~ one's *words, way, steps*; ~ *& choose,* select fastidiously; ~ (contrive) *a quarrel with.* **6.** ~ (person's) *brains,* extract his ideas for one's own use; ~ (person's) *pocket,* steal its contents; (intr.) ~ *& steal,* pilfer; ~ *a lock,* open it (esp. with intent to rob) with pointed instrument, skeleton key, etc. **7.** Pull asunder, esp. ~ *oakum;* ~ *to pieces,* pull asunder, (fig.) criticize (person etc.) hostilely. **8.** *~ at,* nag at, gird at; ~ *off,* pluck off, (also) shoot (persons etc.) deliberately one by one; *~ on,* = ~ *at;* ~ *out,* select, distinguish from surrounding objects, relieve (ground colour *with* another), make out (meaning of passage etc.), play (tune) by ear on piano etc.; ~ *up,* break up (ground etc.) with pick, lay hold of & take up, (golf, ellipt.) ~ up one's ball, raise one*self* from a fall etc., gain, acquire (livelihood, profit, tricks, information), succeed in seeing or hearing with searchlight, radio, etc., take (person, or thing overtaken) along with one, esp. *train stops to ~ up passengers,* make acquaintance of (person) casually (~*-up* n., such person), regain (lost path etc., *flesh, spirit*), (intr.) recover health, make acquaintance *with,* (of motor engine) accelerate *quickly* etc., (games) select sides by alternate choosing (~*-up* n., game between such sides). **9.** ~*'lock,* person who ~s locks, instrument used for this; ~*'me-up,* stimulating drink after previous depression (also fig.); ~*'pocket,* one who steals from pockets; ‖~*'thank* (arch.), sycophant; ~*-up,* ~ing up (esp. of ball in cricket), device replacing sound--box in a gramophone & enabling a record to be heard through a loud-speaker. [hist.

obsc.; ME *piken, pikken* (rel. to OE *pic(i)an*) prob. infl. by MLG, MDu. *pikken* to pick, peck; cf. PICK¹, PIKE¹]

pick³, n. Picking; selection; *the* best part *of* (*the* ~ *of the bunch,* best of the lot). [f. prec.]

pick'-a-băck, adv. On shoulders or back like a bundle (of the way person or thing is carried). [orig. & form uncert.]

pick'ăx(e), n., & v.t. & i. = PICK¹; (v.t.) break (ground etc.) with ~; (v.i.) work with ~. [ME & OF *picois* rel. to OF *pic* PIKE¹, assim. to AXE]

pick'elhaube (-howbe), n. German spiked helmet. [G, = spike cap]

pick'er, n. One who picks, gathers, or collects, as *hop, rag,* ~; kinds of instrument for picking (in var. senses). [-ER¹]

pick'erel, n. Young pike. [PIKE¹, -REL]

pick'ĕt, n., & v.t. & i. **1.** Pointed stake or peg driven into ground to form palisade, tether horse, etc.; (stake with pointed top on which person stood as) form of military punishment (hist.). **2.** (mil.). (Also *piquet, picquet*) small body of troops sent out (*outlying* ~) to watch for enemy, or (*inlying* ~) held ready in quarters, party of sentries, outpost; (in mod. use, chiefly) camp-guard doing police duty in garrison town etc. **3.** (Usu. pl.) men stationed in a body or singly by trade union to dissuade men from work during strike etc. **4.** vb. Secure (place) with stakes, tether; post (men) as ~; beset (workmen) with ~s; act as ~. [f. F *piquet* pointed stake f. *piquer* prick, see -ET¹]

pick'ing, n. In vbl senses, esp.: ~ *& stealing;* (pl.) gleanings, remaining scraps; (pl.) perquisites, pilferings. [-ING¹]

pic'kle, n., & v.t. **1.** Brine, vinegar, or similar liquor in which flesh, vegetables, etc., are preserved; ROD *in* ~; food, esp. (pl.) vegetables preserved in ~; acid solution for cleaning purposes etc.; *sad, sorry, nice,* etc. ~ (plight); mischievous child. **2.** v.t. Preserve in ~ (esp. in p.p.), treat with ~; (naut.) rub salt or vinegar on (person's back) after flogging; ~*d* (sl.), drunk. [ME *pekille, pykyl,* f. MDu., MLG *pekel;* so MDu., MLG *pekelen* vb]

Pickwick'ian, a. (joc.). (Of words) *used in a* ~ (technical, constructive, or esoteric) *sense.* [see Dickens *Pickwick* ch. i]

pic'nic, n., & v.i. (-ck-). **1.** Pleasure party including meal out of doors; (colloq.) something specially agreeable or easily accomplished (*no* ~, not an easy job). **2.** v.i. Take part in ~. Hence ~KER¹ n., ~KY² a. (colloq.). [18th c., f. F *piquenique*]

picot' (-kō), n. Small loop of twisted thread in edging to lace etc. [F, dim. of *pic* peak, point]

picotee', n. Carnation of which flowers have light ground with darker edging to petals. [f. F *picoté* p.p. of *picoter* prick, as prec.]

picquet. See PICKET.

pic′ric, a. ~ *acid*, yellow very bitter substance used in dyeing & surgery, & in explosives. [f. Gk *pikros* bitter +-IC]

Pict, n. One of an ancient people in N. Britain. Hence **Pic′tish**[1] a. [ME, f. LL *Picti* perh. f. *pingere pict-* paint]

pic′tograph (-ahf), n. Pictorial symbol; primitive record consisting of these. Hence **pictogräph′ic** a., **pictŏg′raphy**[1] n. [f. L *pingere pict-* paint +-GRAPH]

pictōr′ial, a. & n. **1.** Of, expressed in, picture(s); illustrated; picturesque. **2.** n. Journal of which pictures are main feature. Hence ~LY[2] adv. [f. LL *pictorius* (*pictor* painter, as foll.) +-AL]

pic′ture, n., & v.t. **1.** Painting, drawing, of objects esp. as work of art; portrait; cinematograph film; beautiful object, as *her hat is a* ~; scene, total visual impression produced, (fig.) conjuncture or affair (*out of, come into, the* ~, irrelevant, become interesting etc.); *she looks the very* ~ (a perfect type) *of health*. **2.** ~-*book* (consisting chiefly or wholly of ~s); ~-*card*, court--card; ~-*gallery*, (hall etc. containing) collection of ~s; ~-*hat*, lady's wide-brimmed & highly decorated hat as in ~s of Reynolds & Gainsborough; ~ *postcard* (with ~ on back); ~-*writing*, mode of recording events etc. by ~s, as in early hieroglyphs etc.; ‖ *moving* ~s or ellipt. *the* ~s (cinematographic); ‖ ~-*palace*, -*theatre*, -*drome*, building etc. in which moving ~s are shown. **3.** v.t. Represent in ~, describe graphically, imagine (*to oneself*). Hence **pic′turIZE** (-kcher-) v.t., = FILM v. [ME, f. L *pictura* (*pingere pict-* paint, see -URE)]

picturesque′ (-kcherĕsk), a. Like, fit to be the subject of, a striking picture; (of language etc.) strikingly graphic, vivid. Hence ~LY[2] adv., ~NESS n. [f. F *pittoresque* f. It. *pittoresco* (*pittore* painter, as PICTORIAL, see -ESQUE)]

pic′ul, n. Chinese weight (133⅓ lb.); ~--*stick* (for carrying weights across shoulders). [Malay]

pid′dle, v.i. (Arch.) work, act, in trifling way; (colloq. or childish) make water. [(1) cf. PEDDLE (2); (2) prob. imit.]

pidd′ock, n. Bivalve mollusc used for bait. [orig. unkn.]

pidg′in, pi′geon (-jn), a. & n. **1.** ~ *English*, jargon chiefly of English words used between Chinese & Europeans. **2.** n. ‖ (colloq.). (A person's) business, job. [corrupt. of *business*]

pie[1], n. = MAGPIE; *French, rain-, wood-,* ~, kinds of woodpecker; SEA-~. [ME, f. OF, f. L *pica*]

pie[2], n. Dish of meat, fruit, etc., enclosed in or covered with paste & baked; APPLE--~ (fig.); *have a finger in the* ~, be (esp. officiously) concerned in the matter; *bran* ~, tub of bran with toys etc. hidden in it to be drawn at random at Christmas festivities etc.; MUD ~; ~′*crust*, baked paste of ~, (prov.) *promises are like* ~-*crust, made to be broken*; ~′*man* (-an),

vendor of ~s. [ME, perh. = prec., f. miscellaneous contents compared to piebald appearance of magpie]

pie[3], n., & v.t. (print.). (Also *printers′* ~) confused mass of type; (fig.) chaos; (v.t.) mix (type). [17th c., of obsc. orig.; perh. as prec.]

pie[4], n. Pakistani coin. [f. Hind. *pa′i* f. Skr. *pad* quarter, prob. orig. same as PICE]

piebald (pīb′awld), a. Of two colours irregularly arranged, esp. black & white (usu. of animal, esp. horse), cf. SKEWBALD; (fig.) motley, mongrel. [PIE[1]+BALD]

piece[1], n. **1.** One of the distinct portions of which thing is composed; *in* ~s, broken; *break to* ~s (fragments); *go to* ~s (fig.), collapse; *pick up the* ~s (said to fallen child etc.). **2.** Enclosed portion (of land). **3.** Detached portion (*of* a substance); *a* ~ *of* one's *mind*, one's candid opinion, rebuke. **4.** Definite quantity (*of* wallpaper = 12 yds, *of* muslin = 10 yds, etc.) in which thing is made up. **5.** Cask (*of* wine etc.) varying in capacity. **6.** ~ (product) *of work*; example, specimen, as *a* ~ *of impudence, fine* ~ *of painting, cricket,* etc.; ~ *of* GOODS. **7.** Fire-arm, (barrel of) artillery weapon. **8.** Man at chess, draughts, etc. **9.** Coin, as *crown, penny*, ~; ~ *of eight* (i.e. REAL[1]s), Spanish dollar. **10.** Picture; literary or musical composition, usu. short; drama. **11.** *Paid by the* ~ (according to amount done); *of a* ~, uniform, consistent, in keeping (*with*); ~-*goods*, textile fabrics (esp. Lancashire cotton goods) woven in recognized lengths; ~-*work* (paid for by the ~). [ME & OF *pece* = It. *pezza*, -*zo*, med. L *pecia, petia* (-*ium*) fragment, prob. of Gaulish orig.; cf. PEAT[1]]

piece[2], v.t. Put together, form into a whole; join threads in spinning, whence **pie′cer**[1] n.; fit *on* (thing *to* another); eke *out*; make *out* (story, theory, chain of evidence) by combination of parts; join *together*; patch *up*. [f. prec.]

pièce de résistance (see Ap.), n. Most substantial dish at meal (also fig.). [F]

piece′meal (-sm-), adv., a., & n. (Also *by* ~) piece by piece, part at a time; (adj.) done etc. ~. [ME (PIECE, OE *mǣlum* suf. f. instr. pl. of *mǣl* MEAL[2])]

pied (pīd), a. Particoloured. [PIE[1], -ED[2]]

pied à terre (pyãd′ahtãr′), n. Rest for the sole of one's foot, somewhere to stay. [F]

pi(e)-dog. See PYEDOG.

pier, n. Breakwater, mole; structure of iron or wood open below running out into sea & used as promenade & landing--stage, whence ~′AGE(4) n.; support of spans of bridge; pillar; solid masonry between windows etc.; ~-*glass*, large mirror orig. used to fill up this. [12th c. *per*, rendering med. L *pera* of. unkn. orig.]

pierce, v.t. & i. (Of sharp instrument etc., also fig. of cold, pain, grief, glance, discernment, discerning person, shriek, etc.) penetrate; prick (substance *with* pin etc.); make hole in (cask etc.); force one's way through or into; penetrate *through*, *into*, etc. Hence **pier′cing**LY[2] adv. [f. OF *percer*, f. Rom. **pertusiare* f. L PER- (*tundere tus-* pound)]

Pier′ian (*or* -ĕ′rĭ-), a. Of Pieria in N. Thessaly, reputed home of Muses. [f. L *Pierius* +-AN]

pierrot (pē′ĕrō, pyĕ′rō), n. (fem. *pierrette*). French pantomime character; itinerant minstrel with whitened face & loose white dress. [F, dim. of *Pierre* PETER[1]]

pietà (pyăt′ah), n. Picture, sculpture, of Virgin Mary holding dead body of Christ on her lap. [It., f. L as PIETY]

pi′et|ism, n. Spener's movement for revival of piety in Lutheran Church in 17th c.; pious sentiment, exaggeration or affectation of this. So ~IST n., ~**is′tic**(AL) aa. [f. G *pietismus* (as PIETY, see -ISM)]

pi′ety̆, n. Quality of being pious. [ME, f. OF *piete* f. L *pietatem* (as PIOUS, see -TY)]

piëzŏm′ěter, n. Kinds of instrument for measuring pressure or the sense of it. [f. Gk *piezō* press +-0- +-METER]

pif′fl|e, v.i., & n. (sl.). **1.** Talk or act feebly, trifle. **2.** n. Twaddle. Hence ~ER[1] n., ~**ing** a., trivial, worthless. [imit.]

pig, n., & v.i. & t. (-gg-). **1.** Swine, hog; flesh of (usu. young or sucking)~ as meat, esp. *roast* ~; GUINEA-~ (lit. & fig.). **2.** (colloq.). Greedy, dirty, sulky, obstinate, or annoying person, whence~**g′ish**[1] a., ~**g′ish**LY[2] adv., ~**g′ish**NESS n., (-g-). **3.** Oblong mass of metal (usu. iron) from smelting-furnace, esp. ~-*iron*. **4.** Segment of orange. **5.** *Buy a ~ in a poke*, buy thing without seeing it or knowing its value; *bring* one's ~*s to a fine, a pretty, the wrong, market*, fail in a venture; ~*s might fly*, wonders might happen; *please the ~s*, joc. substitute for *please God*. **6.** ~'*headed*, obstinate, stupid, whence ~'-*headedly* adv., ~'*headedness* n.; ~'-*jump*, (of horse) jump sportively from all four legs not brought together as in buck-jumping; ~'*nut*, a tuber, kind of EARTH-*nut*; ~'*skin*, (leather made of) ~'s skin, (sl.) saddle; ~'*sticking*, hunting of wild boar with spear, butchering of swine, so ~'**sticker** n. (also, long-bladed pocket-knife); ~'*sty*, sty for~s, (fig.) dirty hovel; ~'s *wash*, ~'*wash*, swill of brewery or kitchen given to ~s; ~'*weed*, kinds of herb eaten by ~s. **7.** v.t. & i. Bring forth (~s, or abs.). **8.** v.i. Herd together like ~s (also ~ *it*). Hence ~'LET, ~'LING[1], nn., ~'LIKE a. (ME *pigge*, f. OE **picga*, **pigga*; cf. DOG, FROG]

pi′geon (-jn), n., & v.t. **1.** Bird with many varieties, wild, domesticated, produced by fancy breeding, trained to carry missives, etc., the dove, (now preferred to *dove* exc. in poet. & rhet. contexts, or of the turtle-dove; *carrier-*~, *homing* ~, (trained to carry home messages tied to its neck etc.). **2.** Simpleton, gull, as

PLUCK[2] *a* ~. **3.** *Clay* ~, clay saucer thrown into air from trap as mark for shooting; ~-*breast*, deformed human chest laterally constricted, so ~-*breasted*; ~ *English*, see PIDGIN; ~-*hole*, small recess for ~ to nest in, one of a set of compartments for papers etc. in cabinet etc., (v.t.) deposit (document) in this, put aside (matter) for future consideration or neglect, assign (thing) to definite place in memory; ~ *pair*, boy & girl twins, or boy & girl as sole children; ~'s *milk*, partly-digested food with which ~s feed their young, ‖ imaginary article for which children are sent on fool's errand; ~-*toed*, having the toes turned inwards. **4.** v.t. Cheat (person *of* thing). [ME, f. OF *pijon* f. LL *pipionem* (nom. -*io*) young cheeping bird (*pipire* cheep)]

pi′geonry̆ (-jn-), n. Pigeon-house. [-RY]

pigg′ery̆ (-g-), n. Pig-breeding establishment; pigsty; dirty place; piggishness. [-ERY]

pigg′y̆ (-g-), n. Little pig; (nursery) ~-*wiggy*, little pig, dirty child; ‖ game of tip-cat. [-Y[3]]

pig′ment, n. Colouring-matter used as paint or dye; natural colouring-matter of a tissue. Hence ~AL (-ĕn[L]), ~ARY[1], aa., ~A′TION n., a colouring of tissue by deposition of ~. [ME, f. L *pigmentum* (*pig-* root of *pingere* paint, -MENT)]

pigmy. See PYGMY.

pig′tail, n. Tobacco twisted into thin roll; plait of hair hanging from back of head, esp. as worn by Chinese under the Manchus, by young girls, & formerly by soldiers & sailors. Hence ~ED[2] (-ld) a.

pike[1], n., & v.t. **1.** Long wooden shaft with pointed steel or iron head, infantry weapon superseded by the bayonet; ‖ (dial.) pickaxe, spike; ‖~'*man*, miner who uses pickaxe. **2.** [perh. diff. wd of Norse orig.]. ‖ Peaked top of hill (in names of hills in Lake district). **3.** [prob. abbr. of ~-*fish*, from its pointed snout]. Large voracious freshwater fish, jack. **4.** v.t. Thrust through, kill, with ~. [in first sense (16th c.) f. F *pique*, in OF *pic* pickaxe, obsc. rel. to OE *pic*, ME *pik*, *pikk* (whence PICK[1]) pickaxe; see PEAK[1]]

pike[2], n. Toll-bar; toll; turnpike road; ~'*man*, keeper of turnpike. [abbr. of TURNPIKE]

pike′lĕt (-kl-), n. Kind of teacake. [f. W (*bara*) *pyglyd* pitchy (bread)]

*pik′er, n. (colloq.). Cautious or timid gambler, a poor sport. [U.S., orig. unkn.]

pike′staff (-kstahf), n. Wooden shaft of pike; *plain as a* ~ [orig. *packstaff*, smooth staff used by pedlar], quite plain. [PIKE[1] +STAFF[1]]

pilăs′ter, n. Rectangular column, esp. one engaged in wall. [f. F *pilastre* f. It. *pilastro* f. med. L *pilastrum* (L *pila* pillar, see -ASTER)]

pilau′, -aw, -äff, n. Oriental dish of rice with meat, spices, etc. [Pers. (-*aw*)]

pilch, n. Infant's wrapper worn over diaper. [OE *pylece*, ME *pilche* outer garment, as PELISSE]

pil'chard, n. Small sea-fish allied to herring. [16th c. *pilcher*, of unkn. orig.]

pil'corn, n. Kind of oat in which husk does not adhere to grain. [= *pilled corn*]

pile¹, n., & v.t. 1. Pointed stake or post; heavy beam driven vertically into bed of river, soft ground, etc. as support for bridge etc.; ~*-driver*, machine for driving ~s. 2. v.t. Furnish with~s, drive~s into. [OE *pil*, OHG *pfil*, f. L *pilum* javelin]

pile², n. 1. Heap of things laid more or less regularly upon one another; (*funeral*) ~, heap of combustibles on which corpse is burnt; (colloq.) heap of money, fortune, as *make a* ~, *make* one's ~ (as much as one wants). 2. Lofty mass of buildings. 3. Series of plates of dissimilar metals laid one upon another alternately for producing electric current; (also *atomic* ~) apparatus designed to contain uranium & a moderating agent for the study or utilization of atomic energy. [ME, f. OF f. L *pila* pillar, pier, mole]

pile³, v.t. Heap up (often *up*, *on*); ~ *arms*, place (usu. four) rifles with butts on ground & muzzles interlocked; ~ *up* (naut.), run (ship) on rocks or aground; (colloq.) ~ *up* (or *on*) *the agony*, intensify painful description etc., ~ *it on*, exaggerate; load (table etc. *with*). [f. prec.]

‖ **pile⁴**, n. (arch.). Reverse of coin; *cross or* ~, heads or tails. [ME, as PILE², orig. = under iron of minting apparatus]

pile⁵, n. Soft hair, down, wool of sheep; nap on cloth, esp. on velvet, plush, etc., or on carpet, as *two, three,* ~ *carpet*. Hence **pil'y²** a. [ME, f. AF *pile* = OF *peil* f. L *pilus* hair]

pile⁶, n. (Pl.) haemorrhoids, disease marked by tumours of veins of lower rectum; (sing.) such tumour; ~*'wort*, lesser celandine (from reputed efficacy against ~s). [ME, prob. f. L *pila* ball]

pil'fer, v.t. & i. Steal (thing, or abs.) esp. in small quantities. Hence ~AGE(3), ~ER¹, nn. [ME, f. OF *pelfre* PELF]

pilgar'lic, n. (arch.). Bald head; bald-headed man; poor creature. [= *pilled* or *peeled garlic*]

pil'grim, n., & v.i. One who journeys to sacred place as act of religious devotion; person regarded as journeying to a future life (*The P~'s Progress*); traveller; *The P~s of Gt Britain, of the U.S.*, societies fostering Anglo-American friendship by mutual hospitality etc.; P~ *Fathers*, English Puritans who founded colony of Plymouth, Massachusetts, in 1620; (v.i.) wander like a ~. Hence ~IZE(2) v.i. [ME *pele-, pilegrim, -grin*, f. OF *pelegrin f. L *peregrinus* stranger f. PER (*egre* f. *ager* field) abroad, -INE¹]

pil'grimage, n., & v.i. Pilgrim's journey, esp. *go on* (*a*) ~; (fig.) mortal life viewed as a journey; (v.i.) go on a~. [ME, f. OF *pelerinage* f. *peleriner* go as a pilgrim (as prec.)]

pilif'erous, a. Having hair (esp. in bot.). So **pil'iform** a. [f. L *pilus* hair, see -FEROUS]

pill¹, n., & v.t. 1. Small ball of medicinal substance for swallowing whole (*a* ~ *to cure an earthquake*, half measures); (fig.) something that has to be done, a humiliation etc., (*swallow the* ~, *a bitter* ~, etc.); ~*'box*, shallow cylindrical box for holding ~s, (joc.) small vehicle or building, (mil.) small isolated chiefly underground concrete fort; GILD¹ *the* ~; (sl. or joc.) ball, e.g. cannon-ball, tennis-ball, ‖ (pl.) billiards; ~*'wort*, kinds of plant with small globular involucres. 2. v.t. (sl.). Blackball, defeat. [f. MDu., MLG *pille* f. L *pilula* dim. of *pila* ball]

‖ **pill²**, v.t. (arch.). Pillage, plunder; (dial.) = PEEL³. [OE *pylian*, ME *pile*, later *pille*, ult. f. Rom. *piliare, perh. f. *pilum* javelin; from 17th c., in sense 'remove the bark etc. from ', different. as PEEL³]

pill'ag|e, n., & v.t. 1. Plunder, esp. as practised in war. 2. v.t. Sack, plunder, (place, person, or abs.). Hence ~ER¹ n. [ME, f. OF, as prec., see -AGE]

pill'ar, n., & v.t. 1. Vertical structure of stone, wood, metal, etc., slender in proportion to height, used as support or ornament; post, pedestal; (fig.) person who is a main supporter, as *a* ~ *of the faith*; upright mass of air, water, etc.; (mining) solid mass of coal etc. left to support roof of the working; *driven from* ~ *to post* (to & fro, from one resource to another); ‖~*-box*, hollow ~ about 5 ft high in which letters may be posted. 2. v.t. Support (as) with ~s. Hence ~ET¹ n. [ME & OF *piler*, f. Rom. *pilare (*pila* pillar, see -AR¹)]

pill'ion (-lyon), n. (Hist.) Woman's light saddle, cushion attached to hinder part of saddle for second rider, usu. woman; (mod.) seating for passenger behind motor-cyclist etc. [f. Gael. *pillean, -in* f. L *pellis* skin]

pill'iwinks, n. (hist.). Instrument of torture for squeezing fingers. [ME *pyrwykes, pyrewinkes*, of unkn. orig.]

pill'ory, n., & v.t. 1. Wooden framework with holes for head & hands of offender exposed to public ridicule etc. 2. v.t. Put in the ~, (fig.) expose to ridicule. [ME, f. OF *pilori*, of unkn. orig.]

pill'ow (-ō), n., & v.t. & i. 1. Cushion of linen etc. stuffed with feathers etc. as support for head in reclining esp. in bed; *take counsel of* one's ~, take a night to reflect; (techn.) ~-shaped block or support; ~*-case, -slip*, washable case of linen etc. for~; ~*-fight*,=BOLSTER²-*fight*. 2. vb. Rest, prop up, on ~; rest on ~. Hence ~Y² (-ōi) a. [OE *pyle, pylu*, = MDu. *pöluwe*, OHG *pfuliwi, pfulwo*, f. WG **pulwi(n)* f. L *pulvinus* cushion]

pil′ōse, -ous, aa. Covered with hair. So **pilŏs′ITY** n. [f. L *pilosus* (*pilus* hair, -OSE¹)]

pil′ot, n., & v.t. **1.** Person qualified to take charge of ships entering or leaving a harbour (*drop the* ~, abandon trusted adviser); steersman (arch.); (aeronaut.) person navigating aircraft or qualified. to do so, (now) one who operates the flying controls of an aircraft (*P*~ *Officer*, rank in AIR¹ Force); (fig.) guide, esp. in hunting-field. **2.** ~ *balloon*, small balloon whose movements are observed as it rises in the air, used to ascertain direction and velocity of currents at various heights; ~- -*cloth*, blue woollen windproof cloth for overcoat used by mariners; ~ *engine* (clearing the way for another and testing the safety. of the permanent way); ~- -*jacket*, = PEA-JACKET; ~-*fish*, small fish said to act as ~ to shark; ~-*light*, small gas-burner kept alight to light another (also ~-*jet*), electric indicator light or control light; ~ *scheme*, preliminary experimental trial of project on small scale. **3.** v.t. Conduct as ~ (lit. & fig.); act as ~ on (way, piece of water); act as ~ of (aircraft). Hence or cogn. ~AGE(3, 4) n., ~LESS a. [f. F *pilote* f. It. *pilota*, -*to*, f. Gk *pēdon* oar]

Pilt′down, n. A Sussex hamlet; ~ *skull* (found in 1913 at ~, & until 1953 believed to belong to a prehistoric type of man).

pil′ūle, pill-, n. Pill; small pill. Hence **pil′ūlAR¹, pil′ūlous,** aa. [F, as PILL¹]

‖ **pim′elōde,** n. Catfish. [f. Gk *pimelōdēs* fatty (*pimelē* fat, see -ODE)]

pimĕn′tō, n. Dried aromatic berries of a certain tree, Jamaica pepper; the tree. [f. Sp. *pimiento* f. L *pigmentum* PIGMENT, (med. L) spice]

pimp, n., & v.i. Pander. [c. 1600, of unkn. orig.]

pim′pernĕl, n. Small annual found in cornfields & waste ground, with scarlet (also blue or white) flowers closing in cloudy or rainy weather. [ME, f. OF *pimprenele*, f. Rom. *piperinella* f. L *piper* PEPPER]

pim′ping, a. Small, mean; sickly. [17th c., of unkn. orig.; cf. dial. *pimpy*]

pim′pl|e, n. Small solid round tumour of the skin, usu. inflammatory. Hence ~ED² (-ld), ~Y², aa. [ME, of unkn. orig.]

pin¹, n. **1.** Thin piece of (usu. tinned brass or iron) wire with sharp point & round flattened head for fastening together parts of dress, papers, etc. **2.** Peg of wood or metal for various purposes (*split* ~, metal cotter to be passed through hole & held there by the gaping of its split end); each of the pegs round which strings of musical instrument are fastened; THOLE², BELAY*ing*, DRAWING, -~, HAIR~, ‖ NINEPIN; *don't care a* ~ (at all). **3.** pl. (colloq.). Legs, as *quick on his* ~s. **4.** ~s *& needles*, tingling sensation in limb recovering from numbness. **5.** Small

cask of 4½ gal. **6.** ~*.cushion*, small cushion for sticking ~s in to keep them ready for use; ~-*feather*, ungrown feather; ~-*fire cartridge* (exploded by means of ~); ~-*head*, (fig.) minute thing; ~-*hole* (made by ~ or into which peg fits); ~- -*money*, annual allowance to woman for dress expenses etc., allowance settled on wife for private expenditure; ~-*point*, point of ~, (fig.) something very small, (attrib., of targets) small & requiring very accurate & precise bombing & shelling, (v.t.) locate or bomb (such target) with the requisite accuracy & precision, designate precisely; ~*-prick*, (fig.) trifling irritation; ~-*table*, kinds of mechanical amusement & gambling device; ~*-tail*, kinds of duck & grouse with pointed tail; ~-*tuck*, very narrow ornamental tuck; ~-*wheel*, small Catherine-wheel. [late OE *pinn*, MDu., MLG *pinne*, G *pinne*, ult. f. L *pinna* point etc.; cf. PINNACLE]

pin², v.t. (-nn-). Fasten (thing to another, *up*, etc., things *together*) with pin(s); ~ *up* (archit.), = UNDERPIN; transfix with pin, lance, etc.; ~ one's *faith* (rely implicitly) *on* (person etc.); seize & hold fast (*against* wall etc.); bind (person etc., often *down*) *to* (promise, arrangement); enclose by bars etc.; ~-*up* n., picture of some favourite or famous person ~ned up on wall etc. (also attrib., esp. ~-*up girl*). [f. prec.]

pin′afor|e, n. Child's washable covering worn over frock to protect it from dirt, apron. Hence ~ED²(-ōrd) a. [PIN² + AFORE]

pinäs′ter, n. A pine indigenous to SW. Europe. [L, = wild pine (*pinus*, -ASTER)]

pince-nez (see Ap.), n. Pair of eyeglasses with spring to clip nose. [F, lit. = pinch--nose]

pin′cers (-z), n. pl. (Also *a pair of* ~) gripping tool made of two limbs pivoted together forming pair of jaws with pair of handles to press them together with; similar organ of crustaceans etc.; ~ *movement*, (mil.) converging movement (also *pincer movement, attack*, etc.). [ME *pinsour(s)*, f. AF f. OF *pincier* PINCH²]

pincette (păⁿsĕt′), n. Small pincers, tweezers. [F]

pinch¹, n. Nip, squeeze; (fig.) stress (*of* poverty etc.); *at a* ~ (critical juncture); as much as can be taken up with tips of finger and thumb, as *a* ~ *of snuff, salt*. [f. foll.]

pinch², v.t. & i. Nip, squeeze, esp. between tips of finger & thumb (also fig. of cold, hunger, etc., esp. ~*ed with cold*); *that is where the shoe* ~*es*, that is the difficulty or trouble; extort (money etc. *from, out of*, person etc.); stint (person etc. *in, of, for*, food etc.); be niggardly; ‖ urge (horse esp. in race); sail (purposely or not) too close to wind; (sl.) steal (thing), rob (person), arrest, take into custody. [ME, f. ONF *pinchier* = OF *pincier*, f. Rom. *pinctiare*]

pinch′běck, n. & a. **1.** Gold-like alloy of copper & zinc used in cheap jewellery etc. **2.** adj. Counterfeit, sham. [f. C. P~, watchmaker, d. 1732]

Pinda′ri (-ahrē), n. Mounted marauder in India in 17th & 18th cc. [f. Hind. *pindari*]

Pinda′ric, a. & n. **1.** Of, supposedly like, the Greek poet Pindar. **2.** n. (usu. pl.). ~ ode(s), metre, verse(s). [f. L f. Gk *Pindarikos* (*Pindaros*, see -IC)]

pine¹, n. Kinds of trees with evergreen needle-shaped leaves growing in sheathed clusters of two or more (cf. FIR), many species of which afford timber, tar, & turpentine; *Chile* ~, MONKEY-puzzle; ~apple; ~'*apple*, large collective fruit of the ananas, so called from resemblance to ~-cone, (sl.) hand-grenade; ~-*beauty*, ~ *carpet*, moths whose larvae feed on ~--trees; ~-*cone*, fruit of the ~; ~ *marten*, dark-brown British marten. [ME, f. OF *pin* f. L *pinus*; OE *pīn* dir. f. L]

pine², v.i. Languish, waste away, from grief, disease, etc.; long eagerly (*for, after, to* do). [OE *pīnian* f. **pīn* pain (ME *pine*) f. L *poena* punishment, pain]

pin′eal, a. (anat.). Shaped like a pine--cone; ~ *gland*, gland of unknown function behind third ventricle of brain. [f. F *pinéal* f. L *pinea* PINE¹-cone, see -AL]

pin′erў, n. Place in which pineapples are grown; plantation of pines. [-ERY]

pin′fōld, n., & v.t. Pound for stray cattle etc.; (v.t.) confine in this. [OE *pundfald* (**pund* POUND² + *fald* FOLD¹)]

ping, n., & v.i. **1.** Abrupt ringing sound as of rifle bullet flying through air. **2.** v.i. Make, fly with, this. [imit.]

ping′pŏng′, n. Table-tennis, game like lawn-tennis played on table with celluloid balls & parchment or wooden bats. [imit. f. sound of bat]

ping′uid (-nggw-), a. (usu. joc.). Fat, oily, greasy. [f. L *pinguis* fat + -ID¹]

ping′uin (-nggw-), n. W.-Ind. plant allied to pineapple; its fruit. [orig. unkn.]

pin′ion¹ (-nyon), n. Terminal segment of bird's wing; (poet.) wing; any flight--feather of wing; (in carving) part of wing corresponding to forearm. [ME, f. OF *pignon* f. L *pinna* PIN¹, -OON]

pin′ion² (-nyon), v.t. Cut off pinion of (wing, bird) to prevent flight; bind the arms of (person), bind (arms); bind (person etc.) fast *to* (thing). [f. prec.]

pin′ion³ (-nyon), n. Small cog-wheel engaging with larger one; cogged spindle engaging with wheel. [f. F *pignon* alt. f. obs. *pignol* f. Rom. **pineolus* f. L *pinea* pine-cone]

pink¹, n. & a. **1.** Garden plant with sweet--smelling white, ~, crimson, or varie-gated flowers. **2.** *The* ~ (embodied per-fection) *of elegance* etc.; *the* ~ (most per-fect condition) *of health* etc. (also sl., *in the* ~, abs., quite well). **3.** (Of a) pale red slightly inclining to purple. **4.** Fox-

-hunter's red coat, cloth of this; fox--hunter. **5.** adj. Of pale red colour of various kinds, as *rose, salmon*, -~, whence ~'ISH¹, ~'Y² aa., ~'NESS n.; (pol.) verging on red; ~-*eye*, contagious fever of horse, contagious ophthalmia in man. [orig. unkn.]

pink², n. Yellowish pigment made by combining vegetable colouring matter with some white base (*brown, French, Dutch*, etc. ~). [orig. unkn.]

pink³, n. (hist.). Sailing-vessel esp. with narrow stern (orig. small & flat-bottomed). [15th c., f. MDu. *pincke, pinke*, of unkn. orig.]

pink⁴, v.t. Pierce slightly with sword etc.; (also ~ *out*) ornament (leather etc.) with perforations; adorn, deck. [ME; cf. LG *pinken* strike, peck, perh. var. of *picken* PICK²]

‖ **pink⁵,** n. Young salmon; (dial.) minnow. [15th c. *penk*, of unkn. orig.; cf. G dial. *pink(e)* in same senses]

pink⁶, v.i. (Of a motor-engine) emit series of high-pitched explosive sounds caused by detonation of mixture following partial combustion. [imit.]

*Pink′ster, n. Whitsuntide; *p~ flower*, pink azalea. [Du., = Pentecost]

pĭnn′a, n. (pl. -ae). Broad upper part of external ear; primary division of pinnate leaf; fin, fin-like structure. [L, = *penna*]

pinn′ace, n. Warship's double-banked (usu. eight-oared) boat now usu. driven by steam or petrol. [16th c., f. F *pinasse* (but cf. ME *spinace* = AF *espynasse*)]

pinn′acle, n., & v.t. Small ornamental turret usu. ending in pyramid or cone, crowning a buttress, roof, etc.; natural peak; (fig.) culmination, climax; (v.t.) set (as) on ~, form the ~ of, furnish with ~s. [ME & OF *pinacle* f. LL *pinnaculum* (*pinna* wing, point, see PIN¹, -CULE)]

pinn′ate, a. (Bot., of compound leaf) with series of leaflets on each side of com-mon petiole; (zool.) with branches, ten-tacles, etc., on each side of an axis. Hence **pinn′ātěd** [-ATE²] a., ~LY² adv. [f. L *pinnatus* feathered (PINNA, see -ATE²)]

pinn′er, n. In vbl senses; also, coif with two long side-flaps pinned on. [f. PIN v. + -ER¹]

pinn′i-, comb. form of L *pinna, penna* wing, fin, as: ~*grade*, ~*ped*, aa. & nn., fin-footed (animal).

pinn′othēre, -tēre, n. Kinds of small crabs commensally inhabiting shells of oyster, mussel, etc. [f. L f. Gk *pinnotērēs* (*pinna* bivalve mollusc, + -*tērĕō* guard)]

pinn′ŭl|e, n. (Bot.) secondary division of pinnate leaf; (zool.) part, organ, like small wing or fin; sight at end of index of astrolabe etc. Hence ~AR¹ a. [f. L *pinnula* dim. of PINNA]

pinn′ў, n. Childish abbr. of PINAFORE.

*pin′oc(h)le (-ŏkl; *or* pē-), n. Game like bezique. [orig. unkn.]

*pinōl′ė, n. Meal made from parched

cornflour mixed with sweet flour, sugar, etc. [Amer.-Sp., f. Aztec *pinolli*]

pint, n. Measure of capacity for liquids etc., ⅛th of gallon. [ME, f. OF *pinte*, of unkn. orig.]

pinta′dō (-ah-), n. (pl. ~s). (Now usu. ~ *bird, petrel*) kind of petrel; guinea-fowl. [f. Port. *pintado* painted, p.p. of *pintar* f. L *pingere* *pinct*- for *pict*-]

pin′tle, n. Kinds of pin or bolt, esp. one on which some other part turns. [OE *pintel* penis, of unkn. orig.; cf. OFris., LG, Du., G *pint*]

***pin′tō** (or pē-), a. & n. Piebald (horse). [Sp.]

***pinx′it, pinxer′unt,** v.t. (So-&-so) painted it (in signature to picture, as FECIT. [L]

pin′y, a. Of, like, abounding in, pines. [-Y²]

piolet (pyōlā′), n. Alpinist's ice-axe. [F]

pioneer′, n., & v.i. & t. **1.** (Mil.) one of body of foot-soldiers marching in advance with spades etc. to prepare road for main body; beginner of enterprise, original explorer, etc. **2.** v.i. Act as ~. **3.** v.t. Open up (road etc.) as ~; act as ~ to, conduct. [f. F *pionnier* foot-soldier, pioneer, (*pion*, f. L as PAWN¹, -IER)]

piou-piou (pyōō-pyōō′), n. (Pop.) typical French private soldier, cf. *poilu*. [F]

pi′ous, a. Devout, religious; ~ *founder* (of college etc. for glory of God & good of man); (arch.) dutiful; ~ FRAUD. Hence ~LY² adv. [f. L *pius* dutiful, pious, -OUS]

pip¹, n. Disease of poultry, hawks, etc., marked by thick mucus in throat & often by white scale on tip of tongue; † (sl.) fit of depression, bad temper, (*he has, gives me, the~*). [ME, f. MDu. *pippe*, MLG *pip* f. WG **pipit* f. Rom. **pipita* corrupt. of L *pituita* phlegm]

pip², n. Each spot on playing-cards, dice, or dominoes; star (1–3 acc. to rank) on army officer's shoulder; single blossom of clustered inflorescence; rhomboidal segment of surface of pineapple. [late 16th c. *peep*, of unkn. orig.]

‖ **pip³,** v.t. (colloq.; -pp-). Blackball; defeat; hit with shot. [f. prec. or foll.]

pip⁴, n. Seed of apple, pear, orange, etc. Hence ~′LESS a. [app. abbr. of PIPPIN]

‖ **pip⁵,** signallers' letter P, as in ~ *emma*, *o.~*.

‖ **pip⁶,** n. Short high-pitched sound, usu. mechanically produced (*the six ~s of the time-signal*). [imit.]

pipal. See PEEPUL.

pipe¹, n. **1.** Tube of wood, metal, etc., esp. for conveying water, gas, etc. **2.** Musical wind-instrument consisting of single tube; each of the tubes by which sound is produced in organ; (pl.) = BAG¹~*s*; boatswain's whistle, sounding of this. **3.** Voice, esp. in singing; song, note, of bird. **4.** Tubular organ, vessel, etc. in animal body. **5.** Cylindrical vein of ore. **6.** Channel of decoy for wild fowl. **7.** (Also *tobacco-~*) narrow tube of clay, wood, etc.,

with bowl at one end for drawing in smoke of tobacco, quantity of tobacco held by this, as *light, smoke, a* ~; PEACE-~~; ‖ *King's* or *Queen's* ~, furnace at London Docks used formerly for burning contraband tobacco; *put that in your* ~ *& smoke it*, digest that fact etc. if you can. **8.** Cask for wine, esp. as measure usu. = 105 gal. **9.** ~′*clay*, fine white clay used for tobacco-~s & (esp. by soldiers) for cleaning white breeches, belts, etc., (fig.) excessive attention to minutiae of dress etc. in regiment, (v.t.) whiten with ~clay; ***~ *dream*, a notion as fantastic as a dream produced by opium-smoking; ~-*fish*, (kinds of) long slender fish with elongated snout; ~-*light*, spill for lighting ~; ~′*line* (esp. for conveying petroleum to a distance), (fig.) continuous flow of goods in transit from producer to retailer or (industrial) consumer etc.; ~ *major*, N.C.O. commanding regimental pipers; ~-*rack* (for tobacco-~s); ~-*rolls* (hist.), records of the old national Exchequer offices (prob. because subsidiary documents were rolled in ~ form); ~-*stone*, hard red clay used by Amer. Indians for tobacco-~s. Hence ~′FUL (-pfŏŏl) n., ~′LESS (-pl-), **pip′Y²,** aa. [OE *pīpe*, OHG *pfīfa*, ON *pipa*, f. Rom. **pipa* f. L *pipare*, *-iare* peep, chirp]

pipe², v.i. & t. **1.** Play (tune etc., or abs.) on pipe; lead, bring, (person etc.) by sound of pipe; summon (crew *up*, to meal, work, etc.) by sounding whistle (~ *away*, give signal for boat to start); whistle; utter in shrill voice; ~ *down*, (naut.) dismiss from duty, (sl.) be less noisy or cocksure; ~ *up*, begin to play or sing; ~ *one's eye(s)*, weep. **2.** Propagate (pinks etc.) by cuttings taken off at joint of stem. **3.** Trim (dress), ornament (cake etc.), with PIPING¹. **4.** Furnish with pipes; convey (oil, water, gas, etc.) by pipes. [OE *pipian* f. as prec.]

‖ **pip emm′a,** adv. (colloq.). Post meridiem. [signallers' former names for letters P, M]

pip′er, n. One who plays on pipe, esp. strolling musician; bagpipe-player; *pay the* ~ (*& call the tune*), bear the cost (& have control) of a proceeding etc.; kinds of fish; broken-winded horse; ‖ decoy-dog. [OE *pipere* (PIPE¹+-ER¹)]

pipette′, n. Slender tube for transferring etc. small quantities of liquids, esp. in chemistry. [F, dim. of PIPE¹]

pip′ing¹, n. In vbl senses, also: ornamentation of dress by means of cord enclosed in pipe-like fold; ornamental cord-like lines of sugar on cake. [f. PIPE²+-ING¹]

pip′ing², a. In vbl senses; *the* ~ *time(s) of peace* (marked by piping as opp. to martial music); ~ (hissing) *hot*. [f. PIPE²+-ING²]

pipistrel(le)′, n. Small kind of bat. [F (-*le*), f. It. *pipistrello, vip-*, f. L *vespertilio* bat (*vesper* evening)]

pip'it, n. Bird like lark. [prob. imit.]

pip'kin, n. Small earthenware pot or pan. [orig. unkn.]

pipp'in, n. Kinds of apple. [ME & OF *pepin* seed, of unkn. orig.]

pip'squeak, n. (sl.). Shell that emits sound so described; insignificant or contemptible person or thing. [imit.]

piquant (pēk'ant), a. Agreeably pungent, sharp, appetizing; (fig.) pleasantly stimulating or disturbing to the mind. Hence **piqu**ANCY (pēk'an-) n., ~LY[2] adv. [F (as foll., see -ANT); F fem. ~e also as E fem.]

pique[1] (pēk), v.t., & n. 1. Irritate, wound the pride of; arouse (curiosity, interest); plume one*self on*. 2. n. Ill-feeling, enmity, resentment, as *in a fit of* ~, *took a* ~ *against me*. [f. F *piquer* vb prick, irritate, *pique* n.]

pique[2] (pēk), n., & v.t. & i. Winning of 30 points in cards and play at piquet before opponent begins to count; (v.t.) score a ~ against; (v.i.) score a ~. [f. F *pic*, of unkn. orig.]

piqué (pēk'ā), n. Stiff ribbed cotton fabric. [F, p.p. of *piquer*, see PIQUE[1]]

piquet'[1] (-kĕt; *or* pĭk[2]), n. Card game for two players with pack of 32 cards (omitting 2–6). [F, of unkn. orig.]

piquet[2]. See PICKET.

pirā'gua, pĕriā'gua (-gwa), n. Long narrow canoe made from single tree-trunk; two-masted sailing-barge. [Sp., f. Carib, = dug-out]

pīr'ate, n., & v.t. & i. 1. (Ship used by) sea-robber; marauder; one who infringes another's copyright; one who broadcasts without official authorization. (freq. attrib., as *a* ~ *broadcast*); ‖ bus that encroaches on recognized routes or overcharges or preys on passengers. 2. v.t. Plunder; reproduce (book etc.) without leave for one's own profit. 3. v.i. Play the ~. Hence or cogn. pīr'ACY n., pīrăt'IC(AL) aa., pīrăt'icalLY[2] adv. [ME, f. L (-ta) f. Gk *peiratēs* (*peiraō* attempt, assault)]

pirogue' (-ōg), n. = PIRAGUA. [F]

pirouětte' (-rŏŏ-), n., & v.i. 1. Ballet-dancer's spin round on one foot or on point of toe. 2. v.i. Dance thus. [F, = spinning top]

***pis aller** (pēzălā', & see Ap.), n. Course etc. taken for want of a better. [F (*pis* worse + *aller* go)]

pis'carỹ, n. *Common of* ~, right of fishing in another's water in common with owner (& others). [ME, f. med. L *piscaria* neut. pl. of L *piscarius* (*piscis* fish, see -ARY[1])]

pis'catorỹ, a. Of fishers or fishing, whence **piscatŏr'iAL** a.; addicted to fishing. [f. L *piscatorius* (*piscator* fisher f. *piscis* fish)]

Pis'cēs (-z), n. pl. The Fishes, 12th zodiacal constellation; 12th sign of zodiac. [L, pl. of *piscis* fish]

pis'cicŭlture, n. Artificial rearing of fish. Hence **piscicŭl'tur**AL a., **piscicŭl-**

---

turIST n., (-cher-). [f. L *piscis* fish + CULTURE]

pisci'na (-sĭ-, -sē-), n. (pl. *-ae*, *-as*). Fish-pond; ancient-Roman bathing-pond; (eccl.) perforated stone basin in church for carrying away water used in rinsing chalice etc. [L, f. *piscis* fish]

pis'cīne[1] (*or* -ēn), n. Bathing-pool. [F, f. prec.]

pis'cīne[2], a. Of fish. [f. L *piscis* fish, -INE[1]]

pisciv'orous, a. Fish-eating. [as prec. + -VOROUS]

***pisé** (pēz'ā), n. Rammed clay or earth (& gravel) as building-material. [F, p.p. of *piser* pound f. L *pi(n)sare* pound]

Pis'gah (-zga), n. Mountain whence Moses viewed the Promised Land (*Deut.* iii. 27); (fig.) ~ *glance, prospect, sight*, etc. [Heb.]

pish, int. expr. contempt, impatience, or disgust; (v.i.) say ~. [natural]

‖ **pishogue'** (-ōg), n. (Ir.). Sorcery; charm, spell. [f. Ir. *pis(r)eog*]

pis'ifŏrm (pīs-, pĭz-), a. Pea-shaped; ~ *bone*, small bone of upper row of carpus. [f. L *pisum* pea + -FORM]

piss, v.i. & t., & n. (not now in polite use). 1. Make water; discharge (blood etc.) with the urine; wet with ᵘrine; (p.p., sl.) drunk. 2. n. Urine. [ME, f. OF *pissier*, f. Rom. *pišare* (imit.)]

pista'chio (-ăshĭŏ, -ăshō, -ăchō), n. (pl. ~*s*). (Tree yielding) nut with greenish edible kernel; colour of this. [f. It. *pistacchio* & Sp. *pistacho* f. L f. Gk *pistakion*; 15th c. *pistace* f. OF]

pis'til, n. Female organ of flower, comprising ovary, style, & stigma. Hence ~LARY[1], ~lATE[2](2), ~līf'erous, ~līNE[1], aa. [f. F *pistile* f. L *pistillum* PESTLE]

pis'tol, n., & v.t. (-ll-). 1. Small fire-arm held & fired by one hand; *within, beyond*, ~*-shot* (range of ~); ~*-grip*, handhold of ~'s butt shape behind trigger-guard on gunstock. 2. v.t. Shoot with ~. [f. obs. F *pistole* (mod. *-let*) f. G *pistole* f. Czech *pišt'al*]

pistōle', n. (hist.). Foreign gold coin, esp. Spanish coin. [f. F *pistole* (as prec.)]

pis'ton, n. Disc or short cylinder of wood, metal, etc., fitting closely within tube in which it moves up & down, used in cylinder of steam or petrol engine to impart motion by means of ~*-rod*; sliding valve in cornet etc. [F, f. It. *pistone* var. of *pestone* PESTLE]

pit[1], n. 1. Natural hole in ground; hole made in digging for mineral etc. or for industrial purposes, as *chalk, clay, gravel, coal, saw, tan,* ~; covered hole as trap for wild beasts or (esp. bibl.) for enemies (*dig a* ~ *for*, fig., try to ensnare); *the* ~ (*of hell*), hell; COCKPIT. 2. Hollow in animal or plant body or on any surface; ~ *of the stomach*, depression between cartilages of false ribs; depressed scar, as after smallpox. **3.** ‖ That part of auditorium of theatre which is on floor of house, now usu. the part of this behind stalls; ‖ people occupying this. **4.** (In motor-racing) place at which cars are refuelled, re-tired, etc. **5.** *Part of floor of an exchange allotted to special trading (*wheat-*~*). **6.**~'*fall*, covered ~ as trap for animals etc., (fig.) unsuspected snare or danger;~'*man*, collier, *connecting rod in machinery; ‖ ~ *pony* (kept underground in coal-mines). [OE *pytt*, OS *putti*, OHG *pfuzzi*, f. L *puteus* well]

pit², v.t. & i. (-tt-). Put into a pit (esp. vegetables etc. for storage); set (cock, dog, etc.) to fight in pit (*against* another), (fig.) match (person *against*); make pits, esp. scars, in (esp. in p.p.); (path., of flesh etc.) retain impression of finger etc. when touched. [f. prec.]

pit'(a-)păt, adv. & n. With the sound ~, palpitatingly, falteringly, as *his heart, feet, went* ~; (n.) the sound ~. [imit.]

pitch¹, n., & v.t. **1.** Black or dark-brown tenacious resinous substance, semi-liquid when hot, hard when cold, got from distillation of tar or turpentine, used for caulking seams of ships etc. (~*-black*, ~ *-darkness*, with no light at all); ~'*blende*, native oxide of uranium, found in ~-like masses, important source of radium; ~*-cap*, cap lined with ~, used as instrument of torture; ~*-pine*, specially resinous kinds of pine; ~'*stone*, old volcanic rock looking like ~. **2.** v.t. Cover, coat, smear, with ~. [OE *pic* (whence vb *pician*), OS *pik*, OHG *peh*, ON *bik*, f. L *pix picis*]

pitch², v.t. & i. **1.** Fix & erect (tent, camp); (abs.) encamp. **2.** (Crick.) ~ *wickets*, fix stumps in ground & place bails; fix, plant, (thing) in definite position; expose (wares) for sale in market etc. **3.** Pave (road) with set stones. **4.** ~*ed battle* (cf. set kind, not casual). **5.** (Mus.) set at particular pitch, (fig.) express in particular style. **6.** Throw, fling; (in games) throw (flat object) towards a mark; (sl.) tell (tale, yarn). **7.** (golf). Play (ball) with pitch shot (see foll.). **8.** Fall heavily (*on* one's head, *into*, etc.); (of ship) plunge in longitudinal direction (cf. ROLL²). **9.** ~ *in* (colloq.), set to work vigorously; ~ *into* (colloq.), assail forcibly with blows, words, etc., make vigorous attack on, (person, food, etc.); ~ *upon*, happen to select; ~*-&-toss*, game of skill & chance in which coins are ~ed at a mark; ~*-farthing*, = CHUCK³-*farthing*. [ME *pic(c)he* (also north. *pikke*, whence (now dial.) *pick*), of obsc. hist. & orig.]

pitch³, n. **1.** Pitching (e.g. of ship). **2.** Mode of delivering cricket-ball in bowling; (golf, also ~ *shot*) lofted approach shot with little run to ball after alighting. **3.** Quantity of commodity pitched in market. **4.** ‖ Place at which one (e.g. street performer, bookmaker) is sta-

tioned; (crick.) place between & about wickets. **5.** Height to which falcon etc. soars before swooping on prey, as *fly a high* etc. ~ (also fig.). **6.** Height, degree, intensity, (*of* quality etc.); (mus.) degree of acuteness or graveness of tone. **7.** Degree of slope; steepness of roof's slope; (mech.) distance between successive points or lines, e.g. between successive teeth of cog-wheel. **8.** ~*-pipe*, small pipe blown by mouth to set ~ for singing or tuning; ~*-wheel*, toothed wheel engaging with another. [f. prec.]

pitch'er¹, n. Large usu. earthenware vessel with handle or two ears & usu. a lip, for holding liquids; jug; *little* ~*s have long ears*, children are apt to overhear; (bot.) modified leaf in ~ form, ~*-plant* (with such leaves). Hence ~FUL(2) n. [ME, f. OF *pichier* f. Rom. *picarium*, var. of *bicarium*, BEAKER]

pitch'er², n. In vbl senses of PITCH², esp.: player who delivers ball, esp. in baseball; ‖ street vendor who pitches stall in fixed place; stone used for paving. [-ER¹]

pitch'fork, n., & v.t. **1.** Long-handled fork with two prongs for pitching hay etc.; tuning-fork. **2.** v.t. Cast (as) with ~, (fig.) thrust (person) forcibly (*into* position, office, etc.). [in ME *pickfork*, prob. f. PICK¹+FORK, assoc. w. PITCH²]

pitch'y, a. Of, like, dark etc. as, pitch. [-Y²]

pit'eous, a. Calling for pity, deplorable. Hence ~LY² adv., ~NESS n. [ME *pitous* f. OF *pitos* f. Rom. *pietosus* (as PIETY, see -ITOUS)]

pith, n., & v.t. Spongy cellular tissue in stems & branches of dicotyledonous plants; similar tissue lining rind of orange etc.; spinal cord; (fig.) essential part, quintessence, (often ~ *& marrow of*); physical strength, vigour; force, energy; *of* ~ (importance) *& moment* (Shakes. *Ham.* III. i. 86); (v.t.) slaughter or immobilize (animal) by severing spinal cord. Hence ~'LESS a. [OE *pitha*,=MDu., MLG *pitte*, *pit*; ult. orig. unkn.]

pithĕcăn'thrōpe, n. Ape-man, hypothetical link between ape & man. [f. Gk *pithēkos* ape+*anthrōpos* man]

pithĕc'oid, a. Ape-like. [as prec., see -OID]

pith'|y, a. Of, like, abounding in, pith; condensed & forcible, terse. Hence ~iLY² adv., ~iNESS n. [-Y²]

pit'iab|le, a. Calling for pity or contempt. Hence ~leNESS n., ~LY² adv. [ME, f. OF (as PITY, see -ABLE)]

pit'iful, a. Compassionate; (of things) calling for pity; contemptible. Hence ~LY² adv., ~NESS n. [ME; -FUL]

pit'iless, a. Showing no pity. Hence ~LY² adv., ~NESS n. [ME; -LESS]

pit'păn, n. Central American dug-out boat. [perh. native]

pitt'ance, n. Pious bequest to religious house for extra food etc. (hist.); allowance, remuneration, esp. scanty one, as *a mere* ~; small number or amount. [ME, f. OF *pitance*, app. same wd as *pitance* pity (as PIETY +-ANCE)]

‖ **pitt'īte**, n. Person occupying seat in pit of theatre. [-ITE¹]

pitū'itary̆, a. Of or secreting phlegm, mucous; ~ *gland*, *body*, a small ductless gland at the base of the brain which has an important influence over the growth of the body. So **pitū'itous** a., **pitū'itrĭn** n., hormone produced by ~ body, solution containing this used medicinally. [f. L *pituitarius* (*pituita* phlegm, see -ARY¹)]

pit'y̆, n., & v.t. **1.** Feeling of tenderness aroused by person's distress or suffering, as *cannot help feeling ~ for him*, *felt no ~ for him*, *in ~ of his fate*; *take ~ on*, feel or act compassionately towards; (as form of entreaty) *for ~'s sake*; regrettable fact, ground for regret, as *what a ~ !*, *more's the ~* (so much the worse), *it is a thousand pities you did not mention it*; (arch.) *it is* or *was ~ of them*, one feels sorry for them. **2.** v.t. Feel (often contemptuous) ~ for, as *he is much to be pitied*, *I ~ you if you think that*. Hence **pit'y̆ingLY²** adv. [ME, f. OF *pite* f. L as PIETY]

pity̆rī'asis, n. (path.). Skin disease characterized by the shedding of bran-like scales. [f. Gk *pituriasis* (*pituron* bran, -ASIS)]

piv'ot, n., & v.t. & i. **1.** Short shaft or pin on which something turns or oscillates; (fig.) cardinal or crucial point. **2.** vb. Furnish with, attach by, ~; turn as on ~, hinge (*upon*, often fig.). Hence ~AL a. [F]

pix'y̆, -xĭe, n. Being akin to fairy. Hence *pix'ĭlātĕd* a. (dial.), slightly crazy. [orig. unkn.]

pizzicato (pĭtsĭkah'tō), adv., a., & n. (mus.). (Played) by plucking string of violin etc. with finger instead of using bow; (n.) passage, note, so played. [It.]

piz'zle, n. (now vulg.). Penis of animal esp. that of bull formerly used as flogging instrument. [16th c., f. LG *pēsel*, dim. of MLG *pēse* (Du. *pees*)]

plăc'|able, a. Easily appeased, mild, forgiving. Hence or cogn. ~ABIL'ITY n., ~abLY² adv. [ME, f. OF, f. L *placabilis* (*placare* appease, see -BLE)]

plăc'ärd, n., & v.t. **1.** Document printed on one side of single sheet for posting up, poster. **2.** v.t. (*also* plakärd'). Set up ~s on (wall etc.) advertise (wares etc.) by ~s, display (poster etc.) as ~. [ME, f. OF, f. *plaquier* vb plaster f. MDu. *plakken*, see -ARD]

placāte' (*or* plăc'āt), v.t. Pacify, conciliate. Hence **plăc'atŏry** a., propitiatory. [f. L *placare*, see -ATE³]

plāce¹, n. **1.** Particular part of space; part of space occupied by person or thing, as *it has changed its* ~. **2.** City, town, village, . etc.; (in names of groups of buildings) *Ely* etc. P~; residence, dwelling; country-house with surroundings. **3.** Building, spot, devoted to specified purpose, as ~ *of amusement*, *worship*, *bathing*-~; ‖ (H. of Commons) *another* ~, H. of Lords; also joc. in Cambridge with ref. to Oxford, and *vice-versa*. **4.** Particular spot on surface etc., as *a sore ~ on his wrist*. **5.** Passage of book etc. **6.** Rank, station, as *servants must know their* ~, *keep him in his* ~. **7.** (In racing) position among placed competitors. **8.** Position of figure in series as indicating its value in decimal or similar notation, as *calculated to 10 decimal* ~s. **9.** Step in progression of argument, statement, etc., as *in the first*, *second*, ~. **10.** Proper or natural position, as *take your* ~s, *there is no* ~ *for doubt*, *is in* or *out of* (*its*, *his*) ~; space, seat, accommodation, for person etc..at table, in conveyance, etc., as *take two* ~s *in the coach*, *always a* ~ *for you at our table*; *in* ~ *of*, instead of; *take the* ~ *of*, be substituted for. **11.** Office, employment, esp. government appointment; duties of office etc., as *it is not my* ~ *to inquire into that*. **12.** *In*, *out of*, ~, (un)suitable, (in)appropriate; *give* ~ *to*, make room for, be succeeded by; *take* ~, happen. **13.** ~-*brick* (imperfectly burnt from being on windward side of kiln); ~ (-*kick*) (footb.), kick made when ball is previously placed for that purpose on ground; ~'*man*, holder of public office, esp. one appointed from motives of interest. [ME, f. OF, f. Rom. **plattia* f. L f. Gk *plateia* (*hodos*) broad (way)]

plāce², v.t. **1.** Put (thing etc.) in particular place; arrange (set of things) in their proper places. **2.** Appoint (person, esp. clergyman) to post; find situation, living, etc., for. **3.** Invest (money); dispose of (goods) to customer; put (order for goods etc.) into hands of firm etc. **4.** Repose (confidence etc. *in*, *on*). **5.** Assign rank to; locate; fully identify, remember circumstances of previous meeting with, assign to a class (*I know that man's face but I can't* ~ *him*). **6.** State position of (usu. any of first 3 horses or runners) in race; *be* ~*d*, be among first three. **7.** Get (goal) by PLACE¹-*kick*. [prec.]

placĕb'ō, n. (pl. ~*s*, ~*es*). (Eccl.) opening antiphon of the vespers for the dead; (med.) medicine given to humour, rather than cure, the patient. [L, = I shall be acceptable (*placēre* please), first word of *Ps.* cxvi. 9 (Vulg.)]

placĕn't|a, n. (pl. ~*ae*). Flattened circular spongy vascular organ in higher mammals, expelled after parturition and helping to nourish foetus, which is attached to it by umbilical cord; (bot.) part of carpel to which ovules are attached. Hence ~AL a. [f. L *placenta*=Gk *plakoeis -entos* flat cake f. root of *plax plakos* flat plate]

plā'cer, n. Deposit of sand, gravel, etc., in bed of stream etc. containing valuable minerals in particles. [Amer. Sp., cogn. w. *placel* sandbank f. *plaza* PLACE[1]]

‖ **plā′cĕt**, sentence & n. (Univ.). ~, *non* ~, it pleases me (not) (forms used in voting for or against measure); (n.) such vote. [L]

plă′cid, a. Mild; peaceful; serene. Hence or cogn. **placid′ITY** n., ~**LY**[2] adv. [f. L *placidus* (*placēre* please, see -ID[1])]

plăck′ĕt, n. Pocket, esp. in woman's skirt; ~*-hole*, opening in outer skirt giving access to this. [var. of PLACARD]

plăc′oid, a. (Of scales) plate-shaped; (of fish) with ~ scales. [f. Gk *plax plakos* plate, -OID]

plafond (plăfawn′), n. Ceiling, esp. one enriched with paintings; such painting. [F]

plāg′al, a. (mus.). (Of ecclesiastical modes) having their sounds comprised between the dominant & its octave; ~ *cadence* (in which chord of subdominant immediately precedes that of the tonic). Cf. AUTHENTIC. [f. med. L *plagalis* f. *plaga* mode, prob. f. med. L f. Gk *plagios* oblique, (med. Gk) plagal, f. *plagos* side]

plage (plahzh), n. Sea beach (esp. at fashionable resort). [F]

plā′giar|īze, **-ise** (-īz), v.t. Take and use another person's (thoughts, writings, inventions, or abs.) as one's own. So ~ISM, ~IST, nn. [f. foll. +-IZE]

plā′giarў̆, n. (arch.). = PLAGIARISM; = PLAGIARIST. [f. L *plagiarius* kidnapper (*plagiare* kidnap)]

plā′gio-, comb. form of Gk *plagios* oblique, as: ~*cephăl′ic*, having anterior part of skull more developed on one side, posterior on the other; ~*clas′tic* (min.), having oblique cleavage; ~*stŏme*, fish with mouth placed transversely beneath snout, as sharks & rays.

plāgue (-g), n., & v.t. **1.** Affliction, esp. as divine punishment; (colloq.) nuisance, trouble; pestilence, esp. *the* (oriental or bubonic)~; (as imprecation)~ *on it!* etc.; ~*-spot*, spot on skin characteristic of ~, locality infected with ~, (fig.) source or symptom of moral corruption. **2.** v.t. Afflict with ~; (colloq.) annoy, bother, whence ~*'SOME* (-gs-) a. (colloq.). [ME, f. L *plaga* stroke (*plag-* root of *plangere* beat breast)]

plāg′u|y (-gi), a. & adv. (arch.). Annoying(ly); exceeding(ly), as *was ~y glad to get back again.* Hence ~**iLY**[2] (-gi-) adv. [f. prec. +-Y[2]]

plaice, n. European flat-fish much used as food. [ME, f. OF *plaïz* f. LL *platessa* app. f. Gk *platus* broad, or *plat-* flat]

plaid (plăd, Sc. plād), n. Long piece of twilled woollen cloth, usu. with chequered or tartan pattern, outer article of Highland costume; cloth used for this. Hence ~′ED[2] a. [Gael. *plaide*, of unkn. orig.]

plain[1], a., adv., & n. **1.** Clear, evident; simple, readily understood, as ~ *words, English*; not in code; not intricate, as ~ *sewing*; unembellished, (of drawings etc.)

not coloured; (of food) not rich or highly seasoned; not luxurious, as~ *living*; outspoken, straightforward, (esp. *be ~ with*, tell home truths to); unsophisticated, as *I am a ~ man*; of homely manners, dress, or appearance; ugly, as *a pity the poor girl is so~*; ~ *as a* PIKESTAFF. **2.** adv. Clearly, as *learn to speak ~*. **3.** ~ *cards* (not court-cards); ~*-chant*, = ~*-song*; ~ *clothes*, unofficial dress; ~ *dealing*, candour, straightforwardness; ~ *sailing*, sailing in a ~ course, (fig.) simple course of action; ~*-song*, vocal music composed in medieval modes & in free rhythm depending on accentuation of the words, and sung in unison; ~*-spoken*, outspoken; ~ *suit* (not trumps); ~ *tile*, flat roofing-tile. **4.** n. Level tract of country; ~*s′man*, inhabitant of a ~. Hence ~′**LY**[2] adv., ~′**NESS** (-n-n-) n. [ME, f. OF *plain* adj. & n., f. L *planus* adj., -*num* n.]

‖ **plain**[2], v.i. (arch., poet.). Mourn; complain; emit plaintive sound. [ME, f. OF *plaindre* (st. *plaign-*) f. L *plangere planct-* beat breast]

plaint, n. ‖ (Law) accusation, charge; (poet.) lamentation, complaint. [ME & OF (1) *plaint* f. L *planctus -ūs*, (2) *plainte* f. med. L *plancta* fem. p.p. as n.; both as prec.]

plain′tiff, n. Party who brings suit into court of law (opp. *defendant*). [ME, f. OF, as foll.]

plain′tive, a. Expressive of sorrow; mournful. Hence ~**LY**[2] adv., ~**NESS** n. [ME, f. OF (-*if*, -*ive*) f. *plaint-*, p.p. of *plaindre* PLAIN[2], see -IVE]

plait (plăt), n., & v.t. **1.** (Now usu. PLEAT) fold, crease, esp. flattened fold in cloth made by doubling it upon itself; (v.t.) fold (cloth etc.) thus. **2.** (Now rarely PLAT[2]) contexture of three or more interlaced strands of hair, ribbon, straw, etc.; (v.t.) form (hair, straw, etc.) into ~. [ME *pleit*, *plait* f. OF *pleit* f. Rom. *plic(i)tum*, p.p. of *plicare* fold; see PLEAT, PLIGHT[2]]

plăn, n., & v.t. & i. (-nn-). **1.** Drawing, diagram, made by projection on flat surface (cf. ELEVATION), esp. one showing relative position of parts of (one floor of) a building; large-scale detailed map of town or district; table indicating times, places, etc., of intended proceedings etc.; scheme of arrangement; project, design; way of proceeding, as *the better ~ is to peel them after boiling*; ~ *of* CAMPAIGN; (perspective) any of the imaginary planes, perpendicular to line of vision,. passing through objects shown in picture. **2.** vb. Make a ~ of (ground, existing building); design (building to be constructed etc.); scheme, arrange beforehand, (procedure etc.), as ~*ned economy*; make ~s. Hence ~′**LESS** a. [F, f. earlier *plant*, f. It. *pianta* plan; see PLANT[1]]

‖ **plănch** (-sh), n. Slab of metal, stone, etc., esp. of baked fire-clay used in enamelling. [late ME & OF *planche* PLANK[1]]

plăn′chĕt (-sh-), n. Plain disc of metal of which coin is made. [prec. +-ET[1]]

plănchĕtte′ (-sh-, & see Ap.), n. Small usu. heart-shaped board supported by two castors & pencil, which when person's fingers rest lightly on board is said to trace letters etc. without conscious direction. [F, dim. of *planche* PLANK[1]]

plǎne[1], n. Tall spreading tree of genus *Platanus* with broad angular palmately- -lobed leaves; ~-*tree* (of this genus). [ME & OF *plane* f. L f. Gk *platanos* (*platus* broad)]

plǎne[2], n., & v.t. **1.** Tool for smoothing surface of woodwork by paring shavings from it, consisting of wooden or metal stock from smooth bottom of which projects a steel blade; similar tool for smoothing metal; *smoothing-*~ (used to finish surface, cf. JACK[1]- & TRY*ing-*~); *moulding-*~ (for making mouldings). **2.** v.t. Smooth (wood, metal) with ~, pare *away* or *down* (irregularities) with ~; (arch.) level, esp. ~ *the way*. [(n.) ME & OF *plane* f. LL *plana*; (vb) ME f. OF *planer*; both f. L *planare* (as PLANE[4])]

plǎne[3], n., & v.i. **1.** Surface such that the straight line joining any two points in it lies wholly in it; imaginary surface of this kind in which points or lines in material bodies lie; level surface; flat thin object such as table-top, supporting part of aeroplane; (also '*plane*) aeroplane; INCLINE[1]*d* ~; each of the natural faces of a crystal. **2.** Main road in mine. **3.** (fig.). Level (*of* thought, knowledge, etc.), as *his superstition places him on the same* ~ *as the savage.* **4.** ~ *sailing*, art of determining ship's position on the theory that she is moving on a ~, (fig., now usu. PLAIN[1] *sailing*) simple course. **5.** v.i. Travel, glide (*down* etc.), in aeroplane. [17th c., different. from PLAIN[1] (n.), after L *planum*, in certain senses]

plǎne[4], a., Perfectly level, as a PLANE[3]; (of angle, figure, etc.) lying in a plane; ~ *chart* (on which meridians & parallels of latitude are represented by equidistant straight lines, used in PLANE[3] sailing); ~- *-table*, surveying instrument used for direct plotting in the field. [late 17th c., different. from PLAIN[1] (adj.), after L *planus*, in certain senses]

plǎn′ĕt[1], n. (Hist.) heavenly body distinguished from fixed stars by having apparent motion of its own (Moon, Mercury, Venus, Sun, Mars, Jupiter, Saturn), esp. (astrol.) with reference to its supposed influence on persons & events; (astron.) *primary* ~*s*, heavenly bodies revolving in approximately circular orbits round sun (*major* ~*s*, Mercury, Venus, Earth, Mars, Jupiter, Saturn, Uranus, Neptune, Pluto; *minor* ~*s*, the asteroids, whose orbits lie between those of Mars & Jupiter); *secondary* ~*s* (also *satellites*), those that revolve round primary; SUN & ~; ~-*struck, -stricken,* bewildered, terrified.

[ME & OF *planete* f. LL f. Gk *planētēs* wanderer, planet, f. *planaomai* wander]

plǎn′ĕt[2], n. Chasuble. [f. med. L *planeta*, also LL *planetica* (*vestis*), f. Gk *planētēs* wanderer (prec.)]

plǎnĕtār′ium, n. Orrery, model of planetary system. [mod. L, see foll.]

plǎn′ĕtarÿ, a. Of planets, as ~ *influence, motions*; ~ *hour*, twelfth part of natural day or night; ~ (solar) *system*; terrestrial, mundane; wandering, erratic. [f. LL *planetarius* (as PLANET[1], see -ARY[1])]

plǎnĕtēs′imal, n. One of a vast number of minute planetoids which, according to the ~ *hypothesis*, formed the bodies of the planets by accretion in a cold state. [f. PLANET[1] after *infinitesimal*]

plǎn′ĕtoid, n. Minor PLANET[1]. [-OID]

plǎn′g|ent (-j-), a. (Of sound) thrilling, vibrating, moaning, insistent. Hence ~ENCY n. [f. L *plangere* beat the breast, see -ENT]

plan|i-, comb. form of L *planus* level, smooth, plane, as: ~*ĭm′ĕter*, instrument for mechanically measuring area of irregular plane figure; ~*ĭm′etrÿ*, measurement of plane surfaces, so *plǎnĭmĕt′ric(al)* aa.; *plǎnĭpet′alous*, with flat petals; *plǎn′isphere*, map formed by projection of (part of) sphere or plane, (*revolving* ~*isphere*, device for showing the part of the heavens visible at given time & place), so *plǎnĭsphĕ′ric* a.

plǎn′ish, v.t. Flatten (sheet metal etc.) with smooth-faced hammer or otherwise; flatten out (coining-metal) between rollers; polish (photograph etc.) with roller etc. Hence ~ER[1] (1, 2) n. [f. obs. F *planir* smooth (*plan* a. as PLANE[4]), see -ISH[2]]

plǎnk[1], n. Long flat piece of timber, 2 to 6 in. thick, 9 or more in. wide (cf. BOARD[1]); item of political or other programme (cf. PLATFORM); *walk the* ~, (of pirates' captive etc.) walk blindfold into sea along ~ laid over side of ship; ~ *bed* (of boards, without mattress, used as prison discipline etc.). [ME, f. ONF *planke* = OF *planche* f. LL *planca* board (*plancus* flat-footed)]

plǎnk[2], v.t. Furnish, cover, floor, with planks, whence ~′ING[1] (2, 3) n.; (colloq.) put *down* roughly or violently, esp. pay (money, or abs.) *down* on the spot. [f. prec.]

plǎnk′tŏn, n. (biol.). The (chiefly microscopic) forms of drifting or floating organic life found at various depths in seas, lakes, rivers, etc., taken collectively (cf. BENTHOS & NEKTON). [G, f. Gk *plagktos* wandering (*plazomai*)]

plǎno-, comb. form of L *planus* level, flat, as: ~*conc′ave,* ~*con′vex*, (of lens etc.) with one surface plane & the other concave, convex; *plǎnŏm′eter*, flat plate, usu. of cast iron, as gauge for plane surfaces.

plant[1] (-ah-), n. **1.** Living organism capable of living wholly on inorganic substances & having neither power of locomotion nor special organs of sensation or digestion, member of the vegetable kingdom (often restricted to the smaller ~s, excluding trees and shrubs). 2. Crop; growth, as *in* ~, growing, *lose* ~, die off, *miss* ~, fail to spring from seed. 3. Mode of planting oneself, pose. 4. Fixtures, implements, machinery, etc., used in industrial process; factory; (fig.) machinery of intellectual work etc. 5. (sl.). Planned swindle or burglary, hoax. 6. ~-*louse*, kinds of insect that infest ~s, esp. aphis. Hence ~'LET n., ~'LIKE a. [OE *plante* (= OHG *pflanza*, ON *planta*), in ME reinforced by OF *plante*; f. L *planta* slip, cutting; partly also f. foll.]

plant[2] (-ah-), v.t. **1.** Place (tree, shoot, bulb, seed, crop, etc.) in ground that it may take root & grow; deposit (young fish, spawn, oysters) in river etc.; ~ *out*, transfer (plant) from pot or frame to open ground, set out (seedlings) at intervals. **2.** Fix firmly (*in, on*, ground etc.); station (person), esp. as spy; ~ one*self*, take up a position. **3.** Establish, found, (community, city, church); settle (person) in a place as colonist etc.; cause (idea etc.) to take root *in* (mind); furnish (land *with* plants, district *with* settlers, etc.). **4.** Deliver (blow, thrust) with definite aim. **5.** (sl.). Conceal (stolen goods etc.); bury; place (gold-dust, ore) in mining claim to encourage prospective buyer, cf. SALT v.; devise (fraudulent scheme). **6.** Abandon, as *there I was, fairly* ~*ed*. Hence ~'ABLE a. [OE *plantian* f. L *plantare*, as prec.]

Plăntă'gĕnĕt, n. & a. (Member) of the family founded by Geoffrey of Anjou, esp. any of the English kings from Henry II to Richard II. [surname, f. sprig of broom (L *planta* plant, *genesta* broom) worn as cognizance]

plăn'tain[1] (-tĭn), n. Kinds of plants, esp. *greater* ~, low herb with broad flat leaves spread out close to ground & seeds much used for cage-birds. [ME & OF, F, L *plantaginem* (nom. -*go*) prob. f. *planta* sole of foot, from its prostrate leaves]

plăn'tain[2] (-tĭn), n. Tree-like tropical herbaceous plant allied to banana and bearing similar fruit; its fruit. [16th c. *pla(n)tan* f. Sp. *plá(n)tano* in same sense, identical in form w. *plá(n)tano* (obs. F *plantain*) PLANE[1]-tree]

plăn'tar (a.anat.). Of the sole of the foot. [f. L *plantaris* (*planta* sole, see -AR[1])]

plăntā'tion, n. Assemblage of planted growing plants, esp. trees; estate on which cotton, tobacco, etc., are cultivated (formerly by servile labour); ~ *song* (of the kind sung by Negroes on American ~s); (hist.) colonization, colony. [ME, f. OF or F. L *plantatio* (as PLANT[2], see -ATION)]

pla'nter (-ah-), n. Cultivator of soil; (in Ireland) English settler on forfeited lands in 17th c., (19th c.) person settled in evicted tenant's holding; occupier of

plantation, esp. in (sub-)tropical countries, as *coffee, cotton, sugar, tobacco,* -~; machine for planting, as *corn, potato,* -~. Hence ~SHIP n. [PLANT[2] + -ER[1]]

plănt'ĭgrāde, a. & n. (Animal) that walks on its soles (cf. DIGITIGRADE). [F, f. L *planta* sole + -*gradus* -walking]

plănx'tÿ, n. (Ir. mus.). Animated harp-tune moving in triplets. [orig. unkn.]

plaque (plahk), n. Ornamental tablet of metal, porcelain, etc., plain or decorated; small tablet as badge of rank in honorary order; (path.) patch of eruption etc. So **plaquETTE'** (-ăkĕt) n. [F, f. Du. *plak* tablet]

plăsh[1], n. Marshy pool; puddle. Hence ~'Y[2] a. [OE *plæsc*, MDu. *plasch*, *plas*, prob. imit., cf. foll.]

plăsh[2], v.t. & i., & n. **1.** Strike surface of (water) so as to break it up; splash (t. & i.). **2.** n. Splash, plunge. Hence ~'Y[2] a. [cf. Du. *plassen*, G *platschen*, prob. imit.]

plăsh[3], v.t. Bend down and interweave (branches, twigs) to form hedge; make, renew, (hedge) thus. [f. OF *plaissier* ult. f. L *plectere* plait; cf. PLEACH]

plăsm, n. Living matter of a cell, protoplasm, esp. general body of this as distinct from nucleus. [f. foll.]

plăs'm|a (-z-), n. **1.** Green variety of quartz. **2.** Colourless coagulable part of blood, lymph, or milk, in which the corpuscles or oil-globules float, so ~**ăt'ic** a. **3.** = prec., whence ~**ic** (-z-) a. [LL & Gk (gen. -*matos*), = thing moulded (*plassō* mould)]

plăsmōd'ium (-z-), n. (biol.; pl. -*ia*). Mass of naked protoplasm formed by fusion or aggregation of amoeboid bodies without fusion of their nuclei; generic name of microscopic parasitic organism whose presence & rapid multiplication in the blood of man constitute malaria. [mod. L, f. PLASMA + -*odium*, see -ODE]

plăsmŏl'ysis (-zm-), n. Loss of water from, & consequent contraction of, protoplasm of vegetable cell due to immersion in a solution stronger than the cell fluid. So **plăs'molÿse** (-zm-) v.t., subject to ~. [f. PLASM, -O-, Gk *lusis* loosing f. *luō* to loose]

pla'ster[1] (-ah-), n. **1.** Curative application consisting of some substance spread upon muslin etc. & capable of adhering at the temperature of the body, as COURT[1], MUSTARD, *sticking-,* ~. **2.** Soft plastic mixture, esp. of lime, sand, & hair, for spreading on walls etc. to form smooth surface; ~ *of Paris*, fine white ~ of gypsum used for making moulds & as cement etc. [prepared from gypsums of Montmartre, Paris]. Hence ~Y[2] a. [(1) OE, f. med. L *plastrum* f. L f. Gk *em-plastron*; (2) f. OF *plastre* f. same source]

pla'ster[2] (-ah-), v.t. **1.** Cover (wall etc.) with plaster or the like, whence ~ER[1] n.; coat, bedaub; (fig.) load to excess (*with* praise etc.). **2.** Apply medical plaster to, (joc.) give compensation for (blow, wound); stick, fix, (thing) like plaster upon surface. **3.** Treat (wine) with gypsum etc. to neutralize acidity. [ME, f. prec.]

plăs′tic, a. Moulding, giving form to clay, wax, etc.; ~ *arts*, those concerned with modelling, e.g. sculpture, ceramics; ~ *surgery* (reparing deficiency of structure); causing growth of natural forms, formative of immaterial things; produced by moulding; capable of being (easily) moulded; ~ *bomb*, one containing ~ explosive of putty-like or dough-like consistency capable of being moulded by hand; ~ *clay* (geol.), middle group of Eocene beds; (fig.) pliant, supple; (biol.) capable of forming living tissue, (also) accompanied by this process, as ~ *bronchitis*. Hence **plăs′ti**CALLY adv., **plăsti′**CITY n., ~IZE(3) v.t., make ~, **plăs′tics** n. pl., group of synthetic resinous or other substances that can be moulded into any form. [f. L f. Gk *plastikos* (*plassō* mould, see -IC)]

plăs′ticine, n. Plastic substance used as substitute for modelling clay. [P; -INE[4]]

plăs′tron, n. Fencer's leather-covered breast-plate; breast-covering of facings-cloth worn by lancers; ornamental front to woman's bodice; man's starched shirt-front; ventral part of shell of tortoise or turtle, corresponding part in other animals; (hist.) steel breast-plate. [F, f. It. *piastrone* (*piastra* breast-plate, as PLASTER; see -OON)]

plăt[1], n. (arch.). Patch, plot, of ground, as *grass-~*. [16th c., collat. form of PLOT]

plăt[2], n., & v.t. (-tt-). = PLAIT (2nd sense).

plat[3] (plah), n. Dish of food. [F, see PLATE[1]]

plăt′an, n. Plane-tree. [ME, f. L *platanus* plane-tree]

plāte[1], n. **1.** Flat thin usu. rigid sheet of metal etc. of even surface and more or less uniform thickness; this as part of mechanism. **2.** Smooth piece of metal etc. for engraving; impression from this; = BOOK[1]-~. **3.** Piece of metal with name or inscription for affixing to something, as *coffin, door, name, -~.* **4.** Thin sheet of metal, glass, etc., coated with sensitive film for photograph (*whole-~*, 8½ × 6½ in., *half-~*, 6½ × 4¾, *quarter-~*, 4¼ × 3¼). **5.** Stereotype or electrotype cast of page of composed movable types, from which sheets are printed. **6.** Horizontal timber laid along top of wall to support ends of joists or rafters, or at top or bottom of a framing, as *roof, wall, window, ~.* **7.** (Also *~-rail*) early form of railroad. **8.** (collect. sing.). ‖ Table & domestic utensils of silver, gold, or other metal, as *pewter ~, electro~.* **9.** Silver or gold cup as prize for (orig. horse-) race, such race; *selling ~*, horse-race winner of which must be sold at fixed price. **10.** Shallow usu. circular vessel, now usu. of earthenware

or china, from which food is eaten, as *dessert, dinner, soup, -~*; contents of this, as *a ~ of strawberries*; similar vessel used for collection in churches etc., as *put a shilling in the ~.* **11.** Thin piece of plastic material, moulded to shape of gums etc., to which artificial teeth are attached. **12.** **Home, pitcher's, ~,* stations of batter, pitcher, in baseball. **13.** Light shoe for racehorse. **14.** ‖ *~-basket* (for spoons, forks, etc.); ~ *glass,* thick glass of fine quality cast in ~s for shop windows etc.; ‖ *~′layer,* man employed in fixing & repairing railway; *~-mark,* = HALL-*mark,* (also) impression left on margin of engraving by pressure of the ~ (hence *~-marked mount* for photographs); *~-powder* (for cleaning silver); ‖ *~-rack* (in which ~s are kept or placed to drain). Hence *~′*FUL(2) (-tfŏŏl) n., *~′*LESS a. [ME & OF *plate,* fem. of *plat* flat, f. Rom. **plattus,* perh. f. Gk *platus* broad; sense 10 is f. OF *plat* n.]

plāte[2], v.t. Cover (esp. ship) with plates of metal for protection, ornament, etc.; cover (other metal) with thin coat of silver, gold, or tin; make a plate of (type) for printing. [f. prec.]

plateau′ (-tō), n. (pl. ~x, ~s, pr. -z). Tableland; ornamented tray or dish; decorative plaque; woman's hat with level top. [F, f. OF *platel* dim. of PLAT[3]]

plăt′en, -tt-, n. Plate in printing-press by which paper is pressed against type; corresponding part in typewriters etc. [f. OF *platine* flat piece (*plat,* see PLATE[1])]

plăt′er, n. One who plates with silver etc.; one who makes or applies plates in shipbuilding; inferior racehorse, competing chiefly for plates. [-ER[1]]

plăt′fŏrm, n., & v.t. & i. **1.** Raised level surface, natural or artificial terrace; ‖ raised surface of planks etc. along side of line at railway station; raised flooring in hall or open air from which speaker addresses audience, (fig.) *the ~,* ~ oratory; (fig.) political basis of party etc., declared policy of political party. **2.** vb. Place (as) on ~; speak on ~. [f. F *plateforme* ground-plan, lit. flat form (as PLATE[1]+*forme* FORM)]

plăt′ing, n. In vbl senses; also or esp.: coating of gold, silver, etc.; plate-racing. [f. PLATE[1,2]+-ING[1]]

plăt′inize, -ise (-īz), v.t. Coat with platinum. [-IZE]

plăt′inoid, n. Alloy of copper, zinc, nickel, & tungsten; kind(s) of metal found associated with platinum. [-OID]

plăt′inotȳpe, n. Process of photographic printing in platinum black. [f. foll. +-O- +-TYPE]

plăt′in|um, n. White heavy ductile malleable metallic element unaffected by simple acids & fusible only at very high temperature; *~um black,* ~um in form of powder like lamp-black; *~um blonde* (colloq., orig. U.S.), woman with gold-

-grey hair; ~um metals, platinoids. Hence **platin'**ic, ~ir'erous, aa. [mod. L (see -ium) f. earlier *platina* f. Sp. dim. of *plata* silver, see -ine[5]]

plät'it|ūde, n. Commonplaceness; commonplace remark, esp. one solemnly delivered. Hence ~ūd'inīze(2) v.i., ~ūd'inous a., ~ūd'inously[2] adv. [F, f. *plat* (see plate[1]) after *latitude* etc.]

plätitūdinār'ian, n. & a. Dealer in platitudes; (adj.) of the nature of platitude. [-arian]

Platōn'ic, a. Of Plato the Greek philosopher (died *c.* 347 b.c.) or his doctrines; ~ *love*, purely spiritual love for one of opposite sex (*p~s*, ~ lovers' talk or relation); (pop.) confined to words or theory, not issuing in action, harmless; ~ *year*, cycle in which heavenly bodies were supposed to go through all their possible movements & return to original positions. So **Platōn'**ically adv., **Plāt'o**nism, **Plāt'**onist, nn., **Plāt'**onīze(2, 3) v.i. & t. [f. L f. Gk *Platōnikos* (*Platōn* Plato, see -ic)]

platoon', n. (Hist.) small infantry detachment, esp. a unit for volley-firing etc., volley fired by it; (in mod. use) subdivision of a company, a tactical unit commanded by a lieutenant & usu. divided into three sections. [f. F *peloton* small ball (as pellet, see -oon)]

plätt'er, n. (chiefly arch. exc. U.S.). Flat dish or plate, often of wood. [ME & AF *plater*, f. *plat* plate[1]]

plät'ÿ-, comb. form of Gk *platus* broad, flat, as: ~*pus*, Australian duck-mole, ornithorhynchus; ~(*r*)*rhine* (-rĭn), (of monkeys) with nostrils far apart & directed forwards or sideways.

plaud'it, n. (usu. in pl.). Round of applause; emphatic expression of approval. [shortened f. L *plaudite* applaud (also as E noun) pl. imperat. of *plaudere* plaus-applaud, said by Roman actors at end of play]

plaus'|ible (-z-), a. (Of arguments, statements, etc.) specious, seeming reasonable or probable; (of persons) fair-spoken (freq. implying deceit). Hence or cogn. ~ibil'ity n.,~ibly[2] adv. [f. L *plausibilis* (as prec., see -ble)]

play[1], v.i. & t. **1.** Move about in lively or capricious manner, frisk, flit, flutter, pass gently (*around, about*, etc.), strike lightly (*upon* etc.), alternate rapidly, as *bees* ~ *about flowers, tresses* ~ *on her neck, smile* ~*ed on his lips, wind* ~*s on water, his fancy* ~*ed round the idea.* **2.** (Of part of mechanism etc.) have free movement. **3.** Wield freely, as ~ *a good knife & fork,* eat heartily; as ~ *a good stick,* fence well. **4.** Allow (fish) to exhaust itself by pulling against line. **5.** Discharge (guns etc. *on*), discharge guns (*on*), (intr., of guns) be fired (*on*). **6.** Direct (light *on, over, along*, etc.), (intr., of light) pass (*over, along*, etc.). **7.** Perform, execute, (trick, prank,

joke, *on* person, or with double object). **8.** Amuse oneself, sport, frolic; ~*boy,* one living for pleasure; ~ *with,* amuse oneself with, trifle with, treat lightly; ~ *upon words,* pun. **9.** (dial.). (Esp. of workmen on strike) abstain from work. **10.** Employ oneself in the game of (cricket, whist, etc., or abs.). **11.** ~*ed out,* exhausted of energy or vitality or usefulness (*our horses were, I felt, Free Trade is,* ~*ed out*); ~ *up,* put all one's energy into the game etc.; ~ duck[1]*s & drakes;* ~ fast[3] *& loose.* **12.** (In cricket, lawn tennis, etc., as bowler's warning to batsman etc.) ~ *!* **13.** Pretend for fun (*that we are gipsies* etc.). **14.** (crick.). (Of ground) ~ *well* etc., be in good rec. condition for play. **15.** ~-*or-pay bet* (holding good whether horse runs or not). **16.** Game, gamble; **~ the market,* gamble in stocks etc. **17.** ~ booty; ~ *fair, foul,* ~ *or* (fig.) act (un)fairly; ~ (*observe* the rules of) *the game* (also fig. of keeping to code of honour); ~ *into the hands of,* act so as to give advantage to (opponent or partner); (sl.) ~ *it on,* ~ *it low on,* ~ (*low*) *down on,* take mean advantage of (person); ~ *upon the* square; ~ *at,* engage in (game), (fig.) engage in (fighting etc.) in trivial or half-hearted way. **18.** Contend against (person) in game; employ (person) to ~ in game, include in team. **19.** Move (piece in chess etc.); take (playing-card) from one's hand & lay it face upwards on table in one's turn; (fig.) ~ *one's cards well,* make good use of opportunities. **20.** (crick. etc.) Strike (ball) in specified esp. defensive manner; (crick.) ~ *on* (abs.), ~ the ball on to one's own wicket and so put oneself out. **21.** ~ *off,* oppose (person *against* another) esp. for one's own advantage; cause (person) to exhibit himself disadvantageously; pass (thing) off as something else; ~*-off* n., additional match to decide a draw or tie. **22.** Perform on (musical instrument, or abs.); perform (*on* instrument); ~*back,* reproduction of sound or picture from magnetic tape etc.; ~ *by ear,* perform on an instrument without technical knowledge of music; perform (music *on* instrument). **23.** ~ (congregation etc.) *in, out,* ~ *on* organ etc. as they come in, go out; ~ (*up*)*on,* make use of (person's fears, credulity, etc.); ~ *first, second,* fiddle. **24.** Perform (drama, or abs.) on stage; act (*in* drama); act (part) in drama, as ~ *Shylock,* (fig.) act in real life the part of (the deuce[2] or *devil* (*with*), *the fool, the man, truant,* etc., also ~ one's *part well* etc.); ~ *up to,* act in drama so as to support (another actor), (fig.) back up, flatter, toady. Hence ~'able a. [OE *plegan* exercise oneself, move briskly, play, corresp. to MDu. *pleyen* dance]

play[2], n. **1.** Brisk, light, or fitful movement. **2.** Activity, operation, as *lively* ~ *of fancy, other forces come into* ~, *are in* full ~, are brought or called into ~; make ~, act effectively, esp. (racing, hunting) exercise pursuers or followers. **3.** Freedom of movement, space for this, scope for activity, as *bolts should have half an inch of* ~, *allow full* ~ *to curiosity*. **4.** Amusement, as *at* ~, engaged in playing; *said it only in* ~ (not seriously); ~ *of words*, trifling with words; ~ *on words*, pun. **5.** Playing of game; manner, style, of this; (crick., footb., etc.) *ball is in* ~ (being used in ordinary course of ~), *is out of* ~ (temporarily removed from ~ according to rules); so ~, part of ground within definite boundaries. **6.** CHILD'S-~; FAIR[2], FOUL, ~. **7.** Cessation from work (of workmen on strike etc.). **8.** Dramatic piece, drama. **9.** Gaming, gambling. **10.** ~-*actor* (usu. derog.); ~*'bill*, bill, placard, announcing theatrical ~; ~-*day*, school holiday, ‖ week-day on which miners etc. do not work; ~-*debt* (incurred in gaming); ~*'fellow*, companion in (usu. children's) ~; ~*'game*, experience that falls short of another (*is a* ~*game in comparison*) or of grim reality (e.g. sham fight); ~*'goer*, frequenter of theatre; ~*'ground*, piece of ground used for ~, esp. at school (*the* ~*ground of Europe*, Switzerland); ~*'house*, theatre; ~*'mate*, ~*fellow*; ~*'thing*, toy, (fig.) person etc. treated as mere toy; ~*'time*; ~*'wright*, dramatist. [OE *plega* as prec.]

play'er, n. In vbl senses, esp.: person engaged at the time, person skilful, in a game; performer on musical instrument; ‖ professional ~ at cricket etc.; actor; (pool, croquet) ball that after present ~ has finished break etc. will play on him; ~-*piano* (fitted with apparatus enabling it to be played automatically). [-ER[1]]

play'ful, a. Frolicsome, sportive; humorous, jocular. Hence ~LY[2] adv., ~NESS n. [ME; -FUL]

play'ing, n. In vbl senses; ~-*cards*, set or pack of cards used in games. [-ING[1]]

pla'za (-ah-), n. Market-place, open square (esp. in Spanish town). [Sp., = place]

plea, n. Pleading, argument, excuse; (law) formal statement by or on behalf of defendant, defence, *special* ~ (alleging new fact); (hist.) action at law. [ME & OF *plaid, plait* f. L *placitum* decree, neut. p.p. of *placēre* please; *plea* = ME *plai, ple* f. AF]

pleach, v.t. Entwine, interlace; esp. = PLASH[3]. [ME *pleche* f. OF **plechier* var. of *plessier* PLASH[3]]

plead, v.i. & t. (~*'ed*; U.S., Sc., dial. *plĕd*). Address court as advocate on behalf of either party, so ~*'ER*[1] n.; maintain (cause) in court; allege formally as plea, (fig.) allege as excuse etc., as *I can only* ~ *inexperience*, so ~*'ABLE* a.; ~ (*not*) *guilty*, deny, confess, liability or guilt; ~ *with*, make earnest appeal to (person *for* person, *for, against*, thing, decision, etc.) whence

~*'INGLY*[2] adv. [ME, f. OF *plaidier* (PLEA)]

plead'ing, n. In vbl senses, esp: (usu. pl.) formal (now usu. written) statement of cause of action or defence; SPECIAL ~. [-ING[1]]

plea'sance (-lĕz-), n. (arch.). Pleasure, enjoyment; pleasure-ground, esp. one attached to mansion (now chiefly surviving in proper names). [ME, f. OF *plaisance* (as foll., see -ANCE)]

plea'sant (-lĕz-), a. Agreeable to mind, feelings, or senses, as *a* ~ *breeze, flavour, discovery, companion*, *has a* ~ *manner, spent a* ~ *evening*; ‖ (arch.) jocular, facetious. Hence ~LY[2] adv., ~NESS n. [ME, f. OF *plaisant* (as PLEASE, see -ANT)]

plea'santry (-lĕz-), n. Jocularity, humorous speech, jest. [f. F *plaisanterie* (prec., -ERY)]

please (-z), v.t. & i. **1.** Be agreeable to, as *meant only to* ~ *the eye, his last book will* ~ *you*; ~ *yourself*, do as you like; *be* ~*d with*, derive pleasure from; *I shall* (or *will*) *be* ~*d* (glad) *to* (do, esp. as polite form of consent or offer). **3.** Think fit, as *take as many as you* ~. **3.** (In formal or iron. deference) *His Majesty has been graciously* ~*d to confer* etc., *your lordship was* ~*d to doubt my veracity*. **4.** (With *it* as subject, expressed or omitted, representing a prec. or foll. infinitive, clause, or sentence, now chiefly as in last use) *it has never* ~*d him to explain*; (*may it*) ~ *your honour, there was no moon that night; the matter will be cleared up some day*, ~ *God* (or, joc., ~ *the pigs*). **5.** Give pleasure, as *he was anxious to* ~. **6.** (As polite form of request esp. for trifling services) *if you* ~, with your permission, as *I will take another cup, if you* ~; (with iron. implication that nothing could be more reasonable) *& now, if you* ~, *he expects me to pay for it!*; (imperat., orig. = may it ~ you) *ring the bell*, ~, *may I come in*, ~?, *coffee for two*, ~, ~ (*to*) *return it soon*, ~ *don't* (or ~ *not to*) *forget the key*. Hence **pleasED**[1] (-ēzd), **pleas'ING**[2], aa., **pleas'INGLY**[2] adv., (-z-). [ME *plaise* f. OF *plaisir* (F *plaire*) f. L *placēre*]

plea'surab|le (plĕzher-), a. Affording pleasure. Hence ~LENESS n., ~LY[2] adv. [f. foll. + -ABLE]

pleasure (plĕzh'er), n., & v.t. & i. **1.** Enjoyment, delight; sensuous enjoyment as chief object of life, as *a life given up to* ~, *man of* ~, profligate; will, desire, as *shall not consult his* ~, *can be postponed during our* ~, *can be altered at* ~; (royal formula) *it is our* ~ *to*, we are graciously pleased to; *to converse with him is a* (source of) ~; *do me the* ~ *of* (gratify me by) *dining with me*; *he takes* (*a*) ~ *in* (likes) *contradicting* or *contradiction*; (arch.) *are now taking their* ~ (enjoying themselves) *at Bath*; ~-*boat* etc. (used for ~, not business); ~-*ground* (laid out for ~). **2.** vb. (arch.). Give ~ to; take ~ (*in* thing, *in* doing). [ME & OF *plesir, plaisir,* PLEASE used as n.; see -URE]

pleat, n., & v.t. = PLAIT (1st sense). [collateral form of PLAIT]

plĕb, n. (sl.). Plebeian, person of lower classes. [abbr.]

*plēbe, n. (colloq.). Member of lowest class at U.S. Naval or Military Academy. [shortened f. PLEBEIAN]

plebei'an (-bēan), n. & a. 1. Commoner in ancient Rome (cf. PATRICIAN); commoner. 2. adj. Of low birth, of the common people, coarse, base, ignoble. Hence ~NESS n., ~IZE(3) v.t. [f. L *plebeius* (*plebs* common people)+-AN]

plĕb'iscite (-sīt), n. (Rom. hist.) law enacted by commonalty in *comitia tributa*; (mod.) direct vote of all electors of State on important public question; public expression of community's opinion, with or without binding force. So **plēbis'ciTARY**[1] a. [f. F *plébiscite* f. L *plebiscitum* (*plebs plebis* commons+*scitum* decree f. *sciscere* vote for)]

plĕc'trum, n. (pl. *-ra*). Small instrument of ivory, quill, etc., for plucking strings of zither etc. [L, f. Gk *plēktron* (*plēssō* strike)]

pled. See PLEAD.

plĕdge[1], n. Thing handed over to person as security (cf. REPLEVIN) for fulfilment of contract, payment of debt, etc., & liable to forfeiture in case of failure; thing put in pawn; (fig.) one's child; thing given as token of favour etc. or of something to come; drinking of a health, toast; promise, as *under ~ of secrecy*; solemn engagement to abstain from intoxicants, as *take, sign, keep, the ~*; (pol.) leader's public promise (not) to adopt some course; state of being pledged, as *goods lying in ~, taken out of ~*. [ME & OF *plege* (mod. *pleige*) f. Frankish L *plevium, plibium* (whence med. L *plevire*) f. Frank. **pligi* surety, poss. rel. to PLIGHT]

plĕdge[2], v.t. Deposit as security, pawn; (fig.) plight (one's honour, word, etc.); drink to the health of. Hence ~'ABLE a. [f. prec.]

plĕdgee', n. One with whom pledge is deposited, pawnee. So **plĕdg'ER**[1] n. [-EE]

plĕdg'ĕt, n. Small wad of lint etc. [16th c., of unkn. orig.]

Plei'ad (plī-), n. (pl. *~s* pr. *-dz, ~es* pr. *-dēz*). (Pl.) cluster of small stars in Taurus, usu. spoken of as 7; (fig., sing.) brilliant group of (usu. 7) persons or things, esp. the French poets of the latter part of 16th c. [f. L *Plēias* f. Gk *Pleias -ados*]

Pleis'tocēne (-līs-), a. & n. (geol.). (Of) the division immediately following the Pliocene formation. [f. Gk *pleistos* most+*kainos* new]

plēn'ar|y̆, a. Entire, absolute, unqualified; (of assembly) fully attended; *~y̆ INSPIRATION.* Hence ~ĭLY[2] adv. [f. LL *plenarius* (*plenus* full, see -ARY[1])]

plĕnĭpotĕn'tiary̆ (-sha-), a. & n. (Person) invested with full power, esp. a diplomatic agent having such power; (of power) absolute. [f. med. L *plenipotentiarius* (*plenus* full+*potens* POTENT), see -ARY[1]]

plĕn'ĭtūde, n. Fullness, completeness; abundance. [ME, f. OF f. L *plenitudo* (*plenus* full, see -TUDE)]

plĕn'tĕous, a. (chiefly poet.). Plentiful. Hence ~LY[2] adv., ~NESS n. [ME & OF *plentivous* f. *plentif* f. *plente* PLENTY; see -IVE, -EOUS; cf. BOUNTEOUS]

plĕn'tiful, a. Abundant, copious. Hence ~LY[2] adv., ~NESS n. [ME, f. foll.+-FUL]

plĕn'ty, n. & adv. 1. Abundance, as much as one could desire, (*of* thing, or abs.), as *~ of cake, here is cake in ~, we are in ~ of time; horn of ~,* cornucopia. 2. adv. (colloq.). Quite, as *it is ~ large enough.* [ME *plenteth, plente* f. OF *plentet, -le* f. L *plenitatem* (*plenus* full, see -TY)]

plĕn'um, n. Space filled with matter (*~ system,* of ventilation by forcing air in); full assembly. [L, neut. of *plenus* full]

plē'on|ăsm, n. Redundancy of expression, e.g. *hear with one's ears, a false lie.* So **~ăs'TIC** a., **~ăs'TICALLY** adv. [f. LL f. Gk *pleonasmos* (*pleonazō* add superfluously f. *pleon* more)]

plĕsiosaur'us, n. (pl. *-rī, -ruses*). Extinct marine reptile with long neck, short tail, & four large paddles. [f. Gk *plēsios* near+*sauros* lizard]

plĕth'ora (*or* plĕthō'r'a), n. Morbid condition marked by excess of red corpuscles in the blood; (fig.) unhealthy repletion. Hence or cogn. **plĕthŏ'ric** a., **plĕthŏ'rically** adv. [LL, f. Gk *plēthōrē* (*plēthō* become full)]

pleur'|a (ploor'a), n. Either of the two serous membranes lining the thorax & enveloping the lungs in mammals; part of the body-wall in invertebrates. Hence ~AL a. [med. L f. Gk, = side of body, rib]

pleur'|ĭsy̆ (ploor-), n. Inflammation of the pleura, usu. caused by chill, & marked by pain in chest or side, fever, etc. So ~ĭt'IC (ploor-) a. [ME, f. OF *pleurisie* f. LL *pleurisis* altered f. L f. Gk *pleuritis* (as prec., see -ITIS), also used in E]

pleuro- (ploor-), comb. form (bef. vowel *pleur-*) of Gk *pleura,* side, pleura, rib, as: *~dy̆n'ia,* pain in side caused by rheumatism in muscles of chest; *~-pneumōn'ia,* pneumonia complicated with pleurisy.

plĕxim'ĕter, n. (med.). Thin plate of ivory etc. placed on part of the body & struck with plexor in medical percussion. [f. Gk *plĕxis* stroke (*plēssō* strike)+-METER]

plĕx'or, n. (med.). Small hammer used with pleximeter. [irreg. as prec.+-OR]

plĕx'us, n. (Anat.) network of nerves or vessels in animal body, as *gastric, pulmonary, SOLAR, ~*; network, complication. Hence **plĕx'iFORM** a. [L, gen. *-ūs,* f. *plectere plex-* plait]

pli'able, a. = foll. Hence pliaBIL'ITY n.,
pli'abLY² adv. [F (*plier* bend f. L *plicare*)]

pli'ant, a. Bending, supple; (fig.) yielding, compliant. Hence pli'ANCY n., ~LY³
adv. [ME, f. OF (as prec., see -ANT)]

plic'a, n. (pl. -ae). Fold, as of skin or
membrane; ~ (*polŏn'ica* Polish), matted
filthy condition of hair due to disease.
[med. L, as foll.]

plic'ate, a. (bot., zool., geol.). Folded.
So **plicāt'ED¹** a. [f. L *plicare* fold,
-ATE²]

plicā'tion, n. Folding; fold, folded condition. [ME, f. OF (as prec., see -ATION)]

pli'ers (-z), n. pl. Pincers having long
jaws with parallel surfaces, for bending
wire etc. [f. (dial.) *ply* bend (see PLIABLE)
+ -ER¹]

plight¹ (plīt), v.t., & n. 1. Pledge (one's
troth, faith, promise, esp. in p.p.); engage
one*self* (*to* person, esp. in p.p., as ~*ed*
lovers). 2. n. Engagement. [OE *pliht*
danger, corresp. to MDu. *plicht*, OHG
pfliht duty, f. *pleh-*, *pleg-*, WG *plegan*,
perh. rel. to PLEDGE]

plight² (plīt), n. Condition, state, esp. a
sorry, evil, hopeless, etc. ~. [ME & AF
plit = OF *pleit* fold, see PLAIT; -*gh*- by
confus. w. prec.]

‖ **plim,** v.t. & i. (dial.; -mm-). Swell, fill
out, make or grow plump. [also *plum*,
perh. cogn. w. PLUMP¹]

Plim'soll, a. & n. ~ *line*, ~'s MARK¹; ‖ (n.
pl.; *p*~*s*) cheap rubber-soled canvas shoes.
[S. ~, agitator for Merchant Shipping
Act of 1876]

plinth, n. Lower square member of base
of column; projecting part of wall
immediately above ground. [f. F *plinthe*
or L (= plinth) f. Gk *plinthos* tile,
brick]

plin'thite, n. Kind of brick-red clay. [as
prec. + -ITE¹]

Pli'ocēne, a. & n. (geol.). (Of) the newest
division of Tertiary formation. [f. Gk
pleiōn more + *kainos* new]

plŏd, v.i. & t. (-dd-), & n. 1. Walk laboriously, trudge, (*on*, *along*, etc.); drudge,
slave, (*at* etc.); make (one's way) laboriously. 2. n. Laborious walk or work.
Hence ~d'ER¹ n., ~d'ingLY² adv. [16th
c., app. imit.]

plom'bé (-awmbā), a. Officially lead-
-sealed. [F]

plŏp, n., adv., & v.t. & i. (-pp-). 1. Sound
as of smooth object dropping into water
without splash; act of falling with this.
2. adv. With a ~. 3. vb. (Cause to) fall
thus. [imit.]

plŏt¹, n. Piece (usu. small) of ground;
plan of play, poem, novel, etc., whence
~'LESS a.; conspiracy (GUN*powder* ~); sly
plan (earlier *complot*). [(?OE) ME *plotte*,
of unkn. orig.; cf. PLAT¹]

plŏt², v.t. (-tt-). Make plan or map of
(existing object, place or thing to be laid
out, constructed, etc.); make (a curve) by
marking out a number of points; plan,

contrive, (evil object, or abs.). Hence
~t'ER¹ n. [f. prec.]

plough¹ (plow), n. 1. Implement for cutting furrows in soil & turning it up, consisting of cutting blade (~'*share*) fixed in
frame drawn by horses etc. & guided by
man (~'*man*); *put* one's *hand to the* ~,
undertake task (*Luke* ix. 62); ploughed
land; kinds of instrument resembling ~,
as *ice-*~ (for cutting up blocks of ice),
snow-~ (for clearing away snow); *the P*~,
CHARLES'S WAIN; ‖ [f. foll.] rejection of
candidate in examination. 2. ~*-beam*,
central beam of ~; ~*-boy*, boy who leads
~-horses etc.; ~*-land* (hist.), as much
land as could be ploughed by one team
of 8 oxen in the year, unit of assessment
in N. & E. counties of England (cf. HIDE³);
P~ *Monday* (first after Epiphany), ~-
-shoe, appliance for protecting or supporting ~*share*; ~*-staff* (ending in small
spade, used to clear coulter etc. from
earth etc.); ~*-tail*, rear of ~, (fig.) farm-
-labour, as *at the* ~*-tail*. [late OE *plōh*
f. ON *plógr*, = OFris. *plōch*, MLG *plōh*,
plūh, OHG *pfluoc*, f. Gmc. **plōg-*, **plōh-*]

plough² (plow), v.t. & i. Turn up (earth,
or abs.) with plough, esp. before sowing
(~ *the sand* or *sands*, labour uselessly);
~ *back*, ~ (grass, clover, etc.) into soil to
enrich it, (fig.) reinvest (profits) in business
etc.; root *out*, cast *up*, thrust *down*, (roots,
weeds) with plough; furrow, scratch,
(surface) as with plough; produce (furrow,
line) thus (~ *a lonely furrow*, fig., take
one's own solitary course); produce
wrinkles in (brow etc.); advance laboriously (*through* snow etc., *through* book
etc.); (of ship etc.) cleave (surface of
water, its way, etc.); ‖ (sl.) reject (candidate) in examination. [f. prec.]

plo'ver (plŭ-), n. Kinds of gregarious gral-
latorial bird, esp. *golden*, *grey*, ~, & (pop.)
lapwing; ~*-page*, ~'s*-page*, dunlin & other
birds said to follow golden ~. [ME & AF
plover, OF -*ier*, f. pop. L **plovarius* (L
pluvia rain)]

‖ **ploy,** n. (colloq.). Expedition, undertaking, occupation, job. [orig. unkn.]

plŭck¹, n. Plucking, twitch; ‖ rejection,
failure, in examination; heart, liver, &
lungs, of beast as food; courage, spirit,
whence (·)~ED² (-kt), ~'LESS, ~'Y² aa.,
~'ILY² adv., ~'iNESS n. [photog. sl.)
boldness of effect. [ME, f. foll.]

plŭck², v.t. & i. Pull off, pick, (flower,
feather, hair); (arch.) pull, drag, snatch,
(*away*, *off*, etc.); pull at, twitch; tug,
(at; strip (bird) of feathers; CROW¹
to ~; plunder, swindle, as ~ a PIGEON;
‖ reject (candidate) in examination; ~ *up*
one's *heart*, *spirits*, *courage*, take courage.
[late OE *plocc-*, *pluccian*, cogn. w. MLG
plucken, MDu. *plocken*, ON *plokka*,
plukka, f. Gmc **plokkōn*, ult. f. Rom.
*piluccare f. *pilus* hair]

plŭg¹, n. Piece of wood etc. fitting tightly
into hole, used to fill gap or act as wedge

(in various techn. uses); natural or morbid concretion acting thus; kinds of stopper for vessel or pipe; pin or other fitting for making electrical contacts; (pop.) release-mechanism of water-closet flushing apparatus; FIRE¹-~; SPARK²ing-~; tobacco pressed into cake or stick, piece of this cut off for chewing; *~-ugly (sl.), street rowdy. [f. MDu. (MLG) plugge, of unkn. orig.]

plŭg², v.t. & i. (-gg-). Stop (hole etc., often up) with plug; (sl.) shoot; (sl.) strike with fist; (colloq.) plod (away at work etc.); (colloq.) endeavour to popularize (a song, theory, policy, etc.) by dinning it into the public ear; ~ in, establish electrical contact by inserting a plug. [f. prec., or early Du. (MLG) pluggen]

plŭm, n. **1.** Roundish fleshy fruit with sweet pulp & flattish pointed stone; (also ~-tree) tree bearing this; dried grape or raisin as used for cakes etc.; SUGAR-~; ‖ French ~, fine kind of prune; (fig.) good thing, best of a collection, prize in life etc. **2.** ~ cake (containing raisins, currants, etc.); ~ duff, plain flour pudding with raisins or currants; ~ pudding, boiled pudding of flour, bread-crumbs, suet, raisins, currants, eggs, spices, etc., eaten at Christmas, (also) ordinary suet-pudding with raisins; ~-pudding (Dalmatian or spotted coach) dog; ~-pudding stone (geol.), conglomerate of flint or other pebbles. [OE plūme, MLG plūme, MHG pflūme, ON plóma, f. Rom. *pruna (whence OHG pfruma, MLG prūme, Du. pruim) f. L prunum PRUNE¹]

plu'mag|e (-ōo-), n. A bird's feathers. Hence (-)~ED²(-ijd) a. [ME,.f. OF (PLUME, -AGE)]

plumassier (plōomasēr'), n. One who trades or works in ornamental feathers. [F (plumasse augment. of PLUME, see -IER)]

plŭmb¹ (-m), n., a., & adv. **1.** Ball of lead, esp. that attached to mason's ~-line (string for testing perpendicularity of wall etc., also fig.); out of ~, not vertical; sounding-lead, plummet; ~-rule, mason's ~-line attached to board. **2.** adj. Vertical; (fig.) downright, sheer, as ~ nonsense;. (crick., of wicket) level, true. **3.** adv. Vertically; (fig.) exactly, as points ~ in the same direction; *(sl.) quite, utterly, (~ crazy, clean mad). [ME; (adj. & adv. f. n.) f. OF plomb f. L plumbum lead]

plŭmb² (-m), v.t. & i. Sound (sea), measure (depth, lit. & fig.), with plummet, whence ~'LESS (-ml-) a.; make vertical; (intr.) work as plumber. [f. prec.]

plumbāg'ō, n. Black lead, graphite, a form of carbon used for pencils etc. & mixed with clay for making crucibles; leadwort, plant with greyish-blue flowers. Hence **plŭmbăg'ĭnous** a. [L, gen. -ginis, f. plumbum lead]

plŭm'bēous, a. Of, like, lead; lead-glazed. [f. L plumbeus (as prec.)+-OUS]

plŭmb'|er (-mer), n. Artisan who fits & repairs pipes, cisterns, etc., with lead, copper, zinc, or tin. So ~ERY(2, 3)(-mer-) n. [ME plummer etc., f. OF plummier f. L plumbarius (as prec., see -ARY)¹]

plŭm'b|ic, a. (Chem.) combined with lead, so ~ĬF'EROUS a.; (path.) due to presence of lead, so ~ISM(5) n. [f. L plumbum lead+-IC]

plume¹ (-ōo-), n. Feather, esp. large one used for ornament; (fig.) borrowed ~s (referring to fable of jackdaw in peacock's ~s); ornamental feather or bunch of feathers or horsehair, esp. as attached to helmet or hat, or worn in hair, as court ~ (of ostrich feathers); (zool.) feather-like part, or formation. Hence ~'LESS, ~'LIKE, aa., ~'LET n., (-ōoml-). [ME, f. OF, f. L pluma down]

plume² (-ōo-), v.t. Furnish with plume(s); dress oneself with borrowed plumes; pride oneself (on esp. something trivial or to which one has no claim); (of bird) trim, dress, (feathers). [f. prec.]

plŭmm'er-blŏck, n. (mech.). Metal case for supporting revolving shaft, with movable cover giving access to bearings. [perh. f. surname+BLOCK]

plŭmm'et, n., & v.i. (Weight attached to) plumb-line; sounding-lead; weight attached to fishing-line to keep float upright; (v.i.) plunge. [ME & OF plommet dim. as PLUMB¹]

plumōse' (-ōo-), a. Feathered; feather-like. [f. L plumosus (as PLUME¹, see -OSE¹)]

plŭmp¹, a., & v.t. & i. **1.** (Esp. of person or parts of body) full, rounded, fleshy, filled out. **2.** vb. Make ~, fatten up; become ~, swell out or up. Hence ~'LY² adv., ~'NESS n., ~'Y² a. [late 15th c. plompe, f. MDu. plomp blunt, MLG plump, plomp unshapen etc.]

plŭmp², v.i. & v.t., n., adv., & a. **1.** Drop or plunge (t. & i.) with abrupt descent (down upon etc.); ‖ plump for (one candidate alone, when one might vote for two); (fig.) go wholeheartedly for one of alternative choices. **2.** n. Abrupt plunge, heavy fall. **3.** adv. With sudden or heavy fall, as came ~ into the river; flatly, bluntly, as I told him ~, I lied ~. **4.** adj. Direct, unqualified, as answer with a ~ No. [ME, of imit. orig.; f. MLG plum-pen, MDu. plompen]

‖ **plŭmp³**, n. (arch.). Company, troop, esp. ~ of spears (spearmen); cluster. [ME, of unkn. orig.; cf. clump (of trees)]

plŭm'per¹, n. Ball, disc, carried in mouth to fill out hollow cheeks. [PLUMP¹ +-ER¹]

plŭm'per², n. In vbl senses, esp.: ‖ (vote of) one who plumps for candidate; (sl.) downright lie. [PLUMP²+-ER¹]

plu'mūl|e (plōo-), n. Rudimentary stem of embryo plant, whence ~AR¹ a.; little feather of down, whence ~A'CEOUS (-āshus) a. [f. L plumula, dim. as PLUME¹]

plu'mў (-ōō-), a. Plume-like; feathery; adorned with plumes. [-Y²]

plŭn'der, v.t., & n. **1.** Rob (place, person) forcibly of goods, esp. as in war; rob systematically; steal, embezzle, (goods, or abs.). **2.** n. Violent or dishonest acquisition of property; property so acquired; (sl.) profit, gain; Hence ~ER¹ n. [c. 1630, f. G *plündern*, lit., rob of household effects (MG, MHG *plunder* clothing &c.), a wd from the Thirty Years' War]

plŭn'derage, n. Plundering, esp. embezzling of goods on shipboard; spoil thus obtained. [-AGE]

plŭnġe (-j), v.t. & i., & n. **1.** Thrust violently (*into* liquid, cavity, etc.); (fig.) thrust (person etc. *into*, *in*, condition, action, etc.; esp. in p.p., as ~*d in gloom*); sink entirely (pot containing plant) in ground; throw oneself, dive, (*into* water, difficulty, discussion, etc.); enter impetuously (*into* room, *up*, *down*, stairs, etc.); (of horse) throw itself violently forward; (of ship) pitch; (sl.) gamble deeply, run into debt; *plunging fire* (from guns at higher level); *plunging neckline* (cut low). **2.** n. Plunging, dive, (~*bath*, large enough to dive into); (fig.) critical step, as *take the ~*. [ME, f. OF *plungier* f. *plumbicare* sound with plummet (*plumbum*)]

plŭn'ger (-j-), n. In vbl senses, esp.: parts of mechanism that work with plunging motion; (sl.) reckless gambler, speculator. [-ER¹]

plŭnk, v.t. & i., & n. **1.** Throw or fall heavily or suddenly; *hit unexpectedly. **2.** n. Sound made by plucking strings of musical instrument (v.i., make such sound). **3.** *(colloq.). Heavy blow; dollar. [imit.]

plu'pĕrf'ĕct (-ōō-), a. & n. (Tense) expressing action completed prior to some past point of time specified or implied (expr. in E by *had* with p.p., as *he had called*). [contr. f. L *plus quam perfectum* more than perfect]

plur'al (-oor-), a. & n. (Form of noun, verb, etc.) denoting more than one (or, in languages with dual, more than two); more than one in number; ~ *vote*, *voter*, *voting* (of one person in more than one constituency). Hence ~LY² adv. [ME, f. OF *plurel* or L *pluralis* (*plus pluris* more, see -AL)]

plur'al|ism (-oor-), n. Holding of more than one office, esp. benefice, at a time; (philos.) system that recognizes more than one ultimate principle (cf. MONISM). So ~IST n., ~is'tIC a. [-ISM]

plurăl'itў (-oor-), n. State of being plural; large number, multitude; holding of two or more benefices or offices; benefice, office, held with another; majority (*of* votes etc.). [ME, f. OF *pluralite* f. LL *pluralitas* (as PLURAL, see -TY)]

plur'alīze (-oor-), -ise (-īz), v.t. & i. Make

plural, express in the plural; hold more than one benefice. [f. F *pluraliser* (as PLURAL, see -IZE)]

pluri- (-oor-), comb. form of L *plus pluris* more, as: ~*lit'eral* (Heb. gram.), having more than 3 letters in the root; ~*pres'ence*, presence in more than one place at same time; ~*sēr'ial*, ~*sēr'iate*, consisting of several series.

plŭs, prep., a., & n. **1.** With the addition of (symbol +), as *3 ~ 4* (cf. MINUS); ~ *1* etc., golfer's handicap; ~*-fours*, long wide knickerbockers (so named because, to produce the overhang, the length is normally increased by four inches). **2.** adj. Additional, extra; (math.) positive; (electr.) positive, positively electrified. **3.** n. The symbol (+); additional quantity, positive quantity. [L, = more]

plŭsh, n. & a. Kind of cloth of silk, cotton, etc., with nap longer & softer than that of velvet; (pl.) footman's ~ breeches; (adj.) of ~, sumptuous. Hence ~'Y² a. [f. obs. F *pluche* contr. f. *peluche* f. Rom. **piluceus* f. *pilus* hair; see PLUCK²]

plu'tärchy (plōō-, -kĭ), n. Plutocracy. [f. Gk *ploutos* wealth + -*arkhia* -rule]

Plu'tō (-ōō-), n. A more remote planet than Neptune (discovered 1930). [f. Gk *Ploutōn* ~, god of infernal regions]

plutŏc'racў (-ōō-), n. Rule of the wealthy; ruling class of wealthy persons. So **plu'tocRAT** n. **plutocrät'ic** a., (-ōō-). [f. Gk *ploutokratia* (as foll., see -CRACY)]

plutŏl'atrў (-ōō-), n. Worship of wealth. [f. Gk *ploutos* wealth, see -LATRY]

Plutōn'ic (-ōō-), a. & n. Of Pluto, infernal; (geol.) igneous, as ~ *rocks*, ~ *theory* (attributing most geological phenomena to action of internal heat, whence **Plu'ton**-ISM(3), **Plu'ton**IST(2), nn.); (n.) ~ rock. So **Plutōn'IAN** (-ōō-) a. [as PLUTO, -IC]

plutōn'ium (-ōō-), n. Element arising from NEPTUNIUM. [f. PLUTO + -IUM]

plutōn'om|ў (-ōō-), n. Political economy. Hence **plutonŏm'ic** a., ~IST n., (-ōō-). [f. Gk *ploutos* wealth + -*nomia* arrangement]

plu'vi|al (-ōō-), a. & n. Of rain, rainy, so ~OUS a.; (geol.) caused by rain; (n., eccl. hist.) long cloak as ceremonial vestment. [(adj.) f. L *pluvialis* (*pluvia* rain, see -AL); (n.) f. med. L *pluviale* rain-cloak]

pluvi|ŏm'ēter (-ōō-), n. Rain-gauge. Hence ~omĕt'ric(AL) aa. [f. L *pluvia* rain + -·O- + -METER]

plў¹, n. Fold, thickness, layer, of cloth etc.; strand of rope etc.; *two, 2, 3, -~*, having 2 etc. thicknesses or strands; (fig.) turn, tendency, esp. *take a ~*; ~*'wood*, strong thin board made by gluing layers with the grains crosswise. [f. F *pli* f. *plier* f. L *plicare* fold]

plў², v.t. & i. Use, wield vigorously, (tool, weapon); work at (one's business, task); supply (person etc.) persistently *with* (food etc.); assail vigorously (person *with* questions, arguments); (naut.) work to windward; (of vessel or its master, bus, etc.) go to & fro *between* (places); || (of boatman, porter, cabman) attend regularly for custom (*at* place). [ME *plye*, aphetic f. APPLY]

Plȳm′outh (-muth), n. ~ *Brethren*, religious body that arose at ~ *c.* 1830, with no formal creed & no official order of ministers, whence ~ISM(3), ~IST(2), ~ITE¹, (-muth-), nn.; ~ *Rock*, large breed of domestic fowl of Amer. origin. [port in England]

pneumăt′ic (n-), a. & n. **1.** Of, acting by means of, wind or air; ~ *tire* (inflated with air); ~ *dispatch*, conveyance of parcels etc. along tubes by compression or exhaustion of air; ~ *trough* (for collecting gases in jars over surface of water or mercury); containing, connected with, air-cavities esp. in bones of birds; spiritual. **2.** n. ~ tire, cycle with such tires; (pl.) science of mechanical properties of air or other elastic fluids or gases. Hence **pneumăt′ICALLY** adv., **pneumati′CITY** n., (n-). [f. F (-*ique*) or L f. Gk *pneumatikos* (*pneuma* wind f. *pneō* breathe, see -IC)]

pneum′at|o- (n-), comb. form of Gk *pneuma -matos* air, breath, spirit, as: ~*ocyst*, air-sac in body of bird etc.; ~*ŏl′ogy*, theory of spiritual beings, doctrine of the Holy Spirit, psychology, so ~*olo′gical* a.; ~*ŏm′eter*, instrument for measuring amount of air breathed at each inspiration; ~*ophore*, part of some compound hydrozoa containing air-cavity.

pneumogăs′tric (n-), a. Of lungs & stomach, esp. ~ *nerves*, tenth pair of cerebral nerves. [irreg. f. Gk *pneumōn -monos* lung + GASTRIC]

pneumōn′ia (n-), n. Inflammation of the substance of one (*single* ~) or both (*double* ~) lungs. So **pneumōn′ic** a., **pneumonIT′IS** n., (n-). [f. Gk *pneumonia* f. *pneumōn* (as prec.); see -IA¹]

pō, n. (pl. *pos*). See POT¹.

poach¹, v.t. Cook (egg) by dropping it without shell into boiling water. Hence ~′ER¹(2) n. [ME, f. OF *pochier* (*poche* POKE¹)]

poach², v.t. & i. Thrust (stick, finger, etc. *into* etc.); trample, cut *up* (turf etc.) with hoofs; (of land) become sodden by being trampled; encroach, trespass, (*on* person's *preserves* often fig., lands, etc.), whence ~′ER¹ n.; trespass on (land etc.), capture (game, fish) by illicit or unsportsmanlike methods; obtain (advantage, start, in race) by unfair means; (lawn tennis) strike (ball, or abs.) in partner's court. [16th c. *poche*, prob. f. F *pocher* in POACH¹, POKE²]

pŏch′ard (*also* -k-), n. European diving-duck with bright reddish-brown head & neck. [orig. unkn.]

pŏck, n. Eruptive spot esp. in smallpox. [OE *poc*, = MDu., MLG *pocke*; see also POX]

pŏck′ĕt¹, n. **1.** Bag, sack, esp. as measure

of hops (168 lb.) or wool (= half sack); small bag inserted in (usu. male) garment for carrying small articles, as *coat, waistcoat, trouser, watch, ticket,* ~; (fig.) pecuniary resources, as *he will suffer in his* ~; *empty* ~, person without money; *be prepared to put your hand in your* ~ (spend some money); *put* one's *pride in* one's ~, submit to doing something that mortifies it; *out-of-*~*-expenses*, actual outlay incurred; *am* 5s. *in* ~, have 5s. available; *am* 5s. *in* ~, *out of* ~, *by the transaction* (have gained, lost); *has him in her* ~ (completely under control); pouch at each corner & on each side of billiard-table into which balls are driven; cavity in earth filled with gold or other ore, whence~Y²a.; cavity in rock esp. (geol.) filled with foreign matter; (mil.) isolated area occupied by enemy, forces occupying this, (*mopping up enemy* ~*s* or ~*s of resistance*); = AIR¹-; (attrib.) of suitable size or shape for carrying in ~. **2.** ~ *battleship*, a ship armoured & equipped like, but smaller than, a battleship; ~*-book*, notebook, book-like case for papers etc. carried in~; ||~*borough* (under control of one person or family); ~ (small personal) *expenses*; ~ *handkerchief* (carried in ~); ~*-money* (for occasional expenses, esp. that allowed to children); ~*-piece*, lucky coin carried in ~ as charm; ~*-pistol*, (joc.) ~ spirit-flask. Hence ~FUL n., ~LESS a. [ME *poket* f. AN *pokete* dim. f. ONF *poke* POKE¹]

pŏck′ĕt², v.t. Put into one's pocket; confine as in pocket; hem in (competitor) in race; appropriate, usu. dishonestly; submit to (affront, injury); conceal, suppress, (feelings); (bill.) drive (ball) into pocket. Hence ~ABLE a. [f. prec.]

pock-pudding. See POKE¹.

pŏcōcuran′t|e (-koorahntā, -kūrănti), a. & n. Indifferent (person). Hence ~(è)ISM n. [It., = caring little]

pŏd¹, n. Socket of brace & bit. [earlier form of PAD³(5)]

pŏd², n., & v.i. & t. (-dd-). **1.** Long seed-vessel esp. of leguminous plants; cocoon of silkworm; case of locust's eggs; narrow-necked eel-net. **2.** vb. Bear ~s; shell (peas etc.). [late 17th c., of unkn. orig.]

pŏd³, n., & v.t. (-dd-). Small herd of seals or whales; (v.t.) drive (seals) into a ~. [of unkn. (U.S.) orig.]

pŏd′agra (*or* podăg²), n. (med.). Gout, esp. in feet. Hence *or* cogn. **pŏd′agrAL**, **podăg′rIC**, **pŏd′agrOUS**, aa. [L, f. Gk *podagra* (*pous podos* foot + *agra* catching)]

pŏdd′ĕd, a. Bearing pods; growing in pod; (fig.) well-off, snug. [-ED²]

pŏdĕstà (-tah′), n. Magistrate in Italian municipalities; (hist.) chief magistrate in medieval Italian towns. [It., f. L *potestatem* power (*potis* able, see -TY)]

pŏdge, n. (colloq.). Short fat person. Hence **pŏdg′Y²** a. [var. of PUDGE]

pōd′ium, n. (pl. *-ia*). Continuous project-ing base or pedestal; raised platform round arena of amphitheatre; continuous bench round room. [L, f. Gk *podion* (*pous podos* foot)]

pŏdophýll′in, n. (chem.). Yellow bitter resin of cathartic properties got from root of wild mandrake. [f. bot. L *podophyllum*, may-apple, wild mandrake, (Gk *pous podos* foot + *phullon* leaf) + -IN]

pō′e-bĭrd, n. = PARSON-bird. [f. Otaheitan wd for 'ear-rings', from tufts under throat]

pō′ĕm, n. A metrical composition, esp. of elevated character; elevated composition in prose or verse, as *prose* ~; (fig.) something (other than a composition of words) akin or compared to a ~, *as their lives are a* ~. [f. F *poème* or L f. Gk *poēma* = *poiēma* (*poieō* make)]

pō′ĕsȳ, n. (arch.). Art, composition, of poetry; poems collectively. [ME, f. OF *poesie* f. Rom. **poesia* f. L f. Gk *poēsis* = *poiēsis* making, poetry, (as prec.)]

pō′ĕt, n. Writer of poems; writer in verse, esp. one possessing high powers of imagination, expression, etc.; *Poets′ Corner*, part of Westminster Abbey containing graves & monuments of several ~s, (joc.) part of newspaper devoted to poetry. Hence ~ESS[1] n. [ME, f. OF *poete* f. L (*-ta*) f. Gk *poētēs* = *poiētēs* maker, poet, (as prec.)]

pōĕtăs′ter, n. Paltry poet. So **pōĕt′ĭcULE** n. [-ASTER]

pōĕt′|ĭc(al), aa. Of, proper to, poets or poetry; (usu. ~*ic*) having the good qualities of poetry; (usu. ~*ical*) written in verse, as ~*ical works*; ~*ic* JUSTICE, LICENCE[1]. Hence ~ICALLY adv., ~ICS n. [f. F *poétique* f. L f. Gk *po(i)ētikos* (as POET, see -IC & -AL)]

pōĕt′ĭcize, -ise (-īz), v.t. Make (theme) poetic. [-IZE]

pō′ĕtize, -ise (-īz), v.i. & t. Play the poet, compose poetry; treat poetically; celebrate in poetry. [f. F *poétiser* (as POET, see -IZE)]

pō′ĕtrȳ, n. Art, work, of the poet; elevated expression of elevated thought or feeling in metrical form; poems; quality (in any thing) that calls for poetical expression; *prose* ~, prose having all the qualities of poetry except metre. [ME, f. OF *poetrie* f. med. L *poetria* (as POET)]

pōg′ō, n. (pl. ~s). Toy like stilt with spring, used to jump on. [app. fanciful]

pogrŏm′, n. Organized massacre orig. or esp. of Jews in Russia. [Russ.]

poign′ant (poin-), a. Sharp, pungent, in taste or smell; painfully sharp, as ~ *hunger, regret, sarcasm*; pleasantly piquant; moving, touching. Hence **poign′ANCY** n., ~LY[2] adv., (poin-). [ME, f. OF part. of *poindre* prick f. L *pungere*]

poilu (see Ap.), n. (sl.). French soldier (nickname, cf. TOMMY). [F, lit. hairy, unshaven]

|| **poind** (pĕnd, pīnd), v.t., & n. (Sc.). Distrain upon, impound; (n.) act of ~ing, beast or chattel ~ed. [late ME f. OE *pyndan* impound; cf. PINFOLD]

poinsĕtt′ia, n. Plant with large scarlet leaves & small yellowish flowers. [f. J. R. *Poinsett* (d. 1851), discoverer, -IA[1]]

point[1], n. **1.** Small dot on a surface. **2.** Stop or punctuation-mark (chiefly now in *full* ~, full stop); dot, small stroke, used in Semitic languages to indicate vowels or distinguish consonants; dot separating integral from fractional parts in decimals, as *four* ~ *six* (4·6). **3.** Single item, detail, particular, as *we differ on these* ~*s, it is a* ~ *of conscience*, STRETCH *a* ~. **4.** *Possession is nine* ~*s of the law* (nine-tenths, almost the whole); *give* ~*s* (odds) *to* (opponent in game), (fig.) be superior to. **5.** Unit in appraising qualities of exhibit in show; unit of value in rationing (*on* ~*s*, rationed on a basis of such units); unit (of varying value) in quoting price of stocks etc. **6.** (print.). Unit of measurement for type bodies (British & U.S.A. 0·0138 in.). **7.** (geom.). That which has position but not magnitude, e.g. ~ *of intersection of two lines.* **8.** Precise place or spot, as ~ *of contact*; ~ *of no return*, ~ in a long-distance flight over the ocean at which an aircraft has not enough fuel to return to its starting--place and must continue onwards; also fig.; (hunt.) spot to which straight run is made, such run, ~-*to*-~ *race* (over course defined only by certain landmarks); (her.) any of nine particular spots on shield used for determining position. **9.** Stage, degree, in progress or increase, esp. of temperature, as *boiling, freezing*, ~ (at which thing boils etc.). **10.** Precise moment for action etc., as *when it came to the* ~, *he declined*; exact moment (*of* death etc.). **11.** Distinctive trait, characteristic, as *singing is not his strong* ~; *the* essential thing, *the* thing under discussion, as *that is just the* ~, *come to the* ~; *to the* ~, relevant(ly) to the purpose; *make a* ~ *of*, regard, treat, as essential; *carry* one's ~, secure one's object; *make a* ~, establish proposition, prove contention. **12.** (Also ~ *lace*) thread lace made wholly with needle; (improp.) pillow lace imitating this. **13.** Sharp end of tool, weapon, pin, pen, etc. (*not to put too fine a* ~ *upon it*, to speak bluntly). **14.** Tip (*the* ~ *of the jaw or the* ~, in boxing, tip of chin as spot for knock-out blow); promontory, esp. in names, as *Start P*~; (mil.) small leading party of advanced guard; (pl.) extremities of horse, as *bay with black* ~*s*. **15.** Sharp--pointed tool, e.g. etching-needle; tine of deer's horn. **16.** || (On railway) tapering movable rail by which train is directed from one line to another; tapered division on backgammon board. **17.** (hist.). Tagged lace for lacing bodice, attaching hose to doublet, etc. **18.** (naut.). Short piece of cord at lower edge of sail for tying up a reef. **19.** ~s *of the compass,* 32 equidistant ~s on compass (N, N by E, NNE, NE by N, NE, NE by E, ENE, E by N, E, E by S, ESE, SE by E, SE, SE by S, SSE, S by E, S, S by W, SSW, SW by S, SW, SW by W, WSW, W by S, W, W by N, WNW, NW by W, NW, NW by N, NNW, N by W), at angular intervals of 11° 15′. **20.** Salient feature of story, joke, etc., as *don't see the* ~; pungency, effectiveness, as *his remarks lack* ~. ·**21.** (crick.). (Position of) fieldsman placed more or less in line with popping-crease a short distance on off-side of batsman. **22.** (Of dog) act of pointing, esp. *make, come to, a* ~; *potatoes & ~,* potatoes to eat & bacon etc. to look at. **23.** *At all* ~s, in every part; *at the* ~ (on the verge) *of death* etc.; *in* ~, apposite, as *the case you take is not in* ~; *in* ~ (as a matter) *of fact*; (*up*)*on the* ~ *of,* on the very verge of (action, do*ing*); ~ *of* (thing that vitally affects one's) *honour,* esp. *the* ~ *of honour* (obligation to demand satisfaction, esp. by duel); ~ *of view,* position from which thing is viewed, (fig.) way of looking at a matter; ‖ ~-*duty* (of constable stationed at particular ~ to regulate traffic etc.); ‖ ~*s'man,* man in charge of railway ~s, constable on ~-duty. [ME (partly thr. F *point, pointe,* & f. foll.) f. L *punctum,* neut. p.p. of *pungere* prick]

point³, *v.t.* & *i.* **1.** Sharpen (pencil etc.). **2.** Punctuate; mark (Psalms etc.) with signs for chanting. **3.** Give point to (words, actions), as ~*ing his remarks with apt illustrations, to* ~ *a moral.* **4.** Fill in joints of (brickwork etc.) with mortar or cement smoothed with trowel. **5.** Prick *in* (manure), turn *over* (soil), with point of spade. **6.** Direct attention (*to, at,* lit. & fig.); ~ *out,* indicate, show, (thing, fact, *that* etc.); (of hound) indicate presence of (game, or abs.) by acting as a POINTER; direct (finger, weapon, etc., *at*); direct attention of (person *to*); aim *at,* tend *towards.* [ME, f. OF *pointer,* as prec.]

point-blănk′, *a.* & *adv.* **1.** (Of shot) fired horizontally, level, at very close range; ~ *distance* (within which gun may be fired horizontally). **2.** *adv.* With direct aim, horizontally, in direct line; (fig.) directly, flatly, as *told him* ~ *it would not do*; offhand, as *refused it* ~. [prob. f. prec.+BLANK, i.e. white spot in centre of target]

point d'appui (pwăn dăpwē′), n. (mil.). Point of support, base, rallying-place. [F]

point-dėvice′, *a.* & *adv.* (arch.). Perfectly correct, extremely neat or precise; (adv.) in ~ manner. [ME *at point devis* app. f. OF *à point devis* to the point arranged, or arranged to the proper point (see POINT¹ & DEVICE)]

point′ėd, *a.* Having, sharpened to, a point; (of remark etc.) having point, penetrating, cutting; emphasized, made

evident. Hence ~LY² *adv.,* ~NESS n. [-ED¹,²]

point′er, n. In vbl senses, esp.: index hand of clock, balance, etc.; rod used for pointing to words etc. on blackboard, map, etc.; (colloq.) hint; dog that on scenting game stands rigidly, with muzzle stretched towards it & usu. one foot raised; (pl.) two stars in Great Bear, straight line through which points nearly to pole-star. [-ER¹]

poin′till|ism (pwăn-), n. Method of producing light effects by crowding a surface with small spots of various colours, which are blended by the eye. So ~IST n. [f. F ~*isme* f. *pointiller* mark with dots f. *point* POINT¹, -ISM]

point′ing, n. In vbl senses, esp.: punctuation; filling up joints of brickwork etc. with cement, facing thus given to the joints; (Psalms etc.) system of signs for Anglican chanting. [-ING¹]

point′lėss, *a.* Without a point, blunt; without point, meaningless; not having scored a point. Hence ~LY² *adv.,* ~NESS n. [-LESS]

poise (-z), *v.t.* & *i.,* & *n.* **1.** Balance; hold suspended or supported; carry (one's head etc. in specified way); be balanced; hover in air etc. **2.** n. Equilibrium (lit. & fig.), carriage (*of* head etc.). [(vb) f. OF *peser* (st. *pois*-) f. L *pensare* frequent. of *pendĕre pens*- weigh; (n.) f. OF *pois* f. L *pensum* weight]

pois′on (-zn), n., & *v.t.* **1.** Substance that when introduced into or absorbed by a living organism destroys life or injures health, esp. (pop.) one that destroys life by rapid action & when taken in small quantity; *slow* ~ (of which repeated doses are injurious); *hate each other like* ~ (bitterly); *what's your* ~? (colloq.), what will you have to drink?; (fig.) baneful principle, doctrine, etc.; ~ GAS; ~ *ivy,* kinds of N.-Amer. sumac with leaves ~ous to touch; ~ *pen,* anonymous writer of libellous or scurrilous letter(s) to a private individual; ~*-tree, -wood,* kinds of tree or plant with ~ous properties. **2.** *v.t.* Administer ~ to (man, animal), kill or injure thus, whence ~ER¹ (-z-) n.; produce morbid effects in (blood etc.), whence (·)~ING¹ (-z-) n.; infect (air, water, etc.) with ~, smear (weapon) with ~ (esp. in p.p.); corrupt, pervert, (person, mind); destroy, spoil, (person's pleasure etc.); render (land, furnace, etc.) foul & unfit for its purpose by noxious application etc. Hence ~OUS *a.,* ~OUSLY² *adv.,* (-z-). [(n.) ME & OF *puison* (as POTION)-; (vb) f. OF *poisonner* f. the n.]

poissărde (pwŏs-), n. Parisian market-woman leading riots during first revolution; French fishwife. [F]

pōke¹, n. Bag, sack, (now dial. exc. *buy a PIG in a* ~). [ME, corresp. in form w. ONF *poke, poque,* = OF *poche*; see POUCH]

pōke², *v.t.* & *i.* Thrust, push, (thing *in,*

up, down, etc.) with hand, arm, point of stick, etc.; stir (fire) with poker; (colloq.) shut (one*self* etc.) *up* in poky place; produce (hole etc. *in* thing) by poking; make thrusts with stick etc. (*at* etc.); thrust forward, esp. obtrusively, as (fig.) *don't* ~ *your nose into my affairs*; ~ *about*, ~ *& pry*, be inquisitive; ~ one *in the ribs*, nudge him with finger or elbows; ~ *fun at*, assail with ridicule; pry (*into*); ~ one's *head*, carry head thrust forward, stoop. [ME, = MDu., MLG *pöken* poke, thrust, whence OF *poquer*, *pocher*; cf. POACH[2]]

pōke[3], n. Poking; thrust, nudge; device fastened on cattle etc. to prevent their breaking through fences; projecting brim or front of woman's bonnet or hat; ~ (*-bonnet*), bonnet with this, esp. as worn by Salvation Army women. [f. prec.]

pōk'er[1], n., & v.t. **1.** Stiff metal rod with handle, for poking fire; (of person's carriage or manner) *as stiff as a* ~; || (Oxf. & Camb. sl.) bedell carrying mace or stave before Vice-Chancellor; kinds of instrument used in ~*-work*; *red-hot* ~, plant with spikes of scarlet or yellow flowers; (joc. asseveration) *by the holy* ~; ~*-work*, burning of designs on white wood with heated implement. **2.** v.t. Execute (design) in, adorn (thing) with, ~*-work*. [-ER[1]]

pōk'er[2], n. (Orig. Amer.) card-game for two or more persons, each of whom if not bluffed into declaring his hand bets on its value; ~*-face*, impassive countenance appropriate to a ~*-player*; so ~*-faced*. [orig. unkn.; cf. G *pochen* to brag, *poch-spiel*]

pōk'ȳ, a. (Of place, room, etc.) confined, mean, shabby; (of occupation etc.) pottering, petty. [f. POKE[2] + -Y[2]]

pola'cre (-ahk*er*), **-ăcc'a**, n. Three-masted Mediterranean merchant vessel. [f. F *polacre -aque*, Polish, Pole, hist. unexpl.]

pōl'ar, a. & n. **1.** Of, near, either pole of the earth or of the celestial sphere; ~ (white) *bear*, *hare*; ~ *circles* (parallel to equator at distance of 23° 28' from the poles); ~ *distance*, angular distance of point on sphere from nearer pole. **2.** Having polarity, magnetic; having positive & negative electricity; (of molecules) symmetrically arranged in definite direction. **3.** (geom.). Relating to a POLE[2]; ~ *curve* (related in particular way to given curve & to fixed point called pole). **4.** (fig.). Analogous to the pole of the earth or to the pole-star; directly opposite in character. **5.** n. ~ curve. Hence ~LY[2] adv. [f. F *polaire* or med. L *polaris* (as POLE[2], see -AR[1])]

polari-, comb. form of prec., as: *pŏlarĭm˘eter*, *polā'riscope*, instruments for showing polarization of light, so *polărĭmĕt'ric*, *polăriscŏp'ic*, aa., *pŏlarĭm'etry* n.

polă'ritȳ, n. Tendency of lodestone, magnetized bar, etc., to point with its ex-

tremities to the magnetic poles of earth; tendency of a body to place its mathematical axis in particular direction; possession of two poles having contrary qualities (also fig.); electrical condition of body as positive or negative; (fig.) magnetic attraction towards an object. [-ITY]

pōl'arīz|e, **-is**|e (-īz), v.t. & i. Modify the vibrations of (light, radiant heat, etc.) so that the ray exhibits different properties on different sides, opposite sides being alike & those at right angles showing maximum difference; (magn., electr.) give polarity to (bar, coil); (fig.) give arbitrary direction, special meaning, etc., to (word etc.), (also) give unity of direction to. Hence or cogn. ~ABLE a., ~A'TION, ~ER[1](2), nn. [(partly thr. F) f. POLAR, see -IZE]

pŏlatouche' (-ōōch), n. Small flying squirrel. [F, f. Russ. *poletuchii* flying]

pōl'der, n. Piece of low-lying land reclaimed from sea or river in Netherlands. [Du.]

pōle[1], n., & v.t. **1.** Long slender rounded tapering piece of wood or (rarely) metal esp. as support for tent, telegraph wires, etc.; wooden shaft fitted to fore-carriage of vehicle & attached to yokes or collars of the horses etc.; *under bare* ~s (naut.), with no sail set; *up the* ~ (sl.), in a fix; (as measure) rod, perch, 5½ yds; ~*-jumping* (with help of ~ held in hands). **2.** v.t. Furnish with ~s; push, move, (*off* etc.) with ~. [OE *pāl*, MDu. *pael*, OHG *pfāl*, ON *páll*, f. L *palus* stake]

pōle[2], n. *North*, *South*, ~, the two points in the celestial sphere about which the stars appear to revolve, (also) N. & S. extremities of earth's axis; *magnetic* ~, points, N. & S., in these extremities where the magnetic needle dips vertically; (geom.) ~*s of a circle of a sphere*, the two points in which axis of that circle cuts surface of sphere; (geom.) fixed point to which others are referred; each of the two opposite points on surface of magnet at which magnetic forces are manifested; each of two terminal points (*positive*, *negative*, ~) of electric cell, battery, etc.; (biol.) extremity of main axis of any spherical or oval organ; (fig.) each of two opposed principles etc.; ~*-star*, a star of Ursa Minor, now about 1° distant from N. ~ of heavens, (fig.) thing serving as guide, lodestar, centre of attraction. Hence ~'WARD a., ~'WARD(S) adv. [ME, f. L f. Gk *polos* pivot, axis, sky]

Pōle[3], n. Native of Poland. [G, f. Pol. *Poljane* lit. field-dwellers (*pole* field)]

pōle'ax(e) (-lă-), n., & v.t. Battle-axe; axe formerly used in naval warfare as weapon & for cutting ropes etc.; halbert; butcher's axe for slaughtering, (vb) slaughter (beast) with this. [ME *pol(l)ax*, *-ex* f. MDu. *pol(l)aex*, MLG *-exe*, as POLL[1] + AXE]

pōle'căt (-lk-), n. || Small brownish-black carnivorous mammal of weasel family, native of Europe. [ME *pol-*, *pulcat*, f. *pol-* (poss. = OF *po(u)le* fowl)+CAT]

pŏl'émärch (-k), n. (Gk hist.). Military commander-in-chief with varying civil functions; (in Athens) third archon orig. with military functions. [f. Gk *polemarkhos* (*polemos* war+*-arkhos* -ruler)]

polěm'ic, a. & n. **1.** Controversial, disputatious. **2.** n. Controversial discussion, (pl.) practice of this, esp. in theology; controversialist. Hence ~AL a., ~alLY² adv., pŏl'émIZE(2) v.i. [f. Gk *polemikos* (*polemos* war, see -IC)]

polěn'ta, n. Italian porridge made of barley, chestnut meal, etc. [It., f. L]

police' (-ēs), n., & v.t. **1.** Civil administration, public order, (arch.); department of government concerned with this (arch.); civil force responsible for maintaining public order; (as pl.) members of this, as *the ~ are on his track*; *~-court* (of summary jurisdiction, dealing with charges preferred by the ~); *~-magistrate* (presiding in ~-court); *~man*, member of ~ force; ‖ *~-office*, headquarters of ~ in city or town; *~-officer*, *~man*; ~ *State*, totalitarian one controlled by political ~; *~--station*, office of local ~ force. **2.** v.t. Control (country etc.) by means of ~, furnish with ~; (fig.) keep order in, control. [F, f. med. L *politia* = L *politia* POLICY¹]

pŏliclin'ic, n. Clinic in private houses, not in hospital; out-patients' department of hospital. [f. G *poliklinik* (Gk *polis* city, CLINIC)]

pŏl'icy¹, n. Political sagacity; statecraft; prudent conduct, sagacity; craftiness; course of action adopted by government, party, etc.; ‖ (Sc.) park round country seat etc.; *Court of P~*, legislative council in British Guiana. [ME, f. OF *policie* f. L f. Gk *politeia* citizenship, polity (*politēs* citizen f. *polis* city); in Sc. sense (earlier=improvement of estate) confused w. L *politus* polished]

pŏl'icy², n. (In full, ~ *of assurance, insurance* ~) document containing contract of assurance or insurance. [f. F *police* bill of lading, contract of insurance, f. Pr. *polissa* f. med. L *apodissa* f. L f. Gk *apodeixis* evidence, proof, f. APO(*deiknumi* show)]

pŏl'iŏ, n. (colloq.). (Person suffering from) poliomyelitis. [abbr.]

pŏl'iŏmyĕlit'is, n. (path.). Inflammation of the grey matter of the spinal cord; infantile paralysis. [f. Gk *polios* grey+MYELITIS]

pŏl'ish¹, v.t. & i. Make, become, smooth & glossy by friction; (fig.) make elegant or cultured, refine, (esp. in p.p.); smarten *up*; ~ *off*, finish off quickly. Hence~ABLE a., ~ER¹ (1, 2) n. [ME, f. OF *polir* (see -ISH²) f. L *polire* -*it*-]

pŏl'ish², n. Smoothness, glossiness, produced by friction; such friction; substance used to produce smooth surface; (fig.) refinement. [f. prec.]

Pŏl'ish³, a. & n. **1.** Of Poland or the Poles. **2.** n. The language of Poland. [-ISH¹]

pŏl'itärch (-k), n. (hist.). Governor of some Oriental cities, e.g. Thessalonica, under Romans. [f. Gk *politarkhēs* (*politēs* citizen+*-arkhēs* ruler)]

polite', a. Of refined manners, courteous; cultivated, cultured; well-bred; (of literature etc.) refined, elegant, as ~ *letters*. Hence ~LY² (-tl-) adv., ~NESS (-tn-) n. [f. L *politus* (POLISH¹)]

pŏl'itic, a. & n. **1.** (Of person) sagacious, prudent, (of actions etc.) judicious, expedient; scheming, crafty; BODY¹ ~. **2.** n. pl. Science & art of government, political affairs or life, political principles, as *what are his~s?*, *talk~s, is not practical* ~*s* (is too remote to be worth discussing). Hence ~LY² adv. [ME, f. OF *politique* f. L f. Gk *politikos* (as POLICY¹, see -IC)]

polit'ical, a. & n. **1.** Of the State or its government; of public affairs; of politics; (of person) engaged in civil administration, as ~ *agent, resident*, (hist., in India) government official advising ruler of native State; having an organized polity; belonging to, taking, a side in politics; ~ ECONOMY; ~ *geography* (dealing with boundaries & possessions of States); ~ *verse*, modern Greek verse composed by accent, not quantity. **2.** n. ~ agent. Hence ~LY² adv. [-AL]

polĭti'cian (-shn), n. One skilled in politics, statesman; one interested or engaged in politics, esp. as profession; one who makes a trade of politics. [f. POLITIC, see -ICIAN]

polit'icīze, -ise (-īz), v.i. & t. Act the politician; engage in, talk, politics; give political character to. [-IZE]

polit'ico- in comb. = politically, political & ~, as ~-*economical*, ~-*geographical*, ~-*moral*, ~-*social*; ~-*religious*, (usu.) pertaining to politics as influenced by religion. [as POLITIC]

pŏl'itÿ, n. Condition of civil order; form, process, of civil government; organized society, state. [f. obs. F *politie* or L *politia* POLICY¹]

pŏlk, v.i. Dance polka. [f. F *polker* as foll.]

pŏl'ka, n. **1.** Lively dance of Bohemian origin in binary time; music for this. **2.** Woman's tight-fitting jacket, usu. knitted. [F & G, f. Czech]

pŏll¹, n. (Now dial. or joc.) human head; part of this on which hair grows, as *grey*, *flaxen*, ~; counting of voters esp. at parliamentary or other election; voting at election, as *exclusion of Negroes from the~*; number of votes recorded, as *heavy*, *light*, ~; questioning of a sample of the population in order to estimate trend of popular opinion, whence ~'STER n. (colloq.); ~*-tax* (levied on every person). [ME, = obs. Du. *polle*, LG *polle*; cf. Da. *puld*, Sw. dial. *pull*]

pŏll², v.t. & i. (Arch.) crop the hair of;

cut off top of (tree, plant), esp. make a pollard of; cut off horns of (cattle, esp. in p.p.); cut evenly edge of (sheet); take the votes of, (pass.) have one's vote taken; (of candidate) receive (so many votes); give (vote); give one's vote. Hence ~'ABLE a. [ME, f. prec.]

pŏll³, a. & n. Polled, cut evenly; (in comb.) hornless, as ~-*beast*, -*ox*; (n.) ~-*beast*, esp. one of a breed of hornless oxen. [short for p.p of prec.]

pŏll⁴, n. (*P*~) conventional proper name of parrot; ~ *parrot*, parrot, user of conventional phrases & arguments. [altered f. *Moll* familiar equivalent of *Mary*]

∥ **pŏll⁵**, n. (Camb. Univ. sl.). The *P*~, the passmen; *go out in the P*~, take pass degree; (attrib.) ~ *degree*, *man*. [perh. f. POLLOI]

pŏll'ack, -**ock**, n. Sea-fish allied to cod. [17th c.; 16th c. (Sc.) *podlock*; orig. unkn.]

pŏll'an, n. Irish freshwater fish. [cf. Gael. *pollag*, Ir. *pollóg*, perh. f. Ir. *poll* inland lake]

pŏll'ard, n., & v.t. **1.** Animal that has cast or lost its horns; ox, sheep, goat, of hornless variety; tree polled so as to produce close rounded head of young branches; bran sifted from flour, (techn.) fine bran containing some flour. **2.** v.t. Make a ~ of (tree). [POLL² +-ARD]

pŏll'ĕn, n., & v.t. **1.** Fine powdery substance discharged from anther of flower, male element that fertilizes ovules. **2.** v.t. Convey~ to, cover with ~. Hence ~LESS, pollin'IC, pollini F'EROUS, aa. [L, gen. -*inis* = fine flour, dust]

pollicita'tion, n. (civil law). Promise not yet formally accepted, & therefore revocable. [f. L *pollicitatio* (*pollicitari* frequent. of *pollicēri* promise, see -ATION)]

pŏll'in|āte, v.t. Besprinkle with pollen, shed pollen upon. Hence ~A'TION n. [-ATE³]

pŏll'oi, n. pl. *Hoi* ~, most people, the majority, the rabble. [Gk, lit. the many]

pollute' (-ōot), v.t. Destroy the purity or sanctity of; make (water etc.) foul or filthy. So **pollu'tion** (-ōo-) n. [ME, f. L *polluere* -*lut*-]

pōl'ō, n. Game of Eastern origin like hockey played on horseback; ~-*stick*, long-handled mallet used; WATER-~. [native]

pŏlonaise' (-āz), n. **1.** Woman's dress consisting of bodice with skirt open from waist downwards. **2.** (Music for) slow processional dance of Polish origin with three beats in bar. [F, fem. (as n.) of *polonais* Polish]

polōn'ium, n. A radio-active metallic element forming the last stage before lead in the radio-active disintegration of radium. [f. med. L *Polonia* Poland, discoverer's country, -IUM]

polōn' y̆, n. (Also *P*~ *sausage*) sausage of partly cooked pork. [app. replacing *Bologna*, -*ian sausage*]

pŏl'tergeist (-gīst), n. (Folklore & spiritualism) noisy mischievous spirit. [G]

pŏlt'-fōōt, n. & a. (arch.). Club-foot(ed). [obs. *polt* pestle, club, orig. unkn., +FOOT]

pŏltrōōn', n. Spiritless coward. So ~ERY(4) n. [f. F *poltron* f. It. *poltrone* f. *poltro* sluggard, see -OON]

pŏly̆-, comb. form of Gk *polus* many, as : ~*adĕl'phous*, with stamens united in 3 or more bundles; ~*ăn'drist*, woman with several husbands or paramours; ~*ăn'drous*, of, practising, (bot.) with numerous stamens; *pol'yandry*, plurality of husbands or paramours; *pol'yarchy* (-kĭ), government by many; ~*atŏm'ic*, containing many (esp. replaceable hydrogen) atoms; ~*autography*, lithography; ~*bās'ic* (chem.), having more than two bases or atoms of a base; ~*carp'ellary*, ~*carp'ous*, having several carpels; ~*chaete* (-kēt) a. & n., ~*chael'an*, ~*chael'ous*, (-kēt-), aa., (worm) with many bristles on the foot-stumps; ~*chrō'ite* (-kr-), colouring-matter of saffron, exhibiting various colours under various reagents; ~*dac'tyl* a. & n., (animal) with more than normal number of fingers or toes; ~*daem'onism*, belief in many supernatural powers; ~*gas'tric*, with many stomachs; ~*gen'esis*, origination of a race or species from several independent ancestors or germs, so ~*genēs'ic*, ~*genĕt'ic*, aa.; ~*gen'ic*, (chem.) forming more than one compound with hydrogen etc., (geol.) = ~*genous*; *poly̆'genism*, theory of ~*geny*; *poly̆'genist*, holder of this, so ~*genis'lic a.*; *poly̆'genous*, (geol.) composed of various kinds of rock, (chem.) = ~*genic*; *poly̆'geny*, origination of mankind from several independent pairs of ancestors; *pol'ygram*, many-lined figure or design; *pol'ygraph*, kinds of copying apparatus, (also) writer of many or various works, so ~*graph'ic* a., *poly̆g'raphy* n.; *poly̆g'y̆nous* (-g-), of, practising, ~*gyny*, (bot.) with many pistils, styles, or stigmas; *poly̆g'y̆ny* (-g-), plurality of wives; ~*hĕd'ron*, many (usu. more than six)-sided solid, so ~*hĕd'ral*, ~*hĕd'ric*, aa.; *pol'ymer*, compound formed by simple chemical addition from a number of identical molecules each of which consists of a number of identical units; ~*mĕ'ric*, (of compounds) composed of same elements in same proportions, but differing in molecular weight; *poly̆m'erism*, condition of being ~meric or ~merous; ~*meriza'tion*, formation of a ~mer by simple chemical addition of a number of identical smaller molecules; *pol'ymerize*, render ~meric or ~merous; *poly̆m'erous* (nat. hist.), composed of many parts; ~*morph'ic*, ~*morph'ous*,

For other words in *poly-* see POLY-.

multiform, esp. (nat. hist., biol.) varying in individuals, passing through
successive variations, so ~morph'ism n.;
~nŏm'ial a. & n. (alg.), = MULTInomial;
~ŏn'ymous, called by several different
names; ~ŏn'ymy, use of different names
for same thing; ~ōp'ia, affection of the
eyes in which one object appears as two
or more; ~pet'alous, having separate
petals; polyph'agous, (zool.) feeding on
various kinds of food or foodplants;
pol'yphone, letter, symbol, standing for
different sounds; ~phŏn'ic, polȳph'onous,
many-voiced, (philol.) standing for different sounds, (mus.) contrapuntal; polȳph'-
ony, quality of being ~phonic, (mus.)
counterpoint; ~phylēt'ic, = ~genetic;
~phȳll'ous, ~sĕp'alous, having separate
perianth-leaves, sepals; pol'ystome a. & n.
(animal) with many mouths or suckers;
~synthĕt'ic, (of languages) combining
several words of a sentence (e.g. verb &
object) into one; ~thăl'amous (nat. hist.),
many-chambered; pol'ytype, kind of
stereotype, copy of engraving etc. made
from this; ~zō'a, class of compound
invertebrates, so ~zō'ic a.; ~zōn'al, (of
lighthouse lens) composed of several
annular segments.

pŏlўăn'thus, n. Kinds of cultivated primula. [f. POLY-+Gk anthos flower]

pŏlўchrŏmăt'ic (-kr-), a. Many-coloured.
[POLY-]

pŏl'ўchrōme (-kr-), a. & n. **1.** Painted,
printed, decorated, in many colours.
2. n. Work of art in several colours, esp.
coloured statue; varied colouring. Hence
pŏlўchrŏm'ic, pŏl'ўchrōmous, aa. [F,
f. Gk polukhrōmos (POLY-, khrōma colour)]

pŏl'ўchrŏmȳ (-kr-), n. Art of painting in
several colours, esp. as applied to ancient
pottery etc. [f. F polychromie (as prec.,
see -Y¹)]

pŏlўclin'ic, n. Clinic devoted to various
diseases, general hospital. [POLY-; altered in sense & form f. POLICLINIC]

pŏlўg'am|ous, a. Having more than one
wife or (less usu.) husband at once, so
pŏlўgăm'ic a., ~ıst, ~ʏ¹, nn.; (zool.)
having more than one mate;(bot.) bearing some flowers with stamens only, some
with pistils only, some with both, on
same or on different plants. [f. late Gk
polugamos (polu- POLY-+-gamos marrying)]

pŏl'ўglŏt, a. & n. Of many languages;
(person) speaking or writing several languages; (book, esp. Bible) with text and
translation into several languages. Hence
polȳglŏtt'al, pŏlȳglŏtt'ic, aa., ~tısm n.
[f. Gk poluglōttos (polu- POLY- + glōtta
tongue)]

pŏl'ўgon, n. Figure (usu. plane rectilineal) with many (usu. more than four)
angles or sides; ~ of forces, ~ illustrating
theorem relating to number of forces act-

ing at a point. Hence **polȳg'on**AL a.,
polȳg'onalLY² adv. [f. LL f. Gk polu-
gōnon neut. adj. as n. (polu- POLY-+-gōnos
-angled)]

Polȳg'onum, n. Genus of plants including knotgrass, snakeweed, etc. [f. Gk
polugonon (polu- POLY-+gonu knee)]

pŏlўhis'tor, n. Man of varied learning,
great scholar. [f. Gk poluistōr (polu POLY-
+histōr, see HISTORY)]

Pŏlўhŷm'nia, n. The MUSE¹ of sacred
song. [L, f. Gk Polumnia (POLY-, HYMN)]

pŏl'ўmăth, n. = POLYHISTOR. So **polȳm'-
athy¹** n. [f. Gk polumathēs (polu-
POLY-+math- st. of manthanō learn)]

Pŏlўnē's|ia (-sha), n. Small islands in
Pacific Ocean east of Australia. Hence
~ıan (-shn) a. [f. POLY-+Gk nēsos island]

pŏlȳn'ia, n. Space of open water in midst
of ice, esp. in arctic seas. [f. Russ. po-
luinya (pole field)]

pŏl'ўp(e), n. Kinds of animal of low organization, e.g. hydra; individual of some
compound organisms. [F (-pe), as POLY-
PUS]

pŏl'ўparȳ, n. Common stem or supporting structure of a colony of polyps. [-ary
= -ARIUM]

polȳp'idom (or pŏl²), n. = prec. [f. POLY-
PUS+L domus house]

pŏl'ўpite, n. Individual polyp. [-ITE¹]

pŏl'ўpŏd, a. & n. (Animal) with many
feet. [f. F polypode f. Gk as POLYPUS]

pŏl'ўpŏdȳ, n. Kinds of ferns, esp. (common ~) species growing on moist rocks,
walls, trees, etc. [f. L f. Gk polupodion,
as POLYPUS]

pŏl'ўp|oid, a. Of, like, a polyp or a poly-
pus. So ~ous a. [-OID]

pŏl'ўpus, n. (pl. -pī). Kinds of tumour,
usu. with ramifications like tentacles. [L,
f. Gk polupous cuttle-fish, polypus in
nose (polu-POLY-+-pous -podos footed)]

pŏlўsȳllăb'|ic, a. (Of word) having many
syllables; marked by polysyllables.
Hence ~ıcally adv. [f. LL f. Gk polusul-
labos (as foll.)+-ıc]

pŏlўsȳll'able, n. Polysyllabic word. [f.
med. L polysyllaba (vox word), see POLY-
& SYLLABLE]

pŏlўtĕch'nĭc (-k-), a. & n. Dealing with,
devoted to, various arts, as ~ school; P~
(Institution), technical school, ‖ esp. one in
London orig. opened 1838. [f. F polytech-
nique f. Gk polutekhnos (polu- POLY-+
tekhnē art), see -IC]

pŏl'ўthė|ism, n. Belief in, worship of,
many gods or more than one god. So
~ıst n., ~ĭs'tıc a. [f. F polythéisme f. Gk
poluthéos of many gods (polu- POLY-+
theos god), see -ISM]

pŏm, n. POMERANIAN dog; POMMY. [abbr.]

pomace (pŭm'ĭs), n. Mass of crushed
apples in cider-making before or after
juice is pressed out; any pulp; refuse of
fish etc. after oil has been extracted, used

as fertilizer. [f. med. L *pomacium* cider f. L *pomum* apple]

pomade' (-ahd, -ād), n., & v.t. **1.** Scented ointment (perh. orig. from apples) for hair & skin of head. **2.** v.t. Anoint with ~. [f. F *pommade* f. It. *pomata* f. med. L (L *pomum* apple, -ADE)]

pŏm'ander (*or* pomăn²), n. (hist.). Ball of mixed aromatic substances carried in box, bag, etc., as preservative against infection; ball of gold, silver, etc., in which ~ was carried. [alt. f. 16th c. *pomamber* f. AF **pome ambre* f. OF *pome d'ambre* (*pome* apple + *ambre* AMBER)]

Pomard', **Pomm-**, (-ahr), n. A red Burgundy wine. [~, village in France]

pomāt'um, n., & v.t. = POMADE. [f. L *pomum* apple + *-atum* -ATE¹]

pŏm'bė, n. Intoxicating drink from various kinds of grain & fruit in Africa. [native]

pŏme, n. (Bot.) succulent INFERIOR fruit with firm fleshy body enclosing carpels forming the core, e.g., apple, pear, quince, so **pomIF'EROUS** a.; (poet.) apple; metal ball. [ME, f. OF, f. Rom. **poma* pl. of *pomum* fruit, apple]

pŏme'grănate (-mg-; *also* pŭm-), n. Fruit of a tree native to N. Africa & W. Asia, a large red berry about size of orange with tough golden or orange rind & acid reddish pulp enveloping seeds; the tree. [ME, f. OF POME *grenale* = L (*malum*) *granatum* (GRAIN, -ATE²); cf. GRENADE]

pom'elō (pŭm-), n. (pl. ~s). Small shaddock or grape-fruit. [orig. unkn.]

Pŏmerān'ian, a. & n. Of Pomerania on S. coast of Baltic; ~ (*dog*), small dog with long silky hair, pointed muzzle, & pricked ears. [-AN]

pŏm'frĕt, n. Fish found in Indian & Pacific Oceans, used as food. [prob. ult. f. Port. *pampo*; cf. PAMPANO]

‖ **pŏm'frĕt-cāke**, n. Liquorice sweetmeat made at Pontefract (earlier Pomfret) in Yorks.

pŏm'iculture, n̄. Fruit-growing. [f. L *pomum* fruit + CULTURE]

Pommard. See POMARD.

pomm'el (pŭm-), n., & v.t. (-ll-). **1.** Rounded knob esp. at end of sword-hilt; upward projecting front part of saddle. **2.** v.t. Strike or beat (as) with ~; beat with fists. [ME, f. OF *pomel* f. Rom. **pomellum* dim. as POME]

*pŏmm'ў, n. (sl.). British immigrant to Australia or New Zealand. [orig. unkn.]

pomŏl'og|ў, n. Science of fruit-growing. Hence **pōmolō'gICAL** a., ~IST n. [as POME + -LOGY]

Pomōn'a, n. (Rom. myth.) goddess of fruits; ~ *green* (in which yellow predominates). [L]

pŏmp, n. Splendid display, splendour; (pl.) *the* ~*s & vanity of this wicked world.* [ME, f. OF *pompe* f. L f. Gk *pompē* procession, pomp, (*pempō* send)]

Pŏm'padour (-ōōr), n. Marquise de ~,

mistress of Louis XV; (attrib., designating) style of hair-dressing, cut of bodice, etc.

pŏm'panō, n. (pl. ~s). Kinds of W.-Ind. & N.-Amer. fish esteemed for food. [f. Sp. *pámpano*]

‖ **Pŏm'pey**, n. (sl.). Portsmouth.

pŏm'pier, a. ~ *ladder*, fireman's scaling ladder. [F, = fireman (as PUMP, see -IER)]

pŏm²-pŏm, n. Long-range Maxim automatic quick-firing gun. [imit.]

pŏm'pŏn (& see Ap.), n. Ornamental tuft or bunch of ribbon, flowers, etc., on women's & children's hats & shoes; round tuft on soldier's cap, front of shako, etc. [F, of unkn. orig.]

pŏm'pous, a. Magnificent, splendid; self-important, consequential, (of language) inflated, so **pŏmpos'ITY** n. Hence ~LY² adv., ~NESS n. [ME, f. LL *pomposus* (as POMP, see -OUS)]

pônce (-ns), n. (sl.). Souteneur. [orig. unkn.]

pŏn'ceau (-sō), n. Poppy colour, bright red. [F]

pŏn'chō, n. (pl. ~s). S.-Amer. cloak, oblong piece of cloth with slit in middle for head; cape for cycling etc. on same plan. [native]

pŏnd, n., & v.t. & i. **1.** Small body of still water artificially formed by hollowing or embanking; (joc.) the sea; cf. HERRING- ~; ~*life*, animals esp. invertebrates that live in ~s; ~*weed*, kinds of aquatic herb growing in still water. **2.** v.t. Hold *back*, dam *up*, (stream); (v.i., of water) form a pool or ~. [ME, app. var. of POUND²]

pŏn'dage, n. Capacity of pond; storage of water. [-AGE]

pŏn'der, v.t. & i. Weigh mentally, think over, (matter, *how*, etc.); think *on*, muse *over*. Hence ~ingLY² adv. [ME, f. OF *ponderer* f. L *ponderare* (*pondus -eris* weight)]

pŏn'der|able, a. Having appreciable weight (lit. & fig.). Hence ~ABIL'ITY n. [f. LL *ponderabilis* (as prec., see -BLE)]

pŏnderā'tion, n. Weighing, balancing, (lit. & fig.). [f. L *ponderatio* (as prec., see -ATION)]

pŏn'derous, a. Heavy; unwieldy; laborious; (of style) dull, tedious. Hence or cogn. **pŏnderos'ITY**, ~NESS, nn., ~LY² adv. [ME, f. OF *pondereus* f. L *ponderosus* (*pondus -eris* weight, see -OUS)]

pōn'e¹, n. Leader('s partner) in some card games. [L, 2nd sing. imperat. of *ponere* place]

pōne², n. Maize bread, esp. as made by N.-Amer. Indians; fine light bread made with milk, eggs, etc.; cake, loaf, of this. [native]

pongee (pŭnjē'), n. Soft unbleached kind of Chinese silk. [perh. f. Chin. *pun-chī* own loom]

pŏn'gō (-ngg-), n. (Early name for) a large anthropoid African ape; (improp.) orang-outang. [native]

pŏn'iard (-yard), n., & v.t. Dagger; (v.t.) stab with ~. [f. F *poignard* (*poing* fist f. L *pugnus*, -ARD)]

pŏns (-nz), n. ~ *ăsĭnor'um*, bridge of asses, i.e. 5th proposition of 1st book of Euclid (' the angles at the base of an isosceles triangle are equal to one another '), hence, anything found difficult by beginners; ~ (*Varol'ĭi*), band of nerve-fibres in brain [f. *Varoli*, Italian anatomist]. [L, = bridge]

pŏn'tifĕx, n. (pl. -*ĭf'ĭces* pr. -ēz). (Rom. ant.) member of principal college of priests in Rome, *P*~ *maximus*, head of this; = foll. [L]

pŏn'tiff, n. (Also *sovereign* ~) the Pope; bishop; chief priest. [f. F *pontife* f. prec.]

pŏntif'ical, a. & n. **1.** Of, befitting, a pontiff; assuming infallibility, pompously dogmatic. **2.** n. Office-book of Western Church containing forms for rites to be performed by bishops; (pl.) vestments & insignia of bishop. Hence~LY[2] adv. [ME, f. L *pontificalis* (as PONTIFEX, see -AL)]

pŏntĭfĭcāl'ia, n. pl. Pontificals. [L, neut. pl. as prec.]

pŏntif'icate, n., & v.i. Office of pontifex, bishop, or pope; period of this; (v.i., pr. -āt) = foll. [f. L *pontificatus* (as PONTIFEX, see -ATE[1])]

pŏn'tify, v.i. Play the pontiff, assume airs of infallibility. [f. F *pontifier* f. med. L *pontificare* (as PONTIFEX), see -FY]

pŏnt-lĕv'ĭs (or pawn levĕ'), n. Drawbridge. [F]

pŏntoneer', -nier (-nēr), n. One who has charge of pontoons or of construction of a pontoon-bridge. [f. F *pontonnier*, see foll. & -EER]

pŏntōōn'[1], n., & v.t. Flat-bottomed boat used as ferry-boat etc.; one of several boats, hollow metal cylinders, etc. used to support temporary bridge; = CAISSON (not in first sense); (v.t.) cross (river) by means of~s. [f. F *ponton* f. L *ponto -onis* (*pons -ntis* bridge, see -OON)]

‖ **pŏntōōn'[2]**, n.=VINGT(-ET)-UN. [prob. corruption]

pŏn'y, n. Horse of any small breed, esp. not more than 13 or (pop.) 14 hands; ‖ (sl.) £25. [f. Sc. *powney* prob. f. OF *poulenet* little foal dim. of *poulain* f. LL *pullamen* (*pullus* foal)]

pŏŏd, n. Russian weight, 36 lb. avoirdupois. [f. Russ. *pudu* f. LG or Norse *pund* POUND]

pŏŏ'dle, n., & v.t. Kinds of pet dog with long curling hair often clipped & shaved fantastically; (v.t.) clip & shave (dog) thus. [f. G *pudel*(*hund*) f. *pudeln* splash in water, see PUDDLE[2]]

pŏŏ'dle-fāk|er, n. (sl.). Youth too much given to tea-parties and ladies' society generally. So ~ing vbl n.

pooh (pōō, pŏŏh), int. expr. impatience or contempt. [imit.]

Pooh-Bah' (pōōb-), n. Holder of many offices at once. [person in W. S. Gilbert's *The Mikado*]

pooh-pooh' (pōōpōō'), v.t. Express contempt for, make light of, as *he ~ed the idea*. [see POOH]

pŏŏ'ja. Var. of PUJA.

‖ **pŏŏ'ka**, n. Hobgoblin. [Ir. *púca*]

pŏŏ'kŏŏ, puku (pōō'kŏŏ), n. Red antelope of S. Central Africa. [f. Zulu *mpuku*]

pŏŏl[1], n., & v.t. **1.** Small body of still water, usu. of natural formation; puddle of any liquid; deep still place in river. **2.** v.t. Make (hole) for insertion of wedge in quarrying, undermine (coal). [OE *pōl*, MLG *pōl*, f. WG *pōlo*-]

pŏŏl[2], n., & v.t. **1.** (In cards) collective amount of players' stake & fines; receptacle for these. **2.** ‖ Game on billiard-table in which each player has ball of different colour with which he tries to pocket the others in fixed order, winner taking the whole stakes. **3.** (Collective stakes in) a joint gambling venture (*football* ~, form of gambling in which a proportion of the entry money for the competition is awarded in 'prizes to those who correctly forecast the results of certain football matches). **4.** Arrangement between competing parties by which prices are fixed & business divided to do away with competition. **5.** Common fund, e.g. of the profits of separate firms; common supply of persons, commodities, etc. (also attrib., as ~ *petrol*). **6.** v.t. Throw into common fund, share in common; (of transport organizations etc.) share (traffic, receipts). [f. F *poule* (= hen) in same sense, in E early assoc. w. prec.]

pŏŏn, n. E.-Indian tree; ~-*oil*, oil from seeds of this, used in medicine & for lamps. [f. Sinhalese *puna*]

pŏŏn'ah (-a), a. ~ *painting* (on rice or other thin paper in imitation of oriental work); ~ *brush*, *paper* (used for this). [*Poona*, Indian city]

pŏŏp[1], n., & v.t. **1.** Stern of ship; aftermost & highest deck. **2.** v.t. (Of wave) break over stern of (ship); (of ship) receive (wave) over stern. Hence (-)~ED[2] (-pt) a. [ME, f. OF *pupe* f. Rom. **puppa* f. L *puppis*]

pŏŏp[2]. See POPE[3].

‖ **pŏŏp[3]**, n. (sl.). Foolish insignificant person. [abbr. NINCOMPOOP]

poor, a. **1.** Wanting means to procure comforts or necessaries of life, needy, indigent; ill supplied, deficient, (*in a possession or quality*); (of soil) unproductive; scanty, inadequate, less than is expected, as *the crop was* ~, *a* ~ *three weeks' holiday*; (of visibility) bad; paltry, sorry, as *that is a* ~ *consolation*; spiritless, despicable, as *he is a* ~ *creature*; humble, insignificant, (often iron. or joc., as *in my* ~ *opinion*); (expr. pity or sympathy) unfortunate, hapless, as ~ *fellow!*, *the* ~ *child is inconsolable*; *the* ~, (esp.) those dependent on charitable or parochial relief. 2. ~-**box**, money-box esp. in church for relief of the ~; ~-**house**, workhouse; ~-**law** (relating to support of paupers; hist.); ~ **man's weather-glass**, pimpernel; ‖ ~-**rate**, rate, assessment, for relief or support of the ~; ~-**spirited**, timid, cowardly. [ME & OF *pov(e)re*, *poure*, f. L *pauper*]

poor′lў, adv. & pred. a. **1.** Scantily, defectively; with no great success; meanly, contemptibly. **2.** adj. Unwell, as *he is (looking) very* ~. [prec.+-LY²; pred. a. prob. orig. adv.]

poor′ness, n. Defectiveness; lack of some good quality or constituent. [POOR + -NESS]

‖ **poort** (pŏrt), n. (S. Afr.). Pass, narrower than a nek. [Du.,= gate(way)]

pŏp¹, v.i. & t. (-pp-). Make small quick explosive sound as of cork when drawn; let off (fire-arm etc.); fire gun (*at* bird etc.); put (thing *in, out, down,* etc.) quickly or suddenly; move, go, come, (*in* etc.) thus; put (question) abruptly, esp. (colloq.)~ *the question,* propose marriage; ‖ (sl.) pawn; *parch (maize) till it bursts open, ~′corn, maize so parched; ~′gun, child's toy gun shooting pellets by compression of air with piston, (derog.) inefficient fire-arm; ‖ ~′shop, pawnbroker's shop. [imit.]

pŏp², n., adv., & int. **1.** Abrupt explosive sound; dot, spot, esp. in marking sheep etc.; (colloq.) effervescing drink, esp. ginger-beer or champagne; ‖ (sl.) pawning, esp. *in* ~, in pawn. **2.** int. or adv. *Heard it go* (make the sound) ~ *!*; ~ *goes the weasel,* country dance in which dancer darted under arms of others to his partner. [as prec.]

pŏp³, n. (colloq.). Popular concert, as *Saturday* ~*s*; popular disc, record, etc. [abbr.]

‖ **Pŏp⁴**, n. Social & debating club at Eton. [said to be so called f. L *popina* cookshop, or E *lollipop shop* (orig. meeting-place)]

pop⁵. See POPPA.

pōpe¹, n. **1.** Bishop of Rome as head of Roman Catholic Church; (fig.) person assuming or credited with infallibility etc. **2.** *P*~ *Joan,* fabulous female ~, a card-game; ~'*s eye,* lymphatic gland surrounded with fat in middle of leg of mutton; ~'*s head,* round long-handled broom; ~'*s nose,* = PARSON'S *nose.* Hence ~′DOM (-pd-) n., ~′LESS (-pl-) a. [OE *pāpa* f. eccl. L *papa* f. late Gk *papas* = Gk *pappas* father, cf. PAPA]

pōpe², n. Parish priest of Greek Church in Russia etc. [f. Russ. *popu* app. f. WG *papo* as prec.]

pōpe³, pōōp, n., & v.t. Place in thigh on which blow is painful or paralysing, esp. *take* person's ~, strike this; (v.t.) take the ~ of. [orig. unkn.]

pōp′erў, n. Papal system, Roman Catholic religion, (in hostile use, esp. *no* ~*!*). [f. POPE¹+-ERY]

*pŏp′eyed** (-īd), a. (colloq.). Having bulging eyes; open-eyed (with surprise etc.). [POP¹]

pŏp′injay, n. (Arch.) parrot; (hist.) figure of parrot on pole as mark to shoot at; conceited person; ‖ (dial.) green woodpecker. [f. OF *papingay* etc., cf. med. Gk *papagas,* Arab. *babagha,* prob. imit. & of Afr. orig.]

pŏp′ish, a. Of popery, papistical. Hence ~LY² adv. [f. POPE¹+-ISH¹]

pŏp′lar, n. Kinds of large trees of rapid growth (often w. allusion to straightness of trunk); *trembling* ~, aspen. [ME, f. OF *poplier* f. L *pōpulus*+-IER]

‖ **Pŏp′larism**, n. Policy of giving extravagant out-relief (as practised by the Poplar Board of Guardians *c.* 1920); any similar policy tending to raise the rates. [-ISM]

pŏp′lin, n. (Formerly) woven fabric of silk warp & worsted weft with corded surface; (now usu.) fabric of mercerized cotton. [f. F *popeline* f. It. *papalina* PAPAL, from the papal town Avignon where it was made]

pŏplit′ĕal, a. Of the ham, of the hollow at back of knee, as ~ *artery,* ~ *tendons* (hamstrings). [f. L *poples -itis* ham, see -AL]

*pŏpp′a**, *pŏp**, n. Papa. [f. *papa*]

pŏpp′ĕt, n. ‖ (Colloq.) small person, esp. as term of endearment; lathe-head; (naut.) short piece of wood for various purposes; ~-*head,* lathe-head, ‖ (mining) frame at top of shaft supporting pulleys for ropes used in hoisting; ~-*valve,* = PUPPET-*valve.* [ME *popet, -elle,* corresp. to F (16th c.) *poupette* doll, dim. f. Rom. *puppa* f. L *pupa* girl; see PUPPET]

pŏpp′ing, n. In vbl senses; (crick.) ~-*crease* [perh. = striking-crease], line 4 feet in front of & parallel to wicket within which batsman must keep one foot grounded. [-ING¹]

pŏp′ple, v.i. & n. (Of water) tumble about, toss to & fro; (n.) rolling, tossing, ripple. Hence **pŏpp′lў²** a. [ME, prob. f. MDu. *popelen,* of imit. orig.]

pŏpp′ў, n. Kinds of herbs having milky juice with narcotic properties & showy flowers of scarlet or other colour; *opium* ~, species from which opium is obtained; *Flanders* poppies (sacred to dead of 1914 -18 war; also as name of those made for & sold on *P*~ *Day,* Saturday nearest 11 Nov.); ~-*head,* seed capsule of ~, (archit.) ornamental top to end of church seat; *Shirley* ~, cultivated variety of common corn ~ [f. Shirley Vicarage, Croydon, where first produced]. Hence **pŏpp′iED²** (-pĭd) a. [OE *popig,* ult. f. L *papaver*]

*pŏp′sўcŏck**, n. (sl.). Nonsense.

pŏp′sў(-wŏpsў), n. An endearing appellation for a girl. [extension of *pop* abbr. of POPPET, with dim. suf.]

pŏp′ūlace, n. The common people; the rabble. [F, f. It. *popolaccio* (*popolo* PEOPLE+-*accio* pejorative suf.)]

Q

pŏp'ūlar, a. Of, carried on by, the people, as ~ *election, meetings, tumult*; adapted to the understanding, taste, or means, of the people, as *in ~ language, ~ science, at ~* (low) *prices*; liked, admired, by the people or by people generally or *with* specified class, as ~ *teachers, the ~ hero, is ~ with his men*, so **pŏpūlā'rity** n.; prevalent among the people, as ~ *fallacies*; ~ *front* (pol.), party representing Left elements. Hence ~LY² adv. [ME, f. AF *populer* or L *popularis* (cf. foll.), as PEOPLE]

pŏp'ūlarīz|e, **-is|e** (-īz), v.t. Make popular, cause (person, principle, etc.) to be generally known or liked; extend (suffrage etc.) to the common people; present (technical subject etc.) in popular form. Hence ~A'TION n. [-IZE]

pŏp'ūlāte, v.t. Inhabit, form the population of, (country, town, etc.); supply with inhabitants, as *a densely ~d district*. [f. med. L *populare* (as PEOPLE)]

pŏpūlā'tion, n. Degree in which place is populated; total number of inhabitants, the people of a country etc.; *the* inhabitants of a place (*the ~ turned out to welcome him*). [f. LL *populatio* (as prec., see -ATION)]

pŏp'ūl|ist, n. Adherent of U.S. political party aiming at public control of railways, graduated income-tax, etc., formed 1892; adherent of Russian political party advocating collectivism. So ~ISM n., ~is'TIC a. [f. L *populus* PEOPLE +-IST]

pŏp'ūlous, a. Thickly inhabited. Hence ~NESS n. [ME, f. L *populosus* (as PEOPLE, see -OUS)]

pŏrb'eagle, n. Mackerel-shark. [Cornish dial., of unkn. orig.]

pŏrce'lain (-slĭn), n. Fine kind of earthenware with translucent body & transparent glaze; thing made of this; (fig., attrib.) delicate, fragile; ~*-shell*, cowrie; ~ *clay*, kaolin. Hence or cogn. ~OUS (-slĭn-), **pŏrcĕllān'EOUS**, **pŏrcĕllān'IC**, **pŏrcĕl-lanOUS**, aa. [f. F *porcelaine* Venus shell, porcelain, f. It. *porcellana* (*porcella* dim. of *porco* hog f. L *porcus*)]

pŏrce'lainize (-slĭn-), **-ise** (-īz), v.t. Convert (clay, shale, etc.) into porcelain or similar substance. [-IZE]

pŏrch, n. Covered approach to entrance of building; *the P~*, colonnade at Athens to which Zeno & his disciples resorted, (hence) Stoic school or philosophy (cf. ACADEMY, GARDEN, LYCEUM). Hence ~ED² (-cht), ~'LESS, aa. [ME, f. OF *porche* f. L *porticus*]

pŏr'cine, a. Of or like swine. [F (-*in*, -*ine*), f. L *porcinus* (*porcus* hog, see -INE¹)]

pŏrc'ūpin|e, n. || Rodent quadruped with body & tail covered with erectile spines; kinds of machine with many spikes or teeth, e.g. for heckling flax etc.; (attrib., applied to animals with spines etc.) ~*e ant-eater, crab, fish, grass*. Hence ~ISH¹,

~Y², **aa**. [ME, f. OF *porc espin* ult. f. L *porcus* hog+*spina* thorn; earlier also **porkenpick** f. F *porc-épic* (L *spicus*=*spica* spike) & *porpentine*]

pōre¹, n. Minute opening (esp. in skin of animal body) through which fluids may pass. [ME, f. OF f. L f. Gk *poros* passage, pore]

pōre², v.i. & t. ~ *over*, be absorbed in studying (book etc.), (fig.) meditate, think intently upon, (subject); (arch.) look intently *at, on, over*; ~ one's *eyes out*, tire them by close reading. [ME *puren, pouren*, of unkn. orig.]

pōrge, v.t. (Jew. ritual). Make (slaughtered beast) ceremonially clean by removing sinews etc. Hence **pŏr'gER¹** n. [app. f. L as PURGE]

*****pŏrg'ȳ** (-g-), n. Perch-like salt-water fish; sea-bream (applied also, esp. locally, to many other fish). [of var. orig.; cf. *porgo, pargo* (Sp.), *paugie* (Amer.-Ind.)]

pōr'ism (*or* pŏ'r-), n. (math.). Proposition concerned with the conditions that will render a given problem capable of innumerable solutions; corollary. So **pōr-ismăt'IC**, **pŏris'tIC**, aa. [f. LL f. Gk *porisma -matos* (*porizō* deduce)]

pŏrk, n. Flesh (esp. fresh) of swine used as food; ~*-butcher*, one who slaughters pigs for sale; ~ *pie* (of minced etc. ~); || ~*-pie hat* (with flat crown & brim turned up all round). [ME & OF *porc* f. L *porcus* hog]

pŏrk'er, n. Pig raised for food; young fattened hog, so **pŏrk'ET¹** n. [-ER¹]

pŏrk'ling, n. Young or small pig. [-LING¹]

pŏrk'ȳ, a. Of, like, pork, esp. (colloq.) fleshy, fat. [-Y²]

pŏrn|o-, comb. form of Gk *pornē* harlot, as : ~*ŏc'racy*, dominant influence of harlots, esp. in government of Rome in 10th c.; ~*ŏg'raphy*, description of manners etc. of harlots, treatment of obscene subjects in literature, inflammatory literature, so ~*ŏg'rapher* n., ~*ograph'ic* a.

pōr'oplăs'tic (*or* pŏ'r-), a. (surg.). (Of felt) both porous & plastic. [as PORE¹+PLASTIC]

pōr'ous, a. Full of pores (lit. & fig.). Hence or cogn. **pōros'ITY**, ~NESS, nn. [ME; -OUS]

pŏrph'yrȳ, n. Hard rock anciently quarried in Egypt, composed of crystals of white or red feldspar in red ground-mass; (geol.) unstratified or igneous rock having homogeneous base in which crystals of one or more minerals are disseminated. [ME; ult. f. Gk *porphuros* purple]

pŏr'poise (-pus), n. Sea animal of the whale order about five feet long with blunt rounded snout. [ME *porpays, peys, -poys*, f. OF *porpeis* f. L *porcus* hog+ *piscis* fish]

pŏrrā'ceous (-shus), a. Leek-green. [f. L *porraceus* (*porrum* leek, see -ACEOUS)]

pŏrrĕct', v.t. (Nat. hist.) stretch out (part of body); (eccl. law) tender, submit, (document). [f. L *porrigere* *-rect-* (*por-* PRO- +*regere* direct)]

‖ **po̅rridge**, n. Soft food made by stirring oatmeal or other meal or cereal in boiling water or milk; *keep* one's *breath to cool* one's ~, keep one's advice etc. for one's own use. [16th c., alt. f. POTTAGE]

po̅rrig′o̅, n. (path.). Scaly eruption of scalp. So **po̅rri′gin**OUS a. [L, gen. *-ginis*]

po̅′rringer (-j-), n. Small basin from which soup etc. is eaten esp. by children. [earlier *potager*, *pottinger* (as PORRIDGE, see -ER[1]); for *-n-* cf. *passenger*]

po̅rt[1], n. Harbour (lit. & fig.); town, place, possessing harbour, esp. one where customs officers are stationed; (in proper names) *P~ Arthur, Said*, etc.; *P~ of London Authority*, corporate body set up by P~-of-London Act 1908 for control of ~ & docks; *free~*, one open for merchants of all nations to load & unload in, (also) exemption for imports or exports; *close* ~ (lying up river); CINQUE PORTS; ~ *admiral* (in command of naval ~). [OE, f. L *portus*; ME reinforced f. OF *port*]

po̅rt[2], n. ‖ Gate, gateway, esp. of walled town (chiefly Sc.); (naut.) opening in side of ship for entrance, loading, etc., (also) = ~*hole*; (mech.) aperture for passage of steam, water, etc.; curved mouthpiece of some bridle-bits; ~*hole*, aperture in ship's side for admission of light & air, or (formerly) for pointing cannon through. [ME & OF *porte* f. L *porta*; OE *port* dir. f. L]

po̅rt[3], n. External deportment, carriage, bearing; (mil.) position taken in porting arms. [ME & OF *port*, as foll.]

po̅rt[4], v.t. (mil.). Carry (rifle, or other weapon) diagonally across & close to the body, with barrel etc. opposite middle of left shoulder, esp. ~ *arms!* [f. F *porter* f. L *portare* carry]

po̅rt[5], n., & v.t. & i. (naut.). **1.** (Also formerly *larboard*) left-hand side of ship looking forward (cf. STARBOARD), as *put the helm to* ~ or *a-*~; (attrib.) *on your* ~ (left) *bow* etc. **2.** v.t. Turn (helm, or abs.) to left side of ship; (v.i., of ship) turn to her ~ side. [orig. obsc.; poss. f. PORT[1] or PORT[2] (naut.), describing the side on which the 'port' was]

po̅rt[6], n. Strong sweet dark-red (occas. white) wine of Portugal. [shortened f. *Oporto*, city of Portugal]

po̅rt′able, a. & n. Movable (article), convenient for carrying, as ~ *furnace, radio*. Hence **po̅rtABIL′ITY** n. [ME, f. OF, f. LL *portabilis* (*portare* carry, -BLE)]

po̅rt′age, n. & v.t. **1.** Carrying, carriage; cost of this; *mariner's* ~, space allowed to mariner for own venture or to be let by him for freight in lieu of wages; carrying of boats or goods between two navigable waters, place at which this is necessary. **2.** v.t. Convey (boat, goods) over a ~. [ME & OF *portage*, = med. L *portaticum*, *-agium*, as PORT[4], -AGE]

po̅rt′al[1], n. Door(way), gate(way), esp. elaborate one. [ME, f. OF, f. med. L *portale* neut. adj. as n. (*porta* gate, see -AL)]

po̅rt′al[2], a. (anat.). Of the *porta* or transverse fissure of the liver, as ~ *vein* (conveying blood to liver). [f. med. L *portalis* as prec.]

portamen′to̅, n. (mus.). Gliding continuously from one pitch to another; (to be played) in a manner intermediate between LEGATO and STACCATO (erron.). [It.]

po̅rt′ative, a. Serving to carry or support. [OF (*-if, -ive*), f. L *portare* carry, see -IVE]

po̅rtcull′is, n. Strong heavy grating sliding up & down in vertical grooves at sides of gateway in fortress etc. Hence ~ED[2] (-st) a. [ME, f. OF *porte coleïce* sliding door (*porte* door f. L *porta*, see COULISSE)]

Po̅rte, n. *The* (*Sublime* or *Ottoman*) ~ (hist.), Ottoman court at Constantinople, Turkish government to 1923. [F (*la Sublime ~*), transl. of Turk. title of central office of Ottoman government]

po̅rte-, comb. form of F *porte-* imperat. of *porter* carry in wds meaning ' -case', ' -holder', as: *port*(*e*)-*cray'on*, metal tube or other holder for crayon; ~*feuille* (-fü′ye), portfolio; ~*-monnaie* (-monē′), flat leathern purse or pocket-book.

porte-cochère (po̅rtkoshār′), n. Gateway & passage for vehicles through house into courtyard. [F]

po̅rtend′, v.t. Foreshow, foreshadow, as an omen; give warning of, as *this* ~*s a renewal of the conflict*. [ME, f. L *portendere* *-tent-* (*por-* PRO- +*tendere* stretch)]

po̅rt′ent, n. Omen, significant sign; prodigy, marvellous thing. So **po̅rtěn′tous** a., **po̅rtěn′tous**LY[2] adv. [f. L *portentum* as prec.]

‖ **po̅rt′er[1]**, n. Gate-keeper, door-keeper. [ME & AF, f. LL *portarius* (*porta* door, see -ER[2])]

po̅rt′er[2], n. **1.** Person employed to carry burdens, esp. railway servant who handles luggage, whence ~AGE (4) n. **2.** Dark-brown bitter beer brewed from charred or browned malt [perh. orig. made esp. for ~s]. **3.** *~-house*, house at which ~ etc. were retailed, (also) one where steaks, chops, etc., were served (~*-house steak*, choice cut of beef from region of undercut); ‖ ~'*s knot*, pad resting on shoulders & secured to forehead used by ~s in carrying loads. [ME, f. OF *porteour* f. LL *portatorem* (*portare* carry, see -OR)]

po̅rt′fire, n. Device for firing rockets, igniting explosives in mining, etc. [after F *porte-feu* (PORTE-, FIRE)]

po̅rtfo̅l′io̅, n. (pl. ~s). Case for keeping loose sheets of paper, drawings, etc.; list of investments held by company etc.; (fig.) office of Minister of State; *Minister without* ~, Cabinet Minister who is not in charge of any Department of State. [18th c., f. It. *portafogli* (*porta* imperat. of *portare* carry +*foglio* leaf f. L *folium*)]

pŏrt'ĭcō, n. (pl. ~s). Colonnade, roof supported by columns at regular intervals, usu. attached as porch to a building. [It., f. L *porticus* PORCH]

portière (pŏrtyār'), n. Curtain hung over door(way). [F]

pŏr'tion, n., & v.t. **1.** Part, share; (in restaurants) amount of a dish served to a customer; dowry, whence ~LESS (-sho-) a.; one's destiny, one's lot; a ~, some (of anything). **2.** v.t. Divide (thing) into shares, distribute *out*, assign (thing *to* person) as share; give dowry to. [ME, f. OF, f. L *portionem*; vb f. OF *portionner*]

Pŏrt'land, n. (Used· for) ~ prison; ~ cement, artificial cement manufactured from chalk and clay, in colour rather like ~ stone, a valuable building limestone obtained from the Isle of ~. [Dorset peninsula]

pŏrt'lĭў̆, a. Bulky, corpulent; of stately appearance. Hence ~ĭNESS n. [PORT³, -LY¹]

pŏrtmăn'teau (-tō), n. (pl. ~s, ~x, pr. -z). || Leather trunk for clothes etc. opening into two equal parts; (fig.) factitious word blending the sounds & combining the meanings of two others (e.g. *slithy*=lithe & slimy). [f. F PORTE-(*manteau* MANTLE)]

pŏrtola'nō (-lah-), n. (hist.). Book of sailing directions with description of harbours etc. [f. It. (*porto* PORT¹)]

pŏrt'rait (-rĭt), n. Likeness of person or animal made by drawing, painting, photography, etc.; (fig.) type, similitude; verbal picture, graphic description. [F, p.p. as PORTRAY]

pŏrt'raitist (-rĭt-), n. One who paints or takes portraits. [-IST]

pŏrt'raiture (-rĭcher), n. Portraying; portrait; graphic description. [ME, f. OF (PORTRAIT +-URE)]

pŏrtray', v.t. Make likeness of; describe graphically. Hence ~AL(2) n. [ME, f. OF *portraire* f. L PRO(*trahere tract*- draw)]

pŏrt'reeve, n. (Hist.) chief officer of town or borough; (now) officer inferior to mayor in some towns. [OE *port-gerēfa* (*port* town (now obs.), = PORT¹ or ²+ REEVE¹)]

pŏrt'ress, n. Female PORTER¹. [-ESS¹]

Pŏrtŭguese' (-gēz), a. & n. (pl. same). (Native, language) of Portugal; ~ *man-of- -war*, dangerous (sub-)tropical jellyfish with sail-shaped crest and poisonous sting, travelling rarely to Britain. [f. Port. *portuguez* f. med. L *portugalensis* (see -ESE)]

pōse¹ (-z), v.t. & i., & n. **1.** Lay down· (assertion, claim, etc.); propound (question); place (artist's model etc.) in certain attitude; assume an attitude, esp. for artistic purposes; set up, give oneself out, *as* (connoisseur etc.); (in dominoes) place first domino on table. **2.** n. Attitude of body or mind, esp. one assumed for effect, as *his philanthropy is a mere* ~; (dominoes) posing, right to ~. [(n. f. F *pose*)

f. F *poser* f. L *pausare* PAUSE; some senses by confus. w. L *ponere* place, cf. COMPOSE]

pōse² (-z), v.t. Puzzle (person) with question or problem. [aphetic f. obs. *oppose* or OPPOSE]

pōs'er (-z-), n. In vbl senses of prec., esp. puzzling question or problem. [-ER¹]

pōseur' (-zēr, & see Ap.), n. Affected person. [F]

|| **pŏsh**, a. (sl.). Smart, tiptop.

pŏs'it (-z-) v.t. Assume as fact, postulate; put in position, place, as ~*ed by natural agency*. [f. L *ponere posit*- place]

posi'tion (-z-), n., & v.t. **1.** Proposition, laying down of this. **2.** Bodily posture; *eastward*~ (of priest at eucharist standing in front of altar & facing east). **3.** Mental attitude, way of looking at question. **4.** Place occupied by a thing; *in, out of,* ~ (proper place); (mil.) place where troops are posted for strategical purposes (*the* ~ *was stormed*), the being advantageously placed (*manœuvring for* ~); *in a* ~ *to do, state*, etc., enabled by circumstances or resources or information to. **5.** Situation of vowel in syllable, esp. (Gk & L pros.) of short vowel before two consonants, making the syllable metrically long. **6.** (fig.). Situation in relation to other persons or things, as *difficult for a person in my* ~. **7.** Rank, status, (*people of* ~, esp. upper & upper-middle classes); official employment. **8.** v.t. Place in~, determine~ of; (mil.) place or post (troops). Hence ~AL (-zĭsho-) a. [ME, f. OF, f. L *positionem* (as prec., see -ION)]

pŏs'itive (-z-), a. & n. **1.** Formally laid down, artificially instituted, (opp. to *natural*), as ~ *laws*. **2.** Explicitly laid down, definite, admitting no question, as ~ *assertion, have no* ~ *proof, here is proof* ~. **3.** (Of person) convinced, confident in opinion, cocksure. **4.** (gram.). ~ (*degree of*) *adjective, adverb*, primary form expressing simple quality without comparison (cf. COMPARATIVE, SUPERLATIVE). **5.** Absolute, not relative; (colloq.) downright, out-&- -out, as *he is a* ~ *nuisance*. **6.** Dealing only with matters of fact, practical, as ~ *philosophy*. **7.** Marked by presence, not absence, of qualities (cf. NEGATIVE). **8.** (Alg., of quantity) greater than zero (cf. NEGATIVE), ~ *sign* (+); tending in the direction naturally or arbitrarily taken as that of increase or progress, as *clockwise rotation is* ~. **9.** ~ *electricity* (of the kind produced by rubbing glass with silk, vitreous); ~ *pole*, (of magnet) north- -seeking pole, (of earth) south pole. **10.** (photog.). Showing lights & shades as seen in nature (opp. NEGATIVE¹). **11.** ~ *organ*, small (orig. portable) organ used to supplement large one in church. **12.** n. ~ *degree*, adjective, quantity, etc. Hence ~LY² adv., ~NESS, pŏsĭtiv'ITY, nn., (-z-). [ME & OF *positif* f. L *positivus* (as POSIT, see -IVE)]

pŏs'itiv|ism(-z-),n. Philosophical system

of Auguste Comte, recognizing only positive facts & observable phenomena; religious system founded on this. So ~IST n., ~IS'TIC a. [f. F *positivisme* (as prec., see -ISM)]

pŏs'ĭtrŏn (-z-), n. A positive electron. [POSI(TIVE ELEC)TRON]

posŏl'ogў, n. Study of the quantities in which drugs should be administered; (Bentham's word for) mathematics. Hence **pŏsolŏ'gICAL** a. [f. F *posologie* f. Gk *posos* how great, see -LOGY]

pŏss'ĕ, n. Body (*of* constables); strong force or company; ~ *cōmĭtāt'us*, body of men above age of 15 in a county, whom sheriff may summon to repress riot etc.; IN⁵ ~. [L, = to be able, (med. L) power]

possĕss' (-z-), v.t. Hold as property, own; have (faculty, quality, etc.), as *they ~ a special value for us*; maintain (oneself, one's mind, soul, *in* patience etc.); (of demon or spirit) occupy, dominate, (person etc.), as *~ed by a devil, you are surely ~ed*, (fig.) *he is ~ed by or with this idea, what~es you to think of such a thing?*; *like all ~ed*, with the utmost vehemence or energy; ~ *oneself of*, take, get for one's own; *be ~ed of*, own, have. So ~OR n., ~ORY a., (-zĕs-). [f. OF *possess(i)er* f. L *possidēre -sess-*]

possĕss'ion (-zĕshn), n. Possessing; actual holding or occupancy; (law) visible power of exercising such control as attaches to (but may exist apart from) lawful ownership; *in ~*, (of thing) possessed, (of person) possessing; ~ *is nine* POINTS *of the law*; *in ~ of*, having in one's ~ (*am in ~ of a fine specimen*); *in the ~ of*, held by (*the specimen is in the ~ of the present writer*); *rejoice in the ~ of*, be so fortunate as to possess; thing possessed; (pl.) property, wealth; subject territory, esp. foreign dominions; DEMONIAC ~; SELF-~. [ME, f. OF f. L *possessionem* (as prec., see -ION)]

possĕss'ive (poz-), a. & n. 1. Of possession; showing a desire to possess; (gram.) indicating possession, as ~ *pronoun* (e.g. *my, mine, his, ours*), ~ *case* (e.g. *John's, the baker's*). 2. n. ~ case or word. Hence ~LY² adv., ~NESS n. [f. L *possessivus* (as POSSESS, see -IVE)]

pŏss'ĕt, n. Drink made of hot milk curdled with ale, wine, etc., often flavoured with spices etc., formerly much used as remedy for colds etc. [ME *poshote*, orig. unkn.]

pŏssib'ilist, n. Member of (esp. Spanish republican or French socialist) political party aiming at those reforms only that are immediately practicable. [f. F *possibiliste* or Sp.-*ista* (as POSSIBLE, see -IST)]

pŏssibil'itў, n. State, fact, of being possible, as *the ~y of miracles, cannot by any ~y be in time, there is no ~y of his coming, it is within the range of ~y*; capability of being used, improved, etc.; thing that may exist or happen, as *what are the ~ies?, there are three ~ies.* [ME, f. OF

possibilite f. L *possibilitatem* (POSSIBLE, -TY)]

pŏss'ible, a. & n. 1. That can exist, be done, or happen, as *that is quite ~, it is scarcely ~ to say, it is ~ (that) he knows* or *may know, there are three ~ excuses* (that may be made), *provide against a ~ loss of* men (that may occur), *get all the assistance ~; come if (it is) ~, come as early as ~* (as you can); tolerable to deal with, reasonable, intelligible, etc., as *only one ~ man among them*, cf. IMPOSSIBLE. 2. n. Highest ~ score esp. in rifle practice, as *scored a ~ at 800 yds*; ~ candidate, member of team, etc. (as in *P~s v. Probables*, teams for football etc. trial match); *do one's ~, do all one can* (imit. of F *faire son ~*). [ME, f. OF, or f. LL *possibilis* (*posse* be able, -BLE)]

pŏss'iblў, adv. In accordance with possibility, as *cannot ~ do it, how can I ~?*; perhaps, maybe, for all one knows to the contrary. [f. prec. + -LY²]

pŏss'um, n. (colloq.). = OPOSSUM; *play ~*, pretend to be unconscious (from ~'s habit of feigning death when attacked). [abbr.]

pōst¹, n., & v.t. 1. Stout piece of timber usu. cylindrical or square & of considerable length placed vertically as support in building; stake, stout pole, for various purposes; BED¹, DOOR, GOAL, KING¹, LAMP, SIGN¹, ~; *starting, winning, ~, ~ that* marks starting, finishing, point in race. 2. Thick compact stratum of sandstone etc.; vertical mass of coal left as support in mine. 3. v.t. Stick (paper etc., usu. *up*) to ~ or in prominent place, advertise (fact, thing, person) by placard; || (in colleges) place in list that is ~ed up the names of (unsuccessful students); publish name of (ship) as overdue or missing; placard (wall etc.) with bills. [OE *post* f. L *postis*; in ME reinforced by OF *post*]

pōst², n. & adv. 1. (hist.). One of a series of men stationed with horses along roads at intervals, the duty of each being to ride forward with letters to next stage; courier, letter-carrier, mail-cart. 2. || A single dispatch of letters, letters so dispatched; letters taken from ~-office or pillar-box on one occasion, as *I missed the morning ~*; || letters delivered at one house on one occasion, as *the ~ has come, had a heavy ~ today*; || official conveyance of letters, parcels, etc., as *send it by ~*; GENERAL, PARCEL, PENNY, ~; ~-office or postal letter-box, as *take it to the ~*; *by return of ~*, (orig.) by same courier who brought the dispatch, (now) by next mail in opposite direction. 3. (As title of newspaper) *Evening P~* etc. 4. Sizes (about 20×16 in.) & kinds of writing-paper. 5. adv. With ~-horses, express, with haste, as *ride ~*. 6. ||~-*bag*, mail-bag; ||~-*boat*, mail-boat, (also) boat conveying travellers between certain points; ||~-*boy*, letter-carrier, (also) postilion; ||~*card*, card for conveyance by ~ at

lower rate than closed letter; ~-*chaise*
(-sh-), (hist.) travelling carriage hired
from stage to stage or drawn by horses so
hired; || ~-*free*, carried free of charge by
~, or with postage prepaid; ~-*haste'*, n.
(arch.) & adv., (with) great expedition;
~-*horse* (kept at inns etc. for use of ~ or
travellers; ~'*man*, one who delivers or
collects letters etc.; ~'*mark*, (n.) official
mark stamped on letter, esp. one giving
place, date, & hour, of dispatch or arrival,
& serving to cancel stamp, (v.t.) mark
(envelope etc.) with this; ~'*master*[1],
official in charge of a ~-office, P~*master
General*, minister at head of the postal
service; ~'*mastership*, office of ~master;
~'*mistress*, woman in charge of ~-office;
~-*office*, public department responsible
for postal & telecommunication services,
house or shop where postal business is
carried on (GENERAL *P*~-*Office*; ~-*office*
ORDER, *savings-bank*, see SAVE[1]); ~-*paid*,
on which postage has been paid; ~-*town*
(with ~-office, esp. one that is not sub-
-office of another). [c. 1500, f. F *poste*
fem. f. It. f. Rom. (= med. L) *posta* =
posita fem. p.p. of *ponere posit-* place]

pŏst[3], v.i. & t. || Travel with relays of
horses; travel with haste, hurry; || put
(letter etc.) into post-office or letter-box
for transmission; *~ (stick) no bills*;
(book-keep.) carry (entry) from auxiliary
book to more formal one, esp. from day-
-book or journal to ledger, (also ~ *up*)
complete (ledger etc.) thus, (fig., esp. in
p.p., also ~ *up*) supply (person) with full
information. [f. prec.]

pŏst[4], n., & v.t. 1. Place where soldier is
stationed, (fig.) place of duty; position
taken by body of soldiers, force occupying this; fort. 2. (Also *trading-*~) place
occupied for purposes of trade esp. in uncivilized country. 3. Situation, employment. 4. (Naval, hist.) commission as
officer in command of vessel of 20 guns or
more; || ~ *captain*, holder of such com-
mission (not of courtesy title or inferior
command). 5. (mil.) *First, last*, ~, bugle-
-call giving notice of hour of retiring for
night (*last* ~ also blown at mil. funerals).
6. v.t. Place, station, (soldiers etc.);
|| (mil., nav.) appoint to a ~ or command.
[f. F *poste* masc. f. It. *posto* f. L neut.
p.p. as POST[2]]

pŏst-, comb. form of L *post* after, behind,
in wds f. L; & as living E prefix, as:
~-*class'ical*, occurring later than the
classical period of (esp. Greek & Roman)
language, literature, or art; ~-*com-
mun'ion*, part of eucharistic office following act of communion; ~-*cŏs'tal*, behind
a rib; ~-*date'*, (v.t.) affix, assign, a later
than the actual date to (document, event,
etc.), (n., ~-*date*) such date; ~-*diluv'ian*,
a. & n., (person) existing, occurring, after
the Flood; ~-*en'try*, late or subsequent
entry (for race, in book-keeping, etc.);
~-*exil'ian*, ~-*exil'ic*, subsequent to the

Babylonian exile; ~-*fix*, (v.t.) append
(letters) at end of word, (n., ~-*fix*) suffix;
~-*glā'cial*, subsequent to the glacial
period; ~-*grăd'uate*, (of course of study)
carried on after taking first degree;
~-*impre'ssionism*, artistic aims & methods
(so named as a reaction from IMPRESSION-
ISM) directed to expressing rather the
individual artist's than the ordinary
observer's presumable conception of the
objects represented; ~-*lūde*, concluding
voluntary [after PRELUDE]; ~-*millenn'ial*,
of the period following the millennium;
~-*millenn'ialism*, doctrine that second
Advent will follow the millennium, so
~-*millenn'ialist* n.; ~-*năt'al*, occurring
after birth; ~-*nup'tial*, subsequent to
marriage; ~-*or'al*, situated behind the
mouth; ~-*Plī'ocene*, of the formation
immediately overlying the Pliocene; ~-
-*post'script* (abbr. P.P.S.), a second POST-
SCRIPT; ~-*Ter'tiary*, of the formations
subsequent to the Tertiary.

pŏs'tăge, n. Amount charged for carriage
of letter etc. by post, now usu. prepaid
by ~ *stamp*, adhesive label to be affixed,
or stamp embossed or impressed on
envelope etc., having specified value.
[-AGE]

pŏs'tal, a. & n. Of the POST[2]; ~ ORDER[1](3);
~ *union*, union of governments of various
countries for regulation of international
postage; *(n., also ~ card)*, postcard with
printed stamp sold by the post-office.
[F (*poste* POST[2], see -AL)]

pŏsteen', n. Afghan sheepskin greatcoat.
[Pers. *postīn*]

pŏs'ter, n. (Also *bill-*~) one who posts
bills; placard displayed in public place;
(rugby football) attempt at goal that
passes straight over a post. [POST[1], -ER[1]]

pŏste rĕstante' ('-tah-, & see Ap.), n.
Department in post-office in which letters
are kept till applied for. [F, = letter(s)
remaining (i.e., at the post-office)]

pŏstēr'ior, a. & n. 1. Later, coming after
in series, order, or time, so ~ITY (-ŏ'r-) I ;
hinder, whence ~LY[2] adv., as viewed from
behind. 2. n. (in sing., or arch. in pl.).
The buttocks. [L, compar. of *posterus*
(*post* after)]

pŏstĕ'ritÿ, n. The descendants of any
person; all succeeding generations, as
deserves the gratitude of ~. [ME, f. OF
posterite f. L *posteritatem* (as prec., see
-TY)]

pŏs'tern, n. (arch.). Back door; side way
or entrance; (attrib.) ~ *door, gate*. [ME,
f. OF *posterne, -rle*, f. LL *posterula* dim. f.
posterus coming after (*post*)]

pŏst hŏc ĕrg'ō prŏp'ter hŏc, L phr.
(after this, therefore on account of this)
ridiculing the tendency to confuse sequence with consequence.

pŏst'humous (-tū-), a. (Of child) born
after death of its father; (of book etc.)
published after author's death; occurring
after death. Hence ~LY[1] adv. [f. L

postumus last (*post* after), in LL *posth-* by assoc. w. *humus* ground, +-ous]

pŏstiche' (-ēsh), n. & a. **1.** Something added after the completion of a work (esp. a superfluous or unsuitable addition to sculpture or architectural work); (shop) coil of false hair, false front. **2.** adj. Counterfeit, artificial. [F, = false f. It. *posticcio*]

pŏstic'ous, a. (bot.). Posterior, hinder. [f. L *posticus* (*post* behind) +-ous]

pŏs'til, n. (hist.). Marginal note, comment, esp. on text of Scripture; commentary. [ME, f. OF *postille* f. med. L *postilla* of unkn. orig.]

postil'ion, -llion, (-lyon), n. One who rides the near horse of the leaders, or near horse when one pair only is used & there is no driver on box. [f. F *postillon* f. It. *postiglione* (*posta* POST[2])]

pŏstlim'iny, n. (Rom. law) right of banished person or captive to resume civic privileges on return; (internat. law) restoration to their former state of persons & things taken in war, when they come again into the power of the nation they belonged to. [f. L POST(*liminium* f. *limen -minis* threshold)]

pŏst'master[1] (-mah-), n. See POST[2].

‖ **pŏst'master[2]** (-mah-), n. Scholar of Merton College, Oxford. Hence ~SHIP n.

pŏst merīd'iem, adv. (usu. abbr. *p.m.,* pr. pē ĕm). After midday, as *3.30 p.m.* [L]

pŏst mōrt'ĕm, adv., **pŏst-mōrt'ĕm,** a. & n. After death; (examination) made after death; (colloq.) subsequent discussion of (esp. card) game. [L]

pŏst-ŏb'it, a. & n. **1.** Taking effect after death. **2.** n. Bond securing to lender a sum to be paid on death of specified person from whom borrower has expectations. [f. L *post* after+*obitus -ūs* decease f. OB(*ire* go) die]

pŏstpōne' (*or* po-), v.t. & i. Put off, defer; treat (thing) as inferior in importance (*to* another); (intr., path., of ague etc.) be later in coming on. Hence ~MENT (-nm-) n. [f. L POST (*ponere posit-*place)]

pŏstposi'tion (-z-), n. Particle, word, placed after another, usu. as enclitic, (e.g. *-wards*). Hence ~AL, **pŏstpŏs'itIVE,** aa., (-z-). [as prec., see -ION]

pŏstpran'dial, a. (usu. joc.). After-lunch or -dinner, as~ *nap, oratory, eloquence.* [f. POST- +L *prandium* lunch +-AL]

pŏst'script (*or* pōsk-), n. (abbr. P.S.). Additional paragraph esp. at end of letter after signature; ‖ talk at the end of some B.B.C. news bulletins. [f. L *postscriptum* neut. p.p. of POST(*scribere* write)]

pŏs'tŭlant, n. Candidate esp. for admission into religious order. [F (as foll., see -ANT)]

pŏs'tŭlate[1], n. Thing claimed or assumed as basis of reasoning, fundamental condition; prerequisite; (geom.) claim to take for granted the possibility of simple operation, e.g. of drawing straight line between any two points. [as foll. see -ATE[2]]

pŏs'tŭl|āte[2], v.t. & i. Demand, require as a necessary condition, claim, take for granted (thing, *that, to* do); stipulate *for*; (eccl. law) nominate or elect subject to superior sanction. So ~A'TION, ~ātor, nn. [f. L *postulare* demand, -ATE[3]]

pŏs'tŭr|e, n., & v.t. & i. **1.** Carriage, attitude of body or mind; condition, state, (*of* affairs etc.); ~*e-maker,* acrobat, contortionist; ~*e-master,* teacher of callisthenics. **2.** vb. Dispose the limbs of (person) in particular way; assume ~e (lit. & fig.). Hence ~AL a., ~ER[1] n. [F, f. It. -*ura* f. L *positura* (*ponere posit-* place, see -URE)]

pŏs'y̆ (-z-), n. (arch.). Short motto, line of verse etc., inscribed within ring (~-*ring*) etc.; nosegay. [= POESY]

pŏt[1], n. **1.** Rounded vessel of earthenware, metal, or glass, for holding liquids or solids, as *flower,* GLUE, *ink, jam,* WATER[2]*ing,* ~~; such vessel for cooking; drinking--vessel of pewter etc.; contents of ~, as a ~ *of porter, honey*; COFFEE-~~; TEA-~; (also, childish, *pō*) = CHAMBER-~; = FLOWER-~; vessel, usu. of silver, as prize in athletic sports, (sl.) any prize in these. **2.** ~ *paper* or ~ (also *pott*), writing or printing paper 15½ in. ×12½, named from the orig. watermark of a ~. **3.** LOBSTER-~~; CHIMNEY-~~. **4.** Large sum, as *made a*~ *or* ~*s of money*; (racing sl.) large sum staked or betted, as *put the* ~ *on,* ‖ (also) favourite. **5.** *Big* ~, important person; *the* ~ *calls the kettle black,* person blames another for fault he too has; *go to* ~ (vulg.), be ruined or destroyed; *make the* ~ *boil,* make a living; *keep the* ~ *boiling,* make a living, keep anything going briskly; *watched* ~ *never boils* (proverb against worrying). **6.**~-*ale,* completely fermented wash in distillation; ~-*belly,* (person with) protuberant belly; ~-*boiler,* work of literature or art done merely to make a living, writer or artist who does this; ~-*bound,* (of plant) whose roots fill flower-~ & want room to expand (also fig.); ~-*boy,* ~'*man,* publican's assistant; ~ *hat,* bowler; ~-*herb,* any of those grown in kitchen-garden; ~-*hole,* (geol.) deep cylindrical hole worn in rock, depression in road surface caused by traffic etc.; ~-*hook,* over fireplace for hanging~ etc. on or for lifting hot ~, curved stroke in handwriting esp. as made in learning to write (cf. HANGER[2]); ~-*house,* (derog.) public house; ~-*hunter,* sportsman who shoots anything he comes across, ‖ person who takes part in contest merely for sake of prize, so ~-*hunting* n. & a.; ~ *lead,* black-lead esp. as used for hull of racing-yacht; ~ *luck,* whatever is to be had for a meal, as *come & take*~ *luck with us*; ~-*metal,* stained glass coloured in melting-~ so that the colour pervades the whole; ~-*roast,* (n.) piece of meat cooked by braising, (v.t.) braise; ~-*shot,*

shot taken at game merely to provide a meal, shot aimed at animal etc. within easy reach, random shot; ~-*still*, kind of STILL[2] (opp. *patent still*) in which heat is applied directly & not by steam-jacket; ~'*stone*, granular variety of soapstone; ~-*valiant*, valiant because drunk, so ~ *valour*; ~'*wall(op)er*, householder voter (before 1832), (naut., ~-*walloper*) cook's assistant [f. *wall(op)* boil]. Hence ~'FUL n. [late OE *pott*, corresp. to OFris., MDu., MLG *pot*, Icel. *pottr*; in ME reinforced by OF *pot* f. Rom. **pottus*]

pŏt[2], v.t. & i. (-tt-). Place (butter, fish, minced meat, etc., usu. salted or seasoned) in pot or other vessel to preserve it (esp. in p.p., as ~*ted ham*); plant (plant) in pot; (billiards) pocket; abridge, epitomize; bag (game), kill (animal) by pot-shot; (intr.) shoot (*at*, or abs.); seize, secure. [f. prec.]

pŏt'able, a. & n. (usu. joc.). Drinkable; (n. pl.) drinkables. [F, f. LL *potabilis* (*potare* drink, see -BLE)]

potăm'ic, a. Of rivers. So pŏtamŏL'OGY n. [f. Gk *potamos* river + -IC]

pŏt'ăsh, (arch.) potăss' (*or* pŏt'-), n. An alkaline substance, crude form of potassium carbonate, orig. got by lixiviating vegetable ashes & evaporating the solution in iron pots; *caustic* ~, hydroxide or hydrate of potassium; PERMANGANATE *of* ~; ~-*water*, an aerated drink. [17th c. *pot-ashes*, f. Du. *pot-asschen*]

potăss'ium, n. Soft white metallic element, one of the alkali metals, used mainly in compounds; ~ *cyanide*, white soluble crystalline salt, extremely poisonous; ~ PERMANGANATE. Hence potăss'IC a. [-IUM]

potā'tion, n. Drinking; (usu. pl.) tippling; draught. So pŏt'atORY a. [ME, f. OF, f. L *potationem* (*potare* drink, see -ATION)]

potāt'ō, n. (pl. ~*es*). Plant with farinaceous tubers used for food; its tuber; *sweet, Spanish*, ~, tropical plant with tuberous roots used for food; ~*es & POINT*[1]; ~-*ring*, Irish (usu. silver) ring used as stand for bowl etc. [f. Sp. *patata* var. of native Amer. BATATA]

poteen', -theen', n. Irish whiskey from illicit still. [f. Ir. *poitín* dim. of *pota* pot]

pŏt'|ent, a. (Chiefly poet. or rhet.) powerful, mighty; (of reasons etc.) cogent; (of drugs etc.) strong. Hence or cogn. ~ENCE, ~ENCY, nn., ~entLY[2] adv. [f. L *potens* part. of *posse* be able]

pŏt'entāte, n. Monarch, ruler. [ME, f. L *potentatus* -*ūs* (as prec., see -ATE[1])]

potĕn'tial (-shl), a. & n. 1. Capable of coming into being or action, latent; (med.) ~ *cautery, corrosive* (agent producing same effect on skin as an actual one); (gram.) ~ *mood*, subjunctive expressing possibility; (electr.) ~ *difference*, difference in electric ~, usu. expressed in volts, between two separate bodies or points on a conductor, being properly the work done when a unit charge is moved from one to the other; ~ *energy* (existing in ~ form, not as motion); (rare) powerful. 2. n. ~ mood; (electr.) degree of electrification, electrical pressure; possibility, as *reached its highest* ~; possible resources. Hence or cogn. ~ITY (-shĭăl[1]) n., ~LY[2] (-sha-) adv. [f. LL *potentialis* (*potentia*, as POTENT, see -AL)]

potĕn'tialize (-sha-), -ise (-īz), v.t. Make potential; convert (energy) into potential condition. [-IZE]

potĕn'tiāte (-shǐ-), v.t. Endow with power; make possible. [f. L as foll. + -ATE[3]]

potĕntiŏm'eter (-shǐ-), n. Instrument for measuring or adjusting electrical potential. [f. L *potentia* power (POTENT) + -O- + -METER]

potheen. See POTEEN.

poth'er (pŏdh-, pŭdh-), n., & v.t. & i. Choking smoke or cloud of dust; noise, din; verbal commotion, as *made a* ~ *about it*; display of sorrow; (v.t.) fluster, worry; (v.i.) make a fuss. [orig. obsc.; 17th c. also *pudder*; alleged identity w. POWDER is phonetically untenable]

pō'tion, n. Dose, draught, of liquid medicine or of poison. [ME, f. OF, f. L *potionem* (*potare* drink, see -ION)]

pŏt'lătch, -*lach(e)*, n. Tribal feast of N.-Amer. Indians given by aspirant to chiefship. [native]

pot-pourri (pōpŏŏrē'), n. Mixture of dried petals & spices kept in jar for its perfume; musical or literary medley. [F, lit. rotten pot]

‖ pŏt'shĕrd, n. Broken piece of earthenware. [POT[1] + SHERD]

pŏtt, n. Var. of POT[1] as applied to paper.

‖ pŏtt'age, n. (arch.). Soup, stew; (fig.) MESS[1] *of* ~. [ME, f. OF *potage* (POT[1] + -AGE)]

pŏtt'er[1], n. Maker of earthenware vessels; ~'s *wheel*, horizontal revolving disc in ~'s *lathe* (machine for moulding clay); ~'s *asthma, bronchitis*, etc. (caused by dust in the pottery industry). [late OE *pottere* (POT[1] + -ER[1])]

pŏtt'er[2], v.i. & t. Work in feeble or desultory manner (*at, in*, subject or occupation); dawdle, loiter, (*about* etc.); trifle *away* (one's time etc.). Hence ~ER[1] n. [f. dial. *pote* push, OE *potian*, + -ER[5]]

pŏtt'er|y, n. Earthenware; potter's work or workshop; ‖ *the P~ies*, district in N. Staffordshire, seat of ~y industry. [15th c., f. OF *poterie* (POT[1], -ERY)]

pŏt'tle, n. ‖ (Arch.) measure for liquids, half gallon, pot etc. containing this; small wicker or chip basket for strawberries etc. [ME & OF *potel* (POT[1], see -LE)]

pŏtt'ō, n. (pl. ~*s*). W.-Afr. lemur; kinkajou. [native]

pŏtt'y, a. (sl.). Insignificant, trivial, (often ~ *little*; ~ *little State, details*; ~ *questions* in examination paper, easy to answer); foolish, crazy, mad *about* (someone or something). [orig. unkn.]

pouch[1], n. Small bag or detachable outside pocket; (arch.) purse; soldier's leathern ammunition bag; bag-like receptacle of marsupials etc.; bag-like cavity, esp. seed-vessel, in plant. Hence ~ED[2] (-cht), ~′Y[2], aa. [ME, f. ONF *pouche* = OF *poche* POKE[1]]

pouch[2], v.t. & i. Put into pouch; take possession of, pocket; ∥ (sl.) give money to, tip; make (part of dress) hang like pouch, (intr., of such part) hang thus. [f. prec.]

poudrette′ (pōō-), n. Manure of night-soil mixed with charcoal etc. [F, dim. of *poudre* POWDER]

pouf(fe) (pōōf), n. Woman's high roll or pad of hair; large cushion used as low seat; soft stuffed couch. [F]

poulp(e) (pōō-), n. Octopus or other cephalopod. [F (-*pe*), as POLYPUS]

poult (pōlt), n. Young of domestic fowl, turkey, pheasant, etc. [ME, contr. f. PULLET]

poult-de-soie (pōōdeswah′), n. Fine corded (now usu. coloured) silk. [F]

poul′terer (pōl-), n. Dealer in poultry. [f. ME *poulter* (still in City Company's name) f. OF *pouletier* (as PULLET, see -ER[2]) +-ER[1]]

poul′tice (pōl-), n., & v.t. **1.** Soft mass of bread, linseed, etc., usu. made with boiling water & spread on muslin etc. & applied to sore or inflamed part. **2.** v.t. Apply ~ to. [ult. f. L *puls -ltis* thick pap etc.]

poul′try (pōl-), n. Domestic fowls, e.g. barn-door fowls, ducks, geese, turkeys. [ME, f. OF *pouletrie* (as PULLET, see -ERY)]

pounce[1], n., & v.t. & i. **1.** Claw, talon, of bird of prey; pouncing, sudden swoop, esp. *make a ~*. **2.** v.t. Swoop down upon & seize; (v.i.) make sudden attack *upon*, (fig.) seize eagerly *upon* (blunder etc.). [*pounce & punch* app. shortened f. *ponson, ponchon*; see PUNCH[1], PUNCHEON[1]]

pounce[2], n., & v.t. **1.** Fine powder used to prevent ink from spreading on unsized paper etc.; powdered charcoal etc. dusted over perforated pattern to transfer design to object beneath. **2.** v.t. Smooth (paper, surface of hat, etc.) with pumice or ~, transfer (design) by use of ~, dust (pattern) with ~. [(vb f. F *poncer*) f. F *ponce* PUMICE]

poun′cet-box, n. (arch.). Small box with perforated lid for perfumes. [in Shakespeare; f. prec., hist. unexpl.]

pound[1], n., & v.i. **1.** (Abbr. *lb.* = L *libra*) measure of weight, 16 oz avoirdupois, 12 oz Troy; ~ *of flesh* (see Shak. *Merchant of Venice*, IV. i), (fig.) any legal but unconscionable demand; (also ~*sterling*) a money of account, 20 shillings, formerly represented by gold sovereign, as *five ~s* (written £5 or 5*l.*), *five ~ ten* (*shillings*); (hist.) ~ *Scots*, 1s. 8*d.*; *pay 5s. in the ~* (for each ~ owing); PENNY *wise & ~ foolish*; ~, *five-~*, *note*, bank-note for one ~, *five ~s*; ~*-cake*, rich cake containing

a ~ (or equal weight) of each of chief ingredients; ~-*day* (on which a charity etc. receives contributions from all comers of a ~ of anything, e.g. £1, 1lb. of tea, etc.). **2.** v.i. ∥ Test the weight of coins by weighing the number that ought to weigh a ~. [OE *pund*, = OS, ON, Goth. *pund*, OHG *pfunt* f. WG f. L *pondo*, orig. instr. abl. of L *pondus -eris* weight]

pound[2], n., & v.t. **1.** Enclosure for detention of stray cattle or of distrained cattle or goods till redeemed; enclosure for animals; (fig.) place of confinement, (hunt.) difficult position; ~-*lock* (with two gates, opp. *flash-lock* with one). **2.** v.t. Shut (cattle etc., often *up*) in ~; (hunt.) ~ *the field*, (of barrier) be impassable, (of rider) clear fence that others cannot. [ME, f. OE *pund (in *pundfald*, cf. PINFOLD); cf. POND]

pound[3], v.t. & i. Crush, bruise, as with pestle; thump, pummel, with fists etc.; knock, beat, (thing *to pieces, into a jelly*, etc.); deliver heavy blows, fire heavy shot, (*at, on, away at*); walk, run, ride, make one's way, heavily (*along* etc.). [OE *pūnian* f. WG **pūn-* whence Du. *puin* rubbish, LG *pūn* chips of stone]

poun′dage, n. Commission, fee, of so much per pound sterling; percentage of total earnings of a business, paid as wages; payment of so much per pound weight; charge on postal order etc.; TONNAGE & ~. [-AGE]

poun′der[1], n. In vbl senses, esp. instrument for pounding with or in, pestle, mortar. [POUND[3]+-ER[1]]

poun′der[2], n. Thing that, gun carrying shell that, weighs a pound or (-~) so many pounds, as *a three-~*; (-~) thing worth, person possessing, so many pounds sterling. [POUND[1], -ER[1]]

pour (pōr), v.t. & i., & n. **1.** Cause (liquid, granular substance, light, etc.) to flow, discharge copiously, as ~ *hot water over it*, ~ *out the tea, river ~s itself into the sea*; ~ *oil upon troubled waters*, (fig.) calm disturbance with soothing words etc.; ~ *cold water on*, (fig.) discourage (person, zeal, plan); discharge (missiles, crowd from building, etc., often *forth, out*) copiously or in rapid succession; send *forth* or *out* (words, music, etc.); (intr., of liquids etc.) flow (usu. *forth, out, down*) in stream, (of rain) descend heavily, whence ~′ING[2] (pōr-) a.; *it never rains but it ~s*, (fig.) events esp. misfortunes always come together; (fig.) come *in, out*, etc., abundantly, as *letters ~ in from all quarters*. **2.** n. Heavy fall of rain, downpour; (found.) amount of molten metal etc. ~ed at a time. [ME *poure*, orig. unexpl.]

pourboire (poorbwahr′), n. Gratuity, tip. [F,=*pour boire* (money) for drinking]

pourparler (poor′pärlā′), n. (usu. in pl.). Informal discussion preliminary to negotiation. [F]

pour′point (poor-), **pūr-**, n. (hist.).

Stuffed & quilted doublet. [ME, f. OF
p.p. of *pourpoindre* perforate (*pour* PRO-
for *par* PER-+*poindre* prick f. L *pungere*)]
poussëtte' (pōō-), v.i., & n. Dance round
one another with hands joined, as two
couples in country dance; (n.) this action.
[F, dim. of *pousse* PUSH]
pou stō (pōō), n. Standing-place, basis of
operation, FULCRUM. [Gk *pou stō* where
I may stand]
pout¹, n. Kinds of fish, as *whiting, eel,
horn-, ~*. [OE **pūta* in *ælepūta*, = MDu.
puyt(e), Du. *puitaal*, G *aalputte*, app. f.
WG **pūt-* inflate]
pout², v.t. & i., & n. 1. Protrude (lips),
protrude lips, (of lips) protrude, esp. as
sign of (mock) displeasure, whence
*~'*ingLY² adv. 2. n. Such protrusion; *in
the ~s*, sulky. [ME, of obsc. hist.; perh.
cogn. w. WG **pūt-* (prec.)]
pout'er, n. In vbl senses, esp.: kind of
pigeon with great power of inflating crop;
(also *whiting-pout*) kind of fish. [-ER¹]
pŏv'ertў, n. Indigence, want; scarcity,
deficiency, (*of*); deficiency *in* (a property);
inferiority, poorness, meanness; *~-
stricken*, poor, esp. fig., as a *~-stricken
language*. [ME, f. OF *poverte* f. L *pauper-
talem* (as PAUPER, see -TY)]
powd'er, n., & v.t. 1. Mass of dry particles
or granules, dust; medicine in the form
of *~*; cosmetic *~* applied to face, skin, or
hair; = GUN*~*, as *smell of ~*, experience
of fighting, FOOD *for ~*; *not worth ~ and
shot*, not worth shooting, or fighting or
striving for. 2. v.t. Sprinkle *~* upon,
cover (*with~* etc.); apply *~* to (nose, hair,
or abs. in same sense); decorate (surface) with spots or small figures; (esp. in
p.p.) reduce to *~ (~ed sugar*). 3. *~ blue,
~*ed small esp. for use in laundry, deep
blue colour of this (also attrib.); *~-down,*
down-feathers found in definite patches
on some birds; *~-flask* (hist.), case for
carrying gun*~*; *~-horn* (hist.), *~-flask*
orig. & esp. of horn; *~-magazine*, place
where gun*~* is stored; *~-monkey* (hist.),
boy employed on board ship to carry *~*
to guns; *~-puff*, soft pad usn. of down for
applying *~* to skin; *~(ing)-room*, ladies'
cloakroom. Hence *~*ĩNESS n., *~*Y³ a.
[ME & OF *poudre*, ult. f. L *pulvis -eris*]
pow'er, n., & v.t. 1. Ability to do or act,
as *will do all in my ~, has the ~ of changing
its colour*; particular faculty of body or
mind, as *taxes his ~s to the utmost, man of
varied ~s*. 2. Vigour, energy, as *more ~ to
your elbow!* (formula of encouragement or
approval). 3. Active property, as *has a
high heating ~*. 4. Government, influence,
authority, (*over*); *in* one's *~*, under one's
control; personal ascendancy (*over*);
political ascendancy, as *the party now in
~*. 5. Authorization, delegated authority, as *a bill to extend & define their ~s;
~ of* ATTORNEY². 6. Influential person,
body, or thing, as *the press had not become
a ~ in the State; the ~s that be*, constituted

authorities; State having international
influence. 7. Deity, as *merciful ~s!*; sixth
ORDER¹ of angels. 8. (vulg.). Large number or amount, as *saw a ~ of people, did a
~ of work*. 9. (math.). Third, tenth, etc., *~*
of a number, product obtained by multiplying the number into itself three, ten,
etc., times, as *the third ~ of 2 is 8*. 10. Instrument for applying energy to mechanical purposes, esp. *the* MECHANICAL *~s*, the
simple MACHINES. 11. Mechanical energy
as opp. to hand-labour, esp. attrib., as
~-lathe, -loom, -mill; ~-station (in which
electric *~* is generated for distribution).
12. Capacity for exerting mechanical
force,' esp. HORSE¹*-~*, whence (-)*~*ED³
(-erd) a. 13. Magnifying capacity of lens.
14. *~-dive* n. & v.i., (of aircraft) dive
without shutting off engine(s); *~ politics*,
diplomacy backed by (the threat of) force.
15. v.t. Supply (vehicle, vessel, etc.) with
~ (esp. of engine). [ME & AF *poër* (vb
inf. as n.) f. Rom. **potere* = L *posse* be
able (*potis*)]
pow'erful, a. Having great (physical or
other) power or influence as *~ grasp,
horse, mind, ally, book, speech, odour*.
Hence *~*LY² adv. [ME; -FUL]
pow'erlĕss, a. Without power; wholly
unable (*to* help etc.). Hence *~*LY² adv.,
*~*NESS n. [-LESS]
pow'wow, pawaw', n., **powwow'**, v.i.
& t. 1. N.-Amer.-Indian medicine-man or
sorcerer; magic ceremonial, conference,
of N.-Amer. Indians; **political or other
meeting; ‖ (sl.) conference of officers
during army manœuvres etc. 2. v.i. Practise medicine or sorcery, hold a *~*, **confer,
discuss, (*about* etc.); (v.t.) doctor, treat
with magic. [f. native *powwaw, powah*]
pŏx, n. Syphilis (colloq.); CHICKEN*~*;
COWPOX; SMALL*-~*. [alt. sp. of POCKS]
pozz(u)olana (pŏtsolah'na, -tswo-), n.
Volcanic ash found near Pozzuoli, much
used for hydraulic cement. [It.]
praam. See PRAM¹.
prăc'tic|able, a. That can be done, feas-
ible; (of road, passage, ford) that can be
used or traversed; (theatr., of windows
etc.) real, that can be used as such. Hence
*~*ABIL'ITY, *~*ableNESS, nn., *~*abLY³ adv.
[f. F *praticable* (*pratiquer* PRACTISE, -ABLE)]
prăc'tical, a. Of, concerned with, shown
in, practice (cf. THEORETICAL), as *~ agriculture, philosophy; ~* JOKE¹; available,
useful, in practice; engaged in practice,
practising; inclined to action rather
than speculation, as *does not appeal to ~
minds*; (derog.) .unimaginative; that is
such in effect though not nominally,
virtual, as *a ~ atheist, has ~ control*;
feasible (*~ politics*). Hence *~*ITY (-ăl-),
*~*NESS, nn. [f. arch. *practic* n. & a. f. obs.
F *practique* f. LL f. Gk *praktikos*+-AL]
prăc'tically, adv. In a practical manner;
virtually, almost, (*~ nothing*). [-LY²]
prăc'tice, n. 1. Habitual action or carrying on, as *the ~ of advertising, makes a ~ of*

saving; method of legal procedure; habit, custom, (*has been the regular* ∼). **2.** Repeated exercise in an art, handicraft, etc., as ∼ *makes perfect*; *in, out of,* ∼ (lately, not lately, practised in thing); *is good* ∼ (improves skill); spell of this (*ball, target,* ∼). **3.** Professional work, business, or connexion, of lawyer or doctor, as *has a large* ∼, *sold his* ∼. **4.** (arch.). Scheming, (usu. underhand) contrivance, artifice, (esp. in pl., & cf. SHARP[1] ∼). **5.** (arith.). Mode of finding value of given number of articles, or of quantity of commodity at given price, when quantity or price or both are in several denominations. **6.** *In* ∼, in the realm of action, as *quite useless, would never work, in* ∼; *put* (plan, method) *in(to)* ∼, carry it out. [ME, earlier *practize* app. f. PRACTISE, replacing earlier *practic* (as PRACTICAL)]

practi′cian (-shn), n. Worker, practitioner. [f. obs. F *practicien* f. med. L *practica* (as PRACTICAL, see -ICIAN)]

prăc′tis|e, v.t. & i. Perform habitually, carry out in action, 'as ∼*e the same method,* ∼*e what you preach*; exercise, pursue, (profession; ∼*ing doctor, barrister,* etc., engaged in actual practice, not retired nor merely qualified); exercise oneself in or on (art, instrument, or abs.), as ∼*e the flute, the piano, music, running*; exercise (person, oneself, in action or subject), whence ∼ED[1] (-st) a.; (arch.) scheme, contrive, as *when first we* ∼*e to deceive*; ∼*e (up)on*, impose upon, take advantage of, (person, his credulity etc.). [ME, f. OF *pra(c)tiser, -tiquer,* or med. L *pra(c)tizare* alt. f. *-care* (as PRACTICAL)]

practi′tioner (-sho-), n. Professional or practical worker, esp. in medicine; *general* ∼ (in both medicine & surgery; abbr. G.P.), opp. *consultant, specialist,* etc.). [irreg. f. PRACTICIAN + -ER[1]]

prae-, pref., the L form of PRE-, kept only in a few wds.

praecō′cial (-shal), a. (Of birds) whose young can feed themselves as soon as hatched. [as PRECOCIOUS, see -AL]

praemūnīr′e, n. (law). Writ charging sheriff to summon person accused of asserting or maintaining papal jurisdiction in England; *Statute of* ∼ (of 16th Richard II, on which the writ is based). [med. L, for L PRAE(*monēre* warn), the wds ∼ *facias* warn (so-&-so to appear) occurring in the writ]

praenōm′ĕn, n. (Rom. ant.). First or personal name (e.g. *Marcus* Tullius Cicero). [PRAE-, cf. COGNOMEN]

‖ **praepŏs′tor,** pre-, (prĭp-), n. (pub. school). = PREFECT, MONITOR. [syncop. f. *praepositor* f. L PRAE(*ponere posit-* place) set over, see -OR; irreg. altered f. L p.p. *-tus*]

praet′or, n. (Rom. hist.). (Orig.) Roman consul as leader of army; (later) annually elected magistrate performing some duties of consul. Hence **praetōr′IAL** a., ∼SHIP D. [L,.f. PRAE(*ire it-* go)]

praetōr′ian, pre-, (prĭt-), a. & n. **1.** Of a praetor; of the bodyguard of Roman general or emperor. **2.** n. Man of ∼ rank, soldier of ∼ guard. [f. L *praetorianus* (as prec., see -AN)]

prăgmăt′|ĭc(al), aa. Meddlesome; dogmatic; of pragmatism; (∼*ic*) treating facts of history with reference to their practical lessons; (∼*ic*) of the affairs of a State (∼*ic sanction,* imperial or royal ordinance issued as fundamental law, esp. that of Charles VI in 1724 settling Austrian succession). Hence ∼**ĭcăl′ITY** n., ∼**ĭcalLY**[2] adv. [f. L f. Gk *pragmatikos* (*pragma -matos* deed), -IC, -AL]

prăg′mat|ism, n. Officiousness; pedantry; matter-of-fact treatment of things; (philos.) doctrine that estimates any assertion solely by its practical bearing upon human interests. So ∼IST n., ∼**ĭs′tĭc** a. [f. Gk *pragma,* see prec. & -ISM]

prăg′matize, -ise (-īz), v.t. Represent as real; rationalize (myth). [as prec., see -IZE]

prair′ie, n. Large treeless tract of level or undulating grass-land; ∼*-chicken, -hen,* N.-Amer. kind of grouse; ∼*-dog,* N.-Amer. rodent with bark like dog's; ∼ *oyster,* raw egg swallowed whole; *∼ -schooner,* early emigrant's white-tilted wagon used in crossing the ∼s. [F, f. Rom. **prataria* (L *pratum* meadow, see -ARY[1])]

praise (-z), v.t., & n. **1.** Express warm approbation of, commend the merits of, (person, thing); glorify, extol the attributes of, (God etc.). **2.** n. Praising, commendation, as *won high* ∼, *was loud in his* ∼*s.* Hence ∼′FUL a., ∼′fulNESS n., (-zf-). [ME, f. OF *preisier* price, prize, praise, f. LL *preciare, pret-,* f. L *pretium* PRICE; see PRIZE]

praise′worth|y (prăz′wẽrdhĭ), a. Worthy of praise, commendable, (often patronizing). Hence ∼**ĭLY**[2] adv., ∼**ĭNESS** n.

Pra′krĭt (prah-), n. Any of the dialects of N. & Central India existing alongside of or growing out of Sanskrit. [f. Skr. *prakrta* unrefined]

pra′line (prah-), n. Sweet made by browning nuts in boiling sugar. [F (*Praslin,* surname)]

pram[1], *praam,* (prahm), n. Flat-bottomed boat used in Baltic etc. for shipping cargo etc.; flat-bottomed boat mounted with guns; Scandinavian ship's boat corresp. to dinghy. [f. MDu., MLG *prame,* f. Slav.]

prăm[2], n. (colloq.). ‖ Perambulator; milkman's handcart. [abbr. of PERAMBULATOR]

prancje (-ah-), v.i. & t., & n. **1.** (Of horse) rise by springing from hind legs; cause (horse) to do this; (fig.) walk, behave, in elated or arrogant manner. **2.** n. ∼*ing,* ∼*ing* movement. [ME, of obsc. orig.; cf. syn. (obs.) *prank* (c. 1500)]

prăn′dial, a. (joc.). Of dinner. [f. L *prandium* lunch, see -AL]

|| prăng, v.t. (R.A.F. sl.). Bomb (target) successfully; crash (aircraft). [imit.]

prănk[1], n. Mad frolic, practical joke; (fig., of machinery etc.) erratic action. Hence ~'FUL, ~'ISH[1], aa., ~'ishNESS n. [c. 1525; goes w. obs. *prank* vb play tricks; orig. unkn.]

prănk[2], v.t. & i. Dress, deck, (person, one*self*, thing, often *out*); adorn, spangle, (field *with* flowers etc.); (v.i.) show oneself off. [c. 1550; cogn. w. Du. *pronken* strut, parade, G *prunken*, & obs. E adj. *prank* smart, showy; cf. PRINK]

prāse (-z), n. Kind of leek-green translucent quartz. [F, f. L f. Gk *prasios* leek--green (*prason* leek); earlier also as L]

prāt|e, v.i. & t., & n. 1. Chatter; talk too much; blab; tell, say, (thing) in ~ing manner. 2. n. ~ing, idle talk. Hence ~'ER[1] n., ~'ING[2] a. [ME, f. MDu., MLG *praten*]

|| prāt'ies (-tĭz), n. (Anglo-Ir. colloq.). Potatoes. [corrupt.]

prăt'incŏle (-ngk-), n. Bird like swallow in appearance & habits, & allied to plover. [f. L *pratum* meadow + *incola* inhabitant]

prăt'ique (-ĭk, or pratĕk'), n. Licence to hold intercourse with port, granted to ship after quarantine or on showing clean bill of health. [F, = PRACTICE, intercourse]

prăt'tle, v.i. & t., & n. 1. Talk in childish or artless fashion; say (thing) thus. 2. n. Childish chatter, small talk. Hence prătt'lER[1] n., prătt'lING[2] a. [f. MLG *pratelen*; see PRATE, -LE(3)]

prăv'itў, n. (rare). Depravity; || badness, corruptness, (of food etc.). [f. L *pravitas* (*pravus* crooked, bad, see -TY)]

prawn, n., & v.i. Marine crustacean like large shrimp; (v.i.) fish for ~s, so ~'ING[1] n. [ME *pra(y)ne*, of unkn. orig.]

prăx'is, n. Accepted practice, custom; (gram.) set of examples for practice. [Gk, = doing, f. *prassō* do]

pray, v.t. & i. Make devout supplication to (God, object of worship); beseech earnestly (God, person, *for* thing, *to do*, *that*); ask earnestly for (permission etc.); engage in prayer, make entreaty, (*to* God, *to* person, *for* thing, *for* or *on behalf of* person, *to do*, *that*); ~ (I beg you to) consider etc.; *what is the use of that*, ~ (tell me)?; ~ *in aid of* (arch.; *in* adv., not prep.), summon to one's support. [ME, f. OF *preier* f. LL *precare* (L *-ri*)]

prayer[1] (prār), n. Solemn request to God or object of worship; formula used in praying, e.g. LORD'S ~; form of divine service consisting largely of ~s, as *morning* ~, *evening* ~, *family* ~s; action, practice, of praying; entreaty to a person; thing prayed for; book of ~, esp. Book of Common P~, public liturgy of Church of England; ~*-meeting*, religious meeting at which several persons offer ~; ~*-wheel*, revolving cylindrical

box inscribed with or containing ~s, used esp. by Buddhists of Tibet. Hence ~'FUL (-ărf-), ~'LESS (-ărl-), aa., ~'fuLLY[2], ~'lèssLY[2], advv., ~'fulNESS, ~'lèssNESS, nn. [ME & OF *preiere* f. med. L *precaria* fem. sing. (orig. neut. pl.) adj. as n. (as PRECARIOUS)]

pray'er[2], n. One who prays. [-ER[1]]

prē-, pref., = med. L *pre-*, L *prae-*, before (in time, place, order, degree, or importance). Occurs not only in wds of L orig., but is (freely) used as a living prefix with E wds, only the more important of which are given in their alphabetical place. In secondary wds such as those here classified, the pron. is (prē-) & the hyphen is usu. written. 1. Vbs & vbl nn. w. sense ' do, doing, thing done, beforehand', as: ~*-acquaint*'; ~*-admi'ssion*; ~*-admon'ish*, ~*-admoni'tion*; ~*-advise*'; ~*-announce*[2] (*ment*); ~*-appoint*'(ment); ~*-arrange*' (ment); || ~*-aud'ience*, right (of lawyer at Bar) to be heard before another; ~*-cal*[2] *culable*, ~*-cal'culate*, ~*-calcula'tion*; ~*-compose*'; ~*-concert*'; ~*-condemn*'; ~*-condi'tion*, prior condition, one that must be fulfilled beforehand; ~*-consid'er*, ~*-considera'tion*; ~*-contract*' v.i., ~*-con'tract* n.; ~*-decease*', (v.t.) die before (person), (n.) such death; ~*-define*'; ~*-digest*', render food easily digestible before introduction into stomach (also fig.), ~*-dige'stion*, this process; ~*-doom*' v.t., ~*-elect*', ~*-elec'tion* (see also in 2); ~*-engage*'(ment), ~*-estab'lish*; ~*-es'timate* v.t., ~*-es'timate* n.; ~*-exist*' v.i., ~*-exis'tence* n., so ~*-exis'tent* a.; ~*-in'dicate*; ~*-in'timate* v.t.; ~*-lim'it* v.t.; ~*-mo'tion*, motion given beforehand, esp. divine act as determining the will of the creature; ~*-ordain*', appoint beforehand, foreordain'; ~*-percep'tion*. 2. Adjj. & nn. w. sense ' (person etc.) existing, dating from, before the time of —', as: ~*-adăm'ic* a., ~*-ad'amite* n. & a., (one of supposed race) existing before the time of Adam; ~*-Chris'tian*, before Christ(ianity); ~*-class'ical*, before the classical age (usu. of Greek & Roman literature); ~*-con'queror*, ~*-con'quest*, before the Norman conquest; ~*-con'scious*, antecedent to consciousness; ~*-elec'tion*, (of acts, promises) done, given, before election; ~*-exil'ian*, ~*-exil'ic*, before (usu. the Babylonian) exile; ~*-glā'cial*, before the glacial period; ~*-hum'an*, existing before man existed; ~*-millenn'ial*(*ism*), (belief that Christ's Second Advent will occur) before the millennium, so ~*-millenar'ian*, ~*-millenn'ialist*; ~*-nat'al*, existing, occurring, before birth; ~*-pran'dial*, before-dinner; ~*-scientif'ic*, before the rise of modern science; ~*-war*' adj. (as ~*-war prices*) & (vulg.) adv. (as *that happened* ~*-war*), before the war. 3. Adjj., chiefly anat. & zool. w. sense 'situated in front of ',

For other words in *pre-* see PRE-.

as: ~-*cord'ial*, in front of or about the heart; ~-*cos'tal*, in front of the ribs; ~-*dors'al*, anterior to the dorsal region; ~-*frŏn'tal*, in front of frontal bone of skull, in fore part of frontal lobe of brain; ~-*maxill'ary*, in front of the upper jaw; ~-*oc'ular*, in front of the eye.

preach, v.i. & n. Deliver sermon or religious address, deliver (sermon); give moral advice in obtrusive way; proclaim, expound, (the Gospel, Christ, *that*, etc.) in public discourse; advocate, inculcate, (quality, conduct, principle, etc.) thus; ~ *up*, extol, commend; ~ *down*, disparage, put down by ~ing or speaking; (n., colloq.) ~ing, sermon, lecture. Hence or cogn. ~'ABLE a., ~'ER¹, ~'erSHIP, ~'MENT (usu. derog.), nn. [ME, f. OF *prechier* f. L PRAE(*dicare* proclaim); in eccl. L 'preach']

preach'ifȳ, v.i. Preach, moralize, hold forth, tediously. [-FY]

preach'lȳ, a. (colloq.). Fond of preaching or holding forth. Hence ~īNESS n. [-Y²]

prĕăm'ble, n., & v.i. Preliminary statement in speech or writing; introductory part of statute, deed, etc.; (v.i.) make ~. [ME, f. OF *preambule* f. med. L *preambulum* f. LL *praecambulus* going before f. LL PRAE(*ambulare* walk)]

prĕb'end, n. Part of revenue of cathedral or collegiate church granted to canon or member of chapter as stipend; portion of land or tithe from which this stipend is drawn; = foll. So ~AL a. [ME, f. OF *prebende* f. LL *praebenda* pension, neut. pl. gerund. of L *praebēre* grant]

prĕb'endarȳ, n. Holder of prebend, honorary canon; ~-*stall*, ~'s stall in cathedral. Hence ~SHIP n. [ME, f. med. L *praebendarius* (as prec., see -ARY¹)]

prĕcār'ious, a. Held during the pleasure of another, as ~ *tenure*; question-begging, taken for granted, as *a ~ assumption*; dependent on chance, uncertain, as *makes a ~ living*; perilous, as *the ~ life of a fisherman*. Hence ~LY² adv., ~NESS n. [f. L *precarius* obtained by entreaty (*prex*, *prec*- prayer, see -ARY¹) +-OUS]

prĕc'atorȳ, a. (Gram., of word or form) expressing entreaty; (in wills) ~ *words* (requesting that a thing be done), ~ *trust*, ~ words that are held to be binding. So **prĕc'ative** a. [f. LL *precatorius* (*precari* pray, see -ORY)]

prĕcau'tion, n. Prudent foresight, measure taken beforehand to ward off evil or ensure good result. Hence ~ARY¹ (-sho-) a. [f. F *précaution* f. LL *praecautionem* f. L PRAE(*cavēre caut*- beware of), see -ION]

prĕcēde', v.t. & i. (Of person or thing) go before in rank or importance, as *such duties ~ all others*, *sons of barons ~ baronets*; come before (thing etc., or abs.) in order, as *the words that ~ (this paragraph)*; walk in front of, as ~*d by our guide*; come before in time, as *in the years preceding his accession*; cause (thing) to be ~*d by*, as *must ~ this*

measure by milder ones. [f. OF *preceder* f. L PRAE(*cedere cess*- go)]

prĕ'cĕdence (or prised²), (rarely) -cȳ, nn. Priority in time or succession; superiority, higher position, as *takes ~ of* (is recognized as superior to) *all others*; right of preceding others in ceremonies & social formalities. [ME, f. PRECEDENT², see -ENCE, -ENCY]

prĕ'cĕdent¹, n. Previous case taken as example for subsequent cases or as justification, as *there is no ~ for this*, *it is without ~*, *do not take this as a ~*; (law) decision, procedure, etc., serving as rule or pattern. [ME, f. OF n., as foll.]

prĕcēd'ent² (or prĕs'ĭ-), a. (now rare). Preceding in time, order, rank, etc., as *condition* ~LY² adv. [ME, f. OF a. & n. f. L as PRECEDE, see -ENT]

prĕ'cĕdĕntĕd, a. Having, supported by, precedent. [-ED²]

prĕcĕnt', v.i. & t. Act as precentor; lead (psalm etc.) in singing. [back form. f. foll.]

prĕcĕn'tor, n. (In some Presbyterian churches etc.) one who leads singing of congregation; (in English cathedrals) member of clergy in general control of musical arrangements, in old foundations ranking next to dean and having succentor as his deputy, and in new foundations being a minor canon. Hence or cogn. ~SHIP, prĕcĕn'TRIX, nn. [f. L *praecentor* f. PRAE(*cinere cent*- = *canere* sing)]

prĕ'cĕpt, n. Command, maxim, so **prĕ-cĕp'tIVE** a.; moral instruction, as *example is better than ~*; divine command; writ, warrant; written order to arrange for & hold election; order for collection or payment of money under a rate. [ME, f. L *praeceptum* neut. p.p. of PRAE(*cipere cept*- = *capere* take) instruct]

prĕcĕp't|or, n. Teacher, instructor. Hence or cogn. prĕcĕp'tor'IAL a., ~or-SHIP, ~ress¹, nn. [f. L *praeceptor* (as prec., see -OR)]

prĕcĕp'torȳ, n. (hist.). Subordinate community of Knights Templars; estate, buildings, of this. [f. med. L *praeceptoria* fem. adj. as n. (as prec., see -ORY)]

prĕcĕ'ssion (-shn), n. (astron.). ~ *of the equinoxes*, (earlier occurrence of the equinoxes in each successive sidereal year, due to) retrograde motion of equinoctial points along ecliptic. Hence ~AL (-sho-) a. [f. LL *praecessio* (as PRECEDE, see -ION)]

prĕ'cĭnct, n. Space enclosed by walls or other boundaries of a place or building, esp. of place of worship; (pl.) *the* environs *of*; boundary; *subdivision of county or city or ward for election and police purposes. [f. med. L *praecinctum* neut. p.p. of PRAE(*cingere* gird)]

prĕ'cious (-shus), a. & adv. **1.** Of great price, costly; ~ *metals*, gold, silver, (occas.) platinum; ~ *stone*, gem; of great non-material worth, as ~ *words, privilege, knowledge, blood of Christ*; affectedly refined in language, workmanship, etc., so **prĕcĭos'ĭty** (-shĭŏs²) n.; (colloq., as intensive) *made a ~ mess of it, a ~ sight more than you think*; (ellipt.) *my ~* (dear etc.). 2. adv. (colloq.). Uncommonly, as *took ~ good care of that, ~ little of it.* Hence ~LY² adv., ~NESS n. [ME, f. OF *precios* f. L *pretiosus* (*pretium* price, see -OUS)]

prĕ'cĭpĭce, n. Vertical or steep face of rock, cliff, mountain, etc. [f. F *précipice* or L *praecipitium* falling headlong, precipice (as PRECIPITOUS)]

prĕcĭp'ĭt|āte¹, n. (Chem.) body precipitated from solution, so ~ABIL'ITY, ~ANT(2), nn., ~ABLE a.; (phys.) moisture condensed from vapour by cooling & deposited, e.g. rain, dew. [as foll.]

prĕcĭp'ĭt|āte², a. Headlong, violently hurried, as ~*ate flight*; (of person or act) hasty, rash, inconsiderate. Hence or cogn. ~ANCE, ~ANCY, ~ateNESS, nn., ~ateLY² adv. [as foll., see -ATE²]

prĕcĭp'ĭtāt|e³, v.t. Throw down headlong; (fig.) hurl, fling, (person etc. *into* condition etc.); hurry, urge on, (course of events etc.); hasten the occurrence of, as *served to ~e his ruin*; (chem.) cause (substance in solution) to be deposited in solid form; condense (vapour) into drops & so deposit. So **prĕcĭpĭtā'tION** (esp., meteorol., fall of rain, sleet, snow, or hail), ~OR, nn. [f. L *praecipitare* (as foll.), -ATE³]

prĕcĭp'ĭtous, a. Of, like, a precipice; dangerously steep; (rare) = PRECIPITATE². Hence ~LY² adv., ~NESS n. [f. obs. F *precipiteux* f. L PRAE(*ceps -cipitis* f. *caput* head) headlong, see -OUS]

précis (prās'ē), n., & v.t. **1.** Summary, abstract. **2.** v.t. Make a ~ of. [F, = foll.]

précīse', a. Accurately expressed, definite, exact; punctilious, scrupulous in observance of rules etc.; *the ~* (exact, identical) *moment* etc. Hence ~NESS (-sn-) n. [f. F *précis, -ise,* f. L PRAE(*cidere cīs-* = *caedere* cut) cut short]

précīse'ly (-sl-), adv. In precise manner; (in emphatic or formal assent) quite so. [-LY²]

précī'sian (-zhn), n. One who is rigidly precise or punctilious, esp. in religious observance. Hence ~ISM (-zha-) n. [-IAN]

précī'sion (-zhn), n. Accuracy; *arm of ~,* fire-arm fitted with sights or other mechanical aids; (attrib.) marked by, adapted for, (~ *bombing, instruments, tools*). Hence ~IST (-zho-) n. [f. F *précision* or L *praecisio* (as PRECISE, see -ION)]

préclūde' (-ōōd), v.t. Exclude, prevent, make impracticable, as *so as to ~ all doubt.* So **préclus'IVE** (-lōō-) a. [f. L PRAE(*cludere clus-* = *claudere* shut)]

précō'cious (-shus), a. (Of plant) flower-

ing or fruiting early; (of person) prematurely developed in some faculty; (of actions etc.) indicating such development. Hence or cogn. ~LY² adv., ~NESS, **prĕcŏ'cĬTY,** nn. [f. L *praecox -cocis* f. PRAE-(*coquere* cook)+-OUS]

prĕcŏgnĭ'tion, n. Antecedent knowledge; || (Sc. law) preliminary examination of witnesses etc., esp. in order to know whether there is ground for trial. [f. LL *praecognitio* f. L PRAE(*cognoscere,* cf. RECOGNIZE), see -ION]

prēconceive' (-sēv), v.t. Conceive beforehand, anticipate in thought. So **prēconcĕp'tion** n. (esp. = *prejudice*). [PRE-]

prĕc'ŏnĭz|e, -ĭs|e (-īz), v.t. Proclaim publicly; commend publicly; summon by name; (Rom. Cath., of pope) approve publicly the appointment of (bishop). So ~A'TION n. [f. med. L *praeconizare* (L *praeco -onis* herald, see -IZE)]

prēcŭrs'or, n. Forerunner, harbinger, esp. John the Baptist; one who precedes in office etc. [f. L *praecursor* f. PRAE-(*currere curs-* run), see -OR]

prēcŭrs'|ory, a. Preliminary, introductory, serving as harbinger (*of*). So ~IVE a. [f. L *praecursorius* (as prec.; see -ORY]

prēdā'cious (-shus), a. (Of animals) naturally preying on others, predatory; pertaining to such animals, as ~ *instincts.* So **prēdā'cITY** n. [as f. L **praedax*: see PREDATORY, -ACIOUS]

prēdāte', v.t. Antedate. [PRE-]

prĕd'ātor, n. Predatory animal. [f. L *praedator* (foll.)]

prĕd'ātory, a. Of, addicted to, plunder or robbery; (of animals) preying upon others. [f. L *praedatorius* (*praedari* plunder f. *praeda* booty, see -ORY)]

prĕd'écĕssor, n. Former holder of any office or position, as *my, William's, ~s, his immediate ~*; thing to which another has succeeded, as *will share the fate of its ~*; forefather. [ME, f. AF, OF *-our* & LL PRAE(*decessor,* see DECEASE, -OR)]

prĕdĕll'a, n. (Painting on vertical face of) altar-step; (painting, sculpture, on) raised shelf at back of altar. [It., = stool]

prēdĕstĭnār'ĭan, n. & a. (Holder of the doctrine) of predestination. [-ARIAN]

prēdĕs'tĭn|āte, v.t. (Of God) foreordain (person) to salvation or to (any fate), *to* (do); determine beforehand. So ~ATE² (-at) a. [f. L PRAE(*destinare* DESTINE), see -ATE³]

prēdĕstĭnā'tion, n. God's appointment from eternity of some of mankind to salvation & eternal life; God's foreordaining of all that comes to pass; fate, destiny. [ME, f. LL *praedestinatio* (as prec., see -ION)]

prēdĕs'tĭne, v.t. Determine beforehand, appoint as if by fate; (theol.) = PRE-DESTINATE. [ME, f. OF *-iner* or L *praedestinare* PREDESTINATE]

prědětěrm'in|e, v.t. Decree beforehand, predestine, so ~ATE² (-at) a.; (of motive etc.) impel (person etc. *to* thing, *to* do) beforehand. Hence ~A'TION n. [f. LL PRAE(*determinare* DETERMINE)]

prěd'ial, a. & n. 1. Of land or farms; rural, agrarian; (of slaves) attached to the land. 2. n. ~ slave. [f. med. L *praedialis* (L *praedium* farm, see -AL)]

prěd'ic|able, a. & n. 1. That may be predicated or affirmed, so ~ABIL'ITY n. 2. n. ~able thing, esp. (pl.) Aristotle's classes of predicates viewed relatively to their subjects (viz. genus, species, difference, property, accident). [f. F, or L *praedicabilis* in med. L sense 'that may be affirmed' (as PREDICATE², see -BLE)]

prěd'icament, n. Thing predicated, esp. (pl.) Aristotle's ten categories, whence **prědicamĕn'tAl** a.; unpleasant, trying, or dangerous situation. [ME, f. LL *praedicamentum* (as foll., see -MENT)]

prěd'icant, a. & n. 1. (Of religious order, esp. Dominicans) engaged in preaching. 2. n. = PREDIKANT. [as foll., see -ANT]

prěd'icate¹, n. (Log.) what is predicated, what is affirmed or denied of the subject by means of the copula (e.g. *a fool* in *he is a fool*): (gram.) what is said of the subject, including the copula (e.g. *is a fool* in prec. ex.); quality, attribute. [as foll. see -ATE²]

prěd'icate², v.t. Assert, affirm, as true or existent, as *many truths may be* ~*d about humanity, we* ~ *goodness or badness of a motive,* ~ *of a motive that it is good or bad*; (log.) assert (thing) about subject. So **prědicA'TION** n. [f. L PRAE(*dicare* declare) proclaim, see -ATE³]

prědic'ative, a. Making a predication; (gram., of adj. or n., opp. *attributive*) forming part or the whole of the predicate, as in 'This is *absurd*', cf. 'an *absurd* notion'. Hence ~LY² adv. [f. L *praedicativus*, as prec., see -IVE]

prěd'icatory, a. Of, given to, marked by, preaching. [f. LL *praedicatorius* (prec., -ORY)]

prědict', v.t. Forecast, prophesy, (thing, that, who, etc.). Hence or cogn. ~ABIL'ITY, **prědic'tion,** nn., ~ABLE, ~IVE, aa., ~ively² adv. [f. L PRAE(*dicere dict-* say)]

prědic'tor, n. In vbl senses; also instrument for determining the height, direction, speed, and range of aircraft and the fuse-setting etc. required in engaging hostile aircraft with anti-aircraft fire. [-OR]

prědikant' (-ahnt), n. Minister of Dutch Protestant church, esp. in S. Africa. [Du., as PREDICANT]

prědilĕc'tion, n. Mental preference, partiality, (*for*). [f. F *prédilection* f. med. L PRAE(*diligere*), see DILIGENT & -ION]

prědispōse' (-z), v.t. Render liable, subject, or inclined (*to* feeling, disease, etc., *to* do). [PRE-]

prědisposi'tion (-zi-), n. State of mind

or body favourable *to* (mercy, malaria, etc.). [PRE-]

prědŏm'in|āte, v.i. Have or exert control (*over* person etc.), be superior; be the stronger or main element, preponderate, as *garden in which dahlias* ~*ate*. Hence or cogn. ~ANCE n., ~ANT a., ~antLY², ~ātingLY², advv. [f. med. L *PRAE-(dominare* DOMINATE)]

prě-ĕm'in|ent, a. Excelling others; distinguished beyond others in some quality. Hence or cogn. ~ENCE n., ~entLY² adv. [f. L PRAE(*eminens* EMINENT)]

prě-ĕmpt', v.t. & i. Obtain by preemption; *occupy (public land) so as to have right of pre-emption; (fig.) appropriate beforehand; (bridge) make preemptive bid. [back formation f. foll.]

prě-ĕmp't|ion, n. Purchase by one person etc. before opportunity is offered to others; right so to purchase. So ~IVE a. (~*ive bid,* bid at bridge intended to be high enough to prevent further bidding). [f. med. L *PRAE(emere empt-* buy), -ION]

preen, v.t. Trim (feathers) with beak; (of person) trim one*self*. [ME, app. var. of PRUNE³, assoc. w. Sc. & dial. *preen* pierce, pin]

prěf'ăb, n. (colloq.). Prefabricated house. [abbr.]

prěfăb'ric|āte, v.t. Manufacture component parts of (building etc.) prior to their assembly on a site. So ~A'TION n. [PRE-]

prěf'ace, n., & v.t. & i. 1. Introduction to book stating subject, scope, etc.; preliminary part of a speech; introduction to central part of eucharistic service. 2. v.t. Furnish (book etc.) with ~; introduce (act, speech, *with*), as ~*d his remarks with a snort;* (of event etc.) lead up to (another); (v.i.) make preliminary remarks. So **prěfatŏr'IAL, prěf'atORY,** aa. [ME, f. OF, app. f. med. L *prefatia* for L *praefatio* f. PRAE(*fari* speak), see -ION]

prěf'ĕct, n. (Rom. ant.) title of various officers, civil & military; chief administrative officer of French department; ~ *of police,* head of Paris police; (in some public schools) senior pupil authorized to maintain discipline. So **prěfĕc'torAL,** ~ōr'IAL, aa. [ME, f. OF, f. L *praefectus* f. PRAE(*ficere fect-* = *facere* make) set over]

prěf'ĕctūre, n. (Period of) office, official residence, district under government, of a prefect. Hence **prěfĕc'turAL** (-cher-) a. [F, or f. L *praefectura* (as prec., see -URE)]

prěfer', v.t. (-rr-). Promote (person *to* office), whence ~MENT n.; bring forward, submit, (statement, information, etc., *to* person in authority etc., *against* offender etc.); choose rather, like better, as *gentlemen* ~ *blondes,* ~ *water to wine,* ~ *to leave it alone,* ~ *that it should be left (than* is unidiomatic after ~ unless *rather* is inserted, as ~*red to die rather than pay*), so **prěf'erABLE** a., **prěf'erabLY²** adv. [ME, f. OF *preferer* f. L PRAE(*ferre* latbear)]

prĕf'erence, n. Liking of one thing better than another (*of* A *to* or *over* B); thing one prefers; prior right esp. to payment of debts; || ~ *bond, share, stock*, (on which dividend is paid before any is paid on ordinary stock); favouring of one person or country before others in business relations, esp. favouring of a country by admitting its products at lower import duty. [f. F *préférence* f. med. L *praeferentia* (prec., -ENCE)]

prĕferĕn'tial (-shl), a. Of, giving, receiving, preference; (of duties etc.) favouring particular countries, whence ~ISM, ~IST, nn., (-sha-). Hence ~LY² adv. [as prec. +-AL]

preferred' (-érd), a. In vbl senses; ~ *shares, stock*, etc., preference shares etc. [-ED¹]

prĕfig'ure (-ger), v.t. Represent beforehand by figure or type, picture to oneself beforehand. Hence or cogn. **prĕfigūrā'TION, ~MENT** (-germ-), nn., **prĕfig'ūratIVE a.** [ME, f. LL PRAE (*figurare* FIGURE)]

prĕf'ix¹, n. Verbal element placed at beginning of word to qualify meaning or (in some languages) as inflexional formative; title placed before name, e.g. *Mr, Mrs, Sir, Dr.* [f. mod. L *praefixum*, p.p. of L PRAE(*figere* FIX)]

prĕfix'², v.t. Add (chapter, paragraph, etc., to book etc.) as introduction; join (word, verbal element) as prefix (*to* word), so **prĕfi'xION, prĕfix'TURE**, nn. [ME, f. OF PRE(*fixer* FIX¹)]

prĕfŏrm', v.t. Form beforehand. [f. L PRAE(*formare* FORM²)]

prĕfŏrmā'tion, n. Previous formation; (biol.) *theory of* ~ (that all parts of the perfect organism exist in the germ & are merely developed). [PRE-]

prĕfŏrm'ative, a. & n. Forming beforehand; (syllable, letter) prefixed as formative element. [PRE-]

prĕg'nable, a. Not impregnable. [late ME & OF *prenable*, see IMPREGNABLE]

prĕg'nant, a. (Of woman or female animal) with child, gravid; teeming with ideas, imaginative, inventive; fruitful in results, big *with* (consequences etc.); (of words or acts) having a hidden meaning, significant, suggestive, whence ~LY² adv.; (gram.) ~ *construction* (in which more is implied than the words express). Hence **prĕg'nANCY** n. [ME, f. L *praegnans -ntis*]

prĕhĕn'sile, a. (zool.). (Of tail or limb) capable of grasping. Hence **prĕhĕnsil'ITY** n. [f. F *préhensile* f. L PRAE(*hendere hens-* grasp), see -ILE]

prĕhĕn'sion (-shn), n. Grasping, seizing; mental apprehension. [f. L *prehensio* (prec., -ION)]

prĕhistŏ'r|ic, a. Of the period antecedent to history; (colloq.) antediluvian. Hence ~ICALLY adv. [PRE-]

prĕhĭs'torў, n. Prehistoric matters or times. [PRE-, after prec.]

prē-ĭgnī'tion, n. Premature firing of explosive mixture in internal-combustion engine. [PRE-]

prējūdge', v.t. Pass judgement on (person) before trial or proper inquiry; form premature judgement upon (person, cause, action, etc.). So ~MENT (-jm-), prējudicā'TION (-jŏŏ-), nn. [f. F *préjuger* or L PRAE(*judicare* JUDGE)]

prĕj'udice (-jŏŏ-), n., & v.t. 1. Preconceived opinion, bias, (*against, in favour of*, person or thing), as *divest your mind of* ~, *has a* ~ *against foreigners, has a* ~ *in our favour, this is mere* ~; injury that results or may result from some action or judgement, as *to the* ~ *of; without* ~, without detriment to existing right or claim. **2. v.t.** Impair the validity of (right, claim, statement, etc.); cause (person) to have a ~ (*against, in favour of*), esp. in p.p. [ME, f. OF *prejudice* f. L PRAE(*judicium* judgement); vb f. OF *prejudicier*]

prĕjudi'cial (-jŏŏdĭshl), a. Causing prejudice, detrimental, (*to* rights, interests, etc.). Hence ~LY² adv. [ME, f. prec. (n.) +-AL (as to sense); corresp. in form to OF *prejudicial, -el*, f. LL *-alis*]

prĕl'acў, n. Office, rank, see, of a prelate; *the* prelates; church government by prelates (usu. hostile for EPISCOPACY). [ME, f. AF *prelacie* f. med. L *praelatia* (as foll. see -ACY)]

prĕl'ate, n. High ecclesiastical dignitary, e.g. (arch)bishop, metropolitan, patriarch, (hist.) abbot or prior. Hence **prĕlăt'ic(AL) aa., prĕlăt'icalLY² adv.** [ME, f. OF *prelat* f. L *praelatus* (as PREFER)]

prĕl'atĕss, n. Abbess, prioress; (joc.) prelate's wife. [-ESS¹]

prĕl'atīze, -ise (-īz), v.t. Bring (church) under prelatical government. [f. PRELATE +-IZE]

prĕl'ature, n. Office of prelate; *the* prelates. [f. F *prélature* f. med. L *praelatura* (as PRELATE, see -URE)]

prĕlĕct', v.i. Discourse, lecture, (*to* audience on subject, esp. in univv.). So **prĕlĕc'tION, prĕlĕc'tOR**, nn. [f. L PRAE(*legere lect-* read)]

prĕlibā'tion, n. Foretaste (usu. fig.). [f. LL PRAE(*libatio* LIBATION)]

prĕlim', n. (colloq.). Preliminary examination; (pl.; print.) pages preceding text. [abbr.]

prĕlim'inar|ў, a. & n. 1. Introductory, preparatory. **2.** n. ~y arrangement (usu. in pl.). Hence ~ĭLY² adv. [f. mod. L *praeliminaris*, pl. *-ia*, or F *préliminaire(s)* (both 1648); f. L *limen -minis* threshold, see -ARY¹]

prĕl'ūde¹, n. Performance, action, event, condition, serving as introduction (*to* another); introductory part of poem etc.;

For other words in *pre-* see PRE-.

(mus.) introductory movement esp. one preceding fugue or forming first piece of suite. Hence **prēlŭd′ɪaʟ** a., **prēl′ŭdɪᴢᴇ(2)** v.i. [f. F *prélude* or med. L *praeludium,* as foll.]

prēl′ūde² (*or* prīlūd′), v.t. & i. Serve as prelude to, introduce, foreshadow; introduce with a prelude; be, give, a prelude *to*; (mus.) play a prelude. So **prēlū′sɪoɴ** (-zhn) n., **prēlūs′ɪᴠᴇ** a. [f. L ᴘʀᴀᴇ(*ludere lus-* play)]

prēmatūre′ (*also* prěm!), a. & n. Occurring, done, before the usual or proper time, too early, hasty, as ~ *decision, decay*; (n.) ~ explosion of shell. Hence or cogn. ~ʟʏ² adv., ~ɴᴇss, **prēmatūr′ɪᴛʏ**, nn. [f. L ᴘʀᴀᴇ(*maturus* ᴍᴀᴛᴜʀᴇ)]

prēmĕd′it│āte, v.t. Think out, design, (action etc.) beforehand (esp. in p.p.). Hence or cogn. ~ātĕdʟʏ² adv., ~ᴀ′ᴛɪoɴ n. [f. L ᴘʀᴀᴇ(*meditari* ᴍᴇᴅɪᴛᴀᴛᴇ)]

ɩ **prēm′ier** (*or* prē-), a. & n. **1.** (Now chiefly sl.) first in position, importance, order, or time, as *secured* ~ *place* (in race). **2.** n. Prime Minister in Great Britain or some British dominions. Hence ~sʜɪᴘ n. [ME, f. OF = first, f. L as ᴘʀɪᴍᴀʀʏ]

première′ (prŭmyār′), n. First performance of play. [F, fem. adj. as prec.]

prēm′ise¹, -ss (as below), n. **1.** (log.). (Often -ss) previous statement from which another is inferred, esp. ᴍᴀᴊoʀ², ᴍɪɴoʀ, ~ in syllogism. **2.** (pl.). The aforesaid, the foregoing, esp. (law) the aforesaid houses, lands, or tenements. **3.** (pl.). House, building, with grounds & appurtenances, as *to be drunk on the* ~s. [ME, f. OF *premisse* f. med. L *praemissa* (*propositio* proposition) set in front f. L ᴘʀᴀᴇ(*mittere miss-*send)]

prēmīse′² (-z), v.t. Say, write, (thing, *that*) by way of introduction. [f. prec.]

prēm′ium, n. Reward, prize, (chiefly now in *put a* ~ *on*, provide or act as incentive to, as *you, this, will put a* ~ *on fraud*); *P*~ (*Savings*) *Bond,* government security with cash prizes drawn monthly in place of regular interest; amount to be paid in consideration of contract of insurance; sum additional to interest, wages, etc., bonus; fee for instruction in profession etc.; charge for changing one currency into another of greater value, agio; *at a* ~, at more than nominal value (cf. ᴅɪsᴄoᴜɴᴛ¹), (fig.) in high esteem. [f. L *praemium* booty, reward, f. ᴘʀᴀᴇ- +*emere* buy, take]

prēmōl′ar, n. Tooth in front of true molars (in man, ʙɪᴄᴜsᴘɪᴅ). [ᴘʀᴇ-]

prēmoni′tion, n. Forewarning. So **prēmŏn′itor** n., **prēmŏn′itorɪʟʏ²** adv., **prēmŏn′itorʏ** a. [f. obs. F *premonicion* or LL *praemonitio* f. L ᴘʀᴀᴇ(*monēre -it-*warn), -ɪoɴ]

Prēmŏnstratēn′sian, a. & n. (Member) of order of regular canons founded at Prémontré in 1119, or of corresponding order of nuns. [f. med. L *Praemonstra-*

tensis (*Praemonstratus* Prémontré, see -ᴇsᴇ) + -ᴀɴ]

prēmōrse′, a. (bot., entom.). With the end abruptly truncate. [f. L ᴘʀᴀᴇ-(*mordēre mors-* bite) bite off in front]

prēn′tice, n., & v.t. (arch.). = ᴀᴘᴘʀᴇɴᴛɪᴄᴇ, esp. ~ (tiro's) *hand.* Hence ~sʜɪᴘ n. (arch.). [aphetic]

prēŏccŭpā′tion, n. Prepossession, prejudice; occupation of a place beforehand; occupation, business, that takes precedence of all others; mental absorption. [F, or f. L *praeoccupatio* (foll., -ᴀᴛɪoɴ)]

prēŏcc′ŭp│y̆, v.t. Engage beforehand, engross (mind etc.); (p.p., esp.) distrait, with thoughts elsewhere, whence~iedʟʏ² (-pīd-) adv.; appropriate beforehand. [f. ᴘʀᴇ- +oᴄᴄᴜᴘʏ, after L *praeoccupare*]

prēp, n. (school sl.). ‖Preparation. [abbr.]

prēparā′tion, n. Preparing; (usu. pl.) thing(s) done to make ready (*for*); *make* ~s, prepare (*for*); ‖ (abbr. *prep*) ~ of lessons as part of school routine; substance, e.g. food or medicine, specially prepared; (mus.) preparing of a discord. [ME, f. OF f. L *praeparationem* (as ᴘʀᴇ-ᴘᴀʀᴇ, see -ɪoɴ)]

prēpă′rative, a. & n. Preparatory; (n.) ~ act, (mil., naut.) signal on drum, bugle, etc., as order to make ready. Hence ~ʟʏ² adv. [ME, f. OF (-*if, -ive*), f. med. L *praeparativus* (as ᴘʀᴇᴘᴀʀᴇ, see -ɪᴠᴇ)]

prēpă′rator│y̆, a. & n. Serving to prepare, introductory (*to*); ~*y* (*school*), ‖where pupils are prepared for higher school; (quasi-adv.) *am packing it up* ~*y to sending it by post.* Hence ~ɪʟʏ² adv. [ME, f. LL *praeparatorius* (as foll., see -oʀʏ)]

prēpāre′, v.t. & i. Make (person, thing) ready (*for*); make ready (food, meal) for eating; make (person) mentally ready or fit (*for* news, *to* hear, etc.); get (lesson, speech, sermon) ready by previous study, get (person) ready by teaching (*for* college, examination, the army, etc.); make preparations (*for, to do*, etc.); *be*~*d,* be ready or willing (*to* do); make(chemical product etc.) by regular process; (mus.) lead up to (discord) by sounding the dissonant note in it as consonant note in preceding chord. Hence **prēpăr′ĕdɴᴇss** n., readiness (esp. of nav. and mil. preparations for possible hostilities). [ME, f. OF *preparer* or L ᴘʀᴀᴇ(*parare* make ready)]

prēpay′, v.t. Pay (charge) beforehand; pay (postage), pay postage of (parcel, &c.) beforehand, e.g. by affixing stamp. Hence ~ᴀʙʟᴇ a., ~ᴍᴇɴᴛ n. [ᴘʀᴇ-]

prēpēnse′, a. Deliberate, intentional, chiefly in *malice* ~, intention to injure, *of malice* ~, with intent to injure. Hence ~ʟʏ² adv. [earlier *prepensed* p.p. of obs. *prepense* altered f. earlier *purpense* f. OF ᴘᴜʀ(*penser,* see ᴘᴇɴsɪᴠᴇ)]

prēpŏn′der│āte, v.i. Weigh more, be heavier; ~*ate over,* exceed in number, quantity, etc.; be of greater moral or intellectual weight; be the chief element, predominate; (of scale of balance) sink. So ~ANCE n., ~ANT a., ~antLY² adv. [f. L PRAE(*ponderare* PONDER), -ATE³]

prĕposi′tion (-z-), n. Word serving to mark relation between the noun or pronoun it governs & normally precedes & another word (e.g. the italic wds in: found him *at* home, wait *in* the hall, what did you do it *for*? the bed (that) he slept *on*, won *by* waiting, came *through* the roof, that is what I was thinking *of*). Hence ~AL a., ~alLY² adv., (-zĭsho-). [ME, f. L *praepositio* f. PRAE(*ponere posit-* place)]

prĕpŏs′itive (-z-), a. (gram.). (Of word, particle, etc.) proper to be placed before or prefixed. [f. LL *praepositivus* (as prec., see -IVE)]

prĕpŏs′itor (-z-). See PRAEPOSTOR.

prĕpossĕss′ (-z-), v.t. Imbue, inspire, (person *with* notion, feeling, etc.); (of idea etc.) take possession of (person, usu. pass.); prejudice, usu. favourably, whence ~ING² a., ~ingLY² adv., ~ingNESS, prĕposse′ssION (-zĕshn), nn. [PRE-]

prĕpŏs′terous, a. Contrary to nature, reason, or common sense; perverse, foolish; absurd. Hence ~LY² adv., ~NESS n. [f. L PRAE(*posterus* coming after) reversed, absurd, +-OUS]

prĕpŏt′|ent, a. Very powerful; more powerful than others; (biol.) having stronger fertilizing influence or power of transmitting hereditary qualities. So ~ENCE, ~ENCY, nn. [ME, f. L *praepotens* part. of PRAE(*posse* be able)]

‖ **prē-prĕf′erence**, a. (Of shares, claims, etc.) ranking before preference shares etc. [PRE-]

prĕp′uce, n. Foreskin, loose integument covering end of penis. So prĕpū′tIAL (-shl) a. [ME, f. OF, f. L *praeputium*]

Prē-Răph′aēlīte, n. Artist who aims at producing work in the spirit that prevailed before the time of Raphael; ~ *Brotherhood* (abbr. *P.R.B.*), group of English artists including Holman Hunt, Millais, D. G. Rossetti. So prē-Răph′aēl a., Prē-Răph′aēl(it)ISM n. [PRE-+*Raphael*+-ITE¹]

prĕrĕ′quisite (-z-), a. & n. (Thing) required as previous condition. [PRE-]

prĕrŏg′ative, n. & a. 1. (Also *royal* ~) right of the sovereign, theoretically subject to no restriction; peculiar right or privilege, as *it is our* ~ *to* (do), *we have the* ~ *of* (doing), *the* ~ *of* (right to show) *mercy*; natural or divinely-given advantage, privilege, or faculty, as *it is the* ~ *of man to drink without thirst*; ‖(pedantic) right of giving first vote and thus influencing those that follow; (hist.) ~ *court*, archbishop's court for probate of wills etc. 2. adj. Privileged, enjoyed by privilege; (Rom. hist.) having the right to vote first. [adj. f. L PRAE(*rogativus* f.

rogare ask, see -IVE) asked first; n. f. AF, OF, f. L *praerogativa* previous choice, prognostic, privilege, fem. adj. as n.]

prĕs′age¹, n. Omen, portent; presentiment, foreboding. Hence prĕsā′ge′FUL (-jf-) a. [ME & OF *presage* f. L *praesagium* f. PRAE(*sagus* predicting)]

prĕsā′ge′², v.t. Portend, foreshadow; give warning of (event etc.) by natural means, as *such ideas are held to* ~ *insanity*; (of person) predict, (also) have presentiment of. [f. F *présager*, as prec.]

prĕsbў|ŏp′ia (-s-, -z-), n. Form of long-sightedness incident to old age. Hence ~ŏp′IC a. [f. Gk *presbus* old man +*ōps* *ōpos* eye, see -IA¹]

prĕs′bўter (-s-, -z-), n. (In early Church) one of several officers managing affairs of local church; (in Episcopal church) minister of second order, priest; (in Presbyterian church) elder. Hence or cogn. prĕsbўt′erAL, prĕsbўtē̆r′IAL, aa., prĕsbўt′erATE¹ (-at), ~SHIP, nn. [LL, f. Gk *presbuteros* elder]

Prĕsbўtē̆r′ian (-s-, -z-), a. & n. 1. ~ *Church*, one governed by elders, all (including ministers) of equal rank; *United* ~ *Church*, that formed in 1847 by union of United Secession & Relief churches, later embodied in the United Free Church of Scotland & from 1929 in the Church of Scotland. 2. n. Adherent of ~ system, member of ~ Church. Hence ~ISM n., ~IZE(3) v.t. [f. LL as foll. +-AN]

prĕs′bўterў (-s-, -z-), n. Eastern part of chancel beyond choir, sanctuary; body of presbyters, esp. court next above KIRK-session, district represented by this; (R.--C. Ch.) priest's house. [ME, f. OF *-terie* f. LL f. Gk *presbuterion* (as PRESBYTER)]

prĕ′scient (-shyent), a. Having foreknowledge or foresight. Hence or cogn. prĕ′sciENCE (-shyens) n., ~LY² adv. [F. f. L PRAE(*scire* know), see -ENT]

prĕscĭnd′, v.t. & i. Cut off (part *from* whole) esp. prematurely or abruptly; ~ *from*, leave out of consideration. [f. L PRAE(*scindere* cut)]

prĕscrībe′, v.t. & i. Lay down or impose authoritatively, as *do not* ~ *to me what I am to do or how to do it, the statutes* ~ *the practice*; (med.) advise use of (medicine etc., or abs.; *to* or *for* patient, *for* complaint; also fig.); assert prescriptive right or claim (*to, for*, thing). [f. L PRAE-(*scribere script-* write) direct in writing]

prĕs′crĭpt, n. Ordinance, law, command. [as prec.]

prĕscrĭp′tion, n. Prescribing; physician's (usu. written) direction for composition & use of medicine; (law) (*positive*) ~, uninterrupted use or possession from time immemorial or for period fixed by law as giving title or right, such title or right, *negative* ~, limitation of the time within which action or claim can be raised; (fig.) ancient custom viewed as authoritative, claim founded on long use. [ME, f. OF or L *praescriptio* (as prec., see -ION)]

prescrip′tive, a. Prescribing; based on prescription, as ~ *right*; prescribed by custom. Hence ~LY[2] adv. [f. LL *praescriptivus* (as PRESCRIBE, see -IVE)]

prĕsĕlĕc′tive, a. (Of motor-car gears) that can be selected and set in advance. [PRE-]

prĕs′ence (-z-), n. Being present, as *your* ~ *is requested, in the* ~ *of a large company*; REAL[2] ~; place where person is, as *admitted to, banished from, his* ~, *in this* (*august* etc.) ~, *in the* ~ *of this* (etc.) person; ‖ *the* ~, ceremonial attendance on person of high esp. royal rank, as *remained in, retired from, the* ~; carriage, bearing, as *a man of (a) noble* ~; ~ *of mind*, calmness & self-command in sudden emergencies; ~-*chamber* (in which great personage receives guests etc.). [ME, f. OF, f. L *praesentia* (as foll., see -ENCE)]

prĕs′ent[1] (-z-), a. Being in the place in question (chiefly pred.), as *no one else was* ~ (*in* place, *at* proceedings etc.); being dealt with, discussed, etc., as *no excuse in the* ~ *case, the* ~ *volume* (the book you are reading or I am reviewing), *the* ~ *writer* (I) *could not verify this*; ~ *to* (felt, remembered, by) *the mind, the imagination*; ‖ (arch.) ready at hand, ready with assistance, as *a very* ~ *help in trouble*; existing, occurring, being such, now, as *the* ~ *Duke of York, in the* ~ *fashion; the* ~ *worth of* (sum that with compound interest dating from now will amount to) *£100 in 12 years*; (gram.) ~ *tense* (denoting action etc. now going on). [ME, f. OF, f. L *praesens -ntis* part. of PRAE(*esse* be) be at hand]

prĕs′ent[2] (-z-), n. *The* present time, the time now passing; *at* ~, now, as *do not want any more at* ~, *is at* ~ *in Egypt; for the* ~, just now, as far as the ~ is concerned, as *that will do for the* ~; = ~ *tense*; (*know all men* etc.) *by these* ~*s*, by this document (now legal or joc.). [ME, as prec.]

prĕs′ent[3] (-z-), n. Gift; *make a* ~ *of*, present (thing *to* person). [ME, f. OF (as prec.), orig. in phr. *mettre une chose en* ~ *à quelqu'un*, put a thing into the presence of a person]

prĕsĕnt′[4] (-z-), v.t. & i., & n. 1. Introduce (person *to* another); introduce (person) to sovereign at court; ~ *oneself*, appear esp. as candidate for examination etc. 2. (Of theatr. manager) cause (actor) to take part in play, produce (play). 3. Recommend (clergyman) to bishop for institution (*to* benefice). 4. Exhibit (thing *to* person etc.), as ~ *a ragged appearance,* ~*ed its front to me*; show (quality etc.), as *cases that* ~ *some difficulty*. 5. (mil.). Hold (fire-arm) in position for taking aim ; (also ~ *arms*) hold fire-arm etc. in deferential

position in saluting. 6. (Of idea etc.) offer, suggest *itself*. 7. (law). Bring formally under notice, submit, (complaint, offence, *to* authority). 8. Aim (weapon *at*), hold out (weapon) in position for aiming (also abs. ~ *l* as word of command). 9. Offer, give, (thing *to* person) as present; offer (compliments, regards, *to*); deliver (bill etc. *to* person etc.) for acceptance etc.; ~ *person with thing,* ~ *it to him*. 10. n. Act of aiming weapon esp. fire-arm, position of weapon when aimed, position of 'P~ arms' in salute. [ME, f. OF *presenter* f. L *praesentare* (as PRESENT[1])]

prĕsĕn′t|able (-z-), a. Of decent appearance, fit to be introduced or go into company; suitable for presentation as a gift etc. Hence ~ABIL′ITY n., ~ABLY[2] adv. [-ABLE]

prĕsĕntā′tion (-z-), n. Presenting; ~ (gratis) *copy* of book etc.; exhibition, theatrical representation, etc.; formal introduction esp. at court; (philos.) all the modification of consciousness directly involved in the knowing or being aware of an object in a single moment of thought, whence ~AL (-sho-) a. [ME, f. OF or LL *praesentatio* (PRESENT[4], -ATION)]

prĕsĕntā′tion|ism (-z-, -sho-), n. (philos.). Doctrine that in perception the mind has immediate cognition of the object. So ~(al)IST nn. [prec. + -ISM]

prĕsĕn′tative (-z-), a. (Of benefice) to which patron has right of presentation; serving to present an idea to the mind; (philos.) of (the nature of) presentation. [-ATIVE]

prĕsĕntee′ (-z-), n. Clergyman presented to benefice; person recommended for office; person presented at court; recipient of present. [ME, f. AF (PRESENT[4], -EE)]

prĕsĕn′tient (-shǐ-), a. Having a presentiment (*of* event etc., or abs.). [f. L PRAE-(*sentiens* SENTIENT)]

prĕsĕn′timent (-z-, -s-), n. Vague expectation, foreboding, (*of* coming event esp. evil). [f. obs. F PRE(SENTIMENT)]

prĕsĕn′tive (-z-), a. (Of word) presenting an object or conception directly to the mind (opp. to *symbolic*). [-IVE]

prĕs′ently (-z-), adv. Soon, after a short time; (chiefly Sc.) at the present time, now. [PRESENT[1] + -LY[2]]

prĕsĕnt′ment(-z-),n. (Law) statement on oath by jury of fact within their knowledge; formal complaint of offence made by parish authorities to bishop or archdeacon at his visitation; theatrical representation; delineation, portrait; statement, description, (*of*); act, mode, of presenting to the mind. [ME, f. OF *presentement* (as PRESENT[3], see -MENT)]

prĕservā′tion (-z-), n. Preserving, being preserved, from injury or destruction; state of being well or ill preserved, as *in an excellent state of* ~, *in* (*a state of) fair* ~.

[late ME, f. OF *preservation* or med. L *praeservatio* (as PRESERVE, see -ATION)]

prèsèrv'at|ive (-z-), a. & n. (Drug, measure, etc.) tending to preserve; chemical substance for preserving perishable foodstuffs, whence~IZE(5) v.t. [ME, f. OF *preservatif* or med. L *praeservativus* (as prec., see -ATIVE)]

prèsèrve'¹ (-z-), n. Jam; ground set apart for protection of game (often fig.); piece of water for fish; (pl.) goggles used as protection from dust etc. [f. foll.]

prèsèrv|e'² (-z-), v.t. Keep safe (*from* harm etc.); keep alive (name, memory, etc.); maintain (state of things); retain (quality, condition); prepare (fruit, meat, etc.) by boiling with sugar, pickling, etc., to prevent decomposition or fermentation; keep from decomposition by chemical treatment etc.; keep (game, game-run, river, or abs.) undisturbed for private use; *well ~ed*, (of elderly person) showing little sign of age. Hence ~'ABLE a., ~'ER¹ n., (-z-). [ME, f. OF *preserver* f. LL PRAE- (*servare* keep)]

prèsìde' (-z-), v.i. Occupy chair of authority at meeting of society or company (often *over*), sit at head of table; exercise control, sit or reign supreme, (often fig.); *~ at the organ, piano*, etc., act as organist etc. [f. F *présider* f. L PRAE(*sidēre* = *sedēre* sit)]

près'idencỳ (-z-), n. Office of president; period of this; district administered by president, esp. (formerly) division of E. India Company's territory (*Bengal, Madras, Bombay, P~*). [f. Sp., Pg. *presidencia* f. med. L *praesidentia* (prec., -ENCY)]

près'ident (-z-), n. Head of temporary or permanent body of persons, presiding over their meetings & proceedings; head of some colleges & U.S. universities; person presiding over meetings of academy, literary or scientific society, etc.; *person presiding over proceedings of bank or company; head of advisory council, board, etc., as *P~ of the Board of Trade*; *Lord P~ of the Council*, Cabinet Minister presiding at meetings of Privy Council; elected head of government in U.S. & other modern republics; (hist.) governor of province, colony, etc. Hence or cogn. près'iden'tial (-z-, -shl) a., près'iden'tiallỳ² adv., ~SHIP n. [ME, f. OF f. L as PRESIDE, see -ENT]

près'identèss (-z-), n. Female president; wife of president. [-ESS¹]

presìd'iarỹ, a. Of, having, serving as, a garrison. [f. L *praesidiarius* (*praesidium* garrison, as PRESIDE, see -ARY¹)]

presìd'iō, n. (pl. ~s). (In Spain & Sp. America) fort, garrison town. [Sp., as foll.]

presìd'ium, n. Standing committee in various Communistic organizations. [L (*praesidium*), = garrison]

près¹, n. 1. Crowding; crowd (*of* people etc.); throng, crush, in battle; pressure, hurry, of affairs, as *the ~ of modern life*. 2. Pressing, as *give it a slight~*. 3. (naut.). *~ of sail, canvas* (as much as wind etc. will allow). 4. Kinds of instrument for compressing, flattening, or shaping, or for extracting juice etc. 5. (Also *printing-~*) machine for printing; printing-house or establishment; publishing firm etc., esp. *University P~*; *the* art, practice, of printing; *in the ~*, being printed, *send, go, come, to (the) ~* (to be printed), *correct the ~* (errors in printing); *freedom of the ~*, right to print & publish anything without censorship; *the* newspapers generally, as *favourably noticed by the ~* (have a good etc. ~, receive such notice); *the* GUTTER, YELLOW, ~ ; ~ *campaign* or *stunt*, prosecution of political or other aims by newspaper letters & articles; (as name of newspaper) *Aberdeen P~ and Journal*. 6. Large usu. shelved cupboard for clothes, books, etc., esp. in recess in wall. 7. ~ *agent*, person employed by theatre, actor, etc., to attend to advertising and ~ *publicity*; ~*-box*, shelter for newspaper reporter at cricket match etc.; ~ *conference*, interview given to the ~ by some person to make announcement or answer questions; ||~ CUTTING; ~*-gallery* (for reporters esp. in House of Commons); ~*'man*, journalist, operator of printing-~ ; ~*'mark*, mark, number in book showing its place in library (now usu. *shelf-mark*). [ME & OF *presse* f. *presser* (foll.); also ME *prēs*, later *preace*, of obsc. form.]

près², v.t. & i. 1. Exert steady force against (thing in contact), as *let a heavy weight ~ it, ~ it under* or *with a stone, ~ the two plates together*; ~ *the button*, set electric machinery in motion, (fig.) take decisive initial step; ~*-button warfare* (carried on by means of guided missiles whose flight is controlled by ~ing a button); (as sign of affection etc.) *he ~ed my hand, ~ed her to his side*; move (thing *up, down, against*, etc.) by ~ing. 2. Exert pressure, bear with weight or force, (*on, against*, etc.). 3. Squeeze (juice etc. *out of, from*, etc.); compress, squeeze, (thing) to flatten or shape or smooth it, or to extract juice etc., as *~ed beef*. 4. (Of enemy, attacking force, etc.) bear heavily on, esp. in p.p. *hard ~ed*; weigh down, oppress, (feelings, mind, spirits); (pass.) *am ~ed for* (have barely enough) *space, time, funds*, etc. 5. Produce strong mental or moral impression, esp. weigh heavily, (*up*)*on* (mind, person). 6. Be urgent, demand immediate action, as *time ~es, nothing remains that ~es*. 7. Urge, entreat, (person *to do*, person or without object *for* answer etc.). 8. Insist on strict interpretation of (words, metaphor). 9. Urge (course, opinion,

For other words in *pre-* see PRE-.

upon person); force (offer, gift, etc. *upon*).
10. Crowd, throng, (*up, round*, etc.);
hasten, urge one's way, *on, forward*, etc.
[ME *presse* f. OF *presser* f. L *pressare*
frequent. of *premere press-*; also ME
prēse (cf. prec.)]

press[3], v.t., & n. (hist., exc. fig.). Force
(man, or abs.) to serve in army or navy
(also fig., esp. ~ thing *into the service of*);
take (horses, boats, etc.) for royal or
public use; (n., hist.) compulsory enlistment in navy or (less usu.) army; ~*-gang*,
body of men employed to ~ men. [alt.
f. 16th c. (obs.) *prest* (by assoc. w. PRESS[2])
f. OF *prest* loan, advance, f. *prester* f. L
PRAE(*stare* stand) vouch for, furnish]

press'ing, a. In vbl senses, esp.: urgent,
as ~ *need, danger*; importunate, persistent, as *a* ~ *invitation, since you are so* ~.
Hence ~LY[2] adv. [PRESS[2]+-ING[2]]

prē'ssure (-sher), n. **1.** Exertion of continuous force, force so exerted, upon or
against a body by another in contact
with it; amount of this, expressed by the
weight upon a unit area. **2.** *Atmospheric* ~
(of the ATMOSPHERE; *high, low,* ~, local
atmospheric condition sending barometer
up, down); *blood-*~, varying tension, now
measured for diagnosis etc., of blood-
-vessels. **3.** Affliction, oppression; trouble,
embarrassment, as *financial* ~. **4.** Urgency, as *wrote hastily & under* ~; constraining influence, as ~ *must be brought
to bear upon him*. **5.** *High* ~, (orig.) ~
higher than atmospheric (now indefinite,
used esp. of compound engines in which
steam is used at different ~s in different
cylinders, so *low* ~), (fig.) high degree of
activity, speed, etc., as *working at high*~,
high-~ *work*; ~*-cooker*, apparatus for
cooking under high ~ at high temperature, so ~*-cooking*; ~ *group*, group exerting ~ on a government for their own
special purpose. Hence **prē'ssurize**
(-sher-) v.t., (esp. in p.p.) construct (aircraft, cabin) so that air-~, temperature,
etc. can be controlled in such a way that
high-altitude flying is possible without
discomfort and without the use of oxygen
apparatus. [ME, f. OF, f. L *pressura* (as
PRESS[2], see -URE)]

Prēs'ter John (jŏn), n. Alleged Christian
priest & king in Abyssinia or some eastern
country in Middle Ages. [ME, f. OF
prestre (as PRESBYTER) *Jehan* priest John]

prēstidī'gĭtātor, n. Juggler, conjurer.
So **prēstidīgĭtA'TION** n. [f. F *prestidigi-
tateur* (*preste* nimble, as PRESTO +L *digitus*
finger, see -OR); earlier *prestigiator* f. L]

prēstĭge' (-ēzh), n. Influence, reputation,
derived from past achievements, associations, etc. [F, = illusion, glamour, f. LL
prestigium (= L *-ia* fem.) f. PRAE(*stringere*
bind) blindfold, dazzle]

prēstĭss'ĭmō, a., adv., & n. (mus.). Very
quick (piece, movement). [It., superl. as
foll.]

prēs'tō[1], a., adv., & n. (mus.). Quick

(piece, movement). [It., f. LL *praestus*
f. L *praesto* ready]

prēs'tō[2], adv. & a. (In conjurer's formulae) quickly, as *hey* ~*, pass!* ; (adj.) rapid,
juggling. [= prec.]

prēsūm|e' (-z-), v.t. & i. Take the
liberty, venture, (*to* do); assume, take for
granted, as *I* ~*e that he has seen them,
I* ~*e this decision to be final, you had better
* ~*e no such thing,* whence ~'ABLE a.,
~'abLY[2],~'ēdLY[2], advv.,(-z-); ~*e* (*up*)*on*,
take advantage of, make unscrupulous
use of, (person's good nature, one's acquaintance with him, etc.), whence
~'ingLY[2] (-z-) adv. [ME, f. OF *presumer*
or L PRAE(*sumere sumpt-* take)]

prēsŭmp'tion (-z-), n. Arrogance, assurance; taking for granted, thing taken for
granted, as *this was a mere* ~; *the* (only
natural) ~ *is that he had lost it*; ground
for presuming, as *there is a strong* ~
against its truth; (law) ~ *of fact*, inference of fact from known facts, ~ *of law,*
(1) assumption of truth of thing until the
contrary is proved, (2) inference established by law as universally applicable
to certain circumstances. [ME, f. OF *pre-
sumpcion* f. L *praesumptionem* (as prec.,
see -ION)]

prēsŭmp'tĭve (-z-), a. Giving grounds for
presumption, as ~ *evidence*, whence ~LY[2]
adv.; *heir* ~ (whose right of inheritance
is liable to be defeated by birth of nearer
heir, cf. APPARENT). [f. F *présomptif* f. LL
praesumptivus (as PRESUME, see -IVE)]

prēsŭmp'tūous (-z-), a. Unduly confident, arrogant, forward. Hence ~LY[2]
adv., ~NESS n. [ME, f. OF *presuntueus* f.
LL *praesumptiosus* (-*uosus*) (as PRESUME,
see -IOUS)]

prēsŭppōse' (-z), v.t. Assume beforehand
(thing, *that*); involve, imply, as *effects* ~
causes. [ME, f. OF *presupposer*, after
med. L *praesupponere* (PRE-, SUPPOSE)]

prēsŭpposi'tion (-zĭ-), n. Presupposing;
thing assumed beforehand as basis of
argument etc. [f. med. L PRAE(*suppositio*
SUPPOSITION)]

prētĕnce', n. Claim (*to* merit etc.);
ostentation, display, as *devoid of all* ~;
false profession of purpose, pretext, as
under the ~ *of helping, on the slightest* ~;
pretending, make-believe. [ME, f. late
AF *pretense*, as foll.]

prētĕnd', v.t. & i. Feign, give oneself out,
(*to* be or do), as *does not* ~ *to be a scholar*;
make believe (*to* do, *that*) in play; profess
falsely to have, as *you should* ~ *illness*;
allege falsely (*that*); venture, aspire, presume, (*to* do); lay claim *to* (right, title,
etc.); ~ *to* (arch.), try to win (person,
person's hand) in marriage; ~ *to*, profess
to have (quality etc.). Hence~ēdLY[2] adv.
[ME, f. OF *pretendre* or f. L PRAE(*tendere
tent-* later *tens-* stretch)]

prētĕn'der, n. One who makes baseless
pretensions (*to* title etc., or abs.); *Old,
Young, P*~, son, grandson, of James II as

claimants to British throne. Hence ~- SHIP n. [-ER[1]].

preten'sion (-shn), n. Assertion of a claim (to thing, or abs.); justifiable claim (to thing, to be or do), as he has no ~s to the name, has some ~s to be chosen as the site, what ~ has he?; pretentiousness. [f. med. L praetensio, -tio, (as PRETEND, see -ION)]

preten'tious (-shus), a. (Of person, book, speech, etc.) making claim to great merit or importance; ostentatious. Hence~LY[2] adv., ~NESS n. [f. F prétentieux (as prec., see -IOUS)]

preter-, pref. = L praeter past, beyond, in senses 'beyond, outside the range of, more than ', as: ~can'ine, more than ca-nine; ~hum'an, beyond what is human, superhuman; ~na'tural, outside the ordinary course of nature, (also) super-natural, whence ~na'turally adv.; ~ na'turalism, system, doctrine, of the ~natural; ~sen'sual, beyond the domain of the senses.

pret'erite, -it, a. & n. (Gram.) ~ (tense), one expressing past action or state, ~-present (tense), one originally ~ but now used as present (e.g. can, may, shall); (joc.) past, bygone, whence ~NESS n. [ME, f. OF or f. L praeteritus p.p. of praeterire pass (ire it- go, see prec.)]

preteri'tion, n. Omission, dis-regard, (of); (theol.) passing over of the non-elect. [f. LL praeteritio (as prec., see -ION)]

preter|mit', v.t. (-tt-). Omit to mention (fact etc.); omit to do or perform, neglect; leave off (custom, continuous action) for a time; (improp.) leave off. So ~mi'ssion (-shn) n. [f. L praetermittere (mittere miss-let go, see PRETER-)]

pret'ext[1], n. Ostensible reason, excuse; on or under, or upon, the ~ of or that, professing as one's object etc. [f. L PRAE-(texere text- weave)]

pretext'[2], v.t. Allege (thing, that) as pretext. [f. F prétexter, as prec.]

pret'one, n. Syllable, vowel, preceding the stressed syllable. So **preton'ic** a. [PRE-]

pretor etc. See PRAETOR etc.

pre'ttify (prĭ-), v.t. Make pretty, repre-sent with finicking prettiness. [-FY]

pre'ttily (prĭ-), adv. In a way that pleases the eye, ear, or aesthetic sense, as ~ dressed; (nursery) eat, ask, behave, ~ (in the approved manner). [f. PRETTY + -LY[2]]

pre'ttiness (prĭ-), n. Beauty of a dainty or childish kind; pretty thing, ornament, etc.; affected or trivial beauty of style in literature or art, so **pre'ttyism** (prĭ-) n. [-NESS]

pre'tty (prĭ-), a., adv., & n. 1. (Of woman or child) beautiful in dainty or diminutive way; attractive to eye, ear, or aesthetic sense, as ~ cottage, song, scene, story; fine,

good of its kind, as has a ~ wit, very ~ sport, (iron.) a ~ mess you have made; || (arch.) fine, stout, as a ~ fellow; || (arch.) considerable in amount or extent, as earned a ~ sum; (ellipt.) my ~ (one, child). **2.** adv. Fairly, moderately, as am ~ well, find it ~ difficult, that is ~ much (very nearly) the same thing; sitting ~ (colloq.), comfortably placed. **3.** n. || Fluted or cut part of wine-glass or tumbler, as fill it up to the ~; (golf) fairway (colloq.). **4.** ~-~, overdoing the ~, aiming too much at prettiness, (n. pl.) ~-pretties, ornaments, knick-knacks. Hence ~ISH[1] a. [late OE prættig f. præt (obs. prat) trick, wile, +-Y[2]; cf. Icel. prettu(g)r, Du. pret(tig) in similar senses]

pret'zel, b-, n. Crisp knot-shaped biscuit flavoured with salt, used esp. by Ger-mans as relish with beer. [G]

preux chevalier (prer̄ shĕvǎlyā'), n. Gal-lant knight. [F]

prevail', v.i. Gain the mastery, be vic-torious, (against, over); ~ (up)on, persuade (to do); be the more usual or prominent, predominate; exist, occur, in general use or experience, be current, whence or cogn. ~ingLY[2], prev'alentLY[2], advv., prev'-alence n., prev'alent a. [ME, f. L PRAE-(valere have power), infl. by obs. vail = AVAIL]

preva'ric|āte, v.i. Speak, act, evasively; quibble, equivocate. So ~A'TION, ~ātor, nn. [f. L PRAE(varicari straddle f. varus bent, knock-kneed) walk crookedly, practise collusion, (eccl. L) transgress]

preven'ient, a. Preceding, previous; having in view the prevention (of); (theol.) ~ grace (preceding repentance & predisposing the heart to seek God). [as foll., see -ENT]

prevent', v.t. Hinder, stop, as this may ~ him from writing, ~ his (pop. him) writing, wish to ~ all dispute; || (arch.) meet, deal with, (wish, question, etc.) before it is expressed etc.; (theol.) God ~s (goes before, guides) us with His grace. Hence or cogn. ~ABLE, ~IBLE, aa. **preven'tion** n. [f. L PRAE(venire vent-come) come before, hinder]

preven'ter, n. In vbl senses, also; (naut.) rope, chain, bolt, etc., used to supplement another. [-ER[1]]

preven'tive, a. & n. **1.** Serving to prevent, esp. (med.) to keep off disease; || ~ deten-tion (to which a persistent offender may be sentenced for not less than 5 nor more than 14 years); || P~ (Coastguard) Service. **2.** n. ~ agent, measure, drug, etc. Hence or cogn. **preven'tative** a. & n., ~LY[2] adv. [-IVE]

prev'iew (-vū), n., & v.t. View or exa-mination of a film, play, book, etc., before it is submitted to the general public; (v.t.) view in advance of public presentation. [PRE-]

For other words in *pre-* see PRE-.

prĕv'ious, a. & adv. **1.** Coming before in time or order; prior *to*; done or acting hastily, as *you have been a little too* ~, whence ~NESS n.; (Parl.) ~ *question*, question whether vote shall be taken on main question (put to avoid putting of main question); || *P~ Examination*, = LITTLE-*go*. **2.** adv. ~ *to*, before, as *had called* ~ *to writing*. Hence ~LY² adv. [f. L PRAE(*vius* f. *via* way)+-OUS]

prĕvise' (-z), v.t. Foresee, forecast, (event etc., or abs.). So prĕvi'sION (-zhn) n., prĕvi'sionAL a., prĕvi'sionalLY² adv., (-zho-). [f. L PRAE(*vidēre vis-* see)]

prey¹ (prā), n. Animal hunted or killed by other animal for food (also fig.); *beast, bird, fish, of* ~, kinds that kill & devour other animals; (bibl.) what one brings away safe from contest etc. (*Jer.* xxi. 9); person, thing, that falls a victim (*to* enemy, disease, fear, etc.). [ME, f. OF *preie, proie*, f. L *praeda*]

prey² (prā), v.i. ~ *upon*, seek, take, (animal etc.) as prey, plunder (persons); (of disease, emotion, etc.) exert baneful or wasteful influence *upon*. [ME, f. OF *preer* f. LL *praedare* (L -*ari*) as prec.]

pri'apism, n. Licentiousness; (path.) persistent erection of penis. [f. LL f. Gk *priapismos* (*Priapos*, god of procreation, see -ISM)]

price, n., & v.t. **1.** Money for which thing is bought or sold, as *what is the* ~ *of this?*, *try our superb tea,* ~ *10/- per lb.*, *offered at reduced* ~*s*; ~ *current*, ~-*list*, list of current ~s of commodities; LONG¹, COST¹, ~ ; *above, beyond, without,* ~, so valuable that no ~ can be stated; *at a* ~, at a relatively high~ ; *set a* ~ *on* person's *head*, offer reward for his capture or death; (betting) odds, as *the starting* ~ *of a horse*; (fig.) what must be given, done, sacrificed, etc., to obtain a thing, as *must be done at any* ~ ; *peace at any* ~ ; *every man has his* ~ (can be won over by some inducement); *would not have it, do it,* etc., *at any* ~, on any terms, for any consideration; || *what* ~ *the Concert of Europe* etc. ? (sl.), taunting allusion to the failure of something vaunted; || (arch.) preciousness, value, as *a pearl of* (*great*) ~. **2.** v.t. Fix, inquire, the ~ of (thing for sale); (fig.) estimate the value of; ~ one*self out of the market*, charge a prohibitive ~. [(n.) f. OF *pris* f. L *pretium*; ME *pris* became *prise* to secure ī, and *price* to avoid z sound of *s* between vowels; (vb) earlier *prise* PRIZE¹ assim. to *price* n.; *price, prize, praise*, are all variants of same wd]

priced (-īst), a. To which a price is assigned, esp. in comb., as *high, low,* ~ ; ~ *catalogue* etc. (in which prices are named). [-ED¹˒²]

price'lèss, a. Invaluable; (sl.) most amusing, incredibly absurd. Hence ~NESS n. [-LESS]

prick¹, n. Pricking, puncture; (fig.) ~*s* (stinging reflections) *of conscience*; mark

made by pricking; || (arch.) goad for oxen, esp. (fig.) *kick against the* ~*s*, hurt oneself by useless resistance (*Acts* ix. 5); (vulg.) penis; ~-*ears*, erect pointed ears of some dogs etc., conspicuous ears of person, esp. of Roundheads, ~-*eared*, having such ears. [OE *prica, -ce,* = MLG *pricke*; goes w. foll.]

prick², v.t. & i. **1.** Pierce slightly, make minute hole in; ~ *a* or *the bladder* (or *bubble*, show the emptiness of a person or thing that has passed for important; (fig.) cause sharp pain to, as *my conscience* ~*ed me*. **2.** Make a thrust (*at, into,* etc.). **3.** (arch.). Spur, urge on, (horse); (intr.) advance on horseback. **4.** Mark off (name etc. in list) with a prick, || select (sheriff) thus; mark (pattern *off, out*) with dots. **5.** ~ *in, out,* plant (seedlings etc.) in small holes ~ed in earth; ~ *up* one's *ears,* (of dog) erect the ears when on the alert, (fig., of person) become suddenly attentive. [late OE *prician,* = MDu., MLG *prikken* f. WG *prik(*k*)-, perh. imit.]

prick'er, n. In vbl senses, esp., pricking instrument, e.g. awl. [-ER¹]

prick'ĕt, n. || Buck in second year, with straight unbranched horns; ||~'*s sister*, female fallow deer in second year; spike to stick candle on. [ME, f. AL *prikettus, -um* f. PRICK, see -ET]

prick'le¹, n., & v.t. & i. **1.** Thorn-like process developed from, & capable of being peeled off with, epidermis of plant; (pop.) small thorn; hard-pointed spine of hedgehog etc. **2.** vb. Affect, be affected, with sensation as of pricks, whence prick'lING¹ n., prick'lING² a. [(n.) OE *pricel,* = MDu., MLG *prickel;* (vb) 16th c. f. prec. & PRICK, = MDu., MLG *prikkeln*] || prick'le², n. Kinds of wicker basket or measure. [orig. unkn.]

prick'lÿ, a. Armed with prickles (esp. in names of plants & animals); (fig., of person) ready to give or take offence; tingling; ~ *heat*, inflammation of sweat glands with eruption of vesicles & ~ sensation, common in hot countries; ~ *pear,* (~ plant bearing) pear-shaped edible fruit. Hence prick'liNESS n. [-Y²]

pride, n., & v. refl. **1.** Overweening opinion of one's own qualities, merits, etc., a deadly SIN, often personified, as *P~ will have a fall*; arrogant bearing or conduct; ~ *of place*, exalted position, consciousness of this, arrogance; (also *proper* ~) sense of what befits one's position, preventing one from doing unworthy thing, *false* ~, mistaken feeling of this kind; feeling of elation & pleasure, as *take a* ~ *in*, be proud of (person, thing, doing); object of this feeling, as *he is his mother's* ~, esp. in names of plants, as LONDON ~ ; (her.) *peacock in his* ~ (with tail expanded and wings drooping); company (of lions); best condition, esp. ~ *of* GREASE¹; ~ *of the morning*, mist or shower at sunrise. **2.** v. refl. ~ one*self* (*up*)*on*, be

proud of (thing, quality, do*ing*). Hence
~'FUL (chiefly Sc.), ~'LESS, aa., ~'fuLLY²
adv. [late OE *prŷtu, prŷde* f. *prút, prŭd*
PROUD; hence vb, ME *priden*]

prie-dieu (prēdyér′, & see Ap.), n. Kneeling-desk; (also ~ *chair*) chair with tall
sloping back for use in praying. [F, lit.
pray God]

priest, n., & v.t. **1.** Ordained minister of
R.C. and Anglican churches; in Established church one above deacon & below
bishop with authority to administer
sacraments & pronounce absolution;
(fig.) ~ *of nature, science*, etc.; minister
of the altar, esp. officiant at Eucharist;
HIGH ~; official minister of non-Christian
religion, whence ~'ESS¹ n. **2.** ‖ Mallet
used to kill fish when spent (chiefly in
Ireland). **3.** ~'*craft*, ambitious or worldly
policy of ~s; ~'s *hood*, ~-*in-the-pulpit*,
wild arum; ~-*ridden*, held in subjection
by ~s; ‖~ *vicar*, minor canon in some
cathedrals. **4.** v.t. Make (person) a ~.
Hence ~'HOOD (-t-h-), ~'LING¹, nn., ~'LESS,
~'LIKE, aa. [OE *prēost*, = OHG *prēst*, ON
presir, ult. f. L PRESBYTER]

priest'l̄|y̆, a. Of, like, befitting, a priest;
(O. T. criticism) ~*y code*, one of the constituent elements in the Hexateuch, ~*y
writer* (of this). Hence ~ĪNESS n. [-LY¹]

prig, n., & v.t. (-gg-). **1.** Precisian in
speech or morals or manners, conceited
or didactic person, whence ~g'ERY(2),
~g'ishNESS, ~g'ISM, nn., ~g'ISH¹ a.,
~g'ishLY² adv., (-g-); (sl.) thief. **2.** v.t.
(sl.). Steal. [16th c. cant, of unkn. orig.]

prim, a., & v.i. & t. (-mm-). (Of persons,
manner, speech, etc.) formal, demure;
(esp. of women) prudish; (v.i.) assume ~
air; (v.t.) form (face, lips, etc.) into ~
expression. Hence ~'LY² adv., ~'NESS n.
[f. 17th c., orig. cant]

pri'ma (prē-) a. First, chief; as : ~ *buff'a*
(bŏŏ-), chief female comic singer or actress; ~ *dŏnn'a*, (pl. ~ *donnas*, *prime
donne* pr. prēm'ā dŏn'ā), chief female
singer in opera, (transf.) temperamental
person. [It., fem. adj.]

prim'acy̆, n. Office of a primate; pre-
-eminence. [ME, f. OF *primacie* f. med. L
primatia (as PRIMATE, see -ACY)]

pri'ma fā'cie (-shǐe), adv. & a. (Arising)
at first sight, (based) on the first impression, as *has ~ a good case, see a ~
reason for it*. [L]

prim'age¹, n. Percentage addition to
freight, paid to owners or freighters of
vessels. [AL *primagium*, of obsc. orig.]

prim'age², n. Amount of water carried
off suspended in steam from boiler. [f.
PRIME v. + -AGE]

prim'al, a. Primitive, primeval; chief,
fundamental. Hence ~LY² adv. [f. med.
L *primalis* (as PRIME a., see -AL)]

prim'ary̆, a. & n. **1.** Earliest, original; of
the first rank in a series, not derived, as
the ~ vowel sounds, ~ meaning of a word;
of the first importance, chief; (geol.) of

the lower series of strata; (biol.) belonging to first stage of development; ~ *amputation* (performed before inflammation
supervenes); ~ *education*, that which begins with the rudiments of knowledge,
elementary, so ~ *school, scholar* (cf.
SECONDARY); (Lat. & Gk gram.) ~ *tenses*,
present, future, perfect, & future perfect,
(cf. HISTORIC); ~ *assembly, meeting* (for
selection of candidates for election); ~
COLOUR; ~ *planets* (revolving directly
round sun as centre); ~ *battery* (in which
current is produced). **2.** n. ~ planet,
meeting, etc. Hence prim'ariLY² adv.
[ME, f. L *primarius* (as PRIME a., -ARY¹)]

prim'ate, n. Archbishop; *P~ of England*,
Archbishop of York, *P~ of all England*,
Archbishop of Canterbury; (zool.) sing.
of foll. Hence **prima'**TIAL (-āshl) a. [ME,
f. OF *primat*, f. L *primas -atis* adj. (as
PRIME a.); in med. L = primate]

primāt'ēs (-z), n. pl. (zool.; for sing., see
prec.). Highest order of mammals, including man, monkeys, apes, & lemurs.
[as prec.]

prime¹, n. State of highest perfection, as
in the ~ of life, manhood, etc.; *the* best
part (*of* thing); beginning, first age, of
anything; a canonical hour of monastic
rule, appointed for first hour of day (i.e.
6 a.m.), (arch.) this time; (arch.) GOLDEN
number; prime number; (chem.) single
atom as unit in combination; a position
in fencing. [OE *prim* f. L *prima* (*hora*)
first (hour); in ME reinforced by OF
prime (as foll.)]

prime², a. Chief, most important, as ~
agent, motive; first-rate (esp. of cattle
& provisions), excellent, whence ~'LY²
adv., ~'NESS n.; primary, fundamental;
(arith., of a number) having no integral
factors except itself and unity (e.g. 2, 3,
5, 7, 11), (of numbers) having no common
measure but unity; ~ COST¹, MOVER¹; ~
vertical (*circle*), great circle of the heavens
passing through E. & W. points of
horizon & through zenith, where it cuts
meridian at right angles; ~ *minister*,
principal minister of any sovereign or
State (now official title of first minister &
head of Government in Great Britain).
[ME, f. OF *prime* or L *primus* first]

prime³, v.t. & i. (Hist.) supply (fire-arm,
or abs.) with gunpowder for firing charge;
wet (pump) to make it start working;
inject petrol into (cylinder or carburettor
of internal-combustion engine); equip
(person *with* information etc.); fill (person
with liquor); cover (wood etc.) with first
coat of paint or with oil etc. to prevent
paint from being absorbed; (of engine
boiler) let water pass with steam into
cylinder in form of spray. [orig. unkn.]

prim'er¹, n. **1.** (*usu.* pri-). Elementary
school-book for teaching children to
read; small introductory book, as *P~ of
Evolution, Latin P~*; (hist.) prayer-book
for use of laity esp. before Reformation

primer (prī-). **2.** (prī-). *Great, long,* ~, *sizes of* TYPE. [ME, AL, f. med. L *primarius, -arium,* f. L *primus* first, see -ER²(2)]

prim'er², n. In vbl senses of PRIME³, esp. cap, cylinder, etc., used to ignite powder of cartridge etc. [-ER¹]

prīmēr'ŏ, n. (hist.). Gambling card-game fashionable in 16th & 17th cc. [f. Sp. *primera* fem. of *primero,* as PRIMARY]

primēv'al, -aeval, a. Of the first age of the world; ancient, primitive. Hence ~LY² adv. [f. L *primaevus* (*primus* first + *aevum* age) + -AL]

prim'ing¹, n. In vbl senses of PRIME³; also or esp.: gunpowder placed in pan of fire-arm; train of powder connecting fuse with charge in blasting etc.; mixture used by painters for preparatory coat; preparation of sugar added to beer; imparting of information. [-ING¹]

prim'ing², n. Acceleration of the tides taking place from neap to spring tides (cf. LAG¹). [f. *prime* vb f. PRIME¹,²]

primip'arous, a. Bearing child for the first time. [f. L *primipara* ~ woman (also used in E) f. *primus* first + *parĕre* bring forth; see -OUS]

prim'itive, a. & n. **1.** Early, ancient, as *the P~ Church* (Christian Church in its earliest times); old-fashioned, simple, rude; uncivilized or of rudimentary civilization; original, primary; (gram., of words) radical, not derivative; (math., of line, figure, etc.) from which another is derived, from which some construction begins, etc.; (of colours) primary; (geol.) of the earliest period; (biol.) appearing in earliest or very early stage of growth etc.; *P~ Methodist Connexion,* society of Methodists founded 1810 by Hugh Bourne by secession from main body, *P~ Methodist, Methodism,* member, principles, of this. **2.** n. Painter of period before Renascence, picture by such painter; ~ *word, line,* etc.; P~ Methodist. Hence ~LY² adv., ~NESS n. [ME & OF *primitif* f. L *primitivus* (as PRIME²)]

prī'mō¹ (prē-), n. (mus.). Upper part in duet etc. [It.]

prīm'ō², adv. ~, *secŭn'dŏ, ter'tiō* (-shǐ-), in the first, second, third, place (written 1°, 2°, 3°). [L]

primŏgĕn'itor, n. Earliest ancestor; (loosely) ancestor. [med. L, f. L *primo* (at) first + *genitor* begetter (*gignere genit-* bring forth, see -OR), after L *primogenitus* first-born]

primŏgĕn'it|ure, n. Fact of being the first-born of the children of the same parents; (*right of*) ~*ure,* right of succession belonging to the first-born, esp. feudal rule by which whole real estate of intestate passes to eldest son. So ~AL, ~ARY¹, aa. [f. med. L *primogenitura* (as prec., see -URE)]

primŏrd'ial, a. Existing at or from the beginning, primeval; original, fundamental. Hence ~ITY (-ăl²) n., ~LY² adv.

[ME, f. LL *primordialis* (L *primordium* f. *primus* first + *ordiri* begin, see -AL)]

prim'rōse (-z), n. Plant bearing pale yellow flowers in early spring; flower of this; (attrib.) of the colour of this flower; *the ~ path,* the pursuit of pleasure (w. ref. to *Haml.* I. iii. 50); ‖ *P~ Day, League,* anniversary of the death (Apr. 19th, 1881) of, Conservative association formed in memory of, Benjamin Disraeli Earl of Beaconsfield; *P~ dame, knight, habitation,* (of the P~ League); ~ *peerless,* two-flowered narcissus. Hence **prim'rōsy²** (-z-) a. [ME *primerose,* corresp. to OF *primerose* & med. L *prima rosa* lit. first rose, sense unexpl.]

prim'ūla, n. Kind of herbaceous perennial with flowers of various colours. [med. L, fem. adj. as n., dim. as PRIME², see -ULE]

prīm'um mōb'ĭlĕ, n. Outermost sphere added in Middle Ages to Ptolemaic system, supposed to revolve round earth in 24 hours carrying with it the contained spheres; (fig.) prime source of motion or action. [med. L, lit. first moving thing]

prim'us¹, a. & n. **1.** ‖ (In boys' school) eldest (or of longest standing) of the name, as *Jones* ~ (usu. written *Jones* i.; similarly *secundus* ii., *tertius* iii., *quartus* iv., *quintus* v., *sextus* vi., *septimus* vii., *octāv'us* viii., *nōnus* ix., *dĕ'cimus* x.); (L) ~ *ĭn'ter pār'ēs* (-z), first among equals, senior or spokesman of a board of colleagues. **2.** n. ‖ Presiding bishop in Scottish Episcopal Church. [L, = first]

prim'us², n. Brand of stove burning vaporized oil for cooking etc. [P]

prince, n. **1.** (Now rhet.) sovereign ruler; *P~ of Peace,* Christ; ~ *of darkness, the air, the world,* etc., Satan. **2.** Ruler of small State, actually or nominally feudatory to king or emperor. **3.** Male member of royal family, esp. (in Great Britain) son or grandson of king or queen (also ~ *of the blood*). **4.** *P~ of Wales,* (title conferred on) heir apparent to British throne (*P~ of Wales's feathers,* triple ostrich plume); *P~ Consort,* (title conferred on) husband of reigning female sovereign being himself a ~; *P~ of Denmark,* Hamlet. (*Hamlet without the P~ of Denmark,* thing robbed of its essence). **5.** (As English rendering of foreign titles) noble usu. ranking next below duke; (as courtesy title in some connexions) duke, marquis, earl; (title of cardinal) ~ *of the* (*Holy Roman*) *Church.* **6.** (fig.). Chief, greatest, (of novelists, liars, etc.). **7.** **P~ Albert* (colloq.), frock-coat; ~ *bishop,* bishop who is also a ~; *P~ Regent,* ~ who acts as regent, e.g. George (afterwards IV); ~ *royal,* eldest son of reigning monarch; *P~ Rupert's drops,* pear-shaped lumps of glass bursting to pieces when thin ends are broken off; ~*'s feather,* kinds of plant, esp. tall plant with feathery spikes of small red flowers; ~*'s metal,* alloy of copper & zinc. Hence

~'DOM (-sd-), ~'KIN (-sk-), ~'LET, ~'LING[1]
(2), (-sl-), nn., ~'LIKE (-sl-), a. [ME, f. OF,
f. L *princeps -cipis* first, prince, (*primus*
first + *-cipere = capere* take)]
prince'l|ў (-sl-), a. (Worthy) of a prince;
sumptuous, splendid. Hence ~ĭNESS n.
[-LY[1]]
prin'cĕss (or -ĕs' *exc. when followed by
name*), n. (Arch.) queen; wife of prince;
(also ~ *of the blood*) daughter, grand-
daughter, of sovereign; ~ *royal*, (title con-
ferrable on) sovereign's eldest daughter;
P~ Regent, ~ acting as regent, (also) wife
of prince regent; ~ *dress, petticoat, slip*,
(made without a seam at the waist). [ME
& OF *princesse* (as PRINCE, see -ESS[1])]
prin'cipal, a. & n. 1. First in rank or importance, chief, as *their* ~ *food is potatoes,
the* ~ *town of the district, the* ~ *persons
concerned*; ~ *boy, girl*, actress who takes
leading male, female, part in pantomime;
main, leading, as *a* ~ *cause of his failure*.
2. (Of money) constituting the original
sum invested or lent. 3. (gram.). ~ *sentence, clause*, one to which another is
subordinate; ~ *parts* of verb, those from
which the others can be derived. 4. n.
Head, ruler, superior; head of some
colleges & universities, whence ~SHIP n.
5. Person for whom another acts as agent
etc., as *I must consult my* ~; person
directly responsible for crime, either (~
in the first degree) as actual perpetrator or
(~ *in the second degree*) as aiding; person
for whom another is surety; combatant in duel (opp. *second*). 6. Any of the
main rafters on which rest the purlins
that support the common rafters. 7.
Capital sum as distinguished from interest
or from income. 8. Organ diapason stop
sounding octave above normal. [ME, f.
OF, or L *principalis* adj. (as PRINCE, see
-AL)]
principăl'itў, n. Government of a prince;
State ruled by a prince; || *the P~*, Wales;
(pl.) an ORDER[1] 1 of angels. [ME, f. OF
principalite f. LL *principalitatem* (as prec.,
see -TY)]
prin'cipallў, adv. For the most part,
chiefly. [-LY[2]]
prin'cipate, n. (Rom. hist.) rule of
early emperors while some republican
forms were retained; State ruled by a
prince. [ME, f. L *principatus* (as PRINCE,
see -ATE[1])]
prin'ciple, n. 1. Fundamental source,
primary element, as *held water to be the
first* ~ *of all things*. 2. Fundamental truth
as basis of reasoning etc., as (*first*) ~s *of
political economy*; (phys.) general law
(often with discoverer's name, as *Pascal's*
~); general law as guide to action, as
moral, conservative, ~s, *a dangerous* ~,
whence -prin'cipl|ED[2] (-ld) a.; *in* ~, dist.
from *in detail*; (pl. & collect. sing.) personal
code of right conduct, as *a man of high* ~,
has ability but no ~s, ~ *is everything*; *on* ~,
from settled moral motive, as *I refuse on

~ (not from selfish motive etc.). 3. Law
of nature seen in working of machine etc.,
as *in all these instruments the* ~ *is the same*.
4. (chem.). Constituent of a substance,
esp. one giving rise to some quality etc.,
as *bitter, colouring,* ~. [ME, f. OF *principe*
f. L *principium*, after *manciple, participle*]
prink, v.t. & i. Make (oneself etc.) spruce;
dress oneself *up*; (of bird) trim (feathers);
dress oneself up. [16th c., cf. PRANK[2]]
print[1], n. 1. Indentation in surface preserving the form left by pressure of some
body, as *finger*-~, *foot'*~, whence ~'LESS
a. 2. Printed cotton fabric, as (attrib.)
~ *dress*. 3. Language embodied in printed
form, printed lettering, as *large, small,
clear*, ~; state of being printed; *book is
in* ~, (1) in printed form, (2) on sale, not
out of ~ (sold out); (of writer) *rush into*
~, publish book, write to newspaper etc.,
on insufficient grounds; (chiefly U.S.)
printed publication, esp. newspaper; picture, design, printed from block or plate;
(photog.) picture produced from negative. 4. ~ *hand, letters* (imitating ~); ~-
seller, dealer in engravings etc.; ~-*shop*,
his shop; ~-*works*, factory where cotton
fabrics are printed. [ME, f. OF *priente,
preinte*, f. p.p. of *preindre* press f. L
premere]
print[2], v.t. 1. Impress, stamp, (surface,
e.g. pat of butter, *with* seal, die, etc.; a
mark or figure *on, in*, yielding or other
surface); (fig.) impress (idea, scene, etc.,
on mind, memory). 2. Produce (book,
picture, etc., or abs.) by applying inked
types, blocks, or plates, to paper, vellum,
etc.; (of author or editor) cause (book,
MS.) to be so ~ed; express, publish, in
print, as *not bound to* ~ *every opinion you
hold*; write (words, or abs.) in imitation
of typography. 3. Mark (textile fabric)
with decorative design in colours; transfer (coloured design) from paper etc. to
unglazed surface of pottery. 4. (photog.).
(Also ~ *out, off*) produce (picture) by
transmission of light through negative.
Hence ~'ABLE a. [ME *prente, printe*, app.
f. prec.]
prin'ter, n. In vbl senses, esp.: one who
prints books; owner of printing business;
printing instrument; *P~s' Bible* (with
P~s for *Princes*, Ps. cxix. 161); ~'s DEVIL[1];
~'s *mark* (device, trade-mark); ~'s *pie*,
= PIE[3] n. [-ER[1]]
prin'ting, n. In vbl senses; ~-*ink*, ~-
press, (for ~ on paper etc. from types
etc.). [-ING[1]]
pri'or[1], n. Superior officer of religious
house or order, (in abbey) officer next
under abbot, so ~ESS[1] n. Hence or cogn.
~ATE[1](1), ~SHIP, nn. [late OE *prior* f. L
prior (foll.); in ME also f. OF *pri(o)ur*]
pri'or[2], a. & adv. 1. Earlier; antecedent
in time, order, or importance, (*to*). 2. adv.
~ *to*, before, as *existing* ~ *to his appointment*. So priŏ'RITY n. (also, an interest
having a ~ claim to consideration; in

recent use freq. with qualification, as *a first*, *top*, *~ity*). [L, f. OL *pri* before]

pri′orў, n. Monastery, nunnery, governed by prior(ess); *alien ~*, *~ alien*, (dependent on abbey in foreign country). [ME, f. AF *priorie*, med. L *prioria* (as prec., see -Y[1])]

‖ **prise.** See PRIZE[3].

pri′sm, n. Solid figure whose two ends are similar, equal, & parallel rectilineal figures, & whose sides are parallelograms; transparent body of this form, usu. triangular, with refracting surfaces at acute angle with each other; (loosely) spectrum produced by refraction through *~*, (pl.) prismatic colours; *~-glasses*, *binoculars* (in which triangular *~*s are used to shorten the instrument); PRUNE[1]*s & ~*. Hence **pris′m**AL (-z-) a. [f. LL f. Gk *prisma* -*matos* thing sawn (*prizō* saw)]

prismăt′ic (-z-), a. Of, like, a prism; *~ compass*, hand-compass used in survey work, with attached prism enabling the dial to be read while the sight is taken; *~ powder*, gunpowder whose grains are hexagonal prisms; (of colours) formed, distributed, etc., by transparent prism, (also) brilliant, so **pris′m**Y[2] (-z-) a.; *the ~ colours*, seven into which ray of light is separated by prism. Hence **prismăt′ICALLY** (-z-) adv. [as prec., see -IC]

pris′moid (-z-), n. Body like prism, with similar but unequal parallel polygonal ends. Hence **prismoid′**AL (-z-) a. [-OID]

pris′on (-zn), n., & v.t. **1.** Place in which person is kept in captivity, esp. building to which person is legally committed while awaiting trial or for punishment; custody, confinement, as *lie*, *put* (person), *in ~*; *~-bird*, = GAOL-bird; *~-breaking*, breaking out of lawfully confined person from *~*, so *~-breaker*; *~ editor* (hist.), editor of newspaper taking legal responsibility for its contents & serving terms of imprisonment entailed by conviction; *~-house* (usu. rhet.), *~*. **2.** v.t. (poet.). Imprison. [ME & OF *prisun*, *-on*, f. L *prensionem* (*pre(he)ndere prens-* seize, see -ION)]

pris′oner (-zn-), n. Person kept in prison; *~ (at the bar)*, person in custody on criminal charge & on trial; *~ of State*, *State ~*, (confined for political reasons); (also *~ of war*, abbr. *P.O.W.*) one who has been captured in war; *take* (person) *~*, seize & hold as *~*; (fig.) *am a ~* (confined by illness etc.) *to my room* or *chair*, *made her hand a ~* (secured it); *~s′ bars*, *base*, game played by two parties of boys etc., each occupying distinct base or home. [ME, f. OF *prisonier*, as prec., see -ER[2](2)]

pris′tine, a. Ancient, primitive, good old. [f. L *pristinus* former]

‖ **prith′ee** (-dhĭ), int. (arch.). Pray, please, as *tell me*, *~*. [= (I) pray thee]

priv′acў (*also* prī-), n. Being withdrawn from society or public interest, as *lived in absolute ~*, *must disturb your ~*; avoidance of publicity, as *in such matters ~ is impossible*. [ME ; PRIVATE, -ACY]

privat-docent, *-zent*, (prĕvaht′ dōtsĕnt′), n. (In German univv.) private teacher or lecturer recognized by university but not on salaried staff. [G]

priv′ate, a. & n. **1.** (Of person) not holding public office or official position; ‖ *~* (*soldier*), ordinary soldier without rank, one below non-commissioned officers (freq. prefixed, as *P~ Smith*); *~ member* of House of Commons (not member of Government). **2.** Kept, removed, from public knowledge, as *the matter was kept ~*, *had ~ reasons*. **3.** Not open to the public, as *~ door*, *news*, *came through ~ channels*, *~ boarding-house*, *carriage*, *hotel*, *theatricals*; *~ view* (of exhibition of pictures esp. before it is opened to the public). **4.** *~ eye*, *~ detective*; *~ house*, dwelling-house of *~* person (opp. to his shop or office, to public house, or to public building); *~ parts*, genitals (*~-protector*, guard worn at cricket etc.); *~ school* (‖ carried on for owner's profit, cf. PUBLIC; *~ schoolmaster*, of or in this). **5.** One's own, as *my ~ goods*, *property*; individual, personal, not affecting the community, as *motives of ~ malice*; (Parl.) *~ bill*, *act* (affecting individual or corporation only). **6.** Confidential, as *asked for some ~ conversation*; *this is for your ~ ear* (confidential). **7.** (Of place) retired, secluded; (arch., of person) given to retirement. **8.** *In ~*, *~ly*, in *~* company or life. **9.** n. pl. *~* parts. Hence *~*LY[2] adv. [ME, f. L *privatus*, orig. p.p. of *privare* deprive]

privateer′, n. Armed vessel owned & officered by private persons holding commission from government (*letters of* MARQUE) & authorized to use it against hostile nation esp. in capture of merchant shipping, whence *~*ING[1](1) n.; commander, (pl.) crew, of this. [f. prec. +-EER, prob. after *volunteer*]

privā′tion, n. Loss, absence, (of quality), as *cold is the ~ of heat*; want of the comforts or necessaries of life, as *died of ~*, *suffered many ~s*. [ME, f. L *privatio* (PRIVATE, -ATION)]

priv′ative, a. Consisting in, marked by, the loss or removal or absence of some quality or attribute, as *cold is merely ~* (cf. prec.); (of terms) denoting privation or absence of quality etc.; (gram., of particles etc.) expressing privation, as (Gk gram.) *alpha ~* (*a-* = not-). Hence *~*LY[2] adv. [f. F (*-if*, *-ive*) or L *privativus* (as PRIVATE, see -IVE)]

priv′ĕt, n. Bushy evergreen shrub with small white flowers & small shining black berries, much used for hedges; *~-hawk*, large species of moth depositing eggs on *~*. [16th c., of unkn. orig.]

priv′ilĕge, n., & v.t. **1.** Right, advantage, immunity, belonging to person, class, or office (*~ of Parliament*, those of either House or its members; *breach of ~*, esp., infringement of any of these); special advantage or benefit, as *to converse with him was a ~*; *~* (BENEFIT[1]) *of clergy*; *bill of ~*, petition of peer demanding to be tried by his peers; *writ of ~*, writ to deliver *~d* person from custody when arrested in civil suit; monopoly, patent, granted to individual, corporation, etc.; || *~ cab* (admitted to stand for hire in private places esp. railway station). **2.** v.t. Invest with *~*, allow (person *to* do) as *~*; exempt (person *from* burden etc.). Hence **priv′ileg**ED[1] (-ĭjd) a. [ME; (n.) f. L *privilegium* bill, law, affecting an individual (*privus* private + *lex legis* law), & OF *privilege*; (vb) f. med. L *privilegiare* & OF *privilegier*]

priv′ity̆, n. (Law) any relation between two parties that is recognized by law, e.g. that of blood, lease, service; being privy (*to* designs etc.). [ME, f. OF *privete* f. L *privus* private, see -TY]

priv′y̆, a. & n. **1.** (Of things, places, etc.) hidden, secluded; *~ parts*, genitals; (of action) secret, whence **priv′ILY**[2] adv.; *~ to*, in the secret of (person's designs etc.). **2.** || *P~ Council*, sovereign's private counsellors, (in Great Britain) body of advisers chosen by sovereign (now chiefly as personal dignity, most functions being performed by Cabinet, committees, etc.) together with princes of blood, archbishops, etc.; || *~ counsellor, -cillor*, private adviser, esp. (abbr. *P.C.*) member of P~ Council; || *~ purse*, allowance from public revenue for monarch's private expenses, keeper of this; || *~ seal*, seal affixed to documents that are afterwards to pass, or that do not require, the Great Seal; *Lord* (keeper of the) *P~ Seal*. **3.** n. Latrine (arch., exc. U.S.); (law) person having a part or interest in any action, matter, or thing. [ME & OF *prive* PRIVATE]

prize[1], n., & v.t. **1.** Reward given as symbol of victory or superiority to student in school or college who excels in attainments; to competitor in athletic contest, to exhibitor of best specimen of manufactured products, works of art, etc., in exhibition; (fig.) anything striven for or worth striving for, as *many ~s in the Church, missed all the great ~s of life*; money or money's worth offered for competition in lottery etc. **2.** (attrib.). *~ ox, poem*, etc. (to which~ is adjudged in show, competition, etc.). **3.** || *~ fellowship* (given as reward for eminence in examination), *~ fellow*, holder of this; *~-fight*, boxing--match for money, so *~-fighter, ~-fighting*, nn.; *~′man*, winner of (often specified) *~*, as *Smith's ~man*, winner of Smith's P~; *~-ring*, enclosed area (now usu. square) for, (fig.) practice of, *~-fighting*. **4.** v.t. Value highly, as *we~ liberty more than life*. Hence *~′*LESS a. [(n.) diff. sp. of PRICE;

(vb) ME, f. OF *prisier*, var. of *preisier* PRAISE]

prize[2], n., & v.t. Ship, property, captured at sea in virtue of rights of war; || *~-court*, department of admiralty court concerned with *~s*; || *~-money* (realized by sale of *~*, esp. hist., such money as awarded to crew of capturing ship); *make~ of* (cargo, ship, etc.), seize thus; *become* (*lawful* etc.) *~*, be thus seized; (fig.) find or windfall (*see what a~ I have found!*); (v.t.) make *~ of*. [ME & OF *prise* taking, fem. p.p. of *prendre* f. L *prehendere -hens-* seize; 16th c. sp. *prize* & later identified w. PRIZE[1]]

|| **prize**[3], *-se*, v.t., & n. Force (lid etc. *up, out*, box etc. *open*) by leverage; (n.) leverage, purchase. [ME & OF *prise* levering instrument, as prec.; 17th c. vb f. n.]

pro[1], prep. *~ bŏn′ŏ pŭb′lĭcō*, for the public good; *~ form′a* adv. & a., (done) for form's sake; *~ hăc vĭ′ce*, for this occasion only; *~ rāt′a* adv. & a., proportional(ly); *~ rē nāt′a* adv. & a., for an occasion as it arises, as *a meeting held~ re nata, a~ re nata meeting*; *~ tăn′tŏ*, so far, to that extent; *~ tĕm′porĕ* adv. & a. (abbr. *pro tem.*), for the time, as *made secretary pro tem., the pro tem. secretary*. [L]

pro[2], n. (colloq.; pl. *~s*). A PROFESSIONAL. [abbr.]

pro-[1], pref. (before vowel) = L *pro* in front of, for, on behalf of, instead of, on account of. As living E pref. **1.** In sense ' substitute(d) for ', as *~-cathed′ral* a. & n., (church) used as substitute for cathedral, || *~-proc′tor*, assistant or deputy proctor in univv., *~-rec′tor*, vice-rector in univv. etc.; *~-leg*, fleshy abdominal limb of larvae of some insects, e.g. caterpillars. **2.** In sense ' (person) favouring or siding with ' (cf. ANTI-), as *~-Bo′er* a. & n., *~-Brit′ish*, *~-educational*, *~-Neg′ro* a. & n., *~-pap′ist* a. & n., *~-slav′ery*, *~-ta′riff reform*.

pro-[2], pref. = Gk *pro* before (in time, place, order, etc.) in wds f. Gk & in mod. scientific wds.

prō′a, n. Malay boat, esp. a type of sailing-boat. [f. Malay *pra*(*h*)*u*, also used in E]

prō and cŏn, adv. & n. **1.** (Of arguments or reasons) for & against, on both sides. **2.** n. pl. *Pros & cons*, reasons for & against. [f. L *pro et contra*]

prŏbabil′ior|ism, n. (R.-C. casuistry). Doctrine that the side on which evidence preponderates ought to be followed (cf. foll.). So *~*IST n. [f. L *probabilior* more PROBABLE + -ISM]

prŏb′abil|ism, n. Doctrine that where authorities differ any course may be followed for which recognized doctor of the Church can be cited (cf. prec.); theory that there is no certain knowledge, but may be grounds of belief sufficient for practical life. So *~*IST n. [as PROBABLE + -ISM]

For other words in *pro-* see PRO-[1].

prŏbabil'it|ў, n. Quality of being probable ; *in all ~y*, most likely ; *there is no ~y* (likelihood) *of his coming* ; (most) probable event, as *what are the ~ies, the ~y is that he will come* ; (math.) likelihood of an event, measured by the ratio of the favourable cases to the whole number of cases possible, as *from a bag containing 3 red balls & 7 white the ~y of a red ball's being drawn first is* 3|10. [f. F *probabilité* or L *probabilitas* (as foll., see -TY)]

prŏb'able, a. & n. 1. That may be expected to happen or prove true, likely, as *reckon the ~ cost, it is ~ that he forgot, gives a ~ account of the matter.* **2.** n. A ~ candidate, member, selection, etc. Hence **prŏb'abLY² adv.** [ME, f. OF, or f. L *probabilis* (*probare* PROVE, see -BLE)]

prŏb'ăng, n. Surgeon's strip of whalebone with sponge, button, etc., at end for introducing into throat. [altered f. inventor's wd *provang* (orig. unkn.), perh. on *probe*]

prŏb'ate, n. Official proving of will; verified copy of will with certificate as handed to executors ; ~ *duty*, tax on personal property of deceased testator. [ME, f. L *probatum* neut. p.p. of *probare* PROVE]

proba'tion, n. Testing of conduct or character of person esp. of candidate for membership in religious body etc. (*on ~*, undergoing it before full admission etc.); moral trial or discipline; system of releasing young criminals esp. first offenders on suspended sentence during good behaviour under supervision of person (~ *officer*) acting as friend & advisor. [ME, f. OF *probacion* or L *probatio* (as PROVE, see -ATION)]

proba'tion|arў (-sho-), **a.** Of, serving for, done in the way of, probation, so ~AL **a.**; undergoing probation. [-ARY¹]

proba'tioner (-sho-), **n.** Person on probation, e.g. hospital nurse at early stage of training; offender under PROBATION. Hence ~SHIP n. [-ER¹]

prŏb'ative, a. Affording proof, evidential. [f. L *probativus* (as PROVE, see -IVE)]

prŏbe, n., & v.t. 1. Blunt-ended surgical instrument usu. of silver for exploring wound etc.; *(fig.; f. vb) investigation. **2.** v.t. Explore (wound, part of body) with ~, penetrate (thing) with sharp instrument; (fig.) examine closely, sound, (person, motive, report, etc.). [(vb f. n.) f. LL *proba* PROOF, med. L examination]

prŏb'itў, n. Uprightness, honesty. [f. L *probitas* (*probus* good, see -TY)]

prŏb'lěm, n. 1. Doubtful or difficult question, as *how to prevent it is a ~, the ~ of ventilation* ; (attrib.)*~ child* (difficult to control, unruly), *~ play, novel* (in which social or other ~ is treated). **2.** Thing hard to understand, as *his whole conduct is a ~ to me.* **3.** (Geom.) proposition in which something has to be constructed (cf. THEOREM); (phys., math.) inquiry starting from given conditions to

investigate a fact, result or law, as *Kepler's ~* ; (chess) arrangement of pieces on the board in which player is challenged to accomplish specified result, often under prescribed conditions. [f. ME & OF *probleme* f. L f. Gk *problēma -matos* f. PRO²(*ballō* throw)]

prŏblěmăt'ĭc(al), aa. Doubtful, questionable, as *its success is ~, the whole question is ~* ; (log.) enunciating or supporting what is possible but not necessarily true. Hence **prŏblěmăt'ĭcaLLY² adv.** [f. F *problématique* or LL f. Gk *problēmatikos* (as prec., see -IC)]

prŏb'lěm(at)ĭst, nn. One who studies or composes (esp. chess) problems. [-IST]

prŏbŏscĭd'ean, -ian, aa. & nn. Having a proboscis ; of, like, a proboscis ; (mammal) of the order *Proboscidea*, containing elephant & extinct allies. [f. mod. L *Proboscidea* +-AN]

probŏs'cĭs, n. Elephant's trunk ; long flexible snout of tapir etc.; elongated part of mouth of some insects; sucking organ in some worms; (joc.) human nose; *~-monkey* (with nose projecting far beyond mouth). So **probŏscĭdĭf'EROUS, probŏscĭd'ĭFORM, aa.** [L, gen. *-cidis*, f. Gk *proboskis* f. PRO²(*boskō* feed)]

procěd'ur|e (-dyer), **n.** Proceeding; mode of conducting business (esp. in parliament) or legal action. Hence ~AL (-dyer-) **a.**, of or relating to ~**e.** [f. F *procédure* (as foll., see -URE)]

proceed', v.i. Go on, make one's way, (*to* place); go on (*with, in*, action, investigation, remarks, etc., *to* another subject, *to* do); adopt course of action, as *how shall we ~?*; take legal proceedings *against* person; (abs.) go on to say, as '*in either case*' *he ~ed* '*our course is clear*'; || ~ *to* (take) *the degree of M.A.*, ~ (take degree of) *M.A.*; (of action) be carried on, take place, as *the case, the play, will now ~*; come forth, issue, originate, as *sobs heard to ~ from next room, volumes ~ from the Pitt Press, exertions ~ from a false hope.* [ME, f. OF *proceder* f. L PRO¹(*cedere* cess-go)]

proceed'ĭng, n. In vbl senses, esp.: action, piece of conduct, as *a high-handed ~*; *legal ~s*, (steps taken in) legal action, as *shall institute legal ~s* (go to law); (as title) *P~s of Royal Society* etc. [-ING¹]

prŏ'ceeds, n. pl. Produce, outcome, profit, as *the ~ will be devoted to charity.* [f. PROCEED v.; sing. now obs.]

procěleusmăt'ĭc, a. & n. (prosody). ~ (*foot*), metrical foot of four short syllables. [f. LL f. Gk *prokeleusmatikos* f. *prokeleusma* exhortation f. PRO²(*keleuō* command), see -IC]

procěllar'ian, a. & n. (Bird) of the genus or family to which petrels belong. [f. L *procella* storm, see -ARIAN]

prŏ'cěss¹, n., & v.t. 1. Progress, course, esp. *in ~ of construction* etc., being constructed etc., *in ~ of time*, as time goes on; course of action, proceeding, esp. method of operation in manufacture, printing, photography, etc.; natural or involuntary operation, series of changes. 2. (Print from block produced by) method other than simple engraving by hand. 3. Action at law, formal commencement of this, summons or writ (~-*server*, sheriff's officer). 4. (anat., zool., bot.). Outgrowth, protuberance. 5. v.t. Institute legal ~ against (person); treat (material), subject (food) to special ~, reproduce (drawing), by a ~. Hence ~ER[1], ~OR, nn. [ME & OF *proces* f. L *processus* -*ūs*, as PROCEED; vb f. n., exc. legal use f. OF *processer*]

process'[2], v.i. (colloq.). Walk in procession. [back formation f. foll.]

proce'**ssion** (-shn), n., & v.i. & t. Proceeding of body of persons (or of boats etc.) in orderly succession, esp. as religious ceremony or on festive etc. occasion, as *go, walk, in* ~; body of persons doing this; (fig.) ill-contested race; (theol.) emanation of the Holy Ghost; ~ *caterpillars*, kinds that go in ~, so ~ *moth*, whence ~ARY[1] (-shŏ) a.; (v.i.) go in ~; (v.t.) walk along (street) in ~. [ME, f. OF f. L *processionem* (as PROCEED, see -ION)]

proce'**ssional** (-sho-), a. & n. 1. Of processions; used, carried, sung, in processions. 2. n. ~ hymn; (eccl.) office-book of ~ hymns etc. [f. med. L *processionalis* a., -*le* n., (as prec., see -AL)]

proce'**ssion**|**ist** (-sho-), n. One who goes in procession. So ~IZE v.i. [-IST]

procès verbal (prŏsă'vărbahl'), n. (pl. -*baux* pr. -bō). Written report of proceedings, minutes; (Fr. law) written statement of facts in support of charge. [F]

prŏ'**chronism** (-k-), n. Referring of event etc. to an earlier than the true date, as *races held in June & called by a ~ the Mays*. [f. PRO-[2] on ANACHRONISM]

proclaim', v.t. Announce publicly & officially (thing, *that*); declare (war, peace); announce officially the accession of (sovereign); declare (person, thing) officially to be a (traitor etc.); declare publicly or openly (thing, *that*); place (district etc.) under legal restrictions, prohibit (meeting etc.), by declaration, as *the whole county is ~ed*. So **prŏclamā**'TION n., **proclăm**'**atory** a. [ME -*clame* f. L PRO[1](*clamare* cry out), sp. after CLAIM]

proclit'**ic**, a. & n. (gram.). (Monosyllable) closely attached in pronunciation to following word & having itself no accent, as *at home*'. [f. PRO-[2] on ENCLITIC]

procliv'**itў**, n. Tendency (*to, towards*, action or habit, esp. bad one, *to* do). [f. L *proclivitas* f. PRO[1](*clivis* f. *clivus* slope), see -TY]

prŏcŏn'**sul**, n. (Rom. hist.) governor of Roman province, in later republic usu. an ex-consul; (under empire) governor of senatorial province; ‖ (rhet.) governor of modern colony etc.; (*pro-consul*) deputy consul. Hence or cogn. ~AR[1] a., ~ATE[1](1), ~SHIP, nn. [ME, f. L, earlier *pro consule* (one acting) for consul]

procrăs'**tin**|**āte**, v.i. & t. Defer action, be dilatory; (rare) postpone (action). Hence or cogn. ~**āting**LY[2] adv., ~A'TION, ~**ātor**, nn., ~**ātive**, ~**ātory**, aa. [f. L PRO[1](*crastinare* f. *crastinus* of tomorrow f. *cras*), see -ATE[3]]

prŏc'**rē**|**āte**, v.t. Beget, generate, (offspring, or abs). Hence or cogn. ~ANT, ~**ātive**, aa., ~A'TION n. [f. L PRO[1](*creare* CREATE)]

Procrŭs'**tēan**, a. Tending to produce uniformity by violent methods. [f. Gk *Prokroustēs*, lit. stretcher, name of fabulous robber who fitted victims to his bed by stretching or mutilation, see -AN]

‖ **prŏc**'**tor**, n. (Camb. & Oxf. Univv.) each of two officers (*senior, junior, ~*) appointed annually & charged with various functions esp. discipline of persons *in statu pupillari*; (law) person managing causes in court (now chiefly eccl.) that administers civil or canon law; *King's, Queen's, P~*, official who has right to intervene in probate, divorce, & nullity cases when collusion or suppression of facts is alleged. Hence **prŏctor**'IAL a., ~SHIP n. [late ME syncopation of PROCURATOR]

‖ **prŏc**'**toriz**|**e**, -**is**|**e** (-īz), v.t. Exercise proctor's authority on (undergraduate etc.). Hence ~A'TION n. [-IZE]

procŭm'**bent**, a. Lying on the face, prostrate; (bot.) growing along the ground. [f. L PRO[1](*cumbere* lay oneself) fall forwards, -ENT]

prŏcŭrā'**tion**, n. Procuring, obtaining, bringing about, so **procūr**'AL(2), **procūr**'ANCE, nn.; function, authorized action, of attorney; ‖ (eccl.) provision of entertainment for bishop or other visitor by incumbent etc., now commuted to money payment; (fee for) negotiation of loan; procurer's trade or offence. [ME, f. OF, or f. L *procuratio* (as PROCURE, see -ATION)]

prŏc'**ūrātor**, n. (Rom. hist.) treasury officer in imperial province; agent, proxy, esp. one who has power of attorney; magistrate in some Italian cities; ‖ ~ *fiscal*, public prosecutor of district in Scotland. Hence or cogn. **prŏcūrātor**'IAL a., ~SHIP n. [ME, f. OF (-*tour*) or L *procurator* (as PROCURE, see -OR)]

prŏc'**ūratorў**, n. Authorization to act for another, esp. *letters of* ~. [f. LL *procuratorium* neut. adj. (as PROCURE, see -ORY)]

prŏc'**ūrātrix**, n. Inmate of nunnery managing its temporal concerns. [L, as foll., -TRIX]

procure', v.t. & i. Obtain by care or effort, acquire, as *must ~ a copy, cannot ~ employment*; (arch.) bring about, as ~*d his*

death by poison; act as procurer or procuress. Hence **procŭr′ABLE** a., **~MENT**
(-ŭrm-) n. [ME, f. OF *procurer* f. L PRO¹-
(*curare* see to)]

procŭr′|er, n. In vbl senses, esp. man or
woman who procures women for gratification of another's lust. So **~ess¹** n. [ME
& AF *procurour* f. L as PROCURATOR]

prŏd, v.t. & i. (-dd-), & n. **1.** Poke with
pointed instrument, end of stick, etc.;
(fig.) stimulate to action; make **~ding**
motion *at.* **2.** n. Poke, thrust, pointed
instrument. [16th c., perh. imit.]

prŏdĕli′sion (-zhn), n. Elision of initial
vowel (as in *I'm* for *I am*). [f. L *prod-* =
PRO-¹+ELISION]

prŏd′igal, a. & n. Recklessly wasteful
(person); lavish *of*; **~** *son*, repentant
sinner, returned wanderer, etc. (*Luke* xv.
11–32). Hence or cogn. **~ITY** (-ăl⊱) n.,
~LY² adv. [obs. F, or f. LL *prodigalis* f.
L *prodigus* wasteful, see -AL]

prŏd′igalize, -ise (-īz), v.t. Spend
lavishly. [-IZE]

prodi′gious (-jus), a. Marvellous, amazing; enormous; abnormal. Hence **~LY²**
adv., **~NESS** n., (-jus-). [f. L *prodigiosus*
(as foll., see -OUS)]

prŏd′igy̌, n. Marvellous thing, esp. one
out of the course of nature; wonderful
example *of* (some quality); person endowed with surprising qualities, esp. precocious child, as (attrib.) *a ~ violinist.*
[f. L *prodigium* portent]

prŏd′rom|e, n. Preliminary book or
treatise (*to* another); (med.) premonitory
symptom (*of*), whence **~AL**, **prodrŏm′ic**,
aa. [F, f. mod. L f. Gk PRO² (*dromos*
running)]

prŏd′ūce¹, n. Amount produced, yield,
esp. in assay of ore; (also *raw ~*) agricultural & natural products collectively; result (*of* labour, efforts, etc.). [f. foll.]

produce′², v.t. Bring forward for inspection or consideration, as *will ~ evidence,
witnesses, reasons, ~ your tickets*; bring
(play, performer, book, etc.) before the
public; (geom.) extend, continue, (line *to*
a point); manufacture (goods) from raw
materials etc.; bring about, cause, (a sensation etc.); (of land etc.) yield (produce);
(of animal or plant) bear, yield, (offspring,
fruit). So **prodūcIBIL′ITY** n., **prodŭ′cIBLE**
a. [ME, f. L PRO¹(*ducere duct-* lead)]

prodū′cer, n. In vbl senses, esp.: (pol.
econ.) one who produces article of consumption (cf. CONSUMER); (cinemat.) person generally responsible for production
of a film (apart from direction of the acting);*~ gas*, combustible gas, properly that
formed by passing air through red-hot
carbon, but often used for the 'semi-water
gas' formed by passing steam and air
through red-hot carbon. [f. prec.+-ER²]

prŏd′uct, n. Thing produced by natural
process or manufacture; result, as *the ~
of his labours*; (math.) quantity obtained
by multiplying quantities together;

(chem.) compound not previously existing in a body but formed during its decomposition. [ME, as PRODUCE²]

produc′tion, n. Producing; total yield;
thing produced, esp. literary or artistic
work. [ME, f. OF, f. L *productionem* (as
prec., see -ION)]

produc′tive, a. Producing, tending to
produce, as *~ of figs, ~ of great annoyance*; (pol. econ.) producing commodities
of exchangeable value, as *~ labour(er)*;
producing abundantly, as *a ~ soil, mine,
writer.* Hence **~LY²** adv., **~NESS** n., **prŏ-
ductiv′ITY** n., capacity to produce,
quality or state of being *~*, production
per man-hour, (loosely) intensified production. [f. F (-*if*, -*ive*), or LL *productivus*
(as PRODUCE², see -IVE)]

prō′em, n. Preface, preamble, to book or
speech, beginning, prelude. Hence **prō-
ēm′IAL** a. [ME, f. OF *pro(h)eme* f. L f. Gk
prooimion]

profāne′¹, v.t. Treat (sacred thing) with
irreverence or disregard; violate, pollute,
(what is entitled to respect). So **prŏfan-
A′TION** n. [ME *prophane* f. OF *prophaner*
f. L *profanare*, as foll.]

profāne′², a. Not belonging to what is
sacred or biblical, as *~ history, literature,
writer, sacred and~ love*; not initiated into
religious rites or any esoteric knowledge;
(of rites etc.) heathen; irreverent, blasphemous, so **profān′ITY** n. Hence **~LY²**
adv., **~NESS** n. [ME, f. OF *prophane* or
med. L *-phanus* f. L PRO¹(*fanus* f. *fanum*
temple) before i.e. outside the temple]

profess′, v.t. & i. Lay claim to (quality,
feeling), pretend (*to* be or do), as *they ~
extreme regret, does not ~ to be a scholar*;
openly declare, as *they ~ themselves quite
content, I ~ (that) this is news to me*;
affirm one's faith in or allegiance to (religion, God, Christ); make (law, medicine,
flute-playing, the flute, etc.) one's profession or business; teach (subject) as
professor; perform duties of a professor.
[ME, f. L PRO¹(*fitēri fess-* = *falēri* confess;]

professed′ (-st), a. Self-acknowledged, as
a~ Christian; alleged, ostensible, whence
profess′edLY² adv.; claiming to be duly
qualified, as *a ~ anatomist*; *~ monk, nun*
(that has taken vows of religious order).
[p.p. of prec.]

profe′ssion (-shn), n. Declaration, avow-
al, as *in practice if not in ~, accept my
sincere ~s of regard, spare me these ~s*;
declaration of belief in a religion; vow
made on entering, fact of being in, a
religious order; vocation, calling, esp.
one that involves some branch of learning
or science, as *the learned~s* (divinity, law,
medicine), *the military~, a carpenter by~,*
whence *~LESS* a.; *the* body of persons engaged in this, esp. (theatr. sl.) actors, as
lets apartments to the ~. [ME, f. OF, f. L
professionem (as PROFESS, see -ION)]

profe′ssional (-sho-), a. & n. **1.** Of,

belonging to, connected with, a profession, as ~ *men, etiquette, jealousy*; ~ *politician, agitator*, etc. (making a trade of politics etc.); ~ *cricketer, golfer*, etc. (playing for money, cf. AMATEUR). **2. n.** ~ man, esp. (abbr. *pro*)~ cricketer, golfer, etc. Hence ~LY² adv. [-AL]

profe'ssional|ism (-sho-), n. Qualities, stamp, of a profession; practice of employing professionals. So ~IZE(3) v.t. [-ISM]

profess'or, n. ‖ One who makes profession (*of* a religion); public teacher of high rank, esp. holder of a chair in university (prefixed as title, abbr. *Prof.*), whence ~ATE¹(1), ~ESS¹, **prŏfessŏr'iATE**¹(1), ~SHIP, nn., **prŏfessŏr'IAL** a., **profèssŏr'iaLLY²**adv.; (as grandiose title)*P~ Smith's Boxing Dormice* etc.; (sl.) professional. [ME, f. AF -*our* or L (as PROFESS, see -OR)]

prŏff'er, v.t., & n. 1. Offer (gift, services, etc., arch. *to* do; esp. in p.p.). **2. n.** Offer. [ME; (n. f. AF *profre*) f. AF *proffrir* (PRO-¹ +*offrir* OFFER)]

profi'cient (-shnt), a. & n. Adept, expert, (*in, at,* an art etc., *in doing*). Hence **profi'ciENCY** n., ~LY² adv., (-shn-). [f. L as PROFIT¹, see -ENT]

prŏf'ile (-fēl, -fîl), n., & v.t. **1.** Drawing, silhouette, or other representation, of side view esp. of human face, whence ~IST n.; drawn etc. *in* ~*e* (as seen from one side); side outline esp. of the human face; (journalism) short biographical or character sketch; (fortif.) transverse vertical section of fort, comparative thickness of earthwork etc.; flat outline piece of scenery on stage. **2. v.t.** Represent in ~*e*, give a ~*e* to. [(n. f. It. *profilo* now *proff-*) f. It. (now *proff-*) PRO¹(*filare* spin f. L *filare* f. *filum* thread)]

prŏf'it¹, n. Advantage, benefit, as *have studied it to my* ~, *no* ~ *in such pursuits*; pecuniary gain, excess of returns over outlay; (book-keep.) ~ *& loss account*, account in which gains are credited & losses debited so as to show net ~ or loss at any time;~-*sharing*(of~s esp. between employer & employed).· Hence ~LESS a., ~lèssLY² adv., ~lèssNESS n. [ME, f. OF, f. L *profectus -ûs* f. PRO¹(*ficere fect-= facere* do) advance]

prŏf'it², v.t. & i. (Of thing) be of advantage to (person etc. orig. indirect object), as *it will not* ~ *him, what will it* ~ *him?*; be of advantage; (of person etc.) be benefited or assisted, as *hope to* ~ *by your advice,* ~*ed by the confusion to make my escape.* [ME, f. OF *profiter* as prec.]

prŏf'itable, a. Beneficial, useful, as ~ *conservation*; yielding profit, lucrative, as *a* ~ *speculation.* Hence ~NESS n., **prŏf'itabLY²** adv. [ME, f. OF (PROFIT¹+-ABLE)]

profiteer', v.i., & n. 1. Make inordinate profits out of the State's or the consumer's straits (esp. of contractors & traders in times of scarcity). **2. n.** ~ing person. [PROFIT, -EER]

prŏf'lig|ate, a. & n. 1. Licentious, dissolute; recklessly extravagant. **2. n.** ~ate person. Hence ~ACY n., ~ateLY² adv. [f. L PRO¹(*fligare* = *fligere* strike down) overthrow, ruin, see -ATE³]

profound', a. & n. 1. Having, showing, great knowledge or insight, as ~ *statesman, inquiry, treatise*; demanding deep study or thought, as ~ *doctrines*; (of state or quality) deep, intense, unqualified, as *fell into a* ~ *sleep, take a* ~ *interest, simulated a* ~ *indifference*; having, coming from, extending to, a great depth, as ~ *crevasses, a* ~ (deep-drawn) *sigh,* ~ (deep-seated) *gangrene.* **2. n.** (poet.). *The* vast depth (*of* ocean, futurity, the soul, etc.). Hence or cogn. ~LY² adv., ~NESS, profŭn'DITY, nn. [ME, f. OF *profound, -fond* f. L PRO¹(*fundus* bottom) deep]

profūse', a. Lavish, extravagant, (*in, of,* gifts, promises, expenditure, etc.); (of things) exuberantly plentiful. Hence or cogn. ~LY² (-sl-) adv., ~NESS (-sn-), profū'SION (-zhn), nn. [f. L PRO¹(*fundere fus-* pour)]

prŏg¹, n. (sl.). Food, esp. for journey or excursion. [17th c.; prob. f. obs. (exc. dial.) *prog* to forage etc.]

‖ **prŏg²,** ‖ **prŏgg'ins** (-gĭnz), nn. & vv.t. (sl.). Proctor at Oxford or Cambridge; (v.t.) proctorize. [abbr.]

progĕn'itive, a. Capable of, connected with, the production of offspring. [as foll., -IVE]

progĕn'it|or, n. Ancestor of person, animal, or plant; (fig.) political or intellectual predecessor, original of a copy. Hence ~ŏr'IAL a., ~orSHIP, ~rESS¹, nn. [ME, f. OF *progeniteur* or L *progenitor* f. PRO¹(*gignere genit-* beget), see -OR]

progĕn'iture, n. (Begetting of) offspring. [as prec., see -URE]

prŏ'gĕny̆, n. Offspring of person, animal, or plant; descendants; (fig.) issue, outcome. [ME, f. OF *progenie* f. L *progenies* f. PRO¹(*gignere* beget)]

‖ **prŏggins.** See PROG².

proglŏtt'|is, n. (pl. ~*ĭdēs*). Segment of tapeworm. [f. Gk PRO²(*glōssis* f. *glōssa, -tta*, tongue), from its shape]

prŏg'nath|ous (*or* -nă²-), a. With projecting jaws; (of jaws) projecting. So **prŏgnăth'IC** a., ~ISM(2) n. [f. PRO-² +Gk *gnathos* jaw+-OUS]

prŏgnŏs'is, n. (pl. ~*osēs*). Prognostication, esp. (med.) forecast of course of disease. [LL, f. Gk PRO²(*gnōsis* f. *gnō-* know)]

prŏgnŏs'tic, n. & a. **1.** Pre-indication, omen, (*of*); prediction, forecast. **2. adj.** Foretelling, predictive, (*of*). [(n. ME, f. OF *pronostique*) f. L f. Gk *prognōstikon* f. PRO²(*gignōskō* learn), -IC]

prŏgnŏs'tic|āte, v.t. Foretell (event, *that*); (of things) betoken. Hence or cogn.

~ABLE, ~ATIVE, ~ATORY, aa., ~A'TION, ~ATOR, nn. [f. med. L *pro(g)nosticare* (as prec.), see -ATE[3]]

prŏg'rămme, -ăm, n., & v.t. **1.** Descriptive notice of series of events, e.g. of course of study, concert, etc.; definite plan of intended proceedings; (colloq.) *what is the ~ for* (what are we going to do) *today?*; *~-music* (intended to suggest series of scenes or events); *~ picture* (cinemat.), film of some length forming part, but not the main feature, of the ~. **2.** v.t. Make a ~ or definite plan of. [f. LL f. Gk *programma* f. PRO[2](*graphō* write) write publicly; *-me* now usu., but cf. *diagram, telegram,* etc.]

prŏg'rèss[1], n. Forward or onward movement in space, as *made slow ~, continued his ~*; *an inquiry is now in ~* (going on); advance, development, as *made no ~ in his studies, the ~ of civilization, disease made rapid ~*; ‖ (arch.) state journey, official tour, esp. *royal ~.* [ME, app. f. OF *progresse,* f. L PRO[1] (*gredi gress-* = *gradi* walk)]

progrèss'[2], v.i. Move forward or onward; be carried on, as *the controversy still ~es;* advance, develop, as *we ~ in knowledge, science~es.* [f. prec.; Amer. revival of obs. E, later re-adopted into E]

progrè'ssion (-shn), n. Progress, as *mode of ~;* (math.) ARITHMETICAL, GEOMETRICAL, HARMONIC, ~; (mus.) passing from one note or chord to another. Hence ~AL (-sho-) a. [ME, f. OF or L *progressio* (as PROGRESS[1], see -ION)]

progrè'ssionist (-sho-), n. Advocate of progress e.g. in political or social matters (also **prŏg'rèssist** n.); one who holds that life on the earth has been marked by gradual progression to higher forms. [-IST]

progrèss'ive, a. & n. **1.** Moving forward, as ~ *motion;* proceeding step by step, successive; ~ *whist* etc. (played by several sets of players at different tables, certain players passing after each round to next table); advancing in social conditions, character, efficiency, etc., as *a ~ nation;* (of disease) continuously increasing; favouring progress or reform, as ~ *principles, party,* whence **progrèss'ivism** n. **2.** n. Advocate of ~ policy. Hence ~LY[2] adv., ~NESS n. [F (-*if, -ive,* as PROGRESS[1], see -IVE]

prohib'it, v.t. Forbid, debar, (action, thing, person *from doing*). Hence or cogn. ~ER[1], ~OR, nn. [ME, f. L PRO[1](*hibēre hibit-* = *habēre* hold)]

prohibi'tion (-õib-), n. Forbidding; edict, order, that forbids; forbidding by law of sale of intoxicants, whence ~IST (-õibĭsho-) n.; (law) writ from High Court of Justice forbidding inferior court to proceed in suit as being beyond its cognizance. [ME, f. OF, or L *prohibitio* (as prec., see -ION)]

prohib'itive, a. Prohibiting; serving to prevent the use or abuse or purchase of a thing, as ~ *tax, published at a ~ price.* Hence or cogn. ~LY[2] adv., ~NESS n., **prohib'itory** a. [F (-*if, -ive*), as PROHIBIT, see -IVE]

projĕct'[1], v.t. & i. Plan, contrive, (scheme, course of action, etc.); cast, throw, impel, (body *into* space etc.); ~ *oneself,* go out of oneself *into* another's feelings, the future, etc., (spirit.) make a phantom of oneself visible to a distant' person; (chem.) cast (substance *into, on,* etc.); cause (light, shadow) to fall on surface etc.; (fig.) cause (idea etc.) to take shape; (geom.) draw straight lines from a centre through every point of (given figure) to produce corresponding figure on a surface by intersecting it, draw (such lines), produce (such corresponding figure); make projection of (earth, sky, etc.); (intr.) protrude. [f. L PRO[1](*jicĕre ject-* = *jacĕre* throw)]

prŏj'ĕct[2], n. Plan, scheme. [ME, as prec.]

projĕc'tile, a. & n. **1.** Impelling, as ~ *force;* capable of being projected by force, esp. from gun. **2.** n. ~ missile. [as prec. +-ILE]

projĕc'tion, n. **1.** Throwing, casting. **2.** Transmutation of metals, as *powder of ~,* alchemists' powder of philosophers' stone. **3.** Planning. **4.** Protruding; protruding thing; thrusting forward. **5.** (geom.). Projecting of a figure (see PROJECT[1]); ~ *of a point,* point in derived figure corresponding to point in original figure. **6.** Representation on plane surface of (any part of) surface of earth or of celestial sphere, as *Mercator's ~* (in which points of compass preserve same direction all over the map). **7.** Mental image viewed as objective reality. **8.** (cinemat.). Display of films by throwing image on screen, whence ~IST (-sho-) n. [f. L *projectio* (as prec., see -ION), or f. F]

projĕc'tive, a. (Geom.) of, derived by, projection, ~ *property* of a figure (unchanged after projection); mentally projecting or projected, as ~ *imagination.* Hence ~LY[2] adv. [[as prec., see -IVE]

projĕc'tor, n. One who forms a project; promoter of speculative companies; apparatus for projecting rays of light or throwing image on cinematograph screen. [as prec., see -OR]

prolăpse', v.i., & n. (path.). Slip forward or down out of place; (n.) = foll. [f. L PRO[1](*labi laps-* slip); n. f. foll.]

prolăp'sus, n. (path.). Slipping forward or down of part of organ esp. of uterus or rectum. [LL, gen. *-ūs,* as prec.]

prōl'āte a. (Geom., of spheroid) lengthened in direction of polar diameter (cf. OBLATE); growing, extending, in width; (fig.) widely spread; (gram.)=foll. Hence ~LY[2] adv. [f. L PRO[1](*ferre lat-* carry) prolong]

prolāt'ive, a. (gram.). Serving to extend or complete predication, as *in ' you can go ' go is a ~ infinitive.* [f. LL *prolativus* (prec., -IVE)] prŏlĕgŏm'ĕn|on, n. (usu. in pl. ~a). Preliminary discourse or matter prefixed to book etc., introduction. Hence ~ARY², ~OUS, aa. [Gk *prolegomenon* neut. pass. part. of PRO²(*legō* say)]

prolĕp'sĭs, n. (pl. *-psēs*). Anticipation; (gram.) anticipatory use of adjectives, as in *So those two brothers & their murdered man Rode past fair Florence*. Hence or cogn. prolĕp'tic a., prolĕp'tICALLY adv. [L, f. Gk *prolēpsis* f. PRO²(*lambanō* take)]

prŏlĕtaire', n. = foll. n. Hence prŏlĕtair'ISM(2) n. [f. F *prolétaire*, as foll.]

prŏlĕtār'ian, a. & n. (Member) of the proletariate. Hence or cogn. ~ISM(2) n., prŏl'ĕtARY¹ n. [f. L *proletarius* one who served the State not with property but with offspring (*proles*), see -ARY¹ & -AN]

prŏlĕtār'iat(e), n. (Rom. hist.; & mod. freq. derog.) lowest class of community; (pol. econ.) indigent wage-earners, labouring classes; *dictatorship of the ~*, Communist ideal of domination by the ~ after the suppression of capitalism & the *bourgeoisie*. [f. F *prolétariat* (as prec., see -ATE¹)]

prŏl'icĭde, n. Killing of offspring, esp. before or soon after birth. Hence prŏlicid'AL a. [f. L *proles* offspring + -CIDE]

prolif'er|āte, v.i. & t. Reproduce itself, grow, by multiplication of elementary parts; produce (cells etc.) thus; increase rapidly. So ~A'TION n., ~ātIVE a. [back form. f. *proliferation* f. F *prolifération* (as foll., see -ATION)]

prolif'erous, a. (Bot.) producing leaf or flower buds from leaf or flower, (also) producing new individuals from buds; (zool.) multiplying by budding; (path.) spreading by proliferation. [f. L *proles* offspring, see -FEROUS]

prolif'ic, a. Producing (much) offspring; abundantly productive *of*, abounding *in*. Hence ~ACY [irreg.], prōlifi'cITY, ~NESS, nn. [f. F *-ique* or med. L *prolificus* (as prec., see -FIC)]

proli'gerous, a. Bearing offspring, generative. [as prec. + L *-ger* -bearing + -OUS]

·prŏl'ix (*or* prolīks'), a. Lengthy, tediously wordy, as ~ *speech, writer*. Hence or cogn. prolix'ITY n., ~LY² adv. [ME, f. OF *prolixe* or L *prolixus* (*liquēre* be liquid)]

prŏl'ocūtor (*or* prolŏ²-), n. Chairman ‖ esp. of lower house of convocation of either province of Church of England. Hence ~SHIP n. [ME, L, f. PRO¹(*loqui locut-* speak), -OR]

prŏl'ogīze (-j-), -guīze (-gīz), -ise (-īz), vv.i. Write, speak, a prologue. [(-*gize*) f. Gk *prologizō* as foll., (-*gu*-) f. foll. + -IZE]

prŏl'ogue (-ŏg), n., & v.t. Preliminary discourse, poem, etc., esp. introducing play (cf. EPILOGUE); (fig.) act, event, serving as introduction (*to*); (v.t.) introduce, furnish, with a ~. [ME, f. OF, f. L f. Gk PRO²(*logos* speech)]

prolŏng', v.t. Extend (action, condition, etc.) in duration; extend in spatial length; lengthen pronunciation of (syllable etc.). So ~ABLE (-nga-) a., prōlongA²TION (-ngg-) n. [ME, f. LL PRO¹(*longare*, as LONG¹)]

prolu'sion (-ōŏzhn), n. Preliminary essay, article, or attempt. So prolus'ORY (-ōŏ-) a. [f. L *prolusio* f. PRO¹(*ludere lus-* play) practise beforehand]

prŏm, n. (colloq.). = PROMENADE concert. [abbr.]

prŏmĕnade' (-ahd, -ād), n., & v.i. & t. 1. Walk, ride, drive, taken for exercise, amusement, or display, or as social ceremony; place, esp. paved public walk, for this; ~ *concert*, one at which (part of) audience is not seated and can move about; ~ *deck*, an upper deck on a liner, where passengers may ~. 2. v.i. Make a ~, whence prŏmĕnad'ER¹ (-ahd-, -ād-) n. 3. v.t. Make a ~ through (place); lead (person) about a place esp. for display. [F, f. *promener* take for walk f. L PRO¹*(minare* threaten) drive (beasts), -ADE]

Promēth'ēan, a. Of, like, Prometheus in his skill or punishment. [f. Gk *Promētheus* (demigod who made man from clay, stole fire from Olympus & taught men the use of it & various arts, & was chained by Zeus to rock in Caucasus), see -AN]

prŏm'in|ent, a. Jutting out, projecting; conspicuous; distinguished. Hence or cogn. ~ENCE, ~ENCY, nn., ~entLY² adv. [f. L PRO¹(*minēre*, see EMINENT)]

promĭs'cŭous, a. Of mixed & disorderly composition, as *a ~ mass*; (w. pl. n.) of various kinds mixed together; indiscriminate, as ~ *massacre, hospitality*; ~ *bathing* (of both sexes together); ~ *sexual relations* (unrestricted by marriage or cohabitation); (colloq.) casual, as *took a ~ stroll*. Hence or cogn. prōmĭscu'ITY n., ~LY² adv. [f. L PRO¹(*miscuus* f. *miscēre* mix) + -OUS]

prŏm'ĭse¹, n. Assurance given to a person that one will do or not do something or will give or procure him something; thing promised, as *I claim your ~*; BREACH¹ *of ~*; *land of ~* (see foll.); (fig.) ground of expectation of future achievements or good results, as *book, writer, of great ~*. [ME, f. L *promissum* p.p. of PRO¹(*mittere* send) put forth, promise]

prŏm'ĭse², v.t. & i. Make (person) a promise to give or procure him (thing), as *I ~ you a fair hearing*; make (person) a promise (*to do, that* thing shall be done etc.); (abs.) *cannot positively ~*; ~ oneself, look forward to (a pleasant time etc.); (colloq.) *I ~* (assure), *it will not be so easy*; (fig.) afford expectation of, as *these discussions ~ future storms*, seem likely (*to* do); (abs.) ~ *well* etc., hold out good etc. prospect; ~*d land* (also *land of promise*), Canaan (*Gen.* xii. 7 etc.), heaven, any place of expected felicity. Hence **prŏm'isER¹** n. [ME, f. prec.]

prŏmisee', n. (law). Person to whom promise is made. So **prŏm'isOR** n. [-EE]

prŏm'ising, a. Likely to turn out well, hopeful, full of promise, as ~ *boy*, *sky*, *beginning*. Hence ~LY² adv. [-ING²]

prŏm'issorў, a. Conveying or implying a promise; (rare) full of promise (*of*); ~ *note*, signed document containing written promise to pay stated sum to specified person or to bearer at specified date or on demand. [f. med. L *promissorius* (as PROMISE¹, see -ORY)]

prŏm'ontor|ў, n. Point of high land jutting out into sea etc., headland; (anat.) kinds of protuberance in the body. Hence ~iED² (-rĭd) a. [f. med. L *promontorium* altered (on *mons -ntis* mount) f. L *promunturium*]

promōte', v.t. Advance, prefer, (person *to* position, higher office; *was* ~*d major*, *to be major*, *to the rank of major*, *to majority*, not *to major*); help forward, encourage, (process, result); support actively the passing of (law), take necessary steps for passing of (local or private act of parliament); *publicize & sell (product); (chess) raise (pawn) to rank of queen etc. Hence or cogn. **promō'tion** n., **promōt'ive** a. [ME, f. L PRO¹(*movēre mot*- move)]

promōt'er, n. In vbl senses, esp. (also *company*-~) one who promotes formation of joint-stock company (freq. derog., whence ~ISM n.). [-ER¹]

prŏmpt¹, a. & n. **1.** Ready in action, acting with alacrity, as *a* ~ *assistant*, made, done, etc., readily or at once, as ~ *reply*, *decision*, *payment*, whence or cogn. ~'ITUDE, ~'NESS, nn., ~'LY² adv.; *for* ~ *cash* (on the spot); (commerc., of goods) for immediate delivery ,& payment, as ~ *iron*. **2.** n. Time limit for payment of account, stated on ~*note*, as *what is the* ~ ? [ME ; (n. f. adj.) OF, or f. L *promptus* f. *promere prompt*- produce (PRO-¹ +*emere* take)]

prŏmpt², v.t., & n. **1.** Incite, move, (person etc. *to* action, *to* do); supply (actor, reciter, or abs.) with the words that come next, assist (hesitating speaker) with suggestion; inspire, give rise to, (feeling, thought, action). **2.** n. Thing said to help the memory esp. of actor; ~*book*, copy of play for prompter's use;~-(prompter's) *box* on stage; ~ *side* of stage (usu. to actor's left; abbr. *p.s.*). [ME, f. med. L *promptare*, as prec.]

prŏmpt'er, n. One who prompts, esp. (theatr.) person stationed out of sight of audience to assist actor's memory. [-ER¹]

prŏmp'ting, n. In vbl senses, esp. *the* ~*s of conscience* etc. [-ING¹]

prŏm'ulg|āte, v.t. Make known to the public, disseminate (creed etc.), proclaim

(decree, news). Hence or cogn. ~A'TION, ~ātoR², nn. [f. L *promulgare*, see -ATE³]

promŭlge' (-j), v.t. (arch.). = prec. [as prec.]

pronā'ŏs, n. (Gk ant.). Space in front of body of temple, enclosed by portico & projecting side walls. [L, f. Gk PRO²(*naos* temple)]

prŏn'|āte, v.t. (physiol.). Put (hand, fore limb) into prone position (cf. SUPINATE). So ~A'TION n. [f. LL *pronare* (as PRONE), see -ATE³]

prōnāt'or, n. (anat.). Muscle that effects or helps pronation. [med. L (as prec., see -OR)]

prōne, a. Having the front or ventral part downwards, lying face downwards, (loosely) lying flat, prostrate, as *fell* ~, whence ~'LY² (-nl-) adv.; (of ground) having downward aspect or direction, (loosely) steep, headlong; disposed, liable, (*to* quality, action, or condition, *to* do). Hence ~'NESS (-n-n-) n. [ME, f. L *pronus*]

prōneur' (-nẽr), n. Extoller; eulogist. [F]

prŏng, n., & v.t. Forked instrument, e.g. hay-fork; each pointed member of fork, whence (-)~ED² (-ngd) a.; (v.t.) pierce, stab, turn up (soil etc.), with ~; ~-*buck*, *-horn*, *-horned antelope*, N.-Amer. deerlike ruminant. [*c.* 1500, of unkn. orig.]

pronŏm'inal, a. Of (the nature of) a pronoun. Hence ~LY² adv. [f. LL *pronominalis* f. L PRO¹(*nomen -minis* noun), see -AL]

prŏn'oun, n. Word used instead of (proper or other) noun to designate person or thing already mentioned or known from context or forming the subject of inquiry (used also to include pronominal & other adjectives, see below); *personal* ~*s* (I, we, thou, you, he, she, it, they); *interrogative* ~*s* (who, what, which); *relative* ~*s* (who, that, which); *possessive* ~*s*, adjectives representing possessive case (*my*, *her*, *our*, etc., with absolute forms *mine*, *hers*, *ours*); *demonstrative* ~*s* (this, that); *distributive* ~*s* (each, every, either, etc.); *indefinite* ~*s* (any, some, etc.). [PRO-¹ + NOUN, after F *pronom*, L *pronomen* (prec.)]

pronounce', v.t. & i. **1.** Utter, deliver, (judgement, sentence, curse, etc.) formally or solemnly, state, declare, as one's opinion, as *I* ~ *the pears unripe*, *cannot* ~ *him* (or *that he is*) *out of danger*, whence ~MENT (-sm-) n. **2.** Pass judgement, give one's opinion, (*on*, *for*, *against*, *in favour of*). **3.** Utter, articulate, (words, or abs.), as ~ *more distinctly*, esp. with reference to different modes, as *how do you* ~ *'fulsome'*?, *cannot* ~ *French*, whence ~ABLE (-sabl) a. [ME, f. OF *pronuncier* f. L PRO¹-(*nuntiare* announce f. *nuntius* messenger)]

pronounced' (-st), a. In vbl senses, also, strongly marked, decided, as ~ *tendency*, *magenta*, *flavour*. Hence **pronoun'cēdLY²** adv. [-ED¹]

pronoun'cing, n. In vbl senses; (attrib.)

~ *dictionary* (in which pronunciation is indicated). [-ING¹]

*prŏn'tō, adv. (sl.). Promptly, quickly. [Sp.]

prŏn'tosĭl, n. One of the sulphonamide group of drugs. [P]

pronŭnciamĕn'tō, n. (pl. ~*s*). Proclamation, manifesto, esp. (in Spanish-speaking countries) one issued by insurrectionists. [f. Sp. *pronunciamiento,* also used in E, f. L as PRONOUNCE, see -MENT]

pronŭncia'tion, n. Mode in which a word is pronounced; a person's way of pronouncing words, as *his ~ is often faulty.* [ME, f. OF, or f. L *pronuntiatio* (as PRONOUNCE, see -ATION)]

proof¹, n. 1. Evidence sufficing or helping to establish a fact, as *this requires no ~, as a ~ of his esteem, ~ positive of his intention* or *that he intended,* whence ~'LESS a.; spoken or written legal evidence. 2. Proving, demonstration, as *not capable of ~, in ~ of my assertion.* 3. ‖ (Sc. law). Trial before judge instead of by jury. 4. Test, trial, as *must be brought to the ~, will stand a severe ~, the ~ of the pudding is in the eating.* .5. (Place for) testing of fire-arms or explosives. 6. (arch.). Proved impenetrability, as *armour of ~.* 7. Standard of strength of distilled alcoholic liquors. 8.. (*First*) ~, trial impression taken from type, in which corrections etc. may be made (cf. REVISE); ~*reader, -reading,* (person employed in) reading & correcting~s; ~*-sheet,* sheet of ~. 9. Each of a limited number of careful impressions made from engraved plate before printing of ordinary issue & usu. (also ~ *before letters*) before inscription is added; *artist's, engraver's,* ~ (taken for examination or alteration by him); *signed* ~, early ~ signed by artist. 10. Test-tube. 11. ~*plane,* conductor fixed on insulating handle & used in measuring electrification of a body. [ME & OF *proeve, preve,* later *prŏf,* f. LL *proba,* as PROVE]

proof², a., & v.t. 1. (Of armour) of tried strength; impenetrable, as ~ *against the severest weather, the pricks of conscience,* esp. in comb., as *bomb, bullet, burglar, fire,* FOOL¹, *rain, sound, weather,* -~, WATER¹-~. 2. v.t. Make (thing) ~, esp. make (fabric etc.) waterproof. [adj. f. prec., app. by ellipsis of *of*; vb f. prec., or f. adj.]

prop¹, n., & v.t. & i. (-pp-). 1. Rigid support, esp. one not forming structural part of thing supported, e.g. pole; ‖ CLOTHES-~; (fig.) person etc. who upholds institution etc. 2. v.t. Support (as) by ~ (lit. & fig.), hold *up* thus. 3. v.i. (Of horse etc.) come to a dead stop with forelegs rigid. [15th c., prob. f. MDu. *proppe*; vb f. n., or MDu. *proppen*]

prop², See PROPORTION.

prop³, n. (colloq.). Aircraft propeller. [abbr.]

prop⁴, n. (theatr.). Stage property. [abbr.]

prŏpaedeut'ic, a. & n. (Subject, study) serving as introduction to higher study; (n. pl.) preliminary learning. Hence ~AL a. [f. Gk PRO²(*paideuō* teach f. *pais paidos* child), see -IC]

prŏpagăn'da, n. 1. (*Congregation, College, of*) *the P~,* committee of cardinals in charge of foreign missions. 2. Association, organized scheme, for propagation of a doctrine or practice; doctrines, information, etc. thus propagated; efforts, schemes, principles, etc of propagation. [It., f. mod. L *congregatio de propaganda fide* congregation for propagation of the faith]

prŏpagăn'd|ist, n. Member, agent, of a propaganda, whence ~ISM n., ~ĭs'TIC a., ~IZE(2, 4) v.i. & t.; proselytizer; missionary, convert, of the Propaganda. [-IST]

prŏp'ag|āte, v.t. 1. Multiply specimens of (plant, animal, disease, etc.) by natural process from parent stock; (of plant etc.) reproduce (*itself,* or abs.). 2. Hand down (quality etc.) from one generation to another. 3. Disseminate, diffuse, (statement, belief, practice). 4. Extend the operation of, transmit, (vibration, earthquake, etc.). Hence or cogn. ~A'TION, ~ātor, nn., ~ātivE a. [f. L *propagare* multiply plants from LAYERS, f. PRO¹(*pago* f. root of *pangere* fix, set), see -ATE³]

prŏparŏx'ўtone, a. & n. (Gk gram.). (Word) with acute accent on antepenult. [f. Gk PRO²(*paroxutonos* PAROXYTONE)]

propĕl', v.t. (-ll-). Drive forward, give onward motion to, (lit. & fig.); JET²-~*led.* [ME, f. L PRO¹(*pellere puls-* drive)]

propĕll'ant, -ent, a. & n. Propelling (agent); explosive that propels bullet or shell from fire-arm. [-ANT, -ENT]

propĕll'er, n. In vbl senses, esp., revolving shaft with blades usu. (*screw* ~) set at an angle & twisted like thread of screw, for propelling ship or aircraft; ~ *turbine* or *prop'-jet engine,* aircraft engine having a turbine-driven-~. [-ER¹]

propĕn'sitў, n. Inclination, tendency, (to condition, quality, thing, *to do, for doing*). [f. now rare *propense* f. L *propensus* inclined, p.p. of PRO¹(*pendēre* hang) + -ITY]

prŏp'er, a. 1. (arch.). (Usu. w. possessive pron. & occas. w. *own*) own, as *with my own ~ eyes.* 2. (astron.). ~ *motion,* that part of the apparent motion of fixed star etc. supposed to be due to its actual movement in space. 3. Belonging, relating, exclusively or distinctively (*to,* or abs. as ~ *psalms, lessons,* ~ to particular day). 4. (gram.). ~ *noun* or *name,* name used to designate an individual person, animal, town, ship, etc. (e.g. Jane, Neddy, London, Victory). 5. Accurate, correct, as *in the~ sense of the word.* 6. (Usu. foll. its noun) strictly so called, real, genuine, as *within the sphere of architecture ~; ~*

For other words in *pro-,* see PRO-¹.

fraction (less than unity). **7.** (colloq.). Thorough, complete, as *will be a ~ row about this*. **8.** (arch.). Handsome, as *a ~ man*. **9.** Fit, suitable, right, as *choose the ~ time, do it the~ way*. **10.** In conformity with demands of society, decent, respectable, as *she is so distressingly ~, would it be quite ~?* **11.** (her.). In the natural, not conventional, colours, as *a peacock~*. [ME & OF *propre* f. L *proprius*]

prŏpĕrispōm'ĕnon, a. & n. (Gk gram.). (Word) with circumflex accent on penult. [Gk PRO²(PERISPOMENON)]

prŏp'erlў, adv. Fittingly, suitably, as *do it ~ or not at all*; rightly, duly, as *he very ~ refused*; with good manners, as *behave ~*; (colloq.) thoroughly, as *puzzled him~*. [-LY²]

prŏp'ertў, n. **1.** Owning, being owned, as *~ has its duties*; thing owned, possession(s), as *the book is his ~, regards him as her exclusive ~, a man of* (great) *~*, *has a small ~* (estate) *in Norfolk*, PERSONAL, REAL², *~*; *~ qualification* (based on possession of *~*), *~ tax* (levied directly on *~*). **2.** (theatr.; abbr. *prŏp*). Article of costume, furniture, etc., used on stage; *~-man, -master*, man in charge of stage properties. **3.** Attribute, quality, as *the properties of soda, has the ~ of dissolving grease*; (log.) quality common to a whole class but not necessary to distinguish it from others, cf. DIFFERENTIA. [ME, f. OF *propriete* f. L *proprietatem* (as PROPER, see -TY)]

prŏph'ĕcў, n. Faculty of a prophet, as *the gift of ~*; prophetic utterance; foretelling of future events. [ME, f. OF *profecie* f. LL f. Gk *prophēteia* (as PROPHET)]

prŏph'esў, v.i. & t. Speak as a prophet; foretell future events; (arch.) expound the Scriptures; foretell (event, *that, who*, etc.). [ME, f. OF *profecier*, as prec.]

prŏph'ĕt, n. Inspired teacher, revealer or interpreter of God's will; *the ~s*, prophetical writers of O.T., *major~s*, Isaiah, Jeremiah, Ezekiel, Daniel, *the 12 minor ~s*, Hosea to Malachi; *the P~*, Mohammed, (also) Joseph Smith, founder of Mormons; *Saul among the ~s*, person revealing unexpected gifts or sympathies (see 1 *Sam.* x. 11); spokesman, advocate, (*of* principle etc.); one who foretells events, as *am no weather-~*; (sl.) tipster. Hence ~ESS¹, ~HOOD, ~SHIP, nn. [ME, f. OF *prophete* f. L (-*ta*) f. Gk PRO²(*phētēs* speaker f. *phēmi* speak) spokesman]

prophĕt'ĭc, a. Of a prophet; predicting, containing a prediction *of* (event etc.). Hence ~AL a., ~alLY² adv. [f. F (-*ique*) or LL f. Gk *prophētikos* (prec., -IC)]

prŏphўlăc'tĭc, a. & n. (Medicine, measure) tending to prevent disease. [f. Gk *prophulaktikos* f. PRO²(*phulassō* guard)]

prŏp.lўlăx'ĭs, n. Preventive treatment of diseas.. [f. PRO-²+Gk *phu.axis* a guarding, after prec.]

propin'quitў, n. Nearness in place; close kinship; similarity. [f. ME & OF *pro~ pinquite* f. L *propinquitatem* (*propinquus* near f. *prope* near, see -TY)]

propi'tiāte (-shǐ-), v.t. Appease (offended person etc.); make propitious. [f. L *pro~ pitiare* (as PROPITIOUS, see -ATE³)]

propitiā'tion (-shǐ-), n. Appeasement; atonement; (arch.) gift etc. meant to propitiate, as *he is the~ for our sins*. [ME, f. LL *propitiatio* (as prec., see -ATION)]

propi'tiator|ў (-sha-), a. & n. Serving, meant, to propitiate, as *a ~y smile*; (n.) the mercy-seat (esp. fig. of Christ). Hence ~ĭLУ² adv. [ME, f. LL *propitiatorius* (as PROPITIATE, see -ORY)]

propi'tious (-shŭs), a. Well-disposed, favourable, as *the fates were~*; (of omens etc.) favourable; (of weather, occasion, etc.) suitable *for*, favourable *to*, (purpose). Hence ~LY² adv. [late ME, f. OF *propicieus* f. L *propitius*, -OUS]

prŏp'olis, n. Red resinous substance got by bees from buds to stop up crevices with. [L, f. Gk PRO²(*polis* city) suburb, bee-glue]

propŏn'ent, a. & n. (Person) that puts forward a motion, theory, or proposal. [f. L as PROPOUND, see -ENT]

propŏr'tion, n., & v.t. **1.** Comparative part, share, as *a large ~ of the earth's surface, of the profits*; comparative relation, ratio, as *the ~ of births to the population, price will be raised in ~* (*to the labour* etc., or abs.); due relation of one thing to another or between parts of a thing, as *windows are in admirable ~, his success bore no ~ to his abilities*, whence ~LESS (-sho-) a.; *was out of* (*all*) *~ to*, too great *for*; (pl.) dimensions, as *athlete, building, of magnificent ~s*; (math.) equality of ratios between two pairs of quantities, as *3, 5, 9, & 15 are in ~*, set of such quantities, (arith.) RULE of three. **2.** v.t. Make (thing etc.) proportionate *to*, as *must ~ the punishment to the crime*, whence (-)~ED¹ (-shond) a., ~MENT (-sho-)n. [ME; n. OF, or L PRO(*portio* PORTION); vb f. OF *proporcioner* or med. L -*are*]

propŏr'tion|al (-sho-), a. & n. **1.** In due proportion, corresponding in degree or amount, as *a ~al increase in the expense, resentment ~al to his injuries, ~al* REPRESENTATION, SO ~ABLE, ~ATE², aa., ~ablУ³, ~ateLУ², advv. **2.** n. One of the terms of a proportion, as *5, 3, 10, 6, are ~als, 6 is a mean ~al between 3 & 12*. Hence or cogn. ~ăl'ITY n., ~alLУ² adv. (-sho-). [f. L *proportionalis* (as prec., see -AL)]

propŏr'tionalist (-sho-), n. One who plans proportions; advocate of proportional representation. [-IST]

propōs'al (-z-), n. Act of proposing something; offer of marriage, as *have had a ~*; scheme of action etc. proposed, as *the ~ was never carried out*. [-AL]

propōse' (-z), v.t. & i. Put forward for consideration, propound; set up as an

aim, as *the object I ~ to myself*; nominate
(person) as member of society etc.; offer
(person's health, person) as toast; make
offer of marriage (*to*); put forward as a
plan, as *we ~* (to make) *a change, that a
change should be made*; intend, purpose,
(*to* do, doing); (abs.) *man ~s, God disposes*.
[ME, f. OF PRO¹(*poser*, see COMPOSE)]

prŏposi'tion (-z-), n. Statement, assertion, as *a ~ too plain to need argument*,
esp. (log.) form of words consisting of
predicate & subject; (math., abbr. *prŏp*)
formal statement of theorem or problem,
often including the demonstration, as
Euclid, Book I, ~ 5; proposal, scheme
proposed; (sl.) task, job, problem, objective, occupation, trade, opponent,
prospect, etc. Hence ~AL (-zisho-) a.
[ME, f. OF, or L *propositio* (as foll., see
-ION)]

propound', v.t. Offer for consideration,
propose, (question, problem, scheme,
matter, etc., *to* person); produce (will)
before proper authority in order to
establish its legality. Hence ~ER¹ n.
[replacing *propone* f. L PRO¹(*ponere posit-*
place), cf. *compound* etc.]

propraet'or, n. (Rom. hist.). Ex-praetor
with authority of praetor in province not
under military control. [L, earlier *pro
praetore* (one acting) for praetor]

propri'étary, a. & n. 1. Of a proprietor,
as *~ rights*; holding property, as *the ~
classes*; held in private ownership, as *~
medicines* (sale of which is restricted by
patent etc.). 2. n. Proprietorship, as *an
exclusive ~*; body of proprietors, as *the
landed ~*. [f. LL *proprietarius* (as PRO-
PERTY, see -ARY¹)]

propri'ét|or, n. Owner. Hence ~ŏr'IAL
a., ~ŏr'ialLY² adv., ~orSHIP, ~rESS¹, nn.
[altered in 17th c. f. prec.]

propri'ét|ў, n. Fitness, rightness, as
doubt the ~y of the term, of refusing him;
correctness of behaviour or morals, as *a
breach of ~y*; (pl.) details of correct conduct, as *must observe the ~ies*. [ME; (in
earlier senses ' ownership, peculiarity ') f.
OF *propriete* PROPERTY]

prŏp'rĭŏ mŏt'ŭ (or *mŏt'ŭ prŏp'rĭŏ*), n.
Form of papal bull without seal & used
in the administration of the papal court.
[L, = of our own motion, wds included in
the formula]

prŏptōs'|is, n. (path.). Prolapse, protru-
sion, esp. of eye. Hence ~ED¹ (-st) a.
[LL, f. Gk *proptōsis* f. PRO²(*piptō* fall)]

propŭl's|ion (-shn), n. Driving or pushing
forward; JET² *~ion*; (fig.) impelling influence. So ~IVE a. [F (as PROPEL, see -ION)]

prŏpŭlae'|um, n. (pl. *~a*). Entrance to
temple; *the P~a*, entrance to Acropolis at
Athens. [L, f. Gk PRO²(*pulaion* f.· *pulē*
gate)]

prŏp'ўl|īte, n. Volcanic rock found in
some silver-mining regions. Hence ~it'IC

a. [f. foll. +-ITE¹, as opening a volcanic
epoch]

prŏp'ўlŏn, n. (pl. -*ons*, -*a*). = PROPYLAEUM.
[L, f. Gk PRO²(*pulon* f. *pulē* gate)]

prorŏgue' (-g), v.t. & i. Discontinue
meetings of (British parliament etc.)
without dissolving it; (of parliament etc.)
be ~d. So prŏrogā'TION n. [ME *proroge*
f. OF *proroger*, *-guer* f. L PRO¹(*rogare* ask)
prolong]

pros- in comb. = Gk *pros* to, towards, in
addition.

prŏsā'ic (-z-; *also* pro-), a. Like prose,
lacking poetic beauty; unromantic, commonplace, dull, as *a ~ life, person, view
of ' things*. Hence **prŏsā'ICALLY** adv.,
~NESS n. [f. F (-*ique*) or LL *prosaicus* (as
PROSE, see -IC)]

prŏs'ā|ist (-z-), n. Prose writer; prosaic
person. So ~ISM(4) n. [as PROSE, see -IST]

prŏscēn'ium (*or* pro-), n. (pl. -*ia*). (In
ancient theatre) the stage; (mod.) space
between curtain or drop-scene & orchestra, esp. with the enclosing arch. [L, f.
Gk PRO²(*skēnion* f. *skēnē*, as SCENE)]

proscribe', v.t. Put (person) out of protection of law; banish, exile, (esp. fig.);
reject, denounce, (practice etc.) as dangerous etc. So **proscrip'**TION n., **proscrip'**TIVE a. [f. L PRO¹(*scribere script-*
write)]

prōse (-z), n., & v.i. & t. 1. Ordinary non-
-metrical form of written or spoken
language (*Milton's ~ works*); (eccl.)=
SEQUENCE; *~ poem*, = work of poetical
style; plain matter-of-fact quality, as *the
~ of existence*; tedious discourse. 2. v.i.
Talk prosily (*about* etc.), whence **prōs'ER¹**
(-z-) n. 3. v.t. Turn (poem etc.) into *~*.
[ME, f. OF, f. L *prosa* (*oratio*) straightforward (discourse), fem. of *prosus*, earlier
prorsus]

prosec'tor, n. One who dissects dead
bodies in preparation for anatomical lecture etc. [LL, = anatomist, f. PRO¹(*secare
sect-* cut), prob. after F *prosecteur*]

prŏs'ecūte, v.t. Follow up, pursue, (inquiry, studies); carry on (trade, pursuit);
institute legal proceedings against (person), as *trespassers will be ~d*, (abs.) *shall
not ~*. [ME, f. L PRO¹(*sequi secut-* follow)]

prŏsecū'tion, n. Prosecuting (*of* pursuit
etc.); (law) institution and carrying on
of criminal charge before court; carrying
on of legal proceedings against person;
prosecuting party, as *the ~ denied this*;
|| *director of public ~s*, public prosecutor.
[ME, f. OF, or f. LL *prosecutio* (prec.,
-ION)]

prŏs'ecūtor, n. One who prosecutes esp.
in criminal court; *public ~*, law officer
conducting criminal proceedings in public
interest. Hence **prŏsecūt'RIX** n. (pl.
-*ices* pr. -ĭsēz). [med. L (as PROSECUTE, see
-OR)]

prŏs'elŷt|e, n., & v.t. 1. Convert from

one opinion, creed, or party, to another, as *made many* ~*es*; Gentile convert to Jewish faith, ~*e of the gate* (not submitting to circumcision etc.). **2.** v.t. (now rare). Make a ~e of (person, or abs.). Hence ~ISM(1, 2), ~ĪZER¹, nn., ~IZE(2) v.t. (often abs.). [ME, f. LL f. Gk PROS(*ēlutos* f. st. *eluth*- come) one who has come, convert]

prŏsĕn'chȳma (-ngk-), n. (bot.). Tissue of elongated cells placed with their ends interpenetrating (cf. PARENCHYMA), esp. fibro-vascular tissue. Hence ~tous (-ĕngkĭm²) a. [f. Gk *pros* toward, as PARENCHYMA]

prŏs'ifȳ (-z-), v.t. & i. Turn into prose, make prosaic; write prose. [-FY]

prŏs'it, int. used in drinking person's health, wishing him success, etc., lit. = may it benefit you. [f. G f. L]

prŏs'od|ȳ, n. Science of versification, laws of METRE¹. Hence ~ī'ACAL, prosŏd'IAL, prosŏd'IC, aa., ~IST n. [ME, f. L f. Gk PROS(*ōidia* as ODE)]

prŏsōpopoe'ia (-pē'a, -pē'ya), n. (rhet.). Introduction of pretended speaker; personification of abstract thing. [L, f. Gk *prosōpopoiia* (*prosōpon* person + *poieō* make)]

prospect, n., & v.i. & t. **1.** (prŏs'pĕkt). Extensive view of landscape etc., as *a fine, striking, ~*; mental scene, as *opened a new ~ to his mind*; expectation, what one expects, as *offers a gloomy ~*, *his ~s were brilliant, no~ of success, have nothing in~ at present*, whence ~LESS a.; (mining) spot giving ~s of mineral deposit, sample of ore for testing, resulting yield; possible or probable customer, subscriber, etc. **2.** (prospĕkt'). v.i. Explore region (*for* gold etc.), so **prospĕc'tor** (*or* prŏs²) n.; (fig.) look out *for*, (of mine) promise (*well, ill*); (v.t.) explore (region) for gold etc., work (mine) experimentally, (of mine) promise (specified yield). [ME; (vb f. n.) as PROSPECTUS]

prospĕc'tive, a. Concerned with, applying to, the future (cf. RETROSPECTIVE), as *the law was held to be exclusively ~, implies a~ obligation*; expected, future, some day to be, as ~ *peer, bridegroom, profit*. Hence ~LY² adv., ~NESS n. [f. obs. F (-*if, -ive*) or LL *prospectivus* (as foll., see -IVE)]

prospĕc'tus, n. (pl. ~es). Circular describing chief features of school, commercial enterprise, forthcoming book, etc. [L, gen. -*ūs*, = prospect, f. PRO¹(*spicere* = *specere* look)]

prŏs'per, v.i. & t. Succeed, thrive, as *cheats never ~, nothing will ever ~ in his hands*; make successful, as *Heaven ~ our attempt*. [ME, f. OF *prosperer* or L *prosperare*, as foll.]

prŏs'perous, a. Flourishing, successful, thriving, as *a ~ merchant, enterprise*, whence or cogn. **prŏspĕ'rITY** n., ~LY² adv.; auspicious, as *a ~ gale, in a ~ hour*. [ME, f. OF *prospereus* f. L *prosper(us)*, see -OUS]

prŏs'tăte, n. Large gland, each of several small glands, accessory to male generative organs in mammals. Hence **prostăt'IC** a. [F, or f. mod. L (-*la*) f. Gk PRO²(*statēs* f. *sta*- stand) one who stands before]

prŏs'thĕsĭs, n. (Gram.) addition of letter or syllable at beginning of word; (surg.) making up of deficiencies (e.g. by false teeth or ·wooden leg) as a branch of surgery. So **prŏsthĕt'IC** a. [LL, f. Gk *prosthesis* f. PROS(*tithēmi* put)]

prŏs'titūte, n., & v.t. **1.** Woman who offers her body to indiscriminate sexual intercourse esp. for hire. **2.** v.t. Make a ~ of (one*self*); (fig.) sell for base gain (one's honour etc.), put (abilities etc.) to infamous use. So **prŏstitū'tion** n. [f. L PRO¹(*stituere -ut-* = *statuere* set up, place) offer for sale; n. = L *prostituta*]

prŏs'trăte¹ (*or* -at), a. Lying with face to ground, esp. as token of submission or humility; lying in horizontal position; overcome, overthrown, as *had laid the Tory party ~*; physically exhausted; (bot.) lying flat on ground. [ME, f. L p.p. as foll.]

prostrăte'² (*or* prŏs²), v.t. Lay (person etc.) flat on ground; cast one*self* down prostrate (*at* shrine, *before* person etc.); (fig.) overcome, make submissive; (of fatigue etc.) reduce to extreme physical weakness. So **prostrā'tion** n. [ME, f. L PRO¹(*sternere strat*- lay flat)]

prŏs'tȳle, n. & a. Portico of not more than four columns in front of Greek temple; (adj.) having a ~. [f. L (-*os*) f. Gk PRO²(*stulos* STYLE²)]

prŏs'|ȳ (-z-), a. Commonplace, tedious, dull, as ~*y talk*(*er*). Hence ~ILY² adv., ~ĪNESS n. [f. PROSE + -Y¹]

prŏtăg'onist, n. Chief person in drama or plot of story, cf. DEUTERAGONIST; leading person in contest, principal performer; (erron.) advocate, champion, of course, method, etc. [f. Gk *prōtagōnistēs* (*prōtos* first + *agōnistēs* actor, as AGONIZE)]

prŏt'asis, n. (pl. -*asēs*). Introductory clause, esp. clause expressing condition (cf. APODOSIS). So **protăt'IC** a. [L, f. Gk PRO²(*tasis* f. *teinō* stretch) proposition]

prŏt'ean (*or*-ē'an), a. Variable, versatile; of or like PROTEUS. [-AN]

protĕct', v.t. Keep safe, defend, guard, (person, thing, *from*, *against*, danger, injury, etc.); (pol. econ.) guard (home industry) against competition by imposts on foreign goods; (commerc.) provide funds to meet (bill, draft); provide (machinery etc.) with appliances to prevent injury from it, as ~*ed rifles*. [f. L PRO¹(*tegere tect*- cover)]

protĕc'tion, n. Protecting, defence, as *is safe under your ~, affords ~ against weather*; patronage, as *book was indebted to your kind ~*; protecting person or thing, as *man, dog, is a great ~ against burglars*; *live under X's ~*, (of a woman) be kept by X; safe-conduct; U.S.

certificate of American citizenship issued to seamen; (pol. econ.) system of protecting home industries, whence ~ISM(3), ~IST(2), nn., (-sho). [ME, f. OF, or LL *protectio* (as prec., see -ION)]

protěc'tive, a. Serving or intended to protect; (of foods) protecting against deficiency diseases; ~ *custody*, (usu.) detention of persons in order to protect the State from their (real or suspected) subversive activities. Hence ~LY[2] adv., ~NESS n. [-IVE]

protěc'tor, n. Person who protects; regent in charge of kingdom during minority, absence, etc., of sovereign, *Lord P~ of the Commonwealth*, title of Oliver Cromwell (1653-8) & Richard Cromwell (1658-9), whence ~AL a., ~SHIP n.; thing, device, that protects, as CHEST-~, point-~ (for pencil). Hence **protěc'tress**[1] n. [ME, f. OF *protectour* f. LL *protector* (as PROTECT, see -OR)]

protěc'torate, n. Office of protector of kingdom or State; period of this, esp. of the ~ of O. & R. Cromwell; protectorship of weak state by stronger one, esp. of territory inhabited by backward tribes; such territory. [-ATE[1]]

protěc'tory, n. (Rom. Cath.). Institution for care of destitute or vicious children. [as PROTECT, see -ORY]

protégé (prŏt'ĕzhā), n. (fem. ~e). Person to whom another is (usu. permanent) protector or patron. [F, p.p. of *protéger* PROTECT]

prŏt'eid, n. = PROTEIN (1st sense). [-ID[4]]

prŏt'eiförm, a. Very changeable in form. [f. PROTEUS + -FORM]

prŏt'ein (*or* -tēn), n. (chem.). (Now preferred in scient. use to *proteid*) albuminoid, kinds of organic compound (containing carbon, hydrogen, oxygen, & nitrogen, freq. also sulphur, occas. phosphorus) forming an important part of all living organisms, and the essential nitrogenous constituent of the food of albuminoids, (orig.) supposed basis of albuminoids. Hence ~A'CEOUS (-āshus), **prŏtěin'ic**, **prŏtě'in-ous**, aa. [f. F *protéine*, G *proteïn*, f. Gk *proteios* primary, see -IN]

prŏter|(o)-, comb. form of Gk *proteros* former, anterior, as ~*an'drous*, ~*o'gynous*, having stamens (pistil) mature before pistil (stamens).

prŏt'ěst[1], n. Formal statement of dissent or disapproval, remonstrance, as *made a ~*, *paid it under ~*; ‖ written statement of dissent from motion carried in H. of Lords signed by any peer of minority (hist.); written declaration usu. by notary public that bill has been duly presented & payment or acceptance refused; solemn declaration. [ME, f. OF *protest* f. *protester* (foll.)]

protěst'[2], v.t. & i. Affirm solemnly (one's innocence etc., *that*, or abs.); write a

protest in regard to (bill, see prec.); make (often written) protest *against* (action, proposal), whence ~ER[1], ~OR, nn., ~ingLY[2] adv. [ME, f. OF *protester* f. L PRO[1](*testari*) aver f. *testis* witness)]

prŏt'ěstant, P-, n. & a. (Member, adherent) of any of the Christian bodies that separated from the Roman communion in the Reformation (16th c.) or their offshoots, whence P~ISM(3) n., P~IZE(3) v.t. & i.; (hist., pl.) those who dissented from decision of Diet of Spires (1529), adherents of reformed doctrines in Germany; (*also* protěs[2]) making, maker of, a protest. [1539, G or F (as prec., -ANT)]

prŏtěstā'tion, n. Solemn affirmation (*of*, *that*); protest (*against*). [ME, f. OF, f. LL *protestatio* (as prec., see -ATION)]

Prŏt'eus (-tūs), 'n. Changing or inconstant person or thing; (earlier name for) amoeba; kinds of bacteria; kinds of tailed amphibian with eel-like body & four short legs. [L, f. Gk *Prōteus* sea-god taking various shapes]

prŏthalăm'ium, -iŏn, n. (pl. *-ia*). Preliminary nuptial song. [(-on) made by Spenser on EPITHALAMIUM (PRO-[2])]

prŏth'ěsis, n. (Placing of eucharistic elements on) credence-table, part of church where this stands; (gram.) = PROSTHESIS, so **prothět'ic** a. [Gk *prothesis* f. PRO[2](*tithemi* place)]

protis'ta, n. pl. Kingdom of organized beings not distinguished as animals or plants. [Gk *prōtista*, neut. pl. superl. f. *prōtos* first]

prŏt'ium, n. (chem.). Ordinary hydrogen as dist. from heavy hydrogen (DEUTERIUM). [f. PROT(O)-, -IUM]

prŏto- (bef. a vowel *prot-*), comb. form of Gk *prōtos* first. **1.** = chief, original, primitive, as: ~-*A'rabic*, ~-*Cel'tic*, etc., of the original Arabs etc.; ~*genět'ic*, ~*gěn'ic*, of first period of formation or growth; *prŏt'ogīne*, kind of granite found in Alps, assumed to be the most ancient; ~*hipp'us*, extinct quadruped related to horse; *prŏ'tomartyr* (-ter), first martyr (esp., of Christians, St Stephen); *prōtŏph'yta* n. pl., the most simply organized plants, each consisting of a single cell, *prŏt'ophyte*, such plant; ~*ther'ia* n. pl., mammals of the lowest subclass, their hypothetical ancestors; ~*zō'a* n. pl., great division of animal kingdom comprising animals of simplest type consisting of single cell & usu. microscopic, ~*zō'on*, such animal; ~*zō'al* a., ~*zō'an* a. & n., (animal) of the ~zoa, (of disease) caused by parasitic ~zoon; ~*zō'ic*, (geol., of strata) containing earliest traces of living beings, (also) = ~*zoal*; ~*zōöl'ogy*, study of ~zoa. **2.** In chem. names of compounds in which the element or radical combines in smallest proportion with another element, as ~*chlor'ide*, ~-

sulph'ide, *prōt'oxide*, compound containing minimum of chlorine, sulphur, oxygen.
prōt'ocŏl, n., & v.i. & t. (-ll-). **1.** Original draft of diplomatic document, esp. of terms of treaty agreed to in conference & signed by the parties; formal statement of transaction; (in France etc.) etiquette department of Ministry of Foreign Affairs; diplomatic. etiquette; official formulas at beginning & end of charter, papal bull, etc. **2.** vb. Draw up ~s; record in ~. [16th c. *prothocol* f. OF *-cole* f. med. L f. Gk PROTO(*kollon* f. *kolla* glue) fly-leaf glued to (book-)case]
prōt'ŏn, n. (phys.). Unit of positive electricity, forming part (or, in hydrogen, whole) of the nucleus of the atom (cf. ELECTRON). [neut. of Gk *prōtos* first]
prŏtŏnŏt'ar|ÿ, prŏtho-, (or *protŏn'o*-), n. Chief clerk in some law courts, esp. (hist.) Chancery, Common Pleas, & King's Bench, (orig. in Byzantine court); *P~ies Apostolic(al)*, twelve prelates who register papal acts, direct canonization of saints, etc. [f. LL f. late Gk PROTO(*notarios* NOTARY)]
prŏt'oplăsm, n. Semifluid semitransparent colourless substance consisting of certain complex organic compounds, basis of life in plants & animals. Hence **prŏtoplăsmăt'ic, prŏtoplăs'mic, aa.,** (-z-). [f. G PROTO(PLASMA)]
prŏt'oplăst, n. The first created man; original, model; unit or mass of protoplasm. Hence **prŏtoplăs'tic a.** [f. F *-plaste* or LL f. Gk PROTO(*plastos* moulded, as PLASMA)]
prŏt'o|type, n. The original thing or person in relation to any copy, imitation, representation, later specimen, improved form, etc. Hence **~type̅AL, ~tÿp'ic(al), aa.** [F, f. Gk PROTO(*tupon* f. *tupos* TYPE)]
protrăct', v.t. Prolong, lengthen out, as *~ed their stay for some weeks*, whence **~edLY²** adv.; draw (plan of ground etc.) to scale. [f. L PRO¹(*trahere tract-* draw)]
protrăc'tile, a. (zool.). (Of organ etc.) that can be extended. [-ILE]
protrăc'tion, n. Protracting; action of protractor muscle; drawing to scale. [F, or LL *protractio* (as PROTRACT, see -ION)]
protrăc'tor, n. Instrument for measuring angles, usu. in form of graduated semicircle; muscle serving to extend limb etc. [med. L (as prec., see -OR)]
protrude' (-ōōd), v.t. & i. Thrust forth, cause to project; (fig.) obtrude; stick out, project. Hence or cogn. **protru'dent, protru'sible, protru'sive, aa.,** (-ōō-), **protru'sion** (-ōōzhn) n. [f. L PRO¹(*trudere trus-* thrust)]
protru'sile (-ōō-), a. (Of limb, etc.) that may be thrust forth. [as prec., see -ILE]
protūb'er|ant, a. Bulging out, prominent (lit. & fig.). Hence **~ANCE n.** [f. LL PRO¹- (*tuberare* f. *tuber* hump), see -ANT]
prŏt'ÿle, n. (chem.). Supposed original undifferentiated matter of which chemi-

cal elements may be composed. [f. PROTO- +-YL]
proud, a. & adv. **1.** Valuing oneself highly or too highly, esp. on the ground of (qualities, rank, possessions, etc.); (also *~-hearted*) haughty, arrogant; feeling oneself greatly honoured, as *am ~ of his acquaintance, of knowing him, to know him*; having a proper PRIDE, as *too ~ to complain*; HOUSE¹-~; (of actions etc.) showing pride; (of which one is or may be *justly ~*, as *a ~ day for us, a ~ sight*; (of things) imposing, splendid; (of waters) swollen, in flood; *~ flesh*, overgrown flesh round healing wound. **2.** adv. (colloq.). *You do me ~* (honour me greatly). Hence **~'LY²** adv. [late OE *prūt, prūd,* = ON *prúthr.* f. OF *prud, prod* (mod. *preux*) valiant, f. LL *prode* f. L *prodesse* be of value; cf. PROW², PRUDE, PRIDE]
prov|e (prōōv), v.t. & i. (arch. p.p. ~*en*). (Arch.) test qualities of, try; subject (gun etc.) to testing process; (arith.) test accuracy of (calculation); *the* EXCEPTION ~*es the rule*; take proof impression of (stereotype plate etc.); make certain, demonstrate, (*fact, the truth of,* thing etc. *to be, that*), whence **~'ABLE a., ~'ableNESS n., ~'abLY²** adv., (-ōōv-); (Sc. law, as verdict in criminal trial) *not proven*; establish genuineness & validity of (will); (intr.) turn out (*to be, to do*), turn out to be, as *will ~e (to be) the heir, to know nothing about it.* [ME, f. OF *prover* f. L *probare* test]
provĕd'itor, provĕdōre', nn. (-*tor*) officer of Venetian republic; caterer, purveyor. [f. obs. It. *proveditore*, Port. *provedor*, ult. f. L as PROVIDE, see -OR]
prōv'ĕnance, n. (Place of) origin, as *vases of doubtful ~*. [F, f. *provenir* f. L PRO¹- (*venire* come), see -ANCE]
Provençal (see Ap.), a. & n. (Inhabitant, language) of Provence. [F, as PROVINCIAL]
prŏv'ĕnder, n. Fodder; (joc.) food for human beings. [ME, f. OF *provend(:)e,* ult. f. LL *praebenaa,* see PREBEND]
provĕn'ience, n. = PROVENANCE. [f. L as PROVENANCE, see -ENCE]
prŏv'ĕrb, n. Short pithy saying in general use, adage, saw; *ignorant etc. to a ~* (notoriously); *their fickleness is a ~* (notorious), *he is a ~* (byword) *for inaccuracy*; play (usu. French) based on *~*; (pl.) kinds of round game; (*Book of*) *P~s* (in O.T.). [ME, f. OF *proverbe* or L PRO¹- (*verbium* f. *verbum* word)]
provĕrb'ial, a. Of, expressed in, proverbs, as *~ wisdom*; that has become a proverb, notorious. Hence **~ITY** (-ăl¹) **n., ~LY²** adv. [f. L *proverbialis* (as prec., see -AL)]
prŏv'iant, n. Food supply esp. of army. [17th c., f. G; ult. as PROVENDER]
provid|e (-), v.i. & t. **1.** Make due preparation (*for* person's safety, entertainment, etc., *against* attack etc., occas. *for* undesirable thing); (of person, law, etc.)

stipulate (*that*); supply, furnish, (person *with* thing, thing *for* or *to* person); equip with necessaries, as *you must ~e yourselves*; make provision, esp. secure maintenance, (*for* oneself, family, etc.). **2.** (hist.). Appoint (incumbent *to* benefice); (of pope) appoint (successor *to* benefice not yet vacant). **3.** *~ing* (*that*) conj., = foll. [ME, f. L PRO¹(*vidēre vis-* see)]

provid'ĕd, a. & conj. **1.** In vbl senses, as ‖ *~ school*, public elementary school ~ by local authority. **2.** conj. On the condition or understanding, as ~ (*that*) *all is safe*, ~ (*that*) *he does no harm*. [-ED¹]

prŏv'idence, n. Foresight, timely care; thrift; beneficent care of God or nature, *special~*, particular instance of this; (*P~*) God. [ME, f. OF, or L *providentia* (as foll., see -ENCE)]

prŏv'ident, a. Having or showing foresight; thrifty. Hence ~LY² adv. [ME, f. L, as PROVIDE, see -ENT]

prŏvidĕn'tial (-shl), a. Of, by, divine foresight or interposition; opportune, lucky. Hence ~LY² (-sha-) adv. [f. as PROVIDENCE + -IAL]

provid'er, n. In vbl senses; *lion's ~*, jackal (lit. & fig.); ‖ *universal ~*, tradesman dealing in all or many kinds of goods etc. [-ER¹]

prŏv'ince, n. (Rom. hist.) territory outside Italy under Roman governor; principal division of country etc.; (eccl.) district under archbishop or metropolitan, e.g. Canterbury, York; *the ~s*, whole of a country outside the capital; sphere of action, business, as (*is not within*) *my ~*; branch of learning etc., as *in the ~ of polite letters*. [ME, f. OF, f. L *provincia* charge, province]

provin'cial (-shl), a. & n. **1.** Of a province; of the provinces; having the manners, speech, narrow views, etc., prevalent in these, whence ~ITY (-shiăl-) n. **2.** n. Inhabitant of a province or the provinces (also ~IST n.); countrified person; (eccl.) head of, chief of religious order in, a province. Hence ~IZE v.t., ~LY² adv., (-sha-). [ME, f. OF, or f. L *provincialis* (as prec., see -AL)]

provin'cialism (-sha-), n. Provincial manner, fashion, mode of thought, etc.; word, phrase, peculiar to county etc.; attachment to one's province rather than country. [-ISM]

provi'sion (-zhn), n., & v.t. **1.** Providing (*for*, *against*), esp. *make ~*; provided amount of something. **2.** pl. Supply of food, eatables & drinkables, whence ~LESS (-zho-) a. **3.** Legal or formal statement providing for something, clause of this. **4.** (hist.). Appointment to benefice not yet vacant; *P~s of Oxford*, ordinances for checking king's misrule drawn up by barons under Simon de Montfort in 1258. **5.** v.t. Supply with ~s,

whence ~MENT (-zho-) n. [ME, f. OF, f. L *provisionem* (as PROVIDE, see -ION)]

provi'sional (-zho-), a. For the time being, temporary. Hence **provisional'**ITY, ~NESS, nn., ~LY² adv., (-zho-). [-AL]

provis'o (-zō), n. (pl. ~s). Stipulation; clause of stipulation or limitation in document. [L, neut. abl. p.p., = PROVIDED *that*]

provis'or (-z-), n. **1.** (hist.). Holder of a PROVISION; *Statute of P~s* (preventing pope from granting provisions). **2.** (R.-C. Ch.) vicar general. [ME, f. AF *provisour* f. L *provisorem* (as PROVIDE, see -OR)]

provis'or|**ў** (-z-), a. Conditional; making provision, as ~ly *care*. Hence ~ILY² adv. [f. F *provisoire* (as prec., see -ORY)]

prŏvocā'tion, n. Incitement, instigation, irritation, as *did it under severe ~*. [ME, f. OF, or L *provocatio* (as PROVOKE, see -ATION)]

provŏc'ative, a. & n. (Thing) tending to provocation (*of* curiosity etc.); intentionally irritating. [f. F (-*if*, -*ive*), or LL *provocativus* (foll., -IVE)]

provŏk|**e'**, v.t. Rouse, incite, (person *to* anger, *to* do); irritate; instigate, tempt, allure; call forth (indignation, inquiry, a storm, etc.); cause, as *will~e fermentation*. Hence ~'ING² a., ~'ingLY² adv. [ME, f. OF *provoker* f. L PRO¹(*vocare* call)]

prŏv'ost (*in mil.* senses provō'), n. **1.** ‖ Head of some colleges at Oxford, Cambridge, etc.; (hist.) head of chapter or religious community. **2.** ‖ Head of Scottish municipal corporation or burgh (in some cities, *Lord P~*). **3.** Protestant clergyman in charge of principal church of town etc. in Germany etc. **4.** *~ marshal*, head of military police in camp or on active service, master-at-arms of ship on which court martial is to be held, chief police official in some colonies; (hist.) French semi-military officer; *~ sergeant*, sergeant of military police. Hence ~SHIP n. [OE *profost*, *pra-*, in ME reinforced by AF & OF *provost*, *pre-*, f. med. L *propositus* for *praepositus*, see PRAEPOSTOR]

prow¹, n. Fore-part immediately about stem of boat or ship; (zool., also *prora*) ~-like projection in front. [f. F *proue* f. L *prora* f. Gk *prō(i)ra*]

‖ **prow²**, a. (arch.). Worthy, gallant. [ME, . f. OF *prou*, *prod*, (F *preux*) f. LL as PROUD]

prow'ĕss, n. Valour, gallantry. [ME, f. OF *proece* (as prec., see -ESS²)]

prowl, v.i. & t., & n. **1.** Go about in search of plunder or prey (also fig.); traverse (streets, place) thus. **2.** n. ~ing, esp. *on the ~*. Hence ~'ER¹ n. [ME *prolle*, of unkn. orig.]

prŏx'imal, a. (anat.). Situated towards centre of body or of point of attachment (cf. DISTAL). Hence ~LY² adv. [f. L *proximus* nearest + -AL]

For other words in pro- see PRO-¹.

prŏx′imate, a. Nearest, next before or after (in place, order, time, connexion of thought, etc.); approximate. Hence ~LY² adv. [f. L *proximare* draw near (as prec.), see -ATE²]

‖**prŏx′imė accēss′ĭt** (aks-), sent., & n. (pl. -*ĕssēr′unt*). (Placed in list after name of candidate for prize etc.) he came very near (the winner); (n.) *I was, he got a,* ~ (was very near). [L]

prŏxim′itў̆, n. Nearness in space, time, etc. (*to*); ~ *of blood*, kinship; ~ *fuse*, radio device causing projectile to explode when near target. [f. F *proximité* f. L *proximitatem* (as PROXIMAL, see -TY)]

prŏx′ĭmō, a. (abbr. *prox*.). Of next month, as *the 3rd prox.* [L, = in next (*mense month*)]

prŏx′ў̆, n. Agency of substitute or deputy, as *married, voted, by* ~ ; person authorized to act for another, as *made me his* ~; writing authorizing person to vote on behalf of another, vote so given; (attrib.) done, given, made, by ~. [15th c. contr. f. obs. *procuracy* f. med. L *procuratia* (as PROCURATION, see -ACY)]

prud|e (prōōd), n. Woman of extreme (esp. affected) propriety in conduct or speech. Hence or cogn. ~′ERY(4), ~′ish-NESS, nn., ~′ISH¹ a., ~′ishLY² adv., (-ōō-). [c. 1700, as adj. & n., f. F *prude*, in OF *prude, prode*, back formation f. *prude-femme*; see PROW², PROUD]

pru′d|ent (-ōō-), a. (Of person or conduct) sagacious, discreet, worldly-wise. Hence or cogn. ~ENCE n., ~entLY² adv. [ME, f. OF or L *prudens* = *providens* PROVIDENT]

prudĕn′tial (-ōō-, -shl), a. & n. Of, involving, marked by, prudence, as ~ *motives, policy*; (n. pl.) ~ considerations or matters. Hence ~ISM(2), ~IST(2), nn., ~LY² adv., (-ōō-, -sha-). [f. L *prudentia* PRUDENCE + -AL or med. L -*alis*]

pru′inōse (-ōō-), a. (nat. hist.). Covered with white powdery substance, frosted. [f. L *pruinosus* (*pruina* hoar-frost, see -OSE¹)]

prune¹ (prōōn), n. Dried plum; colour of its juice, dark reddish purple (esp. attrib.); ~*s & prism* (of mincing way of speaking etc., Dickens' *Little Dorrit* II.v). [ME, f. OF *prune* f. Rom. **pruna* f. L *prunum* PLUM]

prune² (prōōn), v.t. Trim (tree etc., often *down*) by cutting away superfluous branches etc.; hence **prun′ER¹** (-ōōn-) n.; lop *off, away* (branches etc.); (fig.) remove (superfluities); *pruning-hook* (used for this purpose); clear (book etc. *of* what is superfluous. [ME *prouyne* f. OF *prooing-(n)ier, proignier*]

prune³ (prōōn), v.t. (now rare). = PREEN. [ME *prune, pruyne, proyne*, prob. of OF orig.; cf. PREEN]

prunĕll′a¹ (prōō-), n. Strong silk or worsted stuff used formerly for barristers' gowns etc. & later for uppers of women's shoes; LEATHER *&* ~. [17th c., = mod. F *prunelle*, of obsc. orig.]

prunĕll′a² (prōō-), n. Kinds of fever & of throat disorder; ~ *salt*, preparation of fused nitre used for ~; kinds of plants including the weed self-heal used to cure ~. [17th c., f. mod. L, earlier *br*-, dim. of med. L *brunus* BROWN]

prunĕll′ō (prōō-), n. (pl. ~s). Finest kind of prune, made esp. from greengages. [f. obs. It. *prunella* dim. of *pruna* PRUNE¹]

prŭnt, n. Piece of (esp. blackberry--shaped) ornamental glass laid on to vase etc., tool for applying this. [perh. dial. form of *print*]

prur′i|ent (-oor-), a. Given to indulgence of lewd ideas; (rare) having morbid desire or curiosity. Hence ~ENCE, ~ENCY, nn., ~entLY² adv. [f. L *prurire* itch, be wanton, see -ENT]

prurig′ō, -īt′us, (-oor-), nn. (Diseased state of skin marked by) violent itching (-*tus*). So **pruri′ginous** (-oor-) a. [L (gen. -*ginis, -tūs*), = itching, as prec.]

Prŭ′ssian (-shn), a. & n. (Native, inhabitant) of Prussia; ~ *blue*, a deep blue pigment, ~ *brown, green* (derived from or allied to this); ~ (small kind of) *carp*. Hence ~IZE(3)(-sha-) v.t., (esp.) assimilate to the ~ system of sacrificing the individual to the State. [17th c., f. mod. L *Prussianus* f. *Prussia*, see -AN]

prŭss′ic, a. Of, got from, Prussian blue; ~ *acid* (HYDROcyanic). [f. F *prussique* (*Prusse* Prussia, see -IC)]

prў̄¹, v.i. Look, peer, inquisitively (often *into, about* adv.); inquire impertinently *into* (person's affairs, conduct, etc.). Hence ~′ING² a., ~′inGLY² adv. [ME *prie*, of unkn. orig.]

prў̄², v.t. Var. of PRIZE³.

prў̄tanē′um, n. (Gk ant.). Public hall, esp. one in Athens for entertainment of ambassadors, presidents of senate, & specially honoured citizens. [L, f. Gk *prutaneion* f. *prutanis* president etc.]

psalm (sahm), n. Sacred song, hymn; *the* (*Book of*) *P*~s, (pop.) the *P*~s *of David*, book in O.T.; ~-*book*, book containing the P~s, metrical version of these for public worship. [OE (*p*)*sealm* f. LL f. Gk *psalmos* song sung to harp (*psallō* twang, sing to harp)]

psalm′ist (sahm-), n. Author of a psalm (also as title of book of psalmody); *the P*~, David or author of any of the Psalms. [f. LL *psalmista* (as prec., see -IST)]

psal′mod|ў̆ (sahm-, sălm-), n. Practice, art, of singing psalms, hymns, anthems, .etc., esp. in public worship, whence **psalmod′IC** (săl-) a., ~IST n., ~IZE(2) v.i., (sahm-, sălm-); arrangement of psalms for singing, psalms so arranged. [ME, f. LL *psalmodia* f. Gk *psalmōidia* singing to harp (as PSALM + *ō*(*i*)*dē* song)]

psal′ter (sawl-), n. The Book of Psalms; version of this, as *Latin, English, Prayer--book, Scotch Metrical, P*~; copy of the Psalms esp. for liturgical use. [ME & AF *sauter*, OF -*ier*, f. L f. Gk *psalterium*

psaltery stringed instrument (*psallō* twang), in eccl. L Book of Psalms; OE (*p*)*sallere* dir. f. LL]

psal'terý (sawl-), n. Ancient & medieval instrument like dulcimer but played by plucking strings with fingers or plectrum. [ME, f. OF *sauterie* etc. f. L as prec.]

psēph'ism (or s-), n. (Gk ant.). Decree enacted by vote of (esp. Athenian) public assembly. [f. Gk *psēphisma* (*psēphizō* vote f. *psēphos* pebble)]

psēph|ŏl'ogý (or s-), n. Study of elections and voting. Hence ~ŏL'OGIST n. [f. Gk *psēphos* pebble, vote, -LOGY]

pseud'ēchis (s- or ps-, -k-), n. (zool.). Kinds of venomous snakes, as ~ *poisoning*. [f. PSEUDO- + Gk *ekhis* viper]

pseudēpig'raph|a (s- or ps-), n. pl. Spurious writings, esp. Jewish writings ascribed to various O.T. prophets etc. Hence ~AL, **pseudĕpigrăph'ic**(AL), aa. [neut. pl. of Gk PSEUD(*epigraphos*, see EPIGRAPH)]

pseud|(o)- (s- or ps-), comb. form f. stem of meaning false(ly), seeming(ly) or professed(ly) but not real(ly), in compp. f. Gk, & as living pref. (occas. written separately without hyphen as adj., as *the~o penitent*), as : ~*o-archa'ic*, artificially archaic in style etc., so ~*o-arch'aism*, ~*o-arch'aist*; ~'*o-carp* (bot.), fruit formed from other parts besides the ovary; ~*o-cath'olic*; ~'*o-Christ*; ~*o-Chris'tian*; ~*o-class'ic*, pretending or wrongly held to be classic; ~*o-Goth'ic*, sham Gothic in style; ~*o-mart'yr*; ~*o-proph'et*.

pseud'ograph (s- or ps-, -ahf), n. A spurious literary work. [f. LL f. Gk PSEUDO-(*graphos* -GRAPH)]

pseudŏl'og|er (s- or ps-), n. (joc.). Systematic liar. So **pseudolŏ'ǵICAL** a., ~IST n. [f. Gk PSEUDO(*logos*, see -LOGER)]

pseud'o|mŏrph (s- or ps-), n. False form, esp. (mineral.) crystal etc. consisting of one mineral with form proper to another. Hence ~mŏrph'IC, ~mŏrph'OUS, aa., ~mŏrph'ISM(2), ~mŏrphO'IS, nn. [f. PSEUDO- + Gk *morphē* form]

pseud'onўm (s- or ps-), n. Fictitious name, esp. one assumed by author. [f. F (-*me*), f. Gk neut. adj. as foll.]

pseud|ŏn'ўmous (s- or ps-), a. Writing, written, under a false name. Hence ~onўm'ITY n. [f. Gk PSEUD(*ōnumos* f. *onoma* name) + -OUS]

pseud'o|scōpe (s- or ps-), n. Optical instrument making convex object seem concave & vice versa. Hence ~scŏp'IC a. [SCOPE]

pshaw (psh-, sh-), int., n., & v.i. & t. Int. expr. contempt or impatience; (n.) this exclamation; (v.i.) say ~ (often *at*); (v.t.) show contempt for (thing etc.) thus. [natural]

psī, n. Greek letter (Ψ, ψ) = ps. [Gk]

psīlăn'throp|ism (or s-), n. Doctrine that Christ was a mere man. So **psilanthrŏp'IC** a., ~IST n. [f. eccl. Gk *psilan-* *thrōpos* merely human (*psilos* bare, mere, + *anthrōpos* man) + -ISM]

psīlōs'is (or s-), n. (path.). Stripping bare, e.g. of hair or flesh; = SPRUE[2]. [Gk (prec., -OSIS)]

psĭtt'acīne (or s-), a. Of parrots, parrot-like. [f. L *psittacinus* (*psittacus* parrot, see -INE[1])]

psĭttacōs'is (s- or ps-), n. Epidemic disease somewhat resembling typhoid fever and pneumonia said to be caught by human beings from parrots. [f. L *psittacus* parrot + -OSIS]

psō'ās (or s-), n. ~ *magnus*, *parvus*, two hip muscles. [Gk, acc. pl. of *psoa*, taken as sing.]

psōr'a (or s-), n. A contagious skin disease, itch. [L, f. Gk *psōra*]

psōrī'asis (s- or ps-), n. Skin disease marked by red patches covered with scales. [Gk, see prec. & -ASIS]

psyche (sīk'ī, ps-), n. 1. Soul, spirit, mind, (in Gk myth. personified as beloved of Eros, & represented with butterfly wings). 2. Kinds of dayflying moths. [f. Gk *psukhē* breath, life, soul]

psychī'atr|ist (sīk-, psīk-), n. One who treats mental disease. So **psychiăt'rI-**c(AL) aa., ~Y[1] n., (sīk-, psīk-). [f. Gk as prec. + *iatros* physician + -IST]

psych'ic (sīk-, psīk-), a. & n. 1. = foll. ~ *force*, non-physical force assumed to explain spiritualistic phenomena. 2. n. Person susceptible to ~ influence, medium; (pl.) psychology; psychical research. [f. Gk *psukhikos* (PSYCHE, -IC)]

psych'ical (sīk-, psīk-), a. Of the soul or mind, whence ~LY[2] adv.; of the animal life of man; of phenomena & conditions apparently outside domain of physical law, esp. ~ *research*, so **psych'ic**ISM, **psych'ī**CIST, nn., (sīk-, psīk-). [AL-]

psych|o- (sīk-, psīk-), comb. form of Gk *psukhē* soul, mind, as : ~*ō-anăl'ўsts*, the psychology of Freud, Jung, & Adler, dividing the mind into conscious & unconscious elements, & investigating the interactions of these (so ~*ō-ăn'alўse* v.t., ~*ō-ăn'alўst* n., ~*ō-analўt'ic* a.); ~*ō-dўnăm'ic*(s), (science) of the mental powers; ~*ogen'esis*, ~*ŏg'ony*, genesis of soul or mind, so ~*ōgenĕt'ic*(al), ~*ōgŏn'ical*, aa.; ~'*ogram*, writing supposed to come from a spirit, ~'*ograph*, instrument for writing this; ~*ŏg'raphy*, descriptive branch of psychology, (also) spirit-writing; ~'*ōmancy*, occult communication between souls or with spirits; ~*ōm'etry*, faculty of divining from physical contact or proximity the qualities of an object or of persons etc. that have been in contact with it, so ~*ōmĕt'ric*(al) aa., (also) measurement of mental states or processes, so ~*ōmĕt'rics* n. pl.; ~*ōmŏt'or* a., inducing movement by psychic action; ~*ōneurōs'is*, mental disease consisting in loss of balance between instincts & controlling power; ~'*ōpath*, mentally deranged person, ~*ōpath'ic*,

~ŏp′athist,~ōpathŏl′ogy,~ŏp′athy, of, one who treats, science of, mental disease; ~ōphys′ics, science of general relations between mind & body, so ~ōphys′ical a., ~ōphys′icist n.; ~ōphysiŏl′ogy, branch of physiology dealing with mental phenomena, so ~ōphysiolo′gical a., ~ōphysiŏl′ogist n.; ~ōsomăt′ic a., of mind & body, (of bodily disease) caused or made worse by worry; ~ōtherapeut′ic,~ōthĕ′rapy,(of) treatment of mental illness.

psycholŏ′gical (sĭk-, psĭk-), a. Of psychology; ~ moment [f. F mistransl. of G moment neut. potent element as moment masc. moment of time], the ~ly appropriate moment, (improp., esp. joc.) nick of time. Hence~LY² adv. [-ICAL]

psychŏl′og|y̆ (sĭk-, psĭk-), n. Science of nature, functions & phenomena, of human soul or mind; treatise on, system of, this. So ~IST n., ~IZE(2, 3) v.t. & i. [f. mod. L psychologia (PSYCHO-, -LOGY)]

psychōs′is (sĭk-, psĭk-), n. (pl. -osēs). Severe mental derangement involving the whole personality, mental disease. Hence psychOT′IC (sĭk-, psĭk-) a. & n., of or relating to, (person) suffering from, a ~. [f. late Gk psukhōsis (psukhoō give life to, as PSYCHE, see -OSIS)]

psychrŏm′eter (sĭk-, psĭk-), n. Wet-&-dry-bulb thermometer. [f. Gk psukhros cold+-METER]

ptărm′igan (t-), n. Bird of grouse family, with black or grey plumage in summer & white in winter. [= Gaelic tarmachan; p- is pseudo-etym. after Gk wds in pt-]

pterid|ŏl′ogy̆ (pt-, t-), n. Study of ferns. So ~olō′gical a., ~ŏl′ogist n. [f. Gk pteris -idos, a feathery fern (pteron wing) +-o-+LOGY]

ptĕr|o- (pt-, t-), comb. form of Gk pteron wing, as: ~odac′tyl, extinct winged reptile;~ŏg′raphy, description of feathers, so ~ograph′ic(al) aa.; ~′opod, mollusc with middle part of foot expanded into pair of wing-like lobes; ~′osaur, extinct flying saurian reptile.

ptĕ′ropus (pt-, t-), n. (pl. -pī). FLYING fox. [f. Gk PTERO(pous foot) wing-footed]

ptĕ′ry̆goid (pt-, t-), a. ~ process, each of two processes descending from junction of body & great wing of sphenoid bone; connected with these. So ptĕ′ry̆go- (pt-, t-) comb. form. [f. Gk pterugoeidēs wing-like (pterux -ugos wing, -OID)]

ptisan (ti′zn, tĭzăn′), n. Nourishing decoction, esp. barley-water. [ME & OF tizanne etc. f. L f. Gk ptisanē peeled barley]

Ptŏlĕmā′ic (t-), a. Of Ptolemy, Alexandrine astronomer of 2nd c., esp.~ system (of astronomy, in which earth was held to be the stationary centre round which sun and stars revolved, cf. COPERNICAN); of the Ptolemies, rulers of Egypt from death of Alexander the Great to Cleopatra. [f. L f. Gk Ptolemaios+-IC]

ptomaine (tōm′ān, tomăn′), n. Kinds of (often poisonous) alkaloid body in putrefying animal & vegetable matter, esp. ~ poisoning. [f. It. ptomaina irreg. f. Gk ptōma corpse (piptō fall), -INE⁵]

ptōs′is (pt-, t-), n. Drooping of upper eyelid from paralysis of a muscle. [Gk ptōsis f. piptō fall]

‖ pŭb, n. (colloq.). Public house. [abbr.]

pŭb′erty̆, n. Being functionally capable of procreation; age of ~ (at which ~ begins; in England, legally, 14 in boys, 12 in girls). [ME, f. L pubertas (puber of the age of ~, see -TY)]

pūbĕs′c|ence, n. Arrival at puberty; soft down on leaves & stems of plants, downiness; soft down on parts of animals esp. insects. So ~ENT a. [F, or f. L pubescere, see -ENCE]

pŭb′lic, a. & n. 1. Of, concerning, the people as a whole, as ~ offence, holiday, (Parl.) ~ act, bill; ~ utility, a supply or undertaking usu. available in large towns, e.g. water, gas, electricity, etc. 2. Done by or for, representing, the people, as ~ prosecution, prosecutor, assembly. 3. ‖ (Univv.) of, for, acting for, the university, as ~ orator, lecture, examination. 4. Open to, shared by, the people, as ~ baths, library, road. 5. ‖~ house, inn, tavern, providing food & lodging, esp. alcoholic liquors to be consumed on premises; ~ education (at school, also, at ~ school); ~ school, one under ~ management, ‖ esp. endowed grammar (usu. boarding-) school preparing pupils chiefly for universities or ~ services, often maintaining discipline with help of pupils. 6. Open to general observation, done or existing in~, as made a ~ protest, gave it ~ utterance, whence ~LY² adv. 7. Of, engaged in, the affairs or service of the people, as ~ life, a ~ man, notary ~; ~ relations, relations of a department, organization, etc. with the general ~ (~ relations officer, abbr. P.R.O., person who gives out information to the ~ in connexion with some department etc.); ~ spirit, patriotism, so ~-spirited a., -spi′ritedly adv., -spi′ritedness n. 8. Of the nations, international, as proscribed Napoleon as a ~ enemy. 9. n. The (members of the) community in general, as the ~ is the best judge, are the best judges, the British, American, ~; section of the community, as the reading ~, the most gullible of~s; ‖~ house (colloq.); in ~, openly, ~ly. [ME, f. OF (-ique), or f. L publicus, see -IC]

pŭb′lican, n. (Rom. hist., & in N.T.) tax-farmer, tax-gatherer; ‖ keeper of public house. [ME & OF publicain f. L publicanus (as prec., see -AN)]

pūblicā′tion, n. Making publicly known; issuing of book, engraving, music, etc., to the public; book etc. so issued. [ME, f. OF, or f. L publicatio (as PUBLISH, see -ATION)]

pŭb′lic|ist, n. Writer on, person skilled

in, international law; writer on current public topics, esp. journalist. So ~ism n., ~is'tic a., ~ize v.t. [f. F *publiciste* f. L (*jus*) *publicum* public law, see -IST]

pŭbli'cĭtў, n. Openness to general observation, notoriety, (*avoid, court, ~; give ~ to*); the business of advertising (both goods and persons); ~ *agent*, person employed to keep the name of an actor etc. constantly before the public. [f. F -*ité* f. med. L *publicitatem* (PUBLIC, -ITY)]

pŭb'lish, v.t. Make generally known, noise abroad; announce formally, promulgate (edict etc.); ask, read, (banns of marriage); (of author, editor, or publisher) issue copies of (book, engraving, etc.) for sale to the public. Hence ~ABLE a. [ME *puplise, -ish, publisce*, etc. f. OF *puplier, publier* f. L *publicare* (as PUBLIC), see -ISH[2]]

pŭb'lisher, n. In vbl senses, esp. one who produces copies of book etc. & distributes them to booksellers or to the public. [-ER[1]]

pŭccoon', n. N.-Amer. plant yielding red or yellow dye. [native]

pūce, a. Flea-colour, purple-brown. [F, = flea (-colour), f. L *pulicem* (nom. -*ex*)]

pŭck[1], n. (*P~*) the goblin *Robin Goodfellow* or *Hobgoblin*; any mischievous sprite or (fig.) child. Hence ~'ISH[1], ~'LIKE, aa. [OE *pūca* = ON *pūki* mischievous demon; ult. orig. unkn.]

pŭck[2], n. (Disease in cattle attributed to) nightjar, goatsucker. [orig. unkn.]

pŭck[3], n. Rubber disc used for ice hockey. [orig. unkn.]

pŭck'a, pŭkk'a, a. (Anglo-Ind.). Of full weight; genuine; permanent, solidly built. [Hind. (*pakkā*), = cooked, ripe]

pŭck'er, v.i. & t., & n. 1. Contract, gather, (t. & i. of brow, seam, material, often *up*) into wrinkles, folds, or bulges, intentionally or as fault e.g. in sewing. 2. n. Such bulge etc. Hence ~Y[2] a. [vb c. 1600, prob. rel. to POKE[1], POCKET (cf. PURSE[2]), see -ER[5]]

pŭd, n. (nursery). Child's hand; fore-foot of some animals. [orig. unkn.; cf. PAD[3] (4)]

pu'dding (pŏŏ-), n. Soft or stiffish mixture of animal or vegetable ingredients, esp. mixed or enclosed in flour or other farinaceous food, cooked by boiling, steaming, or baking (*batter, beefsteak, bread-&-butter, currant,* HASTY, *lemon,* MILK[1], PLUM, *suet,* YORKSHIRE, ~); intestine of pig etc. stuffed with oatmeal, blood, etc. (BLACK, *hog's, white,* ~); *more praise than* ~ (material reward); *the* PROOF[1] *of the* ~ etc.; thing of ~-like appearance etc.; (sl.) drugged liver etc. given by burglars etc. to dogs; (naut., also *pu'ddening*) pad, tow binding, to prevent chafing etc.; ~-*cloth*, cloth in which some ~s are tied up for boiling; ~ *face*, large fat face; ~-*head*, dolt; ~-*heart*, coward; ‖ ~ *pie*, forms of pastry; ~-*stone*, composite rock of rounded pebbles in silicious matrix.

Hence ~Y[2] a. [ME *poding*, of obsc. orig.; cf. syn. OF *bodin*, mod. F *boudin*]

pŭd'dle[1], n. Small dirty pool esp. of rain on road etc.; (colloq.) muddle, mess; clay (& sand) mixed with water as watertight covering for embankments etc. Hence pŭdd'LY[1] a. [ME *podel, puddel*, dim. of OE *pudd* ditch; cf. LG *pudel*, G *pfudel*]

pŭd'dle[2], v.i. & t. Dabble, wallow, (often *about*) in mud or shallow water; busy oneself in untidy way; make (water, also fig.) muddy; knead (clay & sand) into, make, line (canal etc.) with, PUDDLE[1]; stir about (molten iron) to produce wrought iron by expelling carbon. Hence pŭdd'ler[1] (1, 2) n. [ME f. prec.; cf. Du. *poedeln*, LG *pud(d)eln* splash in water (see POODLE)]

pŭd'encў, n. Modesty. [f. LL *pudentia* (as foll., see -ENCY)]

pūdĕn'dum, n. (usu. in pl. -*da*). Privy parts. Hence or cogn. pūdĕn'dAL, pūd'ic, aa. [L (*pudēre* be ashamed)]

pŭdge, n. (colloq.). Short thick or fat person, animal, or thing. Hence pŭdg'Y[2] a. [cf. PODGE]

pŭd'sў (-z-), a. Plump. [cf. prec. & PUD]

pue'blō (pwĕ-), n. (pl. ~s). Spanish (-Amer.) town or village, esp. settlement of Indians. [Sp.]

pū'erile, a. Boyish, childish; trivial, whence or cogn. ~LY[2] adv., pūeril'ITY n.; ~ *breathing* (with loud pulmonary murmur as in children, usu. sign of disease in adult). [F, or f. L *puerilis* (*puer* boy, -ILE)]

pūĕrp'eral, a. Of, due to, childbirth. [f. L *puerperus* (*puer* child + -*parus* bearing) + -AL]

pŭff[1], n. 1. Short quick blast of breath or wind; sound (as) of this; small quantity of vapour, smoke, etc., emitted at one ~. 2. Round soft protuberant mass of material in dress, of hair of head, etc. 3. (Also *powder-~*) small pad of down or the like for applying powder to skin. 4. Piece, cake, etc., of light pastry esp. of ~ *paste*. 5. Unduly or extravagantly laudatory review of book, advertisement of tradesman's goods etc., esp. in newspaper. 6. ~-*adder*, large venomous African viper inflating upper part of body when excited; ~-*ball*, fungus with ball-shaped spore-case; ~-*box* (containing powder & ~); ~ *paste*, light flaky paste; ‖ ~-~ (nursery), steam-engine, train. [ME *puf*, imit., see foll.]

pŭff[2], v.i. & t. 1. Emit puff of air or breath; (of air etc.) come *out, up,* in puffs; breathe hard, pant, esp. ~ *& blow*; put out of breath, as *was rather ~ed*; ~ *out,* utter pantingly; (of steam-engine, person smoking, etc.) emit puffs, move with puffs, as ~*ed away at his cigar, ~ed out of the terminus.* 2. Blow (dust, smoke, light object, *out, up, away,* etc.) with puff; smoke (pipe) in puffs. 3. Blow *out, up,* inflate; become inflated, swell *up, out*; ~ *up,* elate, make proud, (esp. in p.p.

with pride etc.). **4.** Advertise (goods) with exaggerated or false praise; ‖ bid at auction to raise price. Hence ~'ER¹ n. [ME *puffe*, imit., see prec.]

pŭff'erўy, n. Advertisement, puffing; puff frilling, puffs. [-ERY]

pŭff'in, n. N.-Atlantic sea-bird with large furrowed particoloured bill. [ME *poffin*, of unkn. orig.]

pŭff'|ўy, a. Gusty; short-winded; puffed out; corpulent. Hence ~īNESS n. [-Y²]

pŭg¹, n. **1.** (Also ~-*dog*) dwarf squat-faced breed of dog like bulldog, whence ~g'ISH¹, ~g'Y², aa., (-g-); ~-*nose*(*d*), (with) short squat or snub nose. **2.** ‖ (Among servants) upper servant in large establishment. **3.** (Quasi-proper name for) fox. **4.** ‖ Small locomotive for shunting etc. [orig. unkn.]

pŭg², n., & v.t. (-gg-). Loam or clay mixed & prepared for brickmaking etc.; (v.t.) prepare (clay) thus, pack (space esp. under floor, to deaden sound) with ~, sawdust, etc.; ~-*mill* (for preparing ~). Hence ~g'ING¹(3) (-g-) n. [orig. unkn.]

pŭg³, n., & v.t. (Anglo-Ind.). Footprint of beast; (v.t.; -gg-) track by ~s. [f. Hind. *pag* footprint]

pŭg⁴, n. (sl.). Pugilist. [abbr.]

pŭgg'(a)ree (-rĭ), n. Indian's light turban; thin scarf of muslin etc. worn round hat & sometimes falling down behind to keep off sun. Hence **pŭgg'(a)reED²** (-rĭd) a. [f. Hind. *pagri* turban]

pū'gil|ĭst, n. Boxer, fighter; (fig.) vigorous controversialist. So ~ISM n., ~ĭs'TIC a., ~ĭs'TICALLY adv. [f. L *pugil* boxer (*pugnus* fist) +-IST]

pŭgnā'cious (-shŭs), a. Disposed to fight, quarrelsome. Hence or cogn. ~LY² adv., **pŭgnā'cITY** n. [f. L *pugnax* (*pugnare* fight, see -ACIOUS)]

puisne (pūn'ĭ), a. & n. ~ (*judge*), judge of superior court inferior in rank to chief justice; (law) later, subsequent (*to*), as ~ *mortgagees*, *mortgagees* ~ *to the plaintiff*. [OF (*puis* after f. L *postea* +*né* born f. L *natus*); cf. PUNY]

pū'iss|ant (*or* pūĭs⁴ *or* pwĭs⁴), a. (arch.). Having great power or influence, mighty. Hence or cogn. ~ANCE n., ~antLY² adv. [ME, f. OF f. Rom. **possiantem* f. *posse*; see POTENT]

pu'ja (pōō-), pōō'ja, n. Hindu religious rites (generally); (Anglo-Ind. sl., usu. pl.) prayers. [Hind. f. Skr. *pūjā*]

pūke, v.i. & t., & n. Vomit. [16th c., orig. unkn.]

pukka(h). = PUCKA.

pŭl'chritude (-kr-), n. Beauty. [ME, f. L *pulchritudo* (*pulcher* beautiful, -TUDE)]

pūle, v.i. Cry querulously or weakly, whine. Hence **pūl'ingLY²** adv. [16th c., imit., perh. f. F *piauler*]

pull¹ (pŏol), v.t. & i. Exert upon (thing) force tending to draw it to oneself, as *don't* ~ *my hair*, ~ *his ears* or *him by the ear* (as chastisement), ~ *his nose* or *him by the nose* (as insult), ~ *his sleeve* or *him by the sleeve* (to gain attention), ~ *the* (bell-rope or handle to ring the) *bell*, ~ person's LEG, ~ (= *draw*) *the* LONG¹-*bow*, ~ *the* STRINGS, WIRES. **2.** Draw (thing etc.) towards oneself or in direction so regarded, as ~ *it nearer*, ~ *him into the room*, ~ *your cap over your ears*, ~ *off* one's *hat* (as salutation), ~ *on* one's *stockings*. **3.** Attract or secure (support, custom). **4.** ~ (thing) *to pieces*, separate its parts forcibly, (fig.) criticize (person, thing) unfavourably. **5.** Exert ~ing force, as *horse* ~s *well*, ~*ed* (*away*) *at the handle*; exert influence in favour of person. **6.** Proceed with effort (*up* hill etc.); (of horse) strain, esp. habitually, against bit; ~ *devil*, ~ BAKER. **7.** Draw, suck, *at* (pipe, tankard). **8.** Pluck (plant, often *up*) by root. **9.** ~*ed*, reduced in health or spirits; ~*ed bread*, pieces from inside of new loaf, rebaked till crisp. **10.** ~ *caps*, *wigs*, scuffle, quarrel. **11.** Tear, pluck, *at* (thing). **12.** Print upon (sheet), print (copy, proof), orig. in old hand-press by ~ing bar towards one. **13.** Move boat, move (boat), by ~ing oar; (of boat) be rowed, be rowed by (so many oars), as *she* ~*ed inshore*, ~*s 6 oars*; ~ (row with effect in proportion to) one's *weight*. **14.** (sl.). Arrest; make raid on (gambling-house etc.). **15.** Check (horse) esp. so as to make him lose .*race*; ~ one's *punches* (boxing), fail to give full force to one's blows, also fig. **16.** (Crick.) strike (ball, or abs.), strike ball bowled by (bowler), from off to leg; (golf) drive (ball, or abs.) widely to left (of right-handed player). **17.** ~ *a* FACE¹, ~ *a sanctimonious* etc. *face*, assume such expression. **18.** ~ *about*, ~ from side to side, treat roughly; ~ *down*, demolish (building etc.), lower in health, spirits, price, etc.; ~ *in*, (of train) enter station; ~ *off*, win (prize, contest); ~ *out*, row out, (of train) move out of station; ~ *out of the fire*, save (game etc.) when the case seems hopeless; ~-*out* n., page or plate in book that folds out from front edge of leaves to facilitate reference; ~-*over* n., sweater put on over head; ~ *through* adv. & prep., get (person), get oneself, safely through (danger, illness, etc., or abs.); ~-*through* n., cord with which cleaning-rag is drawn through rifle; ~ one*self together*, rally, recover oneself; ~ *together*, work in harmony; ~ *up*, cause (person, horse, vehicle) to stop, reprimand, check oneself, advance one's relative position in race etc.; ~-*up* n., house of call for travellers. **19.** ~-*back*, retarding influence, check, contrivance for ~ing fullness of woman's skirt to back. [late OE *pullian*, of unkn. orig.]

pull² (pŏol), n. **1.** Act of pulling, wrench, tug; force thus exerted; (fig.) means of exerting influence, interest with the powerful. **2.** (print.). Rough proof. **3.** Pulling at bridle to check horse esp. in racing. **4.** Spell of rowing. **5.** (Crick., golf) pulling stroke. **6.** ‖ (In public house) supply of beer etc. exceeding that asked for. **7.** *Have the*~ (advantage) *of* (person). **8.** Deep draught of liquor. **9.** Handle etc. by which ~ is applied, as BEER¹, BELL¹, ~~. [f. prec.]

pu'ller (pŏŏ-), n. In vbl senses, esp.: kinds of instrument or machine for pulling; horse that pulls esp. against bit. [-ER¹]

pu'llèt (pŏŏ-), ·n. Young fowl, esp. hen from time she begins to lay till first moult. [ME, f. OF *poulet* dim. of *poule*]

pu'lley (pŏŏ-), n. (pl. ~s), & v.t. **1.** Grooved wheel(s) for cord etc. to pass over, mounted in block & used for changing direction of power, one of the simple mechanical powers; wheel, drum, fixed on shaft & turned by belt, used esp. to increase speed or power. **2.** v.t. Hoist, furnish, work, with~. [ME & OF *polie* ult. f. Gk *pòlidion* pivot dim. of *polos* POLE²]

Pu'llman (pŏŏ-), a. & n. ~ (*car*), railway saloon carriage usu. arranged for use as sleeping-car. [G. M.~, designer (d. 1897)]

pŭll'ŭl|āte, v.i. (Of shoot, bud) sprout out, bud; (of seed) sprout; (fig., of doctrines etc.) develop, spring up. Hence ~ANT a., ~A'TION n. [f. L *pullulare* sprout (*pullulus* dim. of *pullus* young of animal), see -ATE³]

‖ **pu'llȳ-haul'ȳ** (pŏŏ-), a. & n. (colloq.). (Of) pulling & hauling. So **pu'llȳ-haul** (pŏŏ-) v.t. & i. [-Y²]

pŭlm|o-, shortened f. *pulmoni-*, comb. form of L *pulmo -monis* lung, as: ~*obranch'iate*, with gills modified for air--breathing; ~*òm'eter*, instrument measuring capacity of lungs, so ~*òm'etry*.

pŭl'monarȳ a. Of, in, connected with, the lungs, as ~ *artery*, main artery conveying blood from heart to lungs, ~ *disease*; having lungs or lung-like organs, so **pŭl'monATE²** a.; affected with, subject to, lung-disease. So **pŭlmŏn'ıC** a. [f. L *pulmonarius* (prec., -ARY¹)]

pŭlp, n., & v.t. & i. **1.** Fleshy part of fruit; any fleshy or soft part of animal body, e.g. nervous substance in interior cavity of tooth; soft formless mass, esp. that of rags, wood, etc., from which paper is made; ore pulverized &. mixed with water. **2.** vb. Reduce to ~, remove ~ from (coffee-beans), whence ~'ER¹(2) n.; become ~y. Hence or cogn. ~'ıFY v.t., ~'ıNESS n., ~'LESS, ~'OUS, ~'Y², aa. [f. L *pulpa*]

pu'lpıt (pŏŏ-), n. Raised enclosed platform usu. with desk & seat from which preacher in church or chapel delivers sermon; *the* profession of preaching; preachers; (in title of book) collected sermons; (attrib.) ~ *eloquence, orator, style.* [ME, f. L *pulpitum* scaffold, platform]

pulpit|eer' (pŏŏ-), n., & v.i. Professional preacher (usu. derog.), so ~AR'IAN a. &

n.; (v.i.) preach, whence ~eer'ıNG¹ n. [-EER]

pulque (pŏŏl'kĕ), n. Mexican fermented drink from sap of agave etc.; ~ *brandy*, intoxicant made from ~. [Sp.-Amer.]

pŭlsāte' (*or* pŭl'-), v.t. & i. Expand & contract rhythmically, beat, throb (lit. & fig.); vibrate, quiver, thrill; agitate (diamonds) with machine (**pŭlsāt'oR** n.) to separate them from earth in which they are found. Hence or cogn. **pŭlsA'TION** n., **pŭl'satorȳ** a. [f. L *pulsare* frequent. of *pellere puls-* drive, beat, see -ATE³]

pŭl'satile, a. Of, having the property of, pulsation; (of musical instrument) played by percussion. [as prec. +-ıLE]

pŭlsatill'a, n. The pasque-flower, its extract used in pharmacy. [med. L; dim. of *pulsata* fem. p.p. (as prec.), as quivering in wind]

pŭlse¹, n., & v.i. & t. **1.** Rhythmical throbbing of arteries as blood is propelled along them esp. as felt in wrists, temples, etc.; *feel* person's ~ (as indicating by its rate & character his state of health, fig., sound his intentions etc.); each successive beat of arteries or heart; (fig.) throb, thrill, of life or emotion; rhythmical recurrence of strokes e.g. of oars; (mus.) beat; single beat or vibration of sound, light, etc. **2.** v.i. Pulsate (lit. & fig.); (v.t.) send *out, in*, etc., by rhythmic beats. Hence ~'LESS a., ~'lèssNESS n. [(n.) ME & OF *pous* f. L *pulsus -ūs* f. *pellere puls-* drive; vb f. L *pulsare* (as PULSATE)]

pŭlse², n. (Collective sing., sometimes with pl. vb) edible seeds of leguminous plants e.g. peas, beans, lentils; (with pl.) any kind of these. [ME, f. OF *po(u)ls* f. L *puls -ltis* pottage of meal etc.]

pŭlsim'ēter, n. Instrument for measuring rate or force of pulse. [f. PULSE¹+-ı-+ -METER]

pŭlsŏm'ēter, n. Steam-condensing vacuum pump, so called from pulsatory action of the steam. [P; irreg. as prec., -o-]

pŭltā'ceous (-shŭs), a. Of (the nature of) pap or a poultice, soft, pulpy. [as PULSE², see -ACEOUS]

pŭl'verIz|e, -is|e (-ız), v.t. & i. Reduce to powder or dust, divide (liquid) into spray, whence ~ātoR, ~ER¹(2), nn.; (fig.) demolish, crush, smash; (intr.) crumble to dust. Hence ~ABLE a., ~A'TION n. [f. LL *pulverizare* (*pulvis -eris* dust, see -IZE)]

pŭlvĕ'rulent (-rŏŏ-), a. Powdery, of dust; covered with powder; (of rock etc.) of slight cohesion, apt to crumble. [f. L *pulverulentus* (as prec., see -LENT)]

pŭl'vinate, -ātĕd, aa. (Archit., -*ed*) swelling, esp. (of frieze) with convex face; (bot., entom.) cushion-like, having cushion-like swelling. [f. L *pulvinatus* (*pulvinus* cushion), see -ATE²(2)]

pūm'a, n. = COUGAR. [Sp. f. Peruv.]

pŭm'ıce(-stōne), n., & v.t. (Piece of) light spongy kind of lava used for removing stains from hands etc., polishing, etc.; (v.t.) rub, clean, with ~ ; ~ *hoof* of horse, made spongy by disease. So pūmi′cĕous a. [ME & OF *pomis* f. Rom. **pŏmicem*, L *pŭmex*; cf. POUNCE²]

pŭmm′el, v.t. (-ll-). Strike repeatedly esp. with fist. [altered f. POMMEL]

pŭm(m)′elō. Var. of POMELO.

pŭmp¹, n. 1. Machine, usu. cylinder in which piston etc, is moved up & down by rod, for raising water; kinds of machine for raising or moving liquids, compressing or rarefying gases, etc. (fig. of heart, insect's suckers, etc.); AIR¹, FORCE¹, STOMACH, -~ ; *bicycle*-~ (for inflating tires); pumping, stroke of ~ ; attempt, person skilful, at pumping others. 2. ~-*brake*, handle of ship's ~ esp. with transverse bar for several persons to work at; ~-*handle* v.t. (colloq.), shake (person's hand) effusively; ~-*room*, building where ~ is worked esp. at spa where medicinal water is dispensed. [ME *pumpe, pompe*, = early mod. Du. *pompe*, LG *pump(e)*; prob. imit.]

pŭmp², v.i. & t. Work a pump; remove, raise, (water etc., usu. *out, up*) thus; make (ship, well, etc.) *dry* by ~ing; ~ *up*, inflate (pneumatic tire), inflate tires of (bicycle etc.); bring out, pour forth, (abuse etc. *upon*) as by ~ing; elicit information from (person), elicit (information, usu. *out of* person), by artful or persistent questions; (of exertion) put completely out of breath (esp. pass.); (of mercury in barometer) rise & fall instantaneously; ~'*ship* (not in polite use), (v.i.) make water, (n.) urination. Hence ~'ER¹ n. (esp., rail TROLLEY). [f. prec.]

pŭmp³, n. Kind of light shoe now usu. of patent leather & without fastening, worn with evening dress & for dancing. [orig. unkn.]

pu′mpernĭckel (pŏŏ-), n. German wholemeal rye bread. [G, f. earlier sense boor, 'stinker']

pŭmp′kin, n. (Cucurbitaceous plant bearing) large egg-shaped or globular fruit with edible layer next to rind, used in cookery & for cattle. [alt. f. 16th c. *pompon, pumpion*, f. obs. F *po(m)pon* f. L f. Gk *pepōn*]

pŭn¹, n. & v.i. (-nn-). 1. Humorous use of word to suggest different meanings, or of words of same sound with different meanings, play on words. 2. v.i. Make ~s (*upon* word, subject). Hence ~n′ing-LY² adv. [17th c., of obsc. orig.]

‖ pŭn², v.t. (-nn-). Consolidate (earth, rubble) by pounding or ramming; work *up* to proper consistency with PUNNER. [dial. var. of POUND³]

pu′na (pŏŏ-), n. High bleak plateau in Peruvian Andes; difficulty in breathing caused by rarefied atmosphere. [Peruv., in first sense]

pŭnch¹, n. Instrument or machine for cutting holes in leather, metal, paper, etc.,

driving bolt etc. out of hole (*starting*-~), enlarging hole, forcing nail beneath surface (*driving*-~), etc.; tool or machine for impressing design or stamping die on material; *bell*-~, conductor's ticket-~ with bell to announce punching of ticket. [app. var. of POUNCE¹, or short f. PUN-CHEON¹]

pŭnch², v.t., & n. 1. Strike esp. with closed fist, as ~ *his head*; ~*ing-ball*, inflated ball held by elastic bands etc. & ~ed as form of exercise; prod with stick etc., esp. *drive (cattle) thus; pierce (metal, leather, bus-ticket, etc.) as or with punch; pierce (hole) thus; drive (nail etc. *in, out*) with punch. 2. n. Blow with fist (*a* ~ *on the head*; PULL¹ one's ~*es*; ~-*drunk*, dazed through being severely ~ed, also transf.); (sl.) vigour, momentum, effective force. Hence ~′ER¹(1, 2) n, [vb var. of POUNCE¹ (16th c. in same senses), see prec.; n. f. vb]

pŭnch³, n. Drink usu. of wine or spirits mixed with hot water or milk, sugar, lemons, spice, etc., as *brandy, rum, milk*, ~ ; bowl of ~ ; party at which ~ is drunk; ~-*bowl*, bowl in which ~ is mixed, round deep hollow in hill(s). [f. 1632, orig. unkn.; perh. abbr. of PUNCHEON²]

pŭnch⁴, n. 1. ‖ (*Suffolk*) ~, short-legged thickset draught horse; ‖ (dial.) short fat man or thing. 2. (P~) grotesque humpbacked figure in puppet-show called *P~ & Judy*, esp. as title of a London weekly comic paper; *as pleased, as proud, as P~* (much, very). [abbr. of PUNCHINELLO]

pŭn′cheon¹ (-shn), n. Short post esp. one supporting roof in coal-mine; (now rare) = PUNCH¹. [ME, f. OF *poinçon, poinchon*, f. Rom. **punctionem* or **punctiare* (L *pungere* punct- prick), see -ION]

pŭn′cheon² (-shn), n. (hist.). Large cask for liquids etc. holding from 72 to 120 gals. [ME, f. OF *poinçon, poinchon*, etc., of unkn. orig.]

Pŭnchinĕll′ō, n. (pl. ~s). Chief character in Italian puppet-show; short stout person. [17th c. *polichinello* f. Neapolitan dial. *Polecenella*, of uncert. orig.]

pŭnc′t|āte, a. (nat. hist., path.). Marked or studded with points, dots, or spots. So ~A′TION n. [f. L as POINT¹, see -ATE²(2)]

pŭnctil′io (-lyō), n. (pl. ~s). Nice point of ceremony or honour; petty formality. [ř. It. *puntiglio* & Sp. *puntillo* dim. of *punto* POINT¹]

pŭnctil′ious (-lyus), a. Attentive to punctilios. Hence ~LY² adv., ~NESS n. [f. F *pointilleux* f. *pointille* (f. It. as prec., see -OUS]

pŭnc′tual, a. Observant of appointed time; in good time, not late; (arch.) punctilious; (geom.) of a point. Hence ~ITY (-ăl²-) n., ~LY² adv. [ME, f. med. L *punctualis* (*punctus* -ūs POINT¹ see -AL)]

pŭnc′tŭāt|e, v.t. Insert stops in (writing), mark or divide with stops; (fig.) interrupt (speech) *with* exclamations etc.; (improp.)

emphasize, accentuate, as *flung it on the ground to* ~*e his refusal*. Hence or cogn. ~IVE a., ~OR n. [f. med. L *punctuare* (as prec.), see -ATE[3]]

pŭnctuā′tion, n. Insertion of vowel & other points in Hebrew etc.; practice, art, of punctuating. [f. med. L *punctuatio* (prec., -ATION)]

pŭnc′t|um, n. (pl. ~*a*). Speck, dot, spot of colour or elevation or depression on surface. So ~ULE n., whence ~ŭlATE[2](2) a., ~ŭlA′TION n. [L, = POINT[1]]

pŭnc′ture, n., & v.t. & i. 1. Pricking, prick, esp. accidental pricking of pneumatic tire; hole thus made. 2. v.t. Prick, pierce; (v.i. of tire, bicycle etc., rider etc.), experience a ~. [ME, f. L *punctura* (*pungere punct-*, see POINT[1], -URE)]

pŭn′dit, n. Hindu learned in Sanskrit & in philosophy, religion, & jurisprudence, of India; (joc.) learned teacher. [f. Hind. *pandit*]

pŭn′gent (-j-), a. (Nat. hist.) sharp-pointed; (of reproof, satire, etc.) biting, caustic; mentally stimulating, piquant; affecting organs of smell or taste, or skin etc., with pricking sensation, as ~ *gas, smoke, sauce*. Hence **pŭn′gENCY** n., ~LY[2] adv., (-j-). [f. L *pungere* prick, -ENT]

Pūn′ic, a. & n. Carthaginian; ~ *Wars* (between Rome & Carthage); ~ FAITH; (n.) ~ language. [f. L *Punicus, Poen-* (*Poenus* f. Gk *Phoinix* Phoenician, see -IC)]

pŭn′ish, v.t. 1. Cause (offender) to suffer for offence; chastise; inflict penalty on (offender); inflict penalty for (offence). 2. (colloq.). Inflict severe blows on (opponent in boxing); (of race, competitor) tax severely the powers of (competitor); take full advantage of (weak bowling, bowler, stroke at tennis); make heavy inroad on (food etc.); whence ~ING[2] a. Hence ~ABIL′ITY, ~ER[1], ~MENT, nn., ~ABLE a., ~ablY[2] adv. [ME, f. OF *punir* (-ISH[2]) f. L *punire* (*poena* PAIN)]

pŭn′itive, a. Inflicting punishment, retributive, as ~ *justice, expedition*; ~ *police* (India), detachment of police sent to a particular district and paid for by the inhabitants as punishment for lawlessness. So **pŭn′itORY** a. [f. F (-*if, -ive*) or med. L *punitivus* (as prec., see -IVE)]

‖ **pŭnk[1]**, n. (arch.). Prostitute. [c. 1600, of unkn. orig.]

*****pŭnk[2]**, n. & a. 1. Rotten wood, fungus growing on wood, used as tinder; worthless stuff, rubbish, tosh. 2. adj. (sl.). Worthless, rotten. [16th c., of obsc. orig.; cf. SPUNK]

pŭnk′a(h) (-kə), n. (E.-Ind.). Portable fan usu. of leaf of palmyra; large swinging cloth fan on frame worked by cord. [f. Hind. *pankha*]

pŭnn′er, n. Tool for ramming earth about post etc. [f. PUN[2]+-ER[1]]

pŭnn′ĕt, n. Small chip basket for fruit or vegetables. [orig. unkn.]

pŭn′ster, n. Inveterate maker of puns. [-STER]

pŭnt[1], n., & v.t. & i. 1. Flat-bottomed shallow boat, broad & square at both ends, propelled by long pole thrust against bottom of river etc. 2. vb. Propel with or use ~-pole; convey in a~. Hence **pŭn′ter[1]** [-ER[1]], **pŭn′tIST**, nn. [ME, f. MLG *punte*, MDu. *ponte*, f. L *ponto*, kind of Gallic transport, whence OE *punt*]

pŭnt[2], v.t., & n. 1. Kick (football) after it has dropped from the hands & before it reaches ground. 2. n. Such kick; ~-*about*, kicking about of football for practice, ball so used. [prob. dial. orig.]

pŭnt[3], v.i., & n. 1. (At faro & other card-games) lay stake against bank; (colloq.) bet on horse etc. 2. n. Player who ~s; point in faro. Hence **pŭn′ter[2]** [-ER[1]] n. [c. 1700, f. F *ponte(r)*]

pŭn′tỹ, pŏ-, n. Iron rod used in glass-blowing. [app. f. F *pontil* f. It. *puntello* dim. of *punto* POINT[1]]

pŭn′|ỹ, a. Undersized; weak, feeble; petty. Hence ~iNESS n. [f. 16th c., phonetic sp. of PUISNE]

pŭp, n., & v.t. & i. (-pp-). 1. Young dog; *in* ~, pregnant; *conceited* etc. ~ (boy, young man); *sell* person *a*~, swindle him esp. by selling thing on prospective value. 2. vb. Bring forth ~s; give birth to. [shortened f. PUPPY]

pūp′|a, n. (pl. ~*ae*). Chrysalis. Hence ~AL a. [L, = girl, doll]

pūp′|āte, v.i. Become a pupa. Hence ~A′TION n. [-ATE[3]]

pūp′il, n. 1. One who is taught by another, scholar; (law) person below age of puberty & under care of guardian; ~-*teacher*, boy, girl, teaching in elementary school under head teacher & concurrently receiving general education from him or elsewhere. 2. Circular opening in centre of iris of eye regulating passage of light to the retina. So ~(l)AR[1], ~(l)ARY[2], aa. [f. OF *pupille* f. L *pupillus, -la*, ward, minor, (-*la*) ~ of eye]

pūp′il(l)|age, n. Nonage, minority (fig. of country, language, etc.), so ~ā′rITY n. (law); being a pupil. So **pūp′ilSHIP** n. [-AGE[3]]

pūp′il(l)īze, -ise (-īz), v.t. & i. Take pupils; coach (pupil). [-IZE]

pūpip′arous; a. (entom.). Bringing forth young already advanced to pupal state. [f. PUPA+L -*parus* -bearing]

pŭpp′et, n. Figure, usu. small, representing human being, esp. one with jointed limbs moved by wires etc. in ~-show; person whose acts are controlled by another; ~-*play*, -*show* (with ~s as characters); ~-*clock*, -*valve*, disc valve opened by lifting bodily from its seat, not hinged; ~ *state*, country professing to be independent but actually under the control of some greater power, so ~ *king, ruler*. Hence ~RY(4, 5) n. [16th c., var. of POPPET]

pŭpp′y̆, n. Young dog (also, childish, ~-*dog*); vain empty-headed young man, coxcomb, whence ~ISM n. Hence ~DOM, ~HOOD, nn., ~ISH¹ a. [ME, perh. f. OF *poupée* doll, plaything, toy]

pur-, pref. AF form of OF *por-, pur-,* f. L *por-,* PRO-¹ (*purchase, purport, pursue*).

pŭrā′na (poorah-), n. Any of a class of Sanskrit sacred poems. Hence **pura′nıc** (poorah-) a. [f. Skr. *puraṇa* of former times (*pura* formerly)]

Pŭrb′ĕck, a. ~ *stone,* hard limestone from ~ in Dorset; ~ *marble,* finer qualities of this.

pŭrb′lind, a., & v.t. Partly blind, dim-sighted; (fig.) obtuse, dull; (v.t.) make ~. Hence ~NESS n. [ME *pur*(e) *blind; pur-* = PURE in sense ‘quite’, w. assim. to PUR-]

pŭrch′ase¹, n. **1.** Buying; ~-*money,* price (to be) paid; (hist.) practice of buying commissions in army; thing bought; annual return from land, as *sold at 20 years'* ~; (fig.) *life is not worth an hour's* ~, cannot be trusted to last an hour; (law) acquisition of property by one's personal action, not by inheritance. **2.** Mechanical advantage, leverage, (often fig.); appliance for gaining this, esp. (naut.) rope, windlass, pulley (*single, double, treble,* -~ *pulley,* with 1, 2, 3, sheaves). [ME, f. OF *porchas, pur-,* as foll.]

pŭrch′as|e², v.t. **1.** Buy; acquire (victory, freedom, etc., *with* one's blood, toil, etc.). **2.** (naut.). Haul up (anchor etc.) by means of pulley, lever, etc. So ~ABLE a., ~ER¹ n. [ME, f. AF PUR(*chacer* CHASE¹) procure, bring about]

pŭrd′ah(-da), n. (E.-Ind.). Curtain, esp. one serving to screen women from sight of strangers; (fig.) Indian system of secluding women of rank; striped material for curtains. [f. Hind. & Pers. *pardah*]

pūre, a. **1.** Unmixed, unadulterated, as ~ *white, air, alcohol, water;* (of sounds) not discordant, esp. (mus.) perfectly in tune. **2.** Of unmixed descent, ~-blooded; ~ *mathematics* (not including practical applications, opp. to *applied, mixed*); (gram., of vowel) preceded by another vowel, (of stem) ending in vowel, (of consonant) not accompanied by another. **3.** Mere, simple, nothing but, sheer, as *knowledge* ~ *& simple,* ~ *nonsense,* prejudice. **4.** Not corrupt, as *his taste was severe & ~;* morally undefiled, guiltless, sincere; sexually undefiled. Hence ~′LY² (-ūrl-) adv. (rare exc. in senses exclusively, solely, entirely), ~′NESS (-ūrn-) n. [ME, f. OF *pur,* fem. *pure,* f. L *purus*]

purée (pūr′ā, & see Ap.), n. Soup of vegetables, meat, etc., boiled to pulp & passed through sieve. [F]

pūr′fle, n., & v.t. (arch.). **1.** Border, esp. embroidered edge of garment. **2.** v.t. Adorn (robe) with ~; ornament (edge of building *with* crockets etc.); beautify.

Hence **pūrf′lıng¹** n., (esp.) inlaid bordering on back & belly of fiddles. [ME, f. OF *porfil*(er), as PROFILE]

pŭrgā′tion, n. Purification; purging of bowels; spiritual cleansing, esp. (R.-C. Ch.) of soul in purgatory; (hist.) clearing of oneself from accusation or suspicion by oath or ordeal. [ME, f. OF *purgacion* or L *purgatio* (as PURGE, see -ATION)]

pŭrg′ative, a. & n. Aperient (medicine); serving to purify. [ME, f. OF (-*if,* -*ive*), or LL *purgativus* (as PURGE, see -ATIVE)]

pŭrg′atory̆, n. & a. **1.** Condition, place, of spiritual purging, esp. (R.-C. Ch.) of souls departing this life in grace of God but requiring to be cleansed from venial sins etc.; place of temporary suffering or expiation. **2.** adj. Purifying. So **pŭr-gatŌr′ıAL** a. [ME, f. AF -*orie,* OF -*oire* f. med. L *purgatorium,* neut. of LL -*orius* adj. (as foll., see -ORY)]

pŭrge, v.t., & n. **1.** Make physically or spiritually clean (*of, from,* impurities, sin, etc.); remove by cleansing process (lit. & fig., often *away, off, out*); (of medicine) relieve (bowels, or abs.) by evacuation; clear (person, one*self, of* charge, suspicion); (law) atone for, wipe out, (offence, sentence) by expiation & submission; rid (political party, army, etc.) of persons regarded as undesirable. **2.** n. Such clearance, purgation, (*Pride's* P~, hist., exclusion by Col. Pride of Presbyterian & Royalist members from Long Parliament); aperient. [ME; vb f. OF *purger* f. L *purgare;* n. f. vb, partly f. F *purge*]

pūrifıcā′tion, n. Purifying; ritual cleansing, esp. that of woman after childbirth enjoined by Jewish law, as *the* P~ (*of the Virgin Mary*), Feb. 2nd (*Luke* ii. 22). So **pūr′ificātory** a. [ME, f. OF, or f. L *purificatio* (as PURIFY, see -ATION)]

pūr′ificātor, n. (eccl.). Cloth used at communion for wiping chalice & paten & fingers & lips of celebrant. [as foll., see -OR]

pūr′if|y̆, v.t. Make pure, cleanse, (*of, from,* impurities, sin, etc.); make ceremonially clean; clear of foreign elements, whence ~ıER¹(2) n. [ME, f. OF *purifier* or L *purificare* (as PURE, see -FY)]

Pūr′im, n. Jewish festival commemorating defeat of Haman's plot (*Esth.* ix). [Heb., pl. of *pur,* perh. = lot]

pūr′|ist, n. Stickler for, affecter of, scrupulous purity esp. in language. So ~ISM n., ~ıs′tıc(AL) aa. [f. F *puriste* (PURE, -IST)]

pūr′itan, n. & a. **1.** (Hist.; P~) member of the party of English Protestants who regarded reformation of Church under Elizabeth as incomplete & sought to abolish unscriptural & corrupt ceremonies etc.; member of any non-religious purist party; person of or affecting extreme strictness in religion or morals. **2.** adj. Of the P~s; scrupulous in religion or morals. Hence **pūrităn′ıc**(AL) aa., **pūri-tăn′icalLY²** adv., ~ISM n., ~IZE(2, 3) v.i.

& t. [f. L *puritas* (foll.)+-AN; cf. F *puritain*]

pūr′ity, n. Pureness, cleanness, freedom from physical or moral pollution. [ME & OF *pur(e)te* f. LL *puritatem* (PURE, -TY)]

purl¹, n., & v.t. & i. **1.** Cord of twisted gold or silver wire for bordering; chain of minute loops, each loop of this, ornamenting edges of lace, ribbon, etc.; (knitting, also *pearl*) inversion of stitches, producing ribbed appearance. **2.** vb. Border (material or abs.) with ~; invert (stitches or abs.); invert stitches of (stocking etc.). [cord sense app. Sc. *pirl* twist; other senses perh. different wds]

purl², v.i., & n. **1.** (Of brook etc.) flow with whirling motion & babbling sound. **2.** n. Such motion or sound. [16th c., prob. imit.; cf. Norw. *purla* bubble up]

purl³, n. (hist.). Ale or beer with wormwood infused; hot beer mixed with gin as morning draught, dog's-nose. [orig. unkn.]

purl⁴, v.t. & i., & n. (colloq.). **1.** Turn (t. & i.) upside down, upset. **2.** n. Cropper, heavy fall. [prob. var. of *pirl* (see PURL¹)]

purl′er, n. (colloq.). Throw, blow, that hurls one head foremost (*come, take, a* ~, fall headlong). [prec.+-ER¹]

purl′ieu (-lū), n. Tract on border of forest esp. one earlier included in it & still partly subject to forest laws; one's bounds, limits; (pl.) outskirts, outlying region (lit. & fig.); squalid street or quarter of town. [ME, prob. altered after LIEU f. *pur(a)ley* f. obs. & AF PUR(*alé* ALLEY) perambulation to settle boundaries]

purl′in, n. Horizontal beam running along length of roof, resting on principals & supporting common rafters or boards. [ME, orig. unkn.]

purloin′ (per-), v.t. Steal, pilfer. Hence ~ER¹ n. [ME, f. AF PUR(*loigner* f. *loing* far f. L *longe*) put away, do away with]

pur′ple, n., a., & v.t. & i. **1.** (Of) a colour mixed of red & blue in various proportions with some black or white or both; (anciently, also *Tyrian* ~) (of) the colour got from the molluscs *purpura* & *murex*, crimson; ~*-red* etc., red etc. inclining to ~. **2.** ~ robe, esp. as dress of emperor, king, consul, etc., as *born in the* ~, or of cardinal, as *raised to the* ~ (cardinalate). **3.** pl. Swine fever; disease in wheat. **4.** ~ *emperor*, a butterfly; ~ *patch*, ornate passage in literary composition. **5.** vb. Make, become, ~. Hence pūr′p′lish¹, pūrp′ly², aa. [OE *purple*, ME *purpul* etc., altered f. OE *purpure*, ME *purpur* etc. f. L PURPURA; cf. *marble* f. *marbre*]

purpoint. See POURPOINT.

pūrp′ort¹, n. Meaning, sense, tenor, of document or speech; (rare) object, purpose. [ME, f. AF, as foll.]

purpŏrt′² (per-), v.t. (Of document or speech) have as its meaning, convey,

state, (fact, *that*); profess, be intended to seem (*to do*), as *a letter* ~*ing to be written by you, to contain your decision*. Hence ~**ēdLY²** adv., professedly. [ME, f. AF & OF PUR*porter* f. med. L *proportare* f. PRO-+L *portare* carry]

pūrp′ose¹, n. Object, thing intended, as *could not effect my* ~, *this will answer* (or *serve*) *our* (or *the*) ~, *what was the* ~ *of this law?*; fact, faculty, of resolving on something, as *honesty of* ~, *is wanting in* ~; *novel with a* ~, ~*-novel*, (written to defend some doctrine etc.); *on* ~, in order (*to do, that*), (abs., also *of set* ~) designedly, not by accident, whence ~LY² (-sl-) adv.; *to the* ~, relevant, useful for one's ~; *to little, some, no,* ~, with such result or effect. Hence ~FUL (-sf-), ~LESS (-sl-), aa., ~fulLY², ~lèssLY², advv., ~fulNESS, ~lèssNESS, nn. [ME, f. AF & OF *purpos*, f. *purposer*, as foll.]

pūrp′ose², v.t. Design, intend, as *I* ~ (*arranging* or *to arrange*) *an interview*, ~ *that an interview shall be arranged*; (arch.) *am* ~*d*, intend (*to do, doing, that*). [ME, f. OF PUR*poser* = *proposer* PROPOSE]

pūrp′osive, a. Having, serving, done with, a purpose; (of person or conduct) having purpose & resolution. [-IVE]

pūrp′ura, n. Disease marked by purple or livid spots on skin; kinds of molluscs including some from which purple dye was derived. [L, f. Gk *porphura* (shell-fish yielding) purple]

purpūr′ic (per-), a. Of purpura, as ~ *fever*; ~ *acid*, an acid the salts of which are purple. [-IC]

pūrp′urin, n. Red colouring-matter orig. got from madder. [f. PURPURA+-IN]

purr, v.i. & t., & n. **1.** (Of cat or other feline animal, fig. of person) make low continuous vibratory sound expressing pleasure; utter, express, (words, contentment) thus. **2.** n. Such sound. [imit.]

pū′rree, n. Yellow colouring-matter from India & China. [f. Hind. *peori*]

pur sang (see Ap.), adv. (appended to classifying n. or adj.). Of the full blood, without admixture, through & through, genuine, (*is Welsh* or *a Welshman, militarist, a cynic,* ~; *the artist* ~ *is a rarity*). [F]

pūrse¹, n. **1.** Small pouch of leather etc. for carrying money on the person, orig. closed by drawing strings together; (fig.) money, funds, as *a common* ~ (fund), *heavy* or *long* ~, wealth, *light* ~, poverty, *the public* ~, national treasury; ‖ PRIVY ~; sum collected, subscribed, or given, as present or as prize for contest, as *will any gentleman give* or *put up a* ~?; bag-like natural or other receptacle, pouch, cyst, etc. **2.** ~*-bearer*, one who has charge of another's or a company's money, ‖ official carrying Great Seal before Lord Chancellor in ~; ~*-net*, bag-shaped net for catching rabbits etc., mouth of which can be closed with cords; ~*-proud*, puffed up by wealth; ~-*seine*, ~-net for fishing; ~-*strings*, strings for closing mouth of ~, (*hold the* ~-*strings*, have control of expenditure; *tighten, loosen, the* ~-*strings*, be sparing, generous, of money). Hence ~'FUL (-sf-) n., ~'LESS (-sl-) a. [OE *purs* app. f. LL *bursa* purse f. Gk *bursa* hide]

pŭrse², v.t. & i. Contract (lips, brow, often *up*) in wrinkles; become wrinkled; (rare) put (often *up*) into one's purse. [f. prec.]

pŭrs'er, n. Officer on ship who keeps accounts esp. in passenger vessel. Hence ~SHIP n. [f. PURSE¹+-ER¹]

pŭrs'lane (-ĭn), n. Low succulent herb used in salads & pickled. [ME, f. OF *porcelaine* altered f. L *porcil(l)aca, portulaca*, on PORCELAIN]

pursū'ance (per-), n. Carrying out, pursuing, (*of* plan, object, idea, etc.), esp. *in* ~ *of*. [as foll., see -ANCE]

pursū'ant (per-), a. & adv. Pursuing; (adv.) conformably *to* (*the Act* etc.), whence ~LY² adv. [f. OF *porsuiant* part. as foll.]

pursūe' (per-), v.t. & i. Follow with intent to capture or kill; (fig., of consequences, penalty, disease, etc.) persistently attend, stick to; seek after, aim at, (pleasure etc., one's object); proceed in compliance with (plan etc.); proceed along, continue, (road, inquiry, conduct); follow (studies, profession); go in pursuit (*after*, or abs.). Hence **pursū'able** (per-) a. [ME, f. AF PURS*iuer*, -*suer*, = OF *porsiver*, -*sivre* etc., f. pop. L *pro-, persequere* f. L *sequi* follow; see SUE]

pursū'er (per-), n. In vbl senses, also || (civil & Sc. law) prosecutor. [-ER¹]

pursuit' (persūt), n. Pursuing, esp. *in*~*of* (animal, person, one's object); ~ *plane*, fighter aircraft; profession, employment, recreation, that one follows. [ME, f. AF *purs(e)ute*, OF *porsuite* f. *porsuivre* PURSUE after *suite* SUIT]

|| **pŭrs'uivant** (-sw-), n. Officer of College of Arms below herald; (poet.) follower, attendant. [ME, f. OF *porsivant* (as PURSUE, see -ANT)]

pŭrs'y̆¹, a. Short-winded, puffy; corpulent. Hence~ĭNESS n. [ME & AF *porsif* f. OF *polsif* f. *polser* breathe with labour (as PULSATE, see -IVE)]

pŭrs'y̆², a. Puckered. [f. PURSE¹+-Y²]

pŭrt'énance, n. (arch.). Inwards, pluck, of animal. [earlier form of PERTINENCE]

pūr'ul|ent (-rŏŏ-), a. Of, full of, discharging, pus. Hence for cogn. ~ENCE, ~ENCY, nn., ~entLY² adv. [f. L *purulentus* (PUS, see -LENT)]

purvey' (pervā), v.t. & i. Provide, supply, (articles of food) as one's business; make provision, act as purveyor, (*for* person, army, etc.). [ME, f. AF PUR*veier* f. L *providere* PROVIDE]

purvey'ance (pervā'ans), n. Purveying; || right of crown to provisions etc. at fixed price & to use of horses etc. [ME, f. AF *porveance* f. L *providentia* PROVIDENCE]

purvey'or (pervā'er), n. One whose business it is to supply articles of food, esp. dinners etc. on large scale, as *P*~ *to the Royal Household*; (hist.) officer making purveyance for sovereign. [ME, f. AF *purveour* (as PURVEY, see -OR)]

pŭrv'iew (-vū), n. Enacting clauses of statute; scope, intention, range, (*of* act, document, scheme, book, occupation, etc.); range of physical or mental vision. [ME, f. AF *purveu* provided, p.p. as PURVEY]

pŭs, n. Yellowish viscid matter produced by suppuration. [L, gen. *puris*]

Pūs'ey|ism (-zĭ-), n. (Hostile term for) TRACTARIANISM. So ~ITE¹ (-zĭīt) n. [E. B. *Pusey* d. 1882+-ISM]

push¹ (pŏŏsh), v.t. & i. 1. Exert upon (body) force tending to move it away; move (body *up, down, away, back*, etc.) thus; exert such pressure, as *do not* ~ *against the fence*; (billiards) make push-stroke; (of person in boat)~ *off*, ~ against bank with oar to get boat out into stream etc. 2. (bibl.). Butt (t. & i.) with the horns. 3. (Cause to) project, thrust *out, forth*, etc., as *plants* ~ *out new roots, cape* ~*es out into sea*. 4. Make one's way forcibly or persistently, force (one's *way*) thus. 5. Exert oneself esp. to surpass others or succeed in one's business etc., whence ~'ING² a., ~'ĭngLY² adv., (pŏŏ-). 6. Urge, impel, (often *on, to* do, *to* effort etc.). 7. Follow up, prosecute, (claim etc., often *on*); engage actively in making (one's *fortune*); extend (one's *conquests* etc.); ~ (matter) *through*, bring it to a conclusion. 8. Press the adoption, use, sale, etc. of (goods etc.) esp. by advertisement. 9. Press (person) hard, as *do not wish to* ~ *him for payment*, esp. in pass., as *am* ~*ed for* (can scarcely find) *time, money*. 10.~-*button war*, = PRESS²- *button war*; *~over* n., an opponent easily defeated, a gullible person, an easy problem; ~-*pin*, a child's game, *draw-ing-pin*. Hence ~ER¹ (1, 2) (pŏŏ-) n. (~er *aeroplane*, with air-screw behind, opp. *tractor*). [ME, f. OF *pousser*, earlier *polser* f. L *pulsare* as PULSATE]

push² (pŏŏsh), n. 1. Act of pushing, shove, thrust; (billiards) stroke in which ball is pushed, not struck; exertion of influence to promote person's advancement. 2. Thrust of weapon or of beast's horn. 3. Vigorous effort, as *must make a* ~ *to get it done, for home*, (mil.) attack in force. 4. Continuous pressure of arch etc.; pressure of affairs, crisis, pinch. 5. Enterprise, determination to get on, self-assertion, whence ~'FUL (pŏŏ-) a. 6. (sl.). Gang of thieves, convicts, etc. 7. (sl.). *Give, get, the* ~, dismiss, be dismissed. 8. ~-*ball*, game played with enormous ball, pushed, not kicked, towards opponents' goal; || ~-*bike* (sl.), bicycle worked by pedalling (opp. *motor-bike*). [f. prec.]

Pŭsh'tōō, -tu (-ōō), n. Afghan language. [f. Pers. *pashto*]

pūsillăn'imous (-z-), a. Faint-hearted, mean-spirited. Hence or cogn. **pūsillanim'ITY** n., ~LY² adv. [f. eccl. L *pusillanimis* (*pusillus* petty + *animus* soul) + -OUS]

puss (pŏŏs), n. Cat (esp. as call-name); (quasi-proper name for) hare, tiger; (colloq.) girl, as *sly* ~ ; ~ *moth*, large European moth. [prob. f. MLG *pūs*, Du. *poes*, cf. Norw. *puse*, perh. orig. a call]

pu'ssy̆ (pŏŏ-), n. (nursery). ~(-*cat*), cat; (nursery) soft furry thing, e.g. willow catkin; (sl.) ~*foot*, P~*foot*, liquor-prohibition, advocate of this, (from nickname of a U.-S. prohibitionist), *(v.i.)* move stealthily, act cautiously. [-Y³]

pŭs'tūl|āte, v.t. & i. Form into pustules. So~ATE² (-*at*) a.,~A'TION n. [f. LL *pustulare*, as foll.]

pŭs'tūl|e, n. Pimple; *malignant* ~*e*, disease caused by anthrax bacillus; (bot., zool.) wart, wart-like excrescence. Hence or cogn. ~AR¹, ~OUS, aa. [ME, f. L *pustula*]

put¹ (pŏŏt), v.t. & i. (*put*). **1.** General senses. **1.** Propel, hurl, (*the weight, stone*) from hand placed close to shoulder as athletic exercise. **2.** Thrust (weapon), send (missile), as ~ *a knife into*, stab, *put a bullet through*, shoot. **3.** (coal-mining). Propel (tram or barrow of coal). **4.**(naut.). Proceed, take one's course, *back, forth, in* (*to* harbour etc.), *off* (*from* shore etc.), *out*, in ship. **5.** Move (thing etc., lit. & fig.) so as to place it in some situation, as ~ *it in your pocket, on the table, up the chimney, down the well*; ~ (mark, write) *a tick against his name, your signature to it*; ~ *the horse to* (*the cart*), harness him; ~ *bull to cow* or *cow to bull* (for breeding); ~ (convey) *him across the river*, ~ *the children to bed*, ~ *him in prison*; *has* ~ (infused) *new life into him*; *will* ~ (present) *the matter clearly before her*; ~ *a* SPOKE *in his wheel*, ~ *the words into his* MOUTH¹,~ one's FOOT¹ *in it*, one's SHOULDER *to the wheel, hand to the* PLOUGH¹, *the* LID *on*. **6.** (With less or no idea of physical motion in space) bring into some relation or state, as ~ *yourself, the matter, in(to) my hands; time he was ~* (began to go habitually) *to school* ; ~ *it to* (offer it for) *sale, on the market*; ~ *'Othello' on* (*the stage*), produce it; ~ (add) *milk to your tea; should* ~ (price) *it at 2/6*; ~*s* (estimates) *the circulation at 60,000*; ~ (translate) *it into Dutch; cannot* ~ *it into* (express it in) *words; what a way you have of* ~*ting things!*; ~*s* (sets) *no value on my advice; I* ~ (base) *my decision on the grounds stated*; ~ (apply) *it to a good use*; ~ (imagine) *yourself in his place*; ~ (substitute) *the will for the deed*; ~ *a good* FACE¹ *on it*; ~ *an end, period, stop, to it, stop it*; ~ *a check* or *stopper on it, a veto on it*, check it, forbid it; ~ *an end to* (destroyed) *himself* or *his life*; ~ *the wind*

up one (sl.), frighten him; ~ (stake) *money on a horse*; ~ *his money into* (invested it in) *land*; ~ *& take* (name of a gambling game with teetotum); ~ (submit) *the case to him, to the vote; I* ~ *it* (appeal) *to you*; (esp. of examining counsel) *I* ~ *it to you* (invite you to acknowledge) *that you were after no good; dues were* ~ (imposed) *on cattle; every insult was* ~ (inflicted) *on him; don't be* ~ *upon* (victimized) *by him*; ~ (lay) *the blame on me*; ~ *him* (caused him to be) *at his ease, in fear of his life, out of temper, on his guard, on his mettle*; ~ *him* (make him speak) *on* (*his*) *oath*; ~ *the servants on* (allow them) *board wages*; ~ *the proposal into shape*; ~ *his* NOSE¹ *out of joint*; ~ *thing out of court* (make it not worth discussing etc.); ~ *thing out of* one's *head* (forget, make him forget, it); *a few words will* ~ (make) *the matter right; always manages to* ~ *me* (make me appear) *in the wrong*; ~ *out of* COUNTENANCE¹; *must have* ~ (made) *the clock fast* (by advancing hands); **~ wise* (sl.), disabuse or enlighten; ~ (subject) *them to death, torture, ransom, expense, inconvenience, the test* or *trial, the rack, the sword, confusion, shame; land was* ~ *into* or *under* (sown with) *turnips*; ~ (set) *him to mind the furnace*; ~ *my horse to* or *at* (invited him to jump) *the fence*; (of horse & fig. of person) *must be* ~ (made to perform) *his paces*; ~ *him* (make him read) *through a book of Livy; was* ~ (forced, driven) *to flight, to his shifts, to the* BLUSH²; *was* ~ *to* (forced to play) *his trumps; surprising what he can do when he's* ~ *to it* (pressed); *was hard* ~ *to it* (could scarcely) *keep them off*. **II.** Special senses with advv. **1.** ~ *about*: lay (sailing vessel) on opposite tack, cause (horse, body of men) to turn round, (of vessel) go about; (chiefly Sc.) trouble, distress. **2.** ~ *across*, execute or establish successfully (~ *it across*, succeed in doing). **3.** ~ *away*: (arch.) divorce; lay by (money etc.) for future use; (sl.) consume (food, drink); (sl.) imprison; (sl.) pawn. **4.** ~ *back*: check the advance of, retard; move back the hands of (clock); restore to former place. **5.** ~ *by*: evade (question, argument); ~ *off* (person) with evasion; lay aside esp. for future use. **6.** ~ *down*: suppress by force or authority; take down, snub, put to silence; cease to maintain (expensive thing); account, reckon, as *I* ~ *him down for nine years old, at nine, as a fool, for a fool*; attribute, as ~ *it down to his nervousness*; ~ one's FOOT¹ *down*. **7.** ~ *forth*: exert (strength, effort, eloquence); ~ *in* circulation; (of plant) send out (buds, leaves, or abs.). **8.** ~ *forward*: thrust (oneself etc.) into prominence; advance, set forth, (theory etc.). **9.** ~ *in*: install in office etc., as ~ *in a caretaker, bailiff*, (hence) *distress, execution*; present formally (document, evidence, plea, claim, bail) as in law-court; ~ *in* (make) *an appearance*; make a claim (*for* election etc.); interpose (blow, shot, remark, quoted words), ~ *in* one's OAR; throw in (additional thing); perform (piece of work) as part of a whole; (colloq.) pass, spend, (time). **10.** ~ *off*: postpone; postpone engagement with (person); evade (person, demand, often *with* excuse, compromise); hinder, dissuade, *from*; foist (thing *upon* person); remove, take off, (clothes); (of boat, crew, etc.) leave shore; ~-*off* n., evasion, postponement. **11.** ~ *on*: clothe oneself or another with; (colloq.) ~ *it on*, overcharge, simulate exaggerated emotion, suffering, etc.; assume, take on, (character, appearance); develop additional (flesh, weight); add (so much *to* price, runs etc. *to* score); stake (money *upon* horse etc.); advance the hands of (clock); bring into action, exert, (force, pressure, speed, STEAM[1], *the* SCREW[1]); appoint, arrange for, (person) to bowl etc., (train) to run etc. **12.** ~ *out*: dislocate (shoulder etc.); (crick.) cause (batsman) to be out; extinguish (candle, gas, fire, etc.); disconcert, confuse; annoy, irritate; ~ to inconvenience; exert (strength etc.); lend (money) at interest, invest; give (work) to be done off the premises. **13.** ~ *over*, secure appreciation for (film, play, etc.); ~ (one*self*) *over*, impress one's personality on (an audience). **14.** ~ *through*: carry out (task); place (person) in telephonic connexion with (*to*) another through exchange(s). **15.** ~ *together*: form (whole) by combination of parts; ~ TWO *& two together*; ~ (*our* etc.) *heads together*, consult; (crick.) compile (score). **16.** ~ *up*: ~ person's *back up*, enrage him; ~ one's HAIR *up*; employ (person) as jockey; produce (play) on stage; cause (game) to rise from cover; raise (price); offer (prayer), present (petition); propose for election; publish (banns); offer for sale by auction or for competition; pack up in parcel, place in receptacle for safe keeping; sheathe (sword); lodge & entertain (man, horse); take up one's lodging (*at* inn etc.); ~ *up a* (*good* etc.) *fight*, make a good etc. fight of it; ~ *up with* (arch. ~ *up*), submit to, tolerate, (insult, annoying person or thing); ~ (person) *up to*, inform him of, instruct him in, (also) instigate him (*to do*, to *doing*, or action); construct, build; concoct (underhand piece of work); ~-*up* a., fraudulently concocted. Hence **pu'tter** (pŏŏ-) n. [late OE *putian* (? *pūtian*), also (ā)*pȳtan*, *potian*, of unkn. orig.]

put² (pŏŏt), n. **1.** Throw, cast, of the weight or stone. **2.** Option of delivering fixed amount of a stock at fixed price within fixed time. [f. prec.]

pŭt³, pŭtt, v.i. & t. (*pŭtted*), & n. **1.** Strike golf-ball, strike (golf-ball) gently with club to make it into hole on smooth piece of ground called *putting-green*. **2.** n. Such stroke. Hence **pŭtt'er¹** (1, 2) n. [differentiated f. PUT¹·²]

pŭt⁴, n. (old sl.). Duffer, queer person, countryman, etc. [17th c., of unkn. orig.]

pūt'ative, a. Reputed, supposed, as *his* ~ *father*. Hence ~LY² adv. [ME, f. OF (-*if*, -*ive*), or LL *putativus* (*putare* think, see -ATIVE)]

pūte, a. (arch.). *Pure* (*&*) ~, mere. [f. L *putus* in phr. *purus ac putus*]

pūt'eal, n. (Rom. ant.). Stone curb round mouth of well. [L (*puteus* well, see -AL)]

pūt'lŏg, -lŏck, n. Short horizontal timber on which scaffold-boards rest. [orig. unkn.]

pūt'rėfy̆, v.i. & t. Become putrid, rot, go bad; fester, suppurate; become morally corrupt; (rare) cause to ~fy. So ~FAC'TION n., ~fāctive a. [ME, f. L *putrefacere* (*putrēre* be rotten, see -FY)]

pūtrēs'c|ent, a. In process of rotting; of, accompanying, this process. Hence ~ENCE n., ~IBLE a. [f. L *putrescere* incept. of *putrēre* rot, see -ENT]

pūt'rid, a. Decomposed, rotten; foul, noxious; (fig.) corrupt; (sl.) of poor quality, highly distasteful; ~ *fever*, typhus; ~ *sore throat*, gangrenous pharyngitis, diphtheria. Hence ~ITY (-Id²), ~NESS, nn., ~LY² adv. [f. L *putridus* (*putrēre* rot, -ID¹)]

putsch (-ŏŏ-), n. Revolutionary attempt, *coup de main*. [G (Swiss)]

putt. See PUT³.

pŭtt'ee (-ĭ), n. Long strip of cloth wound spirally round leg from ankle to knee for protection & support. [f. Hind. *paṭṭī* bandage]

pŭtt'ŏŏ, n. (Anglo-Ind.). Fabric, plain or patterned, produced in Cashmere from coarse goat-wool. [native name]

pŭtt'y̆, n., & v.t. **1.** (Also *jewellers'* ~) powder of calcined tin (& lead) for polishing glass or metal; (also *plasterers'* ~) fine mortar of lime & water without sand; (also *glaziers'* ~) cement of whiting, raw linseed oil, etc., for fixing panes of glass, filling up holes in woodwork, etc.; ~ *medal*, fit reward for small service (*you deserve a ~ medal*). **2.** v.t. Cover, fix, join, fill up, with ~. [f. F *potée* lit. POTful, see -Y⁴]

puy (pwē), n. Small volcanic cone esp. in Auvergne. [F]

pŭz'zle¹, n. Bewilderment, perplexity; perplexing question, enigma; problem, toy, contrived to exercise ingenuity & patience, as *Chinese* ~; ~-*head(ed)*, -*pate(d)*, (person) with confused ideas; || ~-*peg*, piece of wood so fixed to dog's lower jaw as to prevent him from putting nose close to ground. [app. f. foll.]

pŭz'zle², v.t. & i. Perplex; be perplexed (*about*, *over*, problem etc.); make *out* (solution of problem etc.); MONKEY~~. Hence ~DOM (-ld-), ~MENT (-lm-), pŭzz'lER¹(2), nn., pŭzz'lingLY² adv. [orig. unkn.]

puzzolana. See POZZOLANA.

pȳaem'|ia, n. Blood-poisoning marked

by formation of pus-foci. Hence ~ɪc a. [f. Gk *puon* pus + *haima* blood + -ɪᴀ¹]

pȳc′no-, comb. form of Gk *puknos* thick, dense, as ~*style* a. & n., (building) with close arrangement of columns, i.e. at interval of one diameter & a half.

pȳe′dŏg, pī(e)-, n. Ownerless mongrel of the East. [f. Anglo-Ind. *pye, paë*, Hind. *pāhī* outsider]

pȳg′m|ў̄, pī-, n. & a. **1.** One of a diminutive race of men said to have inhabited parts of Ethiopia or India; *the P~ies*, a dwarf people in equatorial Africa; dwarf (fig. of intellectual inferiority etc.); elf, pixy. **2.** adj. Of the ~ies, dwarf. So **pȳgm(a)e′ᴀɴ** (-ē′*an*) a. [ME, f. L f. Gk *pugmaios* (*pugmē* length from elbow to knuckles, also the fist)]

‖ **pȳja′mas, *paj-**, (-ahmaz), n. pl. Loose silk or cotton trousers tied round waist, worn by both sexes among Mohammedans & adopted esp. for night wear by Europeans; sleeping-suit of loose trousers & jacket; also attrib. in sing. form *pȳja′ma* (-ah-), as *pyjama jacket, trousers*. [f. Pers. *pae jamah* (*pae, pay*, foot, leg, + *jamah* clothing)]

pȳk′nic, a. & n. (anthrop.). (Person) characterized by a thick neck, large abdomen, and relatively short legs. [f. Gk *pyknos* compact + -ɪc]

pȳl′ŏn, n. Gateway esp. of Egyptian temple; tall compound structure erected as support (esp. for power-cables) or boundary or decoration. [f. Gk *pulōn* (*pulē* gate)]

pȳlŏr′us, n. (anat.). Opening from stomach into duodenum; part of stomach where this is. Hence **pȳlō′rɪc** a. [LL, f. Gk *pulōros* gatekeeper (*pulē* gate + *ouros* warder)]

pȳo-, comb. form of Gk *puon* pus, as ~*gen′esis*, formation of pus; ~*rrhoe′a* (-rēa), purulent discharge (esp. as a dental disease). So **pȳ′oɪᴅ** a.

pȳr′acănth, n. Evergreen thorny shrub with white flowers & scarlet berries. [f. Gk *purakantha*]

pȳ′ramid, n. **1.** Monumental (esp. ancient Egyptian) structure of stone etc. with polygonal or (usu.) square base, & sloping sides meeting at apex. **2.** Solid of this shape with base of three or more sides. **3.** ~-shaped thing or pile of things; fruit-tree trained in ~ shape. **4.** Poem whose successive lines increase or decrease in length. **5.** ‖ pl. (billiards). Game played with (usu. 15) coloured balls & one cue-ball. Hence or cogn. **pȳrăm′idᴀʟ** a., **pȳrăm′idᴀʟʟʏ²**, ~ᴡɪsᴇ, advv. [f. L f. Gk *puramis -idos*, perh. of Egypt. orig.]

pȳ′rāmidĭst, n. Student of structure & history of Egyptian pyramids. [-ɪsᴛ]

pȳre, n. Heap of combustible material, esp. funeral pile for burning corpse. [f. L f. Gk *pura* (*pur* fire)]

pȳr′ĕth′rum, n. Name of kinds of chrysanthemum. [L, f. Gk *purethron*]

pȳrĕt′ic (*or* pī-), a. Of, for, or producing, fever. [f. Gk *puretos* fever + -ɪc]

pȳrĕx′|ia (*or* pī-), n. (path.). Fever. Hence ~ɪᴀʟ, ~ɪc(ᴀʟ), aa. [f. Gk *purexis* (*puressō* be feverish, as prec.)]

pyrhĕliŏm′ĕter (per-), n. Instrument for measuring heat given off by sun. [f. Gk *pur* fire + *hēlios* sun + -ᴍᴇᴛᴇʀ]

pȳr′idine (*or* pī-), n. (chem.). A volatile liquid alkaloid from dry distillation of bone-oil, used for asthma. [f. Gk *pur* fire + -ɪᴅ⁴ + -ɪɴᴇ⁵]

pȳrīt′ēs (-z), n. (Also *iron* ~) either of two sulphides of iron; *copper* ~, double sulphide of copper & iron. Hence **pyrit′ɪc**, **pyritĭf′ᴇʀous, pyr′ĭtous**, aa., **pyr′ĭtɪᴢᴇ** v.t., (pīt-, *or* pī-). [L, f. Gk *puritēs* of fire (*pur*, see -ɪᴛᴇ¹)]

pyro. See ᴘʏʀᴏ*gallic*.

pȳr|o-, comb. form of Gk *pur* fire, as: ~*o-elec′tric*, ~*o-electri′city*, (property of) becoming electrically polar when heated; ~*ogall′ic acid* (abbr. *pyro*), acid used as reducing agent in photography etc.; ~*ogenĕt′ic*, productive of heat, esp. in the body, or (also ~*ogĕn′ic*) of fever; ~*ŏ′genous*, (of rock) igneous, (of substance) produced by combustion of another; ~*ŏg′raphy*, = ᴘᴏᴋᴇʀ¹ *-work*; ~*ogravure′*, piece of poker-work; ~*ŏl′atry*, fire-worship; ~*olig′neous*, produced by action of fire or heat on wood, as ~*oligneous acid*; ~*omān′ia*, incendiary mania, so ~*omān′iac* n., ~*omanī′acal* a.; ~*ŏm′eter*, instrument for measuring high temperatures, so ~*omet′ric(al)* aa., ~*omet′rically* advv., ~*ŏm′etry* n.; ~*ŏph′orus*, substance that takes fire spontaneously on exposure to air, so ~*ophŏ′ric*, ~*ŏph′orous*, aa.; ~*ophŏt′ograph*, one burnt in on glass or porcelain, so ~*ophotŏgrăph′ic* a., ~*ophotŏg′raphy* n. Also in scientific wds denoting (chem.) new substance formed from another by destructive distillation etc., (min.) minerals etc. showing some property or change under action of heat, or having fiery red or yellow colour.

pȳr′ope, n. A deep-red garnet. [ME, f. OF *pirope* f. L f. Gk *purōpos* gold-bronze, lit. fiery-eyed (*pur* fire + *ōps* eye)]

pȳrōs′is, n. (med.). Burning sensation in the stomach with eructation of watery fluid, water-brash. [mod. L f. Gk *purōsis* f. *pur* fire]

pȳrotech′n|ic (-tĕk-), a. & n. **1.** Of (the nature of) fireworks, as ~*ic display*; (fig., of wit etc.) brilliant, sensational. **2.** n. pl. Art of making, display of, fireworks (lit. & fig.). Hence or cogn. ~ɪcᴀʟ a., ~*ically²* adv., ~ɪsᴛ, **pȳr′otechny¹**, nn., (-tĕk-). [f. ᴘʏʀᴏ- + Gk *tekhnikos* (*tekhnē* art, see -ɪc)]

pȳr′ŏxēne, n. (Kinds of) mineral composed mainly of the silicates of calcium and magnesium, a common component of igneous rocks. [f. ᴘʏʀᴏ- + Gk *xenos* stranger (because supposed alien to igneous rocks)]

pȳrŏx′ўlin, n. Nitrates of cellulose, esp.

the explosive, gun-cotton, or the lower nitrate which when dissolved in ether & alcohol forms collodion & serves as the basis of varnishes, artificial leather, etc. [f. F (-*ine*) f. PYRO- +Gk *xulon* wood +-IN]

Pȳ'rrhic[1] (-rĭk), p-, n. & a. **1.** ~ (*dance*), war dance of ancient Greeks. **2.** The metrical foot ‿‿ ; (adj.) consisting of such feet. [(1) f. L or Gk *purrhikhē*, said to be named from one *Purrhikhos*, the inventor; (2) f. L f. Gk *purrhikhios* (*pous*) pyrrhic foot]

Pȳ'rrhic[2] (-rĭk), a. ~ *victory* (gained at too great cost, like that of Pyrrhus king of Epirus over the Romans at Asculum in 279 B.C.). [f. Gk *purrhikos* (*Purrhos* Pyrrhus, see -IC)]

Pȳ'rrhon|ism (-ro-), n. Sceptic philosophy of Pyrrho of Elis (c. 300 B.C.), doctrine that certainty of knowledge is unattainable; scepticism, philosophic doubt. Hence or cogn. **Pȳrrhon'IAN** (-rō-), **Pȳrrhon'IC** (-rō-), aa. & nn., ~IST (-ro-)n. [f. GkPurrhōn Pyrrho +-ISM]

Pȳr'us, n. Genus of rosaceous trees & shrubs including pear & apple, esp. ~ *japonica*, scarlet or crimson ~. [med. & mod. L erron. sp. of L *pirus* pear-tree]

Pȳthăgorē'an, a. & n. (Follower) of Pythagoras, philosopher of Samos (6th c. B.C.) said to have believed in transmigration of souls; ~ *proposition*, Euclid I. 47. [f. L f. Gk *Puthagoreios* +-AN]

Pȳth'ian (-dh-), a. & n. Of (Apollo's oracle & priestess at) Delphi; *the* ~, Apollo, his priestess at Delphi. [f. L f. Gk *Puthios* (*Puthō*, older name of Delphi) +-AN]

pȳth'on[1], n. (Gk myth.) huge serpent or monster slain near Delphi by Apollo; large snake that crushes its prey. So **pȳthŏn'ic**[1] [-IC] a. [f. L f. Gk *Puthōn*]

pȳth'on[2], n. Familiar spirit; person possessed by this. Hence or cogn. ~ESS[1] n., **pȳthŏn'ic**[2] [-IC] a. [f. LL *pytho* or late Gk *puthōn*]

pȳx, n., & v.t. **1.** (eccl.). Vessel in which consecrated bread is kept. **2.** ∥ Box at Royal Mint in which specimen gold & silver coins are deposited to be tested at the annual *trial of the* ~ by jury of Goldsmiths' Company; ∥ (v.t.) deposit (coin) in ~, test (coin) by weight & assay. [ME, f. L PYXIS]

pȳxid'ium, n. (bot.; pl. -*ia*). Capsule of which the top comes off like lid of box. [f. Gk *puxidion*, dim. as foll.]

pȳx'is, n. Small box, casket; = prec. [L, f. Gk *puxis* f. *puxos* box-tree]

Q

Q (kū), letter (pl. *Qs*, Q's). (Skating) change of edge followed by turn (*reverse Q*, turn followed by change of edge); *mind* one's Ps *& Qs*, see P; *Q-boat, Q-ship*, = MYSTERY[1]-*ship*; *Q department*, that of Q.M.G.

quā, conj. As, in the capacity of, (*objects to the Church not* ~ *Church, but* ~ *Establishment*). [L, abl. fem. sing. of *qui* rel. pron.]

quäck[1], v.i., & n. (Utter) harsh sound made by ducks; talk loudly & foolishly; ~-~ (nursery), duck. [imit.; cf. Du. *kwakken*, G *quacken* croak, quack]

quäck[2], n., & v.i. & t. **1.** Ignorant pretender to skill esp. in medicine or surgery, one who offers wonderful remedies or devices, charlatan, (often attrib., as ~ *doctor, remedies*); hence ~'ERY(4) n., ~'ISH[1] a. **2.** vb. Play the ~; talk pretentiously; puff or advertise (cure etc.). [abbr. of foll.]

quäck'sälver, n. (Orig. form, now rare, of) quack[2] n. [Du. (QUACK[1], SALVE, -ER[1])]

quad (kwŏd), n. See QUADRANGLE, QUADRAT, QUADRUPLET.

qua'drable (-ŏd-), a. (math.). Capable of being represented by an equivalent square or expressed in finite number of algebraic terms. [as QUADRATE[2], -ABLE]

quadragēnăr'ian (-ŏd-), a. & n. (Person) forty years old. [f. L *quadragenarius* (*quadrageni* distrib. of *quadraginta* forty, -ARY[1])]

Quadragĕs'ima (-ŏd-), n. (Also ~ *Sunday*) first Sunday in Lent. [LL (Lent, first Sunday in Lent), fem. of L -*us* fortieth (*quadraginta* forty)]

quadragĕs'imal (-ŏd-), a. Lasting forty days (of fast, esp. Lent); Lenten. [f. med. L *quadragesimalis* (prec., -AL)]

quadrangle (kwŏd'răngg̱l), n. Four-sided figure, esp. square or rectangle; so **quadrăng'ūlAR**[1] a., **quadrăng'ūlarLY**[2] adv., (-ngg-); ∥ (also *quad*, pr. kwŏd) four-sided court (partly) enclosed by parts of large buildings, such court with buildings round it. [ME, f. OF f. LL *quadrangulum* square (QUADRI-, ANGLE)]

qua'drant (-ŏd-), n. Quarter of circle's circumference; plane figure enclosed by two radii of circle at right angles & arc cut off by them; quarter of sphere; thing, esp. graduated strip of metal, shaped like quarter-circle, instrument properly so shaped & graduated for taking angular measurements. Hence **quadrăn'tAL** a. [ME, f. L *quadrans -antis* (QUADRI-)]

qua'drat (-ŏd-), n. (Also *quad*, pr. kwŏd) small metal block used by printers in spacing (*em* ~, *en* ~, broader, narrower, size). [var. of foll.]

qua'drate[1] (-ŏd-), a. & n. **1.** Square, rectangular, (chiefly in anat. names, as ~ *bone* in birds' & reptiles' heads, ~ *muscle* in loins, thigh, forearm, etc.). **2.** n. Rectangular block or plate (rare); ~ bone or muscle. [ME, f. L *quadratus* (foll., -ATE[2])]

quadrāte'[2] (*or* kwŏd[2]), v.t. & i. (rare). Make square; (math.) square (circle etc.); correspond or conform (*with*, or abs. of pl. subj.); make conform *with* or *to* or abs. [f. L *quadrare* (QUADRI-), -ATE[3]]

quadrăt'ic, a. & n. **1.** Square (rare); (math.) involving second & no higher power of unknown quantity or variable (esp. ~ *equation*). **2.** n. ~ equation; (pl.) branch of algebra dealing with these. [QUADRATE¹, -IC; perh. f. F -*ique*]

qua′drature (-ŏd-), n. (Math.) finding of square with area precisely equal to that of figure bounded by curve (esp. ~ *of the circle*); (astron.) one of two points in space or time at which moon is 90° from sun, position of heavenly body in relation to another 90° away. [f. F, or L *quadratura* (QUADRATE², -URE)]

quadrĕnn′ial, a. Occurring every, lasting, four years. [irreg. f. L *quadriennium* four-year period (foll., *annus* year), -AL]

qua′dri- (-ŏd-), (bef. a vowel *quadr*-; in a few wds *quadru*- bef. *p*), L comb. form = four-, in a few L words (*quadriduum* period of four days, *quadripartitus* ~-partite), & in many of later L & mod. formation, esp. in scientific use: ~**fid**, a., cleft into four divisions or lobes; ~-**lăt′eral**, a. & n., four-sided (figure or area; *the Q~lateral*, four fortresses in N. Italy & district protected by them); ~**ling′ual** (-nggw-), a., using, in, four languages; **quadrill′ion** (kwadrĭl′yon), n., ‖ fourth power of million (1 followed by 24 ciphers), *fifth power of a thousand (cf. BILLION); ~**nŏm′ial**, a., consisting of four algebraic terms; ~**pārt′ite**, a., consisting of four parts, shared by or involving four parties; ~**rēme**, n., ancient galley with four banks of oars; ~**sy̆llăb′ic**, a., four--syllabled; ~**sy̆ll′able**, n., word of four syllables; **quadriv′alent** (kwa-), a. (chem.), capable of combining with four univalent atoms; **quadriv′ium** (kwa-), n. (hist.), medieval university course of arithmetic, geometry, astronomy, & music (cf. TRIVIUM).

qua′dric (-ŏd-), a. & n. (solid geom.). (Surface) of second degree. [as prec., -IC]

quadrīg′a, n. (pl. -*ae*). Ancient chariot with four horses abreast. [L (QUADRI-, *jugum* yoke)]

quadrille′¹ (ka-, kwa-), n. Fashionable 18th-c. game for four persons with forty cards. [F, perh. f. Sp. *cuartillo* w. assim. to foll.]

quadrille′² (ka-, kwa-), n. Square dance for four couples & containing five figures (also *set of* ~*s*); piece of music for such dance. [F, f. Sp. *cuadrilla* (*cuadra* square) squadron, band]

quadrōōn′, n. Offspring of white & mulatto, person of quarter-Negro blood; hybrid of similarly proportioned descent between other human, animal, or vegetable stocks. [f. Sp. *cuarteron* (*cuarto* fourth) w. assim. to QUADRI-]

quadru′manous (-rōō-), a. Four-handed, belonging to the order *Quadrumana* of mammals with opposable digit on all four limbs. [after foll. f. L *manus* hand]

qua′drupĕd (-ŏdrŏŏ-), n. & a. **1.** Four--footed animal, esp. four-footed mammal; so **quadru′pĕdAL** (-rŏŏ-) a. **2.** adj. Four-

-footed. [f. F -*pède*, or L *quadrupes* -*pedis* a. & n. (*quadru*- form of QUADRI- occas. used before p-, *pes* foot)]

qua′druple (-ŏdrŏŏ-), a., n., & v.t. & i. **1.** Fourfold, consisting of four parts or involving four parties, (~ *algebra*, using four independent units; ~ *rhythm* or *time*, with four beats to a measure; ~ *alliance* etc.); amounting to four times the amount or number *of*, equivalent to fourfold the amount of, superior by four times in amount or number *to*, (*has a light & heat* ~, or ~ *of* or *to*, *that of the earth*); hence **qua′drupLY²** (-ŏdrŏŏ-) adv. **2.** n. Number or amount four times greater than another (esp. *the* ~ *of*). **3.** vb. Multiply (t. & i.) by four. [F, f. L *quadruplus* (prec., -*plus* as in *duplus* DOUBLE)]

qua′druplĕt (-ŏdrŏŏ-), n. (Pl. four children at a birth (colloq. *quads*, pr. kwŏdz); four things working together; bicycle for four. [f. prec. after TRIPLET]

quadru′plicate¹ (-ōō-), a. & n. **1.** Fourfold, four times repeated or copied. **2.** n. *In* ~, in four exactly similar examples or copies; (pl.) four such copies. [f. L *quadruplicare* (*quadruplex* fourfold, cf. QUADRUPED, DUPLEX), -ATE²]

quadru′plic|āte² (-ōō-), v.t. Multiply by four; make four specimens of. Hence ~A′TION n. [as prec., -ATE³]

quadrupli′city (-ŏdrŏŏ-), n. Fourfold nature, being fourfold. [as prec., -TY]

quaere (kwēr′ĭ), v.t. imperat., & n. (abbr. *qu.*). **1.** Inquire (imperat.), it is a question, I should like to know, (*most interesting, no doubt; but* ~, *is it true?*). **2.** n. A question, query. [L, imperat. of *quaerere* ask]

quaes′tor, n. Ancient-Roman official, state-treasurer, paymaster, etc.; treasurer. Hence or cogn. **quaestōr′IAL** a., ~SHIP n. [L (*quaerere quaesit*- seek, -OR)]

quaff (-ah-), v.i. & t. Drink (t. & i.), drain (cup etc.), in copious or long draughts. [prob. imit.]

quăg, n. Marshy or boggy spot, quaking bog. Hence ~**g′Y¹** (-g-) a. [rel. to dial. *quag* vb, prob. imit.; cf. *wag*, *swag*]

quăgg′a, n. S.-Afr. quadruped related to ass & zebra, less striped than latter; Burchell's zebra. [S.-Afr.]

quăg′mīre, n. Quaking bog, fen, marsh, slough (lit. & fig.). [app. f. QUAG, MIRE]

***quahog′, -haug′**, (kwahŏg), n. Edible round clam of Atlantic coast of N. America. [abbr. of Amer.-Ind. *poquauhock*]

‖ **quaich, quaigh**, (kwāx), n. (Sc.). Kind of drinking-cup, usu. of wood & having two handles. [f. Gael. *cuach* cup]

Quai d'Orsay′ (kādōr-), n. (Used for) the French Foreign Office.

quail¹, n. Kinds of migratory bird allied to partridge esteemed as food; ~-*call*, ~--*pipe*, whistle with note like ~'s for luring. Hence ~′ERY(3) n. [ME, f. OF *quaille* f. med. L *coacula* (imit.); cf. MDu., MLG *quackele*]

quail[2], v.i. & t. (Of person, or his heart, courage, spirit, or eyes) flinch, be cowed, give way *before* or *to*; (rare) cow, daunt. [ME *quayle*, of unkn. orig.]

quaint, a. Attractive or piquant in virtue of unfamiliar, esp. old-fashioned, appearance, ornamentation, manners, etc., daintily odd. Hence ~'LY[2] adv., ~'NESS n. [earlier senses *wise, cunning*; ME, f. OF *cointe* f. L *cognitus* p.p. of *cognoscere* learn]

quāk|e, v.i., & n. **1.** Shake, tremble, rock to & fro, (of earth with earthquake, person usu. *for* or *with* fear or cold, bog when trodden on, etc.); ~*ing-grass*, kinds with slender foot-stalks trembling in wind. **2.** n. Act of ~ing, (colloq.) earthquake. Hence ~'ingLY[2] adv., ~'Y[2] a. [OE *cwacian*]

quăk'er, n. **1.** (*Q*~). (Outsiders' name for) member of Society of Friends founded by George Fox 1648–50, & devoted to peace principles, plainness of dress (esp. the use of drab or grey), simplicity of speech (esp. the use of *thee* & avoidance of titles & words, such as the names of the days, suggestive of paganism), & peculiar priestless religious meetings. **2.** *Dummy gun in ship or fort. **3.** (Also ~*-bird*, *-moth*) kinds of plain-coloured bird & moth. **4.** ~, or ~*s'*, *-meeting*, religious meeting of Friends, silent till some member is moved by the spirit, (transf.) silent meeting, company in which conversation flags. Hence ~DOM, ~ESS[1], ~ISM (3,4), nn., ~ISH[1], ~LY[1], aa. [f. prec. + -ER[1]]

qualifica'tion (-ŏl-), n. **1.** Modification, recognition of contingency, restricting or limiting circumstance, detraction from completeness or absoluteness, (*statement with many* ~*s*; *hedged with* ~*s*; *requires* ~; *his delight had one* ~). **2.** Quality fitting person or thing (*for* post etc., or abs.); condition that must be fulfilled before right can be acquired or office held (*the* ~ *for citizenship may be a certain income*), document attesting such fulfilment. **3.** Attribution of quality (*the* ~ *of his policy as opportunist is unfair*). So **qua'lificā**TORY (-ŏl-) a. [f. F, or med. L *qualificatio* (foll., -FICATION)]

qua'lify (-ŏl-), v.t. & i. **1.** Attribute some quality to, describe as, (~ *documents as heretical, person as a scoundrel, proposal as iniquitous*; *adjectives* ~ *nouns*). **2.** Invest or provide with the necessary qualities, make competent, fit, or legally entitled, (*for being* or *doing, to be or do, for* post or sphere, or abs.; ~*ing examination*, to ascertain that candidates are not below a fixed standard, often followed by competitive; (intr.) fulfil some condition, esp. pass examination or take oath, to make oneself eligible (*for* office, or abs.). **3.** Modify (statement, opinion), make less absolute or sweeping, subject to reservations or limitation. **4.** Moderate, mitigate, make less complete or pleasing or un-pleasing; diminish strength or flavour of (spirit etc. with water, also joc. water with spirit). [f. F *qualifier* or med. L *qualificare* (L *qualis* such as, -FY)]

qua'litative (-ŏl-; *or* -tā-), a. Concerned with, depending on, quality (opp. QUANTITATIVE; esp. ~ *analysis*). [f. LL *qualitativus* (foll., -ATIVE)]

qua'lit|ў (-ŏl-), n. **1.** Degree of excellence, relative nature or kind or character, (opp. QUANTITY; *of good, high, poor*, etc., ~*y*; *is made in three* ~*s*; ~*y matters more than quantity*); general excellence (*has* ~*y*, is excellent). **2.** Faculty, skill, accomplishment, characteristic trait, mental or moral attribute, (*give a taste of* one's ~*y*, show what one can do; *has many good* ~*ies, the* DEFECTS *of his* ~*ies, the* ~*ies of a ruler, the* ~*y of inspiring confidence* or *of courage, the* ~*y of mercy*). **3.** (arch. or vulg.). High rank or social standing (*people of, the*, ~*y*, the upper classes). **4.**(log.). (Of proposition) being affirmative or negative. **5.** (Of sound, voice, etc.) distinctive character apart from pitch & loudness, timbre. [ME & OF *qualite* f. L *qualitatem* (*qualis* of what kind, -TY)]

qualm (-ahm, -awm), n. Momentary faint or sick feeling, queasiness; misgiving, sinking of heart; scruple of conscience, doubt of one's own rectitude in some matter. Hence ~'ISH[1] a. [16th c., of obsc. orig.; cf. G *qualm*, MLG *quallem*, Du., LG *kwalm* (G *qualm*) vapour, smoke]

quandār'ў (-ŏn-; *also* kwŏn'darī), n. A state of perplexity, difficult situation, practical dilemma, (*am in a* ~). [16th c., of unkn. orig.]

quand même (see Ap.), adv. Despite consequences, even so, all the same. [F]

|| **quant** (kwŏnt), n., & v.t. & i. Punting-pole with prong to prevent its sinking in mud, used by E.-coast bargemen etc.; (vb) propel (boat), propel boat, with ~. [15th c., perh. f. L f. Gk *kontos* pole]

qua'ntic (-ŏn-), n. (math.). Rational integral homogeneous function of two or more variables. [f. L *quantus* how much, -IC]

qua'nti|fў (-ŏn-), v.t. (Log.) define application of (term, proposition) by use of *all, some*, etc.; determine quantity of, measure, express as quantity. Hence ~fīABLE a., ~FICA'TION n. [f. med. L *quantificare* (Lrec., -FY)]

qua'ntitative (-ŏn-; *or* -tā-), a. Measured or measurable by, concerned with, quantity (opp. QUALITATIVE; esp. ~ *analysis*); of, based on, the quantity of syllables (~ *scansion, verse*, etc.). Hence ~LY[2] adv. [f. med. L *quantitativus* (QUANTITY, -ATIVE)]

qua'ntitive (-ŏn-), a. = prec. (rare). [foll., -IVE]

qua'ntit|ў (-ŏn-), n. **1.** The property of things that is estimable by some sort of measure, the having of size, extension, weight, amount, or number, (*mathematics is the science of pure* ~*y*; *stated in* *terms of ~y*). **2.** Amount, sum, (*the ~y of the current depends on the size of the plates*). **3.** Specified or considerable portion or number or amount of something, *the amount of something present*, (*a small ~y of blood*; *a ~y of baskets*; *buys in large ~ies*; *the ~y of heat in an animal body*); (pl.) large amounts or numbers, abundance, (*is found in ~ies on the shore*). **4.** Length or shortness of vowel sounds (see LONG[1]; *~y-mark*, put over vowel to indicate ~y; FALSE *~y*). **5.** (log.). Extension given to subject of proposition. **6.** (math.). Thing having ~y, figure or symbol representing it, (*incommensurable ~ies have no aliquot parts*; *unknown ~y*, transf., person or thing whose action cannot be foreseen; *negligible ~y*, transf., person etc. that need not be reckoned with). **7.** || BILL[4] *of ~ies*; || *~y surveyor*, one whose business it is to prepare bills of ~ies, measure and price work done, etc. [ME & OF *quantite* f. L *quantitatem* (*quantus* how much, -TY)]

quantiv'alence (-ŏn-, -ăn-), n. (chem.). Extent to which one of element's atoms can hold other atoms in combination. [f. L *quantus* how much, after *equivalence* see EQUIVALENT]

qua'ntum (-ŏn-, *in* L *phrr.* -ăn-, -ŏn-), n. (pl. *-a*, rare). Amount; share, portion; required, desired, or allowed amount; ~ *lib'ĕt* or *plă'cĕt*, abbr. *q.l.*, *q.p.*, as much as is desired (in prescriptions); ~ *sŭff'ĭcĭt*, abbr. *quant. suff.*, or *q.s.*, as much as suffices (in prescriptions), (gen.) sufficient quantity, to sufficient extent; ~ *theory* (phys.), the hypothesis, accounting for the stability of the atom & other phenomena, that in radiation the energy of electrons is discharged not continuously but in discrete amounts or quanta. [L, neut. of *quantus* how much]

quāquavĕrs'al, a. (geol.). Pointing in every direction. [f. LL *quaquaversus* (*quaqua* wheresoever, *versus* towards)]

quarantine (kwŏ'rantēn), n., & v.t. **1.** (Period of) isolation imposed on voyagers, travellers, sick persons, or infected ship, that might spread contagious disease. **2.** v.t. Impose such isolation on, put in ~. [prob. f. It. *quarantina* forty days f. *quaranta* forty]

quăr'ĕ ĭm'pĕdĭt, n. Writ issued in cases of disputed presentation to benefice against objector. [L, = why does he hinder?]

|| **qua'renden, -der**, (kwŏ-), n. Kind of Devonshire & Somerset apple. [15th c., of unkn. orig.]

qua'rrel[1] (kwŏ-), n. (hist.). Short heavy arrow or bolt used in crossbow or arbalest. [ME, f. OF *quarel*, f. Rom. **quadrellus* dim. of *quadrus* square (L *-um*)]

qua'rrel[2] (kwŏ-), n. **1.** Occasion of complaint against person or his actions (*have no ~ against* or *with him*; *find ~ in a straw*, be captious; *pick a ~*, invent or

eagerly avail oneself of such occasion to commence hostilities; *espouse* one's ~, *fight* one's *~s for him*, assist him in getting redress; *in a good ~*, justly taken up). **2.** Violent contention or altercation between persons, rupture of friendly relations. Hence ~SOME a., ~SOMELY[2] adv., ~SOMENESS n. [ME, f. OF *querele* f. L *querela* complaint (*queri* complain)]

qua'rrel[3] (kwŏ-), v.i. (-ll-). Take exception, find fault *with* (*I never ~ with Providence*; ~ *with* one's *bread & butter*, abandon employment by which one lives); contend violently (*with* person, *about* or *for* thing), fall out, have dispute, break off friendly relations. [ME, f. prec.]

qua'rry[1] (kwŏ-), n. Object of pursuit by bird of prey, hounds, hunters, etc.; intended victim or prey. [ME, f. OF *cuiree* (*cuir* skin f. L *corium*, -Y[4]), orig. sense, parts of deer placed on hide & gi\ en to hounds]

qua'rry[2] (kwŏ-), n., & v.t. & i. **1.** Excavation made by taking stone for building etc. from its bed; place whence stone, or fig. information etc., may be extracted; floor-tile; *~man*, worker in ~. **2.** vb. Extract (stone) from ~; extract (facts etc.) laboriously from books etc.; expend toil in searching documents etc. (*~ing in the Harleian MSS.*). [ME, f. med. L *quarcia* etc. f. OF *quarriere* f. **carre* f. L *quadrum* square]

qua'rry[3] (kwŏ-), n. Diamond-shaped pane of glass as used in lattice-windows. [later form of QUARREL[1]]

quart[1] (kwôrt), n. Measure of capacity, quarter of gallon or two pints (*put ~ into pint pot*, make less contain greater); pot or bottle containing this amount (*~ bottle* of wine or spirit, ¼ gal.); (abs. for) ~ of beer (*still takes his~*); *~-pot*. [ME, f. OF *quarte* f. fem. of L *quartus* fourth]

quart[2] (kärt), n., & v.i. & t. **1.** A position in fencing, CARTE, (*~ & tierce*, fencing-practice); sequence of four cards in piquet etc. (*~ major*, ace, king, queen, knave). **2.** vb. Use the position ~; draw back (head etc.) in this. [f. F *quarte* f. fem. L as prec.]

quar'tan (kwôr-), a. & n. (Ague or fever) with paroxysm every third (by inclusive reckoning fourth) day. [ME & OF *quartaine* f. L (*febris*) *quartana* (*quartus* fourth, -AN)]

quartā'tion (kwôr-), n. Combining of three parts of silver with one of gold as preliminary in purifying gold. [L *quartus* fourth, -ATION]

quarte (kärt). Var. of QUART[2] (see etym.)

quar'ter[1] (kwôr-), n. **1.** Fourth part, one of four equal or corresponding parts, fourth part of, (*divide the apples into ~s*; ~ *of a century*, any period of 25 years; *second etc. ~ of the century*, 26th to 50th etc. years of it; ~ *of an hour*, any consecutive 15 minutes; *bad ~ of an hour*, short unpleasant experience; *can get it at *the stores for a ~ the* or *of the,* or *for ~ the, price; is not a ~ as good as it should be; ~ mile, yard,* etc., *~ of a mile* etc.). **2.** (U.S., Can.). 25 cents or *~* dollar, as amount or coin. **3.** One of four parts, each including leg or arm, into which beast's or bird's carcass is divided (of beast, often *fore, hind, ~*); (pl.) similar parts of traitor quartered after execution; (usu. in pl., often *hind-~s*) haunch(es) of living animal or man. **4.** Either side of ship aft of main-chains (*on the ~,* between astern & on beam). **5.** (her.). One of four divisions of quartered shield (*dexter* & *sinister chief, dexter* & *sinister base*); charge occupying *~* placed in chief. **6.** ‖ Grain-measure of eight bushels, used in stating large quantities, prices, etc.; (abbr. *qr*) fourth of cwt, 28 lb. **7.** Fourth of fathom (& *a ~ five,* 5¼ fathoms; *a ~ less five,* 4¾). **8.** Fourth of year for which payments become due on *~*-day; instalment of allowance etc. for the *~*; school term. **9.** Fourth of lunar period; moon's position between first & second or third & fourth of these. **10.** Point of time 15′ before or after any hour o'clock (*at a ~ to, past, six; it is not the ~ yet, strikes the hours, half-hours,* & *~s; it has gone the ~,* clock has sounded for it). **11.** ‖ (Channel I.). Unit of property or income, reckoned as £25, for assessment of taxes etc. **12.** (Region lying about) point of compass, direction, district, locality, source of supply or help in information, (*wind blows from all four ~s at once; what ~ is the wind in?* lit., & fig. how are things going? etc.; *flocked in from all ~s; no help to be looked for in that ~; had the news from a good ~*). **13.** Division of town, esp. one appropriated to or occupied by special class (*the Jewish, manufacturing, residential,* etc., *~*). **14.** pl. Lodgings, abode, esp. place where troops are lodged or stationed (HEAD*~s; winter ~s,* occupied, esp. by troops, for winter; *take up one's ~s,* lodge *in, with,* etc.; BEAT[1] *up ~s of; beat to ~s,* naut., summon crew to appointed stations as for action; *at* CLOSE[1] *~s).* **15.** Exemption from death offered or granted to enemy in battle who will surrender (*give, receive, ~; ask for* or *cry ~; no ~ to be given).* **16.** *~*-mile race or running-distance (*won the ~; has done the ~ in 50″).* **17.** *~*-*bell,* sounding the *~*-hours; *~ binding* of book, with narrow leather at back & none at corners, so *~*-*bound* a.; *~*-*butt* in billiards, cue shorter than half-butt; ‖*~*-*day,* on which quarterly payments are due, tenancies begin & end, etc. (Lady Day 25 Mar., Midsummer Day 24 June, Michaelmas 29 Sep., & Christmas 25 Dec.; in Scotland, Candlemas 2 Feb., Whitsunday 15 May, Lammas 1 Aug., Martinmas 11 Nov.); *~*-*deck,* part of upper deck between stern & after-mast, *the* officers (cf. LOW[1]*er deck*) of ship or navy; *~*-*ill,*

cattle & sheep disease causing putre-faction in one or more of the *~s; ~ left, right,* (mil.), *~* of a right angle to left, right; *~*-*light,* window in body of closed carriage apart from door-window; *~*-*line* (naut.), disposition in which bow of each ship is abaft beam of one in front; *~*-*master,* (naut.) petty officer or rating in charge of steering, binnacle, signals, hold-stowing, etc., (mil., abbr. Q.M.) regimental officer with duties of assigning *~s,* laying out camp, & looking after rations, clothing, etc. (*Q~master*-*General,* abbr. Q.M.G., military member of the Army Council and head of department controlling quartering, equipment, etc.); *~*-*miler,* runner whose distance is the *~; ~*-*plate,* photographic plate 3¼ in. ×4¼, photograph produced from it; ‖*~ sessions,* court of limited criminal & civil jurisdiction & of appeal held quarterly by justices of peace in counties & by recorder in cities and boroughs; *~*-*staff,* stout pole 6–8 ft long formerly used by peasantry as weapon; *~*-*tone* (mus.), half a semitone; *~*-*wind,* blowing on ship's *~* (most favourable sailing wind). [ME, f. AF *quarter,* OF -*ier,* f. L *quartarius* fourth part (of a measure) f. *quartus* fourth, see -ER²(2)]

quar'ter² (kwôr-), v.t. **1.** Divide into four equal parts, divide (traitor's body) into quarters. **2.** (her.). Place or bear (charges or coats of arms) quarterly on shield; add (another's coat) to one's hereditary arms; place in alternate quarters *with;* divide (shield) into quarters or into divisions formed by vertical & horizontal lines. **3.** Put (esp. soldiers) into quarters, station or lodge in specified place. **4.** (Of dogs) range or traverse (ground) in every direction. [ME, f. prec.]

quar'terage (-ŏr-), n. Quarterly payment, a quarter's wages, allowance, pension, etc. [-AGE]

quar'tering (-ŏr-), n. In vbl senses; esp. (her., pl.) coats marshalled on shield to denote alliances of family with heiresses of others; square lengths of timber made by sawing planks into four lengths. [-ING¹]

quar'terly (-ŏr-), a., n., & adv. **1.** Occurring every quarter of a year. **2.** n. *~* review or magazine. **3.** adv. Once every quarter of a year; (her.) in the four, or in two diagonally opposite, quarters of shield (*~*-*quartered,* with one or more quarters divided in four). [-LY¹,²]

‖ **quar'tern** (-ŏrt-), n. (Also *~*-*loaf*) four-pound loaf. [f. AF *quartrun,* OF *quart(e)ron,* f. *quart(e)* fourth]

quartĕt(te)′ (-ŏr-), n. Musical composition for four voices or instruments, players or singers rendering this (*piano~,* 3 stringed instruments with piano); set of four. [F (-*te*), f. It. *quartetto* (*quarto* fourth f. L *quartus*) -ET¹]

quar'tile (-ŏr-), a. & n. (astrol.). **1.** Connected with or relating to an aspect of two heavenly bodies which are 90° distant from each other. **2.** n. A ~ aspect. [f. med. L *quartilis* f. L *quartus* fourth]

quar′tŏ (-ôr-), n. (also written 4to, 4°; pl. ~s). Size given by folding sheet of paper twice; book consisting of sheets so folded; ~ *paper*, so folded. [L (*in*) *quarto* (in) fourth (of sheet); abl. of *quartus* fourth]

‖ **quar′tus** (-ôr-). See PRIMUS¹.

quartz (-ôr-), n. Kinds of mineral, massive or crystallizing in hexagonal prisms, consisting in pure form of silica or silicon dioxide, & occas. containing gold. [f. G *quarz*, of unkn. orig.]

quash (kwŏsh), v.t. Annul, make void, reject as not valid, put an end to, (esp. by legal procedure or authority). [ME, f. OF *quasser* (now *casser*) f. L *quassare*]

Qua′shee (kwŏ-), n. Negro (as national nickname). [f. Ashantee or Fantee *Kwasi* common personal name]

quăs′i, conj. & pref. **1.** (Introducing etymological explanation, abbr. *qu.*) that is to say, as if it were, (*Earls of Wilbraham*, ~ *Wild boar ham*). **2.** (Hyphened esp. to noun or adj.) seeming(ly), not real(ly), practical(ly), half-, almost, (*engaged in a* ~-*war*; *the* ~-*art of making enemies*; *has a* ~-*episcopal position*). [L, = as if]

quăss′ia (*or* -ăsh′a, -ŏsh′a), n. S.-Amer., esp. Surinam, tree; (wood, bark, or root of this & other trees, yielding) bitter medicinal decoction. [f. name of Negro (cf. QUASHEE) who discovered its virtues 1730]

quăt′ercĕntĕn′arў, n. Four-hundredth anniversary. [L *quater* four times]

quatĕrn′arў, a. & n. **1.** Having four parts, esp. compounded of four chemical elements or radicals; concerned with the number four; (geol.) (*Q*~) belonging to most recent period, subsequent to Tertiary. **2.** n. Set of four things; the number four; *the Pythagorean* ~, 1 + 2 + 3 + 4 = 10, with mystic significance in Pythagoreanism. [ME, f. L *quaternarius* (*quaterni* distrib. of *quatuor* four, -ARY¹)]

quatĕrn′ion, n. Set of four; quire of four sheets folded in two; Pythagorean quaternary, mystic number 4 or 10 (see prec.); (math.) quotient of two vectors or operator that changes one vector into another (named as depending on four geometrical elements), (pl.) form of calculus of vectors in which this operator is used. [ME, f. LL *quaternio* (prec.)]

quatĕrn′itў, n. Being four; set of four persons (esp. of the Godhead in contrast to *Trinity*). [f. LL *quaternitas*]

quatorzain (kăt′erzān), n. Fourteen-line poem, irregular sonnet. [f. F *quatorzaine* (*quatorze* fourteen f. L *quatuordecim*)]

quatrain (kwŏt′rīn), n. Stanza of four lines occas. with alternate rhymes. [F (*quatre* four f. L *quatuor*)]

quatre (kăt′er), n. = CATER¹.

quat′refoil (kătre-, kāter-), n. Four-cusped figure, esp. as opening in archi-tectural tracery, resembling symmetrical four-lobed leaf or flower. [ME, f. AF *quatrefoil* (*quatre* four, FOIL¹)]

quattrocĕn′tist (-ahtrŏch-), n. & a. (Artist etc.) of the quattrocento. [-IST]

quattrocĕn′tŏ (-ahtrŏch-), n. Fifteenth century as period in Italian art. [It., lit. 400, but used = 1400]

quāv′er¹, v.i. & t. Vibrate, shake, tremble, (esp. of voice or musical sound); use trills in singing; sing (note, song) with trills, say (usu. *out*) in trembling tones. Hence ~**inġLY²** adv. [15th c., f. ME (obs.) *quave* + -ER⁵; orig. imit., cf. QUIVER²]

quāv′er², n. Trill in singing; tremulousness in speech, whence ~Y¹ a.; ‖ (mus.) note equal in length to half crotchet. [f. prec.]

quay (kē), n. Solid stationary artificial landing-place usu. of stone or iron lying alongside or projecting into water for (un)loading ships. Hence ~AGE(1, 4) (kē′ij) n. [ME *key*(*e*), *kay* f. OF *kay* f. Gaulish *kagio*, *kajo*]

quean, n. (arch.). Impudent or ill-behaved girl, jade, hussy. [OE *cwene*, OS, OHG *quena*, ON *kvenna*, Goth. *qino* woman f. Gmc *kwenōn* cogn. w. QUEEN]

queas′lў (-z-), a. (Of food) unsettling the stomach, causing or tending to sickness, fulsome; (of person, his stomach, or his conscience) easily upset, weak of digestion, over scrupulous or tender or delicate, in fastidious condition. Hence ~iNESS n. [15th c. *coisy*, of obsc. orig.; cf. OF *coisier* hurt]

quebra′chŏ (kābrah-), n. (Kinds of) American tree yielding very hard timber and medicinal bark; bark of this tree. [Sp., = axe-breaker]

queen¹, n. **1.** King's wife (also ~ *consort* for distinction from next sense; ~ *dowager*, wife of late king; ~ *mother*, ~ dowager who is mother of sovereign, & see next sense; also prefixed as title, as *Q*~ *Elizabeth*). **2.** Female sovereign of kingdom (~*mother*, ~ having child or children; also prefixed as title, as *Q*~ *Victoria*; *Q*~ *Anne is dead*, retort to stale news; *Q*~ *Anne's* BOUNTY; *Q*~-*Anne*, in the architectural or decorative style of Q~ Anne's time; *Q*~ *of Scots*, Mary Stuart). **3.** Worshipped female, e.g. the Virgin Mary (*Q*~ *of grace* etc.); ancient goddess (*Q*~ *of heaven*, Juno, *of love*, Venus, *of night*, Diana, etc.); person's sweetheart or wife or mistress; majestic woman; belle, mock sovereign, on some occasion (*Q*~ *of the* MAY³ etc.). **4.** Personified best example of anything that can be regarded as fem. (*the* ~ *of watering-places, roses, nurses*). **5.** Person, country, etc., regarded as ruling over some sphere (~ *of hearts*, any beautiful woman; ~ *of the Adriatic*, Venice; ~ *of the seas*, Gt Britain; ~ *of the meadows*, meadowsweet). **6.** (Also ~ *bee, wasp, ant*) perfect female of bee etc. **7.** Piece in chess (~'*s bishop, knight,* pawn, etc., those placed nearest ~ at start; ~'s GAMBIT). **8.** One of court-cards in each suit. **9.** ~-*cake*, small soft currant cake often heart-shaped; ~-*posts*, two upright timbers between tie-beam & principal rafters of roof-truss; ‖ *Q*~'*s* BENCH, BOUNTY; ‖ *Q*~'*s* COLOUR[1], COUNSEL[1], ENGLISH[1], EVIDENCE, HEAD[1]; ~'*s pin-cushion*, flower of guelder rose; ‖ ~'*s* SHILLING; ~-*stitch*, fancy stitch in embroidery; ~'*s-ware*, cream-coloured Wedgwood; ‖ ~'*s weather*, sunshine. Hence ~'DOM, ~'HOOD, ~'SHIP, nn., ~'LESS, ~'LIKE, aa. [OE *cwēn*, OS *quân*, ON *kvǽn*, *kvân*, Goth. *qēns* wife f. Gmc *kwæniz* cogn. w. QUEAN]

queen[2], v.t. & i. Make (woman) queen; ~ *it*, play the queen; (chess) advance (pawn) to opponent's end of board & have it converted to queen or other piece, (intr., of pawn) be converted thus. [f. prec.]

‖ **queen'ing**, n. Kind of apple. [-ING[3]]

queen'ly, a. Fit for, appropriate to, queen; majestic, queenlike. Hence ~ĪNESS n. [-LY[1]]

Queens'berry (-z-), n. ~ *Rules*, standard rules of boxing drawn up by 8th Marquis of ~ in 1867.

queer, a., n., & v.t. **1.** Strange, odd, eccentric; of questionable character, shady, suspect; homosexual (also as n.); out of sorts, giddy, faint, (esp. *feel* ~); ‖ (sl.) drunk; in *Q~ Street* (sl.), in a difficulty, in debt or trouble or disrepute; hence ~'ISH[1] a., ~'LY[2] adv., ~'NESS n. **2.** v.t. (sl.). Spoil, put out of order, (‖ esp. ~ *the pitch for* one, spoil his chance beforehand; make feel ~. [(1) orig. unkn.; (2) thieves' cant, orig. unkn.]

quell, v.t. (poet. & rhet.). Suppress, forcibly put an end to, crush, overcome, reduce to submission, (fear, opposition, rebellion, rebels, etc.). Hence (-)~'ER[1] n. [OE *cwellan* kill, OS *quellian*, OHG *quellen*, ON *kvelja* f. Gmc *kwaljan*]

quench, v.t. Extinguish (fire, light, eyesight; chiefly poet. or rhet.); ~ *smoking flax*, cut short promising development (see *Is.* xlii. 3); cool, esp. with water (heat, heated thing; poet. or rhet.); stifle, suppress, (desire, speed, motion; poet. or rhet.); slake (thirst); (sl.) reduce to silence, shut up, (opponent); cool (hot metal) in water. Hence ~'ABLE, ~'LESS, aa. [ME, f. OE -*cwencan* causative f. -*cwincan* (= Fris. *kwinka*) be extinguished]

quen'cher, n. In vbl senses; esp. (sl.) something to drink (usu. *a modest* ~). [-ER[1]]

quenelle' (ke-), n. Seasoned ball of fish or meat reduced to paste. [F, orig. unkn.]

quer'ist, n. Person who asks question. [f. L *quaerere* ask, -IST]

quern, n. Hand-mill for grinding corn; small hand-mill for pepper etc.; ~-*stone*, millstone. [OE *cweorn*, OS *quern*, OHG *quirn*, ON *kvern*, Goth. -*qairnus*]

que'rulous (-rŏŏ-), a. Complaining, peevish. Hence ~'LY[2] adv., ~'NESS n. [f. LL *querulosus* (L *querulus*, f. *queri* complain, -OSE[1])]

quer'y, n., & v.t. & i. **1.** (Used abs. to introduce question; abbr. *qu.*) pray, one would like to know, (*Q*~, or *qu.*, *was the money ever paid?*). **2.** A question, esp. of the nature of objection (*was prepared to suppress all queries*); mark of interrogation or the word ~ or *qu.* written against statement, or the word ~ interjected in speech, to question accuracy. **3.** vb. Ask, inquire, (*whether, if*, etc.); put a question; call (thing) in question in speech or writing, question accuracy of. [17th c., anglicized form of QUAERE]

quest[1], n. **1.** ‖ Official inquiry or jury etc. making it (now only in vulg. *crowner's* ~, coroner's inquest). **2.** Seeking or thing sought by inquiry or search, esp. object of medieval knight's pursuit (*in* ~ *of*, seeking). [ME, f. OF *queste* f. Rom. *quæsita* p.p. of L *quaerere* seek]

quest[2], v.i. & t. (Of dogs etc.) search for game (often *about*); go (*about*) in search of something; (poet.) search for, seek *out*. [ME, f. OF *quester* (prec.)]

ques'tion[1] (-chon), n. **1.** Sentence adapted by order of words, use of interrogative pronoun or stop, or other means, to elicit answer, interrogative sentence, (*put a* ~ *to* one, ask him something; ~ *& answer*, alternation of ~s & answers, catechetic procedure; LEADING[2], RHETORICAL, ~; *indirect, oblique*, ~, made into dependent clause; ~-*mark* or -*stop*, mark of interrogation). **2.** (Raising of) doubt about or objection to thing's truth, credibility, advisability, etc. (*allowed it without* ~; *beyond all* or *beyond, out of, past, without*, ~, certainly, undoubtedly; *call in* ~, raise objections to; *make no* ~ of fact etc., *but that it is so* etc., admit it; *there is no* ~ *but that* . . .), whence ~LESS (-cho-) adv. & a. **3.** Problem requiring solution, matter or concern depending on conditions of, (*a difficult* ~; BEG *the* ~; *success is merely a* ~ *of time*, will certainly come, but may come sooner or later; *it is only a* ~ *of putting enough coffee in*). **4.** Subject being discussed or for discussion, thing to be voted on, (*the person in* ~, that we are referring to; *come into* ~, be discussed, become of practical importance; *that is not the* ~, is irrelevant; *the* ~ *is*, introducing or recalling exact matter of debate; *Q*~ *!* in public assemblies, used to recall speaker from digression; *the* PREVIOUS ~; *out of the* ~, too impracticable to be worth discussing; *put the* ~, require supporters & opponents of proposal to record their votes, divide meeting etc.; OPEN ~). **5.** (arch.). Torture to elicit confession (*was put to the* ~. [ME, f. OF f. L *quaestionem* (*quaerere* seek, -TION)]

ques'tion[2] (-chon), v.t. Ask questions of, interrogate, subject to examination, (person); seek information from study of (phenomena, facts); call in question, throw doubt upon, raise objections to, (~ *the honesty, accuracy, fitness*, etc., *of*; *it cannot be ~ed but that that or but*, it is certain that), whence ~ABLE a. (esp., doubtfully true, not clearly consistent with honesty or honour or wisdom), ~ably² adv., (-cho-). Hence~ingly² (-cho-) adv. [ME, f. OF *questionner* (prec.)]

questionnaire' (kĕstĭŏ-,kwĕscho-),**quĕs'-tionary** (rare; -cho-), n. Formulated series of questions, an interrogatory. [(-*aire* F) f. med. L *questionarium*, see QUESTION, -ARY¹]

quĕt'zal, n. Beautiful Central-Amer. bird. [Sp., f. Aztec *quetzalli* the bird's tail--feather]

queue (kū), n., & v.t. & i. **1.** Hanging plaited tail of hair or wig, pigtail; line of persons, vehicles, etc., awaiting their turn to be attended to or proceed. **2.** vb. Dress (hair) in ~; (of persons etc.) form *up* in, join *on* to, a ~. [F, f. L *cauda* tail)]

quib'ble, n., & v.i. **1.** Play on words, pun; equivocation, evasion, unsubstantial or purely verbal argument etc. esp. one depending on ambiguity of word. **2.** v.i. Use ~s; hence **quibb'ler¹** n., **quibb'ling²** a. [perh. dim. of obs. *quib* f. L *quibus* abl. pl. of *qui* who (familiar f. use in legal documents)]

quick, a., n., & adv. **1.** Living, alive, (arch.; esp. *the ~ & the dead*, *go down ~ into hell*; *~ with child*, orig. *with ~ child*, at stage of pregnancy when motion has been felt). **2.** Vigorous, lively, ready, sensitive, prompt to act, perceive, be affected, learn, think, or invent, (*a ~ child*, intelligent; *~ temper*, easily irritated, whence.~temperED² a.; *~ sight*, acute or alert, whence ~sightED² a.; *has a ~ eye, ear*, etc., whence ~eyED², ~--earED², aa.; *is ~ to take offence*; *has ~ wits*, is ready at grasping situation, making repartees, etc., whence ~wittED² a.; N.B. these compounds have ~ stressed when attrib., unstressed when pred.). **3.** Moving rapidly, rapid, swift, done in short time or with little interval, (*~ succession*; *at a ~ trot*; *a ~ way of doing it*; *his ~ growth*; *a ~ one*, a ~ drink; *be ~*, make haste; *did a ~ mile*; *was followed by ~ vengeance*), whence ~'ly² adv. **4.** ~*-change*, (of actor etc.) ~ly changing costume or appearance to play another part; ~'lime¹; *~ march* (mil.), march in ~ time (see below; esp. as word of command for starting at usual pace); ~'*sand*, (bed of) loose wet sand readily swallowing up ships, animals, etc.; ~'*set*, (adj., of hedge) formed of living plants esp. hawthorn, (n.) live slips of plants esp. hawthorn set in ground to grow, hedge formed of these; ~'*silver*, (n.) mercury, (fig.) mobility of temperament or mood, (v.t.) coat (mirror-glass) with amalgam of

tin; *~ step*, step used in *~ time* (mil.), rate of marching reckoned at 128 paces of 33 in. to the minute or four miles an hour, the usual British-army rate; *~step* (dancing), a fast foxtrot. **5.** n. Tender or sensitive flesh below skin or esp. nails, tender part of wound or sore where healthy tissue begins, seat of feeling or emotion, (*bites his nails to the ~*; *probed it to the ~*; *the insult stung him to the ~*; *is a Tory to the ~*, through & through); = ~*set* a. & n. **6.** adv. (~*er*, ~*est*, always after vb). At rapid rate, in comparatively short time, (*ran as ~ as I could*; *who will be there ~est?*); (ellipt. for imperat. of *go, come, be*, ~) make haste; ~-(prefixed to partt. esp. in -*ing*) ~ly, soon, (~*-fading*, -*forgotten*, etc.; ~*-firing gun*, or ~-**fir'**ER¹ n., gun with special mechanism for firing shots in ~ succession); ~*-freeze*, freeze (food) rapidly so as to preserve its natural qualities (also as n. & attrib.). [OE *cwicu*, OS *quik*, OHG *quec*, ON *kvikr*, f. Gmc **kwikwaz* f. **kwiw-*, cogn. w. Goth. *qius*, L *vivus*]

quick'en, v.t. & i. Give or restore natural or spiritual life or vigour to, animate, stimulate, rouse, inspire, kindle, whence ~ING² a.; receive, come to, life; (of woman or embryo) reach QUICK stage in pregnancy; accelerate, make or (of pace, motion, etc.) become quicker. [-EN⁶]

quick'ie, n. (colloq.). Cheap film made to satisfy the Films Quota Act. [QUICK, -Y³]

quick'ness, n. Readiness or acuteness of perception or apprehension; speed, rapidity, suddenness, (rare; esp. of single gesture or motion); hastiness *of temper*. [-NESS]

quicūn'què vŭlt, n. The~, the Athanasian creed. [initial L wds, = whosoever will]

‖ **quid¹**, n. (sl.; pl. ~). A sovereign, £1, (*at two ~ a week*). [17th c., of unkn. orig.]

quid², n. Lump of tobacco held in mouth & chewed. [var. of CUD]

quidd'itў, n. Essence of a thing, what makes a thing what it is; quibble, captious subtlety. [f. med. L *quidditas* (L *quid* what, -ITY)]

quid'nunc, n. Newsmonger, person given to gossip. [f. L *quid* what, *nunc* now]

quid prō quō, n. Blunder made by using or putting one thing for another (now rare); compensation, return made, consideration, (*must get, must find him, a ~*). [f. L *quid* something *pro* for *quo* something]

quiĕs'c|ent, a. Motionless, inert, silent, dormant. Hence or cogn. ~ENCE, ~ENCY, nn., ~ently² adv. [f. L *quiescere* (*quies* QUIET¹, -ESCENT)]

qui'et¹, n. Undisturbed political condition, public tranquillity; silence, stillness; being free from disturbance or agitation or urgent tasks, rest, repose, peace of mind; unruffled deportment, calm. [ME, f. AF *quiete* f. OF *quiet* (as foll.)]

qui'et², a. (~*er*, ~*est*). With no or slight or gentle sound or motion; of gentle or inactive disposition; (of colour, dress, etc.) unobtrusive, not showy; not overt, private, disguised, (~ *resentment*; *had a* ~ *dig at him*; esp. *on the* ~, or sl. abbr. *on the q.t.*, secretly); undisturbed, not interfered with or interrupted, free or far from strife or uproar; informal (*a* ~ *dinner--party*); enjoyed in quiet, tranquil, not anxious or remorseful. Hence ~LY² adv., ~NESS, quí'ĕTUDE, nn. [ME, f. OF *quiet(e)* or L *quietus* p.p. f. *quiescere* (QUIESCENT)]

qui'et³, v.t. & i. Reduce to quietness, soothe, calm; become quiet (rare; usu. ~ *down*). [f. LL *quietare* (partly f. prec.)]

qui'eten, v.t. & i. = prec. [-EN⁶]

qui'et|ism, n. Passive attitude towards life with devotional contemplation & abandonment of the will as form of religious mysticism, non-resistance principles. So ~IST(2) n. & a., ~ĭs'TIC a. [f. It. *quietismo* (QUIET², -ISM)]

quiēt'us, n. Acquittance, receipt, given on payment of account etc. (now rare); release from life, death, extinction, final riddance, (*got, gave him, his* ~). [f. med. L *quietus* (*est* he is) quit (QUIET²) used as receipt form]

‖ **quiff**, n. Curl plastered down on the forehead, tuft of hair over forehead. [orig. unkn.]

quill¹, n. Hollow stem of feather, (also ~*-feather*) whole large feather of wing or tail; pen (also ~ *pen*), plectrum, fishing--float, or toothpick, made of this; one of porcupine's spines; bobbin of hollow reed, any bobbin; musical pipe made of hollow stem; curled-up piece of cinnamon or cinchona bark; ~*-coverts*, feathers covering base of ~*-feathers*; ~*-driver*, clerk or journalist or author. [prob. f. (M)LG *quiele*; cf. MHG *kil*, G *kiel*]

quill², v.t. & i. Form into quill-like folds, goffer, whence ~'ING¹(2) n.; wind thread or yarn on bobbin. [f. prec.]

‖ **quill'ĕt**, n. (arch.). Quibble, nice distinction. [perh. abbr. of obs. *quillity* alt. of QUIDDITY]

quilt, n., & v.t. **1.** Bed-coverlet made of padding enclosed between two layers of linen etc. & kept in place by cross lines of stitching; any coverlet or counterpane (PATCHwork ~). **2.** v.t. Cover with padded material; make or join together after the manner of a ~; sew up (coin, letters, etc.) between two layers of garment etc.; ‖ compile (literary work) out of extracts or borrowed ideas; (sl.) thrash. Hence ~'ING¹(1, 3) n. [ME, f. OF *cuilte* f. L *culcita* cushion]

quin'arў, a. Of the number five; consisting of five things. [f. L *quinarius* (*quini* distrib. of *quinque* five, -ARY¹)]

quin'ate, a. (bot.). (Of leaf) composed of five leaflets. [f. L *quini* (prec.), -ATE²]

quince, n. Hard acid yellowish pear--shaped fruit used as preserve or as flavouring, tree bearing it. [ME; orig. pl.

of obs. *coyn*, f. OF *cooin* f. L *cotoneum* var. of *cydonium* neut. of *Cydonius* of Cydonia in Crete]

quincĕntĕn'arў, irreg. for quing-.

quinc'ŭnx, n. (Arrangement of) five objects set so that four are at corners of square or rectangle & the other at its centre (e.g. the five on dice or cards; *plantation is laid out in* ~*es*, in the diagonal cross lines given by combining ~es). So quincŭn'cial (-shl) a., quincŭn'cialLY² (-sha-), adv. [L, = 5/12 (*quinque* five, *uncia* OUNCE), also ~ pattern]

quingĕntĕn'arў (-j-; or -jĕn'te-), a. & n. Of, in, 500th year; (n.) 500th anniversary. [f. L *quingenti* 500 after CENTENARY]

quin'ia, n. (med.). = QUININE. [f. Sp. *quina* f. Peruv. *kina* bark]

quinine' (-ēn, -in), n. Alkaloid found esp. in cinchona bark & used as febrifuge and tonic; (pop.) sulphate of ~, the usu. form in which ~ is taken. So quin'IZE(4) v.t., quin'ISM(5) n. [as prec., -INE⁵]

quinquagēnăr'ian, a. & n. (Person) fifty years old. [f. L *quinquagenarius* (*quinquageni* distrib. of *quinquaginta* fifty, -ARY¹), -AN]

quinquagēn'arў (or -kwăj'e-), a. & n. = prec. a. & n.; fiftieth anniversary. [prec.]

Quinquagēs'ima, n. (Also ~ *Sunday*) Sunday before Lent. [f. LL fem. of L *quinquagesimus* fiftieth]

quinqu|(e)-, comb. form of L *quinque* five, in some wds taken f. L, & in many mod., esp. bot. & zool., formations. So ~-ăng'ŭlar (-ngg-) five-angled; ~èccōs'tāte five-ribbed; ~ĕnn'iad, ~ĕnn'ium (pl. -*a*), five-year period; ~ĕnn'ial five-year--long, five-yearly, whence ~ĕnn'ialLY² adv.; ~ĕlăt'eral a. & n., five-sided (figure or object); ~ĕlōb'āte five-lobed; ~ĕpărt'ite divided into, consisting of, five parts; quin'quĕrēme ancient galley with five banks of oars; ~ĕvăl'vŭlar five-valved; quin'quifĭd cleft in five; ~iv'alent capable of combining with five univalent atoms.

quinqui'na (kĭnkē², kwĭnkwĭ²), n. (Kinds of tree producing) Peruvian bark yielding quinine & other febrifuge alkaloids. [f. Peruv. *kinkina* redupl. form as QUINIA]

quins (-z), n. pl. (colloq.). Five children at a birth. [short for QUINTUPLETS]

quin's|ў (-z-), n. Inflammation of throat, suppuration of tonsils. Hence ~iED² (-id) a. [ME, f. med. L *quinancia* f. Gk *kunagkhē* (*kun-* dog, *agkhō* throttle)]

quint (*in sense 2* usu. kĭnt), n. **1.** Musical interval of fifth; organ-stop of tone one--fifth above normal. **2.** (piquet). Sequence of five of same suit (~ *major*, of ace to ten; ~ *minor*, of knave to seven). [f. F *quinte* f. L fem. of *quintus* fifth]

quin'tain (-tĭn), n. (hist.). (Medieval military exercise of tilting at) post set up as mark & often provided with sandbag to swing round & strike unskilful tilter.

R

[ME, f. OF *quintaine* perh. ult. f. L *quin-tana* (*quintus* fifth) camp market]

quin'tal, kin-, n. 100 lb.; 112 lb. or hundredweight; 100 kilograms. [ME, f. OF, f. Arab. *qintar*]

quin'tan, a. & n. (Ague or fever) with paroxysm every fourth (by incl. reckoning fifth) day. [f. L (*febris*) *quintana* (*quintus* fifth, -AN) fifth-day (fever)]

quinte (kahnt), n. Fifth fencing thrust or parry. [as QUINT]

quintèss'ence, n. 1. (Ancient philos.) fifth substance, apart from four elements, composing the heavenly bodies entirely & latent in all things. 2. Most essential part of any substance, refined extract; purest & most perfect form, manifestation, or embodiment, *of* some quality or class. Hence **quintèssĕn'tiAL (-shl)** a. [ME, f. OF or med. L *quinta essentia*]

quintĕt(te)', n. (Performers of) piece for five voices or instruments (*piano, clarinet,* etc. ∼, four stringed instruments plus instrument named); set of five. [F (*-te*), f. It. *quintetto* (*quinto* fifth f. L *quintus*)]

quintill'ion (-lyon), n. ‖ Fifth power of. million (1 with 30 ciphers); (U.S. & France) cube of million (1 with 18 ciphers). [L *quintus* fifth, BILLION]

quin'tŭp|le, a., n., & v.t. & i., **∼lÿ,** adv., **∼lèt,** n., **quintŭp'licate** (-*at*), a. & n. (-āt), v.t., **quintŭplicā'tion,** n. Fivefold etc. (for detailed senses see QUADRUPLE & wds in *quadrupl-*, substituting *five* for *four*). [-*uple* F, f. L *quintus* fifth, after QUADRUPLE]

‖ **quin'tus.** See PRIMUS[1].

quip, n., & v.i. (-pp-). Sarcastic remark, clever hit, smart saying, verbal conceit; equivocation, quibble; (v.i.) make ∼s. [var. of obs. *quippy* perh. f. L *quippe* forsooth]

quipu (kē'pōō, kwē-), n. Ancient-Peruvian substitute for writing by variously knotting threads of various colours. [Peruv., = knot]

quīre[1], n. Four sheets of paper etc. folded to form eight leaves as in mediaeval MSS.; any collection of leaves one within another in MS. or book (*in ∼s,* unbound, in sheets); 24 sheets of writing-paper. [ME, f. OF *quaer* (now *cahier*) f. Rom. *quaternum* f. L *quaterni* set of four, see QUATERNION]

quīre[2], n. & v.t. & i. See CHOIR.

Qui'rinal, n. (Used for) the Italian Government (esp. as opp. VATICAN). [name of palace]

quirk, n. Quibble, quip; trick of action or behaviour; twist or flourish in drawing or writing; (archit.) acute hollow between convex part of moulding & soffit or fillet. [16th c., of unkn. orig.]

quirt, n., & v.t. Short-handled riding-whip with braided leather lash; (v.t.) lash with this. [perh. f. Sp. *cuerda* CORD]

quis'ling (-z-), n. Person co-operating with an enemy who has occupied his country, (pop.) traitor. Hence ∼ITE[1] a. & n. [f. *Q∼,* renegade Norwegian Army officer]

quit[1], pred. a. Free, clear, absolved, (arch.; *the others can go ∼; was ∼ for a ducking,* got off with that); rid *of* (*glad to be ∼ of the trouble*); *∼'claim,* (n.) renunciation of right, (v.t.) renounce claim to, give up (thing) *to; ∼'rent,* (usu. small) rent paid by freeholder or copyholder in lieu of service. [ME, f. OF *quit(t)e* f. L *quietus* QUIET[2]]

quit[2], v.t. (∼*ted,* rarely ∼ exc. U.S.). 1. Rid oneself *of* (arch.). 2. (refl.). (Usu. w. archaic refl. pron. without *self*) behave, acqtuit, conduct, oneself *well* etc. (esp. ∼ *you like men;* arch.). 3. Give up, let go, abandon, (∼ *hold of,* loose; ∼ *office* etc.); *∼cease,* stop, as ∼ *grumbling.* 4. Depart from, leave, (place, person, etc.; ∼*ted Paris at midnight; ∼ted him in anger*); (abs., of tenant) leave occupied premises (esp. *give, have,* etc., *notice to ∼*). 5. (poet.). Requite, repay, clear off, (∼ *love with hate; death ∼s all scores*). Hence *∼t'ER[1]* n., one who deserts his job or his post, shirker, poltroon. [ME, f. OF *quit(t)er* QUIET[3]]

qui tăm, n. (legal). (Action brought by) informer. [L, = who as well (for the King as for himself sues)]

quitch, n. (Also ∼-*grass*) COUCH[3]-*grass.* [OE *cwice* = MLG *kwēke,* Du. *kweek,* cogn. w. QUICK]

quite, adv. Completely, wholly, entirely, altogether, to the utmost extent, nothing short of, in the fullest sense, positively, absolutely, (∼ *covers it; was ∼ by myself; ∼ other,* very different; ∼ *another,* a very different; *is ∼ a hero, disappointment, good thing; I ∼ like him; is ∼ too delightful,* colloq., i.e. to be done justice to in words; *is ∼ the thing,* fashionable; *not ∼ proper,* rather improper); rather, to some extent, (*it took ∼ a long time; ∼ a few,* a fair number); ‖ (ellipt., colloq.) *he, she, isn't ∼,* he, she, isn't ∼ a gentleman, lady; ∼ *so* (& improp. ∼), I grant the truth of that. [ME, f. obs. *quite* a. = QUIT[1]]

quits, pred. a. On even terms by retaliation or repayment (*will be ∼ with him yet,* will have revenge; *now we are ∼; cry ∼,* acknowledge that things are now even, agree not to proceed further in quarrel etc.; DOUBLE[2] *or ∼*). [perh. abbr. of med. L *quittus=quietus* QUIT[1]; or=QUIT[1] +-ES]

quitt'ance, n. (arch., poet.). Release *from* something; acknowledgement of payment, receipt, (*omittance is no ∼,* debt is not annulled by not being pressed); requital. [ME, f. OF *quitance* (*quiter* QUIT[2])]

quiv'er[1], n. Case for holding arrows (*have an arrow, shaft, left in* one's ∼, not be resourceless; ∼ *full of children,* large family, see Ps. cxxvii. 5). Hence ∼FUL(2) n. [ME, f. OF *quivre* f. WG **kokar* (OE *cocer,* OS *cocăre,* OHG *kochar*)]

quiv'er[2], v.i. & t., & n. 1. Tremble or

vibrate with slight rapid motion (of person, leaf, wing, voice, light, etc.; *with* emotion, *in* the wind etc.); (of birds, esp. skylark) make (wings) ~; hence ~**ing**LY[2] adv. **2.** n. ~**ing** motion or sound. [prob. imit.; cf. QUAVER]

qui vive (kĕvēv′). On the ~, on the alert, watching for something to happen. [F, = lit. (*long*) live *who?*, i.e. *on whose side are you?*, as sentry's challenge]

Quix′ote, n. Enthusiastic visionary, pursuer of lofty but impracticable ideals, person utterly regardless of his material interests in comparison with honour or devotion. Hence **quix**ŏt′**ic** a. (*quixotics* n. pl., quixotic sentiments), **quix**ŏt′**I**-CALLY adv., **quix′ot**ISM(2), **quix′ot**RY(4), nn., **quix′ot**IZE(2, 3) v.t. & i. [hero of Cervantes's *Don* ~]

quiz, n., & v.t. (-zz-): **1.** ¶ Odd or eccentric person, person of ridiculous appearance, (now rare); person given to ~zing; (orig. U.S.) interrogation, questionnaire, examination; test of general knowledge in radio or television programme; hoax, ridicule, thing done to expose or burlesque another's oddities, (now rare); hence ~**z′**ICAL a., ~**z′**ICALLY[2] adv. **2.** v.t. Make sport of (person or his ways), whence ~**z′**ABLE a.; regard with mocking air; look curiously at, observe the ways or oddities of, survey through an eye-glass or (now rare) ~*zing-glass*; *examine by questioning; hence ~**z′**ing**LY[2] adv. [appears as a vogue-word (n. 1782, vb 1796, of unkn. orig.]

quō′ăd, prep. As regards; ~ *hŏc*, in this respect, so far as this goes. [L (*quo* whither, *ad* to)]

quŏd[1], n., & v.t. (sl.; -dd-). Prison (*in, out of*, ~); (v.t.) imprison. [c. 1700, orig. unkn.]

quŏd[2], neut. of L *qui* which (~ *ē′răt dēmŏnstrăn′dum* abbr. Q.E.D., ~ *ē′răt faciĕn′dum* (-shĭ-) abbr. Q.E.F, ~ *ē′răt invĕnĭĕn′dum* abbr. Q.E.I., which was the thing to be proved, made or done, found; formulae in geometrical demonstrations, &, esp. Q.E.D., in gen. use; ~ *vid′ē*, abbr. *q.v.*, which see, in cross & other references).

quoin (koin), n., & v.t. **1.** External angle of building; stone or brick forming angle, corner-stone, whence ~′ING[1](3) n.; internal corner of room; wedge for locking type in forme, raising level of gun, keeping barrel from rolling, etc. **2.** v.t. Secure or raise with ~s. [var. of COIN]

quoit (koit, kwoit), n., & v.t. & i. Heavy flattish sharp-edged iron ring thrown to encircle iron peg or to stick in ground near it in game of ~s; (vb; rare) fling like ~, play ~s. [ME, of unkn. (prob. F) orig.]

quŏn′dăm, a. That once had but no longer has the specified character, sometime, former, (*a* ~ *friend of mine*). [L, = formerly]

quōr′um, n. Fixed number of members

that must be present to make proceedings of assembly or society or board valid. [L, = of whom (we will that you etc. be)]

quŏt′a, n. Share that individual person or company is bound to contribute to or entitled to receive from a total; quantity of goods which under government controls must be manufactured, exported, imported, etc.; number of yearly immigrants allowed to enter the United States from any one country; ~ QUICKIE. [f. med. L *quota* (*pars*) how great (a part); fem. of *quotus* (*quot* how many)]

quotā′tion, n. (Print.) quadrat used for filling up blanks; quoting, passage quoted; amount stated as current price of stocks or commodities; ~*-marks*, inverted commas & apostrophes, single (' ') or double (" "), used to mark beginning & end of quoted passage. [f. med. L *quotatio* (QUOTE, -ATION)]

quŏt′ative, a. Of quoting; given to quotation. [foll., -ATIVE]

quōte, v.t., & n. **1.** Cite or appeal to (author, book) in confirmation of some view, repeat or copy out passage(s) from; repeat or copy out (borrowed passage) usu. with indication that it is borrowed, (abs.) make quotations, (*from* author, book, speech, etc.); enclose within quotation-marks; adduce or cite *as*; state price of (usu. *at* figure); hence **quŏt′**ABLE, ~′ WORTHY, aa. **2.** n. (colloq.). Passage quoted; (usu. pl.) quotation-mark(s). [earlier (ME) sense *mark with numbers*, f. med. L *quotare* (QUOTA)]

quŏth, v.t. 1st & 3rd pers. past indic. (arch.). Said *I*, *he*, *she*, & rarely *we* or *they* (placed amidst, after, or before the words quoted; *quŏth′a*, arch. for ~ *he*, used in quoting contemptuously = forsooth). [past of obs. *quethe*, OE *cwethan*]

quotid′ian, a. & n. **1.** Daily, of every day, (~ *fever, ague*, recurring every day); commonplace, trivial. **2.** n. ~ ague or fever. [ME, f. OF *cotidien, -ian*, or L *cot-*, *quotidianus* (*quotidie* daily, -AN)]

quō′tient (-shnt), n. Result given by dividing one quantity by another; INTELLI-GENCE ~. [erron. f. L *quotiens* how many times, by confusion w. -ENT]

quō warrăn′tō (wŏ-), n. (hist.). Writ formerly issued by the King's Bench Division calling on a person to show by what warrant he held or exercised an office or franchise. [med. L, = by what warrant]

R

R (är), letter (pl. *R*s, R's). *The* r *months*, those with *r* in their names (Sep.–Ap.) as season for oysters; *the three* Rs, reading, (w)riting, & (a)rithmetic, as basis of elementary education.

răbb′ĕt, n., & v.t. **1.** Step-shaped reduction cut along edge or face or projecting angle of wood etc. usu. to receive edge or tongue of another piece. **2.** Elastic beam arranged to give rebound to hammer striking it in ascent. **3.** v.t. Join or fix with ~, make ~ in. [ME, f. OF *rabat* abatement, recess, (*rabattre* REBATE¹)]

răbb'i, n. Jewish doctor of the law (as form of address by itself or prefixed to name, or as ordinary noun), esp. one authorized by ordination to deal with law & ritual & perform certain functions; *Chief R~,* ‖ ecclesiastical head of British Jewish communities. [ME; LL f. Gk f. Heb. = my master (*rabh* master + pronom. suf.)]

răbb'in, n. Rabbi (usu. *the~s,* chief Jewish authorities on law & doctrine, most of them between 2nd & 13th cc.). Hence ~ATE¹, ~ISM(3), ~IST(2, 3), nn., **răbbin'-ICAL** a., **răbbin'icAL**LY² adv. [f. F *rabbin* or med. L *rabbinus* (prec.; *-n* obsc.)]

răbb'it¹, n., & v.i. **1.** Burrowing rodent of hare family, brownish grey in natural state, also black or white or pied in domestication; ‖ (colloq.) a poor performer at any game (esp. cricket, golf, or lawn tennis); *~-hutch, -warren;* WELSH¹ *~;* hence ~Y² a. **2.** v.i. Hunt ~s. [ME, app. f. northern F; cf. dial. *rabotte,* Walloon *robett,* Flem. *robbe*]

răbb'it², v.t. (vulg.). *Odd~ it* etc., form of imprecation. [perh. alt. of *-rat* in *od rat,* DRAT]

răb'ble¹, n. Disorderly crowd, mob; contemptible or inferior set of people; *the* lower part of the populace. [orig. unkn.; ME sense *pack* or *string of animals* etc.]

răb'ble², n. Iron bar with bent end for stirring molten metal. [f. F *râble* f. L *rutabulum* (*ruere rut-* rake up) fire-shovel]

răb'blement (-lm-), n. (now rare). (Tumult as of) a rabble. [-MENT]

Răbĕlais'ian, -aes'ian, (-zyan), a. & n. **1.** Of, like, Rabelais or his writings, marked by exuberant imagination & language & coarse humour & satire. **2.** n. Admirer or student of Rabelais. [*Rabelais,* French humorist (d. 1553), -IAN]

răb'id, a. Furious, violent, (~ *hate*); unreasoning, insensate, headstrong, (~ *democrat*); (esp. of dog) affected with rabies, mad; of rabies. Hence **rabid'**ITY, ~NESS, nn., ~LY² adv. [f. L *rabidus* (*rabere* rave)]

răb'ies (-bēz, -biēz), n. Canine madness, hydrophobia. [L (prec.)]

răce¹, n. **1.** Onward sweep or movement, esp. strong current in sea or river (*tide set with a strong ~; the R~ of Alderney* etc.). **2.** Course of sun or moon, course of life, (*ere he had run half his~*). **3.** Channel of stream (esp. in comb., as *mill-~*); channel along which shuttle moves. **4.** Contest of speed between runners, ships, horses, etc., or persons doing anything; (pl.) series of these for horses at fixed time on regular course (SELL*ing ~*); *~ ball,* dance held in connexion with *~s; ~-card,* programme of *~s; ~'course,*

ground for horse-racing; *~'horse,* bred or kept for racing; *~-meeting,* horse-racing fixture. [ME, f. ON *rás* running, race, etc., = OE *ræs*]

răce², v.i. & t. Compete in speed *with;* indulge in horse-racing (*a racing man; the racing world,* the turf); go at full speed, (of propeller, paddle-wheel, etc.) work violently from diminished resistance when out of the water; have race with, try to surpass in speed; cause (horse etc.) to ~ (*~d his bicycle against a motor-car*); make (person, thing) move at full speed (*~d me along at five miles an hour; ~d the Bill through the House*). [f. prec.]

răce³, n. **1.** Group of persons or animals or plants connected by common descent, posterity *of* (person); house, family, tribe or nation regarded as of common stock; distinct ethnical stock (*the Caucasian, Mongolian,* etc., ~); genus or species or breed or variety of animals or plants, any great division of living creatures (*the human, feathered, four-footed, finny,* etc., ~). **2.** Descent, kindred, (*of noble, Oriental,* etc., ~; *separate in language & ~*). **3.** Class of persons etc. with some common feature (*the ~ of poets, dandies,* etc.). [F, f. It. *razza* of unkn. orig.]

răce⁴, n. Root (of ginger). [f. OF *rais* f. L *radicem* nom. *-ix* root]

racème', n. (bot.). Flower-cluster with the separate flowers attached by short equal stalks at equal distances along central stem. Hence **ră'cèm**OSE¹ a. (bot., also anat. of compound glands). [f. L *racemus* grape-bunch]

ră'cer, n. In vbl senses; esp: racehorse, yacht, bicycle, etc., used for racing; circular horizontal rail along which the traversing-platform of a heavy gun moves. [-ER¹]

ră'chis, rhă-, (-k-), n. (pl. *-ĭdes* pr. -ēz). Stem of grasses etc. bearing flower-stalks at short intervals; axis of pinnately compound leaf or frond; vertebral column or cord from which it develops, whence **ră'chĭ**(o)- (-k-) comb. form; feather-shaft, esp. the part that bears the barbs. [f. Gk *rhakhis* spine; the E pl. *-ides* is erron.]

rachit'is (-k-), n. (Learned form for) RICKETS. [f. Gk *rhakhitis* (prec., -ITIS)]

ră'cial (-shl), a. Of, in regard to, due to, race. Hence ~ISM (-sha-) n., tendency to ~ feeling, antagonism between different races of men, ~LY² adv. [RACE³, -IAL]

răck¹, n., & v.i. **1.** Driving clouds. **2.** v.i. (Of clouds) drive before wind. [ME, prob. of Scand. orig.; cf. Norw. & Sw. dial. *rak* wreckage etc., f. *reka* drive]

răck², n., & v.t. & i. **1.** Fixed or movable frame of wooden or metal bars for holding fodder; framework with rails, bars, pegs, or shelves, for keeping articles on or in (*plate, hat, tool, pipe,* etc., *~*); cogged or indented bar or rail gearing with wheel or pinion or worm, or serving with pegs etc. to adjust position of something; ~--railway, with cogged rail between bearing rails; ~-wheel, cog-wheel. **2. vb.** Fill up stable-~ with hay or straw (also trans., ~ up horse, provide it thus); fasten (horse) up to ~; place in or on ~. [ME, f. Du. rak, also MDu. rec, MLG rek(ke) rail etc., f. recken (foll.)]

răck³, v.t., & n. **1.** Stretch joints of (person) by pulling esp. with instruments of torture made for the purpose; (of disease or bodily or mental agony) inflict torture on (a ~ing headache; ~ed with pain); shake violently, injure by straining, task severely, (cough that seemed to ~ his whole body; ~ one's brains for something to say, a plan, etc.). **2.** Exact utmost possible amount of (rent), oppress (tenants) with excessive rent, exhaust (land) with excessive use; ~-rent, (n.) full economic rent, (also) excessive rent, (v.t.) exact this from (tenant) or for (land); ~-renter, tenant paying or landlord exacting ~-rent. **3.** tr. Instrument of torture, a frame with roller at each end to which victim's wrists & ankles were tied so that his joints were stretched when rollers were turned (on the ~, being ~ed, lit., or fig. of person in distress or under strain). [ME, f. MDu., MLG recken stretch (= OE reccan); n.f. prec.]

răck⁴, n. Arrack (esp. ~ punch). [for ARRACK]

răck⁵, n., & v.i. **1.** Horse's gait between trot & canter, both legs of one side being lifted almost at once, & all four feet being off ground together at moments. **2. v.i.** Progress thus. [orig. unkn.]

răck⁶, v.t. Draw off (wine etc.) from the lees (often off). [ME, f. Pr. arracar (raca stems & husks of grapes, dregs)]

răck⁷, n. Destruction (usu. go to ~ & ruin). [var. of WRACK, WRECK]

răck'ĕt¹, răc'quet (-kĭt), n. Cat-gutted bat used in tennis, rackets, etc.; (pl.) ball-game for two or four persons played in plain four-walled court with ~s; snow-shoe resembling ~; ~-ball, small hard kid-covered ball of cork & string; ~-press, for keeping ~s taut & in shape; ~-tail, kinds of small bird with ~-shaped tail. [f. F raquette f. It. racchetta f. Arab. rāha palm of hand]

răck'ĕt², n., & v.i. **1.** Disturbance, uproar, din; social excitement, gaiety, dissipation. **2.** (sl.). Dodge, game, line of business, lay; (orig. U.S.) scheme for obtaining money, or effecting some other object, by illegal (and often violent) means, so ~eer'ING¹ n., organized blackmail of traders etc. by intimidation & violence, ~EER' n., one who practises this. **3.** Ordeal, trying experience, (stand the ~, come successfully through test, face consequences of action). Hence ~Y², a. **4.** v.i. Live gay life (often about), move about noisily. [prob. imit.]

raconteur (see Ap.), n. (fem. -euse). Teller,

of anecdotes (usu. good, skilful, etc., ~). [F]

rac(c)oon', n. Greyish-brown furry bushy-tailed sharp-snouted American nocturnal carnivore. [Algonquin]

ra'c|y̆, a. Having the qualities that characterize the kind in high degree (esp. ~y flavour); of distinctive quality or vigour, not smoothed into sameness or commonness, retaining traces of origin (esp. ~y of the soil, of homely directness. spirited, lively, piquant). Hence ~iLY² adv., ~iNESS n. [RACE³, -Y²]

‖ **răd.** See RADICAL n.

răd'ăr, n. System for ascertaining direction & range of aircraft, ships, coasts, and other objects, by means of the electromagnetic waves which they reflect; apparatus used for this. [f. initial letters of radio detection and ranging]

răd'dle, n., & v.t. **1.** Red ochre. **2.** v.t. Paint with ~; plaster with rouge. [var. of RUDDLE]

răd'ial, a. & n. **1.** Of, in, rays; arranged like rays or radii, having position or direction of a radius (~ axle, maintaining such direction to curve of track as car etc. travels round it); having spokes or radiating lines, whence ~ized (-zd) a., ~izā'tion n.; acting or moving along lines that diverge from a centre; relating to the radius of the forearm (~ artery, vein, nerve); hence ~LY² adv. **2.** n. nerve or artery. [f. med. L radialis, or RADIUS +-AL]

răd'ian, n. Angle at centre of circle subtended by an arc whose length is equal to the radius. [RADIUS, -AN]

răd'iant, a. & n. **1.** Emitting rays of light, (of eyes or looks) beaming with joy or hope or love, (of light) issuing in rays, (of beauty) splendid or dazzling, whence or cogn. **răd'iANCE, răd'iANCY** (rare), nn., ~LY² adv.; operating radially (esp. ~ heat); (bot. etc.) extending radially, radiating; ~ point, from which rays or radii proceed, (astron.) apparent focal point of meteoric shower. **2.** n. Point or object from which light or heat radiates; (astron.) ~ point. [ME, f. L radiare (RADIUS), -ANT]

răd'iate¹, a. Having divergent rays or parts radially arranged. Hence ~LY² adv. [as foll., -ATE²]

răd'i|ate², v.i. & t. Emit rays of light or heat, (of light or heat) issue in rays; emit electromagnetic waves; diverge or spread from central point; emit (light or heat) from centre; disseminate (life, love, joy, etc.). Hence or cogn. ~A'TION n., ~ATIVE a. [f. L radiare (RADIUS), -ATE³]

răd'iātor, n. In vbl senses; esp.: apparatus for heating room etc. consisting of metal case containing winding pipe through which hot water circulates; oil or electric stove, usu. portable; engine-cooling apparatus in motor-car. [-OR]

răd'ical, a. & n. **1.** Of the root(s). **2.**

Naturally inherent, essential, fundamental,(~ *humour, heat,* etc., in mediaeval philos., moisture, heat, etc., essential to life; *a* ~ *error; the* ~ *rottenness of human nature*). **3.** Forming the basis, primary, (*the* ~ *idea* or *principles of a system*). **4.** Affecting the foundation, going to the root, root-&-branch, (~ *change, cure, reform*); (of politicians) desiring such reforms, ‖ belonging to extreme section of Liberal party (hist.), (of measures etc.) advanced by or according to principles of ~ politicians, whence ~ISM(2) n.,~IZE(3) v.t. & i., ~ĪZA'TION n. **5.** (math.). Of the root of a number or quantity (~ *sign*, √, ³, ⁴, etc., indicating that square, cube, fourth, etc. root of number following is to be extracted). **6.** (philol.). Of the roots of words (~ *word*, not analysable into root & other known element). **7.** (mus.). Belonging to the root of a chord. **8.** (bot.). Of, springing direct from, the root or the main stem close to it. Hence ~LY² adv. **9.** n. (Philol.) root; fundamental principle; (math.) quantity forming or expressed as root of another, also the ~ sign; (chem.) element or atom, or group of these, forming base of compound & remaining unaltered during compound's ordinary chemical changes; (pol.) person holding ~ views or belonging to ~ party. [ME, f. LL *radicalis* (*radix -icis* root, -AL)]

răd'icle, n. Part of plant embryo that develops into primary root; rootlet; (anat.) rootlike subdivision of nerve or vein; (chem.) = prec. n. Hence **radic'ūl**AR¹ a. [f. L *radicula* (prec., -ULE)]

răd'iŏ, n. (pl. ~s), & v.t. & i. (orig. U.S.). **1.** Wireless telegraphy or telephony; message so sent; broadcasting; a wireless receiving-set. **2.** (attrib.). Of or relating to, sent by, used in or using,~ (~ *altimeter, beacon, compass*, navigational aids; ~ *cab, car,* vehicles equipped with ~; ~ *direction-finder,* abbr. R.D.F., instrument for determining direction of ~ waves from a ~ transmitter, so *-finding*); of stars or extra-terrestrial sources from which ~ waves are received (~ *source*); ~ *telescope,* used in ~ *astronomy* (dealing with ~ waves transmitted to or received from celestial objects; so ~ *astronomer*). **3.** vb. Send (message), send message to (person), communicate, broadcast, by ~. [short for *radio-telegraphy* etc.]

răd'i|o-, comb. form of RADIUS. **1.** (anat.). Belonging to the radius in conjunction with some other part, as ~*o-carp'al,* of radius & wrist, ~*o-di'gital,* ~*o-ul'nar.* **2.** (phys.). Connected with rays or radiation, as ~*o-balance,* instrument for measuring intensity of heat radiation; ~*o-caesium,* ~*o-cobalt,* radio-active isotopes, prepared artificially; ~*o-carbon,* radio-active isotope of carbon, esp. = carbon 14, an isotope decaying in dead organic matter at a fixed rate, used by archaeologists to determine date of ancient deposits; ~*o-* (radio-active) *element;* ~*o-fre'quency,* (of) the frequency of radio waves; ~*ogĕn'ic,* produced by radio-activity, suitable for being broadcast by radio; ~*ogoniom'eter,* apparatus for finding the direction of ships & aircraft from their radio signals; ~*ogram,* picture obtained by X-rays, (also) = ~*o-telegram,* (also, in full ~*o-gram'ophone*) combined radio receiving-set & gramophone reproducing records through loud speaker; ~*ograph,* instrument recording intensity & duration of sunshine, (also) picture obtained by X-rays, (v.t.) secure such image of, & so ~*ŏg'rapher,* ~*ŏg'raphy,* ~*ogrăph'ic*(*ally*); ~*o-* (radio-active) *isotope;* ~*o-loca'tion,* = RADAR; ~*o'ogy,* scientific study of X-rays, ~*o-activity,* ~*o-therapy,* etc., so ~*ŏl'ogist,* ~*olŏ'gical;* ~*ŏm'eter,* instrument illustrating conversion of radiant energy into mechanical force, (also) instrument for measuring intensity of radiation; ~*ŏph'ony,* production of sound by radiant light or heat; ~*ŏs'copy,* examination by X-rays; ~*osŏnde,* miniature radio transmitter, carried aloft in a balloon and descending by parachute, for broadcasting pressure, temperature, & humidity at various levels [G *sonde* sounding-line]; ~*o-tel'egram,* message by wireless telegraphy; ~*o-the'rapy,* treatment of disease with X-rays or other forms of radiation, so ~*o-thĕrapeut'ic*(*s*).

răd'iŏ(-)ăc'tive, a. Capable of emitting spontaneously rays consisting of material particles travelling at high velocities. So **răd'iŏ(-)ăctiv'itў** n. [f. prec. + ACTIVE]

răd'ish, n. (Cruciferous plant with) fleshy pungent root often eaten raw as relish in salads. [OE *rǣdic* f. L *radicem* (nom. *-ix*) root; in 15th c. readopted f. OF *radis*]

răd'ium, n. Radio-active metallic element obtained from pitchblende, widely used in radio-therapy; ~ *emanation,* RADON; ~*-therapy,* treatment of disease by the use of ~ or its products. [f. L *radius* ray, see -IUM]

răd'ius, n. (pl. *-ii*). **1.** Thicker & shorter bone of forearm in man, corresponding bone in beast's foreleg or bird's wing. **2.** (math.). Straight line from centre to circumference of circle or sphere; radial line from focus to any point of curve (~ *vector,* variable line drawn to curve from fixed point, esp. in astron. from sun or planet to path of satellite). **3.** Any of a set of lines diverging from a point like radii of circle; object of this kind, e.g. spoke. **4.** Circular area as measured by its ~ (*knows everyone within a* ~ *of 20 miles;* ‖ *the four-mile* ~, that of which Charing Cross is centre). **5.** (bot.). Outer rim of composite flowerhead, e.g. daisy, also radiating branch of umbel. [L, = staff, spoke, ray]

răd'ix, n. (pl. *-ices* pr. -ĭsĕz). Number or symbol used as basis of numeration scale *(len is the ~ of decimal numeration, & of common logarithms)*; source or origin *of*. [L, = root]

rād'ōme, n. Dome or covering on outer surface of aircraft protecting radar equipment. [f. RA(DAR), DOME]

rād'ŏn, n. Gaseous radio-active element arising from the disintegration of radium (formerly known as *niton*). [f. RADIUM after *argon* etc.]

rāff. = RIFF-RAFF.

Raffaelesque. = RAPHAELESQUE.

rǎff'ia, n. Kind of palm; fibre from its leaves used for tying up plants and making hats, baskets, mats, etc. [Malagasy]

rǎff'ish, a. Disreputable, dissipated, fast--looking. Hence ~LY² adv., ~NESS n. [-ISH¹]

rǎf'fle¹, n., & v.i. & t. **1.** Sale of article by taking entrance-fee from any number of persons & assigning it by lot to one of them. **2.** vb. Enter one's name in ~ *for* article; sell by ~. [ME, kind of dice--game, f. OF *rafle* of unkn. orig.]

rǎf'fle², n. Rubbish, refuse, lumber, debris. [ME; cf. OF *ne rifle, ne rafle* nothing at all]

raft (-ah-), n., & v.t. & i. **1.** Collection of logs, casks, etc., fastened together in the water for transportation; flat floating structure of timber or other materials for conveying persons or things, esp. as substitute for boat in emergencies; floating accumulation of trees, ice, etc.; ~s'*man*, worker on ~. **2.** vb. Transport as or on ~; form into a ~; cross (water) on ~(s); work ~. [ME, f. ON *raptr* RAFTER²]

ra'fter¹ (-ah-), n. Man who rafts timber. [-ER¹]

ra'fter² (-ah-), n., & v.t. **1.** One of the sloping beams forming framework on which slates etc. of roof are upheld. **2.** v.t. (Usu. in p.p.) provide with ~s; || plough (land) so that contents of furrow are turned over on same breadth of unploughed ground next it, half-plough. [OE *ræfter*, = MLG *rafter*, rel. to ON *raptr* RAFT]

rǎg¹, n. **1.** Torn or frayed piece of woven material, one of the irregular scraps to which cloth etc. is reduced by wear & tear (*in* ~s, torn); (pl.) tattered clothes (*in* ~s, in old clothes); GLAD ~s; (usu. with neg.) smallest scrap of cloth or sail (*not a* ~ *to cover him; spread every* ~ *of sail*); (collect.) ~s used as material for paper, stuffing, etc. **2.** Remnant, odd scrap, irregular piece, (*flying* ~s *of cloud*; *cooked to* ~s, till it falls to pieces; *not a* ~ *of evidence*). **3.** (derog.). Flag, handkerchief, curtain, newspaper, etc. **4.** Jagged projection (rare). **5.** ~-*baby*, doll made of ~s; ~-*bag*, in which scraps of linen etc. are kept for use; ~-*bolt*, (n.) with barbs to keep it tight when driven in, (v.t.) join together with these; ~ *paper*, made of ~s; ~-*tag*, ~-*tag & bob-tail*, the riff-raff, ragged or low or disreputable people;

~-*lime*, popular music of U.S. Negro origin with much syncopation, (attrib.) farcical (*a* ~-*time army*); ~-*wheel*, with projections catching in links of chain that passes over it, sprocket-wheel; ~-*wort*, yellow-flowered ragged-leaved plant. [ME, perh. repr. OE *ragg* f. ON *rogg* tuft or strip of fur]

rǎg², n. Large coarse roofing-slate; || kinds of hard coarse stone breaking up in thick slabs (esp. CORAL-~, *Kentish*, *Rowley*, ~). [ME, of unkn. orig.]

|| rǎg³, v.t. & i. (-gg-), & n. (sl.). **1.** Scold, reprove severely; tease, torment, play rough jokes upon, disarrange (person's room etc.) by way of practical joke; engage in bally-ragging, be noisy & riotous. **2.** n. Noisy disorderly scene. [cf. BALLYRAG, BULLYRAG]

rǎg'amǔffin, n. Ragged dirty fellow. Hence ~LY¹ a. [prob. f. RAG¹ w. fanciful termination]

rāge¹, n. **1.** (Fit of) violent anger; violent operation of some natural force or some sentiment (*the* ~ *of the wind, of faction*). **2.** Vehement desire or passion *for* (*has a* ~ *for*, or *for collecting, first editions*); object of widespread temporary enthusiasm or fashion (*Mrs Siddons, the open-air cure, was the or all the* ~). **3.** Poetic or prophetic or martial ardour. [ME, f. OF f. Rom. *rabia* f. L RABIES]

rāge², v.i. & refl. Rave, storm, speak madly or furiously, (*at, against*, or abs.), be full of anger; (of wind, sea, passion, feeling, battle, pain, disease, etc.) be violent, be at the height, operate unchecked, prevail, whence **rā'gingLY²** adv.; (refl., esp. of storm etc.) ~ it*self out*, cease raging. [ME, f. OF *rager* (prec.)]

rǎgg'ed (-g-), a. Rough, shaggy, hanging in tufts; of broken jagged outline or surface, full of rough or sharp projections; faulty, imperfect, wanting finish or smoothness or uniformity, (~ *rhymes*, *time* in rowing, etc.); rent, torn, frayed, (of persons) in ~ clothes; ~ *robin*, crimson-flowered campion with tattered petals; || ~ *school* (obs.), free school for poor children. Hence ~LY² adv., ~NESS n. [RAG¹, -ED²]

rag(g)ee (rah'gē), n. A coarse kind of millet, the staple food in parts of India. [Hind. *rāgī*]

Rǎg'lan, n. Overcoat without shoulder seams, the sleeve running up to the neck; also attrib., as ~ *sleeve*. [f. Lord ~ (d. 1855), commander in Crimean war]

ragout' (-ōō), n., & v.t. Meat in small pieces stewed with vegetables & highly seasoned; (vb) cook thus. [f. F *ragoût* (*ragoûter* revive taste of, see RE-, GUST²)]

raid, n., & v.i. & t. **1.** Sudden attack made by military party (orig. of mounted men), ship(s), or aircraft; predatory incursion in which surprise & rapidity are usu. relied upon, foray, inroad; sudden descent of police etc. upon suspected premises or illicit goods. **2.** vb. Make ~ *into* etc.; make ~ on (person, place, cattle); hence ~'ER¹ n. [Sc. form of OE *rād* ROAD¹]

rail¹, n., & v.t. & i. **1.** Horizontal or inclined bar or continuous series of bars of wood or metal used to hang things on, as top of banisters, as part of fence, as protection against contact or falling over, or for similar purpose. **2.** Any horizontal piece (cf. STILE²) in frame of panelled door. **3.** Iron bar or continuous line of bars laid on ground as one side or half of ~way track (*off the* ~s, disorganized, out of order, not working right; *by* ~, by ~way). **4.** ~*-chair*, iron holder, attached to sleeper, in which railway ~ rests; ~'*head*, farthest point reached by a ~way under construction, (mil.) point on ~way at which road transport of supplies begins; ~*-motor*, self-propelled ~way coach (also attrib.); ***~'*road*, (n.) ~way, (v.t.) rush (person, thing) *to, into, through*, etc.; ~'*way*, ‖ road laid with ~s for heavy horse-carts, track or set of tracks of iron or steel ~s for passage of trains of cars or trucks drawn by locomotive engine & conveying passengers & goods, (also ~*way line*) the tracks of this kind worked by single company or the whole of the organization & persons required for their working, (attrib. in many phrr., as ~*way accident*; ~*way act*, regulating duties & rights of ~way companies; ~*way bill*, proposal in Parliament esp. for constructing new ~way; ~*way bridge, carriage, company, contractor, director, engine, journey, shares*; *at* ~*way speed*, very quickly; ~'(*way*)*man*, ~way employee; ~*way rug, station, stock, system, train, travelling, tunnel*), whence ~'**way**LESS a., ~*way* v.i., travel by ~; hence ~'AGE(4) n., ~'LESS a. **5.** vb. Furnish or enclose (place) with ~ (often *in, off*), provide (bench etc.) with ~, whence ~'**ing**¹ [-ING¹(3, 4)] n.; lay (~way route) with~s; convey (goods), travel, by ~. [ME, f. OF *reille* (L *regula* RULE)]

rail², n. Kinds of bird, esp. LAND¹~, *water-*~. [ME, f. OF *raale* (now *râle*), f. Rom. **rascula*, prob. imit.]

rail³, v.i. Use abusive language (usu. *at* or *against*, or arch. *upon*). Hence ~'ER¹ n., ~'**ing**² [-ING¹(1)] n., ~'**ing**³ [-ING²] a., ~'**ing**LY² adv. [ME, f. OF *railler* (RALLY²), f. Rom. **ragulare*]

raill'erў, n. (Piece of) good-humoured ridicule, rallying. [f. F *raillerie* (prec., -ERY)]

raim'ent, n. (poet. & rhet.). Clothing, dress, apparel. [ME; aphetic f. obs. *arrayment* (ARRAY¹, -MENT)]

rain¹, n. **1.** Condensed moisture of atmosphere falling visibly in separate drops, fall of such drops (~ *or shine*, whether it rains or not); (pl.) showers of ~, esp. *the* ~s, rainy season in tropical countries, (naut.) *the R~s*, rainy region of Atlantic 4–10° N. lat.; (~-like descent of) falling

liquid or solid particles or bodies (*a* ~ *of* ashes, frogs, pearls, rice, fire*; also fig. *a* ~ *of melody, kisses, congratulations*). **2.** ~*-bird*, kinds of bird, esp. green woodpecker; ~*-box*, theatre contrivance imitating sound of ~; ~'*coat*, waterproof; ~*-doctor*, producer of ~ by magic; ~'*drop*, single drop of ~; ~'*fall*, shower, quantity of ~ falling within given area in given time (usu. in inches of depth per annum); ~*-gauge*, instrument measuring ~fall; ~*-water*, collected from ~, not got from wells etc.; ~*-worm*, common earthworm. Hence ~'LESS. ~'PROOF², ~'TIGHT, aa. [OE *regn*, OS, OHG *regan*, ON *regn*, Goth. *rign*]

rain², v.i. & t. *It* ~s, rain comes down (*it* ~*ed blood, frogs, invitations, tracts*, etc., *there was a shower of them*; *it* ~*s cats & dogs*, violently; *it never* ~*s but it pours*, events usu. happen several together; *it* ~*s in*, rain penetrates house etc.; *it has* ~*ed itself out*, rain has ceased); *God, the sky, the clouds*, ~, send down rain; fall or send down in showers or like rain (*flowers* ~*ed from their hands*; *tears* ~*ed down her cheeks*; *blows* ~ *upon him*; *his eyes* ~ *tears*; ~ *influence*; *he* ~*ed benefits upon us*). [OE *regnian* (prec.)]

rain'bow (-ō), n. Arch showing prismatic colours in their order formed in sky (or across cataract etc.) opposite sun by reflection, double refraction, & dispersion of sun's rays in falling drops of rain (*lunar* ~, similar effect from moon's rays, rarely seen; *sea* ~, formed on sea spray; *secondary* ~, additional arch with colours in reverse order formed inside or outside of ~ by double reflection & double refraction; *all the colours of the* ~, many colours); (attrib.) many-coloured; ~ *trout*, Californian kind. [OE *rēnboga* (RAIN¹, BOW¹)]

rain'|ў, a. In or on which rain is falling or much rain usually falls (~*y weather, climate, day, month, county*, etc.; ~*y day*, fig., time of esp. pecuniary need, as *provide against a* ~*y day*); (of clouds, wind, etc.), laden with, bringing, rain. Hence ~ILУ² adv., ~INESS n. [-Y²]

raise (-z), v.t. (often followed by *up* in most senses), & n. **1.** Set upright, make stand up, restore to or towards vertical position, rouse, (~*d him from his knees*; ~ *the standard of revolt*; ~*d pastry, pie*, etc., standing without support of dish at sides; ~ *one from the dead*, restore him to life; ~ *the country, city*, etc., rouse inhabitants in some emergency, often *against* or *upon* enemy etc.; *the danger* ~*d his spirits*; ~ *the wind*, fig., procure money for some purpose; ~ *a dust*, lit., & fig. cause turmoil, also obscure the truth). **2.** Build up, construct, create, produce, breed, utter, make audible, start, give occasion for, elicit, set up, advance, (~ *palace, large family, blister*, one's *own vegetables, storm, shout, hymn, controversy, prejudice, claim, demand, objection, question*; *a deliverer* *was* ~*d up*, caused by Providence to appear; ~ *a laugh*, cause others to laugh; *no one* ~*d his voice*, spoke). **3.** Elevate, put or take into higher position, extract from earth, direct upwards, promote to higher rank, make higher or nobler, cause to ascend, make (voice) louder or shriller, (naut.) come in sight of (land, ship), increase amount of, heighten level of, (~ one's *hat*, bow; ~ one's *glass to*, drink health of; *thousands of tons of coal were* ~*d*; ~ one's *eyes*, look upwards; ~ one's *eyebrows*, look supercilious or shocked; ~*d him to the see of York*; *trying to* ~ *a degraded class*; *undertook to* ~ *the spirit of King Solomon*, cf. LAY³; ~ *Cain, hell, the devil, the mischief*, etc., make disturbance; *their voices were* ~*d as in anger*; ~ *income-tax from 8s. 6d. to 10s.*; ~ *cloth*, make nap on it; ~ *bread*, cause it to rise with yeast; ~ one's *reputation*, add to it; *the price of the 2lb. loaf is* ~*d a penny*; ~ *colour* in dyeing, brighten it). **4.** Levy, collect, bring together, procure, manage to get, (~ *tax, loan, subscription, money, army, fleet*). **5.** Relinquish, cause enemy to relinquish, (siege, blockade); remove (embargo). **6.** p.p. *(vulg.). Brought up, educated. **7.** n. Increase in salary, stakes at poker (also as vb), bid at bridge, etc. [ME, f. ON *reisa* f. Gmc **raizjan* (whence OE *rǣran* REAR²), causative of *rīsan* RISE¹]

rais′in (-zn), n. Partially dried grape. [ME, f. OF *raisin* f. L as RACEME]

raison d'être (see Ap.), n. Purpose etc. that accounts for or justifies or originally caused thing's existence. [F]

rait. See RET.

raj (rahj), n. (Anglo-Ind.; hist.). Sovereignty (*the British* ~ *in India*). [Hind.]

raja(h) (rah′jǎ), n. Indian king or prince (also as title of petty dignitary or noble in India, or Malay or Javanese chief). Hence **ra′jah**SHIP (rahj′ǎsh-) n. [Hind. *rājā* f. Skr. *rājan* king (*rāj* to reign)]

Rajpoot, -put, (rahj′pōot), n. Member of Hindu soldier caste claiming descent from Kshatriyas. [Hind. (-*ut*), f. prec., *putra* son]

rāke¹, n. Implement consisting of pole with cross-bar toothed like comb at end for drawing together hay etc. or smoothing loose soil or gravel, wheeled implement for same purpose; kinds of implement resembling ~ used for other purposes, e.g. by croupier drawing in money at gaming-table. [OE *raca*, MLG, MDu. *rāke*, cogn. w. MLG *rēke*, OHG *recho*, ON *reka* spade]

rāke², v.t. & i. Collect, draw *together*, gather *up*, pull *out*, clear *off*, (as) with rake (~ *out the fire*; ~ *up* or *together all possible charges*; ~ *off the leaves*); clean or smooth with rake; search (as) with rake, ransack, (*has* ~*d all history for proofs*); make *level, clean*, etc., with rake; scratch, scrape; sweep with shot,

enfilade, send shot along (ship) from stem to stern, sweep with the eyes, (of window etc.) have commanding view of; use rake, search as with rake (*have been raking among* or *in* or *into old records*); ~*-off* (colloq.), commission, rebate, share of profits (usu. in bad sense). [ME, f. ON *raka* cogn. w. prec.]

rāke³, n. Dissipated or immoral man of fashion. [for RAKEHELL]

rāke⁴, v.i. & t., & n. **1.** (Of ship or its bow or stern) project at upper part of bow or stern beyond keel; (of masts or funnels) incline from perpendicular towards stern; give backward inclination to (*bicycle's front forks are* ~*d*). **2.** n. Amount to which thing ~s, raking position or build; slope of stage or auditorium in theatre. [17th c., of unkn. orig.]

‖ **rāke′hell** (-kh-), n. (arch.). = RAKE³. Hence ~Y² a. (arch.). [RAKE², HELL]

rāk′ish¹, a. (As) of, like, a RAKE³. Hence ~LY² adv., ~NESS n. [-ISH¹]

rāk′ish², a. (Of ship) smart & fast-looking, seeming built for speed & therefore open to suspicion of piracy. [perh. = prec., assoc. w. RAKE⁴]

râle (rahl), n. (path.). Sound additional to that of respiration heard in auscultation of unhealthy lungs. [F, f. *râler* to rattle]

rǎllentǎn′dō, mus. direction. Gradually slower. [It.]

‖ **rǎll′icar(t),** n. Light two-wheeled driving-trap for four. [*Ralli*, first purchaser, 1885]

rǎll′y¹, v.t. & i., & n. **1.** Reassemble, get together again, (t. & i.; esp. of army or company) after rout or dispersion, (cause to) renew conflict; bring or come together as support or for concentrated action (*rallied his party, his party rallied, round* or *to him*); revive (faculty etc.) by effort of will, pull oneself together, assume or rouse to fresh energy; throw off prostration or illness or fear, regain health or consciousness, revive. **2.** n. Act of ~ing (intr.), reunion for fresh effort; recovery of energy after or in the middle of exhaustion or illness; (in tennis, rackets, etc.) series of strokes before point is decided. [n. f. vb, f. F *rallier* (RE-, ALLY¹)]

rǎll′y², v.t. Banter, chaff. Hence ~ing-LY² adv. [f. F *railler* RAIL³]

rǎm¹, n. **1.** Uncastrated male sheep, tup. **2.** (*Ram*) zodiacal sign Aries. **3.** = BATTER¹-ing-~; (battleship with) projecting beak at bow for charging side of other ships; falling weight of pile-driving machine; rammer; hydraulic water-raising or lifting machine; piston of hydrostatic press; plunger of force-pump. **4.** ~'s-horn, lit., also scroll ornament imitated from ~'s head & horns. [OE *ram*(*m*), *rom*(*m*), = MDu., MLG, OHG *ram* (*ramm-*), perh. rel. to ON *ramm* strong]

rǎm², v.t. (-mm-). Beat down (soil etc.) into solidity with wooden block etc., (abs.) use ~mer; make (post, plant, etc.) firm by ~ming soil round it; drive (pile etc.) down, in, into, by heavy blows; force (charge) home, pack (gun) tight, with ~rod; squeeze or force into place by pressure (~med his clothes into a bag, his hat down on his head; had the list ~med into me by repetition; ~ the argument home, lay sufficient stress on it); cram with stuffing etc.; (of ship) strike (as) with ram; dash or violently impel (thing) against, at, on, or into (~med his head against the wall, his horse at a fence); ~'rod, for ~ming home charge of muzzle--loader. Hence ~m'ER¹(2) n. [ME, f. prec.]

ram³, n. (naut.). Boat's length over all. [orig. unkn.]

Rămadăn', n. Ninth month of Moham-medan year, during all daylight hours of which rigid fasting is observed. [Arab. (ramada be hot); perh. orig. one of hot months, now passing through all seasons owing to lunar reckoning]

răm'al, a. (bot.). Of, proceeding from, a branch. [f. L ramus branch, -AL]

răm'ble, v.i., & n. 1. Walk (v. & n.) for pleasure, with or without definite route. 2. Wander in discourse, talk or write dis-connectedly. [17th c., of unkn. orig.]

răm'bler, n. In vbl senses: also, kinds of climbing rose, esp. the crimson ~. [-ER¹]

răm'bling, a. Peripatetic, wandering; disconnected, desultory, incoherent; (of plants) straggling, climbing; (of house, street, etc.) irregularly planned. Hence ~LY² adv. [-ING³]

rămbut'an (-ōōt-), n. Red fruit of an E.--Indian tree, covered with soft spines and with pleasant sub-acid pulp. [Malay, f. rambut hair, in allusion to spines]

răm'ĕkĭn, -quin (-kĭn), n. Small quantity of cheese with bread-crumbs, eggs, etc., baked in small mould. [c. 1700, F rame-quin, of Gmc orig.; cf. LG ramkin cheese--cake]

răm'ie (-mē), n. Fine strong fibre ob-tained from a Chinese and E.-Indian nettle-like plant, woven into a durable material. [Malay rāmī]

rămĭfĭcā'tion, n. Ramifying, (arrange-ment of) tree's branches; subdivision of complex structure comparable to tree's branches (the ~s of a river, society, trade, plot, inquiry, etc.). [as foll., -ATION, perh. after F]

răm'if|y̆, v.i. & t. Form branches or sub-divisions or offshoots, branch out; (usu. pass.) cause to branch out, arrange in branching manner (railways were ~ied over the country). [f. F ramifier f. med. L ramificare (L ramus branch, -I-, -FY)]

rămm'ĭsh, a. Rank-smelling. [RAM¹, -ISH¹]

ramōse' (or răm'ōs), a. Branched, branch-ing. [f. L ramosus (ramus branch, -OSE¹)]

rămp¹, n. Slope, inclined plane joining two levels of ground esp. in fortification, or of wall-coping; difference in level be-tween opposite abutments of rampant arch; upward bend in stair-rail. [18th c., f. F rampe f. ramper (foll.)]

rămp², v.i. & t. 1. (Chiefly of lion) stand on hind-legs with fore-paws in air, assume or be in threatening posture; (now usu. joc.) storm, rage, rush about. 2. (Archit., of wall) ascend or descend to different level; (archit., mil.) furnish or build with ramp. [ME, f. OF ramper creep]

‖ rămp³, n., & v.i. & t. (sl.). Attempt to extort payment of fictitious debt from bookmaker; (transf.) levying of exorbi-tant prices, as the black-market ~ in whisky; swindle, racket; (vb) engage in, subject (person etc.) to, ~. [orig. unkn.]

rămpāge', v.i., & n. 1. Behave violently, storm, rage, rush about. 2. Violent be-haviour (esp. be on the ~). Hence ~OUS (-jus) a., ~OUSLY² adv., ~OUSNESS n., (-jus-). [prob. f. RAMP²]

rămp'ant, a. (Chiefly of lion, esp. in her.) ramping (in her., & in allusive imitations, placed after nouns, as lion ~, the snob ~); violent or extravagant in action or opinion, arrant, aggressive, unchecked, prevailing, (is a ~ theorist; popery is ~ among us); rank, luxuriant, (a rich soil makes nasturtiums too ~); (of arch etc.) having one abutment higher than the other, climbing. Hence rămp'-ANCY n., ~LY² adv. [ME & OF rampant (RAMP², -ANT)]

rămp'ărt, n., & v.t. Broad-topped & usu. stone-parapeted walk on top of defensive wall; (fig.) defence, protection; (vb) fortify or protect (as) with ~. [f. F rempart (remparer fortify, f. RE-, emparer take possession of, f. L ante before, parare prepare)]

rămp'ion, n. Kind of bell-flower with white tuberous roots used as salad. [cf. F raiponce, It. ramponzolo]

‖ rămp'īre, n., & v.t. (arch.). = RAMPART.

răm'shăckle, a. Tumbledown, crazy, rickety, (usu. of house or vehicle). [earlier -ed, p.p. of obs. ransackle RANSACK]

răm'son (-sn), n. (Root, eaten as relish, of) broad-leaved garlic. [pl. in -en of OE hramsa, cogn. w. G rams]

răn¹, n. A certain length of twine. [orig. unkn.]

răn². See RUN¹.

rănce, n. Kind of red marble with blue & white veins & spots. [prob. of F orig.]

rănch, n., & v.i. 1. Cattle-breeding estab-lishment in U.S. & Canada. 2. v.i. Con-duct ~. [f. Sp. rancho mess, persons feeding together]

răn'cid, a. Smelling or tasting like rank stale fat. Hence răncid'ITY, ~NESS, nn. [f. L rancidus stinking]

rănc'our (-ker), n. Inveterate bitterness, malignant hate, spitefulness. Hence rănc'orOUS a., rănc'orousLY² adv. [ME, f. OF, f. LL rancorem (prec., -OR)]

rănd, n. **1.** Strip of leather between heel & shoe or boot. **2.** (S.-Afr.) highlands on either side of river valley (*the R~*, district round Johannesburg). [OE *rand* = OHG *rant*, ON *rönd* bank, rim]

răndăn'[1], n. Style of rowing for three men, the middle using sculls & the others oars; boat for such use. [orig. unkn.]

răndăn'[2], n. Spree (esp. *on the ~*). [var. of RANDOM]

răn'dem, adv. & n. With three horses harnessed tandem; (n.) carriage or team so driven. [prob. formed on *random* & *tandem*]

răn'dom, n. & a. **1.** *At ~*, at haphazard, without aim or purpose or principle, heedlessly. **2.** adj. Made, done, etc., at *~* (*~ sample, selection*); (of masonry) with stones of irregular size & shape; hence *~*LY[2] adv. (rare). [ME & OF *randon* etc. great speed (*randir* gallop); *-m* as in *ransom*]

răn'd|y̆, a. ‖ Loud-tongued, boisterous, lusty, (Sc.); (of cattle etc.; dial.) wild, restive; lustful, in lustful mood. Hence *~*INESS n. [perh. f. obs. *rand* var. of RANT, -Y[2]]

ranee (rahn'ī), n. Hindu queen. [f. Hind. *rani* f. Skr. *rajni* fem. of RAJAH]

rang. See RING[2].

rānge[1] (-j), v.t. & i. **1.** Place or arrange in a row or ranks or in specified situation or order or company (usu. pass. or refl.; *~d their troops*; *~d themselves on each side*; *was~d against, among, on the side of, with*, etc.; *trees ~d in an ascending scale of height*; *~ oneself*, imit. F, take up definite position in society, settle down, e.g. by marrying). **2.** Run in a line, reach, lie spread out, extend, be found or occur over specified district (often *from . . . to*), vary between limits, (*~s north & south, along the sea*; *nightingale ~s from the Channel to Warwickshire*). **3.** Be level (*with*; *a 12mo does not ~ well with a folio*); rank or find right place *with* or *among* (*~s with the great writers*). **4.** Rove, wander, (often *over, along, through*, etc., district or coast; *his thoughts ~ over past, present, & future*; *ranging fancy*, inconstant affections). **5.** (Of gun) throw projectile over, (of projectile) traverse, (distance; *~s over a mile*). **6.** Go all about (place), sail along or about (coast, sea). [ME, f. OF *ranger* (*rang* RANK[1])]

rānge[2] (-j), n. **1.** Row, line, tier, or series, of things, esp. of buildings or mountains. **2.** Lie, direction, (*the ~ of the strata is east & west*; *keep the two buoys in ~ with the lighthouse*). **3.** Stretch of grazing or hunting ground. **4.** Piece of ground with targets for shooting. **5.** Area over which plant etc. is distributed, area included in or concerned with something, sphere, scope, compass, register, limits of variation, limited scale or series, distance attainable by gun or projectile, distance between gun etc. & objective, (*gives the ~s of all species*; *the thorniest question in the whole ~ of politics*; *the ~ of her voice is astonishing*; *his reading is of very wide ~*; *the ~ of the barometer readings is about 2 in.*; *Hebrew is out of my ~*; *there is a lower ~ of prices today*; *the enemy are out of ~, have found the ~ of our camp*). **6.** Cooking fireplace usu. with oven(s), boiler(s), & iron top plate with openings for saucepans etc. **7.** *~-finder*, instrument for estimating distance of object, esp. one to be shot at. [ME, f. OF, = row, rank, (prec.)]

rān'ger (-j-), n. In vbl senses: also: keeper of a royal park, whence *~*SHIP n.; *(R~)* member of U.S. COMMANDO; (pl.) body of mounted troops or other armed men; senior girl guide. [-ER[1]]

rănk[1], n. **1.** Row, line, queue, (now chiefly of cabs standing; in chess, row of squares across board, opp. FILE[3]). **2.** Number of soldiers drawn up in single line abreast (*the ~s were broken*, could not keep the formation; *the ~s* or *the ~ & file*, common soldiers, i.e. privates & corporals, & transf. lower classes or ordinary undistinguished people; *rise from the~s*, said of common soldier or sergeant who is given commission, or of selfmade man). **3.** Order, array, (*keep ~, break ~*, remain, fail to remain, in line). **4.** Distinct social class, grade of dignity, station, high station, (*people of all ~s*; *persons of ~*, members of nobility; *~ & fashion*, high society; *the pride of ~*). **5.** Place in a scale. [f. obs. F *ranc* (mod. *rang*), OF *renc*, f. WG *hring* RING[1]]

rănk[2], v.t. & i. Arrange (esp. soldiers) in rank; classify, give certain grade to; *take precedence of (person) in respect to rank; have rank or place (*~s among the Great Powers, next to the king*, etc.); have a rightful place on the list of claims on, or claimants against, a bankrupt estate; (mil.) march *past* or *off*. [f. prec.]

rănk[3], a. Too luxuriant, gross, coarse, over-productive, choked with or apt to produce weeds, (*roses are growing ~*, running too much to leaf; *land too ~ to grow corn*); foul-smelling, offensive, rancid; loathsome, indecent, corrupt; strongly marked, unmistakable, flagrant, virulent, gross, (*~ treason, pedantry, poison, nonsense*). Hence *~*'LY[2] adv., *~*'NESS n. [OE *ranc*, = ON *rakkr* bold, slender; cf. MLG *rank* long & thin]

rănk'er, n. (Commissioned officer who has been) a soldier in the ranks. [-ER[1]]

rankle (răng'kl), v.i. (Of wound, sore, etc.) fester, continue painful, (arch.); (of envy, disappointment, etc., or their cause) be bitter, give intermittent or constant pain. [ME, f. OF *rancler* (*rancle, drancle, draoncle*, festering sore f. med. L *dracunculus* dim. of *draco* serpent)]

răn'săck, v.t. Thoroughly search (place, receptacle, person's pockets, one's conscience, etc.); pillage, plunder, (house, country, etc.). [ME, f. ON *rannsaka* (*rann* house, *sękja* seek]

** răn'som**, n., & v.t. **1.** (Liberation of prisoner of war in consideration of) sum of money or value paid for release (*hold one to ~*, be willing to release him for such consideration; *worth a king's ~*, of immense value); blackmail, sum etc. exacted in return for privilege or immunity, (*graduated income-tax & death-duties are no more than a fair ~ paid by the rich*); *~-bill*, *-bond*, undertaking, esp. on part of captured ship, to pay ~; hence *~LESS* a. **2.** v.t. Redeem, buy freedom or restoration of; atone for, expiate; hold to ~, release for a ~; exact ~ from. [ME, f. OF *ranson(ner)* f. L *redemptionem* REDEMPTION]

rănt, v.i. & t., & n. **1.** Use bombastic language; declaim, recite theatrically; preach noisily, whence (esp. of Primitive Methodists) *~'ER*[1] n. **2.** n. Piece of *~ing*, tirade; empty turgid talk. [f. obs. Du. *randten*, *ranten*, *randen* (cf. RANDY) rave]

ranŭnc'ŭl|us, n. (pl. *~uses*, *~ī*). Kinds of plants including the buttercups, crowfoot. Hence *~A'CEOUS* (-āshus) a. [L, orig. dim. of *rana* frog]

ranz-des-vaches (see Ap.), n. Swiss herdsmen's melody made of harmonic notes of Alpine horn. [Swiss dial.]

răp[1], n., & v.t. & i. (-pp-). **1.** Smart slight blow (*a ~ on the knuckles*, punishment inflicted on child, also fig. reproof); (sl.) blame, punishment, etc., esp. *take the ~* (freq. in another's place); sound made by knocker on door etc., or by some agency on table or floor in spiritualistic seances. **2.** vb. Strike (esp. person's knuckles) smartly; make the sound called a ~ (*~ped at the door, on the table*, etc.); *~ out* (oath, pun, etc.), utter abruptly or on the spur of the moment, (v.i.) use strong language; (of spirits) *~ out* (message, word), express by *~s*. [ME, prob. imit.]

răp[2], n. Skein of 120 yds of yarn. [orig. unkn.]

răp[3], n. An atom, the least bit, (*don't care a ~*). [earlier sense *18th-c.* Irish counterfeit halfpenny*, short. f. Ir. *ropaire*]

rapā'cious (-shus), a. Grasping, extortionate, predatory. Hence or cogn. *~LY*[2] adv., **rapā'CITY** n. [f. L *rapax* (*rapere* seize, -ACIOUS)]

răpe[1], v.t., & n. **1.** Take by force (poet.); ravish, force, violate, (woman). **2.** n. Carrying off by force (poet.); ravishing or violation of a woman (also fig. of a country, as *the ~ of Austria*). [ME, f. AF f. L *rapere* seize]

|| **răpe**[2], n. Any of six divisions of Sussex. [first in Domesday Book; orig. unkn.]

răpe[3], n. Plant grown as food for sheep; plant cultivated for its seed from which oil is made, coleseed; *wild ~*, charlock; *~-cake*, *~-seed* pressed into flat shape after extraction of oil & used as manure; *~-oil*, made from *~-seed* & used as lubri-

cant & in making soap & indiarubber. [ME, f. L *rapum, rapa* turnip]

răpe[4], n. Refuse of grapes after wine-making used in making vinegar; vessel used in vinegar-making. [f. F *râpe*, = Pr. *raspa*, It. *raspo*, med. L *raspa*]

Răphaëlēsque' (-sk), **Răff-**, a. In style of Raphael. [*Raphael* (It. *Raffaello*), -ESQUE]

răph'ia, n. (Bot. name of) RAFFIA.

răp'id, a. & n. **1.** Speedy, quick, swift; acting or completed in short time; (of slope) descending steeply; hence or cogn. **rapid'ITY** n., *~LY*[2] adv. **2.** n. (usu. pl.). Steep descent in river-bed, with swift current. [f. L *rapidus* (*rapere* seize)]

răp'ier, n. Light slender sword for thrusting only, small-sword, (*~-thrust*, often fig. of delicate or witty repartee). [prob. f. Du. *rapier*, f. F *rapière*, of unkn. orig.]

răp'ine, n. (rhet.). Plundering, robbery. [ME, f. OF, or L *rapina* (*rapere* seize, -INE[4])]

răpparee', n. (hist.). 17th-c. Irish irregular soldier or freebooter. [f. Ir. *rapaire* short pike]

răppee', n. Coarse kind of snuff. [f. F (*tabac*) *râpé* RASPed (tobacco)]

rappôrt' (or *rapôr*), n. Communication, relationship, connexion, (*be in*, or F *en* pr. ahn, *~ with*). [F (*rapporter* f. RE-, AP-, *porter* f. L *portare* carry)]

rapprochement (see Ap.), n. Re-establishment or recommencement of harmonious relations, esp. between States. [F]

răpscăll'ion (-lyon), n. (arch.). Rascal, scamp, rogue. [earlier *rascallion*, f. RASCAL]

răpt, p.p., & a. Snatched away bodily or carried away in spirit from earth, from life, from consciousness, or from ordinary thoughts & perceptions (often *away, up*, etc.); absorbed, enraptured, intent, (esp. *listen with ~ attention*). [ME, f. L *raptus* p.p. of *rapere* seize]

răptôr'ial, a. & n. (zool.). Bird (usu. large) which preys upon other birds, mammals, etc.; bird of prey as eagle, falcon, owl, etc.; predatory (animal or bird); adapted for seizing prey. [f. L *raptor* (prec., -OR) plunderer +-IAL]

răp'ture, n. Mental transport, ecstatic delight, (*be in, go into, ~s*, be enthusiastic, talk enthusiastically; *~s*, vehement pleasure or the expression of it); (esp. theol.) act of transporting a person from one place to another (esp. heaven). Hence **răp'turous**, a., **răp'turousLY**[2] adv., (-tyer-). [f. med. L *raptura* (RAPT, -URE)]

răp'tured (-tyerd), a. Enraptured, in ecstasy. [f. obs. *rapture* vb (prec.), -ED[1]]

rar'a āv'is, n. Rarity, kind of person or thing rarely encountered. [L,=rare bird]

rāre[1], a. **1.** Of loosely packed substance, not dense, (*the ~ atmosphere of the mountain tops*). **2.** Few & far between, uncommon, unusual, exceptional, seldom found or occurring, (*it is ~ for* person etc. *to do*, or *it is ~ly that* he etc. does). **3.** Of uncommon excellence, remarkably good, very amusing, (a miracle of ~ device; had ~ fun with him). **4.** ~ earths, oxides of certain metals (e.g. cerium, lanthanum, yttrium) found in a few ~ minerals. Hence ~'LY² (-ār̄l-) adv., (esp.) seldom, not often, finely, in an unusual degree, ~'NESS (-ār̄n-) n. [ME, f. L rarus]

*rāre², a. (Of meat) underdone. [var. of obs. rear half-cooked (of eggs), f. OE hrēr]

rare'bĭt (rār̄b-), n. See WELSH¹ rabbit.

rār̄'ee-show (-ō), n. Show carried about in a box; any show or spectacle. [app. = rare show as pronounced by Savoyard showmen]

rār̄'e|fy̆, v.t. & i. Lessen density or solidity of (esp. air); purify, refine, (person's nature etc.); make (idea etc.) subtle; become less dense. So ~FAC'TION, ~FICA'TION, nn., ~făctIVE a. [ME, f. OF rarefier or L rarefacere (rarus rare, facere make)]

rār̄'ĭty̆, n. Rareness (see RARE¹); uncommon thing, thing valued as being rare. [f. F rareté, or L raritas (RARE¹, -TY)]

ra'scal (rah-), n. & a. **1.** Rogue, knave, scamp, (often playfully to child etc.; you lucky ~ !). **2.** adj. Belonging to the rabble (arch.; the ~ rout, the common people). Hence ~DOM, ~ISM(2), răscăl'ITY nn., ~LY¹ a. [ME, f. OF rascaille rabble]

rase. See RAZE.

răsh¹, n. Eruption of the skin in spots or patches. [c. 1700, corresp. to OF rache scurf, eruptive sores, = It. raschia itch]

răsh², a. Hasty, impetuous, overbold, reckless, acting or done without due consideration. Hence ~'LY² adv., ~'NESS n. [ME, =MDu. rasch, OHG rasc, ON rǫskr]

răsh'er, n. Thin slice of bacon or ham. [orig. obsc.; perh. f. obs. rash to slash]

rasp (rah-), v.t. & i., & n. (Scrape with) coarse kind of file having separate teeth raised with pointed punch; scrape roughly; grate upon (person or his feelings), irritate; scrape off or away; make grating sound. Hence ra'spER¹ (rah-) n., (esp., hunting) high difficult fence. [ME, f. OF raspe(r), now râpe(r), f. WG *hraspōn scrape together]

ra'spatory (rah-), n. Rasp used in surgery. [f. med. L raspatorium (raspare RASP, -TORY)]

ra'spberry̆ (rahzb-), n. **1.** (Plant bearing) yellow or red berry of numerous drupels on conical receptacle. **2.** (sl.). Sound, gesture, or sign expressing dislike, derision, or disapproval; dismissal. **3.** ~-canes, the plants; ~ vinegar, kind of syrup. [f. 16th c. rasp (now Sc. & north.) & raspis (obs.; pl. -es) of unkn. orig.]

rasse (răs'ĭ, răs), n. Kind of civet-cat. [f. Javanese rase]

răt¹, n., & v.i. (-tt-). **1.** Rodent of some larger species of the mouse kind (MUSK, WATER, ~; black or old-English~, variety now largely ousted by common grey, brown, or Norway ~; smell a ~, have suspicions; like a drowned ~, said of

person wet through; Rats!, sl., nonsense!, incredible!, etc.). **2.** (pol.). Person who deserts his party in difficulties as ~s are said to desert doomed house or ship, turncoat. **3.** Workman who refuses to join strike, takes striker's place, or accepts less than trade-union wages. **4.** ~-catcher (who rids houses of ~s), (sl.) unorthodox hunting dress; ~s'bane, ~-poison (now only in literary fig. use); ~ race, fiercely competitive struggle; ~'s-tail, thing shaped like ~'s tail, e.g. kind of file; ~-tail, (horse with) hairless horse's tail, whence ~'tailED² a. (~-tail spoon, with tail-like prolongation of handle along back of bowl); ~-trap, lit., also (cycle pedal) made of two parallel iron plates with teeth; hence ~t'y̆² a. (in n. senses, & sl., snappish, irritable, touchy). **5.** v.i. Hunt or kill ~s (of person or dog); play the ~ in politics; ~ on (desert) person; hence ~t'ER¹ n. [OE rǣt; in ME f. OF rat f. Rom. *rattus]

răt², v.t. 3rd sing. pres. subj. (vulg.). = DRAT.

ra'ta (rah-), n. Large handsome New Zealand tree with crimson flowers & hard red wood. [Maori]

răt'|able, a. Proportional (arch.); || liable to payment of local rates, whence ~abIL'ITY n. Hence ~abLY² adv. [RATE², -ABLE]

rătafi'a (-ēa), -fee', n. Liqueur flavoured with almonds or kernels of peach, apricot, or cherry; kind of biscuit similarly flavoured; kind of cherry. [F (-ia), prob. rel. to TAFIA (Creole)]

răt'al, n. Amount on which rates are assessed (also attrib., as the ~ qualification for vestries). [f. RATE¹, prob. after RENTAL]

rătaplăn', n., & v.t. & i. (-nn-). **1.** Drumming sound. **2.** vb. Play (as) on drum; make ~. [F, imit.]

rătch'ĕt, rătch, nn., & vv.t. **1.** Set of teeth on edge of bar or wheel in which a pawl engages to ensure motion in one direction only; (also ~-wheel) wheel with rim so toothed. **2.** v.t. Provide with ~, give ~ form to. [f. F rochet kind of lancehead, (later) ratchet etc.]

rāte¹, n. **1.** Statement of numerical proportion prevailing or to prevail between two sets of things either or both of which may be unspecified, amount etc. mentioned in one case for application to all similar ones, standard or way of reckoning, (measure of) value, tariff charge, cost, relative speed, (going at the ~ of six miles an hour; can have them at the ~ of 1/- a thousand; the death-~ was 19 per mille; the ~ of interest, wages, etc., is to be regulated; the high~s charged by the railways; at that ~, colloq., if this is a fair specimen, if this assumption is true, etc.; at any ~, in each or any possible case, even if a stronger statement is doubtfully true, etc.; the low ~ at which you value it; sell at a high ~; win success at an easy ~;

went off at a great ~, speed; *pauperism increases at a fearful ~).* **2.** ‖ Assessment levied by local authorities for local purposes (*~s & taxes; a 6d. ~ is raised for the public library service).* **3.** Class (in FIRST, SECOND, THIRD, etc., *-~).* **4.** ‖ *~'payer,* person liable to have municipal *~s* exacted from him. [ME, f. OF, f. med. L *rata* (L *pro rata parte* according to the proportional share), f. *ratus* p.p. of *rēri* reckon]

rāte², v.t. & i. **1.** Estimate worth or value of (*I do not ~ his merits high; each offence is ~d at a fixed sum by way of penalty*; esp. in *over~, under~*), assign fixed value to (coin, metals) in relation to monetary standard (*the copper coinage is ~d much above its real value*); consider, regard as, (*I ~ him among my benefactors).* **2.** ‖ (Usu. in pass.) subject to payment of a local rate, value for purpose of assessing rates on, (*we are highly ~d for education*, have to pay a high rate; *houses are ~d at a sum smaller than the rent*, the sum on which rates are charged is less). **3.** *~ up*, impose higher insurance rate on (persons etc., liable to exceptional risks). **4.** (naut.). Class under a certain RATING¹, (intr.) rank or be *~d as*. [ME, f. prec.]

rāte³, v.t. & i. Scold (trans.) angrily; (rare) storm *at*. [ME, of unkn. orig.]

rate⁴. See RET.

rateable. Var. of RATABLE.

rāt'el, n. African and Indian nocturnal carnivorous burrowing mammal, honey--badger. [Afrikaans, orig. unkn.]

-rāt'er, n. Racing yacht of specified tonnage (*10-~, 2½-~*, etc.). [RATE¹, -ER¹]

‖ **rath** (rahth), n. (Ir. ant.). Prehistoric hill-fort. [Ir.]

‖ **rāthe** (-dh), a. (poet.). Coming, blooming, etc., early in the year or day; *~-ripe, răth'ripe*, ripening early, precocious, (n.) early kinds of pea, apple, etc. [OE *hrǣth* adj., quick, eager]

ra'ther (rahdh-), adv. **1.** More truly, to a greater extent, as a more accurate description or preferable account of the matter, *or* to be more precise, (*is ~ good than bad; derived ~ from imagination than reason; orderliness is not the result of law, ~ it is the cause of it; late last night, or ~ early this morning*); the *~ that*, so much the more because. **2.** In a modified way, to some extent, slightly, somewhat, (*I ~ think you know him; the performance was ~ a failure, was ~ good, fell ~ flat).* **3.** By preference, for choice, sooner, as an alternative chosen sooner *than* another of same grammatical form or *than* to (*would much ~ not go; he would ~ have died than refused; use soft water ~ than hard; the desire to seem clever ~ than honest; he resigned ~ than stifle his conscience; also with had, as I had ~ err with Plato than be right with ―).* **4.** ‖ (colloq.). (In answers) most emphatically, yes without doubt, assuredly, (*Have you been here before?―*

R~!); freq. pr. rahdhêr'. [ME, f. OE *hrathor*, comp. of *hrǣthe* adv. f. *hrǣth* adj.; see prec.]

***ra'thskeller** (rahts-), n. Beer-saloon or restaurant in basement. [G, = town-hall cellar]

rāt'i|fy, v.t. Confirm or make valid (compact made in one's name) by formal consent, signature, etc. So *~FICA'TION* n. [ME, f. OF *ratifier* f. med. L *ratificare* (RATE¹, -FY)]

ratine' (-ēn), n. Dress fabric resembling sponge cloth. [F]

rāt'ing¹, n. In vbl senses of RATE²; also or esp.: ‖ amount fixed as municipal rate; (naut.) person's position or class on ship's books, ‖ non-commissioned sailor, ‖ (collect.) all persons of a particular *~*; any of the classes into which racing yachts are distributed by tonnage. [RATE², -ING¹]

rāt'ing², n. Angry reprimand. [RATE³, -ING¹]

rā'tio (-shĭŏ), n. (pl. *~s*). Quantitative relation between two similar magnitudes determined by the number of times one contains the other integrally or fractionally (*are in the ~ of three to two or 3 : 2; the ~s 1 : 5 & 20 : 100 are the same).* [L (RATE¹, -ION)]

rătiŏ'cin|āte (*or* -shī-), v.i. Go through logical processes, reason formally, use syllogisms. So *~A'TION* n., *~ATIVE* a. [f. L *ratiocinari* (prec.), -ATE³]

rā'tion (*rā-), n., & v.t. **1.** (Usu. pl.) fixed daily allowance of food served out esp. for members of Services (& formerly of forage for animals); fixed allowance of food etc. for civilians in time of shortage (*~ book, card,* entitling holder to *~*); single portion *of* provisions, fuel, clothing, etc.; (pl.) provisions. **2.** v.t. Limit (persons, food, clothing) to fixed *~*. [f. F, or L RATIO]

rā'tional (-shŏ-), a. & n. **1.** Endowed with reason, reasoning; sensible, sane, moderate, not foolish or absurd or extreme; of, based on, reasoning or reason, rejecting what is unreasonable or cannot be tested by reason in religion or custom, (*~ dress,* esp. formerly of knickerbockers worn by women instead of skirts; *has ~ leanings in religion,* has doubts about the truth of revelation, the possibility of miracles, etc.). **2.** (math.). (Of quantity or ratio) expressible without radical signs (opp. SURD); hence or cogn. *~ITY* (-ăl²) n., *~LY²* adv. **3.** n. pl. *~* dress. [ME, f. L *rationalis* (prec.), -AL)]

rătionāl'e (-shŏ-), n. Reasoned exposition, statement of reasons, (now rare); fundamental reason, logical basis, *of.* [L, neut. as prec.]

rā'tional|ism (-shŏ-), n. Practice of explaining the supernatural in religion in a way consonant with reason, or of treating reason as the ultimate authority in religion as elsewhere; theory that reason is the foundation of certainty in knowledge (opp. *empiricism, sensationalism*). So ~IST(2) n. & a., ~IS'TIC a., ~IS'TICALLY adv. [-ISM]

ră'tionaliz|e (-sho-), **-is|e** (-īz), v.t. & i. Explain, explain *away*, by rationalism, bring into conformity with reason; be or act as a rationalist; (math.) clear from surds; (econ.) reform (an industry) by eliminating waste in labour, time, & materials, whence ~A'TION n. [-IZE]

răt'ite, a. (ornith.). Belonging to the *Ratitae*, a genus including ostrich, emu, cassowary, etc., with keelless breastbone (opp. CARINAte). [f. L *ratis* raft, -ITE²]

răt'lin(e), -lĭng, n. (usu. pl.). (One of) small lines fastened across ship's shrouds like ladder-rungs. [ME; orig. unkn.]

ratōōn', n., & v.i. New shoot springing from sugar-cane root after cropping; (vb) send up ~s. [f. Sp. *retoño* sprout]

rat(t)ăn', n. Kinds of E.-Indian climbing palm with long thin many-jointed pliable stems; piece of ~ stem used as cane or for other purposes; ~s used as a material in building etc. [f. Malay *rotan* (*raut* pare)]

răt-tăt', rătatăt', răt-tat-tăt', n. Rapping sound, esp. of knocker. [imit.]

‖ **rătt'en**, v.t. Molest (workman or employer) by abstracting or injuring tools or machinery etc. in disputes. [orig. unkn.]

răt'tle¹, v.i. & t. Give out rapid succession of short sharp hard sounds, cause such sounds by shaking something (*he ~d at the door*); talk in lively thoughtless way (often *on, away, along*); move or fall with rattling noise, drive vehicle or ride or run briskly, (usu. *down, along, past*, etc.); (part.) brisk, vigorous, (*a rattling wind, pace*), (preceding *good* etc.) remarkably (*had a rattling good run, dinner*, etc.); make (chain, window, crockery, etc.) ~ (~ *the sabre*, threaten war); say or recite (verses, stories, lists, oaths) rapidly (usu. *off, out, over, away*, etc.); stir *up* from dullness; (sl.) excite, agitate, fluster, make nervous, frighten; make move quickly (~ *fox*, hunt it close; ~ *up the anchor*; ~ *bill through the House*). [ME, -prob. f. MDu., LG *ratelen* (imit.)]

răt'tle², n. **1.** Instrument or plaything made to rattle esp. in order to give alarm or to amuse babies; set of horny rings in ~snake's tail; kinds of plant with seeds that rattle in their cases when ripe (esp. *yellow, red, ~*); rattling sound, uproar, bustle, noisy gaiety, racket, (*death-~*, such sound in throat immediately before death; *the ~s*, croup); noisy flow of words, empty chatter, trivial talk; lively incessant talker. **2.** ~*-bag, -bladder, -box*, ~s constructed of bag etc. with objects inside to rattle; ~*-brain, -head, -pate*, (person with) empty brain etc., whence ~**brain**-ED², ~**head**ED², ~**pat**ED², aa.; ~*snake*, venomous American snake with rattling apparatus in tail; ~*trap* n. & a., rickety (vehicle etc.), (pl.) curiosities, odds & ends. [f. prec.]

rătt'ler, n. In vbl senses; esp.: remarkably good specimen of anything; *rattle-snake. [-ER¹]

ratty. See RAT¹.

rauc'ous, a. Hoarse, harsh-sounding. Hence ~LY² adv. [f. L *raucus*, -OUS]

‖ **raughty.** See RORTY.

‖ **rauque** (rawk), a. (rare). Raucous. [F (RAUCOUS)]

răv'age, v.t. & i., & n. **1.** Devastate, plunder, (t. & i.), make havoc. **2.** n. Devastation, damage; (esp. pl.) destructive effects *of*. [f. F *ravager, ravage*, alt. f. *ravine* rush of water; see -AGE]

rāve¹, n. Rail of cart; (pl.) permanent or removable framework added to sides of cart to increase capacity. [also *rathe* (dial.), of unkn. orig.]

rāve², v.i. & t., & n. **1.** Talk wildly or furiously (as) in delirium (often *about, against, at, of, for*; *raving mad*, uncontrollably, so as to ~); (of sea, wind, etc.) howl, roar; speak with rapturous admiration *about*, go into raptures; utter with ravings (~ *one's grief* etc.); ~ *oneself hoarse, to sleep*, etc.; *storm ~s itself out*, to an end; hence (often pl.) **răv'**ING¹(1) n. **2.** n. Raving sound *of* wind etc.; (sl.) enthusiastic review (of film, play, etc.); (sl.) infatuation, 'crush'. [ME, perh. f. OF *raver*, rel. to (M)LG *reven* be senseless, rave]

răv'el, v.t. & i. (-ll-), & n. **1.** Entangle or become entangled, confuse, complicate, (thread etc., or fig. question, problem; esp. in p.p., *as the ~led skein of life*); fray (i. & t.) *oul*, whence ~ING¹(2) n.; disentangle, unravel, distinguish the separate threads or subdivisions of, (often *out*). **2.** n. Entanglement, knot, complication; frayed or loose end. [app. f. Du. *ravelen, raf-*, tangle, fray out, unweave, LG *rebbeln* to ripple flax]

răv'elin (-vl-), n. (fortif.). Outwork of two faces forming salient angle outside main ditch before curtain. [F, f. It. *ravellino*, now *riv-*, of unkn. orig.]

răv'en¹, n. & a. **1.** Large glossy blue--black-plumaged hoarse-voiced bird of crow kind feeding chiefly on flesh, often kept tame, & popularly held of evil omen. **2.** adj. Of glossy black (esp. ~ *locks*, black hair). [OE *hræfn*, OHG (*h*)*raban*, ON *hrafn* f. Gmc **hrabhnaz*]

răv'en², v.i. & t. Plunder (intr.), go plundering *about*, seek *after* prey or booty, prowl for prey; eat (t. & abs.) voraciously; have ravenous appetite (*for*). [f. OF *raviner* f. *ravine* RAVIN]

răv'enous, a. Rapacious (now rare); voracious (esp. ~ *hunger, eagerness*, etc.); famished, very hungry. Hence ~LY² adv., ~NESS n. (rare). [ME, f. OF *ravineus* (foll., -OUS)]

răv'in, n. (poet., rhet.). Robbery, rapine; seizing & devouring of prey (*beast of ~, of prey*); spoil. [ME & OF *ravine* (this sense obs. in mod. F) f. L *rapina* RAPINE]

ravin|e' (-ēn), n. Deep narrow gorge, mountain cleft. Hence ~ED² (-ēnd') a. [= mod. F *ravine*, = prec.]

răv'ish, v.t. 1. Carry off (person, thing) by force (now rare); (of death, circumstances, etc.) take from life or from sight. 2. Commit rape upon, violate, (woman), whence ~ER¹ n. 3. Enrapture, charm, entrance, fill with delight, whence ~ING² a., ~ingLY² adv., so ~MENT n. [ME, f. OF *ravir* f. Rom. *rapire* f. L *rapere*, see -ISH²]

raw, a., n., & v.t. 1. Uncooked (~ *cream*, got without scalding of milk; ~ *brick*, not hardened by fire); unripe; in unwrought state, not or not completely manufactured, (~ *silk*, as reeled from cocoons; ~ *cloth*, unfulled; ~ *hide*, untanned leather, also rope_or whip of this; ~ *spirit*, undiluted; ~ *grain*, unmalted; ~ *material*, that out of which any process of manufacture makes the articles it produces, as *the finished product of one industry is the ~ material of another*; *the ~ material of an army is men*); artistically crude; inexperienced, untrained, unskilled, fresh to anything, (*is a ~ lad*; ~ *recruits*); stripped of skin, having the flesh exposed, excoriated, sensitive to a touch from being so exposed; ~ *edge* of cloth, without hem or selvage; (of atmosphere, day, etc.) damp & chilly occas. with fog; ~-*boned*, with bones almost exposed, gaunt; ~ DEAL²; ~ *head & bloody bones*, nursery bugbear, death's-head & cross-bones, (attrib., of narrative style etc.) crudely horrible; hence ~'ISH¹ (2) a., ~'NESS n. 2. n. ~ place on person's or esp. horse's skin; *touch* one *on the* ~, wound his feelings on the points on which he is sensitive. 3. v.t. Rub (esp. horse's back) into ~ness. [OE *hrēaw*, OS, OHG *(h)rāo*, OHG *rāu-*, ON *hrár* f. Gmc *hrawaz*, cogn. w. Gk *kreas* flesh]

ray¹, n. 1. Single line or narrow beam of light; (in scientific use) straight line in which radiant energy capable of producing sensation of light is propagated to given point (*Röntgen*, pr. rŭn'tyen, or *X*, ~s, form of radiation penetrating many substances impervious to ordinary light; *Becquerel* ~s, ~s emitted by RADIO-ACTIVE bodies). 2. Analogous propagation-line of heat or other non-luminous physical energy; (fig.) fragment or remnant or beginning of enlightening or cheering influence (*a ~*, *not a ~*, *of hope, truth, genius*, etc.). 3. Radius of circle (rare); any of the lines forming a pencil or set of straight lines passing through one point, any of a set of radiating lines or parts or things. 4. (Bot.) marginal part of composite flower, as daisy; radial division of starfish. Hence ~ED² (rād), ~'LESS aa., ~'LET n. [ME, f. OF *rai*, acc. of *rais*, f. L RADIUS]

ray², v.i. & t. (Of light etc., or fig. of thought, hope, etc.) issue, come *forth*, or off or out, in rays; radiate (t. & i.; poet.). [f. prec., or F *rayer*, f. L *radiare* (RADIUS)]

ray³, n. Kinds of large sea-fish allied to shark, with broad flat body, used as food, esp. the skate. [ME, f. OF *raie* f. L *raia*]

ray⁴. See RE¹.

ray'ah (rī'a), n. Non-Moslem subject of the Ottoman Empire. [f. Arab. *ra'iyah* flock (*ra'a* feed)]

ray'on, n. Artificial silk made from cellulose. [P; arbitr. f. RAY¹]

răze, rāse (-z), v.t. Wound slightly, graze, (rare); erase, scratch *out*, (rare exc. fig. as ~ *person's name from remembrance*); completely destroy, level with the ground, (town, house, walls, etc.; usu. *to the ground*). [ME *rase* (f. 16th c. *raze*) f. OF *raser* f. Rom. *rasare* f. L *radere* rasscrape]

razee', n., & v.t. (hist.). Ship reduced in height by removal of upper deck(s); (vb) turn into a ~. [f. F *rasée* fem. p.p. as prec.]

răz'or, n., & v.t. 1. Instrument used in shaving hair from skin (*safety ~*, kinds with guard to obviate risk of gashing skin). 2. ~-*back*, back sharp as ~'s edge (often attrib., as ~-*back whale* or RORQUAL, ~-*back hill*, etc.), whence ~-backED² a.; ~-*bill*, kinds of bird with ~ *bill* (bill shaped like ~), whence ~-billED² a.; ~-*edge*, keen edge, sharp mountain ridge, critical situation, sharp line of division (*keep on the ~-edge of orthodoxy*; *be on a ~-edge or ~'s edge*, imit. Gk, be in great danger); ~-*fish*, -*shell*, kinds of bivalve with shell like handle of ordinary ~; ~-*grinder*, lit., || also kinds of bird; ~-*strop*. 3. v.t. (rare). Use ~ upon, shave, cut *down* close. [ME, f. OF *rasor* (prec., -OR)]

răzz'ia, n. Raid, plundering or slave-collecting expedition, esp. as carried out by African Mohammedans. [F, f. Algerian Arab. *ghaziah* (*ghasw* make war)]

răz'zle(-dăz'zle), n. (sl.). Excitement, bustle, stir, spree; undulating merry-go-round. [redupl. of DAZZLE]

R-boat, n. Fast German motor minesweeper. [R f. G *räumen* to clear]

re¹ (rā), ray, n. Second note of octave; (rare) note D, the second in natural scale of C major. [See GAMUT]

rē², abl. of RES. (As prep.) in the matter of (chiefly in legal & business use as first word of headline stating matter to be dealt with; also vulg. as substitute for *about*, *concerning*, in ordinary use); *re infēc'tā*, without having accomplished one's object (esp. *return re infecta*).

re- (see †Pronunciation, **Hyphen, below), pref. f. L *rĕ-*, *rĕd-*, again, back, un-. *Re-* both forms part of large numbers of already compounded words borrowed f. L or Rom., & is treated as a living pref. In the latter capacity it may be prefixed for the occasion to any vb or vbl derivative; this is esp. common in such phrr. as *traverse & re-traverse* = traverse again & again, *reckoning & re-reckoning*, *translation & re-translation*; but many vbs etc. that originated as nonce-wds have become established, often with restriction to one or some only of the simple word's senses; the more common or important words of this class, & others whose simplicity of meaning allows them to be grouped with it, are given with any necessary information under senses 8, 9, below. Those senses are the simple ones, found also in many of the wds compounded before being adopted by E; but in others of the pre-E compds the sense of the pref. has been so developed as to be obscure or unrecognizable, & senses 1–7 are given as a rough classification.

†Pronunciation:—rĕ in all wds (esp. all given under senses 8, 9) that are historically, or are capable of being taken for, simple modifications of existing E wds by one of those senses (even when a similarly spelt compd exists in senses not capable of being so regarded; so *rĕcover* = cover again, cf. RECOVER[1], *rĕcount* = count again, cf. RECOUNT[1], *rĕcreation* second or new creation, cf. *recreation* in RECREATE[1]); rē before vowels, and before h (exc. in *rehearse*); rē also in *reflex, regress* n., *rescript, retail* n.; rē also in *recalesce, recrudesce, regelate*, & their derivv., & *recantation, retardation, retraction,* *retractility*: elsewhere, rĭ when the next syllable bears the word-accent (*reflect', repos'itory*), & otherwise rĕ (*recollect', rev'ocable*).

**Hyphen:—The hyphen is often used when a writer wishes to mark the fact that he is using not a well-known compd vb, but *re-* as a living prefix (senses 8, 9) attached to a simple vb (*re-pair* = pair again, cf. *repair* mend); also usu. before e (*re-emerge*), & occas. before other vowels (*re-assure*, usu. *reassure*); also when the idea of repetition is to be emphasized, esp. in such phrr. as *make & re-make*.

1–7 : Special senses chiefly in pre-E compds.

1. In return, mutual(ly); *react, reciprocal, recompense, recrimination, rejoinder, remunerate, repartee, repay, requite, result, revenge,* etc.

2. Opposition: *rebel, recalcitrant, recusant, reluctance, remonstrate, repugnant, resist, revolt,* etc.

3. Behind, after: *relic, relinquish, relish, remain, remorse,* REST[3, 4], etc.

4. Retirement, secrecy: *recluse, recondite, recourse, refuge, remote, repository, reticent,* etc.

5. Off, away, down: *rebate, relax, release, relegate, remiss, renounce, repress, repudiate, rescind, reside, resolve, retail,* etc.

6. Fréquentative or intensive: *redolent,*

redouble, redoubtable, redound, reduplicate, refine, refulgent, regard, rejoice, remark, renown, repine, repute, research, respect, resplendent, revere, revile, revolve, etc.

7. Negative, un-: *reproach, reproof, reprobate, resign, reveal.*

8, 9 : Ordinary senses as living prefix.

8. Once more, again, anew, afresh, repeated, (often with implication that previous doing etc. was deficient or erroneous or now requires alteration or improvement or renewal; many wds may be classed indifferently under 8 or 9); *readdress'* v.t., change address of (letter); *readjust'* v.t.; so *readjust'ment* n.; *reaffirm'* v.t.; so *reaffirma'tion* n.; *reappa'rel* v.t.; *reapprais'al* n., second or fresh appraisal, revaluation; *rearm'* v.i. & t., provide (troops) with arms of new pattern, restore (country) to military strength; so *rearm'ament* n.; *rearrange'* v.t.; so *rearrange'ment* n.; *reassert'* v.t.; so *reasser'tion* n.; *reassess'* v.t.; so *reassess'ment* n.; *reassign'* v.t.; *rebaptize'* v.t., lit., & fig. give new name to; so *rebap'tism* n.; *rebirth'* n., esp. fresh incarnation; so *reborn'* p.p.; *rebite'* v.t., (defective parts of etched etc. plate with acid); *rebuild'* v.t.; *recapit'ulate* v.t., go over headings of, summarize, go quickly through again; so *recapitula'tion* n. (spec. in biol., reproduction in embryos of successive type-forms in line of development), *recapit'ulative, recapit'ulatory*, aa.; *recast'* v.t., & n., (put into) new shape, improve(d) arrangement etc. (of); *rechri'sten* v.t., = *rebaptize* above; *reclothe'* v.t.; *recoal'* v.t.; *recoal'* v.t., put new coat of paint on; *recoin'* v.t.; so *recoin'age* n.; *recol'onize* v.t.; so *recoloniza'tion* n.; *recol'our* v.t.; *recombine'* v.t.; so *recombina'tion* n.; *recommence'* v.t. & i.; so *recommence'ment* n.; *recommit'* v.t., esp. refer back (bill etc.) for further consideration to committee; so *recommit'ment, recommit'al*, nn.; *recompose'* v.t.; *recompound'* v.t.; *reconsid'er* v.t.; so *reconsidera'tion* n.; *reconstit'uent* a. & n., (remedy) that builds up strength or tissue anew; *recon'stitute* v.t., esp. piece together (past events) into an intelligible whole; so *reconstitu'tion* n.; *reconstruct'* v.t.; so *reconstruc'tion* n., *reconstruc'tive* a.; *re-count'* v.t., (esp. votes at election as security against error), & see RECOUNT[1]; so *re-count'* n.; *re-cov'er* v.t., (esp. umbrellas etc.), & see RECOVER[1]; *recreate'* v.t., create over again, & see RECREATE[1]; so *recrea'tion* & see in RECREATE[1]; *redirect'* v.t., esp. = *readdress* above; so *redirec'tion* n.; *redistrib'ute* v.t.; so *redistribu'tion* n., esp. of seats in Parliament or voting-power in elections, *redistrib'utive* a.; *redivide'* v.t.; so *redivi'sion*, n.; *redo'* v.t.; *redye'* v.t.; *re-ed'it* v.t.; so *re-edi'tion* n.; *re-enforce'* v.t. (cf. REINFORCE); *re-en'gine* v.t., supply (ship etc.) with new engine(s); *re-exam'ine* v.t., esp. of opening side's second examination of witness after opponents' cross-examination; so *re-examina'tion* n.; *reface'* v.t., put new facing on (building); *refa'shion* v.t.; so *refa'shionment* n.; *refit'* v.t. & i., restore (ship) by, (of ship) undergo, renewal & repairs; so *refit'*, *refit'ment*, nn.; *refoot'* v.t., supply new foot to (stocking); *refurn'ish* v.t.; *regen'esis* n.; *regroup'* v.t.; *rehan'dle* v.t., esp. = *recast* above; *rehang'* v.t., (esp. pictures, curtains); *rehash'* v.t., & n., (put) stale materials esp. of literary kind in new shape; *rehear'* v.t., (case in lawcourt); *rehear'ing* n.; *rehouse'* v.t., provide with new house(s); *reincarn'ate* v.t.; so *reincarna'tion* n., entrance of the soul, after death, into another human (or animal) body, *reincarn'ate* (-at) a.; *reink'* v.t.; *reinsure'* v.i. & t. (esp. of underwriter etc. devolving risk upon another); so *reinsur'ance* n.; *reinter'* v.t.; *reinvest'* [1] (see also sense 9) v.t., shift (money) to other investment; so *reinvest'ment* n.; *reiss'ue* v.t.; so *reiss'uable* a. (esp. of bills or notes), *reiss'ue* n., esp. part of already published edition to be sold with change of form or price; *reit'erate* v.t., say or do over again or several times, repeat; so *reitera'tion* n., *reit'erative* a.; *relab'el* v.t.; *relive'* v.i. & t.; *reload'* v.t.; *remake'* v.t.; *reman'* [1] (see also sense 9) v.t., equip with fresh men; *remar'gin* v.t., (esp. of secondhand bookseller repairing worn book); *rema'rry* v.i. & t.; so *rema'rriage* n.; *remast'* v.t.; *remint'* v.t.; *remod'el* v.t.; *remould'* v.t.; *remount'* (see also REMOUNT[2]) v.t., esp. provide with fresh horse etc.; *rēm'ount* n., supply of fresh horses for regiment etc., fresh horse; *rename'* v.t.; *renum'ber* v.t., esp. change numbers of series etc.; *reorg'anize* v.t.; so *reorganiza'tion*, *reorg'anizer*, nn.; *repap'er* v.t., *reparti'tion* v.t.; *reperuse'* v.t.; so *reperu's'al* n.; *replant'* v.t.; so *replanta'tion* n.; *repot'* v.t. (esp. plant into larger pot); *reprint'* v.t.; *rep'rint* n., book, article, etc., reprinted; *reproduce'* v.t. & i., esp. (trans.) produce copy or representation of, (intr.) multiply by generation; so *reproduc'tion* n., *reproduce'able*, *reprodu'cible*, *reproduc'tive*, aa., *reproduc'tively* adv., *reproduc'tiveness* n.; *reprovi'sion* v.t.; *republ'ish* v.t. (esp. book etc.); so *republica'tion* n.; *reread'* v.t.; *reseat'* v.t., esp. provide church, theatre, etc., with fresh seats; *reseek'* v.t.; *reset'* v.t. (esp. gems); *reset'tle* v.t.; so *reset'tlement* n.; *reshape'* v.t.; *reshuf'fle* v.t. (esp. cards, also n.); *resole'* v.t.; *respell'* v.t., esp. spell phonetically; *restamp'* v.t.; *restart'* v.t. & i., & n.; *restate'* v.t., esp. put into more intelligible or convincing words; so *restate'ment* n.; *restock'* v.t. & i., provide with or take in fresh stock; *resumm'ons* n., renewed legal summons; *resurvey'* v.t.; so *resurv'ey* n.;

retaste' v.t.; *retell'* v.t.; *retouch'* v.t. (esp. composition, picture, etc.), & n.; *retrim'* v.t.; *retry'* v.t., = *rehear* above; so *retri'al* n.; *returf'* v.t.; *reurge'* v.t.; *revac'cinate* v.t.; so *revaccina'tion* n.; *reval'ue* v.t., assess value of anew; so *revalua'tion* n.; *revic'tual* v.t.; *revis'it* (often rī-) v.t.; *reword'* v.t., change wording of; *rewrite'* v.t.

9. Back, with return to previous state after lapse or cessation or occurrence of opposite state or action, (often corresponding to compounds in DIS- or UN-; many words may be assigned indifferently to 9 or 8); *reaffo'rest* v.t.; so *reafforesta'tion* n.; *rean'imate* v.t.; so *reanima'tion* n.; *reappear'* v.i.; so *reappear'ance* n.; *reappoint'* v.t.; so *reappoint'ment* n.; *rearise'* v.i.; *rearouse'* v.t.; *reascend'* v.i. & t.; *reassem'ble* v.i. & t.; *reassume'* v.t. (now rare, ousted by RESUME); so *reassump'tion* n.; *reassure'* v.t., restore to confidence, dispel apprehensions of; so *reassur'ing* a. (of words, manner, etc.), *reassur'ingly* adv.; *rebarb'arize* v.t.; *rebind'* v.t. (esp. book); *recap'ture* v.t., & n.; *recede'* v.t.; so *rece'ssion* n.; *recharge'* v.t.; *rē'charge* n., amount of substance, actual piece, used in recharging; *reciv'ilize* v.t.; so *reciviliza'tion* n.; *recom'fort* v.t.; *reconduct'* v.t.; *recon'quer* v.t.; so *recon'quest* n.; *reconvert'* v.t.; so *reconver'sion* n.; *recross'* v.t.; *redescend'* v.i. & t.; *redisco'ver* v.t.; so *redisco'very* n.; *re-elect'* v.t.; so *re-elec'tion* n.; *re-el'igible* a.; *re-embark'* v.i. & t.; so *re-embarka'tion* n.; *re-emerge'* v.i.; so *re-emer'gence* n., *re-emer'gent* a.; *re-ena'ble* v.t.; *re-enact'* v.t.; so *re-enact'ment* n.; *re-en'ter* v.i. & t. (part. occas. = RE-ENTRANT); *re-en'trance* n.; *re-establ'ish* v.t.; so *re-estab'lishment* n.; *re-exist'* v.i.; *re-export'* v.t.; *re-ex'port* n., commodity imported & then exported esp. without further manufacture; so *re-exporta'tion* n.; *refill'* v.t.; *rēf'ill* n., = *recharge* above; *refloat'* v.t. (stranded ship); *rēf'lux* n., backward flow; *refo'rest* v.t., turn into forest again; so *reforesta'tion* n.; *refurb'ish* v.t.; *regerm'inate* v.i.; so *regermina'tion* n.; *regild'* v.t.; *rehabil'itate* v.t., restore to privileges, reputation, or proper condition; so *rehabilita'tion* n.; *rehum'anize* v.t.; *reignite'* v.t. & i.; *reimport'* v.t., import (same goods) after exporting; so *reim'port* n.; *reimpose'* v.t.; so *reimposi'tion* n.; *reincorp'orate* v.t.; *reingra'tiate* v.t.; *reinsert'* v.t.; so *reinser'tion* n.; *reinvest'* [2] (see also sense 8) v.t., replace in office, with privilege; so *reinves'titure* n.; *reinvig'orate* v.t.; so *reinvigora'tion* n.; *rekin'dle* v.t. & i.; *reline'* v.t., renew lining of (esp. garment); *reman'* [2] (see also sense 8) v.t., restore to manhood or courage; *remigrate* v.i., esp. return after migrating; so *remigra'tion* n.; *reocc'upy* v.t.; so *reoccupa'tion* n.; *reop'en* v.t. & i.; *repag'anize* v.t.; *repaint'*

v.t., restore paint or colouring of; *repass'* **v.t.** & **i.**, esp. pass again on way back; so *repass'age* n.; *repeo'ple* v.t.; *repercu'ssion* n., echo, recoil after impact, indirect effect or reaction of event or act; so *repercuss'ive* a.; *repiece'* v.t., put pieces of together again, reconstruct; *repoint'* v.t. (joints of masonry); *repol'ish* v.t.; *repop'ulate* v.t.; *repossess'* v.t.; so *reposse'ssion* n.; *repurch'ase* v.t., & n.; *repur'ify* v.t.; *requick'en* v.t.; *resad'dle* v.t. & abs.; *resale'* n., esp. sale of thing bought; so *resal'able* a.; *reseize'* v.t.; so *reseiz'ure* n.; *resell'* v.t., esp. sell after buying; *reship'* v.t. & i., put, go, on board ship again; so *reship'ment* n.; *restuff'* v.t.; *retake'* v.t.; *ret'ake* n. (cinemat.), a second photograph(ing) of a scene; *retransfer'* v.t.; so *retrans'fer* n.; *retransform'* v.t.; *retranslate'* v.t. (esp. back into the original language); so *retransla'tion* n.; *retread'* v.t.; *reunite'* v.t. & i.; *revit'alize* v.t.; *rewin'* v.t.

're, colloq. abbr. of *are* appended to *we*, *you*, & *they* (*we're*, *you're*, *they're*).

reach[1], v.t. & i. **1.** Stretch out, extend, (t. & i.; often *out* etc.; *~ed out his hand, its branches*; *a dominion ~ing from the Ebro to the Carpathians*). **2.** Stretch out the hand etc., make *~ing* motion or effort lit. or fig., (*you must ~ out further*; *mind ~es forward to an ideal*; *ship ~es ahead in race*). **3.** Get as far as, attain to, arrive at, (specified point or object of destination; also abs.), succeed in affecting, either simply or with the hand or instrument or missile or influence, (*~* BOTTOM[1]; *~ed land*; *could not ~ his enemy*, esp. in fencing, boxing; *how is her conscience to be ~ed?*; *libels that the ordinary law ~es*; *the steps by which you ~ the entrance*; *your letter ~ed me today*; *every syllable ~ed the audience*; *has ~ed middle age, its eighth edition*; *cannot ~ so high, far enough, down, up to it*, etc.; *as far as eye could ~*; *my income will not ~ to it*). **4.** Hand, pass or take with outstretched hand, (*~ed him the book*; *~ed down his hat*). **5.** (naut.). Sail with the wind abeam. **6.** ‖*~-me-down* a. & n. (sl.), ready-made (garment). Hence *~'*ABLE a. [OE *rǣcan*, MDu., MLG *reiken*, OHG *reichen* f. WG *raik-jan*]

reach[2], n. **1.** Act of reaching out. **2.** Extent to which hand etc. can be reached out, influence be exerted, motion be carried out, or mental powers be used, range, scope, compass, (*within, above, out of, beyond*, one's *~*, possible, impossible, of attainment or performance; *has a wide ~*; *within easy ~ of the railway*; *no help was within ~*). **3.** Continuous extent, esp. part of river that can be looked along at once between two bends. **4.** (naut.). Length of tack. [f. prec.]

rěăct', v.i. **1.** Produce reciprocal or responsive effect, act upon the agent, (*they ~ upon each other*; *tyranny ~s upon the tyrant*, has effects upon him as well as upon his victims); (chem., of substance applied to another) call out activity, cause manifestation, (*nitrous oxide ~s upon the metal*). **2.** Respond *to* stimulus, undergo change due to some influence. **3.** (mil.). Make counter-attack(s). **4.** Be actuated by repulsion *against*, tend in reverse or backward direction. Hence **rěăc'tIVE** a., **rěăctiv'ITY** n., **rěăc'tor** n., atomic PILE[2] (also *nuclear ~or*). [RE- 1]

rěăc'tance, n. (electr.). That component of the impedance of an alternating--current circuit due to capacitance or inductance or both. [f. prec., -ANCE]

rěăc'tion, n. **1.** Responsive or reciprocal action (esp. *action & ~*); (chem.) action set up by one substance in another; CHAIN *~*. **2.** Response of organ etc. to external stimulus; responsive feeling (*what was his ~ to this news?*); immediate or first impression. **3.** Return of previous condition after interval of opposite (e.g. glow felt after cold bath, depression after excitement). **4.** (mil.). Counter-stroke. **5.** Retrograde tendency esp. in politics, whence *~*ARY[1] (-sho-) a. & (= *~ary* person) n., *~*IST(2) (-sho-) n. & a. **6.** (radio). Method by which weak signals are strengthened. [RE- 1]

rěăc'tiv|āte. v.t. Restore to a state of activity. Hence *~*A'TION n. [RE- 8]

read (rěd), v.t. & i. (*read*, pr. rěd), & n. **1.** Interpret mentally, declare interpretation or coming development of, divine, (*~ dream, riddle, omen, futurity, men's hearts or thoughts or faces*; *~ person's hand*, as palmist; *~ the sky*, as astrologist or meteorologist). **2.** (Be able to) convert into the intended words or meaning (written or printed or other symbols or things expressed by their means, or abs.; *~s or can ~ hieroglyphs, shorthand, the clock, the Morse system, music, several languages*; *does not ~ or write*). **3.** Reproduce mentally or (often *aloud, out, off*, etc., or with ind. obj.) vocally, while following their symbols with eyes or fingers, the words of (author, book, tale, letter, etc., or abs.; often *over, through*, advv.; *~s well*, with good intonation etc., expressively; *was ~ing Plato*; *~ it through six times*; *does he preach extempore or ~?*; *have no time to ~*; *the Bible is the most ~ of all books*; *~ one a lesson*, admonish him; *the Bill was ~ for the first etc. time*, was allowed its first etc. READING; *invalid is ~ to for several hours daily*; *seldom ~s French*, anything written in it). **4.** Study (t. & i.) by *~ing* (often *up*; *is ~ing law*; *shall not ~ for honours*; ‖*~ing man*, who devotes most of his time to study; *has ~ much*); (p.p. in active sense as adj. with *well, deeply, slightly, little*, etc.) versed *in* subject by *~ing*, acquainted with literature. **5.** Find (thing) stated, find statement, in print etc. (*revenge, we ~, is wild justice*; *I have ~ somewhere that . . . , have*

~ *of it*). **6.** Interpret (statement, action) in certain sense (*may be ~ several ways*; *my silence is not to be ~ as consent*). **7.** Assume as intended in or deducible from writer's words, find implications, (*you~ too much into the text*; *in their pleas for reform I ~ Protection*; *~ between the lines*, search for or discover hidden meanings). **8.** (Of editor or text) give as the word(s) probably used by author (*Bentley ~s* peraeque; also joc. in correcting statements, as *for* white ~ black, *& the account may be accepted*). **9.** Bring into specified state by ~ing (*~ me to sleep*, *himself stupid, hoarse*, etc.; ‖*~* one*self in*, of incumbent, enter upon office by public reading of xxxix articles etc.). **10.** (Of recording instrument) present (figure etc.) to one ~ing it (*thermometer ~s* 33°). **11.** Sound or affect hearer or reader *well*, *ill*, etc., when ~ (*play ~s better than it acts*; *~s like a threat, translation*, etc.). **12.** n. Time spent in ~ing (*have a short*, *long, good, quiet, ~*). [OE *rǣdan* consider, discern, = OS *rādan*, OHG *rātan*, ON *rātha*, Goth. *-rēdan* f. Gmc **rǣdhan*]

read'ab|le, a. Capable of being read with pleasure or interest; (rare) legible. Hence read**a**BIL′ITY, ~le**NESS**, nn., ~**LY**[2] adv. [-ABLE]

readdress. See RE- 8.

read'er, n. In vbl senses; also or esp.: person employed by publisher to read & report on offered MSS.; printer's proof--corrector; person appointed to read aloud, esp. (often *lay~*) parts of service in church; ‖ higher grade of lecturer in some universities etc. (*~ in Roman law* etc.); book of selections for use by students of a language etc. Hence~SHIP, n. [-ER[1]]

rea'dily (rĕd-), adv. Without showing reluctance, willingly; without difficulty (*the facts may ~ be ascertained*). [READY, -LY[2]]

rea'diness (rĕd-), n. Prompt compliance, willingness; facility, prompt resourcefulness, quickness in argument or action; ready or prepared state (*all is in ~*). [READY, -NESS]

read'ing, n. In vbl senses; also or esp.: literary knowledge (*a man of vast ~*); *first, second, third, ~*, successive occasions on which Bill must have been presented for acceptance to each House before it is ready for royal assent (*first ~*, permitting introduction; *second*, approving general principle; *third*, accepting details as amended in committee); entertainment at which something is read to audience (‖*penny ~*, formerly for poor of parish etc.); word(s) read or given by an editor or found in text of a passage (*the right*, *true, best, MS.*, etc., ~; *various ~s*) (specified quality of) matter to be read (*is good, dull, ~*; *there is plenty of ~ in it*); figure etc. shown by graduated instrument (*40° difference between day & night ~s*);

interpretation, view taken, rendering, (*what is your ~ of the facts ?*; *his ~ of Iago was generally condemned*); *~-desk*, for supporting book etc., lectern; *~-room*, in club, library, etc. for persons wishing to read. [-ING[1]]

readjust etc. See RE- 8.

rea'dy (rĕd-), a., adv., n., & v.t. **1.** With preparations complete, in fit state, with resolution nerved, willing, apt, inclined, about *to*, prompt, quick, facile, provided beforehand, within reach, easily secured, unreluctant, easy, fit for immediate use, (*Are you ~?* *Go!*, formula for starting race; ~, *present, fire*, successive orders, the first = make rifle ~; *dinner is ~*; *are ~ to march*; *am ~ to risk my life*; *is too ~ to suspect*; *was ~ to swear with rage*; *a bud just ~ to burst*; *is ~ for death*; *the ~ ministers of vengeance*; *is very~ at excuses*, *has a ~ pen, wit*, whence ~-*witt*ED[2] a., etc.; *gave a ~ consent*; *found ~ acceptance*; *its ~ solubility in water*; *found an instrument ~ to hand*, *a ~ source of revenue*; *the readiest way to do it*; *make ~*, prepare i. & t., as *they made ~ for the attempt* or *to fight*, or *made everything ~*; *~ money*, actual coin, also payment on the spot); *~reckoner*, book of ~-reckoned (see adv.) computations of kind commonly wanted in business. **2.** adv. (chiefly with p.p., usu. hyphened, prop. a pred. use of adj.). Beforehand, so as not to require doing when the time comes, (*please pack everything ~*; *boxes are ~ packed* or *packed ~*; *~-built houses*; *~--made clothes*, made in standard shapes & sizes, not to customer's individual measure; *~-made shop*, selling these); (rare exc. in comp. & superl.) quickly (*the child that answers readiest*). **3.** n. Position in which rifle is held before the present (*come to the ~* etc.); (sl.) ~ money (*planked down the ~*). **4.** v.t. Make ~, prepare. [ME *rǣdi(g), re(a)di*, f. OE *rǣde + -*Y[2], f. Gmc **raidh-* put in order, prepare; cf. OHG *bireiti* (G *bereit*) prepared]

reaffirm etc., see RE- 8; **reafforest** etc., RE- 9.

rēā'gency, n. Reactive power or operation (see REACT).

rēā'gent, n. (Chem.) substance used to detect presence of another by REACTION; reactive substance or force (see REACT).

re'al[1] (rē-, rā-), n. Former silver coin & money of account used in Spain and Spanish-speaking countries (the ~ *de plata* being worth 6½d., and the ~ *de vellon*, of base metal, 2½d.). [Sp., n. use of adj. f. L *regalis* REGAL]

rē'al[2], a. **1.** Actually existing as a thing or occurring in fact, objective, genuine, rightly so called, natural, sincere, not merely apparent or nominal or supposed or pretended or artificial or hypocritical or affected, (~ *money*, coin, cash; *the ~*

presence, of Christ's body & blood in the Eucharist as disputed by theologians; *a ~ object & its image*; *~ & paper roses*; *effected a ~ cure*; *should like a ~ fine day*; *~ life*, that lived by actual people, opp. fictitious & dramatic imitations; *there is no ~ doubt about it*; *who is the ~ manager?*; *is a ~ man*, unaffected, also worthy of the name; *the ~ thing*, not a makeshift or inferior article). **2.** (law; cf. PERSONAL). Consisting of immovable property such as lands or houses (esp. *~ estate*). **3.** (philos.). Having an absolute & necessary & not merely contingent existence. **4.** abs. *The ~*, what is *~*, esp. opp. the ideal (also rarely as n. with pl. *= ~ thing*, as *I deal only with~s*). [f. OF *real, reel*, or LL *realis* (*res* thing, -AL)]

rĕăl'gar, n. Disulphide of arsenic, red arsenic, red orpiment, used as pigment & in fireworks. [ME, f. med. L, f. Arab. *rehj alghār* powder of the cave]

rē'al|ism, n. **1.** Scholastic doctrine that universals or general ideas have objective existence (cf. *nominalism, conceptualism*). **2.** Belief that matter as object of perception has real existence (cf. *idealism*). **3.** Practice, of regarding things in their true nature & dealing with them as they are, freedom from prejudice & convention, practical views & policy, (cf. *idealism*). **4.** Fidelity of representation, truth to nature, insistence upon details. So~IST(2) n. & a.,~īs'tIC a.,~īs'tICALLY adv. [-ISM]

rĕăl'itў, n. Property of being real; resemblance to original (*reproduced with startling ~*); real existence, what is real, what underlies appearances, (*in~*, in fact, opp. *in words, in appearance,* etc.); existent thing; real nature of. [f. med. L *realitas*, or F *réalité* (REAL[2], -TY)]

rē'aliz|e, -is|e (-īz), v.t. **1.** Convert (hope, plan, etc.) into fact (usu. pass.). **2.** Give apparent reality to, make realistic, present as real, (*these details help to~e the scene*); conceive as real, apprehend clearly or in detail (noun, *that, how,* etc.). **3.** Convert (securities, property) into money (often abs., = sell one's property); amass (fortune, specified profit); fetch as price. Hence ~ABLE a.,~A'TION n. [-IZE, after F *réaliser*]

really (rĭ'alĭ), adv. In fact, in reality, (often *~ & truly*); positively, indeed, I assure you, I mean what I say, I protest; *~?*, do you mean it?, is that so? [ME, after med. L *realiter*; see -LY[2]]

realm (rĕlm), n. Kingdom (chiefly rhet., & in some legal phrr., as *the laws of the~, persons who are out of the ~*); sphere, province, domain, (*the~s of fancy, poetry*, etc.). [ME, f. OF *realme, reaume*, f. L *regiminem* REGIMEN infl. by *reial* ROYAL]

real-politik (rāahl' pŏlĭtĕk'), n. Policy of· placing the material greatness and success of one's own nation before all other considerations. [G]

•rē'ăltŏr, n. Real-estate agent (prop. one who is a member or affiliated member of the National Association of Real Estate Boards). [U.S., f. foll.+-OR]

rē'altў, n. Real estate (cf. *personalty*). [-TY]

ream[1], n. Twenty quires or 480 sheets of paper (often 500, to allow for waste; *printers'~*, 516); (often pl.) large quantity of paper (*wrote ~s & ~s of verse*). [ME *rem* (= OF *rayme, reyme*), *rim* (= Du. *riem*), ult. f. Arab. *rizmah* bundle (cf. It. *risma*)]

ream[2], v.t. Widen (hole in metal) with borer or *~'ER[1](2)* n.; turn over edge of (cartridge-case etc.); (naut.) open (seam) for caulking. [19th c., of obsc. orig.]

|| **ream[3],** n. (dial., esp. SW. Eng.). Raw cream. [OE *rēam*, MHG *roum*, G *rahm*]

reanimate etc. See RE- 9.

reap, v.i. & t. Cut (grain or similar crop), cut grain etc., with sickle in harvest; gather in thus or with machine or fig. as harvest (*~ as one has sown, sow wind & ~ whirlwind, ~ the fruits of*, take consequences of one's actions; *~ where one has not sown*, profit by others' toil); harvest crop of (field etc.); *~ing-hook*, sickle; *~ing-machine*, for cutting grain & often binding sheaves without manual labour. Hence *~'ER[1](1, 2)* n. [OE *rīpan, reōpan*, excl. E]

reapparel, see RE- 8; **reappear** etc., **reappoint** etc., RE- 9; **reappraisal,** RE- 8.

rear[1], n. Hindermost part of army or fleet (*hang on the ~, of*, follow with view to attacking); back of, space behind, position at back of, army or camp or person (*bring, close, up the ~*, come last; *take enemy in~*, attack from behind; *saw them far in the ~*, behind; *was sent to the~ for safety*); back part of anything (*at the ~ of*, behind); || (colloq.) water-closet or latrine; *~·, ~* attrib., hinder, back-; so *~'MOST* a.; *~-admiral*, flag-officer below vice-admiral; *~'guard*, body of troops detached to protect ~ esp. in retreats (*~guard action*, engagement between ~-guard & enemy); *~'ward* n. [f. AF *rerewarde* = *~guard*], ~ (esp. in prep. phrr., as *to ~ward of, in the ~ward*); *~'ward* a. & adv., *~'wards* adv., towards the ~ [-WARD(S)]. [aphetic f. ARREAR]

rear[2], v.t. & i. **1.** Raise, set upright, build, uplift, hold upwards, (rhet.; *~ a pillar, cathedral,* etc.; *~ed his mighty stature*; *~ one's head*, one's voice, a hand, etc.). **2.** Raise, bring up, breed, foster, nourish, educate, cultivate, grow, (cattle, game, children, crops, etc.). **3.** (Of horse etc.; intr. & rarely refl.) rise, raise it*self*, on hind legs. Hence *~'ER[1]* n. [OE *rǣran*, = ON *reisa*, Goth. ·*raisjan*; see RAISE]

rear-'arch, rēre'-, n. Inner arch of window or door opening distinct from the outer.

rearise, see RE- 9; **rearm** etc., RE- 8; **rearouse,** RE- 9; **rearrange** etc., RE- 8.

rear-vault, n. Vault between arched

window or door head and arch in inner face of wall.

reascend. See RE- 9.

reas'on[1] (-z-), n. **1.** (Fact adduced or serving as) argument, motive, cause, or justification (*give ~s for; prove with ~s; the woman's ~*, repetition of fact as its own explanation, as in *I love him because I love him; for no other ~ than that I forgot, but this; there is no ~ to suppose*; *~ of State*, political justification esp. for immoral proceeding; *the ~ of your isolation, of eclipses, is that —; failed by ~ of its bad organization; there was ~ to believe; I saw ~ to suspect him; he complains with ~*, not unjustifiably). **2.** (log.). One of premisses of syllogism, esp. minor premiss when given after conclusion. **3.** The intellectual faculty characteristic esp. of human beings by which conclusions are drawn from premisses (*whether dogs have ~ is really a question of definition; there can be no opposition between ~ & common sense*). **4.** Intellect personified (*God & ~ are identical*); (as transl. of G *Vernunft* in Kant) faculty transcending the understanding (*Verstand*) & providing *a priori* principles, intuition. **5.** Sanity (*has lost his, is restored to, ~*). **6.** Sense, sensible conduct, what is right or practical or practicable, moderation, (*without* RHYME *or ~; bring to ~*, induce to cease from vain resistance; *will do anything in ~*, within the bounds of moderation; *it stands to ~*, cannot be denied without paradox, would be generally admitted; *hear* or *listen to ~*, suffer oneself to be persuaded; *as ~ was*, as good sense bade; *have ~*, arch. or transl. of F, be right; *there is ~ in what you say*). Hence ~LESS a. [ME, f. OF *raisun* f. L *rationem* (*rēri rat-* consider, -ION)]

reas'on[2] (-z-), v.i. & t. **1.** Use argument *with* person by way of persuasion. **2.** Form or try to reach conclusions by connected thought silent or expressed (*from premisses; about, of, upon*, subject), whence ~ER[1] n.; discuss *what, whether, why*, etc.; conclude, assume as step in argument, say by way of argument, *that* (or parenth.). **3.** Express in logical or argumentative form (*a ~ed exposition, manifesto, article; ~ed amendment*, in which reasons are embodied with a view to directing course of debate). **4.** Persuade by argument *out of, into* (*tried to ~ him out of his fears; ~ed himself into perplexity*). **5.** Think *out* (consequences etc.). Hence ~ING[1](1) n. [ME, f. OF *raisoner* f. Rom. **rationare* (prec.)]

reas'onab|le (-z-), a. **1.** Endowed with reason, reasoning, (rare). **2.** Sound of judgement, sensible, moderate, not expecting too much, ready to listen to reason. **3.** Agreeable to reason, not absurd, within the limits of reason, not

greatly less or more than might be expected, inexpensive, not extortionate, tolerable, fair. Hence ~leNESS n., ~LY[2] adv. [ME, f. OF *raisonable* (REASON[1], -ABLE), after L *rationabilis*]

reassemble, see RE- 9; **reassert, reassess** etc., **reassign,** RE- 8; **reassume** etc., **reassure** etc., RE- 9.

Réaumur (see Ap.), n. Name of French physicist appended (abbr. R.) to readings of the thermometer introduced by him with freezing-point 0° & boiling-point 80° (*a temperature of more than 55° R.* or ~). [F]

‖ **reave, reive,** (rēv), v.i. & t. (arch., poet.; *reft*). Commit ravages (usu. *reive*), whence **reiv'ER**[1] (rēv-) n.; forcibly deprive *of* (esp. in p.p.); take by force, carry off, (*away, from*). [OE *rēafian*, OS *rōbōn,* OHG *roubōn,* Goth. *-raubōn* f. Gmc **raubhōjan*]

rebaptize etc., see RE- 8; **rebarbarize,** RE- 9.

rebarb'ative, a. Repellent, unattractive. [f. F *rébarbatif, -ive* f. *barbe* beard]

‖ **rebate'**[1], v.t. (arch.). Diminish, reduce force or effect of; blunt, dull. [f. OF *rabattre* (RE- 5, ABATE)]

reb'ate[2] (*also* ribāt'), n. Deduction from sum to be paid, discount, drawback. [f. F *rabat* (prec.)]

rebate[3] (rāb'it, ribāt'), n., & v.t. = RABBET.

reb'ec(k), n. Medieval three-stringed instrument, early form of fiddle. [f. F *rebec* var. of OF *rebebe* f. Arab. *rebab*]

reb'el[1], n. Person who rises in arms against, resists, or refuses allegiance to, the established government; person or thing that resists authority or control; (attrib.) rebellious, of ~s, in rebellion. [orig. & n.; the pred. a. use now obs.; f. ME, f. OF *rebelle* f. L *rebellis* (RE- 2, *bellum* war)]

rebel'[2], v.i. (-ll-). Act as rebel (*against*), feel or manifest repugnance to some custom etc. (*against*). [ME, f. OF *rebeller* f. L *re(bellare* make war), revolt, RE- 2]

rebell'ion (-lyon), n. Organized armed resistance to established government (*the Great R~*, period of English history 1642--60); open resistance to any authority. [ME, f. OF f. L *rebellionem* (REBEL[1], -ION)]

rebell'ious (-lyus), a. In rebellion, disposed to rebel, insubordinate, defying lawful authority; (of diseases, things) difficult to treat, unmanageable, refractory. Hence ~LY[2] adv., ~NESS n. [as REBEL[1] or prec. +-OUS]

rebell'ow (-ō), v.i. & t. (poet.). Re-echo loudly. [RE- 6; after L *re(boare* bellow), *'RE- 6*]

rebind, see RE- 9; **rebirth** etc., **rebite,** RE- 8.

reb'ŏant, a. (poet.). Rebellowing, resounding, re-echoing. [f. L *reboare* RE-BELLOW, -ANT]

rebound'[1], v.i. Spring back after impact; have reactive effect, recoil upon agent, (*our evil example will ~ upon ourselves*). [ME, f. OF *rebonder* (RE- 1, BOUND[3])]

rebound'[2], n. Act of rebounding, recoil; reaction after emotion (*take* one *on* or *at the ~*, utilize such reaction to persuade him to contrary action etc.). [f. prec.]

rebuff', n., & v.t. **1.** Check given to one who makes advances, proffers help or sympathy, shows interest or curiosity, makes request, etc., repulse, snub. **2.** v.t. Give ~ to. [f. obs. F *rebuffe(r)* f. It. *rabbuffo, rabbuffare*, (RE- 2, *buffo* puff)]

rebuild. See RE- 8.

rebuke|e', v.t., & n. **1.** Reprove, reprimand, censure authoritatively; hence ~'**ing**LY[2] adv. **2.** n. ~ing or being ~ed; a reproof. [ME, f. ONF *re(buker* = OF *bucher* beat), RE- 5]

reb'us, n. Enigmatic representation of name, word, etc., by pictures etc. suggesting its syllables. [prob. = abl. pl. of L *res* thing; origin of sense (in F & E) doubtful]

rebut', v.t. (-tt-). Force or turn back, give check to; refute, disprove, (evidence, charge), whence ~t'**AL**(2), ~**MENT**, ~t'**ER**[4] (see SURREBUT), nn. [f. OF *re(buter* BUTT[4]), RE- 9]

recal'citr|āte, v.i. Kick *against* or *at* rules etc., refuse compliance, be refractory. So ~**ANT**(1) a. & n., ~**ANCE**, ~**A'TION**, nn. [f. L *re(calcitrare* strike with heel f. *calx -cis* heel), RE- 2, -**ATE**[3]]

recal|ēsce', v.i. Grow hot again (esp. in techn. use of iron allowed to cool from white heat, which recovers heat at certain point for short time). Hence ~**ēs'**CENCE n. [f. L *re(calescere* grow hot), RE- 9]

recall'[1] (-awl), v.t. Summon back from a place or from different occupation, inattention, digression, etc.; cancel appointment of (official sent to distance, esp. overseas); bring back to memory, serve as reminder of, recollect, remember; revive, resuscitate; revoke, annul, (action, decision), take back (gift). Hence ~**ABLE** a. [RE- 9]

recall'[2] (-awl), n. Summons to come back; cancelling of appointment abroad; signal to ship etc. to return; possibility of recalling esp. in sense of annulling (esp. *beyond, past, ~*). [RE- 9]

recant', v.t. & i. Withdraw & renounce (opinion, statement, etc.) as erroneous or heretical; disavow former opinion, esp. with public confession of error. Hence **recant**A'TION n. [f. L *re(cantare* sing) revoke, RE- 7]

re'cap, v.t. & n. (colloq.). Recapitulate; (n.) recapitulation. [abbr.]

recapitulate etc., see RE- 8; **recapture**, RE- 9; **recast**, RE- 8.

recce (rĕk'ĭ), n. (mil. sl.). Reconnaissance. [abbr.]

recēde', v.i. Go or shrink back or farther off; be left by observer's motion at in-

creasing distance; slope backwards; withdraw (*from* engagement, opinion, etc.); decline in character or value. [f. L *re(cedere* go), RE- 5]

receipt' (-sēt), n., & v.t. **1.** = RECIPE. **2.** Amount of money received. **3.** Fact or action of receiving or being received into person's hands or possession (*on ~ of a postal order for 10/- the goods will be sent*; *beg to acknowledge ~ of your book*; *entrusted with the ~ of subscriptions*); written acknowledgement of such ~ esp. of payment of sum due. **4.** (arch.). Place where money is officially received, esp. ~ *of custom*, custom-house. **5.** v.t. Write or print ~ on (bill). [ME *receit* f. ONF *receite* f. L *recepta* fem. p.p. of *recipere* RECEIVE w. -*p*- inserted on L]

receive' (-sēv), v.t. Accept delivery of, take (proffered thing) into one's hands or possession, (*Lord, ~ my soul*, dying man's prayer; ~ *stolen goods*, as thief's accomplice; ~ person's *confession, oath*, consent to hear; ~ *a petition*, take it to consider; ~ *the sacraments*, eat & drink the bread & wine, also abs., as *attend without receiving*). **2.** Bear up against, stand force or weight of, encounter with opposition, (~*d his body in their hands*; *arch ~s weight of roof*; ~*d the sword-point with his shield*; *prepare to ~ cavalry*, order to infantry). **3.** Admit, consent or prove able to hold, provide accommodation for, submit to, serve as receptacle of, (*had to ~ the visits, attentions, of*; ~ *an impression, stamp, mark*, etc., be marked lit. or fig. more or less permanently with it; *sensitive paper ~s the record of signals*; *the basin that ~d his blood*; *the house ~d a new guest*; *hole large enough to ~ two men*; *fitted to ~ the knowledge of God*; *has ~d our yoke*; *town ~s a French garrison*; *was ~d into the Church*, admitted to membership). **4.** Entertain as guest, greet, welcome, give specified reception to, (*shall not be ~d at my house*; *he that ~th me ~th him that sent me*; *you stay here & ~ him*; *how did she ~ his offer?*; *was ~d with cries of Judas*; *news was ~d with horror*; *I ~ it as certain, as a prophecy*, regard it in that light); (abs.) ~ *company*, hold reception. **5.** Give credit to, accept as true, (*an axiom universally ~d*; *they ~ not our report*), whence **receiv**ED' (-sēvd') a. (~*d pronunciation*, abbr. *R.P.*, form of speech used, with local variations, by the majority of cultured people). **6.** Acquire, get, come by, be given or provided with, have sent to or conferred or inflicted on one, (*have not yet ~d my dividend*; ~ *a letter, news*; *a window that has not ~d a frame*; ~ *the name of John*; ~ *Christ in baptism*, have Christian character conferred; *pleasant to ~ sympathy*; *deserves more attention than it ~s*; ~ *orders to march*; ~*d many insults, a thrust, a broken jaw, the contents of his pistol*); partake of. Hence **receiv'**ABLE (-sēv-) a. [ME, f. ONF receivre f. L re(cipere = capere take) recover, RE- 9]

receiv′er (-sēv-), n. In vbl senses, esp.: person appointed by court's receiving- -order to administer property of bankrupt or property under litigation, whence ~- SHIP n.; person who receives stolen goods, fence; receptacle etc. for receiving something in machine or instrument, esp. earpiece of telephone; apparatus for transforming broadcast waves into sound or light, wireless receiving-set. [ME, f. AF *receivere, -our; later, prec. +-ER¹]

recen′sion (-shn), n. Revision of, revised, text. [f. L recensio f. re(censēre review), RE- 8]

re′cent, a. Not long past, that happened or existed lately, late; not long established, lately begun, modern. Hence re′CENCY n., ~LY² adv., ~NESS n. [f. L recens -entis or F récent]

recep′tacle, n. Containing vessel, place, or space; (bot.) common base of floral organs, axis of cluster. [ME, f. OF, or L receptaculum (recept- p.p. st. of recipere RECEIVE]

recep′tion, n. 1. Receiving or being received (rare in gen. sense); receiving esp. of person, being received, into a place or company (the rooms were prepared for his ~; was honoured by ~ into the Academy; ‖~ order, authorizing ~ of lunatic in asylum). 2. Formal or ceremonious welcome (the ~ of the delegates is arranged for Monday next); occasion of receiving guests, assembly held for this purpose, (after the review there will be a ~; ~-room, available for receiving company, esp. opp. bedroom). 3. Receiving of ideas or impressions into the mind (has a great faculty of ~, but little originative power); (rare) mental acceptance, recognition of something as true or advisable, (the general ~ of the Newtonian hypothesis). 4. Welcome or greeting of specified kind, demonstration of feeling towards person or project, (warm ~, vigorous resistance or enthusiastic welcome; his ~ was frigid, all that he could desire; proposal, book, had a favourable ~). 5. Receiving of wireless signals, or the efficiency with which they are received. Hence-~IST (3) (-sho-) n., person employed by photographer, dentist, etc., to receive clients. [ME, f. OF, or f. L receptio (as prec., -ION]

recep′tive, a. Able or quick to receive impressions or ideas (a mind more ~ than retentive or creative); (rare) concerned with receiving. Hence ~LY² adv., ~NESS, recěptiv′ITY, nn. [f. med. L receptivus (as prec., -IVE)]

recess′, n., & v.t. & i. 1. Temporary cessation from work, vacation, esp. of Parliament; receding of water, land, glacier, etc., from previous limit, amount by which it recedes, recession, (rare);

retired or secret place (in the inmost ~es of the Alps, of the heart); receding part of mountain chain etc., niche or alcove of wall; (anat.) fold or indentation in organ. 2. vb. Place in a ~, set back; provide with ~(es); *(v.i.) take a ~, adjourn. [f. L recessus (recess- p.p. st. of RECEDEre)]

recě′ssion (-shn), n. Receding, withdrawal, from a place or point; receding part of object, recess; *slump in trade. So recess′IVE a. & n., (also, Mendelism, of a) characteristic appearing in the second or later generation of hybrids, inherited from one of the original parents but suppressed in the first generation (cf. DOMINANT). [f. L recessio (as prec., -ION)]

recě′ssional (-sho-), a. & n. ~ hymn or ~, hymn sung while clergy & choir withdraw after service; of the parliamentary recess. [-AL]

Rěch′abīte (-k-), n. Total abstainer. [Rechab, see Jer. xxxv. 6, -ITE¹(1)]

recharge. See RE- 9.

réchauffé (rīshōf′ā, & see Ap.), n. Warmed-up dish; rehash (RE- 8). [F]

recherché (reshārsh′ā, & see Ap.), a. Devised or got with care or difficulty, choice, far-fetched, thought out, (esp. of meals or words). [F]

rechristen. See RE- 8.

recid′iv|ist, n. One who relapses into crime. So ~ISM n. [f. F récidiviste f. L rccidivus f. re(cidere = cadere fall), RE- 9, -IVE, -IST]

re′cipě, n. Medical prescription or remedy prepared from it; statement of ingredients & procedure for preparing dish etc.; expedient, nostrum, device for effecting something. [2nd sing. imperat. as used (abbr. R.) in prescriptions of L recipere RECEIVE].

recip′i|ent, a. & n. 1. Receptive, whence ~ENCY n. 2. n. Person who receives something. [f. L recipere RECEIVE, -ENT]

recip′rocal, a. & n. 1. In return (if I helped him, I had ~ help from him); mutual (~ love, protection, injuries); inversely correspondent, correlative, (I took the chamois for a man, & it made the ~ mistake); (gram.) expressing mutual action or relation ('each other' is a ~ pronoun), (formerly also) reflexive; hence ~LY² adv. 2. n. (math.). Function or expression so related to another that their product is unity (1/5 is the ~ of 5). [f. L reciprocus (prob. f. re- back & pro forward), -AL]

recip′roc|āte, v.t. & i. (Mech.) go with alternate backward & forward motion (~ating engine etc., with work done by part that moves thus, opp. rotatory see ROTATE²), give such motion to; give & receive mutually, interchange, (influence etc.); return, requite, (affection etc.), make a return (often with thing given in return). So ~A'TION n. [f. L *reciprocare* (prec.), -ATE[3]]

rĕcĭprŏ'cĭtў, n. Reciprocal condition, mutual action; principle or practice of give-&-take, esp. interchange of privileges between States as basis of commercial relations. [f. F *réciprocité* (RECIPROCAL, -ITY)]

rĕcĭt'al, n. **1.** Detailed account *of* a number of connected things or facts, relation *of* the facts of an incident etc., a narrative. **2.** Part of document stating facts. **3.** Act of reciting; performance of programme by one musician (*vocal, pianoforte*, etc., ~). [RECITE, -AL]

rĕcĭtative' (-ēv), n. Musical declamation of kind usual in narrative & dialogue parts of opera & oratorio; words, part, given in ~. [f. It. *recitativo* (foll., -IVE)]

rĕcĭte', v.t. & i. Repeat aloud or declaim (poem, passage) from memory esp. before audience, give recitation (*reciting-note*, that held on for indefinite number of syllables in chanting); (law) rehearse (facts) in document; mention in order, enumerate. So **rĕcĭtA'TION** n. [ME, f. OF *reciter* or L *re(citare* CITE), RE- 8]

rĕcĭt'er, n. Person who recites; book of passages for recitation. [-ER[1]]

recivilize etc. See RE- 9.

rĕck, v.i. & t. (rhet., poet., in neg. & interrog. sentences only). ~ *of*, pay heed to, take account of, care about; care, be troubled, concern oneself, (*if, though, that, how, whether*, etc., or abs.; also impers. with same construction following, as *what* ~*s it him that . . .?*). [OE *reccan*, OS *rōkjan*, OHG *ruoh(h)en*, ON *rœkja* f. Gmc *rōkjan*]

rĕck'lĕss, a. Devoid of caution, regardless of consequences, rash; heedless *of* danger etc. Hence ~LY[2] adv., ~NESS n. [OE *receleās* (prec., -LESS)] ,

rĕck'on, v.t. & i. **1.** Ascertain (number, amount), ascertain number or amount of, by counting or usu. by calculation, compute; start *from*, go on *to*, in counting (t. & i.); count *up*, sum *up* character of; arrive at as total (*I* ~ *53 of them*). **2.** Include in computation, count *in*, place in class *among* or *with* or *in*, take *for*, regard *as*, consider *to be* (or with obj. & compl. as ~ *him wise, beyond redemption*). **3.** Conclude after calculation, be of the confident opinion, (*that*; also, chiefly U.S., parenth., cf. *calculate, guess*). **4.** Make calculations, cast up account or sum, (~ *without* one's HOST[2]), settle accounts *with* person. **5.** Rely or count or base plans *upon*. [OE (*ge)recenian*, MDu., MLG *rekenen*, OHG *rechenōn* f. WG **rekenōjan*]

rĕck'oner (-kn-), n. In vbl senses; esp., READY~. [-ER[1]]

rĕck'oning (-kn-), n. In vbl senses; esp.: tavern bill; *day of* ~, time when something must be atoned for or avenged; DEAD ~; *out in* one's ~, mistaken in a calculation or expectation. [ME; -ING[1]]

rĕclaim', v.t. & i., & n. **1.** Win back or away from vice or error or savagery or waste condition, reform, tame, civilize, bring under cultivation esp. from flooding by sea or marsh, whence ~ABLE a. ; make protest, say in protest, (rare); so **rĕclam-A'TION** n. **2.** n. ~ing, reclamation, (rare, chiefly in *past* or *beyond* ~). [ME, f. OF *reclamer* f. L *re(clamare* shout) cry out against, RE- 2]

rĕclame (rāk'lahm, & see Ap.), n. Art or practice by which notoriety is secured. [F]

rĕc'linate, a. (bot.). Bending downwards. [f. L *reclinatus* (foll., -ATE[2])]

rĕcline', v.t. & i. Lay (esp. one's head, body, limbs) in more or less horizontal or recumbent position (p.p., of person, lying thus); assume or be in recumbent position, lie or lean, sit with back or side supported at considerable inclination; (fig.) rely confidently *upon*. [ME, f. OF *recliner* or L *reclinare* (RE- 9), see DECLINE[1]]

reclothe. See RE- 8.

rĕcluse' (-lōōs), a. & n. (Person) given to or living in seclusion or retirement or isolation, esp. as religious discipline, hermit, anchorite or anchoress. [ME, f. OF *reclus, -use* p.p. of *reclure* f. L *re(cludere= claudere* shut), RE- 4]

recoal, recoat. See RE- 8.

rĕcŏgni'tion, n. In vbl senses (RECOGNIZE). So **rĕcŏg'nitORY** a. (rare). [f. L *recognitio* (RECOGNIZE, -ION)]

rĕcŏg'nizance (*or* -kŏn[4]), n. Bond by which person engages before court or magistrate to observe some condition, e.g. to keep the peace, pay a debt, or appear when summoned; sum pledged as surety for such observance. [ME, f. OF *reconoissance* (*reconoistre* RECOGNIZE, -ANCE)]

rĕcŏg'nizant (*or* -kŏn[4]), a. Showing recognition (*of* favour etc.), conscious or showing consciousness of something. [as foll., see -ANT]

rĕc'ogniz|e, -is|e (-īz), v.t. **1.** Acknowledge validity or genuineness or character or claims or existence of, accord notice or consideration to, discover or realize nature of, treat *as*, acknowledge *for*, realize or admit *that*. **2.** Know again, identify as known before. Hence ~ABLE a., ~ABIL'ITY n., ~ABLY[2] adv. [ME, f. OF *reconiss-*part. st. of *reconoistre* f. L *re(cognoscere -gnitum* learn), RE- 8, w. assim. to -IZE]

rĕcoil', v.i., & n. **1.** Retreat before enemy (now rare); start or spring back, shrink mentally, in fear or horror or disgust; rebound after impact, (of gun) be driven backwards by discharge, spring back. **2**, n. Act or fact or sensation of ~ing. [ME, f. OF *reculer* (RE- 9, *cul* posteriors f. L *culus*)]

recoin etc. See RE- 8.

rĕcŏllĕct', v.t. Succeed in remembering, recall to mind, remember. [f. p.p. st. of L *re(colligere* COLLECT[2]), RE- 8]

rĕcollĕc′t|ion, n.. Act, power, of recollecting; thing recollected, reminiscence; person's memory, time over which it extends, (*it is in my ~ion that*, I remember that; *happened within my ~ion*). So ~IVE a. [F, or f. med. L *recollectio* (prec., -ION)]

recolonize etc., **recolour**, **recombine** etc., see RE- 8; **recomfort**, RE- 9; **recommence** etc., RE- 8.

rĕcommĕnd′, v.t. **1.** Give (one*self*, one's spirit, a child, etc.) in charge *to* God or a person or his care etc. **2.** Speak or write of or suggest as fit for employment or favour or trial (*to* person, or with ind. obj. as *can you ~ me a cook, a book?*; *as* servant etc.; *for* post, promotion, decoration). **3.** (Of qualities, conduct, etc.) make acceptable, serve as recommendation of. **4.** Advise (course of action or treatment, person *to* do, *that* thing should be done). Hence or cogn. ~A′TION n., ~ABLE, ~atORY, aa. [ME, f. med. L *re(commendare* COMMEND), RE- 5]

recommit etc. See RE- 8.

rĕc′ompĕnse, v.t., & n. **1.** Requite, reward or punish, (person, action, person *for* action, action *to* person or with ind. obj.); make amends to (person) or for (another's loss, injury, etc., or rarely one's own misconduct). **2.** n. Reward,.requital, atonement or satisfaction given for injury, retribution. [ME, f. OF *recompenser* f. LL *re(compensare* COMPENSATE), RE- 1]

recompose, recompound. See RE- 8.

rĕc′oncil|e, v.t. **1.** Make friendly after estrangement (persons to one another, person *to* or *with* another, person to oneself). **2.** Purify (consecrated place etc.) by special service after desecration. **3.** Make resigned or contentedly submissive (*to* disagreeables, to *doing*, or abs.; usu. in pass.). **4.** Heal, compose, (quarrel etc.). **5.** Harmonize, make compatible, show compatibility of by argument or in practice, (apparently conflicting facts, statements, qualities, actions, or one such *with* or *&* or rarely *to* another). Hence or cogn. ~ABLE a., ~ABIL′ITY, ~eMENT (-lm-), **rĕconciliA′TION**, nn. [ME, f. OF *reconcilier* or f. L *re(conciliare* CONCILIATE), RE- 9]

rĕc′ondīte (*or* rĭkŏn²), a. (Of subjects or knowledge) abstruse, out of the way, little known; (of author or style) dealing in ~ knowledge or allusion, obscure. Hence ~LY² adv., ~NESS n. [f. L *re(conditus* p.p. of *condere* hide), RE- 4]

rĕcondī′tion, v.t. Overhaul & refit, rehabilitate, renovate. [RE- 8]

reconduct. See RE- 9.

rĕcŏnn′aissance (-nĭs-), n. Military, naval, etc. examination of tract by detachment to locate enemy or ascertain strategic features (*~ in force*, made by strong party); reconnoitring party; preliminary survey made by anyone for any purpose. [F (earlier -*oissance*), as foll., -ANCE]

rĕconnoi′tr|e (-*ter*), v.t. & i., & n. **1.** Make reconnaissance of (enemy, district), approach & try to learn position & condition etc. of; make reconnaissance. **2.** n. (rare). Reconnaissance. Hence ~ER¹ n. [f. F *reconnoître* (now -*aître*) f. L *recognoscere* RECOGNIZE]

reconquer etc., see RE- 9; **reconsider** etc., **reconstitute** etc., **reconstruct** etc., RE- 8; **reconvert** etc., RE- 9.

rĕcŏrd′¹, v.t. **1.** (Of birds) practise (tune, or abs.) by singing in an undertone. **2.** Register, set down for remembrance or reference, put in writing or other legible shape, represent in some permanent form, (*his thoughts have been ~ed for us by himself, his features by Watts, & his voice by the phonograph*; *~ing angel*, who registers men's good & bad actions; *minimum thermometer ~ed 10° below zero*); (radio) register & reproduce (item, programme) by RECORDING. Hence ~ABLE a. [ME, f. OF *recorder* f. L *recordari* remember (RE-, *cor* heart)]

rĕc′ŏrd², n. **1.** State of being recorded or preserved in writing esp. as authentic legal evidence (*is on ~*, legally or otherwise recorded; *matter of ~*, something established as fact by being recorded; *court of ~*, whose proceedings are recorded & valid as evidence of fact). **2.** Official report of proceedings & judgement in cause before court of ~, copy of pleadings etc. constituting case to be decided by court (*travel out of, keep to, the ~*, introduce, abstain from introducing, irrelevant matter). **3.** ‖ (*Public*) *R~ Office*, building in London in which State papers and other public documents are stored, calendared, etc. **4.** Piece of recorded evidence or information, account of fact preserved in permanent form, document or monument preserving it; **off the ~*, unofficial(ly); object serving as memorial of something, portrait etc.; series of marks etc. given by recording instrument or plate etc. containing these (*second-hand gramophone ~s for sale*); *~-player*, gramophone, esp. one with electrical pick-up. **5.** Facts known about person's past (*has an honourable ~ of service*; *his ~ is against him*). **6.** Best performances or most remarkable event of its kind on ~ (*break or cut or beat the ~*, outdo all predecessors; (attrib.) best hitherto recorded (*at ~ pace*; *the ~ height*). [ME, f. OF *record*, f. *recorder* (prec.)]

rĕcŏrd′er, n. In vbl senses; also: city or borough magistrate with criminal & civil jurisdiction ‖ & holding court of Quarter sessions, whence ~SHIP n.; recording-apparatus in instruments; vertical (English) flute. [orig. f. AF *recordour*; later, partly f. RECORD¹ + -ER¹]

rĕcōrd'ing, n. ·In ʋbl senses, esp. (radio) process of registering sound for subsequent reproduction, material (disc,· film, magnetic steel or plastic tape) on which sound has been registered, sound-programme registered & reproduced. [-ING [1]]

rĕcount' [1], v.t. Narrate, tell in detail. [f. ONF & AF re(conter COUNT [2]), RE- 8]

rē-count' [2]. See RE- 8.

rĕcoup' (-ōop), v.t. & i. (Law) deduct, keep back, (part of sum due), make such deduction; compensate (person loss, person *for* loss, loss; ~ one*self*, recover what one has expended or lost). Hence ~MENT n. [f. F re(couper cut, see COUP), RE- 5]

rĕcourse' (-ōrs), n. Resorting or betaking of oneself *to* possible source of help (~ *to brandy is deprecated*; usu. in phr. *have* ~ *to, adopt as adviser, helper, or expedient*); thing resorted to (rare; *their usual* ~ *is perjury*); *without* ~ (commerce, law), formula used by indorser of a bill etc. to indicate that he disclaims responsibility for non-payment. [ME, f. OF *recours* f. L *re(cursus* COURSE [1]), RE- 9]

rĕco'ver [1] (-kŭ-), v.t. & i., & n. 1. Regain possession or use or control of, acquire or find (out) again, reclaim, (*has* ~*ed his kingdom, his friends' affection, the meaning of the hieroglyphs, the track, health, his appetite, his voice, much land from the sea*; ~ one*self*, regain consciousness or calmness or control of limbs or senses; *horse* ~*s itself after stumble*; ~ one's *legs*, stand up after fall). 2. Secure restitution or compensation, secure (damages), by legal process (*plaintiff shall* ~ *according to verdict*; *his remedy is to* ~ *in a court of law*; *an action to* ~ *damages for false imprisonment*). 3. Bring or come back to life, consciousness, health, or normal state or position (*he* ~*ed slowly*; *the mention of a bucket of water* ~*ed her*; *I* ~*ed the heat of his body with fomentations*; *corpse cannot be* ~*ed to life*; ~*ed me from a lingering illness*; *am quite* ~*ed from my cold*; *sat down to* ~ *from his agitation*; ~ *sword*, bring it back after thrust etc., or, mil., hold it upright with hilt opposite .mouth*). 4. Retrieve, make up for, get over, cease to feel effects of, (*must try to* ~ *bst time*; *never* ~*ed the blow, his losses, this* faux pas). 5. Make one's way back to (rare; ~*ed the shore with difficulty*); hence ~ABLE a. 6. n. Position to which sword etc. is brought back in fencing or drill, act of coming to this. [ME, f. AF, OF *recov(e)rer* f. L *recuperare* RECUPERATE]

re-cover [2]. See RE- 8.

rĕco'verȳ (-kŭ-), n. Act or process of RECOVER [1]ing or being recovered.· [ME, f. AF *recoverie* or OF *recovree*(RECOVER [1], -Y [4])]

rĕc'rĕ|ant, a. & n. (rhet., poet.). Craven, coward(ly), apostate. Hence ~ANCY n., ~antLY [2] adv. [ME, f. OF, part. of *recroire* f. med. L (*se*) *recredere*, RE- 6, yield in trial by combat]

rĕc'rĕ|āte [1], v.t. & i. (Of pastime, relaxation, holiday, employment, etc., or refl. of person indulging in them) refresh, entertain, agreeably occupy, (*it* ~*ates him to invent histories for his neighbours*; ~*ates himself with cricket, climbing, lying in a hammock, political argument*); amuse oneself, indulge in ~ation. So ~A'TION n., ~ATIVE a. [f. L re(creare CREATE), RE- 8, -ATE [3]]

re-create [2] etc. See RE- 8.

rĕc'rĕment, n. Waste product, refuse, (now rare); (physiol.) fluid separated from blood & again absorbed in it, e.g. saliva, bile. Hence ~I'TIOUS [1] (-ĭshŭs) a. [f. F *récrément* or L re(crementum f. cernere cret- sift, RE- 5, -MENT)]

rĕcrim'in|āte, v.i. Retort accusation, indulge in mutual or counter charges. So ~A'TION n., ~ATIVE, ~ātORY, aa. [f. med. L re(criminari f. crimen, CRIME), RE- 1]

recross. See RE- 9.

rĕcrud|ĕsce' (-ōō-), v.i. (Of sore, disease, etc., or fig. of discontent etc.) break out again. So ~ES'CENT a., ~ĕs'CENCE n. [f. L re(crudescere f. crudus raw, see -ESCENT), RE- 8]

rĕcruit' [1] (-rōōt), n. Newly enlisted & not yet trained soldier; person who joins a society etc.; tiro (often *raw* ~). [earlier sense *reinforcement*, f. obs. F *recrute*= *recrue* fem. p.p. of re(croitre, OF *creistre*, f. L *crescere* increase), RE- 8]

rĕcruit' [2] (-rōōt), v.t. & i. 1. Enlist recruits for (army, regiment, crew, society, party), enlist ·(person) as recruit, get or seek recruits (esp. ~*ing-sergeant*). 2. · Replenish, fill up deficiencies or compensate wear & tear in, refresh, reinvigorate. 3. (Seek to) recover health etc. (*has gone to the country to* ~), whence ~AL [2] n. Hence ~MENT (-rōō-) n. [f. F *recruter* (obs. *recrute*, see prec.)]

rĕc'tal, a. Of or by the rectum. [-AL]

rĕc'tăngle (-nggl), n. Plane rectilinear four-sided figure with four right angles, esp. one with adjacent sides unequal. [F, or f. LL *rectiangulum* (*rectus* straight, ANGLE [1]) right-angled]

rĕctăng'ūlar (-ngg-), a. Shaped, having base or sides or section shaped, like rectangle; placed, having parts or lines placed, at right angles. Hence ~ITY (-ă'r-) n., ~LY [2] adv. [as prec., -AR [1]]

rĕc'tifȳ, v.t. 1. Put right, correct, amend, reform, adjust, (method, calculation, statement, position, instrument)'. 2. Abolish, get rid of, exchange for what is right, (abuse, anomaly, error, omission, grievance). 3. (chem.). Purify or refine by renewed distillation or other process. 4. (geom.). Find straight line equal to (curve). Hence or cogn. ~fiABLE a., ~FICA'TION n., ~fiER [1] (1, 2) n., (also, radio) thermionic valve or other device transforming an alternating to a direct current. [ME, f. OF *rectifier* f. med. L *rectificare* (L *rectus* right, -FY)]

rĕctilin'|ĕar, -ĕaĺ, aa. In or forming a straight line; bounded or characterized by straight lines. Hence ~ĕā'rĬTY n., ~ĕarLY² adv. [f. LL *rectilineus* (L *rectus* straight, *linea* LINE²), -AR¹, -AL]

rĕc'titūde, n. Moral uprightness, righteousness; (rare) correctness, rightness. [ME, f. OF or LL *rectitudo* (L *rectus* right, -TUDE)]

rĕc'tō, n. (pl. ~s). Right-hand page of open book; front of leaf (opp. VERSO). [f. L *recto* (*folio*) on the right (leaf)]

rĕc'tor, n. 1. ‖ Incumbent of parish still in enjoyment of tithes (cf. VICAR). **2.** Head of university, college, school, or religious institution (esp. abroad; in England only of heads of Exeter & Lincoln Colleges, Oxford; in Scotland of headmasters of some secondary schools etc., & see LORD¹ ~), whence **rĕc'trĕss¹** n. Hence ~ATE¹, ~SHIP, nn., **rĕctōr'IAL** a. (‖ also as n. = ~ial election). [ME, f. L, = ruler (*regere rect-* rule, -OR)]

rĕc'torў, n. ‖ Rector's benefice; rector's house. [f. OF *rectorie* or med. L *rectoria* (prec., -Y¹)]

rĕc'tum, n. Final section of large intestine, terminating at anus. [f. L *rectum* (*intestinum*) straight (intestine)]

rĕcŭm'b|ent, a. Lying down, reclining. Hence ~ENCY n., ~entLY² adv. [f. L *re*(*cumbere* lie), RE- 9, -ENT]

rĕcŭp'er|āte, v.t. & i. Restore, be restored or recover, from exhaustion, illness, loss, etc. So ~A'TION n., ~ATIVE a. [f. L *recuperare* RECOVER, see -ATE³]

rĕcŭr', v.i. (-rr-; *part. pr.* -ŭ'rĭng *or* -ēr'ĭng). Go back in thought or speech to; (of idea etc.) come back *to* one's mind etc., return to mind; (of problem etc.) come up again; occur again, be repeated, (~*ring decimals*, figures in decimal fraction that ~ in same order again & again); ~*ring curve*, that returns upon itself, e.g. circle. So **rĕcŭ'rrENCE** n. [f. L *re*(*currere* run), RE-9]

rĕcŭ'rrent, a. & n. 1. (Of nerve, vein, branch, etc.) turning back so as to reverse direction; occurring again or often or periodically; hence ~LY² adv. **2.** n. ~ artery or nerve, esp. one of the two ~ laryngeal nerves. [as prec., -ENT]

rĕcūrv|e', v.t. & i. Bend backwards. So ~'ATE² a., ~'atURE n. [f. L *re*(*curvare* bend), RE- 9]

rĕc'ūs|ant (-z-), n. & a. (Hist.) (person) who refused to attend Church-of-England services; (person) refusing submission to authority or compliance with regulation (*against*). Hence ~ANCE, ~ANCY, nn. [f. L *recusare* RECUSE]

rĕcūse' (-z), v.t. (now rare). Reject (person, his authority); object to (judge) as prejudiced. [ME, f. OF *recuser* f. *recusare* (RE- 2, *causa* CAUSE) refuse]

rĕd, a. & n. 1. Of or approaching the colour seen at least refracted end of

spectrum, of shades varying from crimson to bright brown & orange, esp. those seen in blood, sunset clouds, rubies, glowing coals, human lips, & fox's hair, (~ *as a rose* etc.; *blood, fiery, yellowish, deep*, etc., ~~; ~ *with anger* etc., flushed in face; *with* ~ *hands*, bloodstained; ‖ *all-*~ *route, line, cable*, etc., traversing British territory or under British control, w. ref. to ~ in maps as British colour; ~ *gold*, arch. & poet., real gold, money; *~ *cent*, smallest coin orig. of copper, esp. *don't care a* ~ *cent;* ~ *eyes*, bloodshot, or with lids sore from weeping, also of bird etc. with ~ iris; as, distinctive epithet with many varieties of animal & plant & mineral, as ~ *deer, partridge, mullet, ant,* CURRANT, *campion*, ARSENIC). **2.** Having to do with bloodshed, burning, violence, or revolution (~ *battle, ruin;* SEE¹~; *a~republican, radical, anarchist).* **3.** Russian, Soviet, (*the Red Army, Air Force*). **4.** ~ ADMIRAL; ~ *bark*, superior kind of cinchona; ~*blind*, colour-blind to~; ‖~ *book* (containing list of nobility & gentry); ~ *box*, used by Ministers for official documents; ~*breast*, the robin; ~*'brick*, (of university) of modern foundation (*Red'brick*, opp. OXBRIDGE); ~*'cap*, ‖ military policeman; ~*'coat*, British soldier; ~ *cross*, St George's cross or national emblem of England, also Christian side in crusades, also (emblem of) ambulance etc. service organized according to Geneva Convention; ‖~ ENSIGN (also, sl., ~ *duster*), used by British merchant ships; ~*-eye*, the fish rudd; ~*-fish*, male salmon in spawning season, also (market name for) salmon (opp. *white fish* of all other kinds); ~ *flag*, symbol of revolution (*the Red Flag*, a modern revolutionary song), danger-signal on shooting-ranges, railways, etc.; ~ *gum*, teething-rash in children, also (kinds of eucalyptus yielding) ~dish resin; ~*'hand'ed*, in the act of crime (*take* ~*'handed*); ~ *hat*, cardinal's, ‖ (also nickname for) British staff-officer; ~ *heat*, being ~-hot lit. & fig., temperature of ~-hot thing; ~ *herring*, herring(s) .~dened by being cured in smoke (*neither fish, flesh, nor good* ~ *herring*, of ambiguous indefinite nature; *draw a* ~ *herring across the track*, divert attention from subject in hand by starting irrelevant but exciting question, with ref. to use of ~ herring in exercising hounds); ~*-hot*, heated to ~ness, highly excited, enthusiastic, furious; ~*-hot poker*, garden plant with flame-coloured spikes of flower; ‖~ *lamp*, night-sign of doctor or chemist; ~ *lane*, (nursery name for) throat; ~ *lead*, pigment made from ~ oxide of lead (v.t., coat with this); ~*-legged*, with ~ legs (of birds etc., esp. the ~*-legged* or *French partridge*); ~*-legs*, kinds of bird, also the plant bistort; ~*-letter*, (of day) marked with ~ letter(s) in calendar as saint's day or festival, (fig.) memorable as date of joyful occurrence, (v.t., record as memorable for joy); ~ *light*, danger-signal on railways etc. (*see the* ~ *light*, fig., realize approach of disaster), brothel; ~ *man*, N.-Amer. Indian; ~ *meat*, beef, mutton, etc. (opp. veal & pork & chicken); ~ *mass*, at which priest wears ~; ~'*poll*, kinds of ~-crested bird similar to linnet, also (pl.) ~-haired polled cattle; ~ *rag*, thing that excites person's rage as ~ object enrages bull (*is a* ~ *rag to him*), || also kind of rust in grain; ~ *rattle*, lousewort; || ~ *ribbon*, ribbon, membership, of Order of Bath; ~ *sanders*, wood of E.-Ind. tree used in dyeing; ~'*shank*, large kind of sandpiper; ~-*short*, (of iron) brittle while ~-hot; ~'*skin*, = ~ *man* above; ~ *snow*, ~denéd by kind of alga & common in Arctic & Alpine regions; ~ *soldier*, (pig affected with) kind of swine fever with ~ness of skin; ~ *spider*, insect infesting hothouse plants esp. vines; ~'*start*, ~-tailed European songbird [OE *steort* tail]; ~-*streak*, kind of cider apple; ~ *tape*, excessive use of or adherence to formalities esp. in public business, whence ~-tāp'ERY, ~-tāp'ISM, ~-tāp'IST, nn.; ~ *triangle*, (emblem of) the Y.M.C.A.; ~-*water*, malarial cattle & sheep disease with ~ urine; ~ *weed*, corn poppy; ~^L *wing*, kinds of thrush & other birds; ~'*wood*, kinds of tree etc. esp. Californian *sequoia* (*sempivirens*); ~ *worm*, kind used as fishing-bait; hence ~d'EN⁶ v.t. & i., ~d'ISH¹(2), ~d'Y², aa., ~'LY² adv. (rare), ~'NESS n. 5. n. ~ colour; *a* shade of ~; the ~ colour in roulette & rouge-et-noir; *the* ~ ball at billiards; *the* debtor side of an account (*in the* ~, in debt); ~ cloth or clothes (*dressed in* ~); one of former three squadrons or divisions (*the* ~, *white, blue*) of British fleet; radical or republican or anarchist or communist. [OE *réad*, OS *rōd*, OHG *rōt*, ON *rauthr*, Goth. *rauths* f. Gmc **rauthaz*, cogn. w. L *rufus*]

red-, pref. = RE-, only in wds of L origin.

rĕdăct', v.t. Put into literary form, arrange for publication, edit. So **rĕdăc'tor** n. [in mod. use a back formation f. foll.]

·rĕdăc'tion, n. Preparing or being prepared for publication, revision, editing, rearrangement; new edition. [f. F *rédaction* f. L *red(igere -act- = agere* bring), RE-8, -ION]

rĕdăn', n. Field-work with two faces forming salient angle. [F *redan* for *redent* (RE-, *dent* tooth)]

|| **rĕdd**, v.t. (Sc.). Clear up, arrange, tidy, put right, settle, compose. [= syn. MLG, Du. *redden*, but in ME perh. independent form rel. to READY]

rĕd'dle, n., & v.t. Red ochre, ruddle; (vb) colour with ~. [var. of RUDDLE]

|| **rēde¹**, n. (arch.). Counsel, advice; resolve, design; narrative. [OE *rǣd*, f. Gmc **rǣdhaz*. **rǣdhan* READ]

|| **rēde²**, v.t. (arch.). Advise (person, with inf. with or without *to*, or with imperat.); read (riddle, dream). [same wd as READ, the common ME sp. being retained for the arch. senses of the wd]

rĕdeem', v.t. **1.** Buy back, recover by expenditure of effort. or by stipulated payment, (~ one's *rights, position, honour, mortgaged land, pledged goods*); compound for, buy off, (charge or obligation) by payment. **2.** Perform (promise). **3.** Purchase the freedom of (another, one*self*), save (one's life) by ransom. **4.** Save, rescue, reclaim; (of God or Christ) deliver from sin & damnation. **5.** Make amends for, compensate, counterbalance, (fault, defect; *has one* ~*ing feature*); save *from* a defect (*the eyes* ~ *the face from ugliness*). Hence ~ABLE a., (esp. of Christ, see above) ~ER¹ n. [ME, f. OF *redimer* or L *red(i-mere -empt- = emere* buy), RE-8]

rĕdĕmp'tion, n. **1.** REDEEMing or being redeemed, esp. the deliverance from sin & damnation wrought by Christ's atonement (*past, beyond, without,* ~, so that ~ is hopeless; *in the year of our* ~ *1963* etc., A.D. 1963 etc.). **2.** Thing that redeems (*that blow was* or *proved his* ~). **3.** || Purchase (*became a member of a livery company by* ~). Hence **rĕdĕmp'tive** a. [ME, f. OF, or L *redemptio* (prec., -ION)]

rĕdeploy'ment, n. Improved physical arrangements in factories as means of increasing output. [RE-8]

redescend. See RE-9.

rĕd'ĭngōte (-ngg-), n. Woman's long double-breasted outer coat with skirts sometimes cut away in front. [F, f. E *riding-coat*]

rĕdin'tĕgr|āte, v.t. Restore to wholeness or unity; renew or re-establish in united or perfect state. So ~A'TION n. [ME, f. L *red(integrare* INTEGRATE²), RE-9, -ATE³]

redirect etc., see RE-8; **rediscover** etc., RE-9; **redistribute** etc., **redivide** etc., **redo**, RE-8.

rĕd'ol|ent, a. Fragrant (now rare); having a strong smell, (fig.) strongly suggestive or reminiscent, *of*. Hence ~ENCE n. [ME, f. OF, or L *red(olēre* smell),· RE-6, -ENT]

rĕdou'bl|e (-dŭbl), v.t. & i., & n. **1.** Intensify, increase, make or grow greater or more intense or numerous, (~*e* one's *efforts; the clamour* ~*ed*). **2.** (bridge). Double again a bid already doubled by adversary; (n.) act or instance of ~ing. [f. F *re(doubler* DOUBLE³), RE-6]

rĕdoubt' (-owt), n. (fortif.). Outwork or fieldwork usu. square or polygonal & without flanking defences. [f. F *redoute* f. It. *ridotto* f. med. L *reductus* refuge f. p.p. of L REDUCE*re*; *-b-* after DOUBT (cf. foll.)]

rĕdoubt'able (-owt-), a. (Of opponent, warrior, controversialist, etc.) formidable. [ME, f. OF *redoutable* f. re(*douter* DOUBT²) fear, RE-6]

rědoubt′ěd ·(-owt-), a. (arch.). Dreaded, redoubtable. [f. obs. *redoubt* f. F as prec.]

rědound′, v.i. Contribute in the end, make great contribution, *to* one's advantage, credit, etc. (*this procedure will ~ to our advantage*; *the tale, fact, ~s to their credit*); come as final result *to*, come back or recoil *upon*, person (*the benefits that ~ to us from his self-sacrifice*). [ME also = *overflow*, f. OF *redonder* f. L *red*(*undare* f. *unda* wave), RE- 6]

rědrěss′, v.t., & n. **1.** Readjust, set straight again, (usu. *~ the balance*, restore equality); set right, remedy, make up for, get rid of, rectify, (distress, wrong, damage, grievance, abuse). **2.** n. Reparation for wrong, ~ing of grievances etc. [ME, f. OF *redrecier* (RE- 8, DRESS)]

rědūce′, v.t. & i. **1.** Restore to original or proper position, remedy by such restoration, (now only surg.; *had the shoulder, dislocation, ~d*); bring back *to* (*~ person to discipline*). **2.** Convert physically or mentally *to* other form, subject to such conversion, make suitable or conformable or adapted *to*, bring by classification or analysis *to*, (*~ rule to practice*, act on it; *observations taken at surface must be ~d to centre*; *~ anomalies to rule*, discover formula covering them; *the facts may all be ~d to three heads*; *~ it to English orthography & spell it* employee; *the unwritten customs were ~d to writing*; *~ dissimilar quantities to one denomination*, *integer to form of fraction*; *can we ~ these ripples to their mechanical elements?*; *~ clods to powder, ore to metal, ·compound to components, surface by harrowing*, or simply *~ clods, compound, etc.*; *~ syllogism of one form to another*). **3.** Compel *to* do (rare); bring by force or necessity *to* some state or action, subdue, bring back to obedience, (*~ the Crown to submission, the revolted towns, all the other Powers of the continent*; *~d him to assert* or usu. *asserting an absurdity*; *was ~d to despair, to weakness, to borrow* or usu. *borrowing clothes, to borrowing*). **4.** Bring down, lower, weaken, impoverish, diminish, contract, (*~ Pope to place of chief bishop*; *N.C.O. was ~d to the ranks*, made a private; *is in a very ~d state*, feeble; *~ liquid to two-thirds of its bulk*; *this ~s the temperature*; *the 16 may be ~d to 5*, by omission of 11, or by reclassification etc.; *have ~d our outfit to almost nothing*; *he ~d himself into the least possible compass*; *to be sold at ~d prices*; *~d circumstances*, poverty after prosperity; *~ the establishment*, dismiss officials or cut down expenses; *~d officers* etc., dismissed in such reduction). **5.** intr. Lessen one's weight. Hence **rědū′CER**[1] n., (esp. photog.) an agent for reducing the density of negatives, **rědū′CIBLE** a. [ME, f. L *re*(*ducere duct*- bring), RE- 9]

rědŭc′tiŏ ăd absŭrd′um (-shǐ-), n. Reduction to absurdity (see foll.). [L]

rědŭc′tion, n. Reducing or being REDUCEd; also: reduced copy of picture, map, etc.; *~ to absurdity*, proof of the falsity of a principle etc. given by producing a logical consequence of it that is absurd, (loosely) pushing of a principle to unpractical lengths. [ME, f. OF, or f. L *reductio* (REDUCE, -ION)]

rěduit (redwē′), n. (fortif.). Keep for garrison to retire to & hold when outworks are taken. [f. F *réduit* REDOUBT]

rědŭn′d|ant, a. Superfluous (freq. of workers in industry), excessive, pleonastic; copious, luxuriant, full. Hence or cogn. ~ANCE, ~ANCY, nn., ~antLY[2] adv. [f. L as REDOUND, -ANT]

rědŭp′lic|āte, v.t. Make double, repeat; (gram.) repeat (letter, syllable), form (tense) by reduplication. So ~ATIVE a. [f. LL *re*(*duplicare* DUPLICATE[2]), RE- 8, -ATE[3]]

rědŭplicā′tion, n. Doubling, repetition; counterpart; (gram.) repetition of syllable or letter in word-formation (esp. in perf. in Gk & L, as *tetigi* from *tango*), part so repeated. [f. LL *reduplicatio* (prec. -ATION)]

redye. See RE- 8.

ree. = REEVE[2].

reeb′ok, n. Small S.-African antelope with sharp horns. [Du., = roebuck]

rē-ĕch′ō (-k-), v.i. & t. Echo (t. & i.), echo (t. & i.) again & again, resound. [RE- 6]

reed, n., & v.t. **1.** (Tall straight stalk of) kinds of firm-stemmed water or marsh plant (*broken ~*, unreliable person or thing; *lean on a ~*, put trust in weak thing or person), whence ~′ED[2] a.; (collect.) ~s growing in a mass or used as material esp. for thatching, ‖ wheat-straw prepared for thatching. **2.** (poet.), Arrow; musical pipe of ~ or straw; pastoral poetry. **3.** Vibrating part, of various shape & material, inserted in some musical wind-instruments (esp. oboe, bassoon, clarinet, bagpipe, & some organ-pipes) to produce the sound; (usu. pl., cf. *strings, brass*) ~ instrument(s). **4.** Weaver's implement for separating warp-threads & beating up weft; (usu. pl.) set of semicylindrical adjacent mouldings like ~s laid together. **5.** ~*-babbler* or -*warbler* or -*wren*, ~-*bunting* or -*sparrow*, two kinds of bird; ‖~-*mace*, cat's-tail; ~-*pheasant*, bearded tit; ~-*pipe*, musical pipe of ~, also ~ed organ-pipe; ~-*stop*, organ-stop consisting of ~-pipes. **6.** v.t. Thatch with ~; make (straw) into ~; decorate with ~-moulding; fit (musical instrument or organ-pipe) with ~. [OE *hrēod*, OS *hriod*, OHG (*h*)*riot* f. Gmc **hreudham*]

rē-ĕd′ify, v.t. Rebuild (house etc.); build up again (hopes, wasted tissue, etc.). [RE- 8]

rē-ĕd′it etc. See RE- 8.

---

reed'ling, n. Bearded tit. [-LING¹]

reed'|lў, a. Abounding with reeds; made of reed (chiefly poet., as ~*y pipe, couch*); like a reed in weakness, slenderness, or (of grass etc.) thickness; (of voice) like reed--instrument in tone, scratchy, not round & clear. Hence ~ĭNESS n. [-Y²]

reef¹, n., & v.t. **1.** One of three or four strips across top of square & bottom of fore-&-aft sail that can be taken in or rolled up to reduce sail's surface (*take in a* ~, lit., & fig. proceed cautiously); ~*-knot,* consisting of two bights each enclosing the other's parallel laid shanks, ordinary double-knot made symmetrically for easy casting off (opp. GRANNY); ~*-point,* one of the short pieces of rope attached to a sail to secure it when ~ed. **2.** v.t. Take in ~ (s) of (sail; *single, double, treble,* ~*ed,* with 1, 2, 3, ~s taken in); shorten (topmast, bowsprit, also paddles of paddle-wheel by shifting them nearer centre). [ME *riff,* f. Du. *reef, rif,* f. ON *rif,* RIB, in same sense (cf. foll.)]

reef², n. Ridge of rock or shingle or sand at or just above or below surface of water; (gold-mining) lode of auriferous quartz, also the bedrock. [16th c. *riff(e)* f. MDu., MLG *rif, ref,* f. ON *rif* (as prec.)]

reef'er¹, n. One who reefs; (sl.) midshipman; REEF¹-knot; (also *reefing-jacket*) close double-breasted stout jacket. [REEF¹, -ER¹]

reef'er², n. See MARIJUANA. [orig. unkn.]

reek¹, n. Smoke (Sc. & literary); vapour, visible exhalation, (chiefly Sc. & lit.); foul or stale odour (the ~ *of tobacco*), fetid atmosphere (*amid* ~ & *squalor*). Hence ~'Y² a. (chiefly Sc. & literary; *Auld Reek'ie,* Edinburgh). [OE *rēc,* OS *rōk,* OHG *rouh,* ON *reykr* f. Gmc *°raukiz*]

reek², v.i. Emit smoke (chiefly of houses after conflagration or object that has been burning in open air); emit vapour, steam, (of hot drink or food, sweating person etc., or shed blood or thing smeared with it); smell unpleasantly (usu. *of*; ~s *of patchouli, tobacco, blood,* or fig. *of murder, affectation,* etc.). [OE *rēocan,* OHG *riohhan,* ON *rjúka,* f. Gmc *°riukan* cogn. w. prec.]

reel¹, n., & v.t. & i. **1.** Kinds of rotatory apparatus on which thread, silk, yarn, paper, wire, etc., are wound at some stage of manufacture; contrivance for winding up & unwinding line as required, esp. in fishing (*off the* ~, fig., straight off, without hitch or pause, in rapid succession); ‖ small cylinder on which sewing-cotton etc. are wound for convenience; revolving part in various machines; (cinemat.) quantity of positive film rolled on one ~ (often as rough unit of length, about 1,000 ft, complete films being termed *two-, three-, four-,* etc., ~*ers*). **2.** vb. Wind (thread, fishing-line, etc.) on ~; take (cocoon silk etc.) *off,* draw (fish, logline, etc.) *in* or *up,* by use of ~; rattle

(story, list, verses) *off* without pause or apparent effort; (of grasshopper etc.) make clicking noise like ~ in motion. [OE *hrēol,* not in cogn. langg.]

reel², v.i., & n. **1.** (Of eyes, mind, head) be in a whirl, be dizzy, swim; sway, stagger, stand or walk or run unsteadily, be shaken physically or mentally, rock from side to side, swing violently, (*his mind, the front rank, the ship, the tower,* ~*ed under the shock;* ~ *to & fro like a drunken man; went* ~*ing down the street; the State was* ~*ing to its foundations*); seem to shake (*the mountains* ~ *before his eyes*); hence ~'ingLY² adv. **2.** n. ~ing motion lit. or fig. (*without a* ~ *or a stagger; the* ~ *of vice & folly around us*). [ME (chiefly north. & Sc.), f. prec.]

reel³, n., & v.i. **1.** Lively esp. Scottish dance, usu. of two couples in line & describing circular figures. **2.** v.i. Dance ~. [f. REEL² n.]

re-elect etc., **re-embark** etc., **re-emerge** etc. See RE- 9.

reen, n. = RHINE¹.

re-enable, re-enact etc., see RE- 9; **re--engine,** RE- 8; **re-enter** etc., RE- 9.

rē-ĕn'trant, a. & n. (Angle) that points inward (opp. SALIENT; esp. in fortification). [RE- 9, ENTRANT]

rē-ĕn'trў, n. Act of entering again, esp. (of space vehicle, missile, etc.) of re--entering earth's atmosphere; (law) a retaking possession; *card of* ~ (whist & bridge), high card that can be relied on to give holder the lead by winning a trick. [RE- 9, ENTRY]

re-establish etc. See RE- 9.

reeve¹, n. (Hist.) chief magistrate of town or district; (Canada) president of village or town council. [OE *gerēfa,* orig. unkn.]

reeve², ree, n. Female of RUFF².

reeve³, v.t. (naut.; past & p.p. *rōve* or ~*d*). Thread (rope, rod, etc.) *through* ring or other aperture; pass rope through (a block etc.); fasten (rope, block, or other object) *in, on, round, to,* something by reeving; (of ship) thread (shoals, ice--pack). [f. Du. *reeven* to reef]

re-examine etc., see RE- 8; **re-exist, re--export** etc., RE- 9; **reface, refashion** etc., RE- 8.

rĕf, n. (colloq.). Football referee. [abbr.]

rĕfĕc'tion, n. Refreshment by food or drink (*milk & eggs were offered for our* ~); slight meal, repast. [ME, f. OF f. L *refectionem* f. *reficere* (foll.), RE- 8]

rĕfĕc'torў (*or in monastic use* rĕf'I-), n. Room used for meals in monasteries etc. [(in ME *fraitur* FRATER) f. LL *refectorium* f. L *re(ficere -fect-* = *facere* make) refresh, RE- 8, -ORY]

refer', v.t. & i. (-rr-). **1.** Trace or ascribe *to* person or thing as cause or source, assign *to* certain date or place or class, (~ one's *victories to Providence, miraculous tales to ignorance, ill temper to indigestion, the lake-dwellings to the sixth century, the* *origins of sculpture to Egypt, barnacles to the molluscs*), whence **rĕf′er**ABLE a. **2.** Commit, hand over, (one*self*, question for decision) *to* person etc. (*I ~ myself to your generosity*; *let us ~ the dispute to Socrates*; *~ to drawer*, abbr. R.D., banker's note suspending payment etc. of cheque). **3.** Send on or direct (person), make appeal or have recourse, *to* some authority or source of information, (abs.) cite authority or passage, (*for my proof I ~ to the facts of human nature, to 1 Kings iii. 7*; *~red to his watch for the exact time*). **4.** (Of statement etc.) have relation, be directed, (of hearer etc.) interpret (statement etc.) as directed, *to* (*these remarks ~ only to deliberate, are not to be ~red to involuntary, offences*). **5.** (Of person speaking etc.) make allusion, direct attention, *to* (*he several times ~red to the modern increase in expenditure*; *found myself on the peak ~red to*). [ME, f. OF *referer* or L *re(ferre latum* bring), RE- 9]

rĕferee′, n., & v.i. & t. **1.** Arbitrator, person to whom dispute is to be or is referred for decision; *Official R~*, attached to Supreme Court, to whom questions arising in an action may be referred for enquiry and report or for trial where parties consent; umpire esp. in football. **2.** vb. Act as ~ (for) esp. in football. [-EE]

rĕf′erence, n., & v.t. **1.** Referring of matter for decision or settlement or consideration to some authority, scope given to such authority, (*the peerage was allowed without ~ to the House of Lords*; *the ~ is very wide, strictly limited*; *the Commission must confine itself to, that is a question outside, the terms of ~*). **2.** Relation, respect, correspondence, *to* (*the parts of a machine all have ~ to each other*; *success seems to have little ~ to merit*; *in, with, ~ to*, regarding, as regards, about; *without ~ to*, irrespective of). **3.** Allusion *to* (~, *a* or *no ~*, *several ~s*, *to a previous conversation was or were made*). **4.** Direction more or less precise to (page etc. of) book etc. where information may be found (*loads his pages with, does not give, ~s*; *cross ~*, to another passage in same book; *~ bible*, with marginal cross ~s; || *legislation by ~*, use in bill-drafting of ~s to previous statutes instead of restatement); mark used to refer reader of text to note or to part of diagram (usual ~ marks; asterisk *, obelisk †, double obelisk ‡, section §, parallel ||, paragraph ¶). **5.** Act of looking up passage etc., or of referring another or applying to person, for information (~ or *a ~ to the dictionary would have enlightened him*; *please give me a ~*, *I should like to make ~*, *to your last employer*; *book of ~*, to be used not for continuous reading but to consult on occasion; *~ library*, where books may be consulted without being taken away, opp.

lending library); person named by one applying for post or offering goods etc. as willing to vouch for him or them (*who are your ~s?*; (loosely) testimonial; hence **rĕferĕn′tɪAL** (-shl) a. **6.** v.t. Provide (book) with ~s to authorities. [-ENCE]

|| **rĕferĕn′darȳ**, n. (rare). Referee; assessor to commission; reporting or revising official. [f. LL *referendarius* (foll., -ARY[1])]

rĕferĕn′dum, n. Referring of certain political questions or of such questions under certain circumstances to the electorate for direct decision by a general vote on the single question. [L (REFERfre)]

refill. See RE- 9.

rĕfīn|e′, v.t. & i. Free from dross or impurities or defects, purify, clarify; make elegant or cultured, imbue with delicacy of taste, polish manners or appearance of; become pure or clear or improved in polish or delicacy; employ subtlety of thought or language, make fine distinctions, discourse subtly (*up*)*on*; improve (*up*)*on* by refinements. Hence ~**′ĕdLY**[2] adv. [RE- 6, FINE[2] v., partly after F *raffiner*]

rĕfīne′ment (-nm-), n. Refining or being refined; fineness of feeling or taste, polished manners etc.; subtle or ingenious manifestation *of*, piece of elaborate arrangement, (*all the ~s of luxury*; *a ~ beyond their skill*); piece of subtle reasoning, fine distinction. [-MENT, after F *raffinement*]

rĕfīn′|er, n. In vbl senses; esp., person whose business is to refine crude oil, metal, sugar, etc., whence ~**ERY**(3) n. [-ER[1]]

refit etc. See RE- 8.

rĕflā′tion, n. Inflation of currency after a deflation, undertaken to restore the system to its previous condition. [f. RE-[9], after INFLATION, DEFLATION]

rĕflĕct′, v.t. & i. **1.** Fold back (rare; *~ the corner of the paper*). **2.** (Of surface or body) throw (heat, light, sound, rarely ball etc.) back, cause to rebound, (*shine with ~ed light*, not one's own, borrowed). **3.** (Of mirror etc., or transf.) show image of, reproduce to eye or mind, exactly correspond in appearance or effect to, (*laws ~ the average moral attitude of a half century earlier*). **4.** (Of action, result, etc.) bring back or cause to redound (credit, discredit, etc.), (abs.) bring discredit, (*up*)*on* person or method responsible. **5.** Go back in thought, meditate, or consult with oneself (*on, upon*, or abs.), remind oneself or consider (*that, how, etc.*), whence ~**ingLY**[2] adv. **6.** Make disparaging remarks *upon*. [ME, f. OF *reflecter* or L *re(flectere flex-* bend), RE- 9]

rĕflĕc′tion, -ĕ′xion (-kshn), n. (-x- etym. correct but now rare exc. in scientific use). **1.** REFLECTING or being reflected (*angle of ~*, made by reflected ray with perpendicular to surface); reflected light, heat, colour, or image. **2.** Reflex action. **3.** (Piece of) censure (usu. *on* or *upon*); thing bringing discredit (*up*) *on*. **4.** Reconsideration (*on ∼, I .doubt whether I was right*). **5.** Mental faculty dealing with products of sensation & perception. **6.** Idea arising in the mind, mental or verbal comment, apophthegm, (often *on* or *upon*). Hence ∼AL, ∼LESS, aa., (-sho-). [ME f. OF, or f. LL *reflexio* (prec., -ION) w. assim. to *reflect*]

reflec′tive, a. **1.** (Of surface etc.) giving back reflection or image; (of light etc.) reflected (rare). **2.** (gram.). Reflexive (now rare). **3.** (Of action) reflex, reciprocal, (now rare). **4.** (Of mental faculties) concerned in reflection or thought; (of person, mood, etc.) thoughtful, given to meditation. Hence ∼LY[2] adv., ∼NESS n. [REFLECT, -IVE]

reflec′tor, n. **1.** Body or surface reflecting rays, esp. piece of glass or metal usu. concave for reflecting in required direction; (telescope etc. provided with) apparatus for reflecting images. **2.** Person, book, etc., that gives or affords conscious or unconscious representation *of* prejudices, habits, etc. [-OR]

reflet′ (-lĕ), n. Lustre, iridescence, esp. on pottery. [F]

ref′lex[1], n. **1.** Reflected light or colour or glory (*the fame of Greece was a ∼ from the glory of Athens*); (paint.) part of picture represented as affected by the light or colour of another part. **2.** Image or reflection in mirror etc. **3.** Reproduction, secondary manifestation, correspondent result, (*legislation should be a ∼ of public opinion; lamb & mint sauce is a popular ∼ of the passover with bitter herbs*). **4.** A reflex action (*doctor tested patient's ∼es*); CONDITIONED ∼. [f. L *reflexus -ūs* (REFLECT)]

ref′lex[2], a. **1.** (rare). Recurved; (of light etc.) reflected. **2.** (Of thought etc.) introspective, directed back upon itself or its own operations; (of effect or influence) reactive, coming back upon its author or source. **3.** (physiol.). ∼ *action*, independent of the will, excited as involuntary response to nerve-stimulation. **4.** (gram.). Reflexive (now rare). **5.** ∼ (*camera*), a hand camera in which, by means of a pivoted surface-silvered mirror, the reflected image can be seen and focused up to the moment of exposure. Hence ∼LY[2] adv. [f. L *reflexus* p.p. (REFLECT)]

reflexed′ (-kst), a. (bot.). Recurved. [f. obs. *reflex* vb = REFLECT]

reflex′|ible, a. Capable of being reflected. Hence ∼IBIL′ITY n. [as prec., -IBLE]

reflexion. See REFLECTION.

reflex′ive, a. & n. (gram.). (Word, form) implying agent's action upon himself; (verb) indicating identity of subject & object; (pers. pronoun or poss. adjective) referring to subject. Hence ∼LY[2] adv. [f. mod. L *reflexivus* (as REFLECT, -IVE)]

refloat. See RE- 9.

ref′luent (-ŏŏ-), a. Flowing back (∼ *tide, blood*). Hence **ref′luence** (-ŏŏ-) n. [f. L *re(fluere* flow), RE- 9, see -ENT]

reflux, see RE- 9; **refoot,** RE- 8; **reforest** etc., RE- 9.

reform′[1], v.t. & i. Make (person, institution, procedure, conduct, one*self*) or (of person or body of persons) become better by removal or abandonment of imperfections, faults, or errors (∼*ed churches*, see REFORMATION[2]); abolish, cure, (abuse, malpractice). Hence ∼ABLE a. [ME, f. OF *reformer* or L *re(formare* FORM[2]), RE- 8]

reform′[2], n. Removal of abuse(s) esp. in politics (*R∼ Bill, Act*, esp. those of 1831–2 amending parliamentary representation); improvement made or suggested. [f. prec. or F *réforme*]

reform′[3], v.t. & i. Form again. So **reforma′tion**[1] n. [RE- 8]

reforma′tion[2], n. Reforming or being reformed, esp. radical change for the better in political, religious, or social affairs; *the R∼*, 16th-c. movement for reform of abuses in Roman Church ending in establishment of Reformed or Protestant Churches, whence ∼AL (-sho-) a. [ME, f. OF or L *reformatio* (REFORM[1], -ATION)]

reform′ative a., **reform′atory** a. & n. **1.** Tending or intended to produce reform. **2.** n. Institution to which juvenile offenders are sent for ∼ purposes, approved school. [REFORM[1], -ATIVE, -ORY]

reform′er, n. In vbl senses; esp.: leader in the 16th-c. REFORMATION[2]; advocate of the REFORM[2] bill. [-ER[1]]

refract′, v.t. (Of water, air, glass, etc.) deflect (light) at certain angle when it enters obliquely from another medium of different density (∼*ing telescope*, with object--glass converging rays to focus). Hence or cogn. **refrac′tion** n., **refrac′tional** (-sho-), **refrac′tive**, aa. [f. L *re(fringere -fract- = frangere* break), RE- 5]

refrac′tor, n. Refracting medium or lens or telescope. [-OR]

refrac′tory, a. & n. **1.** Stubborn, unmanageable, rebellious; (of wound, disease, etc.) not yielding to treatment; (of substances) hard to fuse or work. **2.** n. Substance specially resistant to heat, corrosion, etc. Hence ∼ILY[2] adv., ∼INESS n. [alt. of obs. *-ary* (after -ORY), f. L *refractarius* (REFRACT, -ARY[1])]

refrain′[1], n. Recurring phrase or line esp. at end of stanzas. [ME, f. OF, ult. f. Rom. **refrangere* = *refringere* REFRACT]

refrain′[2], v.t. & i. Put restraint upon, curb, (oneself, one's tears, soul, etc.; arch.); abstain from doing something, abstain *from* act or do*ing*. [ME, f. OF *refrener* f. L *re(frenare* f. *frenum* bridle), RE- 9]

refran′g|ible (-j-), a. That can be refracted. Hence ∼IBIL′ITY n. [RE- 5, L *frangere*, -IBLE; cf. FRANGIBLE]

refresh′, v.t. & i. Make cool again (rare); reanimate, reinvigorate, (of food, drink, rest, amusement, etc., or person providing these esp. in ~ one*self*; ~*ing innocence* etc., interesting to blasé observer); freshen up (memory); restore (fire, electric battery, etc.) with fresh supply; take esp. liquid refreshment. Hence ~ing-LY² adv. [ME, f. OF *refreschier*, see FRESH, RE- 9]

refresh′er, n. In vbl senses; esp.: extra fee to counsel in prolonged case; (colloq.) a drink; attrib., as ~ *course* (of instruction in modern methods etc.). [-ER¹]

refresh′ment, n. Refreshing or being refreshed in mind or body; thing, esp. (usu. in pl.) drink or food, that refreshes (*the sight was a ~ to him*; *take some ~* or ~*s*; ~ *room* at railway station or *car* on train); *R~ Sunday*, 4th in Lent with gospel f. *John* vi. [ME, f. OF *refreschement* (RE-FRESH, -MENT)] |

refri′ger|āte, v.t. & i. **1.** Make, rarely become, cool or cold. **2.** Expose (provisions) to extreme cold in order to freeze or preserve, whence ~ātor n. Hence or cogn. ~ant(2) a. & n., ~a′tion n. [f. L *re(frigerare* f. *frigus -oris* cold), RE- 9, -ATE³]

refri′geratory̆, n. & a. **1.** Cold-water vessel attached to still for condensing vapour; refrigerator. **2.** adj. Refrigerant. [f. L *refrigeratorius* (prec., -ORY)]

reft. See REAVE.

ref′ūge, n., & v.t. & i. **1.** (Place of) shelter from pursuit or danger or trouble (*seek ~*; *has found a ~*; *take ~ in a cave, in lying*; *city of ~*, see Josh. xx; *house of ~*, institution for the homeless etc.); person, thing, course, that gives shelter or is resorted to in difficulties (*he is the ~ of the distressed*; *books are the ~ of the destitute*); raised piece in middle of busy road for crossers to halt on. **2.** vb (rare). Give ~ to; take ~. [ME, f. OF f. L *re(fugium* f. *fugere* flee), RE- 4]

refūgee′, n. Person escaped to foreign country from religious or political persecution. [f. F *réfugié* p.p. of *réfugier* (prec.)]

reful′g|ent, a. Shining, gloriously bright. Hence or cogn. ~ence n., ~ently² adv. [f. L *re(fulgēre* shine), RE- 6, -ENT]

refūnd′, v.t. & i., & n. **1.** Pay back (money received or taken, expenses incurred by another); reimburse; make repayment; hence ~ment n. **2.** n. (rē′fŭnd). ~ment. [ME sense *pour back*, f. OF *refunder* or L *re(fundere fus-* pour), RE- 9]

refurbish, see RE- 9; **refurnish**, RE- 8.

refūs′al (-z-), n. In vbl senses (*will take no ~*, is importunate); also, right or privilege of deciding to take or leave a thing before it is offered to others (*have, stipulate for, give* person, *the ~ of*). [-AL(2)]

refūs|e′¹ (-z), v.t. & i. **1.** Say or convey by action that one will not accept or submit

to or give or grant or gratify or consent (~*e offer, gift, chance, office, candidate*, person as husband, etc.; *horse ~es fence* etc., or abs., will not jump, whence ~′ER¹ (-z-) n.; ~*e orders, control*, etc.; ~*e obedience, compliance*; ~*ed me satisfaction, tribute to suzerain, my request*; ~*e* one, not grant his request; *have never been* ~*ed*, had request rejected; ~*e to* do). **2.** Make refusal; (cards) not follow suit. Hence ~ABLE (-z-) a. [ME, f. OF *refuser* f. Rom. **refusare* f. L *refundere*, see REFUND]

ref′ūse², a. & n. (What is) rejected as worthless or left over after use. [ME, app. OF *refuse* p.p. as prec.]

re-fūse′³ (-z), v.t. Fuse again. [RE- 9]

refūt|e′, v.t. Prove falsity or error of (statement, opinion, argument, person advancing it), rebut or repel by argument. Hence or cogn. **ref′ūtABLE** a., ~′AL(2), refūta′TION, nn. [f. L *re(futare* see CONFUTE), RE- 9]

regain′, v.t. Recover possession of (esp. ~ *consciousness*); reach (place) again; recover (one's *feet* or *footing* or *legs*). [f. F *re(gagner* GAIN²), RE- 9]

reg′al, a. Of or by kings (~ *government, title, office*); fit for a king, magnificent, (*lives in ~ splendour*). Hence ~LY² adv. [ME, f. OF *regal* or L *regalis* (*rex regis* king, -AL)]

regāle′¹, n. Choice repast lit. or fig., feast of some dainty; a dainty (rare); choice flavour (rare; *viands of higher ~*). [f. obs. F *régale* (mod. -al) f. OF *gale* pleasure]

regāle′², v.t. & i. **1.** Entertain choicely (often iron.) with food or *with* talk etc.; (of beauty, flowers, etc.) give delight to; feed oneself choicely (usu. *on*). Hence ~MENT (-lm-) n. [f. F *régaler* (prec.)]

regāl′ia¹ (-lya), n. pl. Royal privileges (now rare); insignia of royalty used at coronations; insignia of an order, e.g. of Freemasons. [med. L, f. L, neut. pl. of REGALis]

regāl′ia² (-lya), n. Large cigar of good quality. [f. Sp. *regalia* royal privilege]

reg′alism, n. Doctrine of sovereign's ecclesiastical supremacy. [-ISM]

regāl′ity̆, n. Attribute of kingly power, being king, (*things that touch his ~*); monarchical State, kingdom, (rare); royal privilege. [ME, f. AF, OF *regalite* or med. L *regalitas* (REGAL, -ITY)]

regārd′¹, v.t. & i. **1.** Gaze upon (usu. with adv. phr. or adv.; *found him ~ing me with curiosity, intently*). **2.** Give heed to, take into account, let one's course be affected by, (esp. in neg. context; *fears not God nor ~s man*; *does not ~ my advice*); give heed, pay attention, take notice.. **3.** Look upon or contemplate mentally *with* reverence, horror, etc., or with adv. specified sentiment (*I still ~ him kindly*). **4.** Consider (usu. *as* with compl., also *in*

For pronunciation & hyphening of *re-* see RE-; for words in *re-* not given see RE- 8, 9.

the light of, under an aspect, etc., also vulg. with compl. & without *as*=consider; *is to be ~ed as a wild beast*; ~ *it as madness or indispensable, him as among my friends*). **5.** (Of things) concern, have relation to, (*does not ~ me* etc., has nothing to do with; esp. *as ~s*, or *~ing* as part. or prep., = about, touching; *as ~s wheat, prices are rising*; *considerations ~ing peace*; *am innocent ~ing the former*). [ME, f. F re(*garder* GUARD²), RE- 6, cf. REWARD]

rĕgărd´², n. **1.** Gaze, steady or significant look. **2.** Respect, point attended to, (*in this* etc. ~; esp. *in ~ to* or *of, with ~ to, regarding,* as touching, about; *in* one's ~, concerning or about or towards him). **3.** Attention, heed, care, (*lo, for*; *~ must be had or paid to general principles*; *the next object of ~ is his conduct*; *act without ~ to or for decency*; *pays no ~ to expostulations or adviser*), whence ~FUL a. (*of*), ~LESS a. & adv. (*of*; also sl. as ellipt. adv. = ~less of expense, as *got up ~less,* expensively dressed*), ~fulLY² (rare), ~lÉss-LY², advv., ~fulNESS (rare), ~lÉssNESS, nn. **4.** Esteem, kindly feeling or respectful opinion, (*for*; *have little, a great, ~ for him, no, a high, ~ for his judgement or advice*); (pl.) expression of friendliness in letter etc., compliments, (*kind ~s to you all*; *give him my ~s* or *best* etc. *~s*). [ME & OF *regard* f. *regarder* (prec.)]

rĕgărd´ant, a. (Her.) looking backward; observant, with steady or intent gaze. [AF & OF (REGARD¹, -ANT)]

rĕgătt´a, n. Meeting for boat or yacht races. [It. (Venetian)]

rĕgĕl|āte´, v.i. (Of fragments of ice, heaped snow, etc.) be fused by temporary thawing of surfaces into frozen mass. Hence ~A´TION n. [RE- 9, L *gelare* freeze, -ATE³]

rĕ´gency, n. Rule, control, (rare); office of regent; commission acting as regent; regent's or regency-commission's period of office (*the R~* in Eng. Hist., 1810–20). [ME, f. LL *regentia,* or REGENT +-ENCY]

rĕgĕn´er|āte, v.t. & i. Invest with new & higher spiritual nature; improve moral condition of, breathe new & more vigorous & higher life into, (person, institution, etc.); generate again, bring or come into renewed existence, (*must ~ate his self-respect*; *polypus ~ates after extraction*); reform oneself. Hence or cogn. ~ATE² (-*at*), ~ATIVE, aa., ~A´TION n. [f. L *re*(*generare* GENERATE), RE- 8]

rĕgĕn´erātor, n. In vbl senses; also, fuel-saving fire-brick device in furnaces. [-OR]

regenesis. See RE- 8.

rĕ´gent, n. & a. **1.** Ruler, ruling principle, (rare); person appointed to administer kingdom during minority, absence, or incapacity of monarch; ‖ (Oxford and Cambridge Univ.) Master of Arts who presided over disputations in the Schools (hist.); *member of the governing body of a State University. **2.** adj. (following n.). Acting as ~ (*Queen, Prince,* etc., *R~*).

[ME, f. OF *regent* or L *regere* rule, -ENT; n.f.adj.]

regerminate etc. See RE- 9.

rĕ´gĭcĭde, n. Killer or participator in killing of a king (*the ~s,* those concerned in trying & executing Charles I); king-killing. Hence **rĕgĭcid´AL** a. [L *rex regis* king, -CIDE]

régie (räzhē´), n. State monopoly or control of tobacco, salt, etc. [F]

regild. See RE- 9.

régime, regime (räzhēm´), n. Method of government, prevailing system of things, (*ancien régime,* see Ap., system of government in France before the revolution, also transf. any now abolished or past method); *under the ~ of purchase, privilege, protection, competition, Tory ascendancy,* etc. [F (*ré-*) f. L REGIMEN]

rĕ´gimen, n. Rule, system of government, régime, (now rare); (med.) prescribed course of exercise, way of life, & esp. diet; (gram.) relation of syntactic dependence between words, government. [L (*regere* rule, -MEN)]

rĕ´giment (or -jm-), n., & v.t. **1.** Rule, government, (now rare). **2.** Permanent recruiting & training unit of army usu. commanded by (Lieut.-)Colonel & divided into several companies or troops or batteries & often into two, or in wartime into many, battalions; operational unit of artillery, tanks, armoured cars, etc.; *Royal R~* (*of Artillery*), Royal Artillery; (often pl.) large array or number, legion, (usu. *of*). **3.** v.t. Form (men) into ~ or ~s; organize (workers, labour) in groups or according to a system, whence **rĕgĭmĕntA´TION** n. [ME, f. OF f. LL *regimentum* (prec., -MENT)]

rĕgimĕn´tal, a. & n. **1.** Of a regiment; hence ~LY² adv. **2.** n. pl. Dress worn by regiment, military uniform. [-AL]

Rĕgĭn´a, n. (abbr. *R*.) Reigning queen (in signatures to proclamations, as *V.R.,* Victoria ~, titles of crown law-suits, as ~ *v. Jones,* ~ versus Jones, etc.). [L (*rex regis* king, -INA¹)]

rĕgĭn´al, a. (rare). Queenly, of or befitting a queen. [f. med. L *reginalis* (prec., -AL)]

rĕ´gion (-jn), n. Tract of country, space, place, or more or less definitely marked boundaries or characteristics (*a desert, fertile, ~*; *the ~ between the Elbe & the Rhine*; *earth is divided into ~s characterized by different fauna & flora*); separate part of world or universe (often pl.; *lower ~s,* hell, realm of the dead; *upper ~s,* sky, heaven; *the ~ beyond the grave*); sphere or realm of (*you are getting into the ~ of metaphysics*; *upper, middle, lower,* layer of atmosphere or sea; part of the body round or near some organ etc. (the *lumbar, abdominal,* etc., ~; *the ~ of the eyes*). Hence ~AL (-jo-) a. [ME, f. OF *region* f. L *regionem* nom. *-o* direction (*regere* direct, -ION)]

re̅′gister¹, n. **1.** Book in which entries are made of details to be recorded for reference; official or authoritative list kept e.g. of births, marriages, & burials or deaths, of shipping, of qualified voters in constituency (~ *office*, or in mod. use ~, a registry). **2.** Slider in organ controlling set of pipes; compass of voice or instrument, part of voice-compass (*head*, *chest*, *throat*, *upper*, *middle*, *lower*, ~). **3.** Adjustable plate for widening or narrowing an opening & regulating draught esp. in fire-grate; recording indicator of speed, force, etc. **4.** (Print.) exact correspondence of printed matter on two sides of leaf (*in* ~, so corresponding); (photog.) correspondence of focusing screen with plate or film. [ME & OF *regestre*, *-istre*, or f. med. L *regestrum*, *-istrum* for *regestum* (LL *regesta* things recorded f. RE- 8, L *gerere* carry)]

re̅′gister², v.t. & i. **1.** Set down (name, fact, etc.) formally, record in writing; (fig.) make mental note of. **2.** Enter or cause to be entered in particular register (~ *letter*, entrust to post-office with special precautions for safety; ‖ ~ *luggage*, on railway etc.; ~ one*self* or abs., put one's name on electoral register). **3.** (Of instrument) record automatically, indicate; (cinemat.) express facially or by gesture (emotion). **4.** (print. etc.). Correspond, make correspond, exactly. Hence or cogn. **re̅′gistrABLE** a., **re̅gistra′TION** n. [ME, f. OF *registrer*, or f. med. L *registrare* (prec.)]

re̅′gistrar, n. Official recorder, person charged with keeping register. Hence ~SHIP n. [prec., -AR²]

re̅′gistrary̆, n. Registrar of Cambridge University. [f. med. L *registrarius* (REGISTER¹, -ARY¹)]

re̅′gistry̆, n. Registration; place, office, where registers are kept; *married at a* ~ or ~ *office* or *register office*, i.e. without religious ceremony; *servants'* ~ (*office*), shop etc. where lists of vacant situations & servants seeking them are kept; register (rare). [REGISTER¹, -RY]

‖ **Re̅′gius**, a. ~ *professor* of Greek etc., holder of chair at Oxf. or Camb. instituted by Henry VIII, (or, in Scotland, by the Crown), or of later one placed on same footing. [L, = royal (*rex regis* king)]

re̅g′nal, a. Of a reign (~ *year*, beginning with king's accession or an anniversary of it; ~ *day*, anniversary of accession). [f. med. L *regnalis* (REIGN, -AL)]

re̅g′nant, a. Reigning (*Queen R*~, ruling in her own right & not as consort); (of things, qualities, opinions, etc.) predominant, prevalent. [f. L *regnare* REIGN², -ANT]

re̅gŏrge′, v.t. & i. Bring or cast up again, vomit, disgorge; gush or flow back from pit, channel, etc.; swallow again. [f. F *regorger*, or RE- 9 + GORGE²]

re̅grāt|e′, v.t. (hist.). Buy up (goods, esp. victuals) with view to retailing at a profit (a practice formerly prohibited). Hence ~′ER¹, ~′OR, nn. [ME, f. OF *regrater* (now *regratter*) of obsc. orig.]

re̅g′re̅ss¹, n. Going back; declension, backward tendency. [ME, f. L *regressus* (foll.)]

re̅gre̅ss′², v.i. Move backwards (chiefly astron.). [f. L *re*(*gredi*=*gradi* gress- step), RE- 9]

re̅gre̅′ssion (-shn), n. Backward movement, retreat; return of curve; relapse, reversion. So **re̅gre̅ss′IVE** a., **re̅gre̅s-s′IVELY²** adv., **re̅gre̅ss′IVENESS** n. [f. L *-io* (prec., -ION)]

re̅gre̅t′, v.t. (-tt-), & n. **1.** Be sorry for loss of, wish one could have again; be distressed about or sorry for (event, fact), grieve at, repent (action etc.); be sorry *to* say etc. or *that* (esp. in polite refusal of invitation etc.); hence ~t′ABLE a., ~t′ABLY² adv. **2.** n. Sorrow for loss of person or thing (often *for*); repentance or annoyance concerning thing (left un)done (*has no* ~*s*; *express* ~ *for*, esp. make apology or ask pardon for); vexation or disappointment caused by occurrence or situation (*hear with* ~ *of* or *that*; *refuse with much* ~ or *many* ~*s*); hence (of person or feeling) ~FUL a., ~fulLY² adv. [(1) ME, f. OF *regreter*, perh. f. ON *grāta* GREET²; (2) 16th c., f. F *regret*, f. (1)]

re̅group. See RE- 8.

re̅g′ulable, a. Admitting of regulation. [f. med. L *regulabilis* (REGULATE, -ABLE)]

re̅g′ular, a. & n. **1.** (eccl.). Bound by religious rule, belonging to religious or monastic order, (cf. SECULAR; *the* ~ *clergy* in R.-C. countries, monks as opp. parish priests etc.). **2.** (Of shape, structure, arrangement, or objects in these respects) following or exhibiting a principle, harmonious, consistent, systematic, symmetrical, (~ *nomenclature*, *formation*, *features*, *curve*, *figure*, *flower*; *the five* ~ *solids*, tetrahedron or triangular pyramid bounded by 4 equal triangles, hexahedron or cube by 6 equal squares, octahedron by 8 equal triangles, dodecahedron by 12 equal pentagons, & icosahedron by 20 equal triangles). **3.** Acting, done, recurring, uniformly or calculably in time or manner, habitual, constant, not capricious or casual, orderly, (~ *working*, *steps*, *procedure*, *sequence*, *pulse*, *bowels*, *salary*, *orbit*, *bedtime*, *employ*; *keep* ~ *hours*, do same thing at same time daily; *a* ~ *life*, lived in orderly manner, esp. without excesses; ~ *people*, living ~ *lives*; also vulg. as adv., as *comes*, *happens*, ~). **4.** Conforming to a standard of etiquette etc., not transgressing conventions, in order, (*had no* ~ *introduction*; *the attitude of the Foreign Office has been quite* ~).

5. (gram.). (Of verbs, nouns, etc.) following a normal type of inflection. **6.** Properly constituted or qualified, not defective or amateur, devoted exclusively or primarily to its nominal function, (*cooks as well as a ~ cook; has no ~ profession; ~ soldiers,* opp. volunteers or militia or temporary levies; *~ army,* of *~* soldiers); (colloq.) complete, thorough, indubitable, (*is a ~ rascal, brick, hero; a ~ royal queen; had a ~ smash, overhauling,* etc.; also vulg. as adv., as *is ~ angry*); hence **rĕg̅u̅lă′**RITY n., **~**IZE(3) v.t., **~**I̅ZA̅**-**TION n., **~**LY[2] adv. **7.** n. One of the *~* clergy; *~* soldier; (colloq.) *~* customer, visitor, etc.; (colloq.) person permanently employed. [ME & OF *reguler* f. L *regularis* (*regula* rule); later dir. f. L; see -AR[1]]

rĕg̅′u̅l|āte, v.t. Control by rule, subject to restrictions, moderate, adapt to requirements; adjust (machine, clock) so that it may work accurately. Hence **~ā̅t**OR n., **~**ATIVE a. [f. LL *regulare* (*regula* rule, f. *regere* direct), -ATE[3]]

rĕg̅u̅lā̅′tion, n. Regulating or being regulated; prescribed rule, authoritative direction; (attrib.) fulfilling what is laid down by **~**s, of correct pattern etc., ordinary, usual, formal, (*of the ~ size; exceed the ~ speed; a ~ sword, cap; the ~ mourning*). [prec., -ATION]

rĕg̅′u̅l|us, n. (pl.**~**i̅). **1.** (*R~us*) bright star in Leo. **2.** (chem.). Purer or metallic part of mineral separated by sinking to bottom in crucible, impure metallic product of smelting various ores, whence **~**INE[1] a. **3.** Golden-crested wren. [L, dim. of *rex regis* king; sense 2 orig. of metallic form of antimony, perh. as title of honour due to its readiness to combine with gold]

rĕg̅u̅r′git|āte, v.i. & t. Gush back; (of stomach or crop or receptacle) pour or cast up again. Hence **~**A′TION n. [f. med. L *re*(*gurgitare* f. L *gurges -itis* whirlpool), RE- 9, -ATE[3]]

rehabilitate. [f. med. L *rehabilitare* (RE- 9, HABILITATE)]; **rehandle, rehang, rehash, rehear,** etc., RE- 8.

rehears′al (-hĕr-), n. Rehearsing; preparatory performance of play or other entertainment (*dress ~,* such *~* in costume, i.e. when practice is far advanced). [-AL (2)]

rehearse′ (-hĕrs), v.t. Recite, say over, repeat from beginning to end, give list of, recount, enumerate; have rehearsal of (play etc. or part in it), practise for later public performance. [ME, f. OF *rehercer,* app. f. RE- 8, *herser* harrow f. *herse*; see HEARSE]

rehouse, see RE- 8; **rehumanize,** RE- 9.

Reich (rīk), n. The German commonwealth as a whole (*First ~,* Holy Roman Empire, 962–1806; *Second ~,* 1871–1918; *Third ~,* Nazi regime, 1933–45); *~s′wehr* (-vār), (formerly) German armed forces. [G, = empire]

Reichstag (rīks′tahk), n. (hist.). The German parliament; parliament of the late Transleithan Austria-Hungary. [G]

rē′ify̅, v.t. Convert (person, abstract concept) into thing, materialize. So **rēi̅FI**CA′TION n. [f. L *res* thing, -I-, -FY]

reign[1] (rān), n. Sovereignty, rule, sway, (*under the ~ of Queen Victoria; his ~ was a gentle one; the ~ of law in nature; reign resumes her ~; R~ of* TERROR); realm, sphere, (rare); period during which sovereign reigns (*in the ~ of John; during five successive ~s*). [ME, f. OF *regne* f. L *regnum* (*regere* rule)]

reign[2] (rān), v.i. Hold royal office, be king or queen lit. or fig., (*~ed over Great Britain for 60 years; a king who desired to rule as well as ~; better to ~ in hell than serve in heaven; ~ing beauty,* acknowledged as supreme for the time); hold sway, prevail, (*dissension & improvidence ~ed; silence ~s,* all is quiet). [ME, f. OF *regner* f. L *regnare* (prec.)]

reignite. See RE- 9.

reimburse′, v.t. Repay (person who has expended money, out-of-pocket expenses, person expenses). Hence **~**MENT (-sm-) n. [RE- 9, obs. *imburse* put in purse f. med. L *imbursare* (IM-[1], BOURSE)]

reimport, reimpose etc. See RE- 9.

rein (rān), n., & v.t. **1.** Long narrow strap with each end attached to bit used to guide or check horse etc. in riding or driving, (fig.) means of control, (often pl. in same senses; *draw ~,* stop one's horse, pull up, abandon effort, retrench expenditure, etc.; *give horse the ~s* or *~,* let it go its own way; so *throw the ~s to; give ~* or *the ~s to* one's *imagination* etc., let it have free scope; *assume, drop, the ~s of government,* enter upon, resign, office); hence **~′**LESS a. **2.** v.t. Check or manage with **~**s; (fig.) govern, restrain, control; pull *up* or *back* with **~**s, hold *in* with **~**s or fig. [ME, f. OF *rene,* earlier *resne,* f. Rom. **retina* f. L *retinere* RETAIN]

reincarnate etc., see RE- 8; **reincorporate,** RE- 9.

rein′deer (rān-), n. (collect. sing. usu. for pl.). Subarctic deer used for drawing sledges & kept in herds for its milk, flesh, & hide. [ME, f. ON *hreindy̅ri* (*hreinn* reindeer, DEER)]

rēinforce′, v.t., & n. **1.** Strengthen or support by additional men or material or by increase of numbers, quantity, size, thickness, etc. (*~ fortress, army, provisions, party, the basses* etc. in band or chorus, person's *health* etc. with food etc., one's *argument* with fresh points); *~d concrete* (with metal bars, gratings, or wire, embedded in it); (rare) enforce again, re-enforce. **2.** n. Thicker part of gun next breech; strengthening part, band, etc., added to object. [RE- 8, *inforce* = ENFORCE]

rēinforce′ment (-sm-), n. Reinforcing or being reinforced; (often pl.) additional men, ships, etc., for military or naval force; anything that reinforces. [-MENT]

reingratiate, see RE- 9; **reink**, RE- 8.

‖ **reins** (rānz), n. pl. (arch.). The kidneys; the loins. [ME, f. OF, f. L *renes* pl.]

reinsert etc. See RE- 9.

rëinstäte′, v.t. Restore to, replace *in*, lost position, privileges, etc.; restore to health or proper order. Hence ~MENT (-tm-) n. [RE- 9, obs. *instate* (IN-¹, STATE n.)]

reinsure etc., **reinter**, see RE- 8; **reinvest** etc., RE- 8, 9; **reinvigorate** etc., RE- 9.

reis (räs), n. pl. Former Portuguese and Brazilian money of account of very small value. [Port. (pl. of *real* REAL¹)]

reissue etc., **reiterate** etc. See RE- 8.

reiver. See REAVE.

reject, v.t., & n. **1.** (rĭjĕkt′). Put aside as not to be accepted, practised, believed, chosen, used, complied with, etc. (~ *doctrine, custom, evidence, candidate, literary contribution, food, request, suitor, vote*; *sorting-machine* ~s *all defective specimens*); cast up again, vomit, evacuate. **2.** n. (rĕj′ĕkt). Somebody or something that has been ~ed (e.g. person unfit for military service, article sold cheaply as not up to standard). Hence or cogn. **rejĕct′ABLE** a., **rĕjĕc′tER¹, rĕjĕc′tION, rĕjĕc′tOR**, nn. [ME, f. L *re(jicĕre -ject-* = *jacĕre* throw), RE- 9]

rĕjĕctamĕn′ta, n. pl. Refuse, waste matters; things cast up by the sea; excrements. [mod. L (prec., -MENT)]

rĕjoice′, v.t. & i. Cause joy to, make glad, (*the news* ~*d him*; *I am* ~*d to hear it, that it should be so, at it*, etc.); feel great joy, whence **rĕjoi′cingLY²** adv.; be glad *that* or *to do*, take delight *in* or *at*, (~ *in*, be blessed in the possession of, often joc. for *have*); make merry, celebrate some event, whence **rĕjoi′cings** (-z) [-ING¹] n. pl. [ME, f. OF *re(joir -iss-* JOY²), RE- 6]

rĕjoin′¹, v.i. & t. (Law) reply to charge or pleading, esp. to plaintiff's replication; say in answer, retort; join (one's companion, regiment, etc.) again. [ME, f. OF *rejoindre* JOIN), RE- 9]

rē-join′², v.t. & i. Join (t. & i.) together again, reunite. [RE- 9 + JOIN, or as prec.]

rĕjoin′der, n. What is REJOIN¹ed or said in reply, retort. [as REJOIN¹, see -ER⁴]

rĕjuv′ĕn|āte, rĕjuv′ĕn|ize, -|ise (-ōō-; -iz), vv.t. & i. Make or become young again. Hence ~A′TION, ~ātOR, nn., (-ōō-). [RE- 9, L *juvenis* young, -ATE³, -IZE]

rĕjuvĕn|ĕsce′ (-ōō-), v.i. & t. Become young again (biol., i. & t. of cells) get, fill with, fresh vitality. So ~ĕs′CENT a., ~ĕs′CENCE n., (-ōō-). [f. LL *re(juvenescere* f. L *juvenis*, -ESCENT), RE- 9]

rekindle. See RE- 9.

-rel, also -*erel*, suf. of dim. & depreciating tendency, occas. repr. OF -*erel*, mod. F -*ereau*, but usu. in native wds of obscure origin.

relabel. See RE- 8.

rĕlăps|e′, v.i., & n. **1.** Fall back, sink again, into wrong-doing, error, heresy, weakness or illness, quiescence or indolence, (often *into*). **2.** n. Act or fact of ~ing, esp. deterioration in patient's condition after partial recovery. [f. L *re(labi laps-* slip), RE- 9]

rĕlāt|e′, v.t. & i. **1.** Narrate, recount, whence ~ER¹ n. **2.** Bring into relation, establish relation between, (*to, with*, or abs.; *cannot* ~*e the phenomena with* or *to anything we know* or *to each other*); (p.p.) connected, allied, akin by blood or marriage, (*the law extends to several* ~*ed groups*; *is* ~*ed to the royal family*), whence ~′ĕdNESS n. **3.** Have reference *to*, stand in some relation *to*, (*notices nothing but what* ~*es to himself*; *how parts* ~*e to parts*). [f. L *relat-* (REFER)]

rĕlā′tion, n. **1.** Narration, a narrative; (law) laying of information before Attorney-General for him to take action upon (*proceeding at the* ~ *of the Board of Trade*). **2.** What one person or thing has to do with another, way in which one stands or is related to another, kind of connexion or correspondence or contrast or feeling that prevails between persons or things, (*the* ~s *primarily expressed by prepositions are those of place & time; the outlay seems to bear no* ~, *is out of all* ~, *to the object aimed at; the* ~ *between them is that of guardian & ward;* ~s *are rather strained*, cordiality is impaired; *the report has* ~ *to a state of things now past; in* or rarely *with* ~ *to*, as regards), whence ~AL a., ~ALLY² adv., (-sho-). **3.** Kinship lit. or fig. (rare, now usu. ~SHIP n.). **4.** Kinsman, kinswoman, relative (occas. with mixture of prec. sense, as *is he any* ~, *what* ~ *is he, to you?; he is no* ~). Hence ~LESS (-sho-) a. [ME, f. OF, or L *relatio* (prec., -ION)]

rĕl′ative, a. & n. **1.** (gram.). Referring, & attaching a subordinate clause, to an expressed or implied antecedent (~ *pronoun*, as in *The man whom you saw;* ~ *adjective*, as in *Which things are an allegory;* ~ *adverb*, as in *The place where he died*); (of clause) attached to antecedent by ~ word. **2.** Having mutual relations, corresponding in some way, related to each other, (*different yet* ~ *designs*). **3.** Pertinent, relevant, related to the subject, (*without some more* ~ *proof*). **4.** Comparative (*what are the* ~ *merits of the two?; made the next attempt with* ~ *coolness*); in relation to something else (*their* ~ *positions are the same though they are miles apart*); proportioned to something else (*supply is* ~ *to demand*); implying comparison (heat, speed, strength, *are* ~ *words*); correlative or essentially involving a different but corresponding idea (*the conceptions of husband & wife are*

~ *to each other*); not having absolute existence but conditioned (*she is beautiful to me, but beauty is ~ to the beholder's eye*). **5.** Having reference, relating, *to* (*detailed the facts ~ to the matter*; also loosely as adv., as *I wrote to him ~ to renewal of the lease*); hence ~LY² (-vl-) adv. **6.** n. (Gram.) ~ word, esp. pronoun (*the principal ~s are* who, which, that, what), whence **rĕlativ′AL** a.; (philos.) ~ thing or term. **7.** Kinsman, kinswoman, relation by blood or marriage. [ME, f. OF (-*if*, -*ive*), or LL *relativus* (RELATE, -IVE)]

rĕl′ativ|ism, n. Doctrine that knowledge is of relations only. So ~IST(2) n. [prec., -ISM]

rĕlativ′itў, n. Relativeness; (philos.) Einstein's theory of the universe, based on the principle that all motion is relative, regarding space-time as a four--dimensional continuum, & invalidating previous conceptions of gravitation, geometry, & other matters. [-ITY]

rĕlāt′or, n. Relater (now rare); (law) maker of RELATION (legal sense). [L (RELATE, -OR)]

rĕlăx′, v.t. & i. Cause or allow to become loose or slack or limp, enfeeble, enervate, mitigate, abate, (~ *the bowels, the muscles,* one's *grasp, discipline, a rule,* one's *attention,* one's *efforts*; ~*ed throat,* form of sore throat; *place has a* ~*ing climate,* opp. *bracing*); grow less tense or rigid or stern or ceremonious or energetic or zealous (*his hold, hands, severity, features, manner, endeavours,* ~*ed*; *must not* ~ *in* one's *efforts*). [ME, f. L *re*(*laxare* see LAX), RE- 9]

rĕlaxā′tion, n. Partial remission *of* penalty, duty, etc.; cessation from work, recreation, amusements; diminution of tension, severity, precision, etc. [f. L *relaxatio* (prec., -ATION)]

rĕlay′¹, n., & v.t. & i. **1.** Set of fresh horses substituted for tired ones; gang of men, supply of material, etc., similarly used (~-*race,* between teams of which each person does part of the distance, the 2nd etc. members of teams starting when the 1st etc. end); (teleg.) instrument reinforcing long-distance current with local battery. **2.** vb. Arrange in, provide with, replace by, get, ~(s); (radio) broadcast (a message, programme, originating at, and received from, another station). [ME, f. OF *relai* n., *relaier* vb, ult. f. L *laxare,* cf. DELAY]

rē-lay′², v.t. Lay again. [RE- 8]

rĕleas|e′¹, v.t. **1.** (law). Remit, surrender, make over to another, (debt, right, property), whence ~EE′, ~′OR, nn. **2.** Set free, liberate, deliver, unfasten, (*from*); (cinemat.) issue (film etc.) for general exhibition. Hence ~′ABLE a. [ME, f. OF *relesser* f. L RELAX*are*]

rĕlease′², n. **1.** Deliverance, liberation, from trouble, sorrow, life, duty, confinement, or fixed position. **2.** Written dis-

charge, receipt; legal conveyance of right or estate to another, document effecting this. **3.** Handle, catch, etc., that releases part of machine etc. [ME, f. OF *reles* (prec.)]

rĕl′ég|āte, v.t. Banish *to* some place of exile; consign or dismiss *to* some usu. inferior position, sphere, etc.; transfer (matter) for decision or execution, refer (person) for information etc., *to.* Hence ~ABLE a., ~A′TION n. [f. L *re*(*legare* send), RE- 5, -ATE³]

rĕlĕnt′, v.i. Relax severity, become less stern, abandon harsh intention, yield to compassion. Hence ~ingLY² adv., ~LESS a., ~lessLY² adv., ~lessNESS n. [ME, ult. f. RE- 9, L *lentus* soft; cf. L *relentescere* slacken]

rĕl′ĕv|ant, a. Bearing upon, pertinent *to,* the matter in hand. Hence ~ANCE, ~ANCY, nn., ~antLY² adv. [f. med. L *relevans,* part. of L *relevare* RELIEVE, -ANT]

rĕli′|able, a. That may be relied upon, of sound & consistent character or quality. Hence ~abIL′ITY n. (~*ability trials,* long--distance trials of motor vehicles designed to test dependableness, endurance, etc. rather than speed), ~ablenESS n., ~ablLY² adv. [RELY, -ABLE; from 16th c.; an established wd avoided by some purists as of irreg. formation]

rĕli′ance, n. Trust, confidence, (usu. *upon, on, in*; *have, place, feel,* ~ *upon* etc.; *my* ~ *is upon God*); thing depended upon (*the well is our chief* ~). So **rĕli′ANT** a. [RELY, -ANCE]

rĕl′ic, n. **1.** Part of holy person's body or belongings kept after his death as object of reverence; memento, souvenir. **2.** pl. Dead body, remains, of person; what has survived destruction or wasting, remnant, residue, scraps. **3.** Surviving trace or memorial *of* a custom, belief, period, people, etc.; object interesting for age of associations. [ME *relike* etc., f. OF *relique,* f. RELIQUIAE]

rĕl′ict, n. Widow (usu. *his* etc. ~, or ~ *of*); geological or other object which has survived in a primitive form; animal or plant known to have existed in the same form in previous geological ages; (rare) = prec. [f. p.p. of L *re*(*linquere* -*lict*-leave), RE- 3]

rĕlief′¹, n. **1.** Alleviation of or deliverance from pain, distress, anxiety, etc. (*the medicine brought* ~; *it is a* ~ *to come across an optimist*). **2.** Feature etc. that diversifies monotony or relaxes tension (*a blank wall without* ~; *a comic scene follows by way of* ~). **3.** Assistance given to the poor esp. || formerly under the Poor Law (*recipients of public* ~ *shall not be eligible*) or to persons in special danger or difficulty (*a* ~ *fund for the earthquake victims*; ~-*works,* building etc. operations started to give work to the unemployed). **4.** Reinforcement & esp. raising of siege *of* besieged town. **5.** (Replacing of person or persons on duty by) person(s) appointed to take turn of duty. **6.** Redress of hardship or grievance. [ME, f. *relef*, OF *relief* (*relever* RELIEVE)]

rĕlief'², n. Method of moulding or carving or stamping in which design stands out from plane or curved surface with projections proportioned & more or less (*high*, *low*, ~) closely approximating to those of objects imitated (*the profile of Julius in* ~); piece of sculpture etc, in ~; appearance of being done in ~ given by arrangement of line or colour or shading, distinctness of outline lit. or fig., vividness, (*stands out in* ~; *bring out the facts in full* ~); ~ *map*, map-model showing the elevations and depressions of the area dealt with, usu. on an exaggerated relative scale, (also) ordinary map indicating hills and valleys by shading, colouring, or hachures, rather than by contour lines alone. [f. F *relief* & its source It. *rilievo* (*rilevare* raise f. L as RELIEVE)]

rĕliev̦|e', v.t. **1.** Bring, give, be a, RELIEF¹ to (*town was* ~*ed*; *am much* ~*ed to hear it*; *devotes himself to* ~*ing distress* or *the distressed*; ‖ ~*ing officer*, official charged with care of the poor; ~*ing arch*, built in substance of wall to ~e part below from weight; ~*e* one's *feelings*, by strong language or some ebullition; ~*e nature*, evacuate bladder or bowels; *a black bodice* ~*ed with white lace*; ~*e guard*, come & take one's turn on guard; *you shall be* ~*ed at 10.30*; ~*e* one *of load*, take it off him, also joc., as *a tramp* ~*ed him of his purse*). **2.** Bring into RELIEF², exhibit with appearance of solidity or detachment, (esp. in p.p., often *against* background). Hence ~'ABLE a. [ME, f. OF *relever* f. L *re(levare* f. *levis* light), RE- 9]

rĕliev'ō, n. (pl. ~*s*). = RELIEF² esp. in lit. senses (ALTO, BASSO, MEZZO, ~~). [f. It. *rilievo* RELIEF² w. anglicized spelling & pronunc.]

rĕli'gion (-jn), n. **1.** Monastic condition, being monk or nun, (*enter into*, *be in*, ~); (rare) a monastic order. **2.** (rare). Practice of sacred rites. **3.** One of the prevalent systems of faith & worship (*the Christian, Mohammedan*, ~; *established* ~, that of established CHURCH¹; NATURAL, REVEAL'*ed*, ~; *all* ~*s are the same to him*). **4.** Human recognition of superhuman controlling power & esp. of a personal God entitled to obedience, effect of such recognition on conduct & mental attitude, (*get* ~, vulg. or joc., be converted to such belief). **5.** Action that one is bound to do (*make a* ~ *of doing*). Hence~LESS (-jon-) a. [ME, f. AF *religiun*, OF -*ion*, or L *religio*)]

rĕli'gioner (-jon-), n. Member of monastic order; person zealous for religion. [-ER¹]

rĕli'gion|ism (-jon-), n. Excessive religious zeal. So ~IST(2) n. [-ISM]

rĕli'gionīze (-jon-), **-ise** (-īz), v.t. & i. Convert to or imbue with religion; exhibit religious zeal. [-IZE]

rĕli'gĭōse, a. Morbidly religious. [as RELIGIOUS, -OSE¹]

rĕligĭŏs'ĭtў, n. Being religious or religiose. [ME, f. L *religiositas* (foll., -ITY)]

rĕli'gious (-jus), a. & n. **1.** Imbued with religion, pious, god-fearing, devout; of, belonging to, a monastic order; of, concerned with, religion; scrupulous, conscientious, (*with* ~ *care, exactitude*, etc.); hence ~LY² adv., ~NESS n., (-jus-). **2.** n. (As sing. with *a* etc., & as pl. in same form with *the, some, several*, etc.) person bound by monastic vows. [ME, f. AF *religius*, OF -*ieus*, or L *religiosus* (RELIGION, -OUS)]

reline. See RE- 9.

rĕlin'quish, v.t. Give up, abandon, cease from, resign, surrender, (habit, plan, hope, belief, right, possession); loose hold of (object held). Hence ~MENT n. [ME, f. OF *relinquir* f. L *re(linquere* leave), RE- 3, -ISH²]

rĕl'iquarў, n. Receptacle for relic(s). [f. F *reliquaire* (RELIC, -ARY¹)]

rĕl'ique (-īk; or relēk'), n. (arch.). Relic. [F]

rĕl'iqu̦iae, n. pl. Remains; (geol.) fossil remains of animals or plants; (bot.) withered remains of leaves decaying on stem. [L (*reliquus* remaining, f. *relinquere* RELINQUISH, -IA¹)]

rĕl'ish¹, n. **1.** Flavour, distinctive taste *of*; slight dash or tinge of some quality. **2.** Appetizing flavour, attractive quality, (*meat has no* ~ *when one is ill*; *horseplay loses its* ~ *after childhood*); thing eaten with plainer food to add flavour. **3.** Enjoyment of food or other things, zest, liking for, (*eat, read, appreciate jest*, etc., *with great* ~; *has no* ~ *for poetry*). [16th c. alt. (w. assim. to -ISH²) of obs. *reles* f. OF *reles* remainder f. *relaisser* (RELEASE¹)]

rĕl'ish², v.t. & i. Serve as relish to, make piquant etc.; get pleasure out of, like, be pleased with, (*thought he could* ~ *a lobster*; *does not* ~ *the prospect*), whence ~ABLE a.; taste, savour, smack, suggest presence, *of*; affect the lit. or fig. taste *well, badly*, etc. [f. prec.]

relive, reload. See RE- 8.

rĕlu'cent (-ōō-), a. (rare). Shining, bright. [f. L *re(lucēre* shine), RE- 6, -ENT]

rĕlŭct', v.i. (now rare). Feel or show reluctance, make opposition, (*at, against*). So ~ATE³ (in same sense) v.i., **rĕlŭctA'TION** n. [f. L *re(luctari* struggle), RE- 2]

rĕlŭc'tant, a. Struggling, offering resistance, hard to work or get or manage, (esp. poet.); unwilling, disinclined, *to do* or abs. (*am very* ~ *to admit*; *gave me* ~ *assistance*). Hence **rĕlŭc'tANCE** n., ~LY² adv. [as prec., -ANT]

rĕlūme' (*or* -ōōm), v.t. (poet.). Rekindle (light or flame lit. or fig.); make (eyes etc.) bright again; light (sky etc.) up again. [RE- 9, & as ILLUME]

rely'*, v.i. Put one's trust, depend with confidence, (up)on person or thing (is ~ing upon a broken reed; I ~ upon you to do it, its being done, today; you may ~ upon it that he will be here). [ME; earlier senses rally, be vassal of; f. OF relier bind together, f. L re(ligare bind), RE- 9]

remain'¹, v.i. 1. Be left over after abstraction or use of or dealing with the rest (the few pleasures that ~ to an old man; worse things ~ to be told; nothing ~s but to draw the moral). 2. Abide, stay in same place or condition, continue to exist, be extant, be left behind, (~ three weeks in Paris; let it ~ as it is; as things have been they ~; the Parthenon ~s to attest or as a proof of it; this visit will always ~ in my memory; the luggage unfortunately ~ed on the platform; victory ~ed with the Thebans). 3. (With compl.) continue to be (one thing ~s certain; ~ faithful etc.; I ~ yours truly etc., formula concluding letter). [ME, f. AF remeyn- f. OF remanoir (also remaindre) f. L re(manēre stay), RE- 3]

remain'², n. 1. (Usu. pl.) what remains over, surviving members or parts or amount, (the ~s of a nation, family, meal, stock, building, of one's conscience or strength, etc.; also in pl. as sing., & in sing., as here there is the ~s, a ~, of a temple); (usu. pl.) relics or relic of obsolete custom or of antiquity (Roman ~s). 2. pl. Works, esp. those not before or yet published, left by author (rarely in sing. of single work). 3. pl. Dead body, corpse. [ME, f. OF (prec.)]

remain'der, n., & v.t. 1. (law). Residual interest in estate devised to another (cf. REVERSION) simultaneously with creation of estate (~ man, devisee of ~), right of succession to title or position on holder's decease, whence ~SHIP n. 2. Residue, remaining person or things; (arith.) number left after subtraction or division; (bookselling) copies left unsold when demand has ceased & often offered at reduced price, (vb) treat or dispose of (edition) as ~; (attrib.) left over. [ME & AF, = OF remaindre, see REMAIN¹, -ER⁴]

remake, see RE- 8; reman, RE- 8, 9.

remand' (-ah-), v.t., & n. 1. Send back to, reconsign, (now rare in gen. sense); send back (prisoner) into custody to allow of further inquiry. 2. n. Recommittal to custody; ~ home, temporary institution for juvenile offenders. [ME, f. OF remander or LL re(mandare commit), RE- 3]

rem'anent, a. Remaining, residual, (now rare exc. in ~ magnetism, that left in iron after electric excitation). [ME, f. L part. as foll., see -ENT]

rem'anet, n. Remaining part, residue; postponed lawsuit or parliamentary bill. [L, 3rd sing. of L remanere (REMAIN¹)]

remargin. See RE- 8.

remark'¹, v.t. & i. Take notice of, perceive, regard with attention, observe, (person, thing, fact, that etc.); say by way of comment; make comment (up)on. [f. F re(marquer MARK²), RE- 6]

remark'², n. Noticing, observing, (worthy of ~, remarkable), commenting (is the theme of general ~; let it pass without ~; this ~s are often interesting; make a ~, speak). [f. F remarque (prec.)]

remark'ab|le, a. Worth notice, exceptional, striking, conspicuous. Hence ~leNESS n., ~LY² adv. [f. F remarquable (REMARK¹, -ABLE)]

remarque (rim̄ark'), n. Mark, usu. marginal sketch, indicating certain state of engraving plate. [F]

remarry etc., remast. See RE- 8.

remblai (rahṅblā'), n. (Fortif.) earth used to form ramparts, parapets, etc.; earth brought to form railway embankments etc. [F, f. remblayer embank]

Rembrandtesque' (-sk), a. & n. (After) the style of Rembrandt (d. 1669), with marked effects of light & shade. [-ESQUE]

rem'edy, n., & v.t. 1. Cure for disease, healing medicine or treatment, means of removing or counteracting or relieving any evil (for), redress, legal or other reparation, whence or cogn. remed'IAL a., remed'iaLLY² adv. (now poet. or rhet.) rem'ediLESS (or rimēd'²) a., rem'edilèss-LY² adv. 2. Margin within which coins as minted may differ from the standard fineness and weight. 3. v.t. Cure medically (now rare); rectify, make good; so remed'iABLE a. [ME; vb f. OF remedier or L remediare, n. f. AF remedie, f. L re(medium f. medēri heal), RE- 1]

remem'ber, v.t. 1. Retain in the memory, not forget, recall to mind, recollect, know by heart, (person, thing, fact, that, to do, how to do, when, why, etc., or abs.; ~ oneself, bethink oneself of one's manners or intentions after a lapse; also refl. with me, him, etc., arch., as I ~ me that, they ~ed them of), whence ~ABLE a. 2. Make present to, tip, (~ed me in his will; ~ the waiter). 3. Mention in one's prayers. 4. Convey greetings from (person) to another (~ me kindly to them; begs to be ~ed to you). [ME, f. OF remembrer f. LL re(memorari f. L memor mindful), RE- 9]

remem'brance, n. 1. Remembering or being remembered, memory, recollection, (has escaped my ~; have in, call to, ~; put in ~, remind; have no ~ of it; more than once within my ~; a pillar in ~ of the exploit); R~ Day, day (11th November, ARMISTICE Day, or the Sunday immediately preceding it) commemorating those who fell in the wars of 1914–18 & 1939–45. 2. Keepsake, souvenir, memorial. 3. pl. Greetings conveyed through third person. [ME, f. OF (prec., -ANCE)]

rèmĕm′brancer, n. **1.** ′‖ *King's, Queen's, R~,* officer collecting debts due to sovereign; ‖ *City R~,* representing Corporation of City of London before parliamentary committees etc. **2.** Reminder, memento, *of.* [ME, f. AF (prec., -ER¹)]

remigrate etc. See RE- 9.

rèmind′, v.t. Put (person) in mind *of, to* do, *that, how,* etc., or abs. [RE- 8, MIND vb]

rèmin′der, n. Thing that reminds or is memento, *of.* [ME, f. AF (prec., -ER¹)]

rèmind′ful, a. Acting as a reminder, reviving the memory, *of.* [-FUL]

rĕminis′cence, n. **1.** Remembering, recovery of knowledge by mental effort, (*Platonic doctrine of* ~, that all knowledge is such recovery of things known to the soul in previous existences). **2.** Remembered (& related) fact or incident; (pl.) collection in literary form of incidents that person remembers. **3.** Point in thing reminding or suggestive *of* other thing (*there is a* ~ *of the Greek type in her face*). Hence **rĕminiscĕn′t**IAL (-shl) a. [F, or f. LL *reminiscentia* f. *reminisci* remember, RE- 9, -ENCE]

rĕminis′cent, a. Recalling past things, given to or concerned with retrospection, mindful or having memories *of;* reminding or suggestive *of.* Hence ~LY² adv. [as prec., -ENT]

remint. See RE- 8.

rèmise′¹ (-ēz), n., & v.i. **1.** (arch.). Coach-house, carriage hired from livery-stable. **2.** (fenc.). Second thrust made for recovery from first; (v.i.) make ~. [F, vbl n. f. *remettre* REMIT]

rèmise′² (-ēz), v.t. (legal). Surrender, make over, (right, property). [f. F *remis(e)* p.p. as prec.]

rèmiss′, a. Careless of duty, lax, negligent; lacking force or energy. Hence ~LY² adv., ~NESS n. [f. L *remissus* p.p. of REMIT(*tere*)]

rèmiss′ible, a. That may be remitted. [F, or f. LL *remissibilis* (REMIT, -IBLE)]

rèmi′ssion (-shn), n. **1.** Forgiveness *of* sins etc., forgiveness of sins; remitting of debt, penalty, etc. **2.** Diminution of force, effect, degree, violence, etc. **3.** Act of remitting in other senses (rare). So **rèmiss′ive** a. [ME,. f. OF, f. L *remissionem* (foll., -ION)]

rèmit′, v.t. & i. (-tt-), & n. **1.** (Usu. of God) pardon (sins etc.); refrain from exacting or inflicting or executing (debt, punishment, sentence). **2.** Abate (t. & i.), slacken, mitigate, partly or entirely cease from or cease, (~ *one's anger or efforts, the siege; pain, enthusiasm, begins to* ~). **3.** Refer (matter for decision etc.) *to* some authority, send back (case) to lower court. **4.** Send or put back (*in)to* previous state; postpone, defer, *to* or *till.* **5.** Transmit (money etc.), get conveyed by post etc., whence ~t′er¹ [-ER¹], ~tEE′, nn. Hence

~t′AL(2) n. **6.** n. (*Also* rĕm′ĭt) item ~ted for consideration. [ME, f. L *re(mittere miss-* send), RE- 5]

rèmitt′ance, n. Money sent to person; consignment of goods sent (rare); sending of money; ~-*man,* emigrant subsisting on ~s from home, person paid to stay abroad. [prec., -ANCE]

rèmitt′ent, a. & n. (Fever) that abates at intervals (cf. INTERMITT*ent*). [REMIT, -ENT]

rèmitt′er², n. (legal; for *remitter¹* see REMIT). Substitution, in favour of holder of two titles to estate, of the more valid for the other by which he entered on possession; remitting of case to other court; restoration to rights, rehabilitation, (rare). [-ER⁴]

rĕm′nant, n. *The* little or few that remain(s), small remaining quantity or piece or number of persons or things; surviving trace *of;* fragment, scrap, esp. piece of cloth etc. offered at reduced price when greater part has been used up. [ME, contr. f. obs. & OF *remenant, -manant,* (*remanoir* REMAIN¹, -ANT)]

remodel. See RE- 8.

rèmŏn′ĕtiz|**e** (*or* -mūn²), **-is**|**e** (-īz), v.t. Restore (metal etc.) to former position as legal tender. Hence ~A′TION n. [RE- 9]

rèmŏn′strance, n. (Hist.) formal statement of public grievances (*the Grand R~,* from House of Commons to Crown 1641); remonstrating, expostulation, a protest. [OF (foll., -ANCE)]

rèmŏn′str|**āte** (*or* rĕm′on-), v.i. & t. Make protest, expostulate, (*against* course, *with* person, *on* or *upon* matter, or abs.); urge in remonstrance (*that* or parenth.). Hence or cogn. ~ANT a. & n., ~antLY², ~āt**ing**-LY², advr., ~ative a., ~āt**o**R n. [f. med. L *re(monstrare* show), RE- 2, -ATE³]

rèmŏn′tant, a. & n. (Rose) blooming more than once in year. [F (*remonter* REMOUNT², -ANT)]

rĕm′ora, n. The sucking-fish, formerly supposed to stay course of ship to which it adhered; · obstruction, impediment, (now rare). [L (RE- 2, *mora* delay), = impediment, sucking-fish]

rèmŏrse′, n. Bitter repentance for wrong committed, whence ~FUL (-sf-) a., ~fulLY² adv.; compunction, compassionate reluctance to inflict pain or be cruel, (chiefly in *without* ~), whence ~LESS (-sl-) a., ~lèssLY² adv., ~lèssNESS n. [ME, f. OF *remors* f. LL *re(morsus -ūs* f. *mordēre mors-* bite), RE- 3]

rèmōte′, a. (~*r,* ~*st*). **1.** Far apart. **2.** Far away or off in place or time, not closely related, distant or widely different or by nature separate *from,* (*lies* ~ *from the road; came from the* ~*st parts of the earth; memorials of* ~ *ages; a* ~ *ancestor, descendant, kinsman;* ~ *causes, effects; introduces considerations* ~ *from the subject);* ~ *control,* control of apparatus etc.

For pronunciation & hyphening of *re-* see RE-; for words in *re-* not given see RE- 8, 9.

from a point some distance away by means of electrically operated device, radio waves, etc. **3.** Out-of-the-way, secluded, (a ~ *village; lives* ~). **4.** (Chiefly superl., of idea etc.) slight(est), faint(est), least, (*have not the* ~*st, have only a very* ~, °*conception of what he means*). Hence ~LY[2] (-tl-) adv., ~NESS (-tn-) n. [ME, f. L *remotus* (REMOVE[1])]

remould, remount[1]. See RE- 8.

remount'[2], v.t. & i. Go up, get on to, (hill, ladder, horse, etc.) again; go up again, get on horseback again, make fresh ascent; go back *to* specified date, period, source. [ME, f. OF *re(monter* MOUNT[2]), RE- 9; later dir. f. MOUNT[2]]

remo'v|able (-moo-), a. In vbl senses; esp., (of magistrate or official) subject to removal from office, holding office during pleasure of Crown or other authority. Hence ~ABIL'ITY n. [foll., -ABLE]

remove'[1] (-oov), v.t. & i. **1.** Take off or away from place occupied, convey to another place, change situation of, get rid of, dismiss, (~ one's *hat, the tea-things, all traces*; ~ *mountains*, do miracle; *cardinal was* ~*d by poison*; ~ *magistrate from office; boy is* ~*d from school*, taken away by parents etc.; *this will* ~ *all apprehension, the last doubts*; ~ *furniture*, for persons changing house, as special trade, whence **remo'VER**[1] (-moo-) n.); ‖ (pass., of course at dinner etc.) be succeeded *by* (*boiled haddock* ~*d by hashed mutton*). **2.** Change one's residence, go away *from*, (*am removing from London to Oxford; truth has* ~*d from earth*). **3.** p.p. Distant or remote *from* (*is not many degrees* ~*d from the brute*; (of cousins) *once, twice*, etc., ~*d*, with difference of one, two, etc., generations (*my first cousin once, twice,* ~*d*, cousin's child or parent's cousin, cousin's grandchild or grandparent's cousin). Hence **remo'VAL** (-moo-) n. (not of cousinship). [ME, f. OF *removeir* f. L *re(movēre* MOVE), RE- 1]

remove'[2] (-oov), n. **1.** ‖ Dish that succeeds another at table. **2.** ‖ Promotion to higher-form at school (*has not got his* ~); ‖ (in some schools) a certain form or division. **3.** (rare). Change of residence, departure, removal; distance (*at a certain* ~ *its shape seems to change*). **4.** Stage in gradation, degree, (*is but one* ~, *few* ~s, *from*), esp. in consanguinity (cf. prec.). [f. prec.]

remūn'er|āte, v.t. Reward, pay for service rendered; serve as or provide recompense for (toil etc.) or to (person). Hence or cogn. ~A'TION n., ~ATIVE a., ~atively[2] adv., ~ativeNESS n. [f. L *re(munerari* f. *munus -eris* gift), RE- 1, -ATE[3]]

renaiss'ance (& see Ap.), n. Revival of art & letters under influence of classical models in 14th–16th cc., period of its progress, style of art & architecture developed by it, (often attrib., as ~ *painters,*

architecture, church); any similar revival. [F (*renaître* be born again) after *naissance* birth, cf. RENASCENCE]

rēn'al, a. Of the kidneys. [f. F *rénal* or LL *renalis* (*renes* kidneys, -AL)]

rename. See RE- 8.

rēnās'cence, n. Rebirth, renewal; = RENAISSANCE. [foll., -ENCE]

rēnās'cent, a. Springing up anew, being reborn. [f. L *re(nasci* be born), RE- 8, -ENT]

rĕncoun'ter, rĕncŏn'tre (-ter, & see Ap.), n. (now rare). Encounter, battle, skirmish, duel; casual meeting. [f. F *rencontre* (*rencontrer*, see RE-, ENCOUNTER)]

rĕnd, v.t. & i. (*rĕnt*). **1.** Tear or wrench (*off, away, out of, from, asunder, apart*, etc., or abs.; arch. or rhet.; *a province rent from the empire*; ~ one's *garments, hair*, in sign of grief etc.; *turn & ~* one, fig., abuse him unexpectedly). **2.** Split or divide (t. & i.) in two or in pieces or usu. into factions (~ *laths*, make them by splitting wood; *Europe was rent in two by the question*; *shouts* ~ *the air*, sound explosively; *heart is rent by contending emotions; the veil was rent*). [OE *rendan*, = OFris. *renda*, not otherwise represented]

rĕn'der, v.t., & n. **1.** Give in return (~ *thanks, good for evil*). **2.** Give back (arch.); hand over, deliver, give *up*, surrender, (chiefly arch.; ~ *to Caesar the things that are Caesar's*; *grave* ~s *up its dead*; *fortress was* ~*ed on terms*). **3.** Pay (tribute etc.), show (obedience etc.), do (service etc.), (usu. *to* or with ind. obj.). **4.** Produce for inspection, submit, present, send in, (account, reason, etc.; *will have to* ~ *an account of*; *account* ~*ed*, bill previously sent in & not yet paid, phr. used as substitute for repetition of items). **5.** Reproduce, portray, give representation or performance or effect of, execute, translate, (*painter has hardly* ~*ed the expression; the quartet, Iago, the dramatist's conception, were well* ~*ed*; *how would you* ~ *solvitur ambulando?*; *poetry can never be adequately* ~*ed in another language*), whence ~ING[1] (1, 2) n. **6.** (With obj. & compl.) make, cause to be, convert into, (*age had* ~*ed him peevish; the tone* ~*ed it an insult*). **7.** Melt (fat) down, extract by melting, clarify, also ~ *down*. **8.** Cover (stone, brick) with first coat of plaster; ~*-set* v.t., plaster (wall etc.) with two coats, n. & a., (plastering) of two coats. **9.** n. (legal). Return in money or kind or service made by tenant to superior. [ME, f. OF *rendre* f. Rom. **rendere* f. L *reddere reddit-* (RE- 1, *dare* give)]

rendezvous (rŏn'dĭvōō), n. (pl. same, pr. -ōōz), & v.i. (~es, ~ed, ~ing, pr. -ōōz, -ōōd, -ōōing). **1.** Place appointed for assembling of troops or ships; place of common resort; meeting-place agreed on, meeting by agreement (*place of* ~). **2.** v.i. Meet at ~. [F, f. *rendez vous* (*rendre*, see prec.) betake yourselves]

rĕndi′tion, n. **1.** Surrender of place or person (now rare). **2.** A translation; interpretation, rendering, of dramatic role, musical piece, etc. [F (obs.), f. *rendre* RENDER, -ION]

rĕn′ĕgāde, n. & v.i., **rĕnĕgād′ō** (arch.), n. **1.** Apostate, esp. from Christianity to Mohammedanism; deserter of party or principles, turncoat. **2.** v.i. Turn ~; so **rĕnĕgA′TION** n. [Sp. (-*o*), f. med. L *re*(*negatus* f. *negare* deny), RE- 9]

rĕneg(u)e′ (-ēg), v.i. & t. (Cards) revoke; (arch.) deny, renounce, abandon. [f. med. L *renegare* f. RE-+*negare* deny]

rĕnew′, v.t. & i. **1.** Restore to original state, make (as good as) new, resuscitate, revivify, regenerate, (*nature dies & is* ~*ed*; ~ person's *life, sorrow, energy*; ~ *the golden age*; *rose from her knees* ~*ed by the Holy Spirit*; ~*ed by baptism*). **2.** Patch, fill up, reinforce, replace, (*coat* ~*ed in places*; ~ *the water in the bowl*; ~ *garrison, tires*, etc.). **3.** Get, begin, make, say, or give, anew, continue after intermission, (~ one's *youth, strength*, etc., grow young etc. again; ~ *attack, correspondence, speech, game, efforts*; ~ one's *vows, statements*, etc.; ~ *lease, bill*, grant or be granted continuation of it); (abs.) ~ lease or bill. **4.** (rare) Become new again (*the clamour* ~*ed*; *feel my youth* ~*ing*). Hence ~ABLE a., ~AL(2) n. [RE-, NEW]

rĕn′ifōrm, a. Kidney-shaped. [REINS, -FORM]

rĕnn′ĕt¹, n. Curdled milk found in stomach of unweaned calf, or preparation of stomach-membrane or of kinds of plant, used in curdling milk for cheese etc. [ME, f. *renne* obs. form of RUN¹]

‖ **rĕnn′ĕt²**, n. Kinds of dessert apple. [f. F *reinette*, f. *reine* queen f. L REGINA, -ETTE]

rĕnounce′, v.t. & i., & n. **1.** Consent formally to abandon, surrender, give up, (claim, right, possession). **2.** Repudiate, refuse to recognize longer, decline association or disclaim relationship with, withdraw from, discontinue, forsake, (~ *treaty, principles*, person's *authority*, all *thought of, design, attempt, son* etc., *friend, friendship*; ~ *the world*, abandon society or temporal affairs). **3.** (law). Refuse or resign right or position esp. as heir or trustee. **4.** (cards). Follow with card of another suit for want of right one (cf. REVOKE); (n.) playing of such card, opportunity of doing so. Hence ~MENT (-sm-) n. [ME, f. OF *renoncer* f. L *re*(*nuntiare* ANNOUNCE), RE- 5]

rĕn′ovǀāte, v.t. Make new again, repair, restore to good condition or vigour. So ~A′TION, ~ātor, nn. [f. L *re*(*novare* f. *novus* new), RE- 9, -ATE³]

rĕnown′, n. Celebrity, fame, high distinction, (*man, town*, etc., *of* ~ or *great* etc. ~, famous). [ME, f. AF *renoun* = OF *renon*

f. *renomer* make famous f. L *re*- RE- 8 + *nominare* NOMINATE]

rĕnowned′ (-nd), a. Famous, celebrated. [ME, f. prec.+-ED², after OF *renome* (p.p.)]

rĕnt¹. See REND.

rĕnt², n. Large tear in garment etc., opening in clouds etc. resembling tear; cleft, fissure, gorge. [f. obs. *rent* vb, var. of REND]

rĕnt³, n., & v.t. & i. **1.** Tenant's periodical payment to owner or landlord for use of land or house or room; payment for hire of machinery etc.; ~*charge*, periodical charge on land etc. reserved by deed to one who is not the owner; ~*free* a. & adv., with exemption from ~; ~*roll*, register of person's lands etc. with ~s due from them, sum of one's income from ~; ‖ ~*service*, (tenure by) personal service in lieu of or addition to ~; hence (of land etc., with *low, high*, etc.) -**rĕn′tED²** a. **2.** vb. Take, occupy, use, at a ~; let or hire for ~; be let *at* specified ~; impose ~ on (tenant; ~*s his tenants low*); hence ~′ABLE a., **rĕn′tER¹** n., (esp.) wholesaler in the film trade. [ME, f. OF *rente* f. Rom. **rendita* fem. p.p. as RENDER]

rĕn′tal, n. Income from rents; amount paid or received as rent. [AF (prec., -AL)]

rente (rahṅt), n. Income, esp. that consisting of life-annuity or dividends. [F]

rentier (rahṅ′tiā), n. Person living on *rente*, person not needing to earn his living. [F]

renŭm′ber. See RE- 8.

renŭnciā′tion, n. Renouncing, document expressing it; self-denial, giving up of things. So **renŭn′ciANT**(1) n. & a. (-shǐ-), **renŭn′ciATIVE** (-sha-), **renŭn′ciatory** (-shatrǐ), aa. [ME, f. L *renunciatio* (RENOUNCE, -ATION)]

reo-. See RHEO-.

reoccupy etc., **reopen**, see RE- 9; **reorganize** etc., RE- 8.

rĕp¹, **rĕpp**, **rĕps**, n. Textile fabric with ..corded surface used in upholstery. [f. F *reps* of unkn. orig.]

rĕp², n. (school sl.). Verse etc. learnt by heart. [abbr. of *repetition*]

rĕp³, n. (sl.). Person of loose character. [perh. for REPROBATE²; cf. RIP¹]

rĕp⁴, n. (sl.). Repertory theatre or company. [abbr.]

repaganize etc., **repaint**. See RE- 9.

rĕpair′¹, v.i., & n. **1.** Resort, have recourse, go often or in numbers, *to*. **2.** n. (arch.). Resort (*have* ~ *to*); haunt; being visited by numbers (*a place of great, little,* ~). [ME, f. OF *repaire*(r) f. LL *re*(*patriare* f. L *patria* native land), RE- 9]

rĕpair′², v.t. Restore (building, machine, garment, tissue, strength, etc.) to good condition, renovate, mend, by replacing or refixing parts or compensating loss or exhaustion, whence ~ABLE a.; remedy, set right again, make amends for, (loss, wrong, error). [ME, f. OF *reparer* or L *re(parare* make ready), RE- 9]

rĕpair'[3], n. Restoring to sound condition (*health, bicycle, house, boots, need* ~; *shop is closed during* ~*s*; ~*s done while you wait*; *running* ~*s*, minor replacements); good condition, relative condition, for working or using (*is in, out of,* ~; *must be kept in good, is in bad,* ~). [f. prec.]

rĕpănd', a. (bot., zool.). With undulating margin, wavy. Hence ~o- comb. form. [f. L *re(pandus* bent), RE- 9]

repaper. See RE- 8.

rĕp'arable, a. (Of loss etc.) that can be made good. [F, f. L *reparabilis* (REPAIR[2], -ABLE)]

rĕparā'tion, n. **1.** Repairing or being repaired, repair, (pl.) repairs, (now usu. *repair, repairs*). **2.** Making of amends, compensation (esp., pl., for war damages). So **rĕp'ar**ATIVE (*or* rĭpă'r-) a. [ME, f. OF *reparacion* f. LL *reparationem* (REPAIR[2], -ATION)]

rĕpartee', n., & v.i. Witty retort; (making of) witty retorts (*a great power, a storehouse, of* ~); (vb, now rare) make ~s. [f. F *repartie* fem. p.p. of *re(partir* PART[2]) start again, reply promptly, RE- 8]

repartition, see RE- 8; **repass** etc., RE- 9.

rĕpast' (-ah-), n. (Food supplied for or eaten at) meal (usu. *rich, plentiful, slight, delicate, luxurious,* etc., ~). [ME, f. OF, f. *repaistre* f. LL *re(pascere past-* feed), RE- 8]

rĕpăt'ri|āte, v.t. & i. Restore or return to native land. Hence ~ATE[1] (-at) n., one who has been ~ated, ~A'TION n. [f. LL *re(patriare* f. L *patria* fatherland), RE- 9]

rĕpay', v.t. & i. (-paid). Pay back (money); return, retaliate, (blow, visit, service, etc.); give in recompense *for*; make repayment to (person); make return for, requite, (action); make repayment. Hence ~ABLE a., ~MENT n. [f. OF *re(paier* PAY[2]), RE- 9]

rĕpeal', v.t., & n. **1.** Revoke, rescind, annul, (law etc.); hence ~ABLE a. **2.** n. Abrogation, ~ing; (Irish pol.) cancelling of the Union of .1801 demanded by O'Connell etc., whence ~ER[1] n. (hist.). [ME, f. AF *repel(l)er* = OF *rapeler* (RE- 9, APPEAL[1])]

rĕpeat', v.t. & i., & n. **1.** Say or do over again, recite, rehearse, report, reproduce, give imitation of, (~ *action, statement, poem, conversation, attempt, pattern, signal,* etc.; *action was* ~*ed several times,* whence ~ĕDLY[2] adv.; *language will not bear* ~*ing,* is too foul etc. to ~); (of watch etc., abs.) strike last quarter etc. over again when required (so ~*ing watch* etc. or ~ER[1] n.); (of fire-arms) fire several shots without reloading (~*ing rifle* etc.). **2.** Recur, appear again or ~edly; (*the last three figures* ~; *food* ~*s,* is tasted intermittently for some time). **3.** (refl.). Recur in same form, say or do same thing over again, (*history*

~*s itself; does nothing but* ~ *himself*); hence ~ABLE a. n. ~ing, esp. of item in programme in response to encore; (radio) ~ed programme; (mus.) passage intended to be ~ed, mark indicating this; pattern ~ed in wallpaper etc.; (commerc.) fresh consignment similar to previous one, order given for this. [ME, f. OF *repeter* f. L *re(petere* seek), RE- 8]

rĕp'échage (-eshahzh), n. (rowing). Extra race in which runners-up in the eliminating races compete for a place in the final. [F]

rĕpĕl', v.t. (-ll-). **1.** Drive back, repulse, ward off, refuse admission or acceptance or approach to, (~ *assailant, attack, temptation, weapon, blow, suggestion, plea, offer,* person's *advances*; *first attracts & then* ~*s the magnet*). **2.** Be repulsive or distasteful to, exert mental repulsion upon, whence ~l'ENT a. & n., ~l'entLY[2] adv. [ME, f. L *re(pellere* puls- drive), RE- 2]

rĕp'ent[1], a. (chiefly bot.). Creeping, esp. growing along or just under surface of ground. [f. L *repere* creep, -ENT]

rĕpĕnt'[2], v.t. & i. **1.** (arch.). (Refl., with arch. refl. pron.) feel regret or penitence about something or *of* (*I now* ~ *me*; *he* ~*eth him of the evil*); (impers.) affect with penitence or regret (*it* ~*s me that I did it*). **2.** Think with contrition *of,* think with contrition of, be regretful about or *of,* be contrite, wish one had not done, (*you shall* ~ *this, of this,* or abs.; *have nothing to* ~ *of;* ~ *my kindness, setting off when I did*). So **rĕpĕn'**tANCE n., **rĕpĕn'**tANT a., **rĕpĕn'tant**LY[2] adv. [ME, f. OF *repentir* f. re- RE- 3 + *pentir* f. Rom. **penitire* f. L *poenitēre*]

repeople. See RE- 9.

repercussion etc. See RE- 9.

rĕp'ertoire (-twăr), n. Stock of pieces etc. that company or performer knows or is prepared to give. [F (ré-), f. L as foll.]

rĕp'ertory, n. **1.** Place for finding something, store or collection, esp. of information, instances, facts, etc. **2.** = prec. (~ *theatre, company, system,* relying on ~ & not on long runs). [f. LL *repertorium* f. L *reperire -pert-* find]

reperuse etc. See RE- 8.

rĕpĕtĕnd', n. Recurring figures of decimal; recurring word or phrase, refrain. [f. L as REPEAT]

rĕpĕti'tion, n. REPEATing or being repeated; piece set to be learnt by heart; copy, replica; ability of musical instrument, to repeat note quickly. Hence ~ionAL, ~ionARY[1], (-sho), ~ioUS (-shᵘs), **rĕpĕt'itIVE,** aa. (rare). [f. F, or L *repetitio* (RE- 8, PETITION)]

repiece. See RE- 9.

rĕpīn|e', v.i. Fret, be discontented, (*at, against,* or abs.). Hence ~'ingLY[2] adv. [RE- 6, PINE[2]]

rĕpique' (-ēk), n., & v.t. & i. **1.** Winning

of 30 points on cards alone before beginning to play in piquet. **2.** vb. Score ~ against (opponent); make ~. [f. F *repic* (RE-, PIQUE²)]

replāce′, v.t. Put back in place; take place of, succeed, be substituted for, (pass.) be succeeded or have one's or its place filled *by*, be superseded; fill up place of (*with, by*), find or provide substitute. for. Hence ~ABLE (-sa-) a., ~MENT (-sm-) n., (also) person or thing that ~s another. [RE- 9, PLACE²]

replant etc. See RE- 8.

replay′, v.t. Play (a match) over again; hence **rĕp′lay** n., a ~ed match. [RE- 8]

replĕn′ish, v.t. Fill up again (*with* or abs.); (p.p.) filled, fully stored, full, (*with* or abs.). Hence ~MENT n. [ME, f. OF *re(plenir* ult. f. L *plenus* full), RE- 9, -ISH²]

replēte′, a. Filled, stuffed, fully imbued, well stocked, *with*; gorged, sated, (*with*). So ~ē′TION n. (esp. *full to* ~*etion*). [ME, f. OF *replet* or L *re(plēre plet-* fill), RE- 6]

replĕv′in, n. Restoration or recovery of distrained goods on security given for submission to trial & judgement; writ granting ~; action arising out of ~. [ME, f. AF, f. OF as foll.]

replĕv′y̆, v.t. Recover by replevin. [f. OF *re(plevir* f. Frank. *pligi PLEDGE¹), RE- 9]

rĕp′lica, n. Duplicate made by original artist of his picture etc.; facsimile, exact copy. [It. (*replicare* REPLY)]

rĕp′licate¹, n. Tone one or more octaves above or below given tone. [as foll.]

rĕp′licate², a. (bot.). Folded back on itself. [as foll., -ATE²]

rĕp′licāte³, v.t. (rare). Repeat; make replica of; fold back. [L *re(plicare* fọld), RE- 9, -ATE³]

rĕplicā′tion, n. **1.** Folding back, fold, (rare). **2.** Replying, rejoinder, answer, esp. reply to answer; (law) plaintiff's reply to defendant's plea. **3.** Echo. **4.** Copy, copying. [ME, f. OF, f. L *replicationem* (prec., -ATION)]

replȳ′, v.i. & t., & n. **1.** Make answer, respond, in word or action (*to*; abs., *that* etc., or parenth.; *rose to* ~ *for the ladies*, represent them in returning thanks for toast; *the batteries replied to our fire*; *he replied that I must please myself*; '*Please yourself*' *he replied*). **2.** n. Act of ~ing (*what he says in* ~); what is replied, response; ~ *paid*, (of telegram) with cost of ~ prepaid by sender. [ME, f. OF *replier* f. L as REPLICATE³]

repoint, repolish. See RE- 9.

répondez s'il vous plaît (see Ap.), formula appended (usu. in abbr. *R.S.V.P.*) to invitation or other letter,=please answer. [F]

repopulate. See RE- 9.

rĕpōrt′¹, v.t. & i. **1.** Bring back account of, state as ascertained fact, tell as news,

narrate or describe or repeat esp. as eye--witness etc. (*to*), relate as spoken by another, make official or formal statement about, inform against (offence, offender) *to* authorities or abs., announce oneself or abs. as returned or arrived, (~*s open water at pole, pole to be accessible, that he reached pole*; *it is* ~*ed*, commonly said; ~*ed all details of the scene to me*; *my actual words & those* ~*ed to you were quite different*; ~*ed speech*, oblique oration; *chairman of committee* ~*s bill to House*, announces conclusion of committee's dealings with it between 2nd & 3rd, reading; ‖~ *progress*, state what has been done so far, *move to* ~ *progress* in House of Commons, propose that debate be discontinued, often for obstructive purposes; *all variations are to be* ~*ed daily*; *shall* ~ *you, your unpunctuality, to senior partner*). **2.** Take down word for word or epitomize or write description of for publication (~ *law case, proceedings, meeting*; also abs., as *reports for* The Times). **3.** Make, draw up, or send in report. **4.** Give report of conveying that one is *well* or *badly* impressed (~*s well of the prospects*; *is badly* ~*ed of*). Hence ~ABLE a., ~AGE n., (typical style of) ~ing events for the press, ~ER¹ n. [ME, f. OF *reporter* f. L *re(portare* bring), RE- 9]

rĕpōrt′², n. **1.** Common talk, rumour, (*mere* ~ *is not enough to go upon*; *the* ~ *goes*, it is said); way person or thing is spoken of, repute, (*things of good* ~; *faithful through good & evil* ~). **2.** Account given or opinion formally expressed after investigation or consideration, description or epitome or reproduction of scene or speech or law case esp. for newspaper publication, ‖(~ *stage* in House of Commons, treatment of bill when committee has reported, see prec.); periodical statement on a pupil's work, conduct, etc. at school. **3.** Sound of explosion (*went off with a loud* ~). [ME, f. OF, f. *reporter* (see prec.)]

rĕpōs⎮e′¹ (-z), v.t. Place (trust etc.) *in*. Hence ~′AL (-zl) n. [f. RE- 4 + POSE¹, after L *re(ponere posit-* place)]

rĕpōse′² (-z), v.t. & i., & n. **1.** Rest (oneself or abs.); lay (one's *head* etc.) to rest (often *on* pillow etc.); give rest to, refresh with rest; lie, be lying or laid, esp. in sleep or death (*in, on*, or abs.), be supported or based *on* (*the whole system* ~*s on fear*); (of memory etc.) dwell *on*. **2.** n. Rest, cessation· of activity or excitement, respite from toil, sleep, peaceful or quiescent state, stillness, tranquillity; restful effect, harmonious combination in art, composure or ease of manner, (esp. in *lacks* ~); hence ~FUL (-zf-) a., ~fulLY² adv. [ME, f. OF *repos(er*) f. LL *re(pausare* PAUSE; RE- 5); meaning infl. by prec.]

rĕpŏs′itŏrȳ (-z-), n. **1.** Receptacle; place

where things are stored or may be found, museum, warehouse, store, shop, (*book, person, etc., is a ~ of curious information*); burial-place. **2.** Recipient *of* confidences or secrets. [f. obs. F *repositoire* or L *repositorium* (REPOSE[1], -ORY)]

repossess etc. See RE- 9.

repost. See RIPOSTE.

repot. See RE- 8.

repoussé (repōōs'ā), a. & n. (Ornamental metal work) hammered into relief from reverse side. [F, p.p. of *re(pousser* PUSH[1]), RE- 3]

repp. See REP.[1]

repped (-pt), a. Having surface like rep. [-ED[2]]

rĕprĕh|ĕnd', v.t. Rebuke, blame, find fault with. So ~ĕn'SIBLE a., ~ĕn'sibLY[2] adv., ~ĕn'SION (-shn) n. [ME, f. L *re(prehendere* seize), RE- 2]

rĕprĕsĕnt' (-z-), v.t. **1.** Call up by description or portrayal or imagination, figure, place likeness of before mind or senses, serve or be meant as likeness of, (*can you ~ infinity to yourself?*; *can only ~ it to you by metaphors*; *picture ~s murder of Abel*; *is ~ed in hunting costume*). **2.** Try to bring (facts influencing conduct) home (*to*), state by way of expostulation or incentive, (~*ed the rashness of it, that it could not succeed*). **3.** Make out *to* be etc., allege *that*, describe or depict *as*, (*am not what you ~ me to be* or *as*; *in the corner is the Pope ~ed as a beggar*; *~s that he has* or *himself to have seen service*). **4.** Act (play etc.), play part of on stage. **5.** Symbolize, act as embodiment of, stand for, correspond to, be specimen of, (*sovereign ~s majesty of State*; *inch of rain ~s 100 tons to acre*; *globe ~s totality*; *camels are ~ed in the New World by llamas*; *Welsh football is ~ed in the team by Morgan*). **6.** Fill place of, be substitute or deputy for, be entitled to speak for, be sent as member to House of Commons by, (*King was ~ed by the Duke of Norfolk*; *members ~ing urban constituencies*). Hence or cogn. ~ABLE a., ~A'TION (-z-) n. (*proportional ~ation*, electoral system so arranged that minorities are ~ed in proportion to their strength; ~ā'tionAL (-shon-) a. [ME, f. OF *representer* or L *re(praesentare* PRESENT[4]), RE- 8]

rĕprĕsĕn'tative (-z-), a. & n. **1.** Serving as portrayal or symbol *of* (*a group ~ of the theological virtues*); that presents or can present ideas to the mind (*imagination is a ~ faculty*); typical of a class or classes, containing typical specimens of all or many classes, (*the truth of an allegory is ~, not literal*; *call a meeting of ~ men*; *a very ~ selection, collection*); consisting of elected deputies or ~s (~ *chamber, house,* etc.), based on representation by such deputies (~ *government, institutions*); hence ~LY[2] adv., ~NESS n. **2.** n. Sample, specimen, typical embodiment, analogue, *of*; person's agent, delegate, substitute,

successor, or heir; deputy in ~ chamber (*House of R~s*, lower house of U.S. Congress). [ME, f. OF (-*if*, -*ive*) or med. L *repraesentativus* (REPRESENT, -ATIVE)]

rĕprĕss', v.t. Check, restrain, put down, keep under, quell, suppress, prevent from sounding or bursting out or rioting. So **rĕprĕ'ssION** (-shn) n. (esp., in psych., of natural promptings), ~IVE a. [ME, f. L *re(primere = premere* PRESS[2]), RE- 5]

rĕpriev|e', v.t., & n. **1.** Suspend or delay execution of (condemned person); (fig.) give respite to. **2.** n. ~ing or being ~ed; (warrant for) remission or commutation of capital sentence; respite. [15th c. as p.p. *repryed*, app. f. AF *repris* p.p. of *re(prendre* f. L *prehendere* take), RE- 8; -*v-* unexpl.]

rĕp'rimand (-ah-), n., & v.t. Official(ly) rebuke (*for* fault). [f. F *réprimande* f. L *reprimanda* f. *reprimere* REPRESS]

reprint. See RE- 8.

rĕpris'al (-zl), n. **1.** (hist.). Forcible seizure of foreign subjects' persons or property in retaliation (*letters of ~*, official warrant authorizing this). **2.** Act of retaliation (usu. *make ~s* or ~). [ME, f. OF *reprisaille* as foll. +-AL(2)]

rĕprise' (-z), n. **1.** (law). Rent-charge or other payment to be made yearly out of estate (*beyond, besides, above, ~s*, remaining after all ~s have been paid). **2.** (rare). Resumption of action, one of the times devoted to something not done all at once. [F, fem. of *repris* see REPRIEVE]

rĕproach', v.t., & n. **1.** Upbraid, censure, (person, often *with* offence); rebuke (offence); (of look etc.) convey protest or censure to (*his eyes ~ me*); hence ~ingLY[2] adv. (rare for ~*fully*). **2.** n. Thing that brings disgrace or discredit (*to*; *the state of the roads is a ~ to civilization*); whence ~LESS a. (rare for *irreproachable*); opprobrium, disgraced or discredited state, (*live in ~ & ignominy*; *the things that had brought ~ upon him*; *has taken away my ~*); upbraiding, rebuke, censure, (*abstain from ~*; *heap ~s on*; *the mute ~ in his eyes*; *term of ~*, word implying censure), whence ~FUL a., ~fulLY[2] adv., ~fulNESS n.; (pl.) Good-Friday chiefly R.-C. set of antiphons & responses representing ~es of Christ to people. [ME, f. OF *reproche(r)* f. Rom. *repropiare (*prope* near)]

rĕp'rob|āte[1], v.t. Express or feel disapproval of, censure; (of God) cast off, exclude from salvation. So ~A'TION n. [f. L *re(probare* approve), RE- 7, -ATE[3]]

rĕp'robate[2], a. & n. (Person) cast off by God, hardened in sin, of abandoned character, immoral. [as prec., -ATE[2]]

reproduce etc. See RE- 8.

rĕprōōf'[1], n. Blame (*a word, glance, of ~*; *spoke in ~ of idleness*); a rebuke or expression of blame. [ME, f. OF *reprove* (*re-prover* REPROVE)]

rĕprōōf'[2], v.t. Render (coat etc.) waterproof again. [RE- 9]

reprov|e' (-ŏŏv), v.t. Rebuke, chide, (person, rarely sin etc.). Hence ~'ingLY² (-ŏŏv-) adv. [ME, f. OF *reprover* f. L *reprobare* disapprove, as REPROBATE¹]

reprovision. See RE- 8.

reps. See REP¹.

rĕp'tant, a. (nat. hist.). Creeping. [f. L *reptare* frequent. of *repere* crawl, -ANT]

rĕp'tile, n. & a. **1.** Member of the *Reptilia* or class of animals including snakes, lizards, crocodiles, turtles, & tortoises, whence **rĕptil'IAN** (-lyan) a. & n., **rĕptilIF'EROUS, rĕptil'IFORM,** aa.; mean grovelling person. **2.** adj. (Of animals) creeping; mean & grovelling (*the* ~ *press,* subservient semi-official newspapers). [ME, (n. f. *reptile* neut.) f. LL *reptilis* (*repere* rept- crawl, -IL)]

rĕpŭb'lic, n. A State in which the government is carried on nominally & usu. in fact also by the people or through its elected representatives, commonwealth; (in France) *Third R~* 1871–1940, *Fourth R~* 1947–58, *Fifth R~* 1958–; (fig.) society of persons or animals with equality between members (*the* ~ *of letters,* literary men, literature). [f. F *république* or L *respublica* (abl. *republica*) f. *res* concern, PUBLICus]

rĕpŭb'lican, a. & n. **1.** Of, constituted as, characterizing, republic(s). **2.** (Person) advocating or supporting ~ government. **3.** (*R~*). *(Member) of U.-S. political party favouring liberal interpretation of constitution, extension of central power, & protective tariff, opp. DEMOCRAT(IC). **4.** (Of birds) social, living in large communities. Hence ~ISM(3) n., ~IZE(3) v.t. [-AN]

republish etc. See RE- 8.

rĕpŭd'i|āte, v.t. & i. **1.** Divorce (one's wife; esp. of the ancients or non-Christians). **2.** Disown, disavow, reject, refuse dealings with, deny. **3.** Refuse to recognize or obey (authority) or discharge (obligation, debt); (of State) ~ate public debt. So ~A'TION, ~āTOR, nn. [f. L *repudiare* (*repudium* divorce, -ATE³)]

rĕpugn' (-ūn), v.i. & t. (rare). Offer opposition; strive *against*; strive against; affect disagreeably, be repugnant to. [ME, f. OF *repugner* or L *re(pugnare* fight) oppose, RE- 2]

rĕpŭg'nance, n. Inconsistency, incompatibility, of ideas, statements, tempers, etc. (*of, between, to, with*); antipathy, dislike, aversion, (*to, against*). [ME, f. OF or L *repugnantia* (prec., -ANCE)]

rĕpŭg'nant, a. Contradictory (*to*), incompatible (*with*); (poet.) refractory, resisting; distasteful (*to*). [ME, f. OF or L as REPUGN +-ANT]

rĕpŭll'ŭl|āte, v.i. (rare). Sprout afresh, shoot out again; (of diseases) start again, recur. Hence ~A'TION n. [f. L *re(pullulare* PULLULATE), RE- 9, -ATE³]

rĕpŭls|e', v.t., & n. **1.** Drive back, (attack, attacking enemy) by force of arms, (fig.) foil in controversy; rebuff (friendly advances or maker of them), refuse (request, offer, or maker of it). **2.** n. ~ing or being ~ed, rebuff, (*inflict, meet with, suffer,* etc., ~*e* or usu. *a* ~*e*). [(n. f. L *repulsus* or *-sa*); vb f. *repuls-* as REPEL]

rĕpŭl'sion (-shn), n. **1.** Repulsing (rare). **2.** (phys.). Tendency of bodies to repel each other or increase their mutual distance (opp. ATTRACTION; also fig.); *capillary* ~, tendency in some liquids (e.g. quicksilver in glass) to shrink from wall of capillary tubes so that upper surface is convex. **3.** Dislike, aversion, repugnance. [f. LL *repulsio* (REPEL, -ION)]

rĕpŭl'sive, a. **1.** Offering resistance (poet.). **2.** (phys.). Exercising repulsion. **3.** (Of behaviour etc.) repellent, cold, unsympathetic, (arch.). **4.** Exciting aversion or loathing, loathsome, disgusting, whence ~LY² adv., ~NESS n. [f. F (-*if,* -*ive*), or REPULSE v. +-IVE]

repurchase, repurify. See RE- 9.

rĕp'ūtab|le, a. Of good repute, respectable. Hence~LY² adv. [REPUTE n., -ABLE]

rĕpūtā'tion, n. What is generally said or believed about a person's or thing's character (*has not justified his* ~); state of being well reported of, credit, distinction, respectability, good fame, (*persons of* ~; *has a* ~ *for integrity*); the credit or discredit of doing or of being (*has the* ~ *of racking his tenants, of being* or *of the best shot in England*). [ME, f. L *reputatio* (REPUTE, -ATION)]

rĕpūte', v.t., & n. **1.** (Rare in active) consider or reckon, (pass.) be generally considered or reported of, (with compl., *to* be, or *as; is* ~*d the best doctor* or *to be* or rarely *as the best*); (pass.) be generally *well, ill,* etc., thought or spoken *of*; (p.p.) passing as but probably not being (*his* ~*d father, clemency,* etc.; ||~*d pint* etc., bottle of beer etc. sold as pint etc. but not guaranteed as imperial pint etc.); hence **rĕpūt'ĕd**LY² adv. **2.** n. Reputation. [ME, f. OF *reputer* or L *re(putare* think), RE- 6]

rĕquĕst', n., & v.t. **1.** Act of asking for something, petition made, thing asked for, (*came at his* ~; *shall make two* ~*s; you shall have your* ~; *make* ~ *for*; *by* ~, in response to expressed wish); state of being sought after, demand, (*is now in great, came into,* ~). **2.** v.t. Seek permission *to* do; ask to be given or allowed or favoured with (~ *candid consideration,* person's *presence,* etc.); ask *that*; ask (person) *to* do. [ME, f. OF *requeste(r),* see RE- 6, QUEST]

requicken. See RE- 9.

rĕ'quiĕm, n. Special mass for repose of souls of the dead; musical setting for ~;

dirge. [ME; initial L wd (= rest) of the mass]

rĕquĭĕs′c|ăt, n. Wish for dead person's repose; ~*ăt,* ~*ănt, ĭn pā′ce,* abbr. R.I.P., inscription = may he or she, they, rest in peace, used esp. on R.-C. tombs. [L, = may he rest]

rĕquīre′, v.t. & i. **1.** Order (person), demand (*of* or *from* person), *to do* (*they ~ me* or *of me to appear*); demand or ask in words (person's action, act *of* person, thing *at* person's *hands, that,* etc.) esp. as of right (*they ~ my appearance, an oath of me, a gift at my hands, that I should appear*). **2.** Lay down as imperative (*had done all that was ~d by the Act*). **3.** Need, call for, depend for success etc. on, (*the emergency ~s it, that it should be done; irony ~s care in its use; land ~s 10 lb. of seed to the acre; place would ~ an army to take it; machine ~s no attention; it ~d all his authority to keep them in hand*). **4.** (rare). ‖ Be neces′sary (*do not tie it more tightly than ~s*). Hence ~MENT (-īrm-) n. [ME, f. OF *requerre* f. L *rc*(*quirere -quisit-* = *quaerere* seek), RE- 6]

rĕ′quisite (-z-), a. & n. **1.** Required by circumstances, necessary to success etc., called for; hence ~NESS (-zĭtn-) n. **2.** n. Requirement, thing needed for accomplishment of some purpose (*for*). [ME, f. L p.p. as prec.]

rĕquisi′tion (-z-), n., & v.t. **1.** Requiring, demand made, esp. formal & usu. written demand that some duty should be performed; order given to town etc. to furnish certain military etc. supplies; being called or put into service (*is under* or *in ~,* being used or applied; *put in, call into, ~,* have recourse to). **2.** v.t. Demand use or supply of esp. for war purposes; demand such supplies etc. from (town etc.); press into service, call in for some purpose. [F, or f. L *requisitio* (REQUIRE, -ION)]

rĕquit|e′, v.t. Make return for, reward or avenge, (service, wrong, injury, treatment; often *with*); make return to, repay with good or evil, (person; often *for* treatment received, *with* treatment given); give in return (*~e like for like*). Hence ~′AL(2) n. [RE- 1, *quite* var. of QUIT²]

re-read. See RE- 8.

rere′dŏs, n. (rēŕd-), n. Ornamental screen covering wall at back of altar. [ME, f. AF *reredos (REAR¹, F *dos* back f. L *dorsum*)]

rēs (-z), n. Thing (*~ judĭcāt′a* (jōō-), = CHOSE JUGÉE); property (*~ ăngŭs′ta* (-ngg-) *domĭ′,* poverty). [L]

resaddle, resale etc. See RE- 9.

rĕscind′, v.t. Abrogate, annul, revoke, cancel. So **rĕsci′ssION** (-zhn) n. [f. L *rc*(*scindere sciss-* cut), RE- 5]

rĕs′cript, n. **1.** Roman emperor's written reply to appeal for guidance esp. from magistrate on legal point; Pope's decretal epistle in reply to question, any

papal decision. **2.** Ruler's or government's or official edict or announcement. **3.** Thing rewritten, rewriting; palimpsest. [f. L *rescriptum,* p.p. neut. of *re*(*scribere script-* write), RE- 1]

rĕs′cū|e, v.t., & n. **1.** Deliver from or *from* attack, custody, danger, or harm; (law) unlawfully liberate (person), forcibly recover (property); hence ~ER¹ n. **2.** n. ~ing or being ~ed, succour, deliverance, illegal liberation, forcible recovery; *~e* (*bid*), a bid at bridge made to get one's partner out of a difficult situation. [ME *rescowe* f. OF *rescoure* f. Rom. *rexcutere (L RE-, EX*cutere* = *quatere* shake)]

rĕsearch′ (-sêr-), n., & v.i. **1.** Careful search or inquiry *after* or *for*; (usu. pl.) endeavour to discover new facts etc. by scientific study of a subject, course of critical investigation, (*his ~es have been fruitful; is engaged in ~*). **2.** v.i. Make ~es; hence ~ER¹ n. [f. obs. F *recerche*(*r*), now *recherche*(*r*), see RE- 6, SEARCH]

reseat. See RE- 8.

rĕsĕct′, v.t. (surg.). Pare down (bone, cartilage, etc.). So **rĕsĕc′tION** n. [f. L *re*(*secare sect-* cut), RE- 5]

rĕsēd′a, n. **1.** Kinds of plants including mignonette & dyer's weed. **2.** (usu. *rēsēda* F, pr. rāzădăh′). Pale green colour as of mignonette. [L]

reseek, see RE- 8; **reseize** etc., **resell,** RE- 9.

rĕsĕm′bl|e (-z-), v.t. Be like, have similarity to or feature(s) in common with or same appearance as, & so ~ANCE (*to, between, of*) n., ~ANT (*to*) a. (rare); (arch.) liken *to*. [ME, f. OF *re*(*sembler* f. L *simi-lare, simulare,* f. *similis* SIMILAR), RE- 1]

rĕsĕnt′ (-z-), v.t. Show or feel indignation at or retain feelings about (insult or injury sustained). Hence ~FUL [perh. through obs. *resent* ~ment] a., ~fuLLY² adv., ~MENT n. [f. F *ressentir* (RE- 1, L *sentire* feel)]

rĕservā′tion (-z-), n. In vbl senses; also or esp.: (eccl.) right reserved to Pope of nomination to vacant benefice, power of absolution reserved to superior, practice of retaining for some purpose a portion of the Eucharistic elements (esp. the bread) after celebration; (law) right or interest retained in estate being conveyed, clause reserving it; *tract of land reserved esp. for exclusive occupation by native tribe; express or tacit limitation or exception made about something (*mental ~,* qualification tacitly added in making statement, oath, etc.); *booking (of berth on steamer, room in hotel, seat in train, etc.). [ME, f. OF, or f. LL *reservatio* (foll., -ATION)]

rĕsérv|e¹ (-z-), v.t. **1.** Postpone use or enjoyment or treatment of, hold over, keep back for later occasion, (*~e oneself for,* not put forth one's energies till). **2.** Secure or retain possession or control of esp. by legal or formal stipulation (*for* or *to* oneself or another; *~ed seats* at entertainment etc., that may be booked; ‖ *~ed list*, of naval officers removed from active service but liable to be called out); .(pass.) be left by fate *for*, fall first or only *to*. **3.** Set apart, destine, *for* some use or fate. **4.** (p.p. as adj.). Reticent, slow to reveal emotions or opinions, uncommunicative, whence *~'*ĕdLY² (-z-) adv. [ME, f. OF *reserver* f. L *re*(*servare* keep), RE- 3]

rĕsĕ́rve'² (-z-), n. **1.** Something reserved for future use, extra stock or amount, (*banker's ~*, amount kept on hand to meet probable demands; *has a great ~ of energy*; often attrib., as *his ~ strength*). **2.** (Mil., sing. or pl.) troops withheld from action to reinforce or cover retreat, forces outside regular army & navy & air force liable to be called out in emergencies, member of such forces (also **rĕsĕ́rv'IST** (-z-) n.); (in games) extra player chosen in case substitute should be needed. **3.** Being kept unused but available (*has it in ~*). **4.** Place reserved for some special use (*game ~*). **5.** (At exhibitions) distinction conveying that exhibit will have prize if another is disqualified. **6.** Limitation, exception, restriction, or qualification, attached to something (*I accept your statement without ~*, fully; *sale* or *auction without ~*, not subject to a fixed price's being reached; *~ price*, than which less will not be a█████; *we publish this with all ~*, *all prope**r** ~s*, without endorsing it). **7.** Self-restraint, abstinence from exaggeration or ill-proportioned effects, in artistic or literary expression; reticence, avoidance of plain speaking, coolness of manner, lack of cordiality; intentional suppression of truth. [f. prec., partly thr. F]

rĕs'ervoir (-zervwâr), n., & v.t. **1.** Receptacle constructed usu. of earthwork or masonry in which large quantity of water is stored. **2.** Any natural or artificial receptacle esp. for or of fluid, place where fluid etc. collects; part of machine or organ of body holding fluid (*~ pen*, containing its own supply of ink); reserve supply or collection of something e.g. knowledge or facts, etc. **3.** v.t. Store in *~*. [F, f. *réserver* see prec., -ORY(2)]

‖ **rĕsĕ́t'¹**, v.t. & i. (-tt-). Receive (stolen goods); receive stolen goods. So **~t'ER¹** n. [ME, f. OF *receter* f. L *receptare* frequent, of *recipere* RECEIVE]

reset², **resettle** etc., **reshape**, see RE- 8; **reship** etc., RE- 9; **reshuffle**, RE- 8.

rĕside' (-z-), v.i. (Of persons) have one's home, dwell permanently, *at, in, abroad*, etc.; (of officials) be 'in residence; (of power, rights, etc.) rest or be vested *in* person etc.; (of qualities) be present or inherent *in*. [ME, f. OF *resider* or L *re*(*sidēre* = *sedēre* sit), RE- 3]

rĕs'ĭdence (-z-), n. **1.** Residing (*have, take up*, one's *~*, dwell, begin to dwell; *honoured the place with her~*; *~ is required*,- official etc. must live on the spot for certain periods or altogether; so *in ~*). **2.** Place where one resides, abode *of*; house esp. of considerable pretension, mansion, (*desirable family ~ for sale*). [ME, f. OF f. med. L *residentia* (prec., -ENCE)]

rĕs'ĭdency (-z-), n. (hist.). Official residence of Governor-general's representative at Indian native court. [as prec., -ENCY]

rĕs'ĭdent (-z-), a. & n. **1.** Residing (*whether ~ at home or abroad*; *the ~ population*); (of birds etc.) non-migratory; bound to residence, having quarters on the spot, (*~ surgeon, tutor, political agent*); inherent, located, *in* (*a right ~ in the nation*; *powers of sensation ~ in the nerves*). **2.** n. Permanent inhabitant of town or neighbourhood (opp. *visitor*); Indian Governor-general's political agent residing at native's court (hist.), British government agent in other semi-dependent State, whence *~SHIP* n. [ME, f. OF or L (RESIDE, -ENT)]

rĕsĭdĕn'tial (-z-, -shl), a. Suitable for or occupied by private houses (*~ estate, street, quarter*); connected with residence (*the ~ qualification for voters*). [RESIDENCE, -AL]

rĕsĭdĕn'tiary̆ (-z-, -sha-), n. & a. **1.** Ecclesiastic bound to residence. **2.** adj. Bound to, requiring, of or for, official residence (usu. after n.; *Canon, Canonry, ~*; *at his ~ house*). [f. med. L *residentiarius* (RESIDENCE, -ARY¹)]

rĕsĭd'ŭal (-z-), a. & n. **1.** (math.). Resulting from subtraction (n., *~ quantity*). **2.** Remaining, left over, left as residuum, (n., remainder, substance of the nature of a residuum). **3.** (Of error in calculations) still unaccounted for or not eliminated. [f. RESIDUE + -AL]

rĕsĭd'ŭary̆ (-z-), a. Of the residue of an estate (*~ bequest, clause, legatee*, etc.); of, being, a residuum, residual, still remaining, (*mere ~ substances*; *the ~ aberration*; *some ~ odds & ends*). [RESIDUUM, -ARY¹]

rĕs'ĭdŭe (-z-), n. Remainder, rest, what is left or remains over; what remains of estate after payment of charges, debts, & bequests; (chem. etc.) residuum. [ME, f. OF *residu* f. L RESIDUUM]

rĕsĭd'ŭum (-z-), n. (pl. -*dua*). What remains, esp. (chem. etc.) substance left after combustion or evaporation, (in calculations) amount not accounted for or residual error; lowest stratum or dregs of population. [L, neut. of *residuus* remaining (RESIDE)]

rĕsĭgn'¹ (-zīn), v.t. & i. **1.** Relinquish, surrender, give up, hand over, (office, right, claim, property, charge, task, life, hope; often *to* person, *into* person's hands etc.; ~ one*self to* another's *guidance, to sleep, rest, meditation,* etc.). **2.** Reconcile one*self*, one's *mind*, etc. (*to* one's *fate* etc., *to doing,* or abs. =.accept the inevitable without repining), whence ~ED[1] (-zīnd′) a., ~êdLY[2] (-zĭn-) adv. **3.** Give up office, retire. [ME, f. OF *resigner* f. L *re(signare* seal) unseal, cancel, RE- 7]

rē′-sign′[2] (-sīn), v.t. & i. Sign again. [RE- 8]

rĕsignā′tion (-z-), n. In vbl senses (RE-SIGN[1]); esp.: resigning of an office, document conveying it (*give, send·in,* one's ~); being resigned, uncomplaining endurance of sorrow or other evil. [ME, f. OF f. med. L *resignatio* (RESIGN[1], -ATION)]

rēsile′ (-z-), v.i. (Of elastic bodies) recoil, rebound, resume shape & size after stretching or compression; have or show elasticity or buoyancy or recuperative power. Hence or cogn. **rēsil′iENCE**, **rēsil′iENCY**, nn., **rēsil′iENT** a., (-zĭlyen-). [f. obs. F *résiler, -ir,* or L *re(silire = salire* -jump), RE- 9]

rĕs′in (-z-), n., & v.t. **1.** Adhesive substance insoluble in water (cf. GUM[2]) secreted by most plants & exuding naturally or upon incision esp. from fir & pine; kinds of similar substance got by chemical process. v.t. Rub or treat with ~. Hence ~ĬF′EROUS ~ĬFORM, ~OUS, aa., ~OID a. & n., ~ATE[1](3) n., ~ĬFY v.t. & i., ~ĬFICA′TION n., ~O- comb. form. [ME *resyn, rosyn,* f. L *resina,* med. L *rosina*]

rĕsipis′c|ence, n. Recognition of error, return to good sense. So ~ENT a. [F, or f. LL *resipiscentia* f. *re(sipiscere* f. *sapere* see SAPIENT), RE- 9]

rĕsist′ (-z-), v.t. & i., & n. **1.** Stop course of, successfully oppose, keep off or out, prevent from penetrating, repel, be proof against or unaffected or uninjured by, abstain from, (projectile, weapon, edge, frost, heat, moisture, attack, temptation, power, infection, influence, suggestion, etc.; *who can ~ God's will?; cannot ~ a joke,* must make it if it suggests itself, or must be amused by it); whence ~IBLE a., ~LESS a. (poet.), ~lèssLY[2] adv. **2.** Strive against, oppose, try to impede, refuse to comply with, as ~ *arrest.* **3.** Offer resistance, make opposition, whence or cogn. ~ANT, ~ENT, ~IVE, aa., ~ER[1] n. (‖ *passive ~er,* person refusing on grounds of justice to pay education rate imposed by Act in 1902), ~OR n., device offering electrical resistance. **4.** n. Composition applied to surfaces for protection from some agent employed on them, esp. to parts of calico that are not to take dye. [ME, f. OF *resister* or L *re(sistere* redupl. of *stare* stand), RE- 2]

rĕsis′tance (-z-), n. **1.** (Power of) resisting (*passive ~,* refusal to comply; *something with greater ~ for its weight than steel*); ~ *movement* (esp. of unconquered people in a conquered country). **2.** Hindrance,

impeding or stopping effect, exercised by material thing upon another (*overcome the ~ of the air; ~ of fluids varies with their specific gravity; line of ~,* direction in which it acts; *take line of least ~,* fig., adopt easiest method or course). **3.** (Electr.,magnet., heat) non-conductivity; (electr.) part of apparatus used to offer definite ~ to current. [ME, f. OF *resist-ance* f. LL *resistantia* (prec., -ANCE)]

rĕsistibil′itў (-z-), n. Being resistible; power of offering resistance. [RESIST*ible,* -BILITY]

resole. See RE- 8.

rĕs′oluble (-zolŏō-, -lū-), a. That can be resolved, (usu.) analysable *into,* resolvable. [f. LL *resolubilis* (RESOLVE, & see SOLUBLE)]

rĕs′olute (-zolŏōt, -ūt), a. (Of person or his temper or action) determined, decided, bold, not vacillating, unshrinking, firm of purpose. Hence ~LY[2] adv. [f. L *resolutus* p.p., see RESOLVE]

rĕsolu′tion (-zolŏō-, -lū-), n. **1.** Separation into components, decomposition; analysis, conversion *into* other form; (med.) disappearance of inflammation without suppuration; (pros.) substitution of two short syllables for one long; (mus.) making of discord to pass into concord; (mech.) replacing of single force by two or more jointly equivalent. **2.** Solving of doubt, problem, question, etc. **3.** Formal expression of opinion by legislative body (cf. MOTION) or public meeting, form proposed for this. **4.** Resolve, thing resolved on, (*good ~s,* intentions that one formulates mentally for virtuous conduct). **5.** Determined temper or character, boldness & firmness of purpose. [ME, f. OF or L *resolutio* (RESOLVE, -ION)]

rĕs′olutive (-zolŏō-, -lū-), a. & n. **1.** Having dissolving power, disintegrating, (chiefly med.); (n.) ~ application or drug. **2.** (law). ~ *condition,* whose fulfilment terminates contract etc. [f. med. L *resolutivus* (as prec., -IVE)]

rĕsŏlve′ (-z-), v.t. & i., & n. **1.** Dissolve (t. & i.; *into*),·disintegrate, analyse, break up into parts, dissipate, convert or be converted *into;* reduce by mental analysis *into,* (used *vinegar to ~ the rocks; blood first coagulates & then ~s; ~ thing, thing is ~d or ~s itself or ~s, into its elements; telescope ~s nebula into stars; inflammation, tumour, is ~d* or ~s, passes away without suppuration; *House ~s itself into a committee; might ~ Christianity into a system of morality*); (mus.) convert (discord) or be converted into concord. **2.** Solve, explain, clear up, settle, (*all doubts were ~d;* as *me this,* arch., answer this question; *the problem of its origin has not yet been ~d*). **3.** Decide upon, make up one's mind *upon* action or *doing* or *to do,* form mentally or (of legislative body or public meeting) pass by vote the resolution *that,* (of circumstances etc.) bring (person) to resolution *to do* or *upon*

action or doing, (he ~d upon or rarely ~d
amendment; ~d that nothing should induce
him, that he would do, upon doing; the
House began by resolving that . . .; this
discovery ~d us on going or to go; p.p.
used in minutes of meeting, = the following resolution was passed, namely that;
p.p. as adj., resolute, whence **rĕsŏl'vĕd-
ly²** (-z-) adv.); hence **rĕsŏl'vable** (-z-) a.
4. n. Resolution come to in the mind (&
she kept her ~); (poet.) resolution, steadfastness, (a mind, deeds, of high ~). [ME,
f. L re(solvere solut- SOLVE), RE- 5]

rĕsŏl'vent (-z-), a. & n. (chiefly med. &
chem.). (Drug, application, substance)
effecting resolution of tumour etc. or
division into component parts. [prec.,
-ENT]

rĕs'on|ant (-z-), a. (Of sound) echoing,
resounding, continuing to sound, reinforced or prolonged by vibration or reflexion; (of bodies, rooms, etc.) tending to
reinforce or prolong sounds esp. by vibration; (of places) resounding with. Hence
or cogn. **~ANCE** n., **~antly²** adv. [F, or
f. L re(sonare sound), RE- 6, -ANT]

rĕs'onātor (-z-), n. Instrument responding to single note & used for detecting it
in combinations; appliance for giving
resonance to sounds. [as prec., -OR].

rĕsŏrb', v.t. Absorb again. Hence **~ENCE**
n., **~ENT** a. [f. L re(sorbēre sorpt- ABSORB),
RE- 9]

rĕsŏr'cin (-z-), n. Compound got by action of potash on resin used chiefly as
dye-stuff. [RESIN, ORCIN]

rĕsŏrp'tion, n. Resorbing or being re-
sorbed. [RESORB, -ION]

rĕsŏrt'¹ (-z-), v.i. 1. Turn for aid to (~ to
force, experiment, etc., or rarely concrete
object or person). 2. Go in numbers or
often to (visitors ~ed to him, to the shrine,
by the hundred; watched the inn to which he
was known to ~). [ME, f. OF re(sortir
come or go out) rebound etc., RE- 8]

rĕsŏrt'² (-z-), n. 1. Thing to which recourse
is had, what is turned to for aid, expedient, (a carriage, repetition. of the experiment, was the only ~). 2. Recourse (cannot
be done without ~ to compulsion; in the
last ~, when all else has failed, as final
attempt). 3. Frequenting or being frequented (encouraged the ~ of scholars; a
place of great~). 4. Place frequented usu.
for specified purpose or quality (health,
holiday, ~; mountain, seaside, ~). [ME, f.
OF f. resortir (prec.)]

rĕ-sŏrt'³, v.t. Sort again. [RE- 8]

rĕsound' (-z-), v.i. & t. 1. (Of place) ring
or echo (with); (of voice, instrument,
sound, etc.) produce echoes, go on sounding, fill place with sound. 2. (Of fame,
event, etc.) be much talked of, produce
sensation, (often through Europe ·etc.).
3. Repeat loudly (usu. the praises etc. of);
(of place) give back (sound). Hence

~ingly² adv. [ME; RE- 9, SOUND, after
OF resoner or L resonare (RESONANT)]

rĕsource' (-sōrs), n. 1. (Usu. in pl.) means
of supplying a want, stock that can be
drawn on; (pl.) country's collective means
for support & defence. 2. (after French;
now rare). Possibility of aid (lost without
~). 3. Expedient, device, shift, (flight was
his only ~; am at the end of my ~s). 4.
Leisure occupation (reading is a great ~;
a man of no ~s). 5. Skill in devising
expedients, practical ingenuity, quick
wit, (is full of ~). Hence **~FUL** (-ōrsf-),
~LESS (-ōrsl-), aa., **~fulNESS**, **~lĕssNESS**,
nn., **~fully²** adv. [f. F ressource f. OF
re(s)sourdre f. RE- 9, L surgere rise]

rĕspĕct'¹, n. 1. Reference, relation, (to;
the terms have ~ to position alone; is true
with ~ to the French; with ~ to possible
routes, there are three; ablative, accusative,
of ~ in Lat. gram., those translatable by
with ~ or as to). 2. Heed or regard to or
of, attention to, (have not had or paid ~ to
anything but colour; did it quite without ~
to the results; ~ of persons, partiality or
favour shown esp. to the powerful).
3. Particular, detail, point, aspect, (of; is
admirable in ~ of style; in all, many, some,
~s; in one, this, ~). 4. (arch.). Consideration that (is out of the question, in ~ that
it stultifies the whole plan). 5. Deferential
esteem felt or shown towards person or
quality (has won the ~ of all; have the
greatest ~ for him; is held in ~; SELF-~).
6. pl. (With my, his, etc.) polite messages
or attentions (give him my, sends his, ~s;
went to pay his ~s to). [ME, f. OF or L
respectus -ūs (respicere see foll.)]

rĕspĕct'², v.t. 1. Pay heed to (arch.; ~
persons, discriminate unfairly between
them under influence of wealth etc.,
whence **~ER¹** of persons). 2. Relate
to, be concerned with, (now rare exc. in
part., as legislation ~ing property, also
used as prep., as am at a loss ~ing his
whereabouts). 3. Regard with deference;
avoid degrading or insulting or injuring
or interfering with or interrupting, treat
with consideration, spare, (~ oneself,
refrain from unworthy conduct or
thoughts, have self-respect; ~ innocence or
the innocent, refrain from offending or corrupting or tempting; ~ed my silence, let
me remain silent; ~ privileges, property,
neutral territory, etc.). [f. L re(spicere
spect- = specere look at), RE- 6]

rĕspĕctabil'ity, n. Being, those who are,
·a person who is, socially respectable.
[foll., -BILITY]

rĕspĕc'table, a. & n. 1. Deserving respect
(did ·it from ~ motives). 2. Not inconsiderable in amount etc., of some merit
or importance, fairly good or many or
much, tolerable, passable, (a ~ hill,
antiquity, painter, minority; ~ talents).
3. Of fair social standing, having the

qualities necessary for such standing, not disreputable, honest & decent in conduct; (of pursuits, clothes, etc.) befitting ~ persons; hence **rěspěc′tably²** adv. **4. n. A** ~ person (usu. in pl.). [-ABLE]

rěspěct′ful, a. Showing deference (~ behaviour; stood at a ~ distance). Hence ~LY² adv., ~NESS n. [-FUL]

rěspěc′tive, a. Each's own, proper to each, individual, several, comparative, (go to your, put them in their, ~ places; were given places according to their ~ rank or ranks; A & B contributed the ~ sums of 4d. & 3d.; the election depends on the ~ popularity of the candidates). Hence ~LY² (-vl-) adv. [f. med. L respectivus (RESPECT², -IVE)]

respell. See RE- 8.

rěs′pirable (or rĭspīr′-), a. (Of air, gas, etc.) that can, fit to, be breathed. [f. RESPIRE + -ABLE, or F respirable]

rěspirā′tion, n. Breathing; single inspiration & expiration; plant's absorption of oxygen & emission of carbon dioxide. [ME, f. OF or L respiratio (RESPIRE, -ATION)]

rěs′pirātor, n. Apparatus of gauze etc. worn over mouth (& nose) to warm or filter inhaled air; (mil.) kinds of chemical filtering-apparatus worn for defence against poison-gas. [as foll.; see -OR]

rěspire′, v.i. & t. Breathe, inhale & exhale, air, whence **rěs′pirātory** (or rĭspīr′at-) a.; breathe (air etc.); (rare) exhale (perfume, amiability, etc.); breathe again, take breath, recover hope or spirit, get rest or respite. [ME, f. OF respirer or L re(spirare breathe), RE- 9]

rěs′pīte, n., & v.t. **1.** Delay permitted in the discharge of an obligation or suffering of a penalty; interval of rest or relief. **2.** v.t. Grant ~ to, reprieve, (condemned person); postpone execution or exaction of (sentence, obligation); give temporary relief from (pain, care) or to (sufferer). [ME, f. OF respit f. L RESPECT¹us]

rěsplěn′d|ent, a. Brilliant, dazzlingly or gloriously bright. Hence or cogn. ~ENCE, ~ENCY, nn., ~ently² adv. [ME, f. L re(splendēre glitter), RE- 6, -ENT]

rěspǒnd′¹, v.i. **1.** Make answer (esp. of congregation making set answers to priest etc.); perform answering or corresponding action (~ed with a drop-kick, left-hander, etc.). **2.** Show sensitiveness to by behaviour or change (does not ~ to kindness; nerve ~s to stimulus, string to note, etc.). **3.** (rare). Correspond, be analogous, whence or cogn. ~ENCE, ~ENCY, nn. [f. L re(spondēre spons- pledge) answer, RE- 1]

rěspǒnd′², n. **1.** (eccl.). = RESPONSORY, also response to versicle. **2.** (archit.). Half-pillar or half-pier attached to wall to support arch. [ME, f. OF (respondre answer, as prec.)]

rěspǒn′dent, a. & n. **1.** Making answer; responsive to; in position of defendant. **2.** n. One who makes answer, defends

thesis, etc.; defendant esp. in divorce case. [as RESPOND¹, -ENT]

rěspǒnse′, n. Answer given in word or act, reply, retort, (in ~ to; made no ~; the ~s of the oracles; his ~ was the proclamation of martial law); feeling, movement, etc., elicited by stimulus or influence (called forth no ~ in his breast); (eccl.) = RESPONSORY, also any part of liturgy said or sung in answer to priest. [ME, f. OF respons(e); later f. L responsum neut. p.p. (RESPOND¹)]

rěspǒnsibil′it|y̌, n. Being responsible (declines all ~y for it; will take the ~y of doing it; did it on his own ~y, without authorization; is not afraid of ~y, of having to act without detailed guidance); charge for which one is responsible (a family is a great ~y; asked to be relieved of his ~y or ~ies). [foll., -BILITY]

rěspǒn′sib|le, a. Liable to be called to account, answerable (to person, for thing, or abs.; ~le ruler, government, not autocratic), morally accountable for actions, capable of rational conduct; of good credit or position or repute, respectable, apparently trustworthy; involving responsibility (a ~le office). Hence ~LY² adv. [obs. F (L RESPOND¹ērĕ, -IBLE)]

‖ **rěspǒn′sions** (-shnz), n. pl. First of three examinations for Oxford B.A. degree, abolished in 1960 (also smalls colloq.; cf. moderations, greats, final schools). [f. L responsio (RESPOND¹, -ION)]

rěspǒn′sive, a. Answering, by way of answer, (of liturgy etc.) using responses; responding readily to or to some influence, impressionable, sympathetic. Hence ~LY² adv., ~NESS n. [f. F responsif, -ive or LL responsivus (RESPOND¹, -IVE)]

rěspǒn′sory, n. Anthem said or sung by soloist & choir after lesson. [f. LL responsorium (RESPOND¹, -ORY)]

rěst¹, v.i. & t. **1.** Be still, cease or abstain or be relieved from exertion or action or movement or employment, lie in sleep or death, be tranquil, be let alone, (waves that never ~; ~ (up)on one's oars, temporarily cease rowing or any exertion; never let your enemy ~; let us ~ here, cease walking etc.; ~ from one's labours; actor is ~ing, is out of work; ~s in the churchyard, lies buried; let her ~ in peace; is too feverish to ~; could not ~ under an imputation, till he got his wish; land was allowed to ~, left fallow; the matter cannot ~ here, must be further examined etc.); give relief or repose to (stayed a day to ~ myself; ~ your men for an hour; says the goggles ~ his eyes; must ~ the ground; ~ or God ~ his soul, may God give it repose); (p.p.) refreshed or reinvigorated by ~ing (are you quite ~ed?). **2.** Lie, be spread out, be supported or based, depend, rely, (of eyes etc.) alight or be steadily directed, (up)on (shadow, light, ~s on his face; roof ~s on four arches; their left ~ed on the river; hand ~ing on the table; science ~s on *phenomena*; *I* ~ *upon your promise*; *his gaze* ~*ed on a strange object*); *repose trust in* (*be content to* ~ *in God*); place for support or foundation (*up*)*on* (~ one's *elbow*, *load, on the table*; ~ one's *case on equity, unimpeachable evidence*). **3.** ~*ing-place*, provided or used for ~*ing* (*last* ~*ing-place*, the grave). [OE *ræstan*, = OS *restian*, OHG *restan*]

rěst², n. **1.** Repose or sleep esp. in bed at night (*go, retire, to* ~; *take* ~ or one's ~). **2.** Abstinence or freedom from or absence of exertion or activity or movement or care or molestation, a period of such abstinence etc., (*day of* ~, Sunday; *a* ~ *from work* etc.; *give person, horse, machine*, etc., *a* ~; *take a short* ~; *at* ~, still, not agitated or troubled, often of the dead; *set question*, person's *mind, at* ~, settle, relieve; *lay to* ~, bury). **3.** Lodging-place or shelter provided for sailors, cabmen, or other class. **4.** Prop or support or steadying-piece, e.g. for gun in aiming, telephone-receiver, billiard-cue, cutting--tool in lathe, or foot on bicycle. **5.** (Mus.) appointed interval of silence or sign denoting 'it; pause in elocution, caesura in verse. **6.** ~-*balk*, ridge left unploughed between furrows; ~-*cure*, ~ usu. of some weeks in bed as medical treatment; ~-*day*, day spent in ~, (rare) Sunday; ~-*house*, (in India) DAWK bungalow. [OE *ræst*(e), = OS, OHG *resta* etc.]

rěst³, v.i. Remain over (arch.; *whatever* ~*s of hope*); ~ *with*, be left in the hands or charge of (*it* ~*s with you to propose terms*; *the management of affairs* ~*ed with Wolsey*); remain in specified state (*the affair* ~*s a mystery*; ~ *assured, satisfied*, etc.; also arch. in epistolary forms, as *I* ~ *your devoted friend*). [ME, f. OF *rester* f. L *re*(*stare* stand), RE- 3]

rěst⁴, n. **1.** The remaining part(s) or individuals *of*, *the* remainder of some quantity or number, *the* others, (*& the* or *all the* ~ *of it*, all else that might be mentioned; *for the* ~, as regards anything beyond what has been specially mentioned). **2.** ‖ (Banking) reserve fund; (commerc.) stocktaking & balancing; (tennis etc.) spell of continuous returns. [ME, f. OF *reste* f. *rester* (prec.)]

rěst⁵, n. (hist.). Check holding butt of mediaeval tilter's spear when couched for charging (*with, lay*, or *set* one's, *lance in* ~). [ME, aphetic f. ARREST¹]

restamp, restart, restate etc. See RE- 8.

rěs'taurant (-tor-, & see AP.), n. Place where meals or refreshments may be had. [F (*restaurer* RESTORE, -ANT)]

restaurateur (rěstoratěr'), n. Restaurant--keeper. [F]

rěst'ful, a. Favourable to repose, free from disturbing influences, soothing. Hence ~LY² adv., ~NESS n. [-FUL]

rěst'-harrow .(-ō), n. A tough-rooted

shrub, cammock. [obs. *rest* v. as REST⁵, HARROW¹]

‖ **restiff**. See RESTIVE.

rěs'titūte, v.t. & i. (rare). Make restitution (of). [f. L *re*(*stituere* -*lut*- = *statuere* set up), RE- 8]

rěstitū'tion, n. Restoring of or of thing to proper owner, reparation for injury, (esp. *make* ~; ~ *of conjugal rights*, name of a matrimonial lawsuit); restoring of thing to its original state (esp. theol. *the* ~ *of all things*); resumption of original shape or position by elasticity. [ME, f. OF or L *restitutio* (prec., -ION)]

rěs'tive, ‖ **rěs'tiff** (arch.), a. (Of horse) refusing to advance, stubbornly standing still or moving backwards or sideways, jibbing, refractory; (of person) unmanageable, rejecting control; (erron.) restless. Hence **rěs'tively²** (-vl-) adv., **rěs'tiveness** (-vn-) n. [ME *restif* f. OF (REST³, -IVE)]

rěst'lĕss, a. Finding or affording no rest, uneasy, agitated, never still, ever in motion, unpausing, fidgeting. Hence ~LY² adv., ~NESS n. [REST², -LESS]

restock. See RE- 8.

rěstorā'tion, n. In senses of RESTORE; also or esp.: (period of) re-establishment of monarchy in 1660 (*the R*~); model or drawing representing supposed original form of extinct animal, ruined building, etc. [17th c. alt. (after *restore*) f. ME *restauracion*, f. OF, or LL *restauratio* (RESTORE, -ION)]

rěstorā'tion|**ism** (-shon-), n. Doctrine that all men will ultimately be restored to happiness in the future life. So ~IST(2) n. [-ISM]

rěstō'rative, a. & n. **1.** Tending to restore health or strength. **2.** n. ~ food, medicine, or agency. Hence ~LY² adv. [ME also -*au*- f. OF *restauratif, -ive* (foll., -ATIVE)]

rěstōr|**e'**, v.t. **1.** Give back, make restitution of. **2.** (Attempt to) bring back to original state by rebuilding, repairing, repainting, emending, etc. (*church, picture, text, has been* ~*ed, spoilt in* ~*ing,* ~*ed out of all recognition*, etc.); make representation of supposed original state of (extinct animal, ruin, etc.). **3.** Reinstate, bring back *to* dignity or right; bring back to or to health etc., cure (person). **4.** Re--establish, renew, bring back into use. **5.** Reinsert by conjecture (missing words in text, parts of extinct animal, etc.). **6.** Replace, put back, bring *to* former place or condition. Hence ~'ABLE a., ~´ER¹ n. [ME, f. OF *restorer* f. L *restaurare*]

rěstrain|**'¹**, v.t. Check or hold in *from*, keep in check or under control or within bounds, repress, keep down; confine, imprison. Hence ~ABLE a., ~ĕdLY² adv. (esp., with self-restraint). [ME, f. OF *re*-*strai*(*g*)*n*- st. of *restraindre* f. L *re*(*stringere strict-* tie), RE- 2]

rĕ-strain'[2], v.t. Strain again. [RE- 8]

rėstraint', n. Restraining or being restrained, stoppage, check, controlling agency or influence, confinement esp. in asylum, (*without* ~, freely, copiously; *is under* ~, esp. as lunatic); constraint or reserve of manner; self-control, avoidance of excess or exaggeration, austerity of literary expression. [ME, f. OF *restraint(e)* (RESTRAIN[1])]

rėstrict', v.t. Confine, bound, limit, (*to, within*; *has a very* ~*ed application*; *am* ~*ed to advising*; *is* ~*ed within narrow limits*). Hence or cogn. **rėstric'tion** n., **rėstric'tive** a. (~*ive practices*, ~*ing* output in industry),~**ėdLY**[2], **rėstric'tiveLY**[2], advv. [f. L *restrict*-, see RESTRAIN[1]]

rėstuff'. See RE- 9.

rėsult' (-z-), v.i., & n. 1. Arise as actual or follow as logical consequence (*from* conditions, causes, premisses, etc., or abs.); have issue or end in specified manner esp. *in* failure etc. (~*ed badly, in a large profit*). 2. n. Consequence, issue, or outcome of something (*without* ~, in vain, fruitless), whence ~**FUL**, ~**LESS**, aa.; quantity, formula, etc., given by calculation. [ME, f. med. L f. L *re(sultare* = *saltare* frequent. of *salire* jump), RE- 8]

rėsul'tant (-z-), a. & n. 1. Resulting, esp. as total outcome of more or less opposed forces. 2. n. Composite effect of two or more forces acting in different directions at same point (esp. in mech., also transf.). [prec., -ANT]

rėsume' (-z-), v.t. & i. 1. Get or take again or back, recover, reoccupy, (~ one's *spirits, sway, liberty, seat*; ~ *gift, grant, territory*). 2. Begin again (upon), go on (with) after interruption, begin to speak or work again, recommence t. & i., (*the House* ~*d work* or *its labours*, or ~*d*; ~ *thread of* one's *discourse*; ~ *pipe*, go on smoking again; '*No, it is hopeless' he* ~*d*). 3. Make resumé of, recapitulate, summarize. [ME, f. OF *resumer*, or L *re(sumere sumpt-* take), RE- 8]

résumé (rāz'ŏŏmā, & see Ap.), n. Summary, epitome, abstract. [F, p.p. of *résumer* RESUME]

rėsummons. See RE- 8.

rėsump't|ion (-z-), n. Resuming. So ~**IVE** a., ~**iveLY**[2] adv. [ME, f. OF, or LL *resumptio* (RESUME, -ION)]

rėsup'in|ate, a. (bot.). (Of leaf etc.) inverted, bottom up. Hence ~**A'TION** n. [f. L *re(supinare* make SUPINE[1]), RE- 9]

rėsŭrge', v.i. (rare exc. joc.). Experience resurrection, revive, rise or arise again. So (in ordinary use) **rėsŭr'gent**(1) n. & a., **rėsŭr'gence** n. [f. L *re(surgere surrect-* rise), RE- 9]

rėsurrĕct' (-z-), v.t. (colloq.). Raise from the dead (rare); revive practice or memory of; take from grave, exhume. [back form. f. foll.]

rėsurrĕc'tion (-z-), n. 1. (*R*~). (Festival in memory of) rising of Christ from the grave; rising again of men at the last day. 2. Exhumation lit. or fig., resurrecting (~ *man*, BODY-snatcher), whence ~**IST**(1) (-sho-) n. 3. Revival from disuse or inactivity or decay, restoration to vogue or memory. Hence ~**AL** (-sho-) a. [ME, f. OF, or LL *resurrectio* (RESURGE, -ION)]

rėsurvey. See RE- 8.

rėsŭs'cit|āte, v.t. & i. Revive, return or usu. restore to life, consciousness, vogue, vigour, or vividness. Hence or cogn. ~**A'TION**, ~**ātoR**, nn., ~**ATIVE** a. [f. L *re(suscitare* CITE), RE- 9, -ATE[3]]

rĕt, **rāte**, **rait**, v.t. & i. Soften (flax, hemp) by soaking or exposing to moisture; (of hay etc., in pass. or intr.) be spoilt by wet, rot. [hist. obsc.; 15th c. *ret(t)en* corresp. to MDu. *re(e)ten*]

rėtā'ble, n. Shelf, or frame enclosing decorated panels, above back of altar. [f. F *rétable*, cf. med. L *retrotabulum* rear table]

rėt'ail'[1], n. Sale of goods in small quantities (esp. *by* ~, or attrib., as ~ *trading, dealer*; also adv., esp. in conjunction w. *wholesale*, as *do you buy wholesale or* ~?). [ME, f. OF *retail(le)* piece cut off f. *re(tailler* cut, see TAIL[2]), RE- 5]

rėtail'[2], v.t. & i. 1. Sell (goods) by retail; (of goods) be ~ed (esp. *at* or *for* specified price). 2. Recount, relate details of. Hence ~**ER**[1] n. [ME, prob. f. prec.]

rėtain', v.t. 1. Keep in place, hold fixed, (~*ing wall*, supporting & confining mass of earth or water; ~*ing force*, mil., posted to keep part of enemy inactive etc.). 2. Secure services of (esp. barrister) by engagement & preliminary payment (~*ing fee*, retainer). 3. Keep possession of, not lose, continue to have; continue to practise or recognize, allow to remain or prevail, not abolish or discard or alter. 4. Succeed in remembering, not forget. Hence ~**ABLE** a. [ME, f. OF *retenir* f. L *re(linēre tent-* = *tenēre* hold), RE- 3]

rėtain'er, n. 1. (Law) formal retention of something as one's own, authorization to retain thus; being retained to serve in some capacity; fee paid to barrister etc. for right to his services if required. 2. In vbl senses; esp. (hist.), dependant or follower of person of rank; *old* ~ (joc.), old and faithful servant. [RETAIN+(sense 1) -ER[4], (sense 2) -ER[1]]

rėtake. See RE- 9.

rėtăl'i|āte, v.t. & i. 1. Repay (injury, insult, etc., rarely kindness etc.) in kind; retort (accusation) *upon* person. 2. Do as one is done by, esp. return evil, make reprisals, (pol. econ.) impose duties on imports from foreign State in return for its import duties. Hence or cogn. ~**A'TION** n., ~**ATIVE**, ~**atoRY**, (-lya-), aa. [f. L *re(taliare* f. *talis* such), RE- 1]

rėtärd', v.t. & i., & n. 1. Make slow or late, delay progress or development or arrival or accomplishment or happening of. 2. (Esp. of physical phenomena, e.g.

motion of tides, waves, or celestial bodies) happen, arrive, behind normal or calculated time; hence or cogn. rētārdaˈTION, ~MENT, nn., ~ATIVE, ~atoRY, aa. 3. n. ~ation (~ *of tide* or *high water*, interval between full moon & following high water). [f. F *retard(er)* or L *re(tardare* f. *tardus* slow), RE- 3]

retaste. See RE- 8.

rĕtch, v.i., & n. 1. Make motion of vomiting esp. ineffectually & involuntarily. 2. n. Such motion or sound of it. [16th c., var. of (now dial.) *reach*, f. OE *hrǣcan* spit f. *hrāca* spittle]

retell. See RE- 8.

rĕtĕnˈtion, n. RETAINing; esp. (med.) failure to evacuate urine or other secretion. [ME, f. OF, f. L *retentionem* (RETAIN, -ION)]

rĕtĕnˈtive, a. (Of memory, or rarely of person in that respect) tenacious, not forgetful; (of substances) ~ *of* moisture etc., apt to retain it (also ~ abs., ~ of moisture); (surg., of ligature etc.) serving to keep something in place. Hence ~LY[2] adv.,~NESS n. [ME, f. OF (-*if*, -*ive*), see RETAIN, -IVE]

retenue (-nōō), n. Reserve, self-control. [F].

rēˈtiarȳ (-sha-), n. Net-making or geometrical spider. [f. L *retiarius* (gladiator) with net (*rete* net,-ARY[1])]

rĕtˈiс|ence, n. Reserve in speech, avoidance of saying all one knows or feels, abstinence from over-emphasis in art; holding back of some fact; disposition to silence, taciturnity. So ~ENT a. (*on, upon, about*), ~entLY[2] adv. [F, or f. L *reticentia* f. *re(ticēre* = *tacēre* be silent), RE- 4]

rĕtˈicle, n. Network of fine threads or lines in object-glass of telescope to help accurate observation. [f. L RETICULUM]

retícˈul|āte, v.t. & i. Divide or be divided in fact or appearance into a network, arrange or be arranged in small squares or with intersecting lines. So (see etym.) ~ATE[2] (-*at*) a., ~ateLY[2] adv., ~AˈTION n., ~āto- comb. form. [vb by back form. f. *reticulated* f. *reticulate* a. f. L *reticulatus* (RETICULUM, -ATE[2])]

rĕtˈicūle, n. 1. = RETICLE. 2. Lady's netted or other bag carried or worn to serve purpose of pocket. 3. (astron.). A Southern constellation. [f. F *réticule* f. L (foll.)]

retíc ́úl|um, n. (pl. ~a). 1. Ruminant's second stomach or honeycomb. 2. Netlike structure, reticulated membrane etc., whence ~AR[1], ~OSE[1], aa.,~o- comb. form. [L (*rete* net, -CULE)]

rĕtˈifōrm, a. Netlike, reticulated. [f. *rete* net, -I-, -FORM]

rĕtˈin|a, n. (pl. ~as, ~ae). Layer at back of eyeball sensitive to light. Hence ~AL a., ~IT́IS n. [ME, f. med. L, f. L *rete* net]

rĕtˈiнūe, n. Suite or train of persons in attendance upon someone. [ME, f. OF *retenue* fem. p.p. of *retenir* RETAIN]

retíreˈ, v.i. & t., & n. 1. Withdraw (intr.), go away, retreat, seek seclusion or shelter, recede, go (as) to bed, (~ *from the world*, become recluse; ~ *into oneself*, be uncommunicative or unsociable, whence retírˈINGa., retírˈinGLY[2]adv.,retírˈingNESS n.; *the ladies* ~, leave dining-room after dessert; *always* ~s *before midnight*, often *to rest, to bed, for the night*, etc.; *general, army, was forced to* ~, ~d *in good order*, often *from* position, to place, *before enemy*, etc.; *background does not* ~ *as it should*; *retiring-room*, for retiring to, esp. lavatory); (p.p., f. obs. trans. use; pr. rītīrd') withdrawn from society or observation, secluded, (*lives* ~d; *a* ~d *life*; *in a* ~d *valley*, whence ~d'NESS (-īrdn-) n. 2. Cease *from* or give up office or profession or employment or candidature, (crick.) voluntarily terminate one's innings, compel (officer, employee) to ~, (~ *from the army, from business, on a pension*; *batsman* ~d *hurt*; *was compulsorily* ~d *as incompetent*; *retiring age*, age at which person ~s; *retiring pension*, allowed to one who ~s at normal time); (p.p., see -ED[1](2) for sense) that has ~d (*a* ~d *general, grocer*; ~d *pay*, pension; ~d *list*, of ~d officers). 3. (Mil.) order (troops) to ~; (finance) withdraw (bill, note) from operation or currency. 4. n. (mil.). Signal to troops to ~ (usu. *sound the* ~). [f. F *retirer* f. *tirer* draw, RE- 9]

retíreˈment (-īrm-), n. In vbl senses; also: seclusion, privacy; secluded place. [F (prec., -MENT)]

retōrtˈ'[1],v.t. & i., & n. 1. Requite (humiliation, insult, attack) in kind; turn (mischief etc.), fling (charge, sarcasm, jest), back (*on* or *upon* author or aggressor), make (argument) tell against or *against* its user; make, say by way of, repartee or counter-charge or counter-argument; (p.p.) recurved, twisted or bent backwards. 2. n. Incisive reply, repartee; turning of charge or argument against its author; piece of retaliation. [f. L *re(torquēre tort-* twist), RE- 9]

retōrtˈ'[2], n., & v.t. 1. Vessel usu. of glass with long downward-bent neck used in distilling liquids; kinds of receptacle of various shapes & materials used in purifying mercury & making gas & steel. 2. v.t. Purify (mercury) by heating in ~. [f. F *retorte* f. med. L *retorta* fem. p.p. as prec.]

retōrˈtion, n. Bending back (lit. & fig.); (Internat. law) retaliation by State upon subjects of another. [f. med. L *retortio, -sio* (RETORT[1], -ION)]

retouch. [prob. f. F *retoucher* (RE- 8, TOUCH)]

retrāceˈ, v.t. Trace back to source or

beginning; look over again; recall the course of in memory; go back over (one's *steps* or *way*; often fig. of undoing actions). [f. F *retracer* (RE- 8, TRACE v.)]

rĕtrăct', v.t. & i. **1.** Drăw (esp. part of one's body) back or in, (of such part etc.) shrink back or in or be capable of being ~ed, (*snail* ~s *its horns*; *cat's claws* ~ *or can be* ~ed; *surgeon* ~s *skin with instrument, organ is* ~ed *by muscle, called* **rĕtrăc'tor** n.; *if the piston is suddenly* ~ed); hence or cogn. **rĕtrăc'table**[1] [-ABLE] & (in same sense) **rĕtrăc'tile** aa., **rĕtrăctil'ity** n., **rĕtrăc'tive** a., **rĕtrăc'tion**[1] [-ION] n. **2.** Withdraw, revoke, cancel, refuse to abide by, acknowledge falsity or error of, expressly abandon, (statement, promise, opinion), (abs.) ~ opinion or statement; hence or cogn. **rĕtrăc'table**[2] [-ABLE] a., **rĕtrăcta'tion**, **rĕtrăc'tion**[2] [-ION], nn. [sense 1 f. L *re(trahere tract-* draw), RE- 4; sense 2 partly as 1, but chiefly f. L *re(tractare* draw, frequent. of *trahere* draw), RE- 9, & L *re(tractare* pull about or handle), RE- 8, as in arch. *retractation* rehandling, now only in title of Augustine's *Retractations*]

rĕt'ral, a. (nat. hist. etc.). Hinder, posterior, at the back. [RETRO-, -AL]

retransfer, retransform, retranslate etc., **retread**[1]. See RE- 9.

rē-tread'[2] (-ĕd), v.t., & n. Furnish (tire) with a new tread; (n.) tire so renewed. [RE- 9]

rĕtreat', v.i. & t., & n. **1.** Go back, retire, relinquish a position, (esp. of army etc.); (trans., chiefly in chess) move (piece) back from forward or threatened position; recede (*a* ~*ing chin, forehead*). **2.** n. Act of, (mil.) signal for, ~ing (*sound the* or *a* ~, mil.; *beat a* ~, ~, abandon undertaking; *make good* one's ~, get safely away; *intercept* ~ *of*, cut off; *are in full* ~); (mil.) bugle-call at sunset. **3.** Withdrawing into privacy or security, (place of) seclusion; (eccl.) temporary retirement for religious exercises; asylum for inebriates or lunatics or pensioners; lurking-place, place of shelter. [vb (15th c.) f. OF *retraiter*; n. ME & OF *retret(e)* f. p.p. of *retraire* f. L *retrahere* (RETRACT)]

rĕtrĕnch', v.t. & i. **1.** Cut down, reduce amount of, (expenses, things causing outlay); cut off, deduct, (~ed *a year from the established period*); make excisions in or of, shorten or remove, (literary work or passages in it); cut down expenses, introduce economies. **2.** (fortif.). Furnish with inner line of defence usu. consisting of trench & parapet. Hence ~MENT n. [f. obs. F *retrencher*, mod. *retrancher* (RE-, TRENCH)]

retrial. See RE- 8.

rĕtribū'tion, n. Recompense for evil or rarely for good done, vengeance, requital. So **rĕtrib'ūtive** a., **rĕtrib'ūtively**[2] adv. [ME f. OF, or f. LL *re(tributio* f. *tribuere* -*ut-* assign, -ION), RE- 1]

rĕtriev|e', v.t. & i., & n. **1.** (Of dogs, esp. of special breed) find & bring in (killed or wounded bird etc., or abs.), whence ~'ER[1] n. **2.** Recover by investigation or effort of memory, restore to knowledge or recall to mind. **3.** Regain possession of. **4.** Rescue *from* bad state etc.; restore to flourishing state, revive, (esp. one's fortunes etc.). **5.** Make good, repair, set right, (loss, disaster, error); hence ~'ABLE a., ~'AL(2) n. **6.** n. Possibility of recovery (*beyond, past,* ~*e*). [ME, f. OF *retroeve*-stressed st. of *re(trover* find), RE- 9]

retrim. See RE- 8.

retro- (usu. rē- exc. in the commoner wds, esp. *rĕtrograde, rĕtrospect*), pref. f. L *retro* adv. & pref.: (1) chiefly in L derivatives (~*act,* ~*grade*) or wds formed on L anal. of L elements (~*flex,* ~*ject*) with senses *backwards, back again, in return;* (2) chiefly in anat. and path. terms with sense *behind* (~*sternal* a., behind the breast-bone), *situated behind*.

rĕtro|ăct', v.i. React; operate in backward direction; have retrospective effect. Hence or cogn. ~ăc'tIVE a., ~ăc'tively[2] adv., ~ăctiv'ity, ~ăc'tion, nn. [f. L RETRO(*agere act-* act)]

rĕt'ro|cēde'[1], v.i. Move back, recede; (of gout) strike inward. So ~cēd'ENCE n., ~cēd'ENT a. [f. L RETRO(*cedere cess-* go)]

rĕtrocēde'[2], v.t. Cede (territory) back again. [f. F *rétrocéder* (RETRO-, CEDE)]

rĕtrocĕ'ssion (-shn), n., **rĕtrocĕss'ive**, a. In vbl senses (RETROCEDE[1], [2]). [f. LL *retrocessio* (RETROCEDE[1], -ION)]

rĕt'rochoir (-kwīr), n. Part of cathedral or large church behind high altar. [f. med. L RETRO(*chorus* CHOIR)]

rĕtroflĕc'tĕd, rĕt'roflĕx, -flĕxed (-kst), aa. (anat., path., bot., etc.). Turned backwards. So **rĕtroflĕx'xion** (-kshn) n. [f. L RETRO(*flectere flex-* bend)]

rĕtrogradā'tion, n. (Astron.) apparent backward motion of planet in zodiac, motion of heavenly body from E. to W., backward movement of lunar nodes on ecliptic; = (the now usu.) RETROGRESSION. [f. LL RETRO(*gradatio* f. LL -*gradare* walk), -ATION]

rĕt'rogrāde, a., n., & v.i. **1.** (Astron.) in or showing RETROGRADATION; directed backwards (~ *motion*), retreating; reverting esp. to inferior state, declining; inverse, reversed, (*in* ~ *order*; ~ *imitation* in music, with notes of passage repeated backwards); hence ~LY[2] adv. **2.** n. (rare). Degenerate person; backward tendency. **3.** v.i. (Astron.) show RETROGRADATION; move backwards, recede, retire, decline, revert. [a. (& n.) f. L RETRO*gradus* (*gradus* step); vb f. L *retrogradi* or LL -*gradare* (prec.)]

rĕtrogrĕss', v.i. Go back, move backwards, deteriorate. Hence ~IVE a., ~ively[2] adv. [f. L RETRO(*gradi gress-* walk)]

rĕtrogrĕ'ssion (-shn), n. (Astron.) retrogradation; backward or reversed movement; return to less advanced state, reversal of development, decline, deterioration. [as prec., -ION]

rĕt'rojĕct, v.t. Cast back (chiefly as opp. *project* in lit. senses). [RETRO-, & as PRO- JECT¹]

rĕtropŭl'sion (-shn), n. (path.). Shifting of external disease to internal part. [RETRO-, L *pellere puls-* drive, -ION]

rĕt'ro-rŏck'ĕt, n. Auxiliary rocket for slowing down space vehicle etc. when re-entering earth's atmosphere. [RETRO-, ROCKET²]

rĕtrōrse', a. (nat. hist.). Turned back, reverted. Hence ~LY² (-sl-) adv. [f. L *retrorsus*=RETRO(*versus* p.p. of *vertere* turn)]

rĕt'rospĕct, n. Regard (to be) had *to* precedent or authority or previous conditions; (rare) retrospective force, retroaction; backward view (rare); survey of past time or events (*is pleasant in the ~*, when looked back on; *a short ~ is now necessary*). [f. L RETRO(*spicere spect-* = *specere* look) after PROSPECT n.]

rĕtrospĕc'tion, n. Action of looking back esp. into the past, indulgence or engagement in retrospect. [as prec., -ION]

rĕtrospĕc'tive, a. Of, in, proceeding by, retrospection; (of statutes etc.) not restricted to the future, licensing or punishing etc. past actions, having application to the past, retroactive; (of view) lying to the rear. Hence ~LY² adv. [as prec., -IVE]

retroussé (retrōōs'ā), a. Turned up (of nose). [F]

rĕt'rovĕrt, v.t. Turn backwards (esp. path. in p.p., of womb). So **rĕtrovĕr'sion** (-shn) n. [f. LL RETRO(*vertere vers-* turn)]

retry etc. See RE- 8.

rĕtt'erў, n. Flax-retting place. [RET, -ERY]

returf. See RE- 8.

rĕtŭrn'¹, v.i. & t. **1.** Come or go back (*gone never to~*; *~ home, the way* one came; p.p. occas. as in -ED¹(2), as *a ~ed emigrant*, *they are* or usu. *have ~ed*). **2.** Revert (*shall ~ to the subject*; *unto dust shalt thou ~*; *~ to* one's *old habits*; *properly ~s* to *original owner*). **3.** Bring, convey, give, yield, put, send, or pay, back or in return or requital (*fish must be ~ed to the water*; *~ borrowed book* or *sum*; *investments ~ a profit*; *~ sword to scabbard*, or *~ swords* (mil.); *~ ball*, strike etc. it back in tennis etc.; *~ like for like, the compliment, a blow, an answer*; *~ thanks*, express them esp. in grace at meals or in response to toast; *~ person's love, greeting*, etc., reciprocate it; *~ed empties*, packing-cases etc. sent back; *~ clubs* etc. or *partner's lead* at cards, lead from same suit). **4.** Say in reply, retort. **5.** State, mention, or describe, officially esp. in answer to writ or formal demand (*liabilities were ~ed at*

£5000; *were all ~ed guilty, unfit for work*; ||*~ing officer*, official conducting election & announcing name of person elected); (of constituency) elect as M.P. Hence ~ABLE a. [ME, f. OF *re(torner* TURN), RE- 9]

rĕtŭrn'², n. **1.** Coming back (*his ~ was the signal for riots*; *~ of* POST²; ||*~ ticket* or *~*, ticket for there-&-back journey, as *took a first-class ~ to Leeds*; *~ passenger, voyage, cargo*, etc.; *many happy ~s of the day* or *~s*, birthday or festival greeting; *have had u, no, ~ of the symptoms*). **2.** (archit.). Part receding from line of front, e.g. side of house or of window-opening (*~ angle, side, wall*, etc.); termination of dripstone. **3.** (Coming in of) proceeds or profit of undertaking (often pl.; *the ~s were large*; *brings an adequate ~*; *small profits & quick ~s*, motto of cheap shop etc. relying on large trade). **4.** Giving, sending, putting, or paying, back, or thing so given etc., ||esp. sheriff's report on writ, (returning officer's announcement of) candidate's election as M.P., or formal report with statistics etc. compiled by order (*sheriff made a ~ of nulla bona*; *secured his ~ for Colchester*; *table littered with ~s & pamphlets*; *must ask for the ~ of the book* or *loan*; *received a ticket in ~ for his fare, neglect in ~ for attention*; *fencer's ~*, i.e. riposte, *is slow*; *fielder has a good ~* in cricket, sends ball in fast & straight; *~ match* or *game*, or *~*, between same sides as before). **5.** pl. || Kind of mild pipe-tobacco (orig. sense *refuse of tobacco*). Hence ~LESS a. [ME, f. AF (prec.)]

retūse', a. (bot., entom.). With broad end & central depression (of leaf or similar part). [f. L *re(tundere tus-* beat), RE- 9]

reūn'ion (-nyon), n. **1.** Reuniting or being reunited, reunited state. **2.** Social gathering, esp. of intimates or persons with common interest. [RE- 8, UNION; cf. F *réunion*]

reūn'ionĭst, -ĭsm, (-nyon-), nn. Seeker, seeking, of reunion between R.-C. & Anglican Churches. [-IST, -ISM]

reunite, see RE- 9; **reurge, revaccinate** etc., see RE- 8.

rĕv, n., & v.i. & t. (colloq.; -vv-). **1.** = REVOLUTION (of engine). **2.** vb. Revolve (with *up*, to increase in speed of revolution); (often with *up*) cause (engine) to run quickly (esp. when first starting). [abbr.]

rĕvalĕn'ta, n. Food prepared from lentil & barley flour. [orig. *erv-* (L *ervum lens* LENTIL)]

rĕvălorizā'tion, -is- (-īz-), n. Restoration of the value of a country's currency. [RE- 9 +VALORIZATION]

revalue etc. See RE- 8.

reveal'¹, v.t. **1.** (Esp. of God) make known by inspiration or supernatural means (*~ed religion*, opp. *natural*). **2.** Disclose, divulge, betray; display, show, let appear (~ *itself*, come to sight or knowledge). Hence ~**ABLE** a. [ME, f. OF *reveler* or L *re(velare* f. *velum* VEIL), RE- 7]

reveal'², n. Internal side surface of opening or recess, esp. of doorway or window--aperture. [f. obs. vb *revale* lower f. OF *re(valer* f. *avaler* VAIL¹), RE- 4]

revei'lle (-vĕlĭ, -vălĭ), n. Military waking--signal sounded in morning on bugle or drums etc. [f. F *réveillez* imperat. pl. of *réveiller* (RE-, *veiller* f. L *vigilare* watch)]

rĕv'el, v.i. & t. (-ll-), & n. 1. Make merry, be riotously festive, feast, carouse, whence ~**lER**¹ n.; take keen delight *in*; throw *away* (money, time) in ~ry. 2. n. ~ling, (occasion of indulgence in) merry-making, (often pl., as *the ~s began*; ~ *rout*, party of ~lers, f. obs. ~-*rout* ~ry); hence ~**RY**(4, 5) n. [ME, f. OF *revel(er* riot f. L REBEL²- *lare*]

rĕvĕlā'tion, n. Disclosing of knowledge, knowledge disclosed, to man by divine or supernatural agency (*the R~*, also pop. *R~s* or the *R~s*, abbr. *Rev.*, last book of N.T., Apocalypse, whence ~**AL** (-shon-) a.; striking disclosure (*it was a ~ to me*; *what a ~!*); revealing *of* some fact. [ME, f. OF, or LL *revelatio* (REVEAL¹ -ATION)]

rĕvĕlāt'ionist (-shon-), n. *The R~*, author of Apocalypse; believer in divine revelation. [-IST]

revenant (rev'enahn), n. One returned from the dead or from exile etc. [F]

rĕvĕndĭcā'tion, n. (diplom.). Formal claiming back, or recovery by such claim, of lost territory etc. [F (RE-, VINDICA-TION)]

rĕvĕnge'¹ (-j), v.t. & i. Satisfy one*self*, (pass.) be satisfied, with retaliation (*for* offence, *on*, *upon*, *of*, offender); retaliate, requite, exact retribution for, (offence to oneself or another; *on*, *upon*, offender); avenge (person); take vengeance. [ME, f. OF *re(venger* f. L *vindicare* VINDICATE), RE- 1]

rĕvĕnge'² (-j), n. 1. Revenging, act done in revenging; desire to revenge, vindictive feeling, whence ~**FUL** (-jf-) a., ~**ful**-**LY²** adv., ~**fulNESS** n. 2. (In games) opportunity given for reversing former result by return game (*give* one his ~). [f. prec. or obs. F *revenge* (as prec.)]

rĕv'ĕnūe, n. 1. Income, esp. of large amount, from any source (pl. collective items of it, usu. w. possess. as *his* ~s). 2. State's annual income from which public expenses are met (INLAND ~; ~ *tax*, imposed to raise ~, not to affect trade, opp. *protective*; ~ *cutter*, *officer*, etc., employed to prevent smuggling; department of civil service collecting it. [ME, f. OF, p.p. of *revenir* f. L *re(venire* come) return, RE- 9]

rĕvĕrb'er|āte, v.t. & i. 1. Return, beat back, echo, reflect, (t. & i. of sound, light, heat; ~*ating furnace* or *kiln*, constructed to ~ate heat on substance dealt with,

whence ~**atORY** a. & n.). 2. (rare). (Of emotion etc.) react *upon*; (of ball etc.) rebound. So ~**A'TION** n., ~**ATIVE**, ~**ANT** (poet.), aa. [f. L RE- 9(*verberare* lash), -**ATE**³]

rĕvĕrb'erātor, n. Reflector, reflecting lamp. [-OR]

rĕvēre', v.t. Regard as sacred or exalted, hold in deep & usu. affectionate or religious respect, venerate. [f. F *révérer* or L, RE(*vereri* fear)]

rĕv'erence, n., & v.t. 1. Revering (see prec.; *hold in, regard with, ~*; *feel ~ for*, *pay ~ to*); capacity for it (*the rising generation lacks ~*); (arch.) gesture showing it, bow, curtsy, obeisance; so **rĕverĕn'tIAL** (-shl) a., **rĕverĕn'tialLY²** adv. 2. Being revered (*saving your ~*, arch., apology for use of coarse term; *your, his, ~*, arch. or vulg. or joc., titles used to, of, clergyman). 3. v.t. Regard with ~, venerate. [ME f. OF, or L *reverentia* (prec., -ENCE)]

rĕv'erend, a. & n. 1. Deserving reverence, revered, (esp. as title, abbr. *Rev.*, or otherwise, of clergyman; *Very R~*, of dean; *Right R~*, of bishop; *Most R~*, of archbishop; *the Right R~ John Smith* or *the Right R~ the bishop of —*; *Rev.* or *the Rev. John* or *J. Smith*, or *the Rev. Mr Smith*; *the ~ gentleman*, the clergyman in question; as n., usu. pl., = clergyman etc., as ~*s & right* ~*s*, clergy & bishops). 2. Of the clergy (~ *utterances* etc.). 3. (arch.). = foll. [ME, f. OF or L *reverendus* (REVERE, -ND¹)]

rĕv'erent, a. Feeling or showing reverence. Hence ~**LY²** adv. [ME, f. L *reverens* (REVERE, -ENT)]

rĕv'erie, n. (Fit of) musing, day-dream(ing), (*was lost in ~* or *a ~*); (arch.) fantastic notion or theory, delusion; (mus.) dreamy instrumental piece. [ME, f. OF, f. *rever* to revel (mod. *rêver* dream), of obsc. orig.; see -ERY & cf. RAVE²]

revers (revăr'), n. (pl. the same). Turned--back edge of coat, bodice, etc., displaying lining. [F]

rĕvĕrse'¹, a. Opposite or contrary (*to*, or abs.) in character or order, inverted, back or backward, upside down, (*in the ~ direction to the time before*; *the ~ side* etc. *of a coin, picture*, etc.; ~ *fire*, *battery*, etc., playing on enemy's rear or into works from rear; ~ *flank*, opposite to pivot end in wheeling). Hence ~**LY²** (-sli) adv. [ME, f. OF *revers* or L *reversus* p.p. of *re(vertere vers-* turn), RE- 9]

rĕvĕrs|e'², v.t. & i. 1. Turn (trans.) the other way round or up or inside-out, invert, transpose, convert to opposite character or effect, (~*e arms*, hold rifles butt upwards; ~*e motion*, *policy*, *order*, etc.; ~*e engine*, make it work backwards; ~ *the charge*, make recipient of telephone call responsible for payment. 2. Revoke, annul, (decree, attainder, etc.). 3. (Danc., esp. in waltz) begin to

revolve in opposite direction. Hence
~'AL(2) n., ~'IBLE a., ~IBIL'ITY n. [ME, f.
OF *reverser* f. LL RE(*versare* frequent. of
vertere turn)]

rĕvẽrse'³, n. 1. *The* contrary (*of*, or abs. ;
with others the ~ of this or *the ~ happens*;
'in ~ in motoring, with car moving backwards; often w. adj. as periphr. for
its opposite, as *made remarks the ~ of
complimentary*). 2. (Device on) subordinate side of coin etc. (opp. OBVERSE);
= VERSO. 3. = REVERSE¹ *side* (*take in ~*,
subject to REVERSE¹ *fire*). 4. Piece of
misfortune, disaster, esp. defeat in battle
(*the ~s of fortune*; *suffered a ~*). [ME, f.
OF (*-rs, -rse*) as REVERSE¹]

rĕvẽr'si, n. Game on draught-board with
counters coloured differently above &
below. [F]

rĕvẽr'sion (-shn), n. 1. (Return to
grantor or his heirs or passing to ultimate
grantee or ~ER¹ (-sho-) n. of, also right of
ultimate succession to) estate granted till
specified date or event, esp. death of
original grantee (*in~*, on such conditions).
2. Sum payable on person's death esp. by
way of life-insurance. 3. Thing to which
one has a right or expects to succeed
when relinquished by another. 4. Return
to a previous state, habit, etc., esp. (biol.)
to ancestral type. Hence ~AL, ~ARY¹,
aa., ~alLY² adv., (-sho-). [ME, f. OF, or L
reversio (as REVERSE¹, -ION)]

rĕvẽrt', v.i. & t., & n. 1. Go back (rare).
2. (Of property, office, etc.) fall in by
REVERSION; whence ~ER⁴ n. (legal).
3. Return *to* former state etc. (cf. prec.;
n. after *convert, pervert*, person who
readopts his original faith); (abs.) fall
back into wild state. 4. Recur *to* subject
in talk or thought. 5. Turn (eyes, rarely
steps) back. [ME, f. OF *revertir* or L as
prec.]

rĕvẽrt'ible, a. (Of property) subject to
reversion. [ME, f. med. L *revertibilis*
(prec., -IBLE)] ·

rĕvẽt', v.t. (-tt-). Face (rampart, wall,
etc.) with masonry etc. esp. in fortification. [f. F *revêtir* f. LL *re(vestire* clothe f.
VESTis), RE- 8]

rĕvẽt'ment, n. Retaining-wall or facing
(as prec.). [f. F *revêtement* (prec., -MENT)]

revictual. See RE- 8.

rĕview'¹ (-vū), n. 1. Revision (esp. legal;
is not subject to ~; *court of ~*, before
which sentences etc. come for revision).
2. Display & formal inspection of troops,
fleet, etc. (*~ order*, dress & arrangement
usu. at *~s*, & transf., full fig; *pass in ~*,
fig. t. & i., examine or be examined).
3. Retrospect, survey of the past. 4.
Critique of book etc.; periodical publication with articles on current events, new
books, art, etc. 5. Second view. [16th c.
f. F *reveue* (now *-vue*) f. *revoir* (RE- 9, VIEW)]

rĕview'² (-vū), v.t. & i. 1. View again.

2. Subject to esp. legal revision. 3. Survey, glance over, look back on. 4. Hold
review of (troops etc.). 5. Write review of
(book etc.), write reviews, whence ~ER¹
(-vūer) n. Hence ~ABLE a., ~AL(2) n.,
(-vūa-). [f. RE- 9+VIEW, after F *revoir*]

rĕvile', v.t. & i. Call by ill names, abuse,
rail at; talk abusively, rail. Hence ~'ER¹,
~'ING¹(1), nn., ~'inGLY² adv. [ME, f. OF
reviler (RE- 6, VILE)]

rĕvise' (-z), v.t., & n. 1. Read or look
over or re-examine or reconsider & amend
faults in (literary matter, printers' proofs,
law, constitution, etc.; *R~ed Version*,
abbr. R.V., revision made 1870–84 of
Authorized or 1611 Version of Bible);
hence or cogn. ~'ABLE, ~'ORY, (-z-), aa.,
~'AL(2) (-z-), rĕvi'SION (-zhn), nn., rĕvi-
sionAL (-zho-) a., ~'ER¹ (-z-) n. (esp. in pl.
of authors of R.V.). 2. n. Revision, ~ing,
(rare); ~ed form (rare); (print.) proof-
-sheet embodying corrections made in
earlier proof. [f. F *reviser* look at, or f. L
revisere (*vidēre* vis- see), RE- 8]

revisit, see RE- 8; **revitalize**, RE- 9.

rĕviv'al, n. 1. Bringing or coming back
into vogue (*~ of learning, letters*, etc., at
Renaissance; *~ of architecture*, 19th-c.
reversion to Gothic; *~ of book, play, word,
custom*, etc.). 2. (Special effort with
meetings etc. to promote) reawakening of
religious fervour, whence ~ISM(3), ~IST(2),
nn. 3. Restoration to bodily or mental
vigour or to life or consciousness. [foll.,
-AL(2)]

rĕviv|e', v.i. & t. Come or bring back to
consciousness, life, existence, vigour, notice, activity, validity, or vogue; (chem.)
restore (metal, esp. mercury) to natural
form. Hence ~'ABLE a. [ME, f. OF
revivre or LL *re(vivere* live), RE- 8]

rĕviv'er, n. In vbl senses; esp.: (sl.)
stimulating drink; preparation for restoring faded colour etc. [-ER¹]

rĕviv'i|fȳ, v.t. Restore to animation, ac-
tivity, vigour, or life; (chem.) = REVIVE.
Hence ~FICA'TION n. [f. F *revivifier* or LL
re(vivificare VIVIFY), RE- 8]

rĕvivis'cence, n., **rĕvivis'cent**, a. Returning to life or vigour. [f. LL *revivis-
centia* f. *re(viviscere* incept. of *vivere* live)
RE- 8, -ENCE, -ENT]

|| **rĕviv'or**, n. (law). Proceeding for
revival of suit after death of party etc.
[REVIVE, -OR]

rĕvōke', v.t. & i., & n. 1. Repeal, annul,
withdraw, rescind, cancel, (decree, consent, promise, permission; also rarely
abs., withdraw promise etc.), whence ~'oc-
ABLE, rĕv'ocatORY, aa., rĕvoca'TION n.;
(cards) make ~. 2. n. Card-player's
failure to follow suit though he could;
(rare) revocation (*beyond ~*). [ME, f. OF
revoquer or L *re(vocare* call), RE- 9]

rĕvolt', v.i. & t., & n. 1. Cast off allegiance,
make rising or rebellion, fall away *from*

or rise *against* ruler, go over *to* rival power, (n., act of ~ing or state of having ~ed, rising, insurrection; so *in* ~ ; p.p. as -ED[1](2), as *his* ~*ed subjects*). **2.** Feel revulsion or disgust *at*, rise in repugnance *against*, turn in loathing *from*, (*common sense*, *nature*, one's *heart*, ~s *at* or *against* or *from it*; n., sense of loathing, rebellious or protesting mood). **3.** Affect with strong disgust, nauseate, whence ~ING[2] a., ~ing**LY**[2] adv. [f. F *révolte*(r) f. Rom. *revolvitare* intensive of *revolvere* REVOLVE; RE-2]

rĕv'olute[1] (-ōōt, -ūt), a. (bot. etc.). With back-rolled edge. [f. L REVOLVE*re*]

rĕvolute'[2] (-ōōt), v.i. (sl.). Engage in political revolution. [back formation f. foll.]

rĕvolu'tion (-lōō-, -lū-), n. **1.** Revolving, motion in orbit or circular course or round axis or centre, rotation, single completion of orbit or rotation, time it takes, cyclic recurrence. **2.** Complete change, turning upside down, great reversal of conditions (INDUSTRIAL ~), fundamental reconstruction, esp. forcible substitution by subjects of new ruler or polity for the old (*the R~*, expulsion of James II 1688; *French R~*, overthrow of monarchy 1789 etc.; *American R~*, overthrow of British rule 1775 etc.), whence ~IZE(1, 3) v.t., ~ISM(3), ~IST(2), nn., (-ōōsho-, -ū-). [ME f. OF, or LL *revolutio* as REVOLVE, -ION]

rĕvolu'tionarў (-ōōsho-, -ū-), a. & n. (Instigator) of revolution; involving great & usu. violent changes; (rare) of rotation or revolving. [-ARY[1]]

rĕvolve', v.t. & i. Turn (t. & i.) round or round & round, rotate, go in circular orbit, roll (intr.) along, (~ *problem*, *fact*, *in the mind* etc. or abs., ponder over it; *mechanism for revolving the turntable*; *Earth* ~s *both round* or *about sun & on its axis*; *seasons*, *years*, ~). [ME, f. L re(volvere volut- roll), RE-6]

rĕvŏl'ver, n. Pistol with revolving chambers enabling user to fire several shots without reloading (*policy of the big* ~, of threatening foreign States with retaliatory tariff). [-ER[1]]

rĕvūe', n. Loosely constructed play or series of scenes or spectacles presenting or satirizing current events. [F]

rĕvŭl'sion (-shn), n. **1.** Counter-irritation, treatment of one disordered organ etc. by acting upon another. **2.** (rare). Drawing or being drawn away (*the* ~ *of capital from other trades*). **3.** Sudden violent change of feeling, sudden reaction in taste, fortune, trade, etc. [F, or f. L *revulsio* (*vellere vuls-* pull), RE-9]

rĕvŭl'sive, a. & n. (chiefly med.). **1.** Of, producing, revulsion. **2.** n. Counter-irritant application. [prec., -IVE]

rĕward' (-wŏrd), n., & v.t. **1.** Return or recompense for service or merit, requital

for good or evil, retribution; sum offered for detection of criminal, restoration of lost property, etc.; hence ~LESS a. **2.** v.t. Repay, requite, recompense, (service or doer of it, offender, offence). Hence ~ING[2] a., (of task, book, etc.) well worth doing, reading, etc. [ME, f. ONF *re-ward*(er) = OF REGARD[1](er)]

rewin, see RE- 9; **reword**, **rewrite**, RE- 8.

Rĕx, n. (abbr. *R.*). Reigning king (in use as REGINA). [L]

Rey'nard (rĕn-, rān-), n. (Proper name for) the fox; a fox. [ME, f. OF *Renart* name of fox in the *Roman de Renart*]

rhăb'domăncў, n. Use of divining-rod, esp. for discovering subterranean water or ore. [f. Gk *rhabdomanteia* (*rhabdos* rod, -MANCY)]

Rhădamăn'th|us, n. Stern & incorruptible judge. Hence ~INE[2] a. [name of judge in Gk Hades]

Rhae'tian (rēshn), a. & n. ~ *Alps*, part of Alps about the Engadine; = RHAETO--ROMANIC a. & n. [L *Rhaetia*, -IAN]

Rhaet'ĭc, a. & n. (Of) *the* set of strata intermediate between Lias & Trias prevailing in Rhaetian Alps. [f. L *Rhaeticus* (prec., -IC)]

Rhaeto-Rŏmăn'ĭc, **-ănce'**, aa. & nn. (Of, in) any of the Romance dialects of SE. Switzerland & Tyrol, esp. Romansh & Ladin. [L *Rhaetus* Rhaetian, -O-]

rhăp'sōde, n. Ancient-Greek minstrel or reciter of epic poems. [f. Gk *rhapsō(i)dos* (*rhaptō* stitch, ODE)]

rhăp'sod|ize, -**|ise** (-īz), v.t. & i. Recite (t. & i.) as rhapsode; talk or write rhapsodies (usu. *about*, *on*, etc.). So ~IST(1) n. [foll., -IZE]

rhăp'sodў, n. **1.** (Gk ant.) epic poem, or part of it, of length for one recitation. **2.** Enthusiastic extravagant high-flown utterance or composition, emotional irregular piece of music, whence **rhăp'sŏd'**ICAL a., **rhăpsŏd'ical**LY[2] adv. Hence **rhăpsŏd'ıc** a. [f. L *rhapsodia* f. Gk *rhapsōidia* (RHAPSODE, -IA[1])]

rhăt'anў, n. (Extract, used medicinally & in adulterating port, of root of) S.--Amer. shrub. [f. Port. *ratanhia* f. native *rataña*]

rhe'a (rēa), n. S.-Amer. three-toed ostrich. [name of Gk goddess]

Rhēm'ish, a. Of Rheims (~ *Bible*, *Testament*, *version*, *translation*, N.T. translated by Roman Catholics of English College at Rheims 1582). [obs. E *Rhemes*, -ISH]

Rhēn'ish, a. & n. (arch.). **1.** Of the Rhine & districts on its banks (now usu. *Rhine* attrib.). **2.** n. ~ wine (now usu. *Rhine wine* or *hock*). [14th c. *rynis*, *-isch*, etc., f. MDu. *rijnisch*, G *rheinisch*, w. assim. to L *Rhenus* Rhine]

rhēn'ium, n. Rare metallic element of manganese group, discovered in 1925. [f. L *Rhenus* Rhine, -IUM]

rhĕo-, rēo-, comb. form in chiefly electr. terms of Gk *rheos* stream, = current-, as *rheŏL'OGY,* study of flow & deformation of matter; *rhe'ostat,* apparatus for controlling supply of current, esp. to electric motors when starting up, by introducing variable resistance.

rhĕs'us, n. Small catarrhine monkey common in N. India; *R~ factor* (abbr. *Rh-factor*), substance occurring in red blood cells of most persons and some animals (as in the ~ monkey, in which it was first observed). Subjects in which this substance is present, absent, are said to be *Rh-positive, Rh-negative.* [arbitr. use of Gk *Rhēsus,* mythical king of Thrace]

rhĕt'or, n. Ancient Greek or Roman teacher or professor of rhetoric; (mere) orator (rare). [ME, f. L f. Gk *rhētōr*]

rhĕt'oric, n. (Treatise on) the art of persuasive or impressive speaking or writing; language designed to persuade or impress (often w. implication of insincerity, exaggeration, etc.); persuasiveness of or *of* looks or acts. [ME, f. OF *rethorique* or L f. Gk *rhētorikē (tekhnē* art) of RHETOR, -IC]

rhĕtŏ'rical, a. Expressed with a view to persuasive or impressive effect, artificial or extravagant in language, of the nature of rhetoric, (~ *question,* asked not for information but to produce effect, as *who cares?* for *nobody cares*); of the art of rhetoric; given to rhetoric, oratorical. Hence ~LY² adv. [ME, f. L f. Gk *rhētorikos* (RHETOR, -IC) + -AL]

rhĕtori'cian (-shn), n. = RHETOR; rhetorical speaker or writer. [ME, f. OF *rethoricien* (RHETORIC, -ICIAN)]

‖ **rheum** (rōōm), n. (arch.). Watery secretion or discharge of mucous membrane etc. such as tears, saliva, or mucus; catarrh; (pl.) rheumatic pains. [ME, f. OF *reume* f. LL f. Gk *rheuma -atos* stream (*rheŏ* flow)]

rheumăt'|ic (-ōō-), a. & n. **1.** Of, suffering from, subject to, producing, or produced by, rheumatism (~*ic fever,* non-infectious fever with inflammation & pain in joints; ~*ic walk* etc., impeded by ~ic stiffness); hence ~ICALLY adv., ~**icky²** a. (colloq.). **rheu'mato-** comb. form, **rheu'matoID** a., (-ōō-). **2.** n. ~ic patient; (pl., colloq.) rheumatism. [ME, f. OF *reumatique* or L f. Gk *rheumatikos* (prec., -IC)]

rheu'matism (-ōō-), (vulg.) **-tiz,** n. Disease marked by inflammation & pain in joints (*acute* ~, rheumatic fever). [f. L f. Gk *rheumatismos* (*rheumatizō* f. RHEUMA, -IZE, -ISM)]

‖ **rheu'mУ** (-ōō-), a. (arch.). Consisting of, flowing with, rheum; (of air) damp, raw. [-Y²]

rhin'al, a. (anat. etc.). Of nostril or nose. [f. Gk *rhis rhinos* + -AL]

‖ **rhine¹** (rēn), n. (SW. dial.). Large open ditch. [app. repr. OE *ryne* stream]

Rhine², n. German river (~ *wine,* kinds esp. of white wine from ~ vineyards, cf. RHENISH; ~*'stone,* kind of rock-crystal, also paste gem imitating diamond).

rhin'ō¹, n. (sl.). Money (often *ready* ~).

rhin'ō², n. (sl.; pl. ~*s*). (Short for) rhinoceros.

rhin|o-, comb. form of Gk *rhis rhinos* nostril, nose, as ~*opharyn'geal,* of nose & pharynx; ~*oplas'tic, rhin'oplasty,* (of) plastic surgery of the nose; *rhin'oSCOPE,* ~*oscŏp'ic,* ~*ŏs'copY¹.*

rhinŏ'ceros, n. Large pachydermatous African & S.-Asian quadruped with horn or two horns on nose & thick folded & plated skin. So **rhinŏcerŏt'ic** a. [ME, f. L f. Gk RHINO(*kerōs* f. *keras* horn)]

rhiz'o-, comb. form of Gk *rhiza* root chiefly in bot. terms as ~*carp,* plant with perennial root but perishing stems.

rhiz'ōme, n. Prostrate rootlike stem emitting roots, rootstock. [f. Gk *rhizōma* (*rhizoomai* take root, as prec.)]

rhō, n. Greek letter (*P,* ρ) = r. [Gk]

Rhōde Isl'and (īl-) **Rĕd,** n. American breed of reddish-black domestic fowl. [f. *Rhode Island,* State of U.S.]

Rhodes schŏl'ar (rōdz sk-), n. Holder of any of a number of scholarships awarded annually & tenable at Oxford by candidates from certain Commonwealth countries, South Africa, and the United States. [Cecil *Rhodes,* founder]

Rhŏd'ian, a. & n. (Native) of Rhodes. [L *Rhodius* f. L f. Gk *Rhodos* Rhodes + -AN]

rhŏd'ium¹, n. (Also ~*-wood*) scented wood of Canary convolvulus, (*oil of* ~, oil got from it). [mod. L, neut. adj. (sc. *lignum* wood) = roselike f. Gk *rhodon* rose]

rhŏd'|ium², n. Hard white metal of platinum group (~*ium pen,* steel pen tipped with it). Hence ~IC, ~OUS, aa. (chem.). [Gk *rhodon* rose, -IUM, from colour of solution of its salts]

rhŏdo-, comb. form of Gk *rhodon* rose, found chiefly in names of mineral and chem. substances, as ~*chrŏ'site* (-kr-), carbonate of manganese occurring in rose-red crystals.

rhŏdodĕn'dron, n. Kinds of large-flowered evergreen shrubs akin to azalea. [L f. Gk (prec., *dendron* tree)]

rhŏmb (-b usu. mute exc. before vowel), n. Oblique equilateral parallelogram, as ace of diamonds on playing-card, object or part with such outline; (cryst.) rhombohedron. Hence **rhŏm'bIC** a., **rhŏm'bo-** comb. form. [f. F *rhombe,* or L f. Gk *rhombos*]

rhŏmbohĕd'r|on, n. (chiefly cryst.; pl. ~*a,* ~*ons*). (Crystal in shape of) solid bounded by six equal rhombs. Hence ~AL a. [RHOMBO- (prec.), Gk *hedra* base]

rhŏm'boid, a. & n. **1.** Of or near the shape of a rhomb (~ *muscle,* connecting

In words beginning with **rh-** h is mute.

scapula with vertebrae). **2.** n. Quadrilateral of which only opposite sides & angles are equal; ~ muscle. [f. F *rhomboïde* or LL f.˙Gk *rhomboeidēs* (RHOMB, -OID)]

rhŏmboid′al, a. Having shape of a rhomboid (prec., n.); = prec. (adj.). Hence ~LY² adv.˙[prec., -AL]

rhŏm′bus, n. (pl. *-buses, -bī*). **1.** = RHOMB. **2.** Kinds of flat-fish including turbot & brill. [L (RHOMB)]

rhŏt′acism, n., **rhŏt′acīze** (*or* -ise, *pr.* -īz), v.i. (Speak with) excessive or peculiar pronunciation of *r*; conversion of, convert, other sounds into *r*. [f. Gk *rhōtakizō* (RHO, -IZE, -ISM)]

rhu′bȧrb (rōō-), n. **1.** (Purgative made from) root of Chinese & Tibetan plant (usu. *Chinese, East Indian, Russia,* or *Turkey* ~, from channels of importation). **2.** (Fleshy leaf-stalks of) kinds of garden plant, cooked in spring as substitute for fruit (occas. *English, French, common,* or *garden*~). **3.** attrib.(Of colour) yellowish-brown like Chinese ~. Hence ~Y² a. [ME, f. OF *rubarbe* f. med. L *rhabarbarum* foreign 'rha' or rhubarb (*rha* Gk, perh. f. *Rha* the Volga, BARBAROUS), w. assim. to L f. Gk *rhēon* rhubarb]

rhŭmb (-m), n. (naut.). (Also ~-*line*) line cutting all meridians at same angle, line followed by ship sailing on one course; angular distance between two successive points of compass, 11° 15′. [f. F *rumb* or Sp. *rumbo*. L RHOMBUS]

rhŷme¹, rime, n. **1.** Identity of sound between words or verse-lines extending from the end to the last fully accented vowel & not further (greet & deceit, shepherd & leopard, quality & frivolity, stationary & probationary, is it & visit, give ~s, but seat & deceit, station & crustacean, visible & invisible, do not; single or male or masculine, double or female or FEMININE, treble or triple, quadruple,~, according to number of syllables included; imperfect ~, as in love & move, phase & race; without ~ or reason, quite unaccountable, -bly). **2.** Verse marked by ~s (pl. or sing.), a poem with ~s, the employment of ~, (should be written in ~; prefer blank verse to ~; am sending you some ~s; NURSERY ~; was reading an old ~; ~ royal, stanzas of seven ten-syllable lines with ~s as ababbcc, as˙in Chaucer's Clerkes Tale etc.). **3.** Word providing a ~ (to another; can't find a ~ to teacups; English is badly off for double ~s). Hence ~′LESS (-ml-) a., ~′lèssNESS n. [17th c. var. (w. assim. to RHYTHM) of ME f. OF *rime* f. L f. Gk *rhuthmos* RHYTHM]

rhŷme², rime, v.i. & t. Write rhymes, versify (intr.), whence **rhȳm′ER¹, rhȳme′- STER** (-ms-), nn.; put or make (story etc.) into rhyme (~d verse, opp. blank verse); while (time) away in rhyming; (of words or lines) exhibit rhyme, (of word) supply or act as rhyme to or with, (of person)

treat (word) as rhyming with, select rhymes, (~s carelessly; ~s law with four; rhymING¹-dictionary, of words arranged by terminations for versifiers' use), whence **rhȳm′IST**(1) n. [17th c. var. of ME *rime* f. OF *rimer* (see prec.)]

rhȳ′thm (-dhm, -thm), n. **1.** Metrical movement determined by various relations of long & short or accented & unaccented syllables, measured flow of words & phrases in verse or prose. **2.** That feature of musical composition concerned with periodical accent & the duration of notes. **3.** (art). Harmonious correlation of parts. **4.** (Phys., physiol., & gen.) movement with regular succession of strong & weak elements. Hence or cogn. **rhȳth′mIC(AL)** aa., **rhȳth′micALLY²** adv., **rhȳthm′LESS** a., **rhȳth′mIST**(3) n., (-dh-, -th-). [f. L f. Gk *rhuthmos* cf. *rheō* flow]

rī′ant, a. Smiling, cheerful, (of face, eyes, etc., & esp. of landscape). [F *rire* f. L *ridēre* laugh, -ANT]

rib, n., & v.t. (-bb-). **1.** One of curved bones reaching from spine round upper part of body (*true, sternal,* ~, joined also to breastbone, opp. *false, floating, short,* ~; *poke one in the* ~s, to draw his attention facetiously; *smile under fifth* ~, bibl., *stab mortally;* ~ *or* ~s *of beef* etc., as joint of meat; SPARE-~); (joc. w. ref. to *Gen.* ii. 21) wife, woman. **2.** Ridge or long raised piece often of thicker material across thinner surface serving to support as part of framework or strengthen or adorn, e.g. vein of leaf, shaft of feather, spur of mountain, vein of ore, ridge between furrows, wave-mark on sand, raised line in knitting, one of ship's curved timbers to which planks are nailed or corresponding ironwork, arch supporting vault, groin, raised moulding on groin or across ceiling etc., wooden or iron beam helping to carry bridge, hinged rod of umbrella-frame. **3.** ~-*grass,* ~′*wort,* PLANTAIN¹ with long narrow leaves. Hence (-)~BED² (-bd), ~′LESS, aa. **4.** v.t. Provide with ~s, act as ~s of, whence ~b′ING¹(3, 6) n.; mark with ridges; plough with ~s between furrows, half-plough, rafter; (sl.) make fun of, tease. [OE *rib(b)*, OHG *rippi*, ON *rif*, also OS *ribba,* OHG *rippa,* f. Gmc **rebja-*]

rib′ald, n. & a. **1.** Irreverent jester, user of scurrilous, blasphemous, or indecent language; so ~RY(4, 5) n. **2.** adj. (Of language or its user) scurrilous, obscene, irreverent. [ME, earlier sense *low-born retainer,* f. OF *ribaut, ribault,* f. *riber* pursue licentious pleasures]

rib′and n., **rib′andèd** a. = RIBBON(*ed*). [ME, f. OF *riban* (now *ru-*)]

ribb′and, n. Wale, strip, scantling, or light spar, of wood, used esp. in shipbuilding to hold ribs in position, launching, & making of gun-platform or pontoon-bridge. [f. RIB, BAND¹, or f. prec.]

ribb'on, n. **1.** (Piece or length of) silk or satin or other fine material woven into narrow band esp. for adorning costume; ~ of special colour etc. worn to indicate membership of knightly order, club, college, athletic team, etc. (BLUE[1] ~; R~ Society (hist.), Irish R.-C. secret society formed in early 19th c. & associated with agrarian crime, whence R~ISM n.). **2.** Long narrow strip of anything, ~-like object or mark, (pl.) driving-reins, (hang in, torn to, ~s, ragged strips; handle, take, the ~s, drive). **3.** ~ building, ~ development, the building of houses along a main road, extending outwards from a town; ~-fish, long slender flat kinds; ~-grass, slender-leaved kind; ~-man, member of R~ Society. Hence (-)~ED[2] (-nd) a. [ME, var. of RIBAND]

rib'es (-z), n. (bot.). Currant or gooseberry plant; (pop.) flowering currant. [med. L, = sorrel, f. Arab. ribas]

Rib'ston pipp'in, n. Kind of dessert apple. [Ribston Park in Yorks.]

Ricärd'ian, a. & n. (Adherent) of the political economist Ricardo (d. 1823), according to his views. [-IAN]

rice, n. (Pearl-white seeds, used as staple food in many Eastern countries, & in Britain in puddings, cakes, etc., or as table-vegetable, of) chiefly oriental plant grown in marshes; ~-bird, Java sparrow, also bobolink; ~-milk, boiled & thickened with ~; ~-paper, kind made from pith of a Formosan plant & used by Chinese artists for painting on (named after ~ in error). [ME, f. OF ris f. It. riso f. Rom. *orizum f. L f. Gk oruza of Oriental orig.]

rich, a. **1.** (Of persons, societies, States, etc.) wealthy, having riches, (also as n. in the ~, ~ & poor). **2.** (Of countries, periods, soil, etc.) abounding in or in natural resources or some valuable possession or production, fertile. **3.** Valuable (~ offerings, a ~ harvest). **4.** (Of dress, furniture, buildings, banquets, etc.) splendid, costly, elaborate, (with lace, sculpture, etc.). **5.** (Of food or diet) containing or involving large proportion of fat, oil, butter, eggs, spice, etc. **6.** (Of colours, sounds, smells) mellow, deep, full, not thin. **7.** Abundant, ample. **8.** (Of incidents) highly amusing, full of entertainment or material for humour. **9.** (Of mixture in internal-combustion engines) highly combustible. **10.** ~-, richly (~-clad, -bound, -glittering, etc.). Hence ~'EN[6] v.i. & t. (rare), ~'NESS n. [OE rice, OS riki, OHG richi, ON rikr, Goth. reiks, f. an early Gmc adoption of Celt. *rix = L rex king]

Rich'ard, pers. name. ~ Röe, fictitious character in law (cf. JOHN Doe); ~'s himself again (f. interpolation in Cibber's version of Shaks. ~ III), said by or of person recovered from despondency, fear, illness, etc.

rich'es (-ĭz), n. (usu. as pl.). Abundant means, wealth, valuable possessions,

being rich. [ME richesse f. OF (riche RICH, -ESS[2]), apprehended as pl.]

rich'lỹ, adv. In adj. senses; also (chiefly with deserve) fully, thoroughly, (~ deserves a thrashing, to succeed). [-LY[2]]

rick[1], n., & v.t. **1.** Stack of hay, corn, peas, etc., esp. one regularly built & thatched; ‖ ~-barton, = ~-yard; ~-cloth, canvas cover for unfinished ~; ~-stand, short wooden or stone pillars bearing joists to raise ~ from ground; ~-yard, enclosure for ~s. **2.** v.t. Form into ~(s). [OE hrēac = MDu. rooc, ON hraukr, of unkn. orig.]

rick[2]. See WRICK.

rick'ets, n. (as sing. or pl.; -et in comb. etc., as ricket-producing, rickety). Children's disease with softening of bones, esp. of spine, & bow-legs etc., rachitis. [described as 'The Rickets' by D. Whistler (1645); assoc. w. Gk RACHITIS, adopted as its scientific name]

rick'ėt|ỹ, a. **1.** Suffering from, of (the nature of), rickets. **2.** Feeble, shaky, tottering, weak-jointed, fragile, insecure, (of persons or things, esp. furniture). Hence ~ INESS n. [-Y[2]]

ricksha(w). See JINRICKSHA.

ric'ochet (-shā, -shĕt), n., & v.i. & t. (-t- or -tt-, pr. -shăd or -shĕtíd, -shāïng or -shĕtïng etc.). **1.** Skipping on water or ground of projectile esp. shell or bullet, hit made after it, (often attrib., as ~ fire, shot). **2.** vb. (Of projectile) skip once or more; (of gun, gunner, etc.) hit or aim at with ~ shot(s). [F, of unkn. orig.]

ric'tus, n. Expanse or gape of person's or animal's mouth, bird's beak, or flower with two-lipped corolla. [L (ringi open the mouth)]

rid, v.t. (past ridded, rid; p.p. rid, rarely ridded). Make (person, place) free, disencumber, of (usu. in p.p. with be or get; glad to be, must get, ~ of him); (arch.) abolish, clear away, get ~ of, (pest). Hence ~d'ANCE n. (esp. a good ~dance, as excl. of joy; person etc. is a good ~dance, better away). [ME, earlier sense clear (land etc.); f. ON rythja]

rid(d)'el, n. (eccl.). Altar-curtain. [ME, f. OF ridel (F rideau) curtain]

ridden. See RIDE.

rid'dle[1], n., & v.i. & t. Question, statement, or description, designed or serving to test ingenuity of hearers in divining its answer or meaning or reference, conundrum, enigma; puzzling or mysterious fact, thing, or person. **2.** vb. Speak in, propound, (part.) expressed in, ~s, whence **ridd'lingLY[2]** adv.; solve (~; often ~ me as challenge). [OE rǣdels(e) (= OS rādisli, -lo, OHG rādisle) f. rǣdan READ + -els as in BURIAL]

rid'dle[2], n., & v.t. **1.** Coarse sieve for corn, gravel, cinders, etc.; plate with pins used in straightening wire. **2.** v.t. Pass (corn etc.) through ~, sift, (fig.) test (evidence, truth); fill (ship, person) with holes esp. of gunshot, (fig.) pelt with questions, refute (person, theory) with facts. [OE *hriddel*, earlier *hrid(d)er* f. *hrid*-shake, cogn. w. OHG *(h)ritera* sieve]

ride, v.i. & t. (*rōde*, arch. *rid*; *ridden* pr. ri'dn, arch. *rid*), & n. **1.** Sit on & be carried by horse etc., go on horseback etc. or on bicycle etc. or in train or other public conveyance (cf. DRIVE[1]), sit or go or be *on* something as on horse etc. astride, sit on & manage horse, lie at anchor, float buoyantly, (of sun etc.) seem to float, (of things normally level or even) project or overlap, (~ *a-*COCK-HORSE, BODKIN, ROUGH-shod, *50 miles, full speed, a race*; ~ *to hounds*, hunt; ~ *for a fall*, ~ or fig. act recklessly, court defeat; ~ *12 st.* etc., weigh that in riding-trim; ~ *over*, in horse-racing as WALK *over*; ~ one *down*, overtake him by riding, also put one's horse at him; ~ one *off* at polo, edge him away; ~ *off on* a side issue, use it to evade the main point; ~ & *tie*, of two or more travellers sharing horse, one riding ahead & then leaving it tied to await the other; *riding on his father's shoulders, back, knee, foot*; ~*s well, cannot* ~, *learn to* ~, *riding*-*lessons* or *-school*; *bird, ship*, ~*s on the wind, waves; ship rode at anchor*; ~ *out the storm* lit. & fig., come safely through it; *moon was riding high; bone* ~*s* in fracture, one part overlaps other; *rope* ~*s*, has one turn crossing over another); traverse on horseback etc., ~ over or through, (~ *the country, desert,* etc.; ~ *a ford,* pass through it on horseback). **2.** ~ on, sit heavily on, oppress, haunt, dominate, tyrannize over, (~ *horse;* ~ one's *horse at* fence or enemy, urge it forward; ~ one's *horse,* & fig. hobby or method or jest, *to death,* kill or overdo it; *nightmare* ~*s* sleeper; ~ *the whirlwind,* direct it; *ship* ~*s the waves; ridden by fears, prejudices,* etc.; *priest dead. -ridden*). **3.** Give ~ to, cause to ~, (~ *child on* one's *back;* ~ one *on rail,* carry him astride on it as torture). **4.** (Of ground) be of specified character for riding on (~*s well, soft, hard,* etc.); hence **rid'**ABLE a. **5.** n. Journey in public conveyance, spell of riding on horse, bicycle, person's back, etc.; **take for a* ~ (sl.), drive (person) away in a motor-car prior to murdering him. **6.** Road esp. through wood for riding on. **7.** (mil.). Batch of mounted recruits. [OE (OS) *rīdan,* OHG *rītan,* ON *rītha* f. Gmc **rīdan*]

rid'el. See RIDDEL.

rid'er, n. In vbl senses; also or esp.: **1.** (naut.). (Pl.) additional set of timbers or iron plates strengthening ship's frame; (sing.) overlying rope or rope-turn. **2.** (curl.). Stone that ousts another. **3.** Additional clause amending or supplementing document, esp. parliamentary bill at third reading; corollary, naturally arising supplement; expression of opinion, recommendation etc., added to verdict.

4. (math.). Problem testing student's mastery of principles on which its solution depends. **5.** Piece in machine etc. that surmounts or bridges or works over others. Hence ~LESS a. [OE *rīdere* (RIDE)]

ridge, n., & v.t. & i. **1.** Line of junction of two surfaces sloping upwards towards each other (*the* ~ *of a roof, the nose,* etc.); long narrow hill-top, mountain range, watershed; (agric.) one of a set of raised strips separated by furrows; (gard.) raised hotbed for melons etc.; any narrow elevation across surface; ~*-piece,* beam along ~ of roof; ~*-pole,* horizontal pole of long tent, also = ~*-piece;* ~*-tile,* used for roof-~; ~*-tree,* = ~*-piece;* ~*'way,* road along ~; hence **ridg'**Y[2] a. **2.** vb. Break up (land) into ~s; mark with ~s; plant (cucumbers etc.) in ~s; gather (t. & i. esp. of sea) into ~s. [OE *hrycg,* MDu. *rugghe,* MLG *rugge,* OHG *hrucci,* ON *hryggr* f. Gmc **hrugjaz*]

rid'icule, n., & v.t. **1.** Ridiculous thing, ridiculousness, (arch.); holding or being held up as laughing-stock, derision, mockery. **2.** v.t. Make fun of, subject to ~, laugh at. [F, or f. L *ridiculum* neut. of *ridiculus* laughable (*ridēre* laugh)]

ridic'ulous, a. Deserving to be laughed at, absurd, unreasonable. Hence ~LY[2] adv., ~NESS n. [as prec. + -OUS, or f. L *ridiculosus*]

rid'ing[1], n. In vbl senses; also, road for riders, esp. green track through or beside wood; ~*-breeches;* ~*-*HABIT[1]; ~*-lamp, -light* (borne by ship at anchor). [-ING[1]]

|| **rid'ing**[2], n. Administrative division (*East, W.,* or *N., R*~) of Yorkshire; similar division of other U.-K. or colonial county. [for *thriding* (f. ON *thrithjungr* THIRD, -ING[3]) third part, with loss of *th*-owing to preceding -t(h) of *east* etc.]

Ries'ling (ree-), n. A dry white table--wine. [G]

rifacimen'tō (-ahch-), n. (pl. *-ti* pr. -tē). Remodelled form of a literary work or the like. [It.]

rife, pred. a. Of common occurrence, met with in numbers or quantities, prevailing, current, numerous, (usu. be, also *grow, wax,* etc., ~); well provided *with* (*language is* ~ *with maxims*). Hence ~'NESS (-fn-) n. [OE *rỹfe* = MDu., MLG *rive,* ON *rīfr*]

Riff, a. & n. (Of) a Berber of the *Rif* district of Morocco. So ~'IAN a. & n.

rif'fle, n. (In gold-washing) groove or slat set in the trough or sluice to catch the gold particles. [orig. unkn.]

riff'-raff, n. *The* rabble, disreputable persons. [ME *rif & raf* f. OF *rif et raf*]

ri'fle[1], v.t. & i. **1.** Search & rob, esp. of all that can be found in various pockets or storing-places; carry off as booty. **2.** Make spiral grooves in (gun or its barrel or bore) to produce rotatory motion in projectile (p.p. of projectile, with projections fitting such grooves). **3.** Shoot (t.

S

& i.) with rifle. Hence **rīf′**ᴵᴺᴳ¹ n. [(1)ME,
f. OF *rifler* graze, scratch, plunder; (2)
from 1635, f. obs. Flem. *rijffelen* scrape,
LG *rifeln* to groove f. *rife* groove; (3) f.
foll.]

ri′fle², n. **1.** One of the grooves made in
rifling a gun (obs.). **2.** (Formerly ~-*gun*)
fire-arm with rifled barrel esp. one fired
from shoulder; (pl.) troops armed with
~s. **3.** ~-*bird*, dark-green Australian
bird; || *R~ Brigade*, regiment of British
army; ~-*corps*, of volunteer ~men;
~(-)*green* n. & a., (of) dark green as in
~man's uniform; ~-ᏀᎡᎬNᎪᎠᎬ; ~*man*,
soldier armed with ~, esp. member (*R~
man* when prefixed = Private) of some
~ regiments in British army, also = ~-
-*bird*; ~-*pit*, excavation as cover for ~-
men firing at enemy; ~-*range*, distance
~ carries, place for ~-*practice*; ~-*shot*,
distance~ carries, *good* etc. ~-*marksman*,
shot fired with~. [f. prec.; cf. obs. Flem.
rijffel, LG *riffel* groove]

rift, n., & v.t. **1.** Cleft, fissure, chasm, in
earth or rock; rent, crack, split in an
object, opening in cloud etc. (*little ~
within the lute*, often fig. of incipient madness or dissension); ~-*valley*, steep-sided
formed by subsidence of earth's crust;
hence ~′ʟᴇss, ~′ʏ², aa. **2.** v.t. (Usu. in
p.p.) rend apart, cleave. [ME, of Scand.
orig.; cf. Da., Norw. *rift* cleft, OIcel. *ript*
breach; cogn. w.˙ʀɪᴠᴇ]

rig¹, v.t. & i. (-gg-), & n. **1.** Provide (ship),
(of ship) be provided, with necessary
spars, ropes, etc., or ~ġ′ɪɴɢ¹(3) (-g-) n.,
prepare (t. & i.) for sea in this respect;
assemble & adjust parts of (aircraft);
fit (*out*, *up*, or rarely abs.) with or *with*
clothes or other equipment; set *up*
(structure) hastily or as makeshift or by
utilizing odd materials; ~*ging-loft*, gallery
in dockyard for fitting ~ging, (theatr.)
space over stage from which scenery is
manipulated. **2.** n. Way ship's masts,
sails, etc., are arranged, whence -~ġᴇᴅ²
(-gd) a.; (transf.) person's or thing's look
as determined by clothes etc. (~-*up*, -*out*,
such accessories); *in full* ~ (colloq.),
smartly dressed. [ME, of unkn. orig.; the
syn. Norw., Sw. *rigga*, Da. *rigge* are prob.
f. E]

rig², n., & v.t. (-gg-). **1.** Trick, dodge, way
of swindling; (commerc.) = ᏟᎾᎡNᎬᎡ. **2.**
v.t. Manage or conduct fraudulently (~
the market, cause artificial rise or fall in
prices). [orig. unkn.]

|| **rig³**, n. Imperfectly developed or
partially castrated male animal. [late
ME, f. ON *hyrggr* = OE *hrycg* back,
ʀɪᴅɢᴇ]

Rī′ga (*or* rē-), n. A port of the Baltic (~
deal, *hemp*, etc.; ~ *balsam*, essential oil
distilled from kind of pine & used
medicinally).

rigadoon′, n. Lively dance for two persons; music for this dance. [F *rigaudon*]

rigĕs′c|ent, a. Growing rigid, rather stiff.

So ~ᴇɴᴄᴇ n. [f. L *rigescere* (*rigĕre* be stiff,
-ᴇsᴄᴇɴᴛ)]

rigg′er (-g-), n. In vbl senses (ʀɪɢ¹˒²); also
or esp.: one who attends to the rigging
of aircraft; (mech.) band-wheel; = ᴏᴜᴛ-
ʀɪɢɢᴇʀ; = ᴛʜɪᴍʙʟᴇ-~; -~, ship rigged in
specified way. [-ᴇʀ¹]

right (rīt), a., v.t. & i., n., & adv. **1.** (arch.).
Straight (now only in ~ *line*, ~-*lined*).
2. (Of angle) neither acute nor obtuse,
of 90°, made by lines meeting not
obliquely but perpendicularly, (*at ~
angles*, turning or placed with such angle),
whence ~-*z̄*ᴀ̄ɴɢʟᴇᴅ² (-nggld) a.; involving
~ angle(s), not oblique, (~ *sailing*, due
N., S., E., or W.; ~ ᴀsᴄᴇɴsɪᴏɴ; ~ *cone*,
cylinder, *prism*, etc., with ends or base
perpendicular to axis). **3.** (Of conduct
etc.) just, morally good, required by
equity or duty, proper, (*acted a ~ part*;
*it is only ~ to tell you, that you should
know*), whence ~-*mind*ᴇᴅ² a., ~-
-*mind′ed*ɴᴇss n. **4.** Correct, true, (~ *use
of words*; *did not give a ~ account of the
matter*; *your opinions are ~ enough*);
the preferable or most suitable, the less
wrong or not wrong, (*which is the ~ way
to* —?; *the ~ man in the ~ place*; *does not
do it the ~ way*; *the ~ heir*; *took the ~
way to offend us*; *a fault on the ~ side*; *the
~ side of a fabric* etc., that meant for
show or use; so ~ *side up*; *on the ~ side of
forty* etc., not yet 40 years old). **5.** In
good or normal condition, sound, sane,
satisfactory, well-advised, not mistaken,
(*in one's ~ mind*, not mad etc.; *is not ~ in
his head*; *are you ~ now?*, comfortable,
recovered, etc.; *all's ~ with the world*; *is
as ~ as a trivet, as rain*, etc., quite; *set or
put ~*, restore to order, health, etc., also
correct mistaken ideas of, also justify
one*self* usu. *with* person; *get ~*, bring or
come into ~ state; ~, ~ *you are*, forms of
approval, or, & so also *all ~*, || ~ *oh!* sl.,
of assent to order or proposal), whence
|| ~′ᴇɴ⁶ (rīt-) v.t. (rare). **6.** (arch.). Right-
ful, real, veritable, properly so called, (~
ᴡʜᴀʟᴇ; ~ *cognac* etc.). **7.** (Of position)
having the relation to front & back that
equinoctial sunrise has to north & south,
on or towards that side of human body of
which the hand is normally more used,
on or towards that part of an object
which is analogous to person's ~˙side or
(with opposite sense) hand, which is nearer to
spectator's ~ hand, (cf. ʟᴇғᴛ¹; ~ *side*, *eye*,
etc.; ~ *wing* or *flank* of army etc.; ~ *bank*,
on ~ side of one looking down stream; ~
ᴄᴇɴᴛʀᴇ¹). **8.** ~ *& left*: adv., to or on both
sides, on all hands, as *the crowd divided,
he was abused*, ~ *& left*; adj., with or of or
to both hands or sides, as *a ~-&-left shot*,
with both barrels, ~-*&-left screw*, with
contrary threads at two ends; n., ~-&-
-*left shot*, also pugilist's two blows in
quick succession with different hands.
9. ~ *arm*, (fig.) one's most reliable helper.
10. ~ *hand*: hand of ~ side; this as the

better hånd, as *put* one's ~ *hand to the work*; this w. ref. to handshaking, as *give the* ~ *hand of fellowship*; region or direction on this side of person, as *at, on, to*, one's ~ *hand*; one's indispensable or chief assistant; ~-*hand*, placed on the ~ hand; ~-*hand man*, soldier on one's ~ hand in line, also assistant as above; ~-*hand screw*, with thread turning to ~ ; ~-*handed*, using ~ hand more than left; ~-*handed blow* etc., struck with ~ hand; ~-*handed tool* etc., made to suit ~ hand; ~-*handed rotation* etc.; ~-*hander*, ~-*handed* blow or person. **11.** ~ *turn*, that brings one's front to face as one's ~ side did before; ~-*about turn* or *face*, ~ turn prolonged to rear (see ABOUT¹ for mil. use); ~-*about*, = ~-about turn, reversal of front, hurried retreat as in *send to the* ~-*about*, send packing; also as v.t. & i. = reverse or make reverse front; hence ~'NESS (rīt-) n. **12.** vb. Restore to proper or straight or vertical position (~ *helm*, put it amidships; *boat* ~*s herself*; *could not* ~ *the boat, car*); ~ *oneself*, recover balance, (of ship) recover vertical position. **13.** Make reparation for or to, avenge, (wrong, wronged person); vindicate, justify, rehabilitate. **14.** Correct (mistakes etc.), correct mistakes in, set in order, (often refl., as *that is a fault that will* ~ *itself*); hence ~'ABLE (rīt-) a. **15.** n. What is just, fair treatment, (~ *& might*, ~ *& wrong*; *do one* ~, treat or think of him fairly; *by* ~ or now usu. ~*s*, if ~ were done; *the* ~, the juster cause, as *God defend the* ~ ; *be in the* ~, have justice or truth on one's side). **16.** Justification, fair claim, being entitled to privilege or immunity, thing one is entitled to, (*has a, the, no,* ~ *to* thing, *to do, of doing, of search* etc.; ~ *divine* or DIVINE ~ ; *claims in* ~ *of his wife*; *reigns by* ~ *of worth*; *belongs to him of or by* ~ ; ~*s & duties*; *woman's* ~*s*, of equality with men; ~ *of way*, ~ established by usage to pass over another's ground, also path subject to such ~, precedence in passing granted to one vehicle etc. over another; *Declaration* or *Bill of R*~*s*, constitutional settlement of 1689; *assert* or *stand on* one's ~*s*, refuse to relinquish them; *peeress in her own* ~, not by marriage; *admiration is her* ~), whence ~'LESS (rīt-) a. **17.** pl. ~ condition, true state, (*set* or *put to* ~*s*, arrange properly; *have not heard, do not know, the* ~*s of the case*). **18.** ~-hand part or region or direction (*is on your* or *the, to the,* ~ ; *to, from,* ~ *& left*; *work round the enemy's* ~); (pol., usu. *R*~) conservative members of (orig. continental) parliament etc., whence ~'WARD a. & adv., ~'WARDS adv., (rīt-). **19.** adv. Straight (*wind was* ~ *behind us*; *go* ~ *on*; *went* ~ *at him*); ~ *off, away*, chiefly U.S., immediately, without pause). **20.** All the way *to, round*, etc., completely *off, out*, etc., (*sank* ~ *to the bottom*; *veranda* ~ *round house*; *took gate* ~ *off hinges*;

turned ~ *round*). **21.** Exactly, quite, (~ *in the middle*). **22.** Very, to the full, (*know* ~ *well*; *banqueted* ~ *royally*; *was* ~ *glad to hear*; ‖ ~ HONOURABLE, REVEREND; ~-*down*, thorough, -ly, as *is a* ~-*down scoundrel*, *was* ~-*down sorry*). **23.** Justly, properly, correctly, aright, truly, satisfactorily, (*whether they act* ~ *or wrong*; *does not hold his pen, do the sum,* ~ ; *serves him* ~, is no worse than he deserves; *nothing goes* ~ *with me*; *if I remember* ~ ; *guessed* ~). **24.** To ~ hand (*eyes* ~ *!*, order to soldiers dressing; *looks neither* ~ *nor left*). [OE *riht* adj., = OS, OHG *reht*, ON *réttr*; Goth *raihts*, rel. to L *rectus*]

righteous (rīch'ŭs), a. Just, upright, virtuous, law-abiding, (of person, life, action). Hence ~LY² adv., ~NESS n. [OE *rihtwis* (prec. n. + WISE a., or prec. a. + WISE n.) w. assim. to *bounteous* etc.]

right'ful (rīt-), a. (Of actions etc.) equitable, fair; (of persons) legitimately entitled to position etc. (*the* ~ *king, heir, owner*), (of office, property, etc.) that one is entitled to. Hence ~LY² adv., ~NESS n. [-FUL]

right'ly (rīt-), adv. Justly, fairly, properly, correctly, accurately, justifiably. [-LY²]

ri'gid, a. Not flexible, stiff, unyielding, (*a* ~ *bar, stem, frame, airship*); inflexible, harsh, strict, precise, punctilious, (~ *justice, principles, Catholics, adherence to rules, economy*). Hence or cogn. **rigid'ity** n., ~LY² adv. [f. L *rigidus* (as RIGOR)]

rig'marole, n. Rambling or meaningless talk or tale; (attrib.) incoherent. [alt. f. obs. *ragman roll* = catalogue, orig. unkn.]

rig'or, n. (path.). Sudden chill with shivering before fever etc.; ~ *mort'is*, stiffening of body after death. [L *rigēre* be stiff, -OR)]

rig'our (-ger), n. Severity, strictness, harshness, (pl.) harsh measures; strict enforcement of rules etc. (*with the utmost* ~ *of the law*); extremity or excess of weather, hardship, famine, etc., great distress; austerity of life, Puritanic strictness of observance or doctrine, so **rig'orism**(3), **rig'orist**(2), nn.; logical accuracy, exactitude. So **rig'orous** a., **rig'orously²** adv. [ME, f. OF f. L (prec.)]

rigs'dåg (-z-), n. Former name of Danish parliament (now *folketing*). [Da.]

Rig-ve'da (-vä-), n. The chief VEDA. [f. Skr. *ṛigveda* (ric praise)]

riks'dåg, n. Swedish parliament. [Sw.]

rilie'vo (rēlyā-), n. = RELIEF², RELIEVO. [It.]

rile, v.t. (sl.). Raise anger in, irritate. [var. of obs. & U.S. *roil* make muddy]

rill, n., & v.i. **1.** Small stream, runnel, rivulet; hence ~'ET¹ n. **2.** v.i. Issue or flow as ~. [ME, f. LG *ril, rille*]

rille, n. (astron.). Trench or narrow valley of moon's surface. [G, as prec.]

rilĕtts', **-ĕttes'** (-ĕts), n. pl. Preparation of minced ham, chicken, fat, etc. [F (-cs)]

rim¹, n., & v.t. (-mm-). **1.** Outer ring of

wheel's framework, not including tire; frame of sieve; (poet.) circular object (*golden* ~, crown); (naut.) surface of the water; raised edge or border, margin, verge, esp. of something more or less circular; ~*-brake*, acting on ~ of wheel; hence ~'LESS, (-)~mED² (-md), aa. **2.** v.t. Furnish with ~, serve as ~ to, edge, border. [OE *rima*, = ON *rimi* ridge]

‖ **rim²**, n. (arch.). ~ (*of the belly*), peritoneum. [OE *rēoma*, OS *reomo*, OHG *riumo*, strap]

rime¹, n., & v.t. & i. = RHYME¹,². [ME *rime*, now normally RHYME¹,², but revived in literary use since *c.* 1870]

rime², n., & v.t. (chiefly poet.). **1.** Hoar-frost; hence **rim'**Y² a. **2.** v.t. Cover with ~. [OE *hrim*, MDu. *rijm*, ON *hrim*]

rim'er, n. = REAM²*er*. [dial. *rime* var. of REAM², -ER¹]

Rimm'on, n. Ancient deity worshipped at Damascus (*bow down in the house of* ~, compromise one's convictions). [2 *Kings* v. 18]

rim'ose, rim'ous, aa. (bot. etc.). Full of chinks or fissures. [f. L *rimosus* (*rima* chink, -OSE¹), -OUS]

rind, n., & v.t. Bark of tree or plant (vb, strip ~ from); peel of fruit or vegetable; harder enclosing surface of cheese or other substance; skin of bacon etc.; external aspect, surface. Hence -~'ED² a. [OE *rind*, OS, OHG *rinda*]

rin'derpĕst, n. Disease of ruminants esp. oxen, cattle-plague. [G (*rinder* pl. of *rind* ox)]

ring¹, n., & v.i. & t. **1.** Circlet usu. of precious metal & often set with gem(s) worn round finger as ornament or token (esp. of betrothal or marriage) or signet, or (usu. *nose, arm,* etc., -~) hung to or encircling other part of body. **2.** Circular appliance of any material & any (but esp., cf. *hoop,* no great) size. **3.** Raised or sunk or otherwise distinguishable line or band round, rim of, cylindrical or circular object. **4.** Circular fold, coil, bend, structure, part, or mark (~*s* of tree, concentric bands of wood corresponding in number to tree's years; *has livid* ~*s round his eyes; puffing out* ~*s of smoke*; ~*s* in water, circular ripples expanding from centre of agitation). **5.** Persons, trees, etc., disposed in a circle, such disposition; (commerc. etc.) combination of traders or politicians acting together for control of market or policy. **6.** Circular enclosure or space for circus-riding, prize-fighting (PRIZE-~; ~'*side seat* or *view,* also fig.), betting at races (*the* ~, bookmakers), showing of cattle, etc. **7.** Circular or spiral course (*make* ~*s round,* go or do things incomparably quicker than). **8.** ~*-bark* v.t., cut ~ in bark of (tree) to kill it or to check its growth & bring it into bearing; ~*-bolt,* bolt with ~ attached for fastening rope to etc.; ~*-bone,* (horse-disease with) deposit of bony matter on

pastern-bones; ~*-cartilage,* CRICOID; ~*-dove,* wood-pigeon; ~*-fence,* completely enclosing estate etc., also fig.; ~*-finger,* third esp. of left hand; ~*-goal,* game in which light hoop is thrown towards goal with sticks; ~*-hunt,* in which beasts are driven inwards by ~ of fire; ~'*leader,* (one of) chief instigator(s) in mutiny, riot, etc.; ~*-lock,* opened by right adjustment of several grooved ~s; ‖ ~*-man,* bookmaker; ~'*master,* manager of circus performance; ~*-neck,* ~*-necked* plover or duck; ~*-necked,* with band(s) of colour round neck; ~*-net,* kind of salmon net, also of lace; ~ *ouzel,* kind of bird allied to blackbird; ~*-snake,* common European grass-snake (from coiling); ~*-stand,* for keeping finger-~s on; ~'*tail,* female of hen-harrier, also golden eagle till its third year, also ~*-tailed* opossum or phalanger; ~*-tailed,* with tail ~ed in alternate colours, also (of phalanger) with tail curled at end; ~*-law,* game with marbles in ~; ~*-wall,* as ~*-fence;* ~'*worm,* skin-disease esp. of children in circular patches; hence (-)~ED² (-ngd), ~'LESS, aa. **9.** vb. (Of hawk etc.) rise in spirals; (of hunted fox) take circular course. **10.** Encompass (usu. *round, about, in*; often in p.p.), hem in (game, cattle) by riding or beating in circle round them. **11.** Put ~ upon, put ~ in nose of (pig, bull), (~*-the-bull,* game with ~ to be thrown or swung on to hook). **12.** =~*-bark* above. **13.** Cut (onions, apples) into ~s. [OE, OS, OHG *hring,* ON *hringr* f. Gmc **hrengaz*]

ring², v.i. & t. (*rang,* now rarely *rung; rung*), & n. **1.** Give forth clear resonant sound (as) of vibrating metal (*bell, trumpet, coin, sound,* ~s, often *out* etc.; *with a* ~*ing laugh; a shot rang out; a* ~*ing frost,* in which ground ~s under foot; ~ *true, false,* of coin tested by throwing on counter, & fig. of sentiments etc.); (of bell) ~ *to* or *for* prayers, dinner, etc., convey summons by ~ing. **2.** (Of place) resound, re-echo, (*with* sound, *to* sound or its cause, *with* fame etc. or its theme, *with talk of;* often *again*). **3.** (Of utterance or other sound) ~ *in* one's *ears, heart,* etc., linger in one's hearing, haunt the memory. **4.** (Of ears) be filled with sensation as of bell-~ing (so *has a* ~*ing in the ears*) or *with* sound. **5.** Make (bell) ~ (~ *the bell,* esp. as summons to servant; ~ *the bell* (colloq.), be successful [from use of bell in machines for testing strength or skill], (also) strike a sympathetic note; ~ *up bell,* raise church bell over beam & ~ it there; ~*ing engine,* pile-driver worked by ropes like peal of bells); throw (coin) on counter to test it. **6.** ~ bell as summons (~ *at door,* to get admittance etc.; ~ *for* servant, coffee, etc.; *did you* ~, *sir ?*). **7.** Sound (peal, knell, BOB⁴ · *major, the* CHANGE's) on bells (or with *bell* or *bells* as subj.; ~ *the knell of,* announce or herald abolition etc. of). **8.** Announce (hour etc.)

by sound of bell(s). **9.** Summon *up* etc. by ~ing bell (~ *up* on telephone, get or seek communication with; ~ *off*, terminate telephone interview;~ *curtain up* or *down* in theatre, direct it by bell to be raised or lowered. **10.** Usher *in*, *out*, with bell-~ing, esp. *new, old, year*. **11.** n. Set *of* (church) bells. **12.**~ing sound, ~ing tone in voice etc., resonance of coin or vessel. **13.** Act of ~ing bell, sound so produced, (*three ~s for the hall porter*; *give bell a* ~; *heard a loud* ~ *at the door*); call on the telephone (*give me a* ~). [OE *hringan*, ON *hringja*, perh. imit.]

rin′gent (-j-), a. Gaping, grinning, (esp. bot. of wide labiate corolla). [as RICTUS, -ENT]

ring′er, n. **1.** Quoit that falls round pin; fox that runs in ring when hunted. **2.** Bell-~; device for ringing bell. [RING¹'², -ER¹]

ring′let, n. **1.** (rare). Small ring, fairy ring on grass, ring-shaped mark etc. **2.** Curly lock of hair, curl, whence ~ED², ~Y², aa. [-LET]

rink, n., & v.i. **1.** Stretch of ice used for game of curling; sheet of natural or artificial ice, floor, for (roller-)skating. **2.** v.i. Skate on~ esp. with roller-skates, whence ~′ER¹ n. [orig. North ME, = *jousting-ground*; app. f. OF *renc* RANK¹]

rinse, v.t., & n. **1.** Wash out or *out* (vessel, mouth) by filling with water etc., shaking, & emptying; pour liquid over, or wash lightly; put (clothes) through clean water to remove soap; clear (impurities) *out* or *away* by rinsing; wash (food) *down* with liquor. **2.** n. Rinsing (*give it a* ~); kind of hair tint. [ME, f. OF *rincer, reincier*]

ri′ot, n., & v.i. & t. **1.** Loose living, debauchery. **2.** Loud revelry, a revel; unrestrained indulgence in or display or enjoyment of something.(*a* ~ *of emotion, colour, sound*). **3.** (hunt.). Following of any scent indiscriminately (*run* ~, orig. of hounds doing this, now usu. fig. of person or his tongue or fancy throwing off all restraint). **4.** Disorder, tumult, disturbance of the peace, outbreak of lawlessness, on part of a crowd || (*R~ Act*, by which persons not dispersing after official reading of part of it incur guilt of felony; *read the R~ Act*, lit., & joc. of parent etc. announcing that noise etc. is to cease); hence or cogn. ~OUS a., ~OUSLY² adv., ~OUSNESS, (rare) ~RY(2), nn. **5.** vb. Live wantonly, revel. **6.** Throw *away* (time, money), wear *out* (life), in dissipation. **7.** Make or engage in a political ~ or offence against the R~ Act, whence ~ER²(4) n. [ME, f. OF *riote(r)*, orig. unkn.]

rip¹, n. Worthless horse, screw; dissolute person, rake. [perh. var. of REP³]

rip², v.t. & i. (-pp-), & n. **1.** Cut or tear (thing) quickly or forcibly away from something (~ *out the lining*; ~ *the boards off*); make long cut or tear in, cut or tear

vigorously apart (often *up*; *had his belly* ~*ped up*). **2.** Split (wood, rock), saw (wood) with the grain (~*-saw*, used thus). **3.** Strip (roof) of tiles or slates & laths. **4.** Make (fissure, passage) by ~ping. **5.** Open *up* (wound, quarrel, sorrow, the past) again. **6.** Come violently asunder, split (intr.). **7.** Rush along (of ship, & transf.; so *let her* ~, do not check speed or interfere). **8.** || (part.; sl.; cf. *rattling*). Fine, splendid, enjoyable, first-rate, (also as adv. with *good* etc., as *a* ~*ping good time*), whence ~p′ingLY² adv. **9.** ~*-cord* (aeron.), cord for releasing parachute from its pack. **10.** n. Act of ~ping; long tear or cut. [orig. obsc.; cf. Fris. *rippe*]

rip³, n. Stretch of broken water in sea or river, overfall. [perh. rel. to RIPPLE²]

ripār′ian, a. & n. **1.** Of, on, river-bank (esp. ~ *proprietor, rights*). **2.** n. ~ proprietor. [L *riparius* (*ripa* bank, -ARY¹) + -AN]

ripe, a., & v.t. & i. **1.** Ready to be reaped, gathered, eaten, drunk, used, or dealt with, fully developed, mellow, mature, prepared or able *to* undergo something, in fit state *for*, (~ *corn, fruit, cheese, wine, seed*; ~ *lips*, red & full like ~ fruit; ~ *beauty*, of grown woman; ~ *scholar, scholarship, judgement, experience, understanding*; *die at a* ~ *age*, old; *persons of* ~*r years*, not immature; *opportunity* ~ *to be seized*; *is* ~ *to hear the truth*; *mood* or *person, plan, disease,* ~ *for mischief, execution, treatment*; *soon* ~ *soon rotten*, prov. depreciating precocity); hence **rip′**EN⁶ v.t. & i., ~′LY² (-pl-) adv., ~′NESS (-pn-) n. **2.** vb. (chiefly poet.). = ~n. [OE *ripe*, OS *rīpi*, OHG *rīfi*; perh. rel. to REAP]

ripŏste′, n., & v.i. **1.** Quick return thrust in fencing; (transf.) counterstroke, retort. **2.** v.i. Deliver ~. [F, f. It. *risposta* RESPONSE]

ripp′er, n. In vbl senses; esp.: tool for ripping roof; rip-saw; (sl.) ripping person or thing. [-ER¹]

rip′ple¹, n., & v.t. **1.** Toothed implement used to clear away seeds from flax. **2.** v.t. Treat with ~. [corresp. to MDu., MLG *repel(en)*]

rip′ple², n., & v.i. & t. **1.** Ruffling of water's surface, small wave(s); wavy or crinkled appearance in hair, ribbons, etc.; gentle lively sound that rises & falls (esp. *a* ~ *of conversation*); ~*-cloth*, soft woollen washing fabric with ~d surface used for dressing-gowns etc.; ~*-mark*, ridge, ridged surface, left on sand or mud or rock by water or wind; hence **ripp′**IET¹ n., **ripp′**LY² a. **2.** vb. Form, flow in, show, agitate or mark with, sound like, ~s. [vb 17th c., orig. unkn.; n. f. vb]

Ripuār′ian, a. Of the ancient Franks living on Rhine between Meuse & Moselle (esp. ~ *law*, code observed by them). [f. med. L *Ripuarius* (*Ribu-*) + -AN; connex. w. L *ripa* very doubtful]

Rip văn Winkle (wĭng′kl), n. Person of

utterly antiquated ideas or information. [hero of tale by W. Irving who slept 20 years]

rise¹ (-z), v.i. & t. (*rose* pr. rŏz; ~*n* pr. rï′zn; p.p., see -ED¹(2), often with *is* etc.). **1.** Get up from lying or sitting or kneeling position, get out of bed, (of meeting etc.) cease to sit for business, recover standing or upright position, become erect, leave ground, come to life again or usu. *again* or *from the dead*, (~ *from table*, leave meal; *all rose to receive him*; *house*, i.e. theatre audience, ~*s at* actress etc., in universal applause; *found he could not, was too weak to*, ~; ~, *Sir Thomas* etc., formula in knighting; ~ *betimes, at 5 a.m., with the lark*; ~ *up early*; *Parliament will* ~ *next week*; *fell never to* ~ *again*; *the hair rose on his head*; *horse* ~*s on its hind-legs*; *horse* ~*s to a fence*, takes off for leap; *birds* ~ *well today*). **2.** Cease to be quiet, abandon submission, make revolt, (*if a wind should* ~; ~ *in arms, rebellion*, etc., *against oppression, oppressor*; *town rose on its garrison*; *gorge, stomach*, ~*s*, indignation or disgust is felt; *my whole soul* ~*s against it*, finds it intolerable). **3.** Come or go up, grow upwards, ascend, mount, soar, project or swell upwards, become higher, reach higher position or level or amount, increase, incline upwards, come to surface, become or be visible above or *above* surroundings, develop greater energy or intensity, be progressive, (*sun, star, morning, dawn*, ~*s*; *the* ~*n sun*; *rising cupboard*, kitchen lift; *the rising generation*, the young; *smoke* ~*s straight up*; *tree* ~*s 20 ft*, attains that height; *building rose like a dream*; *blisters* ~, form; *bread will not* ~, swell with yeast; *balloon* ~*s*; *should* ~ *above petty jealousies*, be superior to; *picture, idea*, ~*s before the mind*; *river, tide, flood, level, rose 6 ft, is rising*; *the mercury, barometer* or *glass, is rising*; *spirits* ~, become more cheerful; *prices, demands*, ~; *a rising lawyer*; *a man likely to* ~; ~ *in the world*, attain higher social position; ~ *to greatness*; *rising ground*, sloping up; *in a rising series*; ~*s in a gentle curve*; *the interest* ~*s with each act*; *bubbles* ~; *fish* ~*s*, comes to surface to feed; *drowning man* ~*s three times*; *in the foreground* ~*s a castle*; *does not* ~ *above mediocrity*; *the wind is rising*; *her colour rose*, became bright or deeper; ‖ *rising 5, 14*, getting on for that age). **4.** Develop powers equal to (*does not* ~ *to an occasion*; *rose to the emergency, requirements*, etc.). **5.** Have origin, begin to be, flow, *from, in, at*, etc. (*river* ~*s from a spring, in the Grampians*, etc.; *earth & heaven rose at His word*; *the difficulty* ~*s from misapprehension*). **6.** (rare, usu. poet.). Arise (*a feud, rumour, rose*). **7.** (Causative in spec. senses) make or see ~ (*did not* ~ *a fish, a bird, all day*; ~ *ship*, see it appear from top downwards in approaching it). [OE *risan*, OS, OHG *risan*,

ON *risa*, Goth. *-reisan* f. Gmc *°risan*; see RAISE, REAR²]

rise² (-z), n. **1.** Coming up of sun etc. (rare; *at* ~ *of sun, day*; cf. *sun*~ etc.). **2.** Ascent, upward slope, knoll, hill, (*came to a* ~ *in the road*; *chapel stands on a* ~). **3.** Social advancement, upward progress, increase in power, rank, value, price, amount, height, pitch, ‖ *wages*, etc., (*has had a* ~ *in life*; *the* ~ *& fall of statesmen*; *the* ~ *of the tide is 30 ft*; ‖ *asks for a* ~, higher wages; *prices are on the* ~, increasing). **4.** Movement of fish to surface (*not a sign of a* ~; fig., *get* or *take a* ~ *out of* one, draw him into display of temper or foible). **5.** Vertical height of step, arch, incline, etc., (also **rïs′ER**¹ (-z-) n. f. prec.) vertical piece connecting two treads of staircase. **6.** Origin, start, (*has, takes, its* ~ *in, from*; *give* ~ *to*, occasion, suggest). [f. prec.]

ris′ible (-z-), a. Inclined to laugh, so **risiBIL′ITY** (-z-) n.; of laughter (~ *nerves, faculties*, etc.); (rare) laughable, ludicrous. [f. LL *risibilis* (*ridēre ris-* laugh, -IBLE)]

ris′ing (-z-), n. In vbl senses; esp.: ~ (*-again*), resurrection; insurrection, revolt; boil, pimple. [-ING¹]

risk, n., & v.t. **1.** Hazard, chance of or of bad consequences, loss, etc., exposure to mischance, (*there is the* ~ *of his catching cold*; *run* ~*s, a* ~, *the* ~, often of, expose oneself or be exposed to loss etc.; *take* ~*s* etc., expose oneself so; *at the* ~ *of his life*; *at owner's* etc. ~, he to bear any contingent loss); ~*-money*, allowance to cashier to cover accidental deficits; hence ~′FUL, ~′LESS, aa. **2.** v.t. Expose to chance of injury or loss; venture on, take the chances of, (~ *the jump, a battle, a sprained ankle*). [f. F *risque(r)* f. It. *risco, riscare*]

ris′k|ỹ, a. **1.** Hazardous, full of risk. **2.** (Also, & after, F *risqué* pr. rïs′kā) involving suggestion of indecency, offending against propriety, (of story, dramatic situation, etc.). Hence ~ïLY²adv., ~ïNESS n. [-Y²]

risótt′ō (rē-), n. Stew made with rice, chicken, onions, etc. [It.]

risqué, See RISKY.

riss′öle, n. Fried ball or cake of meat or fish mixed with bread-crumbs etc. [F, OF *ruissole*, f. LL *russeolus* reddish]

ritärdän′dō (rē-), mus. direction. Slower. [It.]

rite, n. (Form of procedure, action required or usual, in) a religious or solemn ceremony or observance (*the* ~*s of hospitality*; *the* ~ *of confirmation*; *burial* or *funeral* ~*s*; *conjugal* or *nuptial* ~*s*, sexual intercourse between husband & wife; *the Latin, Anglican*, etc.*, ~*, body of usages characteristic of a Church). Hence ~′LESS (-tl-) a. [ME, f. OF *rit(e)* or L *ritus -ûs*]

rit′ual, a. & n. **1.** Of, with, consisting in, involving, religious rites; hence ~LY² adv. **2.** n. Prescribed order of performing religious service; book containing this;

performance of ~ acts, whence (w. implication of excess) ~ISM(3), ~IST(2), nn., ~is'tic a., ~is'tically adv., ~IZE(2, 3) v.i. & t. [f. L *ritualis* (prec., -AL)]

|| riv'age, n. (poet.). Coast, shore, bank. [ME, f. OF, f. *rive* f. L *ripa* bank, -AGE)]

riv'al, n., attrib. a., & v.t. & i. (-ll-). 1. Person's competitor for some prize (esp. a woman's or man's love) or in some pursuit or quality (also of things; *without a ~*, unapproached for excellence etc.); hence ~RY(2, 4), ~SHIP, nn. 2. adj. That is a ~ or are ~s. 3. vb. Vie with, be comparable to, seem or claim to be as good etc. as; (rare) be in ~ry. [f. L *rivalis* (*rivus* stream, -AL) orig. = on same stream]

rive, v.t. & i. (~*d*; ~*n* pr. ri'vn, rarely ~*d*). Rend, cleave, wrench *away* or *off* or *from*, strike asunder, (arch., poet.); (of artisan) split (wood, stone), make (laths) by splitting, whence riv'er[1] [-ER[1](1))] n.; be split, gape under blow etc., (of wood etc.) admit of splitting. [ME, f. ON *rifa*]

|| riv'el, v.i. & t. (arch., -ll-). Wrinkle, crumple, shrivel. [ME, back formation f. *rivelled*, OE *rifelede* app. f. **rifel* a wrinkle +-ED[2]]

riven. See RIVE.

riv'er[2], n. (for *river*[1] see RIVE). Copious stream of water flowing in channel to sea or lake or marsh or another~ (|| *the~* often prefixed to name, as *the ~ Thames*); *the* boundary between life & death; copious flow or stream *of* (*a ~ of lava*; *~s of blood*, much bloodshed); (attrib., prefixed to many names of animals, plants, & things) living in, situated or used on, ~(s); ~-BED[1](2); ~*god*, mythological being dwelling in & personifying a ~; ~*horse*, hippopotamus; ~*side*, ground along ~'s bank (often attrib., as *a ~side villa*). Hence (-)~ED[2] (*-erd*), ~LESS aa. [f. AF *rivere*, OF *-iere* f. Rom. **riparia* (L *ripa* bank, -ARY[1])]

riv'erain, a. & n. 1. Of river or its neighbourhood; situated, dwelling, by river. 2. n. Person dwelling by river. [F (*rivière* as prec., -AN)]

riv'erine, a. Of, on, river or its banks, riparian. [-INE[1]]

riv'ĕt, n., & v.t. 1. Nail or bolt for holding together metal plates etc., its headless end being beaten out or pressed down after passing through two holes. 2. v.t. Clinch (bolt); join or fasten with ~s (*together*, *down*, *to*, *into*, *on* adv. or prep., etc.); fix, make immovable, (~ *error* etc.); concentrate, direct intently, (eyes, attention, etc., *upon*); engross (attention), engross attention of; hence ~ER[1](1, 2) n. [ME, f. OF, f. *river* clinch, of unkn. orig.]

riv'ière (-ĭắr, or rēvyằr'), n. Gem necklace, esp. of more than one string. [F, as RIVER[1]]

riv'ūlĕt, n. 1. Small stream. 2. Kinds of

moth. [perh. f. It. *rivoletto* (L *rivus* stream, -UL-, -ET[1])]

rix'-dŏllar, n. (hist.). Silver coin & money of account (4/6–2/3) of 16th–19th cc. in some continental States. [f. Du. *rijcksdaler*, see REICH, DOLLAR]

roach[1], n. Small freshwater fish allied to carp (*sound as a ~*, in first-rate health etc.); ~*backed*, *-bellied* (convex in profile). [ME, f. OF *roche*, of unkn. orig.]

roach[2], n. (naut.). Upward curve in foot of square sail. [18th c., orig. unkn.]

roach[3], n. = COCKROACH. [abbr.]

road[1], n. 1. (Usu. pl.; also ~*'stead*) piece of water near shore in which ships can ride at anchor. 2. Line of communication between places for use of foot-passengers, riders, & vehicles (*on the ~*, travelling, esp. as a commercial traveller; *take the ~*, set out; *the ~*, the highway; || *take to the ~*, arch., become highwayman; *rule of the ~*, custom regulating side to be taken by vehicles, riders, or ships, meeting or passing each other). 3. Way of getting to (*the ~ to York*, *ruin*, *success*; *royal ~ to*, way of attaining without trouble). 4. One's way or route (*in the*, *my*, etc., *~*, colloq., obstructing someone or something; so *get out of the*, *my*, etc., *~*). 5. ~*bed*, foundation structure of a railway, whole material laid down of an ordinary ~; ~*book*, describing ~s of country etc., itinerary; ~ *fund* (for construction & maintenance of~s & bridges); ~*hog*, reckless or inconsiderate motorist or cyclist; ~ *house*, inn on main ~ in country district; ~'*man* (repairing ~s); ~*metal*, broken stone for ~*making*; ~*sense*, capacity for safe handling of vehicles on the ~; ~'*side*, border of ~ (esp. attrib., as ~*side plants*, *inn*); ~'*stead*, see sense 1; ~'*way*, ~, central part of ~ (opp. *side-path*), part of bridge or railway used for traffic; ~'*worthy*, fit to be used on the ~, (of person) fit to travel. Hence (-)~'ED[2], ~'LESS, aa. [OE *rād* (*rīdan* RIDE); cf. RAID]

road[2], v.t. (Of dog) follow up (game-bird, or abs.) by foot-scent. [19th c.; orig. unkn.]

road'ster, n. Ship at anchor in roadstead; horse, bicycle, etc., for use on the road; experienced traveller. [-STER]

roam, v.i. & t., & n. Ramble (v., & rarely n. as *a half-hour's ~*), wander; walk or travel unsystematically over or through or about (country, seas). [ME, orig. unkn.]

roan[1], a. & n. 1. (Of animal) with coat of which the prevailing colour is thickly interspersed with another, esp. bay or sorrel or chestnut mixed with white or grey (often with chief colour prefixed, as *black*, *blue*, *red*, ~). 2. n. ~ horse, cow. [OF *roan* (now *rouan*), f. Sp. *roano*]

roan[2], n. Soft sheepskin leather used in bookbinding as substitute for morocco. [ME, perh. *Roan*, old name of *Rouen*]

roar (rōr), v.i. & t., & n. **1.** (Utter, send forth) loud deep hoarse sound (as) of lion, person or company in pain or rage or loud laughter, the sea, thunder, cannon, furnace, etc. (*the ~ of the waves*; *~s of laughter*; *lions ~ing after their prey*; *~ed with pain or laughter or for mercy*; *you need not ~*, talk so loud; *set table in a ~*, make company laugh loud). **2.** (Of horse) make loud noise in breathing due to disease, whence *~ER*[1], *~ING*[1], (rōr-), nn. **3.** (Of place) be full of din, re-echo, (often *again*). **4.** Say, sing, utter, (words, chorus, oath, etc., often *out*) in loud tone. **5.** Make *deaf*, *hoarse*, etc., put *down*, by *~ing*. **6.** (part.). Riotous, noisy, boisterous, brisk, (*a ~ing night*, stormy, also spent in revelry; *a ~ing blade*, arch., fast liver; *the ~ing game*, curling; *~ing forties*, see FORTY; *in ~ing health*; *drive a ~ing trade*). [OE *rārian*, = MDu. *reeren*, MLG *rāren*, *rēren*, OHG *rēren*, prob. imit.]

roast, v.t. & i. (p.p. in vb forms *~ed*, as adj. *~*), & n. **1.** Cook (esp. meat) by exposure to open fire or now usually in oven (*prefers ~ beef*, *his meat ~ed*); heat or calcine (ore) in furnace; heat (coffee-beans) as preparation for grinding; expose (victim for torture, one*self* or some part for warmth) to fire; ridicule, banter, chaff; undergo *~ing*; (part.) very hot; *~ing-jack*, appliance keeping meat in motion while *~ing*. **2.** n. *~* meat or a dish of it (*rule the ~*, be master); *joint of meat; operation of *~ing*. [ME; n. partly f. OF *rost*, partly f. vb, f. OF *rostir* f. WG (OFrank. *hraustian*; cf. OHG *rōsten* f. *rōst(e)* gridiron)]

roast′er, n. In vbl senses; esp.: kind of oven for roasting; ore-roasting furnace; coffee-roasting apparatus; pig, potato, etc., fit for roasting. [-ER[1]]

rŏb, v.t. (-bb-). Despoil (person etc.) of or *of* property by violence, feloniously plunder (person, place, often *of*), deprive *of* what is due; *~ PETER*; (abs.) commit *~bery*. So *~b′er* [-ER[1], -ER[2](4)], *~b′ERY*(2, 4), nn. [ME, f. OF *rob(b)er* f. Gmc *raubh-* (cf. OS *rōbon*) REAVE]

rōbe, n., & v.t. & i. **1.** Any long loose outer garment (rare, poet., metaph.); (trade name of) kind of lady's dress in one piece; *dressing-gown; outer garment of baby in long-clothes; (often pl.) longer outer garment worn as indication of wearer's rank, office, profession, etc., gown, vestment, (*the long ~*, legal or clerical dress; *gentlemen of the ~*, lawyers); *~-de-chambre* (F, see Ap.), dressing-gown, wrapper. **2.** vb. Invest (person) in *~*, dress; assume one's *~s* or vestments. [ME, f. OF, conn. w. prec., orig. sense *booty*]

‖ **Rŏb′ert**, n. (colloq.). A policeman. [see BOBBY]

rŏb′in, **R-**, n. (Also *~ redbreast*) small red-breasted bird; (with or without distinctive epithet) kinds of Amer., Colonial,

& Indian bird; *~-*, *~'s-*, in plant names, as ‖ *R~-run-the-hedge*, ground-ivy, ‖ *~'s-eye*, kind of geranium; *R~ Goodfellow*, a mischievous sportive sprite, alias *Puck*; *R~ Hood*, (type of) medieval forest outlaw; ROUND[1] *~*. [ME, f. OF, fam. for *Robert*]

rŏb′orant, a. & n. (med.). Strengthening (drug). [L *roborare* (*robur -oris* strength), -ANT]

rŏb′ŏt, n. **1.** An apparently human automaton, an intelligent & obedient but impersonal machine; (transf.) machine-like person. **2.** Automatic traffic signal. **3.** Flying bomb. [term in Capek's play *R.U.R.* (*Rossum's Universal Robots*), 1920; f. Czech *robota* forced labour]

rŏb′urite (-ber-), n. A strong flameless explosive. [L *robur* strength, -ITE[1](2)]

robŭst′, a. (*~er*, *~est*). Of strong health & physique, not slender or delicate or weakly, (of persons, animals, plants, body, health, etc.); (of exercise, discipline, etc.) tending to or requiring strength, invigorating, vigorous; (of intellect etc.) sensible, straightforward, not given to nor confused by subtleties. Hence *~LY*[2] adv., *~NESS* n. [f. F *robuste*, or L *robustus* (*robur* strength)]

robŭs′tious, a. Boisterous, self-assertive, noisy. [earlier in common use = prec.; now chiefly w. ref. to *Hamlet* III. ii. 10]

rŏc, n. Gigantic bird of Eastern tales. [f. Arab. *rokh*]

rŏc′ambōle, n. Kind of leek used for seasoning. [F]

rŏch′ĕt, n. Surplice-like vestment used chiefly by bishops & abbots. [ME, f. OF, dim. f. WG (cf. OE *rocc*, OS, OHG *rok*, ON *rokkr*); cf. FROCK]

rŏck[1], n. **1.** Solid part of earth's crust underlying soil (*dug down to the living ~*; often *bed-~*; *built*, *founded*, *on the ~*, lit., & fig., secure; *R~ of ages*, Christ); mass of this projecting & forming a hill, cliff, etc., or standing up into or out of sea etc. from bottom (*the R~*, Gibraltar; *run upon the ~s*, see *~s ahead*, etc., of lit. or fig. shipwreck or danger of it; *on the ~s*, sl., hard up; *~ of water* etc., ref. to *Numb.* xx. 11). **2.** Stone as a substance (*a mass*, *needle*, *of ~*); large detached stone, boulder; (geol.) any particular igneous or stratified mineral constituent of earth's crust including sands, clays, etc. **3.** Kinds of hard sweetmeat (usu. *almond. ~*). **4.** (Also *blue ~*) = *~-pigeon*. **5.** *~-bed*, base of *~*, rocky bottom; *~-bird*, esp. puffin; *~-bottom*, (colloq., of prices etc.) very lowest; *~-cake*, bun with hard rough surface; *~-cork*, variety of asbestos; *~-crystal*, transparent colourless silica or quartz usu. in hexagonal prisms; *~-dove*, *~-pigeon*; *~-drill*, *~-boring tool or machine*; *R~ English*, mixed language of Gibraltar; *R~ fever*, kind of enteric prevalent at Gibraltar; *~-fish*, kinds of goby, bass, wrasse, etc.; *~-garden*, artificial mound or bank of stones with ~-plants etc. planted in the interstices, garden in which ~eries are the chief feature; ~-*goat*, ibex; ~-*hewn*, cut out of the ~; ~-*leather*, as ~-*cork*; ~'*ling* [-LING¹], kinds of fish esp. sea-loach; ~-*oil*, native naphtha; ~-*paper*, as ~-*cork*; ~-*pigeon*, kind of dove haunting ~s & supposed source of domestic pigeon; ~-*rabbit*, hyrax; ~--*ribbed*, (of earth, coast, etc.) with ribs of ~; ~-*rose*, kinds of cistus with yellow, rose, or salmon flowers; ~-*salmon*, (trade name for) dogfish; ~-*salt*, found stratified in free state; *R*~ *scorpion*, (nickname for) person born at Gibraltar; ~-*silk*, as ~--*cork*; ~-*sucker*, sea lamprey; ~-*tar*, petroleum; ~-*whistler*, Alpine marmot; ~-*wood*, as ~-*cork*; ~-*work* or ~'*ERY*(3)n., pile of rough stones with soil in interstices for growing ferns etc. on, also natural group or display of ~s. Hence ~'*LESS*, ~'*LIKE*, aa., ~'*LET* n. [ME, f. OF *roke*, *roque* (also *roche*), f. Gallo-Rom. *rocca*]

rŏck², n. (hist.). Distaff. [ME, f. MDu. *rocke*, MLG *rocken*, OHG *rocco*, ON *rokkr*]

rŏck³, v.t. & i., & n. **1.** Move (t. & i.) gently to & fro (as) in cradle, set or keep (cradle etc.) or (of cradle etc.) be in such motion, (~ *him to sleep*; *ship* ~*ing on*, ~*ed by, the waves*; *sat* ~*ing himself* or ~*ing in his chair*; ~*ed in security, hopes*, etc.); (gold-min.) work (CRADLE), work cradle, shake in cradle; sway (t. & i.) from side to side, shake, oscillate, reel, (*earthquake* ~*s house, house* ~*s, a* ~*ing gait*). **2.** ~'*ing--chair*, mounted on rockers, or with seat arranged to ~; ~'*ing-horse*, wooden horse on rockers for child; ~'*ing-stone*, poised boulder easily ~ed; ~'*ing-turn* in skating, from any edge to same in opposite direction with body revolving away from convex of first curve (*counter-*~'*ing-turn* or -*rocker* or *counter*, same turn with body revolving away from concave); ~-*shaft*, that oscillates about axis without making complete revolutions; ~-*staff*, part of apparatus working smith's bellows. **3.** n. ~ing motion, spell of ~ing; ~-'*n'* (= *and*) -*roll*, (dancing to) kind of swing music. [OE *roccian*, app. f. Gmc *rukk-* to move; cf. MDu., MLG *rocken, rucken*]

rŏck'er, n. In vbl senses; esp.: one of the curved bars on which cradle etc. rocks (*off* one's ~, sl., crazy); gold-miner's cradle; skate with highly curved blade; (skat.)~, *counter-*~, = (*counter-*)ROCK³*ing--turn*. [ROCK³, -ER¹]

rŏck'ĕt¹, n. Kinds of plant of which some are used as salad & some grown for flowers (*base* ~, wild mignonette; *blue* ~, kinds of wolfsbane & larkspur, also bluebell; *yellow* ~, winter cress). [f. F *roquette* f. It. *ruchetta* (*ruca* f. L *eruca*, -ETTE)]

rŏck'ĕt², n., & v.t. & i. **1.** Cylindrical paper or metal case that can be projected to height or distance by ignition of contents, used in firework displays, for signalling, to carry line to ship in distress,

etc.; projectile containing its own propellant & depending for its flight on the reaction set up by a continuous jet of rapidly expanding gases released in the propellant by ignition (e.g. of cordite) or by the mixture of two liquids (e.g. alcohol & liquid air), whence ~RY n., study or use of ~s; ~ *engine, jet, motor,* (operated on same principle); ~-*propelled*, ~ *propulsion*; ~ *range* (for testing ~ missiles). **2.** (sl.). Reprimand. **3.** vb. Bombard with ~s; (of horse or its rider) bound upwards or dart like ~; (of prices etc.) rise steeply; (of pheasant etc.) fly straight upwards, fly fast & high, whence ~ER¹ n. [f. F *roquet(te)* f. It. *rocchetta* (*rocca* ROCK², w. ref. to cylindrical shape), -ETTE]

rŏck'|y̆, a., & n. (pl.). **1.** Of rock, full of or abounding in rocks, (*the R*~*y Mountains*, or as n. *the R*~*ies*, western N.-Amer. range); like rock in ruggedness, firmness, solidity, etc. **2.** (sl.). Unsteady, tottering. Hence ~ILY² adv., ~INESS n. [ROCK¹, ³, -Y²]

rococ'ō, a. & n. **1.** Of a style of art prevalent in Europe *c.* 1730–80. **2.** (Of furniture, architecture, etc., also of literary style) highly ornamented, florid. **3.** (obs.). Antiquated, out of date. **4.** n. The ~ style of art. [F, joc. alt. f. *rocaille* pebble-work]

rŏd, n. **1.** Slender straight round stick growing as shoot on tree or cut from it or made from wood, switch, wand, (occas. as symbol of office etc., see esp. BLACK¹ ~; AARON'S- ROD; *divining, dowsing*, -~, see DOWSING). **2.** Such stick, or bundle of twigs, for use in caning or flogging (*the* ~, use of this; *spare the* ~ *& spoil the child*; *make* etc. *a* ~ *for* one's *own back*, prepare trouble for oneself; *kiss the* ~, take punishment meekly or gladly; *have a* ~ *in pickle for*, be ready to punish when time comes). **3.** = FISH²*ing-*~. **4.** (Also ~'*man* & ~'STER n.) angler. **5.** (As measure)=PERCH². **6.** Slender metal bar, connecting bar, shaft, (*curtain, piston,* etc., -~). **7.** *(sl.). Pistol or revolver. **8.** (physiol.). ~-shaped structure. Hence ~'LESS, ~'LIKE, aa., ~'LET n. [OE *rodd,* prob. rel. to ON *rudda* club]

rōde¹. See RIDE.

rōde², v.i. (Of wildfowl) fly landward in the evening, (of woodcock) fly in the evening during breeding season. [orig. unkn.]

rŏd'ent, a. & n. **1.** (Animal) of the order *Rodentia* with strong incisor & no canine teeth (e.g. rat, mouse, rabbit, squirrel, beaver, porcupine), whence **rodĕn'tIAL** (-shl) a. **2.** Gnawing (esp. in path. of ulcers). [f. L *rodere ros-* gnaw; see -ENT]

rōde'o (-dāō, *or* rōd'iō; pl. ~s), n. A round-up of cattle on a western American ranch for branding etc., enclosure for this; exhibition of cowboys' skill; (transf.) exhibition of motor-cycle feats etc. [Sp., f. *rodear* go round]

rŏdomontāde′, n., a., & v.i. **1.** Boastful, bragging, (saying or talk). **2.** v.i. Brag, talk big; hence~'ER[1]n. [F (*Rodomont* f. It. *Rodomonte* character in *Orlando Furioso*, -ADE)]

rōe[1], n. (collect. sing. occas. for pl.). Small kind of European & Asian deer; ~'*buck*, male ~; ~-*deer*, ~. [OE *rāha*, OS, OHG *rēho*, ON *rá*]

rōe[2], n. Mass of eggs (also *hard* ~) in female fish's ovary (~-*corn*, one egg); *soft* ~, male fish's milt; ~-*stone*, oolite. Hence (-)rOED[2](rōd) a. [ME *roughe*, MLG *rogen*, OHG *rogo, rogan*, ON *hrogn*]

rogā′tion, n. **1.** (eccl.). (Usu. pl.) litany of the saints chanted on the three days before Ascension Day (*R*~ *days*, these; *R*~ *week, Sunday*, including, preceding, them; ~ *flower*, milkwort), whence ~AL (-shon-) a. **2.** (Rom. ant.). Law proposed before the people, by consul or tribune (*Licinian* etc. ~s, proposed by Licinius etc.). [f. L *rogatio* (*rogare* ask, -ATION)]

Rŏ′ger, n. Male name (*the jolly* ~, pirates' black flag; ~ or *Sir* ~ *de Coverley* (de küv′erli), a country-dance & tune).

rŏgue (-g), n., & v.t. **1.** Idle vagrant (arch.); knave, rascal, swindler, (often playfully of mischievous child or waggish or arch-mannered person). **2.** Inferior plant among seedlings (vb, weed out ~s from). **3.** (Also ~ *elephant, buffalo*, etc.) wild beast, esp. elephant, driven or living apart from the herd & of savage temper. **4.** Shirking racehorse or hunter. Hence rŏg′uERY(4) (-ge-) n., rŏg′uISH[1] (-gī-) a., rŏg′uISHLY[2] adv., rŏg′uISHNESS n. [16th-c. cant wd, of unkn. orig.]

roi (rwah), n. (F for) king; ~ *fainéant* (see Ap.; lit. = King Do-nothing), ruler, chairman, etc., who is a mere figure-head like the Merovingian kings whose power was usurped by mayors of the palace; *le* ~ *le veult, le* ~ *s'avisera*, (see Ap.), forms of giving, refusing, the royal assent to parliamentary bill, = the king wills it, will consider.

roi′nĕk. See ROOINEK.

rois′ter, v.i. Revel noisily, be uproarious, (esp. in part. as adj.). Hence~ER[1], ~ING[1], nn. [f. obs. *roister* roisterer f. F *rustre* var. of *ruste* f. L RUSTICus]

Rŏl′and, n. Name of nephew of Charlemagne celebrated in legend often with his comrade Oliver (*a* ~ *for an Oliver*, effective retort).

rōle, rôle (rōl), n. Actor's part; one's function, what one is appointed or expected or has undertaken to do. [F *rôle*, = foll.]

rŏll[1], n. **1.** Cylinder formed by turning flexible fabric such as paper or cloth over & over upon itself without folding (~s *of carpet, paper*, etc.; SWISS ~); (in Ionic capital) volute. **2.** Document, esp. official record, in this form (|| *Master of the R*~*s*, one of the judges of the Court of Appeal, Keeper of the Records at the Public

Record Office; || *the R*~*s*, buildings in which these were formerly kept now superseded by Public Record Office); register or catalogue (*in the* ~ *of saints*; *a long* ~ *of heroes*; *on the* ~*s of fame*; RENT[3]-~; ~ *of honour*, esp. list of those who have died for their country in war); || the official list of qualified solicitors (*strike off the* ~*s*, debar from practising for dishonesty etc.); a list of persons esp. soldiers or schoolboys used to detect absentees (~-*call*, calling over of this). **3.** More or less (semi)cylindrical straight or curved mass of anything however formed (*a* ~ *of butter, soap, straw, tobacco, hair; has* ~*s of fat on him;* ~ *of bread* or usu. ~, small loaf esp. for breakfast use); (archit., also ~-*moulding*) moulding of convex section. **4.** Turned-back edge of something, e.g. coat-collar. **5.** (bookbind.). Revolving patterned tool for marking cover. **6.** Cylinder or roller. [ME, f. OF *rolle, role* (now *rôle*) f. L *rotulus*]

rŏll[2], v.t. & i., & n. **1.** Move (t. & i.) or send or go in some direction by turning over & over on axis often with aid of gravitation (~ *barrel; barrel started* ~*ing; ball, coin*, ~*ed under the table, into a hole; river* ~*s down stones;* ~*ing stone* GATHERS *no moss; planets* ~ *on their courses; years* ~ *on or by*, go smoothly; ~ *one over*, send him ~*ing* or sprawling); make revolve between two surfaces (~*ing a marble between his palms*); wrap usu. *up in* by ~*ing* motion (~*ed himself up in the blankets*). **2.** Change direction (of) with rotatory motion (*his eyes* ~ *strangely;* ~*ed his eyes on us*). **3.** Wallow, turn about in fluid or loose medium, (of horse etc.) lie on back & kick about, (*porpoise, swimmer*, ~*s in the water;* ~*ing in money, luxury, ease; mule tried to* ~, as way of getting rid of rider or load). **4.** Sway or rock (t. & i.), walk with swaying gait as of sailor, reel, (~*ed himself from side to side; ship* ~*s & pitches; he* ~*ed up to her*). **5.** Undulate, show undulating surface or motion, go or propel or carry with such motion, (*sea, river*, ~*s; river* ~*s its waters to sea; waves* ~ *in; smoke* ~*s up; chimney* ~*s up smoke; the mist* ~*ed away; a* ~*ing expanse* or *plain*). **6.** Utter or be uttered, sound, with vibratory or undulating or trilling effect (~ *out verses, song*, etc.; *thunder, drum, organ, voice, echo*, ~*s;* ~ *one's rs*). **7.** (Of wheeled vehicle) advance or convey usu. *along, by*, etc., (of person) be so conveyed, (*carriage* ~*ed along*, ~*ed them by; he* ~*ed past in his carriage;* ~*ing-stock*, railway engines and vehicles). **8.** Flatten by passing roller over or by passing between rollers (~ *lawn, metal, paste for pies*, etc.; ~*ed gold*, thin coating so applied; ~*ing-pin*, roller for paste; ~*ing-press*, copperplate-printer's press with revolving cylinder, also press with rollers for various purposes).

9. Turn (t. & i.) over & over upon itself into more or less cylindrical shape (usu. *up*; *the way to* ~ *a greatcoat*; *hedgehog* ~*s itself into a ball* or ~*s up*). 10. Form (t. & i.) in(to) cylindrical or spherical shape, or accumulate into mass, by ~ing (~ *cigarettes, a huge snowball, snow into ball*; *the reckoning is* ~*ing up*, increasing. in amount; *saint & philosopher* ~*ed into one*). 11. ~*-top desk*, with flexible cover sliding in curved grooves. 12. ~ *up*, (mil.) drive flank of (enemy line) back & round so that line is shortened or surrounded, (intr., colloq.) appear on the scene, turn up; hence ~'ABLE a. 13. n. ~ing motion (*the* ~ *of the sea, ship*); (aeron.) complete revolution about the longitudinal axis; spell of ~ing (*a* ~ *on the grass*); ~ing gait; ROCK³ -'*n*'- ~. 14. Quick continuous beating of drum; long peal of thunder or shout; rhythmic flow of words. [ME, f. OF *roll(l)er* f. Rom. **rotulare* f. *rotula* (-*us*) dim. of ROTA]

rŏll'er, n. In vbl senses; esp.: cylinder of wood, stone, metal, etc., & of various proportions used alone or as rotating part of machine for lessening friction, smoothing ground, pressing, stamping, crushing, spreading printer's ink, rolling up cloth on, etc.; (usu. ~ *bandage*) long surgical bandage rolled up for convenience of applying; kind of tumbler-pigeon; long swelling wave; brilliant-plumaged bird allied to crows, also German breed of canary, [G, f. *rollen* to roll]; ~ SKATE², *skating*; ~ *towel*, endless, working on ~. [-ER¹]

rŏll'ey, n. See RULLEY.

rŏll'ick, v.i., & n. 1. Be jovial, indulge in high spirits, enjoy life boisterously, revel, (esp. in part. as adj.). 2. n. Exuberant gaiety; frolic, spree, escapade. [orig. unkn.]

rŏl'y̆-pŏl'y̆, n. & a. 1. (Also ~ *pudding*) pudding made of sheet of paste covered with jam etc., formed into roll, & boiled. 2. adj. (Usu. of child) podgy, plump. [prob. formed on ROLL²]

Rŏm, n. (pl. ~*a*). Male gipsy, (pl.) gipsies. [Romany wd]

Rŏmā'ic, a. & n. (Of, in, etc.) the vernacular language of modern Greece. [f. Gk *Rōmaikos* Roman (used esp. of Eastern empire)]

Rŏmā'ika, n. National dance of modern Greece. [mod. Gk (-*kē*), orig. fem. adj. (prec.)]

Rŏm'an¹, n. 1. Citizen, soldier, native, or inhabitant, of ancient Rome, member of ancient-~ State, (*King, Emperor, of the* ~*s*, sovereign head of Holy Roman Empire); inhabitant of medieval or modern Rome. 2. pl. Christians of ancient Rome (~*s*, or in full *Epistle to the* ~*s*, N.-T. book, abbr. *Rom.*). 3. (print.). ROMAN² type (abbr. in press-correcting, *rom.*). 4. = ROMAN CATHOLIC. [f. L *Romanus* (ROME, -AN); ME *romain(e)* f. OF *romain*]

Rōm'an², a. 1. Of ancient Rome or its territory, people, or (rarely; usu. *Latin*) language (~ *Empire*, that established by Augustus 27 B.C. & divided by Theodosius A.D. 395 into WESTERN or Latin & eastern or Greek empires, of which the eastern lasted till 1453, & the western, after lapsing in 476, was revived 800 by Charlemagne & continued to exist as the *Holy* ~ *Empire* till 1806; ~ *law*, code developed by ancient Romans & forming basis of many modern codes; ~ *pottery, bricks, road*, etc., surviving from period of ~ rule; ~ *cement*, trade name for a hydraulic cement named after ancient-~ kind; ~ *balance, beam*, or *steelyard*, ordinary steelyard; ~ *simplicity, honesty, virtue, patriotism*, etc., as of Romans of early Republic; ~ *nose*, with high bridge, aquiline, whence, of person or horse, ~-nōSED² (-zd) a.; ~ *letters* or *type*, of the plain upright type used in ordinary print, opp. *Gothic* or *black letter & italic*; ~ *alphabet*, that used by Romans & still with slight modifications in W. Europe; ~ *numerals*, the letters I, V, etc. used in composing number-symbols, see below† for mod. use, & cf. ARABIC; ~ *architecture*, COMPOSITE, & see ORDER¹; ~ *history, historian*, etc., of ancient Rome). 2. Of papal Rome, esp. = ROMAN CATHOLIC, whence ~ISH¹(2) a., ~izER¹ n. 3. Of medieval or modern Rome (~ *school*, painting school of Raphael; ~ *fever*, malaria, formerly prevalent at Rome; ~ SNAIL; ~ *vitriol*, sulphate of copper; ~ CANDLE). Hence ~ISM(3, 4), ~IST(2, 3), -nn., ~is'tic a., ~IZE(2, 3, 4) v.t. & i., ~iza'tion n., Romān'o- comb. form. †Mod. use of ~ numerals, differing in some respects from the ancient: The only symbols now used are I = 1, V = 5, X = 10, L = 50, C = 100, D = 500, M = 1000; the letters composing a number are ranged in order of value, & the number meant is found by addition, e.g. MDCLXVI = 1666; if a letter or set of letters is placed before a letter of higher value, it is to be subtracted from it before the addition is done, e.g. IX = 9, MCM = 1900; IIII is usu. preferred to IV on clock-faces. [ME *romain(e)*, later *roman* (as prec.)]

roman-à-clef (rômahn' ah klā'), n. Novel in which real persons or events appear in disguise. [F, = novel with a key]

Rōm'an Căth'olic, a. & n. (Member) of the Church of Rome. Hence **Rōman--Căthŏl'ICALLY**, **Rōman-Căth'olicLY²**, advv., **Rōman-Cathŏl'ICISM**(3) n. [f. c. 1600, perh. orig. as non-controversial compromise between *Roman(ist), Romish*, etc., & *Catholic*]

romănce', n. & a., & v.i. 1. (*R*~). Vernacular language of old France mainly developed but distinguished from Latin; corresponding language of Italy, Spain, Provence, etc.; (collect.) the languages descended from Latin. 2. adj. (*R*~; of languages) thus descended. **3.** Medieval tale usu. in verse of some hero of chivalry (named as written in R~). **4.** Prose or rarely verse tale with scene & incidents remote from everyday life, class of literature consisting of such tales; set of facts, episode, love affair, etc., suggesting such tales by its strangeness or moving nature; atmosphere characterizing such tales, mental tendency to be influenced by it, sympathetic imaginativeness, whence ~LESS (-sl-) a. **5.** (An) exaggeration, (a) picturesque falsehood. **6.** (mus.). Short piece of simple character. **7.** v.i. Exaggerate or distort the truth, draw the long-bow. [ME, f. OF *romanz* f. Rom. *•romanice* (opp. *Latine* in Latin) adv. f. ROMANICUS]

rŏmăn′cer, n. Medieval or other writer of romances; fantastic liar. [f. *romance* vb (prec.) partly in obs. sense]

Rŏm′anĕs, n. Gipsy language. [Gipsy (adv.)]

Rōmanĕsque′ (-k), a. & n. = ROMANCE 1 & 2. **2.** (archit.). (In) style of building prevalent in Romanized Europe between the classical & Gothic periods. [-ESQUE]

Rōmăn′ian, Roum- (rōō-), **Rum-** (rōō-), n. & a. (Native or language) of Romania. [-AN]

Rōmăn′ic, a. & n. **1.** Descended from Latin, Romance (a. & n.). **2.** Descended from, inheriting civilization etc. of, the Romans, Romance-speaking. [f. L *Romanicus* (ROMAN 1, -IC)]

Rōmăn′itȳ, n. (rare). Civilization & influence of Roman empire. [f. LL *Romanitas* (ROMAN 2, -ITY)]

Rōmănsh′, Rou-, Ru- (ro-, rōō-), n. & a. (In) the RHAETO-ROMANIC dialect spoken in the Grisons, E. Switzerland; = *Rhaeto-Romanic.* [as ROMANCE]

rŏmăn′tic, a. & n. **1.** Characterized by or suggestive of or given to romance, imaginative, remote from experience, visionary, (*a* ~ *story, scene, adventure, girl*). **2.** (Of music) subordinating form to theme, imaginative, passionate. **3.** (Of projects etc.) fantastic, unpractical, quixotic, dreamy. **4.** (Of literary or artistic method etc.) preferring grandeur or picturesqueness or passion or irregular beauty to finish & proportion, subordinating whole to parts or form to matter, (opp. CLASSIC, CLASSICAL), whence ~IST(2) n.; hence **rŏmăn′tICALLY** adv., ~ISM(2, 3) n., ~IZE(2, 3) v.i. & t. **5.** n. A ~ist; (pl.) ~ ideas or talk. [f. ROMAUNT, f. OF *romant* (mod. *roman*) f. *romanz* ROMANCE, -IC)]

Rŏm′anȳ, n. & a. **1.** Gipsy (n. & a.); (pl., also collect. sing.) *the* gipsies, (pl.) gipsies. **2.** The gipsy language. [f. Gipsy *Romani* fem. & pl. of *Romano* adj. (ROM)]

romaunt′, n. (arch.). A romance or tale of chivalry etc. [f. OF *romant* see ROMANTIC]

Rōme, n. **1.** City or ancient State of ~ (~

was not built in a day, encouragement to fainthearted; *do in* ~ *as* ~ *does, as the Romans do,* adapt oneself to surroundings); Roman empire. **2.** Church of ~, whence ~′WARD a. & adv., ~′WARDS adv., (-mw-), **Rōm′ISH** 1 a. (chiefly derog.). [ME, f. OF, f. L *Roma*; OE f. L]

rŏmp, v.i. & n. **1.** (Of children etc.) play about together, chase each other, wrestle, etc.; (racing sl.) get *along, past,* etc., without effort, come *in* or *home* as easy winner. **2.** n. Child or woman fond of ~ing, tomboy; spell of ~ing, boisterous play, (often *game of* ~*s*); hence ~′Y 2 a. [perh. (n. f. vb) var. of RAMP 2]

rŏmp′er, n. (Sing. or pl.) child's overall. [prec., -ER 1(2)]

rŏn′deau (-dō), n. Ten-line or thirteen-line poem with only two rhymes throughout & opening words used twice as refrain. [F, earlier RONDEL]

rŏn′del, n. (Special form of) RONDEAU. [ME, f. OF, f. *rond* ROUND 1, -LE(2); cf. ROUNDEL]

rŏn′dō, n. (pl. ~s). Piece of music with leading theme which returns from time to time. [It., f. F RONDEAU]

rŏn′dure, n. (poet.). Round outline or object. [f. F *rondeur* (ROUND 1, -URE), after *roundure*] •

|| **rōne,** n. (Sc.). Gutter to carry off rain from roof. [orig. unkn.]

|| **Rŏn′ĕō,** n., & v.t. Machine for duplicating letters, circulars, etc., in numbers; (v.t.) reproduce with a ~. [P]

Rönt′genogrăm (rŭntyen-), n. Photograph taken by Röntgen rays. [foll., -O-, GRAM]

Röntgen rays. See RAY 1. .

rōōd, n. **1.** The cross of Christ (arch.; often in oaths, as *by the* R~); crucifix, esp. one raised on middle of ~-*screen,* wooden or stone carved screen separating nave & choir; ~-*arch,* between nave & choir; ~-*beam,* cross-beam, usu. as head of ~-*screen,* supporting ~; ~-*cloth,* veiling ~ in Lent; ~-*loft,* gallery on top of ~-*screen.* **2.** Quarter of an acre (esp. as loose term for small piece of land; *not a* ~ *remained to him*). [OE *rōd,* OS *rōda,* cross; also, in sense 'rod, pole ', OE *rōd,* OS *rōda,* OHG *ruota* (cf. OE *seglrōd* sail-yard)]

rōōf, n., & v.t. **1.** Upper covering of house or building usu. supported by its walls (*under* one's ~, in one's house, esp. w. ref. to hospitality; *a* ~ *over* one's *head,* somewhere to live; also fig., as *the* ~ *of heaven;* ~ *of the world,* high mountain range; ~ *of the mouth,* palate; *under a* ~ *of foliage*); top of covered vehicle esp. when used for outside passengers; ~-*garden,* on flat ~ of building; ~-*tree,* ridge-pole of ~; hence ~′AGE(1)n., (-)~ED 2 (-ft), ~′LESS, aa. **2.** v.t. Cover with ~, be ~ of, (often *in, over*); hence ~′ING 1(3) n. [OE *hrōf,* = OFris. *rhoof,* MDu. *roof*]

|| **rōōf′er,** n. (colloq.). Letter of thanks

for entertainment sent by departed
visitor. [prec., -ER[1]]

roo′inĕk, roi′nĕk, n. Newcomer, esp.
British or European immigrant, in S.
Africa; (in Boer war) British soldier.
[Afrikaans (*rooi-*), = red-neck]

rook[1], n., & v.t. 1. Black hoarse-voiced
bird of crow tribe nesting in colonies;
sharper, esp. at dice or cards, person who
lives on inexperienced gamblers etc., (cf.
PIGEON); ~ *pie*, of young ~s; ~*-rifle*, of
small bore for ~-shooting; hence ~′LET,
~′LING[1], nn., ~′Y[2] a. 2. v.t. Win money
from at cards etc. esp. by swindling;
charge (customer) extortionately.· [OE
hrōc, MDu. *roec*, MLG *rōk*, OHG *hruoh*,
ON *hrókr*, prob. imit.]

rook[2], n. (chess). = CASTLE[1]. [ME, f. OF
roc(*k*) ult. f. Pers. *rukh*]

rook′erȳ, n. 1. (Clump of trees with)
colony of rooks. 2. Colony of penguins
etc. or seals. 3. Crowded cluster of mean
houses or tenements. [-ERY]

rook′ie, n. (army sl.). Recruit.

room, n., & v.i. 1. Space that is or might
be occupied by something, capaciousness
or ability to accommodate contents,
(*takes up too much* ~; *there is plenty of* ~;
no ~ *to turn in, to swing a* CAT[1]; *would
rather have his* ~ *than his company*, wish
him away; *we have no* ~ *here for idlers*;
make ~, vacate standing-ground etc. or
post etc. for or *for* another, withdraw,
retire, also clear a space *for* person or
thing by removal of others; ~ *for*, arch.,
ellipt. command to make way for some
one; *in one's* ~, *in the* ~ *of*, instead of, in
succession to, as substitute for), whence
~′Y[2] a., ~′INESS n., ~′ILY[2] adv. 2. Opportunity, scope, *to do or for* (~ *to deny
ourselves*; *no* ~ *for dispute*; *leave* ~ *for
evasion*; *there is* ~ *for improvement*, things
are not as good as they should be). 3.
Part of house enclosed by walls or partitions, floor, & ceiling; (pl.) set of these
occupied by person or family, apartments
or lodgings; (transf.) the company in a
~ (*set the* ~ *in a roar*); whence ~′FUL(2) n.,
·~·ED[2] (·md) a. 4. [2]v.i. Have ~(s), lodge,
board, whence ~′ER[1] n.; ~*ing-house*,
lodging-house. [OE *rūm*, OS, OHG, ON,
Goth. *rūm*]

roost[1], n., & v.i. & t. 1. Bird's perching
or resting place, esp. hen-house or part of
it in which fowls sleep, (transf.) sleeping-
-accommodation, bed(room), (*go to* ~, retire for the night; *at* ~, perched, in bed;
curses come home to ~, recoil upon curser).
2. vb. (Of birds or persons) settle for
sleep, be perched or lodged for the night;
provide with sleeping-place. [OE *hrōst*,
= MDu. *roest*; cf. OS *hrōst* roof-spars]

‖ **roost**[2], n. Tidal race about Orkneys &
Shetlands. [f. ON *rost*]

roos′ter, n. Domestic cock. [-ER[1]]

root[1], n. 1. Part of plant normally below
earth's surface & serving to attach it to
earth & convey nourishment from soil to

it, (pl.) such part divided into branches
or fibres, corresponding organ of epiphyte,
part attaching ivy to its support (also.
~′LET n.), permanent underground stock
of plant, small plant with ~ for trans-
planting, (plant, such as turnip or carrot,
with) edible ~, (*pull up by the* ~s, uproot
lit. & fig.; *take, strike,* ~, begin to draw
nourishment from soil, fig. get established; *lay axe to* ~ of tree or institution,
set about destroying it; ~ *&* BRANCH[1]).
2. (bibl.). Scion, offshoot, (*there shall be a
~ of Jesse*). 3. Imbedded part of some
bodily organ or structure, part of these
attaching it to greater or more fundamental whole, (~ *of tongue, tooth, nail*,
etc.; ~ *of a gem*, esp. of emerald, cloudy
part by which it adhered to stone; ~s of
mountain, its base). 4. Source or origin
(*of*; *love of money is the* ~ *of all evil*; *a* ~
of bitterness; ~ *fallacy, idea*, etc., the one
from which the rest originated). 5. Basis,
dependence, means of continuance or
growth, (*has its* ~ or ~s *in selfishness*; *has
no* ~ *in the nature of things*). 6. Bottom,
essential substance or nature, (*get at the
~s of things*; *has the* ~ *of the matter in him*,
is essentially sound, w. ref. to *Job* xix.
28). 7. (math.). ~ *of*, number or quantity
that when multiplied by itself a usu.
specified number of times gives (specified
number etc.; *square or second* ~ *of 4*, or
ellipt. ~ *of 4* or ~ *4*, symbol √*4*, is *2*; √*3
is irrational*; *cube or third* ~ *of 27*, symbol
∛*27, is 3*). 8. (philol.). Ultimate unanalysable element of language, basis (whether
itself surviving as a word or not) on which
words are made by addition of prefixes or
suffixes or by other modification, (symbol
√, as *sopor is from* √SWEP). 9. (mus.).
Fundamental note of chord. 10. ~*-stock*,
= RHIZOME, also primary form whence offshoots have arisen. Hence ~′AGE(1, 3) n.,
~′LESS, ~′ȳ[1] [-Y[2]], aa. [OE *rōt* f. ON *rót*
f. **wrōt-* cogn. w. WORT & L *radix*]

root[2], v.t. & i. 1. (Cause to) take root, fix
firmly to the spot, establish, (*some kinds
~ freely*; *take care to* ~ *them firmly*; *fear
~ed him to the ground*; esp. in p.p., as
her affection was deeply ~*ed*, ~*ed* objec-
tions to, obedience ~*ed in fear*, whence
~′ĕDLY[2] adv., ~′ĕDNESS n.). 2. Drag or
dig *up* by the roots; ~ *out*, exterminate;
uproot, tear away, *from* (poet.). [ME, f.
prec.]

root[3], **rout**, v.i. & t. 1. (Of swine etc.)
turn up ground with snout, beak, etc., in
search of food; turn *up* (ground) thus.
2. (transf.). Search *out*, hunt *up*, rummage (*among, in*). 3. *(sl.). Be active *for*
another by giving encouraging applause
or support. [alt. (w. assim. to ROOT[1]) f.
wroot f. OE *wrōtian* f. *wrōt* snout; cf.
ROUT[2]]

root′erȳ, n. Pile of roots & stumps for
growing garden plants on (cf. ROCK[1]*ery*).
[-ERY]

‖ **roo′tle,** v.i. & t. = ROOT[3]. [-LE(3)]

‖ **rōōt'ў²**, n. (for *rooty*¹ see ROOT¹). (mil. sl.). Bread.· [Anglo-Ind., f. Hind. *rōṭī*]

rōpe, n., & v.t. & i. **1.** (Piece of) stout cordage (prop. over 1 in. in circumf., cf. CABLE¹, CORD) made by twisting strands of hemp, flax, hide, or wire, into one (*the* ~, halter for hanging person, also = TIGHT-~ ; *on the* HIGH~*s* ; *the* ~*s*, those enclosing prize-ring or other area; *know', learn, put* one *up to, the* ~*s*, the conditions in some sphere of action; *give* one ~, ~ *enough to hang* himself, *plenty of* ~, etc., not check him, trust to his bringing about his own discomfiture; ~ *of sand,·* delusive security; ~ *of onions, ova, pearls*, these strung together; *on the* ~, of mountaineers,.~d together). **2.** Viscid or gelatinous stringy formation in beer or other liquid. **3.** ~-*dancer, -dancing*, performer, performing, on tight-~ ; ~-*drill*, in which a ~ stretched by two men' represents company etc.; ~-*ladder*, two long ~*s* connected by short cross-~*s* as ladder; ~'*manship*, skill in ~-walking or ~--climbing; ~-*moulding*, cut spirally in imitation of ~-strands; ~-*quoit*, ring of ~ used in quoits played on board ship; ~'*s-end*, short piece of ~ used to flog (esp. sailor) with ; ~-*walk*, long piece of ground used for twisting ~ ; ~-*walker, -walking*, = ~-dancer, -dancing; ~-*yard*, ~-making establishment; ~-*yarn*, (piece of the) material (esp. when unpicked) of which ~-strands consist, mere trifle; hence **rōp'ING**¹(6) n., **rōp'ў²** a., **rōp'iNESS** n. **4.** vb. Fasten or secure with ~ ; (mountaineering) connect (party) with ~, attach (person) to ~, put on ~ ; use ~ s in towing etc.; enclose, close *in*, (space) with ~ ; ~ *in*, secure adherence of, decoy. **5.** ‖ (In racing) check (horse), check horse, (of athlete) not put forth full powers, in order to lose race. **6.** Become ropy or viscid. [OE *rāp*, MDu., MLG *rēp*, OHG *reif*, ON *reip*, Goth. *raip* f. Gmc **raip*-]

Rŏ'quefort·(-kfôr), n. Kind of French cheese of goats' & ewes' milk. [~ in France]

rŏ'quelaure (-kelōr), n. (hist.). Man's cloak reaching to knees (18th c.). [F (Duke of *R*~)]

rō'quet (-kĭ), v.t. & i. (~*ing*, ~*ed*, pr. -ĭing, -ĭd), & n. **1.** Cause one's ball to strike, (of ball) strike, another ball at croquet; strike another ball thus. **2.** n. Act or fact of ~*ing*. [arbitrary f. CROQUET² & orig. in same sense]

rŏr'qual, n. Whale with dorsal fin, finback. [F, f. Norw. *röyrkval*, repr. OIcel. *reythr* the specific name + *hvalr* whale]

rōrt'ў, raught'ў (-awt-), a. (sl.). Enjoyable (*had a* ~ *time*); fond of amusement & excitement. [orig. unkn.]

rōs'āce (-z-), n. Rose-window; rose--shaped ornament or design. [F (ROSE)]

rosā'ceous (-zāshus), a. Of the family Rosaceae, of which the rose is the type.

So **rosA'CEAN** (-zāshan) n. [f. L *rosaceus*]
(ROSE, -ACEOUS)]

rōsăn'iline (-z-), n. (Kinds of red dye obtained from) an organic base derived from aniline. [ROSE, ANILINE]

rosār'ian, n. **1.** Rose-fancier. **2.** (R.-C. Ch.). Member of a Confraternity of tho Rosary. [f. L *rosarium* ROSARY, -AN]

rosār'ium, n. Rose-garden. [L (foll.)]

rōs'arў (-z-), n. **1.** Rose-garden, rose-bed. **2.** (R.-C. Ch.) form of prayer in which fifteen decades of Aves are repeated, each decade preceded by Paternoster & followed by Gloria; book containing this; string of 165 beads for keeping count in this (*lesser* ~, of 55). [15th c., f. L *rosarium* (ROSE, -ARIUM) ; R.-C. sense f. LL sense *chaplet*]

Rŏs'cian (-shĭ-), a. Like or worthy of Roscius, famous Roman actor of 1st c. B.C. [-AN]

rōse¹ (-z), n., a., & v.t. **1.** (Prickly bush or shrub bearing) a beautiful & usu. fragrant flower usu. of red or yellow or white colour (BLUSH², BRIER¹, CABBAGE, DAMASK, DOG¹, MONTHLY, MOSS¹, MUSK, TEA, etc., -~ ; also in names of other flowering plants, as ROCK¹~, CHRISTMAS ~, ~ *of Jericho*, the Resurrection plant with dried fronds unfolding under moisture, ~ *of Sharon*, unidentified eastern flower, ~ *of May*, white narcissus; ATTAR, OTTO, *of* ~*s* ; *red as a* ~ ; *gather* ~*s* or *life's* ~*s*, seek pleasure; *path strewn with* ~*s*, life of delights; *bed of* ~*s*, pleasant easy post or condition, esp. in *is no bed of* ~*s* ; so *is not all* ~*s* ; ~ *without a thorn*, impossible happiness, unalloyed delight; *the white* ~ *of virginity, innocence*, etc.; *the* ~ *of* with place-name, most beautiful girl or woman in; *Wars of the R*~*s*, 15th-c. civil wars between Yorkists with white & Lancastrians with red ~ as emblem; *under the* ~, = SUB² *rosa*, whence **rōs'ERY**(3) (-z-) n. **2.** Representation of the flower in heraldry or decoration (esp. as national emblem of England, cf. THISTLE, SHAMROCK, LEEK or DAFFODIL; *Golden* ~, ornament blessed by Pope on 4th Sunday in Lent & sent as compliment to some R.-C. sovereign, city, etc.); ~-shaped design. **3.** Rosette worn on shoe or clerical hat. **4.** Protuberance round base of animal's horn or some birds' eyes. **5.** Sprinkling--nozzle of watering-pot or hose, whence (-)**rōsED²** (-zd) a. **6.** = ~ *diamond*; = ~-*window*. **7.** Light crimson colour, pink, (usu. pl.) rosy complexion (*has quite lost her, spoiled her natural*, ~*s*). **8.** *The* ~, erysipelas. **9.** ~-*apple*, tropical tree cultivated for foliage & fruit, its fruit; ~-*bay*, oleander, rhododendron, azalea, species of willow-herb; ~'*bud*, bud of ~ (often attrib., as ~*bud mouth*), pretty girl, *débutante; ~-*bush*, ~ plant; ~--*chafer*, green or copper-coloured beetle frequenting ~*s* ; ~-*colour*, rosy red, pink, (fig.) pleasant state of things or outlook *(life is not all ~-colour)*; ~*-coloured*, rosy, (fig.) optimistic, sanguine, cheerful, *(takes* ~*-coloured views*; *see things through* ~*- -coloured spectacles)*; ~*-cut*, cut as a ~ *diamond*, hemispherical with curved part in triangular facets; ~*-drop*, skin-disease with red blotches; ~*-engine*, appendage to lathe for engraving curved patterns; ~*-gall*, excrescence on dog-~ etc. made by insect; ~*-leaf*, leaf, usu. petal, of ~ *(crumpled* ~*-leaf*, slight vexation alloying general felicity); ~*-lipped*, with rosy lips; ~*-mallow*, hibiscus; ~ (or ~*-head*) *nail*, with head shaped like ~ diamond; ~ *noble*, 15th–16th c. gold coin of varying value stamped with ~ ; ~*-pink*, pigment of chalk or whiting coloured with Brazil-wood decoction, also = ~*-colour(ed)* lit. & fig.; ~*-rash*, = ROSEOLA; ~*-red* a. & n., red as (of) a~ ; ~*-root*, kinds of plant with root smelling like~ when dried or bruised; ~*-tree*; ~ *vinegar*, infusion of ~s in vinegar for application in headache etc.; ~*-water*, perfume made from~s, (fig.) compliments, gentle handling, etc. (~*-water surgery*; *revolutions are not made with* ~*-water*); ~*-window*, circular, usu. with spokelike tracery; ~'*wood*, kinds of cabinet wood named from their fragrance; hence ~'LESS, ~'LIKE, (-z-), aa. **10.** adj. Coloured like a pale red~, of warm pink. **11.** v.t. Make (face, snow-slope, etc.) rosy (esp. in p.p.). [OE *rose, rōse*, f. L *rosa*; in ME reinforced f. OF *rose*]

rose². See RISE¹.

rōs'ēate (-z-), a. = ROSE-*coloured* (lit. & fig.). Hence ~ly, ~Y² adv. [f. L *roseus* (ROSE¹) rosy +-ATE²]

rōse'marȳ (-zm-), n. Evergreen fragrant shrub with leaves used in perfumery etc. & taken as emblem of remembrance. [ME, earlier *rosmarine* f. L *rosmarinus* (*ros* ,dew, MARINE) w. assim. to ROSE & the name of the Virgin]

rōs'ĕo- (-z-), comb. form in names of salts & alkalis of L *roseus* rose-coloured, as ~ :-*cobalt*.

rōsē'ol|a (-z-), n. Rosy rash in measles etc.; German measles. Hence ~AR¹, ~ous, aa. [mod. L (prec, -*ola* dim. termination)]

rosĕtt|e' (-z-), n. Rose-shaped ornament for dress or harness made of ribbons, leather strips, etc.; (archit.) carved or moulded conventional rose on wall etc., also rose-window; (biol.) roselike cluster or organs, markings resembling rose; = ROSE *diamond*; roselike object or arrangement of parts. Hence ~'ED² a. [F (ROSE¹, -ETTE)]

Rōsicru'cian (-zikrōŏshn), n. & a. (Member) of an order devoted to occult lore said to have been founded 1484 by Christian Rosenkreuz. Hence ~ISM(3) n. [f. mod. L *rosa crucis* (or *crux*), as latinization of G *Rosenkreuz*, +-IAN]

rōs'in (-z-), n., & v.t. **1.** = RESIN (esp. of solid residue after distillation of oil of

turpentine from crude turpentine); hence ~Y² a. **2.** v.t. Smear, seal up, rub (esp; bow or string of fiddle etc.), with~. [ME, alt. f. RESIN]

Rōsinăn'tĕ (-z-), Rŏz-, n. Worn-out .horse, jade. [f. Sp. *Rocinante* (*rocin* jade, cf. obs. E *rouncy* riding-horse), Don Quixote's horse]

rosōl'iō (-z-), n. A S.-Europ. sweet cordial. [It., f. L *ros* dew, *solis* of the sun, cordial being orig. made from plant sun-dew] .

rōs'ter, n. List or plan showing turns of duty for individuals or companies esp. of a military force. [f. Du. *rooster* list, orig. gridiron (*roosten* ROAST), w. ref. to parallel lines]

rōs'tral, a. (Of column etc.) adorned with beaks actual or sculptured etc. of ancient war-galleys; (zool. etc.) of, on, the rostrum. [f. LL *rostralis* (ROSTRUM, -AL)]

rŏstrāt'ĕd, a. (Of column etc.) = prec.; (zool. etc.) having, ending in, a rostrum. [f. L *rostratus* (ROSTRUM, -ATE²)]

rŏs'tr|um, n. (pl. ~*a*, ~*ums*). **1.** (Sing., or pl. ~*a* of single specimen but usu. w. pl. constr.; pl. in pl. sense, ~*a* or ~*ums*) platform for public speaking (orig. that in Roman forum adorned with beaks of captured galleys; pulpit, office, etc. that enables one to gain the public ear, esp. *auctioneer's* ~. **2.** (Rom. ant.). Beak of war-galley (pl. usu. ~*a*). **3.** (zool., entom., bot.). Beak, stiff snout, beaklike part, whence ~ATE², ~ĭF'EROUS, ~ĭFORM, aa., ~o- comb. form. [L, = beak (*rodere* gnaw)]

rŏs'ūlate (-z-), a. (bot.). (Of leaves) packed over each other like rose-petals. [LL *rosula* (ROSE¹, -ULE), -ATE², see -UL-]

rōs'ȳ (-z-), a. Coloured like a red rose (esp. of complexion as indicating health, of blush, wine, sky, light, etc.), (fig.) = ROSE- -*coloured*; (now rare) smelling like a rose, made of or covered or strewn with roses; ~ *cross*, emblem of ROSICRUCIANS; ~- -*fingered*, epithet of *dawn* etc. Hence rōs'ĭLY² adv., rōs'ĭNESS n., (-z-). [ME; -Y²]

rŏt¹, n. & int. **1.** Decay, putrefaction, rottenness, (esp. in timber, cf. DRY¹-~). **2.** Virulent liver-disease of sheep (usu. *the* ~). **3.** (sl.). (Also *tommy* ~) nonsense, absurd statement or argument or proposal (often as int. of incredulity or ridicule), foolish course, undesirable state of things, *(don't talk* ~ ; *it is perfect* ~ *to trust him*; *what tommy* ~ *that it is not open on Sundays!)*. **4.** (crick., war, etc.). Sudden series of (freq. unaccountable) failures on one side (*a* ~ *set in*). [ME, prob. f. Scand.; cf. Icel., Norw. *rot*]

rŏt², v.i. & t. (-tt-). **1.** Undergo natural decomposition, decay, putrefy, (~ *off*, drop from stem etc. through rottenness); (fig., of society, institutions, etc.) gradually perish from want of vigour or use, (of prisoner) pine away (*left to* ~ *in gaol*).

2. Cause to ~, make rotten; (sl.) spoil or disconcert (has ~ted the whole plan). **3.** ‖ (sl.). Chaff, banter, tease; (abs.) talk ironically (he is only ~ting). **4.** ~-gut a. & n., (liquor) injurious to stomach. [OE rotian, = MDu., MLG roten, OS rotōn, OHG rozzēn; see RET, ROTTEN]

rōt'a, n. **1.** List of persons acting, or duties to be done, in rotation, roster. **2.** (R.-C. Ch.; R~). Supreme ecclesiastical & secular court. [L, = wheel]

rōt'arȳ, a. & n. **1.** Acting by rotation. **2.** n. ~ machine; *traffic roundabout. **3.** (The) R~, R~ Club(s), a world-wide society with many branches for international service to humanity, orig. named from clubs entertaining in rotation, whence **Rotār'ian** a. & n., (member) of R~. [f. LL rotarius (prec., -ARY[1])]

rōt'ate[1], a. (bot.). Wheel-shaped. [ROTA, -ATE[2]]

rotāt|e'[2], v.i. & t. Move (t. & i.) round axis or centre, revolve; arrange (esp. crops) or take in rotation. So **rōt'ative, rōt'atory,** ~'able, aa. [f. L ROTAre, -ATE[3]]

rotā'tion, n. Rotating; recurrence, recurrent series or period, regular succession in office etc., (often in, by, ~; ~ of crops, growing of different crops in regular order to avoid exhausting soil). Hence ~AL (-sho-) a. [f. L rotatio (prec., -ATION)]

rotāt'or, n. (Anat.) muscle that rotates a limb etc.; revolving apparatus or part. [L (ROTATE[2], -OR)]

rōtch(e), n. The little auk. [later form of Du., Fris. rotge of unkn. orig.]

rōte, n. Mere habituation, knowledge got by repetition, unintelligent memory, (only by ~, as say, know, do, by ~). [ME rote, of unkn. orig.]

rōt'ifer, n. Wheel-animalcule, member of class Rotifera with rotatory organs used in swimming. [L ROTA, -FEROUS]

rōt'ograph (-ahf), n. Print of MS. page etc. got by sensitized roll. [prec., -GRAPH]

rōt'or, .n. Rotary part of machine; horizontally-rotating vane of helicopter. [irreg. for ROTATOR]

rŏtt'en, a. **1.** Decomposed or decomposing, putrid, perishing of decay, falling to pieces or friable or easily breakable or tearable from age or use. **2.** (Of sheep). affected with the rot. **3.** Morally, socially, or politically corrupt, effete, (‖~ BOROUGH; something is ~ in the state of Denmark, Haml. I. iv. 90, things are unsatisfactory). **4.** Inefficient, worthless; (sl.; of state of things, plan, etc.) disagreeable, regrettable, beastly, ill-advised. **5.** ~-stone, decomposed siliceous limestone used as polishing-powder. Hence ~LY[2] adv., ~NESS n. [ME, f. ON rotinn cogn. w. ROT[2], RET]

Rŏtt'en Row (rō), n. (Now usu. the Row) track in Hyde Park, fashionable resort for riding. [app. f. prec.]

‖ **rŏtt'er,** n. (sl.). One who is objectionable on moral or other grounds, useless or inefficient or disliked person. [ROT[2], -ER[1]]

rotŭnd', a. Circular, round, (rare), whence **rotŭn'dATE[2]** a., **rotŭn'di-, rotŭn'do-,** comb. forms, (bot.); (of mouth) rounded in speaking etc., (of speech, literary style, etc.) as from ~ mouth, sonorous, sounding, grandiloquent; (of persons) plump, podgy. Hence or cogn. **rotŭn'diTY** n., ~LY[2] adv. [f. L rotundus cogn. w. ROTA]

rotŭn'da, n. Building of circular ground-plan, esp. one with dome; circular hall or room. [earlier rotonda, It., fem. of rotondo = prec.]

rotŭrier (see Ap.), n. Plebeian. [F (roture plebeian tenure, f. L ruptura breaking, -IER)]

rou'ble (rōō-), **ru-** (rōō-), n. Russian monetary unit and silver coin, = 100 copecks. [F, f. Russ. ruble]

roucou (rōōkōō'), n. (W.-Ind. tree yielding) orange dye. [F, f. Braz. urucú]

roué (rōō'ā), n. Debauchee, rake. [F, p.p. of rouer break on wheel, = one deserving this]

rouge[1] (rōōzh), a., n., & v.t. & i. **1.** Red (only in R~ Croix pr. krwah, R~ Dragon, two pursuivants of English College of Arms, & in ~-royal marble, reddish Belgian kind). **2.** n. Fine red powder made from safflower & used for colouring cheeks & lips; plate-powder of oxide of iron; revolutionary politician; ~-et-noir (-ā-nwah'r), card-game played on table with red & black marks on which money staked is laid (~, the red in this). **3.** vb. Colour, adorn oneself, with ~. [F, f. L rubeus cogn. w. RED]

‖ **rouge[2]** (rōōj), n. Scrummage, also touch-down counting as point to opponents, in Eton football (field game). [orig. unkn.]

rough (rŭf), a., adv., n., & v.t. **1.** Of uneven or irregular surface, not smooth or level or polished, diversified or broken by prominences, hairy, shaggy, coarse in texture, rugged, (~ skin, hands, paper, bark, road, cloth, country; book with ~ edges, in which edges of original sheets are left untrimmed; ~ leaf, ‖ first true leaf of springing plant after the smooth leaves or cotyledons, in the ~ leaf, at this stage; ~ rice, unhusked rice, paddy). **2.** Not mild or quiet or gentle, unrestrained, violent, stormy, boisterous, disorderly, riotous, inconsiderate, harsh, unfeeling, drastic, severe, grating, astringent, (~ manners, soldier, play; ~ water, sea, weather, wind; ~ words; ~ element of the population, quarter of the town; ~ usage, handling; ~ remedies; ~ baritone voice; ~ claret; ~ tongue, habit of rudeness; gave him a lick with the ~ side of my tongue, spoke severely to him; ~ passage, crossing over ~ sea; ~ work, violence, also task requiring it, & see below; have a ~ time, suffer ~ handling or hardship; horse has ~ paces, jolts rider; fact etc. is ~ luck, or ~, on person, worse luck than he deserves; ~ MUSIC). **3.** Deficient in finish or elaboration or delicacy, incomplete, rudimentary, entirely or partly unwrought, merely passable, inexact, approximate, preliminary, (~ *nursing, style, welcome, kindness, plenty, accommodation, sketch, drawing*; ~ *work*, & see above; ~ *state, attempt, makeshift, circle*; ~ *stone*, not dressed; ~ DIAMOND; ~ *justice*; ~ *translation, estimate*; ~ *copy* of picture etc., reproducing only essentials; ~ *draft*; ~ COPY[1]; ~ *coat*, first coat of plaster laid on; ~ *coating*, ~*cast*; ~ *& ready*, not elaborate, just good enough, not over-particular, ~*ly* efficient or effective). **4.** ~-*& -tum'ble*, (adj.) irregular, scrambling, disorderly, regardless of procedure-rules, (n.) haphazard fight, scuffle; ~'*cast*, (adj., of wall etc.) coated with mixture of lime & gravel, (of plan etc.) imperfectly elaborated, (n.) plaster of lime & gravel for walls, (v.t.) coat (wall) with ~*cast*, prepare (plan, essay, etc.) in outline; ~-*dry*, dry (clothes) without ironing etc.; ~-*footed*, with feathered feet (in names of birds); ~-*grind*, give preliminary grinding to (edged tool etc.); ~-*hew*, shape out ~ly, give crude form to, (p.p., uncouth, unrefined); ~-*hound*, kind of dogfish; ~ *house* (sl.), disturbance, row, horseplay; ~-*house*, (v.t.) handle (person) ~ly, (v.i.) make a disturbance, act violently; ~-*legged*, with hairy or feathered legs (of breeds of horse & bird); *·~-neck* (sl.), a rowdy; ~-*rider*, horsebreaker, man who can ride unbroken horses, (mil.) irregular cavalryman; ~'*shod*, (of horse) having shoes with the nail-heads projecting (*ride* ~*shod*, domineer *over*); ~- -SPOKEN; ~-*wrought*, with the earlier processes done; hence ~EN[6] (rŭ'fn) v.t. & i., ~'ISH[1](2) a., ~'LY[2] adv. (~*ly* SPEAKi*ng*), ~'NESS n., (rŭf[2].). **5.** adv. In ~ manner (*land should be ploughed* ~ ; *play* ~ ; chiefly in compds, of which some are given above). **6.** n. ~ ground (esp. '*over* ~ *& smooth*), (golf) *the* ~ ground outside the fairway between tees &·greens; one of the spikes inserted in ~ing horse; hard part of life, piece of hardship, (usu. *take the* ~ *with the smooth, the* ~*s & the smooths*); ‖ rowdy, hooligan, man or boy of lower classes ready for lawless violence; *the* unfinished or *the* natural state, *the* general way, (*shape it from the* ~ ; *have seen it only in the* ~ ; *is true in the* ~). **7.** v.t. Turn *up* (feathers, hair, etc.) by rubbing against the grain (~ one *up the wrong way*, irritate *him*); secure (horse or its shoes) against slipping by insertion of spikes or projecting nails in shoes; ~ *it*, do without ordinary conveniences of life; break in (horse); shape or plan *out* ~ly; sketch *in* ~ly; tune *up* (piano) ~ly; give first shaping to (gem, lens, etc.). [OE *rūh*, MLG *rūch*, OHG *rūh*, f. Gmc **rūh(w)a-*]

roughage (rŭf'ĭj), n. (In dietetics) bran of cereals and other forms of cellulose considered valuable as a mechanical stimulant to the bowels. [-AGE (1)]

roulade (rōōlahd'), n. Florid passage of runs etc. in solo vocal music, usu. sung to one syllable. [F (*rouler* ROLL[2], -ADE)]

rouleau (rōōlō'), n. (pl. ~*x* or ~*s*, pr. -z). Cylindrical packet of coins; coil or roll. [F (*rôle* ROLL[1])]

roulette' (rōō-), n. **1.** Gambling game on table with revolving centre. **2.** (math.). Curve generated by point on rolling curve. **3.** Device for keeping hair in curl. **4.** Revolving toothed wheel used in engraving, similar wheel for perforating postage stamps. [F, dim. of *rouelle* dim. of *roue* f. L *rota* wheel]

Roumān'ian (rōō-), n. & a. See ROMANIAN.

Roumansh. See ROMANSH.

R(o)umēl'iōte (rōō-), n. Native of R(o)umelia. [-OT[2]]

roun'cival, n. (Also ~ *pea*) large variety of pea. [from 16th c.; perh. f. *Roncesvalles* place-name]

round[1], a. **1.** Spherical or circular or cylindrical or approaching these forms, presenting convex outline or surface, (*the* ~ *world*; ~ *shot* (hist.), spherical ball for smooth-bore cannon; ~ *buckler, hole, mat*, of circular outline; ~ *table*, with disc top; *the R~ Table*, at which Arthur & his knights sat that none might have precedence; ~-*table conference*, held at ~ table for same purpose, (also) any informal confidential conference; ~ *game*, proper for ~ table, players being of any number & without sides or partners; ~ *face*, as broad as long; ~ *jacket*, cut level below, without skirts; ~ *hand* or *text*, writing with bold curves; ~ *tower, post, limbs*; ~ *arch*, semicircular as in Romanesque, opp. *pointed*; ~ *cheeks*, plump, not hollow; ~ *shoulders*, so bent forward that back is convex, whence ~*-shoul'derED*[2] (-shŏl'derd) a.; ~ *vowel* in phonet., pronounced with rounded lips). **2.** Done with or involving circular motion (~ *dance*, waltz; ~ *trip, voyage*, with return to starting-point; ~ *or* ~-*arm or* ~-*hand bowling*, with arm swung horizontally, cf. *underhand, overhand*: ~ *towel*, endless on roller; ~ *robin*, written petition with signatures in circle to conceal order in which they were written). **3.** Entire, continuous, all together, not broken or defective or scanty, sound, smooth, plain, genuine, candid, outspoken, (~ *dozen, score*, that & no less, so many together; ~ *numbers*, tens, hundreds, etc., with neglect of minor denominations, whence = roughly correct; *a* ~ *sum*, considerable; *a* ~ *style*, flowing; *at a* ~ *trot*, vigorous; *a* ~ *voice*, not harsh; ~ *unvarnished tale*, the plain truth; *be* ~ *with* one, arch., speak home-truths to him; *a* ~ *oath*, unmistakable). **4.** ~'*head*, member of Parliament party in 17th·c. civil war (from custom of wearing hair close cut); ~-*house*, (hist.) lock-up or place of detention, (naut.) cabin or set of cabins on after part of quarterdeck chiefly in old sailing-ships; ~-*top*, platform about masthead, formerly circular; ~ *turn* (naut.), single turn of rope round post etc. (hence, transf., *bring up with a* ~ *turn*, check with a sudden jerk, check abruptly). Hence ~'ISH[1](2) a., ~'NESS n. [ME, f. OF *rund, round*, f. L ROTUNDus]

round², n. **1.** Round object (*this earthly* ~, *earth*; ~*s* of *ladder*, rungs; ~ of *beef*, thick disc from haunch as joint; ~ of *toast*, disc etc. cut across loaf). **2.** (sculpt.). Solid form as opp. *relief*; *in the* ~ (fig.), with all the features etc. fully shown. **3.** Circumference, bounds, extent, *of* (*in all the* ~ of *Nature*). **4.** Revolving motion, circular or circuitous or recurring course, circuit, cycle, series, (*the earth in its daily* or *yearly* ~; *a milk* (milkman's) ~; *the daily* ~, ordinary occupations of the day; *go for a good* ~, long walk out & home; *a* ~ *of days, pleasures, visits*; *make, go,* one's ~*s*, take customary walk esp. of inspection; *make the* ~ *of,* go round; *news, story, goes the* ~, is passed on); (mil., pl.) watch that goes round inspecting sentries or circuit it makes (*visiting, grand,* ~*s*, orderly, field, officer's inspection of guard & sentries); (golf) playing of all holes in course once; (mus.) kind of perpetual canon at the unison for equal voices. **5.** Allowance of something distributed or measured out, one of set or series, one bout or spell, one stage in competition (*serve out a* ~ of *spirit*, 20 ~*s* of *ball cartridge*; *never fired a single* ~; ~ *after* ~ of *cheers*; *a fight of ten* ~*s*; *threw up the sponge after the third* ~; *the winners in the first* ~ *are paired for the second*). **6.** ‖ ~*s'man*, tradesman's employee going round for orders & with goods. [ME, f. OF *rond*(*e*) n. (as prec.), partly f. ROUND¹]

round³, adv. & prep. **1.** With more or less circular motion, with return to starting-point after such motion, with rotation, with change to opposite position lit. or fig., (*sun goes, summer comes,* ~; *brings us* ~ *to winter*; *sleep the clock* ~, for twelve or twenty-four hours; *all the year* ~; *6 in.* ~, in girth; *wheels go* ~; *he turned short* ~; *soon won him* ~). **2.** To or at or affecting all or many points of a circumference or area or members of a company etc., in every direction from a centre or within a radius, (*glasses* ~, for all present to drink; *tea was served* ~; *send* ~ *the* HAT; *Home Rule all* ~, for each nationality; *an all-~ man*, one of varied talents; *show* one ~, take him to all points of interest; *room hung* ~ *with portraits*; *spread destruction* ~; *all the neighbours for a mile* ~). **3.** By circuitous way (*will you jump or go* ~?; *go a long way* ~; *ask* one ~, out of his house into one's own; *order the car* ~, from garage to door). **4.** *All* ~, *right* ~, ~ *&* ~, emphatic forms of ~; ~ *about*, in a ring (about), all ~ (adv. & prep.); on all

sides (of), with change to opposite position, circuitously, approximately (*it will cost* ~ *about £10*); ~'*about*, (n.) circuitous way, place where all traffic has to follow a circular course (also attrib.), piece of circumlocution, ‖ *merry-go-*~ (‖ *lose on the swings what you make on the* ~*abouts*, end where you began after ups & downs), (adj.) circuitous, circumlocutory, plump or stout. **5.** prep. So as to encircle or enclose (*tour* ~ *the world*; *has a wrapper* ~ *her*). **6.** With successive visits to, at or to points on the circumference of, (*hawks them* ~ *the cafés*; *station them* ~ *the field*; *seated* ~ *the table*). **7.** In various directions from or with regard to (*diffuses cheerfulness* ~ *her*; *shells bursting* ~ *me*). **8.** Having as axis of revolution or central point (*turns* ~ *its centre of gravity*; *argue* ~ *&* ~ *subject*, not come to close quarters with it; *write book* ~ *a subject*). **9.** So as to double or pass in curved course, having thus passed, in the position that would result from thus passing, (*go, be, find* person, ~ *the corner*; GET ~). **10.** *All* ~, *right* ~, ~ *&* ~, emphatic forms of ~. [ME, f. ROUND¹,², perh. partly aphetic f. AROUND]

round⁴, v.t. & i. **1.** Invest with, assume, round shape (~*ed eyes, mouth*; *her form is* ~*ing*; ~ *vowel*, pronounce it with ~*ed lips*; ~ *off* or ~ *the angles*, make them less sharp; ~ *dog's ears*, crop them). **2.** Bring to complete or symmetrical or well-ordered state (often *off*; ~ *off* or ~ *a sentence, estate, career*). **3.** Gather *up* (cattle, & transf.) by riding round, gather *up* (stragglers, criminals, etc.), whence ~'-**ŭp** n. **4.** Pass round, double, (cape etc.). **5.** Turn (t. & i.) round (rare, chiefly naut.; ~*ed on his heel to look at me*; ~ *boat off* etc., turn her to meet wave etc.; *ship* ~*s to*, comes to wind & heaves to). **6.** ~ *on*, make unexpected retort to (friend etc.), (of informer) peach upon. [f. ROUND¹; in ME perh. after OF *rondir*]

‖ **round⁵**, v.i. & t. (arch.). Whisper (t. & i.; chiefly w. double obj., as ~*ed him in the ear that*, told him secretly that). [OE *rūnian* (= OS *rūnōn*, OHG *rūnēn*) f. *rūn* RUNE; -*d* as in SOUND²]

roun'del, n. Small disc, esp. decorative medallion etc.; rondeau or rondel. [ME, f. OF *rondel*(*le*), see ROUND¹, -LE(2)]

roun'delay, n. Short simple song with refrain; bird's song. [f. F *rondelet* (RONDEL, -ET¹) w. assim. to LAY¹]

roun'der, n. In vbl senses of ROUND⁴; ‖ also, (pl.) game with bat & ball between two sides with ~ (or complete run of player through all the bases arranged in a round) as unit of scoring. [ROUND⁴,², -ER¹]

round'ly, adv. In thorough-going manner (*go* ~ *to work*); bluntly, with plain speech, without qualification, severely, (*told him* ~ *that he would not*; ~ *asserts that it is true*; *was* ~ *abused*); in circular way (*swells out* ~). [-LY²]

‖ **roup**[1] (rowp), v.t., & n. (Sc. & north.). **1.** Sell by auction. **2.** n. An auction. [ME 'to shout', of Scand. orig.; cf. Icel. *raupa* boast, M Swed. *röpa* shout]

roup[2] (rōōp), n. Kinds of poultry-disease (a) with swelling on rump, (b) with purulent catarrh. Hence **rou′py**[2] (rōō-) a. [(a) orig. unkn., (b) prob. imit.]

‖ **rouse**[1] (-z), n. (arch.). Draught of liquor, bumper, toast, revel, drinking-bout, (*take* one's ~, carouse; *give a* ~, propose or drink toast). [prob. for CAROUSE, perh. f. wrong division of *drink carouse*]

rouse[2] (-z), v.t. & i., & n. **1.** Startle (game) from lair or cover. **2.** Wake or stir up or startle (person) from sleep or inactivity or confidence or carelessness (often *up*, *from*, *out of*, *to* action, *to* energy, *to* do, etc.; ~ *oneself*, overcome one's indolence; *wants rousing*, is indolent; *a rousing cheer*, *song*, *sermon*, *lie*). **3.** Provoke temper of, inflame with passion, (*is terrible when* ~*d*). **4.** Evoke (feelings). **5.** Stir (liquid, esp. beer while brewing). **6.** (naut.). Haul vigorously *in*, *out*, *up*. **7.** Cease to sleep, become active, (usu. *up*). **8.** n. (mil.). ‖ The reveille. [orig. as hunting term, so prob. f. AF or OF; orig. unkn.]

rouse[3] (-z), **röose** (-z), v.t. Sprinkle (herring etc.) with salt in curing. [aphetic f. *arrouse* f. OF *arouser* f. pop. L *arrosare* f. LL AD(*rorare* f. *ros roris* dew)]

rous′er (-z-), n. In vbl senses of ROUSE[2]; esp.: implement for rousing beer; outrageous or rousing lie. [-ER[1]]

Rousseau′‖ism (rōōsō-), n. (Adherence to) views on religion, politics, education, etc., of Jean-Jacques Rousseau, French author 1712–78. So ~IAN, ~ISH[1], ~AN, aa., ~IST(2), ~ITE(1), nn. & aa. [-ISM]

roust′about, n. *Wharf labourer; deck hand; (Austral., also *rouseabout*) handy man. [f. dial. ROUST rout out]

rout[1], n., & v.t. **1.** Assemblage or company esp. of revellers or rioters, (law) assemblage of three or more persons engaged in unlawful act; riot, tumult, disturbance, clamour, fuss. **2.** (arch.). ‖ Large evening party or reception (~-*seat*, light bench hired out for ~s). **3.** Disorderly retreat of defeated army or troops (*put to* ~, utterly defeat). **4.** v.t. Put to ~. [ME, f. OF *route*, see ROUTE]

rout[2], v.i. & t. = ROOT[3]; also, force or fetch *out* (*of bed* or from bed or house or hiding-place). [var. of ROOT[3]]

route (rōōt, *mil. freq.* rowt), n., & v.t. **1.** Way taken in getting from starting-point to destination; (mil.) marching orders (*get*, *give*, the ~), column of ~, formation of troops on the march, ~-*march*, training march of battalion etc.; *en* ~ (F; pr. ahn), on the way (*is*, *did it*, *en* ~). **2.** v.t. Send, forward, direct to be sent, by a certain ~. [ME, f. OF *route* road f. L *rupta* (*via*) fem. p.p. of *rumpere* break; see ROUT[1]]

routin‖e′ (rōōtēn), n. Regular course of

procedure, unvarying performance of certain acts, (theatr.) dancer's or comedian's act; (attrib.) performed by rule (~*e duties* etc.). Hence ~ISM(3), ~IST(2), nn., (-ĕn[2]). [F (prec., -INE[4])]

röve[1], v.i. & t., & n. **1.** Wander without settled destination, roam, ramble (*roving sailor*, kinds of creeper), (of eyes) look in changing directions; wander over or through; *roving commission*, authority given to person(s) conducting an inquiry to travel as may be necessary; (angling) troll with live bait. **2.** n. Act of roving (esp. *on the*~). [ME; orig. term in archery = shoot at casual mark with range not determined; of Scand. orig.]

röve[2], n., & v.t. **1.** Sliver of cotton, wool, etc., drawn out & slightly twisted. **2.** v.t. Form into ~s; hence **röv′er**[1] [-ER[1]] n. [orig. unkn.]

röve[3], n. Small metal plate or ring for rivet to pass through & be clinched over. [f. ON *ró*, w. excrescent *v*]

rove[4]. See REEVE[3].

röv′er[2] (for *rover*[1] see ROVE[2]), n. **1.** (Archery) mark chosen at undetermined range, also mark for long-distance shooting, (usu. *shoot at* ~*s*); wanderer; (croquet) ball that has passed all hoops but not pegged out, its owner. **2.** Sea robber, pirate; senior boy scout. [ME ; (1) f. ROVE[1], -ER[1]; (2) f. MDu., MLG *rover* (*roven* rob cogn. w. REAVE, -ER[1])]

row[1] (rō), n. Number of persons or things in a more or less straight line (*in a* ~, ~*s*, so arranged); ~ of houses, street with this on one or each side (‖ often in street names); *•~-house*, terrace-house; ‖ *the Row*, ROTTEN ROW; line of seats in theatre etc. (*in the front*, *third*, etc., ~); ~ of plants in garden (*•a hard* ~ *to hoe*, difficult task). [ME *raw*, *row*, f. OE *•raw*, poss. rel. to M Du. *rîe*, G *reihe*]

row[2] (rō), v.i. & t., & n. **1.** Propel boat, propel (boat), convey (passenger) in boat, with oars or sweeps (~ *over*, WALK over in boat-race; also with cogn. obj., as ~ *a race*, *a few strokes*, *a fast stroke*, *30 to the minute*; ~ race with; ~ *down*, overtake in ~ing, esp. bumping, race; ~ *out*, exhaust by ~ing (*the crew were completely* ~*ed out at the finish*); be oarsman of specified number in boat (~*s 5 in the Oxford crew*); (of boat) be fitted with (so many *oars*); ~-*boat*, ~ing-boat. **2.** n. Spell of ~ing, boat-excursion. Hence ~ER[1] (rō′er) n. [OE *rōwan*, =MDu., MLG *rojen*, ON *róa*; cogn. w. RUDDER, L *remus* oar]

row[3], n., & v.t.(colloq.). **1.** Disturbance, commotion, noise, dispute, (*what's the* ~?, what is the matter ?; *make*, *kick up*, *a* ~, raise noise, also make protest); shindy, free fight, (*town-&-*GOWN ~); being reprimanded (*shall get into a* ~). **2.** v.t. Reprimand, rate; hence ~′ING[1](1) n. [sl., *c*. 1800, of unkn. orig.]

row′an (rō-, row-), n. (Sc. & north.).

(Scarlet berry of) mountain ash (also ~: -tree). [f. Scand., corresp. to Norw. raun, Sw. rön]

row-de-dow', n. Din, uproar. [imit.]

rowd'|ȳ, n. & a. Rough & disorderly & noisy (person); so ~y-dowdy a. Hence ~ĭNESS, ~ȳISM(2), nn., ~ȳISH¹(2) a. [U.S., orig. unkn.; orig. sense backwoodsman]

row'ĕl, n., & v.t. (-ll-). **1.** Spiked revolving disc at end of spur (vb, urge with ~). **2.** Circular piece of leather etc. with hole in centre inserted between horse's skin & flesh to discharge humours (vb, insert ~ in). [ME, f. OF ro(u)el f. LL rotella f. L rota wheel, -LE(2)]

row'lock, n. Pair of thole-pins or other contrivance on boat's gunwale serving as fulcrum for oar. [alt. of earlier oarlock, OE ārloc (OAR, LOCK²), to ROW²]

Rŏx'burghe (-ŭru), n. Style of bookbinding with plain leather gilt-lettered backs, cloth or paper sides, & leaves with untrimmed edges & bottoms. [Duke of ~ 1740–1804]

roy'al, a. & n. **1.** Of, from, suited to, worthy of, belonging to family of, in service or under patronage of, a king or queen (after its noun in some phrr., as the blood~, ~ family, RHYME¹~, PRINCESS R~, cf. R~ Princess used of any of ~ family; ~ charter, warrant, etc.; the ~ anger, hands, etc., the sovereign's; R~ ACADEMY; R~ AIR¹ Force; R~ Armoured Corps, armoured fighting vehicles and tanks; R~ Army ORDNANCE Corps; R~ Army Service Corps, commissariat and transport branch of army; R~ Artillery; ~ blue, a deep pure vivid shade; ~ burgh, holding charter from Crown; ~ COMMISSION; R~ Corps of Signals, army organization dealing with communication in the field; R~ Courts of Justice, building in Strand, London, in which superior courts of law & appeal are held; R~ Electrical & Mechanical Engineers, instituted in 1942 to do some of the work previously done by the R~ Army Ordnance Corps & the R~ Army Service Corps; R~ Engineers, engineer branch of army; ~ evil, =KING¹'s evil; R~ Exchange, building in Cornhill, London, for dealings between merchants; R~ Flying Corps, now absorbed by R~ Air Force; R~ HIGHNESS; R~ HORSE¹ Artillery; R~ HUMANE Society; R~ Institution, founded 1799 for diffusion of scientific knowledge; R~ Irish Constabulary, Imperial semi--military police in Ireland, disbanded 1921; R~ Marine Artillery, R~ Marine Light Infantry, now united in R~ Marines, corps trained for service at sea and on land; R~ Military Academy, formerly at Woolwich for Engineer & Artillery cadets, R~ Military College, formerly at Sandhurst for infantry & cavalry cadets, now amalgamated into R~ Military Academy at Sandhurst; R~ Naval Air Service, former naval branch of R~ Air Force; R~ Naval Division, military force raised

in the 1914–18 war from surplus sailors & marines; R~ Naval Reserve, drawn from mercantile marine; R~ Naval Volunteer Reserve, drawn from landsmen used to the sea; R~ Navy; ~ oak, in which Charles II hid after Worcester; R~ Observer Corps, civilian organization for reporting & tracking aircraft movements & radio-active fall-out; ~ ROAD to; R~ SOCIETY; ~ standard, square banner with ~ arms). **2.** Kingly, majestic, stately, splendid,⁻ first-rate, on great scale, of exceptional size etc., (~ magnanimity; gave us ~ entertainment; in ~ spirits; had a ~ time; BATTLE¹ ~; ~ paper, 24 × 19 in. for writing & 25 × 20 for printing; ~ octavo etc., folded from this; ~ fern, osmund; ~ stag, with head of 12 or more points; ~ sail, mast, above topgallant sail & mast; ~ arch, degree in freemasonry); hence ~LY² adv. **3.** n. Member of ~ family (colloq.); ~ stag; ~ sail or mast; the R~s, the R~ Scots, (also) the R~ Marines. [ME, f. OF roial f. L regalis (rex king, -AL)]

roy'al|ist, n. **1.** Monarchist, supporter of monarchy as an institution or of the royal side in civil war etc. (also attrib.). **2.** *Die-hard (esp. in phr. economic ~ist). So ~ISM(3) n., ~ĭS¹TIC a. [-IST]

roy'altȳ, n. **1.** Office or dignity or power of king or queen, sovereignty; royal persons; member of royal family (usu. in pl.); (usu. in pl.) prerogative(s) or privilege(s) of the sovereign. **2.** Royal right (now esp. over minerals) granted by sovereign to individual or corporation; (hist.) lessee's payment to land-owner for privilege of working mine; sum paid to patentee for use of patent or to author etc. for each copy of his book etc. sold. [ME, f. OF roialte (ROYAL, -TY)]

‖ **Roy'ston crow** (-ō), n. Hooded or grey crow. [place-name]

rŭb¹, v.t. & i. (-bb-), & n. **1.** Subject to friction, slide one's hand or an object along over or up & down the surface of (~ one's hands, each with the other usu. in sign of keen satisfaction; ~ shoulders, come into contact with other people; ~ noses, of some savages & animals, greet each other; ~ the wrong way, stroke against the grain, irritate or repel as by stroking cat upwards). **2.** Polish, clean, abrade, chafe, make dry, sore, bare, etc., by ~bing. **3.** Reproduce design of (sepulchral brass or stone) by ~bing paper laid on it with coloured chalk etc., whence ~b'ING¹(2) n. **4.** Slide (hand, object) against or on or over something, (objects) together or together, with friction. **5.** Bring (stain etc.) out, (nap etc., or fig. novelty, shyness, etc.) off or away, force (liniment etc., or fig. lesson, humiliating fact, etc.) in or into, reduce to powder etc., force through sieve, bring size or level of down, spread (ointment etc.) over, groom (horse, oneself) down, freshen or brush (tarnished object, or fig. one's memory,

Greek, etc.) *up*, mix (chocolate, pigment, etc.) *up* into paste, by ~ bing lit. or fig. **6.** Come into or be in sliding contact, exercise friction, *against* or *on*. **7.** (Of bowl) be retarded or diverted by un-evenness of ground, (fig., of person, process, etc.) go *on, along, through*, with more or less restraint or difficulty. **8.** (Of cloth, skin, etc.) get frayed or worn or sore or bare with friction. **9.** ~*-stone*, (piece of) stone used for sharpening, smoothing, etc. **10.** n. Spell of ~bing (*give it a* ~, ~*-up*, ~*-down*, etc.). **11.** (Bowls) inequality of ground impeding or diverting bowl, the being diverted etc. by this (prov., *those who play at bowls must look for* ~*s*); (transf.) impediment or difficulty) *there's the* ~, that is the point at which doubt or difficulty arises; *the* ~*s & worries of life*); (golf) ~ *of* or *on the green*, accidental interference with course or position of ball. [ME *rubben* prob. f. LG *rubben*; orig. unkn.]

rub². See RUBBER².

rŭb′a-dŭb, n., & v.i. (Make) rolling sound of drum. [imit.]

ruba′tō (rōōbah-), a. & n. (mus.). (*Tempo*) ~, time varied for expression. [It., = robbed]

rŭbb′er¹, n., & v.t. In vbl senses; also or esp.: masseur or masseuse; Turkish-bath attendant; implement used for, part of machine operating by, rubbing; caout-chouc or india-~ (often attrib.; vb, coat with ~); superior soft brick that can be rubbed down to any desired shape; *(pl.)* galoshes; *~neck* (sl.), gaping sightseer, inquisitive person. [-ER¹, india-~ sense from use in rubbing out pencil-marks]

rŭbb′er², n. Three successive games between same sides or persons at whist, bridge, cribbage, backgammon, etc. (*have a* ~ *of whist* etc. or *a* ~); *the* ~ (also abbr. *the rub*), winning of two games in ~, third game when each side has won one. [orig. unkn.; as term in bowls from *c.* 1600; in early use often *a rubbers*]

rŭbb′ish, n. & int. Waste material, debris, refuse, litter; worthless material or ar-ticles, trash, (*a good riddance of bad* ~, esp. at departure of person one dislikes), absurd ideas or suggestions, nonsense (often as excl. of contempt), whence ~Y² & colloq. in same sense ~**ing**, aa. [ME & AF *rubbous, robous(e)*, etc.; app. rel. to RUBBLE, w. unexpl. diff. ending; orig. unkn.]

rŭb′ble, n. Waste fragments of stone, brick, etc., from old houses; pieces of un-dressed stone used, esp. as filling-in, for walls; (geol.) loose angular stones etc. as covering of some rocks, also water-worn stones. Hence **rŭbb′lY²** a. [ME *robyl, rubel*, of unkn. orig.; see prec.]

***rube** (rōōb), n. (colloq.). Country bump-kin, hick. [abbr. of *Reuben*]

ru′bĕfy̆, -ĭfy̆, (rōō-), v.t. Make red; (med., of counter-irritant) stimulate (skin etc.)

to redness, so **rubĕFA′CIENT** (-ăshent) a. &, see -ENT(2), n., **rubĕFAC′TION** n., (rōō-). [ME, f. OF *rubifier* f. L *rubefacere* (*rubēre* be red, -FY)]

ru′bicĕlle (rōō-), n. Orange-red precious stone, kind of spinel ruby. [F, prob. dim. of *rubis* or *rubace* RUBY]

Ru′bicon (rōō-), n., & v.t. **1.** *The* boundary by passing which one becomes committed to an enterprise (usu. *pass* or *cross the* ~). **2.** (*r*~; in piquet) winning of game before opponent has scored 100; (v.t.) defeat (opponent) thus. [name of stream limiting Caesar's province & crossed by him before war with Pompey]

ru′bicŭnd (rōō-), a. (Of face, complexion, or person in these respects) ruddy, high-coloured. Hence ~ITY (-ŭn²) n. [f. F *rubicond* or L *rubicundus* (*rubēre* be red)]

rubid′ium (rōō-), n. Soft silvery metallic element grouped with caesium, lithium, potassium, & sodium. [L *rubidus* red (w. ref. to spectrum lines), -IUM]

rubi′ginous (rōō-), a. Rust-coloured. [f. LL *rubiginosus*, f. L *rubigo -inis* rust, -OUS]

ru′bious (rōō-), a. (poet.). Ruby-coloured. [RUBY, -OUS]

ru′ble (rōō-), n. See ROUBLE.

ru′bric (rōō-), n. **1.** Heading of chapter, section, etc., also special passage or sen-tence, written or printed in red or in special lettering. **2.** Direction for conduct of divine service (prop. in red) inserted in liturgical book, whence ~AL a., ~alLY² adv., rubrī′CIAN (-ĭshn) ~ISM(3), ~IST(2), nn., (rōō-). **3.** (Red-letter entry in) calen-dar of saints (now rare). [ME, f. OF *ru-brique* or L *rubrica* (*ruber rubr-* red)]

ru′bricāte (rōō-), v.t. Mark with, print or write in, red; furnish with rubrics. Hence ~A′TION, ~ātOR, nn. [L *rubricare, -ATE³*]

ru′bỹ (rōō-), n. & a., & v.t. **1.** Rare precious stone (also *true* or *Oriental* ~) of colour varying from deep crimson or purple to pale rose (*balas, spinel*, ~, stones of less value resembling ~; *above rubies*, of inestimable value). **2.** (Of) glowing purple-tinged red colour. **3.** Red pimple on nose or face. **4.** Red wine; (pugil.) blood. **5.** A size of TYPE. **6.** ~ *glass*, coloured with oxides of copper, iron, lead, tin, etc.; ~*-tail*, insect of deep metallic bluish-green with upper side of abdomen bright red (also *gold wasp*); ~ *wedding*, fortieth anniversary. **7.** v.t. Dye or tinge ~-colour. [ME, f. OF *rubi(s)*, obsc. rel. to L *rubeus* red]

ruche (rōōsh, & see Ap.), n. Frill or quilling of gauze, lace, etc. Hence **ruchED²** (rōōsht) a. [F]

rŭck¹, n. Main body of competitors left out of the running. [ME 'stack of fuel, heap, rick '; app. Scand., = Norw. *ruka* w. same meanings]

rŭck², ‖ **rŭc′kle¹**, nn., & vv.i. & t. Crease,

wrinkle, (as vb usu. ~ *up*). [*ruck* vb f. n., f. ON *hrukka*; *ruckle* f. *ruck*, -LE(3)]

rŭc′kle², v.i., & n. (Make) gurgling sound esp. in throat of dying person. [f. Scand. (Norw. dial. *rukla* vb)]

ru′cksăck (rŏŏ-), n. Bag slung by straps from both shoulders & resting on back for carrying walker's or climber's necessaries. [G]

rŭc′tion, n. (sl.). Disturbance, tumult, row, (*there will be* ~*s*, things will not be allowed to proceed quietly). [1825, of unkn. orig.]

rŭdbĕck′ia, n. (Kinds of) composite garden plant of the aster family native to N. America. [f. *Rudbeck*, surname of two Swedish botanists (*c.* 1700), -IA¹]

rŭdd, n. Freshwater fish resembling roach, red-eye.· [app. rel. to *rud* red colour]

rŭdd′er, n. Broad flat wooden or metal piece hinged to vessel's stern-post for steering with, (fig.) guiding principle etc.; (brewing) paddle for stirring malt in mash-tub; ~-*fish*, kinds that follow ships. Hence ~LESS a. [OE *rōthor*, MDu., MLG *roder*, OHG *ruodar* f. Gmc *rōthra*- f. st. of ROW²]

rŭd′dle, n., & v.t. 1. Red ochre, esp. of kind used for marking sheep. 2. v.t. Mark or colour (as) with ~. [rel. to obs. *rud* (see RUDD)]

rŭdd′ock, n. Robin redbreast. [OE *rudduc*, as prec., -OCK]

rŭdd′|ý̆, a., & v.t. & i. 1. (Of face or its owner) freshly or healthily red, rosy, (~*y health, youth*, etc., marked by ~iness); (of light, fire, sky, object lighted up, etc., also in animal names as~*y plover, squirrel*) reddish; ‖ (sl.) bloody, damnable; hence ~ILY² adv., ~iNESS n. 2. vb. Make or grow ~y. [OE *rudig* (*rud* see RUDD, -Y²)]

rude (rŏŏd), a. 1. Primitive, simple, unsophisticated, in natural state, rugged, unimproved, uncivilized, uneducated, roughly made or contrived or executed, coarse, artless, wanting subtlety or accuracy, (~ *times, men, simplicity, ignorance, chaos*; ~ *produce, ore*; ~ *scenery*; ~ *plough, beginnings, methods*; ~ *path, verses, drawing*; ~ *fare, plenty*; ~ *writer, style*; ~ *observer, version, classification*). 2. Violent, not gentle, unrestrained, startling, sudden, abrupt, (~ *passions, blast, shock, awakening, reminder*). 3. Vigorous, hearty, (~ *health*). 4. Insolent, impertinent, offensive, (~ *remarks*; *say* ~ *things*; *be* ~ *to*, insult). Hence ~′LY² adv., ~′NESS, (colloq.) ru′dERY(4), nn., ru′d-ISH¹(2) a., (rŏŏ-). [ME, f. OF *ru*(*i*)*de* or L *rudis*]

Ru′desheimer (rŏŏdés-hī-), n. A white Rhine wine. [G (*Rü-*)]

ru′diment (rŏŏ-), n. (Pl.) elements or first principles of or of knowledge or some subject; (pl.) imperfect beginning *of* something that will develop or might under other conditions have developed,

(sing.) part or organ imperfectly developed as having no function (e.g. the breast in males). Hence **rudimĕn′tAL** (rare), **rudimĕn′tARY¹**, aa., (rŏŏ-). [F, or f. L *rudimentum* (RUDE, -MENT)]

rue¹ (rŏŏ), v.t., & n. 1. Repent of, bitterly feel the consequences of, wish undone or non-existent, (*you shall* ~ *it*; ~ *the day, hour*, etc., *when* —). 2. n. (arch.). Repentance, dejection at some occurrence, whence (in ordinary & esp. joc. use) ~′FUL (rŏŏf-) a. (*Knight of the* ~*ful countenance*, Don Quixote), ~′fuLLY² adv., ~′fulNESS n.; compassion, ruth. [OE *hrēow*(*an*), OS *hrewan*, OHG *hriuw*(*an*)]

rue² (rŏŏ), n. Perennial evergreen shrub with bitter strong-scented leaves formerly used in medicine. [ME, f. OF *rue* f. L *ruta* f. Gk *rhutē*]

‖ **rue′-răddy̆** (rŏŏ-), n. Belt or rope passed over shoulder to drag something with. [orig. unkn.]

rufĕs′cent (rŏŏ-), a. (zool. etc.). Reddish. [L *rufescere* (*rufus* red, -ESCENT)]

rŭff¹, n. 1. Deep projecting frill of several folds of linen or muslin starched & separately goffered worn round neck esp. in 16th c.; projecting or conspicuously coloured ring of feathers or hair round bird's or beast's neck; whence (-)~ED² (-ft) a. 2. Kind of domestic pigeon. [perh. f. ROUGH; cf. RUFFLE]

rŭff², n. (fem. *reeve*). Bird of sandpiper kind of which male has RUFF¹ & ear-tufts in breeding season. [perh. f. prec., but that leaves the similarity to the fem. REEVE² unexpl.]

rŭff³, n. Small freshwater fish of perch family with prickly scales. [perh. f. ROUGH]

rŭff⁴, n., & v.i. & t. Trump(ing) at cards; (also *cross* or *double* ~) state of game in which partners out of different suits give each other alternate chances of trumping. [perh. f. *ruff* obs. card-game f. OF *roffle, ronfle*, perh. corrupt. of *triomphe* TRIUMPH, cf. TRUMP²]

rŭff′ian, n. Brutal violent lawless turbulent person, desperado, bully, rough. Hence ~ISM(2) n., ~LY¹ a. [f. F *rufian, -en* = Pr. & Sp. *rufian*, f. It. *ruffiano*]

rŭf′fl|e, v.t. & i., & n. 1. Disturb smoothness or tranquillity of (feathers, hair, water, temper or person in regard to it, brow; *bird* ~*es up its feathers*, in anger or to keep off cold; *nothing ever* ~*ed him*); (of sea,· hair, temper, etc.; rare) suffer ~ing, lose smoothness or calmness; swagger about, behave arrogantly or quarrelsomely, whence ~ER¹ n. 2. n. Perturbation, bustle, (rare; *without* ~*e or excitement*); rippling effect on water; ornamental gathered or goffered frill of lace etc. worn at opening of garment esp. about wrist or breast or neck, RUFF¹ of bird etc., whence ~ED² (-feld) a.; (now rare) a contention, dispute; (mil.) vibrating drum-beat. [ME, of unkn. orig.]

ru'f|ous (rōō-), a. (chiefly nat.-hist.). Reddish-brown. So ~I-, ~O-, comb. forms. [L *rufus*, -OUS]

rŭg, n. **1.** Large wrap or coverlet of thick woollen stuff. **2.** Floor-mat of shaggy material or thick pile, esp. (often hearth-~) laid down before fireplace. [perh. f. Scand. (Norw. dial. *rugga* coverlet, Sw. *rugg* ruffled hair)]

Rŭgbei'an (-bēan), n. & a. (Member) of Rugby School.

Rŭg'by, r-, n. ~ *football* or ~, also **rŭgg'ER**[1] (-g-) n. (sl.), one of the two chief forms of football, distinguished from *Association* or *soccer* esp. by players' being permitted to carry the ball & to hold opponent doing this; ~ *Union*, of clubs using ~ football rules. [~ school]

rŭgg'ĕd (-g-), a. Of rough uneven surface (~ *bark*; ~ *ground, country*, full of abrupt ups & downs, craggy, wooded, etc.; ~ *features*, strongly marked, of irregular outline); unsoftened, unpolished, lacking gentleness or refinement, harsh in sound, austere, unbending, involving hardship, (~ *manners, grandeur, individualist, kindness, honesty, character, verse, times, life*); robust, sturdy. Hence ~LY[2] adv., ~NESS n. [ME, prob. f. Scand.; cf. RUG, & Sw. *rugga* roughen]

rugger. See RUGBY.

rugōse' (rōō-), a. (chiefly nat.-hist.). Wrinkled, corrugated. Hence or cogn. ~LY[2] adv., **ru'gATE**[2], **ru'gOUS**, aa., **rugŏs'ITY** n., (rōō-). [f. L *rugosus* (*ruga* wrinkle, -OSE[1])]

ru'in (rōō-), n., & v.t. & i. **1.** Downfall or fallen or wrecked or impaired state, lit. (of building or structure; *the crash of* ~; *tumble, lie, lay, in* ~) or fig. (*the* ~ *of my hopes*; *bring to* ~, complete loss of property or position; *dates her* ~ *from his arrival*; RACK[7] *&* ~); (often pl.) what remains of building, town, structure, etc., or fig. of person, that has suffered ~ (*the* ~*s of Rome*, remains of ancient Rome or of the Roman imperial system; *is but the* ~ *of what he was*; *lies in* ~*s*; *is a* ~; *lives in an old* ~); what causes ~, destroying agency, havoc, (*will be the* ~ *of us*, BLUE[1] ~; *rapine & red* ~), so [f. obs. *ruinate* vb] **ruina'TION** (rōō-) n. **2.** vb. Reduce (place) to ~s (esp. in p.p.); bring to ~ (*her extravagance* ~*ed him*; so ~ *oneself*; ~ *girl*, seduce her; ~ *one's new hat, prospects*); (poet.) fall headlong or with a crash. [ME; (1) f. OF *ruine* f. L *ruina* (*ruere* fall, -INE[4]); (2) f. F *ruiner* or med. L *ruinare*]

ru'inous (rōō-), a. In ruins, dilapidated; bringing ruin, disastrous, (~ *folly, expense*), whence ~LY[2] adv. Hence ~NESS n. [ME, f. OF *ruineux* or L *ruinosus* (prec., -OSE[1])]

rule (rōōl), n., & v.t. & i. **1.** Principle to which action or procedure conforms or is bound or intended to conform, dominant custom, canon, test, standard, normal state of things, (*deduce* ~*s of action*; *the*

~*s of decorum, cricket*, etc.; ~ *of the* ROAD[1]; *there was a* ~ *that* —; *standing* ~, made by corporation to govern its procedure; ~ *of thumb*, based on experience or practice, not theory, often ~*-of-thumb* attrib.; ~ *of three*, method of finding number that bears same ratio to one given as exists between two others given, also attrib., as ~*-of-three sum*; GOLDEN ~; *by* ~, in regulation manner, mechanically; WORK[2] *to* ~; *hard & fast* ~, rigid formula; EXCEPTION *proves* ~; *large families are the exception & not the* ~; *as a* ~, usually, more often than not). **2.** Sway, government, dominion, (*bear* ~, hold sway; *under British* ~; *the* ~ *of force*; *entrusted with the* ~ *of half the tribe*). **3.** (eccl.). Code of discipline observed by religious order. **4.** (law). Order made by judge or court w. ref. to particular case only (~ NISI; ~ *absolute*, making ~ *nisi* no longer contingent). **5.** (hist.). *The* ~*s*, limited area outside Fleet & King's-Bench prisons in which prisoners were allowed to live on certain terms. **6.** Graduated often jointed straight measure used by carpenters etc. (often *foot*~, *2 ft* ~, etc.); SLIDE[1]-~. **7.** (print.). Thin slip of metal for separating headings, columns, etc., also short (*en* ~) or long (*em* ~) dash in punctuation etc. **8.** ~*-joint*, of kind usual in jointed carpenter's ~; hence ~'LESS (rōōl-l-) a. **9.** vb. Exercise sway or decisive influence over, keep under control, curb, (person, conduct, one's passions; *ruling passion*, motive that habitually directs one's actions); (pass.) consent to follow advice, be guided *by*. **10.** Be the ruler(s) or have the sovereign control of or over, bear~, (~ *the* ROAST; ~*s over many millions*; *kings should* ~ *by love*). **11.** (Of prices, or goods etc. in regard to them or to quality etc.) have a specified general level, be for the most part, (*corn, prices, the market*, ~*d high* etc.; *crops* ~ *good*; *ruling prices*, those current). **12.** Give judicial or authoritative decision (usu. *that*; also ~ person or thing *out of order*; ~ *out*, exclude, pronounce, irrelevant or ineligible), whence **ru'lING**[1](2) (rōō-) n. **13.** Make parallel lines across (paper), make (straight line), with ruler or mechanical help. [ME, f. OF *riule(r)* f. L *regula*, LL *regulare*, see REGULAR]

ru'ler (rōō-), n. **1.** Person or thing bearing (esp. sovereign) rule (often *of*), whence ~SHIP n. **2.** Straight strip or cylinder of wood or metal or plastic material used in ruling paper or lines. [ME; -ER[1]]

‖ **rŭll'ey, rŏl-**, n. (pl. ~s). Flat four-wheeled dray, lorry. [orig. unkn.]

rŭm[1], n. **1.** Spirit distilled from sugarcane; ~*-SHRUB*[2]. **2.** *Any intoxicating liquor (usu. with hostile sense); *~*-runner* (colloq.), smuggler of intoxicants, or ship engaged in the traffic; *~* *row* (colloq.), position outside the prohibited area taken up by ~-running vessels.

[c. 1650, perh. abbr. of contemporary forms *rumbullion, rumbustion*; orig. unkn.]

rŭm², **rŭmm'ў¹**, aa. (sl.). Odd, strange, queer; ~ *customer*, (esp.) person or animal that is dangerous to meddle with; ~ *start* (sl.), surprising occurrence. Hence **rŭm'-LY²**, **rŭmm'ILY²**, advv., **rŭm'NESS**, **rŭmm'INESS**, nn. [16th-c. cant, orig. = *fine, spirited*, perh. var. of ROM; -Y²]

Rŭmān'ian (rŏŏ-), a. & n. See ROMANIAN.

Rŭmansh. See ROMANSH.

rŭm'ba (or rŏŏ-), n. Cuban Negro dance; ballroom dance imitative of this. [Sp.]

rŭm'ble¹, v.i. & t., & n. 1. Make sound (as) of thunder, earthquake, heavy cart, air in the bowels, etc.; go *along, by,* etc., making or in vehicles making such sound; utter, say *out,* give *forth,* with such sound. 2. n. Rumbling sound; hind part of carriage arranged as extra seat or for luggage; ~-*tumble,* lumbering vehicle, rough motion. [ME *romble,* prob. f. MDu. *rommelen* (imit.)]

‖ **rŭm'ble²**, v.t. (sl.). Get to the bottom of, see through, detect. [orig. unkn.]

rŭmbŭs'tious, a. (colloq.). Boisterous, uproarious. [prob. var. of ROBUSTIOUS]

Rŭmeliote. See R(O)UMELIOTE.

ru'mĕn (rŏŏ-), n. Ruminant's first STOM-ACH. [L, = throat]

ru'minant (rŏŏ-), n. & a. 1. Animal that chews cud. 2. adj. Belonging to the ~s; contemplative, given to or engaged in meditation. [foll., -ANT]

ru'min|āte (rŏŏ-), v.i. & t. Chew the cud; meditate, ponder, (i., rarely t.; often *over, about, of, on*), whence or cogn. ~ATIVE a., ~**ātively²** adv., ~**ātor** n. So ~A'TION (rŏŏ-) n. [f. L *ruminari* (RUMEN), -ATE³]

rŭmm'ag|e, v.t. & i., & n. 1. Ransack (ship, house, pockets, records, book), make search in or *in,* make search; fish *out* or *up* from among other things; disarrange, throw *about,* in searching. 2. n. Things got by ~ing, miscellaneous accumulation; ~ing, search (esp. of ship by Customs officer); ~*e sale,* clearance sale of unclaimed articles at docks etc., sale of odds & ends contributed to raise money for charity bazaar. [n. in mod. senses f. vb; vb (16th c.) f. n. in obs. sense *arranging of casks etc. in hold,* f. F *arrumage* (now *arri-*) f. *arrumer* to stow]

rŭmm'er, n. Large drinking-glass. [f. WFlem. *rummer* or Du. *roemer* (= G *römer*) f. *roemen* extol, boast]

rummy¹. See RUM².

rŭmm'ў², n. Simple card game resembling COON-CAN, played with two packs. [orig. unkn.]

rumour (rŏŏm'er), n., & v.t. 1. General talk, report, or hearsay, of doubtful accuracy; *a* or *the* current but unverified statement or assertion (often *that, of*). 2. v.t. (usu. in pass.). Report by way of ~ (*it is* ~*ed that*—; *he is* ~*ed to* be etc.; *the* ~*ed*

disaster). [ME, f. OF, f. L *rumorem* nom. *-or*]

rŭmp, n. 1. Tail-end, posterior, buttocks, of beast or bird or rarely of person, whence (of tailless fowl) ~'LESS a. 2. Small or contemptible remnant of a parliament or similar body, esp. *the R*~ (hist.), that of Long Parliament either after its restoration 1659 or from Pride's Purge 1648 to its first dissolution 1653. 3. ~ *steak,* cut from ox's ~. [ME, prob. f. Scand.; cf. MDa. *rumpe,* MSw. & Norw. *rumpa*]

rŭm'ple, v.t. Wrinkle, crease, tousle, disorder, (fabric, leaves, garment, hair, etc.). [f. obs. *rumple* n. (f. MDu.), or MDu. *rompelen,* MLG *rumpelen*]

rŭm'pus, n. (sl.). Disturbance, brawl, row, uproar. [prob. fanciful]

‖ **rŭm'pў**, n. Manx tailless cat. [RUMP, -Y²]

rŭm'-tŭm', n. Light sculling-boat on lower Thames. [fanciful]

rŭn¹, v.i. & t. (*răn, rŭn*; p.p. rarely as -ED¹(2), as *a fresh-*~ *salmon*). I. General senses. 1. (Of men) progress by advancing each foot alternately never having both on ground at once (cf. WALK¹; ~*ning jump,* in which jumper ~s to the take--off); (of animals) go at quicker than walking pace, amble, trot, canter, gallop, etc. 2. (Start to) cross cricket pitch to score run. 3. Flee, abscond, (chiefly now in ~ *for it, cut &~* sl.; ~*ning fight,* naut., kept up by retreating ship or fleet with pursuer). 4. Go or travel hurriedly, precipitately, etc. (~ *to meet* one's *troubles,* anticipate them; ~ RIOT; ~ *to help* another; ~ *over* or *down* or *up,* to place for flying visit; *he who* ~*s may read,* said of easily intelligible exposition etc.). 5. Be allowed to grow or stray *wild.* 6. Compete in or *in* race (~ *second* etc., come in so); seek election etc. (*for* parliament, president, etc.). 7. (Of fish, ship, etc.) go straight & fast (*a* ~*ning whale; salmon* ~, go up river from sea; *ship* ~*s before the wind, into port, ashore, on the rocks,* FOUL *of* or *aboard* another). 8. Advance (as) by rolling or on wheels, spin round or along, revolve (as) on axle, go with sliding or smooth or continuous or easy motion, be in action, work freely, be current or operative, (*ball, carriage, wheel, spindle, sledge, time,* ~*s; rope* ~*s in pulley; his life* ~*s smoothly;* ~*ning knot,* that slips along rope & enlarges or diminishes ~*ning noose;* ~*ing hand,* writing in which pen etc. is not lifted after each letter; *how your tongue* ~*s!,* how incessantly you talk!; *verse* ~*s,* is smooth; *tune* ~*s in head,* seems to be heard over & over again; *lease, contract,* ~*s for seven* etc. *years; play ran* 100 *nights,* was kept on stage; *courage* ~*s in the family,* is found in all members of it; *the works have ceased* ~-*ning; place where writs do not* ~, are not valid or respected). 9. (Of public conveyance by land or water) ply (*from, to,* *between*); (of fire, news, enthusiasm, etc.) spread rapidly from point to point (*news ran like wildfire*; *a cheer ran down the line*; *~ning fire*, successive shots from different points). **10.** (Of colour in fabric) spread from the dyed to the undyed parts, (of ink) spread beyond proper place. **11.** (Of thought, eye, memory, etc.) pass in transitory or cursory way (*thoughts ~ through one's head*; *eyes ~ over object*; *~ning commentary*, touching on a point here & there, broadcast report by eye-witness of ceremonial, sporting event, etc.; *~ back over the past*, survey it summarily). **12.** (Of liquid, grain, sand, etc., also of vessel containing or object emitting etc., & fig.) flow, be wet, drip, flow with, (*till the blood ran*; *ran blood*; *fountains ~ wine*; *is ~ning with oil*; *tide ~s strong*; *river ~s clear, thick*; *feeling ran high*; one's *blood ~s cold*, he is horrified; *the sands are ~ning out*, time of grace etc. is nearly up; *~ning sore*, suppurating; *nose, eyes, ~*, drop mucus or tears; *~ at the nose*; *~ with sweat*; *~ dry*, cease to flow, be exhausted; *~ low, short*, become scanty; *candle ~s*, gutters). **13.** Extend, be continuous, have a certain course or order, progress, proceed, have a tendency or 'common characteristic or average price or level, (*fence ~s round the house*; *~ning headline, head*, or *title*, repeated or different heading of page; *whereof the memory of man ~neth not to the contrary*, phr. applied to immemorial tradition or custom; *~ning account*, = *current* ACCOUNT[2]; *road ~s at right angles to, along, the ridge*; *story, title, document, ~s in these words*; *must not ~ to extremes*; *~s to sentiment*; *our pears ~ big this year*, are so for the most part; *prices ~ high*; *oats ~ 44 lb. to the bushel*); (in part., placed after pl. n.) following each other without interval, in succession, (*happened three days, hit the bull's-eye seven times, ~ning*). **14.** (With cogn. obj.) pursue, follow, traverse, cover, make way swiftly through or over, wander about in, perform, essay or be exposed or submit to, (course, way, race, a mile, run at cricket; *things must ~ their course*, be left to themselves; *~ a scent*, follow it up; *~ the streets*, be street arab; *~ errands, messages*, be a messenger; *the Derby was ~ in a snow-storm*; *~ the* GAUNTLET[2]; *~ RISKS*; *~s a chance of being*, may be; *~ rapids*, shoot them; *~ croquet-hoop*, send ball clear through it; *~* BLOCKADE[1]). **15.** Sew (fabric) slightly. **16.** Chase, hunt, have *~ning race* with, (*~ fox five miles*; *~ to earth*, chase to its lair, & often fig. = discover after long search; *will ~ you for £50 a side*; *~* one *hard* or *close*, press him severely in race, competition, or comparative merit etc.). **17.** (In causative senses) make *~* or go (*~ cattle* etc., turn out to graze; *~ brandy* etc., smuggle it in by evading coastguard etc.; *~ ship aground, to New York*; *~ boat* down *to the water*; *~ train through*; *~* one's *head against*; *~ cart into wall*; *~ sword, pin, into*; *~* one's *hand, eye, along, down, over*, something; *~ rope through eyelet*; *~ coach, steamer, business, person*, keep them going, manage them, conduct their operations; *~ the show*, sl., dominate in an undertaking etc.; *~ horse*, send him in for race, so *~ candidate*; *~ metal into mould*; *~ the water off*; *~ parallel, simile*, etc., *too far*; *ran his fingers, comb, through his hair*; *~ thing fine*, leave very little margin of time or amount concerning it). **18.** Allow (account, bill) to accumulate for some time before paying. **19.** *~'about*, (a.) roving, (n.) light motor-car; *~'away* n. & a., fugitive, bolting (horse), *~away match* or *marriage*, after elopement, *~away ring* or *knock*, given at door by practical joker who immediately makes off. II. With prepp. **1.** *~ across*, fall in with. **2.** *~ after*, pursue with attentions, seek society of, give much time to (pursuit etc.). **3.** *~ against*, fall in with. **4.** *~ at*, assail by charging or rushing. **5.** *~ in* (incur) *debt*. **6.** *~ into*, fall into (practice, absurdity, etc.), be continuous or coalesce with, have collision with, reach or attain (*some length, five editions*, etc.). **7.** *~ on*, be concerned with (*talk, mind, ~s on* a subject). **8.** *~ over*, review, glance over, peruse, recapitulate; touch (notes of piano etc.) in quick succession; (of vehicle) pass over (prostrate person). **9.** *~ through*, examine cursorily, peruse, deal successively with; consume (estate etc.) by reckless or quick spending, pervade. **10.** *~ to*, reach (amount, number, etc.); have money or ability or (of money etc.) be enough for (some expense or undertaking); fall into (ruin); (of plants) tend to develop chiefly (seed); (of persons) indulge inclination towards (coarseness etc.). **11.** *~ upon*, (of thoughts etc.) be engrossed by, dwell on; (of person) encounter suddenly. III. With advv. **1.** *~ about*, bustle, hurry from one person etc. to another, (esp. of children) play or wander without restraint. **2.** *~ away*, flee, abscond, elope; (of horse) bolt, (of horse or person) get clear away *from* competitors in race. **3.** *~ away with*, carry off (person, stolen property, etc.); accept (notion) hastily; (of expense etc.) consume (money etc.); (of horse etc.) bolt with (rider, carriage or its occupants). **4.** *~ down*, (of clock etc.) stop for want of winding; (of person or his health etc.) become enfeebled from overwork, poor feeding, etc. (also in p.p. as *is, feels, much ~ down*); knock down or collide with (person, ship, etc.); overtake (game, person) in pursuit, discover after search; disparage. **5.** *~ in*, (of combatant) rush to close quarters; (rugby footb.) carry ball over opponents' goal-line & touch it down; pay short visit (*to* person or house); (colloq.) arrest & take to prison; (colloq.) secure election of (candidate); bring (new machinery) into good working order by ~ning it. **6.** ~ *off*, flee, flow away, digress suddenly; write or recite (poem, list, etc.) fluently; drain (liquid) off; decide (race) after tie or trial heats. **7.** ~ *on*, be joined together (of written characters); continue in operation; elapse; speak volubly, talk incessantly; (print.) begin (t. & i. of sentence etc.) in same line as what precedes. **8.** ~ *out*, come to an end (of period, also of stock of something or its owner; ~ *out of*, exhaust one's stock of); escape from containing vessel; advance from block to hit ball in cricket; pass or be paid out (of rope); jut out; come out of contest in specified position etc. or complete required score etc.; complete (race); advance (gun etc.) so as to project; put down wicket of (batsman while ~ning); exhaust one*self* by ~ning. **9.** ~ *over*, overflow (of vessel or contents); recapitulate, review, glance over. **10.** ~ *through*, pierce with sword etc.; draw line through (written words). **11.** ~ *up*, grow quickly, rise in price, amount *to*; be RUNNER-up; accumulate (number, sum, debt) quickly; force (rival bidder) to bid higher, force up (price or commodity in that respect); erect (wall, house) to great height or in unsubstantial or hurried way; add up (column of figures). [OE rare *rinnan* (usu. metath. *irnan*) intr., & *ærnan*, *earnan* (metath. f. *°rennan*) trans., f. Gmc *°rinnan* & *°rannjan*; ME *rinne*, *renne* prob. f. ON]

run², n. **1.** Act or spell of RUN¹ning (*have a* ~ *for* one's *money*, get some enjoyment etc. out of expenditure or effort, orig. w. ref. to scratching of horse after bets; *had a good* ~, esp. in hunting or on ship, train, etc.; *on the* ~, fleeing, also bustling about; *at a* ~, running; *a* ~ *on the Continent*, *to Paris*, etc., short excursion or visit); distance travelled by ship in specific time (usu. 24 hours). **2.** (crick.). Traversing of pitch by both batsmen without either's being put out, point scored thus or otherwise. **3.** Rhythmical motion, way things tend to move, direction, (*cannot get the* ~ *of the metre*, or of some process or operation, see how it goes; *the* ~ *of the market was against us*; *the* ~ *of the hills is NW*.). **4.** Rapid fall (*come down with a* ~, of building etc., person, mercury in barometer etc., prices, etc.). **5.** (mus.). Rapid scale passage. **6.** Continuous stretch or spell or course, long series or succession, general demand, (*a 500 ft* ~ *of pipe*; *a long* ~ *of power, office*; *a* ~ *of luck*; *in the* LONG¹ ~; *a* ~ *on the bank*, sudden demand from many customers for immediate payment; ~ *on rubber, book*, etc., great demand for it; so *book* etc. *has a considerable* ~; ~ *on the red* in rouge-et-noir, its coming many times running; *play has a* ~ *of 50 nights, a long* ~, etc.). **7.** Common, general,

average, or ordinary type or class (*the common* ~ *of men*, average men; ~ *of the mill* or *mine*, ordinary or average product or specimen, not specially selected or distributed); class or line of goods; batch or drove of animals born or reared together, shoal of fish in motion. **8.** Regular track of some animals, enclosure for fowls etc., range of pasture (usu. *sheep* etc. ~). **9.** Trough for water to run in. **10.** Part of ship's bottom narrowing towards stern. **11.** Licence to make free use of (*allowed him the* ~ *of their books, house*; *the* ~ *of* one's *teeth*, free board). **12.** (Of aircraft) flight on a straight and even course at a constant speed before or while dropping bombs (also ~-*in* or ~-*up*). **13.** ~-*down*, reduction in numbers esp. of armed forces by demobilization; ~-*in*, act of running in (see prec.) at football, see also sense 12; ~-*off*, deciding race after dead heat; ~-*up*, race between greyhounds up to hare's first turn, see also sense 12. [f. prec.]

rŭn'agāte, n. (arch.). Vagabond. [assim. of RENEGADE to *run* & obs. *agate* away]

rŭn'cible spoon, n. Kind of fork with three broad prongs, one with a cutting edge, and hollowed out like a spoon. [*runcible*, nonsense word of Edward Lear (d. 1888), SPOON¹]

rŭn'cinate, a. (bot.). Saw-toothed, with lobes curved towards base. [L *runcina* plane (formerly taken to mean saw), -ATE²]

‖ **rŭn'dāle**, n. Joint occupation of (esp. Irish) land, each holder having several strips not contiguous. [RUN¹, obs. *dale* north. var. of DOLE¹]

rune (roōn), n. **1.** Any letter of earliest Teutonic alphabet used esp. by Scandinavians & Anglo-Saxons, dating from as early as 2nd c. & formed by modifying Roman or Greek characters to suit carving; similar mark of mysterious or magic significance. **2.** (Division of) Finnish poem. **3.** ~-*staff*, magic wand inscribed with ~s, also runic calendar. [f. ON & Icel. *rún*, cogn. w. OE *rún*, OS, OHG, Goth. *runa*; see ROUND⁵]

rŭng¹, n. Short stick attached at each end as rail, spoke, or cross-bar in chair etc. or esp. in ladder (often fig., as *the lowest, topmost*, ~ *of Fortune's ladder*). Hence ~ED² (-gd), ~'LESS, aa. [OE *hrung*, = MLG *runge*, Goth. *hrugga*]

rŭng². See RING².

ru'nic (roō-), a. & n. **1.** Of, in, marked with, runes; (of poetry etc.) of the ancient--Scandinavian type; (of ornament) interlacing as on ~ monuments & metal-work. **2.** n. ~ inscription; kinds of moth; (print.) ornamental type of thick face & condensed form. [-IC]

rŭn'lĕt¹, n. (arch.). Cask of varying size for wine etc. [f. OF *rondelet* dim. of *rondelle* dim. of *ronde* (ROUND¹)]

rŭn'lĕt², n. Small stream. [RUN², -LET]

rŭnn'el, n. Brook, rill; gutter. [later form (after *run*) of *rinel*, OE *rynel* (RUN[1], -LE(1))]

rŭnn'er, n. In vbl senses; also or esp.: **1.** Messenger, scout, collector, or agent for bank etc., tout; (hist., esp. BOW-STREET ~) police-officer. **2.** The bird water-rail. **3.** = BLOCKADE[1]-~. **4.** Revolving millstone. **5.** (naut.). Rope in single block with one end round tackle-block & other having hook. **6.** Creeping stem that issues from main stem of strawberry etc. & takes root; (also ~ *bean*) kinds of twining bean, esp. SCARLET ~. **7.** Ring etc. that slides on rod, strap, etc.; one of the long pieces of wood etc. on which sledge etc. slides, (blade of) FEN[1]-~; groove or rod for thing to slide along; roller for moving heavy article. **8.** ~-*up*, dog beaten only in final heat at coursing, competitor similarly beaten at golf etc. [ME; -ER[1]]

rŭnn'ing, n. In vbl senses; esp.: (w. ref. to racing) *make, take up, the* ~, take the lead, set the pace, (lit., & fig. of talk etc.), *in, out of, the* ~, (of competitor) with good, no, chance of winning; ~-*board*, footboard on either side of a locomotive, motor-car, etc.; ~ *commentary*, oral description of event(s) in progress; ~ *powers*, right granted by railway to another to run trains over its line. [-ING[1]]

‖ **rŭn'rĭg**, n. (Sc.). = RUNDALE. [RUN[1], Sc. & north. *rig* RIDGE]

rŭnt, n. Ox or cow of small esp. Scottish-Highland or Welsh breed; large breed of domestic pigeon; small pig; weakling or undersized person. [orig. unkn.]

rŭn'way, n. **1.** Trail to animals' watering-place. **2.** Incline down which logs are slid. **3.** Gangway (usu. of special kind). **4.** Specially prepared surface in airfield, for taking off and landing. [RUN[1]]

rupee' (roo-), n. Monetary unit; in India = 100 *Naye Paise*; in Pakistan formerly = 16 annas; in Ceylon = 100 cents; pl. abbr. *Rs*; *Rx*, tens of ~s, in statistics etc, [f. Hind. *rupiyah* f. Skr. *rupya* wrought silver]

rŭp'ture, n., & v.t. & i. **1.** Breach of harmonious relations, disagreement & parting; (path.) tumour formed by protrusion of part of an organ through breach in wall of containing cavity esp. in abdomen, hernia; breaking, breach. **2.** vb. Burst, break, (cell, vessel, membrane); sever (connexion, marriage, etc.); affect with hernia; suffer ~. [ME, f. OF, or f. L *ruptura* (*rumpere rupt-* break, -URE)]

rŭr'al (roor-), a. In, of, suggesting, the country (opp. URBAN), pastoral or agricultural, (~ DEAN[1]; *in* ~ *seclusion*; ~ *policeman, constituency, sports*, etc.). Hence **rŭrăl'ITY** n., ~IZE(2, 3) v.i. & t., ~ĪZA'TION n., ~LY[2] adv. [ME f. OF, or f. LL *ruralis* (*rus ruris* country, -AL)]

rurĭdĕcăn'al (roor-; *also* -dĕk'a-), a. Of

rural DEAN[1] or deanery. [L *rus* (prec.), -I-]

Rurĭtān'|ia (roor-), n..Imaginary Central-European kingdom, the novelist's and dramatist's locale for court romances in a modern setting; hence ~IAN a. & n. [scene of Anthony Hope's novel *The Prisoner of Zenda* (1894)]

ru'sa (roo-), n. Large E.-Ind. deer. [Malay]

ruse (rooz, & see Ap.), n. Stratagem, feint, trick. [ME, f. OF, f. *ruser*, see RUSH[2]]

rusé (see Ap.), a. (fem. -*ée*). Given to ruses, sly, cunning, (of person, procedure, look, etc.). [F]

rŭsh[1], n., & v.t. **1.** Marsh or waterside plant with naked slender tapering pith-filled stems (prop. leaves) formerly used for strewing floors & still for making chair-bottoms & plaiting baskets etc., *a* stem of this, (collect.)~es as a material; thing of no value (*don't care, not worth, a* ~). **2.** ‖ ~-*bearing*, annual northern festival on occasion of carrying ~es & garlands to strew floor & decorate walls of church; ~ *candle*, made by dipping pith of a ~ in tallow; ~'*light*, ~ candle (usu. fig. of feeble glimmer of intelligence, scanty information, etc.); ~ *ring*, made of ~(es) formerly used in (esp. mock) weddings; hence ~'I:KE, ~'Y[2], aa. **3.** v.t. Supply (chair-bottom), strew (floor), with ~es. [OE *risc* & rare *rysc*, corresp. to MDu., MLG *risch* etc. & *rusch*, MHG *rusch(e)*; ult. orig. unkn.]

rŭsh[2], v.t. & i., & n. **1.** Impel, drag, force, carry along, violently & rapidly (~*ed them into danger, round the sights*; *ball is* ~*ed down the field*; ~ *bill through*, get it hurriedly passed; *refuse to be* ~*ed*, insist on doing things at one's own pace). **2.** (mil.). Take by sudden vehement assault. **3.** Pass (obstacle, stream, fence, etc.) with a rapid dash. **4.** Swarm upon & take possession of (goldfield, platform at meeting, etc.). **5.** (sl.). Charge (customer) exorbitant price (*they* ~ *you shockingly*, ~*ed us £1 a head*). **6.** Run precipitately, violently or with great speed, go or resort without proper consideration (*in)to*, (~ *into, out of, the room*; ~ *at*, charge; *dark horse* ~*ed past the favourite*; ~ *into extremes*; ~ *into print*, write to newspaper, publish book, etc.). **7.** Flow, fall, spread (intr.), roll (intr.), impetuously or fast (*river* ~*es past*; *a* ~*ing mighty wind*; *avalanches* ~ *down*; *blood* ~*ed to his face*; *his past life* ~*ed into his memory*). **8.** n. Act of ~ing, violent or tumultuous advance, spurt, charge, onslaught, (*the* ~ *of the tide*; *carry the citadel with a* ~; *a* ~ *of blood to the head*; *a great* ~ *of business*); (cinemat.) first print or preliminary showing of film before cutting; (footb.) combined dash of several players with the ball; sudden migration of large numbers esp. to new goldfield; strong run *on* or *for* some commodity; ~-*hours* (at which

traffic is busiest). [ME, f. AF *russcher*,
= OF *re(h)user*, *ruser*; ult. orig. unkn.]

rŭsk, n. Piece of bread pulled or cut from
loaf & rebaked. [f. Sp. or Port. *rosca*
twist, coil, roll of bread]

Rŭsk̆|in′ian, a. & n. After the manner
or principles, follower, of John Ruskin
writer on art & social subjects d. 1900.
So ~**ĭnese′** (-ēz), ~**ĭnesque′** (-ĕsk), aa. &
nn., ~′**ĭnism**(3) n., ~′**ĭnize**(2, 3, 4) v.i. & t.
[-ian]

Rŭss, n. & a. (arch.). **1.** A Russian; the
Russian language. **2.** adj. Russian.
Hence ~′**ĭfy** v.t., ~**ĭfica′tion** n., ~′**o**-
comb. form,~′**ophil** n. & a.,~**ŏph′ĭlism**(3)
n., ~′**ophobe** n. & a., ~**ophob′ia** n. [f.
Russ. *Rusi* Russian people or country]

Rŭss′ell (cŏrd), n. Ribbed fabric of cotton & wool used for scholastic gowns etc.
[orig. unkn.]

rŭss′ĕt, n. & a. **1.** (Hist.) coarse homespun reddish-brown or grey cloth worn by
peasants; reddish brown; kind of rough-
-skinned ~-coloured apple. **2.** adj. Reddish-brown (also ~y² a.); (arch.) rustic,
homely, simple. [ME, f. OF *rousset* (*rous*
red f. L *russus*, -et¹)]

Rŭ′ssia (lea′ther) (-sha; lĕdh-), n. Durable bookbinding leather from skins impregnated with birch-bark oil. [*Russia*]

Rŭ′ssian (-shn), n. & a. **1.** Native,
language, of Russia. **2.** adj. Of or from
Russia (~ *boots*, loosely enclosing calf); of
or in ~; hence ~**ize**(3) (-sha-) v.t. [f. med.
L *Russianus* (prec., -an)]

Rŭss′niăk, n. & a. (Member, language) of
the Little Russian or Ruthenian people in
Galicia. [f. native *Rusnyak*]

rŭst, n., & v.i. & t. **1.** Yellowish-brown
coating formed on iron or steel by oxidation esp. as effect of moisture & gradually
corroding the metal, similar coating on
other metals; (fig.) impaired state due to
disuse or inactivity, inaction as deteriorating influence. **2.** (Plant-disease with
~-coloured spots caused by) kinds of
fungus, blight, brand; hence ~′**less** a.
(~*less steel*, esp. ferro-chromium alloys
used for stainless cutlery etc.). **3.** vb.
Contract ~, undergo oxidation or blight;
(of bracken etc.) become ~-coloured ; lose
quality or efficiency by disuse or inactivity (*better wear out than* ~ *out*, exhortation to maintain activity in old age etc.);
affect with ~, corrode. [OE *rŭst*, = OS,
OHG *rost* f. Gmc *rudhs-to-*, f. *rudh-*,
cogn. w. red]

rŭs′tic, a. & n. **1.** (Now less usual for)
rural. **2.** Having the appearance or
manners of country-people, characteristic of peasants, unsophisticated, unpolished, unrefined, uncouth, clownish.
3. Of rude or country workmanship (~
seat, *bridge*, *work*, of untrimmed branches
or rough timber); (of lettering) irregularly
formed; (archit.) with rough-hewn or
roughened surface or with chamfered
joints (~-*work*, such masonry); hence or

cogn. **rŭs′tically**, ~**ly²** (rare), advv.,
rŭstĭ′cĭty n. **4.** n. Countryman, peasant.
[ME, f. L *rusticus* (*rus* the country)]

rŭs′tic|āte, v.i. & t. **1.** Retire to, sojourn
in, the country, lead a rural life; send
down temporarily from university as
punishment; countrify. **2.** Mark (masonry) with sunk joints or roughened surface.
Hence ~**a′tion** n. [f. L *rusticari* live in
the country (prec.), -ate³]

rŭ′stl|e (-sl), v.i. & t., & n. **1.** (Give forth)
sound (as) of dry leaves blown, rain pat-
tering, or silk garments in motion; go
with ~e (*along* etc.; ~*e in silks*, be clad in
silk); cause to ~e by shaking etc.; hence
~**ingly²** (-sl-) adv. **2.** *(colloq.).* Hustle,
move energetically; steal (cattle or
horses); hence~**er¹**(-sl-) n. [ME *rustel* etc.,
imit.; cf. Flem. *ruysselen*, Du. *ridselen*]

rŭs′t|y̆¹, a. Rusted, affected with rust; of
antiquated appearance; (of voice) croaking, creaking; stiff with age or disuse,
antiquated, behind the times, impaired
by neglect, in need of furbishing, (*his
Greek is a little~y*); (of black clothes) discoloured by age; rust-coloured. .Hence
~**ĭly²** adv.,~**ĭness** n. [ME; -y²]

rŭs′ty̆², a. Rancid (esp. of bacon). [dial.,
= obs. *resty* & dial. *reasty* f. OF *reste* left
over, stale]

rŭt¹, n., & v.t. (-tt-). **1.** Track sunk by
passage of wheels; established mode of
procedure, beaten track, groove; hence
~**t′y²** a. **2.** v.t. Mark with ~s (usu. in
p.p.). [16th c., perh. f. OF *rote* route]

rŭt², n., & v.i. (-tt-). **1.** Periodic sexual
excitement of male deer (also of goat, ram,
etc.), heat. **2.** v.i. Be affected with ~.
Hence~**t′ish**¹(1) a. [ME, f. OF, also *ruit*,
f. L *rugitus -ūs* (*rugire* roar)]

ruth (rōoth), n. (arch.). Pity, compassion.
Hence (mod.) ~′**less** a., ~′**lèssly²** adv.,
~′**lèssness** n., (rōo-). [ME, f. rue¹ vb
+ -th¹]

ruthĕn′ium (rōo-), n. Rare metallic element of the platinum group. [f. med.
L *Ruthenia* Russia (from its discovery in
the Urals)]

|| **rŭx** n. (school sl.). Temper, passion.

-ry, suf., shortened form of -ery (which
see for numbered meanings), as in *chantry*
(ME *chaunterie*), *jewry*, *bottomry*, *foundry*,
poultry, *jewel(le)ry*; occas. also in direct
formations, as *rivalry*.

ryĕ, n. (Grain of) a N.-Europ. cereal used
for bread in northern Continental countries & for fodder in U.K. ; (also~ *whisky*)
whisky distilled from~. [OE *ryge*, = ON
rugr f. Gmc *rugiz*; cogn. w. OS *roggo*,
OHG *rocko*]

rye̓′grass (rīgrahs), n. Kinds of fodder
grass. [f. obs. *ray-grass*; orig. unkn.]

|| **rye-pĕck** (rīp-), n. Ironshod pole for se-
curing punt etc. [orig. unkn.]

|| **rȳm′er**, n. One of the posts in weir or
lock holding paddles. [orig. unkn.]

rȳ′ot, n. Indian peasant. [f. Hind. *raiyat*
f. Arab. as rayah]

S

S (ĕs), letter (pl. *Ss*, S's). (Also) S-shaped object (COLLAR¹ *of S, Ss, SS,* or *esses*) or curve (*river makes a great S*).

's, used for (1, arch.) *God's* in *'sblood &* other oaths; (2, colloq.) *is* in *he's, she's, it's, Smith's*, etc.; (3, colloq.) *has* as in (2), esp. before p.p. as *he's done it*; (4, colloq.) *us* in *let us*, as *let's go*; (5, colloq.) *does*, as *what's he say about it?*

Sab(a)e'an (-bē-), a. & n. (Native) of ancient Yemen; (erron.)=SABIAN. [f. L f. Gk *Sabaios* (*Saba* f. Arab. *Saba'* people of Yemen) +-AN]

Sāb'aism, n. Star-worship. [f. Heb. *çābā* host, -ISM]

Săb'āŏth, n. pl. *Lord of* ~ in N.T. & *Te Deum*, Lord of Hosts. [LL, f. Gk f. Heb. pl. (prec.)]

săbbatār'ian, n. & a. 1. Sabbath-keeping Jew; Christian who accepts (& inculcates) the obligation to observe Sunday strictly as sabbath; Christian individual or member of sect observing Saturday as sabbath, seventh-day baptist etc.; hence ~ISM(3) n. 2. adj. Of ~ tenets. [f. L *sabbatarius* (foll., -ARY¹) +-AN, see -ARIAN]

săbb'ath, n. 1. (Also ~ *day*) seventh day of week as day of religious rest appointed for Israel (~-*day's journey*, distance Israelite might travel on ~, about ⅔ m. also transf. easy journey). 2.(Also ~ *day*) Christian Sunday esp. as day of obligatory abstinence from work & play (chiefly in Presbyterian, nonconformist, & distinctively protestant use, or joc.; *keep, break, the* ~ ; ~-*breaker*), whence ~LESS a. 3. Period of rest. 4. (Usu. *witches'* ~) general meeting of the devil and witches. [f. L *sabbatum* & OF *sab*(*b*)*at*, f. Gk -*ton*, f. Heb. *shabbāth* (*shābath* to rest)]

sabbăt'ic|(al), aa. Of, appropriate to, the sabbath (~*al river*, one in Jewish legend flowing except on sabbath; ~*al year*, seventh year in which Israelites were to cease tilling & release debtors & Israelite slaves, (also) year's leave granted to university professor etc. for study, travel, etc.). Hence ~alLY² adv. [f. F *sabbatique* or LL f. Gk *sabbatikos* (prec., -IC), -AL]

săbb'atize, -ise (-īz), v.i. & t. Keep the, have a, sabbath; make (day) into, keep as, a sabbath. [f. LL *sabbatizare* f. Gk *sabbatizō* (SABBATH, -IZE)]

Sabĕll'ian¹, a. & n. (Rom. hist.). (Member) of the group of tribes in ancient Italy including Sabines, Samnites, Campanians, etc. [f. L *Sabelli* SABINES + -IAN]

Sabĕll'ian², a. & n. (Holder) of the doctrine of Sabellius (3rd c.) that the three Divine persons are merely aspects of one, [f. LL *Sabellianus* (-AN)]

Sāb'ian, a. & n. 1. (Member) of a sect classed in Koran with Moslems, Jews, & Christians, as believers in the true God.

2. (erron.). (Adherent) of SABAISM. [f. Arab. *çabi'* +-AN]

săb'īcu (-kōō), n. Cuban timber-tree; its valuable hard durable wood. [Cuban Sp.]

Săb'īne, a. & n. (One) of the ~*s*, ancient Italians of central Apennines. [f. L *Sabinus*]

sā'ble¹, n. Small brown-furred arctic & subarctic carnivorous quadruped allied to martens; its skin or fur; fine paint-brush made of ~ hair. [ME, f. OF, prob. f. Slav., cf. Pol. & Czech *sobol*]

sā'ble², n. & a. 1. Black as a heraldic colour; (poet., rhet.) the colour black; (poet. & rhet.; pl.) mourning garments, whence **sā'bl**ED² (-beld) a. 2. (Also ~ *antelope*) large stout-horned antelope of which male is black. 3. adj. (poet. & rhet.). Black, dusky, gloomy, dread, (of Negro, sky, sea, night, Fate, etc.; *his* ~ *Majesty*, the devil); hence **săb'L**Y² adv. [ME, f. OF (her.), perh. f. prec.]

săb'ot (-ō), n. 1. Shoe hollowed out from one piece of wood worn by French lower classes; wooden-soled shoe. 2. (mil.). Wooden disc riveted to spherical, metal cup strapped to conical, projectile; (mech.) shoe or armature of pile, boring-rod, etc. Hence ~ED² (-bōd) a. [F, alt. f. *savate* shoe]

săb'otage (-ahzh, -ĭj), n., & v.t. & i. 1. Malicious or wanton destruction, esp. doing of damage to plant etc. by workmen on bad terms with their employers (*the derailing of the train is attributed to* ~ ; *acts of* ~). 2. vb. Commit ~ (on); (fig.) destroy, render useless, as ~ *a scheme*. [F, f. *saboter* (prec., -AGE)]

săb'oteur (-tĕr), n. One who commits sabotage. [F]

sā'bre (-ĕr), n., & v.t. 1. Cavalry sword with curved blade (*the* ~, military force or rule); (in pl., hist.) cavalry unit (cf. *rifle*), cavalry soldier & horse, (*had 3,000* ~*s*); copper tool for skimming molten glass; ~-*bill, -wing*, kinds of bird; ~-*cut*, blow with ~, wound made or scar left by it; ~-*toothed lion* or *tiger*, extinct mammal with long ~-shaped upper canines. 2. v.t. Cut down or wound with ~. [F, earlier *sable* f. G *sabel* f. Pol. *szabla* or Magyar *száblya*]

sā'bretache (-ĕrtăsh), n. Cavalry officer's satchel on long straps from left of waist-belt. [F, f. G *säbeltasche* (prec., *tasche* pocket)]

sabreur (sahbrĕr'), n. Cavalryman with sabre, esp. (often *beau* ~) cavalry officer of dashing appearance. [F]

săb'ūlous, a. Sandy, of sand, (pedant.); (med., of secretions esp. in urinary organs) granular. [f. L *sabulosus* (*sabulum* sand, -OSE¹)]

sabū'rra, n. (med.). Foul granular matter deposited in stomach. [L, = sand, ballast, cf. prec.]

săc, n. Baglike membrane-enclosed cavity in animal or vegetable organism;

membranous envelope of hernia, cyst, tumour, etc.; (of dress) = SACK¹. [F, or f. L saccus SACK¹]

sacc′āte, a. (Bot.) dilated into bag; contained in sac. [f. mod. L saccatus (prec., -ATE²)]

sacc′har|(o)- (-ka-), comb. form of med. L f. Gk sakkharon SUGAR, of many words chiefly in scientific use; ~ATE¹(3), salt of sacchá′rIC acid, a dibasic acid formed by the action of nitric acid on dextrose; ~IDE, (now more commonly used in chem. for) ~ose; ~IF′EROUS, sugar-bearing; ~IFY, convert (starch) into sugar; ~IFICA′TION; ~IM′ETER, instrument for testing sugars by polarized light; ~IM′ETRY; ~IN(e) n., intensely sweet substance got from coal-tar & used to sweeten food for the gouty, diabetic, etc.; ~INE¹ a., sugary, of or containing or like sugar; ~O-, sugar-&-; ~OID a. (geol.), granular like sugar, (n.) sugarlike substance; ~O-M′ETER, hydrometer used, esp. in brewing, to estimate amount of sugar in solution by specific gravity; ~OSE², ordinary sugar, cane-sugar.

sắc′cifórm (-ks-), a. Sac-shaped. [SAC, -FORM]

sắcc′ül|e, n. Small sac or cyst. Hence (see -UL-) ~AR¹, ~ATE², ~āted, aa., ~A-TION n. [f. L sacculus (SAC, -ULE)]

să′cerdócў, n. (rare). Sacerdotalism; priestly function. [f. L sacerdotium (sacerdos -otis priest lit. sacrifice-giver f. sacer holy, dare give)]

să′cerdōtage, n. (joc.). Sacerdotalism; priest-ridden state. [as prec. w. ref. to dotage, cf. anecdotage]

sắcerdōt′al, a. Of priest(s) or priesthood, priestly; (of doctrines etc.) ascribing sacrificial functions & supernatural powers to ordained priests, claiming excessive authority for the priesthood. Hence ~LY² adv., ~ISM(3), ~IST(2), nn., ~IZE(3) v.t. [ME, f. OF, or f. LL sacerdotalis as SACERDOCY, -AL)]

sắch′ĕm, n. Supreme chief of some Amer.-Ind. tribes; big-wig, eminent person. [Amer.-Ind.]

să′chet (-shā), n. Small perfumed bag; (packet of) dry perfume for laying among clothes etc. [F, dim. of sac f. L saccus]

sắck¹, n., & v.t. **1.** Large usu. oblong bag for storing & conveying goods usu. open at one end & made of coarse flax or hemp (give one, get, the ~, dismiss him, be dismissed, from service, cf. ' On luy a donné son sac, hee hath his pasport given him ' in Cotgrave), whence ~′ING¹(3) n.; ~ with contents (usu. of; also ~′FUL n.); amount (of corn, coal, flour, wool, potatoes, etc.) usu. put in ~ as unit of measure or weight (at 12/- the ~). **2.** (Of dress; also as pseudo-F sacque, sac) kind of lady's loose gown (arch.); pleated silk appendage attached to shoulders of dress & falling to ground & forming train; man's or woman's loose-hanging coat not shaped to

back. **3.** ~′cloth, coarse fabric of flax or hemp, ~ing, (fig.) mourning or penitential garb (esp. in ~cloth & ashes bibl.); ~-race, between competitors tied in ~s up to the neck. **4.** v.t. Put into ~(s); (colloq.) give the ~ to, dismiss from service; (colloq.) defeat in match or fight. [OE sacc f. L f. Gk sakkos f. Heb. saq]

sắck², v.t., & n. **1.** (Of victorious army or its commander) plunder, give over to plunder, (captured city etc.); (of burglars etc.) carry off contents of. **2.** n. ~ing of captured place. [16th c., f. F sac in phr. mettre à sac put to sack, f. It. sacco; vb f. n.]

sắck³, n. (hist.). Kinds of white wine formerly imported from Spain & the Canaries (sherry, Canary, etc., ~; ~ posset, whey, etc., beverages containing it; halfpennyworth of bread to intolerable deal of ~, absurd excess of the unessential, w. ref. to 1 Henry IV, II. iv. 592). [16th c. wyne seck, f. F vin sec dry wine]

sắck′but, n. (Old name for) trombone. [f. F saquebute sackbut from 15th c., = ONF saqueboute hook for pulling man off horse (saquer pull, boute as BUTT⁴)]

‖ **sắck′lèss**, a. (arch., Sc. & north.). Innocent (of), harmless, feeble-minded. [OE saclēas f. ON saklauss (SAKE, -LESS)]

sacque (săk). See SACK¹.

sắc′ral, a. (Anat.) of the sacrum; (anthropol.) of or for sacred rites. [SACRUM, -AL]

sắc′rament, n., & v.t. **1.** Religious ceremony or act regarded as outward & visible sign of inward & spiritual grace (applied by the Eastern, pre-Reformation Western, & R.-C. Churches to the seven rites of baptism, confirmation, the eucharist, penance, extreme unction, orders, & matrimony; restricted by most Protestants to baptism & the eucharist; the ~, the ~ of the altar, the Blessed or Holy S~, the eucharist, also the consecrated elements esp. the bread or Host; take, receive, the ~ to do or upon, as confirmation of some promise or oath). **2.** Thing of mysterious & sacred significance, sacred influence, symbol, etc. **3.** Oath or solemn engagement taken. **4.** v.t. (esp. in p.p.). Bind by oath. [ME, f. OF sacrement f. L sacramentum military oath, legal caution-money, f. sacrare (sacer sacr-SACRED), -MENT, used in Christian L as transl. of Gk mustērion MYSTERY¹]

sắcramĕn′tal, a. & n. **1.** Of (the nature of) a or the sacrament, whence ~ITY (-ăl²) n.; (of doctrine etc.) attaching great importance to the sacraments, whence ~ISM(3), ~IST(2), nn.; hence ~LY² adv. **2.** n. Observance analogous to but not reckoned among the sacraments, e.g. use of holy water or sign of the cross. [ME, f. OF, or f. LL sacramentalis (prec., -AL)]

sắcramentār′ian, a. & n. **1.** (hist.). (Also sacramentary) denying, denier of, the Real Presence (as holding that 'body &

blood of Christ' was used only in a sacramental, i.e. symbolic, sense). **2.** Holding or involving, holder of, high sacramental doctrine, whence ~ISM(3) n. [f. med. L SACRAMENT(*arius* -ARY[1]), see -ARIAN]

sacrār'ium, n. (pl. *-ia*). (Rom. ant.) shrine, adytum, room of Penates in house; (also *sanctuary*) part of church within altar-rails; (R.-C.) piscina. [L (*sacer sacr-* holy, -ARIUM)]

sāc'rĕd, a. (rarely ~*est*). **1.** Consecrated or held dear *to* a deity, dedicated or reserved or appropriated *to* some person or purpose; made holy by religious association, hallowed, (~ *book, writings*, embodying laws etc. of a religion; ~ *history*, related in Bible; ~ *number*, associated with religious symbolism, e.g. 7; ~ *poetry, music*, on religious themes; ~ *concert*, of ~ music; as specific epithet of beasts etc. now or once ~ to some god, as ~ *ibis, monkey, beetle*). **2.** Safeguarded or required by religion or reverence or tradition, indefeasible, inviolable, sacrosanct, (*His most S~ Majesty the King; the ~ right of insurrection; regards it as a ~ duty; their property, persons, will be held ~; no place was ~ from him, from outrage*). Hence ~LY[2] adv., ~NESS n. [ME, p.p. of obs. *sacre* consecrate f. OF *sacrer* f. L *sacrare* (*sacer sacr-* holy)]

sāc'rifice, n., & v.t. & i. **1.** Slaughter of animal or person, surrender of a possession, as offering to a deity, (fig.) act of prayer or thanksgiving or penitence as propitiation; what is thus slaughtered or surrendered or done, victim, offering; (theol.) the Crucifixion, the Eucharist as either a propitiatory offering of the body & blood of Christ or an act of thanksgiving. **2.** Giving up of thing for the sake of another that is higher or more urgent, thing thus given up, loss thus entailed, (*will gain nothing by the ~ of your principles; at some ~ of regularity; surplus stock for sale at a large ~; his health was the ~ demanded of him; the great or last ~*, esp., death for one's country in war; SELF-~); so **sācrifi'cial** (-shl) a., **sācrifi'cialLY**[2] (-sha-) adv. **3.** vb. Offer (as) ~ (*to*); give up, treat as secondary or of inferior importance, devote, *to* (*has ~d herself, her whole life, her pleasures, to his interest; ~ accuracy to vividness*); resign oneself to parting with. [ME, f. OF f. L *sacrificium* (*sacrificus* as prec., -FIC); vb f. n.]

sāc'rilĕge, n. Robbery or profanation of sacred building, outrage on consecrated person or thing, violation of what is sacred. Hence **sācrilĕ'giOUS** (-jus; or -ij'us) a., **sācrilĕ'giousLY**[2] (-jus-) adv., **sācrilĕ'giST**(1) n. (rare). [ME, f. OF f. L *sacrilegium* f. *sacrilegus* (SACRED, *legere* collect)]

sāc'ring, n. (arch.). Consecration of elements in the mass; ordination & consecration of bishop, sovereign, etc.; ~-

~-*bell*, rung at elevation of Host. [ME, f. obs. *sacre* (SACRED, -ING[1])]

sāc'rĭst, n. Official keeping sacred vessels etc. of religious house or church. [OF (-e), or f. med.L *sacrista* (SACRED, -IST)]

sāc'ristan, n. Sexton of parish church (arch.); = prec. [ME, f. med. L SACRIST*anus* SEXTON]

sāc'rĭstў, n. Repository for vestments, vessels, etc., of a church. [F (-*ie*), or f. med. L *sacristia* (SACRIST, -IA[1])]

sāc'rosănct, a. (Of person, place, law, etc.) secured by religious sanction against outrage, inviolable. Hence **sācrosănc'tITY** n. [f. L *sacrosanctus* (*sacro* abl. of *sacrum* SACRED rite, SAINT a.)]

sāc'r|um, n. Composite triangular bone of anchylosed vertebrae forming back of pelvis. Hence ~AL a., ~O- comb. form. [f. L *os sacrum* sacred bone (from sacrificial use)]

săd, a. (-dd-). Sorrowful, mournful, showing or causing sorrow, (*a ~der & a wiser man*, of one who has had distressing experience; *in ~ earnest*, seriously); (derog., usu. joc.) shocking, deplorably bad, incorrigible, (*is a ~ slut, coward*, etc.; ~ *dog*, rake, scapegrace; *writes ~ stuff*); (of pastry, bread, etc.) heavy, doughy; (of colour) dull, neutral-tinted; ~-*iron*, solid flat-iron. Hence ~d'EN[3] v.t. & i., ~'LY[2] adv., ~'NESS n., ~d'ISH[1](2) a. [OE *sæd*, OS *sad*, OHG *sat*, ON *sathr*, Goth. *saths* f. Gmc **sadhaz* full, cogn. w. L *satis*]

săd'dle, n., & v.t. **1.** Rider's seat placed on back of horse etc. (usu. concave-shaped of leather with side-flaps & girths & stirrups) or forming part of bicycle etc. or of some agricultural machines (PACK[1], SIDE, ~~; *in the ~*, mounted, fig. in office or control; *put ~ on right, wrong, horse*, blame right, wrong, person). **2.** Part of shaft-horse's harness that bears shafts. **3.** ~-shaped thing, e.g. ridge between two summits, support for cable or wire on top of suspension-bridge pier or telegraph-pole, joint *of* mutton or venison consisting of the two loins. **4.** ~*back*, (archit.) tower roof with two opposite gables, ~backed hill, kinds of bird (esp. the grey crow) & fish, (adj.) ~backed; ~*backed*, with upper outline concave, (archit.) having ~back; ~*bag*, one of pair of bags laid across horse behind ~, kind of carpeting (in imitation of Eastern ~-bags of camels) used in upholstering chairs etc.; ~-*boiler*, of concave form used in heating-apparatus; ~-*bow* (-bō), arched front of ~ [BOW[1]]; ~-*cloth*, laid on horse's back under ~; ~*fast*, firmly seated in ~; ~-*horse*, for riding; ~-*pin*, by which bicycle etc. ~ fits into socket; ~-*tree*, frame of ~, also N.-Amer. tulip-tree (with ~-shaped leaves); hence ~LESS a. **5.** v.t. Put ~ on (horse etc.); burden (person) *with* task, responsibility, etc.; put (burden) *on* or *upon* (person). [OE *sadol*, OHG *satal*, ON *sothull* f. Gmc* *sadhulaz*; vb f. OE *sadolian*]

sadd'l|er, n. Maker of or dealer in saddles & other equipment for horses; (mil.) man in charge of mounted regiment's ~ery. Hence ~ERY(1, 2, 3) n. [-ER¹]

Sadd'ucee, n. Member of a Jewish sect or party (cf. PHARISEE, ESSENE) of time of Christ that denied resurrection of the dead, existence of spirits, & obligation of the traditional law. Hence or cogn. **Sădducē'AN** a., ~ISM(2) n. [f. LL f. Gk *Saddoukaios* f. Heb. *Çadduqi* prob. = descendant of *Zadok* (2 Sam. viii, 17)]

sadhu (sah'dōō), n. (India) holy man. [Skr., = pious]

sa'd|ism (sah-), n. Form of sexual perversion marked by love of cruelty; pleasure derived from inflicting or watching cruelty. So ~IST(2) n., ~is'tIC a. [f. F *sadisme* (Count de *Sade* 1740–1814, -ISM)]

safa'ri (-ahr-), n. Hunting expedition in Africa (esp. in phr. *on* ~); sportsman's or traveller's caravan. [Swahili, f. Arab. *safar* journey]

safe¹, n. (Also *meat-*~) ventilated cupboard for provisions; fireproof & burglar-proof receptacle for valuables. [orig. *save*, f. SAVE¹]

safe², a. 1. (Pred., after *come, arrive, bring, keep*, etc.) uninjured (*parcel came* ~; *saw them* ~ *home*; often ~ *& sound*); secure, out of or not exposed to danger (*from*), (*now we are, can feel,* ~; *is* ~ *from his enemies*). 2. Affording security or not involving danger (*put it in a* ~ *place*; *is it* ~ *to leave him?*; ~ *custody, convoy*, etc.; *err, error, on the* ~ *side*, with margin of security against risks; *dog is not* ~ *to touch*; *it is* ~ *to say*, may be said without risk of exaggeration or falsehood); debarred from escaping or doing harm (*have got him* ~). 3. Cautious & unenterprising, consistently moderate, that can be reckoned on, unfailing, certain *to do* or be, sure to become, (*a* ~ *critic, statesman*; ~ *methods*; *a* ~ CATCH², *winner*; *is a* ~ *first*, sure to take a first class; *is* ~ *to win, be there*); hence ~'NESS (-fn-) n. 4. ~ *conduct* (document conveying) privilege granted by sovereign, commander, etc., of being protected from arrest or harm on particular occasion or in district; ~ *deposit*, building containing strong-rooms and safes let separately; ~'*guard*, = ~ *conduct*, (also & usu.) proviso or stipulation or quality or circumstance that tends to prevent some evil or protect, (v.t.) guard, protect, (esp. rights etc.) by precaution or stipulation (|| ~*guarding duties*, on imports, against competition held to be unfair); ~ *keeping*, custody. Hence ~'LY² (-fl-) adv. [ME & OF *sauf* f. L *salvus*]

safe'ty, n. (-ft-), n. 1. Being safe, freedom from danger or risks, (*there is* ~ *in numbers* prov.; *is in* ~; *cannot do it with* ~; *play for* ~, avoid risks in game or fig.; ~ *first!*, motto inculcating caution). 2. Safeness, being sure or likely to bring no danger, (*is the* ~ *of the experiment certain?*; *factor* or *coefficient of* ~ in engineering, ratio of material's strength to strain to be allowed for). 3. (Also ~*-catch*) contrivance for locking gun-trigger, gun with this. 4. (Also ~*-bicycle*) bicycle of usual low-saddled modern form (opp. *ordinary*). 5. ~*-bell*, strap securing occupant to seat, in aeroplane, motor-car, etc.; ~ *curtain*, fireproof curtain cutting off the auditorium in a theatre from the stage; ~ *film*, cinematographic film on slow-burning or non-inflammable base (esp. in sub-standard sizes); ~ *fuse*, FUSE² containing a slow-burning composition for firing detonators from a distance, (electr.) protective FUSE¹; ~*-glass*, TRIPLEX glass; ~ *lamp*, miner's so protected as not to ignite fire-damp; ~ *match*, only igniting on prepared surface; ~*-pin*, with point that returns to head & is caught in a guard so that wearer may not be pricked nor pin come out; ~ *razor*, kinds with guard to prevent cutting skin; ~*-valve* in steam-boiler, opening automatically to relieve excessive pressure, (fig.) means of giving harmless vent to excitement etc. (*sit on the* ~*-valve*, follow policy of repression). [ME, f. OF *sauvete* f. med. L *salvitatem* (prec., -TY)]

säff'ian, n. Leather of goatskin or sheepskin tanned with sumach & dyed in bright colours. [f. Russ. *safiyanu*]

säf'flower (-owr), n. A thistle-like plant yielding red dye used esp. in rouge; its dried petals; the dye made from them. [f. Du. *saffloer* f. OF *saffleur* f. early It. *saffiore*, orig. unkn.]

säff'ron, n., a., & v.t. 1. Orange-coloured stigmas of the autumnal crocus used for colouring & flavouring confectionery & liquors (*bastard* ~, the plant safflower); MEADOW ~. 2. adj. & n. ~*-colour(ed)*, whence ~Y² a.; ~ *cake*, cake flavoured with ~, also tablet of pressed ~. 3. v.t. Colour with.or like ~. [ME, f. OF *safran* ult. f. Arab. *za'faran*]

säff'ranin, n. Colouring-matter of saffron; yellowish-red coal-tar colour. [prec., -IN]

säg, v.i. & t. (-gg-), & n. 1. Sink or subside under weight or pressure; hang sideways, be lopsided, (*gate, bridge,* ~*s*); have downward bulge or curve in middle (*ceiling, beam, stretched rope, ladder,* ~*s*), (trans.) cause to curve thus; (commerc.) decline in price; (of ship) drift from course (esp. ~ *to leeward*); hence ~**g'Y²** (-g-) a. 2. n. Amount that rope etc. ~s, distance from middle of its curve to straight line between supports; sinking, subsidence; decline in price; (naut.) tendency to leeward. [15th c., app. rel. to MLG *sacken*, Du. *zakken* subside]

sa'ga (sah-), n. A medieval Icelandic or Norwegian prose narrative, esp. one embodying history of Icelandic family or

Norwegian king, (transf.) story of heroic achievement or adventure; series of connected books giving the history of a family etc. [ON, = narrative, cogn. w. SAW²]

saga'cious (-shus), a. Mentally penetrating, gifted with discernment, practically wise, acute-minded, shrewd; (of sayings, plans, etc.) showing sagacity; (of animals) exceptionally intelligent, seeming to reason or deliberate. Hence or cogn. ~LY² adv., sagA'CITY n. [f. L sagax (sagire discern acutely), -ACIOUS]

săg'amŏre, n. = SACHEM (1st sense). [f. Amer.-Ind. sagamo]

sāge¹, n. Aromatic herb with dull greyish-green leaves; its leaves used in cookery (~ & onions, stuffing used for goose, duck, pork, etc.); ~-brush, growth of alkaline plants characterizing some sterile districts of U.S. (~-cock, -grouse, -hare, etc., found in this); ~ cheese, flavoured & mottled by addition of ~-infusion to the curd; ~-green, colour of ~-leaves; ~ tea, medicinal infusion of ~-leaves. Hence sā'gy² a. [ME & OF sauge f. L salvia]

sāge², a. & n. 1. Wise, discreet, judicious, having the wisdom of experience, of or indicating profound wisdom, (often iron.) wise-looking, solemn-faced; hence ~'LY² (-jl-) adv., ~'NESS (-jn-) n. 2. n. Profoundly wise man (often iron.), esp. any of the ancients traditionally reputed wisest of their time (the seven ~s, 7 Greeks each credited with a notable saying); hence ~'SHIP (-jsh-) n. [ME & OF, f. Gallo-Rom. *sapius (L sapere bc SAPIENT)]

săg'ar, n. Case of baked fireproof clay enclosing pottery while it is baked. [prob. contr. of safeguard]

Sagitt'a, n. A northern constellation, the Arrow. [L, = arrow]

Săgittār'ius, n. Constellation & ninth sign of zodiac, the Archer. [L (prec., -ARY¹)]

sā'gittāte, -ātĕd, aa. (bot., zool.). Shaped like arrow-head. [SAGITTA, -ATE²]

săg'ō, n. (pl. ~s). (Kinds of palm & cycad with pith yielding) kind of starch used as food in puddings etc. [f. Malay sagu]

‖ **sahaa'** (sa-hah'), int. Goodbye. [Maltese]

Sahār'|a (sa-h-), n. Great Libyan desert; arid tract (lit. & fig.). Hence ~AN, ~IAN, ~IC, aa. [f. Arab. çahra]

Sah'ib, n. (fem. mĕm'sahib). 1. (India). European as spoken of or to by Indians; an honorific affix (Colonel ~, Jones ~, Raja ~, Khan ~). 2. (colloq.; s~). Gentleman (pukka s~). [Hind., f. Arab. çahib friend]

said¹. See SAY².

Said² (săd). Var. of SEID.

saig'a (or sī-), n. Antelope of steppes. [Russ.]

sail¹, n. 1. Piece of canvas or other textile material extended on rigging to catch wind & propel vessel, (collect.) some or all of ship's ~s (CARRY, CROWD², hoist,

lower, MAKE¹, SET¹, SHORTEN, STRIKE, ~; take in ~, fig., moderate one's ambitions; take WIND¹ out of ~s; full ~ adv., with all ~ spread lit. & fig.; under ~, with ~s set). 2. (collect.). Ships (in giving number of ships in squadron or company; a fleet of twenty ~). 3. Ship (esp. in ~ ho!, cry announcing that ship is in sight). 4. pl. (naut. sl.; hist.). ‖ Chief petty officer in charge of rigging; one who makes or repairs ~s. 5. Wind-catching apparatus, now usu. set of boards, attached to arm of windmill. 6. ~-fish's dorsal fin, tentacle of nautilus. 7. (Also wind-~) funnel-shaped bag on ship's deck or above mine giving ventilation. 8. ~-arm, arm of windmill; ~-axle, on which ~-arms revolve; ~-cloth, canvas for ~s, also dress-material; ~-fish, kinds with large dorsal fin, esp. basking shark. Hence (-)~ED² (-ld), ~'LESS, aa. [OE, OS segel, OHG segal, ON segl, f. Gmc *saglam]

sail², v.i. & t., & n. 1. (Of vessel or person on board) travel on water by use of sails (~-ing-ship, -vessel, opp. steamer; ~ close to or near the wind, nearly against it, also fig. come near transgressing a law or moral principle); (of vessel or person on board) travel on water by use of sails or engine-power, start on voyage, (we ~ next week; list of ~ING¹s from London; ~ing orders, instructions to captain for departure, destination, etc.). 2. (Of bird, cloud, moon, etc.) glide in air; (esp. of women) walk in stately manner. 3. Travel over or along, navigate, glide through, (the sea, Spanish main, sky, etc.). 4. Control navigation of (ship; plain ~ING¹, used pred. to describe task etc. that is not perplexing; ~ing-master, officer navigating yacht); set (toy-boat) afloat. 5. ~ into (sl.), inveigh against, scold, rate, attack. 6. n. Voyage or excursion in ~ing-vessel (go for a ~); voyage of specified duration (is ten days' ~ from Plymouth); ~'plane, glider. [OE siglan, segl(i)an, (prec.)]

sail'er, n. Ship of specified sailing-power (fast, good, bad, ~). [-ER¹]

sail'or, n. Seaman, mariner, esp. one below rank of officer (good, bad, ~, person not, very, liable to sea-sickness); ~ hat, of straw with straight narrow brim & flat top worn by women, also with turned-up brim in imitation of ~'s worn by children; ~-man, (vulg. & joc. for) ~; ~s' home, institution for lodging ~s cheaply ashore; ~'s knot, way of tying necktie. Hence ~ING¹(1) n., ~LESS, ~LY¹, aa. [var. of prec., see -ER¹, -OR]

‖ **sain**, v.t. (arch.). Make sign of the cross on, bless, protect by divine power or enchantment. [OE segnian, = OS segnŏn, OHG signŏn, ON signa, f. L signare mark (SIGN¹um)]

sain'foin, n. Plant of pea family grown for forage. [F (sain SANE, foin hay f. L faenum)]

saint, a. (*unstressed* sent, snt; *abbr*. St, S., *in pl*. Sts, SS.), n., & v.t. **1.** Holy, canonized or officially recognized by the Church as having won by exceptional holiness a high place in heaven & veneration on earth, (usu. as prefix to name of person or archangel as *St Paul, St Michael*, whence ellipt. names of churches as *St Peter's*, & of towns called after their churches often with loss of possessive sign as *St Andrews* & *St Albans*, & many Christian & family names taken either from patron ~ or from local names as above; also in some names of churches not called after ~s, as *St Saviour's, Sepulchre's, Faith, Cross*); *St* —*'s day*, Church festival in memory of particular ~. **2.** *St Andrew*, patron ~ of Scotland (*St A.'s day*, 30th Nov.); *St Anthony's, Elmo's*, FIRE[1]. *St Bartholomew*; *St B.'s*, (used for) St B.'s Hospital in London, abbr. *Bart's*; *massacre of St B.*, of Huguenots in France on St B.'s day, 24 Aug., 1572. *St Bernard* (*the Great, Little, St B.*, Alpine passes); *St Bernard dog* or *St Bernard*, breed kept by monks of Hospice on Great St Bernard pass for rescue of travellers. *St Cecilia*, patron ~ of music; *St Charles*, King Charles I as canonized martyr; *St David*, patron ~ of Wales (*St D.'s day*, 1st Mar.); *St Denis*, patron ~ of France. *St George*, patron ~ of England (*St G.'s day*, 23rd Ap.); *St G.'s*, (used for) St G.'s Hospital in London; *St G.'s, Hanover Square*, London church at which many West-end weddings take place; *St G.'s cross*, the *Greek* CROSS[1]. *St Germain* (or *Faubourg St G.*), aristocratic quarter of Paris; *St Gotthard* (*the St G.*, the Alpine pass of St G. or the tunnelled railway used instead of it). *St Helēn'a*, (used for) place of exile (w. ref. to Napoleon, 1815–21). *St James's* (or *the Court of St James's* or *St James*), the British court (esp. in distinction from foreign courts; w. ref. to St James's Palace in London); (also) fashionable district in London about St James's Palace. *St-John's-wort*, kinds of yellow-flowered wild & garden plant. *St Leger*, horse-race at Doncaster for three-year-olds, f. founder's name; *St Lubbock's day*, any of the BANK[3]-holidays instituted 1871 by Sir J. Lubbock's Act; *St Luke's* SUMMER. *St Mark's*, (used for) St M.'s church in Venice; *St Martin's-le-Grand*, (used for) the General Post Office; *St* MARTIN'S *summer*; *St Michael & St George*, order of knighthood; *St Michael*, kind of orange, f. one of the Azores so called; *St* MONDAY. *St Patrick*, patron ~ of Ireland (*St P.'s Day*, 17th Mar.; *order of St P.*, Irish order of knighthood); *St Paul's*, cathedral of see of London; *St Peter's*, (used for) the church of St Peter in the Vatican in Rome; *St Peter's chair*, (used for) the office of Pope. *St Sophia* (used for) the mosque of St S. in Constantinople; *St*

Stephen's, (used for) Parliament (w. ref. to former use of St S.'s chapel, Westminster, for meetings of House of Commons); *St Swithin's*, the day (15th July) whose rain or absence of rain is said to presage the same for 40 days. *St Thomas's*, (used for) St Thomas's Hospital in London. *St* VALENTINE'S *day*; *St Vitus's* DANCE[2]. **3.** n. One of the blessed dead or other member of the company of heaven (*departed* ~, phr. used by or attributed to mourners, = deceased person); canonized person (see adj. sense; *patron* ~, selected as heavenly protector of person or place, esp. church, often named after him); (bibl., arch., & with some mod. sects) one of God's chosen people, member of the Christian Church or speaker's branch of it; person of great real or affected holiness (*would provoke, try the patience of, a* ~; *young* ~s *old devils* or *sinners*, early piety is no good sign; LATTER-*day* ~s); ~'s-*day*, Church festival in memory of a ~, often observed as holiday at schools etc.; hence ~'DOM, ~'HOOD (-t-h-), ~'SHIP, ~'LING[1], nn., ~'LIKE, ~'LY[1], aa., ~'lINESS n. **4.** v.t. Canonize, admit to the calendar of ~s; call or regard as a ~; (p.p.) worthy to be so regarded, of ~ly life (of place etc.) sacred. [ME, f. OF, f. L *sanctus* p.p. of *sancire* consecrate]'

Saint-Simōn'ian, a. & n. (Advocate) of the socialism of the Comte de Saint-Simon (1760–1825) with State control of property & distribution of produce. So **Saint-Sim'on**IST(2), **Saint-Sim'on**ITE[1] (1), **Saint-Sim'on**ISM(3), ~ISM(3), nn. [-IAN]

saith. See SAY[2].

saithe (sāth), n. (Sc.). Coal-fish. [f. ON *seithr*]

Sāīt'ic, a. Of Sais, ancient capital of Lower Egypt (~ *dynasties*, 26th–30th of Egyptian kings). [f. L f. Gk *Saïtikos* (*Saïtēs* f. *Sais*, -ITE[1])]

sāke, n. *For the* ~ *of* —, *for* —*'s* or *my* etc. ~, out of consideration for, in the interest of, because of, owing to, in order to please or honour or get or keep, (common n. with sibilant ending does not take the extra syllable of the possessive before ~, but has usu. the apostrophe, as *for peace', conscience'; goodness', ~*, cf. *for God's, the children's, Phyllis's, ~*; *for my own ~ as well as yours*; *for both, all, our* ~s or rarely ~; *for his name's ~*, because he bears the name he does or in the interest of his reputation; *persecuted for opinion's* ~; *for any* ~ in entreaties, for one reason if not for another; *for old* ~*'s* ~, in memory of old days). [OE *sacu* contention, charge, fault, sake, = OS *saka*, OHG *sahha*, ON *sǫk*, also OE *sæc*(c), Goth. *sakjō*]

sā'ké (-ā), n. Japanese fermented liquor made from rice. [f. Jap. *sake*]

sāk'er, n. **1.** Large lanner falcon used in hawking, esp. the female larger than the male or ~ET[1] n. **2.** (hist.). Old form of cannon. [ME, f. OF *sacre* (in both senses) f. Sp., Port., *sacro*, f. Arab. *çaqr*]

sa′ki (sah-), n. S.-American monkey with long non-prehensile tail, and neck-ruff. [native name, through F]

sa′kĭa (sah-), n. Eastern water-wheel for irrigation. [Arab. *sāqiya* (*saqā* irrigate)]

sal (sahl), **saul**, n. Valuable Indian timber (tree). [Hind.]

salaam′ (-lahm), n., & v.i. & t. **1.** Oriental salutation ' Peace '; Indian obeisance with or without this, low bow of head & body with right palm on forehead. **2.** vb. Make ∼ (to). [f. Arab. *salam*]

sāl′able, **-lea-**, a. Fit for sale, finding purchasers ; ∼ *price*, that article will fetch. Hence **sālabIL′ITY** (*or* **-lea-**) n. [-ABLE]

salā′cious (-shus), a. Lustful, lecherous. Hence or cogn. ∼LY² adv., ∼NESS, salA²-CITY, nn. [f. L *salax* (*salire* leap), -ACIOUS]

săl′ad, n. Cold dish of various mixtures of raw or cooked vegetables or herbs usu. seasoned with oil, vinegar, etc., & eaten with or including cold fish, meat, hard--boiled eggs, etc. ; vegetable or herb suit-able for eating raw ; ∼*-days*, inexperi-enced youth ; ∼*-dressing*, mixture of oil, vinegar, cream, etc., taken with ∼ ; ∼*-oil*, kinds of oil for ∼-dressing. [ME, f. OF *salade* ult. f. L *sal* salt, -ADE(1)]

săl′amănder, n. **1.** Lizard-like animal supposed to live in fire ; person who can endure great heat, fire-eating soldier etc. ; spirit living in fire (cf. *sylph*, *gnome*, *nymph*) ; (zool.) kinds of tailed amphibian, whence **sălamăn′drOID** a. & n. **2.** Red--hot iron for firing gunpowder, hot iron plate for browning omelettes etc. Hence **sălamăn′drIAN**, **sălamăn′drINE¹**, aa. [ME, f. OF (*-dre*), f. L f. Gk *salamandra*]

sala′mĕ (-lah-), n. Italian sausage highly salted and flavoured often with garlic. [It.]

săl-ammōn′iăc, n. Ammonium chloride. [L *sal* salt, AMMONIAC]

săl′angāne (-ngg-), n. Swallow making edible nest. [F, f. *salamga* name in Luzon]

salār′iăt, n. The salaried class. [F]

săl′arÿ, n., & v.t. **1.** Fixed periodical payment made to person doing other than manual or mechanical work (cf. *wages*). **2.** v.t. Pay ∼y to (chiefly in p.p. ∼*ied* pr. -rĭd). [ME, f. AF (*-ie*), = OF *salaire* f. L *salarium* orig. soldier's salt-money (*sal* salt, -ARY¹)]

şāle, n. Exchange of a commodity for money or other valuable consideration, selling (*on*, *for*, ∼, offered for purchase ; ∼ *&*, or *or*, *return*, arrangement by which retailer takes quantity of goods with right of returning all that he fails to sell), amount sold (*the* ∼*s were enormous*); public auction (*put up for* ∼, offer at auction) ; rapid disposal at reduced prices of shop's stock at end of season ; BILL³ *of* ∼ ; ∼*-ring*, ring of buyers at auction ; ∼*s′man*, ∼*s′woman*, person engaged in

selling goods in shop or as middleman between producer & retailer, whence ∼*s′man*SHIP (-lz-) n., skill in this art ; ∼*s resistance*, the opposition or apathy of the prospective customer etc., to be overcome by ∼smanship ; ∼*s tax*, tax on (receipts from) ∼s. [OE *sala* prob. f. ON *sala* f. root *sal*- SELL]

saleable. Var. of SALABLE.

‖ **Sāl′em**, n. Nonconformist chapel. [*Heb.* vii. 2]

săl′ep, n. Nutritive meal from dried tubers of some orchidaceous plants. [F f. Turk., f. Arab. *tha′leb*]

*****sălerăt′us**, n. Impure bicarbonate of potash or sodium bicarbonate as in-gredient in baking-powders. [f. mod. L *sal aeratus* AERATED salt]

Săl′ian¹, a. Of the Salii or priests of Mars. [L *Salii* pl. (*salire* leap), -AN]

Săl′ian², a. & n. (Member) of Frankish tribe near Zuyder Zee from which the Merovingians were descended. [LL *Salii* the tribe, -AN]

Săl′ĭc, **Salique′** (-ĕk), aa. (Form *-ic*) = prec., adj. (∼ *law*, Frankish law-book extant in Merovingian & Carolingian times); (*-ic*, *-ique*) ∼ *law*, law excluding females from dynastic succession, esp. as alleged fundamental law of French monarchy (based on a quotation, not re-ferring to such succession, from the law--book above). [f. F *Salique* or med. L *Salicus* f. *Salii* (prec.), -IC]

săl′icĭn, n. Bitter crystalline principle got from willow-bark & used medicinally. So **săl′icYL** n., **sălicÿl′IC** a. (*salicylic acid*, used as antiseptic & for rheumatism), **sali′cÿlATE¹**(3) n., **sali′cÿlIZE**(5) & in same sense **sali′cÿlATE³** vv.t., **sali′cÿl-ISM**(5) n., **sali′cÿlOUS** (chem.) a. [F (*-ine*), f. L *salix* *-icis* willow, -IN]

sali′cional (-shon-), **săl′icĕt**, nn. Organ stop of soft reedy tone as of willow pipe. [G, f. L *salix* (prec.) w. suff.]

săl′ient, a. & n. **1.** Leaping or dancing (pedant., joc.), (of water etc., poet.) jetting forth, (∼ *point*, arch., initial stage or origin or first beginning, from old med. use = heart as it first shows in an embryo); (of angle, esp. in fortif., opp. RE-ENTRANT) pointing outwards ; jutting out, promi-nent, conspicuous, most noticeable, (∼ *points*, *features*, *characteristics*). **2.** n. A ∼ angle or part in fortification (*the S*∼, that at Ypres in the 1914–18 war). Hence **săl′ĭENCE**, **săl′ĭENCY**, nn., ∼LY² adv. [f. L *salire* leap, -ENT]

salif′erous, a. (geol.). (Of strata) con-taining much salt. [L *sal* salt, -I-, -FEROUS]

săl′īne (*or* salĭn′), a. & n. **1.** (Of natural waters, springs, etc.) impregnated with salt or salts, whence **sălinōM′ETER** n. ; (of taste) salt ; (of chemical salts, of the nature of a salt ; (of medicines) containing salt(s) of alkaline metals or magnesium ; hence **salin′ITY** n., **salīn′o-** comb. form. **2.** n.

Salt lake, spring, marsh, etc.; salt-pan, salt-works; ~ substance; ~ purge; solution of salt & water. [ME; prec., -INE¹]

Salique. See SALIC.

saliv'a, n. Colourless liquid given by mixed secretions of salivary & mucous glands discharged into mouth & assisting mastication, spittle. So **săl'ivARY¹** a. [L]

săl'iv|āte, v.t. & i. Produce unusual secretion of saliva in (person) usu. with mercury; secrete or discharge saliva esp. in excess. So ~A'TION n. [f. L SALIVAre, -ATE³]

salle (sahl), n. Hall, room, (of foreign countries); ~-à-manger (see Ap.), dining-room, coffee-room; ~-d'attente (see Ap.), waiting-room at station. [F]

săll'enders, n. pl. Dry eruption inside hock of horse's hind-leg (cf. MALANDERS). [orig. obsc.; in F solandre]

săll'ow¹ (-ō), n. Willow-tree, esp. of low--growing or shrubby kinds, whence ~Y² (-ōi) a.; a shoot, the wood, of this. [OE sealh, f. Gmc *salhaz, cogn. w. OHG salaha, ON selja, L salix]

săll'ow² (-ō), a. (~er, ~est), n., & v.t. & i. 1. (Of human skin or complexion or person in these respects, rarely of foliage) of sickly yellow or pale brown; hence ~ISH¹(2) (-ŏi-) a., ~NESS (-ōn-) n. 2. n. ~ hue. 3. vb. Make or grow~. [OE salo, = MDu. salu, OHG salo, ON sǫlr f. Gmc *salwa-]

săll'y¹, n., & v.i. 1. Rush of besieged upon besiegers, sortie; a going forth, excursion; sudden start into activity, outburst; escapade (rare); witticism, piece of banter, lively remark esp. by way of attack upon person or thing or of diversion in argument; ~-port, opening in fortification for making ~ from. 2. v.i. Make military ~ (often out); go forth or out on a journey, for a walk, etc.; issue, come out, suddenly (rare). [vb f. n., f. F saillie (saillir issue, f. L salire leap)]

săll'y², n. First movement of bell when set for ringing (also hand-stroke), opp. back-stroke), bell's position when set; part of bell-rope prepared with inwoven wool for holding; ~-hole, through which bell-rope passes. [perh. f. prec. in sense leaping motion]

Săll'y³, fam. for Sarah (AUNT~; || ~ Lunn, sweet light tea-cake served hot, perh. f. name of girl hawking them at Bath c. 1800).

sălmagŭn'dǐ, n.. Dish of chopped meat, anchovies, eggs, onions, etc., & seasoning; general mixture, miscellaneous collection, of articles, subjects, qualities, etc. [f. F salmigondis of unkn. orig.]

săl'mi (-ē), n. Ragout esp. of game-birds. [F, short for prec.]

salmon (săm'on), n. (collect. sing. usual for pl.), & a. 1. Large silver-scaled pink--fleshed anadromous fish much prized for food & sport; ~-colour(ed), (of) the orange-

-pink colour of ~-flesh; ~-ladder, -leap, -pass, -stair, series of steps or other arrangement for allowing ~ to pass dam & ascend stream; ~ peel (or peal), (in Ireland) grilse, (in England) sea-trout; ~ steak, fried slice of ~; ~ trout, N.--Europ. fish resembling ~; hence săl'monOID a. & n. 2. adj. ~-coloured, orange-pink. [ME, f. AF samoun f. L salmonem (-mo)]

Sălomŏn'ic, Sălomōn'ian, aa. Of, as of, Solomon. [LL Salomon Solomon, -IC, -IAN]

salon (see Ap.), n. Reception-room in continental, esp. French, house; (re-union of notabilities in) reception-room of (esp. Parisian) lady of fashion (hist.); the S~, annual exhibition of living artists' pictures in Paris; ~ music, light music for drawing-room. [F]

saloon', n. 1. Hall or large room, esp. in hotel or place of public resort, fit for assemblies, exhibitions, etc. 2. Large cabin for first-class or for all passengers on ship; cabin for passengers in large aircraft. 3. || (Also ~car, carriage) luxurious railway carriage without compartments furnished as drawing-room etc. (also sleeping, dining, -~). 4. || Public room(s) or gallery for specified purpose (billiard, dancing, shaving, shooting, etc., -~). 5. *Drinking-bar. 6. || ~ bar, first--class bar in English public-house; || ~ car, (also) motor-car with closed body and no partition behind driver; ~ deck, reserved for ~ passengers; *~-keeper, of bar; || ~ pistol, rifle, adapted for short--range practice in shooting-~. [f. prec., f. It. salone (sala hall f. Gmc, -OON)]

saloop', n. = SALEP; hot drink of salep or sassafras formerly sold as substitute for coffee at London street-stalls. [var. of SALEP]

Salōp'ian, a. & n. (Native) of Shropshire; (member) of Shrewsbury school. [Salop Shropshire f. AF Sloppesberie corrupt. of OE Scrobbesbyrig Shrewsbury, -IAN]

sălpĭglŏss'is, n. Herbaceous showy--flowered garden-plant allied to petunia. [irreg. f. Gk salpigx trumpet, glōssa tongue]

săl'sify, n. British & Continental plant with long cylindrical fleshy roots eaten as vegetable, purple goat's-beard. [f. F salsifis, app. f. It. sassefrica of unkn. orig.]

salt (sawlt, sŏlt), n., a., & v.t. 1. (Also common ~) substance that gives sea--water its characteristic taste got in crystalline forms from strata consisting of it or by evaporation of brine pumped from these or of sea-water & used for seasoning or preserving food & other purposes, sodium chloride, (BAY-SALT, SEA-~, ROCK¹-~; white ~, refined for household use from the brownish rock-~; table ~, powdered or easy to powder for the ~--cellar; in ~, sprinkled with ~ or immersed in brine as preservative; eat ~ with, be guest of; eat one's ~, be his guest or dependant; *is not, any one, worth his* ~, efficient, worth keeping; *drop pinch of* ~ *on tail of,* capture, w. ref. to directions given children for catching bird; *take with a grain of* ~, regard as exaggerated, be incredulous about, believe only part of; *am not made of* ~, can go out in rain without fear of dissolving; *the* ~ *of the earth,* people or classes for whose existence the world is better, moral élite, see *Matt.* v. 13). **2.** Sting, piquancy, pungency, wit, *(no* ~ *in such tears; talk full of* ~; ATTIC[1]~). **3.** (Old chem.) solid soluble non-inflammable sapid substance (obs. exc. in some compd names, as ~ *of* LEMON[1], GLAUBER'S SALT, SMELL*ing* ~*s*, EPSOM ~); (chem.) compound of basic & acid radicals, acid with whole or part of its hydrogen replaced by a metal. **4.** =~- -*cellar* (chiefly now in trade use; & hist. in *above, below,* etc., *the* ~, seated at table among the family & their equals, among the servants & dependants). **5.** (Also ~- -*marsh,* ~'ING[1] n.) marsh overflowed by sea, often used as pasture or for collecting water for ~-making. **6.** pl. Exceptional rush of sea-water up river. **7.** Experienced sailor (esp. *old* ~). **8.** ~-*cat* [*cat* unexpl.], mass of ~ mixed with gravel, urine, etc., to attract pigeons & keep them at home; ~-*cellar* [assim. of obs. *saler* cf. OF *salier* ~-*box* f. L as SALARY) to *cellar*), vessel holding ~ for table use, (also, colloq.) specially deep hollow above collar-bone in woman's neck (regarded as disfigurement; usu. pl.); ~-*glaze,* glaze on stoneware made by throwing ~ into furnace; ~-*lick,* place where animals collect to lick earth impregnated with ~; ~-*mine,* yielding rock-~; ~-*pan,* depression near sea, vessel, used for getting ~ by evaporation; ~-*pit,* pit yielding ~; ~-*pond,* natural or artificial for evaporating sea-water; ~-*spoon,* usu. with short handle & roundish deep bowl for helping ~; ~- -*well,* bored well yielding brine; ~-*works,* ~ manufactory; ~-*wort,* kinds of maritime & ~-marsh plants; hence ~'LESS, ~'Y[2], aa., ~'INESS n. **9.** adj. Impregnated with, containing, tasting of, cured or preserved or seasoned with, ~ (cf. FRESH); (of plants) growing in sea or ~-marshes; (of tears, grief, etc.) bitter, afflicting; (of wit etc. pungent; (of stories, jests, etc.) indecent, spicy; (of bill, charge, etc.; sl.) exorbitant; ~ *horse* (naut. sl.), ~ *beef;* ~ JUNK[1]; ~ *water,* sea-water, (sl.) tears; ~-*water, of,* living in, the sea; hence ~'ISH[1](2) a., ~'LY[2] adv., ~'NESS n. **10.** v.t. Cure or preserve with ~ or brine (~ *down money* or *stock,* sl., put it by); sprinkle (esp. snow to melt it in street) with ~; make ~, season, (lit. & fig.); (p.p.; of horses or persons) proof against diseases incident to climate or special conditions by habituation, hardened; treat (esp. paper in photog.) with solution of ~ or mixture of ~*s*; (commerc., sl.) ~ *an account* etc., put

down extreme price for articles, ~ *the books,* represent receipts as larger than they have been; (mining, sl.) ~ *a mine,* introduce extraneous ore etc. to make it seem rich. [OE *sealt,* OS, ON, Goth. *salt,* OHG *salz* f. Gmc **saltam;* cogn. w. L *sal,* Gk *hals;* vb f. OE *sealtan*]

săltaréll'ō, n. Italian & Spanish dance with sudden skips for one couple. [It. & (-*elo*) Sp.]

sältā'tion, n. Leaping, dancing, a jump; sudden transition or movement. So **săl'tatory, săltatō̌r'IAL,** aa. [f. L *saltatio* (*saltare* frequent. of *salire salt-* leap, -ATION)]

salt'er (sawl-, sŏl-), n. Manufacturer of, dealer in, salt; = DRY[1]-~; workman at salt-works; person who salts fish etc. [OE *sealtere* (SALT n. & v., -ER[1])]

salt'ern (sawl-, sŏl-), n. A salt-works; set of pools for natural evaporation of sea-water. [OE *sealtærn* (SALT, *ærn* hut)]

săl'tigrāde, a. & n. (Spider) with legs adapted for jumping. [L *saltus -ūs* leap (*salire salt-),* -*gradus* -*gradus* -walking]

săltĭmban'cō, n. Mountebank, quack. [It.]

săl'tīre, n. (her.). Ordinary formed by bend & bend sinister crossing like a St Andrew's cross (*in* ~, *per* ~, so arranged). Hence ~WISE (-īrwīz) adv. [ME, f. OF *sautoir* stile, saltire, f. med. L *saltatorium* (SALTATION, -ORY)]

saltpetre (sawltpět'er, sŏl-), n. Potassium nitrate, nitre, white crystalline salty substance used as constituent of gunpowder, in preserving meat, & medicinally (*Chili* or *cubic* ~, sodium nitrate); ~- -*paper,* TOUCH-paper; ~ *rot,* white efflorescence on new or damp walls. [ME & OF *salpetre* f. med. L *salpetra* prob. for *sal petrae* salt of stone (i.e. found as incrustation) w. assim. to *salt; petrae* f. LL f. Gk *petra* rock]

săl'tus, n. (pl. -*ūs*). Sudden transition, breach of continuity. [L, = leap]

salu'brious (-lōō-, -lū-), a. Healthy (chiefly of climate, air, etc.; rarely of food, exercise, etc.). Hence or cogn. ~LY[2] adv., **salu'brITY** n. (-lōō-, -lū-). [L *salubris* (as SALUTARY), -OUS]

Salu'ki (-lōō-), n. Breed of dog, Arabian gazelle-hound. [Arab.]

săl'ūtarў, a. Salubrious (now rare); producing good effects, beneficial. [f. F *salutaire* or L *salutaris* (*salus -utis* health, -AR[1]), -ARY[2]]

sălūtā'tion, n. (Use of) words spoken or written to convey interest in another's health etc., pleasure at sight of or communication with him, or courteous recognition of his arrival or departure, (rarely, now usu. *salute*) gesture of similar import, (*the Angelic S*~, the Ave Maria). Hence or cogn. ~AL (-sho-), **salu'tatory** (-lōō-, -lū-), aa. [ME, f. OF (-*cion*), or L *salutatio* (foll., -ATION)]

salute' (-ōōt, -ūt), v.t. & i., & n. **1.** Make

salutation to, greet; (rare) hail as (king etc.); perform ~ to or *to*, perform ~; (arch.) kiss (person, cheek, hand) esp. at meeting or parting; accost or receive *with* a smile, oath, volley, etc.; become perceptible to (eye, ear, person arriving). **2.** n. Gesture expressing respect, homage, or courteous recognition, to person esp. when arriving or departing; (mil., naut.) prescribed movement or position of body or weapons, or use of flag(s) or discharge of gun(s) in sign of respect, (*a ~ of 7 guns was fired*; *the ~*, attitude taken by individual soldier, sailor, policeman, etc., in saluting; *take the ~*, esp. of highest officer present, acknowledge it as meant for him by gesture); (fenc.) formal performance of certain guards etc. by fencers before engaging; kiss given, prop. as greeting (arch. or joc.; often *a chaste ~*). [ME; vb f. L *salutare* (*salus -utis* health); n. f. OF *salut*, partly f. E vb]

salutif'erous (-lōō-, -lū-), a. (now rare). Promoting health. [f. L *salutifer* (prec., -FEROUS)]

săl'vage, n., & v.t. **1.** (Payment made or due for) saving of a ship or its cargo from loss by wreck or capture (also attrib., as *~ money*); rescue of property from fire etc.; property ~d; saving & utilization of waste paper, scrap-metal, etc.; materials ~d. **2.** v.t. Make ~ of, save from wreck, fire, etc. [f. med. L *salvagium* or OF *salvage* (LL *salvare* SAVE[1], -AGE)]

săl'varsăn, n. Drug used esp. in syphilis. [P]

sălvā'tion, n. **1.** Saving of the soul; deliverance from sin & its consequences & admission to heaven brought about by Christ (*find ~*, be converted, also joc. discover formula that will enable one to abandon one's principles etc.). **2.** Preservation from loss, calamity, etc., thing that preserves from these (esp. *be the ~ of*). **3.** *S~ Army*, organization on military model for revival of religion among the masses, welfare work, etc., whence (& w. ref. to religious revivals in general) ~ISM(3), ~IST(2), nn., (-sho-. [ME & OF *sau-*, *salvation* f. LL *salvationem* (SAVE[1], -·ATION)]

salve[1] (sahv, sălv), n., & v.t. **1.** Healing ointment for sores or wounds (now chiefly poet. & in *lip-~*). **2.** Mixture of tar & grease for smearing sheep. **3.** Something that soothes wounded feelings or uneasy conscience or (arch.) glozes over discrepancy or palliates fault (usu. *for*). **4.** v.t. Anoint (wound etc.; arch. exc. in fig. use=*soothe* as below). **5.** Smear (sheep). **6.** Smooth over or make good (defect, disgrace, etc.; arch.); soothe (pride, self-·love, conscience, etc.). **7.** Account for, dispose of, harmonize, vindicate, (difficulty, doubt, discrepancy, person's honour). **8.** Save (ship, cargo) from loss at sea or (property) from fire, whence

săl'vable a. [OE *sealf*, OS *salba*, OHG *salba* f. Gmc **salbŏ·*; vb f. OE *sealfian*, in senses 6 & 7 partly f. L *salvare* SAVE[1] & in last sense back formation f. SALVAGE]

săl've[2], n. (Also *S~ regina*) R.-C. antiphon beginning with ~ recited after Divine Office from Trinity Sunday to Advent, music for it. [L (vb imperat.= hail)]

săl'ver, n. Tray usu. of gold, silver, brass, or electroplate, on which servants hand refreshments, letters, cards, etc. [f. F *salve* tray for presenting certain things to king f. Sp. *salva* assaying of food (*salvo* SAFE[2]) + -ER[1]]

săl'via, n. (Kinds of) plant of the sage family (including several garden flowering plants). [L, = SAGE[1]]

săl'vō[1], n. (pl. ~*s*). Saving clause, reservation, (often *of*; *with an express ~ of their rights*); tacit reservation, quibbling evasion, bad excuse; expedient for saving reputation or soothing pride or conscience. [f. L abl. of *salvus* SAFE[2] as used in *salvo jure* etc. without prejudice to the right etc.]

săl'vō[2], n. (pl. ~*es*, ~*s*). Simultaneous discharge of pieces of artillery or other fire-·arms esp. as salute, or in seafight; number (*of bombs*) released from aircraft at the same moment, cf. STICK; round or volley of applause. [earlier & It. *salva* salutation, as SAVE[2]]

săl volăt'ilĕ, n. (Aromatic solution, taken for faintness etc., of) ammonium carbonate. [mod. L, = volatile salt]

săl'vor, n. Person, ship, making or assisting in salvage. [SALVE[1] vb, -OR]

Săm, n. (sl.). *Stand ~*, bear the expense esp. of drink; || *upon my ~*, asseveration. [orig. unkn.]

Samă'ritan, n. & a. **1.** Native, language, of Samaria (*good ~*, genuinely charitable person, w. ref. to *Luke* x. 33 etc.); adherent of the ~ religious system. **2.** adj. Of Samaria or the ~s (*the ~ pentateuch*, recension used by ~s of which MSS. are in ~ or archaic-Hebrew characters). Hence ~ISM(2, 3, 4) n. [f. LL *Samaritanus* f. Gk *Samareitēs* (*Samareia* Samaria) + -AN]

săm'ba, n. Brazilian native dance; ball-·room dance imitative of this. [Braz.]

săm'bō, n. (pl. ~*s*, ~*es*). Half-breed esp. of Negro & Indian or European blood; (*S~*; nickname for) Negro. [1st sense f. Sp. *zambo* perh. = *zambo* bandy-legged; 2nd sense prob. a diff. wd]

Săm Browne, n. Army officer's belt & straps. [f. Gen. Sir *S. J. Browne* (d. 1901)]

săm'būr, n. Kinds of large S.-E.-Asian deer. [f. Hind. *sa(m)bar*]

săme, a. **1.** Monotonous, uniform, unvarying, (*the life is perhaps a little ~*; *the ~ old story*), whence ~'NESS (-mn-) n.; (with *this*, *these*, *that*, *those*; often w. depreciatory intention) aforesaid, previously alluded to or thought of, (*what is the use of this ~ patience?*); (vulg. or commerc.) = *the ~*

(pron. & adv., as specified below). **2.** *The* ~, a., pron., & adv.: (adj.) identical, not different, indifferent, unchanged, (also *the very* ~, *just the* ~, & in sing. *one & the* ~; *the* ~ *causes produce the* ~ *effects*; *the difference between a body in motion & the* ~ *body at rest*; *the* ~ *observations are true of the others also*; *all planets travel in the* ~ *direction*; *belong to one & the* ~ *class*; *say the* ~ *thing twice over*; *several of the very* ~ *birds*; *bigotry is the* ~ *in every age*; *she was always the* ~ *to me*; *it is all, just, the* ~ *to me*, makes no difference; *much the* ~, not appreciably different; *at the* ~ *time*, often introducing fact etc. in apparent conflict with what precedes but also true or to be remembered; *by the* ~ TOKEN); identical with (*words of the* ~ *nature with those he had first heard*; *expectation of pleasure is the* ~ *thing with desire*); (emphatic substitute—before full or elliptical relative clause with *that, where*, etc., or esp. *as* which often replaces *that* under its influence—for) the, that, those, (*at the* ~ *time that I am endeavouring*; *to the* ~ *place where I had found it*; *on the* ~ *grounds that he would defend suicide*; *I have the* ~ *Bible my mother gave me*; *Rhenish wine at the* ~ *price as French is sold at*; *sailors received the* ~ *pay as soldiers*; *gave the* ~ *answer as before*); (pron.) the ~ person (now rare exc. in *To, From, the* ~ as heading of letter or poem addressed to or coming from ~ person as the preceding one), the ~ thing (*we must all say, do, the* ~; *would do the* ~ *again*), the aforesaid thing or person (arch., legal, commerc., & vulg.; occas. in commerc. & vulg. use with omission of *the*; *grace & power faithfully to fulfil the* ~; *he that shall endure unto the end, the* ~ *shall be saved*; *& never met, found, the* ~ *again*; *to repairing sleeve of* ~ 1/3); (adv.) in the ~ manner (*think the* ~ *of, feel the* ~ *to*, remain in the ~ mind regarding; *we take what pleasure we can get, the* ~, or vulg. ~, *as you do*; *all the* ~, nevertheless, notwithstanding, even under different circumstances; *just the* ~, in spite of changed conditions). [ME, f. ON *same*, = OHG, Goth. *sama*, cogn. w. Gk *homos*]

săm'el, a. (Of brick, tile) imperfectly baked, soft, from being outmost in the baking. [perh. f. OE *sam*- half, cogn. w. SEMI-, *ælan* burn]

Săm'ian, a. & n. (Native) of Samos (~ *ware*, fine pottery found on Roman sites). [L f. Gk *Samios* (*Samos*), -AN]

săm'isĕn, n. Long three-stringed Japanese guitar, played with plectrum. [Jap., f. Chin. *san-hsien* (*san* three, *hsien* string)]

săm'ite, n. (arch.). Rich medieval dress-fabric of silk occas. interwoven with gold. [ME, f. OF *samit* f. med. L f. med. Gk *hexamiton* f. *hex* six + *mitos* thread; cf. DIMITY]

săm'lĕt, n. Young salmon. [SALMON, -LET]

Săm'nite, n. & a. **1.** Member of an ancient-Italian people at war with republican Rome. **2.** adj. Of the ~s. [ME, f. L *Samnites* pl.]

Samō'an, a. & n. (Native, language) of Samoa. [-AN]

sămovar', n. Apparatus with interior heat-tube for keeping water at boiling--point for making tea. [f. Russ. *samovar* = self-boiler]

Săm'oyĕd (-mo-), n. Member of a people of Siberian Mongols (also attrib.); their language; white Arctic breed of dog. [f. Russ. *Samoyedu*]

Sămoyĕd'ic (-mo-), a. & n. Of the Samoyeds; (n.) their language. [-IC]

săm'păn, n. Any small boat of Chinese pattern. [f. Chin. *san-pan* (*san* three, *pan* board)]

săm'phīre, n. Cliff plant with aromatic saline fleshy leaves used in pickles. [16th c. *sampere* f. F (*herbe de*) *St Pierre* St Peter('s herb)]

sa'mple (sah-), n., & v.t. **1.** Small separated part of something illustrating the qualities of the mass etc.; it is taken from, specimen, pattern, (esp. as offered by dealer in commodities sold by weight or measure; also of immaterial things, as *if that is a fair* ~ *of his proceedings*); ~-*card*, card with ~(s) of goods attached. **2.** v.t. Take or give ~s, try the qualities, get a representative experience, of; hence **sa'mpler¹** [-ER¹] n. [ME; aphetic f. OF *essample* EXAMPLE]

sa'mpler² (sah-), n. **1.** Piece of embroidery worked by girl as specimen of proficiency & often preserved & displayed on wall etc. **2.** Young tree left standing when others are cut down. [aphetic f. OF *essamplaire* f. LL *exemplarium* (EXAMPLE, -ER²)]

Săm'son, -pson, n. Person of great strength or resembling ~ (*Judg.* xiii-xvi) in some respect; (naut.) ~'s-*post*, strong pillar passing through hold or between decks, post in whale-boat to which harpoon rope is attached. [LL, f. Gk (-*psōn*) f. Heb. *Shimshon*]

săm'urai (-ōori), n. (Jap.; pl. same). Military retainer of daimios, member of military caste, (hist.); army officer. [Jap.]

săn'ative, -torў, aa. Healing, of or tending to physical or moral health, curative. [(1) ME, f. OF (-*if*, -*ive*) or LL *sanativus* (*sanare* cure, -IVE); (2) mod. .form. as (1), -ORY, cf. LL *sanatorius*]

sănatōr'ium, n. (pl. -*ia*). Establishment for treatment of invalids esp. convalescents & consumptives; place with good climate etc. frequented by invalids. [mod. L, as prec., -ORY(2)]

sănbĕni'tō (-nē-), n. (pl. ~s). Penitential scapular-shaped yellow garment with red St Andrew's cross before & behind worn by confessed & penitent heretic under Spanish Inquisition; similar black garment painted with flames & devils worn by impenitent heretic at auto-da-fé. [Sp.

(*samb-*), f. *San Benito* St Benedict (shaped like scapular introduced by him)]

sånc'ti|fȳ, v.t. Consecrate, set apart or observe as holy; purify or free from sin (p.p. often iron. = *sanctimonious*; *such ~fied airs*); impart sanctity to, make legitimate or binding by religious sanction, give colour of innocence to, justify, sanction (*the end ~fies the means*); make productive of or conducive to holiness. So ~FICA'TION n. [ME, f. OF *saintifier* f. eccl. L *sanctificare* (L *sanctus* holy, -FY)]

sånctimōn'ious, a. Making a show of sanctity or piety. Hence ~LY² adv., ~NESS n. [foll., -OUS]

sånc'timonȳ, n. Sanctimoniousness. [f. OF (-*ie*), or L *sanctimonia* sanctity (*sanctus* SAINT, -MONY)]

sånc'tion, n., & v.t. 1. Law, decree, (hist.; PRAGMATIC ~). 2. Penalty (also *vindicatory* or *punitive* ~) or reward (also *remuneratory* ~) for (dis)obedience attached to a law, clause containing this; (eth.) consideration operating to enforce obedience to any rule of conduct. 3. Confirmation or ratification of law etc. by supreme authority, express authoritative permission, countenance or encouragement given to action etc. by custom etc.; hence ~LESS a. 4. v.t. Ratify, invest with authority, make binding; authorize; countenance (action etc.); attach penalty or reward to (law). [F, or f. L *sanctio* (*sancire sanct-* make sacred, -ION)]

sånc'titūde, n. (now rare). Saintliness. [ME, f. L *sanctitudo* (SAINT, -TUDE)]

sånc'tit|ȳ, n. Holiness of life, saintliness, (ODOUR *of~y*); sacredness, being hallowed, right to reverence, inviolability; (pl.) sacred obligations, feelings, etc. (*the ~ies of the home*). [ME, f. OF *sain(c)tete* or L *sanctitas* (SAINT, -TY)]

sånc'tūarȳ, n. 1. Place recognized as holy, church, temple, tabernacle, HOLY place, HOLY of holies. SACRARIUM, penetralia, inmost recess, (lit. & fig.); part of chancel between altar rails and east window or screen, containing high altar. 2. Sacred place by retiring to which fugitive from law or debtor was secured by medieval Church law against arrest or violence, place in which similar immunity was established by custom or law, asylum or place of refuge (*London, the ~ of political refugees*); (right of affording) such immunity (*violate* or *break ~*; arrest or use violence to person in a ~; *take, seek*, etc., ~; *resort to a ~*; *rights* etc. of ~). 3. Place for preservation and protection of birds & wild animals. [ME, f. OF *sain(c)tuarie, -aire* f. L *sanctuarium* (eccl. L=shrine), irreg. f. *sanctus* (SAINT, -ARY¹)]

sånc'tum| (**sånctōr'um**), n. 1. Holy place (~), HOLY of holies (~ *sanctorum*), in Jewish temple (usu. transf. of inner retreat, esoteric doctrine, etc.). 2. Person's private room, study, den. [eccl. L, transl. of Heb.]

sǎnc'tus, n. The hymn 'Holy, holy, holy' closing the Eucharistic preface, music for this; ~ *bell*, bell in turret at junction of nave & chancel, or handbell, rung at the ~. [L, = holy]

sǎnd, n., & v.t. 1. Minute fragment resulting from wearing down of esp. silicious rocks & found covering parts of the seashore, riverbeds, deserts, etc., (also pl.) shoal or submarine bank of ~, (usu. in pl.) grain of ~, (pl.) expanse or tracts of ~, (*numberless as the ~ or ~s*; ROPE of ~; *built* etc. *on ~*, unstable; PLOUGH *the ~* or *~s*; *the ~s are running out* etc., time of grace etc. is nearly at end, w. ref. to hour-glass etc.; *children playing on the ~s*; scour saucepan, adulterate sugar, dry ink or writing, with ~). 2. *(colloq.).* Firmness of purpose, grit. 3. *~bag* n., filled with ~ for use (a) in fortification for making temporary defences, (b) as ballast esp. for boat or balloon, (c) as ruffian's weapon inflicting heavy blow without leaving mark, (d) as support for engraving-place, (e) to stop draught from window or door; ~'bag v.t., barricade or defend, provide (window, chink), with ~-bag(s), fell with blow from ~-bag; ~'bank, shoal in sea or river; ~-bar, ~ bank at mouth of harbour or river; ~-bath, vessel of heated ~ as equable heater in chem. processes; ~-bed, stratum of ~; ~-blast, jet of ~ impelled by compressed air or steam for giving rough surface to glass etc.; ~-box, castor for sprinkling ~ over wet ink (hist.), mould of ~ used in founding, box of ~ on locomotive for sprinkling slippery rails; ~'boy, (prob.) boy hawking ~ for sale (now only in *jolly as a ~boy*); ~-cloud, driving ~ in simoom; ~-crack, disease of horses' hoofs, crack in human foot from walking on hot ~, crack in brick due to imperfect mixing; ~-eel, an eel-like fish; ~-fly, kind of midge, kind of fishing-fly; ~-glass, wasp-waisted reversible glass with two bulbs containing enough ~ to take a definite time (*hour, minute*, etc., *-glass*) in passing from upper to lower bulb; ~-hill, dune; ~-hopper, small marine crustacean, common on seashore; ~'man, (also *dustman*) power causing children's eyes to smart towards bedtime; ~-martin, kind nesting in side of ~-pit or sandy bank; ~'paper, with ~ stuck to it for polishing, (v.t.) polish with ~paper; ~'piper, kinds of bird haunting open wet sandy places; ~-pump, for clearing drill-hole, caisson, etc., of wet ~; ~-shoes, usu. of canvas with rubber or hemp soles for use on ~s; ~-spout, pillar of ~ raised by desert whirlwind; ~'stone, rock of compressed ~ (*old, new, red, ~stone*, series of British rocks below, above, carboniferous); ~-storm, desert storm of wind with clouds of ~. 4. v.t. Sprinkle with ~; overlay with, bury under, ~; adulterate (sugar, wool, etc.) with ~; polish with ~. [OE,

OS *sand-*, OHG *sant*, ON *sandr* f. Gmc **sand-*]

săn′dal[1], n., & v.t. (-ll-). **1.** Sole without uppers attached to foot by thongs passing over instep & round ankle (worn chiefly by ancient Greeks & Romans, by some Orientals, & as modern revival esp. by children & women); strap for fastening low shoe passing over instep or round ankle. **2.** v.t. Put ~s on (feet, person; esp. in p.p.); fasten or provide (shoe) with ~. [ME, f. L f. Gk *sandalion*]

săn′dal[2]**(wŏŏd)**, n. Kinds of scented wood (*white, yellow, red*, ~); *sandal-tree*, the white ~ tree of S.W. India. [ME, f. med. L *sandalum*, ult. f. Skr. *čandana*]

săn′darăc, n. Orpiment (arch.); resin of N.-African conifer, used in making varnish. [f. L f. Gk *sandarakē*]

sănd-blind, a. (arch.). Dim-sighted, purblind. [ME, prob. f. OE **samblind* (cf. SAMEL) after SAND]

săn′derling, n. A small wading bird. [perh. f. OE **sand-* (*yrthling* ploughman, also name of some bird)]

săn′ders, saun-, n. ‖=SANDALWOOD; RED ~. [ME, f. OF *sandre* var. of *sandle* SANDAL[2]]

Sănd′hŭrst (-d-h-), n. (Used for) Royal Military College or Academy, ~, for army cadets. [~ in Berkshire]

săn′diver, n. Glass-gall, liquid saline matter given off in glass-making. [ME, corresp. to F *suin de verre* exhalation (*suer* sweat) of glass]

sănd′wich, n., & v.t. **1.** Two slices of bread with meat or other relish between (*ham, egg, caviare, cucumber*, etc., ~; also fig., as *a ~ of good & bad*); (usu. *~-man*, *-boy*, etc.) man etc. walking street with two advertisement-boards hung one before & one behind; *~-board*, one of such boards; ‖*~-boat* in bumping race, boat rowing last in higher & first in lower division on same day; *~ course* of training (with alternate periods of practical & theoretical instruction). **2.** v.t. Insert (thing, statement, etc.) between two of another character. [f. Earl of *S*~ (said to have eaten slices of bread & meat while gaming for 24 hrs)]

sănd′ȳ[1], a. In n. senses; also, (of hair) yellowish-red, (of person) with such hair. Hence ~INESS n., ~ȲISH[1](2) a. [-Y[2]]

Săn′dȳ[2], n. (Nickname) for Scotsman. [usual Sc. shortening of *Alexander*]

sāne, a. Of sound mind, not mad; (of views etc.) moderate, sensible. Hence ~LY[2] (-nl-) adv. [f. L *sanus* healthy]

sang. See SING.

săng′a(r) (-ngg-), n. Stone breastwork used by Indian hill-tribes. [f. Hind. *sunga*]

săngaree′ (-ngg-), n. Cold drink of wine diluted & spiced. [f. Sp. *sangria* (lit. bleeding) drink of lemon-water & red wine]

sang-de-bœuf (sahŭdebŭf′), n. & a. (Of)

a deep red colour found on old Chinese porcelain. [F, = bullock's blood]

sang-froid (see Ap.), n. Composure, coolness, in danger or under agitating circumstances. [F, = cold blood]

sangrail, -real. See GRAIL[2].

sănguifĭcā′tion (-nggwī-), n. Formation of, conversion of food into, blood. [F, or f. mod. L (L *sanguis* blood, -FICATION)]

săng′uinar|ȳ (-nggwī-), a. Attended by, delighting in, bloodshed or slaughter, bloody, bloodthirsty, (of laws) inflicting death lightly; ‖ (euphem., substituted in reporting strong language, or used orig. as milder form, for) bloody. Hence ~ILY[2] adv.,~iNESS n. [f. L *sanguinarius* (*sanguis -inis* blood, -ARY[1])]

săng′uine (-nggwĭn), a., n., & v.t. **1.** Blood-red (literary, & in nat. hist. = L *sanguineus*, as ~ *ant, sponge, turtle*); of blood (rare; ~ *rain*), sanguinary (rare; ~ *slaughter*); (hist.) of the temperament in which the blood predominates over the other HUMOUR[1]s, with ruddy complexion & courageous hopeful amorous disposition; (of complexion) bright, ruddy, florid; habitually hopeful, confident, expecting things to go well, whence (& rarely in other senses) ~LY[2] adv., ~NESS n. **2.** n. Crayon coloured red with iron oxide; a drawing in red chalk. **3.** v.t. (poet.). Stain with blood, stain red. [ME, f. OF *sanguin* f. L *sanguineus* (prec.)]

sănguin′eous (-nggwĭ-), a. Of blood (med.); blood-coloured (esp. bot.); full-blooded, plethoric. [f. L as prec., -OUS]

săn′hědrim (-nĭ-), **-ĭn**, n. Highest court of justice & supreme council in ancient Jerusalem, of 71 members. [f. late Heb. *sanhedrin* f. Gk *sunedrion* (SYN-, *hedra* seat)]

săn′icle, n. An umbelliferous plant of parsley family formerly believed to have healing properties. [ME, OF, f. med. L *sanicula* prob. f. L *sanus* SANE]

săn′ifȳ, v.t. Make healthy, improve sanitary state of, (place). [f. L *sanus* healthy, -I-, -FY]

săn′itar|ȳ, a. Of the conditions that affect health esp. with regard to dirt & infection; free from or designed to obviate influences deleterious to health; ~*y towel* (of kind used in menstruation). Hence **sănĭtAR′IAN** (-ār-) n. & a., ~ILY[2] adv., ~iNESS, ~IST(2), nn. [f. F *sanitaire* (L as SANITY, -ARY[1])]

sănĭtā′tion, n. (Improving of) sanitary conditions. Hence ~IST(2) (-sho-) n., (by back formation) **săn′itāte** v.t. & i. [irreg. f. SANITARY, -ATION]

săn′itȳ, n. Being sane, mental health; tendency to avoid extreme views. [ME, f. OF *sanite* or f. L *sanitas* (SANE, -TY)]

săn′jăk, n. (hist.). One of the administrative districts of a Turkish vilayet. [Turk.]

sank. See SINK[1].

san(n)yasi (sŭnyah′sĭ), n. (Also *sunnyasee*) Indian religious mendicant. [Hind., f. Skr. *saṃnyāsin* laying aside]

sans, prep. Without (as E wd, pr. sănz, now chiefly w. ref. to Shaks. *A. Y.* L. II. vii: 166, ~ *teeth*, ~ *eyes*, ~ *taste*, ~ *everything*. As F wd, pr. as F, in phrr. & compounds, for pronunc. of which see Ap.: ~ *cérémonie* adv., with rude or hurried or kindly neglect ·of usual ·formalities; ~*culôtte'*, pr. as F or E, lit. = breechless, republican of Parisian lower classes in French Revolution, any extreme republican or revolutionary, whence~*culôtt'erie* [-ERY(4, 5)] n., ~*culôtt'ıc* a., ~*culôtt'ısm* n.; ~ *façon* adv., outspokenly, unceremoniously; ~*-gêne* n., absence of constraint, familiarity, making oneself at home; ~ *peur et* ~ *reproche* a., of chivalrous character, cf. BAYARD; ~ *phrase* adv., in a word, without qualification; ~*-souci* n., gay carelessness, unconcern). [ME *sa(u)n, sa(u)ns*, f. OF, f. L *absentia* AB-SENCE, perh. infl. by *sine* without]

sănsě'rif, n. & a. (Form of type) without serifs. [app. f. prec.+SERIF]

Săn'skrit, -scrit, n. & a. (Of, in) the ancient & sacred language of India, oldest known member of INDO-European family. Hence **Sănskrit'ıc** a., **Săn'skrītıst(3)** n. [f. Skr. *saṃskṛta* composed (*saṃ* together, cogn. w. SAME, *kṛ* make)]

Săn'ta Claus' (-z), n. Personage who fills children's stockings with Christmas presents by night. [U.S., f. Du. dial. *Sante* (Du. *Sint) Klaas* St Nicholas]

săn'tŏn, n. Mohammedan monk or hermit. [f. F or Sp. *santon* (Sp. *santo* SAINT)]

săntŏn'ica, n. Kind of wormwood. [L (*Santones* Aquitanian tribe, -IC)]

săn'tonin, n. Extract of santonica used as anthelmintic. [-IN]

Saorstat Eireann (sayŏr'stath āɪr'an), n. Republic of Ireland. [Ir.]

săp¹, n., & v.t. (-pp-). **1.** Vital juice circulating in plants (also fig., as *the ~ of youth, there is no ~ in a written constitution*); (also ~*-wood*) soft outer layers of wood, alburnum; ~*-green* n. & a., pigment made from buckthorn berries, (of) colour of this; ~*-lath*, made of ~*-wood*; hence ~FUL, ~'LESS, ~*-*p'Y², aa., ~*-*p'INESS n. **2.** v.t. Drain or dry (wood) of ~; (fig.) exhaust vigour of (*his energy, constitution, belief, had been ~ped by*; cf. foll.); remove ~*-wood* from (log). [OE *sæp*, MDu., MLG *sap*, OHG *saf*, p erh. cogn. w. L *sapere* taste]

săp², n., & v.i. & t. (-pp-). **1.** Making of trenches to cover assailants' approach to besieged place, (fig.) insidious or· slow undermining of belief, resolution, etc.; covered siege-trench; ~*-head*, front end of ~; ~*-roller*, large gabion covering ~*-head*. **2.** vb. Dig ~, approach (i. & t.) by ~; undermine, make insecure by removing foundations, (fig.) destroy insidiously (cf. prec.), (*walls, cliffs, ~ped by the stream, tide; health ~ped by the damp climate; science was ~ping old beliefs*). [(vb f. F *saper*) f. F *sappe* & It. *zappa* spade, sap]

săp³, v.i. (-pp-), & n. (school sl.). **1.** ‖ Be studious, work hard at books or lessons. **2.** n. ‖ Studious or hardworking person; ‖ tiresome task, trouble, grind, (*it is such a, too much*, ~); *(sl.)* simpleton. [prob. fig. use of prec.]

săp'ajou (-jo͞o), n. Small S.-Amer. monkey often kept as pet. [F, earlier *-iou*, said to be Cayenne wd]

săp'an-wo͞od, -pp-, n. A red dye-wood obtained from an E.-Ind. tree. [f. Du. *sapan*, f. Malay *sapang*, cf. Tamil *shap-pangam*]

săp'id, a. Having (esp. agreeable) flavour, savoury, palatable, not insipid; (of talk, writing, etc.) not vapid or uninteresting. So **sapid'ıty** n. [f. L *sapidus* (*sapere* taste, -ID¹)]

săp'ient, a. Wise (now rare); would-be wise, of fancied sagacity, aping wisdom. Hence or cogn. **săp'ience** n., ~LY² adv. [ME, f. OF, or L part. st. of *sapere* be wise]

săpiĕn'tial (-shl), a. Of wisdom (esp. *the ~ books*, Prov., Eccl., Ecclus., Cant., Wisd., etc.). [ME, f. OF, or eccl. L *sapientialis* (L *sapientia* wisdom as prec., -AL)]

săp'ling, n. Young tree; (fig.) a youth, greyhound in first year (~ *stakes* in coursing). [SAP¹, -LING¹]

săpodill'a, n. Large evergreen tropical-·Amer. tree with durable wood & edible fruit (~ *plum* or NASEBERRY). [f. Sp. *zapotilla* dim. of *zapote* f. Mex. *zapotl*]

săponā'ceous (-shŭs), a. Of, like, containing, soap, soapy (lit. &, in joc. use, fig.). [f. L *sapo -onis* soap, -ACEOUS]

sapŏn'i|fy, v.t. & i. Turn (t. & i. of fat or oil) into soap by decomposition with alkali. Hence or cogn. ~fIABLE a., ~FICA-TION n. [f. F *saponifier* (prec., -FY)]

săp'ŏr, n. Quality perceptible by taste, e.g. sweetness; distinctive taste of substance; sensation of taste. [ME, f. L (*sapere* taste, -OR)]

săpp'er, n. In vbl senses of SAP¹, ², ³; also, ‖ officer or man of Royal Engineers, as official term, private (*Royal S~s & Miners*, former title of R.E.). [-ER¹]

Sapphic (săf'ĭk), a. & n. **1.** Of Sappho (Lesbian lyric poetess 600 B.C.); ~ *vice*, also **Sapph**ISM (săf'ızm) n., unnatural sexual relations between women; ~ *verse, stanza*, in Gk metres invented by Sappho & imitated in L by Horace, esp. the four-·line stanza with short fourth line incorrectly copied in E light verse as *Needy knife-grinder, whither do you wander?*). **2.** n. pl. Verse in ~ stanzas. [f. F *saphique* f. L f. Gk *Sapphikos* (*Sapphō*, -IC)]

sapphire (săf'ĭr), n. & a. **1.** A transparent usu. blue precious stone, (mineral.) any precious native crystalline alumina including ~ & *ruby*; bright blue of ~, azure; kinds of humming-bird; so **sapphir**INE¹ (săf'ĭr-) a. **2.** adj. Of ~ blue. [ME, f. OF *safir* f. L f. Gk *sappheiros* lapis lazuli]

sappy. See SAP[1].

săp'r|(o)-, comb. form of Gk *sapros* rotten in scient. terms : ~*aem'ia,* septic poisoning, so ~*aem'ic* a., [Gk *haima* blood]; ~*ogen'ic,* causing or produced by putrefaction; ~*ophile* a. & n., (bacterium) inhabiting putrid matter; ~*ophyte,* vegetable organism living on decayed organic matter.

¶ **săr,** n., A fish, the sea bream. [F, f. L *sargus*]

să'rabănd, n. Stately old Spanish dance; music for this or in its rhythm, in triple time freq. with long note on second beat of bar. [F (-*de*), f. Sp. *zarabanda*]

Să'racen, n. & a. 1. (General name among later Greeks & Romans for) nomad of Syro-Arabian desert; Arab or Moslem of time of crusades; ‖~ *corn,* buckwheat; ~*'s head,* as heraldic charge or inn-sign; hence (esp. of Moslem archit.) **Săracĕn'ic** a. 2. adj. = ~ic. [ME, f. OF *Sar(r)acin* f. LL f. late Gk *Sarakēnos*; OE f. LL]

Săratŏg'a (trŭnk), n. Lady's large travelling-trunk. [prob. f. *Saratoga* Springs, New York watering-place]

sărc'ăsm, n. Bitter or wounding remark, taunt, esp. one ironically worded; language consisting of, faculty of uttering, use of, such remarks; so **sărcăs'tic** a., **sărcăs'tically** adv. [f. LL f. late Gk *sarkasmos* (*sarkazō* gnash the teeth, tear flesh, see SARCO-, -*asm* corresp. to -ISM)]

sărcĕlle', n. Kinds of small duck or teal. [ME, f. OF *cercelle* f. L *querquedula*]

sarcenet. See SARSENET.

sărc'|o-, comb. form of Gk *sarx sarkos* flesh ; ~*ol'ogy,* anatomy of fleshy parts of body; ~*oplasm,* interfibrillar substance of muscle.

sărc'ŏde, n. Animal protoplasm. [prec., -ODE]

sărcŏm'a, n. (pl. ~*ta*). Tumour of embryonic connective tissue. [f. Gk *sarkōma* (*sarkoō* see SARCO- become fleshy); see -OMA]

sărcŏph'agus, n. (pl. -*gi,* pr. -gī, -ji). Stone coffin usu. adorned with sculpture in inscription. [L, f. Gk *sarkophagos* orig. = flesh-consuming (stone) as SARCO- + -*phagos* -eating]

sărc'ous, a. Consisting of flesh or muscle. [SARCO-, -OUS]

sărd, n. Yellow or orange cornelian. [f. F *sarde* f. L *sarda* = LL *sardius* f. Gk *sardios* (*Sardis* in Lydia)]

Sărdanapăl'ian, a. As of, like, Sardanapalus king of Nineveh notorious for effeminate luxury. [-IAN]

sărdĕlle', n. Fish like & treated like sardine. [f. It. *sardella* dim. of L *sarda* SARDINE[2]]

sărd'ine[1], n. Precious stone in *Rev.* iv. 3. [ME, f. LL (Vulg.) *sardinus* transl. Gk *sardios* (whence R.V. *sardius*)]

sărdine'[2] (-ēn), n. Small fish of herring kind found off Sardinia & Brittany, or young pilchard of Cornish coast, cured & tinned in oil (*packed like* ~*s,* of crowded company). [ME, f. OF, f. It. f. L *sardina* (*sarda* f. Gk *sardē* perh. f. *Sardō* Sardinia)]

Sărdin'ian, a. & n. (Inhabitant) of the island or of the kingdom (1720–1861, including also Piedmont etc.) of Sardinia. [-AN]

sărdŏn'|ĭc, a. Bitter, scornful, mocking, sneering, cynical, (of laugh, laughter, affected merriment, etc.). Hence ~*I*-CALLY adv. [f. F (-*ique*) f. L f. Gk *sardonios* (= Sardinian) alt. of *sardanios,* Homeric epithet of bitter or scornful laughter]

sărd'onyx, n. Onyx with white layers alternating with sard. [ME, f. L f. Gk *sardonux* (SARDios, ONYX)]

sărgăss'ō, n. (pl. ~*s,* ~*es*). (Also *gulf--weed*) kinds of seaweed with berry-like air-vessels found floating in island-like masses in the Gulf-stream & esp. in N.--Atlantic region called S~ *Sea.* [f. Port. *sargaço*]

sa'ri (sah-), n. Length of cotton or silk wrapped round body, worn as main garment by Hindu women. [Hind. *sārī*]

sariss'a, n. (Gk ant.; pl. -*ae*). Long lance of ancient Macedonians. [Gk]

‖ **sărk,** n. (Sc.). Shirt or chemise. Hence ~*'ING*[1] n., boarding between rafters & roof. [ME *serk* f. ON *serkr* f. Gmc *sarkiz*]

Sărmā'tian (-shn), a. & n. (Inhabitant) of ancient Sarmatia (Russia & Poland); (poet.) Pole, Polish. [-AN]

sărm'entōse, -ĕn'tous, aa. (bot.). With long thin trailing shoots. [f. L *sarmentosus* (*sarmenta* pl. twigs, brushwood, f. *sarpere* prune, -MENT, -OSE[1], -OUS)]

sarŏng', n. Malay national garment, a long strip of (often striped) cotton or silk worn by both sexes tucked round waist. [Malay *sārung*]

sărsaparill'a, n. Kinds of tropical--American smilax esp. the Jamaica ~ (so called as chief source of the medicinal ~ for which Jamaica was emporium); dried roots, or extract of these used as tonic etc., of (esp. Jamaica) ~. [f. Sp. *zarzaparilla* (*zarza* bramble, perh. + dim. of *parra* vine)]

sărs'en, n. Sandstone etc. boulder, relict carried by ice in glacial period. [prob. f. SARACEN]

sărs'enĕt, săr'c-, (-sn-), n. Fine soft silk material now used chiefly for linings. [ME, f. AF *sarzinett* (prob. f. *sarzin* SARACEN + -ET[1] after OF *drap sarrasinois* Saracen cloth)]

sărtŏr'ial, a. Of tailor, tailoring, or men's clothes. [f. L *sartor* tailor + -IAL]

Săr'um, eccl. name of Salisbury (~ *use,* order of divine service used in diocese of Salisbury from 11th c. to Reformation). [med. L, prob. f. misread abbr. of L *Sarisburia* Salisbury, cf. *viz* for *videlicet*]

sǎsh¹, n. Ornamental scarf worn by man usu. as part of uniform or insignia over one shoulder or round waist or by woman or child round waist. Hence ~ed¹ [-ED²] (-sht) a. [16th c. *shash* f. Arab. *shāsh* muslin, turban]

sǎsh², n. Frame u̇su. of wood holding pane(s) of glass & usu. made to slide up & down in grooves of window aperture, glazed sliding light of ' glȧsshouse or garden-frame, (opp. CASEMENT); (rare)= casement; ~-cord, -line, strong cord attaching ~-weights to ~; ~-pocket, space on each side of window-frame in which .~-weights run; ~-pulley, for ~-cord to work over; ~-tool, kinds of glazier's & painter's brush; ~-weight, attached to each end of~ to balance it at any height; ~-window, with ~ or usu. two ~es, of which one or each can be slid over the other to make opening. Hence ~ed² [-ED²] (-sht), ~'LESS, aa. [corrupt. of CHASSIS app. mistaken for pl.]

sǎs'in, n. Indian antelope. [Nepalese]

sassǎb'ӯ, n. Large S.-Afr. antelope. [native] ⸱

sǎss'afrǎs, n. (Small N.-Amer. tree yielding) a bark used medicinally; infusion of this. [Sp. *sasafras*, of unkn. orig.]

Sǎssǎn'ian, Sǎss'anid, nn. & aa. (Member, esp. a king) of family of Sa(s)san, rulers of Persian empire A.D. 211–651. [-IAN, -ID³]

Sǎss'enach (see Ap.), n. & a. (Sc. & Ir. for) English(man). [thr. Gael. & Ir. f. *Saxon*]

sastru'gi (sahstrōō'gī), n. pl. Wavelike irregularities on the surface of hard snow caused by winds. [Russ.]

sat. See SIT.

Sǎt'an, (arch.) **Sǎt'anǎs**, n. The Devil, Lucifer. [LL f. Gk, f. Heb. *ṣatan* enemy]

Satǎn'ic, a. Of, like, or befitting Satan, diabolical, hellish, (*his* ~ *majesty*, Satan; ~ *school*, orig. Byron, Shelley, etc., also any set of writers accused of defiant impiety etc.). Hence ~alLY² adv. [-IC, -ICAL]

Sǎt'an|ism, n. Deliberate wickedness, pursuit of evil for its own sake, diabolical disposition, so ~IZE(3) v.t.; characteristics of SATANIC school; (esp. French 19th-c.) professed 'worship of Satan. So ~IST(2) n. [-ISM]

Sǎtanöl'ogӯ, n. (History or collection of) beliefs concerning the Devil. [-O-, -LOGY]

satǎr'a, n. Heavy broadcloth with horizontal rib. [S~ in India]

sǎtch'el, n. Small bag usu. of leather & hung from shoulder with strap for carrying books etc. esp. to & from school. Hence ~lED² (-ld) a. [ME, f. OF *sachel* f. L *saccellus* (SACK¹, -EL)]

sāte¹, v.t. Gratify (desire, person feeling it) to the full; cloy, surfeit, weary with over-abundance (~d with). Hence ~'LESS (-tl-) a. (poet.). [f. (now dial.) *sade*, OE *sadian* (SAD), assim. to L *sat(is)* enough]

sate² (sǎt, sāt). Arch. past & p.p. of SIT.

sateen', n. Cotton or woollen fabric with glossy surface. [f. SATIN after VELVETEEN]

sǎt'ell|ite, n. Person's follower or henchman or hanger-on, member of great man's retinue, underling; heavenly body revolving round another (often fig.), whence ~it'IC a.; artificial body launched from and encircling the· earth; (attrib.) minor, secondary; ~ *state*, country subservient to or controlled by a greater power; ~ *town*, smaller town dependent on a larger town a short distance away. [F, or f. L *satellit*- nom. *-les* guard]

sati. See SUTTEE.

sā'tiate¹ (-shyat), a. Satiated. [L *satiare* (SATIS), -ATE²]

sā'tiate² (-shı-), v.t. = SATE¹. So **sā'tiABLE** (-sha-) a. (rare), **satiA'TION** (sāsı-, sāshı-) n. [as prec., -ATE³]

sati'etӯ, n. Glutted or satiated state, feeling of having had too much of something, cloyed dislike *of*, (*to* ~, to extent beyond what is desired); (rare) over-abundance. [f. F *satiété* f. L *satietatem* (*satis* enough, -TY)]

sǎt'in, n. & a., & v.t. **1.** Silk fabric with glossy surface on one side got by catching warp-threads only at intervals (*Denmark* ~, smooth worsted material used for ladies' slippers); *white*~, the plant honesty, also kind of moth; ~ or *white*~, sl., gin. **2.** adj. Smooth as ~. **3.** ~ *beauty, carpet,* kinds of moth; ~ *cloth*, a woollen cloth woven like ~; ~ *finish*, polish given to silver with metallic brush; ~-*flower*, honesty, also greater stitchwort; ~ *gypsum*, fibrous kind with pearly lustre; ~ *paper*, fine glossy writing-paper; ~ *pug, pygmy,* kinds of moth; ~ *sheeting*, fabric of waste silk & cotton; ~-*spar*, fibrous carbonate of lime; ~-*stitch*, giving appearance of ~ in embroidery & woolwork; ~-*stone*, ~ gypsum; ~-*straw*, soft & flexible for hats; ~ *white*, artificial sulphate of lime; ~-*wood*, choice timber of a tropical tree; hence ~Y² a., ~ETTE'(2) & in same sense ~ET¹ nn. **4.** v.t. Give glossy surface to (paper). [ME, f. OF, f. Arab. *zaituni*]

sǎt'ire, n. (Rom. ant.) poetic medley, esp. poem aimed at prevalent vices or follies; a composition in verse or prose holding up vice or folly to ridicule or lampooning individual(s), this branch of literature, (often *upon*); thing that brings ridicule upon something (*our lives are a* ~ *upon our religion*); use of ridicule, irony, sarcasm, etc., in speech or writing for the ostensible purpose of exposing & discouraging vice or folly. [F, or f. L *satira* later form of *satura* medley]

sati'ric, a. Of satires or satire, containing satire, writing satires, (~ *verse, poem*; *poet, writer, intent, stroke*). [F (*-ique*), or f. L *satiricus* (prec., -IC)]

sati'rical, a. = prec.; given to the use of satire in speech or writing or to cynical observation of others, sarcastic, humorously critical. Hence ~LY² adv. [as prec., see -ICAL]

sät'irist, n. Writer of satires; satirical person. [-IST]

sät'irize, -ise (-īz), v.t. Assail with satire, write satire(s) upon, describe satirically. .[f. F satiriser (SATIRE, -IZE)]

såt'ĭs, Latin adv. & n. = enough, used in phrr. jäm ~, already enough, ~ superque (pr. sŭpĕrk'wĭ), enough & too much.

sätisfăc'tion, n. **1.** Payment of debt, fulfilment of obligation, atonement (for), thing accepted by way of ~, (eccl.) performance of penance, (theol.) atonement made by Christ for sins of men, (make ~; in ~ of; enter ~, legal, place on record of court that payment ordered has been made; Christ is the ~ for our sins). **2.** Opportunity of fighting duel with person one complains of (give, demand, ~). **3.** Satisfying or being satisfied in regard to desire or want or doubt, thing that satisfies desire or gratifies feeling, (find ~ in; give ~; to the ~ of; heard it with great ~; their ~ at or with the results; if you can prove it to my ~; the ~ of not having to do it; it is a great ~ that it need not be done; would be a ~ to me; .thinks only of present ~). [ME, f. OF, f. L satisfactionem (SATISFY)]

sätisfăc'tor| y, a. **1.** (theol.). Serving as atonement for sin. **2.** Satisfying expectations or needs, leaving no room for complaint, causing satisfaction, adequate, (~y proof, method, result, pupil, pair of boots, expedition, marriage, compromise). Hence ~ILY² adv., ~iNESS n. [f. F satisfactoire or LL satisfactorius (SATISFY, -ORY)]

sät'isf|y, v.t. & i. **1.** Pay (debt, creditor), fulfil (obligation), comply with (demand); (of Christ) make atonement for sins of men. **2.** Meet the expectations or desires of, come up to (notion, preconception, etc.), be accepted by (person, his taste, etc.) as adequate, content, (~y the examiners at univ., receive pass without honours). **3.** pass. Be content or pleased (with), demand no more than or consider it enough to do, (rest ~ied, make or take no further demands or steps). **4.** intr. Give satisfaction, leave nothing to be desired. **5.** Dispose of (an appetite or want), rid (person) of an appetite or want, by sufficient supply. **6.** Furnish with adequate proof, convince, (of fact, that it is so; ~y oneself, attain to practical certainty). **7.** Adequately meet (objection, doubt, request, conditions). Hence ~ī-ABLE, ~ȳING,² aa., ~ȳing̣LY² adv. [ME, f. OF satisfier f. L SATISfacere fact- (-FY)]

satrangi (sŭt'ranjĭ, satrŭn'jĭ), n. Cheap Indian cotton carpet. [Hindi]

sät'răp, n. Holder of provincial governor-.ship or ~Y¹ n. in ancient-Persian empire, viceroy; modern subordinate ruler, colonial governor, etc. (rhet. with implication of luxury or tyranny). [ME, f.

OF, or L f. Gk satrapēs f. OPers. khsatra-pava province-guardian]

Sät'sŭma, n. (Also ~ ware) cream--coloured Japanese pottery. [name of province]

sät'ūr|āte (or -cher-), v.t. Impregnate, soak thoroughly, imbue with; overwhelm (defences, target area) by concentrated bombing; (chem. etc.) charge (substance, air, vapour, metal) with or cause to combine with or absorb or hold the greatest amount possible of another substance, moisture, magnetism, electricity, etc.; (p.p., of colour) free from admixture of white, full, rich. Hence or cogn. ~ATE² (-at) a. (poet. exc. of colour), ~ABLE a., ~A'TION n. [f. L saturare (satur full cogn. w. SATIS), -ATE³]

Sät'urday (-erdǐ), n. Seventh day of week (HOLY, HOSPITAL, ~; ~-to-Monday, = the now usu. WEEK-end). [OE Sætern(es)dæg transl. of L Saturni diẹs day of SATURN]

Sät'ŭrn, n. **1.** (Rom. ant.). Italic god of agriculture later identified with Greek Cronos father of Zeus, ruler of the world in a golden age of innocence and plenty. **2.** A planet, the farthest off of the 7 anciently known, with 10 moons & broad flat ring, credited in astrology with producing cold sluggish gloomy temperament in those born under its influence. [f. L Saturnus (serere sat- sow)]

säturnāl'ia (-ter-), n. pl. & (see below) sing. Ancient-Roman festival of Saturn in December observed as time of unrestrained merrymaking extending even to slaves, predecessor of modern Christmastide (S~); scene or time of wild revelry or tumult (also S~; often as sing. as a ~ of crime). Hence **säturnāl'ian** (-ter-) a. [L, neut. pl. of Saturnalis (prec., -AL)]

Satŭrn'ian, a. & n. **1.** Of the god or the planet Saturn; ~ age, GOLDEN age; ~ metre, verse, metre used in early Latin poetry before introduction of Greek metres. **2.** n. Inhabitant of Saturn; (pl.) ~ verse. [f. L SATURNius, -AN]

satŭrn'ic, a. (path.). Affected with lead--poisoning. So **Sät'urn**ISM(5) (-ter-) n. [SATURN in alch. sense lead, -IC]

sät'urnīne (-ter-), a. Of sluggish gloomy temperament, (of looks etc.) suggestive of or produced by such temperament, whence ~LY² adv.; of lead (a ~ poultice etc.); of, affected by, lead-poisoning (~ patients, symptoms). [ME, f. OF -ine f. med. L -inus (as prec., -INE¹)]

satyagraha (sahtyah'grahah), n. (Indian pol.). Passive resistance. [Skr., f. satya truth + āgraha firm grasping]

sät'yr (-er), n. One of a class of Greek woodland deities in human form with horse's ears & tail (or, as represented by Romans, with goat's ears, tail, legs, & budding horns); lustful or beastly--minded man; (rare) orang-utan. [ME, f. OF satyre or L f. Gk saturos]

sätyrī'asis (-ter-), n. Excessive sexual

desire in males. [f. LL f. Gk *saturiasis* (prec., -ASIS)]

saty′ric, a. Of satyrs (esp. ~ *drama*, kind of Greek comic play with chorus of satyrs, see TETRA*logy*). [f. L f. Gk *saturikos* (SATYR, -IC)]

sauce, n., & v.t. **1.** Liquid preparation taken as relish with some article of food (*bread, egg, mint, parsley, tomato,* etc., ~, with these as prominent ingredient; *white* ~, of melted butter, flour, etc.; *hunger is the best* ~ ; ~ *for the* GANDER; *serve with the same* ~, subject to same usage); (fig.) something that adds piquancy (*is tame without the* ~ *of danger*). **2.** Solution of salt & other ingredients used in some manufacturing processes. **3.** Sauciness, impertinent speech, cheek, (*none of your* ~ *!*). **4.** ~-*alone,* hedge-weed formerly used to flavour salads &~s; ~-*boat,* vessel in which ~ is served; ~′*box,* impudent person; ~′*pan* (-ăn), metal vessel usu. cylindrical with long handle projecting from side for boiling things in cookery; hence ~ LESS a. **5.** v.t. Season with ~s or condiments (rare); (fig.) make piquant, add relish to; (vulg.) be impudent to, cheek, (person). [ME, f. OF f. Rom. **salsa* fem. of *salsus* (*salere sals-* to salt f. *sal* salt)]

sau′cer, n. Shallow vessel for standing cup on to intercept spillings of tea etc. (~ *eye,* large & round as a ~, whence ~- -EYED[2] a.); vessel placed under flowerpot to prevent water from running away at once; any small shallow round vessel resembling tea-~. Hence ~ FUL(2) n., ~ LESS a. [ME = *condiment-dish,* f. OF *saussier* f. LL *salsarium* (SAUCE, -ARY[1])]

sau′c|y̆, a. Impudent to superiors, cheeky; (sl.) sprightly, smart, stylish. Hence ~ ĬLY[2] adv., ~ ĬNESS n. [earlier sense *savoury*; SAUCE, -Y[2]]

sauerkraut (sowr′krowt), n. German dish of pickled cabbage. [G]

saul. See SAL.

saumur (sōm′ū̇r), n. White wine produced near ~ in France.

saunders. See SANDERS.

saun′ter, v.i., & n. **1.** Walk in leisurely way or without destination, stroll, (also fig., as ~ *through life*); hence ~ ER[1] n., ~ ing LY[2] adv. **2.** n. Leisurely ramble or gait. [orig. unkn.]

saur′|ian, a. & n. (One) of the *Sauria* or order of lizards including crocodiles, alligators, & extinct kinds such as ichthyosaurus & plesiosaurus. So ~ O- comb. form, ~ OID a. & n. [Gk *sauros* lizard, -IAN]

saur′y̆, n. A long-billed sea-fish. [prob. f. mod. L f. Gk *sauros* lizard]

sau′sage (sŏs-), n. Pork or other meat minced, seasoned, & stuffed into long cylindrical cases prepared from entrails & divided when full into lengths of a few inches by twisting or tying, a length of this, (*Bologna* ~, large kind made of

bacon, veal, pork-suet, etc., & sold ready for eating cold); ~-*filler,* -*grinder,* -*machine,* ~-*making* appliances; ~-*meat,* meat & bread etc. minced & seasoned for use in ~s or as a stuffing etc.; ~ *roll,* ~-*meat* enclosed in pastry & cooked. [ME, f. ONF *saussiche* f. LL *salsicia* (L *salsus* see SAUCE)]

sauté (sōt′ā), a. (in fem. -*ée;* pl. -*és,* fem. -*ées;* pronunc. the same in all forms). Quickly fried in hot pan with little grease. [F]

Sauterne(s) (sōtŭrn′), n. 'Kinds of sweet white French wine. [f. *Sauternes,* name of district]

sauve-qui-peut (sōvkĕpĕr′), n. Precipitate flight in various directions. [F *sauve qui peut* save (himself) who can]

săv′age, a., n., & v.t. **1.** Uncultivated, wild, (arch.; *a* ~ *scene*); uncivilized, in primitive state, (~ *tribes, life*); fierce, cruel, furious, (~ *persecution, persecutor, revenge, criticism, blow*); (colloq.) angry, out of temper; (her.; of human figure) naked; hence or cogn. ~ LY[2] (-ĭjlĭ) adv., ~ NESS (-ĭjn-), săv′ag ERY(2, 4) (-ĭjrĭ), nn. **2.** n. Member of ~ tribe esp. of one living by hunting & fishing, whence ~ DOM (-ĭjd-) n.; brutally cruel or barbarous person. **3.** v.t. (Of horse) attack & bite or trample (person; *was ~d by his horse*). [ME & OF *sal-, sauvage* f. LL *salvaticum* (L *sil-*) f. *silva* a wood, -ATIC]

savănn′a(h) (-na), n. Grassy plain with scattered trees in tropical & subtropical regions. [f. Sp. *zavana* perh. of Carib orig.]

savant (see Ap.), n. Man of learning, esp. distinguished scientist. [part. of F *savoir* know, as SAPIENT]

savate′ (-aht), n. French boxing, in which feet & head are used as well as fists. [F]

sāve[1], v.t. & i., & n. **1.** Rescue, preserve, deliver, from or *from* danger or misfortune or harm or discredit (~*d my life, me from drowning, the State;* ~ *me* or *God* ~ *me from my friends* etc., comment upon well-meant inopportune officiousness; ~ *us!,* excl. of surprise; ~ *one's* BACON, FACE[1]; ~ *the situation,* find or provide way out of difficulty, avert disaster; ~ *appearances,* put a good face on something; (footb. etc.) prevent opponents from scoring. **2.** Bring about spiritual salvation of, preserve from damnation, (*who then can be ~d?; the saving of souls*); (part.) redeeming (*by the saving grace of God; has the saving grace of humour*). **3.** Keep for future use, husband, reserve, abstain from expending, lay by money, live economically, (~ *one's breath,* be silent; *a saving housekeeper; is saving his strength; has never ~d,* put by money; ~ *up,* try to accumulate money by economy; *you may* ~ *your pains* or *trouble,* need not take, will take in vain), whence săv′ ER[1](1) n., săv′ ING[1](2) n. (usu. in pl.), săv′ ing LY[1] adv. **4.** Relieve (person) from need of expending (money, trouble, etc.) or from exposure to (annoyance etc.), obviate need of, reduce requisite amount of, (*that will ~ me £50*; *his secretary ~d him much time or labour, many interviews*; ~ *the follow-on* in cricket, get enough runs to prevent it; *stitch in time ~s nine*; *soap ~s rubbing*), whence (-)sāvER¹(2) n. (*time-~r*), (-)sāvING² a. (*labour-saving*). 5. Avoid losing, be in time for, succeed in catching, (*write hurriedly to ~ the post*; *shall we ~ the tide?*, get in or out while it serves). 6. Make reservation concerning, make reservation, (esp. *saving clause*, containing stipulation of exemption etc.; *saving your reverence*, apology for unseemly expression etc., cf. ~ *the* MARK¹); (part. as prep.) except, with the exception of, SAVE². 7. n. (Footb. etc.) act of preventing opponents from scoring; (bridge) action taken to prevent heavy losses. 8. ~-*all* (hist.), pan with spike for burning up candle-ends; *savings-bank*, receiving small deposits & conducted solely in depositors' interests (*Post-office savings-bank*, with branches at local post offices). Hence sāv'ABLE a. [ME, f. OF *salver*, *sauver* f. LL *salvare* (*salvus* safe)]

sāve², prep. & conj. 1. Except, but, (with n. in obj. case, or with *that* clause; arch., poet., or with formal or pretentious effect in ordinary writing, also pleonast, in ~ *& except*; *forty stripes ~ one*; *all ~ him*, & see conj.; *I am well ~ that I have a cold*). 2. conj. (arch.). Unless, but, (*thou seest no beauty ~ thou make it*; *all the conspirators ~ only he*; *happy ~ for one want*). [ME, f. OF *sauf*, *sauve* f. L *salvō* (see SALVO¹), *salvā* SAFE²]

sāv'eloy, n. Highly seasoned dried sausage. [corrupt. of F *cervelas*, *-at*, f. It. *cervellata* (*cervello* brain)]

sāv'in, n. (Kind of juniper with) tips of shoots yielding a volatile oil used medicinally. [ME, f. OF *savine* f. L *sabina* (*herba*) SABINE (herb)]

sāv'iour (-vyer), n. Deliverer, redeemer (*the*, *our*, *S~*, Christ), person who saves a State etc. from destruction etc. [ME & OF *sauveour* f. LL *salvatorem* (*salvare* SAVE¹), see -IOUR]

savoir faire (săv'wăr făr'), n. Quickness to see & do the right thing, address, tact. [F]

savoir vivre (săv'wăr vē'vr), n. Good breeding, being at home in society. [F]

sāv'ory, n. Herb of mint family used in cookery. [ME *saverey*, ult. f. L *satureia*]

sāv'our (-ver), n., & v.i. & t. 1. Characteristic taste, flavour, relish, or (now rare) smell, power to affect the taste (lit. or fig.); quality suggestive, perceptible admixture, suspicion, smack, of (*a not unpleasing ~ of preciosity*); hence ~LESS (-ver-) a. 2. vb. Appreciate or perceive the lit. or fig. taste of (arch.); give flavour to

(rare); smack, offer suggestion, suggest presence, *of* (*the offer ~s of impertinence*). [ME; (1) OF, f. L *saporem* (*sapere* taste, -OR); (2) f. OF *savourer* f. LL *saporare*]

sāv'our|ỹ (-verĭ), a. & n. 1. With appetizing taste or smell; (of places etc.; only w. neg.) free from bad smells; (of dishes etc.) of salt or piquant & not sweet flavour (*sweet or ~y omelette*); hence ~ILY² adv., ~INESS n. 2. n. ‖ ~y dish, esp. one served at beginning or end of dinner as stimulant or digestive. [ME, f. OF *savoure* p.p. (prec.); see -Y⁴]

savoy', n. Kind of cabbage with wrinkled leaves. [S~ in France]

Savoy'ard (-oi-), n. & a. 1. (Native) of Savoy. 2. Member of the Savoy Theatre company who acted in the original productions of the Gilbert and Sullivan operas. [F (*Savoie* Savoy, -ARD)]

sāvv'ỹ, corrupt. of Sp. *sabe* knows, in sl. use = do you understand ? (*no ~*, I do, he etc. does, not know or understand), also as n. = understanding, wits, savoir faire.

saw¹, n., & v.t. & i. (p.p. ~*n*, rarely ~*ed*). 1. Implement usu. of steel worked by hand or mechanically & with variously shaped blade or edge having teeth of various forms cut in or attached to it for dividing wood, metal, stone, etc., by reciprocating or rotatory motion (*annular*, *crown*, *cylinder*, ~, cylinder with toothed edge for making circular hole; BAND¹, BOW¹, FRAME², FRET¹, -~; CIRCULAR ~; *cross-cut*, *rip-*, ~, for cutting wood across, along, the grain; *hand-*~, held with one hand; HACK²-~; *jig'*~, frame-~ worked mechanically in connexion with table holding the wood etc. (*jig~ puzzle*, of pieces sawn with jig~ to be put together); *musical or singing ~*, ordinary ~ played on by performer by means of violin bow; *pit-*~, worked by two men one above & one in pit; *reciprocating ~*, worked mechanically with backward & forward strokes; *stone-*~, toothless frame--~ cutting stone by friction with sand & water). 2. (zool. etc.). Serrated organ or part. 3. ~*-doctor*, machine for making teeth of ~; ~'*dust*, wood fragments produced in ~ing used in packing, pugging, stuffing, drying moisture, etc. (*let the ~dust out of*, fig., expose pretentiousness or unsubstantial character of, w. ref. to doll's stuffing); ~'*fish*, large kind with toothed snout used as weapon; ~-*fly*, kinds injurious to plants with serrated ovipositor; ~-*frame*, in which ~-blade is held taut; ~-*gate*, ~-frame; ~-*gin*, cotton--GIN¹ with ~-teeth; ~-*horse*, rack supporting wood for~ing; ~'*mill*, driven by water or steam for mechanical ~ing; ~-*pit*, in which lower of two men working pit-~ stands; ~-*set*, tool for wrenching ~-teeth in alternate directions to give kerf wider than blade & let ~ work freely; ~-*wort*, plant yielding yellow dye named from serrated leaves; ~-*wrack*, a serrated sea-weed; ~-*wrest*, ~-*set*. **4.** vb. Cut (wood etc.) with, make (boards etc.) with, use, ~; move (t. & i.) backward & forward, divide (the air etc.), with motion as of ~ or person ~ing; (quasi-pass.) admit of being ~n *easily, badly*, etc.; (bookbind.) make incisions to receive binding-bands in (gathered sheets); ~'*bones* (sl.), surgeon. [OE *sagu, saga*, OHG *saga*, ON *sǫg* f. Gmc *sagō; cogn. w. L *secare* cut]

saw², n. Proverbial saying, old maxim, (usu. *old* or *wise* ~). [OE *sagu*, OHG, ON *saga*, f. Gmc **sag-* SAY²; cf. SAGA]

saw³. See SEE¹.

sawd'er, n. *Soft* ~, compliments, flatter-ing speeches, blarney. [= SOLDER]

Sawn'ey, n. (Nickname for) Scotsman; simpleton. [prob. as SANDY²]

saw'yer, n. Man employed in sawing timber (TOP-~); * uprooted tree floating or stranded in river (named as sawing up & down); kinds of wood-boring larva. [-YER]

säx, zäx, n. Slater's chopper, with point for making nail-holes. [OE *seax*, OS *saks*, OHG *sahs*, ON *sax* f. Gmc **sah-*, **sag-* cogn. w. SAW¹]

säx'atile, a. (nat. hist.). Living, growing, on or among rocks. [F, or f. L *saxatilis* (*saxum* rock, -ATILE)]

säxe, n. ‖ Kind of photographic paper; a colour, = SAXON *blue*. [F, = Saxony (place of origin)]

säx'hŏrn, n. Brass instrument made in seven sizes, the lowest three being con-sidered tubas. [A. *Sax*, inventor (d. 1894)]

säxic'oline, -lous, aa. (nat. hist.). = SAXATILE. [f. mod. L *saxicolus* (*saxum* rock, *colere* inhabit) +-INE, -OUS]

säx'ifrage (*or* -äj), n. Kinds of Alpine or rock plant with tufted foliage & panicles of white or yellow or red flowers. [ME, f. OF, or LL *saxifraga* (*herba*) f. *saxum* rock +*frangere* break]

Säx'on, n. & a. **1.** Member, language (often *Old* ~), of the Germanic people by which Britain was conquered in 5th & 6th cc.; = ANGLO-SAXON, whence ~DOM n.; native of modern Saxony; Germanic (opp. Latin or Romance) elements of English. **2.** adj. Of the ~s (~ *architecture*, rude Romanesque preceding Norman in England); in ~ (~ *words* in English, of Germanic origin), whence ~ISM(2, 4), ~IST(2), nn.; ~ *blue*, solution of indigo in sulphuric acid as dye; hence ~IZE(2, 3) v.i. & t. [ME, f. OF f. LL *Saxonem* f. WG **Saxon-* (OE *Seaxan, Seaxe* pl.)]

säx'onȳ, n. Fine kind of wool, cloth made from it. [f. *S*~ in Germany]

säx'ophōne, n. Keyed brass instrument in several sizes, having a reed like that of a clarinet. [as SAXHORN, Gk *phōnē* sound]

säx'tūba, n. Large SAXHORN. [TUBA]

say¹, n. (now rare). Fine serge-like cloth. [ME, f. OF *saie* f. L *saga* pl. of *sagum* military cloak]

say², v.t. & i. (*said* pr. sĕd; 3rd sing. pres. *says* pr. sĕz, arch. *saith* pr. sĕth; arch. 2nd sing. pres. ~*st* or ~*est*, past *saidst* rarely *saidest*), & n. **1.** Utter, make (speci-fied remark), recite, rehearse, in ordinary speaking voice (~ *the word*, give the order etc.; ~ WHEN; ~ *no more*, cease speaking; ~ *a good word for*, commend or excuse; *to be said or sung*; ~ *no, yes*, refuse, grant, request,' also deny, confirm or accept, statement; ~ *out*, express fully or candid-ly; ~ one *nay*, refuse him something; *has said his* ~, finished what he had to ~; ~ *lesson*, repeat it to teacher; ~ *grace, prayer*; ~ *something*, make a short speech; *that is to* ~, in other words, as *the whole family, that is to* ~ *four persons*, also = or at least, as *he never went, that is to* ~ *it is not recorded that he did*, also ellipt. ~ in giving sum in words after figures, as *£500* ~ *five hundred pounds; he said 'You lie'*; ~*s* or *said he* etc., *said I*,~*s I* colloq., forms inserted in repeating conversation; ~*ing & doing*, speech & action; ‖ *I* ~, excl. used to draw attention, open a con-versation, or express surprise, as *I* ~, *who was that?, I* ~, *what a beauty!*, or in same sense *I* ~ *!* colloq. (See also ~). **2.** State, promise, prophesy, (*he* ~*s all men* or *that all men are liars; you said you would*; DARE ~; *they* ~, *it is said*, forms introducing rumour; *it* ~*s in the Bible*, the Bible ~s; *goes without* ~*ing*, is too obvious to need mention; *hear* ~, hear it reported; *so he* ~*s, he* ~*s so; you may well* ~ *so*, your statement is fully justified). **3.** Speak, talk, (rare; ~ *away*, ~ what you have to ~; *he said, & turned his back*, in narrative poetry etc.). **4.** Put into words, express (*that was well said*). **5.** Adduce or allege in argument or excuse (*there is much to be said on both sides; have you anything to* ~ *for yourself?*). **6.** Form & give opinion or decision as to or abs. (*there is no* ~*ing, it is hard to* ~, *who it was; I cannot* ~, do not know *whether* etc. or abs.; *do* ~ *which you will have; what* ~ *you to a theatre?*, are you inclined for it ? ; *& so* ~ *all of us*, & that is our opinion too). **7.** Select as example, assume, take (specified number etc.) as near enough, (*let us* ~, or usu. ellipt. ~; *any country, let us* ~ *Sweden, might do the same; well,* ~ *it were true, what then? ; a few of them,* ~ *a dozen or so*). **8.** n. (Oppor-tunity of ~ing) what one has to ~, share in decision, (~ *your* ~; *let him have his* ~; *had no* ~ *in the matter*). [OE *secgan*, OS *seggian*, OHG *sagēn*, ON *segja*, f. Gmc *sagjan, *sagǣjan]

say'ing, n. In vbl senses; esp., sententious remark, maxim, adage, (*as the* ~ *is* or *goes*, form used in quoting proverb or phrase). [-ING¹]

Say(y)id (sā'yĭd), **Said** (sād), nn. Varr. of SEID. [f. Arab., see SIDI, SEID]

sbĭr'rō (zb-), n. (pl. -*ri* pr. -ē). Italian policeman. [It.]

scăb, n., & v.i. (-bb-). **1.** Dry rough

incrustation formed over sore in healing, cicatrice; mange, itch, or similar skin--disease; kinds of fungous plant-disease; mean dirty fellow (arch.); (trade unionism) workman who refuses to join strike or union or takes striker's place, blackleg; ~'*wort*, elecampane; hence ~**bed**[2] (-bd), ~**b'y**[2], aa., ~**b'ily**[2] adv., ~**b'iness** n. **2.** v.i. (Of sore) form ~, heal over. [ME, f. ON *skabbr* = OE *sceabb*, see SHABBY]

scăbb'ard, n. Sheath of sword, bayonet, etc. (*fling, throw, away the* ~, commit oneself to fighting a matter out to the end); ~-*fish*, silvery-white sea-fish shaped like sword-~. [ME *scauberc* etc., f. AF, OF *escauberc, escauberge* of WG orig.]

scăb'iĕs (-z), n. The itch. [L (*scabere* scratch)]

scăb'ious, a. & n. **1.** Scabby, affected with mange, itch, etc. **2.** n. Kinds of wild & cultivated annual or perennial herb with blue, pink, or white, pincushion-shaped flowers, as *devil's-bit*. [(n. f. med. L *scabiosa herba*, named as specific against itch) f. F *scabieux* or L *scabiosus* (prec., -OUS)]

scăb'rous, a. (Zool., bot., etc.) with rough surface, scurfy; (literature; of subject, situation, etc.) requiring tactful treatment, hard to handle with decency. Hence ~NESS n. [f. F *scabreux* or LL *scabrosus* (L *scaber* rough, -OUS)]

scăd, n. Kind of fish called also horse--mackerel. [orig. unkn.]

scăff'old, n., & v.t., **scăff'old|ing**, n. **1.** Elevated platform of timber usu. for execution of criminals (~; *the* ~, death by executioner's hands) or rarely (~, ~*ing*) for display of something or accommodation of spectators; (usu. ~*ing*) temporary structure of poles & planks providing workmen with platform(s) to stand on while building or repairing house etc., (~*ing*) materials for this; (anat., embryol.; ~, ~*ing*) framework outlining parts to be formed on it later (*the* ~ *of the skull*); ~*ing-pole*, mastlike pole helping to support building-platform. **2.** v.t. Attach ~ing to (house). [ME, f. NF forms corresp. to OF *eschaffaut*, earlier *escadafaut* f. EX- + Rom. *catafalcum CATAFALQUE]

scăg'lĭa (or skăl'ya), n. Reddish Italian limestone. [It.]

scagliola (skălyōl'a), n. Imitation stone of plaster mixed with glue & variously coloured or diversified. [It. (-*iuola*)]

scăl'able, a. In vbl senses of SCALE[1, 2, 3]. [-ABLE]

scală'rifôrm, a. (bot., zool.). Ladder--shaped (of veins in insect's wings, or of alternating thick & thin strips in structure). [f. mod. L *scalariformis* f. *scalaris* SCALE[3], -AR[1], -FORM]

scăl'awăg, scăll'a-, scăll'y̆-, n. Undersized or ill-fed animal; good-for-nothing person, scamp, scapegrace. [U.S. sl., of unkn. orig.]

scald[1] (-aw-), v.t., & n. **1.** Injure or pain (skin, or person or animal or part in regard to it) with hot liquid or vapour (*was* ~*ed to death by the steam*; ~*ing tears*, of bitter grief); raise (milk) to near boiling--point (~*ed cream*, from milk ~ed & allowed to stand), whence ~'**er**[1](2) n.; cleanse (vessel; often *out*) by rinsing with boiling water. **2.** n. Injury to skin by ~ing (*for* ~*s & burns*). [ME, f. ONF *escalder* f. LL EX(*caldare* f. L *calidus* hot)]

scald[2] (-aw-), sk-, n. Ancient-Scandinavian composer & reciter of poems in honour of great men. Hence **sca'ldic** (-awl-) a. [ON *skáld*, of unkn. orig.]

scald'head (-awld-hĕd), n. Scalp-disease of children. [SCALL, -ED[2]]

scāle[1], n., & v.t. & i. **1.** One of the thin horny overlapping plates protecting the skin of many fishes & reptiles. **2.** Plate or thin outer piece with some resemblance to fish-~ in organic or other object, e.g. pod, husk, rudimentary leaf or feather, bract, metamorphosed hair of lepidoptera, bulb-layer, flake of skin, scab, lamina on surface of rusty iron. **3.** (Without *a*) incrustation inside boiler etc., tartar on teeth. **4.** ~-*armour*, of metal ~s attached to leather etc.; ~-*board*, very thin for back of mirror, picture, etc.; ~-*borer*, machine for removing ~ from boiler-tubes; ~-*fern*, ceterach; ~-*insect*, kinds that cling fast to plants & secrete a shieldlike ~ as covering; ~-*moss*, kinds of plant with ~like leaves resembling moss; ~-*winged*, lepidopterous; ~-*work*, overlapping arrangement, imbrication; hence (-)scāl**ed**(-ld), ~'**less**(-l-l-), **scāl'y̆**[2], aa., **scāl'iness** n. **5.** vb. Take away ~(s) from (~ *fish, almonds, teeth, iron*); (of skin, metal, etc.) form, come off in, drop, ~s; (of ~s) come *off*. [ME, f. OF *escale* f. WG *skala, see foll.]

scāle[2], n., & v.t. **1.** Dish of simple balance (*throw sword into* ~, back claim with arms; *turn the* ~, of motive or circumstance, be decisive); (astron.) *the S~s*, = LIBRA; (pl.) a simple balance (also *pair of* ~*s*) or weighing-instrument (*hold the* ~*s even*, be impartial judge). **2.** v.t. Weigh in ~s (rare); (of thing weighed) show (specified weight) in the ~s (~*s 10 st.*, *100 lb.*). [ME, f. ON *skál* bowl = OHG *skâla* f. Com *skêlô var. of *skalô whence OE *scealu* SHALE; see also SHELL[1]]

scāle[3], n., & v.t. & i. **1.** Series of degrees, ladderlike arrangement or classification, graded system, (*is high in the* ~ *of creation* or *social, intellectual*, etc., ~; *sink in the* ~, fall to lower rank or level; *at the top, bottom, of the* ~; *sliding* ~, see SLIDE[1]). **2.** (mus.). Steplike ordered arrangement of all notes used in any system of music (DIATONIC, CHROMATIC, MAJOR[2], MINOR, ~; *play, sing, run over* one's, ~*s*, as exercise for fingers or voice). **3.** (Often ~ *of notation*) basis of numerical system as shown in ratio between units in different places of number (the *ordinary* or *denary* or *decimal* ~, with successive places denoting units, tens, hundreds, etc.; *binary* ~, denoting units, twos, fours, etc.; *ternary* ~, denoting units, threes, nines, etc.; thus fourteen is written in binary ~ 1110 i.e. nought + two + four + eight, in ternary ~ 112 i.e. two + three + nine in septenary ~ 20 i.e. nought + two sevens, & in denary ~ 14 i.e. four + ten). **4.** Relative dimensions, ratio of reduction & enlargement in map etc., (*philanthropy, armies, on a vast* ~; *a building of small* ~ *but fine proportions*; *large, small, ~ map*; *to* ~, with uniform reduction or enlargement; *the* ~ *to be one to fifty thousand, an inch to the mile, 1/1000,* etc.). **5.** Set of marks at measured distances on a line for use in measuring or making proportional reductions & enlargements, rule determining intervals between these, piece of metal etc. or apparatus on which they are marked (GUNTER'S ~). **6.** vb. Climb (wall, steep place, or abs.) with latter (*scaling-ladder*) or by clambering. **7.** Represent in dimensions proportional to the actual ones, reduce to common ~, (~ *up, down*, make larger, smaller, in due proportion; increase, reduce, in size). **8.** (Of quantities etc.) have common ~, be commensurable. [ME (= ladder), f. L *scala* (*scandere* climb)]

scalēne′, a. & n. **1.** Unequal-sided (~ *triangle*, with no two sides equal; ~ *cone, cylinder*, with axis inclined to base; ~ *muscle*, any of several connecting spine & ribs). **2.** n. ~ triangle or muscle. [f. LL f. Gk *skalēnos*]

scall (-awl), n. (arch.). Scaly eruption on skin (*dry* ~, the itch; *moist* ~, eczema). [ME, prob. f. ON *skalli* bald head, f. Gmc *skal-* (SHALE, SHELL[1])]

scallawag. See SCALAWAG.

scǎll′ion (-yon), n. Kind of onion or shallot. [ME, f. AF *scal(o)un* = OF *eschalo(i)gne*, see SHALLOT]

scǎll′op, scŏ-, n., & v.t. **1.** Bivalve mollusc with shell divided into grooves & ridges radiating from middle of hinge & edged all round with small semicircular lobes; (also ~*-shell*) one valve of this (hist.) as pilgrim's badge, (mod.) as utensil in which oysters, shredded fish, mince, etc., are cooked & served, small shallow pan similarly used; (pl.) ornamental edging cut in material in imitation of ~*-edge.* **2.** v.t. Cook in ~; ornament (edge, material) with ~s or ~ING[1](6) in. [ME, f. OF *escalope* f. Gmc; cf. MDu. *schelpe, schulpe* shell]

scallywag. See SCALAWAG.

scǎlp, n., & v.t. **1.** Top of head; skin with hair etc. of head excluding face; this or part of it cut as trophy from enemy's head by Red Indians (*take* ~; *out for* ~*s*, on the warpath, often fig. = in aggressive or pugnacious or savagely critical mood); bare rounded hill-top; whale's

head without lower jaw; ~*-lock*, single lock on Red Indian's shaven head left as challenge to enemies; hence ~*′LESS* a. **2.** v.t. Take ~ of; criticize savagely. [north. ME, app. f. Scand.; cf. ON *skđlpr* sheath, Da. dial. *skalp* shell, husk]

scǎl′pel, n. Surgeon's small light knife shaped for holding like pen. [F, or f. L *scalpellum* (*scalprum* chisel, f. *scalpere* scrape, -EL)]

scǎl′per, scaup′er, n. Gouge used by engravers. [f. L *scalprum* (prec.)]

scǎl′priförm, a. Chisel-shaped (of incisor teeth). [as prec., -I-, -FORM]

scǎmm′ony, n. (Kind of Asian convolvulus yielding) a gum resin used as drastic purgative. [ME, f. OF *scamonee, escamonie* f. L f. Gk *skammōnia*]

scǎmp[1], n. Rascal, knave, (also in playful use as term of endearment). Hence ~*′ISH*[1] a. [prob. of same orig. as SCAMPER]

scǎmp[2], v.t. Do (work etc.) in perfunctory or inadequate way. [prob. dial.; cf. SKIMP]

scǎm′per, v.i., & n. **1.** Run impulsively like (or of) frightened animal or playing child; take ~ *through.* **2.** n. Hasty run; gallop on horseback for pleasure; rapid tour or course of reading (*through Normandy, Dickens,* etc.). [f. 16th c. (obs.) *scamp,* f. MDu. *schampen* decamp + -ER[5]]

scǎn, v.t. & i. (-nn-). **1.** Test metre of (line etc.) by examining number & quantity of feet & syllables, read over with emphasis on rhythm; be metrically correct (*line does not* ~), admit of rhythmic reading (*line will not* ~, ~*s smoothly, badly*). **2.** Look intently at all parts successively of (face, horizon, etc.). **3.** (television). Resolve (a picture) into its elements of light and shade for purposes of transmission. **4.** (radar). Cause (a particular region) to be traversed by a controlled beam. [ME, f. L *scandere* climb, in LL scan verses]

scǎn′dal, n. (Thing that occasions) general feeling of outrage or indignation esp. as expressed in common talk, opprobrium, (*it is a ~ that such things should be possible*; *a grave* ~ *occurred*; *gave rise to* ~); malicious gossip, backbiting, whence ~MONGER n.; (law) public affront, irrelevant abusive statement in court, (cf. LIBEL, SLANDER). So ~OUS a., ~OUSLY[2] adv., ~OUSNESS n. [ME *-dle,* f. ONF *escandle* f. eccl. L f. Gk *skandalon* snare, stumbling-block]

scǎn′dalize[1], -ise (-īz), v.t. Offend moral feelings, sense of propriety, or ideas of etiquette, of, shock. [f. F *scandaliser* f. eccl. L f. Gk (*-izō*) as prec., see -IZE]

scǎn′dalize[2], -ise (-īz), v.t. (naut.). Reduce area of (a sail). [alt. f. obs. *scantelize* = obs. *scantle* (SCANT vb + -LE(3))]

scǎn′dalum mǎgnāt′um, n. (hist.). Defamation of magnates. [med. L]

Scǎndināv′ian, a. & n. (Native, family of

languages) of Scandinavia (Denmark, Norway, Sweden, & Iceland). [-AN]

scăn'sion (-shn), n. Metrical scanning, way verse scans. [f. L *scansio* (LL of metre) f. *scandere scans-* climb, -ION]

scănsŏr'ial, a. Habitually climbing, adapted for climbing, (of birds, their feet, etc.). [L *scansorius* (prec., -ORY), -AL].

scănt, a., & v.t. **1.** Barely sufficient, deficient, with scanty supply *of*, (arch., poet., & in isolated phrr., as *with ~ courtesy, ~ of breath*); hence *~'LY*[2] adv. **2.** v.t. (arch.). Skimp, stint, provide grudgingly, (supply, material, person). [ME, f. ON *skamt* short]

scăn'ties (-tĕz), n. pl. (colloq.). Abbreviated panties. [f. prec., after PANTIES]

scănt'ling, n. Specimen, sample, (arch.); modicum, small amount, one's necessary supply *of*; small beam under 5 in. in breadth & depth; size to which stone or timber is to be cut; set of standard dimensions for parts of structure esp. in shipbuilding; trestle for cask. [alt. f. obs. *scantillon* (after -LING[1]) f. OF *escantilon*]

scăn't|ў̆, a. Of small extent or amount, barely sufficient, (opp. *ample*). Hence *~ĭLY*[2] adv., *~ĬNESS* n. [-Y[2]]

scăpe[1], n., & v.t. (arch.). Escape (still in *hairbreadth ~s*). [aphetic f. ESCAPE]

scăpe[2], n. (Bot.) radical stem bearing fructification & no leaves as in primrose; (entom.) base of antenna; shaft of feather; spring, usu. with curve, of column from base. [f. L f. Gk *skapos* cogn. w. SCEPTRE]

scăpe'goat (-pg-), n. (O.T.) goat allowed to escape when Jewish chief priest had laid sins of people upon it (*Lev.* xvi); person bearing blame due to others. [SCAPE[1]]

scăpe'grăce (-pg-), n. Harebrained person, esp. child, who constantly gets into trouble. [= one who escapes the grace of God (SCAPE[1])]

scapement. = ESCAPEMENT.

scăph'oid, a. & n. (anat.). **1.** Boat-shaped (*~ bone*, one in tarsus & one in carpus). **2.** n. *~* bone. [f. Gk *skaphoeides* (*skaphē, skaphos*, bowl, boat, -OID)]

scăp'ŭla, n. (pl. *-ulae*). SHOULDER-blade. [LL, sing. of L *scapulae*]

scăp'ŭlar, a. & n. **1.** Of shoulder or shoulder-blade (*~ arch, = shoulder--GIRDLE[1]; ~ feathers*, growing near insertion of wing). **2.** n. Monastic short cloak covering shoulders; badge of admission to an ecclesiastical order, consisting of two strips of cloth hanging down breast &.back & joined across shoulders (also *~y*); bandage for shoulder-blade; *~* feather. [n. f. LL *scapulare* (prec., -AR[1]); adj. f. mod. L *scapularis*]

scăp'ŭlo-, comb. form of SCAPULA, as *~-hŭm'eral, ~-răd'ial, ~-ŭl'nar*, of scapula & humerus, & radius, & ulna. [-O-]

scăr[1], n., & v.t. & i. (-rr-). **1.** Mark left after healing of wound or burn or sore, cica-

trice, (also fig. of abiding effects of grief etc.); mark on plant left by fall of a leaf etc., hilum; hence *~'LESS* a. **2.** vb. Mark with *~* or *~s* (esp. in p.p.); heal (i. & t.) over, form *~*. [ME, f. OF *escare* f. LL *eschara* (also *scara*) scar]

scăr[2], scaur (-ŏr), n. Precipitous craggy part of mountain side; sea-cliff. [ME, f. ON *sker* low reef in sea, cogn. w. SHEAR[1]]

scă'rab, n. Sacred beetle of ancient Egypt; =foll.; ancient-Egyptian gem cut in form of beetle & engraved with symbols on flat side. [f. L f. Gk *scarabaeus*]

scărabae'id, n. Member of *Scarabacidae*, family of beetles including prec., cockchafer, etc. [prec., -ID[3]]

scărabae'oid, a. & n. Like a·scarab or a scarabaeid; (n.) counterfeit scarab. [-OID]

scă'ramouch, n. (arch.). Boastful poltroon, braggart. [17th c., f. It. *Scaramuccia* stock character in Italian farce (= SKIRMISH); pres. sp. f. F *-mouche*]

scărce, a. & adv. **1.** Insufficient for the demand or need, not plentiful, scanty, (usu. pred., & of food, money, or other necessaries of life), whence **scăr'CITY** n. (*of*, or abs.=dearth of food); seldom met with, rare, hard to find, (a *~ book*, *moth*; *make* oneself *~*, colloq., retire, make off, keep out of the way), whence *~'NESS* (-sn-) n. **2.** adv. (arch., poet., rhet.). Scarcely. [ME & ONF *skars* f. Rom. **excarpsus* f. L *excerptus* EXCERPT]

scărce'lў̆ (-slI), adv. Hardly, barely, only just, (*is ~ seventeen years old; had ~ arrived when he was told that —; I ~ know him*); surely not; not unless the unlikely happens or is true, (*you will ~ maintain that; he can ~ have said so*); (mild or apologetic substitute for) not (*I ~ think so, know what to say*). [-LY[2]]

scărce'ment (-sm-), n. Set-back in a wall, ledge resulting from this. [SCARCE + -MENT]

scăre, v.t., & n. **1.** Strike (esp. child, foolish person, or animal) with sudden terror, frighten (as) with a bugbear, (*~d face, expression*, etc., betraying terror; *~ away*, drive off by fright); keep (birds) away from sown land etc.; *~'crow*, figure of man hung with old clothes & set up in field to keep birds away, bugbear, badly dressed or grotesque-looking or skinny person. **2.** n. Unreasoning terror, esp. baseless general apprehension of war, invasion, etc., whence *~'MONGER* n.; commercial panic; *~-head(ing)*, extravagantly sensational newspaper headline. [ME *skerre*, f. ON *skirra* (*skjarr* timid)]

scărf[1], n. (pl. *-fs, -ves*). Long narrow strip of material worn for ornament or warmth round neck, over shoulders, or baldric--wise; man's necktie (|| *~-pin, -ring*, usu. of gold or jewelled for holding ends of this together); *~-loom*, for weaving narrow fabrics; *~-skin*, outermost layer of skin constantly scaling off (esp. of that adhering to base of nails); *~-wise,* baldric-wise. Hence ~ED² (-ft) a. [f. ONF *escarpe* = OF *escharpe* sash etc., prob. same wd as *escharpe* SCRIP¹]

scarf², v.t., & n. **1.** Join ends of (pieces of timber, metal, or leather) by bevelling or notching so that they overlap without increase of thickness & then ·bolting, brazing, or sewing them together; flench (whale). **2.** n. Joint made by ~ing timber or leather (also ~-*joint*) or metal (also ~--*weld*); notch, groove. [n. ME, perh. f. Scand., cf. Sw. *skarf*, Norw. *skarv* joint or seam; vb f. n.]

scă′rificātor, n. In vbl senses; esp., surgical instrument for scarifying, in which several lancet-points protrude at once from plane surface on touching of trigger. [mod. L, see SCARIFY, -OR]

scă′rifier, n. In vbl senses; esp.: = prec.; agricultural machine with prongs for stirring without turning soil; spiked road-breaking machine. [foll., -ER¹]

scă′ri|fȳ, v.t. (Surg.) make superficial incisions in, cut off skin from, (fig.) pain by severe criticism etc.; stir (soil) with scarifier. So ~FICA′TION n. [f. F *scarifier* f. LL *scarificare* f. L *scarifare*]

scār′ious, a. (bot.). Thin, dry, & membranaceous (of bracts etc.). [f. F *scarieux*]

scārlati′na (-tē-), n. Scarlet fever. [It. (-*tt*-), f. *scarlatto* SCARLET]

scārl′et, n. & a. (Of) brilliant red colour inclining to orange; ~ *cloth* or *clothes* (*dressed in* ~); ~ *fever*, infectious fever with ~ rash, (joc.) tendency to fall in love with soldiers; ~-*grain*, scale-insect from which red dye is made in Russia & Turkey; ~ *hat*, cardinal's, (allus.) cardinalate; ~ *rash*, roseola; ~ *runner*, ~-*flowered* climbing bean-plant; ~ *woman*, *whore*, pagan Rome, papal Rome, or the worldly spirit (acc. to interpretation put on *Rev.* xvii). [ME, f. OF *escarlate*, med. L *scarlatum*; ult. orig. unkn.]

scă′roid (*or* skār-), a. & n. (Fish) of scarus genus, resembling scarus. [-OID]

scārp, n., & v.t. **1.** Inner wall or slope (cf. COUNTERSCARP) of ditch in fortification; any steep steep. **2.** v.t. Make (slope) perpendicular or steep, provide (ditch) with steep ~ & counter~; (p.p.), of hillside etc.) steep, precipitous. [f. It. *scarpa* ESCARP]

scār′us, n. Kinds of bright-hued fish with parrotlike beak (also *parrotfish*) of wrasse family. [L, f. Gk *skaros*]

scăt, int., & v.i. & t. (-tt-; colloq.). Begone!; (vb) say ~, drive away thus. [perh. abbr. of *scatter*]

scăth|e (-dh), v.t., & n. **1.** Injure esp. by blasting or withering up (now rare exc. in part. used by exag. of severe speech, as ~*ing* sarcasm, *ridicule*, *remarks*, whence ~′ingLY² (-dh-) adv.); (in neg. context) do the least harm to (*shall not be* ~*ed*; esp. *unscathed*). **2.** n. (rare, & usu. in neg. context). Harm, injury, (*without*, *guard from*, ~*e*), whence ~e′LESS (-dhl-) a. (usu. pred.). [ME, f. ON *skathi* n., *skatha* vb,

= OE *sc(e)atha*, -*ian*, OHG *skado*, -*ōn* f. Gmc **skath-*]

scatŏl′ogȳ, n. Study of coprolites or of obscene literature. [Gk *skōr skatos* dung, -LOGY]

scatŏph′agous, a. Feeding on dung. [prec., Gk -*phagos* -eating]

scătt′er, v.t. & i., & n. **1.** Throw here & there (~ *seed*), strew (~ *gravel on road*, *road with gravel*), sprinkle; disperse (t. & i.), turn (t. & i.) in dispersed flight, rout, be routed; dissipate (cloud, hopes); diffuse (light); (of gun) send charge, send (charge), in spreading manner; (p.p.) not situated together, wide apart, sporadic, (~*ed hamlets*, *garrisons*, *instances*); ~-*brain*, heedless person; ~-*brained*, heedless, desultory. **2.** n. Act of ~ing, extent of distribution esp. of shot. Hence ~ingLY² adv. [ME, prob. var. of SHATTER]

scătt′ȳ, a. (sl.). Feeble-minded, hare-brained. [orig. unkn.]

scaup(-dŭck, n. Kinds of duck named from frequenting mussel-scaups or beds of mussels exposed at low tide. [perh. f. *scaup*, Sc. var. of SCALP]

scaup′er. Var. of SCALPER.

scaur. See SCAR².

scăv′eng|er (-j-), n., & v.i. **1.** Person employed to keep streets clean by carrying away refuse; animal feeding on carrion (esp. ~*er-beetle*, *-crab*), writer etc. delighting in filthy subjects or dealing in scandal; hence ~e (-j; by back formation) v.t. & i., (also) expel exhaust gases etc. from cylinder of internal-combustion engine, ~ERY (2, 5) (-j-) n. **2.** v.i. Be, act as, ~er. [ME *scavager* (cf. *messenger*) inspector of imports f. AF *scawager* f. *scawage* f. ONF *escauwer* inspect f. Flem. *scauwen* cogn. w. SHOW¹]

scăz′on, n. Greek & Latin iambic, ending with ∪ − ⌣ instead of ⌣ − ∪, used in short poems, choliamb; other metres of limping character. [L f. Gk *skazōn* (*skazō* limp)]

scena (shā′nah), n. (mus.). Scene or portion of opera; elaborate dramatic solo usu. including recitative. [It.]

scenār′iō (shā-), n. (pl. ~*s*). (Table of) scene-distribution, appearances of characters, etc., in dramatic work, skeleton libretto; (*usu. pr.* sēnär′iō) written version of play, details of scenes, etc., in film production. [It.]

scend. See SEND².

scēne, n. **1.** Stage of theatre (arch.; still in fig. use *quit the* ~, esp. = die); place on which something is exhibited as on the stage (*this world is a* ~ *of strife*). **2.** Place in which events set forth in drama or tale are supposed to occur, locality of event, (*the* ~ *is laid in India*; *the* ~ *of the disaster was the North Sea*). **3.** Portion of a play during which action is continuous or (esp. of French plays) in which no intermediate entries or exits occur, subdivision (or rarely the whole) of an act, (*in the* *third ~ of Act II*; *Act II, ~ iii, l. 220*; *the famous duel ~*; CARPENTER-~); (transf.) description with more or less abrupt beginning & end of an incident or part of person's life etc. (*~s of clerical life, from a goldfield*, etc.), actual incident that might occasion such description (*distressing ~s occurred*), agitated colloquy esp. with display of temper (*now don't make a ~*). **4.** Any of the pieces of painted canvas, woodwork, etc., used to help in representing ~ of action on stage, or whole of these together (*behind the ~s*, among the stage machinery or the actors off the stage, usu. fig. = having information not accessible to the public; CARPENTER-~; *~s painted by —*; *set ~*, made up of many parts fitted together; DROP-SCENE); (transf.) landscape or view spread before spectator like ~ in theatre (*a silvan, desolate, ~*; *a ~ of destruction*; *change of ~*, variety of surroundings esp. secured by travel). **5.** *~-dock*, space near stage where ~s are stored; *~-painter, -painting*, of theatre ~s; *~-shifter*, person helping to change ~s in theatre. [f. F *scène* f. L f. Gk *skēnē* tent, stage]

scēn'erў, n. Accessories used in theatre to make stage resemble supposed scene of action; spectacles presented by natural features of a district (*the ~ is imposing, tame*). [17th c. *scenary* f. It. *scenario* f. L LL *scenarius* (prec., -ARY [1]) of the stage, assim. to -ERY]

scēn'ic, a. Of, on, the stage (*~ performances*); of the nature of a show, picturesque in grouping; (of picture etc.) telling a tale, crystallizing an incident; (of emotion etc.) dramatic, affected, put on; *~ railway*, miniature railway running through artificial picturesque scenery, as attraction at large fairs etc. Hence **scēn'ICALLY** adv. [f. F *scénique*, or f. L f. Gk *skēnikos* (SCENE, -IC)]

scēn|ŏg'raphў, n. Drawing or painting in perspective (esp. of representing building not in ground-plan or elevation, but as spectator sees it). So ~'OGRAPH(1), ~ŏG'RAPHER nn., ~OGRAPH'IC a., ~ŏgrăph'ICALLY adv. [f. F (-*ie*) or L f. Gk *skēnographia* (SCENE, -GRAPHY)]

scĕnt, v.t. & i., & n. **1.** Discern by smell (*~ game* etc.), (fig.) begin to suspect presence or existence of (*~ treachery, a job*); *~ out*, discover by smelling about or search; make fragrant or rank (*rose, carrion, ~s the air*), apply perfume to (handkerchief etc.; *~ed soap, tobacco*); exercise sense of smell, apply this to, (*goes ~ing about; lifts its head & ~s the air*). **2.** n. Odour, esp. of agreeable kind, proceeding from or belonging to something (*the ~ of hay*), whence ~'LESS a.; (hunt.) trail perceptible to hounds' sense of smell left by animal (often fig.; *follow up, lose, recover*, etc., *the ~*, lit., & of investigation; *on the ~*, having clue; *put off the ~*, deceive by false indications;

COLD [1], HOT [1], ~), paper strewn by paper-chase hares (*false ~*, laid to deceive about course, also fig.); power of detecting or distinguishing smells or of discovering presence of something, flair, (*some dogs have practically no ~; keen-~ed; has a wonderful ~ for snobbery, young talent*, etc.); liquid perfume distilled from flowers etc. **3.** *~-bag*, pouch containing special odoriferous substance in some animals, also bag of aniseed etc. as substitute for fox in hunting; *~-bottle*, for perfume; *~-gland*, secreting musk, civet, etc.; *~-organ*, *~-bag* or *~-gland*; hence (-)~'ED [2] a. (*~ed caper*, kind of tea; *~ed fern*, kind smelling like citron). [ME *sent* f. OF *sentir* perceive, smell, f. L *sentire*]

scĕp'sis (sk-), *sk-, n. Philosophic doubt, sceptical philosophy. [f. Gk *skepsis* inquiry (*skeptomai* examine)]

scĕp'tic (sk-), *sk-, n. Ancient or modern holder of PYRRHONISM; person who doubts truth of the Christian or of all religious doctrines, agnostic, (pop.) atheist; person of sceptical habit of mind, or unconvinced of truth of particular fact or theory, or who takes cynical views. So ~ISM(3) (sk-) n. [f. F *sceptique* or L f. Gk *skeptikos* (prec., -IC)]

scĕp'tical (sk-), *sk-, a. Inclined to suspense of judgement, given to questioning truth of facts & soundness of inferences, critical, incredulous; accepting PYRRHONISM, denying possibility of knowledge; holding, designed to support, inspired by, the ideas of SCEPTICS. Hence ~LY [2] adv. [-AL]

scĕp'tr|e (-ter), n. Staff borne as symbol of personal sovereignty; royal or imperial authority. Hence ~ED [2] (-*terd*), ~eLESS (-*terl-*), aa. [ME, f. OF, f. L f. Gk *skēptron*]

schadenfreude (shah'denfroide), n. Malicious enjoyment of others' misfortunes. [G, f. *schade* damage + *freude* joy]

schappe (shăp, shah'pe), n. Fabric or yarn made from waste silk. [G, = silk waste]

schĕd'ūle (‖ sh-, *sk-), n., & v.t. **1.** Tabulated statement of details, inventory, list, etc., esp. as appendix or annexe to principal document; *time-table*; ~ *time*, that stated in time-table (*on ~*, to ~ time). **2.** v.t. Make ~ of, include in ~. [ME & OF *cedule* f. LL *scedula* (L *sceda* papyrus-strip, -ULE) *sch-* f. med. L]

scheel'ite (sh-), n. (min.). Calcium tungstate, found in varicoloured brilliant crystals. [K. W. *Scheele* (d. 1786), -ITE [1](2)]

scheik. = SHEIKH.

schēm'|a (sk-), n. (pl. *~ata*). Synopsis, outline, diagram; (log.) syllogistic figure; (gram., rhet.) figure of speech; (Kantian philos.) general type, essential form, conception of what is common to all members of a class. So ~ăt'IC a., ~ăt'ICALLY adv., (sk-). [L, f. Gk *skhēma -atos*] scheme 1126 school

schĕm|e (sk-), n., & v.i. & t. **1.** Systematic arrangement proposed or in operation (~*e of colour*, principle on which colours have been chosen & grouped in picture etc.), table of classification or of appointed times, outline, syllabus; plan for doing something; artful or underhand design. **2.** vb. Make plans, plan esp. in secret or underhand way (*to do, for*, or abs.), intrigue, whence ~'ER[1] n., ~'ING[2] a., (sk-); plan to bring about. [f. L SCHEMA]

scherzăn'dŏ (skärts-), mus. direction. In playful manner. [It.]

scherzo (skārt'sō), n. (pl. ~s). Vigorous (prop. light & playful) composition, independent or as movement in works of sonata type. [It., f. Gmc (G *scherz* jest)]

Schiedăm' (skĭd-), n. Holland gin. [place]

schill'ing (sh-), n. Austrian monetary unit and coin, = 100 groschen. [G]

schipp'erke (sk-, sh-), n. Kind of lapdog. [Du.]

schism (sĭ'zm), n. Division of a community into factions (rare in gen. sense), esp. separation of a Church into two Churches or secession of part of a Church owing to difference of opinion on doctrine or discipline; offence of causing or promoting such separation. [ME & OF *scisme* f. LL f. Gk *skhisma* -*atos* (*skhizō* split)]

schismăt'ic (sĭz-), a & n., -ic|al, a. **1.** Tending or inclined to, guilty of, schism; hence ~alLY[2] adv. **2.** n. Holder of ~ opinions, member of ~ faction or seceded branch of a Church. [ME, f. OF *scismatique* f. LL f. Gk *skhismatikos* (prec., -IC), -AL]

schist (sh-), n. Kinds of foliated rock presenting layers of different minerals & splitting in thin irregular plates. Hence **schis'tOSE[1]** (sh-) a. [f. F *schiste* f. L f. Gk *skhistos* split (SCHISM)]

schizăn'thus (sk-), n. Kinds of plant with handsome white, violet, or crimson flowers & much-divided leaves. [Gk *skhizō* split, *anthos* flower]

schiz'oid (sk-), a. & n. Of or resembling schizophrenia or a schizophrenic; (n.) ~ person. [as prec., -OID]

schizomỹcĕte' (sk-), n. Any of the *Schizomycetae*, a class of minute often single-cell vegetable organisms between algae & fungi multiplying by fission, including bacilli, bacteria. microbes, etc. [Gk *skhizō* split, *mukēs -ētos* mushroom]

schĭzophr|ĕn'ia (sk-), n. Mental disease marked by disconnexion between thoughts, feelings, & actions. Hence ~ĕn'IC a. & n. [as prec., Gk *phrēn* mind]

***schmaltz** (shmawlts), n. (sl.). Sugary sentimentalism in art. [thr. Yiddish f. G *schmalz* dripping, lard]

schnăp(p)s (shn-), n. A spirit resembling Holland gin. [G]

schnauzer (shnow'tser), n. German breed of house-dog with close wiry coat. [G]

Schneid'er Trōph'ỹ (shnī-), n. International trophy open to seaplanes of all nations presented in 1913 by Jacques Schneider, in 1931 won outright by Great Britain.

Schnȯrk'el (shn-), n. (German name for) SNORT[2]. [G *schnorchel*]

schnŏ'rrer (shn-), n. Jewish beggar. [Yiddish, f. G dial. *schnurrer* beggar]

schŏl'ar (sk-), n. **1.** Schoolboy, schoolgirl, (arch. or vulg.). **2.** Person's disciple (rhet.). **3.** Person who learns (*proved an apt, dull, ~; at 90 he was still a ~*). **4.** Learned person, person versed in literature esp. that of ancient Greece & Rome, (*a ~ & a gentleman*, person of good education & breeding), whence ~LY[1] a., ~SHIP (3) n. **5.** (Univv., pub. schh.) undergraduate or child admitted to foundation usu. after competitive examination & receiving education gratis or for reduced fees (RHODES ~), whence ~SHIP(1) n. [ME, f. AF *escoler* (OF -*ier*) f. LL *scholaris* (SCHOOL, -AR[1]); OE dir. f. L]

scholăs'tic (sk-), a. & n. **1.** Of universities, schools, schooling, dons, or schoolmasters, educational, academic, pedantic, formal, (*a ~ education, post; ~ attire, manners, precision, life; ~ agent*, finding posts for teachers). **2.** (As) of the SCHOOL[1]men, dealing in logical subtleties, (*~ theology*, much concerned with precise definition of & deduction from dogma); hence or cogn. **scholăs'tICALLY** adv., ~ISM (2, 3) n. **3.** n. SCHOOL[1]man; modern theologian of ~ tendencies; Jesuit between novitiate & priesthood. [f. L f. Gk *skholastikos* (*skholē*, see SCHOOL[1], -IC)]

schŏl'ĭ|ăst (sk-), n. Commentator, esp. ancient grammarian who wrote scholia on the classics. Hence ~ăs'tIC a. [f. med. L f. Gk *skholiastēs* (*skholiazō* write scholia) (foll.)]

schŏl'ĭum (sk-), n. (pl. -*ia*). Marginal note, explanatory comment, esp. one by ancient grammarian on passage in classical author. [f. med. L f. Gk *skholion* (*skholē* see foll.)]

school[1] (sk-), n., & v.t. **1.** Institution for educating children or giving instruction usu. of more elementary or more technical kind than that given at universities (APPROVED, BOARD[1], BOARDING, COMPREHENSIVE, DAY, GRAMMAR, MIXED, NIGHT, NORMAL, PRIMARY, PRIVATE, PUBLIC, SECONDARY, SUNDAY, ~; || *national ~*, one founded by the National Society started 1811 to promote education of the poor; *continuation ~*, at which those who have left esp. primary ~ for an occupation can have further teaching in leisure time; *evening-~*, = night-~; *free ~*, open without fees; *high ~*, secondary ~, or chief ~ of a town etc.; *technical ~*, giving TECHNICAL education; *keep a ~*, manage private ~); buildings of such institution, any of its rooms used for teaching in (*the fifth-form, chemistry, ~*), its pupils (*the whole ~*

knows); time during which teaching is done (*there will be no ~ today*; *go to ~*, attend lesson). **2.** Being educated in a ~ (*go to, leave, ~*, begin, cease, this; *go to ~ to*, transf., imitate or learn from); (fig.) circumstances or occupation serving to discipline or instruct (*in the ~ of adversity*; *learnt his generalship in a severe ~*; *the duel is a good ~ of manners*). **3.** Medieval lecture-room (*the~s*, medieval universities & their professors & teaching & disputations; *the theology of the ~s*; *~ doctors, ~men*); ‖ any of the branches of study with separate examinations at university (*the history, mathematical, Greats, ~*); hall in which university examinations are held; (pl.) such examination (*in the ~s*, undergoing or conducting this at Oxford; ‖ *in for his ~s*, of candidate). **4.** Disciples or imitators or followers of philosopher, artist, etc., band or succession of persons devoted to some cause or principle or agreeing in typical characteristics, (*left no ~ behind him*; *~ of Epicurus, Raphael*, etc.; *Bolognese, Venetian, Roman, British*, etc., *~*, of painters; *lake, romantic*, etc., *~*, of literature; *peripatetic, Hegelian*, etc., *~*, of philosophy; *laissez-faire, blue-water*, etc., *~*, of politics, strategy; *Tübingen ~*, of rationalistic theological criticism; *a gentleman of the old ~*, according to the older acceptation of the word). **5.** (mus.). Manual of (*—'s violin ~, ~ of counterpoint*). **6.** ‖ *Old ~ tie*, necktie worn by former members of a ~, (fig.) sentimental or excessive local or class loyalty; *~--board*, local education authority ‖ responsible (1870–1902) for providing BOARD[1].*~s*; *~-book*, for use in *~s*; *~'boy*, boy at ~ (often attrib., as *~boy slang, mischief, spirits*); ‖ *~-dame*, keeper of old-fashioned DAME-*~*; *~-days*, time of being at ~ esp. as looked back upon; *~ divine*, scholastic theologian, so *~ divinity*; *~ fee(s)*, amount periodically paid by pupil's parent etc.; *~'fellow*, member past or present of same ~; *~'girl* (as *~boy*); *~'house*, building or esp. village ~; ‖ *~ house*, headmaster's or central boarding-house at public ~; *~-inspector*, reporting on efficiency of *~s*; **~-ma'am, -marm* colloq., *~mistress*); *~'man*, teacher in medieval European university, theologian dealing with religious doctrines by rules of Aristotelian logic; *~'master*, head or assistant male teacher in ~, pedagogue; *~'mate*, contemporary at same ~; *~ miss*, inexperienced or bashful girl; *~'mistress* (as *~master*); ‖ *~ pence*, money formerly brought weekly by elementary-*~* child as fee; *~'room*, used for lessons in ~ or private house; *~-ship*, training-ship; *~-teacher*, master or mistress esp. in primary ~; *~-teaching*; *~-time*, lesson-time at ~ or home, also = *~-days*. **7.** v.t. Send to ~, provide for education of, (rare), whence (in common use)*~'ING*[1] n.;

discipline, bring under control, deliberately train or accustom *to*, induce to follow advice, (*must ~ his temper*; *~ oneself to patience, to take an interest in*; *will not be ~ed*). [OE *scōl* f. L *schola* school f. Gk *skholē* leisure, philosophy, lecture--place]

school[2] (sk-), n., & v.i. **1.** Shoal of or *of* fish; *~-fish*, kinds that *~*, esp. the menhaden. **2.** v.i. Form *~s*. [ME, f. MDu. *schole*, = OS *scola*, OE *scolu* troop]

school'able (sk-), a. Liable by age etc. to compulsory education. [-ABLE]

schoon'er (sk-), n. **1.** Fore-&-aft-rigged vessel with two or more masts; PRAIRIE-*~*. **2.** *Tall beer-glass; ‖ measure for beer. [orig. *scooner*, supposed to have been given by the first designer (*c.* 1713) f. an alleged New-England vb *scun, scoon* skim or skip]

schörl (sh-), n. Black tourmaline. [f. G *schörl*]

schöttische (shŏtēsh'), n. (Music for) kind of slower polka. [G (-*sch*), = *Scottish*]

sciäg'raphy (sī-), **ski-**, n. Art of shading in drawing etc.; photography by X-rays (usu. *sk-*); (archit.; also & usu. *-graph*) vertical section showing interior of house etc.; (astron.) finding of time by shadows as in sundial. So **sci'agräm** n., X-ray picture, **sci'agrammät'ic** a., **-icallÿ** adv., **sci'aGRAPH**(1, 2, 3) n. & v.t., **sciä-GRAPHER** n., **sciaGRAPH'IC** a., **sciagräph'-ICALLY** adv., (-sī-). [f. F (*-ie*) f. L f. Gk *skiagraphia* (*skia* shade, -GRAPHY)]

sciäm'achy (sī-, -kī), **sciŏ-**, n. Fighting with shadows, imaginary or futile combat. [f. Gk *skiamakhia* (prec., *-makhos* -fighting f. *makhomai* fight, -IA[1])]

sciät'ic (sī-), a. Of the hip (*~ nerve, artery*, etc.); of, affecting, the *~ nerve*; suffering from or liable to sciatica. Hence **sciät'IC-ALLY** adv. [f. F *sciatique* f. LL *sciaticus* f. L f. Gk *iskhiadikos* subject to sciatica (*iskhias -ados* loin-pain f. *iskhion* socket of thigh-bone)]

sciät'ica (sī-), n. Neuralgia of hip & thigh, pain in sciatic nerve. [ME, f. med. L *sciatica* (*passio*), fem. of LL as prec.]

sci'ence (sī-), n. **1.** Knowledge (arch.), whence (in mod. use) **sciěn'tIAL** (-shl) a., **sciěn'tialLÿ**[2] adv. **2.** Systematic & formulated knowledge (*moral, political, natural*, etc., *~*, such knowledge in reference to these subjects); pursuit of this or principles regulating such pursuit (*man of ~*). **3.** (Also *natural ~*) the physical or natural *~s* collectively (*~ now shares the curriculum with literature, history, & mathematics*). **4.** (With *a* & pl.) branch of knowledge, organized body of the knowledge that has been accumulated on a subject, (*the ~ of optics, ethics, philology*; *exact ~*, admitting of quantitative treatment; *pure ~*, one depending on deductions from self-evident truths, as mathematics, logic; *natural, physical, ~*, one dealing with material phenomena &

based mainly on observation, experiment, & induction, as chemistry, biology, whence esp. sci′entIST, sci′entISM, nn.; *the dismal* ~, political economy). **5.** Expert's skill as opp. strength or natural ability, esp. in pugilism or other fighting. **6.** ~ *fiction*, fanciful fiction dealing with space travel, life on other planets, etc. [ME, f. OF f. L *scientia* (*scire* know, -ENCE)]

scien′ter (sī-), adv. (legal). Wittingly. [L (prec., -ENT, -*er* adv. term.)]

scientif′|ic (sī-), a. (Of investigations etc.) according to rules laid down in science for testing soundness of conclusions, systematic, accurate; of, used or engaged in, esp. natural science (~*ic instruments, books, terminology, men*); (of act or agent) assisted by expert knowledge (*a*~*ic boxer, game*; ~*ic cruelty*). Hence ~ICALLY adv. [f. LL *scientificus*, see SCIENCE, -FIC]

scil′icĕt (sī-), adv. (abbr. *sc.*, *scil.*). To wit, that is to say, namely, (introducing word to be supplied or explanation of ambiguous one). [L, = *scire licet* it is permitted to know]

Scillōn′ian (sī-), a. & n. (Native, inhabitant) of the Scilly Isles. [f. *Scill(y)* + -*onian* (perh. after *Devonian*)]

scim′itar (sī-), n. Oriental curved sword usu. broadening towards point. [16th c. f. Pers. *šešmīr* sabre, F *cimeterre*, It. *scimitarra* etc.; ult. orig. unkn.]

scintill′a (sī-), n. Spark, atom, (esp. *not a* ~ *of evidence* etc.). [L]

scin′till|āte (sī-), v.i. Sparkle, twinkle, emit sparks; also fig. of witty talk etc. So ~ANT a., ~A′TION n. [f. L *scintillare* (prec.), -ATE[3]]

sci′ol|ist (sī-), n. Superficial pretender to knowledge, smatterer. Hence or cogn. ~ISM(2) n., ~is′tIC a. [f. LL *sciolus* smatterer (*scire* know), -IST]

sciol′tō (shō-), mus. direction. In free manner, according to taste; staccato. [It.]

sciomachy. See SCIAMACHY.

sci′on (sī-), n. Shoot of plant, esp. one cut for grafting or planting; descendant, young member of (esp. noble) family. [ME, f. OF *cion*, *sion*, (mod. *scion*), ult. f. Frank. *kitho* KID[1]]

Sci′ŏt(e) (sī-), a. & n. (Inhabitant) of Scio, the ancient Chios. [-OT[2]]

seir′e fā′ciăs (sīrī, -shī-), n. Writ to enforce or annul judgement, patent, etc. [L, = *let* (party) know]

scirocco. See SIROCCO.

scirrh|us (sī′rus, skī-), n. Hard tumour as early stage of cancer. Hence or cogn. ~′OID, ~OUS, aa., ~ŏs′ITY, n. [L, f. Gk *skir(r)os* (*skiros* hard)]

sciss′el (sī-), n. Waste clippings of metal or remainder of metal plate from which discs have been punched in coining. [f. F *cisaille* f. *ciseau* CHISEL, -AL(2)]

sciss′ile (sī-), a. Able to be cut. [f. L *scissilis* (*scindere sciss-* cut, -IL)]

scission (sī′shn), n. Cutting, being cut, division, split. [F, f. LL *scissionem* (prec., -ION)]

sciss′or (sīz′or), v.t. Cut (*off, up, into*, etc.) with scissors; clip out or *out* (cutting from book etc.), whence ~ING[1](2) n. [f. foll.]

sciss′ors (sīz′orz), n. pl. Instrument for cutting fabrics, paring nails, etc., made of two blades with handles for thumb & one finger or the fingers & so pivoted that their cutting edges work by leverage against each other (often *pair of* ~; *I want a pair of, some,* ~; *where are my* ~?; *buttonhole* ~, with gaps in blades near pivot so that cutting begins inside edge of cloth; *lamp, nail,* ~, of special shapes for trimming wicks, nails; ~ *& paste*, compiling of books out of cuttings from others); *scissor-bill*, the bird SKIMMER; *scissor-bird* or *-tail*, kinds of bird with long forked tail esp. fork-tailed fly-catcher; *scissor-tooth*, tooth in carnivora acting like ~ against one in other jaw. Hence **sciss′or**WISE (sīz′or-) adv. [ME *sisoures* f. OF *cisoires* f. LL *cisoria* pl. of *cisorium* (as CHISEL, -ORY)]

sci′ūr|ine (sī-), a. Of the squirrel tribe; squirrel-like. So ~OID a. [f. L f. Gk *skiouros* squirrel + -INE[1]]

Sclav, Sclavonic, etc. See **Slav** etc.

sclĕr′|a, n. = SCLEROTIC n. (anat.). Hence ~IT′IS, ~ŎT′OMY, nn. [f. fem. of Gk *sklēros* hard]

sclĕrī′asis, n. (path.). Hardening of tissue. [mod. L (foll., -ASIS) after *elephantiasis*]

sclĕr′|(o)-, comb. form of Gk *sklēros* hard: ~*ench′yma* (-ngk-), hard tissue of coral, tissue forming hard parts of plants such as nut-shell or seed-coat; ~*oderm′(at)ous*, with hard outer skin (of reptiles, fish, etc.); ~′*ogen*, hard matter deposited on inner surface of plant-cells, e.g. that lining walnut shell; ~*omēn′inx*, DURA MATER; ~*oskel′eton*, hard parts resulting from ossification of tendons as in turkey's leg etc.; ~*os′teous*, of the nature of ~o-skeleton.

sclĕr′oid, a. (bot., zool.). Of hard texture. [f. Gk *sklēros* hard + -OID]

sclĕrōm′a, sclĕrōs′is, nn. (pl. *-mata, -sēs*). Morbid hardening of tissue; (bot.; -*sis*) hardening of cell-wall by SCLEROgen. Hence **sclĕr′ōSED**[2] (-st) a. [Gk (*sk-*), SCLERO-, -OMA, -OSIS]

sclĕrŏt′ic, a. & n. **1.** Of, with, sclerosis; of the ~. **2.** ′n. Membrane coating eye round iris, white of eye; hence **sclĕrot**IT′IS n. [SCLERO-, -OTIC]

sclĕr′ous, a. (path., anat., bot.). Indurated, bony. [Gk *sklēros* hard, -OUS]

scŏbs, n. Sawdust, shavings, filings, dross. So scŏb′IFORM a. (bot., of seeds). [L]

scŏff[1], n., & v.i. **1.** Mocking words, taunt, gibe; object of ridicule, laughing-stock. **2.** v.i. Speak derisively esp. of religion or object of respect; aim ~s or mockery *at*; hence ~'ER¹ n., ~'inġLY² adv. [vb f. n., ME *scof*, perh. f. Scand.; cf. early mod. Da. *skuf*, *skof* jest, mockery]

scöff², n., & v.t. & i. (sl.). **1.** Food, meal, grub. **2.** vb. Eat greedily. [(1) Afrikaans (now *skof*), repr. Du. *schoft* quarter of a day (hence, meal); (2) vb orig. a var. of dial. *scaff* (16th c.) & assoc. w. (1)]

scöld, v.i. & t., & n. **1.** Find fault noisily, rail; rate, rebuke, (chiefly of parent, employer, speaking to child, servant), whence **scöl'dinġ¹**(1) n. **2.** n. Railing or nagging woman. [vb f. n., ME, app. f. ON *skäld* SCALD²]

scöl'ex, n. (pl. *-ē'cēs*). Head of larval or adult tapeworm. [f. Gk *skōlēx* worm]

scöli|ōs'is, n. Lateral curvature of spine. Hence ~ōT'IC a. [mod. L, f. Gk f. *skolios* crooked, -OSIS]

scollop. See SCALLOP.

scŏlopā'ceous (-shus), scŏl'opacine, aa. Of, like, the snipes. [f. LL f. Gk *skolopax* snipe, see -ACEOUS, -INE¹]

scŏlopĕn'drine, a. Of, like, related to, centipede(s). [f. L f. Gk *skolopendra* millepede, -INE¹]

scŏlopĕn'drium, n. Kinds of fern, hart's--tongue etc. [L, f. Gk *skolopendrion* (prec.)]

scŏm'b|er, n. Mackerel or kinds of fish allied to it. Hence ~rID³(1) n., ~roID a. & n. [L, f. Gk *skombros*]

scŏn. Var. of SCONE.

scönce¹, n. Flat candlestick with handle; bracket candlestick to hang on wall. [ME, f. OF *esconse* lantern or med. L *sconsa* f. L *absconsa* fem. p.p. of ABSCOND-*ere* hide]

scönce², n. (Old joc. term for) head, crown of head (*a crack on the* ~). [perh. a use of prec. or foll.]

scönce³, n. Small fort or earthwork, usu. covering a ford, pass, etc.; (arch.) shelter, screen. [16th c., f. Du. *schans*]

∥ **scönce⁴**, v.t., & n. **1.** (At Oxford) inflict forfeit of beer n. for offence against table etiquette upon (member of company or his offence; *Jones was, Latin quotations are, ~d*); (hist., of university officials etc.) fine for breach of discipline (*Vice-Chancellor ~d all that were without their hoods*). **2.** n. The forfeit. [orig. unkn.]

∥ **scöne**, n. Soft cake of barley-meal or wheat-flour of size for single portion cooked on griddle. [perh. f. MDu. *schoon(brot)*, MLG *schon-* fine (bread)]

scoōp, n., & v.t. **1.** Short-handled deep shovel for taking up & transferring such things as grain, sugar, coal, specie; large long-handled ladle-shaped dipping-vessel for liquids; gouge-like instrument e.g. for surgical use or for helping cheese; coal-scuttle; motion as of, act of, ~ing (*with a, at one,* ~); large profit made quickly or by anticipating competitors; exclusive piece of news for newspaper;

~*-net*, formed for sweeping river-bottom, also hand-net for catching bait; ~*-wheel*, with buckets on circumference raising water for irrigation etc. **2.** v.t. Lift (usu. *up*), hollow (usu. *out*), (as) with ~; secure (large profit etc.) by sudden action or stroke of luck; forestall (rival newspaper, reporter, etc.) with ~. [ME, f. MDu., MLG *schŏpe* bucket etc., & MDu. *schoppe*, MLG *schuppe* shovel]

scoōp'er, n. In vbl senses; esp.: engraver's tool; kind of avocet. [-ER¹]

scoōt, v.i. (sl.). Run, dart, make off. Hence ~'ER¹(2) n., child's toy propelled by foot and consisting of a footboard with two wheels set tandemwise and a long steering-handle, (also, in full *motor* ~*er*) simple motor cycle. [18th c. (naut.) *scout*; later *scoot* from U.S.]

scöp'a, scöp'ŭla, nn. (entom.; pl. *-ae*). Small brushlike tuft of hairs esp. on bees' legs. Hence **scöp'ATE²**, **scöp'ŭlATE²**, **scöp'iFORM, scöp'ŭliFORM, scöpir'EROUS**, aa. [*scopa* sing. of L *scopae*, = twigs, broom; *-la* LL dim.]

scöpe, n. **1.** End aimed at, purpose, intention, (now rare). **2.** Outlook, purview, sweep or reach or sphere of observation or action, tether, extent to which it is permissible or possible to range, opportunity, outlet, vent, (*mind, undertaking, of wide* ~; *is beyond my* ~; *gives no, ample,* ~ *for expatiating, to ability; seeks* ~ *for his energies*). **3.** (naut.). Length of cable out when ship rides at anchor. [f. It. *scopo* f. Gk *skopos* target (*skeptomai* look at)]

-scope, suf. repr. L f. Gk *-skopion* f. *skopein* observe. *Horoscope* is f. Gk *hŏroskopos*, (watcher of) a nativity. *Telescope* is f. Gk *tēleskopos*, far-seeing. In wds of mod. formation the suf. usu. has the sense *instrument for observing or showing*, as *stetho~*, *gyro~*, *laryngo~*, and the hybrid *muto~*. Hence *-scŏp'ic*, adj. suf., pertaining to the -scope, occas. w. extended meaning also, as in TELESCOPIC, MICROSCOPIC; *-scopy*, n. suf., use of or examination by the -scope, as *laryngoscopy*.

scörbūt'|ic, a. & n. Of, like, (person) affected with, scurvy. Hence ~ICALLY adv. [f. obs. *scorbut(e)* f. F *scorbut* scurvy prob. f. MLG *schorbūk* (*schoren* break, *būk* belly) +-IC]

scörch, v.t. & i., & n. **1.** Burn surface of with flame or heat-rays so as to discolour or injure or pain, affect with sensation of burning (*a wit that ~es*), whence ~'ING² a., ~'inġLY² adv.; ~*ed earth policy*, burning crops etc. and removing or destroying anything that might be of use to an enemy occupying the country; become discoloured etc. with heat. **2.** (sl.). (Of motorist or cyclist) go at utmost speed; (n.) spell of such driving or riding. [ME, of obsc. orig.; cf. ME *skorken*, *skorkle* in same sense]

scŏrch′er, n. In vbl senses; (also, (sl.) fine specimen of its kind. [-ER¹]

scōre, n., & v.t. & i. **1.** Notch cut or line cut or scratched or drawn (*rock covered with ~s or striations*; *the ~s of the whip showed on his back*; *made a ~ in the tally*; *lightning had made ~s in the mountain side*); mark showing starting-point in race or standing-place in shooting-match (now rare; hence perh. *go off at ~*, start off vigorously esp. to discourse on pet subject); (naut.) groove in block or dead--eye to hold strap. **2.** Running account kept by ~s against customer's name esp. for drink in old inns, reckoning esp. for entertainment, (*pay · one's ~*, settle reckoning; *death pays all~s*; *pay off old~s*, fig., pay person out for past offence; so *quit ~s with*). **3.** Number of points made by player or side in some games, register of items of this, (*make a good ~*; *what is the~ now?*; *~-book, -card, -sheet*, prepared for entering esp. cricket-~ in; *keep ~*, register it as it is made). **4.** (mus.). Copy of a composition on set of staves braced & barred together (named from bar drawn through all staves; *full ~*, with separate staff for each part; *compressed*, *close*, *short, ~* in vocal music, with treble & alto on one staff, tenor & bass on another; *in ~*, with parts arranged below each other & corresponding). **5.** Twenty, set of twenty, (for use of ~, ~s, see DOZEN; *three ~ & ten*, phr. for normal length of human life; *~s of people*, great numbers); weight of twenty (or twenty-one) pounds, esp. in weighing pigs or oxen. **6.** Category, head, (*rejected on the ~ of absurdity*, as being absurd; *you may be easy on that ~*, so far as that matter is concerned). **7.** ‖ (sl.). Remark or act by which person ~s off another (*given to making cheap ~s*); piece of good fortune (*what a ~!*). **8.** vb. Mark with notches or incisions or lines, slash, furrow, make (line etc.) with something that marks, (*~ out words*, draw line through them; *~ under*, underline); *criticize severely. **9.** Mark *up* in inn-~, enter (item of debt *against* or *to* customer; often *up*); (fig.) mentally record (offence *against* or *to* offender); record (point in cricket etc. ~; abs., keep the ~, whence **scōr′ER**¹ n.). **10.** Win & be credited with (*has ~d a success, a century at cricket*), make points in game (*failed to ~*), secure an advantage or have good luck (*that is where he ~s*; *we shall ~ by it*); ‖ *~ off* (sl.), worst in argument or repartee, inflict some humiliation on. **11.** (mus.). Orchestrate, whence **scōr′ING**¹ (6) n., arrange *for* another instrument, write out in ~. [OE *scoru* f. ON *skor* notch, tally, twenty, f. Gmc *skur-*, *sker-*, see SHEAR]

scŏr′|ia, n. (pl. *~iae*). Cellular lava or fragments of it. Hence~**iA′CEOUS** (-āshus) a. [L, f. Gk *skŏria* refuse (*skŏr* dung)]

scŏr′i|fȳ, v.t. Reduce to dross, assay (precious metal) by~fying a portion of its ore fused with lead & borax. Hence~**FICA**- TION, ~**fIER**¹ (2), nn. [prec., -FY]

scŏrn, n., & v.t. **1.** Disdain, contempt, derision, (*think ~ of*, despise; LAUGH *to ~*), whence~′**FUL** a., ~′**fulLY**² adv., ~′**fulN**ESS n.; object of contempt, (usu. *a ~ to*, the *~ of*, persons etc.). **2.** v.t. Hold in contempt, consider beneath notice, abstain from or refuse *to* do as unworthy (*~s lying, a lie, to lie*); hence ~′**ER**¹ n. (arch. exc. w. *of*). [ME *skarn*, *scorne*, etc. f. OF *esc(h)arn(ir)* f. WG, cf. OS, OHG *skern* mockery]

Scōrp′iō, n. Zodiacal constellation & eighth sign of zodiac, the Scorpion. [L, also *scorpius* f. Gk *skorpios* scorpion]

scōrp′ioid, n. & a. (bot.). (Inflorescence) curled up at end like scorpion's tail & uncurling as flowers develop. [f. Gk *skorpioeidēs* (prec., -OID)]

scōrp′ion, n. **1.** Arachnid with lobster-like claws & jointed tail that can be bent over to inflict poisoned sting on prey held in claws, falsely reputed to sting itself to death if encircled with fire & to contain a substance serving as antidote for its poison. **2.** (bibl.). Whip armed with metal points (1 *Kings* xii. 11). **3.** (*S~*)=SCORPIO. **4.** Kind of ballista. **5.** *~-broom*, kind of genista; *~-fish*, kind with spines on head & fins; *~-plant*, Javan orchid with creamy white flower, also *~-broom*; *~- -shell*, kind of shellfish with long spines fringing outer lip of aperture; *~-thorn*, *~-broom*. [ME, f. OF, f. L *scorpionem* SCORPIO]

scōrzonēr′a, n. Black salsify or viper's--grass, a plant with parsnip-like root used as vegetable. [It., f. *scorzone* venomous snake]

scŏt¹, n. (hist.). Payment corresponding to modern tax, rate, or other assessed contribution (*pay ~ & lot*, share pecuniary burdens of borough etc.); *~-free* (in mod. use), not having to pay (rare), (usu.) unharmed, unpunished, safe, (esp. *go ~- -free*). [ME, f. ON *skot* (also, partly, f. OF *escot* f. same Gmc orig.), corresp. to OE *sc(e)ot*, see SHOT³]

Scŏt², n. (Pl.) Gaelic tribe that migrated from Ireland to Scotland about 6th c. (often PICTS *& ~s*); native of Scotland. [OE *Scottas* pl., f. LL *Scottus*]

Scŏtch¹, a. & n. **1.** Of Scotland or its inhabitants, in the dialect(s) of English spoken in Lowlands of Scotland, (the ~ themselves usu. prefer the form *Scottish* also used by the English esp. in dignified style or context, or *Scots* rare in Engl. use exc. in compliment to ~ hearers; *the ~*, ~ people or nation; *~* FIR, KALE, MIST; POUND¹ *Scots*; *~ broth*, soup or liquid stew with pearl barley and vegetables; *~ cap*, of shapes worn with Highland costume, Glengarry, Tam-o′-Shanter, etc.; *~ catch* or *snap* in music, short note on the beat followed by long one occupying remainder of beat; ~ *collops*, steak & onions; ~ *pebble*, kinds of agate & jasper, cairngorm, etc.; ~ *terrier*, small rough--haired short-legged kind; ~ *whisky*, kind distilled in Scotland esp. from malted barley; ~ *woodcock*, eggs on anchovy toast; ‖ ~-*&-English*, prisoners' base); ~*'man*, Scots*'man*, ~*'woman*, Scots*-woman*, natives of Scotland (*Flying Scotsman*, a London–Edinburgh express). **2.** n. The ~ dialect of English (Sc. *Scots*; also *Lowland* ~; BROAD ~); ~ whisky (~ *& soda*, glass of this with soda-water). [contr. of SCOTTISH]

scotch², v.t., & n. (arch.). **1.** Make incisions in, score, wound without killing, slightly disable, (esp. ' We have ~'d the snake, not killed it ', see *Macbeth* III. ii. 13). **2.** n. Slash, mark on ground for HOP²-~. [ME; orig. unkn.]

scotch³, n., & v.t. **1.** Wedge or block placed before wheel etc. to prevent motion downhill. **2.** v.t. Hold up (wheel, barrel) with ~. [orig. unkn.]

scot'er, n. Large sea-duck. [orig. unkn.]

sco'tia (-sha), n. Concave moulding esp. in base of column. [L, f. Gk *skotia* darkness (SCOTO-) w. ref. to shadow produced]

Scot'|ism, n. (hist.). Metaphysical doctrines of Duns Scotus (d. 1308). So ~IST(2) n. [L *Scotus* the Scot, -ISM]

Scot'land Yard. (Used for) the Criminal Investigation Department of the Metropolitan Police, the headquarters of the detection of crime. [*Great, New*, ~, successive headquarters of Metropolitan Police]

scot'o-, comb. form of Gk *skotos* darkness; ~*din'ia*, giddiness [Gk *dinē* whirl]; ~*graph*, machine for writing in darkness.

scotom'a, n. (path.; pl. ~*ta*). Obscuration of part of the field of vision. [LL, f. Gk *skotōma* f. *skotoō* darken (prec., -OMA)]

Scots. See SCOTCH¹; (in regimental titles) *Royal* ~, *Royal* ~ *Fusiliers*, ~ *Greys*, ~ *Guards*. [orig. *Scottis*, north. var. of SCOTTISH]

Scot(t)ice (skŏt'ĭsē), adv. In Scotch. [mod. L (LL *Scot(t)icus* Scotch)]

Scott'icism, -**ŏti**-, n. Scotch phrase, word, or idiom. [as prec., -ISM(4)]

Scott'icize, -ise (-īz), -**ŏti**-, v.i. & t. Imitate the Scotch in idiom or habits; imbue with, model on, Scotch ways. [prec., -IZE]

Scott'ish, a. See SCOTCH¹; (in regimental titles) *King's Own* ~ *Borderers*, ~ *Rifles*, *London* ~. [SCOT², -ISH¹]

scoun'drel, n. Unscrupulous person, villain, rogue, rascal. Hence ~·DOM, ~ISM(3), nn., ~LY¹ a. [16th c., of unkn. orig.]

scour¹ (-owr), v.t., & n. **1.** Cleanse or brighten by friction (~ *metal*, with sand etc.; ~ *clothes* etc., with soap or chemicals); (of water, or person with water) clear out (channel, harbour, pipe, etc.) by

flushing or flowing through or over; (of drug, physician, etc.) purge (bowels) drastically (~ *worms*, purge them by placing in damp moss etc. to fit them for bait); clear (rust, stain, etc.) *away, off*, by rubbing etc. (also fig.); ~*ing-rush*, kind of HORSE¹-*tail* with silicious coating used for polishing wood etc.; hence (-)~'ER¹(1, 2) n. **2.** n. Clearing action of swift current on channel etc. (*the* ~ *of the tide*); diarrhoea in cattle; substance used for ~ing fabrics. [ME; prob. f. MDu., MLG *schüren* f. OF *escurer* f. LL *excurare* clean (off) (EX-, L *curare* CURE)]

scour² (-owr), v.i. & t. Rove, range, go along hastily, esp. in search or pursuit; hasten over or along, search rapidly, (~ *the plain, coast, woods*). [ME, of obsc. orig.; cf. Norw. *skura* rush violently]

scourge (skêrj), n., & v.t. **1.** Whip for chastising persons (arch.); person or thing regarded as instrument or manifestation of divine or other vengeance or punishment (e.g. barbarian conqueror, pestilence, war; *the white* ~, consumption as an endemic disease). **2.** v.t. Use whip on (arch.); chastise, afflict, oppress, harass. [ME; n. f. AF *escorge*, rel. to OF *escorgiee*; vb f. OF *escorgier*; both ult. f. L *corrigia* thong, whip]

scout¹, n., & v.i. **1.** (Mil. etc.) man sent out to get information about enemy or surroundings (*boy* ~, member of organization intended to develop character, resourcefulness, & public spirit); ‖ A.A. or R.A.C. patrol-man; ship designed for reconnoitring; small fast aircraft; ‖ (Oxf.) college servant (cf. GYP¹, SKIP²); ‖ (crick.; arch.) fielder; act of seeking (esp. mil.) information (*on the* ~); kinds of bird, auk, guillemot, puffin; ~*'master*, officer directing ~s or boy ~s. **2.** v.i. Act as ~ (esp. *out* ~*ing*). [ME, f. OF *escouter* listen, f. L as AUSCULTATION; n. f. vb]

scout², v.t. Reject (proposal, notion) with scorn or ridicule. [f. Scand.; cf. ON *skúta, skúti* taunt]

scow, n. Kind of flat-bottomed boat. [f. Du. *schouw* ferry-boat]

scowl, v.i. & t., & n. **1.** Wear sullen look, look sour, frown ill-temperedly; ~ *down*, master or overbear (person, opposition, etc.) with ~; hence ~'ingLY² adv. **2.** n. ~ing aspect, angry frown. [ME, prob. f. Scand.; cf. Da. *skule*]

scrab'ble, v.i. Scrawl, scribble, (bibl.); scratch or grope about to find or collect something (usu. *about*). [f. Du. *schrabbelen* frequent. of *schrabben* SCRAPE]

scrag, n., & v.t. (-gg-). **1.** Lean skinny person, animal, plant, etc.; bony part of animal's carcass as food, ‖ esp. neck of mutton or inferior part of it; (sl.) person's neck; hence ~g'Y² (-gĭ) a., ~g'ĭLY² adv., ~g'iNESS n., (-gĭ-). **2.** v.t. Put to death by hanging, garotte, wring neck of, (sl.); (footb.) tackle by the neck; (school sl.) squeeze neck of with arm by way of torture. [prob. **alt. f.** (now dial.) *crag* neck, rel. to MDu. *krāghe*, MHG *krage*]

*scräm, int. (sl.). Be off! [f. foll.]

scräm'ble, v.*t.* & t., & n. **1.** Make way as best one can over steep or rough ground by clambering, crawling, etc.; take part in physical or other struggle to secure as much as possible of something from competitors (usu. *for*; ~ *for pennies*, of children etc. among whom coin is thrown; ~ *for place, wealth, a living*); (of aircraft) take off; throw (coins etc.) to be ~d for; cook (eggs) by breaking into pan with butter, milk, etc., stirring slightly, & heating; alter frequency of transmitted speech of (telephone conversation) so as to make it unintelligible to an eavesdropper; hence **scräm'bling**LY² adv. **2. n.** Climb or walk over rough ground etc.; kind of motor-cycle race or trial over fields etc., eager struggle or competition for or *for* something. [f. 16th c., symbolic, cf. dial. *scamble, cramble*]

scrän, n. (sl.). Food, eatables, broken victuals; *bad ~ to* —! (Anglo-Ir.), bad luck to —. [18th c., of unkn. orig.]

‖ **scränn'el**, a. (arch.). (Of sound) weak, reedy, feeble, (chiefly w. allus. to Milton, *Lycidas* 124). [cf. Norw. *skran* thin, lean]

scränn'ÿ, *scrawn'ÿ, a. (chiefly dial.). Lean, scraggy. [cf. prec.]

scräp¹, n., & v.t. (-pp-). **1.** Small detached piece of something, fragment, remnant, (pl.) odds & ends, useless remains, whence ~p'Y² a., ~p'ILY² adv., ~p'INESS n.; picture, paragraph, etc., cut from book or newspaper for keeping in a collection (~-*book*, for pasting these into); ~ *of paper*, negligible promise etc. (w. ref. to violation of Belgian neutrality 1914); (collect.) rubbish, waste material, metal collected for reworking (also ~-*iron*, -*metal*), (~-*heap*, collection of waste stuff, also fig.; ~-*heap policy*, practice of discarding promptly what is past its prime); (sing. or pl.) residuum of melted fat or of fish with the oil expressed (~--*cake*, compressed fish ~). **2.** v.t. Consign to ~-heap, condemn (ships, supplies, etc.) as past use, discard. [ME, f. ON *scrap* f. *scrapa* SCRAPE]

scräp², n., & v.i. (sl.; -pp-). **1.** Fight, scrimmage, esp. of unpremeditated kind (*had a bit of a ~ with*). **2.** v.i. Have a ~.

scräpe, v.t. & i., & n. **1.** Level surface of, clear of projections, abrade, smooth, polish, shave, or graze, by drawing sharp or angular edge breadthwise over or by causing to pass over such edge (~ *ship's bottom*, clear of barnacles etc.; ~ one's *chin*, shave; ~ one's *boots*, remove dirt from soles by drawing over scraper; ~ one's *plate*, leave no food on; *ship* ~d *her side*, *paint*, *against the pier*; ~ *away*, reduce by scraping; ~ *down*, ~ *away*, also ~ *all over*, & see below). **2.** Take (projection, stain, etc.) *off*, *out*, or *away*, by scraping (~ *off the paint*). **3.** Excavate

(hollow) by scraping (often *out*). **4.** Draw along with scraping sound, produce such sound from, emit such sound, (~ one's *feet*, in restlessness or to drown speaker's voice, also ~ abs., esp. = draw back foot in making clumsy formal bow; ~ *down*, silence by scraping feet; ~ *bow across fiddle-strings*, ~ *fiddle*, also ~ abs. = play fiddle etc.; *branches scraping against the window*). **5.** Pass along something so as to graze or be grazed by it or just avoid doing so (~d *against*, *along*, *the wall*; ~ *through* adv. or prep., get through with a squeeze or narrow shave, often fig. of passing examination etc.). **6.** Amass by scraping or with difficulty or by parsimony, contrive to gain, (usu. *up, together*; *must* ~ *up enough for*; ~-*penny*, miser; ~ *acquaintance with*, thrust one's acquaintance on); (abs.) practise economy (*work & ~ as one may*); hence **scräp'ING**¹ (esp. 2), **scräp'ER**¹(1, 2), nn. **7.** n. Act or sound of scraping (*a ~ of the pen*, writing of a, esp. important, word or two e.g. signature); scraping of foot in bowing; awkward predicament esp. resulting from escapade. [ME, repr. OE *scrapian* or f. ON *skrapa* f. Gmc **skrap-*, **skrep-*]

scrätch¹, v.t. & i., n., & a. **1.** Score surface of, make long narrow superficial wounds in, with nail, claw, or something more or less pointed (*threatened to ~ my face*; ~ *the surface of*, not penetrate far into, also fig.; ~ *a Russian*, *& you find a Tartar*; *stones* ~*ed with rude letters or pictures*; *much* ~*ed with thorns*), get (some part of one) ~ed (*have* ~*ed my hands badly*); form (letters, representation), excavate (hole), by ~ing, scribble (*a few lines* etc.); scrape without marking esp. with nails to relieve itching (~ one's *head*, esp. as sign of perplexity; ~ *my back & I will* ~ *yours*, = CLAW² *me*), (abs.) ~ oneself, ~ ground etc. in search (~ *about for stray seeds*, *evidence*, etc.); scrape *together* or *up*; score (written words etc.) *out* or *through*, strike *off* with pencil etc., ‖ erase (horse's name in list of entries for race, competitor's name), withdraw (horse, candidate, or intr. for refl.) from competition; ~ *along*, sl., manage to live etc. **2.** n. Mark or sound made by ~ing (*a ~ of the pen*, signature or written order easily given); spell of ~ing oneself; slight wound (*got off with a ~ or two*); line from which competitors in race start (*toe*, *come to* or *up to*, *the ~*, put in appearance at right time, not shirk, often transf.; ~ *race*, with all on equal terms, opp. handicap; ~ *man* or ~, competitor in handicap receiving no start); (pl.) horse-disease with dry chaps above heel; (also ~-*wig*) wig covering part only of head; ~-*cat*, spiteful child or woman; ~-*work*, graffito decoration. **3.** adj. Collected by haphazard, ~ed together, heterogeneous, (*a ~ crew*, *lot*, *team*). [15th c., app. confus. syn. ME (now dial.) *scrat*, & ME (now obs.)

cratch, both of obsc. orig.; cf. MLG *kratsen*, OHG *krazzōn*]

Scrätch², n. *Old* ~, the devil. [f. obs. *scrat* hermaphrodite = ON *skrat(t)i* goblin]

scrätch'|y̆, a. (Of drawing etc.) done in scratches, careless or unskilful; (of pen) making sound of scratching or given to catching in paper; (of crew etc.) of scratch character, not well matched or working well together. Hence ~ĭLY² adv., ~ĭNESS n. [-Y²]

scrawl, v.i. & t., & n. 1. Write (t. & i.) in hurried more or less illegible way; mark (paper etc.) *over, all over*, with bad writing or lines like writing. 2. n. Piece of bad writing, hurried note or letter. [perh. alt. f. CRAWL²]

|| **scray**, n. Common tern, sea swallow. [cf. W *yscraen*]

scream, v.i. & t., & n. 1. Utter piercing cry expressing terror, pain, or pretence of these, (of steam-engine etc.) whistle or hoot shrilly; laugh uncontrollably (usu. ~ *with laughter*; ~'ING¹ *farce, fun*, etc., causing spectators to ~, intensely funny); utter, say, in ~ing tone (usu. *out*; ~*ed that she did not dare jump*; ~ *out a curse, order*, etc.); hence ~'ingLY² adv. 2. n. ~ing cry or sound (~*s of pain, laughter*); (sl.) irresistibly comical affair. [ME *scrǣme*, perh. f. OE *scrǣman*; cf. WFris. *skrieme* weep]

scream'er, n. In vbl senses; also or esp.: kinds of bird, e.g. the swift; (sl.) tale etc. that raises screams of laughter, extraordinarily fine specimen of anything. [-ER¹]

|| **scree**, n. (Mountain slope covered with) small stones that slide down when trodden on (often pl. in same sense). [f. ON *skritha* (*skrítha* glide)]

screech, v.i. & t., & n. Scream (vb & n.) with, of, fright or pain or anger, or in harsh or uncanny tones (usu. derog. or joc., & esp. w. ref. to disagreeable nature of sound); ~*-owl*, kinds that ~ instead of hooting, || esp. the BARN-owl. [16th c. var. of ME *scritch* (imit.)]

screed, n. Long tiresome harangue (esp. list of grievances) or letter; || one of the fillets of mortar or strips of wood by which a surface to be plastered is divided into compartments. [ME, var. of SHRED]

screen, n., & v.t. 1. Partition of wood or stone separating without completely cutting off one part of church or room from another, esp. that between nave & chancel '(ROOD-~), decorated wall enclosing court etc. 2. Movable piece of furniture designed to shelter from excess of heat, light, draught, etc., or from observation (*fire, window, folding*, etc., ~~). 3. Any object utilized as shelter esp. from observation, expression of face or measure adopted for concealment, protection afforded by these, (*prepared the attack behind a* ~ *of trees*; *put on a* ~ *of indifference*; *a cavalry* ~, cavalry thrown out to keep enemy's scouts from getting in touch with main body; *under* ~ *of night*). 4. Board, often with wire-netting or glass cover, on which notices are posted. 5. White surface on which moving or televised pictures or lantern slides are projected; *the* ~, moving pictures collectively. 6. Body proof against electric or magnetic induction or having property of interrupting other such physical processes. 7. Large sieve or riddle esp. for sorting coal etc. into sizes. 8. (photog.). Transparent finely-ruled plate used in process of half-tone reproduction. 9. (crick.). One of two large movable white wood or canvas erections placed near boundary in line with wicket to assist batsman's sight of the ball. 10. v.t. Afford shelter to, hide partly or completely, (*from*; often fig. of protecting another from deserved censure etc. by taking blame upon oneself or diverting it). 11. Show (object, scene) on lantern or cinema~. 12. Riddle (coal etc.; ~*ed coal*, from which dust etc. has been removed; ~*ings*, refuse separated by sifting); (fig.) sift & investigate (persons). 13. Prevent from causing electrical interference. [of obsc. orig.; perh. f. AF var. of OF *escran* in same sense]

screeve, v.i., **screev'er**, n. (sl.). (Be) pavement artist. [ult. f. L *scribere* write]

screw¹ (-ōō), n., & v.t. & i. 1. Cylinder with spiral ridge called the thread running round it outside (MALE or *exterior* ~) or inside (FEMALE or *interior* ~), metal male ~ with slotted head & sharp point for fastening pieces of wood together with more security than nail (also *wood-, common*, ~) or with blunt end to receive nut & bolt things together (also ~*-bolt*), wooden or metal male or female ~ as part of appliance or machine acting as one of the MECHANICAL powers to exert pressure in various ways, (ARCHIMEDEAN ~; *endless* or *perpetual* ~, threaded revolving shaft engaging with & working cogwheel; *differential* or *Hunter's* ~, arrangement of ~s with threads of different pitch working inside each other giving great lifting-power; *left-handed* ~, advanced by turning leftwards contrary to usu. arrangement; *right-&-left* ~, cylinder with threads in opposite directions at the two ends; *interrupted* ~, with parts of thread cut away; *have, there is, a* ~ *loose*, phrr. suggesting that something, esp. person's brain, is out of working order; *put the* ~ *on*, exert pressure esp. in way of extortion or intimidation). 2. (Also ~*-propeller*) revolving shaft with spiral blades projecting from ship or airship at stern & propelling it by acting on ~ principle upon water or air. 3. (Also ~ *steamer*, abbr. *s.s.*) steamer propelled by ~ or ~s. 4. One turn of a ~ (*give it another* ~). 5. || Oblique curling motion or tendency as of billiard-ball struck sideways. **6.** ‖ Small twisted-up paper *of* tobacco etc. **7.** Miser, stingy or extortionate person. **8.** ‖ (sl.). Amount of salary or wages. **9.*** ~'*ball* (sl.) a. & n., mad, crazy (person); ~ *coupling*, right-&-left female ~ for joining ends of pipes or rods; ~-*cutter*, hand-tool for cutting ~s; ~'*driver*, tool like blunt chisel for turning ~s by the slot; ~-*eye*, ~ with loop for passing cord etc. through instead of slotted head; ~ *gear*, endless ~ with cogwheel or pinion; ~-*hook*, hook to hang things on with ~ at end of shank to fasten it in with; ~-*jack*, dentist's implement for regulating distance between crowded teeth, (also) carriage JACK[1] worked by ~; ~-*pile*, with ~ at lower end, & sunk by rotation; ~-*pine*, plant with leaves arranged spirally & resembling those of pineapple; ~-*plate*, metal plate for holding ~-cutting dies, also steel plate with threaded holes for making male ~s; ~-*pod*, kind of mesquit with spirally twisted pods; ~ *press*, press worked by simple ~ used esp. by printers & binders; ~-*tap*, tool for making female ~s; ~ *valve*, stopcock opened & shut by ~, valve moved by ~; ~-*wheel*, worked by endless ~; ~-*wrench*, for turning ~s with angular head or nuts, also wrench with jaws worked by ~. **10.** vb. Fasten, tighten, etc., by use of ~ or ~s (~ *up door*, make fast, esp. as practical joke at university; ~ *up* person, ~ up his door; *boards are* ~*ed down*; *his head is* ~*ed on the right way*, he has sense). **11.** Turn (~), twist round like ~, (w. ref. to twisting pegs of fiddle; usu. *up*) make tenser or more efficient (~ one's *courage to the sticking-place*, ~ *up* one's *courage*, gather resolution; *he, the management, wants* ~*ing up*). **12.** Put the ~ upon, press hard on, oppress. **13.** Be miserly. **14.** Squeeze, extort, (consent, money, etc.) *out of*. **15.** Contort, distort, contract, (~ one's *face into wrinkles*; ~ *up* one's *eyes*). (Of ~) revolve (~ *stiffly, to the right*, etc.). **17.** (Of rolling ball, also of person etc.) take curling course, swerve; hence ~'ABLE (-ŏŏa-) a. [app. f. OF *escroue*, (mod. *écrou*), female screw, nut, f. L *scrofa* sow]

screw² '(-ŏŏ), n. Vicious, unsound, or worn-out horse. Hence ~'Y² (-ŏŏ͞i) a. (also, sl., slightly crazy, having a screw loose). [perh. f. prec.]

screwed (-ŏŏd), a. (sl.). Drunk, drunken. [prob. f. SCREW¹, -ED¹]

scribā'cious (-shŭs), a. (rare). Given to writing. [f. L *scribere* write, -ACIOUS]

scrīb'ble¹, v.t. & i., & n. **1.** Write (t. & i.) hurriedly or carelessly in regard either to handwriting or composition; be a journalist or author (w. implication, often mock-modest, of inferiority), whence **scribb'ler¹** [-ER¹] n.; ‖ *scribbling-paper*, -*diary*, for casual jottings; hence ~MENT n. (rare). **2.** n. Careless handwriting or thing written in it, scrawl,

hasty note, etc. [ME, f. med. L *scribillare* dim. of L *scribere* write]

scrīb'ble², v.t. Card (wool, cotton) coarsely, pass through scribbling-machine or **scribb'ler²** [-ER¹] n. [prob. f. LG, cf. syn. G *schrubbeln*, see SCRUB²]

scribe, n., & v.t. **1.** Person who writes or can write (rare; *am no great* ~, do not write well); ancient or medieval copyist of manuscripts. **2.** (bibl.). Ancient-Jewish maker & keeper of records etc., also Jewish theologian & jurist of type prevalent in time of Christ; hence **scrib'AL** a. **3.** (Also ~-*awl*) pointed instrument for marking lines on wood, bricks, etc., to guide saw etc., or writing words on barrel etc. **4.** v.t. Mark with ~; *scribing-compass*, for scratching circles etc.; *scribing-iron*, **scrib'ER¹** n., = ~ (sense 3). [ME, f. L *scriba* (*scribere* write)]

scrim, n. Lining-cloth in upholstery etc. [orig. unkn.]

scrimm'age, scrŭ-, n., & v.i. & t. **1.** Tussle, confused struggle, row, brawl, skirmish, (usu. *scri*-). **2.** (Rugby footb.; usu. *scru*-; also abbr. *scrum*) tight mass of all the forwards with ball on ground in middle; *scrum half*, the half-back who puts the ball into the scrum. **3.** vb. Engage in a ~; put (ball) in a ~. [varr. of SKIRMISH]

scrimp, v.t. & i. Skimp. Hence **scrim'**PY² a. [18th c., of obsc. orig.; cf. MHG *schrimpfen* contract, wrinkle, & see SHRIMP]

‖ **scrim'shănk**, v.i. (mil. sl.). Shirk duty. Hence ~ER¹ n. [orig. unkn.]

scrim'shaw, v.t. & i., & n. **1.** Adorn (shells, ivory, etc.), adorn shells etc., with carved or coloured designs (as sailors' amusement at sea). **2.** n. Piece of such work. [perh. f. person's name]

scrin'ium, n. (Rom. ant.; pl. -*ia*). Cylindrical or other box for rolled MSS. [L, see SHRINE]

‖ **scrip¹**, n. (arch.). Beggar's or traveller's or pilgrim's wallet, satchel. [ME, f. OF *escrep(p)e* wallet, var. of *escherpe*, mod. *écharpe* SCARF¹, f. WG *skerpa*]

scrip², n. Provisional certificate of money subscribed to bank or company entitling holder to formal certificate in due time & to dividends etc.; (collect.) such certificates. [abbr., = (sub)scrip(tion) receipt)]

script, n. **1.** (In law) original document (opp. *copy*). **2.** Handwriting, written characters (opp. *print*); printed cursive characters, imitation of handwriting in type; kind of non-cursive handwriting imitating print. **3.** Text of broadcaster's announcement or talk; typescript of film-play. **4.** ‖ Examinee's written answer. [ME, f. L *scriptum* thing written (*scribere* write)]

scriptōr'ium, n. (pl. -*s*, -*ia*). Room set apart for writing esp. in monastery. [med. L (prec., -ORY)]

scrip'tural (-chŏŏ-), a. Founded on,

reconcilable with, laying stress on, appealing to, doctrines contained in the Bible, whence ~ISM(3), ~IST(2), nn.; of, taken from, the Bible (rare; usu. now *scripture* attrib.). Hence ~LY² adv., ~NESS n. [foll., -AL]

scrip'ture, n. **1.** The Bible with or without the Apocrypha (usu. without article; also *Holy S*~ or *the S*~*s*; *a doctrine not found in S*~ or *the S*~*s*); *a* or *the* quotation from the Bible; (attrib.) taken from or relating to the Bible (*a* ~ *text, lesson*; cf. SCRIPTURAL). **2.** Sacred book of non--Christian community. **3.** (arch.). ‖ Inscription. **4.** ~*-reader,* person employed to read the Bible to the poor in their homes. [ME, f. L *scriptura* (SCRIPT, -URE)]

scriv'ener, n. (hist.). Copyist, drafter of documents, notary, broker, money--lender; (in mod. use) ~*'s palsy,* WRITER'S cramp. [ME, f. obs. *scrivein* f. OF *escrivain* (SCRIBE, -AN) + -ER¹]

scrobic'ulate, -āted, aa. (bot., zool.). Pitted, furrowed. [L *scrobiculus* (*scrobis* ditch, -CULE), -ATE²]

scrŏf'ul‖a, n. Morbid constitutional condition with glandular swellings & tendency to consumption. Hence ~OUS a., ~OUSLY² adv., ~OUSNESS n. [ME, f. med. L sing. f. LL *scrofulae* scrofulous swelling, dim. of *scrofa* a sow]

scrŏll, n., & v.t. & i. **1.** Roll of parchment or paper, book or volume of the ancient roll form; (arch.) schedule or list. **2.** Ornamental design esp. in architecture carved or drawn or otherwise made to imitate ~ of parchment more or less exactly, volute of Ionic capital or of chair etc., head of fiddle, flourish in writing, ribbon bearing heraldic motto, etc. **3.** Any tracery of spiral or flowing lines. **4.** ~*-bone,* turbinated; ~ *gear,* with ~*-wheel*; ~*-head,* volute at ship's bow; ~*-lathe,* for spiral work; ~*-saw,* fretsaw; ~*-wheel,* cogwheel in shape of disc with cogs in spiral lines on one side causing variation of pace according as outer or inner parts are in action; ~*-work,* ornament of spiral lines esp. as cut by ~*-saw*. **5.** vb. Curl up (t. & i.; rare) like paper; adorn with ~s (chiefly in p.p.). [15th c. *scrowle* alt. f. ME *scrowe* aphetic f. AF *escrowe* (ESCROW), OF *escro(u)e* strip of parchment etc., f. Gmc, cogn. w. SHRED]

scrŏŏp, n., & v.i. (Make) grating noise. [imit.]

scrŏt'‖um, n. (pl. ~*a*). Bag containing testicles. Hence ~AL a., ~IT'IS, ~OCELE, nn. [L]

scrounge (-j), v.t. & t. (sl.). Appropriate things, cadge; acquire thus. Hence **scroun'gᴇʀ¹** (-j-) n. [cf. dial. *scrunge* steal]

scrŭb¹, n. (Ground covered with) brushwood or stunted forest growth; worn or short-bristled brush or moustache; stunted or insignificant person, animal, or plant; ~*-oak,* American dwarf kinds.

Hence ~**b'ʏ²** a., ~**b'ɪNESS** n. [var. of SHRUB¹]

scrŭb², v.t. & i. (-bb-), & n. **1.** Rub hard to clean or brighten esp. with soap & water applied with ~bing-brush; use such brush (*would rather* ~ *for my living*); (sl.) cancel, scrap; eliminate, or extract for use, certain components from (coal--gas); hence ~**b'ER¹** (esp., apparatus for ~bing gas), ~**b'ɪɴɢ¹,** nn. **2.** n. ~bing or being ~bed (*give it, he wants, a good* ~). **3.** *(colloq.).* Player not belonging to regular team; second or weaker team; game of baseball with less than full complement of players; also attrib., as ~*-team.* [ME, prob. f. MLG, MDu. *schrobben, schrubben,* perh. rel. to SCRAPE]

scrŭbb'er, n. In vbl senses: also, apparatus for purifying coal-gas from ammonia & tar by spraying with water. [-ER¹(1, 2)]

scrŭff, n. Back *of the neck* as used to grasp & lift or drag animal or person by (*take by the* ~ *of the neck*). [corrupt. of SCUFF²]

scrum(mage). See SCRIMMAGE.

scrŭmp'tious (-shŭs), a. (sl.). Delightful, delicious, firstrate. [arbitrary; cf. GOLUPTIOUS]

scrŭnch. = CRUNCH. [s- as in SCRAG etc.]

scru'ple (-ŏŏ-), n., & v.i. & t. **1.** Weight--unit (in apothecaries' wt) of 20 grains; very small quantity (arch.); feeling of doubt or hesitation on grounds of morality or propriety about acting or approving of action, conscientious objection, (*make no* ~ *to do,* do without such hesitation or with easy conscience; *have* ~*s about doing; man of no* ~*s,* unscrupulous; *did it without* ~). **2.** vb. Feel or be influenced by ~s (rare); be deterred from or hindered in (*doing* or n. of action; arch.; *would* ~ *lying* or *a lie*) by ~s; hesitate owing to ~s *to* do (esp. w. neg.; *does not* ~ *to say*). [f. L *scrupulus* (*scrupus* pebble, -ULE); fig. sense thr. F *scrupule*]

scru'pulous (-ŏŏp-), a. Careful to offend in nothing, conscientious even in small matters, not neglectful of details, punctilious, marked by extreme thoroughness, unfailing, (~ *persons*; ~ *honesty, cleanliness, care, methods, respect, attention,* etc.); over-attentive to details, esp. to small points of conscience, whence **scrupulos‖ITY** (-ŏŏp-) n. Hence ~LY² adv., ~NESS n. [f. F *scrupuleux* or L *scrupulosus* (prec., -OSE¹)]

scrutāt'or (-ŏŏ-), n. Person given to scrutiny (chiefly as signature to newspaper letters etc.). [L (SCRUTINY, -OR)]

scrutin (skrŏŏtăň'), n. ~ *d'arrondissement, de liste,* (dărawňdĕsmahň', de lĕst'), contrasted methods by which voter votes for one or more representatives of small district only, or for large number representing wide area. [F]

‖ scrutineer' (-ŏŏ-), n. Person examining ballot papers for irregularities. [SCRUTINY, -EER]

scru'tiniz|e (-ōō-), **-is|e** (-ĭz), v.t. Look closely at, examine in detail. Hence ~**ing**LY² adv. [foll., -IZE]

scru'tiny (-ōō-), n. Critical gaze, close investigation, examination into details; official examination of votes cast in election to test their validity when closeness of contest or suspicion of irregularity makes it desirable (demand a ~). [ME, f. L scrutinium (scrutari search)]

scry, v.i. Use the crystal in CRYSTAL--gazing. Hence ~'ER¹ n. [= (DE)SCRY]

scŭd, v.i. (-dd-), & n. **1.** Run or fly straight & fast esp. with smooth or easy motion, skim along; (naut.) run before the wind. **2.** n. Spell of ~ding; vapoury driving clouds. [16th c., of obsc. orig.]

scŭ'dō (or -ōō-), n. (pl. -di pr. -dē). Old Italian silver coin of about 4/-. [It., f. L scutum shield]

scŭff¹, v.i. Walk with dragging feet, shuffle with the feet. [18th c., of obsc. orig.]

scŭff², n. Nape (now usu. scruff). [18th c., of obsc. orig.]

scŭf'fle, v.i., & n. (Engage in) confused struggle in which disputants chiefly push each other about, disorderly fight. [perh. f. Scand.; cf. Sw. skuffa to push, cogn. w. SHOVE]

‖ **scŭg**, n. (school sl.). Person lacking spirit, sociability, manners, sportsmanship, etc. [orig. unkn.]

sculduggery. See SKUL(L)DUGGERY.

scŭll, n., & v.t. & i. **1.** One of pair of small oars used by single rower each with one hand; oar resting in nick on boat's stern & worked with twisting strokes to propel like ship's screw. **2.** vb. Propel (boat), propel boat, with ~(s). [ME, of unkn. orig.]

scŭll'er, n. User of scull(s); boat intended for sculling. [-ER¹]

scŭll'erў, n. Back kitchen, room for washing up dishes etc. [ME, f. AF squillerie, OF escuelerie f. escuele dish f. L scutella, see -ERY]

‖ **scŭll'ion** (-yon), n. (arch., poet., rhet.). Cook's boy, washer of dishes & pots. [ME; perh. assim. to prec. of F souillon scullion, orig. dirty fellow (as SOIL²)]

scŭlp, v.t. (Colloq. for) SCULPTURE. [f. L sculpere; now regarded as abbr.]

scŭl'pin, n. Kinds of small American sea--fish with large spiny head. [perh. f. obs. scorpene f. L f. Gk skorpaina a fish]

scŭlp'sĭt, scŭlpser'ŭnt, (abbr. sc. or sculps.), v. sing. & pl. 3rd pers. (So-&-so) carved or sculptured or engraved (this work; used with artist's signature). [L]

scŭlp't|or, n. One who sculptures. Hence ~**ress**¹ n. [L (foll., -OR)]

scŭlp'tur|e, n., & v.t. & i. **1.** Art of forming representations of objects in the round or in relief by chiselling stone, carving wood, modelling clay, casting metal, or similar processes; a work of ~e; (zool., bot.) raised or sunk markings on

shell etc.; hence ~**AL**, ~**ESQUE** (-ĕsk'), aa., ~**al**LY² adv., (-cher-). **2.** vb. Represent in ~e; adorn with ~e; be a sculptor, do ~e; (p.p., zool. & bot.) having ~e. [ME, f. L sculptura (sculpere sculpt-, -URE)]

scŭm, n., & v.t. & i. (-mm-). **1.** Impurities that rise to surface of liquid esp. in boiling or fermentation, floating film; (fig.) worst part, refuse, offscouring, (of); hence ~**m'ў²** a. **2.** vb. Take ~ from, skim; be or form a ~ on; (of liquid) develop ~. [ME, f. MLG, MDu. schūm (= OHG scūm), f. Gmc *skūma-; vb f. n.]

scŭm'ble, v.t., & n. **1.** Modify (oil--painting) by painting a thin tint or colour over a darker one. **2.** n. Thin layer of paint over a darker one, modifying the underlying paint. [perh. frequent. of scum vb (-LE(3))]

scŭn'cheon (-chn), n. Stones or arches across angles of square tower supporting alternate sides of octagonal spire. [ME, f. OF escoinson (EX-, COIN¹)]

‖ **scŭnn'er**, n., & v.t. & i. (Sc.). **1.** Strong dislike (esp. take a ~ at, against), object of loathing. **2.** vb. Sicken, disgust; feel sick, be nauseated. [n. f. vb, ME, of obsc. orig.]

scŭpp'er¹, n. Hole in ship's side to carry off water from deck. [ME, perh. f. OF escopir spit; cf. G speigat]

‖ **scŭpp'er²**, v.t. (sl.). Surprise & massacre, sink (ship, crew), do for. [orig. unkn.]

scŭrf, n. Flakes on surface of skin cast off as fresh skin develops below, esp. those of head (also dandruff); any scaly matter on a surface. Hence ~**'ў²** a., ~**'iness** n. [late OE scurf f. Scand. (cf. OSw. skorver), earlier sceorf (= OHG scorf) f. root of sceorfan gnaw]

scŭ'rril|ous, (arch.) **scŭ'rril|(e),** aa. Grossly or obscenely abusive (of person or language), given to or expressed with low buffoonery. Hence or cogn. ~**ously²** adv., ~**ITY** (-ĭl'-) n. [f. obs. scurrile, f. F, or L scurrilis (scurra buffoon), -OUS]

scŭ'rrў, v.i., & n. **1.** Run hurriedly esp. with short quick steps, scamper, (the ~ing mice). **2.** n. Act or sound of ~ing; short fast horse-race (polo-~, race for polo--ponies). [perh. shortened f. hurry-scurry redupl. of hurry]

scŭrv'|ў, a. & n. **1.** Paltry, low, mean, dishonourable, contemptible, (a ~y trick, fellow); hence ~**iLY²** adv. **2.** n. Deficiency disease with swollen gums, livid spots, & prostration, attacking sailors & any who feed on salt meat & lack vegetables; ~**y-grass** [corrupt. of -cress], plant of mustard family used against ~y; hence ~**ieD²** (-vĭd) a. [-adj. f. SCURF+-Y²; n. subst. use of adj., perh. assoc. w. obs. scorbut(e) (SCORBUTIC)]

scŭt, n. Short tail esp. of hare, rabbit, or deer. [orig. unkn.]

scŭt'age, n. (hist.). Money paid by feudal landowner in lieu of personal service. [ME, f. med. L *scutagium*, after OF *escuage* f. *escu* (L *scutum*, shield) +-AGE]

scútch, v.t., & n. 1. Dress (fibrous material, esp. retted flax) by beating; ~-*blade*, ~*ing-sword*, ~'ER¹(2) n., implements for ~ing flax. 2. n. ~er; coarse tow separated in ~ing flax. [vb f. OF **escoucher, escousser*, f. pop. L **excussare* f. L EX(*cutere cuss-* = *quatere quass*-shake); n. f. OF *escouche*]

scútch'eon (-chon), n. = ESCUTCHEON; ornamented brass etc. round keyhole; plate for name or inscription. [ME; aphetic f. ESCUTCHEON]

scute. See SCUTUM.

scútéll'|um, n. (nat. hist.; pl. ~*a*). Small shield, plate, or scale, in plants, insects, birds, etc., esp. one of the horny scales on birds' feet. Hence **scút'ěllATE²**, ~AR¹, aa., ~A'TION n. [mod. L, dim. of SCUTUM]

|| **scút'er**, v.i., & n. Scurry. [perh. alt. of SCUTTLE³ (-ER⁵)]

scút'tle¹, n. (Usu. *coal*-~) metal or other vessel in which small supply of coal etc. for single fireplace is brought & kept. [OE *scutel* = ON *skutill*, OHG *scuzzila* f. L *scutella* dish]

scút'tle², n., & v.t. 1. Hole with lid in wall or roof of house or ship's deck, side, or hatchway-covering; section of motor-car connecting bonnet and body; ~-*butt*, -*cask*, water-butt usu. on deck with hole in top for dipping from. 2. v.t. Make hole(s) in (ship), open sea-cocks of (ship), esp. for purpose of sinking. [ME; identical w. F *escoutille* = Sp. *escotilla* hatchway]

scút'tle³, v.i., & n. 1. Hurry along, scurry, run away, make off, fly from danger or difficulty. 2. n. Hurried gait, precipitate flight or departure. [cf. dial. *scuddle* f. SCUD +-LE(3)]

scút'|um, n. (pl. ~*a*). (Rom. ant.) legionary's shield of oblong, oval, or semicylindrical shape; (anat.) knee-pan; (zool. etc.; also *scute*) shieldlike plate or scale, piece of bony armour in crocodile, sturgeon, turtle, armadillo, etc., whence ~AL, ~ATE², aa. Hence ~íFORM a. [L]

Scýll'a, n. ~ & *Charybdis*, six-headed monster living on a rock, & whirlpool, so placed on opposite sides of Straits of Messina that it was hard to steer clear of one without being caught by the other (see Homer, *Od.* xii); *between* ~ & *Charybdis*, between two dangers, between the devil & the deep sea.

scýph'|us, n. (pl. ~*ī*). (Gk ant.) footless drinking-cup with two handles not higher than rim; (bot.) cup-shaped part as in narcissus flower or in lichens; whence ~OSE¹ a. Hence ~íFORM a. [L, f. Gk *skuphos*]

scythe (sīdh), n., & v.t. 1. Mowing & reaping implement of long slightly curved blade swung over ground by usu. crooked pole about 5 ft long with two short handles projecting at right angles from it; blade continuing axle of ancient war-chariot at each end, whence **scýthED²** (-dhd)'a. 2. v.t. Cut with ~. [OE *sīthe*, ON *sigthr* f. Gmc **segithjaz* f. **seg-* cut, cogn. w. L *secare*]

Scyth'ian (sīdh-, -th-), a. & n. (Inhabitant) of ancient Scythia, the region north of the Black Sea; = TURANIAN. [L f. Gk *Skuthia* (*Skuthēs* a~), -AN]

|| **'sdeath** (zdĕth), int. (arch.) expressing anger, surprise, etc. [short for *God's death*]

se-, L pref. = apart, without.

sea, n. 1. Expanse of salt water that covers most of earth's surface & encloses its continents & islands, the ocean, any part of this as opposed to dry land or fresh water, (*by* ~ & *land*; *at the bottom of the* ~; *jumped into the* ~; *on the* ~, in ship etc., also situated on ~shore; *go to* ~, become sailor; *follow the* ~, be sailor; *put to* ~, leave port or land; *arm of the* ~, deep gulf; *at* ~, away from & esp. out of sight of land, also fig. = perplexed, not knowing conditions etc. or what to do; *between* DEVIL¹ & *deep* ~; *as good* FISH¹ *in the* ~; *when the* ~ *gives up its dead*, at the resurrection; also pl. in same sense, as *beyond, over*, ~ or ~s, to or in countries separated by ~; *the high* ~s, the open ~ outside the three-mile limit to which nearest country's jurisdiction extends; *mistress of the* ~ or ~s, chief naval power at any time). 2. Particular tract of ~ partly or sometimes wholly enclosed by land & usu. distinguished by special name (*the North, Mediterranean, Caspian, Dead, Sea*; *inland* ~, entirely landlocked as the Caspian, also rarely of great freshwater lakes; *closed* ~, = MARE¹ *clausum*; *the seven* ~s, Arctic, Antarctic, N. Pacific, S. Pacific, N. Atlantic, S. Atlantic, & Indian, Oceans; || *the four* ~s, those enclosing Great Britain). 3. Local motion or state of the ~, swell, great billow, (*a heavy* ~, with great waves; ~s *mountains high*; (of boat etc.) *ship a* ~, be flooded by a wave; *long* ~, with long regular waves; *short* ~, choppy & irregularly agitated; ~ *like looking-glass* or *sheet of glass*, quite smooth; *half* ~s *over*, having drunk too much). 4. Vast quantity or expanse *of* (*a* ~ *of troubles, care, flame, upturned faces*; also pl., *as* ~s *of blood*, ruthless bloodshed). 5. (bibl.). *Brazen* or *molten* ~, =LAVER². 6. (attrib. & in comb.). Living or used in or on, of, near, like, the ~ (often prefixed to name of animal, fruit, etc., to form name of marine thing with merely superficial resemblance to what it is named after, as ~ *canary, cucumber, -fox, raven*, below); ~ *acorn*, barnacle; ~ *air*, air at ~side esp. as recommended for invalids etc.; ~-*anchor*, DRAG²-anchor; ~ ANEMONE; ~ *-angel*, ANGEL-fish; ~-*arrow*, flying squid; ~ *asparagus*, kind of soft-shelled crab;

~-*barrow*, skate's egg-case; ~ *bathing*, in ~; ~ *bear*, polar bear, also kind of fur--seal; ~-*bells*, ~shore bindweed; ~-*belt*, sweet fucus, a ~weed with beltlike fronds; ~'*board*, ~shore, coast region, line of coast; ~-*boat*, ship etc. of specified ~going qualities (*is a good, bad*, etc., ~-*boat*), boat which can be lowered quickly in an emergency at ~; ~-*born*, born of the ~ (poet., esp. of Aphrodite); ~-*borne*, conveyed by ~ (~-*borne commerce, goods*); ~-*bow*, rainbow effect in ~-spray; ~'-*breeze*, blowing landward from~ esp. during day in alternation with land-breeze at night; ~ *breeze*, any breeze at ~; ~-*calf*, common seal; ~ *canary*, white whale (from its whistling); ~ *captain*, (poet., rhet.) great sailor or commander at ~, (in ord. use, chiefly where army-captain is to be excluded) past or present captain of ship in navy or merchant service; ~ *change*, transformation (w. ref. to *Tempest* I. ii. 400); ~ *chestnut*, ~-urchin; ~-*cloth*, used in theatre to represent shore; || ~ *coal*, arch., coal (orig. of coal brought from Newcastle by ~, opp. charcoal etc.); ~ *coast*; ~-*cock*, kinds of bird & fish, also valve by which ~-water can be let into ship's interior; ~ *colander*, brown~weed with fronds perforated like colander; ~ *cook*, naut. term of abuse; ~-*cow*, sirenian, also walrus; ~ *crow*, kind of gull; ~ *cucumber*, any holothurian, esp. *bêche-de--mer*; ~-*devil*, kinds of fish; ~-*dog*, kinds of seal, also dogfish, also old sailor (esp. of the Elizabethan ~-captains), & see ~-DOG[1]; ~ *eagle*, kinds of fishing eagle; ~-*ear*, ormer; ~ *elephant*, large kind of seal with proboscis; ~-*fan*, kind of coral; ~'*faring* a. & n., traversing the ~ esp. habitually (~*faring man*, sailor), so ~'far**ER**[1] n. (rare); ~ *fennel*, samphire; ~-*fight*, between warships; ~-*flower*, ~ anemone; ~ *fog*, caused by difference of land & ~ temperature & extending only short way inland; ~-*food*, edible salt-water (shell)fish; ~-*fowl*; ~-*fox*, long-tailed shark; ~ *front*, part of town facing ~; ~ *furbelow*, kinds of brown~weed; ~-*gauge*, ship's draught, also kind of sounding--instrument; ~ *gherkin*, ~ cucumber; ~ *gilliflower*, ~ pink; ~-*girt*, surrounded by ~ (poet., rhet., of island etc.); ~-*god*(dess); ~'*going*, (of ship) for crossing ~, not coasting, (of person) ~faring; ~ *grape*, glasswort, also gulf-weed, also (pl.) cuttle--fish eggs; ~-*green* a. & n., (of) bluish green as of ~; ~-*gull*; ~ *hedgehog*, ~-urchin; ~-*hog*, porpoise, also ~-*horse*, creature harnessed to ~-god's chariot having horse's head & fish's tail, also walrus, also hippocampus; ~-*island cotton*, fine quality of long-stapled cotton originally grown on islands off Georgia and S. Carolina; ~ *kale*, kind of perennial with young shoots used as table vegetable; ~ *kidney*, kidney-shaped polypidom; ~-*king*, medi-

eval Scandinavian pirate chief; ~ *lace*, kind of~weed with long cordlike fronds; ~ *lawyer*, (naut. term of contempt for) captious person; ~-*legs*, ability to walk on deck of rolling ship (*has not yet got his* ~-*legs*); ~ *lemon*, a yellow oval mollusc; ~ *leopard*, kinds of spotted seal; ~--*letter*, official protective letter carried by neutral ship in wartime, describing her cargo, crew, etc.; ~ of ~ *level*, level continuous with that of ~ halfway between high & low water (also *mean* ~ *level*) as used in reckoning height of hills etc. & for barometric standard (*corrected to* ~ *level*); ~ *lily*, crinoid; ~-*line*, horizon at ~; ~ *lion*, kinds of large eared seal, esp. one with mane; || *Sea Lord*, naval member of the Board of Admiralty; ~'*man* (pl. -*men*), sailor, (nav.) rating of executive or upper-deck branch (**ABLE**-*bodied*~*man*; *ordinary* ~*man*, below rating of A.B.), person expert in the practice of nautical matters, whence~'man**LIKE**, ~'man**LY**[1], aa., ~'man**SHIP**(3) n.; ~-*mark*, beacon, lighthouse, etc., or elevated conspicuous object, used to direct course at~; ~-*mat*, polyzoan forming flat matted coralline; ~ *melon*, kind of holothurian; ~-*mew*, gull; ~ *mile*, geographical **MILE**; ~ *monster*, any huge, terrible, or strange ~--*animal*; ~ *moss*, mosslike polyzoan or ~weed; ~-*mouse*, an iridescent ~-*worm*; ~ *mud*, saline deposit of salt marshes etc. used as manure; ~ *necklace*, string of whelk egg-cases; ~ *needle*, garfish; ~ *nettle*, jellyfish; ~-*nymph*; ~ *oak*, kind of ~weed; ~ *ooze*, ~ mud; ~ *orange*, globose orange-coloured holothurian; ~-*orb*, globe-fish; ~ *otter*, kind with very valuable fur; ~-*owl*, = **LUMP**[2]; ~-*ox*, walrus; ~-*pad*, starfish; ~ *parrot*, puffin; ~ *pass*, neutral ship's passport in time of war; ~-*pay*, for active service at ~; ~ *peach*, pear, kinds of ascidium; ~-*pen*, feather--shaped polyp; ~ *pie*, sailors' pie of salt meat etc., || also a shore-bird, the oyster--catcher; ~-*piece*, picture of scene at ~; ~*pi'et*, ~ pie (bird); ~-*pig*, porpoise, also dugong; ~-*pike*, garfish, hake, & other fish; ~ *pilot*, ~ pie (bird); ~ *pincushion*, skate's egg-case; ~ *pink*, ~shore or alpine plant with bright pink flowers, thrift; ~'*plane*, aeroplane constructed for rising from & alighting on water; ~ *poacher*, a small fish; ~'*port*, town with harbour; ~ *power*, ability to control and make successful use of the ~; ~ *pumpkin*, ~ melon; ~-*purse*, skate's egg-case; ~ *raven*, sculpin; ~ *robin*, red gurnard; ~-*room*, clear space at ~ allowing ship to turn etc.; ~ *rover*, pirate or piratical ship; ~-*salt*, got by evaporating ~-*water*; ~-*scape*, ~-*piece*; ~ *scouts*, maritime auxiliary to *boy* **SCOUT**[1]*s*; ~ *serpent*, kinds of snake living in ~, also (*the* ~ *serpent*) enormous serpentine ~ monster occasionally reported as seen but disbelieved in by naturalists; ~ *shell*, shell of any salt-

-water mollusc; ~-*shore'*, land close to ~, (law) space between high & low water marks; ~'*sick*, vomiting or inclined to vomit from motion of ship etc., whence ~'sickNESS n.; || ~*side'*, places or some unspecified place close to ~ as permanent or esp. as holiday residence (*do you like the ~side?*; *must go to the ~side*); ~-*sleeve*, cuttlefish; ~ *slug*, ~ cucumber; ~ *snail*, small slimy fish, the unctuous sucker, also periwinkle or similar shellfish; ~ *snipe*, the dunlin, also the snipefish; ~ *squirt*, any ascidium; ~ *strawberry*, kind of polyp; ~ *sunflower*, ~ *anemone*; ~ *swallow*, tern; ~-*tang(le)*, kinds of ~weed; ~-*toad*, the angler; ~*trout*, kinds of salt-water trout; ~-*urchin*, echinus; ~-*wall*, wall or embankment made to check encroachment of ~; ~-*ware*, ~weed collected for manure or other uses; ~-*water*; ~-*way*, ship's progress, also place where ship lies in open water (*in a ~-way*), also inland waterway; ~'*weed*, any alga or other plant growing in ~; ~-*whip*, whip-shaped coral; ~ *whipcord*, kind of ~-weed; ~-*wife*, fish allied to wrasse; ~-*wind*, = ~-*breeze*; ~-*wing*, a bivalve mollusc; ~'*withwind*, ~-bells; ~-*wolf*, ~ elephant, also kinds of fish, also viking or pirate; ~'*worthy*, (of ship) in fit state to put to ~, strong & well rigged etc., whence ~'worthiness n. Hence ~'WARD a., adv., & n., ~'WARDS (-z) adv. [OE *sǣ*, OS, OHG *sēo*, ON *sǽr*, Goth. *saiws* f. Gmc **saiwiz*]

seal[1], n., & v.i. **1.** Kind of carnivorous amphibious marine mammal with short limbs modified to serve chiefly for swimming but having fur or hair & beastlike face (*eared* ~ or *otary*, distinguished from *common* ~ by having visible external ears, & including the larger kinds, as sea bear, sea lion, sea elephant, & the fur-~s); = ~ *skin*; ~-*fishery* or ~'ERY n.; ~-*rookery*, ~s' breeding-place; ~'*skin*, skin of ~, or usu. prepared fur of ~s as material for women's jackets etc., jacket of this. **2.** v.i. Hunt ~s. [OE *seolh*, MLG *sēl*, OHG *selah*, ON *selr* f. Gmc **selhaz*]

seal[2], n., & v.t. **1.** Piece of wax, lead, or other such material, impressed with device & attached in some way to document usu. in addition to signature as guarantee of authenticity (*given under my hand & ~*, signed & ~ed by me; *set* one's ~ *to*, authorize or confirm) or to envelope or to any receptacle such as box or room or house to prevent its being opened without knowledge of owner etc. (*leaden ~*, stamped piece of lead holding ends of a wire used as fastening; *under ~ of confession, confidence, secrecy, silence*, etc., fig. of communications for which secrecy is stipulated or obligatory); impression stamped on or paper disc stuck to document as symbol equivalent to wax ~. **2.** (fig.). Significant or prophetic mark (*has the ~ of death in his face*). **3.** Gem,

piece of metal, etc., serving as stamp to produce ~ on wax etc. or paper (*~-ring*, finger-ring with ~; || *the ~s*, those held during tenure of office by Lord Chancellor or Secretary of State; || *Great S~*, ~ in charge of Lord Chancellor or Lord Keeper used in ~ing Parliament-writs, treaties, & important State papers; || PRIVY *S~*; *Fisher's S~*, papal ~ with St Peter fishing as device). **4.** Act done, thing given, event regarded, as confirmation or guarantee of (~ *of love*, kiss, birth of child, etc.; *baptism & the Lord's Supper are ~s of God's covenant with us*). **5.** Substance used to close aperture etc., esp. water standing in drain-trap to prevent ascent of foul air (*~-pipe*, DIP[2]-pipe). **6.** ~-*wort*, SOLOMON'S ~. **7.** v.t. Affix ~ to, stamp or fasten with ~, certify as correct with ~ or stamp (*S~ed Book*, one of the presumed perfect copies of Book of Common Prayer certified by Great S~ in 1662 under Charles II); show genuineness of (devotion etc.) *with* one's life etc. **8.** Close securely or hermetically, stop up or *up*, (*my lips are ~ed*, I must not speak; *sleep ~ed his eyes*; *is a ~ed book to me*, is something of which I have & can get no knowledge; *windows must be ~ed up*, e.g. by pasting paper along all crevices; ~ *up tin*, solder it so that air has no access; ~ *pipe* etc., provide it with water~ by means of trap etc.). **9.** Set significant mark on, set apart, destine, decide irrevocably, (*death has ~ed her for his own*; *is ~ed to or for salvation, damnation*, etc.; *his fate is ~ed*); (of Admiralty etc.) officially adopt (design); ⸿ ~*ed pattern*, standard pattern of equipment, clothing, etc., approved for issue by the Admiralty etc. (also fig.). **10.** Confine securely (often *up*); fix (staple etc.) into wall etc. with cement etc. **11.** ~-*ing-wax*, mixture of shellac & rosin with turpentine & pigment used for ~s. [ME, f. AF *seal*, OF *seel* f. L *sigillum*]

seal'er, n. In vbl senses of SEAL[1], [2]; esp., ship or man engaged in seal-hunting. [-ER[1]]

Seal'yham (-liam), n. ~ (*terrier*), a breed of terrier. [place]

seam, n., & v.t. **1.** Line of junction between two edges esp. those of two pieces of cloth etc. turned back & sewn together or of boards fitted edge to edge, fissure left by gaping of parallel edges (*ship's ~s want caulking*); scar, cicatrice; line of separation between two strata; stratum of coal etc.; (anat.) suture; ~ *bowler* in cricket, one who makes the ball move off the ~ when it bounces (also ~'ER[1]); ~-*lace*, ~-ing-lace; ~-*presser*, agricultural implement for flattening down furrow-ridges after the plough, also tailors' goose; hence ~'LESS a. **2.** v.t. Unite with ~ (rare); mark or score with ~, fissure, or scar (chiefly in p.p.; ~*ed with wounds, cracks*, etc.); (knitting) make ridges in (stocking etc.); ~*ing-lace*, galloon or other trimming sewn over ~s in upholstery etc. [OE *séam*, MDu. *sōm*, OHG *soum*, ON *saumr* f. Gmc **saumaz* f. **sau-*, **su-* SEW]

seam′stress, semp′, (sĕms-), n. Sewing- -woman. [OE *séamestre* (prec., -STER)+ -ESS[1]]

seam′y̆, a. Showing seams (~ *side*, inside of garment etc. where turning-back of seams is visible; chiefly fig. of the less presentable or attractive aspect of life etc.). [-Y[2]]

Seanad Eireann (shăn′adh āī′an), n. Upper Chamber of the legislature of Eire. [Ir., = senate of Ireland]

se′ance (sā-), *séance* (see Ap.), n. Sitting of a society or deliberative body; meeting for exhibition or investigation of spiritua- listic phenomena. [F, f. L *sedére* sit]

sear[1]; a. & v.t., **sēre**, a. **1.** (Of leaves, flowers, etc., & fig. of age etc.) withered, dried up (*the* ~, *the yellow leaf*, old age). **2.** v.t. Wither up, blast, (rare); scorch surface of esp. with hot iron, cauterize, brand; make callous (*a seared conscience*); *searing-iron*, for cauterizing. [OE *séar*, MLG *sōr* f. Gmc **sauzra-*; hence OE *séarian* = OHG *(ar-)sōrēn* vb]

sear[2]. See SERE[1].

search (sĕr), v.t. & i., & n. **1.** Look or feel or go over (person or his face or pockets, receptacle, place, book) for what may be found or to find something of which presence is suspected, probe (lit. & fig.; ~ *a wound*, *men's hearts*); **~ me!*, int. implying that the speaker does not know (the answer to some inquiry, what to do, etc.); (of shrapnel, gunners) pene- trate all recesses of (trench etc.); (arch.) look for, seek out or (still current) *out*; make ~ or investigation (*for* or abs.); (part., of examination etc.) thorough, leaving no loopholes, whence ~′ingLY[3] adv.; hence ~ER[1](1, 2) n., ~′LESS a. (poet.). **2.** n. Act of ~ing, investigation, quest, (*am in* ~ *of*, trying to find; *the* ~ *for* or *of*; *right of* ~ in internat. law; belligerent's right to stop neutral vessel & ~ it for contraband); ~′*light*, electric arc-light with concentrated beam that can be turned in any direction for use esp. for discovering hostile aircraft, enemy movements, etc.; ~*-party*, persons going out to look for lost or concealed person or thing; ~*-warrant*, granted by justice of peace to enter premises of person suspected of concealing stolen property etc. [ME, f. OF *cerchier* (F *chercher*) f. LL *circare* go round (CIRCUS)]

search′ing (sĕr-), n. In vbl senses; esp., ~*s of heart*, misgivings caused by guilt or otherwise. [-ING[1]]

seas′on (-zn), n., & v.t. & i. **1.** Proper time, favourable opportunity, time at which something is plentiful or in vogue or active, (*a word in* ~, advice given when it is likely to be taken or is needed;

in ~ *& out of* ~, at all times without selection; *oysters*, *venison*, *strawberries*, *are in* ~, to be had in good condition & without special difficulty; *the holiday* ~, any of the times when most people keep holiday, ‖ esp. Christmas, Easter, Whit- suntide, or August; *the London*, *Brighton*, *Parisian*, ~, when society is busy or visitors many there; *London in the* ~, *the theatrical*, *publishing*, *cricket*, ~; *close*, *open*, ~, when hunting etc. of some animal is prohibited, permitted). **2.** Period of indefinite or various length (*may endure for a* ~; *a* ~ *of inaction*; ‖ ~*-ticket*, issued at reduced rates for any number of journeys taken, performances at- tended, etc., within a year, six months, or other period). **3.** One of the divisions of the year with distinguishable charac- teristics of temperature, rainfall, vegeta- tion, etc. (*the four* ~s, spring, summer, autumn, winter, beginning astronomic- ally each at an equinox or solstice but popularly having different dates in differ- ent countries; *the dry*, *rainy*, ~, two ~s recognized in the tropics instead of the four of temperate countries); hence ~AL, ~LESS, aa., ~ALLY[2] adv., (-z-). **4.** vb. Bring into efficient or sound condition by habituation, acclimatization, exposure, special preparation, use, or lapse of time, inure, mature, (~*ed soldiers*, *timber*). **5.** Make palatable or piquant by intro- duction of salt, condiments, wit, jests, etc., give zest to, flavour, (*highly* ~*ed dishes*; *conversation* ~*ed with humour*), whence ~ER[1](2), ~ING[1](4), nn., (-z-); temper, moderate, (*let mercy* ~ *justice*). **6.** Become fit for use by being ~ed. [ME, f. OF *seson*, f. L *sationem* (*serere sat-* sow, -ION) in Rom. sense *season*]

seas′onab‖le (-z-), a. Suitable to, of the kind usual at, the season (esp. ~*le weather*, frost etc. in winter); opportune, meeting the needs of the occasion, (~*le aid*, *caution*, etc.; *the* ~*le arrival of*). Hence ~le**NESS** n., ~LY[2] adv. [ME; prec., n., -ABLE]

seat, n., & v.t. **1.** Thing used, esp. one made, for sitting on, chair, throne, stool, bench, or other sitting-accommodation, (*the* ~*s are uncomfortable*), occupation of a ~ (*took his* ~ *on the throne*, *a rock*; *pray take a* ~, sit down), whence ~′ING[1](6) n., -~ER[1] n. (motor-car, aeroplane, etc., with ~s for specified number). **2.** Part of chair etc. on which sitter's weight directly rests, part of machine that supports another part (~ *of valve*, surface etc. on which it slides or works). **3.** The but- tocks, part of trousers etc. covering them. **4.** Site or location, temporary or perman- ent scene, abiding-place, *of* (*the liver is the* ~ *of disease*; *the disease has its* ~ *in the liver*; *the* ~ *of war is mountainous*; *an ancient* ~ *of learning*). **5.** Country mansion esp. with park or large grounds (*has a* ~ *in Norfolk*; *the country* ~s. *of England*). **6.** Right to sitting-accommodation or to sit as member of board or esp. House of Commons (*have taken two ~s for* Macbeth; *has a ~ on the Board*; *lost his or the ~*, failed to secure re-election to Parliament). **7.** Manner of sitting horse, bicycle, etc. (*has a good, firm, graceful, ~*); hence *~'LESS* a. **8.** v.t. Make sit, place one*self* in sitting posture, (p.p.) sitting, (*took up the child & ~ed him on the bookcase*; *~ candidate*, elect him to Parliament; *~ed himself in state*; *found him ~ed on a reversed bucket*; *pray be ~ed*, sit down). **9.** Fit or provide (church, room, etc.) with *~s* (*is ~ed for 5000*); (of room etc.) have *~s* for (number). **10.** Mend *~* of (chair, trousers). **11.** Establish in position, fix in particular place (*~ machinery*, put it on its supports; *a deep-~ed disease*). [ME, f. ON *sæti* = MDu. *gesæte*, OHG *gasāzi* f. Gmc. *(ga)sætjam* cogn. w. SIT]

sëbā'ceous (-shŭs), a. Of tallow or fat, fatty, (*~ gland, follicle, duct*, secreting or conveying oily matter or *~ humour* to lubricate hair & skin). [L *sebaceus* (*sebum* tallow), -OUS]

sëbës'tan, -en, n. Plumlike fruit of the tree *Cordia Myxa*, used medicinally in the East & formerly in Europe. [Arab. *sabastān*]

sëc, a. (Of wine) dry. [F]

sëc'ant, a. & n. (math.). **1.** Cutting. **2.** n. *~* line, esp. radius of circle produced through end of arc to meet tangent to other end, ratio of this to radius, *~ of angle*, ratio of greater to less of its containing lines as bounded by a perpendicular to either (abbr. *sec*; *sec 60° = 2*). [L *secare* cut, -ANT]

secateurs (sĕk'atērz), n. Pair of pruning clippers. [F, irreg. f. L *secare* cut]

sëcc'o̅, n. Tempera-painting. [It.]

sëcc'otine (-ēn), n., & v.t. A liquid substitute for glue; (v.t.) stick with *~* (*on, together*, etc.). [P]

sëcëd|e', v.i. Withdraw formally from membership of some body, esp. a Church or federal or other State. Hence *~'ER[1]* n. [f. L SE(*cedere cess-* go)]

sëcërn'ent, a. & n. (physiol.). **1.** That secretes or can secrete. **2.** n. Secreting organ; drug that promotes secretion. [as SECRETE, -ENT]

sëcë'ssion (-shn), n. Act of seceding (*War of S~*, American civil war of 1861–5 caused by *~* of eleven Southern States). Hence *~ISM*(3), *~IST*(2), nn., (-shon-). [f. L *secessio* (SECEDE, -ION)]

sëclud|e' (-o̅o̅d), v.t. Keep (person, place, esp. one*self*) retired or away from company or resort (*~e* one*self from society*; *a ~ed spot, life*, etc.). Hence *~'EDLY[2]* (-o̅o̅-) adv. [ME, f. L SE(*cludere -clus-=claudere* shut)]

sëclu'sion (-o̅o̅zhn), n. Secluding or being secluded, retirement, privacy, avoidance of intercourse, whence *~IST*(2) n.; secluded place. [f. med. L *seclusio* (prec., -ION)]

sëc'ond, a., n., & v.t. **1.** Next after first (*the, a, ~*, often as n. with ellipse of n., esp. = *~* day of month; often further defined, as *the ~ man you meet, was the ~ to come*; *in the ~ place*, secondly; *~ to none*, surpassed by no other; *~* CLASS; *~ cabin, ~ -class accommodation in passenger-ship*; *come in, finish, ~*, be *~* in race; *~ floor*, that two floors above ground-floor; ∥ *~ distance*, space in landscape between foreground & background). **2.** Other besides one or the first, additional, supplementary, (*~ advent*, return of Christ, esp. as preliminary to His expected personal reign on earth, whence *~-ăd'ventIST* n.; *~ ballot*, electoral method by which, if the winner on the first ballot has not polled more than half the votes cast, a *~* is taken in which only he & the next candidate are eligible; *~ chamber*, upper House in bicameral parliament; *~ coming, ~* advent; *~ DIVISION*; *~ nature*, acquired tendency that has become instinctive, as *habit is ~ nature, self-sacrifice is now ~ nature with him*; *~* SELF; *~ teeth*, those of adults, cf. MILK[1]-*teeth*; *~ thoughts*, opinion or resolution formed on reconsideration; *~* WIND[1]). **3.** Of secondary kind, subordinate, derived, unoriginal, imitative, metaphorical, (*~ cause*, that is itself caused; *~* CHILDHOOD, COUSIN; *~ Daniel, Solomon*, etc., person comparable to these; *~ fiddle, violin*, etc., lower of two employed in score, esp. fig. in *play ~ fiddle*, be of only secondary importance, often *to* other person; *at ~ hand*, by hearsay, not actual observation etc.; *~* INTENTION, SIGHT[1]). **4.** *~-best*, of *~* quality (*come off ~-best*, get the worst of it); *~ -class*, of *~* or of inferior position or quality (∥ *~-class passenger, ticket*, using, entitling to use of, *~*-class railway- -carriage etc.); ∥ *~-hand*, (of clothes, books, furniture, etc.) bought after use by a previous owner, (of information etc.) taken on another's authority & not got by original observation or research; *~ lieutenant*, army OFFICER; ∥ *~-pair back, front*, room on *~* floor in back, front, of house (see PAIR[1]); *~* PERSON (gram.); *~ -rate*, not of superior quality, (of ship; also as n.) rated in *~* class. **5.** n. *~* person etc. in race etc. (*a good ~*, close up); ∥ *~* class in examination for honours, person who takes this. **6.** Another person or thing besides the previously mentioned or principal, whether regarded as next, inferior, or equal. **7.** (mus.) Interval of which the span involves only two alphabetical names of notes, harmonic combination of the two notes thus separated. **8.** pl. Goods of *~* quality, esp. coarse flour or bread made from it. **9.** Supporter chosen by principal in duel or pugilism to see fair play etc. **10.** Sixtieth part of a MINUTE of time or angular measurement (see etym.), (loosely) short time (*wait a ~*). **11.** *~ in command*, officer next in

rank to commanding officer; ~ *of* EX-
CHANGE[1]; ~*-hand*, extra hand in some
watches & clocks recording ~s; ~*-mark*,
mark (″) used with ~-figures in statements of angular measurement or time
(*1° 6′ 40″ ; 1 h. 35′ 15″*), or denoting linear
inches. **12.** v.t. Supplement, support,
back up, (~ *words with deeds*; *will you* ~
me if I ask him?). **13.** (Of member of
debating body) give the necessary formal
support to (motion etc. or its proposer)
by rising with or without speech to show
that mover is not isolated, whence ~ER[1]
n. **14.** (*pr.* sĭkŏnd′). ‖ (Mil.) put (officer)
into temporary retirement with a view to
staff or other extra-regimental appointment; ‖ transfer (official) temporarily to
another department. [(adj.) ME f. OF
second f. L *secundus* (*sequi* follow); (time
etc.) ME f. OF *seconde* f. med. L *secunda
minuta* secondary minute, i.e. minute of
a minute; (vb) f. F *seconder* f. L *secun-
dare*]

sĕc′ondar‖ÿ, a. & n. **1.** Next below,
coming in place or time after, depending
on or derived from, of less importance or
originality than, what is primary, of the
second rank etc., supplementary, of inferior rank or importance *to,* (~*y* COLOUR[1];
~*y education, school,* for those who have
received elementary or primary instruction but not yet proceeded to university
or occupation, esp. boys & girls from
11 to 15 years old; ~*y grammar school*
(giving an academic education); ~*y
modern school* (giving a general and practical education); ~*y technical school* (for
those whose abilities are of a more
practical character); ~*y planet,* planet's
satellite); (geol.) = MESOzoic; hence ~ĭLÿ[2]
adv. **2.** n. Deputy or delegate; ‖ minor
cathedral dignitary; ~y planet; feather
growing on second joint of wing; insect's
hind wing; ~y strata. [ME, f. L *secun-
darius* prec., -ARY[1])]

seconde′ (-awnd), n. Fencing-position.
[F (SECOND)]

sĕc′ondlÿ, adv. In the second place (in
enumerations). [-LY[2]]

sécŏn′dō, n. Second performer or lower
part in duet (cf. PRIMO[1]). [It. (as SECOND)]

sĕc′recÿ, n. Keeping of, ability to keep or
habit of keeping, secrets (*he promised* ~;
can rely on his ~; *the gift of* ~; *done with
great* ~); tendency to concealment, se-
cretiveness; unrevealed state, being kept
secret, (*there can be no* ~ *about it*; *in* ~, in
secret). [alt. f. 15/16th c. *secretee, -tie*
app. f. obs. *secre* or *secret* adjj. + -TY or -Y]

sĕc′rĕt, a. & n. **1.** (To be) kept private,
not (to be) made known or exposed to
view, privy, (~ *treaty, understanding,
errand, door, passage, sin, process, influence*; *the* ~ *parts,* parts of body of which
exposure is avoided, esp. the genitals;
‖ ~*-service money,* applied by Government to securing information etc. without
obligation to state details of expendi-

ture), whence ~LY[2] adv.; **given to** or
having faculty of secrecy (~ or ~*-service
agent,* superior kind of spy), secretive,
close, rĕticent, not leaky; (of place etc.)
secluded, retired. **2.** n. Thing (to be) kept
~ (*keep a* or *the* ~, abstain from revealing
it); thing known only to a limited number (*in the* ~, among the number of those
allowed to know it; *open* ~, thing ~ only
to those who do not trouble to learn it);
mystery, thing of which explanation is
sought in vain, (*the* ~*s of nature*); true but
not generally recognized method for attainment *of* (*the* ~ *of health, success, happiness, salvation, is temperance, to try again,*
etc.); secrecy (only in *in* ~, ~ly); (R.-C.
Ch.) celebrant's private prayer in Mass;
(pl.) ~ parts of body. [ME, f. OF f. L
secretus f. SE(*cernere cret-* sift) put apart]

sĕcrĕtaire′, n. Escritoire. [F, as foll.]

sĕcrĕtār′iat(e), n. Office of secretary;
members of a government administrative
office collectively; administrative office
collectively; administrative office building. [F, as foll., -ATE[1]]

sĕc′rĕtarÿ, n. **1.** Person employed by
another to assist him in correspondence,
literary work, getting information, &
other confidential matters (often *private*
~; *unpaid* ~, esp. of person acting as ~ to
prominent politician for sake of experience). **2.** Official appointed by society or
company or corporation to conduct its
correspondence, keep its records, & deal
in the first instance with its business
(‖ *honorary* ~, abbr. *hon. sec.,* unpaid ~
usu. of society not conducted for profit).
3. Minister in charge of a Government
Office (‖ *the S~ of State for Air, the
Colonies, Commonwealth Relations, Foreign
Affairs, Home Affairs, Scotland, War,* or
the Colonial, Foreign, Home, etc., *S~*;
under~, ‖ one of two attached to each
S~ of State, one as permanent manager
of the connected office, the other usu. as
representative in other House of the S~
of State; ‖ *permanent* ~, under-~ as
above; ~ *of legation* or *embassy,* ambassador's chief subordinate & deputy); *S~
of State,* (in U.S. & Vatican) chief ~ &
foreign minister. **4.** Secretaire, escritoire.
5. (print.). Script type imitating en-
grossing-hand. **6.** ~*-bird,* African bird
preying on snakes, with crest likened to
pen stuck over writer's ear. Hence
sĕcrĕtār′IAL a., ~SHIP(1) n. [ME, f. LL
secretarius (SECRET, -ARY[1])]

sĕcrĕt‖e′, v.t. Put (object, person, one-
self) into place of concealment; (physiol.;
of gland or organ or the person etc. of
which it is part) produce by secretion,
whence ~′OR n., ~′ORY a. [f. L *secret-
(as SECRET); partly f. foll.]

sĕcrē′tion, n. Act of concealing (*the* ~ *of
stolen goods*); (physiol.) process by which
special substances are separated from
blood or sap for service in the organism or for rejection as excretions, any

substance produced by such process, as saliva, urine, resin. [F (*sécré-*), or f. L *secretio* (SECRET, -ION)]

sĕc′rĕtive (*or* sĭkrē⁴), a. Given to making secrets, intentionally uncommunicative, needlessly reserved. Hence ~LY² adv., ~NESS n., (*or* sĭkrē⁴). [f. SECRET + -IVE]

sĕct, n. Body of persons agreed upon religious doctrines usu. different from those of an established or orthodox Church from which they have separated & usu. having distinctive common worship, nonconformist or other Church as described by opponents, party or faction in a religious body, religious denomination, so ~ARˈIAN a. & n., ~arˈianISM(2, 3) n., ~arˈianIZE(3) v.t.; followers of a particular philosopher or philosophy or school of thought. [ME, f. OF *secte*, or f. L *secta* f. stem of *sequi secut-* follow]

sĕcˈtary, n. (arch.). Member of a sect, esp. of the Independents, Presbyterians, etc., at time of the Civil War. [f. F *sectaire* or med. L *sectarius* (prec., -ARY¹)]

sĕcˈtile, a. Able to be cut (esp. of soft minerals such as talc). [F, f. L *sectilis* (*secare sect-* cut, -IL)]

sĕcˈtion, n., & v.t. 1. Separation by cutting. 2. Part cut off from something, one of the parts into which something is divided arbitrarily or may naturally be considered as divided (e.g. length of cane-stem between two rings), one part of a structure such as boat or wooden house that is made in parts for transportation, one of the minor subdivisions of a book usu. indicated by the ~*mark* (§; § 20), (mil.) subdivision of the platoon, part of community having separate interests or characteristics (whence ~alISM n., ~alIZE v.t.), (*microscopic* ~, thin slice cut from something for examination with microscope; *subject falls into five* ~s; *last* ~ *of the journey*; *conveyed to Tanganyika in* ~s; ~s *have been preferred to chapters*; ~-*commanders will be responsible*; *popular with all* ~s & *classes*). 3. Cutting of solid by plane (*conic* ~s, study of curves of intersection produced by allowing plane to cut cone at various angles), representation of internal structure of something supposed to be cut thus (*vertical, horizontal, longitudinal, oblique,* etc., ~, according to position chosen for plane). 4. (nat. hist.). Group, esp. sub-genus. 5. The ~ mark (see above) used as mark of marginal reference or with or without number to indicate beginning of ~; hence ~AL (-shon-) a., ~alLY² adv. 6. v.t. Arrange in, divide into, ~s. [F, or f. L *sectio* (prec., -ION)]

sĕcˈtor, n. 1. Plane figure enclosed between two radii of circle, ellipse, etc., & the arc cut off by them (~ *of sphere* etc., solid generated by revolution of plane ~ round one radius). 2. (mil.). Any of the parts into which the space occupied by opposing armies is distributed according

as each lies within the tactical purview of a headquarters at the focus or centre in rear (also transf., as *the private* ~ *of industry*). 3. Mathematical rule of two flat pieces working on rule-joint with lines representing sines, tangents, etc., radiating from centre of joint for use in making diagrams etc. Hence ~AL a. [LL, = sector f. L = cutter (prec., -OR)]

sĕctōrˈial, a. & n. (Carnivore's tooth) acting with tooth in opposite jaw like scissors (of specialized molar or premolar). [prec., -IAL]

sĕcˈular, a. & n. 1. Occurring once in or lasting for an age or a century (~ *games*, ancient-Roman festival held at long intervals; ~ *hymn*, composed for this; *the* ~ *bird*, phoenix). 2. Lasting or going on for ages or an indefinitely long time (opp. *periodical, cyclic*; ~ *change*, going on slowly but persistently; ~ *cooling* or *refrigeration*, that of the earth from fluid state; ~ *acceleration*, slow increase in motion of heavenly body; ~ *fame*, enduring; *the* ~ *rivalry between France & England, Church & State*, etc.). 3. Concerned with the affairs of this world, worldly, not sacred, not monastic, lay (~ *affairs, education, music*; *the* ~ *clergy*, parish priests etc., opp. *regular*; *the* ~ *arm*, hist., civil jurisdiction to which criminal was transferred by ecclesiastical courts for severer punishment); sceptical of religious truth or opposed to religious education etc., whence ~ISM(3)n., ~IST(2)n. & a., ~IZE(3) v.t., ~IZAˈTION n.; hence sĕcŭlăˈrITY n., ~LY² adv. 4. n. ~ priest. [ME; (in senses lay, worldly, f. OF *seculer*) f. L *saecularis* (*saeculum* generation, age)]

sĕcŭnd′, a. (bot., zool.). Arranged on one side only (as flowers in lily-of-the-valley). Hence ~LY² adv. [f. L as SECOND]

sĕcŭn′dō. See PRIMO³.

sĕcŭn′dum, L prep. = according to: ~ *art′ĕm*, artificially, also skilfully or scientifically; ~ *natūr′ăm*, naturally, not artificially; ~ *quid*, in some respect only, not absolutely or generally, with limitations. sĕcŭn′dus. See PRIMUS¹.

sĕcūre′, a., & v.t. 1. Untroubled by danger or apprehension (*a quiet* ~ *existence*; *dwell* ~); (arch.) confident or unsuspecting (*a* ~ *fool*, dupe etc.; *the* ~ *hope of salvation*); safe against attack, impregnable; reliable, certain not to fail or give way, (*a* ~ *foundation, fastening, foothold, grasp*); (usu. pred.) in safe keeping, firmly fastened, (*have got him* ~; *are you sure it is* ~?); having sure prospect of, safe against or from, (~ *of victory*; ~ *against assault*; ~ *from interruption*); hence ~LY² (-rlĭ) adv. 2. v.t. Fortify (town, harbour, etc., usu. *with* wall etc.); confine, enclose, fasten, or close, ~ly (~ *prisoner, valuables, buckle, window*; ~ *vein* etc. in surgery, compress to prevent bleeding; ~ *arms*, mil., hold rifles with lock in armpit to guard from rain); guarantee, make safe against loss, (*loan ~d on landed property* etc.; *how can I ~ myself against the consequences?*; *to ~ the labourer the* or *in the fruits of his labour*); succeed in getting, obtain, (esp. something coveted or competed for, as *have ~d front places, a first-class cook, the prize, my ends*); hence **sĕcūr'**ABLE a. [vb f. a., f. L SE(*curus* f. *cura* care)]

sĕcūr'ifórm, a. (esp. nat. hist.). Axe-shaped. [L *securis* axe (*secare* cut), -I-, -FORM]

sĕcūr'itў, n. In adj. senses; also or esp.: over-confidence; thing that guards or guarantees (*pride should at least be a ~ against meanness*; *in ~ for,* as guarantee for); organization for preventing leakage of information to enemy (*~-minded*; *~ police* etc.; *~ risk,* person of doubtful loyalty whom it is considered risky to employ on state service); *S~ Council,* a body of the United Nations set up to maintain peace and *~,* consisting of five permanent members (China, France, U.K., U.S.A., U.S.S.R.) and six non-permanent members elected for a two-year term; thing deposited or hypothecated as pledge for fulfilment of undertaking or payment of loan to be forfeited in case of failure, document as evidence of loan, certificate of stock, bond, exchequer bill, etc. [ME, f. L *securitas* (SECURE, -TY)]

sĕdăn', n. (Also *~-chair*) 17th & 18th c. vehicle seated for one & carried by two chairmen with poles; enclosed motor-car for four or more persons including driver. [17th c., of obsc. orig.]

sĕdāte', a. (Of person or his manner, look, speech, or writing) tranquil, equable, composed, settled, not impulsive or lively. Hence ~LY[2] adv., ~NESS n. [L *sedare* settle (*sedēre* sit), -ATE[2]]

sĕd'ative, a. & n. (Drug, influence, etc.) tending to soothe. [ME, f. OF *sedatif* or med. L *sedativus* (as prec., -IVE)]

sē dēfĕndĕn'dō, adv. In self-defence (as plea in cases of homicide). [L]

sĕd'entar|ў, a. & n. 1. Sitting (*~y posture, statue*); (of person) inclined by nature or driven by occupation to, (of occupation) involving, (of life etc.) characterized by, much sitting, whence ~iLY[2] adv., ~iNESS n.; (zool. etc.) not migratory, free-swimming, etc., (of spider) lying in wait till prey is in web. 2. n. ~y person; ~y spider. [f. F *sédentaire* or f. L *sedentarius* (*sedēre* sit, -ENT, -ARY[1])]

sed'er (sā-), n. Ritual for the first night of the Passover. [Aram.]

sĕdēr'ŭnt, n. Sitting of ecclesiastical assembly or other body, or of a company over the wine or in talk (*had a long ~*). [L, = (the following persons) sat]

sĕdge, n. Kinds of grasslike plant with jointless stems growing in marshes or by waterside, bed of such plants; *~-warbler, -wren,* kind of warbler frequenting *~.*

Hence **sĕdg'ў**[2] a. [OE *secg* (cf. LG *segge*) f. Gmc *sagjaz* f. *sag-,* cf. SAW[1]]

sĕdil'ia, n. pl. (sing. *sĕdil'ĕ,* rare). Set of usu. three stone seats for priests in S. wall of chancel often canopied & otherwise decorated. [f. L *sedile* seat (*sedēre* sit)]

sĕd'iment, n. Matter that settles to bottom of liquid, lees, dregs. Hence ~ARY[1] (-ĕn[2]) a. [F (*sé-*), or f. L *sedimentum* (prec., -MENT)]

sĕdi't|ion, n. Agitation directed against the authority of a State's executive, conduct or speech tending to rebellion or breach of public order. So ~iOUS (-shŭs) a., ~iousLY[2] adv., ~iousNESS n. [ME, f. OF, or f. L *seditio* (*sed-* = SE-, *ire it-* go, -ION)]

sĕdūc|e', v.t. Lead astray, tempt into sin or crime, corrupt; persuade into surrender of chastity, debauch. Hence ~'IBLE a., ~'ingLY[2] adv., ~e'MENT (-sm-; rare), ~'ER[1], nn. [f. L SE(*ducere duct-* lead)]

sĕdūc't|ion, n. Seducing or being seduced; thing that tends to seduce, tempting or attractive quality of (often with merely playful or no imputation of blame), (*the ~ions of a great capital, beauty, the country,* etc.), so ~IVE a., ~iveLY[2] adv.,~iveNESS n. [F (*sé-*), or f. L *seductio* (prec., -ION)]

sĕd'ūlous, a. Diligent, persevering, assiduous, (of action etc.) deliberately & consciously continued, painstaking, (*with ~ care; ~ flattery, attentions; play the ~ ape,* acquire literary style by imitation). Hence or cogn. ~LY[2] adv., **sĕdūl'ITY,** ~NESS, nn. [L *sedulus,* -OUS]

see[1], v.i. & t. (*saw, seen*). 1. Have or exercise the power of discerning objects with the eyes (*~s best at night*; *cannot ~ till the ninth day*; *~ into millstone, through brick wall,* fig. of preternatural acuteness of intelligence; *~ing is believing,* one's own observation is the best evidence; *~ DOUBLE*[1] adv.; *~ red, ~* things as blood-coloured, be filled with fury ; *~ing ye shall ~ & shall not perceive* ; *~ through,* fig., not be deceived by, penetrate, detect nature of). 2. Descry, discern by sight, observe, look at or over, (*come where we cannot be ~n; children should be ~n & not heard; please ~ whether it is there, where it is; ~ the light,* be born or alive, also of conversion etc.; *things ~n,* not imaginary etc.; *~ visions,* be a seer etc. ; *~ things,* have hallucinations etc.; *~ stars,* have dancing lights before eyes from blow on head; *was ~n to fall* or *falling; saw him fall* or *falling; ~ the back,* be quit of visitor, invader, etc.; *cannot ~ my way; ~* one's *way to do* or *to doing,* manage, contrive; *~ the sights, town,* etc., as SIGHT[1]-seer; *~ over* house etc., go round examining; *worth ~ing,* notable; *~ p. 15* etc., look at, *vide; ~ thing done,* supervise doing of it). 3. Learn from newspaper etc. (*I ~ that another speed record was broken yesterday*). 4. Discern mentally, attain to comprehension of, apprehend, excogitate, ascertain by search or inquiry or reflection, consider, (*cannot ~ a* or *the joke, point; do you ~ what I mean?*, also *~?* ellipt. in same sense colloq.; *you ~,* parenth., as you no doubt understand, also = I must explain; *I ~,* now that you have explained I understand; *as far as I can ~,* to the best of my understanding or belief; *must ~ what can be done; do not ~ the good, fun, advantage,* etc., *of doing; do not ~ how to do it; you ~ what it is to have faith*); (part. as prep. or conj.) considering or inasmuch as (*~ing that you do not know it yourself; ~ing no other course is open to us*). **5.** Experience, go through more or less observantly, have presented to one's attention, contemplate & abstain from interference with, (*shall never ~ death; have ~n five reigns; will never ~ 50* etc. *again,* is over that age; *~ life,* gain experience of men & manners esp. by dissipation etc.; so perh. *well ~n,* arch., accomplished *in,* as intr. p.p.; *have ~n the day when,* in drawing attention to past state of affairs; *never saw such doings; has ~n service,* is expert or worn; *has ~n better,* or *its* etc. *best, days,* has declined; *you will not ~ me shot like a dog?;* ~ person or thing *blowed* or *damned first,* before one will do what he asks or trouble about it; *~ thing through* or *out,* not abandon undertaking before it is completed). **6.** Grant interview or be at home to, pay visit to, secure interview with, (*refused to ~ me; can I ~ you on business?; when will you come & ~ us?; must ~ the lawyer, doctor,* etc.; *can ~ you for five minutes*). **7.** Call up picture of, imagine, (*cannot ~ myself submitting to it*). **8.** Recognize as tolerable, consent willingly to, (*do not ~ being made use of*). **9.** Escort, conduct, stand by & countenance, (*may I ~ you home?; mind you ~ him off the premises; saw him off by the Mauretania; will you ~ me through,* or *through the difficulty?*). **10.** Take view of, have opinion, (*I ~ life, things, it, differently now; ~ good,* consider it right or expedient *to* do; *~* EYE¹ *to eye*). **11.** Make provision, take care, give attention, make sure, (*~ that it is done; ~ you don't catch your foot; ~ to* one's *business; will ~ about it,* & see below; *~ after,* take care of; *~ to it that,* take care that). **12.** Make examination, hold inquiry, (*must ~ into it*). **13.** Reflect, take time to consider, (esp. *let me ~,* appeal for time to think before making answer or giving particulars, or confession that coming statement may need reconsideration; *will ~ about it,* form for declining to act at once, & see above). **14.** (In gambling etc.) accept or take on (challenge to bet or competition, person offering it). **15.** *~-bright,* the plant clary (w. ref. to use as eye-salve founded on pop. etym. of *clary* as = clear-eye). Hence **sē′ER¹** n. [OE

sēon, OS, OHG *sehan,* ON *sjd* (f. *séa*), Goth. *saihwan* f. Gmc **sehw-*]

see², n. What is committed to (arch)-bishop, (archi-)episcopal unit, (usu. *the ~ of Norwich, Canterbury, Rome,* etc.; *Holy See, See of Rome,* the Papacy or Papal court; cf. BISHOPRIC, DIOCESE; *several new ~s were created*). [ME, f. AF *se(d)* = OF *sie(d)* f. Rom. *sēdes f. L *sēdes* (*sedēre* sit)]

seed, n., & v.i. & t. **1.** Flowering plant's unit of reproduction or germ capable of developing into another such plant, (collect.) *~s* in any quantity esp. as collected for sowing, (*its ~s are, ~ is, black; is full of ~; drops its ~s* or *~ everywhere; to be kept for* or *as ~; go, run, to ~,* cease flowering as *~* comes, fig. grow shabby etc.). **2.** Male fecundating fluid, semen, milt. **3.** (bibl.). Offspring, progeny, (*raise up ~,* beget children; *the ~ of Abraham,* Hebrews). **4.** Germ, prime cause, beginning, *of* (*~s of strife, vice; sow the ~s of,* initiate). **5.** (colloq.). ~ed competitor. **6.** *~-cake,* containing whole *~s* esp. caraway as flavouring; *~-coral,* in small *~*like pieces; *~-corn,* reserved for *~; ~-drill,* DRILL²; *~-eater,* kind of bird; *~-fish,* ready to spawn; *~-leaf,* primary leaf or developed cotyledon; *~-lobe,* cotyledon; *~-oysters,* young ones for planting; *~-pearl,* small; *~-plot,* piece of nursery-ground, (fig.) hotbed *of* sedition etc.; *~s'man,* dealer in *~s; ~-time,* sowing season; *~-vessel,* pericarp; *~-wool,* raw cotton before *~s* have been removed from fibre; hence *~'LESS* a. **7.** vb. Go to *~,* produce or let fall *~;* sprinkle (as) with *~.* **8.** Remove *~s* from (fruit etc.). **9.** Separate *~* from straw of (flax); (sport) sort stronger from weaker (competitors) to secure good later matches in tournament. **10.** *~ing-machine,* mechanical *~-sower; ~ing-plough,* with hopper depositing *~* in furrow as made. [OE *sǣd,* OS *sād,* OHG *sāt,* ON *sáth,* Goth. *-sēths* f. Gmc **sǣdh-* f. **sǣ-* SOW]

seed′er, n. Seed-drill; apparatus for seeding raisins etc.; ‖ spawning fish. [-ER¹]

seed′ling, n. Plant raised from seed & not from cutting etc.; young tender plant. [-LING¹]

seed′|y̆, a. Full of seed, going to seed; (of brandy) having flavour attributed to weeds among the vines; (colloq.) shabby-looking, in worn clothes, ‖ out of sorts, feeling ill, whence *~ILY²* adv.; *~y-toe,* disease of horse's foot. Hence *~INESS* n. [-Y²]

seek, v.t. & i. (*sought* pr. sawt). **1.** Make search or inquiry for, try or be anxious to find or get, ask (thing *of* person), aim at, pursue as object, endeavour *to* do, make for or resort to (place, person, for advice, health, etc.), (*what are you ~ing?; ~s a situation as cook, wealth, scope for his energies,* etc.; *sought of him a sign; ~s my aid; ~s my life* or *to kill me; came ~ing advice; sought his bed, a fortune-

-teller, the shore ; ~ dead ?, order to retriever to find killed game ; ~ *out*, single out for pursuit etc., esp. make special efforts to secure society of). 2. Search (place, receptacle) *through*. 3. Make search or inquiry *after* or *for* (*sought-after*, much in demand, generally desired or courted). 4. (arch.). Resort in numbers *to* (person, place). 5. *Is* etc. *to* ~ or *much to* ~, is deficient, wanting, or not yet found (*politeness is much to* ~ *among them; is to* ~ *in intelligence, grammar; an efficient leader is yet to* ~). Hence (-)~′ER[1] n. [OE *sēcan*, OS *sōkian*, OHG *suohhan*, ON *sœkja*, Goth. *sōkjan* f. Gmc **sōk-*; cf. BESEECH]

seel, v.t. (arch.). Close (eye), close eyes of (hawk), by sewing up lids; (fig.) hoodwink. [later form of obs. *sile* f. OF *siller* f. *cil* eyelash f. L as CILIA]

seem, v.i. 1. Have the air or appearance or sensation of being, appear or be apparently perceived or ascertained *to* do or have done, (*be what you* ~ *to be* or ~ ; *the man who* ~ed *the ringleader;* ~s *to be tired, a hopeless absurdity;* ~s *to be a good fellow, saint, etc.; I* ~ *to be* or ~ *deaf today,* ~ *to see him still; do′ not* ~ *to,* colloq., somehow do not, as *I do not* ~ *to like him, fancy it;* ~ *good to,* be adopted as best course by ; *what* ~*eth him good,* arch., what he chooses; ~*s to have died at 35*). 2. Appear to be true or the fact (with anticipatory *it* & following *that*-clause, or parenth. with *it* only, often with implication of anger or remonstrance; *it* ~*s to me that it will rain, such talk is absurd, we had better make up our minds to it; so we are to get nothing, it* ~*s; it* ~*s you were lying*; also *it should* or *would* ~ in same senses; *me* ~*s,* ~*eth,* ~*ed,* arch., it ~*s,* ~ed, to me). 3. (part.). Ostensible, apparent only, apparent but perhaps not real, apparent & perhaps real, (*the* ~*ing & the real; a* ~*ing friend; with* ~*ing sincerity;* ~*ing-virtuous* etc., usu. with suggestion of falsity), whence ~′ingLY[2] adv. [ME *seme* f. ON *sœma* f. *sœmr* seemly ; cogn. w. SAME]

seem′l|ỹ, a. & adv. 1. Decent, decorous, becoming ; hence ~iNESS n. 2. adv. (rare). Decorously. [ME, f. ON *sœmiligr* (prec., -LY[2])]

seen. See SEE[1].

seep, v.i. Ooze out, percolate slowly ; also fig. Hence ~′AGE(3) n. [with *sipe,* of dial. orig. ; cf. OE *sipian* to soak]

seer[1], n. Prophet, person who sees visions, person of preternatural insight esp. as regards the future. [ME; f. SEE[1] + -ER[1]]

seer[2], n. Indian (varying) measure of weight (in most parts = 2 lb.); Indian liquid measure (about one litre). [Hind. *ser*]

seer′-fish, seir- (sēr-), n. Common Indian scombroid fish. [corruption of Port. *serra* saw]

seer′sucker, n. Crimped striped material

of linen or cotton. [f. Pers. *shīr o shakkar* lit. milk & sugar]

see′saw, a., adv., n., & v.i. 1. With backward & forward motion as of a saw (~ *motion; go* ~, vacillate or alternate). 2. n. Game in which two persons sit one at each end of long board balanced on central support & move each other up & down alternately, board thus balanced. 3. v.i. Play at ~ ; move up & down as in ~ ; vacillate in policy etc. [redupl. of SAW[1]]

seeth|e (-dh), v.t. & i. (~*ed*; arch. past *sod*; arch. p.p. SODDEN). Cook (t. & i.) by boiling (arch.; prov. *thou shalt not* ~*e a kid in his mother's milk*); (fig.) boil, bubble over, be agitated, (the ~*ing waters; India was* ~*ing with discontent; madness, enthusiasm,* ~*ing in his brain*). [OE *sēothan,* OHG *siodan,* ON *sjótha* f. Gmc **seuth-*]

segar. (Incorrect for) CIGAR.

seg′ment, n., & v.i. & t. 1. Part cut off or separable or marked off as though separable from the other parts of something (e.g. one ring of a worm, one division of a limb or the skull, one wedge of orange-pulp); (geom.) part cut off by line or plane from any figure (~ *of circle,* part enclosed between arc & chord; ~ *of sphere,* part cut off by any plane not passing through centre), ~ *of line,* part included between two points; ~*-gear, -rack, -wheel,* with cogs occupying arc of circle only; ~*-saw,* with teeth extending over ~ of circle, also circular saw made up of ~al saw-plates, also saw for cutting into ~al shapes; ~*-valve,* closed by slide turning radially across seat; hence ~AL (-ĕn[2]), ~ARY[1], aa., ~aLLY[2] (-ĕn[2]) adv. 2. vb. Divide (i. & t.) into ~s, (of embryo) undergo cleavage or divide into parts; (physiol.) reproduce by gemmation; hence ~A′TION n., (esp.) formation of many cells from a single cell. [f. L *segmentum* (secare cut, -MENT)]

seg′reg|āte[1], v.t. & i. Put apart from the rest, isolate; (intr.; crystallog.) separate from a mass & collect about centres or lines of fracture. Hence or cogn. ~A′TION n., ~ATIVE a. [f. L SE(gregare f. grex gregis flock), -ATE[3]]

seg′regate[2], a. Set apart, separate, (arch.); (zool.) simple or solitary, not compound; (bot.) ~ *polygamy,* inflorescence in which each floret within common calyx has its own perianth also. [prec., -ATE[2]]

seiche (sāsh), n. Oscillation of lake waters due to changes in barometric pressure. [Swiss F, perh. = G *seiche* sinking (of water)]

Se′id (sā-, or sēd), n. Descendant of Mohammed through Fatima & Ali. [f. Arab. *sayyid* prince, see SAYYID, SIDI]

Seid′litz powd′er (sĕd-), n. Aperient medicine of two powders mixed separately with water & then poured together.

[named as substitute for mineral water of *Seidlitz* in Bohemia]

seigneur (sānyêr'), **seignior** (sān'yor), n. Feudal lord, lord of manor, whence **seignior'IAL** (sānyôr'-) a.; *grand seigneur* (see Ap.), person of high rank or whose demeanour etc. correspond to popular ideal of great nobleman; *the Grand Seignior,* = GRAND *Signior.* [ME, f. L *seniorem* SENIOR]

seign(i)orage (sān'yorĭj), n. (hist.). Something claimed by sovereign or feudal superior as prerogative, esp. Crown's right to percentage on bullion brought to mint for coining. [ME, f. OF (*-norage*), see prec., -AGE]

seigniory (sān'yorĭ), n. Lordship, sovereign authority; seignior's domain; municipal council of medieval Italian republic. [ME, f. OF *seignorie* (SEIGNEUR, -Y[1])]

seine (sān, sēn), n., & v.t. & i. **1.** Fishing-net for encircling, with floats at top & weights at bottom edge, & usu. hauled ashore; ~*-gang,* set of men working ~; ~*-needle,* for netting~s;~*-roller,* cylinder over which ~ is hauled. **2.** vb. Fish, catch, with ~, whence **sein'ER**[1] n. [OE *segne,* OS, OHG *segina* f. L f. Gk *sagēnē*]

seise, seisin. See *seiz-.*

seis'mic, seis'mal (rare), (sīz-), aa. Of earthquake(s). [Gk *seismos* earthquake (*seiō* shake), -IC]

seis'm|o- (sīz-), comb. form of Gk *seismos* (prec.); ~*ogram,* record given by ~OGRAPH (2) or ~ŏM'ETER or ~OSCOPE, instruments showing force, place, etc., of earthquake; so ~*ŏg'raphy,* ~*ŏg'rapher,* ~*ogrăph'ic(al),* ~*ŏm'etry,* ~*omĕt'ric(al),* ~*oscŏp'IC* ;~*ŏl'ogy,* ~*ŏl'ogist,* ~*olŏ'gical(ly).*

seize (sēz), v.t. & i. **1.** (law). (Also *seise*) put in possession *of* (chiefly in p.p. ~*d* or *seised of,* having in legal possession, &, fig., aware or informed of; often *stand* ~*d of*). **2.** Take possession of (contraband goods, documents, etc.) by warrant or legal right, confiscate, impound, attach, whence **seiz'OR** n. (legal), **seiz'ABLE** a., (sēz-). **3.** Lay hold of forcibly or suddenly, snatch, grasp with hand or mind, comprehend quickly or clearly, (~ *fortress, sceptre,* person *by the neck* etc., person's *hand, opportunity* or *occasion, an idea, a distinction, the point, the essence of the matter; was* ~*d by apoplexy, with remorse* or *panic*). **4.** Lay hold eagerly *upon* (~ *upon a chance* or *pretext*). **5.** (naut.). Lash, fasten with several turns of cord, (~ one *up,* lash him to rigging for flogging; ~ *ropes together*), whence **seiz'ING**[1](4) (sēz-) n. (usu. pl.). **6.** (Of machinery) becóme stuck, jam, from undue heat or friction. [ME, f. OF *saisir* give seizin f. Frankish L *sacire* f. **sakjan* quarrel, claim at law, cf. OS *sakan* (*saka* lawsuit) SAKE]

seiz'in, seis'in (sēz-), n. (legal). Possession of land by freehold; act of taking such possession; what is so held. [ME, f. OF *saisine* (prec.)]

seizure (sēzh'er), n. In vbl senses; esp., sudden attack of apoplexy etc., stroke. [ME, f. SEIZE + -URE]

sej'ant, a. (her.). (Of animal) sitting upright on haunches. [prop. *seiant* f. OF var. of *seant* f. *seoir* f. L *sedēre* sit, -ANT]

sek'ŏs, n. (archaeol.). Sacred enclosure esp. of ancient temple, adytum. [Gk]

selăch'ian (-k-), n. & a. **1.** Any fish of shark or dogfish kind. **2.** adj. Of or like such fishes. [Gk *selakhos* shark, -IAN]

sela'dăng (-ahd-), n. Large wild ox of Malay countries; Malayan tapir. [native name]

sel'ah, Hebrew word of unknown meaning retained in Bible version of Psalms & supposed to be a musical direction.

sěla'mlĭk (-ah-), n. Men's part of Mohammedan house. [Turk.]

sěl'dom, adv. (rarely ~*er,* ~*est*). Rarely, not often, (~ *or never; very* ~; *not* ~). [OE *seldan* (OHG *seltan,* ON *sjaldan*), alt. to *-um* after adv. dat. ending as in WHILOM]

sělěct', a., & v.t. **1.** Chosen for excellence, choice, picked, got by rejection or exclusion of what is inferior; (of society etc.) exclusive, cautious in admitting members; hence ~NESS n.; ‖ ~ *committee,* small parliamentary committee appointed to conduct some special investigation; ~*man,* one of the annually elected councillors in a New England town(ship). **2.** v.t. Pick out as best or most suitable; hence **sělěc'tIVE** a. (*~ive service,* conscription), **sělěc'tIVELY**[2] adv., **sělěc'tOR** n. [f. L SE(*ligere lect-* = *legere* pick)]

sělěc'tion, n. Selecting, choice; what is selected (*a fine* ~ *of summer goods; what is your* ~ *for the Derby?; the new headmaster is a good* ~); (biol.) sorting out in various ways (*natural, sexual, physical, artificial, methodical, unconscious,* ~) of the types of animal or plant better fitted to survive or multiply regarded as a factor in evolution. [f. L *selectio* (prec., -ION)]

sělěctiv'ity, n. (Of wireless receiving-sets etc.) power to respond to any particular wave-length without interference from others. [SELECTIVE + -ITY]

selenite, n. **1.** (sĕl'in-). Sulphate of lime or gypsum occurring as transparent crystals or thin plates; (chem.) salt of selenium. **2.** (S~; sīlē'). Inhabitant of moon. Hence **sělěnit'ic** a. [(1) f. L f. Gk *selēnitēs* (*lithos*) moon(-stone) f. *Selēnē,* -ITE[1]; (2) f. Gk *selēnitēs*]

sělěn'ium, n. Non-metallic element of sulphur-tellurium group, characterized by the fact that its electrical resistance varies with the intensity of the illumination falling on it. Hence **sělěn'ic** a., **sěl'ěnATE**[1](3) n., **sělěn'ious** (chem.) a. [Gk *Selēnē* moon, -IUM; named w. ref. to TELLURIUM]

sělěn'|(o)-, comb. form of Gk *sclēnē* moon;

~*ocen'tric*, as seen etc. from centre of moon; ~*odont*, (mammal) with crescent- -ridges on crowns of teeth; *sĕlĕnŏg'*RAPHY, study or mapping of the moon, so ~*o*- GRAPH(1), *sĕlĕnŏg'rapher*, ~*ograph'ic*; *sĕlĕnŏL'*OGY, *sĕlĕnŏl'ogist*; ~*otrŏp'ic*, curv- ing towards the moon (of plant-organs influenced in growth thus), so *sĕlĕnŏt'rop- ism*, *sĕlĕnŏt'rop*Y[1].

Sĕleu'cid, n. (pl. ~*s*, ~*ae*). One of the dynasty founded by Seleucus that gov- erned Syria *c*. 312–64 B.C. [-ID[3]]

sĕlf, n. (pl. *-ves*) & a. 1. Person's or thing's own individuality or essence, person or thing as object of introspection or re- flexive action, (*the study of the* ~; *the con- sciousness of* ~; one's *former, better*, etc., ~, oneself as one formerly was, one's nobler impulses etc.; one's *second* ~, intimate friend, right-hand man; chiefly *his, its*, etc., *own* or *very* ~ as form of *himself* etc. when divided; *Caesar's, pity's*, etc., ~, rhet. for *Caesar himself, pity it- self*); one's own interests or pleasure, concentration on these, (*cares for nothing but, refers everything to*, ~; ~ *is a bad guide to happiness*); flower of uniform, or of the natural wild, colour; (commerc., vulg., joc.) = *myself, yourself, himself*, etc. (*cheque drawn to* ~; *a ticket admitting* ~ *& friend*); *our noble selves* (joc., as toast). 2. adj. (Of colour) uniform, the same throughout, (of flower)~*-coloured*. 3. HER- SELF, HIMSELF, ITSELF, MYSELF, ONE~, OUR- SELF, THEMSELVES, YOURSELF. [OE, OS *self*, OHG *selb*, ON *sjalfr*. Goth. *silba*; orig. appended, as adj. or in apposition, to pronoun & declined with it, *he self, his selfes*, dat. *him selfum*, acc. *hine selfne*; in ME also adj. = same, very]

sĕlf-, pref. (prec.) expr. direct or indirect reflexive action, automatic or indepen- dent action, or sameness; freely used as living pref.; the more established wds are given alphabetically with references to the numbered classes following: 1. Expressing direct reflexive action with part. of any vb that can have *self* for object, & hence with the p. in sense *by oneself* or *itself*, & with vbl nn. & adjj. & advv. in sense of *-self*; so from 'I ac- cuse myself' come ~*-accusing, -accused*, aa., *-accuser, -accusation*, nn., *-accusatory* a., *-accusingly, -accusatorily*, advv.

2. By extension it is prefixed also to any word, whether participle or other vbl deriv. or not, to which *self* might be at- tached by a preposition; in a large class (2a) the sense is *without external agency or assistance*; so from 'acts by or of itself' come ~*-acting*, ~*-action*, ~*-activity*; from 'evident of itself' comes ~*-evident*; in other wds (2b) the relation expressed is various; so from 'conceited about one self' ~*-conceited* & ~*-conceit*, from 'be absorbed, confide, in oneself' ~*-absorbed, -absorption, -confidence*, from 'inflict on oneself' ~*-inflicted*, from 'be conscious,

despair, of oneself' ~*-consciousness, -despair*, from 'depend on oneself' ~*- -dependence*, from 'righteous as seen by oneself' ~*-righteous*, from 'seek things for oneself' ~*-seeker, -seeking* a. & n., from 'suffice, use violence, to oneself' ~*-sufficing, -sufficient*, ~*-violence*. 3. To a few nn. & their derivv. in -ED[2] *self-* is prefixed with sense *uniform*, or *natural & not artificially produced*.

~*-aban'donment*,~*-abase'ment*,~*-abho'r- rence*, ~*-abnega'tion*, 1; ~*-absorbed'*, ~*- -absorp'tion*, 2b ;~*-abuse'* 1,solitary sexual indulgence; ~*-accusa'tion*, ~*-accus'atory*, etc.,1;~*-ac'ting*,~*-ac'tion*,~*-activ'ity*, 2a, automatic. (action); ~*-adjust'ing*, ~*- -adjust'ment*, 1, of machinery etc.; ~*- -admira'tion* 1 ; ~*-affirma'tion* 1 (psych.), recognition and assertion of the existence of the conscious self; ~*-aggran'dizement, -appoin'ted, -apprecia'tion, -approv'al, -ap- proba'tion*, 1; ~*-*ASSERT'*ing, -assert'ive, -asser'tion*, etc., 1; ~*-assumed'* 2b, of title etc. not conferred but taken esp. without right; ~*-begott'en* 1, by exag. for *not begotten by another*; ~*-betray'al* 1; ~*- -bin'der* 2a, reaping-machine with auto- matic arrangement for binding sheaves; ~*-blind'ed* 1; ~*-born* 1, as ~*-begotten*; ~*- -cen'tred(ness)* 2b, preoccupied with one's own personality or affairs; ~*-clos'ing* 1; ~*-cock'ing* 1, of gun in which hammer is raised by trigger, not by hand; ~*-col- lect'ed* 2b, having or showing presence of mind or composure; ~*-col'our(ed)* 3, of flower or material in which colour is uni- form throughout, or flower whose colour has not been changed by cultivation etc.; ~*-command'* 1, power of controlling one's emotions; ~*-commun'ion* 2b, meditation esp. upon one's own character or conduct; ~*-compla'cent, -compla'cency*, 2b, of person too easily pleased with himself; ~*-con- ceit'(ed)* 2b ; ~*-condemned', -condemna'tion*, 1; ~*-con'fidence, -con'fident(ly)*, 2b ; ~*- -congratula'tion, -con'quest*, 1; ~*-con- scious(ness)* 2b, esp. of person embar- rassed or made theatrical by inability to forget himself in society, also philos. etc. of man as having faculty of ~*-con- templation*; ~*-consis'tent, -consis'tency*, 2b; ~*-con'stituted* 1, esp. of person who assumes function without right to it; ~*- -consum'ing* 1; ~*-contained'* 1, not com- municative, also compact or complete in itself; ~*-contempt', -contemp'tuous(ly)*, 1; ~*-content'* n., *-conten'ted*, 2b; ~*- -contradic'tion, -contradic'tory, -control', -convict'ed*, 1; ~*-creat'ed, -crea'tion*, 1, as ~*-begotten*; ~*-crit'ical, -crit'icism, -cul- ture, -deceiv'ing, -deceiv'er, -deceit', -decep'tion*, 1; ~*-defence'* 1 (in ~*-defence*, not by way of aggression; *art of* ~*- -defence*, boxing); ~*-delu'sion* 1; ~*- -*DENY'*ing* (~*-denying ordinance*, resolu- tion of Long Parliament 1645 depriving members of Parliament of civil & mili- tary office; also often used allusively),

-deni'al, 1; ~-depen'dent, -ence, 2b; ~-de-
precia'tion, -depre'ciative, 1; ~-despair' 2b;
~-destroy'ing, -destruc'tion, etc., 1; ~-
-determ'ining, -determina'tion, etc., 1, esp.
w. ref. to free will as opp. fatalism etc., &,
in pol., of a nation's right to determine its
own polity; ~-devel'opment 1; ~-devo'tion
1, devoting of oneself to person or cause;
~-dis'cipline, -dispa'ragement, -display',
-dispraise', -distrust'(ful), -ed'ucated,
-educa'tion, -efface'ment, 1; ~-elec'tive 1,
esp. = proceeding etc. by co-optation; ~-
-esteem' 1; ~-ev'ident(ly) 2a, without need
of demonstration; ~-examina'tion 1; ~-
-ex'ecuting 1, not needing legislation etc.
to enforce it; ~-exis'tent 2a; ~-explain-
ing, -explan'atory, 1; ~-faced 3, (of stone)
unhewn, undressed; ~-feed'ing, -feed'er,
1, (furnace, machine, etc.) that renews its
own fuel or material automatically; ~-
-fert'ilizing, -fert'ilized, 1, -fert'ile, -fertil-
ity, 2a, of plants fertilized by their own
pollen, not from others; ~-flatt'ering,
-flatt'ery, 1; ~-forget'ful(ness) 1, unselfish-
(ness); ~-gen'erating 1; ~-glazed 3, (of
porcelain) covered with glaze of one tint;
~-glorifica'tion 1; ~-go'verning (esp. the
~-governing colonies opp. CROWN¹-colony),
-go'vernment, 1; ~-gratula'tion 1; ~-heal 1,
kinds of plant named as enabling patient
to do without doctor; ~-help' 1, working
for oneself without waiting for external
aid; ~-humilia'tion, -immola'tion, 1; ~-
-import'ant, -import'ance, 2b, in one's own
eyes, & hence pompous etc.; ~-imposed'
2b, of task etc.; ~-im'potent 2a, opp. ~-
-fertile; ~-improve'ment 1; ~-induc'tive,
-induc'tion, 2a, (electr.) (capable of) production of extra current in circuit by
variation of current in that circuit; ~-
-indul'gent, -indul'gence, etc., 1, yielding
to temptations of ease or pleasure; ~-in-
flict'ed 2b; ~-in'terest(ed) 2b, (actuated by
or absorbed in) what one conceives to
be for one's own interests; ~-invit'ed 1,
having had to ask for, having come without, an invitation; ~-involved' 2b, wound
up in oneself; ~-justifica'tion, -kind'led,
-know'ledge, -lauda'tion, 1; ~-love' 1,
selfishness, impulse towards ~-indulg-
ence, vulnerable conceit, also rarely desire
of ~-development etc.; ~-lum'inous 2a;
~-made 1, of person who has risen by his
own exertions, often with implication of
vulgarity etc.; ~-mas'tery, -mortifica'tion,
1; ~-mov'ing, -mo'tion, -murd'er(er), 1; ~-
-opin'ion, -opin'ioned, -opin'ionated, 2b,
of stubborn adherence to one's own opinions; ~-par'tial, ~-partial'ity, 2b; ~-
-pit'y, -pleas'ing a. & n., 1; ~-poised' 2a;
~-pollu'tion 1, ~-abuse; ~-port'rait 2a,
portrait (literary or pictorial) made by
a person of himself; ~-possessed', -posse's-
sion, 1, cool(ness), composed, composure,
in agitating circumstances etc.; ~-praise'
1 (~-praise is no recommendation);
~-preserva'tion 1, esp. the primary instinct impelling conscious beings to go
on living & avoid injury; ~-prof'it 1;
~-prop'agating 1; ~-propelled' 1; ~-rak'er
2a, reaping-machine with set of rakes
automatically preparing corn for binding;
~-realiza'tion 1, development of one's
faculties esp. as ethical first principle;
~-record'ing 2a, of scientific instrument
etc.; ~-regard'ing, -regard', 1, opp.
altruism etc. without the censure implied
in selfish etc.; ~-re'gistering 2a, as ~-
-recording; ~-reg'ulating 1, of machinery;
~-reli'ant, -ance, 2b; ~-renuncia'tion 1,
unselfishness; ~-repre'ssion, -reproach-
(ful), 1; ~-repug'nant 2b, inconsistent;
~-respect'ing, -respect', -respect'ful, 1, of
person who has & acts up to a standard
of worthy conduct; ~-restrained', -re-
straint', -reveal'ing a., -revela'tion, 1;
~-rev'erent, -rev'erence, 1, rhet., poet.,
theol., etc., for ~-respect etc.; ~-right-
eous(ness) 2b; ~-right'ing a. 1, of boat; ~-
-sac'rificing a., -sac'rifice, 1, postponing
private interest & desires to those of
others; ~-same 3, emphatic form of same;
~-sat'isfied, -satisfac'tion, 2b, conceit(ed);
~-scorn' 1; ~-seek'ing a. & n., -seek'er,
2b; ~-service 1, (attrib., of restaurant,
shop, etc.) in which customers help themselves to food or goods & afterwards pay
a cashier, thereby reducing the need for
sales assistants, (n.) this kind of service;
~-slaught'er 1; ~-sown' 1, sprung from
seed that has dropped without human
agency; ~-start'er 2a, electric appliance
for starting motor-car without use of
crank-handle; ~-ste'rile, -steril'ity, 2a,
as ~-impotent; ~-styled' 1, having taken
the name without right etc., pretended,
would-be; ~-suffi'cing 2b, requiring
nothing from outside, independent; ~-
-suffi'cient, -ency, 2b, = ~-sufficing, also
& usu. sufficient in one's own opinion,
presumptuous; ~-sugges'tion 2b, reflexive
suggestion of the mesmeric or hypnotic
kind; ~-support'(ing), -surren'der, -sus-
tain'ing, -sustained', -taught', -torment'ing
etc., -tor'ture etc.,·1; ~-vi'olence 2b, esp.
suicide; ~-will(ea) 2b, as ~-opinion etc.;
~-wind'ing 1, of clock with automatic
winding apparatus; ~-wor'ship 1.

sělf'hŏŏd, n. (rare). Personality, separate
& conscious existence. [-HOOD]

sělf'fĭsh, a. Deficient in consideration for
others, alive chiefly to personal profit or
pleasure, actuated by self-interest, (of
motives etc.) appealing to self-interest
(~ theory of morals, that pursuit of
pleasure of one kind or another is the
ultimate spring of every action). Hence
~-LY² adv., ~-NESS n. [-ISH¹]

sělf'lĕss, a. Oblivious of self, incapable of
selfishness. Hence ~-NESS n. [-LESS]

sělf'nĕss, n. (rare). = SELFHOOD. [-NESS]

Sěljuk' (-ook), n. Member of 11th-13th-c.
Mohammedan dynasties in central &
Western Asia descended from the chief-
tain Seljuk. Hence ~-IAN a. & n.

sěll, v.t. & i. (sold), & n. 1. Make over or

dispose of in exchange for money (cf. BUY, BARTER; ~ one's *life dearly*, fig., kill or wound assailants before being killed; ~*ing-race, -handicap*, etc., in which winning horse must be sold to highest bidder; ~ one *a pup*, sl., swindle him). 2. Keep stock of for sale or be a dealer in (*do you* ~ *candles?*; *bookselling* etc.). 3. Betray for money or other reward (~ one's *country* etc.), also ~ *down the river*. 4. Prostitute for money or other consideration, make a matter of corrupt bargaining, (~ *justice*, one*self*, one's *honour* or *chastity*). 5. (sl.). Disappoint by not keeping engagement etc., by failing in some way, or by trickery (*sold again!*, excl. used by or to disappointed person). 6. Advertise or publish merits of; give (person) information *on* value of something, inspire with desire to possess something; *be sold on*, be enthusiastic about. 7. (Of goods) find purchasers (*will never* ~ ; ~*ing like wildfire, hot cakes*). 8. ~ *off*, ~ remainder of (goods), clear out stock, at reduced prices; ~ *out*, leave army by ~ing commission (hist.), ~ (all or some of one's shares in company, whole stock-in-trade, etc., or abs.); ~*-out* n., betrayal, ~ing of all tickets etc. for a show etc., commercial success; ~ *up*, ~ goods of (debtor) by distress or legal process. 9. n. (colloq.). Disappointment (*what a* ~*!*). Hence (-)~'ER[1] n. (~*ers' market*, one in which goods are scarce and high prices favour ~ers). [OE *sellan*, OS *sellian*, OHG *sellen*, ON *selja*, Goth. *saljan*, cf. SALE]

sellanders. See SALLENDERS.

sĕlt′zer, n. (Also ~ *water*) medicinal mineral water from *Selters* in Germany; artificial substitutes for this, soda-water.

sĕlt′zogĕne, n. = GAZOGENE. [f. F *selzogène* (prec., -GEN)]

sĕl′vage, -ĕdge, n. Edge of cloth so woven that it cannot unravel, border of different material or finish along edge of cloth intended to be torn off or hidden, list; edge-plate of lock with opening for the bolt. Hence **sĕl′vagED[2]** (-ĭjd) a. [15th c., f. SELF + EDGE, after MDu. *selfegge*]

sĕlvagee′ (-j-), n. Hank of rope-yarn bound together, used as a sling etc. [f. prec.]

selves. See SELF.

sĕmăn′tic, a. & n. 1. Relating to meaning in language. 2. n. pl. Branch of philology concerned with meanings. [f. F (-*ique*) f. Gk *sēmantikos* significant (*sēmainō* mean)]

sĕm′aphōre, n., & v.i. & t. 1. Signalling apparatus of post with oscillating arms, arrangement of lanterns, etc., for use (esp. now on railways) by day or night; military signalling by operator's two arms or two flags. 2. vb. Signal, send, by ~. Hence **sĕmaphŏ′rIc** a., **sĕmaphŏ′rICALLY** adv. [F, f. Gk *sēma* sign + -PHORE]

sĕmăsi|ŏl′ogȳ, n. Semantics. So ~o-

lŏ′gĭcal a. [G, f. Gk *sēmasia* meaning + -LOGY]

sĕmăt′ic, a. (nat. hist.). (Of colour or markings in animals) significant, serving to warn óff enemies or attract attention. [f. Gk *sēma-atos* sign + -IC]

|| **sĕm′blable,** a. (arch.). Having semblance of something, seeming. [ME, f. OF (foll., -ABLE)]

sĕm′blance, n. What looks like, the outward appearance of, something (*put on a* ~ *of anger*; *bears the* ~ *of an angel & the heart of a devil*). [ME, f. OF f. *sembler* f. L *simulare* SIMULATE]

semée, semé, (sĕm′ĭ), a. (her.). Covered with small bearings of indefinite number (e.g. stars, fleurs-de-lis) arranged over field. [F, p.p. of *semer* sow (SEMEN)]

semeiology, semeiotics. See semio-.

sĕm′ĕn, n. Generative fluid of male animals. [L, genit. *-inis*, = seed (*serere* sow, -MEN)]

sĕmĕs′ter, n. Half-year course or term in German & other universities. [G, f. L *semestris* six-monthly (*sex* six, *mensis* month)]

sĕm′i-, pref. = L *semi-* half, cogn. w. Gk *hēmi-* HEMI-, attached to any E wd as living pref. (cf. BI-, DI-[2], DEMI-, HEMI-); the more established or illustrative wds are given alphabetically w. reff. to the following numbered senses: 1. the half of (~*circle*); 2. on one of two sides (~*-detached*), in one of two directions (~*-infinite*), in some particular (~*vowel*); 3. little more or better than (~*-barbarism*); 4. rather less than (~*-official*), in low degree (~*civilized*), not quite deserving the description (~*-smile*); 5. imperfect(ly)(~*-bull*, ~*-double*); 6. occurring, published, etc., each half — or twice in a — (~*-annual*; cf. BI- 1e): ~*-ann′ual(ly)* 6; ~*-barbār′ian, -barb′arism,* 3; || ~*′brève* 1, longest note in common use, equalling two minims (see BREVE); ~*-bull* 5, issued by Pope after election & before coronation with one side of seal left blank; ~*-centenn′ial* 6, occurring etc. every fifty years; ~*-chor′us* 1, half or part of choir, passage given by it; ~*-circle, ~circ′ular* a., 1, (amounting to, arranged as or in, shaped like) half of a circle or of its circumference, set of objects ranged in or object forming a ~-circle, instrument for measuring angles; ~*-côl′on* 4, punctuation-mark (;) now used as the chief stop (the colon being mostly reserved for special uses) of intermediate value between comma & full stop; ~*-cyl′inder, ~cylin′drical,* 1, (of, forming, etc.) half of a cylinder cut longitudinally; || ~*-demi-semiquaver* 1; ~*-detâched′* (-cht) 2, (of house) joined to another by party-wall on one side only; ~*-documen′tary* a. & n. 1, (cinema film) having an actual background and a fictitious story; ~*′dome* 1, 4, half-dome formed by vertical section, part of structure more or less resembling dome; ~*-dou′ble* 5 (bot.), having outer stamens only converted to petals; ~*fin'al* 4, match or round preceding the final (~*fin'alist*, competitor in this); ~*·flu'id* a. & n. 4, viscous (fluid); ~*·fused* 5; ~*·in'fidel* 3; ~*·in'finite* 2, limited in one direction & stretching to infinity in the other; ~*·lun'ar* 1, 4, half-moon-shaped, crescent-shaped, (esp. in anat. names, as ~*·lunar bone, cartilage, fold, fossa, lobe, valve*); ~*·month'ly* 6; ~*·mute* a. & n. 3, (person) practically dumb owing to (esp. congenital) deafness; ~*·offi'cial(ly)* 4, esp. of communications made to newspapers by official with stipulation that they shall not be formally attributed to him; ~*·plume* 2, feather with firm stem but downy web; ~*pre'cious* 4, of stones; || ~*'quaver* 1 (mus.), note half length of quaver; ~*·ri'gid* 4, (of airship) having a stiffened keel attached to a flexible gas container; ~*·smile* 4; ~*'tone* 1 (mus.), smallest interval in normal European music, half length of tone (*diatonic* ~*tone*, occurring in major or minor scale; *chromatic* ~*tone*, not so occurring); ~*transpār'ent* 4; ~*trop'ical* 4, (as) of regions bordering on the tropics; ~*·tūb'ular* 1, shaped like half a tube cut longitudinally; ~*·un'cial* 5, between uncial & minuscule; ~*'vowel*, ~*vōc'al* a., 2, sound, or letter representing it, intermediate between vowel & consonant (e.g. *y, w*), consonant that is not mute (e.g. *l, m, z*); ~*week'ly* 6.

sĕm'inal, a. Of seed or semen or reproduction, germinal, reproductive, propagative, (~ *fluid, semen*; *in the* ~ *state*, rudimentary, still undeveloped; ~ *principles*, pregnant with consequences). Hence ~LY² adv. [ME, f. OF, or f. L *seminalis* (SEMEN, -AL)]

sĕm'inār, n. Small class at university for discussion and research; *conference of specialists; short intensive course of study. [G, as foll.]

sĕm'inar|y̆, n. Place of education (formerly in pretentious use for *school*, cf. ACADEMY; now rare exc. either fig. as *a*~*y of vice* etc., or of R.-C. & esp. Jesuit schools, whence ~IST n.). [ME, f. L *seminarium* seed-plot (SEMEN, -ARY¹)]

sĕminā'tion, n. (bot.). Process, plant's manner, of seeding. [f. L *seminatio* (*seminare* f. SEMEN, -ATION)]

sĕminif'erous, a. Bearing seed; conveying semen. [SEMEN, -I-, -FEROUS]

sĕmiŏl'ŏgy̆, sĕmiŏt'ics, -meio- (-mĭŏ-), nn. Branch of pathology concerned with symptoms. [Gk *sēmeion* sign (*sēma* mark), *sēmeiōtikos* of signs, -LOGY, -ICS]

Sĕm'|īte, n. & a. (Member) of any of the races supposed to be descended from Shem (*Gen.* x. 21 foll.) including esp. the Hebrews, Arameans, Phoenicians, Arabs, & Assyrians. So **Sĕmit'ic** a. (also n. = ~itic languages), ~**itism**(2, 4), ~**itist**(3), nn., ~**itize**(3) v.t. [f. mod. L *semita*, f. LL f. Gk *Sēm* Shem, -ITE¹]

|| **sĕmm'it**, n. (Sc.). Undershirt.

sĕmoli'na (-lē-), **sĕm'ola**, n. Hard grains left after bolting of flour, used in puddings etc. [-*ina* f. It. *semolino* dim. of *semola* bran]

sĕmpitĕrn'al, a. (Rhet. for) eternal; everlasting, never to end, (rare). [ME, f. OF (-*el*) or LL *sempiternalis*, f. L *sempiternus* (*semper* always +*aeternus* eternal), -AL]

sĕm'plĭce (-chā), mus. direction. Simple in style of performance. [It., = SIMPLE]

sĕm'pre (-ā), mus. direction. Throughout (with other direction, as ~ *forte*). [It.]

sempstress. See SEAMSTRESS.

sĕn, n. Japanese copper coin, 1/100 of yen.

sĕnār'ius, n. (pl. *-iī*). Latin verse of six feet, usu. iambics. [f. L (*versus*) *senarius* (*seni* six each, -ARY¹)]

sĕn'ary̆, a. On basis of six, by sixes, (~ SCALE³, cf. BINARY). [f. L as prec.]

sĕn'ate, n. 1. State-council of the ancient-Roman republic & empire dividing legislation with the popular assemblies, administration with the magistrates, & judicial power with the equites. 2. Upper & less numerous branch of the legislative assembly in various countries; (rhet.) any legislature or its proceedings or members (*the* ~, *the pulpit, & the press*). 3. Governing body of Cambridge Univ. & other institutions; *S*~*-house* (esp. at Cambridge). [ME, f. OF *senat, senaz* f. L *senatus* (*sen-* old, -ATE¹)]

sĕn'ator, n. Member of senate. Hence or cogn. **sĕnatŏr'ial** a., **sĕnatŏr'ialLY²** adv., ~SHIP n. [ME, f. OF (-*eur*), f. L *senatorem* nom. -*or* (prec., -OR)]

sĕnāt'us, n. 1. The ancient-Roman senate (~ *pŏp'ulusque Rōman'us*, the senate & people of Rome, abbr. S.P.Q.R., official name of ancient Rome as a State; ~*consult'*(*um*), decree of the ~). 2. || (In full ~ *acadēm'icus*) governing body in some universities. [L, = SENATE]

sĕnd¹, v.t. & i. (*sent*). 1. Bid go, secure conveyance of, to some destination (destination given by *to* or other prep. or by ind. obj. of person, or merely implied; ~ *message* or *messenger to*; *sent me a book*; *will* ~ *an army*; ~ *goods all over* or *round the world*; ~ COALS *to Newcastle*; ~ *word*, have message taken *that, to* do, etc.; ~ *up* or *in* one's name, an exhibit, etc., enter oneself or it for competition). 2. (Of God, providence, etc.) grant, bestow, inflict, bring about, cause to be so-&-so, (~ *rain, a judgement, pestilence*; *God* ~ *it may not be so!*; ~ *her victorious!*). 3. Propel, cause to move, (~ *bullet*; *sent his temperature up, down*; ~ *out* or *forth leaves, steam, odour*). 4. Dismiss, with or without force (with *off, away*, or compl. or adv. phr.; *sent him away, packing, flying, about his business, to the right-about*; ~ *to* COVENTRY; || ~ *down*, rusticate or expel from university; ~ *off letter, parcel*, etc., get it off one's own hands & started on

its way; ~ *off* person, witness his departure as sign of respect etc., so ~⌐*off* n., also laudatory review of book etc.). 5. Drive *mad* or *crazy*; (jazz sl.) put into ecstasy. 6. ~ message or letter (*sent to warn me, depose him, to me to take care*; ~ *for him*, telling him to come; ~ *for the book*, ordering it as purchase). Hence ~'ER[1] n. [OE *sendan*, OS *-ian*, OHG *-en*, ON *-a*, Goth. *sandjan* f. Gmc **sandh-*]
sĕnd[2], sc-, n., & v.i. (naut.; ~*ed*). 1. Impulse given by the down slope of a wave (usu. ~ *of the sea*). 2. v.i. (Of vessel) plunge or pitch owing to this. 3. n. Such plunge. [f. prec.]
sĕn'dal, n. Medieval silken fabric used for rich dresses, pennons, etc. [ME, f. OF *cendal*, *sen-*, prob. f. Gk *sindōn* fine linen]
sĕn'ĕga, -ka, n. (Drug, used in cough--mixtures, made from root of) American plant called also *S~-snake-root*. [f. name of *Seneca* Indians]
sĕnĕs'c|ent, a. Growing old. Hence ~ENCE n. [f. L *senescere* (SENIOR, -ESCENT)]
sĕn'ĕschal (-shl), n. Steward or major--domo of mediaeval great house. [ME, f. OF, f. med. L *seniscalcus* f. WG **siniskalk* (**sini-* old, **skalk* servant); cf. MARSHAL]
sĕn'green (-n-g-), n. = HOUSE[1]-*leek*. [OE *singrēne* evergreen]
senhor, senhora, senhorita, (sănyōr', -ōr'a, -orēt'a), used of or to Portuguese as SIGNOR etc.
sĕn'ile, a. Showing the feebleness etc. of, incident to, old age (~ *atrophy, apathy, garrulity, dementia*, etc.). Hence **sĕnil'ITY** n. [f. L *senilis* (foll., -IL)]
sĕn'ior, a. & n. 1. More advanced in age or older in standing, superior in age or standing *to*, of higher or highest degree, (opp. JUNIOR; || *the ~ service*, Navy as opp. Army; *the ~ members of the family, university*, etc.; *the ~ partner*, head of firm; ||~ *optime*, see WRANGLER; ||~ *classic*, competitor placed highest in classical tripos when names were arranged according to merit; ||~ WRANGLER; ||~ *man* at university, opp. FRESHman; *is two years ~ to me*), so **sĕniŏ'rITY** n. 2. (Appended to name for distinction; abbr. *sen., sr*; opp. JUNIOR) ~ to another of same name (esp. with father's Christian name & surname when son has same, as *John Smith sen.*, or at school with surname when two or more boys have same, as *Smith sen.*). 3. n. Person of advanced age or comparatively long service etc.; one's elder or superior in length of service, membership, etc. (*is my ~*); ||~ wrangler, || classic or man. [L, = older, old(ish) man, compar. f. st. of *senex senis* old (man)]
sĕniŏr'ĕs priŏr'ĕs (-z, -z), L sentence (= elders first) used in reminding the young of precedence due to seniority.
sĕnn'a, n. (Dried leaflets, used as laxative, of) kinds of cassia. [f. Arab. *sanā*]
sĕnn'ĕt, n. (hist.). Signal call on trumpet

(in stage-directions of Shaksperean & other plays). [app. var. of SIGNET 'sign'] **sĕn'ight** (-īt), n. (arch.). Week (esp. *Tuesday* etc. ~). [OE *seofon nihta* seven nights]
sĕn'it, sĭnn'ĕt, n. (naut.). Braided cordage made in flat or round or square form from 3–9 cords (*common* i.e. flat, *round, square*, ~). [c. 1600 *sinnet*, of unkn. orig.]
señor, señora, señorita, (sĕnyōr', -ōr'a, -orēt'a), used of or to Spaniards as SIGNOR etc.
Sĕnous(s)'i (-ōō-), n. Religious & political Mohammedan fraternity in N. Africa named after founder (usu. *the* ~ as sing. or pl.).
sĕnsā'tion, n. 1. Consciousness of perceiving or seeming to perceive some state or affection of one's body or its parts or senses or of one's mind or its emotions, contents of such consciousness, (*had a ~ of giddiness, heat, pain, comfort, thirst, falling, squrness, deafness, pride, stupidity*; *pressing the eyeball in the dark will produce the ~ of light* or *of seeing light*; *in search of a new ~*). 2. Stirring of the emotions common to many people or of eager interest among them, display of intense common emotion or interest, literary or other use of material calculated to excite it, (*made a great ~*, was eagerly discussed or viewed; ~ *among the audience*, shown by deep silence, applause, or other general manifestation; *a three--days' ~*; *what is the latest ~?*; *the essence of melodrama is ~*; *deals largely in ~*). Hence ~AL(-shon-) a., ~aLY[2] adv. [f. LL *sensatio* (in med. L sense) f. L *sensus* SENSE, -ATION]
sĕnsā'tional|ism (-shon-), n. (Philos.) theory that ideas are derived solely from sensation; pursuit of the sensational in literature, political agitation, etc. So ~IST(2) n. [-ISM]
sĕnse, n., & v.t. 1. Any of the special bodily faculties by which sensation is roused (*the five ~s*, sight, hearing, smell, taste, & touch; *sixth* or *muscular ~*, producing sensation of muscular effort; *has quick, keen, ~s, a dull ~ of smell*); (pl.) person's sanity or ordinary state of mind regarded as secured by possession of these (*have you taken leave of, are you out of, your ~s?*, are you mad?; *he will soon come, we must bring him, to his ~s*, out of mad folly; *frightened out of his ~s*, into loss of faculties; *in* one's *~s*, sane). 2. Ability to perceive or feel or to be conscious of the presence or properties of things, sensitiveness of all or any of the ~s, (~*-perception*; *errors of ~*, mistakes in perception; *the pleasures of ~*, those depending on sensation; *has a plant ~?*). 3. Consciousness of (*a* or *the ~ of pleasure, pain, gratification, having done well*, one's *own importance, shame, responsibility*; *labouring under a ~ of wrong*, feeling wronged). 4. Quick or accurate apprecia-

tion *of*, instinct regarding or insight into specified matter or habit of squaring conduct to such instinct, (~ *of locality, distance, the ridiculous, humour, duty, beauty, gratitude; a keen ~ of honour; the religious, moral, aesthetic,*~). **5.** Practical wisdom, judgement, common ~, conformity to these, (*sound, good,* COMMON[1], ~ ; *a man of* ~, sagacious; *had not the* ~ *to* do; *has plenty of* ~ ; *what is the* ~ *of talking like that? ; has more* ~ *than to* do; *now you are talking* ~). **6.** Meaning, way in which word etc. is to be understood, intelligibility or coherence or possession of a meaning, (*in what exact* ~ *we shall rise again is doubtful; the* ~ *of the word is clear; does not make* ~, is unintelligible; *in the strict, limited, literal, figurative, moral, metaphorical, legal,* PICKWICKIAN, *proper, full,* ~ ; *in a vague, in every,* ~ ; *in a* ~, provided the statement is taken in a particular way, under limitations, as *what you say is true in a* ~ ; *make* ~ *out of nonsense*). **7.** Prevailing sentiment among a number of people (*take the* ~ *of the meeting*, ascertain this by putting question etc.). **8.** ~-*body, -capsule, -cavity, -cell, -centre, -organ*, parts of animals concerned in producing sensation; hence ~'LESS (-sl-) a. (esp.=foolish; *knock* ~*less*, stun), ~'**lèssLY**[2] adv., ~*lèssNESS* n. **9.** v.t. Perceive by ~, (esp.) be vaguely aware of. [ME, f. OF *sens* or L *sensus -ūs* (*sentire* sens- feel)]

sènsibil'itỹ, n. Capacity to feel (*skin lost its* ~); exceptional openness to emotional impressions (*sense & ~*), delicacy of feeling, susceptibility (~ *to kindness* etc.), over-sensitiveness; (pl.) susceptibility in various directions. [ME, f.LL *sensibilitas* (foll., -TY)]

sèn'sible, a. Perceptible by the senses (~ *phenomena, things*); great enough to be perceived, appreciable, (*a* ~ *difference, increase*); (arch.) sensitive (*to*); aware, not unmindful, *of*, (*was* ~ *of his peril, your kindness*); of good sense, reasonable, judicious, moderate, practical, (*a* ~ *man, course, compromise; that is very* ~ *of him*). Hence **sèn'sibLY**[2] adv., ~**NESS** n. [ME f. OF, f. L *sensibilis* (SENSE, -IBLE)]

sèn'sit|ive, a. & n. **1.** Of the senses, sensory, (rare); having sensibility *to*, very open *to* or acutely affected by external impressions esp. those made by the moods or opinions of others in relation to oneself; (of instrument etc.) readily responding *to* or recording slight changes of condition (~*ive market*, liable to quick changes of price); (chem.) readily affected by or responsive *to* appropriate agent, (photog.) ~*ive paper*, prepared to receive impressions from light, whence ~IZE(3) v.t., ~**ĪZA'TION**, ~**ĪZER**[1](2), ~**ŎM'ETER**, nn.; ~*ive plant*, kind of mimosa whose leaves curve downwards & leaflets fold together at nightfall or when touched; hence ~**ĭveLY**[2] adv., ~**ĭveNESS**, ~**ĭv'ITY** (chem.,

photog., physiol., **psychol.**), nn. **2.** n. (hypnotism etc.). Person ~ive to hypnotic etc. influences. [ME f. OF, or f. med. L *sensitivus*, irreg. f. L *sentire* sens- feel, -IVE]

sènsōr'ium, n. (pl. -*ia*, -*s*). The seat of sensation, the brain, brain & spinal cord, or grey matter of these; (biol.) whole sensory apparatus including nerve-system etc. [LL *sensorium* (SENSE, -ORY)]

sèn'sorỹ, sènsōr'ial, aa. Of the sensorium or sensation or the senses. [after prec.; see -ORY]

sèn'sŭal (*or* -shŏŏ-), a. Of sense or sensation, sensory, (rare); of or depending on the senses only & not the intellect or spirit, carnal, fleshly, (~ *pleasures*); given to the pursuit of ~ pleasures or gratification of the appetites, self-indulgent in regard to food & sexual enjoyment, voluptuous, licentious; (philos.) holding the doctrine of, according to, of, sensationalism. Hence or cogn. ~IZE(3) v.t., ~**ĪZA'TION**, ~ISM(2, 3), ~IST(1, 2), ~ITY (-ăl[2]-), nn., ~LY[2] adv. [ME, f. L *sensualis* (SENSE, -AL)]

sèn'sŭous, a. Of, derived from, affecting, the senses (chiefly as substitute, free of implied censure, for prec.; cf. *non-moral & immoral*). Hence ~LY[2] adv., ~**NESS** n. [f. L *sensus* SENSE +-OUS]

sent. See SEND[1].

sèn'tence, n., & v.t. **1.** (arch.). One's opinion for or against some course or conclusion (*my* ~ *is for war*); pithy saying, briefly expressed thought, maxim, proverb. **2.** Verdict (rare); (declaration of) punishment allotted to person condemned in criminal trial (also transf.). **3.** (gram.). Set of words complete in itself, containing subject & predicate (either, or part of either or both, occas. omitted by ellipsis), & conveying a statement, question, or command (e.g. *I go, will you go?, go*=go thou or you, *what?* = what did you say ?, *hearts trumps*=hearts are trumps; *simple* ~, with single subject & predicate; *compound* ~, with more than one of either or both; *complex* ~, with subordinate clause or clauses), so **sèntèn'tiAL** (-shl) a. (rare) ; (loosely in gram.; usu. *subordinate* ~) subordinate clause. **4.** Amount of speech, usu. that between two full stops often including several grammatical ~s (e.g. *I went & he came*). **5.** v.t. State ~ of (condemned criminal, or transf.), declare condemned *to*. [ME, f. OF, f. L *sententia* f. *sentire* be of opinion, -ENCE]

sèntèn'tious (-shus), a. Aphoristic, pithy, given to the use of maxims, affecting a concise' impressive style; (of style) affectedly 'formal; (of persons) fond of pompous moralizing. Hence ~LY[2] adv., ~**NESS** n. [f. L *sententiosus* (as prec., -OUS)]

sèn'tient (-shi-), a. Having the power of sense-perception. Hence **sèn'tiENCE** (-shi-) n., ~LY[2] adv. [L *sentire* feel, -ENT]

sèn'timent, n. **1.** A mental feeling, the sum of what one feels on some subject, a tendency or view based on or coloured with emotion, such feelings collectively as an influence, (*the ~ of pity, patriotism*; *animated by noble ~s*; *my ~ towards him is one of respect*; ~ *unchecked by reason is a bad guide*; *these are*, often joc. *them's*, *my ~s*, that is what I think about it). **2.** (In art) moving quality resulting from artist's sympathetic insight into what is described or depicted. **3.** Tendency to be swayed by feeling rather than by reason, emotional weakness, mawkish tenderness or the display of it, nursing of the emotions, whence **sĕntimĕn'tăl** a., **sĕntimĕn'talLY²** adv., **sĕntimĕntăl'ITY**, **sĕntimĕn'talISM**, **sĕntimĕn'talIST**, nn., **sĕntimĕn'talIZE**(2, 3) v.i. & t. **4.** (Sense intended to be conveyed by) the expression of some desire or view esp. as formulated for a toast etc. (*the ~ is good though the words are injudicious* etc.; *conclude one's speech with a ~*; *I call upon Mr Jones for a song or a ~*). [ME, f. OF (-*tement*), f. med. L *sentimentum* (L *sentire* feel, -MENT)]

sĕn'tinel, n., & v.t. (-ll-). **1.** Soldier posted to keep guard (cf. foll.); (also ~ *crab*) Indian-Ocean crab with long eye-stalks. **2.** v.t. Keep guard over or in (poet.); station ~s at or in (rare). [16th c., f. F *sentinelle* f. It. *-ella*; orig. unkn.]

sĕn'trЎ, n. (Term in ordinary mil. use for) sentinel; ~-*board*, platform for ~ outside ship's gangway; ~-*box*, wooden cabin large enough to hold ~ standing; ~-*go*, duty of pacing up & down as ~. [perh. f. *centrinel* 16th-c. var. of prec.]

Sĕnuss'ī (-ōō-), n. (Now usu. form of) SENOUS(S)I.

sĕn'za (-tsa), It. prep. = without, in mus. directions as ~ *tĕm'pō*, not in strict time.

sĕp'al, n. One of the divisions of the calyx, calyx-leaf, (cf. PETAL). [f. F *sépale* mod. L *sepalum*, formed by H. J. de Necker 1790 after *petalum* PETAL f. Gk *skepē* covering]

sĕp'arate¹,· a. & n. **1.** Physically disconnected, forming a unit that is or may be regarded as apart or by itself, distinct, individual, of individuals, (*from*, or abs.; *the ~ members of the body*; *the ~ volumes may be had singly*; *live in ~ rooms*; *live ~*; *the two questions are essentially ~*; *one is quite ~ from the other*; ~ *& corporate or common ownership*; ~ *estate*, married woman's property when not subject to husband's control; ~ *maintenance*, husband's allowance to wife from whom he lives ~ by consent, cf. *alimony*; hence ~LY² adv., ~NESS n., & (esp. w. ref. to political or ecclesiastical independence, opp. *unionism*, *-ist*) **sĕp'aratISM**(3) n., **sĕp'aratIST**(2) n. & a. **2.** n. Copy of single article etc. reprinted from proceedings of society, magazine, etc., for ~ distribution; either of the articles of women's dress (blouse or jumper, or skirt or slacks) that may be worn ~ly or with the other. [f. L SE(*parare* arrange), -ATE²]

sĕp'ar|āte², v.t. & i. Make separate, sever, disunite, keep (trans.) from union or contact, part (t. & i.), secede *from*, go different ways, disperse (intr.); sort or divide (milk, grain, ore, fruit, light, etc.) into constituent parts or sizes, get (cream etc.) by such process for use or rejection, whence ~ātOR n. Hence ~ABLE, ~ATIVE, ~atORY (rare), aa., ~abLY² adv., ~·abIL'ITY, ~ablENESS, nn. [as prec., -ATE³]

sĕparā'tion, n. In vbl senses; esp. partial divorce, divorce from bed & board without dissolution of marriage tie (*judicial ~*, ordered by court); ~ *allowance*, that made by soldier etc., with larger Government augmentation, to his wife etc. [ME, f. OF, f. L *separationem* (prec., -ION)]

Sĕphard'ī, n. (pl. *-īm*). Spanish or Portuguese Jew. [f. Heb. *Sephārād* (see *Obad.* xx) Spain]

sĕp'ia, n. Black fluid of CUTTLE-fish; brown pigment prepared from this used in monochrome drawing & in water-colours (*warm ~*, mixture of this with some red), dark reddish-brown colour; (also ~*-drawing*) a drawing done in ~. [L f. Gk (*sē-*), = cuttle or its ink]

sĕp'oy, n. Indian soldier disciplined by European methods, esp. one of those serving in British-Indian army (~ *mutiny*, = *Indian* MUTINY). [f. Hind. f. Pers. *sipahi* soldier (*sipah* army)]

sĕps, n. Kinds of skink, serpent lizard. [L, f. Gk *sēps* (*sēpō* make rotten)]

sĕp'sis, n. (med.). Putrefaction, contamination from festering wound etc., blood-poisoning. [Gk *sēpsis* (as prec.)]

sĕpt, n. Clan, esp. in Ireland; in Scotland, tribe within a clan. [prob. 16th c. var. of SECT; cf. obs. F *septe*]

sĕpt-, sĕpt|ĕm-, sĕpt|i-, comb. forms of L *septem* seven: *sĕp'tan*, (of fever) recurring every 6th (inclus. 7th) day; *sĕp'tangle*, ~*ang'ular*, heptagon(al); ~*ĕmpart'ite*, divided into 7 parts; ~*ĕnn'ial(ly)*, of, for, (recurring) every, 7 years; ~*ĕnn'ium* (pl. *-ia*), period of 7 years; ~*ilat'cral*, seven-sided; ~*isyll'able*, word of 7 syllables.

sĕpta. See SEPTUM.

sĕp'tal, a. Of sept(s), septum, or septa. [·AL]

sĕp't|āte, a. (bot., zool., anat.). Having septum or septa, partitioned. Hence ~A'TION n. [SEPTUM, -ATE²]

Sĕptĕm'ber, n. Ninth month of year. [ME, f. L *september* (*septem* seven) the seventh month of the old Roman year]

Sĕptĕm'brist, n. Participator in the massacres in Paris Sept. 2, 3, 1792. [F (*-e*), see -IST]

sĕptĕnār'ius, n. (pl. *-rĭi*). Verse (esp. Latin) of 7 feet esp. trochaic tetrameter catalectic. [L, f. *septeni* seven each]

sĕptĕn'arЎ (*or* sĕp'tĭn-), a. & n. Of or

involving the number 7, on basis of 7, by sevens; (n.) a 7, group or set of 7 (esp. years), a septenarius. [f. L *septenarius* (prec.), -ARY]

sĕp′tĕnate, a. (bot.). Growing in sevens, having 7 divisions. [f. L *septeni* seven each, -ATE²]

sĕptĕnn′ate, n. (Arrangement made for) period of 7 years. [f. F (*-at*) f. L *septennis* (*septem* seven, *annus* year), -ATE¹]

sĕptĕt(te)′, n. (Composition for) group of 7 singers or players, (transf.) any set of 7. [G (*-ett*), f. L *septem*, see -ET¹, -ETTE]

sept′foil (sĕt⁴), n. The plant tormentil (now rare); seven-lobed figure esp. as R.-C. symbol of the 7 sacraments. [f. LL *septifolium* as if thr. OF; see SEPTI-, FOIL¹]

sĕp′tic, a. & n. (med.). 1. Of or involving sepsis, putrefying; ~ *tank* (in which sewage is disintegrated through bacterial activity); hence **sĕp′tICALLY** adv., **sĕp-ti′CITY** n. 2. n. ~ substance. [f. L f. Gk *sēptikos* (*sēptos* f. *sēpō* rot, -IC)]

sĕpticaem′|ia (-sēm-), n. (path.). Blood-poisoning. Hence~IC a. [mod. L, f. Gk *sēptikos* see prec., *haima* blood, & -IA¹]

sĕptill′ion (-yon), n. ‖ Seventh power of a million, 1 with 42 ciphers; *eighth power of a thousand, 1 with 24 ciphers. [f. F f. L *septem* seven, after *million*]

sĕp′timal, a. Of the number 7. [f. L *septimus* seventh (*septem* seven) +-AL]

sĕp′time (-ēm), n. Fencing-position. [f. L *septimus* (prec.)]

sĕp′timus. See PRIMUS¹.

sĕptūagĕnār′ian, a. & n. (Person) between 69 & 80. [foll., -AN]

sĕptūagĕn′arў, a. Of seventy. [f. L *septuagenarius* (*septuageni* seventy each f. *septuaginta* seventy, -ARY¹)]

Sĕptūagĕs′ima, n. (Also ~ *Sunday*) Sunday before Sexagesima. [ME, f. L, = seventieth (day), prob. named loosely as before SEXAGESIMA]

sĕp′tūagint, n. Greek version of O.T. including the Apocrypha said to have been made about 270 B.C. by seventy-two translators. [f. L *septuaginta* seventy]

sĕp′tum, n. (anat., bot., zool.; pl. *-ta*). Partition such as that between the nostrils or the chambers of a poppy-fruit, dissepiment. [L (also *sae-*), = fence (*saevire saept-* f. *saepes* hedge)]

sĕp′tūple, a. & n., & v.i. & t. Sevenfold (amount); (vb) multiply by 7, increase sevenfold. [f. LL *septuplus* f. L *septem* seven]

sĕpŭlch′ral (-kral), a. Of sepulchre(s) or sepulture (~ *mound*, *pillar*, etc.; ~ *customs*); suggestive of the tomb, funereal, gloomy, dismal, (*a* ~ *look*, *voice*). Hence ~LY² adv. [f. L *sepulcralis* (foll., -AL)]

sĕp′ulchre (-ker), n., & v.t. 1. Tomb esp. cut in rock or built of stone or brick, burial vault or cave, (*the Holy S*~, in which Christ was laid; *whited* ~, hypocrite, w. ref. to *Matt.* xxiii. 27). 2. v.t.

Lay in ~, serve as ~ for. [ME, f. OF (*-cre*), f. L *sepulc(h)rum* (*sepelire sepult-* bury)]

sĕp′ulture, n. Burying, putting in the grave. [ME, f. OF, f. L *sepultura* (prec., -URE)]

sĕquā′cious (-shus), a. (pedant.). Inclined to follow, lacking independence or originality, servile; (of reasoning or reasoner) not inconsequent, coherent. Hence ~LY² adv., **sĕquā′CITY** n. [L *sequax* (*sequi* follow), -ACIOUS]

sē′quel, n. What follows after, continuation or resumption of a story or process or the like after a pause or provisional ending, (*in the* ~, as things developed afterwards); after effects, upshot; (rare) result of a chain of argument, logical inference, conclusion. [ME, f. OF (*-lle*), or f. L, as foll.]

sĕquĕl′a, n. (path.; usu. in pl. *-ae*). Morbid condition or symptom following upon some disease. [L (*sequi* follow)]

sē′quence, n. 1. Succession, coming after or next, set of things that belong next each other on some principle of order, series without gaps, (*shall follow the* ~ *of events, give the facts in historical* ~; *calamities fall in rapid* ~; *a* ~ *in clubs* etc. in cards, three or more next each other in value; *the* ~ *spring, summer, autumn, winter*). 2. Mere succession without implication of causality (~ *is related to* consequence *as post hoc to* propter hoc; *is causality, is a law of nature, anything beyond invariable* ~?), so (& rarely in other senses) **sē′quent**, **sĕquĕn′tIAL** (-shl), aa., **sĕquĕn′tiaLY²** adv., **sĕquĕn-tiăl′ITY** (-shĭ-) n. 3. (cinemat.). ·Incident in a film story recorded consecutively (corresponding to a scene in a play). 4. (mus.). Succession of similar melodic phrases at different pitches. 5. (gram.). ~ *of tenses* or *moods*, accommodation of subordinate vb in tense or mood according to certain rules to tense or mood of principal vb (e.g. *I think you* are, *thought you* were, *wrong*). 6. (eccl.). Hymn said or sung after the Alleluia that precedes the Gospel (also *prose*). [f. LL *sequentia* f. part. of *sequi* follow, see -ENCE]

sĕquĕn′tēs, **sĕquĕn′tia** (-shĭa), (abbr. *seq.* or *seqq.*), L wds = (&) the following lines, (&) what follows, appended (with or without *et* and) to line or page numbers in references. [pl. part. of L *sequi* follow]

sĕquĕs′ter, v.t. & i. 1. Seclude, isolate, set apart, (~ *oneself from the world*; esp. in p.p.; as *a* ~*ed life, retreat, cottage*). 2. (law). (Also **sĕquĕs′trATE³**, or sĕk⁴-wis-, v.t.) seize temporary possession of (debtor's estate etc.), remove (debatable property) from control of party to lawsuit, (intr.; of widow) renounce concern in husband's estate. 3. (Also *sequestrate*) confiscate, appropriate; hence or cogn. **sĕquĕstra′TION**, **sē′quĕstrātOR**, nn., **sĕquĕs′trABLE** (or sĕk⁴wĭs-) a. [f. LL

sequestrare commit for safe keeping (L *sequester* trustee, agent, cf. *secus* apart)]

sèquès′tr|um, n. (pl. ~a). Piece of dead bone detached from living bone but remaining in place. Hence ~AL a., **sèquès-trŏt′OMY** n. [neut. of L *sequester* adj. standing apart]

sè′quin, n. (Hist.) Venetian gold coin of about 9/4; coinlike ornament of silver, jet, etc., sewn on to dresses etc. [F, f. It. *zecchino* (*zecca* mint f. Arab. *sikka* die)]

sèquoi′a, n. Kinds of Californian coniferous tree of great height, redwood. [f. *Sequoiah*, a Cherokee pers. name]

sérac (sĕrăk′), n. One of the castellated masses into which a glacier is divided at steep points by the crossing of crevasses (usu. in pl.). [Swiss F, orig. name of a cheese]

sera′glio (-ahlyō), n. (pl. ~s). Walled palace, esp. (hist.) that of Sultan with government offices etc. at Constantinople; harem. [f. It. *serraglio*, f. Turk.-Pers. *serāi* palace; cf. foll.]

serai′ (-rī, -rah′ī), n. = CARAVANSERAI.

seräng′, n. (Anglo-Ind.). Native head of a Lascar crew. [f. Pers. *sarhang* commander]

sèra′pe (-ahpā), n. Shawl or blanket worn by Spanish-Americans. [Sp.]

sè′raph, n. (pl. ~im, ~s). Celestial being; one of the highest ORDER¹ of ninefold celestial hierarchy gifted esp. with love & associated with light, ardour, & purity; *(Order of the S~im,* Swedish order of knighthood). Hence **seräph′IC** a. *(the S~ic Doctor,* St Bonaventura), **seräph′IC-ALLY** adv. [back formation f. *seraphim* (cf. CHERUB) f. LL f. Gk f. Heb. *seraphim* pl. of *saraph*]

sè′raphine (-ēn), n. Early form of harmonium. [prec., -INE¹]

sèraskier′, n. Turkish general commanding, commander-in-chief, or minister of war; ~*ãt,* war office. [Turk. f. Pers. *ser′asker* head of army]

Sĕrb, a. & n., **Sĕrb′ian**, a. & n. (Native, language) of Serbia. Hence **Sĕrbo-** comb. form. [f. Serb. *Srb, Serb*]

Serbōn′ian bŏg, n. Treacherous bog formerly existing between delta of Nile & isthmus of Suez, (fig.) situation from which escape is difficult. [Gk *Serbōnis,* -IAN]

sère¹, sear², n. Catch of gun-lock holding hammer at half or full cock. [of uncert. orig.; usu. referred to OF *serre* lock, bolt, grasp, f. *serrer* (LL *serare*, bolt, bar)]

sere². See SEAR¹.

serein (serăn′), n. Fine rain falling in tropical climates from cloudless sky. [F]

sèrènād|e′, n., & v.t. **1.** Evening song or instrumental piece sung or played by lover at his lady's window; = foll. **2.** v.t. Sing or play ~e to; hence ~′ER¹ n. [F, f. It. *serenata* (*sereno* open air f. L as SERENE); see -ADE]

sèrèna′ta (-nah-), n. (mus.). Cantata with pastoral subject; simple form of orchestral or wind-band suite. [It. (prec.)]

sèrèndip′ĭtў, n. The faculty of making happy and unexpected discoveries by accident. [coined by Horace Walpole after *The Three Princes of Serendip* (Ceylon), a fairy-tale]

serene′, a. & n., & v.t. **1.** (Of sky, air, etc.) clear & calm, (of sea etc.) unruffled; placid, tranquil, unperturbed, (*a ~ temper, look, life*); ‖ (sl.) *all* ~, all right; *His, Her, Their, Your, S~ Highness(es),* abbr. H.S.H., T.S.H., titles used of or to certain continental princes; hence or cogn. ~LY² adv., **serēn′ITY** n. (*your* etc. *Serenity, S~* Highness). **2.** n. ~ expanse of sky, sea, etc. **3.** v.t. (poet.). Make (sky, brow, etc.) ~. [f. L *serenus*]

sèrf, n. Villein, person whose service is attached to the soil & transferred with it (cf. SLAVE); oppressed person, drudge. Hence ~′AGE, ~′DOM, ~′HOOD, nn. [OF, f. L *servus* slave]

sèrge, n. Kind of durable twilled worsted fabric used esp. for rough wear (*silk ~,* used for tailor's linings). [ME, f. OF *sarge, serge* f. pop. L *sarica f. L *serica* (*lana*), see SILK]

sergeant, -j-, (särj′ant), n. **1.** (hist.). *Serjeant-at-law,* barrister of superior rank. **2.** (mil.; -g-; abbr. *Sgt*). Non--commissioned officer above corporal, employed to teach drill, command small detachments, etc. (~*-major* or *regimental ~-major,* R.S.M., warrant officer assisting adjutant of regiment or battalion; *company ~-major,* C.S.M., highest non-comd officer of company; *lance-~,* corporal acting as ~). **3.** Police officer ranking between inspector & constable (-*g*-). **4.** *Serjeant-at-arms,* title of certain court, parliamentary, & city officials with mainly ceremonial duties; *Common Serjeant,* judicial officer of City of London; ~*-fish* (-*g*-), sea-fish with lateral stripes suggesting chevron. Hence ~SHIP n. [ME, f. OF *sergent* f. L *servientem* nom. *-ens* accus. f. L *servire* SERVE, -ENT)]

sèrgétte′ (-j-), n. Thin serge. [F (SERGE, -ETTE)]

sèr′ial, a. & n. **1.** Of, in, forming, a series, whence ~ITY (-ăl²) n.; (of story etc.) issued in instalments (~ *rights,* copyright in regard to story etc. so issued), whence ~IST (1) n.; (of publication) periodical; hence ~LY² adv. **2.** n. ~ story; a ~ publication, periodical, (rare). Hence ~IZE v.t. [SERIES, -AL]

sèr′iate, -ātèd, aa., **sèr′iāte,** v.t (Arrange) in the form of a series, in orderly sequence. So **sēria′TION** n. [L SERIES, -ATE², ³]

sèriāt′im (*or sèr-*), adv. Point by point, taking one subject etc. after another in regular order, (*consider, examine, discuss, take,* etc., ~). [med. L f. L *series* after *gradatim,* LITERATIM]

Sēr′ic, a. (rhet. etc.). Chinese. [f. L *sericus,* see SERGE, SILK]

sèri′ceous (-shus), a. (bot., zool.). Of

silky or satiny surface, soft & shiny, covered with glossy down [as prec., see -EOUS; cf. LL *sericeus*]

se'ri(ci)|culture, n. Silkworm-breeding, production of raw silk. Hence~**cul'turAL** a., ~**cul'tur**IST(3) n., (-cher-). [F (-ci-), see prec., -I-, CULTURE]

seriem'a, n. Sonorous-voiced Brazilian bird of heron size preying on serpents. [native]

ser'ies (sēr'ēz), n. (pl. same). 1. Number of things of which each is similar to the preceding or related to it as it to its predecessor, sequence, succession, order, row, set, (a ~ *of kings, misfortunes*; *in* ~, in ordered succession; ~ *of stamps, coins*, etc., of different denominations but issued at one time, in one reign, etc.; *the whole* ~ *of reform acts*). 2. (bibliog.). Set of successive issues of a periodical, of articles on one subject or by one writer, etc., esp. (*first, second*, etc., ~) when numbered differently from a preceding or following set, also set of independent books in common *format* or under common title or supervised by common general editor, (*Guesses at Truth, 2nd S~*; *the Men-of-Letters* ~). 3. (geol.). Set of strata with common characteristic. 4. (chem.). Set of elements with common properties or of compounds with common radical. 5. (math.). Set of terms constituting a progression or having the several values determined by a common relation (*arithmetical, geometrical*, ~, one in ARITHMETICAL, GEOMETRICAL, progression). 6. (electr.). Set of batteries etc. having positive electrode of each connected with negative of next. 7. (zool.). Number of connected genera, families, etc. (used vaguely like GROUP). [L *series* row, chain, f. *serere* join, connect]

se'rif, (now rare) **ce'riph**, n. Cross-line finishing off a stroke of a letter (esp. in SANSERIF; This has ~s: This is' sanserif). [orig. unkn.]

serig'raph|y̆, n. Art or process of printing designs by means of a silk screen, silk screen printing. So **se'rigraph** (-ahf) [-GRAPH], ~**ER**[1], nn. [irreg. f. L *sericum* silk, -GRAPHY]

se'rin, n. Central-Europ. finch related to canary. [F, of unkn. orig.]

serinette', n. Instrument for teaching cage-birds to sing; kind of small barrel-organ, musical box, etc. [F (*seriner* teach to sing f. prec., -ETTE)]

sering'a (-ngg-), n. = SYRINGA; kinds of Brazilian rubber-tree. [F, = Pg. *seringa* f. mod. L; see SYRINGA]

serio-com'|ic, a. Combining the serious & the comic, jocular in intention but counterfeiting seriousness or vice versa. Hence ~**ICALLY** adv. [-O-]

sěriŏs'ō, mus. direction. With solemnity. [It.]

ser'ious, a. 1. Thoughtful, earnest, sober, sedate, responsible, not frivolous or reck-

less or given to trifling, (*has a* ~ *look, air*; *a* ~ *young person*; ~ *politician*, who gives his best energies to politics; ~ *thought*, real deliberation). 2. Important, demanding consideration, not to be trifled with, not slight, (*this is a* ~ *matter, question, step*; *made a* ~ *alteration*; *have a* ~ *rival in her affections*; ~ *illness, danger, wound, damage, accident, defeat*). 3. Sincere, not ironical or jesting in earnest, (*are you* ~?, do you mean what you say?; *made a* ~ *attempt*, not merely perfunctory; *& now to be* ~). 4. Concerned with religion or ethics, not worldly or secular, (~ *subjects* etc.); (now chiefly joc.) religious-minded, with thoughts concentrated on salvation. Hence ~**LY**[2] adv. (esp. as preface to sentence implying that irony etc. is now to cease), ~**NESS** n. [ME, f. OF *seriôus* or LL *seriosus* (L *serus*, see -OUS)]

se'riph, n. = SERIF.

serjeant. See SERGEANT.

serm'on, n., & v.t. 1. Extempore or written discourse delivered from the pulpit by way of religious instruction or exhortation, similar discourse (often *lay* ~) on religious or moral subject delivered elsewhere or published, (*S~ on the Mount*, discourse of Christ reported *Matt.* v-vii); moral reflection suggested by natural objects etc. (esp. ~*s in stones*); piece of admonition or reproof, lecture. 2. v.t. Administer such ~ to. Hence ~**ETTE'**, ~**ET**[1], nn., ~**IZE**(1, 2) v.t. & i., ~**IZER**[1] n. [ME, f. AF *sermun*, OF -*on*, f. L *sermonem* nom. -o speech]

se'ro-, comb. form of SERUM: ~*pūr'ulent*, of serum & pus; ~*sanguin'olent*, & blood; ~**THERAPY**.

se'rotine, n. Chestnut-coloured European bat. [F (*sé-*), f. L *serotinus* late (*serus* late)]

serŏt'inous, a. (bot.). Appearing late in season. [f. L *serotinus* (prec.) + -OUS]

ser'ous, a. Of or like serum, watery, whey-like. Hence **serŏs'ITY** n. [f. F *séreux* f. L SERUM + -*eux* -OUS)]

serp'ent, n. Scaly limbless reptile, snake esp. of the larger kinds, (preferred to SNAKE chiefly in rhet. use; *the, the old, S~*, the devil, w. ref. to *Gen.* iii, *Rev.* xx), (fig.) treacherous person esp. one who worms himself into favour for base ends; *the S~*, a northern constellation; obsolete wind-instrument, a wooden tube with several bends giving powerful note; *Pharaoh's* ~, chemical toy of small cone that when ignited issues in long coiling ~like ash; ~*charmer*, person who charms ~s esp. by music; ~*eater*, SECRETARY-bird; ~*grass*, Alpine bistort; ~ *lizard*, seps; ~*'s-tongue*, ADDER's-*tongue*. Hence **serpĕn'ti**FORM, ~**LIKE**, aa. [ME, f. OF, f. L *serpentem* nom. -*ens*, part. of *serpere* creep; see -ENT]

serp'entine, a. & n., & v.i. 1. Of or like a serpent lit. or fig., writhing, coiling, tortuous, sinuous, meandering, cunning, subtle, treacherous, (~ *windings*, of stream, road, etc., or of insinuation; ~ *motion*; ~ *wisdom*, profound, w. ref. to *Matt.* x. 16; ~ *dance*, with sinuous movements enhanced by special drapery; ~ *verse*, line beginning & ending with same word; ‖ *the S*~, ornamental water in Hyde Park). **2. n.** Kinds of hydrous silicate of magnesium, soft rocks of dark green & other colours sometimes mottled or spotted like serpent's skin, taking high polish & used as decorative material; (skating) wavy line produced by changes of edge. **3. v.i.** Move sinuously, meander. [(1) ME, f. OF *serpentin* f. LL *serpentinus* (prec., -INE[1]); (2) OF *serpentin(e)* f. med. L *serpentina*, *-um* abs. use of adj.]

serpi′ginous, a. (path.). Affected with herpes; (of skin-disease etc.) creeping from one part to another. [f. med. L *serpigo -ginis* ringworm (L *serpere* creep), -OUS]

serp′ula, n. (pl. *-ae*). Kinds of marine worm inhabiting beautifully coloured tortuous calcareous tubes often massed together. [LL, = small serpent (L *serpere* creep)]

se′rra, n. (anat., bot., zool.; pl. *-ae*). Serrated organ, structure, or edge. [L, = saw]

se̱rradill′a, n. Kind of clover grown as fodder. [Port., dim. of *serrado* SERRATE a.]

se′rrate, a., **se̱rrāte′**, v.t. (chiefly anat., bot., zool.). **1.** Notched like saw. **2.** v.t. (usu. in p.p. as adj.) provide with sawlike edge. Hence **se̱rrA′TION** n. [f. L SERRA*tus* (-ATE[2]), -ATE[3]]

se′rrefile, n. (mil.; usu. in pl.). Person in, (pl.) the line of supernumerary & non-commissioned officers in, rear of squadron or troop of cavalry. [F, f. *serrer* (see SERRIED)+*file* (see FILE[3])]

se′rri-, comb. form (-I-) of SERRA: ~*corn*, (beetle) with serrate antennae; ~F′EROUS; ~FORM; ~*ros′trate*, (of bird) with serrated bill.

se′rried (-rĭd), a. (Of ranks of soldiers, rows of trees, etc.) shoulder to shoulder, without gaps, close. [f. 16th c. *serry* (app. f. F *serré* p.p. of *serrer* close f. LL *serare*) +-ED[1]]

se′rrul|āte (-rŏŏ-), -āted, aa. Finely serrate, with series of small notches. Hence ~A′TION n. [L *serrula* (SERRA, -ULE), -ATE[2]]

sēr′um, n. Whey; amber-coloured liquid which separates from clot when blood coagulates; blood ~ as anti-toxin or therapeutic agent; watery animal fluid; ~ *sickness*, skin eruption, fever, etc., sometimes following injections of ~. [L, = whey]

se̱rv′al, n. Tawny black-spotted African tiger-cat. [F, f. Port.]

se̱rv′ant, n. **1.** Person who has undertaken usu. in return for stipulated pay to carry out the orders of an individual or corporate employer, esp. one who lives in house of master or mistress receiving board & lodging & wages & performing domestic duties (*public*~s, State officials; *civil* ~, member of the civil service; *outdoor* ~, groom, gardener, etc.; *indoor* ~, cook, butler, footman, housemaid, etc.; *domestic*, GENERAL, LIVERY[1], ~; ~*-girl*, *-maid*; *the* ~ *question*, problem of getting & controlling ~s; *keeps three* ~s; ~*s′ hall*, room in which ~s of large household have meals etc.; ~ *of* ~s, lowest of dependants, esp. as title assumed by Popes, transl. of *servus servorum Dei*; a *good* ~ *but a bad master*, of things that should be treated as means & not ends). **2.** Devoted follower, person willing to serve another, (a ~ *of Jesus Christ*; ‖ *your humble* ~, arch., form of ironical courtesy; ‖ *your obedient* ~, epistolary form preceding signature now used only in letters of official type). [ME, f. OF (SERVE, -ANT)]

se̱rve, v.t. & i., & n. **1.** Be servant (to), do service (to), be useful (to), (~ *two masters*, be divided between two conflicting principles etc.; ~ *the Lord* or *God*, be religious or virtuous; ~ *the devil*, be wicked; ~ *tables*, postpone spiritual to bodily needs, see *Acts* vi. 2; ~ *at table*, act as waiter; *has* ~*d his generation*; *would do much to* ~ *you*; *indiscretion sometimes* ~*s us well*; ~ *in army*, *navy*, etc., be employed in it; *has* ~*d in India*, been employed esp. as soldier). **2.** Meet needs (of), avail (t. & i.), suffice (t. & i.), satisfy, perform function, be suitable, do what is required for, (~ *a purpose*; ~ *the purpose of*, take place of, be used as; *to* ~ *some private ends*; ~*s the* or *one's turn* or *need*, does well enough; *it will* ~, do what is absolutely necessary; *that excuse will not* ~ *you*; *it* ~*s to show the folly of*; *1 lb.* ~*s him for a week*; *nothing would* ~ *him* or ~ *but absolute submission*; *a sofa serving him*, or *serving*, *as* or *for (a) bed*; *as memory* ~*s*, whenever one remembers; *as occasion* ~*s*, when it is favourable; *the tide* ~*s*, is suitable for getting out of harbour etc.; *curate* ~*s two parishes*, does the work; ~ *an office*, go through a tenure of it; ~ *one's apprenticeship*, go through training; ~ *a sentence*, undergo it for the full time; ~ *one's time*, hold office for normal period, also ~ *a sentence*; ~ *time*, undergo imprisonment etc.; ~ *gun*, *battery*, keep it firing; ~ *mare* etc., cover, esp. of stallion etc. hired for purpose; ~ *rope* etc., naut., bind with small cord to save fraying). **3.** Dish *up*, set (food) on table, set out ready, distribute (trans. & abs.), supply (person *with*), make legal delivery of (writ etc.), set ball or set (ball) in play, (*fish* ~*d up nearly cold*; *asparagus* ~*d with butter*; ~ *up dinner*; *dinner is* ~*d*, servant's announcement that it is ready; ~ *ammunition*, *rations*, etc., *out* or *round*; *was serving a customer with stockings*, *serving in the shop*; *have them* ~*d with soup*; ~ *with the same sauce*, fig., retaliate upon; ~ *person*, *the town*, etc., *with gas*, *water*; ~ *with* *writ* etc., = ~ writ etc. on; ~ *warrant, writ, notice, process, attachment,* etc., usu. on person, deliver document to person concerned in legally formal manner; *tennis, racquet,* etc., *player* ~*s a ball,* ~*s well, badly,* etc., sends ball to opponent in first stroke of round). **4.** Treat, treat to, pay (person) *out, (has* ~*d me shamefully; you may* ~ *me as you will;* ~*d them a trick,* played it on them; ~ or ~*s him right!,* excl. of satisfaction at sight of offender getting his deserts; *shall manage to* ~ *him out,* retaliate). **5.** ‖ *Serving-man,* male servant. Hence (-)**sĕrv′**ER¹(1, 2) n., (also, eccl.) celebrant's assistant, **sĕrv′**ERY (3) n., room from which meals etc. are ~d & in which utensils are kept. **6.** n. (In tennis etc.) first stroke of round, turn for delivering this (*whose* ~ *is it?*). [ME, f. OF *servir* f. L *servire* (*servus* slave)]

Sĕrv′ian¹. Var. of, & till 1914 more usual than, SERBIAN.

Sĕrv′ian². a. (Rom. ant.). Of Servius Tullius sixth king of Rome (~ *wall,* built by him & still existing in parts). [-AN]

sĕrv′ice¹, n., & v.t. **1.** Being servant, servant's status, master's or mistress's employ, (*girl etc. goes out to, goes into, tries, is in,* ~ ; *take* ~ *with,* become servant to; *take into* one's ~, employ). **2.** Department of royal or public employ or of work done to meet some general need, persons engaged in it, employment in it, (*the fighting,* or *the,* ~*s,* navy, army, & air force; *the public* ~*s; the* CIVIL, COVENANTED, *consular,* SECRET, *bus, railway,* etc., ~ ; *the preventive* ~, coastguards, custom-house, etc.; *is on* ~, *in active* ~, actually engaged in such employ; *see* ~, have experience esp. as soldier or sailor); (attrib.) of the kind issued to the ~ (*the* ~ *rifle*). **3.** Person's disposal or behalf (*at your etc.* ~, ready to obey orders or be used; ‖ *on his, her, Majesty's* ~, abbr. O.H.M.S., frank stamped on official letters etc.). **4.** What employee or subordinate is bound to, work done or doing of work on behalf of employer, benefit conferred on or exertion made on behalf of someone, expression of willingness to confer or make these, (*personal* ~, feudal obligation of homage etc.; *feudal, menial, willing,* YEOMAN('s), ~ ; *has a right to my* ~ ; *asks for my* ~*s; will you do me a* ~*?; exaggerates his own* ~*s; has seen* ~, been much used, shows signs of wear; *my* ~ *to him,* form of respectful message). **5.** Use, assistance, (*can I, will it, be of* ~ *to you?*). **6.** Liturgical form or office appointed for use on some occasion, (whole proceedings, usu. including one such ~ or more, of) single meeting of congregation for worship, musical setting of all or several of the invariable parts of a liturgy adapted for such treatment, (*the communion, burial,* etc., ~ ; *special* ~*s; divine* ~ usu. without *a,* meeting for worship; *holds four* ~*s every Sunday; are you going to* ~ or *the* ~?; —*'s* ~, setting by particular composer; *full* ~, performed by choir without solos, also ~ with music wherever possible; *plain* ~, read or monotoned; ~*-book,* book of offices of a Church, e.g. the Book of Common Prayer; CHURCH¹-~). **7.** Legal serving of or of writ etc. (*personal* ~, delivery with announcement of contents to person affected; ~ *by publication, substitution,* publishing of writ etc. by posting up or insertion in newspaper or by handing to neighbour etc. recognized as sufficient under some conditions; ACCEPT ~). **8.** Set of dishes, plates, etc., required for serving meal (*dinner, dessert, tea,* etc., ~). **9.** Set of trains, steamers, buses, etc., plying at stated times. **10.** (Single act of) serving in tennis etc., serve, manner of serving, person's turn to serve, game in which one serves, (*his* ~ *is weak, terrific; whose* ~ *is it?; he lost his* ~; ~*-line,* marking limit short of which serve must fall). **11.** Expert assistance or advice given to customers after sale by manufacturers or vendors of an article, e.g. a motor-car or wireless set (so . ~ *department, depot, station*). **12.** ~ *area,* area round broadcasting station within which satisfactory reception may be expected; ~ *dress,* ordinary uniform (opp. *full* dress); ~ *flat* (in which domestic ~ and meals are provided by the management); ‖ ~ *hatch* (through which dishes are passed to dining-room); ~ *pipe* (conveying water or gas from the main to a building). **13.** v.t. Maintain or repair (car etc.) after sale. [ME, f. OF, f. L *servitium* (*servus* slave)]

sĕrv′ice², n. (Usu. ~*-tree*) European tree rare in England with leaves like those of mountain-ash, cream-coloured flowers, & small pear-shaped fruit (~*-berry* or ~) eaten when over-ripe. [orig. *serves,* pl. of obs. *serve,* OE *syrfe,* f. L *sorbus* SORB]

sĕrv′iceab‖le (-sabl), a. Of use, useful, willing & able to render or capable of rendering service, (*a* ~*le person, reminder, instrument*); durable, suited for rough use or ordinary wear rather than for ornament. Hence ~LY² adv., ~leNESS n. [ME, f. OF *servisable* (SERVICE¹, -ABLE)]

sĕrviĕtte′, n. Table-napkin. [F]

sĕrv′ile (or -īl), a. Of, being, a slave or slaves, slave-, (~ *war,* between revolted slaves & their owners; ~ *class, labour;* ~ *letter,* fig., having no other function than to indicate pronunciation of another, as *e* in manageable, saleable); as of a slave, slavish, cringing, mean-spirited, menial, completely dependent, (~ *spirit, creature, submission, flattery, fear, imitation*), so **sĕrvil′**ITY n.; ~ *works* (eccl.), menial or mechanical work forbidden on Sundays and major Church festivals. Hence ~LY² adv. [ME, f. L *servilis* (*servus* slave, -IL)]

Sĕrv′ite, n. One of the order of 'Servants of Blessed Mary'. [f. med. L *Servitae* f. L *servus* servant, see -ITE¹(1)]

sĕrv'ĭtor, n. Attendant, henchman, servant, (arch., poet.); ‖ (Oxf. Univ.; hist.) undergraduate assisted from college funds & performing menial duties in return, whence ~SHIP n. [ME, f. OF f. LL (SERVE, -OR)]

sĕrv'ĭtŭde, n. Slavery lit. or fig., subjection esp. involuntary to a master, bondage (PENAL ~); (law) subjection of tenement to an easement. [ME, f. OF f. L servitudinem (servus slave, -TUDE)]

sĕrv'o-mōt'or, n. Auxiliary motor, esp. one for operating the reversing gear of a large marine engine. [f. F servo-moteur (L servus slave)]

sĕs'amė, n. Annual herbaceous tropical & subtropical plant with seeds used in various ways as food & yielding an oil used in salads & as laxative; its seeds; open ~, (w. ref. to Arabian-Nights tale) magical or mysterious means of commanding access to what is usu. inaccessible. [f. L f. Gk sēsamē]

sĕs'amoid, a. & n. 1. Shaped like a sesame-seed, nodular, (esp. of small independent bones developed in tendons passing over angular structure, as the knee-pan & the navicular bone). 2. n. Such bone. [f. L f. Gk sēsamoeidēs (prec., -OID)]

sĕs'elĭ, n. Kinds of white-flowered umbelliferous perennial plants. [f. L f. Gk seselis, sescli, cf. CICELY]

sĕs'qui-, L pref. (perh. f. semis-que & a half), = one & a half (~pedalis a foot & a half long), proportioned as 1½:1 or 3:2 (~alter), proportioned as n+1: n (~tertius, ~quartus, etc., in ratios 4:3, 5:4, etc.). Hence in E: 1. Chem. wds for compounds in which there are three equivalents of the named element to two others, as ~ox'ide, ~sulph'ide; ~bas'ic, (of salt) with three of base to two of acid. 2. Math. wds expressing ratios as above, ~al'teral 3:2, ~ter'tial 4:3, ~quar'tal, ~quin'tal, ~sex'tal, ~sep'timal, ~octav'al, ~non'al 10:9. 3. Mus. wds in -a corresponding to the above & expressing intervals (~al'tera interval having ratio 2:3, ~ter'tia 3:4, etc.). 4. Miscellaneous wds, as ~centenn'ial, (of) a one-hundred--&-fiftieth anniversary; ~ocell'us (entom.), large spot with smaller one within it (also ~alter); ~pedāl'ian, (of word) 1½ ft long, cumbrous & pedantic; sesquip'licate, in ratio of cube to square; ~tone, musical interval of 1½ tone.

sess. See CESS.

sĕss'ile, a. (bot., zool.). (Of flower, leaf, eye, etc.) attached directly by the base without stalk or peduncle. [f. L sessilis (sedēre sess- sit, -IL)]

sĕ'ssion (-shn), n. 1. Being seated, sitting posture, (rare). 2. Being assembled esp. for transaction of deliberative or judicial business, single uninterrupted meeting for such purpose, period during which such meetings are held daily or at short or regular intervals, period (usu. one in a year) between meeting & prorogation of Parliament, (in ~, sitting or assembled for business, not keeping vacation; had a long ~, sat assembled a long time; autumn ~, resumption of ~ of Parliament occas. required by pressure of business after long adjournment in summer without prorogation); (esp. Sc. & U.S.) university term. 3. ‖ QUARTER-~s; ‖ BREWSTER-SESSIONS: ‖ petty ~s, meeting of two or more justices of the peace for summary trying of certain offences; ‖ Court of S~, supreme civil court of Scotland; KIRK-~. Hence ~AL (-shon-) a. (~al order, Parl., valid only for, renewable each, ~). [ME, f. OF, or f. L sessio (prec., -ION)]

sĕs'tĕrce, sĕstĕr'tius (-shus; pl. -iī), nn. Ancient-Roman silver (& later bronze) coin & money of account = ¼ denarius or 2½ (later 4) asses. [f. L (-ius) orig. adj. with nummus coin = 2½ (*semistertius half-third)]

sĕstĕr'tium (-shm), n. (pl. -ia). Ancient--Roman money of account = 1000 sesterces. [orig. gen. pl. of prec. after millia thousands]

sĕstĕt', n. = SEXTET; last six lines of sonnet. [f. It. sestetto (sesto f. L sextus sixth, -ET[1])]

sĕsti'na (-tē-), n. Form of rhymed or unrhymed poem with six stanzas of six lines & final triplet, each stanza having same words as the others ending its lines but in different order. [It. (prec., -INE[4])]

sĕt[1], v.t. & i. (set). I. General senses. 1. Put, lay, stand (trans.), (usu. with adv. or advl phr.; ~ load or passenger down, statue up, meat before person, flowers in water, one brick on another; ~ foot, tread on; ~ thing against another, balance, reckon as counterpoise or compensation; ~ apart, reserve, separate; ~ aside, reserve, reject, disregard, annul; ~ by, reserve, save for future use; ~ stone out, lay it with edge projecting beyond one below; ~ person over others or thing, put in authority). 2. Apply (thing) to (~ pen to paper, bugle to one's lips, spurs to horse; ~ one's hand, seal, to document, sign, seal; ~ one's hand to task, begin; ~ fire to, kindle; ~ the axe to, begin to cut down or destroy; ~ one's wits to question, try to solve; ~ one's wits to another's, argue with him; ~ SHOULDER to wheel). 3. Station, place ready, place or turn in right or specified position or direction, dispose suitably for use or action or display, (~ a or naut. the watch, put sentinels etc. in place; ~ chairs, etc. for visitors etc.; ~ clock or watch, put hands to right time; ~ alarum, provide for its sounding at desired time; ~ hen, cause to sit on eggs; ~ eggs, place for hen to sit on; ~ seed, plant, put in ground; QUICK~; ~ butterfly etc., arrange as specimen; ~ sail, hoist, also = start on voyage; ~ trap; ~ razor, give even edge to after grinding;

~ *saw*, give teeth alternate outward inclination; ~ *table*, lay for meal; ~ or ~ *up type*, arrange it in words etc.; ~ *up book* etc., put it in type; ~ *close, wide,* etc., print with small, large, spaces between words or letters; ~ *out*, ~ wide; ~ one's CAP[1] *at*). 4. Join, attach, fasten, fix, determine, decide, appoint, settle, establish, (~ *leg, bone, joint,* put parts into right relative position after fracture or dislocation, also by extension ~ *fracture* or *dislocation*; ~ *eyes on,* catch sight of; ~ *diamond* etc., insert in gold etc. as frame or foil; ~ *stake in ground; close-~,* with little interval; ~ one's *heart, mind, hopes,* etc., *on,* long for, expect, be resolved to get; ~ one's *life on a chance* etc. metaph. from gambling, risk it; ~ *price on,* announce salable value of; ~ person *against* another or a thing, fill with settled dislike for; ~ *price on* one's *life* or *head,* offer specified reward for his killing; ~ *store* or *much by,* & ellipt. ~ *by,* estimate or value highly; ~ one's *face* or one*self against,* steadfastly oppose or discountenance; ~ one's *teeth,* clench them, esp. fig. = make up one's mind inflexibly; often in p.p., = unmoving, fixed, as ~ *smile, eyes, look, purpose; of ~ purpose,* intentionally, deliberately; ~ *time,* prearranged; ~ *scene,* built up of more or less solid material; ~ *piece* in fireworks, built up on scaffolding; ~ *forms of prayers* etc., not extempore; ~ *speech,* composed beforehand; ~ *fair,* of weather, fine without sign of breaking; ~ *on* or *upon,* determined to get, absorbed in; *batsman is* ~, has got his eye in). 5. Fix (hair) when damp so that it dries in waves. 6. Bring by placing, arranging, impelling, or other means, into specified state (~ *things right, to rights, in order, in motion;* ~ one's *house in order,* often fig., introduce reforms; ~ *question,* person's *heart, at rest;* ~ *machine going, cask abroach;* ~ person *on his feet* lit. & fig., *box on its end;* ~ one *in the way,* direct him; ~ one *on his way,* arch., go part way with him; ~ one *right,* disabuse him of error, correct, often with implication of officiousness etc.; ~ one *at ease,* relieve his anxieties or bashfulness; ~ *at liberty,* ~ *free,* release; ~ persons *by the ears, at variance* or *loggerheads,* produce quarrel; ~ *on fire,* kindle; ~ *Thames on* FIRE[1]; ~ *movement* etc. *on foot,* start it; ~ *table, company,* etc., *laughing* or *on* or *in a roar,* stir laughter; ~ *teeth on* EDGE[1]); ~ *at defiance,* defy; ~ *at naught,* mock, disregard. 7. Make sit down *to* task, order to apply energies *to* do*ing,* cause *to* work, apply oneself *to* work, (~ *him to dictation, wood--chopping, work at his Greek; shall ~ to work now,* begin; ~ one*self to* do, make up one's mind, resolve or undertake). 8. Exhibit or arrange as pattern or as material to be dealt with (often w. ind. obj.; ~, ~ person, *an example, task, prob-*

lem, etc., to be followed, done, solved, by him; ~ *the fashion, the pace,* determine it by leading; ~ *paper,* draw up questions to be answered by examinees; ~ *the* TEMPERAMENT in piano-tuning, arrange intervals of one octave as standard for the rest). 9. ~ (*to music*), provide (song, words) with music usu. composed for the purpose. 10. Make insertions in (surface) *with* (*gold, field, sky,* ~ *with gems, daisies, stars; shall* ~ *top of wall with broken glass, this bed with geraniums*). 11. Turn (i., rarely t.) to solid or hard or rigid from liquid or soft or mobile state, curdle, solidify, harden, take shape, develop (usu. intr.) into definiteness or maturity, (*egg* ~*s,* by cooking or incubation; HARD-~; *blossom* ~*s,* forms into fruit; *fruit* ~*s,* develops out of blossom; *tree* ~*s,* develops fruit; *plaster of Paris* ~*s quickly; the jelly, junket, has* or *is* ~; *when his body, character, has* ~; THICK~; *over-exercise* ~*s a boy's muscles prematurely; face* ~*s,* takes hard expression; *eyes* ~, become motionless in death, swoon, etc.). 12. Sink below horizon (*sun, moon,* ~*s; the star of Rome, his star, has* or *is* ~, greatness is departed). 13. (Of tide, current, etc., & transf. of feelings, customs, etc.) have motion, gather force, sweep along, show or feel tendency, (*tide* ~*s in, out; current* ~*s strongly, eastwards; opinion is* ~*ting against it; his soul* ~ *to grief*). 14. (Of sporting dog) take rigid attitude indicating presence of game; (of dancers) take position facing partners (often ~ *to partners*). 15. (Of garment) adapt itself to figure, sit, *well, badly,* etc. 16. (In some games) fix the number of points to decide the game. 17. SHARP[1] ~. II. Special senses with advv. & prepp. 1. ~ *about,* begin, take steps towards, (task, do*ing*). 2. ~ *back,* impede or reverse progress of, *(sl.)* cost (person) so much. 3. ~ *down,* put in writing, attribute *to,* explain or describe to oneself *as.* 4. ~ *forth,* make known, declare, expound, adorn, begin journey or expedition. 5. ~ *forward,* assist progress of, begin going forward (arch.). 6. ~ *in,* arise, get vogue, become established, (*reaction, rain,* ~ *in; it* ~ *in to rain*). 7. ~ *off,* act as adornment or foil to, enhance, make more striking, start (person) laughing or talking on pet subject, begin journey. 8. ~ *on* adv., instigate, advance to the assault; ~ *on* prep., urge (dog etc.) to attack (person etc.), attack. 9. ~ *out,* embellish, demonstrate, exhibit, declare, begin journey. 10. ~ *to* adv., begin doing something vigorously, esp. (usu. w. pl. subj.) fighting or arguing. 11. ~ *up,* develop figure of by physical training (esp. in p.p., as *a well* ~*-up man*), start (institution, business, one's carriage, etc.), occasion (soreness etc.), establish (person) or provide with means of establishment or establish oneself in some capacity (*his* *father, £500, ~ him up as a tobacconist or in the tobacco trade; shall ~ up as a dentist),* provide adequately *in* or *with* some article (*am ~ up with novels for the winter*), place (standard, notice, etc.) in view, begin uttering (protest, shriek, etc.) loudly, propound (theory), restore from ill-health or depression; *~ up for* (colloq.), make pretensions to the character of (*~s up for a scholar, moralist,* etc.). **12.** *~ upon,* = *~ on* prep. [OE *settan*, OS *-ian*, OHG *sezzan*, ON *setja*, Goth. *saljan* causal of Gmc *setjan (*sitjan) SIT]

sĕt², n. **1.** Number of things or persons that belong together as essentially similar or as complementary to each other, group, clique, collection, (*~ of studs, chairs, golf-clubs, fire-irons, lectures*; *~ of teeth,* natural or artificial; *a fine ~ of men, players, officers,* etc.; *dinner ~,* dinner SERVICE[1]; *toilet ~,* vessels of wash-hand-stand; *the fast, best, racing, smart, literary, political,* etc., *~,* sections of society consorting together; *~ of quadrilles* or *~,* figures that make up a quadrille; *~ of dancers* or *~,* number needed to make up square dance; *a, the first,* etc., *~* in tennis etc., group of games counting as unit to side that wins more than half the games in it; *~ point,* state of a *~* in lawn tennis when one side needs only one more point to win it; *~ of exchange,* first etc. of EXCHANGE[1] collectively). **2.** Slip or shoot for planting; young fruit just set. **3.** Setting *of* sun or day (poet.). **4.** Way current or wind or opinion etc. sets, drift or tendency *of,* (*the ~ of the current, public feeling,* etc.; *the ~ of his mind is towards intolerance*). **5.** Configuration, conformation, habitual posture, way head etc. is set on or carried, way dress etc. sits or flows, (usu. *of; the ~ of the hills, his head, the drapery*); warp or bend or displacement caused by continued pressure or position (*has got a ~ to the right*). **6.** (Amount of) alternate defection of saw-teeth. **7.** Last coat of plaster on wall. **8.** Timber frame supporting gallery etc. in coal-mine. **9.** Amount of margin in type causing letters to be close or wide set. **10.** Number of eggs in nest, or number laid before bird sits, clutch. **11.** Setter's pointing in presence of game (often *dead ~*; *make a dead ~ at,* transf., attack esp. by argument or ridicule). **12.** ‖ Badger's burrow. **13.** Granite paving-block. **14.** Kinds of wrench & punch. **15.** (Theatr.) set scene; (cinemat.) built-up scene. **16.** Radio receiving apparatus. **17.** *~-back,* reversal or arrest of progress, relapse; *~-down,* rebuff, snub; *~-off,* thing set off against another, thing of which the amount or effect may be deducted from that of another of opposite tendency, counterpoise, counter-claim, thing that embellishes, adornment *to* something, (archit.) sloping or horizontal member connecting lower and thicker

part of wall etc. with upper receding part; *~-out,* commencement or start (esp. *at the first ~-out*), things set out, equipment, display of food or utensils or goods; *~-to,* combat esp. with fists; *~-up,* erectness or carriage of body, (colloq., orig. U.S.) structure, or arrangement of an organization etc. [sense 1 f. OF *sette* f. L *secta* SECT; remainder f. prec.]

sētā′ceous (-shus), a. Bristly, having bristles, shaped like a bristle. Hence **~LY²** adv. [f. L *seta* bristle, -ACEOUS]

sētif′erous, sēti′gerous, sētōse′, aa. Having bristles. [L *seta* bristle, *setiger, setosus,* bristly, -FEROUS, -GEROUS, -OSE[1]]

sĕt′on, h. (surg.). Skein of cotton or the like passed below skin and left with ends protruding to maintain an artificial issue as counter-irritant etc. esp. in veterinary practice; *~-needle,* for inserting *~.* [f. med. L *seto* silk, app. f. L *seta* bristle, med. L also silk]

sĕt squāre, n. Draughtsman's appliance consisting of a triangular plate of wood or metal or plastic with angles of 90°, 60°, 30°, or of 90°, 45°, 45°, for drawing lines at such angles. [p.p. of SET[1]]

sĕtt. Arbitrary var. of SET² in some of its more technical senses.

sĕttee′¹, n. Long seat variously constructed to seat more than one person, esp. kind of double armchair or short sofa with ends alike for tête-à-tête. [perh. fanciful var. of SETTLE[1]; see -EE]

sĕttee′², n. Mediterranean sharp-prowed lateen-sailed vessel with two or three masts. [f. It. *saettia* (*saetta* f. L SAGITTA)]

sĕtt′er, n. In vbl senses: esp., breeds (*English, Irish, Gordon, ~*) of long-haired dog trained to stand rigid on scenting game; dog named from native habit of crouching on same occasion; *~-on,* instigator. [SET[1], -ER[1]]

sĕtt′erwort (-êrt), n. A plant, bear's-foot or fetid hellebore. [f. MLG *siterwort* etc.; first element of unkn. orig.]

sĕtt′ing, n. In vbl senses; esp.; the music of a song etc.; the metal or other frame in which a gem is set, (transf.) surroundings of any object regarded as its framework or as accessories setting it off, environment, (theatr.) way a play is put on the stage, scenery, properties, costumes, etc.; *~-board,* on which entomological specimens are set; *~-box,* in which *~-boards* are kept like shelves or drawers; *~-lotion,* used to damp the hair before it is set; *~-needle,* needle in wooden handle used in setting specimens; *~-rule,* brass rule or steel plate with which type is kept temporarily in place as it is set up; *~-stick,* used in setting type. [-ING[1]]

sĕt′tle¹, n. Bench with high back & arms & often with chest from seat to floor. [OE *setl,* OHG *sezzal,* Goth. *sitls* f. Gmc **set-* SIT]

sĕt′tle², v.t. & i. **1.** Establish or become established in more or less permanent abode or place or way of life (often *down*), (cause to) sit down o: *down* to stay for some time, cease from wandering or motion or change or disturbance or turbidity (often *down*), bring to or attain fixity or composure or certainty or clarity or decision, determine, agree upon, decide, appoint, (*he ~d detachments of Jews in Assyria*; *shall ~ in London, Australia*; *~ feet in stirrups, plant's root well down in ground, invalid among pillows,* oneself *in chair*; *~ down to dinner, whist, reading, married life*; *~d down to defensive play, a series of skirmishes*; *marry & ~ down*; *cannot ~ to work, to anything,* of restless or excited or desultory person; *bird ~s on tree,* alights; *stand beer to ~,* get clear; *let the excitement ~ down*; *things will soon ~ into shape*; *must get it ~d up,* finally arranged; *~ coffee, soup, with white of egg,* clarify; *man, expression, of ~d convictions, melancholy*; *~d order, state, habitation, government, weather*; *a liqueur to ~* one's *dinner,* facilitate digestion; *~ the day,* fix date; *~ quarrel, question, doubts, the pattern of, waverers*; *what have you ~d on or ~d?*; *~ the succession,* determine who shall succeed; *that ~s the matter or question,* there is no more to be said; *~* one's *affairs,* esp. before death by making will etc.). **2.** Colonize, establish colonists in, *~* as colonists in, people, (country); ***thickly *~d*** (built-up) *area.* **3.** Subside, (*the solid matter soon ~s*; *soil, house, foundation, ~s,* comes gradually to lower level; *ship ~s,* shows loss of buoyancy, begins to sink). **4.** Deal effectually with, dispose or get rid of, do for, pay (bill), pay bill, (*~* person, get rid of his importunity or obstruction by argument or conflict or killing; *let us ~ up our accounts or ~ up,* draw up & liquidate balance; *~* person's HASH² or *business*; *~d,* written on paid bill in acknowledging payment; *will you ~ for me?,* pay the bill; *~ with creditors,* pay their bills or such proportion as they will agree to accept; || *settling-day,* esp. fortnightly account day at Stock Exchange). **5.** Bestow legally for life on (*~d an annuity on him*; *~d all his property on his wife*; *~d estate,* held by tenant for life under specified conditions). [OE *setlan* f. *setl* (prec.)]

sĕt'tlement (-tlm-), n. In vbl senses; esp.: (law) conveyance of, or creation of estate(s) in, property to make provision for one or more beneficiaries differing from what would result from simple conveyance or statutory inheritance (*marriage ~,* usu. made in favour of wife, her children, etc.); company of persons aiming at social reform who establish themselves in a poor district to live in intimate relations with the working class; newly settled tract of country, colony; subsidence of wall, house, etc.; *Act of S~,* statute of 1701 vesting crown in Sophia of Hanover & her heirs. [-MENT]

sĕtt'ler, n. In vbl senses; esp.: one who settles in new colony, early colonist; (sl.) decisive blow, argument, or event. [-ER¹]

sĕtt'lor, n. (law). One who makes a settlement esp. of property. [-OR]

sĕt'wall (-awl), n. Kind of valerian formerly in medicinal use. [ME & AF *zedewal* = OF *citoual* f. med. L ***zedoale,** var. of *zedoarium* ZEDOARY]

sĕv'en, a. & n. **1.** One more than six, 7, vii, VII, (often agreeing with understood n., as *~ of the men, ~ of them, ~ o'clock* or *~*; *one & ~,* 1/7; *~ & six,* 7/6; *twenty-~* or *~·&·twenty,* & so on to *~·&·* ninety; *was ~ last birthday,* years old; *one·&·~penny* etc., costing 1/7 etc.; *the ~* SAGE²*s* or *wise men*; *the ~ sleepers,* Christians who fell asleep in a cave while hiding from Decian persecution & woke 200 years later when Roman Empire was Christian; *the ~* VIRTUES, *deadly* SINS, WONDER¹*s of the world*; *~-league boots,* giving wearer power of going 7 leagues at each stride; *seventy times ~,* large indefinite number, w. ref. to *Matt.* xviii. 22); *~-gills,* kind of shark; hence *~*FOLD a. & adv., *~*TEEN' a. & n. (*sweet ~teen,* age of girlish beauty), *~*teenTH'² a. & n. **2.** n. The number 7, the symbol 7, set of 7 persons or things esp. 7-pipped card, (*twice ~ is 14*; *make a large ~*; *by ~s,* in sets of 7; *at* SIXes *& ~s*). [OE *seofon,* OS, OHG *sibun,* ON *sjau,* Goth. *sibun* f. Gmc ***sebhun** cogn. w. L *septem*]

sĕv'enth, a. & n. **1.** Next after sixth (*the, a, ~,* often as n. with ellipse of n., esp. *the ~* = 7th day of month; *~ day,* Saturday in Quaker speech & with sects keeping Saturday instead of Sunday as sabbath (*~-day,* sabbatarian; *S~-day Adventists,* a millenarian sect); *in the ~* HEAVEN, in the greatest happiness or satisfaction; *~ part,* one of 7 equal parts into which thing may be divided). **2.** n. *= ~* part; (mus.) interval of which the span involves 7 alphabetical names of notes, harmonic combination of notes thus separated. [OE *seofunda,* ME *sevende*; ME *seventhe* f. prec. + -TH²]

sĕv'enthlÿ, adv. In the 7th place (in enumerations). [-LY²]

sĕv'entĬÿ, a. & n. **1.** Seven times ten, 70, lxx, LXX, (*~y-one* etc., or *one-&-~y* etc.; *~y-first* etc.; *the ~y,* the disciples of Luke x, also the sanhedrim, also the Septuagint translators); *~y-four* (hist.), warship with 74 guns; *~y-five,* French 75 mm. gun, = *soixante-quinze*; hence *~*ĬETH a. & n. **2.** n. The number or symbol 70; *the ~ies,* years between 69 & 80 in life or century. [OE *-seofontig* (SEVEN, -TY²)]

sĕv'er, v.t. & i. Separate, divide, part, disjoin, disunite, (t. & rarely i.: *~ husband & wife, friends or friendship, rope, neck, connexion*; *sea ~s England & or from France*; *the rope ~ed under the strain*); cut or break off, take away, (part) from or *from* whole (*~ed his head, his head from his body*; *~* oneself *from the Church*); (law; of person in joint action) conduct case independently of the rest. Hence ~ABLE a., ~ANCE n. [ME, f. AF, OF *severer* f. pop. L **seperare* f. L *separare* SEPARATE]

sěv'eral, a. & pron. **1.** Separate, diverse, distinct, individual, respective, (*all of us in our ~ stations*; *each has his ~ ideal*; *went their ~ ways*; *indictment of three ~ counts*; *the ~ members of the Board*; *each ~ ship sank her opponent*; *collective & ~ responsibility*, of persons as a body & as individuals; *joint & ~ bond* etc., signed by more than one person, of whom each is liable for whole sum; ~ *estate*, not shared with others), whence ~LY[2] adv.; *a few*, more than two but not many, (*have called ~ times*; *myself & ~ others*). **2.** pron. A moderate number, more than two but not many, of the previously mentioned or implied persons or things (~ *of you have seen him*; *went mushroom- -hunting & found~*). [ME, f. AF, f. med. L *separalis* (L *separ* SEPARATE, -AL)]

sěv'eraltӯ, n. Individual or unshared tenure of estate etc. (usu. *in ~*). [ME, f. AF *severalte* (as prec., -TY[2])]

sěvēre', a. (*-er, -est*). **1.** Austere, strict, harsh, rigorous, unsparing, (~ *look, discipline, critic, master, sentence, inspection, self-control*; ~ *upon*, hard on). **2.** Violent, vehement, extreme, (~ *weather*, very cold or stormy; *a ~ winter*; ~ *attack of gout*). **3.** Trying, making great demands on endurance, energy, skill, or other quality, (~ *test, pain, competition, requirements*). **4.** Unadorned, stripped of all that is unessential, without redundance, restrained, terse, (~ *architecture, beauty, simplicity, style*). **5.** Sarcastic or satirical (~ *remarks*; *you are pleased to be ~*). Hence or cogn. ~LY[2] (*-rlĭ*) adv. (*leave or let ~ly alone*, abstain from dealing with as mark of disapproval, also joc. avoid meddling with as too formidable or difficult), sěvē'rĬTӯ n. (w. pl. = ~ treatment). [F, or f. L *severus*]

sěv'erӯ, n. (archit.). Compartment of vaulted celing. [f. AF **civorie*, OF *civoire* CIBORIUM]

Sěv'ille ŏ'range (*-ĭnj*), n. The bitter orange, used for marmalade. [*Seville*, in Spain]

Sèvres (see Ap.), n. Porcelain made at ~.

sew (sō), v.t. & i. (p.p. *sewn, sewed*, pr. sōn, sōd). Fasten (material, pieces) by passing thread again & again through holes made with threaded needle or with awl etc. (~ *cloth, calico, leather, pieces together, sheets of book*), whence ~'ING[1] (5) (sōĬ-) n.; make by ~ing (~ *seam, pleat, shirt, book, boot, buttonhole*); fasten *on* or *in*, attach, by ~ing (~ *on a button*; *can you~ buttons?*; ~ *in a patch, band, gusset, rib*, etc.); close *up* (hole, rent, wound, bag) by ~ing; enclose, fasten *up*, by

~ing receptacle (~ *up money in a bag*; ~ *money into* one's *belt*); ~ one *up*, sl., utterly exhaust, (esp. in p.p.) intoxicate; use needle & thread or ~ing-machine; *~ing-machine*, apparatus in which needle is worked mechanically by crank or treadle; *~ing-press*, apparatus for ~ing books. Hence ~'er[1] [-ER[1]] (sō'er) n. [OE *si*(o)*wan*, OHG *siuwen*, ON *sӯja*, Goth. *siujan* f. Gmc **siwjan* cogn. w. L *suere*]

sew'age, n., & v.t. **1.** Matter conveyed in sewers; *~-farm*, on which ~ is used as manure, esp. one that utilizes & disposes of a town's ~; *~-grass*, grown on ~d land. **2.** v.t. Manure with ~. [formed f. SEWER[3] by change of (supposed) -ER[1] to -AGE]

sěwěll'el, n. Small burrowing rodent of the W. coast of U.S. [Amer.-Ind.]

sewer[1]. See SEW.

sew'er[2], n. (hist.). Person who set out table, placed guests, carried & tasted dishes, etc. [ME, f. AF *asseour* f. OF *asseoir* to seat, set, f. L AS(*sidēre=sedēre* sit) sit beside]

sew'er[3], n., & v.t. **1.** Conduit or channel usu. covered over for carrying off the drainage & excrementitious matter of a town, public drain; *~-gas*, foul air of ~s; ~ *rat*, common brown or Norway rat; hence ~AGE(1) n. **2.** v.t. Drain, provide, with ~s. [ME, f. AF, ONF *se*(*u*)*wiere* channel to carry off overflow from a fishpond f. L **EXaquaria* (*aqua* water, -ARY[1]); cf. EWER]

sew'in, -ěn, n. Kind of bulltrout. [orig. obsc.]

sewn. See SEW.

sěx, n. Being male or female or hermaphrodite (*what is its~?*; ~ *does not matter*; *without distinction of age or ~*), whence ~'LESS a., ~'lěssNESS n., ~'ӯ[2] a., immoderately concerned with ~; males or females collectively (*all ranks & both~es*; *the fair, gentle, softer, weaker, ~*, & joc. *the ~*, women; *the sterner ~*, men; *is the fairest of her ~*); (attrib.) arising from difference, or consciousness, of ~ (~ *antagonism, ~ instinct, ~ urge*); ~ *appeal*, attractiveness arising from difference of ~. [f. L *sexus -ūs*; partly thr. F]

sěx-, also occas. **sěx|i-**, comb. forms of L *sex* six, in derivatives of L compds & in mod. formations: ~'*angle*, hexagon; ~*ang'ular*(*ly*), hexagonal(ly); ~*centēn'ary* (or *-sē*[2]) a. & n., of 600, 600- -year, 600th anniversary; ~*dĭ'gitate*, six- -fingered; ~*enni'al*(*ly*), lasting, (occurring) once in, six years; ~'*ifid*(bot.), cleft in 6; ~'*foil*, 6-lobed figure in architectural or other decoration, also 6-leaved plant; ~*isyllab'ic*, ~*isyll'able*, (word) of 6 syllables; ~ (*i*)*vāl'ent* (chem.), combining with 6 atoms of hydrogen, having 6 combining equivalents; ~*part'ite*, divided in 6.

sěxagēnār'ian, a. & n. (Person) between 59 & 70. [L *sexagenarius* (foll.), -AN]

sĕxagĕn′arў, a. Of 60, going by sixties. [f. L *sexagenarius* (*sexageni* 60 each f. *sexaginta* 60, -ARY¹)]

Sĕxages′ima, n. (Also ~ *Sunday*) Sunday before Quinquagesima. [ME (-*ime*), f. L, fem. adj. = 60th (day), prob. named loosely as preceding QUINQUAGESIMA]

sĕxages′imal, a. & n. Sixtieth, of 60, proceeding by sixties, (~ *fractions*, or ~s n., with denominators proceeding in ratio of 60 as in the divisions of the circle & hour). Hence ~LY² adv. [f. med. L *sexagesimalis* f. L *sexagesimus* 60th (*sexaginta* 60), -AL]

sĕxill′ion (-lyon), n. ‖ 6th power of a million, 1 with 36 ciphers; *7th power of a thousand, 1 with 21 ciphers. [f. SEX-, after *million*]

sĕxt, sĕxte, n. (eccl.). The office of the 6th hour, recited at noon. [ME, f. fem. *sexta* (*hora* hour) of L *sextus* sixth]

sĕx′tain, n. = SESTINA. [perh. alt. f. obs. F *sestine*, after *quatrain*, *sixain*]

sĕx′tan, a. (Of fever etc.) recurring every fifth (by inclusive reckoning sixth) day. [f. mod. L *sextana* (*febris* fever) f. *sextus* sixth, -AN]

sĕx′tant, n. Sixth part of circle (obs.); instrument used in navigation and surveying for measuring the angular distance of objects by means of reflection. [f. L *sextans* -*ntis* sixth part (*sextus* sixth, -ANT)]

sĕxtĕt(te)′, n. (Musical work for) 6 voices, singers, instruments, or players, in combination; (transf.) any set of 6. [alt. of SESTET after L *sex* six]

sĕxtill′ion (-lyon), n. = SEXILLION. [F, f. L *sex* six, after *septillion*]

sĕx′tō, n. (pl. ~s). Book formed by folding sheets in six. [f. L *sextus* sixth, as QUARTO]

sĕxtodĕ′cimō, n. (*abbr.* 16mo, usu. read *sixteenmo*). Sheet of paper folded in 16 leaves; this way of folding (*in* ~); book made by folding thus. [orig. *in* ~ L (IN⁵, *sextus decimus* 16th)]

sĕx′ton, n. Officer charged with care of church & churchyard, & often with duties of parish clerk & grave-digger; ~ *beetle*, kinds that bury carrion to serve as nidus for eggs. [ME *segerstane* f. AF *segerstaine*, OF *segrestein* f. med. L *sacristanus* SACRISTAN]

sĕx′tūple, a. & n., & v.t. & i. Sixfold (amount); (vb) multiply by 6. [f. med. L *sextuplus*, irreg. f. L *sex* six. after LL *quintuplus* QUINTUPLE]

‖ **sĕx′tus**. See PRIMUS¹.

sĕx′ūal (*or* -kshōŏ-), a. Of sex, a sex, or the sexes (~ *organs*, *genitals*); ~ *intercourse* or *commerce*, copulation; ~ *affinity*, mutual attraction of two individuals of opposite sexes; ~ SELECTION; ~ *appetite*, *indulgence*, for, in, ~ *intercourse*; (bot.; of classification) based on the distinction of sexes in plants, whence ~IST(2) n. Hence ~ITY (-ăl⁴) n., ~LY² adv. [f. LL *sexualis* (SEX, -AL)]

sĕx′ūalīz|e (*or* -kshōŏ-), -**is|e** (-īz), v.t. Attribute sex to. Hence ~A′TION n. [-IZE]

sfŏr̄zăn′dō (-ts-), mus. direction. With sudden emphasis. [It.]

sfuma′tō (-ōōmah-), a. (paint.). With indistinct outlines. [It., lit. smoked]

shăbb′|ў, a. Scurvy, contemptible, paltry, dishonourable, (*played me a* ~*y trick*); close-fisted, mean; worn, threadbare, dilapidated, seedy, in bad repair or condition; ~*y-genteel*, retaining traces of better days, attempting to keep up appearances. Hence ~ILY² adv., ~INESS n., ~ŸISH¹(2) a. [f. (now dial.) *shab* f. OE *sceabb* (Gmc *skabh-* SHAVE)+-Y²; cf. SCAB]

shăb′răck, n. Cavalry saddlecloth. [f. G *schabracke* of E.-Europ. orig.]

shăck, n. Rough hut. [orig. unkn.]

shăc′kle, n., & v.t. 1. Metal loop or staple, bow of padlock, link closed by bolt for connecting chains etc., coupling link; long link joining pair of wrist or ankle rings, (pl.) fetters, impediments, or restraints (*the* ~*s of convention*); kind of insulator for telegraph wires; ~*-bolt*, for closing ~, also bolt with ~ at its end; ~*-joint*, in some fishes, formed by bony ring passing through hole in other bone. 2. v.t. Fetter, impede, trammel. [OE *sceacul*, fetter, corresp. to LG *schake*, *schäkel* link, coupling]

shăd, n. Kinds of anadromous deep-bodied fish, of which the American or white ~ is much esteemed as food. [OE *sceadd*, of unkn. orig.]

shădd′ock, n. (Fruit, sometimes weighing 15 lb., of) orig. Malayan & Polynesian tree of orange kind. [*S*~, introducer to W. Indies]

shade¹, n. 1. Comparative darkness (& usu. coolness) caused by interception of light (& usu. heat) rays; (fig.) comparative obscurity (*throw into the* ~, outshine). 2. (Often pl.) place sheltered from sun, cool or sequestered retreat; (pl.) wine vaults; (pl.) darkness *of* night or evening. 3. Darker part of picture (*without light &* ~, of paintings, also fig. of descriptions or characters, monotonous, uniformly glaring or sombre). 4. A colour esp. with regard to its depth or as distinguished from one nearly like it, gradation of colour, material so coloured, (*in all* ~*s of purple*; *I want the same colour in a lighter* ~; *all the newest* ~*s in stock*; also fig., as *people of all* ~*s of opinion*, *delicate* ~*s of meaning*). 5. Slight difference, small amount, (*am a* ~ *better today*). 6. Unsubstantial or unreal thing (*is the shadow of a* ~, delusive). 7. Soul after death (*spoke with the* ~ *of Homer*; *went down to the* ~*s*, died, visited Hades; *S*~ *of Priscian* etc. *!*, exclamation at grammatical blunder etc., that would have outraged person invoked). 8. Screen excluding or moderating light, heat, etc. (usu. in comb., as SUN, *candle*, *lamp*, ~), eye-shield, glass

cover for object; *window-blind. Hence
~'LESS (-dl-) a. [ME *schade* f. OE *sceadu*,
OS *scado*, OHG *scato*, Goth. *skadus* f.
Gmc *skadhw- cogn. w. Gk *skotos*; see
SHADOW]

shāde², v.t. & i. **1.** Screen from excessive
light (~*d his eyes with his hand*; *trees* ~
the street). **2.** Cover, keep off, or moderate
power of (luminous object, light) with
or as intervening object. **3.** Make dark
or gloomy (*a sullen look* ~*d his face*). **4.**
(In drawing) darken (parts of object represented) esp. with parallel pencil lines to
give effects of light & shade or gradations
of colour, whence **shād'ING¹**(6) n. **5.** (Of
colour or light, & fig. of opinion, practice,
etc.) pass *off* by degrees into (or *into*)
other colour or variety, make (colour etc.)
pass thus *into* another. **6.** Modify pitch
of (organ-pipe). [ME, f. prec.]

shadoof', n. Pole with bucket & counterpoise used esp. in Egypt for raising water.
[f. Arab. *shādūf*]

shăd'ow¹ (-dō), n. **1.** Shade (*sitting in the*
~; *the* ~ *of death is on his face*; VALLEY of
the ~ *of death*; *the* ~*s of night*; *under the*
~ *of misfortune*); dark part of picture,
room, etc. **2.** Patch of shade, dark figure
projected by body that intercepts light
rays, this regarded as person's or thing's
appendage (*may your* ~ *never grow less!*);
(fig.) one's inseparable attendant or companion. **3.** Reflected image. **4.** Type,
faint representation, adumbration, pre-
monition (*coming events cast their* ~*s*
before). **5.** Slightest trace (*without a* ~ *of*
doubt). **6.** Unsubstantial or unreal thing
or counterfeit (*what* ~*s we are!*; *catch at*
~*s*; *having only the* ~ *of freedom*); phantom, ghost, (*is but the* ~ *of his former self*;
worn to a ~; *a terrible* ~ *with uplifted hand*).
7. Privacy, obscurity, (*content to live in*
the ~). **8.** Shelter, protection, (*under the*
~ *of the Almighty*). **9.** ~-*boxing* (against
imaginary opponent as form of training);
|| ~. CABINET; ~ *factory*, one planned or
built for possible reserve production
against the emergency of war; ~-*stitch*,
kind of ladder-work in lace-making.
Hence ~LESS (-ōl-), ~Y² (-ōi), aa., ~ĪNESS
(-ōī-) n. [repr. OE *scead*(*u*)*we*, obl. case of
sceadu SHADE¹]

shăd'ow² (-dō), v.t. Overspread with
shadow (chiefly poet.); set *forth* dimly, in
outline, allegorically, or prophetically;
dog, secretly watch all movements of.
[ME, f. prec.]

shād'|y̆, a. Giving, situated in, shade; (of
actions, conduct, etc.) shunning the light,
disreputable, of dubious honesty; *on the*
~*y side of forty* etc., more than. Hence
~ILY² adv., ~ĪNESS n. [-Y²]

shaft (-ah-), n. **1.** (Slender pole of) lance
or spear. **2.** Long-bow arrow (often
CLOTH-*yard* ~; also fig., as ~*s of satire*,
ridicule, *envy*). **3.** Ray of light, bolt or
stroke of lightning. **4.** Stem, stalk,
column between base & capital, one of

group of clustered columns, spire, part of
chimney above roof, rib of feather, part
more or less long & narrow & straight
supporting or connecting part(s) of greater
thickness etc. **5.** (mech.). Large axle,
revolving bar transferring force by belts
or cogs, whence ~'ING¹ (3, 6) n. **6.** Handle
of tool etc. **7.** One of pair of bars between
which horse of vehicle is harnessed (~-
-*horse*, so placed, opp. LEADER in tandem).
8. Vertical or inclined excavation giving
access to mine; tunnel of blast-furnace;
(also · *ventilating* ~) upward vent for
smoke or bad air from tunnel, drain, etc.
[OE *sceaft*, OS *skaft*, OHG *scaft*, ON *skapt*
f. Gmc *skaft-; cf. L *scapus*]

shăg¹, n. **1.** Rough growth or mass of
hair etc., whence ~g'ED² (-gĭd) a. (rare);
(arch.) long-napped rough cloth. **2.**
Coarse kind of cut tobacco. [OE *sceacga*,
cogn. w. ON *skegg* beard, OE *sceaga*
coppice, SHAW; f. Gmc *skag-]

shăg², n. Crested cormorant. [prob. f.
prec.]

*shăg'bärk, n. The white hickory.
[SHAG¹]

shăgg'|y̆ (-g-), a. Hairy, rough-haired;
(of hair) coarse, wildly abundant, unkempt; (of land etc.) overgrown with
forest or rough vegetation; (of trees etc.)
with rough branches or twigs; (bot.,
biol.) villous; ~ *dog* (long rambling would-
be funny) *story*. Hence ~ILY² adv., ~ĪNESS
n., (-g-). [-Y²]

shagreen', n. Kind of untanned leather
with artificially granulated surface made
from skin of horse, ass, camel, etc., & usu.
dyed green; shark-skin rough with natural papillae used for rasping & polishing.
[var. of CHAGRIN]

shah, n. King of Persia, padishah. [Pers.,
= ruler; cf. CHECK¹]

shāke¹, v.t. & i. (*shŏŏk*, *shāken*). **1.** Move
(thing, person) violently or quickly up &
down or to & fro with the hand(s) etc.
(*like a terrier shaking a rat*; *deserves a*
good shāk'ING¹(1) n.; ~ *hands*, ~ *one by*
the hand, clasp right hands with or without shaking at meeting or parting, in
reconciliation or congratulation, or over
concluded bargain; ~ *a mat*). **2.** (Make)
tremble or rock or quiver or vibrate or
wave, jolt, jar, brandish, (~ *the house*;
the earth shook; *hand* ~*s*, is unsteady;
~ *one's fist*, *stick*, etc., *in* person's *face* or
at, threaten with fist etc.; ~ *a* LEG; ~
one's head, move it from side to side in
refusal, denial, disapproval, or concern
over or *at* or abs.; ~ *with fear*, *cold*, etc.,
tremble violently; ~ *in* one's *shoes*,
tremble with apprehension). **3.** Agitate,
shock, disturb, (*was much* ~*n by*, *with*, *at*,
the news; ~ *him out of his lethargy*; *shook*
my composure); (colloq.) upset composure
of (person). **4.** Weaken, impair, make
less convincing or firm or stable or
courageous, (*the firm's credit was* ~*n*;
shook the witness's evidence; *his faith in*

Providence was greatly ~*n; the ranks were* ~*n but not broken*). 5. (Of voice, musical note, singer, etc.) make tremulous sounds, change pitch or power with rapid alternations, trill, (*his voice shook with emotion; must learn to* ~). 6. (imperat.; colloq., chiefly U.S.). ~ *hands*. 7.~*down*, fetch or send down by shaking (fruit from tree; straw or blankets etc. on floor for bed, whence ~'*down* n.; grain etc. in vessel into least compass, (intr.) become compact, get comfortably settled or into harmony with associates or circumstances (~*down cruise* of new ship, made to run in the engines and accustom the crew to the ship); ~ *off*, get rid of (dust etc., & fig. undesirable companion or worry) by shaking (~ *off the* DUST[1] *from* one's*back*);~*out*, empty (vessel, garment, etc.) of contents or dust, (contents) from vessel etc., spread or open (sail, flag, reef); ~ *up*, mix (ingredients), restore (pillow etc.) to shape, by shaking, rouse from stagnant or lethargic or convention-ridden state. Hence shāk'ABLE a. [OE *scacan*, = OS *skakan*, ON *skaka* f. Gmc **skakan*]

shāke², n. 1. Shaking or being shaken (see prec.; *with a* ~ *of the head*; *give it, had, a* ~; *all of a* ~, trembling; *the* ~*s*, ague); jolt, jerk, shock. 2. *A glass of milk, or milk and egg, flavoured and shaken up (short for *milk*~~). 3. Trill, quick alternation of two notes with voice or on instrument. 4. Moment (*in two* etc. ~*s of a lamb's tail* etc. or ~*s*, very quickly, in no time; *in a brace of* ~*s*). 5. Crack in growing timber. 6. (sl.). *Is no great* ~*s*, not very good or efficient. 7. ~-*out* (St. Exch.), crisis in which weaker speculators are driven out of market; ~-*up*, shaking or being shaken up. [f. prec.]

shāk'er, n. In vbl senses; also (*S*~) member of religious sect founded in Manchester, & still existing in U.S., holding that Christ's second coming has taken place (named from religious dances), whence **Shāk'erESS**[1], **Shāk'erISM**(3), nn. [-ER²]

Shāk(e)spe(a)r'i|an (-kspēr-), a. & n. (In the style) of Shakespeare; (n.) student of Shakespeare. So ~AN'A n. pl. [-IAN]

shāk'ō, n. (pl. ~s). Form of military hat, more or less cylindrical with peak & upright plume or tuft. [f. Magyar *csdkó*]

shāk'|y̆, a. Unsteady, apt to shake, trembling, unsound, infirm, unreliable, tottering, wavering, (*a* ~*y hand, table, old man, house*; ~*y credit, voters, courage*; *feel, look,* ~*y*). Hence ~ILY² adv., ~INESS n. [-Y²]

shāle, n. Kinds of clayey stone splitting readily into thin plates & resembling slate but softer & less solid; ~-*oil*, kind of naphtha got from bituminous ~. Hence shāl'y² a. [perh. = dial. *shale* scale f. OE *scealu* cogn. w. ON *skal* SCALE²]

shall (*unstressed* shal, shl), v. aux. (pres.

I, he, we, you, they, ~, *thou shalt*; past & condit. *I, he, we, you, they, should* pr. shŏŏd, *thou shouldst* pr. shŏŏdst, *or shouldest* pr. shŏŏd'Ist; neg. forms *shall not or shan't* pr. -ah-, *should not or shouldn't*; no other parts used). ~ & *should* are used: 1 in first person (the others having *will, would*) to form a plain future or conditional statement or question (*we* ~ *hear about it tomorrow; I should have been killed if I had let go;* ~ *I hear from you soon?*); 2 in 2nd & 3rd persons (1st having *will, would*) to form a future or conditional statement expressing speaker's will or intention (*you* ~ *not catch me again; he should not have gone if I could have prevented it*); 3 alternatively with *will, would*, in sentences of type 1 changed in reporting from 1st to other person (*he says or said, you say or said, that he, you,* ~ *or should never manage it*; now more usu. *will, would*) or from other person to 1st (*he says I* ~ *or will never manage it*, reporting *you will never; will* now rare); 4 in reporting sentences of type 2 that contained ~ *or should* (*you promised I, he, should not catch you at it again*); 5 in 2nd-person questions corresponding to type 1, by attraction to expected answer (~ *you be going to church?*); 6 in any person to form statements or questions involving the notions of command & future or conditional duty, obligation, etc. (*thou shalt not steal; I, you, he, should really have been more careful;* ~*I, he, open the door?*; *why should I, you, he, obey?*); 7 in all persons to form conditional protasis or indefinite clause (*if, when, we* ~ *be defeated or defeat* ~ *overtake us; any one who should say; if you should happen to be there;* & with inversion *should I, you, he, be there, it would·be talked about*); 8 alternatively with *may, might*, in all persons in final clauses (*to the end that I, you, he* ~ *or should not be able*); 9 in some miscellaneous idioms (*it should seem*, it seems; *you* ~ *find*, arch., be sure you will find; *it is surprising* etc. *that I, you, he, should be or have been so foolish*. [OE *sceal*, OHG *scal, sal*, OS, ON, Goth. *skal*, a preterite-present vb f. Gmc **skal-*, **skul-* owe]

shallōōn', n. Light cloth for coat-linings & women's dresses. [f. *Châlons* in France]

shǎll'op, n. Light open boat. [f. F *chaloupe* SLOOP]

shal(l)ŏt', n. Plant of onion kind with cloves like, but of milder flavour than, those of garlic. [aphetic f. 18th c. *eschalot* f. F *eschalotte* alt. of *escaloigne* (SCALLION) f. L *ascalonia* f. *Ascalon* in Palestine]

shǎll'ow (-ō), a. (~*er*, ~*est*), n., & v.i. & t. 1. Of little depth (lit. & fig.; ~ *water, a* ~ *stream, dish; a* ~ *mind, argument, love, man*, superficial, trivial; so ~-*brained, -hearted, -pated*); hence ~LY² adv., ~NESS n. 2. n. ~ *place*, shoal. 3. vb. Become

~er, make ~. [15th c. *schalowe*, prob. rel. to *schald*, OE *sceald* SHOAL¹]

shalt. See SHALL.

shăm, v.t. & i. (-mm-), n., & a. **1.** Feign, simulate, (~ *illness, sleep, a faint, fear*; *is only ~ming*); pretend to be (~*med ill, dead, asleep*); hence ~m′ER¹ n. **2.** n. Imposture, pretence, humbug, (*this age of ~s*); person or thing pretending or pretended to be something that he or it is not; (also *sheet, pillow*, ~) embroidered linen laid on bed in day for show. **3.** adj. Pretended, counterfeit, (~ *fight*, imitation battle for training troops; ~ *plea* etc. in law, advanced only to gain time). [17th-c. sl. of obsc. orig.]

Shăm′anĭsm, n. Religion of Siberian tribes involving belief in secondary gods & in power of shamans or priests to influence these. [f. G *schamane* of Mongol origin, -ISM]

shăm′bl|e, v.i., & n. **1.** Walk or run in shuffling or awkward or decrepit way (~*ing gait*, of person who ~es). **2.** n. ~ing gait. [prob. f. *shamble* adj. straddling, wry, perh. f. *shamble* bench (see foll.) w. ref. to straddling trestles]

shăm′bles (-lz), n. pl. (often w. sing. constr.). Butchers' slaughter-house; scene of carnage (*the place became a ~*); (loosely, esp. in journalistic use) mess, muddle (with no implication of blood or death). [pl. of *shamble* stool, stall, OE *sc(e)amel*, OS *skamel*, OHG *scamel* f. WG f. L *scamellum* dim. of *scamnum* bench]

shāme¹, n. **1.** Feeling of humiliation excited by consciousness of guilt or shortcoming, of having made oneself or been made ridiculous, or of having offended against propriety, modesty, or decency, (*flushed with ~*; *begin with ~ to take the lowest room*). **2.** Restraint imposed by, desire to avoid, such humiliation (*for ~!*, appeal to person not to disregard or reproof for disregarding this; *cannot do it for very ~*; *is quite without or lost to ~*), whence ~′LESS (-ml-) a., ~′lĕss-LY² adv., ~′lĕssNESS n. **3.** State of disgrace or ignominy or discredit (~ *on you!*; *put one to ~*, disgrace him esp. by exhibiting superior qualities etc.), person or thing that brings disgrace (*is a ~ to his parents*; *would think ~ to do it*; *is a sin & a ~*), whence ~′FUL (-mf-) a., ~′fulLY² adv., ~′fulNESS n [OE *sc(e)amu*, OS *skama*, OHG *scama*, ON *skomm* f. Gmc *skamō*]

shāme², v.i. & t. Be ashamed, refuse from shame, *to* (arch.; usu. with negative, as *he ~d not to say*); bring shame on, be a shame to, make ashamed; put (superior) to the blush by outdoing (*a dog's fidelity ~s us*); frighten by shame *into* or *out of* doing, conduct, etc. [OE *sc(e)amian*, Goth. *skaman* (prec.)]

shāme′faced (-āmfāst), a. Bashful, shy; (poet., of virtue, flowers, etc.) modest, retiring, inconspicuous. Hence ~LY²

adv., ~NESS n., (-āmfāsĭd-, -āst-). [16th c. etym. misinterpretation of *shamefast* f. OE *sceamu* SHAME¹ + *fæst* FAST³]

shămm′ў, shăm′oy, n. = CHAMOIS(2).

shămpōō′, v.t., & n. **1.** Subject (body etc.) to kneading or massage after hot bath (orig. sense, now rare); lather, wash, & rub (head, hair). **2.** n. A ~ing of the head; *dry* ~, alcoholic saponaceous preparation for cleaning the hair, powder for similar purpose, ~ing with these. [prob. f. Hind. *shāmpo*, imper. of *shāmpnā* to press]

shăm′rŏck, n. Kinds of trefoil or clover serving as national emblem of Ireland (cf. ROSE, THISTLE, LEEK). [f. Ir. *seamróg* trefoil, dim. of *seamar* clover]

shăn′drydăn, n. Light two-wheeled cart; old rickety vehicle. [orig. unkn.]

shăn′dў(găff), n. Mixed drink of beer & ginger-beer or lemonade. [orig. unkn.]

shănghai′ (-hī), v.t. (naut. sl.). Drug & ship as sailor while unconscious. [S~ in China]

shănk, n., & v.i. & t. **1.** Leg (S~*s's mare*, one's own legs as opp. riding etc.); leg from knee to ankle; shin-bone; upright part of bird's foot; footstalk of flower; ‖ leg of stocking; shaft of pillar etc., shaft of tool·between head etc. & handle, stem of key, spoon, anchor, etc., straight part of fish-hook, narrow middle of boot-sole; hence (-)~ED² (-kt) a. **2.** vb. ~ *off*, (of flowers) fall off by decay of ~; (golf) strike (ball) with heel of club. [OE *sc(e)anca* (WG **skank-*) cogn. w. MHG *schenkel*, OHG *scinko* thigh (G *schinken* ham)]

shănn′ў, n. Oblong olive-green European sea-fish, the smooth blenny. [also (18th c.) *shan*; orig. unkn.]

shan't. See SHALL.

shăn′tŭng′, n. A soft undressed Chinese silk (usu. undyed). [S~, Chin. province]

shăn′tў¹, n. Hut, cabin, mean dwelling. [f. Canad.-F *chantier* log hut f. F = workshop]

shăn′tў², n. Sailor's song (with alternating solo by ~*man*, & chorus) in heaving. [perh. a corrupt. of F *chantez*, imperat. pl. of *chanter* CHANT]

shāpe¹, v.t. & i. (p.p. ~*d*, arch. ~*n*). Create, form, construct; model, mould, fashion, bring into desired or definite figure or form (p.p., having such figure, as ~*d like a pear*); adapt, make conform, *to*; plan, devise; direct, aim, (one's course etc.); frame mentally, imagine, call up image of; assume form, develop into shape, give signs of future shape (~*s well*, is promising). Hence **shăp′ABLE** a. [OE *scieppan*, OS *sceppian*, Goth. *gaskapjan* create, f. Gmc **skapjan*; *shape* is a new ME form after the p.p.]

shāpe², n. **1.** Configuration, form, total effect produced by thing's outlines, (*spherical in ~*; *has the ~ of a boat*). **2.** Appearance, guise, (*monster in human*

~). 3. Concrete presentment, embodiment, (*intention took ~ in action*; *showed me politeness in the ~ of an invitation*). 4. Kind, description, sort, (*made no overtures in any ~ or form*). 5. Symmetrical or definite form, orderly arrangement, proper condition, (*get one's ideas into ~*; LICK *into ~*; *give ~ to*), whence ~'LESS (-pl-) a., ~'lĕssLY² adv., ~'lĕssNESS n. 6. Person considered as impressing the sight, & esp. as indistinctly seen or imagined, apparition, ghost, (*a ~ loomed through the mist*; *a grim mysterious ~ stalked towards me*). 7. Pattern for workman etc., mould for shaping hats etc.; jelly, blancmange, etc. shaped in mould; padding worn by.actor. Hence (-)shāp-ED² (-pt) a. [OE *gesceap* (Y-, prec.)]

shāpe'l|y (-plǐ), a. Well formed or proportioned, of the right or a pleasing shape. Hence ~ĭNESS n. [ME; -LY¹]

shāp'er, n. In vbl senses; esp., kinds of machine for turning, planing, stamping, moulding, etc. [-ER¹].

shār̃d, shĕr̃d, n. (arch.). Potsherd (still used by gardeners of fragment put over hole of flowerpot); beetle's wing-cover. [OE *sceard*, ON *skarthr* f. Gmc *skardaz notched f. *skar-* SHEAR¹;'cf. SHARE]

shāre¹, n. 1. Portion detached for individual from common amount (*must get a ~ of the plunder*). 2. Part one is entitled to have or bound to contribute, equitable portion, (*that is your fair~*; *took, bore, my or more or less than my ~ of the burden*; *go ~s*, make equitable division with others; *~ & ~ alike*, with equal division; LION's ~). 3. Part one gets or contributes (*had a large ~ in bringing it about, but no ~ of the credit*). 4. Part-proprietorship of property held by joint owners (*has a ~ in the bank, estate*, etc.), esp. one of the equal parts into which company's capital is divided entitling holder to proportion of profits (*hold 50 ~s in*; *an issue of 10,000 ~s*); *deferred~s*, on which lower dividend or none is to be paid till fixed date or contingent event; *preference* or *preferred ~s*, on which fixed dividend is guaranteed before payment begins on *ordinary ~s*; ~'*holder*, owner of ~s; ‖ ~*list*, of current prices of ~s in various companies; ~*-pusher*, colloq., pedlar of (usu. worthless) ~s. 5. *~'cropper*, tenant farmer who pays his rent with a part of his crop. [ME *share* f. OE *scearu* division f. WG *skarō* f. *skar-* SHEAR¹]

shāre², v.t. & i. Apportion (food, property, task, etc.) among others, give each a share of; give away part of (*would ~ his last crust*); get or have share of, possess or use or endure jointly with others; have share(s), be sharer(s), (*will ~ with you in the undertaking*; *we must ~ alike*); ~ *out*, distribute, whence ~'*out* n., provident club's distribution. Hence shār'ER¹ n. [16th c., f. prec.]

shāre³, n. Ploughshare; blade of seeding-machine or cultivator; ~*-beam*, part of plough in which ~ is fixed. [OE *scear*, *scær*, OHG *scar*, f. Gmc *skar-*, *sker-* SHEAR¹]

shārk, n., & v.i. & t. 1. Kinds of long-shaped lateral-gilled inferior-mouthed sea-fish many species of which are large & voracious (*basking-, man-eating, while, blue, dusky, bonnet-headed*, etc., ~); rapacious person, swindler, (LAND-~); *(college sl.) brilliant student; ~*-moth*, kinds of moth named from shape; ~*-oil*, got from ~'s liver & used like cod-liver oil; ~'*s-mouth*, opening in awning for mast etc. 2. vb. Play the swindler, adventurer, etc. (*~s for a living*), whence ~'ING² a.; gather *up* by dishonest or dishonourable means; swallow voraciously. [f. 16th c., of unkn. orig.]

shārp¹, a., n., & adv. 1. With fine edge or point, not blunt; peaked, pointed, edged, (~ *gable, summit, ridge*). 2. Well-defined, clean-cut, (~ *outline, distinction, impression, features*; so ~*-cut*). 3. Abrupt, angular, (~ *turn, incline*). 4. Keen, pungent, acid, tart, shrill, piercing, biting, harsh, acrimonious, severe, intense, painful, (~ *flavour, wine, voice, cry, frost, air, words, tongue, temper, reproof, contest, attack of gout*). 5. Acute, sensitive, quick to see or hear or notice, keen-witted, vigilant, clever, (~ *eyes, ears, intelligence, attention*; ~*-sighted, -witted*, etc.; *keep a ~ look-out*; *a ~ remark, child*; *as ~ as a needle*, very intelligent). 6. Quick to take advantage, bent on winning, artful, unscrupulous, dishonest, (*was too ~ for me*, overreached me; ~ *practice*, barely honest dealings). 7. Vigorous, speedy, not loitering, impetuous, (*take a ~ walk*; ~'*s the word*, exhortation to be quick; ~ *work*, said of matter quickly dispatched or fight etc. that takes all one's energy). 8. (phonet.). (Of mutes) unvoiced, hard. 9. (mus., opp. FLAT²). Above true pitch (*piano is ~*; *B, D*, etc., ~, a semitone higher than B, D, etc.), (of key) having ~(s) in signature. 10. ~'*shooter*, skilled shot posted where marksmanship is required; hence ~'EN⁶ v.t. & i., (-)~'en-ER¹(1, 2) n., ~'LY² adv., ~'NESS n. 11. n. Sewing-needle of slender make; (mus.) note raised a semitone above pitch, symbol indicating this raising, ~s & FLAT²s; ~ *consonant*; (colloq.) swindler, cheat (*billiard-~*); *(joc.) expert (*mining-~*); ‖ (pl.) middlings (between flour & bran). 12. adv. Punctually (*at six o'clock ~*); (mus.) above true pitch (*is singing ~*); LOOK¹ ~; ~*-set*, hungry; ~*-shod*, calked. [OE *scearp*, OS *skarp*, OHG *scarpf*, ON *skarpr* f. Gmc *skarpaz*]

shārp², v.t. & i. Sharpen, whet, (arch. or vulg.); raise pitch of (note) or mark as sharp; play unfairly, swindle, at cards etc., whence ~'ER¹ n. [OE *scierpan*, f. prec.]

Sha'stra (-ah-), n. One of the sacred Hindu writings. [Skr. *çāstra*]

shatt′er, v.t. & i. Break (t. & i.) suddenly & violently in pieces; utterly derange, destroy, dissipate, (~ed nerves, constitution, hopes). [14th c., obsc. rel. to earlier SCATTER]

shave¹, v.t. & i. (p.p. ~d &, chiefly as adj., ~n). **1.** Remove (hair), free (chin etc.) of hair, relieve (person) of hair on chin etc., with razor (has ~d off or ~d his beard, now wears none; a ~n chin); (intr.) ~ oneself (he does not ~ every day). **2.** Pare surface of (wood etc.) with SPOKE⁻shave, plane, etc., whence **shāv′ING¹**(2) n. **3.** Pass close to without touching, skirt, miss narrowly, nearly graze. **4.** ~-hook, tool for scraping surface of metal before soldering; shaving-brush, for lathering chin etc. before shaving; shaving-horse, bench with clamp for holding wood to be ~d. [OE sceafan, OS scavan, OHG scaban, ON skafa, Goth. skaban f. Gmc *skabh-]

shāve², n. **1.** Having one's beard etc. shaved (must have a ~; shilling ~). **2.** Close approach without contact, narrow miss or escape or failure, (had a close ~ of it). **3.** Knife-blade with handle at each end for shaving wood etc. **4.** ‖ Trick, deception, hoax. [(the tool f. OE sceafa) f. prec.]

shāve′ling (-vl-), n. (arch.). Shaven person, monk, friar, priest. [-LING¹]

shāv′er, n. In vbl senses; also (colloq.), lad, youngster, (usu. young ~). [-ER¹]

Shāv′ian, a. (In the manner) of G. B. Shaw, dramatist (d. 1950). [-IAN]

‖ **shaw¹**, n. (arch. & poet.). Thicket, wood. [OE sc(e)aga = ON skagi; see SHAG¹]

‖ **shaw²**, n. (Sc.). Stalks and leaves of some plants, esp. potatoes and turnips. [of obsc. orig.]

shawl, n., & v.t. **1.** Rectangular garment, often square to be folded into triangle, chiefly worn by women as outer covering for shoulders; ~-dance, in which dancer waves a ~; ~-pattern, variegated design like that of Oriental ~. **2.** v.t. Put ~ on (person). [f. Pers. shdl]

shawm, n. Obsolete musical instrument with reed. [ME, f. OF chalemie f. L f. Gk kalamos reed]

shay, n. (Arch. joc., or vulg., for) CHAISE. [back form. f. chaise taken for pl.]

shē, pron. (obj. HER¹, possess. HER², HER²s, pl. THEY etc.), n., & a. **1.** The female (or thing personified as female, e.g. ship or train) previously mentioned or implied or easily identified. **2.** n. Female, woman, (the not impossible ~, woman one might love; is the child a he or a ~?; had a litter of two ~s & a he, two bitches & a dog). **3.** adj. (usu. hyphened). Female (~ -goat, -ass, -bear, etc.; ~-devil, -cat, malignant or spiteful woman; ~-oak, kinds of Australian shrub, esp. BEEFwood; ~-pine, Australian conifer). [prob. an alt. form of OE fem. demonstr. pron. sio, sēo, sie]

shea (shē), n. W.-Afr. tree yielding a vegetable butter (~-butter). [native si, se, sye]

shead′ing, n. Any of the six administrative divisions of the I. of Man. [SHED¹, -ING¹]

sheaf, n. (pl. -ves), & v.t. **1.** Bundle of things laid lengthwise together & usu. tied (~ of papers, arrows, etc.), esp. armful of corn-stalks tied after reaping (~ -binder, tool for tying these). **2.** v.t. Make into sheaves, sheave. [OE scéaf, OS skóf, OHG scoub, ON skauf f. Gmc *skaubh-, see SHOVE]

sheal′ing. Var. of SHIELING.

shear¹, v.t. & i. (past ~ed & arch. shore; p.p. shorn, rarely ~ed). **1.** Cut with sword etc. (poet.; t. & i.; shore off his plume; shore through the bone); clip, cut with scissors or shears, (trans.; ~ sheep, clip its wool; also abs., shall be ~ing, i.e. my sheep, tomorrow; ~ cloth, remove or reduce nap by clipping); (fig.) fleece, strip bare, (come home shorn; shorn of wool, glory, etc.). **2.** (Of structure, material, etc.) be distorted or broken by the strain called a shear, (of pressure) distort or break thus. **3.** ~water, kinds of low-flying sea-bird. Hence ~ER¹ n. [OE, OS, OHG sceran, ON skera f. Gmc *sker-, *skar-, *skǣr-, *skur-, cogn. w. SHARD, SHARE, SCAR², etc.]

shear², n. **1.** (Pl.) clipping-instrument with two meeting blades pivoted as in scissors or connected by spring & passing close over each other edge to edge (want a pair of ~s; ~ in comb. or attrib., as ~bill, the bird scissorbill or skimmer; ~-grass, kind with sharp-edged leaves; ~-legs, SHEER⁴s; ~ steel, of special quality fit for ~s & other cutting tools; ~tail, humming-bird with tail like ~s). **2.** (mech.). Kind of strain produced by pressure in structure of a substance, its successive layers being shifted laterally over each other. [OE scēar, OHG scāra, also OE scērero pl., f., Gmc *skǣr- (prec.)]

shear′ling, n. Sheep once shorn. [-LING¹]

sheat′fish, n. Largest European freshwater fish. [c. 1600, f. G scheidfisch of unkn. orig.; 16th c. sheath-fish prob. f. SHEATH]

sheath, n. (pl. pr. -dhz). Close-fitting cover, esp. for blade of weapon or tool; (bot., zool., anat.) investing membrane, tissue, skin, horny case, etc.; structure of loose stones for confining river within banks. Hence ~LESS a. [OE scǣth, scēath, OS skēdia, OHG sceida, ON skeithir pl. f. Gmc *skaithjō; cf. SHED¹]

sheathe (-dh), v.t. Put into sheath (~ the sword, cease from war, & fig.); encase, protect with casing or sheath′ING(3) n. [ME, f. prec.]

sheave¹, n. Grooved wheel in pulley etc. for rope to run on. [ME, cogn. w. OS sciva, OHG sciba]

sheave², v.t. Gather (corn etc.) into sheaves, sheaf. [f. SHEAF]

sheaves. See SHEAF.

*shĕbăng′, n. (sl.). House (esp. gambling--house), store, saloon; any matter of present concern; business (*the whole* ~). [orig. unkn.]

‖ **shĕbeen′**, n. Pot-house, unlicensed house selling drink. [Ir.]

shĕd¹, v.t. (*shed*). Part with, let fall off, (*tree, stag, snake, crab, Prime Minister,* ~*s leaves, horns, skin, shell, colleagues*); drop (~ *tears*, weep; ~ one's *blood for* one's *country*, be wounded or killed); cause (others' *blood*) to flow; disperse, diffuse, spread abroad, (~ *light on*, illuminate, esp. fig.; ~ *love, radiance, perfume*, etc., *around* one); (electr.) reduce (the LOAD¹). Hence ~d′ER¹ n. [OE *sc(e)ădan*, OS *skĕdan*, OHG *sceidan*, Goth. *skaidan* f. Gmc **skaith*- etc., prob. cogn. w. Gk *skhizō*, L *scindere*]

shĕd², n. One-storeyed shelter for storing goods or vehicles or keeping cattle etc. or for use as workshop etc. & consisting of roof with some or all or no sides open. Hence ~d′ING¹(3) n. [app. var. of SHADE]

sheen, n. Splendour, radiance, brightness. Hence ~′y̆¹ [-Y²] a. (poet.). [f. obs. adj. *sheen* beautiful, OE *scīene*, OS, OHG *skōni*, Goth. *skauns* f. Gmc **skau-* SHOW¹; sense assim. to unrelated *shine*]

sheen′y̆², n. (sl.). Jew (derog.). [orig. unkn.]

sheep, n. (pl. the same). **1.** Kinds of wild or domesticated timid gregarious woolly occas. horned ruminant of which male is named *ram*, female *ewe*, & young *lamb* (~ *& goats*, the good & the bad, see *Matt.* xxv. 33; BLACK¹ ~; cast ~'s *eyes*, glance amorously *at*; *follow like* ~, said of persons with no initiative or independence; *as well be hanged for a* ~ *as a* LAMB¹; ~ *that have no shepherd*, helpless crowd etc.; WOLF *in* ~'*s clothing*). **2.** Bashful embarrassed person (so ~'ISH¹ a., ~′ishLY² adv., ~′ishNESS n.). **3.** (Usu. pl., now chiefly joc.) member(s) of minister's flock, parishioners etc. **4.** = ~-skin leather. **5.** ~-*bot*, fly & larva injurious to ~; ~-*cote* (arch.), -*fold*, -*pen* (rare), enclosure for penning ~; ~-*dip*, preparation for cleansing ~ of vermin or preserving their wool; ~-*dog*, collie, also breed of rough-coated short-tailed dog used by shepherds; ‖ ~-*farmer, -master*, breeder of ~; ~-*hook*, shepherd's crook; ~-*louse*, -*tick*, kinds of parasite on ~; ~-*pox*, ~-disease resembling smallpox; ~-*run*, extensive ~-*walk*, esp. in Australia; ~'*s-bit*, plant resembling scabious; ~'*s fescue*, a pasture grass; ~'*shank*, bight & hitches used to shorten rope's length temporarily; ~'*s-head* lit., also kind of sea-fish used for food; ~-*shearing*, (festival at) shearing of ~; ~'*skin*, garment or rug of ~'s skin with wool on, also leather of ~'s skin used in bookbinding etc., also parchment of it or deed or diploma engrossed on this; ~-*walk*, tract of land on which ~ are pastured; ~-*wash*, lotion for killing vermin or preserving wool on ~. [OE *scēap*, OS *scáp*, OHG *scáf*, WG f. Gmc **skǣpam*]

sheer¹, a. & adv. **1.** Mere, simple, unassisted, undiluted, uncompounded, neither more nor less than, absolute, (*did it by* ~ *force; is* ~ *waste, nonsense, folly; a* ~ *impossibility*); (of rock, fall, ascent, etc.) perpendicular, unrelieved by slope; (of textiles) diaphanous. **2.** adv. Plumb, perpendicularly, outright, (*fell 3000 ft* ~; *torn* ~ *out by the roots; rises* ~ *from the water*). [ME *schēre* prob. f. ON *skærr* f. Gmc **skairjaz* f. **ski-* SHINE (cf. OE *scīr* bright)]

sheer², v.i. (Naut.) deviate from course; (also in gen. use) ~ *off*, part company, depart, esp. from person or topic one dislikes or fears or is offended by. [perh. a use of SHEAR¹, but sense development is obsc.; cf. (M)LG *scheren*]

sheer³, n. Upward slope of ship's lines towards bow & stern; deviation of ship from course. [perh. f. SHEAR²,¹]

sheer⁴, n. (Pl.; also ~-*legs* or *shear-legs*) hoisting-apparatus of two (or more) poles attached at or near top and separated at bottom for masting ships or putting in engines etc., used in dockyards.or on ~-*hulk*, dismasted ship used for the purpose. [var. of SHEAR²; named from resemblance to pair of shears]

sheet¹, n. **1.** Rectangular piece of linen used in pairs as inner bed-clothes (*between the* ~*s*, in bed), whence ~′ING¹(3) n.; WHITE¹~. **2.** Broad more or less flat piece of some thin material (*a* ~ *of iron, glass,* etc.). **3.** Wide expanse of water, snow, ice, flame, colour, etc. **4.** Complete piece of paper of the size in which it was made (*book is in* ~*s*, printed but not bound; ~ *of notepaper*, freq. folded once for writing on; ~ *of quarto* etc., the four etc. leaves given by folding a ~ twice etc.); newspaper (*a penny, scurrilous*, etc., ~). **5.** Rope or chain at lower corner of sail for regulating its tension etc. (*flowing* ~, not close-hauled, eased for free wind; *a* ~, *three* ~*s, in the wind*, sl., rather, very, drunk). **6.** ~-*anchor*, second anchor orig. carried outside waist of ship for use in emergencies, (fig.) main dependence or security, something that may hold when all else has failed; ~ *copper, iron, metal*, etc., spread by rolling, hammering, etc., into thin ~*s*; ~ *glass*, kind made first as hollow cylinder, which is cut open & flattened in furnace; ~ LIGHTNING; ~ *music* (published in ~*s*, not in book form). [(1-4) OE *scīete* f. Gmc **skautjōn* f. **skaut-* SHOOT¹; (5) OE *scēata* f. same source; (6) ~-*anchor* of obsc. orig.]

sheet², v.t. Furnish with sheets; cover with sheet (*the* ~*ed dead*); form into sheets (~*ed rain*); secure (sail) with sheet (esp. ~ *home*). [f. prec.]

sheik(h) (-ĕk, -āk), n. Chief, head of Arabian or Mohammedan tribe, family, or village; (transf.) masterful husband or lover, (sl.) dashing or attractive man; *S~ ul Islam* (hist.), grand mufti at Constantinople, chief authority on sacred law in Turkey. [Arab. *shaikh*, = elder, chief]

shekarry. See SHIKAREE.

shĕk'el, n. Ancient Jewish weight & silver coin; (pl., colloq.) money, riches, pelf. [f. Heb. *sheqel* (*shāqal* weigh)]

Shĕkin'ah, -ch-, n. Visible glory of Jehovah resting over mercy-seat. [Heb. (-k-), f. *shākan* dwell]

shĕl'drāke, n. (fem. & pl. *shelduck*). Kinds of (usu. bright-plumaged) wild duck. [ME, prob. f. dial. *sheld* (f. or cogn. w. MDu. *schillede* variegated) +DRAKE]

shĕlf, n. (pl. *-ves*). Projecting slab of stone or board let into or hung on wall to support things, one of the boards in cabinet, bookcase, etc., on which books etc. stand, (*on the ~*, put aside, done with, esp. of person past work and of woman now unlikely to be married); ledge, horizontal steplike projection in cliff face etc.; reef or sandbank under water. Hence **shĕlvED²** (-vd) a., **~'FUL**(2) n. [ME, f. (M)LG *schelf*, cogn. w. OE *scylfe* (? ledge, floor), *scylf* crag]

shĕll¹, n. **1.** Hard outer case enclosing nuts, kinds of seed or fruit, eggs, some animals or parts of them, etc., husk, crust, pod, carapace, scale, conch, wing-case, pupa-case, (*come out of* one's ~, throw off reserve, become communicative). **2.** Walls of unfinished or gutted house, ship, etc. **3.** Outline of plan etc. **4.** Inner coffin. **5.** Light racing-boat. **6.** Hollow metal or paper case to contain explosives for fireworks, cartridges, etc.; explosive projectile or bomb for use in big gun or mortar, whence **~'PROOF²** a.; *cartridge. **7.** Handguard of sword. **8.** Lyre (poet.). **9.** ‖ (At schools) intermediate form. **10.** Outward show, mere semblance. **11.** (Short for) ~-jacket. **12.** *~'back* (naut. sl.), old sailor; *~-bark*, kinds of hickory; *~-bit*, gouge-shaped boring-bit; ~ *button*, made of two metal discs enclosed in cloth etc.; *~'fish*, aquatic ~ed mollusc (oyster etc.) or crustacean (crab, shrimp, etc.); *~-heap* or *-mound*, kitchen MIDDEN; *~-jacket*, army officer's undress jacket reaching only to waist behind; *~-lime*, fine quality produced by burning sea-~s; *~-marble*, kinds containing fossil ~s; *~-shock*, disorganization of mental faculties, power of speech, etc., resulting from exposure to bombardment & other war strains; *~-work*, ornamentation of ~s cemented on wood etc. Hence (-)~ED² (-ld), ~ᴸLESS, ~'Y², aa. [OE *sci(e)ll*, MDu., MLG *schelle*, ON *skel*, Goth. *skalja* f. Gmc *skaljō* f. *skal-* SCALE¹·², SHALE]

shĕll², v.t. & i. **1.** Take out of shell,

remove shell or pod from, (~ *peas*). **2.** Provide, cover, or pave, with shell(s). **3.** Bombard (town etc.), fire at (troops), with shells, whence **~'ING¹**(1) n. **4.** (Of metal etc.) come *off* in scales. **5.** ~ *out* (sl.), pay up (t. & i.), hand over required sum; *~-out*, n., the game of pyramids played by three or more persons. [f. prec.]

shellăc', n., & v.t. (~*king*, ~*ked*). **1.** LAC¹ melted into thin plates, used for making varnish. **2.** v.t. Varnish with ~. [transl. F *laque en écailles* LAC in thin plates]

shĕl'ta, n. Ancient hybrid cant language of Irish gipsies and pipers, Irish and Welsh travelling tinkers, etc. (largely BACK¹-slang). [orig. unkn.]

shĕl'ter¹, n. Thing serving as shield or barrier against attack, danger, heat, wind, etc. (ANDERSON, MORRISON, ~); screen or cabin built to keep off wind & rain (*cabman's* ~); place of safety or immunity; shielded condition (*find, take,* ~). Hence ~LESS a. [16th c., of obsc. orig.; perh. f. *sheld* SHIELD + -TURE, after *jointure*]

shĕl'ter², v.t. & i. Act or serve as shelter to, protect, conceal, harbour, defend *from* blame, screen, shield; ~ one*self under, beneath, behind,* etc., use the protection afforded by; take shelter *under, in, from*; ‖ *~ed trades*, those not exposed to foreign competition, e.g. building & inland transport. [f. prec.]

‖ **shĕl'tÿ, -tie,** n. (Sc.). Shetland pony. [prob. repr. ON *Hjalti* Shetlander]

shĕlve¹, v.t. Put on shelf (books etc.), (fig.) abandon or defer consideration of (plan etc.), cease to employ (person); fit (cupboard etc.) with shelves, whence **shĕl'vING¹**(3) n. [f. *shelves* pl. of SHELF]

shĕlve², v.i. Slope gently. [16th c., of obsc. orig.; cf. WFris. *skelf* oblique]

shelves. See SHELF.

Shema' (-ah), n. The *Hear, O Israel,* Jews' confession of faith. [the initial wd, Heb. = hear]

shĕmŏz'zle, n. (sl.). Rumpus, brawl, muddle. [Yiddish]

*shĕnăn'igan, n. (colloq.). Nonsense, trickery.

She'ŏl, n. Hebrew Hades, place of the dead, the grave. [Heb.]

shĕp'herd (-perd), n., & v.t. **1.** Man who tends sheep at pasture, pastor (lit., & fig. esp. of minister in relation to his flock; *the good S~*, Christ); ~*'s crook*, staff with hook at one end used by ~s; ~*'s needle,* white-flowered common weed; ~*'s pie,* minced meat baked under mashed potatoes; ~*'s plaid*, small black & white check pattern in cloth; ~*'s purse*, white-flowered cornfield weed; hence ~ESS¹ (-per-) n. **2.** v.t. Tend (sheep, also fig.) as ~, marshal or conduct, or drive (crowd etc.) like sheep. [OE *scēaphirde* (SHEEP, HERD²)]

Shĕ'raton, n. Severe 18th-c. style of

furniture (often attrib., as ~ *chairs*). [T. ~ maker & designer (d. 1806)]

sherb'et, n. Eastern cooling drink of diluted fruit-juices (in pop. Engl. use, made effervescent). [Turk. & Pers., f. Arab. *shariba* to drink]

sherd. See SHARD.

sherif' (-ēf), -eef, n. Descendant of Mohammed through Fatima, entitled to wear green turban or veil; chief magistrate of Mecca. [f. Arab. *sharif* noble]

she'riff, n. ‖ Chief officer of crown in county or shire, charged with the keeping of the peace, administering justice under direction of the courts, executing writs by deputy, presiding over elections, etc.; (in Scotland) chief judge of county or district; *elective officer responsible for keeping the peace in his county. [OE *scīr-gerēfa* (SHIRE, REEVE[1])]

she'riffalty, she'riffdom, she'riffhŏŏd, she'riffship, nn. Shrievalty, office of sheriff. [-*alty* after *shrievalty*; -DOM, -HOOD, -SHIP]

Shĕr'pa, n. One of a Himalayan people living on the borders of Nepal and Tibet. [native]

she'rrў, n. White wine from Jeres in Southern Spain (*brown* ~, dark varieties); ~-*glass*, wineglass containing about four table-spoons; ~ COBBLER. [16th c. *sherris* f. Sp. (*vino de*) *Xeres* (now *Jerez de la Frontera*); cf. CHERRY]

Shĕt'land, n. Group of islands NNE of Scotland (~ *lace*, openwork woollen trimming; ~ *pony*, small hardy breed; ~ *wool*, fine kind).

shew. See SHOW[1]; ~*bread*, see SHOW[1].

Shi'ah, Shi'īte, (shē-), nn. Member of the Mohammedan sect (cf. *Sunni*, see SUN-NAH) that regards Ali as first imam or successor of Mohammed & rejects first three Sunni Caliphs. [Arab., = sect]

shibb'olĕth, n. Test word or principle or behaviour or opinion, the use of or inability to use which betrays one's party, nationality, etc. (see *Judg.* xii. 6); old-fashioned & generally abandoned doctrine once held essential. [Heb.]

shield, n., & v.t. 1. Variously shaped & sized detached piece of armour made of leather, wood, or metal, for wearing on left arm to receive thrust or stroke, esp. (cf. *buckler*, *target*) one of elongated form large enough to cover most of body (*the other side of the* ~, the aspect of a question etc. that is less obvious, or that is not the one lately presented); protective plate or screen in machinery etc.; person or thing that protects one; ~like part in animal or plant; (her.) drawing etc. of ~ used for displaying person's coat of arms; ~-*fern*, common handsome fern with ~-shaped covers to fruit-dots; ~-*hand* (arch.), left hand; hence ~LESS a. 2. v.t. Protect, screen, esp. from censure or punishment (often with implication of illegitimate concealment of facts). [OE

sceld, OS, OHG *scild*, ON *skjǫldr*, Goth. *skildus* f. Gmc *skelduz*]

‖ **shiel'ing,** ·n. (Sc.). Grazing-ground for cattle; cottage with earth floor; roughly constructed hut for shepherds or sportsmen; sheep-shelter. [f. Sc. *shiel* hut, of obsc. orig., +-ING[1]]

shi'er, -est. See SHY[1].

shift[1], v.t. & i. 1. Change or move (t. & i.) from one position to another, substitute one specimen of for another, undergo such substitution, change form or character, (~ one's *ground*, take up new position in argument etc.; ~ one's *lodging*; ~ *load into other hand*; ~ *the scene*, *the scene* ~*s*, in theatre, novel, etc.; ‖ ~ one's *shirt* etc., arch., change it; *cargo* ~*ed*, got shaken out of place; often ~ *about*; ~ *off* responsibility etc., get rid of, transfer to another; *wind* ~*s round to the E*). 2. Use expedients, take whatever course is available, contrive to do something, manage or get along or make a livelihood, (*must* ~ *as I can, for himself*). 3. Equivocate, practise evasion, (rare; ~*s & prevaricates*). [OE *sciftan* arrange, divide, etc., = MLG *schiften*, ON *skipta* f. Gmc *skiftjan*]

shift[2], n. 1. Change of place or character, substitution of one thing for another, vicissitude, rotation, (rare; *the* ~*s & changes of life*; ~ *of crops*, rotation). 2. Relay of workmen, time for which it works. 3. New device, expedient, resource, whence ~LESS a., ~'lĕssLY[2] adv., ~'lĕssNESS n. 4. Dodge, trick, artifice, piece of evasion or equivocation, whence ~'Y[2] a. (~*y eyes*, deceitful), ~'ilY[2] adv., ~'iNESS n. 5. *Make* ~ or *a* ~, manage or contrive (*to do*, or abs.), get along somehow (*must make* ~ *without it*). 6. (arch.). Chemise. 7. Arrangement by which joints of successive tiers in brickwork etc. do not coincide. [ME *schift*, f. prec.; cf. ON *skipti*]

Shiite. See SHIAH.

shikar', n. (Anglo-Ind.). Hunting. [Hind.]

shikar'ee (-rī), -ri, **shĕkă'rrў,** n. (Anglo-Ind.). Hunter. Hund. (-*i*), f. prec.]

shille'lagh (-āla), -ālah, n. Irish cudgel of blackthorn or oak. [*Shillelagh* in Ireland]

‖ **shill'ing,** n. (abbr. *s.*, as 3*s.*). British silver coin & money of account=1/20 of pound or twelve pence (1/6, a ~ & sixpence; £1 1*s.* 1*d.*; *take King's* or *Queen's* ~, enlist as soldier, w. ref. to now obs. method of recruiting; *cut off* one's heir etc. *with a* ~, leave one's property to others; ~*s'*-WORTH[1]). [OE, OS, OHG *scilling*, ON *skillingr*, Goth. *skilliggs* f. Gmc *skillingaz*]

shill'ў-shăllў, n., a., & v.i. 1. Inability to make up one's mind, indecision, vacillation. 2. adj. Vacillating. 3. v.i. Vacillate, be undecided, hesitate to act or choose one's course. [orig. *shill I, shall I*; cf. *dilly-dally*]

shily. See SHY[1].

shim, n., & v.t. (-mm-). Thin slip or wedge used in machinery etc. to make parts fit; (vb) fit or fill up thus. [orig. unkn.]

shimm'er, v.i., & n. (Shine with) tremulous or faint diffused light. [OE *scymrian*, MDu. *schēmeren*, G *schimmern*; rel. to obs. *shim*, OE *scimian* shine]

shimm'ȳ[1], n. (Colloq., nursery, etc., for) CHEMISE.

*****shimm'ȳ**[2], n., & v.i. **1.** Kind of fox-trot accompanied by tremulous motions of body; vibration of (front) wheels of car. **2.** v.i. Dance a ~; vibrate. [orig. unkn.]

shin, n., & v.i. & t. (-nn-). **1.** Front of leg below knee (~-*bone*, tibia; ~ *of beef*, ox's shank); ~-*guard*, worn at football. **2.** vb. Climb *up* (tree, wall, ladder, etc.; or with *up* adv.); kick ~s of, hack. [OE *scinu*, MDu. *schēne*, OHG *scina*]

shin'dȳ, n. Brawl, disturbance, row, noise, (often KICK[2] *up* a ~). [perh. alt. f. SHINTY]

shine[1], v.i. & t. (*shōne*). Emit or reflect light, be bright, glow, (lit. & fig.; *face shone with soap* or *with gratitude* etc.); be brilliant, be a luminary, excel, in some respect or sphere (*does not ~ in conversation, society; is a shining example*); (colloq.) make bright, polish, (boots, fireplace, brass, etc.). [OE (OS, OHG) *scinan*, ON *skina*, Goth. *skeinan* f. Gmc *skinan* f. *ski-*]

shine[2], n. Light, brightness, (chiefly colloq.; *rain or* ~, whatever the weather; *put a good ~ on* boots etc.; *take the ~ out of*, impair brilliance or newness of, also throw into the shade by surpassing); (sl.) disturbance, shindy, sensation; *take a ~ to* (sl.), take a fancy for. [f. prec.]

shin'er, n. (sl.). A coin, esp. sovereign, (pl.) money. [SHINE[1], -ER[1]]

shingle[1] (shĭng'gl), n., & v.t. **1.** Rectangular slip of wood used like roof-tile on roofs, spires, etc.; *small signboard*; ~d hair, this style of hairdressing. **2.** v.t. Roof with ~s; cut (hair of head) so that all ends are exposed like roof-~s, cut hair of (head, person) thus. [ME, app. f. L *scindula*, earlier *scandula*]

shingle[2] (shĭng'gl), n. Small rounded pebbles lying on sea-shore. Hence **shing'lȳ**[2] (-ngg-) a. [16th c. *chingle* (cf. SHIVER[1]), of obsc. orig.; perh. imit.]

shingles (shĭng'glz), n. pl. Acute skin-inflammation occurring along nerve-tracks. [ME, f. med. L *cingulus* f. L *cingulum* girdle (*cingere* gird)]

*****shinn'ȳ**[1], v.i. (colloq.). Shin tree etc., usu. *up*. [SHIN]

Shin'tō, n. Japanese religion partly ousted by Buddhism. Hence ~ISM, ~IST, nn. [f. Chin. *shin tao* way of the gods]

shin'tȳ, **shinn'ȳ**[2], n. Variation of hockey played in Scotland and N. England; stick or ball used in it. [17th c. *shinny*, app. f. the cry used in the game *shin ye*, *shin you*, of unkn. orig.]

shin'|ȳ, a. Glistening, polished, rubbed bright, (~*y hat*, *boots*, etc.; ~*y coat*, *seams*, with nap worn off). Hence ~INESS n. [-Y[2]]

ship[1], n. (regarded as fem., w. pron. *she*, *her*). **1.** Vessel with bowsprit & three, four, or five square-rigged masts (cf. BARQUE, BRIG, SCHOONER, SLOOP); any sea-going vessel of considerable size (BATTLE[1]-~, ~ *of the* LINE[2], MERCHANT-~, SAIL[2]*ing*-~, WAR[1]~; *sister* ~, built on same plan as another; ~ *of the desert*, camel; ABOUT[2]~; PUMP[3]-~;*take* ~, embark; *on* BOARD[1] ~; *when my* etc. ~ *comes home*, when I etc. make my etc. fortune); (sl.) boat, esp. racing-boat; *aircraft*; *on* ~*board*, *on* board ~. **2.** ~('s) *biscuit*, hard coarse kind made for keeping used on board ~; ~-*breaker*, contractor who breaks up old ~s; ~-*broker*, agent in buying and selling and insuring ~s; ~'*builder*, ~'*building*; ~-*canal*, for conveying ~s inland; ~-*CHANDLER(y)*; ~-*fever*, typhus; ~'*load*, quantity of something forming whole cargo; ~'*mate*, person belonging to or sailing on same ~ as another, esp. fellow sailor; ~-*money* (hist.), impost for providing ~s for navy, revival of which by Charles I was a cause of Great Rebellion; ~'*owner*, person owning (shares in) ~(s); ~-*railway*, for transportation of ~s overland from water to water; ~-*rigged*, as ~ in first sense; ~'*s articles*, terms on which seamen take service on her; ~'s COMPANY[1]; ‖ ~'s CORPORAL[3]; ~'*shape* adv. or pred. a., in good order (& see BRISTOL); ~'*s husband*, agent appointed by the owners to see that a ~ in port is well found in all respects; ~'*s papers*, documents establishing ownership, nationality, nature of cargo, etc., of ~; ~-*way*, inclined structure on which ~ is built & down which it slides to be launched; ~-*worm*, mollusc boring into ~ timbers; ~'*wreck* n., destruction of ~ by storm, foundering, stranding, striking rock, etc., (fig.) ruin (*make* ~*wreck*, be ruined; *make* or *suffer* ~*wreck of* one's *hopes* etc.); ~'*wreck* v.t. & i., inflict ~wreck lit. or fig. on (person, hopes, etc., rarely ~), suffer ~wreck; ~'*wright*, ~-*builder*; ~'*yard*, ~-building establishment. Hence ~'LESS a. [OE *scip*, OHG *scif*, OS, ON, Goth. *skip*; ult. orig. unkn.]

ship[2], v.t. & i. (-pp-). Put, take, or send away (goods, passengers, sailors) on board ship; (commerc.) deliver (goods) to forwarding agent for conveyance by land or water; step (mast), fix (rudder etc.), in its place on ship (~ *oars*, take from rowlocks & lay inside boat); (of ship or boat) ~ *a sea*, be flooded by wave; take ship, embark, (of sailor) take service on ship. [OE *scipian* f. prec.]

-ship, suf. f. OE *-scipe* (cogn. w. (M)Du. *-schap*, OHG *-scaf*, (G *-schaft*), ON *-skapr*) f. Gmc *skap-* SHAPE[1], forming abstract nn. on adjj. as *hard*~, *wor*~ (*worth* adj.),

& on nn. as *lord~, friend~, scholar~, apprentice~*; in the latter use it is a living suf.; meaning, (1) being so-&-so, status, office, honour, (2) tenure of office, (3) skill in certain capacity. *Landscape* also contains the suf.

ship′ment, n. Putting of goods etc. on ship; amount shipped, consignment. [SHIP², -MENT]

‖ **shipp′en, -on,** n. (chiefly dial.). Cowhouse, cattleshed. [OE *scypen* f. Gmc **skup-* (see SHOP)+-EN²; cf. MLG (G) *schuppen*]

shipp′er, n. Merchant etc. who sends or gets goods by ship. [-ER¹]

shipp′ing, n. In vbl senses; also: ships, esp. the ships of a country, port, etc.; *~-agent,* person acting for ship or line of ships at a port etc.; *~-articles,* agreement between captain & seamen as to wages etc.; *~-bill,* manifest of goods shipped; ‖ *~-master,* official in whose presence *~-articles* are signed, paying off is done, etc.; *~-office, ~-agent's* or *~-master's.* [-ING¹]

‖ **shire** (*as suf. pr.* -sher), n. County (chiefly now as suf. in names of certain counties & districts, as *Hamp~, Hallam~,* with some of which it is omissible, as *Devon~* or *Devon,* & in pl. *the ~s,* band of counties stretching NE from Hamp~ & Devon~ ending in *~,* also loose term for midland counties, & for the hunting district including Leics. & Rutland & Northants.); *~-bred horse,~-horse,* largest breed of draught horse raised esp. in Lincoln~ & Cambridge~; KNIGHT *of the ~.* [OE *scir,* OHG *scira* care, official charge; orig. unkn.]

shirk, v.t., & n. 1. Avoid meanly, get out of, shrink selfishly from, (duty, responsibility, fighting, etc.; also abs.); hence *~′ER¹* n. 2. n. *~er.* [f. obs. *shirk* n. sponger, sharper, perh. f. G *schurke*]

****shirr(r),** n., & v.t. 1. Elastic webbing; elastic thread woven into fabric; gathered trimming, gathering in costumery. 2. v.t. Gather (material) with parallel threads run through; hence **shir′ring¹** n. [orig. unkn.]

shirt, n. Man's sleeved under-garment worn under cloth clothes, extending from neck to thighs, usu. visible at collar & wristbands, & made of linen, cotton, flannel, or silk (NIGHT-~; *in* one's *~-sleeves,* without coat; *near is my ~, but nearer is my skin,* self is the first consideration; *keep* one's *~ on,* sl., keep one's temper; *get* one's *~ off,* sl., make him angry; *put* one's *~ on, upon,* sl., bet all one has upon; *give* one *a wet ~,* work him till he sweats); woman's blouse with stiff collar & cuffs; *~-front,* breast of *~,* usu. stiffened & starched (*~-front wicket,* absolutely true & smooth cricket pitch), also dicky. Hence *~ED², ~′LESS,* aa., *~′ING¹(3)* n., *~′Y²* a. (sl.), in a rage, annoyed. [OE *scyrte,* corresp. to ON

skyrta (whence SKIRT) f. Gmc **skurtjon* prob. f. **skurt-* SHORT]

shit, v.i., & n. (vulg.). 1. Evacuate bowels. 2. n. Ordure (& as term of abuse). [OE **scitan,* MLG *schiten,* OHG *scizan,* ON *skita* f. Gmc **skit-*]

shiv′er¹, v.i., & n. 1. Experience or show quick slight vibrating movement (such as is) caused by sensation of cold, tremble with cold; *~ing-fit,* as in ague; hence *~ingLY²* adv. 2. n. Momentary *~ing* movement (often pl., as *gives me the ~s*), whence *~Y²* a. [ME *chivere,* orig. obsc.]

shiv′er², n. (usu. pl.), & v.t. & i. 1. (One of) the many small pieces into which thing is shattered by blow or fall. 2. vb. Break (t. & i.) into *~s* (*~ my timbers,* reputed naut. imprecation). [ME *scifre,* cogn. w. OHG *scivero* splinter (G *schiefer(stein)* slate) f. Gmc **skif* to split; cf. dial. *shive* slice]

shoal¹, a., n., & v.i. 1. Shallow, not deep, (only lit., of water). 2. n. Shallow place, submerged sandbank esp. one that shows at low water, (fig., usu. pl.) hidden danger(s) or impediment(s), whence *~′Y²* a., *~′INESS* n. 3. v.i. Get shallower. [OE *sceald* f. **skaldaz,* rel. to SHALLOW]

shoal², n., & v.i. 1. Multitude, crowd, great number, esp. of fish swimming in company (also SCHOOL²), (*~s of people*; *gets letters in ~s*). 2. v.i. (Of fish) form *~s.* [16th c., perh. re-adoption of MDu. *schole* SCHOOL²]

shock¹, n. 1. Violent collision, concussion, or impact (*three ~s of earthquake were felt*; *clashed with a mighty ~*; *~ tactics,* (orig.) use of cavalry to charge in masses, (fig.) sudden violent action; *~-troops,* troops specially trained for the offensive). 2. Sudden & disturbing physical or mental impression (*news came upon me with a ~, was a great ~*; *electric ~,* stimulation of nerves by passage of current through body); (path.) state of prostration following overstimulation of nerves by sudden pain as of wound etc. or violent emotion (*died of ~*; *the ~ is more dangerous than the loss of blood*); *~ therapy, treatment,* method of treating certain mental disorders by means of an electrical shock or powerful drug. 3. Injury inflicted on credit, stability, etc., great disturbance of organization or system. 4. *~-brigade, -workers,* (in U.S.S.R.) body of workers selected or volunteering for some specially arduous task; *~ stall,* excessive strain produced by air resistance on aircraft when speed approximates to that of sound. [app. f. F *choc* f. *choquer* (foll.)]

shock², v.t. & i. Affect with indignation, sorrow, disgust, or horror, appear improper or outrageous or scandalous to (*was ~ed at, by, to hear,* etc.), whence *~′ING²* a. & adv. (*~ing bad* etc. colloq.), *~′ingLY²* adv., *~′ingNESS* n.; collide violently (poet.). [f. F *choquer,* of obsc. orig.]

shŏck³, n., & v.t. **1.** Group of usu. twelve corn-sheaves stood up close together in field. **2.** v.t. Arrange (corn) in ~s. [ME, = OS *scok*, MDu., MLG *schok* shock of corn, sixty; cf. MHG *schoc* heap, sixty]

shŏck⁴, n. Unkempt or shaggy mass of hair; ~ *head*, rough head of hair, whence ~-headED² a. [cf. obs. 17th c. *shock(-dog)*, (16th c. *shough*) shaggy-haired poodle]

‖ shŏck′er, n. (colloq.). Very bad specimen of anything; sensational cheap novel. [-ER¹]

shod. See SHOE².

shŏdd′y, n. & a. **1.** Fibre made from old cloth etc. shredded; inferior cloth made partly of such fibre; anything of worse quality than it claims or seems to have. **2.** adj. Counterfeit, pretentious, trashy. [19th c., of unkn. orig.]

shoe¹ (-ōō), n. **1.** Outer foot-covering not reaching above ankle (*that's another pair of ~s*, another matter; *dead men's ~s*, property or position as looked forward to by expectant successor; *be in person's ~s*, in his plight; *die in one's ~s*, by violence, esp. hanging; *where the ~ pinches*, hardships of one's own lot; *put the ~ on the right foot*, apportion blame etc. truly). **2.** Metal rim nailed to hoof of horse etc. **3.** Thing like ~ in shape or use, e.g. wheel-drag, socket, ferrule, mast-step. **4.** ~s *& stockings*, bird's-foot trefoil; ‖ ~'*black*, boy or man who blacks ~s of passers-by; ~'*buckle*, for fastening ~ over instep (now usu. worn only as ornament); ~'*horn*, instrument of horn, metal, etc., for helping ~ on to foot; ~'*lace*, -*string*, for lacing up ~; ~-*latchet* (bibl.), fastening of ~; ~'*leather*, leather for ~s, ~s (*as good a man as ever trod ~-leather*, lived); ~'*-lift*, = ~*horn*; ~'*maker*, maker of boots & ~s; ~'*string*, *(also, colloq.) a small or inadequate amount of money, (attrib.) precarious, just adequate, as *a ~-string majority*. Hence ~'LESS (-ōōl-) a. [OE (OS) *scōh*, OHG *scuoh*, ON *skór*, Goth. *skohs* f. Gmc *skōh(w)az*]

shoe² (-ōō), v.t. (*shŏd*; part. ~*ing*). Fit with shoe(s) (esp. with *horse* etc. as obj., or in p.p. as *neatly shod (feet)*, *pole shod with iron*). [OE *scōgan*, f. prec.]

shŏg′un (-ōōn), n. (hist.). Japanese hereditary commander-in-chief & virtual ruler for some centuries until the office was abolished 1868. Hence ~ATE¹ n. [Jap., = general]

shone. See SHINE¹.

shoō, int., & v.i. & t. (Utter) sound used to frighten birds away; drive *away* thus. [imit.]

shook¹. See SHAKE¹.

shook², n., & v.t. **1.** Set of staves & headings for cask ready for putting together. **2.** v.t. Pack in ~s. [prob. p.p. of *shake*; *shaken cask* is used in same sense]

shoot¹, v.i. & t. (*shŏt*). **1.** Come vigorously or swiftly *out*, *forth*, *along*, *up*, etc., or abs., sprout, dart, (*boat shot out from the creek*; ~*ing* STAR¹; *flash* ~s *across sky*; ~ *ahead*, come quickly to front of competitors etc.; *buds are* ~*ing*; *tree* ~s, puts forth buds; *fountain*, *flame*, ~s *up*; *prices shot up*, rose suddenly; *cricket-ball* ~s, darts along ground when it touches, instead of bouncing; *child is* ~*ing up*, growing tall; *pain* ~s *through nerves* etc.; *corn*, *tooth*, ~s, inflicts intermittent pain). **2.** Project abruptly *out* (*mountain-spur*, *cape*, ~s *out*). **3.** Send out, discharge, propel, emit, violently or swiftly (~ *rubbish* etc., let it slide from cart or receptacle; *bow*, *gun*, ~s *arrow*, *shell*; *passengers were shot out of coach*; *sun* ~s *its rays*; ~ *out one's lips*, bibl., protrude in scorn; ~ *one's linen*, display wristbands by shaking them down; ~ *the cat*, sl., vomit; ~ *fishing-net*, extend it across river etc.; ~ *bolt* of door, send it home; *tree* ~s *out branches*; *~! (sl.), say what you have to say. **4.** Discharge (bullet etc.) from gun etc., cause (bow, gun, etc.) to discharge missile, discharge gun etc., make use well etc. of gun etc., kill or wound (person, animal) with missile from gun etc., hunt game etc. habitually or on one occasion with gun, ~ *the game over estate etc.*, ~ *game on (estate etc.)*, (*of gun etc.*) go off, send missile *straight* etc., (*fool's* BOLT¹ *is soon shot*; *I'll be shot if* —, form of negative asseveration; *can army or sportsman, does gun*, ~ *straight?*; *was shot for a day*; ~ *a match*, engage in ~*ing-match*; *will* ~ *the coverts tomorrow*; *neither rides nor* ~s; *was out* ~*ing*; *have shot away all our ammunition*). **5.** (cinemat.). Photograph. **6.** (assoc. footb., hockey, etc.). Take a shot at goal. **7.** ~ *up*, terrorize (village, district) with punitive rifle-shooting, firing of houses, etc.; ~ *a line* (sl.), tell a tall story; ~ *the sun*, take its altitude with the sextant at noon; ‖ ~ *the moon* (sl.), remove one's goods by night to avoid paying rent. **8.** Be, have one's boat, swept swiftly under or down (bridge, rapid fall; ~ *Niagara*, attempt desperate enterprise). **9.** (joinery). Plane (edge of board) accurately (hence *shot edges*). **10.** p.p. (Of coloured material) so woven etc. as to show different colours at different angles (*shot silk*; *crimson shot with maize-colour*). **11.** ‖ ~*ing-box*, sportsman's lodge for use in ~*ing-season*; ~*ing-brake*, ESTATE car; ~*ing-coat*, -*jacket*, -*boots*, of patterns useful in ~*ing game*; ~*ing-iron* (sl.), fire-arm; ~*ing-range*, ground with butts for rifle practice; ~*ing-stick*, walking-stick which may be adapted to form a seat; ~*ing war*, one in which there is ~*ing* (opp. *cold war* or WAR¹ *of nerves*). Hence ~'ABLE a. [OE *scēotan*, OS *skietan*, OHG *sciozzan*, ON *skjóta* f. Gmc *skeut-*, *skaut-*, *skut-*, cf. SHEET¹, SHOT¹, SHUT]

shoot², n. Young branch or sucker; rapid in stream; inclined plane down which water etc. may flow or things slide, chute;

shooting party or expedition or practice or (= SHOOTING) land. [f. prec.]

shōōt′er, n. In vbl senses; esp.: ball that shoots at cricket; (in comb.) shooting-implement (PEA-~; six etc. -~, revolver firing six etc. shots). [ME, -ER¹]

shōōt′ing, n. In vbl senses (for compounds see SHOOT¹); esp.: right of ~ over particular land; estate etc. rented to shoot over. [-ING¹]

shŏp, n., & v.i. & t. (-pp-). **1.** Building, room, etc., for retail sale of some commodity (chemist's, butcher's, fruit-, ~; come to the wrong ~, transf., apply to wrong person etc.), or in which manufacture or repairing is done (engineering-~; fitting, pattern, etc., -~, departments of manufactory). **2.** ‖(sl.). Institution, establishment, etc., (e.g. one's school, university, etc.; esp. formerly of R.M.A., Woolwich; the other ~, rival institution). **3.** One's profession, trade, or business, things connected with it, or talk about it, (CLOSE³d ~; shut up ~, cease doing something; talk ~; sink the ~, refrain from talking ~, also conceal one's occupation; SMELL of the ~), whence ~p′y² a. **4.** All over the ~ (sl.), in disorder, in every direction, wildly, (have looked for it all over the ~; my books are all over the ~; hitting, steering, etc., all over the ~). **5.** ~-bell, on door to give notice of customer's entrance; ~-boy, -girl, assistants in ~; ~′keeper, owner of ~ (nation of ~-keepers, the English); ~-lifter, pretended customer who steals goods in ~; ~′man ~keeper or his assistant; ~-soiled, = ~-worn; ‖~-steward, person elected by his fellow workmen in a factory or branch of it as their spokesman on conditions of work etc.; ‖~′walker, attendant in large ~ who directs customers; ~ window, window of ~ used for display of wares (has everything in the ~ window, transf., is superficial); ~-worn, soiled or faded by being shown in ~. **6.** vb. Go to ~(s) to make purchases (*or inspect goods), whence ~p′ING¹ n.; (sl.) imprison, (of informer) cause (accomplice) to be imprisoned. [ME, f. OE sceoppa (cf. OHG scopf) f. Gmc *skuppan-, cf. SHIPPEN]

shore¹, n. Land that skirts sea or large body of water (in ~, on the shore near or nearer to ~); (law) land between ordinary high & low water marks. Hence ~′LESS (-ōrl-) a., ~′WARD (-ōrw-) a. & adv. [ME schore f. MDu., MLG schore, prob. f. root of SHEAR¹]

shore², n., & v.t. **1.** Prop, beam set obliquely against ship, wall, tree, etc., as support. **2.** v.t. Support, hold up, with ~(s). Hence shōr′ING¹(3) n. [ME schore, f. MDu., MLG schōre, prop, of unkn. orig.; cf. syn. ON skortha]

shore³, shorn. See SHEAR¹.

shŏrt, a., adv., n., & v.t. **1.** Measuring little from end to end in space or time, soon traversed or finished, (a ~ way off;

a ~ time ago; ~ story, of the character of a novel but less length; ~ CUT¹; ~ circuit, electric circuit made through a small resistance, esp. one acting as a shunt to one of greater resistance, form of this due to a fault that allows current's escape to earth; ~-circuit v.t., establish ~ circuit in, cut off current from thus; ~ DIVISION; ~ drink, cocktail etc. esp. before a meal; ~er CATECHISM; ~ rib, = false RIB; ~ SHRIFT; ~ WHIST³; a ~ sea, ~ broken waves; make ~ work of, dispose of or destroy or consume quickly; he, his joy etc., had but a ~ life, whence ~-liveD² a.; ~ temper, self-control that is soon or easily lost, whence ~-temperED² a.; ~ waist in dress, made high up, whence ~-waistED² a.; ~ wind, easily exhausted breathing-power, inability to run long or fig. to talk or write at any length, whence ~-windED² a., ~-wind′edNESS n.; ~ clothes or coats, dress of child too old for long-clothes, whence ~ᶜcoat v.t.). **2.** Of small stature, not tall, (usu. of human beings, or of upright things, as chimney, tower, tree). **3.** Not far-reaching, acting near at hand, deficient, scanty, in want of, below the degree of, abruptly finished, (~ sight, not seeing clearly at distance or fig. into the future, whence ~-sightED² a., ~-sight′edLY² adv., ~-sight′edNESS n.; at ~ range; take ~ views, consider the present only; ~ date, early date for maturing of bill etc., whence ~-datED² a.; ~ bill, paper, etc., dated for early payment; ~ LEG, SLIP, in cricket; has a ~ memory; are ~ of hands, have not enough workmen, whence ~-handED² a.; ~ of breath, panting, ~-winded; ~ COMMONS; in ~ supply, scarce; ~ weight, less than it is represented to be; a ~ ten miles, mile, hour, etc., less or seeming less than that; cut ~, bring to end before natural time; come ~, disappoint expectations etc., fail of one's duty or proper development, whence ~ᶜcomING¹ n.; fall ~, be insufficient or inadequate; run ~, have or be too little, as our tea ran ~, we ran ~ of tea; an escape nothing ~ of marvellous). **4.** Concise, brief, curt, sullenly or snappishly reticent, (the LONG¹ & the ~ of it; in ~, to use few words, without circumlocution, to give the conclusion briefly; is called Bob for ~, by way of ~ name; was very ~ with me, uncivil). **5.** (phonet., pros.). (Of vowel or syllable) (prop.) having the less of the two recognized durations, (pop.) unstressed, (also, of vowel) having the one or an other sound, than that called LONG¹ (e.g. those in met, pill, but). **6.** (Of pastry, clay, etc.) friable, crumbling, not tenacious, (cf. COLD-SHORT). **7.** (St. Exch. etc.; of stocks, stockbroker, crops, etc.) sold, selling, etc., when the amount is not in hand in reliance on getting the deficit in time for delivery. **8.** Something ~, a drink of spirits etc.; ~′bread, ~′cake, brittle dry cake made

with flour & much butter & sugar; ~'*fall*,
deficit; ~'*hand*, methods of compendious
writing used for taking verbatim reports
of speeches etc., stenography; ~ *head*
(racing), distance of less than length of
horse's head (also ~-*head* v.t., beat by
this distance); ~'*horn*, name of ~-horned
breed of cattle; ~ *metre*, hymn stanza of
4 lines (6, 6, 8, 6 syllables); ~ *suit* (of
less than four cards); ~ *time*, condition
of working less than the regular number
of hours per day or days per week;
~ TON[1]; ~ *wave* (radio), having a wave-
·length of from 10 to 100 metres; hence
~'ISH[1] (2) a., ~'NESS n. **9.** adv. Abruptly,
before the natural or expected time, in ~
manner, (*look him up* ~, interrupted him;
stop ~, suddenly cease, not go on to the
end; *bring*, or *pull*, *up* ~, check or pause
abruptly; *be taken* ~, have sudden motion
of bowels; ~-*spoken*, given to brevity
of speech; *sell* ~, when one has not the
articles in hand, see the adj.); ~ *of*, except, putting out of the question, (*all aid
~ of war*; ~ *of committing suicide he does
his best to keep out of the way*). **10.** n. ~
syllable (LONG[1]s & ~s) or vowel; mark
indicating that vowel is ~, as ă; ~ *film*;
(colloq.) a ~ circuit; (colloq.) a ~ drink
esp. of spirits; (pl.) garment like trousers
cut ~ worn by athletes, boys, etc. **11.** v.t.
(colloq.). To ~-circuit. [OE *sc(e)ort*,
OHG *scurz*, f. Gmc **skurtaz*, perh. alt.
f. L *curtus* (whence OS, OHG *kurt*,
OHG(G) *kurz*); cf. SHIRT, SKIRT]

short'**age**, n. (Amount of) deficiency
(*there is no ~, a ~ of 100 tons*). [-AGE]
short'**en**, v.i. & t. Become or make
actually or apparently shorter or short,
curtail; reduce the amount of *sail* spread;
put (child) into short clothes. Hence
~ING[1](3) n., fat used for making pastry
crisp. [-EN[6]]
short'**ly**, adv. Before long, a short time
before or *after*; in few words, briefly;
curtly. [ME; -LY[2]]
shot[1], n. (pl. ~s, also ~ see below), & v.t.
(-tt-). **1.** Single missile for fire-arm or big
gun, non-explosive projectile, (usu. with
qualification or in comb., as *round*, *solid*,
CHAIN, GRAPE-, CASE[2]-, BUCK[1]-, ~; *chilled*
~, case-hardened for armour-piercing;
a ~ in the LOCKER); (pl. usu. ~) small lead
pellets of which a quantity is used for
single charge or cartridge esp. in sporting
guns, such pellets collectively, (~ *does* or
do well for cleaning decanters; *put three* ~
or ~s *of different sizes on the gut*; ~ *is
made in various ways*; *about a dozen n° 10
~ were extracted from his leg*). **2.** Discharge
of fire-arm or big gun (*several ~s were
fired*, *heard*, etc.); attempt to hit with
projectile or missile or fig. to make stroke
in game or guess or do something (*at each
~ he was nearer the bull's-eye*; *a beautiful
~ from cover-point took off the bails*; *a
lucky ~ at goal*; *like a ~*, willingly; *made
a bad ~*, guessed wrong; *am going to have

a good ~ at winning; *snap ~*, discharging
of rifle etc. with momentary aim, cf.
SNAP*shot*; *flying ~*, at bird on wing or
moving object; PARTHIAN, *random*, ~;
(·)~, range, reach, distance to or at which
thing will carry or act, as *bow*, *rifle*, *ear*
·~). **3.** Possessor of specified skill with
rifle, gun, pistol, etc. (*is a good, bad, crack
or first-class*, or *no*, ~). **4.** Dose of cocaine,
injection of morphine, etc.; (colloq.) dram
of spirits. **5.** Photograph taken with
cinematograph camera. **6.** ~-*firer*, one
who fires the ~ in blasting; ~-*gun*,
smooth-bore gun. for firing small ~ at
short range; ~-*tower*, in which ~ was
made from molten lead poured through
sieves at top & falling into water at
bottom; hence ~'PROOF[2] a. **7.** v.t. Load,
weight, etc.; with ~. [OE *sc(e)ot*, *gesc(e)ot*,
OHG *scoz*, ON *skot* f. Gmc **skut-* SHOOT[1]]
shot[2], p.p. of SHOOT[1].
shot[3], n. Reckoning, (one's share of) bill
at inn etc., (usu. *pay* one's ~). [ME, =
SHOT[1] (cf. OE *scēotan* SHOOT, pay, contribute); cf. SCOT[1]]
should. See SHALL.
shoul'**der** (shōl-), n., & v.t. & i. **1.** Part of
body at which arm or foreleg or wing is
attached, either lateral projection below
or behind neck, (also ~-*joint*) combination of end of upper arm with those of
collarbone & blade-bone, (pl.) upper part
of back, (pl.) body regarded as bearing
burdens, (of slaughtered animal) foreleg
with parts usu. kept with it in dismem-
bering, (HEAD[1] & ~s; *dislocate* one's ~;
~ *to* ~, with closed ranks or united effort;
has broad ~s, is strong, can bear much
weight or responsibility; *old head on
young* ~s, youthful wisdom, wise young
person; *put*, *set*, ~ *to wheel*, make effort;
straight from the ~, said of well-delivered
blow or telling invective; ~-*of-mutton
sail*, triangular fore-&-aft sail hoisted
abaft mast; COLD[1] ~; COLD[1]-~ v.t.; *lay
the blame*, *burden*, etc., *on the right* ~s).
2. Part of mountain, bottle, tool, etc.,
projecting like human ~. **3.** (mil.). Position of soldier who has ~ed arms (see vb).
4. ~-*belt*, baldric, bandolier, or other
band passing over one~ & under opposite
arm; ~-*blade*, either large flat bone of
upper back, scapula; ~-*brace*, contrivance for flattening round back of child
etc.; ~-*knot*, of ribbon or metal lace worn
on ~ by livery servant; ~-*pegged*, (of
horse) stiff in ~s; ~-*strap*, band from ~-
-tip in soldier's uniform, keeping ~-belts
in place & bearing name or number of
regiment etc., (also) one of two strips of
cloth suspending a garment from the
wearer's ~s; hence (·)~ED[2] (-erd) a. **5.** vb.
Push (t. & i.) with ~, jostle, make way
thus; take (burden lit. or fig.) on one's
~s; (mil.) ~ *arms*, hold rifle vertical
supported by right hand at lock (cf.
SLOPE v.). [OE *sculdor*, OFris. *skuldere*,
OHG *sculter(r)a*; orig. unkn.]

shout, v.i. & t., & n. **1.** Make loud articulate or inarticulate cry or vocal sound, speak loudly, (~*ed with laughter*; ~ *for joy*; ~ *at*, speak loudly to etc.; *the ~ing is over but the ~ing*, contest is virtually decided); say loudly, call out, express in loud tones, (~ *approbation*; ~*ed that the coast was clear*; ~*ed to* or *for me to come*; '*Go back*' *he* ~*ed*). **2.** n. Loud utterance or vocal sound from individual or company expressing joy, (dis)approval, defiance, etc., or calling attention (*my etc.* ~, sl., turn to order drink etc. for the company). [ME, formally corresp. to ON *skúta* SCOUT[2]; prob. f. root of SHOOT[1]]

shove (-ŭv), v.t. & i., & n. **1.** Push (t. & i.) vigorously, move (t.) along by hard or rough pushing; make one's way *along*, *past*, *through*, etc., by pushing, jostle (person); ~*-halfpenny*, modern gambling form of shoveboard; (colloq.) put somewhere (~ *it in the drawer*); ~ *off*, start from shore in boat. **2.** n. Push (*give one a* ~ *off*, help him to start); woody centre of flax-stem. [OE *scúfan*, MDu. *schúven*, OHG *scioban*, ON *skúfa*, Goth. *-skiuban* f. Gmc **skeubh-*, **skaubh-*, **skŭb-*]

sho'vel (-ŭv-), n., & v.t. (-ll-). **1.** Scooping implement for shifting coal, earth, etc., often in form of spade with sides of blade turned up; ~ *hat*, broad-brimmed as worn by Anglican dignitaries; ~*-head*, kinds of sturgeon & shark, also ~*-nose*; hence ~FUL(2) (shŭv'elfŏŏl) n. (pl. ~*fuls*). **2.** v.t. Shift (coal etc.) with or as with ~ (~ *food into one's mouth*, eat greedily). [OE *scofl*, MLG *schuffel*, cogn. w. OS, OHG *skúfla* (G *schaufel*), f. Gmc **skăbh-* (prec.)]

shovelboard (shŭv'elbŏrd), n. Game played (now esp. on ship's deck) by impelling discs (formerly coins) with hand or mace over marked surface. [earlier *shoveboard*, *-groat* (SHOVE)]

sho'veller (-ŭv-), n. In vbl senses; also, kind of duck with broad shovel-like beak. [-ER[1]]

show[1] (-ō), v.t. & i. (p.p. ~*n*, rarely ~*ed*; also spelt, now rarely, *shew*, *shewn*, *shewed*, w. pron. shō etc.). **1.** Let be seen, disclose, manifest, offer (thing, person *thing*, thing *to* person) for inspection, exhibit, produce, give (treatment, person treatment, treatment *to* person), reveal, (*clothes* ~ *signs of wear*; *an aperture* ~*s the inside*; ~*ed neither joy nor anger, that he was annoyed, how much he felt it*, etc.; ~ *oneself*, be seen in public; ~ *me, I was* ~*n, a specimen*; *has nothing to* ~ *for it*, no token of achievement etc.; ~ *your tickets, please*; *got prizes for all the dogs he* ~*ed*; ~ CAUSE[1]; ~ *favour*, *mercy*, *to*; ~*ed me kindness* or *unkindness*; ~ *fight*, not yield tamely; ~ *one's* COLOUR[1]*s*; ~ *one's hand* orig. in cards, let out one's designs; ~ *the hoof* or *cloven hoof*, see CLEAVE[1]; ~ *the white* FEATHER[1]; ~ *a* CLEAN[1] *pair of heels*; ~ *a leg*, get out of bed; ~ *thing the fire*, slightly heat it). **2.** Be visible

or noticeable, come into sight, appear in public, have some appearance, (*the blood* ~*s through her skin*; *stain will never* ~; *buds are just* ~*ing*; *her husband never* ~*s* (*up*) *at her at-homes*, colloq.; ~*s white, like a disc, from here*). **3.** Demonstrate, prove, expound, point out, cause (person) to understand (thing), (*has* ~*n the falsity of the tale, that it is false, how false it is, it to be false*; ~ *one the way*, by words, pointing, or going with or before him, also encourage by doing thing first; ~ *person how to write, what to do*, etc.; ~ *person the* DOOR; *it only* ~*s how little you know*; *on your own* ~*ing*, even according to your own admission or contention). **4.** Conduct (~*ed us round the house*; ~ *one out* or *in*, esp. open door for his exit or entrance). **5.** ~*-down*, (poker) laying down of cards with faces up, (fig.) final test, disclosure of achievements or possibilities; ~ *forth* (arch.), exhibit, expound; ~ *off*, (trans.) display to advantage, (intr.) try to make impression by exhibiting one's wealth or skill; ~ *up*, make or be conspicuous or clearly visible, expose (fraud, impostor), (colloq.) appear, be present; *shew'bread*, twelve loaves displayed in Jewish temple & renewed each sabbath; ~*-case*, glazed case for exhibiting goods, curiosities, etc.; ~*-room*, *-window*, in which wares are kept, hung up, for inspection; ~*-place*, that tourists etc. go to see. [OE *scēawian*, OS *skawon*, OHG *scouwōn* f. WG **skauwōjan* f. Gmc **skau-*, see SHEEN]

show[2] (-ō), n. **1.** Showing (*voted by* ~ *of hands*; DUMB[1] ~). **2.** Spectacle, exhibition, pageant, display, collection of things shown esp. for money to entertain, (*flower, horse*, etc., *-~*; || *Lord Mayor's* ~, procession of symbolic cars etc. in London; *a fine* ~ *of blossom*); (colloq.) any kind of public entertainment. **3.** Outward appearance, semblance, impression produced, parade, ostentation, pomp, display, (*pierce beneath the* ~*s of things*; *there is a* ~ *of reason in it*; *good enough in outward* ~; *did it for* ~; *is fond of* ~), whence ~'Y[2] (-ŏĭ) a., ~'ILY[2] adv., ~'INESS n. **4.** (sl.). Concern, undertaking, organization, (RUN[1] or BOSS[3] *the* ~; *give away the* ~, betray its inadequacy or pretentiousness; *good* ~!, well done!). **5.** (sl.). Opportunity of acting, defending oneself, etc. (*had no* ~ *at all*; *give him a fair* ~). **6.** (obstetr.). Discharge indicating approach of labour. **7.** ~'*boat* (orig. U.S.), (river) steamboat in which theatrical performances are given; ~'*girl*, actress whose role is decorative rather than histrionic; ~'*man*, proprietor or manager of menagerie or other such ~; ~'*manship*, the art of the ~*man*, (fig.) capacity for exhibiting one's wares or oneself to the best advantage. [ME, f. prec.]

show'er, n., & v.t. & i. **1.** Brief fall of rain, hail, sleet, or snow, or *of* arrows, bullets, dust, stones, etc. (also fig., as *a* ~ *of gifts, honours*; *letters come in* ~*s*); ~-*bath* (colloq. ~), in which water descends from above through perforated plate; hence ~Y² a., ~iNESS n. 2. vb. Discharge (water, missiles, etc.) in a ~, bestow (gifts etc. usu. *upon*); descend or come in a ~. [OE (= OS, OHG, ON) *scūr*, Goth. *skūra* f. Gmc **skūr-*, of unkn. orig.]

‖ **shräm**, v.t. (dial.; -mm-; usu. in p.p.). Benumb with or *with* cold. [cf. 15th c. (now dial.) *scram*, dial. *shrim* (OE *scrimman*) shrivel]

shrank. See SHRINK.

shräp'nel, n. Bullets or pieces of metal contained in shell timed to burst slightly short of objective & let them fly on in shower; part of fragmentation bomb etc. so scored as to break & scatter. [f. inventor H. *S*~ (d. 1842)]

shrĕd, n., & v.t. (~*ded*, arch. ~). 1. Scrap, fragment, rag, strip, torn or broken piece, small remains, least amount, (*tore it to* ~*s*; *without a* ~ *of clothing on him*; *not a* ~ *of evidence, reputation*, etc.; *tear* an argument etc. *to* ~*s*, completely refute it). 2. v.t. Tear or cut into ~. [OE *scrēade* (= OHG *scrōt*) piece cut off, *scrēadian* (= OHG *scrōtan*) f. Gmc **skraudh-*, (**skreudh-*, **skrūdh-*): see SHROUD, SCREED]

shrew (-ōō), n. 1. Scolding woman, whence ~'ISH¹ (-ōō-) a., ~'ishLY² adv.; ~'ishNESS n. 2. (Also ~-*mouse*) small long-snouted mammal, like mouse, feeding chiefly on insects. [OE *scrēawa* ~- -mouse, not found elsewhere in Gmc]

shrewd (-ōōd), a. (Of pain, cold, etc.) sharp, biting, (literary, esp. ~ *blow, knock, thrust, turn*); sagacious, sensible, discriminating, astute, judicious, (*can make a* ~ *guess*; *a* ~ *observer*; ~ *face* etc., sagacious-looking). Hence ~'LY² adv., ~'NESS n. [ME *shrewed* (prec., -ED², cf. *dogged, crabbed*)]

shriek, v.i. & t., & n. (Utter) shrill & usu. inarticulate cry of terror, pain, etc., screech, scream; laugh uncontrollably (usu. ~ *with laughter*); ~ *out*, say in shrill agonized tones. [16th c. parallel to *screak* (f. ON *skrækja*, imit.); cf. ME (now dial.) *shrike, scrike, scritch*, SCREECH]

shriev'altў, n. Sheriff's office or jurisdiction, tenure of this. [f. *shrieve*, obs. var. of SHERIFF, +-*alty* as in *admiralty* etc.]

shrift, n. (Arch.) confession to priest, confession & absolution, (now only in *short* ~, little time between condemnation & execution or punishment). [OE *scrift*, vbl n. f. SHRIVE; so OHG *scrift*, ON *skrift*]

shrike, n. Kinds of bird called also *butcher-bird* with strong hooked & toothed bill & habit of impaling its prey of small birds & insects on thorns. [app. repr. OE *scríc*, *scrēc* (imit., cf. SHRIEK) thrush or perh. any shrill-voiced bird]

shrill, a., & v.i. & t. 1. Piercing & high--pitched in sound; (fig.) importunate; hence **shril'LY²** (-l-lĭ) adv., ~'NESS n. 2. vb. (poet. or rhet.). (Of cry etc.) sound ~y; (of person etc.) utter, send *out*, (song, complaint, etc.) ~y. [ME, rel. to LG *schrell* of sharp tone or taste]

shrimp, n., & v.i. 1. Small aquatic (esp. marine) edible crustacean, grey-green when alive, pink when boiled; diminutive person. 2. v.i. Go catching ~s; hence ~'ER¹ n. [ME, prob. cogn. w. MHG (MG) *schrimpen* shrink up; cf. SHRAM]

shrine, n., & v.t. 1. Casket, esp. one holding sacred relics; tomb usu. sculptured or highly ornamented of saint etc.; altar or chapel of special associations; place hallowed by some memory. 2. v.t. (poet.). Enshrine. [OE *scrín*, OHG *scrini*, ON *skrin*, f. L *scrinium* case for books etc.]

shrink, v.i. & t. (*shrănk*; *shrŭnk* & rarely in vbl, commonly in adj., use *shrŭnken*), & n. 1. Become of less dimensions, grow smaller, whence ~'AGE(3) n.; recoil, retire from observation, (~ *into* oneself, become reserved), flinch *from*, whence ~'ingLY² adv.; be averse *from doing*; make smaller (esp. in pass.; *his face has a shrunken look*), make ~ (flannel etc., in order that it may not do so later; ~ *wheel-tire* etc. *on*, slip it on while expanded with heat & let it tighten as it cools), whence ~'ABLE a. . 2. n. (rare). ~ing (*how much must we allow for the* ~?). [OE *scrincan*, cf. Sw. *skrynka* to wrinkle]

shrive, v.t. (arch.; *shrōve*, *shrĭven*). Hear confession of, assign penance to, & absolve; (of penitent) submit one*self* to priest for this purpose. [OE *scrífan*, OS *skríban*, OHG *scríban*, ON *skrifa* f. L *scribere* write]

shriv'el, v.i. & t. (-ll-). Contract or wither (i. & t.) into wrinkled, folded, rolled-up, contorted, or dried-up state. [16th c., perh. of Scand. orig.; cf. Sw. dial. *skryfla* to wrinkle]

shröff, n., & v.t. 1. Banker or money--changer in the East; (Far East) native expert employed to detect base coin. 2. v.t. Examine (coin). [Anglo-Ind. corrupt. of Pers. *saraf*]

shroud, n., & v.t. 1. Winding-sheet, garment for the dead, whence ~'LESS a.; concealing agency (*wrapped in a* ~ *of mystery*); (pl.) set of ropes forming part of standing rigging & supporting mast or topmast. 2. v.t. Clothe (corpse) for burial; cover & conceal or disguise. [OE *scrūd*, ON *skrúth* f. Gmc **skrūdh-* see SHRED]

Shröve Tues'day (tūz'dĭ), n. Day before Ash Wednesday, on which & the preceding days or *Shrovetide* it was customary to be shriven. [rel. to SHRIVE]

shrŭb¹, n. Woody plant of less size than tree & usu. divided into separate stems from near the ground. Hence ~b'Y² a., ~b'ERY(3) n. [ME, app. repr. OE *scrubb*,

scrybb; cf. NFris. *skrobb*, WFlem. *schrobbe*, Norw. *skrubba*; cf. SCRUB[1]]
shrŭb², n. Cordial made of fruit-juice & spirit (usu. *rum·~*). [f. Arab. *sharāb*; cogn. w. SHERBET, SYRUP]
shrŭg, v.t. & i. (-gg-), & n. 1. Slightly & momentarily raise (shoulders), raise shoulders, to express indifference, helplessness, contempt, vexation, etc. 2. n. This motion (*of the shoulders*, or abs.). [c. 1400, of unkn. orig.]
shrunk(en). See SHRINK.
shŭck, n., & v.t. 1. Husk, pod; *~s!*, int. of disgust or regret. 2. v.t. Remove ~s of, shell. [17th c., of unkn. orig.]
shŭdd'er, v.i., & n. (Experience) sudden shivering due to fear, horror, repugnance, or cold; feel strong repugnance etc. (*I ~ to think what might happen*). Hence~**ing**-LY² adv. [ME *shod(d)re*, rel. to MDu. *schŭderen*, MLG *schöderen* f. *skŭdh-* shake, +-ER⁵]
shŭf'fle, v.i. & t., & n. 1. Move (t. & i.) with scraping or sliding or dragging or difficult motion (*~s along rheumatically*; *~s his* or *with his feet*; *~ cards*, slide them over one another so as to change their relative positions; so ~ *things of any sort*, intermingle, confuse; ~ *the cards*, fig., change the parts, try new policy, etc.); slip (clothes, burden) *off* or *on* (~ *off responsibility upon others*; *~d on his clothes*); keep shifting one's position lit. or fig., fidget, vacillate, prevaricate, whence **shŭff'ler¹** n.; *~board*, =SHOVELBOARD; hence **shŭff'ling**LY² adv. 2. n. Shuffling movement; shuffling of cards, general change of relative positions; piece of equivocation or sharp practice; quick scraping movement of feet in dancing (*double ~*, executed twice with one & then the other foot). [f. or cogn. w. LG *schüffeln*, f. Gmc root *skuf-* (*skubh-*) SHOVE]
shŭn, v.t. (-nn-). Avoid, keep clear of, eschew. Hence ~LESS a. (poet.). [OE *scunian*, not found in other Gmc langg.]
'shun!, abbr. of *attention!* as word of command.
shŭnt, v.t. & i., & n. 1. Divert (train, electric current, etc.), ‖ (of train etc.) diverge, on to a side track, esp. to clear line for more important traffic, whence ~'ER¹ n.; postpone or stifle discussion of (subject), lay aside (project), leave (person) inactive. 2. n. Turning or being turned on to side track; (electr.) conductor joining two points of circuit, over which more or less of current may be diverted. [ME, perh. f. SHUN]
shŭt, v.t. & i. (*shut*). 1. Move (door, sash, lid, lips, etc.) into position to stop an aperture (*~ the door upon*, refuse to consider, make impossible). 2. ~ door etc. of (room, window, box, eye, mouth, etc.; ~ *your eyes*; ~ one's *eyes* or by extension *ears to*, pretend not or refuse to see or hear). 3. Become or admit of being closed,

swing or fall or contract into closed position, (*the door ~ with a bang*; *lid ~s automatically*; *pimpernels ~ in rainy weather*). 4. Keep (person, sound, etc.) *out* or *in* by ~ting door etc., send (person) *into* or *out of* room etc. & fasten door etc. against him, bar (person) *out from* hope etc. 5. *Be ~ of* person (sl.), be rid of. 6. Catch or pinch (finger, dress, etc.) by ~ting something on it (~ *his finger into the door-hinge*). 7. Bring parts of together (~ *his teeth, a knife*, etc.). 8. ~ *down*, push or pull (window-sash etc.) down into closed position, (of factory etc.) cease working; ~ *in*, (of hills, houses, sea, etc.) encircle, prevent free prospect or egress from or access to; ~ *off*, stop flow of (water, gas, etc.) by ~ting valve, separate *from* society etc.; ~ *out*, exclude (landscape etc.) from view, prevent (possibility etc.); ~*out bid* (bridge), pre-emptive bid; ~ *to* adv., close (door etc., or intr. of door etc.) tight; ~ *up*, close all doors & windows of or bolt & bar (house; ~ *up shop*, cease business for the day or permanently), close (box etc.) securely or decisively or permanently, imprison (person), put (thing) away in box etc., desist (colloq.; esp. ~ *up* imperat.), reduce to silence by rebuke or refutation. [OE *scyttan* f. *skultjan* f. Gmc *skut-* SHOOT¹; cf. MDu., MLG *schutten*]
shŭtt'er, n., & v.t. In vbl senses of prec.; esp.: one of a set of wooden panels or iron plates, hinged, sliding, folding, or detachable, placed inside or outside glass of window to keep out light or burglars (*put up the ~s*, cease business for the day or permanently); structure of jointed laths or metal slats on rollers serving same purposes; blind of swell-box or organ for regulating loudness; piece that opens & closes lens of photographic camera; hence ~LESS a.; (v.t.) provide with ~s, put up ~s of. [-ER¹]
shŭt'tle, n. Weaving-implement shaped like cigar with two pointed ends by which weft-thread is carried or shot across between threads of warp; carrier of lower thread in lock-stitch sewing-machine; ~ *armature* (electr.), armature with a single coil wound on an elongated iron bobbin; ~*cock*, cork stuck with feathers & struck to & fro in BATTLEDORE *& ~* [-*cock* prob. f. flying motion]; ~ *train* (running a short distance to and fro, usu. on branch-line), so ~ *service*. [OE *scytel* f. Gmc *skut-* SHOOT¹+-LE(1)]
shy¹, a. (~*er*, ~*est*, rarely *shi-*). (Of beasts, birds, fish, etc.) easily startled, timid, avoiding observation; bashful, coy, uneasy in company; avoiding company *of* person, chary *of* doing, (FIGHT¹~*of*); elusive, hard to find, catch, interpret, etc.; (sl.) short (*of*), in the position of having lost *(I'm ~ three quid*); *-shy*, (in combb.) indicating fear of or distaste for (first element of comb.), as in GUN-~,

WORK¹·~. Hence ~'LY² adv., ~'NESS n. [OE *scēoh*, = MHG *schiech*, f. Gmc *°skeuhw-* fear, terrify]

shy², v.i., & n. Start suddenly aside (*at* object or noise, or fig. *at* proposal etc.) in alarm (usu. of horse, or fig. of person). Hence ~'ER¹ n. [f. prec.]

shy³, v.t. & i., & n. (colloq.). **1.** Fling, throw, (stone etc., or abs.). **2.** n. Act of ~ing (*have a* ~ *at*, try to hit with missile, jeer at, make an attempt to get). [18th c., of unkn. orig.]

Shy̆l'ŏck, n. Hard-hearted money-lender. [character in *Merchant of Venice*]

°shy̆s'ter, n. (sl.). Person without professional honour, esp. tricky lawyer. [orig. unkn.]

si (sē), n. (mus.). Seventh note of octave. [added perh. *c.* 1600 to names of hexachord; see GAMUT; perh. f. initials of *Sancte Johannes* in sapphics given under *gamut*]

si'amăng (*or* sē-), n. Kind of gibbon from Sumatra & Malay peninsula. [Malay]

Siamese' (-z), a. & n. (pl. same). (Native, language) of Siam (Thailand); ~ *twins*, two ~ (d. 1874) joined by cartilaginous band from one's right to other's left side, any similar monstrosity, (fig.) inseparable friends etc.; ~ *cat*, cream-coloured short-haired breed with brown or blue points. [-ESE]

sib, a. (chiefly Sc.), & n. (genetics; usu. pl.). **1.** Related, akin, (*to*). **2.** n. A brother or sister (disregarding sex). Hence ~'LING¹ n., one of two or more children having one or both parents in common (usu. pl.), ~'SHIP n., the group of children (disregarding sex) from the same two parents. [OE *sib(b)*, MDu. *sib(be)*, OHG *sippi*, Goth. *-sibjis*]

Sibēr'ian, a. & n. (Inhabitant) of Siberia (~ *dog*, of breed much used for sledging). [-AN]

sib'il|ant, a. & n. **1.** Hissing, sounded with a hiss (esp. of letter or set of letters, as s, sh); hence ~ANCE, ~ANCY, nn. **2.** n. ~ant letter(s). [f. L *sibilare* hiss, -ANT]

sib'il|āte, v.t. & i. Pronounce with hissing sound. Hence ~A'TION n. [as prec., -ATE³]

sib'y̆l, n. One of the women who in ancient times acted at various places (*Cumaean*, *Erythraean*, etc., ~) as mouthpiece of some god, & to whom many collections of oracles & prophecies were attributed, pagan prophetess; old fortune-teller, sorceress, or hag. [ME, f. OF *Sibile* or med. L *Sibilla* f. L f. Gk *Sibulla*]

sib'y̆lline, a. Issuing from an ancient sibyl, oracular, mysteriously prophetic; *the* ~ *books*, collection of oracles belonging to ancient-Roman State & often consulted by magistrates for guidance, (fig., with ref. to story of their acquisition) thing that one refuses & is afterwards glad to get on worse terms. [f. L *Sibyllinus* (prec., -INE¹)]

sīc, Latin adv. = so, appended in brackets after a word or expression in a quoted passage as guarantee that it is quoted exactly, though its incorrectness or absurdity would suggest that it was not. Also in the phrr. ~ *vŏl'ō* ~ *jŭb'eō* (jōō-; such is my will & command) used as n. = arbitrary order; ~ *vōs nŏn vōb'īs* (so ye not for yourselves) used w. ref. to work of which the credit etc. falls to another than the doer.

sicc'ative, a. & n. (Substance etc.) of drying properties, esp. one mixed with oil-paint to dry it. [f. LL *siccativus* f. *siccare* dry, see -ATIVE]

sice¹, n. The six on dice. [ME, f. OF *sis* SIX]

sice², **sy̆ce**, n. (Anglo-Ind.). Groom. [f. Hind. f. Arab. *sā'is*]

Sicil'ian, a. & n. **1.** Of Sicily or its inhabitants (~ *Vespers*, massacre of French residents by natives in 1282, with vesper bell as signal). **2.** n. Native of Sicily. [f. L *Sicilia* Sicily +-AN]

sick¹, a. **1.** Ill, incapacitated by illness, feeling effects of some disease, (*a* ~ *man*; *the S*~ *Man* (*of Europe*), Turkish Empire (hist.); ~ *of a fever*; *the* ~, those who are ill; ‖ *be*, *feel*, *make*, ~ in mod. use, vomit, be disposed or cause to vomit; *turn* ~, feel as if about to vomit). **2.** Disordered, perturbed, suffering effects of, disgusted, pining *for*, (*am* ~ *at heart*; ~ *of love*, love~; *makes me* ~ *to think of it*; *is awfully* ~ *at being beaten*; ~ *for a sight of home*). **3.** Surfeited & tired of (~ *of flattery*, *rain*, *waiting*). **4.** (Of ship) needing repair (esp. of specified kind, as *nail-* ~, *paint-*~). **5.** ~-BAY³; ~-*bed*, invalid's bed, invalid state; ~-*benefit*, allowance made to person absent from work through illness; ~-*call*, military summons on bugle etc. for ~ men to attend; ~-*flag*, yellow, indicating presence of disease at quarantine station or on ship; ~ *headache*, due to biliousness; ~-*leave*, leave of absence granted for reason of health; ~-*list*, of the ~ esp. in regiment, ship, etc. (*on the* ~-*list*, laid up); ~-*making* (colloq.); ~-*room*, occupied by ~ person, or kept ready for the ~. Hence ~'ISH¹(2) a. [OE *sēoc*, OS *siok*, OHG *sioh*, ON *sjúkr*, Goth. *siuks*]

sick², v.t. Set upon (usu. in imperat. ~ *him!* etc. urging dog to worry rat etc.). [19th c., dial. var. of SEEK]

sick'en, v.i. & t. Begin to be ill, show symptoms of illness (*child is* ~*ing for something*); feel nausea or disgust *at*, *to see*, etc.; affect with inclination to vomit, loathing, or disgust (*a* ~*ing sight*) or with weariness or despair *of* (*was* ~*ed of trying to make peace*), whence ~ER¹(2) n., ~ingLY² adv. [ME, f. SICK¹ +-EN⁶]

sic'kle, n. Reaping-hook, short-handled semicircular-bladed implement now chiefly used for lopping & trimming, formerly for cutting corn; *the* constellation Leo; ~*bill*, kinds of bird with ~-

-shaped bill; ~-*feather*, one of long middle
feathers of cock's tail; ~-*wort*, the plant
heal-all. [OE *sicol*, -*el*, MDu., MLG *sekele*,
OHG *sihhila*, f. L *secula* f. *secare* cut]

sick'l|y̆, a., & v.t. **1.** Apt to be ill,
chronically ailing, of weak health; suggesting sickness, as of sick person,
languid, faint, pale, (~*y look*, *smile*,
complexion); causing ill health, inducing
or ˙connected with nausea, (~*y climate*,
smell, *taste*); mawkish, weakly sentimental. **2.** v.t. Cover *over* or *o'er* with a
~*y* hue (w. ref. to *Haml*. III. i. 85). Hence
~ĬNESS n. [ME; -LY[1]]

sick'nĕss, n. **1.** Being ill, disease. **2.** A
disease (FALL[1]*ing* ~; *sleeping*-~, fatal
African disease, *morbus dormitivus*,
marked by somnolence & nerve-paralysis,
caused by certain trypanosomes introduced by kinds of tsetse; *sleepy* ~, epidemic encephalitis or *encephalitis lethar-
gica*, acute inflammation of the brain, not
yet traced to a parasitic cause, but distinct
from sleeping-~, though lethargy is a
mark of both). **3.** Vomiting or inclination
to vomit. [ME; -NESS]

Sic'ŭlo-, comb. form of L *Siculi* Sicilians,
as ~-*Arabian*, Arabian as modified in
Sicily. [-O-]

side[1], n. **1.** One of the flat(tish) surfaces
bounding an object (*cube has six* ~*s*), esp.
a more or less vertical outer or inner surface (~ *of house*, *cave*, *mountain*, etc.; so
perh. COUNTRY~); such surface as distinguished from top & bottom, or front &
back, or ends (*four*, or *two*, ~*s of box*; *two*
~*s of house*). **2.** Either surface of thing
regarded as having only two (*two* ~*s of
sheet of paper*, *board*, etc.; *sent him six* ~*s
of argument*, pages of notepaper so filled;
the INSIDE *&* OUTSIDE *of a bowl*; *right*,
wrong, ~ *of cloth* etc., surface, meant, not
meant, to be visible; BACK[1]*side*; SHADY,
SEAMY, SILVER[1], ~). **3.** (math.). Bounding
line of plane rectilinear figure (*opposite* ~*s
of a parallelogram*). **4.** Part of person or
animal that is on his or its right or left,
esp. that of it which extends from armpit
to hip or from foreleg to hindleg (~ *of
mutton*, *bacon*, etc., this part of carcass;
BLIND[1]~; ~ *by* ~, standing close together,
esp. for mutual support; *shake one's* ~*s*,
laugh heartily; ~-*splitting*, causing
violent laughter, amusing). **5.** Part of
object turned in same direction as observer's right or left & not directly towards or away from him, or turned in
specified direction (*right*, *left*, ~; *debit*,
credit, ~, in account book; *epistle*, *gospel*,
~, south, north, end of altar; DECANI,
CANTORIS, ~; *the north*, *landward*, ~).
6. Part or region near margin and remote
from centre or axis of thing, subordinate
or less essential or more or less detached
part, (~ *of room*, *road*, *table*, etc.); (attrib.)
subordinate (~ *issue*, point that distracts
attention; ~ *line*, work etc. carried on
apart from one's main work, see also

sense 14); *on the* ~, as a ~ line, in addition
to one's regular work. **7.** Region external
but contiguous to, specified direction
with relation to, person or thing (*on one*
~, aside; *look on all* ~*s*; *came from all* ~*s*
or *every* ~; *standing at my* ~; *on the north*
~ *of*). **8.** Partial aspect of. thing, aspect
differing from or opposed to other aspects
(*study all* ~*s of the question*; *has many*
~*s to his character*; *the* ~ *of the moon
visible to us*); *on the* (so-and-so) ~, rather
(so-and-so), as *prices were on the high* ~.
9. (Cause represented by, position in
company with) one of two sets of opponents in war, politics, games, etc. (*the Lord
is on my* ~; *there is much to be said, there
are faults, on both* ~*s*; *take* ~*s*, decide to
espouse one or other cause; *join the winning* ~; ON[1], OFF, ~; *Cambridge has a
strong* ~, team for cricket, football, etc.).
10. Position nearer or farther than, right
or left of, dividing line (*on this* ~ *of*, or *on
this* ~, *the Alps*; *on this* ~ *the grave*, in
life; *on the right*, *wrong*, ~ *of forty*, below,
above, 40 years of age; *on the wrong* ~
of the door, shut out; *on the wrong* ~ *of
the* BLANKET[1]). **11.** Line of descent
through father or mother (*well descended
on the mother's* or *maternal* ~; DISTAFF or
spindle, SPEAR, ~). **12.** ‖ (bill.). Spinning
motion given to ball by striking it on ~.
13. ‖ (sl.). Assumption of superiority,
swagger; (*puts on*, *has too much*, ~),
whence **sīd'y̆**[2] a. **14.** ~-*arms*, swords or
bayonets; ~-*bet*, bet between opponents,
freq. in card-games, over & above the
ordinary stakes; ~-*board*, table or flat-
-topped chest at ~ of dining-room for
supporting and containing dishes, decanters, etc., (pl., sl.) ~-*whiskers*; ~-*bone*, (in
carving fowls) either small forked bone
under wing; °~-*burns*, short ~-whiskers;
~-*car*, = JAUNTing-*car*, (also) car for
passenger(s) attachable to ~ of (motor-)
cycle; ~-*chapel*, in aisle or at ~ of church;
~-*dish*, extra dish often of elaborate kind
at dinner etc.; ~-*drum*, small double-
-headed drum in military band hung at
drummer's ~; ~-*light*, light from ~, (fig.)
incidental illustration etc., (naut.) red
port or green starboard light on ship under
way; ~-*lines*, (space immediately outside)
lines bounding football-pitch, tennis-
-court, etc., at the ~s, see also sense 6;
~-*note*, marginal note; ~-*saddle*, for rider,
usu. woman, with both feet on same ~ of
horse; ~-*seat* in vehicle etc., in which
occupant has back against ~ of vehicle;
~-*show*, minor show attached to principal
one; ~-*slip*, skid v. & n., (aeron.)·move
(vb) or motion broadside on instead of
forward, also shoot of tree & (fig.) illegitimate child, also (theatr.) division at ~
of stage for working scenery; ~*s'man*,
deputy churchwarden; ~-*step*, (n.) step
taken sideways, step for getting in & out
of carriage etc., (v.t.) avoid by stepping
sideways (esp. in football), (fig.) evade;

~-**stroke**, stroke towards or from a ~, incidental action, kinds of swimming action opp. breast-stroke; ~-*track*, siding, (v.t.) turn into siding, shunt, postpone treatment or consideration of; ~-*view*, view obtained sideways, profile; ~'*walk*, path at ~ of road for foot-passengers (chiefly U.S.); *~-*wheeler*, steamer with paddle-wheels; ~ *wind*, wind from a ~, indirect agency or influence. Hence (-)**sid**'ED²a., (-)**sid**'ĕdLY²adv., (-)**sid**'ĕd-NESS n., ~'LESS (-dl-) a. [OE (OS) *side*, OHG *sita*, ON *sitha*; perh. f. the adj., OE *sid*, ON *sithr* extensive etc.]

side², v.i. Take part, be on same side, *with* disputant etc. [f. prec.]

side'lŏng (-dl-), adv. & a. Inclining to one side, oblique(ly), (*move*~; *a*~ *glance*). [-LONG]

sidēr'ĕal, a. Of the constellations or the fixed stars (~ *day*, time between successive meridional transits of star, esp. of first point in Aries, about 4' shorter than solar day; ~ *year*, time in which earth makes one complete · revolution round sun, longer than tropical year by difference due to precession; ~ *time*, measured by apparent diurnal motion of stars). [f. L *sidereus* (*sidus -eris* star), -AL]

siderŏg'raphy̆, n. A process of engraving on steel. [f. Gk *sidēros* iron, -GRAPHY]

side'ward(s) (-dw-), adv. & a. Lateral(ly), ·to or from a side, (*moved* ~; ~ *motion*). [-WARD(S)]

side'ways (-dwāz), adv. & a. = prec. [-WAYS]

sid'ing, n. Short track by side of railway line & opening into it at one end or both for shunting purposes. [-ING¹]

si'dle, v.i. Walk obliquely, esp. in timid or cringing manner (often *along*, *up*). [back formation f. obs. *sideling* (now SIDELONG)]

siege, n., & v.t. **1.** Operations of encamped attacking force to take or compel surrender of fortified place, period during which these last, besieging or being besieged, (often fig.; *raise the* ~ *of*, abandon attempt to take; *lay* ~ *to*, begin besieging; ~ *lasted 100 days*; *stood a long* ~, before or without surrendering); persistent attempt to force or persuade reluctant person to do something; ~-*basket*, gabion; ~-*gun* (hist.), used in ~s, too heavy for field use; ~-*train* (hist.), artillery & other appliances for besieging; ~-*works*, trenches, shelters, etc., of besiegers. **2.** v.t. (arch.). Besiege. [ME & OF *sege* seat f. pop. L *sedicum* f. L *sedem*]

Sieg'fried line, n. German fortified line along Franco-German border, constructed prior to 1939-45 war. [person]

Sien(n)ĕse' (-z), a. & n. (pl. same). (Inhabitant) of Sienna (~ *school*, of 13th--14th-c. painters). [-ESE]

siĕnn'a, n. Ochrous earth used raw or burnt as pigment of brownish-yellow (*raw* ~) or reddish-brown (*burnt* ~) colour.

[f. It. (*terra di*) Sienna (earth of) Sienna]

siĕ'rra, n. Long jagged mountain-chain; Spanish mackerel. [Sp., f. L *serra* saw]

siĕs'ta, n. Midday nap or rest in hot countries. [Sp., f. L *sexta (hora)* sixth hour]

sieve (sĭv), n., & v.t. **1.** Sorting utensil with network or perforated bottom through which liquids or fine particles can pass while solid or coarser matter is retained; coarsely plaited basket often used as measure; person who cannot keep secrets. **2.** v.t. Put through, sift with, ~. [OE *sife*, MDu., MLG *seve*, OHG *sib*; cf. SIFT]

siffleur (sēflĕr'), n. (fem. *-euse*, pr. *-ĕrz*). Whistling artiste. [F]

sift, v.t. & i. Separate into finer & coarser parts with sieve, separate (finer parts) *from* material or its coarser parts or *out*, sprinkle (sugar etc.) from perforated spoon etc.; closely examine details of (evidence, facts, etc.) with regard to credibility or authenticity or relevance, analyse character of; (of snow, light, etc.) fall as from sieve. Hence (-)~'ER¹ (1, 2) n. [OE *siftan*, MDu., MLG *siften*, cf. SIEVE]

sigh (sī), v.i. & t., & n. **1.** Draw deep audible breath expressive of sadness, weariness, aspiration, relief from tension, cessation of effort, etc.; yearn *for* (person or thing desired or lost); utter or express with ~s (usu. *out*); (of wind etc.) make sound like ~ing; hence ~'ingLY² (sī'ĭ-) adv. **2.** n. Act of, sound made in, ~ing (*a* ~ *of relief*). [ME *sihen*, prob. back form. on *sihte* past of obs. *siche* f. OE *sīcan*]

sight¹ (sīt), n. **1.** Faculty of vision (*long*, *short* or *near*, ~, requiring objects to be unusually far, near, for clear definition; *short* ~, fig., lack of discernment or foresight; *has good*, *bad*, ~; *know by* ~, be familiar with appearance only of; *loss of* ~, becoming blind; *second* ~, power of internal vision by which future or distant occurrences are presented), whence (-)~'ED² (sīt-), a., (-)~'ĕdLY² adv., (-)~'ĕdNESS n. **2.** Seeing or being seen, way of looking at or considering thing, (*catch*, *lose*, ~ *of*, begin, cease, to see; *have lost* ~ *of Jones*, no longer know his movements etc.; *get a* ~ *of*, manage to see; *take a* ~ (*of*, *at*), sl., cock a snook; *at*, *on*, ~, as soon as person or thing has been seen; *plays music at* ~, without preliminary study or practice of piece; ~-*singing*, reading vocal music at ~; *payable at* ~, of draft etc.; *at first* ~, prima facie; *the* ~ *of her distress unmanned him*; *she found favour in his* ~; *do what is right in* one's *own* ~). **3.** Range or unobstructed space within which person etc. can see or object be seen (*is in*, *out of*, ~, visible, not visible; HEAVE¹ *in* ~; *the millennium is in* ~, clearly near at hand; *put out of* ~, hide, ignore; *came in* ~ *of the fort*, so as to see it or be seen from it; *out of ~ out of mind*, we forget the absent; *out of my ~ !*, rhetorical order to depart). **4.** Thing seen, visible, or worth seeing, display, show, spectacle, (*a sad ~ awaited us; a ~ for sore eyes*, person or thing one is glad to see, esp. welcome visitor; *went to see the ~s*, noteworthy features of town etc., whence ~'**sēER**[1], ~'**seeING**[1], nn.; *the daffodils were a ~ to see* or *a ~*; *his face is a perfect ~*, disfigured with wounds etc.; *make a ~ of oneself*, dress in bizarre fashion etc.). **5.** (colloq.). Great quantity (*will cost a ~ of money*; *is a long ~ better*). **6.** (Kinds of device for assisting) precise aim with gun or observation with optical instrument (*forgot to put up the leaf of his back ~*, in rifle-shooting; *took a careful ~ before firing*; *the ~s of, a ~ with*, quadrant or compass). **7.** ~'*worthy*, worth seeing. [OE (*ge*)*sihth*, MDu., OHG *siht*, f. sih-stem of SEE[1]+-TH[1]]

sight[2] (sīt), v.t. Get sight of, esp. by coming near (~ *land, game*); take observation (of star etc.) with instrument; provide (gun, quadrant, etc.) with sights; adjust sights of (~*ing shot*, experimental one to guide rifleman etc. in this); aim (gun etc.) with sights. [f. prec.]

sight'lĕss (sīt-), a. Blind; (poet.) invisible. [ME; -LESS]

sight'l|ў̆ (sīt-), a. Not unsightly. Hence ~**iNESS** n. [-LY[1]]

si′gillate, a. (Of pottery) with impressed patterns; (bot.) having seal-like marks. [f. L *sigillatus* (*sigillum* seal dim. of SIGNUM, -ATE[2])]

sig′ma, n. Greek letter (Σ or ς, σ or, when final, ς) corresponding to s. [Gk]

sig′mate[1], a. Sigma-shaped; S-shaped. [-ATE[2]]

sig′m|āte[2], v.t. Add sigma or s to. Hence ~**A′TION** n. [-ATE[3]]

sigmăt′ic, a. Formed with sigma (esp. ~ *aorist*). [SIGMA *-atos*, -IC]

sig′moid, a. & n. **1.** (Chiefly anat.) curved like the uncial sigma (ᴄ), or (now usu.) like S. **2.** n. Reversed or inverted curve. [-OID]

sign[1] (sīn), n. **1.** Mark traced on surface etc. (esp. *the ~ of the cross*, made by Christian priests in blessing or laymen in reverence with finger on forehead or breast; ~ *manual*, signature written with person's own hand). **2.** Written mark conventionally used for word or phrase, symbol, thing used as representation of something, (*positive sign ~, + ; negative or minus ~, − ; words are the ~s of ideas*; *a sacrament is an outward & visible ~ of an inward & spiritual grace*). **3.** (Thing serving as) presumptive evidence or indication or suggestion or symptom *of* or *that*, distinctive mark, token, guarantee, password, miracle evidencing supernatural power, portent, (*violence is a ~ of weakness* or *that one is weak*; *shows all the ~s of decay*; *gave earth & water in ~*

of submission; *by this ~ ye shall know them*; *did ~s & wonders*; ~ & *counter~*, secret words etc. by which confederates recognize each other; ~*s of the times*, things showing the tendency of affairs); (path.) objective evidence or indication of disease (often with defining word, as *Babinski's, Oppenheim's*, ~). **4.** (Often ~'*board*) fanciful device usu. painted on a board displayed formerly by traders of any sort & still by many inns & some barbers etc. as advertisement of their business (*at the ~ of the White Hart* etc., arch., formerly used as address). **5.** Natural or conventional motion or gesture used instead of words to convey information & esp. order or request (*gave him a ~ to withdraw*; *deaf-&-dumb ~s*, those used in finger-talk; *make no ~*, seem unconscious, not protest, etc.). **6.** Any of twelve divisions of ZODIAC named from constellations formerly situated in them. **7.** ~-*painter, -writer*, of ~*boards*, shop-front inscriptions, etc.; ~'*post*, at cross-roads etc. with names of places on each road. [ME & OF *signe* f. L *signum*]

sign[2] (sīn), v.t. & i. **1.** Mark with sign (esp. ~ *infant* etc. *with the sign of the cross* in baptism). **2.** Acknowledge or guarantee (letter, deed, picture, book, article, petition, etc., or abs.) as one's own production or as having one's authority or consent by affixing or having affixed one's name or initials or recognized mark (*the will had never been ~ed*; *a ~ed masterpiece of Turner's*; ~*ed as usual with a dicky-bird*; *does not ~ his contributions to the press*; *nothing shall induce me to ~*), whence ~'**ABLE** (sīn-) a. **3.** Write (one's name) as signature; convey (right, property, etc.) *away* by ~ing deed etc.; take, acknowledge being taken, *on* for some employment to which employee binds himself by signature. **4.** Communicate by gesture (~ *assent*), give order or make request by gesture *to* person *to do* (~*ed to me to come*). **5.** ~ *off*, (bridge) indicate by a conventional bid that one is ending the bidding, (radio) cease transmitting; so ~-*off* n. [ME, f. OF *signer* or L *signare* (*signum*, see prec.)]

sig′nal[1], a. Remarkably good or bad, conspicuous, noteworthy, exemplary, condign, (~ *victory, defeat, reward, punishment, virtue, example*). Hence ~**LY**[2] adv. [f. F *signalé* f. It. p.p. *segnalato* distinguished (foll., *-ato* -ATE[2])]

sig′nal[2], n., & v.t. & i. (-ll-). **1.** Preconcerted or intelligible sign conveying information or direction esp. to person(s) at a distance, message made up of such signs, (*the ~ was to be the dropping of a handkerchief*; ~*s are made by day with flags & by night with lights*; *gave the ~ for advance*; FOG[2]-~; ~ *of distress*, appeal for help, esp. from ship made by firing guns; *storm-~*, cone etc. hoisted at meteorological station; *code of ~s*, ~-*book*, body of ~s arranged for sending complicated messages esp. in naval & mil. use); immediate occasion *for* some general movement (*the earthquake was the ~ for an outbreak of the primitive instincts*); ‖ ROYAL Corps of S~s; ~-*box*, hut on railway with ~ling-apparatus; ~-*man*, ~ler; ~ *strength*, strength of reception of radio ~s (varying with the time of day etc.). **2. vb.** Make ~(s), make ~(s) to, transmit (order, information) by ~, announce (event, *that*) by ~, direct (person *to* do) by ~; hence ~1ER¹ n. [ME, f. OF, f. med. L *signale* (LL *signalis*) f. L *signum* SIGN¹, -AL]

sig′nalize, -ise (-īz), v.t. Make noteworthy or remarkable, lend distinction or lustre to, (*his accession was ~d by an amnesty*). [SIGNAL¹, -IZE]

sig′nator|y̆, a. & n. (Party, esp. State) that has signed an agreement esp. a treaty (*the ~ies or ~y powers to the treaty of Berlin*). [f. L *signatorius* of sealing (*signare* mark, -TORY)]

sig′nature, n. **1.** (arch.). Significant appearance or mark (*has the ~ of passion, of early death, in his face; herb's yellow flowers are a ~ indicating that it will cure jaundice*). **2.** Person's name or initials or mark used in SIGN²ing. **3.** Letter or figure placed by printer at foot of (now, usu. only first) page of each sheet of book as guide in making up for binding, such sheet after folding. **4.** (mus.). *Key ~*, clef with sharps or flats at beginning of each staff; *time ~*, fraction placed at beginning of composition, numerator giving number of beats in each bar and denominator duration of each. **5.** ~ *tune*, special tune used in broadcasting to announce a particular turn etc. [f. med. L *signatura* (LL = marking of sheep), or F *signature*; (as prec., -URE)]

sig′nēt, n. Private seal for use instead of or with signature as authentication (*the ~, royal seal formerly used for special purposes*; ‖ WRITER *to the ~*); ~-*ring*, finger-ring with seal set in it. [ME, f. AF, OF *signet*, or med. L *signetum* (SIGN¹, -ET¹)]

signif′icance, n. Being significant, expressiveness, (*there is no ~ in his eyes; with a look of deep ~*); covert or real import, what is meant to be or may be inferred, (*those were the words, but what is their ~?*); importance, noteworthiness, (*what he thinks about it is of no ~*). [OF, or f. L *significantia* (SIGNIFY, -ANCE)]

signif′icant, a. Having a meaning (-kin *is a ~ termination*); expressive, suggestive, with pregnant or secret sense, inviting attention; noteworthy, of considerable amount or effect or importance, not insignificant or negligible, (usu. in negative contexts, as *the only ~ event was ~*). Hence ~LY² adv. [as SIGNIFY, -ANT]

significā′tion, n. Act of signifying (rare); exact meaning or sense (usu. *of* something, esp. of a word or phrase). [ME, f. OF, or f. L *significatio* (SIGNIFY, -ATION)]

signif′icătive, a. Offering signs or presumptive evidence *of*. [ME, f. OF (-*if*, -*ive*), or f. LL *significativus* (as foll., -ATIVE)]

sig′nif|y̆, v.t. & i. Be a sign or indication or presage of (*a long upper lip ~ies obstinacy; a halo ~ies rain*); mean, have as meaning, (*D.D. ~ies doctor of divinity*); communicate, make known, (*he ~ied his reluctance, that he could not consent*); be of importance, matter, (esp. in negative contexts, as *it does not ~y*). [ME, f. OF *signifier* f. L *significare* (SIGN¹, -FY)]

Signor, Signora, Signorina, (sēn′yor̄, sēnyor̄′a, sēnyorēn′a*l*, nn. (pl. -*ri* pr. -rē, -*re* pr. -rā, -*ne* pr. -nā). Titles used of or to Italians corresponding to Sir & Mr, Madam & Mrs, young lady & Miss. [It.]

Sikh (sēk, sĭk), n. Member of Hindu community founded as monotheistic sect *c.* 1500 in Punjab & after achieving independence annexed 1849 to British India. Hence ~′ISM n., the (religious) tenets of the ~s. [Hind., = disciple]

sil′age, n., & v.t. **1.** = ENSILAGE. **2.** v.t. Put into silo. [alt. f. ENSILAGE after SILO]

sil′ence, n., & v.t. **1.** Abstinence from speech or noise, being silent, taciturnity, non-betrayal of secret etc., fact of not mentioning a thing, (*the ~ of Scripture on the subject*; ~ *gives consent*; ~ *is golden*; *keep, break, ~*, abstain from speaking, speak; *put to ~*, esp. refute in argument); absence of sound, stillness, (*in ~*, without speech or other sound); oblivion, state of not being mentioned, (*have passed into ~*); *S~!* (order to cease from speech or noise). **2.** v.t. Make silent by force, superior argument, etc. (*~d the enemy's batteries, the best debaters in the House, the voice of conscience*). Hence **sil′encER¹** n., kinds of device for rendering (comparatively) noiseless the escape of gas from gun, oil-engine, etc. [ME, f. OF, f. L *silentium* (*silēre* be silent)]

sil′ent, a. Not speaking, not uttering or making or accompanied by any sound, (~ *letter*, one written but not pronounced, e.g. *b* in *doubt*; ~ *film*, without sound accompaniment; ~ *partner*, with no voice in management of business; *the ~ system* in prisons, by which prisoners are never allowed to speak); taciturn, speaking little; saying nothing on some subject (*history is ~ upon it*). Hence ~LY² adv. [f. L *silēre* be silent, -ENT]

Silēn′us, n. Rollicking drunken bloated old man. [L, f. Gk *Seilēnos* name of one of Bacchus's attendants]

silē′sia (-sha), n. Kinds of thin cloth used for blinds & dress-linings. [orig. made in Silesia]

silhouëtte′ (-lŏŏ-), n., & v.t. **1.** Portrait of person in profile showing outline only, all inside the outline being usu. black on white ground or cut out in paper; appearance of person or object as seen against light so that outline only is distinguishable (*in* ~, so seen or placed). **2. v.t.** Represent or (usu. pass.) exhibit in ~. [f. Etienne de *Silhouette* (1709–67), French author & politician]

sil'ic|a, n. Silicon dioxide, occurring as quartz & as principal constituent of sandstone & other rocks (~ŏs'IS n., disease caused by inhalation of quartz dust, so ~ŏT'IC a. & n.). Hence **sili'c**IC, ~IF'EROUS, **sili'c**IOUS or **sili'c**EOUS (-sh*u*s), aa., ~ATE¹(3) n., ~I-, ~O-, comb. forms. [f. L *silex -icis* flint]

sil'icāt̀ed, a. Coated, mixed, combined, or impregnated, with silica. [prec., -ATE³, -ED¹]

sili'ci|fy̆, v.t. & i. Impregnate with silica, turn (t. & i.) into silica, petrify. Hence ~FICA'TION n. [SILICA, -FY]

sil'icon, n. Non-metallic element of very common occurrence in the compound SILICA. [f. L *silex -icis* flint, (after *carbon, boron*), replacing *silicium*]

sil'iqua (pl. *-ae*), **silique'** (-ēk), n. Pod of plants of mustard family. Hence **sil'iqu-**OSE¹, **sil'iqu**OUS, (-kw-), aa. [L]

silk, n. · **1.** Fine soft thread produced in making cocoon by ~'*worm* or larva of kinds of moth feeding esp. on mulberry leaves (*spun* ~, see SPIN ; *thrown* ~, ORGANZINE); similar thread spun by some spiders etc. or (*artificial* ~, now usu. *rayon*) thread or yarn made from cellulose. **2.** Cloth woven of ~ (‖ *take* ~, become K.C. or Q.C. & exchange stuff for ~ gown); (pl.) kinds, or garments made, of such cloth. **3.** ‖ (colloq.). K.C. or Q.C. **4.** Peculiar lustre seen in some sapphires & rubies. **5.** (attrib., now usu. preferred to *silken*). Made of ~ (~ *stockings* etc.; *make a* ~ *purse out of a sow's ear*, get better results from a person than his qualities admit of). **6.** ‖~-*fowl*, breed with silky plumage; ~-*gland*, secreting the substance produced as ~; ~-*reel*, -*winder*, for unwinding ~ from cócoon & winding it as thread; ~-*screen printing*, a stencil printing process. [OE *sioloc* (cf. ON *silki*) prob. ult. f. L, or Gk *sērikos* f. *Sēres*, prob. the Chinese, -IC]

sil'ken, a. Made of silk (arch., poet.); clad in silk; soft, lustrous, as silk; (of ~ manner etc.)suave, insinuating. [ME; -EN⁵]

sil'k|y̆, a. Like silk in smoothness, softness, fineness, or lustre (~*y manner* etc., suave). Hence ~ĭNESS n. [-Y²]

sill, n. Shelf or slab of stone or wood at foot of door or esp. window; horizontal timber at bottom of dock or lock entrance, against which the gates close. [OE *syll*(e), = MDu., MLG *sulle*, cogn. w. ON *syll*, OHG *swelli*, Goth. *gasuljan* to found]

sill'abūb, n. Dish made of cream or milk mixed with wine etc. into soft curd & sometimes whipped or solidified with gelatine. [16th c. also *sillibucke, sillub*, etc., of unkn. orig.]

‖ **sill'er,** n. (Sc.). Silver; money. [=SILVER]

Sill'er̆y̆, n. Kinds of sparkling & still champagne. [place-name]

sill'|y̆, a. & n. **1.** ‖ Innocent, simple, helpless, (arch.); foolish, weak-minded, imprudent, unwise, imbecile; ‖ *the* ~*y season*, August & September as the season when newspapers start trivial discussions for lack of news; ~*y point, short leg* (placed close up to batsman). **2.** n. (colloq.). A ~*y* person. Hence ~ILY² adv., ~ĭNESS n. [later form of ME *sely* (dial. *seely*) f. OE **sælig*, OS, OHG *sālig*, f. WG **sæli* luck, happiness]

sil'ō, n. (pl. ~*s*), & v.t. **1.** Pit or airtight structure in which green crops are pressed & kept for fodder, undergoing fermentation. **2.** v.t. Make ensilage of. [Sp., f. L f. Gk *siros*]

silt, n., & v.t. & i. **1.** Sediment deposited by water in channel, harbour, etc. **2.** vb. Choke or be choked with ~ (usu. *up*; *the passage has* or *is* ~*ed up*). [ME, of obsc. orig.; cf. Da., Norw. *sylt*, OLG *sulla*, OHG *sulza* salt marsh, cogn. w. SALT]

Silūr'ian, a. & n. **1.** Of the Silures, a people of ancient Britain. **2.** (Of) a series of rocks forming a subdivision of the Palaeozoic immediately underlying the Devonian, named as first investigated in district of the Silures. [f. L *Silures*, -IAN]

sil'van, sy̆-, a. Of the, having, woods; rural. [16th c., f. L *silva* wood +-AN, thr. F *sylvain*; cf. L *Silvanus* woodland deity]

sil'ver¹, n. **1.** A white lustrous precious metal used chiefly with alloy of harder metals for coin, plate, & ornaments, & in chem. combinations for photography etc. (*German* ~, *nickel* ~, etc., white alloys used as substitutes for ~ in table articles etc., or for coating with ~; *fulminating* ~, an explosive powder; OXIDIZED ~). **2.** ~ coins (*have you any* ~ *on you?*). **3.** ~ vessels or implements or articles of furniture (*melted down all his* ~ *in the king's service*). **4.** Any of the salts of ~ used in sensitizing photographic paper. **5.** attrib. or adj. (usu. now preferred to ~**n** a. arch. see -EN⁵). Made of ~, second-best, (*the* ~ *age*, see BRAZEN¹, also spec. the period of Latin literature that followed the Augustan; *so* ~ *Latin*; *a* ~ *cup*; *speech is* ~ or ~*n, but silence is golden*, better be silent than speak); (as substitute for ~Y² a.,..whence ~ĭNESS n.) resembling ~ in whiteness, lustre, ringing sound, etc. (~ *hair*, white & lustrous; *has a* ~ or ~*y tone*; *has a* ~ *tongue*, is eloquent, whence ~-*tongu*ED² a.; *every cloud has a* ~ *lining*, misfortune has its consolations). **6.** ~-*bath*, (tray for holding) solution of ~ nitrate used for sensitizing; ~ *fir*, kind with two ~ lines on under side of leaves; ~-*fish*, kinds of fish, esp. a colourless variety of goldfish, (also)~*y* insect found in books & mouldy places;~ FOIL¹;~ *fox*, variety of common fox with black grey-tipped fur; ~ *gill*, ~ gilded over, also imitation gilding of yellow lacquer over ~ leaf; ~-*grey*, lustrous grey; ~ LEAF; ~ *paper*, fine white tissue-paper, (loosely) tin foil; ~ *plate*, vessels, spoons, etc., of ~; ~ *point*, (process of sketching on prepared paper with) ~-pointed style (*a head in* ~ *point*); ~ *print*, photographic positive on paper sensitized by a salt of ~; ~ *sand*, fine kind used in gardening; ~ *screen*, superior type of cinematographic screen, (also) film-pictures collectively; ~*side*, best side of round of beef; ~*smith*, worker in ~, manufacturer of ~ articles; ~ *solder*, solder for joining ~; ~ *standard*, use of ~ money alone as full legal tender; ‖~-*stick*, field-officer of Life Guards on palace duty; ‖ ~ *streak*, the English Channel; ~ *thaw*, glassy coating on the ground, exposed woodwork, etc., caused when rain freezes as it falls, or when a sudden thaw (after hard frost) is succeeded by a light frost; ~-*top*, a disease in grasses; ~ *wedding*, twenty-fifth anniversary; ~*weed*, yellow--flowered roadside plant with ~y lower leaf-surfaces. [OE *seolfor*, OS *sil(u)bar*, OHG *sil(a)bar*, Goth. *silubr*, of obsc. orig.]

sil′ver², v.t. & i. Coat or plate with silver; provide (mirror-glass) with backing of tin foil, mercury, etc.; (of moon or white light) give silvery appearance to; (with *hair* as obj. or subj.) turn (t. & i.) grey or white. [f. prec.]

sil′vicŭlture, sў-, n. The growing and tending of trees as a branch of forestry. [f. L *silva* wood +CULTURE]

sim′i̇|an, a. & n. **1.** (zool.). (Of) one of the *Simiidae* or anthropoid apes. **2.** Ape-(like), monkey(-like). So ~OID a. [f. L *simia* ape, -AN]

sim′ilar, a. & n. **1.** Like, alike, having mutual resemblance or resemblance *to*, of the same kind; (geom.) shaped alike; hence or cogn. ~ITY (-ă′r-) n., ~LY² adv. **2.** n. Thing resembling another; (pl.) ~ things. [f. F *similaire* or med. L *similaris* (L *similis* like, -AR)]

sim′il̇e, n. The introduction, esp. in poetry or poetical style, ostensibly for explanatory or illustrative purposes but often in fact for ornament only, of an object or scene or action with which the one in hand is professedly compared & usu. connected by a comparative con-junction such as *as* (*a style rich in* ~ *& metaphor*); a comparison of this kind (*the* ~ *of the dome of many-coloured glass*; cf. METAPHOR, ALLEGORY, PARABLE). [f. L neut. of *similis* like]

simil̇′itŭde, n. Likeness, guise, outward appearance, (*in, assume, the* ~ *of*); simile, comparison, (*talks in* ~*s*); counterpart, facsimile, (rare; *is the very* ~ *of*). [ME, f. OF, or f. L *similitudo* (prec., -TUDE)]

sim′ilize, -ise (-īz), v.i. & t. Use simile; illustrate by simile(s). [SIMILE, -IZE]

simm′er, v.i. & t., & n. **1.** Be, keep (trans.), on the point of boiling, boil (t. & i.) very gently; (fig.) be in a state of sup-pressed anger, indignation, or laughter.

2. n. ~ing state (esp. *at a* or *on the* ~). [alt. f. 16th c. (now dial.) *simper*, prob. imit.]

‖ **sim′nel-căke,** n. Rich ornamental boiled cake made esp. at Easter, Christ-mas, and Mid Lent. [ME, f. OF *simenel*, rel. in some way to L *simila* finest flour]

simōn′iăc, n. Person guilty of simony. [ME, f. OF, or f. med. L *simoniacus* (SIMONY, -AC)]

simoni̇′acal, a. Guilty, of the nature, of simony. Hence ~LY² adv. [-AL]

Sim′on Pūre, n. The real or genuine per-son or article (usu. *the real* ~). [character in Centlivre's *Bold Stroke for a Wife*]

sim′ony̆, n. Buying or selling of ecclesias-tical preferment. [ME, f. OF *simonie* f. LL *simonia* f. *Simon (Magus)*, see *Acts* viii. 18, -Y¹]

simōōm′, n. Hot dry suffocating dust--laden wind moving in straight narrow track and passing in a few minutes, chiefly in Arabian desert. [f. Arab. *semūm samm* to poison)]

*****simp,** n. (colloq.). Simpleton. [abbr.]

sim′per, v.i. & t., & n. **1.** Smile affectedly, smirk; express by or with ~ing (~*ed consent*); hence ~ingLY² adv., ~ER¹ n. **2.** n. Affected smile. [16th c., orig. obsc.; cf. Da., Norw., Sw. dial. *semper, simper*, MDu. *simperlijk* nice, affected]

sim′ple, a. & n. **1.** Not compound, con-sisting of one element, all of one kind, involving only one operation or power, not divided into parts, not analysable, (~ SENTENCE; ~ INTEREST¹; *a* ~ *quantity*, expressible by single number; *induction by* ~ *enumeration*, based merely on ran-dom examples without selection or tests; ~ *addition*, of numbers of one denomina-tion; ~ *equation*, not involving the second or any higher power of unknown quan-tity, cf. QUADRATIC; ~ *machine*, any of the MECHANICAL powers; ~ *leaf*, of one blade; ~ *pistil*, of one carpel; ~ *eye* of insect, OCELLUS; ~ *fracture*, breaking of bone only, cf. COMPOUND²; ~ *idea*, that cannot be analysed into elements). **2.** Not com-plicated or elaborate or adorned or in-volved or highly developed (*the style is* ~ *and devoid of ornament*; ~ *diet*; *the* ~ *life*, practice of doing without servants & luxuries, attempt to return to more primitive conditions; *the greatest works of art are the* ~*st*; *in* ~ *beauty*, unadorned; *a* ~ *form of pump*; ~ *forms of life*, creatures low in scale of evolution). **3.** Absolute, unqualified, mere, neither more nor less than, just, (*to give an infant alcohol is* ~ *murder* or *madness*; *his* ~ *word is as good as an oath*; *pretends to be no more than a* ~ *gentleman*; FEE ~). **4.** Plain in appear-ance or manner, unaffected, unsophisti-cated, ingenuous, natural, artless, (*a* ~ *person*; ~ *attire*; *a* ~ *heart* or *mind*, whence ~-**heart**ED², ~-**mind**ED², aa., ~-**mind**-edNESS n.). **5.** Foolish, ignorant, inex-perienced, (*am not so* ~ *as to suppose*).

6. Easily understood or done, presenting no difficulty, (*gave a* ~ *explanation*; *the problem is very* ~; *can be cured by a* ~ *device*). **7.** Of low ránk, humble, insignificant, trifling, (GENTLE *&* ~; *her* ~ *efforts to please*); hence or cogn. ~NESS (rare), simpli'CITY, nn., sim'PLY² adv. **8.** n. A herb used medicinally, the medicine made from it; *be cut for the* ~s, undergo operation for cure of folly. [ME, f. OF, f. L *simplus* or *simplex*]

sim'pleton (-plt-), n. Foolish, gullible, or half-witted person. [fancy noun f. prec.]

slmplǐ'cǐter, adv. Absolutely, universally, without limitation, not relatively or in certain respects only (cf. SECUNDUM *quid*). [L]

sim'pli|fӯ, v.t. Make simple, make easy to do or understand. So ~FICA'TION n. [f. F *simplifier* f. med. L *simplificare* (SIMPLE, -FY)]

sim'plism, n. Affected simplicity. [-ISM]

simulāc'rum, n. (pl. *-ra*). Image of something; shadowy likeness, deceptive substitute, mere pretence. [L (SIMULATE)]

sim'ūlant, a. Having the appearance *of* (esp. biol., as *stamens* ~ *of petals*). [foll., -ANT]

sim'ūlāte, v.t. Feign, pretend to have or feel, put on, (~ *virtue, indignation,* etc.); pretend to be, act like,. resemble, wear the guise of, mimic, (of word) take or have an altered form suggested by (word wrongly taken for its source), (*actor* ~s *king* etc.; *chameleon* ~s *its surroundings*; amuck, *for* amok, ~s *the English* muck). So simūlA'TION n. [f. L *simulare* (*similis* like), -ATE³]

simultān'éous, a. Occurring or operating at the same time (*with*); ~ *equation* (involving two or more variables). Hence simŭltane'ITY, ~NESS, nn., ~LY² adv. [f. L *simul* together, -ANEOUS after *instantaneous* or (obs.) *momentaneous*]

simūrg', n. Monstrous bird of Persian myth. [f. Pers. *sīmurgh*]

sin, n., & v.i. & t. (-nn-). **1.** Transgression, a transgression, against divine law or principles of morality (ORIGINAL ~; *living in open* ~; *deadly* or *mortal* ~, such as kills the soul or is fatal to salvation; *the seven deadly* ~s, pride, covetousness, lust, anger, gluttony, envy, sloth; one's *besetting* ~, to which one is especially tempted; *for my* ~s, joc., as a judgement for something or other; *the unpardonable* ~, that described *Matt.* xii. 31–32; *man of* ~, arch. or joc., reprobate, also Antichrist; *like* ~, sl., vehemently); offence *against* good taste, propriety, etc.; ~- *-eater*, one hired to take on himself a dead person's ~s by eating bread and drinking ale placed on the bier; ~-*offering*, sacrifice etc. in expiation of ~; hence ~'FUL, ~²LESS, aa., ~'fulLY², ~'lèssLY², advv., ~'fulNESS, ~'lèssNESS, nn. **2.** vb. Commit ~; offend *against* (*more* ~*ned against than* ~*ning*, see *King Lear* III. ii. 60, often

of victim of seduction); ~ one's *mercies*, be ungrateful for good luck; hence ~n'ER¹ n. (often joc., as *you young* ~*ner*; *as I am a* ~*ner*, form of asseveration). [OE *syn*(*n*), rel. to OS *sundea*, OHG *sunt*(*e*)*a*, ON *synth*; cf. L *sons sontis* guilty]

Sināit'ic, a. Of Mount Sinai or the peninsula of Sinai. [f. mod. L *Sinaiticus*]

Sinānthrŏp'us, n. Apelike man of the type represented by remains found near Peking. [mod. L, f. SINO- + Gk *anthrōpos* man]

sin'apism, n. Mustard plaster. [f. F *-isme* or LL f. Gk *sinapismus* f. *sinapi* mustard]

since, adv., prep., & conj. **1.** After specified or implied past time, throughout (usu. *ever* ~) or at some or any point in the period between such time & that which is present or being dealt with, (*has* or *had been healthy ever* ~; *then more flourishing than ever before or* ~; *has* ~ *been cut down*; *have* or *had not seen him* ~); ago (*happened many years* ~; *how long* ~ *is it?*; *saw him not long* ~). **2.** prep. After (specified past time or event), through or in period between time present or being dealt with & (such time), (*has* or *had been going· on, has happened,* ~ *1900* or *Christmas*; *have eaten nothing* ~ *yesterday*; ~ *seeing you I have* or *had heard* ~). **3.** conj. From the past time when, through or in the period between time present or being dealt with & that when (*what have you done* ~ *we met?*; *nothing has happened, there had been a disturbance,* ~ *we parted*); seeing that, inasmuch as, (~ *that is so, there is no more to be said*); (ellipt.) as being (*a more dangerous,* ~ *unknown, foe*). [reduced form of obs. *sithence* (or f. dial. *sin* (f. *sithen*) adv. + -ES), f. OE *siththon* (prop. *sith thon* after that) + -ES; cf. OHG *sīd* since etc., Goth. *seithus* late]

sincēre', a. Free from pretence or deceit, the same in reality as in seeming or profession, not assumed or put on, genuine, honest, frank. Hence or cogn. **since'rITY** n., ~LY² (-rlī) adv. (esp. in *yours* ~*ly* before signature of letter). [f. L *sincerus*]

sin'cǐpŭt, n. Head from forehead to top (cf. OCCIPUT). [L (*semi-* half, *caput* head)]

sine¹, n. (trigon.). (~ *of arc*) line drawn from one extremity of arc perpendicularly to radius which meets other extremity; (~ *of angle*) ratio of above line to radius (abbr. *sīn,* as *sin A,* ratio of the perpendicular subtending the angle A to the hypotenuse; *versed* ~, abbr. *vers,* unity minus the cosine). [f. L *sinus* curve]

sin'ě², L prep. Without (~ *dī'ě,* without date, of business indefinitely adjourned; ~ *quā nŏn,* indispensable condition or qualification).

sin'ecūr|e, n. Office of profit or honour without duties attached, esp. benefice without cure of souls. Hence ~ISM (3), ~IST(2), nn. [f. L *sine cura* without care]

sin'ew, n., & v.t. **1.** (Piece of) tough fibrous tissue uniting muscle to bone, tendon; (pl., loosely) muscles, bodily strength, wiriness, (fig.) what forms the strength of or sustains or holds together, framework, resources, (esp. *the* ~s *of war*, money, armaments, etc.); hence ~LESS, ~Y², aa., ~iNESS n. **2.** v.t. (poet.). Serve as ~s of, sustain, hold together. [OE *seon(o)we* obl. form of *si(o)nu* f. Gmc *senawō; = OS *senewa*, OHG *-awa*, ON *sin*]

sinfoni'a (-ē'a), n. (In early Italian operas) overture. [It., = symphony]

sing, v.i. & t. (*sǎng* or, now rare, *sǔng*; *sung*). **1.** Utter words, utter (words), in tuneful succession, esp. in accordance with a set tune (~ *one's praises*, be always praising him), whence ~'ABLE a. **2.** Produce vocal melody, utter (song, tune), (*birds were* ~*ing*; ~ *another song* or *tune*, ~ *small*, become more humble, be crestfallen). **3.** Make inarticulate melodious or humming or buzzing or whistling sounds (*wind, kettle, bee*, ~s); (of ears) be affected as with buzzing sound (also *have a* ~*ing in* one's *ears*). **4.** Compose poetry, celebrate (hero, beauty, great event, etc.) in verse. **5.** Usher (esp. old or new year) *out* or *in* with ~ing; put *to sleep, into good humour*, etc., with ~ing; ~ *out* t. & i., call out loudly, shout. **6.** ‖ ~*ing-man* [-ING²], paid ~er; ~*ing-master* [-ING¹], teacher of ~ing; ~*ing-voice* [-ING¹], voice as modulated in ~ing. Hence ~'ER¹ n. [OE (= OS, OHG) *singan*, ON *syngva*, Goth. *siggwan* f. Gmc *singwan*]

singe (-j), v.t. & i. (~*ing*), & n. **1.** Burn (t. & i.) superficially (~ person's *hair*, burn off tips as hairdressing operation; ~ *pig, fowl*, burn off bristles, down, after killing or plucking; *your dress is* ~*ing*; *his reputation is a little* ~*d*; ~ one's *feathers* or *wings*, take some harm esp. in venturesome attempt). **2.** n. Superficial burn (rare). [OE *sencgan*, = OFris. *senga*, MLG, MHG *sengen*, perh. causative f. SING (Gmc *sangjan*), w. ref. to hissing sound produced in burning]

Singhalese (-nggalēz'), a. & n. Var. of SINHALESE.

single¹ (sīng'gl), a. & n. **1.** One only, not double or multiple, united, undivided, designed for or used or done by one person etc. or one set or pair, (~ COMBAT, ENTRY, FILE³; ~ *flower*, that grows one on a stem, also that has not DOUBLE¹ corolla; ~ *game*, with one player on each side; ~ *wicket*, rudimentary form of cricket; ~ *court* in lawn tennis, fives, etc., of size etc. for ~ game; ~ *bed, room*, for one person; ~ *eye-glass*, for one eye, monocle; *a multitude inspired with a* ~ *purpose*; (of ticket) valid for outward journey only). **2.** Solitary, lonely, unaided, (a ~ *tree stands on the ridge*; *paid either by instalments or in a* ~ *sum*; ~ *life, state, man, woman*, unmarried; ~ *blessedness*, joc., unmarried

state). **3.** (In negative contexts) not to speak of more (*did not see a* ~ *one, a* ~ *person*; *can a* ~ *argument be advanced for it?*). **4.** Free from duplicity, sincere, consistent, guileless, ingenuous, (*a* ~ *eye*, devotion to one purpose, whence ~-eyED² a.; ~ *heart* or *mind*, simplicity of character, whence ~-**heart**ED², ~-**mind**ED², aa., ~-**mind'ed**NESS n.). **5.** ~-*acting*, (of engine etc.) with steam admitted only to one side of piston; ~-*breasted*, (of coat etc.) with only one set of buttons & buttonholes, not overlapping; ~-*cut*, (of file) with grooves cut in one direction only, not crossing; ~-*fire*, (of cartridge) not meant to be recharged after use; ~-*handed* a. & adv., (*done* etc.) without help from other persons (*by his* ~-*handed efforts; cannot be done* ~-*handed*), also with or for one hand (*the men played* ~-*handed against the women with both hands; two-handed* & ~-*handed swords*); ~-*loader*, breechloading rifle without magazine; ~*stick*, (fencing with) basket-hilted stick of about sword's length; hence ~NESS n., **sing'**LY² adv., (-ngg-). **6.** n. ~ game; ~ ticket; hit for one in cricket; (short whist) game won by 5-4; (pl.) twisted ~ threads of silk. [ME, f. OF, f. L *singulus*]

single² (sĭng'gl), v.t. Choose *out* as an example or as distinguishable or to serve some purpose. [f. prec.]

‖ **sing'let** (-ngg-), n. Garment worn below shirt, vest. [SINGLE¹, -ET¹; prob. orig. = unlined garment on anal. of DOUBLET]

sing'leton (-ngglt-), n. The only card of a suit at bridge etc.; single thing, only child, etc. [f. SINGLE on anal. of *simpleton*]

sing'sŏng, a. & n., & v.i. & t. **1.** In, recited with, monotonous rhythm. **2.** n. Monotonous rhythm; monotonous cadence in speaking; ‖ impromptu vocal concert, meeting for amateur singing. **3.** vb. Recite (verse etc.), speak, in ~ manner. [SING, SONG]

sing'ūlar (-ngg-), a. & n. **1.** (Gram.) of the form used in speaking of a single person or thing, not dual or plural; single, individual, (esp. *all* & ~, all whether taken together or separately); unexampled, unique, (now rare); unusual, remarkable from rarity, much beyond the average in degree, extraordinary, surprising; eccentric, unconventional, strangely behaved. **2.** n. (gram.). The ~ NUMBER¹; a word in the ~ number. Hence ~LY² adv. [ME, f. OF *singuler, -ier, -aire*, or f. L *singularis* (*-arius*), as SINGLE, -AR¹]

singūlă'rity (-ngg-), n. In adj. senses; esp., uncommonness, being remarkable, odd trait or peculiarity. [ME, f. OF *singularite* or LL *singularitas* (prec., -TY)]

sing'ūlariz|e (-ngg-), **-is**|e (-iz), v.t. Strip (word) of termination mistaken for that of plural (*pease* & *Chinese are* ~*d into* pea, Chinee). Hence ~A'TION n. [-IZE]

Sinhalese' (-nalĕz'), a. & n. (Member, language) of an Aryan people deriving from N. India and now living in Ceylon. [f. Skr. *Sinhala* Ceylon +-ESE]

sin'ister, a. (Her.) on left side of shield etc. (i.e. on right as seen by observer; BATON, BEND¹, ~; cf. DEXTER); (joc.) left; of evil omen; (usu. of person in regard to his appearance, or of his face or look) ill-looking, of malignant or villainous aspect; wicked, flagitious, (*a ~ design*). Hence ~LY² adv. [ME, f. OF *sinistre* or L *sinister* left]

sin'istral, a. Of, on, the left (rare); (of spiral shells) with whorls going to left & not as usu. to right. Hence ~LY² adv. [f. med. L *sinistralis* (prec., -AL)]

sin'istro-, comb. form of L *sinister* left, as ~*ce'rebral*, of the left hemisphere of the brain; ~*rse*, with leftward motion or aspect (esp. in bot. of climbing plants etc.).

sink¹, v.i. & t. (*sănk* or now rarely *sŭnk*; *sŭnk* or in adj. use usu. *sŭnken*). 1. Fall slowly downwards, decline, disappear below surface of liquid or below horizon, come gradually to lower level or pitch, droop, despond, subside, settle down, gradually expire or perish or cease, (*sun is ~ing, sank; my heart, spirits, sank; ship ~s*, goes to the bottom; *her eyes sank*, were turned downwards; *his head, chin, sank on his shoulder, chest; voice ~s*, becomes lower-pitched, or quieter; *sick man, life, is ~ing*, becoming weaker, dying; *prices ~*, become lower; *storm, river, ~s*, subsides; *ground ~s*, slopes down, also comes to lower level by subsidence; *darkness sank upon the scene*, descended; *~ into feebleness, degradation, the grave, a quicksand, a chair; ~ in* one's *estimation*, lose credit with him; *his eyes, cheeks, have sunk in* or *sunk*, fallen inwards, become hollow; so *sunken cheeks, eyes; here goes, ~ or swim*, said in running risks & taking chances). 2. Penetrate (intr.), make way, in or *into* (*bayonet sank in to the hilt; impression, lesson, ~s into the mind* or *memory*, becomes fixed; *dye ~s in*, is absorbed). 3. Cause or allow to ~, send below surface of liquid or ground, lower level of, keep (trans.) in obscurity or background, conceal, put out of sight, make no reference to, excavate, make by excavating, engrave, (*would sooner ~ the ship than surrender; ~ shaft, well*, dig or bore it; *~* one's *head on* one's *chest*, let it droop; *drought had sunk the streams; ~* one's *title, name, office*, etc., keep it temporarily secret, not obtrude it; *~ the* SHOP; *~ a fact*, keep it quiet; *~ one*self or one's *own interests*, be altruistic; SINKING-*fund*; *~ a die*, engrave it; *~ money*, invest it in undertaking from which it cannot be readily withdrawn, also lose it by such investment; *sunk* FENCE¹). Hence ~'ABLE a. [OE *sincan*, OS, OHG *sinkan*, ON *søkkva*, Goth. *sigqan* f. Gmc *sinkwan*]

sink², n. Place in which foul liquid collects (now usu. fig.; *the Chinese quarter is a ~ of iniquity*); basin or box of porcelain etc. with outflow pipe into which slops are thrown in kitchens etc.; pool or marsh in which river's water disappears by evaporation or percolation; opening in stage through which scenery is raised & lowered. [f. prec.]

sink'er, n. In vbl senses; esp.: weight used to sink fishing or sounding line (HOOK¹, *line*, & ~); DIE¹-~. [-ER¹]

sink'ing, n. In vbl senses; also: internal bodily sensation caused by hunger or apprehension; ~*-fund*, moneys set aside for the purpose of sinking or wiping out a State's or corporation's debt by degrees (*the ~-fund*, surplus of revenue over expenditure, devoted to reduction of national debt; *raid the ~-fund*, use such surplus in any year for other purposes). [-ING¹]

sinn'er. See SIN.

sinn'et. See SENNIT.

Sinn Fein (shĭn fān), n. A 20th-c. patriotic movement & party in Ireland aiming at national revival in language etc. as well as political independence. [Ir., = we ourselves]

Sin'o-, comb. form of Gk *Sinai*, the Chinese; ~PHOBE n. & a., hater of, hating, the Chinese; ~PHOB'IA; also with another adj. of nationality, with the meaning 'Chinese and' (~*-Japanese*).

Sin'ologue (-ŏg, -ŏg), n. Person versed in Sinology. [F (foll., -LOGUE)]

Sinŏl'ogў, n. Knowledge of the Chinese language, history, customs, etc. Hence SinŎL'OGIST n. [SINO-, -LOGY]

sin'ter, n. Siliceous or calcareous rock formed by deposit of springs. [G, = Eng. *sinder*; see CINDER]

sin'ŭate, a. (esp. bot.). Wavy-edged, with distinct inward & outward bends along edge. Hence ~LY² adv., sinŭA'TION n. [f. L *sinuare* (SINUS) bend, -ATE²]

sinŭŏs'itў, n. Being sinuous; a bend, esp. in a stream or road. [f. med. L *sinuositas* or F *-ité* (foll., -ITY)]

sin'ŭous, a. With many curves, serpentine, tortuous, undulating. Hence ~LY² adv. [f. L *sinuosus* (SINUS, -OUS)]

sin'us, n. (pl. *-uses, -ūs*). (Anat., zool.) cavity of bone or tissue, pouch-shaped hollow; (path.) fistula; (bot.) curve between lobes of leaf. [L, = bosom, recess]

-sion (-shn, -zhn), suf. of nn. of action or condition thr. F *-sion* (or direct) f. L *-sionem* (nom. *-sio*) a compd suf. of p.p. stems in *-s-* +-ION (e.g. *mansion, mission*).

Sioux (sōō, sū), n. (pl. the same, pr. sōō, sū, sōōz, sūz), & a. 1. Member of a N.-Amer.-Indian tribe. 2. adj. Of the ~. [F, f. native name]

sip, v.t. & i. (-pp-), & n. 1. Drink (t. & i.) in repeated tiny mouthfuls or by spoonfuls. 2. n. Small mouthful of liquid imbibed (*a ~ of brandy*). [ME, perh. a modification of SUP]

sīph'on, n., & v.i. & t. **1.** Pipe or tube shaped like inverted V with unequal legs for conveying liquid over edge of vessel & delivering it at lower level by utilizing atmospheric pressure; (also ~-*bottle*) aerated-water bottle from which liquid is forced out by pressure of gas through ~-tube; (zool.; also *siphuncle*) canal or conduit etc. in molluscs or shells, sucking-tube of some insects etc.; ~ *barometer*, with tube bent at bottom like inverted ~; ~*cup*, lubricating apparatus with oil led over edge of reservoir by capillary action through wick; ~ *gauge*, glass ~ attached to reservoir & containing mercury for indicating pressure etc. inside reservoir; hence ~AL, **sīphon'IC**, aa. **2.** vb. Conduct or flow (as) through ~ (*water is* ~*ing from the vase on to the tablecloth*); hence ~AGE(3) n. [f. F, or L f. Gk *siphōn* tube]

sīph'onĕt, n. One of two tubes through which aphides exude honeydew. [prec., -ET¹]

sīph'uncle (-ŭngkl), n. See SIPHON. [f. L *siphunculus* (SIPHON, -UNCLE)]

sĭpp'ĕt, n. Small piece of bread etc. soaked in liquid; one of the pieces of toast or fried bread served round mince etc. [app. dim. of SOP, see -ET¹]

sĭ quĭs, n. Notice posted in ordination-candidate's parish church serving similar purpose to banns. [L, = if anyone (know an impediment)]

sĭr, n., & v.t. (-rr-). **1.** Used as vocative in addressing the king, a royal prince, archduke, a master or superior, the Speaker of the House of Commons either in his own person on points of order or as embodiment of the House in ordinary debate, any male whose name is or is to be understood to be unknown to speaker, or boy etc. who is to be rebuked (pl. ~*s*, for which *gentlemen* is usu. substituted). **2.** Used as titular prefix to name of knight or baronet, always followed by Christian name, or its initial & surname, or the whole name (esp. *Sir John Moore*, *Sir J. Moore*, or, in familiar use esp. as vocative, *Sir John*). **3.** v.t. Address as ~ (*don't* ~ *me*). [ME; reduced form of SIRE]

sĭrc'ar, n. (Anglo-Ind.). Government; head of government or household; house-steward; native accountant. [f. Hind. f. Pers. *sarkār* (*sar* head, *kār* work)]

sĭrd'ar, n. (In India etc.) person in command, leader; (in Egypt) commander-in-chief (formerly a British officer) of army. [f. Hind. f. Pers. *sardār* (prec.), -*dār* possessor)]

sīre, n., & v.t. **1.** Father or male ancestor (poet.): male parent of beast, esp. stallion kept for breeding. **2.** v.t. Beget (esp. of stallions). [ME, f. OF, f. pop. L **seior* f. L SENIOR]

sĭr'ĕn, n. **1.** (Gk myth.; pl.) 'women, or half women & half birds, living on a rocky isle to which they lured unwary seafarers

with enchanting music. **2.** Sweet singer. **3.** Dangerously fascinating woman, temptress, tempting pursuit etc.; (attrib.) irresistibly tempting, as of a ~. **4.** = SIRENIAN. **5.** Instrument used in acoustic experiments & for making loud sound as warning etc. by revolution of perforated disc over jet of compressed air or steam; instrument for giving warning of air raids. [ME, f. OF *sereine* & LL *Sirena* f. L f. Gk *Seirēn*]

sīrēn'ian, a. & n. (Member) of the *Sirenia*, an order of fishlike ·mammals resembling cetaceans, including manatee & dugong. [mod. L *Sirenia* (prec.), -AN]

sīrg'ăng, n. Bright-green Asian bird, the green jackdaw. [E.-Ind.]

sirī'asis, n. Sunstroke; sun-bath as medical treatment. [L, f. Gk *seiriasis* (*seiriaō* be hot, -ASIS)]

Sĭr'ius. See DOG¹. [L, f. Gk *Seirios*]

sĭrk'ar. = SIRCAR.

sĭrl'oin, n. ‖ Upper part of loin of beef, with meat both above & (*undercut* or *fillet*) below the bone. [16th c. *surloin* f. OF **surloigne* var. of *surlonge* (SUR-², LOIN)]

sirŏcc'ō, **sci-**, n. (pl. ~*s*). (Italian name for) Sahara wind or simoom when it reaches Italy, (also for) warm sultry rainy wind prevailing in winter. [It., f. Arab. *sharq* the East]

si'rrah (arch.), ***sir(r)ee'** (U.S. & dial.), nn. voc. replacing *sir* in imperious or contemptuous use. [f. SIR; -*ah* of uncert. orig.; w. -*ee* cf. dial. *sirry*, *surry*, etc.]

sirup. See SYRUP.

sĭrvente (sěrvahnt'), n. Medieval usu. satirical lay of special metrical form. [f. F *sirvente* f. Prov. *sirventes*, ser-; E & F sp. due to taking -*es* as pl.]

sĭs'al, n. Fibre prepared from leaves of agave, used for cordage, ropes, etc.; the plant. [S~, port of Yucatan]

sĭs'kĭn, n. Olive-green songbird, kind of finch, often kept in cage. [16th c., f. MDu. *siseken*, dim. of *sijs*]

sĭss'oo, n. Valuable Indian timber (-tree). [Hind. *sīsū*]

sĭss'ȳ. See CISSY.

sĭs'ter, n. **1.** Daughter of same parents (also ~ *german*), or (strictly *half-*~) parent, as another person (the latter usu. specified by *my* etc. or possessive case; *the Fatal S~s* or *S~s three* or *three S~s*, the Fates; *S~ Anne*, person watching on behalf of another for an arrival, w. ref. to *Bluebeard*); (prop. ~-*in-law*) one's husband's or wife's ~ or brother's wife. **2.** Close female friend, female fellow member of class or sect or human race. **3.** Member of religious community of women (~ *of* CHARITY; ~ *of mercy*, member of nursing sisterhood, esp. of R.-C. one founded in Dublin 1827; *little S~s of the poor*, French R.-C. charitable sisterhood; LAY² ~). **4.** Hospital nurse in authority over others. **5.** Personified quality or thing regarded as female that closely resembles another (*prose, younger ~ of verse; ~ ships*, built on same design). **6.** ~*-hook*, double hook that opens to admit rope etc. & closes into a figure 8. Hence ~LESS, ~LY [1], aa., ~liNESS n. [OE *sweoster*, OS *swestar*, OHG *-ter*, Goth. *swistar* f. Gmc **swestr-*, cogn. w. L *soror*; the current form *sister* is ME f. ON *systir*]

sis'terhōōd, n. Being a sister or sisters, relation between sisters; society of women bound by monastic vows or devoting themselves to religious or charitable work. [-HOOD]

Sis'tine, a. Of one of the popes called *Sixtus* (~ *chapel*, in Vatican, with frescoes by Michelangelo; ~ *Madonna*, picture by Raphael removed from church of San Sisto in Piacenza). [f. It. *Sistino* (*Sisto* Sixtus, -INE [1])]

sis'trum, n. (pl. *-tra*). Jingling instrument or rattle used by ancient Egyptians esp. in rites of Isis. [L, f. Gk *seistron* (*seiō* shake)]

sisȳphē'an, a. As of Sisyphus, Greek condemned in Tartarus to push a stone up hill & begin again when it rolled down, everlastingly laborious. [f. L f. Gk *Sisupheios* (*Sisuphos*), -AN]

sit, v.i. & t. (*săt*, arch. *săte*). **1.** Take or be in position in which body is supported more or less upright by buttocks resting on ground or raised seat (*~s well*, has good seat in riding; *~ tight*, colloq., remain firmly in one's place, not be shaken off or move away or yield to distractions); be engaged in some occupation in which this position is usual (*~ in judgement*, assume right of judging others, be censorious; *~ for one's portrait*, give painter interviews or sittings; || *~ for fellowship* etc., undergo examination for it; *~ for borough* etc., represent it in Parliament; *Parliament, Courts, are ~ting*, in session; *~ at home*, be inactive). **2.** (Of birds & some animals) rest with legs bent & body close to ground or perch (*shoot bird, hare, ~ting*, when not on wing or running); remain on nest to hatch eggs (*~ting hen*, engaged in hatching; *wants to ~*, is broody). **3.** (Chiefly of inanimate things) be in more or less permanent position (*~s the wind there?*, is it in that quarter?, is that the state of affairs?; *food ~s heavy on the stomach*, is not soon digested; *her dress, imperiousness*, etc., *~s well on her*, suits, fits; *~ting tenant*, one in present occupation; *his principles ~ loosely on him*, do not bind him much). **4.** Keep one's seat on (horse etc.; *he could not ~ his mule*). **5.** Undergo, be a candidate at, (examination etc.). **6.** *~ down*, take seat after standing (also refl. arch., as *sat him, pray ~ you, down*), (mil.) encamp *before* place to besiege it; *~-down strike*, one in which strikers refuse to leave the place where

they are working; *~ down under*, submit tamely to (insult etc.). **7.** *~ in* (colloq.), act as *~ter-in* (= BABY-*~ter*). **8.** *~ on* or *upon*, (of jury etc.) hold session concerning; *~ on his head* (as way of keeping fallen horse quiet); (sl.) repress or rebuke or snub (*he wants ~ting upon*). **9.** *~ out*, take no part in something, esp. in particular dance (also trans., as *sat out the next dance*), also *~ outdoors*, (trans.) outstay (other visitors) or stay till end of (performance). **10.** *~ over* (player), (bridge) be on his left hand (and so in advantageous position). **11.** *~ under*, be one of congregation preached to by (minister). **12.** *~ up*, rise from lying to *~ting* posture, remain (*late, nursing*, etc.) out of bed, *~ erect* without lolling (*make one ~ up*, colloq., subject him to hard work, pain, surprise, etc.); *~ up & take notice* (colloq.), have one's interest (suddenly) aroused. **13.** *~'fast* n., horny sore on horse's back. [OE *sittan*, OS *-ian*, OHG *sizzan*, ON *sitja* (Goth. *sitan*), f. Gmc **sitjan* f. **set-* cogn. w. L *sedēre*]

site, n., & v.t. **1.** Ground on which town or building stood, stands, or is to stand. **2.** v.t. Locate, place. [ME, f. AF, or f. L *situs*]

|| **sith,** conj. (arch., bibl.). Since. [see SINCE]

siti|o-, sīt|o-, comb. form of Gk *sitos, sition*, food, as *~ŏl'ogy* dietetics, *~ophŏb'ia* morbid aversion to food.

sitt'er, n. In vbl senses; esp.: person sitting for portrait; *good, bad, ~*, hen that sits well etc.; (sl., from *to shoot bird sitting*) easy shot, thing easily done. [-ER [1]]

sitt'ing, n. In vbl senses; esp.: time during which one sits continuously (*wrote the whole poem at a ~*; *all-night ~ of House of Commons*; *can you give me six ~s?*, for portrait); clutch of eggs; seat in church appropriated to a person; *~-room*, space enough to accommodate seated persons, also a room used for sitting in (opp. *bedroom*). [-ING [1]]

sit'ūātėd, sit'ūate (arch.), aa. In specified situation (*situated on the top of the hill; awkwardly situated*, in a difficulty). [f. LL *situatus* (L *situs* SITE, -ATE [2, 3])]

sitūā'tion, n. Place, with its surroundings, occupied by something (*house stands in a fine ~; unrivalled for ~*); set of circumstances, position in which one finds oneself, (*came out of a difficult ~ with credit*); critical point or complication in drama (*curtain falls on a strong ~*); employee's, esp. domestic's, place or paid office (*cannot find a ~*). [F, or f. med. L *situatio* (as prec., -ATION)]

sitz-bath. See BATH [1].

Si'va (sē-), n. Hindu god held supreme by his special votaries, & by others associated as principle of destruction with Brahma & Vishnu in a triad. Hence ~**is'tic** [-IST, -IC] a., ~**ITE** [1](1) n. & a. [Hind., f. Skr. *çiva* propitious]

six, a. & n. **1.** One more than five, 6, vi, (often agreeing with understood noun, as ~ *of the men*, ~ *of them*, ~ *o'clock* or ~; ~ *to one*, long odds; *two & ~*, half-a--crown; ‖ ~ *& eight(pence)*, common item in solicitors' bills; ‖ ~ *& ~*, 6/6; *it is ~ of one & half-a-dozen of the other*, difference is merely nominal; *twenty-~* or ~-*&--twenty*, & so on to ~-*&-ninety*; *am not ~ yet*, years old); ~-*footer*, person 6 ft in height, thing 6 ft long; ‖ ~'*pence*, (silver coin worth) 6*d. (have not got a ~pence)*; ‖ ~'*penny* a., costing or worth 6*d.* (~-*penny bit*, or ~*penny* as n., the coin ~-pence; ‖ *seven-&-~penny* etc., costing 7/6 etc.); ~-*shooter*, ~-chambered revolver; hence ~'FOLD a. & adv. **2.** n. The number ~ *(twice ~ is twelve; at ~es & sevens*, in confusion); card or die-face of ~ pips *(the ~ of spades; (double)~es*, die--throw of two ~es); ‖ (pl.) candles made ~ to the lb. [OE, ON *sex*, OS, OHG *sehs*, Goth. *saihs*, cogn. w. L *sex*]

six'ain, n. Six-line stanza. [F, see -AN]

six'er, n. Hit for six in cricket. [-ER¹]

sixte, n. One of the positions in fencing. [F, f. L *sextus* sixth]

sixteen', a. & n. **1.** One more than fifteen, 16, xvi; ~*mo* or *16mo*, = SEXTODECIMO; hence ~TH² a. & n. **2.** n. The number ~ *(twice ~ is thirty-two).* [-TEEN]

sixth, a. & n. **1.** Next after fifth *(the, a,~,* often as n. with ellipse of noun, esp. *the ~* = 6th day of month; ‖ ~ FORM¹); ~ *part*, one of six equal parts into which thing may be divided. **2.** n. = ~ part; ‖ *the* ~ form; (mus.) interval of which the span involves six alphabetical names of notes, harmonic combination of notes thus separated. [OE *sixta*, see -TH²]

sixth'ly̆, adv. In the sixth place (in enumerations). [-LY²]

six'tў, a. & n. **1.** Six times ten, 60, lx, (~-*one, -eight*, etc.; ~-*first, -fourth*, etc.); ~-*four-mo*, (size of) book or page given by folding sheet six times into 64 leaves (for L *in quarto et sexagesimo*); hence **six'ti**-ETH a. & n. **2.** n. The number ~; *the sixties*, years between 59 & 70 in life or century. [OE *siextig* (-TY²)]

siz'able, a. Of large size; (angling) above prescribed size limit. [SIZE¹, -ABLE]

‖ **siz'ar**, n. Student at Cambridge or Trinity College, Dublin, paying reduced fees & formerly charged with certain menial offices, cf. SERVITOR. Hence ~SHIP n. [foll. = ration, -ER¹ (cf. *scholar*)]

size¹, n., & v.t. & i. **1.** (hist.). Standard of weight or measure for some article esp. of food or drink; ‖ (Camb. Univ.; also siz'ING¹ n.) ration of food or drink from buttery. **2.** Dimensions, magnitude, (*is of vast, diminutive*, ~, very large or small; ~ *matters less than quality*; *are both of a*, i.e. the same, ~; *is the ~ of*, i.e. as big as, *an egg; what ~*, i.e. how big, *is it?; that's about the ~ of it*, colloq., a true account of the matter); one of the usu. numbered

classes into which things, esp. garments, otherwise similar are divided in respect of ~ *(is made in several ~s; takes ~ 7 in gloves; is quite a ~, three ~s, too big*; OUT ~). **3.** Implement for sizing pearls. **4.** ~-*stick*, shoemaker's measure for taking length of foot; hence (-)SIZED² (-zd) a. **5.** v.t. Group or sort in ~s or according to ~, whence siz'ER¹(2) n.; ~ *up*, estimate ~ of, (colloq.) form judgement of (person etc.); **6.** v.i. ‖ (Camb. Univ.) order ~. [ME, f. OF *sise* aphetic f. *assise* ASSIZE]

size², n., & v.t. **1.** Gelatinous solution used in glazing paper & stiffening textiles & in many manufacturing processes; hence siz'y² a. **2.** v.t. Glaze or stiffen or treat with ~. [ME, perh. = prec.]

siz'zle, v.i., & n. (colloq.). **1.** Make sputtering sound as in frying. **2.** n. Such noise. [imit.]

sjäm'bŏk (sh-), n., & v.t. **1.** Rhinoceros--hide whip. **2.** v.t. Flog with ~. [Afrikaans (now *sambok*) f. Malay *chamboq* f. Urdu *chābuk*]

skald. See SCALD².

skat (-aht), n. A three-handed card-game popular in Germany. [G, f. It. *scarto* a, discard]

skāte¹, n. Kinds of ray-fish, esp. rhomboidal long-tailed kind. [ME, f. ON *skata*]

skāt|e², n., & v.i. & t. **1.** One of pair of implements, each with steel blade or set of rollers, attached beneath boots & enabling wearer to glide in curves over ice or *(roller-~e*) hard floor. **2.** vb. Move, perform (specified figure), on ~es (~*e over thin ice*, talk on subject needing tactful treatment); ~*ing-rink*, piece of ice artificially made, or floor reserved, for ~ing; hence ~'ER¹ n. [17th c. *schates* pl. f. Du. *schaats* (pl. *schaatsen*) f. ONF *escache* stilt]

skean, skēne, skain, n. Gaelic dagger used in Ireland & Scotland; ~-*dhu* (-dōō), dagger stuck in stocking as part of Highland costume. [f. Gael. *sgian* knife, *dubh* black]

skĕdăd'dle, v.i., & n. (colloq.). **1.** Run away, disperse in flight. **2.** n. Hurried flight or dispersal. [U.S., of unkn. orig.]

skee. See SKI.

skein (-ān), n. Bundle of yarn or thread or silk made by coiling it many times, drawing it out to the coil's length, & folding it; flock of wild geese etc. in flight; (fig.) tangle, confusion. [ME, f. OF *escaigne*, of unkn. orig.]

skĕl'ĕton, n. **1.** Hard internal or external framework of bones, cartilage, shell, woody fibre, etc., supporting or containing an animal or vegetable body, whence skĕl'ĕtAL a., skĕl'ĕto- comb. form, skĕlĕtŏG'RAPHY n., etc. **2.** Dried bones of human being or other animal fastened together in same relative positions as in life (~ *at the feast*, something that alloys pleasure, intrusive care; ~ *in the cup-*

board, family ~, discreditable or humiliating fact concealed from strangers); part of anything that remains after its life or usefulness is gone. **3.** Framework or essential part of anything (~ *crew, regiment,* etc., permanent nucleus ready for filling up, cadre; ~ *drill,* with companies etc. represented by two men separated by long rope; ~ *key,* fitting many locks by having interior of bit hollowed; ~ or ~-*face type,* with thin strokes). **4.** Outline sketch, epitome, abstract. **5.** (By exag.) thin person. [f. Gk neut. of *skeletos* dried-up, whence L *sceletus*]

skĕl'ĕtonize, -ise (-ĭz), v.t. Reduce to skeleton or abstract by destroying flesh, the tissue between veins of leaves, etc., or by omitting details. [-IZE]

‖ **skĕlp,** v.t. & i., & n. (chiefly Sc.). **1.** Slap, smack; (v.i.) hurry along. **2.** n. (Noise made by) a slap or smack. [ME, prob. imit.]

skene. See SKEAN.

skĕp, skip, n. Kinds, varying locally, of wooden or wicker basket; straw or wicker beehive. [ME, f. ON *skeppa,* rel. to OHG *sceffil* (G *scheffel* bushel)]

skepsis, skeptic, etc. See **sce-.**

skĕ'rrў, n. Reef, rocky isle. [f. ON *sker*]

skĕtch, n., & v.t. & i. **1.** Preliminary, rough, slight, merely outlined, or unfinished drawing or painting often as experiment for, or memorandum for use in, regular picture; brief account without many details conveying general idea of something, rough draft, general outline; slight play often of musical kind or short descriptive article; musical composition of single movement; ~-*block, -book,* arrangements of drawing-paper leaves for doing series of ~es on; ~-*map,* with outlines but little detail; hence ~'ɏ² a., ~'ĭLɏ² adv., ~'ĭNESS n. **2.** vb. Make or give ~ of; make ~es esp. of landscape (*went out* ~*ing*); hence ~'ER¹ n. [f. Du. *schets* or G *skizze* f. It. *schizzo,* perh. f. L f. Gk *skhedios* extempore]

skew, a. & n. **1.** Oblique, slanting, sideways, distorted, (now chiefly in archit., mech., & math.; ~ *bridge,* with line of arch not at right angles to abutment; ~ *chisel,* with oblique edge; ~ *wheel,* bevel wheel with oblique teeth; ~ *curve,* in three dimensions); (math.) having symmetry distorted by reversal of some element on opposite sides; ~'*back,* sloping face of an abutment on which the extremity of an arch rests; ~'*bald,* (esp. of horse) with irregular patches of white & some colour (prop. not black, cf. *piebald*); ~-*eyed,* squinting; ‖~-*whiff* (colloq. & dial.), askew. **2.** n. Sloping top of buttress; coping of gable; stone built into bottom of gable to support coping. [17th c., rel. to ME *skew* vb ' turn aside ' etc., f. ONF *eskiu(w)er* = OF *eschiver,* see ESCHEW; cf. ASKEW]

skew'er, n., & v.t. **1.** Pin of wood or iron for⸢ holding meat compactly together while cooking; (joc.) sword etc. **2.** v.t. Fasten together, pierce, (as) with ~. [17th c., var. of dial. *skiver,* of unkn. orig.]

ski (skē, shē), n. (pl. ~, ~s), & v.i. (~'d pr. skēd, shĕd; ~*ing* pr. skē'ĭng, shē'-). **1.** One of pair of wooden runners about 8 ft long & 4 in. broad fastened under feet for travelling over snow esp. in Scandinavia; ~-*joring* (-yĕr'ĭng), winter sport in which the skier is towed by a horse. **2.** v.i. Go on ~. [Norw., f. ON *skith* billet, snowshoe]

skiagraphy etc. See **scia-.**

skid, n., & v.t. & i. (-dd-). **1.** Piece of frame or timber serving as buffer, support, inclined plane, etc.; wooden or metal shoe preventing wheel from revolving used as drag (also ~-*pan*), other kinds of wheel-locking contrivance; slip or slide of wheel on muddy ground. **2.** vb. Support or move or protect or check with ~; (of wheel or vehicle) slide forwards or backwards or sideways on slippery ground. [17th c., of obsc. orig.]

skier (skē'er, shē'er), n. Person using ski (cf. SKYER). [-ER¹]

skiff, n. Light rowing or sculling boat. [16th c., f. F *esquif,* Sp., Port. *esquife,* or It. *schifo,* of Gmc origin.]

skif'fle, n. Kind of music played by a ~ *group* (a band accompanying a single singing guitarist or banjoist on a variety of instruments). [perh. imit.]

skil'ful, a. Having or showing skill (*at, in*), practised, expert, adroit, ingenious. Hence ~Lɏ² adv. [foll., -FUL]

skill, n. Expertness, practised ability, facility in doing something, dexterity, tact. [ME, f. ON *skil* distinction, cf. SKILLS]

skilled (-ld), a. Having or showing skill, skilful, (rare exc. in phrr. ~ *labour, workman,* etc., = highly-trained, or followed by *in*). [-ED²]

skill'ĕt, n. Small metal pot with long handle & usu. legs used in cooking. [ME, of unkn. orig.]

skill-lĕss, a. (rare). Without skill, knowing nothing *of.* [-LESS]

skills, v.i. 3rd sing. impers. (arch.). *It* ~ *not,* makes no difference, is of no use, (usu. *to* do). [ME, f. ON *skilja* distinguish, or *skila* decide, see SKILL]

‖ **skill'ў,** n. Thin broth or soup or gruel (usu. of oatmeal & water flavoured with meat. [abbr. f. *skilligalee,* prob. fanciful]

skim, v.t. & i. (-mm-), & a. **1.** Take scum or cream or floating layer from surface of (liquid), take (cream etc.) from surface of liquid, (~ *the cream off,* often fig., take best part of; ~*ming-dish,* sl., flat-bottomed racing yacht, fast light motor-boat); keep touching lightly or nearly touching (surface) in passing over; (intr.) go thus over ⸢or *along* surface, glide along in air; read (bk. & i.) superficially, look over cursorily, gather salient facts

contained in. **2.** adj. ~ *milk*, from which
cream has been ~med. [ME, back form.
f. SKIMMER, or f. OF *escumer* f. *escume* f.
WG *skŭm* SCUM]

skimm'er, n. In vbl senses; esp.: ladle
etc. for skimming liquids; fast light
motor-boat; kinds of water-bird, esp.
black ~, with flat mandibles. [ME, f. OF
escumoir, -eur (prec.); later f. prec. + -ER[1]]

skimp, v.t. & i. Supply (person with or in
food, money, etc.; material, expenses,
etc.) meagrely, stint; be parsimonious.
Hence ~'Y[2] a., ~'INGLY[2] adv. [19th c.;
also 18th c. *skimp* adj. scanty; orig. unkn.,
cf. SCRIMP]

skin[1], n. **1.** Flexible continuous covering
of human or other animal body (*with a
whole* ~, unwounded; *save* one's ~, get
off safe; *change* one's ~, undergo impossible change of character etc.; *get under*
one's ~, colloq., take strong hold on one,
interest or annoy one intensely; *would not
be in his* ~, should not like to be he; *is
only* ~ & *bone*, very thin, & so ~n'Y[2] a.,
~n'INESS n.; *escape with the* ~ *of* one's *teeth*,
narrowly; *thick, thin*, ~, imperviousness,
sensitiveness, to affront or criticism; *fair,
dark*, etc., ~, complexion; *near is my*
SHIRT, *nearer my* ~); (anat.) one layer of
this (*true* or *inner* ~, derma; *outer* ~,
epidermis). **2.** Hide of flayed animal
with or without the hair etc.; material
prepared from ~s esp. of smaller animals
(cf. *hide*). **3.** Vessel for wine or water
made of animal's whole ~. **4.** Outer
coating of plant, fruit, etc., rind. **5.**
Planking or plating of ship or boat inside
or outside ribs. **6.** GOLD-*beaters'* ~; ~-
bound, with ~ tightly stretched over
flesh; ~-*deep*, (of wound, also of emotion,
impression, beauty, etc.) superficial, not
deep or lasting; ~-*diver*, one who dives
without a diving-suit, usu. in deep water
with AQUALUNG; ~-*effect* (electr.), tendency
of high-frequency alternating current to
flow through the outer layer only of a
conductor; ~-*friction*, lateral resistance
to way of ship etc. passing through water;
~'*ful* (*of wine* etc., or abs.), as much liquor
as one can hold; * ~-*game* (sl.), swindle; ~-
grafting, surgical substitution of ~ cut
from another part or person for damaged
part. Hence (-)**skinnED**[2] (-nd), ~'LESS, aa.
[ME, f. ON *skinn*; cf. OHG *scindan* flay]

skin[2], v.t. & i. (-nn-). Cover (sore etc.,
usu. *over*) as with skin, (of wound etc.)
form or become covered with new skin,
cicatrize, (usu. *over*); strip of skin, withdraw skin from, flay, (*keep your eyes
~ned*, sl., be watchful or cautious);
(colloq.) strip oneself, strip (another), of
tight garment such as jersey; (sl.) fleece,
swindle; ~'*flint*, niggard, miser. [f. prec.]

skink, n. Kinds of small-limbed lizard.
[f. older F *scinc*, or L f. Gk *skingkos*]

skinn'er, n. In vbl senses; esp., (now
chiefly in name of a CITY company) dealer
in skins, furrier. [-ER[1]]

skip[1], v.i. & t. (-pp-), & n. **1.** (Of lambs,
kids, children, etc.) jump about, gambol,
caper, frisk, move lightly from one foot
on to the other; (of children, esp. girls)
use ~ping-rope; shift quickly from one
subject or occupation to another, be desultory, (usu. *off, from*, etc.); (sl.) make
off, disappear; omit, make omissions, in
dealing with a series or in reading (*do
them all without* ~ping any or ~ping;
always ~ *the descriptions*; ~s *as he reads*;
~ *every tenth row*); ~'*jack*, jumping toy
made of bird's merrythought, also kinds
of fish & butterfly & beetle named from
their movements; || ~*ping-rope*, length of
rope with two wooden handles used in
girls' game of ~ping; hence ~p'ingLY[2]
adv. **2.** n. ~ping movement, esp. quick
shift from one foot to other (HOP[3], ~, &
jump). [ME, app. f. Scand., cf. MSw.
skuppa, skoppa in same sense]

|| **skip[2],** n. College servant, scout, esp. at
Trinity College, Dublin. [prob. f. obs.
skip-kennel lackey (prec.)]

skip[3], n. Captain or director of side at
bowls & curling. [abbr. of SKIPPER[2]]

skip[4], n. Cage, bucket, etc., in which men
or materials are lowered & raised in mines
& quarries. [var. of SKEP]

skip[5]. See SKEP.

skipp'er[1], n. In vbl senses of SKIP[1]; esp.
(zool.) kind of usu. small brown butterfly.
[-ER[1]]

skipp'er[2], n. Sea captain, esp. master of
small trading vessel; ~'s *daughters*, (with
pun on prec.) tall white-crested waves;
captain of an aircraft; (transf.) captain of
side in games. [ME, f. MDu. or MLG
schipper (*schip* SHIP[1], -ER[1])]

skipp'et, n. (hist.). Small cylindrical
wooden box used to enclose and protect
large seal attached by ribbon to deed.
[ME, with var. *skibbet* (now dial.), of
unkn. orig.]

|| **skirl,** v.i., & n. (Make) sound character-
istic of bagpipes. [prob. Scand., cf. Norw.
dial. *skrylla*]

skirm'ish, n., & v.i. **1.** Piece of irregular
or unpremeditated fighting esp. between
small or outlying parties, slight engagement; encounter of wit, argument, etc.
2. v.i. Fight in small parties, loose order,
or unpremeditated way; hence ~ER[1] n.
[ME, f. OF *eskirmir*, also *escremir*, f. WG
skirmjan (cf. OHG *scirmen* f. *scirm*
shield), see -ISH]

ski'rret, n. Kind of water parsnip formerly much used as table vegetable.
[ME *skirwhit(e)*, app. alt. f. OF *eschervis*,
var. of *carvi* CARAWAY]

skirt, n., & v.t. & i. **1.** Part of coat or
shirt that hangs below waist; woman's
outer garment shaped like petticoat from
waist downwards (*divided* ~, loose
trousers resembling ~), whence ~'ING[1](3)
n.; (vulg. sl.) woman (esp. in *bit of* ~);
edge, border, extreme part, (often pl.; *on
the* ~s *of London*, just inside or outside of

it); ~ *of beef* etc., the diaphragm & other membranes as cheap food-material; ~- -*dance*(r), -*dancing*, with full ~ waved about giving graceful effects; hence -~ED², ~'LESS, aa. 2. vb. Go along or round or past the edge of, be situated along; go *along* coast, wall, etc.; ~*ing* or ~*ing-board*, along bottom of room-wall. [ME, f. ON *skyrta*, corresp. to OE *scyrte* SHIRT]

skit¹, n. Light piece of satire, burlesque, literary squib, (often *upon*). [18th c., rel. to 17th c. *skit*, fig. meaning, (unkn. orig.), perh. f. ON **skyt-* cogn. w. *skjóta* SHOOT]

skit², n. (colloq.). A number, crowd (esp. in pl., heaps, lots). [orig. unkn.]

skitt'er, v.i. (Of wild-fowl) go splashing along water in rising or settling; fish by drawing bait along surface. [app. frequent. of dial. *skite*, perh. f. ON **skýt-* modified stem of *skjóta* shoot; cf. SKIT¹]

skitt'ish, a. (Of horses etc.) nervous, inclined to shy, excitable, playful, fidgety; (chiefly of women) capricious, coquettish, flirting, lively, given to amusement, gadding about, affecting youthfulness. Hence ~LY² adv., ~NESS n. [ME, of obsc. orig., perh. f. ON **skyt-* SKIT¹+-ISH]

skit'tle, n., & v.t. 1. ‖ ~*s*, game played with nine pins (~*s* or ~-*pins*) set up at end of ~-*alley* or ~-*ground* to be bowled down with ~-*ball* (*beer & ~s*, amusement, as *life is not all beer & ~s*); (in full *table* ~*s*) game played with nine pins set up on board to be knocked down by swinging suspended ball; (sl., as int.) ~*s!*, rubbish, nonsense. 2. v.t. ~ *out*, (crick.) get (batsmen) out rapidly in succession. [17th c. (also *kittle-pins*), of unkn. orig.]

skive, v.t. Split or pare (hide, leather); grind away surface of (gem). [f. ON *skifa*, rel. to ME *schive* (now dial. *shive*), slice]

skiv'er, n. Knife for skiving leather; thin leather got by skiving. [-ER¹]

‖ **skivv'y**, n. (colloq.). Female domestic servant (usu. derog.). [alt. f. *slavvy*, SLAVEY]

skū'a, n. Kinds of gull-like predatory sea-bird which pursue other birds and make them disgorge the fish they have caught. [f. ON *skūfr*]

*skŭldŭgg'ery (-g-), sc-, n. (joc.). Trickery; corrupt behaviour. [orig. unkn.]

skŭlk, v.i. Lurk, keep oneself concealed esp. in cowardice or with evil intent, stay or sneak away in time of danger, shirk duty, avoid observation. Hence ~'ER¹ & (in same sense) **skŭlk**, nn., ~'ingLY² adv. [ME, app. f. Scand., cf. Norw. *skulka* lurk, Da. *skolke*, Sw. *skolka* shirk, play truant]

skŭll, n. Bony case of the brain, frame of the head, cranium, (~ & *cross-bones*, representation of bare ~ with two thigh-bones crossed below it as emblem of death); ~-*cap*, close-fitting cap usu. of velvet worn indoors chiefly by old men, also kinds of plant with helmet-shaped flower. Hence (-)~ED² (-ld) a. [ME *scolle*, of unkn. orig.]

skŭnk, n. Black white-striped bushy-tailed American carnivorous animal about size of cat able to emit powerful stench from liquid secreted by anal glands as defence; its fur; stinking or contemptible fellow. [f. Amer.-Ind. *segankw*, *segongw*]

Skup'shtĭna (-ŏŏp-), n. Jugoslav parliament. [Serb., = assembly]

skỹ, n., & v.t. 1. (The vault of) heaven (*blue, clear, cloudy, overcast*, etc., ~; *if the ~ fall we shall catch larks*, unlikely cataclysms are not worth providing against; *under the open ~*, out of doors; often pl., as *laud to the skies*, highly; *was raised to the skies*, taken up to heaven). 2. Climate, atmosphere, (*try what a warmer ~*, *warmer skies, will do for you*). 3. ~-*blue* a. & n., colour(ed) like clear ~; ~-*born*, poet., of divine birth; ~-*clad*, joc., naked; ~-*high* adv. & a., so as to reach, reaching, the ~; ~'*lark* n., lark that flies spirally upwards singing, v.i. (with pun on LARK¹,², & perh. of naut. orig., w. ref. to clambering about rigging), frolic, play tricks or practical jokes, ballyrag, etc.; ~'*light*, window set in plane of roof or ceiling; ~'*line*, outline of hill etc. defined against ~ (*is on the* ~*line*, seen outlined on ~); ~ *marker*, parachute flare dropped to mark target area; ~ *pilot*, sl., parson; ~-*rocket*, discharged upwards, (v.i., fig., of prices etc.) rise steeply; ~'*sail*, light sail above royal in square-rigged ship; ~-*scape*, picture chiefly representing ~; ~ *scraper*, = ~*sail*, also very tall building, tall chimney, etc.; ~'*way*, airways; ~-*writing*, legible smoke-trails made as advertising method by aeroplane; hence ~'eY², ~'LESS, aa., ~'WARD(s) adv. & a. 4. v.t. Hit (cricket-ball) high up; hang (picture) high on wall, treat picture of (artist) so. [ME *ski(es)* cloud(s) f. ON *skỹ* (f. **skiuja*), rel. to OS *skio*, OE *scēo*]

Skỹe (tĕ'rrier), n. Small long-bodied short-legged long-haired slate or fawn coloured variety of Scotch terrier, named from Skye.

skỹ'er, n. High hit at cricket (cf. SKIER). [*sky* + -ER¹]

slăb¹, n., & v.t. (-bb-). 1. Thin flat usu. square or rectangular piece of stone or other rigid material; (of timber) outer cut sawn from log; ~-*sided*, long & lank; ~-*stone*, kinds of stone that split readily into ~s. 2. v.t. Remove ~s from (log, tree) to prepare it for sawing into planks; ~*bing-gang*, set of saws for doing this. [ME, of unkn. orig.]

‖ **slăb**², a. (arch.). Viscous, (of liquid) thick & sticky, (chiefly w. ref. to *Macbeth* IV. i. 32). [rel. to *slab* ooze, sludge, app. f. Scand., cf. older Da. *slab* mud, Norw., Sw. *slabb* wet filth]

slabber. = SLOBBER. [16th c., prob. of Du. or LG orig., cf. Du., LG *slabber(e)n*]

slăck, a., adv., n., & v.t. & i. **1.** Sluggish, remiss, relaxed, languid, loose, inactive, negligent, (~ *water*, about turn of tide, esp. low tide; ~ *in stays*, naut., slow in going about; *a* ~ *rope*, not taut; *keep a* ~ *hand* or *rein*, ride, or fig. govern, carelessly; ~ *trade*, *business*, *market*, with little doing; ~ *weather*, inclining to indolence); ~ *lime*, slaked lime; hence ~'EN⁶ v.t. & i., ~'LY² adv., ~'NESS n. **2.** adv. (In comb. w. *dry*, *bake*, etc.) slowly, insufficiently, (~*-dried hops*; *to* ~*-bake bread*). **3.** n. ~ part of rope (*haul in the* ~); ~ time in trade etc.; (colloq.) spell of inactivity or laziness (*I'm going to have a good* ~ *this afternoon*); (dial.) check, impertinence; (pl.) trousers; coal-dust used chiefly for making briquettes etc. **4.** vb. ~en; make loose (rope; often *off*, *away*); (colloq.) take a rest, be indolent, whence ~'ER¹ n.; = SLAKE (lime); ~ *off*, abate vigour; ~ *up*, reduce speed of train etc. before stopping. [OE *sleac*, *slæc*, adj., = MDu., MLG *slak*, OHG *slach*, ON *slakr*, cogn. w. L *laxus*; the sense 'coal-dust' is of obsc. orig.]

slăg, n., & v.i. (-gg-). **1.** Dross separated in fused state in reduction of ores, vitreous smelting-refuse, clinkers; BASIC ~; volcanic scoria; ~*-wool*, = mineral WOOL; hence ~g'Y²(-g-) a. **2.** v.i. Form~, cohere into ~like mass. [16th c., f. MLG *slagge* of obsc. orig.]

slain. See SLAY.

slāke, v.t. Assuage, satisfy, (thirst, & rhet. revenge etc.), whence ~'LESS (-kl-) a. (poet.); (also *slack*) combine (lime) chemically with water. [OE *sleac-*, *slacian* f. *slæc* SLACK adj.]

sla'lom (-ah-), n. Ski-race down course defined by artificial obstacles; obstacle race in canoes. [Norw.]

slăm, v.t. & i. (-mm-), & n. **1.** Shut (t. & i., of door etc; often *to* adv.) with loud bang; put *down* (object) with similar sound; (sl.) hit, beat, gain easy victory over. **2.** n. Sound (as) of ~med door; gaining of every trick in whist, bridge, etc. (*grand*, *little*, ~, winning of 13, 12, tricks in bridge). [perh. f. Scand., cf. Sw., Norw., Icel. *slamra*]

sla'nder (-ah-), n., & v.t. **1.** False report maliciously uttered to person's injury; uttering of such reports, calumny; (law) false oral defamation (cf. LIBEL, SCANDAL); hence or cogn. ~OUS a., ~OUSLY² adv., ~OUSNESS n. **2.** v.t. Utter ~ about, defame falsely; hence ~ER¹ n. [ME *sclaundre* f. AF (OF) *escla(u)ndre*, alt. f. OF *escandle* f. LL SCANDALum]

slăng, n., & v.t. **1.** Words & phrases in common colloquial use, but generally considered in some or all of their senses to be outside of standard English; words & phrases either entirely peculiar to or used in special senses by some class or profession, cant, (*racing*, *thieves'*, *artistic*,

schoolboy, etc., ~). **2.** v.t. Use abusive language to. [18th c. cant, of unkn. orig.]

slăng'| y̆, a. Of the character of, given to the use of, slang. Hence ~iLY² adv., ~iNESS n. [-Y²]

slant (-ah-), v.i. & t., a., & n. **1.** Slope (i. & t.), diverge from a line, lie or go obliquely to a vertical or horizontal line; *present* (news) from a particular angle; hence ~'ingLY² adv., (joc. on *perpendicular*) ~in(g)dic'ular or ~endic'ular a. **2.** adj. (chiefly poet.). Sloping, inclined, oblique. **3.** n. Slope, oblique position, (*on the* or *a* ~, aslant), whence ~'WISE (-ahntwiz) adv.; || (arch.) indirect censure, disparaging remark; (naut.) *a* ~ *of wind*, favourable breeze; *way of regarding a thing, point of view. [1 vb: later var. of ME (now dial.) *slent*, f. ON *slenta* (Norw. *slenta*) to slant, slope, prob. infl. by ASLANT; 2 adj.: 17th c. aphetic f. ME *aslonte*, *o-slante* ASLANT adv.; 3 n.: 17th c., goes w. (1) & (2) (cf. Norw. *slent*); relation of forms is obsc.]

slăp, v.t. (-pp-), n., & adv. **1.** Strike with palm of hand, smack; (colloq., also ~ *down*) reprimand; (part. as adj. & adv.) very fast, big, good, etc. (*a* ~*ping pace*, *great girl*, *dinner*). **2.** n. Such stroke (~ *in the face* lit., also fig. rebuff, insult). **3.** adv. With the suddenness or effectiveness or true aim of a blow, suddenly, just quite, full, (*ran* ~ *into him*; *hit me* ~ *in the eye*). **4.** ~*-bang'*, violently, noisily, headlong; ~*dash'* adv., vehemently, recklessly; ~*dash*, (adj.) impetuous, random, happy-go-lucky, (n.) such action or work, also = ROUGHcast, (v.t.) = ROUGHcast; ~*-happy* (sl.), recklessly happy; ~*-up* a, (sl.), quite up to date, in the latest fashion, with all modern appliances. [17th c.: n. & adv. f. LG *slapp* (imit.); vb f. the E n. or adv.]

*****slăp'jăck,** n. Kind of pancake cooked on a griddle; = FLAPJACK. [SLAP v. + JACK]

slăp'stick, n. Flexible divided lath used by harlequin; (fig.) boisterous low comedy of the roughest kind (also attrib.). [SLAP v. +STICK]

slăsh, v.i. & t., & n. **1.** Make sweeping or random cut(s) with sword, knife, whip, etc. (~*ing criticism*, with outspoken condemnation); make long narrow gashes in (~*ed sleeve* etc., with slits cut to show lining or puffing of other material); reduce or cut drastically (prices etc.); lash (person etc.) with whip, crack (whip); (mil.) fell (trees) to form abatis. **2.** n. (Wound or slit made by) ~ing cut; debris resulting from the felling or destruction of trees. [ME, perh. f. OF *esclachier* break in pieces]

slăt¹, n. Thin narrow piece of wood, esp. used in sets in Venetian blinds, lath. [ME *s(c)lat* f. OF *esclat* splinter etc., rel. to *esclater* burst; cf. SLATE¹]

slăt², v.i. & t. (-tt-). (Of sails, cordage,

etc.) flap against mast etc. with reports; strike noisily with or on a surface. [orig. unkn.]

slāte¹, n., a., & v.t. **1.** Kinds of grey, green, or bluish-purple rock easily split into flat smooth plates; piece of such plate used as roofing-material; piece of it usu. framed in wood used for writing on with ~-*pencil* or small rod of soft ~ (*clean the* ~, rid oneself of or renounce obligations); ~-*black*, -*blue*, -*grey*, modifications of these tints such as occur in ~; || ~-*club*, mutual benefit society with small weekly contributions; ~-*colour(ed)*, (of) dark bluish or greenish grey; hence **slāt'Y²** a. **2.** adj. (Made) of ~. **3.** v.t. Cover with ~s esp. as roofing; hence **slāt'ER¹** n. [ME *s(c)late* f. OF *esclate*, fem. of *esclat* SLAT¹]

slāte², v.t. (colloq.). Criticize severely (esp. author in reviews), scold, rate; *nominate, propose for office etc. Hence **slāt'ING¹**(1) n. [app. f. prec.]

slätt'ern, n. Sluttish woman. Hence ~LY¹ a., ~LĬNESS n. [17th c., rel. to *slattering* (woman etc.) slovenly, f. dial. *slatter* to spill, slop, waste]

slaught'er (-awt-), n., & v.t. **1.** Slaying, esp. of many persons or animals at once, carnage, massacre, (~ or *massacre of the* INNOCENTS); ~-*house*, shambles, place for killing cattle or sheep, place of carnage; hence ~OUS a. (rhet.), ~OUSLY² adv. **2.** v.t. Kill (people) in ruthless manner or on great scale; butcher, kill for food; hence ~ER¹ n. [ME *slahter* f. ON **slahtr* (ON *slátr* butcher-meat), f. *slah-* see SLAY]

Slav (-ahv), n. & a. **1.** One of a people spread over most of Eastern Europe and including Russians, Bulgarians, Illyrians, Poles, Silesians, Pomeranians, Bohemians, etc.; hence ~'OPHIL, ~'OPHOBE, nn. & aa., ~'ISM(2, 3) n., (-ahv-). **2.** adj. Of the ~s, Slavonic, Slavonian. [ME *Sclave* f. med. L *Sclavus*, late Gk *Sklabos*, f. Slavonic]

slāve, n., & v.i. **1.** Person who is the legal property of another or others and is bound to absolute obedience, human chattel (WHITE¹ ~); helpless victim *to* or *of* some dominating influence (*is a* ~ *to drink, the* ~ *of his wife's caprices*, etc.; *the* ~s *of fashion*); drudge, person of no leisure; mean contemptible person. **2.** ~-*bangle* (of gold, glass, etc., worn by ladies above elbow); ~-*born* (in slavery, of ~ parents); ~-*driver*, overseer of ~s at work, (transf.) hard taskmaster; ~-*grown*, (of commodities) produced by ~-*labour*; ~-*holder*, owner of ~s; ~-*hunter*, person who hunts esp. Negroes to sell them as ~s; ~-*ship*, employed in ~-*trade*; ~ *States* (hist.), southern States of N. America in which slavery prevailed before civil war; ~-*trade*, procuring, transporting, & selling as ~s, of human beings, esp. African Negroes; so ~-*trader*. **3.** v.i. Work like ~, drudge. [ME, f. OF *esclave* = med. L *sclavus, sclava* Slav (captive), see prec.]

slāv'er¹, n. Ship or person engaged in slave-trade. [-ER¹]

slāv'er², v.i. & t., & n. **1.** Let spittle flow from mouth; let one's spittle fall upon (garment etc., or another's cheek in kissing). **2.** n. Spittle running from mouth, (fig.) fulsome or servile flattery; hence ~Y¹ [-Y²] a. [ME, app. Scand., cf. Icel. *slafra*, rel. to LG *slabber* SLABBER, SLOBBER]

slāv'erY², n. Condition of a slave; slave-holding; exhausting labour, drudgery. [-ERY]

|| **slāv'ey**, n. (sl.; pl. ~s). Maid-servant, esp. in lodgings or boarding-house. [-Y³]

Sla'vic (-ah-), a. & n. (Language) of the Slavs, Slavonic. [-IC]

slāv'ish, a. As of, having the characteristics of, slaves, abject, servile, base, (~ *imitation*, without any attempt at development or originality). Hence ~LY³ adv., ~NESS n. [-ISH¹]

Slavōn'ian, a. & n. (Language, member) of the Slav people; (inhabitant) of the former Austrian district Slavonia. [f. med. L *S(c)lavonia* country of Slavs, -AN]

Slavōn'ic, a. & n. (Language) of the Slavs. Hence ~IZE(3) v.t. [as prec., -IC]

*slaw, n. Salad of sliced cabbage. [Du. *sla*, shortened f. *salade* SALAD]

slay, v.t. (*slew* pr. -ōō, *slain*). Kill (chiefly poet., rhet., or joc.; often abs., as *went forth* ~*ing & spoiling*). Hence (-) ~'ER¹ n. [OE *slēan*, OS, OHG *slahan*, ON *slá*, Goth. *slahan*]

sleaz'y, a. (Of textiles, & rarely transf.) flimsy; (colloq.) slatternly. [17th c., of unkn. orig.]

slĕd, slĕdge¹, sleigh (slā), nn., & vv.i. & t. **1.** Vehicle on runners instead of wheels for conveying loads or passengers esp. over snow, drawn by horses or dogs or reindeer or pushed or pulled by hand, toboggan, (*sled* now little used in England except of structure on runners for dragging loads in agriculture; *sleigh* chiefly of runner-carriage for driving over snow; *sledge* in all senses); *sleigh-bell*, one of the tinkling bells often attached to harness of ~-horse etc. **2.** vv.i. & t. Travel, go, convey, in ~. [14th c. *sled* f. MFlem. or MLG *sledde*; 17th c. *sledge* f. MDu. *sleedse*, rel. to *slede*, whence E dial. *slead*; *sleigh*, orig. U.S., f. Du. *slee*, contr. f. *slede*]

slĕdge², n. (Also ~-*hammer*) blacksmith's lárge heavy hammer (~-*hammer* often attrib. & fig., as ~-*hammer blows, arguments, style*). [OE *slecg*, = MDu. *slegge*, cogn. w. ON *sleggja*, f. stem of SLAY]

sleek, a., & v.t. **1.** Smooth & soft & glossy (of hair, fur, skin, or animal or person with such hair etc.); hence ~'LY² adv., ~'NESS n. **2.** v.t. Make ~ esp. by stroking or pressing down. [later var. of SLICK]

sleep¹, n. Bodily condition, normally recurring every night & lasting several hours, in which nervous system is inactive, eyes are closed, muscles relaxed, & consciousness nearly suspended, prolonged similar condition of hibernating animals, (BEAUTY ~; *in* one's ~, while asleep; *the ~ of the just*, sound; ~ *that knows not breaking*, death; *broken* ~, with disturbed intervals; *go to* ~, fall asleep; *fall on* ~, arch., go to ~, fig. die); a period of or single indulgence in ~ (*shall try to get a* ~); (fig.) rest, quiet, negligence, death, etc.; ~*-walker, -walking*, somnambulist, -ism. Hence ~'LESS a., ~'lèssLY[2] adv., ~'lèssNESS n. [OE *slēp, slǣp*, OS *slāp*, OHG *slāf*, Goth. *slēps*]

sleep[2], v.i. & t. (*slĕpt*). 1. Be immersed in sleep, fall or be asleep, (*let* ~*ing dogs lie*, avoid stirring up trouble; ~ *like a log* or *top*, soundly; ~ *in*, live in, (Sc.) ~ *late*, over~ oneself; ~ *on, upon, over*, a question, leave it till tomorrow). 2. Spend in or affect by ~ing (~ *the hours away*; *slept off his vexation, headache, etc.*). 3. Be inactive or dormant (*sword* ~*s in the scabbard; top* ~*s*, spins so steadily as to seem motionless; ~*ing partner*, not sharing management). 4. Lie in the grave. 5. Sojourn for the night *at, in*, etc.; have sexual intercourse *with*; ~ *around*, be sexually promiscuous. 6. Provide ~ing accommodation for (*lodging-house* ~*s 300 men*). 7. ~*ing-bag*, for ~ing out of doors in; ~*ing-car(riage)*, railway coach provided with beds;~*ing-draught*, opiate; ~*ing*-SICKNESS; ~*ing-suit*, pyjamas. [OE *slēpan, slǣpan*, OS *slāpan*, OHG *slāfan*, Goth. *slēpan*]

sleep'er, n. In vbl senses; also, || wooden beam or piece of other material used as support for rails etc.; = (berth in) SLEEP[2]-*ing-car*. [ME; -ER[1]]

sleep'|y̆, a. Drowsy, ready for sleep; habitually indolent, unobservant, etc.; without stir or bustle (*a* ~*y little town*); (of fruit, esp. pears) insipid & dry with incipient decay; ~*yhead*, ~y or inattentive person (esp. in voc.); ~*y* SICKNESS. Hence ~ĭLY[2] adv., ~ĭNESS n. [ME; -Y[2]]

sleet, n., & v.i. impers. 1. Snow and rain together, or snow melting while falling. 2. vb. *It* ~*s* etc., ~ *falls*. Hence ~'Y[2] a., ~'iNESS n. [prob. repr. OE **slet* (f. **slĕatj-*), rel. to MLG *slōte*, MHG *slōz(e)* (G *schlosse*)]

sleeve, n. 1. Part of garment that covers arm (LAWN[1] ~*s*; LEG-*of-mutton* ~; *mandarin* ~, loose & open below elbow; *laugh in* one's ~, slyly, secretly; *have card, plan*, etc., *up* one's ~, in reserve, concealed but ready for use; *turn, roll, up* one's ~*s*, prepare to fight or work; *wear* one's HEART *upon* one's ~). 2. Tube enclosing rod or smaller tube. 3. = WIND[1]-*sock*. 4. ~*-coupling*, tube for connecting shafts or pipes; ~*-fish*, kind of cuttlefish, squid; ~*-link*, two buttons linked for fastening wristband; ~*-nut*, long nut with right-hand & left-hand screw-threads for drawing together pipes or shafts conversely

threaded; ~*-valve* (in the form of a cylinder with sliding movement). Hence (-)sleeveD[2] (-vd), ~'LESS (-vl-), aa. [OE *slieve, slȳf*, = NFris. *slēv, slīv*]

sleigh. See SLED.

sleight (slīt), n. Dexterity, cunning, deceptive trick or device or movement, (arch.); ~*-of-hand*, juggling, legerdemain, prestidigitation, quickness of hand in fencing etc. [ME *slĕgth* f. ON *slǣgth (slǣgr* SLY, -TH[1])]

slen'der, a. Of small girth or breadth, slim, not stout, (~ *stem, waist, pillar, girl, hand*); scanty, slight, meagre, inadequate, relatively small, (~ *hopes, means, store, income, acquaintance with subject, foundations for belief*). Hence ~LY[2] adv., ~NESS n. [ME *s(c)lendre*, of unkn. orig.]

slept. See SLEEP[2].

sleuth'hound (-loō-, -lū-), n. Bloodhound (lit. & fig.); (also *sleuth*, esp. U.S.) detective. [ME *sleuth* f. ON *slóth* track, trail; see SLOT[2]]

slew[1], slue, (sloō), v.t. & i., & n. 1. Turn or swing forcibly or with effort out of the forward or ordinary position (often *round, to the left*, etc.). 2. n. Such change of position. [18th c. naut., of unkn. orig.]

slew[2]. See SLAY.

slice, n., & v.t. & i. 1. Thin broad piece or wedge cut off or out esp. from meat, bread, or cake; share, part taken or allotted, (*a* ~ *of territory, of the profits*, etc.); kinds of implement with thin broad blade e.g. (also *fish*-~) for helping fish, (also ~*-bar*) for clearing furnace-bars of clinker, or for lifting things out of frying-pan etc. 2. vb. Cut (often *up*) into ~s, cut (piece) *off* adv. or prep., go through (air etc.) with cutting motion; make incorrect slicing motion with oar (also trans. ~ *the water*) or golf-club (also trans. ~ *the ball*, hit it a glancing blow so that it curves off to the right of a right-handed player). [ME, f. OF *esclice* splinter, f. *esclicer* f. WG **slītjan*, see SLIT]

slick, a. & adv. (colloq.), & v.t. 1. Dextrous, not marred by bungling, carried smoothly through; superficially or pretentiously smooth and dextrous. 2. adv. Directly, exactly, completely, (*came* ~ *into the middle of them; hit him* ~ *in the eye; bowled his middle stump* ~ *out of the ground*). 3. v.t. Make sleek. Hence ***~'ER n., plausible cheat, (also) waterproof coat. [ME *slike(n)*, f. OE **slice, -slician*; cf. SLEEK]

slid|e[1], v.i. & t. (*slĭd*). 1. Progress along smooth surface with continuous friction on same part of object progressing (cf. ROLL; *slid sitting down a grassy slope; piston* ~*es noiselessly up & down*), make move thus (~*e the drawer into its place*). 2. Glide over ice on both feet without skates with momentum got by running (~*e over delicate subject*, barely touch upon it); glide, go smoothly along. 3. Take its own course (*let it* ~*e*). 4. Go unconsciously or by imperceptible degrees (~es into sin; ~e from one note to another in music). 5. ~ing door, drawn across aperture on slide instead of turning on hinges; ‖ ~ing keel, CENTRE-board; ~ing, ~e-, rule, graduated, with ~ing part for doing certain mathematical processes automatically; ~ing scale, schedule for automatically varying one thing (esp. tax, wages, prices) in direct or inverse proportion to fluctuations of another; ~ing seat, mounted on runners esp. in racing boats to lengthen rower's or sculler's stroke. Hence ~'ER¹ (1, 2) n., ~'ABLE a. [OE slīdan, older LG slīden, MHG slīten]

slide², n. 1. Track on ice made by persons sliding; slope prepared with snow or ice for tobogganing. 2. Act of sliding. 3. Inclined plane down which goods etc. slide to lower level, chute. 4. (Also ~-way) part(s) of machine on or between which sliding part works. 5. Part of machine or instrument that slides, (also ~-valve) sliding piece that opens and closes aperture by sliding across it. 6. Thing slid into place, esp. glass holding object for microscope or magic-lantern picture. [f. prec.]

slight¹ (-it), a. Slender, slim, frail-looking, (saw a ~ figure approaching; supported by a ~ framework); a or some inconsiderable (has a ~ cold; took a ~ repast; have made a ~ inquiry, some ~ inquiries, into it); not much or great or thorough, inadequate, scanty, not even the smallest, (after ~ inquiry; did it with ~ inconvenience to himself; there is not the ~est excuse for it; a conclusion based on very ~ observation; a structure raised on ~ foundations; paid him ~ attention). Hence ~'ISH¹(2) a., ~'LY² adv., ~'NESS n., (-it-). [ME slight, sleght, f. ON *slehtr, sléttr = OS sliht, OHG sleht, Goth. slaihts]

slight² (-īt), v.t., & n. 1. Treat or speak of (person, branch of study, etc.) as not worth attention, fail in courtesy or respect towards, markedly neglect; hence ~'ingLY² (-it-) adv. 2. n. Marked piece of neglect, omission of due respect etc., (put a ~ upon, slight). [f. prec.]

sli'ly. Var. of SLYly.

slim, a., & v.i. (-mm-). 1. Of small girth or thickness, slenderly built, of slight shape; clever in stratagem, crafty, unscrupulous. 2. v.i. Reduce one's figure by dieting and exercises. Hence ~'LY² adv., ~m'ISH¹(2) a., ~'NESS n. [17th c., f. Du. or LG slim, = MHG slim (G schlimm) crooked, bad, etc.]

slime, n., & v.t. & i. 1. Fine oozy mud or other substance of similar consistence, e.g. liquid bitumen or mucous exudation of fish etc.; ~-gland in molluscs etc., secreting ~; ~-pit, of liquid bitumen. 2. vb. Cover with ~ (esp. of snake preparing prey for gorging; ‖ (sl.) get through, away, past, out of it, etc., by physical or moral slipperiness. [OE slīm,

MDu.; MLG, MHG slīm, ON slím, prob. cogn. w. L limus mud]

slim'y, a. Of the consistence of slime; covered or smeared with or full of slime; slippery, hard to hold; cringingly dishonest; repulsively meek or flattering. Hence ~ILY² adv., ~INESS n. [ME; -Y²]

sling¹, v.t. & i. (slŭng), & n. 1. Throw (rare; ~ ink, sl., be an author or journalist, write); hurl (stone etc.) from ~, use ~, whence ~'ER¹ n.; suspend with ~, allow to swing suspended, arrange so as to be supported from above, hoist or transfer with ~; ~ one's HOOK¹; ~-cart, in which load is slung from axletree; slung shot, metal ball attached by thong etc. to wrist & used esp. by criminals as weapon. 2. n. Strap or string used with the hand to give impetus to small missile; kinds of apparatus used to support hanging weight, e.g. injured arm, rifle, ship's boat, goods being transferred; ~-dog, one of pair of hooks used to grapple goods for hoisting. [vb f. ON slyngva; n. app. f. LG or Scand.]

sling², n. (chiefly U.S.). Kind of toddy (esp. gin-~). [orig. unkn.]

slink¹, v.i. (slŭnk or rarely slank, slunk). Go in secretive manner or with guilty or ashamed or sneaking air (usu. off, away, by, etc.). Hence ~'Y² a., gracefully slender and flowing, sinuous. [OE slincan = LG slinken]

slink², v.t. & i., & n. 1. (Of animal) miscarry, produce (young, or abs.) prematurely. 2. n. Animal, esp. calf, so born; its flesh; ~-butcher, who deals in ~; [app. = prec.; cf. cast, sling]

slip¹, v.i. & t. (-pp-). 1. Slide unintentionally for short distance, lose footing or balance or place by unintended sliding, (~ped in the mud or over the edge and fell; blanket ~ped off bed; foot ~s out of stirrup, ring off finger). 2. Go with sliding motion (as the door closes the catch ~s into place; ~ along, sl., go at great speed; ~ into, sl., pummel, belabour, eat heartily of). 3. Escape restraint or capture by being slippery or hard to hold or by not being grasped (eel, opportunity, ~ped through his fingers; let reins ~ out of his hands; let ~ the dogs of war, poet., begin war). 4. Make way unobserved or quietly or quickly (how time ~s away!; ~ by, past; ~ out of the room; ~ off or away, depart without leave-taking etc.; just ~ across to the baker's; errors will ~ in). 5. Make careless mistake (~s now & then in his grammar); deteriorate, lapse; ~ up (colloq.), fail, make a mistake. 6. Let go from restraint of some kind (~ greyhounds, from leash; ~ anchor, detach ship from it; cow ~s its calf, produces it prematurely). 7. Pull (garment etc.) hastily on, off. 8. Insert stealthily or casually or with gliding motion (~ped half a crown into the porter's hand, a white powder into her glass, the papers into his pocket, a marker between *the pages*). **9.** Escape from, give the slip to, (*dog ~s his collar, prisoner his guard*; *the point had ~ped my attention*). **10.** ~*ped disc*, layer of cartilage between vertebrae that has ~ped from its place. [ME. prob. f. MLG *slippen*, = OHG *slipfan*; cf. SLIPPERY]

slip², n. **1.** Act of slipping, blunder, accidental piece of misconduct, (*a ~ on a piece of orange-peel may be fatal*; *there's many a ~ 'twixt the cup & the lip*, nothing is certain till it has happened; *give one the ~*, escape from him; *~ of the tongue, pen*, thing said or written accidentally for something else; *a few ~s in youth are inevitable*). **2.** Kinds of loose covering or garment,. e.g. pillow-case, under-bodice, petticoat, pinafore. **3.** Leash for slipping dogs, device for suddenly loosing clip or attachment. **4.** Artificial slope of stone as landing-stage; inclined plane on which ships are built or repaired. **5.** Long narrow strip of thin wood, paper, etc.; printer's proof on such paper (see GALLEY). **6.** Cutting taken from plant for grafting or planting, scion (*a ~ of a boy*, slim boy). **7.** One of the fielders (*short, long, ~*) stationed for balls glancing off bat to off side behind batsman; (sing. or pl.) this part of ground (*was caught in the ~s* or *at~*). **8.** (Without pl. or article) semifluid clay for coating or making pattern on earthenware. **9.** (theatr.; pl.). Part from which scenes are slipped on, part where actors stand before entering. **10.** pl. Bathing-drawers. **11.** Small sole (flat-fish). **12.** Loss of distance travelled by aircraft arising from nature of medium in which its propeller revolves. [chiefly f. prec.; sense 8 f. OE *sly(p)pe* (cf. COWSLIP); senses 5, 6, 11 app. f. MDu. or MLG *slippe* cut, strip, etc.]

slip-, the stem of SLIP¹ in comb.: ‖ ~*-carriage, -coach*, railway carriage on express for casting loose at station where rest of train does not stop; ~*-cover*, of calico etc. for furniture out of use; ~*-galley*, long narrow tray for holding composed type; ~*-hook*, with contrivance for loosing it readily at need; ~*-knot*, that can be undone by a pull, also knot that slips up & down string & tightens or loosens loop; ~*-road*, minor & local by-pass; ~*-rope*, with both ends on board so that casting loose either end frees ship from moorings; ~'*shod*, having shoes down at heel, slovenly, (fig., of speech, writing, speaker, writer, method of work, etc.) negligent, careless, unsystematic, casual, loose in arrangement; ~'*slop*, = ~*shod* (fig.), (as n.) ~shod writing etc., also (as redupl. of *slop*) washy stuff lit. or fig., weak drink, slops, sentimental talk or writing; ~*-stream*, stream of air driven astern by aircraft's propeller(s); ~*-up* n. (colloq.), blunder; ~'*way*, shipbuilding or landing slip.

slipp'er, n., & v.t. **1.** Loose comfortable

indoor shoe (HUNT¹*-the-~*; *bed-~*, ~*-shaped* BED¹*-pan*), whence ~ED² (*-erd*) a.; skid or shoe placed under wagon-wheel as drag; person who slips greyhounds in coursing-match; ~*-bath*, shaped like ~, with covered end; ~*-wort*, calceolaria. **2.** v.t. Chastise (child etc.) with ~; hence ~ING¹(1) n. [ME.; -ER¹]

slipp'er|y̆, a. (Of ground) hard to stand on, causing slips by its smoothness or muddiness, (fig., of subject) requiring tactful handling; (of object or person) hard to hold firmly owing to polish or sliminess or elusive motion, (fig.) unreliable, incalculable, shifty, unscrupulous. Hence ~ILY² adv., ~INESS n. [alt. (perh. after LG *slipperig*) f. (now dial.) *slipper* (OE *slipor*)+-Y²]

slipp'y̆, a. Slippery (colloq.); *look or be ~* (sl.), look sharp, make haste. [-Y²]

slit, v.t. & i. (*slit*), & n. **1.** Cut or (t. & i.) tear lengthwise, make slight incision or rent in, cut into strips, (*threatened to ~ his nose, tongue*, etc.; ~ *one's weasand*, cut his throat; ~ *hide into thongs, sheet of metal into strips or rods*; *if you strain it too hard it will ~*; *has ~ my coat-sleeve from shoulder to wrist*); ~*ling-rollers*, ribbed pair fitting into each other & ~ting metal sheet by pressure. **2.** n. Long incision; long narrow opening comparable to cut (*a ~ is provided for the coin to drop through*; *the windows are mere ~s*; *the ~s on the neck are gill-openings*); ~ *trench*, narrow trench for soldier or weapon. [ME *slitte*, rel. to OE *slitan* (dial. *slite*), OHG *sliz(z)an* (G *schleissen*), ON *slita*; cf. SLICE]

slith'er (-dh-), v.i. (colloq.). Slide unsteadily, go with irregular slipping motion. [ME var. of (now dial.) *slidder* (cf. *hither*) f. OE *slid(e)rian* frequent. f. *slid-* weak grade of *slid-* SLIDE]

sliv'er, n., & v.t. **1.** Piece of wood torn from tree or timber, splinter (esp. of exploded shell), (vb, break t. & i. off as~, break t. & i. up into ~s). **2.** (In fishing) side of small fish cut off as bait (vb, cut~s from). [ME, f. (now dial.) *slive* cleave (OE *slifan*)+-ER¹]

slŏbb'er, v.i. & t., & n. **1.** Run at the mouth in infantile helplessness or maudlin emotion; wet (clothes, other person in kissing) with saliva; do (task) badly, botch, bungle. **2.** n. Running saliva; maudlin talk, emotion, or kisses; hence ~Y² a., ~INESS n. [rel. to SLABBER, SLUBBER; cf. Du. *slobberen*]

slŏb'-ice, n. (Newfoundland). Floating ice mixed with snow. [*slob* var. of *slab* mud, cf. SLAB²]

slŏe, n. (Small bluish-black wild plum, fruit of BLACK¹*thorn* (~*-gin*, liqueur of ~s steeped in gin). [OE *slā(h)*, MDu., MLG *slee*, OHG *slēha*]

‖ **sloe-worm**. Var. of SLOW-WORM.

slŏg, v.i. & t. (-gg-), & n. **1.** Hit (i. & t.) hard & wildly esp. in boxing & at cricket;

walk or work doggedly (usu. *on*, *away*); hence ~g′ER¹ (-g-) n. **2**. n. Hard random hit. [orig. mil.; cf. SLUG²]

slŏg′an, n. Highland war-cry; party cry, watchword,·motto; short catchy phrase used in advertising. [f. Gael. *sluagh-ghairm* (*sluagh* host, *gairm* outcry)]

sloid, sloyd, n. A system (orig. Swedish) of manual training, esp. by means of wood-carving, used in schools. [f. Sw. *slöjd*, corresp. to ON *slægth* SLEIGHT]

slŏŏp, n. Small one-masted fore-&-aft-rigged vessel with mainsail & jib, & usu. gaff topsail & forestaysail; || small warship used for general purposes & esp. for police work on foreign stations; ||~ *of war* (hist.), cutter-rigged ship mounting guns; ~-*rigged*, rigged like ~. [17th c., f. Du. *sloep*, older *sloepe*, LG *slūp(e)*, whence F *chaloupe*; see SHALLOP]

sloot. Var. of SLUIT.

slŏp¹, n. (in pl. only), & v.i. & t. (-pp-). **1**. (Pl.) dirty water or liquid, waste contents of kitchen or bedroom vessels; (pl.) liquid food, as broth, gruel, etc., non-alcoholic drinks; ~-*basin*, for receiving dregs of cups at table; ~-*pail*, for removing bedroom ~s. **2**. vb. Spill (i. & t.), (allow to) flow over edge of vessel, (often *over*, *out*); make mess with ~s (or with ~s as subj.) upon (clothes, floor); ~ *over* (fig.), gush, be maudlin. [earlier ' slush ', prob. repr. OE *sloppe*, rel. to *slyppe*; see SLIP²(8)]

slŏp², n. (in pl. only). (Arch.) wide knickerbockers; ready-made clothing, clothes & bedding supplied to sailors in navy; ~-*room*, from which ~s are issued aboard ship; ~-*seller*, -*shop*, of ready-made clothes. [ME; cf. OE *overslop* surplice, MDu. (*over*)*slop*, OIcel. *sloppr* gown]

|| **slŏp³**, n. (sl.). Policeman. [f. *ecilop*, back sl. for *police*]

slŏpe, n., & v.i. & t. **1**. Inclined position or direction, the having of one end or side at higher level than the other, difference in level between two ends or sides of thing, the lying in a line neither parallel nor perpendicular to level ground or a line serving as standard, (*there is always a certain* ~ *in a ship's deck*; *cut this side straight & the other with a* ~ *to the right*; *the whole* ~ *may amount to 2 ft*); piece of rising or falling ground, incline; position of soldier with rifle ~d (*come to the* ~); hence ~′WISE (-pwīz) adv. **2**. vb. Have or show ~, lie or tend obliquely esp. to ground level, slant esp. up or down, whence **slŏp′ingLY²** adv.; place or arrange or make in or at a ~ (~ *arms*, place rifle at a ~ over shoulder; *must* ~ *the sides of the pit*); (sl.) make *off*, go away, also saunter, walk about. [n. (17th c.) aphetic f. ASLOPE; vb (16th c.) f. (now poet.) *slope* adj. (16th c.) f. as n.]

slŏpp′lÿ̆, a. (Of road) wet with rain, full of puddles; (of floor, table, etc.) wet with slops, having water etc. spilt on it; (of work) unsystematic, not thorough; (of sentiment or talk) weakly emotional; maudlin. Hence ~ILY² adv., ~INESS n, [SLOP¹,-Y²]

slŏsh, n., & v.t. **1**. = SLUSH. **2**. v.t. (sl.). Beat, thrash. [see SLUSH]

slŏt¹, n., & v.t. (-tt-). **1**. Groove, channel, slit, or long aperture, made in machine etc. to admit some other part, esp. slit for penny or other coin that sets working a ~-*machine* or automatic retailer of small wares; stage trapdoor. **2**. v.t. Provide with ~(s). [f. OF *esclot* hollow of the breast, of unkn. orig.]

slŏt², n. Track of deer etc. esp. as shown by footprints. [f. AF & OF *esclot* 'hoof-print prob. f. ON *slóth*, trail, cf. SLEUTH-HOUND]

slŏth, n. **1**. Laziness, indolence, whence ~′FUL a., ~′fulLY² adv., ~′fulNESS n. **2**. Kinds of S.-Amer. mammal with curved long-clawed feet living entirely in trees & capable only of very slow motion on ground. **3**. ~-*bear*, large-lipped black shaggy honey-eating bear of India & Ceylon; ~-*monkey*, kind of loris. [ME *slowthe* (SLOW, -TH¹)]

slouch, v.i. & t., & n. **1**. Droop, hang down negligently; go or stand or sit with loose ungainly attitude; bend one side of brim of (hat) downwards (opp. *cock*); hence ~′ingLY² adv. **2**. n. ~ing attitude or walk, stoop, downward bend of hat-brim (opp. *cock*); (sl.) incompetent or slovenly worker or operator or performance (esp. *is no* ~ *at*, *this show* etc. *is no* ~); ~ *hat*, with ~ed brim. [16th c., of unkn. orig.; cf. dial. *slouk*, Norw. *slōk*, Icel. *slókr*; vb app. f. n.]

slough¹ (slow), n. Quagmire, swamp, miry place, (*the S*~ *of Despond*, state of hopeless floundering in sin). Hence ~′y¹ [-Y²] (-owi) a. [OE *slōh*, of unkn. orig.]

slough² (slŭf), n., & v.i. & t. **1**. Snake's cast skin, any part that an animal casts or moults; dead tissue that drops off from living flesh etc.; (fig.) habit etc. abandoned; hence ~′y² [-Y²] (slŭfi) a. **2**. vb. Drop off (t. & i.; often *off*, *away*, esp. in intr. sense) as ~; cast off ~. [ME *slo(u)h*, perh. rel. to LG *sluwe*, *slu* husk]

Slŏv′ăk, n. & a. (Member) of a formerly Hungarian Slavic people. [Slovak & Czech]

slo′ven (-ŭv-), n. Personally untidy or dirty, careless & lazy, or unmethodical person. Hence ~LY¹ a., ~liNESS n., ~LY² adv. (arch.), ~RY n., (-ŭv-). [ME, perh. an AF formation on Flem. *sloef* dirty, or Du. *slof* careless]

Slovēne′ (*or* slŏv⸗), n., Slovĕn′ian, a. & n. (Member) of a southern Slavic people in Jugoslavia; (-*ian*) language of the Slovenes. [G, f. OSlav. (*slovo* word), whence also SLAV]

slow (-ō), a., adv., & v.i. & t. **1**. Not quick, deficient in speed, taking a long time to

traverse a distance or do a thing, (~ *&
steady wins the race*; ~ *& sure*, haste is
risky; ~ *march*, of troops in funeral procession etc.; ~ *music*), gradual (~ *growth,
progress*), whence ~'LY[2] (-ŏlĭ) adv.; tardy,
reluctant, lingering, (*was not* ~ *to defend
himself*), not hasty or easily moved (*is* ~
to anger); (of clock etc., usu. pred.) behind
correct time (*is 20'* ~); dull-witted, stupid,
(*is* ~ *of speech, of wit*); deficient in interest
or liveliness, dull, tedious, (*entertainment
was voted* ~); (of a photographic lens)
of small aperture (and so necessitating
long exposure); (of surfaces) tending to
cause ~ness (*a* ~ *pitch, tennis-court,
billiard-table*); ~'*coach*, person~ in action,
dull of wit, or behind the times in opinions
etc.; ~-*match*, ~-burning for igniting
explosives; ~-*motion*, (attrib., of a film)
with the number of exposures per second
greatly increased (~ing down the motion
when projected at the normal rate);
~-*worm*, see foll.; hence ~'NESS (-ŏn-) n.
2. adv. (~*er*, ~*est*). At ~ pace, ~ly,
(being ousted by ~*ly*, but still common
when the adv. & not the vb gives the
essential point, as *how* ~ *he climbs!,
please read* or *go* ~ or ~*er, watch goes*~,
cf. *I saw a man climb* ~*ly up*; placed
always after vb exc. in excl. with *how* or
in comb. with part. as ~-*going, -moving*).
3. vb. Reduce one's speed, reduce speed
of (train, ship, etc.), (usu. *down, up, off*).
[OE *slāw*, OS *slēu*, OHG *slēo*, ON *slǽr,
sljár* f. Gmc *slaiwaz]

slow-worm (slō'wĕrm), n. Small harmless reptile between snakes & lizards,
blindworm. [OE *slā-wyrm*; first element
obsc., cf. MSw. *slā*, Norw. *slo*, etc., slow-
-worm]

sloyd. See SLOID.

slub, n., & v.t. (-bb-). 1. Wool slightly
twisted as preparation for spinning.
2. v.t. Twist thus. [orig. unkn.]

slubb'er, v.t. & i. Do carelessly or bung-
lingly; slaver, slobber. [16th c., prob. f.
Du. or LG, cf. LG *slubbern*; cf. SLOBBER]

sludge, n. Thick greasy mud; sewage.
Hence **sludg'y**[2] a. [see SLUSH]

slue. See SLEW[1].

slug[1], n., & v.i. (-gg-). 1. Kinds of shell-
less snail destructive to small plants;
(vb) collect & destroy ~s in garden etc.
2. Bullet of irregular shape; roundish
lump of metal; line of type in linotype
printing. [ME *slugg(e)* sluggard, perh.
f. Scand.; cf. Norw. dial. *sluggje* heavy
slow person, Sw. dial. *slogga* be slow]

*slug[2], v.t. & i. (-gg-), & n. = SLOG. [orig.
unkn., cf. SLOG]

slug'-abĕd, n. (arch.). Person who lies
late in bed. [f. *slug* vb (foll.)+ABED]

slugg'ard, n. Lazy sluggish person.
[ME, f. *slug* vb be slothful (perh. f. Scand.,
see SLUG[1])+-ARD]

slugg'ish (-gĭ-), a. Inert, inactive, torpid,
indolent, slow-moving, (*a* ~ *stream, circulation, temper, person*). Hence ~LY[2] adv.,

~NESS n. [ME, f. SLUG[1] or *slug* vb (see
prec.)+-ISH[1]]

sluice (-ōōs), n., & v.t. & i. 1. (Also ~-
-*gate*, -*valve*) sliding gate or other contrivance for changing level of a body of
water by controlling flow into or out of it,
floodgate; water above or below or issuing
through floodgate; (also ~-*way*) artificial
water-channel; *a* rinsing. 2. vb. Provide
with ~(s); flood with water from ~;
rinse; pour or throw water freely upon;
(of water) rush *out* etc. (as) from ~. [ME,
f. OF *escluse* f. LL *exclusa, sclusa* flood-
gate (orig. fem. p.p. see EXCLUDE)]

sluit (-ōōt), slōōt, n. (S. Africa). Narrow
water-channel. [Du. *sloot* ditch]

slŭm[1], n., & v.i. (-mm-). 1. Overcrowded
and squalid back street or court or alley
or district in city. 2. v.i. Go about the
~s to visit or examine condition of
inhabitants; hence ~m'ER[1] n. [c. 1800,
cant wd of unkn. orig.]

slŭm[2], n. Non-lubricating part of crude
oil; gummy residue formed in lubricating
oil during use. [orig. unkn.]

slŭm'ber, v.i. & t., & n. Sleep (distinguished in sense only by an implication
of comfort or ease, which is not invariable,
e.g. *fell into a troubled* ~; & in use by a
rhet. or poet. tinge; the n. is often in pl.,
as *his* ~*s were interrupted by a knock*); ~
away, waste (time) in ~; ~-*wear* (shop),
pyjamas. Hence **slŭm'b(e)rous** a.,
slŭm'b(e)rously[2] adv., ~ER[1] n. [ME
slūmeren, slombre, etc., f. *slūmen* vb or *slūme*
n. (OE *slūma*)+-ER[5]; -*b*- as in NUMBER; cf.
MDu. *slummeren*, MHG *slum(m)ern*]

slŭmm'ock, v.t. & i. (colloq.). Swallow
greedily, wolf down; move or speak in
awkward disorderly way. [var. of dial.
slommack, slammack]

slŭmp, n., & v.i. 1. Sudden or rapid
or great fall in prices or values, or
diminution of demand for commodity or
interest taken in subject or undertaking.
2. v.i. Undergo ~, fall in price, fall
through, fail utterly; subside limply (*he
~ed into a chair*). [in 17th c. ' fall into a
bog ', prob. imit., cf. PLUMP[2]]

slung. See SLING[1].

slunk. See SLINK[1].

slŭr, v.t. & i. (-rr-), & n. 1. Write (t. & i.)
or pronounce (t. & i.) indistinctly with
letters or sounds running into one another; (mus.) perform legato, mark
(notes) as to be so performed; pass (fault,
fact, etc.) lightly *over*, conceal or mini-
mize; (arch.) put ~ upon (person, character), make insinuations against. 2. n.
Imputation, blame, stigma, (*he put a* ~
upon me; it is no ~ *upon his reputation
that he should have* or *to say that*); piece
of ~*ring* in handwriting, pronunciation,
or singing; curved mark used in music-
-writing to show that two or more notes
are to be sung to one syllable or played
or sung legato. [17th c., f. 15th c. (now
dial.) *slur* thin mud, of unkn. orig.]

slŭ′rrў, n. Liquid mixture of materials for Portland cement manufacture; sticky muddy residue separated from coal at the pithead washing plants; semi-fluid mixture of ganister and fire-clay used in repairing converter-linings etc. [rel. to prec.]

slŭsh, n. Watery mud or thawing snow (cf. SLUDGE); (fig.) silly sentiment. Hence ~′ʏ² a. [f. 17th c., w. varr. *sludge* & *slutch*, also 19th c. *slosh*; orig. unkn.]

slŭt, n. Slovenly woman, slattern; (joc.) girl. Hence ~t′ERY(4) n., ~t′ISH¹ a., ~t′ishLY² adv., ~t′ishNESS n. [ME; orig. unkn.]

slȳ, a. (~*er*, ~*est*). Cunning, wily, hypocritical; practising concealment (~ *dog*, person who keeps his peccadilloes or pleasures quiet), done etc. in secret (*on the* ~, privately, without publicity); knowing, arch, bantering, insinuating, ironical; ~′*boots*, ~ person (in playful use, esp. to or of child or animal). Hence ~′LY² adv., ~′NESS n. [ME *slégh* f. ON *slǽgr* cunning, orig. ' able to strike ' f. *slóg-* pret. stem of *slá* SLAY; cf. SLEIGHT]

slȳpe, n. Covered way or passage from cathedral transept to chapter-house. [cf. WFlem. *slipe, slijpe* secret path]

smack¹, n. & v.i. 1. Flavour, taste that suggests presence of something; barely discernible amount *of* some food-material etc. or *of* a quality etc. present in dish or person's character, tinge, tincture, spice, dash, *of*, (*has a* ~ *of ginger, of the cask, in it, of recklessness, of the old Adam, in him*). 2. v.i. Have a slight curious or unexpected or secondary taste (rare); taste slightly *of*, suggest by taste or otherwise the presence or effects *of*, (*wine* ~*ing of the cork*; *his manner* ~*ed of superciliousness*). [OE *smæc*, = MDu., OHG *smac*; vb f. n.]

smäck², n., v.t. & i., & adv. 1. Slight explosive report as of surface struck with palm, of lips parted suddenly, or of whip cracked; blow with palm, slap; hard hit at cricket; loud kiss (*gave her a hearty* ~); *have a* ~ *at* (colloq.), make trial of (something), have a go at. 2. vb. Slap (person's face etc.) with palm; part (t. & i. of lips) noisily in eager anticipation or enjoyment of food or other delight; crack (t. & i. of whip). 3. adv. (colloq.). With a ~, in sudden direct violent way, outright, exactly, (*went* ~ *through windows, into ditch*; *hit him* ~ *on the nose*). [16th c., prob. init.; cf. MDu. *smak*, MDu., MLG *smacken*]

smäck³, n. Sloop esp. for fishing; ~*s*-*man*, sailor on ~. [f. Du. *smak*, earlier *smacke*, LG *smak(ke)*]

smäck′er, n. (sl.). Loud kiss; sounding blow; ‖ large or remarkable specimen of anything; *dollar. [SMACK², -ER¹]

small (-awl), a., n., & adv. 1. Not large, of deficient or comparatively little size or strength or power or number, consisting

of minute units (~ *rain*), (of agent) not doing thing on large scale, (usu. without emotional implications of LITTLE, e.g. not *a dear* ~ *pony* or *a dirty* ~ *scoundrel*; ~ *farmer, shopkeeper*, on ~ scale; *has a* ~ *voice*; ~ FRY¹; ~ HOURS; ~ *& early*, party with few guests & not kept up late; *the still* ~ *voice*, conscience; *coat is* ~ or *too* ~ *for me*; ~ *craft*, boats; *came in* ~ *numbers*; *this beer is very* ~, weak, watery). 2. (As distinctive epithet) of the ~er kind (~*-sword*, rapier or sword for thrusting only; ~ *beer*, arch., of light kind; *think no* ~ *beer of oneself*, be conceited; *chronicle* ~ *beer*, talk of trifles as important; *look, feel*, ~, be humiliated; ~ *change*, copper & silver coins, (transf.) trivial remarks; ~ *gross*, ten dozen; ~*-ARM²s*, portable fire-arms; ~ *letters*, not capitals; ~ *capitals*, of less height than the fount's regular capitals; ~ *pica*, size of TYPE; ~ *hand*, ordinary writing, opp. *text-hand*; ‖ ~ *debt*, not above largest amount recoverable in county court; ~*-clothes*, arch., knee-breeches; ‖ ~ *holding*, piece of land between one and fifty acres in extent let or sold by a county council to a ~ *holder* for cultivation. 3. Not much of (*& ~ blame to him, & ~ wonder*, comments on conduct etc. just described; *there was no* ~ *excitement about it*; *has* ~ *Latin*, knows little of it). 4. Unimportant, trifling, (~ *talk*, ordinary society conversation; *the* ~ *worries of life*; *is great in* ~ *matters*). 5. Socially undistinguished, poor, obscure, humble, (*great & ~*, all classes; *lives in a* ~ *way*, unpretentiously; *have experimented with radium in a* ~ *way*; ~ *people love to talk of great*). 6. Morally mean, ungenerous, petty, paltry, (*his* ~ *spiteful nature*; *only a* ~ *man would think of that at such a time*; *I call it* ~ *of him to remind me of it*), whence ~′mind′ED² a. 7. ~′*pox*, highly contagious & fatal disease with fever & pustules; hence ~′ISH′(2) a., ~′NESS n., (-awl-). 8. n. *The* slenderest part of something, esp. ~ *of the back*, hinder part of waist; ‖ (pl., at Oxford) former responsions; ‖ (pl., colloq.) ~ articles of laundry. 9. adv. SING~. [OE *smæl*, OS, OHG *smal*, ON *smalr*, Goth *smals*]

small′age (-awl-), n. Wild celery. [ME, f. SMALL +obs. *ache* f. OF *ache* f. L f. Gk *apion* parsley]

smalt (-awlt), n. Glass coloured blue with cobalt; pigment made by pulverizing this. [F, f. It. *smalto* f. Gmc, cogn. w. SMELT¹]

‖ smärm′ў, a. (colloq.). Unctuously ingratiating, fulsome. [f. *smarm* var. of dial. *smalm* smooth down (as with grease), -ʏ²]

smärt¹, v.i., & n. 1. (Of person or part of him, or of wound lit. or fig. or the missile or insult etc. that has inflicted it) feel or give acute pain, rankle, (*my finger* ~*s*; *rushed off* ~*ing with nettle-stings, under disappointment*, etc.; *with the gibe yet*

~*ing in his brain*; ~ *for*, be paid out for, suffer consequences of, esp. as threat *you shall* ~ *for this*). **2.** n. Bodily or mental sharp pain, stinging sensation. **3.** ~-*money*, paid or exacted as penalty or compensation; ~'*weed*, the water-pepper. [vb f. OE *smeortan* = MDu., LG *smerten*, OHG *smerzan*; n. ME, app. f. OE *smiertu f. *smeart* adj. (foll.)]

smart², a. **1.** Severe, sharp, vigorous, lively, brisk, (*gave him a* ~ *rap over the knuckles*; *had a* ~ *skirmish, walk, bout of toothache*; *went off at a* ~ *pace*). **2.** Clever, ingenious, showing quick wit or ingenuity, keen in bargaining, quick to take advantage, (*a* ~ *talker, retort, saying, device, invention*; *a* ~ *officer, servant, lad*, ready & intelligent; ~ *dealing*, selfishly clever to verge of dishonesty); unscrupulously clever; *~ *alec*(*k*), a would-be clever person. **3.** Bright & fresh in appearance, spruce, in perfect order or repair, in gay or fashionable clothes, well groomed, showing bright colours or new paint, (~ *clothes, a* ~ *garden*; *person, house, ship, looks quite* ~). **4.** Conspicuous in society, leading the fashion, stylish, (~ *people*; *the* ~ *set*). Hence ~'EN⁶ v.t. & i., ~'LY² adv., ~'NESS n. [OE *smeart*, rel. to *smeortan* (prec.)]

smash, v.t. & i., n., & adv. **1.** Break (t. & i.) utterly to pieces (often *up*), shatter, bash *in* with crushing blow, (*a* ~*ing blow*, of irresistible force); utterly rout & disorganize (enemy); hit (lawn-tennis ball) downwards over net with great force; (of business firm) break, go bankrupt, come to grief; (of vehicle etc.) crash *into* another or an obstacle; (sl.) utter false coin; ~-*and-grab raid* (in which thief ~es shop-window· and grabs valuables behind it). Hence~'ING²a.(sl.), unusually good, superlative. **2.** n. Breaking to pieces; violent fall or collision or disaster (*go to* ~, be spoilt or disorganized or ruined); ~ing stroke in lawn tennis (see vb); violent blow with fist etc.; bankruptcy, series of commercial failures; drink of spirit & water·iced & flavoured (usu. *brandy-*~); ~-*hit* (sl.), success; ~-*up*, complete ~. **3.** adv. (With vbs of motion) with a ~ (*went* ~ *into a goods train*). [prob. imit.]

smash'er, n. In vbl senses; esp. (sl.), someone or something excellent, convincing argument or smashing blow or heavy fall. [-ER¹]

‖ **smatch**, n. (now rare). = SMACK¹ n. [ME var. of SMACK¹ n.]

smätt'er|ing, n. Slight superficial knowledge of a language or subject. So ~ER¹ n. [f. ME *smatter* talk ignorantly, prate, of unkn. orig.]

smäze, n. Mixture of smoke and haze, cf. SMOG. [portmanteau wd]

smear, v.t. & i., & n. **1.** Daub with greasy or sticky substance or with something that stains, (of grease etc.) make

marks on, make a ~; blot, obscure outline of, (writing, drawing); defame, sully. **2.** n. Blotch made by ~ing; defamation; hence ~'Y² a., ~'iNESS n. [OE *smerian* f. *smeoru* fat = OS, OHG *smero*, ON *smjǫr*]

smĕc'tīte, n. Kind of whitish clay used for taking out grease from cloth etc. [f. Gk *smēktis* fuller's earth, -ITE¹(2)]

‖ **smeech, smitch**, n. (dial.). Smell of burning or smouldering. [OE *smĕc, smic*, cogn. w. *smoke*]

smĕǵ'|ma, n. Sebaceous soaplike secretion in folds of the skin, esp. of the prepuce. Hence ~*mǎt*'IC a. [f. Gk *smēgma* -*atos* soap (*smēkhō* = cleanse)]

smĕll, n., & v.t. & i. (*smĕlt* or rarely ~*ed*). **1.** Nasal sense by which odours are perceived (~ *is less acute in man than in most animals*; *has a fine sense of* ~; *is perceptible to* ~ *as well as sight*); quality in substances that affects this sense, odour, (*has no, a sweet, pungent, disgusting, peculiar, close*, ~; *the* ~ *of thyme, carrion*); bad odour, whence ~'Y² a. (colloq.); act of inhaling in order to ascertain ~ (*take a* ~ *at it*); hence ~'LESS a. **2.** vb. Perceive ~ of, detect presence of by ~, (*am sure I* ~ *gas*; *horses smell the water a mile off*; ~ *a rat*, fig., suspect foul dealing etc.), whence ~'ABLE a.; inhale ~ of, set one's sense of ~ to work at (*smell it* or *at it to see if it was high*; *came up &* smell *at my calves*); (of dog) hunt out by ~, (fig. of person) find *out* (secret, plotter, etc.) by investigation, (of dog or fig. of person) sniff or search *about*; perceive ~s, have sense of ~ (*can, do, fishes* ~?); emit ~ usu. of kind specified by adj. or adv., suggest or recall the ~ *of*, (*flowers that do not* ~; ~s *sweet, nice, disgustingly, of garlic, of brandy*; ~ *of the lamp*, seem to have been composed laboriously at night; ~ *of the shop*, be over-technical; ~ *of jobbery, nepotism*, etc., suggest these); stink, be rank; seem from the ~ to be (*dish, milk*, ~s *good, sour*); ~*ing-bottle*, pocket phial of ~*ing-salts*, ammonium carbonate mixed with scent to be sniffed as cure for faintness etc. [ME *smel(len)*, excl. E]

smĕll'er, n. In vbl senses; (also) the nose (sl.). [-ER¹]

smĕlt¹, v.t. Extract metal from (ore) by melting; extract (metal) from ore by melting. [f. MDu. or MLG *smelten*; cogn. w. MELT²]

smĕlt², n. Small fish allied to salmon & prized as food. [OE, = obs. G *schmelt, schmelz*, Da. *smelt*]

smĕlt³. See SMELL.

smew, n. Kind of fishing duck. [also *smee, smeath*, orig. unkn.]

smil'ax, n. Kinds of climbing shrubs some of which yield sarsaparilla; climbing kind of asparagus much used in decoration. [L f. Gk]

smil|e, v.i. & t., & n. **1.** Relax features often by parting lips into pleased or kind or gently amused or indulgently contemptuous or sceptical expression or forced imitation of these, look (up)on or at with such expression, (~e *sweetly, indulgently, cynically, bitterly*; ~e *at the claims of,* ridicule or show indifference to them), whence ~'**ingLY**[2] adv.; express by ~ing (~e *welcome, consent, appreciation,* etc.); give a~e of specified kind (~ed *an ironical, a curious,* ~e); drive (person's vexation etc.) *away,* bring (person) *into* or *out of* a mood, by ~ing; *come up* ~*ing,* face fresh difficulty (w. ref. to boxer beginning new round); be or appear propitious, have bright aspect, seem to look propitiously (up)on, (*fortune, occasion,* ~es *on us; all nature looks* ~*ing & gay*). **2.** n. Act of ~ing, ~ing expression or aspect; hence ~e'**LESS** (-l-l-) a. [ME, perh. f. MLG **smilen* = OHG *smilan*]

smirch, v.t., & n. Stain, soil, smear, spot, (lit., & fig. as a ~ed *reputation*). [15th c., of unkn. orig.]

smirk, v.i., & n. (Put on or wear) affected or silly smile, simper. [OE *sme(a)rcian;* f. **smar-, *smer-* as in OE *smerian* laugh at; for *-k* cf. TALK]

smite, v.t. & i. (*smôte* & arch. *smît, smitten* & arch. *smit*), & n. **1.** Strike, hit, (chiefly arch. or joc.; *whosoever shall* ~ *thee on thy right cheek; smote his hands together; smote the harpstrings;* ~ *off his head; smote the first ball for four; an idea smote him,* suddenly came); inflict severe defeat on (~ *them hip & thigh,* utterly defeat them; *we hope to* ~ *them*); chastise (*God shall* ~ *thee; his conscience smote him*); (chiefly in p.p.) strike or seize or infect or possess *with* disease or desire or fascination (*city, person, smitten with plague, palsy; am smitten with her charms* or *her* or abs.; *smitten with a desire to*); come forcibly or abruptly (up)on (*wave smote upon the cliff; sun's rays smiting upon him; sound* ~s *upon the ear*); hence **smit'ER**[1] n. **2.** n. (colloq.). Blow, stroke, attempt. [OE *smitan,* MDu., MLG *smiten,* OHG *smizan,* Goth. *-smeitan*]

smith, n. Worker in metal esp. one who forges iron, blacksmith, (the gen. sense chiefly in comb., as *gold, silver, tin, white,* -~). [OE *smith,* MDu., MLG *smit,* OHG *smid, smit,* ON *smithr,* Goth. *smitha*]

smithereens' (-dherēnz), **smith'ers** (-dh-), nn. pl. Small fragments (*smash* etc. *to* or *into* ~). [f. syn. *smithers* + *-een* (Ir. dim. ending); orig. unkn.]

smith'erỹ, n. Smith's work; (esp. in Admiralty dockyards) smithy. [-ERY]

Smith'field, n. (Used for) the London meat market. [~ in London]

smi'thy (-dhi), n. Blacksmith's workshop, forge. [ME, f. ON *smithja,* = OE *smiththe,* (Gmc **smithjōn*) whence obs. *smithe*]

smitten. See SMITE.

smock, n., & v.t. **1.** Chemise (arch.); child's overall; blouse worn by artists etc.; ~(-*frock*), field-labourer's former outer linen garment of shirtlike shape & with upper part closely gathered; ~-*mill* (hist.), windmill of which the cap only & not the body revolves. **2.** v.t. Adorn with SMOCKING. [OE *smoc,* OHG *smoccho,* ON *smokkr,* prob. rel. to OE *smūgan* creep, ON *smjúga* put on a garment]

smock'ing, n. Honeycomb ornamentation on garment of which the basis is close gathers as on smock-frock. [-ING[1]]

smŏg, n. Mixture of smoke and fog, cf. SMAZE. [portmanteau wd]

smoke[1], n. **1.** Volatile products of combustion, esp. visible vapour with carbon etc. in suspension emitted by burning substance (*a column, cloud, of* ~; *end, go up, in* ~, come to nothing; *no* ~ *without* FIRE[1]; *from* ~ *into smother,* from one evil to another or a worse; *like* ~, sl., without check or difficulty, rapidly, easily; *the big* ~, sl., London or any large town). **2.** Spell of tobacco-smoking (*must have a* ~). **3.** (sl.). Cigar(ette). **4.** ~-*ball,* projectile filled with material emitting dense ~ used to conceal military operations etc., also ball used in trap-shooting & giving puff of ~ when struck, also medical appliance for inhaling vapour from in asthma etc.; ~-*bell,* suspended over lamp etc. to protect ceiling; ~-*consumer,* apparatus for utilizing instead of releasing ~ of furnace or fireplace, & so ~-*consuming* a.; ~-*dried,* cured in ~; ~-*jack,* machine for turning roasting-spit by use of current of hot air in chimney; ~-*plant, -tree,* ornamental shrub with feathery ~like fruit-stalks; ~-*rocket,* contrivance for injecting ~ into drain to discover leak; ~-*screen* (mil., nav.), ~ diffused to hide operations; ~-*stack,* funnel & steam-escape pipes of steamer; ~-*stone,* cairngorm. Hence **smŏk'ō** n. (Australia & New Zealand), break for a ~ during working hours, ~'LESS (-kl-) a., ~'lĕssLY[2] adv., ~'lĕssNESS n. [OE *smoca,* f. weak grade of stem of *smēocan, smēcan;* see SMEECH]

smŏk|e[2], v.i. & t. **1.** Emit smoke or visible vapour, reek, steam, (*his* ~*ing blade, steeds; meat* ~*ing on the board; lamp is* ~*ing,* not burning clear), (of chimney or fire) discharge smoke into room. **2.** Colour or darken or obscure, spoil taste of in cooking, preserve or cure, suffocate, rid of insects etc., with smoke (*lamp* ~*es ceiling;* ~*ed wood,* fumed; ~*ed glass,* darkened with smoke for looking at sun etc.; *the porridge is* ~*ed;* ~*ed ham, haddock,* etc.; ~*e insects, plants,* kill, cleanse, them by fumigation; **~e out,* discover by thorough investigation; ~*e out wasps, wasps'-nest,* etc., destroy by injecting smoke). **3.** Breathe in and out smoke of (tobacco-pipe, cigar, cigarette, tobacco, opium, stramonium, cane, brown paper; *put that in your pipe &* ~ *it,* reflect upon what has been said, esp. some admonition or rebuke), whence ~'ABLE a.; ~e tobacco (~*es too much* or *like a chimney; will you*

~*e?*), bring one*self* into specified state by ~ing (*has ~ed himself ill, sick, stupid, into tranquillity*). **4.** Get inkling, become suspicious or aware, of; ‖ (arch.) quiz, make fun of, (person etc.). **5.** ‖ ~*e-room*, ~ing-room; ~*ing-cap, -jacket*, of ornamental kind formerly worn while one ~ed; ~*ing-car(riage)* or *compartment*, reserved for smokers on railway-train; ‖ ~*ing-concert*, concert at which ~ing is allowed; ~*ing-mixture*, blend of tobaccos for ~ing in pipe; ~*ing-room*, in hotel or house kept for ~ing in (~*ing-room talk* etc., esp. such as is suited for men only). [OE *smocian* f. *smoca* (prec.)]

smōk'er, n. In vbl senses; also or esp.: person who habitually smokes tobacco (~*'s heart, throat*, ailments due to excessive smoking; CHAIN-~); smoking-compartment on train; ‖ smoking-concert. [-ER[1]]

smōk'|ȳ, a. Emitting, veiled or filled with, obscure (as) with, stained with or coloured like, smoke (*a ~y fire, city, room, hue, ceiling*). Hence ~ĭLY[2] adv., ~ĭNESS n. [-Y[2]]

smōlt, n. Migratory stage of young salmon or sea-trout whilst leaving fresh water for first visit to sea. [ME; orig. unkn.]

smōōth[1] (-dh), a. **1.** Of relatively even & polished surface, free from perceptible projections or lumps or indentations or roughness or (of liquid) undulations, not wrinkled or pitted or scored or hairy, that can be traversed without check, (~ *skin, surface, morocco, brow, chin*; *am now in ~ water*, have passed obstacles or difficulties; *bring the paste to a ~ consistence*; *had a ~ passage*, across sea; *course of true love never did run ~*; ~ *hair*, esp. flattened down on head). **2.** Free from harshness of sound or taste (~ *verse*, with easy & correct rhythm; ~ *claret, spirit*, etc.; ~ BREATHING). **3.** Equable, unruffled, polite, conciliatory, complimentary, flattering, (~ *temper, manners*; ~ *face*, esp. hypocritically friendly, whence ~**fac**ED[2] a.; ~ *things*, esp. flattery or insincere encouragement, whence ~SPOKEN, ~**-tongu**ED[2], aa.). **4.** ~*-bore*, gun with unrifled barrel. Hence ~'LY[2] adv., ~'NESS n., (-dh-). [OE *smōth* (once, usu. *smēthe* whence dial. *smeeth*); not in cogn. langg.]

smōōth[2] (-dh), v.t. & i., & n. **1.** Make smooth (often *out, over, down, away*; ~ *over* or *away differences, perplexities, difficulties*, etc., reduce or get rid of in fact or appearance); free from impediments or discomfort (~ *the way*; *will ~ his declining years*); cloak *over* faults etc.; become smooth (usu. *down*; *sea presently ~ed down*). **2.** n. ~ing touch or stroke (*gave his hair a ~*); ~*ing-iron*, implement usu. heated to ~ linen etc.; ~*ing-plane*, small plane for finishing the planing of wood. [ME, f. prec.]

smörgåsbord (smer'gōsboord), **smōr'gasbōrd**, n. Scandinavian hors-d'œuvres. [Sw., f. *smör* butter, *gås* goose, *bord* table]

smote. See SMITE.

smo'ther (-ŭdh-), n., & v.t. & i. **1.** Smouldering ashes etc. (arch.; *from the* SMOKE[1] *into the ~*); cloud of dust, spray, smoke etc., or obscurity caused by it (rare). **2.** vb. Suffocate, stifle, kill by stopping breath of or excluding air from, (~*ed mate* in chess, when king having no vacant space to move to is checked by knight); overwhelm *with* kisses, gifts, kindness, etc.; put out or keep down (fire) by heaping with ashes etc.; suppress, conceal or secure concealment of, keep from notice or publicity, burke, (often *up*; ~ *a yawn, with ~ed curses*; *the facts, the recommendations of the committee, were ~ed up*); cover entirely *in* (*strawberries ~ed in cream*); (rare) perish of suffocation, have difficulty in breathing. [ME *smorther* f. st. of *smorian* suffocate (dial. *smore*, = MDu., MLG *smoren*, G *schmoren*); vb f. n.]

smo'therȳ (-ŭdh-), a. Stifling. [-Y[2]]

smoul'der (smōl-), v.i., & n. **1.** Burn without flame, burn inwardly or in suppressed way or unseen; (of feelings etc.) exist, operate, be nursed, undetected or without conspicuous effects (~*ing discontent, hatred, rebellion*). **2.** n. ~ing combustion (*the ~ will soon be a flame*). [ME *smolder* n., of obsc. orig.; vb f. n.]

smŭdge[1], **smŭtch** (arch.), v.t. & i., & n. **1.** Smear or blot or blur lines of (writing, drawing); make dirt-mark or confused blot or smear on (face, paper, surface); (usu. *-tch*) defile, sully, stain with disgrace, impair purity of, (person's record, fame, etc.); (of ink, drawing, etc.) become blurred (*smudges easily*). **2.** n. Dirt-mark lit. or (esp. *-tch*) fig., blotted line, blurred mark; hence **smŭdg'**Y[2] a., **smŭdg'**ĭLY[2] adv., **smŭdg'**ĭNESS n. [*-ge* older as vb (1430), *-tch* as n. (1530); orig. unkn.]

smŭdge[2], n. Outdoor fire with dense smoke made to keep off insects etc. [rel. to prec.]

smŭg, a. & n. **1.** Of commonplace respectable narrow-minded self-satisfied comfortable unambitious unimaginative character or appearance; hence ~'NESS n. **2.** n. (chiefly univ. sl.) ‖ Person ill fitted for society or without athletic pursuits or interests. [16th c., of unkn. orig.]

smŭg'gl|e, v.t. Import or export (goods, or abs.) illegally, esp. without payment of customs duties (often *in, out, over*), whence ~ER[1], ~ING[1], nn.; convey secretly *in, out*, etc., or put *away* etc. into concealment. [17th c. *smuckle, smuggle*, f. LG *smukkeln* (Du. *smokkelen*), *smuggeln* (G *schmuggeln*)]

smŭt, n., & v.t. & i. (-tt-). **1.** (Spot or smudge made by) small flake of soot; *ditto, brother ~* (nursery etc.), tu quoque retort to criticism; lascivious talk or words or stories; disease of corn by which parts of the ear change to black powder; ~-*ball*, kinds of fungus; ~-*mill*, machine for cleansing grain from ~; hence ~t′Y² a., ~t′ILY² adv., ~t′INESS n. **2. vb.** Mark with ~(s); infect (corn) with, (of corn) contract, ~. [rel. to LG *smutt*, G *schmutz* the corn-disease, MHG *schmuz*, G *schmutz* dirt]

smutch. See SMUDGE.

Smyrn′iot(e) (-ĕr-), a. & n. (Native or inhabitant) of Smyrna. [-OT²]

snäck, n. Slight or casual or hurried meal (~ *bar* or *counter*, place where ~s are served); *go* ~s, go shares (~s!, claim to share). [orig. (15th c.) a snap or bite, f. *snack* vb; f. MDu. *snac(k)*, *snacken* snap (of a dog)]

snäf′fl|e¹, n. Bridle consisting of ~*e-bit*, or plain slender jointed bit without curb, & single rein; *ride* one *on the* ~*e* (fig.), manage him gently. Hence ~ED² (-ld) a. [16th c., perh. conn. w. (M)Du., (M)LG *snavel* beak, mouth]

|| **snäf′fle²**, v.t. (sl.). Appropriate, purloin, pinch. [*c.* 1700, cant of unkn. orig.]

snäfu′ (-fōō), a. & n. (Service sl.). 1. Chaotic. 2. n. Utter confusion. [f. initial letters of 'situation normal, *all fouled up*']

snäg, n., & v.t. (-gg-). **1.** Jagged projecting point, e.g. irregular or broken tooth, stump of branch remaining on tree, pointed root or stump poking out of ground, piece of rough timber or rock embedded in river or sea bottom & impeding navigation; (fig.) unexpected obstacle or drawback; hence ~gED² (-gd), ~g′Y² (-gĭ), aa. **2. v.t.** Run (ship) on ~; clear (land, waterway, tree-trunk) of ~s. [prob. f. Scand. (Norw. *snag* spike)]

snail, n., & v.t. & i. 1. Kinds of slimy slow-creeping gasteropod mollusc, most of them with spiral shell & horns or retractile eye-stalks, some used as food esp. in France, whence ~′ERY(3) n., & many destructive in gardens (*Roman* ~, the chief edible kind; ~′s *gallop*, *pace*, very slow locomotion); (also ~-*wheel*) notched wheel in clock resembling ~ in outline determining number of strokes in striking the hours; (also ~-*clover*, -*trefoil*) kinds of leguminous plant including lucerne with spiral pods; ~-*fish*, with ventral sucker for clinging; ~-*slow*, slow as a ~; hence ~′LIKE a. **2. vb.** Rid (garden) of, hunt for, ~s. [OE *snægel* etc., MLG *sneil*, OHG *snegil* (G dial. *schnegel*), ON *snigill*]

snäke, n., & v.i. 1. Serpent (commoner in ordinary speech, more loosely applied so as to include ~like lizards etc., & specially used of the common British harmless kind; ~ *in the grass*, hidden danger or secret enemy; *warm*, *cherish*, etc., *a* ~ *in* one's *bosom*, meet with ingratitude or receive evil for good; SCOTCH² *the* ~; see ~s, have delirium tremens; *raise* or *wake* ~s, make disturbance, start violent quarrel; *S~s!*,

int. of anger). **2.** Treacherous cold-hearted person. **3.** ~-*bird*, fish-eating bird with long slender neck; ~-*charmer*, -*charming*, see SERPENT; ~-*fence* (of horizontal tree-trunks only, laid zigzag with overlapping ends to support each other); ~ *lizard*, kinds of lizard with rudimentary or no legs; ~-*locked*, with ~s instead of hair; ~(-)*root*, one of several American plants having roots reputed to be ~-poison antidotes; ~*s′head*, the fritillary plant (from resemblance of bud to head of ~); ~-*stone*, ammonite; ~-*weed*, bistort; ~-*wood*, (wood of) a S.-American timber-tree (from its ~like markings). **4. v.i.** Move, twist, etc. like a ~. [OE *snaca*, = MLG *snake*, ON *snåkr*, *snókr*]

snäk′|ў, a. Infested with snakes; snake-like in appearance or in such attributes as venom, guile, coldness, ingratitude; ~*y* hair (of the Furies with snakes for hair). Hence ~INESS n. [-Y²]

snäp, v.t. & i. (-pp-), & n. **1.** Make sudden audible bite (*dog* ~*ped viciously*; ~ *at*, try to bite, also speak irritably to; ~ *at* bait, offer, chance, etc., accept eagerly), (fig.) say ill-tempered or spiteful things (~ *out*, say irritably), whence ~p′ISH¹ a., ~p′ishLY² adv., ~p′ishNESS n.; bite *off* (~ *off* one's *nose*, esp. fig. interrupt him angrily or rudely). **2.** Pick *up* (scraps, or fig. bargain etc.) hastily, whence ~p′ER¹-up n.; take *up* (interlocutor) without letting him finish. **3.** (crick.). Catch (batsman) smartly at the wicket. **4.** Break (t. & i.) with sharp crack (~ *the string*, *a stick*; *oar*, *wire*, ~s). **5.** Produce report from, emit report or crack, (~ *pistol*, *whip*; ~ one's *fingers*, make audible fillip esp. *at* person etc. in contempt; ~ one's *fingers at*, fig., defy; *pistol* ~s, either in going off or in missing fire); close (t. & i.) etc. with ~ping sound (~ *the clasp*, one's *teeth together*; *the door* ~*ped to*). **6.** Take instantaneous photograph of (esp. unconscious or unwilling subject). **7.** *~ into it* (sl.), start moving quickly; *~ out of it* (sl.), get rid of a mood, habit, etc. **8.** ~*ping turtle*, ferocious American freshwater kind. **9. n.** Act or sound of ~ping (also quasi-adv., as ~ *went an oar*). **10.** Spring-catch fastening bracelet etc. **11.** || Kinds of small crisp cake; BRANDY-~. **12.** A card-game. **13.** (Usu. *cold* ~) sudden spell of frost. **14.** Crispness of style, fresh vigour or liveliness in action, go, dash, spring, whence ~p′Y² a. (*make it* ~*py*, colloq.; be quick about it). **15.** = ~*shot* n. (see below). **16.** *(sl.).* Easy task (esp. *soft* ~). **17.** (theatr.). Short engagement as actor. **18.** attrib. (Esp. of parliamentary or other deliberative proceedings) taken by surprise, brought on without notice, etc. (*a* ~ *division*, *debate*, *crisis*, *vote*, etc.). **19.** ~-*bolt*, -*lock*, going home automatically with spring on closing of door etc.; ~′*dragon*, kinds of plant with bag-shaped flower like a dragon's mouth, antirrhinum, also Christmas game of plucking raisins from dish of burning brandy; ~-hook, -link, with spring allowing entrance but barring escape of cord, link, etc.; ~ shot n., shot taken with little or no delay in aiming; ~'shot, (n.) instantaneous photograph taken with hand camera, (v.t., also -shoot) take such photograph of. [f. MDu. or MLG snappen; partly echoic]

snare, n., & v.t. **1.** Trap for catching birds or animals, esp. one made with wire; (surg.) wire loop for catching & extracting polypi etc.; device for tempting enemy or dupe to expose himself to capture, defeat, failure, disgrace, loss, etc.; thing that acts as a temptation (popularity is often a ~); (pl.) twisted strings of gut or hide stretched across lower head of side-drum to produce rattling sound. **2.** v.t. Catch (bird etc.) in ~, whence (-)snarER[1] n.; get (person) into ~ (less common, & with more of the lit. sense, than ensnare). [ME, f. ON snara, rel. to OS snari, OHG snar(ahha); sense 'drum-snare' prob. f. Du.. or LG]

snark, n. Chimerical animal of ill-defined characteristics and potentialities. [from The Hunting of the S~ by 'Lewis Carroll' (1876)]

snarl[1], v.i. & t., & n. **1.** (Of dog) make high-pitched quarrelsome growl; (of person) speak cynically, make ill--tempered complaints or criticisms; ~ out, utter in ~ing tone; express (discontent etc.) by ~ing; hence ~'ER[1] n., ~'ingLY[2] adv. **2.** n. Act or sound of ~ing; hence ~'Y[2] a. [frequent. of 16th c. snar, f. MDu., (M)LG snarren; see -LE(3)]

snarl[2], v.t. & i., & n. **1.** Twist, entangle, become entangled, (a ~ed skein, intricate business); adorn exterior of (narrow metal vase) with raised work made by indirect internal hammering with ~-ing--iron. **2.** n. Knot, tangle. [ME; n..f. SNARE n. or vb (see -LE(3)); vb f. n.]

snatch, v.t. & i., & n. **1.** Seize quickly, eagerly, or unexpectedly, esp. with suddenly outstretched hand(s), rescue narrowly from, secure with difficulty, carry suddenly away or from, (~ed his gun up, down; wind ~ed my cap off; child ~es its food; ~ kiss, opportunity, etc.; was ~ed from the jaws of death; ~ a half-hour's repose; ~ victory out of defeat; ~ed away, from us, from premature death); shoot out hand(s) at to seize (also fig., as ~ at offer, take it eagerly); ~-block (naut.), block with hinged flap admitting rope to sheave. **2.** n. Act of ~ing (made a ~ at it); (usu. pl.) fragment(s) or short burst(s) of song or recitation or talk, short spell(s) of action (only works by ~es, fits & starts), whence ~'Y[2] a., ~'iLY[2] adv. [ME snecchen, sna(c)che, of unkn. orig.; perh. rel. to SNACK]

sneak, v.i. & t., & n. **1.** Slink, go furtively, (often in, out, past, round, about, off, away, etc.), whence ~'ers n. pl. (sl.), silent shoes; (part.) furtive, not avowed, (have a ~ing kindness for him, an affection that one cannot justify by reason); || (school sl.) peach, tell tales; (sl.) make off with, steal; hence ~'ingLY[2] adv. **2.** n. Mean cowardly underhand person; || (school sl.) informer, telltale; (crick.) ball bowled along the ground; ~-thief (stealing from open doors or windows). [16th c., obsc. rel. to ME snike, OE snikan creep]

|| **sneck**, n., & v.t. (chiefly Sc.). Latch. [ME; cf. ME snatch in same sense]

sneer, v.i. & t., & n. **1.** Smile derisively (often at); utter derisive words esp. of a covert or ironical kind (usu. at); put (person) down, out of countenance, etc., take away (person's reputation etc.), by ~ing; hence ~'ER[1] n., ~'ingLY[2] adv. **2.** n. ~ing look or remark. [16th c., prob. imit.]

sneeze, v.i., & n. **1.** Make explosive sound in involuntarily expelling anything that irritates interior of nostrils (not to be ~d at, passable, not contemptible); ~ into a basket (euphem.), be guillotined. **2.** n. Act or sound of sneezing. [c. 1500 snese, app. alt. f. obs. fnese (OE *fnēosan) due to misreading or misprinting f as ſ after the initial combination fn- had become unfamiliar, & fnese had been replaced (early 15th c.) by (now dial.) neese]

snib, n., & v.t. (-bb-; chiefly Sc.). **1.** Bolt, fastening, catch, of door, window, etc. **2.** v.t. Bolt, fasten. [Sc.; orig. obsc.]

snick, v.t., & n. **1.** Cut small notch or make small incision in; (crick.) slightly deflect course of (ball) with bat. **2.** n. Slight notch or cut; (crick.) ~ing touch with bat. [18th c., prob. suggested by SNICKERSNEE etc.]

snick'er, v.i., & n. Whinny, neigh; = SNIGGER. [imit.]

snickersnee', n. (joc.). Knife, esp. one usable as weapon. [alt. f. earlier snick-or--snee a fight with knives, earlier stick or snee, f. Du. steken thrust, snijen cut]

snide, a. & n. (sl.). **1.** Counterfeit, bogus; insinuating, slyly derogatory. **2.** n. ~ jewellery or coin(s); ~s'man, utterer of false coin. [19th c. cant, of unkn. orig.]

sniff, v.i. & t., & n. **1.** Draw up air audibly through nose to stop it from running or as expression of contempt (~ at, try the smell of, also show contempt for or discontent with, also, of dog, show disposition to bite person's calves); draw up or up (air, liquid, scent), draw up scent of (flower, brandy, meat, etc.), into nose. **2.** n. Act or sound of ~ing, amount of air etc. ~ed up. [ME, imit.; cf. SNUFF[1]]

sniff'y, a. (colloq.). Disdainful, contemptuous; (of thing that should be odourless) slightly malodorous. [-Y[2]]

snift'ing-valve, n. Air-escape valve in

steam-engine cylinder. [f. (now dial.) *snift* = SNIFF]

snigg'er (-g-), v.i., & n. (Give) half--suppressed secretive laugh. [imit., cf. SNICKER]

snig'gle, v.i. Fish *for eels* by pushing bait into hole. [f. *snig* small eel; orig. unkn.]

snip, v.t. & i. (-pp-), & n. **1.** Cut with scissors or shears esp. in small quick strokes (~ *cloth, a hole*; ~ *off the ends*; ~ *at*, make ~ping strokes at), whence ~p'ING¹(2) n. **2.** n. Act of ~ping; piece ~ped off; (sl.) tailor; (racing sl.) certainty (also *dead* ~). [16th c., f. Du. or LG *snippen*]

snipe, n. (collect. sing. usu. for pl.), & v.i. & t. **1.** Kinds of gamebird with long straight bill & angular flight frequenting marshes (*common* or *whole, great* or *double* or *solitary, small* or *half* or *jack*, ~, British kinds); GUTTER-~; ~*-eel, -fish*, etc., kinds with long slender snout; hence **snip'**y² a. **2.** vb. Go ~-shooting; (mil.) fire shots from hiding usu. at long range into enemy's camp or at individuals, kill or hit thus, whence **snip'ER¹** n. [ME *snipe*, corresp. to Scand. *snipa* in Icel. *mȳrisnīpa*; cf. MDu., MLG *snippe*, OHG *snepfa*]

snipp'et, n. Small piece cut off, snipping; (pl.) detached fragments of knowledge or information, short extracts from books, odds & ends, whence ~y² a., ~iNESS n. [-ET¹]

snip-snăp-snŏr'um, n. A round card--game. [18th c., f. LG *snipp-snapp--snorum*]

sniv'el, v.i. (-ll-), & n. **1.** Run at the nose; be lachrymose, show maudlin emotion; hence ~IER¹ n., ~liNG² a. **2.** n. Running mucus; whining & weeping; hypocritical talk, cant. [ME, f. OE *snyflan* f. *snofl* mucus; n. f. vb]

snŏb, n. ‖ Man of low birth or breeding or social position (arch.); ‖ (at universities & public schools; arch.) townsman; person with exaggerated respect for social position or wealth & a disposition to be ashamed of socially inferior connexions, behave with servility to social superiors, & judge of merit by externals, whence ~b'ISH¹ a., ~b'ishLY² adv., ~b'ishNESS, ~b'ERY(4, 5), ~'liNG¹(2), ~ŏc'RACY, nn. [18th c. (still colloq.) *cobbler*; orig. unkn.]

snoek (-ōōk), n. (S. Afr.). Large edible sea-fish (cf. SNOOK¹). [Du.]

snŏŏd, n. **1.** (Sc. & literary) fillet worn by maidens in Scotland to confine hair, whence ~'ED² a. **2.** Any of the short lines attaching hooks to a main line in sea fishing. [OE *snōd*, of unkn. orig.]

snŏŏk¹, n. Kinds of fish esp. the sea pike (cf. SNOEK). [f. Du. *snoek*]

snŏŏk², n. (sl.). Contemptuous gesture with thumb to nose & fingers spread out (*cock, cut, make, a* ~ or ~*s*; *S~s!*, int. of contempt). [orig. unkn.]

snŏŏk'er, n. Game on billiard-table combining pool & pyramids (~*ed*, having one's object-ball covered by another; (fig.) beaten, defeated). [orig. unkn.]

snŏŏp, v.i. & t. (orig. U.S., colloq.). Pry into matters one is not concerned with; sneak *around* looking for infractions of the law; steal. Hence ~'ER¹ n. [f. Du. *snoepen* enjoy stealthily]

snooty. See SNOUT.

snŏŏze, v.i. & t., & n. (Take) short sleep esp. in day-time; pass time in lazy indifference; ~ *time* etc. *away*, spend it indolently. [18th c. cant, of unkn. orig.]

snŏr|e, v.i. & t., & n. (Make) hoarse rattling or grunting noise in breathing esp. during sleep; pass time *away* in ~ing; bring one*self awake, into a nightmare*, etc., by ~ing. Hence ~'ER¹ n. [ME, prob. imit.; cf. foll.]

snŏrt¹, v.i. & t., & n. (Make) explosive noise due to sudden forcing of breath through nose & usu. expressing anger or indignation or incredulity, or (of steam--engine etc.) noise resembling this; express (defiance etc.) by ~ing (often *out*), throw *out* (words) with ~ing. [ME, prob. imit.; cf. prec.]

Snŏrt², n. Device for enabling submarines to take in air for engines & crew when submerged to periscope depth. [orig. unkn.]

snŏrt'er, n. In vbl senses; also (sl.): boisterous gale; performance etc. conspicuous for vigour or violence. [-ER¹]

snŏt, n. (vulg.). Mucus of the nose (also of person as low term of abuse); ~*-rag*, handkerchief. [ME *snot(te)* (cf. OE *gesnot*), prob. f. MDu., MLG *snotte*]

snŏtt'|y̆, a. & n. **1.** Running or foul with snot (vulg.; also as low abusive epithet); (colloq.) annoyed, short-tempered; hence ~iLY² adv., ~iNESS n. **2.** n. (nav. sl.). Midshipman. [-Y²]

snout, n. Nose (& mouth) of animal or (derog.) human being; pointed front of something, nozzle, (~ *of glacier, of battleship's ram*, etc.); ~*-beetle*, kinds with beaked head; ~*-ring*, inserted in pig's ~ to prevent rooting. Hence (-)~ED² a., ~'Y², like 'a ~, having a (prominent) ~, (colloq., also snooT'y̆) supercilious, conceited. [ME, f. MDu., MLG *snūte*]

snow¹ (-ō), n., & v.i. & t. **1.** Atmospheric vapour frozen into ice crystals & falling to earth in white flakes or spread on it as a white layer (*red* ~, ~*-plant*, see below); (pl.) falls or accumulations of ~ (*where are the* ~*s of yester-year?*). **2.** Substance etc. resembling ~ esp. in whiteness (*her breast of* ~ ; *the* ~*s of seventy years*, white hair; *apple, chestnut*, etc., ~, kinds of pudding); (sl.) cocaine. **3.** ~'*ball*, (n.) mass of ~ pressed into hard ball esp. for use as missile, ‖ fund each subscriber to which finds *n* others, ‖ kinds of pudding e.g. apple enclosed in rice, (v.t. & i.) pelt or have pelting-match with ~balls;

~*ball-tree*, guelder-rose; ~*-berry*, garden shrub with white berries; ~*-bird*, kinds of white or partly white finch, esp. the ~ *bunting*; ~*-blind(ness)*, unable, inability, to see owing to exhaustion of retina by reflection of light endured in traversing ~-fields etc.; ~*-blink*, reflection in sky of ~ or ice fields; ~*-boots*, over-boots of rubber & cloth; ~*-bound*, kept from going out or travelling by ~; ~*-cap*, white-crowned humming-bird; ~*-capped*, (of móuntain) covered at top with ~; ~*-drift*, bank of ~ heaped by wind; ~*'drop*, early spring white-flowered plant; ~*-fall*, esp. amount of ~ that falls on one occasion or in a year at any place as measured by ~*-gauge*; ~*-field*, esp. permanent wide expanse of ~ in mountainous or polar regions; ~*-flake*, one of the small collections of crystals in which ~ falls; ~*-goggles*, darkened spectacles worn by mountaineers etc. to prevent ~-blindness; ~*-goose*, arctic white goose with black-tipped wings, the wavy; ~*-grouse*, ptarmigan; ~*-ice*, opaque white ice formed from ~-slush; ~*-leopard*, ounce; ~*-line*, level above which ~ lies permanently at any place; ~ *man*, figure made of ~ by children etc. & set up (*Abominable Snowman*, (sub)-human animal alleged to have been seen, or supposed to leave tracks in the ~, on the higher Himalaya mountains, YETI); ~*-on-the-mountain*, kinds of white-flowered garden plant; ~-, or usu. ~*y*, owl, the great white owl; ~*-plant* or *red*~, microscopic alga growing in~ & colouring it red; ~*-plough*, contrivance for clearing road or track by pushing ~ aside; ~ *plume*, fringe of blown ~ wind-driven from mountain-top or ridge; ~*-shoes*, racket-heads or (also SKI) long narrow boards attached to feet & enabling wearer to traverse ~ without sinking in; ~*-shovel*, large wooden shovel for~; ~*-slip*, avalanche; ~*-storm*, heavy fall of ~ esp. with wind; ~*-white*, white as ~; hence ~'LESS (-ŏl-), ~'Y² (-ŏi), aa., ~'iLY² adv., ~'iNESS n., (-ŏi-). **4.** vb. (Impers.) *it ~s*, *will*~, etc., ~ falls etc.; sprinkle or scatter, come, like~; *°*~ *under*, cover (as) with~, overwhelm with numbers etc. (esp. in pass. of election cándidate defeated by huge majority); ~*ed up*, *in*, ~-bound, blocked up with ~*s*. [OE *snāw*. OS *snēu*, OHG *snēo*, ON *snær*, Goth *snaiws* f. Gmc *°snaiwaz*, cogn. w. L *nix nivis*]

snow² (-ŏ), ·n. Small brig-like sailing vessel with supplementary trysail mast. [f. Du. *sna(a)uw* or LG *snau*]

snŭb¹, v.t. (-bb-), & n. **1.** Rebuff, reprove, put down, humiliate, with sharp words or marked want of cordiality, whence ~b'ING(1) n., ~b'ingLY² adv.; check way of (ship) esp. by rope wound round ~*(bing)-post* or bollard. **2.** n. ~bing, rebuff. [ME, f. ON *snubba* chide]

snŭb², a. & n. **1.** (Of nose) short & stumpy

or turned up, whence ~-NOSED² a. **2. n.** (rare). ~ nose. [f. prec. vb in old sense *check growth of*]

snŭff¹, v.i. & t., & n. **1.** = (the now more usu.) SNIFF vb; also, take ~, whence ~'ER¹ n. **2. n.** = (the now·more usu.) SNIFF n.; also: powdered tobacco taken by sniffing as stimulant or sedative (*give person ~*, deal sharply with him; *take thing in ~*, arch., take offence at it; *up to ~*, sl., not childishly ignorant or innocent*, whence ~'Y² a., ~'iNESS n.; medicinal powder taken by sniffing; ||~*-&-butter*, brownish-yellow; ~*-box*; ~*-colour(ed)*, (of) dark yellowish-brown; ~*-mill*, for grinding ~, || also ~-box; ~*-taker*, *-taking*. [vb prob. f. MDu. *snoffen*, *snuffen*; n. 'tobacco ' f. Du. *snuf*, *snuif*, app. abbr. f. *snuiftabak* snuffing-tobacco]

snŭff², v.t. & i., & n. **1.** Trim ~ from (candle or its wick) with fingers or scissors or esp. ~'ers n. pl., kind of scissors with box to catch ~ (~ *out* v.t., extinguish by trimming, also fig. as *I was nearly*, *his hopes were*, ~*ed out*; ~ *out* v.i., sl., die; *can* ~ *a candle with a pistol*, shoot off top of wick without putting flame out); ~*er-tray*, holding ~ers. **2.** n. Charred part of candle-wick, esp., in bad wick; ~*-dish*, ~er-tray. [ME *snoffe*, *snuffe*, of unkn. orig.; cf. LG *snuppe*; vb f. n., cf. LG *snuppen*]

snŭf'fl|e, v.i. & t., & n. **1.** Sniff (intr.), make sniffing sounds; speak nasally, whiningly, or like one with a cold, esp. as form of religious affectation ascribed to puritans & dissenters, whence ~ER¹ n.; ~*e out*, utter with ~ing; hence ~ingLY² adv. **2.** n. Sniff; ~ing sound, tone, or talk. [prob. f. Du., Flem. *snuffelen*; see SNUFF¹, -LE(3)]

snŭg, a. Sheltered from weather & cold, well enclosed or packed in or fixed in place, comfortably situated, cosy, (*as ~ as a bug in a rug*); (of income, dinner, etc.) good enough for modest requirements. Hence ~'LY² adv.,~'NESS n. [16th c., orig. naut.; orig. unkn.]

snŭgg'erÿ (-g-), n. Snug place, esp. person's private room or den; bar-parlour of inn. [-ERY]

snŭg'gle, v.i. & t. Shift one's position or lie close *up to* for warmth; draw (child etc.) close *to* one, cuddle. [f. 16th c. vb *snug* (of unkn. orig., later assoc. w. SNUG) +-LE(3)]

sō, adv., conj., int., & pron. **1.** To the extent or in the manner set forth by preceding or following *as*-clause or implied in context, thus, equally, similarly, analogously, (now used to express degree before an-clause only with negative, as *I am not so eager*, but *I am as eager*, *as you*; *as the tree falls*, *so must it lie*; *as bees love sweetness*, *so flies love rottenness*; rarely used twice correlatively, as *so many men so many minds*; *when he saw her so frightened*; *why are you panting* *so?*; *so & so only can it be done*; *stand just so*; *did not expect to live so long*; *did not get it by force & ought not to be so deprived of it*; often in sentence appended as explanation, as *I paid him double, I was so pleased*; *ever or never so bad* etc. in condit. clause, as *bad* etc. as possible; *so far*, up to this time or point or extent, as *so far it has not happened*, *so far you are right*; *so or in so far as* or arch. *so far forth as*, to whatever extent; *& so forth, & so on*, et cetera, & the like; *so long as*, with the proviso, on the condition, that; *so be it*, form of acceptance, resignation, etc.; *so long*, good-bye till we next meet; *so much for*, that is all that need be done or said about; *is only so much rubbish*, all rubbish; *at so much a week, a head*; etc., a definite but unspecified sum etc.; similarly *so much of one ingredient & so much of another*; *not so much as*, less than, not even; *is not so much discontented as unsatisfied*. **2.** To the degree or in the manner or with the intent or result set forth by following *that*-clause or *but*-clause or *as to* (*so high that you cannot reach it*; *so run that ye may obtain*; *warned him so that he might avoid the danger*; *all precautions have been taken, so that we expect to succeed*; *not so deaf but he can hear a gun*; *was so fortunate as to escape*; *put it so as not to offend him*; *it so happens that he was not there*). **3.** To a degree that demands exclamatory emphasis (*so many worlds, so much to do!*; *I am so glad, tired!*; *she is so beautiful!*; *so kind of you!*; also colloq. or vulg. with *ever*, as *that is ever so much better, he is ever so angry!*). **4.** On condition that or *that*, on condition set forth in *as*-clause or implied, (*so that or so it is done, it matters not how*; *so may you find forgiveness as now you forgive me!*; *so help me God!*, form of asseveration). **5.** Accordingly, consequently, therefore, as appears or results from preceding or implied statements or fact, (*he says he was not there, so he doubtless was not*; *so or and so I cannot come*; *so you are back again*; *so that's that*, colloq. winding up of statement or discussion; *so WHAT?*; *so look to yourself*). **6.** (Accompanying emphasis on some later word) moreover, also, as well, in actual fact, (*well, so I did*; *you said it was good, & so it is*; *yes, I denied it, but or & so did you*; '*your birthday? yes, so it is*'). **7.** (As substitute, often preceding vb, for obj. of *say, call, speak, tell, think, hope, suppose, do*, etc.) it, this, that, the same, this is what, (*so he said*; *so spake Achilles*, i.e. what precedes, *& Patroclus so*, i.e. what follows; also ellipt., as *So Satan, whom the archangel thus rebukes*; *do you think so?*; *& so say all of us*; *I suppose so*, form of agreement; *I told you so*, warned you in vain; *she is ill & he thinks himself so*; *so-called*, epithet questioning accuracy

of description; *so to say or speak*, apology for exaggeration, metaphor, neologism, etc.; *you don't say so?*, formula of surprise). **8.** In that state or condition, actually the case, (*he, it, is better so*; *God said Let there be light, & it was so*; *must it be so?*; *but perhaps it is not, even if it were, so*; *though it was*, or *things were, ever or never so*, vulg., however bad the state of things; also with omission of *it is* etc., as *how so?, why so?, if so, not so*; also ellipt. for *is that so?* chiefly in imit. of German, as 'He went off yesterday'. 'So?'; *quite so, just so*, forms of agreement). **9.** (arch.). *And so*, after which I, they, etc., proceeded (*& so to dinner, to bed*, etc.); *so please you*, by your favour, if you please. **10.** (Ellipt. after conditional clause; arch.) let it be so, very well, (*if you are content, so*). **11.** (As int., also *soh*) that will do, stay as you are, stand still, be quiet. **12.** (In comb. with relative words) *-ever* (also with *-ever* appended, as *whoso, whosoever*). **13.** *So-&-so* (pl. *so-&--so's*), particular person or thing not needing to be specified (*never mind what so-&--so says*; *tells me to do so-&-so*); *so so*, pred. adj. or adv., not more than passable, *-bly*; *or so*, or thereabouts (after expressions of quantity or numbers; *send me ten or so*; *1 lb. or so will do*). [OE *swā* etc., OS, OHG *sō*, ON *svā*, Goth. *swa, swē*]

soak, v.t. & i., & n. **1.** (Of absorbent substance) take *up* or suck *in* (liquid); place or leave or lie in or *in* liquid for saturation, steep t. & i., make or be wet through, (of rain etc.) drench, whence *~'ING*[1] n.; (of moisture) make way *in(to)* or *through*, make its *way*, by saturation, whence *~'AGE*[3] n.; (sl.) extract money from by extortionate charge, taxation, etc. (*~ the rich*); drink persistently, booze. **2.** n. *~ing*; drinking-bout; hard drinker. [OE *socian* cogn. w. *sūcan* SUCK]

soak'er, n. In vbl senses; esp.: hard drinker; drenching shower. [-ER[1]]

soap, n., & v.t. & i. **1.** Compound of fatty acid with soda or potash or (*insoluble ~s*) with an earth or metallic oxide, of which the soluble kinds yield when rubbed in water a lather used in washing (*soft ~*, made with potash & remaining liquid, also fig. flattery); *~-berry, -nut, -plant, -pod, -root, -wort*, kinds of plant yielding substances serving purpose of *~*; *~-boiler, -boiling*, manufacture(r) of *~*; *~-box*, box for holding *~*, makeshift stand for street orator; *~-bubble*, iridescent globe of air enclosed in film of soapy water made by blowing through pipe dipped in *~*-suds; *~-earth, -stone*, steatite; **~ opera* (sl.), radio serial; *~--SUDS*; *~-works, ~* manufactory; hence *~'LESS* a. **2.** vb. Apply *~* to, scrub or rub with *~*; use *~* upon oneself. [OE *sāpe*, MDu. *seepe*, OHG *seifa* f. Gmc **saipōn* whence. L *sapo*]

soap′|ў, a. Like, smeared or impregnated with, suggestive of, soap; (of person or his manners or talk) unctuous, flattering. Hence ~ĭLY² adv., ~ĭNESS n. [-Y²]

soar (sōr), v.i. Fly high (lit. & fig.), mount to or be at a great height above earth, hover or sail in the air without flapping of wings, (~ing eagle, spire, thoughts, ambition, ideals). Hence ~′ĭngLY² adv. [ME, f. OF essorer f. pop. L *EX (aurare f. aura breeze)]

sŏa′vĕ, sŏavĕmĕn′tĕ, (-ah-), mus. direction. With tenderness. [It.]

sŏb, v.i. & t. (-bb-), & n. **1.** Draw breath in convulsive gasps usu. with weeping under mental distress or physical exhaustion; ~ out, utter with ~s; hence ~b′ingLY² adv. **2.** n. Convulsive drawing of breath esp. in weeping; *~-stuff, pathos, sentimental writing. [ME sobbe(n), prob. imit.]

sŏb′er, a., & v.t. & i. 1. Not drunk (as ~ as a judge; appeal from Philip drunk to Philip ~, suggest that opinion etc. represents passing mood only); temperate in regard to drink (is a ~ man); moderate, well-balanced, sane, tranquil, self-controlled, sedate, not vehement or passionate or excited or wayward or fanciful or exaggerated, (of colour) quiet & inconspicuous, (in ~ fact, in fact as opp. fancy; a ~ estimate; ~-minded; ~-sides, sedate person; ~-suited, poet., clad in ~ colours), whence ~LY² adv. **2.** vb. Make or become ~ or less wild, reckless, enthusiastic, visionary, etc. (often down). [ME, f. OF sobre f. L sobrius]

Sŏbra′nje (-ahnyĕ), n. Bulgarian national assembly. [Bulg.]

sobri′ĕtў, n. Being SOBER. [ME, f. OF sobriete or L sobrietas (SOBER, -TY)]

sŏb′riquet (-kā), **sou-** (sōō-), n. Nickname, assumed name. [F]

sŏc(c)′age, n. Feudal tenure of land involving payment of rent or other service to superior. [AF, f. soc f. OE sōcn SOKE +-AGE]

sŏcc′er (-k-), n. (colloq.). ASSOCIATION football. [ASSOCIATION, -ER¹]

sŏ′ciab|le (-sha-), a. & n. **1.** Fitted for companionship, ready & willing to converse, not averse to society, communicative, liking company; (of meeting etc.) marked by friendliness, not stiff or formal; hence sŏciaBIL′ITY n., ~LY² adv., (-sha-). **2.** n. Open carriage with facing side seats; tricycle for two riders side by side; S-shaped couch allowing two occupants to face each other. [F, or f. L sociabilis (sociare to unite, -ABLE)]

sŏ′cial (-shl), a. & n. **1.** Living in companies, gregarious, not fitted for or not practising solitary life, interdependent, co-operative, practising division of labour, existing only as member of compound organism, (man is a ~ animal; ~ bees, wasps, kinds having common nests etc.; ~ birds, building near each other in com-

munities; ~ plants, kinds that grow thickly together & monopolize ground they grow on; ~ polyp etc.). **2.** Concerned with the mutual relations of men or classes of men (~ problems, science, morality, students, philosophers; the ~ contract or rarely compact, agreement among men to exchange the individual freedom of the state of nature for legal restriction, assumed by 18th-c. thinkers as basis of political society; ~ democrat, politician aiming at improving condition of lower classes by gradual advance towards socialism; ~ security, freedom from unemployment & want; ~ services, education, health, housing, insurance, pensions; the ~ evil, prostitution). **3.** Of or in or towards society (~ intercourse, life, code, etiquette, pleasures, duties; one's ~ superiors & inferiors; ~ rank, position, distinctions; has ~ tastes; a ~ evening, gathering). **4.** Of or with allies (the S~ war in Rom. hist.). **5.** n. ~ gathering, esp. one organized by club, congregation, etc. Hence or cogn. ~ITE¹ (-sha-) n., prominent society person, sŏciăl′ITY (-shĭ-) n., ~LY² adv. [F, or f. L socialis (socius friend, -AL)]

sŏ′cial|ism (-sha-), n. A political and economic theory of social organization which advocates State ownership and control of the means of production, distribution, and exchange; a policy or practice based on this theory; Christian ~ism, attempt to apply Christian precepts in ordinary life resulting in some approximation to the aims of ~ism. Hence ~IST(2) n. & a., ~is′TIC a., ~is′TICALLY adv., (-sha-). [f. F -isme, or f. prec. +-ISM]

sŏ′cializ|e (-sha-), **-is|e** (-īz), v.t. Make social; arrange socialistically. Hence ~A′TION n. [-IZE]

soci′ĕtў, n. 1. Social mode of life, the customs & organization of a civilized nation, (the progress of ~ is an evolution; pests of ~, persons who prey on the community). **2.** Any social community (no ~ can retain members who flout its principles). **3.** The upper classes of a community whose movements & entertainments & other doings are more or less conspicuous, the socially distinguished, fashionable & well-to-do & well-connected people, (was welcomed by ~; the customs of polite ~; ~ does not approve; leaders of ~; often attrib., as ~ lady, people, gossip, news, journal; ~ verse, of light topical witty kind). **4.** Participation in hospitality, other people's houses or company, (goes a great deal into, avoids, is at his best or embarrassed in, ~). **5.** Companionship, company, (~ & solitude; always enjoy his ~; seek, avoid, the ~ of). **6.** Association of persons united by a common aim or interest or principle (S~ of Friends, Quakers; S~ of Jesus, abbr. S.J., see JESUIT; BUILDING, CO-OPERATIVE, FRIENDLY ~; Royal S~, founded

1662 for improving natural knowledge; DORCAS ~). [f. F *société* f. L *societatem* (*socius* friend, -TY)]

Socin'ian, a. & n. (Follower, following or according to doctrine) of the 16th-c. Italian theologians Laelius & Faustus Socinus, whose opinions resemble those of modern unitarians. Hence ~ISM(3) n. [-IAN]

sociŏl'ogy̆, n. Science of the development & nature & laws of human society. Hence **sŏcioLO'GICAL** a., **sŏciolŏ'gicaLLY²** adv., (-sho-), **sŏciŏl'OGIST** n. [F (-*gie*), f. L *socius* see SOCIABLE, -LOGY]

sŏck¹, n. (shop pl. *sox*). Short stocking not reaching knee (||*pull up your ~s!*, brace yourself for an effort); removable inner sole put into shoe for warmth etc.; ancient comic actor's light shoe (also used allusively for comedy etc., cf. BUSKIN). [OE *socc* f. L *soccus* comic actor's shoe]

sŏck², v.t., n., & adv. (sl.). **1.** Fling (ball, stone) *at*; hit (person) with hand-flung missile. **2.** n. Blow inflicted by missile or fist (esp. *give him ~s!*). **3.** adv. With such blow, plump, right, (*hit him ~ in the eye*). [*c.* 1700, cant, of unkn. orig.]

|| **sŏck³**, n., & v.t. & i. (school sl.). **1.** Sweets, pastry, etc., eaten at odd times, tuck, grub. **2.** vb. Treat to ~, indulge in ~; give (person thing). [orig. Eton sl., of unkn. orig.]

***sŏckdŏl'oger**, -lag-, n. (sl.). Decisive blow or argument. [prob. fanciful]

sŏck'ét, n., & v.t. **1.** Natural or artificial hollow for something to fit into or stand firm or revolve in (*eye~*; ~ *of the hip*; *candle too large for ~*; BALL¹ & ~); ~-*joint*, = BALL¹-&-~ *joint*; ~-*pipe*, with enlarged end to receive another. **2.** v.t. Place in, fit with, ~; (golf) hit (ball) with heel of club. Hence ~ED² a. [15th c., AF, dim. of *soc* ploughshare, prob. of Celt. orig.]

sŏck'eye (-kĭ), n. The blue-back salmon. [Amer.-Ind. *sukai*]

sŏ'cle, n. (archit.). Plain low rectangular block serving as support for pedestal, vase, statue, etc. [F, f. It. *zoccolo* f. L *socculus* (*soccus* SOCK¹, -ULE)]

Socrăt'|ĭc, a. & n. **1.** Of, like, following, etc., Socrates (~*ic method*, dialectic, procedure by question & answer; ~*ic irony*, pose of ignorance assumed in order to entice others into display of supposed knowledge). **2.** n. Follower of Socrates. Hence~ICALLY adv. [f. L f. Gk *Sōkratikos* (*Sōkratēs*, -IC)]

sŏd¹, n., & v.t. (-dd-). **1.** Turf, upper layer of grass land including blades & roots & earth, (*under the ~*, in the grave); piece of turf pared off; hence ~d'y̆² a. **2.** v.t. Cover (ground) with ~s (~*ding mallet*, *spade*, implements used); pelt with ~s. [15th c., f. MDu. or MLG *sode*, = OFris. *sātha*, *sāda*, of unkn. orig.]

sŏd². See SEETHE.

sŏd³, n. (vulg.). Sodomite (esp. as vague term of abuse). [abbr.]

sōd'a, n. **1.** One of the compounds of sodium in common use, esp. sodium carbonate or bicarbonate. **2.** (Also ~-*water*) water made effervescent by impregnation with carbonic acid under pressure & used alone or with spirit or wine or milk as a drink (orig. made with sodium bicarbonate; *some ~-water*; *some* or *a brandy & ~*; ~-*fountain*, vessel in which ~-water is stored under pressure to be drawn out, shop, *store, or counter equipped with this apparatus). [med. L, f. *sodanum* glasswort, f. Arab. *suda'*]

sodăl'ity̆, n. A confraternity or association esp. of religious character (chiefly in titles of R.-C. societies). [f. F -*ité* or L *sodalitas* (*sodalis* comrade, -TY)]

sŏdd'en, a., & v.t. & i. **1.** Saturated with liquid, soaked through; (of bread) doughy, heavy & moist; stupid or dull in fact or appearance with habitual drunkenness; hence ~NESS n. **2.** vb. Become or make ~. [orig. p.p. of SEETHE]

sōd'ium, n. A soft silver-white metallic element found in soda, salt, & other compounds, which in its pure form decomposes water; ~ *bicarbonate*, baking powder; ~ *carbonate*, washing soda; ~ *chloride*, common salt; ~ *silicate*, water-glass; ~ *sulphate*, Glauber's salt. Hence **sōd'IC** a. [SODA, -IUM]

Sŏd'om, n. (Type of) wicked town. [*Gen.* xviii, xix]

sŏd'omite, n. Person practising sodomy. [ME, f. OF, orig. f. LL f. Gk *Sodomitēs* inhabitant of Sodom, see -ITE¹(1)]

sŏd'omy̆, n. Copulation between male persons; unnatural connexion between human beings and animals. [ME, f. OF *sodomie* (LL *Sodoma*, -IA¹)]

soěv'er, suf. occas. separable usu. appended to relative pronouns, adverbs, or adjectives, but sometimes following them at an interval, to give indefinite meaning (*whosoever, howsoever*, etc.; *how great ~ it may be*; *with what end ~ he did it*). [SO, EVER]

sōf'a, n. Couch with raised ends & back on which several persons can sit or one lie; ~ *bed*(*stead*), piece of furniture serving as ~ by day & bed by night. [F, f. Arab. *suffah*]

sŏff'it, n. Lower surface of architrave, arch, balcony, etc. [f. It. *soffitta*, -*itto*, & F *soffite*, ult. f. L SUB² (*figere* fix)]

sofi(sm). See SUFI(*sm*).

sŏft (or saw-), a., n., adv., & int. **1.** Comparatively wanting in hardness, yielding to pressure, malleable, plastic, easily cut, (~ *as butter*; ~ *stone, iron*; ~ *coal*, bituminous, opp. *anthracite*; ~ *corn*, moist thickening of skin between toes confused with CORN³; ~ (opp. HARD) *currency*; ~ *tissues* of body, not bony or cartilaginous; ~ *palate*, hinder part of palate; ~ *wicket* at cricket, moist or sodden turf; ‖~ *goods*, textiles; ~ *solder*, kinds used for easily fusible metal, cf. ~ SAWDER; ~ SOAP; ~ *tack*, naut., bread, opp. *hard tack* or biscuit; ~ *roe*, of male fish; ~ *wood*, (wood of) coniferous tree). **2.** Of smooth surface or fine texture, not rough or coarse, (~ *skin, hair, raiment*). **3.** Mellow, mild, balmy, not noticeably cold or hot, (~ *air*; *a* ~ *winter*). **4.** ‖ Rainy or moist or thawing (~ *weather*; *a* ~ *day*). **5.** (Of water) free from mineral salts & so good for washing or cooking. **6.** Not astringent or sour or bitter (~ *claret* etc.). **7.** Not crude or brilliant or dazzling (~ *colours, light, eyes*); not sharply defined (~ *outline*); not strident or loud, low-toned, (*a* ~ *voice*; ~ *music*; ~ PEDAL[1]; ~-*pedal* v.i. & t., play with ~ pedal down, tone down, refrain from emphasizing; ~ *whispers, murmurs*); (phonet.) sibilant (*g is* ~ *in* gin), voiced (*b, g, d, are* ~ *mutes*), unaspirated (~. or *smooth* BREATHING[1]). **8.** Gentle, quiet, conciliatory, complimentary or amorous, (~ *rain*; ~ *drink*, colloq., non-alcoholic; ~ *manners*; *a* ~ *answer*, esp. a good-tempered one to abuse or accusation; ~-*spoken*, see SPEAK; ~ *nothings*, amorous talk). **9.** Sympathetic, compassionate, (*has a* ~ *heart*, whence ~-**heart**'ED[2] a., ~-**heart**'edNESS n.). **10.** Tranquil (~ *slumbers*). **11.** (sl.). Easy (*has a* ~ *job*; *a* ~ *option*; ~ *thing*, light well-paid office etc.). **12.** Flabby, weak, feeble, unstrung, effeminate, silly, (*the national character has gone* ~; *a* ~ *luxurious people*; ~ *muscles*; ~-*headed*, ~-*witted*, half idiotic); hence ~'ISH[1] a., ~'LY[2] adv., ~'NESS n. **13.** n. Silly weak person, also ~'Y[3] n. **14.** adv. (commoner in compar. than in posit.). ~ly (*play* ~, ~*er*; ~-*whispering* etc.). **15.** int. (arch.). Wait a moment; hush! [OE *sŏft(e)*, older *sĕft(e)*, = OHG *semfti*; cf. also MDu., MLG *sacht*, MHG *sanft*]

sŏf'ta, n. Moslem student of sacred law & theology. [Turk.]

soften (sŏ'fn, saw⁴), v.i. & t. Become or make SOFT or softer; (also ~ *up*) reduce strength of (defences) by bombing etc.; ~*ing* (morbid degeneration) *of the brain*. Hence ~ER[1](1, 2) n. [ME; -EN[6]]

sŏgg'|ў (-g-), a. Sodden, saturated, dank. Hence ~iNESS n. [f. dial. *sog* a swamp]

soh. See SOL[2].

sohō'[1], int. used in quieting horse etc. [AF hunting-cry]

Sohō'[2], n. District in London associated with foreign restaurants etc.

soi-disant (see Ap.), a. Self-styled, pretended. [F]

soigné (swahn'yā), (fem. ~*e*), a. (Chiefly of a woman's toilet) exquisite in detail, carefully finished or arranged. [p.p. of F *soigner* take care of (*soin* care)]

soil[1], n. The ground, upper layer of earth in which plants grow consisting of disintegrated rock usu. with admixture of organic remains, mould, (*good, poor, clayey, alluvial, light, rich,* etc., ~; NIGHT-~; one's *native* ~, ground of one's native land or place). Hence (-)~ED[2] (-ld) a. [ME, f. AF, app. f. L *solium* taken in sense of L *solum* ground]

soil[2], v.t. & i., & n. **1.** Make dirty, smear or stain with dirt, tarnish, defile, (~*ed linen*; *would not* ~ *my hands with it* fig.), so ~'URE n. (arch.); admit of being ~ed (~*s easily*). **2.** n. Dirty mark, stain, smear, defilement. **3.** ~-*pipe*, discharge-pipe of water-closet; hence ~'LESS (-l-l-) a. [ME, f. OF *suill(i)er, soill(i)er*, etc., f. Rom. **suculare* f. *sucula* dim. of *sus* pig; cf. SULLY]

soil[3], v.t. Feed (cattle) on fresh-cut green fodder (orig. for purging). [perh. f. SOIL[2] in sense *dung* (cf. NIGHT-*soil*)]

soirée (swär'ā), n. Social evening, evening gathering esp. for music, conversation, the advancement of some society's objects, or the like. [F]

soixante-quinze (see Ap.), n. French 75 mm. gun. [F]

sojourn (sŏj'ern, sŏ-, sŭ-), v.i., & n. (Make) temporary stay in or *in* place or *with* or *among* person(s). Hence ~ER[1] n. [ME, f. OF *sojorner* etc., f. Rom. **subdiurnare* (SUB-, *diurnum* daily, day); n. f. OF *sojorn* etc.]

‖ **sōke**, n. A right of local jurisdiction (hist.); district under a particular jurisdiction and administration, as the *S~ of Peterborough*. [f. OE *sōcn*]

Sōl[1], n. (joc.). The sun. [L]

sŏl[2], **soh** (sō), n. (mus.). Fifth note of octave. [1st syl. of L *solve*, see GAMUT]

sŏl'a, n. Pithy-stemmed tropical swamp plant (~ *tŏp'i*, Indian sun-helmet of the pith). [f. Hind. *sholá*]

sŏl'ace, n., & v.t. Comfort (v. & n.) in distress or disappointment or tedium (~ *oneself with*, find compensation or relief in; *tobacco, once the poor man's* ~; *found* ~ *in religion*). [ME, f. OF *solas* f. L *solacium* (*solari* CONSOLE[1])]

sōl'an(-gōose), n. The gannet. [f. ON *súla* gannet, perh. + *ǫnd, and-* duck]

Solān'um, n. Large genus of plants including potato, nightshade, & many kinds (often spoken of as ~) cultivated as ornamental creepers or for flowers or foliage. [L, = nightshade]

sōl'ar, a. Of, concerned with, determined by, the sun (~ *DAY, eclipse, spectrum, time,* YEAR; ~ *flowers*, that remain open only for some hours in the day; ~ *month*, an exact twelfth of the year; ~ *myth*, tale explained as symbolizing ~ phenomena; ~ *plexus*, the complex of nerves at pit of stomach; ~ *system*, our sun & the heavenly bodies whose motion is directly or indirectly determined by it). [ME, f. L *solaris* (*sol* sun, -AR[1])]

sōl'ar|ism, n. Belief in solar myths as chief source of mythology. So ~IST(2) n. [-ISM]

solār'ium, n. (pl. *-ia*). Place often enclosed in glass for enjoyment or esp. medical use of sun's rays. [L, =sun-dial, sunning-place (SOLAR, -ARY¹)]

sŏl'ariz|e, -is|e (-īz), v.i. & t. (photog.). Spoil (i. & t.) by. long exposure. Hence ~A'TION n. [-IZE]

solā'tium (-shĭ-), n. (pl. *-tia*). Thing given as compensation or consolation. [L, = SOLACE]

sold. See SELL.

sŏldanĕll'a, n. Kinds of Alpine plant some of which are grown in gardens. [mod. L, f. It.]

sŏl'der (*or* sŏd'er), n., & v.t. **1.** Kinds of fusible alloy used to join edges of less fusible metals (*hard*, SOFT, ~, fusible at higher, lower, temperature & so serving for different metals), (fig.) cementing agency. **2.** v.t. Join with ~; ~*ing-iron*, tool used hot for applying ~. [ME, f. OF *soudure* (*souder* f. L *solidare* f. SOLIDUS, -URE)]

sŏl'dier (-jer), n., & v.i. **1.** Member of army (lit. & fig.; ~*s & sailors*; *play at* ~*s*, of children, also of volunteers etc.; *tin, toy,* ~*s*; ~ *of Christ*, active or proselytizing Christian; *the unknown S*~, see WARRIOR; *old* ~, lit., also person of experience, also empty bottle, also cigar-end; *come the old* ~ *over*, claim to dictate to in virtue of greater experience, seek to impose on; ~ *of fortune*, ready to take service under any State or person that will hire him; *red* ~, pig-disease; ~*'s wind*, naut., fair wind for going & returning); private or N.C.O. in army (*both officers &* ~*s*; often *common* ~); military commander of specified ability (*a great, fine, poor,* ~; *no* ~), whence ~SHIP(3) n.; hence ~LIKE a., ~LY¹,² a. & adv., (-jer-). **2.** (sl.). (Naut.) man, esp. sailor, who shirks work; red herring. **3.** (Also ~ *ant*) one of fighting section of ant or termite colony; (also ~ *beetle*) kinds of reddish-coloured insect with carnivorous larvae; (also ~ *crab*) kind of hermit crab; ~ *orchis*, kind with helmet-shaped sepals. **4.** v.i. Serve as ~ (chiefly in gerund, as *go, tired of,* ~*ing*) (naut., sl.) shirk work; ~ *on*, persevere doggedly. [ME *souder* etc., f. OF *soud(i)er, soldier* (*soude* pay f. SOLIDUS, -ARY¹); cf. med. L *solidarius*]

sŏl'diery (-jerĭ), n. *The* soldiers (of a State, in a district, etc.); a set of troops of specified character (*a wild, licentious,* etc., ~). [-ERY]

sŏl'do, n. (pl. *-di*, pr. -dē). Italian coin, one-twentieth of lira. [It., f. SOLIDUS]

sōle¹, n., & v.t. **1.** Lower surface of human or other plantigrade foot; part of shoe, sock, etc. below foot; bottom or foundation of various things, e.g. plough, carpenter's plane, wagon, golf-club head; ~*-channel*, groove in ~ of boot etc. in which sewing is sunk; ~*-leather*, compressed for use in ~s; ~*-plate*, bed-plate of engine etc.; hence **-sōlED²** (-ĭd) a.

2. v.t. Provide (shoe etc.) with ~. [ME, f. OF, f. Rom.-*sola f. L solea sandal]

sōle², n. Kind of flat-fish much esteemed as food (LEMON² ~). [ME, f. OF, same wd as prec., in sense = L *solea* flat-fish]

sōle³, a. On° & only, exclusive, (*his* ~ *reason is this*; *on my own* ~ *responsibility*); (law) unmarried (only in FEME SOLE); ‖ (arch.) alone, unaccompanied, (*went forth* ~; CORPORATION ~). Hence ~'LY² (-l-l-) adv. [ME, f. OF *so(u)l* f. L *solus*]

sŏl'éc|ism, n. Offence against grammar or idiom, blunder in the manner of speaking or writing; piece of ill breeding or incorrect behaviour. So ~IST(1) n., ~is'tic a. [f. L f. Gk *soloikismos* f. *soloikos* speaking incorrectly]

sŏl'emn (-m), a. Accompanied with ceremony, done etc. in due form, formally regular, (~ *feast-day, sacrifice, oath*; *the S*~ *League & COVENANT*; *probate in* ~ *form*); mysteriously impressive (~ *silence*; *a* ~ *cathedral*); sacred, full of importance, weighty, (*a* ~ *occasion, truth, warning*); grave, sober, deliberate, slow in movement or action, (~ *music, a* ~ *promise,* ~ *looks*; *a* ~ *pace*); pompous, affecting gravity or importance, dull, (*put on a* ~ *face*; *a* ~ *fool*). Hence ~LY² (-mlĭ) adv., ~NESS n. (rare). [ME & OF *solem(p)ne*, or f. L *so(l)lemnis* customary etc.]

solĕm'nitý, n. Rite, celebration, festival, piece of ceremony; being solemn, solemn character or feeling or behaviour. [ME, f. OF *solem(p)nite* f. L *sollemnitatem* (prec., -TY)]

sŏl'emniz|e, -is|e (-īz), v.t. Celebrate (festival etc.); duly perform (marriage ceremony); make solemn. Hence ~A'TION n. [ME, f. OF *solem(p)niser* or med. L *solemnizare* (SOLEMN, -IZE)]

sŏl'en, n. A bivalve, the razor-shell. [L, f. Gk *sōlēn* tube, shellfish]

sŏl'enoid, n. Cylindrical coil of wire which, when an electric current is passed through it, behaves as a bar magnet, & can magnetize a piece of iron or steel placed inside it. [f. F *solénoïde* (prec., -OID)]

sŏl'-fa' (-ah), v.i. & t., & n. = SOLMIZATE, SOLMIZATION; TONIC ~. [SOL², FA]

sŏlfĕ'ggio (-jō), n. (pl. *-gi*, pr. -jē). Solmization, sol-fa; sol-fa exercise for voice. [It., (prec. +suf. *-eggio*)]

sŏlferi'nō (-rē-), n. A purplish-red colour made from rosaniline. [discovered in year of battle of *S*~ (1859), cf. MAGENTA]

soli'cit, v.t. & i. Invite, make appeals or requests to, importune, (*marvels* ~ *his attention* or *senses*; *we* ~ *you for your custom*; *was known to have* ~*ed the judges*), (of prostitute) entice (man, or abs.) in public place; ask importunately or earnestly for (~ *favours, office, custom*). So ~A'TION n. [ME, f. OF *sol(l)iciter* or L *sollicitare* (*sollicitus* anxious)]

soli'citor, n. One who solicits (rare); ‖ member of the legal profession competent to advise clients & instruct &

prepare causes for barristers but not to appear as advocate except in certain lower courts (cf. BARRISTER, LAWYER, ATTORNEY); *canvasser; || S~-*General*, Crown law officer below Attorney-General (in Scotland below Lord Advocate), & like him appointed by the Government of the day & advising & representing it in legal matters. [ME, f. OF *sol(l)iciteur* (prec., -OR)]

soli′citous, a. Eager *to* do; desirous *of*; anxious, troubled, (*about*, *concerning*, *for*, etc., or abs.). Hence ~LY[2] adv. [f. L *sol(l)icitus* see SOLICIT, -OUS]

soli′citūde, n. Being solicitous, anxiety, concern. [ME, f. OF, or f. L *sol(l)icitudo* (prec., -TUDE)]

sŏl′id, a. & n. **1.** Of stable shape, not liquid or fluid, having some rigidity, (~ *food*; *water becomes* ~ *at 32° F.*). **2.** Of ~ substance throughout, not hollow, without internal cavities or interstices, uninterrupted, whole (~ *sphere* or *ball*; ~ *tire*, without central tube; ~ *square*, mil., formation of equal depth & length; ~- *-hoofed*, *-horned*, etc.; ~*-drawn*, of tubes etc., pressed or drawn out from a ~ bar of metal; ~ *printing*, without leads between lines; *a* ~ *hour*, *day*, etc.). **3.** Strongly constructed, not flimsy, (~ *house*, *pier*, *furniture*; *man of* ~ *build*). **4.** Homogeneous, alike all through, (*of* ~ *silver* etc.; ~ *colour*, covering the whole of an object, without pattern etc.; *a* ~ *vote* etc., unanimous, undivided; *go or be* ~ *for*, be united in favour of; *the* ~ *South*, southern States of U.S. consistently voting for Democratic party). **5.** Well grounded, sound, reliable, real, genuine, not fancied or pretended or showy, (~ *arguments*, *sense*, *comfort*; *a* ~ *man*, sensible but not brilliant, also of sound financial position; *have* ~ *grounds for supposing*; ~ *consideration*, thing that can fairly be regarded as an inducement in contracts etc.). **6.** Of three dimensions (~ *foot* etc., cubic; ~ *angle*, formed by three or more plane angles in different planes meeting at point; ~ *number*, integer with three prime factors). **7.** Concerned with ~s (~ *geometry*; ~ *measure*; ~ *problem*, math., involving curves that are sections of ~s & requiring cubic equation); hence or cogn. solid′IFY v.t. & i., solidIFICA′TION n., solid′ifiABLE a., solid′ITY n., ~LY[2] adv. **8.** n. Body consisting of particles that maintain their relative positions against some degree of pressure; (geom.) body or magnitude having three dimensions (cf. *point*, *line*, *surface*; REGULAR ~). [ME; adj. f. OF *solide* or L *solidus*; n. f. adj. or f. F *solide* f. L *solidum*]

sŏlidă′ritÿ, n. Holding together, mutual dependence, community of interests, feelings, & action. So **sŏl′idarÿ** a. [f. F *solidarité* (*solidaire* f. *solide* = prec., -ARY[1], -TY)]

sŏlĭdŭng′ūlar (-ngg-), **-ate**, aa. Solid--hoofed, of horse family, equine. [f. L SOLIDus, *ungula* hoof, -AR[1], -ATE[2]]

sŏl′idus, n. (pl. *-dī*). (Hist.) gold coin introduced by Roman Emperor Constantine; (only in abbr. *s.*) shilling(s), as 7*s.* 6*d.*, £1. 1*s.*; the shilling line (for ∫ or long s) as in 7/6, used also in writing fractions as in 3/4. [L, a noun use of SOLIDus]

sōlifid′ian, a. & n. (Holder) of doctrine that faith by itself suffices for salvation. [L *solus* alone, *fides* faith, +-IAN]

solil′oquÿ, n. Talking without or regardless of the presence of hearers (*a* ~*y*, piece of this esp. on part of character in play). Hence ~IZE(2) v.i., ~IST(1) n. [f. LL *soliloquium* (*solus* alone, -I-, *loqui* speak)]

sŏl′ipĕd, a. & n. Solidungulate (animal). [L *solus* alone, *pes pedis* foot, or alt. f. L *solidipes* (SOLID); cf. F *solipède*]

sŏl′ips|ism, n. (metaphys.). View that the self is the only knowable, or the only existent, thing. So ~IST n. [f. L *solus* alone, *ipse* self, -ISM]

sŏlitaire′, n. Ear-ring, shirt-stud, etc., having a single gem; shirt-cuff fastening in one piece; game played by one person with marbles on special board; (now usu. *patience*) kinds of card-game for one player; kinds of W.-Ind. & Amer. thrush; (now rare) a recluse. [F, f. L *solitarius* (foll.)]

sŏl′itarÿ, a. & n. **1.** Living alone, not gregarious, without companions, unfrequented, secluded, single, lonely, sole, (~*y ants*, *bees*, etc., kinds not living in communities; *a* ~*y life*, *walk*, *valley*, *instance*; ~*y confinement*, isolation in separate cell); hence ~iLY[2] adv., ~iNESS n. **2.** n. Recluse, anchorite. [ME, f. L *solitarius* (*solus* alone)]

sŏl′itūde, n. Being solitary; lonely place. [ME, f. OF, or f. L *solitudo* (SOLE[3], -TUDE)]

sŏl′mizāte, v.i., **sŏlmizā′tion**, n. (Use) system of associating each note of scale with particular syllable (see GAMUT), in *fixed-do* system C always being do & other syllables accordingly, in *movable-do* system key-note always being do & other syllables accordingly. [f. F *solmiser*, *-ation* (SOL[2], MI, -IZE)]

sōl′ō, n. (pl. *-os*, in sense 1 also *-i* pr. *-ē*), a., & adv. **1.** Vocal or instrumental piece or passage performed by one person with or without subordinate accompaniment (also attrib., as ~ *passage*; ~ *stops* on organ, stops specially suitable for playing ~ passages accompanied by other stops; ~ *organ*, fourth manual on large organ, with stops of this kind); whence ~IST(1) n. **2.** (cards). Kind of whist in which one player opposes three or undertakes other tasks; similar varieties of other games; declaration or playing to win five tricks at ~ whist. **3.** (aviation). An unaccompanied flight; (adj. & adv.) unaccom-

panied, alone, (a ~ *flight*; *flying* ~). [It.,
f. L *solus* SOLE[3]]

Sŏl'omon, n. King of Israel reputed
wisest of men (*is no* ~; SONG *of* ~),
whence **Sŏlomŏn'ıc** a.; ~'*s seal*, kinds
of flowering plant of family of lily of the
valley

Sŏl'on, n Sage, wise legislator. [name of
Athenian lawgiver (d. 558 B.C.)]

sŏl'stice, n. Either time (*summer, winter*,
~, about 21st June, 22nd Dec.) at which
sun is farthest from equator & appears
to pause before returning; (also *solstitial
point*) point in ecliptic reached by sun at
~. So **sŏlsti'tıAL** (-ĭshl) a. [ME, f. OF, f.
L *solstitium* (SOL[1] *sistere* -*stit*- make stand
f. *stare* stand)]

sŏl'ŭble, a. That can be dissolved in
some fluid; that can be solved; ~ *glass*,
(also WATER-*glass*) preparation of silicate
of soda used for hardening artificial stone,
preserving eggs, etc. Hence **sŏlŭbıL'ıTY** n.
[ME, f. OF, f. LL *solubilis* (SOLVE, -BLE)]

sŏl'us, pred. a. (fem. *sola*). Alone, unaccompanied, (esp. in stage directions,
as *enter king* ~; also joc., as *found myself*
~). [L]

solu'tion (-lōō-, -lū-), n., & v.t. 1. Separation, dissolution, abolition of union,
(chiefly in ~ *of continuity*, surg., separation of tissues by fracture etc., & transf.).
2. Dissolving or being dissolved, esp. conversion of solid or gas into liquid form by
mixture with liquid called the solvent or
menstruum (*chemical* ~, involving change
in chem. properties of components;
mechanical ~, without such change);
state resulting from this (*held in* ~ etc.;
his ideas are in ~, in a state of flux,
unsettled); liquid & solid or gas so mixed
(a ~ *of alum*; *strong, weak*, ~, with small,
large, proportion of solvent). 3. Resolution, solving, answer, method for the
solving, of a problem, puzzle, question,
doubt, difficulty, etc. (*of, for, to*). 4. (In
full *rubber* ~) dissolved caoutchouc. 5.
v.t. Coat with rubber ~. [ME, f. OF, or f.
L *solutio* (as SOLVE, -ION)]

solu'tionist (-lōōshon-, -lū-), n. Professional solver of newspaper puzzles. [prec.
+ -IST (3)]

Solŭt'rian, a. (archaeol.). Of the palaeolithic period represented by remains
found at the Solutré cave, Saône-et-
-Loire, France.

sŏlve, v.t. Untie, loosen, unravel,
dissolve, (knot, tangle, cohesion, etc.;
arch.); find answer to (problem) or way
out of (difficulty). Hence **sŏl'vABLE** a.,
sŏlvabıL'ıTY n. [ME, f. L *solvere solut*-]

sŏl'vent, a. & n. 1. Having the power
of dissolving or forming SOLUTION with
something or fig. of weakening the hold
of traditions or beliefs; having money
enough to meet all pecuniary liabilities,
whence **sŏl'vENCY** n. 2. n. ~ liquid or
substance, menstruum, (see SOLUTION;
water is the commonest ~; *alcohol is the*

~ *of resinous substances*); dissolving or
weakening agent (*science as a* ~ *of
religious belief*). [f. L SOLVEre, -ENT]

-som. See -SOME.

somăt'ic, a. Of the body, corporeal,
physical, (opp. *mental, spiritual, psychic*;
~ *death*, of the body as a whole). [f. Gk
sōmatikos (*sōma* -*atos* body, -IC)]

sŏm'at|o-, comb. form of Gk *sōma* (prec.,
-o-) used in a number of scientific terms,
= of body or the human body, as
~*ogĕn'ic*, originating in the body, ~ŏL'OGY,
science of living bodies physically considered.

sŏm'bre (-ber), a. Dark, gloomy, dismal,
as *a* ~ *sky*, ~ *prospect, man of* ~ *character*.
Hence ~LY[2] adv., ~NESS n., **sŏm'broŭs**
(poet.) a. [F, app. f. *sombrer* to shade f.
LL *subumbrare* (SUB-, *umbra* shade)]

sŏmbrer'o (-ā́rō), n. (pl. ~s). Broad-
-brimmed felt hat common in America.
[Sp., f. *sombra* shade, see prec.]

some (sŭm, sum), a., pron., & adv.
1. Particular but unknown or unspecified
(person or thing), as ~ *fool has locked the
door, saw it in* ~ *book* (or *other*), *ask* ~
experienced person, ~ (*people*) *say yes &*
~ (or *others* or *other people*) *say no*. 2. A
certain quantity or number of (~thing),
as *drink* ~ *water, eat* ~ *bread, bring* ~
pens, I have ~ *already, have* ~ *more*, ~ *of
it is spoilt*, ~ *of them were late, can we* or
can't we have ~ *milk?* (but *we cannot have
any milk*), *if I find* ~ (or *any*) *I will send
them*; **& then* ~ (sl.), & plenty more
than that. 3. An appreciable or considerable quantity of, as *went* ~ *miles
out of our way, had* ~ *trouble in arranging
it*, ~ *years ago, that is* ~ *help*. 4. Such to
a certain extent, as *that is* ~ *guide, test,
proof*; (emphat. in meiosis, U.S. & sl.)
such in the fullest sense, ~thing like
(a), as *this is* ~ *war!, I call that* ~ *poem*.
5. (Usu. stressed) not quite no, as *do have*
~ *mercy on our nerves, has after all* ~
sense of decency. 6. Approximately so
many or much of (~thing), as *waited* ~ *20
minutes, scales* ~ *15 stone, we were* ~ *60
in all*; ALL *&*~. 7. adv. (sl.). In ~ degree,
as *he seemed annoyed* ~. 8. ~'*body*, ~
person, (w. pl. -*dies*) person of consequence. 9. ~'*how*, in ~ unspecified or
unexplained manner, for ~ reason or
other, as *he* ~*how dropped behind*, ~*how
or other I never liked him*, (stressed) no
matter how, as *must get it finished* ~*how*.
10. ~'*one*, = ~*body* (not in pl.); ~ *one*,
any particular (one), as *choose* ~ *one
place as a centre, take* ~ *one as a type*.
11. ~'*thing*, ~ thing (esp. or ~*thing* as
vague substitute for noun, adj., vb, or
adv.), as *have* ~*thing to tell you*; *we hope to
see* ~*thing of* (occasionally meet) *them, has
lost* ~*thing or other, take a drop of* ~*thing*
(liquor), *he is* or *has* ~*thing* (~ official,
~ employment) *in the record office, can
spare* ~*thing out of so much, there is*
~*thing* (truth, point) *in what you say*,

thinks himself ~thing (of ~ consequence), *felt there was a little ~thing wanting*, *~-thing of preciosity in his style*, *am ~thing of* (am in ~ sense or degree) *a carpenter, it is ~thing* (~ comfort) *to be safe home again*, *his temper is, his fads are, ~thing awful, was made a bishop or ~thing, has sprained his ankle or ~thing* (~ other part), *is neurotic or ~thing, lost his train or* (did) *~thing, turned the tap too soon or too hard or* (too) *~thing*; (adv., arch. exc. *~thing like*) in ~ degree, as *was ~thing impatient, ~thing troubled, shaped ~thing like a cigar*; (colloq., w. stress on *like*) *this is ~thing like a* (is a large or good) *pudding, that's ~thing like* (is capital)*!* **12.** ~ *time* adv., for ~ time, as *have been waiting ~ time*, at ~ time, as *must see him about it ~ time*; *~'time* adv. & a. (arch.), *former*(ly), as *was ~time mayor of Barnstaple*, (the) *~time sheriff*; *~'times* adv., at ~ times, as *have ~times thought, is ~times hot & ~times cold*. **13.** *~'way*, in ~ way. **14.** *~'what*, (adv.) in ~ degree, as *it is ~what difficult, was ~what puzzled, answered ~what hastily*, (pron., arch. exc. when indisting. f. adv.) *found ~what to detain him, loses ~what* (perh. adv.) *in the telling, loses ~what of its force*. **15.** *~'when* (rare, affected), at ~ time or other. **16.** *~'where*, in, at, to, ~ place, as *lives ~where near us, sent him ~where, Burton says ~where in the Anatomy, will see him ~where* (in hell etc.) *first*. **17.** *~'whither* (arch.), to ~ place. [OE, OS, OHG *sum*, ON *sumr*, Goth. *sums*]

-some, **-som**, suf. forming adjj., OE *-sum*, cogn. w. OS, OHG *-sam*; joined to nn. w. sense 'adapted to, productive of', as *quarrelsome, gladsome* (f. obs. *glad* n.), to adjj., as *lithesome* (also *lissom*), *blithesome, fulsome*, & to trans. vbs w. sense 'apt to', as *tiresome, winsome, wearisome, gruesome* (f. *grue* in impers. trans. use *it grues me*). Written *-om* in *lissom, buxom*, etc.; in *two, three, four, -some* the suf. was orig. the pronoun OE *sum* some; *-som* in RANSOM is of diff. orig.

so'mersault, -sĕt[1], (sŭ-), n., & v.i. **1.** Spring, bound, in which person turns heels over head (*double, treble*, ~, twice, thrice) in the air; *turn a* ~, make such spring. **2.** v.i. Turn ~. [f. OF *sombresau*(l)*t* alt. f. *sobresault* f. L *supra* above + *saltus -ūs* leap (*salire*)]

‖ **so'mersĕt**[2] (sŭ-), n. Padded saddle esp. for one-legged rider. [f. Lord F. *S~* (d. 1855), who used one]

So'mersĕt House (sŭ-), n. Building in London containing chief place of deposit of proved wills, & inland revenue offices, & often mentioned allusively in these connexions.

sōm'ite, n. Each body-division of a segmented animal, metamere. Hence **sōmit'ic** a. [f. Gk *sōma* body + -ITE[1](2)]

sŏmnăm'bŭl|ism, n. Walking or performing other action during sleep; con-

dition of brain inducing this; *artificial ~ism*, hypnotism. Hence or cogn. ~ANT (rare), **~is'tic**, aa., ~ATE[3] v.i. (rare), ~IST n. [f. L *somnus* sleep + *ambulare* walk]

sŏmni-, comb. form of L *somnus* sleep, as: *~f'erous*, inducing sleep, narcotic; *~l'oquence*, *~l'oquism*, *~l'oquy*, habit of talking in sleep; *~l'oquous*, *~l'oquist*, (person) given to this; *~p'athist*, hypnotic subject; *~p'athy*, hypnotic sleep.

sŏm'nol|ent, a. Sleepy, drowsy; inducing drowsiness; (path.) in state between sleeping & waking. Hence or cogn. ~ENCE, ~ENCY, nn., **~ently**[2] adv. [ME, f. OF, or f. L *somnolentus* (*somnus* sleep, -LENT)]

sŏm'nolism, n. Hypnotic sleep. [f. prec. + -ISM]

son (sŭn), n. **1.** Male child of a parent (~ *& heir*, esp. eldest ~); *~-in-law*, one's daughter's husband; *he is his father's ~* (like, worthy of, his father). **2.** *The Son of Man*, (N.T.) Christ, the Messiah, (O.T.) descendant of Adam, esp. as form of address in *Ezekiel*; *the ~s of men*, mankind; *the Son* (*of God*), = GOD[1] *the Son*. **3.** ~ *of a* GUN; *every* MOTHER[1]*'s* ~. **4.** Descendant, as ~*s of Abraham*. **5.** (As form of address esp. of old man to young man, confessor to penitent, etc.) *my* ~. **6.** ~ *of the soil*, recognizable native of a district, worker on the land, dweller in the country. **7.** Native of a country, as *Britain's ~s*. **8.** Person viewed as inheriting an occupation, quality, etc., as ~ *of toil*, ~ *of Mars* (soldier), ~ (= *man*) *of* BELIAL, ~*s of light, darkness*, etc.; *Sons of Liberty, of the* (American) *Revolution*, etc., American patriotic etc. organizations. Hence ~'LESS a., ~'SHIP n. [OE, OS, OHG *sunu*, ON *sunr*, Goth. *sunus* f. Gmc **sunuz*]

sŏn'|ant, a. & n. (Sound, letter) accompanied by vocal vibration, voiced, not surd, (e.g. *b, d, g, j, v, z*). Hence ~ANCY n. [f. L *sonare* sound (*sonus*, -ANT)]

***sŏn'ăr**, n. = ASDIC. [sound *na*vigation *ra*nging]

sona'ta (-nah-), n. Composition for one instrument (e.g. piano) or two (e.g. piano & violin), normally with three or four movements (one or more being usu. in ~ form) contrasted in rhythm & speed but related in key; ~ *form*, type of composition in which two themes ('subjects') are successively set forth, developed, & restated. [It. (as SONANT, see -ADE)]

sōnati'na (-tē-), n. Simple or short form of sonata. [It., dim. of prec.]

sŏng, n. **1.** Singing, vocal music, as *burst forth into* ~; musical cry of some birds (~*-birds*). **2.** Short poem set to music or meant to be sung; short poem in rhymed stanzas; poetry, verse, as *renowned in* ~. **3.** (mus.) ~ *form*, mode of composition usu. in three sections, the first & third being nearly the same & the second contrasted with the first. **4.** *Bought, sold, it for a* ~ or *an old* ~ (mere trifle); *nothing to make a* ~ *about* (colloq.), of very trifling importance; *S*~ *of* DEGREES or *ascents* (in O.T., Psalms 120-134); *S*~ *of S*~*s*, *S*~ *of Solomon*, O.T. book once attributed to Solomon; ~-PLUG[2]*ging*;~-THRUSH[1];~-*sparrow*,hedge--sparrow & other birds. Hence ~'LESS a. [OE, OS *sang*, OHG *sang-*, ON *sǫng*, Goth. *saggws* f. Gmc **sangwaz* f. pret. stem of **singwan* SING]

sŏng'st|er, n. Singer; song-bird; poet. Hence ~FESS[1] n. [ME; -STER]

sŏn'ic, a. Of or relating to sound or sound-waves (~ *boom*, loud noise made when aircraft crashes the sound barrier; ~ *barrier*, excessive resistance offered by air to objects moving at speed near that of sound). [f. L *sonus* sound, -IC]

sonif'erous, a. Conveying or producing sound. [f. L *sonus* sound +-FEROUS]

sŏnn'ĕt, n. Poem of 14 lines (usu. rhyming thus; *pig bat cat wig jig hat rat fig*; *lie red sob die bed rob* or *lie red die bed pie wed*; or otherwise e.g. as in Shakespeare's ~s); ~ *sequence*, a set of ~s connected in theme; (now rare) any short lyric. So ~EER' (usu. derog.), (n.) composer of ~s, (v.i. & t.) compose ~s, celebrate in ~s, address ~s to. [F, or f. It. *sonetto* (*suono* SOUND[2] n., -ET[1])]

so'nny (sŭ-), n. Familiar form of address to a boy. [f. SON +-Y[3]]

sŏn'obuoy (-boi), n. Buoy for detecting submarines, dropped by parachute from aircraft and equipped with hydrophone and radio for transmitting sounds to aircraft and surface vessels. [f. L *sonus* sound +BUOY[1]]

sonŏm'ĕter, n. Kinds of instrument for testing deaf person's hearing, measuring sounds, etc. [f. L *sonus* sound +-METER]

sŏnorĕs'c|ent, a. (Of hard rubber etc.) emitting sounds corresponding to pulsations of radiant heat or light. So ~ENCE n. [as SONOROUS +-ESCENT]

sŏnorif'ic, a. Producing (esp. other than vocal) sound. [as foll. +-FIC]

sonōr'ous (*or* sŏn'o-), a. Resonant; loud--sounding; (of speech, style, etc.) high--sounding, imposing; ~ *figures* (formed in layer of sand etc. by sound-vibration); ~ *râle* (heard in some diseases). Hence or cogn. sonōr'ITY, ~NESS, nn., ~LY[2] adv. [f. L *sonorus* (*sonor* sound) +-OUS]

‖ **sŏn'sў**, a. (Sc.). Plump, buxom; of cheerful disposition (esp. in phr. ~ *lass*). [ult. f. Gael. *sonas* good fortune]

sŏon, adv. **1.** Not long after the present time or time in question or *after* specified time, in a short time, as *shall* ~ *know the result, was* ~ *convinced of his error, arrived* ~ *after four,* ~ *after the gate was closed, least said* ~*est mended.* **2.** *As* (or *so*, esp after negative, or when causality or other close connexion is suggested)

~ *as*, the moment that, not later than, as early as, as *came as* (or *so*) ~ *as I heard of it, will get there as* ~ *as they* (do), did not arrive *so* (or *as*) ~ *as I expected, drops his fine theories so* (or *as*) ~ *as they clash with his interests, so* ~ *as* (ever) *there is any talk of paying he cools down.* **3.** (With expressed or implied comparison) willingly, as *I would just as* ~ *stay at home* (as *go*), *would* ~*er die than let him* (or *than that he should*) *find it out, which would you* ~*est do*? **4.** Early, as *what makes you come so* ~?; *you spoke too* ~; *we had no* ~*er sat down than* (the moment we sat down) *she burst into tears; no* ~*er said than done*, it was done the moment it was proposed etc.; *the* ~*er the better; you will repent it* ~*er or later* (some day). [OE *sōna*, OS, OHG *sān(o)*]

sŏŏt, n., & v.t. **1.** Black substance rising in fine flakes in the smoke of wood, coal, oil, etc., during combustion & sticking to sides of chimney etc., used as fertilizer; ~-*cancer*, -*wart*, disease of scrotum in sweeps. Hence ~'ILY[2] adv., ~'INESS n., ~'LESS, ~'Y[2], aa. **2.** v.t. Cover with ~. [OE, MLG *sōt*, MDu. *soet*, ON *sót*]

‖ **sŏŏt'erkin**, n. (arch.). Dutch woman's false birth produced by sitting over stove; (fig.) abortive scheme. [perh. f. prec.; there is app. no similar term in Dutch]

‖ **sŏŏth**, n. (arch.). Truth, fact, esp. *in* (*good*) ~, really, truly. [OE, f. *sōth* adj. (= OS *sōth*, ON *sannr*, *sathr*), f. **santh-*, cogn. w. Goth. *sunjis* true]

sŏŏth|e (-dh), v.t. Calm (person, nerves, passions); soften, mitigate, (pain); flatter, humour, (person, his vanity). Hence ~'ER[1] (-dh-) n. (in vbl senses, & esp. rubber teat for child to suck), ~'ingLY (-dh-) adv. [OE *sōthian* verify, f. *sōth* adj. (prec.)]

‖ **sŏŏth'fast** (-ah-), a. (arch.). Truthful; true; loyal, steadfast. [OE *sōthfæst* (SOOTH, FAST[3]), cf. STEADFAST]

sŏŏth'sayer, n. One who foretells the future, diviner. Hence sŏŏth'say v.i. [ME; SOOTH +SAY +-ER[1]]

sŏp, n., & v.t. & i. (-pp-). **1.** Piece of bread etc. dipped in broth etc. (~ *in the pan*, fried bread); MILK[1]~; something given (*to* formidable or troublesome animal, person, etc., esp. *to Cerberus*) to pacify, bribe. **2.** v.t. Soak (bread etc. in broth etc.), take *up* (water etc.) by absorption in towel etc., wet thoroughly. **3.** v.i. Be drenched, as *am* ~*ping with rain, clothes are* ~*ping* (vbl n. as adj.) *wet*, whence ~**p'Y**[2] a., ‖ also (colloq.) full of mawkish sentiment. [OE *sopp*, corresp. to MLG *soppe*, OHG *sopfa*, f. weak grade of *sūpan* SUP]

sŏph'ism, n. False argument intended to deceive (cf. PARALOGISM). [ME, f. OF *sophi*(*s*)*me* f. L f. Gk *sophisma* (foll.)]

sŏph'ist, n. Ancient-Greek paid teacher of philosophy & rhetoric; captious or fallacious reasoner, quibbler. Hence or cogn. **sophis'tic**(AL) aa., **sophis'ticaly²** adv., ~RY(4, 5) n. [f. L f. Gk *sophistēs* (*sophizō* instruct f. *sophos* wise, -IST)]

sŏph'ister, n. (hist.). Student of varying seniority at some English & American universities. [ME, f. OF *sophistre* as prec.]

sophis'tic|āte, v.t. & i. Involve (subject) in sophistry; mislead (person) thus; deprive (person, thing) of simplicity; make artificial; (p.p., of person) worldly--wise; tamper with (text etc.) for purposes of argument etc.; use sophistry; adulterate (wine etc.). So ~A'TION n. [f. OF (-*quer*), or med. L *sophisticare* (*sophisticus* sophistic), see -ATE³]

*****sŏph'omŏre**, n. Second-year university student. [app. f. *sophom* obs. var. of SOPHISM + -OR]

Sŏph'ỹ, n. (hist.). Ruler of Persia in 16th & 17th cc. [f. Pers. *Çafī* surname of dynasty]

sŏpor|if'ic, a. & n. (Drug) tending to produce sleep. So ~IF'EROUS a. [f. L *sopor* sleep + -I- + -FIC; cf. L *soporifer*]

sopra'n|ō (-rah-), n. (pl. -*nos*, -*ni* pr. -nē). (Music for) highest female or boy's voice, treble (often attrib.); (also ~IST n.) singer with this. [It. (*sopra* above f. L *supra*)]

sŏr'a, n. Bird frequenting marshes of Carolina etc. in autumn & used as food. [native]

sŏrb, n. Service-tree; (also ~-*apple*) its fruit. Hence ~'ATE¹(3) n., ~'IC a., (chem.). [f. F *sorbe*, or L *sorbus* service-tree]

sŏrbēfā'cient (-shnt), a. & n. (med.). (Drug etc.) causing absorption. [f. L *sorbēre* suck in + -FACIENT]

sŏrb'ĕt, n. Flavoured water-ice; = SHER-BET. [F, as SHERBET]

Sŏrbŏnne', n. Theological faculty in University of Paris having great influence in 16th & 17th cc. (hist.); the seat of the *Académie* of Paris & of the faculties of science & literature. [F, f. R. de *Sorbon*, founder about 1250]

sŏr'cer|er, n. User of magic arts, wizard, enchanter (often fig.). So ~ESS¹, sŏr'CERY (4, 5), nn. [f. obs. *sorcer* f. OF *sorcier* f. Rom. *sortiarius* caster of lots (*sors* -*tis* lot, see -ARY¹) + -ER¹]

sŏrdamĕn'tĕ, adv. (mus.). In a muffled manner. [It.]

sŏrd'id, a. Mean, niggardly; ignoble, base; (bot., zool., of colours) impure, muddy, as ~ *blue*; dirty, squalid. Hence ~LY² adv., ~NESS n. [f. F *sordide* or L *sordidus* (*sordēre* be dirty, *sordes* filth, see -ID¹)]

sŏrd'ine (-ēn), n. (mus.). Mute for bowed or wind instruments; damper of piano string. [f. It. *sordina* f. L as SURD]

sŏre, a., n., & adv. 1. (Of parts of body, person) morbidly tender, as *has a* ~ *arm, is* FOOT¹~, (*clergyman's*) ~ THROAT, *touched him on a* ~ *place* (often fig.), *a sight for* ~ *eyes* (welcome, pleasant), *like a bear with a* ~ *head* (grumpy); irritated,

aggrieved, touchy, as *is very* ~ *about his defeat*; arousing painful feelings, irritating, esp. a ~ *subject*; (arch., poet.) distressing, grievous, severe, as *in* ~ *distress, a* ~ *struggle, affliction* ~ *long time he bore*, whence ~LY² (-rl-) adv. 2. n. ~ place on body e.g. where skin or flesh is bruised or inflamed; (fig.) ~ subject, painful memory, esp. *re-open old* ~s; BED¹~; EYE¹~. 3. adv. Grievously, severely, as ~ *oppressed, bested, afflicted*. Hence ~'NESS (-rn-) n. [(n. & adv. f. adj.) OE *sār* painful, OS, OHG *sēr*, ON *sárr* (Goth. *sair* n.), f. Gmc **sairaz*]

sorel. See SORREL².

sŏr'ghum (-gum), n. Kinds of tropical cereal grasses including millet. [mod. L, f. It. *sorgo*]

sŏr'icine, a. Of, related to, the shrew--mouse. [f. L *soricinus* (*sorex* -*icis* shrew--mouse, -INE¹)]

sorit'ēs (-z), n. Chain-syllogism (e.g. a cat is a quadruped, quadruped is an animal, animal is a substance; therefore a cat is a substance); form of sophism leading by gradual steps from truth to absurdity & based on the absence of precise, esp. numerical, limits to terms (e.g. a man with only 1 hair is bald, therefore a man with 2, 3, 4, . . . 10,000, hairs is bald). So **sorit'ICAL** a. [L f. Gk *sōritēs* lit. heaper (*sōros* heap, see -ITE¹)]

|| **sŏrn**, v.i. (Sc.). Obtrude oneself *on* (person) for bed & board. Hence ~'ER¹ n. [f. obs. Ir. *sorthan* free quarters]

sorŏp'timist, n. Member of an international association of women's clubs. [app. f. L *soror* sister + OPTIMIST]

sorŏ'ritỹ, n. Devotional sisterhood; *women's society in college or university. [f. med. L *sororitas* (L *soror* sister), after *fraternity*]

sorŏs'is, n. (bot.). Fleshy compound fruit, e.g. pineapple, mulberry. [mod. L f. Gk *soros* SORUS + -OSIS]

|| **sŏr'ra**, adv. (Ir., sl.). Not, never, (~ *a one, a bit*, etc., = the devil a). [= *sorrow*]

sŏ'rrel¹, n. Kinds of acid-leaved herb allied with dock. [ME, f. OF *surele, sorele* f. *sur* f. WG **sūr* SOUR]

sŏ'rrel², a. & n. (Of) reddish-brown colour; ~ animal esp. horse; (also *sorel*) buck of third year. [ME, f. OF *sorel* f. *sore* (mod. *saur*) f. WG **saur* dry, yellowish; see -LE(2)]

sŏ'rrow (-ō), n., & v.i. 1. Grief, sadness, caused by loss of good or occurrence of evil, whence ~FUL (-rof-) a., ~fulLY² adv., ~fulNESS n.; occasion of this, misfortune, trouble, as *has had many* ~s, *much* ~; *the Man of S*~s, Christ; ~-*stricken* (with ~); lamentation, as *his* ~ *was loud & long*. 2. v.i. Grieve, feel ~, (*at, over, for*, misfortune etc., *for*, i.e. on behalf of, person etc.), mourn (*after, for*, lost person or thing), whence ~ER¹ (-ōer) n., ~ING² (-rōi-) a. [OE *sorh, sorg*, OS, OHG *sorga*, ON *sorg*, Goth. *saurga*]

sŏr′rў, a. Feeling regret, regretful, as *will be ~ for this some day, fell ~ for him* (on his account), *~ for* oneself (colloq. = depressed), *am ~ for* (regret) *that, am so ~ (that) you must go, am ~ to hear it,* (as informal apology for trifling offence) *~ !*; (literary) wretched, paltry, shabby, of poor quality, as *a ~ fellow, in a ~ plight, in ~ clothes, a ~ excuse,* whence **sŏ′rrĭLY**[2] adv., **sŏ′rrĭNESS** n. [OE *sārig* (SORE, -Y[2])]

sŏrt[1], n. **1.** Group of things etc. with common attributes, class, kind, species, as *biscuits of several ~s, a new ~ of bicycle, people of every ~ & kind; of ~s,* (in inventories etc.) unassorted, mixed. **2.** (In foll. uses = KIND[1]) *nothing of the ~, coffee of a ~, what ~ of tree?,* (colloq.) *these ~ of men, a ~ of stockbroker* etc., *I ~ of expected it; a ~ of war* etc., *a war* etc. *of a ~* or colloq. *of ~s,* not fully deserving the name; (colloq.) *an awfully good ~* (of person), *that's your ~* (the way to do it). **3.** (arch.). Manner, way, as *in seemly, courteous,* etc., *~; after or in a ~* (= FASHION); *in some ~* (literary), to a certain extent. **4.** (print.). Any letter or piece in fount of type, as *copy is hard* (or *runs*) *on ~s* (requires many of some ~s). **5.** *Out of ~s,* out of health, spirits, or temper, (print.) short of ~s. [ME, f. OF *sorte* f. Rom. *sorta alt. f. L *sors* sort- lot]

sŏrt[2], v.t. & i. **1.** Separate into sorts (often *over, out*); select (things of one sort) from miscellaneous group, as *~ed out those of the largest size.* **2.** (arch.). Correspond or agree *with* (*his actions ~ ill, well, with his professions*). Hence *~′ABLE* a., *~′ER*[1] n. [ME, f. OF *sortir,* L *sortire,* & prec.]

sŏr′tēs (-z), n. pl. *~ Virgiliān′ae, Bĭb′licae* or *Sāc′rae, Homē′ricae,* divination by chance selection of passages from Virgil, the Bible, or Homer. [L, pl. as SORT[1]]

sŏr′tie (-tē), n. **1.** Sally esp. of beleaguered garrison. **2.** Operational flight by one aircraft. [F, f. *sortir* go out]

sŏr′tilêge, n. Divination by lots. [ME, f. OF *sortilege* or med. L *sortilegium* f. L *sortilegus* a. (as SORT[1] + *legere* choose)]

sŏrti′tion, n. Casting of lots. [f. L *sortitio* (*sortiri* cast lots)]

sŏr′us, n. (bot.; pl. *sŏr′ī*). Heap, cluster, esp. of spore-cases on back of fern-frond. [f. Gk *sōros* heap]

-sory, suf., a spec. form of -ORY in aa. or nn. f. L vbs that form p.p. in -s-, as *accessory* (*cedere cess-*), *promissory* (*mittere miss-*).

S O S (ĕs′ōĕs′), n. Radio code-signal of extreme distress; broadcast appeal to (otherwise untraceable) person (to visit dying relative etc.); (transf.) any despairing cry or action. [Morse ᴗᴗᴗ---ᴗᴗᴗ]

sō′sō, pred. a. & adv. Not very good. [SO]

sŏstenu′tō (-nōō-), adv. (mus.). In sustained or prolonged manner. [It.]

sŏt, n., & v.i. (-tt-). **1.** Confirmed drunkard, person stupefied by habitual drunkenness. **2.** v.i. Tipple. Hence *~t′ISH*[1] a., *~t′ishLY*[2] adv., *~t′ishNESS* n. [f. OF *sot, sote* fool(ish), of unkn. orig.]

Sŏth′ebў's (sŭdhe-), n. A sale-room in London for books, MSS., etc.

Sŏth′ic, a. Of the dog-star, esp. *~ year* (Egyptian, fixed by heliacal rising of dog-star), *~ cycle* (of 1460 ~ or 1461 solar years). [f. Gk *Sōthis* f. Egypt. name of dog-star]

sŏtt′ō vō′ce (-chĕ), adv. In an undertone, aside. [It. *sotto* under + *voce* voice]

sou (sōō), n. (pl. -s pr. -z). (Hist.) French coin of various values; (loosely) five-centime piece; (colloq.) *hasn't a ~* (a farthing, any money). [F, f. L as SOLIDUS]

soubrette (sōōbrĕt′), n. Maid-servant or similar character (esp. w. implication of pertness, coquetry, intrigue, etc.) in comedy. [F]

sou′cār (sow-), **sow′kār**, n. Hindu banker or money-lender. [Hind. *sāhūkār* great merchant]

sou′chŏng (sōōsh-), n. Kind of black tea made from youngest leaves. [F, f. Chin. *siao* small + *chung* sort]

Soudanese′ (sōō-; -ēz). = SUDANESE.

souffle (sōō′fl), n. (med.). Low murmur heard in auscultation of various organs etc. [F, f. *souffler* blow f. L SUF(*flare* blow)]

soufflé (sōōf′lā), a. & n. **1.** Made light & frothy, as *omelet ~.* **2.** n. Such dish, usu. made with beaten whites of eggs. [F, p.p. as prec.]

sough (sŭf, sow, Sc. sōōχ), n., & v.i. (Make) moaning, whistling, or rushing sound as of wind in trees etc. [OE *swōgan,* OS *swōgan,* move with a rushing sound]

sought. See SEEK.

soul (sōl), n. **1.** The immaterial part of man, as *immortality of the ~, commend one's ~ to God* (of person at point of death), *'pon my ~* (asseveration). **2.** Moral & emotional part of man, as *his whole ~ revolted from it,* CURE[1] *of ~s, has a ~ above sherry & bitters.* **3.** Intellectual part of man, vital principle & mental powers of animals including man, as *keep* BODY[1] *& ~ together, cannot call his ~ his own* (is dominated by another). **4.** Animating or essential part, person viewed as this, as *he was the* (*life &*) *~ of the enterprise, of the party.* **5.** Person viewed as embodying moral or intellectual qualities, as *the greatest ~s of antiquity, left that to meaner ~s.* **6.** (Often without *a*) emotional or intellectual energy e.g. as revealed in work of art, as *the fellow has no ~, his pictures lack ~.* **7.** (Of persons) personification or pattern of (*is the ~ of honour,* is incapable of dishonourable conduct). **8.** Departed spirit, as ALL *S~s' Day*; disembodied spirit. **9.** Person, as *not a ~ to speak to for miles round, ship went down with 200 ~s*; (expr. familiarity, patronage, pity, contempt, etc.) *my good ~, there's a good ~, the poor little ~ had lost her way,* *a simple* ~. **10.** (In comb.) ~*-destroying, -stirring, -subduing,* etc. Hence (-)~ED² (sōld), ~'LESS (sōl-l-), āa., ~'lèssLY² adv., '~'lèssNESS n. [OE *sāwol* = Goth. *saiwala*; cf. OS *sēola*, OHG *sē(u)la*, ON *sdla*]

soul'ful (sōl-), a. Having, expressing, appealing to, the (esp. higher) emotional or intellectual qualities (occas. derog.). Hence~LY² adv., ~NESS n. [-FUL]

sound¹, a. & adv. **1.** Healthy, not diseased nor injured nor rotten, as *a* ~ *body*, ~ *mind*, ~ *in wind & limb*, ~ *fruit, timbers, ship*; correct, logical, well--founded, judicious, as ~ *doctrine, theologian, argument, views, policy, is he* ~ *on free trade?*; (commerc., of company etc.) solvent; thorough, unqualified, as *a* ~ *sleep(er), flogging*. **2.** adv. ~ly, as ~ (fast) *asleep, will sleep the* ~*er for it.* Hence ~'LY² adv., ~'NESS n. [ME *sund*, repr. OE (= G) *gesund*; cf. MDu. *ghesont*, MLG (*ge*)*sunt*]

sound², n., & v.i. & t. **1.** The sensation produced through the ear, what is or may be heard; vibrations causing this sensation; *musical* ~ (produced by continuous & regular vibrations, opp. to *noise*); any of a series of articulate utterances, as *vowel, consonant*, ~s; mere words (~ *& fury*); (fig.) mental impression produced by oral or other statement etc., as *will have a queer* ~, *don't like the* ~ *of it.* **2.** ~*-board*, ~*-ing--board*; ~*-bow*, thick edge of bell against which tongue strikes; ~*-film*, cinema film with audible dialogue, songs, etc. recorded on ~*-track*; ~*-hole, -post*, hole in belly, small prop between belly & back, of some stringed instruments; ~*-PROOF²*; ~*-track*, on side of cinema film recording ~; ~*-wave* (of condensation & rarefaction, by which ~ is propagated in elastic medium e.g. air). **3.** vb. Give forth ~, as *the trumpets* ~; (w. ref. to impression created, often fig.) ~*s to me like something cracking*, ~*s as if a tap were running*, ~*s as if he wanted to back out of it, will* ~ *very strange to say you hadn't time, that* (excuse etc.) ~*s very hollow, that* (report, explanation) ~*s all right* (promising, plausible, etc.); (part.) having more ~ than sense or truth, as ~*ing rhetoric, promises*, imposing, as ~*ing titles*; make (trumpet etc.) ~; utter, as ~ *a note of alarm*; pronounce (*the h in hour is not* ~*ed*); give notice of (*an alarm, the retreat*, etc.) with bell etc.; cause to resound, make known, as ~ *his praises far & wide*; test (railway-carriage wheel etc., lungs etc.) by noting ~ produced by hammer, by auscultation. **4.** ~*ing-board*, canopy over pulpit etc. serving to direct ~ towards audience, thin plate of wood in musical instrument increasing ~. Hence ~'LESS a. [ME; (n.) AF *soun* f. OF *son* f. L *sonus*, for *-d* cf. LEND, ROUND⁵, HIND²; (vb) f. OF *soner* f. L *sonare*]

sound³, v.t. & i., & n. **1.** Test the depth of (sea, channel, pond, etc., or abs.) & the quality of its bottom with ~*ing-line* or *-apparatus* or *-machine* (often furnished with cup etc. for bringing up sample); find depth of water in (ship's hold) with ~*ing-rod*; get records of temperature, humidity, pressure, etc. from (upper atmosphere) with ~*ing-balloon*; (med.) examine (bladder etc.) with probe; (of fish, esp. whale) dive to the bottom; inquire esp. in cautious or reserved manner into the sentiments or inclination of (person *about, on, as to*). **2.** n. Surgeon's probe. [ME, f. OF *sonder* f. Rom. *subundare*, f. sub- SUB-+*unda* wave]

sound⁴, n. **1.** Narrow passage of water connecting two seas or sea with lake etc., strait. **2.** Fish's air-bladder; cuttle-fish. [partly OE *sund*, partly f. ON *sund* swimming, sea, strait, f. stem of SWIM]

sound'er¹, n. ‖ (Arch.) herd of wild swine; (pseudo-arch.) young wild boar. [ME, f. OF *sundre* f. Gmc, cf. OE *sunor*, OHG *swaner*, ON *sonar*]

sound'er², n. In vbl senses of SOUND³, esp. telegraphic receiving instrument for reading message by sound. [-ER¹]

sound'er³, n. In vbl senses of SOUND³; *echo-*~, apparatus for sounding by measuring time-interval between transmission of a note & receipt of its echo from the sea-bed; *flying* ~, sounding--apparatus that can be used without reducing ship's speed. [-ER¹]

sound'ing, n. In vbl senses of SOUND³, also (pl.) place near enough to shore to admit of ~, as *be in, come into*, ~*s*. [-ING¹]

soup (sōōp), n. Liquid food made of stock & other ingredients (*in the* ~, sl., in difficulties); ‖ (legal sl.) prosecution brief given to junior barrister at Quarter Sessions etc.; ~*-kitchen*, public establishment for supplying ~ gratis to the poor; ~*-ticket* (entitling holder to ~ at ~*-kitchen*); ~ *maigre* (-ger), thin ~ chiefly of vegetables; ~*-plate*, deep kind for ~; PEA ~. Hence ~'Y² a. [f. F *soupe* sop, broth, f. LL *suppa*; rel. to OE *sopp* (SOP) not clear]

soupçon (see Ap.), n. Very small quantity, dash, (of flavouring, quality, etc.). [F]

sour (sowr), a., & v.i. & t. **1.** Of acid taste, esp. as result of unripeness, as ~ *apples*, ~ GRAPES, or of fermentation, as ~ *milk, bread*; (of smell) suggestive of fermentation; (of soil) dank; (of person or temper) harsh, peevish, morose; ~ *dock*, common sorrel; ~'*puss* (sl.), ~-tempered person. **2.** vb. Make, become, ~ (esp. fig.), as ~*ed by misfortune*. Hence ~'ISH¹ a., ~'LY² adv., ~'NESS n. [OE *sūr*, OS, OHG *sūr*, ON *surr*]

source (sōrs), n. Spring, fountain-head, from which stream issues, as *the* ~*s of the Nile*; origin, place from which thing comes or is got, as *the* ~ *of all our woes, reliable* ~ *of information, drawn from all*

~s; ~-*book* [transl. of G *quellenbuch*], book or collection of original documents serving as material for the historical study of a subject. [ME, f. OF *sors, sourse*, p.p. as n. of *sourdre* rise f. L *surgere*]

sourdine (soordĕn'), n. Harmonium stop producing soft effect; = SORDINE. [F, cf. SORDINE]

*****sourdough** (sowr'dō), n. One who has spent one or more winters in Alaska; old-timer. [dial., = leaven; SOUR + .DOUGH]

sour-sŏp (sowr-), n. A W.-Ind. fruit & tree. [SOUR+SOP]

souse[1], n., & v.t. & i. 1. Pickle made with salt; food in pickle, esp. head, feet, & ears, of swine; dip, plunge, drenching, in water. 2. vb. Put in pickle, as ~*d mackerel*; plunge (t. & i., *into* liquid), soak (thing *in* liquid), throw (liquid *over* thing); (p.p.) drunk (sl.). [ME; vb f. n., OF *souz* pickle f. WG *****sultja* (= OS *sultia*, OHG *sulza*), cogn. w. SALT]

souse[2], adv. With swift descent, headlong, as *came ~ into our midst*. [f. obs. *souse* swoop, alt. f. obs. SOURCE (in hawking)]

soutache (soo'tahsh), n. Ornamental braid for sewing on fabric in designs. [F, f. Magyar *sujtás*]

soutane (sootahn'), n. (R.-C. Ch.). Priest's cassock. [F]

soûteneur (sootenĕr'), n. Man cohabiting with & living on the earnings of a prostitute. [F, = protector]

|| **sout'er** (soo-), n. (Sc. & north.). Shoemaker, cobbler. [OE *sûtere* f. L *sutor* (*suere*, *sut*- sew)]

south, adv., n., a., (abbr. *S*.), & v.i. 1. (Towards, at, near) point of horizon directly opposite to north; point of compass opposite north; DUE[1] ~; ~ BY[1] *east* or *west*; ~ *of*, farther ~ than; ~-*east*, ~--*west*, etc., advv., aa., & nn., POINT[1]s of the compass, corresponding regions, (with uses & derivatives corresp. to those of ~, e.g. ~-~-*easterly*); || *southern* part of England, Scotland, Wales, Ireland, or Europe; the Southern STATE[1]s; ~ (*wind*), wind from the ~. 2. adj. Situated or dwelling in, looking towards, the ~; S~ *Downs* (of Hampshire & Sussex); ~'*down* a. & n., (sheep) of a breed originating on S~ Downs esteemed for their flesh; *S~ Kensington*, (used for) the museums of S~ Kensington or the atmosphere of culture & art & instruction associated w. them; ~'*paw* a. & n. (sl.), left-handed (person), esp. in sport; *S~ Sea* (hist.), the Pacific; *S~ Sea Bubble*, scheme for trading in Spanish America, which collapsed in 1720. 3. v.i. Move towards ~, (of moon etc.) cross the meridian of a place. Hence ~'WARD a. & n., ~'WARD(s) adv. [OE *sûth*, OS *sûth*, OHG *sund*-, ON *sûthr*]

southeas'ter, south'er, nn. Wind from SE, from S. [-ER[1]]

sou'therly (sŭdh-), a. & adv. Towards the south; (of wind) blowing from the south. [f. SOUTH, as EASTERLY]

sou'thern (sŭdh-), a. & n. 1. Of, in, the south; S~ HEMISPHERE, CROSS[1], CONFEDERACY, STATES; looking south, as *a ~ aspect*; (of wind, rare)=prec. 2. n. Inhabitant of the south, esp. of the S~ States, whence ~ER[1] n.; ~*wood*, kind of wormwood with scented leaves. Hence ~MOST a. [OE; -ERN]

south'ing, n. In vbl senses, also (naut.) difference of latitude made in sailing south. [-ING[1]]

sou'thron (sŭdh-), a. & n. (arch. Sc.). English, Englishman, (usu. derog.). [var. of SOUTHERN]

southwĕs'ter, n. (Also *sou'wĕs'ter*) wind from SW.; (usu. *sou'wĕs'ter*) waterproof hat with broad brim behind to protect neck. [-ER[1]]

souvenir (soov'enĕr), n. Thing given, kept, etc., to recall the past, memento (*of* occasion, place, etc.). [F, f. vb = remember, f. L SUB(*venire* come) occur to the mind]

sŏv'ereign (-vrĭn), a. & n. 1. Supreme, as ~ *power, the ~ good* (= SUMMUM BONUM); lofty, as *with ~ contempt*; possessing ~ power, as ~ *States*, royal, as *our ~* LORD, whence ~TY (-vrĭn-) n.; very good, esp. *a ~ remedy*; hence ~LY[2] adv. (arch.). 2. n. Supreme ruler, esp. monarch; || (colloq. abbr. *sov*) British gold coin (now hardly in use) worth nominally £1. [(n. f. adj.) f. OF *soverain* f. Rom. *****SUPER-(*anus* -AN); -*g*- by assoc. w. *reign*]

sŏv'iĕt, S-, n. Any of the councils elected by the workers & soldiers of a district in revolutionary Russia, or of a smaller number elected by these, or the all--Russian congress of delegates from these latter; *Union of S~ Socialist Republics* (abbr. U.S.S.R.), the revolutionary government of Russia; *the S~*, Russia; (attrib., usu *S~*) Russian. [Russ.]

sow[1] (sō), v.t. (~*ed*, ~*n* or ~*ed*). Scatter (seed, or abs.) on or in the earth for purpose of growth; (fig.) ~ (*the seeds of*) *dissension* etc., *must reap what you have* ~*n*, ~ *the wind* (see WHIRL); plant (field etc. *with* seed) by ~ing; (fig.) cover thickly *with*. Hence ~'ER[1](1, 2), ~'ING[1], nn. [OE *sâwan*, OS *sâian*, OHG *sâjan*, ON *sd*, Goth. *saian* f. Gmc *****sǣ*-, cf. SEED]

sow[2], n. 1. Adult female hog; *get the wrong* ~ *by the ear*, fix on wrong person or thing, reach wrong conclusion; *as drunk as a* ~ (completely). 2. (Also ~-*bug*) wood-louse. 3. Main trough through which molten iron runs into side-channels to form pigs, large block of iron that solidifies in this. 4. ~'*back*, low ridge of sand etc.; ~'*bread*, kind of cyclamen; ~'*thistle*, plant with small yellow flowers & milky juice. [OE *sugu*, MDu., MLG *soge*, rel. to OHG *sû*, ON *sŷr*, L *sus*]

soy, n. Kind of sauce made in Japan & China from the SOYA BEAN. [f. Jap. *shoyu*]

soy'a, (now rarely) **soy, bean**, n. (Seed of) a leguminous plant of south-eastern Asia, yielding an edible oil (~ *oil*) & *soya meal* or *flour* used for cattle & human food. [prec.]

söz'zled (-ld), a. (sl.). Very drunk. [p.p. of *sozzle* dial., to mix sloppily (prob. imit.)]

spa (-ah, -aw), n. (Place where there is a) mineral spring. [*Spa*, place in Belgium]

spāce¹, n. 1. Continuous extension viewed with or without reference to the existence of objects within it. 2. Interval between points or objects viewed as having one, two, or three dimensions, as *separated by a* ~ *of 10 ft, clear a* ~ (area), *box occupies too much* ~, *would take up too much* ~ (on paper) *to go into detail*; large region (*the wide open* ~*s*). 3. (print.). Blank between words etc., type securing this. 4. Interval of time, as *in the* ~ *of an hour, after a short* ~, *let us rest a* ~. 5. ~*-bar*, bar in type-writer for making ~ between words; ~ *craft* (for travelling through inter-planetary ~ beyond the earth's atmo-sphere); ~ *fiction*, fanciful fiction about travel through ~; ~ *flight, flying*; ~ *helmet, suit*, worn by ~*man* (traveller in outer ~); ~ *ship*, = ~ *craft*; ~*-time* (philos.), a fusion of the concepts of ~ & time, regarded as a continuum in which the existent exists; ~ *travel(ler), travelling*; ~ *vehicle*, = ~ *craft*; ~*-writer, -writing* (in newspaper, paid according to area occupied). Hence ~'LESS (-sl-) a. [ME, f. OF *espace* f. L *spatium*]

spāce², v.t. & i. Set at intervals, put spaces between, (esp. words, letters, lines, in printing); make a space between words on typewriter etc., *as don't forget to* ~, whence spā'CER¹(2) n.; ~ *out* (print.), put more or wider spaces between. Hence spā'CING¹(1) n. [f. prec.]

spā'cious (-shus), a. Enclosing a large space, roomy. Hence ~LY² adv., ~NESS n. [ME, f. L *spatiosus* (as SPACE¹, see -OUS)]

spāde¹, n., & v.t. 1. Tool for digging & cut-ting ground, turf, etc., with sharp-edged iron blade & wooden handle used with both hands; *call a* ~ *a* ~, call things by their names, speak plainly or bluntly; tool of similar shape for various purposes, e.g. for removing blubber from whale; ~ *bayonet* (with broad blade, used as both ~ & weapon); ~ *husbandry* (with deep ~-digging instead of subsoil-ploughing). 2. ~*-work*, (fig.) hard preparatory work. 3. v.t. Dig over (ground), cut blubber from (whale), with ~. Hence ~'FUL (-dfŏŏl) n. [OE *spadu, spada*, = OFris. *spada*, OS *spado*, rel. to Gk *spathē* blade, whence L *spatha*]

spāde², n. (Playing-card with) black figure(s) shaped like heart with small handle; (pl.) suit of these cards; ~ *guinea* (of George III with shield shaped like ~ on cards). [f. It. *spade* pl. of *spada* sword f. L *spatha*, as prec.]

|| **spādg'er**, n. (sl.). Fanciful alt. of SPAR-ROW.

spadille', n. Ace of spades in ombre & quadrille. [F, f. Sp. *espadilla* dim. of *espada* sword, see SPADE²]

spād'|ix, n. (bot.; pl. ~*ices* pr. -ĭs'ēz). Spike of flowers closely arranged round fleshy axis & usu. enclosed in a spathe. Hence or cogn.~ĭ'CEOUS (-ĭshus),~ĭCOSE¹, aa. [L f. Gk, = palm-branch]

spād'ō, n. (law). Person incapable of pro-creation. [L, f. Gk *spadōn* eunuch]

|| **spae** (spā), v.i. & t. (Sc.). Foretell, prophesy; ~'*wife*, female fortune-teller. [f. ON *spá*]

spaghett'i (-gĕ-), n. Kind of macaroni. [It.]

spahi, -ee (spah'hē), n. (hist.). Member of 14th-c. Turkish irregular cavalry; member of native Algerian cavalry in French service. [f. Turk. f. Hind. *sipahi* SEPOY]

spake. See SPEAK.

spall (-awl), v.t. & i., & n. Splinter, chip; (mining) prepare (ore) for sorting by breaking it up. Hence spal'DER¹ (-awl-) n. [also *spale* (both 15th c.), of unkn. orig.; cf. LG *spellen*, LG *spellen* to split]

|| **spālpeen'**, n. (Ir.). Mean fellow, rascal.

spăm, n. Tinned foodstuff imported from U.S. [P; f. *spiced ham*]

spăn¹, v.t. & i. (-nn-). (Of bridge, arch, etc., fig. of memory etc.) stretch from side to side of, extend across, (river etc., fig. period etc.), (of builder etc.) bridge (river etc.); measure, cover, the extent of (thing) with one's grasp etc.; (naut.) confine (booms etc.) with ropes; move in distinct stretches like span-worm. [ME, f. MDu. or MLG *spannen*, = OE, OHG *spannan*; see foll.]

spăn², n. 1. Full extent from end to end, as ~ *of a bridge, of an arch, our brief* ~ (of life), *the whole* ~ *of Roman history*. 2. Each part of a bridge etc. between piers or supports. 3. Greenhouse or similar struc-ture with ~ roof. 4. Maximum distance between tips of thumb & little finger, esp. as a measure = 9 in. 5. Short distance, as *our life is but a* ~. 6. (naut.). Rope fastened by both ends to take a purchase in the loop, double rope connected with thimbles. 7. Pair of horses or mules, yoke of oxen. 8. ~*-dogs*, pair of iron bars with claws for grappling timber; ~ *roof* (with two inclined sides, opp. to pent-roof or lean-to); ~*-worm*, larva of geometer. [OE *span(n)*, MDu. *spanne*, OHG *spanna*, ON *spann-* rel. to OE *spannan* (prec.); in ME prob. reinforced by OF *espan*; senses 6 & 7 f. (M)Du., (M)LG *span*]

spăn'drel, n. Space between shoulder of arch & surrounding rectangular moulding or framework, or between shoulders of adjoining arches & moulding above; ~ *wall* (built on curve of arch, filling in ~).

[app. a dim. of AF *spaundre, -dere*, perh. identical w. *(e)spaundre* expand]

spangl|e (spăng'gl), n., & v.t. **1.** Small piece of glittering material esp. one of many as ornament of dress etc.; any small sparkling object;˙ (also *oak-~e*) spongy excrescence on oak-leaves, oak- -apple. **2.** v.t. Cover with ~es (esp. in p.p.; STAR¹*-~ed*). Hence ~Y² a. [ME, f. *spang*, f. MDu. *spange*, +-LE]

Spăn'iard (-yard), n. Native of Spain. [f. OF *Espaignart* (*Espaigne* Spain, -ARD)]

spăn'iel (-yel), n. Kinds of dog with long silky coat, drooping ears, & docile & affectionate disposition, some used by sportsmen & some kept as pets (*King Charles's ~*, small black-&-tan kind); (fig.) fawning or cringing person. [ME, f. OF *espaignol, -eul* Spanish (dog) f. Rom. **hispaniolus* f. *hispania* Spain]

Spăn'ish, a. & n. **1.** Of Spain or the Spaniards or their language; ~ (= *Invincible*) ARMADA; ~ *black, brown, red, white*, pigments; ~ CHESTNUT; ~ *fly*, bright green insect dried & used for raising blisters, as aphrodisiac, etc.; ~ *fowl*, breed of domestic fowl with glossy greenish-black plumage; ~ *grass*, esparto; ~ *main* (hist.), NE coast of S. America between Orinoco river & Panama, & adjoining part of Caribbean sea; ~ *windlass*, use of stick as lever for tightening cord or bandage. **2.** n. ~ language. [ME *Spainisc* (*Spain*, see SPAN¹)]

spănk, v.t. & i., & n. **1.** Slap on buttocks with open hand or slipper etc., whence ~'ing¹ [-ING¹] n.; urge forward esp. by slapping or whipping; (of horse etc.) move briskly esp. at a step between trot & gallop. **2.** n. Slap, blow with open hand etc., on buttocks. [imit.]

spănk'er, n. In vbl senses; also or esp.: fast-going horse; (colloq.) person or thing of notable size or quality, stunner, whopper; (naut.) fore-&-aft sail set on after side of mizzenmast. [-ER¹]

spanking¹. See SPANK.

spănk'ing², a. & adv. In vbl senses; also: (colloq.) striking, notable, excellent, as *had a ~ time, a ~* (strong) *breeze*, (adv.) *a ~ fine woman*. [-ING², cf. *whacking, thumping, whopping*]

spăn'less, a. (poet.). Beyond measure. [-LESS]

spănn'er, n. Instrument for turning nut on screw etc. (*throw a ~ into the works*, fig., introduce an upsetting element or influence); cross-brace of bridge etc.; connecting-rod in parallel motion of engine; = SPAN²*-worm*. [f. G *spanner*, f. *spannen* draw tight (see SPAN²)]

spăr¹, n., & v.t. (-rr-). **1.** Stout pole esp. such as is used for mast, yard, etc., of ship; ~*-buoy* (made of a ~ with one end moored so that other stands up); ~*-deck*, upper deck extending from bow to stern, including quarterdeck and forecastle. **2.** v.t. Furnish with ~, help (ship) over

shallow bar with ~s. [ME *sparre, sperre*, f. MDu., MLG *sparre*, MDu. *sperre*, = OS, OHG *sparro*, ON *sparri, sperra*; poss. also f. OF *esparre*, f. Gmc]

spăr², n. Kinds of crystalline mineral, easily cleavable & non-lustrous, as *calcareous ~*, calcite, *Derbyshire* (= FLUOR) ~, *Iceland ~*, transparent calcite much used for optical purposes. [f. MLG *spar*, cogn. w. OE *spæren* gypsum]

spăr³, v.i. & (-rr-), & n. **1.** Make motions of attack & defence with closed fists, use the hands (as) in boxing, (often *at* opponent; ~*ring partner*, boxer employed to practise with another in training for a fight); (fig.) bandy words, as *they are always ~ring (at each other)*; (of cocks) fight esp. with protected spurs. **2.** n. ~*-ring* motion, boxing-match, cock-fight. [ME, f. OE *sperran*, of unkn. orig.]

spă'rable, n. Headless nail for soles & heels of boots. [reduced f. *sparrow-bill*]

spāre¹, a. & n. **1.** Scanty, frugal, as ~ *diet*, lean, thin, as *man of ~ frame*, whence ~'LY² (-rl-) adv., ~'NESS (-rn-), n.; ~'*rib*, upper part of row of ribs of pork with small amount of meat adhering; that can be spared, not required for ordinary use, as *how to use your ~ time, have no ~ cash*; reserved for emergency or extraordinary use, as *always take a ~ cap, ~ room* (bedroom for visitor). **2.** n. ~ part for substitution in machine. [ME, corresp. to OE *spær*, OHG *spar*, MDu. *spaer* sparing, f. **spar* (foll.) n. f. adj. & vb]

spāre², v.t. & i. Be frugal or grudging of, as ~ *the rod & spoil the child, must not ~ expense*, whence **spār'ingLY²** adv., **spār'ingNESS** n.; dispense with, do without, as *cannot ~ him just now, ~ me a pound, could have ~d the explanation*; || (arch.) forbear (*to* do); abstain from inflicting (with double object), as ~ *me these protestations*; abstain from killing, hurting, wounding, etc., as ~ (do not kill) *me, ~ my life, ~ his feelings*, (loosely) ~ (do not provoke) *his blushes*; be frugal. [OE *sparian*, OS, OHG *sparōn*, ON *spara* f. Gmc **spar-* (prec.)]

spăr'ger, n. Sprinkling-apparatus, esp. in brewing. [f. *sparge* to sprinkle (L *spargere*) +-ER¹]

spărk¹, n. **1.** Fiery particle thrown off from burning substance, or still visibly alight in ashes, or struck out by impact from flint etc. (*as the ~s fly upward*, with the certainty of a law of nature). **2.** Small bright object or point e.g. in gem. **3.** (fig.). Brilliant emanation of wit etc., esp. *strike ~s out of* person, provoke him to lively or original conversation. **4.** (Usu. neg. or quasi-neg.) particle of fire or. (fig.) of a quality etc., as *not a ~ of life remained, if you had a ~ of generosity in you*. **5.** (electr.). Luminous effect of sudden disruptive discharge, electric ~ serving to fire explosive mixture in oil-engine of motor etc., as *advance, retard, the ~* (in

the cycle of operation in the engine).
6. *S~s*, (nickname for) radio operator;
fairy ~s, phosphorescent light from decayed vegetable matter etc.; *~-arrester*,
device for preventing (injury from)
SPARK[2]ing in electrical apparatus, netting
etc. to catch *~s* on steam-engine. Hence
~'LESS a., *~'LET* n., small *~*, carbonic-acid
charge for use in some gazogenes. [OE
~spærca, spearca, = MDu., MLG *sparke*,
of unkn. orig.]

spark[2], v.i. & t. Emit sparks of fire or
electricity; || *~(ing)-plug*, device for firing
explosive mixture in motor-engine;
(electr.) produce sparks at point where
continuity of circuit is interrupted; (v.t.;
also *~ off*) stir into activity. [ME, rel. to
prec.; cf. MDu., MLG *sparken*]

spark[3], n., & v.i. 1. Gay fellow; gallant.
2. v.i. Play the gallant. Hence *~'ISH[1]* a.
[(vb f. n.) prob. fig. use of SPARK[1]]

spar'kl|e, v.i., & n. 1. Emit sparks, (of
gems etc. & fig. of wit etc.) glitter, glisten,
scintillate, whence *~ER[2]* n., *~ingLY[2]*
adv.; *~ing wines* (giving out carbonic-
-acid gas in small bubbles, cf. STILL). 2. n.
~ing, gleam, spark. [ME, f. SPARK[1,2]
+ -LE (1,3); cf. MDu. *sparkelen* vb]

spa'rrow (-ō), n. Kinds of small plain-
-coloured bird, esp. *house ~*, European
kind noted for attachment to human
dwellings, prolificness, and pugnacity;
~-bill, = SPARABLE; *~-grass* (vulg.), asparagus; *~-hawk*, kinds of small hawk preying on *~s* etc. [OE *spearwa*, MHG
sparwe, Goth. *sparwa*; also OHG *sparo*,
ON *spǫrr*]

spar'ry, a. Of, like, rich in, SPAR[2].
[-Y[2]]

sparse, a. (Of population etc.) thinly
scattered, not dense; (bot., zool.) placed,
occurring, at distant or irregular intervals. Hence *~'LY[2]* (-sl-) adv., *~'NESS*
(-sn-) n. [f. L *sparsus* (*spargere spars-
scatter*)]

Spart'acist, a. & n. (Member) of the
Spartacus group of extremists in the
German revolution in 1918. [*Spartacus*,
leader in anc.-Roman servile war, -IST]

Spart'an, a. & n. (Native) of Sparta (esp.
w. allusion to supposed characteristics
of *~s*, as *~ endurance, simplicity*). [ME, f.
L *Spartanus*, f. Gk *Spartā*, -*tē*, see -AN]

spa'sm, n. Excessive muscular contraction (CLONIC, TONIC, *~*); sudden convulsive
movement, wrench, or strain, as *a ~ of
coughing*, (fig.) *~s of grief* etc.; *functional
~*, nervous disorders caused by occupation, e.g. writer's cramp. Hence *~ŏL'OGY*
(-ăz-) n. [ME, f. OF *spasme* or L f. Gk
spasmos (*spaō* draw)]

spasmŏd'|ic (-ăz-), a. Of, caused by,
subject to, spasm(s), as *a ~ic jerk*, *~ic
asthma*; occurring, done, by fits & starts,
as *~ic efforts*. Hence *~ICALLY* adv. [f. Gk
spasmōdēs (as SPASM, see -ODE) + -IC]

spas'tic, a. & n. (med.). 1. = prec. 2. n.
Person suffering from cerebral palsy. [f.

L f. Gk *spastikos* drawing (*spaō* draw, see
-IC)]

spat[1], n., & v.i. & t. (-tt-). 1. Spawn of
shellfish esp. oyster. 2. vb. (Of oyster
etc.) spawn; shed (spawn). [AN *spat*
(14th c.), of unkn. orig.]

spat[2], n. (usu. pl.). Short gaiter covering
instep & reaching little above ankle.
[abbr. of (17th c.) SPATTER*dash*]

spat[3]. See SPIT[2].

spatch'cŏck, n., & v.t. 1. Fowl killed &
cooked in a hurry. 2. v.t. (colloq.). Insert
(words) hastily in telegram etc. [orig. in
Ir. use, expl. by Grose (1785) as f. *dispatch-
-cock*; cf. SPITCHCOCK]

spāte, n. || River-flood, esp. *river is in ~*;
(fig.) excessive amount, as *a ~ of words*.
[ME, Sc. & north., of unkn. orig.]

spāthe (-dh), n. (bot.). Large bract or pair
of bracts enveloping spadix or flower-
-cluster. Hence **spāth'ose**[1], **spāth'ous**,
aa. [f. L f. Gk *spathē* broad blade etc.]

spāth'ic, a. Of SPAR[2], like spar esp. in
cleavage. So **spāth'iFORM** a. [f. obs.
spath, f. G *spath* spar + -IC]

spā'tial (-shl), a. Of space, as *~ relations,
extent*. Hence **spātiǎl'ITY** (-shǐ-) n., *~LY[2]*
adv. [f. L *spatium* SPACE + -AL]

spättee', n. Woollen legging worn by
women and children over shoes and
stockings. [f. SPAT[2] after *puttee*]

spätt'er, v.t. & i., & n. 1. Scatter (liquid,
mud, etc.) here & there in small drops;
splash (person *with* mud, slander, etc.)
thus; (of liquid) fall here & there in
drops. 2. n. *~ing*, splash (of mud etc.),
quick succession of light sounds, patter-
ing. 3. *~dashes* (or now usu. *späts*), cloth
or other leggings to protect stockings etc.
from mud etc. [app. frequent. of stem
found in Du., LG *spatten* etc.; cf. WFlem.
spetteren spatter]

spät'ūla, n. Broad-bladed instrument
for working pigments etc.; surgeon's
instrument for pressing tongue down or
to one side. [L, dim. of *spatha* SPATHE]

spät'ūl|e, n. (zool.). Broad racket-shaped
formation or part, esp. end of bird's tail-
-feather. Hence *~AR[1]*, *~ATE[2]*, *~iFORM*, aa.
[ME, f. OF, f. L as prec.]

späv'in, n. Disease of horse's hock-joint;
blood, bog, ~, distension of the joint by
effusion of lymph within it; *bone ~*, deposit of bony substance uniting the bones.
Hence *~ED[2]* (-nd) a. [ME, f. OF *espavain*,
var. of *esparvain*, perh. of Gmc orig.]

spawn, v.t. & i., & n. 1. (Of fish, frog,
mollusc, crustacean, derog. of human
being or other animal) produce (eggs, or
abs.), generate; (of eggs or young of fish
etc.) be produced, issue. 2. n. Eggs of
fish etc.; (derog.) human or other offspring (*~ of the devil, of Cobden*, scoun-
drels, free-traders); white fibrous matter
from which fungi are produced, myce-
lium, as *mushroom ~*. [ME, f. AF
espaundre, OF *espandre* EXPAND; n. f.
vb]

spay, v.t. Castrate, remove ovaries of, (female animal). [ME, f. AF *espeier*, OF *espeer* cut with a sword (*espee* sword)]

speak, v.i. & t. (*spŏke*, arch. *spăke*; *spŏken*). **1.** Use articulate utterance in ordinary (not singing-) voice, as *child is learning to ~, wish you would ~ distinctly*; (p.p., as stage direction) to be said, not sung (also as n., such part). **2.** Hold conversation (*with, to*, person, *of, about*, thing), as *have heard him ~ of it, will ~ to him about it*; *portrait ~s* (is lifelike), so *~ing likeness*. **3.** Make oral address, deliver speech, before assembly, magistrate, tribunal, etc. **4.** Utter (words); make known (one's opinion, *the truth*, etc.) thus, esp. *~ one's mind* (bluntly etc.). **5.** Use (specified language) in *~*ing, as *cannot ~ French*, whence **French'** etc. *~*ER[1] n., *~*ING[2] a. **6.** *Strictly, roughly, generally, ~ing* (quasi-adv.), in the strict, rough, etc., sense of the word(s), as *am not strictly ~ing a member of the staff*; *legally* etc. *~ing*, from the legal etc. point of view. **7.** (As an apology for loose or strong or figurative expression) *so to ~*, if I may use such an expression. **8.** Hail & hold communication with (ship). **9.** (arch.). (Of conduct, circumstance, etc.) show (person) to be (so-&-so), as *his conduct ~s him generous*; be evidence of, as *this ~s a little mind*. **10.** (Of fact etc.) *~ volumes*, be very significant; *~ volumes* etc. *for, ~ well for*, be abundant evidence of, place in favourable light, as *~s volumes for his forbearance*. **11.** (Of dog) bark esp. when ordered. **12.** fig. (Of mus. instrument etc.) sound. **13.** Make mention in writing *of*. **14.** *~ by the* or *like a* BOOK[1]; *~* (person) *fair*, use polite language to; *~ for*, act as spokesman of, state the sentiments of; *~ of*, mention; *nothing to ~ of*, nothing worth mentioning, practically nothing; *~ out* (also *up*), *~ freely, ~ one's whole opinion; ~ to*, address (person etc.), in confirmation of or in reference to, as *I can ~ to his having been there, will ~ to that point later; ~ up* (also *out*), *~* loud(er); *~ without book*, give facts etc. from memory; *fair, smooth, ill, well,* etc., *-spoken* [as if *-speech*ED[2]], (given to) using such language; *~-easy* (sl.), illicit liquor shop. [OE *sprecan*, later *specan*, OS *sprekan*, OHG *sprehhan*]

speak'er, n. One who speaks esp. in public; (*S~*) presiding officer in House of Commons charged with preservation of order etc. & having casting vote in case of equal division, similar officer in U.S. House of Representatives etc., whence *S~*SHIP n.; LOUD *~*. [ME; -ER[1]]

speak'ing, n. In vbl senses: *~ acquaintance*, person one knows well enough to exchange conversation with him, this degree of familiarity; *not on ~ terms*, not, esp. no longer, having *~* acquaintance *with* (usu. implying estrangement); *~-trumpet*, instrument for conveying voice

to a distance; *~-tube*, tube for conveying voice from one room or building to another. [ME; -ING[1]]

spear, n., & v.t. & i. **1.** Hunter's or foot-soldier's thrusting or hurling weapon consisting of stout staff with point usu. of steel (cf. LANCE, PIKE); (poet.) = *~man*; sharp-pointed & barbed instrument for stabbing fish etc.; *~* (long stiff) *grass*; *~'head*, (esp. fig.) individual or group chosen to lead a thrust or attack, (v.t.) act as *~*head of (attack etc.); *~'man*, person esp. soldier who uses *~; ~'mint*, common garden mint; *~ side*, male branch of family (cf. DISTAFF). **2.** v.t. Pierce, strike, with *~*. **3.** v.i. Shoot into a long stem. [OE *spere*, OS, OHG *sper*, ON *spjǫr*]

spĕc, n. (colloq.). Speculation, speculative enterprise, as *it turned out a good ~, did it on ~*. [abbr. of SPECULATION]

spĕ'cial (-shl), a. & n. **1.** Of a particular kind, peculiar, not general, (cf. ESPECIAL), as *lacks the ~ qualities required, word used in a ~ sense, what is your ~ work?, its ~ charm did not appeal to him, ~ anatomy* (of particular organs of human body), *~* JURY, *~ hospital* (for particular class of diseases). **2.** For a particular purpose, as *appointed ~ agents, received ~ instructions*. **3.** (Also *especial*) exceptional in amount, degree, intensity, etc., as *took ~ trouble, find no ~ excellence in his work*. **4.** *~ case*, written statement of facts submitted by litigants to court, (also) exceptional or peculiar case; *~ constable* (sworn in to assist in maintaining public peace in time of emergency); *~ correspondent* (appointed by newspaper to report on *~* facts); *~ edition* (including later news than ordinary edition of newspaper); || *~ licence* (enabling priests to marry parties without publication of banns or at time or place other than those usually necessary); *~ logic*, rules for thinking concerning *~* class of objects; *~ pleader*, member of Inns of Court whose business it is to give verbal or written opinions on matters submitted to him & to deal with various proceedings out of usual course; *~ pleading*, (law) allegation of *~* or new matter as opp. to denial of allegations of other side, (pop.) specious but unfair argument, statement of case designed to favour speaker's point of view rather than to discover the truth; *~ train*, extra train for *~* purpose; *~* VERDICT. **5.** n. *~* constable, train, examination, edition of newspaper (esp. EXTRA-*~*), etc. Hence *~*LY[2] (-sha-) adv. [ME, f. OF *especial* .(ESPECIAL) or L *specialis* (SPECIES, -AL)]

spĕ'cial|ist (-sha-), n. One who devotes himself to particular branch of a profession, science, etc. Hence or cogn. *~*ISM n., *~*is'tic a. [-IST]

spĕciăl'ity (-shi-), n. Special feature or characteristic; (also *specialty*) special pursuit, product, operation, etc., thing to which a person gives special attention, as *jam*(-*making*) *is our* ~. [ME, f. OF (*e*)*specialite* or LL *specialitas* (as SPECIAL, see -TY)]

spe'cializ|e (-sha-), **-is|e** (-īz), v.t. & i. Make specific or individual; modify, limit, (idea, statement); (biol.) adapt, set apart, (organ etc.) for particular purpose, differentiate; be differentiated, become individual in character; be(come) a specialist. Hence ~A'TION n. [f. F *spécialiser* (SPECIAL, -IZE)]

spe'cialty (-shl-), n. (Law) instrument under seal, sealed contract; = SPECIALITY (2nd sense). [ME, f. OF (*e*)*specialte* SPECIALITY]

spēciā'tion (*or* -shī-), n. (zool.). Formation of SPECIES by evolutionary process. [-ATION]

spē'cie (-shĭē, -shē), n. (no pl.). Coin as opp. to paper money, as ~ *payments, paid in* ~, *shortness of* ~. [f. L abl. of foll. in phr. *in specie*]

spē'cies (-shĭēz, -shēz), n. (pl. same). 1. (Nat. hist.) group subordinate in classification to *genus* (cf. CLASS) & having members that differ only in minor details; *the* or *our* ~, mankind. 2. (log.). Group subordinate to GENUS & containing individuals agreeing in some common attribute(s) & called by a common name. 3. Kind, sort, as *has a* ~ *of cunning, a* ~ *of dogcart.* 4. (law). Form, shape, given to materials. 5. (eccl.). The sensible form of each of the elements of consecrated bread and wine used in the Eucharist. [L, = appearance, kind, beauty, f. *specere* look]

specif'ic, a. & n. 1. Definite, distinctly formulated, as *a* ~ *statement, has no* ~ *aim*; of a species, as *the* ~ *name* of plant etc.; ~ *difference* (what differentiates a species); possessing, concerned with, the properties that characterize a species, as *the* ~ *forms of animals, draws a* ~ *distinction between them*; relating to particular subject; peculiar, as *has a* ~ *charm, a style* ~ *to that school of painters*; (of a duty or tax) assessed by quantity or amount, not *ad valorem*; ~ *cause* (producing a particular form of disease); ~ *centre*, place or period at which differentiation from a common stock takes place; ~ GRAVITY, HEAT[1]; ~ *medicine*, having distinct effect in curing a certain disease. 2. n. ~ medicine or remedy. Hence **specif'ICALLY** adv., **spĕcifi'CITY**, ~NESS, nn. [f. LL *specificus* (as SPECIES, see -FIC)]

spĕcificā'tion, n. Specifying; specified detail, esp. (pl.) detailed description of construction, workmanship, materials, etc., of work undertaken by architect, engineer, etc.; description by applicant for patent of the construction & use of his invention; (law) working up of materials into a new product not held to be the property of the owner of the materials. [f. med. L *specificatio* (foll., -FICATION)]

spe'cif|y̆, v.t. Name expressly, mention definitely, (items, details, ingredients, etc.; often abs.); include in (e.g. architect's) specifications, as *a slate-course was not* ~*ied*. Hence ~IABLE a. [ME, f. OF *specifier* f. LL *specificare* (as SPECIFIC, see -FY)]

spĕ'cimĕn, n. Individual or part taken as example of a class or whole, esp. individual animal or plant or piece of a mineral etc. used for scientific examination, as ~*s* of copper ore, *zoological* ~*s, fine* ~ *of the swallow-tail, of mosaic work, a* ~ *of his skill, generosity,* ~ *page* (of book, printed in prospectus etc.); (colloq. derog.) *what a* ~ (person)*!* [L, (*specere* look, -MEN)]

spĕci|ŏl'ogy̆ (-shĭ-), n. Science of (origin etc. of) species. Hence ~olō'gICAL a. [-LOGY]

spē'cious (-shŭs), a. Of good appearance, plausible, fair or right on the surface, as ~ *argument, tale, pretence, person, appearance.* Hence or cogn. **spēcios'ITY** (-shĭ-), ~NESS, nn., ~LY[2] adv. [f. L *speciosus* beautiful (SPECIES, see -OUS)]

spĕck[1], n., & v.t. 1. Small spot, dot, stain; particle (*of* dirt etc.); spot of rottenness in fruit. 2. v.t. Mark with ~s (esp. in p.p.). Hence ~'LESS a. [OE *specca*, not in cogn. langg.; cf. SPECKLE]

spĕck[2], n. (U.S. & S. Afr.). Fat meat, bacon, pork; fat of seals, whales, etc., blubber. [f. Du. *spek* or G *speck*, rel. to OE *spic* bacon]

spĕc'kle, n., & v.t. 1. Small spot or stain. 2. v.t. Mark with ~s or patches (esp. in p.p.). [ME, corresp. to MDu. *speckel*, see SPECK[1], -LE]

spĕcktioneer', **-si-**, (-shon-), n. (whaling). Chief harpooner. [f. Du. *speksnijer*, for -*snijder*, (SPECK[2], *snijden* cut, -ER[1])]

spĕcs, n. pl. (colloq.). Pair of spectacles. [abbr.]

spĕc'tacle, n. 1. Public show, whence **spĕctăc'ŭlAR**[1] a., **spĕctăc'ŭlarLY**[2] adv. 2. Object of sight, esp. of public attention, as *a charming* ~, *drunken woman is a deplorable* ~, *sure to make a* ~ (= EXHIBITION) *of himself.* 3. (*Pair of*) ~*s* or colloq. specs, pair of lenses to correct or assist defective sight, set in frame without spring (cf. EYE[1]-*glass*) constructed to rest on nose & ears; (fig.) *sees everything through rose-coloured* etc. ~*s*, takes cheerful etc. views; (crick.) *pair of* ~*s*, two DUCK[1]s. [ME, f. OF, or f. L *spectaculum* (*spectare* look)]

spĕc'tacled (-ld), a. Wearing spectacles; (of animals) marked in a way that suggests spectacles, esp. ~ *bear*, the S.-Amer. bear. [-ED[2]]

spĕctāt'or, n. One who looks on esp. at a show, game, etc., as *the* ~*s were moved to tears, was a mere* ~, *an unconcerned* ~, (as title of paper) *The S*~. Hence **spĕctāt'rESS**[1] n. [L (*spectare*, see SPECTACLE & -OR)]

spĕc′tral, a. Ghostlike, of ghosts; of spectra or the spectrum, as ~ *colours, analysis.* Hence~LY² adv. [f. L *spectrum* SPECTRE + -AL]

spĕc′tre (-*ter*), n. Ghost; haunting presentiment (*of* ruin, war, madness, etc.); ~ *of the Brocken*, huge shadowy image of the observer projected on mists about mountain-top, first observed on the Brocken; (in names of animals compared to ~ from thinness of body etc.) ~-*bat*, -*crab*, -*insect*, -*lemur*, -*shrimp*. [F, or f. L SPECTRUM]

spĕc′tr|o- in comb. = SPECTRUM, as : ~*o-graph*, apparatus for photographing or otherwise reproducing the spectrum, ~*ogram*, representation obtained by this, so ~*ograph′ic* a., ~*ŏg′raphy* n.; ~*ohĕl′iograph*, instrument for taking photographs of the sun from light of one wave-length only; ~*ohĕl′ioscope*, spectroscope provided with a pair of oscillating slits which exclude from the observer's eye all light except that of the red hydrogen line; ~*ŏm′eter*, instrument for measuring refraction of light-rays in passing through prism.

spĕc′tr|oscōpe, n. Instrument for forming & analysing the spectra of rays, consisting usu. of collimating tube, prism or diffraction grating, small telescope, & measuring apparatus. Hence ~oscŏp′IC(AL) aa., ~oscŏp′icaLY¹² adv., ~ŏs′copIST (*or* spĕ²), ~ŏs′copY¹ (*or* spĕ²), nn. [F (SPECTRO- + -SCOPE)]

spĕc′trum, n. (pl. -*ra*). (Also *ocular* ~) image of something seen continuing when the eyes are closed or turned away; image formed by rays of light or other radiation in which the parts are arranged in a progressive series according to their refrangibility, i.e. according to wave-length; *diffraction, prismatic,* ~ (produced by means of diffraction grating, by means of prism); *solar* ~ (formed from rays of sun); ~ (or *spectral) analysis*, chemical analysis by means of spectroscope. [L; = appearance, image, f. *specere* look]

spĕc′ular, a. Of (the nature of) a speculum, esp. reflecting, as ~ *surface.* [f. L *specularis* (SPECULUM, see -AR¹)]

spĕc′ūlăt|e, v.i. 1. Pursue an inquiry, meditate, form theory or conjectural opinion, (*on, upon, about,* subject, the nature, cause, etc., of a thing, or abs.). 2. Make investment, engage in commercial operation, that involves risk of loss, as *has been* ~*ing in stocks, in rubber,* (esp. w. implication of rashness) *is believed to* ~*e a good deal.* Hence or cogn. ~IVE² a., ~ĭveLY² adv., ~ĭveNESS, ~OR, nn. [f. L *speculari* spy out, observe, (*specula* watch-tower as SPECULUM, see -ATE³]

spĕcūlā′tion, n. 1. Meditation on, inquiry into, theory about, a subject, as *much given to* ~, *sorry to disturb your* ~*s.* 2. Speculative investment or enterprise,

practice of speculating, in business, as *ruined by (a single unlucky)* ~, *bought it as a* ~ (or *on* SPEC, rarely *on* ~). 3. Game in which cards are bought & sold. [ME, f. LL *speculatio* (as prec., see -ATION)]

spĕc′ūlum, n. (pl. -*la*). (Surg.) instrument for dilating cavities of human body for inspection; mirror, usu. of polished metal e.g. ~-*metal* (alloy of copper & tin), esp. in reflecting telescope; (ornith.) specially coloured area on wing of some birds, also = OCELLUS. [L, = mirror (*specere* look)]

sped. See SPEED.

speech, n. 1. Faculty of speaking. 2. Thing said, remark, as *after this unlucky* ~ *he remained silent.* 3. Public address, as *after-dinner*, MAIDEN, ~, ~ *for the defence, a set* ~ (studied, prepared), *make* (deliver) *a* ~; ‖ *Queen's* or *King's* (*gracious*) ~, ~ *from the throne*, brief statement of foreign & domestic affairs & of the chief measures to be considered by Parliament, prepared by Government & read by sovereign in person or by commission at opening of Parliament. 4. Language of a nation. 5. Act of sounding in organ-pipe etc. 6. FIGURE¹ *of* ~; PART¹ *) of* ~; ~-*reading*, deaf person's interpretation of ~ by watching speaker's lips; ‖ ~-*day*, annual day for delivering prizes in schools usu. marked by ~es etc. [OE *sprǣc, sprēc*, later *spǣc, spĕc*, OS *sprāka*, OHG *sprāhha* f. st. of *sprecan* SPEAK]

speech′i|fy̆, v.i. (derog.). Make speeches, hold forth in public. Hence ~FICA′TION, ~fiER¹, nn. [-FY]

speech′lĕss, a. Dumb; temporarily deprived of speech by emotion etc., as ~ *with rage*; (sl.) dead drunk. Hence ~LY² adv., ~NESS n. [OE *spǣclēas*, see -LESS]

speed, n., & v.t. & i. (*spĕd*, exc. as below). 1. Rapidity of movement, as *with all* ~, *more haste less* ~, *at full* ~; rate of progress or motion, as *attains a high* ~, *depends on the* ~ *required, three-* ~ *engine, bicycle*, etc. (with adaptable gear for going at different ~s); AIR¹, GROUND¹, ~. 2. (arch.). Success, prosperity, as *send me good* ~ (cf. GOD¹-~). 3. ~-*boat*, motor-boat designed for high ~; ~-*cone*, contrivance for adjusting ratio of ~ between parallel shafts by means of belt; ~-*cop* (orig. U.S., sl.), police motor-cyclist detailed to check motorists' ~; ~′*way*, arena for motor-cycle racing, *road or track reserved for fast motor traffic; ~′*well*, kinds of herb with creeping or ascending stems & bright-blue flowers. 4. vb. Go fast, as *sped down the street* (now chiefly literary); (arch.) send fast, send on the way, as ~ *an arrow from the bow,* ~ *the parting guest.* 5. (arch.). Be or make prosperous, succeed, give success to, as *how have you sped?, God* ~ *you!* 6. (past & p.p. ~*ed*). Regulate ~ of (engine etc.), cause to go at fixed ~; ~ *up*, cause to work at greater ~ (*the train service wants* ~*ing up*); (of motorists) travel at illegal or dangerous ~. [(n.) OE *spēd*, earlier *spœd*, (OS *spōd*, OHG *spuot*) f. OE *spōwan* (OHG *spuon*) prosper; (vb) OE *spēdan* (OS *spōdian*, OHG *spuolen*) f. st. *spōd*-(as n.)]

speed'er, n. Kinds of device for regulating or increasing speed of machinery. [-ER¹]

speedōm'eter, n. Appliance indicating the speed of a vehicle etc. [SPEED, -O-, -METER]

speed'|ȳ, a. Rapid; expeditious, prompt, coming without delay, as ~*y answer, vengeance.* Hence ~ĭLY² adv., ~ĭNESS n. [ME; -Y²]

speiss (-ĭs), n. Compound of arsenic, iron, etc., found in smelting some lead ores. [f. G *speise* food, amalgam, f. pop. L *spesa* EXPENSE]

spēlae'|an, a. Of, dwelling in, caves. So ~ŏL'OGIST, ~ŏL'OGY, nn. [f. L f. Gk *spēlaion* cave +-AN]

spelicans. See SPILLIKIN.

spĕll¹, n. Words used as charm, incantation or its effect (*under a* ~, mastered by or as by a ~); attraction, fascination, exercised by person, pursuit, quality, etc.; ~*'binder,* political speaker who can hold audiences ~bound; ~*'bound,* bound (as) by a ~. [OE *spel(l)*, OS, OHG *spel*, *spell*-, ON *spjall*, Goth. *spill*]

spĕll², v.t. (spelt or ~ed pr. -lt). Write or name the letters that form (a word), as *how do you ~ ' analyse '?, must not be spelt with a z, can't ~ his own name,* (abs.) *wish you would learn to ~* (*correctly*); ~ *out* or *over,* make out (words, writing) laboriously letter by letter; ~ *backward,* repeat or write the letters of (word) in reverse order, (fig.) misinterpret, pervert meaning of; (of letters) make up, form, (word), as *what does* c a t ~?; (fig., of circumstances, scheme, etc.) have as necessary result, involve, as *these changes ~ ruin to the farmer.* [ME, f. OF *espeler* f. WG *spellōn* discourse f. *spell*- (prec.)]

spĕll³, n., & v.t. 1. Turn of work, as *did a ~ of carpentering;* short period, as *wait* (*for*) *a ~.* 2. v.t. (rare). Relieve, take the place of, (person) in work etc. [later form of dial. *spele* f. OE *spelian,* of unkn. orig.; n. f. vb]

spĕll'er, n. In vbl senses of SPELL²; also = SPELLING-book. [-ER¹]

spĕll'ing, n. In vbl senses, as *his ~ is weak, not sure of the ~ of ' aneurysm ', another ~ of the same word;* ~*-bee,* competition in ~; ~*-book* (for teaching ~); ~*-pronunciation,* artificial pronunciation based on ~ (as *forehead* pron. fŏr'hĕd instead of fŏ'rĕd). [15th c.; -ING¹]

spĕlt¹, n. Kind of wheat giving very fine flour, German wheat. [OE *spelt,* OS *spelta,* OHG *spelza* f. LL *spelta*]

spĕlt². See SPELL².

spĕl'ter, n. (now commerc.). Zinc.

[corresp. to OF *espeautre,* MDu. *speauter,* LG *spialter;* rel. to PEWTER]

‖ **spĕnce, -se,** n. (arch.). Buttery, larder. [ME; aphetic f. OF *despense* (see DISPENSE)]

spĕn'cer¹, n. Short woollen jacket. [perh. f. Mr Knight S~ (fl. 1803)]

spĕn'cer², n. (naut.). = TRYSAIL. [orig. unkn.]

Spĕn'cerism, n. Doctrine of Herbert Spencer (d. 1903) referring the ordered universe to the necessary laws of mechanics, synthetic philosophy. So **Spĕncēr'IAN** a., **Spĕncēr'ianISM** n. [-ISM]

spĕnd, v.t. & i. (spent). 1. Pay out (money) for a purchase etc. (also abs., as ~ *profusely*); ~ *a penny* (colloq.), evacuate bladder or bowels; **~ing money,* pocket-money. 2. Use, use up, consume, as *our ammunition was all spent, shall ~ no more breath, trouble,* etc., *on him, how do you ~ your time?, spent a pleasant day;* exhaust, wear out, as *his anger will soon ~ itself, storm is spent, spent cannon-ball* (with little impulse left). 3. (naut.). Lose (mast). 4. Be consumed, as *candles ~ fast in draught.* 5. Emit spawn; *spent herring* etc. (that has deposited its spawn). 6. ~*'thrift,* extravagant person, prodigal, (often attrib.). Hence ~*'ABLE* a., ~*'ER¹* n. [OE *spendan,* (OS), OHG *spendōn,* ON *spenna,* f. L EX(*pendere* weigh); ME *spende* perh. also aphetic f. OF *despendre* (obs. *dispend,* cf. DISPENSE)]

Spĕn'low and Jŏrk'ins (-lō, -z), n. Plan of attributing one's (S.'s) hard dealings to a supposed hard partner (J.) kept in background. [persons in Dickens's *David Copperfield*]

‖ **spense.** See SPENCE.

Spĕnsēr'ian, a. & n. 1. Of the poet Edmund Spenser (d. 1599), esp. ~ *stanza,* that used in the *Faerie Queen.* 2. n. pl. ~ stanzas. [-IAN]

spent. See SPEND.

spĕrm¹, n. Male generative fluid. [ME, f. OF *esperme* or LL f. Gk *sperma -matos* seed]

spĕrm², n. (Also ~*-whale*) cachalot, whale yielding spermaceti; = foll.; ~*-oil,* lubricant from ~-whale. [abbr.]

spermacet'i, n. White brittle fatty substance contained in solution in heads of sperm-whale etc., used for candles & ointments. [med. L, f. *sperma* SPERM¹ + *ceti* of whale f. Gk *kētos* (~ being regarded as whale-spawn)]

spĕrm'ary, n. Male germ-gland, testicle or equivalent organ. [SPERM¹ +-ARY¹]

spĕrmăt'ic, a. Of SPERM¹ or the spermary. [f. OF *spermatique* or LL f. Gk *spermatikos* (as SPERM¹, see -IC)]

spĕrm'at|o-, comb. form of Gk *sperma* SPERM¹, as: ~*o- blast,* germ of a ~ozoon; ~*ogen'esis,* development of ~ozoa, so ~*ŏ'genous* a., ~*ŏ'geny* n.; ~*ŏl'ogist,* ~*ŏl'ogy,* student, study, of sperm, so ~*olō'gical* a.; ~*ophore,* capsule containing

~ozoa; ~orrhoe′a (-rēa), involuntary seminal discharge; ~ozō′ŏn (pl. -zōa), male fertilizing element contained in semen of animals, similar element in lower plants, so ~ozo′al, ~ozo′an, aa.

spěrm′|o-, irreg. comb. form (for prec.) of Gk sperma seed, semen, as: ~oblast = SPERMATOblast; ~ŏl′ogy, = SPERMATOlogy, (bot.) study of seeds, so ~olŏ′gical a., ~ŏl′ogist n.

spew, spūe, v.t. & i. Vomit (t. & i.); (of gun) droop at muzzle from too quick firing. [OE spīwan, spēowan, OS, OHG spīwan, ON spȳja, Goth. speiwan, cogn. w. L spuere]

sphă′cěl|āte, v.t. & i. Affect, be affected, with gangrene or necrosis. Hence ~A′TION n. [f. Gk sphakelos gangrene + -ATE³]

sphaer(o)-, comb. form of Gk sphaira SPHERE, in many scientific esp. nat. hist. terms.

sphăg′num, n. (bot.; pl. -na). Kinds of moss growing in bogs and peat, and used as packing etc. [mod. L, f. Gk sphagnos a moss]

sphěn′|(o)-, comb. form of Gk sphēn wedge, chiefly in sense 'of the sphenoid bone'; also: ~ogram, cuneiform character, so ~ograph′ic a.

sphěn′oid, a. & n. (anat.). Wedge-shaped, esp. ~ (bone), compound bone at base of skull. Hence sphēnoid′AL a., sphē- noid′o- comb. form. [f. Gk sphenoeidēs (sphēn wedge, -OID)]

sphēre, n., & v.t. 1. Solid figure gene- rated by revolution of semicircle about its diameter, every point on whose sur- face is equidistant from a point within called the centre. 2. Ball, globe; (poet.) the heavens, the sky; any heavenly body; globe representing the earth or the apparent heavens. 3. Each of the revolv- ing globe-shaped shells in which the heavenly bodies were formerly supposed to be set, esp. music, harmony, of the ~s (produced by movements of the ~s). 4. One's field of action, influence, or existence, one's natural surroundings, one's place in society, as has done much within his peculiar ~, earnest young lady in search of a ~, great mistake to take him out of his ~, moves in quite another ~, State's ~ (claimed or recognized area) of influence in Africa. 5. Celestial ~, surface on which heavenly bodies appear to lie; doctrine of the ~, spherical geometry & trigonometry; great, small, circle of ~, section made by plane passing, not pass- ing, through its centre; oblique, right, parallel, ~, ~ of apparent heavens at a place where there is oblique angle, right angle, no angle, between equator & horizon. 6. v.t. Enclose (as) in ~, make ~-shaped; (poet.) exalt to the (celestial) ~. Hence sphēr′y² a. (poet.). [ME sper(e) f. OF espere or LL sphera, L f. Gk sphaira ball]

sphě′ric, a. & n. 1. (Poet.) of the heavens,

celestial, exalted; (rare) = foll. 2. n. pl. Geometry & trigonometry of the sphere. [f. LL f. Gk sphairikos (as prec., see -IC)]

sphě′rical, a. Shaped like a sphere, globular, whence or cogn. ~LY² adv., sphěri′CITY n.; of spheres, as ~ geometry; ~ lune, triangle, polygon (bounded by arcs of great circles of sphere). [-AL]

spher′ograph (-ahf), n. Stereographic projection of the earth on disc, with meridians & parallels of latitude marked in single degrees. [SPHERE + -O- + -GRAPH]

spher′oid, n. Sphere-like but not per- fectly spherical body; solid generated by revolution of ellipse about its major (pro- late or oblong ~) or minor (oblate ~) axis, as the earth is an oblate ~. Hence sphē- roid′alLY² adv., sphěroid′(IC)AL aa., ~i′CITY n. [f. L f. Gk sphairoeidēs (as SPHERE, see -OID)]

sphěrŏm′eter, n. Instrument for finding radius of sphere & for exact measure- ment of thickness of small bodies. [f. F sphéromètre, see SPHERE, -METER]

sphě′rul|e (-ōōl), n. Small sphere. Hence ~AR¹, ~ATE²(2) (entom.), aa. [f. LL sphaerula (as SPHERE, see -ULE)]

sphě′rul|ite (-rōō-), n. Vitreous globule as constituent of some rocks. Hence ~it′IC a., ~itIZE(3) v.t. [f. prec. + -ITE¹]

sphinc′ter, n. Muscle surrounding & serv- ing to close an opening or tube. Hence ~AL, sphinctēr′IAL, sphinctě′rIC, aa. [LL, f. Gk sphigktēr (sphiggō bind tight)]

sphinx, n. 1. (Gk myth., S~) winged monster of Thebes with woman's head & lion's body who proposed a riddle to the Thebans, killed all who could not guess it, & on Oedipus' solving it threw herself from the rock on which she sat & died. 2. (Egypt. ant.) figure with lion's body & man's or animal's head (the S~, colossal ~ near the pyramids at Gizeh). 3. Enig- matic person (the ~ is silent). 4. Hawk- -moth; kind of baboon. [L, f. Gk sphigx, app. f. sphiggō draw tight]

sphragis′tics, n. pl. (often treated as sing.). Study of engraved seals. [f. F -ique or Gk sphragistikos (sphragis seal, -IC(2))]

sphyˇg′m|o-, comb. form of Gk sphugmos SPHYGMUS, as: ~ograph, instrument for showing character of pulse in series of curves, ~ogram, record so produced, so ~ograph′ic a., ~ŏg′raphy n.; ~ŏl′ogy, study of the pulse; ~omanŏm′eter, instru- ment for measuring blood-pressure; ~ophone, ~oscope, instrument for making audible, visible, the action of the pulse.

sphyˇg′mus, n. (physiol.). Pulse, pulsa- tion. [f. Gk sphugmos f. sphuzō throb]

spic′|a, n. (Bot.) spike, whence ~ATE², ~ātěd, aa.; (surg.) spiral bandage with reversed turns. [L, = spike, ear of grain]

spice, n., & v.t. 1. = Aromatic or pungent vegetable substance used to flavour food, e.g. cloves, pepper, mace; ~s collectively, as dealer in ~, sugar & ~ & all that's nice, so **spi'**CERY(1) n.; (fig.) smack, dash, flavour, (of malice etc. *in* person's character, writings, etc.); ~*'bush*, aromatic American shrub of laurel family. **2.** v.t. Flavour with ~. [ME, f. OF *espice* spice f. L SPECIES]

spick, a. ~ *&* *span*, smart & new, brand--new. [16th c. *spick & span new*, emphatic extension of ME *span new* f. ON *spán-nýr* = chip-new]

spic'ul|e, n. Small sharp-pointed body; (zool.) small hard body esp. in framework of sponge; (bot.) small or secondary spike. Hence ~AR[1], ~ATE[2](2), aa. [F, or f. mod. L *spicula*, L *spiculum*, see -ULE]

spi'c|y̆, a. Of, flavoured or fragrant with, spice; (fig.) piquant, pungent, improper (~*y story*), showy, smart. Hence ~ILY[2] adv., ~INESS n. [-Y[2]]

spid'er, n. **1.** Eight-legged animal of the order *Araneida*, many species of which spin webs esp. for capture of insects as food (~ *& fly*, fig., ensnarer & ensnared); kinds of arachnid like ~. **2.** Thing compared to ~ esp. as having prominent legs, e.g. kind of three-legged gridiron. **3.** Sulky with very large light wheels. **4.** ~-*catcher*, kinds of bird; ~-*crab*, crab with long thin legs; ~-*line*, thread of ~'s web substituted for wire in scales etc. for minute work; ~-*monkey*, kind with long limbs & long prehensile tail; ~-*wasp*, wasp that stores its nest with ~s for its young. Hence ~LIKE a., ~Y[2] a. (esp. of writing, legs, spokes, etc.) very thin. [OE *spīthra* (SPIN[1] + -*ther* agent suf.)]

spieg'eleisen (-līzn), n. Kind of cast iron containing manganese, much used in Bessemer process. [G (*spiegel* mirror f. L *speculum* + *eisen* iron)]

***spiel**, n., & v.i. & t. (sl.). **1.** Speech, story. **2.** v.i. Hold forth, orate; reel off (patter, yarn, tale of misfortune). [G, = play, game]

spif(f)'lic|āte, v.t. (sl.). Trounce, do for. Hence ~A'TION n. [fanciful]

spig'ot, n. Small peg or plug esp. one for insertion into gimlet-hole in cask; plain end of pipe fitting into socket of next one. [ME, perh. f. OPr. *espigot* f. *espiga* SPICA]

spike[1], n., & v.t. **1.** Sharp point; pointed piece of metal e.g. one of a set forming top of iron fence etc. or worn in bottom of shoe to prevent slipping; large stout nail esp. as used for railways; || (colloq.) a 'spiky' Anglican [back formation f. *spiky*]; ~ *plank*, bridge before mizzen--mast of vessel meant for arctic service. **2.** v.t. Fasten with ~s, furnish with ~s; fix on or pierce with ~; plug up vent of (gun) with ~, (fig.) make useless, *put an end to (idea etc.). Hence ~'WISE (-kw-) adv., **spik'y̆**[1] [-Y[2]] a. (also, colloq.) of hard unyielding ' high-church ' views. [ME, ult. f. L *spīca*, perh. thr. MSw. *spik*, Sw. & Norw. *spīk* nail]

spike[2], n. (bot.). Flower-cluster of many sessile flowers arranged closely on long common axis; separate sprig of any plant in which flowers form ~like cluster; [f. F *spic*] kind of lavender; ~ *oil* (got from lavender). Hence ~'LET (-kl-) n., **spik'y̆**[2] [-Y[2]] a. [f. L *spica* ear of corn, plant~]

spike'na̅rd (-kn-), n. (Ancient costly aromatic ointment made chiefly from) perennial herb allied to valerian; *plough-man's* ~, composite fragrant plant with purplish-yellow flower-heads; kinds of fragrant oil. [ME, f. med. L SPICA *nardi* (NARD)]

spile, n., & v.t. **1.** Wooden peg, spigot; large timber for driving into ground, pile. **2.** v.t. Make ~-hole in (cask). [f. MDu. or MLG *spile* wooden peg etc.; in sense *pile* app. alt. f. PILE[1]]

spil'ing, n. Set of piles; (naut.) edge--curve of plank in vessel's hull. [f. prec. +-ING[1]; naut. sense, earlier *spoiling*, orig. unkn.]

spill[1], v.t. & i. (*spilt* or ~*ed*), & n. **1.** Allow (liquid, substance in small particles) to fall or run out from vessel, as *spilt the salt*, *no use crying over spilt milk*, (of liquid etc.) fall or run out; ~ *blood*, be guilty of bloodshed, ~ *the blood of*, kill; ~ *money* (sl.), lose it in betting etc.; (naut.) empty (belly of sail) of wind; *~ *the beans* (sl.), give the show away, divulge information indiscreetly; throw from saddle or vehicle, as *horse spilt him*, *was spilt from a cycle*; ~ *over* (of surplus population of towns), cf. *overspill* n. **2.** n. Such throwing, as *had a nasty* ~; fall (e.g. from cycle); ~'*way*, passage for surplus water from dam. [OE *spillan*, = MDu., MLG *spillen*, rel. to syn. OE *spildan*, = OS *spildian*, OHG *spilden*]

spill[2], n. Thin strip of wood, spiral tube etc. of paper for lighting candles etc. [ME, of unkn. orig.; app. rel. to SPILE]

spill'er, n. Seine put into a larger one to take out fish when the larger cannot be hauled ashore. [orig. unkn.]

spill'ikin, n. Splinter of wood, bone, etc., used in some games; (pl., also *spĕl'icans*) game played with~s. [f. SPILL[2], see -KIN)]

spilt. See SPILL[1].

spilth, n. (arch.). What is spilt; excess, surplus. [-TH[1]]

spin[1], v.t. & i. (*spun* or *span*, *spun*). **1.** Draw out & twist (wool, cotton, or abs.) into threads; make (yarn) thus. **2.** (Of spider, silkworm, etc.) make (web, gossamer, cocoon, or abs.) by extrusion of fine viscous thread. **3.** Form (cup etc.) in lathe or similar machine. **4.** (fig.). Produce, compose, (narrative, literary article, etc.; often *out* i.e. at great length), esp. ~ *a yarn* (orig. naut.), tell a story. **5.** ~ *out*, spend, consume, (time, one's life, etc., *by* discussion etc., *in* occupation etc.), prolong (discussion etc.), (crick.) dismiss (batsman, side) by spin bowling. **6.** Cause (top etc.) to whirl round, (of top) whirl round, turn (person, thing) quickly round; (of person etc.) turn thus, e.g. as result of blow, as *sent him~ning*. **7.** Fish in (stream, pool) with swivel or spoon-bait. **8.** ‖ (sl.). Reject (candidate) after examination. **9.** p.p. (sl.). Tired out, done. **10.** *Spun glass* (spun when heated into filaments that remain pliant when cold); *spun gold, silver*, gold, silver, thread prepared for weaving; *spun silk*, cheap material of short-fibred & waste silk often mixed with cotton; *spun yarn* (naut.), line formed of rope-yarns twisted together. [OE, OHG, Goth. *spinnan*, ON *spinna*]

spin², n. Spinning motion, whirl; (aviation) diving descent combined with rotation; secondary revolving motion esp. as developed in rifle bullet, or in billiard or tennis ball struck aslant; (crick.) twisting motion given to ball when bowled (~ *bowler*, expert at this); brisk or short run or spell of driving, rowing, cycling, etc., as *went for a* ~; ~ *drier*, machine which dries clothes etc. by rapid spinning in a rotating aerated drum. [f. prec.]

spin'ach, -age, (-nǐj), n. Garden vegetable with thick succulent leaves used when boiled as food; other plants similarly used; ~ *beet*, kind of beet used like ~. Hence **spina'ceous** (-āshus) a. [prob. f. MDu. *spinaetse, spinag(i)e*, f. OF *espinage; (e)spinache*]

spin'al, a. Of the spine, as ~ *curvature, complaint*; ~ *column*, spine; ~ *cord*, cylindrical structure within ~ canal, a part of the central nervous system. [f. LL *spinalis* (SPINE, -AL)]

spin'dle, n., & v.i. **1.** Pin in spinning-wheel used for twisting & winding the thread; small bar serving same purposes in hand-spinning; pin bearing bobbin of spinning-machine; pin, axis, that revolves or on which a thing revolves; *live* (revolving) ~, *dead* (non-revolving) ~; slender thing or person; varying measure of length for yarn. **2.** ~*-shanked*, with long thin legs, ~*-shanks*, person with such legs; ~*-shaped*, of circular cross-section & tapering towards each end; ~*-tree*, shrub or small tree with greenish-white flowers and hard wood used for ~s; hence **spind'ly²** a., slender, attenuated. **3.** v.i. Have, grow into, long slender form. [OE *spinel*, = OHG *spin(n)ila*, f. SPIN¹ +-LE(1); cf. MHG, G *spindel*]

spin'drift, n. Spray blown along surface of sea; ~ *clouds*, light feathery clouds. [Sc. var. of *spoon-*, (*spoom-*) *drift*, f. (16th c., now obs.) *spoon* run before wind or sea, +DRIFT]

spin|e, n. The series of the vertebrae, backbone; (bot.) stiff sharp woody process due to degeneracy or modification of some organ; sharp ridge or projection; the part of a book's cover or jacket

visible when it is in place on a shelf; ~*e'back*, kinds of fish with ~es in or in front of dorsal fins. Hence ~ED² (-nd), ~'OSE¹, ~'OUS, aa., ~OS'ITY n. [ME, f. OF *espine* or L *spina* thorn, backbone]

spin'el, n. Kinds of mineral of various colours occurring in regular crystals; ~ *ruby*, valuable red variety. [f. F *spinelle*, f. It. *spinella*]

spine'less (-nl-), a. Having no spine, invertebrate; (fig.) limp, weak, having no backbone; (of fish) having no fin-spines. [-LESS]

spin'et (*or* -ĕt'), n. (hist.). Small wing-shaped harpsichord with one string to each note. [f. obs. *espinette* f. It. *spinetta*, prob. f. G *Spinetti*, inventor]

spin'|i-, comb. form of L *spina* thorn, backbone, as: ~*ice'rebrate*, having brain & spinal cord; ~*if'erous*, having or producing spines; ~*iFORM*.

spinn'aker, n. Large jib-shaped sail carried on mainmast of racing-yacht running before wind. [fanciful f. *Sphinx*, name of yacht first using it]

spinn'er, n. In vbl senses, esp.: thread-spinning machine; person who shapes vessels etc. in lathe; (also ~ET¹ n.) spinning-organ in spider, silkworm, etc. [ME; -ER¹]

‖ **spinn'ey,** n. (pl. ~s). Small wood, thicket. [f. OF *espinnei* (*espine*, see SPINE)]

spinn'ing, n. In vbl senses; ~*-house* (hist.), house of correction for prostitutes; ~*-jenny*, mechanism for spinning more than one strand at a time; ~*-machine*, (esp.) machine that spins fibres continuously; ~*-wheel* (hist.), household implement for spinning yarn or thread, with fly-wheel driven by crank or treadle. [ME; -ING¹]

Spinŏz'|ism, n. Doctrine of B. de Spinoza, a Spanish Jew (d. 1677), that there is one sole & infinite substance of which extension & mind are attributes & individual beings are changing forms. So ~IST n., ~is'TIC a. [-ISM]

spin'ster, n. Unmarried (esp. elderly in pop. use) woman. Hence ~HOOD n. [ME, orig.=woman who spins (SPIN¹, see -STER)]

spinthă'riscōpe, n. Screen of zinc blende showing incidence of alpha particles (of ALPHA *rays*) by fluorescent flash. [irreg. f. Gk *spintharis* spark +-SCOPE]

spin'ül|e, n. (bot., zool.). Small spine. Hence ~IF'EROUS, ~OSE¹, ~OUS, aa. [f. L *spinula* (as SPINE, see -ULE)]

spin'|y, a. Full of spines, prickly, esp. in names of animals, as ~*y crab, lobster, rat*; (fig.) perplexing, troublesome, thorny. Hence ~iNESS n. [-Y²]

spir'acle, n. (zool.). External orifice of trachea in insects; blow-hole of whales etc. Hence **spirăc'ūlAR¹, spirăc'ū-**lATE²(2), aa. [f. L *spiraculum* (also used in E) f. *spirare* breathe]

spirae'a, n. Kinds of rosaceous plant

with white or pink flowers. [L, f. Gk *speiraia* meadowsweet (*speira* coil)]

spir'al, a., n., & v.t. & i. (-ll-). **1.** Coiled; winding continually about & constantly receding from a centre, whether remaining in same plane like watch-spring or rising in a cone; winding continually & advancing as if along cylinder, like thread of screw; ~ *balance* (measuring weight by torsion of ~ spring); ~ *wheel* (with teeth cut at angle to axis). **2.** n. Plane or other ~ curve, ~ spring, ~ formation in shell etc.; (fig.) gradual but progressive rise or fall (*the vicious ~ of rising prices and wages*). **3.** vb. Make ~; move in a ~ course. Hence ~ITY (-ăl⁴) n., ~LY² adv. [f. med. L *spiralis* (as SPIRE², see -AL)]

spir'ant, a. & n. (phonet.). (Consonant) uttered with perceptible expulsion of breath & in producing which the organs are near together but not wholly closed, continuable (consonant) (cf. EXPLOSIVE), e.g. *f*, *v*, *th*, *dh*, & occas. *w*, *y*, & others. [f. L *spirare* breathe, see -ANT]

spire¹, n., & v.i. & t. **1.** Tapering structure in form of tall cone or pyramid rising above tower; continuation of tree trunk above point where branching begins; any tapering body, e.g. stalk of grass. **2.** v.i. Shoot up. **3.** v.t. Furnish with ~. Hence **spir'y²** a. [OE *spir*, MDu. *spier*, MLG, MHG *spir*]

spire², n. Spiral, coil; single twist of this. Hence **spir'y²** a. [F, or f. L f. Gk *speira* coil]

spirill'um, n. (pl. *-la*). Group of bacteria characterized by a spiral structure; any member of this. [mod. L, dim. of L *spira* SPIRE²]

spi'rit¹, n. **1.** Intelligent or immaterial part of man, soul; *in (the) ~*, inwardly, as *groaned in ~*, *was vexed in ~*, *shall be with you in (the) ~*. **2.** Person viewed as possessing this, esp. w. reference to particular mental or moral qualities, as *one of the most ardent ~s of his time*, *a meeting of choice ~s*; *a master-~*, person of commanding intellect etc. **3.** Rational or intelligent being not connected with material body, disembodied soul, incorporeal being, elf, fairy, as *God is a ~*, *the Holy S~* (third person of the Trinity), *has seen a ~*, *~s must have been at work*, ASTRAL~s, FAMILIAR~, *peace to his departed ~*. **4.** Person's mental or moral nature or qualities, as *a man of an unbending ~*; *the poor in ~*, the meek. **5.** Courage, self-assertion, vivacity, energy, dash, as *if you had the ~ of a mouse*, *do show a little ~*, *went at it with ~*, *infused ~ into his men*, *people of ~*. **6.** Person viewed as supplying this (= *soul*, but usu. w. adj.), as *was the animating ~ of the rebellion*. **7.** Mental or moral condition or attitude, mood, as *took it in a wrong ~*, *depends on the ~ in which it is done*, *did it in a ~ of mischief*, *objections made in a captious ~*. **8.** Real meaning opp. to verbal expres-

sion, as *must consider the ~ of the law*, *not the letter*, *have followed out the ~ of his instructions*. **9.** Animating principle or influence, mental or moral tendency, as *cannot resist the ~ of the age or times*. **10.** (Formerly) immaterial principle governing vital phenomena, whence (mod.) ANIMAL ~s; *high* or *great* ~s, cheerfulness & buoyancy; *poor* or *low* ~s, depression. **11.** (Usu. pl.) strong distilled liquor esp. alcohol, e.g. brandy, whisky, gin, rum, as *glass of ~s & water*, ARDENT~s, *touches no ~ but gin*. **12.** Solution (*of* volatile principle) in alcohol, tincture; ~s *of salt*, hydrochloric acid; ~ *or* ~s *of wine*, alcohol; METHYLATED ~. **13.** ~ *blue*, aniline blue soluble in alcohol; ~ *duck*, kinds of duck diving rapidly at flash of gun etc.; ∥~-*lamp* (burning methylated ~ instead of oil); ~-*level*, glass tube partly filled with ~ for testing horizontality; ~-*rapper*, person professing to hold intercourse with departed ~s by means of their raps on table etc., so ~-*rapping*; ~-*room* (naut.), paymaster's store-room, formerly used for ~s. [ME, f. AF *spirit(e)*, OF *esperit*, or L *spiritus* breath, spirit, f. *spirare* breathe]

spi'rit², v.t. Convey (usu. *away*, *off*, etc.) rapidly and secretly (as) by agency of spirits; cheer (person, usu. *up*). [f. prec.]

spi'rited, a. Full of spirit, animated, lively, brisk, courageous, as *a ~ translation*, *attack*, *reply*; having specified spirit, as *high*, *mean*, *proud*, *jealous*, *~*; having specified spirits, as *low-~*. Hence (-)~LY² adv., ~NESS n. [-ED²]

spi'ritless, a. Wanting in courage, vigour, or vivacity. Hence ~LY² adv. [-LESS]

spiritoso'õ, adv. (mus.). With spirit. [It.]

spi'ritual, a. & n. **1.** Of spirit as opp. to matter; of the soul esp. as acted on by God, as ~ *life*; of, proceeding from, God, holy, divine, inspired, as ~ *songs*, *the ~ law*; *the ~ man*, inner nature of man, (also esp. in N.T.) regenerate man (opp. to *natural*, *carnal*); concerned with sacred or religious things, as *our ~ interests*, ~ (ecclesiastical) *courts*, ~ *corporations*; *lords ~*, bishops & archbishops in House of Lords, cf. TEMPORAL; having the higher qualities of the mind. **2.** n. Religious song peculiar to American Negroes (also (*Negro ~*). Hence ~LY² adv., ~NESS n. [ME, f. OF *spirituel* or L *spiritualis* (as SPIRIT, see -AL)]

spi'ritual|ism, n. Belief that departed spirits communicate with & show themselves to men, esp. (also *modern ~ism*) at seances by means of spirit-rapping, -handwriting, etc., so **spi'ritism, spi'ritist**, nn.; (philos.) doctrine that spirit exists as distinct from matter or that spirit is the only reality (cf. MATERIALISM). Hence or cogn. ~IST n., ~is'tic a. [-ISM]

spiritual'it|y̆, n. Spiritual quality; (usu. pl.) what belongs or is due to the Church or to an ecclesiastic as such, as *the ~ies of his office, ~y of benefices*, tithes of land etc. [ME, f. OF (*e*)*spiritualite* or LL *spiritualitas* (as SPIRITUAL, see -TY)]

spi′ritūaliz|e, -is|e (-īz), v.t. Make spiritual, elevate, (character, person, thoughts); (rare) infuse life into, animate; attach spiritual as opp. to literal meaning to. Hence ~A′TION n. [f. SPIRITUAL +-IZE, or f. F *spiritualiser*]

spiritūĕl(le)′, a. (Chiefly of women) marked by refinement, grace, or delicacy of mind. [F, as SPIRITUAL]

spi′ritūous, a. Containing much alcohol, distilled not fermented, as ~ *liquors* (also used loosely of beer etc.). Hence ~NESS n. [f. L *spiritus* SPIRIT +-OUS, or f. F *spiritueux*]

spi′rĭtus, n. (Gk gram.). ~ *ăs′per, lēn′is*, = *rough, smooth,* BREATHING[1]. [L]

spīr′ivălve, a. Having spiral shell; (of shell) spiral. [F, f. L *spira* SPIRE[2] + *valva* VALVE]

spĭrk′ĕtĭng, n. (naut.). Inside planking between top of waterways & lower sills of ports. [f. obs. *spurkett* (17th c.), *spirkett* (18th c.), of unkn. orig.]

spīro-[1], comb. form of Gk *speira* coil, as ~*chaete* (-kēt′ē), spiral-shaped bacterium.

spīr′|o-[2] in comb. (irreg.)=L *spiro* breathe in sense 'breath', as: ~*ograph*, instrument for marking breathing movement; ~*ŏm′eter,* ~*oscope,* instrument for measuring lung capacity, so ~*omet′ric* a., ~*ŏm²etry* n.; ~*ophore,* instrument for inducing respiration in cases of suspended animation.

spĭrt, spŭrt, v.i. & t., & n. **1.** Gush out in a jet or stream; cause (liquid etc.) to do this. **2.** n. Sudden gushing out, jet. [vb 16th c., of unkn. orig.]

spit[1], n., & v.t. (-tt-). **1.** Slender bar on which meat that is to be roasted is made to rotate before fire; skewer; small point of land running into sea; long narrow underwater bank. **2.** v.t. Thrust a ~ through (meat etc.); (fig.) pierce, transfix, with sword etc. [OE *spitu*, MDu., MLG *spit*, OHG *spiz* (G *spiess*)]

spit[2], v.i. & t. (*spat* or arch. *spit*), & n. **1.** Eject saliva (|| ~ & *polish*, furbishing work of soldier etc.); eject (saliva, blood, food, etc. *out*) from mouth; (fig.) utter (oaths, threats, etc.) vehemently (~ *it out*, sl., exhortation to speak or sing louder); (of cat etc., fig. of person) make noise as of ~*ting* as sign of anger or hostility; (of rain) fall lightly, (of fire, candle, pen) send out sparks, stray ink, etc.; ~ *at* or *upon*, (fig.) treat with ignominy; ~*′fire,* person of fiery temper, (also ~*′devil*) toy cone of wet gunpowder ~*ting* when ignited. Hence ~t′ER[1] n. **2.** n. ~*ting* (esp. of cat), spawn of some insects; spittle; *the (very)* ~ *of* (exact counterpart of, likeness of, as *he is the very* ~ *of his father*). [OE *spittan* = G dial. *spitzen,* of imit. orig.; cf. OE *spætan* (whence

past & p.p. *spat*); ON *spŷta* = MHG *spiutzen*]

spit[3], n. Spade-depth (*dig it two ~s* or ~ *deep*). [f. MDu., MLG *spit,* also *spitten* dig, = OE *spittan,* dial. *spit* vb]

spitch′cŏck, n., & v.t. **1.** Eel split & broiled. **2.** v.t. Prepare thus (eel, fish, bird). [16th c., of unkn. orig.; cf. SPATCH-COCK]

spite, n., & v.t. **1.** Ill will, malice, as *did it from pure* ~ or *in* or *out of* ~; grudge, as *has a* ~ *against me*; *(in)* ~ *of,* notwithstanding. **2.** v.t. Thwart, mortify, annoy, as *does it to* ~ *me, cut off* one's *nose to* ~ one's *face,* injure oneself by vindictive or resentful conduct. Hence ~′FUL (-tf-) a., ~′fulLY² adv., ~′fulNESS n. [ME; aphetic f. *despite* n. & vb]

spit′tle, n. Saliva esp. as ejected from mouth. [alt. f. ME (now dial.) *spattle* (OE *spätl*), *spettle,* after SPIT²]

spittoon′, n. Vessel to spit into, usu. round metal or earthenware vessel with funnel-shaped top. [irreg. f. SPIT² +-OON]

spitz, n. (Also ~*-dog*) small kind of dog with pointed muzzle, Pomeranian. [G *spitz*(*hund*) f. *spitz* pointed, *hund* dog]

|| **spiv**, n. (sl.). Shady character who avoids honest work & lives by his wits esp. in black-market traffic. [orig. unkn.]

splänch′n|ic (-ngk-), a. Of the entrails, intestinal. So ~*o-* comb. form, ~*ŏl′ogy,* ~*ŏt′omy,* nn. [f. Gk *splagkhnikos* (*splagkhna* entrails, see -IC)]

splåsh, v.t. & i., & n. **1.** Bespatter (person etc. *with* water, mud, etc.); dash, spatter, (liquid *about, on* or *over* person etc.); (of liquid) fly about in drops or scattered portions; (of person) cause liquid to do this, make one's *way,* move *across, along,* etc., thus; step, fall, plunge, etc., *into* (water etc.) so as to ~ it; decorate with scattered ornamentation. **2.** n. ~*ing*; quantity of liquid ~ed; resulting noise, as *we heard a* ~; WATER¹~; || (colloq.) small quantity of soda-water etc. (diluting whisky etc.); spot of dirt etc. ~ed on to things; patch of colour esp. on animal's skin; *make a* ~, (fig.) attract much attention, create sensation; complexion powder usu. of rice-flour; ~*-board,* guard over or beside wheel of vehicle to keep mud off occupants; ~ *headline* (conspicuous, designed to attract attention). Hence ~′Y² a.[alt. f. PLASH²]

splåsh′er, n. In vbl senses; also : kinds of guard placed over wheels of locomotive etc. to keep off mud etc.; screen behind wash-stand to protect wall. [-ER¹]

splätt′er, v.i. & t. Make continuous splashing sound; speak (a language, or abs.) unintelligibly; ||~*-dash,* noise, clamour; ||~*-dashes,* = SPATTER*dashes.* [imit.]

splay, v.t. & i., n., & a. **1.** Construct (aperture) with divergent sides (~*ed loop-hole, window, doorway,* with opening wider at one side of wall), (of aperture or its sides) be so shaped or set; dislocate (esp. horse's shoulder). **2.** n. Surface making oblique angle with another, e.g. ~ed side of window, embrasure. **3.** adj. Wide & flat, turned outward; ~-*foot* n. & a., (having) broad flat foot turned outward; ~ *mouth*, wide mouth, mouth stretched wide in grimace. [aphetic f. DISPLAY vb]

spleen, n. **1.** Organ producing certain modifications in the blood of most vertebrates, situated in mammals at left of stomach. **2.** Lowness of spirits, ill temper, spite, as *a fit of* ~, *vented his* ~, whence ~'FUL, ~'ISH[1], ~'Y[2], aa., ~'fuLY[2], ~'ishLY[2], advv. **3.** ~'*wort*, kinds of fern formerly used for ~ disorders. Hence ~'LESS a. [ME, f. OF *esplen*, or L f. Gk *splēn*]

splēn|(o)-, comb. form of Gk *splēn* spleen, as : ~*āl'gia*, pain in (region of) spleen, so ~*āl'gic* a.; ~*ĕc'tomy*, excision of spleen; ~*ĭt'is*, inflammation of spleen, so ~*ĭt'ic* a.; ~*ŏl'ogy*, study of spleen, so ~*olō'gical* a.; ~*ŏt'omy* incision into, dissection of, spleen.

splĕn'dent, a. (mineral., entom.). Having bright metallic lustre. [ME, f. L *splendēre* shine, see -ENT]

splĕn'did, a. Magnificent, gorgeous, sumptuous, glorious, brilliant, as *a* ~ *palace, gift, achievement, victory*; (of person) affecting splendour (*in* surroundings etc.); (colloq.) excellent, capital, as *here is a* ~ *chance of escape.* Hence ~LY[2] adv. [f. F (-*ide*) or L *splendidus* (prec., -ID[1])]

splĕndif'erous, a. (colloq.). Splendid. [irreg. f. foll. + -FEROUS]

splĕn'dour (-der), n. Great or dazzling brightness; magnificence, grandeur; (her.) *sun in* ~ (with rays & human face). [ME, f. AF (*e*)*splend*(o)*ur* or L *splendor* (as SPLENDENT, see -OR)]

splĕnĕt'|ic, a. & n. **1.** Ill-tempered, peevish, whence ~ICALLY adv.; of the spleen. **2.** n. Medicine for, sufferer from, disease of the spleen. [f. LL *spleneticus* (as SPLEEN, see -ETIC)]

splĕn'ial, a. (anat.). Acting like a splint; of the splenius muscle. [f. L f. Gk *splēnion* + -AL]

splĕn'ĭc, a. Of, in, the spleen, as ~ *fever*, anthrax. So ~'OID a. [f. L f. Gk *splēnikos* (as SPLEEN, see -IC)]

splĕn'ius, n. (pl. -*iī*). (Either section of) muscle on back & sides of neck serving to draw back the head. [f. Gk *splēnion* bandage]

splēnizā'tion, -is-, n. Conversion of lung into substance resembling spleen. [f. F *splénisation* or mod. L *splenisatio* (SPLEEN, -IZE, -ATION)]

splice, v.t., & n. **1.** Join ends of (ropes) by interweaving strands; join (pieces of timber etc.) in overlapping position; (colloq.) join in marriage, as *when did he or they get* ~*d?*; ~ *the* MAIN[3] *brace.* **2.** n. Junction of two ropes or pieces of wood etc. by splicing; EYE[1]-~; *sit on the* ~ (crick.

sl.), play a cautious defensive game, stonewall. [f. MDu. *splissen* of uncert. orig.; perh. rel. to SPLIT]

spline, n., & v.t. **1.** Rectangular key fitting into grooves in hub & shaft of wheel & allowing longitudinal play; slat; flexible wood or rubber strip used in drawing large curves esp. in railway work. **2.** v.t. Fit with ~. [orig. E. Angl. dial., perh. for *splind*, & rel. to *splinder*, SPLINTER]

splint, n., & v.t. **1.** Strip of rigid or flexible material for holding broken bone when set or for basketwork etc.; (anat., also ~-*bone*) either of two small bones in horse's foreleg lying behind & in close contact with cannon-bone, (in man) fibula; tumour on, callus due to disease of, ~-bone of horse; ~-*coal*, cannel coal of slaty structure. **2.** v.t. Confine (broken limb etc.) with ~s. [ME *splent*(*e*), f. MDu. *splinte* or MLG *splinte, splente* metal plate or pin; cf. prec.]

splin'ter, v.t. & i., & n. **1.** Split (t. & i.) into long thin pieces, shiver. **2.** n. Sharp-edged or thin piece broken off from wood, stone, etc.; || ~-*bar*, cross-bar in vehicle supporting springs or to which traces are attached; ~-*bone*, fibula; ~ *party* (pol.), a party that has broken away from a larger one, esp. when very small in numbers; ~-*proof* (against ~s of bursting shells or bombs). [ME, f. MDu. (= LG) *splinter, splenter*; rel. to prec. & dial. *splinder*]

splin'tery, a. Of splinters; splinter-like; apt to splinter. [-Y[2]]

split[1], v.t. & i. (*split*). **1.** Break forcibly, be broken, into parts esp. with the grain or plane of cleavage. **2.** Divide into parts, thicknesses, etc., as ~ *it into three layers, the job, sum, etc., was* ~ (usu. *up*) *among 6 of us,* ~ *one's vote,* vote for opposed candidates, ~ *the difference,* take mean quantity etc. between two proposed; ~ *hairs,* draw over-subtle distinctions, so HAIR-~*ting.* **3.** Divide (t. & i.) into disagreeing or hostile parties (*on* question etc.). **4.** ~ (one's *sides* or intr.), be convulsed with laughter, so *side-*~*ting* a. & n., *side-*~*ter* (person or joke); *head is* ~*ting* (feels acute pain), *a* ~*ting* (acute) *headache.* **5.** ~ *on* (sl.), betray the secrets of (accomplice etc.). **6.** ~ *cloth* (surg.), bandage with several tails esp. for head & face; ~ *gear, wheel* (made in halves for removal from shaft); ~ *infinitive* (with adverb etc. inserted between *to* and verb, e.g. *seems to partly correspond*); ~ *moss,* kinds of which capsules ~ at maturity; ~*peas*(*e*) (dried & ~ in half for cooking); ~ *personality,* alteration or dissociation of personality such as may occur in some mental illnesses esp. schizophrenia and hysteria; ~ PIN[1]; ~ *ring* (usu. of steel on the pattern of those used for bunches of keys); ~ *second,* a very short period of time; ~ *shot, stroke,* stroke at croquet driving two touching balls in different directions. Hence (-)~tER¹(1, 2) n. [16th c., orig. naut., f. MDu. *splitten*, obsc. rel. to *spletten*, *spliten* (G *spleissen*), & E dial. *splet*, *spleet*]

split², n. **1.** Splitting; fissure, rent, crack. **2.** Separation into parties, schism, rupture. **3.** Split osier etc. for parts of basket-work; each of the strips of steel, cane, etc., of reed in loom; single thickness of split hide. **4.** (In faro) turning up of two cards of equal value so that stakes are divided. **5.** Half bottle of aerated water, half glass of liquor. **6.** pl. Trick of sitting on ground with legs spread out, as *do the* ~*s*. [f. prec.]

splŏsh, n. (colloq.). A quantity of water suddenly dropped or thrown down; ‖ (sl.) money. [imit.]

splŏtch, splŏdge, nn. Daub, smear. Hence **splŏtch′y**² a. [*-tch* f. 17th, *-dge* 19th, c.; perh. imit.]

*splŭrge, n., & v.i. (Make) noisy display or effort. [U.S. wd, prob. imit.]

splŭtt′er, v.i. & t., & n. = SPUTTER. Hence ~ER¹ n. [imit.; for *-l-* cf. SP(L)ATTER]

Spŏde, n. A fine pottery. [J. ~, maker, d. 1827]

spŏff′ish, a. (sl.). Bustling, fussy. [orig. unkn.]

spoil¹, n. **1.** (Usu. pl. or collect. sing.) plunder taken from enemy in war, (fig.) profit, advantage accruing from success in contest etc., (joc.) emoluments of public office etc. **2.** *~*s system*, practice of giving public offices to adherents of successful party, whence ~*s′man*, advocate of, one who seeks to profit by, this. **3.** A draw in the game of ~*-five*, in which each player has five cards. **4.** Earth etc. thrown or brought up in excavating, dredging, etc. [ME, f. OF *espoille*, or f. foll.]

spoil², v.t. & i. (~*t* or ~*ed*). **1.** (arch., literary) never ~*t*). Plunder, deprive (person *of* thing), by force or stealth, as ~ *the Egyptians* (persons regarded as one's natural enemies etc.; *Exod.* xii. 36). **2.** Impair the qualities of, or person's enjoyment of, as *was quite* ~*t by the rain*, *will* ~ *all the fun*, *always* ~ *a joke in the telling*, *the news* ~*t his dinner*, ~ *one's beauty for him* (with black eye etc.). **3.** Injure character of (person etc.) by indulgence, as *spare the rod & ~ the child*, *are determined to ~ me*, *is the ~t child of fortune*. **4.** Maim or kill or do for (person). **5.** (Of fruit, fish, etc., fig. of joke etc.) decay, go bad, as *will not* ~ *with keeping*, (only in part.) *dog is ~ing* (ripe, eager) *for a fight*. **6.** ~*-sport*, one who ~s sport. Hence ~′ER¹ n. [ME, f. OF *espoillier* f. L *spoliare* f. *spolium* spoil, plunder]

spoil′age, n. Paper spoilt in printing. [-AGE]

spŏke¹, n., & v.t. **1.** Each of the bars running from hub to rim of wheel, whence ~′WISE (-kw-) adv.; rung of ladder; each

radial handle of steering-wheel of vessel; bar used to prevent wheel from turning esp. in going down hill, as (fig.) *put a ~ in* person's *wheel*, thwart his purposes; ~*-bone*, radius of forearm; ~′*shave*, plane-bit between two handles, used for ~s & other esp. curved work where ordinary plane is not available. **2.** v.t. Furnish with ~s, check (wheel) with ~; *spoking-machine* (for giving uniform inclination to ~s of wheel). [OE *spāca*, OS *spēca*, OHG *speicha*]

spoke², spoken, -spoken. See SPEAK.

spōkes′man (-ks-), n. (pl. *-men*). One who speaks for others, representative. [irreg. f. SPOKE² + -ES + MAN]

spŏl′ia opīm′a, n. (Rom. ant.) arms stripped from hostile general by Roman commander in single combat; (fig.) supreme achievement or distinction. [L, = rich spoils]

spōliā′tion, n. Plunder, pillage, esp. of neutral vessels by belligerent, (fig.) extortion; (eccl.) taking of fruits of benefice under pretended title, *writ of ~* (for recovery of these); (law) destruction, mutilation, alteration, of document to prevent its being used as evidence. Hence or cogn. **spōl′iātŏr** n., **spŏl′iatory** a. [ME, f. L *spoliatio* (as SPOIL², see -ATION), or f. OF]

spŏndā′ic, a. Of spondees; (of hexameter) having spondee as fifth foot. [f. F *spondaique* or *spondaicus* = LL f. Gk *spondeiakos* (as foll., see -AC)]

spŏn′dee (-dī), n. Metrical foot – –. [ME, f. L f. Gk *spondeios* (*pous* foot) f. *spondē* solemn drink-offering; or f. OF *spondee*]

*spŏndŭl′icks, n. pl. (sl.). Money.

spŏn′dȳl‖(e), n. Joint of backbone, vertebra. Hence ~(o)- comb. form. [OF (*-le*), or f. L f. Gk *sp-*, *sphondulos*]

sponge¹ (-ŭnj), n. **1.** Aquatic animal of low order with pores in the body-wall, whence **spŏngŏL′OGIST, spŏngŏL′OGY,** (-ngg-), nn. **2.** Skeleton of a ~ or colony of ~s (whence **spo′ngiFORM** (-ŭnj-) a.), esp. elastic kind chiefly from the Levant used as absorbent in bathing, cleansing surfaces, etc.; *throw up the ~*, (of boxer or his attendant) throw into the air as token of defeat the ~ used between rounds, (fig.) abandon contest, own oneself beaten; *pass the ~ over*, agree to forget (offence etc.). **3.** Thing of ~like absorbency or consistence, e.g. piece of leavened dough, ~*-cake*, absorbent pad used in surgery, kind of mop for cleaning bore of big gun, iron or other metal in finely divided condition. **4.** (fig.) Parasite, person who contrives to live at another's expense. **5.** ~-BATH; ~*-cake*, light cake of ~like consistence; ~ *cloth*, soft loosely woven fabric with wrinkled surface; ~ *cucumber*, ~*-gourd*, *vegetable* ~, kind of gourd used in Turkish baths as rubber or towel, loofah; ~ *tent*, compressed ~ for keeping wound etc. open; ~*-tree*, spiny tropical leguminous shrub with globose heads of fragrant yellow flowers. [OE *sponge*, *spunge*, f. L f. Gk *spoggia* later var. of *spoggos*]

sponge[2] (-ŭnj), v.t. & i., & n. **1.** Wipe, cleanse, with sponge; sluice water over (parts of body etc., or abs., often *down*, *over*) with sponge; wipe out, efface, (writing, fig. memory of thing etc., usu. *out*) with sponge; absorb, take *up*, (water etc.) with sponge; gather sponges; procure by sycophantic arts; ~ *on*, live as the parasite of, be meanly dependent on (person *for* thing). **2.** n. Sponging, bath with sponge, as *had a ~ down*. Hence **spo'ng**ER[1](1, 2) (-ŭnj-) n. [ME, f. prec., or OF *esponger* f. LL *spongiare* (as prec.)]

spo'nging (-ŭnj-), n. In vbl senses; ~-*house* (hist., in arch. sense *squeezing*), bailiff's house for temporary lodging of arrested debtor. [-ING[1]]

spongiopil'ine (spŭnj-), n. Substitute for poultice made of sponge & fibre backed with rubber. [as SPONGE[1] + Gk *pilos* felt + -INE[4]]

spo'ng|y (-ŭnjĭ), a. Like sponge; porous, compressible, elastic, absorbent, as sponge; (of metal) finely divided & loosely coherent. Hence ~**iNESS** n. [-Y[2]]

spŏn'sion (-shn), n. Being surety for another; (internat. law) engagement made on behalf of State by agent not specially authorized. [f. L *sponsio* (*spondēre spons-* promise, see -ION)]

spŏn'son, n. Projection from side of warship to enable gun to be trained forward & aft; triangular platform before & abaft paddle-box. [orig. unkn.]

spŏn'sor, n., & v.t. **1.** Godfather or godmother; person who makes himself responsible for another; advertiser who pays for a broadcast or televised programme into which advertisements of his wares are introduced. **2.** v.t. Be~ for. Hence **spŏnsŏ'r**IAL a., ~**SHIP** n. [L (*spondēre spons-* promise, see -OR)]

spŏntān'eous, a. **1.** Acting, done, occurring, without external cause; voluntary, without external incitement, as *made a ~ offer of his services*; (of sudden movements etc.) involuntary, not due to conscious volition; growing naturally without cultivation; (biol., of structural changes in plants, muscular activity in esp. young animals) instinctive, automatic, prompted by no motive; (of bodily movements, literary style, etc.) gracefully natural & unconstrained. **2.** ~ *combustion*, ignition of mineral or vegetable substance (e.g. heap of rags soaked with oil, mass of wet coal) from heat engendered by rapid oxidation; ~ *generation*, production of living from non-living matter as inferred from appearance of life (due in fact to bacteria etc.) in some infusions; ~ *suggestion* (from association of ideas without conscious volition). Hence or cogn. **spŏntanē'**ITY, ~NESS, nn., ~LY[2]

adv. [f. LL *spontaneus* (*sponte* of one's own accord, see -ANEOUS)]

spŏntoon', n. (hist.). Kind of halberd used by some British infantry officers. [f. F *sponton* f. It. *spontone* f. *puntone*, *punto*, point]

spoof, v.t., & n. (sl.). Swindle, humbug, hoax; (attrib.) faked or fabricated. Hence ~**ER**[1] n. [invented by Arthur Roberts (d. 1933), comedian]

spook, n. (joc.). Ghost. Hence ~**'ISH**[1], ~**'Y**[2], aa. [f. Du. *spook*, G *spuk*]

spool, n., & v.t. **1.** Reel for winding yarn, photographic film, etc., on; revolving shaft of angler's reel. **2.** v.t. Wind on ~. [ME, f. ONF *espole* or its source, MDu. *spole*, *spoele*, (M)LG *spōle*]

spoon[1], n., & v.t. & i. **1.** Utensil consisting of round or usu. oval bowl & a handle for conveying esp. liquid food to mouth, usu. of silver or plated metal for table use (*tea*, *dessert*, *table*, ~~, of small, medium, large, size, esp. as recognized measure for medicine; APOSTLE ~, EGG[1], *salt*, *mustard*, ~~; *marrow*-~, for getting marrow from bones) & of wood or iron for cooking etc.; BORN *with silver ~ in mouth*; *long ~ & the devil* (see SUP); *wooden ~*, (wooden ~ given to) last man in Cambridge mathematical tripos (hist.), (fig.) booby prize; EGG[1]-*&*-~ *race*; ~-shaped thing, esp. (oar with) broad curved blade, wooden golf-club with more loft than driver & brassie. **2.** ~ (-*bait*), bright revolving ~-shaped piece of metal used as lure in fishing; ~'*beak*, -*bill*, kinds of bird; ~-*drift*, see SPINDRIFT; ~-*fed*, (fig., of industries etc.) artificially encouraged by bounties or import duties, (of pupil) crammed with information; ~-*meat*, liquid food, food for infants (also fig.); ~-*net*, angler's landing-net. **3.** vb. Take (liquid etc., usu. *up*, *out*) with ~; fish with ~-*bait*; (croquet) make pushing stroke; (crick.) strike (ball) feebly, send *up* (ball, a catch) thus, with bat. Hence (-)~'FUL n. [OE *spōn* chip of wood, = (M)LG *spān*, ON *spónn*; cf. OHG *spān*, ON *spánn*]

spoon[2], n., & v.i. & t. (sl.). **1.** Simpleton; silly or demonstratively fond lover; *be ~s on*, be sillily in love with. **2.** vb. Behave amorously, behave thus towards (girl etc.). [f. prec.]

spoon'er(ism), n. Accidental transposition of initial letters etc. of two or more words (e.g. *has just received a blushing crow*, for real enjoyment give me a well-*boiled icycle*). [f. Rev. W. A. Spooner (d. 1930), esteemed for ~s, +-ISM]

spoon'|y, a., & n. (sl.). 1. Soft, silly; sentimental, amorous, sweet (*up*)on. **2.** n. Mild simpleton. Hence ~**iLY**[2] adv., ~**i**-NESS n. [prob. f. SPOON[2], -Y[2]]

spoor, n., & v.t. & i. **1.** Track, scent, of animal. **2.** vb. Follow by ~. Hence ~**'ER**[1] n. [Du. (S.A.) *spoor*, = G *spur*]

sporăd'ic, a. Occurring only here & there,

separate, scattered. Hence ~AL a. (rare), ~ALLY² adv., ~alNESS n. [f. med. L f. Gk *sporadikos* (*sporas -ados* scattered, cf. *speirō* sow, see -IC)]

sporăn'gium, n. (bot.). Case in which spores are produced. [f. Gk *spora* SPORE + *aggeion* vessel]

spōre, n. (Bot., in cryptogamous plants) single cell that becomes free & capable of individual development; (biol.) minute organic that develops into new individual; (fig.) seed, germ, of anything. [f. Gk *spora* sowing, seed, f. *speirō* SOW]

spōr|o-, comb. form of Gk *spora* SPORE, as: ~*ogen'esis*, spore-formation; ~*ŏ̆'genous*, producing spores.

spö'rran, n. Pouch, usu. covered with fur etc., worn by Highlander in front of kilt. [f. Gael. *sporan*]

spŏrt, n., & v.i. & t. **1.** Amusement, diversion, fun; *in* ~, jestingly; *make* ~ *of*, turn into ridicule, make fun of; *be the* ~ (plaything, butt) *of Fortune* etc.; pastime, game; outdoor pastime, e.g. hunting, fishing, racing; *have good* ~, esp. make good bag or basket when shooting etc.; *athletic* ~s, running, jumping, putting weight, etc., meeting of athletes to compete in these, as *school* ~s, *inter-university* ~s (~s *coat*, *jacket*, giving freedom of movement; ~s *field*; ~s *car*, for racing); animal, plant, deviating suddenly or strikingly from normal type; (sl.) good fellow, ~sman; ~s'man, ~s'woman, person fond of ~s esp. hunting, shooting, or fishing, (fig.) person who regards life as a game in which opponents must be allowed fair play, person ready to play a bold game, whence ~s'manship n.; ~s'man-like, befitting, worthy of, a ~sman. **2.** vb. Divert oneself, take part in pastime; (part.) interested in ~, as *a* ~*ing man*, ~smanlike, as ~*ing conduct*, ~*ing offer*, whence ~'ingLY² adv.; (bot., zool.) become or produce a ~; wear, exhibit, produce, esp. ostentatiously, as ~*ed a gold tie-pin*; || ~ *one's* OAK. [ME; aphetic f. DISPORT]

spŏrt'ive, a. Playful. Hence ~LY² adv., ~NESS n. [-IVE]

spö'rŭl|e, n. Spore; small spore. Hence ~AR¹ a. [F, or f. mod. L *sporula* (SPORE, -ULE)]

spŏt¹, n. **1.** Particular place, definite locality, as *dropped it on this precise* ~, *the* ~ *where William III landed*; *a tender* ~, (fig.) subject on which one is touchy. **2.** Small part of the surface of a thing distinguished by colour, texture, etc., usu. round or less elongated than a streak or stripe, small mark or stain, pimple, as *a blue tie with pink* ~s, SUN-~, *can the* LEOPARD *change his* ~s?; (fig.) moral blemish, stain, as *without a* ~ *on his reputation*. **3.** Kinds of fish & domestic pigeon. **4.** (sl.). Act of spotting winner etc.; horse etc. so spotted. **5.** (colloq.).

Small quantity of anything (*a* ~ *of leave*, *lunch*); a drink. **6.** (billiards). Small round black patch near each end of table equidistant from sides; || ~-*stroke*, pocketing red ball when placed on ~ remote from balk; || ~-*barred game* (in which successive ~-strokes are not allowed); ~ (*-ball*), white ball distinguished from the other by black ~. **7.** *On the* ~, without delay or change of place, then & there, (of person) wide awake, equal to the situation, in good form at game etc.; *put on the* ~ (sl.), decide on the assassination of, murder. **8.** (commerc.). ~ *cash*, *cotton, wheat, prices* (to be paid or delivered immediately on sale); ~s, commodities sold for ~ cash. **9.** ~'*light* (theatr.), beam of light thrown on a particular actor, or the projector used for this purpose (also fig., as LIMELIGHT). Hence ~'LESS, ~t'Y², aa., ~'lessLY² adv., ~'lessNESS, ~t'iNESS, nn. [ME = MDu. *spotte*, *spot*, ON *spotti*]

spŏt², v.t. & i. (-tt-). **1.** Mark, stain, soil, with spots (lit., & fig. of character etc.); (of material etc.) be (liable to be) marked with spots. **2.** (colloq.). Single out beforehand (winner of race etc., horse etc. as winner *for* event); detect, recognize nationality etc. of, as ~*ted him at once as an American, can always* ~ *a dun*. **3.** (mil.). Locate (enemy's position), esp. from the air; whence ~t'ER¹ n., airman detailed for such work, also person trained in aircraft recognition. **4.** (p.p.). Marked with spots, esp. in names of animals; || ~*ted dog* (sl.), = PLUM *duff*; ~*ted fever*, cerebro-spinal meningitis. Hence ~t'édNESS n. [ME, f. prec.]

spouse (-z), n. Husband or wife. [ME & OF *sp(o)us*, *sp(o)use*, varr. of OF *espus* masc., -*se* fem., f. L p.p. of *spondēre*, see ESPOUSE]

spout, v.t. & i., & n. **1.** Discharge, issue, forcibly in a jet, as *blood* ~s *from wound*, *wounds* ~ *blood*, *whale* ~s *water*; utter (verses etc., or abs.) in declamatory manner, speechify; (sl.) pawn. **2.** n. Projecting tube through which liquid etc. is poured from teapot, kettle, gutter of roof, etc.; sloping trough down which thing may be shot into receptacle, esp. shoot in pawnbroker's shop, as *his watch is up the* ~ (in pawn); jet, column, of liquid or grain etc.; WATER¹-~; (also ~-*hole*) spiracle of whale. Hence ~'ER¹ n., ~'LESS a. [ME, of doubtful orig.; cf. Du. *spuit*, MDu. *spouten*; stem *spūt*- also in ON *spyta* SPIT²]

spräg, n. Billet of wood or similar device for checking wheel of car etc. [orig. unkn.]

sprain, v.t., & n. **1.** Wrench (ankle, wrist, etc.) violently so as to cause pain & swelling but not dislocation. **2.** n. Such wrench, resulting inflammation & swelling. [17th c., of unkn. orig.]

|| **spraints**, n. pl. Otter's dung. [ME, f.

OF *espraintes* f. *espraindre* squeeze out f. L EX(*primere* = *premere* press)]

sprang. See SPRING[1].

sprăt, n., & v.i. (-tt-). **1.** Small European herring-like fish much used as food; other kinds of fish, e.g. sand-eel, young herring; *throw a ~ to catch a herring* or *mackerel* or *whale*, risk a little to gain much; (joc.) thin child; ‖ *~-day*, Nov. 9, on which *~* season begins in England. **2.** v.i. Fish for *~*s, whence *~*t*'ER*[1], *~*t*'ING*[1], nn. [later form of OE *sprot*, = MDu., MLG *sprot*]

sprawl, v.i. & t., & n. **1.** Spread oneself, spread (one's limbs), out in careless or ungainly way; (of writing, plant, etc.) be of irregular or straggling form; open out (troops) irregularly. **2.** n. *~*ing movement or attitude. [OE *spreawlian*, = NFris. *spraweli*]

spray[1], n. Branch of tree with branchlets or flowers, esp. slender or graceful one, sprig of flowers or leaves; ornaments in similar form, as *a ~ of diamonds* etc.; *~-drain*, drain in field etc. made by filling trench with branches. Hence *~'ey*[1] a. [cf. CLAYEY]. [ME, of unkn. orig.]

spray[2], n., & v.t. **1.** Water or other liquid flying in small drops from force of wind, dashing of waves, or action of atomizer etc.; medical or other liquid preparation to be applied in this form with atomizer etc. **2.** v.t. Throw (liquid, or abs.) in form of *~*, sprinkle (object) thus, esp. fruit-trees etc. with insecticides. **3.** *~'board* (on boat's gunwale to keep off *~*). Hence *~'ER*[1](1, 2) n., *~'ey*[2] a. [n. (17th c.) app. rel. to MDu. *sprayen*, = MHG *spræjen*, to sprinkle]

spread[1] (-ĕd), v.t. & i. (*spread*). **1.** Extend the surface of, cause to cover larger surface, by unrolling, unfolding, smearing, flattening out, etc., (fig.) display thus to eye or mind, as *peacock ~s its tail*, *~ oneself* (sl., = talk bumptiously), *~ a banner*, *~ out a rug on the grass*, *~ butter on bread*, *map lay ~ out on the table*, *the view ~ out before us*, whence *~'ER*[1](2) n. **2.** Show extended or extensive surface, as *river here ~s out to a width of half a mile*, *on every side ~ a vast desert*, *~ing yews*. **3.** Diffuse, be diffused, as *his name ~ fear in every quarter*, *rumour ~ from mouth to mouth*, *has ~ a malicious report*. **4.** Cover surface of, as *slices of bread ~ with jam*, *a table ~ with every luxury*, *meadow ~ with daisies*. **5.** *~ eagle*, figure of eagle with legs & wings extended as seen on coins etc., skating movement on both inside edges at once one forward & the other back, (colloq.) fowl split open down the back & broiled, (naut.) person lashed in rigging with arms and legs *~* out as punishment, (v.t., *~-eagle*) lash (man) thus, *~ out*, outrun, (adj., *~-eagle*) bombastic, esp. noisily patriotic, whence *~-ea'gleism* n. **6.** *~-over* (*system*), elasticity in accommodating restricted work-hours

to special needs. [OE *sprǣdan*, MDu., MLG *sprēden*. OHG *spreitan*; ult. orig. unkn.]

spread[2] (-ĕd), n. Spreading; capability of expanding, as *inferior to the eagle in ~ of wings*; increased bodily girth, as *middle--age(d) ~*; breadth, compass, as *arches of equal ~*; diffusion (*of* education etc.); (colloq.) feast, meal, as *had no end of a ~*; *(commerc.) difference between cost of manufacture & selling price. [f. prec.]

spree, n., & v.i. Lively frolic, bout of drinking etc., as *is on the* (having a) *~*; *buying ~*, bout of lavish spending; (v.i.) *háve a ~*. [19th-c. sl., orig. unkn.]

‖ **sprĕnt,** a. (arch.). Sprinkled, overspread, (*with* drops, particles, etc.). [p.p. of obs. *sprenge* f. OE *sprengan* make SPRING[1]]

sprig, n., & v.t. (-gg-). **1.** Small branch, shoot; ornament of *~* form; small tapering headless tack; (usu. derog.) youth, young man, as *who is this ~?*, *a ~ of* (*the*) *nobility*. **2.** v.t. Ornament with *~*s, as *~ged muslin*. **3.** *~'tail*, kinds of duck & grouse with pointed tail. Hence *~g'r*[2] (-g-) a. [sense *nail* f. 14th, *shoot* f. 15th, c.; two unrelated wds of unkn. orig.]

spright'l|ỹ (-ĭt-), a. Vivacious, lively, gay. Hence *~*iNESS n. [f. *spright*, var. of SPRITE + -LY[1]]

spring[1], v.t. & t. (*sprang*, *sprung*). **1.** Leap, jump, move rapidly or suddenly, (often *up*, *down*, *out*, *over*, *through*, *away*, *back*, etc.), as *sprang* (*up*) *from his seat*, *sprang through the gap*, *at his throat*, *to their assistance*, *blood sprang to her cheeks*. **2.** Move rapidly as from constrained position or by action of a spring, as *branch sprang back*, *door sprang to*. **3.** Come into being (usu. *~ up*), arise (often *from* source), appear, as *a breeze sprang up*, *the piers from which the arches ~*, *is sprung from* or *of a royal stock*, *the buds are ~ing*, *the belief has sprung up*, *his actions ~ from a false conviction*; (to person arriving suddenly or unexpectedly or whose presence is only now realized) *where do* or *did you ~ from?* **4.** (Of wood) warp; (t. & i. of wood) split, crack, as *bat is* or *has sprung*, *have sprung my racket*. **5.** p.p. (colloq.). Tipsy. **6.** Rouse (game) from earth or covert. **7.** Cause to act suddenly by means of a spring, produce or develop suddenly or unexpectedly, as *~ a trap*, *has sprung a new theory*, *loves to ~ surprises on us*. **8.** Provide (motor vehicle etc.) with springs (usu. as p.p.). **9.** Cause (mine) to burst. **10.** (naut.). (Of ship) *~ a butt*, loosen end of plank by labouring in heavy sea, *~ a leak*, develop leak from starting of timbers, ‖ *~ the* or *her luff*, yield to helm & sail nearer to wind. [OE, OS, OHG *springan*, ON *springa*]

spring[2], n. **1.** Leap, as *took a ~*, *rose with a ~*. **2.** Season in which vegetation begins, the first season of the year, (astron., from vernal equinox to summer solstice). **3.** Place where water or oil wells up from earth, basin so formed, as *hot, mineral,* ~*s.* **4.** Backward movement from constrained position, recoil, e.g. of bow. **5.** Elasticity, as *his muscles have no* ~ *in them.* **6.** Elastic contrivance usu. of bent or coiled metal used esp. as motive power in clockwork etc. or for preventing jar as in vehicle, as *bow* ~ (bow-shaped), CEE ~, *air* or *pneumatic* ~ (working by compression of air), HAIR-~, MAIN²-~. **7.** (fig.). Motive actuating person etc., source, origin, as *the* ~*s of human action, the custom had its* ~ *in another country.* **8.** Upward curve of beam etc. from horizontal line. **9.** Starting of plank. **10.** Springing of leak. **11.** Mooring-rope. **12.** pl. Period of ~ tide. **13.** ~ *balance* (measuring weight by tension of ~); ~-*beam,* beam stretching across wide space without intermediate support, elastic bar used as ~ in tilt-hammer etc.; ~ *bed, mattress,* mattress formed of spiral ~s in wooden frame; ~-*board,* elastic board giving impetus in leaping, diving, etc.; ~-*carriage, -cart* (mounted on ~s); ~-*clean* v.t., clean (house, room) thoroughly, esp. in ~; ~-*cleaning* n.; ~ *gun* (contrived to go off when trespasser or animal stumbles on it); ~-*halt,* convulsive movement of horse's hind leg in walking; ~ *tide,* high tide occurring shortly after new & full moon in each month; ~'*tide* (poet.), ~'*time,* season of ~; ~ *water* (from ~, opp. to river or rain water). Hence ~'LESS, ~'LIKE, aa., ~'LET n. [OE, f. prec.]

|| **spring'al(d),** n. (arch.). Youngster. [15th c., perh. f. SPRING¹]

spring'bŏk, n. S.-Afr. gazelle with habit of springing in play or when alarmed; S~s, (nickname for) S. Africans, S.-African football team etc. [Afrikaans]

springe (-j), n. Noose, snare, for small game. [ME, app. repr. OE *sprencg,* rel. to obs. *sprenge* factitive f. SPRING¹]

spring'er, n. In vbl senses; also or esp.: (archit.) part of arch where curve begins, lowest stone of this part, bottom stone of coping of gable, rib of groined roof or vault; kind of field spaniel used to spring game; grampus; springbok. [-ER¹]

spring'|y̌, a. (Of movement or substance) elastic. Hence ~INESS n. [-Y²]

sprinkle (spring'kl), v.t. & i., & n. **1.** Scatter (liquid, ashes, crumbs, etc.) in small drops or particles, whence **sprink-**LER¹(2) n.; subject (ground, object) to sprinkling (*with* liquid etc.); (of liquid etc.) fall thus on. **2.** n. Light shower (*of* rain etc.), so **sprink'ling¹**(2) n. (esp., fig., *a* few here & there) *of*. [ME also *sprenkle,* rel. to Du. *sprenkelen,* LG *sprinkeln,* MDu. *sprenkel, sprinkel*]

sprint, v.i. & t., & n. **1.** Run short distance, run (specified distance), at full speed. **2.** n. Such run. Hence ~'ER¹ n. [f. early Scand. *sprinta,* cf. ON *spretta*]

sprit, n. Small spar reaching diagonally from mast to upper outer corner of sail; ~'*sail* (-săl, -sl), sail extended by ~, (formerly) sail extended by yard set under bowsprit. [OE *sprēot* pole, MDu., MLG *spriet, sprel,* cogn. w. SPROUT]

sprite, n. Elf, fairy, goblin. [ME, f. OF *esprit,* or similarly reduced f. OF *esperil(e), AF *spiril(e)* SPIRIT]

sprŏck'ĕt, n. Each of several teeth on wheel engaging with links of chain; ~-*wheel,* such wheel, e.g. for engaging bicycle chain. [16th c., of unkn. orig.]

sprout, v.i. & t., & n. **1.** Begin to grow, shoot forth, put forth shoots; spring up, grow to a height; produce by ~ing, as *has* ~*ed horns, a moustache.* **2.** n. Shoot of plant; BRUSSELS ~*s.* [OE *sprūtan,* MDu., MLG *spruten,* MHG *spriezen;* rel. to OE *spryttan*]

spruce¹ (-ōos), a., & v.t. **1.** Neat in dress & appearance, trim, smart. **2.** v.t. Smarten (oneself etc., usu. *up*). Hence ~'LY² adv., ~'NESS n. [perh. f. foll., in the collocation *spruce (leather) jerkin*]

spruce² (-ōos), n. Coniferous tree related to pine; (also ~ *fir*) kinds of fir; ~-*beer* (made from leaves and small branches of ~, useful as antiscorbutic). [alt. f. AF (ME, now obs.) *Pruce* Prussia; cf. med. L *Sprucia*]

sprue¹ (-ōo), n. Passage through which metal is poured into mould; metal filling ~. [19th c., of unkn. orig.]

sprue² (-ōo), n. Tropical disease (also *psilosis*) with ulcerated mucous membrane of mouth & chronic enteritis. [f. Du. *spruw* THRUSH² (*Indische spruw* = psilosis)]

spruit (-răt), n. (S. Africa). A small watercourse, usu. almost dry except in the wet season. [Du. *spruit* cogn. w. SPROUT]

sprung. See SPRING¹.

sprȳ, a. (~*er,* ~*est*). Active, lively. [18th c., dial. & U.S., of unkn. orig.]

spŭd, n., & v.t. (-dd-). **1.** Kinds of small spade for cutting roots of weeds etc.; short thick thing, whence ~d'Y³ a.; (sl.) potato. **2.** v.t. Remove (weeds, often *up, out*) with ~. [ME; orig. unkn.]

|| **spŭd'dle,** v.i. (dial.). Dig lightly, dig about, (of amateur gardeners etc.). [orig. alt. of *puddle;* now assoc. w. prec.]

spue. See SPEW.

spŭm|e, n., & v.i. Froth, foam. Hence ~ēs'CENCE, ~'INESS, nn., ~ES'CENT, ~'OUS, ~'Y², aa. [ME, f. OF (e)*spume* or L *spuma*]

spun. See SPIN¹.

spunge. (Arch. for) SPONGE.

spŭnk, n. (colloq.). Courage, mettle, spirit; anger. Hence ~'Y² a. [16th c. 'spark, tinder', prob. rel. to obs. *funk* & PUNK²]

spŭr, n., & v.t. & i. (-rr-). **1.** Pricking instrument with point or (also *rowel-*~) rowel worn on horseman's heel (*put or *set* ~*s to*, = ~ vb; *need the* ~, be sluggish, also of persons); *win* one's ~*s*, (hist.) gain knighthood, (fig.) gain distinction, make a name; (fig.) stimulus, incentive; *on the* ~ *of the moment*, impromptu, on a momentary impulse; ~-shaped thing, e.g. hard projection on cock's leg, steel point fastened to this in cockfight, projection from mountain (range), climbing-iron, wall crossing part of rampart and joining it to interior work, slender hollow projection from some part of flower. **2.** ‖ ~ *royal*, coin of James I bearing ~like sun with rays; ~-*wheel*, cog-wheel with radial teeth; ~'*wort*, plant with whorls of leaves like rowel of ~. **3.** vb. Prick (horse) with ~s (~ *a willing horse*, fig., be needlessly importunate), incite (person *on to* effort, *to* do, etc.), furnish (person, boots, gamecock, esp. in p.p.) with ~s; (intr.) ride hard (*on*, *forward*, etc.). Hence ~'LESS a. [OE *spora*, *spura*, OS *spora*, OHG *sporo*, ON *spori*; cf. SPURN]

spŭrge, n. Kinds of plant with acrid milky juice. [ME, f. OF *espurge* (*espurgier* purge, as EXPURGATE)]

spŭr′ious, a. Not genuine, not being what it pretends to be, not proceeding from the pretended source, as ~ *coin*, (*reading in*) *MS.*, *affection*; (zool.) resembling an organ etc. but not having its function, having the function of organ etc. but morphologically different, as ~ *eyes*, *legs*. Hence ~LY² adv., ~NESS n. [f. L *spurius* + -OUS]

‖ **spŭrl′ing-line**, n. (naut.). Line from steering-wheel to telltale in cabin for showing position of helm. [orig. unkn.]

spŭrn, v.t. & i., & n. **1.** Repel, thrust back, with foot; (also arch. ~ *at*) reject with disdain, treat with contempt, (offer, advances, person, rejection, etc.). **2.** n. ~ing, contemptuous rejection. [OE *spurnan*, *spornan*, prob. f. stem of SPUR]

spŭr′rier (*or* spŭ²), n. Spur-maker. [-IER]

spŭ′rrÿ, **-rey**, n. Kinds of herb of pink family, esp. *corn*-~, a weed in cornfield etc. [f. Du. *spurrie*, prob. rel. to med. L *spergula*]

spŭrt¹, v.i., & n. (Make) short sudden violent effort esp. in racing. [var. of SPIRT in same sense]

spurt². See SPIRT.

sput′nik (-ōot-), n. Russian earth SATELLITE. [Russ., = travelling companion]

spŭtt′er, v.t. & i., & n. **1.** Emit with spitting sound; speak, utter, (words, threats, a language, etc.) rapidly or incoherently; speak in hurried or vehement fashion (often *at* person etc.). **2.** n. Such speech. Hence ~ER¹ n., ~ingLY² adv. [16th c., = Du. *sputteren*, imit.]

spū′tum, n. (pl. *-ta*). Saliva, spittle; expectorated matter esp. as diagnostic of disease. [L, neut. p.p. of *spuere* spit]

spÿ, n., & v.t. & i. **1.** Person who goes, esp. in disguise, into enemy's camp or

territory to inspect works, watch movements, etc., & report the result; person who keeps (esp. secret) watch on movements of others, as *refuse to be a* ~ *on his conduct*. **2.** v.t. Discern, make out, esp. by careful observation, as *spied a horseman approaching*, *is quick at* ~*ing his neighbours' faults*, *I* ~ STRANGERS; ~ *out*, explore secretly, discover by this means; (v.i.) play the ~, keep close & secret watch (*upon* person, movements, etc., *into* secret etc.); ~'*glass*, small telescope; ~'*hole*, peep-hole. [ME *spie* n., *spien* vb, f. OF *espie* n., *espier* vb ESPY]

squab (-ŏb), a., adv., & n. **1.** Short & fat, squat, whence ~b′y² (-ŏ-) a. **2.** adv. With heavy fall, as *come down* ~ *on the floor*. **3.** n. Short fat person; young esp. unfledged pigeon; stuffed cushion; ottoman; ~-*chick*, unfledged bird; ~ *pie*, pigeon-pie, pie of mutton, onions, & apples. [17th c., of unkn. orig.; cf. obs. *quab* shapeless thing, Sw. dial. *squabba*, Norw. dial. *skvabb* in similar senses]

squa′bbl|e (-ŏ-), v.i. & t., & n. **1.** Engage in petty or noisy quarrel (*with* person *about* thing); (print.) disarrange (composed type). **2.** n. Petty or noisy quarrel. Hence ~ER¹ n. [prob. imit., cf. Sw. dial. *skvabbel* n. dispute]

squăcc′ō, n. (pl. ~s). Small crested heron of S. Europe, Africa, & Asia. [f. It. *sguacco*]

squad (-ŏd), n. (Mil.) small number of men assembled for drill etc. (~ *drill*, elementary); *awkward* ~ (of recruits not yet competent to take place in regimental line, also fig.); small party of persons; FLYING ~. [f. F *escouade* var. of *esquadre* f. It. *squadra* SQUARE]

squa′dron (-ŏd-), n., & v.t. **1.** Principal division of cavalry regiment or mechanized formation, consisting of two troops. **2.** Any orderly body of persons. **3.** Detachment of warships employed on particular service, as *flying* ~ (equipped for rapid cruising). **4.** Unit of Royal Air Force (10 to 18 machines); ~-*leader* (see AIR¹ *Force*). **5.** v.t. Form (men) into ~s. [f. It. *squadrone* (prec., -OON)]

‖ **squail**, n. (Pl.) game with small wooden discs (~s) on round table or board (~-*board*). [orig. unkn.]

‖ **squail′er**, n. Stick with leaded knob for striking or throwing at squirrels etc. [f. dial. *squail* strike with ~ + -ER¹]

squa′lid (-ŏl-), a. Dirty, mean, poor, in appearance. Hence or cogn. ~ITY (-ĭd²), ~NESS, **squa′lor**¹, nn., ~LY² adv., (-ŏl-). [f. L *squalidus* (*squalēre* be stiff or dirty, -ID¹)]

squall (-awl), v.i. & t., & n. **1.** Cry out, scream, violently as in fear or pain; utter in screaming or discordant voice. Hence ~'ER¹ n. **2.** n. Sudden & violent gust or successive gusts of wind, esp. with rain or snow or sleet (*arched* ~, ~ occurring near equator with sudden collection of black clouds in form of arch & usu. violent thunderstorm; *black*~, with dark cloud; *white* ~, arising in fair weather without formation of clouds), whence ~'Y² (-aw-) a.; *look out for* ~*s*, (fig.) be on one's guard against danger or trouble; [f. the vb] discordant cry, scream. [imit.]

squāl'oid, a. Like a shark. [f. L *squalus*, kind of sea-fish, (mod. L) genus of sharks, +-OID]

squăm'|a, n. (bot., zool.; pl. ~*ae*). Scale, scalelike feather or part of bone. Hence or cogn. ~I-, ~O-, comb. forms, ~OSE¹, ~OUS, aa., ~ULE n. [L]

squa'nder (-ŏn-), v.t. Spend (money, time, etc.) wastefully; dissipate (fortune etc.) thus. Hence ~ER¹ n., ~ingLY² adv., ~MAN'IA n. (craze for extravagant expenditure). [16th c., of unkn. orig.]

squāre, n., a., adv., & v.t. & i. **1.** Equilateral rectangle; object (approximately) of this shape; (usu. quadrilateral) area planted with trees etc. or ornamentally laid out & surrounded with buildings esp. dwelling-houses, as *Trafalgar S~, Russell S~, lives in the next* ~; block of buildings bounded by four streets; L-shaped or (T'~) T-shaped instrument for obtaining or testing right angles; *out of* ~, not at right angles; standard, pattern, (usu. fig., & arch. exc. *on the* ~, fairly, honestly, as *can be trusted to act on the* ~, *by the* ~, exactly); product of a number multiplied by itself, as *the* ~ *of 9 is 81, of x² is x⁴, 9 is a perfect* ~ (has rational root); body of infantry drawn up in rectangular form, *hollow* ~ (hist.), so drawn up with space in middle; (also *word*-~) set of words (to be guessed from description &) arranged in a ~ so as to read alike across & downwards (e.g. *cab ace bed*); (sl.) old-fashioned person; MAGIC ~; 100 ~ ft as measure of flooring etc. **2.** adj. Of ~ shape; ~ *foot, inch,* etc., (area equal to that of) ~ whose side is a foot, inch, etc.; ~ *measure* (expressed in ~ feet etc.); *a table 4 ft* ~ *has an area of 16* ~ *ft*; rectangular, as *table with* ~ *corners*; at right angles *to*; ~ *number,* ~ of an integer, e.g. 1, 4, 9, 16, etc.; ~ *root* of a given number, number of which it is the ~, as *the* ~ *root of 9 is 3, of x⁶ is x³, of 2 is irrational*; ~ *dance, game* (in which four couples, players, face inwards from four sides); having the breadth more nearly equal to the length or height than is usual, as *a man of* ~ *frame*; angular, not round, as ~ *peg in round* HOLE¹, *has a* ~ *jaw*; properly arranged, in good order, as *must tidy up & get things* ~; thorough, uncompromising, as *was met with a* ~ *refusal, made a* ~ *meal*; fair, honest, as *his play is not always quite* ~, *a* ~ *deal*, fair bargain, fair treatment; (sl.) old-fashioned; *be on the* ~, be a freemason; on a proper footing, even, quits, as *am now* ~ *with all the world, get* ~ *with* (pay, compound with) *our creditors*; (golf) *they were* ~ *or all* ~ (had won the same

number of holes) *at the turn.* **3.** ~-*built,* of comparatively broad shape; ||~'*face* (sl.), gin; *~'head*, Scandinavian in U.S. or Canada; ~ *leg* (crick.), fielder at some distance on batsman's leg-side & nearly opposite wicket, his place, as *was put at* ~ *leg*; ~-*rigged*, with principal sails at right angles to length of ship & extended by horizontal yards slung to mast by the middle, opp. to *fore-&-aft rigged*; ~ *sail*, four-cornered sail extended on yard slung to mast by middle; ~-*shouldered*, with broad & not sloping shoulders, esp. opp. to *round-shouldered*; ~-*toed*, (having boots) with ~ toes, (fig.) formal, prim; ~-*toes*, ~-*toed* person. Hence ~'LY² (-rl-) adv., ~'NESS (-rn-) n., squaR´ISH¹ a. **4.** adv. ~-*ly*, as *sat* ~ *on his seat, hit him* ~ *on the jaw, do you think he plays* ~ (fair)?, FAIR² *&* ~. **5.** vb. Make ~; make rectangular, give rectangular edges to (timber); multiply (number) by itself, as *3* ~*d is 9, x* ~*d is written x²*; adjust, make or be suitable *to* or consistent *with*, reconcile, as *decline to* ~ *my conduct to* or *with his interests, his practice does not* ~ or *he does not* ~ *his practice with his principles*; settle, pay, (bill etc.), esp. ~ *accounts with* (fig. have revenge on), (abs. in some senses) ~ *up*; (colloq.) pay, esp. bribe, as *can you* ~ *the porter?, has been* ~*d to hold his tongue*; secure acquiescence etc. of (person) thus; assume attitude of boxer, move *up to* (person) thus; ~ *up to difficulties* or *problems*, face and tackle them resolutely; ~ *the circle*, construct ~ equal in area to given circle, express area of circle exactly in ~ measure, (fig.) perform demonstrable impossibility; (golf) make the score of (a match) equal, make the scores equal; (naut.) lay (yards) at right angles with keel making them at same time horizontal, get (dead-eyes) horizontal, get (ratlines) horizontal & parallel to one another; *~ away*, tidy up (orig. naut.). [ME, f. OF *esquarre* etc., n., *esquarrer* vb; *esquarre* p.p. adj.; f. pop. L *EX(quadra* n., -*are* vb, square; cf. QUADRI-)]

squa'rrōse, -ous, (-ŏr-), aa. (bot., zool.). Rough with scalelike processes. [f. L *squarrosus* scurfy, scabby]

||**squa'rs'on**, n. (joc.). Squire & parson in one. [portmanteau wd]

squash¹ (-ŏ-), v.t. & i., & n. **1.** Crush, squeeze flat or into pulp; pack tight, crowd; (fig.) silence (person) with crushing retort; squeeze one's way (*into* etc.). **2.** n. ~ed thing or mass, whence ~'INESS n., ~'Y² a.; crowd, crowded assembly; (sound of) fall of soft body; (also ~ *rackets*) game played with rackets & soft ball in fives-court; LEMON¹ ~; ~ *hat* (of soft felt etc.). [f. OF *esquasser* f. pop. L *EX(quassare* see QUASH)]

squash² (-ŏ-), n. Kinds of gourd. [f. Amer.-Ind. *askutasquash*]

squat (-ŏt), v.i. & t. (-tt-), a., & n. **1.** Sit

on ground etc. with knees drawn up & heels close to or touching hams, crouch with hams resting on backs of heels; put (one*self*, person) into this position; (of animals) crouch close to ground; (colloq.) sit (*down, on*, etc.). **2.** adj. In ~ting posture; (of person etc.) short & thick, dumpy. **3.** n. ~ting posture; *hot ~ (sl.), electric chair; ~ person. [ME; (adj. & n. f. vb) f. OF *esquatir* flatten (es- EX- +*quatir* f. L *coactus*, see COGENT)]

squa′tter (-ŏt-), n. In vbl senses; also: (Austral.) person who gets right of pasturage from government on easy terms, also, any stock-owner; person who settles on new esp. public land without title; person who takes unauthorized possession of unoccupied premises. [f. prec.+-ER¹]

squaw, n. Amer.-Indian woman or wife; ~*man*, white married to ~. [Amer.-Ind. *squaws, squa*, etc.]

squawk, v.i. & n. **1.** (Chiefly of birds) utter harsh cry of pain or fear. **2.** n. Such cry. [imit.]

squeak, v.i. & t., & n. **1.** Utter short shrill cry as of mouse or unoiled hinge; utter (words) shrilly; (sl.) turn informer, peach. **2.** n. Short shrill sound, whence ~′ILY² adv., ~′Y² a.; (*narrow*) ~, narrow escape, success barely attained; BUBBLE¹- -*and*-~. [ME; imit., cf. Sw. *sqväka* croak]

squeak′er, n. In vbl senses; also, young bird esp. pigeon. [-ER¹]

squeal, v.i. & t., & n. **1.** Utter shrill cry as of child from pain, fear, anger, joy, etc.; utter (words) thus; (sl.) protest excitedly e.g. against taxation; (sl.) turn informer; *make* one ~ (sl.), blackmail him. **2.** n. Shrill cry of child, pig, etc. [ME; imit.]

squeal′er, n. In vbl senses; also, young bird esp. pigeon. [-ER¹]

squeam′ish, a. Easily nauseated; fastidious, overnice, overscrupulous in questions of propriety, honesty, etc. Hence ~LY² adv., ~NESS n. [ME var. of (now dial.) *squeamous*, f. AF *escoymo*(*u*)*s*, of unkn. orig.]

squee′gee (or -ē′), **squil′gee**, nn., & vv.t. **1.** Rubber-edged implement for sweeping wet deck or road; small similar instrument or roller used in photography. **2.** v.t. Treat with ~. [*squeegee* perh. f. *squeege*, strengthened form of SQUEEZE; *squil-* unexpl. var.]

squeeze, v.t. & i., & n. **1.** Exert pressure upon (sponge, lemon, etc.) esp. in order to extract moisture, compress with hand or between two bodies, as ~ person's *hand* (as sign of sympathy, affection, etc.), ~*d orange* (fig.), person, thing, from whom or which no more is to be had, *was* ~*d to death in the crowd*; thrust (one*self*, person, thing, *into* vehicle, room, etc., *out of*, etc.) forcibly; make one's way by squeezing (*into* etc.); harass by exactions, extort money etc. from; constrain, bring pressure to bear on, as *could* ~ *the government to any extent*; get (money etc. *out of*

person etc.) by extortion, entreaty, etc.; produce with effort (*a tear* etc.); take impression of (coin etc.) esp. with sheets of damp paper or prepared wax. **2.** n. Application of pressure, as *gave him a* ~ (*of the hand*); crowd, crush, as *we all got in, but it was a* (*tight*) ~; a restriction; impression of coin etc., esp. as above; forced exaction by Asian official, illicit commission, percentage on goods purchased extorted by native servant. **3.** ~ *play*, (bridge) leading winning cards until opponent is forced to discard important card, (baseball) hitting ball short to infield to enable runner on third base to get home as soon as ball is pitched. Hence **squeez-ABIL′ITY** n., **squeez′ABLE** a. [c. 1600, perh. strengthened form of (15th c., now obs.) *quease*, of unkn. orig.; cf. obs. *squiss, squize*]

squeez′er, n. In vbl senses; also or esp.: machine for expressing air-bubbles etc. from puddled iron; (pl.) playing-cards with value shown at top right-hand corner so that they need not be opened out. [-ER¹]

squelch, v.t. & i., & n. (colloq.). **1.** Stamp on, crush flat, put an end to; disconcert, silence; make sucking sound as of hoof drawn out of thick mud. **2.** n. Act or sound of ~ing. [imit.]

squib, n., & v.t. & i. (-bb-). **1.** Firework thrown by hand & exploding like rocket or burning with hissing sound; tube of gunpowder used to fire a charge; short satirical composition, lampoon. **2.** vb. Write, attack with, lampoons. [16th c., of unkn. orig.; perh. imit.]

squid¹, n., & v.i. (-dd-). **1.** Kind of cuttle--fish used as bait; kinds of artificial bait. **2.** v.i. Fish with ~. [17th c., of unkn. orig.]

squid², n. Anti-submarine mortar with several barrels firing depth-charges ahead of ship. [orig. unkn.]

‖ **squiff′er**, n. (sl.). Concertina. [orig. unkn.]

squiff′y, a. (sl.). Slightly drunk. [fanciful]

squilgee. See SQUEEGEE.

squill, n. Plant of lily family; its bulb, used as diuretic, purgative, etc.; (also ~*-fish*) a crustacean. [f. L *squilla* f. Gk *skilla*]

squinch, n. Straight or arched structure across interior angle of square tower as support for side of octagon. [var. of obs. *scunch* abbr. of SCUNCHEON]

squint, v.i. & t., n., & a. **1.** Have the eyes turned in different directions, have strabismus; look obliquely (*at* etc.); close (eyes) quickly, hold (eyes) half-shut. Hence ~′ER¹ n. **2.** n. Affection of eyes in which their axes are differently directed, as *has a fearful* ~; stealthy or sidelong glance; (colloq.) glance, look, as *let's have a* ~ *at it*; leaning, inclination, (*to, towards*, policy etc.); oblique opening through wall of church affording view of altar. **3.** adj. ~ing, looking different ways; ~*-eyed*, (fig.) malignant. [vb aphetic f. *asquint*; n. f. adj. or vb; adj. f. obs. *squint* adv. (f. ASQUINT) or inferred f. ~*-eyed*]

squire, n., & v.t. **1.** Country gentleman, esp. *the* chief landed proprietor in a district; woman's escort or gallant; ~ *of dames*, man who is attentive to or frequents company of women; attendant on knight (hist.). **2.** v.t. (Of man) attend upon, escort, (woman). Hence ~'HOOD, ~'LET, ~'LING[1], ~'SHIP, nn., ~'LY[1] a. [ME, f. OF *esquier* ESQUIRE]

squir(e)'|archy (-kǐ), n. Government by, influence of, landed proprietors esp. before Reform Bill of 1832; the class of landed proprietors, so ~**arch** (-k) n. Hence ~**archAL**, ~**arch'ICAL**, aa., (-k-). [f. prec. + Gk -*arkhia* rule f. *arkhō*]

‖ **squireen'**, n. Small landed proprietor esp. in Ireland. [f. SQUIRE + -*een* dim. suf.]

squirm, v.i., & n. **1.** Wriggle, writhe; (fig.) show, feel, embarrassment or discomfiture. **2.** n. Wriggling movement; (naut.) twist in rope. [imit.]

squi'rrel, n. Kinds of rodent of arboreal habits with bushy tail carried over back & pointed ears; *barking* ~, prairie-dog; ~*-fish*, kinds of fish covered with sharp spines; ~*-hawk*, large hawk preying on ~s; ~*-monkey*, marmoset & other small monkeys; ~*-tail*, kinds of grass allied to barley. [ME, f. AF *esquirel*, OF -*euil*, f. Rom. *scuriulus*, dim. of L f. Gk *skiouros*]

squirt, v.t. & i., & n. **1.** Eject (liquid, powder) in a jet as from syringe; (of liquid etc.) be discharged thus. **2.** n. Syringe; jet of water etc.; (also ~*-gun*) kind of toy syringe; (colloq.) insignificant self-assertive fellow. [ME, prob. imit.; cf. LG *swirtjen*, EFris. *kwirtjen*]

squish, n. (colloq.). Marmalade. [imit.]

squit, n. (sl.). Small insignificant person. [cf. dial. *squit* vb 'to squirt', & *squirt* in same sense]

St. For St Andrew etc. see SAINT.

stab, v.t. & i. (-bb-), & n. **1.** Pierce, wound, with (usu. short) pointed weapon e.g. knife or dagger; aim blow with such weapon (*at*); (fig.) inflict sharp pain on (person, his feelings, conscience, etc.), aim blow *at* (reputation, person, etc.); ~ (vb & n.) *in the back*, slander; roughen (brick wall) with pick before plastering. ' **2.** n. Blow, thrust, with knife etc., wound thus made, blow or pain inflicted on person's feelings; (sl.) an attempt, try. Hence ~**b'ER**[1] n. [n. 15th c., vb 16th c., rel. to syn. (now dial.) *stob* vb, prob. f. *stob*, cogn. w. STUB]

Stab'at Mat'er (*or* stah-, mah-), n. (Musical setting for) Latin hymn on agony of the Virgin Mary at the crucifixion. [f. the opening wds, L *stabat*

mater dolorosa 'Stood the Mother, full of grief']

sta'ble[1], a. Firmly fixed or established, not easily to be moved or changed or destroyed, as *doubt whether the structure is* ~; firm, resolute, not wavering nor fickle, as *the only* ~ *politician of his day*; ~ EQUILIBRIUM. Hence or cogn. sta-BIL'ITY, **stabiliza'TION** (also, esp.) maintenance of the purchasing power of a country's currency by fixing its value in terms of gold, ~NESS, nn., **stab'ilIZE(3)** v.t., **stab'ilizER**[1] n. (esp., one of a pair of retractable fins on sides of ship's hull below water-line to prevent rolling, aircraft's horizontal tailplane), **sta'bLY**[2] adv. [ME, f. AF *stable*, OF *estable* f. L *stabilis* (*stare* stand, see -BLE)]

sta'ble[2], n., & v.t. & i. **1.** Building set apart & adapted for lodging & feeding horses or (less usu.) cattle; racehorses of particular ~; (pl., mil.) duty or work in the ~s, (also) = ~*-call*; AUGEAN ~ *s*; ~*-boy*, *-man* (-mn), (employed in ~); ~*-call*, cavalry signal for grooming & watering horses; ~*-companion*, horse of same ~, (colloq.) member of same school, club, etc. **2.** v.t. Put, keep, (horse) in ~, as *where can we* ~ *our horses?*; (v.i., of horse etc., fig. of person) be ~d, as *must* ~ *where they can.* [ME, f. OF *estable* f. L *stabulum* (*stare* stand)]

sta'bling, n. In vbl senses of prec., esp. accommodation for horses etc. [-ING[1]]

‖ **stab'lish**, v.t. (arch.). Fix firmly, establish, set up. [var. of ESTABLISH]

stacca'to (-aht-), a. & adv. (To be played) in abrupt sharply detached manner, cf. LEGATO; ~ *mark*, dot above or below ~ note. [It.]

stack, n., & v.t. **1.** Circular or rectangular pile of grain in sheaf or of hay, straw, etc., usu. with sloping thatched top; ~*-funnel*, pyramidal frame ventilating centre of ~; ~*-stand* (on which ~ is built for dryness & exclusion of vermin); (as measure of wood) pile of 108 cub. ft; pile, heap, of anything; (colloq.) large quantity, as *have* ~*s, a whole* ~, *of work to get through first*; pyramidal group of rifles, pile; number of chimneys standing together; isolated tall factory chimney; (also *smoke-*~) chimney, funnel, of locomotive or steamer; ‖ high detached rock esp. off coast of Scotland & Orkneys. **2.** v.t. Pile in ~; arrange (cards) secretly for cheating; instruct to fly round at different levels (aircraft waiting to land at aerodrome); ~ (= PILE[3]) *arms*. [ME, f. ON *stakkr* haystack]

stac'te, n. A sweet spice used by ancient Jews in making incense. [ME, f. L f. Gk *staktē* (*stazō* drip)]

stactom'eter, n. Tube for measuring a liquid in drops. [f. Gk *staktos* vbl adj. f. *stazō* drip + -METER]

sta'dium, n. (pl. -*ia*). **1.** (Gk ant.) measure of length, about 202 yds; course for foot-race and chariot-race. **2.** Modern athletic or sports ground. **3.** (med.). Stage, period, of disease. **4.** Interval between moults of an insect. [L, f. Gk *stadion* (*sta-* stand)]

stad(t)'hölder (stahd-, staht-, stå-), n. (hist.). Viceroy or governor of province or town in Netherlands; chief magistrate of United Provinces. Hence ~SHIP n. [f. Du. *stadhouder* deputy (*stad* STEAD + *houder* HOLDER)]

staff¹ (-ahf), n. (pl. now ~s exc. mus. *ståves*), & v.t. **1.** Stick, pole, for use in walking or climbing or as weapon (now chiefly fig.), as *bread is the ~* (support) *of life, you are the ~ of his old age*, QUARTER¹-~. **2.** This as sign of office or authority, a*s* *pastoral ~* (borne by or before bishop etc.). **3.** Shaft, pole, as support or handle, as FLAG⁴~. **4.** Stick used in surveying etc., esp. JACOB's ~. **5.** Kinds of instrument for taking altitude at sea, as *back, cross, fore,* -~. **6.** Surgeon's steel instrument for guiding knife into bladder. **7.** Token delivered to engine-driver on single-line railways as authority to proceed over a given section of line (~ *system*, this method of working). **8.** (mil.). Body of officers assisting officer in high command & concerned with army or regiment as a whole, as *regimental ~*; *general ~* (at main headquarters of army, acting as personal ~ of commander-in--chief); ~ *captain, officer,* (serving on ~); ~ *college* (in which officers are prepared for ~ as opp. to regimental duties). **9.** Body of persons carrying on work under manager etc., as *editorial ~ of newspaper, diplomatic ~*; those in authority, opp. students, pupils, etc.; whence (-)~ED² (-ahft) a. **10.** (mus.). Set of five parallel lines on any one or between any two of which a note is placed to indicate its pitch; ~ *notation* (by means of ~, esp. opp. to TONIC *sol-fa*). **11.** v.t. Provide (institution etc.) with ~. [OE *stæf*, OS *staf*, OHG *stab*, ON *stafr* f. Gmc *stabhaz*]

staff² (-ahf), n. Mixture of plaster of Paris, cement, etc., as building-material. [orig. unkn.]

ståg, n. **1.** Male of red deer or of other large kinds of deer; bull castrated when (nearly) full-grown. **2.** ‖ (St. Exch.) person who applies for allotments in new concerns with a view to selling at once at a profit; ‖ (sl.) irregular dealer in stocks. **3.** ~*-beetle* (with branched mandibles like ~'s antlers); ~*-evil*, lockjaw in horses; ~*-horn*, kinds of club-moss & coral; ~*-hound*, large kinds of hound hunting deer by sight or scent; ~*-party* (of men only). [prob. repr. OE *stacga*, *stagga*, cf. *docga* dog, *frocga* frog, *picga* pig]

ståge¹, n. **1.** Raised floor or platform, e.g. scaffold for workmen's use in building, *hanging ~* (suspended on ropes for painters' use), *landing ~* (at quay etc.

for landing from vessel); surface on which object is placed for inspection through microscope. **2.** Platform on which plays etc. are exhibited. **3.** (fig.). The drama, dramatic art or literature, actor's profession, as *went on the ~*, became actor, *the French ~*. **4.** (fig.). Scene of action, as *quitted the ~ of politics, the ~ of his operations, a larger ~ opened to him*. **5.** Point or period in development etc., as *reached a critical ~, at this ~ an interruption occurred, passed through a lòng ~ of inactivity, is in the hoyden ~, larval ~*. **6.** Regular stopping-place in route, distance between two of these, as *travelled by easy ~s, got down at the next ~*. **7.** ~*-coach*, coach running regularly by ~s between two places, ~*-coachman*, driver of this; ~*'craft*, skill or experience in writing or staging plays; ~ *direction*, written or printed instruction in play as to movement, position, tone, etc. of actor; ~ *door*, actors' & workmen's entrance at back of ~; ~ *effect*, effect produced in acting or on the ~, artificial or theatrical effect produced in real life; ~ *fever*, inordinate desire to go on the ~; ~ *fright*, nervousness on facing audience esp. for first time; ~ *manager*, person responsible for lighting and other mechanical arrangements, costumes, etc. of play; ~ *rights*, exclusive rights to perform particular play; ~*-struck*, struck with ~ fever; ~ *whisper*, aside, whisper meant to be heard by others than the person addressed. [ME, f. OF *estage* f. Rom. *staticum* (*stare* stand)]

ståge², v.t. & i. Put (play) on stage; arrange to take place dramatically (~ *a* COME¹*-back, recovery*); (of play) lend itself to representation, as *does not ~ well*. [f. prec.]

stå'ger, n. *Old* ~, experienced person, old hand. [STAGE¹ + -ER¹]

stågg'ard, -t, n. Stag four years old. [ME ; -ARD]

stågg'er (-g-), v.i. & t., & n. **1.** Walk or stand unsteadily, totter; hesitat*o*, waver in purpose; cause to totter, as *received a ~ing blow*; cause to hesitate or waver, as *the question ~ed him, his resolution*; arrange in zigzag order, esp. set (spokes of wheel) leaning alternately to right & left; arrange (holidays, hours of work, etc.) so that they differ from those of others. Hence ~ingLY² adv. **2.** n. Tottering movement; (mech.) overhanging or slantwise or zigzag arrangement of like parts in a structure etc.; (pl., also *blind ~s*) kinds of disease of brain & spinal cord esp. in horses & cattle; (pl.) giddiness. [alt. of ME (now dial.) *stacker* f. ON *stakra* frequent. of *staka* push, stagger]

stågg'erer (-g-), n. In vbl senses, esp. disconcerting argument, objection, event, etc. [-ER¹]

stå'ging, n. Putting play on stage; driving or running stage-coaches;

scaffolding; ~ *post*, regular stopping place on air route. [-ING¹]

Stä′girite, n. *The* ~, Aristotle. [f. L f. Gk *Stageirītēs* native of *Stageira* (-ITE¹)]

stăg′n|āte, v.i. (Of liquid) be(come) motionless, have no current, cease to flow; (of life, action, mind, business, person) be(come) dull or sluggish. Hence or cogn. ~ANCY, ~A′TION, nn., ~ANT a., ~antLY² adv. [f. L *stagnare* (*stagnum* pool), -ATE³]

stăg′nic′olous, a. Living in swamps or stagnant water. [f. L *stagnum* pool + *colere* inhabit + -OUS]

stā′g|y̆, a. Theatrical in manner, style, appearance, etc. Hence ~iNESS n. [f. STAGE¹ + -Y²]

staid, a. Of steady & sober character; sedate. Hence ~′LY² adv., ~′NESS n. [= *stayed* p.p. of STAY]

stain, v.t. & i., & n. 1. Discolour, make foul, soil, as *cigarettes* ~ *the fingers, wine will* ~ *the cloth, warranted not to* ~ *clothes*; (fig.) sully, blemish, (reputation, name, person; p.p. often in comb., as *guilt, sin, -~ed*); colour (wood, glass, etc.) by process other than painting or covering the surface; impregnate (substance) for microscopic examination with colouring matter that acts more powerfully on some parts than on others; print colours on (wallpaper). Hence ~′ABLE a., ~′ER¹ n. 2. n. Discoloration, spot or mark caused esp. by contact with foreign matter, as *cloth is covered with tea-~s*; ~ing-material; (fig.) blot, blemish, as *without a* ~ *on his character.* Hence ~′LESS a. (usu. of reputation, also of kind of chromium-steel alloy immune to rusting & corrosion),· ~′lèssLY² adv. [ME; aphetic f. OF *desteign-, desteindre* (obs. E *distain*), f. DIS- + *teindre* (L *tingere* dye)]

stair, n. Each of a set of (now usu. indoor) steps, as *the top* ~ *but one*; (now usu. pl.) set of these, as *passed him on the* ~*s, down a winding* ~; *flight, pair, of* ~*s*, set of ~s in continuous straight line or from one landing to another; *below* ~*s*, in the basement of house esp. as part belonging to servants, as *was coolly discussed below* ~*s* (by the servants); *down, up,* ~*s*, on, to, the lower, upper, floor(s) of house; BACK¹~; ~′*case*, (part of building containing) flight of ~s, *corkscrew*~*case* (winding round NEWEL); ~*rod* (for securing ~-carpet in angle between two steps); ~′*way*, way up a flight of ~s, ~*case.* [OE *stæger* f. Gmc *staig-, *stig*to climb; cf. (M)Du., LG *steiger* landing-stage, WFlem. *steeger* ~*case*]

|| **staith, staithe** (-dh), n. Waterside coal depot equipped for loading vessels. [ME, f. ON *stǫth* (f. *stathwō*) landing-stage]

stāke, n., & v.t. 1. Stick sharpened at one end & driven into ground as support, boundary mark, etc.; post to which person is bound to be burnt alive, (fig.) death by burning, as *was condemned to,*

suffered at, the ~. 2. Tinsmith′s small anvil fixed on bench by pointed prop. 3. Money etc. wagered on an event, esp. deposited with third party·(~′*holder*) by each of those who make a wager, (pl.) money to be contended for esp. in horse-race, (pl.) such race, as *maiden, trial,* ~*s*; *have a* ~ *in the country*, be materially concerned in its welfare, e.g. as landowner; (fig.) principle etc. contended for, as *consider the immensity of the* ~; *at* ~, at issue, in question, risked, as *life itself is at* ~. 4. ~*-boat* (anchored to mark course for boat-race etc.); ~*-net*, fishing-net hung on ~s. 5. v.t. Fasten, secure, support, with ~ or ~s; mark *off, out* (area) with ~s, as ~ *out a claim.* 6. Wager, risk, (money etc. *on* event etc.). [OE *staca*, = MDu., (M)LG *stake*, f. WG *stak-*, *stek-* pierce, cogn. w. STICK]

stăkhan′ovite (-kahn-), n. A (Russian) worker who increases his output to an exceptional extent; also attrib. [f. *Stakhanov*, a Russian miner, + -ITE¹(1)]

stăl′actite (*or* stală̆-), n. Deposit of carbonate of lime, usu. in form like large icicle, hanging from roof of cave etc. & formed by trickling of water. Hence **stalăc′tıc, stalăc′tiform, stălactit′ıc**, aa. [f. mod. L *stalactitēs* (Gk *stalaktos* vbl adj. f. *stalassō* drip, see -ITE¹)]

Stăl′ăg, n. German prison camp, esp. for non-commissioned officers and men. [G]

stăl′agmite (*or* stală̆-), n. Deposit as STALACTITE on floor of cave etc. often uniting with stalactite. Hence **stălagmit′ıc** a., **stălagmit′ıcALLY** adv. [f. mod. L *stalagmitēs* (Gk *stalagmos* dripping, as STALACTITE)]

stāle¹, a., & v.t. & i. 1. Musty, insipid, or otherwise the worse for age, not fresh; ~ *bread* (musty; also, not of the day′s baking, as ~ *bread is best for toast*); (fig.) lacking novelty, trite, as ~ *joke,. news, devices*; (of athlete) overtrained, also transf., e.g. of a crammed pupil. Hence ~′LY² (-l-lĭ-) adv., ~′NESS (-ln-) n. 2. vb. Make or become ~ or common. [prob. ult. f. the Gmc root *stā-* STAND]

|| **stāle²**, n. (arch.). Decoy bird; dupe, laughing-stock. [prob. f. AF *estale* of Gmc orig. cf. OE *stæl(hrān* reindeer) decoy reindeer f. *stellan* to place]

stāle³, v.i. (arch. & dial.), & n. 1. (Esp. of horses and cattle) urinate. 2. n. Urine of horses and cattle. [late ME, perh. f. OF *estaler* = It. *stallare*]

stāle′māte (-lm-), n., & v.t. 1. (In chess) a draw resulting from a player′s having no move available, his king not being in check; (fig.) deadlock. 2. v.t. Reduce (player) to ~; (fig.) bring to a standstill. [f. obs. *stale* (f. AF *estale* perh. f. *estaler*; cf. STALL²), + MATE¹]

Stal′in|ism (-ah-)·; n. Political theories and practices of the Russian Communist dictator Josef V. *Stalin* (d. 1953). So ~IST n. & a., ~ITE¹ n. & a. [-ISM]

stalk[1] (-awk), v.i. & t., & n. 1. Stride, walk in stately or imposing manner (often *along* etc.); steal up to game under cover; pursue (game) stealthily; ~*ing-horse*, horse behind which hunter conceals himself, (fig.) pretext. 2. n. ~ing of game, imposing gait. Hence (-)~ER[1] n. [ME *stalke* f. OE **stealcian* frequent. of **stal-*, **stel-* STEAL]

stalk[2] (-awk), n. (Bot.) stem, main axis, of plant, (loosely) any support of an organ; ~like support of organ etc. in animals; stem of wineglass etc.; (archit.) ornament like ~ of plant; tall chimney of factory etc.; ~*-eyed*, (of crab etc.) having the eyes mounted on ~s. Hence (-)~ED[2] (-awkt), ~'LESS, aa., ~'LET n. [ME *stalke*, app. dim. f. *stal-* in OE *stalu* side or rung of ladder, now dial. *stale* long handle]

stall[1] (-awl), n., & v.t. & i. 1. (Single com-partment for one animal in) stable, cow--house; FINGER-~; booth in bazaar, market, etc., compartment in a building, for sale of goods, table in this on which goods are exposed, as *picked it up in* or *on a book*~; fixed seat in choir or chancel of church more or less enclosed at back & sides & often canopied, esp. one appropriated to clergyman, as *canon's, dean's*, ~, (fig.) office, dignity, of canon etc., as *how long has he had his* ~?; ‖ each of a set of seats in theatre usu. between pit & stage; working-compartment in coal-mine; ~*-feed*, fatten (cattle) in ~, so ~*-fed* a. 2. vb. Place, keep, (cattle etc.) in ~ esp. for fattening, as *a* ~*ed ox*; furnish (stable etc.) with ~s; (of horse or cart) stick fast as in mud or snow, (of motor-engine) stop working, (of aeroplane or airman) become unstable by loss of air-speed. [OE *steall*, MDu., MLG, OHG *stal*, ON *stallr* f. Gmc **stalla-* f. **sta-* STAND]

stall[2] (-awl), n., & v.i. & t. 1. Pickpocket's confederate who diverts attention during theft & assists thief's escape etc. 2. vb. **Fence conversationally; **block, delay, obstruct, (~ *off*, get rid of by evasive tactics or trick). [var. of STALE[2]]

‖ **sta'llage** (-awl-), n. Space for, rent for, right to erect, stall(s) in market etc. [ME, f. AF *estalage* (*estal* STALL[1], -AGE)]

stall'ion (-yon), n. Uncastrated male horse, esp. one kept for breeding. [ME, f. OF *estalon* = It. *stallone* f. Rom. **stallonem* f. Gmc **stalla-* STALL[1]]

sta'lwart (-awl-), a. & n. 1. Strongly-built, sturdy; courageous, resolute, deter-mined, as ~ *supporters*. 2. n. (pol.). Strong party man. Hence ~LY[2] adv., ~NESS n. [16th c. Sc. var. of obs. *stal-worth*, OE *stælwierthe* (*stæl* place, WORTH[1])]

stăm'en, n. Male organ of flowering plants, organ containing pollen. Hence (-)~ED[2] (-nd), **stamin'ÉAL**, **stamin'ÉOUS**, **stăminif'EROUS**, aa. [L, gen. *-minis*, = warp in upright loom, thread]

stăm'ĭna, n. Staying-power, power of en-durance. [L pl. of prec. now usu. as sing.]

stăm'ĭnal, a. Of stamens or stamina. [-AL]

stăm'ĭnate, a. Having stamens but no pistils; having stamens. [-ATE[2](2)]

stămm'er, v.i. & t., & n. 1. Speak (habi-tually, or on occasion from embarrass-ment etc.) with halting articulation esp. with pauses or rapid repetitions of same syllable, whence ~ER[1] n., ~ĭngLY[2] adv.; utter (words) thus, as ~*ed out an excuse*. 2. n. ~ing speech, tendency to ~. [OE *stamerian* f. Gmc **stam-*, see STEM[2]]

stămp, v.t. & i., & n. 1. Impress pattern, name, mark, upon (metal, butter, paper, etc.) with die or similar instrument of metal, wood, rubber, etc.; affix postage or other ~ to (envelope, document); crush, pulverize, (ores etc.); bring down one's foot, bring down (foot), heavily on ground; ~ *out*, put an end to, crush, destroy, (rebellion etc.); assign a character to, characterize, as *this alone* ~*s the story* (as) *a slander*; impress *on* the memory. Hence (-)~ER[1](1, 2) n. 2. n. Instrument for ~ing pattern or mark; mark made by this; impression of official mark required to be made for revenue purposes on deeds, bills of exchange, etc., as evidence of payment of tax; piece of paper impressed with official mark as evidence of payment of tax or fee &' meant to be affixed to letter, postcard, receipted account, etc.; POSTAGE ~; mark impressed on, label etc. affixed to, commodity as evidence of quali-ty etc., (fig.) characteristic mark, impress, as *bears the* ~ *of genius*; character, kind, as *avoid men of that* or *his* ~; block that crushes ore in ~-mill; heavy downward blow with foot. 3. *S~ Act*, act concerned with ~-duty, esp. that imposing duty on American colonies in 1765 & repealed in 1766; ~*-collector* (of postage-~s as curio-sities); ~*-duty* (imposed on certain kinds of legal instrument); ~*-machine* (for issuing postage-stamps); ~*-mill* (for crushing ore etc.); ~*-office* (for issue of government ~s & receipt of ~-duty etc.). [(vb) ME *stampen* f. Gmc **stampaz* pestle f. **stamp-*, prob. cogn. w. **stap-* STEP; (n.) partly f. vb, partly f. OF *estampe* f. same Gmc source]

stămpēde', n., & v.i. & t. 1. Sudden fright & scattering of a number of horses or cattle; sudden flight or hurried move-ment of people due to panic; **(pol.) unconcerted movement of many persons by common impulse. 2. vb. (Cause to) take part in ~. [f. Sp. *estampida* crash]

stănce, n. (golf, crick.). Position taken for stroke. [F, f. It. STANZA]

stanch[1], **staunch**, (-ah-, -aw-), v.t. Check the flow of (esp. blood); check the flow from (esp. wound). [ME, f. OF *estanchier* (mod. F *étancher* dam up, make water-tight), of disputed orig.]

stanch[2] etc. See STAUNCH[1] etc.

sta'nchion (-ahnshn), n., & v.t. **1.** Post, pillar, upright support, vertical strut; upright bar, pair of bars, for confining cattle in stall. **2.** v.t. Supply with ~, fasten (cattle) to ~. [15th c., f. OF *estanchon*, *-son*, f. *estance* prop, f. Rom. *stantia; see STANZA]

stand[1], v.i. & t. (*stŏŏd*). **1.** Have or take or maintain upright position, be set upright, as *tell him to ~ up*, ~ *at* EASE[1], || ~ EASY, ~ *in* person's LIGHT[1], *in the* BREACH[1], *stood there till I was tired, was too weak to ~, chair will not ~ on two legs, hair ~s on end* (with terror). **2.** Be of specified height, as ~*s six foot three*. **3.** Be situated, be, as *on each side ~ two pillars, a stranger stood in the doorway, the cups ~ on the top shelf, here once stood a huge oak.* **4.** Assume stationary position, as ~ *still, was commanded to ~*; ~ (*& deliver*)!, highwayman's order. **5.** Maintain position, avoid falling or moving or being moved, as *don't ~ there arguing, house will ~ another century, whether we ~ or fall, has stood through worse storms, ~ on* one's *own* BOTTOM[1], ~ *fast*, ~ *firm*; *all ~ing* (naut. & transf.), without time to lower sails or prepare, taken by surprise. **6.** *It ~s to reason*, it is logically demonstrable (*that*), (pop.) *I shall lose my temper if you deny* (*that*). **7.** Hold good, remain valid or unaltered, as *the former conditions may ~, the passage must ~, the same remark ~s good.* **8.** Be, find oneself, in specified situation, rank, etc., as ~*s convicted of treachery, in need of help, in an awkward position, under heavy obligations*; *I ~ corrected* (accept correction); *thermometer stood at 90°* ; *corn ~s higher* (is dearer) *than ever*;. *the matter ~s thus*; *he ~s first on the list, alone among his contemporaries, in the same relation to both parties, ~s well* (is on good terms or in good odour) *with the authorities*; *how do we ~ in the matter of* (have we enough or suitable) *horses?*; *I ~ prepared to dispute it, ~ in awe of, have often stood his friend, ~ at* BAY[4]. **9.** Move to & remain in specified position, as ~ *back, clear, aside, aloof, away*; (naut.) hold specified course, as ~ *in for the shore*; (of dog) point, set. **10.** Place, set, in upright or specified position, as ~ *the jug on the table, ~ it against the wall, shall ~ you in the corner* (as punishment). **11.** Endure without succumbing or complaining, as *nerves could not ~ the strain, how does he ~ pain?, could never ~ the fellow, shall ~ no nonsense, can't ~ these French matches*; ~ *fire* (receive fire of enemy without giving way); *failed to ~ the test*; ~ one's *ground*, maintain one's position (lit., & fig. of argument etc.). **12.** Undergo (trial), be faced with (CHANCE[1]). **13.** Provide at one's expense, as *stood him a drink, stood a bottle to the company, who is going to ~ treat?* **14.** ~ *by* (prep.), uphold, support, side with, (person), adhere to, abide by,

(terms, promise), (naut.) take or ~ ready to take hold of (anchor etc.); ~ *by* (adv.), ~ near, be a bystander, ~ & look on, as *will not ~ by & see him ill-treated*, (orig. naut.) ~ ready, be on the alert; ~*-by*, thing, person, that one can depend upon, machine etc. kept for emergency. **15.** ~ *down*, retire from witness-box or similar position, (mil.) go off duty after ~ing to. **16.** ~ *for*, represent, signify, imply, as *P.O. ~s for postal order, tariff reform ~s for a great deal more than that*, || be candidate for (office), be candidate for representation of (constituency) in Parliament, espouse the cause of (free trade etc.), (colloq.) endure, tolerate, acquiesce in. **17.** ~ (person) *in* (sum), cost, as *coat stood me in £20, wife ~s him in £50 yearly for motor tires*; ~ (person) *in good* STEAD; ~ *in*, deputize for (~*in* n., deputy, substitute); ~ *in with*, be in league with. **18.** ~ *off*, move away, keep one's distance, (v.t.) dispense with the services of (employee) temporarily; ~*-off* (*half*), (rugby football) half-back who forms a link between the scrum-half and the three-quarters; ~ *off & on* (naut.), sail alternately away from & towards shore so as to keep a point in sight. **19.** ~ *on* (prep.), insist on, observe scrupulously, esp. ~ *on ceremony*; ~ *on* (adv., naut.), continue on same course. **20.** ~ *out*, hold out, persist in opposition (*against*) or endurance, be prominent or conspicuous or outstanding. **21.** ~ *over*, be postponed. **22.** ~ *to* (prep.), abide by (promise, etc.), stick to, not desert, (one's *post, guns*, esp. fig., *duty*, etc.), ~ *to it*, maintain stoutly (*that*), ~ *to sea* (naut.), sail out to sea; ~ *to* (adv.), (arch.) fall to, set to work, (mil.) take post in preparation for an attack (esp. before dawn & after dark); ~ *to win, lose*, have one's bets or other dispositions so made that one is sure to win or lose something or a specified amount (*whoever loses, I ~ to win; how much do you ~ to lose?*). **23.** ~ *up*, rise to one's feet from sitting or other position, maintain erect position; ~ *up for*, side with, maintain, support, (person, cause); ~ *upon*, = ~ *on*; ~ *up to*, meet, face, (opponent) courageously, (of things) remain unimpaired despite the effects of (hard wear etc.). **24.** ~*-off'ish* a., distant, reserved, not affable, whence ~*-offishly* adv., ~*-offishness* n.; ~*-up* a., (of collar) upright, high, opp. to *turn-down*, (of fight) thorough, fair & square. [OE, OS, Goth. *standan*, OHG *stantan*, ON *standa* f. Gmc **sta-*, **stō-*, cogn. w. L *stare*]

stand[2], n. **1.** Cessation from motion or progress, stoppage, as *came, was brought, to a ~*; *be at a ~* (arch.), be unable to proceed, be in perplexity. **2.** Stationary condition assumed for purpose of resistance, esp. *make a ~* (*against* enemy, *for, against*, principle etc.). **3.** Position taken up, as *took his ~ near the door, I take my ~* (base argument etc., rely) *on the precise* *wording of the act.* **4.** Table, set of shelves, rack, etc., on or in which things may be placed, as *music, hat, umbrella,* ~; INK~; (WASH-*hand-*)~. **5.** Stall in market etc., as *fruit-*~. **6.** Standing-place for vehicles etc., as CAB¹-~. **7.** Raised structure for persons to sit or stand on, as BAND¹~, GRAND ~; *witness-box, as *take the* ~. **8.** Standing growth (*of* clover etc.). **9.** (theatr.). Each halt made on a tour to give performances (*a one-night* ~). **10.** (Austral.). A forest, or its timber, regarded commercially. **11.** ~ *of arms,* complete set for one man; ~ *of colours,* regiment's flags. **12.** ~ *camera* (for use on a tripod); ~*pipe,* vertical pipe for various purposes; ~*point,* point of view; ~*rest,* high stool with sloping top for supporting person standing at easel etc.; ~*'still,* stoppage, inability to proceed, as *am brought to a~still.* [ME, f. prec.]

stǎn'dard, n. **1.** Distinctive flag, esp. flag of cavalry regiment (opp. to *colours* of infantry); *the Royal* ~, flag with Sovereign's personal coat of arms; rallying principle (*raise the* ~ *of revolt, free trade*). **2.** Weight or measure to which others conform or by which the accuracy of others is judged (often attrib., as~*pound, yard,* etc.); thing serving as basis of comparison. **3.** Degree of excellence etc. required for particular purpose (*does not come up to the* ~; *must set a low* ~; ~ *of living,* minimum of material comfort with which a person or class or community may reasonably be content); thing recognized as model for imitation etc., esp. attrib., as *the* ~ *work on the subject,* ~ *novels* (those of admitted merit); grade of classification in primary schools. **4.** Average quality, as *work was of a low* ~. **5.** *Monetary* ~, proportion of weight of fine metal & alloy in gold or silver coin (*gold, silver,* ~) or in both (*double*~); *multiple, tabular,* ~, ~ of value obtained by averaging prices of a number of products. **6.** Measure (165 cub. ft) of timber. **7.** Upright support (often attrib., as ~ *lamp,* set on tall freq. telescopic pillar); upright water or gas pipe; tree, shrub, that stands alone without support; shrub grafted on upright stem & trained in tree form. **8.** ~*bearer,* soldier who bears~, (fig.) prominent leader in a cause; ‖~ *bread* (wheaten, of mixed flours). [ME, f. OF *estandard* prob. f. Rom. *estendere* (f. L as EXTEND +-ARD); partly assoc. w. STAND¹]

stǎn'dardiz|e, -is|e (-ĭz), v.t. Make to conform to standard; (chem.) obtain by analysis specific value of (solution etc.) for purposes of comparison. Hence ~A'TION n. [-IZE]

stǎn'ding¹, n. In · vbl senses; esp.: estimation in which one is held, repute, position, as *men of high* ~, *is of no* ~; duration, as *a dispute of long* ~; ~*rocm,* space to stand in. [ME; -ING¹]

stǎn'ding², a. In vbl senses, esp.: established, as *a* ~ *rule, has become a* ~ (stock) *jest*; permanent, not made, raised, etc., for the occasion, as ~ *army,* ~ *orders* (esp. those respecting manner in which business shall be conducted in Parliament), ~ *rigging* (fixed stays); ~ *corn* (not cut); ~ *jump* (performed without preliminary run); ~ (stagnant) *water.* [ME: -ING²]

stǎn'dish, n. (arch.). Inkstand. [ME, commonly thought to be f. STAND² + DISH]

*stǎnd'pǎtter,** n. Politician who is for strict adherence to party platform, esp. on tariffs. [f. *stand* PAT³]

stǎn'hope (-nop), n. Light open carriage of 2 or 4 wheels; (also *S*~ *press*) iron printing press invented by Lord S~; *S*~ *lens* (with convex surfaces of different curves). [name of inventors]

stǎn'iel (-yel), n. Kestrel. [OE *stǎngella* (*stǎn* stone + *gcllan* YELL)]

stank. See STINK v.

‖ **stǎn'ary,** n. & a. Tin-mine; tin-mining district; ~ *court* (hist.; for regulation of tin-mines in Cornwall & Devon). [f. med. L *stannaria* n. (LL *stannum,* tin, see -ARY¹)]

stǎnn'|ic, a. (chem.). Of tin esp. in its higher valence, as ~*ic acid.* So ~ATE¹(3) n., ~IF'EROUS, ~OUS, aa. [f. LL *stannum* tin +-IC]

stǎn'za, n. Group of (usu. four or more) rhymed lines, as SPENSERIAN ~; group of four lines in some Greek & Latin metres, esp. *Alcaic, Sapphic,* ~. Hence (-)~'d, ~ED² (-ad), **stǎnzǎ'ic,** aa. [It., = chamber, stanza, f. Rom. *stantia* abode (*stare* stand, see -ANCE)]

stǎphўlocǒcc'us, n. (bacteriol.; pl. -*cocci,* pron. -kŏk'sī). Form of pus-producing bacteria characterized by grapelike clusters. [mod. L, f. Gk *staphulē* bunch of grapes +*kokkos* berry]

stā'ple¹, n., & v.t. **1.** U-shaped piece of metal bar or wire with ends pointed for driving into wood etc. to take hasp of padlock or hook, or to secure netting, electric wire, etc.; metal tube holding the reeds of oboe & similar instruments; bent wire used in wire-stitching. **2.** v.t. Furnish, fasten, with ~; *stapling- -machine,* bookbinder's wire-stitching machine. [OE *stapol,* OS *stapal,* OHG *staffal,* f. Gmc *stapulaz* f. *stap-* STEP]

stā'ple², n., a., & v.t. **1.** Important or principal article of commerce, as *the* ~s *of that country, of British industry*; raw material; (fig.) chief element or material, as *formed the* ~ *of conversation*; fibre of cotton, wool, etc., viewed as determining its quality, as *cotton of fine, short,* ~. **2.** adj. Principal, as ~ *commodities.* **3.** v.t. Sort, classify, (wool etc.) according to fibre, whence **stā'p'lER¹** n. [ME, f. OF *estaple* market f. MLG, MDu. *stapel* market]

stār¹, n. **1.** Celestial body appearing as luminous point; (also *fixed* ~) such body so far from earth as to appear motionless except for diurnal revolution of the heavens; *double, multiple,* ~, group of two, of three to six, fixed ~s appearing to naked eye as one; *binary* ~, two ~s revolving round one another; EVENING, MORNING, ~; *day'*~ (poet.), morning ~, sun; LODE~; *north, polar,* (= POLE²·) ~; *shooting* ~, small meteor appearing like ~ moving rapidly and disappearing. **2.** Thing suggesting ~ by its shape, esp. figure or object with radiating points e.g. as decoration of an order; *S~s & Stripes,* U.S. national flag; asterisk; white spot on forehead of horse etc. **3.** ‖ (pool). Additional life bought by player whose lives are lost. **4.** Principal actor or actress in a company (*film* ~; *the* ~ *system,* of relying on a ~ or two to make up for weak company); ~ *turn,* principal item in an entertainment or performance; brilliant or prominent person, as *literary* ~, *bright particular* ~ (object of one's devotion). **5.** Heavenly body considered as influencing person's fortunes etc., as *born under an unlucky* ~, *his* ~ *was in the ascendant, you may thank your* ~s *you were not there, the* ~s *were against it* (cf. ILL-~*red*). **6.** ~*-apple,* edible applelike fruit of W.-Indian tree, with a stellate section; *S~ Chamber* [perh. diff. wd], court of civil & criminal jurisdiction primarily concerned with offences affecting crown interests, noted for summary & arbitrary procedure, & abolished 1640; ~*-drift,* common proper motion of a number of fixed ~s in same region; ~*'finch,* redstart; ~*'fish,* echinoderm with five or more radiating arms; ~*-gazer* (joc.), astronomer; ~*'light,* light of ~s, as *walked home by* ~*light,* (adj., also ~*'lit*) lighted by the ~s, as *a* ~*light night*; ~ *of Bethlehem,* plant of lily family with ~-like white flowers striped with green on outside; *S~ of India* (hist.), order instituted 1861 to commemorate assumption of direct government of India; ~ *shell,* kind designed to burst in air & light up enemy's position; ~*-spangled,* spangled with ~s (esp. of U.S. flag); ~*-stone,* kind of sapphire; ~*-stream,* either of two systematic drifts of ~s (one of which comprises the nearer ~s and moves towards Orion). Hence ~'LET n., little ~, young film actress who shows promise of becoming a ~, ~'LESS, ~'LIKE, ~'r'Y², aa. (~*ry--eyed,* colloq., visionary, impractical). [OE *steorra,* OS, OHG *sterro* f. Gmc *sterron* f. *ster*-, cogn. w. Gk *astēr*]

star², v.t. & i. (-rr-). **1.** Set, adorn, (as) with stars (esp. in p.p.); affix asterisk to (name in list etc.). **2.** Appear as star actor; present as a theatrical, film, etc., star. **3.** ‖ (pool). Buy additional life. [f. prec.]

starb'oard (-berd), n., & v.t. **1.** Right side of vessel looking forward (cf. PORT⁵, LAR-BOARD; often attrib.). **2.** v.t. Turn, put, (helm) to ~. [OE *stēorbord (stēor* rudder,

see STEER¹, +*bord* BOARD), early Teut. ships being steered with a paddle over the right side]

starch, a., n., & v.t. **1.** (now rare). Precise, prim, whence ~'LY² adv., ~'NESS n. **2.** n. White odourless tasteless powder procured chiefly from corn & potatoes but found in all plants except fungi & valuable in digestion; preparation of this with usu. boiling water for stiffening linen etc. before ironing; (fig.) stiffness of manner, formality. Hence ~'iNESS n., ~'Y² a., (lit. & fig.). **3.** v.t. Stiffen with ~ (often fig. esp. in p.p., whence ~'ĕDLY² adv., ~'ĕdNESS n.); CLEAR¹·~. Hence (·)~ER¹ n. [adj. f. n. f. vb ME *sterche* f. OE **stercan* stiffen f. *stearc* STARK]

star|e, v.i. & t., & n. **1.** Look fixedly with eyes wide open (*at, upon,* etc., or abs.) from surprise, admiration, bewilderment, stupidity, horror, impertinent curiosity, etc.; (chiefly in part.) be unpleasantly prominent or striking, as *a* ~*ing waistcoat, tie was of a* ~*ing red,* (adv.) *stark* ~*ing mad;·* reduce (person) to specified condition by ~ing, as ~*ed him out of countenance, into silence, dumb;* ~*e down,* outstare; ~*e* (person) *in the face,* be evident or imminent, as *the facts* ~*e us in the face, ruin* ~*ed him in the face.* Hence ~'ingLY² adv. **2.** n. ~ing gaze. [OE *starian,* OHG *starēn,* ON *stara* f. Gmc **star*- be rigid]

stark, a. & adv. **1.** Stiff, rigid, as ~ & *stiff, lies* ~ *in death*; (poet.) strong; (poet.) stubborn, resolute; downright, sheer, as ~ *madness*; = foll. **2.** adv. Quite, wholly, as ~ *crazy.* [OE *stearc,* OS, OHG *stark,* ON *sterkr* f. Gmc **starkuz*]

stark nāk'ĕd, a. Utterly naked, absolutely without clothing. [16th c. alt. f. ME (now dial.) *start naked (start = tail,* as in RED*start*]

starl'ing¹, n. Small gregarious partly migratory bird with blackish-brown speckled plumage inhabiting chiefly cultivated areas, a good mimic. [OE *stærlinc* f. *stær* (now dial. *stare*) = OHG *star,* f. Gmc **staraz, *starōn* cogn. w. L *sturnus*; see -LING¹]

starl'ing², n. Protective piling round pier of bridge. [perh. corrupt. of (now dial.) *staddling* in same sense]

starry. See STAR¹.

start¹, v.i. & t. **1.** Make sudden movement from pain, surprise, etc., as ~*ed in his seat,* ~*ed at the sound of my voice*; change position abruptly as from shock or sudden impulse, as ~ *aside, from* one's *chair.* **2.** (Of timbers etc.) spring from proper position, give way. **3.** Set out, begin journey, as *we* ~ *at six*; make a beginning (*on* journey, enterprise, book, cigar, etc.); begin, commence, (*work* etc., do*ing, to* do). **4.** ~ *in* (colloq.), begin (*to* do); ~ *out* (colloq.), take steps as intending (*to* do); ~ *up,* rise suddenly e.g. from seat, arise, come into existence or action, occur to the mind, as *many difficulties, rivals, have*

~ed up, (trans.) cause (engine) to begin running. **5.** Rouse (game) from lair etc. **6.** Originate, set going, (enterprise, newspaper, business, clock after winding, objections, quarrel, etc.); cause to begin doing (this ~ed me coughing); cause or enable (person) to commence business etc.; give signal to (persons) to ~ in race. **7.** Cause or experience the starting of (timbers, tooth, etc.). **8.** (naut.). Pour out (liquor) from cask. **9.** To ~ with, in the first place, as you have no right to be here, to ~ with; at the beginning, as had 6 members to ~ with. [OE styrtan = OHG sturzen; ME sterte = MHG sterzen; f. Gmc *sturt-, *stert-]

start², n. **1.** Sudden movement of surprise, pain, etc.; (pl.) intermittent or spasmodic efforts or movements, esp. (works) by fits & ~s. **2.** Beginning of journey or action or race, as shall make an early ~ for town, is difficult work at the ~, the ~ is fixed for 3 p.m.; starting-place of race. **3.** Advantage conceded in race, as will give you 60 yards ~, 15 seconds ~; advantageous position gained in business etc., as got a good ~ in life, got the ~ of (gained advantage over) his rivals. **4.** A rum ~ (colloq.), surprising occurrence. [ME stert(e), f. prec.]

start'er, n. In vbl senses, esp.: one who gives signal to start in race; horse, competitor, starting in race, as list of probable ~s; SELF-~. [-ER¹]

start'ing, n. In vbl senses; ~-gate, removable barrier for securing fair start in horse-races; ~-post (from which competitors start in race); ~ prices in horse-races, final odds at start. [-ING¹]

star'tle, v.t. Cause (person etc.) to start with surprise or sudden alarm, give shock to, take by surprise, whence (of person, news, etc.) start'ler¹ n.; (part.) surprising, alarming, as startling news, discovery, development, whence start'lingly² adv. [ME stertle f. START¹ + -LE(3)]

starve, v.i. & t. **1.** Die of hunger; suffer from lack of food; suffer extreme poverty; (colloq.) feel hungry, as am simply starving; || (now rare) perish with, suffer from, cold; (fig.) suffer mental or spiritual want, feel strong craving for (sympathy, amusement, knowledge, etc.). **2.** Cause to perish with hunger; deprive of, keep scantily supplied with, food (lit. & fig.); compel (garrison etc. into surrender etc.) thus; || cause to perish, affect severely, with cold. Hence starva'tion n. [OE steorfan die, OS sterban, OHG sterban f. Gmc *sterbh-]

starve'ling (-vl-), n. & a. **1.** Starving or ill-fed person or animal. **2.** adj. Starving. [-LING¹]

stas'is, n. (path.). Stoppage of circulation of any of the fluids of the body. [Gk, = standing]

-stat, terminal element in names of cer-

tain instruments, f. Gk statos stationary; as AERO-~, PHOTO-~, THERMO-~.

state¹, n. & a. **1.** Condition in which a thing is, mode of existence as determined by circumstances, as ~ of life (one's rank & occupation), a precarious ~ of health, found him in the same ~, in a ~ of deep depression, things were in an untidy ~, in a bad ~ of repair, what a (dirty, untidy) ~ you are in!, (colloq.) he was in quite a ~ (quite excited or anxious) about it. **2.** (Often S~) organized political community with government recognized by the people, commonwealth, nation; such community forming part of federal republic, esp. the United S~s (of America). **3.** pl. Legislative body in Jersey, Guernsey, and Alderney. **4.** Civil government, as Church & S~. **5.** Rank, dignity, as in a style befitting his ~. **6.** Pomp, as arrived in great~; keep~, maintain one's dignity, be difficult of access; in ~ (with all due ceremony). **7.** (arch.). Throne (also chair of ~), dais, canopy over throne. **8.** (Of dead person) lie in ~, be placed on view in public place. **9.** (bibliog.). One of two or more differing portions of a single edition of a book. **10.** (Impression taken from) an etched or engraved plate at a particular stage of its progress. **11.** *Free, slave, S~, S~ in which slavery did not, did, exist; Southern S~s (in southern part of U.S.); S~s of the Church, Papal S~s, former temporal dominions of Pope chiefly in central Italy; S~s General, legislative bodies of (1) the Netherlands (2) France before 1789; ~'craft, art of conducting affairs of S~. Hence ~'HOOD (-āt'h-) n. **12.** adj. Of, for, concerned with, the S~, as ~ criminal, political offender; ~ documents, service; ~ prisoner, person under arrest for felony, also political prisoner; ~ trial, prosecution by S~ esp. for political offence; *S~ Department (of foreign affairs); *S~ rights, rights & powers not assumed by United S~s but reserved to individual S~s; S~ socialism, socialist, policy, advocate, of S~ control of manufactures, railways, etc. for the benefit of the masses. **13.** Reserved for, done on, occasions of ceremony, as ~ apartments, carriage; ~ call (colloq.), formal visit; ~ room, room so reserved, also, private sleeping-apartment on steamer. [ME; partly var. of ESTATE, partly dir. f. L STATUS]

state², v.t. Express, esp. fully or clearly, in speech or writing, as have ~d my opinion, must ~ full particulars, this condition was expressly ~d, no precise time was ~d, did not ~ why, ~s that arrangements are complete; fix, specify, (date etc.), as at ~d intervals, whence stat'edly² adv.; (alg.) express the conditions of (problem, relation, etc.) in symbols. Hence stat'ABLE a. [f. prec.]

state'ly (-tl-), a. (Of manner, language,

person, literary style, rhythm, building, proportions, etc.) dignified, imposing, grand. Hence~iNESS n. [ME, f. STATE[1] + -LY[1]]

state'ment (-tm-), n. Stating, expression in words, as *requires clearer* ~; thing stated, as *the* ~ *is unfounded*; formal account of facts, e.g. of liabilities & assets, as *the Bank issues monthly* ~*s*. [-MENT]

stat'er, n. Ancient Greek coin of various values, esp. gold coin worth 20 drachmae. [LL, f. Gk *statēr*]

states'man (-ts-), n. Person taking prominent part, person skilled, in management of State affairs; sagacious far-sighted practical politician; || (north.) small working landowner; *the Elder Statesmen*, the Japanese statesmen who mainly directed the evolution of Japan between the re-establishment of the Mikado (1868) & the end of the 19th c., also transf. Hence ~LIKE, ~LY[1], aa., ~SHIP(3) n. [= *state's man*]

stat'ic(al), a. Concerned with bodies at rest or forces in equilibrium, whence **stat'ics** n. pl. (or as sing.), also = atmospherics; acting as weight but not moving, as ~ *pressure*; ~ *electricity* (at rest); *static ataxia*, inability to stand without falling or swaying; *static water*, local supply not under pressure. Hence **stat'ically**[2] adv. [f. Gk *statikos* (*sta-* stand, see -IC & -AL)]

sta'tion, n., & v.t. 1. Standing, being still, (opp. *motion*; now rare; *a* ~ *like the herald Mercury*). 2. Place, building, etc., in which person or thing stands or is placed esp. habitually or for definite purpose, as *was assigned a* ~ *in the valley, returned to their several* ~*s*, *took up a convenient* ~, *coastguard* ~ (occupied by coastguardsmen), POLICE ~, || *lifeboat* ~ (where lifeboat is kept); *naval* ~, place affording shelter or harbour for ships with dockyard etc.; (pl., nav.) posts assigned to members of ship's complement in readiness for battle. 3. Subordinate depot or office serving local needs. 4. Stopping--place on railway with buildings for accommodation of passengers & goods or || (*goods-*~) of goods only. 5. Position in life, (high) rank, status, employment, as *occupied a humble* ~, *men of (exalted)* ~, *the duties of his* ~. 6. (surv.). Point from which measurements are made, standard distance usu. 100 or 66 ft. 7. Military post esp. in India, officers or society residing there. 8. (Austral.). Sheep-run or its building. 9. (eccl.). Fast on Wed. & Frid. (hist.); (also ~ *of the cross*) each of series of 14 images or pictures representing Christ's passion before which devotions are performed in some churches; church esp. in Rome to which pilgrims etc. go for devotions. 10. (bot., zool.). Nature of the habitat of plant or animal in respect of climate, soil, etc. 11. ~*-bill* (naut.), list of appointed posts of ship's

company; || ~*-calendar*, board showing successively the starting-time of trains at each platform; ~*-house*, police-station; || ~*-master*, official in charge of railway-~; ~*-pointer*, three-armed protractor for locating place on chart from certain data; ~*-wagon*, = ESTATE *car*. 12. v.t. Assign ~ to, place (person, one*self*) in ~. [ME, f. OF f. L *stationem* (*stare* stand, -ATION)]

sta'tionary (-sho-), a. & n. 1. Remaining in one place, not moving, as *balloon was now* ~; not meant to be moved, not portable, as ~ *engine, troops*; (of planet) having no apparent motion in longitude; not changing in magnitude, number, quality, efficiency, etc., as ~ *temperature, population, intelligence*; ~ *air* (remaining in lungs during ordinary respiration); ~ *diseases*, local diseases due to atmospheric conditions & disappearing after a period. 2. n. ~ person, esp. (pl.) ~ troops. Hence **sta'tionariness** (-sho-) n. [ME, f. L *stationarius* (as prec., see -ARY[1])]

sta'tioner (-sho-), n. One who sells writing-materials etc.; || *S~s' Hall* (of S~s' Company in London, at which book was formerly *entered*, i.e. registered, for purposes of copyright). ·Hence **sta'tionery** (1) (-sho-) n. [ME = bookseller (as prec. in med. L sense *shopkeeper* (esp. *bookseller*) as opp. pedlar)]

stat'ist, n. Dealer in statistics. [16th c.= politician, f. L *status* STATE[1] + -IST]

statis't|ics, n. pl. Numerical facts systematically collected, as ~*ics of population, crime*; (treated as sing.) science of collecting, classifying, & using ~ics. So ~IC(AL) aa., ~ically[2] adv. **statisti'cian** (-Ishn), **statistŏl'ogy**, nn. [f. G *statistik* n., -*isch* adj., f. mod. L *statisticus* f. *°statista* STATIST]

stat'or, n. (electr.). Stationary portion of a generator or motor; ~ *armature* (non-rotating). [mod. L, f. *stare* stand + -OR]

stat'oscope, n. Aneroid barometer for showing minute variations of pressure. [f. Gk *statos* fixed (*sta-* stand) + -SCOPE]

stat'uary, a. & n. 1. Of or for statues, as ~ *art*, ~ *marble* (fine-grained white). 2. n. Sculptor; (art of making) statues. [f. L *statuarius* (as foll., see -ARY[1])]

stat'u|e, n. Sculptured or cast or moulded figure of person or animal (esp. one not much below life size, opp. to ~ETTE' n.); EQUESTRIAN ~*e*. Hence ~ED[2] (-ūd) a. [ME, f. OF, f. L *statua* (*stare* stand)]

statuesque' (-k), a. Like, having the dignity or beauty of, a statue. Hence ~LY[2] (-kl-) adv., ~NESS (-kn-) n. [-ESQUE]

stat'ur|e (-yer), n. Height of (esp. human) body, as *increased in* ~*e, of mean* ~*e*; (fig.) stage of advancement. Hence (-)~ED[2] (-yerd) a. [ME, f. OF, f. L *statura* (*stare stat-* stand, see -URE)]

stat'us, n. (pl. prob. not used). Social position, rank, relation to others, relative importance, (*his* ~ *is a matter of doubt, their* ~ *is wholly different, his* ~ *among* *novelists*; ~ *symbol*, possession etc. denoting person's ~); (law) person's relation to others as fixed by law; position of affairs, esp. ~ (*in*) *quo*, unchanged position (cf. IN[5] *statu quo*) or (also ~ *quo ante*) the previous position. [L, gen. *-ūs*, = standing (*stare* stand)]

stăt'ūtab|le, a = STATUTORY. Hence~LY[2] adv. [-ABLE]

stăt'ūte, n. A written law of a legislative body, e.g. Act of Parliament; *S*~ *of Westminster* (in 1931, conferring equality of status on the self-governing British Dominions); ~ *law*, a ~, (collect.) the ~s (opp. to CASE[1] *law* and COMMON[1] *law*); ordinance of corporation, founder, etc., intended to be permanent, as *University* ~*s*; (bibl.) divine law, as *kept thy* ~*s*; *declaratory* ~ (fixing interpretation of existing law); *private* ~ (affecting individuals, opp. to *general, public*, ~); ~-*book*, book(s) containing the ~ law; ~-*roll*, engrossed ~, ~-*book*; ~*s at large* (in full as originally enacted). [ME, f. OF *statut* f. LL *statutum* neut. p.p. as n. of L *statuere* set up (*stare* stand)]

stăt'ūtorў, a. Enacted, required, imposed, by statute, as ~ *provisions, minimum*. [-ORY]

staunch[1], stanch, (-aw-, -ah-), a. Trustworthy, loyal, as ~ *friend, supporter*; (of ship, joint, etc.) watertight, airtight. Hence ~'LY[2] adv., ~'NESS n. [ME, f. OF *estanche* fem. of *estanc* f. *estanchier* STANCH[1]]

staunch[2]. See STANCH[1].

staur'oscōpe, n. Instrument for examining effects of polarized light on crystals. [f. Gk *stauros* cross + -SCOPE]

stāve[1], n. Each of the curved pieces of wood forming sides of cask etc.; each of the boards forming curb of well or hollow cylinder; rung of ladder; stanza, verse; (mus.) = *STAFF*; ~-*rhyme*, alliteration esp. in old Teut. poetry. [var. of STAFF, due to pl. *staves*]

stāve[2], v.t. (*stōve* or ~*d*). Break a hole in (cask, boat; often *in* adv.); (usu. ~ *in*) crush or bash (hat, box) out of shape; furnish, fit, (cask etc.) with staves; ~ *off*, avert, ward off, defer, (ruin, exposure, etc.); make (metal etc.) firm by compression. [f. prec.]

stāves'acre (-văker), n. Kind of larkspur whose seeds are used as poison for vermin. [back form. f. *staves* pl. of STAFF[1]]

stay[1], v.t. & i., & n. 1. (Now chiefly literary) check, stop, (progress, inroads of disease etc.). 2. ~ one's *stomach*, appease hunger esp. temporarily. 3. Postpone (judgement, decision). 4. Support, prop (often *up*) as or with buttress etc. 5. Remain, as ~ *here till I return, will not* ~ *where it is put* (also, *will not* ~ *put*), *has come to* ~ (colloq.), must be regarded as permanent; (w. adv.) ~ *away, on, out*, etc.; ~-*in strike*, (of miners)~-*down strike*, = SIT-*down strike*; (colloq.) wait long en-

ough to partake of (*can you* ~ *to supper?*); dwell temporarily (*at* hotel etc., *in* town etc., *with* person). 6. Pause in movement, action, speech (esp. in imperat.), etc., as *get him to~ a minute*, ~ *!—you forget one thing*. 7. Show endurance esp. in race, as *does not seem able to* ~, whence ~'ER[1] n. . 8. ~-*at-home* a. & n., (person) remaining habitually at home. 9. n. Remaining, esp. dwelling, in a place, duration of this, as *made a long* ~ *in London, your* ~ *has been very short*. 10. Suspension of judicial proceedings (esp. ~ *of execution*, i.e. of carrying out judgement given). 11. (Chiefly literary) check, restraint, (*will endure no* ~, *a*~ *upon his activity*). 12. Endurance, ~ing-power. 13. Prop, support, (*you have been the* ~ *of my old age*). 14. pl. Corset, whence ~-LESS a. 15. ~-*bar, -rod*, support in building or machinery; ~-*lace, -maker* (of corsets). [senses *remain, endure*: n. prob. f. vb f. OF *ester* f. L *stare* stand; sense *support* (4, 13–15) ult. f. OF *estaye*(r) prop, prob. = naut. vb *estayer* f. Gmc (foll.)]

stay[2], n., & v.t. (naut.). 1. Rope supporting mast or spar; *ship is* (*hove*) *in* ~*s* (going about from one tack to another); *miss* ~*s*, fail in endeavour to tack; ~'*sail* (-sāl, *naut*. -sl), any sail extended on ~. 2. v.t. Support (mast etc.) by ~s; put (ship) on other tack. [vb f. n., OE *stæg*, LG (G), ON *stag*, f. Gmc *stag-, *stah-* be firm, cf. STEEL]

stead (stĕd), n. (now chiefly literary). *Stand* (person) *in good* ~, be advantageous or serviceable to; *in* person's ~, instead of him, as his substitute. [OE *stede*, OS *stedi*, OHG *stat*, ON *stathr*, Goth. *staths* f. Gmc *stadhiz* f. *sta-* STAND]

stead'fast (stĕd-), a. Constant, firm, unwavering. Hence ~LY[2] adv., ~NESS n. [OE *stedefæst* (prec., FAST[3])]

|| **stea'ding** (stĕd-), n. Farmstead. [-ING[1]]

stea'dў (stĕd-), a., n., & v.t. & i. 1. Firmly fixed or supported or standing or balanced, not tottering, as *not* ~ *on his legs, must level table's legs to make it* ~, ~ *as a rock, has not acquired a* ~ *seat on bicycle*; done, moving, acting, happening, in uniform & regular manner, as *went off at a* ~ *pace, had a* ~ *wind behind us, requires a* ~ *light, observe a* ~ *increase in the numbers*; (as command or warning) ~ *!*, be ~, abstain from erratic or boisterous behaviour, premature action, hasty inference, etc., (naut., also *keep her* ~) keep direction of ship's head unchanged; ~ *on !*, stop !; constant in mind or conduct, not changeable, as ~ *in his principles, allegiance*; of industrious & temperate habits. 2. n. Kinds of support for hand or tool; *~*(colloq.) regular sweetheart. Hence stea'diLY[2] adv., stea'diNESS n., (stĕd-). 3. vb. Make, become, ~, as ~ *the boat, boat steadied, adversity will* ~ *him, ĥe will soon* ~ (*down*). [STEAD + -Y[2]]

stēak (stāk), n. Slice of beef, pork, venison, or fish, cut for broiling etc., as *beef~*, RUMP-, PORTER²-*house*, ~, *fillet* ~ (from undercut of sirloin); *Hamburg* ~, cake of chopped & seasoned beef cooked in covered frying-pan. [ME, f. ON *steik*, cogn. w. *steikja* roast on spit]

steal, v.t. & i. (*stōle, stōlen*). **1.** Take away (thing, or abs.) secretly for one's own use without right or leave, take feloniously, as *who ~s my purse ~s trash, stolen fruit*; obtain surreptitiously or by surprise, as *stole a kiss, a stolen interview*; ~ one's THUNDER; (also ~ *away*) win, get possession of, (esp. person's *heart*) by insidious arts, attractions, etc.; ~ *a march on*, get the start of, anticipate. **2.** intr. Move (*in, out, away, up, by*, etc.) secretly or silently, as *stole out of the room, mist stole over the valley*. Hence (·)~-ER¹ n. [OE (= OS, OHG) *stelan*, ON *stela*, Goth. *stilan* f. Gmc *stel-*]

stealth (stěl-), n. Secrecy, secret procedure, esp. *by* ~, surreptitiously. Hence ~'ILY² adv., ~'INESS n., ~'Y² a. [ME; -TH¹]

steam¹, n. **1.** Vapour of water, esp. the gas into which water is changed by boiling, largely used as motive power owing to its elasticity; *saturated* ~ (in contact with, & at same temperature as, boiling water); *superheated* ~ (having higher temperature at given pressure, & greater volume for a given weight, than saturated ~); *wet, dry*, ~ (containing, not containing, mechanically suspended particles of water); visible particles of water resulting from condensation of ~; any vaporous exhalation. **2.** (colloq.). Energy, as *get up* ~, summon energy for special effort, so *put on, let off, work off*, ~. **3.** ~'*boat*, vessel propelled by ~; ~-*boiler*, vessel in which water is boiled to generate ~ esp. for working engine; ~-*box, -chest* (through which ~ passes from boiler to cylinder); ~ *brake, crane, gun, hammer, plough, whistle, winch*, etc. (worked by ~); ~-*coal* (used in heating ~-boilers); ~-*colour* (fixed on printed cloth by action of ~); ~-*cylinder* (in which piston of ~-engine moves); ~-*engine*, locomotive or stationary engine in which the motive power depends on elasticity & expansion or rapid condensation of ~; ~-*gas*, superheated ~; ~-*gauge* (attached to boiler to show pressure of ~); ~-*heat*, heat required to produce ~ from water at freezing-point, also, heat given out by ~ from radiators etc.; ~-*jacket*, casing round cylinder etc. with space between to be filled by ~ for heating the cylinder etc.; || ~ *navvy*, excavating machine; ~-*port*, each of two oblong passages from ~-chest into cylinder, any passage for ~; ~-*power*, force of ~ applied to machinery etc.; ~ *radio* (sl.), sound radio; ~-*roller*, heavy slow-moving locomotive with wide wheels used in road--making, (fig.) a crushing power or force

(v.t., crush as with a ~-roller); ~'*ship* (propelled by ~); ~-*tight*, capable of resisting passage of ~; ~ *tug*, steamer for towing ships etc.; ~ *turbine* (in which a high-velocity jet of ~ rotates a bladed disc or drum). Hence ~'INESS n., ~'Y² a. [OE *stēam* = WFris. *steam*, Du. *stoom* f. Gmc *staumaz*]

steam², v.t. °; i. Cook (food) by steam; treat with steam, soften (timber) for bending by steam; give out steam or vapour, as *a sirloin ~ed on the table, water ~ing hot*; rise in vapour; move by agency of steam, as *we, the vessel, ~ed down the river*; (colloq.) work vigorously, make great progress, esp. ~ *ahead, away*. [OE *stēman, stȳman* rel. to prec.]

steam'er, n. In vbl senses; also or esp.: vessel propelled by steam; vessel in which things are steamed, esp. cooked by steam; *boiler is a bad* ~ (generator of steam). [-ER¹]

stē'arin, n. Chief ingredient of suet & tallow; (pop.) stearic acid separated from ~ by steam & used for candles. Hence **stē'arATE¹**(3) n., **steā'rIC** a. [f. F *stéarine* f. Gk *stear* stiff fat +-IN]

stē'atite, n. Kind of talc, soapstone. Hence **steatit'IC** a. [f. L *steatites* (f. Gk as foll., -ITE¹)]

stēat|(ō)-, comb. form of Gk *stear -atos* fat, as: ~*ōpȳ'gia* n., excessive development of fat on the buttocks, esp. of women [Gk *pȳgē* buttock], ~*ōpȳ'gous* (or -ōp'īgus) a.; ~*ōs'īs*, fatty degeneration.

steed, n. (poet., rhet., or joc.). Horse, esp. war-horse. Hence ~'LESS a. [OE *stēda* stallion cogn. w. *stōd* STUD²]

steel, n. & v.t. **1.** Kinds of malleable alloy of iron & carbon largely used as material for tools, weapons, etc., & capable of being tempered to many different degrees of hardness (often attrib., as ~ *pen*), whence ~'IFY a.; BESSEMER ~; *cold* ~, sword etc. as opp. to fire-arm; *a grip, muscles, a heart, of* ~ (very tight, strong, hard); rod of ~, usu. tapering & roughened, for sharpening knives; strip of ~ for stiffening corset or expanding skirt; (poet., rhet., not in pl.) sword (*a foe worthy of* one's ~). **2.** ~ *cap*, simple form of helmet; ~-*clad*, clad in armour; ~ *engraving*, engraving on, impression taken from, ~ plate; ~ *wool*, fine shavings of ~ massed together, used esp. for cleaning pots and pans; ~'*work*, ~ articles, ~ for these. **3.** v.t. Harden (one*self*, one's *heart*, etc., *to do, to* action, *against* compassion etc.). [OE *stȳle*, OS *stehli*, also OHG *stahal*, ON *stāl*, ult. f. Gmc **stahla-* f. **stah-*, **stag-* be rigid, see STAY²]

steel'|y, a. Of, hard as, steèl; inflexibly severe, as ~*y glance, composure*. Hence ~-INESS n. [-Y²]

steel'yārd, n. Kind of balance with short arm to take the thing weighed & long graduated arm along which a weight is

moved till it balances this. [f. STEEL+
YARD[1], prob. suggested by the *steelyard
beam* or public scales at the Hanseatic
' steelyard ' (mistranslation of MLG
stålhof = sample-house) in London]
steen'bŏk (stän-, stĕn-), n. Kinds of small
African antelope. [Du., lit. stone buck]
steen'ing, n. Stone lining of well. [f.
(now dial.) *sleen* (OE *stǣnan* to STONE)+
-ING[1]]
steen'kĭrk, n. (hist.). Cravat, other articles of dress etc., named in allusion to
Battle of *Steenkerke* in Belgium 1692.
steep[1], a. & n. **1.** Having decided slope,
sheer, as ~ *hills*; (colloq., of demand,
price, etc.) exorbitant, unreasonable, as
*seems a bit ~ that we should have both the
trouble & the expense,* (of story etc.) exaggerated, incredible. **2.** n. ~ slope, precipice. Hence ~'EN[6] v.i. & t., ~'LY[2] adv.,
~'NESS n., ~'Y[2] (poet.) a. [OE *stéap* adj.
f. Gmc **staupaz-* cogn. w. STOOP[1]]
steep[2], v.t., & n. **1.** Soak in liquid; bathe
with liquid; ~ *in* (fig.), impregnate with,
pervade with, as ~*ed in Greek & Latin,
misery,* slumber. **2.** n. Process of ~ing
(esp. *in* ~), liquid in which thing is ~ed.
[ME *stepe, stipa,* repr. OE **stiepan,
stēpan* f. *stéap* STOUP]
steep'er, n. Vessel in which things are
steeped. [-ER[1]]
stee'ple, n. Lofty structure, esp. tower
surmounted with spire, rising above roof
of church; ~*chase,* horse-race (perh. orig.
with ~ as goal) across tract of country
with ditches, hedges, etc., to jump, (also)
cross-country foot-race; ~*chaser,* rider in
~chase, horse trained for ~chase; ~*-
chasing,* the sport of riding in ~chases;
~*-crowned hat* (with tall pointed crown);
~*jack,* man who climbs ~s etc. to do
repairs etc.; ~*-top,* polar whale with
spout-holes ending in cone. Hence
stee'plED[2] (-ld) a., ~WISE adv. [OE
stēpel & *stŷpel* (as STEEP), see -LE(1)]
steer[1], v.t. & i. Guide (vessel) by rudder
or helm, guide vessel in specified direction,
(~*ing-wheel,* vertical wheel with handles
along rim for controlling rudder, wheel
for controlling front wheels of motor-car);
guide (motor, aircraft, etc.) by wheel etc.;
(chiefly colloq. or poet.) direct (one's
course), direct one's course, in specified
direction, as ~*ed his flight heavenwards,
we ~ed (our course) for the railway station,
~ clear of* (avoid) *the local meteorologist;*
~*s'man,* one who ~s vessel, ~*s'manship,*
skill in ~ing. Hence ~'ABLE a., ~'ER[1]
(1, 2) n., ~'ING[1] n. (~*ing committee,* one
that decides in what order items of
business are to be dealt with). [OE
stîeran, OHG *stiuren,* ON *stýra* f. Gmc
*steurjan f. **steurō* (OE *stéor*) rudder]
steer[2], n. Young male of ox kind, esp.
castrated bullock raised for beef. [OE
stéor, OHG *stior,* Goth. *stiur,* f. Gmc
*steuraz]
steer'age, n. (Now rare) steering; (naut.)

effect of helm on ship, as *ship went·with
easy ~*; part of ship allotted to ~ *passengers* (travelling at cheapest rate),
variously placed; (hist.; in warship) part
of berth-deck just forward of wardroom,
quarters of junior officers, clerks, etc.;
~*-way,* amount of headway required by
vessel to enable her to be controlled by
helm. [ME;-AGE]
steeve[1], v.i. & t., & n. (naut.). **1.** (Of bowsprit) make angle with horizon; cause
(bowsprit) to do this. **2.** n. Such angle.
[orig. .unkn.]
steeve[2], n., & v.t. (naut.). **1.** Long spar
used in stowing cargo. **2.** v.t. Stow with
this. [ME, f. OF *estiver* or Sp. *estivar* f. L
stipare pack tight; cf. STEVEDORE]
stein (stín), n. Beer mug. [G, = stone]
Stein'bĕrger (stín-, -ger), n. White wine
grown on Rhine near Wiesbaden.
stein'bŏck (stín-), n. A wild goat, the
Alpine ibex. [G, = stone buck]
stĕl'ē, n. (Gk archaeol.; pl. -*ae*). Upright
slab or pillar usu. with inscription &
sculpture, esp. as gravestone. [Gk]
stĕll'|ar, n. Of stars. So ~ĭF'EROUS, ~ĭ-
FORM, aa. [f. LL *stellaris* (*stella* star, see
-AR[1])]
stĕll'ate, -ātĕd, aa. Arranged like a star,
radiating, esp. (bot.) ~ *leaves* (surrounding stem in a whorl). Hence **stĕll'atELY[2]**
adv. [f. L *stellatus* (*stella* star, -ATE[2])]
‖ stĕll'enbŏsch (-sh), v.t. (hist.; mil. sl.).
Supersede without formal disgrace by
appointing to unimportant command.
[f. *S~* in S. Africa, military base so
utilized]
stĕll'ŭl|ar, a. Shaped like, set with, small
stars. So ~ATE[2] a. [f. LL *stellula* dim. of
stella star+-AR[1]]
stĕm[1], n., & v.t. & i. (-mm-). **1.** Main
body or stalk (usu. rising into light & air
but occas. subterranean) of tree, shrub,
or plant; slender stalk supporting fruit,
flower, or leaf, & attaching it to main
stalk or branch or twig. **2.** ~-shaped
part, e.g. slender part of wineglass
between body & foot, vertical line rising
or falling from head of note in music,
various winding-parts of watch (~*-winder,
watch wound by turning head on end of
~,* not by key), tubular part of tobacco-
-pipe. **3.** Part of noun, verb, etc. (derived
from & occas. identified with a root) to
which case-endings etc. are added, part
that appears or would originally appear
unchanged throughout the case of a
noun, persons of a tense, etc. **4.** Line of
ancestry, branch of family, as *descended
from an ancient, a collateral,* ~. **5.** Curved
timber or metal piece to which ship's
sides are joined at fore end, piece joined
to & forming upright continuation of keel
at fore end, as *from~ to stern,* from end to
end; *false* ~, sharp-edged piece in front
of ~ serving as cutwater. **6.** vb. Remove
~ of (esp. tobacco, whence ~m'ER[1](1)
n.); **spring from,* originate *in.* Hence

~'LESS, (-)~MED² (-md), aa., ~'LET n. [OE *stemn, stefn* f. Gmc *stamniz, cogn. w. OHG *stam*, ON *stamn, stafn*; f. root STA-STAND]

stĕm², v.t. (-mm-). Check, dam up, (stream etc., lit. & fig.); make headway against (tide, current, etc., lit. & fig.). [(1) *check*: f. ON *stemma* (= OHG, G *stemmen*) f. Gmc *stamjan f. **stam-*, cf. STAMMER; (2) *make headway* f. STEM¹(5)]

stĕmm'a, n. (pl. ~*ta*). Family tree, pedigree; lineal descent;˙ (zool.) simple eye, facet of compound eye. [L, f. Gk *stemma* wreath (*stephō* wreathe)]

stĕm'ple, n. Each of several cross-bars in shaft of mine serving as supports or steps. [orig. obsc.; cf. MHG *stempfel*, (G) *stempel* in similar sense]

Stĕn (gŭn), n. A light-weight machine-gun. [f. *S* and *T* (initials of inventors' surnames, Shepherd and Turpin)+ -*en* after BREN)]

stĕnch, n. Offensive smell; ~-*trap* (in sewer etc., to prevent upward passage of gas). [OE *stenc* (any) smell, = OS *stanc*, OHG *stanch*, f. Gmc *stankw- var. of *stinkw- STINK]

stĕn'cil, n., & v.t. (-ll-). 1. (Also ~-*plate*) thin plate of metal etc. in which pattern (interrupted when necessary by a thin bar of the material left to prevent piece from falling out) is cut out; decoration, lettering, etc., produced by ~. 2. v.t. Produce (pattern) on surface, ornament (surface) with pattern, by brushing paint etc. over a ~-*plate* laid on the surface. Hence ~IER¹ n. [f. OF *estanceler* sparkle, cover with stars, f. *estencele* f. Rom. *stincilla, see TINSEL]

stĕno-, comb. form of Gk *stenos* narrow, chiefly in scientific wds.

stĕnŏch'romў (-k-), n. Art of printing in several colours at one impression. [f. STENO- + Gk *khrōma* colour + -Y¹]

stĕn'ograph (-ahf), n. Character used, piece of writing, in shorthand; kinds of machine for writing in shorthand. So stĕnŏg'raphER¹, stĕnŏg'raph-IST, stĕnŏg'raphY¹, nn.,˙stĕnŏgrăph'IC a., stĕnŏgrăph'ICALLY adv. [STENO- + -GRAPH]

Stĕn'tŏr, n. Person with powerful voice. Hence stĕntŏr'IAN a. [L f. Gk *Stentōr*, herald in Trojan war]

stĕp¹, v.i. & t. (-pp-). 1. Shift & set down foot or alternate feet (~ *out, short*, take long, short, steps; ~ *through a dance*, perform its steps; ~ *high*, lift feet high esp. of trotting horse, so HIGH-*stepp'er*); go short distance or progress in some direction by ~ping (~ *back, forward, across the road, into the boat*; ~ *this way*, polite formula for *come here*; ~ *in, out*, enter, leave, room or house; ~ *in*, fig., intervene to help or hinder; ~ *up, down*; ~ *aside*, lit., & fig. = make digression); ~ *on the* GAS; hence ~ *on it* (sl.), hurry. 2. Perform (dance; also ~ *it*, dance),

measure (distance), by ~ping. 3. (naut., prob. f. n.). Set up (mast) in step. 4.~'*in* n. & a., (garment, esp. woman's undergarment) put on by being ~ped into; ~*ping-stone*, raised usu. as one of set in stream or muddy place to enable passengers to cross dryshod, (fig.) means to an end; ~ *up* (trans.), increase the rate, volume, etc. of, (electr.) increase voltage of (current) by transformer. [OE *stæppan, steppan* = OHG *stepfen* f. Gmc *stapjan f. *stap- (foll.)]

stĕp², n. 1. Complete movement of one leg in walking or running or dancing, distance gained by it, mark left by foot on ground, sound made by setting foot down, manner of stepping as seen or heard, simultaneous stepping with corresponding legs by two or more persons or animals, (fig.) measure taken˙esp. as one of a series in some course of action, (*took a* ~ *back or forward*; ~ *by* ~, gradually, cautiously; by degrees; *that is a long* ~ *towards success*; *it is but a* ~ *to my house*, *from life to death*, exagg. for short distance or quick transition; *do not move a* ~; *turn one's* ~*s*, go in a specified direction; *found his* ~*s* or usu. *foot*~*s in the soil*; *in his* etc. ~*s*, following his etc. example; *do you hear a, know her*, ~?; *walks with a rapid* ~; *one*-~, *two*-~, dance names; *in, out of*, ~, stepping, not stepping, in time with others or with drum-beat etc.; *keep, break*, ~, keep in, get out of, ~; *keep* ~ *with* person, *to* band etc.; FALSE ~; *must take* ~*s in the matter, to prevent it*, etc.; *a rash, ill-advised, prudent*, etc., ~; *mind, watch, your* ~, be careful). 2. Surface provided or utilized for placing foot on in ascending or descending, e.g. tread or riser & tread of staircase, block of stone or other platform before door or altar etc., rung of ladder, notch cut for foot in ice climbing, attached piece of vehicle for stepping up or down by, (pl., also ~-*ladder* or *pair* or *set of* ~*s*) kind of short ladder with flat ~s & prop used without being leant against wall etc., (fig.) one of the degrees in some scale of precedence or advancement, advance from one of these to another, (*staircase of 50* ~*s*; *stone, oak*, ~*s*; *door, altar*, -~; *on the top* ~ *of the ladder*; *run down the* ~*s*; *cutting* ~*s with his ice-axe*; *when did you get your* ~?, promotion esp. in army; *give him a* ~ *in the peerage*). 3. (Naut.) socket or platform supporting mast; (carpentry) piece of timber with another fixed upright in it; (mech.) lower socket or bearing for shaft. 4. ~-*dance*, in which the ~s are peculiar or difficult or of more importance than the figure, usu. danced as display by one performer. Hence ~PED² (-pt) a., ~'WISE adv. [OE *stæpe, stepe* f. *stapiz* f. Gmc *stap-]

stĕp-, pref., = holding nominal relationship analogous to that specified owing to death of one and remarriage of the other of a married pair; ~'*child*, ~'*son*, ~'*daughter*, one's wife's or husband's child by previous marriage; ~'*father*, ~'*mother*, ~'*parent*, one's parent's later husband or wife; ~'*mother* or arch. ~ *dame*, harsh or neglectful mother lit. or fig., whence ~'**mother**LY[1] a.; ~'*brother*, ~'*sister*, child of previous marriage of one's ~parent. [OE *steop*-, = OHG *stiof*-, ON *stjúp*- f. Gmc *steupo-]

stĕphanōt'is, n. Climbing hothouse plant with fragrant waxy flowers. [Gk fem. adj. = fit for a wreath (*stephanos*)]

stĕp'ney, n. (hist.; pl. ~s). Spare spokeless wheel formerly carried by motorists. [said to be from *S*~ Street, Llanelly, where made]

stĕppe, n. Level plain devoid of forest esp. in Russia & Siberia. [f. Russ. *stepi*]

-ster, suf. forming agent nn.; OE -*estre*, cf. Du. & Fris. -*ster*. In OE the suf. was orig. confined to the fem., but this restriction appears in mod. E only in *spinster*. EXX.: *brew*~, *huck*~ (which however seems to have existed before the obs. vb *huck*), *game*~, *malt*~, *pun*~, & perh. *hol*~, *bol*~. In *seamstress* -ESS[1] is added to -*ster*; -*ster* in *lobster* is of different orig., but perh. assimilated.

stĕrcorā'ceous (-shŭs), **stĕrc'oral**, aa. Of ordure or faeces. [L *stercus* -*oris* dung, -ACEOUS, -AL]

stēre, n. A cubic metre (about 35·3 cu. ft). [F (-*ère*), f. Gk *stereos* solid]

stĕ'rĕŏ, n. & a. (colloq.; pl. ~s). Stereotype (often attrib., as ~ *plate*); stereoscope; (adj.) stereoscopic. [shortening]

stĕ'rĕo- (or stēr[1]), comb. form of Gk *stereos* solid, stiff: ~*bate*, solid platform on which a building is erected; ~*chem'istry*, branch dealing with composition of matter as affected by relations of atoms in space; ~*gram*, ~*graph*, (one of) a pair of photographs for use in a ~scope; ~*phŏn'ic* a., (of sound reproduced) giving the effect of coming from more than one direction; ~*scope*, instrument for viewing pair of photographs of scene, object, etc. taken at slightly different angles, each with one eye, thus producing by the combination of these images an impression of depth & solidity, so ~*scŏp'ic*(ALLY), ~*scopy*[1] (-ŏs[2]).

stĕ'rĕŏtȳp|e (or stēr[2]), n., & v.t. 1. Printing-plate cast from a papier-mâché or other mould of a piece of printing composed in movable type; making, use, of such plates; (fig.) fixed mental impression; ~*e-block*, on which ~e is mounted for use; hence ~IST(1), ~Y[1], ~ŏG'RAPHY, nn. 2. v.t. Make ~es of; print by use of ~es; (fig.) make unchangeable, impart monotonous regularity to, fix in all details, formalize; hence ~ER[1] n. [f. F *stéréotype* a. (prec., TYPE)]

stĕ'ril|e, a. Unfruitful, unproductive, barren, not producing crop or fruit or young or complete seed or result (~*e land, cow, plant, year, effort, discussion*);

free from living germs esp. bacilli or bacteria or microbes (usu. ~*ized*); (of style) jejune, bald. Hence or cogn. ~IZE(3) (-il-) v.t., (esp.) render free from micro-organisms, render incapable of producing offspring, ~IZA'TION, ~IZER[1](2), steril'ITY, nn. [f. F *stérile* or L *sterilis*]

stĕrl'ĕt, n. Kind of small sturgeon. [f. Russ. *sterlyadi*]

stĕrl'ing, a. & n. 1. (Of coins & precious metals) genuine, of standard value or purity, (abbr. *stg*; with coins, chiefly appended to sum expressed in pounds without odd money, as *£20 stg*; *is of ~ gold, silver*); (transf.) of solid worth, not showy, that is what it seems to be, (*is a ~ fellow*; ~ *sense, qualities, character*; the ~ *nature of*). 2. n. Genuine British money; British money as dist. from foreign money; ~ *area*, group of countries keeping their reserves in ~ and not in gold or dollars, and transferring money freely between each other. [of uncert. orig., but prob. a late OE formation in -LING[1], perh. *steorling coin with a star (OE *steorra*), some of the early Norman pennies having on them a small star]

stĕrn[1], a. Severe, grim, rigid, strict, enforcing discipline or submission, not compassionate or indulgent or yielding, (~ *countenance, ruler, treatment, rebuke, virtue, father, tutor*; made of ~er *stuff*; ~er SEX). Hence ~'LY[2] adv., ~'NESS n. [OE *styrne*, f. Gmc *sternjaz, repr. only in E]

stĕrn[2], n. 1. Hind part of ship or boat (opp. *bow, stem*; *from stem to* ~, throughout ship; ~ *chase*, pursuit of ship by another straight behind it; ~ *foremost*, moving backwards; ~ *on*, with ~ presented; BY[1] the ~). 2. Buttocks, rump; tail esp. of foxhound. 3. ~*fast*, rope or chain securing ~ to quay etc.; ~*post*, central upright timber or iron of ~ usu. bearing rudder; ~ *sheets*, space in boat aft of rowers' thwarts often with seats for passengers [perh. f. SHEET in naut. sense *rope*]; ~*way*, backward motion or impetus of ship; ~*wheel'er*, steamer propelled by one large paddle-wheel at ~. Hence (-)~ED[2] (-nd), ~'MOST, aa., ~'WARD a. & adv., ~'WARDS (-z) adv. [prob. f. ON *stjórn* steering f. Gmc *steurjan STEER[1]]

stĕrn|(o)-, comb. form of foll. esp. in names of muscles etc. connecting sternum with other part; ~*al'gia*, chest-pain, esp. angina pectoris; ~*oclavic'ular*, of sternum & clavicle; ~*ofa'cial*; ~*othyr'oid*.

stĕrn'|um, n. (pl. ~*a*). Bone running from neck to stomach & having ribs articulated with it, the breastbone. Hence ~AL a. [mod. L, f. Gk *sternon* chest]

stĕrnūtā'tion, n. Sneezing, sneeze. [f. L *sternutatio* (*sternutare* frequent. of *sternuere* sneeze) cf. Gk *ptarnumai*, -ATION)]

sternūt'ative, sternūt'atorȳ, a. & n. (Substance, e.g. snuff) causing to sneeze. [L *sternutare* (prec.), -IVE, -ORY]

stĕrt'orous, a. (Of breathing or breather,

esp. in apoplexy etc.) making snorelike sounds. Hence ~LY² adv., ~NESS n. [L *stertere* snore, -OR, -OUS] .

stet, proof-correcting direction, & v.t. **1.** Let it (i.e. the original form) stand (in margin to cancel a correction). **2.** v.t. Write ~ against, cancel correction of. [L, 3 sing. subj. of *stare* stand]

stĕth'|oscōpe, n., & v.t. **1.** Instrument used in auscultation esp. of the heart. **2.** v.t. Examine with ~oscope. Hence ~-ŏs'copIST, ~ŏs'copy¹, nn., ~oscŏp'IO a., ~oscŏp'ICALLY adv. [F (*sté-*), f. Gk *stéthos* breast, -SCOPE]

stĕt'son, n. Broad-brimmed slouch hat. [*S~*, maker's name]

stĕv'ĕdōre, n. Man employed in loading & unloading ships. [f. Sp. *estivador* f. *estivar* stow a cargo (L *stipare* see STEEVE²)]

stew¹, n. (arch.). Brothel (usu. *the ~s*). [ME; orig. bath-room or house (cf. BAGNIO), f. OF *estuve*, rel. to foll.]

stew², v.t. & i., & n. **1.** Cook (t. & i.) by long simmering in closed vessel with little liquid (*let* person, thing, ~ *in his* etc. *own juice* or *grease*, abstain from helping etc. ; ~ING¹ *pears* etc., fit for eating ~ed, not raw; *the tea is ~ed*, is bitter or strong with too long soaking) ; (fig.) be oppressed by close or moist warm atmosphere, (sl.) = SWOT; ~*-pan*, *-pot*, shallow saucepan, covered crock, used for ~ing. **2.** n. Dish made by ~ing (*Irish ~*, of mutton, potato, & onion) ; (fig., colloq.) *in a ~*, agitated with perplexity, anxiety, or anger. [ME, f. OF *estuver*, rel. to prec.]

stew³, n. ‖ Fishpond, tank for keeping fish alive in ; artificial oyster-bed. [ME, f. OF *estui* (*estuier* shut up)]

stew'ard, n. **1.** Person entrusted with management of another's property, esp. paid manager of great house or estate. **2.** Purveyor of provisions etc. for a college, club, guild, ship, etc. **3.** Passengers' attendant & waiter on ship or aircraft. **4.** Any of the officials managing a race--meeting, ball, show, etc. **5.** ‖ *Lord High S~ of England*, high officer of state; ‖ *Lord S~ of the Household*, high court officer. Hence ~ESS¹, ~SHIP, nn. [OE *stiweard* f. *stig* (prob.) house, hall, +*weard* WARD¹; cf. STY¹]

sthĕn'ĭc, a. (path.). (Of disease etc.) with morbid increase of vital action esp. of heart & arteries. [Gk *sthenos* strength +-IC, after *asthenic*]

stich'omўth, stichomўth'ĭa, (-k-), n. Dialogue in alternate lines of verse as employed in Greek plays. [f. Gk *stikho-muthia* (*stikhos* line, MYTH)]

stick, v.t. & i. (*stuck*), & n. **1.** Thrust point of *in(to)* or *through* (~ *the spurs in* ; ~ *bayonet, pin, into* or *through*). **2.** Insert pointed thing(s) into, stab, (~ *pigs*, of butcher, also of mounted sportsman spearing wild pig; *will pull out a knife & ~ you* ; *tipsy-cake stuck over* or *stuck with almonds* ; *cushion stuck full of pins*). **3.** Fix

(*up*)*on* pointed thing, be fixed (as) by point *in(to)* or *on* (*to*), (colloq.) put in specified position, (*heads were stuck on spikes of gateway* ; *arrows ~ in target* ; *work with needle ~ing in it* ; ~ *feather, rose, in cap, buttonhole* ; ~ *pen behind* one's *ear* ; ~ *up a target*, erect it ; ~ *your cap on* ; ~ *them in your pocket* ; ~ *a few commas in* ; *just ~ it on the table, down anywhere*). **4.** (With *out*, *up*) protrude, (cause to) project, be or make erect, (~ one's *head out of window* ; *his hair ~s straight up* ; ~*-up collar*, not turned down ; ~ *out* one's *chest* ; ~ one's *chin* (or *neck*) *out* (colloq.), ask for trouble, expose oneself to danger ; *how his stomach ~s out!* ; *this ~s out a mile*, sl., is very obvious ; *stuck--up*, conceited, insolently exclusive, prob. f. carriage of head ; ~ *up to*, not humble oneself before, offer resistance to ; ~ *up for*, maintain cause or character of esp. absent person). **5.** Fix or become or remain fixed (as) by adhesion of surfaces, (cause to) adhere or cleave, (~ *postage--stamp on* ; *this envelope will not ~* ; *if you throw MUD enough, some of it will ~*, innocence is not proof against scandal ; *limpet ~s to rock* ; ~ *to the point*, not digress ; ~ *to business*, avoid distractions ; *the name stuck to him* or *stuck*, was not forgotten ; *friend that ~eth closer than a brother* ; *can you ~ on a horse?*, escape being thrown ; *some of the money stuck in* or *to his fingers*, was appropriated or embezzled by him ; *friends should ~ to--gether* ; ~ *to friend, resolve, promise, word*, etc., abide by, remain faithful to ; ‖~ *bills*, post placards on wall etc., esp. ~ *no bills*, notice forbidding placarding of wall ; ~ *to it*, persist, not cease trying ; ~ *in photographs*, paste them in book etc. ; ~*s like a bur*, is not to be got rid of ; *are you going to ~ in* or *indoors all day?*, remain at home ; so perh. ~ *out for higher price, better terms*, etc., refuse to take lower). **6.** ~ *it out* or ~ *it* (sl.), endure the conditions (*could not ~ it any longer*). **7.** ~ *it on* (sl.), make high charges, exaggerate in narration. **8.** Lose or deprive of power of motion through friction, jamming, suction, difficulty, or other impediment (~ *in the mud* lit., & fig. be unprogressive ; ~*-in-the-mud*, (adj.) slow, unprogressive, (n.) person of such kind ; also sl. *Mrs* etc. *S~-in-the-mud*, Mrs. etc. So-&-so ; ~*s in my throat*, I cannot swallow it lit. or fig. ; ~*s in* one's *gizzard*, cannot be digested fig. ; ~ *fast*, be hopelessly bogged etc. ; *is stuck on a sandbank* ; *got up to the fourth form, through some ten lines, & there stuck* ; ~ *at nothing*, allow nothing, esp. no scruples, to deter one ; ‖ *stuck up*, sl., completely at a loss ; *that will ~ him up*, puzzle him ; ~ *up bank, mail-van*, etc., sl., terrorize officials etc., in order to rob). **9.** Provide (plant) with ~ as support or to climb up. **10.** Set (type) in COMPOSING-~, whence ~'FUL(2) n.

11. ~*ing-place*, -*point*, at which screw becomes jammed (usu. fig. w. ref. to *Macbeth* I. vii. 60); ~*ing-plaster*, adhesive plaster for wounds etc.; || ~*jaw* (sl.), toffy etc. hard to masticate. **12. n.** Shoot of tree cut to convenient length for use as walking-cane or bludgeon, staff, wand, rod, piece of wood whether as part of something or separate more or less resembling these in shape & size, (*cut a* ~ *from the hedge*; *cannot walk without a* ~; *gathering* ~*s to make a fire*, twigs; *any* ~ *to beat a dog*, hatred makes unscrupulous; BROOM, DRUM[1], FIDDLE, GOLD, *rocket*, SHOOTING, SINGLE[1], SWORD, *umbrella*, -~; *riding on broom*~, witch's way of transporting herself through air; *house was pulled down & not a* ~ *left standing*; *a few* ~*s of furniture*, chairs etc. of simple kind; *wants the* ~, should be caned; *as* CROSS[3] *as*, DEVIL[1] *on*, *two* ~*s*; *in a cleft* ~, see CLEAVE[1]; CUT[2] *one's* ~); (naut., joc.) mast or spar; (mus.) conductor's baton; (fig.) person of no vigour or intelligence or social qualities, incompetent actor or actress. **13.** Slender more or less cylindrical piece *of* sugar-candy, sealing-wax, shaving-soap, etc. **14.** (Short, with aid of context, for) fiddle-~, drum-~, composing-~, etc. **15.** Number (*of bombs*) released in rapid succession from aircraft, cf. SALVO[2]. **16.** ~-*insect*, = WALKing-~ *insect*. [(vb) OE *stician* (= OHG *stehhōn*) f. Gmc *stik-* cogn. w. Gk STIGMA; (n.) OE *sticca*, OHG *stecko* f. *stikkon* f. Gmc *stik-*]

stick'er, n. In vbl senses; also or esp.: *pig*-~, long-bladed sharp-pointed knife; BILL[4]-~; batsman who scores slowly & is hard to get out; person who stays too long on visit; *adhesive label; (organ-build.) wooden rod transmitting motion between ends of two reciprocating levers. [-ER[1]]

|| **stick'it,** a. (Sc.). ~ *minister*, licentiate who has failed to get a pastoral charge. [Sc. form of p.p. of STICK]

stic'kleback (-klb-), n. Small fish with sharp spines on back. [ME, f. OE *sticel* a prickle, sting, see STICK, -LE(1), BACK[1]]

stick'ler, n. ~ *for*, person who insists on or pertinaciously supports or advocates (*is a great, am no*, ~ *for authority, precision*, etc.). [f. obs. *stickle* be umpire, ME *stightle* frequent. of *stight* f. OE *stihtan* (= OHG *stiften*) set in order]

stick'ly, a. Tending to stick to what is touched, glutinous, viscous; unbending, critical, making or likely to make objections (*he was very* ~*y about giving me leave*); (sl.) highly unpleasant & painful (*he'll come to a* ~*y end*); ~*y-back*, small photograph with gummed back. Hence ~ILY[2] adv., ~INESS n. [-Y[2]]

stiff, a. & n. **1.** Rigid, not flexible, unbending, unyielding, uncompromising, obstinate, (~ *shirt-front*; *lies* ~ *in death*; *has a* ~ *leg*, incapable of bending at knee; ~-*necked*, stubborn; *keep a* ~ *upper lip*,

show firmness of character; ~ *ship*, heeling little under sail, not crank; ~ *market*, with prices remaining firm; *met the charge with a* ~ *denial*). **2.** Lacking ease or grace or graciousness or spontaneity, constrained, reserved, haughty, formal, (~ *manners*; *a* ~ *reception, bow*, etc.; ~ *movement, attitude*, etc.; *writes in a* ~ *style*). **3.** Not working freely, sticking, offering resistance, (*a* ~ *hinge, piston*, etc.; ~ *un*, veteran athlete etc., (sl.) corpse; ~ *neck*, rheumatic affection in which patient cannot turn head without pain); (of muscle, limb, etc., or person in regard to them) aching when used as result of previous exertion. **4.** Hard to cope with, calling for strength or capacity of some kind, trying, (~ *examination, climb, slope, breeze*; *a* ~ *price*, high; *a* ~ *glass of rum*, strong; *a* ~ *subject*, requiring application to master it). **5.** (Of moist clay, batter, etc.) thick & viscous, not fluid, in or approaching plastic state. **6.** (colloq.). (In pred. use) to the point of exhaustion, almost to death, as *bore, scare*, ~. **7.** ~-*bit*, horse's bit made of unjointed bar with rings at ends; hence ~'LY[2] adv., ~'NESS n., ~'ISH[1](2) a., ~'EN[6] v.t. & i., ~'enER[1] (2), ~'enING[1](1, 4), nn. **8.** n. (sl.). Negotiable paper; corpse; hopeless or incorrigible person. [OE *stif*, = MLG *stif* f. Gmc *stīfaz*, cogn. w. L *stīpare* to crowd]

sti'fle[1], v.t. & i. = SMOTHER vb. Hence (preferred to corresp. wds f. *smother*) **stif'lING[1]** a., **stif'lingLY[2]** adv. [orig. obsc.; w. 14th c. form *stuf(f)le* cf. OF *estouffer* smother]

sti'fle[2], n. (Also ~-*joint*) joint of horse's hind leg between hip & hock; disease of ~-joint or ~-bone, whence **stif'lED[2]** (-ld) a.; ~-*bone*, bone of ~-joint, horse's knee-pan; ~-*shoe*, kind with which ~d horse is shod on sound leg to make it use & so strengthen the weak one. [orig. unkn.]

stig'ma, n. (pl. ~*s*, & ~*ta* as specified below). **1.** (arch.). Mark branded on slave, criminal, etc. **2.** Imputation attaching to person's reputation; stain on one's good name. **3.** (Path.) definite characteristic of some disease; (anat., zool.) spot, pore, small natural mark on skin etc., small red spot on person's skin (pl. ~*ta*) that bleeds periodically or under mental stimulus; (bot.) part of style or ovary-surface that receives pollen in impregnation, so **stigmăt'IC, ~tosE[1],** aa. **4.** (eccl.; pl. ~*ta*; usu. in pl.). Mark(s) corresponding to those left by the nails & spear at the Crucifixion said to have been impressed on the bodies of St Francis of Assisi & others (whence ~TIST n.) & attributed to divine favour. [L f. Gk *stigma -atos* mark made by pointed instrument, brand]

stig'matiz|e, -is|e (-īz), v.t. Use opprobrious terms of, describe opprobriously as, (*shall not* ~*e him as he deserves*; ~*e him, it, as a coward, cowardice*); produce stigmata on (person) by hypnotic suggestion etc. Hence ~A'TION n. [f. F -iser or med. L f. Gk stigmatizō (prec., -IZE)]

stile[1], n. Steps or some provision other than gate enabling passengers to get over or through fence or wall but excluding cattle etc. (help lame DOG[1] over ~). [OE stigel f. stīgan climb, -LE(1); cf. STIRRUP]

stile[2], n. Vertical piece (cf. RAIL[1]) in frame of panelled door, wainscot, etc. [perh. f. Du. stijl pillar, door-post]

stilĕtt'ō, n. (pl. ~s), & v.t. 1. Small dagger (vb, stab with ~). 2. Pointed implement for making eyelets etc.; ~ heel of shoe (long and pointed). [It., dim. of stilo f. L stilus STYLE[1], -ET[1]]

still[1], a., n., v.t. & i., & adv. 1. Without or almost without motion or sound or both (stand, sit, lie, keep, ~, motionless; a ~ lake, unruffled; ~ WATER[1]s run deep; ~ as the grave; a ~ evening; how ~ everything is!; in ~ meditation; ~ small voice, that of conscience, w. ref. to 1 Kings xix. 12; all sounds are ~, hushed; ~ life in painting, representation of inanimate things such as fruit & furniture; ~ hock etc., not sparkling; ~ birth, delivery of dead child, so ~-born); ~-bugle, naval call requiring crew to remain motionless till next call; ~-fish v.i., fish from anchored boat; hence ~'ȳ[1] (-l-ll) [-LY[2]] adv. (rare), ~'NESS n. 2. n. Deep silence (in the ~ of night); an ordinary photograph, as distinct from a motion picture. 3. vb. Quiet, calm, appease, assuage, silence; (rare) grow calm (when the tempest ~s). 4. adv. Constantly, habitually, (arch.); then or now or for the future as before, even to this or that past or present or future time; nevertheless, for all that, on the other hand, all the same; (with compar.) even, yet. [OE stille adj., OS, OHG stilli f. Gmc *stell-, *stilljaz f. *stel- be fixed; vb f. OE stillan]

still[2], n., & v.t. 1. Distilling-apparatus, esp. for making spirituous liquors, consisting essentially of a boiler & a condensing chamber, the vapour from the former passing into a spiral tube or worm surrounded by cold water or other refrigerating matter that fills the latter & issuing in drops as it condenses; || ~-room, room for distilling, housekeeper's store-room in large house. 2. v.t. Distil (poet.); make (spirit) in ~. [aphetic f. DISTIL; n. f. vb]

still'age, n. Bench, frame, etc., for keeping articles off floor while draining, waiting to be packed, etc. [app. f. Du. stellagie, -age (stellen to place, -AGE)]

still'ing, **still'ion** (-yon), n. Support for cask. [perh. f. Du. stelling scaffold (as prec., -ING[1])]

stilly[1]. See STILL[1].

still'ȳ[2], a. (poet.). Still, quiet. [STILL[1], -LY[1]]

stilt, n. Pole with rest for foot used generally in pairs with upper part of pole bound to leg or held with hand & raising

user from ground (on ~s lit., & fig. = bombastic, stilted); (also ~-bird or -plover or -walker) long-legged bird resembling plover in having three-toed feet; ~-petrel, -sandpiper, long-legged kinds. [ME stille, cogn. w. MDu., (M)LG stelte, OHG stelza]

stil'tĕd, a. (As) on stilts; (of literary style etc.) pompous, bombastic, whence ~LY[2] adv., ~NESS n.; (of arch) with pieces of upright masonry between imposts & feet of the true arch. [-ED[2]]

Stil'ton, n. Superior kind of veined cheese named from ~ in Huntingdonshire.

stilus. See STYLUS.

stim'ulant, a. & n. 1. Stimulating (rare in gen. sense); (med.) producing rapid transient increase of vital energy in organism or some part of it. 2. n. ~ agent or substance, as warmth, electricity, joy, etc., or exciting drug or article of food esp. alcoholic drink; never takes ~s, usu. = drinks no alcohol. [f. L as foll., -ANT]

stim'ŭlāte, v.t. Apply stimulus to, act as stimulus upon, animate, spur on, excite to (more vigorous) action. Hence or cogn. ~āting[2], ~ATIVE, aa., ~A'TION, ~ātor, nn. [L stimulare (foll.), -ATE[3]]

stim'ŭlus, n. (pl. ~ī). 1. Thing that rouses to activity or energy (so lethargic that no ~us affects him); rousing effect (under the ~us of hunger). 2. (Physiol.) thing that evokes functional reaction in tissues; (bot.) sting, whence ~OSE[1] a. 3. (eccl.). Point at end of crosier, pastoral staff, etc. [L, = goad]

stim'ȳ, n., & v.t. (Var. of) STYMIE.

sting, v.t. & i. (stung), & n. 1. Wound with ~ (a bee, nettle, stung him, his finger); affect with tingling physical or sharp mental pain (pepper ~s one's tongue; the cane, his bat-handle, the blow, his conscience, the imputation, stung him; stung by reproaches, with envy or desire; a ~ing insult), whence ~'ingLY[2] adv.; (of part of one's body) feel acute pain or communicate it to sensorium (my hand, tooth, ~s); be able to ~, have a ~ (some bees do not ~; ~ing-nettle, opp. DEAD-nettle); (sl.) involve in expense, (usu. pass.) be caught, swindled, involved in expense (he was stung for a fiver). 2. n. Sharp-pointed weapon often tubular & connected with poison-gland in some insects & other animals (in tail as with bee; also of snake's poison-fang) & plants (projecting as hair from surface as in nettle); infliction of wound with ~, wound so made, pain caused by it, wounding quality or effect, rankling or acute pain of body or mind, keenness or vigour, (was hurt by a ~; face covered with ~s; the ~ of hunger, ~s of remorse; the ~ is in the postscript; this air, bowling, has no ~ in it, is relaxing, feeble). 3. ~-bull or -fish, kind of weever; ~-nettle, ~ing-nettle; ~-ray, kinds of fish with flexible tail having sharp serrated projecting spine used as weapon;

~-*winkle*, beaked shellfish that bores holes in other shellfish; hence ~'LESS a. [OE *stingan*, ON *stinga*, f. Gmc *stengpierce*]

sting'aree (-ngg-), n. = STING-*ray*. [corrupt.]

sting'er, n. In vbl senses; esp., smart painful blow. [-ER¹]

sting'o (-nggō), n. (arch.). Strong beer. [STING, w. ref. to pungency, with fancy ending]

stin'g|y (-jĭ), a. Meanly parsimonious, niggardly. Hence ~ĭLY² adv., ~ĭNESS n. [17th c. also = stinging, perh. f. dial. *stinge* sting]

stink, v.i. & t. (*stank* or *stunk*, *stunk*), & n. 1. (Have or emit) strong offensive smell (~ *in* NOSTRILS *of*; ~ one *out*, drive him from room etc. by ~), whence ~'ingLY² adv.; (sl.) ~ *of money*, be notoriously rich; (sl.) perceive ~ of (*can ~ it a mile off*); || (n. pl., sl.) chemistry, natural science, as subject of study; (part., sl.) objectionable in any way, that one dislikes; (part., as distinctive epithet of animals or plants) having recognizable & usu. disagreeable smell (~*ing camomile*; ~*ing cedar* or *yew*, savin & allied trees; ~*ing crane's-bill*, *hellebore*, *horehound*, *nightshade*, etc.; ~*ing-weed* or -*wood*, kind of cassia; ~*ing badger*, teledu). 2. ~-*alive*, the fish bib (from rapid putrefaction after death); ~-*ball*, vessel containing explosives etc. generating noxious vapours used formerly in naval warfare; ~-*bomb* (emitting nauseating smell on exploding); ~-*horn*, kinds of ill-smelling fungus; ~'*pot*, any receptacle containing something that ~s, also = ~-*ball*, also as abusive term for person or thing; ~-*stone*, kind of limestone giving off fetid smell when quarried; ~-*trap*, appliance to prevent escape of effluvia from drains when opened. [OE *stincan*, (M)Du., (M)LG, G *stinken*, OHG *stinkan* f. Gmc *stinkw-*; cf. STENCH]

stink'ard, n. Stinking person or animal, esp. the teledu. [-ARD]

stink'er, n. Stinkard, stinkpot; kinds of large petrel; ˙(sl.) anything peculiarly offensive, irritating, or rousing (esp. of a letter, as *I wrote him a* ~). [-ER¹]

stint, v.t., & n. 1. Cease *doing* or *to* do (arch.); keep on short allowance (~ one*self* or person or animal *in* food etc.); supply or give in niggardly amount or grudgingly (~ *food, money, service*, etc.); hence ~'ingLY² adv. 2. n. Limitation of supply or effort (usu. *without*, *no*, ~; *laboured without* ~, ψithout sparing effort), whence ~'LESS a. 3. Fixed or allotted amount of or *of* work (*do* one's *daily* ~); area of coal-face to be worked in a shift. 4. Kinds of small sandpiper, (pop.) dunlin. [OE *styntan* to blunt, dull, f. Gmc *stuntjan* f. *stuntaz* adj. STUNT¹]

stip'āte, a. (bot.). Crowded, close-set. [L *stipare* pack, -ATE²]

stipe, **stip'ēs** (-z), n. (bot., zool.). Stalk or stem (in bot. esp. support of carpel, stalk of frond, stem of fungus). Hence **stip'i**FORM,˙**stip'i**TATE², **stip'i**TIFORM, aa. [F *stipe*, L *stipes* tree-trunk etc.]

stip'el, n. (bot.).˳Secondary stipule at base of leaflets of compound leaf. Hence ~lATE² a. [f. F *stipelle* (prec., -EL)]

stip'ēnd, n. Fixed periodical money allowance for work done, salary, esp. clergyman's official income. [ME, f. OF *stipende* f. L *stipendium*]

stipěn'diary, a. & n. (Person) receiving stipend, paid, not serving gratuitously; || ~ (*magistrate*), paid magistrate in large provincial towns, cf. METROPOLITAN. [f. L *stipendiarius* (prec., -ARY¹)]

stipes. See STIPE.

stip'pl|e, v.t. & i., & n. 1. Engrave (plate, thing portrayed), paint or draw, in dots, not lines; use this method; hence~ER¹(1, 2), ~ING¹, nn. 2. n. Dotted work; ~*e-graver*, engraver's ~ing-tool. [f. Du. *stippelen* (*stippen* to prick, f. *stip* point)]

stip'ūl|āte¹, v.i. & t. ~*ate for*, mention or insist upon as essential part of agreement; demand as part of bargain or agreement *that*; (p.p.) laid down as part of the terms of an agreement (*is not of the* ~*ated quality*). So ~**ā'tion**¹ [-ATION], ~**āt**OR, nn. [f. L *stipulari*, -ATE³]

stip'ūle, n. Small leaflike appendage to leaf usu. at base of leaf-stem. Hence ~A'CEOUS (-āshŭs), ~AR¹, ~ARY¹, ~ate² [-ATE²], ~iFORM, aa.,~ā'tion² [-ATION] n. [F, f. L *stipula*, see STUBBLE]

stir¹, v.t. & i. (-rr-), & n. 1. Set, keep, or (begin to) be, in motion (*not a breath* ~*s the lake, leaves*; *sit without* ~*ring a foot* etc. or~*ring*; *if you* ~, *I shoot*; *never*~*red abroad* or *out of the house*, went out; *is not* ~*ring yet*, is still in bed; ~ *the fire*, use poker; ~ *your stumps*, colloq., make haste, walk etc. faster; ~ *tea, porridge, soup*, etc., move spoon etc. round & round in to mix ingredients, keep from burning in pot, etc.; *there is no news*~*ring*, going about; *lead* ~*ring life*, be busy; ~ *up*, mix well by ~*ring*; ~ *up the mud, sediment*, etc., make it rise from bottom of liquid by ~*ring*); rouse (*up*), excite, animate, inspirit,.(~ *up strife, mutiny, discontent, curiosity*; person *wants* ~*ring up*, is indolent or torpid; ~ one's *blood*, excite him to enthusiasm, desire, etc.; ~ one's *wrath, bile*, etc., enrage, disgust, etc.; ~*ring events, times, music*, etc., exciting, stimulating; *a* ~*ring speech, picture, tale*, whence ~'**ring**LY² adv.; ~-*about*, (n.) porridge, (adj.) bustling; hence ~'ReR¹(1, 2) n. 2. n. Commotion, bustle, disturbance, excitement, sensation, (*full of* ~ *& movement*; *person, event, makes a great* ~, is much discussed etc.); slightest movement (*not a* ~), whence ~'LESS a.; act of ~ring (*give the fire a* ~). [OE *styrian*, MSw. *styra* f. Gmc *sturjan*; cogn. w. OHG *stōren*]

stir², n. (sl.). Prison. [orig. unkn.]

stirk, n. (Sc. & dial.). Yearling bullock or heifer. [OE *stirc*, app. dim. of *stēor* STEER²]

stirp'iculture, n. Breeding of special stocks or strains. [foll., -I-, CULTURE]

stirps, n. (Law) progenitor of family; (zool.) classificatory group. [L, = stock]

stir'rup, n. Rider's foot-rest usu. consisting of iron loop with flattened base hung by a strap or ~-*leather* from ~-*bar*, iron attachment let into saddle; ~ & ~- -*leather* as a whole; (naut.) rope with eye giving hold in reefing; ~-*bone*, small bone, ~-shaped .in man, in mammal's ear; ~- -*cup*, of wine etc. presented to person mounted for departure; ~-*iron*, ~ without ~-leather; ~-*piece* in carpentry etc., hanging support; ~-*pump* (with foot-rest & nozzle for producing either jet or spray of water, used for extinguishing small fires). [OE *stirāp* (*stīgan* climb, cf. STILE, ROPE)]

stitch, n., & v.t. & i. **1.** Acute internal pain in the side such as often results from running etc. soon after eating. **2.** Single pass of needle in sewing (a ~ *in time* SAVE¹s *nine*); result of it or of single complete movement in knitting, crochet, embroidery, etc. (*if one* ~ *gives the rest will*; *what long* ~*es !*; *has not a dry* ~ *on him*, is wet through; *drop a* ~ in knitting, let loop fall off needle-end spoiling the continuity; *put a* ~ or ~*es in* in surgery, sew up wound with gut, silk, wire; etc.); method followed in making ~es or kind of work produced (*am learning a new* ~; LOCK³, *buttonhole*, HERRING-*bone*, etc., ~, CROSS-STITCH). **3.**~-*wheel*, harness-maker's notched wheel for pricking leather in places where ~es are to go; ~'*wort*, kinds of chickweed, esp. one with erect stem & white star flowers (named as cure for ~ in side). **4.** vb. Sew (t. & i.; ~ *up*, usu. mend by sewing; ~-*ing-horse*, harness- -maker's clamp for holding work). [OE *stice*, OS *stiki*, OHG *stih*, Goth. *stiks* f. Gmc **stikiz* f. **stik-* STICK; vb f. n.]

stith'y (-dhĭ), n. (arch. & poet.). Smith's shop, forge. [ME, f. ON *stethi* f. **stathjon* (*sta-* STAND)]

stiv'er, n. Even the smallest coin (usu. *don't care, has not, a* ~). [f. Du. *stuiver* small obsolete coin]

stō'a, n. (pl. -*ae*). Portico in ancient- -Greek architecture (*the* ~, the PORCH, see STOIC). [Gk]

stoat¹, n. Kinds of ermine, esp. in its summer coat. [orig. of unkn. orig.]

stoat², v.t. Sew up (tear, cloth edges) with invisible stitches. [orig. unkn.]

stock, n., & v.t. & i. **1.** Stump, butt, main trunk, plant into which graft is inserted, body-piece serving as base or holder or handle for working parts of implement or machine, (source of) family or breed, raw material of manufacture, store ready for drawing on, equipment for trade or pur-

suit, (*they nest in the* ~*s of trees*, arch. use; ~*s & stones*, inanimate things, lethargic persons; *laughing, gazing*, etc., -~, butt for ridicule etc.; *must be grafted on a sound* ~; ~ *of rifle, plane, plough*, main part, usu. of wood, into which barrel, blade, share, etc., are fastened; ~ *of bit*, brace; ~ *of anvil*, base it rests on; ~ *of anchor*, cross-bar; *lock*, ~, *& barrel*, fig., completely, root & branch; *comes of a good, Puritan, treacherous*, etc., ~, family of distinct character; *polyp* etc. -~ in zool., aggregate organism; *paper* etc. ~, rags etc. from which paper etc. is made; *soup*~ or usu. ~, liquor made by stewing bones etc. as basis for any sort of soup; *has a great* ~ *of information, hardware*; ROLL²*ing* ~; *take over a farm with the* ~, its animals, also *live*~, & implements, also *dead* ~; *fat* ~, ~ fit for slaughter as food; ~-*in-trade*, all requisites for a trade, also fig., as *the politician's* ~-*in-trade of a dozen catchwords*; *renew one's* ~; *lay in a* ~ *of*; *have in* ~, have ready without need of procuring specially; *take* ~, review one's ~ for accurate knowledge of what one has in ~; so ~- -*taking* n.; *take* ~ *of*, fig., observe with a view to estimating character etc. of; ~ *argument, comparison, response, joke*, etc., one that requires no fresh thought but is always at hand & perpetually repeated whether by individual or by people in general). **2.** Kinds (*common* or *ten-weeks, Virginia*, etc., ~) of fragrant-flowered usu. hoary-leaved garden plant (orig. ~- -*gilliflower*, named as having stronger stem than clove-gilliflower or pink). **3.** pl. (hist.). Timber frame with holes for feet & occas. hands in which petty offenders were confined in sitting position. **4.** pl. Timbers on which ship rests while building (*on the* ~*s*, in construction or preparation, often transf.). **5.** Stiff wide band of leather or other material formerly worn round neck, now displaced in general use by collar & tie, but surviving in some military uniforms & clerical dress & occas. revived in modified forms by fashion. **6.** ‖ (Finance) money lent to a government & involving payment of fixed interest to lenders or whomsoever their rights have passed to by purchase etc. (*buy, hold*, ~, the right to receive such interest on some amount of ~; ‖ *the* ~*s*, State's funded debts as a whole; *has money, £50,000, in the* ~*s*; *take* ~ *in*, fig., concern oneself with); capital of corporation or company contributed by individuals for prosecution of some undertaking & divided into shares entitling holders to proportion of profits (also JOINT²-~; *bank, railway*, etc., ~; PREFERENCE or *preferred* ~; ~ *certificate*; WATER² ~). **7.** Best quality clamp-burnt brick (also of certain kiln-burnt bricks, as *malm* ~). **8.** ‖ ~-*account, -book*, showing amount of goods laid in & amount disposed of;

‖ ~*-breeder*, raiser of live~; ~*'broker*, ~*-broking*, (person engaged in) buying & selling for clients on commission of ~s 'held by ~jobbers; ~*-car*, cattle-truck; ~*-car racing*, motor-racing in which ordinary cars, not racing-cars, are used; ~ *company*, one semi-permanently engaged at a particular theatre; ~*'dove*, European wild pigeon smaller & darker than wood-pigeon [perh. from breeding in ~s of trees]; ~ *exchange*, place where ~s & shares are publicly bought & sold, ‖ esp. *the S~ Exchange*, (building in London occupied by) association of dealers in ~s conducting business according to fixed rules (*is on the S~ Exchange*, a member of this association); ~*-farm(er)*, that breeds live~; ~*'fish*, cod & similar fish split & dried in sun without salt; ~*-gang*, gang of saws in frame cutting log into boards at one passage; ~*'jobber*, ~*'jobbing*, ~*'jobbery*, ‖ (person engaged in) speculating in ~s with view of profiting by fluctuations in price, cf. ~*broker*; ~*'list*, daily or periodical ~*-*exchange publication giving current prices of ~s etc.; ~ *lock* (enclosed in wooden case, usu. on outer door); ~*'man* (Austral.), man in charge of live~; ~*-market*, ~ exchange or transactions on it; ‖ ~*-owl*, the great eagle owl; ~*'piling*, accumulating ~s of commodities, raw materials, etc. to be held in reserve, so ~*'pile* in. & v.t.; ~*-pot*, for making or keeping soup~; ~*'rider* (Austral.), herdsman on unfenced station; ~*-still*, motionless; ~*-whip*, with short handle & long lash for herding cattle; ~*'yard*, enclosure with pens etc. for sorting or temporary keeping of cattle; hence ~*'LESS* a. (esp. of gun, anchor, etc.). 9. vb. Fit (gun etc.) with ~. 10. (hist.). Confine in the ~s. 11. Provide (shop, farm, etc.) with goods or live~ or requisites (*a well~ed larder, library*, etc.); keep (goods) in ~ (*we do not ~ the out sizes*). 12. Fill or cover (land) with permanent growth esp. of pasture-grass; (of plant) = TILLER³. [OE *stoc(c)*, OS *stok*, OHG *stoc*, ON *stokkr* f. Gmc *stukkaz*]

stockāde', n., & v.t. (Fortify with) breastwork or enclosure of upright stakes. [f. obs. F *estocade*, alt. of *estacade* f. Sp. *estacada* (rel. to STAKE)]

Stŏck'holm tǎr (-hōm), n. Kind of tar prepared from resinous pinewood, used esp. in shipbuilding. [*Stockholm* in Sweden]

stŏck'inĕt, n. Elastic knitted material used esp. for underclothing. [prob. perversion of *stocking-net*]

stŏck'ing, n. Tight covering usu. knitted or woven of wool or cotton or silk or nylon for foot & leg (usu. in pl., esp. *pair of ~s; is or stands six feet in his ~s or ~-feet*, when measured without his shoes; *elastic ~*, surgical appliance of elastic webbing like ~ or part of it worn for

varicose veins, strained muscles, etc.; *white* etc. ~ in horse etc., lower part of leg differently coloured from rest); ~*-frame*, -*loom*, -*machine*, knitting-machine. Hence ~LESS a. [f. STOCK, in 16th c. (now dial.) sense 'stocking', +-ING³]

stŏck'ist, n. One who stocks (certain) goods for sale. [-IST (3)]

stŏck'|ў̄, a. Thickset, short & strongly built, (of person; also in bot. & zool.). Hence ~*iLY²* adv., ~*iNESS* n. [f. STOCK +-Y²]

stŏdge, n., & v.i. & t. (school sl.). 1. Food esp. of heavy kind; full meal, feast; greedy eater. 2. vb. Eat greedily. [n. f. vb, of unkn. orig.; perh. imit.]

stŏdg'|ў̄, a. (Of food) heavy, filling, indigestible; (of receptacle) packed, bulging; (of book, style, etc.) over-full of facts or details, wanting in lightness or interest. Hence ~*iNESS* n. [-Y²]

stoep (-ōop), n. (S. Afr.). Terraced veranda in front of house. [Du., cogn. w.'STEP]

*stŏg'y, -gie, (-gĭ), n. Kind of heavy boot or shoe; long roughly-made cigar. [orig. *stoga*, short for *Conestoga* (Pa.)]

stō'ic, n. Philosopher of the school founded at Athens *c.* 308 B.C. by Zeno making virtue the highest good, concentrating attention on ethics, & inculcating control of the passions & indifference to pleasure & pain (*S~*; often attrib., as *S~ philosopher, doctrines, indifference*); person of great self-control or fortitude or austerity, whence ~AL a., ~aLLY² adv. Hence S~ISM(2, 3), ~ISM, n. [f. L f. Gk *stŏikos* (*stoa* porch, w. ref. to Zeno's teaching in *Stoa Poekile* Painted Porch at Athens, -IC)]

stōke, v.t. & i. Feed & tend (furnace), feed furnace of (engine etc.), act as stoker; (fig.; colloq.) take food esp. in hurried way; ~*'hole*, ~*'hold*, compartment in which steamer's fires are worked. [back form. f. foll.]

stōk'er, n. Man who tends furnace esp. that of steamer or steam-engine (*mechanical ~*, automatic feeder for furnace). [17th c., Du., f. *stoken* stoke]

stōle¹, n. (Rom. ant.; also L *stola* pl. -*ae*) outer dress of ancient-Roman matron; ecclesiastical vestment, a strip of silk or other material hanging from back of neck over shoulders & down to knees (worn by deacon over left shoulder only); woman's wrap similarly worn; ‖ *groom of the ~* [orig. *stoole*, i.e. king's close-stool], first LORD of the Bed-chamber. Hence (-)stōlED² (-ld) a. [ME, f. L f. Gk *stolē* robe (*stellō* array)]

stōle². = STOLON.

stōle³, stolen. See STEAL.

stŏl'id, a. Phlegmatic, unemotional, lacking animation, not easily agitated, hard to stir, obstinate, apparently stupid. Hence or cogn. **stolid'iTY** n., ~LY² adv. [f. F *stolide* or L *stolidus*]

stŏl'on, stōle, n. Reclined or prostrate

branch that strikes root & develops new plant; underground shoot of mosses developing leaves; (zool.) rootlike creeping growth. Hence stŏl'onATE², stŏloniF⁴EROUS, aa. [f. L *stolo -onis*]

sto'mach (-ŭmak), n., & v.t. **1.** Internal organ in which chief part of digestion is carried on, being in man a pear-shaped enlargement of the alimentary canal extending from end of gullet to beginning of gut (*coat of the* ~, its mucous inmost lining; *coats of the* ~, the peritoneum or serous coat, the muscular, submucous, & mucous layers); (in some animals, esp. ruminants), one of several digestive organs either of similar character or differing in action or function (*ruminant's* ~*s*, first ~ or paunch or rumen, second ~ or honeycomb or reticulum, third ~ or psalterium or omasum, fourth or true ~ or reed or abomasum; *muscular* ~, acting by grinding or squeezing, as the gizzard; *glandular* ~, acting esp. by gastric juices); (loosely) belly, abdomen, lower front of body, (*pit of the* ~, depression below bottom of breastbone; *what a* ~ *he has got!*, corporation). **2.** Appetite for or for food (STAY¹ one's ~). **3.** Taste or readiness or sufficient spirit for (or arch. *to*) controversy, conflict, danger, or an undertaking (*had no* ~ *for the fight*), proud or high ~, haughtiness. **4.** ~*-ache*, pain in belly, esp. in bowels; ~*-cough*, caused by irritation of ~ or small intestine; ~*-pump*, kind of syringe for emptying ~ or forcing liquid into it; ~*-staggers*, apoplexy in horses due to paralysis of ~; ~*-tooth*, lower canine milk-tooth in infants, cutting of which often disorders ~; ~*-tube*, for introducing through gullet into ~ to wash it out or empty it by siphon action; hence ~AL, ~LESS, aa., ~FUL (2) n. **5.** v.t. Eat with relish or toleration, find sufficiently palatable to swallow or keep down, (fig.) pocket or put up with (affront etc.), (usu. w. neg., as *cannot* ~ *it*). [ME *stomak* f. OF *estomac* f. L f. Gk *stomakhos* gullet f. *stoma* mouth]

sto'macher (-ŭmach-), n. (hist.). Front--piece of 15th-17th-c. woman's dress covering breast & pit of stomach, ending downwards in point often lapping over skirt, & often set with gems or richly embroidered. [ME, app. f. prec. +-ER¹; but pronunc. supports deriv. f. an AF *esto-machier*]

stomăch'ic (-k-), a. & n. **1.** Of the stomach; aiding ~ action, promoting digestion or appetite. **2.** n. ~ draught or drug, bitters etc. [f. L f. Gk *stomakhikos* (STOMACH, -IC)]

stŏmatit'is, n. Inflammation of the mucous membrane of the mouth. [as foll. +-ITIS]

stŏmato-, comb. form of Gk *stoma -atos* mouth, as ~*gas'tric*, of mouth & stomach; ~*logy* (-ŏl⁴) n. (med.), science of (diseases of) the mouth.

stōne, n., a., & v.t. **1.** Piece of rock of any shape usu. detached from earth's crust & of no great size, esp. a pebble, a cobble, or a single piece used or usable in building or roadmaking or as missile (STOCKs & ~s; *built of great* ~*s*; *as hard as a* ~; ROLL³*ing* ~; ROCK³*ing* ~; SERMONS *in* ~*s*; ~*s will cry out*, wrong is great enough to move inanimate things; *give a* ~ *for bread*, offer a mockery of help; *mark with a white* ~, record as a joyful day, w. ref. to ancient-Roman use of chalk; *meteoric* ~, meteorite; *leave no* ~ *unturned*, try every possible means, often *to* do; *break* ~*s*, get.living by preparing road metal, as phr. for being reduced to extremities; *cast, throw,* ~*s or a* ~ *at,* or *the first* ~, lit., & = make aspersions on character etc. of; *those who live in glass houses should not throw* ~*s*, aspersion provokes retort; *shower of* ~*s*, thrown, or rolling down hill etc.; *kill two* BIRDS *with one* ~; ~*'s cast* or *throw,* distance ~ can be thrown). **2.** (Usu. *precious* ~) a gem (*no* ~ *in it worth less than £100*; *Bristol* ~, Bristol DIAMOND; CAIRNGORM ~). **3.** ~*s or rock as a substance* or material (often with defining pref., as SAND, LIME¹, ~; *Bath, Caen, Portland,* ~, kinds of building-; *built of* ~; ~ *buildings* etc.; ~ *jar* etc., of ~ware; ~ JUG¹; HOLYSTONE; *artificial* ~, kinds of concrete; *Cornish* ~, kaolin; *has a heart of* ~, is hard--hearted; *harden into* ~, petrify lit. or fig.; *the* ~ *age*, stage of civilization at which implements & weapons were of ~, not metal; PHILOSOPHERS' ~). **4.** Piece of ~ of definite & designed shape (often with purpose specified by word in comb., or easily supplied from context; GRIND, GRAVE¹, HEARTH, MILL¹, WHET, -~; *Moabite, Rosetta,* ~, stelae with historically important inscriptions. **5.** Thing resembling ~ in hardness or pebble in shape, e.g. calculus (as single concretion or as the malady), hard case of kernel in drupe or ~-fruit, seed of grape, testicle, pellet of hail, (GALL¹-~; *underwent an operation for* ~ or *the* ~, remove the ~*s from plums, grapes,* etc.; *hail-storm with* ~*s as big as marbles*). **6.** ∥ Weight of 14 lb. or of other amounts varying with the commodity (*rides 12* ~, weighs that in the saddle; *give a* ~ *& a beating to*, orig. racing sl., surpass easily; ~ *of meat or fish 8 lb.*, ~ *of cheese 16 lb.*, etc.). **7.** ~*-axe*, with two obtuse edges for hewing ~; ~*-blind* (quite); ~*-blue*, compound of indigo with starch or whiting; ~*-boiling*, primitive method of boiling by putting heated ~s into water; ~*-borer*, kinds of mollusc; ~*-break*, saxifrage; ~*-buck*, steenbok; ~*-butler*, kind of alum; ~*-cast*, = ~*'s cast* above; ~*-CHAT²*; ~*-coal*, anthracite; ~*-cold* (quite); ~*'crop*, kinds of low creeping plant growing esp. on walls & rocks; ~*--curlew*, thick-knee or thick-kneed plover; ~*-dead, -deaf,* (quite); ~*-eater,* = ~*-borer*; *~-fence* (sl.), whisky & cider, or similar mixed drink; ~-*fern*, ceterach; ~-*fly*, insect with aquatic larvae found under ~s, used as bait for trout; ‖~ *frigate*, naval establishment ashore bearing name of ship; ~-*fruit*, with seeds enclosed in hard shell surrounded by pulp, drupe, e.g. plum, peach, cherry; ~-*gall*, round mass of clay in variegated sand~; ~-*horse* (arch.), stallion; ~ *man*, cairn; ~ *marten*, = BEECH *marten*; ~'*mason*, dresser of or builder in ~; ~-*parsley*, umbelliferous hedge plant of carrot family; ~-*pine*, S.-Ital. kind with branches at top spreading like umbrella; ~-*pit*, quarry; ~ *pitch*, inspissated pitch; ~-*plover*, large kind called also *thick-knee* & ~-*curlew*; ~-*race* (of runners who must pick up ~s laid at intervals); ‖~-*rag*, kind of lichen; ~-*rue*, kind of fern; ~-*saw*, untoothed iron blade stretched in saw-frame for cutting ~ with aid of sand; ~-*weed*, gromwell; ~-*snipe*, large N.-Amer. kind; ~*wall*' v.i. & t., obstruct by ~walling; ~*wall*'*ing*, (crick.) excessively cautious batting, (pol., esp. Austral.) parliamentary obstruction; ~'*ware*, pottery made from very silicious clay or from composition of clay & flint; ~'*work*, masonry; ~'*wort*, kinds of plant, esp. ~-parsley; hence (-)stōnED² (-nd), ~'LESS (-nl-), aa. 8. adj. Made of ~. 9. v.t. Pelt with ~s (~ *to death*). 10. Free (fruit) from ~s. 11. Face, pave, etc., with ~. [OE *stān*, OS *stēn*, OHG *stein*, ON *steinn*, Goth. *stains* f. Gmc **stainaz*]

stŏn'/y̆, a. & adv. 1. Full of, covered with, having many, stones; hard, rigid, fixed, as stone (*a ~y stare*, refusing response or recognition; ~*y heart*, obdurate or unfeeling heart, also hard core or interior, whence ~y̆-heartED² a.); hence ~ı̆LY² adv., ~ı̄NESS n. 2. adv. Utterly (only in ~*y*-BROKE²). [ME; -Y²]

stood. See STAND.

stōŏge, n., & v.i. (sl.). 1. *Butt, foil, esp. for a comedian; a deputy; subordinate, puppet; person learning to fly. 2. v.i. Move, esp. fly, *about*, *around*, etc. [orig. unkn.]

stŏŏk, n., & v.t. (chiefly Sc. & north.). = SHOCK³. [ME *stouk*, f. or cogn. w. MLG *stūke*, WFlem. *stuik*]

stŏŏl, n., & v.i. 1. Backless seat for one, often consisting of wooden slab on three legs (*office ~*, high ~ used by clerks etc.; MUSIC, CAMP¹, ~*~*; *three-legged ~*; *folding ~*, made to fold up; ~ *of repentance*, orig. that on which fornicators etc. were set to receive rebuke in churches in Scotland, & now transf.; *fall between two ~s*, fail from vacillation between two courses etc.); low bench for kneeling on; = FOOT-~. 2. (archit.). Window-sill. 3. (Place for) evacuation of bowels, faeces evacuated, (*go to ~*; CLOSE¹, NIGHT¹, ~*~*). 4. Root or stump of plant from which shoots spring. 5. Piece of wood to which decoy-bird is attached. 6. ~-*ball*, old game resembling cricket still played in Sussex esp. by girls;

~-*pigeon*, pigeon used, person acting, as decoy. 7. v.i. Throw up shoots from root; (arch.) go to ~, evacuate bowels. [OE *stōl*, OS *stōl*, OHG *stuol*, ON *stóll*, Goth. *stōls* f. Gmc **stōlaz* (**stō-*, **sta-* STAND)]

stōŏp¹, v.i. & t., & n. 1. Bring one's head nearer the ground by bending down from standing position, (fig.) deign or condescend *to* do, descend or lower oneself *to* some conduct (~ *to conquer*, gain power or one's end by preliminary self-abasement); carry one's head & shoulders bowed forward, whence ~'ınGLY² adv.; (of hawk etc., & transf.) swoop, pounce; incline (head, neck, shoulders, back) forward & down; tilt (cask) forward. 2. n. ~ing carriage of body; (arch.) swoop of hawk etc. [OE *stūpian*, MDu. *stūpen*, ON *stúpa* rel. to Gmc **staupo-* STEEP¹]

stōŏp², n. = STOUP.

stōŏp³, n. (U.S., Can.). Unroofed platform in front of house. [f. Du. STOEP]

stŏp¹, v.t. & i. (-pp-). 1. Stuff up or *up*, prevent or forbid passage through, make impervious or impassable, close, bar, stifle, stanch, (~ *a leak*, *hole*, etc.; ~*ped pipe* in organ, with upper end plugged, giving note an octave lower; ~ *one's ears*, put fingers in to avoid hearing, also fig. refuse to listen; ‖~ *a tooth*, fill cavity in it with ~p'ıNG¹ n. of gold, amalgam, cement, etc.; ~ *a wound*, stanch its bleeding; ~ *one's mouth*, fig., induce him by bribery or other means to keep silence about something; ~ *a gap*, serve to meet a temporary need; ~ *the way*, be or act as obstruction, prevent progress). 2. Put an end to (motion etc.), completely check progress or motion or operation of, effectively hinder or prevent, (~ *progress* etc.; ~ *horse* etc., esp. when running away; ~ *ball*, esp. of batsman or field in cricket; ~ *thief*!, cry of pursuer; ~ *blow*, parry it in boxing; ~ *blow with* one's *head* etc., joc., receive it, esp. ~ *a bullet*, (sl.) ~ *one*, be shot; *thick walls* ~ *sound*, render it inaudible; ~ *one's breath*, kill him by smothering or otherwise; ~ *clock*, *factory*, etc., make it cease working; ~ *person's doing*, person *from doing*; *shall* ~ *that nonsense*, not allow it to go on). 3. Cut off, suspend, decline customary giving of or permission for, (*shall* ~ *your wages*, *holidays*, *meetings*; *the cost must be* ~*ped out of his salary*; ~ *payment of a cheque*, direct one's banker not to cash; ~ *payment*, declare oneself unable to meet obligations, break financially; *why has our gas*, *water*, *been* ~*ped?*). 4. Obtain desired note from (string of violin etc.) by pressing finger, so shortening vibrating length. 5. Cease, come to an end, cease from doing, discontinue (one's action), cease from motion or speaking or action, make a halt or pause, (*noise*, *annuity*, ~*s*; *do not* ~, go on, continue; ~ *dead* or *short*, cease abruptly; *shall* ~ *playing*, *subscribing*, *my visits*, *my endeavours*; *do*~

grumbling, your complaints, that noise; he ~*ped in the middle of a sentence*; *my watch has* ~*ped*; *train does not* ~ *at, before,* *Exeter*; *he never* ~*s to think*). **6.** (colloq.). Remain, stay, sojourn, (*shall* ~ *in bed, at home*; ~ *up,* not go to bed; *shall you* ~ *for the sermon?*; *have been* ~*ping in Cornwall with friends*). **7.** Provide with stops, punctuate, (*a badly spelt & ~ped letter*). **8.** (Naut.) make fast, stopper, (cable etc.); (etching) ~ *out,* cover (parts that are to be protected from action of acid) with defensive coating (~*ping-brush,* for doing this); (photog.) ~ *down,* obscure part of (lens) with diaphragm; (founding) ~ *off,* fill in (part of mould not to be used) with sand. ***9.** ~ *off,* ~ *over,* break one's journey; ~*'off,* ~*'over,* nn., a break in one's journey. Hence ~p'AGE(3) n. (also, path., obstruction in bodily organ). [ME, f. OE *-stoppian* = OLFrank. *-stuppōn,* MDu., MLG. *stoppen* f. WG **stoppōn* f. Rom. ***stuppare** (L *stuppa* tow; see STUFF]

stŏp², n. **1.** Stopping or being stopped, pause, check, (*put a* ~ *to*; *make, come to, bring to, a* ~; *is at a* ~, not proceeding or unable to proceed; *train runs from London to Crewe without a* ~). **2.** Punctuation-mark, esp. comma, semicolon, colon, or period (*full* ~, period; *come to a full* ~, transf., cease completely). **3.** (Mus.) change of pitch effected by stopping (see prec.), (in organ) row of pipes of one character brought into action by a ~*-knob* or small ~*-key*; (fig.) manner of speech adopted to produce particular effect (*can put on* or *pull out the pathetic, blustering, virtuous,* etc., ~ *at will*). **4.** Batten, peg, or the like, meant to stop motion of something at fixed point. **5.** (Opt., photog.) diaphragm; (phonet.) mute consonant sound made by closure of organs concerned (as k, t, p); (naut.) small line used as lashing, also projection of lower mast-head supporting trestle-trees. Hence ~'LESS a. [f. prec.]

stŏp-, comb. form of STOP¹·²: ~*'cock,* externally-operated valve inserted in pipe to regulate passage of contents; ~*-collar,* ring checking motion of shaft; ~*-cylinder,* kind of printing-press; ~*-drill,* with shoulder limiting depth of penetration; ~*'gap,* ·temporary substitute; ~*-key, -knob,* see prec. (sense 3); ~*-order,* order to stockbroker to buy or sell on stock's reaching specified price; ~*-plate,* limiting play of axle on bearings; ‖ ~*-press,* (news) inserted in paper after printing has begun; ~*-valve,* closing pipe against passage of liquid; ~*-volley* (lawn tennis), checked ⸲ volley close to net, dropping ball dead on other side; ~*-watch,* with mechanism for starting & stopping it at will, used in timing races etc.

stŏpp'er, n., & v.t. In vbl senses; esp.: plug for closing bottle etc. usu. of same material as the vessel (*put a* ~ *on* something, bring about cessation of it); *tobacco·*

~, implement for pressing down tobacco in pipe-bowl; (naut.) rope, clamp, double claw, etc., for checking & holding rope cable or chain cable; ~ *bolt,* ring-bolt in deck to which ~s are secured; ~*-knot,* finishing of end of ~*-rope* made by interlacing its strands; (vb) close or secure with ~. [-ER¹]

stŏp'ple, n., & v.t. **1.** Stopper of bottle or other vessel. **2.** v.t. Close with ~. [ME; partly f. STOP¹ + -LE(1), partly aphetic f. ESTOPPEL]

stōr'age, n. Storing of goods, method of doing this (*cold* ~, in refrigerators etc., also transf.); space available for it; cost of warehousing; ~ *cell, battery* (electr.), apparatus for storing electrical energy in a chemical form, accumulator. [STORE + -AGE].

stōr'ax, n. (Tree yielding) a resinous vanilla-scented balsam formerly much used in medicine & perfumery; *liquid* ~, a balsam got from the Oriental sweet-gum-tree. [ME; LL var. of STYRAX]

stōre, n., & v.t. **1.** Abundance, provision, stock of something ready to be drawn upon, (sing. with or, arch. exc. of intangible things, without *a,* & pl.; *has* ~, *good* ~, *a* ~, or ~s, *of wine, wit, anecdote, wisdom*; *in* ~, laid up in readiness, about to come, destined, as *I have, tomorrow has, a surprise in* ~ *for you*). **2.** Place where things are kept for sale, ***ordinary shop* (~ *clothes* etc., esp. = ready-made; *book* etc. ·~), ‖ large commercial establishment selling goods of many different kinds (*the* ~s, these opp. ordinary shops, as *I get most things at the* ~s; CHAIN, DEPARTMENT, ~; CO-OPERATIVE ~ or ~s; *Army & Navy,* etc., ~s, orig. selling only to members, who must have specified qualification). **3.** pl. Articles of particular kind or for special purpose accumulated for use, supply of things needed, (*military, naval,* etc., ~s; *marine* ~s, old ship materials). **4.** attrib. Kept for future use (~ *cattle* etc., not yet being fattened). **5.** *Set* ~ *by,* reckon precious or important, esp. *set no great* ~ *by.* **6.** ~⸲ *house,* place where things are ~d up, granary etc., esp. fig. (*person, book, is a* ~*house of information* etc., cf. MINE¹); ~*'keeper,* *shopkeeper; ~*-room,* in which household supplies are kept; ~*-ship,* carrying ~s for fleet, garrison, etc. **7.** v.t. Stock or furnish with or *with* something (usu. with knowledge or the like; ~ *your mind with facts*; *a well·~d memory*). **8.** Lay up or *up* for future use (*harvest has been* ~*d,* got in; ~ *up a saying in* one's *heart*); deposit (furniture etc.) in a warehouse for temporary keeping. **9.** (Of receptacle) hold, keep, contain, have storage-accommodation for (*a single cell can* ~ *2,000,000 foot-pounds of energy*); hence **stōr'ABLE** a. [ME; aphetic f. obs. *astore* sb f. OF *estore,* f. *estorer* (whence E vb), f. L *instaurare,* cf. RESTORE]

stōr'|ey (pl. ~eys), **stōr'|ў** (pl. ~ies), n. Any of the parts into which a house is divided horizontally, the whole of the rooms etc. having a continuous floor, (*fell from a third-~ey window; a house of five ~eys; upper ~ey* or *~eys*, fig., the brain, as *is a little wrong in the upper ~ey*); *~ey-post*, upright supporting a beam on which rests a floor or wall. Hence (-)~ **eyED²**, **~ied**, (-rĭd), a. [aphetic f. Anglo-L *historia* (perh. orig. meaning a tier of STORIED windows or sculpture), hence prob. same wd as STORY¹]

stōr'iātĕd, a. (Of title-pages etc.) with elaborate decorative designs. [for HIS-TORIATED]

stōr'ied (-rĭd), a. Celebrated in legend, associated with legends or stories or history; adorned with legendary or historical representations. [f. STORY¹ & *story* vb +-ED²]

stork, n. Tall stately wading bird allied to heron, the best-known species pure white except for black wing-tips & reddish bill & feet, occas. half domesticated & nesting on buildings, & credited with peculiar affection both to its young & its parents (*King S~*, oppressively active ruler, cf. *King* LOG¹); *~'s-bill*, kinds of geranium. [OE *storc*, OS *stork*, OHG *storah*, ON *storkr* f. Gmc *sturkaz*]

storm, n., & v.i. & t. **1.** Violent disturbance of the atmosphere with thunder, strong wind, or heavy rain or snow or hail, a tempest, (*cyclonic ~; thunder, rain, snow, wind, -~; ~ in a teacup*, great excitement over small matter); (meteorol.) atmospheric disturbance intermediate between whole gale & hurricane. **2.** Violent disturbance of the established order in human affairs, tumult, agitation, war, invasion, dispute, etc. (*~ & stress*, period of fermenting ideas & unrest in person's or nation's life, f. G *Sturm und Drang*, name of a play characteristic of the literary movement in Germany 1770–82). **3.** Vehement shower *of* missiles or outbreak of hisses, applause, indignation, etc. **4.** Direct assault by troops on fortified place, capture *of* place by such assault, (*take by ~*, of such capture, & transf. of captivating audience or person rapidly). **5.** *~-beaten*, battered by lit. or fig. *~s*; *~-bell*, tract in which *~s* are frequent; *~-bird*, stormy petrel; *~'bound*, prevented from leaving port or continuing voyage by *~s*; *~-card*, chart assisting navigator of ship in *~* to conjecture position of *~-centre* & so to direct course; *~-centre*, point to which wind blows spirally inward in cyclonic *~*, (fig.) subject etc. upon which agitation or disturbance is concentrated; *~-cloud*, heavy rain-cloud, state of affairs that threatens disturbances; ‖ *~-cock*, kinds of bird, esp. missel-thrush, fieldfare, or green woodpecker; ‖ *~-cone*, tarred-canvas cone hoisted as warning of high wind, upright for north & inverted for south; *~-door*, additional outer door for protection in bad weather or winter; *~-drum*, cylinder added to *~-cone* for expected *~* of great violence; ‖ *~-finch*, stormy petrel; *~-glass*, sealed tube containing a solution of which the clarity is affected by temperature, formerly regarded as efficient weather-glass; *~-petrel*, stormy petrel; *~-sail*, of smaller size & stouter canvas than the corresponding one used in ordinary weather; *~-signal*, *~-cone*, *~-drum*, or other device for warning of an approaching *~*; *~-tossed*, lit. & fig.; *~-troops*, shock-troops, (also) a Nazi semi-military organization (*~-trooper*, member of this); *~-wind*; *~-window*, as *~-door*; *~-zone*, *~-belt*; hence *~'LESS*, *~'PROOF²*, aa. **6.** vb. (Of wind, rain, etc.) rage, be violent. **7.** Talk violently, rage, bluster, fume, scold (intr.), (often *at* object of displeasure). **8.** Take by *~* (*~ing-party*, detachment told off to begin assault; so *~'ER¹* n.). [OE, ˙OS *storm*, OHG *sturm*, ON *stormr* f. Gmc *sturmaz* f. *stur-* STIR¹]

storm'|ў, a. Of marked violence, raging, vehement, boisterous, (*~y wind, sea, waves, passions, temper, abuse*); infested or troubled with lit. or fig. storms (*a ~y coast, sea, night, debate, life*); associated with or threatening storms (*~y petrel; a ~y sunset*). Hence *~ILY²* adv., *~INESS* n. [ME; -Y²]

stōr'tĭ(h)ing (-tĭ-), n. Norwegian Parliament. [Norw. (-*ti*-), f. *stor* great, *t(h)ing* assembly]

stōr'ў¹, n. **1.** History (arch.; *versed in classic ~*). **2.** Past course of person's or institution's life (*his ~ is an eventful one; in our rough island-~*). **3.** Account given of an incident (*they all tell the same ~; according to his own ~*, suggestion of doubt as to his veracity; *to make a long ~ short*, formula excusing omission of details; *it is quite another ~ now*, we now hear a different account, esp. = things have changed; *the ~ goes*, it is said); any narrative or descriptive article in a newspaper. **4.** Piece of narrative, tale of any length told or printed in prose or verse of actual or fictitious events, legend, myth, anecdote, novel, romance, (*tell me a ~; but is the ~ true?; short ~*, relating usu. a single incident & published as article in magazine or as one of a collection; *good, funny, ~*, amusing anecdote often embodying witticism or ludicrous situation; *but that is another ~*, formula for breaking off & tantalizing reader with allusion). **5.** Main facts or plot of novel or epic or play (*reads only for the ~; the ~ is the least part of the book*). **6.** Facts or experiences that deserve narration (*that face must have a ~ belonging to it*). **7.** (nursery). Lie, fib, liar (*oh you ~!*). **8.** *~-book*, containing *~* or stories; *~-teller*, Eastern making a living by telling stories to audience, writer of stories, retailer of anecdotes in society, (nursery) liar. [ME *storie* f. AF *estorie* (OF *estoire*) f. L as HISTORY]

story², See STOREY.

‖ **stŏt**, n. (north. dial.). Young ox, steer. [OE *stot(t)*; cf. ON *stutr* bull]

stoup (-ōop), n. (arch.). Flagon, beaker, drinking-vessel; holy-water basin. [f. ON *staup* = OE *stēap*, OHG *stouf* f. Gmc **staupaz, -am*]

stout, a. & n. **1.** Brave, doughty, resolute, vigorous, sturdy, stubborn, staunch, strongly built, (~ *fellow*, arch., also colloq., good at fighting etc.; *a* ~ *heart*, courage, whence ~**heart'**ED² (-hăr-) a., ~-**heart'**ĕdLY² adv., ~-**heart'**ĕdNESS n.; *made a* ~ *resistance*; *a* ~ *opponent*; *a* ~ *stick, ship*, etc.); corpulent, bulky, tending to fatness; hence ~'ISH¹(2) a., ~'LY² adv., ~'NESS n. **2.** n. Kind of strong dark-brown beer brewed (esp. in Dublin) with roasted malt. [ME *st(o)ute*, f. OF *estout* adj. f. WG **stulta-* (= MHG, G *stolz* proud)]

stōve¹, n., & v.t. **1.** Kinds of closed apparatus in which heat is produced by consumption of wood, coal, charcoal, oil, gas, or other fuel, for use in warming rooms, cooking, etc.; (gardening) hot-house with artificial heat; ~-*pipe*, conducting smoke & gases from~ to chimney (**~-pipe hat*, tall silk hat). **2.** v.t. Force, raise, (plants) in ~. [ME = sweating-room; f. MDu., MLG *stove*, corresp. to OE *stofa*, OHG *stuba*]

stove², See STAVE².

stow (-ō), v.t. Pack (goods etc.) in right or convenient places without waste of room (~ *thing away*, place it where it will not cause obstruction); fill (receptacle) with articles compactly arranged; (sl., usu. in imperat.) abstain from, cease to indulge in, (~ *larks, that nonsense*, etc.); ~'*away*, person getting free passage by hiding aboard ship (~ *away* as v.i., do this); ~-*wood*, billets used for chocking casks in ship's hold. Hence ~'AGE(1, 3, 4) (-ōij) n. [ME *stow, stouwe*, etc., f. OE *stōw* a place; in (16th c.) naut. sense perh. infl. by Du. *stouwen*]

strabis'm|us (-z-), n. Squinting, squint, (*cross-eyed* ~*us*, with eye or eyes turning inward; *wall-eyed* ~*us*, outward). Hence ~IC, ~AL, aa. [mod. L, f. Gk *strabismos* (*strabos* squinting, -ISM)]

strabŏt'omy̆, n. Operation of cutting eyeball muscle to cure squint. [prec., -TOMY]

străd'dl|e, v.i. & t., & n. **1.** Take or be in attitude with legs wide apart; stand or sit across (thing) thus (*cannot~e his horse*; *stood* ~*ing the ditch*); part (one's legs) widely; (nav.) drop shots short of & beyond (target, enemy) esp. to find range; drop bombs from side to side across (target); (fig.) vacillate between two policies etc., sit on the fence. **2.** n. Act of ~ing lit. or fig.; (St. Exch.) contract giving holder the right of either calling for or

delivering stock at fixed price. [frequent. of *străd-*, var. of *strĭd-* STRIDE, see -LE(3)]

Strădivār'ius (*or* -ăr-), (colloq.) **Străd**, n. Violin or other stringed instrument made by ~ of Cremona (d. 1737).

strafe (-ahf; ***-āf), v.t., & n. (sl.). **1.** Bombard, worry with shells, bombs, sniping, etc.; reprimand or abuse or thrash. **2.** n. Piece of strafing (*the morning* ~, gunfire at dawn). [joc. adaptation of G 1914 catchword *Gott* ~ (God chastise) *England*]

străg'gl|e, v.i. Stray from the main body, fail to remain compact, get dispersed, proceed in scattered irregular order, be sporadic, occur here & there, (*crowd* ~*ed along*; *plant* ~*es*, grows long & weedy; ~*ing village, houses*, etc.). Hence ~ER¹ n., ~ingLY² adv., ~Y² a. [perh. alt. f. **strackle* frequent. of dial. *strake* rel. to STRETCH]

straight (-āt), a., n., & adv. **1.** Without curve or bend, extending uniformly in same direction, (~ *line* in geom., lying evenly between any two of its points; ~ *arch*, shaped like inverted V, without curves; *a* ~ *back*, not bowed; *a* ~ *knee*, not bent; ~ *.legs*, not bandy or knock-kneed; ~ *hair*, not curly; (of aim, look, blow, course) going direct to the mark; upright, honest, candid, (~ *dealings*, *speaking*; *is perfectly* ~ *in all his dealings*; ~ *thinking*, logical, not swayed by emotion); in proper order or place, level, symmetrical, (*are the pictures* ~?; *put things* ~, get rid of disorder; *accounts are* ~, made up in due form; *a* ~ *race* etc., in which competitors do their best to win); direct from source (~ *tip*, hint esp. as to likely winner of race or prospects of investment got from good authority); **neat* (*a whisky* ~), undiluted, unmixed; **the* ~ *ticket*, the party programme without modification; ~ *jet*, jet aircraft with no propeller; ~*for'ward*, honest, open, frank, (of task etc.) presenting no complications; so ~*for'wardly* adv., ~-*for'wardness* n.; ~'*way* (arch.), at once, immediately; hence~'EN⁶ v.t. & i., ~'NESS n., (-āt-). **2.** n. ~ condition (*is out of the* ~, crooked); ~ part of something, esp. concluding stretch of racecourse (*they were even as they reached the* ~); sequence of five cards in poker. **3.** adv. In a ~ line, direct, without deviation or circumlocution, (*go* ~; *hit* ~ *from the shoulder*, in boxing, also fig.; *ride* ~, taking fences etc. instead of going round; *come* ~ *from Paris*; *is making* ~ *for a precipice*; *told it him* ~ *out*)»; in right direction, with good aim, (*shoot* ~); correctly (*does not see* ~); (arch.) at once (also in ~ *away*, sl., immediately); ~ *off*, without hesitation, deliberation, etc., as *cannot tell you* ~ *off*). **4.** ~-*cut*, (tobacco) cut lengthwise into long silky fibres; ~-*edge*, bar with one edge accurately ~, used for testing; ~-*eight*, motor vehicle with eight cylinders in line; ~ *eye*, ability to detect deviation from the ~; ~ *face* (intentionally inexpressive); ~ *fight* (pol.), direct contest between two candidates. [ME *streǥt*, p.p. of *strecche* STRETCH]

strain[1], v.t. & i. **1.** Stretch tightly, make taut, exercise to greatest possible or beyond legitimate extent, press to extremes, wrest or distort from true intention or meaning, (~ *parchment across the aperture*; ~ *rope to breaking-point*; ~ *every nerve*, do one's utmost; ~ *one's ears, eyes, voice*, etc., listen etc. to best of one's power, & see below; ~ *one's authority, powers, rights*, etc., or *the law* etc., apply them beyond their province or in violation of their true intention; ~ *a point*, go further than one is entitled or can be expected to, esp. in the way of concession, to effect a purpose; *a ~ed interpretation* or *sense*, got by pressing some rule of grammar etc. too far; *~ing-beam, -piece,* horizontal beam used as strut between tops of queen-posts). **2.** Hug (person) *to* oneself or one's breast etc. **3.** p.p. Produced under compulsion or by effort, artificial, forced, constrained, not spontaneous, (*the quality of mercy is not ~ed,* mercy should be spontaneous; *~ed manner, laugh, cordiality,* etc.). **4.** Overtask, injure or try or imperil by over-use or making of excessive demands, (*take care not to ~ your eyes, voice,* etc.; *for fear of ~ing his followers' loyalty*; *has ~ed a muscle, his leg, his heart,* etc.; *ship is ~ed,* has had parts wrenched out of rigid state; *~ed relations,* over-sensitiveness between parties who have tried each other's forbearance too far). **5.** Make intense effort, strive intensely *after,* tug *at,* hold out with difficulty under or *under* pressure, (*the ~ing horses, masts; plants ~ing upwards to the light; dogs, horses, rowers, ~ at the leash, collar, oar; porter ~ing under his load ; ~s too much after epigram, effect,* etc.). **6.** Clear (liquid) of solid matter by passing through sieve or other ~ 'ER[1](2) n.; filter (solids) *out* from liquid; (of liquid) percolate. **7.** ~ *at a gnat,* be over-scrupulous (ref. to *Matt.* xxiii. 24, prop. ~ *out,* see R.V., in prec. sense). Hence ~'ABLE *a.* [ME *streine* f. OF *estreindre estreign-* f. L *stringere strict-*]

strain[2], n. **1.** Pull, stretching force, tension, demand upon or force that tries cohesion or strength or stability or resources, exertion required to meet such demand or to do something difficult, injury or change of structure resulting from such exertion or force, (*the ~ on the rope was tremendous; was a great ~ on my resources, attention, credulity; the ~ of modern life; is suffering from ~ or over-~; all his senses were on the ~,* exerted to the utmost; *is epigrammatic without ~,* appearance of undue effort; *has a ~ in his leg*). **2.** (phys., mech.). Condition of a body subjected to stress, molecular displacement. **3.** (poet. & rhet., usu. in pl.).

Burst or snatch or spell of music or poetry (*martial, inspiriting, pathetic,* etc., ~*s,* music or poetry of such character; *the ~s of the harp, of the Elizabethan poets,* etc.). **4.** Tone or style adopted in talking or writing, tendency of discourse, (*he went on in another ~; & much more in the same ~*). **5.** Moral tendency forming part of a character (*there is a ~ of weakness, ferocity, mysticism, in him*). **6.** Breed of animals, human stock or family, (*comes of a good ~*). [ME; senses 1–5 f. prec.; sense 6 f. OE *strēon* gain, progeny]

strait, a. & n. **1.** Narrow, limited, confined or confining, (arch. exc. in ~ *gate* w. ref. to *Matt.* vii. 14, ~ *jacket* or usu. *waistcoat,* strong garment put on maniacs to confine arms, which are either in sleeves so long that the ends can be tied or are strapped within body of jacket, & in ~*-laced* now fig. only, severely virtuous, morally scrupulous, puritanic). **2.** Strict (arch. exc. in ~*est sect of* w. ref. to *Acts* xxvi. 5); hence ~'LY[2] adv. (arch.), ~'NESS n. (arch.), ~'EN[6] v.t. (~*ened circumstances,* poverty; *is ~ened for,* ill supplied with). **2.** n. Narrow passage of water connecting two seas or large bodies of water (usu. in pl. when used of particular ~ with name, as *the S~s of Messina, Dover; S~s Settlements,* former Crown colony on S~s of Malacca & Singapore; *the S~s,* formerly of Gibraltar, now usu. of Malacca); (usu. pl.) difficult position, need, distress, (esp. *in ~s*). [ME *streit,* f. OF *estreit* f. L *strictus* STRICT]

strāke, n. Continuous line of planking or plates from stem to stern of ship (GARBOARD ~). [ME, app. f. *strak-* whence Gmc **strakkjan* STRETCH]

stramin'eous, a. (arch.). Of, light or worthless as, coloured like, straw. [f. L *stramineus* (*stramen -inis* straw) + -OUS]

stramōn'ium, n. (Drug, much used in asthma, from seeds or leaves of) kind of datura. [mod. L, of uncert. orig.]

strand[1], n., & v.t. & i. **1.** Margin of sea, lake, or river (rhet., poet.). **2.** vb. Run (t. & i. of ship) aground; (p.p.) in difficulties, unable to get along esp. for want of funds or other resources, left behind while others advance. [OE *strand,* MLG *strand-,* ON *strǫnd*]

strănd[2], n., & v.t. **1.** One of the strings or wires by twisting which a rope is made; (fig.) element or strain in any composite whole. **2.** v.t. Break a ~ in (rope). [15th– –18th c. also *strond*; orig. unkn.]

strānge (-j), a. **1.** Foreign, alien, not one's own, not familiar or well known (*to*), novel, queer, peculiar, eccentric, singular, surprising, unaccountable, unexpected, (*in a ~ land; worship ~ gods; cannot play on a ~ ground, with a ~ racket; the place, work, handwriting, is ~ to me; it is a ~ thing, story; how ~ that you should not have heard!; wears the ~st clothes; is very ~ in his manner,* seems mad etc.; *truth is*

~r *than fiction*; *repeating the question with* ~ *persistency*; *feel* ~, not in one's usual condition, esp. dizzy etc.; *it feels* ~, is a novel sensation, whence ~'LY² (-jlĭ) adv. **2.** Fresh or unaccustomed *to*, unacquainted, bewildered, (*am* ~ *to the work*; *am quite* ~ *here*, do not know my way about or the people etc.; *feel* ~, not at home, out of one's element etc.). Hence ~'NESS (-jn-) n: [ME *strang, straung*(e), f. OF *estrange* f. L EXTRAN*eus*]

strän'ger (-j-), n. Foreigner, person in a country or town or company that he does not belong to, person unknown to or *to* one (in U.S. as rustic voc. = *sir* etc.), person entirely unaccustomed *to* some feeling or practice or experience, (*am a* ~ *here*, do not know my way about etc.; ‖ *spy* or *see* ~*s* in House of Commons, demand withdrawal of all but members or officials; *make a, no,* ~ *of,* treat distantly, cordially; *you are quite a* ~, seldom show yourself here; *is no, a,* ~ *to me,* I know, do not know, him; *is no,* ~ *to fear, court-intrigues,* has had no, much, experience of; *the little* ~, newborn child). [ME *straunger*(e), f. OF *estrangier,* as prec., -ER²(2)]

strangle (sträng'gl), v.t. Throttle, kill by squeezing windpipe; (of collar etc.) squeeze (neck); (fig.) suppress (movement, impulse, etc.); ~*hold,* deadly grip (usu. fig. in pol. or commerce). [ME *strangel, -ul,* f. OF *estrangler* f. L *strangulare* f. Gk *straggalaō*]

strangles (sträng'glz), n. pl. (usu. treated as sing). Infectious catarrh in horse, ass, etc. [f. prec.]

sträng'ul|āte (-ngg-), v.t. Strangle (rare); (path., surg.) prevent circulation through (vein, intestine, etc.) by compression. Hence ~A'TION n. [f. L as STRANGLE, -ATE³]

sträng'ūrў (-ngg-), n. Disease in which urine is passed painfully & in drops; disease produced in plants by bandaging. So **strängūr'ious** (-ngg-) a. [f. L f. Gk *straggouria* (*stragx -ggos* drop squeezed out, *ouron* urine)]

sträp, n., & v.t. (-pp-). **1.** Strip of leather; strip of leather or other flexible material with buckle or other fastening for holding things together or other purpose (SHOULDER-~; *rug, umbrella,* etc., -~, pair of ~s with holder joining them for making bundle); strip of metal used to secure or connect, leaf of hinge, etc.; (bot.) tongue-shaped part in ligulate floret; *the* ~, chastisement with a ~. **2.** ~'*hanger,* bus or train passenger who has to stand & hold on by ~ for want of sitting space; ~-*laid,* (of rope) made by laying ropes side by side & joining them into a flat band; ~-*oil,* beating given with ~; ~-*work,* ornamentation imitating plaited ~s; ~-*wort,* kind of white-flowered knotgrass. Hence ~'LESS a., (of dress) without shoulder-~s. **3.** v.t. Secure with ~ (often *up, down,* etc.; ~*ped*

trousers, held down by ~ passing below instep for riding etc.); strop, whet, (razor, knife); (surg.) close (wound), bind (part), up or *up* with adhesive plaster or ~p'ING¹(4) n.; flog with ~; (part. as adj., cf. *thumping, whacking, whopping* big, lusty, tall, (*a* ~*ping girl, fellow*), whence ~p'ER¹ n. [dial. form of STROP]

strappād'ō, n. (pl. ~*s*), & v.t. **1.** Torture inflicted by securing person's hands or other part in ropes, raising them, & letting him fall till brought up by taut rope. **2.** v.t. Subject to ~. [f. F *strapade* f. It. *strappata* (*strappare* pull); for -*o* see -ADO(2)]

sträss, n. Paste used in making artificial gems. [G, f. name of inventor, Josef *Strasser*]

strata. See STRATUM.

străt'agĕm, n. (An) artifice, trick(ery), device(s) for deceiving enemy, (*devised a* ~; *must be effected by* ~). [15th c., f. F *stratagème* f. L f. Gk *stratēgēma* (*stratēgeō* be STRATEGUS)]

stratĕ'gic, a. Of, dictated by, serving the ends of, strategy (~ *skill, considerations, movement, position*); (of bombing) designed to disorganize the enemy's internal economy & to destroy morale. Hence ~AL a. (now rare), ~ALLY² adv., **strate'gics** n. [f. F -*ique* f. Gk *stratēgikos* (foll., -IC)]

stratēg'us, n. (Gk ant.; pl. -*gi* pr. -gī *or* -jī). Military commander, esp. one of annually appointed board of ten at Athens. [L, f. Gk *stratēgos* (*stratos* army, *agō* lead)]

străt'ĕg|ў, n. Generalship, the art of war, (lit. & fig.); management of an army or armies in a campaign, art of so moving or disposing troops or ships or aircraft as to impose upon the enemy the place & time & conditions for fighting preferred by oneself, (cf. TACTICS). Hence ~IST(3) n. [f. F *stratégie* f. Gk *stratēgia* (prec., -IA¹)]

sträth, n. (Sc.). Broad mountain valley; ~*spey'* (-ā), (music for) a lively Scottish dance (named f. *Strathspey* valley of the Spey. [f. Gael. *srath*]

stratic'ūlate, a. (geol.). Arranged in thin layers. [STRATUM, -I-, -CULE, -ATE²]

străt'i|fў, v.t. Arrange in strata (esp. p.p.). So ~FICA'TION n. [f. F *stratifier* f. med. L *stratificare* (STRATUM, -FY)]

strāto-, comb. form of STRATUS, as ~*ci'rrus,* ~*cŭm'ulus.*

stratŏc'racў, n. Military government, domination of soldiers. [Gk *stratos* army, -CRACY]

străt'osphēre, n. The layer of atmospheric air lying above the TROPOSPHERE, in which the temperature ceases to fall with height, remaining constant. [STRATO-+SPHERE]

străt'|um, n. (pl. ~*a*). (Geol.) layer, or set of successive layers, of any deposited substance; (transf.) social grade (*the various* ~*a of society*). Hence ~AL, **străt'ĭFORM, aa., stratĭG'RAPHY(2) n.,**

strătĭgraph'ic a., **strătĭgräph'ically** adv. [L, = something spread or laid down, neut. p.p. of *sternere* strew]

strāt'us, n. (pl. *-tī*). Continuous horizontal sheet of cloud. [assim. of prec. to termination of *cumulus* & other CLOUDS]

straw, n., & v.t. **1.** Dry cut stalks of kinds of grain as material for bedding, thatching, packing, hats, etc. (*made of, thatched* etc. *with,* ~ ; *a load of* ~ ; ~ *mattress, hat, rope,* etc.; *in the* ~, arch., in childbed; *man of* ~, stuffed effigy, imaginary person set up as opponent etc., person without substantial means); ~ hat; single stalk or piece of ~, insignificant trifle, (*with a* ~ *in his mouth*; *lemonade sucked through* ~s; *draw* ~s, draw lots with ~s of different lengths; *make bricks without* ~, of persons set to work without adequate means, see *Exod.* v. 7; *catch at a* ~, resort to utterly inadequate expedient like drowning man; *the last* ~, slight addition that makes something no longer tolerable as with camel's load; *a* ~ *shows which way the wind blows,* slight hint may suggest much; *is not worth, don't care, a* ~). **2.** ~*-board,* coarse cardboard made of ~ ; ~*-colour(ed),* (of) pale yellow; ~*-stem,* wineglass with stem not made separately & attached but drawn out of bowl; *~ *vote* (pol.), unofficial balloting as test of strength; ~*-worm,* caddis; hence ~'y² a. **3.** v.t. (arch.). Strew. [OE *strēaw,* OS, MDu., MLG, OHG *strō,* ON *strá* f. Gmc *strāwam f. **strau-, *strew-* STREW]

straw'berry, n. (Kind of perennial plant throwing out runners & producing) pulpy red fruit having surface studded with yellow seeds (*crushed* ~, kind of dull crimson; ‖ *the* ~ *leaves,* ducal rank, w. ref. to ornamentation of duke's coronet); ~*-mark,* soft reddish birthmark; ~ *pear,* (fruit of) W.-Ind. cactaceous plant; ~ *roan,* red ROAN¹; ~*-tree,* evergreen arbutus bearing ~-like fruit. [OE *strēaw-, strēowberige* (STRAW, BERRY)]

stray, v.i. (p.p. as -ED¹, 2), n., & a. **1.** Wander, go aimlessly, deviate from the right way or from virtue, lose one's way, get separated from flock or companions or proper place. **2.** n. ~ed domestic animal; WAIFS & ~s; ‖ property of deceased person escheating to crown in default of heirs; (radio, usu. in pl.) = ATMOSPHERICS. **3.** adj. (no comp. & sup.). ~ed; scattered, sporadic, occurring or met with now & then or casually or unexpectedly, (*a few* ~ *instances*; *a customer or two came in*; *hit by a* ~ *bullet*). [(vb) ME, aphetic f. *astray, estray* vbs f. OF *estraier* f. Rom. *estravagare f. L *extra vagari* EXTRAVAGATE; (n.) ME, f. AF *stray, estrai,* f. *estraier,* partly f. the vb; (adj.) 17th c., partly f. ASTRAY, partly f. n.]

streak, n., & v.t. & i. **1.** Long narrow irregular line or band or layer-edge, esp. one distinguished by colour, visible on a surface (*black with red* ~s; *a* ~ *of light*

above the horizon; *bacon with* ~s *of fat & lean*; ~ *of lightning,* flash; *like a* ~ *of lightning,* or *a* ~, swiftly; ‖ *the silver* ~, English Channel; *has a* ~ *of humour, superstition,* etc., *in him,* strain or element); hence ~'y² a., ~'ily² adv., ~'iness n. **2.** vb. (Usu. in p.p.) mark with ~(s); (intr.) move very rapidly (like a ~ of lightning). [OE *strica,* = OHG *strich,* Goth. *striks,* f. Gmc **strik-* STRIKE]

stream, n., & v.i. & t. **1.** Body of water running in bed, river, or brook, (*on the banks of a* ~; *up, down,* ~, moving or situated upwards, downwards, on river; whence ~'LESS a., ~'LET n.; flow of any liquid, onward moving fluid mass or crowd, (sing. or pl.) large quantity of or of something that flows or moves along, (*saw a* ~ *of lava*; *came out, went by, in a* ~ or ~s; *a* ~, ~s, *of blood, tears, people*); current, direction of flow, (GULF-~; *with, against, the* ~; *go with the* ~, do as others do; *the* ~ *of tendency, thought, is the other way*). **2.** ~*-anchor,* intermediate between bower & kedge esp. for use in warping; ~'*line,* (n.) natural course of water or air currents (~*line* shape in aircraft, motor-car, etc., that calculated to cause least resistance), (v.t.) give a ~line form to; hence ~'y² a. (rare). **3.** vb. Flow or move as a ~; run with liquid (~*ing eyes, windows, umbrella*); (of banner, loose hair, etc.) float or wave in the wind; emit ~ of (blood etc.). [OE *strēam,* OS *strōm,* OHG *stroum,* ON *straumr* f. Gmc *straumaz]

stream'er, n. Pennon, ribbon attached at one end & floating or waving at the other; column of light shooting up in aurora. [ME; -ER¹]

street, n. Town or village road that has (mainly) contiguous houses on one side or both, this with the houses, (*go down, across, the* ~; *main, side, broad,* etc., ~; *live in the* ~, be constantly outside one's house; *lives in a fashionable* ~; MAN¹ *in the* ~; *not in the same* ~ *with,* colloq., utterly inferior to in ability etc.; *window looks on the* ~; *in the* ~, said of St.-Exch. business done after closing hours; *on the* ~s, living by prostitution; KEY¹ *of the* ~; GRUB-STREET; HIGH, LOMBARD, QUEER, ~; ~ ARAB; ‖ ~ *cries,* of hawkers; ‖ ~ *orderly, scavenger*; (arch.) paved road, highway (as *Watling S*~); WALL STREET; *the* ~, = *Fleet S*~, *Wall S*~; *~'*car,* tram-car; ~*-door,* opening on ~; ~*-sweeper,* machine with revolving brush for cleaning ~s; ~'*walker,* common prostitute. Hence (-)~ED² a., ~'WARD adv. & a. [OE *strǣt,* OS *strāta,* OHG *straza,* f. LL *strata* (ellipt. f. *via strata* paved road), f. *sternere* strat- lay]

strĕngth, n. **1.** Being STRONG, degree in which person or thing is strong, (*the* ~ *of a man, rope, beam, fortress, current, argument, fleet*; *the* ~ *of wine, acid, tea, evidence*; ~ *of body, mind, will, memory, judgement*; *his* ~ *is in endurance*; *has the*

~ *of a horse*, is as strong; *has not the ~ to lift a cup, walk upstairs; that is beyond human, too much for my*, ~; MEASURE² one's ~ *with*; *on the ~ of*, encouraged by or relying on or arguing from, as *I did it on the ~ of your promise*). **2.** What makes strong (*God is our ~*; *his ~ is patience*). **3.** Proportion of whole number present (*were there in great, full*, ~); full complement (*up to, below*, ~). **4.** ‖ (mil. etc.). *On the ~*, on the muster-roll (*was taken, is, on the ~*). Hence ~'LESS a. [OE *strengthu* (*strang* STRONG, -TH¹)]

strĕng'then, v.t. & i. Make or become stronger; ~ one's *hands* (fig.), encourage him to vigorous action. [-EN¹]

strĕn'ūous, a. Energetic, unrelaxing, ardently persistent; requiring exertion. Hence ~LY² adv., ~NESS n. [f. L *strenuus* +-OUS]

Strĕph'on, n. Fond lover (~ *& Chloe*, pair of lovers). [character in Sidney's *Arcadia*]

strĕpĭtŏs'ō, mus. direction. Noisily. [It.]

strĕptocŏcc'us, n. (pl. -cī). Any of a group of bacteria which, as they remain attached after fission, are usu. found in chains. [Gk *streptos* twisted (*strephō* turn), *kokkos* a grain]

strĕptomy'cin, n. An antibiotic produced by the *Streptomyces* group of bacteria, effective against some groups of disease- -producing bacteria which are immune to penicillin. [f. Gk *streptos* (prec.), *mukēs* fungus, -IN]

Strĕp'yan, a. Of the stage of palaeolithic culture represented by remains found at Strépy in Belgium. [-AN]

strĕss, n., & v.t. **1.** Constraining or impelling force *of* (*under, driven by*, ~ *of weather, poverty*, etc.). **2.** Effort, demand upon energy, (STORM *& ~*; *subjected to great ~*; *times of slackness & times of* ~). **3.** Emphasis (*lay ~ on*, convey that one attaches importance to); accentuation, emphasis laid on syllable or word, *a* or *the* accent, (~ *& quantity are different metrical principles*; *the ~ is on the first syllable, on the word 'permissive'*). **4.** (mech.). Force exerted between contiguous bodies or parts of a body. Hence ~'LESS a. **5.** v.t. Lay the ~ on, accent, emphasize; subject to mechanical ~. [ME; vb in present sense f. n., which is prob. aphetic f. DISTRESS¹]

strĕtch, v.t. & i., & n. **1.** Make taut, tighten, straighten, place somewhere in tight-drawn or outspread state, (*the rope must be ~ed tight*; ~ *a wire across the road*; *with a canopy ~ed over them*; ~ *trousers*, remove creases etc. by pulling out in frame; ~ *oneself* or ~ abs., tighten muscles after sleeping etc. by extending limbs etc. in various directions; ~ one's *legs*, straighten them by walking as relief from sitting etc.; ~ one *on the ground*, knock him sprawling; (p.p.) lying *at full length, on the lawn*, etc.; ~ *out hand, foot,*

etc., extend it by straightening arm or leg; ~ *out*, abs., reach out hand, also begin to lengthen stride). **2.** Strain, exert to utmost or beyond legitimate extent, make the most of, do violence to, exaggerate, (~ *a point, a principle*, one's *powers*, one's *credit*,=strain; ~ *the truth* or ~ abs., exaggerate, lie). **3.** Have specified length or extension, be continuous between points or to or from a point, (~es *from end to end*, across *the sky, to infinity*; *road ~es away, memory ~es down, from* or *to* place or period). **4.** Draw, be drawn or admit of being drawn, out into greater length or extension or size (*gloves, boots, want ~ing*; *it ~es like elastic*); (sl.) hang (person). **5.** n. ~ing or being ~ed (*with a ~ & a yawn*, whence ~'Y² a., ~'INESS n.; *by a ~ of authority, language*, etc.; *with every faculty on the ~*). **6.** Continuous expanse or tract or spell (*a ~ of road, open country*, etc.; *works ten hours at a ~*); (naut.) distance covered on one tack; (sl.) imprisonment for a year, any term of imprisonment. [OE *streccan*, OHG *strecken*, f. WG *strakkjan* f. *strak-* straight]

strĕtch'er, n. In vbl senses; esp.: brick or stone laid with side in face of wall (cf. HEADER); board in boat against which rower presses feet; appliance, often of canvas stretched on oblong frame, for carrying disabled person on; wooden frame over which canvas of picture is stretched; (sl.) exaggeration, lie; ~*-bond*, method of building in which all bricks are ~s but joints of contiguous courses do not coincide. [-ER¹]

strew (-ōō), v.t. (p.p. ~n, ~ed). Scatter (sand, flowers, small objects) over a surface; (partly) cover (surface, object) with small objects scattered. [OE *strewian* etc., OS *stroian*, OHG *strouwen*, ON *strá*, Goth. *straujan* f. Gmc *strau-*, perh. rel. to L *sternere strat-*; cf. STRAW]

stri'|a, n. (anat., zool., bot., geol.; pl. ~ae). Linear mark on surface, slight ridge or furrow or score. Hence ~ATE² a., ~ATE³ v.t., ~ateLY² adv., ~A'TION, ~atURE, nn. [L]

stricken. See STRIKE.

stric'kle, n. Rod used in STRIKE-*measure*; whetstone. [OE *stricel* (STRIKE)]

strict, a. Precisely limited or defined, accurate, tense, without irregularity or exception or deviation, requiring implicit obedience or exact performance, not lax, (*in the ~ sense*; *keep ~ watch*; *lives in ~ seclusion*; *was told me in ~ confidence*; *gave ~ orders*; *a ~ code of laws or customs*; ~ *morals*, admitting no laxity; ~ *parents, schoolmaster, discipline*). Hence ~LY² adv. (~*ly speaking*, if one is to use words in their ~ sense), ~'NESS n. [f. L *strictus* STRAIT (*stringere strict-* tighten)]

stric'tur|e, n. (Usu. in pl.) piece of censure, critical remark, (usu. *on* or *upon*); (path.) morbid contraction of some canal or duct in the body, whence ~ED²

(-kcherd) a. [ME, f. L *strictura* (prec., -URE)]

stride, v.i.. & t. (past *strōde*, rare p.p. *stridden* or *strid*), & n. **1.** Walk with long steps; pass over (ditch etc.) with one step; bestride, straddle (trans.). **2.** n. Single step esp. in respect of length, gait as determined by length of ~, (*walks with vigorous* ~*s* or *a vigorous* ~; *take obstacle in* one's ~, clear it without changing step to jump, (fig.) find no serious impediment in it; *get into* one's ~, (fig.) settle down steadily to the job in hand); distance between feet parted either laterally or as in walking. [OE *strīdan* = (M)LG *striden* in same sense; formally rel. to & prob. identical w. OS *strīdian*, OHG *strītan*, ON *strītha* strive, quarrel]

strid'ent, a. Loud & harsh in sound. Hence ~LY² adv. [L *stridere* creak, -ENT]

strid'ūl|āte, v.i. (entom.). Make shrill jarring sound (of cicadas, grasshoppers, etc.). So ~ANT a., ~A'TION, ~ātoR, nn. [L *stridulus* creaking (prec.), -ATE³]

strife, n. Contention, state of conflict, struggle between opposed persons or things. [ME, aphetic f. OF *estrif*, cf. *estriver* STRIVE]

stri'gil, n. Skin-scraper used by ancients at bath. [f. L *strigilis* (*stringere* graze)]

strig'ōse, **strig'ous**, aa. (bot.). With short stiff hairs or scales. [L *striga* swath, -OSE¹, -OUS]

strike, v.t. & i. (*struck*, *struck* & as specified below *stricken*), & n. **1.** Hit, hit upon or (*up*)*on*, deliver blow(s) or stroke(s), (*struck me in the mouth, with his fist*; ~ *ball out of court* etc., send it with blow; ~ *weapon up* or *down* or *aside*, divert it by blow; ~ one's *foot against a stone*, one's *hand on the table*; ~ *while* IRON¹ *is hot*; *striking- -force*, esp. military body ready to deliver blow at short notice; *within striking- -distance*, near enough to ~; ~ *a blow*, or ~, *for freedom*; *hammer* ~*s on* or ~*s bell*; *ship* ~*s rock* or *on rock* or ~*s*, runs on it; ~ *hands*, arch., touch or clasp them in sign of agreement made; *was struck by a stone*, *lightning*; *a stricken heart*, afflicted by strokes of grief; *stricken with fever, pesti- lence, paralysis*, etc.; *a stricken field*, pitched battle or scene of it; *stricken in years*, enfeebled by age; ~ *out*, hit from the shoulder, also use arms & legs in swimming or feet in skating; ~ *upon an idea, plan*, etc., have it luckily occur to one; ~ OIL¹; *light* ~*s upon* object, illu- minates it; ~ *at*, aim blow at; ~ *at the root of*, threaten destruction to; ~ *back*, return blow; ~ *home*, get blow well in; ~ *all of a heap*, colloq., dumbfound; ~ *fish* or ~ abs., jerk tackle in order to secure hook in mouth; ~ *the track*, come upon it). **2.** Produce or record or bring into speci- fied state by stroke(s) or striking (~ *coin*, make it by stamping; ~ *bargain*, make it as by striking hands; ~ *sparks, fire,*

light, out of flint; ~ *a match*, ignite by striking against something; ~ *a light*, produce by striking match; *match will not* ~, give light when struck; *clock* ~*s the hour, five*, etc.; *the hour has struck*, clock has struck it, & fig. the critical moment has come or gone; ~ one *blind*, *deaf*, etc., blind, deafen, etc., him at one stroke; ~ *me dead!*, vulg., form of as- severation; ~ *down*, fell with blow lit. or fig.; ~ *his head off*, behead; ~ *out plan* etc., forge or devise; ~ *out a line for one- self*, be original; ~ *item* or *name out* or *off*, ~ *word through*, expunge with pen-stroke; ~ *up an acquaintance*, start it rapidly or casually; band or person ~*s up a tune* or ~*s up*, starts playing or singing as by stroke of drum). **3.** Arrest attention of, occur to mind of, produce mental im- pression on, impress as, (*what struck me was the generosity of the offer*; *it* ~*s me he* or *that he may have misunderstood*; *an idea suddenly struck me*; *how does it* ~ *you?*, what do you think about it?; *it* ~*s me as. ridiculous, absolutely perfect*); (part.) sure to be noticed, arresting, impressive, whence **strik'ingLY²** adv., **strik'ingNESS** n. **4.** Lower or take down (flag, sail, tent), signify surrender by striking flag, sur- render, (~ one's *flag*, surrender ship or fortress to enemy, also resign a naval command; ~ *tents*, break up camp; *town*, *ship*, ~*s*, surrenders). **5.** Cease (work), cease work, (of workmen) refuse to go on working unless employer accedes to some demand (cf. LOCK³ *out*; ~ *for higher pay*, *against long hours*, etc.). **6.** (Cause to) penetrate (*struck a knife, terror, into his heart*; *cold* ~*s through his clothes, into his marrow, the wind* ~*s cold*; *plant* ~*s its roots into the soil*; ~*s root*, or ~*s* abs.; *oysters* ~, attach themselves to bed; *rays* ~ *through fog*; *struck with terror, panic, dizziness*, etc., suddenly filled with). **7.** Direct one's course somewhere, take specified direction, diverge *to*, start *into*, (*then* ~ *to the right*; ~ *into* or *out of a track*, *subject*, etc.; ~ *in*, intervene in talk, often *with* suggestion etc.; *gout* ~*s in*, attacks interior instead of extremities; ~ *into a gallop*, begin galloping). **8.** Level (grain etc. or the measure) in ~ *measure* (see n.); ascertain (balance) by deducting credit or debit from the other; arrive at (average) by equalizing all items; compose (jury) by allowing both sides to reject same number. **9.** Suddenly & dramatically assume (attitude). **10.** ~*-a-light*, appara- tus for getting light from flint. Hence **strik'ER¹** (1, 2) n. **11.** n. Concerted refusal to work by employees till some grievance is remedied (*on* ~, acting on such refusal; ~'*bound*, immobilized by ~; ~*-breakers*, workmen brought in to replace strikers; ~ *pay*, allowance for subsistence made by trade union to workmen who have struck; *general* ~, by workmen of all or most trades with a view' to securing some

common object by paralysing business;
SIT-*down*, STAY[1]-*in*, ~; *sympathetic* ~, by
unaggrieved trade to give moral support
to one on ~). **12.** = STRICKLE (~ *measure*,
when grain etc. is measured by passing a
rod across top of heaped vessel to secure
that it shall be full & no more). **13.**
*Sudden success at finding petroleum,
gold, etc., or in financial operations.
14. (In baseball) batsman's actual or
constructive attempt to hit pitched ball.
15. Attack, esp. from the air. [OE *strican*
go, OHG *strîhhan*, f. WG *strîk-* cogn.
w. L *stringere strict-* touch lightly]

string, n., & v.t. & i.(*strung*). **1.** Twine or
fine cord, piece of this or of leather,
ribbon, webbing, or other material, used
for tying up, lacing, drawing or holding
together, actuating puppet, etc., (*want
some* ~ *& brown paper*; APRON, *bonnet*,
BOW[1], *kite*, etc., ~ ; *two* ~*s to* one's BOW[1];
first, second, ~, person or thing that one's
chief, alternative, reliance is set on, w.
ref. to prec. phr.; *pull the* ~*s*, be the real
actuator of what another does; *have* person *on a* ~, have under one's thumb;
HEART~*s*). **2.** Tough piece connecting
two halves of pod in beans etc. **3.**
Stretched piece of catgut, cord, or wire,
yielding musical tone(s) in piano, harp,
violin, & other instruments (*harp-, fiddle-,
-*~; *touch the* ~*s*, play; *harp on one* ~,
dwell on single subject; *touch a* ~, fig.,
excite particular feeling in person's heart;
the ~*s*, the ~ed instruments in a band or
part contributed by them to the effect,
cf. *the* WIND[1]), whence (-)~ED[2] (-ngd) a.
4. Set of or usu. *of* objects strung together
or persons or things of one kind coming
one after another (*a* ~ *of beads, onions,
pearls; filed past in a long* ~; *a* ~ *of
porters, horses, oaths, lies*). **5.** (billiards).
Scoring-board with buttons sliding on
wires. **6.** The racehorses, collectively,
under training at a particular stable.
7. pl. *Conditions attached to a gift, offer,
etc. **8.** ~ *alphabet*, code for the blind in
which special knots on~ represent letters;
~ *band*, (prop.) of ~ed instruments only;
~-*bark*, STRINGY-bark; ~-*board*, supporting timber in which ends of staircase
steps are set; ~-*course*, (also ~) raised
horizontal band or course on a building;
~-*halt*, = SPRING[2]-*halt*; ~-*piece*, long
timber supporting & connecting the parts
of a framework; ~ *tie*, very narrow tie.
Hence ~*LESS* a. **9.** vb. Supply with ~(s),
tie with ~. **10.** Secure (bow) in state
ready for use by bending it & slipping
loop of ~ into notch; (fig., chiefly in p.p.)
tighten *up·* or make ready or sensitive
or excited (senses, nerves, resolution, or
person in regard to them; *was strung up
to do the deed*; *high-strung* or *highly strung
nerves* or *person*, neurotic, susceptible,
over-sensitive). **11.** Thread (beads etc.)
on a ~; strip ~s from (beans). **12.**
*(colloq.). Hoax. **13.** (colloq.). ~ (*per-

son) *along*, deceive; ~ *along with*, accompany; ~ *up*, kill by hanging. **14.** (Of glue
etc.) become stringy. **15.** (billiards).
Make the preliminary strokes that decide
which player shall begin. [OE *streng*,
MLG *strenge*, ON *strengr* f. Gmc *strangiz*;
cf. OHG *stranc* rope; see STRONG]

strĭngĕn'dō (-j-), mus. direction. With
increasing speed. [It.]

strĭn'g|ent (-j-), a. (Of rules, stipulations,
etc.) strict, precise, requiring exact performance, leaving no loophole or discretion; (of money-market etc.) tight,
hampered by scarcity, unaccommodating,
hard to operate in. Hence ~ENCY n.,
~ently[2] adv. [L *stringere* draw tight,
-ENT]

string'er (-ng-), n. In vbl senses; also,
STRING-board. [-ER[1]]

string'|y (-ngi), a. Fibrous, like string,
(~*y-bark*, kinds of gum-tree); (of liquid)
viscous, ropy. Hence ~*iNESS* n. [-Y[2]]

strip[1], v.t. & i. (-pp-). **1.** Denude, lay
bare, deprive of covering or appurtenance
or property, (~ one *to the skin*, leave him
no clothes; ~*ped*, naked; ~*ped of fine
names, it is a swindle*; ~ *house, ship,
tree*, remove furniture, rigging, bark &
branches; ~ *cow*, milk to last drop; ~
tobacco, remove stems from; ~ *screw*, tear
thread from it); pull or tear (covering lit.
or fig., appurtenance, property) off or *off*
from or *from* something; put off one's
clothes, undress (~-*tease*, an entertainment in which a woman gradually ~s
before an audience, also as vb). **2.** (Of
screw) lose thread; (of projectile) issue
from rifled gun without spin. **3.** ~-*leaf*,
tobacco with stems removed. Hence
~p'ER[1](1, 2) n. [ME, f. OE -*strŷpan*
despoil, = MDu., MLG *strōpen*, OHG
stroufen f. WG *strauppan*]

strip[2], n. Long narrow piece (*a* ~ *of card,
paper, cloth, garden, territory, board*);
narrow space in newspaper for small
pictures telling a comic or serial story (~
cartoon); AIR[1] ~. [ME, f. or cogn. w.
MLG *strippe* strap, thong, prob. rel. to
STRIPE]

stripe, n. **1.** Long narrow band usu. of
uniform breadth on a surface from which
it differs in colour or texture (*black with
a red* ~; STAR[1]*s & ~s*; ~*s on soldier's
trousers*; *sergeant's, corporal's*, ~*s*, chev-
rons on sleeves denoting rank; *get, lose,
a* ~, be promoted, degraded; *zebra's* ~*s*),
whence (-)stripED[2] (-pt), strip[Y][2], aa.,
strip'iNESS n. **2.** (arch.). Blow with
scourge (usu. in pl.); (pl.) flogging. **3.** pl.
(colloq.). Tiger. [17th c., perh. back
form. f. an earlier *striped*, f. MDu., MLG
strïpe = MHG *strïfe*, ON *strip* f. Gmc
strïp- (cf. prec.); sense 2 ME, perh. f.
Du. or LG; cf. MLG *strippe* whip-lash]

strip'ling, n. Lad, young man whose
figure has not yet filled out. [ME, prob.
f. STRIP[2], -LING[1]]

strive, v.i. (*strōve, striven*). Struggle,

endeavour, try hard, make efforts, contend, vie (to do, for or after desired end,
with or against opponent or temptation
or difficulty; ~ together, or with each other,
quarrel, dispute pre-eminence etc.). [ME,
aphetic f. OF estriver, of disputed orig.]

strŏb'ĭle, n. Cone of pine etc. [f. LL f. Gk
strobilos (strephō twist)]

strode. See STRIDE.

strōke¹, n., & v.t. **1.** Blow, shock given
by blow, (to receive 20 ~s of the birch;
with one ~ of his sword; killed by a ~
of lightning or lightning-~; finishing ~,
coup de grâce, final & fatal blow; ~ of
paralysis or apoplexy, or ~, sudden dis-
abling attack; SUN~). **2.** Single effort
put forth, one complete performance of
a recurrent action or movement, time
or way in which such movements are
done, (has not done a ~ of work; ~ of
wing, oar, etc., whole of motion till
starting-position is regained; ~ of piston,
whole motion in either direction; golfer
does hole in five ~s, successive single
dealings with ball; row a fast, slow, long,
etc., ~; vary the ~; second boat is gaining
at every ~ or ~ by ~). **3.** Method of striking in games etc., specially successful or
skilful effort, (invented a new ~ in cricket;
~ of genius, original idea; ~ of wit,
diplomacy, etc.; ~ of business, profitable
transaction; a clever ~; MASTER¹-~); ~ of
luck, unforeseen opportune occurrence.
4. Mark made by movement in one
direction of pen or pencil or paint-brush,
detail contributing to general effect in
description, (up, down, -~, part of letter
so written; HAIR-~; thick, thin, horizontal,
etc., ~; dash off picture with a few ~s;
could do it with a ~ of the pen by exag.,
by writing signature; finishing ~s, finishing touches; description is full of ~s from
the life). **5.** Sound made by striking clock
(it is on the ~ of nine, nine is about to
strike; was there on the ~, punctually).
6. (Also, now rarely, ~ oar) oarsman rowing nearest stern & setting time of ~ (row,
pull, ~, act as ~). **7.** v.t. Act as ~ to
(boat, crew). [ME, f. OE *strāc =
(M)LG strēk, MHG streich f. Gmc *straik-
var. of *strik- STRIKE]

strōke², v.t., & n. **1.** Pass the hand
gently, & usu. repeatedly in same direction, along surface of (~e one or one's hair
the wrong way, irritate him; ~e one down,
mollify his anger etc.); hence ~'ingLY²
adv. **2.** n. Act or spell of ~ing. [OE
strācian, = MDu., MLG strēken, OHG
streihhōn f. Gmc *straik- (prec.)]

strōll, v.i. & t., & n. **1.** Saunter, go for
short leisurely walk; go from place to
place giving performances etc., traverse
the country thus, (~ing players; a ~ing
company). **2.** n. Short leisurely walk (go
for, take, a ~). Hence ~'ER¹ n. [c. 1600,
perh. a soldier's wd f. obs. G (17th c.)
strollen, strolchen (strolch vagabond)]

strōm'a, n. (biol.; pl. ~ta). Framework

of an organ or cell, usu. of connective
tissue. Hence **stromăt'ic** a. [LL, f. Gk
strōma coverlet]

strŏng, a. (comp. & sup. pr. -ngg-).
1. Having power of resistance, not easily
broken or torn or worn or injured or
captured, tough, healthy, firm, solid, (~
china, stick, cloth; a ~ constitution, not
liable to, able to overcome, disease; ~
nerves, proof against fright, irritation,
etc.; ~ fortress, town, etc.; ~-box, -room,
proof against burglars etc. for keeping
valuables in; ~ conviction, faith, character; the ~, those who have good health;
are you quite ~ again?, restored to health;
a ~ foundation; a ~ market, steadily high
or rising prices; ~ meat, doctrine or
measures acceptable only to vigorous or
instructed minds; ~ suit, suit at cards
that is able to take tricks, (fig.) thing at
which one excels). **2.** Capable of exerting
great force or doing much, muscular,
powerful by size or numbers or resources
or quality or ability, convincing, striking,
powerfully affecting the senses, (~ to do,
suffer, labour, save, etc.; is ~ enough to; ~
in judgement, Greek, numbers, health, well
equipped in these respects; ~ eyes,
memory, etc.; a ~ man, muscular; by the
~ arm or hand, by force; is as ~ as a
horse, can do or stand much work; the
~, those who have might on their side;
~ army, fleet, etc., numerous & well
equipped; a ~ detachment, numerous; a
company 200 ~, numbering 200; how
many ~ are you?, what are your numbers?; a ~ combination, set capable of
doing much when united; a ~ candidate,
formidable, likely to win; ~ drink,
waters, alcoholic liquors; ~ tea, toddy,
made with large proportion of the
flavouring element; ~ situation, conjuncture in play or story calculated to
move audience deeply; ~ voice, loud or
penetrating; ~ mind, capable of sound
reasoning; ~-minded, having such mind;
~ evidence, argument, case; ~ light,
shadow, colour, flavour; ~ cheese, onion,
pungent; ~ butter, bacon, rancid; ~
breath, ill-smelling). **3.** Energetic, effective, vigorous, decided, (a ~ tide, attraction; have a ~ hold upon or over, be able to
influence; a ~ literary style, vivid & terse;
has a ~ inclination to; ~ language, forcible
expressions esp. of abusive or blasphemous kind; ~ wind, very fresh; give ~
support to, support with all one's power;
a ~ partisan, Tory, advocate; ~ man,
administrator who acts without hesitation, masterful person; ~ measures,
drastic action; is ~ against compromise,
will have nothing to do with it; going
~, sl., continuing race or other occupation
vigorously, also in good health or trim;
come or go it ~, sl., go to great lengths in
something). **4.** (gram.). (Of vbs) forming
inflections by vowel-change within stem
rather than by addition of suffix (e.g.

swim swam, give gave, break broke, cf. *float floated).* 5. ~'*hold,* fort, fastness, citadel, place where some cause or sentiment prevails (*Liverpool was a ~hold of protestantism*). Hence ~'ISH[1](2) a., ~'LY[3] adv. [OE *strang, strong* = OS *strang,* ON *strangr* f. Gmc *strangaz*; cf. STRING]

strön'tia (-sha), n., **strön'tian** (-shn), n. & a. An oxide of strontium of which the nitrate is used in fireworks to colour flame red; (adj.) of strontia or strontium. [*-an* (orig. adj.) f. *Strontian* in Argyll; hence *-ia* (-IA)]

strön'tium (-shm), n. A soft silver-white metallic element; ~ *90,* product of atomic fission, concentrating selectively on the bones. [f. STRONTIA, see -IUM]

strŏp, n;, & v.t. (-pp-). 1. Strip of leather on which razor is sharpened, implement or machine serving same purpose; collar of leather or spliced rope or iron used in slinging pulley etc. 2. v.t. Sharpen on or with ~. [ME, f. (M)Du., (M)LG *strop,* OHG *strupf,* WG f. L *stroppus, struppus* STRAP]

strophän'thin, n. Poisonous drug extracted from varieties of the tropical plant *Strophanthus,* used as a heart-tonic. [f. Gk *strophos* twisted cord + *anthos* flower +-IN]

strŏph'ė, n. (Lines sung during) turn made in dancing by ancient-Greek chorus (~, *antistrophe, epode,* three sections of a choral ode or of one division of it, ~ & antistrophe exactly corresponding in metre). So **strŏph'IC** a. [Gk (-ē), orig.= turning (*strephō* turn)]

strove. See STRIVE.

strow (-ō), v.t. (p.p. ~*n* or ~*ed).* (Arch. for) STREW.

struck, See STRIKE.

strŭc'tur|e, n. Manner in which a building or organism or other complete whole is constructed, supporting framework or whole of the essential parts of something, make, construction, (*the ~e of a house, machine, animal, poem, sentence, society; a sentence of loose, a rock of columnar,* ~*e; its ~e is ingenious; ornament should emphasize & not disguise the lines of* ~e), whence ~AL (-cher-), ~eLESS, (-)~ED[3] (-cherd), aa., ~alLY[2] adv.; thing constructed, complex whole, a building, (*a fine marble* ~*e; a lumbering* ~*e drawn by six horses).* [f. L *structura* (*struere* struct-build, -URE)]

strŭg'gl|e, v.i., & n. 1. Throw one's limbs about in violent effort to get free or escape grasp (*child* ~*ed & kicked*); make violent or determined efforts under difficulties, strive hard *to* do, contend *with* or *against* opponent or obstacle or difficulty, (~*ed to express himself, control his feelings;* ~*ing with his infirmity, against superior numbers* or *the forces of nature*); make one's way with difficulty *through, up, along, in,* etc. (*light* ~*ed in through dirty panes*); (part.) experiencing difficulty

in making a living or getting recognition (*a* ~*ing artist* etc.); hence ~ingLY[2] adv., ~ER[1] n. 2. n. Spell of ~ing, confused wrectle or jostling, mêlée, hard contest, effort under difficulties; *the* ~*e for existence,* the competition between organisms esp. as an element in natural selection. [ME *strugle, strogel,* etc., frequent. formation of obsc. orig.]

strüld'brŭg, n. One of those cursed with immortality in Swift's *Gulliver's Travels.* [arbitrary]

strŭm, v.i. & t. (-mm-), & n. 1. Touch notes or twang strings of piano or other stringed instrument (esp. unskilfully); ~ on (piano, guitar, etc.). 2. n. Sound made by ~ming (*the* ~ *of a guitar).* [imit., cf. THRUM]

strum'|a (-ōō-), n. (pl. ~*ae*). Scrofula; goitre; (bot.) cushion-like dilatation of an organ. So ~OSE[1], ~OUS, aa. [L, = scrofulous tumour]

strŭm'pėt, n. Prostitute. [ME, of unkn. orig.]

strung. See STRING.

strŭt[1], v.i. (-tt-), & n. (Walk with) pompous or affected gait. Hence ~t'ingLY[2] adv. [ME ' bulge, swell, strive ', OE *strūtian* prob. f. **strūt* = OHG *strūz* strife]

strŭt[2], n., & v.t. (-tt-). 1. Piece of wood or iron inserted in a framework & intended to bear weight or pressure in the direction of its length, brace, esp. one set obliquely from rafter to king-post or queen-post. 2. v.t. Brace with ~(s). [16th c., ult. rel. to OE **strūt* (prec.); cf. LG *strutt* rigid]

struth'ious (-ōō-), a. Of or like an ostrich, of the ostrich tribe. [L *struthio* f. Gk *strouthiōn* ostrich (*strouthos* sparrow), -OUS]

strých'n|ine, (arch.) **strých'n|ia,** (-k-), nn. Vegetable alkaloid got from plants of genus *Strychnos,* very bitter to the taste & highly poisonous & used in minute doses as nerve-stimulant. Hence ~IC a., ~(in)ISM(5) nn. [L *strychnos* f. Gk (*s)trukhnos* kind of nightshade, -INE[5]]

Stū'art, n. The ~s, sovereigns James I, Charles I & II, James II, Mary & Anne, & members of their families.

stŭb, n., & v.t. (-bb-). 1. Stump of tree, tooth, etc., left projecting; remnant of pencil, cigar, dog's tail, or similar object; **counterfoil;* ~*-iron,* used for gun-barrels & made of old horseshoe or other nails; ~*-mortise, -tenon,* going only part of the way through; hence ~b'Y[2] a. 2. v.t. Grub up (~) by the roots; clear (land) of ~s; ~ one's *toe,* hurt it by striking against something; (also ~ *out*) extinguish (cigar, cigarette) by pressing lighted end of ~ against some object. [OE *stub(b)=*MDu., (M)LG *stubbe,* ON *stubbr, stubbi*]

stŭb'ble, n. Short stalks of cereal plants left sticking up after harvest, cropped hair or beard, hair on unshaved chin or cheek.

Hence **stŭbb'ly²** a. [ME, f. OF (e)stuble f. L stup(u)la var. of stipula straw]

stŭbb'orn, a. Obstinate, unyielding, obdurate, inflexible, refractory, intractable, (facts are ~ things, will not adapt themselves to theory). Hence~LY² adv.,~NESS n. [ME stiborn, stoburn, etc., of unexpl. orig.]

stŭcc'ō, n. (pl. ~es), & v.t. **1.** Kinds of plaster or cement used for coating wall surfaces or moulding into architectural decorations. **2.** v.t. Coat with ~. [It., perh. f. Gmc (cf. OHG stukki crust)]

stuck(-up). See STICK.

stŭd¹, n., & v.t. (-dd-). **1.** Large-headed nail, boss, or knob, projecting from a surface esp. for ornament, rivet, cross-piece in each link of chain-cable; two-headed button for use with two button-holes ‖ esp. in shirt-front (collar-~, long kind going through two or four holes); post to which laths are nailed, whence ~d'ING¹ n., woodwork of lath-&-plaster wall. **2.** v.t. Set with ~s by way of strengthening or usu. of decorating, (p.p.) thickly set or strewed with (door, lawn, sea, sky, ~ded with nails, daisies, islands, stars); be scattered over or about (surface). [OE studu, stuthu, MHG stud, ON stoth f. Gmc *studh-, *stuth- prop]

stŭd², n. Number of horses kept for some purpose as breeding, racing, hunting, coaching; ~-book, containing pedigrees of horses; ~ farm, place where horses are bred; ~-horse, stallion. [OE stōd, OHG stuot (G stute mare), ON stóth f. Gmc *stōdh- f. *stō-, *sta- STAND]

studding-sail (stŭn'sl), n. Sail set on small extra yard & boom beyond leech of square sail in light winds. [16th c., of unkn. orig.]

stŭd'ent, n. **1.** Person studying in order to qualify himself for some occupation or devoting himself to some branch of learning or under instruction at university or other place of higher education or technical training (medical, theological, historical, ~; ~ interpreter, civil servant qualified or qualifying for consular service in China, Persia, etc., by study of the language required; a ~ of archaeology, law, botany, manners; numbers its ~s by the thousand). **2.** Person of studious habits. **3.** ‖ (At some colleges) recipient of stipend from foundation, fellow or scholar, whence ~SHIP n. [f. L studēre (studium STUDY¹), -ENT; ME studiant, aphetic f. OF estudiant]

stŭd'iō, n. (pl. ~s). Working-room of painter, sculptor, photographer, etc., often with skylights or windows specially designed to secure suitable light; room in which cinema-play is staged; (pl.) cinema-~s of a film company with auxiliary buildings; one of the rooms in a broadcasting station used for transmissions. [It., f. L as STUDY¹]

stŭd'ious, a. Given to study, occupied

with reading; taking care to do (more ~ to divide than to unite—Pope), anxiously desirous of doing; studied, deliberate, intended, zealous, anxious, painstaking, (with ~ care, attention, politeness). Hence ~LY² adv., ~NESS n. [ME, f. L studiosus (foll., -OUS)]

stŭd'y¹, n. **1.** Thing to be secured by pains or attention (it shall be my ~ to please, to write correctly; your comfort was my ~; make a ~ of, try to secure). **2.** (Now usu. brown ~) fit of musing, reverie, (there he stood for an hour in a ~; is in a brown ~, too intent on his thoughts to observe what is passing). **3.** Devotion of time & thought to acquiring information esp. from books (often pl.), pursuit of some branch of knowledge, (gives his hours to ~; make a ~ of, investigate carefully; my studies have convinced me that; the ~ of mathematics, morals; continue your studies, go on with your lessons). **4.** Thing that is or deserves to be investigated (the proper ~ of mankind is man; his face was a ~). **5.** (Paint. etc.) sketch made for practice in technique or as preliminary experiment for picture or part of it (his studies are exquisite, but his finished work disappointing; a ~ of a head); (mus.) composition designed to develop skill in some particular branch of execution; (theatr.) good, slow, etc., learner of parts (UNDERSTUDY). **6.** Room used for literary occupation, transaction of business, etc. (you will find him in his, the,~). [ME studie, f. AF & OF estudie f. L studium zeal, study]

stŭd'y², v.t. & i. **1.** Make a study of, take pains to investigate or acquire knowledge of (subject) or to assure (result sought), scrutinize or earnestly contemplate (visible object), (~ law, French, philosophy; ~ book, read it attentively; ~ one's part, try to learn it by heart; ~ up, get up for examination etc.; ~ out, succeed in finding out by hard thinking; studies others' convenience, his own interests; ~ person's face or character, a map, the stars). **2.** Apply oneself to study esp. reading (~ for the bar, read law). **3.** (arch.). Meditate, muse. **4.** Be on the watch, try constantly to manage, to do (studies to avoid disagreeable topics). **5.** p.p. Deliberate, intentional, affected, (a studied insult; with studied politeness, rudeness, unconcern, abandon), whence **stŭd'ied**LY² (-dĭd-) adv. [ME studie, f. OF estudier f. med. L studiare f. L as prec.]

stŭff, n., & v.t. & i. **1.** Material that thing is made of or that is or may be used for some purpose (the ~ that dreams, heroes, are made of; has good ~ in him, sterling qualities; some ~ they call beer; this punch, book, is good, sorry, ~; household ~, arch., furniture etc.; bread, food, ~s, things made of bread, used as food; green, garden, ~, vegetables; doctors' ~, physic; inch ~, boards 1 in. thick; thick ~, planking over 4 in. thick; the ~, colloq., available supply of something, e.g. timber, money, shells). **2.** Any woollen fabric (opp. silk, cotton, linen; ‖ ~ *gown*, worn by barrister who has not taken SILK). **3.** Valueless matter, refuse, trash, nonsense (n. & int.), (*take that* ~ *away*; *Smith a liar?* ~ *& nonsense!*; *what* ~ *he writes!*). **4.** (sl.). *Do your* ~, perform your tricks, get on with your job; HOT ~; *know* one's ~, be a master of one's subject, trade, etc.; *the* ~ *to give* 'em *or the troops*, the way to proceed etc. **5.** vb. Pack, cram, stop *up*, fill, distend, (~ one's *ears with wool*, *cushion with down*; ~*ed birds, beasts*, skin with interior removed & replaced by enough material to restore original shape; ~*ed fowl, turkey, haddock, veal*, with minced seasoning inserted before cooking; *~ed shirt*, colloq., a pompous nonentity; ~ *child, goose*, etc., make it eat largely; *a head* ~*ed with romance, facts, folly*), whence ~'ING¹(4) n. (~*ing-box*, chamber in machinery through which rod can work without allowing passage of air etc., all vacant space being filled with ~ing). **6.** Ram or press into receptacle (~*ed his necessaries into a small bag, his fingers into his ears, the food into his mouth*). **7.** Gull with lies, hoax. **8.** Gorge oneself, eat greedily; hence (-)~ER¹ n. [ME *stoffe* f. OF *estoffe* f. *estoffer* equip, furnish f. Rom. **stuppare* STOP¹ up]

stuff'| y̆, a. (Of valley, room, etc., or atmosphere in it) lacking fresh air or ventilation, close, hard to breathe in, fusty; angry, sulky; narrow-minded. Hence ~iNESS n. [-Y²]

stŭl'tĭ|fy̆, v.t. (Of act, statement, agent, speaker) reduce (previous act etc.) to absurdity, exhibit (act etc. or one*self*) in ridiculous light, make (act etc.) of no effect, neutralize (one*self*) as agent, by later inconsistent act etc. Hence ~FICA'TION n. [f. LL *stultificare* (L *stultus* foolish, -I-, -FY)]

stŭm, n., & v.t. (-mm-). **1.** Unfermented grape-juice, must. **2.** v.t. Prevent from fermenting, secure (wine) against further fermentation in cask, by introduction of antiseptic. [17th c., f. Du. *stom* n., *stommen* vb, f. *stom*.adj. dumb]

stŭm'bl|e, v.i. & t., & n. **1.** Lurch forward, have partial fall, from catching or striking foot or making false step (~*e along*, go with frequent ~es); make blunder(s) in doing something (~*es in his speech*; ~*e through a recitation*); be offended, feel scruples, *at*; come accidentally (*up*)*on* or *across*; (arch.) give pause to, excite scruples in; ~*ing-block*, obstacle, circumstance that causes difficulty or hesitation or scruples; hence ~iNGLY² adv. **2.** n. Act of ~ing. [ME *stomble*, *stumble* (-b- is euphonic) corresp. to Norw. *stumla*, cogn. w. *stam*- STAMMER]

‖ **stŭm'er**, n. (sl.). Worthless cheque, counterfeit coin or note. [orig. unkn.]

stŭmp, n., & v.i. & t. **1.** Projecting remnant of cut or fallen tree, corresponding remnant of broken branch or tooth or amputated limb, useless end of cigar or pencil, worn-down brush or other implement, stub; (pl., joc.) legs (usu. STIR one's ~s). **2.** ~ of tree used by orator to address meeting from (*on the* ~, colloq., engaged in political speech-making or agitation; ~ *oratory*, of kind suitable for such speeches). **3.** (crick.). One of the three uprights of a wicket (OFF, *middle*, LEG, ~). **4.** Cylinder of rolled paper or other material with conical ends for softening pencil-marks & other uses in drawing. **5.** vb. Walk stiffly & noisily as on wooden legs. **6.** (Of question etc.; colloq.) pose, be too hard for, (*am* ~*ed*, at a loss, at my wits' end), whence ~'ER¹(2) n. **7.** (crick.). Put (batsman who is not in his ground) out by disturbing wicket while holding ball, whence ~'ER¹(1) n. (sl., = wicket--keeper). **8.** Make ~ speeches, traverse (district) doing this. **9.** Use~ on (drawing, line, etc.). **10.** ‖~ *up* (sl.), pay over the money required, produce (sum). [ME *stompe*, f. (M)Du. *stomp*, MLG *stump(e)*, corresp. to OHG (G) *stumpf* stump]

stŭmp'|y̆, a. Thickset, stocky, of small height or length in proportion to girth, (*a* ~*y man, book, tail, pencil*). Hence ~iLY² adv.,~iNESS n. [-Y²]

stŭn, v.t. (-nn-). (Of sound) deafen temporarily, bewilder; (of blow lit. or fig.) knock senseless, reduce to insensibility or stupor, benumb, overwhelm; (part. as adj., sl.) ravishingly good in some respect, splendid, delightful, ripping, whence ~n'ingLY² adv., & so ~n'ER¹ n. [ME; aphetic f. OF *estoner* ASTONISH]

Stun'dism, Stun'dist, (-ōō-), nn. Doctrines, adherent, of a religious body in Russia, orig. of peasants, rejecting ceremonies of Orthodox Church & basing itself on the Bible as translated 1861 into modern Russian. [G *stunde* hour, lesson (the movement originating with German colonists), -ISM, -IST]

stung. See STING.

stunk. See STINK.

stŭn'sail, stŭns'l, n. = STUDDING-SAIL.

stŭnt¹, v.t. Check growth or development of, dwarf, cramp, (esp. in p.p.). [f. OE *stunt* adj. foolish, corresp. to MHG *stunz*, ON *stuttr* short]

stŭnt², n., & v.i. (colloq.). **1.** Special effort, feat, show performance, display of concentrated energy; advertising device. **2.** v.i. Perform ~s esp. aerobatics. [orig. unkn.; first in U.S. college athletics]

stūpe¹, n., & v.t. **1.** Flannel etc. wrung out of hot water & applied as fomentation; pledget of soft material used as surgical dressing. **2.** v.t. Apply ~ to, foment. [ME, f. L *stup(p)a* tow]

stūpe², n. (sl.). Fool. [for STUPID]

stŭp'ė|fy̆, v.t. Make stupid or torpid, deprive of sensibility, (~*fied with drink, narcotics, grief*, etc.). Hence or cogn.

~FA'CIENT (-āshnt) a. & n. (med.), ~FAC-
TION, ~FIER¹(1, 2), nn., ~fáctive a. [f. F
stupéfier f. L *stupefacere* (*stupēre* be
amazed, -FY)]

stūpĕn'dous, a. Amazing, prodigious,
astounding, esp. by size or degree (*a ~
structure, error, achievement*; ~ *folly*).
Hence ~LY² adv., ~NESS n. [L *stupendus*
(*stupēre* be amazed at), -OUS]

stŭp'id, a. & n. **1.** In a state of stupor or
lethargy; dull by nature, slow-witted,
lacking in sensibility, obtuse, crass,
characteristic of persons of this nature,
(*a ~ person, joke, idea, book*; *what a ~
place to put it in!*), so **stūpĭd'ĭTY** n.;
uninteresting, dull, (*a ~ place, visit, time*).
2. n. (colloq.). ~ person. Hence ~LY²
adv. [f. F *stupide* or L *stupidus* (as
STUPENDOUS, -ID¹)]

stūp'or, n. Dazed state, torpidity, whence
~OUS a. (med.); helpless amazement. [L
(as STUPENDOUS, -OR)]

stŭrd'|ў¹, a. Robust, hardy, vigorous,
lusty, strongly built, (~*y child, opponent,
legs, frame, resistançe, courage*; ~*y beggar*,
arch., able-bodied but not working).
Hence ~ĭLY² adv., ~ĭNESS n. [ME ' reckless, violent ', aphetic f. OF *estourdi* p.p.
of *estourdir* stun, daze]

stŭrd'|ў², n. Vertigo in sheep caused by
tapeworm in brain. Hence ~ĭED² (-ĭd) a.
[f. OF *estourdie* giddiness (prec.)]

stŭr'geon (-jn), n. Kinds of large anadromous fish resembling shark in general
shape, having mailed body & head, yielding caviare & isinglass, & esteemed as
food. [ME, f. AF (*e*)*sturgeon* f. Rom.
sturionem nom. *-o* f. WG *sturjo* whence
OHG *sturjo*, OE *styrga*]

Sturm und Drang (shtoorm ŏont
drahng'). See STORM & *stress*.

stŭtt'er, v.i. & t., & n. **1.** Keep repeating
parts, esp. initial consonants, of words
in effort to articulate; utter in this
way (often *out*); hence ~ER¹ n., ~ĭnGLY²
adv. **2.** n. Act or habit of ~ing. [f. ME
(now dial.) *stutt*, cogn. w. OHG *stōzen*
knock, +-ER⁵; cf. MDu., MLG
stoteren]

stȳ¹, n. (pl. *-ies*), & v.t. & i. **1.** (*Pig!*)~, enclosure for keeping pig(s) in, (fig.) mean or
dirty hovel or room, place of debauchery.
2. vb. Lodge (t. & i.) in ~. [OE *stī*, prob.
= *stīg* (see STEWARD), ON (*svin*) *stī*]

stȳ² (pl. *-ies*), **stȳe**, n. Inflamed swelling
on edge of eyelid (usu. *a ~ in one's eye*).
[prob. f. obs. *styany* (= *styan eye* f. OE
stīgend sty, lit. riser, f. *stīgan* rise + *eye*)
shortened as though = sty on eye]

Stȳ'gian, a. (As) of the Styx or of Hades,
murky, gloomy. [L f. Gk *Stugios* (STYX),
-AN]

stȳle¹, n., & v.t. **1.** Ancient writing-
-implement, a small rod with pointed end
for scratching letters on wax-covered
tablets & blunt end for obliterating
(whence **stȳl'ĭFORM** a.); (poet.) pen or
pencil; (transf.) thing of ~-like shape as

etching-needle or styloid process in anat.
2. Manner of writing, speaking, or doing,
esp. as opposed to the matter to be expressed or thing done (*the ~ is better than
the matter*; *written in a florid, cumbrous,
lucid, delightful,* ~; *different ~s of rowing*;
slashed about him in fine ~; *good, bad,* ~,
= *good, bad,* FORM¹). **3.** Collective characteristics of the writing or diction or
artistic expression or way of presenting
things or decorative methods proper to
a person or school or period or subject,
manner exhibiting these characteristics,
(*in the~ of Shakespeare, Raphael, Wagner*;
the epic, lyric, dramatic, ~; *lapidary or
monumental* ~, fit or resembling that fit
for inscriptions on stone; *pre-Raphaelite,
impressionist,* ~, in painting; *baroque,
Louis XIV, rococo, renaissance,* ~, in
architecture or furniture or dress; GOTHIC,
classical, ROMANESQUE, ~, in architecture;
*Norman, early English, decorated, per-
pendicular,* ~*s*, kinds of esp. ecclesiastical
architecture prevailing successively in
England 1066–1189, 1189–1272, 1272–1377,
1350–1600, & marked respectively by
round arches & heavy pillars, pointed
arches & lancet windows & simple tracery,
flowing tracery & elaborate ornament,
slender pillars & vast windows divided
by vertical & horizontal lines; *Tudor,
Jacobean, Queen Anne,* ~*s*, kinds of
esp. domestic architecture). **4.** Descriptive formula, designation of person
or thing, full title, (*is entitled to the
~ of* Right honourable, King, Esquire;
did not recognize him under his new ~;
my ~ is plain John Smith; *regret that
I am not acquainted with your proper ~*;
old, new, ~, abbr. *O.S., N.S.*, appended
to dates, = so called when reckoned
by the Julian, GREGORIAN, CALENDAR¹).
5. Noticeably superior quality or manner
esp. in regard to breeding or fashion,
distinction, (*there is no ~ about her*, she
looks commonplace; *let us do the thing
in ~ if we do it at all*), whence **stȳl'ISH**¹ a.,
stȳl'ishLY² adv., **stȳl'ishNESS** n. **6.** Kind,
sort, esp. with regard to appearance (*what
~ of house, servant, do you require?*; *a
gentleman of the old ~*). **7.** Make, shape,
pattern, (*this ~ 2/6*; *in all sizes & ~s*).
8. v.t. (usu. pass.). Use specified designation of (*is ~d king, folly*). [ME & OF
stile, style f. L *stilus*; sp. *style* w. assim. to
foll.]

stȳle², n. Gnomon of sun-dial; (bot.)
narrowed extension of ovary supporting
stigma. [app. f. Gk *stulos* pillar]

stȳle³, n. (Incorrect spelling for) STILE.

stȳl'ét, n. Slender pointed instrument,
stiletto; (surg.) stiffening wire of catheter,
probe. [F, f. It. STILETTO]

stȳl'ist, n. Person with or aiming at good
literary style. [-IST]

stȳlĭs't|ĭc, a. Of literary style. Hence
~ICALLY adv. [-IC]

stȳl'ĭte, n. Medieval ascetic living on top

of a pillar. [f. late Gk *stulilēs* (STYLE², -ITE¹)]

stȳl′ize, -ise (-īz), v.t. (Usu. in p.p.) conform (artistic representation) to the rules of a conventional style. [-IZE (G *stilisieren*)]

stȳl′ō, n. (colloq; pl. ~s). Stylograph. [abbr.]

stȳlo-, comb. form of *styloid* in names of muscles = of the styloid process & —, as ~*hy′oid*,~*maxill′ary*. [f. L as STYLE¹, -O-]

stȳl′obāte, n. Continuous basement supporting a row or rows of columns. [f. L f. Gk *stulobatēs* (STYLE², *bainō* walk)]

stȳl′o|graph (-ahf), n. Kind of pen containing reservoir of ink & marking with point instead of split nib. Hence ~**gr̄āph′ıc** a., ~**gr̄āph′ıcALLY** adv. [STYLE¹, -O-, -GRAPH]

stȳl′oid, a. & n. ~ (*process*), spine projecting from base of temporal bone. [STYLE¹, -OID]

stȳl′us, stil′us, n. **1.** = STYLE¹ (writing--implement). **2.** = STYLE². [see STYLE¹]

stȳm′ie, n., & v.t. (golf; ~ abolished in 1952). **1.** Condition on putting-green when a player's ball lay between opponent's ball & the hole, if the balls were at least six inches apart, as *I laid him a ~*. **2.** v.t. Put (opponent, opponent's ball, one*self*) into the position of having to negotiate a ~; also fig. [orig. unkn.]

stȳp′tic, a. & n. (Substance) that checks bleeding. [f. L f. Gk *stuptikos* (*stuphō* contract)]

stȳr′ăx, n. Kinds of tree & shrub, some of which yield valuable gums. [L, f. Gk *sturax*; cf. STORAX]

Stȳ′rian, a. & n. (Native) of Styria. [-AN]

Stȳx, n. (Gk myth.). River encompassing Hades (*cross the ~*, die; *black* etc. *as ~*). [L, f. Gk *Stux -ugos*]

Suabian. See SWABIAN.

sū′able, a. That can be sued. Hence **sūabil′ıty** n. [-ABLE]

suasion (swā′zhn), n. Persuasion as opposed to force (esp. *moral ~*). So **suas-́ ıve** (swā-) a. [ME, f. OF or L *suasio* (*suadēre suas-* urge)]

suave (swāv), a. Bland, soothing, mollifȳing, polite, (~ *person, speech, manners, wine, medicine*). Hence or cogn. ~′**LY²** adv., **suăv′ıty** (sw-) n. [F, or f. L *suavis* cogn. w. SWEET]

suav′iter (swā-). ~ *in mŏd′ō, fŏrt′iter in rē*, gently but firmly, with iron hand in velvet glove. [L]

sŭb¹, n., & v.i. (-bb-; colloq.). **1.** Subaltern; submarine; subscription; substitute. **2.** v.i. Act as substitute *for* someone. [abbr.]

sŭb², L prep., = under, in some L phrr.: ~ *fin′em* (abbr. *s.f.*), towards the end (of the chapter etc. referred to); ~ *ju′dĭcĕ* (jōō-), under judicial consideration (*newspaper comment on cases ~ judice is prohibited*), not yet decided, still debatable (*the matter is still ~ judice*; cf. RES *judicata*); ~ *rōs′a* (-z-), (of communications, consultations, etc.) in confidence, under express or implied pledge of secrecy [lit. under the rose, as emblem of secrecy]; ~ *silĕn′tio* (-tĭō, -shĭō), in hushed-up manner, privately; ~ *vō′cĕ*, abbr. *s.v.*, (in references to dictionaries etc.) under the word in question, under the word —.

sub- (sŭb, sub), pref. f. L *sub* prep. & *sub-* pref. = under.

1. Many words are from L compounds, in which ~ (or often by assim. etc. *suc-, suf-, sug-, sum-, sup-, sur-, sus-*) expresses clearly or obscurely the ideas of lower position (~*jacent*, ~*ordinate*, ~*scribe*, ~*sist*, ~*stance*), motion to this (~*ject*, ~*jugate*, ~*junctive*, ~*merge*, ~*mit*, ~*side*, succumb, suppose, suppress) or from this (~*tract*, succinct, suspect, suspend, suspire), covertness or secrecy or tacitness (~*audition*, ~*orn*, summon, surreptitious), inclusion (~*sume*), closeness (~*join*, ~*junctive*, ~*lime*, ~*sequent*, ~*urb*, succeed), inferiority (~*altern*, ~*serve*, *succentor*), support (~*sidy*, ~*vention*, *succour*, *suffer*, *suffice*, *sustain*), addition (*suffix*, *supplement*), or substitution (~*stitute*, *supplant*, *surrogate*).

2. ~, without the above changes into *suc-* etc., is also used as a living pref. after L models or prefixes to wds of E or other orig.:

a. Adjj. are formed from *sub*, the abl. of any L noun, & an adj. ending, esp. as anat. terms with sense *situated under the* — (~*sternal* below the breastbone); in others ~ has the secondary sense *below in degree* (~*normal* below normal), & in some having this sense, as in b below, ~ is prefixed directly to a derived E adj. (~*human* less than human).

b. Adjj. & rarely nn. are formed by prefixing ~ to E adjj. & nn., the pref. having an effect equivalent to rather (~*acid*), more or less (~*aquatic*), roughly (~*cylindrical*), incipient (~*delirium*), not quite (~*conscious*), approaching the specified character (~*erect*), on the borders of (~*alpine*).

c. ~ is prefixed to nn. & vv. with sense *under-, subordinate(ly), secondary -ily, further*, (~*prefect*, ~*heading*, ~*species*, ~*divide*, ~*let*).

d. ~ is rarely prefixed to E nn. with sense *underlying* (~*soil*, ~*way*).

The following list contains, with letters of reference & further explanation when necessary, the words in ~ whether compounded in L or in E that fall under 2; the L wd needed to give the meaning of wds marked *a* will be found by reference to the simple adj. that is left when ~ is removed, or to wd added in brackets:— ~*abdom′inal*, a; ~*a′cid*, ~*acid′ity*, b, (lit., & fig. of words etc.); ~a'gent, ~ä'gency, c; ~al'pine, b; ~ān'al, a; ~ande'an, b (of Andes mountains); ~ap'ennine, b; ~apostol'ic, b, of period after that of apostles; ~aquat'ic, b, of more or less aquatic habits or kind, also a, underwater; ~āq'ueous, a; ~arc'tic, b; ~as'tral, a, terrestrial; ~aur'al, a; ~ax'illary, a; ~ᴸbranch, ~ᴸbreed, nn., c; ~caudᴸ al, a; ~cen'tral, a, b; ~ce'rebral, a (esp. of reflex action in which the spinal cord is concerned, but not the brain); ~'class, c; ~clāv'ate, b; ~clāv'ian, ~clavic'ular, a (CLAVICLE); ~ᴸcommi'ssion(er), ~committ'ee, c; ~conc'ave, ~con'ical, ~con'scious(ly, -ness), b; ~con'tinent n., b, region whose size & importance would justify the name continent if it were not part of one, e.g. India, S. Africa; ~con'tract n., ~contract' v.i., ~contrac'tor n., c; ~con'trary a. & n. pl., ~contrari'ety n., b, contrary in some degree only (esp. in logic, as ' some men are mortal ' & ' some men are not mortal ' are ~contraries, whereas ' all men are mortal ' & ' no man is mortal ' are contraries); ~con'vex, b; ~cord'ate, b; ~corn'eous, b, rather horny, also a, placed under horn, nail, etc.; ~cort'ical, ~cos'tal, ~crān'ial, a; ~crys'talline, b; ~cūtān'e-ous(ly), ~cutic'ular, a; ~cylin'drical, b; ~deac'on, ~deac'onship, ~dean', ~dean'ery, ~decān'al, c; ~deli'rium, b, incipient or mild or intermittent; ~derm'al, a (DERM); ~dīac'onate, c; ~divide' v.t. & i. [f. L subdividere], -divi'sion, c; ~dom'i-nant n. (mus.), a, note below dominant, fourth of diatonic scale; ~dors'al, a; ‖~ed'it, ~ed'itor, c; ~epiderm'al, a (EPIDERMIS); ~e'qual, b (esp. of quantities in a group such that no one is as large as the sum of the rest); ~equi-lat'eral, b; ~erect', b; ~fam'ily, c (in zool. classif.); ~feb'rile, b; ~'flavour, d; ~'form, c; ~'fusc, b, dusky, dull-coloured [f. L suffuscus see FUSCOUS]; ~gelat'inous, b; ~gēnus, ~gene'ric, c; ~gla'cial, a; ~glob'ular, ~grallator'ial, b; ~'group, ~'head (in classif.), ~head'ing, c; ~hep-at'ic, a, b; ~himalay'an, b; ~hām'an, a; ~hŭm'eral, a (HUMERUS); ~infeuda'tion, ~inspec'tor, c; ~intes'tinal, a (INTESTINE[1]); ~'joint, c, one of ~divisions of regular joint in leg etc. of insect etc.; ~'kingdom, c, main division of animal or vegetable kingdom; ~lan'ceolate, b; ~'lease n., ~'lease' v.t., ~lessee', ~less'or, ~let' v.t., ~librar'ian, ‖~lieuten'ant, c; ~ling'ual, a; ~litt'oral, b; ~lun'ar (poet.), ~lun'ary, a, of this world, earthly; ~-machine-gun, a, large automatic pistol; ~mamm'ary, a (MAMMA[2]); ‖~'master, c, second master in some schools; ~maxill'ary, a (MAXILLA); ~mēd'iant n. (mus.), a, sixth note of diatonic scale; ~mem'branous, b; ~men'tal, a (MENTAL[2]); ~metall'ic, b; ~monᴸ tane, a; ~muc'ous, b; ~narcot'ic, b;

~nās'al, ~na'tural (opp. supernatural), ~norm'al, ~occip'ital (OCCIPUT), ~ocean'ic, a; ~ocell'ate, b (OCELLUS); ~oc'ular, ~oesopha'geal(OESOPHAGUS), ~orb'ital(ORBIT), a; ~'order, ~ord'inal, c (in bot. & zool. classif.); ~ov'al, b; ~pari'etal, ~pharyn'-geal (PHARYNX), ~phren'ic, a; ~pil'ose, b; ~pleur'al, a; ~pol'ar, b, of nearly polar character or situation, also a, directly below pole of heavens (astron.); ~prēf'ect(ure), ~prī'or, c; ~pyram'idal, ~quadran'g'ular, ~quad'rate, b; ~ram'ose, b; ‖~'reader, c (in Inns of Court); ~rec-tang'ular, b; ~'rector, c, rector's deputy; ~'region, c, division of faunal region; ~'rent v.t., c; ~ret'inal, a (RETINA); ~rhomboid'al, b; ~sac'ral, a (SACRUM); ~sat'urated, ~satura'tion, b; ~scap'ular, a; ~'section, c; ~sen'sible, a, below the reach of the senses; ~ser'ous, ~sess'ile, b; ~'soil, d; ~'species, ~specif'ic a., c; ~sphe'rical, ~spin'ous (SPINE), b; ~'station, c; ~stern'al, a (STERNUM); ~strāt'um (pl. -ta rare), d, what underlies something, lower layer, foundation, basis, (often fig., as it has a ~stratum of truth); ~struc'tion or ~struc'ture, ~struc'tural, d; ~tem'perate, b (of climate etc.); ~'tenant, ~'tenancy, c; ~term'inal, b, nearly at the end; ~terrā-n'ean, a, underground (lit. & fig.), so ~terran'eously; ~thora'cic, a (THORAX); ~ᴸ title, c, (also) film-caption; ~ton'ic n. (mus.), a, note next below tonic; ~trans-par'ent, ~triang'ular, b; ~'tribe, a (zool. & bot. classif.); ~trop'ical, b (of climate, fauna, flora, etc.); ~ung'ulate, b, hoofed, but with several digits; ~urs'ine, b; ~'variety c, (in classif.); ~vert'ebral, a; ~vert'ical, ~vit'reous, b; ~'way, d, ‖ covered usu. underground way, *under-ground railway.

subahdār' (sōōba-), n. (Anglo-Ind.). Chief Indian officer of company of sepoys. [Hind. (subah province, dār master)]

sub'altern, a. & n. **1.** Of inferior rank, (log., of propositions) particular, not universal. **2.** n. (mil.). Officer below rank of captain. [f. LL SUB(alternus ALTERNATE[1])]

subaud'ī, v. imperat. Supply (specified word or words) by way of subaudition. [L]

subaudi'tion, n. Mental supplying of omitted word(s), understanding of what is not expressed, reading between the lines. [f. LL subauditio f. SUB(audīre hear) understand]

‖ **subdūce', subdŭct',** vv.t. (rare). Withdraw, deduct, subtract. So **subdŭc'ᴛɪoɴ** n. [f. L SUB(ducere -duct- draw)]

subdūe', v.t. Conquer, subjugate, over-come, vanquish, master, tame, bring into subjection, discipline, (~ enemies, nature, rough land, one's passions; ~d by kind-ness); soften, make gentle, tone down, mitigate, (esp. in p.p., as ~d colour, light,

tone, effect, mood, manners, satisfaction,
whence ~d'NESS (-dūd-) n.). Hence **subdū'ABLE** a., **subdū'AL**(2) n. [ME *sodewe*
repr. AF **soduer*, **su*(b)*duer* = OF
soduire repr. in form L SUBDUCEre, but in
sense L SEDUCEre, while the E vb has the
sense of L SUB²(*dere* put) conquer]
sūbĕr'éous, sūbĕ'ric, sūb'erōse, aa.
Corky, of or like cork. [(-*ous* f. L
subereus + -OUS) f. L *suber* cork, -IC, -OSE¹]
subjā'cent, a. Underlying, situated below. [f. L SUB(*jacēre* lie), -ENT]
sŭb'jĕct¹, a. & adv. 1. (arch., poet.). Sub-
jacent (*survey the* ~ *plains*). 2. Under
government, not independent, owing
obedience *to*, (*a* ~ *province, tribe; is held*
~, in subjection; *has long been* ~ *to
France; States* ~ *to foreign rule; we are all*
~ *to the laws of nature, the law of the land*).
3. Liable or exposed or prone *to* (thing;
persons ~ *to gout; is very* ~ *to damage,
envy,* etc.). 4. ~ (a. & adv.) *to,* condi-
tional(ly) upon, on the assumption of,
without precluding, (*treaty is* ~ *to ratification,* not valid unless ratified; *the
arrangement is made,* or *is,* ~ *to your
approval;* ~ *to your consent, I propose to
try again;* ~ *to correction, these are the
facts*). [ME & OF *suget* etc., f. L p.p. of
SUB(*jicĕre* -*ject*- = *jacĕre* throw)]
sŭb'jĕct², n. 1. Person subject to political
rule, any member of a State except the
Sovereign, any member of a subject State,
(*rulers & ~s; the ~s of the Sultan; the
liberty of the ~,* such immunities as are
secured to ~s under constitutional rule;
fig., as *the ~s of King Shakespeare*). 2. (log.,
gram.). That member of a proposition
about which something is predicated, the
noun or noun-equivalent with which the
verb of a sentence is made to agree in
number etc., (~ *& predicate are the
essential parts of a sentence; every verb has
a ~ expressed or understood, not every verb
has an object*). 3. (philos.). Thinking &
feeling entity, the mind, the ego, the
conscious self, as opp. all that is external
to the mind (~ *& object,* the ego & the
non-ego, self & not-self, the consciousness
& what it is or may be conscious of); the
substance or substratum of anything as
opp. its attributes. 4. Theme or of *of*
discussion or description or representation, matter (to be) treated of or dealt
with, (*never talks on serious ~s; proposed
a ~ for the debate; on the ~ of,* concerning,
about; *a tabooed, ticklish, interesting,
dull,* ~; *what is the ~ of the poem, story,
picture?; constantly wanders from the ~;
pastoral, genre, marine, historical,* etc., ~
in painting; ~ *of piece of music,* theme of
fugue or sonata, leading phrase, motif;
~ *for dissection,* or ~, dead body; *was
made the ~ of an experiment; could write
if I could think of a ~; change the ~,* talk
of something else, esp. as way out of embarrassment). 5. Circumstance that gives
occasion *for* specified feeling or action

(*is a* ~ *for ridicule, pity, rejoicing, congratulation*). 6. Person of specified usu.
undesirable bodily or mental tendencies
(*a sensitive, bilious, plethoric, hysterical,
ill-conditioned,* etc., ~). 7. ~-*heading,* in
index collecting references to a ~; ~-
-*matter,* matter treated of in book etc.;
~-*object,* object of sense or thought as it is
conceived of (opp. *object-object,* as it is in
fact. Hence ~LESS a. [ME & OF *suget*
etc. f. L masc. & neut. p.p. (prec.)]
subjĕct'³, v.t. Subdue (nation etc. usu. *to*
one's sway etc.); expose, make liable,
treat, *to* (*rudeness ~s one to retorts in kind;
must be ~ed to great heat; shall* ~ *it to
criticism.* So **subjĕc'TION** n. [ME, f. OF
subjecter or L *subjectare* as SUBJECT¹]
subjĕc'tive, a. & n. 1. (Philos.) belonging
to, of, due to, the consciousness or thinking or perceiving subject or ego as opp.
real or external things; (pop.) imaginary.
2. (Of art & artists, literature, & history)
giving prominence to or depending on
personal idiosyncrasy or individual point
of view, not producing the effect of
literal & impartial transcription of external realities, whence ~NESS, **sub-
jĕctiv'ITY,** nn. 3. (gram.). Of the subject (~ *case,* or ~ as n., the nominative;
~ *genitive,* as in ' by the act of *God* ', cf.
OBJECTIVE). Hence ~LY² adv. [ME, f. L
subjectivus (SUBJECT², -IVE)]
subjĕc'tiv|ism, n. Doctrine that know-
ledge is merely subjective & that there is
no external or objective test of truth. So
~IST(2) n. & a. [prec., -ISM, -IST]
subjoin', v.t. Add at the end, append,
(illustration, anecdote, etc.). [f. obs. F
subjoindre f. L SUB(*jungere junct*- join)]
sŭb'jug|āte (-jŏŏ-), v.t. Subdue, van-
quish, bring under bondage or into subjection. Hence or cogn.~ABLE a., ~A'TION,
~ātoR, nn. [ME, f. LL *subjugare* bring
under the yoke (SUB², *jugum* yoke),
-ATE³]
subjŭnc'tive, a. & n. ~ *mood* or ~, a
verbal MOOD², obsolescent in English,
named as being used in the classical
languages chiefly in subordinate or sub-
joined clauses (cf. CONJUNCTIVE; the two
names denote the same forms & are occas.
used indifferently; occas. ~ is restricted
to the subordinate uses while *conjunctive*
either includes all uses or is restricted to
principal-clause verbs, as in apodosis of
conditional sentence). Hence ~LY² adv.
[f. LL *subjunctivus* (SUBJOIN, -IVE)]
sŭblăpsār'ian, a. & n. = INFRALAPSARIAN.
[SUB- 2a]
sŭb'lim|āte¹, v.t. Convert from solid
state to vapour by heat & allow to solidify again; (fig.) refine, purify, idealize.
Hence ~A'TION n. [as foll., -ATE³]
sŭb'limate², a. & n. Sublimated (substance); *corrosive* ~, mercuric chloride.
[f. L *sublimare* SUBLIME², -ATE²]
sublime'¹, a. Of the most exalted kind,
so distinguished by elevation or size or

nobility or grandeur or other impressive quality as to inspire awe or wonder, aloof from & raised far above the ordinary, (~ *mountain, scenery, tempest, ambition, virtue, heroism, self-sacrifice, love, thought, beauty, genius, poet*, etc.; ~ *indifference, impudence*, etc., as of one too exalted to fear consequences; *the S~* PORTE; *the* ~, all that is ~, sublimity), whence or cogn. ~LY² adv., sublim′ITY n.; (anat.) lying near the surface, not deep-sunk. [f. L *sublimis*]

sublim|e′², v.t. & i. Sublimate (lit.), whence~′ER¹(2) n.; undergo sublimation; purify or elevate, become pure, as by sublimation; make sublime. [ME, f. OF *sublimer* f. L *sublimare* in med. L sense *sublimate* (prec.)]

sublim′inal, a. (psych.). Below the threshold of consciousness, (of sensations) so faint that subject is not conscious of them; ~ *advertising*, technique of flashing an advertisement on a screen for a fraction of a second.so that the image penetrates to the viewer's subconsciousness though it makes no impression on his conscious mind; ~ *self*, the subconscious mind as a distinct part of the individual's personality. [f. SUB- 2a, L *limen -inis* threshold, -AL]

sub′măn, n. Man of markedly inferior development or capacity (opp. SUPER-MAN). [SUB- 2c]

sub′marin|e (-ēn; *adj. also* -ēn′), a. & n. 1. Existing, acting, used, constructed, etc., under the surface of the sea, as ~*e plant, volcano, cable*. 2. n. A ~e vessel, esp. a warship capable of operating either on or under the surface, equipped with torpedo-tubes, guns, & periscope, & propelled by diesel engines or electric motors or atomic power. Hence ~ER¹ (-mă′rĭn-) n. [SUB- 2a]

submerge′, v.t. & i. Place below water, flood with water, inundate, (also fig.; *the ~d tenth*, the part of the population that is sunk in poverty or permanently in distress); (of submarine or its crew or commander) dive, go below surface. Hence or cogn. submer′gENCE, submer′sION (-shn), nn. [f. L SUB(*mergere mers-* dip)]

submers|e′, v.t., & a. (rare). 1. Submerge (rare exc. in p.p. used in bot. of parts of plants growing under water). 2. adj. (rare; bot.). ~ed. Hence (in common use) ~′IBLE a. [f. L p.p. (prec.)]

submi′ssion (-shn), n. Submitting or being submitted (*shall be satisfied with nothing short of complete* ~; *demands the* ~ *of the signature to an expert*); (in legal use) theory etc. submitted by counsel to judge or jury (*my* ~ *is that*, I submit that); humility, meekness, resignation, acceptance of authority, obedient conduct or spirit, so submiss′IVE a., submiss′ive-

LY² adv., submiss′IVENESS n. [ME, f. OF, or L *submissio* (foll., -ION)]

submit′, v.t. & i. (-tt-). Surrender oneself for control etc. *to* (*wives* ~ *yourselves unto your own husbands*); present for consideration or decision (*should like to* ~ *it to your inspection*; ~ *a case to the court*); urge or represent deferentially *that* (*I* ~ *that a material fact has been passed over*; also parenth., as *that, I* ~, *is a false inference*); give way, make submission, yield, cease or abstain from resistance, (*will never* ~, ~ *to indignity*, ~ *to being parted from you; had to* ~ *to defeat, God's will*). [ME, f. L SUB(*mittere miss-* send)]

subōrd′inate¹, a. & n. 1. Of inferior importance or rank, secondary, subservient, (*to*; ~ *clause*, sentence made by addition of a conjunction or by position to serve as a noun or adj. or adv. in another sentence); hence ~LY² adv. 2. n. Person working under another (*leaves everything to, never trusts,* ~*s* or *his* ~*s*). [f. med. L SUB(*ordinatus* f. L *ordinare* ORDAIN), -ATE²]

subōrd′in|āte², v.t. Make subordinate, treat or regard as of minor importance, bring or put into subservient relation, (*to*). Hence or cogn. ~A′TION n., ~ATIVE a. [f. med. L *subordinare* (as prec., -ATE³)]

subōrdina′tionism (-sho-), n. (theol.). Doctrine that second & third persons of Trinity are inferior to the Father as regards (orthodox view) order only or (Arian view) essence. [-ISM]

subōrn′, v.t. Induce by bribery or otherwise to commit perjury or other unlawful act. Hence or cogn. subōrnA′TION, ~ER¹, nn. [f. L SUB*ornare* equip or incite secretly]

subpoen′a (-pēn-), n., & v.t. (~*ed* pr. -*ad*, ~′*d*). 1. Writ commanding person's attendance in court of justice. 2. v.t. Serve ~ on. [ME; orig. two words, L, = under penalty, the first in the writ]

subrep′tion, n. Obtaining of something by surprise or misrepresentation. [f. L *subreptio* purloining f. SUB(*ripere rept-* = *rapere* snatch)]

subroga′tion, n. (law). Substitution of one party for another as creditor. [f. LL *subrogatio -onis*, see SURROGATE]

subscrib|e′, v.t. & i. 1. Write (one's name or rarely other inscription) at foot of document etc. (*the ~ed names carry weight*; *someone has ~ed a motto*; also refl.); write one's name at foot of, sign, (document, picture, etc.). 2. Express one's adhesion *to* an opinion or resolution (*cannot~e to that*). 3. Enter one's name in a list of contributors, make or promise a contribution, contribute (specified sum), *to* or *to* a common fund or *for* a common object, raise or guarantee raising of by ~ing thus, (~*e to a charity, for a testimonial, £10*; ~*e for a book*, engage before it is published to take copy or copies; ~e to a newspaper, engage to take it for specified time; *the sum needed was ~ed several times over*). Hence or cogn. ~'ER[1] (*the ~er*, the undersigned), subscrip'TION, nn. [ME, f. L SUB(*scribere script*-write)]

sŭb'script, a. (Gk gram.). Written below (only in *iota* ~, small iota written below ā, ē, & ō). [f. L p.p. (prec.)]

subsĕll'ium, n. (pl. *-ia*). = MISERICORD (last sense). [L (SUB[2], *sella* seat)]

sŭb'sĕqu|ent, a. That follow(s) or followed the event etc. indicated in the context, of later time or date than something, posterior in time *to*. Hence ~ENCE n., ~entLY[2] adv. [ME, f. OF, or f. L SUB[2](*sequi* follow), -ENT]

subsẽrve', v.t. Serve as means in promoting (purpose, end, etc.). [f. L SUB[2](*servire* SERVE)]

subsẽrv'i|ent, a. Useful as means, having merely instrumental relation, (*to*); cringing, obsequious. Hence ~ENCE, ~ENCY, nn., ~entLY[2] adv. [f. L as prec., -ENT]

subside', v.i. (Of water, esp. flood) sink in level, run off, disappear; (of ground) cave in, sink; (of building, ship, etc.) settle down lower in ground or water; (of suspended matter) fall to bottom, be precipitated; (of person, usu. joc.) sink into sitting or kneeling or lying posture (*~d into an armchair*); cease from activity or agitation, become tranquil, abate, (*storm, tumult, apprehension, excitement, ~s*). Hence sŭb'sidENCE (*or* subsī'-) n. [f. L SUB[2](*sidere* settle cogn. w. *sedēre* sit)]

subsid'iar|ў, a. & n. 1. Serving to assist or supplement, auxiliary, supplementary, whence ~ILY[2] adv.; (of company) controlled by another holding more than 50 per cent. of its issued share capital; (of troops) subsidized, hired by another nation. 2. n. (Usu. pl.) ~y thing or person, accessory; ~y company. [f. L *subsidiarius* (SUBSIDY, -ARY[1])]

sŭb'sidize, -ise (-īz), v.t. Pay subsidy to. [foll., -IZE]

sŭb'sidЎ, n. (Hist.) parliamentary grant of money to the sovereign for State needs, tax levied on particular occasion; money grant from one State to another in return for military or naval aid or other equivalent; money contributed by State to keep down price of commodities etc. (*food, housing, ~*) or to expenses of commercial undertaking, charitable institution, etc., held to be of public utility. [ME, f. AF *subsidie* = OF *subside* f. L *subsidium*]

subsist', v.i. & t. Exist, continue to exist, remain in being; keep oneself alive, support life, be kept in life, find sustenance, (*on vegetables, charity*, etc., *by begging* etc.); provide sustenance for (*undertook to clothe, arm, & ~ 1000 men*). [f. L SUB[2]-(*sistere* set, stand, causal f. *stare* stand)]

subsis'tence, n. Subsisting; means of

supporting life, livelihood, what one lives on or by; ~ *money*, allowance or advance of pay granted for maintenance; ~ *wage*, merely enough to provide the bare necessities of life. [f. LL *subsistentia* substance (prec., -ENCE)]

sŭb'stance, n. 1. (Metaphys.) the substratum that the cognizable properties or qualities or attributes or accidents of things are conceived as inhering in or affecting, the essential nature underlying phenomena, (*~ & accidents in metaphysics correspond to subject & predicate in logic; a ~ is a being subsisting in itself & subject to accidents; being of one ~ with the Father*); essence or most important part of anything, pith, purport, real meaning, (*I agree with you in ~*, generally, apart from details; *can give you the ~ of his remarks; the ~ of religion*). 2. Material as opposed to form (*the ~ is good, but the style repellent*). 3. Reality, solidity, solid worth, actual possessions, (*sacrifice the ~ for the shadow; there is no ~ in him; an argument of little ~; a man of ~*, with property, cf. *man of* STRAW; *waste one's ~*, be spendthrift). 4. Particular kind of matter (*a heavy, porous, yellow, transparent, ~; the small number of ~s that make up the world*). [ME, f. OF, f. L *substantia* (SUB[2], *stare* stand, -ANCE)]

substan'tial (-shl), a. Having substance, actually existing, not illusory, (*the ghost proved ~ after all*); of real importance or value, of considerable amount, (opp. *nominal, verbal; a ~ argument, point; made a ~ contribution, ~ progress, ~ concessions*); of solid material or structure, not flimsy, stout, (*a ~ house; a man of ~ build*); possessed of property, well-to-do, commercially sound, (*a ~ yeoman; deal only with ~ firms*); deserving the name in essentials, virtual, practical, (*~ truth, agreement, success, performance of contract*). Hence or cogn. ~ITY (-shiăl[2]) n., ~LY[2] adv. [ME, f. OF *substanciel* or LL *substantialis* (prec., -AL)]

substăn'tial|ism (-sha-), n. (philos.). Doctrine that behind phenomena there are substantial realities. So ~IST(2) n. [-ISM]

substan'tialize (-sha-), -ise (-īz), v.t. & i. Invest with or acquire substance or actual existence. [-IZE]

substan'ti|āte (-shī-), v.t. Prove the truth of, give good grounds for, (charge, statement, claim). Hence ~A'TION (-sī-, -shī-) n. [17th c., see SUBSTANCE, -ATE[3]]

sŭb'stantive, a. & n. 1. Expressing existence (*the ~ verb*, the vb *be*); having a separate & independent existence, not merely inferential or implicit or subservient or parasitic, (*~ enactment, motion*, etc., made in due form as such; *noun ~*, old name for the noun in the now usual sense distinguishing it from the *noun adjective* now called *adjective* simply); ~ *rank* (mil.), permanent rank in the holder's branch of the army (as opp. brevet, honorary, acting, or temporary rank); hence ~LY² adv. (esp. in gram., = *substantivally*). 2. n. Noun ~, noun in the now usual sense excluding adjectives; so **sŭbstantīv′al** a., **sŭbstantīv′alLY²** adv. [ME, f. OF (-*if*, -*ive*), or LL *substantivus* (SUBSTANCE, -IVE)]

sŭb′stit|ūte, n., & v.t. 1. Person or thing performing some function instead of another. 2. v.t. Make (person or thing) fill a place or discharge a function for or *for* another; (vulg.) replace (person or thing) *by* or *with* another; put in exchange (*for*; so ~ū′tION n., ~ū′tionAL (-sho-), ~ū′tionARY¹ (-sho-), ~ūtIVE, aa., ~ū′tionalLY² adv. [ME, f. L SUB(*stituere -ut-* = *statuere* .see STATUTE)]

subsūme′, v.t. Include (instance etc.) under a rule or class. Hence **subsŭmp′TION** n. [SUB-, L *sumere sumpt-* take]

subtĕnd′, v.t. (geom.). (Of chord, side of triangle) be opposite to (arc, angle). [f. L SUB(*tendere tens-* stretch); cf. TEND]

subtĕnse′, n. Line subtending arc or angle. [f. L p.p. (prec.)]

sŭbter-, pref. = under, less than, esp. in wds formed as opposites to compounds of SUPER-, as ~*position*, ~*human*, ~*natural*. [L (SUB², -*ter* as in INTER²)]

sŭb′terfūge, n. Attempt to escape censure or defeat in argument by evading the issue, statement etc. resorted to for such purpose, use of such statements etc. [f. LL -*fugium* f. L SUBTER(*fugere* flee)]

subtil(e) (sŭ′tl, sŭb′tĭl), a. (Arch. for) SUBTLE. Hence or cogn. **subt′ilize**(2, 3) v.t. & i., **subtiliza′TION** n., (sŭt-), **subtilty** (sŭt′ltĭ) n. (arch.). [ME & OF *subtil* f. L *subtilis* f. SUB² + *tela* web]

subtle (sŭ′tl) a. Tenuous or rarefied (arch.), pervasive owing to tenuity, (the ~ *air*, a ~ *vapour*; of ~ *texture*, a ~ *perfume*); evasive, mysterious, hard to grasp or trace, (~ *magic, charm, power, art*; a ~ *distinction*); making fine distinctions, having delicate perception, acute, (~ *senses, perception, insight*; a ~ *observer, philosopher, intellect, mind*); ingenious, elaborate, clever, (a ~ *device, fancy, workman, explanation, policy*; ~ *fingers*); crafty, cunning, (*now the serpent was more ~ than any beast*; a ~ *enemy*). Hence **subt′LY²** (sŭt-) adv. [ME & OF *sotil* f. L as prec.]

subtlety (sŭt′ltĭ), n. In adj. senses; also, a fine distinction, a piece of hair-splitting. [ME, f. OF *s(o)utilte* f. L *subtilitatem* (SUBTIL, -TY)]

sŭbtŏp′i|a, n. (derog.). Term applied to urban and rural areas disfigured by ill-planned and ugly building development; unsightly suburbs regarded as encroaching upon the natural scene; also fig. Hence ~AN a. [f. SUB- 2a +(U)TOPIA]

subtrăct′, v.t. Deduct (part, quantity,

number) from or *from* whole or greater quantity or number, esp. in arithmetic or algebra. Hence or cogn. **subtrăc′tION** n., **subtrăc′tIVE** a. [f. L SUB(*trahere tract-* draw)]

sŭb′trahĕnd, n. What is to be subtracted in a subtraction sum. [L as prec.]

sŭb′ūlate, sŭb′ūlifŏrm, aa. (bot., zool.). Awl-shaped. [L *subula* awl (*suere* sew), -ATE², -I-, -FORM]

sŭb′ûrb, n. Outlying district of city (the ~s, all or one of such districts, as a *house in the ~s*, also the environs). So **subûrb′AN** a. [ME, f. OF *suburbe* or L SUB(*urbium* f. *urbs urbis* city)]

Subûrb′ia, n. (usu. derog.). (Quasi-proper name for) the suburbs (esp. of London) & their inhabitants. [-IA¹]

subvĕn′tion, n. Grant of money in aid, subsidy. [ME, f. OF, f. LL *subventionem* f. SUB(*venire vent-* come) assist, -ION]

subvĕrt′, v.t. Overturn, upset, effect destruction or overthrow of, (religion, monarchy, the constitution, principles, morality). Hence or cogn. **subvĕr′sION** (-shn) n., **subvĕr′sIVE** a. [ME, f. OF *subvertir* or L SUB(*vertere vers-* turn)]

suc-, = SUB- in L compounds of *sub* with words in c- & their derivatives.

succāde′, n. Candied fruit in syrup. [ME, f. AF *sukade* = OF *succade, chuc(c)ade*]

sŭccēdān′é|um (-ks-), n. (pl. ~a). Substitute, thing or rarely person that one falls back on in default of another. So ~ous a. [neut. of L *succedaneus* (foll., -ANEOUS)]

succeed′ (-ks-), v.t. & i. 1. Take the place previously filled by, follow (t. & i.) in order, come next (to), ensue, be subsequent (to), come by inheritance or in due order to or to office or title or property, (*day ~s day* or *to day*; *agitation ~ed calm*; ~*ing ages will reverence his memory*; *Elizabeth ~ed Mary*, ~*ed to the throne*, ~*ed*). 2. Have success (*in doing* etc.), be successful, prosper, accomplish one's purpose; (of plan etc.) be brought to successful issue. [ME, f. OF *succeder* or L SUC(*cedere cess-* go)]

succĕn′tor (-ks-), n. Precentor's deputy in some cathedrals. [LL, f. L SUC(*cinere -cent-* = *canere* sing), -OR]

succès d'estime (see Ap.), n. Passably cordial reception given to performance or work from respect rather than appreciation. [F]

succès fou (see Ap.), n. Success marked by wild enthusiasm. [F]

success′ (-ks-), n. Issue of undertaking (rare; *with good or bad* ~); favourable issue, accomplishment of end aimed at, attainment of wealth or fame or position, (*have inquired for it without* ~; *military* ~*es*; *spoilt by* ~; *nothing succeeds like* ~, one ~ leads to others), whence ~FUL a., ~fulLY² adv.; thing or person that turns out well (*the experiment is a* ~; *was a great*

For words in sub- not given see SUB-.

~ *as a bishop*); pupil who passes his examination. [f. L *successus* -*ūs* (SUCCEED)]

succe'ssion (-ksĕshn), n. **1.** A following in order (esp. *in* ~; *three great victories in* ~, running, without intervening defeat). **2.** Series of things in ~ (*a* ~ *of disasters*, several running). **3.** (Right of) succeeding to the throne or any office or inheritance, set or order of persons having such right, (*laws regulating the* ~; *claimed, was excluded from, the* ~; *in* ~ *to*, as successor of; *the* ~ *must not be broken*; *is second in the* ~; *was left to him & his* ~, heirs; *apostolic* ~, uninterrupted transmission of spiritual authority through bishops from the apostles downwards; *law of* ~, regulating inheritance esp. in cases of intestate decease; *the S*~ *States*, those resulting from the partition of Austria- -Hungary. **4.** (biol.). Order of descent in development of species. Hence ~AL (-ksĕsho-) a. [ME, f. OF, or L *successio* (SUCCEED, -ION)]

succĕss'ive (-ks-), a. Following one after another, in uninterrupted succession, running, consecutive. Hence ~LY² adv. [ME, f. med. L *successivus* (SUCCEED, -IVE)]

succĕss'or (-ks-), n. Person or thing that succeeds to another (*to, of*; cf. PREDECESSOR). [ME, f. OF f. L (SUCCEED, -OR)]

succinct' (-ks-), a. Terse, concise, briefly expressed. Hence ~LY² adv., ~NESS n. [ME, f. L *succinctus* f. SUC(*cingere cinct*-gird) tuck up]

sŭcc'ory̆, n. = CHICORY. [alt. f. *cicoree* etc., old forms of CHICORY]

*****sŭcc'otăsh**, n. Dish of green maize & beans (& salt pork) boiled together. [f. Amer.-Ind. *msiquatash*]

sŭcc'our (-ker), v.t., & n. **1.** Come to the assistance of, give aid to, (person in danger or difficulty). **2.** n. Aid given at time of need; (pl., arch.) reinforcements, troops coming to the rescue; hence ~LESS a. [vb ME, f. OF *sucurre* f. L SUC(*currere curs*- run); n. ME & OF *sucurs* etc. f. med. L *succursus* -*ūs* (*succurrere*)]

sŭcc'ūba, **-bus**, n. (pl. -*bae*, -*bī*). Female demon having sexual intercourse with sleeping men. [LL (-*ba*) & med. L (-*bus*) f. SUC(*cumbere* lie)]

sŭcc'ūl|ent, a. Juicy (of lit. or fig. food); (bot.) thick & fleshy, having such leaves or stems. Hence ~ENCE n., ~entLY² adv. [f. L *succulentus* (*succus* juice, -LENT)]

succŭmb' (-m), v.i. Be overcome, have to cease from resistance or competition or other effort, be forced to give way *to*, die owing *to*, die, (~ *to one's enemies, superior numbers, grief, temptation*). [ME, f. OF *succomber* or f. L SUC(*cumbere* lie)]

succŭrs'al, a. (Of chapel of ease) subsidiary. [f. F (*église*) *succursale* subsidiary (church) f. med. L as SUCCOUR, -AL]

sŭch, a. (no comp. or sup.; placed not between *a* & its n. but before or after them), & pron. **1.** Of the same kind or

degree *as* (~ *people, people* ~, *as these*; ~ *beauty as yours*; *experiences* ~ *as this are rare*; ~ *grapes as you never saw*; ~ *as also* = of the or a kind that, as ~ *a scarlet as makes the eyes ache*). **2.** So great, so natured in some respect, *as to* do or *that* (*is* ~ *as to make one despair*; *had* ~ *a fright that she hardly survived it*). **3.** Of the kind or degree already described or implied or intelligible from the context or circumstances (*never had* ~ *sport*; *there are no* ~ *doings now*; ~ *things make one despair*; ~ *are the privileges of fatherhood*; *don't be in* ~ *a hurry*; *how could you leave him at* ~ *a time?*; *saw just* ~ *another yesterday*; *long may he continue* ~*!*; often colloq. preceding adj. & n. with the effect of *so* modifying the adj., as ~ *horrid language*, language so horrid, *was it* ~ *a long time ago?*, *don't want* ~ *a big one* or ~ *big ones*; also rarely used twice as relative & correl., as ~ *master* ~ *servant*, the servant is ~ as the master is). **4.** (In legal or formal style) the aforesaid, of the aforesaid kind (*whoever shall make* ~ *return falsely*). **5.** So great!, of a kind that demands exclamatory description, (*we have had* ~ *sport!*, ~ *an enjoyable evening!*). **6.** Of a kind or degree sufficient to account for the preceding or following statement (*he cannot come too often, he gives* ~ *pleasure*; *there was* ~ *draught, it is no wonder he caught cold*). **7.** (Also ~-*&-*~) particular, of particular kind, but not needing to be specified (~ *an one*, ~ *a one*, arch., ~-*&-*~ *a person*, someone, so-&-so; ~-*&-*~ *results will follow from* ~-*&-*~ *causes*). **8.** ~'*like*, of ~ kind (now chiefly vulg.; & see below). **9.** pron. ~ *as*, those who (chiefly arch. or poet. or rhet.; ~ *as sit in darkness*). **10.** That, the action etc. referred to, (*I may have offended, but* ~ *was not my intention*). **11.** *As* ~, as being what has been named (*in country places a stranger is welcome as* ~); *all* ~, persons of ~ character (*so perish all* ~*!*). **12.** (Also ~*like*; chiefly vulg.) things of ~ kind (*do not hold with theatres & balls & ~ or ~like*). **13.** (vulg. or commerc.). The aforesaid thing(s), it, they or them, (*those who leave parcels in the train cannot expect to recover* ~). [OE *swylc*, OS *sulik*, OHG *sulih*, ON *slikr*, Goth. *swaleiks* f. Gmc. **swalik*- (SO, ‑LIKE)]

sŭck, v.t. & i., & n. **1.** Draw (milk, liquid) into mouth by making vacuum with muscles of lips etc., (fig.) imbibe or gain (knowledge, advantage, etc.; also ~ *in knowledge*, ~ *advantage out of*); draw milk or liquid or sustenance or advantage from (~ *dry*, exhaust of contents thus; ~ *the breast of*; *the mother whom he* ~*ed*; ~*ed orange*, thing in which there is no goodness left; ~ *one's brains*, extract his ideas for one's own use); roll the tongue about, squeeze in the mouth, (~ *sweets*, *one's teeth*, etc.); (of absorbent substance) ~ *in* or *up*, absorb; (of whirlpool etc.) ~

in, engulf; ~ the breast or udder (part., not yet weaned, as ~*ing child*, ~*ing-pig*; also fig., unpractised, budding, as ~*ing barrister*, *saint*); ~ something, use ~*ing* action, make ~*ing* sound, (*sat* ~*ing at his pipe*; *pump* etc. ~*s*, makes gurgling or drawing sound; ~*ing-disc*, sucker); ~ *in* (sl.), deceive, ~*-in*, n., disappointment; ‖ ~ *up* (schoolboy sl.), play toady (*to*; ~*-up* n., a toady). 2. n. Opportunity of ~*ing* the breast (*give* ~, of mother or nurse or animal suckling child etc.); drawing action of whirlpool etc.; spell of ~*ing* with lips or in mouth (*take a* ~ *at it*); small draught of or of liquor; ‖ (schoolboy sl., pl.) sweets; (sl.; also ~*-in*) disappointment, fiasco, (*what a* ~ *!*, ~*s !*, intt. expr. amusement at another's failure after confidence). [OE *sūcan*, cogn. w. L *sugere*; cf. SOAK]

sŭck′er, n., & v.t. & i. 1. Person or thing that sucks, esp. sucking-pig or new-born whale; (sl.) person of immature mind, greenhorn; kinds of fish that suck in food or have mouth suggesting suction or adhere by sucking-disc. 2. Piston of suction-pump; pipe through which liquid is drawn by suction. 3. (Also *sucking-disc*) flat or concave surface (as organ in some animals, also *acetabulum*, or artificial or rubber etc. in machinery or appliances) that adheres by suction & atmospheric pressure to what it is placed against. 4. (bot.). Shoot springing from subterranean part of stem, from part of root remote from main stem, from axil, or abnormally from bole or branch. 5. vb. (bot.). Remove ~s from; produce ~s. [-ER¹]

sŭc′kle, v.t. Give suck to. [ME, perh. back form. f. foll.]

sŭck′ling, n. Unweaned child or animal (*babes & ~s*, the utterly inexperienced). [ME, f. SUCK vb; -LING¹]

sŭc′rōse, n. Cane-sugar or any of the sugars of the same composition & properties. [F *sucre* SUGAR, -OSE²]

sŭc′tion, n. Sucking; production of partial vacuum by removal of air etc. for purpose of enabling external atmospheric pressure to force in liquid or produce adhesion of surfaces; ~*-chamber*, *-pipe*, in ~*-pump*; ~*-fan*, for withdrawing chaff etc. from grain by ~; ~*-plate*, holding set of artificial upper teeth & adhering to palate by ~; ~*-pump*, drawing water through pipe into chamber exhausted by piston. [f. LL *suctio* (L *sugere* *suct-* SUCK, -ION)]

sŭctōr′ial, a. (zool.). Adapted for or capable of sucking, having sucker for feeding or adhering. [mod. L *suctorius* (prec., -ORY), -AL]

Sudanese (sōōdanēz′), a. & n. (pl. same). (Inhabitant, language) of the Sudan, region of Africa south of Egypt. [-ESE]

sūdar′ium, n. (pl. -*ia*). Kerchief of St Veronica miraculously stamped with face

of Christ; any miraculous portrait of Christ; napkin about Christ's head (*John* xx. 7). [L, = napkin (*sudor* sweat, -ARY¹)]

sūdatōr′ium, n. (pl. -*ia*). Hot-air bath. [L neut. as foll.]

sŭd′atorỹ, a. & n. 1. Promoting perspiration. 2. n. = drug; = prec. [f. L *sudatorius* (*sudare* SWEAT, -ORY)]

sŭdd, n. Floating plants, trees, etc., impeding navigation of White Nile. [Arab., = barrier]

sŭdd′en, a. & n. 1. Occurring or come upon or made or done unexpectedly or without warning, abrupt, abnormally rapid, hurried, (~ *death*, *need*, *fear*; *a* ~ *resolve*, *departure*, *change*, *turn of the wrist*, *bend in the road*; *is very* ~ *in his movements*); ~ *death*, (also, colloq.) decision by a single toss of a coin (as against the best of three), decision of a level set at lawn tennis by the issue of the next game; hence ~LY² adv., ~NESS n. 2. n. *Of* or *on a*, rarely *on the*, ~, ~*ly*. [ME, f. AF *sodein*, *sudein* = OF *soudain* f. L *subitaneus* (*subitus* sudden, -ANEOUS)]

sūdorif′erous, a. Sweat-producing (of glands). [f. LL *sudorifer* (*sudor* sweat, -FEROUS)]

sūdorif′ic, a. & n. (Drug) causing sweat. [L *sudor* sweat, -I-, -FIC]

Sud′ra (sōō-), n. Lowest of four great Hindu castes; cf. BRAHMIN, KSHATRIYA, VAISYA. [Skr.]

sŭds (-z), n. pl. Froth of soap & water (usu. *soap-~*). [16th c. also = fen waters etc., of uncert. orig.; cf. MDu., MLG *sudde*, MDu. *sudse* marsh, bog]

sūe, v.t. & i. Prosecute (person) in lawcourt; entreat (person), make entreaty or application *to* person or law-court, (*for* redress or a favour, esp. woman's hand in marriage); ~ *out*, make petition in lawcourt for & obtain (writ, pardon, etc.). [ME, f. AF *suer*, *siwer* = OF *sivre* etc. f. Rom. **sequēre* f. L *sequi* follow]

suède (swād), n. Kid-skin dressed with flesh side rubbed to a nap (usu. attrib.). [f. F (*gants de*) *Suède* (gloves of) Sweden]

sū′ét, n. Hard fat of. kidneys & loins of oxen, sheep, etc. Hence ~Y² a. [ME, app. f. AF **suet*, **sewet* f. OF *seu*, *sieu* (mod. *suif*) f. L *sebum* tallow, -ET¹]

suf-, = SUB- in L compds with wds in f- & their derivatives.

sŭff′er, v.t. & i. 1. Undergo, experience, be subjected to, (pain, loss, grief, defeat, change, punishment, wrong, etc.); undergo pain or grief or damage or disablement (~*s acutely*; ~*ing mortals*; *was* ~*ing from neuralgia*; *your reputation will* ~; *the engine* ~*ed severely*; *trade is* ~*ing from the war*), whence ~ER¹, ~ING¹(1), nn. (often pl.). 2. (Of condemned man) be executed (*was to* ~ *the next morning*). 3. Permit *to* do, allow to go on, put up with, tolerate, (~ *them to come*; *should not* ~ *it for a moment*; *how can you* ~ *him or his insolence?*, whence, chiefly w. neg., ~ABLE a.). [ME, f. AF *suffrir* = OF *sof(f)rir* f. L SUF(*ferre* bear)]

süff′erance, n. ‖ (Arch.) submissiveness; tacit consent, permission or toleration implied by abstinence from objection, (esp. *on* ~, in virtue of such toleration). [ME, f. AF, OF *suf(f)rance* f. LL *sufferentia* (SUFFER, -ENCE)]

süff′ēte, n. One of two chief magistrates of ancient Carthage. [f. L *sufes -etis* f. Punic]

suffice′, v.i. & t. Be enough (*to do*, *for* person or purpose, or abs.), be adequate, (*your word will* ~; *that* ~*s to prove it*; ~ *it to say that*, I will content myself with saying that); satisfy, meet the needs of, (*half a dozen* ~*d him*). Hence **suffi′cingLY**[2] adv. [ME, f. OF *suffire* (*suffis*-) f. L SUF(*ficere* = *facere* make)]

suffi′ciency̆ (-shn-), n. ‖ (Arch.) being sufficient, ability, efficiency; adequate resources, a competence, a sufficient amount of or of something. [f. OF *sufficience* or LL *sufficientia* (foll., -ENCY)]

suffi′cient (-shnt), a. & n. **1.** Sufficing, adequate esp. in amount or number to the need, enough, (*is* ~ *to feed a hundred men*; *had not* ~ *courage for it*; *has impudence* ~ *for anything*; *have you* ~ *provisions?*), whence ~LY[2] adv.; ‖ (arch.) competent, of adequate ability or resources; SELF-~. **2.** n. Enough, a ~ quantity, (chiefly vulg. for *enough*; *have you had* ~?). [ME, f. OF, or f. L *sufficiens* (SUFFICE, -ENT)]

suffix′[1], v.t. Append (letter, syllable) in word-formation. [f. foll.]

süff′ix[2], n. Suffixed letter or syllable (cf. *prefix*, *affix*). [f. mod. L *suffixum* f. neut. p.p. of L SUF(*figere fix*- fasten)]

süff′oc|āte, v.t. & i. Choke or kill by stopping respiration (of person, superincumbent mass, fumes, etc.); produce choking sensation in, impede breath or utterance of, (~*ated by* or *with grief, excitement,* etc.); feel ~ated, gasp for breath. Hence or cogn. ~**ātingLY**[2] adv., ~**A′TION** n. [f. L *suffocare* (SUB[2], *fauces* throat)]

süff′ragan, a. & n. ~ *bishop* or *bishop* ~ or ~, bishop appointed to help diocesan bishop in administration of diocese, also any bishop in relation to his archbishop or metropolitan (~ *see* etc., of ~ bishop). Hence ~SHIP n. [ME, f. AF, OF *suffragan*, repr. med. L *suffraganeus* assistant (bishop) f. stem of *suffragium* (foll.)]

süff′rage, n. Vote, approval or consent expressed by voting, (*the electors gave their* ~*s for free trade*; also transf., as *the horse has my* ~, I think it preferable); the right of voting in political elections (*the* ~, or *manhood, woman, universal,* etc., ~; *manhood* ~, extended to all adult males without property tests etc.; *woman* ~, extended to women as well as men; *universal* ~, extended to all adults); (eccl.) short petition of congregation, esp. one said in response to priest, (arch.) an inter-

cessory prayer. [ME, f. L *suffragium*, partly thr. F *suffrage*]

süffragëtte′, n. Woman who agitated for woman suffrage. [irreg. f. SUFFRAGE + -ETTE]

süff′ragist, n. One who attaches importance to (esp. some extension of) the suffrage (*woman*-~ etc.). [-IST]

suffūse′ (-z), v.t. (Of colour or moisture) well up from within & colour or moisten (*a blush, tears,* ~*d her cheeks, eyes*; often in p.p., as *skies* ~*d with amethyst*). So **suffū′SION** (-zhn) n. [f. L SUF(*fundere fus*-pour)]

suf′|ĭ (soō-), **sōf′|ĭ**, n. Mohammedan pantheistic mystic. Hence ~IC a., ~ISM (3) n. [f. Arab. *çūfī* man of wool (*çūf* wool)]

sug-, = SUB- in L compds w. wds in g- & their derivatives.

su′gar (shoō-), n., & v.t. & i. **1.** Kinds of sweet crystalline substance prepared from various plants esp. the ~-cane & beet for use in cookery, confectionery, brewing, etc. (*cane, beet, maple,* etc., ~, named from plant of origin; *brown, white, granulated, powdered,* LUMP[1], CASTOR[2], LOAF[1], ~). **2.** Sweet words, flattery, anything serving purpose of ~ put round pill in reconciling person to what is unpalatable. **3.** (chem.). Kinds of soluble sweet-tasting fermentable carbohydrate divided according to their composition into glucoses & saccharoses. **4.** ‖ ~-*basin,* holding ~ for table use; ~-*bean,* kinds of pulse & kidney-bean; ~-*beet,* kinds from which ~ is extracted; ~-*bird,* kinds that suck flowers; ~-CANDY; ~-*cane,* a grass with jointed stems 18-20 ft high from which ~ is made; *~-daddy* (sl.), elderly protector and source of revenue of a (female) GOLD-*digger*; ~-*gum,* Australian gum-tree with sweet foliage; ~-*house,* establishment in which raw ~ is made; ~-LOAF[1]; ~-*maple,* tree from sap of which ~ is made; ~-*mill,* for crushing ~-cane & expressing ~; ~-*mite,* kind infesting unrefined ~; ~-*orchard,* of ~-maples; ~-*plum,* sweetmeat, esp. small ball of boiled ~; ~-*refiner(y),* (establishment of) manufacturer who refines raw ~; ~-*tongs,* small tongs for taking up lump-~ at table; hence ~Y[2], ~LESS, aa., ~INESS n. **5.** vb. Sweeten with ~ lit. or fig. **6.** (sl.). Used in pass. as euphem. imprecation. **7.** ‖ (sl.). Work lazily, not do one's full share of work, not put forth all one's strength, whence ~ER[1] n. [ME, f. OF *çucre, zuchre,* etc., f. med. L *zuc-, succarum,* f. Arab. *sukkar*]

suggëst′ (suj-), v.t. Cause (idea) to present itself, call up the idea of by mention or association, (*thing* ~*s itself,* comes into the mind); propose (theory, plan, often expressed in *that*-clause) for acceptance or rejection, set up the hypothesis *that,* (~*ed a retreat, that they should retreat*; *I* ~ *that,* formula of examining counsel in imputing motives etc. = *I put it to you,* as

I ~ that you had a secret understanding with them). [f. L SUG(*gerere gest*- bring)]

sugges't|ible (suj-), a. That may be suggested; open to hypnotic suggestion. Hence ~**ibil'ity** n. [-IBLE]

sugges'tĭŏ făl'sī (suj-), n. Positive misrepresentation not involving direct lie but going beyond concealment of the truth (cf. SUPPRESSIO VERI). [L]

suggestion (sujĕs'chon), n. Suggesting (*full of ~*, suggesting many ideas, stimulating reflection); theory or plan suggested; suggesting of prurient ideas; insinuation of a belief or impulse into the mind of a hypnotic subject, such belief or impulse. So **sugges'tive** a. (*of*), **suggestively**[2] adv., **sugges'tiveness** n., (suj-). [ME, f. OF, f. L SUGGESTI*onem* (-ION)]

sū'ī, genit. of L *suus* his, her, its, or their, own: ~ *gĕn'erĭs* pred. a., not classifiable with others, unique; ~ *jur'ĭs* (-oor-) pred. a., of full age & capacity, independent.

sū'ĭcĭde, n. **1.** Person who intentionally kills himself; (law) ~ of years of discretion & sane mind. **2.** Intentional self-slaughter (in law, as in 1; esp. *commit ~*, kill oneself); action destructive to one's own interests or continuance in some capacity (*commit political ~*, ruin one's prospects as a politician; *race-~*, failure of a people to maintain its numbers); hence **sŭĭcĭd'al** a., **sŭĭcĭd'ally**[2] adv. [f. mod. L *suicida, suicidium*, f. *sui* of oneself +-CIDE]

sū'ĭlline, a. Of the hog family. [f. LL *suillinus* f. L *suillus* (*sus* pig), -INE[1]]

suit (sūt), n., & v.t. & i. **1.** Suing, petition, seeking of woman's hand in marriage, (*make ~*, urge a humble request; *with lowly ~*; *has a ~ to the king*; *press, push*, etc., one's ~; *prosper in* one's ~). **2.** Legal prosecution of a claim, action in law-court, (also *law~, ~ at law*; *criminal, civil*, etc., ~). **3.** Any of the four sets (spades, hearts, diamonds, clubs) into which pack of cards is divided (*follow ~*, play from ~ that was led, fig. conform to another's movements); player's holding in it (*long, short, ~* in whist, of more than three, less than four, cards). **4.** Set of man's clothes esp. when of same cloth, consisting usu. of coat, waistcoat, & trousers or knickerbockers or breeches (often ~ *of clothes*; *dress ~*, for evening dress; ~ *of* DITTOS; ~'*case*, kind of small portmanteau), whence ~'ING[1](3) n.; (usu. *2, 3, 4, -piece ~*) woman's costume. **5.** Set *of* sails, set *of* armour, for simultaneous use. **6.** vb. Accommodate, adapt, make fitting or appropriate, *to* (~ *the action to the word*, carry out promise or threat at once; ~ *one's style to* one's *audience*); (p.p.) appropriate *to*, well adapted or having the right qualities *for, is not ~ed to be* or *for an engineer*). **7.** Satisfy, meet the demands or requirements or interests of, (*does not ~ all tastes*; *it ~s me* or, prob.

w. ref. to betting, *my book to put up with him*; ~ *yourself*, do as you choose, also find something that satisfies you, esp. as servant's formula in giving warning; (of food, climate, etc.) improve or be consistent with the health of, agree with, (*cold, asparagus, does not ~ me*). **8.** Comport with or *with*, go well with appearance or character of, become, (*red does not ~ with* or ~*s her complexion*; *the part ~s him admirably*; *mercy ~s a king*). **9.** Be convenient (*that date will ~*). [f. AF *siute* etc., = OF *sieute* f. Gallo-Rom. *sequita* f. Rom. *sequere* SUE]

suit'|able (sūt-), a. Suited *to* or *for*, well fitted for the purpose, appropriate to the occasion.• Hence ~**abil'ity**, ~**ableness**, nn., ~**ably**[2] adv. [prec., -ABLE]

suite (swēt), n. Retinue, set of persons in attendance; set of things belonging together, esp. ~ *of rooms* or *furniture*; (mus.) instrumental composition, orig. succession of movements in dance style. [F, as SUIT]

suit'or (sūt-), n. Party to lawsuit; petitioner; wooer, man who asks for woman's hand in marriage. [ME, f. AF *seutor, suitour*, etc., f. L *secutorem* (*sequi, secut-* follow, -OR)]

suivez (swēv'ā), mus. direction instructing accompanist to suit his time etc. to soloist's performance. [F]

sŭl'cāte, a. (bot., anat.). Grooved, fluted, channelled. [f. L *sulcare* (*sulcus* furrow), -ATE[2]]

sŭlk, n., & v.i. **1.** Sulky fit (usu. pl., esp. *in the ~s*). **2.** v.i. Be sulky. [18th c., of unkn. orig.; cf. NFris. *sulke*]

sŭl'k|ў̆, a. & n. **1.** Sullen, morose, silent or inactive or unsociable from resentment or ill temper; hence ~**ily**[2] adv., ~**iness** n. **2.** n. Light two-wheeled one-horse vehicle for single person. [-Y[2]; cf. NFris. *sulkig*]

sŭll'age, n. Filth, refuse, sewage. [16th c., of unkn. orig.]

Sŭll'an, a. (Rom. hist.). Of, enacted by, L. Cornelius Sulla. [-AN]

sŭll'en, a. & n. **1.** Passively resentful, unforgiving, gloomy-tempered, unsociable, not responding to friendliness or encouragement or urging, stubbornly ill-humoured, morose, of dismal aspect; hence ~**ly**[2] adv., ~**ness** n. **2.** n. pl. *The ~s*, ~ frame of mind, ill temper, depression. [16th c. alt. f. ME *solein* f. AF *solein* ult. f. L *solus* SOLE[3], -AN]

sŭll'ў̆, v.t. Soil, tarnish, (chiefly poet.); diminish the purity or splendour of (reputation, character, victory, etc.), disgrace. [c. 1600, app. f. F *souiller*, see SOIL[2]]

sŭl'ph|(o)-, comb. forms of SULPHUR: ~*ăm'ic*, derived from an amic acid of sulphuric acid, so ~*amate*[1](3); ~*āte*, salt of sulphuric acid (~*ate of copper*, blue vitriol; ~*ate of iron*, green vitriol; ~*ate of magnesium*, Epsom salts; ~*ate of sodium*, Glauber's salts; ~*ate of zinc*, white vitriol); ~*īde*, compound of sulphur with element or radical; ~*ile*, salt of sulphurous acid; ~*ocyăn'ic*, containing sulphur & cyanogen; ~*onal*, a hypnotic & anaesthetic drug; ~*ŏn'amĭdes*, group of synthetic chemical compounds acting as anti-bacterial agents when circulating in the blood-stream or applied locally; ~*ŏn'ic acid*, any of a group of acids produced by the action of sulphuric acid (~*ona'tion*) on various aromatic compounds; ~*ovĭn'ic*, of sulphuric acid & alcohol.

sŭl'phur (*-er*), n., a., & v.t. **1.** Pale-yellow non-metallic element occurring in crystalline & amorphous modifications, burning with blue flame & stifling smell, & used in making gunpowder, matches, vulcanite, & sulphuric acid, & in medical treatment of skin-diseases (*flowers, milk, of* ~, yellow, white, powders got by treating ~ in certain ways; *roll, stick,* -~, ~ refined & cast in moulds, brimstone). **2.** Kinds of yellow butterfly. **3.** Material of which hell-fire & lightning were held to consist. **4.** ~*-bottom* (*whale*), Pacific rorqual with yellow belly; ~ *ore*, iron pyrites; ~*-spring*, of water impregnated with ~ or its compounds; ~*wort*, yellow-flowered herb formerly used in medicine; hence ~Y² a. **5.** adj. Of pale slightly greenish yellow. **6.** v.t. Apply ~ to, fumigate with ~. [ME, f. AF *sulf(e)re* = OF *soufre* f. L *sulfur(em)*, *sulphur(em)*]

sŭl'phur|āte, v.t. Impregnate or fumigate or treat with sulphur, esp. in bleaching. Hence ~A'TION, ~ātOR, nn. [f. prec. +-ATE³]

sŭlphŭr'eous, a. Of, like, suggesting, sulphur; (bot.) sulphur-coloured. [L *sulphureus* (SULPHUR), -OUS]

sŭlphŭrĕtt'ĕd, a. Having sulphur in combination (chiefly in ~ *hydrogen*, H₂S, a transparent colourless fetid gas). [f. *sulphuret* (SULPHUR, -URET) +-ED²]

sŭlphŭr'ic, a. (chem.). Containing sulphur in its higher combining proportion (cf. SULPHUROUS; ~ *acid*, H₂SO₄, oil of vitriol, a dense oily colourless highly acid & corrosive fluid much used in many processes in chemical industry; ~ *ether*, = ETHER in chem. sense). [f. F *sulfurique* see SULPHUR, -IC (chem.)]

sŭl'phŭriz|e, -is|e (-īz), v.t. = SULPHURATE. Hence ~A'TION n. [f. F *sulfuriser* (as prec., -IZE)]

sŭl'phŭrous, a. = SULPHUREOUS; (chem.; *pr.* -ŭr'us) containing sulphur in its lower combining proportion (cf. SULPHURIC; ~ *acid*). [f. L SULPHUR(*osus* -OUS), or f. SULPHUR+-OUS]

sŭl'tan, n. **1.** Moslem sovereign (*the S*~, hist., ~ of Turkey), whence ~ATE¹ n. **2.** Kinds of gorgeously coloured bird of rail family; variety of white domestic fowl from Turkey; *sweet, yellow,* ~, kinds of garden flower. [F, or f. med. L *sultanus*, f. Arab.]

sŭlta'na (-tah-), n. **1.** Sultan's mother,

wife, or daughter. **2.** Mistress of king etc. **3.** Sultan-bird. **4.** Kind of seedless raisin used in puddings & cakes. [It., f. *sultano* (prec.)]

sŭl'tanĕss, n.=prec. (first sense). [-ESS¹]

sŭl'tr|y̆, a. (Of atmosphere or weather) hot & close or oppressive; (of temper etc.) passionate. Hence ~ILY² adv., ~iNESS n. [f. obs. *sulter* vb (perh. f. *swulter* cogn. w. SWELTER) +-Y²]

sŭm, n., & v.t. & i. (-mm-). **1.** Total amount resulting from addition of items, brief expression that includes but does not specify details, substance, summary, (also ~ *total*; *the* ~ *of all my wishes is happiness*; *the* ~ *of two & three is five*; ~, *remainder, product, quotient,* results of addition, subtraction, multiplication, division; *the* ~ or ~ *& substance of his objections is this*; *in* ~, briefly & comprehensively put); particular amount of money (*what* ~ *would you give for it?*; *for the* ~ *of 15/-*; *a good, round, considerable,* ~; LUMP¹ ~); (working out of) an arithmetical problem (*good at* ~s; *did a rapid* ~ *in his head*). **2.** vb. Collect into or express or include as one total or whole (often *up*), gather *up* (evidence, points of argument etc., already treated in detail) into brief review; ~ *up* (intr.), make recapitulation of evidence or argument (esp. of judge after both sides have been heard; so ~*ming-up* n.), (trans.) form or express idea of character of (person). [ME, f. AF, OF *summe, somme* f. L *summa* fem. of *summus* highest; vb f. OF *sommer* or LL *summare*]

sŭm'ăc(h) (-k; *also* shŏŏm'ăk), n. (Dried & ground leaves, used in tanning & dyeing, of) kinds of shrub. [ME, f. OF *sumac* f. Arab. *summāq*]

Sŭmēr'ian, a. & n. (archaeol.). **1.** Of the non-Semitic element in the civilization of Babylonia. **2.** n. The ~ language, a ~ person. [f. F (-*ien*), f. *Sumer* in Babylonia]

sŭmm'ar|ize, -|ise (-īz), v.t. Make or be a summary of, sum up. So ~IST(1) n. [foll., -IZE]

sŭmm'ar|y̆, a. & n. **1.** Compendious, brief, dispensing with needless details or formalities, done with dispatch, (*a* ~*y account*; ~*y methods, jurisdiction,* etc.); hence ~ILY² adv. **2.** n. Brief account, abridgement, epitome. [n. f. L *summarium*, adj. f. med. L *summarius*, (L *summa*, -ARY¹)]

summa'tion, n. Addition, finding of total or sum. [f. SUM vb +-ATION]

sŭmm'er¹, n., & v.i. & t. **1.** Second season of the year, June–August (astron., from ~ solstice to autumnal equinox); INDIAN, ‖ *St* MARTIN'S, ~; ‖ *St Luke's* ~, period of fine weather expected about 18th October. **2.** (poet.). (Usu. in pl. with number etc.) year of life or age (*a child of ten* ~s). **3.** attrib. Characteristic of or fit for ~ (~*-house*, light building in garden etc. for sitting in); ~ *lightning*, distant sheet lightning; ~ *school*, long-vacation meeting for lectures etc., esp. at university; ~-*time* or ~*time*, the weather or season of ~; || ~ *time*, that indicated by clocks advanced in ~ to prolong use of daylight; || (*British*) *double* ~ *time*, two hours in advance of Greenwich mean time); hence ~LY¹, ~Y², ~LESS, aa. **4.** vb. Pass the ~ usu. *at* or *in* place; pasture (cattle) *at* or *in*. [OE *sumor*, OS, OHG, ON *sumar*]

summ'er², n. (Also ~-*tree*) horizontal bearing beam, esp. one supporting joists or rafters. [ME, f. AN *sumer, somer* pack-horse, beam, = OF *somier* f. Rom. *saumarius*, LL *sag-*, f. LL f. Gk *sagma* pack-saddle; see BREASTSUMMER]

summersault, -set. = SOMERSAULT.

summ'it, n. Highest point, top, apex, highest degree, (*the icy ~s of the Alps*; *at the ~ of power*; *the ~ of my ambition is*); a ~ meeting; (attrib., of meetings, talks, etc.) taking place between heads of governments. Hence ~LESS a. [ME, f. OF *somet, sommette*, (som top f. L *summum* neut. of SUMMUS, -ET¹)]

summ'on, v.t. Demand the presence of, call upon to appear, esp. as defendant or witness in lawcourt, cite, convoke, invite; call upon (town etc.) to surrender; ~ *up*, gather *courage, spirit*, etc., usu. *to* do or *for* undertaking. [ME, f. OF *somondre* f. L SUB(*monēre*, warn), in med. L = call]

summ'ons (-z), n. (pl. ~*es*), & v.t. **1.** Authoritative call or urgent invitation to attend on some occasion or do something. **2.** Citation to appear before judge or magistrate. **3.** v.t. Serve with ~. [ME, f. OF *somo(u)nse* fem. p.p. of *somondre* as prec.]

summ'um bon'um, n. The chief good, esp. as the end or ultimate determining principle in an ethical system. [L]

sump, n. Pit or well for the reception of (esp. superfluous) water, oil, or other liquid in mines, machines, etc.; cesspool. [ME = *marsh*, f. MDu., MLG *sump*, or (mining) G *sumpf*, rel. to SWAMP]

sump'ter, n. (Arch.) pack-horse or its driver; ~-*horse*, -*mule*, -*pony*, pack-animals. [ME, f. OF *som(m)etier* f. Rom. *sagmatarius* f. LL f. Gk *sagma* -*atos* pack-saddle; see SUMMER²]

sump'tion, n. Major premiss of syllogism. [f. L *sumptio* f. *sumere sumpt-* take, -ION]

sump'tuary, a. Regulating expenditure (~ *law, edict*, etc., limiting private expenditure in the interest of the State). [f. L *sumptuarius* (*sumptus -ūs* cost as prec.)]

sump'tuous, a. Rich & costly, suggesting lavish expenditure. Hence ~LY² adv., ~NESS n. [ME, f. OF *somptueux* or L *sumptuosus* (prec., -OUS)]

sun, n., & v.t. & i. (-nn-). **1.** The heavenly body that the earth travels round & receives warmth & light from, such light or warmth or both, (~ *rises, sets,* is brought by earth's revolution above, below, the horizon; *his, its*, etc., ~ *is set*, time of prosperity or existence is over; *rise with the* ~, get up early; *Order of the Rising Sun*, Japanese order; *hail* or *adore the rising* ~, curry favour with new or coming power; *empire* etc. *on which the* ~ *never sets*, world-wide; *let not the* ~ *go down upon your wrath*, limit it to one day; *the midnight* ~, seen in arctic & antarctic regions; *nothing new under the* ~, in the world; *mock* ~, parhelion; *Sun of righteousness*, Christ; *see the* ~, be alive; *make* HAY *while the* ~ *shines*; *hold a candle to the* ~, prov. of superfluous action; *take*, or sl. *shoot, the* ~ (naut.), ascertain its altitude in order to fix latitude; *with, against, the* ~, CLOCK¹wise, counterclockwise, whence ~'WISE (-z) adv.; ~'s *eyelashes*, ~'s *backstays* (naut.), ~ *drawing water*, phenomenon given by rays piercing aperture in cloud & illuminating suspended particles in parallel lines; ~ *& planet*, system of gearing in which cogged wheel on reciprocating rod both rotates on its axis & travels round the wheel that it engages & communicates motion to; *exclude, let in. the* ~; *in the* ~, exposed to ~'s rays; *a place in the* ~, fig., favourable situation or conditions; *take the* ~, expose oneself to ~light). **2.** Any fixed star with satellite(s). **3.** (poet.). Day or year. **4.** (Also ~ *burner*) set of gas-jets, electric lights, etc., massed as one great light in ceiling. **5.** ~-*bath*, exposure of body to ~; ~'*beam*, ray of ~; ~-*bird*, kinds of small bright-plumaged Old-World birds with resemblance to humming-birds; || ~-*blind*, window-shade; ~-*bonnet*, of linen etc. with projection & pendent back to shade face & neck; ~-*bow*, prismatic bow given by ~light on spray etc.; ~'*burn*, tanning of skin by exposure to ~, so ~'*burnt* or -*burned* a.; ~'*burst*, firework or piece of jewellery imitating ~ and rays; ~-*dance*, of N.-Amer. Indians in honour of ~; ~'*dew*, kinds of small bog-plant with hairs secreting drops of moisture; ~-DIAL; ~-DOG¹; ~'*down*, ~-*set*; ~'*downer*, Australian tramp who times his arrival at a station for the evening, (colloq.) a drink at ~set; ~-*dried*, dried by ~ & not by artificial heat; ~'*fish*, large fish of almost spherical shape; ~'*flower*, kinds of tall garden-plant with showy golden-rayed flowers, plant grown for its seeds which yield an edible oil; ~-*glasses*, for protecting the eyes from direct ~light or glare; ~-*glow*, whitish or faintly coloured corona of light occas. seen round ~; ~-*god*, the ~ worshipped as a deity; ~-*hat*, -*helmet*, adapted by material or shape to keep ~ off; ~'*light*; ~'*lit*; ~-*myth*, SOLAR myth; ~-*rays*, ultra-violet rays used therapeutically as substitute for ~light; ~'*rise*, (moment of) ~'s rising; ~'*set*, (moment of) ~'s setting, western sky with colours characterizing ~set (attrib., resembling these), (fig.) declining period of life; ~'*shade*, parasol, also awning of shop-window; ~'*shine*, light of ~ (~*shine recorder*, instrument recording duration of ~shine; ~*shine roof*, sliding roof of saloon motor-car), surface illuminated by it, fair weather, (fig.) cheerfulness or bright influence, so ~'*shiny* a.; ~-*snake*, ornament found in early N.-Europ. art shaped like S with small circle at centre; ~-*spot*, one of the dark patches, changing in shape & size & lasting for varying periods, occas. observed on ~'s surface; ~-*star*, red starfish with many rays; ~-*stone*, kinds of quartz (esp. cat's-eye) & feldspar; ~'*stroke*, acute prostration from excessive heat of weather; ~-*up* (dial.), ~*rise*; ~-*worship(per)*; hence ~'LESS a., ~'lèssNESS n., ~'LIKE, ~'PROOF², aa., ~'WARD a. & adv., ~'WARDS (-z) adv. **6.** vb. Expose to the ~ (~ one*self*, bask in ~light, also fig.); ~ oneself. [OE *sunne*, also OE; ON -*a*, OS, OHG -*o*, -*a*, Goth. -*ō* f. Gmc **sunnon*, -*ōn*]

*****sun′dae** (-dĭ), n. Portion of ice-cream mixed with crushed fruit, nuts, etc. [arbitrary]

Sun′day (-dĭ), n. First day of week, Lord's day, observed as day of rest & worship (HOSPITAL, LOW¹, PALM¹, ROGATION, SHOW², ~; *month of* ~s, long period; ~ *letter*, DOMINICAL letter; ~ *best*, ~ *go-to-meeting clothes*, usu. joc., best clothes kept for ~ use; ~-*school*, for religious instruction on ~s). [OE *sunnan dæg*, transl. LL *dies solis* day of the sun]

sun′der, v.t. & i. (arch., rhet., poet.). Separate (t. & rarely i.), sever, keep (trans.) apart. Hence ~ANCE n. (rare). [OE *sundrian*, f. *āsundrian*, f. *sundor*, esp. in *on sundran* ASUNDER]

sun′drў, a. & n. **1.** Divers, several, (chiefly arch. & joc.; *all & ~*, each & all, everyone collectively & individually). **2.** n. (Austral.) an extra in cricket; (pl.) oddments, accessories or items not needing special mention. [OE *syndrig* (*sundor* see prec., -Y²)]

sung. See SING.

sunk(en). See SINK¹.

sunn, n. (Also ~ *hemp*) E.-Ind. hemplike fibre. [f. Hind. *san* f. Skr. *sana*]

Sunn′|a(h) (-na), n. Traditional portion of Mohammedan law based on Mohammed's words or acts, but not written by him, accepted as authoritative by the orthodox (~ITE¹ or ~i pr. -ē, nn.) & rejected by the Shiites. [Arab. *sunnaʰ* (*sunnat*) tradition]

sunnud. Var. of SANAD.

sunn′|ў, a. Bright with or as sunlight; of the sun (rare); exposed to, warm with, the sun (*the* ~*y side*, side of house etc. that gets sun, also fig. the more cheerful aspect of circumstances etc.); cheery, bright in disposition, diffusing cheerful-

ness. Hence ~ĭLY² adv., ~ĭNESS n. [ME; -Y²]

sunnyasee. Var. of SAN(N)YASI.

sŭp, v.t. & i. (-pp-), & n. **1.** Take (soup, tea, etc.) by sips or spoonfuls (*he must have a long spoon that* ~*s with the devil*, parleying with doubtful characters is risky); take supper (*on, off*, specified food); (of food or host) provide supper for. **2.** n. Mouthful of liquid (esp. *neither bit or bite nor* ~). [(sense ' sip ') OE *sūpan* (MLG *sūpen*, OHG *sūfan*), **suppan* (OHG *-supphen*, G *supfen*), **sūpian* f. *sŭp*- cf. SOP; (sense ' take supper ') ME f. OF *soper, super* see SUPPER]

sup-, = SUB- in L compds w. wds in p- & their derivatives.

sŭp′er, n. & a. (colloq., shop). **1.** Supernumerary actor, (fig.) extra or unwanted or unimportant person etc.; superintendent; expensively produced film designed for exhibition as the principal item in cinema programmes (in full ~-*film*); (commerc.) superfine cloth or manufacture. **2.** adj. Superfine; (of measure) superficial, in square (not linear or solid) measure (*120* ~ *ft*, or *120 ft* ~); (sl.) splendid. [abbr. *supernumerary*,. *superfine, superficial*]

sŭp′er-, pref. f. L *super* prep., *super-* pref., over, beyond. In **1.** In adjj. & their derivv. varieties of meaning are:
a. situated directly over, as ~*columnar* above columns, ~*humeral* over the shoulder;
b. not in or under but above, as ~*aqueous*, ~*terrene*, ~*celestial*, above water, earth, sky;
c. exceeding, going beyond, more than, transcending, too exalted for contact or connexion with, as ~*normal* beyond the norm, ~*natural* beyond what nature will account for, ~*sensible* out of reach of sense, ~*ethical* above the sphere of ethics. **2.** In vbs & adjj. & their derivv. varieties of meaning are:
a. on the top of something, as ~*impose*, ~*scribe*, ~*stratum*;
b. observation from above, as ~*intend*, ~*stition*, ~*vise*;
c. besides, in addition, as ~*add*. ~*erogation*, ~*fetation*;
d. to a degree beyond the usual or the right, as ~*eminent*, ~*saturate*, ~*subtle*. **3.** In nn. & their derivv. varieties of meaning are:
a. upper or outer, as ~*canopy*, ~*cilious*, ~*hive*;
b. of higher kind, higher in degree, expressing addition, in higher than the ordinary sense, esp. in names of classificatory divisions, as ~*class* group including more than one class;
~*abound* v.i., ~*abūn′dance* n., ~-*abūn′dant* a., ~*abūn′dantly* adv., 2d; ~*ădd′* v.t., ~*addi′tion* n., 2c; ~*altar*

(-awl-) n., 3a, slab of stone consecrated & placed on unconsecrated altar; ~ăn'al a., 1a (ANUS); ~ăngĕl'ic a., 1c; ~ănn'ūāte v.t., 1c (L *annus* year), declare too old for work or use or continuance, dismiss or discard as too old, require the removal from school of (a pupil who has failed to reach a certain educational standard), send into retirement with pension, (p.p.) past work or use, so ~ănnūā'tion n.; ~ā'quĕous a., 1b; ~căl'ĕndered a., 2d; ~căn'opў n., 3a; ~cărgō n. (pl. *-oes*), 1, person in merchant ship managing sales etc. of cargo [f. Sp. *sobrecargo*]; ~cēlĕs'tial a., 1b, also 1c = ~*angelic*; ~chărger n., 2d, pump used in motor-cars & aeroplanes to force an extra quantity of explosive mixture into cylinders of engine & so increase the power output; ~cil'iarў a., 3a (L *supercilium* eyebrow f. *cilium* eyelid), of the brows, over the eye; ~cil'ious a., ~cil'iouslў adv., ~cil'iousnĕss n., 3a [f. L *superciliosus* w. ref. to raised eyebrows, see prec.], contemptuous, showing haughty indifference, assuming superiority; ~civ'ilized (-zd) a., 2d; ~class (-ah-) n., 3b; ~colŭm'nar a., 1a; ~columniā'tion n., 1a, placing of one architectural order over another; ~cōōl v.t., 2d, cool (a liquid) below its freezing-point, without solidification; ~dread'nought (-drĕd'nawt) n., 1c, battleship more powerful than the Dreadnought type (hist.); ~ĕlĕvā'tion n., 3b, amount by which outer rail at a curve is higher than inner; ~ĕm'inent a., 2d; ~ĕrogā'tion n., 2c [f. LL *supererogare* pay out beyond what is expected], doing of more than duty requires (esp. *works of* ~*erogation* in theol., such as form a reserve fund of merit that can be drawn on in favour of sinners), so ~ĕrŏg'atorў a.; ~ĕth'ical a., 1c; ~ĕx'cellent a., ~ĕx'cellence, ~ĕxcitā'tion, nn., 2d; ~fămilў n. (biol.), 3b; ~fătt'ĕd a., 2d (of soap); ~fĕcundā'tion, ~fĕtā'tion, nn., 2c, second conception occurring during gestation; ~fi'cial (-ĭshl) a., ~ficiăl'itў (-shĭ-) n., ~fi'ciallў adv., 3a (foll.), of or on the surface only, not going deep, without depth, (~*ficial colour*, *resemblance, knowledge, wound, accomplishments; a* ~*ficial person*, with no reserve of knowledge or feeling behind what he shows), (of measure) square (see SUPER a.); ~fi'cies (-shĭēz) n. (pl. the same), 3a (L, f. *facies* face), a surface; ~fine a., 2d, (commerc.) of extra quality, (gen.) affecting great refinement; ~flu'itў (-lōō-) n., 2d (foll.), ~fluous amount (*give of* one's ~*fluity*), thing not needed; ~fluous (sōōpĕr'flōō-) a.. ~fluouslў adv., ~fluousnĕss n., 2d (L *superfluus* f. *fluere* flow), more than enough, redundant, needless; ~heat' v.t., 2d, (esp.) heat (steam) to temperature higher than that of boiling water, so ~heat'ER[1](2) n.; ~hive n., 3a, removable upper compartment of hive; ~hŭm'an a., ~hŭm'anlў adv., 1c; ~hŭm'eral n., 1a (L HUMERUS), Jewish ephod, also AMICE[1], also archiepiscopal pallium; ~impōse' (-z) v.t., 2a, lay on or *on* something else; ~imprĕgnā'tion n., 2c, ~fecundation; ~incŭm'bent a., 2a, lying on something; ~indūce' v.t., 2c, develop or bring in as an addition; ~institū'tion n., 2c, institution of person into benefice already occupied; ~intĕnd' v.t. & i., 2b (L INTENDere attend to), have the management (of), arrange & inspect working (of), so ~intĕn'dence n., ~intĕn'dent n., person who ~intends, || police officer above rank of inspector; ~jā'cent a., 2a (L *jacēre* lie), ~incumbent; ~lative (sōōpĕr-) a. & n., 2d [f. LL *super(lativus* f. *ferre lat-* carry)], of the highest degree (~*lative wisdom, beauty,* etc.; ~*lative degree* in gram., the forms of the adjective & adverb by which the highest or a very high degree of a quality is expressed, as *bravest, most absurdly*), so ~lativelў adv., ~lativenĕss n., (n.) the ~lative degree or form (*not used in the* ~*lative*; *what is the* ~*lative of shy?*), a word in the ~lative (*his talk is all* ~*latives,* he exaggerates); ~lun'ar(ў) (-lōō-) a., 1b, (esp.) not of this world; ~man n., 3b, OVERMAN n.; ~mărkĕt, n., 3b, large, usu. self-service, store selling food & domestic goods; ~mĕd'ial a., 1a; ~mŏl'ĕcūle n., 3b, compound molecule, combination of molecules acting as physical unit; ~mŭn'dāne a., 1c, superior to earthly things; ~năc'ūlum adv. & n., 1 [16th c. L rendering of G *auf den Nagel* (*trinken*)], || *drink* ~*naculum*, to the bottom (w. ref. to pouring of the last drop on thumbnail), (n.) choice wine worthy of being so drunk; ~năt'ant a., 2a (NATATION), floating on surface; ~nă'tural (-cher-) a., ~nă'turallў adv., ~nă'turalnĕss n., 1c, due to or manifesting some agency above the forces of nature, outside the ordinary operation of cause & effect, so ~nă'turalism, ~nă'turalist, belief, believer, in the ~natural, ~nă'turalize, -ise (-īz), elevate into the ~natural region; ~nŏrm'al a., 1c; ~nŭm'erarў a. & n., 1c, (person or thing) in excess of the normal number, esp. extra person engaged for odd jobs; ~nūtri'tion n., 2d; ~ŏctave (-ĭv) n., 3b, organ-stop two octaves above open diapason; ~ŏrder n., ~ŏrd'inal a., 3b (in classif.); ~ŏrd'inarў a., 1c; ~ŏrgăn'ic a., 1c (of psychical things considered apart from the organisms in which they are manifested), also, 3b, social, organic in a higher metaphorical sense; ~ŏxўgĕnā'tion n., 2d; ~pă'rasite n., parasite of a parasite, ~părasit'ic a., 3b; ~phŏs'phāte n., 2d, phosphate with greatest possible pro-

portion of phosphoric acid; ~**phys′ical**
(-z-) a., 1c; ~**pōse′** (-z) v.t., ~**posi′tion**
(-z-) n., 2a, lay (thing) on or (up)on
another; ~**sāc′ral** a., 1a (SACRUM);
~**săt′ūrāte** v.t., ~**sătūrā′tion** n., 2d;
~**scrībe** v.t., 2a [f. L super(scribere script-
write)], write (inscription) at top of or
outside something, write inscription over
or on (thing), so ~**script** a., written above
the line, superior, ~**scrip′tion** n.,
~scribed word(s); ~**sēde′** v.t. [f. OF
superseder desist f. L super(sedēre sess-
sit) desist from], set aside, cease to
employ, adopt or appoint another person
or thing in place of, (of person or thing
appointed or adopted) take the place
of, oust, supplant; ~**sĕn′sible** a., 1c;
~**sĕn′sitive** a., 2d; ~**sĕn′sūal**, ~**sĕn′-
sūous**, aa., 1c, ~**sensible**; ~**sĕ′ssion**
(-shn) n., ~seding or being ~seded;
~**sōl′ar** a., 1b; ~**sŏlid** n., 3b, a solid
of more than three dimensions; ~**sŏn′ic**
a. & n., 1c (L sonus sound), relating
to sound-waves of such a high frequency as to be inaudible, (of speed)
greater than that of sound, (of aircraft
etc.) travelling at ~sonic speed, (n. pl.)
high-frequency sound-waves, study of
these; ~**sound** n., 1c, vibrations of same
type as sound but too rapid to be audible;
~**spi′ritūal** a., ~**spiritūāl′itӯ** n., 2d;
~**strāt′um**, ~**strŭc′tion** or ~**strŭcture**
nn., ~**strŭc′tural** (-cher-) a., 2a; ~**sub-
stăn′tial** (-shl) a., 1c; ~**subtle** (-sŭ′tl) a.,
~**subtlety** (-sŭt′ltl) n., 2d; ‖~**tăx** n., 3b,
(1900–29) graduated tax on incomes above
£5,000 p.a. levied in addition to ordinary
income tax; ~**tellūr′ic** a., 1b (L tellus
-uris the earth); ~**tĕm′poral** a., 1a, above
the temples of the head, also 1c, transcending time; ~**tĕrrēne′**, ~**terrĕs′-
trial**, aa., 1b; ~**tŏnic** n., 1c, tone in
musical scale next above tonic; ~**tūberā′-
tion** n., 3b, formation of tubers on tubers;
~**vacān′eous** a., 2d [f. L super(vacaneus
f. vacare be empty)], ~**fluous**, unnecessary; ~**vēne′** v.i., 2a [f. L super(venire
veni- come)], occur as an interruption to
or change from some condition or process,
so ~**vĕn′tion** n.; ~**vīse′** (-z) v.t., 2b (L
vidēre vis- see), direct or watch with
authority the work or proceedings or
progress of, oversee, so ~**vī′sion** (-zhn)
n., ~**visor** (-z-) n., ~**vīs′ory** (-z-) a. [repr.
L super- = adv. & prep. super above,
rel. to OVER, Gk huper, Skr. upari]
sūp′erable, a. Not insuperable. [f. L
superabilis f. superare overcome (super
over, see prec.), -ABLE]
supĕrb′ (sŏŏ-, sū-), a. Of the most impressive or splendid or exalted kind,
grand, (~ beauty, courage, impudence; a~
view, display, collection, specimen, voice,
binding). Hence ~**LY**² adv. [f. F superbe
or L superbus proud]
sūperhĕt′erodӯne, n. & a. (Using) a
system of wireless reception in which a
local variable oscillator is tuned to beat

at a constant ultrasonic rate with carrier-
-wave frequencies, thus making it unnecessary to tune the amplifier & securing
great selectivity; abbr. superhĕt′. [f.
SUPER(SONIC) + HETERODYNE]
supēr′ior (sŏŏ-, sū-), a. & n. **1.** Upper, in
higher position, of higher rank, (~ officer,
rank, court; ~ LIMIT¹; ~ genus, higher in
the classificatory series & so more comprehensive; ~ wings, folding over others;
~ figures or letters, written or printed
above the line; ~ limb of sun etc., upper
edge; (bot., of calyx or ovary) placed
above the ovary or calyx). **2.** Better or
greater in some respect, related as the
better or greater to, (by ~ wisdom,
cunning, etc.; is ~ in speed to any other
machine; ~ numbers, esp. more men or
their presence, as was overcome by ~
numbers). **3.** Of quality or qualities above
the average, having or showing consciousness of such qualities, (made of ~ leather;
my cook is a very ~ woman; ~ persons, the
better educated etc., also & usu. iron.,
prigs; he remarked with a ~ air). **4.** Above
giving attention or yielding or making
concessions to (~ to bribery, temptation,
revenge, fortune; rise ~ to, be unaffected
by); hence or cogn. **supēriŏr′ity** (or -pĕ-)
n., ~**LY**² adv. (chiefly in describing position in bot., anat., etc.). **5.** n. One's
better, person ~ to one, in rank or in
some respect (is deferential to his ~s; you
are my ~ in ability & I yours in application; has no ~ in courage). **6.** Head of
monastery etc. (often Father, Mother,
Lady, S~), whence ~**ESS**¹ n. (rare).
[ME, f. OF, f. L superiorem nom. -or,
comp. of superus high (super above, see
SUPER-)]
sūpērn′al, a. (poet., rhet.). Heavenly,
divine, of the sky, lofty. [ME, f. OF,
or med. L supernalis f. L SUPERnus,
-AL]
sūpersēd′eās, n. Writ staying proceedings. [L 2 sing. pres. subj. as SUPERsede]
sūpersti′t|ion, n. Credulity regarding
the supernatural, irrational fear of the
unknown or mysterious, misdirected
reverence; a religion or practice or
particular opinion based on such tendencies. So ~**IOUS** (-shus) a., ~**iousLY**²
adv., ~**iousNESS** n., (-shus-). [ME, f. OF,
or f. L superstitio f. stare stat- stand]
sūp′in|āte, v.t. Turn (hand) palm upward
(cf. PRONATE). Hence or cogn. ~**A′TION** n.,
~**ātor** n. (as name of two muscles). [L
supinare (foll.), -ATE³]
sūp′ine¹ (or -īn′), a. Lying face upward
(cf. PRONE); disinclined for exertion,
indolent, lethargic. Hence **sūpine′LY**²
adv., **sūpine′NESS** n. [f. L supinus (st. of
SUPER-, -INE¹)]
sūp′ine², n. (L gram.). Verbal noun with
accusative in -um & ablative in -u formed
from p.p. st. of L vbs & used in special
constructions. [f. LL (verbum) supinum,
transl. Gk hyptios passive]

sŭpp′er, n. A meal taken at the end of a day, the last meal of the day when dinner is not the last. Hence ~LESS a. [ME, f. OF. *soper*, *super*, subst. use of inf. (-ER[4]), f. Rom. **suppare* f. Gallo-Rom. *suppa* SOP, SOUP; cf. SUP]

supplant′ (-ah-), v.t. Oust & take the place of esp. by underhand means. Hence ~ER[1] n. [ME, f. OF *supplanter* or L SUP(*plantare* f. *planta* sole) trip up]

sŭp′ple, a., & v.t. & i. 1. Easily bent, pliant, flexible; given to compliance, avoiding overt resistance, wanting in sturdiness of character, artfully submissive, fawning; ~-*jack*, (walking-cane of) kinds of strong twining shrub; hence ~-NESS n., **sŭp′pLY**[2] adv. 2. vb. Make or grow ~ (~ *horse*, train him to obey slightest touch of rein). [ME *souple*, f. OF, f. Rom. **supples* f. L SUP(*plex* -*plicis* f. *plicare* fold) submissive]

sŭp′plĕment[1], n. Thing added to supply deficiencies, esp. fuller treatment of special subject issued with or in addition to newspaper etc.; (math.) the angle that added to another will make the sum two right angles. Hence ~AL, ~ARY[1], aa., (-mĕn²-). [ME, f. L SUP(*plementum* f. *plēre* fill, -MENT)]

sŭpplĕmĕnt′[2], v.t. Make addition(s) to. Hence ~A′TION n. [f. prec.]

sŭpp′liant, a. & n. 1. Supplicating, expressive of supplication; hence ~LY[2] adv. 2. n. Humble petitioner. [ME, f. OF (*supplier* f. L as foll., -ANT)]

sŭpp′lic|āte, v.t. & i. Make humble petition to or *to* person or for or *for* thing. Hence or cogn. ~ātingLY[2] adv., ~A′TION n., ~atORY a. [ME, f. L *supplicare* (*supplex* SUPPLE), -ATE[3]]

supplý′, v.t., & n. 1. Furnish, provide, (thing needed, or person, receptacle, etc., with or *with* thing needed), whence **suppli′ER**[1] n.; make up for, meet, serve to obviate, (deficiency, need, loss); fill (place vacancy, pulpit) as substitute. 2. n. Providing of what is needed (*Committee of S*~, House of Commons discussing details of estimates for public service); stock, store, amount of something provided or at hand or get-at-able, (~ *& demand*, in pol. econ., chief factors regulating price of commodities; *an inexhaustible* ~ *of fish, coal*, etc.; *goods are in short* ~, scarce; *water* etc. ~~), (pl.) collected necessaries for army etc.; (pl.) grant of money by Parliament for cost of government, money allowance to person (*his father cut off the supplies*). [ME, f. OF *so*(*u*)*pleer*, *souplier*, f. L SUP(*plēre* fill)]

support′, v.t., & n. 1. Carry (part of) weight of, hold up, keep from falling or sinking, (*foundation, buttress*, ~s *house, wall*; ~ed *by a lifebelt*; *had to be* ~ed *home*). 2. Enable to last out, keep from failing, give strength to, encourage, (*what* ~ed *him* or *his strength was a glass of*

brandy, *a good conscience, hope, your approval*; *too little food to* ~ *life*). 3. Endure, tolerate, (~s *fatigue well*; *I can* ~ *life, such insolence, no longer*), whence ~ABLE a., ~abLY[2] adv. 4. Supply with necessaries, provide for, (~ *a family*). 5. Lend assistance or countenance to, back up, second, further, (~ *a cause, policy, team, leader, candidate*; ~ *actor* or other performer, take secondary part to him; ~*ing film, picture*, less important one in programme; ~ *resolution* etc., speak in favour of it; ~ *lecturer* etc., appear on his platform; ~ *institution*, subscribe to its funds). 6. Bear out, tend to substantiate, bring facts to confirm, (statement, charge, theory, etc.). 7. Keep up or represent (part, character) adequately. 8. n. ~ing or being ~ed (*give* ~ *to*; *requires* ~; *gets no* ~; *troops stationed in* ~, as reserve; ~ *trench*, the second of three lines, between fire-trench & reserve trench; *speak in* ~ *of*, advocate); person or thing that ~s (*shelf must have another* ~; *he is the chief* ~ *of the cause*); hence ~LESS a. [ME, f. OF *supporter* f. L SUP(*portare* carry)]

support′er, n. In vbl senses; esp., (her.) representation of living creature holding up or standing (usu. as one of pair) beside an escutcheon. [15th c., -ER[1]]

suppose′ (-z), v.t. 1. Assume as a hypothesis (*let us* ~ *a second flood*; *well*, ~ *it was so*; in part. or imperat. with conjunctional force = *if*, as *supposing white were black you would be right*; ~ *your father saw you what would he say?*; also in imperat. as formula of proposal, as ~ *we went for a walk*, ~ *we try another*). 2. (Of theory, result, etc.) require as a condition (*that* ~s *mechanism without flaws*; *design in creation* ~s *a creator*). 3. Take for granted, presume, assume in default of knowledge, be inclined to think, accept as probable, (*I* ~ *we shall be back in an hour*; *you cannot* ~, *it is not to be* ~d, *that*; *I* ~ *he won't* or *I don't* ~ *he will come*; *what do you* ~ *he meant?*; *I* ~ *so*, form of hesitating assent; also abs. in parenth., as *you will not be there, I* ~). 4. *Be* ~d, have as a duty (*he is not* ~d *to clean the boots*). 5. p.p. Believed to exist, believed to have specified character, (*the* ~d *music of the spheres*; *his* ~d *brother, generosity*), whence **suppōs′ĕdLY**[2] (-z-) adv. Hence or cogn. **suppōs′ABLE** (-z-) a., **sŭpposi′TION** (-zĭ-) n. [see below], **sŭpposi′tionAL** (-zĭsho-) a., **sŭpposi′tionaLY**[2] adv.; **sŭpposi′tIOUS**(2) (-zĭshŭs) a., hypothetical, assumed. [ME, f. OF SUP(*poser* POSE[1]); *supposition* etc. f. L SUP(*positio* (in LL ′hypothesis′) f. L *ponere posit-* place, -ION)]

supposi′tious (-zĭtĭshŭs), a. Substituted for the real, spurious, (~ *child, writings*). Hence ~LY[2] adv., ~NESS n. [f. L *suppositicius* f. SUP(*ponere posit-* place) substitute, -ITIOUS[1]]

suppŏs'ĭtorў (-z-), n. (med.). Cone or cylinder of medicinal substance introduced into rectum or vagina or uterus & left to dissolve. [ME, f. med. L *suppositorium*, subst. use of LL *-orius* (as prec., -ORY)]

suppress', v.t. Put down, quell, put an end to activity or existence of, (rebellion, sedition, agitators, conscience, piracy, monasteries, etc.); restrain, keep in, not give vent to, withhold or withdraw from publication, keep secret, not reveal, (groan, yawn, feelings, name, book, evidence, facts); (p.p., of a disease) checked in its normal course (*~ed measles* etc.). So ~IBLE a., **supprĕ'ssION** (-shn) n., ~OR n., (esp.) device for counteracting electrical interference. [ME, f. L SUP- (*primere press- = premere* press)]

suppres'sĭŏ vēr'ĭ, n. Suppression of truth, misrepresentation by concealment of facts that ought to be made known (cf. SUGGESTIO FALSI). [L]

sŭpp'ūr|āte, v.i. Form pus, fester. So ~A'TION n., ~ATIVE a. [L SUP(*purare* f. PUS), -ATE [3]]

sŭp'ra, adv. Above; previously, before (in a book or writing). [L, = above]

sŭpra-, pref. f. L *supra* adv. & prep. above, freely used in forming anat. terms indifferently with SUPER- 1a, as *~clavic'ular* above the clavicle, *~-orb'ital* above the eye-sockets, *~rēn'al* above the kidney, or with SUPER- 3a as *~maxill'ary* a. & n., (of) the upper jaw; also in other wds w. sense *over, beyond, before, after,* often in contrast with compds of INFRA-, SUB-, as *~mun'dane* above or superior to the world, *~lapsar'ian*(ism) a. & nn., (holding, holder of) doctrine that God's decrees of election & reprobation were not due to the Fall but preceded it & his prescience of it (cf. INFRALAPSARIAN); *~prot'est*, acceptance or payment of bill by third person after protest for non--acceptance or non-payment.

suprĕm'acў (sŏŏ-, sŭ-), n. Being supreme, highest authority, (*Act, oath, of ~*, securing ecclesiastical ~ to the Crown & excluding the authority of the Pope). [foll., -ACY(2)]

suprēme' (sŏŏ-, sŭ-), a. & n. Highest in authority or rank (*the S~ Being* or *the S~* as n., God; *S~ Council of the Allies*, small body, also *the Big Four, Five*, settling by conference the Allied common policy 1919-21, each Great Power having a representative; *S~ Court of* JUDICATURE; *~ end* or *good*, SUMMUM BONUM; *~ Pontiff*, the Pope); greatest possible, uttermost, extreme, last & greatest or most important, (*~ wisdom, courage*, etc.; *the ~ test of fidelity; a* or *the ~ hour, moment*, etc.). Hence ~LY[2] adv. [f. L *supremus* superl. of *superus* f. *super* above]

sur-, = SUPER- in many wds taken into E f. OF, as *surcharge, surface, surloin, surprise, surrender,* also sometimes for

super-, supra-, in anat. wds as *surrenal* SUPRARENAL.

sura(*h*[1]) (soor'a), n. Chapter of Koran. [Arab.]

sūr'ah[2] (*-a*), n. Kind of soft twilled usu. one-coloured silk. [f. F pron. of *Surat* in India]

sūr'al, a. Of the calf of the leg (*~ artery* etc.). [L *sura* calf, -AL]

surăt' (sŏŏ-), n. Kind of cotton grown, kind of cotton cloth made, in the Bombay Presidency. [place-name]

surcease' (ser-), n., & v.i. (arch.). 1. Cessation. 2. v.i. Cease. [AF *sursise* delay, [ME, f. OF *sursis*, fem. *-ise* (cf. AF *sursise* omission), p.p. of OF *surseoir* f. L as SUPERSEDE, w. assim. to *cease*]

surcharge, n., & v.t. 1. (sĕr'chärj). Excessive or additional load or burden or amount of money charged; supply of force, electricity, etc., in excess of what is required; additional charge made by assessors as penalty for false returns of taxable property; mark printed on postage-stamp changing its value; amount in official account not passed by auditor & having to be refunded by person responsible; showing of omission in account for which credit should have been given. 2. v.t. (serchärj'). Overload, fill or saturate to excess; (of assessor, auditor) exact ~ from, exact (sum) as ~, fine (person sum) as ~; show omission of credit in (account). [ME, f. OF *surcharge(r)*, see SUR-]

sūr'cingle, n., & v.t. Band round horse's body rarely as saddlegirth, usu. to keep blanket etc. in place; girdle of cassock; (vb) gird (horse), fasten (blanket etc.), with ~. [ME, f. OF SUR(*cengle* girth f. L *cingula* f. *cingere* gird)]

sūrc'oat, n. (hist.). Loose robe worn over armour; 15th-16th-c. woman's jacket. [ME, f. OF SUR(*cot, -cote* COAT)]

sūrc'ūlōse, -lous, aa. (bot.). Producing suckers. [f. L *surculosus* (*surculus* sucker, -OSE[1]), -OUS]

sūrd, a. & n. 1. (math.). Irrational (a. & n.). 2. (phonet.). (Consonant, consonantal sound) uttered with the breath & not the voice (as p, f, s, cf. *voiced* or *vocal* of b, v, z). [f. L *surdus* deaf, noiseless; math. sense by mistransl. into L of Gk *alogos* irrational, speechless thr. Arab. *jaḏr açamm* deaf root]

sure (shoor), a. & adv. 1. Having or seeming to have adequate reason for belief, convinced of or (*that*), having certain prospect or confident anticipation or satisfactory knowledge *of*, free from doubts *of*, (*are you ~?; you may be ~ of his honesty, he is* or *that he is honest; he feels* or *is ~ of success; I did not feel ~ of my company, could not feel ~ about it; I the one could be ~ of living to 70; I'm ~ I didn't mean to hurt you,* form of asseveration; *well, I'm ~!,* excl. of surprise). 2. Safe, reliable, trusty, unfailing, (*sent it by a ~*

hand; *put it in a ~ place*; *a ~ shot*, marksman who never misses; *a ~ draw*, covert certain to yield fox, remark etc. certain to draw person; *~ card*, scheme etc. certain to succeed; SLOW & *~*; *there is only one ~ way*; *~-footed*, never stumbling or making false step lit. or fig.). **3.** To be relied on, certain, *to do* (*is ~ to turn out well*; *would be ~ to dislike him*). **4.** Undoubtedly true or truthful (*one thing is ~*; *to be ~*, formula of concession = to avoid over-statement, as *to be ~ she is not perfect, is pretty*, also as excl. of surprise, as *so it is, to be ~!*, *well, to be ~!*; *make ~*, ascertain absolutely that something is as supposed, take measures to secure that something is as desired; *make ~ of*, establish the truth or ensure the happening of; also *make ~ of or that*, have confident but often false anticipation of or that); hence *~'NESS* n. **5.** adv. (Arch.) I admit, you will admit, (*'tis pleasant, ~, to see one's name in print*); *(colloq.) certainly (*it ~ was cold*); *as* certainly *as* (*as ~ as eggs is eggs, as ~ as a gun*, colloq. forms of asseveration); *~ enough*, in fact as well as in prospect (*I said it would be, & ~ enough it is*), with practical certainty (*he will come~ enough*); **~ thing* (colloq.), a certainty, (as int.) certainly! [ME, f. OF *sur, sëur* f. L *securus* SECURE]

sure'ly (shoor'lĭ), adv. With certainty or safety (*he knows full ~ that*; *will diminish slowly but ~*; *mule plants its feet ~*); if strong belief or experience or probability or right is to count for anything (*it ~ cannot have been he*; *~ I have met you before*; *there is no truth in it, ~*; *~ you will not desert me*); (in answers, arch.) certainly, undoubtedly, (' *Should you be willing to try?* ' *'S~'*). [-LY²]

sure'ty (shoor'tĭ), n. (Arch.) certainty (esp. *of a ~*, certainly); thing pledged as security for payment or performance (now rare); person who makes himself responsible for another's appearance in court or payment of sum or performance of engagement (*stand ~*, become so responsible, go bail, *for* another; *find ~* or *sureties*, said of person primarily liable), whence *~SHIP* n. [ME, f. OF *surte, sëurte* f. L *securitatem* (SURE, -TY)]

surf, n., & v.i. **1.** Foam & commotion of sea breaking on shore or reefs; *~-bird*, coast-bird related to sandpiper; *~-boat*, of buoyant build for use in *~*; *~-man*, skilled in managing *~-boats*; *~-riding* (on boards, as a sport). **2.** v.i. Go *~-riding*. Hence *~'Y²* a. [earlier *suff* (c. 1600), poss. of Indian orig.]

surf'ace (-ĭs), n., & v.t. & i. **1.** The outside of a body, (any of) the limits that terminate a solid, outward aspect of material or immaterial thing, what is apprehended of something upon a casual view or consideration, (*has a smooth, uneven, ~*; *presents a large ~ to view*; *its upper ~ is*

as *cold as ice*; *looks only at the ~ of men & things*; *his politeness is only of* or *on the ~*; *one never gets below the ~ with him*), (attrib.) of the *~* only (*~ plausibility, impressions*, etc.); the *~* of the sea (*~ mail*, opp. air mail; *~ craft, raider, ship*, opp. submarine). **2.** (geom.) That which has length & breadth but no thickness (*plane ~*, that contains the whole of the straight line connecting any two points in it; *curved ~*, that may be so cut by a plane through any point in it that the line of section shall be a curve; *developable ~*, that may be unfolded into a plane without doubling or separation of parts, e.g. *~* of cone or cylinder). **3.** *~-colour*, used in *~-printing*, printing from raised *~* as with ordinary type or woodcuts & not from incised lines; *~-man*, keeping permanent way of railway in order; *~-tension*, tension of a liquid causing it to act as an elastic enveloping membrane seen in drop or bubble; *~-water*, that collects on & runs off from *~* of ground etc.; hence (-)*surfaceD*² a. **4.** vb. Put special *~* on (paper etc.); bring (submarine) to the *~*; (of submarine) rise to the *~*. [F (SUR-, FACE)]

surf'eit (-fĭt), n., & v.t. & i. **1.** Excess esp. in eating or drinking, oppression or satiety resulting. **2.** vb. Overfeed (t. & i.), (cause to) take too much of something, cloy, satiate *with*. [ME, f. OF *sor-, surfeit*, f. SUR- + *fait* p.p. of *faire* (L *facere fact-* do); cf. LL *superficiens* excessive]

surge, v.i., & n. **1.** Move up & down or to & fro (as) in waves (of sea, crowd, standing corn, emotion, etc.); (naut., of rope or chain on windlass) slip back with a jerk; (of wheel) revolve without advancing on rail or road. **2.** n. Waves, a wave, surging motion. [n.: orig. obsc., in sense 2 f. vb; vb partly f. OF *sourdre* (*sorge-*) or obs. F *sorgir* f. L *surgere* rise, partly f. n.]

sur'geon (-jn), n. Medical man treating injuries & deformities & diseases by manual operation (*house-~*, on staff of hospital), person skilled in surgery; medical practitioner having a diploma qualifying him to practise surgery (*~ dentist*, dentist thus qualified); (formerly, opp. *physician*) general practitioner dispensing drugs & attending out-patients & not confining himself to consultation; medical officer in navy or army or military hospital; *~-fish*, kind named from lancet-shaped spines on each side of tail. [ME, f. AF *surgien*, f. OF *ser-, cirurgien* f. *cirurgie* f. L f. Gk *kheirourgia* handiwork, surgery (*kheir* hand, -o-, *ergō* work)]

sur'gery, n. **1.** Manual treatment of injuries or disorders of the body, operative therapeutics, surgical work, (*antiseptic, clinical, plastic*, etc., *~*; *conservative ~*, avoiding amputations etc.). **2.** Doctor's consulting-room & dispensary.

[ME, f. OF *surgerie*, contr. f. *ser-, cirurgerie* (*cirurgie* see prec., -ERY)]

sūr'gical, a. Of surgeons or surgery (~ *skill, operations, instruments*; ~ *fever,* caused by ~ operation through sepsis). Hence ~LY² adv. [as SURGEON, -ICAL]

sūr'icāte, n. S.-Afr. animal resembling polecat & ferret. [f. F *surikate,* f. native African]

surloin, obs. form of SIRLOIN.

sūrl'|y̆, a. Uncivil, given to making rude answers, showing unfriendly temper, churlish. Hence ~ĭLY² adv., ~ĭNESS n. [alt. sp. of obs. *sirly* (SIR, -LY¹)]

∥ **sūrm'aster** (-ah-), n. Second master or vice-master in St Paul's School. [alt. f. orig. *submaster* (*hypodidascalus* in Erasmus lett.) f. med. L *submagister* (SUB- 2b)]

surmise (sermīz'), n., & v.t. & i. **1.** Conjecture, suspicion of the existence or guess at the nature of something. **2.** vb. Infer doubtfully, suspect the existence of; make a guess, try to divine something. [ME, f. OF p.p. of SUR(*mettre* put f. L *mittere miss-* send) accuse]

surmount' (ser-), v.t. Cap, be on the top of, (usu. in pass.: *peaks ~ed with snow*); overcome, get over, (difficulty, obstacle), whence ~ABLE a. [ME, f. OF *so(u)rmonter* f. med. L *supermontare* (SUR-, MOUNT²)]

surmūll'et (ser-), n. The red mullet. [f. F *surmulet*]

sūrn'āme, n., & v.t. **1.** Additional name of descriptive or allusive kind attached to a person & occas. becoming hereditary; the name common to all members of a family (cf. CHRISTIAN *name*). **2.** v.t. Give ~ to; give (person ~); (p.p.) called by way of additional name, having as family name. [ME; SUR-, NAME, after AF, OF *surnum, sornom*]

surpass' (serpahs'), v.t. Outdo, excel. Hence ~ING² a., ~ingLY² adv. [f. F SUR(*passer* PASS¹)]

sūrp'lic|e, n. Loose full-sleeved white--linen vestment descending to hips or knees or ankles & worn usu. over cassock by clergy & choristers at divine service; ~*e choir*, wearing ~es; ∥~*e-fee,* paid to clergy for marriages, funerals, etc. Hence ~ED² (-st) a. [ME, f. AF *surpliz,* OF *sourpeliz,* f. med. L *superpellicium* (SUPER-, *pellicia* PELISSE)]

sūrp'lus, n. What remains over, what is not required for the purpose in hand, esp. excess of public revenue over expenditure for the financial year, (opp. *deficit*; often attrib., as ~ *population*). So ~AGE(1) n. [ME, f. OF, f. med. L SUPER(PLUS)]

surprise (serprīz'), n., & v.t. **1.** Catching of person(s) unprepared (*the fort was taken, the truth must be elicited, by* ~; *determined to attempt a* ~; *a* ~ *visit,* without notice); emotion excited by the unexpected, astonishment, (*full of* ~; *his* ~ *was visible; to my great* ~, much against my expectations; ∥~ *packet,* with unexpected con-

tents, e.g. packet of sweets with coin, also often fig.); event etc. that excites ~ (*was a great* ~ *to me*; *I have a* ~ *for you,* piece of unexpected news, unexpected gift, etc.; *what a* ~ *!*). **2.** v.t. Capture (place, person) by ~, attack at unawares, come upon (person) off his guard (~*d him in the act*); affect with ~, astonish, turn out contrary to expectations of, be a ~ to, (*should you be* ~*d to learn* —?; *I am* ~*d at you,* shocked, scandalized; *more* ~*d than frightened*), whence **surpris'**ING² a., **surpris'ingLY²,** **surpris'edLY²,** advv., (serprīz-); hurry (person) by ~ *into* conduct or act or doing (~*d me into rudeness, consent, dropping the reins*); hence **surpris'AL**(2) (serprīz-) n. [OF, fem. p.p. of SUR(*prendre* f. L *prehendere* take)]

surra (sū'ra, soor'a), n. Form of pernicious anaemia affecting horses & cattle in the tropics. [Marathi *sūra*]

sūrre'al|ism, n. Twentieth-century movement in art & literature purporting to express the subconscious mind by images etc. in sequences or associations such as may occur in dreams. So ~IST a. & n. [SUR-², REAL², -ISM]

sūrrebūt' (-tt-), **sūrrejoin',** vv.i. (Of plaintiff) reply, make **sūrrebūtt'ER⁴,** **sūrrejoin'DER⁴,** nn., to defendant's rebutter, rejoinder (order of pleadings at common law: Plaintiff's *declaration,* Defendant's *plea,* P.'s *replication,* D.'s *rejoinder,* P.'s *surrejoinder,* D.'s *rebutter,* P.'s *surrebutter*). [SUR-]

surrĕn'der, v.t. & i., & n. **1.** Hand over, give one another's power or control, relinquish possession of, esp. upon compulsion or demand (~ *fortress, army, ship, freedom, hopes, chastity, privilege, office,* etc.; ~ *insurance policy,* abandon claim in return for repayment of part of premiums); give one*self* over *to* habit, emotion, influence, etc.; (of fortress, ship, or force, or its commander) accept enemy's demand for submission; give oneself up, cease from resistance, submit, (~ *to* one's *bail,* appear in court after being admitted to bail). **2.** n. ~ing or being ~ed (~ *value,* amount payable to one who ~s insurance policy). [ME, f. OF *sur*(*rendre* RENDER)]

sūrrĕpti'tious (-Ishus), a. Underhand, kept secret, done by stealth, clandestine. Hence ~LY² adv. [ME; L *surrepticius* f. *sur*(*ripere -rept-* f. *rapere* snatch), -ITIOUS¹]

*****sū'rrey,** n. (pl. ~s). Light two-seater four-wheeled carriage. [Engl. county]

sū'rrogate, n. ∥ Deputy, esp. of bishop or his chancellor for granting licences for marriages without banns. Hence ~SHIP n. [L *sur*(*rogare* ask) elect as substitute, -ATE²]

surround', v.t., & n. **1.** Come or be all round, invest, enclose, encompass, encircle, environ, (*the* ~*ing country,* the neighbouring district; ~*ed with* or *by*). **2.** n. Floor-covering between walls &

carpet. [ME = overflow, f. OF suronder f. LL super(undare flow f. unda wave); cf. ABOUND]

surroun'dings (-z), n. pl. Sum total or general effect of all that is in the neighbourhood of a person or thing (picturesque, healthy, degraded, cultured, ~). [-ING¹]

sūrs'um cord'a, L phr. Priest's exhortation to the people before the Preface in the Latin Mass. [in Book of Common Prayer 'Lift up your hearts']

sūrt'ax, n., & v.t. (Impose) additional tax (on); ‖ graduated tax on incomes above a certain figure in addition to ordinary income tax, imposed since 1929--30 in place of supertax. [f. F sur(taxe, -taxer, TAX)]

sūrt'out (-tōō), n. (now rare). Overcoat, esp. of frock-coat shape. [F, f. sur tout over all]

surveill'ance (servāl'ans, -l'yans), n. Supervision, close observation, invigilation, (esp. under~, not trusted to work or go about unwatched). [F, f. SUR(veiller f. L as VIGILANT)]

survey'¹ (servā'), v.t. Let the eyes pass over, take general view of, form general idea of the arrangement & chief features of; examine condition of (building etc.); collect by measurement etc. all facts needed for determining the boundaries, size, position, shape, contour, ownership, value, etc., of (country, coast, district, estate, etc.), whence ~ING¹(1) n. [ME, f. AF surveier = OF -vëeir, f. med. L SUPER-(vidēre see)]

sūrv'ey² (-vā), n. General view, casting of eyes or mind over something; inspection of the condition, amount, etc., of something, account given of result of this; department carrying on, operations constituting, piece of, surveying of land etc. (see prec.), map or plan setting forth results of such ~ (ORDNANCE ~). [f. prec.]

survey'or (servā'er), n. Official inspector of (~ of weights & measures etc.), whence ~SHIP n.; person professionally engaged in SURVEY¹ing. [ME, f. AF surve(i)our (SURVEY¹, -OR)]

surviv'al (ser-), n. Surviving (~ of the fittest, process or result of natural SELECTION); person or thing that has remained as a relic of an earlier time; [foll., -AL(2)]

survive' (ser-), v.t. & i. Outlive, be still alive or in existence after the passing away of, come alive through or continue to exist in spite of, (~ one's children, contemporaries, etc.; ~ one's usefulness; ~ all perils); continue to live or exist, be still alive or existent. Hence **surviv'or** (ser-) n., **surviv'orship** n. (esp. right of joint tenant to whole estate on other's death). [ME, f. AF survivre f. L SUPER-(vivere live)]

sus-, = SUB- in L compds w. wds in c- (also SUC-, cf. succeed, susceptible), in p- (also SUP-, cf. suppose, suspend), & in t-,

& their derivatives. [for subs var. of sub; cf. ABS-]

suscěp'tib|le, a. (Pred.) admitting of (passage is ~le of another interpretation; facts not ~le of proof), open or liable or accessible or sensitive to (very ~le to pain, injury, kindness, female charms); impressionable, sensitive, readily touched with emotion, touchy. Hence or cogn. **suscěptibil'ity** n. (often in pl. = sensitive points of person's nature), ~LY² adv. [f. LL susceptibilis f. L sus(cipere -cept- = capere take), -IBLE]

suscěp'tive, a. Concerned with the receiving of emotional impressions (cf. prec. & receptive; the ~ faculties, nature). [f. LL susceptivus as prec., -IVE]

sus'i (sōō-), n. E.-Ind. cotton fabric with stripes of different-coloured silk. [Hind.]

suspěct'¹, v.t. 1. Have an impression of the existence or presence of (danger, a plot, foul play, collusion, a causal relation); half believe to be (I ~ him to be my brother, a liar, dying); be inclined to think that or that (I ~ you once thought otherwise; also parenth., as you, I ~, don'; care). 2. Incline to mentally accuse of or inculpate, doubt the innocence of, distrust, (I ~ him of lying, of deep designs; a ~ed criminal, person ~ed of being one; ~ed persons; the ignorant ~ everybody). 3. Hold to be uncertain, mistrust, doubt the genuineness or truth of, (~ the authenticity of the evidence). Hence ~ABLE a. (rare). [ME, f. L suspect- (foll.)]

sŭs'pěct², pred. a. & n. 1. Of suspected character, subject to suspicion, not unimpeachable, (the statement of an interested party is naturally ~). 2. n. Suspected person (political ~s are kept under surveillance). [ME, f. L suspectus p.p. of suspicere f. specere look; partly after OF sospet, F suspect]

suspend', v.t. 1. Hang up, (p.p., of solid particles or body in fluid medium) sustained somewhere between top & bottom (a balloon ~ed in mid-air; ~ed particles of dust), so **suspen'sible** a., **suspensibil'ity** n. 2. Keep in undecided or inoperative state for a time, defer, temporarily annul, adjourn, debar temporarily from office or function or privilege or membership, (~ judgement, one's indignation, the rules, the Habeas-Corpus Act, proceedings, a clergyman; ~ payment, fail to meet financial engagements, admit insolvency; ~ed animation, state of insensibility without death). [ME, f. OF suspendre or L sus(pendēre pens- hang]

suspen'der, n. In vbl senses; esp., (pl.) *pair of braces, ‖ pair of (sets of) attachments to which tops of socks or stockings are hung. [-ER¹]

suspense', n. State of usu. anxious uncertainty or expectation or waiting for information (keep one in ~, delay acquainting him with what he is eager to know); (law) suspension, temporary cessation of right etc.; ~ *account* in book-keeping (in which items are temporarily entered till proper place is determined). [ME, f. OF *suspens*, p.p. of L SUSPEND*ere*] **suspĕn'|sion** (-shn), n. In vbl senses (SUSPEND); esp. ~*sion bridge*, in which roadway is hung across stream etc., usu. on wire or chain cables passing over towers & anchored, without support from below. So ~SIVE a. (~*sive veto*, operating only for a time, not definitive), ~SORY a., ~SIVELY² adv. [f. L *suspensio* (SUSPEND, -ION)]

sŭs.pĕr cŏll., n. The entry recording that a person is to be hanged (often joc. = hanged, hanging). [abbr. of L *suspendatur per collum* let him be hanged by the neck]

suspi'cion (-shn), n., & v.t. **1.** Feeling of one who suspects, suspecting or being suspected (*above* ~, too obviously good etc. to be suspected), partial or unconfirmed belief esp. that something is wrong or someone guilty; soupçon *of*; hence ~LESS a. **2.** v.t. (dial.). Have ~ that or *that*. [ME, f. AF *suspecioun* (OF *souspeçon*) f. med. L *suspectionem* f. L *suspicere* SUSPECT, -ION]

suspi'cious (-shŭs), a. Prone to, feeling, indicating, suggesting or justifying, suspicion (*the ignorant are* ~; *he became* ~; *with a~ glance*; *under~ circumstances*). Hence ~LY² adv., ~NESS n. [ME, f. OF f. L *suspiciosus* (prec., -OUS)]

suspïre', v.i. (poet.). Sigh. So **suspïrA‑TION** n. [f. L *suspirare* (SUB-, *spirare* breathe)]

sustain', v.t. **1.** Bear weight of, hold up, keep from falling or sinking (cf. *support*). **2.** Enable to last out, keep from failing, give strength to, encourage, (exx. as in SUPPORT; ~*ing food*, that keeps up the strength). **3.** Endure without giving way, stand, bear up against, (~*ed the shock of the enemy's tanks*; *will not* ~ *comparison with*). **4.** Undergo, experience, suffer, (~ *a defeat, severe contusion, loss*, etc.). **5.** (Of court or other authority) allow validity of, give decision in favour of, uphold, (~ *the objection, the applicant in his claim*, etc.). **6.** Bear out, tend to substantiate or corroborate, confirm, (statement, charge, theory, etc.). **7.** Keep up or represent (part, character) adequately. **8.** Keep (sound, effort, etc.) going continuously (*a* ~*ed note, effort*). Hence ~ABLE a., ~MENT n. (rare). [ME, f. AF, OF *sus-*, *sostenir* f. L SUS(*tinēre tent-* = *tenēre* hold)]

sŭs'tenance, n. Nourishing (now rare; *given for the* ~ *of our bodies*); nourishing quality, subsistence, food lit. or fig., (*there is no* ~ *in it*; *how shall we get* ~?; *lived a week without* ~ *of any kind*). [ME, f. AF *sustenaunce* f. *sustenir* (prec., -ANCE)]

sŭstentā'tion, n. Support of life (rare; ~ *fund*, collected to support indigent clergy). [ME, f. OF, or f. L *sustentatio* (*sustentare* frequent. of *sustinēre* SUSTAIN, -ION)]

sūsŭrrā'tion, n., **sūsŭ'rrous**, a., (rare). Whispering, rustling. [f. LL *susurratio* (L *susurrare*), L *susurrus* a. or n., -ATION, -OUS]

sŭt'ler, n. Camp-follower selling provisions etc. [f. early mod. Du. *soeteler* f. *soetelen* befoul, perform mean duties]

Sut'ra (sōō-), n. Set of aphorisms in Sanskrit literature. [Skr. *sutra* thread, (hence) rule, f. *siv* SEW]

suttee', **sati'** (-ē), n. Hindu widow who immolates herself on her husband's funeral pyre; custom requiring such immolation, also **suttee'**ISM(2) n. [f. Skr. *sati* virtuous wife]

sū'tur|e, n., & v.t. **1.** Seamlike articulation of two bones at their edges, esp. one of those in the skull, similar junction of parts in bot., entom., etc.; (surg.) uniting of edges of wound by stitching, thread or wire used for this. **2.** v.t. Stitch (wound). Hence ~AL (-che-) a., ~alLY² adv., ~A'TION n., ~ED² (-cherd) a. [F, or f. L *sutura* (*suere sut-* SEW, -URE)]

sūz'erain, n. Feudal lord, lord paramount, sovereign or State having nominal sovereignty or right of general control over semi-independent or internally autonomous State. So ~TY n. [F, app. f. *sus* above f. L *su(r)sum* upward, after *souverain* SOVEREIGN]

svĕlte, a. Lightly built, lissom, supple, (chiefly of human, esp. female, figure). [F]

swab (-ŏb), v.t. (-bb-), & n. **1.** Mop or other arrangement of absorbent material on handle for cleaning; absorbent pad used in surgery; specimen of morbid secretion etc. taken with a ~ for bacteriological examination. **2.** (naut. sl.). Officer's epaulet; clumsy fellow, also ~b'ER¹ n. **3.** v.t. Clean with ~, as ~ (*down*) *the deck*; take *up* (moisture) with ~. [n. f. vb, back form. f. *swabber* f. early mod. Du. *zwabber* f. *zwabben* (MLG *swabben*) splash in water or mire]

Swāb'ian, **Sua-**, a. & n. (Inhabitant) of Swabia (~ *emperors*, Hohenstaufens, 1138–1254). [*Suabia* (mod. L f. G *Schwaben*), -AN]

swa'ddl|e (-ŏ-), v.t. Swathe in bandages or many or thick wraps or garments (~*ing-bands, -clothes*, in which infants are wrapped, also fig. influences that restrain freedom of action or thought). [ME; SWATHE, -LE]

Swade'shī (-ahdā-), n. Movement in India, originating in Bengal, advocating the production of home-made, and the boycott of foreign, goods. [Hindi, = own country]

swăg, n. (sl.). Booty carried off by burglars etc., (transf.) gains made by political or other jobbery; (Austral.) tramp's, miner's, or bush-traveller's bundle. [f. now dial. *swag* vb hang swaying (of bundle, fat belly, etc.), prob. Scand., cf. Norw. dial. *svag(g)a*]

swäge, n., & v.t. **1.** Kinds of die or form for shaping wrought iron etc. by hammering or pressure; ~-*block*, with variety of perforations, grooves, etc., for this purpose. **2.** v.t. Shape with ~. [f. F· *suage*, *souage*]

swägg'er (-g-), v.i. & t., & n. & a. **1.** Walk like a superior among inferiors, show self-confidence or self-satisfaction by gait, go *about, in, out*, etc., with such walk; behave in domineering or defiant way; talk boastfully (*about* prep.) or in hectoring manner; bluff (person) *into, out of*, etc.; hence ~ER¹ n., ~ingLY² adv. **2.** n. ~ing gait or manner or talk; dashing or confident air or way of doing something, freedom from tameness or hesitancy, smartness; ‖ ~-*cane*, carried by soldiers when walking out. **3.** adj. (colloq.). Smart, fashionable, (~ *clothes, society*, etc.). [app. f. SWAG vb + -ER⁵]

Swahili (swahhěl'ī), n. A Bantu people (or one of them) inhabiting Zanzibar and the adjacent coasts; (also *Kiswahili*) their language. [f. Arab. *sawāḥil* pl. of *sāḥil* coast]

swain, n. Young rustic; bucolic lover; (joc.) lover, suitor. [ME *swein* f. ON *sveinn* lad = OE *swān* swineherd]

‖ **swäle**, **sweal**, v.t. & i. (dial.). Burn, set fire to (esp. gorse, brushwood, etc.); be scorched; (of candle) melt away. [OE *swǽlan* = (M)LG *swelen* to burn (trans.)]

‖ **swa'llet** (-ŏl-), n. (dial.). Underground stream; hole into which a stream flows, SWALLOW¹-hole. [obsc. f. foll.]

swa'llow¹ (-ŏlō), v.t. & i., & n. **1.** Cause or allow (food etc.) to pass down one's throat (~ *a* CAMEL, make no difficulty about something incredible or impossible or outrageous); engulf, absorb, exhaust, draw in, make away with, (usu. *up; the earth* ~*ed them up; the expenses more than* ~ *up the earnings; death is* ~*ed up in victory*); accept (statement) with ready credulity (*will* ~ *anything you tell him*); put up with, pocket, stomach, (affront); recant (one's words); perform muscular operation of ~ing something. Hence ~-ABLE a. **2.** n. Gullet; act of ~ing; amount ~ed at once; ‖ (also ~-*hole*) funnel-shaped cavity in limestone. [OE, OHG *swelgan*, ON *svelga*, f. Gmc *·swelg-*, *·swalg-*]

swa'llow² (-ŏlō), n. **1.** Kinds of usu. migratory, long-winged, swift-flying, wide-gaped, weak-legged, fork-tailed, insectivorous bird associated with summer (*one* ~ *does not make a summer*, warning against hasty inference). **2.** ‖ ~ *dive* (with arms outspread till close to water); ~-*fish*, kind of gurnard; ~-*hawk*, *-plover*, *-shrike*, etc., fork-tailed kinds of hawk etc.; ~-*tail*, deeply forked tail, kinds of butterfly & humming-bird having this, points of burgee, (sing. or pl.) ~-*tailed coat*; ~-*tailed*, with deeply forked tail (of butter-

flies, birds, etc.; ~-*tailed coat*, kind with tapering tails formerly worn in ordinary costume & still in evening dress); ~-*wort*, milkweed, also celandine. [OE *swealwe*, OS *suala*, OHG *swalwa*, ON *svala* f. Gmc *·swalwōn*]

swam. See SWIM.

swa'mi (-ah-), n. Hindu idol; Hindu religious teacher (esp. as form of address to Brahmin); ~ *work*, silver articles ornamented with figures of Hindu deities. [Hind., – master, prince, f. Skr. *svāmin*]

swamp (-ŏ-), n. & v.t. & i. **1.** Piece of wet spongy ground, bog, marsh, (attrib., in many names of plants & animals found in ~s); hence ~'Y² a. **2.** vb. Entangle in ~ (usu. in p.p.); (of water) overwhelm, flood, soak, (boat or its crew or contents, house, provisions, etc.); make helpless with excessive supply of something (*am* ~*ed with letters, applications, work*); (of greater quantity or numbers) swallow up, make invisible etc., prevent from being noticed or taking effect; (v.i.) become ~ed. [17th c., usu. referred to root *swamp-, swamb-, swamm-* sponge or fungus (as in G *schwamm*); cf. SUMP]

swan (-ŏn), n. **1.** Kinds of large water-bird with long flexible neck, webbed feet, and in most species snow-white plumage, formerly supposed to sing melodiously at point of death (*white, black-necked, black, mute* or *tame* or *common, trumpeter, whooper*, etc., ~; *black* ~, name given before discovery of black species to extreme rarity; *all his geese are* ~*s*, see GOOSE); (fig., w. ref. to sweetness of dying song) poet (esp. *S*~ *of Avon*, Shakespeare). **2.** The constellation Cygnus. **3.** *·*~ *dive*, = SWALLOW² *dive*; ~-*flower*, kind of orchid; ~-*goose*, long-necked China goose; ~-*herd*, royal officer having charge of ~-marks; ~-*mark*, cut in skin of beak to show ownership; ~-*neck*, curved end of discharge-pipe; ~'*s-down*, down of ~ used in trimmings & esp. in powder-puffs, also kind of thick cotton cloth with soft nap on one side; ~-*shot*, of large size; ~-*skin*, kind of fine twilled flannel; ~ *song*, of dying ~, also person's last production etc.; ‖ ~-*upping*, annual taking up & marking of Thames ~s. Hence ~'LIKE a., ~n'ERY(3) n. [OE, OS *swan*, OHG *swan(a)*, ON *svanr* f. Gmc *·swan-*]

swänk, n., & v.i. (sl.). Show(ing) off, swagger, bounce, bluff. Hence ~'Y² a., marked by ~, ostentatiously smart. [c. 1800, orig. midl. & s.w. dial.]

swap. See SWOP.

Swaraj' (-ahj), n. Self-government, independence, for India. Hence **swaraj'**IST (-ahj-) n. & a. [Skr. = self-ruling (RAJ)]

sward (-ôrd), n. Expanse covered with short grass, lawnlike ground; turf, whence ~'ED² a. [OE *sweard*, MDu., MLG *swarde*, MHG *swarte*, ON *svǫrthr* f. Gmc *·sward-, ·swardh-, ·swarth-*]

sware. See SWEAR.

swarf (-ôrf), n. Chips or filings of wood, metal, etc. [f. ON *svarf* file-dust]

swarm[1] (-ôrm), n., & v.i. **1.** Large number of insects, birds, small animals, sharp-shooters, horsemen, etc., moving about in a cluster or irregular body esp. round prey or enemy (~s, great numbers of children, stars, people, bills, etc.); cluster of honey-bees emigrating from hive with queen bee to establish new home; ~-cell, -spore, zoospore. **2.** v.i. Move in a ~ (~ round, about, over, etc., prepp.), (of bees) cluster for emigration; congregate in numbers, be very numerous; (of places) be overrun, be crowded, abound, *with* (road, hills, house, ~ing with beggars, rebels, fleas). [OE *swearm*, OS, OHG *swarm*, ON *svarmr* f. Gmc *swarmaz*]

swarm[2] (-ôrm), v.i. & t. Climb rope or tree or pole (always *up*), climb (rope etc., or *up* rope etc.), by clipping with knees & hands. [16th c., of unkn. orig.]

swart (-ôrt), a. (arch.). Dark-hued, swarthy. [OE *sweart*, OS *swart*, OHG *swarz*, ON *svartr*, Goth. *swarts* f. Gmc *swartaz*]

swar'th|y (-ôrdhĭ), a. Dark-complexioned. Hence ~ĭLY[2] adv., ~ĭNESS n. [obsc. var. of obs. *swarty* (prec. -Y[2])]

swash (-ŏ-), v.t. & i., & n. **1.** (Arch.) strike violently (~'buckler, bully, bravo; ~ing blow, hard); (of water etc.) wash about, make sound of washing or rising & falling; ~-plate, inclined disc revolving on axle & communicating up-&-down motion to bar whose end rests on it. **2.** n. Motion or sound of ~ing water. [imit.]

swäs'tika (or swŏs̆), n. Fylfot. [Skr., f. *svasti* well-being (*sū* good, *asti* being)]

swat (-ŏt), v.t. (-tt-). Slap, crush (fly etc.). [c. 1600 = sit down, north. dial. & U.S. var. of SQUAT]

swatch (-ŏ-), n. (chiefly Sc. & north.). Sample of cloth or fabric. [orig. unkn.]

swath (-aw-; pl. pron. -dhz), n. Ridge of grass, corn, etc., lying after being cut, or space left clear after one passage of mower etc. [OE *swæth*, *swathu*, MDu., MLG *swāde*, G *schwade* f. Gmc *swath-*]

swäthe (-dh), v.t., & n. **1.** Bind with bandages, enclose in wraps or cloths or warm or many garments. **2.** n. (rare). A bandage or fold. [OE *swathian* f. *swæth* n.; cf. SWADDLE]

sway, v.i. & t., & n. **1.** Lean unsteadily to one side or in different directions by turns, have unsteady swinging motion, oscillate irregularly, waver, vacillate; give ~ing motion to, govern the motion of, wield, control direction of, have influence over, govern, rule over, (wind ~s trees; ~ sceptre, cricket-bat, sword; his speech ~ed votes; is too much ~ed by the needs of the moment; ~s a fifth of mankind); (p.p., of horse, also ~-backed) with back abnormally hollowed. **2.** n. ~ing motion or position; rule, government. [c. 1500,

app. f. LG *swājen* be blown to and fro, Du. *zwaaien* swing, wave]

swear (swār), v.t. & i. (*swōre* or arch. *swāre*; *sworn*), & n. **1.** State something on oath, take oath (*to*, that or *that*), promise (conduct, *to* do) on oath, take (oath), (colloq.) say emphatically that, (will you ~, ~ it, to it, ~ you or that you were not there; on the Testament? ; ~ eternal fidelity; had sworn, or sworn a solemn oath, to return; I ~ it is too bad of him; ~ to or by, appeal to as witness & guarantee of oath; ~ by, colloq., profess or have great belief in, regularly resort to or recommend; ~ off drink etc., take oath to abstain). **2.** Use profane oaths to express anger or as expletives (often *at*). **3.** Cause to take oath, administer oath to, (~ witness etc.; ~ person to secrecy; sworn brothers or friends, close intimates; sworn enemies, open & irreconcilable; sworn broker, admitted to profession with oath against fraud etc.; ~ in, induct into office by administering oath); (p.p., of evidence etc.) given on oath. **4.** Make sworn affirmation of (offence) against (~ treason against; ~ the peace against, make oath that one is in danger of bodily harm from); hence ~'ER[1] n. **5.** n. Spell of profane ~ing (relieved his feelings by a hearty ~); (colloq., also ~-word) a profane oath. [OE, OS, OHG *swerian*, ON *sverja*, f. Gmc *swarjan* f. *swar-* (Goth. *swaran*)]

sweat (-ĕt), n., & v.i. & t. **1.** Moisture exuded from the skin, perspiration, (running, dripping, wet, with ~; in or by the ~ of one's brow or face, by dint of toil; bloody ~, exudation of blood mixed with ~); ~ing state, spell of ~ing, piece of exercise that induces ~, (in a, colloq. all of a, ~; nightly ~s; a cold ~, as in death, swoon, terror, etc.; a ~ will do him good); (colloq.) state of anxiety (in a ~); (chiefly colloq.) drudgery, toil, effort, a laborious task or undertaking, (cannot stand the ~ of it; says it is a horrid ~; will not take the ~); old ~ (sl.), old soldier; drops exuding from or condensing on any surface. **2.** ~-band, leather or flannel lining of hat or cap; ~-cloth, esp. thin blanket under horse's saddle or collar; ~-duct, by which ~ exudes from ~-gland, secreting ~ below skin; ~ shirt, short-sleeved sweater; ~-shop, in which ~ed workers are employed; hence ~'LESS, ~'Y[2], aa., ~'ĭLY[2] adv., ~'ĭNESS n. **3.** vb. Exude ~, perspire; (fig.) be in state of terror or suffering or repentance (he shall ~ for it, repent it); emit (blood, gum, etc.) like ~; (of wall etc.) exhibit surface moisture; toil, drudge; make (horse, athlete, etc.) ~ by exercise; employ (labour, workers) at starvation wages for long hours, exploit to the utmost by utilizing competition, (~ed clothes etc., made by ~ed workers), (of workers) work on such terms; subject (hides, tobacco) to fermentation in manufacturing; deprive (coins) of part of metal by shaking in bag; remove ~ from (horse) by scraping; fasten (metal part) on or in by partial fusion. **4.** ~*ing-bath*, for producing ~; ~*ing-iron*, for scraping ~ from horse; ~*ing-room*, in Turkish bath; ~*ing-sickness*, epidemic fever prevalent in 15th & 16th cc. [ME *swet(e)*, alt. (after *swete* vb f. OE *swǣtan* f. *swāt*) f. *swote* f. OE *swāt* (OS *swēt*, OHG *sweiz*, ON *sveiti*) f. Gmc *swait*-]

swea'ter (-ĕt-), n. In vbl senses; esp.: sweating employer; thick woollen jersey worn during or after exercise to reduce weight or prevent chills; ~ *girl* (colloq.), girl or woman with well-developed bust. [-ER[1]]

swēde, n. Native of Sweden (*S*~); Swedish turnip. [MLG, MDu.]

Swēdenbōr'ǵian, a. & n. (Adherent) of the Swedish philosophical & religious mystic Emanuel Swedenborg (1688–1772) or his doctrines or New Church. Hence ~ISM(3) n. [-IAN]

Swēd'ish, a. & n. (Language) of Sweden or its inhabitants. [SWEDE, -ISH[1]]

°sween'ȳ, n. Atrophy of muscle, esp. of shoulder, in horse. [prob. f. dial. G *schweine* atrophy]

sweep, v.i. & t. (*swĕpt*), & n. **1.** Glide swiftly, speed along with impetuous unchecked motion, go majestically, extend (intr.) in continuous curve or line or slope, (*eagle* ~*s past*; *wind* ~*s along*; *cavalry* ~*s down on the enemy*; *she swept out of the room*; *his glance* ~*s from right to left*; *with a* ~*ing stroke*; *coast* ~*s northward*; *plain sweeps away to the sea*). **2.** (part.). Of wide range, regardless of limitations or exceptions, (~*ing remark*, *generalization*, etc.), whence ~'**inGLY**[2] adv., ~'**inG**NESS n. **3.** Impart ~ing motion to, carry *along* or *down* or *away* or *off* in impetuous course, clear *off* or *away* or *out of* existence etc. or *from*, (*swept his hand across*; *river* ~*s away bridge*, ~*s logs down with it*; *was swept away by an avalanche*; *the plague swept off thousands*; ~ *away slavery*, *feudalism*, abolish swiftly; *he swept his audience along with him*, won enthusiastic support; ~ *all obstacles from* one's *path*). **4.** Traverse or range swiftly, pass lightly across or along, pass eyes or hand quickly along or over, scan, scour, graze, (~ *the seas*, traverse in all directions, & see below; *wind* ~*s the hillside*; ~ *the strings*, *lute*, etc., of hand or its owner; ~ *the horizon*, of eyes or their owner; ~ *river-bottom* etc., drag it to find something; *dress* ~*s the ground*). **5.** (Of artillery etc.) include in line of fire, cover, enfilade, rake, (*battery* ~*s the approaches*, *glacis*, *street*). **6.** Clear everything from, clear of dust or soot or litter with broom (often *up*), gather *up* or collect (as) with broom, push *away* etc. (as) with broom, (~ *the seas*, drive all enemies from them, & see above; ~ *floor*, *carpet*,

chimney; ~ *up the room*; ~ *away the snow*; *swept & garnished*, generally renovated, w. ref. to *Luke* xi. 25; ~ *the board*, win all the money on gaming-table, & transf. win all possible prizes etc.; ~ *a constituency* etc., receive nearly all votes, have large majority; ~*s everything into his net*, seizes all that comes; ~ *up litter* etc., whence ~'ING[1](2) n. usu. in pl.). **7.** Propel (barge etc.) with ~s. **8.** ~*-net*, long fishing-net, also entomologist's net; ~*-seine*, large seine; ~'*stake(s)*, form of gambling on horse-races etc. in which the sum composed of participators' stakes goes to the drawer(s) of winning or placed horse(s) etc.; hence ~'ER[1](1, 2) n., (also, India) domestic servant employed on sanitary & scavenging duties. **9.** n. ~ing motion or extension, curve in road etc., piece of curving road etc., (*with a* ~ *of his arm*, *eyes*, *scythe*; *a* ~ *of mountain country*; *river makes a great* ~ *to the left*; *house is approached by a fine* ~ *or carriage* ~). **10.** Range or compass of something that has ~ing motion (*within*, *beyond*, *the* ~ *of the scythe*, *net*, *telescope*, *eye*, *human intelligence*). **11.** Act of ~ing (as) with broom (*give it a thorough* ~ *or* ~*-up or* ~*-out*; *make a clean* ~, have complete riddance of old furniture, officials, etc.); sortie by aircraft. **12.** Long oar worked by standing rower(s) on barge, becalmed sailing-ship, etc. (*had to get out the* ~*s*). **13.** Long pole mounted as lever for raising bucket from well. **14.** Man who ~s chimneys (often *chimney-*~). **15.** (colloq.). =~*stake*. **16.** ~'*back*, angle at which aircraft's wing is set back relatively to the axis; *swept-back wing* or *swept-wing* a., (of aircraft) having the outer portion of the wing aft of the inner portion. [ME *swepe*, replacing obs. *swope* SWOOP f. OE *swāpan*; see SWIFT]

sweet, a. & n. **1.** Tasting like sugar or honey (~ *apples* etc.; ~ *stuff*, ~*meats*; *likes her tea* ~, with much sugar; *a* ~ *tooth*, a liking for ~ things; ~ *wine*, opp. DRY[1]; *tastes* ~, has ~ taste). **2.** Smelling like roses or perfumes, fragrant, (*smells* ~; so ~*-scent*ED[2] a.; *air is* ~ *with thyme*; ~ *violet*, of scented kind, opp. *dog-violet*; ~ *breath*). **3.** Melodious or harmonious in sound (*has a* ~ *voice*; *sounds* ~; ~ *song*, *singer*, etc.). **4.** Fresh & sound, not salt or salted or sour or bitter or rancid or high or stinking, (~ *water*, fit for drinking, neither salt nor bitter nor putrid; *is the meat*, *milk*, *butter*, *still* ~?; *keep the room clean & ~*). **5.** Highly agreeable or attractive or gratifying, inspiring affection, dear, beloved, amiable, gentle, easy, (colloq.) pretty or charming or delightful, ('*tis* ~ *to hear* one's *own praises*; ~ *toil*, that one loves; ~ *love*, *dalliance*, *idleness*, *sleep*; *what a* ~ *blouse*, *moustache*, *collie!*; ~ *temper*, amiability, whence ~*-tem*perED[2] a.; *a* ~ *nature*, *face*, etc.; *a* ~ *girl*, lovable, affectionate; ~ *one*, voc., darling;

$a \sim$ one, sl., painful blow with fist etc.; $\sim$ going, travelling over well-laid road or in smooth-going carriage). **6.** *At* one's own $\sim$ *will*, just as or when one pleases, arbitrarily, at random; $\sim$ (*up*)*on* (colloq.), (inclined to be) in love with, very fond of. **7.** $\sim$'*bread*, pancreas (*belly* $\sim$*bread*) or thymus-gland (*throat* or *neck* $\sim$*bread*) esp. of calf as food; $\sim$BRIER[1]; $\sim$ GALE[1]; $\sim$'*heart*, either of pair of lovers, (vb) be engaged in love-making (esp. *go* $\sim$*hearting*); $\sim$-*john*, kinds of pink or of narrow- -leaved $\sim$-*william*; $\sim$'*meat*, shaped morsel of confectionery usu. consisting chiefly of sugar or chocolate, a fruit preserved in sugar, bonbon, sugarplum, goody; $\sim$ *oil*, (esp.) olive oil; $\sim$ *pea*, garden annual with showy variously-coloured $\sim$-scented flowers; $\sim$ POTATO; $\sim$-*root*, liquorice; $\sim$ *rush*, kind of sedge with thick creeping aromatic rootstock used in medicine & confectionery; $\sim$-*sop*, ($\sim$-pulped fruit of) an evergreen shrub of tropical America; $\sim$ SULTAN; $\sim$-*water*, kind of white hothouse grape; $\sim$-*will'iam*, a garden-plant, kind of pink with close-clustered flowers often particoloured in zones; $\sim$ *willow*, $\sim$ *gale*; hence $\sim$'EN[6] v.t. & i., $\sim$'enING[1](4) n., $\sim$'ISH[1](2) a., $\sim$'LY[2] adv., $\sim$'NESS n. **8.** n. $\sim$ part (*the* $\sim$ *& the bitter* or $\sim$*s & bitters of life*); ‖ a $\sim$meat, bonbon, (also $\sim$'Y[3] n.); $\sim$ dish such as pudding, tart, cream, jelly, forming a course at table; (usu. pl.) fragrance (*flowers diffusing their* $\sim$*s on the air*); (pl.) delights, gratifications, pleasures, (*the* $\sim$*s of office, domestication, flattery, success*); (chiefly in voc.) darling. [OE *swēte*, OS *swōti*, OHG *s(w)uozi*, ON *sœtr* f. Gmc **swōtja-*, **swōti-*, cogn. w. L *suavis*, Goth *suts*]

sweet'ing, n. Kind of sweet apple; (arch.) darling. [-ING[3]]

swell, v.i. & t. (p.p. *swollen*, arch. *swoln*, rarely $\sim$*ed*), & n. & a. **1.** (Cause to) grow bigger or louder, dilate, expand, rise or raise *up* from surrounding surface, bulge *out*, increase in volume or force or intensity, (*river swollen with melted snow; the injured wrist began to* $\sim$ *up* or $\sim$, whence $\sim$'ING[1](2) n.; *the* $\sim$*ing sails*; *toad* $\sim$*ing himself to size of ox*; $\sim$*ing oratory*, of inflated·kind; *sound* $\sim$*s on the breeze*; *murmur* $\sim$*ed into a roar*; *ground* $\sim$*s into an eminence*; *heart* $\sim$*s*, feels like bursting with emotion; $\sim$ *with pride, indignation*, etc., be or seem hardly able to contain it; $\sim$ *like a turkey-cock*, put on blustering air; *wind* $\sim$*s the sails*; *the* $\sim$*ing tide*; *expenditure swollen by extravagance*; *swollen estimates*, inordinately high; *a thousand voices* $\sim$ *the sound*; *items* $\sim$ *the total*; $\sim$ *note* in music, sing or play it with alternate crescendo & diminuendo; *emotion* $\sim$*s & subsides*; $\sim$*ed* or *swollen head*, sl., conceit). **2.** n. Act or condition of $\sim$ing (*the* $\sim$ *of the hymn floated past*; *the* $\sim$ *of the ground*). **3.** Heaving of sea with waves that do not break after storm. **4.** Part of any more

or less cylindrical object that $\sim$s out (*the* $\sim$ *of the fore-arm*). **5.** (mus.). Mechanism in organ (operated by $\sim$-*pedal*) for obtaining crescendo or diminuendo by opening or closing slats in front of $\sim$-*box* containing pipes of the $\sim$-*manual*. **6.** (colloq.). Person of distinction or ability, first-class person, member of good society, person of dashing or fashionable appearance, (*is a* $\sim$ *in politics, at cricket*, etc.; *what a* $\sim$ *you are!*, how finely dressed; *has been asked to dinner by some* $\sim$*s), whence $\sim$'DOM n. **7.** $\sim$-*fish*, kinds that can inflate themselves into nearly globular form; $\sim$ *mob*(*smen*), (class of) pickpockets dressed like gentlemen; $\sim$-*organ*, set of pipes enclosed in $\sim$-box; $\sim$*rule* in printing, dash $\sim$ing into·diamond in middle & tapering towards ends. **8.** adj. (colloq.). Of distinction (*a* $\sim$ *pianist*; $\sim$ *parties, society*, etc.); fine, splendid; smart, finely dressed, ($\sim$ *clothes*; *looks very* $\sim$); hence $\sim$'ISH[1](2) a. [OE, OS, OHG *swellan*, ON *svella* f. Gmc *swellan]

swel'ter, v.i., & n. **1.** Be faint or moist or languid or oppressive with heat (of atmosphere etc., or of things or persons suffering from it; *under a* $\sim$*ing sky*; *city* $\sim$*ed in the plain*; *the* $\sim$*ing horses*). **2.** n. $\sim$ing atmosphere·or conditions (*in the* $\sim$ *of the Indian night*). [f. root of (now dial.) *swelt*, f. OE (= OS) *sweltan* perish, OHG *swelzan*, ON *svelta*, Goth. *swiltan*, see -ER[1]]

swept. See SWEEP.

swerve, v.i. & t., & n. **1.** Diverge from regular line of motion, go off in changed direction, dodge, (*never* $\sim$*s an inch from his duty*; *bird, ball*, $\sim$*s in the air*; *horse, three-quarters* at football, $\sim$*d suddenly*); cause (ball) to $\sim$ in the air. **2.** n. Divergence from course, swerving motion; hence $\sim$'LESS (-vl-) a. [ME *swerve*, repr. OE *sweorfan*, OS, OHG *swerban* wipe etc., ON *sverfa*, Goth. -*swairban*]

swift, a., adv. ($\sim$*er*, $\sim$*est*), & n. **1.** Fleet, rapid, quick, soon coming or passing, not long delayed, (now chiefly poet. & rhet.; $\sim$ *runner, movement, feet, retribution, anger, laughter, response, riddance*; so $\sim$-FOOTED[2], $\sim$-wingED[2], aa.); prompt, quick *to* do, (*has a* $\sim$ *wit*; $\sim$ *to anger*; *be* $\sim$ *to hear, slow to speak*; so $\sim$-handED[2] a.); hence $\sim$'LY[2] adv., $\sim$'NESS n. **2.** adv. $\sim$ly (*he answered* $\sim$; *they that run* $\sim$*est*; esp. in comb., as $\sim$-*coming*, -*passing*). **3.** n. Kinds of very long-winged & $\sim$-flying insectivorous bird with resemblances to swallows, whence $\sim$'LET n. (small kind); kinds of small lizard; the common newt; ‖ breed of pigeons; kinds of moth; revolving frame for winding yarn etc. from. [OE *swift*, prehist. *swipt- f. Gmc *swaip-, *swip-; see SWOOP, SWEEP]

swig, v.t. & i. (-gg-), & n. (sl.). **1.** Take draughts (of). **2.** n. (Act of taking) a draught of liquor. [vb f. n. (16th c.) in obs. sense *liquor*, of unkn. orig.]

swill, v.t. & i., & n. **1.** Rinse, pour water over or through, flush, (often *out*); drink (t. & i.) greedily. **2.** n. Rinsing (*give it a ~ or ~ out*); bout of drinking (rare); inferior liquor; hog-wash, slops. [OE *swillan*, *swilian*, of unkn. orig.]

swim, v.i. & t. (*swăm*, *swŭm*), & n. **1.** Float on or at surface of liquid (SINK[1] *or ~*; *vegetables ~ming in butter*; *with bubbles ~ming on it*). **2.** Progress at or below surface of water by working legs, arms, tail, webbed feet, fins, flippers, wings, body, etc., traverse or accomplish (stream, distance, etc.) thus, compete in (race) thus, compete with thus, cause (horse, dog, etc.) to progress thus, (fig.) go with gliding motion, (*~ on one's chest, back, side*, methods of human *~ming*; *~ across, out, back, the channel, a mile, a race*, person *a hundred yards*, one's *horse across*; *cannot ~ a stroke*; *~ with the tide* or *stream*, act with the majority; *~ to the bottom* or *like a stone* or *tailor's goose*, joc., sink; *she swam into the room*; *moon ~s in sky*), whence *~*m'ER[1] n. **3.** Appear to undulate or reel or whirl, have dizzy effect or sensation, (*everything swam before his eyes*; *my head ~s*; *has a ~ming in the head*). **4.** Be flooded or overflow with or with or in moisture (*eyes, deck, ~ming with tears, water*; *~ming eyes*, *floor ~ming in blood*). **5.** *~ming-bath*, large enough to ~ in; *~ming-bell*, bell-shaped *~ming* organ of jellyfish etc.; *~ming-belt*, to keep learner afloat; *~ming-bladder*, fish's sound; *~ming-stone*, kind of spongy quartz. **6.** n. Spell of *~ming*; *~ming-bladder* (rare); deep pool frequented by fish in river; (fig.) main current of affairs (esp. *in the ~*, engaged in or acquainted with what is going on); *~-suit*, bathing-dress. [OE, OS, OHG *swimman*, ON *svimma*]

swimm'erĕt, n. Swimming-foot in crustaceans. [*swimmer*, -ET[1]]

swimm'inglỹ, adv. With easy & unobstructed progress (esp. *go on ~*). [-LY[2]]

swin'dl|e, v.t. & i., & n. **1.** Cheat (person, *money out of* person, person *out of* money etc., or abs.); so *~-*ER[1] n., *~*ingLY[2] adv. **2.** n. Fraudulent scheme, imposition, piece of *~ing*, person or thing represented as what it is not. [back form. f. *swindler* f. G *schwindler* visionary projector, swindler, (*schwindeln* be dizzy)]

swine, n. (pl. the same). Kinds of ungulate non-ruminant omnivorous mammal, pig (which name has displaced it exc. in poet., rhet., zool., agricult., & U.-S. use), whence **swin'ERY**[3] n.; person of greedy or bestial habits; *~-bread*, the truffle, also = SOW[2]*-bread*; *~-fever, ~-*plague; *~-herd*, tender of *~*; *~-plague*, infectious lung-disease of *~*; *~-pox*, form of chicken-pox; *~'s-snout*, dandelion. Hence **swin'ISH**[1] a., **swin'ishlỹ** adv., **swin'ishNESS** n., (chiefly of persons & their habits).' [OE *swin*, OS, OHG *swin*, ON *svin*,

Goth. *swein* f. Gmc *swinam*, neut. of adj. form, cf. L *suinus* f. *su-* SOW[2]]

swing, v.i. & t. (*swŭng* or rarely *swăng*, *swung*), & n. **1.** Move (t. & i.) with to-&-fro or curving motion of object having fixed point(s) or side but otherwise free, sway (t. & i.) or so hang (t. & i.) as to be free to sway like a pendulum or door or branch or tree or hammock or anchored ship, oscillate, revolve, rock, wheel, (*he shall ~ for it*, be hanged; *door swung to*, closed; *boat, boom, ~s round, across*; *ship ~s at anchor*; *~ child* etc., work the *~* in which he sits; *sat on table ~ing his legs*; *~ one's arms, a bell, Indian clubs, bat, basket*; *~ a hammock*, suspend it by ends; *no room to ~ a* CAT[1]). **2.** part. (Of gait, melody, etc.) vigorously rhythmical (*at a long ~ing trot*; *a ~ing chorus*). **3.** Go with *~ing* gait (*he swung out of the room*; *~ along, past, by*, etc.), whence *~'*ingLY[2] adv. **4.** ‖ *~ the lead* (Service sl.), malinger or scrimshank. **5.** n. Act of *~ing*, oscillation, *~ing* movement, (*work is in full ~*, active; *the ~ of the pendulum*, fig., tendency to alternation, esp. tendency of electorate to put parties in power alternately). **6.** *~ing* gait or rhythm (*goes with a ~*); (also *~ music*) kind of jazz in which time of melody is freely varied, with simple harmonic accompaniment in rigid rhythm. **7.** Normal duration of activity (*let it have its ~*, have free course till it rests of itself like pendulum). **8.** Seat slung by ropes or chains for *~ing* in (*~s & ROUND*[3]*-abouts*), spell of *~ing* in this. **9.** Compass to which thing *~s* (*has a ~ of 3 ft*). **10.** *~-boat*, boat-shaped carriage hung from frame for *~ing* in; *~ bridge*, that can be swung aside as a whole or in sections to let ships etc. pass; *~ plough*, without wheels. [OE, OHG *swingan*, f. Gmc *swingw-*, *swangw-*]

swinge (-j), v.t. (*~ing*). Strike hard, beat, (arch. exc. in *a ~ing blow* etc.); (part.) huge (*~ing majority, lie, damages*; cf. *thumping, whopping*, etc.). [alt. f. ME *svenge* f. OE *swengan*, causal (*swangwjan*) of prec.]

swingle (swing'gl), n., & v.t. **1.** Wooden instrument for beating flax & removing woody parts from it; swinging part of flail; ‖*~tree*, crossbar pivoted in middle to ends of which traces are fastened in cart, plough, etc. **2.** v.t. Clean (flax) with *~*; *swingling-tow*, coarse part of flax. [ME, f. MDu. *swinghel*, as SWING, -LE(1)]

swink, v.i., & n. (arch.). Toil. [OE *swincan* (whence n.), parallel form. to *swingan* SWING]

swipe, v.i. & t., & n. **1.** Hit at or hit cricket-ball etc., hit (cricket-ball etc.), hard & recklessly, slog; (sl.) steal by snatching; hence **swip'**ER[1] n. **2.** n. Reckless hard hit or attempt to hit at cricket etc., slog. [var. of SWEEP]

‖ **swipes** (-ps), n. pl. Washy or turbid or

otherwise inferior beer. [f. prec. in obs. sense *drink off*]

swirl, v.i. & t., & n. **1.** Eddy, carry (object) or be carried with eddying motion. **2.** n. Eddying motion of water, air, etc., commotion made by fish etc. rushing through water. [orig. Sc., of uncert. orig.; cf. Norw. dial. *svirla*, Du. *zwirrelen* to whirl, G dial. *schwirren* totter]

swish[1], v.t. & i., & n. ‖ Flog with birch; audibly cut the air with (cane etc.), cut (flower etc.) *off* thus; make such audible cut *with* cane etc.; (make, move with) sound as of cane or lash or swift bird cutting the air or of scythe cutting grass; ‖ a stroke of a birch or cane or lash. [imit.]

‖ **swish**[2], a. (colloq.). Smart, swagger.

Swiss, a., & n. (pl. the same). (Native) of Switzerland (~ *French, German*, dialects of French & German spoken in Switzerland; *German* ~, a patois; ~ *guards*, ~ mercenaries formerly employed in France etc. & still at the Vatican; ~ *roll*, kind of jam sandwich baked & rolled up). [f. F *Suisse* f. MHG *Swiz*]

switch, n., & v.t. & i. **1.** Flexible shoot cut from tree, tapering rod resembling this. **2.** Tress of dead hair tied at one end used in hairdressing. **3.** Kinds of mechanism for making & breaking connexion between corresponding parts of a system by which railway trains are diverted from one line to another, electric circuits completed or interrupted, etc. **4.** ‖ ~'*back*, zigzag railway for ascending or descending steep slopes, also railway (chiefly used for amusement at fairs etc.) in which train's ascents are effected solely by momentum acquired in previous descents; ~-*bar*, part of railway or electric ~; ~'*board*, arrangement for varying the connexion between a number of electric circuits; ~-*lever*, handle & lever operating a ~; ~-*man*, in charge of railway ~es; ~-*signal*, flag or lantern or semaphore board indicating position of railway ~. **5.** vb. Whip with ~. **6.** Swing (thing) round quickly, snatch suddenly, whisk, (cow ~*es her tail; I* ~*ed my head round; he* ~*ed it out of my hand*). **7.** Transfer (train, current) with ~, (fig.) direct (thoughts, talk) to another subject; race (horse) under another's name; (bridge) change to another suit in bidding. **8.** Turn (electric light, current) *off* or *on*; put (user of telephone) *on* to or cut (him) *off* from another (~ *off* intr., cut off connexion). [early forms *swits*, *switz*, prob. f. Flem. or LG, cf. Hanoverian *swutsche*, LG *zwukse* long thin stick, switch]

‖ **swith'er** (-dh-), v.i., & n. (Sc.). **1.** Hesitate, be uncertain. **2.** n. Flurry, doubt, uncertainty. [16th c. Sc., of unkn. orig.]

Swit'zer, n. (arch.). A Swiss. [f. MHG *Switzer*, or MDu. *Switser* f. *Switz(en)* Switzerland, -ER[1]]

swiv'el, n., & v.i. & t. (-ll-). **1.** Ring & pivot serving as connexion between two

parts of something & enabling one of them to revolve without the other (~ *chain, bookrest, gun, -hook, -joint, rowlock*, etc., provided with ~); ~-*eye(d)*, (with) squinting eye. **2.** vb. Turn (t. & i.) on ~. [ME, f. weak grade *swif-* of OE *swifan* copulate + -LE(1)]

swiz'zle, n. Compounded intoxicating drink (~-*stick*, with brushlike end used for frothing or flattening drinks). [orig. unkn.]

swob(ber), var. of. SWAB(*ber*).

swollen, swoln (arch.), p.p. of SWELL.

swoon, v.i., & n. (Have) fainting-fit (~*ed for joy, with pain*, etc.); (of music etc.) die languidly away, whence ~'*ing*-LY[2] adv. [ME *swoune* perh. back form. f. *swogning* n. f. OE p.p. *geswōgen* in a swoon]

swoop, v.i. & t., & n. **1.** Come down or *down* with the rush of a bird of prey, make sudden attack from a distance, (often *upon* prey, place, etc.); (colloq.) snatch *up*, snatch, the whole of, at one ~. **2.** n. Sudden attack or downward plunge as of bird of prey; snatching action carrying off many things at once; *at one fell* ~ (in describing completeness & extent & suddenness of catastrophe etc., see *Macb.* IV. iii. 219). [app. dial. var. of obs. *swope* f. OE *swāpan*, see SWEEP, SWIFT]

swop, swap (-ŏp), v.t. & i. (-pp-), & n. (sl.). Exchange (v.t. & i., & n.) by way of barter (*never* ~ *horses while crossing the stream*, leave changes till crisis is past; ~*ped my knife for bread; will you* ~ *places* etc.?, or abs.; *shall we try a* ~?). [f. 14th c. in obs. sense *hit*, prob. imit., hence (16th c.) 'strike' a bargain]

sword (sŏrd), n. **1.** Offensive weapon consisting of long variously shaped blade for cutting or thrusting or both & hilt with hand-guard (BROAD~; *cavalry* ~, sabre; *court, dress*, ~, worn with court dress; *double-edged, two-handed*, etc., ~; *duelling, small-*, ~, kind with straight edgeless blade of triangular section used for thrusting only; SCUTCHing-~; ‖ ~ *of State*, borne before sovereign on State occasions; *the* ~ *of the spirit*, the word of God; *cross* or *measure* ~s, have fight or controversy or open rivalry, often *with*; *draw, sheathe, the* ~, begin, cease from, war; *throw* one's ~ *into the scale*, back claim etc. with arms; *put to the* ~, kill, esp. of victors or captors; *fire &* ~, rapine, destruction spread by invading army; *the* ~ *of justice*, judicial authority; *the* ~, war, the arbitrament of war, military power, sovereign power); (army sl.) bayonet. **2.** ~-*arm*, right; ~-*bayonet*, kind with short ~-blade & hilt; ‖ ~-*bearer*, person carrying sovereign's or other great person's ~ on some occasions; ~-*belt*, to which scabbard is attached; ~-*bill*, long-billed humming-bird; ~-*cane*, hollow walking-stick enclosing ~-blade;

~-*cut*, wound given with ~-edge, scar left by it; ~-*dance*, in which ~s are brandished, or women pass under men's crossed ~s, or performer treads about ~s laid on ground; ~-*fish*, fish with upper jaw prolonged into sharp ~like weapon; ~-*flag*, esp. yellow iris; ~-*flighted*, (of birds) having flight-feathers of separate colour & looking when closed like ~ worn at side; ~-*grass*, gladiolus, kinds of sedge with ~like leaves; ~-*guard*, part of ~-hilt that protects hand; ~-*hand*, right; ~-*knot*, ribbon or tassel attached to ~-hilt orig. for securing it to wrist; ~-*law*, military domination; ~-*lily*, gladiolus; ~-*play*, fencing, (fig.) repartee, cut-&-thrust argument; ~*s'man*, person of (usu. specified) skill with ~, whence ~**s'man**-SHIP(3) (sŏrdz-) n.; ~-*stick*, ~-cane. Hence (-)~'ED², ~'LESS, ~'LIKE, ~'PROOF², aa. [OE *sweord*, OS *swerd*, OHG *swert*, ON *sverth* f. Gmc *swerdam*]

swore, sworn. See SWEAR.

‖ **swŏt**, v.i. & t. (-tt-); & n. (school sl.). 1. Work hard esp. at books, sap; ~ (subject) *up*, study it hurriedly. 2. n. Hard study; (thing that demands) effort, a sweat, (*it is too much* ~; *what a* ~!); person who works hard esp. at learning, a sap. [dial. var. of SWEAT]

swum, swung. See SWIM, SWING.

sŷb'ar|īte, n. & a. 1. (S~*ite*). Inhabitant of ancient-Greek colony of Sybaris in Italy noted for luxury. 2. Luxurious & effeminate (person). Hence ~**ĭt'ĭc** a., ~**ītĬSM**(2) n., ~**ĭt'ĬCALLY** adv. [f. L (-*ta*) f. Gk *Subarĭtēs* (*Subaris*, -ITE¹)]

sŷb'ĭl, n. (Erron. for) SIBYL.

sỹc'amĭne, n. (bibl.). The black mulberry-tree. [f. L f. Gk *sukamĭnos* mulberry-tree f. Heb. *shiqmah* sycamore]

sỹc'amōre, n. (Also ~ *fig* or *Egyptian* or *oriental* ~) kind of fig-tree growing in Syria & Egypt; (also ~ *maple*) large timber-tree allied to maple; *plane-tree. [ME, f. OF *sicamore* f. L f. Gk *sukomoros* (*sukon* fig, *moron* mulberry)]

sỹce, sīce, n. (Anglo-Ind.). Groom. [f. Hind. f. Arab. *sā'is*]

sỹcee', n. (Also ~ *silver*) ingots of pure silver bearing banker's or assayer's seal & used in China for payments by weight. [f. Chin. *si sz'* fine silk (as capable of being drawn out fine)]

sỹchnocărp'ous (-k-), a. (bot.). Bearing fruit several times before dying, perennial. [Gk *sukhnos* numerous, *karpos* fruit, -OUS]

sỹcŏn'ium, n. (bot.; pl. ~*ia*). Fleshy hollow receptacle developing into multiple fruit as in fig. [mod. L (Gk *sukon* fig)]

sỹc'oph|ant, n. Flatterer, toady, parasitic person. So ~ANCY n., ~**ăn'tĬc** a. [f. L f. Gk *sukophantēs* informer, f. *sukon* fig, *phainō* show, reason for name unkn.]

sỹcōs'is, n. Skin-disease of bearded part of face or scalp also called *barber's itch*. [f. Gk *sukōsis* (*sukon* fig, -OSIS)]

sỹ'en|īte, n. Grey crystalline rock of feldspar & hornblende with or without quartz. Hence ~**ĭt'ĭc** a. [F (*syé*-), f. L *Syenĭtes* (*lapis* stone) of Syene in Egypt, see -ITE¹]

sỹll'abarў, n. List of characters representing syllables & serving the purpose, in some languages or stages, of an alphabet. [f. mod. L *syllabarium* f. med. L -*ius* adj. (as SYLLABLE, -ARY¹)]

sỹllăb'|ĭc, a. Of syllable(s) (often in comb., as *mono*, *di*, *tri*, *quadri*, ~*ic*, having 1, 2, 3, 4, syllables); (of symbols) representing a whole syllable; articulated in syllables. Hence ~**ĬCALLY** adv. [f. LL f. Gk *sullabikos* (SYLLABLE, -IC)]

sỹllăb'icāte, sỹllăb'ĭfȳ, sỹll'abīze, -ise (-ĭz), vv.t. Divide into or articulate by syllables. Hence **sỹllăbicA'TION, sỹllăbi-FICA'TION**, nn. [Gk *sullabē* see foll., -IC, -ATE³, -FY, -IZE]

sỹll'abl|e, n., & v.t. 1. Unit of pronunciation forming a word or part of a word & containing one vowel sound & often consonant(s) preceding or following or preceding & following this; (transf.) so much as a word, the least amount of speech, (*not a* ~*e!*, do not speak); hence (-)~ED² (-ld) a. 2. v.t. Pronounce by ~es, articulate distinctly; (poet.) utter (name, word). [ME, f. AF *sillable* f. OF *sillabe* (cf. *participle*, *principle*) f. L f. Gk *sullabē* (*syl*-, *lambanō* take)]

syllabub. See SILLABUB.

sỹll'abus, n. (pl. -*bī*, -*buses*). 1. Abstract giving heads or main subjects of a lecture, course of teaching, etc., conspectus or programme of hours of work etc. 2. (R.-C. Ch.) summary of points decided by an ecclesiastical decree, esp. catalogue of eighty heretical doctrines or practices or institutions condemned by Pius IX in 1864. [mod. L *syllabus*, orig. misreading of L f. Gk *sittuba* title-slip or label]

sỹllĕp'|sĭs, n. (gram.; pl. ~*sēs*). Application of a word to two others in different senses (e.g. *in a flood of tears & a sedan-chair*) or to two of which it grammatically suits one only (e.g. *neither you nor he knows*); cf. ZEUGMA. So ~TĬC a., ~TĬCALLY adv. [LL, f. Gk *sullēpsis* (*sullambanō* see SYLLABLE)]

sỹll'og|ism, n. Form of reasoning in which from two given or assumed propositions called the premis(s)es & having a common or middle term a third is deduced called the conclusion from which the middle term is absent (FIGURE¹, MOOD² *of* ~*ism*; *false* ~*ism*, one whose conclusion does not necessarily follow from its premisses because it fails to fulfil the rules of logic regarding the nature & mutual relations of the major & minor & middle terms necessary if the inference is to be sound); (transf.) deductive reasoning as opp. to induction. So ~**is'tĬc** a., ~**ĭs'tĬCALLY** adv. [ME, f. OF *silogi(s)me* or L f. Gk *sullogismos* f. *sullogizomai* (*syl-*, *logizomai* to reason f. *logos* reason), -ISM]

syllˈogize, -ise (-īz), v.i. & t. Use syllogisms; throw (facts, . argument) into syllogistic form. [ME, f. OF *sil(l)ogiser* or LL *syllogizare* f. Gk *sullogizomai* (prec.)]

sylph, n. Elemental spirit of the air (cf. *nymph, gnome, salamander,* of water, earth, fire) in Paracelsus's system, whence ~ˈLIKE a.; (transf.) slender girl; kinds of long-tailed humming-bird. [f. mod. L *sylphes,* G *sylphen* (pl.), prob. invented by Paracelsus]

sylvan. See SILVAN.

sylviculture. See SILVICULTURE.

sym-, = SYN- in Gk compds with words in b-, m-, p-, as : ~ˈbĭon(t), organism living in ~biosis [Gk *biŏn -ountos* part. of *bioŏ* f. *bios* life]; ~ˈbĭosˈis, permanent union between organisms each of which depends for its existence on the other as the fungus & alga composing lichen [f. Gk as *symbion,* -OSIS], whence ~*bĭŏlˈIO* a.,~*bĭŏlˈ*ICALLY adv.; ~*palˈmograph,* apparatus exhibiting sound-curves usu. by double pendulum with style attached [Gk *palmos* vibration f. *pallŏ* brandish]; ~*pelˈmous,* (of bird) having tendons of toe-flexors united at a point [Gk *pelma* sole]; ~*petˈalous,* having petals united; ~*phyllˈous,* with leaves united [Gk *phullon* leaf]; ~*ˈphy̆sis,* growing together, (place or line of) union between two corresponding bones or other parts, coalescence, [Gk *phuŏ* grow], whence ~*physˈ*EAL a.; ~*plĕsŏmˈeter,* instrument for measuring force of current of water, also barometer in which atmospheric pressure is balanced partly by column of liquid & partly by elastic pressure of confined gas [Gk *piesis* pressure f. *piezŏ* press]; ~*pŏdˈium,* stem whose successive sections are strictly branches each springing from the preceding, as in the vine [Gk *pous podos* foot], so ~*pŏdˈ*IAL a., ~*pŏdˈial*LY² adv.

symˈbol, n., & v.t. (-ll-). **1.** = CREDO. **2.** Thing regarded by general consent as naturally typifying or representing or recalling something by possession of analogous qualities or by association in fact or thought (*white, the lion, the thunderbolt, the cross, are* ~s *of purity, courage, Zeus, Christianity; 'values the handle to his name only as a* ~). **3.** Mark or character taken as the conventional sign of some object or idea or process, e.g. the astronomical signs for the planets, the letters standing for chemical elements, letters of the alphabet, the mathematical signs for addition & infinity, the asterisk; hence or cogn. **symbŏlˈ**IC(AL) aa., **symbŏlˈical**LY² adv., **symbŏlˈ**ICS n., ~ISM(3), ~IST(3), nn. (esp. denoting certain schools of painters & of French poets), ~IZE v.t. (see vb), ~IZAˈTION, **symb(ol)ŏlˈ**OGY, **symb(ol)-ŏlˈ**ATRY, nn. **4.** vb (rare, also & usu.~*ize*). Be the ~ of; represent by means of ~, speak of under a ~; (~*ize* only) treat (story etc.) as ~ic & not literal, import ~ism

into. [15th c., f. L f. Gk *sumbolon* mark, token, f. SYM(*ballŏ* throw); in eccl. L 'creed']

symˈmetr|y̆, n. 1. (Beauty resulting from) right proportion between the parts of the body or any whole, balance, congruity, harmony, keeping. **2.** Such structure as allows of an object's being divided by a point or line or plane or radiating lines or planes into two or more parts exactly similar in size & shape & in position relatively to the dividing point etc., repetition of exactly similar parts facing each other or a centre, whence (in art) ~OPHOBˈIA n. **3.** Approximation to such structure, possession by a whole of corresponding parts correspondingly placed; (bot.) possession by flower of sepals & petals & stamens & pistils in (multiples of) the same number. Hence or cogn. **symmĕtˈr**IC(AL) aa., **symmĕtˈrical**LY² adv., ~IZE(3) v.t., ~IZAˈTION n. [f. obs. F -*ie* or L f. Gk *summetria* (SYM-, *metron* measure)]

sympathĕtˈic, a. & n. **1.** Of, full of, exhibiting, expressing, due to, effecting, sympathy (~ *heart, person, conduct, words;* ~ *landscape* etc., that touches the feelings by association etc.; ~ *pain* etc., caused by pain or injury to someone else or in another part of the body; ~ *sound, resonance, string,* sounding by vibration communicated through the air or other medium from vibrating object; ~ STRIKE; ~ *nerve,* any, esp. either of two extending the length of the vertebral column, of a system of nerves uniting viscera & blood-vessels in common nervous action; ~ *ink,* writing done with which is invisible till brought out by warmth or other agency); capable of evoking sympathy, appealing *to* reader etc.; hence **sympathĕtˈical**LY² adv. **2.** n. ~ nerve or system; person peculiarly sensitive to hypnotic or similar influence. [f. mod. L f. Gk *sumpathētikos* (SYMPATHY, PATHETIC)]

symˈpathiz|e, -is|e (-īz), v.i. Feel or express sympathy, share feeling or opinion *with* person etc., agree *with* sentiment. Hence ~ER¹ n. [f. F *sympathiser* (foll., -IZE)]

symˈpathy̆, n. Being simultaneously affected with the same feeling, tendency to share or state of sharing another person's or thing's emotion or sensation or condition (*with*), mental participation in another's trouble (*with*), compassion (*for*), agreement in opinion or desire. [f. L f. Gk *sumpatheia* f. SYM(*pathēs* f. *pathos* feeling) sympathetic]

symˈphony̆, n. (Arch.) harmony, consonance of sounds, whence **symphŏnˈi**ous a. (rare); (mus.) SONATA for full orchestra, (also) opening or closing instrumental passage in song. Hence **symphŏnˈ**IC a. [ME, f. OF *simphonie* f. L f. Gk *sumphōnia* f. SYM(*phōnos* f. *phōnē* sound) harmonious]

sỹmpŏs'iặrch (-k), n. President of symposium, toast-master, feast-master. [f. Gk *sumposiarkhos* (foll., *-arkhos* -ruler f. *arkhŏ* rule)]

sỹmpŏs'ĭ|um (-z-), n. (pl.~*a*). **1.** Ancient--Greek after-dinner drinking-party with music, dancers, or conversation; any drinking-party. **2.** Philosophical or other friendly discussion; set of contributions on one subject from various authors & points of view in magazine etc. Hence ~ᴬᴸ a. [f. L f. Gk *sumposion* f. sʏм(*pinŏ* drink, cf. *posis* drinking) drink together]

sỹmp'tom, n. Perceptible change in the body or its functions indicating disease (*subjective*, *objective*, ~*s*, directly perceptible only to patient, to others); sign or token of the existence of something. Hence or cogn. ~ăt'ɪᴄ a., ~atŏʟ'ᴏɢʏ n. [14th c. f. med. L *sinthoma*; later F *-tome* or LL f. Gk *sumptŏma -atos* chance, symptom, f. sʏм(*piptŏ* fall, -ᴍ)]

sỹn-, pref. (assim. to *syl-* before l, to *sym-* before b, m, p; to *sur-* before r, to *sys-* before simple s, to *sy-* followed by s plus consonant, and before z. The Gk change of *sun-* to *sug-* before gutturals is disregarded in mod. derivatives) repr. Gk *sun* prep. & pref., with, together or alike, in wds derived directly f. Gk wds (*syncope*) or made f. Gk (*syngnathous*):—~(*a)er'esis* (-nē̆r-), contraction of two vowels or syllables into one [Gk *haireŏ* take]; ~*allagmăt'ic*, (of treaty or contract) imposing reciprocal obligations [Gk *allassŏ* exchange]; ~*al*(o)*eph'a* (-lē-), elision or obscuration of final before initial vowel [Gk *aleiphŏ* smear]; ~*an'therous*, with stamens coalescent by the anthers; ~*an'thous*, with flowers & leaves appearing simultaneously [Gk *anthos* flower]; ~*aphe*(i)*'a* (-ēa), continuity between lines in verse, allowing the ordinary rules of elision & quantity to operate with the final syllable [Gk *haptŏ* join]; ~*arthrŏs'is* (pl. *-osēs*), immovable articulation, as in sutures of skull & socketing of teeth; ~*'carp*, aggregate or multiple fruit, e.g. blackberry, fig, so ~*carp'ous* a. [Gk *karpos* fruit]; ~*chondrŏs'is* (-k-), (nearly) immovable articulation of bones by layer of cartilage, as in spinal vertebrae; ~*clas'tic*, concave, or convex, all over (opp. *anticlastic*, partly concave & partly convex) [Gk *klaŏ* break]; ~*clin'al*, (of strata) dipping towards a common line or point (opp. *anticlinal*, dipping away); ~*cotylĕd'onous*, with cotyledons united; ~*'cretism*, attempt to sink differences & effect union between sects or philosophic schools, so ~*crĕt'ic*, ~*'cretist*, ~*cretis'tic*, ~*'cretize* v.t. & i. [Gk *sugkrētizŏ* combine against common enemy]; ~*cŷt'ium* (pl. *-ia*), mass of protoplasm with several nuclei but forming one cell [-ᴄʏᴛᴇ]; ~*dac'tyl*(*ous*) aa., with digits united as in webbed feet etc., so ~*dac'tylism*; ~*desmŏs'is*, articulation by ligaments, so

~*desmŏt'ic*, ~*desmol'ogy*, ~*desmog'raphy* [Gk *desmos* bond f. *deŏ* bind]; ~*dĕt'ic*, of, using, conjunctions [ᴀsʏɴᴅᴇᴛᴏɴ]; ~*'drŏme* (*or* -ᴍĭ), concurrence of, set of concurrent, symptoms in disease; ~*cc'doche* (-kĭ), extended acceptation by which when a part is named the whole it belongs to is understood, as in *50 sail* (for *ships*) [Gk *ek* out *dekhomai* accept]; ~*'esis*, violation of grammatical rule due to influence exerted by the sense (as *neither of them* are *right*) [Gk *sunesis* understanding]; ~*gen'esis*, formation of embryo partly from the male & partly from the female element; ~*'gnathous*, (of fish) with jaws united into tubular snout; ~*izēs'is* (pl. *-esēs*), pronunciation of two vowels not making a diphthong as one syllable [Gk *hizŏ* to seat]; ~*oe'cious* (-nēshus), having male & female organs in one inflorescence or receptacle, as in composite flowers & mosses [Gk *oikos* house]; ~*osteol'ogy*, science of the joints of the body; ~*ost*(e)*ŏs'is*, anchylosis, so ~*ostŏt'ic* a.; ~*ŏv'ia*, albuminous fluid· secreted by membranes in interior of joints & in other places needing lubrication, so ~*ŏv'ial* a. [invented by Paracelsus from unknown elements].

sỹn'agogue (-ŏg), n. Jewish congregation with organized religious observances & instruction, its place of meeting. Hence **sỹnagŏ'ɢɪᴄᴀʟ** (-gĭ-, -jĭ-) a. [ᴍᴇ, f. OF *sinagoge* or LL f. Gk *sunagŏgē* f. sʏɴ(*agŏ* bring)]

sỹnch'romĕsh, a. & n. (System of gear--changing, esp. in motor-cars) in which the sliding gear-wheels are provided with small friction clutches which make contact with the non-sliding wheels before engagement, thus facilitating gear--changing by making both wheels revolve at the same speed. [for *synchronized mesh*]

sỹnchrŏn'ic (-ngk-), a. See ᴅɪᴀᴄʜʀᴏɴɪᴄ.

sỹnch'ron|ize (-ngk-), **|-ise** (-ĭz), v.i. & t. Occur at the same time, be simultaneous or ~ᴏᴜs a. (whence ~ᴏᴜsʟʏ² adv.), (*with*); ascertain or set forth the correspondence in date of (events); cause (clocks) to show, (of clocks) show, a standard or uniform time. Hence or cogn. ~ɪsᴍ(1) n., (also) co-ordination of the audible and visible components in cinematography, television, etc., ~ɪᴢᴀ'ᴛɪᴏɴ n. [f. *synchronism* f. mod. L f. Gk *-ismos* (sʏɴ-, *khronos* time), -ɪᴢᴇ]

sỹn'cop|āte, v. t. Shorten (word) by dropping interior letter(s) or syllable(s), as in *symbology* for *symbolology*, *Gloster* for *Gloucester*; (mus.) displace beats or accents in (passage) so that what was 'strong' becomes 'weak', & vice versa. So ~ᴀ'ᴛɪᴏɴ n. [LL *syncopare* swoon (foll.). -ᴀᴛᴇ³]

sỹnc'opĕ, n. (Gram.) syncopated spelling or pronunciation; (med.) fainting, loss of consciousness from fall of blood-pressure, whence **sўncŏp'(t)ic** a.; (mus.) syncopation, also such combination of voice-parts that two or more notes in one coincide with one in another. [f. LL f. Gk *sugkopē* (SYN-, *koptō* strike)]

sўn'dic, n. Official of kinds differing in different countries & times; ‖ (Camb. Univ.) member of special committee of senate. [F, f. LL f. Gk *sun(dikos* f. *dikē* justice) advocate]

sўn'dicalism, n. A movement among industrial workers having as its object the transfer of the means of production & distribution from their present owners to unions of workers. [f. F -*isme* (prec., -AL, -ISM)]

sўn'dicate, n. (-*at*), & v.t. (-āt). 1. Body of syndics (esp. at Camb.); combination of commercial firms etc. associated to forward some common interest; combination of persons for the acquisition of literary articles etc., and their simultaneous publication in a number of periodicals; group of people who combine to rent a shooting, fishing, etc. 2. v.t. Form (parties) into ~; deal with (news etc.) by ~. Hence **sўndicA'TION** n. [f. F -*at* f. med. L -*atus* (SYNDIC, -ATE[1])]

sŷne, Sc. for *since* (*auld lang* ~, the days of long ago, esp. as title & refrain of song sung at parting etc.).

sўn'od, n. 1. Ecclesiastical council (*oecumenical* or *general*, *national*, *provincial*, *diocesan*, ~, attended by bishop(s) & delegated clergy of all nations, a nation, a province, a diocese); (Presb.) ecclesiastical court above presbyteries & subject to General Assembly; any meeting for debate. 2. (astron.). Conjunction of planets or stars. So ~AL, **sўnŏd'ic**(AL), aa., **sўnŏd'ically** adv. [ME, f. LL f. Gk *sunodos* (SYN-, *hodos* way) meeting]

sўn'onym, n. Word identical & coextensive in sense & usage with another of the same language (as *caecitis*, cf. *typhlitis*); word denoting the same thing(s) as another but suitable to different context (as *leap*, *slay*, cf. *jump*, *kill*) or containing different suggestion (as *blind-worm*, cf. *slow-worm*); word equivalent to another in some only of either's senses (as *ship*, cf. *vessel*). Hence or cogn. **sўnonym'ity** n., **sўnŏn'ўmous** a. (*with*), **sўnŏn'ўmously**[2] adv. [f. L f. Gk *sunōnumon* (SYN-, *onoma* -*atos* name)]

sўnonym'ic, a. Of or using synonyms. [prec., -IC]

sўnŏn'ўmў, n. Synonymity; collocation of synonyms for emphasis (as *in any shape or form*); system or collection of, treatise on, synonyms. [f. LL f. Gk *sunōnumia* (SYNONYM, -Y[1])]

sўnŏp'sis, n. (pl. -*psēs*). Summary, conspectus. [f. LL f. Gk SYN(*opsis* seeing)]

sўnŏp'tic, a. & n. 1. Affording a conspectus or general survey (~ *gospels*, those of Matthew, Mark, & Luke); of the ~ gospels; ~ *chart* (meteor.), weather map;

hence ~AL a., ~alLY[2] adv. 2. n. (Also **sўnŏp'tist**) writer of a ~ gospel. [f. Gk *sunoptikos* (prec., -IC)]

sўnovit'is, n. Inflammation of the membrane that secretes the lubricating fluid in a joint. [f. SYN*ovia* + -ITIS]

sўntăc't|ic, a. Of, according to, syntax. Hence ~ICALLY adv. [f. Gk *suntaktikos* (foll.)]

sўn'tăx, n. Sentence-construction, the grammatical arrangement of words in speech or writing, set of rules governing this, cf. ACCIDENCE. [F (-*xe*), or f. LL f. Gk *suntaxis* (SYN-, *tassō* order) marshalling, syntax]

sўn'thě|sis, n. (pl. ~*sēs*). Combination, composition, putting together, (opp. *analysis*); building up of separate elements esp. of conceptions or propositions or facts, into a connected whole, esp. a theory or system; (chem.) artificial production of compounds (called 'synthetic rubber, indigo, cream', etc.) from their constituents as opp. extraction from plants etc.; (gram.) making of compound & derivative words, preference of composition & inflexion to use of prepositions etc.; (surg.) joining of divided parts. Hence or cogn. **sўnthět'ic**(AL) aa., **sўnthět'ically** adv., ~SIZE(1), ~tize, vv.t., ~tIST(1), ~sist, nn. [L, f. Gk *sunthesis* (SYN-, *tithēmi* put); the irreg. ~*size* more used than the correct ~*tize*]

sŷph'er, v.t. Join (planks) with overlapping edges into flush surface; ~*joint*, thus made. [var. of CIPHER in obs. sense]

sŷph'il|is, n. Pox, a contagious venereal disease affecting first some local part (*primary* ~*is*), secondly the skin & mucous membrane (*secondary* ~*is*), & thirdly the bones & muscles & brain (*tertiary* ~*is*). Hence ~it'ic, ~ous, ~oid, aa., ~IZE(5) v.t., ~ŏL'OGY n. [mod. L, f. title (*Syphilis*, *sive Morbus Gallicus*) of Latin poem (1530), f. *Syphilus*, a character in it, first sufferer from the disease]

syphon, syren, erron. for **si-**.

Sŷ'riăc, n. & a. (In) the language of ancient Syria, western Aramaic. Hence ~ISM(4) n. [f. L f. Gk *Suriakos* (*Suria* Syria f. *Suros* a Syrian, -AC)]

Sŷ'rian, a. & n. (Native) of Syria. [*Syria*, -AN]

sŷring'a (-ngga), n. The mock orange, a shrub with strong-scented white clustered flowers; (bot.) lilac. [mod. L, as SYRINX (w. ref. to use of stems cleared of pith as pipe-stems), -A; cf. SERINGA]

sŷ'ringe (-j), n., & v.t. 1. Cylindrical tube with nozzle & piston into which liquid is first drawn by suction & then ejected in fine stream used in surgery, gardening, etc., squirt, (*hypodermic* ~, needle-pointed for hypodermic injections). 2. v.t. Sluice or spray (ears, plants, etc.) with ~. [f. med. L *siringa* f. Gk as foll.]

sŷ'rinx, n. (pl. -*es*, -*ngēs*). Pan-pipe;

(archaeol.) narrow rock-cut · gallery in Egyptian tombs; (anat.) Eustachian tube from throat to drum of ear supplying latter with air, whence **sўringīt′is** (-j-) n.; lower larynx or song-organ of birds, whence **sўrin′ḡἐal** (-j-) a.; (surg.) fistula, whence **sўringŏt′omy** n. [L, f. Gk *surigx surigg-* pipe]

Sўro-, comb. form f. Gk *Suros* Syrian, as ~*arab′ian*, ~*phoeni′cian*. [-o-]

syr′tis (sẽr-), n. (pl. *-tēs*). Quicksand. [L, f. Gk *surtis* (*surō* draw)]

sў′rup, *si-, n. Water (nearly) saturated with sugar, this combined with flavouring as beverage or with drug(s) as medicine; condensed sugarcane-juice, part of this remaining uncrystallized at various stages of refining, molasses, treacle, (‖ *golden* ~, trade name for pale kind). Hence ~y² a. - [ME, f. OF *sirop* or med. L *siropus* f. Arab. *sharāb* beverage, cf. SHERBET, SHRUB²]

sўssarcōs′is, n. Connexion between bones by intervening muscle. [f. Gk *sussarkōsis* (SYN-, *sarkoō* f. *sarx sarkos* flesh, -osis)]

sўssit′ia, n. pl. (Gk ant.). Public messes of Spartans & some other Dorians at which citizens were required to feed with a view to the promotion of patriotism, military efficiency, discipline, & simplicity. [Gk (*su-*) pl. of *sussition* (SYN-, *sitos* food)]

sўstăl′tic, a. Contracting & dilating by turns, having systole & diastole, pulsatory. [f. LL f. Gk *sustaltikos* (*sy-* =SYN-, *stellō* place, -ic)]

sўs′tĕm, n. 1. Complex whole, set of connected things or parts, organized body of material or immaterial things, (~ *of pulleys*, several arranged to work together; ~ *of philosophy*, set of co-ordinated doctrines; *mountain* ~, range or connected ranges; *river, railway,* ~, river, railway, with its tributaries or branches, also rivers, railways, of a country, continent, etc.; *solar* ~, sun & planets; *nervous, muscular,* etc., ~, the nerves, muscles, of a person's or animal's body; *digestive* etc. ~, all bodily parts subserving digestion etc.; *the* ~, the body as a functional whole, as *the poison has passed into the* ~ or *his* ~; *Ptolemaic* etc. ~, set of hypotheses or principles composing Ptolemy's etc. theory; *Devonian* etc.~, set of strata etc. so named). 2. Method, organization, considered principles of procedure, (principle of) classification, (~ *of government*; ~ *do you go on?*; *lacks, works with,* ~; *Linnaean, natural,* etc.,~, classifications with different criteria), whence ~LESS a. 3. (mus.). Braced staffs of score. [f. F *système* or LL f. Gk *sustēma -atos* (*sy-* = SYN-, *histēmi* set, -M)]

sўstĕmät′ic, a. Methodical, according to a plan, not casual or sporadic or unintentional, classificatory, (~*ic worker, liar, insolence, nomenclature*). Hence or cogn.

~ICALLY adv., **sўs′tĕmatize**(3) v.t., **sўs′tĕmatism**(1), **sўs′tĕmatist**(1), **sўs′tĕmatizer**¹, **sўstĕmatiza′tion**, nn. [f. LL f. late Gk *sustēmatikos* (prec., -ic)]

sўstĕm′/ic, a. (physiol.). Of the bodily system as a whole, not confined to a particular part; (of insecticides, fungicides, etc.) entering the plant via roots or shoots and passing through the tissue. Hence~ICALLY adv. [irreg. f. SYSTEM + -IC]

sўs′tolĕ, n. (physiol.). Contraction of heart etc. alternate with DIASTOLE. Hence **sўstŏl′ic** a. [f. Gk *sustolē* (*sustellō*, see SYSTALTIC)]

sўs′tўle, a. With columns set comparatively close together. [f. L f. Gk SY(*stulos* STYLE²)]

sўs′tўlous, a. (bot.). With styles united. [as prec., -ous]

sўz′ўḡў, n. (astron.). Conjunction or opposition. [f. LL f. Gk *suzugia* f. *suzeugnumi* (*sy-*=SYN-, *zeugnumi* f. *zugon* yoke)]

T

T, t, (tē), letter (pl. *T*s, T's). T-shaped thing, esp. attrib., as *T-bandage, -bar, -bolt, -joint, -pipe,* -SQUARE; *suits me, hit it off*, etc., *to a T*, exactly, to a nicety; *cross the T's*, (fig.) be minutely accurate, also, emphasize a point.

‖ **ta** (tah), int. (nursery, vulg.). Thank you, as *ta muchly, must say ta*.

taal (tahl), n. *The* ~ (hist.), term used for the earlier form of AFRIKAANS. [Du., = language, cogn. w. TALE]

tăb, n., & v.t. (colloq.; -bb-). 1. Small flap, strip, tag, or tongue, as part of or appendage to garment etc., e.g. metallic binding at end of bootlace, (also *ear-*~) flap at side of cap to protect ear; (mil.) mark on collar distinguishing · staff-officer; (colloq.) account, tally, check (esp. in phr. *keep* ~ (or ~s) *on*, keep account of, have under observation or in check; **baggage-*~, luggage-label. 2. v.t. Tabulate, record. [c. 1600, of unkn. orig.]

tăb′ard, n. (Hist.) coarse outer garment worn by the poor, knight's garment worn over armour; herald's coat blazoned with arms of sovereign. [ME, f. OF *tabart*, of unkn. orig.]

tăb′arĕt, n. Upholstery fabric of alternate satin & watered-silk stripes. [mod. trade wd, perh. f. TABBY]

tăbasheer′, -shir (-ẽr), n. Kind of opal found in joints of bamboo & used in E.-Ind. medicine. [f. Pg. or F f. Hind. & Arab. (*-ir*)]

tăbb′ў, n., & v.t. 1. Watered fabric esp. silk (often attrib.). 2.(Also~ *cat*) brindled or mottled or streaked cat, esp. of grey or brownish colour with dark stripes; cat, esp. female. 3. Gossiping woman esp. old maid. 4. (Also ~ *moth*) kinds of moth. 5. Kind of concrete. 6. v.t. Give wavy appearance to (fabric). [sense 1 f. F *tabis*

f. Arab. *'attābiy* a quarter of Baghdad; remaining senses of obsc. orig.]

tăbĕfăc′tion, n. Emaciation due to disease. [f. LL *tabefacere* (*tabēre* f. TABES, see -FACTION)]

‖ **tăb′erdăr,** n. Scholar of Queen's College, Oxford. [= *tabarder* (TABARD + -ER[1]), from former dress]

tăb′ernăcl|e, n., & v.t. & i. **1.** (Bibl.) fixed or movable habitation usu. of slight construction, (fig.) human body; *Feast of T~es*, Jewish autumn festival commemorating the dwelling of the Jews in wilderness; (Jewish hist.) tent used as sanctuary before final settlement of Jews in Palestine. **2.** (freq. derog.). Place of public worship. **3.** Receptacle for pyx or eucharistic elements. **4.** (archit.). Canopied stall, niche, or pinnacle, *~e-work,* series, tracery characteristic, of such *~es,* whence *~*ED[2] (-ld) a. **5.** Socket or double post for hinged mast that requires lowering to pass under bridges. **6.** vb. (fig.). Provide with shelter; dwell temporarily. So **tăbernăc′ūlAR**[2] a. [ME, f. OF, or L *tabernaculum* tent (*taberna* hut, see -CULE)]

tăb′ēs (-z), n. (med.). Emaciation; *dorsal ~,* wasting disease of spinal cord, locomotor ataxia. [L]

tabĕt′ic, a. & n. **1.** Of, affected with, (esp. dorsal) tabes. **2.** n. *~* patient. So **tabēs′CENCE,** **tăb′iTUDE,** nn., **tabēs′CENT,** **tăb′IC, tăb′ID**[1], aa., **tăb′idLY**[2] adv. [irreg. f. prec. + -t- + -IC]

tăb′inĕt, n. Watered fabric of silk & wool. [as TABARET]

tăb′lature, n. (arch.). Mental picture; graphic description. [f. F (foll., -URE)]

tā′ble, n., & v.t. **1.** Article of furniture consisting of flat top of wood or marble etc. & one or more usu. vertical supports esp. one on which meals are laid out, work done, or games played; *breakfast, luncheon, dinner, tea, supper, -~, ~* used for such meals or on which such meal is laid out (*at ~,* while taking meal at *~,* as *refused to talk politics at ~; under the ~,* esp. drunk after dinner); each half of folding backgammon-~; *billiard-~* (for billiards, with slate top covered with green cloth); LORD'S, ROUND[1], KNEE[1]-*hole,* DRESSING-, TOILET-, *~.* **2.** Part of machine--tool on which work is put to be operated on. **3.** Slab of wood, stone, etc. **4.** Matter written on this, esp. *the two ~s or the ~s of the law or covenant or testimony,* ten commandments, *the twelve ~s,* laws promulgated in Rome 451–450 B.C., principal source of Roman jurisprudence. **5.** Level area, plateau. **6.** (archit.). Flat usu. rectangular surface, horizontal moulding esp. cornice. **7.** Flat surface of gem, cut gem with two flat faces. **8.** Palm of hand, esp. part indicating character or fortune. **9.** Each of two bony layers of skull. **10.** Company seated at (dinner- etc.) *~,* as *kept the ~ amused.* **11.** (Quantity &

quality of) food provided at *~,* as *keeps a good ~, expenses of his ~.* **12.** List of facts, numbers, etc., systematically arranged esp. in columns, matter contained in this, as *mathematical~s* of logarithms, trigonometrical ratios, etc.), *~s of weights & measures, knows his multiplication ~ up to 12 times 12, ~ of* (i.e. *prohibited*) DEGREES, *~ of* CONTENT[1]*s.* **13.** *Lay, lie, on the ~,* postpone (measure, report, etc., in Parliament etc.), be postponed, indefinitely; *turn the ~s* (*on* person, or abs.), reverse relations (between), esp. pass from inferior to superior position [f. backgammon sense of *~s*]. **14.** *~-beer,* ordinary beer used at *~; ~-book,* ornamental usu. illustrated book kept on esp. drawing--room *~; ~-clamp* (for fastening thing to *~); ~-cloth* (of white linen etc. for use at meals, of coloured material for use at other times); *~-cut,* (of gem) cut with flat top; *~-flap,* hinged end of *~-top,* lowered when not in use; *~-knife,* steel knife for use at *~; ~-land,* extensive elevated region with level surface, plateau; *~-leaf,* piece that may be inserted in top of *~* to increase its length, also, *~-flap; ~-lifting, -moving, -rapping, -tipping, -turning,* lifting etc. of *~* apparently without physical force, as spiritualistic phenomenon; *~-linen, ~-cloths,* napkins, etc.; *~-money;* allowance to higher officers in army etc. for official hospitality, charge to members of club for use of dining--room; *~-*SPOON; *~-talk,* miscellaneous talk at *~* (often as title of book); *~ tennis,* PING-PONG; *~-tomb,* flat-topped chest-like tomb in Roman catacombs; *~-ware* (for use at *~); ~-water,* mineral water bottled for use at *~.* Hence *~*FUL n. **15.** v.t. Lay (measure etc., as above) on the *~.* **16.** Set (timbers) together with alternate grooves & projections in each to prevent shifting. **17.** Strengthen (sail) with wide hems. Hence **tăb′l**ING[1](1, 2) n. [ME & OF *table* f. L *tabula*; OE *tabule* dir. f. L]

tăb′leau (-lō), n. (pl. *-eaux* pr. -ōz). Picturesque presentation, esp. (also *~ vivant,* see Ap.; pl. *~x vivants;* lit. living picture) silent & motionless group of persons etc. arranged to represent a scene; dramatic or effective situation suddenly brought about; (as int., after description of incident) picture the scene!; *~ curtains* (theatr.), pair of curtains to draw across & meet in the middle of the stage in place of the usual drop-curtain. [F, = picture, dim. of prec.]

table d'hôte (tahbl-dōt′), n. Common table for guests at hotel; *~ dinner* etc. (served in hotel etc. at fixed hour & price), cf. À LA CARTE. [F, = host's table]

tăb′lĕt, n. **1.** Thin sheet of ivory, wood, etc., for writing on, esp. each of a set fastened together; (usu. pl.) such set. **2.** Small slab esp. with or for inscription, as *votive~.* **3.** Small flat piece of prepared substance, esp. fixed weight or measure of a drug brought by pressure or addition of gum into convenient shape. 4. (Also *tablette'*) projecting horizontal coping of wall. [ME, f. OF *tablete* (TABLE, -ETTE)]

tablier' (-lyā), n. Woman's small apron or apron-like part of dress. [F]

tăb'loid, n. 1. = TABLET (sense 3; P). 2. Newspaper, usu. popular in style, printed on sheets of half normal size; also attrib., as ~ *journalism*. [-OID]

taboo', n., a., & v.t. 1. (Among Polynesians etc.) system, act, of setting apart person or thing as accursed or sacred; ban, prohibition. 2. adj. Under a ban, prohibited, consecrated. 3. v.t. Put (thing, practice, etc.) under ~, exclude or prohibit by authority or social influence, as *the subject was ~ed*. [f. Tongan *ta-bu*]

tăb'or, n. (hist.). Small drum, esp. one used to accompany pipe. [ME, f. OF *tabour* f. Arab. *ṭabl*, pl. *ṭubūl*, cf. TAMBOUR]

tăb'ouret (-borīt), n. Small seat usu. without arms or back, stool; embroidery--frame. [F, = stool, dim. as prec.]

tabu. Var. of TABOO.

tăb'ŭla, n. (pl. *-ae*). (Anat.) hard flat surface of bone etc.; ~ *rās'a*, erased tablet, (fig.) human mind at birth viewed as having no innate ideas. [L, = TABLE]

tăb'ŭlar, a. Of, arranged in, computed etc. by means of, tables, as a ~ *statement*, ~ *values, results, computations, arranged in* ~ *form*, ~ *difference* (between successive logarithms etc. in mathematical tables); broad & flat like a table, as ~ *surface*; (formed) in thin plates, as ~ *structure*. Hence ~LY[2] adv. [f. L *tabularis* (prec., see -AR[1])]

tăb'ŭl|āte, v.t., & a. 1. Arrange (figures, facts) in tabular form, whence ~A'TION, ~ātOR, nn.; give flat surface to. 2. adj. (-*at*). Having flat surface, composed of thin plate. [f. LL *tabulare* f. TABULA + -ATE[2, 3]]

tăc'amahăc (-*ama*-), n. Gum resin from some S.-Amer. & other trees; the balsam poplar. [Sp. (-*ca*), f. Aztec *tecomahiyac*]

tăc'-au-tăc' (-ō-), n. (fencing). Parry combined with riposte; rapid succession of attacks & parries. [F, imit.]

tā'cē, v.i. imperat. Be silent (~ *is Latin for a candle*, veiled injunction = MUM[1]). [L]

tā'cĕt, mus. direction indicating silence of voice or instrument. [L, = is silent]

tăch(e), n. (bibl.). A clasp, link. [ME, f. OF *tache* fibula; rel. to *attach*, *detach*; doublet of TACK]

tachŏm'ĕter (-k-), n. Instrument for measuring velocity. So **tachŏm'ETRY** n. [f. Gk *takhos* speed + -METER]

tăchycărd'ia (-kĭ-), n. (path.). Abnormally rapid heart-action as a disease. [f. Gk as foll. & see CARDIAC]

tachỹg'raph|ȳ (-k-), n. Stenography, esp. that of ancient Greeks & Romans. Hence ~ER[1] n., **tăchỹgrăph'IC(AL)** aa. [f. Gk *takhus* swift + -GRAPHY]

tăch'ȳ|lȳte (-k-), n. A vitreous form of basalt. Hence ~lȳt'IC a. [as prec. + -*lutos* f. *luō* loose, from ready fusion under blowpipe]

tachym'ĕter (-k-), n. Surveyor's instrument for rapid location of points. [as prec. + -METER]

tā'cit, a. Understood, implied, existing, without being stated, as ~ *consent*, *agreement*, *understanding*; abstaining from speech or action (~ *speculator*). Hence ~LY[2] adv. [f. L *tacitus* silent (*tacēre* be silent)]

tā'citŭrn, a. Reserved in speech, not given to much speaking. So **tăcitŭr'-ITY** n. [f. F (-*ne*) or L *taciturnus* as prec.]

tăck, n., & v.t. & i. 1. Small sharp flat--headed nail of iron, copper, etc., for securing carpet etc. (*tin-*~, iron ~ coated with tin; BRASS ~*s*). 2. pl. Long stitches as temporary fastening in needlework. 3. (naut.). Rope for securing corner of some sails, corner to which this is fastened; direction in which vessel moves as determined by position of sails (*port*, *starboard*, ~, with wind on port, starboard, side); temporary change of direction in sailing to take advantage of side wind etc., esp. each of several alternate movements to port & starboard (*by* ~ *& * ~, by successive ~*s*). 4. (fig.). Course of action or policy, as *must change our* ~, *am on the right* or *wrong* ~, *try another* ~. 5. = foll. (Parl. sense). 6. Sticky condition of varnish etc., whence ~'INESS n., ~'Y[2] a. 7. [prob. diff. wd]. Food, fare, esp. HARD ~; *soft* ~, bread, good fare. 8. ~-*driver*, machine that automatically places & drives ~*s*; ~-*hammer*, light hammer for driving ~*s*, usu. with claw for extracting ~*s*. 9. vb. Fasten (carpet etc., often *down*) with ~*s*, stitch (pieces or parts of cloth etc.) lightly together; (fig.) annex, append, (thing *to* or *on to* another, esp. as in foll.). 10. Change ship's course (often *about* by shifting ~*s* & sails (cf. WEAR[3]); (fig.) change one's conduct, policy, etc. Hence ~'ER[1](1, 2) n. [ME *tak* etc., of obsc. orig.; doublet of TACH(E), though no forms in *k* or *q* are recorded in OF]

tăck'ing, n. In vbl senses, esp.: (law) priority of a third or subsequent mortgage etc. to a second of which notice was not given; ‖ (Parl.) appending of an extraneous clause to a money bill to secure its passing House of Lords, which cannot amend money bills. [-ING[1]]

tăc'kle, n., & v.t. & i. 1. (Also *block & *~) mechanism esp. of ropes, pulley-blocks, hooks, etc., for lifting weights, managing sails or spars, etc. (*naut. pr.* tā'kl); windlass with its ropes & hooks; requisites for a task or sport, as *fishing-*~; grasping or holding or obstructing esp. of opponent in football; ~-*block*, pulley over which rope runs; ~-*fall*, rope connecting blocks of a ~. 2. vb. Grapple with, grasp with endeavour to hold or manage or overcome, (opponent, awkward thing or business problem); (footb.) obstruct or seize & stop (player running with ball); secure by means of ~; ~ *to* (colloq.), fall to work vigorously, set to. Hence **tăck'**ING¹(1, 3, 6) n. [ME, f. MLG, MDu. *takel*, f. *taken* lay hold of, see -LE(1)]

tăct, n. Intuitive perception of what is fitting esp. of the right thing to do or say, adroitness in dealing with persons or circumstances, whence ~'FUL, ~'LESS, aa., ~'fuLLY² adv., ~'lèssNESS n. [F, f. L *tactus -ūs* (sense of) touch (*tangere tact-* touch)]

tăc'tical, a. Of tactics; (of bombing) carried out in immediate support of military or naval operations; adroitly planning or planned. Hence ~LY² adv. [f. Gk *taktikos* (foll.)+-AL]

tăc'tics, n. (As sing. or pl.) art of disposing military or naval or air forces esp. (cf. STRATEGY, LOGISTICS) in actual contact with enemy; (pl.) procedure calculated to gain some end, skilful device(s), as *cannot approve these* ~; so occas. in sing. form **tăc'tic** n. Hence **tăcti'**CIAN (-ĭshn) n. [f. Gk *taktika* neut. pl. (*tassō* arrange, see -IC)]

tăc'tile, a. Of, perceived by, connected with, the sense of touch, as ~ *impression, organ*, so **tăc'tuAL** a., **tăc'tuAL**LY² adv.; tangible; (paint.) producing or having to do with the effect of solidity (~ *values* etc.). Hence **tăctil'**ITY n. [f. L *tactilis* (*tangere tact-* touch, see -ILE)]

tăd'pōle, n. Larva of batrachian e.g. frog from time it leaves egg till loss of gills & tail; ~*fish*, European fish with large flat head. [ME *taddepolle* (TOAD+POLL¹, f. size of head)]

***taed'ium vit'ae**, n. (path.). Weariness of life with tendency to suicide. [L]

tael (tāl), n. Chinese ounce (= 1⅓ oz avoirdupois) esp. of silver as former monetary unit. [Port., f. Malay *tahil* weight]

taen'i|a, n. (pl. ~ae). (Archit.) fillet on top of Doric epistyle; (anat.) ribbonlike part esp. of brain; roller bandage; tapeworm; (Gk & Rom. ant.) fillet, headband. Hence ~OID a. [L, f. Gk *tainia*]

tăff'èta, n. Kinds of silk or linen fabric esp. thin glossy silk of plain texture. [ME, f. OF *taffetas* f. Pers. *taftah* (*tāftan* shine)]

tăff'rail, **tăff'erel** (-frĭl), n. Rail round stern of vessel; (-*erel*) upper part of stern. [f. Du. *tafereel* panel dim. of *tafel* f. L as TABLE, assim. to RAIL¹]

Tăff'ў¹, n. (colloq.). Welshman. [W pronunc. of *Davy* = *David*]

taffy². See TOFFEE.

tăf'ia, n. (W. Ind.). Kind of rum distilled from molasses etc. [native]

tăg, n., & v.t. & i. (-gg-). 1. Metal point at end of lace. 2. Loop at back of boot used in pulling it on. 3. Address label, esp. one for tying on. 4. Loose or ragged end of anything; ragged lock of wool on sheep. 5. Appendage; (theatr.) closing

speech addressed to audience; trite quotation, stock phrase, refrain of song. 6. (Tip of) animal's tail. 7. [perh. diff. wd]. Children's game in which one chases the rest (*cross-, long*, etc., ~, forms of this). 8. *~ *day*, = FLAG⁴-*day*; ~'*rag*, = RAG¹~; ~-*sore*, pustular disease of sheep; ~'*tail*, kind of worm, sycophant. 9. vb. Furnish (lace etc., literary composition) with a ~. 10. Join (thing, esp. piece of writing, *to* or *on to* another, things *together*), find rhymes for (verses), string (rhymes) together. 11. Shear away ~s from (sheep). 12. (colloq.). Follow closely or persistently. 13. Touch (person pursued) in game of ~. [ME, of unkn. orig.]

tagēt'ēs (-jĕtēz), n. Kinds of plant of aster family with showy yellow or orange flowers. [f. L *Tages*, Etruscan divinity]

tăgg'er (-g-), n. In vbl senses; also or esp.: pursuer (also called *it*) in game of tag; (pl.) thin sheet iron, whether coated with tin or (*black*~s) not. [-ER¹]

tahsil' (-ēl), n. Territorial subdivision in India for revenue purposes. Hence ~**dār** n., native collector of revenue in ~. [Hind. & Arab., = collection; Pers. *dār* holder]

taiga (ti'gah), n. Coniferous forest between tundra & steppe. [Russ.]

tail¹, n., & v.t. & i. 1. Hindmost part of animal esp. when prolonged beyond rest of body, as *dog* WAG¹s *his* ~, *tail* WAG¹s *dog, dog has his* ~ *between his legs* (as sign of alarm or dejection; often fig. of person); ~s *up*, (of persons, fig.) in good spirits; *turn* ~, turn one's back, run away; *twist the* LION's ~, *drop pinch of* SALT *on* ~ *of*, PASHA *of three* etc. ~s. 2. Thing like or suggesting ~ in shape or position, hind or lower or subordinate or inferior part, slender part or prolongation, as ~ (luminous train) *of comet*, ~ (outer corner) *of the eye*, ~ (end) *of procession* etc., ~ (weaker members) *of the cricket XI* (or other sports team), ~ *margin* (at foot of page), *followed by a* ~ (long train) *of attendants*, at the ~ (back) *of a cart*, ~ (string & paper appendage at lower end) *of a kite, cow's*~, frayed end of rope etc., ~ (= STEM¹) *of musical note*, ~ (part below line) *of a g* etc., ~ (exposed end) *of slate* or *tile* in roof, ~ (unexposed end) *of brick* or *stone* in wall, ~ (slender backward prolongation) *of butterfly's wing*, ~ (comparative calm at end) *of a gale*, ~ (calm stretch following rough water) *of a stream*, ~ *of the trenches* (fortif.), part first made by advancing party, *make* HEAD¹ *or* ~ *of*, PIGTAIL. 3. pl. = ~coat, as *boys go into*~s *at sixteen*. 4. (In tossing) ~ or usu. ~s, reverse of coin turned upwards (see HEAD). 5. ~*bay*, part of canal lock between ~-*gate* & lower pond; ~-*board*, hinged or removable back of cart; ~-*braid* (for protecting hem of skirt); ~-*coat*, man's morning or evening coat with long skirt divided at back into ~s & cut away in front; ~-*gate*, lower gate of canal lock; ~-*light* (carried at back of train, car, cycle, etc.); ~'*piece*, decoration in blank space at end of chapter etc., triangular piece of wood to which lower ends of strings are fastened in some musical instruments; ~'*pipe*, suction--pipe of pump, (v.t.) fasten something to ~ of (dog, fig. person); ~-*race*, part of mill-race below water-wheel; ~-*spin* (aviation), kind of spinning dive. Hence (-)~ED[2] (-ld), ~'LESS, aa. **6.** vb. Furnish with ~. **7.** Remove the stalks of (fruit); dock ~ of (lamb etc.). **8.** (colloq.). Shadow, follow closely. **9.** Join (thing *on to* another). **10.** ~ *after*, follow closely; ~ *away* or *off*, (of persons, dogs, etc.) fall behind or away in scattered line; ~ *in*, fasten (timber) by one end into wall etc.; ~ *to the tide*, ~ *up and down stream*, (of anchored vessel) swing up & down with tide. [OE *tægel*, *tægl*, OHG *zagal*, ON *tagl* f. Gmc **taglaz*]

tail², n. & a. (law). **1.** Limited ownership (*in*~, on those terms); estate limited to a person & heirs of his body. **2.** adj. So limited, esp. *estate* ~, FEE-~. [ME, f. OF *taille* notch, cut, tax, f. *taillier* cut f. LL *taliare* (L *talea* slip of wood); see TALLY]

tail'ing, n. In vbl senses of TAIL¹; also or esp.: unexposed end of brick or stone or beam in wall; (pl.) refuse or inferior part of grain, ore, etc.; blur or other fault in calico-printing. [-ING¹]

tail'or, n., & v.i. & t. **1.** Maker of (esp. men's) garments esp. to order (*the*~*makes the man*; *nine*~*s go to a man*; *ride like a* ~, badly); ~-*bird*, kinds of small bird sewing leaves together to form nest; ~-*made*, (esp. of woman's dress) made by ~ usu. w. little ornament & w. special attention to exact fit; ~'*s chair* (without legs), for sitting cross-legged as ~ at work; ~'*s cramp* (in fingers & thumbs); ~'*s twist*, kind of strong silk thread. Hence ~ESS¹ n. **2.** vb. Be, work as, a ~, whence ~ING¹ n.; make clothes for (chiefly in p.p., as *well-~ed*). [ME & AF *taillour*, = OF *tailleor* f. Rom. **taliatorem* f. LL *taliare* TAIL², -OR]

tain, n. Thin tin plate; tin foil for backing mirror. [F, = *étain* tin]

taint, n., & v.t. & i. **1.** Spot, trace, of decay or corruption or disease (lit. & fig.), corrupt condition, infection, as *there was a* ~ *of insanity in the family*, *the moral* ~ *had spread among all classes*, *without* ~ *of commercialism*. **2.** vb. Introduce corruption or disease into, infect, be infected, as ~*ed meat*, ~*s all it touches*, *meat will* ~ *readily in hot weather*, *his mind was* ~*ed*; ~*ed goods* (in trade-unionism), goods that members of a union must not handle because non-union labour has been employed on them or for similar reasons. Hence ~'LESS a., ~'lèssLY² adv. [ME, f.

OF *teint* n. & p.p. of *teindre* TINGE; partly also aphetic f. ATTAINT]

Tai'ping', **Tae-**, (ti-), n. One of those who took part in a rebellion in China (1850-64). [f. Chin. *t'ai p'ing* great peace]

taj (tahj), n. Tall cap of Mohammedan dervish. [Pers. f. Arab.]

tāke¹, v.t. & i. (*tŏŏk*, ~*n*). **I.** General senses. **1.** Lay hold of with the hand(s) or other part of the body or with any instrument (lit. & fig.), grasp, seize, capture, catch by pursuit or surprise, captivate, win, gain, as ~ *it between your finger & thumb*, *took him by the throat*, ~ *it up with the tongs*, ~ *the* BULL¹ *by the horns*, *deuce* ~ *it!*, ~ BIT¹ *between teeth*, ~ *a fortress*, ~ *by* STORM, *took 113 prisoners*, *was* ~*n prisoner* or *captive*, *took his bishop* (at chess), ~ *the odd trick* (at cards), ~*s* (gains, receives in payment) £*40 a week*, *took* (gained) *little by this move*, *took first prize*, ~ *the* CAKE or *biscuit* (sl.), *rabbit* ~*n in trap*, *took* (surprised, caught) *him in the act* or *at a disadvantage*, *was* ~*n ill* or colloq. *bad*, ~*n aback*, *what* ~*s* (captivates) *my fancy*, *was much* ~*n* (charmed) *with* or *by her manners*, *novel did not* ~ (become popular), *vaccine did not* ~ (operate). **2.** (See also 9 below). Assume possession of, procure e.g. by purchase, acquire, avail oneself of, use, use up, consume, require as instrument, material, agent, etc., as ~*s whatever he can lay his hand on*, *wish you would not* ~ *my bicycle*, ~ (assume or enjoy as one's right) *precedence*, *took his degree*, ~ ORDER¹*s*, ‖ ~ SILK, *shall* ~ *a holiday*, (cooking direction) ~ *1 oz of curry-powder*, *do you* ~ (buy regularly, subscribe to) *Punch?*, *am not taking any* (sl.), decline offer, *took* (engaged) *seats in advance*, *must* ~ *lessons*, *lodgings*, *a taxi*, *will* ~ (buy) *2 lb.*, ~ *legal*, *medical*, etc., *advice*, *consult lawyer etc.* (& see below), ~ (as instance) *the French Revolution*, *has* ~*n a partner*, *a wife*, (arch.) *took to* (as) *wife Jane Smith*, ~ *a* BACK¹ *seat*, *took his seat on the* WOOLSACK, *must* ~ *the liberty of differing from you*, *must* ~ *leave to differ*, *took a mean advantage*, *do not* ~ *advantage* (avail yourself unfairly) *of his youth*, ~ *the opportunity*, *will* ~ (drink) *a cup of tea*, ~*s too much alcohol*, *these things* ~ *time*, ~ *your time*, do not hurry, *it* ~*s a lot of doing* (is hard to do), ~*s a poet to translate* Virgil, transitive verbs ~ *an object*. **3.** Cause to come with one, carry with one, conduct, convey, remove, dispossess person etc. of, as ~ *the letters to the post*, *the dog for a walk*, *the children to the pantomime*, *the corkscrew from the shelf*, ~ *for a* RIDE, ~*s his readers with him* (engrosses their attention), ~ *him through* (make him read) *a book of* Livy, *took him into partnership*, ~*s all the fun out of it*, ~ *to* TASK, ~ *in hand*, undertake, start doing or dealing with, undertake the control or reform of (*the boy wants taking in hand*), (see also special uses w. advv. & prepp.).

4. Catch, be infected with, (cold, fever, etc.). **5.** Conceive, experience, indulge, give play to, exert, as ~ *offence, umbrage,* ~ *a fancy to,* ~*s a pride in his work, a pleasure in contradicting,* ~ *pity on him,* ~ *no notice,* ~ *heed, pains, trouble.* **6.** Ascertain (person's measure, height, temperature, address, etc.) by inquiry, measurement, etc. **7.** Apprehend, grasp mentally, infer, conclude, understand, interpret, as *I* ~ *your meaning* or (arch.) *you, I* ~ *this to be ironical, I* ~ *it that we are to wait here,* ~ *person at his* WORD[1], *how would you* ~ (translate, interpret) *this passage?,* ~ *it for granted,* assume it, *do you* ~ *me for* (think me) *a fool?* **8.** Treat or regard in specified manner, adopt specified attitude towards, as ~ *things coolly,* ~ *it easy, should* ~ *it kindly of you* (be obliged) *if you would answer my letter, must not* ~ *it ill of him* (resent his conduct), ~ *to* HEART, ~ *as read,* dispense with the actual reading of (minutes etc.). **9.** (See also 2 above.) Accept, put up with, submit to, adopt, choose, receive, derive, as ~ *the offer,* ~ *what you can get, the bet was* ~*n,* ~*n & offered* (abbr. *t. & o.,* phr. used in recording betting odds), *I took him* (his bet), *must* ~ *us as you find us, will* ~ *no nonsense, will not* ~ *this treatment, took it like a lamb, will not* ~ *a hint,* ~ *advice,* act on it (& see above), *you may* ~ *it from me* or ~ *my word for it,* I, a well--informed person, assure you, ~ *sides,* join one of two parties, ~ (hold, adopt) *a different view,* ~*s its name from the inventor.* **10.** Perform, execute, make, undertake, negotiate, deal with, as *took work for a friend,* ~ *notes,* ~ *a photograph, took a sudden leap, horse will not* ~ *the fence,* ~ *a walk,* ||~ (be examined in) *the mathematical tripos,* ~ (conduct) *the evening service,* ~ *a glance round you, took a deep breath,* ~ *an oath.* **11.** Photograph, come out *well* etc. when photographed, as ~ *him in cap & gown, does not* ~ *well.* **12.** ~ *account of,* include in one's reckoning, not overlook; ~ *aim,* direct weapon or missile (*at* object); ~ *care,* be careful, be on one's guard, not neglect or fail, be cautious in arranging or deciding, as ~ *care!,* ~ *care to leave plenty of room,* ~ *care not to wake the baby,* ~ *care how you speak* or *what you say to him;* ~ *care of,* be careful of, be in charge of, *be adequate provision for, *be able to deal with; ~ *one's chance,* accept risk (*of*); ~ *earth,* (of fox etc., fig. of person) escape into hole; ~ EFFECT[1], EXCEPTION, HEART (*of grace*), HOLD[2]; ~ *it* (colloq.), endure punishment etc.; ~ LEAVE[1] (*of*); ~ *one's life in one's hand,* risk it; ~ *person's* esp. God's *name in vain,* use it lightly or profanely; ~ PART[1]; ~ *place,* happen; ~ STOCK (*of, in*); ~ *the* WALL, ~ WIND[1]. **II.** Spec. uses w. prepp., advv., & adv. phrr. **1.** ~ *after,* resemble (person, esp. parent) in character, feature, etc. **2.** ~ *back* (colloq.), retract (words). **3.** ~ *down*: write down, as ~ *down his name & address, took down the sermon in shorthand;* humble, esp. ~ *person down a* PEG[1] *or two;* swallow (food etc.) esp. with difficulty or reluctance; remove (building, structure) by taking it to pieces. **4.** ~ *from,* diminish, lessen, weaken, as *such faults do not* ~ *from his credit as a historian.* **5.** ~ *in*: admit, receive, (lodgers, guest, etc.); ~ (lady) *in* (often *to dinner*), conduct from drawing--room to dining-room & sit beside; receive (washing, sewing, typewriting, etc.) to be done at home; include, comprise; reduce (garment etc.) to smaller compass, furl (sail); understand, digest mentally; believe (false statement); deceive; cheat; ||~ (newspaper etc.) by subscription; ~*↳in* n., a fraud, deception, piece of humbug. **6.** ~ *into*: ~ *into* one's *confidence,* confide in; ~ *into* one's *head,* conceive, get hold of, (idea), imagine, adopt the belief, (*that, it . . . that*), resolve (*to* do). **7.** ~ *off*: remove (clothes, hat, etc.) from the body (~ *off* one's *hai to,* fig., applaud as admirable); remove, conduct away, as *took him off to the station, took himself off,* went off; deduct (part of price); drink off; ridicule by imitation, mimic; jump, spring, (*from, at,* place); (aviation) start from rest & become airborne; ~*-off* n., caricature, spot from which one jumps, (aviation) becoming airborne, (croquet) stroke causing one's own ball to go forward while touching but scarcely moving another. **8.** ~ *on*: undertake (work, responsibility); ~ *person on at golf* etc., play with him; (colloq.) show violent emotion, make a fuss. **9.** ~ *out*: cause to come out, bring or convey out, as ~ *him out for a walk, books must not be* ~*n out of the library;* remove (stain etc.); (bridge) remove (one's partner) from the suit he has called by bidding a fresh suit or no trumps; ~ *the nonsense* etc. *out of* person, cure him of it; accept payment of (debt etc.) or compensation for (injury etc.) *in,* as *took it out in cigars & drinks;* ~ *it out of,* have revenge on, get satisfaction from, exhaust the strength of; procure, get issued, (patent, summons, etc.). **10.** ~ *over,* succeed to management or ownership of (business etc.); ~*-over bid,* an offer to purchase shares which will secure for the bidder control of a company. **11.** ~ *to*: begin, fall into the habit of, begin to busy oneself with, as *took to humming a tune,* ~ *to bad habits, literature;* conceive a liking for (person etc.). **12.** ~ *up*: lift up; absorb, occupy, engage, as *sponges* ~ *up water,* ~*s up all my time, my attention; train stops to* ~ *up* (admit) *passengers;* ~ *into* custody; adopt as protégé; interrupt or correct (speaker); enter upon (profession, subject); pursue (matter, inquiry) further; secure, fasten, (dropped stitch, artery, etc.); furnish the amount of (loan

etc.); ~ *up with*, consort with; ~ *up the*
CUDGELS, GAUNTLET[1], GLOVE; ~*up* n.
(mech.), kinds of device for tightening
band etc. in machine, drawing up slack
of thread, removing material that has
been operated on, etc. **13.** ~ (*it*) *upon* or
on one *to*, venture, presume, to. [late OE
tacan f. ON *taka*, in ME superseding
niman]

tāke², n. Amount (*of* fish, game, etc.)
taken or caught; (print.) amount of copy
set up at one time; takings, esp. money
received at theatre for seats; (cinemat.)
a scene that has been or is to be photographed; GIVE² & ~. [f. prec.]

tāk'er, n. In vbl senses, esp. one who
takes a bet, as *no ~s, a few ~s at 5 to 4*.
[-ER¹]

ta'kin(tah-), n. Tibetan horned ruminant.
[native]

tāk'ing¹, n. In vbl senses, esp.: (pl.)
money taken in business, receipts; (arch.)
state of agitation, as *was in a great ~*.
[-ING¹]

tāk'ing², a. Attractive, captivating;
catching, infectious. Hence ~LY² adv.,
~NESS n. [-ING²]

tăl'apoin, n. **1.** Buddhist monk in Ceylon, Siam, etc. **2.** Kind of monkey. [f.
Port. *talapão*, of E.-Ind. orig.]

talār'ia, n. pl. Winged boots or sandals as
attribute of Mercury, Iris, & others. [L]

tal'botype (tawl-), n. Photographic process invented by W. H. Fox Talbot in
1840, the basis of that now used. [TYPE]

tălc, n., & v.t. **1.** A magnesium silicate usu.
found in flat smooth often transparent
plates & used as lubricator etc.; (pop.,
commerc.) mica esp. as glazing-material.
Hence tăl(c)k'Y², ~'OID, ~'OSE¹, ~'OUS,
aa. **2.** v.t. Treat with~. [F, or f. med. L
talcum f. Arab. *talq*]

tăl'cīte, n. A massive variety of talc.
[-ITE¹]

tăl'cum, n. = TALC; ~ *powder*, powdered
talc for toilet use, usu. perfumed. [med.
L]

tāle, n. **1.** True or usu. fictitious narrative
esp. one imaginatively treated, story, as
*tell him a ~, a true ~ of the Crusades, old
wives' ~s, marvellous legendary ~s*; ~ *of a
tub*, idle fiction; TELL *the ~*; *prefer to tell
my own ~* (give my own account of the
matter); *thing tells its own ~* (is significant,
requires no comment, explains itself).
2. Malicious report whether true or false,
as *all sorts of ~s will get about, if all ~s
be true* (esp. as preface to scandal); *tell ~s
(out of school)*, report esp. with malicious
intention what is meant to be secret; ~*-
bearer*, person who does this, so ~'*bearing*
a. & n.; ~'*teller*, one who tells ~s (in
either sense). **3.** ‖ (arch., rhet., poet.).
Number, total, as *the ~ is complete,
shepherd tells his ~* (of sheep). [OE *talu*,
OS, ON *tala*, OHG *zala*, f. Gmc *talō* f.
tal- see TELL]

tăl'ent, n. **1.** Special aptitude, faculty,

gift, (*for* music etc., *for* doing; see *Matt.*
xxv. 14–30), high mental ability, whence
~ED², ~LESS, aa. **2.** Persons of ~, as *all
the ~ of the country, looking out for local
~, ministry of all the ~s*; (sport. sl.) *the ~*,
those who take odds etc. relying on their
own judgement & knowledge, opp. to
bookmakers. **3.** Ancient weight & money
of account among Greeks, Romans,
Assyrians, etc., of varying value. **4.** ~*-
money*, bonus to professional cricketer
etc. for especially good performance.
[ME, f. OF f. L *talentum* f. Gk *talanton*
balance, weight, sum of money]

tāl'ēs (-z), n. (law). Writ for summoning
jurors, list of persons who may be so
summoned, to supply deficiency; *pray a
~*, plead for completion of jury thus;
~'*man* (or -lz-), person so summoned.
[ME; L ~ (*de circumstantibus*) such (of
the bystanders), first wds of writ]

Tăliacō'tian (-shn), a. ~ *operation*, formation of new nose by means of flap
taken from upper arm but severed only
after union has taken place. [f. *Taglia-
cozzi*, Italian surgeon d. 1599 +-AN]

tăl'ion, n. (Also L *lēx tăliōn'is*) the law of
retaliation inflicting punishment of same
kind & degree as injury (see *Lev.* xxiv.
20). Hence tăliōn'IC a. [ME, f. OF, f. L
talio -onis (*talis* such)]

tăl'ipĕd, a. & n. **1.** Club-footed; (zool., of
sloth etc.) having feet twisted into unusual position. **2.** n. ~ person or animal.
[as foll.]

tăl'ipēs (-z), n. Club-foot(edness); taliped
formation. [mod. L (TALUS, *pes pedis*
foot)]

tăl'ipŏt, -ŭt, n. A fan-leafed palm. [f.
Hind. *tālpāt* f. Skr. *tālapattra* (*tāla* palm +
paltra leaf)]

tăl'isman (-z-), n. Charm, amulet, thing
capable of working wonders; (astrol.)
magical figure cut or engraved & capable
of benefiting its possessor. Hence tălis-
măn'IC (-z-) a. [F, = Sp., Port. *talisman*,
It. *-mano*, ult. f. Arab. *tilsam* f. Gk *telesma*]

talk (tawk), v.i. & t., & n. **1.** Converse,
communicate ideas, by spoken words,
as *was ~ing with* or *to a friend, what are
you ~ing about?*, ~ BIG, TALL, *people
will ~* (scandal), *now you're ~ing* (sl. = I
welcome that offer etc.), *you can't ~*
(colloq. = you are just as bad yourself);
communicate by radio signals. **2.** Have
the power of speech, as *child is learning to
~, parrots can ~*; use this to excess, as *is
always ~ing*. **3.** Express, utter, discuss,
in words, as *you are ~ing nonsense, ~
treason, philosophy*, SHOP; *~ (cold) turkey*
(colloq.), tell the plain truth. **4.** Use
(language), as *they were ~ing French*.
5. Bring into specified condition etc. by
~ing, as *~ed himself hoarse, ~ person
round*, persuade him, *~ed him out of his
resolution, into his grave, would ~ the hind
leg off a donkey*, is talkative. **6.** ~ *about*,
discuss, as *do not want to be ~ed about*

(made subject of gossip); ~ *at*, address to one of a company remarks covertly hostile to & meant to be heard by (another); ~ *away*, consume (time) in ~ing; ~ *back*, reply defiantly; ~ *down*, silence (person) by superior loudness or persistency, bring (aircraft) to a landing by radioing instructions from the ground; ~ *of*, discuss, mention, as ~ing (while we are on the subject) *of muffins, what time do you have tea?*, express some intention of (doing); ‖ ~ *out* (bill, motion, in Parl.), get rid of it by prolonging discussion till time of adjournment; ~ *over*, discuss at some length, win over by ~ing; ~ *round*, discuss (subject) at length without reaching conclusion, also ~ over (person); ~ *through* one's *hat* (sl.), exaggerate or bluff or make wild statements; ~ *to*, speak to, (colloq.) reprove, give a piece of one's mind to, so *gave him a ~ing-to*; ~ *up*, discuss (subject) in order to rouse interest in it. Hence ~ER² (tawk-) n. **7.** n. Conversation, as *let us have a~*, SMALL-, TABLE-, TALL-, ~, *it will end in* ~ (nothing will be done); short address or lecture in conversational style (esp. when broadcast by radio); theme of gossip, as *they, their quarrels, are the* ~ *of the town*. [ME *talkien, talken*, deriv. vb f. TALE or TELL, w. frequent. -*k* as in *stalk, walk, lurk*]

ta′lkative (tawk-), a. Fond of talking. Hence ~NESS n. [ME; -ATIVE]

ta′lkee-ta′lkee (tawkĭ), n. Incessant chatter; broken English of Negroes etc. [TALK]

ta′lkie (tawkĭ), n. (sl.). = SOUND²-*film*. [f. TALK, after MOVIES]

ta′lking (tawk-), a. In vbl senses, esp.: having the power of speech, as ~ *parrot*; expressive, as ~ *eyes*. [-ING²]

tall (tawl), a. & adv. **1.** (Of person) of more than average height; (of tree, steeple, mast, etc.) higher than the average or than surrounding objects; of specified height, as *he is six feet* ~ (now usu. *high*), *how* ~ *is it?*; ~*boy*, ‖ bedroom chest of drawers 5 ft or more high sometimes in lower & upper sections or mounted on legs or on dressing-table, kind of chimney-pot; (sl.) extravagant, boastful, excessive, as *a* ~ *story*, ~ *talk*, *a* ~ *order* (exorbitant or unreasonable demand). **2.** adv. (sl.). In *a*~ way, as *talk* ~, boast. Hence ~′NESS n. [prob. repr. OE *getæl* swift, prompt]

tall′(i)age, n. (hist.). Form of taxation abolished in 14th c. [ME & OF *taillage* (*tailler* cut, see TAIL² & -AGE)]

tall′ith, n. Scarf worn by Jews esp. at prayer. [Heb.]

tall′ow (-ō), n., & v.t. **1.** Substance got by melting the harder & less fusible kinds of (esp. animal) fat, used for making candles & soap, greasing machinery, etc.; *vegetable* ~, kinds of vegetable fat similarly used; ~-*chandler*, maker, vendor, of ~ candles so ~ER¹ (-ōer) n.; ~-*drop*, style of cutting precious stones with dome on one or both

sides; ~-*face*, pale person; ~-*tree*, kinds of tree yielding vegetable ~. Hence ~ISH¹, ~Y² (-ōi), aa. **2.** v.t. Grease with ~; fatten (sheep). [ME *talg(h)*, MLG (G) *talg*, MIcel. *tōlg, tōlk*; ult. orig. unkn.]

tǎll′y̆, n., & v.t. & i. **1.** Piece of wood scored across with notches for the items of an account & then split into halves of which each party kept one; account so kept, score, reckoning; mark made to register a fixed number of objects delivered or received, such number used as unit, as *buy goods by the* ~ (dozen, hundred, etc.); (in counting goods aloud as delivered) *16, 18,* ~ (20), *96, 98,* ~ (100); ticket, label of wood or metal or paper with name etc. attached to thing for identification, as *horticultural tallies*, plant labels; corresponding thing, counterpart, duplicate, (*of*). **2.** ‖~*man*, one who keeps a ~ or ~-shop, one who sells goods by sample; ~-*sheet*, paper on which ~ is kept; ‖~-*shop*, conducted on ~ system; ‖ ~ *system, trade* (of sales on short credit with account kept by ~). **3.** vb. Record, reckon, by ~; (naut.) haul (sheet) taut; agree, correspond, (*with*), as *goods do not* ~ *with invoice*. Hence **tǎll′iER¹** n. [ME, f. AF *tallie* (= OF *taille*, whence doublet obs. *tail* = TALLY), f. L *talea*, see TAIL²]

tǎll′y̆-hō′, int., n., & v.t. & i. **1.** Huntsman's cry to hounds on viewing fox. **2.** vb. Utter, urge (hounds) with, this. [cf. F *taïaut*]

tǎl′ma, n. Woman's or man's long cape or cloak in first half of 19th c. [F. J. *T~*, French tragedian, d. 1826)]

tǎl′mi-gŏld, n. Brass thinly coated with gold. [f. G *talmi(gold*)]

Tǎl′mud, n. Body of Jewish law & legend comprising the Mishnah (precepts of the elders codified *c.* 200 A.D.) & the Gemara (commentary on the Mishnah in recensions at Jerusalem *c.* 400 & at Babylon *c.* 500), (also, in limited sense) the Babylonian Gemara. Hence **Tǎlmŭd′IC(AL)** aa. [late Heb., = instruction]

Tǎl′mud|ist, n. Compiler, adherent, or (now usu.) student, of the Talmud. Hence ~IS′TIC a. [-IST]

tǎl′on, n. **1.** Claw esp. of bird of prey. **2.** Cards left after deal. **3.** Shoulder of bolt against which key presses in shooting it; ogee moulding; heel of sword-blade. Hence (-)~ED² (-nd) a. [ME, f. OF, = heel, f. Rom. **talo -onis* f. L *talus*]

taluk′ (-ōōk), -**ōōk**, n. District in India subject to revenue collection by native officer; tract of proprietary land in India; ~*dar*, such officer, proprietor of ~. [Hind. *ta′alluq*]

tǎl′us, n. (pl. -*li*). **1.** (Anat.) ankle(-bone); form of club-foot. **2.** Slope of wall that tapers to the top or rests against bank; (geol.) sloping mass of fragments at foot of cliff. [L, = ankle, heel; sense 2 f. F *talus* of unkn. orig.]

tamăn'dūa, tăm'anoir (-wȧr), nn. Kinds of ant-eater. [(-*ua*) Braz., (-*oir*) F corrupt.]

tăm'arăck, n. Kinds of Amer. tree, esp. = HACKMATACK. [Amer.-Ind.]

tăm'arin, n. Kinds of S.-Amer. marmoset. [F, f. native name]

tăm'arĭnd, n. (Tropical tree with) fruit whose pulp is used in making cooling drinks etc.; ∼-*fish*, preparation of fish with ∼ pulp. [ult. f. Arab. *tamr-hindi* date of India]

tăm'arĭsk, n. Kind of plant, esp. *common* or *French* ∼, evergreen shrub with feathery branches & white or pink flowers suitable for planting near sea. [ME, f. LL *tamariscus*, L *tamarix*]

tama'sha (-mah-), n. (Anglo-Ind.). A show or entertainment or function. [Arab.]

tăm'bour (-oor), n., & v.t. **1.** Drum; circular frame on which silk etc. is stretched to be embroidered, stuff so embroidered; (archit.) cylindrical stone in shaft of column, circular part of various structures, ceiled lobby with folding doors in church porch etc. to obviate draught; kinds of fish making drumming noise or like drum in shape; (fortif.) palisaded defence for road, gate, etc. **2.** v.t. Decorate, embroider, (stuff or abs.) on ∼. [F, later f. *tabour* TABOR]

tăm'bourĭn (-bor-), n. Long narrow drum used in Provence; (music for) dance accompanied by this. [F, dim. of prec.]

tămbourine' (-borēn), n. **1.** Small drum made of wooden or metal hoop with parchment stretched over one end & loose jingling metal discs. **2.** Kind of African pigeon. [cf. prec.]

tāme, v.t., & a. **1.** Make gentle & tractable, domesticate, break in, (wild beast, bird, etc.); subdue, curb, reduce to submission, humble, (person, spirit, courage, ardour, etc.). Hence tām(e)a-BIL'ITY, tăm(e)'ableNESS, (-)tāmER[1], nn., tăm(e)'ABLE, ∼'LESS (-ml-; poet.), aa. **2.** adj. Made tractable, domesticated, not wild, (∼ *cat*, fig., person tolerated as useful hanger-on); (colloq., of land or plant) cultivated, produced by cultivation; submissive, spiritless, inert, feeble, flat, insipid, as *the* ∼*st of slaves*, ∼ *acquiescence*, *scenery*, *description*. Hence ∼'LY (-ml-) adv., ∼'NESS (-mn-) n. [OE *tam*, OHG *zam*, ON *tamr* f. Gmc **tamaz* cogn. w. L *domare*; (vb) ME *tame* f. adj.]

Tăm'il, n. Language, member, of a people inhabiting S. India & Ceylon. Hence Tamĭl'IAN a. [native]

Tămm'anў, n. Organization of democratic party in ∼ *Hall*, New York (often implying political corruption). Hence ∼ISM n.

tăm-o'-shăn'ter, tămm'ў, n. Round woollen or cloth cap fitting closely round brows but large & full above. [f. Burns's *Tam o' Shanter*]

tămp, v.t. Pack (blast-hole) full of clay etc. to get full force of explosion, whence ∼'ING[1](3) n.; ram down (road material etc.). Hence ∼'ER[1] (1, 2) n., (also) bricklayer's tool. [perh. back form. f. *tampin* (var. of TAMPION) taken as = *tamping*]

tăm'per, v.i. ∼ *with*: meddle with; make unauthorized changes in (will, MS., etc.); exert secret or corrupt influence upon, bribe. Hence ∼ER[1] n. [var. of TEMPER]

tăm'pion, n. Wooden stopper for muzzle of gun; plug e.g. for top of organ-pipe. [15th c. -*on*, -*ion*, f. F *tampon*, nasalized var. of *tapon*; see TAP[1], -OON]

tăm'pon, n., & v.t. **1.** Plug used to stop haemorrhage; pad for the hair. **2.** v.t. Plug (wound etc.) with ∼. [F, see prec.]

tămponāde', n. Use of tampon for wound etc. So **tăm'pon**AGE, **tăm'pon**MENT, nn. [-ADE]

tamtam. See TOMTOM.

tăn[1], v.t. & i. (-nn-), n., & a. **1.** Convert (raw hide) into leather by soaking in liquid containing tannic acid or by use of mineral salts etc., whence ∼n'ABLE a., ∼n'AGE(3),∼n'er[1] [-ER[1](1)],∼n'ERY(2, 3), nn.; make, become, brown by exposure to sun; treat (imitation marble, fish-nets, etc.) with hardening process; (sl.) beat, thrash. Hence ∼n'ING[1](1) n. **2.** n. Bark of oak or other tree bruised & used for ∼ning hides; colour of this, yellowish-brown; the bronze of sunburnt skin; *the* ∼ (sl.), the circus, floor of riding-school; (also *spent* ∼) ∼ from which tannic acid has been extracted, used for covering roads etc.; ∼-*balls* (of spent ∼, used for fuel); ∼-*liquor*, -*ooze*, -*pickle*, liquid used in ∼ning; ∼-*yard*, ∼nery. **3.** adj. Of ∼ colour; BLACK[1] *&* ∼. [(vb) late OE *tannian*, f. med. L *tan(n)are* f. *tan(n)um*; (n.) *c.* 1600, prob. f. F *tan*, = med. L *tan(n)um*, prob. of Celt. orig., cf. Bret. *tann* oak]

tăn[2]. See TANGENT.

ta'na (tah-), **tănn'a,** n. Military post, police-station, in India; *tan(n)'adar*, chief officer of this. [f. Hind. *thāna*]

tăn'ag|er, n. Kinds of Amer. birds of finch family & mostly of brilliant plumage. Hence ∼rINE[1], ∼rOID, aa. [f. Braz. *tangara*]

Tăn'agra (or tanăg[z]-), n. City of Boeotia in ancient Greece; (in full, ∼ *statuette*, *figurine*) terracotta statuette found, or of the type found, in tombs near ∼.

tăn'dĕm, adv., n., & a. **1.** (Of horses in harness) one behind another; *drive* ∼ (with horses so harnessed). **2.** n. (Carriage with) horses ∼; bicycle or tricycle with seats for two or more one behind another. **3.** adj. (Of bicycle) so arranged. [L, = at length (of time), used punningly]

tăng[1], n., & v.t. **1.** Point, projection, esp. part of chisel etc., that goes into handle. **2.** Strong taste or flavour, characteristic property, whence ~'Y² (-ngĭ) a. **3.** v.t. Furnish or affect with a ~. [ME, f. ON *tangi* point]

tăng², n. Kinds of seaweed. [16th c., f. Scand., = Norw., Da., Færoese *tang*, Icel. *thang*]

tăng³, v.t. & i., & n. **1.** Ring, twang, sound loudly, (t. & i.); induce (bees) to settle by striking pieces of metal together. **2.** n. Twang. [imit.]

tăn'gent (-j-), a. & n. **1.** Meeting a line or surface at a point but not (when produced if necessary) intersecting it. **2.** n. Straight line ~ to a curve at any point; *fly, go, off at a* ~, diverge impetuously from matter in hand or from normal line of thought or conduct; (trig., abbr. *tan*) ~ *of an angle*, ratio of the perpendicular subtending it in any right-angled triangle to the base. **3.** ~-*balance* (showing weight by position of beam as shown on graduated arc). Hence **tăn'gENCY** n., **tăngĕn'tIAL** (-jĕnshl) a., **tăngĕn'tialLY²** a̤dv. [f. L *tangere* touch, see -ENT]

Tăngerine' (-jerēn), a. & n. (Native) of Tangier; ~ (*orange*), small flattened kind. [f. *Tanger,_Tangier* + -INE¹]

tăn'ghin (-nggĭn), n. Madagascar tree the fruit of which has poisonous kernel formerly used in ordeals. [F, f. native *tangena*]

tăn'g|ible (-j-), a. Perceptible by touch; definite, clearly intelligible, not elusive or visionary, as ~*ible advantages, scheme, distinction*; (law) corporeal. Hence or cogn. ~iBIL'ITY, ~ibleNESS, nn., ~ibLY² adv. [F, or f. LL *tangibilis* (*tangere* touch, see -BLE)]

tangle¹ (tăng'gl), v.t. & i., & n. **1.** Intertwine (threads, hair, etc.), become involved, in confused mass; entrap, entangle; complicate, as *a* ~*d affair*; **~foot* (sl.), whisky or intoxicants. **2.** n. Confused mass of intertwined threads etc.; confused state, as *skein, business, is in a* ~; device used in dredging for delicate forms of marine life. Hence ~SOME, **tăng'lY²** (-ngg-), aa. [ME var. of obs. *tagle*, prob. of Scand. orig.; cf. Sw. dial. *taggla* disarrange; 17th c. n. f. vb]

tangle² (tăng'gl), n. = TANG².

tăng'ō (-ngg-), n. (pl. ~s), & v.i. A S.-Amer. dance; (v.i.) dance the ~. [Sp.]

tăn'gram (-ngg-), n. Chinese puzzle square cut into seven pieces to be combined into various figures. [orig. unkn.]

tăn'ist, n. (hist.). Successor apparent to Celtic chief, usu. most vigorous adult of his kin. [f. Ir. *tánaiste* heir]

tăn'istry, n. Celtic mode of tenure according to which a lord's successor was chosen from his family by election (abolished in Ireland under James I). [-RY]

tănk, n. **1.** Large metal or wooden vessel for liquid, gas, etc.; part of locomotive tender containing water for boiler; (E.-Ind.) storage-pond, reservoir for water. **2.** (mil.). Armoured motor vehicle moving on caterpillar tracks & mounted with guns (~-*buster*, sl., aircraft with anti- -~ cannon). **3.** ~ *drama* (theatr. sl.), sensational drama in which water is used for representing rescue from drowning etc.; ~ *engine*, railway engine carrying fuel & water receptacles on its own frame, not in tender. [cf. Gujerati *tänkh*; partly f. Port. *tanque* f. L *stagnum* pool]

tănk'age, n. (Charge for) storage in tanks; cubic content of tank(s); kind of fertilizer got from refuse fats etc. [-AGE]

tănk'ard, n. Large drinking-vessel usu. of silver or pewter & often with cover; contents of, amount held by, this, as *a* ~ *of ale*; COOL¹ ~; ~ *turnip*, kinds with oblong root usu. rising high above ground. [ME, = (M)Du. *tankaert*; orig. unkn.]

tănk'er, n. Ship with tank(s) for carrying liquids, esp. mineral oils, in bulk; road vehicle with large tank for conveying milk etc. in bulk; aircraft for refuelling other aircraft in air. [-ER¹]

tanner¹. See TAN¹.

‖ **tănn'er²,** n. (sl.). A sixpence. [orig. unkn.]

tănn'|ic, a. Of tan; ~*ic acid* (also ~IN n.), astringent substance got chiefly from bark etc. of oak & other trees & used in preparing leather & writing-ink & in medicine. So ~ATE¹(3̇) n. (chem.), ~iF'EROUS a. [f. *tannin* (F, *tan* + -IN) + -IC]

tanrec. See TENREC.

tăn'sy (-zĭ), n. Herb with yellow flowers & finely-toothed bitter aromatic leaves used in medicine & cookery. [ME, f. OF *tanesie* f. med. L f. Gk *athanasia* immortality (*a-* not + *thanatos* death)]

tăn'taliz|e, -is|e (-ĭz), v.t. Torment, tease, (person etc.) with hopes that seem continually on point of fulfilment or with object almost within his grasp or with imperfect information etc. Hence ~A̤L-TION n., ~ingLY² adv. [f. TANTALUS + -IZE]

tăn'talum, n. A rare white metallic element highly resistant to heat & to action of acids. [f. foll. w. ref. to its non--absorbent quality + -UM]

Tăn'talus, n. **1.** (Gk myth.). Son of Zeus condemned in Tartarus to stand up to chin in water that receded whenever he stooped to drink. **2.** (*t*~). Kinds of ibis; spirit-stand in which decanters are locked up but visible. **3.** ~-*cup*, toy cup containing figure of man illustrating principle of siphon. [L, f. Gk *Tantalos*]

tăn'tamount, a. Equivalent, as *his message was* ~ *to a flat refusal*. [orig. as vb, f. AF *tant amunter* AMOUNT to so much ·(*tant* f. L *tantus* so great)]

tăntăr'a, n. Succession of notes on trumpet or horn. [imit.]

tăntiv'y, n., a., adv., & v.i. (arch.). **1.** Hunting cry; swift movement, gallop, rush. **2.** adj. Swift. **3.** adv. Swiftly. **4.** v.i. Hurry, rush. [perh. imit. of hoof--strokes]

tăn′tra, n. Each of a class of Sanskrit religious works dealing chiefly with magic. Hence **tăn′trism**(3), **tăn′trist**(2), nn. [Skr., =loom, groundwork, doctrine]

tăn′trum, n. Display of temper or petulance, as *is in, went into, her* ~*s*. [18th c., of unkn. orig.]

Taoiseach (tē′shăkh), n. Official title of Prime Minister of Eire. [Ir., = chief, leader]

Taoism (tah′ō-, tow²-), n. Religious doctrine of Lao-tsze, Chinese philosopher (*c.* 500 B.C.). [f. Chin. *tao* way +-ISM]

tăp¹, n., & v.t. (-pp-). **1.** ‖ Cock through which liquid is drawn from cask or flows from pipe; plug used to close opening in cask; liquor of a particular brewing etc. w. ref. to quality, as *an excellent* ~, *you know the* ~; = ~*room*, as *found him in the* ~; instrument for cutting threads of internal screws; *on* ~, (of cask) furnished with ~, (of liquor) in such cask, ready to be drawn, also fig., ‖ (of Treasury bills etc.) obtainable when & as required at a fixed rate; ~*-borer*, auger for boring tapering hole in cask; ‖ ~*′room* (in which liquor is sold & drunk); ~*-root*, chief descending root of plant. **2.** v.t. Furnish (cask) with cock; pierce (cask etc.) to let out liquid, let out thus; (surg.) give vent to (fluid accumulated in body), operate thus on (person); draw sap from (tree) by cutting into it; penetrate to, get into communication with, establish trade etc. in, (district etc.); apply to, solicit, (person *for*); broach (subject); divert part of current from (telegraph wires etc.) to intercept message: make internal screw--thread in. [OE *tæppa*, OHG *zapfo*, ON *tappi* f. Gmc **tappon*; vb f. OE *tæppian*]

tăp², v.t. & i. (-pp-), & n. **1.** Strike lightly, as ~ *the door with your knuckles, pavement with your stick,* ~*ped his forehead knowingly*; cause (thing) to strike lightly *against* etc., as ~*ped his stick against the window*; strike gentle blow, rap, (*at* door etc.); apply leather to (heel of shoe). **2.** n. Light blow, rap; sound of this, as *heard a* ~ *at the door*; (pl.) men's dinner-call in barracks, *signal on drum or trumpet for lights to be put out in soldiers' quarters; ~*-dancing*, stage-dancing characterized by rhythmical ~*ping* of the feet. [ME *tappe*, imit., perh. thr. F *taper*]

ta′pa (tah-), n. Bark of a tree used in Pacific islands for clothes, mats, etc. [native]

tāpe, n., & v.t. **1.** Narrow cotton or linen strip used for tying up parcels & in dressmaking etc. (RED ~); such strip stretched across racing-track between winning--posts, as *breast the* ~, win race; narrow band of strong fabric rotating on pulleys etc. in machinery; continuous strip of paper in receiving instrument of recording telegraph; (also *magnetic* ~), metal strip or ribbon for the electromagnetic recording & reproduction of signals;

= ~*-measure,* ~worm. **2.** ~*-line, -measure,* strip of ~ or thin flexible metal marked for use as measure, & often coiled up in cylindrical case; ~ *recorder,* apparatus for recording sounds etc. on magnetic ~ and afterwards reproducing them (~ *recording,* such reproduction); ~*′worm,* kinds of ~-like many-jointed worm infesting alimentary canal of man & most vertebrates. Hence ~*′LESS a.* **3.** v.t. Furnish, tie up, with ~; join sections of (book) with bands of ~; *have person* ~*d* (sl.), have summed him up. [OE *tæppa, -e,* ME *tappe, tāpe,* of unkn. orig.]

tāp′er, n., a., & v.i. & t. **1.** Slender candle, wick coated with wax etc. **2.** adj. (now chiefly poet. or rhet.). Growing gradually smaller towards one end like cone or pyramid, as ~ *fingers,* whence ~NESS n., ~WISE adv. **3.** vb. (Often ~ *off*) make or become ~, (cause to) grow gradually less, as *the upper part* ~*s* or *is* ~*ed off to a point,* whence ~inGLY² adv. [OE *tapur, -or, -er* wax candle; not in cogn. langg.; perh. f. Rom. **papyrus* wick]

tăp′estr|ỹ, n. Textile fabric in which woof is supplied with spindle instead of shuttle, with design formed by stitches across warp, used for covering walls, furniture, etc.; *Bayeux* ~*y,* ancient roll of linen representing scenes in life of William I preserved at Bayeux; *Russian* ~*y,* stout linen or hemp stuff used for blinds etc. Hence (-)~iED² (-rId) a. [15th c. alt. f. *tapissery* f. OF *tapisserie* (TAPIS, -ERY)]

tăpiōc′a, n. Starchy substance in hard white grains got by heating cassava & used for puddings etc. [Port., Sp., F, f. Braz. *tipioca* (*tipi* dregs, *og, ók* squeeze out)]

tāp′ir (-er), n. Hoofed swinelike mammal with short proboscis, allied to rhinoceros. Hence ~OID (-er-) a. & n. [f. Braz. *tapira*]

tăp′is (-ē, -Is), n. (Of subject) *be, come, on the* ~ (under consideration or discussion). [15th c., f. OF *tapiz* f. LL f. Gk *tapētion* dim. of *tapēs -ētos*]

tapōte′ment (-tm-), n. (med.). Percussion as part of massage treatment. [F (*tapoter* to tap, -MENT)]

tăpp′ĕt, n. Arm, collar, cam, etc., used in machinery to impart intermittent motion; ~ *loom* (in which hammers are worked by ~s). [app. f. TAP² +-ET¹]

‖ **tăpp′it,** a. (Sc.). ~ *hen:* crested hen; large drinking vessel with knob on lid. [= *topped* p.p. of TOP²]

‖ **tăp rāte,** n. (financ.). Current rate for Treasury bills etc. [f. phr. *on* TAP¹]

tăp′ster, n. Person employed at a bar to draw & serve liquor. [OE *tæppestre,* orig. fem. (TAP¹, -STER)]

tapu. See TABOO.

tär¹, n., & v.t. (-rr-). **1.** Dark viscid liquid got by dry distillation of wood, coal, etc., & used as preservative of timber & iron, antiseptic, etc.; *a touch of the* ~ *-brush,* admixture of Negro blood as shown by colour of skin; ~-*board*, stout millboard of ~*red* rope etc.; ~ *macad'am*, road--materials of stone or slag with ~; ~-*sealed* (New Zealand), surfaced with ~ macadam, so ~-*seal* n.; ~-*water*, cold infusion of ~ used as medicine, also, tarry ammoniacal water obtained in gas--manufacture. **2.** v.t. Cover with ~; ~ *& feather*, smear with ~ & then cover with feathers as punishment; ~*red with the same brush* or *stick*, having the same faults. [OE *teru*, MLG *ter(e)*, ON *tjara*, f. Gmc **terwa-* f. **trew-* TREE]

tar², n. (Also *Jack* ~) sailor. [abbr. of TARPAULIN]

tă'radĭddle, tarra-, n. (colloq.). Fib, lie. [cf. DIDDLE]

tăr'a(-fĕrn), n. Edible fern of New Zealand etc. [Tasmanian]

taraki'hi (tahrakē'hē), **ter-**, n. A New Zealand sea-fish. [Maori]

tărantăss', n. Springless four-wheeled Russian vehicle. [f. Russ. *tarantasu*]

tărantĕll'a, -ĕlle', n. (Music for) rapid whirling Ital. dance once held a cure for tarantism. [f. It. (-*la*) dim. as foll.]

tă'rantĭsm, n. Dancing mania, esp. that originating in S. Italy among those who (thought they) had been bitten by the tarantula. [f. It. *Taranto* f. L *Tarentum*, S.-Ital. town, -ISM]

tarăn'tūl|a, n. Large spider of S. Europe whose bite was formerly held to cause tarantism; other kinds of spider. Hence ~AR¹ a. [f. med. L *-ula*, It. *-ola*, as prec.]

tăratăn'tara (or *-ăntăr'a*), n. Sound of trumpet or bugle. [imit., cf. TANTARA]

tarăx'acum, n. Kinds of plant of aster family including dandelion; drug prepared from this. [med. L f. Arab. f. Pers.]

tărbŏōsh', n. Cap like fez. [f. Arab. *tarbūsh*]

tardamĕn'tĕ, adv. (mus.). Slowly. [It.]

Tărdenois'ean (-z-), a. (archaeol.). Of the mesolithic period represented by remains in Tardenois, Aisne, France. [-EAN]

tărd'ĭgrăde, a. & n. (zool.). Slow-moving (animal). [F, or f. L *tardigradus* (*tardus* slow +*gradi* walk)]

tărd'o, a. & adv. (mus.). Slow(ly). [It.]

tărd'|y̆, a. Slow-moving, slow, sluggish; late, coming or done late, as ~*y retribution, amends, reform*; (of person etc.) reluctant, hanging back. Hence ~ILY² adv., ~iNESS n. [f. F *tardif, -ive* f. Rom. **tardivus* f. L *tardus* slow, see -IVE]

tāre¹, n. Kinds of vetch, esp. common vetch (in *Matt.* xiii. 25, 36, perh.=darnel). [ME, of unkn. orig.]

tāre², n., & v.t. **1.** Allowance made for weight of box etc. in which goods are packed, as *real, customary, average*, ~; weight of motor vehicle without fuel etc.; ~ *& tret*, arithmetical rule for computing ~ etc.; (chem.) weight of vessel in which substance is weighed. **2.** v.t. Ascertain weight of (box etc.). [15th c., f. OF, f.

med. L *tara* f. Arab. *ţarḥah* what is rejected (*ţaraḥa* reject)]

tărge. See foll.

tărg'ĕt (-g-), n. **1.** Circular stuffed pad with concentric circles painted on surface as mark in archery; similar usu. rectangular mark for fire-arms; anything that is fired at (also attrib., as ~ *area*); (fig.) objective, result aimed at, as *export, fuel, savings*, ~ (also attrib.); (fig.) person, thing, serving as mark *for* (scorn etc.). **2.** Circular railway signal e.g. at a switch. **3.** Neck & breast of lamb as joint. **4.** (Also *targe* arch.) shield, buckler, esp. small round one, whence ~ED² a. **5.** ~-*card* (coloured like ~, for keeping archer's score); ~ *ship*, old ship used as ~. [ME, dim. of ME & OF *targe* f. OFrank. **targa* shield, cogn. w. OE *targe, -a*, OHG *zarga*, ON *targa*]

Tărg'|um, n. Each of various ancient Aramaic or Chaldee paraphrases of the Hebrew scriptures. Hence ~ŪM'IC, ~ŪMIS'TIC, aa., ~UMIST(3) n. [Chald., = interpretation (*targēm* interpret)]

tă'riff, n., & v.t. **1.** List of duties or customs to be paid on imports or exports; such duties collectively; law imposing these; duty on particular class of goods; *preferential* ~, reduced duties on imports from favoured country; *retaliatory* ~, import duties levied by a nation to balance foreign duties imposed on its exports; ~ *reform* (hist.), removal of inequalities etc. in ~ (|| esp. as name given by opponents of free trade in U.K. to their policy); ~ *wall*, ~-created national trade barrier; list of charges, as *railway, telegraph*, || *refreshment-room*, ~. **2.** v.t. Make~ of duties on (goods); put a valuation on. [f. F *tarif* f. It. *tariffa* arithmetic, rate-book, f. Arab. *tar'īf* notification ('*arafa* notify)]

tărl'atan, n. Thin kind of muslin. [f. F *tarlatane* earlier *tarn-*, prob. of Ind. orig.]

tărm'ăc, n.=TAR¹ *macadam*; part of airfield surface made of ~. [abbr., P]

tărn¹, n. Small mountain lake. [ME *terne* f. ON **tarnu, tjǫrn*]

tărn². [dial. form of TERN¹]

*tărn'al, *tărnă'tion, aa. & advv. (sl.). Confounded(ly). [dial. pron. of *eternal*; *-ation* on *damnation*]

tărn'ish, v.t. & i., & n. **1.** Lessen or destroy the lustre of, lose lustre, as *has been* ~*ed by damp, will* ~ *if exposed, does not easily* ~, (fig.) *a* ~*ed reputation*. **2.** n. Loss of lustre, blemish, stain; (mineral.) film of colour formed on exposed surface of mineral. Hence ~ABLE a. [f. F *ternir* (*terne* dark), see -ISH²]

ta'rō (tah-), n. (pl. ~*s*). Kinds of tropical plant of arum family with root used as food esp. in Pacific islands. [native]

tă'rŏc, -ot (-ō), n. Game played with, each card of, a pack of 78 cards. [f. It. *tarocchi*, F *tarot*, of unkn. orig.]

tărp'ăn, n. Wild horse of Tartary. [native]

tărpaul'ĭn, n. Waterproof cloth esp. of tarred canvas; sheet of this as covering; sailor's tarred or oiled hat; (arch.) sailor. [prob. f. TAR + PALL¹ + -ING¹, as in *netting* etc.]

Tārpei'an (-pēan), a. ~ *rock*, cliff from which ancient-Roman criminals were hurled. [f. L *Tarpeius* of Tarpeia (who was buried at foot of ~ rock) + -AN]

tărp'on, n. Large game-fish common on south coast of U.S. [so Du. *tarpoen*; orig. unkn.]

tă'rradĭddle. See tara-.

tă'rragon, n. Plant allied to wormwood & used in salads & in making ~ *vinegar*. [= med. L f. Byzantine Gk f. Arab. *ṭarchōn*, perh. f. Gk *drakōn* DRAGON]

Tārragōn'a, n. Spanish wine like port. [~ in Spain]

tă'rras, n. See TRASS.

tă'rrock, n. Young kittiwake; common tern; guillemot. [orig. unkn.]

tăr'rў¹, a. Of, like, smeared with, tar. [-Y²]

tă'rrў², v.i. & t. (now literary). Remain, stay, lodge, (*at, in,* etc.); wait (often *for*); delay to come or appear; be late; wait for. [ME, orig. unascert.]

tărs'ia, n. Kind of mosaic woodwork. [It.]

tărs'ier, n. Small large-eyed nocturnal lemur. [F (foll., from structure of foot)]

tărs'|us, n. (pl. ~i). **1.** Collection of bones between lower leg & metatarsus, ankle; shank of bird's leg; (entom.) terminal segment of limb. **2.** Plate of connective tissue in eyelid. Hence ~AL a., ~I-, ~O-, comb. forms. [mod. L, f. Gk *tarsos* flat of the foot]

tărt¹, a. Sharp-tasting, acid; cutting, biting, as *a ~ rejoinder*. Hence ~'LY² adv., ~'NESS n. [OE *teart*, of unkn. orig.]

tărt², n., & v.t. & i. **1.** ‖ Pie containing fruit, as *apple, cherry, ~ ~; jam ~*, piece of pastry with jam on top. **2.** (sl.). Girl, woman, esp. of immoral character. So ~'LET n. **3.** vb. ~ *up*, dress up like a ~, deck gaudily; (fig.) smarten up. [ME & OF *tarte*, = med. L *tarta*, of unkn. orig.]

tărt'an¹, n. & a. Woollen fabric with stripes of various colours crossing at right angles esp. as worn by Scottish Highlanders; (other fabric) so striped, as *silk ~, ~ velvet*; Scottish plaid with distinctive pattern of a clan. [c. 1500, perh. f. OF *tertaine, tiretaine*]

tărt'an², n. Kind of single-masted vessel used in Mediterranean. [f. F *tartane* f. It. *tartana*]

tărt'ar¹, n. Pink or red deposit from completely fermented wine, forming hard crust on side of cask, whence tărtă'rĭc, ~ous, aa. (chem.), ~izā'TION n., ~IZE(5) v.t.; CREAM¹ *of* ~; incrustation of saliva, calcium phosphate, etc., forming on the teeth; ~ *emetic*, double tartrate of potassium & antimony used as emetic, purgative, etc. [ME, f. OF *tartre* f. med. L f. med. Gk *tartaron*]

Tărt'ar², Ta'tar (tah-), a. & n. **1.** (Native) of Tartary, (member) of a group of peoples including Turks, Cossacks, etc., so **Tărtā'rIAN** a. **2.** (*Tar-*) intractable or savage person (*catch a ~*, meet with person who is more than a match for one). [ME *tartre* f. OF *tartare* or med. L *Tartarus*; in Pers. *Tātār*, perh. the native form, whence *Tar-*, the usu. spelling, by assoc. w. TARTARUS]

tăr'tar(e) sauce, n. A savoury sauce containing mayonnaise, chopped gherkins, etc. [F *sauce tartare*]

Tărt'arus, n. (Gk myth.). Abyss below Hades where Titans were confined; place of punishment in Hades. So **Tărtā'réAN** a. [L, f. Gk *Tartaros*]

tărt'rate, n. Salt of tartaric acid. [f. TARTAR¹ + -ATE¹]

Tărtuf(f)e' (-ōof), n. Religious hypocrite. Hence ~'ISM n. [character in Molière's ~*e*]

Tăr'zan, n. Man of great agility and powerful physique. [name of a white man reared by African apes, in stories by E. R. Burroughs (d. 1950)]

task (tah-), n., & v.t. **1.** Piece of work imposed; lesson to be learnt at school, as *has done his ~*; a work voluntarily undertaken, as *an arduous ~, undertook the ~ of classification; take person to ~*, accuse him of fault, rebuke him *for* (*doing*); *~ force*, specially organized unit for a special ~; ~'*master, -mistress*, one who imposes ~. **2.** v.t. Assign ~ to; exact labour from, put strain upon, tax, (*powers, intellect,* etc.). [ME, f. ONF *tasque* = OF *tasche* f. med. L *tasca*, perh. metath. f. *taxa* TAX]

Tăsmān'ian (-z-), a. & n. (Inhabitant) of Tasmania; ~ *devil*, DASYURE peculiar to the island; ~ *wolf*, nocturnal carnivorous wolflike marsupial. [after Abel *Tasman*, discoverer in 1642]

‖ **tăss¹,** n. (Sc.). Small draught (*of* brandy etc.). [15th c., f. OF *tasse* cup f. Arab. *tass* basin]

Tăss², n. Telegraph agency of the Soviet Union. [f. initials of Russian title]

tăss'el, n., & v.t. (-ll-). **1.** Tuft of loosely hanging threads or cords as ornament for cushion, cap, etc.; ~-like head of some plants, esp. staminate inflorescence at top of stalk of Indian corn; ribbon sewn into book to be used as bookmark; = TORSEL. **2.** v.t. Furnish with ~; remove ~s of (Indian corn) to strengthen plant. [ME, f. OF *tasel, tassel*, of unkn. orig.]

tăste¹, v.t. & i. **1.** Learn flavour of (food etc., or abs.) by taking it into the mouth, as ~ *this cheese, he ~s teas* (professionally) *for Smith & Co*. **2.** Eat small portion of or arch. of (esp. after negative), as *must just ~ a snack, has not ~d food for 3 days*. **3.** Perceive the flavour of, as *can ~ nothing when you have a cold, fancy I ~ garlic*. **4.** (arch.). Relish, enjoy, as *cannot ~ a joke against himself*. **5.** Experience, have experience *of*, as *shall not ~ (of) death*, *has never ~d (of) success.* **6.** (Of food etc., or fig.) have a flavour *of*, smack *of*, as *~s of mint, his writings ~ of the schools.* Hence **tāst**′ABLE a. [ME, = touch, taste, f. OF *taster* touch, taste, f. Rom. **tastare*, f. **taxitare* f. L *taxare* touch, TAX]

tāste², n. **1.** Sensation excited in certain organs of mouth by contact of some soluble things, flavour, as *cannot endure the ~ of onions, white of egg has no ~.* **2.** Sense by which ·this is perceived. **3.** (rare). Act of tasting. **4.** Small portion (*of* food etc.) taken as sample (*give him a ~ of the whip*, enough to show how it feels). **5.** Liking, predilection, *for*, as *has no ~ for sweet things, a ~ for drawing, scenery, argument, is not to my ~* (liking), *~s differ, there is no accounting for~s, add pepper etc: to ~* (to the amount desired). **6.** Faculty of discerning & enjoying beauty or other excellence esp. in art & literature, as *is a man of~, true, false, ~.* **7.** Disposition or execution of work of art, choice of language, conduct, etc., dictated by or seen in the light of this faculty, as *composed in admirable ~, the remark was in bad ~.* [ME, f. OF *tast*, f. *taster*, as prec.]

tāste′ful (-tf-), a. (Of person, work of art, etc.) having, showing, done in, good taste. Hence ~LY² adv., ~NESS n. [-FUL]

tāste′lĕss (-tl-), a.: Having no flavour; insipid; lacking the physical sense of taste; lacking artistic taste; (of language, conduct, etc.) not in good taste. Hence ~LY² adv., ~NESS n. [-LESS]

tās′ter, n. In vbl senses, esp.: person employed to judge of teas, wines, etc., by taste; (fig.) publisher's reader; (hist.) person employed to taste food before it was touched by his employer; small cup used by wine-~; instrument for extracting small cylindrical sample from a cheese. [-ER¹]

tās′t|ў̆, a. (colloq.). Savoury, of pleasant flavour; (now vulg.; of dress, decoration, etc.) in good taste. Hence ~ĬLY² adv. [-Y²]

tăt¹, v.i. & t. (-tt-). Do tatting; make by tatting. [orig. unkn.]

tăt², **tătt′ōō**¹, nn. (Anglo-Ind.). Pony. [f. Hind. *ṭaṭṭū*]

ta-ta (tätah′), int. Good-bye.

Tatar. · See TARTAR².

Tāte Găll′erў̆, n. London public gallery with permanent exhibition of pictures & sculpture by British & modern foreign artists. [Sir H. *Tate*, donor (d. 1899)]

tatou (tah′tōō), n. An armadillo. [Braz.]

tătt′er, n. Rag, torn piece, of cloth, paper, etc. (usu. in pl.); *~demăl′ion*, ragged person. Hence ~ED² (-erd)~Y², aa. [ME, of Scand. orig.; cf. ON *ṭǫturr* (f. **taṭurr*), pl. *ṭǫtrar* rags]

Tătt′ersall's (-z), n. (Used for) head-quarters of horse-dealing & betting rendezvous (*knows his ~ better than his Greek Testament*). [R. *Tattersall*, founder of firm (d. 1795)]

tătt′ing, n. Kind of knotted work used for trimmings etc. [orig. unkn.]

tăt′tle, v.i. & t., & n. **1.** Prattle, chatter, gossip, whence **tătt′lIng**LY² adv.; utter (words) idly. **2.** n. Trivial talk. [limit.; cf. MFlem. *tatelen*, LG *tateln, täteln* gabble, cackle]

tătt′ler, n. **1.** Prattler, gossip, (arch. *Tatler*, periodical of Steele & Addison). **2.** Sandpiper. [f. prec.+-ER¹]

tattōō¹ (tatōō′), n., & v.i. **1.**. Beat of drum, or bugle-call, at 10 p.m. recalling soldiers to quarters, elaboration of this with music & marching as entertainment; *beat the devil's ~*, drum idly ·with fingers etc. **2.** v.i. Rap quickly & repeatedly, beat the devil's ~. [17th c. *tap-too* f. Du. *taptoe*, lit. ' close the tap ' (of the cask)]

tattōō² (tatōō′), v.t., & n. **1.** Mark (skin etc.) with indelible patterns by inserting pigments in punctures. **2.** n. Such mark. [(n. f. vb) f. Tahitian *tatau* n.]

tătt′ў̆¹, n. (Anglo-Ind.). Matting of cuscus-grass hung & kept wet to cool & perfume the air. [f. Hind. *ṭaṭṭi* wicker frame]

tătt′|ў̆², a. (orig. dial.). Ragged, shabby; fussily ornate. So ~ĬLY² adv., ~ĬNESS n. [app. rel. to OE *tættec* rag, TATTER]

tau (taw, tow), n. Greek letter (*T*, τ) = t; kinds of fish etc. marked with or suggesting this; (attrib.). T-shaped, *as ~ cross.* [Gk]

taught. See TEACH.

taunt¹, v.t., & n. **1.** Reproach, upbraid, (person etc. *with* conduct etc.) contemptuously, whence ~′ingLY² adv. **2.** n. Contemptuous reproach, object of this, as *endured the ~s of, became a ~ to, his neighbours.* [16th c., in phr. *taunt pour* (*for*) *taunt* f. F *tant pour tant* tit for tat, hence, smart rejoinder; hence vb]

‖ **taunt**², a. (naut.). (Of mast) tall. [16th c., of unkn. orig.; cf. obs. *ataunt* adv. with all sails set]

taur′|ine, a. Bull-like, bovine, so ~ĬFORM a.; of the zodiacal sign Taurus. [f. L *taurinus* (*taurus* bull, see -INE¹)]

taurŏm′achy (-kĭ), n. Bull-fight(ing). [f. Gk *tauromakhia* (*lauros* bull + *makhē* fight)]

Taur′us, n. Zodiacal constellation, the Bull; second sign of zodiac. [L, = bull]

taut, a. (naut.). (Of rope) tight, not slack; (of vessel etc.) in good order or condition. Hence ~′EN⁶ v.t. & i., ~′LY² adv., ~′NESS n. [ME *togt*, perh. alt. f. *tigt* (TIGHT) after *togen* drawn,· p.p. of obs. *tee* (OE *tēon* draw]

taut|o-, comb. form of Gk *tauto* = *to auto*, the same, as: ~′*ochrōne* (-k-) [f. Gk *khronos* time], curve on which body starting from state of rest under gravity will reach lowest point in same time from whatever point it starts, so ~*ŏch′ronism* (-k-) n., ~*ŏch′ronous* {-k-) a.; ~*ŏph′ony*, repetition of same sound.

tautŏl′og|ў̆, n. Saying of the same ·thing

twice over in different words (e.g. *arrived one after the other in succession*). Hence **tautolŏ′gĭc**(AL) aa., **tautolŏ′gĭcal**LY[2] adv., ~IST(1) n., ~IZE(2) v.i. [f. LL f. Gk TAUTO(*logia* -LOGY)]

tăv′ern, n. Public house for supply of food & drink. [ME, f. OF *taverne* f. L *taberna* hut, tavern]

taw[1], v.t. Make (hide) into leather without use of tannin, esp. by soaking in solution of alum & salt. Hence ~′ER[1], ~′ERY(3), nn. [OE *tawian*, MDu., MLG *touwen*, OHG *zouwen* f. Gmc **taw-*, **tōw-*, (cf. Goth. *taujan* do, make)]

taw[2], n. Game at marbles; limit line in playing marbles; a marble. [c. 1700; of unkn. orig.]

tawd′r|ÿ, a. & n. **1.** Showy but worthless, gaudy, having too much or ill-judged ornament, whence ~ĭLY[2] adv., ~ĭNESS n. **2.** n. Cheap or excessive or tasteless finery. [as n., short for *tawdry lace*, orig. *St Audrey's lace*, f. *Audrey* = *Etheldrida*, patron saint of Ely]

tawn′|ÿ, a. Brownish-yellow, tan-coloured. Hence ~ĭNESS n. [ME, f. AF *taune*, OF *tane* f. *tan* TAN[1]]

‖ **taws(e)** (-z-), n. sing. or pl. (Sc.). Slit thong for chastising children. [app. pl. of obs. *taw* tawed leather, see TAW[1]]

tăx[1], v.t. Impose tax on (subjects, citizens, etc., commodity, land, etc.), so ~A′TION n.; (N.T.) register (person) for purpose of imposing tribute; make demands upon, demand exertion from, (person's resources, powers, ingenuity, etc.); *cannot ~ my memory*, cannot undertake to recollect the facts wanted; (law) examine & (dis)allow items of (costs etc.); ‖ ~*ed* (also ~-) *cart*, two-wheeled cart usu. for agricultural or trade purposes on which only reduced duty (& later none) was charged; charge (person *with fault*, *with doing*); ‖ ~*ing-master*, law-court official who ~es costs. Hence ~ABIL′ITY, ~′able**NESS**, nn., ~′ABLE a., ~′ablY[2] adv. [ME, f. OF *taxer* f. L *taxare* censure, charge, compute, cf. TASK, TASTE[1]]

tăx[2], n. Contribution levied on persons, property, or business, for support of government, as DIRECT[2], INDIRECT, *capitation*, INCOME, *poll-*, PURCHASE[1], ~; strain, heavy demand, (*up*)*on* (person, his energies etc.); ‖ ~*cart*, see prec.; ~*collector*, official who collects ~es; ~*farmer*, one who buys from government the right to collect certain ~es; ~*free*, exempt from ~es; ~*gatherer*, = ~*collector*; ~′*payer*. Hence ~′LESS a. [ME, f. prec.]

tăx′i, n., & v.i. & t. **1.** Motor-cab plying for hire & fitted with taximeter (also ~-*cab*), other motor-car of similar pattern; ~*man*, driver of ~. **2.** vb. Go or convey in ~; (aeron., of aircraft or pilot) go along ground or water under machine's own power before or after flying. [abbr. TAXI-METER]

tăx′idĕrm|ÿ, n. Art of preparing & mounting skins of animals in lifelike manner. Hence **tăxĭdĕrm′al**, **tăxĭdĕrm′ic**, aa., ~IST(3) n. [f. TAXIS + DERM]

tăxim′eter, n. Automatic device fitted to cab & indicating fare due at any moment. [f. F *taximètre* (*taxe* tariff, TAX[2], -METER)]

tăx′in, n. Resinous substance from yew leaves. [f. L *taxus* yew + -IN]

tăx′is, n. (Surg.) manual pressure applied to restore parts to their place; (Gk ant.) various divisions of troops; (zool.) classification; (gram., rhet.) arrangement. [Gk, f. *tassō* arrange]

tăx|ŏn′omÿ, n. (nat. hist.). (Principles of) classification. Hence or cogn. ~ŏL′OGY, ~ŏn′omIST(3), nn., ~onŏm′ic(AL) aa., ~onŏm′ical**LY**[2] adv. [f. F *taxonomie* (TAXIS + Gk -*nomia* distribution)]

tazza (taht′sa), n. Saucer-shaped cup esp. one mounted on a foot. [It.]

tchĭck, n., & v.i. (Make) sound produced by pressing tongue against roof of mouth & quickly withdrawing it, esp. as used in urging horse. [imit.]

tĕ. See SI.

tea, n., & v.i. & t. **1.** (Also ~-*plant*) shrub or small tree of camellia family grown in China, India, etc.; leaves of this dried & prepared for use (*black, green*, ~, prepared by different processes; *bohea, congou, souchong, pekoe*, etc., ~, kinds of black; *hyson, gunpowder*, etc., ~, kinds of green; *tile* ~, in BRICK form). **2.** Infusion or decoction of ~-leaves as beverage; infusion etc. of leaves of other plants or of other substance, as BEEF, CAMOMILE, ~. **3.** Light afternoon meal with ~; (also *high* ~, *meat* ~) solid evening meal with ~. **4.** ~-CADDY; ‖ ~-*cake*, kinds of cake or bun eaten toasted or otherwise at ~; ~-*chest*, light lead-lined wooden box in which ~ is exported; ~-*cloth* (for ~-table or -tray, also drying-cloth for cups etc.); ~′*cup*, cup in which ~ is drunk (*storm in a ~cup*, commotion in circumscribed circle or about trivial matter), (as measure, also ~′*cupful*) gill; ~-*fight* (colloq.), ~-*party*; ~-*garden* (in which ~ is served to the public); ~-*gown*, woman's loose gown worn at ~ etc.; ~-*house* (in which ~ etc. is served in China & Japan); ~-*kettle* (used in making ~); ~-*leaf*, leaf of ~ esp. (pl.) after infusion or soaking, used in sweeping floors; ~-*party* (at which ~ is served); ~′*pot*, vessel in which ~ is made; ~-*rose*, kinds with scent compared to that of ~; ~-*service, -set*, ~-pot, cups, etc., used in serving ~; ~-SPOON; ~-*table* (often attrib., as ~-*table conversation*); ~-*things*, = ~-*set*; ~-*tray* (on which ~-set is used or carried); ~-*urn*, for boiling or holding water for ~. **5.** vb. Take ~, as *we* ~ *at* 4; give ~ to (person). [17th c. *tay, tee*, prob. f. Du. *thee* f. Chin. (Amoy dial.) *t'e*, = Mandarin dial. *ch'a*]

teach, v.t. & i. (*taught* pr. tawt). **1.** Enable or cause (person etc. *to* do) by instruction

& training, as ~ _him to swim, dog was taught to beg, misfortune has taught him to be thankful for small mercies, this_ (punishment) _will ~ you to speak the truth,_ (colloq.) _I will ~ him_ (not) _to meddle in my affairs._ **2.** Give lessons at school or elsewhere in or on (subject, game, instrument, etc., _to_ person, or w. double object), as _taught him Greek for a living, ~es the violin, ~ me bridge, was never taught music, music was never taught to a more unwilling pupil, it is time the boy was taught something_; *~ _school,_ be a ~er in a school. **3.** Give instruction to, educate; (intr.) be a ~er. **4.** Explain, show, state by way of instruction, (fact etc., _how, that,_ etc., _to_ person or w. double obj.), as _taught that we must forgive our enemies, I was taught that two sides of a triangle were greater than the third, was taught otherwise, was never taught this, who taught you that?_ Hence ~'ER[1], ~'erSHIP, nn. [OE _tǣc(e)an_ f. Gmc *_taikjan,_ f. *_taik-_ TOKEN]

teach'|able, a. Apt to learn, docile; (of subject etc.) that can be taught. Hence ~ABIL'ITY, ~ableNESS, nn. [-ABLE]

teach'ing, n. In vbl senses, esp. what is taught, doctrines, as _the ~s of the Church._ [ME; -ING[1]]

teak, n. (E.-Ind. tree with) heavy durable timber that does not warp or shrink or corrode iron, much used in shipbuilding. [f. Port. _teca_ f. Malayalam _tēkka_]

teal, n. (pl. same). Kinds of small freshwater duck. [ME _tele_ (WG *_taili_), cf. MDu. _tēling_]

team, n., & v.t. **1.** Two or more beasts of burden harnessed together, whence ~'WISE adv.; set of players on one side in some games e.g. football; set of persons working together; ~-_work,_ combined effort, organized co-operation. **2.** v.t. Harness (horses etc.) in ~; give out (work) to contractor who employs~ of workmen, whence ~'ING[1] n. [OE. _tēam_ family, offspring, corresp. to OS _tōm,_ OHG _zoum,_ ON _taumr,_ f. Gmc *_taumaz_ prob. f. *_taug-_ cogn. w. L _ducere,_ cf. TOW[1]]

team'ster, n. Driver of a team. [-STER]

teap'oy, n. Small three- or four-legged table esp. for tea. [f. Hind. _tin_ three + Pers. _pāē_ foot; sense & spelling influenced by TEA]

tear[1] (tār), v.t. & i. (_tore, torn_), & n. **1.** Pull apart, rend, lacerate, as _tore up the letter, has torn his coat, ~ it in half, in two, in pieces, torn to pieces by a tiger,_ (fig.) _country was torn by factions, heart torn by conflicting emotions_; make (hole, rent) thus; ~ _it_ (sl.), spoil one's chances, foil one's plans, put the lid on (_that's torn it_); pull violently (lit. & fig.), as _tore down the notice, ~ out a page, ~ off the cover, tree torn up by the roots, was torn_ (forcibly parted) _from her parents, babe torn from the breast, could not ~ myself_ (make up my mind to go) _away;_ pull violently _at,_ as _tore at the cover of the parcel;_ ~ one's hair,

pull it in anger or perplexity or despair; lend itself to ~ing, as ~s _easily, will not ~._ **2.** Run or walk hurriedly or impetuously, as _tore down the hill, was simply ~ing._ **3.** ~'_away,_ (adj.) impetuous, (n.) street ruffian. **4.** n. Rent in cloth etc. [OE _teran,_ OHG _zeran,_ Goth. _gatairan_ f. Gmc *_teran,_ cogn. w. Gk _derō_ flay]

tear[2] (tēr), n. (Also ~-_drop_) drop of saline liquid ordinarily serving to moisten & wash the eye but falling from it as result of grief or other emotion or of coughing or laughter, as _the ~s fell down her cheeks, wept bitter ~s of remorse, laughed till the ~s came, ~s were her only argument, a ~- -stained face, found her in ~s_ (weeping); ~like thing, e.g. drop of fluid, solid drop of resin etc.; ~s _of strong wine,_ drops forming on inside of partly-filled glass of port etc.; CROCODILE~S; ~-_gas,_ lachrymatory poison gas used in warfare; ~-_jerker_ n. (colloq.), song, story, film, etc. calculated to evoke sadness or sympathy; ~-_jerking_ a.; ~- (= LACHRYMA-TORY) _shell._ [OE _tēar,_ OHG _zahar,_ ON _tār,_ Goth. _tagr,_ cogn. w. L _lacrima_ (OL _dacr_), Gk _dakru_]

tear'ful (tēr-), a. Shedding tears, so tear-LESS a.; (of event, news, etc.) mournful, sad. Hence ~LY[2] adv., ~NESS n. [-FUL]

tear'ing (tār-), a. In vbl senses (TEAR[1]), also, violent, overwhelming (~ _pace, rage_). [-ING[2]]

teas|e (-z), v.t., & n. **1.** Assail playfully or maliciously, vex, with jests, questions, or petty annoyances, whence ~'ingLY[2] (-z-) adv.; importune (person _for_ thing, _to_ do); pick into separate fibres, comb, card, (wool, flax, etc.); dress (cloth etc.) with teasels. **2.** n. Person given to ~ing. [OE _tǣsan_ = MDu. _tēzen,_ MLG _tēsen,_ OHG _zeisan_ f. WG *_taisjan_]

teas'el (-z-), -zel, -zle n., & v.t. **1.** Kinds of plant with large prickly heads used in dressing cloth; such head; machine substituted for ~s. **2.** v.t. Dress (cloth) with ~s, whence ~ER[1] (-zel-), teaz'ler, nn. [OE _tǣs(e)l_ (as prec. + -LE)]

teas'er (-z-), n. In vbl senses, esp. : teasing person; (colloq.) difficult question or problem or task, thing hard to deal with. [-ER[1]]

teat, n. Mammary nipple through which milk passes, pap of woman, dug of beast. Hence ~ED[2], ~'LIKE, aa. [ME _tete, tette_ f. OF _tete,_ replacing OE _tit(t),_ mod. dial. _tit_]

tĕc, n. (sl.). Detective (novel). [abbr.]

techne'tium (tĕknē'shm), n. (chem.). Artificially produced radio-active metallic element. [f. Gk _teknētos_ artificial f. _tekhnē_ art, + -IUM]

tĕch'nic (-k-), a. & n. **1.** adj. (rare). = foll. **2.** n. = TECHNIQUE; (usu. pl.) doctrine of arts in general; (pl.) technical terms, details, methods, etc. Hence **techni'c**IAN (tĕkni'shn) n., person skilled in the technique of a particular craft, or in ~s

Y

generally, ~IST n. [f. L f. Gk *tekhnikos* (*tekhnē* art, see -IC)]

tĕch'nical (-k-), a. Of or in a particular art, science, handicraft, etc., as ~ *terms, skill, difficulty*; of, for, in, the mechanical arts, as ~ *education, school*; legally such, in the eyes of the law, as ~ *assault*. Hence ~LY² adv., ~NESS n. [-AL]

tĕchnicăl'it|y̆ (-k-), n. Technicalness, technical expression, distinction, etc., as *legal ~ies*. [-ITY]

Technicolor (tĕk'nĭkŭlcr), n. (cinemat.). Process of colour photography in which the colours are separately but simultaneously recorded & then transferred to a single positive print; (fig.) vivid colour, artificial brilliance. Hence ~ED² (-*erd*) a. [P; f. TECHNI(CAL) + COLOUR]

technique (tĕknēk'), n. Mode of artistic execution in music, painting, etc.; mechanical skill in art. [F, as TECHNIC]

tĕchnŏc'racy (-k-), n. Organization and management of a country's industrial resources by technical experts for the good of the whole community. Hence **tĕch'no**CRAT (-k-) n., advocate of this. [f. Gk *tekhnē* art + -CRACY]

tĕchnŏl'og|y̆ (-k-), n. Science of the industrial arts; ethnological study of development of arts. Hence **tĕchnolŏ'g**ICAL a., ~IST n. [f. Gk *tekhnologia* (*tekhnē* art, -LOGY)]

techy. See TETCHY.

tĕctŏl'ogy̆, n. Structural morphology, i.e. that which treats an organism as composed of organic individuals. Hence **tĕctolŏ'g**ICAL a. [f. G *tektologie*, f. Gk *tektōn* carpenter + -LOGY]

tĕctŏn'ic, a. & n. **1.** Of building or construction; (geol.) due to a change in structural conditions caused by deformation. **2.** n. pl. Whole art of producing useful & beautiful buildings, furniture, vessels, etc. [f. LL f. Gk *tektonikos* (*tektōn -onos* carpenter, see -IC)]

tĕctōr'ial, a. Forming a covering, esp. ~ *membrane* (of ear). [f. L *tectorius* (as foll., see -ORY) + -AL]

tĕctrī'cēs (-z), n. pl. (ornith.). Covering feathers of wings & tail. [f. L *tegere tect-* cover, -TRIX]

tĕd, v.t. (-dd-). Turn over & spread out (grass, hay) to dry. Hence ~d'ER¹(1, 2) n. [ME, f. ON *tethja* spread manure, rel. to OHG *zetten*; cf. TOD¹]

Tĕdd'y̆, n. Pet-form of Christian name *Edward*; (colloq., also ~ or *t*~ *boy*) youth affecting a style of dress held to be characteristic of reign of Edward VII (1901–10); ~ *girl*, female counterpart in behaviour but not dress.

Tĕdd'y̆ bear (bar), n. Child's toy bear (named after *Theodore* Roosevelt, d. 1919).

Tē Dē'um, n. (Music for) hymn beginning ~ *laudamus*, 'Thee, God, we praise', sung at morning service, or on special occasions as thanksgiving; *sing* ~, (fig.) exult, triumph. [L]

tēd'ious, a. Wearisome, irksome, tiresome. Hence ~LY² adv., ~NESS n. [ME, f. LL *taediosus* (as foll., see -OUS)]

tēd'ium, n. Tediousness. [f. L *taedium* f. *taedēre* to weary]

tee¹, n. Letter T; T-shaped thing esp. pipe.

tee², n., & v.t. & i. **1.** Mark aimed at in quoits, bowls, curling. **2.** (golf). Cleared space from which the ball is struck at beginning of play for each hole (also ~*ing-ground*); small pile of sand or small appliance of wood, rubber, etc. on which ball is placed before being struck. **3.** v.t. Place (ball) on ~; (v.i.) ~ *off*, start from ~, (fig.) start, begin. [f. (17th c.) *teaz*, of unkn. orig.]

tee³, n. Umbrella-shaped usu. gilded ornament crowning tope or pagoda. [f. Burm. *h'ti* umbrella]

teem¹, v.t. & i. ‖ (Arch.) bear (offspring); be prolific, be stocked to overflowing *with*, as *forests ~ with snakes, book ~s with blunders*; be abundant, as *fish ~ in these waters*. [OE *tīeman* etc., f. **taumjan* f. Gmc **taumaz* TEAM]

teem², v.t. (dial., tech.). Empty, discharge, pour out, (vessel, cart, coal, molten metal, etc.). Hence ~'ER¹ n. [ME *teme* f. ON *tœma* (*tómr* adj. empty)]

‖ **teen**, n. (arch.). Grief; trouble; harm. [OE *tēona*, OS *tiono*, ON *tjón*]

-teen, an inflected form of TEN (OE -**tiene, -tȳne, -tēne*) added to the numerals 3 to 9 to form the names of those from 13 to 19.

teens (-z), n. pl. (Also **teen age, years*) years of one's age from 13 to 19, esp. *in* one's ~; **teen-age* a., in the ~; *teen-ager*, person of this age.

teeny. See TINY.

teet'er, v.i., & n. (U.S. & dial.). **1.** Seesaw; move unsteadily. **2.** n. A seesaw. [var. of dial. *titter* totter]

teeth. See TOOTH.

teethe (-dh), v.i. Grow or cut teeth. Hence **teeth'**ING¹ (-dh-) n. [f. prec.]

teetōt'al, a. Of, advocating, total abstinence from intoxicants, as ~ *meeting, pledge*, whence ~ISM n.; (colloq.) total, entire, whence ~LY² adv. [redupl. of *total*; from about 1833]

teetōt'aller, n. Total abstainer. [-ER¹]

teetōt'um, n. Children's four-sided top with sides lettered to determine gain or loss of the spinner; any top spun with the fingers (*like a* ~, spinning). [f. T (the letter on one side) + L *totum* the whole (stakes), for which it stood]

tĕg, n. Sheep in its second year. [16th c., perh. Scand.; cf. OSw. *takka* ewe]

tĕg'ūl|ar, a. Of or like tiles. Hence or cogn. ~arLY² adv., ~**ātėd** [-ATE²] a. [f. L *tegula* tile (*tegere* cover) + -AR¹]

tĕg'ūment, n. Natural covering of (part of) animal body. Hence ~AL, ~ARY¹, aa., (-ĕn'-). [f. L *tegumentum* (*tegere* cover, see -MENT)]

tĕhee', n., & v.i. **1.** Restrained or contemptuous laugh. **2.** v.i. Laugh thus, titter. [imit.]

Tē'ian, Tē'an, a. Of (the poet Anacreon born at) Teos. [f. L *Teius* (L f. Gk *Teōs*) +-AN]

|| **teind** (tēnd), n. (Sc.). Tithe. [ME *tende*, = TEN*th*]

tĕknŏn'ўm|ў, n. (anthrop.). Practice of naming parent from child. So ~OUS a. [f. Gk *tcknon* child + -*ŏnumos* -named +-Y¹]

tĕlaesth|ēs'ia, n. (psych.). Direct perception of distant occurrences or objects not effected by the recognized senses. Hence ~ĕt'IC a. [mod. L, f. TELE-, Gk *aisthēsis* perception, & -IA¹]

tĕl'amon, n. (archit.; pl. ~es pr. -ŏn'ēz). Male figure as bearing pillar (cf. CARYATID). [L, f. Gk *Telamŏn* mythol. person]

tĕlaut'o|graph (-ahf), n. Telegraph that reproduces writing etc. So ~GRAM (5) n. [f. TELE- +AUTOGRAPH, after *telegraph*]

tĕlĕ-, comb. form of Gk *tĕle*- far, esp. in names of instruments producing or recording results etc. at a distance, as ~*barŏm'eter*, ~*thermŏm'eter*; (also) abbr. for TELEVISION, as *tĕl'ecast* n., television broadcast programme or item, also as v.t.; *tĕl'ecaster*, television broadcaster; *tĕl'efilm*, cinema film transmitted by television; ~*gĕn'ic*, suitable for being televised; ~*promp'ter*, electronic device that slowly unrolls (television) speaker's text, in large print, outside the sight of the audience; ~*record'* v.t., record (item or programme to be televised); ~*record'ing* n.

tĕlĕcommūnicā'tion, n. Communication at a distance, as by cable, telegraph, telephone, or radio; (also, freq. in pl.) means or channel of so communicating (also attrib.). [TELE-]

tĕl'edu (-ōō), n. Stinking badger of Java and Sumatra. [native]

tĕlĕg'onў, n. (biol.). Supposed influence of previous sire seen in subsequent sire's progeny by same mother. Hence tĕlegŏn'IC a. [f. TELE- +Gk -*gonia* begetting]

tĕl'ĕgrăm, n. Telegraphic message. [-GRAM]

tĕl'ĕgraph¹ (-ahf), n. **1.** Apparatus for transmitting messages or signals to a distance esp. by electrical impulses. **2.** Semaphore. **3.** (In titles of newspapers) *Daily T*~ etc. **4.** ~ (-*board*), board on which numbers of horses running in race, cricket scores, etc., are put up so as to be visible at distance; ~-*key*, device for making and breaking electric circuit of ~; ~-*line*, -*pole* or -*post*, -*wire* (used in forming telegraphic connexion); ~-*plant*, E.-Ind. plant whose leaves have spontaneous jerking motion. [f. F *télégraphe* (TELE-), -GRAPH]

tĕl'ĕgraph² (-ahf), v.t. & i. Send (message *to* person, or abs.) by telegraph, as ~ *the news to your father,* ~ *me the result,* ~ *to him to come, that we cannot come*; make

signals (*to* person *to* do, *that*, etc.). [f. prec.]

tĕlĕg'raph|er (*or* tĕl'I-), n. Person skilled or employed in telegraphy. So ~IST n. [-ER¹]

tĕlĕgraphēse' (-z), n. & a. (In) the elliptical style usual in telegrams. [-ESE]

tĕlĕgrăph'|ic, a. Of telegraphs or telegrams; of ~ic brevity, economically worded, with unessential words omitted; ~*ic address*, abbreviated or other registered address for use in telegrams. Hence ~ICALLY adv. [-IC]

tĕlĕg'raphў, n. Art of constructing, practice of communicating by, telegraph; *wireless*~, transmission of signals through space by means of electromagnetic waves. [-Y¹]

tĕlĕkinēs'is, n. (psych.). Movement at a distance from the motive cause or agent without material connexion. [mod. L, f. TELE- +Gk *kinēsis* motion (*kineŏ* move)]

tĕl'ĕmărk, n. Expert swing turn in skiing used to change direction or to stop short. [f. *T*~, district in Norway]

tĕlĕmĕchăn'ics (-k-), n. pl. Art of transmitting power by radio, & so controlling machinery from a distance. [TELE-]

tĕl'ĕmĕter, v.i. & t. Record readings of an instrument at a distance usu. by means of radio devices; (freq. ~ *back*) transmit (readings etc.) to a distant receiving set or station. Hence ~ED¹ a., ~ING¹ n., tĕlĕM'ETRY n. [TELE-]

tĕlĕŏl'og|ў, n. Doctrine of final causes, view that developments are due to the purpose or design that is served by them. So tĕlĕolŏ'gic(AL) aa., tĕlĕolŏ'gicalLY² adv., ~ISM, ~IST, nn. [f. mod. L *teleologia* f. Gk *telos -eos* end +-LOGY]

Tĕlĕosaur'us (-sŏr-), n. Genus of fossil crocodiles. [f. Gk *teleos* complete + *sauros* lizard]

tĕlĕp'ath|ў, n. Action of one mind on another at a distance through emotional influence without communication through senses. Hence **tĕlĕpăth'IC** a., **tĕlĕpăth'ICALLY** adv., ~IST(2) n., ~IZE(1, 2) v.t. & i. [TELE- +-PATHY]

tĕl'ĕphōne, n., & v.t. & i. **1.** Apparatus for transmitting sound esp. speech to a distance by wire or cord, esp. by means of electricity; *the* ~, system of communication by a network of ~s (*on the* ~, having an instrument connected with this, also, by use of or while using the ~). **2.** vb. Send (message etc.), speak (*to* person) by ~. Hence **tĕlĕphŏn'IC** a., **tĕlĕphŏn'ICALLY** adv., **tĕlĕph'onIST**(3), **tĕlĕph'onY¹** n. [f. TELE- +Gk *phŏnē* sound]

tĕlĕ|photŏg'raphў, n. Photographing of distant objects by means of a combination of telescope & ordinary photographic lens. So ~**photōgrăph'IC** a. [TELE-]

tĕl'ĕprinter, n. Telegraph instrument for transmitting messages by typing over the telephone exchange system. [TELE-]

tĕl′ergў, n. (psych.). Force conceived as operating on the brain in telepathy. [TELE-+(en)ergy]

tĕl′escōpe, n., & v.t. & i. 1. Instrument for making distant objects appear nearer & larger, whence **tĕlĕs′copist**(3), **tĕlĕs′copy**[1], nn. 2. vb. Press, drive, (sections of tube, colliding trains, etc.) together so that one slides into another like sections of small ∼; close, be driven, be capable of closing, thus. [17th c., f. It. *telescopio* or mod. L *-ium* (TELE-, -SCOPE)]

tĕlescŏp′|ic, a. Of, made with, a telescope, as ∼*ic observations*; visible only through telescope, as ∼*ic stars*; consisting of sections that telescope, as ∼*ic funnel* (of steamer), so ∼**īFORM** a. Hence ∼**ICALLY** adv. [-IC]

tĕl′evision (-zhn), n. A system employing photo-electrical & wireless processes by means of which an actual or recorded scene may be reproduced at a distance on a screen; vision of distant objects obtained thus. Hence **tĕl′eviewer** (-vūer) n., one who uses a ∼ receiver, **tĕl′evīse** (-z) v.t. & i., transmit by∼, be suitable for ∼ (*the play televised well*). [TELE-]

tĕl′ex, T∼, n. System of telegraphy in which printed signals or messages are exchanged by teleprinters connected to public telecommunication network. [f. *teleprinter*+*exchange*]

tĕll, v.t. & i. (*tōld*). 1. Relate in spoken or written words, as ∼ *me a tale, a story*. 2. Make known, divulge, state, express in words, as ∼ *me what you want*, ∼ *me all about it, will* ∼ *you a secret*, ∼ *it not in Gath* (let this news not reach & gladden the enemy, usu. joc. w. ref. to 2 *Sam.* i. 20), ∼ *that to the* (HORSE[1]-)*marines, told him my candid opinion*, ∼ *me your name*, ∼ TALES (*out of school*), *cannot* ∼ *you how glad I was*, ∼ FORTUNES. 3. Utter, as *you told me a lie*, a STORY[1], *are you* ∼*ing the truth?* 4. Give information or description, as *told me of or about his difficulties, he told of foreign lands, that* ∼*s a tale* (is significant, reveals something); (childish) *don't* ∼ *on* (inform against) *me*. 5. Decide, determine, as *how do you* ∼ *which button to press?, you never can* ∼ (appearances & probabilities are deceptive). 6. Distinguish, as *cannot* ∼ *them apart, him from his brother*. 7. Assure, as *I can* ∼ *you, it is not so easy*. 8. Produce marked effect, as *every blow* ∼*s, strain begins to* ∼ *on him*, whence ∼′ING[2] a., ∼′ingLY[2] adv. 9. Count (votes esp. in House of Commons, one's BEAD[1]s; *we were 18 men all told*; ∼ *a hundred*; ∼*s over his money every night*). 10. Direct (person) to do something (∼ *him to wait for me*). 11. •∼ person *good-bye*, say good-bye to; ∼ *off*, count off, detach, for duty, as *6 of us were, I was, told off to get fuel*, || (sl.) ∼ (person) home truths, ·recite misdoings of; ∼ *the tale* (sl.), pitch a pitiful yarn to evoke sympathy; •∼ *the world*,

announce openly, assert emphatically; *you're* ∼*ing me!* (sl.), I am fully aware of that. Hence ∼′ABLE a. [OE *tellan*, OS *tellian*, OHG *zellen*, ON *telja* f. Gmc *taljan* f. *talō* TALE]

tĕll′er, n. In vbl senses, esp.: any of four persons appointed (two for each side) to count votes in House of Commons; person appointed to receive or pay out money in bank etc. ·Hence∼SHIP n. [ME; -ER[1]]

tĕll′tāle, n. One who tells about another's private affairs, tattler; (fig.) thing, circumstance, that reveals person's thoughts, conduct, etc., esp. attrib., as ∼ *blushes, face, the* ∼ *clay on his shoes*; kinds of mechanical device for recording person's attendance at specified time etc., giving warning that cistern is full, etc.; (naut.) index near wheel to show position of tiller, (also∼ *compass*) compass hung usu. in captain's cabin for checking ship's course.

tĕllūr′|ian, a. (Inhabitant) of the earth. So ∼AL a. [as foll.+-IAN]

tĕllūr′ion, n. Instrument for illustrating succession of day & night & changes of seasons. [f. L *tellus -uris* earth]

tĕll|ūr′ium, n. (chem.). A rare brittle silver-white metallic element. Hence ∼′ūrATE[1](3), ∼′ūRET, ∼′ūrIDE, nn., ∼′ūrĕttED[1], ∼ūr′IC, ∼′ūroUS, aa. [as prec. + -IUM]

tĕll′ў, n. (sl.). Television. [abbr.]

tĕ′lotype, n. Printing electric telegraph; telegram so printed. [TELE-, -O-, TYPE]

tĕl′pher, a. Serving to transport (esp. goods) by electric locomotion, as ∼ *line*. Hence ∼AGE(1, 2) n. [for TELE-(PHORE)]

tĕl′son, n. Last joint in abdomen of Crustacea. [Gk, = limit]

tĕm′enōs, n. (Gk ant.; pl. *-nē*). Sacred enclosure, temple precinct. [Gk(*temnō* cut)]

tĕmerār′ious, a. (literary). Reckless, rash. [f. L *temerarius* (*temere* rashly) + -OUS]

tĕmĕ′ritў, n. Rashness. [f. L *temeritas* (*temere* at random, rashly, see -TY)]

tĕmp., abbr. (now usu. as playful pedantry) of L *tempore* in the time of, as ∼ *Henry I*.

Tĕmpē′an, a. Of or like Tempe, beautiful vale in Thessaly celebrated by Gk & L poets. [-AN]

tĕm′per[1], v.t. & i. 1. Prepare (clay etc.) by moistening, mixing, & kneading. 2. Bring (metal, esp. steel), (of metal) come, to proper hardness & elasticity by successive heating & cooling. 3. Modify, mitigate, (justice etc.) by blending *with* (*mercy* etc.); moderate, restrain, tone down. 4.(mus.) Tune, modulate, (piano, organ) in particular TEMPERAMENT. Hence ∼ABLE, ∼ATIVE, aa., ∼ER[1] n. [OE *temprian* f. L *temperare*, in ME reinforced by OF *temprer*; cf. TAMPER]

tĕm′per[2], n. 1. Mixture, esp. suitable combination of ingredients (of mortar etc.); resulting condition or consistence. **2.** Condition of metal as to hardness & elasticity. **3.** Habitual or temporary disposition of mind, as *was of a saturnine, frigid, fiery, placid,* ~, *persons of congenial* ~, *found him ·in ˙a good* ~ (not irritable or angry), *in a bad* ~ (peevish, angry); irritation, anger, as *fit of* ~, *what a* ~ *he is in!, naughty* ~ *!; show* ~, be petulant; *lose* one's ~, become angry; *keep, control,* one's ~, not lose it; *out of* ~, angry. Hence (-)~ED² (-*erd*) a., (-)~edLY² adv. [ME *tempre*, f. prec.]

tĕm′pera, n. = DISTEMPER³. [It.]

tĕm′perament, n. **1.** Individual character of one's physical organization permanently affecting the manner of acting, feeling, & thinking, as a *nervous* ~, *the artistic* ~; *sanguine, lymphatic* or *phlegmatic, choleric* or *bilious, melancholic* or *atrabilious,* ~ (formerly attributed to predominance of blood, lymph, yellow bile, black bile). **2.** (mus.). Adjustment of tuning of piano etc. so as to fit the scale for all keys, esp. *equal* ~, in which the 12 semitones are at equal intervals. Hence ~AL (-ĕn²) a. (in n. senses, & esp., of persons, liable to peculiar moods). [ME, f. L *temperamentum* (as TEMPER¹, see -MENT)]

tĕm′perance, n. Moderation, self--restraint, in speech, conduct, etc., esp. in eating & drinking; moderation in use of, total abstinence from, alcoholic liquors as beverages; ~ *hotel* (not supplying alcoholic drinks); ~ *movement, society, league* (for restriction or abolition of use of alcoholic drinks). [ME, f. AF (-*àunce*), f. L *temperantia* (as TEMPER¹, see -ANCE)]

tĕm′perate, a. Moderate; self-restrained; abstemious; of mild temperature, as *north, south,* ~ *zone* (between tropic of Cancer & arctic circle, Capricorn & antarctic). Hence ~LY² adv., ~NESS n. [ME, f. L TEMPER¹*atus,* -ATE²]

tĕm′perature, n. Degree or intensity of sensible heat of a body or of the atmosphere esp. as shown by thermometer, as *high, low,* ~; (med.) internal heat of the body (*normal* ~ in man, 98.4° F.; *take* one's ~, ascertain his variation from this in illness etc.); (colloq.) *body* ~ above normal; *absolute* ZERO *of* ~; ~ *curve* (showing variations of ~). [F, or f. L *temperatura* (as TEMPER¹, see -URE)]

tĕm′pĕst, n. Violent storm of wind often with rain, snow, etc.; (fig.) violent tumult or agitation. [ME, f. OF *tempeste* f. Rom. *tempesta* = class. L *tempestas* (*tempus* time)]

tĕmpĕs′tŭous, a. (Of weather, time, etc., and fig. of person or mood) stormy, violent. Hence ~LY² adv., ~NESS n. [f. LL *tempestuosus* (prec., -OUS)]

tĕm′plar, n. **1.** (*T*~) member of religious military order (*Knights T*~*s*) for protection of pilgrims to Holy Land, suppressed in 1312. **2.** Lawyer, law student, with

chambers in the Temple. **3.** *Good T*~*s,* temperance society. [ME, f. AF *templer,* OF -*ier,* = med. L -*arius* (TEMPLE¹, -ARY¹)]

template. See TEMPLET.

tĕm′ple¹, n. **1.** Edifice dedicated to service of (esp. ancient Greek, Roman, Egyptian) god. **2.** Any of three successive religious edifices of the Jews in Jerusalem. **3.** Place of Christian public worship, esp. Protestant church in France; (fig.) place in which God resides (1 *Cor.* vi. 19). **4.** *Inner, Middle, T*~, two INNS of Court on site of *the T*~ (establishment of Knights Templars) in London; *T*~ *Bar,* gateway (removed 1879) that marked the westward limit of the City Corporation's jurisdiction, at junction of Fleet Street & Strand in London. [OE *temp(e)l,* reinforced in ME by OF *temple,* f. L *templum*]

tĕm′ple², n. Flat part of either side of head between forehead & ear. [ME, f. OF, f. Rom. **temp(u)là,* f. L *tempora* pl., in same sense]

tĕm′ple³, n. Device in loom for keeping cloth stretched. [15th c., OF, perh. orig. same wd as prec.]

tĕm′plĕt, -āte, n. Pattern, gauge, usu. thin board or metal plate, used as guide in cutting or drilling metal, stone, wood, etc.; timber or plate used to distribute weight in wall or under beam etc.; wedge for building-block under ship's keel; = prec. [prob. f. prec.+-ET]

tĕm′pō, n. (mus. pl. -*pi* pr. -pē). Time, rapidity of movement; (fig.) rate of motion or activity (*the* ~ *of the war is quickening*); characteristic style of movement, as ~ *di menuetto.* [It.]

tĕm′poral, a. & n. **1.** Of this life, secular, esp. opp. to *spiritual,* as ~ *affairs, interests,* whence ~LY² adv., ~NESS n.; || ~ *lords,* peers of realm, cf. SPIRITUAL; ~ *power,* of ecclesiastic esp. Pope in ~ matters. **2.** Of or in or denoting time (~ *& spatial,* of time & space; ~ *conjunctions,* when etc.). **3.** Of the temple(s) of the head, as ~ *artery, bone.* **4.** n. ~ bone. [ME, f. OF, f. L *temporalis* (*tempus -oris,* see TEMPER¹, TEMPLE²+-AL)]

tĕmporăl′ itў, n. A secular possession, esp. properties & revenues of religious corporation or ecclesiastic (usu. pl.); (law) temporariness. [ME, f. LL *temporalitas* (as prec., see -TY)]

tĕm′poraltў, n. The laity; = prec. (1st sense). [ME, app. f. AF **temporelle* = OF *temporalite* as prec.]

tĕm′porar| ў, a. & n. Lasting, meant, only for a time, as ~*y buildings, relief, possession, office*; (n.) person employed ~ily. Hence ~ĭLY² adv., ~ĭNESS n. [f. L *temporarius* (*tempus -oris* time, see -ARY¹)]

tĕm′poriz|e, -is|e (-īz), v.i. Pursue indecisive or time-serving policy; avoid committing oneself, act so as to gain time; comply temporarily with requirements of occasion. Hence ~A′TION, ~ER¹, nn.,

~ing**LY**[2] adv. [f. F *temporiser* f. med. L *temporizare* (*tempus -oris* time, -**IZE**)]

těm'poro-, comb. form of L *tempora* temples of head, as ~*fa'cial*, of temporal & facial regions.

těmpt, v.t. (Arch., bibl.) test, try the resolution of, as *God did* ~ *Abraham*; entice, incite esp. to sin, (*to do, to* action esp. evil one); *I am* ~*ed* (strongly disposed) *to question this*; allure, attract, whence ~'ing**LY**[2] adv.; (arch., bibl.) provoke, defy, as *shalt not* ~ *the Lord*. Hence or cogn. ~a**BIL'ITY** n., ~'**ABLE** a. [ME, f. OF *tenter, tempter*, f. L *temptare* (*tentare* handle, test, try]

těmptā'tion, n. Tempting or being tempted (*the T*~, see *Matt.* iv); incitement esp. to sin; thing that attracts, attractive course. [ME, f. OF *temptacioun* f. L *temptationem* (prec., -**ATION**)]

těmp't|er, n. One who tempts; *the T*~*er*, the devil. So ~**RESS**[1] n. [ME, f. OF *tempteor, -eur*, f. L *temptatorem* (as prec., see -**OR**)]

těn, a. & n. One more than nine, 10, X; (as round number) ~ *times as easy*, ~ *to one he forgets it*; **HART** *of* ~; **UPPER** ~; ~'**PENNY** *nail*; *~'pins*, ninepins; ~*poun'der* (hist.), person having vote in parliamentary election by occupation of property of rental value of £10. Hence ~'**FOLD** a. & adv., ~**TH**[2] a. & n., ~**th'LY**[2] adv. [OE *tien*, OS *tehan*, OHG *zehan*, ON *tíu*, Goth. *taihun* f. Gmc **taihan, -un* cogn. w. L *decem*]

těn'able, a. That can be maintained or defended against attack, as *a* ~ *position, fortress, theory*; (of office etc.) that can be held *for* specified time, *by* person, etc. Hence **těn**a**BIL'ITY**, ~**NESS**, nn. [F (*tenir* hold f. L *tenēre*, see -**ABLE**)]

těn'ace (-ĭs), n. (cards). (Holding of) two cards, one next above, the other next below, the opponents' highest of the suit (*major, minor*, ~, variations of this variously defined). [F, f. Sp. *tenaza* lit. pincers]

těnā'cious (-shŭs), a. Holding fast; keeping firm hold (*of* property, rights, principles, etc.); (of memory) retentive; adhesive, sticky; strongly cohesive. Hence or cogn.~**LY**[2] adv., ~**NESS**, n., **těnǎ'CITY**, nn. [f. L *tenax* (*tenēre* hold, see -**ACIOUS**)]

těnăc'ulum, n. (pl. *-la*). Surgeon's sharp hook for picking up arteries etc. [L, = holding instrument (*tenēre* hold)]

těn'ant, n., & v.t. **1.** One who occupies land or tenement under a landlord; (law) person holding real property by private ownership, also defendant in real action; occupant (*of* any place); ~ *farmer* (cultivating farm he does not own); || ~ *right*, right of ~ to continue tenancy, as long as he pays rent & acts properly, without injurious increase of rent, & to receive compensation from landlord if turned off. **2.** v.t. Occupy as ~ (esp. in p.p.). Hence or cogn. **těn'ANCY** n., ~**LESS** a. [ME, f. OF, f. L *tenēre* hold, see -**ANT**]

těn'antable, a. Fit to be occupied by a tenant. [-**ABLE**]

těn'antry̆, n. Tenants. [-**RY**]

těnch, n. A European freshwater fish of carp family. [ME, f. OF *tenche* f. LL *tinca*]

těnd[1], v.i. Be moving, be directed, hold a course, lit. & fig., as ~*s in our direction, downwards, this way, towards the coast, to the same conclusion*; be apt or inclined, serve, conduce, (*to* action, quality, etc., *to* do). [ME, f. OF *tendre* stretch f. L *tendere* tens- or *tent-*]

těnd[2], v.t. & i. Take care of, look after, (flocks, invalid, machine); wait *upon*; (naut.) watch (ship at anchor) so as to keep turns out of her cable. So **těn'd**-**ANCE** n. (arch.). [ME, aphetic f. **ATTEND**]

těn'dency̆, n. Bent, leaning, inclination, (*towards, to,* thing, *to* do). [f. med. L *tendentia* (as **TEND**[1], see -**ANCE**)]

těndĕn'tious (-shŭs), a. (derog.). (Of writing etc.) having an underlying purpose, calculated to advance a cause. [f. G *tendenziös* (**TENDENCY**, -**OUS**)]

těn'der[1], n. In vbl senses of **TEND**[2]; also: vessel attending larger one to supply her with stores, convey orders, etc.; carriage attached to locomotive & carrying fuel, water, etc.; small water reservoir fixed to mop etc. [-**ER**[1]]

těn'der[2], v.t. & i., & n. **1.** Offer, present, give in, (one's *services, resignation,* etc.); offer (money etc.) as payment; make a ~ (*for* supply of thing or execution of work). **2.** n. Offer, esp. offer in writing to execute work or supply goods at fixed price, as *are open to receive* ~*s for*; *plea of* ~ (that defendant has always been ready to satisfy plaintiff's claim & now brings the sum into court); *legal* ~, currency that cannot legally be refused in payment of debt, as *silver is not legal* ~ *above 40s.* [f. OF *tendre* (**TEND**[1]); for *-er* cf. **RENDER** & -**ER**[4]]

těn'der[3], a. (~*est*). **1.** Soft, not tough or hard, as ~ *steak*; easily touched or wounded, susceptible to pain or grief, as *a* ~ *heart, conscience, place* (in body); delicate, fragile, (lit., & fig. of reputation etc.; *of* ~ *age*, immature, young); loving, affectionate, fond, as ~ *parents, wrote* ~ *verses*; solicitous, considerate, (*of* one's honour, good name, etc.); afraid *of* (do*ing* wrong thing); requiring careful handling, ticklish, as *a* ~ *subject.* **2.** ~-*eyed*, having gentle eyes, weak-eyed; ~*foot* (chiefly U.S. sl.), new-comer in bush etc., novice; ~-*hearted*, having ~ heart, so ~-*heart'edly* adv., ~-*heart'edness* n.; *~loin*, undercut of sirloin, (*T*~*loin*) amusements district of New York & other cities. Hence ~**LY**[2] adv., ~**NESS** n. [ME, f. OF *tendre* f. L *tener*]

těn'don, n. Strong band or cord of tissue forming termination or connexion of fleshy part of muscle; ~ *of Achilles* (akĭl'ēz; L *tendo Achillis*), ~ connecting heel (where alone Achilles was vulnerable) with calf. So **těn′dĭnous** a. [F, or f. med. L *tendo -inis* f. LL f. Gk *tenōn* w. assim. to *tendere* stretch]

těn′dril, n. Slender leafless plant-organ attaching itself to another body for support. Hence ~lED² (-ld) a. [16th c., prob. f. obs. F *tendrillon*, f. obs. *tendron* young shoot]

těn′ébrae, n. pl. (R.-C. Ch.). Matins & lauds for last three days of Holy Week, at which candles ·are successively extinguished. [L, = darkness]

těnèbrif′ĭc, a. Making ·darkness, as ~ *stars* (believed to cause night). [f. prec., see -FIC]

těn′ébrous, a. (arch.). Dark, gloomy. [ME, f. OF *tenebrus* f. L *tenebrosus* (TENEBRAE, -OUS)]

těn′ément, n. Piece of land held by an owner; (law) any kind of permanent property, e.g. lands, rents, peerage, held of a superior, so ~ARY¹ (-měn⁴) a.; dwelling-house; set of apartments used by one family (~-*house*, containing ~s). Hence ~AL (-měn⁴) a. [ME, f. AF, OF, f. med. L *tenementum* (*tenēre* hold, see -MENT)]

těněs′mus (-z-), n. (path.). Continual inclination to void the bowels or bladder accompanied by painful straining. [L, f. Gk *tĕnesmos* straining (*teinō* stretch)]

těn′ét, n. Principle, dogma, doctrine, of a person or school. [L,=he holds; formerly also *tenent*, = they hold]

těnn′er, n. (colloq.). ‖ Ten-pound, *ten--dollar, note. [-ER¹]

těnn′is, n. Game for 2, 3, or 4 persons played by striking ball with rackets over net stretched across walled court; = LAWN ~; ~ *arm, elbow*, affection of arm caused by ~; ~-*ball, -court* (for ~). [c. 1400 *tenetz, tenes*, app. f. OF *tenez* 'take, receive ', called by server to his opponent]

těn′on, n., & v.t. **1.** End of piece of wood fitted for insertion into corresponding cavity (esp. MORTISE) in another piece; ~-*saw* (small, with strong brass or steel back, for fine work). **2.** v.t. Cut into a ~, join by means of ~, whence ~ER¹ (1, 2) n. [ME, f. OF, f. *tenir* hold f. L *tenēre*]

těn′or, n. **1.** Settled or prevailing course or direction, esp. fig. *of* one's *life, way*, etc.; general purport, drift, (*of* speech, writing, etc.); (law) true intent, (also) exact copy. **2.** (mus.). (Music for, singer with) highest ordinary adult male voice, between baritone & alto (often attrib., as ~ *voice*); instrument, esp. viola, of which range is roughly that of ~ voice; ~ *bell* (largest of peal or set). So~IST(3) n. (mus.). [ME, f. OF *tenor*, -*our* f. L *tenorem* (nom. -*or*) f. *tenēre* hold, see -OR]

tenŏt′omў, n. Tendon-cutting, esp. as remedy for club-foot. [f. F -*mie*, irreg. f. Gk *tenōn -ontos* TENDON, see -TOMY]

těn′rěc, tän′, n. Hedgehog-like tailless insectivorous mammal of Madagascar. [F (*tan*-), f. Malagasy *t*(*r*)*àndraka*]

těnse¹, n. (gram.). Form taken by verb to indicate the time (also continuance or completeness) of the action etc., as *present, future, past, (im)perfect, pluperfect, aorist, ~, primary, historic, ~s*; set of such forms for the various persons and numbers; SEQUENCE *of* ~s. Hence ~′LESS a. [ME, f. OF *tens* f. L *tempus* time]

těnse², a., & v.t. & i. **1.** (Of cord, membrane, nerve, fig. of mind, emotion) stretched tight, strained to stiffness. **2.** vb. Make or become ~. Hence ~′LY² adv., ~′NESS, těn′SITY, nn. [f. L *tensus*, p.p. of *tendere* stretch (TEND¹)]·

těn′sile, a. Of tension, as ~ *force*; capable of being drawn out or stretched, whence or cogn. **těnsĭBIL′ITY, těnsĭl′ITY**, nn., **těn′sible** a. [as prec., see -IL]

těn′sion (-shn), n., & v.t. **1.** Stretching, being stretched; tenseness; mental strain or excitement; strained (political, social, etc.) state; (mech.) stress by which· bar, cord, etc. is pulled when it is part of a system in equilibrium or motion; expansive force of gas or vapour; electromotive force. **2.** v.t. Subject to ~. Hence ~AL a. [f. F *tension* or L *tensio* (TEND¹, -ION)]

těn′son, -zon, n. Contest in verse between troubadours; subdivision of poem composed for this. [F *tension*, = Prov. *tenso*, as prec.]

těn′sor, n. (anat.). Muscle that tightens or stretches a part. [mod. L, as TEND¹, see -OR]

těnt¹, n., & v.i. & t. **1.** Portable shelter of canvas, cloth, etc., supported by pole(s) & stretched by cords secured to ~-*pegs* driven into ground; *bell* ~, circular ~ with one pole in middle; (photog., also *dark* ~) portable dark room for outdoor use. **2.** ~-*bed* (with a ~like canopy); ~--*fly*, piece of canvas stretched over ridge pole of ~ leaving open space but keeping off sun & rain; ~-*pegging*, cavalry exercise in which rider tries at full gallop to carry off on point of lance ~-peg fixed in ground; ~-*stitch*, series of parallel diagonal stitches suggesting ~. **3.** vb. Cover (as) with ~; encamp in ~. [ME & OF *tente* f. Rom. **tenta* neut. pl. p.p. as TEND¹]

těnt², n., & v.t. **1.** Piece, bunch, roll, of linen etc. inserted into wound or natural opening to keep it open. **2.** v.t. Keep open thus. [ME, f. OF *tente* f. *tenter* probe, as TEMPT]

těnt³, n. Deep red wine chiefly from Spain, used esp. as sacramental wine. [f. Sp. *tinto* deep-coloured f. L as TINGE]

těn′tacl|e, n. Feeler, long slender flexible process or appendage of animal, used for exploration, prehension, or locomotion; (bot.) sensitive hair or filament. Hence ~ED² (-ld), **těntăc′ŭlAR¹, těntăc′ŭlATE²**, **-ātĕd, těntăc′ŭlIFORM, těntăcŭli′GEROUS**, aa. [f. mod. L *tentaculum*, f. *tentare* = *templare* (TEMPT)+-*culum* -CULE]

tĕn'tative, a. & n. **1.** Done by way of trial, experimental. **2.** n. Experimental proposal or theory. Hence ~LY[2] adv. [f. med. L *tentativus* (as TEMPT, see -IVE)]

tĕn'ter[1], n. Person in charge of something, || esp. of machinery in factory. [f. obs. & Sc. *tent* var. of TEND[2] + -ER[1]]

tĕn'ter[2], n. Machine for stretching cloth to set or dry; ~(*hook*), each of the hooks that hold the cloth; *be on* ~*hooks* or (arch.) *on the* ~*s* (in state of suspense or mental torment). [ME, f. AF **tentur*, f. med. L *tentorium* f. *tent*- TEND[1], see -ER[2], -OR]

tĕn'ŭis, n. (pl. -*es* pr. -ēz). Hard or surd mute (k, p, t), cf. MEDIA. [L, = thin]

tĕnū'itў, n. Slenderness; (of air, fluid) rarity, thinness; (of style) simplicity, absence of grandeur. [f. L *tenuitas* (as prec., see -TY)]

tĕn'ūous, a. (rare). Thin, slender, small; (of distinctions etc.) subtle, over-refined. [f. L TENUIS + -OUS]

tĕn'ure (-yer), n. Kind of right or title by which (esp. real) property is held, as ALLODIAL, FEUDAL, ~, *military* ~ (involving military service); (period of) holding, possession, enjoyment, as *during his* ~ *of office*, *holds life on a precarious* ~; (hist.) ~*-horn*, *-sword* (produced on certain occasions as evidence of ~ of estates). [ME, f. OF (*tenir* hold f. L *tenēre*, see -URE)]

tenu'tō (-ōō-), a. (mus.). Sustained, given its full time value (cf. STACCATO). [It., = held]

tēocăll'ĭ, n. Temple of Mex. & other Amer. aborigines, usu. on truncated pyramid. [Mex. (*teotl* god + *calli* house); also *teopan*]

tĕp'ee, teep'ee, n. Conical tent or lodge of the American Indians, formerly made of skins, now of cloth or canvas. [native name]

tĕp'è|fў, v.t. & i. Make, become, tepid. Hence ~FAC'TION n. [f. L *tepefacere* (as TEPID, see -FY)]

tĕph'igrăm, n. (meteorol.). Diagram showing state of atmosphere at different levels in terms of temperature & entropy. [f. symbol *t* for temperature + symbol *phi* for entropy + -GRAM]

tĕph'rite, n. Kinds of modern volcanic rock. [f. Gk *tephra* ashes, -ITE[1]]

tĕp'id, a. Slightly warm, lukewarm (lit. & fig.). Hence or cogn. tĕpid'ITY, ~NESS, nn., ~LY[2] adv. [f. L *tepidus* (*tepēre* be lukewarm, see -ID[1])]

tĕpĭdār'ĭum, n. (Rom. ant.; pl. -*aria*). Intermediate room of moderate temperature in Roman baths; boiler for heating hot bath. [L (as prec., see -ARIUM)]

tēr, adv. Three times (esp. mus. & med.). [L]

-ter. See -THER.

terai' (-rī), n. Wide-brimmed felt hat, often with double crown, worn by white men in sub-tropical regions. [f. *T*~, belt of marshy jungle between Himalayan foot-hills and plains]

tē'raph, n. (bibl.; only in pl. ~*īm*, used as sing. or collective sing.). Small image(s) as domestic oracle of ancient Hebrews. [Heb.]

tĕrat|o-, comb. form of Gk *teras -atos* monster, as: ~*ogĕn'ic* a., ~*ŏ'genў* n., (of) production of monstrosities; ~*ŏl'ogў*, dealing in the marvellous, (biol.) study of animal or vegetable monstrosities, so ~*olŏ'gical* a., ~*ŏl'ogist* n.

terce. See TIERCE.

tēr'cel, tier'cel, n. Male falcon. [ME, f. OF *terçel* etc., f. Rom. **tertiolus* dim. of L *tertius* third]

tērcĕn'tēnarў (*or* -entēn[2]), -tĕnn'ial, aa. & nn. Of 300 years; (n.) 300th anniversary. [TER]

tēr'cĕt, n. (Mus.; pros., also *tiercet*) = TRIPLET. [f. It. *terzetto* (*terzo* third f. L *tertius*)]

tē'rēbēne, n. A hydrocarbon prepared by treating oil of turpentine with sulphuric acid, used as disinfectant etc. [f. foll. + -ENE]

tē'rĕbinth, n. Turpentine-tree, yielding Chian turpentine; *oil of* ~, oil of turpentine. [ME, f. OF *therebinthe* or L f. Gk *terebinthos*]

tĕrebin'thine, a. Of the terebinth; of turpentine, so **terĕb'ic** a. [f. L f. Gk *terebinthinos* (as prec., see -INE[2])]

tē'rĕbr|a, n. (pl. ~*ae*). Boring ovipositor of some insects. Hence ~ATE[2](2) a. [L, = borer]

terĕd'ō, n. (pl. ~*s*). Ship-worm, mollusc that bores ships etc. [L, f. Gk *terēdōn* (*teirō* rub)]

tērg'al, a. Of the back, dorsal. [f. L *tergum* back + -AL]

tērgĕm'inate, a. (bot.). (Of leaf) having at base a pair of leaflets & forking with a pair on each branch. [f. L TER(*geminus* born together) + -ATE[2]]

tēr'givĕrs|āte, v.i. Turn one's back on oneself, turn one's coat, apostatize, change one's party or principles; make conflicting statements. So ~A'TION, ~ātoR, nn. [f. L *tergiversari* turn one's back (*tergum* back + *vers-* f. *vertere* turn), see -ATE[3]]

tērm[1], n. **1.** (arch.). Boundary, limit, esp. of time, as *set a* ~ *to his encroachments*, *awaited the* ~ *of his existence*, whence ~*'less* a. (poet., rhet.). **2.** Limited period, as *for a* ~ *of 5 years*, *his~ of office expired*. **3.** (Univv., school, law) period during which instruction is given || or court holds sessions, as *Michaelmas, Hilary, Easter, Trinity*, ~ (w. ref. to administration of justice, now *sittings*), *will end it next* ~, *during* ~ (*-time*), || EAT one's ~*s*. **4.** Appointed day, || esp. QUARTER[1]-day. **5.** (law). (Also ~ *of* or *for years*) estate or interest in land to be enjoyed for fixed period. **6.** (math.). Antecedent or consequent of ratio, part of expression joined to the rest by + or − (e.g. *3ax²−b+cz* has *three* ∼s). **7.** (log.). Word(s) that may be subject or predicate of a proposition, as MAJOR², MINOR, MIDDLE¹, ∼. **8.** Word used to express a definite conception esp. in particular branch of study etc., as *technical, scientific, law*, ∼, *in*∼*s of* (in the language peculiar to), CONTRADICTION *in* ∼*s, set* (definite) ∼*s*. **9.** pl. Language employed, mode of expression, as *in the most flattering* ∼*s*. **10.** pl. Conditions, as *cannot accept his* ∼*s, do it on your own* ∼*s*; esp. charge, price, as *his* ∼*s are 2 guineas a lesson*, INCLUSIVE ∼*s; come to* ∼*s*, yield, give way, (also *make*∼*s*) conclude agreement (*with*); *bring* person *to* ∼*s*, cause him to accept conditions; ∼*s of reference*, points referred to an individual or body of persons for decision or report, scope of an inquiry; ∼*s of trade*, ratio between prices paid for imports and received for exports. **11.** pl. Relation, footing, as *am on good, bad, familiar*, ∼*s with him, are not on speaking* ∼*s*. [f. ME & OF *terme* f. L TERMINUS]

term², v.t. Denominate, call, as *the music* ∼*ed plain-song, I forget how* or *what he* ∼*s it, this he* ∼*ed sheer robbery*. [f. prec.]

term'agant, n. & a. **1.** (hist.; *T*∼). Imaginary deity of violent and turbulent character, often appearing in morality plays. **2.** Brawling woman, shrew, scold. **3.** adj. Boisterous, turbulent, shrewish, whence **term'ag**ANCY n., ∼LY² adv. [ME *Tervagant* f. OF *Tervagan*, proper name in *Chanson de Roland*]

term'inable, a. That may be terminated; coming to an end after certain time, as ∼ *annuity*. Hence ∼NESS n. [f. obs. *termine* TERMINATE, see -ABLE; cf. LL *-abilis*]

term'inal, a. & n. **1.** Of, forming, a limit or terminus, as ∼ *station*; (math.) ∼ *value*, most concise form of an expression; (bot.) borne at end of stem etc.; (zool. etc.) ending a series, as ∼ *joints*; of, done etc., each term, as ∼ *accounts, subscription*; ∼ (TERMINUS) *figure*. **2.** n. Terminating thing, extremity, esp. point of connexion in electric circuit; railway or airway terminus. Hence ∼LY² adv. [f. L *terminalis* (TERMINUS, see -AL)]

term'in|ate¹, v.t. & i. Bound, limit; bring, come, to an end; (of word) end *in* (such letters or syllable). Hence or cogn. ∼ativeLY² adv. [f. L *terminare* (TERMINUS), see -ATE³]

term'inate², a. Coming to an end, bounded, as *a* ∼ *decimal*. [as prec., see -ATE²]

termina'tion, n. (In vbl senses, see TERMINATE¹, & esp.) word's final syllable or letter or group of letters esp. as an element in inflexion or derivation; *put a* ∼ *to, bring to a* ∼, make an end of. Hence ∼AL a. (gram.). [ME, f. OF, or L *terminatio* (TERMINATE¹, -ATION)]

term'inātor, n. Person, thing, that terminates; dividing line between light &

dark part of heavenly body. [f. TERMIN-ATE¹ +-OR; cf. LL *terminator*]

term'iner. See OYER.

term'in|ism, n. Doctrine that everyone has limited term for repentance; = NOMINALISM. So ∼IST n. [f. TERMINUS +-ISM]

termin|öl'ogy, n. Science of proper use of terms; terms used in an art etc. Hence ∼olö'gICAL a. (∼*ological inexactitude*, joc., lie), ∼olö'gicalLY² adv. [f. TERMINUS +-LOGY]

term'inus, n. (pl. *-uses, -ī*). **1.** (Now rare) final point, goal. **2.** ‖ Station at end of railway or bus route. **3.** (Rom. ant., *T*∼) god of boundaries. **4.** Figure of human bust ending in square pillar. **5.** ∼ *ăd quĕm, ā quō*, terminating, starting-point (of argument, policy, period, etc.). [L *terminus* end, limit, boundary]

termitār'ium, term'itary, nn. Nest of, cage for, termites. [f. foll. +-ARIUM, -ARY¹]

term'ite, n. Social insect, chiefly tropical & very destructive to timber, pop. but erron. called *white ant*. [f. LL *termes -itis* alt. f. *tarmes* after *terere* rub, bore]

term'ly, a. & adv. (rare). (Occurring, paid, etc.) by the term, terminal(ly). [-LY¹]

term'or, n. (law). One who holds lands etc. for a term of years, or for life. [ME, f. AF *termer* (TERM, see -ER², -OR)]

tern¹, tärn, n. Kinds of sea-bird like gull but usu. smaller & with long forked tail. [f. Scand. orig., cf. Da. *terne*, Sw. *tärna* f. ON *therna*]

tern², n. & a. **1.** Set of three, esp. three lottery numbers that when drawn together win large prize; such prize. **2.** adj. = TERNATE. [f. F *terne*, L *terni*]

tern'|ary, a. Composed of three, so ∼AL a.; (math.) having three variables. [f. L *ternarius* (L *terni* three each, see -ARY¹)]

tern'āte (or *-at*), a. Arranged in threes, esp. (bot., of leaves) having three leaflets, whorled in threes. Hence ∼LY² adv. [mod. L *ternatus* (as prec., -ATE²)]

tërne, n. (Usu. ∼*-plate*) inferior tin plate alloyed with much lead. [prob. f. F *terne* dull, see TARNISH]

Terpsich'orē (-ko-), n. The MUSE¹ of dancing. Hence **Terpsichore'AN** (-ko-) a. [Gk (*-khorē*)]

te'rra, n. Earth (in various L & It. phrr.); ∼ *căriōs'a*, tripoli, rotten-stone; *terrae fīl'ius*, son of the soil, humbly-born person; ∼ *fĭrm'a*, dry land; ∼ *incŏg'nĭta* (in-k-), unknown region; ∼ *Japŏn'ica*, gambier [orig. thought to be earth from Japan]; ∼ *nera* (nār'a), pigment used by ancient artists [It., = black earth]; ∼ *verde* (vär'dā), green earth used as pigment [It.]. [L]

te'rrace, n., & v.t. **1.** Raised level space, natural or artificial; (geol.) raised beach. **2.** ‖ Row of housing along top or face of slope, row of contiguous houses; ∼*-house*, one of row of houses joined by party-

-walls. **3.** v.t. Form into, furnish with, ~;
~*d roof*, flat roof of an Indian or Eastern
house. [F, f. Rom. **terracea* (prec.,
-ACEOUS)]

tĕrracŏtt'a, n. Hard pottery used as
ornamental building-material & in statuary (often attrib.); statue, figurine, of
this; (a. & n.) its brownish-red colour.
[It., = baked earth]

tĕrrain', n. A tract of land as regarded
by the physical geographer or the tactician. [F, f. Rom. **terranum*, f. L *terrenum*
TERRENE]

tĕrramare' (-ahr, -ār), n. Kinds of earthy
deposit containing bones, phosphates,
etc., & useful as fertilizer; S.-Europ. prehistoric deposit like kitchen MIDDEN. [F,
f. dial. It. TERRA (*mara* = *marna* marl)]

tĕrrān'ĕous, a. (bot.). Growing on land.
[f. L *-terraneus* (TERRA, -ANEOUS)]

tĕ'rrapin, n. Kinds of freshwater tortoise,
esp. *salt-marsh* ~ (also *diamond-back*),
kind valued as food. [Algonquin dim. of
torope, *turupe*]

tĕrrā'quĕous, a. (Of the earth) comprising
both land & water. [TERRA, AQUA, -EOUS]

tĕrrēne', a. Of earth, earthy; terrestrial.
[ME, f. AF, f. L *terrenus* (TERRA)]

terreplein (tār'plān), n. (fortif.). Surface
of rampart behind parapet, where guns
are mounted. [F (*terre* earth+*plein* f. L
plenus full); orig. sense *talus*]

terrĕs'trial, a. & n. **1.** Of the earth, esp.
opp. to *celestial*, as *the ~ seasons, the ~
globe*, the earth, *a ~ globe* (representing
earth), ~ MAGNETISM; of this world, worldly, as ~ *aims, interests*; of land opp. to
water; (zool.) living on the ground, opp.
to *aquatic, arboreal, aerial.* **2.** n. Inhabitant of earth. Hence ~LY² adv. [ME, f.
L *terrestris* (TERRA)+-AL]

tĕ'rrĕt, -it, n. Each of loops or rings on
harness-pad for driving-reins to pass
through. [15th c. var. of (now dial.)
torret, turret, f. OF *toret* dim. of TOUR]

tĕ'rrible, a. Exciting or fit to excite
terror, awful, dreadful, formidable;
(colloq.) excessive, as *a ~ bore*; (colloq.)
incompetent; ENFANT TERRIBLE. Hence
~NESS n., **tĕ'rribLY²** adv. (esp., sl., very).
[ME, f. F, f. L *terribilis* (*terrēre* frighten,
see -BLE)]

tĕrric'olous, a. Living on or in the earth,
esp. of the *Terricolae*, group of annelids
including earthworm. [f. L *terricola*
(TERRA+*colere* inhabit)+-OUS]

tĕ'rrier¹, n. **1.** Kinds of active & hardy
dog with digging propensity; *black-&-tan*,
BULL¹, FOX¹, ~, short-haired kinds;
Cairn, Irish, Scotch, Skye, Yorkshire, ~,
rough-haired kinds; *Maltese, toy*,~, small
toy kinds. **2.** (colloq.). ‖ Member of
Territorial Army. [ME, f. OF (*chien*)
terrier (= burrow) f. med. L *terrarius*;
-ium (TERRA, -ER² (2))]

tĕ'rrier², n. Book recording site, boundaries, etc., of land of private persons
or corporations; (hist.) collection of

acknowledgements or vassals or tenants
of a lordship. [ME, f. OF (as prec.) =
rent-roll. = med. L *terrarius* (*liber* book)]

terrif'‖ic, a. Causing terror, terrible.
Hence~ICALLY adv. [f. L *terrificus* (*terrēre*
frighten, see -FIC)]

tĕ'rrify, v.t. Fill with terror, frighten.
[f. L *terrificare* (as prec., see -FY)]

tĕrri'gĕnous, a. Produced by the earth,
as ~ *deposits*; ~ *metals*, metallic bases of
earths, c.g. aluminium. [f. L *terrigenus*
earth-born, +-OUS]

terrine' (-ēn), n. Earthenware vessel
containing and sold with some table
delicacy. [orig. form of TUREEN]

territ. See TERRET.

tĕrritōr'ial, a. & n. **1.** Of territory, as ~
possessions, acquisitions; limited to a
district, as *the right was strictly* ~; (*T~*)
of (any of) the U.S. Territories; (eccl.)
~ *system* (in which civil rule claims supremacy as a natural right, whence ~ISM n.);
‖ *T~ Army*, volunteer force organized on
a ~ basis to provide a reserve of trained
and disciplined manpower for use in any
emergency; ~ *waters*, marginal waters
under the jurisdiction of a State, esp.
that part of the sea within three miles
of the shore measured from low-water
mark. **2.** n. ‖ Member of T~ Army.
Hence ~LY² adv. [f. LL *territorialis* (as
TERRITORY, see -AL)]

tĕrritōr'ialize, -ise (-īz), v.t. Extend by
addition of, reduce to state of, territory.
[-IZE]

tĕ'rritory, n. Extent of land under jurisdiction of sovereign, State, city, etc.;
(commerc.) area over which a commercial traveller operates; large tract of
land; **(T~)* organized division of the
country not yet admitted to full rights of
a State. [ME, f. L *territorium* (TERRA,
-ORY(1))]

tĕ'rror, n. Extreme fear; ~*-stricken,
-struck* (with ~); person, thing, that
causes this, as *a ~ to evildoers*; (colloq.)
here comes this (*holy*) ~ (troublesome child)
again; *king of* ~*s*, death (*Job* xviii. 14);
Reign of T~, *the T~*, period of French
Revolution, 1793–4 (& of similar periods
marked by sanguinary excesses of revolu-
tionaries, also *Red T~*, or reactionaries,
also *White T~*). [ME & AF *terrour*, OF
-or f. L *terrorem* (*terrēre* frighten, -OR)]

tĕ'rror‖ist, n. One who favours or uses
terror-inspiring methods of governing or
of coercing government or community.
Hence or cogn. ~ISM(2, 3), ~IZA'TION, nn.,
~ĬS'TIC a., ~IZE(1) v.t. [F (*-e*), prec., -IST]

tĕ'rry, n. A pile fabric with the loops
uncut (also attrib.). [18th c., of unkn.
orig.]

tĕrse, a. (Of speech, style, writer) free
from cumbrousness and superfluity,
smooth and concise. Hence ~LY² (-sl-)
adv., ~'NESS (-sn-) n. [f. L *tersus* p.p. of
tergere wipe, polish]

tĕr'tian (-shn), a. & n. (Fever, disease)

whose paroxysms occur every other day, as ~ *ague*. [ME (*fevẹr*) *lertiane* f. L (*febris*) *lertiana* (*lertius* third, -AN)]

tĕr'tiary (-sha-), a. & n. **1.** Of the third order, rank, formation, etc. **2.** n. (Ornith.) flight-feather of third row, so **tĕr'tiaʟ** (-shl) a. & n.; (*T*~) member of third order of monastic body; *the T*~, third geological period. [f. L *tertiarius* (prec., -ARY[1])]

tĕr'tio (-shĭō). See PRIMO[2].

tĕr'tium quĭd (-shĭ-), n. A third something, esp. between mind and matter or between opposite things; (joc.) third party in *the* ETERNAL *triangle*. [L]

tĕr'tius (-shus), a. ‖ (In schools) *Jones* etc. ~ (third of the name); ~ *gaud'ens* (L, = glad third), third party expecting to profit by two others' quarrel. [L]

terᴢa rima (tārt'sa rēm'a), n. (pl. -ze -me, pr. -ā). Arrangement of (hen)decasyllabic triplets rhyming thus (bat pig cat fig box wig ox etc.) as in Dante's *Commedia*; such triplets. [It.]

terᴢĕtt'ō (tārts-), n. (mus.). Vocal trio. [It.]

Tĕs'la, n. ~ *coil*, form of induction coil for high-frequency alternating currents such as are used in diathermy. [Nikola ~, Amer. scientist (d. 1943)]

tĕss'ell|ātĕd, a. Formed of tesserae, as ~*ated pavement*; (bot., zool.) regularly checkered. So ~AR[1] a., ~A'TION n. [f. LL *tessellare* (*tessella* dim. of foll., see -ATE[2]), or It. *tessellato*, w. Engl. suf.]

tĕss'er|a, n. (pl. ~*ae*). Small square usu. cubic block used in mosaic, whence ~AL a.; (Rom. ant.) small square of bone etc. used as token, ticket, etc. [L]

tĕssĭtur'a (-oora), n. (mus.). Range within which most tones of a voice-part fall. [It., = TEXTURE]

tĕst[1], n. **1.** Critical examination or trial of person's or thing's qualities, as *has stood* (undergone) *the successive* ~*s of poverty and riches, must put it to the* ~; *a* ~ *case* (serving to show the principle involved). **2.** Means of so examining, standard for comparison or trial, circumstances suitable for this, as *success is not a fair* ~. **3.** Ground of admission or rejection, as *is excluded by our* ~. **4.** (chem.). Reagent, substance employed to reveal presence of an ingredient in a compound, as *galls are a* ~ *of* or *for iron*. **5.** Movable hearth in reverberation furnace used in separating silver from lead. **6.** (colloq.). ~-*match*. **7.** *T*~ *Act* (of 1672, requiring all persons before holding office to *take the* ~, i.e. the oaths of supremacy and allegiance or equivalent ~; repealed in 1828); ~-*match*, one of the matches in a cricket tour etc. that are to count towards the total result; ~-*glass*, -*mixer*, -*paper*, -*tube*, (for ~s or other chem. purposes); ~-*tube baby*, colloq., one conceived by artificial insemination). [ME, f. OF, f. L *testu(m)* earthen pot, collateral form of *testa* TEST[3]; in mod. use mainly f. foll.]

tĕst[2], v.t. Put to the test, make trial of, (person, thing, quality); try severely, tax, (one's powers of endurance etc.); refine (metal); (chem.) examine by means of reagent. Hence ~'ABLE a., **tĕs'ter**[1] [-ER[1](1, 2)] n. [f. prec.]

tĕst[3], n. Shell, hard covering, of some animals. [f. L *testa* tile, jug, shell, etc., cf. TEST[1]]

tĕstā'ceous (-shus), a. Of shells or shellfish, so **tĕstA'CEAN** (-āshn) a. & n., **tĕstāceŏʟ'ogy** n.; with a hard continuous shell; (bot., zool.) of red brick colour. [f. L *testaceus* (TEST[3], -ACEOUS)]

tĕs'tacy̆, n. Being testate. [f. 'TESTATE, after INTESTACY]

tĕs'tament, n. **1.** = WILL[2] (last sense), as MILITARY ~, so ~**arily̆**[2] (-ĕn[2]) adv., ~ARY[1] (-ĕn[2]) a. **2.** (Bibl.) covenant, dispensation; *Old, New, T*~, the portion of the Bible dealing with the Mosaic, Christian, dispensation; (*T*~) copy of the N.T. [ME, f. L *testamentum* will (TESTATE, -MENT); in early Christian L rendering Gk *diathēkē* covenant]

‖ **tĕstām'ur**, n. (univ.). Certificate that one has passed examination. [L, = we testify]

tĕs'tāte (*or* -at), a. & n. (Person) who has made a will (and died leaving it in force). So **tĕstāt'or**, **tĕstāt'rix**, nn. [f. L *testari* testify, make will, (*testis* witness), see -ATE[2]]

tester[1] See TEST[2].

tĕs'ter[2], n. Canopy, esp. over FOUR-poster. [ME; med. L *testerium*, *testrum*, *testura* (Rom. *testa* head); cf. OF *testre*, *testiere*]

‖ **tĕs'ter**[3], n. Shilling of Henry VIII; (arch., joc.) sixpence. [var. of earlier and OF *teston* (as TEST[3], see -OON)]

tĕs'ticle, n. Each of two glands in male that secrete spermatozoa etc. Hence **tĕstic'ulAR**[1] a. [15th c., f. L *testiculus* dim. of *testis* a ~]

tĕstic'ulate, a. Having, shaped like, testicles; (bot.) having a pair of organs so shaped. [f. LL *testiculatus* (prec., -ATE[2])]

tĕs'tify̆, v.i. & t. (Of person or thing) bear witness (*to* fact, state, assertion, *against* person etc., arch. *of* or *concerning* matter); (law) give evidence; affirm, declare, (one's *regret* etc., *that, how,* etc.); (of things) be evidence of, evince. [ME, f. L *testificari* (*testis* witness, see -FY)]

tĕstimōn'ial, n. Certificate of character, conduct, or qualifications; gift, money, presented to person, esp. in public, as mark of esteem, in acknowledgement of services, etc. [ME, f. OF (adj.), f. LL *testimonialis* (TESTIMONY, -AL)]

tĕstimōn'ialize, -ise (-īz), v.t. Present (person) with testimonial. [-IZE]

tĕs'timony̆ n. Evidence, demonstration, as *called him in* ~, *produce* ~ (*to, of*), *we have his* ~ *for that*; (law) oral or written statement under oath, or affirmation; declarations, statements, as *must rely* on the ~ of history, of historians; (arch.) solemn protest, as *for a ~ against them*; (bibl.) the decalogue, esp. *the tables of the ~*, (sing. or pl.) the Scriptures. [ME, f. L *testimonium* (*testis* witness, see -MONY)]

tĕstūdinār′ious, a. Mottled with red, yellow, and black, like tortoise-shell. [f. TESTUDO +-ARIOUS]

tĕstūd′inate, a. Arched like carapace of tortoise. [f. L *testudinatus* (TESTUDO, see -ATE²)]

tĕstūdin′eous, a. Like carapace of tortoise. [f. L *testudineus* (foll., -EOUS)]

tĕstūd′|ō, n. (pl. ~*os*, ~*ines*). 1. (Rom. ant.) screen formed by body of troops in close array with overlapping shields; similar screen used by miners where ground is likely to cave in. 2. Kinds of tortoises, whence ~INAL a. [L, gen. -*dinis*, = tortoise-shell (TEST³)]

tĕs′t|y̆, a. Irritable, touchy. Hence ~ILY² adv., ~INESS n. [ME & AF *testif*, f. *teste* head (TEST³), see -IVE]

tĕtăn′ic, a. & n. 1. Of, such as occurs in, tetanus, as ~ *spasm*. 2. n. Remedy acting on the muscles through the nerves, e.g. strychnine. [f. L f. Gk *tetanikos* (as foll., see -IC)]

tĕt′an|us, n. Disease marked by spasm of many or all muscles of voluntary motion, e.g. lockjaw; *artificial* ~*us* (induced by strychnine etc.). Hence or cogn. ~IZA′TION n., ~IZE(3) v.t., ~OID a. [L, f. Gk *tetanos* f. *teinō* stretch]

tĕ(t)ch′|y̆, a. Peevish, irritable. Hence ~ILY² adv., ~INESS n. [prob. f. *teche, tache* fault or vice, f. OF *teche*+-Y²]

tête-à-tête (tāt′ahtāt′), adv., a., & n. 1. Together in private. 2. adj. Private, confidential. 3. n. Private interview or conversation usu. between two; sofa for two. [F, lit. head-to-head]

tĕth′er (-dh-), n., & v.t. 1. Rope, chain, halter, by which grazing animal is confined; (fig.) scope, extent of one's knowledge, authority, etc. (*was beyond, at the end of, his* ~). 2. v.t. Tie (esp. grazing animal) with ~. [ME, f. ON *tjōthr*]

tĕt′ra-, comb. form of Gk *tettares* four, as: ~*chord* (-k-), scale series of half-octave (esp. in ancient mus.), so ~*chord′al* a.; ~*cyc′lic* (bot.), of four circles or whorls; ~*dac′tyl* a. & n., ~*dac′tylous* a., four-toed (animal); ~*gon*, plane rectilineal figure of four angles & four sides, so *tĕträg′onal* a.; ~*grăm*, word of four letters, quadrilateral figure;~*grămm′aton*, *Jehovah* or other sacred word written in four letters; *tĕträ′gynous* (-j-), of four pistils; ~*hĕd′ron* (-a-h-), four-sided solid, esp. triangular pyramid, so ~*hĕd′ral* (-*a*-h-) a.; *tĕträl′ogy*, group of four literary or operatic works, esp. (Gk ant.) three tragedies & satyric drama; *tĕträm′eral, tĕträm′erous*, having four parts; *tĕträm′eter*, verse of four measures (cf. DIMETER); ~*morph* (Christian art), union of attri-butes of four evangelists in one winged figure; ~*pet′alous*, ~*phyll′ous*, of four petals, leaves; ~*pŏd* a. & n., *tĕträp′odous* a., (butterfly) with only four perfect legs; *tĕträp′ody*, group, verse, of four feet; ~*stich* (-k), group of four lines of verse; ~*style* a. & n., (building) with four pillars esp. forming portico in front or supporting ceiling; ~*syll′able*, word of four syllables, so ~*syllăb′ic* a.

tĕt′răd, n. The number four; set of four; atom, element, with combining-power of four atoms of hydrogen. [f. Gk *tetras* -*ados* (as prec., see -AD)]

tĕtrăn′drous, a. (bot.). Having four stamens. [f. TETRA-+Gk *anēr andros* male+-OUS]

tĕt′rārch (-k), n. (In Rom. empire) governor of fourth part of a country or province, subordinate ruler, whence or cogn. ~ATE(1), ~Y¹, nn., **tĕtrārch′ICAL** a., (-k-); commander of subdivision of ancient Greek phalanx. [f. LL *tetrarcha*, class. L f. Gk *tetrarkhēs* (TETRA-, *arkhō* rule)]

tĕt′er, n. Kinds of skin-disease; ~*wort*, larger celandine (supposed to cure these). [OE *teter*, cf. OHG *zitaroh*, G dial. *zitteroch*]

Teuc′rian, a. & n. Ancient Trojan. [f. L *Teucri*+-AN]

Teut′o-, comb. form (irreg.) of foll., as ~MAN′IA(C), ~PHIL(E), ~PHOBE, ~PHOB′IA.

Teut′on, n. Member of any of the Teutonic nations or (hist.) of the tribe of ~*s* first mentioned in 4th c. B.C. & dwelling perh. near mouth of Elbe. [f. L *Teutones, Teutoni*, ethnic name]

Teuton′ic, a. & n. 1. Of the Teutons; of the Germanic peoples (including, in widest sense, Scandinavians & Anglo-Saxons as well as German races); ~ *languages*, High & Low GERMAN² & Scandinavian. 2. n. Languages of the Teutons collectively. Hence ~ISM(4), **Teut′on**ISM(2, 4), **Teutoniza′TION**, nn., **Teut′on**IZE(3) v.t. [f. L *Teutonicus* (prec., -IC)]

tĕxt, n. Original words of author esp. opp. to paraphrase of or commentary on them, as *there is nothing about this in the* ~, *the* ~ *is hopelessly corrupt* (altered by copyists); passage of Scripture quoted as authority or esp. chosen as subject of sermon etc.; subject, theme; *stick to* one's ~, not digress; main body of book opp. to notes, pictures, etc.; *~book*, (pl.) books prescribed for study; (also ~-*hand*) large kind of handwriting; CHURCH¹, GERMAN², ~; ~′*book*, manual of instruction, standard book in a branch of study. [f. ME & OF *texte* f. L *textus* -*ūs* (in med. L = Gospel) f. L *texere* *text-* 'weave']

tĕx′tile, a. & n. 1. Of weaving, as *the* ~ *art*; woven, suitable for weaving, as ~ *fabrics, materials*. 2. n. ~ material. [F, or f. L *textilis* (as prec., see -ILE)]

tĕx′tūal, a. Of, in, the text, as ~ *criticism*, *errors*. Hence ~LY² adv. [ME & AF *textuel* (as TEXT, see -AL)]

tĕx′tūal|ist, n. One who adheres strictly to the letter of the text, so ~ISM n.; ready quoter of scriptural texts. [-IST]

tĕx′tur|e, n. Arrangement of threads etc. in textile fabric, as *loose* ~ *e*; arrangement of constituent parts, structure, (*of* skin, rock, literary work, etc.); representation of surface of objects in works of art; (biol.) tissue, structure of this. Hence ~AL (-cher-, -tūr-) a. [ME, f. L *textura* (as TEXT, see -URE)]

tĕx′tureless (-cherl-, -tūrl-), a. Without discernible texture, amorphous.. [-LESS]

-th¹, suf. forming nn. (a) f. vbs; in some, as *bath, birth, death*, Gmc, repr. var. Aryan suff. (*-tos* etc.); in others, going back to OE or ON, as *tilth*, or of later form. aş *growth, spilth, stealth*; the suf. appears regularly as *-t* in *flight, gift, thirst* (f. Gmc), & in *sight* (in E). (b) f. adjj. (rarely nn.), OE *-thu, -tho, -th* (= Goth. *-itha*, Gmc*-ithō*), forming nn. of state, as *filth* (*foul*), *length* (*long*), etc., & by analogy *breadth, sloth*, etc. In some, *-th* is repr. by *-t*, as *height, slight, theft*.

-th², **-eth** after *-ty*, suf. forming ordinal numbers with all simple numbers from *fourth* onward in mod. E; repr. OE *-tha, -the*, or *-othå, -othe*, f. Aryan *-tos* (cf. Gk *pemptos*, L *quintus*).

thăl′amus, n. (pl. *-mī*). (Gk ant.) inner room, women's apartment; (anat.) place where nerve emerges from brain, esp. optic ~; (bot.) receptacle of flower. [L, f. Gk *thalamos*]

tha′ler (tah-), n. (hist.). German silver coin. [G, see DOLLAR]

Thali′|a, n. MUSE¹ of comedy & pastoral poetry; one of the Graces. Hence ~AN a. [L, f. Gk *Thaleia* (*thallō* bloom)]

thăll′|ium, n. Rare soft white metallic element used in making a highly refractive optical glass. Hence ~IC, ~OUS, aa.. [f. foll. (from green line given in spectrum) +-IUM]

thăll′|us, n. Plant-body not differentiated into root, stem, and leaves. Hence ~OID a. [L, f. Gk *thallos* green shoot (*thallō* bloom)]

than (dhan, -ăn), conj. (& quasi-prep.) introducing second member of comparison, as *you are taller* ~ *he* (*is*), (colloq.) *taller* ~ *him, I know you better* ~ *he* (*does*), *better* ~ (I know) *him, it is better to use hot water* ~ *cold, do anything rather* ~ *let him get off,* *would do anything rather* ~ *that he should get off, a man* ~ *whom no one is better able to judge*. [OE *thanne* etc., orig. same wd as THEN ; *A is better* ~ *B* orig. = *A is better, then B*; so OS *than*, OHG *danne*]

thăn′age, n. Rank of, land granted to, thane. [ME, f. AF *thanage*, f. THANE +-AGE]

thănat|(o)-, comb. form of Gk *thanatos* death, as ~*ophĭd′ia* n. pl., poisonous snakes.

thăn′atoid, a. Deathlike, apparently dead; deadly. [as prec. +-OID]

thăne, n. (In early Eng. hist.) member of a rank between ordinary freemen and hereditary nobles. Hence ~′DOM, ~′HOOD, ~′SHIP, nn. [OE *theg(e)n, thēn* servant, soldier, = OS *thegan*, OHG *degan*, ON *thegn* f. Gmc **thegnaz* cogn. w. Gk *teknon* child]

thănk¹, v.t. Express gratitude to (person *for* thing); ~ *you*, I ~ you (polite formula acknowledging gift, service, offer accepted or refused); (as contempt. refusal) ~ *you for nothing*; (anticipatory) ~ *you* (*for that ball*)!, please throw it here; (as polite formula, now usu. iron. implying reproach) *I will* ~ *you to shut the door, wipe your boots, leave my affairs alone*; *he may* ~ *himself, has only himself to* ~ *, for that, it is his own fault*. [OE *thancian*, (OS *thankōn*, OHG *dankōn*), f. foll.]

thănk², n. (now only in pl.). (Expression of) gratitude, as *give* ~*s to Heaven, expressed his heartfelt* ~*s, she bowed her* ~*s, small* (iron. *much*)~*s I got for it*; ~*-offering* (bibl.), Jewish offering made as act of thanksgiving; (as formula) ~*s*, thank you; ~*s to* (as the result of) *my foresight, your obstinacy*. Hence ~′WORTHY a. (arch.). [OE *thanc, thonc*, OS *thank*, OHG *dank*, (ON *thǫkk*), Goth. *thagks* f. Gmc **thankaz* cogn. w. THINK]

thănk′ful, a. Grateful; (of words or act) expressive of thanks. Hence ~LY² adv., ~NESS n. [-FUL]

thănk′less, a. Not feeling or expressing gratitude; *a* ~ *task* (not likely to win thanks, unprofitable). Hence ~LY² adv., ~NESS n. [-LESS]

thănks′giving, n. Expression of gratitude esp. to God; form of words for this, as *General T* ~ (in Book of Common Prayer); *T* ~ *day* (set apart in U.S. for ~ to God, usu. last Thursday of November); (bibl.) offering made as ~.

thar (tär), n. Goat antelope of Nepal. [native]

that¹, a., pron., & adv. **1.** demonstr. adj. & pron. (pr. dhăt; pl. *those* pr. dhōz). The (person, thing), the person or thing pointed to or drawn attention to or observed by the speaker at the time, or already named or understood or in question or familiar, as *observe* ~ *dog in the next field, who is* ~ (*woman*) *in the garden?, what was* ~ *noise?, what noise is* ~*?, don't roll your eyes like* ~ (as you are doing) or *in* ~ *imbecile fashion, I knew all* ~ *before, talked about responsibilities & all* ~ (similar commonplaces), ~ (your action, the action you tell me of) *is not fair*, ~'s *right!* (formula of approval, also vulg. = yes), (colloq.; also *there 's*) ~'s (you, in view of present or future compliance etc., are) *a dear!, I use* ~ (or *the*) *term·in a special sense, much to the disgust of* ~ (or *the*) *monarch, was cured from* ~ *hour, things were easier in those* *days, so* ~*'s* ~ (formula closing narrative or discussion), *come out of* ~ (sl. form ordering person etc. to clear out), *wouldn't give* ~ (a finger-snap) *for it,* AT ~; (with feeling) *I will not see* ~ *boy put upon, why will you bring* ~ *woman here?, when you have done thumping* ~ *piano, shall not easily forget* ~ *day*; (coupled or contrasted with *this,* & applied esp. to the farther, less immediate or obvious, etc., of two) *this poker is much heavier than* ~ (*one*), *went to this doctor & * ~ *or to this & * ~ *doctor* (various doctors), *this,* ~, & *the other* (various things), *put this & * ~ (various facts etc.) *together*; (as pron. replacing *the* w. noun, w. sense completed by rel. pron. expressed or, in obj. case & arch. in subj., omitted) *those who drink water think water, those may try it who choose, had* ~ *in his eye which forbade further trifling, all those* (~) *I saw, all those* (usu. *the*) *specimens* ~ *I saw, those* (usu. *the*) *few* (*books*) ~ *I had, a different pattern to* ~ (*which*) *I was used to*; (or by adj. or equivalent) *those unfit for use, those below the standard, a tunic like* ~ *described above, those* (usu. *the*) *persons most injured by the tax, like most of those issuing from German workshops, cost of oil is less than* ~ *of gas*; (foll. by *that* conj.) such, such a, as *has* ~ *confidence in his theory that he would put it into practice tomorrow, was wounded to* ~ *degree that he resigned.* 2. adv. (pr. dhăt). To such a degree, so, as (colloq.) *will go* ~ *far, have done* ~ *much,* (vulg.) *I was* ~ *angry I could have struck him.* 3. rel. pron. (pl. same; pr. dhat; used, exc. arch., rhet., poet., only to introduce defining-clause essential or rhet. viewed as essential to identification; now largely replaced by WHO & to some extent by WHICH, esp. after antecedent ~; in obj. case, & in arch. use in subj., ~ is often omitted; prep. governing ~ is always placed after it & usu. at end of clause). Exx.: *the book* (~ *or which*) *I sent you, the box* (~ *or which*) *you put them in, the man* (~ *or* usu. *whom*) *you stopped, the people* (~) *you got it from or from whom you got it, the meanest flower* ~ (rarely *which*) *blows, the best* ~ (not *which*) *you can do, no one* (~; not *whom*) *I ever heard of could see any difference*; (colloq.) *Mrs Smith, Mary Jones* ~ (not *who*) *was* (=whose maiden name was Mary Jones). [OE *thæt,* nom. & acc. sing. neut. of the demonstr. pron. & adj. *se, sẽo, thæt*; see THE]

that[2] (dhat, *occas.* -ăt), conj. introducing subordinate clauses: (of statement or hypothesis) *they say* (~) *he is better, there is no doubt* (~) *he meant it, it is suggested* ~ *the mistake was intentional, it is hoped* ~ *all will go well, it is monstrous* ~ *he should expect further help, to think* (~) *he should use me so!*; (of purpose) *he lives* ~ *he may eat, he withdrew* (*in order*) ~ *the*

dispute might cease; (of result) *am so sleepy* (~) *I cannot keep my eyes open, his language was such* ~ *we declined further dealings with him, what have I done* ~ *he should cut me?, where is he,* ~ *you come without him?*; (of reason or cause) *it is rather* ~ *he has not the time, not* ~ (I do not say this because) *I have any objection*; (of wish) (O) ~ *that were all!,* (O) ~ *I knew the truth!*; (arch. or literary) *in* ~, since, in so far as: *now* ~, since now, as *you ought to write now* ~ *you know the address.* [uses of THAT[1] demonstr. or rel. pron., in which it becomes a mere relative or conjunctive particle; cf. THE]

thătch, n., & v.t. 1. Roof-covering of straw, reeds, or (in tropical countries) coconut & other leaves; (colloq.) hair of the head. 2. v.t. Cover (roof, house, or abs.) with ~. [(n.) late collateral form of (now dial.) *thack* (after the vb *thatch,* OE *thecc*(e)*an*), OE *thæc,* OHG *dach,* ON *thak*; f. Gmc *thakam* cogn. w. L *tegere* cover]

thaum'atrōpe, n. Disc etc. on which are depicted images that appear to go through various movements when disc revolves. [irreg. f. Gk *thauma* wonder + -*tropos* -turning]

thaum'atǔrg|e, n. Worker of miracles, wonder-worker. Hence or cogn. **thaumatǔr'g**IC(AL) aa., ~IST, ~Y[1], nn. [f. med. L f. Gk *thaumaturgos* a. (*thauma -matos* wonder + -o- + -*ergos* -working)]

thaw, v.i. & t., & n. 1. (Of ice, snow, frozen thing) pass to liquid state, melt, dissolve; (of weather, *it*) become so warm as to melt ice etc., rise above 32° Fahr.; (fig.) be freed from coldness or stiffness, unbend, become genial; cause to ~ (lit. & fig.). 2. n. ~ing, warmth of weather that ~s, as *a* ~ *has set in.* Hence ~'LESS, ~'Y[2], aa. [OE *thawian,* OHG *douwen,* ON *theyja*]

the (*before vowel* dhĭ, *before consonant* dhe, *emphat.* dhē), a. & adv. 1. adj. Applied esp. to person(s) or thing(s) already mentioned or under discussion, or from the nature of the case actually or potentially existent, or unique (as class or individual), or familiar, or otherwise sufficiently identified, as *tried to soothe* ~ *child, gave* ~ *fellow a shilling, shall let* ~ *matter drop, how is* ~ *game or score?, what is* ~ *time?, depends on* ~ *weather,* ~ *Devil, sun, moon, stars, Thames, inflammation of* ~ *lungs, pulled* ~ *trigger, what was* ~ *result?, you will be* ~ *loser, revised by* ~ *author, find their way to* ~ *sea, went to* ~ *baths, theatre, rink,* ~ *King,* ~ *Home Secretary,* ~ M[c]*Gregor* etc. (chief of clan), *story does not lose in* ~ *telling*; to sing. n. as repr. species, class, etc., as ~ *lion, domestic cat, philosopher, cucumber, gavotte, general reader, man in the street, new woman,* (rhet., esp. bibl.) ~ *oppressor, locust*; to some nn. used in restricted sense, esp. fig. repr. a pursuit etc., as ~ *gloves, ribbons, table, stage, theatre, platform, hustings, bottle, pulpit, fancy*;

to names of diseases etc. (now partly arch.), as ~ *smallpox, measles, tooth-ache, gout, fidgets, blues* (depression), *hump,* (vulg.) ~ (habit of) *drink*; to nn. expr. a unit, as *10d.* ~ (or *a* or *per*) *pound, yard,* etc., *£15* ~ *coat & skirt, allow 8 minutes (to)* ~ *mile, 16 oz to* ~ *pound*; with sense completed by ref. clause or adj. or equivalent, as ~ *book (that) you borrowed,* ~ *best (that) I can do for you, has not* ~ *nerve for motoring, wonder you have* ~ *impudence (to ask it* expr. or under-stood), (exclam.)~ *impudence of* ~ *fellow!,* ~ *cup on* ~ *top shelf,* ~ *one with a broken handle,* ~ *bottom of a well,* ~ *best way,* ~ *only way,* ~ *way out,* ~ *upper classes,* ~ *better man of the two*; w. adjj. used abs., as *none but* ~ *brave* (brave men) *deserve* ~ *fair,* ~ *beautiful* (beauty), ~ *sublime*; w. adjj. rhet. viewed as part of definition, as ~ *virtuous & talented Duchess of X., details of* ~ *shocking disaster,* ~ *enraged animal*; (dhē; italics) applied to the person or thing best known or best entitled to the name, as *no relation to the Browning,* the *tobacco is* (advertiser's). **2.** adv. (a) rel., only in comb. w. (b). In whatever degree. (b) In that degree, by that amount, on that account. Exx.: ~ *more he gets,* ~ *more he wants; I play* ~ *worse,* ~ *more I practise; am not* (or *none*) ~ *more inclined to help him because he is poor, on that account, for what you tell me; none* ~ *better for seeing you; that makes it all* ~ *worse* (in the full degree to be expected from what you say etc.); (tautologically) *so much* ~ *worse for him,* ~ worse, so much worse, for him. [late OE *the,* the reduced & flexionless stem of the OE demonstr. *se, sēo, thæt* (= THAT[1]), = ON *sá, sú, that,* Goth. *sa, sō, thata,* cogn. w. Gk *ho, hē, to,* Skr. *sa, sā, tat*; **2.** OE *thȳ, thē,* instrumental case]

theân'dric, a. Of the union, by joint agency, of divine & human nature in Christ. [f. eccl. Gk *theandrikos* (*theos* god, *anēr andros* man, -IC)]

theânthrŏp'ic(al), aa. Both divine & human; tending to embody deity in human form. [f. eccl. Gk *theanthrōpos* god-man f. *theos* god + *anthrōpos* man + -IC]

the'ârchy (-kǐ), n. Government by god(s); class, order, of gods, as *the Olympian* ~. [f. eccl. Gk *thearkhia* rule of god (Gk *theos* god + -*arkhia* f. *arkhō* rule)]

the'atre (-ter), n. Building for dramatic spectacles, playhouse; ‖ *patent* ~ (established by letters patent, not licensed by Lord Chamberlain); room, hall, for lectures etc. with seats in tiers (*operating-* ~, for surgical demonstrations); dramatic literature or art; scene, field, of operation, as *the* ~ *of war; good* ~ (pred.), effective on the stage; ~*goer, -going,* frequenter, frequenting, of ~s. [ME, f. OF, or L f. Gk *theatron* f. *theaomai* behold]

theât'rical, a. & n. **1.** (Of manner, speech,

gesture, person) calculated for effect, showy, affected; of or suited to the theatre, of acting or actors, so **theât'ric** a. (rare). **2.** n. pl. ~ performances, esp. *private* (amateur) ~s. Hence ~ISM(2, 4), ~ITY (-ǎl[2]), nn., ~IZE(3) v.t., ~LY[2] adv. [f. LL f. Gk *theatrikos* (prec., -ICAL)]

Thēbā'id (or thē[2]), n. Territory around Thebes (in Egypt); poem on (siege of) Thebes (in Greece), esp. that of Statius. [f. L f. Gk *Thēbaïs -idos* (*Thēbai* Thebes)]

Thēb'an, a. & n. (Inhabitant) of Thebes. [-AN]

thé dansant (tā dahṅsahṅ'), n. Afternoon tea with dancing. [F]

thee. See THOU.

thĕft, n. Stealing; larceny. [OE *thīefth, thēofth,* later *thēoft* (THIEF, -TH[1])]

thegn (-ān), n. (hist.). Older form of THANE.

thē'ine, n. = CAFFEINE. [f. mod. L *thea* tea + -INE[1]]

their (dhār), possessive case of, & adj. corresponding to, THEY, with absolute form *theirs* (for uses cf. HER[2]). [f. ON *their(r)a* gen. pl. of *sá* = OE *se* THE]

thē'ism, n. Belief in existence of a god supernaturally revealed to man (cf. DEISM) & sustaining a personal relation to his creatures. So ~IST n., ~ĭs'tIC(AL) aa. [f. Gk *theos* god + -ISM]

them. See THEY.

thĕmăt'ic, a. (Mus.) of themes, as ~ *treatment,* ~ *catalogue* (giving opening themes as well as names etc.); (gram.) of, belonging to, a theme, as ~ *vowel, form.* Hence **thĕmăt'ICALLY** adv. [f. Gk *thematikos* (as foll., -IC)]

thēme, n. Subject on which one speaks, writes, or thinks; school composition, essay, on given subject; (gram.) stem of noun or verb, part to which inflexions are added; (mus.) melodic subject usu. developed with variations; (hist.) any of 29 provinces in Byzantine empire; ~ *song,* recurrent melody in musical play or film. [ME, f. L f. Gk *thema -matos* (*tithēmi* set, place, see -M); partly thr. OF]

Thĕm'is, n. (Gk myth.) goddess of law & justice; these personified. [L f. Gk *Themis* law]

themselves (dhemsĕlvz'), pron. Emphat. & reflex. form corresp. to THEY (for use, cf. HIMSELF). [see SELF]

then (dhĕn), adv., conj., a., & n. **1.** adv. At that time, as *was* ~ *too much occupied,* ~ *comes the trouble, the* ~ *existing ordinances*; next, afterwards, after that, as *it must* ~ *soak for two hours, & ~ the operation is complete; now & ~,* at one time & another, from time to time. **2.** conj. In that case, therefore, it follows that, (often *well,* ~), as ~ *you should have said so,* ~ *it is no use your going,* (*but*) ~ (if what you say is true) *why did you take it?*; (of grudging or impatient concession) if you must have it so, as *take it* ~, *between you & I* . . . '*me*', ~; (resumptively, not as first word) accordingly, as *the new Governor*, ~, *came prepared*; NOW ~. **3.** adj. Existing etc. at that time, as *the ~ Duke, secretary*. **4.** n. That time, as *before, till, by, from*, ~; *every now & ~*, from time to time. [OE *thanne, thenne*, etc., = OS *than(na)*, OHG *danne, denne*, (cf. Goth. *than*), adv. formation f. demonstr. root *tha-*; cf. THAT, THE]

then´ar, n. (anat.). Palm of hand, sole of foot; (also attrib. ~ *prominence, eminence*) ball of thumb. [Gk *thenar*]

thence (dh-), adv. (Arch.) from that place, from there; (somewhat arch.) from that source, for that reason, as *a discrepancy ~ results, it ~ appears*; ~*forth'*, ~*for'ward*, advv. & nn., from (or *from*) that time forward. [ME *thannes, thennes*, f. *thenne* adv. (OE *thanon(e)* etc., f. *tha-* as THEN), +-ES]

the|o-, comb. form of Gk *theos* god, as: ~*öc'racy*, government or State governed by God directly or through a sacerdotal class etc., *the Theoc'racy*, Jewish commonwealth from Moses to the monarchy; *thē'ocrat*, ruler in, subject under, ~*ocracy*, so *theōcrăt'ic* a.; ~*öc'ratist*, believer in direct intervention & authority of God through revelation in government of society; ~*öc'rasy* (or *thē'okrāsi*) [f. Gk *krasis* mixture], union of soul with God through contemplation (among Neo--platonists, Buddhists, etc.); ~*öd'icy* [f. Gk *dĭkē* right], vindication of divine providence in view of existence of evil; ~*ög'ony*, (poem dealing with) genealogy of the gods, so *thēogŏn'ìc* a., ~*ŏg'onist* n.; ~*ŏm'achy* (-ki), strife against or among the gods; *thēomăn'ia*, insane belief that one is God, also, religious insanity, so *thēomăn'iac* n.; ~*öph'any*, appearance of God to man, so *thēophăn'ic* a.; *thēophilăn'thropist*, one who professes to unite love to God with love to man, so *thēophilanthrŏp'ic* a., *thēophilăn'thropist*, *thēophilăn'thropy*, nn.; *thēopneus'ly*, divine inspiration, so *thēopneus'tic* a.; *thē'otechny* (-k-), supernatural machinery, so *thēotech'nic* (-k-) a.

thēŏd'ol|ite, n. Surveying-instrument for measuring horizontal and vertical angles by means of telescope. Hence ~*it'IC* a. [16th c. *-delitus*, of unkn. (Engl.) orig.]

Thēodōs'ian, n. Of the emperor Theodosius (I, II, or III), esp. ~ *code* (published under Theodosius II, d. 450). [-AN]

thēolō'ğian, n. Person skilled in, professor of, theology. [F (-*ien*), as foll. + -AN]

thēŏl'ogӯ, n. Science of (esp. Christian) religion; *natural* ~ (dealing with knowledge of God as gained from his works by light of nature & reason); *positive*, *revealed*, ~ (based on revelation); *dogmatic* ~ (dealing with authoritative teaching of the Scriptures & the Church); *speculative* ~ (giving scope to human speculation, not confined to revelation);

systematic ~, methodical arrangement of the truths of religion in their natural connexion. Hence or cogn. **thēolō'ğICAL** a., **thēolō'ğically**[2] adv., **thèŏl'oğIZE**(1, 2) v.t. & i. [ME & OF *theologie* f. L f. Gk THEO(*logia* -LOGY)]

thêŏrb'ō, n. (pl. ~s). Two-necked musical instrument of lute class much used in 17th c. [f. It. *tiorba*, of unkn. orig.; whence F *téorbe, théorbe*]

thē'or|êm, n. (Math.) proposition to be proved by chain of reasoning, a truth to be established by means of accepted truths, (cf. PROBLEM); algebraical or other rule, esp. one expressed by symbols or formulae, as BINOMIAL ~*em*; a speculative truth. Hence~*êmăt'IC*(AL) aa.,~*êm'at*-IST(3) n. [f. F, or LL f. Gk *theōrēma* (*theōreō*, see THEORY & -M)]

thēor|ĕt'ic, a. & n. **1.** = foll. **2.** n. pl. Speculative parts of a science etc., so ~*êti'CIAN* (-ĭshn) n. [f. LL f. Gk *theōrētikos* (as THEORY, see -ETIC)]

thēorĕt'ical, a. Concerned with knowledge but not with its practical application, speculative; based on mere theory, not dealing with facts as presented by experience. Hence~*LY*[2] adv. [-AL]

thē'or|ӯ, n. Supposition explaining something, esp. one based on principles independent of the phenomena etc. to be explained, opp. to HYPOTHESIS, as *atomic* ~*y*, ~*y of gravitation, evolution*; speculative view, as *one of my pet* ~*ies* (often implying fancifulness); the sphere of speculative thought, as *this is all very well in* ~*y, but how will it work in practice?*; exposition of the principles of a science etc., as *the* ~*y of music*; (math.) collection of results designed to illustrate principles of a subject, as ~*y of chances, equations*. Hence ~*IST*(3), ~*IZA'TION*, nn., ~*IZE*(2) v.i. [f. LL f. Gk *theōria* f. *theōros* spectator f. *theōreō* behold]

thēŏs'oph|ӯ, n. Any of various ancient & modern philosophies professing to attain to a knowledge of God by spiritual ecstasy, direct intuition, or special individual relations. Hence or cogn. **thē'o-sŏph**,~*ER*[1],~*IST*(2), nn., **thēosŏph'IC**(AL), **thēosophis'tICAL**, aa., ~*IZE*(2) v.i. [f. med. L f. late Gk *theosophia* f. THEO(*sophos* wise)]

-ther, **-ter**, suf. repr. (a) Aryan compar. suf. *-tero-*, Gk *-teros*, L-*ter* (*alter, neuter*), as in *after, further; either, other, whether*; (b) indicating direction (cf. Goth. *-thrō, -drē*, L *citro, ultro*), as in *hither, thither, whither*.

thĕrapeut'|ic, a. & n. **1.** Curative; of the healing art. **2.** n. pl. Branch of medicine concerned with treatment of disease & action of remedial agents in disease or health. Hence ~*ĭCAL* a., ~*icALLY*[2] adv., ~*IST*(3) n. [f. LL f. Gk *therapeutikos* (*therapeuō* wait on, cure, f. *theraps* servant, use -IC)]

-thē'rapӯ, suf. f. Gk *therapeia* service,

medical treatment, denoting medical treatment as indicated by first element of wd; also as n. (*occupational therapy*).

there (dhār, dher *as below*), adv., n., & int. **1.** In or at that place, as *put it down ~, what is that dog doing ~?, lived ~ some years, have been ~ before* (sl.), know all about it, *all ~* (sl.), in one's senses, sane, *~ it is—on the sofa,* (calling attention) *you ~!*; at that point in argument, progress of affairs, situation, etc., as *~ I agree with you, ~ is* (or *comes in*) *the rub, you had* (the advantage of) *him ~, ~ it* (the trouble) *is, you see*; HERE & *~, neither* HERE *nor ~*; to that place, as *go ~ every day, got ~ in two minutes, get ~* (sl.), succeed; *~ or ~abouts,* (transf.) about that amount, time, etc. ('*was it two years ago?*' '*T~ or ~abouts*'; *will come to £100, ~ or ~abouts*); (merely expletive or introductory, usu. dher; preceding, or in interrog. or neg. or quasi-neg. sentence following, verb that normally precedes its subject, esp. *be*; in poet. or exclam. use subject may stand first) *~ was a cart close by, ~ was nothing ~, ~ was plenty to eat, what is ~ for supper?, not a sound was ~ to indicate their presence, seldom has ~ been more fuss, ~. fell a deep silence, a knight ~ was, a nice mess ~ is* or *seems to be!*; *~'s* (=THAT¹*'s*) *a dear* etc. **2.** n. That place, as *was brought from ~, lives somewhere near ~, tide comes up to ~, passed by ~.* **3.** int. Expr. confirmation, triumph, dismay, etc., as *~! what did I tell you?,* or used to soothe child etc., as *~, ~, never mind.* **4.** *~about(s)', near* that place, as *ought to be somewhere ~abouts,* near that number, quantity, etc., as *two gallons or ~abouts*; *~af'ter* (arch.), after that, according to that rule etc.; *~anent'* (Sc.), about that matter; *~at'* (arch.), at that place, on that account, after that; *~by'* (or dhār'bī), by that means,. as result of that (& *~by hangs a tale,* in which connexion there is something to be told, see *As You Like It,* II. vii. 28); *~for'* (arch.), for that object or purpose; *~'fore,* for that reason, accordingly, consequently; *~from'* (arch.), from that or it; *~in'* (arch.), in that place, in that respect; *~inaf'ter, ~before',* later, earlier, in same document etc.; *~in'to* (arch.), into that place; *~of'* (arch.), of that or it; *~on'* (arch.), on that or it (of motion & position); *~out'* (arch.), out of that, from that source; *~through'* (arch.), through that; *~to'* (arch.), to that or it, in addition, to boot; *~un'to* (arch.), to that or it; *~upon',* in consequence of that, soon or immediately after that, (arch.) upon that (of motion or position); *~with'* (arch.), with that, *~upon; ~withal',* in addition, besides. [OE *thǣr, thēr,* OS *thār,* OHG *dār,* ON, Goth. *thar* f. demonstr. root *tha-* (THAT, THE)]

ther'iăc, n. (Also *therī'aca Andrŏm'achī* pr. -akī, *Venice treacle*) antidote to bites

of poisonous animals compounded of many drugs. [f. L f. Gk *thēriakē* antidote, fem. adj. as n. (*thērion* dim. of *thēr* wild beast, see -AC)]

thēri|ănthrŏp'ic, a. Of, worshipping, beings represented under form of man & beast. So *~ăn'thropISM(3)* n. [f. Gk *thērion* beast + *anthrōpos* man + -IC]

thĕrm, n. Statutory unit of calorific value in gas-supply (100,000 B.Th. units; see THERMAL). [f. Gk *thermē* heat]

thĕrm'ae, n. pl. (Gk & Rom. ant.). Hot springs or (esp. public) baths. [L, f. Gk *thermai* pl. as prec.]

thĕrm'al, a. & n. **1.** Of heat, as *~ unit* (for measuring heat); *British ~ unit* (abbr. *B.Th.U.*), amount of heat required to raise 1 lb. of water at maximum density through 1° Fahr.; *~ equator,* line along which greatest heat occurs on earth's surface; *~ springs,* hot springs; of thermae. **2.** n. Rising current of heated air (used by gliders). Hence *~LY²* adv. [f. F, as THERM + -AL]

thĕrman'tidōte, n. Apparatus for cooling the air, used in India. [as THERM + ANTIDOTE]

thĕrm'ic, a. Of heat, as *~ rays, conditions.* [as THERM + -IC]

Thĕrmidŏr'ian, n. Any of those who effected or favoured Robespierre's overthrow on Thermidor 9th, 1794. [f. F *thermidorien* (*thermidor,* republican month July–August, as THERM + Gk *dōron* gift), see -IAN]

thĕrmi'on, n. An ION emitted by an incandescent substance. Hence **thĕrmiŏn'ic** a. (*~ic valve* or *vacuum tube,* appliance giving copious flow of electrons used esp. in wireless transmission & reception). [THERMO- + ION]

thĕrm'ite, -mit, n. Mixture of finely powdered aluminium and oxide of iron that produces a very high temperature on combustion (used in welding and as a composition for incendiary bombs). [G (-*mit*), f. foll. + -ITE¹]

thĕrm'o-, comb. form of Gk *thermos* warm, *thermē* heat, as: *~chem'istry* (-kĕm-), branch of chemistry dealing with the quantities of heat evolved or absorbed during chemical reactions; *~-(electric) couple,* = *~pile*; *~dynăm'ics,* science of the relations between heat & mechanical work; *~-electri'city,* electricity produced by difference of temperature, so *~-elec'tric* a.; *~gen'esis,* production of heat esp. in human body, so *~genĕl'ic, ~gĕn'ic,* aa.; *~gram,* record made by *~graph* (self-registering thermometer); *~nuclear* (hydrogen) *bomb*; *~pile, ~-electric battery* esp. arranged for measuring small quantities of radiant heat; *~scope,* instrument for detecting differences of temperature without measuring, so *~scop'ic(al)* aa.; *~setting,* (of plastics) setting when heated; *~stat,* automatic instrument for regulating temperature, so *~stăt'ic a.;*

~*stăt′ics*, theory of the equilibrium of heat; ~*tăx′is*, regulation of heat or temperature esp. in warm-blooded animals, so ~*tăc′tic*, ~*tăx′ic*, aa.; *ther-mŏt′ropism*, involuntary movement of animal or plant towards or away from source of heat.

thermŏm′eter, n. Instrument for measuring temperature, usu. glass tube with small bore containing mercury or alcohol, & variously graduated (*Fahrenheit, Réaumur, Celsius* or *Centigrade*, ~, with freezing-point at 32°, 0°, 0°, boiling-point of water at 212°, 80°, 100°); *clinical* ~ (small, with range of 25° or less, for taking temperature of the body); MAXIMUM, MINIMUM, ~. Hence **thermomĕt′ric**(AL) aa., **thermomĕt′rical**LY[2] adv., **thermŏm′etry** n. [THERMO- + -METER]

therm′ŏs, n. *T*~ *flask* or ~, brand of VACUUM flask. [P]

ther′oid, a. (Esp. of idiot) having beast-like propensities. [f. Gk *thēr* wild beast + -OID]

therŏl′og|ў, n. Science of mammals, mammalogy. So ~IST n. [as prec. + -LOGY]

thesaur′us, n. (pl. -*rī*). Elaborate lexicon, cyclopaedia. [L, f. Gk *thēsauros* treasure]

these. See THIS.

thĕs′is (*or* thē- *as below*), n. (pl. *thĕses* pr. -ēz). **1.** Proposition to be maintained; dissertation, esp. one by candidate for degree; school or college exercise. **2.** (*Also* thē-) unaccented syllable in English scansion (cf. ARSIS). [L f. Gk *thesis* putting, placing; a proposition etc., f. *the*- root of *tithēmi* place]

Thĕs′pian, a. & n. **1.** Of Thespis, semi-legendary Greek dramatic poet of 6th c. B.C.; *the* ~ *art*, the drama. **2.** n. Actor or actress. [f. Gk *Thespis* + -AN]

thĕt′a, n. Greek letter (Θ, θ) = th. [Gk]

theŭr′gy|ў, n. Supernatural agency esp. in human affairs; art of securing this; magical science of Neoplatonists; production of effects by supernatural agency opp. natural magic. Hence or cogn. **theŭr′gic**(AL) aa., ~IST(3) n. [f. LL f. Gk *theourgia* f. *theos* god + -*ergos* working]

thews (-z), n. pl. Sinews, muscles; (fig.) mental or moral vigour. Hence **thewED**[2] (-ŭd), **thew′**LESS, **thew′y**[2], aa. [OE *thēaw*, = ·OS *thau*, OHG *dau* usage, custom]

they (dhā), pron. (obj. *them* pr. dhem, -ĕm, poss. THEIR). Pl. of HE, SHE, IT; ~ (the persons) *who*; ~ (people in general) *say*; ~ (those in authority) *have raised the rates*; (joc.) *them′s* (those are) *my sentiments*. [ME *thei* f. ON *their* nom. pl. masc. of *sá, sú, that* THE]

thick, a., n., & adv. **1.** Of great or specified depth between opposite surfaces, as *bread is* (*cut*) *too* ~, *spread the butter* ~, *a board two inches* ~, *how* ~ *was it?*; (of line etc.) broad, not fine, (of script, type, etc.) consisting of ~ lines. **2.** Arranged

closely, crowded together, as ~ *hair, forest, crowd grew* ~*er*; numerous, as *fell* ~ *as peas*; abounding, packed, *with*, as *trees* ~ *with leaves, air* ~ *with snow*; of firm consistence, as ~ *paste, soup*; turbid, muddy, cloudy, not clear, as ~ *puddles, weather is still* ~. **3.** Stupid, dull; (of voice) muffled, indistinct. **4.** (colloq.) Intimate, esp. ~ *as thieves*. **5.** *Lay it on* ~, (sl.) be profuse esp. in compliments; ‖ *a bit* ~, *rather* ~, *a little too* ~, etc. (sl.), going beyond what is reasonable, too much of a good thing; ‖~ *ear* (sl.), external ear swollen as result of blow (esp. in *give* person *a* ~ *ear*). **6.** ~*′head*, blockhead; ~*-headed*, stupid; ~*′sĕt′*, set or growing close together, heavily or solidly built, (n., ~*′set*) kind of stout fustian, (also ~*set hedge*) close-grown hedge; ~*-skinned*, (fig.) not sensitive to reproach, insult, etc., stolid; ~*-skulled*, *-witted*, stupid; ‖ ~*′un* (obs. sl.), sovereign (coin). **7.** n. The ~ part of anything, esp. fig. *in the* ~ *of it* (of fight etc.); (colloq.) stupid person; *through* ~ *& thin*, under all conditions, resolutely, so ~*-&-thin* a., as ~*-&-thin supporters*. **8.** adv. ~ly, as *snow was falling* ~, *blows came fast &* ~, *heart beats* ~. Hence ~ISH[1] a., ~ly[2] adv. [OE *thicce*, OS *thikki*, OHG *dicki*, ON *thykkr* f. Gmc *thik*(*k*)*uz*]

thick′en, v.t. & i. Make or become thick; make (gravy etc.) of stiffer consistence, whence ~ING[1](3) n.; *plot* ~s (becomes more intricate). [-EN[6]]

thick′et, n. Number of shrubs, trees, etc., growing close together. [OE *thiccet* f. THICK + -*et* denominative suf.]

thick′ness, n. Being thick; dimension other than length & breadth; piece of material of known ~, as *three* ~*es of cardboard will suffice*. [-NESS]

thief, n. (pl. -*ves*). **1.** One who steals esp. secretly & without violence, whence **thiev′**ERY(4), **thiev′ish**NESS, nn., **thiev′**ISH[1] a., **thiev′ish**LY[2] adv.; *thieves′* LATIN. **2.** Projection in wick of candle causing it to gutter. [OE *thēof*, OS *thiof*, OHG *diob*, ON *thjófr*, Goth *thiufs* f. Gmc **theubhaz*]

thieve, v.i. & t. Be a thief, practise stealing; steal (thing). [OE *thēofian* (as prec.)]

thigh (thī), n. Part of human leg between hip & knee, corresponding part in other animals; *smile* HIP[1] *and* ~; ~*-bone*, single bone of ~, femur. Hence (-)~ED[2] (-īd) a. [OE *.thēoh*, OHG *dioh*, ON *thjó* f. Gmc **theuham*]

thill, n. Shaft of cart or carriage; (also ~*′ER*[1] n.)~*-horse* (put between~s). [14th c., of uncert. orig.; cf. DEAL[3]]

thim′ble, n. **1.** Metal cap (occas. open at end) worn to protect finger & push needle in sewing; (mech.) short metal tube, as ~ *joint, coupling*; metal ring concave on outside & fitting in rope to prevent chafing. **2.** ~*fŭl* (-bl-fŏŏl), small quantity (of brandy etc.) to drink; ~*-pie*, rapping on head with ~, as punishment;

~**rig** n. & v.i., (play) sleight-of-hand trick with three ~-shaped cups & pea, by-standers betting which cup covers pea, ~*rigger*, one who plays this, sharper. [OE *thȳmel*, as THUMB +-LE(1)]

thin[1], a. Having opposite surfaces close together, of small diameter, slender, as ~ *wire, string, board, sheet*; not dense, as ~ *air*; not full or closely packed, as ~ *house* (theatre); of slight consistency, as ~ *gruel*; lacking in important ingredient, as ~ *beer, blood, voice, humour, eloquence*; (fig.) shallow, transparent, flimsy, as ~ *disguise, excuse*, (colloq.) *that's too* ~; lean, not plump; (of lines) narrow, fine, (of script, type, etc.) consisting of ~ lines; (sl.) uncomfortable, distasteful, (esp. *have a* ~ *time*); *through* THICK *and* ~; ~-*skinned*, (fig.) sensitive. Hence ~'LY[2] adv., ~'NESS n., ~n'ISH[1] a. [OE *thynne*, OS *thunni*, OHG *dunni*, ON *thunnr* f. Gmc *thunnuz* cogn. w. L *tenuis*]

thin[2], v.t. & i. (-nn-). Make or become thin, reduce in bulk or numbers, as *his hair is* ~*ning, nation had* ~*ned under* (or *been* ~*ned by*) *proscription*; remove some young fruit from (vine, tree) to improve growth of rest (also ~ *out seedlings* etc.). [OE *thynnian*, as prec.]

thine. See THY.

thing, n. **1.** Whatever is or may be an object of thought (including or opp. to *person*), as: (of animate objects, esp. persons, expr. contempt, pity, affection, etc.) *poor* ~, *spiteful* ~, *a dear old* ~, *dumb* ~*s*, (sl.) OLD ~, *&* ~*s* (colloq.=*& the like*, etc.); (of inanimate material object) *take those* ~*s off the table, platinum is a costly* ~, *got my* ~*s* (clothes) *wet, pack up your* ~*s* (personal belongings); (of act, fact, idea, course, task, affair, circum-stance) *a foolish* ~ *to do*, SOFT ~, PUT[1]-*up* ~, *strange* ~ *that you cannot hold your tongue, that is not the same* ~, *the only* ~ *now is to take a cab, the* ~ (to aim at) *is to improve the pace*, ~*s begin to look brighter, has made a mess of* ~*s, takes* ~*s too seriously*; (of specimen or type of work etc.) *the latest* ~ *in hats, a little* ~ *of mine I should like to read to you*; *not the* (con-ventionally proper) ~; *am not feeling at all the* ~ (well); (law) ~*s personal, real,* personal, real, property; (pl., with adj. following, often joc.) all that is so describ-able (~*s Japanese, political, feminine, scholastic*, etc.). **2.** *Do the handsome* ~ *by*, treat handsomely; *have a* ~ *about* (colloq.), be obsessed by; *know a* ~ *or two*, be ex-perienced or shrewd; *make a good* ~ *of*, make good profit by. [OE (= OS, ON) *thing*, OHG *ding* public assembly etc.]

thing'amȳ, thing'umajig, thing'um-bŏb, thing'ummȳ, nn.(colloq.). Person, thing, whose name one forgets or treats as known, what's-his-name, what-d'you--call-it. [prec.]

think, v.t. & i. (*thought* pr. thawt). **1.** Consider, be of opinion, as *we* ~ (*that*)

he will come, we do not ~ *it probable, I* ~ *it a shame, it is not thought fair, is thought to be a fraud, I don't* ~ (sl. addition to ironical statement, as *you are a pattern of tact, I don't* ~). **2.** Intend, expect, as ~*s to deceive us.* **3.** Form conception of, as *cannot* ~ *the infinite*, (colloq.) *I can't* ~ *how you do it.* **4.** Recognize presence or existence of, as *the child thought no harm.* **5.** Reduce to specified condition etc. by ~*ing*, as *cannot* ~ *away a toothache, will* ~ *himself silly.* **6.** Exercise the mind otherwise than by passive reception of another's ideas, as *let me* ~ (appeal for time before answering etc.), ~ *twice before doing* (avoid hasty action), ~ *in German* etc. **7.** Have half-formed intention, as *I* ~ *I'll try.* **8.** ~ *about*, consider, esp. consider the practicability of (scheme, doing); ~ *aloud*, utter one's thoughts in the order of their occurrence; ~ *fit* or *good*, choose (*to* do esp. arbitrary or foolish thing); ~ *of*, consider, imagine, propose to oneself, entertain the idea of, hit upon, as *have many things to* ~ *of, to* ~ *of* (one can hardly imagine) *his not guess-ing it!, must be* ~*ing of going, couldn't* ~ *of such a thing*, ~ *of a word beginning with B, would have telephoned if I had thought of it*; ~ *better of*, decide on second thoughts to abandon (intention), (also) have higher opinion of (person, esp. *than to believe* etc.); ~ *little* or *nothing of*, consider insignificant or contemptible, as ~ *nothing of 30 miles a day, I* ~ *nothing of your friend Jones* ; ~ *much, well, highly, meanly, of*, esteem thus, ~ *no small* BEER *of*; ~ *out*, consider carefully, devise (plan etc.); ~ *over* (adv. or prep.), reflect upon, as ~ *over what I have said, will* ~ *it over*; ~ *up* (colloq.), devise. Hence ~'ABLE, ~'ING[2] (*all* ~*ing men*, all who accept my view), aa., ~'ER[1] n. [OE *thenc(e)an*, OS *thenkian*, OHG *denken*, ON *thekkja*, Goth. *thagkjan* f. Gmc *think-*, *thank-* (whence also THANK), *thunk-*]

thi(o)-, comb. form of Gk *theion* sulphur, as ~'*o-acid*, acid in which oxygen is replaced by sulphur.

third, a. & n. **1.** Next after second, whence ~'LY[2] adv. **2.** *~* DEGREE, ‖~ ESTATE, of EXCHANGE[1]; ~-*class*, -*rate*, (loosely) inferior, poor; (crick.) ~ *man*, (place of) fielder between slip(s) and point; ~ *party* or *person* (see PERSON for gram. sense), another besides the two principals, bystander etc., (~-*party risks* in insurance, damage to another than the insured, which the underwriter con-tracts to meet); ~ REPUBLIC. **3.** n. One of three equal divisions of a whole. **4.** Sixtieth of a second of time or angular measurement. **5.** (mus.). Interval of which the span involves three alpha-betical notes, harmonic combination of the notes thus separated. **6.** ~ part of husband's personal property, formerly going to widow in certain cases. [OE *thridda*, OS *-io*, OHG *dritto*, ON *thrithi*, Goth. *thridja* f. Gmc *thridhjaz* cogn. w. Gk *tritos*, L *tertius*]

thīrst, n., & v.i. **1.** Suffering caused by want of drink, desire for drink (*have a ~*, colloq., want a drink); (fig.) ardent desire, craving, (*of, for, after,* glory, person's blood, etc.). **2.** v.i. Feel ~ (now chiefly fig. *for, after*). Hence ~'LESS a. [OE (OS) *thurst*, OHG *durst*, ON *thorsti*, Goth. *thaurstei* f. Gmc *thurs-* cogn. w. L *torrēre* parch; vb f. n., OE *thyrstan*]

thīrs't|ȳ, a. Feeling thirst (*be ~y*, current E for *thirst* vb); fond of drink; (of country or season) dry, parched; (colloq.) causing thirst, as *this is ~y work*. Hence ~ILY[2] adv. [OE *thurstig* (prec., -Y[1])]

thīrteen', a. & n. One more than twelve, 13, xiii; *the ~ superstition* (that ~ as the number of persons at table, or of one's room etc., brings ill luck). Hence ~TH[2] a. & n. [OE *thrēotiene, -tēne* (as THREE, see -TEEN)]

thīrt'ȳ, a. & n. Three times ten, 30, xxx; *~-one* etc., *~-first* etc.; *T~-nine Articles* (subscribed to by person taking orders in Ch. of Eng.); *~-two-mo, 32mo*, book with 32 leaves to the sheet. Hence **thīrt'IETH, ~fold** (see -FOLD), aa. & nn. [OE *thrītig* (*thrī* THREE, see -TY[2])]

this (dh-), a. & pron. (pl. *these* pr. dhēz). The (person, thing), the person or thing, close at hand or touched or pointed to or drawn attention to or observed by the speaker at the time, or already named or understood or in question or familiar (seldom idiomatically interchangeable with THAT[1], but often only equally applicable to the facts, the implication of greater nearness, familiarity, etc., being purely idiomatic), as *observe ~ dog on the hearth-rug, who are these people in the next room?, what is all ~ noise?, fold it like ~, I knew all ~ before, ~* (your action, the action I am speaking of) *is not fair, ~ term is liable to much abuse, things are easier in these days; ~ and* THAT[1]; *~ much, ~ amount* (esp. *= what I am about to state,* as *I know ~ much, that the thing is absurd*); *~,* THAT[1], *& the other*; (of time) *~day,* today, *shall be or have been busy all ~ week, ought to be ready by ~* (time), *before ~* (time), *have been asking for it these* (or *~*) *three weeks* (just past). [OE masc. *thes,* fem. *thēos,* neut. *this,* ult. f. root *tha-* (THAT[1]); OE pl *thās* gave THOSE; the less common pl. *thǣs,* ME *thēs,* later *these,* was ult. different. f. *those*]

this'nĕss (dh-), n. Quality of being this, = HAECCEITY. [-NESS]

thi'stle (-sl), n. Kinds of prickly composite plant with globular or cylindrical heads with purple, yellow, or white flowers, Scottish national emblem (cf. ROSE); *Order of the T~,* a Scottish order of knighthood. Hence **thi'stlȳ**[2] (-sli) a. [OE *thistil, -el,* OHG *distil,* ON *thistell, -ill*]

thith'er (dhĭdh-), adv. (arch.). To that

place, there (of motion). Hence ~WARD(S) adv. [OE *thider,* alt. (after HITHER) f. *thǣder* f. root *tha-* (THAT[1], THE) + suf. -THER denoting motion towards, cf. HITHER, WHITHER]

tho'. See THOUGH.

‖ **thōle**[1], v.t. (arch., exc. Sc.). Undergo, endure, suffer, (pain, grief, etc., or abs.); permit, admit of. [OE *tholian,* OS *-ōn, -ian,* OHG *dolōn,* ON *thola,* Goth. *thulan* f. Gmc *thul-* cogn. w. L *tolerare*]

thōle[2], n. (Also *~-pin*) pin in gunwale of boat as fulcrum for oar; each of two such pins between which oar plays. [OE *thol(l),* MDu., MLG *dolle,* ON *thollr*]

Thom'|ism (tō-), n. Doctrine of Thomas Aquinas (died 1274), a scholastic philosopher and theologian, or of his followers. So ~IST n., ~IS'TIC(AL) aa. [-ISM]

thŏng, n., & v.t. **1.** Narrow strip of leather used as halter, reins, lash of whip, etc. **2.** v.t. Provide with ~, strike with ~. [OE *thwang, thwong* (cf. ON *thvengr*), f. Gmc *thwing-, thwang-, thwung-,* restrain (cf. G *zwingen*)]

Thōr, n. Scandinavian god of thunder, war, & agriculture; *~'s hammer,* flint axe (-hammer). [f. ON *Thórr*]

thōr'ăx, n. (Anat., zool.) part of trunk between neck & abdomen or tail, whence **thōrǎ'CIC** a., **thōrǎ'CI-, thōrǎ'cico-, thōrǎc'o-,** comb. forms; (Gk ant.) breastplate, cuirass. [L, f. Gk *thōrax-akos*]

thōr'īte, n. A black compact mineral found in Norway. [THOR + -ITE[1]]

thōr'ium, n. Radio-active metallic element, the oxide of which is used in gas-mantles. [THOR + -IUM]

thŏrn, n. **1.** Prickle, spiny process on plant, esp. abortive branch; kinds of *~y* shrub or tree, as *haw~, white~, black~; a ~ in* one's *flesh* or *side,* constant source of annoyance; *be, sit, on ~s,* be continuously uneasy esp. in expectation of being detected etc. at any moment. **2.** Name of the obs. E letter þ (th). **3.** *~'back,* ray with spines on back and tail, British spider crab; *~'bill, ~'tail,* kinds of humming-bird; *~'tree* (S. Afr.), kinds of acacia. Hence *~'LESS, ~'Y*[2] (often fig. of affair, = hard to handle),.aa. [OE, OS, ON *thorn,* OHG *dorn,* Goth. *thaurnus* f. Gmc *thurnuz*]

thorough (thŭ'ro), a., n., prep., & adv. **1.** Complete, unqualified, not superficial, out-&-out, as *his work is seldom ~, has caught a ~ chill, wants a ~ change, a ~ scoundrel.* **2.** n. (hist.). Uncompromising policy of Strafford & Laud under Charles I. **3.** prep. & adv. (arch.). Through (*~ bush, ~ brier*). **4.** *~-băss,* bass part accompanied by signs esp. numerals to indicate the general harmony, such system of signs, (loosely) harmonic composition; *~-brace,* strap between C-springs of vehicle; *~-bred* a. & n. (animal, esp. horse) of pure breed, high-spirited, mettlesome, (also fig. of persons); ~*fare*, road, street, esp. one through which much traffic passes; *no* ~*fare*, (as notice at end of obstructed or private road) no passage; ~*going*, uncompromising, out- -&-out; ~*paced*, (lit., of horse) trained to all paces, (fig.) complete, unqualified, as *a* ~*paced rascal*; ~-*pin*, swelling in hollow of horse's hock. Hence~LY[2](-ŭ'rolĭ) adv., ~NESS (-ŭ'ronĕs) n. [later OE *thuruh*, var. of *thurh* THROUGH]

thōrp(e), n. Village, hamlet. [OE, OS, ON *thorp*, OHG *dorf*, Goth. *thaurp* f. Gmc **thorpam*]

those. [pl. of THAT[1]; see THIS]

thou (dhow), pron. (object. *thee*, pl. YE, YOU), & v.t. & i. Sing. pron. of 2nd pers., now arch. or poet. exc. in addressing God & (usu. *thee* as subject. with 3rd pers. vb) as used by Quakers; (v.t.) address (person) as ~; (v.i.) use ~ instead of *you*. [OE, OS *thū*, OHG *dū*, ON *thū*, Goth. *thu* f. Gmc **thū* cogn. w. L *tu*]

though (dhō), **thō'**, conj. (Also *although*) notwithstanding the fact that, as *he finished first* ~ *he began last*, ~ *it was late we decided to go*; (also *although*) on the supposition that, as *it is better to ask him* (*even*) ~ *he* (*should*) *refuse* or *refuses*; *what* ~ (what does it matter if) *the way is* (arch. *be*) *long?*; *as* ~, as if, as *it is as* ~ *a man should ask alms of a beggar, he acts as* ~ *he were mad, it looks as* ~ *he meant* (vulg. *means*) *business*; (introducing what is virtually an independent sentence) & yet, as *I have no doubt he will understand* — ~ *you never know*; (abs. or as adv.) however, as *I wish you had told me*, ~. [ME *thoh* etc. f. ON *thó* (f. **thauh*), corresp. to OE *thēah*, *thēh*, OS *thōh*, OHG *doh* f. Gmc **thauh*]

thought[1] (thawt), n. **1.** Process, power, of thinking; faculty of reason; sober reflection (*in* ~, meditating); consideration, as *take* ~ (consider matters), *after serious* ~, *acts without* ~; idea, conception, chain of reasoning, etc., produced by thinking, as *an essay full of striking* ~*s*, *a happy* ~, well-timed or apposite idea or suggestion; half-formed intention, as *had* (*some*) ~*s of resigning, had no* ~ *of offending him*; (usu. pl.) what one thinks, one's opinion, as *will tell you my* ~*s of the matter*; subject of one's ~, as *his one* ~ *is how to get away*, *a* PENNY *for your* ~*s*; *you are much in my* ~*s*, I often think of you. **2.** *A* ~, a little, somewhat, as *cut it a* ~ *shorter*, *seems to me a* ~ *arrogant*; FREE[1]~; *quick as* ~, very quick; *second* ~*s*, further consideration, as *second* ~*s are best, on second* ~*s I will take a bus*; ~-*reader*, -*reading*, reader, ·reading, of person's ~*s* by telepathy; ~·*transference*, telepathy; ~-*wave*, undulation of the supposed medium of ~-*transference*. Hence (·)~ED[2] (-awt-) a. [OE *thoht* f. **thōht* f. **thanht* f. st. of *thencan* THINK + -*t* suff.]

thought[2]. See THINK.

thought'ful (-awt-), a. Engaged in or given to meditation; (of book, writer, remark, etc.) giving signs of original thought; (of persons or conduct) considerate, not haphazard or unfeeling. Hence ~LY[2] adv., ~NESS n. [ME; -FUL]

thought'less (-awt-), a. Careless of consequences or of others' feelings; due to want of thought. Hence ~LY[2] adv., ~NESS n. [-LESS]

thous'and (-z-), a. & n. Ten hundred, 1000, M (for uses cf. HUNDRED); (loosely) many, as *a* ~ *times easier, one in a* ~ (esp. rare or excellent one); (*a*) ~ & *one*, myriad, numberless (*the* ~ & *one small worries of life*; *made a* ~ & *one excuses*); *a* ~ *thanks, pardons, apologies*, etc. (forms of polite exaggeration); UPPER *ten* ~. Hence ~FOLD a. & adv., (·)~TH[2] a. & n. [OE *thūsend*, OS -*ind*, OHG *dūsunt*, ON *thūsund*, Goth. *thūsundi*]

thrall (-awl), n., a., & v.t. **1.** Slave (*of, to*, person or thing, lit. & fig.); bondage, esp. *in* ~. **2.** adj. (arch.). Enslaved (*to*). **3.** v.t. Enslave. Hence thra'IDOM (-awl-) n. [OE *thræl* f. ON *thræll*]

thrăsh, thrĕsh, v.t. & i. **1.** (usu. -*esh*). Beat out or separate grain from (corn etc.) on *threshing-floor* or in *threshing-machine*; (fig.) ~ *out*, arrive at, obtain, (the truth, rhyme, etc.) by repeated trial. **2.** (Of paddle-wheel, branch, etc.) act like flail, deliver repeated blows, (of ship) keep striking the waves, make way against wind or tide (usu. -*ash*, as ~ *to windward*). **3.** (-*ash*). Beat esp. with stick or whip, conquer, surpass, whence **thrăsh'**ING[1] n. [OE *therscan*, later *threscan*, OHG *dreskan*, ON *threskja*, Goth. *thriskan*]

thrăsh'er, thrĕ-, n. Kind of shark; (usu. *thre-*) person, machine, that threshes; (*thra-*) one who thrashes. [-ER[1]]

thrasŏn'ical, a. Bragging. Hence ~LY[2] adv. [f. L *Thraso -onis*, character in Terence, f. Gk *thrasus* bold, +-ICAL]

thread[1] (-rĕd), n. **1.** Spun-out filament of cotton, flax, silk, wool, etc., yarn, (*has not a dry* ~ *on him*, is wet through); thin cord of twisted yarns; *gold* ~ (of silk etc. with gold wire wound round it); LISLE THREAD; ~ & THRUM[1]; ~-shaped thing, long slender body, e.g. spiral part of screw; thin seam or vein of ore; (fig.) *the* ~ (course) *of life*; *hang by a* ~, (of person's life etc.) be in a precarious state, (of momentous issue etc.) be determinable either way by something still in doubt; *lost the* ~ (chain, connexion) *of his argument*; *resume* or *take up the* ~ *of*, proceed with after interruption; *gather up the* ~*s*, bring the divisions of subject etc. into relation after separate treatment. **2.** ~'*bare*, (of cloth) worn so that nap is lost and ~ visible, wearing such clothes, (fig.) well-worn, hackneyed, whence ~'*bareness* n.; ~ *lace* (made of ~); ~-*mark*, mark made in bank-note paper with highly coloured silk fibres to prevent counterfeiting; ~-*needle*, children's game (OLD *Lady of T~needle St*); ~-*paper*, (strip of) soft thin paper used for rolling up ~; ~'*worm*, kinds of ~like worm, esp. one infesting rectum of children. Hence ~'INESS n., ~'Y² a., (-rĕd-). [OE *thrǣd*, OHG *drāt*, ON *thráthr*, f. Gmc **thrǣdhuz* f. *thrǣ*- THROW]

thread² (-rĕd), v.t. Pass thread through eye of (needle); string (beads etc.) on thread, make (chain etc.) thus; pick one's way through (maze, streets, crowded place, etc.), make one's *way* thus; streak (hair etc.) as with threads. [ME, f. prec.]

threat (-rĕt), n. Declaration of intention to punish or hurt; (law) such menace of bodily hurt or injury to reputation or property as may restrain person's freedom of action; indication of coming evil (*there is a ~ of rain*). [OE *thrēat* affliction etc., f. Gmc **thrautaz* f. **threut-*, **thraut-*, **thrut-* whence OHG *-driozan* (G *verdrie- ssen*), Goth. *-thriutan*]

threa'ten (-rĕtn), v.t. & i. Use threats towards (person etc., or abs.; *with* the evil ~ed), as ~*ed me with death, am ~ed with a visit*; give warning of the infliction of (injury etc., or abs.), announce one's intention (*to do*), as punishment or in revenge etc., as ~*s every kind of torment*, ~ *to resign*, (fig.) *clouds ~ (an interruption* or *to interrupt us), the practice ~s to become general.* Hence~INGLY² adv. [OE *thrēatnian* f. prec. + -EN⁶]

three, a. & n. **1.** One more than two, 3, iii; (skat.) any of four turns in which direction & edge are both changed; (rugby footb.) ~-quarter; ~ *limes* ~, ~ *cheers* thrice repeated; *the ~ R's*, reading, writing, arithmetic; RULE *of* ~. **2.** ~- *-bottle man*, old-fashioned hard drinker; ~-*card trick* (in which bets are made on which is the queen among ~ cards lying face downwards; also *find the lady*); ~- *-colour process* (of reproducing natural colours by combining photographs in red, blue, & yellow); ~-*cornered*, triangular, (of contest etc.) between ~ parties each for himself; ~-*deck'er*, war-vessel with ~ gun-decks, novel in ~ volumes, ~- -storeyed pulpit;~-*handed*, with~ hands, played by~ persons, as ~-*handed euchre*; ~ *halfpence*, 1½*d*.; *T~ in One*, the Trinity; ~-*lane*, wide enough for ~ lines of traffic; ~-*legged race*, of couples each having a right & left leg tied together; ~-*mast'er*, vessel esp. schooner with ~ masts; ‖~-*pair*, (of room) up ~ pair of stairs (usu. ~-*pair back* or *front*); ‖~'*pence* (thrĕp-, -Ip-), sum of ~ pence; ‖~'*penny* (*bit*) (same pron.), coin worth ~ pence; (*the*) ~-*per-cents*, (government) bonds bearing that interest; ~-PHASE; ~-*ply*, of ~ strands, webs, or thicknesses, (as n.) ~-ply wood made by gluing together 3 layers with grain in different directions; ~-*point landing* (aeron.), landing of an aircraft on the two wheels & the tail skid

simultaneously; ~-*quart'er(s)*, (adj.) of ~ fourths of normal size or numbers, (of portrait) going down to hips, showing ~ fourths of face, (n.) any of 3 or 4 players behind HALF-backs; ~*score'*, (age of) sixty (~*score & ten*, age of 70 as normal limit of life). Hence ~'FOLD a. & adv. [OE *thrī*, fem. & neut. *thrio, thrēo* f. Gmc **thrīz* (f. **thrijiz*), **thrijō*, Aryan *treies, treja*, Skr. *trayas*, Gk *treis, tria*, L *tres, tria*]

three'some, n. & a. **1.** Set of three persons; game etc. for three. **2.** adj. Of three. '[-SOME]

thrĕmmatŏl'ogў, n. Science of breeding animals & plants. [f. Gk *thremma -matos* nursling (*trephō* nourish, -M), -O-, -LOGY]

thrĕn'|ōde, -odў, nn. (Song of) lamentation esp. on person's death. Hence or cogn. ~ET'IC, ~ĕt'ICAL, ~ōd'IAL, ~ōd'IC, aa., ~odIST(3) n. [f. Gk *thrēnōidia* (*thrēnos* wailing + *ōidē* ODE)]

thresh etc. See THRASH etc.

thrĕsh'ōld, n. Plank or stone at bottom of door in dwelling-house, church, etc.; (loosely, esp. fig.) entrance, as *at the ~ of a discussion, on the ~ of a revolution, of a new century*; (psych.) limit of consciousness, limit below which a stimulus ceases to be perceptible. [OE *therscold, -wold*, etc., gen. referred to THRESH]

threw. See THROW.

thrice, adv. (arch. or literary). Three times (now chiefly in comb. = highly, as ~-*blessed, -favoured*). [ME *thriĕs* f. *thriĕ* adv. (OE *thriwa, thriga*) + -ES]

thrid, v.t. (arch.; -dd-). = THREAD².

thrid'ace, n. Inspissated juice of lettuce, used as sedative. [f. Gk *thridax -akos* lettuce]

thrift, n. **1.** Frugality, economical management, whence ~'LESS a., ~'lĕSSLY² adv., ~'lĕSSNESS n. **2.** n. Kinds of plant, esp. sea-pink. [ME, f. THRIVE + -*t*; cf. *drift, gift* (-TH¹ (a))]

thrif't|ў, a. Frugal, economical; thriving, prosperous. Hence~ILY² adv. [ME; -Y²]

thrill, v.t. & i., & n. **1.** Penetrate (person etc.) with wave of emotion or sensation, as *his voice ~ed the listeners*; be thus penetrated or agitated (*with* horror etc.); (of emotion etc.) pass *through, over, along*, as *fear ~ed through my veins*; quiver, throb, (as) with emotion. **2.** n. Wave of emotion or sensation, as *a ~ of joy*; throb, pulsation; (med.) kinds of tremor or resonance observed in auscultation; (sl.) sensational story. Hence~'ER¹(2) n. (esp. sensational play or tale), ~'INGLY² adv., ~'INGNESS n. [metathetic f. (now dial.) *thirl* vb f. OE *thyrlian* pierce f. *thȳr(e)l* hole f. *thurh* THROUGH + -EL]

thrips, n. Kinds of insect, esp. (improp.) some injurious to vines etc. [L f. Gk, = woodworm]

thrĭv|e, v.i. (*thrōve* rarely ~*ed*, *thriven* rarely ~*ed*). Prosper, flourish; grow rich; (of animal or plant) grow vigorously.

Hence ~'ingLY[2] adv., ~'ingNESS n. [ME, f. ON *thrifask* refl. thrive]

thro', thro. See THROUGH.

throat, n., & v.t. **1.** Front of neck between chin & collar-bone, jugular region, (*cut one's* ~, esp. with intent to kill him; *take by the* ~, try to throttle); gullet; windpipe, as *words stuck in my* ~; ~*-shaped thing,* e.g. narrow part of river between rocks, (also in many naut. wds); *sore* ~, inflammation of lining membrane of gullet etc., *clergyman's* (*sore*) ~, form of this affecting those who speak much in public, often of nervous origin; *cut* one's *own* ~, *one another's* ~s, adopt suicidal, mutually destructive, policy; *lie in* one's ~, lie grossly; *give* person *the lie in his* ~, accuse him of lying grossly; *thrust* thing *down* one's ~, force it on his attention. **2.** v.t. Channel, groove. Hence (·)~ED[2] a. [OE *throte, -u,* app. f. Gmc. **thrut-, thrŭt* (OE *thrŭtian* to swell); cogn. w. OHG *drozza* (G *drossel*)]

throat'|y̆, a. Guttural, uttered in the throat; having prominent or capacious throat. Hence ~iNESS n. [-Y[2]]

throb, v.i. (-bb-), & n. **1.** (Of heart, bosom, temples, etc.) palpitate, pulsate esp. with more than usual force or rapidity; (fig.) quiver, vibrate, (as) with emotion. **2.** n. Palpitation, pulsation, as *heart-*~s, ~s *of pleasure.* Hence ~b'ing-LY[2] adv. [ME, app. imit.]

throe, n., & v.i. **1.** (Usu. pl.) violent pang(s), esp. of childbirth lit. & fig., anguish; (pop.) *in the* ~s *of* (struggling with) *spring-cleaning.* **2.** v.i. (rare). Be in agony. [17th c. alt. f. obs. *throw(e),* poss. rel. to THROW[1]]

‖ **Thrŏgmŏrt'on Street.** (Used for) the London Stock Exchange or its members or operations.

thrŏmb|ōs'is, n. Coagulation of blood in blood-vessel or organ. Hence ~ŏT'ic a. [Gk *thrombosis* curdling (*thrombos* lump, see -OSIS)]

thrōne, n., & v:t. **1.** Chair of state for sovereign, bishop, etc., usu. decorated & raised on dais; sovereign power, as *came to the* ~, *lost his* ~; (pl.) third ORDER[1] of angels. **2.** v.t. (poet. exc. in p.p.). Enthrone (lit. & fig.). Hence ~'LESS (-nl-) a. [ME, f. OF *trone* f. L f. Gk *thronos* seat, chair]

thrŏng, n., & v.i. & t. **1.** Crowd of people; multitude esp. in small space (*of* people or things). .**2.** vb. Come, go, press, (*round* etc.) in multitudes; fill (street etc.) with a crowd or as crowd does; (arch.) press hard upon (person). [ME *thrang(e), throng(e),* f. st. of OE *thringan -thrang -thrungen* press]

thrŏ'stle (-sl), n. **1.** Song-thrush. **2.** (Also ~*-frame*) machine for spinning wool, cotton, etc. [OE *throstle* f. root of Gmc *thrastuz (ON *throstr*), commonly referred to Aryan **trozdus,* whence L *turdus*]

thrŏt'tle, n., & v.t. **1.** Throat, gullet,

---

windpipe; (also ~*-valve*) valve controlling flow of steam etc. in engine. **2.** v.t. Choke, strangle; control (steam etc., engine) with ~*-valve*; ~ *down,* reduce speed of (engine, car) thus. [vb (f. 1400) perh. f. THROAT + -LE(3); n. (f. 1550) of obsc. hist.; perh. f. vb]

through, thro', thro, (-rōō), prep., & a. **1.** From end to end or side to side of, between the sides or walls or parts of, as *marched* ~ *the town, arrow went* ~ *his arm, see* ~ *a telescope, look* ~ *the window, pass* ~ *the doorway, swam* ~ *the waves, pushes his fingers* ~ *his hair*; (fig.) *went* ~ *many trials, got* ~ *his examinations, saw* ~ *his hypocrisy, wait* ~ *ten long years, flashed* ~ *his mind*; by reason of, by agency, means, or fault of, as *it all came about* ~ *his not knowing the way, concealed it* ~ *shame, it was all* ~ *you that we were late*; **up to and including (*from Friday* ~ *Tuesday*). **2.** adv. From side to side, from end to end, from beginning to end, as *let us stroll* ~, *would not let us* ~ (gate etc.), *ice gave & I went* ~, *read it carefully* ~, *read it* ~ *&* ~ (~ again & again), *looked him* ~ *&* ~ (observed searchingly), *lasted all* ~ (all the time); (colloq.) *are you* ~ (*with that job*)?, have you finished (it)?; CARRY, *drop* or FALL[1], PULL[1], ~; GO[1] ~ *with.* **3.** adj. Going, concerned with going, ~, as *a* ~ *bolt,* ~*-stone,* = BOND[1]*-stone*; esp. (of railway or steamboat travelling) going all the way without change of line etc., going over different companies' lines with same ticket, as ~ *carriage, train, passenger, ticket* (for ~ *passenger*), *fares.* **4.** ~*-put* n., amount of material put ~ in a manufacturing etc. process. [OE, OS *thurh,* OHG *duruh*; cogn. w. Goth. *thairh* (cf. *thairkō* hole), THRILL]

through'ly (-ōōli), adv. (arch.). Thoroughly. [15th c., f. THROUGH + -LY[2]]

throughout' (-rōō-owt), adv. & prep. **1.** Right through, in every part, in all respects, as *timber was rotten* ~, *followed a sound policy* ~. **2.** prep. Right through, from end to end of, as ~ *the length & breadth of the land,* ~ *the 18th century.* [ME; OUT]

throve. See THRIVE.

throw[1] (-ō), v.t. & i. (*threw* pr. -ōō, ~n pr. -ōn). **1.** Release (ball, object) after imparting motion, propel through space, send forth or dismiss esp. with some violence, fling or hurl or cast (lit. & fig.), as *must not* ~ *stones* (lit., & fig. = cast imputations), *threw the ball over his head, learnt to* ~ *a fly* (in fishing), *mortars* ~ *shells, hose* ~s *water, house* ~n *down by earthquake, ship was* ~n *upon the coast,* ~n *from his horse, was* ~n *into a dilemma* or *upon his own resources,* ~ COLD[1] *water on,* ~ *a* SOP *to*; ~ *light on the matter,* help to explain it; ~ *down the* GLOVE, ~ DUST[1] *in* person's *eyes*; ~ *oneself,* one's *daughter, at the head of* (openly seek as husband); ~ (as FLING) *in* one's *teeth*; ~ *good money* *after bad* (lose more in trying to recoup a loss); (w. ind. obj.) *~ me a rope*, *~* one a *kiss* (wave hand to him after kissing it); (crick., of bowler) deliver ball with sudden straightening of elbow (*was no-balled for ~ing*). **2.** (Of wrestler, horse) bring (antagonist, rider) to the ground. **3.** Put (clothes etc.) carelessly or hastily *on, off, over* one's *shoulders* etc.; (of snake) cast (skin). **4.** (Of animals, e.g. rabbits, pigeons) bring forth (young). **5.** Make (specified cast) with dice, as *threw deuce--ace*. **6.** Twist (silk etc.) into threads. **7.** Shape (round pottery) on potter's wheel. **8.** Turn, direct, move esp. quickly (esp. part of body), as *threw his eyes to the ground, a glance backwards, his arms up, his head back*; *~ a chest* (sl.), stand erect with chest expanded. **9.** *Lose (contest, race, etc.) intentionally. **10.** Have (a fit); (sl.) give (a party). **11.** *~ away*, (fig.) part with needlessly or recklessly, lose by neglect, as *threw away all his advantages, an excellent offer*; (theatr.) speak (lines) with conscious under-emphasis; (p.p.) wasted, as *the advice was ~n away upon him*. **12.** *~ back*, revert to ancestral character; *~-back* n., reversion to ancestral character, example of this. **13.** *~ oneself-down*, lie down. **14.** *~ in*, (also *~ into the bargain*) add (thing) to a bargain without extra charge; interpose (word, remark) by way of parenthesis or casually; *~ in* one's *hand*, lit. in card games esp. poker, (fig.) give up, withdraw from a contest; *~ in* one's *lot with*, decide to share the fortunes of. **15.** *~ oneself into*, engage vigorously in. **16.** *~ off*, discard (acquaintance etc.); contrive to get rid of (illness, troublesome companion); abandon (disguise); produce, deliver, (poem, epigram) in offhand manner; (of hounds or hunt, & transf.) begin hunting, make a start, begin speaking, playing, etc.; (& see above). **17.** *~ oneself on, upon*, place one's reliance on (*the mercy of the court* etc.). **18.** *~ open*, open suddenly or wide; make accessible (*to* all comers etc.); *~ open the door to*, make possible. **19.** *~ out*, cast out; build (wing of house, pier, projecting or prominent thing); suggest, put forward tentatively; reject (bill in Parliament); distract (person speaking, thinking, or acting) from the matter in hand so that he blunders or stops; (crick., of fielder) put out (batsman) by *~ing at* & hitting wicket. **20.** *~ over*, desert, abandon. **21.** *~ overboard*, see OVER-(2). **22.** *~ up*, lift up (window-sash); resign (office); vomit (t. & i.); *~* one's *eyes up* (as sign of horror or outraged propriety); *~ up* the SPONGE. Hence (-)*~'ER*[1] (-ŏer) n. [OE *thrāwan* twist, turn, OS *thrāian*, OHG *drāen* f. Gmc *thrǣ- cogn. w. Gk *terō* bore, L *terere* rub; cf. THREAD.]

throw[2] (-ō), n. **1.** Throwing, cast; cast of dice; cast of fishing-line; distance a missile is or may be thrown, as *record ~*

with the hammer; *a stone's ~*, (loosely) slight distance; fall in wrestling; (crick.) bowler's illegitimately delivered ball. **2.** (geol., mining). Fault, leap, in strata. **3.** Machine, device, giving rapid rotary motion. **4.** *~-off*, start in hunt or race; *~-stick*, club, stick, meant to be whirled from the hand, e.g. boomerang. [f. prec.]

throw'ster (-rō-), n. One who throws silk. [-STER]

thrum[1], n., & v.t. (-mm-). **1.** Fringe of threads remaining on loom when web has been cut off; single thread of this; any loose thread or tuft; *thread & ~*, all alike, good & bad. **2.** v.t. Make of, cover with, *~s*. Hence *~m'Y*[2] a. [OE, = OHG *drum*, ON *thrǫmr* f. Gmc *thrum-, *thram-* cogn. w. L *terminus*.]

thrum[2], v.i. & t. (-mm-), & n. **1.** Play monotonously or unskilfully on or *on* (stringed instrument); drum, tap, idly on or *on* (table etc.). **2.** n. Such playing, resulting sound. [imit.]

thrush[1], n. Family or genus of birds, esp. European *song-~*, throstle. [OE *thrȳsce* f. Gmc *thruskjǫn*]

thrush[2], n. Disease, esp. of children, marked by pearl-coloured fungous vesicles in mouth & throat; disease affecting frog of horse's foot. [17th c., of unkn. orig.]

thrust, v.t. & i. (*thrust*), & n. **1.** Push with sudden impulse or with force (lit. & fig.), as *~ his fist into my face, ~ the letter into his pocket, ~ a pin into the cushion, I ~ out my hand, ~ him forth* (out of room etc.), *was ~ from his rights*; *~ oneself* or one's *nose in*, obtrude, interfere; pierce (person etc.) *through*; make sudden push *at* (person etc. *with* dagger etc.); force oneself *through, past*, etc.; make one's *way* thus; hence *~'ER*[1] n. (‖ esp., foxhunter who endangers others or the hounds in securing a forward place). **2.** n. Sudden or forcible push, strong attempt to penetrate enemy's line or territory; attack with point of weapon; remark aimed at a person (*a shrewd*, HOME[1], *~*; *he parried the ~*); stress between two bodies esp. parts of structure, e.g. arch, rafters; crushing of coal-mine pillars by weight of roof; *~-block*, (esp.) casting or frame carrying or containing the bearings on which the collars of a propeller-shaft press; *~-hoe* (worked by *~*, not pull). [ME *thruste, thryste*, f. ON *thrȳsta*]

thud, v.i. (-dd-), & n. (Make, fall with) low dull sound as of blow on soft thing. [*c.* 1500, app. imit.]

thug, n. Member of a religious organization of assassins in India suppressed about 1825; cut-throat, ruffian. [f. Hind. *thag*]

thŭgg'|ee (-gē), n. (hist.). The practice of the thug. So *~ery*, *~ism*, nn., (-g-). [f. Hind. *thagi* as prec.]

Thū'l'ĕ, n. Name given by Pytheas of Massilia to some (is)land north of Gt

Britain; *ul'tima* (= farthest) ~, any far-away unknown region.

thŭmb (-m), n., & v.t. **1.** Short thick finger set apart from & opposite to the others on human hand; digit of other animals corresponding to this in position; ~*s up!* (sl. excl. of satisfaction); RULE *of* ~; *his* FINGERS *are all* ~*s*; *under* person's~ (influence, domination). **2.** ~-*blue*, washing indigo in small lumps; ~-*index*, set of lettered grooves cut in front edges of a book's leaves to facilitate reference; ~-*latch* (raised by pressing end of lever with ~); ~-*mark* (made by ~ esp. on leaf of book); ~-*nail sketch*, portrait of ~-nail size, hasty word-picture; ~-*nut* (shaped for ~ to turn); ~-*print*, impression of ~ esp. as used for identification; ~'*screw*, instrument of torture for squeezing ~*s*; ~-*stall*, sheath, pad, etc., to protect ~; *~-'tack*, drawing-pin. **3.** v.t. Wear, soil, (pages etc.) with ~; handle (piano keys etc.) or play (music) awkwardly; signal (to) with the ~; ~ *a lift*, (try to) get a lift from a passing motorist by such signal; *~ one's nose* (*at*), cock a SNOOK² (at). Hence ~'LESS (-ml-) a. [OE *thūma*, OHG *dūmo* f. Gmc **thūmon* cogn. w. L *tumēre* swell]

thŭmm'im. See URIM.

thŭmp, v.t. & i., & n. **1.** Beat heavily esp. with fist; deliver heavy blows *at*, *on*, etc.; ~ *the* or *a cushion* (of vehement preacher emphasizing his words with blows on pulpit cushion). **2.** n. Heavy blow, bang. [16th c., imit.]

thŭm'p|er, n. In vbl senses, also : (colloq.) large, striking, or impressive person or thing, esp. lie, so ~ING² a. [-ER¹]

thŭn'der, n., & v.i. & t. **1.** Loud noise following flash of . lightning & due to discharge of electricity through the air; ~bolt, as *Jove's* ~*s*; (fig.) loud noise, as ~*s of applause, blood-&-*~, (of novel etc.) sensational, melodramatic; (pl.) authoritative censure or threats (the ~*s of* The Times, *the Church*). **2.** v.i. Give forth ~, usu. *it* ~*s*; make loud noise, as *voice*~*ed in my cars*; utter violent threats etc. *against* etc. **3.** v.t. Emit (threats etc.) in loud or impressive manner. **4.** *Steal* person's ~, (fig.) forestall him (by telling the story he meant to tell, making profit-able use of his invention before he can, & the like; from remark of John Dennis when the stage ~ he had intended for his own play was used for another); ~*bolt*, flash of lightning with crash of ~, imaginary bolt or shaft viewed as substance of lightning, kinds of stone or fossil supposed to be such bolt, formidable threat etc.; ~*clap*, crash of ~ (esp. fig. or in simile of sudden terrible event or news; *the* ~*clap of Napoleon's escape*; *the news came on me like a* ~*clap*); ~*cloud* (producing ~); ~*storm* (with ~ & lightning & usu. heavy rain or hail); ~*struck*, struck by lightning, amazed. Hence ~LESS, ~OUS, ~Y², aa.,

~OUSLY² adv. [OE *thunor*, OS -*er*, OHG *donar*, ON *thórr* f. Gmc **thonaraz* cogn. w. L *tonare*]

thŭn'derer], n. In vbl senses, esp. *the T*~, Jupiter (Tonans), ‖ (joc.) *The Times* newspaper. [-ER¹]

thŭn'dering, a. & adv. In vbl senses, also or esp.: (colloq.) unusual(ly), re-markable, remarkably, decided(ly), as *a* ~ *nuisance, was* ~ *glad to get back, a* ~ *great fish*; *the T*~ *Legion*, Roman legion containing Christian soldiers whose prayers were held to have procured a thunderstorm that terrified the enemy. Hence ~LY² adv. [-ING².¹]

thūr|i-, comb. form of L *thus thuris* frank-incense, as : ~'*ifer*, acolyte who carries censer; ~*if'erous*, producing frankin-cense; ~*ifica'tion*, burning of incense.

thūr'ible, n. Censer. [ME, f. OF, or L *t(h)uribulum* (prec.) f. Gk *thuō* sacrifice]

Thŭrs'day (-zdi), n. Fifth day of week; HOLY, MAUNDY, ~. [OE *thunres-, thur(e)s-dæg*, day of Thor, rendering LL *dies Jovis* day of Jupiter]

thŭs (dh-), adv. In this way, in the way (to be) indicated, whence ~'NESS n. (joc.); accordingly, as a result or inference; to this extent, so, as ~ *far*, ~ *much*. [OE, OS *thus* app. f. *tha*- (THAT¹)]

thwăck, v.t., & n. = WHACK. [imit.]

‖ **thwaite**, n. Piece of wild land made arable. [f. ON *thveit* paddock, f. **thvīta* = OE *thwītan* cut (cf. WHITTLE)]

thwart (-ôrt), adv., prep., & a., (arch.), v.t., & n. **1.** Across, athwart; (naut.) ~-*-hawse*, across the hawse, ~-*ship* a., *-ships* adv., (lying) across ship; (adj.) lying across, transverse. **2.** v.t. Frustrate, cross, (wish, purpose), whence ~'ingLY² adv. **3.** n. Oarsman's bench placed across boat. [ME *thwert* f. ON *thvert* adv., neut. of *thverr* adj., f. **thverh* = OE *thwerh*, OHG *twerh* (G *zwerch*-), Goth. *thwairhs* f. Gmc **thwerhw-* cogn. w. L *torquēre* twist]

thȳ, thine, (dh-), pron. & a. Possessive case of, & adj. corresp. to, THOU (now arch. etc. as THOU; before vowel usu. *thine*), also (*thine* in abs. use, as *it was thy fault, lift thine eyes, the fault is thine, do what thou wilt with thine own*. [ME, reduced f. *thin* (mod. *thine*), OE, OS, ON *thin*, OHG *dīn*, Goth. *theins* f. Gmc **thīnaz*]

thȳl'acine, n. Zebra wolf, a Tasmanian carnivorous marsupial. [F, f. Gk *thulakos* pouch, -INE¹]

thyme (tīm), n. Kinds of plant, esp. *common garden* ~, shrub with pungent aromatic leaves used in cookery, *shepherd's* or *wild* ~, kind with mildly aromatic leaves. Hence **thȳm'oL** n. (a powerful antiseptic), **thym'y²** (tī-) a. [ME, f. OF *thym* f. L f. Gk *thumon* (*thuō* sacrifice)]

thȳm'us, n. (anat.; pl. -*mī*). (Usu. ~ *gland*) a ductless gland situated near the base of the neck (in man disappearing on the approach of puberty). [f. Gk *thumos*]

thyr'oid, a. & n. (anat., zool.). Shield-shaped, as ~ *cartilage*, large cartilage of larynx projection of which in man forms Adam's apple; connected with the ~ cartilage, as ~ *artery*; ~ *gland*, large ductless gland lying near larynx and trachea secreting hormone which regulates rate of metabolism (~ *gland* or ~, extract prepared from the ~ gland of animals and used in treating goitre, cretinism, etc.); having shield-shaped markings, as ~ *woodpecker*. Hence thyro- comb. form (anat.). [f. obs. F *-ide*, irreg. f. Gk *thureoeidēs* (Galen) f. *thureos* shield, see -OID]

thyrox'in(e), n. White active principle of thyroid gland. [f. THYR(OID) + OX- + -IN]

thyrs'us (-ĕr-), n. (Gk ant.; pl. -si). Staff tipped with ornament like pine-cone, an attribute of Bacchus. [L, f. Gk *thursos*]

thyself' (dh-), pron. Reflexive & emphat. form corresp. to *thou*, *thee*. [THY + SELF]

ti[1] (tē), n. Kinds of tree with edible roots. [Polynesian name]

ti[2] (tē). See SI.

tiar'a, n. Ancient Persian turban worn erect by king, depressed by others; Pope's diadem pointed at top & surrounded by three crowns, (fig.) the papal office; ornamental coronet. Hence ~'d [-ED[2]] a. [L f. Gk of unkn. orig.]

tib'i|a, n. (anat.; pl. ~*ae* pr. -ē). The shin-bone; fourth joint of leg in insects; drumstick of fowl. So ~AL a., ~o- comb. form. [L (*tĭ*-), = shin-bone, flute]

tic, n. Habitual spasmodic contraction of muscles esp. of face; (in full ~ *douloureux* pr. dōleroo', & see Ap., lit. painful ~) severe form of facial neuralgia with convulsive twitchings. [F]

tical (*in Siam* tikahl'; *in Burma* tĭ'kl), n. Former Siamese silver coin (roughly = 1 rupee) or its weight; similar Burmese and Chinese weight. [Port. *ticāl* = Ind. *țankā*, *țakā*]

ticc'a, a. (Anglo-Ind.). Engaged on contract, hired (esp. in ~-*gharry*, hackney-carriage). [Hind. *țhikā*, hire, fare]

tice, n. = YORKER. [f. obs. *tice* ENTICE]

tick[1], v.i. & t., & n. **1**. (Make) slight recurring click, esp. that of watch or clock (*to* or *on the* ~, with exact punctuality); (colloq.) moment, instant; ~-*tack*, pulsating sound esp. of the heart (see also TRICK-TRACK), kind of manual semaphore signalling practised by racecourse touts; ~-~, (nursery for) watch. **2**. Small mark set against items in list etc. in checking; (v.t.) mark (item, usu. *off*) with ~. **3**. (Of clock etc.) ~ *away* (time etc.); ~ *off* (sl.), reprimand; (of tape-machine) ~ *out* (news etc.); ~ *over*, (of int.-comb. engine) run slowly with gears etc. disconnected, also fig. [n. 15th c. (*tek*), cf. Du. *tik*, LG *tikk* touch, tick; vb 16th c., cf. Du., LG *tikken*, Norw. *tikke* touch lightly]

tick[2], n. Arachnid or insect parasitic on various animals, as *dog*, *sheep*, *cattle*, -~. [OE *tica*, ME *teke*, *tyke*, of obsc. orig.; cf. MDu., MLG *teke*, OHG *zeho*, G *zecke*]

tick[3], n. Cover, case, of bedding; (also ~'ING[1] n.) stout usu. striped linen or cotton material used for this. [15th c. *tikke*, *teke* (= MDu., MLG *tēke*, OHG *zicha*), f. WG *tēka*, *tīka*, f. L f. Gk *thēkē* case]

tick[4], n., & v.i. & t. (colloq.). **1**. Credit, as *buy goods on* ~. **2**. vb. Give ~; buy or sell (thing) on ~; give (person) ~. [app. abbr. of TICKET in phr. *on the ticket*]

tick'er, n. In vbl senses of TICK[1], esp.: (colloq.) watch, telegraphic tape; (joc.) the heart. [-ER[1]]

tick'et, n., & v.t. **1**. Written or printed piece of card or paper entitling holder to admission to place of entertainment etc., conveyance by train etc., or other right, as *concert*, *theatre*, *bath*, *lottery*, *railway*, *excursion*, SEASON, THROUGH, RETURN, ~; || (mil. sl.) discharge (*get* one's ~); label attached to thing & giving price or other particulars; notice, usu. of card, set up in window etc. of house to let etc.; *the* ~ (colloq.), the proper thing, as *not quite the* ~; *(pol.) list of candidates put forward by a party, (fig.) principles of a party, as *the democratic* ~. **2**. || ~ *of leave* (allowing liberty with certain restrictions to prisoner or convict who has served part of his time), || ~-*of-leave man*, holder of such ~; || ~-*day* (St. Exch.), day before settling-day, when names of actual purchasers are handed to stockbrokers; ~-*night*, performance at theatre proceeds of which are divided among several persons in proportion to number of ~s disposed of by each; || ~-*porter*, licensed porter identified by badge; ~-*punch* (for punching ~s). **3**. v.t. Put ~ on (article for sale etc.). [16th c., f. obs. F *etiquet* or (mod.) *étiquette* f. OF *estiquer* f. MDu. *steken* to STICK]

tick'ey, -kȳ, **tikk'ie**, -kȳ, n. (S.-Afr. colloq.). Threepenny-bit. [orig. unkn.]

tic'kle, v.t. & i., & n. **1**. Apply light touches to (person, part of his body, or abs.) so as to excite the nerves & usu. produce laughter, & in extreme case convulsion, as ~ *him with a feather*, ~ *the soles of her feet*, *don't* ~; feel this sensation, as *my foot* ~s; excite agreeably, amuse, divert, (person, his sense of humour, vanity, etc.), as *I was highly* ~*d at the idea, this will* ~ *his palate*; catch (trout etc.) with the hand. **2**. n. Act, sensation, of tickling. [ME *tikelle*, perh. by metath. f. ON *kitla*, cf. KITTLE]

tick'ler, n. In vbl senses, also: puzzling or delicate question or matter; feather used by revellers to tickle faces. [-ER[1]]

tick'lish, a. Easily tickled, sensitive to tickling; (of question or thing to be dealt with) difficult, critical, delicate, requiring careful handling. Hence ~LY² adv., ~NESS n. [-ISH¹]

ticpolŏng'a (-ngg-), n. Venomous serpent of India & Ceylon. [f. Sinhalese *titpolongā* spot-viper]

tid'al, a. Of tide(s); ~ *air* (passing in & out of lungs at each respiration); ~ *basin, dock, harbour* (subject to rise & fall of tide); ~ *friction* (of ~ wave, retarding diurnal rotation of earth); ~ *river* (affected by tide to some distance from mouth); ~ *wave*, wave following sun & moon from east to west & causing tides, (improp.) any extraordinary ocean wave e.g. one attributed to earthquake, (fig.) widespread manifestation of feeling etc. Hence ~LY² adv. [-AL]

‖ **tidd'ler**, n. (Nursery name for) stickleback. [orig. unkn.]

tidbit. See TITBIT.

tidd'lў-winks, n. Game in which counters are flicked into tray etc. on centre of table. [orig. unkn.]

tide¹, n. **1.** Time, season, (now chiefly in *Whitsun*~, *Christmas*~, *yule*-~, etc., otherwise arch.); period of time, as *work double* ~s (night & day). **2.** Periodical rise (*flood*-~) & fall (*ebb*-~) of sea due to attraction of moon & sun, whence **tidŏ-L'OGY** n.; *high, low,* ~, completion of flood, ebb, -~; *spring, neap,* -~, maximum, minimum, -~ when solar & lunar~s act together, act 90° apart; LAG¹*ging,* PRIMING², *of the* ~s; *meteorological* ~ (due to regular alternations of wind etc.); (fig.) trend of opinion or fortune or events (*go with the* ~, *the* ~ *turns*). **3.** ~*-yule* (opened to admit water or let vessels pass during rising ~, closed to keep water in during ebb); ~*-gauge* (showing extremes or present level of ~); ~*-lock* (between tidal harbour & basin behind it); ~*-rip(s)*, rough water caused by opposing ~s; ~*-waiter*, customs officer who boards ship on arrival to enforce customs regulations; ~*'way*, channel where ~ runs, ebb or flow in such channel. Hence ~'LESS (-dl-) a. [OE, OS *tid* time, OHG *zit,'* ON *tith* f. Gmc *tidiz*, f. root *ti-*, cf. TIME]

tide², v.i. & t. Drift with tide, esp. work in or out of harbour with help of tide; get over (difficulty etc.), as ~ *over this business,* ~ *it over*. [(in obs. sense happen, betide) OE *tidan*; mod. senses direct f. prec.]

tid'ings (-z), n. pl. (now chiefly literary; treated as sing. or pl.). (Piece of) news, as *the* ~ *come(s) too late*. [OE *tidung* (as prec.), ME *tidinde* f. ON *tithindi* f. corresp. ON vb]

tid'ў, a., n., & v.t. **1.** (Of dress, room, person, habits) neatly arranged, neat, orderly; (colloq.) pretty large, considerable, as *left a* ~ *sum behind him, a* ~ *day's work*; (dial.) fairly well in health, as *am feeling pretty* ~. **2.** n. Detachable usu. ornamental cover for chair-back etc., receptacle for odds & ends (*street* ~, bin

for paper etc.). **3.** v.t. Make (room, table, etc., one*self,* or abs.; often *up*) neat, put in good order. Hence **tid'ILY²** adv., **tid'INESS** n. [ME, = timely etc., f. TIDE¹ +-Y²]

tie¹, v.t. & i. (*tҮing*). **1.** Attach, fasten, with cord or the like, as ~ *the dog to the railings,* RIDE *& ~, ~ his legs together, ~ up a parcel*; secure (shoe, bonnet) by tightening & knotting its strings; arrange (string, ribbon, tie, etc.) to form knot, bow, etc., as ~ *your tie, ~ it in a bow*; form (knot, bow) thus; ~ (dress fish-hook to look like) *a fly*; bind (rafters etc.) by crosspiece etc.; restrict, bind, (person etc. *to, down to,* conditions, occupation, etc.). **2.** ~*d* to woman's APRON*-strings*; ~ person's *tongue*, secure, compel, his silence; ~ *up*, restrict, esp. annex conditions to (bequest etc.) to prevent its being sold or diverted from its purpose; ‖ ~*d garage, house*, garage, public house, bound to deal exclusively with one firm. **3.** (mus.). Unite (notes) by tie. **4.** Make equal score or run dead heat or draw game (*with* competitor, *for* place or prize). [OE *tigan* f. **tēagjan* f. *tēag* rope (foll.)]

tie², n. **1.** Cord, chain, etc., used for fastening; = NECK¹-~; *old* SCHOOL¹ ~; (fig.) thing that unites persons, bond, obligation, as ~*s of blood, friendship*; rod, beam, holding parts of a structure together, **rail sleeper*; ~*-beam*, horizontal beam connecting rafters; small fur necklet. **2.** (mus.). Curved line above two notes of same pitch that are to be joined as one. **3.** Equality of score or draw or dead heat among competitors in game or contest; *play, shoot,* etc., *off a* ~, play further game etc. to decide between such competitors; match between any pair of several competing players or teams, as *cup*-~*s* (in competition for cup). **4.** ~*-up*, obstructed situation, standstill, esp. **strike* of railwaymen etc.; ~*-wig* (tied behind with ribbon). [OE *tēah, tēag*, ON *taug* rope f. Gmc **teuh-, *tauh-, *tuh-* to pull]

tier, n., & v.t. **1.** Row, rank, esp. one of several placed one above another as in theatre; ~*s of cable*, circles it forms when coiled. **2.** v.t. Pile (often *up*) in ~s. [16th c. *tire* f. F, f. *tirer* draw, elongate]

tierce, n. .One third of a pipe as old wine-measure, cask containing certain quantity (varying with the goods) esp. of provisions; (mus.) = THIRD; sequence of three cards; (fencing) third position for guard, parry, or thrust (~ *& quart,* fencing); (eccl., also *terce*) office of third hour. [ME, f. OF *terce, tierce,* fem. of *terz, tierz* third f. L TERT*ius*]

tiercel. See TERCEL.

tiercet. See TERCET.

tiers état (tyärz'ätah'), n. = *third* ESTATE. [F]

tiff¹, n., & v.t. Draught of liquor; (v.t.) sip, drink. [17th c., orig. unkn.]

tiff²,· n, & v.i. Fit of peevishness, slight

quarrel; (v.i.) be in a pet. [18th c., orig. unkn.]

tiff[3], v.i. (Anglo-Ind.). = TIFFIN. [abbr.]

tiff'any, n. Kind of gauze muslin. [orig. dress for Twelfth Night, f. OF *tiphanie* f. LL THEO*phania* manifestation of God, EPIPHANY]

tiff'in, n., & v.i. (Anglo-Ind.). (Take) light meal esp. of curried dishes & fruit, lunch. [TIFF[1]+-ING[1]; orig. in sense ' drinking ']

tige (tēzh), n. (Archit.) shaft of column; (bot.) stem, stalk. [F, f. L TIBIA]

tig'er (-g-), n. 1. Large Asian striped feline quadruped, esp. *Bengal* ~; *American* ~, jaguar; *red* ~, cougar; *work* etc. *like a* ~ (with fierce energy); (colloq.) formidable opponent in a game, opp. RABBIT; dissolute swaggerer or bully, whence ~ISM(2) n.; groom accompanying master in light vehicle; *(sl.) yell supplementary to three cheers, final burst. 2. ~-*beetle*, predacious kinds with spotted or striped wing-covers; ~-*cat*, any moderate-sized feline beast resembling the ~, e.g. ocelot, serval, margay; ~*('s)-eye*, a gem of brilliant lustre; ~-*lily*, garden kind with flowers of dull orange spotted with black or purple; ~-*moth*, kinds with richly streaked hairy wings suggesting ~'s skin; ~-*wood* (imported from Brit. Guiana for cabinet-making. So **tig'reSS**[1] n. [ME & OF *tigre* f. L f. Gk *tigris* of oriental orig.]

tig'erish (-g-), a. Like, cruel as, a tiger. [-ISH[1]]

tight (tīt), a., n., & adv. 1. Closely & firmly put together, as ~ *ship*; impermeable, impervious, esp. (in comb.) to specified thing, as *air*, *gas*, *water*, *wind*, ~; closely held, drawn, fastened, fitting, etc., as ~ *knots*, *cork is too* ~, *corn caused by a* (too) ~ *shoe*; neat, trim, compact, as *a* ~ *lass* (arch.), ~ *little island*; tense, stretched so as to leave no slack, as ~ *rope* (~*'rope*, one on which rope-dancers etc. perform); (colloq.) drunk; *money is* ~ (not easily obtainable), *a* ~ *money-market* (in which money is ~); produced by, requiring, great exertion or pressure, as *a* ~ *squeeze*, *am in a* ~ *place* (usu. fig., difficult situation); ~-*fisted*, stingy; *a* ~*wad* (sl.), close-fisted or stingy person. 2. n. pl. Close-fitting garments as used by acrobat, dancer, etc. 3. adv. ~ly, as *squeeze it*, *hold it*, ~. Hence ~'EN[6] (tīt-) v.t. & i. (~*en one's belt*, go without food, also fig.), ~'enER[1](1, 2), ~'NESS, nn., ~'LY[2] adv. [app. alt. f. ME (now dial.) *thight* f. ON *théhtr*, *théttr*, cf. MLG (G) *dicht*]

tig'on, n. Offspring of tiger and lioness. [portmanteau wd]

tike. See TYKE.

tiki (tēk'ē), n. (New Zealand). Large wooden or small greenstone image of creator of man or of an ancestor. [Maori]

tikkie, -ky. See TICKEY.

til (tēl), n. The TILDE in Port. use (over vowel, repr. lost nasal n).

til'bury, n. (hist.). Kind of gig. [maker]

til'de (-ā), n. Swung dash, mark (~) put over Spanish *n* when it is pronounced ny (so *señor*). [Sp., var. of *titulo* TITLE[1]]

tile, n., & v.t. 1. Thin slab of baked clay for roof, pavement, drain, etc.; similar slab glazed & often decorated for hearth, fireplace, wall, etc.; *have a* ~ *loose* (sl.), be rather mad; *on the* ~*s* (sl.), on a debauch; *Dutch* ~ (painted usu. in blue & with scriptural subjects); PANTILE; *plain* ~, flat roofing~ usu. about 10½ × 6¼ in.; (colloq.) silk hat; ~ TEA; ~-*stone*, kinds of flagstone serving when split for ~s. 2. v.t. Cover (roof etc., or abs.) with ~s; (freemasonry) guard (lodge, meeting) against intrusion by placing tiler at door, whence (gen.) bind (person) to secrecy; ~ *in*, enclose in ~s. Hence **til'ING**[1](1, 2, 6) n. [OE *tigule*, -*ele*, OS *tiegla*, OHG *ziagal*, ON *tigl*, f. L *tegula* f. *tegere* cover]

til'er, n. One who makes or lays tiles, whence **til'ERY**(3) n.; (freemasonry, also arch. *tyler*) doorkeeper of lodge. [-ER[1]]

till[1], v.t. Prepare and use (soil) for crops. Hence ~'ABLE a., ~'AGE(3) n. [OE (OS) *tilian* strive, obtain, OHG *zilōn*, Goth. *gatilōn*, see TILL[2]]

till[2], prep. & conj. 1. Up to, as late as, (specified day, hour, season), as *wait* ~ *evening*, *four o'clock*, *then*, *Monday*, *next week*; up to the time of (event expected to happen sooner or later), as *was true* ~ *death*, *waited* ~ *the end*, ~ *his return*, *arrival*, *departure*. 2. conj. Up to the time when, as *ring* ~ *you get an answer*, *walk on* ~ *you come to the gate*. [f. ON *til* to, prob. orig. a noun **til* (prec.) = OE *till* fixed point, OHG *zil* goal, Goth *til*]

till[3], n. Money-drawer in shop counter. [15th c., cf unkn. orig.]

till[4], n. Stiff clay with boulders, sand, etc., boulder-clay. Hence ~'Y[2] a. [orig. unkn.]

till'er[1], n. One who tills. [ME; -ER[1]]

till'er[2], n. Lever fitted to head of rudder for steering; ~-*chain*, ~-*rope* (connecting ~ with wheel). [ME, f. OF *telier* crossbow-stock, orig. weaver's beam, f. L *tela* web, -ARY[1]]

till'er[3], n., & v.i. 1. Shoot of plant springing from bottom of original stalk; sapling; sucker. 2. v.i. Put forth ~s. [app. repr. OE *telgor* extended f. *telga* bough, = ON *tjalga*, MHG *zelg(e)*]

tilt[1], v.i. & t., n. & n. 1. (Cause to) assume sloping position, heel over, as *table is apt to* ~ *over*, *don't* ~ *the table*, *cask wants* ~*ing* (to facilitate emptying); (geol., t. & i. of strata) turn *up* at steep angle. 2. Make a charge with lance (often *at* opponent, esp. fig.); ~ *at the ring* (suspended for horseman to carry off on point of lance). 3. Hammer (steel etc.) with ~. 4. n. ~*ing*, sloping position. 5. Charging with spear against antagonist or mark (~-*yard*, place used for this). 6. Device of crossed sticks etc. for showing when fish has taken hook. 7. *Full* ~, at full speed, with full force, esp. *come, run, full ~ against*. **8.** ~ *(-hammer)*, heavy pivoted hammer used in forging. Hence ~'ER¹ (1, 2) n. [ME *tilte* f. OE *tealt* unsteady, shaky, cf. Norw. *tylten* shaky, Sw. *tulta* waddle]

tilt², n., & v.t. **1.** Covering of canvas etc. esp. for cart. **2.** v.t. Furnish with ~. [collateral form of ME *tild*, OE *teld*, OHG *zelt*, ON *tjald*, perh. infl. by *tent*]

tilth, n. Tillage, cultivation; depth of soil affected by this. [OE (TILL¹+-TH¹)]

tim'bal, -ul, tȳ-, n. Kettledrum. [f. F *timbale*, earlier *attabale* f. Sp. f. Arab. *aṭṭabal* the drum]

timbale (tǎṅbahl'), n. Drum-shaped raised pie in crust of paste or macaroni. [F]

tim'ber, n. **1.** Wood prepared for building, carpentry, etc.; trees suitable for this; woods, forest; piece of wood, beam, esp. (naut.) any of the curved pieces forming ribs of vessel, whence (invoking destruction) *shiver my ~s;·* ‖ (hunting) *fences & gates*. **2.** ‖ ~*-cart* (high-wheeled with tackle for lifting ~); ~*-head*, top end of ~ rising above deck & used for belaying ropes etc.; ~*-hitch*, knot used in attaching a rope to a spar; ~*-toe(s)*, colloq., person with wooden leg; ~*-wolf*, large American grey wolf; ‖ ~*-yard* (lit., &, in cricket sl., batsman's wicket). Hence (·)~ED² (·erd) a., ~ING¹(2, 3) n. [OE *timber* building, OS *-ar*, OHG *zimbar*, ON *timbr*, Goth. **timr* f. Gmc **timram* f. **tem-*, cogn. w. Gk *demō* build, L *domus* house]

timbre (tǎm'ber, & see Ap.), n. Characteristic quality of sounds produced by each particular voice or instrument, depending on the number & character of the overtones. [F, ult. f. L f. Gk as TYMPANUM]

tim'brel, n. Tambourine. [dim. of ME *timbre* f. OF, as prec., see -LE(2)]

time¹, n. **1.** Duration, continued existence; progress of this viewed as affecting persons or things, as ~ *will show who is right, has stood the test of* ~, (personified) *assaults of (old, Father)* T~. **2.** More or less definite portion of this associated with particular events or circumstances, historical or other period, as *the ~s of the Stuarts, the ~ of the Black Death, for the* ~ BEing, *prehistoric ~s, those godless ~s, the good old ~s, things have changed since those~s, the scientists of the~*. **3.** Allotted or available portion of ~, the ~ at one's disposal, as *it will last our ~* (lives), *have no ~ for such frivolities, had no ~ to discuss it, spend, lose, waste*, ~; *will take you all your ~* (colloq. = tax your powers); *give me ~ & I will pay*; (colloq.) *got there ~* (soon) *enough to see him; gain~*; procure it esp. by temporizing measures. **4.** Moment or definite portion of ~ destined or suitable for a purpose etc., as *there is a ~ for everything, will fix a ~ for seeing him, now is the ~ to press your point, now is your ~* (opportunity), *I must bide my* ~, *it is*

(HIGH) ~ *to go,* ~ *for lunch, lunch-~, it is* ~ *I was going* (for me to go), *in the* NICK¹ *of* ~, ~ (for boxing-round etc.) *is up*, (umpire's call) ~*!, is serving his* ~ (as apprentice etc.), *is doing* ~ (in prison), *is far on in her* ~ (of gestation), *is near her* ~ (of childbirth), *my* ~ (death) *is drawing near*. **5.** (Often pl.) conditions of life, prevailing circumstances, of a period, as *hard, bad, good, ~s* (esp. hard etc. to get a living in); *had a good~*, enjoyed myself; *those were* (fine) ~s*!; what a* ~ (trouble) *you will have getting him home!* **6.** Occasion, as *the first* ~ *I saw him, wait till next* ~, *did it seven* ~s *running, have told you a dozen* ~s, ~s *out of number,* ~ *& again, many a* ~, ~ *after* ~, *for the last* ~ *of asking; three, four*, etc. ~s (but *twice*, not *two* ~s) *9 is 27* etc., *is three* ~s *the size of mine, ten* ~s *easier* or *as easy*. **7.** *Past, present, future, ~*, the portions into which *all* ~ may at any moment be accurately or loosely divided (esp., gram., with reference to tenses). **8.** (Amount of) ~ as reckoned by conventional standards, as *the* ~ *allowed was four years, months, minutes, did a mile in record* ~, *astronomical* (mean solar) ~, *apparent* (SOLAR) ~, SIDEREAL~, esp. stated in hours & minutes of the day, as *the.~ fixed was 4.30, what is the* ~*?, is that the correct* (GREENWICH) ~*?, at this* ~ *of day* (fig., at this late stage in history, in the negotiations, etc.). **9.** (mus.). Duration of a note as indicated by semibreve, minim, etc.; style of movement depending on number & accentuation of beats in a bar, as *binary, ternary,* ~ (with two, three, beats in bar), COMMON¹ ~; rate of execution, = *tempo*. **10.** *Against* ~, with utmost speed, as *working, riding, against* ~; *ahead of*, (born) *before*, one's ~ or ~s, having notions too enlightened to be appreciated or put into practice; *all the~*, during the whole of the ~ referred to (*they were laughing all the* ~), *at all* ~s (*is a business man all the* ~); *at the same*~, simultaneously, notwithstanding, *all the same; at~s, now & then; at one ~*, during a known but unspecified past period (*at one* ~ *we met frequently); beat* ~, indicate, follow, ~ of music with stick, hand, etc.; *civil* ~ (expressed by CIVIL year etc.); CLOSE¹~; *from ~ to* ~, occasionally; *in* ~, not late, early enough (*to do, for* thing), eventually, sooner or later, in accordance with, following, the ~ of music etc.; *in no* ~, rapidly, in the twinkling of an eye; *keep* ~, walk, dance, sing, etc., in ~, (of clock etc.) *keep good, bad,* ~, record ~ (in)accurately; *mean* ~ (regulated by average); *one, two*, etc., *at a* ~, each, each two etc., separately; *out of* ~, unseasonable, unseasonably, too late, (of singing etc.) not in ~; ~ *immemorial* or *out of mind*, (for, from) a longer ~ than anyone can remember or trace; *the ~ of day*, hour by clock, (colloq.) *pass the ~ of day*, exchange greeting etc. (*with* person), (sl.) *so that's the ~ of day* (the state of affairs, your little game, etc.)*!*; *the ~ of one's life*, a period of exceptional enjoyment or pleasant or unpleasant excitement (*have the ~ of one's*, *give one the ~ of his*, *life*); *what ~* (poet.), while, when; *The T~s*, the newspaper so named. **11.** *~-ball* (dropped from top of staff at observatory to indicate fixed moment of mean ~); *~-bargain*, contract for sale of stock etc. at future ~ (often a form of gambling); *~ bomb* (designed to explode some ~ after being dropped or put in position); *~-book, -card, -sheet* (for recording workmen's hours of work); *~-fuse* (calculated to burn for or explode at given ~); *~-honoured*, venerable by antiquity; *~'keeper*, one who records ~ esp. of workmen, *watch* etc. *is good, bad, ~keeper* (keeps good, bad, ~); *~ lag*, interval of ~ between cause etc. & result or consequence; *~-limit* (within which something must be done); *~'piece*, *~-measuring* instrument esp. portable but stationary clock; *~-server*, one who, esp. for selfish ends, adapts himself to opinions of the ~s or of persons in power, so *~-serving* a. & n.; *~-table*, scheme of school work etc., table showing ~s of trains; *~-work* (paid for by ~, not PIECE-*work*). [OE *tíma*, ON *tími*, f. Gmc root *tī-*, cf. TIDE]

time², v.t. & i. Choose the time for, do at chosen time, as *must ~ your blows, remark was ill, well, ~d*; arrange time of arrival of, regulate rate of travelling of, (train etc.); ascertain the time taken by (race, runner, etc.), whence **tim'ER**¹(1, 2), **tim'ING**¹, nn.; keep time, harmonize, *with*. [ME; f. prec.]

time'less (-ml-), a. (rare). Unending; untimely. [-LESS]

time'ly (-ml-), a. Seasonable, opportune. Hence ~**NESS** n. [ME; -LY¹]

tím'eō Dán'aös ĕt dōn'a feren'tēs, phr. inculcating or expressing distrust of a conciliatory enemy. [L, = I fear the Greeks, even when they bring gifts]

‖ **time'ous** (-mus), **tim'ous**, a. (chiefly Sc.). Timely. Hence ~**LY**² adv. [f. TIME¹ + -OUS]

tim'id, a. Easily alarmed; shy. Hence or cogn. **timid'ITY**, ~**NESS**, nn., ~**LY**² adv. [f. F *-ide* or L *timidus* (*limēre* fear, -ID¹)]

timŏc'racĭ, n. Form of government in which there is a property qualification for office. So **timocrăt'IC** a. [f. OF *tymocracie* f. med. L f. Gk *timokratia* (*timē* honour, worth, value, see -CRACY)]

tim'orous, a. Timid, easily alarmed. Hence ~**LY**² adv., ~**NESS** n. [ME, f. OF *timoreus*, f. med. L *timorosus*, f. L *timor*, see -OUS]

tim'othĭ, n. (Also ~ *grass*) a fodder--grass. [*T~* Hanson, who introduced it in N. America *c*. 1720]

‖ **timous**. See TIMEOUS.

tim'pan|ō, n. (pl. ~*i* pr. *-ē*). A kettle--drum. So ~**IST** n., one who plays the percussion instruments in an orchestra. [It., see TYMPANUM]

tin, n., & v.t. (-nn-). **1.** White malleable metal, taking high polish & resisting corrosion, used mainly in alloys with lead, copper, or antimony to form solder, white-metal, pewter, bronze, etc., or in plating thin steel sheets to form ~ *plate* to make containers, kitchen utensils, toys, etc.; ‖ vessel etc. of ~, esp. for preserving meat, fruit, etc., as *sardine-~*; (attrib.) made of ~ or of iron covered with ~; (sl.) money; *cry of ~*, crackling sound it makes if bent; *salt of ~*, *~--liquor*, solutions of ~ used as mordants by dyers etc. **2.** *~ fish* (naut. sl.), torpedo; *~ foil*, foil of ~ or alloy; *~ god*, object of mistaken veneration; *~ hat* (army sl.), modern soldier's steel helmet; ‖ *~-opener*, tool for opening ~s; *~-pan alley*, (fig.) the world of the composers and publishers of popular music; *~-plate* v.t., coat with ~; *~'man*, *~-smith*, worker in ~ and ~ plate, so *~n'ER*¹ n.; *~'pot* a. (derog.), cheap, inferior; *~'stone*, one of the ores of ~; *~'ware*, vessels etc. of ~ or ~ plate; *~ whistle*, = *penny* WHISTLE. Hence ~**n'Y**² a. **3.** v.t. Cover, coat, with ~; ‖ pack (meat, fruit, etc.) in ~s for preservation. [OE, ON *tin*, OHG *zin*, f. Gmc **tinam*, not known outside Gmc]

tin'amou (-ōō), n. S.-Amer. quail-like game-bird. [F, of S.-Amer. orig.]

tinc'al, -kal, (-ngkl), n. Unrefined borax. [f. Malay *tingkal* f. Skr. *ṭankaṇa*]

tinctŏr'ial, a. Of colour or dyeing, producing colour. [f. L *tinctorius* (*tinctor* dyer), see TINGE, -ORY, -AL]

tinc'ture, n., & v.t. **1.** Alcoholic solution of some (usu. vegetable) principle used in medicine, as *~ of quinine*; slight flavour, spice, smack, (*of* thing, fig. *of* moral quality etc.); tinge (*of* colour); (her.) inclusive term for the metals, colours, & furs in a coat of arms. **2.** v.t. Colour slightly, tinge, flavour; (fig.) affect slightly (*with* quality). [(vb f. n.) ME, f. L *tinctura* dyeing (as TINGE, see -URE)]

tin'dal, n. (India). Native petty officer or Lascars. [Malayalam *taṇḍal*]

tin'der, n. Dry substance readily taking fire from spark, esp. charred linen etc. used in *~-box* (containing ~, flint, & steel, for kindling fire); *German ~*, = AMADOU. Hence ~**Y**² a. [OE *tynder*, *-re* f. Gmc **tund-*, **lind-* kindle; cf. ON *tundr*, OHG *zuntara*]

tine, n. Point, prong, e.g. of antler, harrow, or fork. Hence (-)**tinED**² (-nd) a. [OE *tind*, ON *tindr* f. Gmc **tindiz*]

ting, n., & v.i. (Make) tinkling sound as of bell. [imit.]

tinge, v.t. (*-j*), v.t. & n. **1.** Colour slightly (*with* red etc.); (fig.) modify by mixture (*with* envy etc.). **2.** n. Tint, slight colouring, flavour (lit. & fig.). [ME, f. L *tingere tinct-* dye, stain]

tingle (tĭng'gl), v.i. & t., & n. (Feel) prickling or stinging sensation; cause this, as *the reply ~d in his ears*; (rare) make (ear etc.) ~. [ME; var. of TINKLE]

tink'er, n., & v.t. & i. **1.** ‖ Mender (esp. itinerant) of kettles, pans, etc. (*don't care a~'s damn* or *cuss,* at all); rough-&-ready worker, botcher; patching, botching, as *had an hour's ~ at it.* **2.** Kinds of fish, bird, & seal. **3.** vb. Repair (metal-work), patch (anything, lit. & fig., often *up*) roughly; work in amateurish or clumsy fashion *at* (thing) in the way of repair or alteration. Hence~LY[1] a. [ME, of unkn. orig.]

tinkle (tĭng'kl), v.i. & t., & n. (Make) succession of clinking sounds; make (bell etc.)~ ; (obs.) tingle. [ME, f. obs. *tink* to chink + -LE(3)]

tink'ler, n. In vbl senses, esp.: (sl.) small bell. [-ER[1]]

tinnit'us, n. (med.). Ringing in the ears. [L, f. *tinnire -it-* ring, tinkle]

tinny. See TIN.

tin'sel, n., a., & v.t. (-ll-). **1.** Kinds of glittering metallic substance made in thin sheets & used in strips, threads, etc., to give sparkling effect; dress-fabric etc. adorned with ~; (fig.) superficial brilliancy or splendour. **2.** adj. Showy, gaudy, cheaply splendid. **3.** v.t. Adorn with ~ (lit. & fig.). [f. OF *estincelle* f. pop. L *stincilla* f. L *scintilla* spark; cf. STENCIL]

tint, n., & v.t. **1.** A variety of a colour, esp. one made by diluting with white; (rare) tendency towards, admixture of, a different colour, as *red of* or *with a blue ~*; *autumn ~s* (of dying leaves); (engrav.) set of parallel lines cut with ~*-tool* to give uniform shading; ~*-block,* block bearing design to be printed in faint colour as background, *ruled, crossed, ~,* surface of this with parallel, crossing, lines. **2.** v.t. Apply ~ to, colour. Hence ~LESS a. [app. alt. ˈf. earlier *tinct* f. L (as TINGE), perh. infl. by It. *tinta*]

tint'er, n. Person who tints; instrument for tinting; magic-lantern slide of plain coloured glass. [-ER[1]]

tintinnăbŭlā'tion, n. Tinkling of bells. [f. foll. + -ATION]

tintinnăb'ŭl|um, n. (pl. ~a). Bell, esp. small tinkling one, whence~AR(Y)[1],~OUS, aa.; rattle made of small bells or metal plates. [L, = bell, f. *tintinnare* redupl. form as TINNITUS]

tintŏm'eter, n. Instrument for determining tints. [-METER]

tint'y, a. Discordantly tinted. [-Y[2]]

tin'y, teen'y (nursery), a. Very small, as *a ~ little boy,ˈlittle ~ boy.* [app. f. 15th c. *tine, tyne* adj. & n., small, a little (of unkn. orig.) + -Y[2]]

-tion, suf. of nn. of action or condition, thr. F *-tion* (or dir.) f. L *-tionem* (nom. *-tio*), a compd suf. f. p.p. stems in *-i-* + -ION. See -ATION, -ITION, -SION.

tip[1], n., & v.t. (-pp-). **1.** Extremity, end, esp. of small or tapering thing, as *the ~s of the fingers, walk on the ~s of your toes, ~ of a cigar, bird measures 15 in. from ~* (of one wing) *to ~* (of other), *had it on the ~ of my tongue,* was just going to say it or was on the point of remembering it; kinds of brush used in gilding; small piece or part attached to end of thing, e.g. ferrule. **2.** ~*'staff* (hist.; pl. ~*staves*), (metal-tipped staff as badge of) sheriff's officer; ~*-tilled,* (of nose) turned up at ~; ~*'toe,* (adv., also *on~toe*) on the~s of the toes, (v.i.) walk ~toe; ~*top', (n.) highest point of excellence, (a. & adv.) first-rate. **3.** v.t. Furnish with ~. [ME (first in p.p.), f. ON *typpi* n., *typpa* vb, *typptr* tipped; prob. reinforced by MDu., MLG *tip* = MHG *zipf*]

tip[2], v.t. & i. (-pp-), & n. **1.** (Cause to) lean or slant, tilt, topple, (*over, up,* etc.) esp. with slight effort. **2.** Strike or touch lightly (~ *& run,* form of cricket in which batsman must run if bat touches ball; ~*-&-run raid,* one in which the raider appears suddenly and makes off immediately after attacking). **3.** Overturn, cause to overbalance, (person *into* pond etc.); discharge (contents of jug etc. *out, into,* etc.) thus. **4.** (sl.). Throw lightly, hand, give, communicate, in informal manner, as ~ (throw) *us a copper,* ~ *us your fin,* shake hands, ~ *us a song, a yarn, might have ~ped me the wink* (given me warning wink); ~ *off,* give (person) warning, hint, inside information, so ~*-off* n., a hint; (sport.) give secret information about horse etc. to. **5.** Make usu. small present of money to, as *must ~ the porter,* ~*ped me* (now rarely *with*) *half-a-crown.* **6.** n. Small money present. **7.** Secret information about horse-racing, money-market, etc., as *will give you the straight* (correct) ~; good dodge or recipe for doing something; *miss one's ~,* fail in one's object. **8.** Slight push; light stroke esp. in baseball. **9.** Place where refuse is ~ped. **10.** ~*-car, -cart* (pivoted for ~ping); ~*'cat,* (game with) short piece of wood tapering at ends & struck with stick; ~*-up seat,* of the kind used in theatres etc. to allow of free passing. Hence~p'ER[1] (1, 2) n. [of various orig.]

Tipperar'y, n. Refrain specially associated with the B.E.F. of 1914. [*It's a long way to ~,* first wds of chorus]

tipp'et, n. Cape, muffler, of fur etc. covering shoulders & coming down to some distance in front, worn by women & as part of official costume by judges, clergy, etc. [ME, of unkn. orig.]

tip'ple, v.i. & t., & n. **1.** Drink strong drink habitually; drink (liquor) slowly & repeatedly. **2.** n. Strong drink. **tipp'l**ER[1] n. [ME *tippler* of unkn. orig.; vb later, prob. by back form.; cf. Norw. dial. *tippla* to drink in small quantities]

tipp'y, a. (Of tea) containing a large

proportion of ' golden tips ' (leaf-buds). [TIP¹ +-Y²]

tip′ster, n. One who gives tips about races etc. [-STER]

tip′sỹ, a. Slightly intoxicated; proceeding from, showing, intoxication, as *a ~y lurch*; *~y-cake*, sponge-cake soaked in wine & served with custard. Hence ~iFY v.t., ~iLY² adv., ~iNESS n. [prob. f. TIP², = inclined to lean, unsteady; for -*sy* cf. *tricksy, flimsy*]

tirāde′ (*or* tīr-), n. Long vehement speech esp. of censure; long passage of declamation etc. [F, = long speech, f. It. *tirata*, f. It. *tirare* draw, see -ADE]

tirailleur′ (-ralér, & see Ap.), n. Sharp-shooter, skirmisher. [F]

tīre¹, v.t. & i. Make or grow weary; *am ~d*, have had enough *of*, am sick *of*, (thing, doing), am exhausted *with*. Hence ~d′NESS (tīrd-) n., also (rhet., poet.) ~′lĕss¹ (tīrl-) [-LESS] a., ~′lĕssLY² adv. [OE *tīorian, tē*-; excl. E]

tīre², ‖ **tȳre**, n., & v.t. 1. Band of metal, rubber, etc., placed round rim of wheel to strengthen it or prevent jar; PNEUMATIC ~. 2. v.t. Place ~ on (wheel). Hence (-)tirED² (tīrd), ~′lĕss² (tīrl-) [-LESS], aa. [15th c., prob. = foll.]

‖ **tīre³**, n., & v.t. (arch.). 1. Head-dress; attire. 2. v.t. Adorn, attire, as *she~d her head*; *~′woman* (arch.), woman employed to dress another. [ME, aphetic f. ATTIRE]

tire′some (tīrs-), a. Tending to tire, fatiguing; tedious; annoying, as *how ~ ! —I have left my watch behind.* Hence~LY² adv., ~NESS n. [TIRE¹+-SOME]

tīr′ō, tȳr′ō, n. (pl. ~s). Beginner, novice. [L (*ti*-), = newly levied soldier]

tīrocin′ium, n. (pedant.). Apprenticeship, first rudiments of an art. [L, = first service of soldier (prec.)]

′tis (-z), arch. or poet. contraction of *it is*.

tisane′ (-zăn), n. = PTISAN. [F]

tiss′ue (-sū, -shū, -shōō), n. Any fine woven fabric; (biol.) substance of an organ, fabric formed of cells & cell-products, as *adipose, connective, muscular, nervous*, ~; (fig.) interwoven series, set, collection, (*of* lies, absurdities, etc.); ~ (-*paper*), thin soft unsized paper for wrapping or protecting delicate articles, engraving in book, etc. Hence (-)tiss′uED² (-sŭd, -shŭd) a. [ME, f. OF *tissu* rich stuff, f.p.p. of *tistre* f. L *texere* weave]

tit¹, n. 1. Kinds of small bird, including ~′lark &~′mouse (both also called~′ling); *bearded, blue, coal* or *cole, crested, great, long-tailed, marsh*,~. 2. (arch.). Small or poor horse; child, girl. [prob. imit. of littleness; cf. Icel. *tittr* pin, titmouse]

tit², n. ~ *for tat*, blow for blow, retaliation. [perh., = earlier *tip for tap*]

tit³, n. (colloq.). = TEAT.

Tit′an, n. (Gk myth.) each of a gigantic race, the children of Uranus & Ge, (also) the sun-god, brother of Helios; person of superhuman size, strength, intellect, etc.,

whence ~ESS¹ n. So ~ESQUE′ (-ĕsk), titān′ic, aa. [L f. Gk]

titān′ium, n. A dark-grey metallic element. Hence **tit′an**ATE¹ (3) n. [prec.+ -IUM]

tit′bit, n. Delicate bit, choice morsel. [17th c. *tid-bit*, f. dial. *tid* adj.]

tithe (-dh), n., & v.t. 1. Tax of one-tenth, esp. one payable in kind; ‖ (often pl.) tenth part of annual proceeds of land (*predial~s*) & personal industry (*personal ~s*) taken for support of clergy & church; ‖ *mixed ~s* (from pigs, sheep, etc., fed on the land); ‖~ *redemption commissioners* (arranging commutation of ~s etc.); ‖~-*pig*, tenth pig set apart for ~; (rhet.) tenth part, esp. *not a ~ of*. 2. v.t. Subject to ~s. Hence **tith′**ABLE (-dh-) a. [ME *tig(e)the, tithe* = OE *teogotha, tēotha* TENTH; vb f. *teogothian*]

tith′ing (-dh-), n. Taking tithe; (hist.) ten householders living near together & bound over as sureties for each other's peaceable behaviour. [as prec., -ING¹]

Ti′tian (-shn), n. Venetian painter (d. 1576); one of his pictures; (attrib., esp. of hair) bright golden auburn. Hence ~ESQUE′ (-shanĕsk) a., in the style of ~.

tit′illāte, v.t. Tickle; excite pleasantly. So~A′TION n. [f. L *titillare*, see -ATE³]

tit′ivate, titt′i-, v.t. & i. (colloq.). Adorn, smarten, (oneself etc.); adorn oneself. [earlier *tid-*, perh. f. *tidy* after *cultivate*]

tit′lark. See TIT¹.

ti′tle, n. 1. Distinguishing appellation placed at head of chapter, poem, etc.; contents of ~-page of book, short essential part of these used in reference (e.g. *Adam Smith's Wealth of Nations*); book or publication. 2. Formula at head of legal document, statute, etc.; division of statute etc. 3. Personal appellation, hereditary or not, denoting or implying office (e.g. *king, queen, judge, mayor, rector, captain*) or nobility (e.g. *duke, marquis, earl, viscount, baron*, any of which exc. *duke* may be COURTESY ~ of son etc. of duke etc.) or distinction or merit (e.g. *baronet, knight*) or (usu. *degree*) qualification (e.g. *D.D., M.A.*), or used in addressing or referring to person (e.g. *Lord, Lady, Sir, Mrs, Miss, Doctor, Professor*, prefixed to name; *your* or *her* or *his Majesty, Grace*, etc.). 4. (Law) right to ownership of property with or without possession, the facts constituting this, (also ~-*deed*) legal instrument as evidence of right; just or recognized claim (*to*), service, merit, etc., that constitutes this. 5. Fineness of gold as expressed in carats. 6. Fixed sphere of work & source of income as condition to ordination. 7. (District attached to) parish church in Rome. 8. ~-*page*, page at beginning of book giving particulars of subject, authorship, publication, etc.; ~-*role*, part in a play that gives it its name (e.g. *Othello*). Hence ~LESS a. [ME & OF *title* f. L *titulus*]

ti′tled (-ld), a. Having title of nobility. [-ED²]

tit′ling¹, n. See TIT¹. [f. TIT¹+-LING; cf. Norw. dial., Icel. *titlingr*]

tit′ling², n. Impressing of title in gold-leaf etc. on back of book. [-ING¹]

tit′mouse, n. (pl. -*mice*). = TIT¹. [ME *titmōse* (TIT¹+OE *māse* ~, = OHG *meisa*, G *meise*]

Tit′o̱lism (tē-), n. President Tito's kind of Communism in Jugoslavia as dist. from that of Russia and her satellite countries. So ~IST(2) n. & a. [*Tito*, assumed name of Josip Broz (b. 1892), -ISM(3)]

tit′r|āte, v.t. Determine quantity of given constituent in (compound) by observing quantity of a standard solution necessary to convert this constituent into another form. So ~A′TION n. [f. F *titrer* (*litre* TITLE), see -ATE³]

titt′er, v.i., & n. **1.** Laugh, giggle, in restrained manner. **2.** n. Such laugh. Hence ~ER¹ n. [imit.]

tit′tle, n. Particle, whit, esp. *not one jot or* ~. [ME, = stroke over word or letter, f. L as TITLE, cf. TILDE]

‖ **tit′tlebăt** (-lb-), n. Stickleback. [var., of childish orig.]

tit′tle-tăttle, n., & v.i. Gossip. [redupl. f. *tattle*]

titt′up, v.i., & n. **1.** Go *along* etc., move, conduct oneself, in lively or frisky fashion; ‖ (naut. etc. sl.) toss for drinks. **2.** n. Spring, prance. Hence ~(p)y² a. [perh. imit. of hoof-beat]

titubā′tion, n. (med.). Fidgetiness esp. as caused by nervous irritation. [f. L *titubatio* (*titubare* totter, see -ATION)]

tit′ular, a. & n. **1.** Held by virtue of a title, as ~ *possessions*; existing, that is such, only in name, as ~ *sovereign(ty)*; ~ *bishop*, (R.-C. Ch.) bishop bearing name of a former Christian see esp. in Mohammedan countries; ~ (*saint*), patron saint of church. **2.** n. Holder of office etc. esp. benefice without corresponding functions or obligations. Hence ~LY² adv. [c. 1600, f. F *titulaire* (TITLE, -AR¹)]

†mēs′is, n. (gram.). Separation of the parts of a compound word by intervening word(s) (e.g. *to* us *ward, what* things *soever*). [LL f. Gk *tmēsis* cutting f. *temnō* cut]

to¹ (*before consonant* te, *before vowel* to͝o, *emphat. or at end of clause* to͞o), prep. **1.** In the direction of (place, person, thing, condition, quality, etc.; with or without the implication of intention or of arrival), *as was walking over to Bath, on his way to the station, fled to Rome, throw it to me, got to the house by four, to bed with you!, fluttered to the pavement, was committed to the flames, house looks to the south, held it to the light, to arms!, hand to hand, told him to his face, was carried to destruction, letter has come to hand, fell to work, fell to musing, tends or has a tendency to indolence, slow to anger, appointed to a post, born to a great*

fortune, all to no purpose, to his shame be it said. **2.** As far as, not short of, as *true to the end, not short to the heart, a Home-ruler to the core, fought to the last gasp, hit it to the boundary, correct to a hair's-breadth, suits him to a T, acted his part to perfection, might run to £5, drank himself to death, might argue to all eternity, & so on to the end of the chapter.* **3.** (Of comparison, ratio, adaptation, reference, etc.) *this is nothing to what it might be, 3 is to 4 as 6 is to 8, ten to one he will find it out, two to one is not fair play, not up to the mark, equal to the occasion, made to order, drawn to scale, not to the point, true to life, will speak to that question later, sang to his guitar, cannot do it to his liking; corresponding, compared, inferior, etc., to.* **4.** (arch.). For, by way of, as *took her to wife, has a duke to his father-in-law.* **5.** (Introducing indirect object of vb, recipient, possessor, etc., or person or thing affected by the action, quality, etc.; alternative constr. as shown) *lend it or them, or this* etc., or *your knife* etc., *to John* or *to him* (also *lend John or him this* etc. or *your knife* or rarely *it or them, lend it or rarely them him* or rarely *John, but not lend this* etc., or *your knife him, or John, nor lend to him or John it or them, nor in ordinary prose lend to him or John this* etc. or *your knife*); *write to me, explain it to me, apply to the secretary, seems to me absurd, to my mind or thinking, revolting to sane minds, pleasant to the taste, impervious to weather, obedient to command, unkind to him, has been a good father to them, what's that to you?, drink to me only with thine eyes, here's to you* (your health), *broken in to the saddle, accustomed to it, next door to us, ready to his hand, has not a shilling to his name, takes no wine to his dinner* (arch.), *there is a moral to it, there is no end to it; would to God* (I wish it were or had been God's will) *that.* **6.** (As sign of infinitive, expressing purpose, consequence, etc., limiting the meaning of adj., or merely forming verbal n.; omitted after *can, do, may, must, shall, will,* & as shown, cf. also DARE, NEED, GO) *he proposes to stay, declines to go, wants to know, began to sing* (or *began singing*), *fail to understand, does it to annoy, the matter is difficult to explain, it is useless to rebel* (rebellion is useless), *allow me to remind* (but *let me remind) you, was seen to fall* (but *I saw him fall), was heard to complain* (but *I heard him complain), floor was felt to tremble* (but *felt the floor tremble), was never known or found to fail, have sometimes known or found it (to) fail, make him repeat it, he was made* (usu. *to*) *repeat it, help me (to) lift this, please* (to usu. omitted) *shut the door, was pleased* (thought fit) *to be angry, I prefer to go* (but *had rather go, had as lief go), had my work to do, had to do my work* (but *will not have you talk such nonsense), was about to protest,* (arch.) *he is much to seek* (deficient) *in that respect*, (arch.) *what went ye out for to see?*, *to* WIT[1]. **7.** (As substitute for infinitive) *meant to call but forgot to, had no time to, you promised to.* **8.** Included, contained, or involved in (*that's all there is to it*, it's that and no more). [OE, (OS) *tō*, OHG *zuo* f. WG **tō*]

to[2] (tōō), adv. To the normal or required position or condition, esp. to a standstill, as BRING, COME, FALL, GO, HEAVE, LIE[3], *to*; *the door is to* (just not shut); *to & FRO.* [f. prec.]

toad, n. **1.** Amphibian like frog but with clumsy & usu. warty body & not aquatic except when breeding; detestable or disgusting person. **2.** ~ *in a* (or *the*) *hole*, beef or sausages baked in batter. **3.** ~-*eater*, sycophant, obsequious parasite, so ~-*eating* a. & n.; ~'*flax*, perennial plant with spurred yellow flowers marked with orange spot (*ivy-leaved* ~*flax*, with lilac flowers & ivy-shaped leaves); ~'*spit*, = CUCKOO-*spit*; ~'*stone*, stone, occas. precious, supposed to resemble or to have been formed in body of ~, formerly used as amulet etc., [f. G *todtes gestein* dead rock] kind of volcanic rock; ~'*stool*, kinds of umbrella-shaped fungus. Hence~'ISH[1] a. [OE *tādige, tadde*, of unkn. orig.]

toad'ў, n., & v.t. **1.** = TOAD-*eater*. **2.** v.t. Fawn servilely upon (person, or abs.). Hence ~ISH[1] a., ~ISM n. [19th c., f. TOAD-*eater*+-Y[3]]

toast, n., & v.t. & i. **1.** (Slice of) bread browned on each side esp. at the fire (*anchovies* etc. *on* ~, so served at table; MELBA ~; *have one on* ~, sl., have him at one's mercy; *as warm as a* ~, glowing with warmth); (arch.) *a* ~, piece of ~ in cup of wine. **2.** Person esp. woman whose health is drunk, thing, sentiment, similarly named in drinking, as *was a great* ~ *in her day.* **3.** ~-*list*, ~-*master*, (person who announces) ~s at public dinner; ‖~-*rack* (for holding slices of ~ at table); ~-*water* (in which ~ has stood, used as cooling drink; also ~ *& water*). **4.** vb. Brown, cook, (bread, muffin, cheese, bacon, or intr. of these) before fire; warm (one's feet etc.) thus. **5.** Drink to the health or in honour of. Hence ~'ER[1] (1, 2) n. [ME, f. OF *toster* f. LL *tostare* grill, roast (L *torrēre tost-* parch); n. f. vb]

toast'ing, n. In vbl senses; ~-*fork*, long fork for making toast, (joc., also ~-*iron*) sword. [-ING[1]]

tobăcc'ō, n. (pl. ~s). **1.** (Also ~-*plant*) plant of Amer. origin with narcotic leaves used for smoking, chewing, or snuff; its leaves esp. as prepared for smoking etc. (abbr. *baccy*). **2.** ~-*cutter*, instrument for shredding ~; ~ *heart*, disorder of heart caused by excessive use of ~; ~-PIPE[1]; ~-*pouch* (for carrying about small quantity of ~); ~-*stopper*, instrument for pressing down ~ in pipe. [f. Sp. *tabaco*, of native orig.]

tobăcc'onĭst, n. Dealer in tobacco. [f. prec. +-IST w. inserted -n-]

tobŏgg'an, n., & v.i. **1.** Long narrow sledge used for going downhill esp. over snow or ice; ~-*shoot, -slide*, slide for ~s, usu. divided into different courses to prevent collision. **2.** v.i. Go in ~. Hence ~ER[1], ~ING[1], nn. [of Canadian Ind. orig.]

tŏb'ў, n. -Jug or mug usu. in form of old man with three-cornered hat (also *T*~ *Fillpot*); ‖~ *collar*, broad turned-down goffered collar like the frill of Punch's dog T~. [pers. name]

tocca'ta (-kah-), n. (mus.). Kind of rapid brilliant composition for piano, organ, etc. [It., f. *toccare* TOUCH, see -ADE]

Tŏc H, n. Society with many branches embodying Christian fellowship and service. [signallers' former letter T, + H, for *Talbot House* started by Rev. T. B. Clayton in Ypres Salient in 1915 in memory of Gilbert Talbot]

Tochār'ian (-k-), a. & n. (Of, in) an extinct Indo-European language. [f. F -*ien*, f. *Tochari* a Scythian tribe. (in Strabo)]

‖**tŏch'er** (-χ-), n. (Sc.). Marriage portion, dowry. [f. Gael. *tochar*]

‖**tŏc'ō, -kō**, n. (sl.). A thrashing; chastisement. [Hind. *thōcō*, imper. of *thocnā* censure]

tŏc'sin, n. (Bell rung as) alarm-signal (now chiefly fig.). [F, in OF *toquassen* f. Pr. *tocascnh* (*tocar* TOUCH + *senh* signal-bell f. L as SIGN)]

‖**tŏd**[1], n. (arch.). Bush; mass of foliage; weight for wool, usu. 28 lb. [ME, app. same wd as EFris., LG *todde* bundle, pack, ON *toddi* bit, piece; see TED]

‖**tŏd**[2], n. (dial.). Fox. [orig. unkn.]

today', to-day', adv. & n. (On) this present day, as *saw* or *shall see him* ~, ~ *is his birthday*. [OE *tō dæg* on (this) day (*tō* TO[1]+DAY); so *tonight, tomorrow*]

tŏd'dl|e, v.i. & t., & n. **1.** Walk with short tottering steps, as child learning to walk; make (one's *way*), perform (distance), thus; take casual or leisurely walk (*round, to*, etc.). **2.** n. ~ing walk; (colloq.) ~ing child. Hence **tŏdd'lER**[1] n. [of obsc. orig.]

tŏdd'ў, n. Sap of some kinds of palm, from which when fermented arrack is obtained; sweetened drink of spirits & hot water. [f. Hind. *tārī* (*tār* palm f. Skr. *tāla* palmyra)]

to-do' (-dōō), n. Bustle, fuss. [f. *to do*, dat. inf. 'to be done', as in *What's to do?*; cf. ADO]

tŏd'ў, n. W.-Ind. bird related to kingfisher. [f. F *todier* f. L *todus*, a small bird]

tōe, n., & v.t. & i. (part. ~*ing*). **1.** Digit of foot; part of stocking, shoe, boot, that covers the ~s. **2.** Fore part of hoof; piece of iron under front of horseshoe to prevent slipping. **3.** Projection from foot of buttress etc. to give stability; outer end of head of golf-club; (mech.) lower end of vertical shaft resting in a step, arm on valve-lifting rod of steam-engine. 4. *Ball* (callous fleshy pad on under side) *of* ~; *great, little,* ~, largest, smallest, ~ of human foot; *tread on* person's ~*s*, offend his feelings or prejudices; *the light fantastic* ~, (joc.) dancing; *on* one's ~*s*, alert, eager; (sl.) *turn up* one's ~*s*, die; *from top to* ~, from head to foot, completely; *heel-&-* ~ WALK[1]*ing*; ~-*cap*, outer covering of ~ in boot or shoe; ~-*drop*, inability to raise ~*s*, from paralysed muscles; ~-*nail*, nail of human ~, metal nail driven obliquely through end of board etc. 5. vb. Furnish with ~, mend ~ of, (stocking, shoe); touch (*the line, mark, scratch*) with ~ before starting in race (~ *the line*, fig., conform esp. under pressure to the requirements of one's party); (golf) strike (ball) with part of club too near ~; ~ *in, out*, turn ~*s* in, out, in walking. Hence (-)toED (tōd), ~'LESS, aa. [OE *tā*, ON *tá*, OHG *zēha* f. Gmc *taih(w)ōn*]

to-fall (tōō'fawl), n. (arch., poet.). Close, decline, (*of* day etc.). [TO[2] + FALL]

‖ **töff**, n. (sl.). Distinguished person, swell. [perh. perversion of TUFT]

‖ **töff'ee** (-fi), -**fy**, n. Kinds of sweet made of sugar, butter, etc., as *almond* ~; *can't shoot* etc. *for* ~ (sl.), is no shot etc. (cf. NUT). [earlier, & still Sc. & U.S., *taffy*, of unkn. orig.]

‖ **töft**, n. (law). Homestead; land once occupied by this; ~'*man* (hist.), occupier of ~. [OE, f. ON *topt*]

tög, n., & v.t. (sl.; -gg-). 1. (Usu. pl.) garment(s); (naut.) *long* ~*s*, shore-clothes. 2. v.t. Dress (person, one*self*, often *out*). Hence ~g'ERY(5) (-g-) n. [app. abbr. of *togeman*(s), *togman*, a 16th c. cant wd]

tög'a, n. Ancient Roman's loose flowing outer garment, esp. w. allusion to Roman citizenship, to civil career, or (also ~ *viril'īs*, manly ~) to its assumption as sign of manhood (at age of 14). Hence ~'d, ~ED[2] (-ad), a. [L, cogn. w. *tegere* cover]

togëth'er (-dh-), adv. In company or conjunction, as *walking* ~, *lived* ~; simultaneously, as *both* ~ *exclaimed*; *compared* ~ (one with another); into conjunction, so as to unite, as *sew them* ~, *tied* ~, GET, HANG[1], ~, *put* TWO *& two* ~; uninterruptedly, on end (*he would keep sober for weeks* ~); ~ *with*, as well as, & also, as *sent a host of foot-soldiers* ~ *with some cavalry*. [OE *tōgædere tō* TO[1] + *gædre* together, cf. GATHER)]

‖ **tögg'er** (-g-), n. (Oxf. sl. for) TORPID n.

tög'gle, n. (Naut.) pin put through eye of rope etc. to keep it in place etc.; pair of rods or plates hinged together by ~-*joint* (knee-joint) so as to transmit pressure at right angles; ~-*iron*, harpoon with movable blade instead of fixed barbs; ~-*press* (acting by means of ~-*joints*); ~-*rope* (with wooden handle at one end & loop at the other). [of unkn. orig.]

toil[1], v.i., & n. 1. Work long or laboriously (*at, on, through*, task); move painfully or laboriously (*up* hill etc., *along*). 2. n. Labour, drudgery; ~-*worn* (by ~). Hence ~'ER[1], ~'SOMENESS, nn., ~'FUL, ~'LESS (-l-l-), ~'SOME, aa., ~'fullY[2], ~'somelY[2], advv. [ME, f. AF *toiler* = OF *tooillier*, f. L *tudiculare* stir about, f. *tudicula* machine for bruising olives]

toil[2], n. (now only in pl.). Net, snare, (lit. & fig.), as *taken in the* ~*s*. [f. OF *toile* cloth, (pl.) toils, f. L *tela* web]

toile (twahl), n. ~ *cirée* (sērā'), fine kinds of oilcloth; ~ *côl'bert* (-bār), canvas for embroidery; ~ *d'Alsace'* (-ahs), *de Vichy* (vēshē'), linen materials for woman's summer dress. [F, see prec.]

toil'ët, n. 1. Process of dressing, arranging the hair, etc., as *make* one's ~; (style of) dress, costume, as *an elaborate* ~, *a* ~ *of white satin*; (also ~-*table*) dressing-table usu. with looking-glass; lavatory or water-closet; ~-*cover*, cover for ~-*table*; ~-*paper* (for water-closet); ~ *powder*, dusting powder used in making one's ~; ~-*roll* (of ~-*paper*); ~-*set* (of utensils for ~); ~ *soap* (for use in ~); ~ *vinegar* (aromatic kind for mixing with washing-water). 2. (med.). Cleansing of a part after operation. [F -*ette*), orig. = cloth, wrapper, dim. of prec.]

toison d'or (twahzawn' dōr'), n. = *Golden* FLEECE. [F]

Tokay', n. Rich aromatic wine made at Tokaj in Hungary; kind of grape.

‖ **töke**, n. (sl.). Food (esp. dry bread).

tök'en, n. 1. Sign, symbol, evidence, (*of* affection etc.; often *in* ~ *of*); memorial of friendship, keepsake; ring, coin, etc., serving as proof of authenticity; BOOK[1] ~. 2. (bibl.). Preconcerted signal (*Mark* xiv. 44). 3. (hist.). Piece of metal like & used instead of coin, but worth much less than nominal value & issued by tradesmen, bank, etc., without sanction of government. 4. (arch. or joc.). *By* (*this, the same*) ~, *more by* ~, in corroboration of what I say. 5. ~ *money*, coins of higher nominal than intrinsic value but exchangeable for full-standard money at the higher rate; ~ *payment*, (pol.) payment of small proportion of sum due (esp. from one country to another) as indication that debt is not repudiated, (loosely) nominal payment; ~ *vote*, Parliamentary vote of money in which the amount stated *pro formâ* is not meant to be binding. Hence ~LESS a. [OE *tāc(e)n*, OS *tēcan*, OHG *zeihhan*, ON *teikn*, Goth. *taikns* f. Gmc *taik-* TEACH]

‖ **tök'ō**. See TOCO.

tōl'a, n. Unit of weight in India, = 180 grains troy. [Hind., f. Skr. *tulā*]

told. See TELL.

Tolēd'ō, n. (pl. ~s). Fine sword(-blade) made at ~ in Spain.

tŏl′erab|le, a. Endurable; fairly good, not bad, as *am in ~le health, had a ~le passage*. Hence ~leNESS n., ~LY² adv. [ME, f. OF, f. L *tolerabilis* (as foll., see -BLE)]

tŏl′er|āte, v.t. Endure, permit, (practice, action, person's do*ing*); forbear to judge harshly or rigorously (person, religious sect, opinion); endure society of or intercourse with; sustain, endure, (suffering etc.), esp. (med.) sustain use of (drug etc.) without harm. Hence or cogn. ~ANCE n., (also) permissible variation in dimension, weight, etc., ~ātOR n., ~ANT a., ~antLY² adv. [f. L *tolerare*, -ATE³]

tŏlerā′tion, n. Tolerating; forbearance; recognition of right of private judgement in religious matters, liberty to uphold one's religious opinions & forms of worship or to enjoy all social privileges etc. without regard to religious differences, whence ~IST(2) n.; *Act of T~* (conditionally freeing Dissenters from some restrictions on the exercise of their forms of worship, 1689). [F (-lé-), f. L *tolerationem* (as prec., see -ATION)]

tŏll¹, n., & v.i. **1.** Tax, duty, paid for use of market, public road, etc., or for service rendered; *road ~* (fig.), road casualties; (law) ‖~ *thorough* (taken by town for use of highway, bridge, etc.), ‖~ *traverse* (for passing over private land); ‖ grain retained by miller as compensation for grinding (still, fig., in *take ~* = abstract a portion *of*). **2.** ~*-bar*, *-gate*, bar or usu. gate across road to prevent passage of person, vehicle, etc., without paying ~; ‖ *tol(l)′booth* (arch., Sc.), town gaol [orig. temporary structure for collection of market ~s & detention of those who did not pay & others]; ~′*house* (occupied by collector at ~-gate). **3.** v.i. Take, pay, ~. [OE *toll, toln,* OS *tol, tolna,* OHG *zoll,* ON *tollr* f. pop. L *toloneum* f. LL f. Gk *telōnion* ~house (*telos* tax)]

tŏll², v.t. & i., & n. **1.** Cause (bell, or abs.) to ring with slow uniform strokes; (of bell or clock) give out (stroke, knell, hour of day), give out measured sounds, ring on account of (person, his death, etc.). **2.** n. ~ing, stroke, of bell. [15th c., spec. use of ME (now dial.) *toll* entice, pull]

tŏll′able, a. (Of person or goods) subject to toll. [TOLL¹ + -ABLE]

‖ **tŏll(l)′bōoth.** See TOLL¹.

tŏl-lŏl′, a. (sl.). In fair state, so-so, middling. [f. *tol(erable)* w. redupl.]

‖ **tŏll′y̆**, n. (school sl.). Candle. [perh. f. TALLOW]

Tŏl′tĕc, n. One of a people traditionally held to have ruled in Mexico before the Aztecs. Hence ~AN a. [Mex.]

tolū′ (*or* tō²), n. Balsam got from a S.-Amer. tree & used in perfumery & medicine. Hence ~IC a., **tŏl′ūENE & tŏl′ūoL** nn., colourless inflammable liquid hydrocarbon of the benzene series, used in the preparation of dyes & T.N.T. [name of place]

tŏm, n. **1.** (*Tom*) abbr. of *Thomas*; *Tom, Dick, & Harry*, persons taken at random, ordinary commonplace people. **2.** Male animal, esp. ~(*-cat*). **3.** *Long ~* (naut.), long gun esp. one carried amidships on swivel-carriage; *Old Tom*, strong kind of gin; PEEP²*ing Tom*; **Tom & Jerry*, rum & water beaten up with eggs etc.; ~′*boy*, romping girl, hoyden; ~′*fool*, fool, trifler, (v.i.) play the fool, act in trifling manner (~*fool′ery*, foolish trifling, foolish knick-knacks etc.); *Tom Fool* (type of witlessness, esp. in proverb *there's more knows Tom Fool than Tom Fool knows* = notoriety is not honour); ~*nodd′y*, blockhead, fool; *Tom Thumb*, a legendary dwarf, any diminutive person, dwarf variety of various plants; *Tom Tiddler's ground*, children's game, place where money can be had for the picking up; ‖ ~*′tit*, kinds of small bird, esp. titmouse.

tŏm′ahawk (*-a-*h-), n., & v.t. **1.** War-axe of N.-Amer. Indian, with head of horn, stone, or steel; *bury the ~* or HATCHET. **2.** v.t. Strike, kill, with ~; criticize savagely in review. [of native orig.]

tomăll′ey, -ly̆, n. Soft greenish substance (called the liver) in lobster, used as sauce. [Carib]

toman′ (*-ahn*), n. Persian gold coin. [Pers. *tuman*]

toma′tō (‖ *-ah-*, **-ā-*), n. (pl. ~*es*). (Plant with) red or yellow pulpy edible fruit; *currant ~* (with small fruit about size of currant); *tree-~*, kind that grows erect & sustains fruit without support. [17th c. *tomate,* = F (2 syll.) or Sp. & Port. (3 syll.), f. Mex. *tomatl*]

tomb (tōōm), n., & v.t. **1.** Hole (made) in earth or rock to receive dead (esp. human) body, grave; subterranean or other vault for the dead; sepulchral monument; (fig.) *the ~,* death; ~′*stone,* monumental stone placed over grave. **2.** v.t. Enclose as or in or as in ~. Hence ~′LESS a. [ME *t(o)umbe* f. AF *tumbe* = OF *tombe* f. LL *tumba* f. Gk *tumbos*]

tŏm′băc, -k, n. Kinds of copper-&-zinc alloy, used under various names as material for cheap jewellery. [F (-c), f. Malay *tambâga* copper]

tŏm′bola, n. Kind of lottery. [F or It., f. *tombolare* TUMBLE]

tōme, n. Volume, esp. large heavy one. [F, f. L f. Gk *tomos* section f. *temnō* cut]

-tome, suf. (1) Gk *tomē* a cutting, or (2) *-tomos* cutting, (1) denoting section, segment, & (2) used in designations of surgical instruments (for corresponding operations in -TOMY).

tomĕn′t|um, n. (Bot.) kind of pubescence composed of matted woolly hairs; (anat.) flocculent inner surface of pia mater. Hence **tōm′entose¹, ~ous,** aa. [L, = padding of wool etc.]

tŏmm′y̆, n. **1.** (*T~*) familiar form of, TOM; ‖ *T~ Atkins,* the British soldier, whence *T~* or ~ (sl.), private in army.

2. (mech.). Kinds of wrench or turn-
-screw, (also ~-*bar*) short bar for working
box-spanners. **3.** Bread, provisions, esp.
as given to workman in lieu of wages;
this system of payment, truck system
(now illegal); ~-*shop*, (formerly) in which
~ was enforced, (now) shop in works
where provisions may be bought, any
baker's shop; ‖ food carried by workmen.
4. *~-*gun*, sub-machine gun [f. inventor
J. T. *Thompson*]; ~ ROT¹; *soft* ~ (naut.),
soft or fresh bread (cf. HARD *tack*). [-Y³]

tomŏ′rrow, to-mŏ′rrow, (-ō), adv. & n.
(On) the day after today, as *will write* ~,
(prov.) ~ *never comes*; (attrib.) ~ *morning,
afternoon,* etc. (used as nn. & advv.; ~
week, eight days hence). [TO¹+MORROW,
cf. TODAY]

tŏm′pion. Var. of TAMPION.

tŏm′tŏm, n., & v.i. (-mm-). **1.** Indian
drum; gong. **2.** v.i. Beat ~. [f. Hind.
tamtam, imit.]

-tomy, suf. = Gk -*tomia* -cutting (*temnō*
cut), chiefly in names of surgical operations (*ana~, phlebo~, tracheo~*).

ton¹ (tŭn), n. **1.** Measure of weight, 2240
or *(also *short* ~) 2000 lb. avoirdupois;
metric ~, 1000 kilograms (2204·6 lb.).
2. Measure of capacity (often varying) for
timber (40 ft), stone (16 cub. ft), salt (42
bushels), lime (40 bushels), coke (28
bushels), wheat (20 bushels), wine (see
TUN), etc. **3.** Unit of internal capacity
(100 cub. ft) or carrying capacity (40 cub.
ft) of ship. **4.** (colloq.). Large number or
amount, as *bag weighs (half)* a ~ (several
pounds, ounces, etc.), ~*s of people, have
asked him ~s of times.* **5.** (sl.). Speed of
100 m.p.h. (~-*up boys,* motor cyclists
who travel at this speed). [diff. f. TUN
in 17th c.]

ton² (tawṅ), n. Prevailing mode, fashion,
as *in the* ~, BON TON. [F]

tŏn′al, a. Of tone or tones; of tonality.
Hence ~LY² adv. [f. med. L *tonalis*
(TONE, -AL)]

tonăl′itỹ, n. (Mus.) character of tone, key;
colour scheme of picture. [-ITY]

‖ **to′năme** (tōō-)(c), n. (chiefly Sc.). Name
added esp. to person's Christian name &
surname for distinction. [OE *tō-nama*
(TO¹, NAME)]

tŏn′dŏ, n. (pl. -*di* pr. -dē). Easel painting, or relief, of circular form. [It., =
round (plate), f. L *rotundus* round]

tōne¹, n. **1.** Sound, esp. w. ref. to pitch,
quality, & strength; *heart* ~s, sounds of
heart heard in auscultation. **2.** Modulation of voice to express emotion, sentiment, etc., as *impatient, lively, imploring,
despondent, bantering, suspicious,* ~.
3. (phon.). Accent on one syllable of
word. **4.** (mus.). Musical sound, esp.
with ref. to pitch, quality, & strength
(FUNDAMENTAL ~); interval of major
second, e.g. C–D, E–F sharp; *whole-*~
scale, consisting entirely of ~s, with no
semitones; ' *Gregorian* ~s, traditional

plain-song chants for psalms. **5.** (med.).
Proper condition of the bodily organs,
state of health in which animal functions
are duly performed, as *has lost, recovered,*
~. **6.** Prevailing character of morals,
sentiments, etc., as *the* ~ *of the nation
must be raised, gave a flippant* ~ *to the
debate.* **7.** General effect of colour or of
light & shade in picture; tint, shade of
colour; degree of luminosity of colour;
(photog.) colour of finished positive
picture. **8.** ~-*arm,* tubular arm connecting sound-box of gramophone to the horn;
~-*poem,* musical composition for orchestra illustrating or translating a poetic
idea, painting in which the ~s are harmonized poetically. Hence ~′LESS (-nl-)
a., ~′lèssNESS n. [ME, partly f. OF *ton*
f. L f. Gk *tonos* f. *teinō* stretch, partly
f. L]

tōne², v.t. & i. **1.** Give tone or quality (of
sound or colour) to (~*d paper,* esp. of
pale amber tint). **2.** (mus.). Adjust (part
of instrument, e.g. padded surface of
hammers of piano) so as to produce
desired quality of sound. **3.** (photog.).
Give (picture), (of picture) receive, altered
colour in finishing by means of chemical
solution. **4.** Harmonize (usu. intr.), as
does not ~ *with the wallpaper.* **5.** ~ *down,*
soften colouring of (picture), render
(statement, expression, etc.) less pronounced or confident, (intr.) become
softer, less pronounced, etc.; ~ *up,* give,
receive, higher tone or character or
greater vigour. [ME, f. prec.]

tŏng, n. A Chinese guild, association, or
secret society. [Chin. *t'ang* meeting-place]

tŏng′a (-ngg-), n. Light two-wheeled
vehicle used in India. [f. Hind. *tāngā*]

tŏngs (-z), n. pl. (Also *pair of* ~) kinds of
instrument for grasping & holding usu.
with two limbs pivoted together near
either end or connected by spring piece,
as *fire-*~ (for grasping coal etc.), *asparagus,
sugar, blacksmith's, wire,* LAZY, ~; HAM-
MER¹ & ~; *would not touch* (repulsive
person or thing) *with a pair of* ~ (still less
without). [OE *tang*(e), OS *tanga,* OHG
zanga, ON *tǫng* f. Gmc *tang-*]

tongue¹ (tŭng), n. **1.** Fleshy muscular
organ in the mouth, serving purposes of
taste, mastication, swallowing, & (in
man) of speech (*put out* one's ~, as
grimace, or for doctor's inspection; *on the
~s of men,* much talked of; *furred* or *dirty
~,* symptom of illness). **2.** This as article
of food, as *ox-, sheep's, reindeer's,* ~;
smoked, rolled, ~. **3.** Faculty of, tendency
in, speech, as *has a ready* or *fluent~, sharp,
caustic, dangerous, long* (talkative), ~;
have, speak with, one's ~ *in* one's *cheek,*
speak ironically, humour one's hearer;
keep a civil ~ *in* one's *head,* avoid rudeness. **4.** Language of a nation etc., as
the German ~, one's *mother* ~; *gift of
~s,* power of speaking in unknown ~s
esp. as miraculously conferred on early

Christians; *confusion of* ~*s* (*Gen.* xi. 1–9).
5. Thing like ~ in shape (esp. tapering) or
function, e.g. long low promontory, strip
of leather closing gap in front of shoe,
clapper of bell, pin of buckle, projecting
edge of MATCH[1]-board, slip connecting two
grooved boards etc., index of scale or
balance, vibrating slip in reed of some
musical instruments, jet of flame, pointed
rail in railway-switch. **6.** *Have lost, find,*
one's ~, be too bashful, recover power of
speech; *give* or *throw* ~, (of hounds) bark
esp. on finding scent; *hold* one's ~, be
silent; *on the* TIP[1] *of* one's ~; *wag* one's ~,
talk indiscreetly or volubly; ~-*bit* (with
plate preventing horse from getting ~
over mouthpiece); ~-*bone*, = HYOID; ~-
-*tie*, impediment in speech due to shortness of fraenum or ~, ~-*tied*, having this,
(fig.) debarred from speaking out. Hence
(-)tongUED[2] (tŭngd), ~'LESS, aa., ~'LET n.
[OE *tunge*, OS, ON *tunga*, OHG *zunga*,
Goth. *tuggō* f. Gmc *tungōn, held to be
cogn. w. L *lingua* (f. *dingua)]

tongue[2] (tŭng), v.t. & i. Produce staccato etc. effects with (flute etc.) by use
of tongue, use tongue thus; ~ & *groove*,
furnish (MATCH[1]-board etc.) with tongue
& groove. [f. prec.]

tŏn′ic, a. & n. **1.** (Of medicine, medical
treatment, etc., fig. of success, misfortune, punishment) serving to in-
vigorate, bracing; (mus.) of tones, esp.
of the keynote; ~ *accent*, accent on
syllable; ~ *sŏl-fa′* (-ah), system of sight-
-singing & notation in which keynote of
all major keys is *doh* (& other notes correspondingly, as *ray, me, fah, sol, lah, te*) &
keynote of all minor keys *lah* (& other
notes correspondingly, as *te, doh,* etc.),
with time-values shown by vertical lines,
colons, etc.; ~ *spasm*, continuous muscular contraction (cf. CLONIC). **2.** n. ~
medicine etc. (lit. & fig.); (mus.) keynote.
Hence **tŏn′ICALLY** adv. [f. Gk *tonikos* (as
TONE[1], see -IC)]

toni′cit̯y, n. Tone; being tonic; healthy
elasticity of muscles etc. [-ITY]

tonight′, to-night′, (-nīt), adv. & n. (On)
the present night, (on) the night of today.
[TO[1] + NIGHT, cf. TODAY]

tŏn′ish, tonn-, a. (now rare). In the TON[2],
modish, stylish. Hence ~NESS n. [-ISH[1]]

tŏn′ite, n. A powerful gun-cotton explosive. [f. L *tonare* thunder + -ITE[1]]

‖ **tŏnk,** v.t. (sl.). Hit (bowling, person)
hard, defeat easily in contest. [orig.
unkn.]

Tŏnk′a bean, t-, n. Fragrant seed of a
tree found in Guiana etc., used in perfumery etc. [native *tonka*, the bean]

to′nnage (tŭ-), n. Internal cubic capacity,
or freight-carrying capacity, of ship in
TON[1]s; total freightage esp. of a country's
merchant marine; duty on vessels
formerly reckoned on ~, now on registered size; charge per ton on cargo or
freight; ~ & *poundage* (hist.), customs

duties on the tun of wine & the pound's-
-worth of merchandise imported or exported, granted as subsidies (orig. for the
defence of the realm) at intervals in the
14th–18th cc. & levied unconstitutionally
by Charles I without consent of Parliament; ~-*deck* (upper of two, second of
three or more). [in hist. sense ME f. OF;
in mod. use f. TON[1] + -AGE]

tŏnn′eau (-nō), n. Part of some motor-
-cars that contains the back seats. [F,
lit. cask, tun]

tonŏm′eter, n. Tuning-fork or other instrument for measuring pitch of tones.
[as TONE[1] + -METER]

tŏn′sil, n. Either of two oral organs on
each side of the fauces. Hence **tŏn′sillAR[1]**
a., **tŏnsillIT′IS** n. [f. L *tonsillae* pl.]

tŏnsōr′ial, a. (joc.). Of a barber or his
work. [f. L *tonsorius* (*tondēre tons-* shave,
see -OR) + -AL]

tŏn′sure (-sher), n., & v.t. **1.** Rite of
shaving the crown (R.-C. Ch.) or whole
head (Gk Ch.) of person entering priesthood or monastic order; bare part of
monk's or priest's head; (fig.) admission
to holy orders. **2.** v.t. Shave head of,
give ~ to. [ME, f. OF, or f. L *tonsura*
(prec., -URE)]

tŏntine′ (-ēn), n. Annuity shared by subscribers to loan, the shares increasing as
subscribers die till last survivor gets all;
~*policy of insurance* (in which associated
policy-holders agree to receive no dividend, return-premium, etc., till end of
fixed period called ~ *period*). [F, f. name
of Lorenzo *Tonti*, originator of ~s in
France c. 1653]

tŏo, adv. & a. **1.** In a higher degree than is
admissible for a specified or understood
purpose, standard, etc. (not used to
qualify vb, cf. VERY), as ~ *ripe for cooking,*
~ *good to be true, allows* ~ *long an interval,*
~ *long intervals,* ~ *large for me, my taste,*
my purpose, is ~ *fond of comfort,* ~ MANY
for; ~ *much (of a good thing),* intolerable
(*this is really* ~ *much* or ~ *much of a good
thing;* (colloq.) very (*you are* ~ *kind; he is
not* ~ *well today*). **2.** (In affected or gushing use) *is quite* ~, *is* ~ ~, (*delightful* etc.,
often omitted). **3.** Also, as well, as *take
the others* ~, *mean to do it* ~ (as well as
threaten). **4.** Moreover, as *achieved,* ~, *at
small cost.* **5.** adj. ~-~, gushing. [stressed
form of TO[1], f. 16th c. sp. *too*]

took. See TAKE.

tŏol[1], n. **1.** Mechanical implement, as
*carpenter's, joiner's, gardener's, engraver's,
mason's,* ~*s*; (pl.) implements & munitions
of war; machine used in making machinery, e.g. lathe. **2.** (fig.) Thing used in
an occupation or pursuit, as *literary* ~*s,
the* ~*s of* one's *trade*; person used as mere
instrument by another, cat's-paw. **3.**
Separate figure in tooling of book. **4.**
Broad ~, = TOOLER; EDGE[1]-, *edged,* ~;
~-*holder,* device for holding ~ in lathe,
handle for use with different ~s; ~-*post,*

-*rest*, holder or support for cutting-~ in lathe. [OE *tōl* = ON *tól* pl., f. Gmc *lō(w)lam* f. *lōw-, see TAW¹]

tool², v.t. & i. Dress (stone) with chisel; ornament (sides & back of book-cover) with tooling; equip with tools; work with ~; (sl.) drive (coach etc.), (intr.) drive, ride, (often *along* etc.) esp. in casual or leisurely manner. [f. prec.]

tool'er, n. In vbl senses, esp.: stone- -mason's broad chisel for tooling. [-ER¹]

tool'ing, n. Stone-dressing in parallel lines; ornamentation of book-cover with designs impressed by heated tools (*blind* ~, without gilding). [-ING¹]

toon, n. E.-Ind. tree with close-grained red wood much used for furniture etc. [f. Hind. *tun*]

toot, v.t. & i., & n. 1. Sound, esp. produce short rapid sound with, (horn, cornet, whistle, etc.); sound horn etc. thus; (of horn etc.) give out such sound; (of grouse) call. 2. n. Sound of horn, trumpet, etc. [c. 1500, imit., or f. (M)LG *tūten*]

tooth, n. (pl. *teeth*), & v.t. & i. 1. Each of several hard dense structures growing in jaws of vertebrates & used for mastica- tion; CANINE, EYE¹-, INCISOR, MILK¹-, MOLAR¹, WISDOM, ~; *false, artificial, ~* (made by dentist). 2. ~-shaped projec- tion or thing, e.g. cog, point, etc., of gear-wheel, saw, comb, rake. 3. SWEET~; *cast* thing *in* person's *teeth*, reproach him with it; *in the teeth of*, in spite of (opposi- tion etc.), in opposition to (directions etc.), in the face of (the wind etc.); *armed to the teeth* (completely, elaborately); *cut* one's *eye-teeth*, gain worldly wisdom; *escape by the skin of* one's *teeth* (narrowly); *fight, struggle, ~ & nail* (with utmost effort); *from the teeth outwards* (arch.), insincerely, not from the heart; LIE² *in* one's *teeth*; *long in the* ~, old (orig. of horses; from recession of gums with age); *put teeth into* (law, regulation, etc.), make it effective; *set* one's *teeth on* EDGE¹; *show* one's *teeth*, take threatening tone; *take the* BIT¹ *between* one's *teeth*. 4. ~'*ache*, ache in ~; ~-*billed*, (of bird) having~like process(es) on cutting edges of bill; ~-*brush* (for cleaning teeth); ‖~-*comb* (with fine close- -set teeth; prop. *fine-~ comb*); ~ *orna- ment*, = DOG¹-~; ~-*paste, -powder*, (for cleaning or preserving teeth); ~'*pick*, small sharp instrument of quill, wood, gold, etc., for removing matter lodged between teeth. 5. vb. Furnish with teeth; (of cog-wheels) interlock. Hence (·)~ED² (·thd), ~'LESS, aa., ~'LET n. [OE *tōth*, OS *tand*, OHG *zan(d)*, ON *tǫnn*, Goth. *tunthus* f. Gmc *tanth-, *tunth- cogn. w. L *dens dentis*, Gk *odous -ontos*]

tooth'ful (·ōōl), n. Small draught of spirit etc., thimbleful. [-FUL]

tooth'ing, n. In vbl senses, esp.: project- ing bricks or stones left at end of wall to provide for continuation; ~-*plane* (with serrated edge for roughing surface). [-ING¹]

tooth'some, a. Pleasant to eat. Hence ~LY² adv., ~NESS n. [-SOME]

too'tle, v.i. Toot gently or repeatedly esp. on flute. [-LE(3)]

toot'sy(-wootsy), n. (nursery). Foot.

top¹, n. & a. 1. Summit, highest part, as ~ *of a hill, hill~, at the ~ of the tree* (fig., of highest rank in profession etc.); *come to the* ~, win distinction; *on* ~, above; *on the* ~ *of*, in addition to. 2. Leaves etc. of plants grown for the root, as *turnip-~s*. 3. Surface (of ground), upper surface (of table etc.). 4. Upper part of shoe; cover of carriage; lid of saucepan etc.; head (of page in book); upper edges of book, as *gilt* ~. 5. (Person occupying) highest rank, foremost place, as *came out* (*at the*) ~ *of the school, the ~* (upper end, head) *of the table*. 6. Utmost degree, height, as *realized the ~ of my ambition, called at the ~ of his voice, ran at the ~ of his speed*; *crown* of the head, as *from ~ to toe*; *the ~ of the morning* (*to you*), Irish morning greeting. 7. (naut.). Platform round head of lower mast serving to extend ~mast shrouds, as *main-~, fore-~, mizzen-~*. 8. pl. Two highest cards of a suit in bridge etc. 9. (In motoring) highest gear (usu. *on* or *in* ~). 10. pl. Metal buttons plated etc. only on face. 11. Bunch of hair, fibres, etc., esp. as measure = 1½ lb. 12. adj. Highest in position or degree, as *the ~ rail, at ~ speed, ~ dog* (sl., = victor, master, opp. *under dog*), whence ~'MOST a. 13. ~-*boot* (also ~), boot with high ~ usu. of different material or colour & made to look as if turned down; ~'*coat*, overcoat; ~-*dress*, apply manure on the ~ of (earth) instead of ploughing it in; ~-*dressing*, this process, manure so applied; ~-*gall'ant* (tŏpg-, tog-), mast, sail, yard, rigging, immediately above ~mast & ~sail; ~ *hamper*, light upper sails & rigging; ~ *hat*, tall silk hat; ~-*heavy*, overweighted at ~ so as to be in danger of falling (often fig. of scheme etc.); ‖~-*hole* (sl.), first-rate; ~'*knot*, knot, bow of ribbon etc., tuft, crest, worn or growing on head; ~- -*lantern*, -*light*, light displayed from mizzen-~ of flagship; ~'*man*, ~-*sawyer* (lit.), (naut., also ~*s'man*) man doing duty in a ~; ~'*mast* (-ast) (next above lower mast); ~'*sail* (-sl), square sail next above lowest; ~-*saw'yer*, sawyer in upper position in saw-pit, (fig.) person in superior or high position; ~'*sides*, sides of ship above water-line. [OE *top*, OHG *zopf*, ON *toppr* f. Gmc **tuppaz*]

top², v.t. (-pp-). 1. Provide with top or cap; (naut.) raise one end of (yard etc.) above the other. 2. Remove top of (plant) to improve growth etc. 3. Reach the top of (hill etc.). 4. Be higher than; be superior to, surpass, as *~s all I ever saw*, whence ‖~p'ING² a., ~p'ing LY² adv.; ~ one's *part*, act or discharge it to perfection. 5. (golf). Hit (ball) at top instead of true. 6. ~ *off* or *up*, put an end or a finishing touch to (thing, or abs.); ~ up, (also) fill up (partly empty container). **7.** Be of (specified height), as *he* ~*s 6 ft.* **8.** ~*ping-lift*, each of a pair of lifts by which a yard may be topped. [ME, f. prec.]

tŏp³, n. Kinds of wooden or metal toy, usu. conical, spherical, or pear-shaped, rotating on sharp point at bottom when set in motion by hand, spring, or string; HUMMING, PEG, WHIP¹*ping* or *whip*, ~ ; SLEEP² *like a* ~ (sound); *old* ~ (sl.), old chap, old fellow; ~*-shell*, kinds of shellfish with ~-shaped shell. [late OE *top*; cf. MDu. *dop*(*pe*), Du. *top*, OHG *topfo*, G dial. *topf*]

tŏp'ăz, n. **1.** A transparent or translucent mineral, a silicate of aluminium, yellow, white, green, blue, or colourless; *false* ~, kind of yellow quartz. **2.** Kind of humming-bird. [ME, f. OF *topaze* f. L f. Gk *topazos, -zion*]

topăz'olite, n. Yellow or green kind of garnet. [prec. + -O- + -LITE]

tōpe¹, v.i. Drink alcoholic liquors to excess esp. habitually. Hence **tōp'ER¹** n. [orig. unkn.; cf. earlier (obs.) *top*]

tŏpe², n. (Anglo-Ind.). Mango or other grove. [f. Tamil *tōppu*]

tŏpe³, n. Buddhist monument, usu. dome or tower. [f. Hind. *tōp* f. Skr. *stūpa* mound]

tōpe⁴, n. Small species of shark, dogfish. [perh. f. Cornish]

tŏph, tŏph'us (pl. -*phi*), nn. Gouty deposit of calcareous matter round teeth & at surface of joints. Hence **tophA'CEOUS** (-āshus) a. [L (-*us*), = sandstone, TUFA]

Tŏph'ĕt, n. Place in Valley of Hinnom near Jerusalem used for idolatrous worship & later for depositing refuse, for consumption of which fires were kept burning; hell. [f. Heb. *topheth*]

tŏp'ĭ, tŏp'ee (-ĭ), n. (Anglo-Ind.). Hat (see SOLA). [Hind. *topī*]

tŏp'ĭa, n. Ancient-Roman style of mural decoration with heterogeneous landscape scenes. [L, f. Gk *topos* place]

tŏp'iar|y, a. The ~*y art* (of clipping shrubs etc. into ornamental shapes). Hence **tōpiār'IAN** a., ~IST n. [f. L *topiarius* landscape gardener (as prec., see -ARY¹)]

tŏp'ĭc, n. Theme for discussion, subject of conversation or discourse; (log., rhet.) class of considerations from which arguments can be drawn. [f. L f. Gk (*ta*) *topika* topics, as title of a treatise of Aristotle (*topos* place, see -IC)]

tŏp'ical, a. Of topics; dealing with esp. current or local topics, as ~ *allusion, song*; local, esp. (med.) affecting a part of the body. Hence ~LY² adv. [-AL]

topŏg'raph|y, n. Detailed description, representation on map etc., of natural & artificial features of a town, district, etc.; such features; (anat.) mapping of surface of body with reference to the parts beneath. Hence ~ER¹ n., **tŏpo-**

grăph'IC(AL) aa., **tŏpogrăph'icalLY²** adv. [f. LL f. Gk *topographia* (*topos* place, see -GRAPHY)]

topŏn'ymȳ, n. Study of the place-names of a region. [f. Gk *topos* place', *onuma* name, -Y¹]

tŏpp'er, n. In vbl senses, also: (colloq.) = TOP¹ *hat*; (colloq.) a good fellow, good sort; (commerc.) fine fruit etc. put at top of stock for show. [f. TOP² + -ER¹]

tŏp'ple, v.i. & t. (Cause to) totter & fall (often *over, down*). [f. TOP² + -LE(3)]

tŏpsȳtŭrv'|ȳ, adv., a., n., & v.t. **1.** Upside down; (in)utter confusion. **2.** v.t. Turn~y; Hence (joc.) ~ȳDOM, ~iFICA'TION, nn., ~iFY v.t. [16th c., of obsc. hist., but app. f. TOP¹ + obs. *terve* overturn]

tōque (-k), n. **1.** Small kinds of man's & woman's cap or bonnet (hist.); woman's small hat with little or no or turned-up brim. **2.** Kinds of monkey with caplike arrangement of hair. [F, app. = It. *tocca*, Sp. *toca*]

tŏr, n. Hill, rocky peak, esp. on Dartmoor. [OE, perh. cogn. w. Gael. *tòrr* hill]

tŏr'ah, n. Revealed will of God, esp., Mosaic law; Pentateuch. [Heb. *torāh* instruction]

tŏrc, n. See TORQUE.

tŏrch, n. Piece of resinous wood or twisted flax etc. soaked in tallow etc. for carrying lighted (~ *of Hymen*, passion of love); other appliance for this purpose, e.g. oil-lamp on pole; *electric* ~, portable electric lamp; ~*-fishing*, (also ~ING¹ n.) mode of catching fish by ~light; ~*-race*, ancient-Greek festival performance of runners handing lighted ~es to others in relays; *~-singer*, woman who sings ~*-songs* (sentimental ditties of unrequited love); *hand on the* ~, keep knowledge etc. alive (w. ref. to ~-race). [ME, f. OF *torche* app. f. Rom. **torca* f. L *torquēre* twist]

torchon (see Ap.), n. attrib. ~ *paper,* paper with rough surface used esp. for water-colours; ~ *board* (covered with ~ paper); ~ *mat*, MAT³ of ~ paper; ~ *lace*, peasants' bobbin lace with geometrical designs. [F, = dish-cloth (*torcher* wipe)]

tore¹. See TEAR¹.

tore². = TORUS (first sense).

tŏ'réadór', n. (hist.). Spanish (usu. mounted) bullfighter. [Sp., f. *toro* f. L *taurus* bull]

toreut'ic (-rōō-), a. & n. **1.** Of chasing, carving, & embossing, esp. metal. **2.** n. pl. This art. [f. Gk *toreutikos* (*toreuō* bore, chase, see -IC)]

tŏrg'ŏch (-x), n. Red-bellied char. [W (*tor* belly + *coch* red)]

torii (tō'rĭĕ, tŏr'ĭĕ), n. Gateway of Shinto temple. [Jap.]

tŏrm'ent¹, n. Severe bodily or mental suffering, as *was in* ~, *suffered* ~*s*; source of this, as (colloq.) *the child is a positive* ~*.* [ME, f. OF, f. L *tormentum* (*torquēre* twist, see -MENT)]

tŏr'mĕnt'², v.t. Subject to torment, as ~ed with neuralgia, suspense, inquiries. Hence ~ingLY² adv. [ME, f. OF tormenter f. LL tormentare f. L tormentum (prec.)]

tŏrm'entĭl, n. Low herb with bright yellow flowers & highly astringent root-stock used in medicine. [ME, = OF tormentille f. med. L -illa dim. of L tormentum TORMENT¹; sense-connexion unkn.]

tŏrmĕn'tǀor, n. Person, thing, that torments, whence ~rESS¹ n.; long fork used on ship for taking meat from coppers; kind of harrow on wheels; [ME & AF tormentour, OF -teur (TORMENT², -OR)]

tŏrm'ina, n. Griping pains in bowels, colic. [L, f. torquēre twist)]

torn. See TEAR¹.

tŏrnăd'ō, n. (pl. ~es). Violent storm of small extent, esp. in W. Africa at beginning & end of rainy season & in U.S. from April to July, having usually a rotary motion, & often accompanied by funnel--shaped cloud; (fig.) outburst or volley of cheers, hisses, missiles, etc. Hence tŏrnăd'ic a. [app. assim. of Sp.. tronada thunderstorm (tronar to thunder) to Sp. tornar to turn]

tŏr'ous, torōse', aa. (Bot.) cylindrical with bulges at intervals; (zool.) knobby. [f. L torosus (TORUS, see -OSE¹, -OUS)]

tŏrpēd'ō, n. (pl. ~es), & v.t. **1.** Electric ray, a fish with electric apparatus for numbing or killing its prey etc. **2.** Kinds of explosive mine or petard; cigar-shaped self-propelling submarine missile that can be aimed at a ship etc. & explodes on touching it (aerial ~, discharged from aircraft); ~-boat, small fast warship for carrying or discharging ~es; ~ gunboat, large vessel intended to catch ~-boat; (~-boat) DESTROYER; ~-net (hung round ship to intercept ~es or ~-boat); ~-tube (from which ~es are discharged). **3.** v.t. Destroy, attack, with ~; (fig.) paralyse, make (policy, institution, etc.) ineffective. [L torpedo electric ray (torpēre be numb)]

tŏrp'ǀid, a. & n. **1.** (Of hibernating animal) dormant; numb; sluggish, dull, apathetic. **2.** n. pl. ‖ Hilary term boat-races at Oxford between (orig. second crews of) colleges; (sing.) boat rowing in these. Hence or cogn. ~ĭd'ITY, ~ĭdNESS, ~OR, nn., ~ĭdLY² adv., ~ĭFY v.t., ~orĭF'ĭc a. [f. L torpidus (prec., -ID¹)]

Tŏrps, n. (nav. sl.). Ship's torpedo officer. [abbr.]

tŏr'quăte, -ātĕd, aa. (zool.). With ring of peculiar colour or texture of hair or plumage about the neck. [f. L torquatus (foll., -ATE²)]

tŏrque (-k), tŏrc, n. Necklace of twisted metal, esp. of Gauls; (mech., -que) twisting-MOMENT. [f. L torques (torquēre twist)]

tŏ'rrěǀfy, v.t. Parch with heat, roast, dry, (metallic ores, drugs). So ~FAC'TION n. [f. F torréfier f. L torrefacere (torrēre parch, see -FY)]

tŏ'rrent, n. Rushing stream of water etc.; (pl.) great downpour of rain (also rain falls in ~s); (fig.) violent flow (of abuse, grief, questions). Hence tŏrrĕn'tIAL (-shl) a., tŏrrĕn'tiaLY² adv. [F, f. It. -ente f. L torrentem (torrēre parch, -ENT)]

Tŏrricĕll'ian, a. ~ experiment (with mercury in tube, leading to principle on which barometer is made); ~ tube (used for this). [E. Torricelli d. 1647 +-AN]

tŏ'rrid, a. (Of land etc.) parched by sun, very hot; ~ zone, part of earth's surface between tropics. Hence ~ITY (-Id²), ~NESS, nn. [f. F -ide or L torridus (torrēre parch, see -ID¹)]

tŏrs'el, n. Twisted ornament e.g. scroll; block of wood in brick wall for joist etc. to rest on. [var. of TASSEL]

tŏr'sion (-shn), n. Twisting; (bot.) state of being spirally twisted, so tŏrs'IVE a.; (med.) twisting of cut end of artery after operation etc. to check haemorrhage; ~ balance (for measuring minute forces by means of fine twisted wire). Hence ~AL, ~LESS, aa., ~aLY² adv., (-sho-). [ME, f. OF, f. LL tortionem, -si- (as TORT, see -ION)]

tŏrsk, n. Fish of cod family. [f. Norw. torsk, tosk f. ON tho(r)skr]

tŏrs'ō, n. (pl. ~s). Trunk of statue apart from head & limbs; human trunk; (fig.) unfinished or mutilated work. [It., = stalk, stump, torso, f. THYRSUS]

tŏrt, n. (law). Private or civil wrong. [ME, f. OF, f. med. L tortum wrong f. L torquēre tort- twist]

tŏrticŏll'is, n. (path.). Rheumatic affection of muscles of neck, stiff neck. [mod. L, f. tortus crooked (prec.) +collum neck]

tŏrt'ile, a. Twisted, curved; (bot.) coiled. Hence tŏrtil'ITY n. [f. L tortilis (TORT, -ILE)]

tŏrtïl'la (-ēlya), n. Flat maize cake, Mexican equivalent of bread. [Sp.]

tŏr'tious (-shus), a. (law). Constituting a tort, wrongful. Hence ~LY² adv. [AF torcious (TORSION, -OUS), assoc. in sense w. tort]

tŏrt'oise (-tus), n. **1.** Land (& freshwater) varieties of turtle, reptile encased in two scaly or leathery shields forming a box; ALLIGATOR ~; (Rom. ant.) = TESTUDO. **2.** Hare & ~, ability beaten by persistence; ~-shell, mottled & clouded outer shell or scale of some sea-turtles used for combs etc., ~-shell cat, butterfly (with black & yellow markings suggesting ~--shell). [ME tortuce etc., tortu (thr. OF tortue) f. med. L tortuca, tortua app. f. L tortus (TORT) w. ref. to ~'s crooked feet]

tŏrt'uous, a. Full of twists or turns, so tŏrt'ūosE¹ a. (bot.); (fig., of policy etc.) devious, circuitous, crooked, not straightforward. Hence or cogn. tŏrtūŏs'ITY, ~NESS, nn., ~LY² adv. [ME, f. AF, f. L tortuosus (tortus -ūs twist, foll., -OUS)]

tŏr'turǀe, n., & v.t. **1.** Infliction of severe

bodily pain e.g. as punishment or means of persuasion, as *was put to the ~e*, *instruments of ~e* (rack, thumbscrew, etc.); severe physical or mental pain. **2.** v.t. Subject to ~e, as *~ed with neuralgia*, *tight boots, anxiety*; (fig.) force out of natural position or state, pervert meaning of (words, passage). Hence ~ABLE, ~OUS, aa., ~ER¹ n., ~inGLY² adv. [F, f. LL *tortura* twisting (*torquēre tort-* twist, see -URE)]

tŏ′rūl|a, n. (pl. ~ae). Kinds of yeastlike fungus; chain of spherical bacteria, whence ~iFORM a.; (bot.) small torus. [mod. L dim. of TORUS]

tŏr′us, n. (pl. *-ri*). Large moulding of semicircular profile esp. as lowest member of base of column; (bot.) receptacle of flower, modified end of stem; (anat.) smooth ridge as of muscle. [L, = swelling, bulge, cushion, etc.]

Tŏr′y̆, n. & a. (now chiefly in colloq. in hostile use). (Member) of the party that opposed the exclusion of the Duke of York (James II), inclined to the Stuarts after 1689, accepted George III and the established order in Church & State, opposed Reform Bill of 1832, & has been succeeded by Conservative party (cf. WHIG). Hence ~ISM n. [orig. = Irish robber, f. Ir. **lóraidhe, -aighe* pursuer (*tóir* pursue)]

-tory, suf., most freq. form of -ORY, in wds f. L vbs w. p.p. stem in *-t-* (*amatory*, *factory*).

tŏsh, n. (sl.). Rubbish, twaddle; (crick., lawn tennis, etc.) easy bowling or service. ‖ tŏsh′er, n. (sl.). Unattached student (see UNATTACHED). [corrupt.]

tŏss, v.t. & i. (~ed or poet. *tost*), & n. **1.** Throw up (ball etc.) with the hand esp. with palm upward, (of bull etc.) throw (person etc.) up with the horns. **2.** Throw (thing *to* person, *away*, *aside*, etc.) lightly or carelessly. **3.** Throw (coin) into air to decide choice etc. by way it falls, settle question or dispute with (person *for* thing) thus, as *will ~ you for* (or *who has*) *the armchair*. **4.** *Toss* (person) *in blanket*, jerk him upwards out of it by pulling suddenly on all corners; ~ one's *head*, throw it back esp. in contempt or impatience; ~ *a pancake*, jerk it up so that it returns upside down to pan. **5.** Throw (thing, one*self*) about from side to side, throw oneself about thus in bed etc., roll about restlessly; (of sea, ship, branch, etc.) roll or swing with fitful to-&-fro motion. **6.** Separate heavy from light parts of (tin ore) by agitation in vessel. **7.** ~ *oars* (of boat's crew bringing oars to upright position blades upward as salute); ~ *off*, drink off at a draught, dispatch (work) rapidly or without apparent effort; ~ *up*, ~ coin as above, prepare (food) hastily; ~*'pot* (arch.), toper. **8.** n. ~ing of coin, head, etc., as *win the~*, have its decision in one's favour; *a contemptu-*

ous ~ of the head; *full ~*, a full pitch at cricket; *~-up*, ~ing up of coin, doubtful question, as *is quite a ~-up whether he comes or not*; PITCH²*-&-~*. **9.** ‖ Throw from horseback etc. (*take a~*, be thrown). [c. 1500, of unkn. orig.]

tŏt¹, n. Small child, esp. *a tiny ~*; (colloq.) dram of liquor. [18th c., of unkn. orig.]

tŏt², n., & v.t. & i. (colloq.; -tt-). **1.** ‖ Set of figures to be added. **2.** vb. Add usu. *up*; (of items) mount *up* (~ *up to*, amount to). [abbr. of foll. or of L *totum* the whole]

tŏt′al, a., n., & v.t. & i. (-ll-). **1.** Complete, comprising the whole, as *the ~ number of persons*, *~ population*, *sum ~*, *~ tonnage*; absolute, unqualified, as *was in ~ ignorance of it*; *resulted in ~ loss of his fortune*, *~ ABSTINENCE, abstainer*; ~ *eclipse* (in which whole surface is obscured); *~ war* (in which all available weapons & resources are employed). **2.** n. ~ number or amount. **3.** vb. Find the ~ of (things, set of figures), amount in number to, as *the visitors ~led 131*; amount to, mount *up to*. Hence totăl′ITY n. (esp., time for which an eclipse is ~), ~LY² adv. [ME, f. OF, f. med. L *totalis* (*tōtus* entire, see -AL)]

tŏtālitār′ian, a. Relating to a polity that permits no rival loyalties or parties; ~ *State* (with only one, the governing, party). [-ARIAN]

tŏt′alizātor, n. Device showing number & amount of bets staked on race with a view to dividing the total among betters on winner. [foll., -ATE³, -OR]

tŏt′aliz|e, -is|e (-īz), v.t. & i. Collect into a total, find the total of; use totalizator in betting. Hence ~A′TION n. [-IZE]

tōte¹, n. (sl.). = TOTALIZATOR. [abbr.]

*tōte², v.t. Carry (a gun, supplies, timber, etc.). [U.S., f. 1676, of unkn. orig.]

tŏt′em, n. Natural object esp. animal assumed among N.-Amer. Indians as emblem of clan or individual on ground of relationship; image of this; ~-*pole*, -*post* (on which ~s are carved or hung);~ *stage*, stage of mental development in which ~s are taken as clan-names & objects of worship. Hence totĕm′IC, ~is′TIC, aa., ~ISM(3), ~IST(2), nn. [Algonquian]

t'o′ther, to′ther, (tŭdh-), a. & pron. The other; *tell ~ from which* (joc. variant of *tell one from the other*). [ME *the tother*, for earlier *thet other* ' the other'; now understood as = *the other* & usu. used without *the*]

tŏt′īdĕm vĕr′bīs, adv. In so many words, in these very words, as *he said, ~, that he would write in either case*. [L]

tŏt′īēs quŏt′īēs (or tōsh′ïēs kwŏsh′ïēs), adv. On each occasion, every time, as *offer was refused~*. [L, = as often as]

tŏt′ō cael′ō (sē-), adv. *Differ ~* (by an immense distance). [L, = by the whole heaven]

tŏtt′er, v.i. Stand or walk unsteadily (esp. of child learning to walk); (part., of steps) unsteady; (of tower etc., fig. of

State, system, etc.) be shaken, be on the point of falling. Hence ~ER[1] n., ~ingLY[2] adv., ~Y[2] a. [ME, perh. f. Norse; cf. Norw. dial. *tutra, totra* quiver, shake]

toucan (tōōkahn', tōō'kn), n. Kinds of tropical American bird with immense beak. [f. Braz. *tucana*]

touch[1] (tŭch), v.t. & i. **1.** Be separated at one or more points by no intervening space or object from (thing etc.), be in or come into contact with, bring part of body esp. hand into contact with, establish this relation towards (thing *with* one's *hand, stick,* etc.), cause (two things) to come into contact, (of two things) be in contact, as *two rocks ~ (each other) at the bases, you are ~ing wet paint, ~ pitch,* have to do with shady transaction or person, *he ~ed me on the shoulder, ~ the table with your stick, wouldn't ~ him* (unpleasant person) *with a barge-pole, just ~ed them together & they cracked, I never ~ed him* (hostilely), *can just ~ bottom* (of water with toes), ~ BOTTOM[1], *~ed his hat* (as salutation), *was ~ed by the king* (to cure KING[1]'s evil), *~ wood* (to propitiate Nemesis after boasting etc.), *~ the spot* (find out, or do, exactly what is requisite). **2.** (geom.). Be a tangent to (circle etc.). **3.** Apply slight force to, as *he ~ed* (rang) *the bell*; strike (keys, strings, of musical instrument), strike keys or strings of. **4.** Delineate, mark lightly, put *in*, (features etc.) with brush, pencil, etc. **5.** Reach, as *can just ~ the ceiling*; (fig.) approach in excellence etc., as *no one can ~ him in light comedy, for purity of style.* **6.** Affect with tender feeling, soften, as *it ~ed me to the heart, was visibly ~ed by her appeal*; rouse painful or angry feeling in, as *~ed him home, ~ed him to the quick,* = *~ed him on a raw* or *tender place* (also lit.). **7.** Treat of (subject) lightly or in passing. **8.** Concern, as the *question ~es you nearly.* **9.** (Chiefly neg.) have to do with, as *refuses to ~* (risk capital in) *breweries, dare not ~* (drink) *beer.* **10.** Injure slightly, as *flowers are a little ~ed with the east wind.* **11.** p.p. Slightly crazy. **12.** Affect slightly, modify, as *morality ~ed with emotion*; (neg.) produce slightest effect on, cope with, as *brass polish won't ~ these candlesticks, couldn't ~ the algebra paper.* **13.** (sl.). ~ one *for*, get (sum) out of him (*~ed me for £5*; cf. TAP[1]). **14.** ~ *at* (naut.), call at (port etc.); ~ *down,* (rugby footb.) ~ ball on ground either behind one's own or the opponents' goal, (of aircraft) alight; ~ *off,* make (sketch) hastily, make hasty sketch of, (obs.) discharge (cannon); ~ *on* or *upon,* treat (subject) briefly; refer to or mention casually; ~ *up,* correct, give finishing touches to (picture, writing, etc.), strike (horse) with whip, jog (memory). **15.** ~'*wood*[1] (see also foll.), children's game in which ~ing wood gives immunity from pursuit. Hence

~'ABLE a. [ME, f. OF *tochier, tuchier,* f. Rom. **toccare,* prob. imit., f. *toc imitating a knock]

touch[2] (tŭch), n. **1.** Act or fact of touching, contact, as *gave him a ~, felt a ~ on my arm, royal ~* (for KING[1]'s evil), *at a ~* (if touched, however lightly). **2.** Sense by which contact is perceived, whence ~'LESS a. **3.** Light stroke with pencil, brush, etc., in drawing etc., as *added a few ~es, finishing ~es,* (often fig. of writing, management of business, etc.). **4.** Small amount, slight tinge or trace, as *wants a ~ of salt, an occasional ~ of irony, felt a ~ of rheumatism.* **5.** Performer's manner of touching keys or strings of musical instrument, manner or degree in which keys etc. respond to this, manner or style of workmanship in carving etc. or in writing, as *has a light* or *firm ~ on piano, piano is wanting in ~, writer has light ~* (produces required effect simply, without laboured emphasis, etc.); *the Nelson ~, Nelson's masterly handling of a situation.* **6.** Mental correspondence, sympathy, communication, esp. *keep in ~,* remain in sympathy or not cease from correspondence or personal intercourse (*with*), so *get in*(to) ~ *with.* **7.** Magnetization of steel bar by repeated contact with magnet. **8.** (arch.). ~stone, test, as *put it to the ~.* **9.** *Near ~,* close shave, narrow escape. **10.** (med.). Exploration of organs etc. by sense of ~. **11.** (footb.). Part of field outside the side limits (*~-lines*) & between goal-lines produced (*~-in-goal,* each of the four outside corners enclosed by ~-lines & goal-lines; ~-*down,* touching down (as in prec.). **12.** ~-*&-go,* (adj.) of uncertain event, risky, placed in risky circumstances, as *it was ~-&-go whether we got past, a ~-&-go business, we were ~-&-go all the time,* (n.) such situation; ~-*body, -corpuscle* (concerned in sense of ~); ~'*hole,* small hole in cannon by which it was fired; ~'*last,* children's game; ~-*needle,* needle of gold alloy of known composition used as standard in testing other alloys on ~stone; ~ *of nature,* natural trait, (pop.) exhibition of feeling with which others sympathize (f. misinterpretation of Shakesp. *T. & C.* III. iii. 175); ~'*paper* (steeped in nitre, for firing gunpowder etc.); ~'*stone,* fine-grained dark schist or jasper used for testing alloys of gold etc., (fig.) standard, criterion; ~'*wood*[2] (see also prec.), soft substance into which wood is changed by some fungi, used as tinder. [ME, f. OF *touche* f. *tochier* (prec.); partly f. vb]

tou'cher (tŭ-), n. In vbl senses, also : || (sl.) *near ~,* close shave, as *near as a ~,* very nearly, almost exactly. [ME; -ER[1]]

tou'ching (tŭ-), a. & prep. **1.** Affecting, pathetic, as *a ~ incident, shows the most ~ confidence in us,* whence ~LY[2] adv., ~NESS n. **2.** prep. (arch. or literary). (Also *as~*) concerning, about. [ME; -ING[2]]

tou′ch|ў (tŭ-), a. .Apt to take offence, over-sensitive. Hence ~ĭLY² adv., ~ĭNESS n. [perh. alt. f. TETCHY]

tough (tŭf), a. & n. **1.** Flexible but not brittle, hard to break or cut, as *a beef-steak as ~ as leather, requires the ~est steel*; (of clay etc.) stiff, tenacious; able to endure hardship, hardy; unyielding, stubborn; difficult, as *found it a ~ job*; (colloq., of luck etc.) hard, severe, unpleasant; *ruffianly, turbulent & criminal. **2.** n. *Street ruffian. Hence ~′EN⁶ v.t. & i., ~′ISH¹ a., ~′LY² adv., ~′NESS n., (tŭf-). [OE *tōh*, OHG *zāh* f. Gmc *tanhuz; cf. OHG *zāhi* (G *zäh(e)*)]

toupee′ (tōō-), n. Wig or artificial patch of hair worn to cover bald spot. [f. F *toupet* dim. of OF *toup* tuft (as TOP¹)]

toupet (tōōp′ā), n. Front of false hair. [F, see prec.]

tour (toor), n., & v.i. & t. **1.** Journey through a country from place to place; *the grand ~* (hist.), journey through France, Italy, etc., as finishing touch to education; rambling excursion, journey, walk, as *a ~ of observation through the town*; ‖ (mil.) spell of duty on service, time to be spent at a station; *~ de force* (de), feat of strength or skill. **2.** vb. Make *~ (through, about*, etc.); make a *~* of, travel through, (country etc.). Hence ~′ER¹ n., ~ing-car. [ME, f. OF *tor, tour*, back form. f. pl. *tors* (cf. TURN), f. L f. Gk *tornos*]

tour′acō (toor-), n. (Kinds of) large African bird with crimson & green plumage & prominent crest. [F, f. native name]

tourbillion (toorbĭl′yon), n. Kind of fire-work spinning in air so as to look like scroll or spiral column of fire. [f. F *tourbillon* whirlwind]

tour′ist (toor-), n. Person who makes a tour, as *place is overrun with ~s*; *~ ticket*, railway etc. ticket issued to ~ on special terms, esp. return ticket available for extended period. So **tour′ISM** (toor-) n., organized touring. [f. TOUR + -IST]

tour′malin(e) (toor-), n. Mineral of various colours possessing powerful electric properties & used as gem; *~ granite* (containing ~). [F, f. Sinhalese *tòramalli*]

tour′nament (toor-, tĕr-), n. **1.** (hist.). Pageant in which two parties of mounted & armed men contended with usu. blunted weapons. **2.** Any contest of skill between a number of competitors, as *chess, lawn--tennis, ~*. [ME, f. OF *torneiement* (*tornei* TOURNEY, see -MENT)]

tour′nay (toor-), n. Printed worsted upholstering-material. [f. *Tournay*, in Belgium]

tournedos (toornedō′), n. Small fillet of beef within strip of suet etc. [F]

tour′ney (tĕr-, toor-), n. (pl. ~*s*), & v.i. (Take part in) tournament (esp. sense 1). [ME, f. OF *tornei* n., (f.) *torneier* vb, ult. f. L *tornus, tornare* see TURN]

tourniquet (toorn′ĭkĕt), n. Instrument for stopping flow of blood through artery by compression effected with screw. [F, f. *tourner* TURN]

tournure (toornūr′), n. Curve, contour; pad etc. worn by women to give rounded outline to hips, back drapery of dress. [F (as TURN, see -URE)]

tou′sle (-zl), v.t. Pull about, handle roughly, make (esp. hair) untidy. [f. *touse* (now dial.) + -LE(3); ME *t(o)use* f. OE *tūsian cogn. w. OHG *-zūsōn* (G *zausen*)]

tous-les-mois (tōōlämwah′), n. Food starch got from tubers of species of canna. [F, lit. =′ every month, prob. corrupt. of S.-Amer. *toloman*]

tous′ў (-z-), a. Rough, shaggy, dishevelled. [f. *touse* (TOUSLE) + -Y²]

tout (towt), v.i., & n. **1.** Solicit custom, pester possible customers with applications (*for* orders); ‖ spy out movements & condition of horses in training. **2.** n. Instance of, (also ~′ER¹ n. rare) person employed in, ~ing. [ME *tūte* look out (OE *tūtian) = ME (now dial.) *toot* (OE *tōtian*) f. Gmc **tūt-, *tōt-* project]

tout court (tōō koor), adv. (Of name etc.) without addition or explanation. [F, lit. = quite short]

tout ensemble (see Ap.), n. See ENSEMBLE. [F]

tow¹ (tō), v.t., & n. **1.** (Of vessel, horse on bank, etc.) pull (boat, barge, etc.) along in water by rope or chain; pull (person, thing) along behind one; drag (net) over surface of water, drag net over (water), to collect specimens. **2.** n. ~ing, being ~ed, esp. *take, have, in* or *on ~*, (fig.) assume direction of, take possession of, (person); ~(*ing*)-*line*, -*rope* (used in ~ing); ~(*ing*)-*net* (for dragging water); ~(*ing*)- -*path* (along river or canal for use in ~ing). Hence ~AGE(3, 4) (tō′ĭj) n. [OE *togian*, OHG *zogōn*, ON *toga* f. Gmc **tog-* cogn. w. L *ducere*; cf. TUG]

tow² (tō), n. Coarse & broken part of flax or hemp. Hence ~Y² (tō′ĭ) a. [ME, f. MLG *touw*, f. OS *tou*, rel. to ON *tó* uncleansed wool or flax]

toward¹ (tō′erd), a. (arch.). Docile, apt. Hence ~LY¹ a., ~NESS n., (arch.). [as foll.]

towards, toward², (tōrdz, tō′erdz, twōrdz, towōrdz′), prep. (-*s* now more usu. in prose & colloq.). In the direction of, as *looks ~ the sea, set out ~ town, I look ~ you* (in drinking health); as regards, in relation to, as *felt some animosity ~ him, his attitude ~ Home Rule*; (arch. esp. bibl.) *to usward, ~ us*; for, for the purpose of, as *saved something ~ his education*; near, as *~ noon, ~ the end of our journey*; (arch., as adv.) *feast is toward* (coming). [OE *tōweard* a. future, OS *tōward*, OHG *zuoward* (TO, -WARD, -ES)]

tow′el, n., & v.t. & i. (-ll-). **1.** Cloth for drying oneself after washing; *throw in the ~* (boxing, & fig.), admit defeat (cf. SPONGE[1]); *röller* ~, endless ~ on revolving bar; ~-*horse*, frame for hanging ~s on; (old sl.) *lead* ~, bullet, *oaken* ~, cudgel. **2.** vb. Wipe (one*self* etc.) with ~; ‖ (sl.) thrash; wipe oneself with ~. Hence ~LING[1] (1, 3) n. [ME, f. OF *toaille* f. WG *thwahlja* f. *thwahan* (= OS, Goth.) to wash]

tow′er, n., & v.i. **1.** Tall usu. equilateral (esp. square) or circular structure, often forming part of church or other large building; (fig.) place of defence, protector (~ *of strength*, champion, comforter, etc.); *ivory* ~, shelter from the harsh realities of life; MARTELLO ~; *water-*~, pipe used to secure high head of water at fires, (also)~ supporting tank for distribution of water at high pressure; ‖ *the T~* (*of London*), assemblage of buildings now used as repository of objects of public interest, orig. a fortress & palace & later used as State prison. **2.** v.i. Reach high (*above* surroundings, often fig. of eminent person, as ~s *above his contemporaries*), (of eagle etc.) soar or be poised aloft, (of wounded bird) shoot straight up; (part.) high, lofty, (fig.) *a* ~*ing* (violent) *rage, passion.* Hence ~ED[2] (-erd), ~Y[2], aa. [ME & OF *tor, tur* f. L *turris*; OE *torr* dir. f. L]

town, n. **1.** (hist.). Collection of houses enclosed by wall or hedge. **2.** Considerable collection of dwellings etc. (larger than *village*; often opp. to *country*), esp. one not created a CITY. **3.** The people of a ~, as *the whole* ~ *knows of it, is the talk of the* ~ (talked about by everyone in the ~). **4.** (Without *the*) London or the chief city or ~ in speaker's neighbourhood, as *went up to* ~ (London) *from York, is not in* ~, *is out of* ~. **5.** *Man about* ~, fashionable idler esp. in London; PAINT[2] *the* ~. *red*; COUNTY ~; ~ *& GOWN.* **6.** ~ *clerk,* official who makes & keeps ~ records; ~ *council*(*lor*), (member of) governing body in municipality; ~ CRIER; ~ *hall*, building for transaction of official business of ~, often also used for public entertainment etc.; ~ *house,* one's ~ (as opp. to *country*) residence; ~ *major* (hist.), chief executive officer in a garrison-~ or fortress; ~*s′-folk*, inhabitants of a particular ~ or of ~s; ~*s′man*, inhabitant of a town, fellow citizen; ~*s′people*, the people of a ~; ~ *talk*, the talk of the ~. Hence ~′LESS, ~′WARD, aa., ~′LET n., ~′WARD(S) adv. [OE, OS *tūn*, ON *tún*, OHG *zūn* (G *zaun* hedge) f. Gmc *tūn-*, cogn. w. Celt. *dūn* camp]

‖ **townee′,** n. (univ. sl.). Inhabitant of university town who is not a member of the university. [-EE]

town′ship, n. (Hist.) community inhabiting a manor, parish, etc., manor or parish as a territorial division, small town or village forming part of a large parish, or being one of the parishes into which a larger one had been divided; (U.S.

& Can.) division of county with some corporate powers, district six miles square; (Austral., New Zealand) small town, town-site. [OE *tūnscipe*, see TOWN, -SHIP]

towy. See TOW[2].

tox̄aem′ia, n. Blood-poisoning. [as TOXIC + Gk *haima* blood + -IA[1]]

tox̄′ic, a. Of poison, as ~ *symptoms*; poisonous; ~ *anaemia, epilepsy*, etc. (caused by poison). Hence tŏx̄′ICALLY, ~olŏ′gicalLY[2], advv., ~ANT a. & n., ~olŏ′gical a., tŏxi′CITY, ~ŏl′ogIST, ~ŏL′OGY, ~oMAN′IA, ~os′IS, tŏx̄ĭPHOB′IA, nn. [f. med. L *toxicus* f. L f. Gk *toxikon* poison for arrows (*toxa* pl. arrows, -IC)]

tox̄′in, n. A poison, esp. one secreted by a microbe & causing some particular disease. [f. TOXIC + -IN]

tox̄ŏph′il|ite, n. & a. (Student, lover) of archery. Hence ~it′IC a., ~y̆ n. [f. Gk *toxon* bow + -PHIL + -ITE[1]]

toy, n., & v.i. **1.** Plaything esp. for child; knick-knack, thing meant rather for amusement than for serious use, as *the spinthariscope is a pretty* ~; occupation followed in trifling or unpractical manner, hobby, as *she makes a* ~ (amuses herself with needless elaboration) *of housekeeping*. **2.** ~-*box* (for keeping one's ~s in); ~ *dog, spaniel, terrier*, small kinds kept as pets or curiosities; ~*'shop*; ~ *soldier* (of lead etc., or of an army that has no fighting to do). **3.** v.i. Trifle, amuse oneself; ~ *with*, deal with, handle, in trifling or fondling or careless manner, as ~*ed with a plate of strawberries*, whence ~′inGLY[2] adv. [16th c.; earlier = dallying, fun, jest, whim, trifle; orig. unkn.]

Toyn′bee Hall (hawl), n. Institution in Whitechapel founded in 1884 by members of Oxf. & Camb. Univv. as a SETTLE-MENT in memory of A. Toynbee, social reformer (d. 1883).

trăbēā′tion, n. Use of beams (not arches or vaulting) in construction. So **trăb′éate** [-ATE[2](2)], **-ātéd,** aa. [f. L *trabs* beam + -ATION]

trabĕc′ŭl|a, n. (pl. ~*ae*). (Anat.) supporting band or bar of connective tissue etc.; (bot.) beamlike projection or process. Hence ~AR[1], ~**ate** [-ATE[2](2)], ~**ātéd,** aa. [L, dim. of *trabs* beam]

tracasseries (trahkahsrē′), n. pl. Petty worries & entanglements & quarrels. [F]

trāce[1], v.t., & n. **1.** Delineate, mark out, sketch, write esp. laboriously, as ~*d* (*out*) *a plan of the district,* ~*d the words with a shaking hand,* (fig.) *the policy* ~*d* (*out*) *by him was never followed*. **2.** (Also ~ *over*) copy (drawing etc.) by following & marking its lines on superimposed sheet (esp. of *tracing-paper* made transparent with oil of turpentine etc.) through which they are visible or on sheet placed below with carbon paper between. **3.** Follow the track or path of (person, animal, footsteps, etc., *along, through, to,* etc.). **4.** Ascertain position & dimensions etc. of (ancient road, wall, etc.) by its remains. **5.** Observe or find vestiges or signs of, as *his resentment can be clearly ~d in many passages, cannot ~* (often = do not think I received) *any letter of that date.* **6.** ~ *back,* go back over the course of, as *have ~d his genealogy back to (the time of) William I, the report has been ~d back to you.* **7.** Pursue one's way along (path etc.). Hence ~**abil'ity** (-sa-), ~**'ablene**ss, nn., ~**'able** a., ~**'ably**[2] adv., **trā'cing**[1] n., reproduction made on tracing-paper or *tracing-cloth* (transparent linen sized on one side). **8.** n. Track left by person or animal walking or running, footprints or other visible signs of course pursued (usu. pl.). **9.** Visible or other sign of what has existed or happened, as *of these buildings no ~ remains, sorrow has left its ~s on her face, ~s of Italian influence abound in his earlier works*; (loosely) small quantity, as *contains ~s of soda*; ~ *elements* (occurring, or required to be present, esp. in soil, in ~s). Hence ~**'less** (-sl-) a., ~**'lessly**[2] adv. [ME; n. f. OF *trace,* vb f. OF *tracier* f. Rom. ***tractiare** ult. f. L *trahere tract-* draw]

trace[2], n. Each of the two side-straps or chains by which horse draws vehicle; *in the ~s,* in harness (lit. & fig.); *kick over the ~s,* (fig., of person) become insubordinate; ~*horse* (that draws in ~s or by single ~, esp. one hitched on to help up hill etc.). [ME *trays* f. OF *trais,* pl. of *trait*; see TRAIT]

trā'cer, n. (Mil.) projectile whose course is made visible by flame etc. emitted, so ~ *bullet, shell*; artificially produced radio-active isotope introduced into human body in food or otherwise and capable of being followed in its course by the radiations it produces. [f. TRACE[1], -ER[1]]

trā'cer|y, n. Stone-ornamental open-work esp. in head of Gothic window; decorative pattern or natural outline (e.g. in insect's wing) suggesting this. Hence ~**ied**[2] (-rid) a. [f. TRACE[1] + -ERY]

trache'a (-kēa; *or* trăk'īa), n. (pl. *-ae*). Principal air-passage of body from larynx to bronchial tubes; each of the passages by which air is conveyed from the exterior in insects, arachnids, etc.; (bot.) duct, vessel. Hence **trăch'eal, trăch'ean, trăch'eate**[2](2), aa., **trăch'eo-** comb. form, **trăch'eocele, trăcheot'omy, trăchēit'is,** nn., (-k-). [med. L, = LL *trachia* f. Gk *trakheia (artēria)* 'rough artery', f. *trakhus* rough]

trachēl'o- (-k-), comb. form of Gk *trakhēlos* neck.

trach|ōm'a (-k-), n. Disease of eye marked by granular excrescences on inner surface of lids. Hence ~**ōm'atous** a. [17th c., f. LL f. Gk *trakhōma (trakhus* rough, see -OMA)]

trăchy̆- (-k-), comb. form of Gk *trakhus* rough, as ~*phōn'ia* hoarseness.

trăch'yte (-kīt), n. Light-coloured volcanic rock rough to the touch. Hence **trachy̆t'ic** (-k-) a. [F, f.. Gk *trakhutēs* (prec.) + -ITE; cf. BARYTES]

trăck[1], n., & v.t. & i. **1.** Continuous line, series of marks, left by person, animal, or thing, in passing along, (pl.) such marks, esp. footprints, as *watched the broad ~ of departing ship, followed his ~ through the snow, am on his ~* (in pursuit of him, fig. in possession of clue to his conduct, designs, etc.), *presently came on some more of his ~s, keep ~ of* (follow the course or development of). **2.** Course taken, as *followed in his ~, indicated the ~ in which we were to go, ~ of a comet.* **3.** Path, esp. one beaten by use, (fig.) course of life or routine, as *a rough ~ runs round the hillside, covered with sheep-~s, afraid to leave the beaten~* (of ordinary life; also lit.). **4.** Prepared racing-path, esp. *cinder-~* (for runners). **5.** Continuous line of railway, as *single, double, ~,* one pair, two pairs, of rails. **6.** Wheelband of tank, tractor, etc., whence (of vehicle) ~**ed**[2] (-kt) a. **7.** Transverse distance between a vehicle's wheels. **8.** *In* one's ~s (sl.), where one stands, there & then; *make~s* (sl.), go or run away, make off; *make ~s for* (sl.), go in pursuit of, go after; *off the ~,* off the scent, (fig.) away from the subject; ~*-clearer,* kinds of device attached to locomotive, mowing-machine, etc., for clearing ~ in front or behind. Hence ~**'less** a., ~**'lessly**[2] adv., ~**'lessness** n. **9.** vb. Follow the ~ of (animal, person, *to* lair etc.); ~ *down,* reach, capture, by ~ing; trace, make *out,* (course, development, etc.) by vestiges. **10.** (Of wheels) so run that the hinder is exactly in the first's ~. [vb f. n., ME, f. OF *trac* of uncert. orig.; cf. MLG & Du. *tre(c)k* draught etc., Du. *trecken* to draw etc.]

trăck[2], v.t. & i. Tow (boat) by rope etc. from bank; (v.i.) travel by towing. [18th c., app. f. Du. *trecken* to draw etc.]

trăck'age, n. Towing; railway-tracks collectively, amount of these. [f. TRACK[1,2] + -AGE]

trăck'er, n. In vbl senses of TRACK[1,2]; wooden connecting-rod in organ mechanism. [-ER[1]]

trăct[1], n. Region, passage, of indefinite (usu. large) extent, as *a ~ of sand, pathless ~s*; (anat.) area of organ or system, as *olfactory, optic, respiratory, ~*; ǁ (arch.) period (*of* time, etc.). [f. L *tractus -ūs,* vbl n. f. *trahere tract-* draw]

trăct[2], n. Short treatise or discourse or pamphlet esp. on religious subject; (R.-C. Ch. etc.) a form of anthem; *T~s for the Times, Oxford T~s,* see TRACTARIANISM. [app. abbr. of L *tractatus* TRACTATE; sense 'anthem' f. med. L *tractus* (prec.)]

trăc't|able, a. (Of persons, rarely of materials etc.) easily handled, manageable, pliant, docile. Hence ~ABIL'ITY, ~ableNESS, nn., ~abLY[2] adv. [f. L *tractabilis* (*tractare* ,handle, frequent. of *trahere tract-* draw, -BLE)]

Tractār'ian, a. & n. (Adherent, promoter) of Tractarianism. [TRACT[2]+-ARIAN]

Tractār'ianism, n. (Also *Oxford movement*) High-Church reaction towards primitive Catholicism & against rationalism & formalism, voiced by Newman, Pusey, Keble, Froude, etc., in 90 tracts (*Tracts for the Times*) published at Oxford 1833–41. [-ISM]

tractāte, n. Treatise. [f. L *tractatus* -*ūs* (*tractare*, see TRACTABLE)]

trac'tion, n. Drawing of a body along a surface, as *electric*, *steam*, ~; *line of* ~, that in which the force of ~ acts, *angle of* ~ (between line of ~ & plane in which body is drawn); contraction e.g. of muscle, as ~ *aneurysm* (produced by ~); ~-*engine*, movable steam-engine for dragging heavy load on ordinary road, or gang of ploughs etc.; ~-*wheel*,. driving--wheel of locomotive etc. Hence or cogn. ~AL (-sho-), **trac'tIVE**, aa. [F, or f. med. L *tractio* f. L *trahere tract-*, -ION]

trac'tor, n. **1.** Traction-engine; stationary or locomotive motor engine for hauling; self-propelled vehicle for hauling other vehicles, farm machines, etc. **2.** Aeroplane with engine in front (opp. *pusher*). [mod. L, as prec., -OR]

trāde, n., & v.i. & t. **1.** Business, esp. mechanical or mercantile employment opp. to *profession*, carried on as means of livelihood or profit; *be in* ~, be a retailer, keep a shop; JACK[1] *of all* ~*s*; *two of a* ~ *never 'gree*; *trick of the* ~, device for attracting custom, gaining advantage of rival, etc.; ‖ *the* ~, (colloq.) the licensed victuallers, (naut. sl.) submarine branch of Navy. **2.** Exchange of commodities for money or other commodities, commerce, as *foreign* ~, exportation & importation of goods from & to home country or exchange of commodities of different countries, *domestic* or *home* ~ (carried on within a country); *is good, bad, for* ~, induces, discourages, buying; *carrying* ~, transportation of goods from one country to another by water or air. **3.** The persons engaged in a ~, as *the* ~ *will never submit to it, is unpopular with the book* ~. **4.** Board of T~, ‖ government department supervising commerce & industry;· BAL-ANCE[1] *of* ~; FREE[1] ~; FAIR[2] ~. **5.** = ~ *wind* (chiefly pl.). **6.** T~ Board, statutory body for the settlement of disputes, wage claims, etc., in certain industries; ~ *cycle*, recurring succession of ~ conditions alternating between prosperity & depression; ~ *hall* (for meetings of traders etc.); ~ *mark*, device or word or words legally registered (or, formerly, established by use) as distinguishing a manufacturer's or trader's goods; ~ *name*, that by which a thing is called in the ~,

(also) name given by manufacturer to proprietary article; ~ *price* (charged by manufacturer etc. to dealer for goods that are to be sold again); ~ *show*, private exhibition of new film to renters & critics; ~*s'man*, person engaged in ~, esp. shopkeeper;~*s'people*,~smen & their families; ~ *union*, organized association of workmen of a ~ formed for protection & promotion of common interests, ~-*un'ionism*, this system of association, ~-*un'ionist*, advocate of this, member of ~ union; ~ *wind*, wind blowing continually towards thermal equator within parallels 30° N. & 30° S. in Atlantic & Pacific & deflected westwardly by rotation of earth, (pl.) the ~ wind & the (30°–60°) ANTI-TRADE. **7.** vb. Buy & sell, engage in ~ (in commodity, with person); have a transaction (with person *for* thing); carry. merchandise (to place); exchange in commerce, barter, (goods); make a ~ of one's political influence, make corrupt bargains in politics, (esp. in part.). **8.** ~ *on*, take (esp. unscrupulous) advantage of (person's good-nature, one's knowledge of a secret, etc.). [ME, f. MLG *trade* track, f. OS *trada* f. *tredan* TREAD]

trād'er, n. Person engaged, vessel regularly employed, in trade. [-ER[1]]

tradi'tion, n. **1.** Opinion or belief or custom handed down, handing down of these, from ancestors to posterity. **2.** (theol.). Doctrine etc. supposed to have divine authority but not committed to writing, esp. (1) laws held by Pharisees to have been delivered by God to Moses, (2) oral teaching of Christ not recorded in writing by immediate disciples, (3) words & deeds of Mohammed not in Koran. **3.** Artistic or literary principle(s) based on accumulated experience or continuous usage, as *stage* ~, *the* ~*s of the Dutch School*. **4.** (law). Formal delivery. Hence or cogn. ~AL, ~ARY[1], aa., ~alLY[2] adv., (-sho-). [ME, f. OF *tradicion* or L *traditio* f. *tra*(*dere dit-* = *dare*, give), -ION]

tradi'tion|alism (-sho-), n. (Excessive) respect for tradition esp. in religion; philosophical system referring all religious knowledge to divine revelation & tradition. So ~(al)IST nn., ~alis'TIC a. [-ISM]

trād'itor, n. (pl. ~*s*, ~*es* pr. -ōr'ēz). Early Christian who to save his life surrendered copies of Scripture or Church property to persecutors. [L (*tradere*, see TRADITION, -OR)]

tradūce', v.t. Calumniate, misrepresent. Hence **tradū'cer**[1], ~MENT (-sm-), nn., **tradū'cible** a. [f. L *tra*(*ducere duct-* lead) disgrace]

tradū'cian|(ist), nn. One who believes that soul as well as body is propagated (cf. CREATIONISM, 1st sense). So ~ISM n. [f. LL *traducianus* f. L *tradux -ucis* vine--shoot trained for propagation (as prec.), see -AN]

traffic, v.i. & t. (-ck-), & n. **1.** Trade (in

commodity lit. & fig.), carry on commerce: barter (esp. fig.). Hence ~KER[1] n. **2.** n. Trade (*in* commodity lit. & fig.), as *the ~ in raw hides, unscrupulous .~ in lucrative appointments*; transportation of goods, coming & going of persons or goods by road, rail, steamship route, etc., number or amount of persons or goods conveyed, as *there is little ~ on these roads, the ~-returns* (periodical statements of ~) *on all railways show marked decrease, apply to the superintendent of ~* (on railway); *•~ circle*, roundabout; *~ lights,* series of coloured lights working automatically and regulating ~ usu. at cross--roads. Hence ~ător n., movable direction-indicator on motor vehicle, ~LESS a. [16th c.; n. f. F traf(f)ic f. It. traffico; vb f. F -iquer f. It. -icare; ult. orig. obsc.]

trăg'acănth, n. White or reddish gum from certain herbs, used in pharmacy, calico-printing, etc. [f. F tragacante or L f. Gk tragakantha, name of shrub (tragos goat + akantha thorn)]

traged'i|an, n. Writer of tragedies; (w. fem. ~ĕnne') actor in tragedy. [ME (TRAGEDY, -AN)]

tră'gĕdy, n. **1.** Drama in prose or verse of elevated theme & diction & with unhappy ending (~ queen, tragic actress); (T~) ~ personified. **2.** Sad event, calamity, serious accident or crime. [ME, f. OF tragedie f. L f. Gk tragŏidia app. goat--song (tragos goat, ōidē song)]

tră'gic|(al), aa. **1.** (-ic). Of, in the style of, tragedy, as ~ drama, thĕ ~ stage, in a ~ voice, ~ actor; ~ irony, used in Gk tragedy of words having an inner esp. prophetic meaning for audience unsuspected by speaker. **2.** Sad, calamitous, distressing, as a ~(al) tale, event, scene. Hence ~alLY[2] adv., ~alNESS n. [f. F -ique f. L f. Gk tragikos (tragos see prec., -IC, -AL)]

trăgĭcŏm'|ĕdy, n. Drama of mixed tragic & comic elements. So~IC a., ~ICALLY adv. [f. F (-édie) f. LL tragicomoedia (L tragico--comoedia) as prec., see COMEDY]

tră'gopăn, n. Horned pheasant. [L f. Gk, reputed bird in Ethiopia (tragos goat, Pan, Gk god)]

trail, n., & v.t. & i. **1.** Part drawn behind or in the wake of a thing, long (real or apparent) appendage, as engine left a ~ of smoke behind it, the ~ of a meteor; lower end of gun-carriage; track left by thing that has moved or been drawn over surface, as slimy ~ of a slug; track, scent followed in hunting, as got on, off, the ~; beaten path esp. through wild region; at the ~ (mil.), with arms ~ed (see vb); ~-net, drag-net. **2.** vb. Draw along behind one esp. on the ground, as was ~ing a toy cart, ~ed her dress through the mud, ~ing clouds of glory; follow the ~ of, pursue; (mil.) ~ arms, let rifles hang balanced in one hand (right, left, ~) parallel to ground; tread down (grass etc.) so as to make path; be drawn along behind, as skirt ~s on the ground; drag (one's limbs) along, walk wearily, lag, straggle; hang loosely; (of plant) grow to some length over ground, wall, etc.; ~ing edge, rear edge of aircraft's wing; ~ing wheel, either hind wheel of carriage. [ME trail(l)e, f. OF trailler to tow, or MLG, MDu. treilen haul, f. Rom. *tragulare f. L tragula drag-net, sledge]

trail'er, n. In vbl senses; also or esp.: trailing plant; set of short extracts from a film exhibited to advertise it in advance; wheeled vehicle drawn by another. [-ER[1]]

train, v.t. & i., & n. **1.** Bring (person, child, animal) to desired state or standard of efficiency etc. by instruction & practice, as ~ up a child in the way he should go, was ~ed for the ministry, a ~ed nurse, soldier, ~ed faculties, did not escape his ~ed eye. **2.** Teach & accustom (person, animal, to do, to action), as dog is ~ed to jump through hoop, ~ed to all outdoor exercises, to obey or obedience. **3.** Bring (horse, athlete, oneself), come, to physical efficiency by exercise & diet, as is ~ing for the boat-race, ~s horses, is only half--~ed, is over, under, ~ed, ~ down (to lower weight), ~ fine (into exact condition required; t. & i.), always ~s on vegetarian diet; cause (plant) to grow in required shape (often up, over, wall etc.). **4.** Point, aim, (gun etc. upon object etc.). **5.** (arch.). ‖ Entice, lure, (away, from post etc.). **6.** (now rare). ‖ Draw along (esp. heavy thing). **7.** (colloq.). Go by ~, perform (journey) thus, as shall ~ from York to Leeds, ~ the rest of the way, we ~ed it all the way. **8.** ~ off, (of shot) go off obliquely. Hence ~'ABLE a., ~EE' n. **9.** n. Thing drawn along behind or forming hinder part, esp. elongated part of woman's skirt trailing on ground or of official robe, long or conspicuous tail of bird. **10.** Body of followers, retinue, as formed part of his ~, a ~ of admirers. **11.** Succession or series of persons or things, as long ~ of sight-seers, of camels, by an unlucky ~ of events, suggested a whole ~ of ideas, painful ~ of thought, in the ~ of (as a sequel of; war with pestilence in its ~). **12.** Series of railway carriages drawn by same engine(s), as missed my ~, put on a special ~, EXPRESS[1], fast, slow, UP, DOWN[3], THROUGH, CORRIDOR, PARLIAMENTARY, ~; train de LUXE (see Ap.). **13.** Line of combustible material to lead fire to mine etc. **14.** (arch.). Ordered arrangement, condition, as matters were in a fine ~. **15.** Series of connected wheels or parts in machinery. **16.** ~'band (hist.), each division of London citizen soldiery esp. in Stuart period; ~-bearer, person employed to hold up ~ of robe; ~-ferry, vessel that conveys a ~ across a piece of water; ~-mile, mile run by a ~, as unit of work in railway accounts. Hence

~'**LESS** a. [ME, f. OF *traïner, traïniner,* f. Rom. **traginare,* ult. f. L *trahere* draw; n. repr. OF *traine, train,* f. *trainer*]

train'er, n. In vbl senses, esp. one who trains horses, athletes, etc., for races etc. [-ER[1]]

train'ing, n. In vbl senses; *be in* (process of)~, *go into* ~, (for race etc.); ~*-bit,* gag- -bit for vicious horse; ~*-college, -school,* (for training teachers); ~*-ship* (on which boys are taught seamanship etc.). [-ING[1]]

train'-oil, n. Oil got from blubber of whale (esp. of the right whale). [*c.* 1500 (now obs.) *trane,* f. syn. (M)LG *trān,* MDu. *traen,* app. = the wd meaning ' tear ', ' drop ', = OS *trahni* (pl.), OHG *trahan* (G *träne*)]

traipse. Var. of TRAPES.

trait (|| -ā, *-āt), n. Distinguishing feature in character, physiognomy, habit, or portrayal; stroke, touch (*of* humour etc.). [F, f. L *tractus* (as TRACT[1])]

trait'or, n. One who violates his allegiance or acts disloyally (*to* country, king, cause, religion, principles, him*self,* etc.). Hence or cogn. ~OUS a., ~OUSLY[2] adv., ~OUSNESS, trait'RESS[1], nn. [ME, f. OF, f. L *traditorem* (*tradere,* see TRADITION & -OR)]

trajec'torў (*or* trāj'e-), n. Path described by projectile moving under given forces; (geom.) curve or surface cutting system of curves or surfaces at constant angle. [f. med. L *trajectorius* f. L *tra(jicĕre ject-* = *jacĕre* throw), see -ORY]

trām[1], n., & v.i. & t. (-mm-). 1. || (Also ~*-car*) passenger car running on rails laid in public road; such rail; || (also ~*'way,* ~*-line*) line consisting of such rails; four- -wheeled car used in coal-mines; || ~*-lines* (colloq.), either pair of long parallel lines bounding a lawn-tennis court, the inner of each pair being the single-court boundary; ~*-road* (hist.), road with wooden, stone, or metal wheel-tracks. 2. vb. Convey in ~, perform (journey) in ~; go in ~. [app. same wd as LG *traam* balk, beam, barrowshaft, MDu., MLG, EFris. *trame*]

trām[2], n. Kind of double silk thread used for some velvets & silks. [f. F *trame* f. L *trama* weft]

trāmm'el, n., & v.t. (-ll-). 1. Kinds of net for fish, esp. (also ~*-net*) triple drag-net; shackle, esp. one used in teaching horse to amble; hook in fireplace for kettles etc.; instrument for drawing ellipses etc.; beam-compass; (usu. pl.) impediment(s) to free movement or action (chiefly fig.), as ~s *of etiquette, official routine.* 2. v.t. Confine, hamper, with ~s (usu. fig.); (p.p.), of horse) with white marks on fore & hind feet of same or (*cross-*~*led*) different sides. [in sense ' net ' ME, f. OF *tramail* f. L *tremaculum usu. expl. as f. tri- triple +*macula* MAIL[1]; other senses obsc.]

tramonta'na (-ah-, -ah-), n. (In Mediter-

ranean) north wind; cold blighting wind in the Archipelago. [It., see foll.]

tramŏn'tāne, a. & n. 1. (Situated, living) on other side of the Alps; (fig., from It. point of view) foreign, barbarous. 2. n. ~ person, also = prec. [f. It. *tramontano* f. L TRANS(*montanus* f. *mons -ntis* mountain) beyond the mountains]

trămp, v.i. & t., & n. 1. Walk heavily, as *heard him* ~*ing about overhead*; walk, go on foot, perform (journey), traverse (country), on foot (usu. w. implication of reluctance, weariness, etc.), as *have* ~*ed up & down all day looking for you,* decline *to* ~ *ten miles in this heat, have* ~*ed the whole country in my time, missed the train & had to* ~ *it.* 2. Be a ~. 3. n. Sound of person(s) walking or marching or of horse's steps. 4. Journey on foot, walk. 5. Iron plate protecting sole of boot from wear & tear of spade in digging. 6. Person who ~s the roads in search of work or as vagrant, this mode of life (esp. *on the* ~). 7. Freight-vessel running on no regular line. 8. ~*-pick,* lever for turning up hard soil. [ME *trampe* f. Gmc **tremp-,* **tramp-,* whence MLG *trampen,* Goth. *ana-trimpan*]

trăm'pl|e, v.t. & i., & n. 1. Tread under foot, crush thus, as ~*ed to death by ele-phants;* ~*e on,* tread heavily on, (fig.) treat roughly or with contempt, show no consideration for, (person, feelings, etc.). 2. n. Sound, act, of ~ing. Hence ~ER[1] n. [ME, f. prec. +-LE(3); cf. LG, MHG *trampeln*]

trăm'pŏline, n. Elastic contrivance resembling spring-mattress used by acrobats etc. [It. *trampolino* spring-board]

trance (-ah-), n., & v.t. 1. State suggesting that the soul has passed out of the body; ecstasy, rapture, extreme exaltation; (path.) state of insensibility to external surroundings with partial suspension of vital functions, catalepsy, also, hypnotic state. 2. v.t. (poet.). = ENTRANCE[2]. [ME; (vb f. n.) f. OF *transe* f. *transir* fall into trance f. L TRANS(*ire* go) over]

trăn'quil, a. Calm, serene, unruffled, not agitated, as *preserved a* ~ *mind,* ~ *scene,* ~ *surface of pond.* Hence or cogn. ~l'ITY, ~liza'TION n., ~lIZE(3) v.t., ~lIZER[1] n., (also) sedative drug, ~lizingLY[2], ~LY[2], advv. [f. F -*ille,* or L *tranquillus*]

trans-, pref., the L prep. & pref. *trans* (in L wds usu. reduced to *tran-* before s, occas. to *tra-* before other consonants, across, beyond, on or to the other side, through, into a different state or place. Occurs in wds f. L, or in those formed on L elements, or on E or other wds of non-L origin; ~*-fer,* ~*-late* (*lation*), ~- *marine,* ~*-ocular, transcribe, transcript(ion),* ~*-uterine;* ~*-border,* ~*-fashion,* ~*-ship;* in many geog. adjj., as ~*-African,* ~*-at-lantic,* ~*-Siberian;* esp. in sense beyond, surpassing, transcending, as ~*-human,* ~- -*material.*

trăns|ăct' (-z-), v.t. & i. Perform, carry

through, (business); carry on business (*with* person). So ~**ăc′to**R (-z-) n. [f. L TRANS(*igere* act-·= *agere* ACT)]

trănsăc′tion (-z-), n. Management of business, as *left the ~ of the matter to him*; piece of esp. commercial business done, *as the ~s of a firm, the ~ will not bear looking into, mixed up in shady ~s*; (pl.) reports of discussions, papers read etc., at meetings of some learned societies, as *Philosophical T~s* (esp. of Royal Society); (law) adjustment of dispute by mutual concessions, any act affecting legal rights. [ME, f. LL *transactio* (as prec., see -ION)]

trănsăl′pine (-z-), a. & n. (Person living) beyond the Alps (usu. from Ital. point of view). [f. L TRANS(*alpinus* ALPINE)]

trănsatlăn′tic (-z-), a. Beyond the Atlantic, American; crossing the Atlantic, as ~ *flight, line, steamer*. [TRANS-]

*•**trănsceiv′er** (-nsĕv-), n. Combined radio transmitter & receiver. [f. *trans-(mitter)* +(*re*)*ceiver*]

trănscĕnd′, v.t. & i. Be beyond the range or domain or grasp of (human experience, reason, description, belief, etc.); (t. & i.) excel, surpass. [ME, f. OF *transcendre* or L *tran(scendere* = *scandere* climb)]

trănscĕn′d|ent, a. & n. **1.** Excelling, surpassing, as ~*ent merit, genius.* **2.** (scholastic philos.). Higher than, not included under any of, the ten categories. **3.** (Kantian philos.). Not realizable in experience. **4.** (Esp. of God) existing apart from, not subject to limitations of, the material universe, cf. IMMANENT. **5.** n. (philos.). ~ent thing. Hence or cogn. ~ENCE, ~ENCY, nn., ~entLY² adv. [as prec., see -ANT, -ENT]

trănscendĕn′tal, a. & n. **1.** = prec. (second sense). **2.** (Kantian philos.). Of *a priori* character, presupposed in & necessary to experience, as ~ *cognition, a priori* knowledge, ~ *object*, real (unknown & unknowable) object, ~ *unity* (brought about by cognition). **3.** Explaining matter & objective things as products of the subjective mind (esp. in Schelling's philosophy). **4.** (pop.). Abstruse, vague, obscure, visionary. **5.** (math.). (Of functions) not capable of being produced by the algebraical operations of addition, multiplication, & involution, or the inverse operations; ~ *curve* (represented by ~ function). **6.** n. ~ term, conception, etc. Hence ~LY² adv. [f. med. L *transcendentalis* (prec., -AL)]

trănscendĕn′tal|ism, n. Transcendental philosophy, esp. that of Schelling & his followers e.g. Emerson. So~IST n.,~IZE(3) v.t. [-ISM]

trănscŏntinĕn′tal (-z-), a. Extending across a continent, as ~ *railway*. [TRANS-]

trănscr|ībe′, v.t. Copy out in writing; (radio) record for subsequent reproduction, broadcast by *transcription* (recorded programme). Hence or cogn. ~**ib′ER**¹,

~**ip′tio**N, nn., ~**ip′tion**AL, ~**ip′tiv**E, aa. [f. L *tran(scribere script-* write)]

trăn′script, n. Written or recorded copy. [as prec.]

trănscŭ′rrent, a. (nat. hist.). Set or running crosswise. [f. L TRANS(*currere* run), -ENT]

trănsĕc′tion, n. Cross-section. [TRANS-]

trăn′sĕpt, n. Transverse part of cruciform church, either arm (*north, south, ~*) of this. Hence **trănsĕp′tal** a. [16th c., f. med. or mod. (Anglo-) L *transseptum* f. TRANS-+SEPTUM]

trănsfĕr′¹, v.t. (-rr-). Convey, remove, hand over, (thing etc. *from* person or place *to* another); make over possession of (property, ticket etc. conferring rights, *to* person); convey (drawing etc.) from one surface to another esp. to lithographic stone by means of transfer--paper; remove (picture) from one surface to another esp. from wood or wall to canvas. Hence **trănsferabi**L′**ITY**, **trănsferEE′**, **trăns′ferENCE**, **trăns′feror**, ~**r′ER**¹, nn., **trăns′ferABLE** a. (*the ~able vote*, electoral method for securing that elected candidate· shall represent a majority, each voter signifying on his ballot-paper to which candidate his vote shall be ~red if no candidate has an absolute majority of first preferences), **trănsferĕn′tial** (-shal) a. [ME, f. OF *transferer* or L TRANS(*ferre lat-* bear)]

trăns′fer², n. **1.** Transferring; conveyance of property or right, document effecting this; design etc. (to be) conveyed from one surface to another; small toy coloured picture or design transferable from paper on which it is sold to other surface; ‖ soldier exchanged from one regiment etc. to another. **2.** ~-*book*, register of ~s of property, shares, etc.; ‖~-*days* at Bank of England, days for ~ of consols etc. free of charge (all but Sat. & Sun.); ~-*ink* (for making designs on lithographic stone or ~-paper); ~-*paper* (specially coated to receive impression of ~-ink & transfer it to stone). [f. prec.]

trănsfigūrā′tion, n. Change of form or appearance, esp. that of Christ (*Matt.* xvii. 1–9); (*T~*) festival of Christ's ~, Aug. 6. [ME, f. OF, or L *transfiguratio* (as foll., see -ATION)]

trănsfĭg′ure (-ger), v.t. Change in form or aspect esp. so as to elevate or idealize. [ME, f. L TRANS(*figurare* FIGURE) or OF *transfigurer*]

trănsfix′, v.t. Pierce with lance etc.; (of horror etc.) root (person) to the spot, paralyse faculties of. [f. L TRANS(*figere fix-* fix)]

trănsfi′xion (-kshon), n. Piercing through; (surg.) amputation by piercing transversely & cutting outwards. [-ION]

trănsfōrm′, v.t. Make (esp. considerable) change in the form, outward appearance, character, disposition, etc., of, as *caterpillar is ~ed into butterfly, 10 years in*

India have ~*ed him* (in character or physique), *a beard may* ~ *a man beyond recognition.* Hence ~ABLE, ~ATIVE, aa. [ME, f. OF, or L TRANS(*formare* FORM²)]

trănsformā′tion, n. Transforming, being transformed, as *has undergone a great* ~; metamorphosis esp. of insects; change from solid to liquid or from liquid to gaseous state or vice versa; (math.) change from one figure or expression to another equal in quantity; change in blood during passage through capillaries of vascular system; morbid change of tissue into form proper to some different part; (shop) woman's artificial head of hair; ~-*scene*, elaborate spectacular scene in which chief pantomime characters are supposed to change into chief actors of the harlequinade that follows. [ME, f. OF, or LL *transformatio* (as prec., see -ATION)]

trănsförm′er, n. In vbl senses, esp. apparatus for reducing or increasing the voltage of an alternating current. [-ER¹]

trănsförm′|ism, n. Fact, doctrine, of the development of one species from another; theory of development of complex animals from free organisms united into a colony & changed into organs of a complex whole. So ~IST n. [F (-*isme*), as TRANSFORM, -ISM]

trăns|fūse′ (-z), v.t. Cause (fluid, fig. quality etc.) to pass from one vessel etc. to another; (med.) transfer (blood) from veins of person or animal to those of another person, inject (liquid) into blood-vessel to replace lost fluid. Hence or cogn. ~fū′SION (-zhn) n., ~fūs′IVE a. [ME, f. L TRANS(*fundere fus*- pour)]

trănsgrĕss′ (-z-, -s-), v.t. Violate, infringe, (commandment, law; often abs.). So trănsgrĕ′ssION (-shn), ~OR, nn. [app. f. F *transgresser* f. L TRANS(*gredi gress*- = *gradi* walk)]

tranship. See TRANS-SHIP.

trănshūm′ance, n. Seasonal moving of live-stock to another region. [F, (TRANS-, L *humus* ground, -ANCE)]

trăns′ient (-z-), a. Not permanent, as *the* ~ *affairs of this life*; of short duration, momentary, hasty, as *a* ~ *gleam of hope, snatched a* ~ *glance*; (mus.) ~ *chord, note* (unessential, serving only to connect). Hence **trăns′iENCE**, -ENCY, nn., ~LY² adv., (-z-). [f. L TRANS(*ire* go), see -ENT]

trănsil′ient, a. Extending across from one point of support to another. [f. L TRAN(*silire* = *salire* leap), see -ENT]

trănsillūminā′tion (-z-), n. (med.). Throwing of strong light through organ etc. for purpose of diagnosis. [TRANS-]

|| **trănsir′é** (-z-), n. Custom-house permit for removal of goods. [L TRANS(*ire* go) go across]

trăns′tor (-z-), n. Non-vacuum electronic device performing functions usu. performed by the thermionic valve; ~ *radio.* [*tran(s)er, re)sistor*]

trăns′it (-z-), n., & v.t. **1.** Going, conveying, being conveyed, across or over or through, as *allowed 2 days for the* ~ *of the lake, improved methods of* ~ *by rail, goods delayed in* ~, *loses quality in* (*the*) ~; passage, route, as *the overland* ~; = ~-*circle, -compass, -instrument*; apparent passage of heavenly body across meridian of place; passage of heavenly body (esp. of Venus as determining solar parallax, or of Mercury) across sun's disc etc. **2.** ~-*circle, -instrument*, instruments for observing ~ of heavenly body across meridian; ~-*compass*, surveyor's instrument for measuring horizontal angle; ~-*duty* (paid on goods passing through a country). **3.** v.t. Cross the disc of (sun etc.). [ME, f. L *transitus* f. TRANS(*ire it*-go)]

trănsi′tion (-z-), n. Passage, change, from one place or state or act or set of circumstances to another, as *came by an abrupt* ~ *into hilly country, made a hurried* ~ *to indifferent topics, is subject to frequent* ~*s from high spirits to depression*; (mus.) modulation of momentary character; (art) change from one style to another, esp. (archit.) from Norman to Early-English, as (attrib.) ~ *stage, period*; ~ *tumour* (tending, on recurrence after removal, to become malignant). Hence ~AL, ~ARY¹, aa., ~aLLY² adv., (-zīsho-). [f. F, or L TRANSITIo (-ION)]

trăns′itive, a. & n. (gram.). (Verb) taking a direct object expressed or understood (e.g. *pick* in: *pick peas, pick till you are tired*; opp. to *intransitive* as in *picked at the hole to make it bigger*). Hence ~LY² adv., ~NESS n. [f. LL *transitivus* (as TRANSIT, see -IVE)]

trăns′itor|y̆, a. Not permanent, lasting only a short time; ~*y action* (law), one that can be brought in any country irrespective of where the transaction etc. occurred. Hence ~ĭLY² adv., ~ĭNESS n. [ME, f. AF *transitorie*, OF *transitoire* f. L *transitorius* (TRANSIT, -ORY)]

trănslāt|e′ (-s-, -z-), v.t. **1.** Express the sense of (word, sentence, book) in or *into* another language, as *has* ~*ed Homer* (*into English, from the Greek*), *his own novels into French*; (fig.) *kindly* ~*e* (say what you mean in plain words); (quasi-pass., of language, style, etc.) lend itself *well* etc. to translation. **2.** Convey, introduce, (idea, principle) *from* one art etc. *into* another. **3.** Infer or declare the significance of, interpret, (signs, movements, conduct, hint, etc.), as *this I* ~*ed as a protest,* ~*ed his gestures to the bystanders.* **4.** Remove (bishop) to another see; (bibl.) convey to heaven without death; (arch.) transform; (teleg.) retransmit (message); (mech.) cause (body) to move so that all its parts follow same direction, impart motion without rotation to. Hence or cogn. ~′ABLE, **trănslā′tion**AL (mech.), aa., **trănslā′tion**, ~′OR, nn. [ME, f. L *trans-latus*, p.p. of TRANSFER¹, see -ATE²,³]

trănslit′er|āte (-z-), v.t. Represent (word, or abs.) in the more or less corresponding characters of a different language. Hence ~A′TION, ~ātoᴙ, nn. [f. TRANS- +L *littera* letter + -ATE³]

trănslu′c|ent (-zlōō-), a. Transmitting light but not transparent; (loosely) transparent. Hence ~ENCE, ~ENCY, nn., ~ID¹ (rare) a. [f. L TRANS(*lucēre* shine), -ENT]

trănsmarine′ (-z-, -ēn), a. Situated beyond the sea. [f. L TRANS(*marinus* MARINE)]

trăns′migr|āte (*or* -īg²), v.i. (Of soul) pass into, become incarnate in, a different body; migrate. So ~ANT a. & n. (esp., alien passing through one country·on way to another), ~ātoᴙ n., **trănsmĭg′-ratoᴙʏ** a. [f. L TRANS(*migrare* MIGRATE)]

trănsmĭgrā′tion, n. = METEMPSYCHOSIS, whence ~ISM(3) n.; migration. [ME, f. LL *transmigratio* (as prec., see -ATION)]

trăns|mĭt′ (-z-), v.t. (-tt-). Pass on, hand on, transfer, communicate, as *will ~mit the parcel, shall ~mit daily dispatches, will ~mit the title, the disease, the faculty, to his descendants, his writings have ~mitted the principle to posterity*; suffer to pass through, be a medium for, serve to communicate, (heat, light, sound, electricity, emotion, news). Hence or cogn. ~MISSI-BIL′ITY, ~mi′ssion (-zmĭshn), ~mĭtt′AL, ~mĭtt′ER¹(1, 2), nn., ~miss′IBLE, ~-mĭss′IVE,~mĭtt′ABLE, aa. [ME, f. L TRANS(*mittere miss-* send)]

trănsmŏg′ri|fy (-z-), v.t. (joc.). Transform esp. in magical or surprising manner. Hence ~FICA′TION n. [17th c., of unkn. orig.]

trănsmūtā′tion (-z-), n. Transmuting; change into another form, nature, or substance; (alch.) change of baser metals into gold etc.; (geom.) change of figure or body into another of same area or content; (biol.) change of one species into another, whence ~IST(2) n.; ~ *glaze*, iridescent porcelain glaze. [ME, f. OF, or f. L *transmutatio* (as foll., see -ATION)]

trănsmūt|e′ (-z-), v.t. Change the form, nature, or substance, of. Hence or cogn. ~abIL′ITY, ~′ER¹, nn., ~′ABLE, ~′ativE, aa.,~′abLY² adv. [ME, f. L TRANS(*mutare* change)]

trănsnŏrm′al (-z-), a. Beyond, exceeding, what is normal. [TRANS-]

trănsocĕăn′ic (-zŏsh-), a. Situated beyond the ocean; crossing, concerned with crossing, the ocean, as ~ *flight* of birds. [TRANS-]

trăn′som, n. ‖ Horizontal (cf. MULLION) bar of wood or stone across window or top of door; ~ *window* (divided by ~ or placed above ~ of door); each of several beams fixed across stern-post of ship; beam across saw-pit; strengthening cross-bar. Hence ~ED² (-md) a. [ME (13th–15th c.) *traversayn*,ˈ*transyn*, *-ing*, app. f. OF *traversin* in same sense, f. *traverse* TRAVERSE]

trăns′padāne, a. Situated beyond (usu. = north of) the Po. [f. L TRANS(*padanus* f. *Padus* Po, see -AN)]

trănspar′encў (*or* -ä′r-), n. Being transparent, so **trănspar′ENCE** (*or* -ä′r-) n.; picture, inscription, etc., painted on canvas or muslin & shown up by light behind, wooden framework supporting such picture; (photog.) positive picture on glass hung in window as ornament or used as lantern slide; porcelain relief whose parts vary in thickness & ~; *his* etc. *T~* (burlesque title = G *Durchlaucht*, cf. SERENITY). [f. med. L *transparentia* (as foll., see -ENCY)]

trănspar′ent (*or* -ä′r-), a. Transmitting rays of light without diffusion so that bodies behind can be distinctly seen (cf. TRANSLUCENT); (fig., of disguise, pretext, etc.) easily seen through, (of motive, quality, etc.) easily seen through attempted disguise; bright, clear, (fig.) free from affectation or disguise, frank; ~ *colours*, (in painting) such as when laid lightly on do not hide underlying colours & forms, (in stained glass) appearing only by transmission of light. Hence ~LY² adv., ~NESS n. [ME, f. OF, f. med. L *transparens* (TRANS-, *parēre* appear, -ENT)]

trănspierce′, v.t. Pierce through. [f. F TRANS(*percer* PIERCE)]

trănspīr|e′, v.t. & i. 1. Emit through excretory organs of skin or lungs, send off in vapour; be emitted thus, pass off as in insensible perspiration. 2. (Of gas or liquid) move through capillary tube under pressure; (bot., of plant or leaf) exhale watery vapour. 3. (fig.). (Of secret etc.) ooze out, come to be known; (vulg.) happen. Hence or cogn. ~′ABLE, ~′atoᴙʏ, aa., **trănspirA′TION** n. [f. med. L *tran-*(*spirare* breathe), or F *transpirer*]

trănsplant′ (-lah-), v.t. Plant in another place; remove & establish, esp. cause to live, in another place; (surg.) transfer (living tissue) & implant in another part of body or in another person's body. Hence or cogn. ~ABLE (-lah-) a., **trănsplănt-A′TION** n. [ME, f. LL TRANS(*plantare* PLANT)]

trănspla′nter (-lah-), n. In vbl senses, esp.: hand-tool for lifting plants, machine for removing trees, with ball of earth about roots. [-ER¹]

‖ **trănspŏn′tine**, a. Of the part of London on Surrey side of Thames; cheaply melodramatic, like the plays formerly popular in ~ theatres. [f. TRANS- +L *pons -ntis* bridge + -INE¹]

trănspŏrt′¹, v.t. 1. Convey (person, goods, troops, baggage, etc.) from one place to another, whence ~ER¹ n. 2. (hist.). Convey (criminal) to penal colony. 3. Carry away by strong emotion (chiefly in pass., as ~*ed with joy, anger, fear*), whence ~ingLY² adv. [ME, f. OF *transporter*, or L TRANS(*portare* carry)]

trăns′pŏrt², n. 1. Conveyance, transportation, from place to place, carriage; means of ~, as *motor* ~. **2.** Vessel employed to carry soldiers, stores, etc., to destination. **3.** (hist.). Transported convict. **4.** Vehement emotion, as *in a* ~ *of rage, was in* ~*s* (usu. of joy). [f. prec.]

trănspŏrt′|able, a. That may be transported, whence ~ABIL′ITY n.; (of offender or offence) punishable by transportation (hist.). [-ABLE]

trănsportā′tion, n. Conveying, being conveyed, from place to place; removal to penal colony (hist.). [-ATION]

trănspŏs|e′ (-z), v.t. Cause (two or more things) to change places; (alg.) transfer (term) with changed sign to other side of equation; change the natural or the existing order or position of (words, a word) in sentence; (mus.) write, play, in different key, as ~*ed from G to B*; ~*ing instrument* (producing notes different in pitch from the written notes), ~*ing piano* (on which transposition may be effected mechanically). Hence ~′AL, ~′ER¹, nn., (-z-). [ME, f. OF TRANS(*poser*, see COMPOSE)]

trănsposi′tion (-zĭ-), n. Transposing, being transposed. Hence or cogn. ~AL, **trănspŏs′itive**, aa., (-zĭ-). [F, or f. LL *transpositio* f. TRANS(*ponere posit-* place), see -ION; assoc. w. prec.]

trăns-ship′ (-nsh-), v.t. (-pp-). Transfer from one ship or conveyance to another. Hence ~MENT n. [TRANS-]

trănsubstăn′tiāte (-shĭ-), v.t. Change from one substance into another (esp. as foll.). [f. med. L TRAN(*substantiare*, as SUBSTANCE), see -ATE³]

trănsubstăntiā′tion (-shĭ-, -sĭ-), n. Change from one substance into another, esp. (theol.) conversion of whole substance of eucharistic bread & wine into body & blood respectively of Christ (cf. CONSUBSTANTIATION). [ME, f. med. L *transubstantiatio* (as prec., see -ATION)]

trănsūd|e′, v.i. (Of fluid) pass through pores or interstices of membrane etc. Hence ~A′TION n., ~′ATORY a. [f. F *transuder* or mod. L, f. *tran-* = TRANS-+ *sudare* sweat]

trănsūrān′ĭc, a. (chem.). (Of elements) having a higher atomic number than uranium. [TRANS-]

trănsvĕrs′al (-nz-), a. & n. **1.** (Of line) cutting a system of lines. **2.** n. ~ line. Hence ~ITY (-ăl̷) n., ~LY² adv. [ME, f. med. L *transversalis* (foll., -AL)]

trănsvĕrse′ (-z-; *also* tră̷-), a. & n. **1.** Situated, arranged, acting, in crosswise direction, as ~ *artery, ligament, magnet* (whose poles are at sides not ends), *section, strain.* **2.** n. ~ muscle. Hence ~LY² adv., **trănsvĕrs′o-** (-z-) comb. form. [f. L TRANS(*vertere vers-* turn)]

trănsvĕst′, v.t. (psychol.). Clothe in other garments, esp. those of opposite sex. Hence ~ISM n. [TRANS-, L *vestire* clothe]

|| **trăn′ter**, n. (dial.). Carrier; hawker. [c. 1500, f. AF *traventer* f. med. (Anglo-) L *travelarius*, perh. f. **tra(ns)vectarius* transporter]

trăp¹, n., & v.t. & i. (-pp-). **1.** Pitfall or enclosure or mechanical structure for catching animals, affording entrance but not exit & often baited & having door or lid actuated by spring; FLY¹, RAT¹, ~; (fig.) trick for betraying person into speech or act, as *is always setting* ~*s for me, walked straight into the* ~, *is this* (question etc.) *a* ~*?* **2.** Contrivance for suddenly releasing bird, or throwing ball etc. into air, to be shot at; shoe-shaped wooden device with pivoted bar that sends ball from its heel into air on being struck at other end with bat, ~-*ball*, game played with this. **3.** U-shaped or other section of pipe so arranged as to prevent return flow of gas by means of liquid replaced whenever ~ is used. **4.** || Kinds of wheeled vehicle, e.g. dogcart. **5.** = ~*door*. **6.** ||~-*cellar*, space under stage of theatre; ~′*door*, door in floor or roof (~*door spider*, kind that makes hinged ~door at top of nest), (fig.) L-shaped tear in cloth etc. **7.** vb. Catch (animal, fig. person) in ~; furnish (stage) with ~s for a play; set ~s in (wood, hedge, etc.); arrest (gas) in ~; supply (drain etc.) with ~; (of steam) be impeded in pipe etc. [OE *treppe, træppe*, ME *trapp(e)*; cf. syn. MDu. *trappe*, WFlem. *traap, trape*, also med. L (Rom.) *trappa*; ult. orig. obsc.]

trăp², n. (min.). Dark-coloured eruptive rock of columnar structure. [f. Sw. *trapp* f. *trappa* stair (the rock freq. presenting a stair-like appearance)]

trăp³, v.t. (-pp-). Furnish with trappings. [f. obs. *trap*, n., ME f. OF *drap*, see DRAPE]

|| **trăp⁴**, n. (Sc.). Ladder leading to a loft. [app. = Du., MFlem. *trap* flight of steps]

trapan. See TREPAN².

trāpes (-ps), **traipse**, n., & v.i. (colloq. & dial.). **1.** Slattern; a tiresome walk. **2.** v.i. (Esp. of women) tramp or trudge wearily or in draggletailed way, go about on errands. [vb earlier (1593), of unkn. orig.]

trapēz|e′, n. Cross-bar(s) suspended by cords used as swing for gymnastic exercises; = foll., whence ~′IFORM a. [f. F *trapeze* f. foll.]

trapēz′ium, n. **1.** Quadrilateral with two sides parallel. **2.** (U.S.) A trapezoid. [mod. L, f. Gk *trapezion* (*trapeza* table)]

trăp′ĕzoid, n. & a. **1.** Quadrilateral with no two sides parallel. **2.** (U.S.) A trapezium. **3.** adj. Of, in the form of, a ~. Hence ~AL (-oid̷) a. [f. late Gk *trapezoeidēs* (prec., -OID)]

trăpp′|ĕan, a. Of the nature of the rock TRAP². So ~OID, ~OSE¹, aa. [-EAN]

trăpp′er, n. One whose business is to trap animals esp. for furs; one who tends air-doors in mines. [f. TRAP¹+-ER¹]

trapp′ings (-z), n. pl. Harness of horse esp. when ornamental; (fig.) ornamental accessories (*of* office etc.). [ME, f. TRAP³ + -ING¹]

Trapp′ist, n. Member of a Cistercian order founded 1140 at Soligny-la-Trappe & noted for silence & other austerities. [-IST]

trapp′istine, n. **1.** Liqueur made at Trappist abbey of Grâce-Dieu in France. **2.** (*T*~). Nun of an order affiliated with Trappists. [-INE¹]

trapp′|y̆, a. (colloq.). Tricky, treacherous, (chiefly of things). Hence ~**iNESS** n. [f. TRAP¹ + -Y²]

träps, n. pl. (colloq.). Personal belongings, baggage. [app. shortened f. TRAPPINGS]

träsh, n., & v.t. **1.** Worthless or waste stuff, rubbish, refuse; loppings of trees etc., (W. Ind.) stripped leaves of sugar-cane used as fuel; thing, e.g. literary production, of bad workmanship or material; nonsensical talk; *cane-*~, refuse of crushed sugar-canes & dried leaves & tops, used as fuel; ~-*house* (on sugar-plantation, for storing bagasse & cane-~); ~-*ice*, broken ice mixed with water; *°white* ~, the poor white population in the Southern States. **2.** v.t. Strip (sugar-canes) of outer leaves. Hence ~′ERY(1), ~′iNESS, nn., ~′iLY² adv., ~′Y² a. [16th c., of unkn. orig.; cf. Norw. dial. *trask* trash etc., Icel. *tros* rubbish, fallen leaves & twigs]

träss, tä′rras, n. A volcanic earth formerly imported as cement-material. [f. Du. *tras*, earlier *terras*, *tiras* f. Rom., cf. TERRACE]

trättori′a (-ēa), n. Italian eating-house. [It.]

traum′a, n. (pl. ~*ta*, ~*s*). Morbid condition of body produced by wound or external violence; (psych.) emotional shock. So ~TISM n. [f. Gk *trauma* -*matos* wound]

traumăt′ic, a. & n. Of, (medicine) for, wounds. [f. LL f. Gk *traumatikos* (as prec., see -IC)]

träv′ail, n., & v.i. (Suffer) pangs of child-birth; (make) painful or laborious effort. [ME; vb f. OF *travaillier* app. f. Rom. *°trepaliare* f. LL *trepalium* instrument of torture (L *tres* three, *palus* stake); n. f. OF n. f. vb]

träv′el, v.i. & t. (-ll-), & n. **1.** Make a journey esp. one of some length to distant countries, as *ordered to* ~ *for his health, spent his life in* ~*ling*; act as COMMERCIAL traveller (*for* firm, *in* commodity); (of machine or part) move (*along* bar etc., *in* groove etc.); pass esp. in deliberate or systematic manner from point to point, as *his eye* ~*led over the scene, mind* ~*s over the events of the day*; (of deer etc.) move onwards in feeding; move, proceed, in specified manner or at specified rate, perform (distance), as *horse* ~*s slowly, light* ~*s faster than sound*,

~*s thousands of miles per second, train* ~*led 1,000 miles a day*; journey through, as ~*led France from end to end*; cause (herds etc.) to ~; (p.p.) experienced in ~*ling*, as *is a* ~*led man*; ~ *out of the record*, wander from subject; ~*ling-cap*, -*dress*, etc. (of form convenient for ~*ling*). **2.** n. ~*ling* esp. in foreign countries, as *is much improved by* ~, *has returned from his* ~*s, is going to publish* (account of) *his* ~*s, cannot read books of* ~ or ~*s*; range, rate, mode, of motion of a part in machinery, as *has extended, improved, the* ~ *of the valves*; (of person, clothes, etc.) ~-*soiled*, -*stained*, -*worn*, etc. (as result of ~). [ME; differentiated f. prec.]

träv′eller, n. in vbl senses, esp.. kinds of moving mechanism (esp. overhead crane on rails); = COMMERCIAL ~; FELLOW-~; *tip person the* ~, impose on him, tell him-lies; ~'*s tale*, presumable lie; ~'*s joy*, a climbing shrub with greenish-white flowers, wild clematis. [ME; -ER¹]

träv′elogue (-ŏg), n. Illustrated lecture-narrative of expedition etc. [f. TRAVEL, after *monologue* etc.]

träv′erse, a., n., & v.t. & i. **1.** (Arch. in gen. use) = TRANSVERSE; (her.) crossing shield from side to side; ~ *sailing* (on zigzag track). **2.** n. Thing, esp. part of structure, that crosses another; (fortif.) earthwork in form of parapet protecting covered way etc., double or quad-ruple right-angle in trench (⌐, ⌐⌐) to prevent enfilading; gallery from side to side of church etc.; (geom.) trans-versal line; single line of survey (usu. plotted from prismatic-compass bearings & chained or paced distances between angular points); (naut.) zigzag line taken by ship owing to contrary winds or currents (*work, solve, a* ~, compute direct distance so covered); sideways movement of part in machine; sideways motion across face of precipice from one practic-able line of ascent or descent to another, place where this is necessary; (law) denial esp. of allegation of matter of fact; ‖ (arch.) thwarting circumstance; turning of gun to required direction; ~-*table*, nautical table used in solving ~s, plat-form for shifting engine etc. from one line of rails to another. **3.** vb. Travel or lie across, as *must* ~ *a vast extent of country, district* ~*d by canals, wall* ~*d by beam*; make a ~ in climbing; (fig.) consider, discuss, the whole extent of (subject); turn (gun); plane (wood) across grain; deny esp. (law) in pleading; thwart, frustrate, oppose, (plan, opinion); (of needle of compass etc.) turn (as) on pivot; (of horse) walk crosswise; *travers-ing pulley* (running over rope etc. that supports it). [n. f. OF *travers* f. pop. L *traversum* f. L *trans-* (TRANSVERSE), partly f. OF *traverse* f. *traverser* (see vb); vb f. OF *traverser* f. *travers* n. or adj.; adj. f. OF *travers* f. pop. L *traversus* (see n.)]

trăv′erṣer, n. In vbl senses, esp. railway traverse-table. [-ER¹]

trăv′ertin(e), n. Porous light-yellow rock, a calcareous deposit from springs, hardening on exposure. [f. It. *travertino* f. L *tiburtinus* (*lapis* stone) of Tibur (Tivoli), see -INE¹]

trăv′ĕstў̆, v.t., & n. 1. Mâke (subject etc.) ridiculous (intentionally or not) by treatment of it; (of person or thing, e.g. literary work) be a ridiculous imitation of (another). 2. n. Such treatment, such imitation, (*of*). [f. F *travesti* p.p. of *travestir* disguise, change the clothes of, f. It. *tra(vestire* clothe f. L *vestire*)]

trawl, v.t. & i., & n. 1. Drag (∼-net), catch fish in ∼-net. Hence ∼′ING¹ n. 2. n. (Also ∼-*net*) large bag-net with wide mouth held open by beam (*beam*-∼) or otherwise, meant to be dragged along the bottom by boat; *(also ∼-*line*) long sea-fishing line buoyed & supporting short lines with baited hooks; ∼-*anchor* (for anchoring ∼-line); ∼-*boat* (for setting ∼-line or drawing ∼-net). [orig. & age obsc.; cf. MDu. *traghelen* to drag, f. *traghel* drag-net]

trawl′er, n. Person who trawls; trawl-boat. [-ER¹]

tray, n. Flat shallow vessel usu. of wood or metal for placing or carrying esp. small articles on, as *tea*-∼, *pen*-∼, *developing*-∼ (in photography); metal or other container on desk for correspondence, as *in*, *out*, -∼; shallow lidless box forming a compartment in trunk. Hence ∼′FUL n. [OE *trig* f. Gmc **traujam*, cogn. w. TREE]

trea′cherous (-ĕch-), a. Violating allegiance, betraying trust, perfidious; not to be relied on, deceptive, as ∼ *memory*, ∼ *ice* (apt to give). Hence or cogn. ∼LY² adv., ∼NESS, **trea′chery**¹ (-ĕch-), nn. [ME, f. OF *trecherous* (*trechour* a cheat f. *trechier*, *trichier* (see TRICK)), -OUS]

‖ **trea′cle**, n. Syrup got in refining sugar; (loosely) = MOLASSES; kinds of saccharine fluid, e.g. sap of birch. Hence **treac′ly**² a. [ME *triacle*, in sense ' theriac ', f. OF f. L *theriaca* THERIAC]

tread (-ĕd), v.i. & t. (*trŏd*, arch. *trode*; *trodden*), & n. 1. Set down one's foot, walk, step, (of foot) be set down, as *do not ∼ on the grass*, *trod on a snake*; ∼ *lightly*, (fig.) deal cautiously with delicate subject; *where no foot may ∼*, *where angels fear to ∼*; ∼ *in* person's (*foot)steps*, (fig.) follow his example; ∼ *on* person's *corns* or *toes*, (fig.) offend him; ∼ *on the heels of*, (lit., & fig. of event etc.) come closely or immediately after; ∼ *or seem to ∼ on air* (of person transported with joy); ∼ *on* or *as on eggs* (of person in situation requiring much tact); ∼ (set one's foot lit. or fig. as sign of supremacy) *on the neck of* person, ∼ AWRY. 2. Walk upon, press or crush with the feet, as ∼*s a perilous path*, *trod the room from end to end*, ∼ *grapes* (in making wine), *wine*. 3. Perform, execute,

in walking etc., as *trod a dozen hurried paces*, ∼ *a measure* (in dancing). 4. (Of cock) copulate with (hen, or abs.). 5. ∼ *down*, press down with feet, trample on, destroy, as∼ *down the earth round the roots*, ∼ *down Satan under our feet*; ∼ *in*, press in or into earth etc. with feet; ∼ *out*, stamp out (fire, fig. insurrection etc.), press out (wine, grain) with feet; ∼ *the stage* or *boards*, be an actor, appear on stage; ∼ *under foot*, (fig.) destroy, treat contemptuously; ∼ *water*, maintain upright position in deep water. 6. n. Manner, sound, of walking, as *recognized his heavy* ∼, *approached with cautious* ∼. 7. (Of male bird) copulation. 8. (Also ∼-*board*) top surface of step or stair, each step of ∼mill. 9. Piece of metal or rubber placed on step to lessen wear or sound. 10. Part of wheel that touches ground or rails, part of rail that wheels touch. 11. Part of stilt on which foot rests. 12. Part of boot-sole that rests on ground. 13. Distance between pedals of bicycle. 14. Cicatricule of egg (formerly supposed to appear only in fecundated eggs). 15. ∼′*mill*, appliance for producing motion by the stepping of man or horse etc. on movable steps on revolving cylinder, esp. kind formerly used in prisons as punishment, (fig.) monotonous routine; ∼-*wheel*, ∼mill or similar appliance. [OE, OS *tredan*, OHG *tretan*, cogn. w. ON *trotha*, Goth. *trudan*, f. Gmc **tredh-*, **tradh-*, **trudh-*]

trea′dle (-ĕdl), n., & v.i. 1. Lever moved by foot & imparting motion to machine, e.g. lathe, sewing-machine, bicycle, reed-organ; ∼-*machine*, -*press*, printing-press worked by ∼. 2. v.i. Work ∼. Hence **tread′lER**¹ (-rĕd-) n. [ME, f. prec. + -LE(1)]

treas′on (-z-), n. 1. (Also *high*∼) violation by subject of allegiance to sovereign or to chief authority of State (e.g. compassing or intending sovereign's death, levying war against him, adhering to his enemies, killing his wife or heir, violating his wife or eldest unmarried daughter or heir's wife, killing chancellor or treasurer or justice, abetting marriage of sovereign under 18 years of age without written consent of regent & parliament). 2. Breach of faith, disloyalty, (*to* cause, friend, etc.). 3. *Constructive* ∼ (held in law as equivalent to ∼ though not intended or realized as such); MISPRISION¹ *of* ∼; ‖∼-*felony*, attempt to depose sovereign or levy war in order to compel change of measures, intimidate parliament, or stir up foreign invasion. Hence∼OUS a. [ME, f. AF *treisoun* etc., OF *traïson*, f. L as TRADITION]

treas′onab‖le (-z-), a. Involving the crime, guilty, of treason. Hence ∼leNESS n., ∼LY² adv. [ME; -ABLE]

trea′sure (-ĕzher), n., & v.t. 1. Precious metals or gems, hoard of these, accumulated wealth, as *buried* ∼, *had amassed* *great* ~ or ~*s, a voyage in quest of* ~, (not now in colloq. use); thing valued for rarity, workmanship, associations, etc., as *art* ~*s, absorbed in his latest* ~ (book, picture, etc.); (colloq.) beloved person esp. child, as (voc.) *my* ~; (colloq.) highly efficient or satisfactory person e.g. servant, as *the girl is a perfect* ~. **2.** v.t. Store (usu. *up*) as valuable; receive, regard, as valuable, store (usu. *up*) in memory, (person's words, looks, etc.). **3.** ~-*city* (bibl.), city for stores & magazines; ~-*house*, place where ~s (esp. fig.) are kept; ~ *trove* [see TROVER], gold etc. found hidden of unknown ownership. [ME, f. OF *tresor* f. Rom. **tresaurus* for L f. Gk *thēsauros*]

trea'surer (-ĕzhe-), n. Person in charge of funds of society, company, club, etc.; officer authorized to receive & disburse public revenues; *Lord High T*~ (hist.), crown officer with duties now discharged by Lords of the Treasury; ‖*T*~ *of the Household*, official ranking next to Lord Steward. Hence ~SHIP n. [ME, f. ONF, AF *tresorer*, OF *-ier* f. *tresor* (prec., see -ARY¹, -ER²), after LL *thesaurarius*]

trea'sury (-ĕzhe-), n. **1.** Place, building, where treasure is stored; (fig.) book, person, etc., viewed as repository of information etc. **2.** Place where public revenues are kept; department managing public revenue of a country, officers of this; ‖ *T*~ *Board, Lords* (*Commissioners*) *of the T*~, board in charge of British public revenue, viz. Prime Minister (who is also *First Lord of the T*~), Chancellor of the Exchequer, & 5 junior lords; *T*~ *bench*, front bench on right hand of Speaker in House of Commons, occupied by Prime Minister, Chancellor of Exchequer, & other members of Government. **3.** ‖ ~ *bill*, bill of exchange issued by the T~ to raise money for temporary needs & sold to highest bidder; ~ *note*, = CURRENCY *note*, *note issued by T~ & receivable for government dues; *T*~ *warrant* (issued by T~ for sums disbursed by Exchequer). [ME, f. OF *tresorie* (as TREASURE, see -Y¹)]

treat, v.t. & i., & n. **1.** Act towards, behave to, as *how did they* ~ *you?,* ~*ed me abominably, kindly, as if I were a child, better* ~ *it as a joke*. **2.** Deal with (person, thing) with view to result, apply process to, subject to chemical agent etc., as ~*ed him for smallpox, how would you* ~ *a sprained ankle?, must next be* ~*ed with sulphuric acid*. **3.** Manipulate, present, express, (subject) in literature or art. **4.** Give (person) food and drink or entertainment at one's expense, as *I will* ~ *you all, think you might* ~ *me to an ice, a theatre*, (of candidate for election) give food etc. or cause these to be given to (electors) in order to influence election, whence ~'ING¹ n. **5.** Negotiate terms (*with* person); ~ *of*, handle, discuss,

(subject). **6.** n. Thing that gives great pleasure, as *pantomime is a great* ~ *to him, what a* ~ *it is not to have to get up early*; entertainment designed to do this, as *school-*~, picnic etc. for (esp. Sunday-) school children; *stand* ~, bear expense of entertainment. Hence ~'ABLE a., ~'ER¹ n. [ME, f. OF *traitier* f. L *tractare* handle frequent. of *trahere tract-* draw]

treat'ise (-z, -s), n. Literary composition dealing more or less systematically with definite subject. [ME, f. AF *tretis* (*traitier* as prec.)]

treat'ment, n. (Mode of) dealing with or behaving towards a person or thing, as *received strange* ~ *from him, must vary the* ~, *is now ready for* ~ *with an acid*. [as TREAT, see -MENT]

treat'y, n. Formally concluded & ratified agreement between nations; agreement between persons (*to do* etc.); *be in* ~ (negotiating) *with* (person *for* purchase etc.); ~ *port*, one that a country is bound by ~ to keep open to foreign trade. [ME, f. AF *trete*, p.p. of *trailer* TREAT, & f. L *tractatum* TRACTATE]

tre'ble, a. & n., & v.t. & i. **1.** Threefold, triple, whence **trĕb'LY²** adv.; multiplied by three, three times (amount etc., as *the enemy had* ~ *our numbers*); (esp. of boy's voice or boy) = SOPRANO; ~ *chance*, method of competing in football pool in which the aim is to pick all draws from a given selection of matches, a draw counting more than a home or away win. **2.** n. (In short whist) game won by 5 to 0 counting three points; = SOPRANO. **3.** vb. Multiply, be multiplied, by three, as *has* ~*d its value, its value has* ~*d*. [ME, f. OF, f. L *triplus* TRIPLE]

trĕb'uchĕt (-sh-), **trĕb'uckĕt**, n. (Hist.) military engine for throwing stones etc.; tilting balance for weighing light articles; kind of trap for small birds etc. [ME, f. OF, f. *trebucher* overthrow etc.]

trecĕn'to (-āch-), n. The 14th century in Italian art & literature. So ~IST(2, 3) n. [It., = three (for thirteen) hundred]

tree, n., & v.t. **1.** Perennial plant with single woody self-supporting stem or trunk usu. unbranched (cf. SHRUB¹) for some distance above ground; piece or framework of wood for various purposes, e.g. AXLE, BOOT¹, ROOF, SADDLE, SWINGLE, -~, CROSS-TREES; (arch.) gibbet, cross used for (esp. Christ's) crucifixion; CHRISTMAS ~; (math.) diagram of branching lines; *family* or GENEALOGICAL ~; *up a* ~, (fig.) cornered, nonplussed; *at the top of the* ~, at the top of one's profession. **2.** ~ *agate* (with ~-like markings); ~ *calf*, calf binding for book stained with ~like design; ~--creeper*, kinds of small bird; ~-*fern*, kinds of fern attaining size of ~; ~-*frog*, (pop. name for) ~-*toad*; ~-*goose*, = BARNACLE² (1); ~-*milk*, juice of a shrub used in Ceylon instead of milk; ~'*nail*, pin of hard wood for securing planks etc.; ~ *of* *heaven*, ornamental Asian ~ with ill-scented flowers; ~ *of knowledge of good & evil* (Gen. iii); ~ *of liberty* (dedicated to liberty & set up in public place); ~ *of life* (Gen. ii. 9); ~*-toad*, arboreal amphibian with adhesive discs on digits enabling it to climb. Hence ~'LESS a., ~'lèssNESS n. **3.** v.t. Force (animal, fig. person) to take refuge in ~; stretch (boot) on boot-~. [OE *trēow*, OS *treo*, ON *tré*, Goth. *triu*, f. Gmc **trewam*, cogn. w. Gk *drus* oak, *doru* spear]

tref'oil, n. & a. Kinds of leguminous plant with leaves of three leaflets & flowers of various colours, clover; kinds of plant with similar leaves; three-lobed ornamentation in tracery etc.; (thing) arranged in three lobes, whence ~ED² (-ld) a. [ME, f. AF *trifoil* & L TRI(*folium* leaf)]

treha'la (-ah-), n. Manna of starch, sugar, & gum, excreted in cocoon form by an insect in Turkey & Persia. [f. native *tīqālah*]

trĕk, v.i. (-kk-), & n. (S.-Afr.). **1.** (Of ox) draw vehicle, pull load; travel by ox-wagon; migrate; proceed slowly. **2.** n. Such journey, each stage of journey; organized migration. Hence ~k'ER¹ n. [f. Du. *trekken* vb, *trek* n.]

trĕll'ĭs, n., & v.t. **1.** (Also ~*-work*) lattice, grating, of light wooden cross-bars nailed together where they cross, similar structure of wire or metal; summer-house, screen, etc., made of ~-work. **2.** v.t. Furnish, support (vine etc.), with ~. [ME, f. OF *treliz*, *-is*, f. Rom. **trilicius* f. L TRI(*lix* f. *licium* warp-thread) three-ply]

trĕm'bl|e, v.i., & n. **1.** Shake involuntarily from fear, agitation, physical weakness, etc., as *he ~ed with anger*, *voice ~ed with excitement*, *hands ~e from oversmoking* etc.; (fig.) be in state of extreme agitation, fear, suspense, etc., as *I ~e to think what has become of him*, *~e at the thought*, *no cause to ~e before his judge*, *hear & ~e* (be duly impressed)*!*, *I ~e* (am alarmed) *for his safety*, *in ~ing uncertainty*; move in quivering manner, as *leaves ~e in the breeze*, *~ing* POPLAR; (fig.) *his fate*, *life*, etc., *~es in the balance* (has reached a critical point, is in extreme danger). Hence or cogn.~eMENT n.(poet., rare), ~ingLY² adv., ~Y² a. **2.** n. ~ing, quiver, as *there was a ~e in her voice*, (colloq.) *was all of a ~e* (~ing all over); (pl.) kinds of (esp. cattle-) disease, with ~ing. [ME, f. OF *trembler* f. med. L *tremulare* f. *tremulus* TREMULOUS]

trĕm'bler, n. In vbl senses; also or esp.: automatic vibrator for making & breaking electric circuit; electric bell. [-ER¹]

trĕm'ellōse, a. (bot.). Jellylike, shaking like jelly. [f. mod. L *Tremella*, genus of jellylike fungi, +-OSE¹]

trĕmĕn'dous, a. Awful, fearful, overpowering, (colloq.) considerable, as *a ~ explosion*, *revolution*, *makes a ~ difference*, *a ~* (huge) *bluebottle*. Hence ~LY² adv.,

~NESS n. [f. L *tremendus* (*tremere* tremble) +-OUS]

trĕmŏlăn'dō, adv. (mus.). Tremulously. [It.]

trĕm'olant, -ŭlant, n. Device in organ for producing tremolo effect. [(-*ol-* f. It. *tremolante*) f. med. L as TREMBLE, see -ANT]

trĕm'olō, n. (mus.). Tremulous effect in singing or in playing bowed instruments etc.; = prec. [It, as TREMULOUS]

trĕm'or, n. (Of leaf, part of body, voice, person) shaking, quivering; thrill (of fear, exultation, etc.); *earth ~*, slight earthquake; *intention ~* (in part of body when it moves to do something); *metallic ~*, trembling palsy of metal-workers. Hence ~LESS a. [ME & OF, f. L *tremorem* (*tremere* tremble, see -OR)]

trĕm'ŭlous, a. Trembling, quivering, as *~ leaves*, *voice*, *hand*; *~ line* (drawn by ~ hand); timid, vacillating. Hence ~LY² adv., ~NESS n. [f. L *tremulus*, LL *-osus*, f. *tremere* tremble, see -OUS]

trenail. Var. of TREE*nail*.

trench, v.t. & i., & n. **1.** Dig ditch in (ground); turn over the earth of (field etc.) by digging succession of contiguous ditches; ‖ cut groove in (wood etc.); proceed, make one's way, (*down*, *along*, etc.) by~ing; encroach (*up*)*on* (person's rights, privacy, etc.); verge or border closely (*up*)*on* (heresy, vulgarity, etc.). Hence ~'er [-ER¹] n. **2.** n. Deep furrow or ditch; (mil.) ditch often 7 ft deep with earth thrown up to form parapet, as *open* (begin digging) *the ~es*, *mount* (guard in) *the~es*. **3.**~*-cart*, hand-cart on low wheels for use in ~es; ~ *coat*, soldier's lined or padded mackintosh; ~ *fever*, form of fever affecting soldiers in ~es, spread by lice; ~ *foot*, affection of feet or legs with sloughing etc. caused by much standing in water; ~ *mortar*, light simple kind throwing heavy charge of high explosive short distance for use in ~es. [ME, f. OF *trenchier* (& *tranche* n.) cut f. Rom. **trincare* f. L *truncare* TRUNCATE]

trench'ant, a. Sharp, keen, as ~ *sword*, *blade*, (now rare in lit. sense); (fig., of style, language, policy, etc.) penetrating, incisive, decisive, vigorous. Hence **trench'ANCY** n., ~LY² adv. [ME, f. OF, part. as prec.]

trencher¹. See TRENCH.

trench'er², n. Wooden platter now chiefly used for cutting bread on at table; (arch.) the pleasures of the table, eating, (chiefly attrib. or in comb., as ~ *companions*, ~*-valiant*; *good*, *poor*, etc., ~*man*, great, small, etc., eater); ~ *cap*, square college cap; ~*-fed*, (of hounds) kept by separate members of the hunt, not all together in hunt kennels. [ME, f. AF *trenchour*, OF *-oir*, f. *trenchier* (prec.) + *-oir* = L *-atorium*]

trend, v.i., & n. **1.** Have specified general direction, bend or turn away in specified direction, as *coast ~s* (*towards the*) *south*;

(fig.) be chiefly directed, have general tendency, (*towards* etc.). **2.** n. General direction & tendency (esp. fig. *of* events, opinion, etc.). [ME ' revolve ' etc., OE *trendan* f. Gmc **trend-*, **trand-*, **trund-*; cf. MLG *trint*, *trent*, *trunt* aa. round, & TRUNDLE]

trĕn′tal, n. Set of 30 successive daily masses for the dead. [ME, f. OF *trentel* & med. L *trentale* f. L *triginta* thirty +-AL]

trente-et-quarante (see Ap.), n. = ROUGE[1]*-et-noir*. [F, = 30 & 40]

trĕpăn′[1], n., & v.t. (-nn-). **1.** Surgeon's cylindrical saw for removing part of bone of skull to relieve brain; borer for sinking shafts. **2.** v.t. Perforate (skull) with~. So **trĕpan**A′TION, ~n′ING[1], nn. [ME, f. OF *trepan(er)* n. & vb f. med. L *trepanum* f. Gk *trupanon* (*trupaō* bore f. *trupa* hole)]

trĕpăn′[2], v.t. (-nn-). Trap, ensnare, beguile, (*into*, *from*, place etc., *into doing*). [17th c., f. earlier *trapan* a decoy, prob. thieves' sl. f. TRAP[1]]

trĕpăng′, n. Edible sea-slug used in China for soup. [f. Malay *trīpang*]

trĕphine′ (-ēn, -īn), n., & v.t. **1.** Improved form of trepan with guiding centre-pin. **2.** v.t. Operate on (skull, eyeball, person) with this. So **trĕphin**A′TION n. [orig. *trafine*, f. L *tres fines* three ends, after TREPAN[1]]

trĕpĭdā′tion, n. Alarm, flurry; trembling of limbs e.g. in paralysis; (hist.) oscillation of ecliptic formerly assumed to account for precession of equinoxes etc. [f. L *trepidatio* (*trepidare* be agitated, tremble, f. *trepidus* flurried, see -ATION)]

trĕs′pass, v.i., & n. **1.** Make unlawful or unwarrantable intrusion (*on*, *upon*, land, rights, etc., or abs.; ~ *on* one's *preserves*, fig., meddle in a matter that he has made his own); make unwarrantable claim *on* (chiefly in polite formulas, as *shall~ on your hospitality*); offend (*against* person, law, principle, rights; now literary), as *forgive them that ~ against us*. Hence ~ER[1] n. **2.** n. Transgression of law or right; (law) any transgression that is not (misprision of) treason or felony; ~ing (see vb, 1st sense) on another's land with damage; (also *action of* ~) common-law action for recovery of damages for ~; ~*-offering*, sacrifice atoning for ~ against Mosaic law. [ME; n. f. OF *trespas* f. *trespasser* pass over, trespass, f. med. L TRANS(*passare* PASS); vb f. n., or OF *trespasser*]

trĕss, n., & v.t. **1.** Portion, lock, plait, of hair of human esp. woman's or girl's head; (pl.) hair of esp. woman's or girl's head. Hence (-)~ED[2] (-st), ~′Y[2], aa. **2.** v.t. Arrange (hair) in ~es (chiefly in p.p.). [ME, f. OF *tresce*, *tresse*; vb. f. OF *trecier*, *tresser* (f. n.)]

trĕ′stle (sl), n. Supporting structure for table or flat form or carpenter's work etc., consisting of bar supported by two divergent pairs of legs or of two frames fixed at an angle or hinged; (also ~*-work*) open braced framework of wood or metal for supporting bridge etc.; (naut., also ~*-tree*) each of a pair of horizontal pieces on lower mast supporting topmast etc. [ME, f. OF *trestel* f. Gallo-Rom. **transtellum* beam, dim. of L *transtrum*]

‖ **trĕt**, n. (hist.). Allowance of extra weight formerly made to purchasers of some goods for waste in transportation. [ME, prob. f. AF, OF *tret*, var. of *trait* draught; see TRAIT]

trevet. See TRIVET.

‖ **trews** (-ōōz), n. pl. Tartan trousers, esp. as worn by some Scottish regiments. [f. Ir. *trius*, Gael. *triubhas* (sing.); see TROUSERS]

trey (trā), n. Card, die, with three spots. [ME, f. AF, OF *treis*, *trei* three f. L *tres*]

tri-, pref. = L & Gk *tri-* three-, comb. form of L *tres*, Gk *treis* three, Gk *tris* thrice, having or composed of three, triple, as : ~*adelph′ous*, with stamens in 3 sets; ~*an′drous*, with 3 stamens; ~*ap′sidal*, with 3 apses; ~*bās′ic*, with 3 hydrogen atoms replaceable by base or basic radical; ~*brāch′ial* (-k-), three-armed implement etc., esp. a flint implement; ~*cap′sular* (bot., zool.), with 3 capsules (to each flower); ~*carp′ous*, bearing 3 fruits or carpels; ~*centĕn′ary*, = TERCENTENARY; ~*chlŏr′ide* (-kl-), compound of element or radical with 3 atoms of chlorine; ~′*chord* (-k-) a. & n., three-stringed (instrument esp. lute), (of piano) with 3 strings to each note; ~*chromat′ic* (-kr-), three-coloured (~*-chromatic photography*, THREE-*colour process*), (of the eye) having the normal three colour sensations, i.e. red, green, & purple, so ~*chrōm′atism* (-kr-) n.; ~′*corn*, having 3 horns, (n., also ~′*corne*) three-cornered cocked hat; ~*corp′oral*, ~*corp′orate*, (her.) having 3 bodies & one head; ~*cotylēd′onous*, with 3 cotyledons; ~*crŏt′ic*, (of pulse) with 3 beats; ~*cŭs′pid*, with 3 cusps or points, as ~*cuspid valve* of heart, ~*cuspid murmur* (heard when this is deranged); ~*dac′tyl* (ous), with 3 fingers or toes; ~*den′late*, with 3 teeth or prongs; ~*di′gitate*, = ~*dactyl*; ~*dimen′sional*, of 3 dimensions; ~*fā′cial* a. & n., (of) the trigeminus; ~*flor′al*, ~*flor′ous*, bearing 3 flowers; ~*fōl′iate*, ~*fōl′iolate* (of compound leaf) with 3 leaflets, (of plants) having such leaves; ~*fōl′iated*, (bot.) = prec., (archit.) trefoiled; ~′*form(ed)*, formed of 3 parts, having 3 forms or bodies; ~*furc′ate* (-at) a., divided into three forks, (v.t. & i., -āt) divide thus; ~*gĕm′inal* a. & n., triple, (of) the ~geminus; ~*gĕm′inus*, cranial nerve with the 3 functions of motion, common sensation, & taste; ~′*glot*, written in 3 languages; ~*goneut′ic* (entom.), having 3

For other words in *tri-* see TRI-.

broods in a year; ~'*gram*, ~'*graph*, group of 3 letters representing one sound; ~*gynous* (trĭj⁴), having 3 pistils; ~*hĕd'ral*, with 3 surfaces; ~*jug'ate*, ~*jug'ous*, (-jōō-), (bot.), having, arranged in, 3 pairs; ~*lăb'iate*, three-lipped; ~*lăm'inar*, of 3 layers; ~*lăt'eral* a. & n. (adv. -*lly*), of 3 sides, (of dealings) to which there are 3 parties, (n.) triangle; ~*lemm'a*, choice between 3 things; ~*lĭn'ear*, of 3 lines; ~*ling'ual* (-nggw-), of, expressed in, 3 languages; ~*lĭt'eral*, of 3 letters, (of Semitic languages) having (most of) their roots in 3 consonants, so ~*lĭt'eralism*, ~*literal'ity*, nn.; ~'*lĭth*, monument of 3 stones, esp. two upright & one across their tops, so ~*lĭth'ic* a.; ~*lŏb'ate*, three-lobed; ~*lŏc'ular*, with 3 cells or compartments; ~*men'sual*, ~*mes'tr*(i)*al*, occurring every 3 months; *trim'erous*, of 3 members or joints (also *3-merous*); ~*morph'ism*, ~*morph'ous*, (biol., bot., crystallog.), existence, existing, in 3 distinct forms; ~*nerv'ate*, three-nerved; ~*nŏd'al* (anat., bot.), having 3 joints; ~*nŏm'ial* a. & n., (technical name, algebraical expression) consisting of 3 terms; ~*nŏm'ialism*, use of 3 terms in naming objects in natural history; ~*oe'cious* (-ēsh-), having male, female, & hermaphrodite flowers each on different plants; ~*ox'ide*, oxide containing 3 oxygen atoms; ~*penn'ate*, = ~*pinnate*; ~*pĕt'alous*, having 3 petals; *trĭph'thong*, 3 vowels forming one sound; *trĭphthong'al* (-nggl), so formed; ~*phyll'ous*, three-leaved; ~*pinn'ate*, having 3 series of leaflets; ~*răd'ial*, ~*răd'iate*(d), radiating in 3 directions; ~*sĕr'ial*, ~*sĕr'iate*, (anat., bot.) disposed in 3 rows; ~*sperm'ous*, containing 3 seeds; ~*spor'ous*, ~*spor'ic*, having 3 spores; *trĭs'tichous* (-k-), arranged in 3 vertical rows; ~*stigmat'ic*, ~*styl'ous*, (bot.), having 3 stigmas, styles; ~*sulc'ate*, (bot.) three-grooved, (zool.) divided into 3 digits or hoofs; ~*tern'ate*, (bot.) thrice ternate, having 27 leaflets; ~'*tone*, (mus.) interval of 3 tones; *trĭv'alent* (chem.), having combining power of 3.

tri'able, a. That may be tried. [ME, f. AF, as TRY + -ABLE]

triacŏntahĕd'ral, a. Having 30 sides or surfaces. [f. Gk *triakonta* 30 + *hedra* base, side, -AL]

tri'ad, n. Group of three; (chem.) element, radical, with combining power of three; (mus.) chord of three notes, common chord; Welsh form of literary composition depending on arrangement in groups of three. Hence **triăd'ic** a. [f. F *triade* or LL f. Gk *trias -ados* (*treis* three, see -AD)]

|| **tri'age**, n. Refuse of coffee-beans. [F, = sifting (as TRY, see -AGE)]

tri'al, n. 1. Process or mode of testing the qualities of a thing, experimental treatment, test, as *made* ~ *of his strength, was found on* ~ *to be incompetent, shall subject* or *put it to further* ~, *will make the* ~ (try the experiment), *has been making* ~*s* or (attrib.) ~ *ascents with an aeroplane*; ~ *of the* PYX; *bicycle is hired, clerk employed, on* ~ (to be retained only if efficient), *will give you a* ~ (employ you on ~); = ~ HEAT[1]; = ~ *match.* 2. Trying thing or experience or person, esp. hardship, trouble, as *old age has many* ~*s, fear you will find the boy, the piano next door, a great* ~. 3. Judicial examination & determination of issues between parties by judge with or without jury or by referee etc., as *was on his* ~ or *stood* or *underwent* ~ *for murder, granted a new* ~ (on ground of error or injustice in former ~, or because of jury's failure to agree). 4. ~ *balance* (of ledger in double-entry book-keeping), comparison of Dr & Cr totals, inequality of which reveals certain errors in posting; ~ *eights*, two experimental crews tried against each other with a view to selection of crew for boat-race; ~ *match*, game of cricket, football, etc., in which players who may be selected for an important team take part; ~ *trip*, new vessel's trip to test sailing qualities etc., (fig.) experiment. [AF *trial, triel* (TRY, -AL)]

tri'ăngle (-nggl), n. 1. Figure (esp. plane) bounded by three (esp. straight) lines, as *equilateral, isosceles, scalene, right-angled.* ~, *spherical* ~ (formed on surface of sphere by intersection of three great circles); any three points not in one straight line together with the imaginary lines joining them. 2. Implement etc. of this shape, e.g. right-angled ~ as drawing-implement, (naut.) device of three spars for raising weights, (mus.) rod of polished steel in form of ~ open at one angle sounded by striking with steel rod, (hist.) frame of three halberds joined at top to which soldier was bound for flogging; *the* ETERNAL ~; ~*s of the neck* (regions into which it is divided for surgical purposes); (*T*~) a northern constellation. 3. *Solution of a* ~, finding of the remaining angles & sides when some are given; ~ *of forces*, ~ whose sides represent in magnitude & direction three forces in equilibrium, fact that such forces can always be represented by a ~. [ME, f. OF, or f. L *triangulum* f. TRI(*angulus* ANGLE) a.]

triăng'ular (-ngg-), a. Of the shape of a triangle, three-cornered, so **triăng'ul**OID (-ngg-) a. ; ~ *treaty, duel,* etc., (between three parties); ~ *compasses* (with three legs); ~ *numbers*, sums of the series 1, 2, 3, etc., taken to any number of terms, e.g. 1, 6, 28, 55 (w. ref. to mode of disposing such number of points in form of equilateral triangle); ~ *pyramid* (with ~ base). Hence ~ITY (-nggŭlă'r-) n., ~LY² adv. [f. LL *triangularis* (as prec., see -AR¹)]

triăng'ul|āte¹ (-ngg-), v.t. Make triangular; divide (area etc.) into triangles for surveying purposes; determine

(height, distance, etc.) thus. Hence ~ᴀᴸ
TION n. [f. L, as TRIANGLE +-ATE³]

triäng′ulate² (-ngg-), a. (zool.). Marked
with triangles. Hence ~LY² adv. [f.
med. L *triangulatus* (prec., -ATE²)]

Tri′ăs, n. (geol.). Division of rocks underlying the Jurassic. Hence **Triäss′ɪC** a.
[as TRIAD, f. threefold subdivision in Ger-
many]

triät′ɪc stay, n. (naut.). Stay connecting
masts in fore-&-aft-rigged ships. [orig.
unkn.]

trib′adism, n. Unnatural vice between
women. [f. L f. Gk *tribas -ados* lewd
woman (*tribō* rub) +-ISM]

trib′al|ism, n. Tribal organization. So
~ɪZE v.t. [-ISM]

tribe, n. 1. Group of primitive clans
under recognized chiefs; (Rom. hist.)
each of the political divisions (orig. three,
probably representing clans, ultimately
35) of the Romans; any similar division
whether of natural or political origin, e.g.
the twelve ~s of the Israelites (*the ten* ~s,
these without Judah & Benjamin; *the
lost* ~s, the ten ~s after deportation by
Shalmaneser). 2. (zool., bot.). Group of
plants or animals usu. ranking between
genus & order. 3. (usu. derog.). Set,
number, of persons esp. of one profession
etc., as *the whole* ~ *of parasites, actors, the
scribbling* ~. 4. ~s′man, member of a ~
or of one's own ~. Hence **trib′ᴀʟ** a.,
trib′ᴀʟLY² adv. [ME *tribu, tribe,* f. OF
tribu or L *tribus*]

trib′lĕt, trib′olĕt, n. Mandrel used in
making tubes, rings, etc. [f. F *triboulet*]

tribōm′ĕter, n. Sledlike apparatus for
measuring friction. [f. F *tribomètre* f. Gk
tribos rubbing +-METER]

trib′răch (-k-), n. Metrical foot ∪ ∪ ∪.
Hence **tribrăch′ɪC** (-k-) a. [f. L f. Gk
TRI(*brakhus* short)]

tribūlā′tion, n. Severe suffering or trial.
[ME, f. OF (-*cion*), f. LL *tribulationem*
(*tribulare* press, oppress, f. *tribulum* sledge
for threshing, f. *terere trit-* rub, see -ATION)]

tribūn′al, n. Judgement-seat, seat or
bench for judge(s) or magistrate(s); court
of justice (rhet., & often fig., as *before the*
~ *of public opinion*); ‖ (in the 1914–18
war) local board hearing claims for
exemption from military service. [f. F, or
L (as TRIBUNE¹, see -AL)]

trib′ūn|e¹, n. 1. (Rom. hist.). (Also ~*e
of the people*) each of (orig. two, ultimately
ten) officers chosen by the people to
protect their liberties against senate &
consuls; kinds of military, fiscal, & other
officers. 2. (transf.). Popular leader or
demagogue (*the T*~*e,* often as newspaper
title). Hence or cogn. ~ATE¹(1), ~eSHIP,
nn., ~ARY¹,~i′CIᴀʟ,~i′tial, (-shl),~i′CIAN
(-ishn), aa. [ME, f. L *tribunus* (as TRIBE)]

trib′ūne², n. Raised floor for magistrate's
chair in apse of Roman basilica; bishop's

throne, apse containing this, in basilica;
platform, pulpit, esp. that used by
speakers in French Chamber of Deputies.
[F, f. It., f. med. L *tribuna* (prec.)]

trib′ūtar|y̆, a. & n. 1. Paying, subject to,
tribute, as ~*y States*; contributory, auxiliary; (of river) serving to swell a larger
river. 2. n̄. ~y State, person, stream.
Hence ~ɪLY² adv., ~iNESS n. [ME, f. L
tributarius (as foll., see -ARY¹)]

trib′ūte, n. Money or equivalent paid
periodically by one prince or State to
another in acknowledgement of submission or as price of peace or protection, or
by virtue of treaty; state of being subject
to ~, as *was laid under* ~; (fig.) contribution, esp. thing done, said, given,
etc., as mark of respect etc., as *the* ~ *of a
tear, will not withhold my* ~ *of praise, the*
~*s* (gifts, compliments, attentions) *of her
admirers, floral* ~*s* (flowers to actress, at
funeral, etc.); ‖ (mining) proportion of
ore, its equivalent, paid to miner for his
work, ~*-work* (so paid). [ME, f. L *tributum*
(*tribuere -ut-* give)]

tric′ar, n. Three-wheeled motor-car.
[TRI-]

trice¹, v.t. (naut.). Haul up (usu. *up*);
haul up & secure in place (usu. *up*); tie up
(usu. *up*). [ME, f. MDu. *trīsen*, MLG
trīssen]

trice², n. *In a* ~, in a moment. [ME,
f. prec.]

tri′cĕps, a. & n. 1. (Of muscle) three-
-headed. 2. n. ~ muscle, esp. large
muscle of back of arm. [L, f. TRI-+-*ceps*
(*caput* head)]

trich′ī. See TRICHINOPOLI.

trichi′asis (-k-), n. Urinary disease in
which hairlike filaments appear in urine;
disease of breasts in child-bearing women;
inversion of eyelashes; disease marked by
matted state of hair. [LL, f. Gk *trikhia-
sis* (as foll., see -ASIS)]

trich′in|a (-k-), n. (pl. ~ae). Hairlike
worm parasitic in body of man, swine,
rat, etc., usu. introduced into human
body by use of imperfectly cooked pork,
& causing often fatal disease. Hence
~ĭ′ASIS, ~ĪZA′TION, ~OS′IS, nn., ~ɪZE(3)
v.t.,~ōSED²(-sd),~OT′ɪC,~OUS, aa. [mod.
L, f. Gk *trikhinos* of hair (TRICHO-, -INE²)]

trichinŏp′oli, trich′ī, n. Kind of Indian
cheroot. [*Trichinopoli* in India]

trich|(0)- (-k-), comb. form of Gk *thrix
trikhos* hair, as: ~*′ogen* n., ~*ŏ′genous* a.,
(preparation) promoting growth of hair;
~*ŏl′ogy,* study of the hair; ~*opath′ic* a.,
~*ŏp′athy* n., (treatment) of diseases of
hair.

trich′ōme (-k-), n. Hair, scale, or other
outgrowth from epidermis of plant. [f.
Gk *trikhōma* (*trikhoō* furnish with hair,
see prec.)]

trichōs′is (-k-), n. Any disease of hair.
[f. Gk *trichosis,* as TRICHO- +-OSIS]

For other words in *tri-* see TRI-.

trĭchŏt'om|ў (-k-), n. Division into three, esp. of human nature into body, soul, & spirit. Hence~ous a. [f. Gk *trikha* three-fold (*treis* three)+-·TOMY]

trick, n., & v.t. & i. 1. Fraudulent device or stratagem, as *I suspect some~, ~ of the* TRADE, *shall not serve me that ~ twice.* 2. Feat of skill or dexterity, knack, precise mode of doing or dealing with a thing, as *conjurer's ~s, do the ~* (sl., = accomplish one's purpose), *my dog knows no ~s, I know a ~ worth two of that* (better expedient), *shall soon get or learn the ~ of it* (best way of doing or handling it), (attrib.) ~ *cyclist* etc. 3. Peculiar or characteristic practice, habit, mannerism, as *has a ~ of repeating himself, these are private-school~s, style is disfigured by ~s, must cure himself of the ~ of archaism.* 4. Mischievous or foolish or discreditable act, practical joke, prank, as *is always playing mad~s, a dirty or shabby or dog's ~ to play on anyone.* 5. (cards). The cards played in a round, as *take up the~*; such round, point gained as result of this, as *won, lost, saved, the ~; the* ODD *~.* 6. (naut.). Man's turn at helm, usu. two hours. 7. ~ *cyclist* (sl.), psychiatrist; ~·*line*, cord used in making changes in pantomime; ~ *scene* (made without dropping curtain); ~ *wig* (of which hair can be made to stand on end). 8. vb. Deceive by ~, cheat, (person, often *out of* thing, *into doing*, etc.); (of thing) foil, baffle, disappoint the calculations of, take by surprise; play~s; (usu. ~ *out* or *up*) dress, decorate, deck. Hence~'ER¹, ~'ERY (4, 5),~'STER, nn.,~'ISH (now rare,=TRICKY) a. [ME, f. OF dial. *trique*, f. *trikier* = OF *trichier* (cf. TREACHEROUS); vb f. n.]

trĭck'kl|e, v.i. & t., & n. 1. (Of liquid) flow in drops or in small stream, as *tears ~ed down her cheeks, water~es through crevice*, (fig.) *the information~ed* (came gradually) *out*; cause (liquid) to do this, pour out in drops; ~*e charger*, accumulator charger that works at a low rate. 2. n. ~ing stream. Hence ~ET¹ n., ~Y² a. [ME *trekel, trikle*, prob. imit.]

trick'sў, a. Playful, frolicsome; quaint. [f. TRICK; for -*sy* cf. TIPSY]

trick'träck, tick'täck, n. Complicated form of backgammon. [f. F *trictrac*, prob. imit. of sound]

trick'|ў, a. Crafty, prone to deceit; skilful at evasion, resourceful, adroit; (of task etc.) requiring adroitness, full of pitfalls, ticklish. Hence ~ĭLY² adv., ~ĭNESS n. [TRICK+-Y²]

triclĭn'ium, n. (Rom. ant.; pl. -*ia*). Dining-table with couches along three sides, room containing this. [L, f. Gk TRI(*klinion* f. *klīnē* couch)]

tric'oline, n. Fine cotton poplin resembling silk. [P]

tri'colour, -or, (-ŭler), a. & n. 1. (Also ~ED² a.) of three colours. 2. n. Flag of three colours in about equal proportions,

esp. French national standard of blue, white, & red, adopted during Revolution. [f. F TRI(*colore* f. LL as COLOUR)]

tricot (trĕk'ō), n. Hand-knitted woollen fabric, imitation of this; kind of ribbed cloth; ~·*stitch*, kind of crochet stitch. [F, = knitting]

tri'cўcl|e, n., & v.i. (Ride on) three-·wheeled pedal-driven vehicle. Hence ~IST(1) n. [F]

trid'ent, n. Three-pronged implement e.g. fish-spear; such spear or sceptre as attribute of Poseidon or Neptune. [f. L TRI(*dens -ntis* tooth)]

Trĭdĕn'tine, a. & n. 1. Of the Council of Trent (1545–63) esp. as basis of Roman Catholic doctrine & practice, as ~ *theology.* 2. n. Roman Catholic. [f. med. L *Tridentum* Trent+-INE¹]

triduo (trĕd'ōō̄), **trid'uum**, n. (R.-C. Ch.). Three days' service of prayer in preparation for saint's day or for obtaining saint's intercession. [(-*o* It.) f. L TRI(*duum* f. *dies* day) three days]

trĭĕnn'ial, a. & n. 1. Lasting, happening or done every, three years, as ~ *plants, parliaments; T~ Act* (requiring ~ parliaments, repealed 1716). 2. n. ~ plant; mass performed daily for three years for soul of dead person; every third anniversary of event. Hence ~LY² adv. [f. L TRI(*ennis* f. *annus* year)+-AL]

tri'er, n. In senses of TRY, esp. (also *trior*) person appointed to decide whether challenge to juror is well founded. [-ER¹]

tri'crärch (-k), n. (Gk ant.). Commander of trireme; wealthy person compelled to build & equip trireme at his own expense. Hence ~AL (-k-) a. [f. L f. Gk *triĕrarkhos* f. *triĕrēs* trireme+*arkhō* rule]

tri'erärchў (-k-), n. Office, duty, of trierarch; (Athenian formation of fleet at expense of) the trierarchs. [f. Gk *triĕrarkhia* (prec., -Y¹)]

trif'id, a. (bot., zool.). Partly or wholly divided into three, three-cleft. [f. L TRI(*fidus* f. root of *findere* cleave)]

tri'fle, n., & v.i. & t. 1. Thing, fact, circumstance, of slight value or importance, as *wastes time on~s, the merest ~ puts him out*, (iron.) *shall probably break our necks, but that is a ~*; small amount esp. of money, as *spare a ~ for the porter*, (adv.) *seems a~* (rather) *angry*; confection of whipped cream or white of eggs, with pastry etc. soaked in wine, fruit, almonds, etc.; common pewter; ~·*ring*, kinds of puzzle-ring. 2. vb. Talk or act frivolously; ~ *with*, treat (person, thing, matter) with flippancy or derision, refuse to take seriously, (also) occupy oneself carelessly with, toy with, (novel, cigarette, etc.); throw or fool *away* (time, energies, money, etc., *on* object); (part.) *a trifling error, correction, circumstance*, etc. (unimportant). Hence **trif'lER¹** n., **trif'lingLY¹** adv. [ME & OF *trufle* parallel form of *truf(f)e* deceit, of unkn. orig.]

trifōr′ium, n. (pl. *-ia*). Gallery, usu. in form of arcade, above arches of nave & choir (& transepts) of church. [*c.* 1185 in Anglo-L, of unkn. orig.]

trig[1], a., & v.t. (-gg-). **1.** Trim, spruce, smart. **2.** v.t. Smarten, deck, (often *up*, *out*). [ME adj., f. ON *tryggr* faithful etc., = Goth. *triggws* TRUE]

trig[2], v.t. (-gg-), & n. **1.** Check, stop, (wheel) with skid, stone, etc.; prop *up*. **2.** n. Obstacle etc. used. [perh. f. ON *tryggja* to secure, f. *tryggr* firm, see prec.]

trig[3], school abbr. of *trigonometry*.

trig′am|ous, a. Thrice married or having three wives or husbands at once; so ~IST, ~Y[1], nn.; (bot.) having male, female, & hermaphrodite flowers in same head (cf. TRIO*ecious*). [f. Gk TRI(*gamos* wedding)+ -OUS]

trigg′er (-g-), n., & v.t. **1.** Device for releasing spring or catch & so setting mechanism in action, esp. projecting tongue in firearm that liberates hammer of lock; agent that sets off a chain reaction; HAIR ~; ~-*happy*, apt to shoot on slight provocation. **2.** v.t. (Also ~ *off*) set in action, initiate or precipitate. Hence (-)~ED[2] (-gerd) a. [17th c. *tricker* f. Du. *trekker* (*trekken* pull, cf. TREK)]

trig′lyph, n. Each of the grooved tablets alternating with metopes in Doric frieze. Hence ~AL, **trĭglўph′**IC(AL), aa. [f. L f. Gk TRI(*gluphos* f. *glupho* carve)]

trig′ŏn, n. (Astrol.) each of four groups (*watery*, *earthly*, *airy*, *fiery*, ~) of three signs of zodiac; triangular instrument used in dialling; = TRINE; (Gk ant., also *trigŏn′on*) triangular lyre or harp; (math.) triangle, whence **trĭgŏn′**IC a. [f. L f. Gk TRI(*gŏnon* f. *gōnia* angle) triangle]

trig′on|al, a. (Math.) triangular; (bot., zool.) triangular in cross-section, as ~*al stem, antennae*. Hence or cogn. ~al**LY**[2] adv., ~OUS a. [f. prec. + -AL]

trigŏnŏm′ĕter, n. Instrument for solution of plane right-angled triangles by inspection; one versed in trigonometry. [TRIGON + -O- + -METER]

trigon|ŏm′ĕtrў, n. Branch of mathematics dealing primarily with relations of sides & angles of a triangle, much used in astronomy, surveying, & navigation. Hence ~omĕt′ric(AL) aa., ~omĕt′ri**cal**LY[2] adv. [f. mod. L *trigonometria* (TRIGON + -O- + -METRY)]

trike, n. & v.i. (colloq.). = TRICYCLE. [abbr.]

tril′bў, n. || ~ (*hat*), soft felt kind (colloq.). [f. G. du Maurier's novel *T*~ (1894)]

trill, v.i. & t., & n. **1.** (Of person or thing) give forth sound with tremulous vibration, as ~*ing laughter*; sing (t. & i.) in quavering manner, esp. (mus.) with shake. **2.** n. Quavering sound, esp. (mus.) quick alternation of two notes a (semi)tone apart, shake; consonant pronounced with ~ing sound, e.g. *r*. [f. It. *trillare* (imit.)]

trill′ing, n. Compound crystal of three individuals; each of three children born at a birth. [f. TRI- + -LING, app. after Da., Sw. *trilling*, Du. *drieling*, G *drilling*]

trill′ion (-lyon), n. & a. || A million million million; *(after F) a million million. Hence ~TH[2] a. & n. [F, f. TRI- on *million*, after *billion*]

tril′obite, n. Member of a large group of extinct arthropods characterized by a three-lobed body. [f. mod. L *Trilobites* (TRI-, Gk *lobos* lobe, -ITE[1])]

tril′ogў, n. (Gk ant.) set of three tragedies to be performed in immediate succession; set of three literary compositions, speeches, etc., each complete in itself but with common theme. [f. Gk TRI(*logia* -LOGY)]

trim, a., v.t. & i. (-mm-), & n. **1.** In good order, well arranged or equipped, neat, spruce, whence ~LY[2] adv., ~′NESS n. **2.** vb. Set in good order, make neat or tidy, remove irregular or superfluous or unsightly parts from, (lamp or strictly its wick, hedge, beard, etc.); remove (such parts, often *off*, *away*) by clipping, pruning, planing, etc.; make (person, one*self*, often *up*) neat in dress &. appearance; ornament (dress etc. *with* ribbon, lace, etc.); (of school of fish) ~ (move along close to) the *shore*; (naut.) adjust balance of (ship, boat) by distribution of cargo or passengers etc., arrange (yards, sails) to suit wind, as ~ BY[1] *the head, stern*; hold middle course in politics or opinion, attach oneself to neither of contesting parties, be a time-server; (colloq.) rebuke sharply, thrash, cheat out of money, worst in bargain etc.; (colloq.) ~ person's *jacket*, flog him. **3.** n. State, degree, of adjustment or readiness or fitness, as *found everything in perfect* ~, *am in no* ~ (state of dress, health, etc.) *for rough work*, *in fighting* ~, (of ship, & fig.) ready for battle; good order (esp. naut.), as *in*, *out of*, ~; (naut.) ~ (relative position) *of the masts*. [formally repr. OE *trymman*, *trymian* make firm, arrange, f. *trum* strong; but the vb is undocumented from OE to 1500]

trim′ĕter, n. & a. (Verse) consisting of three measures (see DIMETER), esp. *iambic* ~, six-foot iambic line usual in ancient Greek dramatic dialogue. Hence **trĭmĕt′**RIC(AL) aa. [f. L f. Gk TRI(*metros* f. *metron* measure)]

trimm′er, n. In vbl senses, esp.: one who trims articles of dress, as *coat*, *hat*, ~; person who stands neutral, time-server, (orig. of party following Marquis of Halifax 1680-90); kinds of instrument for clipping etc.; piece of timber framed across opening (e.g. for hearth) to carry ends of the truncated joists. [-ER[1]]

trimm'ing, n. In vbl senses, esp.: ornamentation of lace etc. on dress etc.; (pl., colloq.) leg of mutton etc. & ~s (accessories). [-ING[1]]

trine, a. & n. 1. Threefold, triple, made up of three parts, whence trin'AL, trin'ARY[1], aa.; ~ aspersion or immersion, thrice sprinkling in baptism; (astrol.) of a ~, in ~. 2. n. (astrol.). Aspect of two planets 120° apart; in ~, so related (to). [ME, f. OF trin(e) f. L trinus threefold (tres three)]

tringle (tring'gl), n. Curtain-rod : supporting rod for canopy of bedstead ; (archit.) small square moulding or ornament; (gunnery) bar on traversing-platform to check recoil. [F, of unkn. orig.]

trinitrotŏl'uēne, -ŭŏl, n. A high explosive (abbr. T.N.T. or TNT). [f. TRI-, NITRO-, TOLU, -ENE, -OL]

trin'ity, n. 1. Being three; group of three; the T~, union of three persons (Father, Son, Holy Spirit) in one Godhead, doctrine of this, whence Trinitār'ian(ism) nn.; symbolical representation of the T~ in art. 2. ~ ring, kinds of ancient bronze ring with three bosses etc. found in Ireland; T~ Sunday, next after Whitsunday ; ‖ T~ Brethren, members of T~ House, association concerned with licensing of pilots, erection and maintenance of lighthouses, etc.; ‖ T~ TERM. [ME, f. OF trinite f. LL trinitatem f. trinus TRINE, see -TY]

trink'ét, n. Trifling ornament, jewel, etc., worn on the person; small fancy article. Hence ~RY(1, 5) n. [16th c., of unkn. orig.]

tri'o (-ĕō, -ĭō), n. (pl. ~s). 1. (mus.). Composition for three vocal or instrumental parts; set of three performers; second division of minuet, march, etc., orig. performed by ~ of instruments; piano ~, for violin, violoncello, & piano. 2. Set of three persons etc.; three aces, kings, queens, or knaves, in piquet. [F f. It., f. tre three, after duo]

tri'ōde, a. (Of radio valves) having three electrodes. [f. TRI- +(ELECTR)ODE]

tri'ōle (trē-), n. (mus.). = TRIPLET. [dim. of TRIO]

tri'olét (or trē-), n. Poem of 8 (usu. 8-syllabled) lines with rhymes as shown, first line recurring as fourth & seventh & second as eighth (cat dog bat cat fat hog cat dog). [F (-LET)]

Trïōn'ĕs (-z), n. pl. = CHARLES'S WAIN, [L, = plough-oxen]

trior. See TRIER.

trip, v.i. & t. (-pp-), & n. 1. Walk or dance with quick light tread, (fig., of rhythm etc.) run lightly, whence ~p'ingLY[2] adv. 2. (arch.). Take journey or excursion, whence (in mod. use) ‖ ~p'ER[1] n., person who goes on a ~ esp. for a day to seaside or other resort. 3. Make false step, stumble, (often over obstacle); make mistake, commit inconsistency or inaccuracy or moral delinquency, as caught

him ~ping in his dates, all apt to ~; (of person or obstacle) cause (person) to stumble by entangling or suddenly arresting his feet (often up); detect (person) in blunder (often up). 4. (Naut.) loose (anchor) from bottom by means of cable, turn (yard etc.) from horizontal to vertical position; release (part of machine) suddenly by withdrawing catch etc. 5. n. Journey, voyage, excursion esp. for pleasure, as round ~ (to a place & back), cheap ~s to the Riviera. 6. Nimble step. 7. Stumble (lit. & fig.); ~ping or being ~ped up. 8. The fish caught during a voyage. 9. ~-hammer, kind of TILT[1]-hammer. [ME, f. OF treper, trip(p)er, f. MDu. trippen skip, hop]

tripārt'ite (or trĭp[2]), a. Divided into 3 parts; (bot., of leaf) divided into 3 segments almost to the base; ~ indenture (with 3 corresponding parts or copies) made, existing, between 3 parties, as ~ treaty. Hence ~LY[2] adv., tripārti'tion n. [f. L TRI(partitus p.p. of partiri divide)]

tripe, n. Principal part of stomach of ox etc. as food, as will stand anything but ~ (arch. a ~); (now vulg., usu. pl.) entrails, belly; ‖ (sl.) inferior stuff, nonsense, easy bowling etc.; ~-de-roche (trĕp'derŏsh') [F, lit. rock-~], bitter nutritive vegetable substance obtained from some lichens & used at a pinch by hunters etc. as food; ~'man, man who prepares & hawks ~. Hence trip'ERY(3) n. [ME, f. OF trip(p)e, of unkn. orig.]

tri'plāne, n. Aeroplane with three planes. [TRI-, PLANE[3]]

tri'ple, a., & v.t. & i. 1. Threefold, of three parts (often in comb., as ~-headed, -nerved); T~ Alliance, (1) between England, Sweden, & Netherlands, in 1668 against Louis XIV, (2) between France, Great Britain, & Netherlands, in 1717 chiefly against Spain, (3) between Germany, Austria, & Italy, in 1882-3 against Russia & France; ~ crown, pope's tiara; T~ ENTENTE; (mus.)~ time (of 3 or 9 beats in bar). 2. vb. Increase (t. & i.) threefold; be three times as great or many as; alter (engine) to ~ expansion. [adj. (16th c.) F, or f. L triplus f. Gk triplous; vb (14th c.) f. LL triplare]

trip'lét, n. Set of three things; 3 verses rhyming together; (mus.) 3 notes performed in the time of two; each of 3 children born at a birth; (naut.) 3 links of chain between cable & anchor-ring. [f. prec. +-ET[1], after DOUBLET]

trip'lĕx, a. & n. 1. Triple, threefold; ~ glass (P; also ~) unsplinterable glass used in motor-cars etc., consisting of a transparent sheet of plastic material between two sheets of glass. 2. n. (mus.). Triple time; composition in three parts. [L TRI(plex -plicis f. plicare fold)]

trip'licate[1], a. & n. 1. Threefold, esp. of which three copies are made, as ~ certificate; ~ ratio of two numbers, ratio of their cubes. **2.** n. Each of a set of 3 copies or corresponding parts, state of being ~, as *document drawn up in* ~. [ME, f. L *triplicare* (TRIPLEX), -ATE²]

trip'lic|āte², v.t. Treble, make triplicate. So ~A'TION, ~āTURE, nn. [-ATE³]

trip'līce (-chā), n. = TRIPLE *alliance* (3). [It., = triple]

tripli'cĭtў, n. State of being triple. [ME, f. OF *-ite* or LL *triplicitas* (TRIPLEX, -ITY)]

trip'ŏd, n. Stool, table, utensil, resting on three feet or legs, whence ~AL a.; three--legged stand for supporting camera etc.; (Gk ant.) bronze altar at Delphi on which priestess sat to utter oracles, imitation of this esp. as prize in Pythian games etc. [f. L *tripus* f. Gk TRI(*pous podos* foot)]

trip'oli, n. = ROTTEN-*stone*. [f. *T*~ in Africa]

‖ trip'ŏs, n. (Camb. Univ.). Honours examination for degree of Bachelor of Arts. [as TRIPOD, w. ref. to stool on which B.A. sat to deliver satirical speech at commencement]

tripper. See TRIP.

trip'tўch (-ĭk), n. Picture or carving on three panels side by side, set of three associated pictures so placed; set of three writing-tablets hinged or tied together; triangular plate on motor-car serving as a customs international pass. [f. TRI- after DIPTYCH]

‖ tripūd'iāte, v.i. (pedant.). Dance for joy; dance in triumph or contempt *upon*. [f. L *tripudiare* (*tripudium* a dance, perh. f. TRI-, *pes pedis* foot), -ATE³]

triquĕt'ra, n. (pl. *-ae*). Symmetrical ornament of three interlaced arcs. [L, fem. of *triquetrus*) three-cornered]

triquĕt'rous, a. Three-cornered, esp. (bot., of stem) having 3 acute angles. Hence ~LY² adv. [f. L as prec. +-OUS]

trir'ēme, n. Ancient esp. Greek warship with three banks of oars. [f. L TRI(*remis* f. *remus* oar)]

Trĭsăg'ĭon (-g-), n. Hymn esp. in Oriental Churches with triple invocation of God as holy. [f. Gk *trisagios* (*tris* thrice +*hagios* holy)]

trisĕct', v.t. Divide into three (usu. equal) parts. Hence **trisĕc'tĭon** n. [f. TRI-+L *secare sect-* cut]

tris'mus (-z-), n. (path.). Lockjaw [mod. L, f. Gk *trismos* = *trigmos* a scream, grinding]

trist'ful, a. (arch.). Sad. [obs. *trist* adj. f. OF *triste* f. L *tristis* sad +-FUL]

trisўll'able, n. Word of three syllables. **trisўllăb'ic** a., **trisўllăb'ically** adv. [f. TRI- + SYLLABLE]

trităg'onist, n. Third actor in Greek play (cf. DEUTERAGONIST). [f. Gk *tritagōnistēs* (*tritos* third +*agōnistēs* actor)]

trite, a. (Of expression, sentiment, quotation, etc.) commonplace, hackneyed,

worn out. Hence ~'LY² adv., ~'NESS n. [f. L *terere trit-* rub]

tri'thĕ|ism, n. Doctrine that there are (esp. that Father, Son, & Holy Spirit are) 3 Gods. So ~IST n., ~IS'TIC(AL) aa. [TRI-]

trit'ium, n. (chem.). Heavy isotope of hydrogen with mass about three times that of ordinary hydrogen, cf. DEUTERIUM. [f. Gk *tritos* third +-IUM]

Trit'on, n. (Gk myth.) son of Poseidon & Amphitrite, each of a race of minor sea--gods usu. represented as men with fishes' tails & occas. with forefeet of horse & carrying shell-trumpet; ~ *among the* MINNOWS; (*t~*) kinds of gastropod & salamander. [L, f. Gk *Tritōn*]

trit'ur|āte, v.t. Grind to fine powder; grind with molar teeth, masticate thoroughly. Hence or cogn. ~ABLE a., ~A'TION, ~āTOR, nn. [f. LL *triturare* f. L *tritura* rubbing, as TRITE, see -URE & -ATE³]

tri'umph, n., & v.i. **1.** (Rom. ant.) procession & ceremony in honour of victory & victorious general; state of being victorious or successful, signal success, great achievement, thing that constitutes this, as *returned home in* ~, *has achieved great* ~s, *the* ~s *of science*, *hat is a* ~ *of ugliness*; joy at success, manifestation of this, exultation, as *great was his* ~ *on hearing* etc., *could detect no* ~ *in his eye*. **2.** v.i. (Rom. ant.) enjoy a ~; gain victory, be successful, prevail, (*over* enemy, opposition, etc.); exult (*over* fallen enemy etc., or abs.), whence ~ingLY² adv. [ME; n. f. OF *triumphe* f. L *triumphus*; vb f. OF *triumpher* f. L *triumphare*]

triūm'phal, a. Of, used in, celebrating, a triumph, as ~ *car*, *progress*, *hymn*; ~ *crown* (Roman general's laurel wreath); ~ *arch* (built to commemorate victory etc.). [ME, f. OF, or L *triumphalis* (as prec., -AL)]

triūm'phant, a. Victorious, successful; (of person, speech, voice, etc.) exulting. Hence ~LY² adv. [ME, f. OF, or L *triumphare* (as prec., -ANT²)]

triūm'vir, n. (pl. ~s, ~ī). (Rom. ant.) each of three men united in office; (Rom. hist.) each member of first or second triumvirate. Hence ~AL a. [L (*trium*, gen. of *tres* three, +*vir* man)]

triūm'virate, n. Office of a triumvir; set of triumviri; (Rom. hist.) first ~, (coalition 60 B.C. between) Pompey, Julius Caesar, & Crassus, second ~, (that in 43 B.C. between) Mark Antony, Octavian, & Lepidus; party, set, of three. [f. L *triumviratus* (prec., see -ATE¹)]

tri'ūne, a. Three in one, as ~ *Godhead*. Hence **triūn'ITY** n. [f. TRI- +L *unus* one]

triv'ĕt, n. Iron tripod for holding cooking--vessels by the fire; iron bracket designed to hook on to bars of grate for similar purposes; *right* (orig. = steady) *as a* ~,

For other words in *tri-* see TRI-.

(colloq.) all right (adj. & adv.), in good health or position or circumstances; ~ *table* (with three feet). [ME *trevet*, app. f. L TRI(*pes pedis* foot) three-footed]

triv′ia, n. pl. Trifles, trivialities [mod. L, see foll.]

triv′ial, a. Of small value or importance, trifling, as ~ *matters*, *a* ~ *loss* (of something ~), *raised* ~ *objections*; (of person) trifling, shallow, lacking ability or moral qualities; commonplace, humdrum, as *the* ~ *round* (of daily life etc.); (bot., zool., of name) popular, not scientific, also, specific opp. to *generic*. Hence or cogn. ~ISM(2, 4), **triviäl′ITY**, ~NESS, nn., ~IZE(3) v.t., ~LY² adv. [f. L *trivialis* commonplace f. TRI(*vium* f. *via* road) place where three ways meet, see -AL]

triv′ium, n. (hist.). (In medieval schools) the first three liberal arts, grammar, rhetoric, & logic. [see prec.]

-trix, suf. forming fem. agent nn. corresp. to masc. nn. in *-tor*, f. L *-trix -tricis*, chiefly in legal terms (*executrix*, *administratrix*).

troat, v.i., & n. (Make) cry of rutting buck. [cf. OF *trout*, *trut*, int. for urging on hunting dogs etc.]

tro̅c′ar, n. (med.). Instrument used in dropsy etc. for withdrawing fluid from body. [f. F *troquart*, *trois-quarts*, *trocart* (*trois* three + *carre* side, face of instrument)]

tro̅chä′ic (-k-), a. & n. 1. (Composed) of trochees, as ~ DIMETER, TETRA*meter*. 2. n. pl. ~ verse. [f. F (*-ique*) or L f. Gk *trokhaïkos* (as TROCHEE, see -IC)]

tro̅ch′al (-k-), a. (zool.). Wheel-shaped. [f. Gk *trokhos* wheel (*trekho̅* run) + -AL]

trochän′ter (-k-), n. (anat., zool.). Each of several bony processes on upper part of thighbone; second joint of insect's leg. [F, f. Gk *trokhantér* (*trekho̅* run)]

tro̅che (-k, -sh, -ch, tro̅k′ē), n. Small medicinal circular cake or lozenge. [back form. f. *troches*, pl. of obs. *trochisk* f. OF *trochisque* f. LL f. Gk *trokhiskos* dim. of *trokhos* wheel]

tro̅ch′ee (-kī), n. Metrical foot – ⌣. [f. f. Gk *trokhaios* (*pous*) running foot (*trekho̅* run)]

tro̅ch′il(us) (-k-), n. Kinds of small bird esp. (1) humming-bird, (2) bird mentioned by ancient writers as picking crocodile's teeth. [f. L f. Gk *trokhilos* (*trekho̅* run)]

tro̅ch′le̍|a (-k-), n. (anat.; pl.~*ae*). Pulley-like part or arrangement. Hence ~AR¹ (anat., bot.), ~ATE² (bot.), aa. [f. L *trochlea* pulley, f. Gk *trokhileia*]

tro̅ch′oid (-k-), a. & n. 1. (Anat.) rotating on its own axis; (of curve) generated by a point in the plane of one curve that rolls on another; (conch.) top-shaped. 2. n. ~ joint, ~ curve, kinds of gasteropod. Hence trochoid′AL (-k-) a. [f. Gk *trokhoeidēs* wheel-like (TROCHAL, -OID)]

trochöm′eter (-k-), n. = HODOMETER. [as TROCHAL + -METER]

trod(den). See TREAD.

trŏg′lody̆t|e, n. Cave-dweller, esp. of prehistoric W. Europe (often attrib.); (fig.) hermit; kinds of wren & anthropoid ape. Hence or cogn. ~ISM(2) n. [f. L (*-ta*) f. Gk *trōglody̆t′*IC(AL) aa., ~ISM(2) n. [f. L (*-ta*) f. Gk *trōglodutés* (*trōglē* cave + *duō* enter)]

troik′a, n. (Vehicle with) team of three horses abreast. [Russ.]

trois-temps (see Ap.), a. & n. ~ (*waltz*), waltz in ordinary time (cf. DEUX-TEMPS). [F, = three-time]

Trōj′an, a. & n. (Inhabitant) of Troy; ~ *War* (between Greeks under Agamemnon & ~s under Priam); (fig.) person who works or fights or endures courageously, esp. *like a* ~. [orig. *Troyan*, *Troian*, f. L *Troianus* f. *Troia* Troy]

trŏll¹, v.t. & i., & n. 1. Sing out in carefree spirit; fish for, fish in (water), fish, with rod & line & dead bait or with spoon-bait (~*ing-spoon*) drawn along behind boat; (arch.) cause (bottle) to circulate at table etc. 2. n. Reel of fishing-rod; ~ing-spoon. [ME ' stroll, roll '; cf. OF *troller* to quest, (M)HG *trollen* roll]

trŏll², n. Supernatural being, giant or (later) friendly but mischievous dwarf, in Scandinavian mythology. [f. ON & Sw. *troll*, Da. *trold*]

trŏll′ey (pl. ~s), **trŏll′y̆**, n. Kind of truck that can be tilted; || costermonger's cart pushed by hand or drawn by donkey; || low truck worked by hand-lever along the rails for conveying railwaymen to work; (also ~*-table*) small table usu. on castors for use in serving food; apparatus consisting of wheel, pole, etc. used for collecting current in electric street-railway (|| ~ *bus*, trackless electric bus running on a highway and collecting current from overhead ~*-wires*; *~-car*, electric street-car); (also ~*-lace*) lace of which the pattern is outlined with thick thread. [of dial. orig., perh. f. TROLL¹]

trŏll′op, n. Slatternly woman; prostitute. Hence ~ISH¹, ~Y², aa. [perh. rel. to TROLL¹, or TRULL]

trŏm′ba, n. (mus.). Trumpet. [It.]

trŏm′bōn|e, n. Large musical instrument of trumpet family with sliding tube or with valves. Hence ~IST(3) n. [It. (as prec., see -OON)]

trŏmm′el, n. (mining). Revolving cylindrical sieve for cleaning ore. [G, = drum]

tromöm′eter, n. Instrument for measuring very slight earthquake shocks. [f. Gk *tromos* trembling + -METER]

trŏmpe, n. Apparatus for producing blast in furnace. [F, = TRUMP¹]

tro̅op, n,, & v.i. & t. 1. Assembled company, assemblage of persons or animals, as *a* ~ *of school-children*, *of antelopes*, *surrounded by ~s of friends*; (pl.) soldiers, as *lost a third of his* ~*s*, HOUSEHOLD ~*s*; cavalry unit consisting of usu. 60 troopers with two lieutenants & captain (cf. COM-PANY), command of this (*get one's ~*, be promoted captain); unit of artillery & armoured formation; particular call of drum as signal for marching; company of performers, troupe; ~-carrier, large aircraft for transporting~s; ~-horse, cavalry horse; ~'ship, transport. 2. vb. Assemble, flock together, (often up, together, etc.); move along in a ~ (along, in, out, etc.); (w. pl. subject) walk hurriedly off, away; form (regiment) into ~s; || ~ing the colour, ceremony at public mounting of garrison guards. [f. F troupe f. med. L troppus flock, of Gmc orig.]

troop'er, n. Horse-soldier, private soldier in cavalry and armoured unit; swear like a ~ (much); cavalry horse; troopship. [-ER¹]

tropae'olum, n. Indian cress, kinds of trailing plant with spurred yellow or scarlet flowers including NASTURTIUM (2nd sense). [mod. L f. Gk tropaion TROPHY, w. ref. to likeness of flower & leaf to helmet & shield]

trope, n. Figurative (e.g. metaphorical, ironical) use of a word; (eccl.) phrase or verse introduced as embellishment into some part of the mass. [f. L f. Gk tropos turn, way, trope, (trepō turn)]

troph'ic, a. Concerned with nutrition, as ~ nerves. [f. Gk trophikos (trophē nourishment f. trephō nourish +-IC)]

tropho-, comb. form of Gk trophē food, as ~neurōs'is, defective nutrition due to nervous derangement.

troph'|ў, n. (Gk ant.) arms etc. of vanquished enemy set up on field of battle or elsewhere to commemorate victory; Roman memorial of victory in imitation of this but usu. permanent; anything, e.g. captured standard, kept as memorial of victory (lit. & fig.); prize; memento; ornamental group of symbolic or typical objects arranged on wall etc. Hence (-)~iED² (-Id) a. [f. F trophée f. L f. Gk tropaion (tropē rout f. trepō turn)]

trop'ic, n. & a. 1. Parallel of latitude 23° 27′ north (~ of Cancer) or south (~ of Capricorn) of the equator; the ~s, region between these; each of the two corresponding circles on celestial sphere where sun appears to turn after reaching greatest declination; ~-bird, kinds of bird like tern seen usu. in the ~s. 2. adj. = foll. exc. last sense. [ME, f. L f. Gk tropikos (kuklos) tropic (circle) f. tropē turning, solstice, (trepō turn), see -IC]

trop'ical, a. Of, peculiar to, suggestive of, the tropics, as ~ plants, diseases, heat, abscess (of liver, induced by residence in hot climate); ~ year (between two successive passages of sun through same equinox); (fig.) fervid, passionate; [f. TROPE] figurative. Hence ~LY² adv. [-AL]

tropicopŏl'itan, a. & n. (Animal, plant) confined & common to the tropics. [f. TROPIC on cosmopolitan]

tropŏl'ogў, n. Figurative use of words; figurative interpretation esp. of the Scrip-

tures, so trŏp'IST(2)n. Hence tropolŏ'gi-CAL a., tropolŏ'gicalLY² adv. [f. LL f. Gk tropologia (TROPE, -LOGY)]

trop'opause (-z), n. Narrow layer between troposphere & stratosphere. [f. Gk tropos turn +PAUSE]

trop'osphēre, n. Layer of atmospheric air extending about seven miles upwards from the earth's surface, in which temperature falls with height (cf. STRATOSPHERE). [f. Gk tropos turn +SPHERE]

trŏpp'o, adv. (mus.). Too, as andante etc. ma non ~ (but not too much so). [It.]

trŏt, v.i. & t. (-tt-), & n. 1. (Of horses etc.) proceed at steady pace faster than walk lifting each diagonal pair of legs alternately with brief intervals during which body is unsupported; cause (horse etc.) to do this; (of person) run at moderate pace esp. with short strides (often along etc.); perform (distance) by ~ting; bring (person, horse, etc.) to specified condition by ~ting, as ~ted him off his legs, to death; ~ out, cause (horse) to ~ to show his paces, (fig.) produce, introduce, (person, thing, superior information, subject) to excite admiration. 2. n. Action, exercise, of ~ting, as proceeded at a ~, went for a ~; (fig.) brisk steady movement or occupation, as kept him on the ~ (busy); || toddling child. [ME, f. OF troter; n. f. OF trot]

trŏth, n. (arch.). Truth, esp. (in)~, truly, upon my word; plight one's ~, pledge one's word esp. in betrothal. [ME trowthe, for OE trēowth TRUTH]

trŏtt'er, n. In vbl senses; also or esp.: horse of special breed noted for trotting; (pl.) animal's feet used as food, as pigs', sheep's, ~s; (joc.) human foot. [TROT, -ER¹]

trŏttoir' (-twahr), n. Side pavement. [F]

trŏt'ўl, n. (chem.). Trinitrotoluene. [(trini)trot(oluene) +-YL]

trou'badour (-ōō-, -oor), n. Lyric poet of a class originating in Provence (cf. TROUVÈRE) in 11th c. [F, f. Pr. trobador f. trobar (F trouver) find, invent, compose in verse]

trou'ble (trŭb-), v.t. & i., & n. 1. Agitate, disturb, be disturbed or worried, as ~d waters, don't let it ~ you, don't ~ about it, has been ~d about or with money matters, a ~d countenance; afflict, as, am ~d with neuralgia, how long has it been troubling you?; subject, be subjected, to inconvenience or exertion (chiefly in polite formulas), as may I ~ you to shut the door?, to mind your own business?, will ~ you for (to pass) the mustard, sorry to ~ you, don't ~ (to explain etc., or abs.), why should I ~ (myself) to explain? 2. n. Vexation, affliction, as has been through much ~, till this great ~ came upon them, life is full of small ~s; disease, as liver, digestive, ~s; inconvenience, unpleasant exertion, source of this, as did it to spare you ~, shall not put you to any ~ in the matter, fear the child is a great ~ to you, will never take the ~ to write, is incapable of taking ~, an omelette is no ~ (to make), French beans are a great ~ to prepare, (as polite formula) no ~ (at all); ask or look for ~ (colloq.), meddle, be rash, etc.; be in, get into, ~, incur censure, punishment, etc.; (mining) small fault; *~-shooter (colloq.), man employed to detect and correct (esp. mechanical) faults. [ME, f. OF trubler etc., f. Rom. *turbulare f. *turbulus = cl. L turbidus; n. f. OF truble (f. vb)]

trou'blesome (trŭbls-), a. (Of person or thing) causing trouble, vexatious. Hence ~LY² adv., ~NESS n. [-SOME]

trou'blous (trŭb-), a. (arch.). Full of troubles, agitated, disturbed, as ~ times. [ME, f. OF troubleus (TROUBLE, -OUS)]

trough (-ŏf, -awf, -ŭf), n. Long narrow open wooden or other receptacle for holding water or food for sheep etc., kneading dough, washing ore, etc.; wooden or other channel for conveying liquid; ~ of the sea, hollow between two waves; ~ of barometric depression, line of greatest depression in area of moving barometric pressure. [OE, OS, ON trog, OHG troc, f. Gmc *trugaz, cogn. w. TREE]

trounce, v.t. Beat severely, castigate, (lit. & fig.). Hence **troun'CING**¹ n. [16th c. ' afflict ', of unkn. orig.]

troup|e (-ōō-), n. Company of actors, acrobats, etc. Hence ~'ER¹ n., member of a theatrical ~e. [F, see TROOP]

trous'er (-z-), n. (Pl., also pair of ~s) two-legged outer garment reaching from waist to ankles; (vulg.) pair of ~s, as here, again, is a smart & dressy ~; ~-button (of certain sizes & materials); ~ or ~s pocket (esp. as holding one's money, or hands when idle); ~-stretcher, apparatus for stretching ~s to preserve shape; early 19th-c. woman's long frilled drawers reaching to ankles. Hence ~ED²(-zerd) a., ~ING¹(3) n. [extended pl. form, after drawers, of arch. trouse sing., f. Ir. (& Sc. Gael.) triubhas TREWS]

trousseau (trōōsō', trōō'sō), n. (pl. ~s, or ~x pr. -z). Bride's outfit of clothes etc. [F, lit. bundle, dim. of trousse TRUSS]

trout, n. (pl. usu. same), & v.i. 1. Kinds of freshwater fish esteemed as food & game; ~-coloured, (of white horse) speckled with black, bay, or sorrel. 2. v.i. Fish for ~. Hence ~'LET, ~'LING¹, nn., ~'Y² a. [OE truht f. LL tructa]

trouvaille (see Ap.), n. Lucky find, windfall. [F]

trouvère (trōōvār'), n. Epic poet of a class originating in N. France (cf. TROUBADOUR) in 11th c. [OF nom. form (acc. trovĕor) used as equivalent of Pr. (acc.) trobador, see TROUBADOUR]

trove. See TREASURE.

trov'er, n. (law). Acquisition of personal property; common-law action to recover value of personal property wrongfully taken or detained. [OF = find (-ER⁴)]

‖ **trow** (-ō, -ow), v.t. (arch.). Think, be-

lieve; (added to question) what ails him, (I) ~ (I wonder)? [OE trūwian (trūwa faith), trēowian (trēowe faith)]

trow'el, n., & v.t. (-ll-). 1. Mason's or bricklayer's flat-bladed tool for spreading mortar etc.; lay it on with a ~, (fig.) flatter grossly; gardener's scoop for lifting plants etc. 2. v.t. Apply (plaster etc.) dress (wall etc.), with ~. [ME, f. OF truele f. med. L truella f. L trulla dim. of trua ladle etc.]

troy, n. (Also ~ weight) system of weights used for gold & silver (cf. AVOIRDUPOIS), as weighs 3 lb. 5 oz ~, ~ pound contains 12 oz, 5760 grains. [ME, prob. f. Troyes, town in France]

tru'ant (-ōō-), n., a., & v.i. 1. One who absents himself from place of work, esp. child who stays away from school without leave; play ~, stay away thus; ~-school (hist.), industrial school for ~ children. 2. adj. (Of person, conduct, character, thoughts, etc.) shirking, idle, loitering, wandering. 3. v.i. Play ~. Hence **tru'ANCY** n., ~LY² adv., (-ōō-). [ME & OF, prob. f. Celt. (W truan, Gael. truaghan, wretched)]

truce (-ōō-), n. (Agreement for) temporary cessation of hostilities (FLAG⁴ of ~); respite from pain etc., rest from work etc. (a ~ to —, arch., demand that — shall cease); ~ of God (hist.), suspension of private feuds esp. during certain church festivals etc. Hence ~'LESS a., **tru'CIAL** (-ōōshl) a., of or bound by a ~ (only in ref. to ~ of 1835 between Britain & certain Sheikhs of Oman Peninsula, as in trucial chiefs). [ME trewes, pl. of trewe, f. OE trēow (Goth. triggwa) compact, faith, see TRUE]

trŭck¹, v.i. & t., & n. 1. Make an exchange, trade, bargain, (with person for thing); exchange (thing for another); hawk (wares) about. 2. n. Exchange, barter, traffic, (have no ~ with, avoid dealing with); small wares; *market-garden produce; (colloq.) rubbish, (fig.) nonsense, as shall stand no ~; (hist.; also ~ system, tommy) practice of paying workmen in goods instead of money or in money on the understanding that they will buy provisions etc. of their employers, T~ Acts (of 1831 & 1870, providing for suppression of or inquiry into ~ system), ~ shop (conducted on ~ system). [ME, f. OF troquer; = med. L trocare; n. f. AF truk, OF troque (f. troquer)]

trŭck², n., & v.t. 1. Strong usu. four or six wheeled vehicle for heavy goods; ‖ open railway wagon; motor vehicle for transporting goods, troops, etc.; porter's two, three, or four, wheeled barrow for luggage at railway station etc.; set of wheels in framework for supporting whole or part of railway-carriage etc.; (naut.) wooden disc at top of mast with holes for halyards; (now rare) small tireless wheel; ~-bolster, crossbeam on car-~

supporting one end. **2. v.t.** Convey on ∼.
Hence ∼'AGE(3, 4) n. [f. L f. Gk *trokhos*
wheel; or short for TRUCKLE in sense
' wheel, pulley ']

trŭc'kle, v.i., & n. **1.** Submit obsequiously, cringe, (*to*), whence **trŭck'IER**[1] n.
2. n. (Usu. ∼-*bed*) low bed on wheels that
may be wheeled under another, esp. as
formerly used by servants etc. [ME =
AF *trocle* f. L TROCHLEA; vb f. (to sleep in
a) *truckle-bed*]

trŭc'ŭl|ent (*or* troo-), a. Of or showing
bellicose aggressive merciless temper.
Hence *or* cogn. ∼ENCE, ∼ENCY, nn.,
∼entLY[2] adv. [f. L *truculentus* (*trux trucis*
fierce, see -LENT)]

trŭdge, v.i. & t., & n. **1.** Walk esp. laboriously, perform (distance) thus. **2.** n. Such
walk. [16th c., of unkn. orig.]

trŭdg'en, n. ∼ (*stroke*), swimming with
alternate right & left over-arm strokes &
ordinary leg action. [J. *T*∼, person]

true (-oo), a., adv., & v.t. **1.** In accordance
with fact or reality, not false or erroneous,
as *his story is* ∼, *that is only too* ∼, *is it* ∼
that he refused?; *a dream came* ∼ (was
realized in fact); (as formula of concession), ∼, *it would cost more*. **2.** In accordance with reason or correct principles
or received standard, rightly so called,
genuine, not spurious or hybrid or
counterfeit or merely apparent, having
all the attributes implied in the name, as
could not form a ∼ *judgement, frog is not a*
∼ *reptile, is a* ∼ *benefactor, the* ∼ *heir,* ∼
ribs (complete, articulating with breast-
bone, not floating), ∼ HORIZON. **3.** Accurately conforming *to* (type etc.). **4.** (Of
voice) in perfect tune. **5.** Loyal, constant,
adhering faithfully, (*to* one's word, friend,
one*self*, etc.; often ∼ *as steel*). **6.** (Of
wheel, post, beam, etc.) in correct position,
balanced or upright or level. **7.** (arch.).
Not given to lying, veracious; honest, as
∼ *men*. **8.** ∼ *bill*, bill of indictment endorsed by grand jury as being sustained
by evidence; ∼-*blue* a. & n., (person) of
uncompromising principles or loyalty;
∼-*born*, of genuine birth, truly such by
birth, as *a* ∼-*born Englishman*; ∼-*bred*, of
genuine or good breed; ∼-*hearted*(*ness*);
∼-*love*, person truly loved or loving,
sweetheart, plant with four leaves
arranged like ∼-*love*(*r's*) *knot* (kind of
double knot with interlacing bows on
each side); ∼'*penny* (arch.), honest fellow.
9. adv. Truly (rare exc. w. certain vbs, as
tell me, aim, breed, ∼). **10.** v.t. Bring
(tool, wheel, frame, etc.) into exact position or form required. Hence ∼'NESS n.
(rare). [OE *treowe*, OS, OHG *triuwi*,
ON *tryggr*, Goth. *triggws*, f. n. repr. by
OE *treow* f. Gmc **triww-*, see TRUCE]

trŭf'fl|e (*or* troo-), n. Subterranean fun-
gus used for seasoning dishes. Hence
∼ED[2] (-ld) a. [prob.: f. MDu. *truffel*, f. obs.
F *truffel* (mod. *truffe*)]

‖ **trŭg,** n. Wooden milk-pan; shallow gar-

den basket made or wood strips. [perh.
dial. var. of TROUGH]

tru'ism (-oo-), n. A self-evident or indisputable truth; proposition that states
nothing not already implied in one of its
terms (e.g. *I don't like my tea too hot* = *I
don't like it hotter than I like it*); hackneyed
truth, platitude. [f. TRUE + -ISM]

trŭll, n. (arch.). Prostitute. [16th c.,
= G *trulle*, TROLLOP]

tru'lÿ (-oo-), adv. Sincerely, genuinely, as
am ∼ *grateful, a* ∼ *alarming state of affairs,
a* ∼ *courageous act*; (as purely neutral
formula for closing letter) *yours* (*very*) ∼
W. Jones, (hence, joc.) *won't do for yours*
∼ (me); (usu. parenthet., & now chiefly
literary or arch.) really, indeed, as ∼, *I
should be puzzled to say*; faithfully, loyally,
as *has served him* ∼; accurately, truth-
fully, as *it has been* ∼ *stated, is not* ∼
represented. [OE *treowlice* (TRUE, -LY[2])]

trumeau (troomo'), n. (archit.; pl. ∼*x*).
Piece of wall, pillar, between two open-
ings, e.g. pillar dividing large doorway.
[F]

trŭmp[1], n. (arch., poet.). Trumpet, its
sound, as *last* ∼, ∼ *of doom*. [ME & OF
trompe, of Gmc. orig.]

trŭmp[2], n., & v.t. & i. **1.** Each card of a
suit temporarily ranking above others, as
a call for ∼s (conventional signal to partner to lead ∼s); ∼ *card*, card turned up to
determine which suit shall be ∼s, any
card of this suit, (fig.) valuable resource;
(colloq.) person of admirable courage, resource, generosity, etc., excellent fellow;
put person to his ∼s, (fig.) reduce him to
his last resources; *turn up* ∼s (colloq.),
turn out better than was expected, (also)
have a stroke of luck. **2. vb.** Defeat (card)
with a ∼, play a ∼ (also fig.); ∼ *up*, fabricate, forge, (story, excuses, etc.). [cor-
rupt. f. TRIUMPH in same (now obs.) sense]

trŭmp'erÿ, n. & a. **1.** Worthless finery;
rubbish; nonsense. **2.** adj. Showy but
worthless, delusive, shallow, as ∼ *furniture, arguments*. [ME, f. OF *tromperie*
(*tromper* deceive, -ERY)]

trŭmp'ĕt, n., & v.t. & i. **1.** Wind instrument of brass, the developed orchestral
form having valves (occas. slides) increasing the sounding length of the tube
& thus giving extra harmonic series, so
making all notes instantaneously available; reed-stop in organ imitating this;
trumpeter, esp. (hist.) one sent as envoy;
EAR, SPEAKING, -∼; ∼-*shaped* thing e.g.
kind of funnel; sound (as) of ∼; *feast of*
∼s, Jewish festival celebrating beginning
of year; FLOURISH[2] *of* ∼s; BLOW[1] one's *own*
∼. **2.** ∼-*call*, call by sound of ∼, (fig.)
urgent summons to action; ∼-*conch*,
-*shell, sea*-∼, kinds of gasteropod with
turreted shell; ∼-*flower*, -*leaf*, kinds of
plant with ∼-*shaped* flowers, leaves;
∼ *major*, head trumpeter of cavalry
regiment. **3. vb.** Proclaim (as) by sound
of ∼ (usu. fig., = celebrate), blow ∼, (of

elephant etc.) make loud sound as of ∼.
[ME, f. OF *trompete* dim. as TRUMP[1]]
trump′eter, n. **1.** One who sounds a
trumpet, esp. cavalry soldier giving
signals with trumpet (*be one's own* ∼,
= BLOW[1] one's *own trumpet*). **2.** Kind of
domestic pigeon with peculiar coo, other
birds making trumpetlike sound, esp.
(also ∼ *swan*) a large N.-Amer. swan. [f.
prec. +-ER[1], or F *trompeteur*]
trŭnc′al, a. Of the trunk of a body or
tree. [f. L *truncus* TRUNK +-AL]
trŭnc′ǀāte, v.t., & a. **1.** Cut the top or
end from (tree, body, cone, pyramid,
fig. quoted passage etc.); (cryst.) replace (edge) by plane. **2.** adj. ∼ated,
(bot., zool., of leaf, feather, etc.) ending
abruptly ɐs if cut off at tip, whence
∼ātelY[2] adv. So∼ʌ′TION, ∼atURE (zool.),
nn. [f. L *truncare* (TRUNK), -ATE[2, 3]]
trŭn′cheon (-shn), n. ǁ Short club or
cudgel e.g. that carried by policeman;
baton, staff of authority, esp. (her.) that
of Earl Marshal. [ME, f. OF *tronchon*
stump f. Rom. *truncionem f. L *truncus*
TRUNK]
trŭn′dle, n., & v.t. & i. **1.** Small broad
wheel, e.g. castor; small wheel with
cylindrical teeth; low-wheeled truck;
(also ∼-*bed*)=TRUCKLE-*bed*; head of lower
drum of double capstan. **2.** vb. Roll (t.
& i., of hoop, truck, etc., often *along*,
down, etc.); (sl.) bowl at cricket; hence
trŭnd′ler[1] n. (esp., sl., bowler). [var. of
obs. or dial. *trendle, trindle,* OE *trendel*
circle, see TREND]
trŭnk, n., & v.t. **1.** Main body of tree opp.
to branches & roots; human or animal's
body without head & limbs & tail; main
part of any structure. **2.** (Also ∼-*line*)
main line of railway or canal, telephone
main line (esp. of lines from town to
town). **3.** Large box with hinged lid, often
covered with leather, for carrying clothes
etc. on journey. **4.** Kinds of shaft, conduit, or trough, usu. rectangular & of
wood, for ventilation, separation of ores,
etc. **5.** Open cylinder used instead of
piston-rod in some marine & other
engines (∼-*engines*). **6.** Proboscis esp. of
elephant. **7.** pl. (Also ∼ *hose*) 16th-17th-c.
breeches from waist to middle of thigh.
8. ǁ ∼-*call*, telephone call on ∼-line with
charges according to distance; ∼ *drawers*,
drawers reaching only to knees; ∼-*nail*,
nail with large ornamental head for ∼,
coffin, etc.; ∼-*road*, main road. Hence
∼′FUL n., ∼′LESS a. **9.** v.t. Separate (ore)
by use of∼. [ME, f. OF *tronc* f. L *truncus*]
trŭnn′ion (-yon), n. Supporting cylindrical projection on each side of cannon
or mortar; hollow gudgeon supporting
cylinder in steam-engine & giving passage
to steam. Hence ∼ED[2] (-yond) a. [f. F
trognon core, stump]
trŭss, v.t., & n. **1.** Support (roof, bridge,
etc.) with ∼ (see below). **2.** Fasten (wings
of fowl etc.), fasten wings etc. of (fowl

etc.), before cooking, tie arms of (person)
to his sides; (arch.) fasten, tighten, (garment, usu. *up*), hang (criminal, usu. *up*),
(of hawk etc.) seize (bird). **3.** n. Supporting structure or framework of roof, bridge,
etc., e.g. pair of rafters with tie-beam,
king-post, & struts (∼-*bridge* etc., so
strengthened). **4.** Bundle of old (56 lb.) or
new (60 lb.) hay or (36 lb.) straw. **5.** Compact terminal flower-cluster. **6.** Large
corbel supporting monument etc. **7.**
(naut.). Heavy iron fitting securing lower
yards to mast. **8.** (surg.). Padded belt or
encircling spring used in rupture. [ME;
vb f. OF *trusser* (mod. *trousser*); n. f. OF
trusse (mod. *trousse*)]
trŭst, n., & v. & i. **1.** Firm belief in the
honesty, veracity, justice, strength, etc.,
of a person or thing, as *our* ∼ *is in God,
I repose considerable* ∼ *in him, put no* ∼ *in
him*; confident expectation (*that*). **2.** Person, thing, confided in, as *he is our sole* ∼.
3. Reliance on truth of statement etc.
without examination, as *takes everything
on* ∼. **4.** Commercial credit, as *supplied
with goods on* ∼. **5.** Responsibility arising
from confidence reposed in one, as *am in
a position of* ∼. **6.** (law). Confidence
reposed in person by making him nominal
owner of property to be used for another's
benefit; right of the latter to benefit by
such property; property so held, legal
relation between holder & property so
held, as *have accepted a* ∼, *the property is
merely a* ∼, *is held in* ∼, (attrib.) ∼-*money*.
7. Thing, person committed to one's
care, resulting obligation, as *would not
desert his* ∼, *have fulfilled my* ∼. **8.** (commerc.). Organized association of several
companies for purpose of defeating competition etc., the shareholders in each
transferring all or most of the stock to
central committee & losing their voting
power while remaining entitled to profits.
9. BRAINS *T*∼; ∼-*deed*, deed by debtor
conveying property to trustee for payment of his debts, deed conveying property to creditor to sell & pay himself &
restore the residue, any instrument of
conveyance that creates a ∼. **10.** vb.
Place∼ in, believe in, rely on the character
or behaviour of, as *have never* ∼*ed him, if
we may* ∼ *this account, do not* ∼ *him with*
(let him use) *your typewriter, cat cannot
be* ∼*ed with* (will steal) *milk, would* ∼ *him
with untold gold,* whence ∼′ingLY[2] adv.
11. Consign (thing *to* person etc.), place
or leave (thing *with* person etc., *in* place
etc.), without misgiving. **12.** Allow credit
to (customer *for* goods). **13.** Entertain
an earnest or (rarely) confident hope, as
I ∼ *he is not hurt*(?), *I* ∼ *to hear better news.*
14. Place reliance *in*; ∼ *to*, place (esp.
undue) reliance on, as *we must* ∼ *to meeting
someone who knows, does not do to* ∼ *to
memory for these things.* [ME *troste,
truste*; n. f. ON *traust* (*traustr* strong); vb
f. ON *treysta,* w. assim. to n.]

trustee', n. Person who holds property in trust for another (‖ *the Public T~*, State official charged, since 1908, with executing wills & trusts when invited); each of a body of men, often elective, managing affairs of college etc. Hence ~SHIP n. [-EE]

trust'ful, a. Full of trust, confiding. Hence ~LY[2] adv., ~NESS n. [-FUL]

trust'worth|y (-ĕrdhĭ), a. Worthy of trust, reliable. Hence ~iNESS n.

trus't|ŷ, a. & n. **1.** (Chiefly arch.) trustworthy, as ~*y steed, sword, servant*, whence ~iLY[2] adv., ~iNESS n.; *trustful. **2.** n. Well-behaved & privileged convict. [ME; -Y[2]]

truth (-ōō-), n. (*pl. pr.* -dhz). Quality, state, of being true or accurate or honest or sincere or loyal or accurately shaped or adjusted, as *the ~ of the rumour is doubted, there is ~ in what he says, may depend on his ~, wheel is out of ~*; what is true, as *have told you the (whole) ~, the ~ is that I forgot, am a lover of ~* (or *T~* personified), *fundamental ~s, home ~s* (unpalatable facts about oneself), GOD'*s ~*, GOSPEL *~*, HALF-~; *in ~* (literary), *of a ~* (arch.), *truly, really; to tell the ~, ~ to tell*, formulas introducing confession. [OE *trēowth* (as TRUE, see -TH[1])]

truth'ful (-ōōth-), a. Habitually speaking truth, veracious; (of tale etc.) true. Hence ~LY[2] adv., ~NESS n. [-FUL]

truth'less (-ōōth-), a. (Of statement) false; (of person) faithless, not adhering to promise etc. Hence ~NESS n. [-LESS]

trŷ, v.t. & i., & n. **1.** Test (quality), test the qualities of (person, thing), by experiment, subject (person etc.) to suffering or hard treatment (as if) for this purpose (whence ~'ING[2] a., ~'ingLY[2] adv.), as *~ (the effect of) soap & water, ~* (buy) *our ginger ale, did you ever ~ quinine* (as cure) *for it?*, *(strength of) rope must be tried before it is used, each machine is tried before it leaves the shops, ~ your hand* (skill) *at, this will ~ his courage, patience has been sorely tried, should not ~ your eyes with that small print*. **2.** Make experiment in order to find out, as *~ how far you can throw, let us ~ which takes longest, whether it will break*; *~* CONCLUSIONS, a FALL[2]. **3.** Investigate (case, issue) judicially, subject (person) to trial (*for* murder etc., also *for* his *life*). **4.** Settle (question, disputed point) by examination or experiment. **5.** Attempt to achieve or perform, as *tried a jump & fell, better ~ something easier*; attempt, endeavour, (*to* do or abs.; colloq. often *&* do, seldom after neg. or quasi-neg. & never after past tense), as *do ~ to* (or *&*) *attend, must ~ to* (or *&*) *get it finished tonight, if at first you don't succeed ~; ~, ~ again, no use ~ing to persuade him, don't ~ to* (rarely *&*) *palliate it, have often tried to mend it*. **6.** (Also *~ up*) dress (roughly-planed board) with *~ing-plane* to give fine sur-

face. **7.** (Also *~ out*) purify (metal, fat, oil) by melting or boiling. **8.** *~ back*, = HARK (intr.) *back*, lit. & fig.; *~ for*, apply or compete for (appointment etc.); *~ on*, put (clothes etc.) on to test fit, begin (*it*, one's *games, tricks*, etc., often *with* person) experimentally to see how much will be tolerated, as *no use~ing it on with me*; *~'on* n. (colloq.), an attempt to deceive; *~ out*, put to the test, test thoroughly; *~'out* n., experimental trial, test of popularity etc. (*he gave the play a ~-out at Brighton*). **9.** *~'sail* (-sl), small fore-&-aft sail set with gaff in heavy weather on mainmast or foremast or supplementary mast instead of mainsail or foresail [f. obs. naut. sense of vb, = lie to]; *~'(ing)-square*, carpenter's square usu. with one wooden & one metal limb; *~works*, apparatus for *~ing* blubber. **10.** n. Attempt (colloq.), as *have* (make) *a ~ at it, for it, to catch it*; (rugby footb.) touching-down of ball by player behind adversaries' goal-line. [ME 'separate, distinguish, etc.' f. OF *trier* of unkn. orig.]

trŷp'anosōme, n. Kinds of blood-parasite some of which cause sleeping-sickness & other diseases. [f. Gk *trupanon* auger, *sōma* body]

trŷp'sin, n. Chief digestive ferment of the pancreatic juice. [f. Gk *tripsis* friction (because first obtained by rubbing down the pancreas with glycerin)+-IN]

trŷst, n., & v.t. & i. (arch.). **1.** Appointed meeting, appointment, as *keep, break, ~*. **2.** vb. Engage to meet (person), appoint (time, place) for meeting; make a *~*. [ME, = obs. *triste* f. OF *triste* appointed station in hunting, of obsc. hist.]

tsar, czar (z-), n. Emperor of Russia.

tsari'na, czarina (-ēna), n. Empress of Russia. [f. G. (*c*)*zarin* f. TSAR]

tsĕt'sĕ, n. African fly whose bite is often fatal to horses, cattle, dogs, etc. [native]

tsuna'mi (tsōōnah'mĭ), n. Sea wave caused by disturbance of ocean floor or seismic movement. [Jap.]

tuan (tōōahn'), n. Sir, master (used by Malayans as a respectful term of address). [Malay *tuan, tuwan*]

tuata'ra (tōōatah'ra), n. Large iguana-like reptile, peculiar to New Zealand, having a dorsal row of yellow spines. [Maori, = spine on the back]

tŭb, n., & v.t. & i. (-bb-). **1.** Open wooden usu. round vessel of staves held together by hoops used for washing (*wash-~*) or holding butter, liquids, etc. (*let every ~ stand on its own bottom*, everyone look to himself); varying measure of capacity for butter, corn, tea, etc. **2.** Sponge-bath, (colloq.) bath of any kind, bath taken in this, as *jumped into his ~, seldom has a ~, a cold ~ would do him good*. **3.** (mining). Kinds of bucket or box for conveying ore, coal, etc. **4.** Clumsy slow boat (derog.); boat used for practice rowing, as *~-pair, -eight*, etc. (for so many oarsmen). **5.** ~-*thumper*, ranting preacher or orator, so ~-*thumping* a. & n.; ~-*wheel*, bowl-shaped water-wheel, rotating drum for washing skins etc. in. Hence ~'FUL n. **6.** vb. Bathe (t. & i.) in ~; plant in ~; row in ~, coach (oarsman, -men) in ~- -pair; (mining) line (shaft) with wood or iron casing. Hence ~b'ING¹(1, 2) n. [ME *tubbe* = MDu., MLG *tubbe, tobbe*]

tūb′a, n. Bass brass instrument of various sizes & pitches; an organ reed-stop. [L, = trumpet]

tŭbb′|ў̄, a. Tub-shaped, fat & round, corpulent, so ~ISH¹ a.; (of musical instrument) sounding dull, lacking resonance. [-Y¹]

tūbe, n., & v.t. **1.** Long hollow cylinder esp. for conveying or holding liquids etc.; cylinder of thin flexible metal with screw cap for holding paint etc. (~ *colours*, kept in ~s). **2.** Main body of wind instrument. **3.** (anat.). Hollow ~-shaped organ, esp. one conveying air, as *bronchial* ~, whence **tūb′AL, tūb′AR¹,** aa. **4.** *Thermionic valve. **5.** ‖ Each of several tubular electric railways in London. **6.** *Crookes's* ~, vacuum ~ for showing certain phenomena connected with gases; *pneumatic* ~ (for pneumatic dispatch); TEST¹-~; ~- *-flower*, ornamental E.-Ind. shrub of vervain family; ~-*shell*, kinds of bivalve forming shelly ~; ~-*well*, iron pipe with sharp point & perforations at bottom for getting water from underground. **7.** v.t. Furnish with, enclose in, ~ or ~s; ~*d horse* (that has had a metallic ~ inserted in the air-passage). Hence **tūb′ING**¹(2) n. [F, or f. L *tubus*]

tūb′er, n. Short thick part of an underground stem covered with modified buds, e.g. potato, artichoke, whence ~IF′EROUS, ~IFORM, aa.; kinds of underground fungus, truffle; (anat.) swelling part, prominence. [L, = bump, tumour]

tūb′ercl|e, n. Small rounded projection esp. of bone; small granular tumour or nodule formed within the substance of an organ tending to degeneration & (in lungs etc.) to production of pulmonary consumption etc.; (bot.) wartlike excrescence, small tuber. Hence ~ED² (-ld), **tūbẽrc′ūlAR¹, tūbẽrc′ūlATE², aa., tūbẽrc′ūlIN** n., liquid prepared from cultures of ~e bacillus, used esp. as a test for tuberculosis, **tūbẽrc′ūlOID, tūbẽrc′ū-lOSE¹, tūbẽrc′ūlOUS,** aa. [f. L TUBER-*culum* (-CULE)]

tūbẽrcūlā′tion, n. Formation, set, system, of tubercles. [-ATION]

tūbẽrc′ūl(ar)iz|e, -is|e (-īz), vv.t. Infect with tuberculosis. Hence ~A′TION n. [-IZE]

tūbẽrcūlōs′is, n. Disease affecting most tissues of the body marked by tubercles & the presence of a characteristic bacillus; *pulmonary* ~, consumption. Hence **tūbẽrc′ūlOSED²** (-st) a. [-OSIS]

tūb′er|ōse, a. & (*pop. pron.* tūb′rōz) n.

1. Covered with tubers, knobby; of the nature of a tuber; bearing tubers. Hence or cogn. ~ŏs′ITY, ~OUSNESS, nn., ~OUS a. **2.** n. Garden & greenhouse bulb with creamy-white fragrant flowers. [(n. f. L fem. adj.) f. L *tuberosus* (TUBER, see -OSE¹)]

tūb′i-, comb. form of L *tubus* tube, as: ~*corn* a. & n., (ruminant) with hollow horns; ~FORM; ~*ling′ual*, with tubular tongue.

tūb′ūl|ar, a. Tube-shaped; having, consisting of, contained in, tube(s), as ~*ar boiler* (in which heat or water to be heated passes through many tubes), ~*ar bridge,* rectangular tube through which railway etc. passes; (of sound in breathing) like sound of air passing through tube. So ~OSE¹, ~OUS, aa. [f. as foll. + -AR¹]

tūb′ūle, n. Small tube. Hence **tūb′ūli-** comb. form. [f. L *tubulus* dim. as TUBE]

tŭck¹, v.t. & i., & n. **1.** Gather (material) into flat folds for stitching; draw or thrust or roll the parts of (cloth etc. *up, in*) close together, as ~ *in the loose ends,* ~*ed up his shirt-sleeves* (so as to leave arms bare); draw together into small compass, as ~*ed his legs under him like a tailor,* bird ~s *his head under his wing*; cover (person, one*self*) snugly & compactly *up* or *in,* as ~*ed himself up in bed*; stow away (thing *in* corner etc., *away,* etc.); (of spare material etc.) be disposed of by ~*ing away*; empty (seine) by means of small one; (sl.) hang (criminal) *up* ; ~ *in* (sl.), eat heartily (*at* food, or abs.). **2.** n. Flat fold, often one of several parallel folds, in fabric fixed in place by stitches as ornament or to dispose of spare stuff, as *make a* ~ *in sleeves* (when too long); (naut.) part of vessel's hull where after planks meet; ‖ (sl.) eatables esp. pastry & sweets, ~-*in,* -*out,* full meal, ‖ ~-*shop* (where ~ is sold); ~-*net,* -*seine,* small net for taking fish from larger one; ~-*point-ing,* method of pointing brickwork with coloured mortar, a central groove in which is filled with fine white lime putty, projecting slightly. [ME *tukke, tokke,* f. MDu., MLG *tucken, tokken,* = OHG *zucken,* pull, pluck]

tŭck², n. (arch.). Blast, flourish, of trumpet; (Sc.) ~ (beat) *of drum.* [f. ME (now dial.) *tuck* vb f. ONF *to(u)ker* (OF *tochier*) TOUCH¹]

tŭck′er¹, n. In vbl senses; also or esp.: piece of lace, linen, etc., covering neck & shoulders of woman in 17th & 18th c. (*best* BIB² *&* ~); part of sewing-machine used in making tucks; ‖ (sl.) food. [TUCK¹ + -ER¹]

***tŭck′er²,** v.t. (colloq.). Tire, weary (usu. ~ *out*). [f. TUCK¹ (vb)]

tŭck′ét, n. (arch.). Flourish on trumpet. [conn. w. TUCK²]

tuc′um (tōō-), n. Brazilian palm with fibre used for cordage etc. [Braz.]

-tude, suf. repr. L -*tudo*, -*tudinem* (F -*tude*), forming abstract nn. f. adjj., p. pp., or vb stems; in E direct f. L (*alti*~), thr. F (*soli*~), or on L anal. (*exacti*~).

Tūd'or, a. Of the (period of the) ~*s*, English sovereigns from Henry VII to Elizabeth I, as ~ (late perpendicular) *style* in architecture, ~ *rose*, five-lobed flower, ~ *flower*, trefoil ornament, used in ~ style. [Owen ~ of Wales, grandfather of Henry VII]

Tuesday (tūz'dī), n. Third day of week; SHROVE ~. [OE *Tiwesdæg* (rendering L *dies Martis*) f. *Tiwes* genit. of *Tiw* ancient Teutonic deity identified w. the Roman *Mars*; so OHG *ziestac*, ON *týsdagr*]

tūf'a, n. Rock of rough or cellular texture of volcanic or other origin. Hence **tūfA⁴-CEOUS** (-āshus) a. [It., as foll.]

tūff, n. Kinds of volcanic fragmentary rock; ~-*cone* (of ashes etc. round volcanic opening). [f. F *tuf(fe)* f. It. *tufo* f. L *tofus* soft sandy stone]

tūft, n., & v.t. & i. **1.** Bunch, collection, of threads, grass, feathers, etc., held or growing together at the base, whence **tūf'tY²** a.; (anat.) bunch of small blood-vessels; imperial (beard); ‖ titled undergraduate [from ~ formerly worn on cap]; ~-*hunter*, -*hunting*, one who seeks, practice of seeking, society of titled persons. **2.** vb. Furnish with ~ or ~s; make depressions at regular intervals in (mattress etc.) by passing thread through; grow in ~s. [ME, of obsc. orig.; perh. repr. F *touffe*]

tŭg, v.t. & i. (-gg-), & n. **1.** Pull with great effort or violently; make vigorous pull *at*; tow (vessel) by means of steam ~, (of steam ~) tow (vessel); (fig.) drag (subject etc. *in* etc.) forcibly. **2.** n. ~*ging*, violent pull, as *gave a ~ at the bell*; violent or painful effort, esp. fig., as *felt a great ~ at parting, parting was a ~, had a great ~ to persuade him.* **3.** ‖ (Eton sl.). Colleger. **4.** (Also ~'*boat*) small powerful steam-vessel for towing others. **5.** Loop from saddle supporting shaft or (in double harness) trace; ~-*spring*, spring-frame to which this is fastened to lessen jerk in starting etc. **6.** (mining). Iron hoop to which a tackle is fixed. **7.** ~ *of war*, contest in which each of two groups of persons holding same rope tries to pull the other across line marked between them, supreme contest. [ME *togge*, *tugge*, intensive f. Gmc **teuh-*, **tauh-*, **tug-*, see TOW¹]

tū'ism, n. Doctrine that all thought is addressed to a second person, esp. to one's future self as this. [f. L *tu* thou + -ISM]

tūi'tion, n. Teaching, esp. as a thing to be paid for; fee for this. Hence ~AL, ~ARY¹, aa., (-sho-). [ME, f. AF, OF, f. L *tuitionem* (*tuēri tuit*- watch, guard, see -ION)]

tul'a (tōō-), n. (Also ~-*work*) = NIELLO. [*Tula*, in Russia]

‖ tūl'chan, **-in**, (-χ-), n. (Sc.). Calf-skin stuffed with straw or spread on mound beside cow to make her give milk; ~ *bishops* (hist.), titular bishops in whose names revenues of Scottish sees were drawn by lay barons after Reformation. [Gael., = mound]

tūl'ip, n. Kinds of plant with brilliant bell-shaped flowers of various colours; bell-shaped outward swell of muzzle of gun; ~-*root*, disease of oats causing base of stem to swell; ~-*tree*, N.-Amer. tree with flowers like large greenish-yellow ~s, marked with orange inside. [16th c. *tulipa*, also -*pan*, -*pant* = F (obs.) *tulipan*, *tulipe*, f. Turk. *tulbant* f. Pers. *dulband* TURBAN]

tūlipo|mān'ia, n. Craze for tulips, esp. that in Holland about 1634. Hence ~MAN'IAC n. [prec. + -O- + -MANIA]

tulle (tōōl, & see Ap.), n. Fine silk net used for veils & dresses. [*T*~, city in⸮France]

tūl'wār, n. Sabre used by some N.-Indian tribes. [Hind. *talwār*]

tŭm, **tŭm'tŭm**, n. Sound of banjo or similar instrument. [imit.]

tŭm'ble, v.i. & t., & n. **1.** Fall (*down, over, off, from*, etc.) suddenly or violently; (of waves, sick person, etc.) roll, toss, up & down or from side to side; move, walk, run, in headlong or blundering fashion (*came tumbling along*, ~*d up the stairs*, ~*d into* or *out of bed*); perform acrobatic feats; pull about, disorder, rumple, (clothes, hair, etc.); overturn, fling headlong, throw or push (*down, out, in*, etc.) roughly or carelessly; bring down (bird, hare, etc.) by shooting; polish (castings etc.) in tumbling-box. **2.** ~ *in*, fit (piece of timber) into another, (naut., also ~ *home*, of ship's sides) incline inwards above extreme breadth, (sl.) go to bed; ~ *to* (sl.), understand, grasp, (idea etc.). **3.** n. Fall, as *had a slight, nasty*, etc., ~ ; somersault or other acrobatic feat; untidy or confused state, as *things were all in a* ~. **4.** ~-*bug*, kinds of dung-beetle; ~*down*, dilapidated. [ME *tumbel*, frequent. f. OE *tumbian* (-LE(3)); cf. MLG *tummeln*, OHG *tumalōn*]

tŭmb'ler, n. In vbl senses; also or esp.; one who turns somersaults etc., acrobat; kind of pigeon that turns somersaults during flight; toy figure of sitting mandarin etc. contrived to rock when touched; flat-bottomed stemless drinking-glass (formerly with rounded bottom so as not to stand upright), whence ~FUL n.; part of the mechanism of a lock or gunlock. [ME; ~ER¹]

tŭmb'ling, n. In vbl senses; ~-*barrel*, -*box*, -*wheel*, revolving box or barrel containing emery-powder etc. in which castings etc. are cleaned by friction against each other or the walls of the box; ~-*bob*, weighted lever reacting when lifted to a certain point. [15th c.; -ING¹]

‖ tŭm'brel, **-il**, n. (hist.). Two-wheeled covered cart for carrying tools, ammunition, etc.; dung-cart; open cart used in French Revolution to convey victims to the guillotine; instrument of punishment perh. the same as CUCKING-STOOL. [ME, f. OF *tumb-*, *tomberel*, f. *tomber* fall]

tŭm′ė|fў, v.t. & i. (Cause to) swell, inflate; be inflated, (lit. & fig.). So ~FA′CIENT (-áshnt) a. (path.), ~FAC′TION n. (path.). [f. F *tuméfier* f. L *lumēre* swell, see -FY]

tŭm′ĭd, a. (Of parts of body etc.) swollen, inflated, so tŭmēs′CENCE n., tŭmēs′CENT a.; (fig., of style etc.) inflated, bombastic. Hence or cogn. tŭmĭd′ITY, ~NESS, nn., ~LY² adv. [f. L *tumidus* (*lumēre* swell, -ID¹)]

tŭmm′ў, n. (nursery). = STOMACH. [-Y³]

tŭm′our (-mer), n. Local swelling esp. from morbid growth; *malignant* ~ (tending to recur after removal & cause death, opp. to *benign* ~). [f. L *tumor* (*lumēre* swell, -OR)]

tŭm′tŭm¹, n. W.-Ind. dish of boiled plantains beaten soft in a mortar; (Anglo--Ind.) light vehicle, dog-cart. [orig. unkn.]

tŭmtum². See TUM.

tŭm′ŭlt, n. Commotion of a multitude esp. with confused cries etc.; noisy uprising of mob etc.; uproar; confused & excited state of mind, as *the* ~ *within him had subsided*. Hence or cogn. tŭmŭl′tūARY¹ (esp. undisciplined, riotous), tŭmŭl′tūous (esp. vehement, uproarious), aa., tŭmŭl′tūousLY² adv., tŭmŭl′tūousNESS n. [ME, f. L *tumultus* f. *tumēre* swell]

tŭm′ŭl|us, n. (pl. ~ī). Sepulchral mound often enclosing masonry. Hence or cogn. ~AR(Y)¹ aa. [L (*lumēre* swell)]

tŭn, n., & v.t. (-nn-). 1. Large cask for wine, beer, etc., esp. formerly as measure of capacity (252 wine gallons); brewer's fermenting-vat; ‖ ~′*dish*, kind of funnel esp. in brewing. 2. v.t. Store (liquor) in ~. [OE *tunne*, = OHG, ON *lvnna*, f. Gaulish *tunna*]

tŭn′a, n. The Californian TUNNY. [f. Sp.--Amer. *atún* TUNNY]

tun′dra (tōō-), n. Barren arctic regions where subsoil is frozen. [Lappish]

tūne, n., & v.t. & i. 1. Melody with or without harmony, air, as *psalm*, *hymn*, ~~; correct intonation in singing or playing, due adjustment of instrument for this, as *piano is out of* ~, *sings out of* ~, *must learn to sing in* ~. 2. Agreement, concord, harmonious relation, as *in*, *out of*, ~ *with* one's *surroundings* or *company*; suitable mood (*for* purpose etc.). 3. Change one's ~, *sing another* ~, assume a different style of language or manner, e.g. change from insolent to respectful tone; *to the* ~ (serious or exorbitant amount) *of £5* etc. 4. vb. Put (violin, piano, etc.) in ~, whence tŭn′ER¹(1, 2) n.; (fig.) adjust, adapt, (thing *to* standard, purpose, circumstances, etc.); be in harmony (*with*, lit. & fig.); (poet.) produce

(music), as *lark* ~*s his song*; express, celebrate, in music. 5. ~ *in*, set wireless instrument to right wave-length; ~ *up*, (of orchestra) bring instruments to common pitch, begin to play or sing, (joc., of child) begin to cry. Hence tŭn′ABLE a., tūn′ableNESS n., tūn′abLY² adv. [ME unexpl. phon. var. of TONE¹]

tūne′ful (-nf-), a. Melodious, musical. Hence ~LY² adv., ~NESS n. [-FUL]

tūne′lėss (-nl-), a. Not in tune; unmelodious; (of mus. instrument) not played, silent. [-LESS]

tŭng′oil, n. An oil used chiefly for varnishing woodwork, obtained from the Chinese *lung-tree*. [Chin. *yu t'ung*]

tŭng′st|en, n. Wolfram, a steel-grey heavy metallic element with very high melting-point, used for the filaments of electric lamps and for alloying steel etc. Hence ~ATE¹(3) n., ~IC, ~OUS, aa. (chem.). [Sw. (*tung* heavy + *sten* stone)]

tūn′ĭc, n. 1. Ancient Greek or Roman short-sleeved body-garment reaching about to knees; woman's loose blouse or coat gathered or belted at waist; close--fitting short coat of uniform of soldier, policeman, etc. 2. (Zool.) leathery envelope of ascidia etc.; (anat.) membrane enclosing an organ; (bot.) any of the layers of a bulb, integument of a part; whence ~ATE¹ a. (zool., anat., bot.), & n. (zool.); (eccl.) = foll. [f. F *tunique* or L *tunica*]

tūn′ĭcle, n. Fine or delicate tunic (esp. bot., zool.); (eccl., esp. R.-C. Ch.) short vestment of subdeacon at eucharist etc., (pl.) this & dalmatic worn by bishop. [ME, f. L *tunicula* dim. as prec.]

tūn′ing, n. In vbl senses; ~*-fork*, two--pronged steel fork designed to give particular note (esp. middle C) when struck; ~*-hammer*, hammer-shaped wrench for altering tension of strings in piano etc. by turning the pegs (~*-pegs*, *-pins*) to which they are attached. [-ING¹]

tunnage. See TONNAGE.

tŭnn′el, n., & v.t. & i. (-ll-). 1. Artificial subterranean passage through hill etc. or under river etc.; subterranean passage dug by burrowing animal; (mining) adit or level open at one end; main flue of chimney; ~*-borer*, kinds of machine for making ~s; ~*-net*, fishing-net wide at mouth & narrow at other end. 2. vb. Make a ~ through (hill etc.); furnish with ~; make one's way (*through*, *into*, etc.), make one's *way*, by ~ling. [ME, f. OF *tonel* & *tonnelle*, dim. of *tonne* TUN]

tŭnn′ў, n. Large oceanic scombroid fish used as food. [f. F *thon* f. Prov. *ton*, f. L f. Gk *thunnos*]

tūn′|ў, a. (Of music) having marked or catchy tunes. Hence ~iNES₀ n. [TUNE, -Y²]

tŭp, n., & v.t. (-pp-). 1. Male sheep, ram; striking-face of steam hammer etc. 2. v.t. Copulate with (ewe). [ME *tope*, *tupe*, of unkn. orig.]

tūque (-k), n. Kind of Canadian cap. [Canad. F form of TOQUE]

tū quó′qué, n. The retort *So are* (or *did* etc.) *you*. [L, = you too]

turacou, turako. Varr. of TOURACO.

Tūrān′ian, a. Of the Asian languages that are neither Semitic nor Indo-European, esp. of the Ural-Altaic group of languages. [f. Pers. *Turān* region beyond Oxus, + -IAN]

tūrb′an, n. Oriental man's head-dress of scarf wound round cap; modification of this, esp. early-19th-c. European woman's head-dress; (later) woman's or child's hat with narrow or no brim; spire of univalve shell; ~-*shell*, kinds of gasteropod or shell ; ~-*stone*, Mohammedan pillar tombstone with ~ carved on top; ~-*top*, kind of mushroom. Hence ~ED[2] (-nd) a. [16th c. also *tulbant* etc., f. Turk. *tulbant* f. Pers. *dulband*; see TULIP]

‖ **tūrb′arȳ**, n. Right of digging turf on another's ground; place where turf or peat is dug. [ME, f. AF *turberie* f. OF *turb-, torberie* f. *tourbe* TURF]

tūrb′id, a. (Of liquid or colour) muddy, thick, not clear; (fig.) confused, disordered. Hence ~ITY (-id[2]), ~NESS, nn., ~LY[2] adv. [f. L *turbidus* f. *turba* crowd, disturbance, see -ID[1]]

tūrb′in|ate, a. Shaped like a top or inverted cone, so ~iFORM, ~OID, aa.; (anat., esp. of some nasal bones) of scroll-like formation; whirling like a top. So ~AL a., ~A′TION n. [f. L *turbinatus* (as foll., see -ATE[2])]

tūrb′ine, n. Kinds of water-wheel driven by impact or reaction or both of a flowing stream of water; *air* ~, wheel of similar form driven by wind or by air from tube, *gas* ~ (driven by gas), *steam* ~ (driven by steam jets); ~ *boat* etc. (driven by ~s). [F, f. L *turbo* -*inis* top, whirlwind]

tūrb′it, n. Kind of domestic pigeon with flat head & short beak. [app. f. L *turbo* top, from its figure; cf. TURBOT]

tūrb′o-, comb. form of TURBINE; ~-*jet engine* (having a turbine-driven compressor for supplying compressed air to the combustion chamber); ~-*prop(eller)-engine* (having a turbine-driven propeller).

tūrb′ot, n. Large kind of flat-fish esteemed as food. [ME, f. OF *turbot*, f. OSw. *törnbut* f. *törn* thorn + *but* BUTT[2]; cf. E *thornback, -but*]

tūrb′ül|ent, a. Disturbed, in commotion; tumultuous; insubordinate, riotous. Hence or cogn. ~ENCE n., ~entLY[2] adv. [f. L *turbulentus* (*turba* tumult, see -LENT)]

Tūrc′ō, n. (hist.; pl. ~s). Algerian tirailleur in French service. [F]

Tūrco-, Tūrko-, in comb. Of the Turks. So **Tūrc′oPHIL, Tūrcŏph′iLISM, Tūrc′oPHOBE**, nn. [f. med. L as TURK, -O-]

tūrd, n. (not in polite lang.). Ball or lump of excrement. [OE *tord*, ON *tord(yfill)*]

tūrd′|ïne, a. Thrushlike. So ~iFORM, ~OID, aa. [f. L *turdus* thrush + -INE[1]]

tūreen′, n. Deep covered dish for holding soup etc. at table. [c. 1700 *terrine, -ene* f. F TERRINE (L *terra*, -INE[1])]

tūrf, n., & v.t. 1. Surface earth filled with matted roots of grass etc.; piece of this cut from the ground, sod; (in Ireland) peat; *the* ~, the race-course, occupation or profession of horse-racing, esp. *on the* ~, so occupied; ~-*bound*, covered with close ~; ~ *drain* (covered with ~); ~-*man*, person interested in horse-racing, so ~'ITE[1] n. 2. v.t. Plant (ground) with ~; (sl.) throw (person or thing) *out*. Hence ~'iNESS n., ~'Y[2] a. [OE, OS *turf*, ON *torf(a)*, OHG *zurf, zurba*, MDu., MLG (G) *torf*, f. Gmc **turbh-*]

tūr′g|id, a. Morbidly swollen or inflated or enlarged, whence ~ĕs′CIBLE a.; (fig., of language) pompous, bombastic, inflated. Hence or cogn. ~ĕs′CENCE, ~id′ITY, nn., ~ES′CENT a., ~idLY[2] adv. [f. L *turgidus* (*turgēre* swell, see -ID[1])]

tūr′ion, n. (bot.). Young scaly shoot rising from ground as in asparagus, hops, etc. Hence ~iF′EROUS a. [f. L *turio* -*onis* shoot]

Tūrk, n. 1. Ottoman, Osmanli; member of the people from whom the Ottomans are derived; (trans.) ferocious, wild, or unmanageable person (now chiefly joc. of children); (arch.) Mohammedan; Turkish horse. 2. ~'s *cap*, kinds of lily & other plants with turban-like flowers; ~'s *head*, head on post for sword displays, turban-like ornamental knot, kinds of round brush or broom, kind of baking-pan for cakes. Hence ~'ISM n. [ME, = F *Turc*, med. L *Turcus*, Pers. & Arab. *Turk*]

tūrk′ey, n. (pl. ~s). 1. Large (esp. domestic) gallinaceous bird native of America related to pheasant, esteemed as food & associated with Christmas festivities. 2. (*T*~). Country of the Turks. 3. ~ *buzzard, vulture*, an American vulture; *T*~ *carpet* (made entirely of wool, & of velvety appearance); ~-*cock*, male of ~ (*red as a* ~-*cock*, of person flushed with anger etc.), (fig.) pompous or self-important person; *T*~ *corn*, maize; ‖ *T*~ *leather*, kind treated with oil before the hair side is removed; ~-*poult*, young of ~; *T*~ *red*, a pigment or colour, cotton cloth dyed with this; *T*~ *stone*, kind of oilstone for sharpening knives etc.; ~ *trot*, kind of dance. [16th c., short for *turkey-cock, -hen*, orig. applied to the guinea-fowl, as imported through Turkey, and then erron. to the American bird]

Tūrk′ish, a. & n. 1. (Language) of Turkey or the Turks. 2. ~ *bath*, hot-air bath followed by soaping, washing, rubbing, kneading, etc., (also pl.) building used for this; ~ (= TURKEY) *carpet*; ~ *delight*, a sweetmeat in gelatinous slabs coated with powdered sugar; ~ *music* (produced with instruments of percussion); ~

pound (usu. written £*T*, as £*T50*), coin formerly worth about 18/2 ; ~ *towel* (rough with long nap usu. of uncut loops). [-ISH[1]]

Tŭrk'oman, Tŭrk'man, Tŭrc'o-, n. (pl. ~s). Member of any of various Turkish tribes in Turkestan, Afghanistan, Persia, & Russia ; ~ *carpet*, rich-coloured kind with soft long nap. [f. Pers. *Turkumān* (TURK, *mān-dan* resemble)]

tŭrm'alin(e). See TOURMALIN.

tŭrm'eric, n. E.-Ind. plant of ginger family : powdered root of this as dye--stuff, stimulant. & condiment esp. in curry-powder ; ~-*paper* (saturated with ~ & used as test for alkalis). [16th c. forms *tarmaret* etc., perh. f. F *terre mérite* & med. L *terra merita*]

tŭrm'oil, n., & v.t. **1.** Agitation, trouble. **2.** v.t, (arch., chiefly in p.p.). Agitate, trouble. [16th c., of unkn. orig.]

∥ **tŭrm'ut,** var. of *turnip* used by writers as characteristic of rustic speech.

tŭrn[1], v.t. & i. **I.** General senses. **1.** Move (t. & i.) on or as on axis, give rotary motion to, receive such motion, as *crank* ~*s wheel*, *wheel* ~*s*, ~ *the key in the lock*, ~ *the tap*, *tap will not* ~, *he* ~*ed on his heel(s)*, ~ person *round* one's FINGER, *everything* ~*s* (depends) *on his answer*. **2.** Execute (somersault etc.) with rotary motion. **3.** Change from one side to another, invert, reverse, (fig.) revolve mentally, as ~*s everything upside down* or *inside out* (into state of confusion), *whole world has* ~*ed topsy-turvy*, *umbrella* ~*s inside out*, ~*ed the body with its face upwards*, ~*ed* (inverted) *comma*, ~*ed period* (·), ~ TURTLE, ~ *the* TABLES *on*, ~ *over pages of book* (to read on other side), ~ *over new* LEAF, *not* ~ *a* HAIR, *dress must be* ~*ed* (the soiled outside becoming the inside), ~ one's COAT, ~ *an honest* PENNY, *have* ~*ed the matter over & over in my mind*. **4.** Give new direction to, take new direction, adapt, be adapted, as ~ *your face this way*, *river* ~*s to the right*, ~*ed his flight northwards*, *scarcely know where* or *which way to* ~ (fig. what course to follow, where to seek help), ~*ed to God in her trouble*, ~ one's BACK[1] *on*, ~ *a* DEAF *ear to*; ~ *the edge of* (knife etc., fig. remark etc.), blunt ; ~ *your attention to this*; *have often* ~*ed my thoughts*, *thoughts have often* ~*ed*, *to the subject* ; *can* ~ *his hand to* (learn to do) *anything* ; ~*s even his errors to account* (profits by them) ; *all* ~*s* (tends) *to his profit* ; *tide* ~*s* (at ebb or flow). **5.** Move to other side of, go round, flank, as ~ *the* CORNER; ~ *the scale*, cause it to sink, (fig.) decide question in suspense ; ~ (*the flank* or *position of*) *an army*, pass round so as to attack it from flank or rear ; ~ person's *flank*, outwit him, defeat him in argument etc. **6.** *Be* ~*ed* (have passed the age) (*of*) *40* etc. **7.** Cause to go, send, put, as *was* ~*ed adrift in the world*, ~ *it out into a basin*, *never* ~*ed* (*away*) *a beggar from his door*, *will* ~ (resist or

divert) *a bullet*. **8.** Change (t. & i.) in nature, form, condition, etc., change for the worse, (cause to) become, as ~*ed water into wine*, *has been* ~*ed into a joint stock company*, *fear he will* ~ *crusty*, *has* ~*ed traitor*, *Mohammedan*, *botanist*, *joy is* or *has* ~*ed to bitterness*, ~ (translate) *it into French*, *how would you* ~ *this passage?*, *milk will* ~ (sour), *thunder will* ~ *milk* (sour), ~*ed pale at the thought*, *very thought* ~*s me pale*, *sight of raw meat* ~*s* (nauseates) *my stomach*, *stomach* ~*s at the sight*, *success has* ~*ed his head* (intoxicated him), *head has* ~*ed with success*, *head* ~*s* (with giddiness), *overwork has* ~*ed his brain*. **9.** Shape (object) in lathe, (of material) lend itself (*easily*, *well*, etc.) to treatment in lathe. **10.** Give (esp. elegant) form to, as *can* ~ *a compliment*, *could* ~ *a Latin verse in my day*, *well*--*ed phrase*, *exquisitely*-~*ed wrist*. **II.** Spec. uses with advv. & prepp. **1.** ~ *about*, or, as mil. command, *about* ~ *!*, ~ so as to face in new direction. **2.** ~ *against*, become hostile to. **3.** ~ *down*, fold down ; place (playing-card) face downwards ; reduce flame of (gas, lamp, etc.) by ~*ing tap* etc. ; reject (proposal, its maker, etc.). **4.** ~ *in*, fold inwards ; hand in, give up ; incline inwards, as *his toes* ~ *in* ; (colloq.) go to bed. **5.** ~ *off*, check passage of (water, gas, etc.) by means of tap etc. ; achieve, produce, (epigram, piece of work) ; dismiss (servant etc.) from employment ; (sl.) hang (criminal), marry (couple). **6.** ~ *on* (adv.), give free passage to (water etc.) by ~*ing tap* ; (colloq.) give free scope to, as ~ *on the waterworks*, begin to cry. **7.** ~ *on* (prep.), depend upon ; face hostilely, become hostile to. **8.** ~ *out*, expel ; cause to point or incline outwards, as ~ *out your toes* ; produce (manufactured goods etc.) ; ~ inside out, bring to view, as *made him* ~ *out his pockets* ; assemble for duty etc., as *15 men* ~*ed out* ; get out of bed ; (mil.) ~ *out the guard*, call them from guard-room ; be found, prove to be the case, as *this* ~*s out to be true*, *he* ~*ed out a humbug*, *it* ~*s out that he was never there*, *we shall see how things* ~ *out*. **9.** ~ *over*, cause to fall over, upset ; transfer the conduct of (thing *to* person) ; do business to the amount of, as ~*s over £500 a week*. **10.** ~ *round*, face about ; adopt new opinions or policy. **11.** ~ *to* (prep.), apply oneself to, set about, (work, *doing*). **12.** ~ *to* (adv.) begin work. **13.** ~ *up*, disinter, as *plough* ~*s up skulls* ; make one's appearance, as ~*ed up an hour late*, *unexpectedly* ; (of event, opportunity, etc.) happen, present itself ; (colloq.) cause to vomit, as *the sight* ~*ed me up*. **14.** ~ *upon*, = ~ *on*. **III.** Comb. ~-*bench*, watchmaker's portable lathe ; ~-*buckle*, device for connecting parts of metal rod ; ~-*cap*, revolving chimney-top ; ~'*coat*, one who ~*s his* COAT ; ~'*cock*, person employed to ~ on water for mains etc.; ~-*down*, (of collar) doubled down; ~'*key*, person in charge of prison keys; ~*out*, ~ing-out esp. for duty, strike of employees, assembly of persons to see spectacle etc., equipage, quantity of goods manufactured etc. in given time; ~'*over*, upsetting of carriage etc., semicircular pie or tart, amount of money ~ed over in business, changing of labour in factories etc., ‖ newspaper article running on to next page; ~'*pike*, defensive frame of pikes (hist.), gate set across road to stop carts etc. till toll is paid, such road; ~-*round*, (of ship) process of entering port, discharging cargo, re-loading, & leaving port; ~-*screw*, screw-driver; ~'*side*, giddiness in dogs; ~'*sole*, kinds of plant supposed to ~ with the sun; ~'*spit*, long-bodied short-legged dog formerly used to ~ spit; ~'*stile*, post at entrance of building esp. where admission fee is charged with four horizontal arms that move round as person passes through; ~'*stone*, bird allied to plover; ~-*table*, circular revolving platform for reversing locomotives etc.; ~-*up*, thing ~ed up, (colloq.) commotion. [OE *tyrnan*, *turnian*, in ME reinforced f. OF *turner*, *torner*, f. L *tornare* turn in lathe (*tornus* f. Gk *tornos*)]

tŭrn[2], n. 1. Rotary motion, changed or change of direction or position or tend-ency, deflection, deflected part, bend, as *a single ~ of the handle*, *a ~ of Fortune's wheel* (change of luck), *with a neat ~ of the wrist*, *took a sudden ~ to the left*, *complaint took a favourable ~*, *milk is on the ~* (just turning sour), *tide is on the ~* (turning), *gave a new ~ to the argument*, *path is full of ~s & twists*, *walked along a ~ of the river*; (mil. as wds of command) *right*, *left*, *about*, *~ !*; any of the THREES (*~ A, B, C, D*) in figure-skating. 2. Character, tendency, disposition, forma-tion, as *was of a humorous ~*, *do not like the ~ of the sentence*, *the ~ of an ankle*; *have a fine*, *pretty*, etc., *~ of speed* etc., *be able to go very fast* etc. *on occasion*. 3. Short walk, stroll, drive, ride, or per-formance, as *take a ~ in the garden*, *on a bicycle*, *took a ~ of work*; *short ~s* (songs, recitations, etc., in music-hall etc.). 4. Opportunity, occasion, privilege, obligation, coming successively to each of several persons etc., as *it is your ~ to watch*, *it was now my ~ to be angry*, *must not speak out of* (before or after) *your ~*, *will hear you all in ~* (succession); *we dug by ~s* (in rotation of individuals or groups); *take ~s*, work etc. alternately; *work ~ & ~ about* (alternately), *went hot & cold by ~s*; *did not serve my ~* (purpose); *did me a good*, *an ill*, *~* (service, disservice); *one good ~ deserves another*. 5. (mus.). Kind of grace consisting of principal note with those above & below it. 6. pl. Menses. 7. Each round in coil of rope etc. 8. (print.). Inverted type as tem-porary substitute for missing letter, letter turned wrong side up. 9. (colloq.). Nervous shock, as *gave me quite a ~*. 10. *To a ~*, exactly, perfectly, as *meat is done to a ~* (enough & not too much). [ME, partly f. AF **tŏrn*, **turn*, = OF *torn* (later *tor*, see TOUR), f. L *tornus* (prec.); partly f. prec.]

tŭrn'|er, n. In vbl senses; also or esp.: one who works with lathe, so ~ERY (1, 2, 3) n.; ‖ kind of tumbler-pigeon. [-ER[1]]

tŭrn'ing, n. In vbl senses, esp.: use of lathe; place where road meets another, such road, as *stop at the next ~*, *take the second ~ to the left*; ~-*point*, point in place, time, development, etc., at which decisive change occurs, as *has reached the ~-point*, *this may be the ~-point of his life*. [ME]

tŭrn'ĭp, n. Biennial plant of mustard family; its fleshy globular root used as vegetable & for feeding cattle etc.; ~-*top*, growing top of ~ used as vegetable. Hence ~Y[2] a. (esp. tasting of ~s). [16th c. *turnep*(e), f. Sc. & dial. *neep* (OE *næp* f. L *napus*); first element uncert., perh. f. F *tour* or E *turn*]

tŭrp'entine, n., & v.t. 1. Oleo-resin secreted by several coniferous trees & (*Chian ~*) by terebinth, used in mixing paints & varnishes & in medicine; (also pop. *turps*) oil or spirit of ~; ~-*tree*, tere-binth. 2. v.t. Apply ~ to. [ME, f. OF *ter(e)bentine* f. L *terebinthina* (sc. *resina* resin) (as TEREBINTH, see -INE[2])]

tŭrp'ĕth, n. Cathartic root of an E.-Ind. plant. [ME, f. OF *turbith* or med. L *tur-bith*(*um*) f. Arab. & Pers. *turbid*]

tŭrp'itŭde, n. Baseness, depravity. [F, or f. L *turpitudo* (*turpis* base, see -TUDE)]

tŭrps. See TURPENTINE.

tŭr'quoise (-koiz, -kwoiz), n. Opaque sky--blue or greenish-blue precious stone; ~ *green*, pale colour between green & blue. [ME *turkeis* etc., f. OF *turqueise*, later -*oise* Turkish (*Turc* TURK, see -ESE)]

tŭ'rrĕt, n. Small tower connected with main building whether rising from ground or projecting from wall or corbels; (mil.) low flat usu. revolving tower for gun & gunners in ship or fort; (hist.) square many-storeyed building on wheels used in attacking fortified place; ~ *gun* (for use in revolving ~); ~-*ship* (with guns in ~s). Hence ~ED[2] a. [ME, f. OF *torete* dim. of *tor* TOWER, see -ET[1]]

tŭrric'ŭlate, -ātĕd, aa. (conch.). (Of shell) having a long spire. [f. L *turricula* (*turris* tower, see -CULE, -ATE[2])]

tŭr'tle[1], n. (Now usu. ~-*dove*) kinds of dove, esp. a common wild kind noted for soft cooing & affection for mate & young. [OE *turtla*, -*le* = OHG *turtulo*, -*la*, dim. or assim. form of L *turtur*]

tŭr'tle[2], n., & v.i. 1. Marine reptile encased as tortoise & with flippers used in swim-ming, esp. (also *green ~*) kind much used for soup; MOCK[2] ~; *turn ~* (naut. sl.), capsize; ~-*shell*, tortoise-shell, esp. dark

kind used for inlaying, (also ~-*cowry*)
large handsome kind of cowry. 2. v.i.
Hunt for~s, whence tŭrt′lᴇʀ¹, tŭrt′lɪɴɢ¹,
nn. [app. correl. of earlier *tortue* (see
TORTOISE), assim. to prec.]

Tŭs′can, a. & n. (Language, inhabitant)
of Tuscany; ~ ORDER¹; ~ *straw*, fine
yellow wheat-straw used for hats etc.
[f. L *Tuscanus* (L *Tuscus*, see -AN)]

tŭsh¹, int., n., & v.i. (arch.). Pshaw.
[ME, imit.]

tŭsh², n. Long pointed tooth, esp. canine
tooth of horse. [ME repr. of rare OE
tusc TUSK]

tŭsh′erў, n. (literary). Use of *Wardour
Street* archaisms such as TUSH¹. [-ERY;
word made by R. L. Stevenson]

tŭsk, n., & v.t. 1. Long pointed tooth,
esp. protruding from closed mouth as
in elephant, walrus, etc.; ~like tooth or
part in harrow, lock, etc. Hence (-)~ᴇᴅ²
(-kt), ~′ʏ², aa. 2. v.t. Gore, thrust, tear
up, with ~ or ~s. [ME alt. of OE *tux*
(*tusc*; see TUSH²)]

tŭsk′er, n. Elephant with developed
tusks. [-ᴇʀ¹]

tŭss′er, -ur, -ōre, n. Oak-feeding silkworm yielding strong but coarse silk; (also
~-*silk*) silk of this & some other silkworms.
[f. Hind. *tasar* f. Skr. *tasara* shuttle]

tŭss′ive, a. (med.). Of a cough. [f. L
tussis cough, see -IVE]

tŭs′sle, n., & v.i. Struggle, scuffle, (*with*
person, *for* thing). [orig. Sc. & north.,
dim. of *touse*, see TOUSLE]

tŭss′ock, n. Clump, hillock, of grass etc.;
tuft, lock, of hair etc.; (also ~-*moth*) kinds
of moth with tufted larvae; ~-*grass*, tall
elegant grass on boggy ground in Pata-
gonia etc. Hence~ʏ² a. [16th c., perh.
alt. f. dial. *tusk* tuft]

tŭss′ōre. See TUSSER.

tŭt¹, tŭt-tŭt′, int., n., & v.i. (-tt-). 1. Int.
expr. impatience, contempt, or rebuke.
2. n. This exclamation. 3. v.i. Exclaim
~. [a natural utterance]

‖ tŭt², n. (mining). Job; ~-*work*, piece-
-work (cf. TRIBUTE). [c. 1700, of unkn.
orig.]

tŭt′elage, n. Guardianship; (period of)
being under this. [f. L *tutela* (*tueri tuit-*
or *tut*- watch) + -AGE]

tŭt′elar(ў), aa. Serving as a guardian,
protective; of a guardian, as ~ *authority*.
[f. LL *tutelaris*, L -*arius*, f. *tutela* (prec.,
-AR¹, -ARY¹)]

tŭt′enăg, n. Zinc imported from China
& E. Indies; white alloy like German
silver. [f. Marathi *tuttināg* perh. f. Skr.
tuttha blue vitriol + *nāga* tin]

tŭt′or, n., & v.t. & i. 1. Private teacher,
esp. one having general charge of person's
education; ‖ (Eng. Univv.) college official,
usu. a fellow, directing studies of undergraduates assigned him; (law) guardian
of a minor. Hence or cogn. ~AGE(2),
~ESS¹, ~SHIP, nn., tŭtŏr′IAL a. (also n.,
period of instruction given by a college

~), tŭtŏr′iaɪʟʏ² adv. 2. vb. Act as ~ to,
instruct; exercise restraint over (one*self*,
one's passions, another); make one's
living as ~. [ME, f. AF, OF *tutour* or L
tutor (*tueri tut*- watch, see -OR)]

tŭt′san, n. St-John's-wort, plant once
held to heal wounds etc. [ME, of AF or
OF (unkn.) orig.]

tutti (tŏŏt′ē), mus. direction, & n. All
(voices, instruments) together; (n.) passage for these. [It.]

tutti-frutti (tŏŏt′ē frŏŏtē), n. Confection,
ice-cream, of mixed fruits. [It., = all
fruits]

tŭtt′ў, n. Impure zinc oxide used as
polishing-powder. [ME, f. OF *tutie* f.
med. L *tutia* f. Arab. *tūtiyā*]

tu′tu (tŏŏ′tŏŏ), n. Ballet dancer's short
projecting skirt. [F]

tū′um.' see MEUM.

tu-whit′ (tŏŏ-) n., tu-whoō′ (tŏŏ-) n., &
v.i. (Make) cry of owl. [imit.]

*tŭxēd′ō, n. (pl. ~*s*, ~*es*). Dinner-jacket.
[*T*~, place-name]

tuyère (twēyär′, tŏŏyär′, twēr), twў′er, n.
Pipe through which air is forced into
furnace etc. [earlier *tewire*, *twire*, *tweer*
f. OF *toiere*, mod. F *tuyère*]

twa′ddl|e (-ŏ-), v.i., & n. (Indulge in)
senseless, feeble, or prosy talk. Hence
~ᴇʀ¹ n., ~ʏ² a. [alt. f. earlier *twattle*]

twain, a. & n. (arch.). Two; two persons
or things; *cut* etc. *in* ~ (in two). [OE
twēgen, masc. nom. & acc. of *twā* TWO]

twăng, v.i. & t., & n. 1. (Cause to) make
ringing metallic sound as of string of
musical instrument or bow when plucked,
(derog.) play on *or* on (fiddle etc.) thus,
as *the fiddles* ~*ed*, ~*ed* (*on*) *his fiddle*,
~*ed his bow*, whence ~LE(3) (-ăng′gl) v.i.
& t.; speak, utter, with nasal sound.
2. n. Sound of tense string when plucked,
nasal tone. [imit.]

twănk′ay, n. Kind of green tea. [f.
Chin. *Tun-ki*, name of a stream]

'twas (-oz), arch. or poet. contr. of *it was*.

tway′blāde, n. Kinds of orchid with green
or purple flowers & single pair of leaves.
[*tway* var. of TWAIN + BLADE]

tweak, v.t., & n. 1. Pinch & twist sharply,
pull with sharp jerk, twitch. 2. n. Twitch,
sharp pull, pinch. Hence ‖ ~′ᴇʀ¹ n. (sl.),
boy's catapult. [prob. alt. f. dial. *twick*,
TWITCH]

tweed, n. Twilled woollen or wool-&-
-cotton fabric with unfinished surface &
usu. two colours combined in the yarn,
used esp. for men's clothes & largely
made in S. Scotland; (pl.) suit of ~. [a
trade name originating in a misreading of
tweel, Sc. form of TWILL, helped by assoc.
w. the river *Tweed*]

twee′dle, n. Sound as of fiddle; ~*dum′* &
~*dee′* (-ld-), things differing only or
chiefly in name. [imit.]

'tween, adv. & prep. Between, esp.
~-*decks*, (space) between decks. [ME
abbr.]

‖ **tween'ȳ,' n.** (colloq.). Servant assisting two others e.g. cook & housemaid. [prec. +-Y³]

tweet, n., & v.i. Chirp (of bird). [imit.]

tweez'er, n., & v.t. **1.** (Pl., also *pair of ~s*) minute pair of tongs for taking up small objects, plucking out hairs, etc. **2.** v.t. Extract (hair, thorn, etc.) with ~s. [extended form of *tweezes* (cf. TROUSERS), pl. of obs. *tweeze*, case for small instruments, aphetic f. *etweese = etuis*, pl. of ETUI]

twelfth, a. & n. **1.** Next in order after eleventh (*the ~*, of August, as beginning of grouse-shooting); *T~-day* (after Christmas, festival of Epiphany); *T~-night*, night of this, celebrated with various festivities etc.; *T~-cake*, prepared for T~-night. **2. n.** Each of 12 equal parts. Hence ~'LY² adv. [OE *twelfta* (foll. -TH²)]

twelve, a. & n. One more than eleven, 12, xii; *the T~* (apostles); *T~* TABLES; *in ~s* (duodecimo); *long, square, ~s,* duodecimo pages of sheet variously folded; ~'FOLD a. & adv.; ~'*mo, 12mo,* = DUODECIMO; ‖~² *month,* year, as *has been there a ~month,* (adv.) *this day ~month,* a year hence or ago; ‖~'*pence* (arch. exc. shop), a shilling; ‖~'*penny*, shilling (adj.). [OE *twelf,* OS *twelif,* OHG *zwelif,* ON *tólf,* Goth. *twalif* f. Gmc **twalibhi-* f. **twa* TWO + **libh-,* prob. rel. to LEAVE² (as if = two over)]

twen'tȳ, a. & n. Twice ten, 20, xx; *have told him ~* (several) *times; ~-one, -two,* etc., or *one, two,* etc., *& ~; ~-five,* 25 (rugby footb., hockey), line drawn across ground 25 yds from each goal, ground between this & goal-line; *~mo, ~four'mo,* (*20mo, 24mo*), leaf of sheet folded into 20, 24, equal parts, book made up of such leaves. Hence **twěn'tiETH a. & n.,** ~FOLD a. & adv. [OE *twentig* f. *twen-* two + *-tig* -TY²]

'twere (*-er*), arch. or poet. contr. of *it were*.

‖ **twėrp, n.** (sl.). Bounder, cad.

twi-, twȳ-, = two, double, f. OE *twi-,* comb. form expr. two, occas. twice, in TWILIGHT & in some arch. or pseudo-arch. forms, as : ~'*bill,* double-bladed battle-axe, kind of mattock; ~'*blade,* = TWAY-BLADE; ~'*fold* a. & adv., twofold; ~'*folded*; ~'*forked*; ~'*formed.* [= OHG *zwi-,* ON *tvi,* cogn. w. L *bi-* BI-, Gk *di-* DI-]

twice, adv. Two times (esp. of multiplication), on two occasions, as *~ 3 is 6, told him ~;* doubly, in double degree or quantity, as *~ as strong, has ~ the strength, is ~ the man he was* (~ as strong etc.); (colloq.) *did it in ~* (two attempts or instalments). [OE *twiges* f. *twige* adv. twice +-ES]

‖ **twi'cer, n.** Compositor who is also pressman; (sl.) one who usu. goes to church twice on Sunday. [f. prec. +-ER¹]

twid'dle, v.t. & i., & n. **1.** Twirl idly, esp. ~ *one's thumbs* (for lack of occupation); trifle *with* (object); *twiddling-line,* string attached to compass-gimbal & pulled to make compass-card play freely. **2. n.** Slight twirl. [app. imit., after *twirl, twist,* & *fiddle, piddle*]

twig¹, n. Small shoot or branch of tree or plant; (anat.) small branch of artery etc.; (electr.) small distributing conductor; divining-rod, esp. *work the ~; hop the ~* (colloq.), die. Hence (-)~ğED² (-gd), ~'LESS, ~ğ'Y² (-g-), aa. [north. OE *twigge,* obsc. rel. to OE *twig, twi;* cf. OHG *zwig, zwi;* all f. stem TWI-]

twig², v.t. (colloq.; -gg-). Understand, catch the meaning of, (person, words, plan, *that* etc., or abs.); perceive, observe. [18th c., of unkn. orig.]

twil'ight (-it), n., & v.t. (~ed). **1.** Light from sky when sun is below horizon in morning or (usu.) evening; faint light; (fig.) state of imperfect knowledge, understanding, etc.; ~ *arc(h)* or *curve* (bounding the brightest region of ~ where atmosphere receives solar rays direct); ~ *of the gods* (Norse myth.), conflict in which gods & giants destroyed each other; ~ *sleep,* name of a method of making child-birth painless. **2.** v.t. (rare). Illuminate faintly. [ME (TWI- +LIGHT¹)]

twill, n., & v.t. **1.** Textile fabric in which weft-threads pass alternately over one warp-thread & under (not one as in plain weaving but) two or more thus producing diagonal lines. **2.** v.t. Weave (material) thus (esp. in p.p.). [Sc. & north. var. of obs. *twilly,* OE *twili* = OHG *zwilih,* f. TWI- after L BI(*lix* f. *licium* thread)]

**'twill, arch. or poet. contr. of *it will.*

twin, a., n., & v.t. & i. (-nn-). **1.** Forming, being one of, a closely related or associated pair esp. of children born at a birth, as *~ children, brother(s), sister(s), the T~ Brothers* or *Brethren,* Castor & Pollux, *~ bed(s);* (bot.) growing in pairs; consisting of two closely connected & similar parts; *~ boat, steamer* (with two hulls supporting one deck & having paddle-wheel between them); *~-screw,* steamer with two propellers on separate shafts having opposite twists; *~ set,* woman's matching cardigan and jumper. **2. n.** Each of a closely related pair esp. of children born at a birth; exact counterpart of person or thing; compound crystal one part of which is in a reversed position with reference to the other; *The T~s,* Gemini; SIAMESE ~s. Hence ~'LING¹, ~'SHIP, nn. **3. vb.** Join intimately together, couple, pair, (*with;* t. & i.); ~*ning-machine, -saw* (for cutting out teeth of combs, these being cut in pairs). Hence ~n'ING¹ n., formation of ~ crystals. [OE *twinn* adj. double, f. TWI-; cf. ON *tvinnr*]

twin|e, n., & v.t. & i. **1.** String of two or more strands of hemp, manilla, etc., twisted together; coil, twist, as *snaky ~es;* interlacing, tangle. **2. vb.** Form (thread) by twisting strands together, whence ~'ER¹(2) n.; form (garland etc.) of interwoven material, garland (brow etc.)

with; interweave; coil, wind, (thing *about*, *round*, another); (of plant, snake) coil itself or it*self* (*round*). Hence ~**'**inGLY[2] adv. [OE *twin*, Du. *twijn*, ult. f. stem of TWI-; vb ME *twine*, Du. *twijnen*, goes w. n.]

twinge (-j), v.t. (rare), & n. (Affect with) sharp darting pain, as *conscience* ~*d him*, *a* ~ *of toothache, rheumatism, conscience, remorse*. [OE *twengan*, = MLG *twengen*, OHG *zwengen*; n. (16th c.) f. vb]

twinkl|e (twĭng'kl), v.i. & t., & n. **1.** (Of light, star, etc.) shine with quick gleams, sparkle; (of eyelids, feet in dancing, etc.) move rapidly up & down or to & fro; blink, wink, (one's eyes, or intr. of person or eye); (of eyes) sparkle (*at* jest etc.); emit (light) in quick gleams. Hence ~ER[1] n. **2.** n. Twitching of eyelid, blink, wink; sparkle, gleam, of the eyes, as *a humorous, ~e*; short rapid movement e.g. of feet in dancing; quick tremulous light, glimmer. [OE *twinclian*, frequent. of **twincan*, repr. by ME *twinke*, MHG *zwinken*]

twink'ling, n. In vbl senses, esp. *in a* ~, *in the* ~ *of an eye, in the* ~ *of a* BED[1]*post*, in a moment, very quickly. [-ING[1]]

twirl, v.t. & i., & n. **1.** Revolve (t. & i.) rapidly, spin, whirl, (often *round*); turn (one's *thumbs* etc.) round & round in purposeless way, twiddle. **2.** n. Rapid or idle circular motion, flourish or curl made with pen etc. [16th c., prob. alt., after *whirl*, f. obs. *tirl* THRILL]

twirp. Var. of TWERP.

twist, n., & v.t. & i. **1.** Thread, rope, etc., made by winding two or more strands etc. about one another; kinds of strong silk thread & of cotton yarn; roll of bread, tobacco, etc. in form of ~; paper packet with screwed-up ends. **2.** Act of ~ing, condition of being ~ed, as *give it a* ~, *has a curious* ~, *full of turns & ~s*; jazzlike dance with vigorous bodily contortions. **3.** Manner or degree in which thing is ~ed, e.g. inclination of rifle-grooves, whirling motion given to ball in cricket etc. to make it take special curve. **4.** Peculiar tendency of mind, character, etc. (freq. derog.). **5.** ~ing strain, (angle showing) amount of torsion of rod etc., forward motion combined with rotation about an axis. **6.** || Kinds of mixed drink, as *gin* ~. **7.** || (colloq.). Appetite, as *had a tremendous* ~. **8.** *Damascus* ~, process of ~ing. Damascus iron to form gun-barrel; ~ *of the wrist*, (fig.) dexterity, knack. **9.** vb. Wind (strands etc.) one about another; form (rope etc.) thus; interweave (thing *with* or *in with* another). **10.** Give spiral form to (rod, column, etc.) as by rotating the ends in opposite directions; receive, grow in, spiral form. **11.** Cause (ball, esp. in billiards) to rotate while following curved path. **12.** Twine (flowers etc. *into* garland etc.), make (garland etc.) thus. **13.** Make one's way,

make one's *way*, (*through* crowd, etc., *along*, etc.) in winding manner; dance the ~. **14.** Wrench out of natural shape, distort slightly, as *limbs* ~*ed on the rack, features* ~*ed with pain*, (fig.) *wants to* ~ *my words into an admission of error*; ~ one's *arm*, force his hand or wrist round as torture. **15.** ~ *off*, break off (piece) by ~ing; ~ *up*, ~ (paper etc.) into spiral form. Hence ~'ABLE a. [ME, f. TWI-]

twis'ter, n. In vbl senses; also or esp.: untrustworthy person, swindler; twisting ball in cricket or billiards; girder; inner part of thigh as proper place to rest upon on horseback. [-ER[1]]

twit, v.t. (-tt-). Reproach, upbraid, taunt, (person *with* fault etc.); tease. Hence ~t'inGLY[2] adv. [16th c. *twite*, aphetic f. *atwite* f. OE *ætwîtan* (*æt* at +*wîtan* blame)]

twitch[1], v.t. & i., & n. **1.** Pull (thing *off* etc.) with light jerk; pull at, jerk at, (person's sleeve etc.) esp. to call attention; (of features, muscles, limbs) move or contract spasmodically. **2.** n. Sudden involuntary contraction or movement, sudden pull or jerk; veterinary appliance for stilling horse during operation. [ME *twicche*, = LG *twikken*, MHG *zwicken*, OE *twiccian*, dial. *twick*]

twitch[2], n. = QUITCH. [dial. var.]

twite, n. Bird like linnet. [perh. imit. of cry]

twitt'er, v.i. & t., & n. **1.** (Of bird) utter succession of light tremulous sounds, chirp; utter, express, thus. **2.** n. Such series of sounds; (colloq., also ~A'TION n.) excited state. [ME, imit.; cf. OHG *zwizirōn*]

'twixt, prep. = BETWIXT. [abbr.]

two (tōō), a. & n. **1.** One more than one, 2, ii; *one or* ~, a few (also lit.); *cut, divide*, etc., *in* ~ (into ~ parts); ~ *can play at that game*, threat of retaliation; *put* ~ *& ~ together*, make inference from data; *in* ~ ~*s*, in a very short time. **2.** ~*-cleft* (bot.), divided nearly to the middle in ~ parts; ~*-edged*, (of sword etc.) having an edge on each side, (fig., of argument, compliment, etc.) cutting both ways, ambiguous; ~*-faced*, (fig.) insincere; ~*'fold* a. & adv., double, doubly; ~*-handed*, having ~ hands, (of sword) requiring to be used with both hands, (of saw, game, etc.) to be worked, played, etc., by ~ persons; ~*-handled*, *-legged*, *-tipped*, *-masted*, *-petalled*, *-toothed*, etc., (having ~ handles etc.); ~*-line* a. (print.), having a depth double that of the size specified, as ~*-line pica*; || ~*pence* (tŭp'ns), sum of, silver coin (now only as maundy money) worth, ~ pence (~*pence coloured*, cheap &, as opp. *penny plain*, gaudy); || ~*penny* (tŭp'enĭ), (adj.) worth or costing ~pence, cheap, worthless, (n.) kind of beer orig. sold at ~pence a quart (hist.), (sl.) *tuck in your* ~*penny* (head, at leap-frog); || ~*penny-halfpenny* (tŭp'enĭ hāp'nĭ), contemptible, insignificant, trumpery; ~-*ply*, of ~ strands, layers, or thicknesses, as ~-*ply rope, carpet*; ~-*sided*, having ~ sides, aspects, etc.; ~-*speed*, adapted for ~ rates of speed, as ~-*speed gear, bicycle*; ~-*step*, kind of round dance in march or polka time; ~-*tongued*, double-tongued, deceitful; ~-*way*, (electr., of switch) permitting current to be switched on or off from either of ~ points, (plumbing, of cock) permitting fluid to flow in either of ~ channels, (math.) having double mode of variation. Hence ~'NESS n. [fem. of the OE numeral *twegen* masc. (TWAIN), *twā* fem. & neut., *tū* neut.; cf. OS *twēne*: *twā, twō*: *twē*, OHG *zwēne*: *zwā, zwō*: *zwei*; cogn. w. Skr. *dwaw, dwē*, Gk & L DUO]

two'some (too-), a. & n. (Game, dance, etc.) for two persons. [-SOME]

'twould, contr. of *it would*.

twy- pref., var. of TWI-.

twyer. See TUYÈRE.

-ty[1], suf. denoting quality or condition, repr. ME -*tie*, -*tee*, -*te* f. OF -*te* (mod. F -*té*) in pop. derivv. f. L -*italem* (nom. -*itas*). Such L types as *bonitatem* became OF *bonte* (w. loss of atonic L -*i*-), whence ME *bonte* bounty; thus ME.*plente* plenty, *poverte* poverty. Many of these older adoptives were refash. after the L, as ME *purte* purity (similarly in F, cf. OF *verte, amablete*, now *vérité, amabilité*). See -ITY.

-ty[2], suf. = tens, as *twenty, thirty, ninety*, (two, three, etc. tens); OE (OS) -*tig*, = OHG -*zug* etc. (G -*zig*), & the independent wds ON *tigr*, Goth. *tigus* TEN.

Tỹb'ūrn, n. (hist.). Place of execution in London on site of Marble Arch; ~ *ticket* (hist.), exemption from parish offices etc. granted to one who prosecuted a felon to conviction; ‖ ~ *tippet*, halter; ‖ ~ *tree*, gallows. Hence **Tỹbūrn'ia** n., fashionable London district north of Hyde Park.

Tỹchŏn'ic (-k-), a. Of the Danish astronomer Tycho Brahe (d. 1601) or his system. [-IC]

tycoon', n. Title applied by foreigners to shogun of Japan 1854–68; *(colloq.) business magnate. [f. Jap. *taikun* great prince]

tying. See TIE[1].

tỹke, ti-, n. Cur; ‖ low fellow: *Yorkshire* ~, Yorkshireman. [ME, f. ON *tik* bitch]

tyler. See TILER.

tỹl'opŏd, a. & n. (Animal) with padded not hoofed digits, e.g. camel. Hence **tỹlŏp'odous** a. [f. Gk *tulos* knob or *tulē* callus, cushion +*pous podos* foot]

tỹlōs'is, n. (Path.) inflammation of eyelids with hardening of the margins; (bot.) kind of growth formed in the cavity of a duct. So **tỹlOT'IC** a. [mod. L, f. Gk f. *tulos* or *tulē* (prec., -OSIS)]

tỹl'ōte, n. (zool.). Cylindrical sponge-spicule knobbed at ends. [as prec.]

tỹmp, n. Crown of opening in front of hearth in blast-furnace; short horizontal roof-timber in mine. [abbr. of foll.]

tỹm'pan, n. Stretched sheet of membrane or thin material; frame for equalizing pressure in some printing-presses; (anat., archit.) = TYMPANUM. [f. F *tympan* or L TYMPANUM]

tỹmpăn'ic, a. Like, acting like, a drum-head; (anat.) of the tympanum; ~ *membrane*, drum-membrane of ear; ~ (*bone*), bone of ear supporting this. [-IC]

tympanist. Var. of TIMPANIST.

tỹmpan|ĭt'ēs (-z), n. Swelling of abdomen caused by air in intestine etc. Hence ~it'ic a. [LL f. Gk *tumpanitēs* of drum (TYMPANUM, -ITE[1])]

tỹmpanĭt'is, n. Inflammation of lining membrane of tympanum. [-ITIS]

tỹm'panum, n. (pl. -*na*). (Anat.) middle ear, (also *tympanic membrane*) ear-drum; modified end of trachea in ducks etc.; (archit.) triangular space forming field of pediment, similar space over door between lintel & arch, door-panel; drum-wheel for raising water from stream; kind of treadmill. [L, f. Gk *tumpanon* drum]

Tỹn'wald (-ôld), n. Isle of Man legislature. [f. ON *thing-vǫllr* place of assembly (*thing* assembly +*vǫllr* field)]

tỹpe[1], n. **1.** Person, thing, event, serving as illustration, symbol, prophetic similitude, or characteristic specimen, of another thing or of a class, as *water may serve as a ~ of instability, paschal lamb is a ~ of Christ, these things are a ~* (have a prophetic significance), *the treatment he received is but a ~ of what patriots must expect, he is an admirable ~ of modern athleticism* or *of the modern athlete.* **2.** Class of things etc. having common characteristics, as *her beauty was of* or *belonged to another ~, dislike men of that ~.* **3.** (biol. etc.). Plan of structure, as *deviates from the ~*; main division of animal or vegetable kingdom characterized by this, as *the vertebrate ~*; organism having the essential characteristics of its group (so ~ *genus*, genus giving its name to & having the characteristics of a higher group, e.g. a family); whence **typ'AL** a. **4.** (chem.). Compound whose structure illustrates that of many others, esp. hydrochloric acid, water, ammonia, & marsh-gas. **5.** Object, conception, work of art, serving as model for subsequent artists. **6.** Device on either side of medal or coin. **7.** (print.). Piece of metal or wood having on its upper surface a letter or character for use in printing, (collect. sing.) set or supply or (with pl.) kind of these, as *wooden ~s are* or *~ is now used only for posters, ran short of ~, short of certain ~s, was printed in various ~s* (kinds or sizes of ~), *printed in large ~, a large-~ Bible*; *brilliant, diamond, pearl, ruby, nonpareil, emerald, minion, brevier, bourgeois, long primer, small pica, pica, English, great primer, canon, ~* (principal sizes in ascending order); BLACK[1]-*letter*, CHURCH[1]-*text*, CLARENDON, GERMAN[2]-*text*,

GOTHIC, ITALIC, ROMAN², RUNIC, SCRIPT, ∼; FOUNT² *of* ∼. 8. ∼*-bar*, line of ∼s in solid bar as cast in some ∼-setting machines; ∼*-high*, (of woodcut etc.) of proper height to print with ∼; ∼*-metal*, alloy used for printing-∼s; ∼*'script*, ∼written matter; ∼*'setter*, compositor, (also) composing machine; ∼*'setting*, setting of∼s in proper order for printing, ∼*-setting machine* (for simplifying this process, occas. including the making of ∼s as they are needed); ∼*-wheel*, wheel bearing letters in relief as used in some ∼writers & telegraphs; ∼*'write*, print (copy etc., or abs.) with ∼*-writer*; ∼*'writer*, machine for producing printed characters on paper as substitute for handwriting, (now rare) typist. [F, or f. L f. Gk *tupos* impression, figure, type, f. *tuptō* strike]

type², v.t. Be a type of; typewrite. [prec.]

typhl|it'is, n. Inflammation of caecum & vermiform appendix. Hence ∼it'IC a. [mod. L, f. Gk *tuphlon* caecum or blind gut (*tuphlos* blind) + -ITIS]

typh'oid, a. & n. Like typhus; ∼ (*fever*), infectious fever with eruption of red points on chest & abdomen & severe intestinal irritation, enteric; ∼ *bacillus*, germ causing ∼; ∼ *condition* (of depressed vitality, occurring in many acute diseases); ∼ *pneumonia* (combined with ∼). Hence **typhoid'AL** a. [f. TYPHUS + -OID]

typhomān'ia, n. Muttering delirium characteristic of typhus. [Gk (*tuphō-*) f. *tuphos* TYPHUS, -MANIA]

typhoōn', n. Violent hurricane in the China seas occurring esp. from July to October. Hence **typhon'IC** a. [partly f. Arab. *tūfān* perh. f. Gk *tuphōn* whirlwind, partly f. Chin. *tai fung* big wind]

typh'us, n. Fever marked by eruption of purple spots, great prostration, & usu. delirium; *malignant*, *simple*, ∼, severe, mild, form of ∼. Hence **typh'ous** a. [mod. L f. Gk *tuphos* smoke, stupor]

typ'ic, a. = foll. (first sense). [f. F *typique* f. LL f. Gk *tupikos* (as TYPE¹, see -IC)]

typ'ical, a. Serving as a type or character-istic example, representative, symbolical, emblematic, (*of*), as *a* ∼ *genus*, *plant*, *Scotsman*, *is* ∼ *of the genus*, *was* ∼ *of* (foreshadowed) *Christ's second coming*; characteristic of, serving to distinguish, a type, as ∼ *markings*, *structure*, *phrase-ology*. Hence ∼LY² advv., ∼NESS n. [f. LL *typicalis* (prec., -AL)]

typ'i|fy̆, v.t. Represent by a type, fore-shadow; be a type of, embody the charac-teristics of. Hence ∼FICA'TION, ∼fīER¹, nn. [f. L *typhus* TYPE¹ + -FY]

typ'ist, n. User of typewriter. [f. TYPE¹ + -IST]

typ'ō, n. (sl.; pl. ∼s). = TYPOGRAPHER. [abbr.]

typ'|o-, comb. form of Gk *lupos* TYPE¹, as: ∼*ograph*, machine for making & setting type; ∼*olite*, stone impressed with figure

of animal etc., fossil; ∼*ŏl'ogy*, doctrine, in-terpretation, of (esp. biblical) types, so ∼*olo'gical* a.; ∼*onym* (biol.), name based on a type, so ∼*ŏn'ŷmal*, ∼*onȳm'ic*, aa.

typŏg'raph|y̆, n. Art of printing, whence ∼ER¹ n.; character, appearance, of printed matter, as *faults of* ∼*y*, *the* ∼*y was admirable*. Hence **typŏgrǎph'IC(AL)** aa., **typŏgrǎph'ically²** adv. [F (-*ie*), = TYPE + -O- + -GRAPHY]

ty̆rǎnn'|ic(al), a. (∼*ic* rare). Acting like, characteristic of, a tyrant; arbitrary, imperious, despotic. Hence or cogn. ∼**icaLLY²**, **ty̆'rannousLY²**, advv., ∼**ical-**NESS n., **ty̆'rann**ous a. [∼*ic* f. L f. Gk *turannikos* (TYRANT, -IC) + -AL]

ty̆rǎnn'i|cīde, n. Killer, killing, of a tyrant. Hence ∼**cid'AL** a. [F, f. L *tyran-nicida*, -*cidium* (as TYRANT, see -CIDE)]

ty̆'rannize, -ise (-īz), v.i. & t. Play the tyrant, rule despotically or cruelly (*over* person etc.); (now rare) rule (person etc.) despotically. [f. F *tyranniser* (TYRANT, see -IZE)]

ty̆'rannȳ, n. Despotic or cruel exercise of power; instance of this, tyrannical act or behaviour; rule of (Greek) tyrant, period of this. [ME, f. OF *tyrannie* f. med. L (-*ia*) f. Gk *turannia*, as foll., -Y¹]

tyr̄'ant, n. Oppressive or cruel ruler; (Gk hist.) absolute ruler usu. owing his office to usurpation, *Thirty T*∼*s*, oligarchs ruling Athens 404-403 B.C.; ∼*-bird*, ∼ *fly-catcher*, kinds of Amer. passerine bird. [ME *tyran*, -*ant*, f. OF *tiran*, *tyrant* f. L f. Gk *turannos*]

tyre¹, n. (Anglo-Ind.). Curdled milk & cream. [Tamil *tayir*]

tyre². See TIRE².

tyr̄'ō. See TIRO.

Tyrolēse' (-z), a. & n. (pl. same). (Native) of the Tyrol. [-ESE]

Ty̆rŏllēnne', n. Dance of Tyrolese pea-sants, song suitable for this. [F]

tyr̄otŏx'icŏn, n. A ptomaine produced in milk or cheese. [f. Gk *turos* cheese + *toxikon* poison]

Ty̆'rrhēne, **Ty̆rrhēn'ian**, (-rē-), aa. & nn. Etruscan. [f. L f. Gk *Turrhēnos* + -IAN]

tzetze. See TSETSE.

Tzigane (tsĭgahn'), a. & n. **1.** Of the Hungarian gipsies or their music. **2.** n. Hungarian gipsy. [F, f. Magyar *czigány*]

U

U, u, (ū), letter (pl. U̇s, 'U's). *U-boat*, German submarine [G *untersee*, under-water]; *U-bolt*, -*tube*, etc. (shaped like U); U.P. (sl. pronunc. of *up* adv., esp. *it's all U.P.*).

ūbi'etȳ, n. Being in definite place, local relation, whereness. [f. L *ubi* where, see -TY]

ūb'ĭ in'fra, adv. In the place (in book etc.) mentioned below. [L, lit. where below]

ŭbiquitār′ian, a. & n. (theol.). Of, believer in, the omnipresence of Christ's body. Hence ~ISM n. [foll., -ARIAN]

ŭbi′quit|y̆, n. Omnipresence; being everywhere or in an indefinite number of places at same time; ‖~y of the king (law), his official presence in courts in the person of his judges. Hence ~OUS a., ~OUSLY² adv., ~OUSNESS n. [f. mod. L ubiquitas f. L ubique everywhere f. ubi where, -ITY]

ŭb′ĭ sŭp′ra, adv. In the place (in book etc.) above mentioned. [L, lit. where above]

ŭd′al, n. Kind of freehold right based on uninterrupted possession prevailing in N. Europe before feudal system & still in Orkney & Shetland (often attrib., as ~ lenure); ~man, holder of property by ~, so ~IER¹ n. [f. ON óthal, = OE æthel, éthel, OHG uodil]

ŭdd′er, n. Mammary glands of cattle etc. esp. when large & having more than one teat. Hence (-)~ED² (-erd), ~LESS, aa. [OE ūder, OS ūdar, OHG ūtar, f. Gmc *ūdhr- cogn. w. L uber, Gk outhar]

ŭdŏm′ēter, n. Rain-gauge. Hence **ŭdomĕt′rio** a. [f. F udomètre f. L udus damp +-o-+-METER]

ŭgh (ōōh), int. expr. disgust or horror.

ŭg′ly̆, a. & n. 1. Unpleasing or repulsive to sight, as an ~ beast of a bulldog, must not make ~ faces, the ugliest man I have seen, has an ~ scar on the forehead; morally repulsive, vile, discreditable, unpleasant, unpleasantly suggestive, threatening, unpromising, as ~ vices, his conduct has an ~ look, ~ rumours are about, an ~ (awkward) job, an ~ customer, formidable person, cloud has an ~ look, have had ~ weather, an ~ gash; ~ duckling, person who turns out the genius etc. of the family after being thought the dullard etc. (w. ref. to cygnet in brood of ducks in an Andersen tale). Hence ŭg′lĭly v.t., ŭg′lĭLY² adv., ŭg′lĭNESS n. 2. n. ‖ Shade worn as appendage to bonnet about middle of 19th c. [ME, f. ON ugglígr to be dreaded, f. ugga to dread, see -LY¹]

Ŭg′rĭan, **Ŭg′rĭc** (ōō-), aa. Finnic. [f. name of a tribe +-IAN, -IC]

ŭh′lan (ōō-, ū-), n. (hist.). Cavalryman armed with lance in some European armies. [F, G, f. Pol. (h)ulan f. Turk. oghlān son, youth, servant]

Ŭitlander (āt′lŏnder), n. (S. Africa). Foreigner, alien. [Du., f. uit out +land land; cf. OUTLANDISH]

ŭkāse′, n. Edict of Tsarist Russian government; any arbitrary order. [f. Russ. ukaz′ ordinance, edict]

ŭkulele (ūkŭlā′lĕ), n. Four-stringed Hawaiian guitar. [native]

-ular, suf. repr. L -ularis (see -ULE, -AR¹), in adjj. f. nn. in -ulus, -ula, -ulum. E adjj. in ~ are usu. f. L, med. or mod. L forms, some (corpusc~, funic~) dir. on L nn.

ŭl′cer, n. Open sore on external or internal surface of body with secretion of pus etc.; (fig.) moral blemish, corrupting influence, etc. Hence or cogn. ~ED² (-erd), ~OUS, aa., ~OUSLY² adv., ~OUSNESS n. [ME, f. OF ulcere, or f. L ulcus -eris, rel. to Gk helkos]

ŭl′cer|āte, v.i. & t. Form, convert or be converted into, affect with, an ulcer (lit. & fig.). Hence or cogn. ~ABLE, ~ATIVE, aa., ~A′TION n. [f. L ulcerare (prec.), -ATE³]

-ule, suf. of dimm. f. L wds in -ulus, -ula, -ulum, as globule (L globulus f. globus), granule, pustule, & in mod. wds on L anal. anguillule.

u′lēma (ōō-), n. Moslem doctors of sacred law & theology esp. in former Turk. empire. [f. Arab 'ulema pl. of 'alim learned i. 'alama know]

-ulent, suf. of adjj. f. L, repr. L -ulentus, the normal form of -lentus -LENT, as in fraud~, turb~, truc~; meaning, 'abounding in, full of'. Hence n. suf. -ulence.

ŭli′ginōse, a. (bot.). Growing in muddy places. [f. L uliginosus (uligo -ginis moisture, see -OSE¹)]

ŭll′age, n. (commerc.). What a cask etc. wants of being full, loss by evaporation or leakage; (sl.) dregs. [ME, f. AF ulliage, OF ouillage (ouiller fill up, -AGE)]

ŭl′m|in, n. (chem.). Black gummy substance found on elm & other trees & in vegetable mould etc. Hence ~IC, ~OUS, aa., (chem.). [f. L ulmus elm +-IN]

ŭl′n|a, n. (pl. ~ae). Inner of two bones of forearm (cf. RADIUS). Hence ~AR¹ a., ~O-comb. form. [L, cogn. w. Gk ōlenē, & ELL]

-ulose, suf. repr. L -ulosus (see -ULE, -OSE¹), forming adjj. on nn. in -ulus, -ula, -ulum. In E dir. f. L (calc~) or on L anal. (glob~). Where forms in ~ are paralleled by forms in -ulous, the former are either older forms now displaced by -ulous, or later forms different. for special senses.

ŭlŏt′rich|an, a. & n., ~ous, a., (-k-). Woolly-haired; (member) of the woolly-haired division of mankind. [f. Gk oulos woolly +thrix trikhos hair +-AN, -OUS]

-ulous, suf. repr. L -ulosus (see -ULOSE), as in fab~, pop~, & L -ulus, as in garr~, trem~.

ŭl′ster, n. Long loose overcoat often with belt orig. of U~ frieze, whence ~ED² (-erd) a.; U~ custom, form of tenant-right in Ireland. [U~ in Ireland]

ŭltēr′ior, a. Situated beyond; more remote, not immediate, in the future, in the background, beyond what is seen or avowed, (~ views, motive, plans). Hence ~LY² adv. [L, compar. adj., corresp. to the advv. ultra, ultro]

ŭl′tĭma, a. Last, most remote, (in phrr.: ~ rā′tiō (-shĭ-), final argument esp. force; ~ ratio rēg′um, last argument of kings, resort to arms; ~ THULE). [L, fem. of ultimus, superl. as prec.]

ŭl′timate, a. Last, final, beyond which

no other exists or is possible, as ~ *result*, *analysis*; fundamental, primary, as ~ *basis*, ~*principles*, *truths*, ~ *cause* (beyond which no other can be found), *the* ~ *facts of nature* (beyond reach of analysis). Hence ~LY[2] adv., ~NESS n. [f. LL *ultimare* come to an end (*ultimus*, as prec.), see -ATE[2]]

ŭltimāt'um, n. (pl. *-tums*, *-ta*). Final proposal or statement of terms, rejection of which by opposite party may lead to rupture, declaration of war, etc.; ultimate conclusion; fundamental principle. [neut. p.p. as prec.]

ŭl'timō, adj. (usu. abbr. *ult.*). In the month preceding that now current (cf. PROXIMO, INSTANT[1]), *as your letters of the 28th ult. & 3rd inst.* [L, = in last (*mense* month), see ULTIMA]

ŭltimogĕn'iture, n. System in which youngest son (cf. PRIMOGENITURE) takes inheritance, = BOROUGH-ENGLISH. [f. L *ultimus* (see ULTIMA) on PRIMOGENITURE]

ŭl'tra, a. & n. Favouring, advocate of, extreme views or measures. [orig. as abbr. of F *ultra-royaliste*]

ŭltra-, pref. = L *ultra* beyond, on the other side of, as ~*montane*, ~*terrestrial*, ~*-violet*; ~*microscope*, instrument devised to reveal objects too minute to be detected by the ordinary microscope; ~*microscopic*, beyond the power of conventional microscopes; ~*short wave* (radio), having a wave-length below 10 metres; ~*son'ic* a., relating to sound waves of such pitch as to be beyond the threshold of human audibility; ~*son'ics* n. pl.; esp. in sense 'excessively or extravagantly, beyond what is usual or natural or reasonable', as ~*classical*, ~*conservatism*, ~*conservative*, ~*cosmopolitan*, ~*critical*, ~*fashionable*, ~*partisan*, ~*Protestant*(*ism*), ~*religious*.

ŭl'tra|ist, n. Holder of extreme opinions in politics, religion, etc. So ~ISM n. [-IST]

ŭltramarine' (-ēn), a. & n. 1. Situated beyond the sea. 2. n. Blue pigment got from lapis lazuli; *artificial* ~ (made by mixing clay, carbonate of soda, sulphur, & resin); ~ *ashes*, residuum of lapis lazuli after extraction of ~, used by old masters for neutral flesh-tints etc. [f. med. L ULTRA(*marinus* MARINE); n. sense from fact that lapis lazuli was brought from beyond sea]

ŭltramŏn't|āne, a. & n. 1. Situated south of the Alps; Italian; favourable to the absolute authority of the Pope in matters of faith & discipline, whence ~anISM, ~anIST, nn. 2. n. One who resides south of the Alps, person holding ~ane views. [f. med. L ULTRA(*montanus* f. L *mons* -*ntis* mountain + -ANE); earlier in senses, 'north of Alps', 'unfavourable to Pope', etc., cf. TRAMONTANE, CIS-*montane*]

ŭltramŭn'dāne, a. Beyond the world or the solar system; of another life. [f. L ULTRA(*mundanus* MUNDANE)]

ŭltra-vī'olĕt, a. (Of invisible rays of the spectrum) beyond the violet rays. [ULTRA-]

ŭl'tra vīr'ēs (-z), adv. or pred. a. Beyond one's power or authority. [L]

ŭl'ŭl|āte, v.i. Howl; hoot. So ~ANT a., ~A'TION n. [f. L *ululare*, see -ATE[3]]

-um. See -IUM.

ŭm'bel, n. (bot.). Flower-cluster in which stalks nearly equal in length spring from common centre & form a flat or convex or concave surface as in parsley. Hence ~IAL, ~IAR[1], ~LATE[2], ~liF'EROUS, ŭmbĕll'iFORM, aa., ~lET[1], ŭmbĕll'ULE, nn. [f. L *umbella* sunshade dim. of UMBRA]

ŭm'ber, n., a., & v.t. 1. Natural pigment like ochre but darker & browner (*raw* ~, this in natural state, of dark yellow colour, *burnt* ~, redder & deeper in colour), whence ~Y[2] a.; grayling; ~*bird* (also *umbrette'*), Afr. bird allied to stork & heron. 2. adj. Of ~ colour, dark, dusky. 3. v.t. Colour with ~. [f. F (*terre d'*) *ombre* or It. (*terra di*) *ombra*, either = shadow (L *umbra*) or f. fem. of L *Umber* Umbrian]

ŭmbĭl'ical (or -ĭk'al), a. Of, situated near, the umbilicus, as ~ *cord*, ropelike structure passing from foetus to placenta; central; connected through the female line, as *an* ~ *ancestor*. [f. med. L *umbilicalis* (UMBILICUS, -AL)]

ŭmbĭl'ic|āte, a. Shaped like a navel, whence ~A'TION n.; having an umbilicus. [f. L *umbilicatus* (UMBILICUS, -ATE[2])]

ŭmbĭl'ic'us (or -bīl'ī-), n. Navel, whence ŭmbĭlIF'EROUS, ŭm'bilIFORM, aa., (bot., zool., conch.) navel-like formation; (geom.) point in a surface through which all lines of curvature pass; (Rom. ant.) boss at each end of stick on which MS. was rolled. [L, cogn. w. Gk *omphalos*, & NAVEL]

ŭm'bles (-blz), n. pl. (obs.). Edible offal of deer; attrib. in *umble-pie* (cf. HUMBLE *pie*). [15th c.; var. of NUMBLES]

ŭm'bō, n. (pl. ~*s*, ~*nes* pr. -ōn'ēz). Boss of shield, esp. in centre; (bot., zool., etc.) boss, knob, protuberance. Hence ŭm'bonAL, ŭm'bonATE[2], ŭmbŏn'IC, aa. [L, gen. -*onis*]

ŭm'br|a, n. (pl. ~*ae*). (Astron.) total shadow (cf. PENUMBRA) cast by the earth or moon in an eclipse; dark central part of sun-spot (cf. PENUMBRA); (Rom. ant.) uninvited guest brought by a guest. Hence ~AL a. [L, = shade]

ŭm'brage, n. Sense of slight or injury, offence, as *give*, *take*, ~; (chiefly poet.) shade, what gives shade, so ŭmbrāge-OUS (-jus) a. [ME, f. OF *ombrage* f. Rom. **umbraticum* (L -*us* adj.), see UMBRA, -AGE]

ŭmbrĕll'a, n. 1. Light circular canopy of silk or other material attached to radiating folding frame sliding on stick carried in the hand as protection against rain or (now usu. *sunshade*, *parasol*) sun; (fig.)

a screen of fighter aircraft or (in full ~ *barrage*) a curtain of fire put up as protection against enemy aircraft; gelatinous disc of jellyfish etc. by contraction & expansion of which it swims; (also ~*-shell*) gasteropod with ~like shell. 2. ~*-bird*, kinds of S.-Amer. bird with radiating crest; ~*-stand* (for holding closed ~s, usu. with pan at bottom to catch drippings); ~*-tree*, small kind of magnolia with leaves in ~like whorl at end of branch, (colloq.) tree so grafted or trained that its branches droop in ~ form. Hence ~'d [-ED²] a. [f. It. *ombrella*, dim. of *ombra* shade f. UMBRA]

umbrette. See UMBER.

Um'brian (ŭ-), a. & n. 1. Of (ancient or modern) Umbria; ~ *school*, school of painting to which Raphael & Perugino belonged. 2. n. Language, inhabitant, of ancient Umbria. [-AN]

ûmbrif'erous, a. Affording shade. [f. L *umbrifer* (UMBRA, see -FEROUS)]

ûmiak (ōōm'yăk), n. Eskimo boat worked by women. [Esk.]

umlaut (ōōm'lowt), n., & v.t. 1. (In Germanic languages) vowel change due to *i* or *u* (now usu. lost or altered) in following syllable (e.g. German *mann männer, fuss füsse,* English *man men*). 2. v.t. Modify (form, sound) by the ~. [G (*um-* about + *laut* sound)]

ûm'pire, n., & v.i. & t. 1. (Law) third person called in to decide between arbitrators who disagree; person chosen to decide question; person chosen to enforce rules & settle disputes in cricket or other game. Hence **ûm'pirAGE**(3), ~SHIP, nn. 2. vb. Act as ~ (*for* persons, *in* game etc.), act as ~ in (game). [ME; later form of *noumpere* f. OF *non-, nomper* not equal, in sense *odd man* (*non* not + *per* PEER¹); for loss of *n-* cf. ADDER]

ûmp'teen, a. (sl.). Several, many, a lot of. [joc. form. on -TEEN]

'un, pron. (colloq.). One, as *that's a good 'un, he's a tough 'un*.

ûn-¹, repr. OE *un-, on-*, (orig. *and-*, see ANSWER), OS *and-*, OHG *ant-, int-* (G *-ent*), Goth. *and-*, cogn. with Gk *anti*; pref. of vbs w. neg. sense & usu. denoting action contrary to or annulling that of the simple vb. The pref. being unlimited in use, only a selection of the existing vbs & derivative wds is here given. Adjj. in *-able, -ed,* & *-ing,* are identical in form with wds in UN-², with or without material difference in meaning; *undoable, unstrappable,* may mean 'that can be undone, unstrapped', or 'that cannot be done, strapped'; *unbracing* may mean 'that unbraces' or 'that does not brace'; an *unbending* person is one fond of or averse to relaxation; an *un²coiled* rope must be coiled before it can be *un¹coiled*; an *unbridlED*¹ horse may (*un-*¹) or may not (UN-²) have been previously bridled, in either case he is now *un²bridlED²*. As a

rule, the UN-² forms of such adjj. are current, the others not. The stress in the foll. wds is not marked, being the same as in the simple vb or n. or, where that is monosyllabic, falling on the second syllable (*undeceive', unsay'*); but p.pp. or adjj. in *-ed,* whether in *un-*¹ or UN-², tend in attrib. use to take stress on *un-* (cf. *-ED*²), as *an un'masked villain, an un²muzzled hound, villain was unma'sked, dog was unmuz'zled*.

1. Wds formed upon a simple verb & with contrary sense (rarely w. intensified negative sense, as *unloose*). The distinction between some of these & the vbs in sections 2, 3, & 4, which appear to be formed rather on a noun, is necessarily arbitrary, the assumed simple vb (identical in form with the noun, from which it is usu. derived) being often rare or non-existent in the required senses of 'furnish with', 'place in', etc.

Exx.: *unanchor* v.t. & i.; *unattire* v.t. & i.; *unbalance* v.t.; *unbank* v.t., cause (fire) to burn briskly by removing ashes from top; *unbar* v.t., remove bar from (gate etc.), unlock, open, (often fig.); *unbear* v.t., take off or relax bearing-rein of (horse); *unbend* v.t. & i., change from bent position, straighten, relax (mind etc.) from strain or exertion, rid oneself of constraint, be affable, whence *unbending*¹ a., (naut.) unfasten (sails) from yards & stays, cast (cable) loose, untie (rope); *unbeseem* v.t., be unbecoming to; *unbias* v.t., free from bias; *unbind* v.t., release from bonds or binding; *unblindfold* v.t.; *unblock* v.i. & t. (cards), play high card to avoid interrupting partner's long suit, give free scope to (partner's suit) by such play; *unbolt* v.t., release (door etc.) by drawing back bolt; *unbonnet* v.i. & t., take off cap etc. e.g. in salutation, remove the bonnet of; *unbosom* v.i. & t., disclose one's secret feelings, disclose (thoughts etc.); *unbrace* v.t., remove the braces of, free from tension, relax (nerves etc.); *unbraid* v.t., separate the strands of; *unbreech* v.t., free the breech of (cannon) from fastenings etc.; *unbridle* v.t., remove bridle from (horse, fig. person, tongue, etc.); *unbuckle* v.t., release the buckle of (strap, shoe, etc.); *unburden* v.t., relieve of burden, relieve (one*self*, conscience, etc.) by confession etc. to person; *unbutton* v.t., open (coat etc.) by withdrawing buttons from buttonholes; *unchain* v.t.; *unchristianize* v.t.; *unclasp* v.t., loosen the clasp of; *unclench, -inch,* v.t. & i.; *unclog* v.t.; *unclose* v.t. & i., open; *unclothe* v.t.; *uncock* v.t., let down hammer of (gun) softly so as not to explode charge; *uncoil* v.t. & i.; *uncord* v.t.; *uncork* v.t., draw cork from (bottle), (colloq.) give vent or expression to (feelings etc.); *uncouple* v.t., release (dogs, railway-cars, etc.) from couples or couplings; *uncover* v.t. & i., remove covering from, lay bare, disclose, take off one's hat or cap; *uncreate*[1] v.t., annihilate; *uncross* v.t., remove (legs, arms, knives, etc.) from crossed position; *uncurb* v.t.; *uncurl* v.t.; *undeceive* v.t., free from deception, whence *undeceived*[1] a.; *undeify* v.t.; *undo* v.t., annul (*cannot* ~ *the past, our past actions*), untie or unfasten or unloose (coat, button, parcel), unfasten the buttons or garments or stays of (person), ruin the prospects or reputation or morals of, whence *undoer, undoing*, nn., *undone*[1] a.; *undomesticate* v.t.; *undrape* v.t.; *undress*[1] v.t. & i., take off the clothes of, take off one's clothes, whence *undressed*[1] a.; *unegoize* v.t.; *unentangle* v.t.; *unequalize* v.t.; *unfasten* v.t., whence *unfastened*[1] a.; *unfetter* v.t., whence *unfettered*[1] a.; *unfeudalize* v.t.; *unfile* v.t., remove (paper) from file; *unfit* v.t., make unsuitable (*for*); *unfix* v.t., whence *unfixed*[1] a.; *unfold*[1] v.t. & i., open the folds of, spread out, (fig.) reveal (thoughts, designs), become opened out, develop; *unform* v.t.; *unfurl* v.t. & i., spread out (sail), become spread out; *ungear* v.t., strip of gear, throw out of gear; *ungild* v.t.; *ungird* v.t.; *unglaze* v.t.; *unhallow* v.t., profane, desecrate; *unhand* v.t., take one's hands off, release from one's grasp; *unhang* v.t., remove from hanging position, strip (wall etc.) of hangings; *unharness* v.t.; *unhasp* v.t., loose from hasp; *unhinge* v.t., take (door) off its hinges, disorder (mind etc.), whence *unhinged* a.; *unhitch* v.t.; *unhook* v.t., remove from hook, open (dress etc.) by detaching its hooks; *unhoop* v.t.; *unhouse* (-z) v.t., deprive of shelter, drive from house; *unhumanize* v.t.; *unjoin* v.t.; *unjoint* v.t., separate joints of (fishing-rod etc.); *unkink* v.t. & i.; *unknit* v.t.; *unknot* v.t.; *unlace* v.t., loose or open by undoing lace(s) of (boot, stays, etc.); *unlade* v.t.; *unlash* v.t. (naut.); *unlatch* v.t., release latch of (door); *unlay* v.t. (naut.), untwist; *unlearn* v.t., expel from one's memory, forget the knowledge of, rid oneself of (esp. false or misleading information, habit, etc.), re-move lining of; *unlink* v.t.; *unload* v.t., remove load from (ship, cart, etc., or abs.), remove (load) from ship etc., (Stock Exch.) get rid of (stocks or shares), sell out, withdraw charge from (gun etc.); *unlock* v.t., release lock of (door, box, etc., fig. mind etc.), (fig.) disclose (secret etc.); *unlodge* v.t., dislodge; *unloose* v.t., loose; *unmake* v.t., destroy, annul; *unmask* v.t. & i., remove the mask from, expose (villain, villainy), take off one's mask, reveal one's true character etc.; *unmew* v.t. (poet., rhet.), release; *unmoor* v.t., loose the moorings of (vessel etc. or fig., also abs.), weigh one of two or more anchors of (vessel); *unmortise* v.t.; *unmould* v.t., change the form of; *unmuffle* v.t. & i., remove muffler from (face, bell,

etc.), remove muffler etc. from one's face; *unmuzzle* v.t., (esp., fig.) relieve of obligation to remain silent; *unnaturalize* v.t., make unnatural; *unnerve* v.t., deprive of nerve or strength or resolution, whence *unnerved* a.; *unpack* v.t., open & remove contents of (package, box, etc., or abs.), take out (contents) from package etc.; *unpeg* v.t., remove the peg(s) from or of, open thus; *unpeople* v.t., depopulate; *unpick* v.t., undo (stitches, garment, etc.) by picking, open with pick; *unpin* v.t., unfasten by removing pins; *unplait* v.t.; *unplug* v.t.; *unpreach* v.t., recant in preaching; *unravel* v.t., separate (threads etc.), separate the threads of (material), disentangle (lit. & fig.); *unreel* v.t. & i., unwind, become unwound, from reel; *unreeve* v.t. (naut.); *unrein* v.t., give the rein to (often fig.); *unriddle* v.t., solve or explain (riddle, mystery); *unrig* v.t. (naut.); *unrip* v.t., rip open or apart; *unrivet* v.t., unroll v.t. & i., open (roll of cloth etc.), (of roll) be opened, display, be displayed; *unromanize* v.t.; *unroot* v.t., pull up by root; *unsaddle* v.t. (often abs.); *unsay* v.t., retract (statement), whence *unsaid*[1] a.; *unscrew* v.t., unfasten by removing screws, loosen (screw); *unseal* v.t., break the seal of, open, (letter etc.); *unseam* v.t., rip open (garment etc.) at seam; *unseat* v.t., remove from seat, throw from seat on horseback, depose (M.P. etc.) from seat, whence *unseated*[1] a.; *unset* v.t., remove (gem) from its setting; *unsettle* v.t., disturb orderly arrangement of, discompose, disincline to routine etc. (*holidays* ~ *me*), derange (intellect), whence *unsettled*[1] a.; *unshackle* v.t.; *unsheathe* v.t.; *unship* v.t., unload (cargo), disembark (passenger), (naut.) remove (oar, tiller, etc.) from place where it is fixed or fitted, whence *unshipped*[1] a.; *unsling* v.t. (esp. naut.); *unspeak* v.t., retract; *unsteel* v.t., soften, relax, (resolution, person); *unstick* v.t., separate (thing stuck to another; *come unstuck*, sl., come to grief, fail); *unstitch* v.t., undo stitches of; *unstock* v.t., deprive of stock, remove (gun-barrel) from stock; *unstop* v.t., free from obstruction, remove stopper from; *unstrap* v.t., remove or undo the strap(s) of; *unstring* v.t., remove the strings of, loosen strings of (harp etc.), take (beads etc.) off string, weaken (nerves), weaken nerves of (person etc.), whence *unstrung* a.; *unswaddle* v.t.; *unswathe* v.t.; *unswear* v.t., recant by oath; *untack* v.t., disjoin, separate, (thing tacked to another); *untangle* v.t.; *unteach* v.t.; *untemper* v.t., take away the temper of (metal etc.); *untether* v.t.; *unthink* v.t., retract in thought; *unthread* v.t., take thread out of (needle), find one's way out of (maze); *untie* v.t., undo (knot etc.), undo the cords etc. of (bundle, package, etc.), liberate from bonds, whence *untied*[1] a.;

untruss v.t.; *untuck* v.t.; *untune* v.t., put out of tune (lit. & fig.); *untwine* v.t. & i.; *untwist* v.t. & i.; *unveil* v.t. & i., remove veil from, remove one's veil, remove concealing drapery from (statue etc.) with ceremonies; *unvote* v.t., retract by vote (what has been voted); *unwarp* v.t., restore from warped state; *unweave* v.t., take to pieces (textile fabric), separate (woven threads); *unwill* v.t., will the reverse of (what one has willed); *unwind* v.t. & i., draw out at length (what is wound), become thus drawn out, whence *unwound*[1] a.; *unwork* v.t., undo, destroy, (fabric etc.); *unwrap* v.t.; *unwrinkle* v.t.; *unyoke* v.t. & i., release (as) from yoke, (fig.) cease work.

2. Vbs formed on n. or vb—see (1)—& having sense ' deprive of ', ' separate from '. A simple vb sometimes exists in same sense, e.g. (*un*)*bone*, (*un*)*husk*, (*un*)*shell*.

Exx.: *unapparel* v.t.; *unarm* v.t., deprive of arms or armour, whence *unarmed*[1] a.; *unballast* v.t.; *unbelt* v.t.; *unbone* v.t.; *unboot* v.t. & i.; *unbowel* v.t.; *uncap* v.t.; *uncloak* v.t.; *uncowl* v.t., uncover (face) by removing cowl, unmonk; *uncrown* v.t., deprive (esp. fig. king etc.) of crown; *unedge* v.t., destroy edge of, blunt; *unface* v.t., expose; *unfeather* v.t.; *unfence* v.t.; *unflesh* v.t.; *unflower* v.t.; *unframe* v.t.; *unfrock* v.t., deprive of frock or (fig.) of ecclesiastical rank; *ungirdle* v.t.; *unglove* v.t. & i., deprive of, take off one's, gloves; *ungown* v.t.; *ungum* v.t.; *unhair* v.t.; *unhat* v.t.; *unhelm* v.t.; *unhusk* v.t.; *unlead* (-lĕd) v.t. (print.), remove leads from (types); *unlimber* v.t. & abs.; *unman* v.t., deprive (esp. ship) of men, see also (4); *unmantle* v.t.; *unnail* v.t., take nails out of, unfasten (box etc.) thus; *unplume* v.t.; *unprop* v.t.; *unring* v.t.; *unrobe* v.t. & i., undress; *unroof* v.t.; *unrumple* v.t.; *unscale* v.t., remove scales of; *unself* v.t., rid of self, unegoize; *unsex* v.t., deprive (usu. woman) of the qualities of the sex; *unshell* v.t.; *unshoe* v.t., take shoe(s) off (horse etc.); *unshot* v.t., remove shot from (gun); *unshutter* v.t.; *unsinew* v.t.; *unsister* v.t.; *unsolder* v.t.; *unspar* v.t.; *unstarch* v.t., free from starch or (fig.) stiffness or reserve; *unstopper* v.t.; *untile* v.t.; *untin* v.t.; *untooth* v.t.; *unturf* v.t.

3. Vbs similarly formed with sense ' release from ', ' take out of ', ' displace from '.

Exx.: *unbag* v.t.; *unbed* v.t.; *unbill* v.t. (naut.); *unbox* v.t.; *uncage* v.t.; *uncart* v.t.; *uncase* v.t.; *unchurch* v.t., excommunicate; *uncloister* v.t.; *uncoop* v.t.; *undock* v.t.; *unearth* v.t., drive (fox etc.) from an earth, dig up, (fig.) bring to light; *unfold*[2] v.t., release (sheep) from fold; *unhive* v.t.; *unhorse* v.t., throw from horse, (of horse) throw (rider), cause

to dismount; *unleash* v.t.; *unnest* v.t.; *unpen* v.t.; *unperch* v.t.; *unroost* v.t.; *unsnare* v.t.; *unspell* v.t., release from spell; *unsphere* v.t.; *unstep* v.t. (naut.); *untent* v.t.; *unthrone* v.t.; *untomb* v.t.

4. Occasional vbs formed f. nouns with sense 'cause to be no longer', 'degrade from the position of '.

Exx.: *unbishop* v.t.; *unduke* v.t.; *unking* v.t.; *unlord* v.t.; *unman* v.t., deprive of manly qualities, break the courage of, dishearten, emasculate, see also (2); *unmonk* v.t.; *unpope* v.t.; *unprelate* v.t.; *unpriest* v.t.; *unprince* v.t.; *unqueen* v.t.; *unsquire* v.t.; *unvicar* v.t.

ŭn-[2], repr. OE *un-*, OS, OHG, Goth. *un-*, ON *ú-*, *ó-*, corresp. to L IN-[2], Gk *an-*, *a-*, Skr. *an-*; pref. giving neg. sense to adjj. with their derivative nn. & advv., & to a miscellaneous group of nn. not formed on adjj.; see (2).

1. Of the many adjj. formed with *un-*, esp. of those in -*able*, -*ed*, -*ing*, for which cf. UN-[1], only a selection is here given. The sense of *un-* is either simply 'not' (as in most adjj. in -*able*, -*ed*, -*ing*, & in some others, as *unofficial*) or more commonly 'the reverse of ', with implication of praise, blame, etc. Between *un-* & IN-[2] a differentiation has been suggested according to which *inartistic* means ' contrary to rules of art ', 'such as an artist would condemn', & *unartistic* means 'not concerned with rules of art'; & pairs of words may be found that bear out the distinction, esp. where one of the pair has long been restricted to the proposed sense & the other has been created or revived to supply its deficiencies (*immoral*, *unmoral*). But the purely neutral sense thus ascribed to *un-* is not that found in many of the most familiar adjj. (*unbeautiful*, *unfair*, *ungraceful*, *ungracious*, *unkind*, *unjust*, *ungenerous*, *untrue*, *unscrupulous*, *unmanly*, *unscholarly*, *unladylike*, *unchristian*), including some of the exact type of *unartistic* (*unscientific*, *unphilosophical*): when we say that a thing is *untrue*, we do not mean that it does not matter for our purpose whether it is true or not, but that it is culpably inconsistent with truth. Apart from the adjj. in -*able*, -*ed*, -*ing*, both *un-* & *in-* more commonly have this implication of blame etc., the purely neutral sense being often given by NON-(5). IN-[2] is preferred to *un-* with certain terminations of L orig., e.g. -*ate*, -*ite*, -*ant*, -*ent*, -*ble* (exc. -*able*, now a living E suf.). It is for the most part arch. with -*ed*[1,2] (*indigested* etc., but cf. *inexperienced*), and is not used with -*ing*, -*ful*, -*like*, -*ly*, etc. Derivatives in -*ly*, -*ness*, -*ily*, etc., are briefly recorded; stress follows that of the simple adj.; but for adjj. in -*ed* see UN-[1].

Exx.: **unabashed**; *unabated*; *unabbreviated*; *unabetted*; *unabiding*; *unable*, not able (*to* do); *unabridged*; *unabsorbable*;

unabsorbed; *unabsorbent*; *unaccented*; *unaccentuated*; *unacceptable*; *unaccommodating*; *unaccompanied*, not accompanied, (mus.) without accompaniment; *unaccomplished*, ·not accomplished or achieved, lacking accomplishments; *unaccordant*; *unaccountable* (*-bility, -bleness, -bly*), that cannot be explained, strange, irresponsible; *unaccoutred*; *unaccredited*; *unaccused*; *unaccustomed*, not accustomed (*to*), not usual (*his ~ silence*); *unachievable*; *unachieved*; *unacknowledged*; *unacquainted*; *unacquirable*; *unacquired*; *unacted*; *unadaptable*; *unadapted*; *unaddicted*; *unaddressed*; *unadjudged*; *unadjusted*; *unadministered*; *unadmired*; *unadmonished*; *unadopted*, ‖ (esp., of new roads) not taken over for maintenance by the local authority; *unadorned*; *unadult̲rated*; *unadventurous*; *unadvisable* (*-bility*); *unadvised* (*-èdly*), indiscreet, rash, without advice; *unaffable*; *unaffected* (*-ly, -ness*), free from affectation, genuine, sincere, not affected (*by*); *unaffiliated*; *unafflicted*; *unaggressive*; *unaided*; *unalarmed*; *unalleviated*; *unallotted*; *unallowable*; *unalloyed*; *unalterable* (*-bility, -bleness, -bly*); *unaltered*; *unamazed*; *unambiguous* (*-ly, -ness*); *unambitious* (*-ly, -ness*); *unamenable*; *unamendable*; *un-American*, not American, foreign to American customs or ideas; *unamiable* (*-bility, -bleness, -bly*); *unamusing*; ∖*unanalysable*; *unanalysed*; *unanimated*; *unannounced*; *unanswerable* (*-bility, -bleness, -bly*), that cannot be answered or refuted; *unanswered*; *unanticipated*; *unapocryphal*; *unapostolic*, contrary to apostolic usage, not having apostolic authority; *unappalled*; *unapparelled*; *unapparent*; *unappeasable*; *unappeased*; *unappetizing* (*-ly*); *unapplied*; *unappreciated*; *unappreciative*; *unapprehended*; *unapprehensive*; *unapprised*; *unapproachable* (*-bility, -bleness, -bly*); *unappropriated* (*~ blessing*, joc., old maid); *unapproved*; *unapproving* (*-ly*); *unapt* (*-ly, -ness*); *unarmed*²; *unarmoured*; *unarranged*; *unarrayed*; *unarrested*; *unartificial* (*-ly*), not artificial, natural; *unartistic*; *unascertainable*; *unascertained*; *unashamed*; *unasked*; *unaspirated*; *unaspiring* (*-ly*); *unassailable*, not assailable, (of statement etc.) against which nothing can be said; *unassayed*; *unassignable*; *unassimilated*; *unassisted*; *unassuming*, making little of one's merits or status; *unattached*, not attached, (law) not seized for debt, (mil.) not assigned to regiment or company, (univv., of student) belonging to no college; *unattainable* (*-ness*); *unattempted*; *unattended*; *unattested*; *unattractive* (*-ly, -ness*); *unaugmented*; *unauthentic* (*-ity*); *unauthenticated*; *unauthorized*; *unavailable*; *unavailing* (*-ly*), ineffectual; *unavenged*; *unavoidable* (*-bly*); *unavowed*; *unaware*, not aware (*of, that*, etc.); *unawares* (ŭnawāᵃz′) [-ES] adv. & n., unexpectedly, by surprise, unintention-

ally, as *was taken ~ by his question, must have dropped it ~*, (n.) *at ~*, unexpectedly; *unbacked*, not supported, having no backers (esp. in betting), (of horse) unbroken, not taught to bear rider; *unbalanced*, (esp., of the mind) disordered, violently impulsive; *unbaptized*; *unbearable* (*-bly*); *unbeaten*, not beaten, not surpassed (*~ record* etc.); *unbeautiful*, ugly; *unbecoming* (*ly, -ness*), indecorous (an *~ speech*), not befitting (person, *to* or *for* person), not suited to the wearer (*an ~ hat*); *unbefitting*; *unbefriended*; *unbegotten*; *unbeknown, -knownst*, (colloq.), not known, esp. *~ to* quasi-adv., without the knowledge of, as *did it ~ to him*; *unbelievable*; *unbelieving* (*-ly*), not believing esp. in divine revelation; *unbeloved* (*-vd*); *unbending*² (*-ly, -ness*), not bending, inflexible, firm, austere; *unbeneficed*; *unbeseeming* (*-ly*); *unbesought*; *unbespoken*; *unbias(s)ed*; *unbiblical*, not in or authorized by the Bible; *unbidden*, not commanded, not invited; *unbigoted*; *unbirthday*, (joc., of a present) given on a day other than a birthday); *unbleached*; *unblemished*; *unblest*; *unblooded*, (of horse etc.) not thoroughbred; *unblushing* (*-ly, -ness*); *unbookish*; *unborn*; *unbounded* (*-ly, -ness*), not bounded (*by*, or abs.), infinite; *unbred*; *unbribable*; *unbridled*, not bridled, esp. fig., as *~ insolence, tongue*; *unbroken* (*-ly, -ness*), not broken, not subdued, not interrupted (*~ slumber, peace*), not surpassed (*~ record*), not broken in (*~ horse*); *unbrotherly*; *unburdened*; *unburied*; *unbusinesslike*;

uncalled, not called, esp. *~ for*, impertinently obtruded, as *the remark was ~ for, his ~-for remark*; *uncandid* (*-ly*); *uncanny* (*-iness*), weird, mysterious, not canny; *uncanonical* (*-ly, -ness*); *uncanonized*; *uncared-for*, disregarded, neglected; *uncarpeted*; *uncastrated*; *uncatalogued*; *uncaused*, not caused, not created, self-existent; *uncauterized*; *unceasing* (*-ly*); *unceremonious* (*-ly, -ness*), informal, familiar, abrupt in manner, wanting in courtesy; *uncertain* (*-ly, -ly*), not certainly knowing or known (*am ~ which he means, ~ of his meaning, is of ~ age, the result is ~*), not to be depended on (*is ~ in his aim*), changeable (*~ temper, weather*); *uncertificated*; *unchallenged*; *unchancy* (chiefly Sc.), unlucky, unseasonable; *unchangeable* (*-bly, ness*); *uncharitable* (*-bly, -ness*), censorious, severe in judgement; *unchartered*; *unchary*; *unchaste* (*-ly, -tity*); *unchastened*; *unchivalrous*; *unchristian* (*-ly, -ness*), not Christian, contrary to the Christian character; *uncircumcised*, (fig.) heathen, unregenerate; *uncircumstantial*, not going into details; *uncivil* (*-ly*), ill-mannered, rude; *uncivilized*; *unclad*; *unclaimed*; *unclean* (*-ness*), not clean, foul, unchaste, ceremonially impure (in Jewish law); *unclerical*; *unclothed*; *unclouded* (esp. of happiness etc., cf. *cloudless*); *uncoined*; *uncoloured*, not coloured, (fig.) not exaggerated or heightened in description (~ *account* etc.); *uncombed*; *uncome-at-able* (-kŭmăt-), colloq., not accessible or attainable; *uncomely* (-*iness*); *uncomfortable* (-*bly*); *uncommercial*, not commercial, contrary to commercial principles; *uncommitted*; *uncommon* (-*ly*, -*ness*) a. & colloq. adv., not common, unusual, remarkable, (adv.) remarkably (*an ~ fine girl*); *uncommunicative* (-*ly*, -*ness*), reserved, taciturn; *uncompanionable*; *uncomplaining* (-*ly*, -*ness*); *uncomplaisant* (-*ly*); *uncomplicated*; *uncomplimentary*; *uncompounded*; *uncompromising* (-*ly*), not admitting of compromise, decided, inflexible, unyielding; *unconcerned* (-*édly*), not concerned (*in*, *with*), easy in mind, free from anxiety or agitation; *uncondemned*; *uncondensed*; *unconditional* (-*ity*, -*ness*, -*ly*), not subject to conditions, absolute, (~ *surrender*, *refusal*); *unconditioned*, not subject to conditions (*the U~*, philos., that which is not subject to the conditions of finite existence; ~ *reflex*, psych., instinctive or inborn response to a stimulus); *unconfirmed* (esp. of rumour etc.); *unconformable* (-*bly*, -*ness*); *uncongenial* (-*ly*); *unconnected*; *unconquerable* (-*bly*); *unconquered*; *unconscientious* (-*ly*, -*ness*); *unconscionable* (-*bly*, -*ness*), wholly unreasonable, not guided or restrained by conscience, (law) ~ *bargain*, contract too grossly unfair to be enforced, [prob. f. *conscion*, formed as sing, of *conscience* taken as pl.]; *unconscious* (-*ly*, -*ness*), not conscious, as *was ~ of any change*, *lay ~ for some hours*, ~ CEREBRATION, *the ~* (as n.; see PSYCHO-*analysis*); *unconsecrated*; *unconsidered*, disregarded; *unconstitutional* (-*ity*, -*ly*), (of measures, acts, etc.) opposed to a country's constitution; *unconstrained* (-*édly*); *unconsumed*; *uncontainable*; *uncontaminated*; *uncontemplated*, not expected; *uncontracted*; *uncontradicted*; *uncontrollable* (-*bly*, -*ness*); *uncontrolled* (-*édly*); *uncontroversial* (-*ly*); *uncontroverted*; *unconventional* (-*ity*, -*ly*), not bound by convention or custom, free in character or action or treatment; *unconversable*; *unconversant*; *unconverted*; *unconvinced*; *uncooked*; *uncorroborated*; *uncorroded*; *uncorrupted*; *uncountenanced*; *uncoupled*; *uncourtly*; *uncovenanted*, not promised by or based on a covenant (~ *mercies* of God), not enjoying a covenant; *uncovered*; *uncoveted*; *uncreated*, not yet created, (also arch. *uncreate²*) existing without being created; *uncritical* (-*ly*), disinclined or incompetent to criticize, not according to principles of criticism; *uncrossed*, not crossed (|| ~ *cheque* etc.), not thwarted; *uncrowned* (~ *king*, not yet crowned, also, having power but not name of king); *unculled*; *uncultivable*; *uncultivated*; *uncultured*; *uncurbed*; *uncurtailed*; *uncushioned*; *uncustomed*, not liable to

duty, having paid no duty; *uncut*, not cut, esp. (of book) with full untrimmed margins, (loosely) unopened;

undamaged; *undated*, not dated; *undaunted* (-*ly*, -*ness*), not daunted, fearless; *undebated*; *undebauched*; *undeceived²*; *undecided* (-*ly*), not settled (*point is still ~*), irresolute (*he stood ~*); *undecipherable*; *undefended*, (esp., of suit) in which no defence is put in; *undefiled*; *undefined*; *undelivered*; *undemonstrated*; *undemonstrative*, not given to showing strong feelings, reserved; *undeniable* (-*bly*), that cannot be denied or disputed, decidedly good; *undenominational* (~ *education*); *undenounced*; *undependable*; *undeplored*; *undeposed*; *undepraved*; *undepreciated*; *undepressed*; *undescried*; *undeserved* (-*édly*); *undeserving*; *undesignated*; *undesigned* (-*édly*), not designed, esp. not intended; *undesirable* (-*bility*, -*bleness*, -*bly*) a. & n., not desirable, unpleasant, inconvenient, (n.) ~ person; *undesired*, not desired or solicited; *undesirous*; *undetachable*; *undetected*; *undetermined*, not settled, irresolute; *undeterred*; *undeveloped*; *undeviating* (-*ly*); *undevout*(-*ly*); *undifferentiated*; *undiffused*; *undigested* (esp. fig., of ill-arranged facts etc.); *undignified*, lacking or inconsistent with dignity; *undiluted*; *undiminished*; *undimmed*; *undiplomatic*; *undirected*; *undiscerned*; *undiscerning* (-*ly*); *undischarged*; *undisciplined*; *undisclosed*; *undiscomfited*; *undisconcerted*; *undiscoverable* (-*bly*); *undiscovered*; *undiscriminating*(-*ly*); *undiscussed*; *undisguised* (-*édly*), not veiled, open, (~ *reluctance* etc.); *undismayed*; *undispelled*; *undispersed*; *undisplayed*; *undisputed*; *undissected*; *undissembled*; *undissolved*; *undistinguishable* (-*bly*, -*ness*); *undistinguished*; *undistracted*; *undistressed*; *undistributed* (~ *middle*, fallacy resulting from failure to DISTRIBUTE middle term); *undisturbed* (-*édly*); *undiversified*; *undiverted*; *undivided*; *undivorced*; *undivulged*; *undomesticated*; *undone²*, not done; *undoubted*; *undoubtedly* adv., without doubt (implying certainty on speaker's part, cf. DOUBTLESS); *undoubting* (-*ly*); *undraped*; *undreamed-of*, -*mt-of*; *undressed²*; *undrilled*; *undrinkable*; *undue* (-*duly*), excessive, disproportionate, (*spoke with ~ warmth*), improper (~ *influence*, by which person, e.g. testator, is induced to do what he would not of his own free will), (of bill etc.) not yet due; *undurable* (-*bly*); *undutiful* (-*ly*, -*ness*); *undying* (-*ly*,) immortal (~ *fame* etc.);

unearned, not earned (~ *increment*, increased value of land due to external causes e.g. increased population, not to owner's labour or outlay); *unearthly* (-*iness*), not earthly, supernatural, ghostly, weird, (~ *cry*, *pallor*), (colloq.) absurdly early (*why call me at this ~ hour?*); *uneasy* (-*ily*, -*iness*), disturbed or uncomfortable in body or mind (*you seem ~*, *passed an ~*

night), disturbing (*had an ~ suspicion*); *uneatable*; *uneaten*; *unecclesiastical*; *uneclipsed*; *uneconomic*, (esp., of rent) too low to repay owner & builder; *uneconomical*; *unedified*; *unedifying*, (esp.) tending, to suggest evil or offend moral delicacy; *unedited*; *uneducated*; *uneffaced*; *uneffected*; *unelated*; *unelected*; *unelucidated*; *unemancipated*; *unembarrassed*; *unemotional* (-*ly*); *unemphatic* (-*ally*); *unemployable* a. & n., (person) unfitted by character, by age, or otherwise, for paid employment; *unemployed*, not used, lacking employment, out of work & wages (~ *capital, energies, the* ~); *unempowered*; *unenclosed*; *unencumbered* (~ *estate*, having no liabilities on it); *unendangered*; *unending* (-*ly*, -*ness*), having no end; *unendorsed*; *unendowed*; *unendurable* (-*bly*); *unenforced*; *unenfranchised*; *unengaged*; *un-English*, not (characteristic of the) English; *unenjoyable*; *unenlightened*; *unenrolled*; *unenslaved*; *unenterprising* (-*ly*, -*ness*); *unentertaining* (-*ly*, -*ness*); *unenthusiastic*; *unenumerated*; *unenviable* (-*bly*); *unenvied*; *unequable*; *unequal* (-*ly*), not equal (*to*), of varying quality; *unequalled*; *unequipped*; *unequivocal* (-*ly*, -*ness*), not ambiguous, plain, unmistakable; *unerased*; *unerring* (-*ly*, -*ness*), not erring or failing or missing the mark (~ *judgement, wisdom, aim*); *unescapable*; *unespied*; *unessayed*; *unessential* a. & n., not essential, not of the first importance, (n.) ~ part or thing; *unestablished*; *unestimated*; *unestranged*; *unethical*; *unevangelical*; *unevaporated*; *uneven* (-*ly*, -*ness*), not level or smooth, not uniform or equable (*makes ~ progress, has an ~ temper*), (of number, rare) odd; *uneventful* (-*ly*); *unexamined*; *unexampled*, without precedent; *unexcelled*; *unexceptionable* (-*bly*, -*ness*), with which no fault can be found; *unexcluded*, not subject to excise; *unexclusive* (-*ly*); *unexecuted*; *unexemplified*; *unexercised*; *unexhausted*; *unexpected* (-*ly*, -*ness*); *unexpensive*; *unexpiated*; *unexpired*, (of lease etc.) still running; *unexplained*; *unexplored*; *unexposed*;· *unexpounded*; *unexpressed*; *unexpurgated*; *unextended*, not extended, occupying no space, dimensionless;

unfadable, that cannot fade; *unfading* (-*ly*, -*ness*); *unfailing* (-*ly*, -*ness*), not failing, not running short (~ *supply*), not disappointing one's expectations etc. (~ *resource, supporter*, etc.); *unfair* (-*ly*, -*ness*), not equitable or honest or impartial (*an ~ advantage, got by ~ means, ~ play*); *unfaithful* (-*ly*, -*ness*), (esp.) not faithful in wedlock; *unfaltering* (-*ly*); *unfamiliar* (-*ity*, -*ly*); *unfashionable* (-*bly*, -*ness*); *unfashioned*, not brought into shape; *unfastened*[2]; *unfathered*, (poet.) fatherless, (fig.) not acknowledged by its author (~ *theory* etc.); *unfatherly*; *unfathomable* (-*bly*); *unfathomed*; *unfavourable* (-*bly*, -*ness*); *unfeasible*; *unfed*; *unfeed*,

not FEED[3]; *unfeeling* (-*ly*, -*ness*), lacking sensibility, harsh, cruel; *unfeigned* (-*edly*); *unfelt*, not FELT[2]; *unfeminine*; *unfermented*; *unfertilized*; *unfettered*[2]; *unfigured*, not marked with figures (~ *muslin, vase*); *unfilial* (-*ly*); *unfilled*; *unfiltered*; *unfinished*; *unfit* (-*ly*, -*ness*), not fit (*to do, for* purpose, *for a doctor* etc., to be one); *unfitted*, not fit, not fitted, not furnished with fittings; *unfitting* (-*ly*); *unfixed*[2]; *unflagging*; *unflattering* (-*ly*); *unflavoured*; *unfledged*, not yet fledged or (fig., of person etc.) developed; *unfleshed*; *unflinching* (-*ly*); *unfordable*; *unforeseen*; *unforgettable*; *unforgivable*; *unforgiven*; *unforgiving* (-*ly*, -*ness*); *unforgotten*; *unformed*, not formed, shapeless; *unformulated*; *unfortified*; *unfortunate* (-*ly*) a. & n., the reverse of fortunate, unlucky, unhappy, (n.) ~ person; *unfounded*, without foundation (~ *rumour, hopes*), not yet founded; *unfrequented*; *unfriended*, lacking friends; *unfriendly* (-*iness*); *unfruitful* (-*ly*, -*ness*); *unfulfilled*; *unfunded*, (of debt) floating, not funded; *unfurnished*, not supplied (*with*), without furniture; *unfused* (FUSE [1,2]);

ungallant (-*ly*), not gallant to women; *ungalvanized*; *ungarbled*; *ungarnered*; *ungarnished*, not decorated; *ungauged*; *ungenerous* (-*ly*); *ungenial*; *ungenteel* (-*ly*); *ungentle* (-*ness*, -*tly*), harsh, rude, ill-bred; *ungentlemanly* (-*iness*), unworthy of a gentleman, rude, ill-bred; *unget-at-able*, inaccessible; *unglazed*; *unglutted*; *ungodly* (-*ily*, -*iness*); *ungovernable* (-*bly*), unruly, licentious, wild, violent, (~ *passions*); *ungraceful* (-*ly*, -*ness*); *ungracious* (-*ly*, -*ness*), not kindly or courteous (~ *reply, reception*); *ungraduated*; *ungrammatical* (-*ly*), contrary to rules of grammar; *ungrateful* (-*ly*); *ungrounded*, (of statement etc.) unfounded; *ungrudging* (-*ly*); *unguarded* (-*ly*), not guarded, incautious, thoughtless (*an ~ expression, admission*);

unhackneyed; *unhallowed*; *unhampered*; *unhandsome* (-*ly*, -*ness*), (of appearance, conduct, etc.) not handsome; *unhandy* (-*ily*, -*iness*), awkward to handle, inconvenient, (of person) clumsy; *unhanged*, (esp.) who has escaped hanging (*the greatest scoundrel* ~); *unhappy* (-*ily*, -*iness*), not happy, unlucky, wretched; *unharmed*; *unhatched* (HATCH[2,3]); *unhealthful* (-*ly*, -*ness*); *unhealthy* (-*ily*, -*iness*), (esp., mil. sl., of places) dangerous, exposed to fire; *unheard*, not heard (~ *of*, unprecedented); *unheeded*; *unheedful* (-*ly*); *unheeding*; *unhelpful* (-*ly*); *unhemmed*; *unheralded*; *unheroic*; *unhesitating* (-*ly*); *unhewn* (lit., & fig.), rough, incondite); *unhidden*; *unhistoric(al)*, (esp.) merely legendary; *unholy* (-*ily*, -*iness*), not holy, impious, wicked, (colloq., as intensive epithet) frightful, hideous (*what an ~ row to kick up !*); *unhonoured*; *unhuman*, not human; *unhung*; *unhurt*;

unidea'd, having no ideas; *unideal,* not ideal, prosaic, ordinary, dull, inferior; *unidentified; unilluminated; unillustrated; unimaginable; unimaginative (-ly, -ness); unimpaired; unimpassioned; unimpeachable (-bility, -bleness, -bly),* giving no opening to censure, beyond reproach or question; *unimpeded; unimportant (-ance); unimposing; unimpressionable; unimpressive (-ly, -ness); unimproved,* (esp. of land) not improved; *unimpugned; unindexed; unindicated; uninflammable; uninflated; uninflicted; uninfluenced; uninfluential; uninformed,* (esp.) ignorant; *uninhabitable; uninhabited; uninitiated; uninjured; uninspired,* (esp., of oratory etc.) commonplace; *uninstigated; uninstructed; uninstructive; uninsulated; uninsured; unintelligent (-ly); unintelligible (-bility, -bly); unintentional (-ly); uninteresting (-ly, -ness); unintermittent (-ly); unintermitting (-ly); uninterpretable; uninterred; uninterrupted (-ly); uninventive (-ly); uninvestigated; uninvited; uninviting (-ly),* unattractive, repellent; *uninvoked; uninvolved; unirrigated; unisolated; unissued; unjaundiced; unjust (-ly),* contrary to justice, not just; *unjustifiable (-bly, -ness);*

unkind (*-ly, -ness*), not kind, harsh, cruel; *unkingly; unkneaded; unknightly (-iness); unknowable (-bility, -bleness, -bly) (the U~,* the First Cause or ultimate reality, which is beyond finite apprehension); *unknowing (-ly),* not knowing, unconscious, (*of,* or abs.); *unknown* a., n., & adv., not known (*he, his purpose, what he wanted, that district, was~ to me, a youth to fame~, of~ ingredients,* x *& y denote~ quantities* in equation etc., *the U~* WARRIOR), (n. or abs. adj.) *we all dread the ~, equation of two~s,* (adv.) *~ to,* without the knowledge of (*did it ~ to me*);

unlabelled; *unlaboured,* (of style etc.) easy, spontaneous; *unladylike; unlamented; unlawful (-ly, -ness); unlearnéd,* not LEARNED; *unlearnt, -ned (pr. -nd),* not learnt; *unleavened* (lit. & fig.); *unlettered,* illiterate; *unlicensed; unlicked,* not licked into shape, unmannerly; *unlike (-ness)* a. & prep., not like (*is ~ both his parents, the two are ~, portrait is utterly ~, ~ signs,* + *& —, plays quite ~ anyone I have heard before*); *unlikely (-ihood, -iness),* improbable, unpromising, (*~ tale, errand*); *unlimited (-ly, -ness),* boundless, unrestricted, very great or numerous (*has ~ scope, possibilities, his powers are ~, ~ expanse of sea, drinks ~ coffee*); *unlined,* (esp.) with no lining, (of face etc.) not wrinkled; *unliquidated; unlit; unlocated; unlooked-for,* not expected; *unlopped; unlovable; unloved; unlovely (-iness),* not amiable or attractive; *unloverlike; unloving; unlucky (-ily),* not lucky or fortunate or successful, hapless, wretched, unsuccessful, bringing bad luck, ill-timed, ill-contrived, (*~ toss of coin, always ~ at*

cards, ~ fellow, asked in an ~ hour, single magpie is ~, his ~ efforts to please, an ~ expedient);

unmade; *unmaidenly; unmailable,* that must not or cannot be sent by post; *unmaimed; unmaintainable; unmalleable (-bility); unmanageable (-bly, -ness),* not (easily) to be managed or manipulated or controlled (*~ child, material, situation*); *unmanful (-ly); unmanlike,* not like a man, esp. womanish or childish; *unmanly (-iness); unmannerly (-iness),* rude, ill-bred; *unmarked,* not marked, not noticed; *unmarketable; unmarriageable (-ness); unmarried; unmartial,* unwarlike; *unmasculine,* not masculine or manly; *unmasticable; unmatchable; unmatched; unmated; unmaterial,* not consisting of matter; *unmatured; unmeaning (-ly, -ness),* without meaning, senseless; *unmeant,* not intended; *unmeasured,* not measured, (poet.) immeasurable; *unmechanical; unmeet (-ly, -ness),* arch., not fit (*to do, for* purpose); *unmelodious (-ly, -ness); unmendable; unmentionable (-ness)* a. & n., that it is improper to mention, (n. pl., joc.) trousers; *unmerchantable; unmerciful (-ly, -ness); unmerited; unmethodical; unmetrical (-ly),* not metrical, violating requirements of metre; *unmilitary; unmindful (-ly, -ness); unminted; unmirthful (-ly); unmistakable (-bly),* that cannot be mistaken or doubted, clear; *unmitigated,* unqualified, absolute, (*~ blackguard, lie*); *unmixed; unmodern; unmodified; unmodulated; unmolested; unmoral (-ity),* non-moral; *unmortgaged; unmotherly; unmounted,* not mounted (*~ police, picture, jewel*); *unmourned; unmoved,* not moved, not changed in purpose, not affected by emotion; *unmown; unmurmuring (-ly),* not complaining; *unmusical (-ity, -ly),* not pleasing to the ear, unskilled in or indifferent to music; *unmutilated;*

unnamable, (esp., of vices) too horrible to be named; *unnamed; unnational; unnatural (-ly, -ness),* contrary or doing violence to nature, monstrous, (*~ crimes, vices*), lacking natural feelings (*~ parent, child*), artificial, forced, affected; *unnaturalized,* not naturalized; *unnavigable; unnecessary (-ily)* a. & n., not necessary, more than is necessary (*with ~ care*), (n., usu. pl.) *~* thing(s); *unneedful (-ly); unnegotiable; unneighbourly (-iness); unnoticed; unnourished; unnumbered,* not marked with number, not counted, countless;

unobjectionable (*-bly*); *unobliging; unobliterated; unobscured; unobservant; unobserved; unobstructed; unobtainable; unobtrusive (-ly, -ness); unoccupied; unoffending,* harmless, innocent; *unoffered; unofficial,* (esp., of news) not officially confirmed; *unofficinal; unopened; unopposed; unordained; unorganized; unoriginal,* not possessing originality, derived;

unornamental, not ornamental, unsightly ; *unornamented* ; *unorthodox* ; *unostentatious* (*-ly*, *-ness*) ; *unowned* ;

unpacified ; *unpaged*, with pages not numbered ; *unpaid*, (of sum, bill, debt, or person) not paid (|| *the great* ~, ~ *magistrates or justices*) ; *unpaired* ; *unpalatable* (*-bly*) ; *unparalleled*, having no parallel or equal ; *unpardonable* (*-bly*, *-ness*) ; *unpared* ; *unparental*, unworthy of a parent ; *unparliamentary* (*-ily*, *-iness*), contrary to parliamentary usage (~ *language*, oaths, abuse) ; *unpatented* ; *unpatriotic* (*-ally*) ; *unpatronized* ; *unpaved* ; *unpawned* ; *unpeaceful* ; *unpedantic* ; *unpedigreed* ; *unpeeled* ; *unpensioned* ; *unperceived* ; *unperforated* ; *unperformed* ; *unperjured* ; *unpersuadable* ; *unpersuaded* ; *unpersuasive* ; *unperturbed* ; *unperused* ; *unperverted* ; *unphilosophical* (*-ly*, *-ness*), not according to philosophical principles, wanting in philosophy ; *unpicked*, not selected, (of flowers) not plucked ; *unpicturesque* ; *unpiloted* ; *unpitied* ; *unpitying* (*-ly*), *unplaced*, not placed esp. in race or list ; *unplagued* ; *unplaned* ; *unplanned* ; *unplanted* ; *unplastered* ; *unplastic* ; *unplated* ; *unplausible* (*-bly*) ; *unplayable* (esp. of ball or serve in games) ; *unpleasant* (*-ly*), not pleasant, disagreeable ; *unpleasantness* n., in adj. senses, also, misunderstanding, quarrel, **the late* ~ (joc.), the American civil war (1861–5) ; *unpleasing* (*-ly*) ; *unpliable* (*-bly*) ; *unpliant* (*-ly*) ; *unploughed* ; *unplucked* ; *unplumbed* ; *unpoetical* (*-ly*, *-ness*) ; *unpointed*, having no point, not punctuated, without vowel points (in Hebrew etc.), (of masonry) not pointed ; *unpolished* ; *unpolitical*, not concerned with politics ; *unpolled*, not polled (~ *elector*, *vote*) ; *unpolluted* ; *unpopular* (*-ity*, *-ly*), not popular, esp. not liked by the public ; *unportioned*, portionless ; *unpossessed*, not possessed, not possessed *of* ; *unposted*, uninformed, || (of letter) not posted ; *unpractical* (*-ity*, *-ly*), (of person, plan, method, etc.) not practical ; *unpractised*, not experienced or skilled, not put into practice ; *unpraised* ; *unprecedented*, for which there is no precedent, unparalleled ; *unprefaced* ; *unprejudiced*, (esp.) impartial ; *unprelatical* ; *unpremeditated* (*-ly*), not previously thought over, not deliberately planned, unintentional ; *unpreoccupied* ; *unprepared* (*-ness*), not prepared (*found everything* ~, *was* ~ *for this objection, delivered an* ~ *speech*) ; *unprepossessing* ; *unprescribed* ; *unpresentable*, not presentable, not fit to be presented to company, not fit to be seen ; *unpresuming* ; *unpresumptuous* ; *unpretending* (*-ly*), *unpretentious* (*-ly*, *-ness*), aa., not given to display, making little show ; *unpreventable* ; *unpriced*, with the price(s) not fixed or marked or stated (~ *goods*, *catalogue*) ; *unpriestly* ; *unprimed* ; *unprincely* ; *unprincipled*, lacking or not dictated by good moral principles (~

person, *conduct*) ; *unprintable*, (esp.) too blasphemous, indecent, etc., to appear in print ; *unprinted* ; *unprivileged* ; *unprized*, not valued ; *unprobed* ; *unproclaimed* ; *unprocurable* ; *unproductive* (*-ly*, *-ness*) ; *unprofaned* ; *unprofessional* (*-ly*), not pertaining to one's profession, not belonging to a profession, contrary to professional etiquette etc., (*knows nothing of* ~ *matters*, *ask any* ~ *man*, ~ *conduct*) ; *unprofitable* (*-bly*, *-ness* ; ~ *servants*, persons content to do no more than their duty) ; *unprogressive* (*-ness*), not progressive, conservative ; *unprohibited* ; *unprolific* ; *unpromising* ; *unprompted*, spontaneous ; *unpromulgated* ; *unpronounceable* ; *unpropagated* ; *unprophetic* ; *unpropitious* (*-ly*, *-ness*) ; *unproportional*, not proportional ; *unproposed* ; *unprosperous* (*-ly*, *-ness*) ; *unprotected* ; *unprotested* ; *unprovable* ; *unproved*, *-en* ; *unprovided*, not supplied (*with* money etc.), not. prepared ; *unprovoked*, (of person or act) without provocation : *unpruned* ; *unpublished*, not made public, (of MS. etc.) not published ; *unpunctual* (*-ity*, *-ly*) ; *unpunctuated* ; *unpunishable* ; *unpunished* ; *unpurified* ;

unquailing (*-ly*) ; *unqualified* (*-ly*), not competent, not legally or officially qualified, not modified, (*am* ~ *to serve, an* ~ *practitioner, gave his* ~ *assent*) ; *unquarried* ; *unquelled* ; *unquenchable* (*-bly*) ; *unquenched* ; *unquestionable* (*-bly*, *-ness*), that cannot be questioned or doubted ; *unquestioned*, not disputed or doubted, not interrogated ; *unquestioning* (*-ly*), asking no questions (~ *obedience* etc., yielded without questions asked) ; *unquiet*, restless, agitated, (~ *spirit, times*) ; *unquilled* ; *unquotable* (as *unprintable*) ; *unquoted* ;

unransomed ; *unrazored*, unshaven ; *unreachable* ; *unread*, (of book etc.) not read, (of person) not well-read ; *unreadable* (*-ness*) ; *unready*, not ready, not prompt in action ; *unreal* (*-ity*, *-ly*), illusive, sham, visionary ; *unrealizable* ; *unrealized* ; *unreaped* ; *unreasonable* (*-bly*, *-ness*), not reasonable, exceeding the bounds of reason (~ *demands, conduct*, etc.), not guided by or listening to reason ; *unreasoned*, not rationally thought out ; *unreasoning* (*-ly*), not using or guided by reason ; *unrebuked* ; *unrecallable* ; *unrecalled* ; *unreceipted* ; *unreceived* ; *unreciprocated* ; *unreckoned* ; *unreclaimed* ; *unrecognizable* (*-bly*) ; *unrecognized* ; *unrecompensed* ; *unreconciled* ; *unrecorded* ; *unrectified* ; *unredeemed*, not redeemed, (of promise) not fulfilled, (of bills etc.) not recalled by payment, not taken out of pawn, (of faults etc.) not mitigated or relieved (*by* merits etc., or abs.) ; *unredressed* ; *unrefined*, not refined (~ *sugar, manners*) ; *unreflecting* (*-ly*) ; *unreformable* ; *unreformed* ; *unrefuted* ; *unregal* ; *unregarded* ; *unregenerate* ; *unregistered* ; *unregretted* ; *unregulated* ; *unrehearsed* (esp. of results that surprise their authors); *unrelated*; *unrelaxed*; *unrelenting* (-*ly*, -*ness*); *unreliable* (-*bility*, -*bleness*, -*bly*); *unrelieved*, (esp.) lacking the relief given by contrast or variation; *unreligious*, not concerned with religion; *unremembered*; *unremitting* (-*ly*), not abating, incessant, (~ *care*, *exertions*); *unremunerative*, not profitable; *unrenewed*; *unrenounced*; *unrepealed*; *unrepentant* (-*ance*); *unrepining* (-*ly*); *unreplenished*; *unreported*; *unrepresentative*; *unrepresented*; *unreproachful*; *unreproved*; *unrequited*, not requited or returned (~ *affection*); *unrescinded*; *unresented*; *unresenting* (-*ly*); *unreserved* (-*edly*, -*ness*), without reservation (~ *compliance* etc.), open, frank, (*an* ~ *nature*), not reserved (~ *seats*); *unresisted*; *unresisting* (-*ly*); *unresolved*, not having formed a decision, not solved or cleared up (~ *doubts*, *problem*), not separated into constituent parts; *unrespected*; *unresponsive* (-*ness*); *unrestful* (-*ly*, -*ness*); *unresting* (-*ly*); *unrestored*; *unrestrainable* (-*bly*); *unrestrained* (-*edly*, -*ness*); *unrestricted* (-*ly*); *unretarded*; *unretentive*; *unrevenged*; *unreversed*; *unrevised*; *unrevoked*; *unrewarded*; *unrhetorical*; *unrhymed*; *unrhythmical*, without (satisfactory) rhythm; *unridable*; *unridden*; *unrighted*; *unrighteous* (-*ly*, -*ness*), not upright or honest or just, evil, wicked; *unripe* (-*ness*), not ripe (lit. & fig.); *unrisen*; *unrivalled*, having no equal, peerless; *unromantic* (-*ally*); *unroofed*; *unroyal* (-*ly*), unlike or unworthy of a king; *unruffled*; *unruled*, not governed, not ruled with lines; *unru'ly* (-*iness*), lawless, refractory, [f. rare *ruly* (RULE, -Y²)];

unsafe (-*ly*, -*ness*), dangerous; *unsaid*²; *unsaintly*; *unsal(e)able* (-*bility*, -*bleness*); *unsalaried*; *unsalted*; *unsanctified*; *unsanctioned*; *unsanitary*, unhealthy; *unsated*; *unsatisfactory* (-*ily*, -*iness*); *unsatisfied*; *unsatisfying* (-*ly*); *unsaved*, not saved (esp. in religious sense); *unsavoury* (-*ily*, -*iness*), uninviting, disgusting, (*an* ~ *dish*, *smell*, *theme*); *unsayable*; *unscalable*, that cannot be climbed; *unscannable*, that cannot be scanned (~ *verses*); *unscared*; *unscarred*; *unscathed*, without injury suffered; *unscented*; *unscheduled*; *unscholarly*; *unschooled*; *unscientific* (-*ally*), (esp.) transgressing scientific principles; *unscoured*; *unscourged*; *unscreened* (esp. of coal); *unscriptural* (-*ly*), not in accordance with Scripture; *unscrupulous* (-*ly*, -*ness*), having no scruples, shameless, unprincipled; *unsculptured*, not covered with sculpture, (zool.) smooth; *unsealed*; *unsearchable*, beyond the reach of search; *unsearched*; *unseasonable* (-*bly*, -*ness*); *unseasoned*; *unseated*², not provided or furnished with seat(s); *unseaworthy* (-*iness*); *unseconded*; *unsectarian* (-*ism*), free from sectarian limitations; *unsecured*; *unseduced*; *unseductive*; *unseeing*, blind, unobservant;

unseemly (-*iness*) a. & (arch.) adv.; *unseen* a. & n., not seen (*the* ~, the world of spirits), ~ (*translation*), translation of unprepared passages as school exercise; *unseizable*; *unselect*, promiscuous, mixed; *unselected*; *unselfish* (-*ly*, -*ness*), regardful of others' interests rather than of one's own; *unsensational* (-*ly*); *unsent*; *unsentenced*; *unsentimental*; *unseparated*; *unserviceable* (-*bly*, -*ness*); *unset*, not set (*sun*, *gem*, *trap*, *broken leg*, *is* ~); *unsettled*², not settled, liable to change, open to further discussion, not paid, having no fixed abode, (of lands) not occupied by permanent inhabitants, (*his mind is still* ~, *a* ~ *weather*; *the point*, *the bill*, *is* ~); *unsevered*; *unshackled*; *unshaded*; *unshadowed*; *unshaken*, not shaken esp. in resolution; *unshapely*; *unshared*; *unshaven*; *unshed*; *unsheltered*; *unshipped*²; *unshocked*; *unshod*; *unshorn*, not shorn or shaven; *unshown*; *unshrinkable*, that will not shrink (~ *flannel*); *unshrinking* (-*ly*), unhesitating, fearless, firm; *unshrunk*; *unshut*; *unshuttered*; *unsifted*; *unsighted*, not sighted (*ship is still* ~), not furnished with sights (~ *gun*), precluded from seeing (*the umpire was* ~ *when Jones was caught*); *unsightly* (-*iness*), repulsive to the sight, ugly; *unsight, unseen, without examination or inspection; *unsigned*; *unsinged*; *unsisterly* (-*iness*); *unsized*, not stiffened with size; *unskilful* (-*ly*, -*ness*); *unskilled*, not possessing or requiring skill or special training (~ *labour*, simple forms of manual labour); *unslaked*; *unsleeping*, *unslumbering*, (fig.) watchful; *unsmoked*; *unsociable* (-*bility*, -*bleness*, -*bly*); *unsocial*; *unsoiled*; *unsolaced*; *unsold*; *unsoldierly*; *unsolicited* (esp. ~ *testimonial*); *unsolicitous*; *unsolid* (-*ity*); *unsolvable*; *unsolved*; *unsoothed*; *unsophistical*; *unsophisticated* (-*ness*), artless, innocent, simple, not adulterated, not artificial; *unsorted*; *unsought*; *unsound* (-*ness*), not sound, diseased, morbid, rotten, ill-founded, erroneous, fallacious, unreliable, (~ *lungs*, *fruit*, *doctrine*, *policy*, *argument*; *of* ~ *mind*, insane); *unsounded*, unfathomed; *unsoured*; *unsown*; *unsparing* (-*ly*, -*ness*), profuse, lavish, (~ *praise*, ~ *of* or *in praise*, ~ *in his efforts*), merciless; *unspeakable* (-*bly*, -*ness*), that words cannot express, good, bad, etc., beyond description (~ *joys*, *an* ~ *bore*); *unspecified*; *unspeculative*; *unspent*; *unspilt*; *unspiritual* (-*ity*, -*ly*); *unspliced*; *unspoiled*, -*lt*; *unspoken*; *unspontaneous*, forced, artificial; *unsportsmanlike* (colloq. also *unsporting*); *unspotted*, not spotted or (fig.) contaminated; *unsprung*, (of vehicles, furniture, etc.) not provided with springs; *unsquared*; *unstable*; *unstaid*; *unstained*, not stained (esp. fig.); *unstamped*, without stamp (~ *deed*, *letter*); *unstarched*; *unstartled*; *unstated*; *unstatesmanlike*; *unstatutable* (-*bly*), not warranted by statute; *unsteadfast* (-*ly*, -*ness*); *unsteady* (-*ily*,

-iness), not steady or firm, shaking, reeling, changeable, fluctuating, of irregular habits, (an ~ hand, walked with ~ steps, ladder is ~, was ~ in his adherence, ~ winds, is notoriously ~, dissipated); unstigmatized; unstimulated; unstinted; unstirred; unstocked, not stocked (with, or abs.); unstopped; unstored; unstrained, not forced, not subjected to strain, not put through a strainer; unstratified; unstressed, not pronounced with stress; unstudied, easy, natural, spontaneous, (~ ease, eloquence); unstuffed; unstung; unsubdued; unsubjugated; unsubmissive (-ly, -ness); unsubscribed; unsubstantial (-ity, -ly), having little or no solidity or reality (~ air, visions, forms, an ~ building); unsubstantiated, not confirmed or established (~ rumours); unsuccessful (-ly); unsugared; unsuggestive; unsuitable (-bility, -bly); unsuited, unfit (for purpose), not adapted (to); unsullied; unsummed; unsummoned; unsung, not sung or (poet.) sung of; unsunned, not lighted by sun; unsupple; unsupplied; unsupportable (-bly, -ness); unsupported; unsuppressed; unsure; unsurgical; unsurmised; unsurmounted; unsurpassable (-bly); unsurpassed; unsurrendered; unsurveyed; unsusceptible; unsuspected (-ly); unsuspicious (-ly, -ness); unsustainable; unsustained; unswallowed; unswayed, not controlled or influenced; unsweetened; unswept; unswerving (-ly); unsworn, not sworn (~ oath, witness); unsymbolical; unsymmetrical (-ly), failing in or not characterized by symmetry; unsympathetic (-ally); unsympathizing (-ly); unsystematic (-ally);

untainted; untalented; untamable(-ness); untamed; untanned; untarnishable; untarnished; untasked; untasted; untaught, (of person etc. or subject etc.) not taught, ignorant; untaxed; unteachable (-ness); untearable; untechnical; untempered, not tempered (~ mortar, steel, severity); untempted; untenable (-bility, -bleness); untenantable, not fit to be occupied; untenanted; untended; untendered, not offered; unterrified; untested; untethered; unthanked; unthankful (-ly, -ness); unthatched; unthinkable, that cannot be conceived in thought, (colloq.) unlikely; unthinking (-ly), thoughtless; unthought, not thought, esp. ~-of; unthoughtful (-ness); unthrashed; unthreadable; unthreaded; unthreshed; unthrifty; unthwarted; untidy (-ily, -iness); untied²; untiled; untillable; untilled; untimbered; untimely (-iness) a. & adv.; ‖ untim(e)ous (Sc.), untimely; untinctured; untinged; untired; untiring (-ly); untithed, not subject to tithes; untitled; untold, not told, not counted, beyond count (~ gold); untormented; untorn; untortured; untouchable, that may not be touched, (n.) a non-caste Hindu (whom a caste man may not touch); untouched; untoward, perverse, refractory, awkward, unlucky, (an ~ generation, accident);

untraceable; untraced; untracked, not followed by means of or marked with tracks; untragic, not tragic or suited to tragedy; untrained, not trained or practised or instructed, not prepared by exercise, diet, etc., for race etc.; untrammelled; untransferable, that cannot or must not be transferred; untranslatable (-bility, -bleness, -bly); untransmutable; untransportable; untravelled, that has not travelled; untraversable; untried, (esp.) inexperienced; untrimmed; untrodden; untroubled, not troubled, calm; untrue (-uly), not true, contrary to the fact, false, not faithful or loyal (to person, principle, etc.), deviating from correct standard; untrussed (~ fowl etc.); untrustworthy (-iness); untruthful (-ly, -ness); untuned; untuneful . (-ly); unturned, not turned (leave no STONE ~); untutored, not taught or schooled;

unused; unusual (-ity rare, -ness, -ly), not usual, remarkable; unutilized; unutterable (-bly), above or beyond description (~ torment, joy, etc., an ~ fool); unuttered; unvaccinated; unvalued, not esteemed or prized, not estimated or priced; unvanquished; unvaried; unvarnished, not varnished or embellished (~ surface, the ~ truth); unvarying (-ly); unvenerable; unvenerated; unvenomous; unventilated; unveracious; unverifiable; unverified; unversed, not versed or skilled (in); unvexed; unvictualled; unvindicated; unviolated; unvisited; unvitiated; unvoiced, not spoken or uttered, (phonet.) not voiced; unvouched, not vouched (usu. -for);

unwak(en)ed; unwanted; unwarlike; unwarmed; unwarned; unwarped; unwarrantable (-bly, -ness), indefensible, unjustifiable, improper; unwarranted, unauthorized, not guaranteed; unwary (-ily, -iness); unwashed, not washed (the great~, the rabble); unwatched; unwatchful (-ness); unwatered, not watered or diluted or supplied with water (~ milk, horse, capital); unwavering (-ly); unweaned; unwearable; unwearied; unweary; unwearying (-ly), not growing weary, persistent, (~ efforts etc.); unwedded; unweeded; unweighed; unwelcome; unwelcomed; unwell, not in good health, indisposed, menstruating; unwept (rhet., poet.), not wept for; unwetted; unwhipped; unwhitened; unwhitewashed; unwholesome (-ly, -ness); unwifely; unwilling (-ly, -ness), not willing or inclined (to do, for thing, for thing to be done, that, or abs.); unwinged; unwinking, not winking, vigilant; unwise (-ly), foolish, imprudent; unwished, not wished (usu. -for); unwithdrawn; unwithered; unwithering; unwitnessed; unwitting (-ly), not consciously or intentionally [see WIT¹]; unwomanly; unwon; unwonted; unwooded; unworkable; unworkmanlike; unworldly (-iness), not worldly, spiritual, (~-minded etc.); unworn, that has not been worn or impaired

by wear; *unworshipped*; *unworthy* (*-ily*, *-iness*), not worthy or befitting the character (*of*), discreditable, unseemly; *unwound*[2]; *unwounded*; *unwoven*; *unwreaked*; *unwrinkled*; *unwritable*; *unwritten*, not written (~ *law*, resting originally on custom or judicial decision, not on written statutes etc., also, assumption that homicide in defence of personal honour etc. is justifiable); *unwrought*; *unwrung*, not wrung (WITHERS ~); *unyielding* (*-ly*, *-ness*), firm, obstinate; *unyoked*; *unyouthful*; *unzealous*.
2. Nouns are occas. formed either directly on a simple noun (*unbelief, unfriend, unrepair*) or by back formation or otherwise on corresp. adj. In these the formation may not be ascertainable, e.g. *unchastity* may be from *un-*+*chastity* or from *unchaste*+*-ity*.
Exx.: *unbelief'*, incredulity, disbelief esp. in divine revelation or in a particular religion, so *unbeliev'er*; *unchas'tity*; *uncircumci'sion*, not being circumcised, (N.T.) *the* ~, the Gentiles; *unconcern'*, freedom from anxiety, indifference, apathy; *unconstraint'*, freedom from constraint; *undress'*[2], ordinary dress opp. to full dress or uniform, loose negligent dress, (often fig. & attrib.); *unease'* (arch.), uneasiness, distress, discomfort; *unemploy'ment*, lack of employment, state of things in which many workers cannot find work or wages (~ *benefit*, payment made to unemployed worker under an insurance act, or by a trade union); *unfaith'* (rare), want of faith; *unfriend'* (arch.), enemy; *unprej'udice*, freedom from prejudice; *unreas'on*, lack of reason, nonsense, folly (ABBOT *of U~*); *unrepair'*, dilapidation, want of repair; *unreserve'*, absence of reserve, frankness; *unrest'*, lack of rest, disturbed or agitated condition of person or nation; *unrestraint'*; *unright'* (arch.), wrong injustice; *unsuccess'*, want of success, failure; *unsuspi'cion* (rare); *unsymm'etry*, absence or violation of symmetry; *un'thrift* (arch.), prodigal(ity); *untruth'*, being untrue, falsehood, lie, (*the manifest* ~ *of this statement, told me an* ~); *unwis'dom*, lack of wisdom, folly, imprudence.

unadopted, see UN-[2](1); **unanchor**, UN-[1] (1).

ūnăn'imous, a. All of one mind, agreeing in opinion, as *we were, the meeting was,* ~ (*for reform, as to the policy to be pursued, in protesting*, etc.); (of opinion, vote, etc.) formed, held, given, with one accord. Hence or cogn. **ūnanim'ITY**, ~NESS, nn., ~LY[2] adv. [f. L *unanimus*, LL *-mis*, (*unus* one+*animus* mind)+-OUS]

unapparel, unarm, unarmed[1], see UN-[1] (2); **unattire**, UN-[1](1).

ŭn'au (*-aw*), n. Brazilian two-toed sloth. [Braz.]

unbag, see UN-[1](3); **unbalance**, UN-[1](1); **unballast**, UN-[1](2); **unbank, unbar, unbear**, UN-[1](1); **unbed**, UN-[1](3); **unbeknown(st)**, UN-[2](1); **unbelief, unbeliever**, UN-[2](2); **unbelt**, UN-[1](2); **unbend, unbending**[1], UN-[1](1).

unberu'fen (ŏŏnberoō-), a. Unsummoned (in E use as deprecating Nemesis after boastful remark etc.). [G]

unbeseem, unbias, unbind, see UN-[1](1); **unbirthday**, UN-[2](1); **unbishop**, UN-[1](4); **unbitt**, UN-[1](3); **unblindfold, unblock, unbolt** UN-[1](1); **unbone**, UN-[1](2); **unbonnet**, UN-[1](1); **unboot**, UN-[1](2); **unbosom**, UN-[1](1); **unbowel**, UN-[1](2); **unbox**, UN-[1](3); **unbrace, unbraid, unbreech, unbridle, unbuckle, unburden, unbutton**, UN-[1] (1); **uncage**, UN-[1](3); **uncanny**, UN-[2](1); **uncap**, UN-[1](2); **uncart, uncase**, UN-[1](3).

uncate. See UNCINATE.

unchain, see UN-[1](1); **unchastity**, UN-[2] (2); **unchristianize**, UN-[1](1); **unchurch**, UN-[1](3).

ŭn'cia (*-shĭa*), n. (Rom. ant.; pl. *-ae*). Twelfth part, esp. (as coin or amount) of the *as*; ounce; inch. [L]

ŭn'cial (*-shl*), a. & n. 1. Of, written in, a kind of majuscule writing found in MSS. of 4th to 8th c. with characters from which modern capitals are largely derived. 2. n. ~ letter or MS. [f. L *uncialis* (prec., see -AL), in LL sense *inch-high, large*]

ŭn'cin|ate, a. (Also **ŭnc'ate**) hooked, crooked. So **ŭncif'EROUS, ŭn'cIFORM**, ~AL, aa. [f. L *uncinatus* (*uncinus* hook f. L *uncus* hook, see -ATE[2])]

uncircumcision, see UN-[2](2); **unclasp**, UN-[1](1).

uncle (ŭng'kl), n. Father's or mother's brother; aunt's husband; *(as familiar mode of address)* *U~ Tom's Cabin* etc., *U~ Sam* (colloq.), federal government or typical citizen of U.S.; (sl.) pawnbroker; (colloq., often w. name added, as voc. or not) elderly friendly person, e.g. B.B.C. announcer; *talk to* (person) *like a Dutch* ~ (with kindly severity). Hence ~SHIP n. [ME, f. AF, f. L *avunculus* maternal uncle (*avus* grandfather, see foll.)]

-uncle, suf. repr. OF *-uncle* (*-oncle*) & L *-unculus*; *-la*, a special form of *-ulus* -ULE. In E thr. (O)F (*carb*~) or dir. f. L (*fur*~); the L form is retained in *ranunculus*.

unclench, -inch, see UN-[1](1); **uncloak**, UN-[1](2); **unclog**, UN-[1](1); **uncloister**, UN-[1](1); **unclose, unclothe**, UN-[1](2).

∥**ŭnc'ō**, a., n. (pl. ~s), & adv. (Sc.). 1. Strange, unusual; notable. 2. n. Stranger; (pl.) news. 3. adv. Remarkably, very; *the* ~ *guid*, rigidly religious people (usu. derog.). [dial. var. of UNCOUTH]

uncock, uncoil, see UN-[1](1); **unconcern**, UN-[2](2); **unconditioned, unconscionable**, UN-[2](1); **unconstraint**, UN-[2](2);

For adjj. in *un-* not given see UN-[2](1).

uncoop, UN-¹(3); uncord, uncork, uncouple, UN-¹(1).

uncouth' (-ōō-), a. (Obs. or arch.) not known of, unfamiliar, unusual; (of places; now literary) unfrequented, desolate, wild, (of life) uncivilized, comfortless; (of persons, looks, conduct, etc.) strange, awkward, clumsy, uncultured, (of language) harsh, rugged, pedantic. Hence ~LY² adv., ~NESS n. [OE *uncūth* unknown (UN-² + *cūth* p.p. of *cunnan* know, CAN²)]

uncover, see UN-¹(1); uncowl, UN-¹(2); uncreate, uncross, UN-¹(1); uncrown, UN-¹(2).

ŭnc'tion, n. Anointing with oil or unguent for medical purposes or as religious rite or ceremonial (EXTREME ~); thing used in anointing, unguent, (fig.) soothing or flattering words or thought or circumstance (see FLATTER); fervent or sympathetic quality in words or tone caused by or causing deep religious or other emotion; simulation of this, affected enthusiasm, gush; excessive suavity; keen or lingering enjoyment in narration, gusto, (*told the story with much* ~). [ME, f. L *unctio* (*unguere unct-* anoint, see -ION)]

ŭnc'tŭous, a. Full of (esp. simulated) unction; greasy, esp. (of minerals) having a soapy feel when touched. Hence ~LY² adv., ~NESS n. [ME, f. med. L *unctuosus* f. L *unctus -ūs* anointing (as prec.), see -OUS]

uncurb, uncurl, see UN-¹(1).

ŭn'dé (-ā), ŭn'dee, a. (her.). Wavy. [f. F *ondé* (L *unda* wave, -ATE²)]

undeceive, undeceived¹, undeify, see UN-¹(1).

ŭn'der, prep., adv., & a. 1. In or to a position lower than, below, as *it lay, fell,* ~ *the table, assembled* ~ (at the foot of) *the castle wall, struck him* ~ *the left eye, nothing new* ~ *the sun* (anywhere), ~ FOOT¹, ~ HATCH¹*es,* ~ one's NOSE, ~ (in & covered by) *water,* ~ one's WING. 2. Within, on the inside of, (surface etc.), as *inserted a knife-blade* ~ *the bark, was seen to blush* ~ *his dusky skin, with a good meal* ~ *his belt* (in his stomach), ~ *the* LEE *of.* 3. Inferior to, less than, as *no one* ~ *a bishop, incomes* ~ *£400, cannot be done* ~ (at less cost than) *£5, total falls* ~ *what was expected, speak* ~ *one's breath* (in a whisper). 4. In the position or act of supporting or sustaining, subjected to, undergoing, liable to, on condition of, subject to, governed or controlled or bound by, in accordance with, in the form of, in the time of, as *sank* ~ *the load* (lit. & fig.), ~ *a* CLOUD, *groaning* ~ *tyranny, is now* ~ *repair,* ~ *examination, a few acres* ~ (planted with) *corn,* ~ FIRE¹, ~ (propelled by) *sail,* ~ WAY, ~ ARM²*s, forbidden* ~ *pain of death, a criminal* ~ *sentence of* (condemned to) *death, have sat* ~ (attended sermons of) *famous preachers, country prospered* ~ *him or his rule, might*

succeed ~ *other conditions, is* ~ *a delusion, was* ~ *the impression,* ~ *the circumstances,* ~ *the rose,* =SUB² *rosa,* ~ FAVOUR¹, ~ (attested by) one's *hand & seal, was* ~ *a vow, known* ~ *an assumed name, appears* ~ *various forms,* ~ *pretence of ignorance, lived* ~ *the Stuarts.* 5. adv. In or to a lower place or subordinate condition, as BRING, KEEP¹, KNOCK¹, KNUCKLE, GO¹, ~, *a cloth should be spread* ~ (usu. ~*neath, beneath*). 6. adj. Lower (now largely merged in foll.), as *the* ~ *jaw,* ~ *layers,* ~ *servants;* ~ *dog* (sl.), dog, person, who has the worst of an encounter, oppressed or (socially) inferior person. Hence ~- MOST a. [OE *under,* OS *-ar,* OHG *untar,* ON *undir,* Goth. *undar*]

ŭnder-, pref. =prec. prep. or adv. or adj. 1. As prep. governing the noun to which it is prefixed, w. sense 'below', *under*- forms a few advv. & adjj., as: *un'derarm* a., (crick.) = UNDERHAND, (lawn tennis, of service or stroke) made by swinging racket below shoulder-level; ~*co'ver* a., surreptitious (~*cover agent,* one trying to secure evidence of illegal activities by associating with the suspected wrongdoers); ~*foot'* adv., under one's feet; UNDERGROUND; UNDERHAND; *un'derproof* a., with less alcohol than proof spirit. 2. *Under-* is prefixed to vbs & their derivatives w. adv. or prep. force in sense ' beneath ', ' lower than ', ' below ', as: ~*bid'* v.t., make lower bid than (person), (bridge) bid less on (a hand) than its strength warrants; ~*cut'*¹ v.t., cut away material of (design etc. in carving) so as to make it stand out in relief, (golf) hit (ball) so that it rises high & does not roll far on alighting, (commerc.) offer lower terms than (competitor); ~*drain'*¹ v.t., drain (ground) by forming channels beneath it; ~*lay'* v.t. & 1., lay something under (thing), esp. (print.) lay paper under (types) to raise them, (mining, intr.) incline from the vertical; *un'derlay* n., paper laid under types, waterproof paper, sheet, etc., for laying under carpet or mattress, (mining) = inclined lode or shaft; ~*let'* v.t., let below true value, sublet; ~*line'*¹ v.t., draw line under (word) to secure emphasis or to indicate italics, stress, emphasize; ~*men'tioned* a.; ~*pin'* v.t., place support of masonry etc. under (wall, overhanging bank, etc.); ~*play'* v.i. (cards), play low card while retaining high one of same suit; *un'derplay* n., ~playing; ~*prop'* v.t., put prop under; ~*quote'* v.t., quote lower prices than (person), quote lower prices than others for (goods etc.); ~*run'* v.t. & i., run or pass under, (naut.) overhaul or examine (a cable etc.) by lifting it on board and passing it along by hand; ~*score'* v.t., =~*line'*¹; ~*sell'* v.t., sell cheaper than (person); *un'derseller* n.; ~*set'*¹ v.t., support (masonry etc.) by prop; *un'dershot* a., (of wheel) worked by water passing under it, = UNDERHUNG; ~signed' a., I, we, the ~signed, (whose signatures appear below). **3.** Under- in sense 'insufficiently', 'incompletely', is prefixed to vbs (used in p.p.) & to some adjj., w. their derivatives. Adjj. & p.pp. tend in attrib. use (cf. UN-[1], -ED[2]) to take stress on first syllable (beef was ~done', hate un'derdone beef; an un'der-exposed or un'der-exposed' negative).

Exx. ~act' v.t., act (a part, or abs.) inadequately; ~bred' a., ill-bred, vulgar; ~charge' v.t., charge too little for (thing) or to (person), put insufficient charge into (gun etc.); un'dercharge n., insufficient charge; ~-devel'op v.t. (photog.); ~do' v.t., cook insufficiently, esp. in p.p. ~done; ~dose' v.t.; ~draw' v.t., depict inadequately; ~dress' v.t. & i., dress too plainly or too lightly; ~employ'ment n., shortage of work; ~es'timāte v.t., form too low an estimate of; ~es'timate (-at), -ation, nn.; ~-expose' v.t., ~-exposure n., (photog.); ~feed' v.t. & i.; ~fired' a., (of pottery) not baked enough; ~grown' a.; ~man' v.t., furnish (ship etc.) with too few men; ~mas'ted a.; ~pay' v.t., pay (workmen etc.) inadequately; ~priv'ileged (-ĭjd) a., less privileged than others, belonging to the lower classes of society; ~produc'tion n., production less than is usual or required; ~rate' v.t., ~estimate; ~-reck'on v.t.; ~-ripe' a.; ~sized' a., of less than the usual size, dwarfish; ~state' v.t.; ~statement n.; ~stock' v.t., supply (farm, shop, etc.) with insufficient stock; ~valua'tion n.; ~val'ue v.t. **4.** Under- in adj. relation with noun replaces or is interchangeable with under a., in senses 'situated beneath', 'subordinate'. In the less-established compounds the hyphen is usu. retained & the stress variously placed on either component or both.

Exx. ~-agent n.; un'derbrush n., = ~growth; un'dercarriage, aircraft's landing gear; un'derclay n., clay bed under coal; ~-clerk(ship) nn.; un'dercliff n., terrace or lower cliff formed by a landslip; un'derclothes, un'derclothing, nn., clothes worn under others esp. next to skin; ~drain[2] n., drain placed underground; un'derflow n., current flowing beneath surface; un'dergarment n., garment worn under others; un'dergrowth n., shrubs or small trees growing under larger ones; ~-king n., inferior or subordinate king; ~-lease n., lease granted by lessee for shorter term than his own; un'derline[2] n., advance announcement of production of subsequent play at foot of play-bill, descriptive line(s) under an illustration; un'derlinen n., linen or (loosely) other ~garments; *un'derpass, subway; un'derplot n., subordinate plot in play or novel; un'der-

-sec'retary(ship) nn.; || (Parliamentary Under-Secretary, member of Government; Permanent Under-Secretary, member of Civil Service & head of a department); ~-servant n.; un'derset[2] n. (naut.), undercurrent in contrary direction to that of wind or surface water; ~-sheriff n., sheriff's deputy; ~shirt n.; un'dershrub n., plant like shrub but smaller; un'derskirt n.; un'dersleeve n., sleeve, esp. detached one, worn under another; un'dersoil n.; un'derstrapper n., inferior agent, underling; ~-stratum n.; ~-tenant n., tenant's tenant; ~-tenancy n.; un'dertint n., subdued tint; un'dertone n., subdued tone esp. in speaking, thin or subdued colour, ~lying quality or element, ~current; un'dertow n., backward flow of wave breaking on beach, = ~set; un'derwear n., (clothes meant for) wearing underneath; un'derwing n., kinds of moth with conspicuous markings etc. on under wings; un'derwood n., = ~growth; un'derworld n., antipodes, infernal regions, lowest social stratum, world of crime.

underact, see UNDER- 3; **under-agent,** UNDER- 4; **underarm,** UNDER- 1; **underbid,** UNDER- 2; **underbred,** UNDER- 3; **underbrush, undercarriage,** UNDER- 4; **undercharge,** UNDER- 3; **underclay, undercliff, underclothes, underclothing,** UNDER- 4; **undercover,** UNDER- 1. **ŭn'dercroft** (-aw-), n. Crypt. [UNDER, ME croft f. L crupta CRYPT]

ŭn'dercurrent, n. Current below the surface; (fig.) unperceived influence or feeling of different or contrary tendency; (mining) large shallow box beside main hydraulic sluice serving to aid in saving gold. [UNDER- 4]

undercut[1]. See UNDER- 2.

ŭn'dercŭt[2], n. || Under side of sirloin; upward blow in boxing. [UNDER- 4]

under-develop, underdo, underdose, see UNDER- 3; **underdrain**[1] v.t., UNDER- 2; **underdrain**[2] n., UNDER- 4; **underdraw, underdress, underemployment, underestimate, underestimation, under-expose, under-exposure, underfeed, underfired,** UNDER- 3; **underflow,** UNDER- 4; **underfoot,** UNDER- 1; **undergarment,** UNDER- 4.

ŭndergō', v.t. Be subjected to, suffer, endure esp. with firmness, as has undergone many trials, underwent a rapid change, an operation. [OE UNDER(gān GO)]

ŭndergrăd'ū|ate, n. Member of university who has not taken his first degree (often attrib.). Hence ~ateSHIP n., ~ETTE[2] n. (joc.), female ~ate. [UNDER- 4]

ŭnderground', adv., a., & n. **1.** Beneath surface of earth. **2.** adj. (in attrib. use ŭn[2]). Situated ~, as ~ railway; (fig.) hidden, secret, as ~ (secret resistance) movement. **3.** n. (ŭn[2]). || ~ railway; ~ movement. [UNDER- 1]

For adjj. in un- not given see UN-[2](1).

For other words in under- see UNDER-.

undergrown, see UNDER- 3; **under-growth,** UNDER- 4.

ŭnderhánd', adv. & a. (*in attrib. use* ŭn²). Clandestine(ly), secret(ly), not above--board; (crick., of bowling) (performed) with hand underneath both elbow & ball, as *bowls ~, ~ bowling.* [UNDER- 1, 4]

ŭnderhŭng' (*in attrib. use* ŭn²), a. (Of lower jaw) projecting beyond upper jaw; having ~ jaw. [UNDER- 2]

under-king, see UNDER- 4; **underlay** v.t. & i., & n., UNDER- 2; **under-lease,** UNDER- 4; **underlet,** UNDER- 2.

ŭnderlíe', v.t. Lie, be situated, under (stratum etc., or abs.); (fig., of principle etc.) be the basis of (doctrine, law, conduct, etc., or abs. esp. in part.). [UNDER- 2]

underline¹ v.t., see UNDER- 2; **underline², underlinen,** UNDER- 4.

ŭn'derling, n. Subordinate (usu. derog.). [ME (-LING¹)]

underman, undermasted, see UNDER- 3; **undermentioned,** UNDER- 2.

ŭndermín|e', v.t. Make mine or excavation under, wear away base or foundation of, as *rivers ~e their banks, ~e the walls*; injure (person, reputation, influence, etc.) by secret means; injure, wear out, (health etc.) insidiously or imperceptibly. Hence ~'ER¹ n. [UNDER- 2]

ŭnderneath', adv., prep., a., & n. **1.** At or to a lower place (than), below (not in fig. senses). **2.** adj. & n. Lower (surface, part). [OE *underneothan* (UNDER, cf. BENEATH)]

*underpass, see UNDER- 4; **underpay,** UNDER- 3; **underpin, underplay** v.i., & n., UNDER- 2; **underplot,** UNDER- 4; **underprivileged, under-production,** UNDER- 3; **underproof,** UNDER-1; **underprop, underquote,** UNDER- 2; **underrate, under-reckon, under-ripe,** UNDER- 3; **underrun, underscore,** UNDER- 2; **under-secretary(ship),** UNDER-4; **undersell(er),** UNDER- 2; **under-servant,** UNDER- 4; **underset¹** v.t., UNDER- 2; **underset²** n., **under-sheriff, undershirt,** UNDER- 4; **undershot,** UNDER- 2; **undershrub,** UNDER- 4; **undersigned,** UNDER- 2; **undersized,** UNDER- 3; **underskirt, undersleeve, undersoil,** UNDER- 4.

ŭnderstánd', v.t. & i. (-*stood*); arch. p.p. -*standed*). **1.** Comprehend, perceive the meaning of, (words, person, or language etc.), as *does not ~ what you say, do you ~ me?, French?; tongue not ~ed of the people,* foreign language. **2.** Grasp mentally, perceive the significance or explanation or cause or nature of, know how to deal with, as *do not ~ why he came, what the noise is about, the point of his remark; quite ~ your difficulty; cannot ~ him, his conduct, his wanting to go; thoroughly ~s children, could never ~ mathematics;* (abs.) *you don't ~* (the situation etc.). **3.** Infer esp. from information received, take as implied, take

for granted, as *I ~ that doors open at 7.30, that they are almost destitute, him to be* or *that he is a distant relation, I quite understood that expenses were to be paid, no one could ~ that from my words, what did you ~ him to say* (~ from his words)? ; (expr. uncertainty or surprise or indignation) *do I ~ (you to say) that* or *am I to ~ that you refuse?;* (introducing warning or threat) *now ~ me, he gave me* or *I was given to ~* (I thought he said or meant) *that it was done.* **4.** Supply (word) mentally, as *the verb may be either expressed or understood.* [OE UNDER(*standan* STAND)]

ŭnderstánd'ing¹, a. Having insight. [ME; -ING²]

ŭnderstánd'ing², n. In vbl senses, esp.: intelligence, as *has an excellent ~, men without ~*; power of apprehension, power of abstract thought, (often opp. to *reason*); agreement, harmony, union of sentiments, convention, thing agreed upon, as *must come to an ~ with him, disturbed the (good) ~ between them, had a secret ~ with other firms, consented only on this ~, on the distinct ~ that;* (pl., sl.) feet, legs, shoes, etc. [ME; -ING¹]

understate(ment), understock, see UNDER- 3; **understrapper, under-stratum,** UNDER- 4.

ŭn'derstŭdȳ, n., & v.t. **1.** One who studies theatrical part in order to play it at short notice in absence of the usual actor. **2.** v.t. Study (part) thus, act as ~ to (actor). [UNDER- 4]

undertáke', v.t. & i. Bind oneself to perform, make oneself responsible for, engage in, enter upon, (work, enterprise, responsibility); accept an obligation, promise, (*to* do); (arch.) engage with (person) in combat, argument, etc.; guarantee, affirm, as *I will ~ that he has not heard a word, that you shall* or *will be no loser by it;* (arch.) be guarantee *for* (person, fact); (colloq.) manage funerals. [ME, repl. OE *underniman*]

ŭn'dertáker, n. In vbl senses, esp.: one who manages funerals; (hist.) influential person who undertook to procure particular legislation esp. to obtain supplies from Commons if king would grant some concession. [-ER¹]

ŭnderták'ing, n. In vbl senses, esp.: work etc. undertaken, enterprise, as *a serious ~;* management of funerals (ŭn²). [-ING¹]

under-tenant, under-tenancy, see UNDER- 4; **undertint, undertone, undertow,** UNDER- 4; **undervaluation, undervalue,** UNDER- 3; **underwear, underwing, underwood, underworld,** UNDER- 4.

ŭnderwríte' (-crít), v.t. & i. Execute & deliver (policy of insurance esp. on marine property), practise marine insurance, engage to buy all stock in (company etc.) not bought by the public, whence **ŭn'derwríTER** n.; undertake to finance;

write below, as *the underwritten names.*
[UNDER- 2]

ŭn'dies (-dĭz), n. pl. (colloq.). (Esp. women's) underclothing. [abbr., -Y³]

ŭndine' (-ēn), n. Female water-sprite who by marrying a mortal & bearing a child might receive a soul. [f. mod. L *Undina* f. L *unda* wave + -INE¹]

undo, see UN-¹(1); **undock,** UN-¹(3); **undoer, undoing, undomesticate, undone¹,** UN-¹(1).

undrape, undress¹ v.t. & i., see UN-¹ (1); **undress²** n., UN-²(2); **undressed¹,** UN-¹(1); **unduke,** UN-¹(4).

ŭn'dŭl|āte¹, v.i. Have wavy motion or look. Hence ~ANT a. (esp. ~*ant fever,* Malta fever), ~**ātĭng**LY² adv. [as foll., -ATE³]

ŭn'dŭlate², a. Wavy, going alternately up & down or in & out, as *leaves with* ~ *margins.* Hence~LY² adv. [f. L *undulatus* (*unda* wave, see -UL-, -ATE²)]

ŭndŭlā'tion, n. Wavy motion or form, gentle rise & fall, each wave of this; set of wavy lines; (path.) sensation of undulating movement in the heart. [as prec. + -ATION]

ŭn'dŭlātory̆, a. Undulating, wavy; of, due to, undulation; ~ *theory of light* (that light is propagated through the ether by wave-motion imparted to the ether by molecular vibrations of the radiant body), so **ŭndŭlā'tion**IST(2) (-sho-) n. [-ORY]

unearth, see UN-¹(3); **unease,** UN-²(2); **unedge,** UN-¹(2); **unegoize,** UN-¹(1); **unemployment,** UN-²(2); **unentangle, unequalize,** UN-¹(1); **unethical,** UN-²(1); **unface,** UN-¹(2); **unfaith,** UN-²(2); **unfasten, unfastened¹,** UN-¹(1): **unfeather, unfence,** UN-¹(2); **unfetter, unfettered¹, unfeudalize, unfile, unfit, unfix, unfixed¹,** UN-¹(1); **unflesh, unflower,** UN-¹(2); **unfold¹,** UN-¹ (1); **unfold²,** UN-¹(3); **unform,** UN-¹(1); **unframe,** UN-¹(2); **unfriend,** UN-²(2); **unfrock,** UN-¹(2); **unfurl,** UN-¹(1).

ŭngain'l|y̆ (-n-g-), a. & adv. (Of persons or animals or their movements) ill-made, awkward-looking, clumsy; (adv.) in ~y manner. Hence ~**ĭ**NESS n. [UN-² + obs. *gain* a. f. ON *gegn* straight + -LY¹; rel. to AGAIN]

ungear, see UN-¹(1); **unget-at-able,** UN-²(1); **ungild, ungird,** see UN-¹(1); **ungirdle,** UN-¹(2); **unglaze,** UN-¹(1); **unglove, ungown,** UN-¹(2).

ŭng'ual (-nggw-), a. Of, like, bearing, a nail or hoof or claw. So **ŭnguĭc'ūl**AR¹, **ŭnguĭc'ūl**ATE², [-CULE, usu. without dim. force], **ŭnguĭf'er**OUS, **ŭng'uĭf**ORM, aa. [f. L *unguis* claw, nail, + -AL]

ŭng'uent (-nggw-), n. Any soft substance used as ointment or for lubrication. So ~ARY¹ a. [f. L *unguentum* (*unguere* anoint]

ŭng'ūl|a (-ngg-), n. (pl. ~ae). Hoof, claw,

For adjj. in *un-* not given see UN-²(1).

talon, whence ~ATE²(2) a. & n. (zool.); hooked instrument for extracting dead foetus; cone, cylinder, with top cut off by plane oblique to base. Hence ~AR¹ a. [L, dim. as UNGUAL]

ungum, unhair, see UN-¹(2); **unhallow, unhand, unhang, unharness, unhasp,** UN-¹(1); **unhat, unhelm,** UN-¹(2); **unhinge(d), unhitch,** UN-(1); **unhive,** UN-¹(3); **unhook, unhoop,** UN-¹(1); **unhorse,** UN-¹(3); **unhouse, unhumanize,** UN-¹(1); **unhusk,** UN-¹(2).

ūni-, comb. form of L *unus* one, as: ~*artic'ulate,* single-jointed; ~*ax'(i)al,* having a single axis, whence ~*ax'ially* adv.; ~*căm'eral,* of only one chamber (of Parliament etc.); ~*cap'sular,* of one capsule; ~*cell'ular,* one-celled; ~*col'our(ed),* of one colour; ~*corn'ous,* one-horned; ~*cos'tate,* single-ribbed; ~*cus'pid* a. & n., (tooth) of one cusp; *ūn'icycle,* single-wheeled vehicle; ~*flor'ous,* bearing one flower; ~*fol'iate,* having one leaf; ~*lăt'eral,* one-sided (~*lateral leaves,* leaning to one side of stem,~*lateral contract,* binding one party only), (of car-parking) restricted to one side of the street; ~*lat'erally* adv.; ~*lĭt'eral,* consisting of one letter; ~*loc'ular,* ~*loc'ulate,* (bot., zool.), single--chambered; *ūnip'arous,* producing one at a birth, (bot.) having one axis or branch; ~*part'ile,* not divided; *ūn'iped,* single--footed; ~*pers'onal,* (of Deity) existing only in one person, (of verb) used only in one person; ~*plăn'ar,* lying in one plane; ~*pol'ar,* (biol., of cell etc.) having only one pole, (electr.) showing only one kind of polarity, whence ~*pola'rity* n.; ~*rād'iate(d),* having only one arm or process; ~*scr'ial,* set in one row; ~*sex'ual,* of one sex, not hermaphrodite, having stamens or pistil but not both, whence ~*sexual'ity* n., ~*sex'ually* adv.; ~*sul'cate* (bot., zool.), single-grooved; *ūnĭv'alent* (chem.), having a combining power of one, whence *ūnĭv'alence, ūnĭv'alency,* nn.; *ūn'ivalve* a. & n., (mollusc) of one valve; *ūnĭv'ocal* a. & n., (word) of only one proper meaning, whence *ūnĭv'ocally* adv.

Un'iat, -āte, (ū-), n. Member of any community of Oriental Christians that acknowledges Pope's supremacy but retains own liturgy etc. [f. Russ. *uniyat* f. *uniya* union f. L *unus* one]

ūn'icŏrn, n. 1. Fabulous animal with horse's body & single straight horn (in *Deut.* xxxiii. 17 mistransl. of Heb. *re'em,* a two-horned animal); heraldic representation of this, with goat's beard & lion's tail. 2. (Also ~*-fish, -whale, sea-*~) narwhal. 3. Kind of single-horned beetle; caterpillar with hornlike prominence on back (~ *moth,* of this). 4. Pair of horses with third horse in front, turn-out with these. 5. (Also ~*-shell*) kinds of gasteropod with spine on lip of shell. [ME, f. OF

For other words in *uni-* see UNI-.

unicorne or LL *unicornis, -uus* n., f. L adj. UNI(*cornis* f. *cornu* horn)]

ūn'ifŏrm, a., n., & v.t. **1.** Not changing in form or character, the same, unvarying, as *present a ~ appearance, of ~ size & shape, keeps a ~ temperature, behaved with ~ moderation, ~ acceleration* (not varying with time); (of tax, law, etc.) not varying with time or place; conforming to same standard or rule. **2.** n. ~ dress worn by members of same body, e.g. by soldiers, sailors, policemen. **3.** v.t. Make ~, clothe in ~. Hence ~LY[2] adv. [f. F *uniforme* adj. or L UNI(*formis* -FORM)]

ūnifŏrm'itў, n. Being uniform, sameness, consistency; *Act of U~* (for securing ~ in public worship, esp. that of 1662); *doctrine of ~* (that ~ has prevailed in physical causes & effects in all ages, opp. to CATA-STROPHISM), whence **ūnifŏrmĭtār'ĭan(ĭsm)** nn. [ME, f. OF *uniformite* or LL *uniformitas* (as prec., see -TY)]

ūn'ĭfў, v.t. Reduce (things, or abs.) to unity or uniformity. Hence or cogn. ~FICA'TION, ~FĬER[1], nn. [f. F *unifier* or LL UNI(*ficare* -FY)]

Ūnĭgĕn'ĭtus (ū-), n. (hist.). Bull of Clement XI against Jansenism in 1713. [LL=only-begotten, rendering Gk *monogenēs*]

unintelligible. See UN-[2](1).

ūn'ion (-yon), n. **1.** Uniting, being united, coalition, junction, as *effected a ~, the ~ of the parts was imperfect, ~ by first or second* INTENTION; *the U~* (of England & Scotland in 1706, also, of Great Britain & Ireland in 1801). **2.** Matrimony, marriage. **3.** Concord, agreement, as *lived together in perfect ~*. **4.** A whole resulting from combination of parts or members, esp. (1) *the* U.S., (2) *the* United Kingdom, (3) South Africa; TRADE ~; POSTAL ~. **5.** ‖ (Formerly) two or more parishes consolidated for administration of poor-laws, (in full ~ *workhouse*) workhouse erected by such ~. **6.** ‖ Association of independent (esp. Congregational or Baptist) churches for purposes of co-operation. **7.** (*U~*) general club & debating society at some universities, buildings of such society. **8.** Part of flag with device emblematic of ~ normally occupying upper corner next staff (*ensign hoisted ~ down*, with ~ below as signal of distress); *U~ Jack* or *flag*, national ensign of United Kingdom formed by ~ of crosses of St George, St Andrew, & St Patrick. **9.** Kinds of joint or coupling for pipes etc.; shallow vat in which beer is left to clear; fabric of mixed materials, e.g. cotton with linen or silk or jute. **10.** *~ *suit*, combinations (garment). [ME, f. OF, f. LL *unio* unity (*unus* one, see -ION)]

ūn'ion|ist (-nyo-), n. **1.** Member of a trade union, advocate of trade unions. **2.** Person opposed to rupture of legislative union between Great Britain & Ireland, opponent of home rule in Ireland, as

LIBERAL ~*ist*, (attrib.) ~*ist party, principles*; *(hist.) one who during the civil war opposed secession. So ~ISM n., ~*is'*TIC a. [-IST]

ūnique' (-ēk), a. & n. **1.** Unmatched, unequalled, having no like or equal or parallel, as *his position was ~, this vase is so far as is known ~*, (vulg.) *the most ~* (remarkable) *man I ever met, rather ~* (unusual). **2.** n. ~ thing. Hence ~LY[2] (-ēk'lĭ) adv., ~NESS (-ēk'n-) n. [F, f. L *unicus* (*unus* one)]

ūn'ĭson, a. & n. **1.** (mus.). Coinciding in pitch, whence or cogn. **ūnĭs'onAL, ūnĭs'onANT, ūnĭs'onous,** aa., **ūnĭs'on-**ANCE n.; ~ *string* (tuned in ~ with another string & meant to be sounded with it). **2.** n. Unity of pitch in sounds or notes, (mus.) this regarded as an interval; state of sounding at same pitch, esp. *in ~*; = ~ *string*; concord, agreement, as *acted in perfect ~*. [f. OF *unison* or LL UNI(*sonus* sound)]

ūn'it, n. Individual thing or person or group regarded for purposes of calculation etc. as single & complete, each of the individuals or groups into which a complex whole may be analysed, as *take the family as the ~ of society*; quantity chosen as a standard in terms of which other quantities may be expressed, as *abstract ~*, the number one (1), *C.G.S. system of ~s* (in which centimetre, gramme, second, are the ~s of length, mass, & time), *electrical, magnetic, thermal, ~*. [1570 (J. Dee), f. L *unus* repl. *unity*, perh. after *digit*]

ūnĭtār'ĭan, n. & a. **1.** (*U~*) one who, member of a religious body that, maintains against the doctrine of the Trinity that God is one person, whence U~ISM n., U~IZE v.t.; advocate of unity or centralization e.g. in politics. **2.** adj. Of the U~s, as *U~ Church*; = foll. [partly f. mod. L *unitarius* (*unitas* UNITY) +-AN, partly f. UNITY +-ARIAN]

ūn'ĭtarў, a. Of a unit or units, as ~ *method*, a rule in arithmetic used for same purpose as rule of three; marked by unity or uniformity. [f. UNIT or UNITY + -ARY[1]]

ūnite', v.t. & i. **1.** Join (t. & i.) together, make or become one, combine, consolidate, amalgamate, as ~ *the parts with cement, give the parts time to ~, the two nations gradually (became) ~d, oil will not ~ with water*; *U~d Brethren*, the MORAVIAN sect; *U~d Irishmen*, Irish society formed in 1791 for purposes of parliamentary reform etc.; *U~d* KINGDOM; *U~d Nations*, (orig., in 1942) those ~d against the AXIS powers in the 1939–45 war, (later) an organization of almost all ‘ peace-loving States ’; *U~d Provinces*, Holland, Zealand, & 5 other provinces ~d in 1579 & forming basis of republic of Netherlands, (also, hist.) one of the major Indian administrative divisions,

comprising Agra and Oudh; *U~d* STATE[1]*s*.
2. Agree, combine, co-operate, (*in senti-*
ment, conduct, do*ing*). Hence ūnit'ĕDLY[2]
adv., ūn'ĭtĭVE a. [f. L *unire -it-* (*unus*
one)]

ūn'ĭtў, n. Oneness, being one or single or
individual, being formed of parts that
constitute a whole, due interconnexion &
coherence of parts, as *disturbs the ~ of
the idea, pictures lack ~, national ~;*
thing showing such ~, thing that forms
a complex whole, as a *person regarded as
a ~*; (math.) the number one, factor that
leaves unchanged the quantity on which
it operates; *the dramatic unities, unities of
time, place, & action,* limitation of supposed time of drama to that occupied in
acting it or to a single day, use of same
scene throughout, & abstention from all
that is irrelevant to development of single
plot; harmony, concord, between persons
etc., as *dwell together in ~, at ~ with;*
(law) joint tenancy of different tenants,
joint possession by one person of different
rights. [ME, f. OF *unite,* or L *unitas*
(*unus* one, see -TY)]

ūnĭvĕrs'al, a. & n. **1.** Of or belonging to
or done etc. by all persons or things in the
world or in the class concerned, applicable to all cases, as *the terror was ~, met
with ~ applause,* has the ~ *sanction of
philosophers, the rule does not pretend to
be ~, ~ agent* (empowered to do all that
can be delegated), ~ PROVIDER, ~ *compass*
(with legs that may be extended for
large circles), ~ *coupling* or *joint* (transmitting power by a shaft at any selected
angle), ~ *legatee* (to whom the whole of
a property is bequeathed), ~ *proposition*
(in which predicate is affirmed or denied
of the entire subject). Hence or cogn.
ūnĭvĕrsăl'ITY, ~īZA'TION, nn., ~IZE(3)
v.t., ~LY[2] adv. **2.** n. (Log.) ~ proposition; (philos.) general notion or idea,
thing that by its nature may be predicated of many. [ME, f. OF *universal,
-el,* or L *universalis* (as UNIVERSE, see -AL)]

ūnĭvĕrs'al|ist, U-, n. One who holds,
esp. member of an organized body of
Christians who hold, that all mankind
will eventually be saved. Hence or cogn.
~ISM n., ~ĭs'tĭc a. [-IST]

ūn'ĭvĕrse, n. All existing things; the
whole creation (& the Creator); all mankind; (log.) all the objects under consideration (usu. ~ *of discourse*). [f. F
univers f. L *universum* neut. of UNI(*versus*
p.p. of *vertere* turn) combined into one,
whole]

ūnĭvĕrs'ĭtў, n. Educational institution
designed for instruction or examination
or both of students in all or many of the
more important branches of learning,
conferring degrees in various faculties,
& often embodying colleges & similar
institutions; members of this collec-

tively; team, crew, etc., representing a
~, as *the ~ had four wickets to fall;* *U~*
EXTENSION; *U~ Test Act* (abolishing
subscription to Thirty-nine Articles etc.
as requisite to taking of degree, 1871).
[ME, f. OF *universite* f. L *universitatem*
the whole (world); in LL college, guild
(as prec., -TY)]

ūnivers|ŏl'ogў, n. Science of all created
things; science of all that is of human
interest. Hence ~olŏ'gĭGAL a., ~ŏl'ogĭST
n. [f. UNIVERSE + -O- + -LOGY]

unjoin, unjoint, see UN-[1](1).

unkĕmpt' (ŭn-k-), a. Uncombed, dishevelled; untidy, of neglected appearance;
(of language) careless, rough, incondite.
[UN-[2] + ME *kempt* p.p. of *kemben* COMB[2]]

unking, see UN-[1](4); unkink, unknit,
unknot, unlace, unlade, unlash, unlatch, unlay, UN-[1](1); unlead, UN-[1](2);

unlearn, UN-[1](1); unleash, UN-[1](3).

unlĕss', conj. If not, except when, as
*shall (not) go ~ I hear from him, ~
absolutely compelled, always walked ~ I
had a bicycle; ~ & until* (verbose for *until*
in condit. use, cf. *if & when*). [f. LESS
preceded by *of, in, upon,* & *on*; unstressed
on assim. to UN-[2]]

unlimber, see UN-[1](2); unline, unlink,
unload, unlock, unlodge, unloose,
UN-[1](1); unlord, UN-[1](4); unmake,
UN-[1](1); unman, UN-[1](2, 4); unmantle,
UN-[1](2); unmask, unmew, UN-[1](1);
unmonk, UN-[1](4); unmoor, unmortise,
unmould, unmuffle, unmuzzle, UN-[1]
(1); unnail, UN-[1](2); unnaturalize, un-
nerve(d), UN-[1](1); unnest, UN-[1](3); unpack, unpeg, UN-[1](1); unpen, UN-[1](3);
unpeople, UN-[1](1); unperch, UN-[1](3);
unpick, unpin, unplait, unplug, UN-[1]
(1); unplume, UN-[1](2); unpope, UN-[1](4);
unpreach, UN-[1](1); unprejudice, UN-[2]
(2); unprelate, unpriest, unprince,
UN-[1](4); unprop, UN-[1](2); unqueen,
UN-[1](4); unravel, UN-[1](1); unreason,
UN-[2](2); unreel, unreeve, unrein, UN-[1]
(1); unrepair, unreserve, unrest, unrestraint, UN-[2](2); unriddle, unrig,
UN-[1](1); unright, UN-[2](2); unring, UN-[1]
(2); unrip, unrivet, UN-[1](1); unrobe,
UN-[1](2); unroll, unromanize, UN-[1]
(1); unroof, UN-[1](2); unroost, UN-[1](3);
unroot, UN-[1](1); unrumple, UN-[1](2);
unsaddle, unsaid[1], unsay, UN-[1](1);
unscale, UN-[1](2); unscrew, unseal,
unseam, unseat, unseated[1], UN-[1](1);
unself, UN-[1](2); unset, unsettle, unsettled[1], UN-[1](1); unsex, UN-[1](2); unshackle, unsheathe, UN-[1](1); unshell,
UN-[1](2); unship, unshipped[1], UN-[1](1);
unshoe, unshot, unshutter, UN-[1](1);
unsight, unseen, UN-[2](1); unsinew,
unsister, UN-[1](2); unsling, UN-[1](1);
unsnare, UN-[1](3); unsolder, unspar,
UN-[1](2); unspeak, UN-[1](1); unspell,
unsphere, UN-[1](3); unsprung, UN-[2](1);

unsquire, UN-¹(4); unstarch, UN-¹(2); unsteel, UN-¹(1); unstep, UN-¹(3); unstick, unstitch, unstock, unstop, UN-¹(1); unstopper, UN-¹(2); unstrap, unstring, unstrung, UN-¹(1); unsuccess, unsuspicion, UN-²(2); unswaddle, unswathe, unswear, UN-¹(1); unsymmetry, UN-²(2); untack, untangle, unteach, untemper, UN-¹(1); untent, UN-¹(3); untether, unthink, unthread, UN-¹(1); unthrift, ÜN-²(2); unthrone, UN-¹(3); untie, untied¹, UN-¹(1).

until', prep. & conj. = TILL² (preferred when its clause or phrase stands first, as ~ *you told me I had no idea of it*, & occas. ín leisurely or dignified style, as *unless* & ~). [orig. north. ME *untill* f. ON (= OS, Goth.) *und* as far as +TILL²]

untile, untin, see UN-¹(2).

ün'to (-o͞o), prep. (arch.). = TO¹ (in all uses except as sign of infinitive). [ME; formed on UNTIL, w. TO¹ repl. north. TILL²]

untomb, see UN-¹(3); **untooth,** UN-¹(2); **untouchable,** UN-²(1); **untruss,** UN-¹(1); **untruth,** UN-²(2); **untuck, untune,** UN-¹(1); **unturf,** UN-¹(2); **untwine, untwist, unveil,** UN-¹(1); **unvicar,** UN-¹(4) ; **unvote, unwarp, unweave,** UN-¹(1).

ünwiel'd|y̆, a. Slow or clumsy of movement, difficult to use or manage, owing to size or weight or shape. Hence ~iLY² adv., ~iNESS n. [UN-² +(now dial.) *wieldy* active f. WIELD +-Y²]

unwill, unwind, see UN-¹(1); **unwisdom,** UN-²(2); **unwitting(ly),** UN-²(1); **unwork, unwound¹, unwrap, unwrinkle, unyoke,** UN-¹(1).

üp, adv., prep., a., n., & v.i. **1.** To or in a high(er) place, position, degree, amount, value, etc., to or in a capital or university or place farther north or otherwise conventionally regarded as high(er), *as bird flew up to the caves, high up in the air, what is he doing up there?, horse might have won with a better jockey up* (in saddle), *lives four floors up, a few feet farther up, flames mount up, total mounts up, tide is coming up, water came up to his chin, a hundred up* (on scoring-board, scored in game), *it is up to* (incumbent on) *us to foot the bill, sums up to £5, lives up to* (spends all) *his income, up to the* MARK¹, *up against* (confronted with) *a hard job, am not up to* (fit for) *travelling, custom is traced up* (back) *to the Stuarts, up to* DATE², *lift up your head, as far up* (north) *as Aberdeen,* || *Oxford men just going up,* || *stayed up* (at Oxford etc.) *for the vacation, ran up to town* (London) *for the day, was had up* (before magistrate) *on a charge of drunkenness, sailed up* (towards source) *as far as the river was navigable, corn is up* (at high price), *is high up in the school, went up three places in class, ran up a bill, have looked for it up & down* (in every direction). **2.** To the place in question or in which the speaker etc. is, as *child came up & asked me the time, went straight up*

to the door, sure to TURN¹ *up late.* **3.** To or in erect or vertical position (lit. & fig.) esp. as favourable to activity, out of bed or lying or sitting or kneeling posture, in(to) condition of efficiency or activity, as *sprang up from his seat, stand up,* (with *get, stand,* etc. understood) *up!, up with you,* get up, *up with it,* put it up, *up* (opp. *down with*) *the Bolsheviks!, was* (already) *up early this morning, was* (still) *up late last night, must be up & doing, Home Secretary is up* (has risen to speak, is speaking), || *Parliament is up* (no longer sitting, prorogued), *stir up sedition,* GET *up, screw up your courage, wind up watch, put the helm up* (so place it as to force ship away from wind), *beer is not up* (is flat), *nation is up in arms* (armed & ready to fight lit. & fig., often *against*), *whole of the west was up* (in rebellion etc.), *his blood is up* (anger or spirit roused), *is well up* (instructed) *in mathematics, what is up* (going on)?, *what tricks have you been up to* (playing)?, *up to* SNUFF¹, *do not feel up* (equal) *to work, this cigar is not up to much* (is poor); || (at Eton Coll.) *he is up to* (in the form of) *Mr A.* **4.** (Expr. complete or effectual result etc.) *eat, drink, burn, dry, tear, up; speak up* (loudly); *hunt up,* find by hunting; *follow up; praise up; save up,* accumulate by saving; *pack,* PUT¹, *bind, store, up; lock, chain, tie, fasten, fix, nail, seal, up* (securely); *time is up* (exhausted); GIVE¹ *up, hurry up,* MAKE¹ *up, cheer up, clear up; it is all up* (& sl. *U.P.*) *with him,* his case is hopeless; HARD-*up.* **5.** prep. To a higher point of, on or along in ascending direction, as *climbed up the ladder, up the hill, smoke goes up chimney, sailed up* (towards source of) *the river, walked up* (towards higher or more central part of, or simply along) *the street, up hill & down dale,* up & down in every direction, taking the country as it comes; at or in a higher part of, as *lives farther up the road, somewhere up the river, saw him sitting half-a- -mile up the hill, up a* TREE, *up the* POLE¹, *up the* SPOUT. **6.** adj. Moving, sloping, going, towards a higher point or to the capital, as *up stroke, line* (of railway); *train;* *up-and-coming,* enterprising, alert. **7.** n. *On the up-&-up* (colloq.), improving, on the level, honest; *ups & downs,* rises & falls, undulating ground, alternately good & bad fortune. **8.** v.i. (colloq. & dial.; -pp-). Start up, begin abruptly to say or do something (*he ups & says*); (with *with*) raise, pick up, as *he upped* (or *up*) *with his fist, with his stick.* [OE *upp, up* adv., OS *up*, ON *upp*, rel. to OHG *üf* (G *auf*), Goth. *iup*]

üp-, pref. = prec. **1.** Adv. pref. to vbs (esp. in p.p.) & vbl ns., chiefly arch., poet., or rhet., exc. a few given separately (UPBRAID etc.), as: *upbear'* v.t. hold up, sustain, aloft, esp. in p.p. *upborne; upbind'* v.t.; *upblaze'* v.i.; *up'bringing* n.

bringing up, education; *upcast'* (-ah-) v.t.; *up'cast* n., casting up, upward throw, (mining) shaft through which air passes out of mine; *up'growth* (-ōth) n., growing up, development, what grows up; *upheap'* (-p-h-) v.t.; *upheav'al* (-p-h-) n., heaving up, esp. (geol.) of part of earth's crust, (fig.) vast social or other change; *upheave'* (-p-h-) v.t. & i.; *up'keep* n. (mod.), (cost, means, of) maintenance; *uplift'* v.t.; *up'lift* n., elevating influence, edifying effect, moral insulation; *upraise'* v.t.; *uprear'* v.t.; *uprise'* v.i.; *upris'ing* n., rising esp. from bed, rebellion, riot; *uproot'* v.t. (mod.), tear up by roots (lit. & fig.); *upstan'ding*, well set up, erect, (of wages) fixed, not variable; *up'take* n., lifting, (orig. Sc.) understanding, apprehension, as *quick in the uptake*; *up'throw* (-ō) n., throwing upward, esp. (geol., mining) upward displacement of rock on one side of fault; *up'thrust* n. (geol.), = *upheaval*; *upturn'* v.t., turn up (ground in ploughing etc.). **2.** Pref. with prep. force forming advv. & adjj. f. nn., as: *up*ᴸ*country* (-kŭ-) a., toward the interior, inland, as *up-country districts* (cf. *up country* adv.); *uphill'* (-p-h-) adv., with upward slope along hill or slope in upward direction, as *road runs uphill, riding uphill*; *up'hill* (-p-h-) a., sloping upwards, (fig.) arduous, difficult, laborious, as *uphill work*; *up'stage* a. (colloq.), stand-offish; *upstairs'* (-z) adv., *up'stair*(s) a., on, to, an upper storey; *up-stream'* adv., *up*ᴸ*stream* a., (moving, done) against the current; *up*ᴸ*town* adv., to, in or the upper (*or residential) part of a town, also as adj. **3.** With adj. force, as: *up'land* a. & n. (sing. or pl.), (of) the higher or inland parts of a country; *up'stroke*, upward line made in writing.

upa'nishad (ōōpah-, ōōpä-), n. Each of a series of Sanskrit philosophical treatises forming an exposition of the Vedas. [Skr.]

ūp'as, n. (Also ~-*tree, antiar*) Javanese tree yielding milky sap used as arrow--poison & held fatal to whatever came beneath its branches, (fig.) pernicious influence, practice, etc.; poisonous sap of this & other trees. [Malay, = poison]

upbraid', v.t. Chide, reproach (person etc. *with, for,* fault etc., or abs.). Hence ~ING[1] n., ~ingLY[2] adv. [OE UP(*bregdan* BRAID[2] in obs. sense)]

up-ĕnd', v.t. & i. (dial.). Set on end; sit, stand, or rise up. [UP adv.]

ūphōld' (-p-h-), v.t. Hold up, keep erect, support; give support or countenance to (person, practice, etc.); maintain, confirm, (decision, verdict). Hence ~ER[1] n, [ME; UP-]

ūphōl'ster (-p-h-), v.t. Furnish (room etc.) with hangings, carpets, furniture, etc.; provide (chair etc.) with textile covering, padding, springs, etc., cover (chair etc. *with, in,* tapestry etc.). [back formation f. foll.]

ūphōl'sterer (-p-h-), n. One whose trade it is to upholster; ~-*bee*, kind that furnishes its cell with cut leaves etc. So **ūphōl'st**ERY(1, 2) n. [f. obs. *upholster* n. (also obs. *upholder*) f. *uphold* (in obs. sense 'keep in repair') + -STER, + -ER[1]]

ūph'rōe, n. (naut.). Long wooden block with holes through which cords are rove for adjusting an awning. [f. Du. *juffrouw* young lady, (naut.) ornamental pulley, etc. (*jong* young + *vrouw* woman)]

upŏn', prep. = ON (*on* & ~ are perhaps always idiomatically interchangeable; *on* is perhaps the commoner word esp. in colloq. use; ~ is perhaps preferred when the prep. follows its object, as *had no evidence to go ~, nothing to depend ~, not enough to live ~,* but cf. *which table did you leave it on?;* other idiomatic preferences are perhaps rightly shown in ~ *my word, on the whole, tier ~ tier of seats, fell ~ him unawares, had him on toast, came at once on receiving your message, take it on trust, will go on the chance, went on the spree, thrown ~ his own resources, stretched ~ the rack*). [formerly also as adv.; ME (UP + ON)]

ūpp'er, a. & n. **1.** Higher in place, situated above, as ~ *lip*, ~ *storey* (of house, also fig. = brain, as *something wrong in his ~ storey*), ~ (right-hand side of) *keyboard*, ~ CASE[2], *have* or *get the ~ hand* (mastery); ~ *works* (naut.), parts of ship above water when she is balanced for voyage; ~-*cut* (boxing), short-arm blow delivered upwards inside opponent's guard, (v.t.) hit with ~-*cut*; ~ PARTIALS. **2.** Higher in rank, dignity, etc., as *the ~ servants, the U~ House,* House of Lords, *the ~ ten* (*thousand*), the aristocracy, *the U~ Bench* (hist.), Court of King's Bench during exile of Charles II; ~ *crust* (colloq.), the aristocracy. **3.** n. ~ part of boot or shoe, as *be on* one's ~*s* (poor, in difficulties); (pl.) cloth gaiters. [ME (UP + -ER[3])]

ūpp'ermost, a. & adv. **1.** Highest in place or rank, so **ūp'**MOST a. **2.** adv. On or to the top, as *said whatever came ~* (first suggested itself). [prec. + -MOST]

ūpp'ish, a. Self-assertive, pert. Hence ~LY[2] adv., ~NESS n. [f. UP + -ISH[1]]

ūp'right (-rīt; *in pred. use also* ūprīt'), a., adv., & n. **1.** Erect, vertical, as *an ~ post, posture,* PIANO[2], (pred. a. or adv.) *stood ~, set it ~;* righteous, strictly honourable or honest, whence ~LY[2] adv., ~NESS n., (-rīt-). **2.** n. Post or rod fixed ~ esp. as support to some structure. [OE UP(*riht* RIGHT)]

ūp'roar ᐟ(-ōr), n. Tumult, violent disturbance, clamour. Hence **ūproar'**ioUS a. (often of laughter, high spirits, etc.), **ūproar'**iousLY[2] adv., **ūproar'**iousNESS

For other words in *up-* see UP-.

n., (-ōr-). [f. Du. *oproer* (*op* up +*roer* confusion, cf. G *aufruhr*); assoc. w. ROAR]

ŭp′rŭsh, n. An upward rush; (esp., psych.) a sudden emergence into consciousness from the subliminal. [UP- 1]

ŭpsĕt′ [1], v.t. & i., & n. **1.** Overturn, be overturned, as *carriage* (*was*) ~; disturb the composure or temper or digestion of, as *the news quite* ~ *him*, *ate something that* ~ *him*; shorten & thicken (metal, esp. tire) by hammering or pressure. **2.** n. (ŭp²). ~ting, being ~. [UP-]

ŭp′sĕt², a. ~ *price*, lowest selling price of property in auction etc., reserve price. [ME; UP-]

ŭp′shŏt, n. Final issue, conclusion; general effect, the long & short, (*of a matter*). [UP-]

ŭp′side-down′, adv. & a. With the upper part under, inverted, in total disorder, as *everything was* (*turned*) ~, *an* ~ *arrangement*. [altered f. ME *up so down*, lit. up as if down]

|| **ŭpsīdes′** (-dz), adv. (colloq.). *Get* ~ *with*, turn the tables on, avenge oneself upon. [UP, SIDE, -ES]

ŭpsīl′on, n. Greek letter (*Y*, *v*) = u. [Gk *u psilon* slender u, w. ref. to its later sound (ü)]

ŭp′stȧrt, n. Person who has risen suddenly from humble position (often attrib.); person who assumes arrogant tone. [UP-]

ŭp′ward, a., **ŭp′ward**|(s) (-z), adv. **1.** Directed, moving, towards a higher place (lit. & fig.), as *an* ~ *glance*, *prices show an* ~ *tendency*, whence ~LY² adv. **2.** adv. In ~ direction, as *look*, *move*, ~(s), *followed the stream* ~(s) (towards source); *children of 6 years old & ~*(s) (more); *found* ~(s) *of* (more than) *40 specimens*. [OE; -WARD(S)]

ur- (oor), pref. repr. G (MLG, MHG) *ur-*, denoting ' primitive, original, earliest '.

ūraem′|ia, n. (path.). Morbid condition of blood due to retention of urinary matter normally eliminated by kidneys. Hence ~IC a. [f. Gk *ouron* urine +*haima* blood]

ūrae′us, n. Serpent as head-dress of Egyptian divinities & kings. [mod. L f. Gk *ouraios* repr. the anc.-Egypt. wd for cobra]

Ur′al-Altā′ic (ūral-ăl-), a. Of (the people of) the Ural & Altaic mountain ranges; (philol.) of a family of Finnic, Mongolian, & other agglutinative languages of N. Europe & Asia.

Urān′ia (ūr-), n. The MUSE¹ of astronomy. [L, f. Gk *ouranos* heaven]

uranian. See VENUS.

ūrān′ium, n. Radio-active white metallic element, the heaviest of the elements occurring in nature, used as a source of atomic energy & (in the isotope U 235) in atomic bombs. Hence **ūrăn′ic**, **ūr′an**ous, aa. [f. URANUS +-IUM]

ūran|o-, comb. form of Gk *ouranos* heaven, as: ~*ŏg′raphy*, descriptive astronomy, so ~*ograph′ic*(al) aa., ~*ŏg′raphist* n.; ~*ŏl′ogy*, astronomy; ~*ŏm′etry*, measurement of

stellar distances, map showing positions and magnitudes of stars.

Ur′anus (ūr-; or ūrān²), n. (Gk myth.) son of Ge (Earth) & father of Cronus (Saturn), the Titans, etc.; planet discovered by Herschel in 1781, outermost of solar system except Neptune & Pluto. [L, f. Gk *ouranos* heaven, Uranus]

ŭrb′an, a. Of, living or situated in, a city or town, as ~ *districts*, *population*. Hence ~IZE (3) v.t., render ~, remove the rural character of (a district), ~īZA′TION n. [f. L *urbanus* (*urbs urbis* city, see -AN)]

ŭrbāne′, a. Courteous, suave, elegant or refined in manner. Hence ~LY² adv. [f. F *urbain* or L *urbanus* (as prec.)]

ŭrbăn′ity̆, n. Courtesy, polished manners; || (arch.) polished wit or humour. [f. F -*ité* or L *urbanitas* (as prec., see -TY)]

ŭr′céolate, a. (bot.). Pitcher-shaped, with large body & small mouth. [f. L *urceolus* dim. of *urceus* pitcher +-ATE²]

ŭrch′in, n. **1.** Roguish or mischievous boy; boy, youngster. **2.** (Usu. *sea*-~) = ECHINUS; || (arch.) hedgehog, goblin. [ME var. of (now dial.) *hurcheon* f. ONF *herichon*, ult. f. L *ericius* hedgehog]

Urdu (oor′dōō), n. An Indic language, allied to Hindi but with large admixture of Persian, etc., widely used in Pakistan & India. [Hindi, lit. = 'camp language']

-ure, suf. repr. (O)F -*ure*, L -*ura* in many E wds of F or L orig. Many are f. OF (*figure*), a few f. L (*aperture*), some f. L stems of L orig. (*composure*). Senses in E: (1) action or process, its result (*enclosure*, *scripture*), (2) function, state, rank, dignity, office (*judicature*, *prefecture*), (3) collective body of agents (*legislature*), (4) that by which the action is effected (*closure*, *ligature*). To this form various (O)F suff. have been assimilated in E, as in *failure*, *leisure*, *pleasure*, *seizure*, *treasure*, *velure*.

ūr′ea, n. (chem.). Soluble colourless crystalline compound contained esp. in urine of mammals. [latinized f. F *uréc* f. Gk *ouron* urine]

-uret, suf. (chem.) of nn. & their derivatives indicating combination, now for the most part replaced by -IDE. [mod. L -*uretum* first applied to F wds in -*ure*]

ūrēt′er, n. Duct by which urine passes from kidney to bladder etc. [f. Gk *ourĕtēr* (*oureō* make water)]

ūrēth′r|a, n. Duct by which urine is discharged from bladder. Hence ~AL a., ~IT′IS, ~OCELE, ~ŏT′OMY, nn. [LL, f. Gk *ourĕthra* (as prec.)]

ūrēt′ic, a. & n. = DIURETIC.

ŭrge, v.t., & n. **1.** Drive forcibly, impel, hasten, cause to proceed with effort, as ~*d his horse forward*, ~*d him on*, *we* ~*d our flight northwards*; entreat or exhort earnestly or persistently, as ~ *him to action*, *to take steps*; advocate (measure etc.) pressingly; ply (person etc.) hard with argument or entreaty; dwell persistently or emphatically upon, as *in vain you~ his youth, ~d the difficulty of getting supplies, argument was ~d in vain*. 2. n. Impulsion, yearning. [f. L *urgēre* press, drive]

ur′gent, a. Pressing, calling for immediate action or attention, as *am in ~ need, the matter is ~, an ~ demand*; importunate, earnest & persistent in demand, as *was ~ with me for* (or *to disclose*) *further particulars*. Hence **ūr′g-ENCY** n., **~LY²** adv. [F (as URGE, see -ENT)]

ūr′ic, a. Of urine; *~ acid* (found in small quantities in healthy urine of man & quadrupeds, chief constituent in that of birds & reptiles). [f. F *urique* (URINE, -IC)]

-urient, suf. f. L -*urient-*, part. stem of desiderative verbs, forming aa. with meaning ' desiring (to do something) ', as ESURIENT.

ūr′im, n. *~ & thŭmm′ĭm*, objects of unknown nature connected with breastplate of high priest (*Exod.* xxviii. 30). [Heb. *urim* pl. of *ōr* light, *tummim* pl. of *tōm* perfection]

ūr′inal, n. Fixed vessel or receptacle for use of persons requiring to pass urine; public or private place containing such receptacles; vessel used by invalid for passing water in bed; glass vessel for containing urine for inspection. [ME, f. OF f. LL *urinal* (URINE, -AL)]

ūr′inarȳ, a. & n. 1. Of urine, as *~ organs, diseases*. 2. n. Reservoir for urine as manure; (mil.) barrack building containing several urinals. [f. med. L **urinarius* (URINE, -ARY¹)]

ūr′in|āte, v.i. Pass urine. Hence **~A′TION** n. [f. med. L *urinare* (as foll.), see -ATE³]

ūr′in|e, n. Pale-yellow fluid secreted from the blood by the kidneys, stored in bladder, & discharged through urethra. So ~OUS a. [ME, f. OF, f. L *urina*, cogn. w. Gk *ouron*, see -INE³]

ūrin|o-, comb. form of prec., as: *~ŏl′ogy*, study of the urine; *~ŏm′eter*, instrument showing specific gravity of urine, so *~omĕt′ric* a., *~ŏm′etry* n.; *~ŏs′copy*, inspection of urine, so *~oscŏp′ic* a.

ūrn, n., & v.t. 1. Vase with foot & usu. with rounded body, esp. as anciently used for storing the ashes of the dead or as vessel or measure; (fig.) anything in which dead body or its remains are preserved, e.g. grave; vase-shaped vessel with tap in which tea, coffee, etc., is kept hot, e.g. by means of spirit-lamp; *~-flower*, kinds of bulbous plant with *~-shaped* flower. Hence *~′FUL* n. 2. v.t. Enclose in *~*. [ME, f. L *urna*]

ūro-¹, comb. form of URINO-, as *ŭrŏl′ogy* etc.

ūro-², comb. form of Gk *oura* tail, in anat. terms.

Urs′a (ĕr-), n. *~ Major, Minor,* Great,

Little, BEAR¹; *~ Major,* (also) Dr Johnson. [L, = she-bear]

ūrs′ine, a. Of, like, a bear. [f. L *ursinus* (*ursus* bear, see -INE¹)]

Urs′uline (ĕr-), a. & n. (Nun) of an order founded in 1537 for nursing the sick & teaching girls. [f. St *Ursula*+-INE¹]

ūrticār′ia, n. (path.). Nettle-rash. [f. L *urtica* nettle]

ūrt′ic|āte, v.t. Sting like a nettle; whip (paralytic limb etc.) with nettles to restore feeling. So *~A′TION* n. [f. med. L *urticare* (L *urtica* nettle) see -ATE³]

urubu (ōō′rōōbōō), n. American black vulture. [Brazilian]

ūr′us, n. Kind of wild bull described by Caesar, = AUROCHS. [L, = Gk *ouros*, Gmc **ūrus*, see AUROCHS]

us (ŭs, *us*), pl. obj. of I² (abbr. 's, as *let's go*; occas. poet. & arch., = ourselves, as *let's get us from the walls*). [OE, OS *ūs*, ON *oss*, = OHG, Goth. *uns*, cogn. w. L *nos*, Skr. *nas*]

ūs′age (-z-), n. Manner of using or treating, treatment, as *met with harsh ~, damaged by rough ~*; habitual or customary practice esp. as creating a right or obligation or standard, as *sanctified by ~, an ancient ~, contrary to the ~ of the best writers, modern English ~*; (law) habitual but not necessarily immemorial practice. [ME, f. OF *usage* f. L *usus* (as USE², see -AGE)]

ūs′ance (-z-), n. (commerc.). Time allowed for payment of foreign bills of exchange, as *the ~ on Indian bills is 4 months, bill drawn at half or double ~*. [ME, f. OF (as USE², see -ANCE)]

use¹ (ūs), n. 1. Using, employment, application to a purpose, as *should recommend the ~ of a file, taught him the ~ of the globes, put it to a good ~, is meant for ~ not ornament, is in daily ~, becomes easier with ~, worn & polished with ~, made ~ of* (employed) *~, a quibble, pray make ~ of my telephone*. 2. Right or power of using, as *stipulated for the ~ of the piano, lost the ~ of his left arm*. 3. Availability, utility, purpose for which thing can be used, as *a blunt knife is of ~ for this work, a footrule will be found of* (great) *~, it is* (of) *no ~ talking* or *to talk, what is the ~ of talking?, talking is no ~, find a ~ for banana-skins, I have no ~ for it*. 4. Custom, wont, familiarity, as *long ~ has reconciled me to it, in such matters ~ is everything, according to his ~ in emergencies, ~ & wont*. 5. Ritual & liturgy of a church, diocese, etc., as *Sarum, Anglican, Roman, ~*. 6. (law). Benefit or profit of lands & tenements in the possession of another who holds them solely for the beneficiary. [ME, f. OF *us* f. L *usus* (as foll.)]

use² (ūz), v.t. & i. 1. Employ for a purpose, handle as instrument, consume as material, exercise, put into operation, avail oneself of, as *seldom ~ a knife,* *should* ~ *oil for frying, we seem to* ~ *a great deal of butter, never* ~ *a dictionary, learn to* ~ *your hands,* ~ *your wits, must* ~ *the services of an agent, shall* ~ *every means, must* ~ *your opportunities,* ~ *your discretion, should at least* ~ *some moderation, may I* ~ *your name* (quote you as authority, reference, etc.)?, *do not fail to* ~ (in argument, pleading, etc.) *this damaging fact, has* ~d *my absence to poison everyone against me.* **2.** Treat in specified manner, as *has* ~d *me like a dog, how did he* ~ *you?,* ~d *me ill, ill-*~d *me.* **3.** (Now only in past, usu. pron. ūst, esp. when followed immediately by *to*) be accustomed, have as one's constant or frequent practice, as *I* ~d *to take the bus, does not come as often as he* ~d (*to*)*, bell* ~d *always to ring at one, what* ~d *he* (colloq. *did he* ~) *to say?,* ~d *not* (colloq. *didn't* ~) *to answer.* **4.** (Now only in p.p., pron. as last sense) accustomed, as *am not* ~d *to this sort of thing, to being called a liar, have become* ~d *to a vegetarian diet.* **5.** ~ *up,* consume the whole of (material etc.), find a use for (remaining material etc.), exhaust, wear out e.g. with overwork. Hence **ūs'ABLE** a., **ūs'er**[1] [-ER[1]] n., (-z-). [ME, f. OF *user* f. Rom. **usare* frequent. of L *uti us-* use]

ūse'ful (-sf-), a. Of use, serviceable, producing or able to produce good result, as ~ *arts, ratchet-brace will be found* ~, *gave me some* ~ *hints, must make himself generally* ~ (perform miscellaneous services); (sl.) highly creditable or efficient, as *pretty* ~ *performance, is pretty* ~ *at Greek iambics.* Hence ~**LY**[2] adv., ~**NESS** n. [-FUL]

ūse'less (-sl-), a. Serving no useful purpose, unavailing, as *a mass of* ~ *erudition, contents were rendered* ~ *by damp, protest is* ~; (sl.) out of health or spirits, unfit for anything, as *am feeling* ~. Hence ~**LY**[1] adv., ~**NESS** n. [-LESS]

user[1]. See USE[2].

ūs'er[2] (-z-), n. (law). Continued use or enjoyment of a right etc.; *right of* ~, (1) right to use, (2) presumptive right arising from ~. [F *user* USE[2], or inferred f. NON-USER]

ūsh'er, n., & v.t. **1.** Officer or servant acting as doorkeeper of a court etc., showing persons to seats in public hall etc., || or walking before person of rank, as (*gentleman* ~ *of the*) BLACK[1] *rod*; || (now usu. derog.) under-teacher, assistant schoolmaster. Hence ~**ETTE'**, ~**SHIP**, nn. **2.** v.t. Act as ~ to, precede (person) as ~, announce, show *in* etc., as *was at length* ~*ed* (*in*)*to his presence, star* ~*s in the dawn.* [ME, f. AF *usser,* OF *u*(*i*)*ssier,* var. of *huisier* f. *huis* door f. pop. L *ūstium* f. cl. L *ostium,* see -ARY[1], -ER[2]]

ūs'quebaugh (-aw), n. Whisky; Irish cordial made of brandy etc. [f. Ir. & Sc. Gael. *uisge beatha* water of life, see WHISKY[1]]

ūstūlā'tion, n. Drying of moist substance to prepare it for pulverizing; burning of wine. [f. LL *ustulatio* f. L *ustulare* scorch f. *urere ust-* burn, -ATION]

ū'sual (-zhŏŏ-), a. Such as commonly occurs, customary, habitual, as *asked the* ~ *questions, with his* ~ *disregard of convention, the courtesy* ~ *with him, it is* ~ *to tip the waiter, came earlier than* (was) ~, *have forgotten something as* (is) ~ or (vulg. joc.) *as per* ~; also abs., as *may I have my* ~ (drink etc.). Hence ~**LY**[2] adv., ~**NESS** n. [ME, f. OF *usual, -el* or LL *usualis* (as USE[1], see -AL)]

ūsūcăp'tion (-z-), **-cāp'ion**, n. (civil law). Acquisition of the title or right to property by uninterrupted & undisputed possession for prescribed term. [f. OF *usucaption* or med. L *usucaptio* f. L *usucapio -onis* f. *usucapere* acquire by prescription (*usu* by USE[1] + *capere capt-* take)]

ūs'ūfrŭct (-z-), n., & v.t. Right of enjoying the use & advantages of another's property short of destruction or waste of its substance; (vb) hold in ~. [f. med. L *usufructus* (cf. foll.) f. L *usus fructus* (*usus* USE[1] + *fructus* FRUIT)]

ūsūfrŭc'tūarў (-z-), a & n. Of, one who has, usufruct. [f. LL *usufructuarius* (prec., -ARY[1])]

ū'surer (-zhu-), n. One who lends money at exorbitant interest. [ME, f. AF *usurer,* OF *-cor,* f. LL *usurarius* n. (as USURY see -ER[2])]

ūsūrp' (-z-), v.t. & i. Seize, assume, (throne, office, power, property, etc.) wrongfully; (rare) encroach (*up*)*on.* Hence or cogn. **ūsurpā'TION** (-zer-), ~**ER**[1], nn., ~**ĭngLY**[2] adv. [ME, f. OF *usurper* f. L *usurpare*]

ū'surў (-zhu-), n. Practice of lending money at exorbitant interest esp. at higher interest than is allowed by law, whence **ūsūr'ĭous** (-z-, -zh-) a., **ūsūr'ĭousLY**[2] adv., **ūsūr'ĭousNESS** n.; such interest; (now usu. fig.) interest, as *the service was repaid with* ~. [ME, f. AF **usurie* or med. L *usuria* (-Y[1]), f. L *usura* (USE[1], -URE)]

ut[1] (ŏŏt), n. Key-note of a scale (now usu. DO[3]). [see GAMUT]

ŭt[2], adv. *Ut săp'ra, ĭn'fra,* as shown or stated above, below. [L]

ūtĕn'sĭl, n. Instrument, implement, esp. one in domestic use, as *kitchen, cooking-,* ~*s.* [f. OF *utensile* f. L *utensilis* usable]

ūt'erine, a. Of the uterus; born of same mother but not same father (*his* ~ *brother*). [15th c., f. OF *uterin*(*e*) or LL *uterinus* (foll., -INE[1])]

ūt'er|us, n. (pl. ~ī). The womb. Hence ~**IT'IS** n. [L]

ūtĭlitār'ian, a. & n. Of, consisting in, utility; (holder) of utilitarianism. [-ARIAN]

ūtĭlitār'ianism, n. Doctrine that actions are right because they are useful; doctrine that greatest happiness of greatest number should be sole end of public action. [-ISM]

útil'itỹ, n. Usefulness, profitableness; useful thing; = public ~;· = prec.; (theatr., also ~-man) actor of the smallest parts in plays; (attrib.) made or serving for ~, severely practical, (~ clothes, furniture). [ME, f. OF utilite f. L utilitatem (utilis useful f. uti use, see -TY)]

ŭt'ilíz|e, -is|e (-īz), v.t. Make use of, turn to account, use. Hence~ABLE a.,~A'TION n. [f. F utiliser f. It. utilizzare, see prec.]

ŭt'ĭ pŏssĭdḗt'ĭs, n. Principle that leaves belligerents in possession of what they have acquired. [L, = as you possess]

ŭt'most, a. & n. **1.** Furthest, extreme, as the ~ limits; that is such in the highest degree, as showed the ~ reluctance. **2.** n. One's ~, all one can do. [OE ūtemest, double superl. of ūt OUT, cf. AFTER-MOST]

Utōp'ia (ū-), n. (Book published by Sir T. More in 1516 describing) imaginary island with perfect social & political system; ideally perfect place or state of things. [= nowhere, f. Gk ou not+topos place]

Utōp'ian (ū-), **ŭ-**, a. & n. (Inhabitant) of Utopia; (characteristic of an) ardent but unpractical reformer etc., whence **ŭtōp'ianısm** n. [-AN]

ŭt'ricle, n. Cell of animal or plant; small bag or cavity in the body, esp. one in the inner ear. Hence **ŭtric'ŭlAR¹** a. [f. F utricule or L utriculus dim. of uter leather bag]

ŭtt'er¹, a. Complete, total, unqualified, as ~ misery, saw the ~ absurdity of it, an ~ denial; || ~ barrister (junior, addressing· court from outside bar within which Q.C. pleads). Hence~LY² adv.,~MOST a., ~NESS n. [OE ūtera, ūttera, compar. adj. f. ūt OUT; cf. OUTER]

ŭtt'er², v.t. Emit audibly·(cry, groan, sigh, etc.); express in spoken or written wds (one's sentiments, a lie, the truth, etc.); put (notes, base coin, etc.) into circulation. [ME utter f. OE ūtor compar. of ūt OUT; cf. OFris. ūtria, MLG ūteren, MHG ūzeren make known]

ŭtt'erance¹, n. Uttering, expressing in words, as gave ~ to his rage; power of speech, as defective ~; spoken words, as his pulpit~s. [ME, f. prec.+-ANCE]

ŭtt'erance², n. (literary). Fight etc. to the ~ (bitter end). [ME, f. OF outrance (outrer surpass, as ULTRA-)]

ŭv'ŭl|a, n. (pl. ~ae). Pendent fleshy part of soft palate; similar processes in bladder & cerebellum. Hence ~AR¹ a. [LL, dim. of L uva grape]

ŭxŏr'ious, a. Excessively fond of one's wife. Hence ~LY² adv., ~NESS n. [f. L uxorius (uxor wife)+ -OUS]

Uz'bĕk, Uz'bĕg (ū-), n. Member of a Turkish people in central Asia. [native]

V

V, v, (vē), letter (pl. Vs, V's, Vees). V--shaped thing, e.g. joint; (Roman numeral) 5, as IV 4, VI 6, viii 8, viiii (now usu. ix) 9, xv 15, lv 55; V sign, made by hand with fingers clenched except the first and second outspread to form the letter V (for Victory).

văc'ancỹ, n. Being vacant or empty or unoccupied; emptiness of mind, idleness, listlessness; unoccupied post, as has a ~ on his staff, in his warehouse, must fill the ~. [f. foll. + -ANCY; or med. L vacantia]

văc'ant, a. Empty, not filled or occupied, as house is still ~, a ~ smoking-compartment, have no ~ space, will amuse your ~ hours, applied for a ~ post in the Treasury; not mentally active, not rationally occupied, empty-headed, thoughtless, listless, stupid, as his mind seems completely ~, received the news with a ~ stare, given up to ~ frivolities, whence ~LY² adv. [ME, f. OF, or f. L vacare (as foll., see -ANT)]

vacāte' (or vā¹-), v.t. Go away from so as to leave empty or unoccupied, give up occupation or possession of, (military position, place, house, throne, office); annul (law, contract, etc.). [f. L vacare be empty (cf. VACUOUS), see -ATE³]

vacā'tion (or vā-), n. Vacating (of house, post, etc.); holiday, fixed period of cessation from work, esp. in law-courts & universities, as Christmas, Easter, Whitsun, long or summer, ~. [ME, f. OF, or f. L vacatio (as prec., see·-ATION)]

văc'cin|āte (-ks-),·v.t. Inoculate with vaccine to procure immunity from smallpox or with modified virus of any disease in order to produce it in mild form & so prevent serious attack. Hence ~A'TION (-ks-), ~ā'tionIST(2) (-ks-, -sho-), ~ātoR (-ks-), nn. [f. foll. + -ATE³]

văc'cine (-ks-), a. & n. **1.** Of cows or cowpox or vaccination. **2.** n. Virus of cowpox as used in vaccination (bovine, humanized, ~), got direct from cow, got from human subject), modified virus of any disease similarly used, whence **văc'cinAL, văccin'IC,** (-ks-), aa. [f. L vaccinus a.; n. f. F vaccine (vacca cow, see -INE¹)]

văccin'ia (-ks-), n. (med.). Cowpox, esp. inoculated. [mod. L, f. prec., -IA¹]

vă'cĭll|āte, v.i. Move from side to side, oscillate, waver; fluctuate in opinion or resolution. Hence or cogn. ~ātingLY² adv., ~A'TION n. [f. L vacillare, see -ATE³]

văc'ū|ōle, n. (biol.). Minute cavity in organ etc. containing air, fluid, etc. Hence ~olAR¹, ~olATE²(2), aa. [F, f. L vacuus empty]

văc'ūous, a. Empty, void; unintelligent, expressionless, vacant, as a ~ stare, remark. Hence or cogn. **văcū'ITY, ~NESS,** nn. [f. L vacuus+ -OUS]

văc'ūum, n. (pl. *-ums, -ua*). **1.** Space entirely devoid of matter, as *nature abhors a* ~ ; space, vessel, from which air has been almost exhausted by air-pump etc. (*Guerickian, Torricellian,* ~, produced by air-pump, by mercury-pump as in mercurial barometer); (loosely) partial diminution of pressure below normal atmospheric pressure; (colloq.) ~ cleaner. **2.** ~ *brake,* continuous train-brake in which pressure is caused by exhaustion of air from bellows pulling brake-rod; ~ *cleaner,* apparatus for removing dust etc. by suction; ~ *flask,* vessel with double wall enclosing ~ so that liquid in inner receptacle retains its temperature; ~-*gauge* (for testing pressure consequent on production of ~); ~-*tube,* sealed glass tube with almost perfect ~ for observing passage of electric charge (see also THER-MION). [L, neut. of *vacuus* empty]

văd'ė-mēc'um, n. Handbook or other thing carried constantly about the person (often in title of book). [L, = go with me]

vae vĭc'tĭs, int. Woe to the vanquished (expressing victor's intention of exacting full fruits of victory). [L]

văg'abŏnd, a., n., & v.i. **1.** Having no fixed habitation, wandering; driven, drifting, to & fro; (of spider) not sedentary. **2.** n. Wanderer, vagrant, esp. idle & worthless one; (colloq.) scamp, rascal. **3.** v.i. (now colloq.). Wander about, play the ~. Hence ~AGE(2, 3), ~ISM(2), nn., ~ISH[1] a., ~IZE(2) v.i. [ME, f. OF, or f. L *vagabundus* (*vagari* wander)]

vagār'y, n. Whimsical or extravagant notion; caprice; freak. [f. L *vagari* wander]

vagīn'a, n. Sheath, sheathlike covering, esp. (anat.) sexual passage in female from uterus to external orifice, whence **văgĭnĭT'ĬS, văgĭnŏT'OMY,** nn.; (bot.) sheath formed round stem by base of leaf. Hence **vă'gĭnAL, vă'gĭnATE²,** **vă'gĭnātėd,** aa. [L]

văg'rant, a. & n. **1.** Wandering, roving, strolling, itinerant, as *a* ~ *musician, indulging in* ~ *speculations.* **2.** n. Wanderer, idle rover, vagabond; (law) idle & disorderly person of any of three grades liable to various terms of imprisonment. Hence **văg'rANCY** n., ~LY² adv. [ME *vag(a)raunt,* perh. alt. f. AF *wakerant,* by assoc. w. L *vagari* wander]

vāgue (-g), a. Indistinct, not clearly expressed or identified, of uncertain or ill--defined meaning or character, as *returned only a* ~ *answer, has some* ~ *idea of going to Canada, have not the* ~*st notion of his reasons, yield to* ~ *terrors, heard a* ~ *rumour to that effect.* Hence ~'LY² (-gl-) adv., ~'NESS (-gn-) n. [F, or f. L *vagus* wandering]

vail¹, v.t. & i. (arch., poet.). ‖ Lower or doff (one's plumes, pride, crown, etc.) esp. in token of submission; yield, give place, uncover as sign of respect etc. [f.

OF *valer,* or aphetic f. obs. *avale* f. OF *avaler* (*a val* down, f. *val* VALE¹) lower]

‖ **vail²,** n. (arch.; usu. pl.). Gratuity, tip; present given for corrupt purpose. [ME, aphetic f. AVAIL²]

vain, a. **1.** Unsubstantial, empty, trivial, as ~ *boasts,* ~ *triumphs, distinctions*; useless, unavailing, followed by no good result, as *in the* ~ *hope of dissuading him, all resistance was* ~, *to resist is* ~, *it is* ~ *to resist*; conceited, having too high an opinion *of* one's beauty, ability, etc. **2.** *In* ~, to no purpose, as *we protested in* ~, *it was in* ~ *that we protested*; TAKE¹ person's *name in* ~. **3.** ~*glor'y,* boastfulness, excessive vanity, whence ~*glor'ious* a., ~*glor'iously* adv., ~*glor'iousness* n. Hence ~'LY² adv., ~'NESS n. (rare). [ME, f. OF, f. L *vanus* empty, vain]

vair, n. (her.). A fur represented by small shield-shaped figures alternately azure & argent. [ME, f. OF, f. L as VARIOUS]

Vaisya (vī'sya), n. (Member of) the third of the four great Hindu castes, comprising the merchants and agriculturists, cf. BRAHMIN, KSHATRIYA, SUDRA. [Skr. *vaiśya* peasant]

văl'ance, văl'ence¹, n. Kind of damask used for furniture; short curtain round frame or canopy of bedstead. Hence **văl'ancED²** (-st) a. [ME, f. AF **valance* f. *valer* = OF *avaler* descend, see VAIL¹]

vāle¹, n. Valley (now chiefly poet. or in names as *V*~ *of the White Horse*). [ME, f. OF *val* f. L *vallis*]

văl'ė², int. & n. Farewell. [L, imperat. of *valēre* be well, be strong]

vălėdĭc't|ion, n. (Words used in) bidding farewell. So ~ORY a., (also, as n., **farewell oration delivered by senior scholar on graduation etc.). [f. L VALE(*dicere dict-* say) bid farewell, see -ION]

valence¹. See VALANCE.

văl'ence², n. (chem.). Combining or replacing power of an atom as compared with standard hydrogen atom, as *hydrogen, carbon, has a* ~ *of one, four.* [f. LL *valentia* strength (as VALE², see -ENCE)]

Valĕn'cia (-sha), n. Province of Spain; (usu. pl.) mixed fabric with wool weft and silk, cotton, or linen warp, usu. striped; (pl.) ~ almonds or raisins.

Valenciennes' (-sēnz, & see Ap.), n. Rich kind of lace. [~, in France]

văl'enc|y, n. (chem.). Unit of combining capacity, as *carbon has 4* ~*ies*; = VALENCE². [-ENCY]

văl'entine, n. *St V*~'s *day,* day on which *St V*~ was beheaded & on which birds were supposed to pair, Feb. 14; sweetheart chosen on this; amatory or satirical letter or picture sent to person of opposite sex on St V~'s day. [ME, f. OF *-in,* or L *Valentinus,* proper name]

valēr'ian, n. Kinds of plant, esp. *common* ~, herb with pink or white flowers & rather unpleasant smell; root of this used as mild stimulant etc., whence

văl'erATE¹(3) n., **valĕ'ric** a., (chem.). [ME, f. OF *valeriane* f. med. L *-ana*]

văl'ĕt (*or* -lā), n., & v.t. **1.** (Also ~ *de chambre*, pr. văl'ā de shahn'br) man--servant who attends on man's person; ~ *de place* (văl'ā de plahs), courier esp. in France. **2.** v.t. Act as ~ to. [F, = OF *valet, vaslet*, rel. to VASSAL; cf. VARLET]

vălĕtūdĭnār'ian, a. & n. **1.** Of infirm health; seeking to recover health; unduly solicitous about health. **2.** n. ~ person. Hence or cogn. ~ISM n., **vălĕtūd'inARY¹** a. & n. [f. L *valetudinarius* (*valetudo -dinis* health f. *valēre* be well, see -TUDE & -ARIAN, -ARY¹)]

văl'gus, n. Deformity involving outward bending of distal part of limb; knock--kneed person. [L]

Vălhăll'a, n. (Norse myth.) palace in which souls of slain heroes feasted; building used as final resting-place of the illustrious, or containing their statues etc. [f. ON *valhǫll*, hall of the slain (*valr* slain + *hǫll* HALL)]

văl'iant (-ya-), a. (Of person or conduct) brave, courageous. Hence ~LY² adv. [ME, f. OF *vaillant* part. of *valoir* be worth f. L *valēre* be strong]

văl'id, a. (Of reason, objection, argument, etc.) sound, defensible, well-grounded; (law) sound & sufficient, executed with proper formalities, as ~ *contract*, *the marriage was held to be* ~. Hence or cogn. **valid'ITY** n., ~LY² adv. [f. F *valide* or L *validus* strong (as prec., see -ID¹)]

văl'id|āte, v.t. Make valid, ratify, confirm. So ~A'TION n. [f. LL *validare* (as prec.), see -ATE³; partly f. F *valider*]

valise' (-ēs), n. Kind of small portman-teau; kitbag. [F, f. It. *valigia* corresp. to med. L *valisia*, of unkn. orig.]

văl'kyr (-ēr), **vălky'ria**, -**ie**, n. (Norse myth.; pl. -*kyrs*, -*kyries*). Each of Odin's handmaidens who selected those destined to be slain in battle. Hence **vălky'riAN** a. [f. ON *valkyrja* lit. chooser of slain (*valr* slain + -*kyrja* chooser cogn. w. *kjósa* CHOOSE)]

văllĕc'ūl|a, n. (anat., bot.; pl. ~*ae*). Groove, furrow. Hence ~AR¹, ~ATE², aa. [LL, dim. of L *vallis* vale]

văll'ey, n. (pl. ~s). Low area more or less enclosed by hills & usu. with stream flowing through it; any depression compared to this; ~ *of the shadow of death*, (period of) extreme affliction (*Ps.* xxiii. 4); (archit.) internal angle formed by intersecting planes of roof. [ME, f. OF *valee* (as VALE¹, see -Y⁴)]

val(l)ōn'ia, n. Acorn-cups of the ~ *oak*, used in tanning, dyeing, & making ink. [f. It. *vallonia* ult. f. Gk *balanos* acorn]

văll'um, n. (Rom. ant.). Rampart. [L]

văl'orize, -**is**|e (-īz), v.t. Raise or stabilize the value of (a commodity etc.) by government action. Hence ~A'TION n. [f. L *valor* worth + -IZE (3)]

văl'our (-ler), n. (now chiefly poet., rhet.,

or joc.). Personal courage esp. as shown in fighting, prowess. So **văl'orous** a., **văl'orousLY²** adv. [ME, f. OF, f. LL *valorem* (*valēre* be strong, see -OR)]

valse (vahls), n. Waltz; ~ *à* DEUX-TEMPS, waltz with two beats (instead of three) in a bar, each divided into three smaller beats. [F, f. G as WALTZ]

văl'ūable, a. & n. **1.** Of great value or price or worth, as ~ *property, land, furniture, information, assistance*; capable of valuation, as *a service not* ~ *in money*. **2.** n. (usu. in pl.). ~ thing(s), esp. small article(s) of personal property, as *sent all her* ~*s to the bank*. [f. VALUE + -ABLE]

vălŭā'tion, n. Estimation (esp. by professional valuer) of a thing's worth, worth so estimated, price set on a thing, as ~ *of land, disposed of at a low* ~, *sets too high a* ~ *on his abilities*. [16th c., f. foll. vb + -ATION]

văl'ūe, n., & v.t. **1.** Worth, desirability, utility, qualities on which these depend, as *now learnt the* ~ *of fresh water, a friend, quinine, accuracy, regular exercise*; worth as estimated, valuation, as *sets a high* ~ *on his time*; commercial, economic, ex-*change(able)* ~, ~ *in exchange*, purchasing power, power of a commodity to purchase others, amount of (pop.) money or (pol. econ.) other commodities for which thing can be exchanged in open market; FACE¹, SURRENDER, ~; *surplus* ~, surplus production of labour after subsistence of labourer & family; the equivalent of a thing, what represents or is represented by or may be substituted for a thing, as ~ *received* (see BILL⁴ *of exchange*), *got good* ~ *for* (something well worth) *his money, paid him the* ~ *of his lost property, the precise* ~ (meaning) *of a word, acute accent has not always the same* ~, *give the note* (in music) *its full time-*~ (the full time indicated by it); (paint.) relation of one part of picture to others in respect of light & shade, as *out of* ~, too light or dark; amount, quantity, denoted by algebraical term or expression; (biol.) rank in classification. **2.** v.t. Estimate the ~ of, appraise (professionally, whence **văl'ūER¹** n., or otherwise), as *should* ~ *the whole at £2000*; have high or specified opinion of, attach importance to, prize, esteem, appreciate, pride oneself *on*, as ~ *sincerity (beyond all things), a* ~*d friend,* ~*s himself on his conversational powers, do not* ~ *that a brass farthing.* [ME, f. OF, fem. p.p. of *valoir* be worth f. L *valēre* be strong; vb f. n.]

văl'ūeless (-ūl-), a. Worthless. Hence ~NESS n. [-LESS]

valve, n. Kinds of automatic or other device for controlling passage of liquid or gas or the like through pipe etc., as *clack, rotary, screw, sliding, throttle,* ~, *key* ~ (of organ, flute, etc.), SAFETY-~, THERMIONIC~; (anat., zool.) membranous part of organ etc. allowing flow of blood etc. in one direction & not in another, as ~s *of the heart, veins, pulmonary* ~s, whence **vălvŭl**IT'IS [-UL-] n.; (conch.) each of two or more separable pieces of which shell consists, whole shell in one piece; (bot.) each of the segments into which a capsule dehisces, each half of an anther after its opening; (now rare) leaf of folding door. Hence or cogn. **văl'**VAL (bot.), **văl'**VAR[1], **văl'**VATE[2] (anat., bot.), (-)**vălvED**[2] (-vd), ~'LESS (-vl-), **vălv**IF'EROUS, **văl'vi**FORM, **văl'vŭlAR**[1] [-UL-], aa., ~'LET (-vl-), **vălvŏr'**OMY (med.), **văl'vULE** (anat., bot.), nn. [f. L *valva* leaf of folding door]

văm'brāce, n. (hist.). Armour for fore--arm. [ME, f. AF *vaunt-bras* (*avaunt* before, see ADVANCE[1], + *bras* arm f. L *brachium*)]

°vamōse', -ōōs(e)', v.i. & t. (sl.). Begone, decamp; decamp from (place). [f. Sp. *vamos* let us go]

vămp[1], n., & v.i. & t. **1.** Upper front part of boot or shoe; patch designed to make old thing look new; improvised accompaniment. **2.** vb. Put new ~ to (boot, shoe); repair, furbish usu. *up*; make *up* (literary article etc.) out of odds & ends; improvise accompaniment to, improvise accompaniments. Hence ~'ER[1] n. [ME, f. AF *°vampe*, *°vanpe*, = OF *avanpie* f. *avan(t)* before +*pie* foot]

vămp[2], n., & v.t. & i. (colloq.). **1.** Adventuress, woman who exploits men; unscrupulous flirt. **2.** vb. Allure, exploit; act as ~. [abbr. of foll.]

văm'pīre, n. Ghost or reanimated body (usu. of wizard, heretic, criminal, etc.) that leaves grave at night & sucks blood of sleeping persons; person who preys on others; = prec. n.; (in full ~ *bat*) kinds of bat, some of which suck blood of horses, cattle, & sleeping persons; (theatr.) small spring trap of two flaps used for sudden (dis)appearances of one person. Hence **vămpi'r**IC a. [F, f. Magyar *vampir* perh. of Turk. orig.]

văm'pīrism, n. Belief in existence of vampires; blood-sucking (lit. & fig.). [-ISM]

văm'plāte, n. (hist.). Iron plate protecting hand when lance was couched. [ME, f. AF *vaunt-* (as VAMBRACE) +PLATE]

‖ **văn**[1], n., & v.t. (-nn-). **1.** (Arch.) winnowing-machine; (arch., poet.) wing. **2.** v.t. Test quality of (ore) by washing on shovel or by machine, whence ~n'ER[1](1, 2) n.; (n.) such test. [ME, southern var. of FAN[1], perh. partly f. OF *van* or L *vannus*]

văn[2], n. Foremost division of army on the march or of fleet when sailing; front of army in line of battle; (fig.) leaders of a movement etc., as *in the* ~ *of civilization*. [abbr. of VANGUARD]

văn[3], n., & v.t. (-nn-). Large usu. covered vehicle for conveying furniture or other goods; ‖ railway carriage for luggage (*luggage* ~) or for use of guard (*guard's*

~); (vb) convey in ~. [abbr. of CARAVAN, cf. *bus, wig*]

vanăd'ium, n. Hard grey metallic element used in small quantities for strengthening some steels. Hence **văn'ad**ATE[1](3) n., **vanăd'**IC, **văn'ad**OUS, aa., (chem.). [f. ON *Vanadis* name of the Scand. goddess *Freyja*, + -IUM]

Văn'dal, a. & n. (Member) of a Germanic people that ravaged Gaul, Spain, N. Africa, & Rome, destroying many books & works of art; (fig., also *v*~) wilful or ignorant destroyer of works of art etc., whence ~ISM(2), v-, n. Hence **Vandăl'**IC, v-, a. [f. LL *Vandalus* of Gmc orig.]

văndÿke', n., a., & v.t. **1.** (*V*~; prop. *Van Dyck*) Flemish painter d. 1641, picture by him; each of a series of large points forming a border to lace, cloth, etc., (also *V*~ *cape, collar*) cape, collar, with ~s. **2.** adj. (usu. *V*~). In the style of dress, esp. with pointed borders, common in *V*~'s portraits; *V*~ (pointed) *beard*; *V*~ *brown*, deep rich brown. **3.** v.t. Cut (cloth etc.) in ~s.

vāne, n. Weathercock; similar device exposed to current of air etc. as in water-meter; (also *dog*-~) cone or other device used on shipboard as weathercock; blade of windmill, screw propeller, etc.; sight of surveying instruments, sight of quadrant etc. Hence **vān**ED[2] (-nd), ~[.]LESS, aa. [ME, southern var. of obs. *fane* f. OE *fana*, banner; cf. GONFALON]

văng, n. (naut.). Each of two guy-ropes running from end of gaff to deck. [f. Du. *vang* in *vanglijn* painter; earlier *fang*]

văn'guard (-gârd), n. Foremost part of army etc.; (fig.) leaders of an intellectual etc. movement. [f. OF *avan(t)garde* (*avant* before), see ADVANCE[1], GUARD, WARD]

vanill'‖a, n. Kinds of tall orchid with fragrant flowers; (also ~*a-bean*) fruit of this; extract obtained from ~a-bean & used for flavouring ices, chocolate, etc. Hence ~ATE[1](3) n., ~IC a., (chem.). [f. Sp. *vainilla* pod dim. of *vaina* sheath, pod, f. L. VAGINA]

vanill'ism, n. Eruptive itching skin--disease common among workers in vanilla. [-ISM(5)]

văn'ish, v.i., & n. **1.** Disappear suddenly; disappear gradually, fade away; pass away; cease to exist; (math.) become zero (~*ing fraction*, one that becomes zero for a particular value of the variable it contains); (perspect.) ~*ing-point*, point in which all parallel lines in same plane tend to meet, ~*ing-line*, that which represents the line at infinity in which given plane cuts all parallel planes; ~*ing cream*, emollient that leaves no trace when rubbed into the skin. **2.** n. (phonet.). Slight sound with which a principal sound ends (e.g. ŏŏ, ĭ, at end of ō, ā). [ME; aphetic f. OF *evanir* EVANISH]

văn'itÿ, n. Futility, unsubstantiality,

unreality, emptiness, unsubstantial or unreal thing, as *the ~ of worldly wealth, of political distinction, of human achievements, these things are ~ or vanities, all is ~, pomps & ~ of this wicked world, V~ Fair*, the world (allegorized in *Pilgrim's Progress*) as a scene of ~; empty pride, conceit, based on personal attainments or attractions or qualities (*~ bag, case*, carried on the person & containing small mirror, powder-puff, etc.); ostentatious display; (O.T.) heathen deity, as *the vanities of the Gentiles*. [ME, f. OF *vanite*, f. L *vanitatem* (as VAIN, see -TY)]

văn'quish, v.t. Conquer, overcome, (lit. & fig.; now chiefly rhet.). Hence ~ABLE a., ~ER[1] n. [ME *venkus, -quis*, etc., f. OF *vencus* p.p., & *-quis* past tense of *veintre* f. L *vincere*; see -ISH[2]]

va'ntage (vah-), n. = ADVANTAGE (now chiefly in tennis use & in *~-ground*, COIGN *of~*). [ME, f. AF aphetic f. OF *avantage* ADVANTAGE]

văp'id, a. Insipid, flat, as ~ *beer, conversation, moralizings*. Hence vapid'ITY, ~NESS, nn., ~LY[2] adv. [f. L *vapidus*]

văp'or|ize, -ise (-īz), v.t. & i. Convert, be converted, into vapour. Hence or cogn. ~ABIL'ITY, ~ĪZA'TION, ~ĪZER[1](2), nn., ~(ĭz)ABLE aa. [-IZE]

văp'our (-per), n., & v.i. 1. Moisture in the air e.g. mist, (loosely) light cloudy substance e.g. smoke, (phys.) gaseous form of a normally liquid or solid substance (cf. GAS), whence **vāporĬF'EROUS, vāporĬF'IC, văp'orĬFORM**, aa., **vāporĬM'ETER** n.; (med.) kinds of remedial agent to be inhaled, as ~ *of iodine*; unsubstantial thing, vain imagination; (arch.) empty boasting; ‖ (pl., arch.) depression, spleen, hypochondria, whence ~ISH[1] (-per-) a., ~ĭshNESS n.; ~ *bath* (also **vāporAR'IUM** n.), bath in ~ or steam, apparatus or apartment for this; ~*-burner*, apparatus for vaporizing a hydrocarbon for lighting or heating purposes; ~*-engine* (driven by steam or other elastic fluid). Hence or cogn. **văp'orOSE[1], văp'orous, ~Y[2]** (-per-), aa., **vāporŏs'ITY, văp'orOUSNESS**, nn., **văp'orOUSLY[2]** adv. 2. v.i. Emit ~; utter idle boasts or empty talk, whence ~ER[1] (-per-) n. [ME, f. OF, or f. L *vapor*; vb f. n. or L *vaporare*]

văpŭlā'tion, n. (rare). Flogging. So **văp'ŭlātORY** a. [f. L *vapulare* be flogged +-ATION]

vaquer'ō (-kār-), n. (pl. ~s). Mex. or U.-S. herdsman. [Sp. (*vaccà* cow, -ARY[1])]

Varăn'gian (-j-), n. Norse rover, esp. of those who ravaged Baltic coasts about 9th c.; ~ *guard*, bodyguard of Byzantine emperors formed partly of ~s. [f. med. L *Varangus* f. ON *Væringi* lit. confederate (*vdrar* oaths)]

vă'rĕc, n. Seaweed; kelp. [f. F *varec, varech*, of Scand. orig.; cf. WRECK]

văr'iable, a. & n. 1. That can be varied or adapted, as *rod of ~ length, the pressure*

is ~, *a word of ~ construction, ~ gear* (designed to give varying speeds, e.g. slow advance & quick return); apt to vary, not constant, fickle, unsteady, as ~ *wind, mood, temper, fortune*; (astron., of stars) periodically varying in brightness or magnitude; (math., of quantity) indeterminate, able to assume different numerical values; (bot., zool., of species) including individuals or groups that depart from the type; (biol., of organism) tending to change in structure or function. Hence **vāriaBIL'ITY, ~NESS, nn., văr'iabLY[2]** adv. 2. n. ~ thing esp. quantity; (naut.) shifting wind, (pl.) region between NE & SE trade-winds. [ME, f. OF, f. L *variabilis* (VARY, -BLE)]

vă'rĭa lĕc'tĭō, n. Variant reading. [L]

văr'iance, n. Disagreement, difference of opinion, dispute, lack of harmony, as *on that point we are at ~ (among ourselves), at ~ with the authorities, have had a slight ~ with him, this theory is at ~ with all that is known on the subject*; (law) discrepancy between pleadings & proof or between writ & declaration. [ME, f. OF, f. L *variantia* difference (as foll., see -ANCE)]

văr'iant, a. & n. 1. Differing in form or in details from the one named or considered, differing thus among themselves, as *a ~ reading in some MSS., 40 ~ types of pigeon*; variable, changing. 2. n. ~ form, spelling, type, reading, etc., as valet *is a ~ of* varlet, *difficult to choose between these ~s*. [ME, f. OF (as VARY, see -ANT)]

vāria'tion, n. Varying, departure from a former or normal condition or action or amount or from a standard or type, extent of this, as *is not liable to ~, repeated ~s of temperature, is subject to a ~ of several degrees, estimates the ~ in value at 20 per cent*; (astron.) deviation of heavenly body from mean orbit or motion (*periodic, secular, ~*, compensated in short, in very long, period); (of magnetic needle) = DECLINATION (*~-chart*, with lines drawn through places that have same ~); (biol.) structural or functional deviation from type; (alg.) (theory of) relation between quantities that VARY as each other; thing that varies from a type, as *the scazon is a ~ of* or *on the ordinary iambic trimeter*, esp. (mus.) tune or theme repeated in a changed or elaborated form. Hence ~AL (-sho-) a. [ME, f. OF, or L *variatio* (VARY, -ATION)]

vă'ricātĕd, a. (conch.). Having varices. So **vărĭca'TION** n. [f. VARIX, see -ATE[2](2)]

vărĭcĕll'|a, n. = CHICKEN-*pox*. Hence ~AR[1], ~OID, aa. [mod. L, irreg. dim. of VARIOLA]

vă'ricocēle, n. Tumour composed of varicose veins of spermatic cord. [as VARIX+-CELE]

văr'icoloured (-kŭlerd), a. Variegated in colour; of various or different colours. [f. L *varius* various+COLOURED]

vă'ricōs|e, a. Of, affected with, designed

for cure of, varix, as ~e *ulcer, vein, bandage,* whence ~ED[1] (-st) a., **vărĭcŏs'ITY** n.; = VARICATED. [f. L *varicosus* (VARIX, see -OSE[1])]

vār'ĭĕg|āte, v.t. Diversify in colour, mark with irregular patches of different colours (chiefly in p.p., esp. bot. of leaves partly pale from suppression of chlorophyll or of plants with such leaves, as ~*ated geranium*). Hence ~A'TION n. [f. L *variegare* f. *varius* VARIOUS, see -ATE[3]]

vari'ĕtў, n. 1. Being various, diversity, absence of monotony or uniformity, many-sidedness, as *was struck by the ~ of his attainments, of his conversation, of the scene, London has for me the charm of ~, cannot live without ~*. **2.** Collection of different things, as *turned over a ~ of silks, for a ~ of reasons; ~ entertainment* or *show* or simply ~ (consisting of dances, songs, acrobatic feats, etc.), ~ *theatre* (for ~ shows etc.). **3.** (Specimen, member, of a) class of things differing in some common qualities from the rest of a larger class to which they belong. **4.** (biol.). Individual or group usually fertile with any other member of the species to which it belongs but differing from the type in some qualities capable of perpetuation, subspecies, as *climatic ~* (produced by climatic influences), *geographical ~* (confined to given area), whence **vari'ĕtAL** a., **vari'ĕtALLY[2]** adv. [f. F *variété* or L *varietas* (as VARIOUS, see -TY)]

vār'ĭfŏrm, a. Having various forms. [-FORM]

vari'ol|a, n. Smallpox. Hence ~AR[1], **vărĭŏl'IC,** ~OUS, aa. [med. L, as VARIOUS]

vărĭolā'tion, n. Inoculation with smallpox virus. [f. prec. + -ATION]

vār'ĭ|ōle, n. (zool., bot.). Shallow pit like smallpox mark. Hence~olATE[2],~olātĕd, aa. [f. med. L VARIOLA]

vār'ĭol|ĭte, n. Rock with concretionary structure causing on surface an appearance like smallpox pustules. Hence ~ĭt'IC a. [as prec. + -ITE[1]]

vār'ĭoloid, a. & n. **1.** Like smallpox. **2.** n. Mild form of smallpox esp. as modified by previous inoculation. [as prec. + -OID]

vărĭŏm'ēter, n. (electr.). Device for varying the inductance in an electric circuit. [as VARIOUS + -METER]

vārĭōr'um, a. & n. **1.** With notes of various commentators, as *a ~* (*edition of*) *Horace.* **2.** n. A ~ edition. [L, gen. pl. as VARIOUS; short for *cum notis ~*]

vār'ĭous, a. Different, diverse, as *the modes of procedure were ~, types so ~ as to defy classification;* separate, several, more than one, as *came across ~ people, for ~ reasons.* Hence ~LY[2] adv.,~NESS n. (rare). [f. L *varius* + -OUS]

vār'ĭx, n. (pl. *vă'rĭcēs*). (Path.) permanent abnormal dilatation of vein or other vessel, vein etc. thus dilated; (conch.) each of the ridges across the whorls of a univalve shell. [L]

vārl'ĕt, n. (Hist.) medieval page preparing to be a squire; (arch., esp. joc.) menial, low fellow, rascal. [ME, f. OF var. of *vaslet,* see VALET]

vărm'int, n. (vulg., joc.). Mischievous or discreditable person or animal; (hunt. sl.) *the* fox. [var. of *varmin,* VERMIN]

vārn'ish, n., & v.t. **1.** Kinds of resinous solution applied to wood, metal, etc., to give hard shiny transparent surface; glaze on pottery etc.; artificial or natural glossiness; superficial polish of manner; favourable appearance given to misconduct etc., palliation, whitewash; ~-*tree,* kinds from which ~ is obtained. **2.** v.t. Apply ~ to (wood, picture, etc., fig. character, person, action, account, or abs.); ~*ing-day,* day before exhibition of pictures on which exhibitors may retouch or ~ their pictures already hung. [ME, f. OF *vernis,* of unkn. orig.; vb f. OF *verniss(i)er* f. *vernis;* see -ISH[2]]

‖ **vărs'al,** a. (colloq., now rare). = UNIVERSAL. [illit. abbr.]

vărs'itў, n. (colloq.). University (often attrib., as *the ~ boat).* [colloq. abbr.]

vărsovienne' (-vyĕn), n. (Music for) dance resembling mazurka. [F, = (dance) of Warsaw (*Varsovie*)]

vār'us[1], n. Deformity involving inward bending of distal part of limb; bandy-legged person. [L, = bent]

vār'us[2], n. = ACNE. [L, = pimple]

vār'|ў, v.t. & i. Change, make different, modify, diversify, as *can~y the* (direction, amount, etc., of) *pressure at will, seldom ~ies the routine, ~ies the treatment according to circumstances, never ~ies his style, style is not sufficiently ~ied, a ~ied scene;* (mus.) make VARIATIONS of (theme); suffer change, be(come) different in degree or quality, be of different kinds, as *he, his mood, ~ies from day to day, climate ~ies, tried with ~ying success, ~ies from the type, opinions ~y on this point; ~y* (directly) *as, ~y inversely as,* increase, decrease, in proportion or correspondingly to the increase of, as *attraction of bodies ~ies* (directly) *as their masses & inversely as the square of their distances, A ~ies as* (symbol ∝) *B, A ~ies as B & C jointly* (as their product). [ME, f. OF *varier* or L *variare* (as VARIOUS)]

vās, n. (anat.; pl. *vās'a*). Vessel, duct, as ~ *def'erens,* excretory duct of testicle. Hence **vās'AL** a., ~EC'TOMY n. [L, = vessel]

văs'cŭlar, a. Of, made up of, containing, vessels or ducts for conveying blood, sap, etc., as ~ *functions, tissue, ~* (circulatory) *system, ~ plants.* Hence ~ITY (-ă'r·ĭ-), ~īZA'TION, nn., ~IZE(3) v.t., ~LY[2] adv. [f. mod. L *vascularis* f. VASCULUM + -AR[1]]

văs'cŭlōse, n. & a. Chief substance of vessels of plants; (adj.) = prec. [foll., -OSE[2,1]]

văs'cŭlum, n. (pl. -*la*). Botanist's (usu.

tin) collecting-case; (anat.) small vessel, penis. [L, dim. of VAS]

vase (vahz; *arch.* vawz, *arch. & U.S.* văs, -z), n. Vessel of baked clay or other material used for various purposes but primarily ornamental, as *flower-~*; large usu. sculptured vessel of marble etc. used to decorate gate-post etc.; *~-painting*, decoration of ~s with pigments esp. among ancient Greeks, instance of this. Hence ~'FUL n. [F, f. L VAS]

văs'elĭne, n. Unctuous substance got from petroleum & used in ointments etc. [P; irreg. f. G *wasser* water + Gk *elaion* oil + -INE³]

văsi-, văso-, comb. forms of VAS, as: *vas'i-form*, tubular; *vasoconstric'tor, -dilat'or, -mot'or*, aa. & nn., (nerve, drug) causing constriction, dilatation, either, of blood--vessels; *vasosen'sory*, supplying sensation to vessels.

văss'al, n. (Hist.) holder of land by feudal tenure (*great, rear, ~*, holding directly from king, holding from great ~); (rhet.) slave, humble dependant. [ME, f. OF, f. med. L *vassallus*, of Celt. orig., the simplex *vassus* corresp. to OBreton *uuas*, W *gwas*, Ir. *foss*; cf. VAVASOUR]

văss'al|age, n. (Hist.) condition, obligations, service, of a vassal; servitude, dependence; fief; (rare; also ~RY n.) vassals collectively. [ME, f. OF *vassal-(l)age* (prec., see -AGE)]

vast (vah-), a. & n. **1.** Immense, huge, very great, as *a ~ expanse of water, ~ plains, shook his ~ frame, a ~ multitude, scheme*; (colloq.) *gave him ~ satisfaction, makes a ~ difference*. Hence ~'LY² adv. (esp. colloq.), ~'NESS n. **2.** n. (poet., rhet.). *~ space*, as *the ~ of ocean, of heaven*. [f. L *vastus* void, immense, or F *vaste*]

văt, n., & v.t. (-tt-). **1.** Large tub, cistern, or other vessel, esp. for holding liquids or holding something in liquid in process of manufacture, as *fermenting, tan, -~, whence ~'FUL n.* **2.** v.t. Place, treat, in~. [ME; southern var. of *fat*, OE *fæt*, OS, ON *fat*, OHG *faz*, f. Gmc **fatam* container]

Văt'ican, n. Palace & official residence of Pope on ~ hill in Rome; (fig.) papal government; *~ Council*, oecumenical council held 1869-70 & proclaiming infallibility of Pope when speaking *ex cathedra*, whence ~ISM(3), ~IST(2), nn. [f. L *Vaticanus ~* hill]

vati'cin|āte, v.t. Prophesy (often abs.). So ~A'TION, ~ātOR, nn. [f. L *vaticinari* (*vates* prophet + *canere* sing), -ATE³]

vaude'vill|e (vōdv-), n. ‖ Slight dramatic music-hall sketch interspersed with songs & dances; variety entertainment; French popular e.g. topical song with refrain; (hist.) convivial song esp. any of those composed by O. Basselin, poet born at Vau de Vire in Normandy, d. 1418. Hence ~IST(3) n. [F, f. *Vau de Vire* Valley of the Vire]

Vaudois¹ (vōdwah'), a. & n. (pl. same). (Inhabitants, dialect) of Vaud in Switzerland. [F (*Vaud + -ois* -ESE)]

Vaudois² (vōdwah'), a. & n. (pl. same). (Member) of the Waldenses. [F, repr. med. L *Valdensis*, see WALDENSES]

vaudoo. See VOODOO.

vault¹, n., & v.t. **1.** (Archit.) arched roof, continuous arch, set or series of arches whose joints radiate from central point or line; ~like covering, as *the ~ of heaven*; arched apartment; arched or other cellar or subterranean chamber as place of storage (*wine-~* etc.), of interment beneath church or in cemetery (*family ~*), etc.; (anat.) arched roof of a cavity. **2.** v.t. Make in form of, furnish with, ~ or ~s (esp. in p.p.). Hence ~'ING¹(6) n. [ME, f. OF *voute, vaulte*, f. Rom. **volvita* fem. p.p. of L *volvere* roll]

vault², v.i. & t., & n. **1.** Leap, spring, esp. while resting on the hand(s) or with help of pole, as *~ over the gate, from the saddle, upon a horse*; spring over (gate etc.) thus; *~ing-horse*, wooden horse for practice in ~ing. Hence ~'ER¹ n. **2.** n. Leap so performed. [app. f. OF *volter* leap, w. assim. to prec.]

vaunt, v.i. & t., & n. **1.** Boast, brag; boast of. **2.** n. Boast. Hence or cogn. ~'ER¹ n., ~'ĭnGLY² adv. [ME; vb f. OF *vanter* f. LL *vanitare* f. L *vanus* VAIN; partly aphetic f. obs. *avaunt* f. OF *a + vanter*]

vaunt'-courier (-kŏŏ-), n. = AVANT-COURIER.

văv'asorȳ, n. (hist.). Tenure, lands, of a vavasour. [f. OF *vavasorie* or med. L *-oria* (foll., -Y¹]

văv'asour (-ōr, -er, -oor), n. (hist.). Vassal holding of a great lord & having other vassals under him. [ME, f. OF *vavas-(s)our* or med. L *vavassor*, app. f. *vassus vassorum* VASSAL of vassals]

've, colloq. abbr. of *have* appended to *I, we, you, they*, & *who* (*I've* etc.).

veal, n. Flesh of calf as food, as *~ cutlet*. Hence ~'Y² a., like ~, *(colloq.) immature. [ME, f. OF *veël* (mod. *veau*) f. L *vitellus* dim. of *vitulus* calf]

věc'tor, n., & v.t. **1.** (In quaternions etc.) line conceived to have fixed length & direction but no fixed position, quantity determining position of one point in space relative to another (*~ quantity*, one that may be represented by a ~); carrier of disease or infection; RADIUS ~. Hence **věctōr'IAL** a. **2.** v.t. Direct (aircraft in flight) to desired point. [L, = carrier (*vehere vect-* convey, see -OR)]

Ve'da (vā-), n. (Also in pl.) ancient Hindu scriptures written in old form of Sanskrit (*Rig, Sama, Yajur, Atharva, -~*, four collections of hymns etc. composing the ~). Hence **Ve'dic**(vā-) a. [Skr., lit. knowledge]

Vedān't|a (vā-), n. Hindu philosophy founded on the Veda. Hence ~IC a., ~IST(3) n. [Skr. (*vēda + anta* end)]

Vĕdd'a, n. Member of primitive race living in the Ceylon forests. [Sinhalese, = hunter]

vĕdĕtte', vĭ-, n. Mounted sentry placed in advance of an outpost. [F (ve-), f. It. vedetta]

veer[1], v.t. (naut.). Slacken, let out, (rope, cable, etc.); ~ & haul, tighten & slacken (rope etc.) alternately. [ME, f. MDu. vieren]

veer[2], v.i. & t., & n. **1.** Change direction esp. (of wind, cf. BACK[2]) clockwise; (naut.) = WEAR[3]; (fig.) change one's mind, turn round in opinion or conduct or language. Hence ~'inGLY[2] adv. **2.** n. Change of direction, shifting round. [f. F viver f. Rom. *virare, alt. f. gyrare GYRATE]

ve'ga[1] (vā-), n. Low moist tract in Spain or Cuba; Cuban tobacco-field. [Sp.]

Vĕg'a[2], n. The brightest star in the constellation Lyra. [Sp. or med. L, f. Arab. wāqi' falling]

vĕ'gĕtable, a. & n. **1.** Of (the nature of), derived from, concerned with, comprising, plants, as ~ colic (caused by use of unripe fruit), IVORY, jelly (= PECTIN), KINGDOM, MARROW, naphtha, oyster (= SALSIFY), physiology, SPONGE[1]. Hence **vĕgĕtabIL'ITY** n. **2.** n. Plant, esp. herbaceous plant or part of one used for food, e.g. cabbage, potato, turnip, bean, (freq. attrib., as ~ diet, soup). [ME adj. f. OF, or f. LL vegetabilis vivifying (as VEGETATE, see -BLE); n.f. adj.]

vĕ'gĕt|al, a. & n. **1.** Of (the nature of) plants, so ~o- comb. form; common to animals & plants, as the ~al functions (of growth, circulation, generation, etc.). **2.** n. Plant, vegetable. Hence ~ăl'ITY n. [f. med. L *vegetalis f. L vegetare VEGETATE + -AL]

vĕgĕtār'ian, n. One who abstains from the use of flesh, fish, and fowl as food, with or without the addition of eggs and dairy produce, and whose diet includes roots, leafy vegetables, cereals, seeds, fruit, and nuts; attrib., as ~ diet, principles. Hence ~ISM n. [irreg. f. VEGETABLE + -ARIAN]

vĕ'gĕtāt|e, v.i. Grow as plants do, fulfil vegetable functions; (fig.) live an idle or monotonous life. So ~IVE a., ~ĭvELY[2] adv., ~ĭvENESS n. [f. L vegetare enliven (vegetus f. vegēre move, quicken), see -ATE[3]]

vĕgĕtā'tion, n. Vegetating (lit. & fig.); plants collectively, plant life, as luxuriant ~, no sign of ~ for miles round; (path.) excrescence of surface of body. [f. med. L vegetatio growth (as prec., see -ATION)]

vĕ'hement (vĕim-), a. Showing or caused by strong feeling, impetuous, ardent, passionate, as a ~ desire, protest, man of ~ character; acting with great force, violent, as a ~ wind, onset. Hence or cogn. **vĕ'hemENCE** (vĕim-) n., ~LY[2] adv. [F, or f. L vehement-, nom. -ns]

ve'hicle (vēi-), n. Carriage, conveyance, of any kind used on land; liquid etc. used as a medium for pigments, drugs, etc.; thing, person, used as a medium for thought or feeling or action, as used the pulpit, the press, as a ~ for his political opinions, will not be used as the ~ of your resentment. So **vĕhic'ūlAR**[1] a. [f. F véhicule or L vehiculum (vehere carry, see -CULE)]

vehmgericht (fām'gerĭχt), n. German system of irregular tribunals prevailing esp. in Westphalia in 14th & 15th cc. & trying the more serious crimes in secret night sessions; such tribunal. Hence **veh'mIC** (fām-) a. [G, also f-, f. feme punishment, tribunal, + gericht judgement, law]

veil (vāl), n., & v.t. **1.** Piece of usu. more or less transparent material attached to woman's bonnet or hat or otherwise forming part of head-dress, esp. one serving to conceal the face or as protection against sun, dust, etc., as raised, dropped, her ~ (so as to uncover, cover, face), took the ~, became nun; curtain (the ~ of the temple; beyond the ~, in the unknown state of after death); (fig.) disguise, pretext, as under the ~ of religion; draw a ~ over, avoid discussing or calling attention to; scarf on pastoral staff; (bot., zool.)= VELUM; slight huskiness of voice, natural or due to a cold etc. Hence ~'ING[1](3) n., ~'LESS a. **2.** v.t. Cover (one's face, oneself, or abs. in same sense) with ~; (fig.) partly conceal, disguise, mask, as ~ed resentment. [ME, f. AF veile (OF voile) f. L vela pl. of VELUM]

vein (vān), n., & v.t. **1.** Each of the membranous tubes that convey blood to the heart (cf. ARTERY; pulmonary ~s, returning oxygenated blood from lungs to left side, systemic ~s, returning venous blood from all parts to right side); (pop.) any blood-vessel; (entom., bot.) rib of insect's wing or of leaf; (geol., mining) fissure in rock filled with deposited matter (~'stone, = GANGUE); streak, stripe, of different colour in wood, marble, etc.; distinctive character or tendency, cast of mind or disposition, mood, as was of an imaginative ~, said in a humorous ~, other remarks in the same ~, am in the ~ for high play, am not in (the) ~ just now. Hence ~'LESS, ~'LIKE, ~'Y[2], aa., ~'LET n. **2.** v.t. Fill or cover (as) with ~ or ~s (esp. in p.p.). Hence ~'AGE(1), ~'ING[1](6), nn. [ME, f. OF veine f. L vena]

vēlām'en (pl. -mina), **vēlamĕn'tum** (pl. -ta), nn. Enveloping membrane esp. of brain. [L, f. velare (VELUM)]

vēl'ar, a. Of a veil or velum, as ~gutturals, sounds produced by aid of soft palate (e.g. gw, kw). [f. L velaris (VELUM, see -AR[1])]

veld (fĕlt), n. S.-Afr. open country neither cultivated nor true forest. [Du., = FIELD]

vēlĭtā'tion, n. (arch.). Slight skirmish, controversy. [f. L velitatio (velitari skirmish, as foll., see -ATION)]

vĕl'īte, n. (Rom. ant.). Light-armed soldier. [f. L *veles -itis*]

vĕllē'itȳ, n. Low degree of volition not prompting to action. [f. med. L *velleitas* (L *velle* vb wish, see -TY)]

vĕll'ic|āte, v.t. & i. (rare). Twitch. Hence or cogn. ~A'TION n., ~ātIVE a. [f. L *vellicare* (*vellere* pluck), see -ATE³]

vĕll'um, n. Fine parchment orig. from skin of calf; manuscript written on this; ~ *paper* (imitating~). Hence~Y²a. [ME *velym*, *-um* f. OF *velin* (*vcl* VEAL, -INE¹)]

vĕlō'ce (-chā), adv. (mus.). With great rapidity. [It.]

vĕlō'cĭpĕd|e, n. Kinds of light vehicle impelled by rider (now chiefly hist. of obs. types e.g. hobby). Hence ~IST(3) n. [f. F *vélocipède* f. L *velox -ocis* swift +*pes pedis* foot]

vĕlō'cĭtȳ, n. Quickness, rate, of motion usu. of inanimate things, as *uniform* ~; (mech.) speed in a given direction; *initial* ~, ~ of a body at starting, esp. (also *muzzle* ~) of projectile issuing from fire-arm. Hence **vĕlocĭM'ETER** n. [f. F *vélo-cité* or L *velocitas* (as prec., -TY)]

velours' (-oor), n. Kinds of plush used for hats etc. [F (OF *-our*, *-ous*), as VELVET]

vĕloutine' (-ōōtēn), n. Kinds of corded fabric & of toilet-powder. [F]

vĕl'um, n. (anat., bot., zool.; pl. *-la*). Kinds of membrane or membranous covering, esp. the soft palate. [L, = sail, curtain, covering, veil]

vĕl'ure, n., & v.t. Velvet or similar fabric; velvet or other pad for smoothing silk hat; (vb) smooth with ~. [f. OF *velour*, see VELOURS]

vĕlūt'ĭnous, a. (bot., entom.). Velvety. [f. med. L as VELVET +-INE¹+-OUS]

vĕl'verĕt, n. Bad kind of velvet. [irreg. dim. of foll.]

vĕl'vĕt, n. & a. **1.** Closely woven fabric wholly (also *silk* ~) or partly (*cotton* ~) of silk with thick short pile on one side (*terry* ~, with pile uncut); furry skin covering a growing antler; (transf.) profit, gain; *on* ~, in an advantageous or prosperous position; ~ *pile*, fabric with pile like that of~. **2.** adj. Of, soft as, ~ (often in names of animals & plants, as ~ *ant, osier*); ~ *glove*, outward gentleness cloaking inflexibility (*with an iron hand in a* ~ *glove*); ~ *paw*, of cat, fig. of cruelty etc. veiled under suave manner; ~ *tread*, soft. Hence ~ED², ~Y², aa. [ME, f. med. L *velvet(t)um*, also *vel(l)utum*, ult. f. L *villus* shaggy hair]

vĕlvĕteen', n. Cotton fabric with pile like velvet; kind of velvet made of silk & cotton; ‖ (pl., transf.) gamekeeper. [prec. +-een -INE⁴]

vĕl'vĕtĭng, n. Velvet goods collectively; pile, nap, of velvet. [-ING¹]

vēn'al, a. (Of person) that may be bought, ready to sell influence or services or to sacrifice principles from sordid motive; (of conduct etc.) characteristic of ~

person. Hence or cogn. **vēnăl'ITY** n., ~LY² adv. [f. L *venalis* (*venum*, sale, see -AL)]

vēnā'tion, n. Arrangement of veins on leaf, insect's wing, etc. Hence ~AL a. [f. L *vena* VEIN +-ATION]

vĕnd, v.t. Sell (now chiefly legal, whence or cogn. ~EE', vĕn'dOR, nn.); offer (small wares) for sale, so (-)vĕn'dER¹ n.; *~ing machine*, SLOT¹-machine. Hence or cogn. ~ĬBIL'ITY n., ~'IBLE a., ~'ĬBLY² adv. [f. F *vendre* or L *vendere* sell]

vĕn'dāce, n. Small & delicate fish found in some British & Continental lakes. [app. f. OF *vendese*, *-oise* dace]

Vĕndē'an, a. & n. (Native) of Vendée, department of W. France; (member) of ~ royalist party in 1793–5. [f. F *Vendéen* (*Vendée*, see -AN)]

vĕndĕtt'a, n. Blood-feud in which family of injured or murdered man seeks vengeance on offender or his family; this practice as prevalent in Corsica etc. [It., f. L *vindicta*, see VINDICTIVE]

vēneer', v.t., & n. **1.** Cover (wood, furniture, etc.) with thin coating of finer wood; cover (pottery etc.) with thin coat of finer substance; (fig.) disguise (character etc.) under superficial polish of manner etc. **2.** n. Thin outer coating, ~ing (lit. & fig.); ~*-moth*, kinds whose colouring suggests ~. [later form of (obs.) *fineer* f. G *furni(e)r, furni(e)ren* f. F *fournir* FUR-NISH]

vĕn'ĕpŭnc'ture, n. (med.). Puncture of vein esp. with hypodermic needle to draw blood or for intravenous injection. [f. L *vena* vein +PUNCTURE]

vĕn'er|able, a. Entitled to veneration on account of character, age, associations, etc., as ~*able priest, relics, beard, ruins, Bede* (also in Ch. of Eng. as title of arch-deacons, abbr. *Ven.*; in R.-C. Ch. as title of one who has attained first of three degrees of sanctity but is not canonized). Hence ~abIL'ITY, ~ableNESS, nn., ~abLY² adv. [ME, f. OF, or L *venerabilis* (as foll., see -ABLE]

vĕn'erāt|e, v.t. Consider worthy of & regard with deep respect or warm approbation; revere. So ~OR n. [f. L *venerari* -ATE³]

vĕnerā'tion, n. Profound respect, reverence; (phren., often joc.) faculty of feeling reverence, as *organ, bump*, of ~. [ME, f. L *veneratio* (as prec., see -ATION]

vēnēr'é|al, a. Of sexual intercourse, as ~*al desire*; ~*al disease*, communicated by sexual intercourse; ~*al remedies* (for ~al disease). Hence~ŏL'OGIST, ~ŏL'OGY, nn. [f. L *Venereus* of VENUS +-AL]

vĕn'erȳ¹, n. (arch.). Hunting. [ME, f. OF *venerie* (*vener* hunt f. L *venari*, see -ERY)]

vĕn'erȳ², n. (arch.). Sexual indulgence. [VENUS, -Y¹]

vĕn'ĕsĕct, v.t. & i., **vĕnĕsĕc'tion**, n. = PHLEBOTOMIZE, PHLEBOTOMY. [vb f. n., f. mod. L *venae sectio* cutting of vein]

Vĕnē'tian (-shn), a. & n. **1.** Of Venice; ~ *blind*, window blind of slats of wood that may be turned so as to admit or exclude light; ~ *carpet* (of worsted, usu. with striped pattern); ~ (=FRENCH) *chalk*; ~ *glass*, glassware made at or near Venice, (also *Venice glass*) cup of this said to be destroyed by contact with poison; ~ *lace*, kind of point lace; ~ *mast*, spirally painted pole for use in street decorations; ~ (solid artificial) *pearl*; ~ *window* (with three separate openings). **2.** n. Native of Venice; (usu. *v*~) ~ blind, whence **vĕnē'tian**ED[2] (-sha-) a., (pl.) kind of tape for holding slats of this. [ME, f. OF *Venicien* or med. L *Venetianus* f. *Venetia* Venice, see -AN]

vĕn'geance (-jans), n. Punishment inflicted, retribution exacted, for wrong to oneself or to person etc. whose cause one espouses, as *will exact ample* ~, *took a bloody* ~ *on the murderer* or *for the murder of his children, you lay yourself open to his* ~; *with a* ~, in a higher degree than was expected or desired, in the fullest sense of the word(s), & no mistake, as *this is punctuality with a* ~. [ME, f. OF (*venger*) avenge f. L as VINDICATE, see -ANCE)]

vĕnge'ful (-jf-), a. Disposed to revenge, vindictive. Hence ~LY[2] adv., ~NESS n. [f. obs. *venge* vb (as prec.) + -FUL]

vĕn'ial, a. (Of sin or fault) pardonable, excusable, not very wrong, (theol.) not mortal. Hence **vĕniăl'**ITY, ~NESS, nn., ~LY[2] adv. [ME, f. OF *venial*, *-el*, or LL *venialis* (*venia* pardon, see -AL)]

Vĕn'ice, n. (attrib.). ~ (= VENETIAN) *glass*; ~ *treacle*, = THERIAC.

vĕnīr'é (*fă'cĭǎs*) (-sh-), n. (law). Writ directing sheriff to summon jury. [L, = make or cause to come]

vĕn'ison (-nzon), n. Deer's flesh as food. [ME, f. OF *veneisun* f. L *venationem* hunting (*venari* hunt, see -ATION)]

Vĕnī't'é, n. (Musical setting of) *Ps.* xcv. [L, = Come ye, first word of psalm]

vĕn'om, n. Poisonous fluid secreted by serpents, scorpions, etc., & introduced into system of victim by bite or sting; (fig.) malignity, virulence, of feeling or language or conduct. Hence or cogn. ~ED[2] (-md), ~OUS, aa., ~OUSLY[2] adv., ~OUSNESS n. [ME, f. AF, OF *venim*, var. of *venin* f. Gallo-Rom. **venimen* f. L *venenum* poison]

vĕnŏs'itў, n. Excess of venous blood in organ etc.; deficient aeration of venous blood in lungs with afflux of venous blood into arteries. [as foll., see -OSITY]

vĕn'ous, **-ōse**, aa. (anat., zool., bot.). Of, full of, contained in, veins, as ~ (opp. to arterial) *blood*, ~ *congestion*, accumulation of ~ blood in organ etc. Hence **vĕn'ous**LY[2] adv. [f. L *venosus*, or f. L *vena* + -OSE[1], -OUS.]

vĕnt[1], n., & v.t. & i. **1.** Hole or opening allowing passage out of or into confined space, e.g. touch-hole of gun, hole in top of barrel to admit air while liquid is being drawn out, finger-hole in musical instrument (also **vĕn'tAGE** n.), flue of chimney; = ~-*faucet*; anus esp. of animals below mammals; (fig.) outlet, free passage, free play, as *gave* ~ *to his indignation, impatience found a* ~; ‖ ~ing of otter etc. (see vb); ~-*faucet*, hollow gimlet for making ~ in cask etc.; ~-*hole*, ~; ~-*peg*, peg for stopping ~ of barrel, also = ~-*faucet*; ~-*plug*, plug for ~ of gun, also = ~-*peg* (1st sense). Hence ~'LESS a. **2.** vb. Make ~ in (gun, cask, etc.); give ~ to, as ~*ed his disgust in an epigram, with a snort, on the office-boy*; ‖ (of otter or beaver) come to surface for breath. [n. partly f. F *vent* f. L *ventus* wind, partly f. F *évent* (*éventer* f. EX- + *vent* wind); vb f. n., & F *éventer*]

vĕnt[2], n. Slit in garment now esp. in back of coat; (obs.) = CRENEL. [ME, var. of *fent* f. OF *fente* f. L *findere* cleave]

vĕn'ter, n. (Anat.) belly, also, protuberant or concave part of muscle or bone; (law) womb, mother, as *a son by, the son of, another* ~. [f. AF *ventre*, *venter*, or L *venter* paunch, womb]

vĕn'tidŭct, n. (archit.). Air-passage, esp. subterranean one. [f. L *ventus* wind + DUCT]

vĕn'til, n. Valve in musical instrument; shutter for regulating air in organ. [G, f. med. L *ventile* shutter f. L *ventus* wind]

vĕn'til|āte, v.t. Cause air to circulate freely in (room etc.); purify by air, oxygenate, (blood); submit (question, subject, grievance, etc.) to public consideration & discussion. Hence or cogn. ~A'TION, ~ātOR (esp., appliance for ~ating room), nn., ~ātIVE a. [f. L *ventilare* blow, winnow (*ventus* wind), see -ATE[3]]

vĕn'tral, a. & n. (zool., bot.). Of the venter; on the belly (opp. DORSAL); ~ (*fin*), either of the abdominal fins. Hence ~LY[2] adv. [F, or f. L *ventralis* (VENTER, see -AL)]

ventre à terre (see Ap.), adv. At full speed (lit. with belly to ground). [F]

vĕn'tricle, n. (anat.). Any cavity of the body, hollow part or organ, as ~*s of the brain, right, left,* ~ (*of the heart*). Hence **vĕntric'ūl**AR[1], **vĕntric'ūl**OUS, aa. [ME, f. L *ventriculus* dim. of VENTER]

vĕn'tricōse, **-ous**, aa. Having a protruding belly; (bot.) distended, inflated. [f. VENTER + -IC + -OSE[1], -OUS]

vĕntril'oqu|ism, n. Act, art, of speaking, or uttering sounds in such a manner that the voice appears to come from some other source than the speaker. So ~IST(1), ~Y[1], nn., **vĕntrilŏ'qui**AL, ~is'TIC, ~OUS, aa., ~IZE(2) v.i. [all ult. f. LL *ventriloquus* ventriloquist (VENTER + *loqui* locut-speak)]

vĕn'tro-, comb. form of VENTER, as ~*dors'al*, extending from belly to back.

věn′ture, n., & v.t. & i. 1. Undertaking of a risk, risky undertaking, as *declined the ~, ready for any ~*; commercial speculation, as *one lucky ~ made his fortune, failed in all his ~s*; (arch.) thing at stake, property risked; *at a ~*, at random. **2. vb.** Dare, not be afraid, make bold, as *did not ~ to stop him, I ~ to differ from you*; dare to make or advance or put forward, hazard, as *would not ~ an opinion, a guess, a step*; expose to risk, stake, as *men who ~ their lives for the cause, will ~ five shillings on it*; (abs.) undertake risk; *~ (up)on*, dare to engage in or grapple with or make, as *shall ~ on a mild protest, will you ~ on a slice of cucumber?* Hence **věn′turer[1] n.**, (esp. hist.) one who undertakes or shares in a trading ~, ~SOME (-chers-) a., ~SOMELY[2] adv., ~SOMENESS n. [aphetic f. ADVEN-TURE]

věn′ūe, n. (law). Country within which jury must be gathered & cause tried (orig. neighbourhood of crime etc.), as *change the ~* (to avoid riot, prejudiced jury, etc.); statement in indictment etc. in-dicating this; (pop.) rendezvous. [F, = coming, f. *venir* come f. L *venire*]

Věn′us, n. (Rom. myth.) goddess of love; a PLANET[1]; sexual love, amorous influences or desires, (*uranian, pandemian, ~*, spiritual, sensual, sex love); a beautiful woman; *Mount of ~* (palmistry), base of thumb; *~′s basin, bath*, common teazel; *~′s comb*, plant of parsley family with comblike fruit; *~′s fly-trap*, herb with leaves that close on insects etc.; *~′s slipper*, = LADY′s-slipper. [L, gen. -*eris*]

verā′cious (-shus), a. Speaking, disposed to speak, the truth; (of statement etc.) true, not (meant to be) false. Hence or cogn. ~LY[2] adv., verā′CITY n. [f. L *verax* (*verus* true, see -ACIOUS)]

verăn′da(h) (-dα), n. Open portico or gallery along side of house with roof sup-ported on pillars. [f. Port. *varanda*]

vě′ratr|ine, n. Poisonous compound from hellebore used esp. as local irritant in neuralgia & rheumatism. So ~ATE[1](3) n., verăt′rIC a. ~IZE(5) v.t. [F (*vé*-), f. L *veratrum* hellebore + -INE[5]]

věrb, n. (gram.). Part of speech that pre-dicates, word whose function is predica-tion (e.g. italicized words in Time *flies, Salt is good, You surprise me); copulative* or *substantive* ~, be ; AUXILIARY, DEPONENT, IMPERSONAL, (IN)TRANSITIVE, NEUTER, RE-FLEXIVE, ~. [ME, f. OF *verbe* or L *verbum* WORD, verb]

věrb′al, a. & n. 1. Of, concerned with, words, as *~ distinctions, subtleties, critic-(ism), accuracy*, INSPIRATION ; (loosely) oral, not written, as *a ~ communication, con-tract, ~ evidence*; (of translation) literal, word for word; *~ note* (diplomacy), un-signed memorandum on matter that is not urgent but must not be overlooked; (gram.) of (the nature of) a verb, as ~

inflexions, used in all the ~ senses (of the verb), *~ noun*, noun derived from verb & partly sharing its constructions (e.g. E nouns in -ING[1]). **2. n.** ~ *noun*. Hence ~LY[2] adv. [F, or f. LL *verbalis* (as prec., see -AL)]

věrb′alism, n. Minute attention to words, verbal criticism. [-ISM]

věrb′alist, n. Person concerned with words only, verbal critic. [-IST]

věrb′aliz|e, -is|e (-ĭz), v.t. & i. Make (noun etc.) into a verb, so **věrb′ifY v.t.**; be verbose. Hence ~A′TION n. [f. F *verbaliser*, or f. VERBAL + -IZE]

verbāt′im, adv. & a. Word for word, as *copied it ~, a ~ reprint*. [med. L (adv.), f. L *verbum* VERB, cf. LITERATIM]

verbĕn′a, n. Kinds of plant of vervain family, as *lemon(-scented)~*. [L, = sacred bough of olive etc., VERVAIN]

věrb′iage, n. Needless accumulation of words, verbosity. [F (as VERB, see -AGE)]

věrb′icide, n. (joc.). Word-butcher(y). [as VERB + -CIDE]

verbōse′, a. Using, containing, more words than are wanted, prolix. Hence ~LY[2] adv., ~NESS, **verbŏs′ITY, nn.** [f. L *verbosus* (as VERB, see -OSE[1])]

věrb′um (săt) săpiĕn′tĭ, sent. (abbr. *verb. sap.*). A word is enough to the wise. [L]

věrd′ant, a. (Of grass etc.) green, fresh-coloured (of field etc.) covered with ~ grass etc.; (of person) unsophisticated, raw, green. Hence **věrd′ancY n.**, ~LY[2] adv. [f. *verd*- (as in *verdure*), perh. partly after L *viridans -ant-* green]

věrd-ăntique′ (-ĕk), n. Ornamental usu. green building-stone formed chiefly of serpentine; green incrustation on ancient bronze. [older F = antique green]

věrd′erer, -or, n. (hist.). Judicial officer of royal forests. [AF *verderer*, f. *verder* (*verd* f. L *viridis* green) + -ER[1], -OR]

věrd′ict, n. Decision of jury on issue of fact in civil or criminal cause, as *brought in a ~ of not guilty, a ~ for the plaintiff, open ~* (reporting commission of crime but not specifying criminal, also, open as between accident and suicide), *partial ~* (finding person guilty of part of the charge), *privy* or *sealed ~* (written ~ de-livered to clerk of court when court has adjourned during deliberation of jury), *special ~* (stating facts as proved but leaving court to draw conclusion from them); decision, judgement, as *the ~ of the public was in its favour, does not dis-pute your ~*. [ME & AF *verdit* (= OF *voirdit*) f. *ver, veir* true + *dit* p.p. of *dire* say]

věrd′igris (or -ēs), n. Green crystallized substance formed on copper by action of acetic acid & used in medicine & as pig-ment etc.; green rust on copper. [ME, f. AF, OF *vert de Grece* green of Greece]

věrd′iter, n. *Blue, green,* ~, pigments got from copper nitrate. [f. OF *vert de terre* green of earth]

vērd'ur|e (-dyer), n. Greenness of vegetation, green vegetation, whence ~ED² (-dyerd), ~ELESS, vērd'ūroŭs, aa.; (fig.) freshness. [ME, f. OF, f. vert f. L viridis green +-URE]

vervein (ferīn'), n. Association of persons or parties, organized body. [G]

Verey. Var. of VERY².

vērge¹, n. Extreme edge, brink, border, (usu. fig.), as drew near to the very ~ of the stream, on the ~ of 70, destruction, betraying his secret; grass edging of flower-bed etc.; wand, rod, carried before bishop, dean, etc., as emblem of office; kinds of shaft or spindle in various mechanisms; (archit.) shaft of column, edge of tiles projecting over gable, ~-board, = BARGE- -board; (hist.) area of jurisdiction of Marshalsea. [ME, f. OF, f. L virga rod]

vērge², v.i. Incline downwards or in specified direction (the now verging sun; ~ towards old age, to a close); ~ on, border on, approach closely, as path ~s on the edge of a precipice, a solemnity verging on the tragic. [f. L vergere bend, incline]

vēr'ger, n. Official in a church who shows persons to their seats etc.; ‖ officer who bears staff before bishop, (vice-) chancellor of university, etc. Hence ~SHIP n. [15th c., prob. f. AF *verger f. verge VERGE¹, see -ER²; cf. med. L virgarius rod-bearer]

vērid'ic|al, a. Truthful (usu. iron.); (psych., spirit.; of visions etc.) coinciding with realities. Hence or cogn. ~alLY² adv., ~OUS a. [f. L veridicus (verus true + dicere say) +-AL]

vē'ri|fÿ, v.t. Establish the truth of, examine for this purpose, as must ~fy the statement, his figures, am now ~fying the items, ~fy your references; (of event, action, etc.) bear out, make good, fulfil, (prediction, promise); (law) append affidavit to (pleadings), support (statement) by proofs. Hence or cogn. ~fīa- BIL'ITY, ~FICA'TION, ~fĭER¹, nn., ~fīABLE a. [ME, f. OF verifier f. med. L verificare (verus true, see -FY)]

vē'rilÿ, adv. (arch.). Really, truly, in very truth (freq. ~ ~). [ME, f. VERY¹ +-LY²]

vĕrisimil'itūde, n. Air of being true, semblance of actuality, (the ~ of the tale; ~ is not proof); a thing that seems true. So **vĕrisim'ilAR¹** a. [f. obs. F, or L verisimilitudo f. verisimilis probable (veri gen. of verus true + similis like), see -TUDE]

vĕ'ritab|le, a. Real, rightly so called, as a ~le boon. Hence ~LY² adv. [OF (as VERITY, see -ABLE)]

vĕ'ritās, n. (Also bureau véritas) French ship register like Lloyd's. [F (vé-), f. L as foll.]

vĕ'rit|ÿ, n. Truth (of statement etc.); true statement; really existent thing, as these things, alas! are ~ies; of a ~y (arch.), in truth, really. [ME, f. OF verite f. L veritatem (verus true, see -TY)]

vēr'juic|e (-ōōs), n. Acid liquor got from crab-apples, sour grapes, etc., & used in cooking. Hence ~ED² (-st) a. [ME, f. OF vertjus (vert, see VERDURE, +jus JUICE)]

vērm'eil (-mǐl), n. Silver gilt; varnish used to give lustre to gilding; orange-red garnet; (poet.) vermilion. [ME, f. OF, see VERMILION]

vērm'|i-, comb. form of L vermis worm, as: ~icide, drug that kills worms, so ~icĭd'al a.; ~iform, worm-shaped (~iform APPENDIX), structurally allied to worms; ~ifuge, drug that expels intestinal worms, so ~if'ugal a.; ~igrade, moving like worm, wriggling along; ~iv'orous, feeding on worms.

vērm'ian, a. Of worms, wormlike. [f. L vermis worm +-AN]

vērmicĕll'i, n. Paste of same materials as macaroni made in slender threads. [It., pl. of vermicello dim. f. L vermis worm]

vermic'ūlar, a. Like a worm in form or movements, as ~ (=VERMIform) appendix; of worm-eaten appearance; marked with close wavy lines. [f. med. L vermicularis (L vermiculus dim. of vermis worm, see -AR¹)]

vermic'ūlate, a. = prec. (rare, usu. fig.). [f. L vermiculari be full of worms (prec.), -ATE³, ³]

vermiculā'tion, n. Being eaten or infested by or converted into worms; vermicular marking; worm-eaten state. [f. L vermiculatio (prec., -ATION)]

vermic'ūlite, n. (min.). Any of a number of hydrous silicates, chiefly resulting from alterations of mica. [as VERMICULATE, -ITE¹ (2)]

vermil'ion (-yon), n., a., & v.t. 1. Cinnabar; brilliant red pigment made by grinding this or artificially; (of) this colour. 2. v.t. Colour (as) with ~. [ME, f. OF verm(e)illon (vermeil f. L vermiculus little worm (LL also ~ scarlet) dim. of vermis worm), see -OON]

vērm'in, n. (usu. treated as pl.). Mammals & birds injurious to game, crops, etc., e.g. foxes, weasels, rats, mice, moles, owls, etc.; noxious insects, e.g. fleas, bugs, lice; parasitic worms or insects; (fig.) vile persons, as the ~ that infest race- -courses. So ~OUS a., ~OUSLY² adv. [ME, f. OF vermin, -ine f. Rom. *verminum, -ina f. L vermis worm]

vērm'in|āte v.i. Breed vermin, become infested with parasites. So ~A'TION n. [f. L verminare (vermis worm), see -ATE³]

vērm'(o)uth (-ōōth; or vār̆m'ōōt), n. White wine flavoured with wormwood; French, Italian, ~, dry, sweet, kind. [f. F vermout f. G wermuth wormwood]

vernăc'ūlar, a. & n. 1. (Of language, idiom, word) of one's native country, native, indigenous, not of foreign origin or of learned formation. 2. n. The language or dialect of the country, as

Latin gave place to the ~. Hence ~ISM(4), ~ITY (-ǎ'r-), ~ĪZA'TION, nn., ~IZE(3) v.t., ~LY² adv. [f. L *vernaculus* native (*verna* home-born slave, see -CULE)+-AR¹]

vẽrn'al, a. Of, appearing or occurring or done in, spring, as ~ *breezes, flowers,* EQUINOX, *migration,* ~ (malarial) *fever;* ~ *grass,* sweet-scented grass grown among hay. Hence ~LY² adv. [f. L *vernalis* (*vernus* f. *ver* spring, see -AL)]

verna'tion, n. (bot.). Arrangement of leaves (cf. AESTIVATION) within leaf-bud. [f. L *vernare* bloom (as prec., see -ATION)]

Verner's law. See LAW¹.

vẽrn'ier, n. Small movable scale for obtaining fractional parts of the subdivisions on fixed scale of barometer, sextant, etc. [F, f. P. *V*~, inventor, d. 1637]

vě'ronal, n. Sedative drug. [P]

Vĕronēse' (-z), a., & n. (pl. the same). (Inhabitant) of Verona. [-ESE]

vĕrŏn'ica, n. **1.** Kinds of herb or shrub with blue, purple, pink or white flowers. **2.** Cloth with respresentation of Christ's face, esp. one miraculously so impressed after being used by St V~ to wipe sweat from Christ's face. [*V*~, woman's name]

vĕrruc'|a (-rŏŏ-), n. (path., zool., bot.; pl. ~*ae* pr. -sē). Wart, wartlike elevation. Hence or cogn. ~ĪFORM (-rŏŏ-), vě'rru-COSE¹ (-rŏŏ-), vě'rrucous (-rŏŏ-), ~ŭlose¹ (-rŏŏ-), aa. [L]

vẽrs'ant, n. Extent of land sloping in one direction, general slope of land. [F, f. L *versare* frequent. of *vertere vers-* turn]

vẽrs'atile, a. Turning readily from one subject or occupation to another, capable of dealing with many subjects, as ~ *author, genius, disposition, mind;* capable of being moved or turned as on hinge, as ~ *spindle;* (bot., zool.) moving freely about or up & down on a support, as ~ *anther, head, antennae;* changeable, inconstant. Hence or cogn. ~LY² adv., vẽrsatil'ITY n. [F, or f. L *versatilis* (as prec., see -ATILE)]

vers de société (vâr de sosiātā'), n. SOCIETY verse. [F]

vẽrse, n., & v.t. & i. **1.** Metrical line containing definite number of feet, as *quoted some* ~*s of the.Iliad, had a good* ~ *here & there,* CAP² ~*s;* group of definite number of ~*s,* stanza; metrical composition in general, particular type of this, as *wrote pages of* ~, *expressed in indifferent* ~, *what is not prose is* ~, *a prize for Latin* ~, BLANK¹, SOCIETY, *elegiac, iambic, trochaic,* etc., ~; each of the short divisions of chapter in Bible (CHAPTER *&* ~); short sentence as part of liturgy; solo part of anthem etc.; ~*-monger*(*ing*), maker, making, of bad ~s. Hence ~'LET (-sl-) n. **2.** vb. Express in ~, make ~s. [OE *fers* (OHG, ON *vers*) f. L *versus* (*vertere vers-* turn); in ME reinforced by AF, OF *vers*]

vẽrsed (-st), a. Experienced, skilled, proficient, (*in* subject, occupation, etc.); reversed (now only in ~ SINE). [f. L

---

versatus p.p. of *versari* be engaged in, see VERSANT; trig. sense f. L *versus* p.p. as prec.]

vẽrs'ĕt, n. (mus.). Short prelude or interlude for organ. [F, dim. of *vers* VERSE]

vẽrs'icle, n. Short verse, esp. of each series of short verses in liturgy said or sung alternately by minister & people. [ME, f. OF *versicule* or L *versiculus* (as VERSE, see -CULE)]

vẽrs'icolour(ed) (-ŭlerd), aa. Variegated; changing from one colour to another in different lights. [f. L *versicolor* (*vertere vers-* turn+*color* COLOUR)]

versic'ular, a. ~ *division* (into verses). [as VERSICLE+-ULAR]

vẽrs'i|fy̆, v.t. & i. Turn (prose) into verse; express in verse; make verses. Hence or cogn. ~FICA'TION, ~fIER¹, nn. [ME, f. OF *versifier* f. L *versificare* (as VERSE, see -FY)]

vẽr'sion (-shn), n. **1.** Book etc. translated into another language, as *Authorized, Revised, V*~ (of the Bible, made 1604–11, 1870–84; abbr. *A.V., R.V.*). **2.** Piece of translation, esp. into foreign language, as school exercise. **3.** Account of a matter from particular person's point of view, as *now let me have your own* ~ *of the affair.* **4.** Turning of child awkwardly placed for delivery so that head or feet may be first presented. Hence ~AL (-sho-) a. [F, or f. med. L *versio* (L *vertere vers-* turn, see -ION)]

vers libre (vârlĕb're), n. Versification or verses in which different metres are mingled, or prosodical restrictions disregarded, or variable rhythm substituted for definite metre. Hence **versli'brist** (vârlĕ-) n., writer of ~. [F]

vẽrs'ō, n. (pl. ~s). Any left-hand page of book (cf. RECTO); reverse of coin. [L, abl. p.p. as VERSE]

vẽrst, n. Russian measure of length, 3,500 feet. [f. Russ. *verstá*]

vẽrs'us, prep. (abbr. *v.*). Against, as (law) *Jones v. Smith,* (crick. etc.) *Surrey v. Kent.* [L, = towards, against]

vẽrt¹, n. (Law, hist.) all that bears green leaves in forest, right to cut this; (her.) the tincture green. [ME, f. OF, f. L *viridis* green]

‖ **vẽrt²,** n., & v.i. (colloq.). Convert or pervert; (vb) leave one Church for another. [short for CONVERT n., PERVERT n.]

vẽrt'ebr|a, n. (pl. ~*ae*). Each segment of backbone (*false* ~*a,* fixed, as os sacrum & coccyx in man, *true* ~*a,* movable; neither expression now used in human anat.). Hence ~AL a., ~ālLY² adv., ~o- comb. form. [L (*vertere* turn)]

vẽrt'ēbr|ate, a. & n. (Animal) having a spinal column or a notochord, esp. (member) of the division *Vertebrāt'a,* including mammals, birds, reptiles, amphibians, & fishes. Hence ~ātĕd [-ATE²] a. [f. L *vertebratus* jointed (as prec., see -ATE²)]

vĕr̆tĕbrā'tion, n. Formation of, division into, vertebrae or similar segments. [-ATION]

vĕr̆t'ĕx, n. (pl. usu. *-ĭcēs*). Highest point, top, apex; (anat.) crown of head; (geom.) each angular point of triangle, polygon, etc., ~ *of an angle*, meeting-point of lines that form it. [L, gen. *-icis*, = whirlpool, head, vertex, (*vertere* turn)]

vĕr̆t'ical, a. & n. **1.** Of, at, the vertex or highest point; at the zenith; perpendicular to plane of horizon; (anat.) of the crown of the head; ~ *angles*, each pair of opposite angles made by two intersecting lines; ~ (= AZIMUTH-) *circle*; ~ *fins* (dorsal, anal, & caudal); ~ *plane*, plane perpendicular to the horizon. Hence ~ITY (-ăl²) n., ~LY² adv. **2.** n. ~ line, plane, or circle; *out of the* ~, not ~. [F, or f. LL *verticalis* (prec., see -AL)]

vĕrt'icil, n. (bot., zool.). Whorl, set of parts radiating from axis. Hence **verti'cillATE²** a., **verti'cillateLY²** adv. [f. L *verticillus* whorl of spindle, dim. of VERTEX]

vĕrt'igŏ (*or verti²*, -tē²), n. (pl. ~s). Giddiness, dizziness, as *subjective*, *objective*, ~ (in which patient feels as if he, as if surrounding objects, were turning round), *essential* ~ (without apparent cause). Hence **verti'ginous** a., **verti'ginousLY²** adv., **verti'ginousNESS** n. [L, gen. *-ginis*, = whirling (*vertere* turn)]

vertu. See VIRTU.

vĕrv'ain, n. Kinds of weedy plant with small blue, white, or purple flowers, formerly believed to have various virtues & used as amulet etc. [ME, f. OF *verveine* f. L VERBENA]

verve (vărv), n. Enthusiasm, energy, vigour, in artistic or literary work. [F]

vĕrv'ĕt, n. A small S.-Afr. monkey freq. carried by organ-grinders. [F]

vĕ'rȳ¹, a. & adv. **1.** Real, true, genuine, that is such in the truest or fullest sense, as ~ *God of* ~ *God, has shown himself a* ~ *knave, the veriest simpleton knows that, must consent from* ~ *shame,* (somewhat arch. exc. in foll. uses); (with *the*, *this*, *that*, or possessive adj., emphasizing identity, coincidence, significance, or extreme degree) *this is the* ~ *spot I found it on, speaking in this* ~ *room, the* ~ *fact of his presence is enough, you are the* ~ *man I am looking for, a needle is the* ~ *thing (for our purpose), come here this* ~ *minute, grieves me to the* ~ *heart, the* ~ *stones cry out, his* ~ *servants bully him, drank it to the* ~ *dregs;* (with *a*) *a* ~ *little more will do, give me only a* ~ *little.* **2.** adv. (Perh. orig. adj., with superl. adj. often abs., or with *my* etc. *own*) in the fullest sense, as *drank it to the* ~ *last drop, the* ~ *last thing I expected, did the* ~ *best I could, did my* ~ *utmost, may keep it for your* ~ *own;* (used with advv. & the opposite of non-verbal adjj.; with partt. established as independent adjj., as *a* ~ *dazzling effect,*

effect was ~ *dazzling, a* ~ *trying time;* with p.pp. in attrib. use applied to what is not the real object of the vbl action, as *wore a* ~ *pained, pleased, puzzled, troubled, vexed, annoyed, surprised,* etc., *expression,* but not *his expression was* ~ *pained* etc.; & colloq. with the same p.pp. in pred. use applied to the true object & fulfilling purely vbl function, as *I was* ~ *pleased, surprised, annoyed,* etc.; not otherwise used with vbs) in a high degree, as *that is* ~ *easily done,* ~ *often fails,* ~ *easy, not* ~ *much use, find* ~ *few instances, gives* ~ *little trouble,* but not ~ *better* etc. **3.** ~ *well* (or, more respectfully, ~ *good*), formula of consent or approval. [ME, f. OF *verai,* f. Gallo-Rom. **veraius,* f. L *verus* true]

Vĕ'rȳ², n. (attrib.). ~ *light* (projected from ~ *pistol* for signalling or temporarily illuminating part of battlefield etc.). [S. W. ~, inventor (1877)]

vĕsic'a, n. (anat., bot.). **1.** Bladder, cyst, sac, esp. (whence **vĕs'icocele, vĕsicōt'OMY,** nn.) urinary bladder. **2.** ~ (*piscis* or *piscium* = fish's or fishes'), the pointed oval (()) used as an aureole in medieval sculpture & painting. Hence **vĕs'icAL** a., **vĕs'ico-** comb. form. [L]

vĕs'icāte, v.t. Raise blisters on. Hence ~ANT(2), ~ātORY, aa. & nn., ~A'TION n. [f. mod. L *vesicare* (prec., -ATE³)]

vĕs'icle, n. (anat., bot., geol.). Small bladder, cell, bubble, or hollow structure. Hence **vĕsic'ūlAR¹, vĕsic'ūlATE², vĕsicūliF'EROUS, vĕsic'ūliFORM, vĕsic'ūlOSE¹, vĕsic'ūlOUS,** aa., **vĕsicūlA'TION** n., **vĕsic'ūlo-** comb. form. [f. F *vésicule,* or L *vesicula* dim. of VESICA]

vĕs'per, n. (*V*~) Venus as evening-star, (poet.) evening; (pl.) sixth of the seven canonical hours of the breviary, EVEN¹- song; ~(-*bell*), bell that calls to ~s; *Sicilian V*~s, massacre of French residents in Sicily in 1282, begun at stroke of ~-bell. [(1) f. L *vesper;* (2) f. F *vespres* (mod. *vêpres*)]

vĕs'pertine, a. Of, done in, the evening; (bot., of flowers) opening, (zool.) flying, in the evening; (astron.) descending towards horizon at sunset. [f. L *vespertinus* (VESPER)]

vĕs'piarȳ, n. Nest of wasps. [irreg. f. L *vespa* wasp, after *apiary*]

vĕs'pine, a. Of wasps. So **vĕs'piFORM** a. [f. L *vespa* wasp + -INE¹]

vĕss'el, n. **1.** Hollow receptacle esp. for liquid, e.g. cask, cup, pot, bottle, dish. **2.** Ship, boat, esp. large one. **3.** (Anat.) duct, canal, holding or conveying blood or other fluid, esp. *blood-*~; (bot.) chain of cells that have lost intervening partitions, duct. **4.** (bibl. or allus. esp. joc.). Person viewed as recipient or exponent, as *chosen* ~ (*Acts* ix. 15), *weaker* ~, woman (1 *Pet.* iii. 7), ~*s of wrath* (*Rom.* ix. 22). Hence ~FUL n. [ME, f. OF *vessel, -elle,* f. LL *vascellum,* (pl.) *-ella,* dim. of VAS]

vĕst¹, n. (Shop) waistcoat; (also *under~*) ‖ knitted or woven undergarment; piece, usu. V-shaped, on front of body of woman's gown; (arch.) clothing, dress; *~-pocket*, (attrib. of small articles, esp. hand-cameras) of a size suitable for the pocket (as a size of plate or film, 6 × 4·5 cm.). Hence *~'ING*¹(3) n. [f. F f. It. *veste* f. L *vestis* garment]

vĕst², v.t. & i. Furnish (person *with* authority, powers, property, etc.); *~* (property, power) *in* (person), confer formally on him an immediate fixed right of present or future possession of it (*~ed rights, interests, estate*, etc., possession of which is determinately fixed in a person & is subject to no contingency); (of property, right, etc.) *~ in* (person), come to him; (poet.) clothe. [ME, f. OF *vestir* f. L *vestire -it-* clothe (as prec.)]

vĕs'ta, n. (Rom. myth., *V~*) goddess of the hearth; (astron., *V~*) an asteroid; short wooden or (*wax ~*) wax match. [L, = Gk *Hestia*]

vĕs'tal, a. & n. Of the goddess Vesta or the *~* virgins; *~* (*virgin*), virgin consecrated to Vesta, vowed to chastity, & charged with care of sacred fire perpetually burning on her altar, hence, woman of spotless chastity, esp. one who devotes her life to religion, nun. [ME, f. L *Vestalis* a. & n. (as prec., see -AL)]

vĕs'tiary, n. (rare or obs.), & a. A vestry, robing-room or cloakroom; (adj.) relating to clothes or dress. [ME, f. OF *vestiarie*, see VESTRY]

vĕs'tibūl|e, n. Ante-chamber, hall, lobby, next to outer door of house & from which doors open into various rooms; porch of church etc.; **~e* (= CORRIDOR) *train*; (anat.) chamber or channel communicating with others, esp. *~e of the ear*, central cavity of labyrinth of internal ear. Hence **vĕstib'ūlAR¹**, **vĕstib'ūlATE²** (anat.), *~ED²* (-ld), aa. [F, or f. L *vestibulum*]

vĕs'tĭge, n. Footprint (now only fig.), track, trace, evidence, sign, as *~s of an earlier civilization, found no ~s of his presence*; (loosely, w. neg.) atom, particle, as *without a ~ of clothing, has not a ~ of evidence for this assertion*; (biol.) part, organ, now degenerate & of little or no utility but ancestrally well developed. Hence **vĕsti'gIAL** (esp. biol.), **vĕsti'gĭARY¹**, aa. [f. L *vestigium* footstep]

vĕs'tĭture, n. (zool.). Hair, scales, etc., covering a surface. [f. med. L *vestitura* f. L as VEST², -URE]

vĕst'ment, n. Garment, esp. official or state robe; any of the official garments of clergy, choristers, etc., worn during divine service, esp. chasuble; altar-cloth. [ME, f. OF *vestement* f. L *vestimentum* (as VEST², see -MENT)]

vĕs'trў, n. Room, building, attached to church & in which vestments are kept & put on; chapel attached to non-liturgical church & used for prayer meetings etc.; ‖ (also *common, general, ordinary, ~*) ratepayers of a parish, (also *select ~*) representatives of these, assembled for dispatch of parochial business; ‖ (room used for) meeting of either of these bodies; ‖ *~-clerk*, officer chosen by *~* to keep parish accounts etc.; *~man*, member of a *~*. [ME, f. AF **vest(e)rie* (f. VEST² + -ERY), repl. OF *vestiarie, vestiaire*, f. L *vestiarium* (VEST¹, -ARIUM)]

‖ **vĕs'trўdom**, n. (Corrupt, inefficient) government by vestry. [-DOM]

vĕs'ture, n., & v.t. (poet., rhet.). 1. Garments, dress, clothes; covering. 2. v.t. Clothe. [ME, f. OF f. med. L *vest(it)ura*, as VEST²; see -URE]

‖ **vĕs'turer** (-cher-), n. Church official in charge of vestments; sub-treasurer of cathedral or church. [f. prec. + -ER¹]

vĕsūv'ian, a. & n. 1. (*V~*). Of Vesuvius; volcanic. 2. n. (Also *~ITE¹* n.) brown or green mineral first found on Vesuvius. [f. L *Vesuvius* + -AN]

vĕt, n., & v.t. (colloq.; -tt-). 1. = VETERINARY. 2. v.t. Examine & pass fit, treat, (beast); (fig.) check & correct. [abbr.]

vĕtch, n. Kinds of plant of pea family largely used, wild or cultivated, for forage, esp. *common ~*, tare; *kidney-~*, perennial herb with red or yellow flowers. Hence *~'Y²* a. [ME, f. ONF *veche* f. L *vicia*]

vĕtch'ling, n. Plant allied to vetch. [-LING¹]

vĕt'eran, n. & a. Person who has grown old in or had long experience of (esp. military) service or occupation, as *Wellington's ~s, a ~ golfer; *ex-service man*; (adj.) of a *~*, composed of *~s*, as *~ service, troops*. Hence *~IZE*(3) v.t. [F, or f. L *veteranus* a. & n. (*vetus -eris* old, see -AN)]

vĕt'erinarў, a. & n. 1. Of, for, (the treatment of) diseases & injuries of domestic animals, as *~ surgeon, science, college*. 2. n. (abbr. *vet*). A *~* surgeon; also **vĕterinār'iAN** n. [f. L *veterinarius* f. *veterinae* cattle]

vĕt'ō, n. (pl. *~es*), & v.t. 1. Constitutional right of sovereign, president, governor, upper house of legislature, etc., to reject a legislative enactment (*suspensory ~*, suspending but not necessarily preventing completion of measure), whence *~IST*(2) n.; (official message conveying) such rejection; prohibition, as *interposed his ~, put a* or *his ~ on the proposal*. 2. v.t. Exercise *~* against (bill etc.), forbid authoritatively. [L, = I forbid, w. ref. to its use by tribune of the people in nullifying measures]

vĕx, v.t. Anger by slight or petty annoyance, irritate, as *this would ~ a saint, how ~ing!*, whence *~'ĕdLY²*, *~'ĭngLY²*, advv.; (arch.) grieve, afflict; (poet., rhet.) put (sea etc.) into state of commotion; *a ~ed* (much discussed) *question*. [ME, f. OF *vexer* f. L *vexare*]

vĕxā'tion, n. Vexing, being vexed; harassing by means of malicious or trivial litigation; state of irritation or distress, as *conceive my ~, in ~ of spirit*; annoying or distressing thing, as *subjected to many ~s*. Hence **vĕxā'tious** (-shŭs) a., **vĕxā'tious-**LY² adv., **vĕxā'tious**NESS n. [ME, f. OF, or f. L *vexatio*]

vĕxill'um, n. (pl. *-illa*). (Rom. ant.) military standard esp. of maniple, body of troops under this; (bot., also **vĕx'il** n.) large upper petal of papilionaceous flower; web of a feather, whence **vĕx'il-**lATE² a.; (eccl.) flag on or wound round bishop's staff, processional banner or cross. Hence or cogn. **vĕx'ill**AR(Y)¹ aa. [L (*vehere vect-* carry)]

vī'a, n. & prep. **1.** *Via Lăc'tĕa*, Milky Way; *~ mĕd'ta*, mean between extremes (esp. of Anglican church as placed between Romanism & extreme Protestantism). **2.** prep. (Also *viā*) by way of, through, as *from Exeter to York ~ London* (also joc. of connected subjects etc.). [L, =way, road]

vī'able, a. (Of foetus or new-born child) capable of maintaining life; (of plant, animal, etc.) able to live or exist in particular climate etc., (of seed) able to germinate. So **vīabil'ity** n. [F (*vie* life f. L *vita*, see -ABLE)]

vī'adŭct, n. Long bridgelike structure, esp. series of arches, for carrying road or railway over valley or dip in ground; such road or railway. [f. L *via* way, after AQUEDUCT]

vī'al, n. Small (usu. cylindrical glass) vessel for holding liquid medicines etc.; LEYDEN ~ (= *jar*); *pour out ~s of wrath*, take vengeance (*Rev.* xv. 7), (colloq.) give vent to anger. Hence ~FUL n. [ME, var. of *fiol, fiall*, etc., see PHIAL]

viăm'ĕter, n. = HODOMETER. [L *via* way +-METER]

vī'and, n. (usu. in pl.). Article(s) of food, victual(s). [ME, f. OF *viande* food f. Rom. **vivanda* for L *vivenda*, neut. pl. gerundive of L *vivere* live]

viăt'icum, n. (Rom. ant.) supplies or sum of money allowed to officer for journey on State service; provisions for journey; Eucharist as given to dying person; portable altar. [L (*via* way, see -ATIC); cf. VOYAGE]

vibrăc'ŭl|um, n. (pl. *~a*). Filamentous appendage of some polyzoa serving to bring food within reach by lashing movements. Hence ~AR¹ a. [mod. L as foll., see -CULE]

vib'rant, a. Vibrating; thrilling *with* something; (of sound) resonant. [f. L *vibrare* (foll.), -ANT]

vibrāte', v.i. & t. Move to & fro like pendulum, oscillate; (of sound) throb (on ear, in memory, etc.); (phys.) move unceasingly to & fro, esp. rapidly; thrill, quiver, (*with* passion etc.); cause to oscillate; (of pendulum) measure (seconds etc.) by vibrating. Hence **vīb'ratt**IvE, **vib'rat**ORY, aa. [f. L *vibrare* shake, swing, see -ATE³]

vīb'ratīle, a. Capable of vibrating. Hence **vibratil'**ITY n. [-ILE]

vibrā'tion, n. Vibrating, oscillation; (phys.) rapid motion to & fro esp. of the parts of a fluid or an elastic solid whose equilibrium has been disturbed (*amplitude of ~*, maximum departure of vibrating body from position of rest; *forced, free, ~*, whose period is, is not, modified by an outside force). Hence ~AL a., **vibrāt'i**UNCLE n. dim. [f. L *vibratio* (as VIBRATE, see -ATION)]

vībra'tō (vēbrah-), n. Effect like TREMOLO in singing & playing stringed instruments. [It.]

vibrāt'or, n. Person, thing, that vibrates, esp. (electr., teleg.) kinds of vibrating reed, (mus.) reed in reed-organ, (print.) inking-roller with vibrating & rotary movements, (med.) electric or other instrument used in massage. [-OR]

vibrīss'ae, n. pl. Stiff coarse hair about mouth of most mammals & in nostrils of man; bristle-like feathers about mouth of some birds. [L (as VIBRATE)]

vib'roscōpe, n. Instrument for observing vibrations. [-SCOPE]

vibūrn'um, n. Kinds of shrub of honey-suckle family. [L]

vic'ar, n. ‖Incumbent of a parish the tithes of which belong to chapter or religious house or layman (cf. RECTOR); *~ of Bray*, systematic turncoat, w. ref. to 17th-c. song; *lay ~*, cathedral officer singing some parts of service; ‖ *~ choral*, clerical or lay assistant in some (esp. musical) parts of cathedral service; ‖ *~ general*, (Ch. of Eng.) official assisting (arch)bishop in ecclesiastical causes etc. (usu. his chancellor), (R.-C. Ch.) bishop's assistant in matters of jurisdiction etc.; (R.-C. Ch.) *cardinal ~*, Pope's delegate acting as bishop of diocese of Rome, *~ apostolic*, missionary or titular bishop (whence **vicār'i**ATE¹(1) n.), *~ fō'rane*, dignitary appointed by bishop to exercise limited local jurisdiction, *V~ of* (*Jesus*) *Christ*, Pope. Hence ~SHIP n. [ME, f. AF *viker(e)*, OF *vicaire* f. L *vicarius* substitute f. *vicis* (VICE⁴, -ARY¹)]

vic'arage, n. Benefice, residence, of vicar. [-AGE]

vicār'ial, a. Of, serving as, a vicar. [-AL]

vicār'ious, a. Deputed, delegated, as *~ authority*; acting, done, for another, as *~ work, suffering, ~ sacrifice* (of Christ in place of sinner). Hence ~LY² adv., ~NESS n. [f. L as VICARI*us* +-OUS]

vice¹, n. Evil esp. grossly immoral habit or conduct, (particular form of) depravity, serious fault, as *has the ~ of gluttony, drunkenness is not among his ~s, ~is duly punished & virtue rewarded in fifth act, has no redeeming ~* (to relieve overpowering rectitude); defect, blemish, (of character, literary style, etc.); fault, bad trick, in horse etc., as *has no ~s, is free from ~, has one ~*; (now rare) morbid state of physical system, as *inherited ~s of consti- tution*; (*V~*) buffoon in a MORALITY. [ME, f. OF, f. L *vitium*]

vice², ***vise***, n., & v.t. 1. Instrument with two jaws between which thing may be gripped usu. by operation of screw so as to leave the hands free for working upon it, as *bench ~* (attached to carpenter's or machinist's bench), *instantaneous-grip ~*, *grips like a ~*. 2. v.t. Secure (material to be worked upon, or fig.) in *~*. [ME, = winding-stair, screw, f. OF *vis* f. L *vitis* vine]

vice³, n. (colloq.). = VICE-*president* etc.

vi'ce⁴, prep. In the place of, as *gazetted as captain ~ Captain Jones promoted*. [L, abl. of **vix vicis* change]

vice-, pref. (= prec.) forming nn. w. sense 'person acting or qualified to act in place of or next in rank to', w. their derivv., as: *~-ad'miral*, ADMIRAL of third grade; *~-ad'miralty*, office of *~*-admiral ‖ (*~-admiralty* courts, tribunals with admiralty jurisdiction in British colonial possessions); *~-a'gent*; *~-chair'man*(*ship*); ‖ *~-cham'berlain* (esp. deputy of lord chamberlain); *~-chan'cellor*, (univv.) deputy chancellor discharging most administrative duties, (law, formerly) judge in chancery division of High Court of Justice, (R.-C. Ch.) cardinal at head of the branch of chancery in charge of bulls etc.; *~-chan'cellorship*; *~-con'sul*(*ship*); *~-dean'*, subdean; *~-go'vernor*; *~-king'*, = VICEROY; *~-pres'ident*(*ship*), *~-pres'i-dency*; *~-prin'cipal*; *~-queen'* (rare), woman acting as viceroy, viceroy's wife; *~-re'gent*; *~'reine* (-srän), viceroy's wife; *~-she'riff*; *~-trea'surer*(*ship*); *~-war'den*.

vicegě'ren|t (-sj-; also -ēr²), a. & n. (Person) exercising delegated power, deputy, as *regard the Pope as God's V~t*. Hence *~*CY n. [f. med. L *vicegerent-nom. -ens* (prec. +L *gerere* carry on, see -ENT)]

vicěnn'ĭal, a. Lasting, happening every, twenty years. [f. LL *vicennium* period of 20 years (*viginti* 20 +*annus* year) +-AL]

vice'roy (-sr-), n. Ruler exercising royal authority in colony, province, etc., as (hist.) *V~ of India*. Hence **vicerěg'AL, viceroy'AL**, aa., **viceroy'alTY**, *~*SHIP, nn., (-sr-). [16th c., f. older F (VICE- + *roy* king f. L *regem* nom. *rex*)]

vi'ce věr's'a, adv. or ellipt. sent. (The same is true, on the corresponding sup-position, etc.) with the order of terms changed, the other way round, as *the man blames his wife & ~* (she him), *cat stole the dog's dinner & ~* (he hers), *calls black white & ~* (white black). [L, (VICE⁴, *versa* abl. fem. p.p. of *vertere* turn)]

Vichy (water) (vē'shē), n. A mineral water. [*Vichy* in France]

vi'cinage, n. Neighbourhood, surround-ing district; relation of neighbours. [ME, f. OF *visenage* w. assim. to the L source *vicinus* f. *vicus* (WICK²)]

vicin'itў, n. Surrounding district; near-ness in place (*to*); close relationship (*to*). [f. L *vicinitas* (as prec., see -TY)]

vi'cious (-shus), a. Of the nature of vice, morally evil or injurious, as *~ tendencies*, *courses*, *life*; addicted to vice, as *~ com-panions*; (of horse etc.) having vices; (of language, reasoning, etc.) incorrect, faulty, unsound, corrupt, as *a ~ style*, *a notoriously ~ manuscript*, *~* CIRCLE¹; *~ union* (surg.), faulty joining of frac-tured ends of bone, resulting deformity; bad-tempered, spiteful, as *~ dog, mood, remarks*. Hence *~*LY² adv., *~*NESS n. [ME, f. OF or f. L *vitiosus* (as VICE¹, see -OUS)]

viciss'itūde, n. Change of circumstances esp. of fortune, as *a life marked by ~s* (arch., poet.) regular change, alterna-tion. Hence **vicissitūd'in**ous a. [F, or f. L *vicissitudo -dinis* (as VICE⁴, see -TUDE)]

vic'tim, n. Living being sacrificed to a deity or in performance of religious rite; person, thing, injured or destroyed in pursuit of an object, in gratification of a passion etc., or as result of event or cir-cumstance, as *the ~s of his relentless am-bition, fell a ~ to his own avarice, the ~s of disease, of a railway accident*; prey, dupe, as *held the ~ in his talons, the numerous ~s of the confidence trick*. [f. L *victima*]

vic'timiz|e, -is|e (-īz), v.t. Make (person etc.) the victim of a swindle etc. or of one's ambition, loquacity, etc.; make (striker etc.) suffer by dismissal or other excep-tional treatment. Hence *~*A'TION n. [-IZE]

vic'tor, n. (rhet.). Conqueror in battle or contest (also attrib., as *~ troops, sword*). Hence **vic'tr**ESS¹ n. [ME, f. AF *victo*(*u*)*r* or L *victor* (*vincere vict-* conquer, -OR)]

victōr'ia, n. 1. Low light four-wheeled carriage with seat for two & raised driver's seat & with falling top. 2. Kinds of gigantic water-lily. 3. Kinds of domestic pigeon. 4. *V~ Cross* (abbr. *V.C.*), decora-tion awarded to members of the armed services for conspicuous act of bravery founded by Queen V~ in 1856. [L, = victory (as prec., see -Y¹)]

Victōr'ian, a. & n. Of, (person esp. author) living in, the reign of Queen Victoria (1837–1901); *~ Order* (founded by Queen Victoria in 1896 & conferred usu. for great service rendered to sovereign). [-AN]

victōr'ious, a. Conquering, triumphant; marked by victory (*~ day* etc.). Hence *~*LY² adv., *~*NESS n. [ME, f. AF f. L *victoriosus* (VICTORIA, -OUS)]

vic'torў, n. Defeat of enemy in battle or opponent in contest, as *battle ended in a decisive ~, fought hard for ~, hero of many victories*, (fig.) *gained a* or *the ~ over his passions*, *Cadmean* or PYRRHIC² *~*, MORAL *~*; (*V~*), (statue of) goddess of *~* (*winged* etc. *V~*). [ME, f. AF *victorie*, = OF *victoire*, f. L VICTORIA, see -Y¹]

victual (vi'tl), n., & v.t. & i. (-ll-). 1. (Usu.

pl.) food, provisions. **2. vb.** Supply with
~s, obtain stores, eat ~s. Hence ~LESS
a. [ME, f. OF *vitaile, -aille*, f. LL
victualia, neut. pl. of L *victualis* f. *victus*
food, see -AL; vb f. OF *vitailler*]
victualler (vĭt'ler), n. One who furnishes
victuals, ‖ esp. *licensed* ~, innkeeper
licensed to sell spirits etc.; ship employed
to carry stores for other ships. [ME, f.
OF *vitaill(i)er* (prec., -OR)]
victualling (vĭt'lĭng), n. In vbl senses;
‖ ~-*bill*, custom-house warrant for ship-
ment of bonded stores; ‖ ~-*note* (nav.),
order authorizing ship's steward to victual
a seaman; ‖ ~-*office* (for supplying provisions to navy); ‖ ~-*yard* (adjoining dockyard, for naval stores). [-ING¹]
vicu'gna, -u'ña, (-kooñya), n. S.-Amer.
mammal allied to llama & hunted for its
flesh & wool; ~ *wool* (commerc.), mixture
of wool & cotton, also wool of the ~. [Sp.
f. Peruv.]
vĭd'ē (*or* -ē), vb imperat. (abbr. *v.*). (In
formal or joc. reference to passage in
book etc.) see, as ~ *supra, infra*, see
above, below, QUOD²~, ~ *the press passim.*
[L, imperat. of *vidēre*]
vĭdēl'ĭcĕt, adv. (abbr. *viz*, usu. spoken as
namely). That is to say, in other words,
namely, (usu. following words that
promise or more or less clearly require
explanation etc. as: *under the following
conditions, viz that* etc.; *a permanent
board of three, viz*, etc.; opp. to *i.e.*, which
explains or elaborates a statement. [L
(*vidēre licet* one may see)]
*****vid'ēō,** a. & n. Of or used in the trans-
mission or reception of television; (n.)
television. [L, = I see]
‖ **vidette.** See VEDETTE.
vĭd'īmus, n. (pl. ~*es*). Inspection of
accounts etc.; abstract of document etc.
[L, = we have seen (*vidēre*)]
vie, v.i. (*vying*). Strive for superiority,
carry on rivalry, (*with* another *in* quality,
in doing). [ult. aphetic f. F *envier* increase the stake, f. L *invilare* INVITE]
Viennēse' (-z), a. & n. (pl. same). (Inhabitant) of Vienna. [-ESE]
vī ĕt ārm'īs, adv. (law). With force &
arms, with violence. [L]
view (vū), n., & v.t. **1.** Inspection by eye,
survey, (*of* surroundings etc.); (law) inspection by jury of place, property, etc.,
concerned in a case, or of dead body.
2. Power of seeing, range of vision, as
stood in full ~ *of* (visible to) *the crowd,
came in* ~ *of* (where one could be seen
from or see) *the castle, passed from our* ~
(sight); what is seen, scene, prospect, as
a superb ~ ; picture etc. representing this.
3. Mental survey, as *take a general* ~ *of
the subject*; manner of considering a subject, opinion, mental attitude, as *takes a
different* ~, *his* ~ *is that we are the aggres-
sors, takes a favourable* ~ *of her conduct,
holds extreme* ~*s* (in politics etc.). **4.** Intention, design, as *will this meet your* ~*s?*,

cannot fall in with your ~*s, cat has* ~*s
upon the larder*. **5.** *In* ~ *of*, having
regard to, considering, as *in* ~ *of recent
developments we do not think this step advisable*, (vulg.) = *with a* ~ *to* (1); *on* ~,
open to inspection; *with a* ~ *to*, (1; also
with the ~ *of*; vulg. *with a* ~ *of*) for the
purpose of, as a step towards, as *with a* ~
to extending (vulg. *extend*) *our trade, with
a* ~ *to further hostilities*, (2) in the hope
or on the chance of getting, with an eye
to, as *said this with a* ~ *to the vacant
secretaryship*, (3, vulg.) = *in* ~ *of*, to the
~, openly, in public. **6.** BIRD'*s-eye* ~;
dissolving ~*s* (see DISSOLVE); *have in* ~,
have as one's object, also, bear (circumstance) in mind in forming judgement
etc.; POINT¹ *of* ~; *private* ~ (of picture
etc. exhibition, open only to exhibitors'
friends, critics, etc.); ~-*finder*, part of
camera showing limits of picture; ~
halloo', huntsman's shout on seeing fox
break cover; ~'*point*, point of ~, standpoint. **7.** v.t. Survey with the eyes;
survey mentally, form mental impression
or judgment of, as *subject may be* ~*ed in
different ways, does not* ~ *the matter in the
right light*, he or the proposal is ~*ed unfavourably*. Hence ~ABLE (vū'abl) a.,
~ER¹ (vū'er) n., (esp.) television watcher.
[ME & AF *vewe, viewe*, OF *veue* p.p. as n.
f. *veoir* see f. L *vidēre*; vb f. n.]
view'lěss (vū-), a. (poet., rhet.). Invisible.
[-LESS]
view'lỹ (vū-), a. (colloq.). Given to odd or
fanciful views, faddy. Hence ~ĭNESS n.
[-Y²]
vi'gil, n. Keeping awake during the time
usually given to sleep, watchfulness, as
keep ~; (usu. pl.) nocturnal devotions;
eve of a festival, esp. eve that is a fast.
[ME, f. OF *vigile* f. L *vigilia* (*vigil* awake)]
vi'gil|ance, n. Watchfulness, caution,
circumspection, so ~ANT a., ~antLY² adv.;
(med.) insomnia; ~*ance committee*, self-
-organized body for maintenance of
order etc. in imperfectly organized community. [F, or f. L *vigilantia* (*vigilare*
watch, as prec., -ANCE)]
*****vigilăn'tě,** n. Member of a vigilance
committee. [Sp.]
vignett|e (vĕnyĕt'), n., & v.t. **1.** (Archit.)
ornament of leaves & tendrils; flourishes
round capital letter in MS.; engraved
illustration, esp. on title-page of book,
not enclosed in definite border; photograph or portrait showing only head &
shoulders with background gradually
shaded off; (fig.) character sketch. **2.** v.t.
Make portrait of (person) in ~e style,
shade off (portrait) thus, whence ~'ER²(2),
~'IST, nn. [F, dim. as VINE]
vigorōs'ō, adv. (mus.). With vigour. [It.]
vig'our (-ger), n. Active physical strength
or energy; flourishing physical condition;
healthy growth, vitality, vital force;
mental strength or activity as shown
in thought or speech or literary style,

forcibleness, trenchancy, animation. Hence or cogn. **vig′orous**, **~less** (-ger-), aa., **vig′orously**[2] adv., **vig′orousness** n. [ME, f. OF, f. L *vigorem* (*vigēre* be lively, see -OR)]

vik′ing, n. Northern sea robber of 8th to 10th c. Hence **~ism**(2) n. [f. ON *vīkingr*, perh. f. OE *wīcing* (*wīc* camp, -ING[3])]

vila′yet (-lahyĕt), n. Province of Turkey. [Turk., f. Arab. *welāyet* district]

vile, a. Worthless; morally base, depraved, shameful, abject, as *the~ trade of an informer*, *sycophant's ~ practices*, *the ~st of mankind*; (colloq.) abominably bad, as *a ~ pen*, *~ pastry*. Hence **~′ly**[2] adv., **~′ness** n. [ME, f. OF (*vil vile*), f. L *vilis*]

vil′ify, v.t. Defame, traduce, speak ill of; (rare) degrade, debase. Hence **~fica′tion**, **~fīer**[1], nn. [ME, f. LL *vilificare* (prec., -FY)]

vil′ipend, v.t. (literary). Treat contemptuously, disparage. [ME, f. OF *vilipender* or L *vilipendere* (as VILE + *pendere* weigh)]

vill′a, n. Country residence; detached suburban house. Hence **~dom** n., suburban society. [L & It. *villa*]

vill′age, n. Assemblage of houses etc. larger than hamlet & smaller than town. [ME, f. OF, f. Rom. *villaticum* neut. sing. as n. f. L *-icus* f. VILLA, see -AGE]

vill′ager, n. Inhabitant of a village (usu. implying rusticity). [-ER[1]]

vill′ain (-ən), n. & a. **1.** Person guilty or capable of great wickedness, scoundrel, as *has played the ~*, *plays the ~s in melodramas*, (colloq., playful) *you little* etc. ~ (rascal); ‖ (arch.) rustic, boor; (hist., also *villein* a. & n.) feudal serf, tenant holding by menial services, so **vill′ai(n)-age** (-lan-), **-e(i)nage** (-lin-), n. **2.** adj. Of, done by, a ~, as ~ *services*. [ME, f. OF *vilein*, *vil(l)ain* f. Rom. *villanus* f. VILLA, see -AN]

vill′ainous (-lan-), a. Worthy of a villain, vile, wicked, so **vill′ainy**[2] (-lan-) n.; (colloq.) abominably bad, as *a ~ scrawl*, *style*, *hotel*. Hence **~ly**[2] adv., **~ness** n. [ME; -OUS]

villanĕlle′, n. Form of (esp. French) poem of 19 lines on two rhymes. [F, f. It. *villanella*]

villĕggiatur′a (-jatoora), n. Stay, retirement, in the country. [It.]

vill′ein (-lin). See a. n. See VILLAIN.

vill′|us, n. (pl. **~i**). (Anat.) each of the short hairlike processes on some membranes esp. on mucous membrane of intestine; (bot., pl.) long soft hair covering fruit, flower, etc. Hence or cogn. **~iform**, **~oid**, **~ose**[1], **~ous**, aa., **~os′ity** n. [L, = shaggy hair]

vim, n. (colloq.). Vigour. [L, acc. of VIS]

vim′inal, a. (bot.). Of, producing, twigs or shoots. So **vimin′eous** a. [f. L *viminalis* (*vimen -minis* osier)]

vi′na (vē-), n. Indian seven-stringed musical instrument with fretted finger-board & a gourd at each end. [Hind.]

vinā′ceous (-shus), a. Of wine or grapes; wine-red. [f. L *vinaceus* (*vinum* wine, -ACEOUS)]

vinaigrĕtte′ (-nĭg-), n. Bottle for holding aromatic vinegar etc., smelling-bottle. [F, dim. of *vinaigre* VINEGAR]

vin′cible, a. (rare). Not invincible. [f. L *vincibilis* (*vincere* conquer, see -BLE)]

vin′culum, n. (pl. *-la*). (Alg.) line drawn over several terms to show that they have a common relation to what follows or precedes (e.g. $\overline{a+b} \times c = ac+bc$, but $a+b \times c = a+bc$; $a - \overline{b+c} = a-b-c$); (print.) = BRACE[1]; (anat.) = FRAENUM. [L, = bond (*vincire* bind)]

vin′dic|āte, v.t. Maintain the cause of (person, religion, etc.) successfully; establish the existence or merits or justice of (one's veracity, courage, conduct, character, assertion). Hence or cogn. **~abil′ity**, **~a′tion**, **~ātor**, **~ātress**[1], nn., **~able**, **~ative**, aa. [f. L *vindicare* lay claim to, see -ATE[3]]

vin′dicatory, a. Tending to vindicate; (of laws) punitive. [-ORY]

vindic′tive, a. Revengeful, given to revenge; **~** (or *exemplary*) *damages* (awarded as punishment to defendant). Hence **~ly**[2] adv., **~ness** n. [f. L *vindicta* vengeance (VINDICATE) + -IVE]

vine, n. Climbing woody-stemmed plant whose fruit is the grape (*under* one's *~ & FIG[1]-tree*); any plant with slender stem that trails or climbs, as *hop*, *melon*, *~*; **~-borer**, kinds of insect destroying **~**; **~-disease**, due to PHYLLOXERA etc. Hence **vin′y**[2] aa. [ME & OF *vigne*, *vine*, f. L *vinea* vineyard (*vinum* wine)]

vin′egar, n., & v.t. **1.** Acid liquid got from wine, cider, etc., by acetous fermentation & used as condiment or for pickling (fig., often attrib.); as type of sourness, as *a ~ countenance*; *aromatic ~* (holding camphor etc. in solution); *toilet ~*, aromatic **~** used for mixing with washing-water etc.; MOTHER[3] *of ~*; *V~ Bible*, 1717 ed. with *parable of the ~* (for *vineyard*) above *Luke* xx; **~-eel**; **~-plant**, microscopic fungus producing fermentation. Hence **~ish**[1], **~y**[2], aa. **2.** v.t. Apply ~ to, make sour like ~ (lit. & fig.). [ME, f. OF *vinegre* (*vin* wine f. L *vinum* + *egre*, see EAGER)]

vin′ery, n. Vine greenhouse. [f. med. L *vinarium* or f. VINE + -ERY]

vine′yard (-ny-), n. Plantation of grape-vines. [ME; VINE + YARD]

vingt-et-un (see Ap.), n. Card game in which the object is to reach the number of 21 pips without exceeding it. [F, = 21]

vini-, comb. form of L *vinum* wine, as: **~cul′ture**, cultivation of vines, so **~cul′turist**; **vinif′erous**, (of district) wine-producing; **~ficā′tor**, apparatus for collecting alcoholic vapours in wine-making.

vinōm′eter, n. Apparatus for measuring alcohol in wine. [f. L *vinum* wine + -METER]

vin ordinaire (see Ap.), n. Cheap (usu.

red) wine as drunk in France mixed with water. [F]

vin′ous, a. Of, like, due to, wine, as ~ *flavour, fermentation, eloquence.* So vīnos⸗ ITY n. [f. L *vinosus* (*vinum* wine, see -OUS)]

‖ **vint¹**, v.t. Make (wine). [f. VINTAGE]

vint², n. A Russian card-game. [Russ., = screw]

vin′tağe, n. Season of gathering grapes; (wine made from) season's produce of grapes; ~ *wines* (of well-known ~s); (poet., rhet.) wine; (attrib.) of a past season, as *a ~ motor-car.* [alt. (after *vint-ner*) f. ME *vendage, vindage* f. OF *vendange* f. L *vindemia*]

vin′tağer, n. Grape-gatherer. [prec., -ER¹]

vint′ner, n. Wine-merchant. [alt. f. ME, AF *vinter* = OF *vinetier* f. L *vinum* wine]

vī′ol, n. Medieval (usu. 6-)stringed musical instrument, predecessor of violin etc. (*treble, tenor, bass, ~*); *bass ~* (mod.), = VIOLONCELLO. [ME *viel* f. OF *viel(l)e,* alt. f. *viole* (whence mod. E sp.) f. pop L *vitula* f. L *vitulari* be joyful; see FIDDLE]

vīŏl′a¹, n. 1. Kind of large violin, alto or tenor violin. 2. (hist.). = prec.; ~ *da braccio, ~,* (alto) violin; ~ *da gamba,* bass viol. [It. & Sp., = F *viole* (prec.)]

vī′ola², n. Kinds of plant including pansy, esp. of single colour, & violet. [L, = violet]

violā′ceous (-shus), a. Of violet colour; of violet family. [f. L *violaceus* (prec., -ACEOUS)]

vī′olāte, v.t. Transgress, infringe, act against the dictates or requirements of (oath, treaty, law, terms, conscience); treat profanely or with disrespect (sanctuary etc.); break in upon, disturb, (person's privacy etc.); commit rape upon, ravish. So ~ABLE a., ~A′TION, ~ātoR, nn. [ME, f. L *violare* (VIS), see -ATE³]

vī′olence, n. Quality of being violent; violent conduct or treatment, outrage, injury, as *was compelled to use ~, did ~ to* (outraged, acted contrary to) *his feelings, our principles;* (law) unlawful exercise of physical force, intimidation by exhibition of this. [ME, f. OF, f. L *violentia* (as foll., see -ENCE)]

vī′olent, a. Marked by great physical force, as *a ~ storm, came into ~ collision,* ~ *blows;* ~ *death* (resulting from external force or from poison, cf. NATURAL); marked by unlawful exercise of force, as *laid ~ hands on him;* intense, vehement, passionate, furious, impetuous, as ~ *pain, sickness, abuse, controversy, discrepancy, revulsion, contrast, dislike, shock, apt to form ~ attachments, is of or was in a ~ temper;* ~ *presumption* (law), one resting on almost conclusive evidence. Hence ~LY² adv [ME, f. OF, f. L *violentus* (VIS, -LENT)]

vī′olet, n. & a. 1. Kinds of plant chiefly of genus VIOLA, with blue, purple, white, or other flowers, as *common blue ~, sweet ~, dog-~.* 2. (Of) the colour seen at end of

spectrum opposite red, produced by slight admixture of red with blue, so VIOLES⸗ CENT a. 3. Kinds of ~ butterfly. 4. ~-*-powder,* toilet powder scented with orris or other perfume; ~*-wood,* myall & other kinds. [ME, f. OF *violette, -et,* dim. of *viole* f. L VIOLA²]

violin′¹, n. Musical instrument with 4 strings of treble pitch played with bow; (also ~IST n.) player on ~, as *first, second,* ~ (playing separate parts in orchestra etc.). [f. It. *violino* dim. of VIOLA¹]

vī′olin², **-ine,** n. Emetic substance contained in sweet violet. [f. F *violine* (VIOLA², -IN, -INE⁵)]

vī′olist, n. Performer on viol(a). [-IST]

violoncell′|ō (vē-, -chĕ-), n. (usu. abbr. *'cello:* pl. ~*os*). Bass violin, 4-stringed instrument held between player's knees. Hence ~IST(3) n. [It., dim. of *violone* large viol (VIOLA¹, see -OON)]

vīp′er, n. Kinds of venomous snake esp. *common ~,* adder, the only poisonous snake in Gt Britain; (fig.) malignant or treacherous person; ~*'s bugloss,* stiff bristly blue-flowered plant; ~*'s grass,* black salsify. Hence or cogn. ~īFORM, ~INE¹, ~ISH¹ (fig.), ~OID, ~OUS (fig.), aa. [f. F *vipère* or L *vipera*]

virāğ′ō, n. (pl. ~*s*). Turbulent woman, termagant; ‖ (arch.) woman of masculine strength or spirit. [OE & ME, f. L, = female warrior (*vir* man)]

vī′relay, n. Kinds of (esp. old French) poem with two rhymes to a stanza variously arranged. [ME, f. OF *virelai, -li*]

virement (vēr′mahn̄), n. Power to transfer items from one account to another. [F]

vī′rēō, n. (Kinds of) small greenish--coloured American singing bird (also *greenlet*). [L, perh. = greenfinch]

vires′c|ence, n. Greenness; (bot.) abnormal greenness in petals etc. normally of some bright colour. So ~ENT a. [f. L *virescere,* see -ESCENT, -ENCE]

vīrg′ate¹, a. (nat. hist.). Slim, straight, & erect. [f. L *virgatus* (*virga* rod, -ATE²)]

vīrg′ate², n. (hist.). A varying measure of land. [f. med. L *virgata* (*terrae*), rendering OE *gierd-land* yard-land, f. L *virga* rod + -ATE¹]

Vīrgil′ian, a. Of, in the style of, the Roman poet Virgil (d. 19 B.C.). [f. L *Virgilianus* (*Virgilius* Virgil, -AN)]

vĭr′ğin, n. & a. 1. Person esp. woman who has had no sexual intercourse, whence or cogn. ~HOOD, vĭrğin′ITY, nn.; member of any order of women under a vow to remain ~s; *the* (Blessed) *V~* (Mary) (abbr. *B.V.M.*), mother of Christ; picture, statue, of the B.V.M.; female insect producing eggs without impregnation; (astron., *V~*) = VIRGO; ~*'s bower,* = TRAVELLER'S *joy.* 2. adj. That is a ~; of, befitting, a ~, as ~ *modesty;* undefiled, spotless; not yet used or tried, as ~ *soil,* ~ *clay* (not fired); (of insect) producing eggs without impregnation; ~ *comb* (that has been used only once for honey & never for brood); ~ *honey* (taken from ~ comb, also, drained from comb without heat or pressure); ~ *queen*, unfertilized queen bee; *the V*~ *Queen*, Queen Elizabeth I. [ME, f. OF *virgine* f. L *virginem*, nom. *-go*]

vir′ginal, a. & n. **1.** That is or befits or belongs to a virgin, whence ~LY[2] adv. **2.** n. (hist.). (Also ~s, *pair of* ~s) square legless spinet used in 16th–17th cc. [(adj., ME) f. OF, or L *virginalis* (as prec., see -AL); origin of n. use unknown]

Virgin′i|a, n. One of the U.S.; tobacco from ~a; ~*a creeper*, a vine cultivated for ornament. Hence ~AN a. & n. [f. VIRGIN (Queen) +-IA[1]]

virgin′ibus puer′is′que, L phr. (Addressed, suited) to girls & boys (i.e. respecting innocence).

Virg′o, n. **1.** Sixth zodiacal sign; a constellation. **2.** *v*~ *intac′ta* (law), virgin with hymen intact. [L, = virgin]

viridës′c|ent, a. Greenish, tending to become green. Hence ~ENCE n. [f. LL *viridescere* (*viridis* green, see -ESCENT)]

virid′itȳ, n. Greenness, esp. of oysters etc. after feeding on certain vegetable organisms. [ME, f. OF *viridite* or L *viriditas* (*viridis* green, see -TY)]

vi′rile (*also* vīr[2]), a. Of man as opp. to woman or child; of, having, procreative power; (of mind, character, literary style, etc.) having masculine vigour or strength. So **viril′ITY** n. [f. F *viril* or L *virilis* (*vir* man, see -ILE)]

virilës′c|ent, a. (Of female animal) assuming in advanced age some male characteristics. So ~ENCE n. [f. L as prec., -ESCENT]

virŏl′og|ȳ, n. Science or study of viruses. So ~IST n. [VIR(US), -O-, -LOGY]

vir′|ōse, a. Poisonous, full of virus, so ~OUS a.; (bot.) having fetid smell. [f. L *virosus* (VIRUS, see -OSE[1])]

virtu′ (′-ōō), n. Love of fine arts; *articles of* ~ (interesting from workmanship, antiquity, rarity, etc.). [f. It. *virtu* VIRTUE, virtu]

virt′ual, a. That is such for practical purposes though not in name or according to strict definition, as *is the* ~ *manager of the business, take this as a* ~ *promise, constitutes a* ~ *exculpation*; ~ *focus* (opt.), point at which the lines of a pencil of rays would meet if produced; ~ *velocity* or *displacement*, infinitesimal displacement of the point of application of a force measured in the direction of that force. Hence ~ITY (-ăl[2]) n., ~LY[2] adv. [ME, f. med. L *virtualis* f. L *virtus* after LL *virtuosus*, see -AL]

virt′ue, n. Moral excellence, uprightness, goodness, as ~ *is its own reward*, *make a* ~ *of necessity*, feign alacrity or sense of duty while acting under compulsion; particular moral excellence, as *patience is a* ~, *she has every* ~, *the*

(*seven*) *cardinal* ~s (*natural* ~s, justice, prudence, temperance, fortitude; *theological* ~s, faith, hope, charity); chastity esp. of women, as *a woman of* ~; good quality, as *has the* ~ *of being adjustable*, *of resisting temperature*; inherent power, efficacy, as *no* ~ *in such drugs*; (pl.) seventh ORDER[1] of angels; *by* or *in* ~ *of*, on the strength of, on the ground of, as *claims it in* ~ *of his long service, is entitled to it by* ~ *of his prerogative*. Hence ~LESS (-ŭl-) a. [ME, f. OF *vertu* f. L *virtutem* nom. *-tus* f. *vir* man]

virtūŏs′ō, n. (pl. *-si* pr. -sē). Person with special knowledge of or taste for works of art or virtu; person skilled in the mechanical part of a fine art. Hence **virtūŏs′ITY**, ~SHIP, nn. [It., as foll.]

virt′uous, a. Possessing, showing, moral rectitude; chaste. Hence ~LY[2] adv., ~NESS n. [ME, f. OF *vertuous* f. LL *virtuosus* f. *virtus* VIRTUE, see -OUS]

vi′rul|ent (*or* -rōō-), a. Poisonous; caused by or containing virus, as ~*ent ulcer*, so [irreg.] ~IF′EROUS a. (med.); malignant, bitter, as ~*ent animosity, tone, abuse*. Hence or cogn. ~ENCE n., ~entLY[2] adv. [f. L *virulentus* (foll., see -LENT)]

vir′us, n. Morbid poison, poison of contagious disease, as *smallpox* ~; (fig.) moral poison; (fig.) malignity, acrimony. [L, = poison]

vis, n. (mech.). ~ INERTIAe; ~ *mōrt′ua*, force that does no work, dead force; ~ *viv′a*, living force (= mass × square of velocity) of moving body. [L, = force]

visa (vēz′a; *-sa'd*), (obs.) **visé** (vēz′ā; *-séd*, *-sé′d*), n., & v.t. **1.** Indorsement on passport etc. showing that it has been found correct. **2.** v.t. Mark with ~. [L *visa* fem. p.p. of *videre* to see; F *visé* p.p. of *viser* to examine]

vis′ag|e (-z-), n. (now chiefly literary). Face, countenance. Hence (-)~ED[2] (-zĭjd) a. [ME, f. OF, f. L *visus* face, see -AGE]

visard. See VISOR.

vis-à-vis (vēz′ahvē′), adv. & n. **1.** In a position facing one another; opposite *to*. **2.** n. Person facing another esp. in some dances; kinds of carriage & couch in or on which persons sit facing each other. [F, =face to face (*vis* face f. L as VISAGE)]

viscăch′a, **viz-**, n. S.-Amer. burrowing rodent with valuable fur. [of native orig.]

vis′cer|a, n. pl. The interior organs in the great cavities of the body (e.g. brain, heart, liver), esp. in the abdomen (e.g. the intestines). Hence ~AL a., ~I-, ~O-, comb. forms. [L, pl. of *viscus -eris*]

vis′cerăte, v.t. Disembowel. [f. prec. +-ATE[3], after *eviscerate*]

vis′cid, a. Sticky; semifluid. So ~ITY (-ĭd[2]) n. [f. LL *viscidus* (L *viscum* mistletoe, birdlime, see -ID[1])]

vis′cin, n. Sticky substance got from mistletoe & used in birdlime. [F, f. *viscum*, prec., -IN]

vis′cōse, n. (In the manufacture of rayon) cellulose reduced to a viscous state (suitable for drawing into yarn) by treatment with sodium hydroxide solution & carbon disulphide. [f. L *viscum* birdlime + -OSE²]

viscŏs′ity, n. Stickiness; (phys., of fluids, semifluids, & gases) internal friction, power of resisting a change in the arrangement of the molecules, whence **viscŏm′eter, viscŏm′etry, viscŏsim′eter**, nn. [ME, f. OF *viscosite* or med. L *viscositas* (as VISCOUS, see -TY)]

visc′ount (vīk-), n. Noble ranking between earl & baron. Hence or cogn. ~CY, ~ESS¹, ~SHIP or ~Y⁴, nn., (vīk-). [ME, f. AF *viscounte*, OF *vi(s)conte* (VICE- + *counte* COUNT³)]

vis′cous, a. Sticky; (phys.) having viscosity. Hence ~NESS n. [ME, f. AF, or f. LL *viscosus* (as VISCID, see -OUS)]

visé. See VISA.

***vise.** See VICE².

vis′ible (-z-), a. That can be seen by the eye; that can be perceived or ascertained, apparent, open, as *has no* ~ *means of support, spoke with* ~ *impatience*; prepared to receive callers (*is she* ~?); *the* ~ *church*, whole body of professed believers; ~ *horizon*, the line that bounds sight; ~ *speech*, system of alphabetical characters designed to represent all possible articulate utterances. Hence or cogn. **visibil′ity** (in adj. senses, & esp., meteorol., naut., conditions of light & atmosphere as regards distinguishing of objects by sight), ~NESS, nn., **vis′ibly²** adv., (-z-). [ME, f. OF, or f. L *visibilis* (*vidēre vis-* see, see -BLE)]

vi′sion (-zhn), n., & v.t. **1.** Act or faculty of seeing, sight, as *beyond our* ~, *has impaired his* ~, *the field of* ~, all that comes into view when the eyes are turned in some direction, *reflected, refracted*, ~ (as affected by reflected, refracted, rays of light); thing seen in dream or trance; supernatural or prophetic apparition, phantom; thing seen in the imagination, as *romantic* ~*s of youth, had* ~*s of roast beef & plum pudding*; (without article) imaginative insight, statesmanlike foresight, political sagacity. **2.** v.t. See, present, (as) in a ~. [ME, f. OF, or f. L *visio* (as prec., see -ION)]

vi′sion|ary̆ (-zho-), a. & n. **1.** Given to seeing visions or to indulging in fanciful theories; existing only in a vision or in the imagination, imaginary, fanciful, unpractical. **2.** n. (Also ~IST n.) ~ary person. Hence or cogn. ~AL a., ~aLLY² adv., ~ariNESS n., (-zho-). [-ARY¹]

vis′it (-z-), v.t., & n. **1.** Go, come, to see (person, place, etc., or abs.) as act of friendship or ceremony, on business, or from curiosity, as *have never* ~*ed us, had no time to* ~ *the Tower, hope to* ~ *Rome*; go, come, to see for purpose of official inspection or supervision or correction; (of disease, calamity, etc.) come upon, attack; (bibl.) punish (person, sin), avenge (his *sins* etc.) *upon* person, comfort, bless, (person *with* salvation etc.). **2.** n. Call on a person or at a place, temporary residence with person or at place, as *was on a* ~ *to some friends, paid him a long* ~, *during his second* ~ *to the East*; formal or official call for purpose of inspection etc., as DOMICILIARY ~, *right of* ~ (see VISITATION). Hence ~ABLE a. [ME, f. OF *visiter* or L *visitare* frequent. of *visare* f. *vidēre vis-* see; n.f. F *visite* or f. Engl. vb]

vis′itant (-z-), a. & n. **1.** (poet.). Visiting. **2.** n. Migratory bird; (poet., rhet.) visitor; (V~) member of an order of nuns concerned with education of young girls. [F, or f. L *visitare* (as prec., see -ANT)]

visitā′tion (-z-), n. Official visit of inspection or the like esp. bishop's examination of the churches of his diocese; (colloq.) unduly protracted visit or social call; boarding of vessel belonging to another State to learn her character & purpose (*right of* ~ or *visit*, right to do this, not including right of search); divine dispensation of punishment or reward, notable experience compared to this; (eccl.) festival in honour of visit of B.V.M. to Elizabeth (*Luke* i. 39); (zool.) unusual & large migration of animals; *Nuns of the V*~, = VISITANTS; *V*~ *of the Sick*, office of Anglican Church. [ME, f. OF, or f. LL *visitatio*; as VISIT, see -ATION]

vis′iting (-z-), n. Paying visits, making calls; *have a* ~ *acquaintance with, be on* ~ *terms with*, know well enough to visit; ~*-book* (for names of persons to be called upon); ||~*-card*, small card with one's name, address, etc., left in making call etc. [-ING¹]

vis′itor (-z-), n. One who visits a person or place; || (in colleges etc.) official with the right or duty of occasionally inspecting & reporting, whence or cogn. **visit- (at)ŏr′ial** aa.; ||~*s' book*, book in hotel, boarding-house, etc., in which ~s write their names and addresses and draw, remarks. [ME, f. AF *visitour*, OF *visiteur* (as VISIT, -OR)]

vis′or (-z-), **-zor**, **vis′ard** (-z-), **-zard**, n. (Hist.) movable part of helmet covering face; projecting front part of cap; (hist.) mask. Hence **vis′orED²** (-zerd), **vis′or-LESS** (-z-), aa. [ME & AF *viser* f. *vis* face (L *visus*)]

vis′ta, n. Long narrow view as between rows of trees; long succession of remembered or anticipated events etc., mental prospect or retrospect, as *opened up new* ~*s or a new* ~ *to his ambition, searched the dim* ~ *of his childhood*. Hence ~'d [-ED²] a. [It., p.p. of *vedere* see (L *vidēre vis-*)]

vis′ual (-zhŏŏ- or -zū-), a. Of, concerned with, used in, seeing, as ~ *nerve, organ*; ~ *angle* (formed at the eye by rays from the extremities of an object viewed); ~

field (of VISION); ~ *rays*, lines of light supposed to come from object to eye; ~ *point*, point in the horizontal line in which the ~ rays unite. Hence ~ITY (-ăl⁻) n., ~LY² adv. [f. LL *visualis* (*visus -ūs* sight f. *vidēre* see, -AL)]

vis′ualiz|e (-zhy͝oŏ- *or* -zū-), **-is|e** (-ĭz), v.t. Make visible to the eye, give outward & visible form to, (mental image, idea, etc.); call up distinct mental picture of (thing imagined or formerly seen, or abs.). Hence ~A′TION n. [-IZE]

vīt′a glass (-ah-), n. Kind of glass by which the ultra-violet vitalizing rays of sunlight are not excluded as by ordinary glass. [P]

vīt′al, a. & n. **1.** Of, concerned with or essential to, organic life, as ~ *energies*, *functions*, ~ *power* (to sustain life), *wounded in a~ part*; essential to existence or to the matter in hand, as *a ~ question*, *question of ~ importance*, *secrecy is ~ to the success of the scheme*; affecting life, fatal to life or to success etc., as *a ~ wound*, *error*; ~ *centre* (med.), part in which wound appears to be instantly fatal, esp. respiratory nerve-centre in medulla oblongata; ~ *force* or *principle* (assumed to account for organic life); ~ *statistics* (of birth, marriage, death, etc.; also, colloq., feminine measurements of bust, waist, and hips). Hence ~LY² adv. **2.** n. pl. ~ parts, e.g. lungs, heart, brain. [ME, f. OF, or f. L *vitalis* (*vita* life, see -AL)]

vīt′al|ism, n. (biol.). Doctrine that life originates in a vital principle distinct from chemical & other physical forces. So ~IST n., ~is′tIC a. [F -*isme*, or f. prec. +-ISM]

vīt′al′ity, n. Vital power, ability to sustain life; (fig., of institution, language, etc.) ability to endure & to perform its functions. [f. L *vitalis* (as VITAL, see -TY)]

vīt′alize, **-ise** (-ĭz), v.t. Endow with life. [-IZE]

vīt′amin, n. Any of a number of accessory food factors chiefly of very complex chemical composition, present in many food-stuffs esp. in the raw state, & essential to the health of man & other animals; their absence from the diet is associated with malnutrition in various parts of the body or deficiency diseases. [f. G -*ine*, f. L *vita* life +AMINE]

vītĕll′in, n. (chem.). Chief protein constituent of yolk of egg. [f. foll. +-IN]

vītĕll′|us, n. (pl. ~*i*). Yolk of egg, protoplasmic contents of ovum. Hence **vīt′ell**ARY¹, ~INE¹, aa., ~I-, ~O-, comb. forms. [L, = yolk]

vī′ti-, comb. form of L *vitis* vine, as :~*cide*, insect etc. destructive to vines; ~*culture*, grape-growing, so ~*cul′tural* a., ~*cul′tur(al)ist* nn.

vi′tiāt|e (-shĭ-), v.t. Impair the quality of, corrupt, debase, contaminate, as *constitution ~ed by excess*, ~*ed air*, *blood*, *mind*,

judgement; make invalid or ineffectual, as *a word may ~e a contract*. So vitiA′TION, ~OR, nn., (-shĭ-). [f. L *vitiare* f. *vitium* (VICE¹), see -ATE³]

vit′reous, a. Of (the nature of) glass; like glass in hardness, brittleness, transparency, structure, etc.; ~ *body* or *humour*, transparent jellylike tissue filling ball of eye; ~ ELECTRICITY. Hence or cogn. **vitrēos′ITY**, ~NESS, **vitrēs′CENCE**, nn., **vitres′cent**, **vit′ri**FORM(1), aa. [f. L *vitreus* (*vitrum* glass) +-OUS]

vit′ri|fy̆, v.t. & i. Convert, be converted, into glass or glasslike substance. Hence or cogn. ~FAC′TION, ~fiaBIL′ITY, ~FICA⁻TION, nn., ~fīABLE a. [f. F *vitrifier* (as prec., see -FY)]

vit′riol, n. Sulphuric acid or any of its salts; (fig.) caustic speech, criticism, etc.; *blue* or *copper* ~, copper sulphate; *white* ~, zinc sulphate; *oil of* ~, concentrated sulphuric acid; ~*-throwing*, throwing ~ in person's face as act of vengeance etc. Hence **vitriŏl′IC**, ~INE¹, aa. [ME, f. OF, or f. med. L *vitriolum* f. *vitrum* glass]

vit′riol|ize, **-ise** (-ĭz), v.t. Convert into a sulphate, so ~ATE³ v.t., ~A′TION n.; poison, burn, with vitriol. Hence ~IZABLE a., ~IZA′TION n. [-IZE]

Vitru′vian (-ōŏ-), a. Of Vitruvius, Roman architect of the Augustan age; ~ *scroll*, scroll pattern in frieze decorations etc. [-AN]

vitt′|a, n. (pl. ~*ae*). (Rom. ant.) fillet, garland, as decoration of priest, victim, statue, etc.; lappet of mitre; (bot.) oil-tube in fruit of some plants; (zool.) strips of colour. So ~ATE² a. [L]

vītŭp′er|āte, v.t. Revile, abuse. Hence or cogn. ~A′TION, ~ātOR, nn., ~atIVE a., ~atIVELY² adv. [f. L *vituperare*, see -ATE³]

vi′va¹ (vē-), int. & n. (The cry) long live —. [It., 3rd pers. subj. of *vivere* live, cf. VIVAT, VIVE]

viva². See VIVA VOCE.

vivace (vēvah′chä), adv. (mus.). In a lively manner. [It.]

vivā′cious (-shŭs), a. Lively, sprightly, animated, whence or cogn. ~LY² adv., **vĭvā′cITY** n.; (bot.) tenacious of life, surviving winter, perennial. [f. L *vivax* (*vivere* live, -ACIOUS)]

vivandière (vīvahndyār′), n. (hist.). Woman attached to continental esp. French regiment & selling provisions & liquor. [F]

vivār′ium, n. (pl. -*ia*). Place artificially prepared for keeping animals in their natural state, zoological garden or the like. [L (*vivus*, see VIVIFY & -ARIUM)]

viv′ăt, int. & n. (The cry) long live, as ~ *rex*, *regina*, long live the king, queen. [L, 3rd sing. subj. of *vivere* live]

viv′a vŏ′cè, adv., a., & n. **1.** Oral(ly). **2.** n. (abbr. *viva*). Oral examination. Hence **vīv′a(-vŏ′cè)** v.t., examine ~. [L, = with the living voice]

vive (vēv), int. Long live, as ~ *le roi* (the

king), QUI VIVE. [F, 3rd sing. subj. of *vivre* live f. L *vivere*]

|| **viv′ers** (-z), n. pl. (Sc.). Food, victuals. [f. F *vivres* (*vivre* live f. L *vivere*)]

vives (-vz), n. Hard swellings of the sub-maxillary glands of a horse. [aphetic f. obs. *avives* f. F *avives* f. Sp. *avivas* f. Arab. *addhibah* (*al* the +*dhibah* she-wolf)]

viv′id, a. (Of light or colour) bright, intense, glaring, as ~ *flash of lightning*, *of a* ~ *green*; (of person) full of life; (of mental faculty or impression) clear, vigorous, strongly marked, as *has a* ~ *imagination*, *gave a* ~ *description*, *have a* ~ *recollection of the scene*. Hence ~LY² adv., ~NESS n. [f. L *vividus* (*vivere* live, see -ID¹)]

viv′ify, v.t. Give life to, enliven, animate, (chiefly fig.). [f. F *vivifier* f. LL *vivificare* (*vivus* living f. *vivere* live, see -FY)]

vivip′arous, a. (Zool.) bringing forth young alive, not hatching by means of egg, (cf. OVIparous); (bot.) producing bulbs or seeds that germinate while still attached to parent plant. Hence **vivipā′rity**, ~NESS, nn., ~LY² adv. [f. L *viviparus* (*vivus*, see prec., +*parĕre* bring forth)+-OUS]

viv′isect, v.t. Dissect (animal, or abs.) while living. [f. foll.]

vivisec′tion, n. Dissection of or (loosely) inoculation etc. tried upon living animals. Hence ~AL a., ~IST(2, 3), viv′isectOR, nn. [f. L *vivi-*, comb. form of *vivus* living +*sectio* cutting]

vi′vo (vē-), adv. (mus.). = VIVACE. [It.]

vix′en, n. She-fox; quarrelsome woman, termagant. Hence ~ISH¹, ~LY¹, aa. [ME *fixen* f. OE *fyxen* (= MHG *vühsinne*, G *füchsin*), fem. of FOX; see -EN³]

viz. See VIDELICET.

vizard. See VISOR.

vizcacha. See VISCACHA.

vizi(e)r′ (-zēr), n. High official, esp. State minister, in Mohammedan countries; *grand* ~, prime minister in Turkish empire & other countries. Hence ~ATE¹(1), ~SHIP, nn., ~IAL a. [f. Turk. *vezir* f. Arab. *wazir* counsellor, orig. porter (*wazara* bear burden); cf. F, Sp. *visir*]

Vlach (-äk), a. & n. Member of a SE. European Latin-speaking people, Walachian or Romanian, Wal(l)ach. [Slav., ult. f. Gmc *Walh* foreigner, Celt, Italian, Latin]

vlei (flā), n. (S. Afr.). Hollow in which water collects during rainy season. [Du. dial., f. Du. *vallei* valley]

vŏc′able, n. Word, esp. w. ref. to form rather than meaning. [F, or f. L *vocabulum* (*vocare* call)]

vocăb′ulary̆, n. (List, arranged alphabetically with definitions, of) the (principal) words used in a language or usu. in a particular book or branch of science etc., or by a particular author, as *a Livy with notes &* ~, *a word not found in the Chaucerian* ~, *the ever-increasing scientific*

~, *his* ~ (range of language) *is limited*. [f. med. L *vocabularius*, *-um* (prec., -ARY¹)]

vŏc′al, a. & n. **1.** Of, concerned with, uttered by, the voice, as *a* ~ *communication*, ~ *auscultation* (of the sounds of the voice as heard through walls of chest), ~ *cords*, folds of lining membrane of larynx about the opening of the glottis, ~ *music* (written for or produced by the voice with or without accompaniment), ~ *thrill*, vibration of wall of chest in audible speech; (poet., of trees, water, etc.) endowed (as) with a voice; (phonet.) voiced, sonant, (also) of vowel character. Hence or cogn. vocăl′ITY n., ~LY² adv. **2.** n. Vowel, whence vocăl′IC a.; (R.-C. Ch.) person entitled to vote in certain elections. [f. L *vocalis* (as VOICE, see -AL)]

vŏc′alism, n. Use of voice in speaking or singing; vowel sound. [-ISM]

vŏc′alist, n. Singer (opp. to *instrumentalist*) [-IST]

vŏc′aliz|e, -is|e (-īz), v.t. & i. Form (sound), utter (word), with the voice, esp. make sonant, as f *is* ~*ed into* v; write (Hebrew etc.) with vowel points; (joc.) speak, sing, hum, shout, etc.; (mus.) sing florid passage to a vowel. So ~A′TION n. [-IZE]

voca′tion, n. Divine call to, sense of fitness for, a career or occupation, as *felt no* ~ (for the ministry), *has never had the sense of* ~, *little or no* ~ *to literature*; employment, trade, profession, as *mechanical* ~*s*, *all* ~*s are overcrowded*, *mistook his* (chose the wrong) ~. Hence ~AL (-sho-) a., ~aLLY² adv. [ME, f. OF, or f. L *vocatio* f. *vocare* call, see -ATION]

vŏc′ative, a. & n. (gram.). (Case) employed in addressing person or thing. [ME, f. OF (-*if*, *-ive*) or L *vocativus* (*vocare*, see VOCABLE & -ATIVE)]

vocif′er|āte, v.t. Utter (words etc., or abs.) noisily, shout, bawl. Hence or cogn. ~ANCE (rare), ~A′TION, ~ātOR, nn., ~ANT(1) a. & n. [f. L *vociferari* (as VOICE +*ferre* bear)]

vocif′erous, a. (Of person, speech, etc.) noisy, clamorous. Hence ~LY² adv., ~NESS n. [as prec. + -OUS]

vŏd′ka, n. Kind of fiery brandy made esp. in Russia by distillation of rye etc. [Russ.]

|| **vŏe**, n. (Shetland). Small bay, creek. [f. Norw. *vaag*, ON *vágr*]

vogue (vōg), n., & v.i. **1.** (Now chiefly literary) the prevailing fashion, as *the* ~ *of large hats*, *large hats are the* ~; popular use or reception, as *has had a great* ~; *in* ~, in fashion, generally current. **2.** v.i. ~ *la galère* (-ār), here goes (lit. let the galley set forth). [F, orig. = course, f. *voguer* f. It. *vogare* row in galley]

voice, n., & v.t. **1.** Sound uttered by the mouth, esp. human utterance in speaking, shouting, singing, etc., as *heard a* ~, *did not recognize his* ~, *cried out in a loud* ~, *has lost her* (esp. singing-) ~, *is not in* ~ (proper vocal condition for singing or speaking), CHEST, HEAD¹, -~, *the ~ of the cuckoo, veiled ~* (due to malformation etc.), (fig.) *sea, storm, lifts up its~,* whence -VOICED² [-st] a. **2.** Use of the ~, utterance esp. in spoken or (fig.) written words, opinion so expressed, right to express opinion, as *gave ~ to his indignation in a pamphlet, dog gave ~ to his joy, took it* (natural phenomenon, calamity, popular outcry, etc.) *for the ~* (expression of the will, resentment, etc.) *of God, I count on your ~* (spoken or written support), *I have no ~ in the matter, refused with one ~* (unanimously); (arch., rhet.) *my ~ is for peace.* **3.** (phonet.). Sound uttered with resonance of vocal cords, not with mere breath. **4.** (gram.). Set of forms of a verb showing relation of the subject to the action, as ACTIVE, PASSIVE, MIDDLE¹, ~. **5.** v.t. Give utterance to, express, as *was chosen to ~ their grievance, believe I am voicing the general sentiment when I say*; (mus.) regulate tone-quality of (organ pipes); (phonet.) utter with ~, make sonant, (esp. in p.p.). [ME, f. OF *vois* f. L *vocem,* nom. *vox*]

voice′ful (-sf-), a.(poet.). Sonorous. [-FUL]

voice′less (-sl-), a. Speechless, dumb, mute; (phonet.) not voiced. Hence ~NESS n. [-LESS]

void, a., n., & v.t. **1.** Empty, vacant, as *a ~ space, interval*; (of office) vacant, as *bishopric fell ~*; (esp. law, of deed, promise, contract, etc.) invalid, not binding, as *null & ~*; (poet., rhet.) ineffectual, useless; *~ of,* lacking, free from, as *a proposal wholly ~ of sense, his style is ~ of affectation.* Hence ~′LY² adv., ~′NESS n. **2.** n. Empty space, as *vanished into the ~,* (fig.) *the aching ~ of his heart, cannot fill the ~ made by death.* **3.** v.t. Render invalid; emit (excrement etc.); (arch.) quit, evacuate. Hence ~′ABLE a. [ME, f. OF *voide,* fem. of *voit, vuit* (mod. *vide*) f. Rom. *vocitus repl. L *vacuus*; vb partly f. OF *voider,* partly aphetic f. AVOID]

void′ance, n. Ejection from benefice; vacancy in benefice; voiding. [ME, f. OF (prec., -ANCE), or aphetic f. AVOIDANCE]

void′ed, a. In vbl senses, also (her., of bearing) having the central area cut away so as to show the field. [-ED¹]

voile (vwahl, voil), n. A thin semi-transparent cotton, woollen, or silken dress material. [F, = VEIL]

vŏl′ant, a. (Zool.) flying, able to fly; (her.) represented as flying; (poet.) nimble, rapid. [F, f. L *volare* fly, see -ANT]

Vŏlapük′ (-ook), **Vŏl′apuk** (-ook), n. Artificial international language invented about 1879 by J. M. Schleyer. Hence ~IST(2, 3) n. [Volapük (*vol* world +-*a-* + *pük* speech]

vŏl′ar, a. (anat.). Of the palm or sole. [f. L *vola* palm, sole, +-AR¹]

vŏl′atile, a. Evaporating rapidly, as *~ salts, ~* (= ESSENTIAL) *oil*; (fig.) lively,

gay, changeable, as *~ wit, writer, disposition.* Hence or cogn. ~NESS, vŏlatil′ITY, nn. [F (-*il, -ile*), or f. L *volatilis* (*volare* -*at-* fly, -ILE)]

vŏlăt′iliz|e, -is|e (-īz), v.t. & i. (Cause to) evaporate. Hence or cogn. ~ABLE a., ~A′TION n. [-IZE]

vol-au-vent (see Ap.), n. Kind of rich raised pie. [F]

vŏlcăn′|ic, a. Of, like, produced by, a volcano; *~ic bomb,* mass of lava usually rounded & sometimes hollow; *~ic glass,* obsidian. Hence ~ICALLY adv., vŏlcani′CITY n. [f. F *-ique,* or f. VOLCANO +-IC]

vŏlcăn′o, n. (pl. *~es*). Mountain, hill, having opening(s) in earth's crust through which lava, cinders, water, gases, etc., are expelled continuously or at intervals (*active, dormant, extinct, ~; submarine ~,* originating beneath sea & rising above surface by accumulation). Hence vŏl′canISM(2), vŏl′canIST(3), vŏlcanŏl′OGY, nn., vŏlcanolŏ′gICAL a. [It., f. L as VULCAN]

vŏle¹, n., & v.i. (In some card-games) winning of all the tricks in a deal; (vb) win all the tricks. [(vb f. n.) F, f. *voler* fly f. L *volare*]

vŏle², n. Kinds of mouselike rodent; *water-~,* large kind. [orig. *~-mouse* f. Norw. **vollmus* (Icel. *vallarmús*) f. *voll* field +*mús* mouse]

vŏl′et (-lā), n. Panel, wing, of triptych. [F, f. *voler* f. L *volare* to fly]

vŏl′itant, a. (zool.). = VOLANT. [f. L *volitare* frequent. of *volare* fly, see -ANT]

voli′tion, n. Exercise of the will; power of willing. Hence ~AL, ~ARY¹, ~LESS, (-sho-), vŏl′ĭTIVE, aa., ~alLY² adv. [F, or f. med. L *volitio* (*velle* wish, pres. *volo,* see -ITION)]

vŏlks′lied (f-, -lēt), n. Folk-song. [G]

vŏlks′raad (f-, -raht), n. (hist.). Legislative assembly of Transvaal & Orange Free State. [Afrikaans]

vŏll′ey, n. (pl. *~s*), & v.t. & i. **1.** Simultaneous discharge of missiles, missiles so discharged; (fig.) noisy emission (*of oaths* etc.) in quick succession; (tennis, lawn tennis) return of ball in play before it touches ground; (crick.) pitching of ball, ball pitched, right up to batsman or wicket without bouncing; *half-~,* (lawn tennis) return of ball as soon as it touches ground, (crick.) ball so pitched that batsman may hit it as it bounces, hit so made, (v.t.) return, send, (ball, or abs.) thus; *~-gun,* machine-gun discharging~. **2.** vb. Discharge (missiles, abuse, etc., or abs.) in ~; (tennis, crick.) return, send, (ball, or abs.) in ~; (of missiles) fly in a ~; (of guns etc.) sound together. [f. F *volée* f. Rom. *volata fem. p.p. as n. f. L *volare* fly, see -Y¹]

vŏl′plāne, n., & v.i. (Of aeroplane or its pilot) descent, descend, by gliding without use of engine. [f. F *vol plané* (*vol* flight, *planer* hover)]

Vŏlt¹, v.i., & n. Make a volte; (n., var. of) VOLTE. [VOLTE]

Vŏlt², n. Unit of electromotive force, the force that would carry one ampere of current against one ohm resistance. Hence ~'METER n., instrument for measuring electric currents in ~s. [as VOLTAIC]

vŏl'ta, n. (mus.; pl. *-te* pr. -tä). *Una* ~, *due* etc. *volte*, once, twice etc.; *prima* etc. ~, first etc. time. [It.]

vŏl'tage, n. Electromotive force expressed in volts. [-AGE]

vŏltā'ic, a. (chiefly hist.). Of electricity produced by chemical action, galvanic, as ~ *battery, cell,* PILE². [f. A. *Volta,* Italian physicist (d. 1827), -IC]

Vŏltair'(ian)ism, nn. Principles of Voltaire (d. 1778), scepticism. [-IAN, -ISM]

vŏltăm'eter, n. Instrument for measuring electric currents by their electrolytic effects. [as VOLTAIC, -METER]

vŏlte, n. (Fenc.) quick movement to escape thrust; circular tread of horse. [F, f. It. *volta* turn]

vŏlte-face' (-tfahs), n. Turning round, esp. (fig.) complete change of front in argument, politics, etc. [F]

vŏl'ūb|le, a. (Of speech or speaker) fluent, glib, whence or cogn. vŏlūBIL'ITY, ~leNESS, nn., ~LY² adv.; (arch.) revolving, rotating; (bot.) twisting round a support, twining. [F, or f. L *volubilis* (*volvere* roll, see -BLE)]

vŏl'ūme, n. 1. Set of (usu. printed) sheets of paper bound together & forming part or the whole of a work or comprising several works (abbr. *vol.*), as *is now issued in 3* ~*s, an odd* ~ *of* Punch, *library of 12,000* ~*s,* SPEAK ~*s* (for); (hist.) scroll of papyrus etc., ancient form of book (cf. CODEX). 2. (usu. pl.). Wreath, coil, rounded mass, of smoke etc. 3. Solid content, bulk, whence volu'minAL (-lōō-) a.; (mus.) fullness of tone. Hence (-)vŏlūmED² (-md) a. [ME, f. OF, f. L *volumen -minis* roll (*volvere,* see prec.)]

volumén|ŏm'eter (-lōō-), n. Instrument for measuring volume of a solid body by quantity of liquid etc. displaced. Hence ~ŎM'ETRY n. [f. L (prec.)+-O-+-METER]

volu'mĕter (-lōō-), n. Kinds of instrument for measuring volume of gas or liquid. Hence vŏlumĕt'rIC(AL) aa., vŏlumĕt'rĭcaLY² adv. [f. VOLUME + -METER]

volūm'inous (*or* -lōō-), a. Having coils or convolutions (of snakes, the brain, etc.; now rare); consisting of many volumes, as *a* ~ *work*; (of writer) producing many books; of great volume, bulky, (of drapery etc.) loose or ample. Hence volūmINOS'ITY, ~NESS, nn., ~LY² adv. [f. LL *voluminosus* (as VOLUME, see -OUS)]

vŏl'untary̆, a. & n. 1. Done, acting, able to act, of one's own free will, not constrained, purposed, intentional, as *a* ~ *gift, there was no* ~ *mis-statement, was a* ~

agent in the matter, ~ (opp. to *compulsory*) *service, army,* ~ *confession* (of criminal, not prompted by promise or threat); brought about, produced, etc., by ~ action, as ‖~ *school* (supported by ~ contributions), ~ *waste* (of property by tenant's deliberate act or order); (of limb, muscle, movement) controlled by the will; (law) ~ *conveyance* (made without valuable consideration), ~ *grantee* (in ~ conveyance), ~ *partition* (by mutual agreement, not by judgement of court). Hence vŏl'untariLY² adv., vŏl'untarĭNESS n. 2. n. Organ solo played before, during, or after service; one who holds that the Church or the schools should be independent of the State & supported by ~ contributions, whence ~ISM (3) n., reliance on ~ subscriptions & not on State aid fŏr the maintenance of education, reliance on ~ enlisting & not on compulsion for raising military etc. forces, ~IST(2) n.; (in competitions) special performance left to performer's choice. *[ME, f. OF *volontaire* or f. L *voluntarius* (*voluntas* will, see -ARY¹)]

vŏlunteer', n., & v.t. & i. 1. Spontaneous undertaker of task etc.; person who voluntarily enters military or other service, esp. member of any of the corps of voluntary soldiers formerly organized in U.K. & provided with instructors, arms, etc., by government (often attrib., as ~ *corps, manœuvres*); (attrib., of vegetation) growing spontaneously. 2. vb. Undertake, offer, (one's services, remark, explanation, etc., *to* do) voluntarily; make voluntary offer of one's services (*for* campaign, purpose), be a ~. [f. F *volontaire* (obs. *-un-*), as prec., w. assim. to -EER]

volŭp'tüary̆, a. & n. Concerned with, (person) given up to, luxury & sensual gratifications. [f. L *volupt(u)arius* (as foll., see -ARY¹)]

volŭp'tüous, a. Of, tending to, occupied with, sensuous or sensual gratification, as ~ *life, liver, music, beauty.* Hence ~LY² adv., ~NESS n. [ME, f. OF *voluptueux* or L *voluptuosus* f. *voluptas* pleasure, see -OUS]

volūt|e', n. & a. 1. Spiral scroll characteristic of Ionic, Corinthian, & Composite capitals, whence ~'ED² a.; kinds of (chiefly tropical) gasteropod often with beautiful shell, whence vŏl'ūtOID a. & n. 2. adj. (bot.). Rolled up. [f. L *voluta* (*volvee volut-* roll), or f. F *volute*]

volu'tion (-lōō-), n. Spiral turn; whorl(s) of spiral shell; (anat.) convolution. [as prec., -ION, after *revolution*]

vōm'er, n. (anat.). The small thin bone partitioning the nostrils in man and most vertebrates. [L, = ploughshare]

vŏm'it, v.t. & i., & n. 1. Eject from stomach through mouth; puke, spew; (fig., of volcano, chimney, etc.) eject violently, belch forth. 2. n. Matter

~ed from stomach; emetic; *black ~*, (black substance ~ed in) yellow fever; *~ -nut*, = NUX VOMICA. [ME; n. f. AF *vomit(e)*, OF *-ite*, or f. L *vomitus* (*-ūs*) f. *vomere*, *-it-*; vb f. L *vomere* or frequent. *vomitare*]

vŏm′itorў, a. & n. **1.** Emetic (a. & n.), so vŏm′itive a. **2.** n. (Rom. ant.). Each of a series of passages for entrance & exit in (amphi)theatre. [f. L *vomitorius* a., *-um* n., (as prec., see -ORY)]

vŏmitūri′tion, n. Ineffectual attempt to vomit, retching; repeated vomiting. [F, or mod. L *vomituritio*]

voō′doō, n., & v.t. **1.** Use of, belief in, witchcraft & the like prevalent among W.-Ind. & U.S. creoles & Negroes; (also *~ doctor*, *~ priest*) person skilled in this. Hence ~ISM, ~IST(2, 3), nn. **2.** v.t. Affect by~, bewitch. [(vb f. n.) Afr. *vodu*]

-vora. See -VOROUS.

vorā′cious (-shus), a. Greedy in eating, ravenous, (lit. & fig.), as *party of ~ trippers, a ~ appetite for scandal, a ~ whirlpool.* Hence or cogn. ~LY² adv., ~NESS, vorā′cITY, nn. [f. L *vorax* (*vorare* swallow, see -ACIOUS)]

-vore. See foll.

-vorous, suf. f. L *-vorus* (*vorare* devour, eat) +-OUS; forming adjj. w. sense ' feeding on ', as *carni~*, *gramini~*; also *-vora*, in L neut. pl. names of animals classified by their food, as *herbivora*; also F & E *-vore* forming name of individual of such class, as *carnivore*.

vŏrt′|ĕx, n. (pl. ~*ĭcēs*, *-exes*). Mass of whirling fluid, esp. whirlpool; (phys.) portion of fluid whose particles have rotatory motion; any whirling motion or mass, esp. (fig.) system, pursuit, etc., viewed as swallowing up or engrossing those who approach it, as *the ~ex of society, ~ex* (spiral arrangement of fibres at apex) *of the heart; ~ex-ring, ~ex* whose axis is a closed curve, e.g. smoke-ring puffed from smoker's lips or pipe. Hence ~ical, ~icose¹, ~ic′ūlar¹ [-UL-], aa., ~icalLY² adv. [L, var. of VERTEX]

vŏrt′icĕl, n. Bell-shaped animalcule found in stagnant water etc. [f. mod. L *vorticella*, dim. of prec.]

vŏrt′ic|ist, n. (Metaphys.) person regarding the universe, with Descartes, as a plenum in which motion propagates itself in circles; (art) painter of school using vortices as the CUBIST uses cubes etc. So ~ISM n. [f. vortic- st. of L VORTEX +-IST]

vorti′ginous, a. Whirling, vortical. [f. L *vortigo*, var. of VERTIGO, +-OUS]

vŏt′ar|ў, n. Person vowed to the service of (God etc.); ardent follower, devoted adherent or advocate, (*of* system, pursuit, etc.). Hence ~ESS¹ n. [f. L *vot-* (see foll.) +-ARY¹]

vŏte, n., & v.i. & t. **1.** Formal expression of will or opinion in regard to election of officer etc., sanctioning law, passing

resolution, etc., signified by ballot, show of hands, voice, or otherwise, as *shall give my ~ to* or *for the Labour candidate, passed without a dissentient ~*, CAST¹ ~, SPLIT¹ one's ~, CASTING-VOTE, TRANSFERABLE ~; opinion expressed, money granted, by majority of ~s, as *Government received a ~ of confidence, the army ~; the* collective ~s given or to be given by a party etc., as *will lose the Labour, Conservative, ~, the floating ~* (of persons not attached to a party); *the right to ~*, as *women now have the ~*; ticket etc. used for recording ~. Hence ~′LESS a. **2.** vb. Give a~ (*for, against*, person or measure); enact, resolve, (*that*), grant (sum), by majority of ~s; (colloq.) pronounce, declare, by general consent, as *was ~d a failure*; (colloq.) propose (*that*); ~ *down*, defeat (measure) by ~s; ~ *in*, elect by ~s. Hence vŏt′ABLE a., vŏt′ER¹ n. [ME, n. f. L *votum*; vb f. same p.p. st. *vot-* of L *vovēre* vow, or f. LL *votare*]

vŏt′ing, n. In vbl senses; ~*-paper* (used in ~ by ballot in election of M.P. etc.); CUMULATIVE ~. [-ING¹]

vŏt′ive, a. Offered, consecrated, in fulfilment of a vow, as *~ offering, tablet, picture*. [f. L *votivus* (as VOTE, see -IVE)]

vouch, v.t. & i. Confirm, uphold, (statement) by evidence or assertion; answer *for*, be surety for, as *will ~ for the truth of this, for him* or *his honesty, can ~ for it that no step was taken*. [ME, f. OF *vo(u)cher* call etc., obsc. f. L *vocare* call]

vouch′er, n. In vbl senses, esp.: document, receipt, etc., establishing the payment of money or the truth of accounts; document which can be exchanged for goods or services as token of payment made or promised. [AF (prec., -ER⁴)]

vouchsāfe′, v.t. Condescend to grant, as *~d me no answer, ~ me a visit*; condescend (*to* do). [ME, f. VOUCH in sense ' warrant ' +SAFE²]

voussoir (voō′swär), n. Each of the wedge-shaped stones forming an arch. [f. OF *vossoir*, ult. f. L *volvere* roll]

vow, n., & v.t. **1.** Solemn promise or engagement esp. in the form of an oath to God, as *baptismal~s* (given at baptism by baptized person or by sponsors), *monastic ~* (by which monk binds himself to poverty, celibacy, & obedience), *lovers' ~s* (promises of fidelity), *am under* (have taken) *a ~ to drink no wine*; action, conduct, etc., promised by ~, as *is this your ~?* **2.** v.t. Promise solemnly (thing, conduct), as *~ed a temple to Apollo, ~ obedience, vengeance against the oppressor*; (arch.) utter, make, *a~*; declare solemnly (*that*); (arch.) declare, as *I ~ you are most obliging*. [ME, f. OF *vou, veu*, f. L as VOTE; vb f. OF *vouer*]

vow′ĕl, n. Each of the more open sounds uttered in speaking, sound capable of forming a syllable, (opp. to, but not sharply divided from, *consonant*); letter representing this, as a, e, i, o, u; *neutral* ~ (heard in second syllable of *cousin*, *reason*, *haddock*); ~ *gradation*, = ABLAUT; ~ *mutation*, = UMLAUT; ~ *point*, each of a set of marks indicating ~s in Hebrew & other Oriental languages. Hence (-)~ lED² (-ld), ~LESS, ~IY², aa. [ME, f. OF *vouel* f. L *vocalis* (*littera*) VOCAL (letter)]

vow'elize, -ise (-iz), v.t. Insert the vowels in (Hebrew etc., shorthand). [-IZE]

vŏx, n. ~ *barb'ara* (anat., bot., etc.), hybrid or incorrectly formed word; ~ *ĕt praetĕ'rĕa ni'hĭl*, a voice & nothing more (i.e., esp. an empty word); ~ *hūma'na* (-mā-, -mah-), organ-stop with tones supposed to resemble human voice; ~ *pŏp'ŭlĭ*, the people's voice (i.e. public opinion, the general verdict, popular belief, or rumour). [see VOICE]

voy'ag|e, n., & v.i. & t. **1.** Journey, esp. long one, by sea or water; *broken ~e*, unsuccessful whaling etc. ~e. **2.** vb. Travel, traverse, by water. Hence ~EABLE (-ija-) a., ~ER¹ n. [ME, f. AF, OF *veage*, *veiage*, *voiage* f. L *viaticum*, see -AGE; vb f. F *voyager*, or f. the n.]

voyageur (vwahyahzhḗr'), n. Man employed in transportation of goods & passengers between trading posts in the Hudson's Bay territory; Canadian boatman. [F]

|| **vraic** (vrăk), n. A seaweed found in the Channel Islands, used for fuel and manure. [F dial.; cf. VAREC]

vraisemblance (vrăsahňblahňs'), n. Appearance of truth, plausible appearance, verisimilitude. [F]

Vŭl'can, n. (Rom. myth.) god of fire & metal-working; ~ *powder*, an explosive. [f. L *Volcanus*, *Vu*-]

vulcanic etc. See **vol-**.

Vŭl'canist, n. (geol.). Holder of PLUTONIC theory. [f. F *vulcaniste* (VULCAN, -IST)]

vŭl'canīte, n. Hard vulcanized rubber, ebonite. [-ITE¹]

vŭl'caniz|e, -is|e (-iz), v.t. Treat (rubber) with sulphur at high temperature to increase elasticity & strength & yield hard or soft flexible rubber. Hence ~ABLE a., ~A'TION, ~ER¹(1, 2), nn. [-IZE]

vŭl'gar, a. Of, characteristic of, the common people, plebeian, coarse, low, as ~ *expressions*, *mind*, *tastes*, *finery*, *an air of* ~ *prosperity*, *the* ~ HERD¹, (abs.) *the* ~, the common people; in common use, generally prevalent, as ~ *errors*, *superstitions*, *the* ~ (national, esp. formerly as opp. to Latin) *tongue*, ~ FRACTION, *the* ~ (Christian) *era*. Hence or cogn. ~ISM(4, 2), vŭlgă'rITY, nn., ~IY² adv. [ME, f. L *vulgaris* f. *vulgus* common people, see -AR¹]

vŭlgār'ian, n. Vulgar (esp. rich) person. [-IAN]

vŭl'gariz|e, -is|e (-iz), v.t. Make (person, manners, etc.) vulgar, infect with vulgarity; spoil (scene, sentiment, etc.) by making too common or frequented or well

known. Hence ~A'TION n. [VULGAR + -IZE (3)]

Vŭl'gate, n. Latin version of the Bible prepared by Jerome late in the 4th c.; (v~) traditionally accepted text of any author. [f. L *vulgata* (*editio* edition), fem. p.p. of *vulgare* make public (*vulgus*, see VULGAR)]

|| **vŭl'gus**, n. (school sl.). Greek or Latin verse-exercise in some schools. [prob. alt. f. 16th-c. *vulgars* = vulgar-tongue (i.e. English) passages for rendering into Latin]

vŭl'ner|able, a. That may be wounded (lit. & fig.), susceptible of injury, not proof against weapon, criticism, etc.; (contract bridge) having won one game towards rubber & therefore being liable to higher penalties. Hence ~aB·L·ITY, ~ableNESS, nn. [f. LL *vulnerabilis* (*vulnerare* wound f. *vulnus* -*eris* wound, see -BLE)]

vŭl'nerary̆, a. & n. (Drug, unguent, etc.) useful or used for healing wounds. [f. L *vulnerarius* (*vulnus*, see prec. & -ARY¹)]

vŭl'p|īne, a. Of (the nature of) a fox, so ~ĪCIDE(1, 2) n.; crafty, cunning. [f. L *vulpinus* (*vulpes* fox, see -INE¹)]

vŭl'tur|e, n. Kinds of large bird of prey with head & neck more or less bare of feathers feeding chiefly on carrion; (fig.) rapacious person. Hence or cogn. ~INE¹, ~ISH¹, ~OUS, aa., (-cher-). [ME, f. AF *vultur*, OF *voltour* etc., or L *vultur*, or L *vulturius*]

vŭl'v|a, n. (anat.). Opening, orifice, esp. of female genitals. Hence ~AR¹, ~ATE², ~IFORM, aa., ~IT'IS n., ~O- comb. form. [L]

vying. See VIE.

W

W (dŭb'elyoŏ), letter (pl. *W's*, W's).

|| **Waac** (wăk), n. (colloq.). Member of the *Women's Army Auxiliary Corps* (organized in 1917). [f. initials]

|| **Waaf** (wăf), n. (colloq.). Member of the *Women's Auxiliary Air Force* (organized in 1939). [f. initials]

wabble. See WOBBLE.

wăc'ke (-ke), n. Kind of greyish-green or brownish clay resulting from decomposition of volcanic rock. [G, f. MHG *wacke* large stone]

wad (wŏd), n., & v.t. (-dd-). **1.** Small lump of soft material used to keep things apart or in place or to stuff up opening, esp. disc of felt etc. keeping powder or shot compact in gun; *roll of notes, money. **2.** v.t. Press (cotton etc.) into ~ or wadding; line (garment, coverlet), protect (person, walls, etc.), with wadding (also fig., as *well ~ded with conceit*); stop up (aperture, gun-barrel), keep (powder etc.) in place, with ~; ram (~) home. [16th c., of unkn. orig.]

wa′dding (wŏd-), n. Spongy material usu. of cotton or wool used to stuff garments, quilts, etc., or to pack fragile articles in, cotton wool; material from which gun-wads are made. [-ING[1]]

waddl|e (wŏ′dl), v.i., & n. **1.** Walk with the rocking motion natural to fat short-legged person or to bird with short legs set far apart as duck or goose; hence ~ing[2] adv. **2.** n. ~ing gait. [WADE + -LE(3)]

wa′ddy (wŏ-), n. Australian war-club. [native]

wāde, v.i. & t., & n. **1.** Walk through water or other impeding medium as snow, mud, sand (also fig., as ~ through slaughter or blood, make one's way by massacre etc.; ~ through book, read it in spite of dullness etc.; ~ in, colloq., intervene, make vigorous attack on one's opponent; ~ into, colloq., attack energetically); ford (stream) on foot, whence wād′ABLE a.; wading bird, long-legged water-bird that ~s (opp. short-legged web-footed swimmers). **2.** n. Spell of wading. [OE wadan, OHG watan, ON vatha f. Gmc *wadhan cogn. w. L vadere go]

wād′er, n. In vbl senses; esp.: wading bird (see prec.); (pl.) high waterproof boots worn in fishing. [-ER[1]]

wa′di, -y, (wah-), n. Rocky watercourse dry except in rainy season (chiefly of Eastern countries). [Arab. wādī]

Wafd (-ah-), n. The extreme Nationalist party in Egypt. Hence ~′IST a. & n. [Arab.]

wāf′er, n., & v.t. **1.** Kind of very thin sweet honeycomb-faced biscuit now chiefly eaten with ices (thin as a~, whence ~Y[2] a.); thin disc of unleavened bread used in Eucharist; small disc of dried paste formerly used for fastening letters, holding papers together, etc.; disc of red paper stuck on law papers instead of seal. **2.** v.t. Attach or seal with ~. [ME & AF vafre (= ONF waufre, F gaufre whence GOF(F)ER), f. MLG wāfel, see foll.]

wa′ffle[1] (wŏ-), n. Small batter cake baked in ~-iron, special utensil. [f. Du. wafel, see prec.]

wa′ffle[2] (wŏ-), v.i., & n. (Indulge in) continual rapid chatter, twaddle. [orig. unkn.]

waft (wah-, wŏ-), v.t., & n. **1.** Convey (as) through air or over water, sweep smoothly & lightly along. **2.** n. Single sweep of bird's wing; whiff of odour; fugitive sensation of peace, joy, etc.; (naut., also weft) distress signal, e.g. ensign rolled or knotted or garment flown in rigging. [c. 1500 ' convoy (ship etc.) ' back form. f. obs. waughter, wafter armed convoy-ship, f. Du. or LG wachter f. wachten to guard]

wăg[1], v.t. & i. (-gg-), & n. **1.** Shake (t. & i., of thing attached by one end, as tail) to & fro, oscillate, (dog ~s his tail, in sign of pleasure; tail was ~ging; tail ~s dog,

least important member of society or section of party has control; ~ one's finger at, in reproof etc.; ~ one's head, in derision or amusement; beards, chins, jaws, tongues, are ~ging, talk going on); (arch., of the world, times, etc.) go along with varied fortune or characteristics (how ~s the world?); ~′tail, kinds of small bird (grey, pied, yellow, etc., ~tail) with long tail in constant motion. **2.** n. Single ~ging motion (with a ~ of his tail, head, etc.). [ME wagge f. root of OE wagian]

wăg[2], n. Facetious person, one given to jesting or practical jokes; ‖ (sl.) truant (esp. play ~ or the ~). Hence ~g′ERY (4) n., ~g′ISH[1] a., ~g′ishLY[2] adv., ~g′ish-NESS n., (-g-). [prob. f. prec.]

wāge[1], n. Amount paid periodically, esp. by the day or week or month, for time during which workman or servant is at employer's disposal (usu. pl. exc. in certain phrr.; gets good ~s; brings his ~s home; at a ~ or ~s of £10 a week; living ~, ~s that allow earner to live without fear of starvation; a fair day's work for a fair day's ~); requital (usu. pl.; the ~s of sin is death); ~ FREEZE; ~(s)-fund in pol. econ., part of community's capital devoted to paying ~s & salaries. [ME, f. AF vage, OF g(u)age, see GAGE[1], WED]

wāge[2], v.t. Carry on (war, conflict). [ME pledge, gage, f. ONF wagier f. vage (prec.)]

wā′ger, n., & v.t. **1.** = BET n. & v.t. **2.** (hist.). ~ of battle, ancient form of trial by personal combat between parties or champions; ~ of law, COMPURGATION. [f. AF wageure f. wager WAGE[2] + -URE; -ER[2] (3)]

wăg′gle, v.i. & t., & n. = WAG[1] (but in more familiar use); esp. (golf) of swinging club-head to & fro over ball before playing shot. Hence **wăgg′lY**[2] a., unsteady. [f. WAG[1] + -LE(3)]

wăg(g)′on, n. Four-wheeled vehicle for drawing heavy loads, often with removable semicylindrical tilt or cover, usu. drawn by two or more horses (hitch one's ~ to a star, utilize powers higher than one's own); ‖ open railway truck; ~-boiler, -ceiling, -roof, -vault, shaped like ~-tilt. [early 16th c. wagan, waghen, f. Du. vag(h)en, cogn. w. OE wægn WAIN]

wăg(g)′oner, n. Driver of wagon; the W~, constellation Auriga. [-ER[1]]

wăg(g)onětte′, n. Four-wheeled open pleasure vehicle (or with removable cover) for one or more horses & with facing side seats. [-ETTE]

wagon-lit (văgawnlē′), n. Sleeping-car on continental railway. [F]

Waha′bi, -ee, (-hahbē), n. One of a sect of Mohammedan puritans following the letter of the Koran. [Abd-el-Wahhab, founder c. 1700]

waif, n. Ownerless object or animal, thing cast up by or drifting in sea or brought by unknown agency; homeless & helpless person, esp. unowned or abandoned child;

~s & strays, odds & ends, unowned or neglected children. [ME, f. AF *waif*=OF *gaif*, prob. of Scand. orig., cf. ON *veif* something flapping or waving; see WAIVE]

wail, v.i. & t., n. (Lament, i. & t., with) prolonged plaintive inarticulate usu. high- -pitched cry; (fig.) lament(ation) in words (often *over*); (of wind etc.) sound (v. & n.) like person ~ing; ~*ing wall*, *place*, part of the Solomonic wall at Jerusalem where the Jews assemble to bewail the destruc- tion of the Temple. Hence ~'FUL a. (poet.), ~'ingLY[2] adv. [ME; prob. f. ON *veila* f. *vei* int., see WOE]

wain, n. Wagon (chiefly poet. or agricul- tural); *Charles's*, *Arthur's*, or *the W*~, CHARLES'S WAIN. [OE *wægen*, *wæn*, OS, OHG *wagan*, ON *vagn* f. Gmc **wagnaz*; cf. WAY, WEIGH]

wain'scot, n., & v.t. **1.** Wooden panelling or boarding on room-wall from floor to a limited height. **2.** v.t. Line with ~, whence ~ING(3) n. [ME, kind of imported oak-wood, f. MLG *wagenschot*, app. f. *wagen* WAGON + *schot* of uncert. meaning]

waist, n. **1.** Part of human body below ribs & above hips (*large*, *small*, ~, of such circumference; *long*, *short*, ~, of such vertical extent). **2.** Contraction marking this in normal figure (*has no* ~, of stout person); analogous contraction in middle of long object, e.g. fiddle or hour-glass. **3.** Part of ship between forecastle & quarter-deck. **4.** Part of garment en- circling ~, band round ~ from which petticoats etc. may be suspended; *bodice. **5.** ~*-band*, *-belt*, worn round ~; ~*-cloth*, = LOIN-cloth; || ~*coat* (wǎs(t)'kōt, wěs'kot), garment reaching down to ~ with front showing when coat is open & usu. without sleeves (*sleeved* ~*coat*, with sleeves for extra warmth or for use with- out coat by workmen); ~*-deep* or *-high* aa. & advv., up to ~. Hence (-)~'ED[2] a. [ME *wast*, perh. repr. OE **wæst*, **weahst* (= Goth. *wahstus* growth), f. root of WAX[2]]

wait[1], v.i. & t. **1.** Abstain from action or departure till some expected event occurs, pause, tarry, stay, kick one's heels, be ex- pectant or on the watch, (often *for*, *till*; ~ *a minute*, shall not ~ here any longer; *kept me* ~*ing* or *made me* ~; *have a month to* ~ *yet*; ~ *till I come*, *for high water* or *a fine day*; *everything comes to those who* ~; *always has to be* ~*ed for*, is unpunctual). **2.** Await, bide, (*is* ~*ing his opportunity*; *you must* ~ *my convenience*; *am only* ~*ing the signal*). **3.** Act as waiter, as servant shifting plates etc. at table, (*are you accustomed to* ~*ing?*; often *at table*), or as attendant (LORD[1], GROOM, *in* ~*ing*). **4.** Defer (meal) till someone arrives (*don't* ~ *dinner for me*). **5.** ~*-a-bit* [tr. Afrikaans *wag-'n-bietjie*], kinds of S.-Afr. shrub with hooked thorns; ~ (*up*)*on*, watch (arch.), await convenience of, serve as attendant esp. at table, pay visit to (person regarded

as superior), escort (arch.), (in race) pur- posely keep close behind (competitor), follow as result; ~*ing-room*, provided for persons to ~ in esp. at railway-station or house of doctor, dentist, etc. [ME, f. AF, ONF *waitier* = OF *guaitier*, f. WG **wahta* watch, f. Gmc **wak-* see WAKE[1]]

wait[2], n. **1.** pl. Official bands of musicians maintained by a city or town (hist.); street singers of Christmas carols. **2.** Act or time of waiting (*had a long* ~ *for the train*); watching for enemy, ambush, (*lie in* or *lay* ~ usu. *for*). [sense 1 f. ONF **wait*, *wet* (= OF *guait*, *guet*) sentinel f. *waitier* (prec.); sense 2 f. prec.]

wait'er, n. In vbl senses; also or esp. : man who takes & executes orders, shifts plates, etc., at hotel or restaurant tables, whence **wait'r**ESS[1] n.; tray, salver; DUMB[1]-~; TIDE-~. [-ER[1]]

waive, v.t. Forbear to insist on or use, tacitly or implicitly relinquish or forgo, (right, claim, opportunity, legitimate plea, etc.). Hence **waiv'ER**[3] n. (legal). [f. AF *weyver* allow to become a ' waif ', abandon, f. *weyf* WAIF]

wāke[1], v.i. & t. (past *wōke*, ~*d*; p.p. ~*d*, *wōken*, *wōke*). **1.** Cease to sleep, rouse from sleep, (often *up*; also fig., as *spring* ~*s all nature*, *nature* ~*s*); be awake (arch. exc. in part. or gerund, as *in his waking hours*, *waking* or *sleeping*; *waking dream*, day-dream, reverie); cease or rouse from sloth, torpidity, inactivity, or inattention (usu. *up*; ~ *up there!*; *wants something to* ~ *him up*; *the insult* ~*d his dull spirit*); rise or raise from the dead. **2.** (chiefly Ir.) Hold wake over. **3.** Disturb (silence, place) with noise, make re-echo. **4.** ~*- -robin*, wild arum, lords-&-ladies. [goes back to two OE forms: (a) strong vb **wacan*; *wōc*; **wacen*; (b) weak vb *wacian* (cf. OS *wakōn*, OHG *wachēn*, -ōn, ON *vaka*, Goth. *wakan*), f. Gmc **wak-*; see WATCH[2]]

wāke[2], n. **1.** Vigil commemorating church dedication, merry-making or fair on the occasion, (hist.); || (usu. pl.) annual holi- day in northern England. **2.** (Ir.). || Watch by corpse before burial, lamenta- tions & merry-making in connexion with it. [partly f. OE **wacu* (= OHG *wacha*, ON *vaka*), rel. to prec.; in ME partly f. prec.; sense ' vigil ' perh. f. ON]

wāke[3], n. Strip of smooth water left be- hind moving ship (*in the* ~ *of*, behind, following, after the example of). [f. ON **vaku*, *vǫk*, hole or opening in ice]

wāke'ful (-kf-), a. Unable to sleep, (of person's night etc.) passed with little or no sleep; vigilant. Hence ~NESS n. [WAKE[1], -FUL]

wāk'en, v.t. & i. Cause to be, become, awake (usu. = *wake up*, but conveying less of abruptness). [OE *wæcnan* = ON *vakna*, Goth. *-waknan* f. Gmc **wak-* WAKE[1]]

Walach, **Wall-**, (wǒl'ak), n. = VLACH.

Hence **Wal(l)achian** (wŏlăk′Ĭan) a. (of the ~s or of Walachia, a principality now forming part of Romania) & n. (= ~, also the language of the ~s). [see VLACH]

Waldĕn′s|ĕs (wŏ-, -z), n. pl. Puritan sect in valleys of Piedmont, Dauphiné, & Provence, started *c.* 1170 & much persecuted in 16th & 17th cc. Hence ~IAN a. & n. [Peter *Waldo* of Lyons, founder]

wāle, weal, n., & v.t. **1.** Ridge raised on flesh by stroke of rod or whip ; || *wale-knot* or *wall-knot,* made at end of rope by intertwining strands to prevent unravelling or act as stopper. **2.** v.t. Raise ~ on ; (mil., *vale*) weave (a hurdle or gabion). Hence **wāl′ING**[1] n., hurdlework used as revetment. [OE *walu* stripe, ridge ; sp. *veal* is mod. var., by assoc. w. obs. *wheal* pustule, suppurate, whence the misspelling *wheal*]

Wāl′er, n. (hist.). Horse imported for Indian army from New South Wales. [N.S. *Wales,* -ER[1]]

Wāles (-lz), n. Principality inhabited by the Welsh (*Prince of* ~, title usu. conferred on heir-apparent of Great Britain). [OE *Wealas* pl. of *wealh* see WELSH[1]]

Walhalla. See VALHALLA.

walk[1] (wawk), v.i. & t. **1.** (Of men) progress by advancing each foot alternately never having both off ground at once (*heel-&-toe* ~*ing,* in which both heel & toe are used, as required in ~ing-races ; ~ *backwards, sideways,* go in those directions with analogous motions ; ~ *over course* or ~ *over,* have WALK[2]-over ; ~ *away from,* easily out-distance), go with the gait usual except when speed is desired (~*ing* DICTIONARY) ; (of animals) go with slowest gait corresponding to human walk. **2.** Travel or go on foot (~ *into shop, up to* person, *down hill,* etc. ; *please* ~ *in,* invitation to enter ; ~ *up,* showman's invitation to circus etc. ; ~ *out with,* have as sweetheart ; ~ *about,* stroll ; ~*s two hours, ten miles, a day* ; *ghost* ~*s,* shows itself (see also GHOST) ; ~ *into,* sl., thrash, abuse, eat heartily of ; ~ *off,* depart, esp. abruptly ; ~ *off* or *away with,* carry off, steal ; *~ *out on* person, leave him). **3.** (arch.). Live with or in specified principle or manner, conduct oneself, (~ *in love, humbly, honestly, after the flesh, by faith, with God,* etc.). **4.** Perambulate, tread floor or surface of, (~ *the streets,* in gen. sense, also be prostitute ; ~ *the hospitals,* be medical student ; ~ *the boards,* be actor ; ~ *the* PLANK[1] ; ~ *the chalk,* prove sobriety to police etc. by ~ing straight between chalked lines), whence ~′ABLE (wawk-) a. **5.** Cause to ~ with one, have ~ing-race with, (~ *horse,* when riding or driving or leading it ; *policeman* ~*ed the man off* ; *Smith will* ~ *Jones for £100 a side* ; *you have* ~*ed me off my legs,* tired out). **6.** (Of farmer etc.) take charge of (hound puppy). **7.** ~*ie-talkie* (wawk′Ĭ-tawk′Ĭ) n., small transmitting and receiv-

ing radio set carried on the person ; ~ING[1] *chair,* = GO[1]-*cart* ; ~ING[2] *delegate,* trade- -union official who visits sick members, interviews employers, etc. ; ~ING[1]-*dress,* for outdoor wear ; ~ING[2]-*fern,* N.-Amer. kind with slender-tipped fronds that bow down to ground & take root ; ~ING[3] *gentleman, lady,* actor, actress, of part requiring good presence but no skill ; ~ING[2]-*leaf,* insect imitating leaf ; ~ING[1]- -*papers* or -*ticket,* sl., dismissal ; ||~ING[1]- -*stick,* carried in ~ing ; ~ING[1]-*tour,* pleasure journey on foot. [OE *wealcan* roll, toss, wander, *wealcian* muffle up, corresp. to OHG *walchan,* (M)Du., (M)LG *walken* to full, cudgel, ON *valka* drag about]

walk[2] (wawk), n. Walking gait, person's action in walking, (see prec., ; *go at, never gets beyond, a* ~ ; *know him a mile off by his* ~) ; excursion on foot, stroll, constitutional, (*go for, take, a* ~ ; *across the hills from X to Z is a good* ~ ; ~-*over,* race in which from absence or inferiority of competitors winner can go at a ~ if he chooses, easy victory) ; person's favourite walking ground, round of hawker etc., place or track intended or suitable for strollers or foot-passengers, promenade, colonnade, footpath, (ROPE-~ ; SHEEP-~ ; ~ *of life,* calling, profession, occupation) ; *~-*out,* workmen's strike ; *~′*way* : passage for walking along, esp. one connecting different sections of a building ; wide path in garden etc. [ME, f. prec.]

wa′lker (wawk-), n. In vbl senses ; esp. : || SHOP-~ ; STREET-~ ; (class-name for) bird such as common fowl that neither flies nor swims, also bird that does not hop but walks on alternate feet. [-ER[1]]

Walkyrie. See VALKYR.

wall (wawl), n., & v.t. **1.** Continuous & usu. vertical & solid structure of stones, bricks, concrete, timber, etc., narrow in proportion to length & height serving to enclose (partly) or protect or divide off town, house, room, field, etc., surface of inner side(s) of room, (*party* or *partition* ~, separating two rooms, houses, fields, etc. ; ~ *of partition,* fig., line of division, gulf ; *blank* ~, without door or gate or window, also without decoration ; *run* one's *head against a* ~, attempt impossibilities ; *see through brick* ~, have miraculous insight ; ~*s have ears,* eavesdroppers are or may be about ; *with* one's *back to the* ~, brought to bay, fighting alone against odds ; RETAIN*ing* ~). **2.** Something resembling ~ in appearance or effect (*mountain*~, line of steep hills ; ~ *of armed men, fire, bayonets,* protection or obstacle consisting of these ; *cell*-~, ~*s of the chest* etc., enclosing tissue or framework in bot. or anat. ; *hanging, foot-,* ~, in mining, upper, lower, rock enclosing lode). **3.** (Position next) ~ as opp. gutter side of street footpath (*give* one *the* ~, allow him cleaner and safer part in passing ; *take* the ~ of, refuse this courtesy to). **4.** Side as opp. centre of road (*the weakest goes to the* ~, is pushed aside, gets the worst in competition). **5.** ~-*creeper*, kinds of bird; ~-*cress*, kinds of plant growing in stony places; ~-*fern*, common polypody; ~-*flower*, yellow-flowered plant growing wild on old ~s, fragrant spring garden--plant with usu. orange or brown clustered flowers, (colloq.) woman sitting out dances for lack of partners; ~-*fruit*, of trees fastened against ~ for protection & warmth; ‖ ~ *game*, an Eton form of football; ~-*painting*, on ~ usu. of room, esp. fresco; ~-*paper*, for pasting over room-~s, freq. with decorative printed patterns; ~-*pepper*, kind of stonecrop; ~-*plate*, timber laid in or on ~ to distribute pressure of girder etc.; ~-*rue*, small fern growing on ~s & rocks; ~-*washer*, plate used with tie-rod in supporting shaky ~; hence ~-LESS (wawl-l) a. **6.** v.t. Provide or protect with ~ (esp. in p.p., as ~*ed towns*); block *up* aperture etc. with ~. [OE *wall* = OFris. *wal*, OS *wal(l)*, f. L *vallum* rampart]

walla(h) (wŏl'a), n. (Anglo-Ind.). Person or thing employed about or concerned with something, -man, (BOX²-~; *competition*-~, Indian civilian appointed by competitive examination; *punkah*-~, servant who works punkah). [f. Hind. -*wālā* suf. = -ER¹(3)]

wa'llabý (wŏ-), n. Kinds of smaller kangaroo; *on the* ~ (*track*), on tramp, unemployed; (pl., colloq.) Australians. [Austral.]

Wallach. See WALACH.

wallaroō' (wŏ-), n. Kinds of larger kangaroo. [Austral.]

wa'llĕt (wŏ-), n. (Arch.) bag for carrying personal necessaries, food, etc., on journey, esp. pilgrim's or beggar's scrip; small leather case holding repairing tools for bicycle etc., fishing-kit, papers, or other small articles; flat case for holding bank-notes etc. [ME *walet*, of unkn. orig.]

wall-eye (wawl'ī), n. Appearance of whitish opacity of eye caused by injury or disease; (loosely) eye showing abnormal amount of white owing to squint etc., or large & glaring as in some fishes. [back formation f. foll.]

wall-eyed (wawl'īd), a. Having wall-eye. [f. ON *vagl-eygr* (*vagl* unexpl., *auga* eye)]

‖ **wall-knot.** See WALE.

Walloōn', n. & a. **1.** Member, language (a French dialect), of people scattered in Belgium & neighbouring parts of France. **2.** adj. Of the ~s or in their language. [f. F *Wallon* f. med. L *Wallonem* f. Gmc *walh*, see WELSH¹; cf. VLACH]

wa'llop (wŏ-), v.t., & n. (sl.). **1.** Thrash, beat, hide; (part.) big, strapping, thumping. **2.** n. A heavy blow; (sl.) beer. Hence ~ING¹(1) n. [earlier senses *gallop*, *boil*, f. ONF *waloper*, f. Frank. *wola lōpan*; see GALLOP]

wallow (wŏl'ō), v.i., & n. **1.** Roll about in mud, sand, water, etc. (~ *in money*, be very rich); take swinish or gross delight *in* sensuality etc. **2.** n. Place to which buffaloes etc. resort to ~. [OE *wealwian* roll, cf. Goth. *walwjan*; cogn. w. L *volvere*]

Wa'llsĕnd (wawlz-), n. Kind of superior house-coal orig. from ~ on Tyne.

Wall Street (wawl), n. (Used for) the New York money-market. [street in New York]

wa'lnŭt (wawl-), n. (Kinds of tree yielding) delicate-flavoured nut in pair of similar boat-shaped shells (*over the* ~*s & the wine*, at dessert); timber of ~-tree used in cabinet-making & for gunstocks. [OE *walhhnutu* f. *wealh* foreign + NUT; cf. WELSH¹]

Walpur'gis-night (vahlpoorgĭs-nĭt), n. Eve of 1st May, when witches meet at the Brocken or elsewhere & hold revels with the devil. [*Walpurgis*, female saint of 8th c.]

wa'lrus (wawl-, wŏl-), n. Kinds of large amphibious arctic long-tusked mammal related to seal, morse, sea-horse. [prob. f. Du. *walrus*, -*ros*, perh. w. metath., after *walvisch*, f. wd repr. by OE *horshwæl*, ON *hross hvalr*]

waltz (wawlts, wawls), n., & v.i. **1.** (Music for) dance in triple time with graceful flowing melody & (usu.) one harmony to each measure. **2.** v.i. Dance ~; dance *in*, *out*, *round*, etc., in joy etc.; hence ~'ER¹ (wawls-) n. [f. G *walzer* (*walzen* revolve)]

wampee' (wŏ-), n. (Tree yielding) grapelike fruit grown in China & E. Indies. [Chin. (*hwang* yellow, *pī* skin)]

wa'mpum (wŏ-), n. Beads made from shells & strung for money or decoration by N.-Amer. Indians. [f. N.-Amer. Ind. *wampumpeag* (*wompi* white, -*ampi* string)]

wan (wŏn), a. Pale, colourless, bloodless, looking worn or exhausted, (chiefly of persons or their complexion or look, or of sky or light); (arch., of night, water, etc.) dark, black. Hence ~'LY² adv., ~'NESS (-n-n-) n. [OE *wann*, *wonn*, dark, black, of unkn. orig.]

wand (wŏ-), n. Slender rod for carrying in hand or setting in ground as temporary mark (chiefly now of conjurer's or music conductor's baton, or of staff symbolizing some officials' authority). [ME, f. ON *vandur*, *vǫndr*, = Goth. *wandus*, prob. f. *wend*-, *wand*-, see WEND¹, WIND³]

wa'nder (wŏ-), v.i. & t. **1.** Rove, stroll, go from country to country or from place to place without settled route or destination, (~*ing Jew*, supposed to be still living from when Christ said 'Thou shalt ~ on the earth till I return' as punishment for an insult, also person who never settles down, also kinds of climbing plant; ~*ing cell*, *abscess*, *kidney*, etc., moving about, normally or abnormally attached to place in body; ~*ing sailor,* kinds of climbing plant), whence ~ER[1] (wŏ-) n. **2.** Stray, diverge from the right way lit. or fig., get lost, depart from home. **3.** Talk or think irrelevantly or disconnectedly or incoherently, stray from subject in hand, be inattentive or delirious, (*his wits are* ~*ing*; ~*s in his talk*). **4.** Traverse desultorily (*you may* ~ *the world*, or usu. *the world through, & not find such another*). Hence ~ING[1](1) n. (usu. pl.), ~ing LY[2] adv., (wŏ-). [OE *wandrian* f. Gmc *wand-* +-ER[5], see prec.; cf. MHG *wandern*]

wanderlust (vahn'derlŏŏst), n. Eager desire or fondness for travelling or wandering. [G]

wanderoo' (wŏ-), n. Kind of Ceylon monkey. [Sinhalese *wanderu*]

wāne, v.i., & n. **1.** Decrease in size or splendour like moon after the full, lose power or vigour or importance or repute, decline. **2.** n. Process of waning (esp. *is on the* ~, declining. [OE *wanian* = OS *wanon*, OHG *-ōn*, *-ēn*, ON *vana* f. Gmc *wano-* lacking, see WANT[1]]

‖ **wangl|e** (wăng'gl), v.t., & n. (sl.). **1.** Secure (favour, desired result) by plausibility or management or other dubious means; show in the desired light, cook, fake, (report etc.). **2.** n. Act of ~ing. [orig. unkn.; first recorded (1888) as printers' sl.]

‖ **wanion** (wŏn'yon), n. *With a* ~ (*to*), imprecation (arch.). [var. of *waniand* part. of WANE (waning moon = unlucky hour)]

want[1] (wŏ-, wah-), n. Lack, absence, deficiency, of (*ship rotting for* ~ *of paint*; *shows great* ~ *of thought, care, sense, judgement*); need *of*, need of sustenance, poverty, (*is in* ~ *of money, a servant*, etc.; *living in the direst* ~; ~ *is a severe but efficient teacher*); desire for thing as necessary to life or happiness or success or completion (whence ~'LESS a.), thing so desired, (*a man of few* ~*s*; *superfluities soon become* ~*s*; *is, supplies, a felt* ~; *can supply your* ~*s*). [ME, f. ON *vant* neut. of *vanr* lacking = OE *wan*, Goth. *wans*, f. Gmc *wana-*, see WANE]

want[2] (wŏ-, wah-), v.i. & t. **1.** Be without or deficiently supplied with, fall short *of*, fall short by (specified amount) *of* specified limit, (part.) lacking *in* quality or unequal *to* requirements or absent or deficient or (orig. dial.) lacking in intelligence, (~*s, is* ~*ing in, judgement*; *fortunately* ~*s the power to do it*; *what was* ~*ing, what we unfortunately* ~*ed, was the will*; ~*s something of perfection; be found* ~*ing*, or ~*ing to the occasion*, one's *duty*, etc.; *head of statue is* ~*ing*; *statue* ~*s the head*; *infinitive* ~*ing*, verb has none; ~*s half a minute of the hour, an inch of the regulation measurement*). **2.** Be in want (*for*; *let him* ~ *for nothing*; *must not be allowed to* ~). **3.** Require (thing, *-ing*, *to be -ed*, to do; *boy* ~*s the whip, whipping, to be whipped, to feel the whip*; *it* ~*s careful handling*). **4.** Desire, wish for possession or presence of, (*to do*, thing, person; *don't* ~ *to go*; *I* ~ *some sugar, it done, you to try*; *call me if I am* ~*ed*; *is* ~*ed by the police*, of suspected criminal etc.; *tell Jones I* ~ *him*, send him to me). [ME, f. ON *vanta* (prec.)]

wa'nting (wŏ-, wah-), quasi- prep. Without, minus, less, (~ *common honesty, nothing can be done*; *made a century* ~ *one run*). [-ING[2]; use of part. either abs., cf. NOTWITHSTANDING, or in ordinary agreement]

wa'nton (wŏ-), a., n., & v.i. **1.** Sportive, gambolling, playful, irresponsible, capricious, (~ *child, kid, wind, mood*); luxuriant, unrestrained, wild, (~ *growth, ringlets, profusion*); licentious, unchaste, lewd, (*a* ~ *woman*; ~ *thoughts*); motiveless, serving no purpose, random, arbitrary, (~*mischief, destruction*); hence ~LY[2] adv., ~NESS n. **2.** n. Unchaste woman or rarely man; (rare) playful child. **3.** v.i. Sport, gambol, move capriciously; (rare) act lasciviously. [ME *wantowen* f. WAN + *towen* (cf. obs. *wanhope* despair), f. OE *togen* p.p. of *tēon* draw, educate; cf. G *ungezogen*]

wap. See WHOP.

wa'pentake (wŏ-), n. (Old name in Yorkshire and some other shires for) hundred or division of shire. [OE *wæpengetæc* f. ON *vápnatak* (*vápn* weapon, *tac* taking f. *taka* TAKE)]

wa'piti (wŏ-), n. N.-Amer. stag resembling red deer but larger. [f. Amer.-Ind. *wapitik* white deer]

‖ **Wappens(c)haw** (wah'penshaw), n. (Sc.). (Hist.) periodical muster & inspection of men under arms in a particular district; (mod.) rifle-meeting. [f. *wapen* obs. form of *weapon* +*schaw* show (n.)]

war[1] (wŏr), n. **1.** Quarrel usu. between nations conducted by force, state of open hostility, & suspension of ordinary international law, prevalent during such quarrel, military or naval attack or series of attacks, (fig.) hostility or contention between persons, (*civil* ~, between parts of one nation for supremacy; *cold* ~, unfriendly relations between nations characterized by hostile propaganda & attempted economic sabotage; ~ *of nerves*, attempt to wear down opponent by gradual destruction of morale, opp. SHOOT*ing* ~; *private* ~, feud between persons or families carried on in defiance of laws of murder etc., or armed attack made by members of one State without government sanction upon another; *holy* ~, waged in support of some religious cause; TOTAL ~; *make* or *wage* ~, begin or carry on hostile operations; *declare* ~, announce that hostilities may be expected, often *upon* another nation, also fig. *upon* institution, party, custom, etc.; so *declaration of* ~; *drift into* ~; *be at* ~, engaged in hostilities *with* enemy or abs., also fig.; *roll back tide of* ~, repel invasion; *go to the* ~*s*, arch., serve as soldier; *carry the* ~ *into the enemy's country*, (fig.) make counter-accusations etc., not confine oneself to defence; *has been in the* ~*s*, usu. fig. of person who has been mauled physically or otherwise; *on a* ~ *footing*, of army, fleet, etc., with full establishment; ~ *to the knife*, struggle to the bitter end usu. between persons; *Secretary of State for War*, also *Secretary for War*, *War Secretary*, ‖ parliamentary head of War Office; *art of* ~, strategy & tactics; *trade of* ~, soldier's profession; *sinews of* ~, money etc. for waging ~ or for effecting any object; TUG, CONTRABAND, COUNCIL, HONOUR¹s, *of* ~; MAN¹-*of*-~; *laws of* ~, those recognized by civilized nations as limiting belligerents' action; *rights of* ~, those similarly permitting to belligerents certain acts illegitimate in peace; *the dogs of* ~, poet., havoc attending ~; ~*s & rumours of* ~*s*, prevalence of the appeal to force among nations; ~ *of the elements*, storms & catastrophes in nature; *all's* FAIR² *in love & ~*). **2.** ~ *baby*, illegitimate child attributable to ~ conditions; ~-*cloud*, position of international affairs that threatens ~; ~-*cry*, phrase or name formerly shouted in charging or rallying to attack, party catchword, savages' battle-shout; ~-*dance*, indulged in by savages before ~; ~-*game*, = KRIEGSPIEL; ~-*god*, one worshipped as giving victory in ~, esp. the Greek Ares or Roman Mars; ~-*head*, explosive head of torpedo or similar weapon; ~-*horse*, charger (arch. & poet. exc. in phr. *like an old* ~-*horse*, of person excited by memories of abandoned pursuit or controversy); ~-*lord* (derog.), military commander (esp. of William II of Germany, & of Chinese civil-war generals); ~'*monger*, one who seeks to bring about ~; ‖ *War Office*, State department in charge of army; ~-*paint*, put on body by savages before battle, (fig.) ceremonial costume, full fig; ~-*path*, (route of) warlike expedition of Amer. Indians (*be*, *go*, *on the* ~-*path*, fig., be engaged in, enter upon, any conflict, have taken, take, up the cudgels); ~'*ship*, for use in ~; ~-*song*, sung by savages before battle, also any song on martial theme; ~-*whoop*, yell esp. of Amer. Indians in charging; ~-*worn*, experienced in or damaged or exhausted by ~. [late OE *werre* f. AF, ONF *werre* (OF *guerre*) f. WG *werra* (cf. OHG *werra* confusion, strife, OS, OHG *werran* embroil), f. Gmc *werz-, *wers- (WORSE)]

war² (wôr), v.i. & t. (-rr-). Make war (arch.); bring or beat *down* by war; (part.) rival, competing, inconsistent, (~*ing creeds, principles*). [ME, f. prec.]

war'bl|e¹ (wôr-), v.i. & t., & n. **1.** Sing (i. & t.) in gentle continuous trilling manner (esp. of birds, also of person or sound); speak, utter, in manner sug-

gestive of bird's song; relate in verse. **2.** n. ~ed song etc.; ~ing voice (*spoke in a* ~*e*). [ME, f. ONF *werble*(*r*) f. WG f. Gmc *hwerbh-* revolve, see WHIRL]

war'ble² (wôr-), n. Hard lump on horse's back from galling of saddle; (tumour produced by) larva of gadfly. [orig. obsc.; cf. MSw. *varbulde* boil (*var* pus, *bulde* tumour)]

war'bler (wôr-), n. In vbl senses; esp., many kinds of small bird including nightingale, whitethroat, and chiff-chaff, some not remarkable for song. [-ER¹]

ward¹ (wôrd), n. **1.** Act of guarding or defending place etc. (now only in *keep watch & ~*). **2.** Guard or parry in fencing (arch.). **3.** Confinement, custody, guardian's control, (arch.; *is under* ~; *put him in* ~; *to whom the child is in* ~). **4.** Minor under care of guardian or Court of Chancery. **5.** Administrative division of city. **6.** Separate room or division in prison (*condemned* etc. ~) or hospital (*isolation* etc. ~) ‖ or workhouse (*casual* etc. ~). **7.** pl. Notches & projections in key and lock designed to prevent opening by wrong key. **8.** ~-*mote* (hist.), meeting of city ~ [OE *mót* meeting]; ~'*room*, in warship for commissioned officers below commanding officer. [OE *weard*, OS *ward*, OHG *wart*, ON *vǫrthr*, Goth. -*wards*, f. Gmc *wardh-* extended form of *war-* WARE²,³; cf. GUARD¹]

ward² (wôrd), v.t. Have in keeping, protect, (chiefly now of God); parry (blow, often *off*), keep *off* (danger, poverty, etc.). [OE *weardian*, OS -*on*, OHG *wartēn*, ON *vartha*, f. Gmc *wardh-* (prec.)]

-ward(s) (-ward, -dz), suf. repr. OE -*weard*, primarily forming adjj., w. sense 'having a specified direction', corresp. to OS -*ward*, OHG -*wart*, f. Gmc *-wardha-* f. *wardh-*, *werth-* to turn, cogn. w. L *vertere* (cf. *versus*). OE adjj. in -*weard* usu. denoted direction of movement. They could be used adv. in the acc., or in the gen. case (-*weardes* (now -*wards*): see -ES). The suf. was occas. attached to a phr. consisting of a n. or pron. governed by a prep., e.g. *tō Lundene weard* 'to Londonward(s)', wh. survives in arch. use, as in '*to us-ward*'. On the anal. of such compds after loss of *to* (e.g. *heavenward*, for *to heavenward*) the suf. has been added to nn. (*Godward, earthward*) esp. in lit. use. -*ward* & -*wards* are so nearly syn. that no hard & fast rules can be given for their use; it is largely a matter of idiom & euphony; e.g. -*wards* is required when manner is indicated as well as direction of movement, as *to walk backwards*; we say *a forward* (adj.) *movement, to come forward* (adv.) but *it is moving forwards, not backwards*. As living suff., -*ward* & -*wards* form extempore adjj. & advv., freq. more or less joc., as *bankwards, bedward, Perthwards*.

war′den[1] (wŏr-), n. Watchman, sentinel, (arch.); member of civilian organization for assisting the civil population in air raids; guardian, president, governor, *of* (in obs. or existent titles, as *W∼ of the Marches, Merton College* etc., *the Cinque Ports*), whence ∼SHIP n. [ME, f. AF, ONF *wardein*, var. of OF *guarden(e)* GUARDIAN]

war′den[2] (wŏr-), n. Kind of cooking pear. [ME, of unkn. orig.]

war′der (wŏr-), n. ‖ Sentinel (arch.); ‖ gaoler, whence **war′dress**[1] (wŏr-) n.; (hist.) staff of authority carried by king or commander & occas. used to give signals. [ME, f. AF *wardere, -our* f. *warder* = OF *guarder* GUARD[2], see -OR]

War′dour Street (wŏrder), n. A London street formerly noted for antique & imitation-antique furniture (∼ *English*, affectedly archaic) but now given over esp. to the film trade; (used for) the film trade.

ward′robe (wŏr-), n. Place where clothes are kept, esp. large cabinet or movable cupboard with pegs, shelves, etc.; person's stock of clothes; ∼ *dealer*, dealer in second-hand clothes; ∼ *mistress*, one who has charge of the professional ∼ of an actor or actress, or of a theatrical company; ∼ *trunk* (fitted with drawers, coat-hangers, etc., & designed to stand on end, serving as ∼). [ME, f. *warderobe*, ONF var. of OF *garderobe* (GUARD[2], ROBE)]

war′dship (wŏr-), n. Tutelage, guardian's care, (*under* ∼; *has the* ∼ *of*). [WARD[1], -SHIP]

ware[1], n. 1. Things manufactured for sale, esp. pottery of any kind (otherwise usu. in comb., as HARD∼, TIN∼); (pl.) articles that person etc. has for sale (usu. *his* etc. ∼*s*); (with distinctive epithet) kind of manufactured material esp. pottery, named from inventor, place of manufacture, or some characteristic (*Wedgwood, Delft* or *Delf, black,* etc., ∼, kinds of pottery; *Tunbridge* ∼, inlaid wood). 2. ∼′*house* (-s) n., building in which goods are stored, bonded, or displayed for sale, repository, wholesale or large retail store; ∼′*house* (-z) v.t., store (esp. furniture or bonded goods) temporarily in respository; ∼′*houseman*, owner of repository. [OE *waru,* MDu., MLG, MHG *ware,* ON *vara*]

ware[2], pred. a. (poet.). Aware. [OE *wær,* OS *war,* ON *varr,* Goth *wars* f. Gmc *war-*, cf. WARD[1]]

ware[3] (wŏr, wār), v.t. (Imperat.) look out for, be cautious about, (∼ *hounds, wire, traps!*; esp. in hunting-field); (colloq., usu. imperat.) decline to have anything to do with, bar, avoid, fight shy of. [OE *warian,* OS *-on,* OHG *-ōn* f. Gmc *war-* (prec.)]

war′fare (wŏr-), n. State of war, campaigning, being engaged in war, (*after long* ∼; *his* ∼ *is over*). [f. WAR[1] + FARE[2]]

war′like (wŏr-), a. Martial, fond of or skilful in war; military, of or for war, (∼ *preparations*); bellicose, threatening war. [ME; -LIKE]

war′lock (wŏr-), n. (arch.). Sorcerer, wizard. [OE *wær-loga* = OS *wâr-logo,* prob. f. *wær* covenant (OHG *wâra* truth) + *loga* liar]

warm[1] (wŏrm), a. & n. 1. Hottish, of or at rather high temperature, (*hot,* ∼, *tepid, cool, cold*; ∼ *water, weather, countries*; ∼ *blood,* that of mammals & birds ranging from 98° to 112° F., also fig. passionate or amorous or emotional disposition, whence ∼-**blood**ED[2] (-lŭd) a.; (of persons etc.) having temperature of skin raised by exercise or excitement or external heat. 2. (Of clothes etc.) serving to keep one ∼. 3. (Of friendly relations or actions or agents) enthusiastic, hearty, zealous, (*a* ∼ *partisan, friend, welcome,* RECEPTION; ∼ *thanks*). 4. Animated, heated, exciting or excited, in or resulting from sanguine or offended or indignant or unreserved mood, (*when* ∼ *with wine; the dispute* or *disputants grew* ∼; ∼ *work,* keen or dangerous conflict). 5. (Of position etc.) difficult or dangerous to maintain or meet (*a* ∼ *corner,* hot part of battle etc.; so ∼ RECEPTION; *make it* or *things* ∼ *for* one, create strong feeling against him). 6. (Of feelings etc.) sympathetic, emotional, affectionate, susceptible, (*has a* ∼ *heart,* whence ∼-**heart**ED[2] (-hărt-) a., ∼-**heart′ed**LY[2] adv., ∼-**heart′ed**NESS n.; *a* ∼ *temperament,* susceptible esp. to amorous impressions; ∼ *descriptions* etc., intended to appeal to amorous feelings, indelicate). 7. (Of colour) suggestive of ∼th, esp. containing rich reds or yellows. 8. (Of scent in hunting) fresh & strong, indicating recent passage of quarry; (of seeker in children's hiding games etc.) near the object sought, on verge of finding. 9. (colloq.). (Of person) comfortably off, rich. 10. (Of official etc.) no longer strange, comfortably established, *in* office. 11. n. Something ∼, esp. BRITISH ∼. Hence ∼′LY[2] adv., ∼TH[1] n., (wŏr-). [OE *wearm,* OS, OHG *warm,* ON *varmr* f. Gmc *warmaz,* prob. cogn. w. L *formus,* Gk *thermos,* Skr. *gharma*]

warm[2] (wŏrm), v.t. & i., & n. 1. Make warm, excite, (*fire* ∼*s room, person,* etc.; *wine to* ∼ *the heart*; ∼ *oneself at fire* etc.; ∼ *person* or *his jacket,* thrash him, whence ∼′ING[1] n., sl.); ∼ *oneself at fire* etc.; become warm or animated or sympathetic (often *up*; *room is* ∼*ing up*; *he* ∼*ed up* or ∼*ed as he got into his subject; my heart* ∼*s to him*); ∼*ing-pan,* flat closed long-handled usu. brass vessel holding live coals formerly used for ∼ing inside of bed before it was occupied, (fig.) person holding office temporarily to keep it for another not yet of age etc.; hence (-)∼ER[1] (2) n. 2. n. Act of ∼ing oneself or something (*must have, give it, another* ∼ *first*).

[OE *werman* (= OS *wermian*, OHG -*en*, Goth. -*jan*), f. Gmc **warm-* (prec.)]

warn (wôrn), v.t. Give notice to, put on guard, caution, admonish, (person *of* danger or consequences or future or unknown present circumstance, *against* person or thing or do*ing*, *that* something impends or must be reckoned with, *that* he is neglecting or has neglected to do something, *to* do, or abs.). Hence ∼ᴸ **inGLY²** adv. [OE *war(e)nian*, *wearnian*, OHG *warnōn*, f. Gmc **war-* WARE²]

war'ning (wôr-), n. In vbl senses (*lake* ∼, have one's caution excited, mentally register danger etc., act on a ∼); also or esp.: thing that serves to warn (*palpitation is a* ∼ *of heart trouble*; *let this be a* ∼ *to you*); *give* (master, servant) ∼, announce that employment is to terminate in specified (e.g. *a month's*) time. [-ING¹]

warp¹ (wôrp), v.t. & i. **1.** Make or become crooked or perverted, change from straight or right or natural state, bias, (*sun had* ∼*ed the boards*; *seasoned timber does not* ∼; *hardship* ∼*ed his disposition*; *judgement* ∼*ed by self-interest*). **2.** (naut.). Haul (ship) in some direction by rope attached to fixed point, progress thus. **3.** Fertilize by inundating with WARP². [OE *weorpan* throw, OS *werpan*, OHG *werfan*, ON *verpa*, Goth. *wairpan*, f. Gmc **werp-*, **warp-*, **wurp-*]

warp² (wôrp), n. **1.** Threads stretched lengthwise in loom to be crossed by weft. **2.** Rope used in towing or warping. **3.** Crooked state produced in timber etc. by uneven shrinking or expansion; (fig.) perversion or perverse inclination in mind. **4.** Sediment or alluvial deposit, esp. that left by turbid water kept standing on poor land. [OE *wearp*, OHG *warf*, ON *varp*, f. Gmc **warp-* (prec.)]

wa'rrant¹ (wŏ-), n. **1.** Thing that bears person out in or authorizes action (*have no* ∼ *for what you do*; *his promise* or *order*, *our strength*, *is our* ∼; *I will be your* ∼; *with the* ∼ *of a good conscience*). **2.** Voucher, written authorization to receive money (*dividend*, TREASURY, ∼), carry out arrest or distress (*a* ∼ *is out against him*), represent principal in lawsuit (∼ *of attorney*), etc. **3.** Certificate from War Office or Admiralty or Air Ministry (cf. COMMISSION) held by ∼-*officer* (between commissioned officers & N.C.O.s, as gunner, boatswain, sergeant-major). [ME, f. ONF *warant*, -*and*, var. of OF *g(u)arant*, -*and*, f. subst. use of part of WG **waren* to warrant]

wa'rrant² (wŏ-), v.t. Serve as warrant for, justify, (*nothing can* ∼ *such insolence*), whence ∼ABLE a., (also, of a stag) of an age to be hunted (5 or 6 years); = GUARANTEE v., esp. in sense *answer for genuineness* etc. *of* (goods; ∼*ed pure* etc., to be so), & in *I* or *I'll* ∼ (*you*) usu. parenthet. = no doubt, whence ∼ER¹, ∼OR, ∼EE' (one to whom warranty is given), nn., (wŏ-). [ME,

f. *warantir*, -*dir*, dial. var. of OF *g(u)arantir*, -*dir*, f. com.-Rom. f. prec.]

wa'rrantỹ (wŏ-), n. Authority or justification (usu. *for* doing or saying or supposing); (law) express or implied undertaking on vendor's part that thing sold is vendor's & is fit for use or fulfils specified conditions. [f. AF (OF) *warantie*, dial. var. of *guarantie* (GUARANTY), f. *warant* WARRANT¹]

wa'rrèn (wŏ-), n. Piece of ground in which rabbits are preserved or abound (*like rabbits in a* ∼, of thick population). [ME, f. AF, ONF *warenne* (OF *garenne*), f. Gmc **war-* (WARE³)]

wa'rrior (wŏ-), n. Distinguished or veteran soldier (rhet., poet.); member of any of the fighting services (*the Unknown W* ∼, or *Soldier*, unidentified body of one killed in the 1914–18 war selected for public burial as symbolizing his country's sacrifice); (attrib., of nation etc.) martial; (of savages) fighting man; ∼ *ant*, of kinds that make slaves of other species. [ME, f. *werreior* etc., ONF var. of OF *guerreior* etc., f. *werreier*, *guerreier*, f. com. Rom. f. WG **werra* WAR¹]

wart (wôrt), n. Small hardish excrescence on skin caused by abnormal growth of papillae (*paint one with his* ∼*s*, without concealment of blemishes), similar lump on stem etc. of plant; ∼-*grass*, -*weed*, -*wort*, kind of spurge with juice used to cure ∼*s*; ∼-*hog*, kinds of African large-headed swine with ∼*y* lumps on face. Hence ∼'ʏ² a. [OE *wearte*, OS *warta*, OHG *warza*, ON *varta* f. Gmc **wartōn*]

wār'|ỹ, a. Given to caution, habitually on the look-out, circumspect; cautious *of doing*; showing, done with, caution. Hence ∼ɪʟʏ² adv., ∼ɪNESS n. [f. WARE³ +-ʏ²]

was. See BE.

wash¹ (wŏ-), v.t. & i. **1.** Cleanse with liquid (∼ one's *face* etc., one*self*, or any object; ∼ thing *out*, clean its inside; ∼ one's *dirty* LINEN; ∼ one's *hands*, fig., decline responsibility usu. *of*), (fig.) purify (∼ *me throughly from mine iniquity*); take (stain, dirt, etc.) *out* or *off* or *away* by ∼*ing*; ∼ *up* (plates etc., or usu. abs.), clean table utensils after use; (abs.) ∼ oneself or esp. one's (*face &*) hands (*must* ∼ *before dinner*), ∼ clothes (∼*es for a living*). **2.** (Of coloured material or dye) bear ∼*ing* without loss of colour (*won't* ∼, fig. of argument etc., stand examination), whence ∼'ɪNG² (wŏ-) a.; ∼*ed out*, (fig.) enfeebled, limp, demoralized, esp. as effect of dissipation. **3.** Moisten (*roses* ∼*ed with dew*); (of river, sea, etc.) touch (coast, bank, country) with its waters. **4.** (Of moving liquid) carry along in specified direction (chiefly in pass.; *a wave* ∼*ed him overboard*; *was* ∼*ed up by the sea*; *bee* ∼*ed down with ale*); denude (*sea-*∼*ed cliffs*); scoop out (*water had* ∼*ed a channel*); go splashing or sweeping *over,* *along, out, in,* or *into.* **5.** Sift (ore) by action of water. **6.** Brush thin coating of watery colour over (paper in water-colour or sepia painting, wall), coat (inferior metal) thinly with gold etc. Hence ~-ABLE (wŏ-) a. [OE *wæscan,* OS, OHG *wascan,* ON *vaska,* f. Gmc **waskan* f. **watskan* f. root **wat-* as in WATER]

wash[2] (wŏ-), n. **1.** Washing or being washed (*give it a good* ~; *must get a* ~; *the* ~, treatment at laundry, as *send the linen to the* ~); quantity of clothes just (to be, being) washed. **2.** Visible or audible motion of agitated water, esp. waves caused by passage of vessel. **3.** Soil swept off by water, alluvium. **4.** Kitchen water & scraps given to pigs. **5.** Thin or weak or inferior liquid food (*this soup, tea, claret, is mere* ~); (fig.) twaddle, wishwash. **6.** Liquid for spreading over surface to cleanse or heal or colour, lotion, cosmetic; thin coating of water-colour, wall-colouring, or metal. [f. prec.]

wash- (wŏ-), comb. form of WASH[1, 2], often = & used as substitute for *wash*ING[1]: || ~-*basin*; ~-*board,* of ribbed wood for use in scrubbing clothes at wash, also board attached to gunwale, port, etc., to prevent water from washing in, also board skirting bottom of room-wall; ~-*boiler,* clothes-washing cauldron; ~-*bottle,* apparatus for purifying gases etc. by passage through liquid; ~-*bowl;* ~-*cloth,* piece of linen etc. used in washing dishes etc.; ~-*day,* on which clothes are washed; || ~-*hand-basin;* || ~-*hand-stand,* piece of furniture with toilet utensils; ~-*house,* laundry; ~-*leather,* chamois or similar leather; ~-*out,* breach in railway or road track caused by flood, heavy rainfall, etc., (sl.) complete failure, fiasco, (sl.) useless or inefficient person; ~-*pot* (arch. exc. of pot with melted tin for final dipping of tinplate); ***~-*rag,* ~-*cloth;* ***~-*room,* lavatory; ~-*stand,* = ~-*hand--stand;* ~-*tub,* esp. for clothes.

wa'sher (wŏ-), n. In vbl senses; also, flat ring or perforated piece of leather, rubber, metal, etc., used to give tightness to joint, nut, fastening, etc.; BOTTLE[1]-~; || ~-*woman,* laundress. [-ER[1]]

wa'shing (wŏ-), n. In vbl senses (& see WASH-); esp., linen etc. sent to the wash; BRAIN-~; ~ *machine,* for the ~ of clothes etc.; ~ *soda,* sodium carbonate, used dissolved in water for ~ & cleaning; ~-*stand,* = WASH-*stand;* ~-*up,* ~ of table utensils after a meal. [-ING[1]]

Wa'shington (wŏ-), n. (Used for) the U.S. Government. [capital of U.S.]

Washingtōn'ia (wŏ-), n. Californian palm-tree named after George Washington. [-IA[1]]

wa'sh|y (wŏ-), a. (Of liquid food etc.) too watery, weak, thin, insipid; (of colour) faded-looking, thin; (of style, sentiment, etc.) diffuse, feeble, lacking vigour or compression. Hence ~ILY[2] adv., ~INESS n. [-Y[2]]

wasn't (wŏznt). See BE.

wasp (wŏ-), n. Kinds of hymenopterous social or solitary insect of which the common kind has black & yellow transverse stripes, very slender waist, taste for fruit & sweets, & powerfully venomous sting (*has a waist like a* ~'s, whence ~-waistED[2] a.); ~-*bee, -beetle, -fly,* kinds having some resemblance to ~. [OE *wæfs, wæps, wæsp,* OS *wepsia,* OHG *wafsa, wefsa,* f. Gmc **wabhis-,* **waps-,* cogn. w. L *vespa* & WEAVE, w. ref. to nests]

wa'spish (wŏ-), a. Irritable, petulant, ill--tempered, sharp in retort. Hence ~LY[2] adv., ~NESS n. [-ISH[1]]

wassail (wŏ'sl, wă'sl), n., & v.i. (arch.). **1.** Festive occasion, drinking-bout; kind of liquor drunk on such occasion; ~-*bowl, -cup, -horn,* etc. **2.** v.i. Make merry, hold festivities. [ME *wæs hæil* etc., f. ON *ves heill,* corresp. to OE *wes hāl* 'be in good health' (*hāl*=WHOLE), form of salutation]

wast. See BE.

wāst'age, n. Amount wasted or that runs to waste, loss by waste. [-AGE]

wāste[1], a. (Of district etc.) desolate, desert, uninhabited, uncultivated, as result of natural barrenness etc. or of ravages or catastrophe (*lay* ~, ravage; *lie* ~, be uncultivated; ~ *land,* not occupied for any purpose); (fig.) monotonous or presenting no features of interest (*the* ~ *periods of history*); superfluous, refuse, no longer serving a purpose, left over after use, (~ *products,* useless by-products of manufacture; ~ *energy, steam,* etc.; ~ *paper,* esp. books or documents that fail or are valueless). [ME, f. AF, ONF *wast,* var. of OF *g(u)ast* f. Rom. **wasto* f. L *vastus* infl. by cogn. WG, as OS *wōsti*]

wāst|e[2], v.t. & i. Lay WASTE[1]; (law) bring (estate) into bad condition by damage or neglect; expend to no purpose or for inadequate result, use extravagantly, squander, (~*e money, time, food,* etc., or abs. as ~*e not, want not;* ~*e breath* or *words,* talk uselessly; wear (t. & i.) gradually away, wither, (arch., of time) pass t. & i., (*his resources were* ~*ed, were rapidly* ~*ing; day* ~*es,* draws to a close; *sorcerer* ~*ed his arm; a* ~*ing disease; is* ~*ing away for lack of food*); run to waste (*that water is* ~*ing*). [ME, f. AF, ONF *waster,* var. of OF *g(u)aster* f. Rom. **wastare* f. L *vastare* infl. by cogn. WG **wōstjan,* see prec.]

wāste[3], n. **1.** Desert, waste region, dreary scene, (*a* ~ *of waters,* unbroken expanse of sea or floods). **2.** Being used up, diminution by wear & tear, (*the* ~ *of tissue is continuous;* ~ *& repair balance each other*). **3.** Waste material or food, useless remains, refuse, scraps, shreds; = COTTON ~. **4.** Act of wasting, throwing away or extravagant or ineffectual use *of* time, money, food, etc., (*wilful* ~ *makes woeful want; it is* ~ *of time to argue further; run* *to* ~, of liquid or fig. of affection etc., be wasted). **5.** (law). Injury to estate caused by act or neglect esp. of life-tenant. [ME, f. AF, ONF *wast(e)*, var. of OF *g(u)ast(e)*, partly f. L *vastum* (WASTE¹), partly f. *waster* (prec.)]

wāste-, comb. form of WASTE¹, ², ³; ~*-basket*, for waste odds & ends esp. of paper; ‖ ~*-book* in book-keeping, book in which rough preliminary entries of transactions are made; **wāste′FUL** (-tf-) a., extravagant, given to or exhibiting waste, whence **wāste′fuLLY**² adv., **wāste′fulNESS** n.; **wāste′LESS** (-tl-) a.; ‖ ~*-pap′er--basket*, receptacle for used paper etc.; ~*-pipe*, for carrying off used or superfluous water.

wāst′er, n. In vbl senses; also, article spoilt or flawed in manufacture; (sl.) good-for-nothing person. [ME; -ER¹]

wāst′rel, n. Thing spoilt in making; stray child, street arab, waif; good-for-nothing fellow; wasteful person. [f. WASTE² + -REL]

watch¹ (wŏ-), n. **1.** Wakefulness at night (now rare; *in the* ~*es of the night*, while one lies awake; *pass as a* ~ *in the night*, be soon forgotten). **2.** Alert state, being on the look-out, vigilance, constant observation, attention to what may come, (*keep* ~, *a* ~, *good* or *a good* ~; ~ *& ward*, orig. guard by night & day, now emphatic reduplication of ~; *on the* ~, waiting usu. *for* expected or desired or feared occurrence), whence ~′FUL a., ~′fuLLY² adv., ~′fulNESS n. **3.** (hist.). Man or body of men charged with patrolling streets at night, guard (BLACK¹ ~, orig. an armed company). **4.** (hist.). One of three or of four parts into which night was anciently divided (*first* etc. or *evening* etc. ~). **5.** Four-hour spell of duty on board ship (DOG-~, 2-hr); one of the halves (*starboard & port* ~ from position of men's bunks) into which ship's crew is divided to take alternate duty. **6.** Small timepiece worked by coiled spring for carrying on person (STOP-~). **7.** ~*-case*, outer metal case enclosing ~*-works*; ~*-chain*, metal ~*-guard*; ‖ *W*~ *Committee*, committee of a (county) borough council dealing with (policing &) lighting etc.; ~*-fire*, at night in camps etc.; ‖ ~*-glass*, disc covering face of ~; ~*-guard*, chain for securing ~ on person; ~*-key*, instrument for winding up ~*-works*; ~*-maker*; ~′*man*, (formerly, & still poet.) sentinel or member of street patrol, (now) man employed to look after empty building etc. at night; ~*-night*, last night of year esp. as celebrated by religious services; ~ *oil*, fine thin kind for lubricating ~*-works* etc.; ~*-pocket*, in garment esp. waistcoat, or separate for attachment to bed etc., holding ~; ~*--spring*, kind used in ~*-works*, also mainspring of ~ (cf. HAIRspring); ~*-stand*, small pillar etc. for hanging ~ on; ~*--tower*, post of observation usu. fortified;

~′*word*, (formerly) military password, (now) phrase expressing briefly the principles of a party etc. (e.g. *Equal pay for equal work*). [OE *wæcce* (*wæccan*, see foll.); cf. WAKE²]

watch² (wŏ-), v.i. & t. Remain awake for a purpose (now rare; ~*ed all night by his side*; ~ *& pray*); be on the watch, keep watch, be vigilant, look out *for* opportunity etc., exercise protecting care *over*; keep eyes fixed on, keep under observation, follow observantly, (*had him* ~*ed by detectives*; *if you don't* ~ *it*, colloq., take care or precautions; ~*ed pot never boils*, strained expectation makes time seem long); look out for, bide, await, (opportunity; ~ *one's time*, wait for right moment). Hence ~′ER¹ n. [OE *wæccan*, doublet of *wacian* (WAKE¹), f. Gmc *wakæjan* (OHG *wahhēn*)]

wa′ter¹ (waw-), n. **1.** Colourless transparent tasteless scentless compound of oxygen & hydrogen in liquid state convertible by heat into steam & by cold into ice, kinds of liquid consisting chiefly of this seen in sea, lake, stream, spring, rain, tears, sweat, saliva, urine, serum, etc., body of ~ as sea or lake or river, (*hot & cold, salt & fresh* or *sweet, smooth* or *still & rough* or *troubled*, HARD or SOFT, *aerated, saline, chalybeate, thermal*, BLUE¹, HEAVY, HOLY, MINERAL, etc., ~; *the upper* ~*s of the Thames*; *strong*~*s*, arch., distilled spirits; *table* ~*s*, esp. mineral ~s bottled for use at meals; *red* ~, bloody urine; *in smooth*~, going easily, past one's troubles; *on the* ~, in boat or ship; *by* ~, using ships, barges, etc., for travel or transport; *in deep* ~ or ~*s*, floundering, in great difficulties, in affliction; *still* ~*s run deep*, quiet manner may cover depths of emotion, knowledge, or cunning; FISH² *in troubled* ~*s*; *cup of cold* ~, symbol of charitable intent; *get into, be in, hot* ~, bring or have brought trouble or rebuke on oneself by indiscretion etc.; *throw cold* ~ *on* scheme etc., discourage or poohpooh it; *written in* ~, of name, achievements, etc., transient; *keep one's head above* ~, chiefly fig., avoid financial ruin; *the* ~*s*, rhet., the sea, as *cross the* ~*s*; *cast* one's *bread upon the* ~*s*, do good without looking for gratitude or immediate or definite return; *drink the* ~*s*, attend spa for health; *brings the* ~ *to* one's *mouth*, makes it water; FISH¹ *out of* ~; BETWEEN *wind & ~*; *pour* OIL¹ *on the* ~*s*; *spend money, shed blood, like* ~, lavishly or recklessly; *go through* FIRE¹ *& ~*; *fire & ~*, arch., symbol of necessaries of life not to be supplied to outlaw; HOLD¹ ~; *make, pass*, ~, void urine; *tread* ~, maintain position in deep ~ by action of marking time; ~ *on the brain, knee*, etc., morbid accumulation of fluid; ~ *bewitched*, very weak tea etc. or spirit-&-~; ~ *of life*, spiritual enlightenment; ~*s of forgetfulness*, Lethe, oblivion, death). **2.** State of tide (*high, low, ~*;

in low ~, fig., in depressed condition, esp. badly off for money; *high, low,* -~ *mark,* highest, lowest, point reached by tidal ~, also fig. of best & worst results of fluctuating process). **3.** Solution of specified substance in ~ (*lavender, rose,* etc., -~, scents; *soda, lithia, dill,* etc., -~, beverages or medicines). **4.** Transparency & brilliance of gem esp. diamond (*of the first* ~, of finest quality, often also transf. as *a genius, blunder, of the first* ~). **5.** (finance). Amount of nominal capital added by watering, see WATER². **6.** ~ (in compounds of which those especially that distinguish varieties of plants & animals are too numerous to be given separately), haunting, growing in, used or employed on, etc., the ~; of, for, worked or effected by, made with, containing, using, yielding, etc., ~. **7.** ‖ ~*-anchor,* = DRAG²- -anchor; ~ AVENS; ‖ ~*-bailiff,* customhouse officer at port (hist.), official who prevents poaching of fish in protected ~s; ~*-bed,* rubber mattress filled with ~ for invalid to avoid bed-sores; ~*-bellows,* blower made by suspension in ~ of inverted valved vessel by raising & lowering of which air is drawn in & expelled; ~*-bird*; ~*-biscuit*; ~*-blister,* containing colourless fluid, not blood; ~*-boatman,* kind of aquatic bug; ~*-borne,* (of goods) conveyed by ~, (of diseases) communicated or propagated by use of contaminated drinking-~; ~*-bottle,* esp. of glass for wash-hand-stand or dining table, also of metal etc. for soldier's kit; ~*-brash,* form of indigestion with eructation of watery fluid; ~*-*BREAKER²; ~*-buffalo,* the common domestic Indian buffalo; ‖ ~ *bus,* river craft carrying passengers on regular run; ~*-butt*; ~*-carriage,* conveyance of goods by ~; *W*~*-carrier,* Aquarius; ~*-cart,* esp. with ~ for sale or for watering roads; ~*- -chute,* slope of boards slippery with running ~ for tobogganing down; ~*-closet,* place for evacuation of bladder or bowels with arrangement for flushing pan with ~; ~*-colour,* pigment mixed with ~ & not oil, picture painted with such colours, (pl. or sing.) art of painting such pictures; ~ COMPRESS²; ~*-course,* brook, stream; ~*- -cracker,* kind of biscuit; ~*-cress,* creeping ~*-plant,* eaten as salad; ~*-cure,* hydropathy; ~*-diviner,* dowser (see DOWSING); ~*-drinker,* (esp.) abstainer from alcohol; ~*-fall,* stream falling over precipice or down steep hillside; ~*-finder,* dowser (DOWSING); ~*-fowl* (usu. collect. as pl.), birds haunting ~, esp. as objects of sport; ~*-gas,* got by decomposing ~ & used after treatment with carbon as illuminant; ~*-gate,* flood-gate, also gate giving access to river etc.; ~*-gauge,* glass tube etc. indicating height of ~ inside reservoir, boiler, etc.; ~*-glass,* tube with glass bottom enabling objects under ~ to be observed, also solution of silicate of soda used as a vehicle for fresco-painting, or

used for preserving eggs; ~*-gruel*; ‖ ~*- -guard,* (member of) Customs and Excise marine anti-smuggling service; ~*-hammer,* percussion made by ~ in pipe when tap is turned off, or by ~ in steam-pipe when live steam is admitted; ~*-hen,* = MOOR¹- hen; ~*-hole,* shallow depression or cavity in which ~ collects (esp. in the bed of a river otherwise dry); ~*-ice,* flavoured & frozen ~ & sugar; ~*-inch,* quantity discharged in 24 hrs through 1 in. pipe under least pressure; ~*-jacket,* case filled with ~ & enclosing part of machine that is to be kept cool; ~*-joint,* proof against leakage; ‖ ~*-junket,* sandpiper; ~*-laid,* (of rope) = CABLE¹-*laid*; ~*-lens,* magnifying lens made of glass-bottomed brass cell filled with ~; ~*-level,* surface of ~ in reservoir etc., also plane below which ground is saturated with ~, also levelling- -instrument made of glass tube to be held horizontal with two upturned graduated open ends in which the contained ~ must be at same height; ~*-lily,* kinds of plant with broad leaves & white or blue or yellow or red flowers floating on surface of ~; ~*-line,* along which surface of ~ touches ship's side (when loaded, *load- -~-line,* when empty, *light-~-line*), also one of the semi-transparent parallel lines formed in some papers in manufacture; ~*logged,* (of wood) so saturated, (of vessel) so filled, with ~ as barely to float; ~*-main,* main pipe in ~-supplying system; ~*man,* boatman plying for hire, also oarsman *good, bad,* etc., at keeping boat truly balanced etc., whence ~*man*SHIP(3) n.; ~*mark,* (n.) faint design seen in some paper when held against light indicating maker, size, etc., (v.t.) impress such mark on in making; ~*-meadow,* kept fertile by being flooded; ~*-melon,* one of two divisions of melon (the other being *musk- -melon*) with ellipse shape, smooth skin, & watery juice; ~*-meter*; ~*-mill,* worked by ~*-wheel*; ~*-monkey,* jar with long narrow neck for ~ used in hot countries; ~*-motor,* ~*-wheel,* turbine, small motor using ~ under pressure; ~*-nymph,* naiad; ~ OUZEL; ~*-pepper,* acrid plant found in wet places; ~*-pillar,* upright with revolving head for feeding steam-engines etc.; ~*-pipe*; ~*-plane,* plane passing through ship's~-line; ~*-plate,* with double bottom to hold hot ~ for keeping food warm; ~*- -platter,* kind of ~-lily with upturned edges to leaves; *W*~ *Poet* (the), John Taylor (d. 1653); ~ *polo,* hand-ball game with goals played by swimmers; ~*-power,* mechanical force got from weight or motion of ~, fall in stream capable of being utilized as force; ~*proof,* (adj.) impervious to ~, (n.) ~proof garment or material, (v.t.) make ~proof with rubber etc., whence ~**proof**ER¹ n.; ~*-ram,* hydraulic ram; ~*-rat,* = ~ *vole*; ~*-rate,* ‖ charge made for use of public ~-supply; ~*-sail,* below lower studding-sail close over ~; ~-*seal*, body of ~ used in bent pipe or about mouth of pipe to prevent passage or escape of gas; ~*shed*, line of separation between~s flowing to different rivers or basins or seas [cogn. w. SHED[1]], (pop.) slope down which ~ flows, (pop.) river basin; ~-*shoot*, pipe or trough throwing off ~ from house etc.; ~*side'*, margin of sea, lake, or river; ~-*skiing*, sport of being towed on skis behind a motor-boat; ~-*skin*, skin bag for carrying ~; ~-*soldier*, aquatic plant with flowers above surface; ~ *souchy* (sōo'shǐ), fish boiled & served in its own liquor; ~--*splash*, part of road submerged by stream or pool; ~*spout*, phenomenon in which whirling cloud forms a funnel-shaped pendant, which descends towards sea & draws up corresponding volume of whirling ~, the whole forming a pillar uniting sea & cloud; ~-*sprite*; ~-*supply*, providing & storing of ~, amount of ~ stored, for use of town, house, etc.; ~-*table*, string-course arranged to throw ~ off building, plane below which the soil or rock is saturated with ~; ~-*tiger*, larva of certain ~-beetles; ~*tight*, (of joint, boots, cask, compartment in ship, etc.) tightly enough fastened or fitted to prevent ingress or egress of ~ (~*tight compartments*, fig., keeping of subjects etc. entirely separate); ~-*tower*, supporting elevated tank to secure pressure for distributing ~-supply; ~-*tube boiler*, in which ~ circulates in tubes exposed to flames & hot gases; ~-*vole*, large vole haunting ~; ~*wag(g)on*, =~-*cart* (*on the* ~-*waggon*, sl., abstaining from alcohol); ~ *wagtail*, common pied wagtail; ~--*wave*, wave in the hair produced by ~--*waving*, a method of waving hair with the use of ~; ~*way*, navigable channel, also thick planks at outer edge of deck along which channel is hollowed for ~ to run off by; ~-*wheel*, kinds of wheel (*overshot*, *undershot*, *breast*, & *turbine*, *wheel*) worked by ~ & working machinery; ~-*wings*, floats fixed behind shoulders of persons learning to swim; ~-*witch*, = ~-*finder*, also kinds of bird; ~-*withe*, W.-Ind. vine so full of sap that branch broken off yields draught of ~; ~*works*, establishment for managing ~-supply, also ornamental fountain (*turn on the* ~*works*, sl., shed tears). Hence ~LESS a. [OE *wæter*, OS *watar*, OHG *wazzar*, (cf. ON *vatn*, Goth. *wato*), f. Gmc **wat*-, cogn. w. WET, L *unda*, Gk *hudōr*]

wa'ter[2] (waw-), v.t. & i. **1.** Sprinkle (road, plants, etc.), adulterate (milk, beer, etc.), with water. **2.** Give drink of water to (horse etc.), (of animals) go to pool etc. to drink. **3.** (Of ship, engine, etc., or persons in charge) take in supply of water. **4.** (Of smarting eyes, or of mouth when food is seen or food or pleasure eagerly anticipated) secrete or run with water (*makes* one's *mouth* ~, excites

desire or envy). **5.** (Chiefly in p.p., as ~*ed silk*) produce irregular wavy damask--like markings on (material) by moistening & pressing in manufacture. **6.** (finance). Increase (company's debt or nominal capital) by issue of new shares without corresponding addition to assets. **7.** ~ *down*, make (details of story etc.) less vivid or horrifying; ~*ing-cart*, with perforated pipe or other device for ~ing road; ~*ing-place*, pool etc. at which animals ~, also spa, also seaside place frequented at certain seasons by holiday--makers & invalids; ~*ing-pot*, with perforated nozzle or rose for ~ing plants. [OE *wæterian* f. *wæter*, see prec.]

Waterloo' (waw-), n. The battle in which Napoleon was finally defeated in 1815; (with *a* or *his*) crushing blow, decisive contest, chiefly in phr. *meet* one's ~.

wa'ter|ў (waw-), a. Containing too much water, over-moist, sodden, (esp. of cooked vegetables or fish); (of eyes or lips) suffused or running with water; (of liquids) too thin, actually or apparently diluted, resembling water, (fig., of expression, talk, style, etc.) vapid, insipid, uninteresting, feeble, (of colour) pale, washed out; indicative of rain (*a* ~*y moon*, *sky*). Hence ~iNESS n. [OE; -Y[2]]

watt (wŏt), n. Unit of electric power, rate of working in circuit when electromotive force is one volt & intensity of current one ampere. Hence ~'AGE n., amount of electrical power expressed in ~s, ~*t* METER n. [J. *W*~, engineer (d. 1819)]

Watteau (wŏt'ō), n. French painter d. 1721 (~ *back*, arrangement of woman's dress-back with broad pleat falling from neck to ground without girdle; ~ *bodice*, with square opening at neck & short ruffled sleeves).

wa'ttle[1] (wŏ-), n., & v.t. **1.** Interlaced rods & twigs as material of fences, walls, or roofs (~ *& daub*, plastered with mud or clay); (sing. or pl.) rods & twigs for such use; kinds of Australian acacia supplying such twigs, having bark used in tanning, & bearing golden flowers adopted as national emblem; (dial.) a wicker hurdle. **2.** v.t. Construct of ~; interlace (twigs etc.); enclose or fill up with ~-work. [OE *watul*, of unkn. orig.]

wa'ttl|e[2] (wŏ-), n. Fleshy appendage on head or throat of turkey & other birds; BARB[1] of fish. Hence ~ED[2] (wŏt'ld) a. [orig. unkn.]

waul, v.i. Squall, cry like cat. [imit.]

wāve[1], v.i. & t. **1.** Vibrate or be stirred with sinuous or sweeping motions like those of flag or tree or field of corn in wind, flutter, undulate; impart waving motion to (~ *sword*, brandish it as encouragement to followers etc.; ~ one's *hand* often *to* person, in greeting or as signal); ~ hand or thing held in it usu. *to* person, give direction thus *to* person *to* do, send (person *away* thus, summon (person) *nearer* thus, direct (person) thus *to* do, express *farewell* etc. thus; ~ aside, dismiss as intrusive or irrelevant. 2. Give undulating surface or course or appearance to (hair of head, lines in drawing, etc.), make wavy, (of hair, line, etc.) have such appearance, be wavy. [OE *wafian*, MHG *waben*, f. Gmc **wabh-* move to and fro; cf. WAVER]

wāve², n. 1. Ridge of water between two depressions or (also *breaker*) long body of water curling into arched form & breaking on shore (*the* ~*s* or ~, poet. & rhet., **the sea**, water; *attack in* ~*s*, mil., in successive lines advancing like sea-~s). 2. Disturbance of the particles of a fluid medium e.g. water, air, ether, into a ridge-&-trough oscillation by which motion is propagated & heat, light, sound, electricity, etc., conveyed in some direction without corresponding advance or without any advance of the particles in the same direction; single curve in the course of such motion. 3. Temporary heightening of some influence or condition or feeling (*a* ~ *of enthusiasm, prosperity, depression*; *heat, cold,* ~, rise or fall of temperature travelling over large area). 4. Undulating line or outline or surface, waviness. 5. Gesture of waving. 6. ~ *length*, distance in any undulation from one crest to the next; corresponding distance between points in the same phase in sound ~s or electromagnetic radiation, i.e. the speed of light divided by the frequency. Hence ~'LESS a., ~'LET n., (-vl-). [f. prec.; in sense 1 repl. ME *wawe*]

wāv'er, v.i. Oscillate unsteadily, flicker, quiver, (rare; chiefly of flame); (of troops) falter, become unsteady, begin to give way; be irresolute or undecided between different courses or opinions, be shaken in resolution or belief. Hence ~ER¹ n., ~ingLY² adv. [ME, f. ON *vafra* corresp. to MHG *waberen*, f. Gmc **wab-* WAVE¹]

wāv'y̌¹, a. Undulating, (of line or surface) consisting of or showing alternate contrary curves, (~ *hair*); ‖ *W*~ *Navy* (colloq., hist.), R.N.V.R. (from ~ line of insignia on sleeve). Hence **wāv'ILY²** adv., **wāv'INESS** n. [-Y²]

wāv'y̌², -ey, n. The snow-goose. [f. Amer.-Ind. *wawa*]

wawl. = WAUL.

wăx¹, n., & v.t. 1. Sticky plastic yellowish substance secreted by bees as material of honeycomb cells, bees~, white translucent scentless tasteless material got from this by bleaching & purifying & used for candles, in modelling, & for other purposes, (*mould* one *like* ~, form his character, on desired lines or induce him to act just as desired); substance resembling ~ in some respect, as the secretion of some other insects esp. *Chinese* ~, *ear-*~ or cerumen, *mineral* ~, esp. ozocerite, bee-bread, *paraffin* ~,

obtained from shale or petroleum, *vegetable* ~ or exudation of certain plants, SEAL²*ing-*~, COBBLERS'-~; (attrib., now usu. preferred to *waxen*) made of ~. 2. ~'*bill*, kinds of small bird with translucent bill; ~ *candle*; ~-*chandler*, maker or seller of ~ candles; ~'*cloth*, floor-cloth; ~ *doll*, with face etc. of ~, also person esp. woman with pretty but unexpressive face; ~-*flower*, HOYA; ~-*insect*, kinds that secrete ~, esp. that collected as Chinese ~ from which superior candles are made; ~-*light*, taper or candle of ~; ~-*myrtle*, candleberry; ~-*painting*, encaustic; ~-*palm*, S.-Amer. palm with stem coated in mixture of resin & ~; ~-*paper*, waterproofed with layer of ~; ~-*pink*, kind of garden-plant; ~-*pocket*, one of bee's ~-exuding apertures; ~-*pod*, = BUTTER-*bean*; ~-*tree*, kinds exuding ~ or encrusted with it by insects; ~'*wing*, kinds of bird with small horny tips like red sealing-~ to some feathers; ~'*work*, modelling-work, objects modelled, in ~, esp. dummies of persons with face & hands of coloured ~ clothed to look like life & be exhibited. 3. v.t. Smear, polish, encrust, treat surface of, with ~. [OE *weax*, OS, OHG *wahs*, ON *vax*, f. Gmc **wahsam*]

wăx², v.i. (Of moon between new & full) have progressively larger part of surface illuminated (cf. *wane*; ~ *&* *wane* also transf. of influence etc., undergo alternations of increase & decrease); (arch. & poet.) grow or increase; (with adj. compl.) pass into specified condition or esp. mood or tone (~ *fat, old, merry, facetious, indignant, pathetic, angry*). [OE *weaxan*, OS, OHG *wahsan*, ON *vaxa*, Goth. *wahsjan* f. Gmc **wahs-* cogn. w. L *augēre*, Gk *auxanō*]

wăx³, n. (sl.). Fit of anger (*is in, got into, put him in, a* ~). [orig. unkn.]

wăx'en, a. Made of wax (being ousted by attrib. use of *wax*); presenting surface as of wax (esp. of complexion, used with less of depreciation than *waxy*); impressible as wax, plastic. [OE; -EN³]

wăx'/y̌, a. Resembling wax in some way, esp. easily moulded or presenting smooth pale translucent surface; (of tissue) having degenerated into consistency resembling wax (so ~*y liver* etc.); ‖ (sl.) angry, quick-tempered. Hence ~iLY² adv., ~iNESS n. [WAX¹, ³, -Y²]

way, n. 1. Road or track lit. or fig. provided for passing along (HIGH~; OVER *the* ~; ‖ *permanent* ~, complete piece of regular railroad track; ‖ *six-foot* ~, space left between each pair of rails & the next on railway; *covered* ~, roofed or in fortif. screened passage; *Appian, Latin*, etc., *Way*, great Roman roads in Italy; MILKY ~; *the* ~ *of the Cross*, series of paintings in church etc., to receive successive attention in certain services, illustrating Christ's progress to Calvary; *go the* ~ *of* all the earth, *of all flesh, of nature*, die; *pave the ~ for*, take steps that will facilitate or prepare people's minds to accept some change); (pl.) structure of timber etc. on which new ship is slid down at launch. **2.** Best route or route taken or contemplated between two places or to place, method or plan for attaining object, person's desired or chosen course of action, (*ask the* or one's ~; *farthest~ about is nearest~ home*, short cuts are delusive; *find* one's or *the* ~, reach destination; *lose* one's or *the* ~, go astray; *parting of the ~s*, usu. fig., time for momentous decision; *take* one's ~, go in some direction, usu. *to* or *towards*; *go* one's ~ or *~s*, depart; *came by ~ of London*, via; *lead the ~*, act as guide or leader, show by example how thing can be done; *put* oneself *out of the ~*, inconvenience oneself to serve another; *is nothing out of the ~*, not uncommon or remarkable; *an out-of-the--~ corner*, remote, inaccessible; *go out of the* or one's ~ *to be rude*, show gratuitous rudeness; *right & wrong ~s of doing a thing; that is the ~ to do it; don't like the ~ she smiles; where there's a will there's a ~; you will never manage it that ~; will find* or *make a ~; will do it one ~ or another; ~s & means*, methods esp. of providing money as in parliamentary *Committee of Ways & Means; go, take*, one's *own* ~, act independently esp. against others' advice; *have* one's *own* or one's ~, get what one wants, see one's orders carried out or desires gratified). **3.** Travelling-distance, length of road etc. (to be) traversed, (*India is a long ~ off; went a little, a good, a long, some, ~* with or *to meet him;* ONCE *in a ~; is still a long ~ off perfection*). **4.** Unimpeded opportunity of advance, room free of obstacles, ground over which advance is desired or would naturally take place, (GIVE[1], MAKE[1], ~; LION *in the ~; stand, be, in the ~ of, in* one's ~, or *in the ~*, be obstacle to, be obstacle; *get out of, in, the* ~, cease, begin, to be impediment; *get* thing *out of the ~*, dispose of, get rid of, settle; *put* person *out of the ~*, confine or secretly kill him; *clear the ~*, remove obstacles, stand aside; RIGHT *of ~; put* one *in the ~ of a good bargain, of doing*, give him opportunity). **5.** Being engaged, time spent, in locomotion lit. or fig. (*with songs to clear the ~; met him on the ~ out* or *home; is on the ~*, travelling or approaching; *by the ~*, during journey, (fig.) incidentally, often used by speaker to introduce more or less irrelevant remark). **6.** Specified direction (usu. in adv. phrr. without prep.; *which ~ is he looking, going?; look the other ~*, avoid meeting person's eye, cut him; appended colloq. to names of places, as *lives somewhere London ~*). **7.** Custom, manner of behaving, personal peculiarity, (*the good old ~s*, old fashions; *the ~ of a man with a maid;*

the ~ of the world, conduct no worse than is justified by custom; *it is not my ~ to desert people in misfortune; has a little~ of leaving his bills unpaid; it is only his ~*, piece of rudeness etc. from him has no special significance, so *pretty Fanny's ~*); specific manner of life (*I soon got into his ~s*). **8.** Scope, sphere, range, line of occupation, branch of business, (*hunting is not, does not lie* or *come* or *fall, in my ~; is in the grocery ~*, a grocer; *want a few things in the stationery ~*). **9.** Advance in some direction, impetus, progress, (*make* one's~ *home, into a shop*, etc.; *make* one's or one's *own ~*, prosper; *make the best of* one's ~, go as fast as one can; *make ~*, advance lit. or fig.; *gather, lose,~*, gain or lose speed; *give~*, of oarsmen, row hard; *~ enough!*, call to boat's crew to complete their stroke & then cease rowing; *ship has ~ on, is under ~*, moves through water). **10.** Respect (*not a bad fellow in some ~s; is satisfactory in one* or *a ~; in a ~*, to a limited extent, not altogether; *no ~ inferior*, not at all). **11.** Ordinary course (*did it in the~ of business*). **12.** Condition, assumption, hypothesis, state, train, degree, (*things are in a bad ~; have it* BOTH *~s;* ‖ *each ~, both ~s*, in backing horse etc., to win, to be placed; *any ~*, in either or any case or event; *we are all in the same~, live in a* SMALL *~; is an author, builds ships, in a small ~*, on small scale; ‖ *be in a ~* or *a great~*, colloq., be agitated; ‖ *be in the family ~*, with child). **13.** *By ~ of*, as substitute for or form of, with intention of, (*carries a stick by ~ of weapon; did it by ~ of apology, of discovering the truth; is by ~ of making an effort*, represents himself to himself or others to be doing so). **14.** *~-bill*, list of passengers or parcels on conveyance; ‖ *~-board*, thin layer separating thicker strata; *~'farer, ~'faring*, traveller, travelling, esp. on foot; *~'faring-tree*, white--flowered shrub common along roadsides, species of viburnum; *~lay'* v.t., lie in wait for, wait about for to rob or interview; *~-leave*, right of ~ rented by mine--owners etc.; *~-shaft* in steam-engine, rocking shaft for working slide-valve from eccentric; *~'side*, side of road (esp. attrib., as *~side flowers, inn*); *~-worn*, tired with travel. [OE, OS, OHG *weg*, ON *vegr*, Goth. *wigs*, f. Gmc **wegaz* f. **weg-*; cogn. w. WAIN, WEIGH, L *vehere*]

-way, orig. adv. acc. of WAY, = foll.; most advv. in *-way* have synonyms in *-ways*: *alway(s), crossway(s)*, etc.

-ways (-z), orig. adv. gen. of WAY (see -ES), now terminal element of advv., as *length~, side~, al~*; freq. used indifferently w. -WISE; see prec.

way'ward, a. Childishly self-willed or perverse, capricious, unaccountable, freakish. Hence *~*LY[2] adv., *~*NESS n. [aphetic f. *away*WARD, cf. *froward*]

‖ **wayz'gōōse**, n. Printing-house's annual

festivity. [1683 *waygoose* (also from 1731 *wayzgoose*), of unkn. orig.]

wĕ, pl. subj. of I[2] (used, besides the ordinary pron. use, by royal person in proclamations etc. instead of *I*, by writer in unsigned article of newspaper etc., & as collective name for speaker & all others of the class that context shows him to be representing for the moment). [OE *wĕ*, OS *wī*, *wĕ*, OHG *wir*, ON *vér*, Goth. *weis*, f. Gmc *wīz*, cogn. w. Skr. *vayām*]

weak, a. 1. Wanting in strength or power or number, fragile, easily broken or bent or defeated, (~ *barrier*, *rope*, etc.; ~ AS *a rat*, *water*; *a ~ eleven*, of poor players; *offer but a ~ resistance*; ~ *vessel*, fig., unreliable person; *a ~ crew*, short-handed; ~ *hand*, deficient in high cards; *the ~er sex*, women; *the ~est goes to the* WALL; ~ *knees*, usu. fig., inability to stand firm, want of resolution, whence ~-kneED[2] (-nĕd) a.; ~ *ending* in blank verse, unaccented or proclitic word such as *if* at end). 2. Wanting in vigour, not acting strongly, sickly, feeble, (~ *constitution*, want of power to resist disease etc.; ~ *stomach*, easily upset; ~ *eyes*, *sight*, easily tired or not seeing well, whence ~-eyED[2] (-īd), ~-sightED[2], aa.; ~ *heart*, acting feebly; ~ *mind*, *head*, below average in intelligence, verging on idiocy, whence ~-mindED[2], ~-headED[2], aa.; so ~ *intellect*; ~ *imagination*; ~ *voice*, easily tired or not reaching far; ~ *demand* for goods or stocks, slack; so *the market was* ~). 3. Wanting in resolution or power of resisting temptation, easily led, (~ *character*, *man*; person's ~ *side* or *point*, at which he is open to temptation); (of action) indicating want of resolution in agent (*a ~ surrender*, *compliance*). 4. Unconvincing, logically deficient, (~ *logic*, *evidence*; *a ~ argument*). 5. (Of mixed liquid or solution) watery, thin, (~ *tea*, *brandy-&-water*, *brine*). 6. (Of style etc.) not nervous or well-knit, diffuse, slipshod. 7. (gram.). Inflected by consonantal additions to, not vowel change in, stem (in English esp. of verbs making past & p.p. by addition of *-ed*). Hence ~'EN[6] v.t. & i., ~'ISH[1](2) a., ~'lȳ[1] [-LY[2]] adv. [ME, f. ON *veikr*, corresp. to OE *wāc* pliant, OS *wēk*, OHG *weih*]

weak'ling, n. Feeble person etc. [-LING[1]]

weak'lȳ[2], a. Sickly, not robust, ailing. [-LY[1]]

weak'nĕss, n. In adj. senses; also or esp.: weak point or defect; inability to resist a particular temptation; foolish liking or inclination *for*. [ME; -NESS]

weal[1], n. Welfare, prosperity, good fortune, (chiefly now in ~ *& woe*, ~ *or woe*, in COMMONWEAL, & in *for the public* or *general* ~). [OE *wela*, OS *welo*, f. Gmc *wel-*WELL[3]]

weal[2], n. Ridge raised on flesh by stroke of rod or whip, WALE. [var. of WALE]

‖ **weald**, n. District including parts of

Kent, Surrey, Hants, & Sussex, with geologically interesting characteristics; ~-*clay*, beds of clay, sandstone, limestone, & iron-stone, forming top of ~ strata, with abundant fossil remains. [OE *weald* forest, the WS equivalent of Anglian *wald* WOLD]

‖ **weal'den**, a. & n. 1. Of the weald, resembling the weald geologically. 2. n. Series of lower-cretaceous freshwater strata above oolite & below chalk best exemplified in the weald. [-EN[3]]

wealth (wĕl-), n. Welfare, prosperity, (arch.; *in health & ~ long to live*); riches, large possessions, opulence, being rich; the rich; abundance, *a* profusion or great quantity or display, *of* (*a ~ of illustration*, *wit*, *fruit*; ~ *of words is not eloquence*). Hence ~'y[2] a., ~'iLY[2] adv. ~'iNESS n. [ME *wellhe*, f. WELL[3] or WEAL[1] + -TH, after *health*; cf. MDu. *we(e)lde*, OHG *welida*]

wean[1], v.t. Teach (sucking child or animal) to feed otherwise than from the breast (often *from* mother or breast); disengage or cure *from* or rarely *of* habit, specified company, etc., by enforced abstinence or counter-attractions. [OE *wenian* accustom, OS *wennian*, OHG *wennen*, ON *venja*, f. Gmc *wanjan* f. *wan-*; cf. WONT]

‖ **wean[2]**, n. (Sc.). Child. [= *wee ane* little one]

wean'ling, n. New-weaned child etc. [-LING[1]]

wea'pon (wĕp-), n. Material thing designed or used or usable as an instrument for inflicting bodily harm, e.g. gun, bomb, rifle, sword, spear, stick, hammer, poker, horn, claw; action or procedure or means used to get the better in a conflict (*irony is a double-edged ~*; *use the ~ of a general strike*; *tears*, *the woman's* ~). Hence ~LESS a. [OE *wǣpen*, OS *vāpan*, OHG *wāfan*, ON *vápn*, Goth. *wēpn*, f. Gmc *wǣpnam*]

wear[1] (wār), v.t. & i. (*wōre*, *wōrn*). 1. Be dressed habitually in, have on, carry or exhibit on one's person or some part of it, (~s *green*, *serge*, *shorts*, etc., as usual colour etc.; *is ~ing diamonds*, on this occasion; *worn clothes*, that have been put on at least once; ~ *the crown*, *sword*, *gown*, *willow*, *breeches* or *trousers*, be a monarch or martyr, soldier, lawyer, desolate lover, husband-ruling wife; ~ *one's hair long*, *short*, etc.; ~ *a face of joy*, *sour look*, etc.; ~ *one's* HEART (*up*)*on one's sleeve*; ~ person or principle *in one's heart*, be devoted to; ~ *one's years well*, remain young-looking), whence ~'ER[1] n.; (of ship) fly (flag). 2. Injure surface of, partly consume or obliterate, damage, attenuate, or alter, by rubbing or use, suffer such injury or consumption or change, come or bring into specified state by use, rub (t. & i.) *off* or *out* or *away* or *down*, (*step worn with pilgrims' knees*; *worn clothes*, the worse for wear; *inscription has been worn*, or *has worn, away ;~ the freshness, the nap, off ; impression soon ~s off ; clothes ~ to one's shape,* fit better with use ; ~ one's *trousers, trousers have worn, into holes* or *bagginess ; seams ~ white, ragged, threadbare ; is worn to a shadow with care ; stick ~s down to a stump ; a worn* or *well-worn joke,* stale ; ~ *out,* use or be used till usable no longer). **3.** Exhaust, tire or be tired *out,* put *down* by persistence, (*worn with travel ; a~ing occupation, companion,* etc. ; ~ *out* one's *welcome,* go too often or stay too long as visitor etc. ; *his patience wore,* or *was worn, out at last* ; *succeeded in ~ing down opposition).* **4.** Endure continued use *well, badly,* etc., remain specified time in working order or presentable state, last long, (*won't ~,* of inferior material, transitory impression, etc. ; ~*s for years* ; person ~*s well,* retains youthful strength or esp. look). **5.** (Of time) go slowly or tediously *on,* pass (t. & i. of time) gradually *away,* (*winter, time, day, ~s on* or *away* ; ~ *away* or *out* one's *life* or *time* or *youth in trifles ;~ through the day,* get through it somehow). **6.** Make (hole, groove, channel) by attrition (usu. of incidental or undesigned action, cf. BORE¹ ; often of water). **7.** ~*ing-apparel,* clothes ; ~*ing-iron* or -*plate,* piece of metal attached to protect surface exposed to friction. Hence ~'ABLE a. [OE *werian,* = OHG *werien,* ON *verga,* Goth. *wasjan* to clothe, f. Gmc **was-,* cogn. w. L *vestis*]

wear² (wār), n. **1.** Wearing or being worn on person, use as clothes, (*the best materials for Sunday, working, spring, seaside,* etc., ~ ; *tweeds were in general ~,* fashionable ; *the coat I have in ~,* am regularly wearing). **2.** Thing to wear, fashionable or suitable apparel, (in phrr. on type of *motley's the only ~* ; also in *foot* etc. ~ chiefly in trade use as collective for things worn on feet etc.). **3.** Damage sustained as result of ordinary use (esp. ~ *& tear ; will stand any amount of ~ ; is the worse for ~,* damaged by use). **4.** Capacity for resisting ~ & tear (*there is a great deal of, no, ~ in it*). [f. prec.]

wear³ (wār), v.t. & i. (naut.; past & p.p. *wore*). Bring (ship), (of ship) come, about by putting up of helm (cf. *tack*). [orig. obsc.; perh. f. VEER by confusion w. WEAR¹]

wear⁴. = WEIR.

wear'|ў, a., & v.t. & i. **1.** Tired, with energy abated, dispirited (~ *Willie,* sl., habitually ~ person, tramp); sick or impatient *of* ; tiring, tedious, irksome ; hence ~ILY²adv., ~iNESS n. **2.** vb. Make ~y (esp. of or with importunity or monotony), whence ~iSOME a., ~iSOMELУ² adv., ~iSOMENESS n. ; grow ~y (esp. *of* importunity or importunate person), whence ~iLESS a. ; (chiefly Sc.) long *to do* or *for.* [OE *wērig,* OS *wōrig,* OHG *wuarag* (drunk), f. WG **wōrīga, -aga* ; vb f. OE *wēr(i)gian*]

weas'and (wĕz-), n. Windpipe, gullet, throat ; (pl.) sausage skins made from the windpipes of cows. [OE (OS) *wāsend,* OHG *weisant,* of unkn. orig.]

weas'el¹ (-zl), n., & v.i. **1.** Small nimble reddish-brown white-bellied slender-bodied carnivorous quadruped allied to stoat & ferret (*catch a ~ asleep,* deceive wide-awake person) ; ~*-faced,* with thin sharp features. **2.** *v.i.* Equivocate, quibble. [OE *wes(u)le,* OHG *wisula,* f. WG **wisulōn* of unkn. orig.]

weas'el² (-zl), n. Tracked amphibious vehicle, snow tractor. [official designation WSL (*water, snow, land*)]

wea'ther¹ (wĕdh-), n. & a. **1.** Atmospheric conditions prevailing at a place & time, combination produced by heat or cold, clearness or cloudiness, dryness or moisture, wind or calm, high or low pressure, & electrical state, of local air & sky, (*April ~,* showers alternating with sunshine, fig. smiles & tears ; FAIR³, FOUL¹, DIRTY, FINE, SOFT, ~ ; || *King's* or *Queen's* or *royal ~,* fine on ceremonial occasion ; *favourable, seasonable, good, bad,* etc., ~ ; *under stress of ~,* owing to storms etc. ; CLERK *of the* ~ ; *make good* or *bad* ~, naut., meet with ; *make heavy~ of,* fig., find trying ; *under the ~,* colloq., indisposed, out of sorts). **2.** ~*-beaten,* seasoned by or bearing the marks of exposure to storms ; ~*-board,* (n.) sloping board attached at bottom of door to keep out rain, (vb) supply with ~*-boarding,* -*boards,* horizontal boards of which each overlaps the next below to throw off rain as protective casing to wall etc. ; ~*-bound,* unable to proceed owing to bad~; ~*-box,* ~-indicator with figures of man & woman, one issuing to foreshow rain, the other fine~ ;~*-bureau,* meteorological office ; ~*-chart,* diagram showing details of ~ over wide area ; ~*cock,* revolving pointer often in shape of cock mounted in high place esp. on church spire to show whence wind blows, (fig.) inconstant person ; ~*-contact* or *-cross,* leakage from one telegraph wire to another due to wet ~ ; ~*-forecast,* prophecy of the day's ~ ; ~*-glass,* barometer ; ~*-map,* = ~*-chart* ; ~*-moulding,* dripstone ; ~*-*PROOF²; ~*-prophet,* person who foretells ~ ; ~*-service, -ship,* organization, ship, for meteorological observations ; ~*-stain,* discoloration of wall etc. by exposure ; so ~*-stained* ; ~*-station,* post of observation in connexion with ~*-service* ; ~*-strip,* piece of material used to make door or window proof against rain or wind ; ~*-tiles,* arranged to overlap like ~*-board-ing* ; ~*-vane,* = ~*cock* ; ~*-wise,* able to forecast ~ ; ~*-worn,* marked by storms etc. **3.** adj. (naut.). Windward (*on the ~ quarter, beam, bow,* etc. ; *have the ~ gage* or GAUGE¹ *of* ; *keep* one's ~ *eye open,* fig., be on the look-out) ; hence ~MOST a. [OE *weder,* OS -*ar,* OHG *wetar,* ON *vethr*

f. Gmc *wedhram, prob. f. root *wĕ- to blow (WIND[1])]

wea'ther[2] (wĕdh-), v.t. & i. **1.** Expose to atmospheric changes; (usu. in pass.) discolour or partly disintegrate (rock, stones) by exposure to air (esp. in geol.); be discoloured or worn thus. **2.** (Of ship or its crew) get to windward of (cape etc.); come safely through (storm lit. or fig.). **3.** Make (boards, tiles) overlap downwards, whence ~ING[2] n. [ME, f. prec.]

wea'therl|ȳ (wĕdh-), a. (naut.). (Of ship) making little leeway, capable of keeping close to wind. Hence ~iNESS n. [-LY[1]]

weave, v.t. & i. (wŏve, wŏv'en &, chiefly in some trade phrr., wove), & n. **1.** Form (thread etc.) into fabric, (fabric) out of thread etc., by interlacing, make fabric thus, work at loom; work up (facts etc.) introduce (details), into a story or connected whole, fashion (tale, poem, etc.); contrive (plot); move to & fro or from side to side; (R.A.F. sl.) dodge, take evasive action; wove(n) paper, with uniform unlined surface given by making in frame of crossed wire-gauze. **2.** n. Style of weaving. [OE wefan, OHG weban, ON vefa, f. Gmc *webh-]

weav'er, n. In vbl senses; esp.: artisan who lives by weaving (~'s knot, kind used esp. for joining cords of different size); (also ~-bird) kinds of bird remarkable for elaborate or dextrously made textile nests. [ME; -ER[1]]

weazen. See WIZENED.

wĕb, n. **1.** Woven fabric, amount woven in one piece, (also fig., as a ~ of lies). **2.** Cob~ (with help of context only; often spider's ~), similar product of any spinning creature, gossamer, etc. **3.** Membrane filling spaces between toes esp. of swimming bird or bat; connective tissue. **4.** Vane of feather. **5.** Large roll of paper used esp. in newspaper-printing. **6.** Thin flat part connecting more solid parts in machinery etc., e.g. part of railway-carriage wheel between nave & rim. **7.** ~-eye, disease of eye with film or excrescence, whence ~'eyED[2] (-ĭd) a.; ~-fingers, -toes, abnormally or normally connected with ~, whence ~-fingerED[2], ~'toED[2] (-tŏd), aa.; ~-foot, with ~-toes, whence ~-footED[2] a.; ~-wheel, with plate or ~ instead of spokes, or with rim, spokes, & centre, in one piece as in watch-wheels; ~-worm, kinds of gregarious larvae spinning large ~s to sleep or to feed on enclosed foliage in. Hence ~bED[2] (-bd) a. [OE web(b), OS webbi, OHG weppi, ON vefr f. Gmc *wabjam f. *wabh- var. of *webh- WEAVE]

wĕbb'ing, n. Strong narrow fabric such as is used for horse-girths, gymnastic belts, etc.; stronger edging of more delicate fabric. [-ING[1]]

wĕd, v.t. & i. (~ded, ~ded or rarely & not in adj. use wed). (Of party, priest, or parent etc.) MARRY[1] (t. & i., rhet. exc. in

p.p. ~ded in adj. use, as a ~ded pair; ~ded life, bliss, etc., in matrimony; newly-~s n., newly-~ded pair); unite (qualities often separated; ~ efficiency to economy); (p.p.) devoted to opinions, pursuits, etc., so as to be unable to abandon them. [OE weddian to pledge, OHG wettōn, ON vethja, Goth. gawadjōn, f. Gmc *wadhjam pledge (whence Goth. wadi, OE (now dial.) wed); cf. GAGE[1]]

wĕdd'ing, n. Marriage ceremony (& festivities); silver, ruby, golden, diamond, ~, 25th, 40th, 50th, 60th or 75th, anniversary of ~; || penny ~, with money contributions from guests; ~ breakfast, entertainment usual between ~ ceremony & departure for honeymoon; ~-cake, distributed to ~-guests & sent in portions to absent friends; ~-cards, with names of pair sent to friends as announcement of ~; ~-day, day or anniversary of ~; ~-favour, white rosette or knot of ribbons worn in honour of ~; ~ garment, qualification for participating in feast of some kind (ref. to Matt. xxii. 11); ~-ring, that put on bride's finger at ~-ceremony & freq. worn constantly as distinctive mark of married woman. [ME; -ING[1]]

wĕdge, n., & v.t. **1.** Piece of wood or metal of which one end is an acute-angled edge formed by two converging planes used to split wood or rock or widen opening or exert force in various ways, one of the MECHANICAL powers (or a special application of the INCLINE[1]d plane), (thin end of the ~, change, measure, action, etc., that will lead to further changes or developments & is therefore of more importance than it seems); anything resembling a ~ in being chiefly outlined by two radial planes or lines converging at acute angle (a ~ of cake etc.; the seats are disposed in ~s; drew up his men in a ~); golf-club with ~-shaped head used for approaching; ~-shaped, like solid ~, also V-shaped; ~-tailed, of birds having middle tail-feathers longest; hence ~-WISE adv. **2.** v.t. Split with ~ (rare); fasten by use of ~; thrust or pack (usu. in) tightly between other things or persons; push off or away like a ~. [OE wecg, OS weggi, OHG wecki, ON veggr, f. Gmc *wagjaz]

Wĕdg'wŏod, n. Kind of superior (semi-) vitrified pottery or ware made by Josiah ~ (d. 1795) and his successors; (attrib.) of the blue colour characteristic of ~. [P]

wĕd'lŏck, n. The married state (born in lawful ~, legitimately, of married parents). [OE wedlāc (wed pledge, lāc n. of action suf.) marriage vow]

Wednesday (wĕnz'dĭ), n. Fourth day of week (ASH[2] ~). [OE wōdnes dæg day of (the god) Woden, transl. of LL Mercurii dies]

wee, a. (~er, ~est). Little, very small, (esp. in nursery, Sc., & Ir. use); Wee Frees, nickname for part of Free Church of

Scotland that refused inclusion in the United Free Church in 1900. [f. north. ME *wei* f. Anglian *wēg*(*e*) = West Saxon **wǣg*(*e*), whence WEIGH rel. to WEY]

weed, n., & v.t. & i. **1.** Wild herb springing where it is not wanted (*ill* ~s *grow apace*, gibe at tall or fast-growing child); *the* (*Indian, soothing*, etc.) ~, tobacco; lanky & weakly horse or person; ~*-grown*, ~y or overgrown with ~s; hence ~'LESS, ~'Y², aa., ~'iNESS n. **2.** vb. Clear (ground) of ~s (also fig.), cut off or uproot ~s, whence ~'ER¹(1, 2) n.; sort *out* (inferior parts or members of a quantity or company) for riddance, rid (quantity or company) of inferior members etc. [OE *wēod*, OS *wiod*, of unkn. orig.; vb f. OE *wēodian* = OS *wiodon*]

weeds (-z), n. pl. Mourning worn by widow (usu. *widow's* ~). [OE *wǣd* garment, = OS *wād*, OHG *wāt*, ON *váth*, f. Gmc **wǣdhiz*]

week, n. **1.** Period of seven days reckoned from midnight on Saturday–Sunday (*what day of the* ~ *is it?*, is it Sunday, Monday, Tuesday, Wednesday, Thursday, Friday, or Saturday?; HOLY, PASSION, EASTER, ~; ~ *of Sundays* ~*s*, seven ~s; *feast of* ~*s*, Jewish PENTECOST; *middle of next* ~, see KNOCK¹). **2.** Period of seven days reckoned from any point (*can you come to us for a* ~*?*; *today* ~, 7 days hence; *tomorrow, yesterday, Friday*, etc., ~, day later, earlier, than such future, past, day by a ~; *have not seen you for* ~*s*; *did it* ~*s ago*). **3.** The six days between Sundays. **4.** ~*-day*, any day other than Sunday; ~*-end*, Sunday & parts of Saturday & Monday (occas. from Friday to Tuesday) as time for holiday or visit, (v.i.) make ~*-end* visit etc., whence ~*-ĕn'dER¹* n. [OE *wice*, OS *-wika*, OHG *wehha, wohha*, ON *vika*, (cf. Goth. *wikō*), f. Gmc **wikōn*]

week'lỹ, a., & adv., & n. **1.** (Occurring, issuing, done, etc.) once a week, every week; of or for or lasting a week. **2.** n. ~ newspaper or periodical. [-LY¹, ²]

ween, v.t. (poet.). Be of opinion (usu. *I* ~ abs. & parenthet. also with *that* expressed or omitted), expect *to* get etc. [OE *wēnan*, OS *wānian*, OHG *wānen*, ON *væna*, Goth *wēnjan*, f. Gmc **wænjan*]

weep, v.i. & t. (*wĕpt*). **1.** Shed tears (*for* person; *for* pain, rage, joy, etc.); shed tears for, lament over, bewail. **2.** Send forth or be covered with drops, come or send forth in drops, exude, sweat, drip, (~*ing eczema*, with exudation; ~*ing pipe*, designed to drip at intervals); *W~ing Cross* (hist.), wayside cross for penitents to pray at (*come home by W~ing Cross*, be made to repent one's conduct etc.). **3.** (Of tree) have drooping branches (chiefly in part. as distinctive epithet of variety, ~*ing birch, willow*, etc.). **4.** ~ *out*, utter with tears; ~ one*self out*, ~ one's fill; ~ *away*, consume (time) in ~*ing*.

[OE *wēpan*, OS *wōpian*, OHG *wuofan*, ON *œpa*, Goth. *wōpjan* f. Gmc **wōp*-lamentation]

weep'er, n. In vbl senses; also or esp.: hired mourner at funeral; crape hat-sash worn by men at funerals; widow's black crape veil; (pl.) widow's white cuffs. [ME; -ER¹]

weev'er, n. Kinds of fish (*dragon & lesser* ~) with sharp dorsal spines inflicting wound that often festers. [f. OF *vivre* weever, orig. = serpent, see WIVERN]

weev'il, n. Kinds of beetle with head extended into a proboscis feeding on grain, nuts, fruit, & leaves; any insect damaging stored grain similarly to corn- -~. Hence (of grain) ~lED² (-vld), ~Y² (-vlī), aa. [OE *wifel*, OS *-wivil*, OHG *wibil*, ON *vifill* f. Gmc **webhilaz* f. **webh*- (**wabh*- WAVE) move about briskly]

wĕft¹, n. Cross-threads woven into warp to make web; (loosely) web. [OE *wefta*, *weft*, = ON *veptr, vipta*, MHG *wift*, f. Gmc **weft*- f. **webh*- WEAVE]

wĕft². Var. of WAFT n. (naut.).

Wehrmacht (vār'mahχt), n. German armed forces. [G, = defensive force]

weigh (wā), v.t. & i., & n. **1.** Find weight of with scales or other machine, whence ~AGE(4) (wā'ij) n., balance in hands (as if) to guess weight of, (~ *sugar, luggage*; *meditatively* ~*ed his stick in his hand*; ~ *out*, take definite weight of, take specified weight from larger quantity, distribute, in definite quantities, by aid of scales, as ~ *out butter, portions* or *3 lb. of butter*); ascertain one's own weight (*when did you* ~ *last?*; ~ *out, in*, of jockey before & after race, & transf. ~ *in*, enter an appearance; ~ *in with* argument etc., produce it triumphantly). **2.** Estimate relative value or importance of, compare *with* or *against* or abs., consider with a view to choice or rejection or preference, (~ *consequences, pros & cons, oath* or *argument with* or *against* another; ~ one's *words*, select such as express neither more nor less than one means; ~ *the* claims, merits, etc., *of rival candidates*). **3.** Be equal to or balance (specified weight) in the scales, (fig.) have specified importance, exercise pressure or influence, have weight or importance, be heavy or burdensome, (~*s a ton, 6 oz*, *little, nothing, light, heavy, heavily*; ~ *heavy* etc., or abs., *upon*, be burdensome or depressing to; *the point that* ~*s with me*). Bring *down* by weight lit. or fig., (of counterweight) force *up*, (*fruit* ~*s down branch*; *one good argument* ~*s down six bad ones*; ~*ed down with* ~*ares*; *bucket is* ~*ed up by mass of iron at end of lever*). **5.** Raise from below water (~ *anchor*, start for voyage; ~ *ship* (rare), refloat it when sunk). **6.** ~*-beam*, portable steelyard suspended in frame; ~*'bridge*, ~ing-machine with plate on to which vehicles etc. can be driven to be ~ed;

~-*house*, building in which goods can be ~ed officially; ~-*lock*, canal lock with provision for ~ing barges; ~*ing-machine*, usu. for great weights or of more complicated mechanism than simple balance. **7.** n. Process or occasion of ~ing; *under* ~, by erron. assoc. with (*under*) WAY. [OE, OS, OHG *wegan*, ON *vega* lift, weigh, Goth. *gawigan* shake, f. Gmc *weg-*, *wag-*, *wäg-*, cf. WAG[1], WAIN, WAY; n. f. OE *wäg(e)*, see WEY]

weight[1] (wāt), n. **1.** Force with which body tends to centre of attraction (*the* ~s *of the planets*); (of terrestrial things) degree of downward tendency in body produced as resultant of earth's gravitation & centrifugal force (*the* ~ *of a body varies with latitude & altitude, its mass does not*). **2.** Relative mass or quantity of matter contained, downward force, heaviness, regarded as a property of bodies (*superior both in size & in* ~; *he is twice your* ~; DEAD ~; ~ *of metal*, total amount that can be thrown by ship's gun at one discharge). **3.** Body's mass numerically expressed in some recognized scale (*what is your* ~?; *reached the* ~ *of 12 st.*); scale or notation for expressing ~s (TROY, AVOIRDUPOIS, ~); BOX[5]*ing* ~s. **4.** Heavy body (*keep papers down with a* ~; *clock is worked by* ~s; *must not lift* ~s); piece of metal etc. of known mass used in scales for weighing articles (*where is the ounce* ~?). **5.** Load to be supported (*the pillars have a great* ~ *to bear*), heavy burden *of* care, responsibility, etc. **6.** Importance, convincing effect, influence, preponderance, (*considerations of no* ~; *men of* ~; *has great* ~ *with me*; *the* ~ *of evidence is against him*). Hence ~LESS a. [OE *wiht*, (M)Du., (M)LG *wicht*, ON *vétt* f. Gmc *wehtiz* f. *weg-* WEIGH]

weight[2] (wāt), v.t. Attach a weight to, hold down with a weight or weights; impede or burden with load lit. or fig.; treat (fabric) with mineral etc. to make it seem stouter; (statistics) multiply components of (average) by compensating factors. Hence ~'ING[1] (wāt-)n., extra pay or allowances given in special cases. [f. prec.]

weight'|ў (wāt-), a. Weighing much, heavy; momentous, important; well--weighed, evidencing thought, deserving of consideration; influential, authoritative. Hence ~iLY[2] adv., ~iNESS n. [-Y[2]]

weir, wear, (wēr), n. Dam across river to raise level of water above it; enclosure of stakes etc. set in stream as trap for fish. [OE (= MLG, MHG) *wer*, f. st. of *werian* dam up f. Gmc *war-*, cf. WARE[3]]

‖ **weird**[1] (wērd), n. Fate, destiny, (chiefly Sc.; DREE one's ~). [OE *wyrd* destiny, = OS *wurd*, OHG *wurt*, ON *urthr*, f. Gmc *werth-*, *warth-*, *wurth-* become, see WORTH[2]]

weird[2] (wērd), a. Connected with fate (*the* ~ *sisters*, the fates, witches); super-

natural, uncanny, unearthly; (colloq.) queer, odd, old-fashioned, strange, incomprehensible. Hence ~'LY[2] adv., ~NESS n. [ME, attrib. use of prec., in ~ *sister(s)*]

Weis'mannism (vīs-), n. A theory of heredity, in which transmission of acquired characters is denied. [A. *Weismann*, German biologist (d. 1914), +-ISM]

Welch[1], a. Obs. var. of WELSH[1] surviving in names of regiments (~ *Regiment, Royal* ~ *Fusiliers*; but *Welsh Guards*).

welch[2]**(er).** See WELSH[2].

wel'come, int., n., v.t., & a. **1.** Hail, know that your coming gives pleasure (often with adv. addition, as ~ *home*, *to Edinburgh!*). **2.** n. Saying *to* person, kind or glad reception or entertainment of person or acceptance of offer, gift, etc., (*bid* one ~, assure him he is ~; WEAR[1] *out* or *outstay* one's ~; *give warm* ~, show great joy at arrival, also make vigorous resistance). **3.** v.t. Say ~ to, greet on arrival, receive (guest, arrival, news, opportunity, event) with pleasure or signs of it. **4.** adj. Gladly received (*a* ~ *guest, interruption, gift, rest, denial, sight, etc.*; ~ *as snow in harvest*, un~; *make* one~, let him feel so); (pred. only) ungrudgingly permitted *to* do or given right *to* thing, absolved of thanking or recompensing, (*you are* ~ *to take what steps you please*; *any one is* ~ *to my share, to any service I can do*; *you are* ~, or ellipt. ~, no thanks required); hence ~NESS n. [orig. OE *wilcuma* (*wil-* desire, pleasure, + *cuma* comer) one whose coming is pleasing, w. later change to *wel-* = WELL[3] after OF *bien venu* (or ON *velkominn*)]

weld[1], n. Dyer's-weed, plant formerly used to dye yellow. [OE **wealde* = MDu. *woude*, MLG *walde*]

weld[2], v.t. & i., & n. **1.** Unite (pieces of metal, esp. iron) into homogeneous mass by hammering or pressure (usu. when iron is softened by heat but not melted), make by ~ing, (of iron etc.) admit of being ~ed *easily* etc.; (fig.) bring (recruits, parts, arguments, etc.) into homogeneous whole (usu. *into*); hence ~'ABLE a., ~ABIL'ITY n. **2.** n. ~ed junction. [alt. f. WELL[2] in obs. (exc. dial.) sense *weld* (heated metal), prob. infl. by p.p.]

wel'fāre, n. Satisfactory state, health & prosperity, well-being, (usu. *of* person, society, etc., or with *my* etc.); ~ *State*, one having national health, insurance, & other social services; ~ *work*, efforts to make life worth living for employees etc. [ME; WELL[1], FARE[2]]

welk, v.i. (arch.). Fade, wither. [ME, prob. of Continental orig., cf. (M)Du., LG *welken*]

wel'kin, n. (poet.). Sky. [OE *wolcen* cloud, sky, = OS *wolcan*, OHG *wolkan*]

well[1], n. **1.** Spring or fountain, (fig.) source, (poet. or arch.; ~ *of English undefiled*, Chaucer). **2.** Shaft sunk in ground

& lined with stone or other protection for obtaining subterranean water, oil, etc. (ARTESIAN ~). **3.** Enclosed space more or less resembling ~-shaft, space in middle of house from floor to roof containing stairs (also ~ *staircase*) or lift or surrounded by stairs (also ~-*hole*) or open for light & ventilation; || railed space for counsel etc. in court; receptacle for ink in inkstand. **4.** ~-*deck*, space on main deck enclosed by bulwarks & higher decks; ~-*dish*, with hollow for gravy to collect in; ~-*grate*, in which fire burns on hearth, receiving its air supply from below; ~-*head*, source, fountain-head; ~-*room*, where spa water is dispensed; ~--*sinker*, person whose occupation is sinking ~s; ~-*spring*, = ~-*head*. [Anglian *wella* = West Saxon *wielle* etc. f. st. of *weallan* to boil, bubble up, cf. OHG *wella* wave]

well², v.i. Spring (as) from fountain (often *up, out, forth*). [Anglian *wellan* (West Saxon *wiellan*) causative of *weallan* (prec.)]

well³, adv. (BETTER, BEST), pred. a. (*better, best*), attrib. a. (no comp.), & n. **1.** In good manner or style, satisfactorily, rightly, (*the work is* ~ *done*; *that is* ~ *said*; *a* ~ *situated house*; ~ *begun is half done*; ~ *done!*, *run!*, etc., cry of commendation; ~ *met!*, greeting to person one has been wanting to see; *come off* ~, have good luck, distinguish oneself; *wish I was* ~ *out of it*, without disaster etc.; *you did* ~, *it was* ~ *done of you, to come*). **2.** Thoroughly, with care or completeness, sufficiently, to a considerable distance or extent, with margin enough to justify description, quite, (*look* ~ *to yourself*; *judge* ~ *& truly*; *smack him, polish it,* ~; *is* ~ *up in the list,* ~ *on in life,* ~ *advanced* or *stricken in years,* ~ *past forty,* ~ *among the leaders of thought*; *as* ~, in addition, to an equal extent, not less truly, as *but he is a Christian as* ~, *he gave me clothes as* ~ *as food*). **3.** Heartily, kindly, laudatorily, approvingly, on good terms, (*love, like*, person ~; *treat* person ~; *think* or *speak* ~ *of*; *it speaks* ~ *for his discipline that he never punishes*, serves as commendation; *stand* ~ *with* one, be in his good graces). **4.** Probably, not incredibly, easily, with reason, wisely, advisably, (*it may* ~ *be that* —; *can, cannot,* ~ *manage it*; *you may* ~ *ask, say, that*; *we might* ~ *make the experiment*; *as* ~, with equal reason, preferably, without worse consequences, as *you might as* ~ *throw your money into the sea as lend it to him, as* ~ *be hanged for a sheep as a lamb, we may as* ~ *begin at once*; *that is just as* ~, need not be regretted; *you might as* ~, nursery formula of request). **5.** pred. adj. (often indistinguishable from adv.). In good health (*is she* ~ *or ill?*; *will soon be better*; *is best in the winter*; *quite* ~, *thank you*; *am perfectly* ~); in satisfactory state or position, satisfactory, advisable, (*am very* ~ *where I am*; *all's* ~; *it is all very* ~, ironical expression of discontent, or rejection of comfort, arguments, etc.; *it is* ~ *with him*; *it would have been, were,* ~ *for him if*; *it would be* ~ *to inquire*; ~ *enough*, tolerably good or good-looking; *as* ~, not unadvisable, as *it may be as* ~ *to explain*; ~ *& good*, formula of dispassionate acceptance of decision, as *if you choose to take my advice,* ~ *& good*; VERY ~). **6.** attrib. adj. (rare). In good health (*a* ~ *man should not be dawdling in bed*; *the* ~ *are impatient of the sick*). **7.** n. Good things (*I wish him* ~); what is satisfactory (*let* ~ *alone*, do not meddle needlessly). [OE *wel*(*l*), OS, OHG *wela, wola*, ON *vel*, Goth *waila*, f. same st. as WILL¹]

well⁴, int. expressing great astonishment (~, *who would have thought it?*; ~*!*; ~ *to be sure!*), relief (~, *here we are at last*), concession (~, *come if you like*; ~, *perhaps you are right*; ~ *then, say no more about it*), resumption of talk (~, *who was it?*; ~, *he says he must see you*), qualified recognition of point (~, *but what about Jones?*), expectation (~ *then?*), resignation (~, *it can't be helped*), etc. [ellipt. uses of prec. adv.]

well-. **1.** In a few words *well-* or *well* is inseparable pref.: ~-*being*, welfare; ~--*doer, -doing*, virtuous person, conduct; ~-*nigh*, rhet., almost; ~-*wisher*, person who wishes well to one. **2.** *Well* may precede any participle or word in -ED²; when the combination is used attrib. with n. following, it is usu. hyphened (*he is a* ~-*known person*); this is done in the pred. use also when the combination ends in -ING² or -ED², but not usu. when it ends in -ED¹ (*the stroke was well timed*, cf. *a* ~--*limed stroke*) unless it has acquired a sense or use other or more restricted than that of the separate elements (*my watch is well regulated*; *I do not think his action was* ~-*advised*, cf. *he is not well advised by his friends*); a list of the commoner combinations follows with special senses or contexts noted; ~-*advised*, prudent, wise, (chiefly of action taken); ~ *aimed*; ~--*appointed*, having all necessary equipment (esp. of expedition fleet, etc.); ~ *armed*; ~ *attested*; ~ *authenticated*; ~--*balanced*, sane, sensible, (esp. of mind); ~-*behaved*; ~ *beloved*; ~-*born*, of good family; ~-*bred*, having good breeding or manners, (of horse etc.) of good or pure stock; ~ *chosen*, esp. of words or phrases; ~-*conditioned*, not querulous; ~-*conducted*, characterized by good conduct; ~-*connected*, connected by blood etc. with good families; ~ *contented*; ~ *contested*; ~ *defined*; ~ *directed*, esp. of blow or shot; ~-*disposed*, having good disposition or kindly feeling (*towards*); || ~ *done*, (of meat) cooked through; ~ *dressed*; ~ *drilled*; ~ *earned*; ~ *educated*; ~-*favoured*, good-looking; ~ *fed*; ~ *fought*; ~-*found,*

= ~-*appointed*; ~*founded*, having foundation in fact (of suspicion or other belief or sentiment); ~ *furnished*; ~-*graced*, possessed of attractive qualities; ~ *grounded*, = ~ *founded*, also ~ trained in rudiments; ~-*informed*, having ~-stored mind or access to best information; ~--*intentioned*, aiming or aimed (usu. unsuccessfully) at good results; ~-*judged*, showing good judgement or tact or good aim (of action taken); ~-*knit*, compact, not loose-made or sprawling, (esp. of person or his frame); ~ *known*; || ~-*liking*, with ~-fed prosperous look (usu. *fat & ~-liking*); ~-*looking*, of attractive appearance; ~ *loved*; ~ *made*, (esp.) of symmetrical bodily make; ~-*mannered*, with good manners; ~ *marked*, distinct, easy to detect; ~-*meaning*, = ~-*intentioned* (of person or attempt); ~ *meant*, = ~--*intentioned* (of attempt); ~ *oiled*, (fig., of expression) complimentary; ~ *ordered*, arranged in orderly manner; ~ *paid*; ~ *painted*; ~ *pleased*; ~-*pleasing*; ~--*proportioned*; ~-*read*, having read much [cf. -ED[1](2)], with mind ~ stored by reading; ~ *regulated*, under proper control, not undisciplined; ~ *remembered*; ~-*reputed*, of good repute; ~-*rounded*, complete & symmetrical; ~-*seeming*, apparently satisfactory or good; || ~-*seen* (arch.), accomplished *in*; ~ *set*, compact, firmly knit, (esp., also ~ *set up*, of bodily frame); ~ *sifted* (esp. of facts or evidence); ~ *spent* (esp. of time or effort); ~-*spoken*, refined in speech; ~-*timbered*; ~ *timed*, opportune; ~ *trained*; ~-*tried*, often tested with good result; ~-*trod*-(*den*), frequented; ~ *tuned*; ~ *turned*, happily expressed (of compliment, phrase, verse); ~-*worn*, (esp.) trite, stale. **3.** ~ *off*, = fortunately situated (*does not know when he is* ~ *off*), sufficiently rich, is two words when used pred., but hyphened when attrib. (~-*off people*); ~-*to-do*, = sufficiently rich, is hyphened when attrib. & usu. when pred. also.

wĕlladay', -away', int. of grief (arch. or joc.). [OE *wei lā wei* alt. f. *wā lā wā* (woe, lo! woe) after OScand. **wei*; *welladay* 16th c. alt. after *lackaday*]

Wĕllingtŏn'ia, n. Kinds of sequoia. [named after Duke of Wellington, -IA[1]]

Wĕll'ingtons (-z), n. pl. Boots coming up or nearly up to knees. [as prec.]

Wĕlsh[1] (& see WELCH[1]), a. & n. (Language, *the* people) of Wales (~ *mutton*, from small ~ mountain sheep; ~ *rabbit* or by pop. etym. *rarebit*, dish of toasted cheese); ~*-man*, ~'*woman*, native of Wales. [OE (Anglian & Kentish) *welisc, wǣlisc* f. *wealh, walh* Celt, Briton, +-ISH[1]]

wĕlsh[2], **wĕlch**, v.t. & i. Decamp without paying (winner of bet on horse-race etc., or abs.). Hence ~'ER[1] n. [orig. unkn.]

wĕlt[1], n., & v.t. **1.** Strip of leather sewn round edge of boot or shoe uppers to serve as attachment to sole; wale; border or edging of garment etc., trimming. **2.** v.t. Provide with ~; raise wales on, beat, flog. [ME *welte, walt,* of unkn. orig.]

Wĕlt[2] (v-), n. (German for) world; ~--*ānschau'ūng* (-show-), philosophical survey of the world as a whole; ~'*politik'* (-ēk), foreign policy on the grand scale; ~'*schmerz* (-shmĕrts), vague yearning & discontent with regard to the constitution of things. [G]

wĕl'ter[1], v.i., & n. **1.** Roll, wallow, be washed about, be soaked or steeped or dabbled *in* blood etc. **2.** n. General confusion, disorderly mixture or aimless conflict *of* creeds, policies, vices, etc. [ME, f. MDu., MLG *welteren*]

wĕl'ter[2], n. **1.** Heavy rider (now rare) (attrib.) ~ *race, cup, stakes, handicap,* etc., horse-races for heavy-weight riders (also ellipt. ~, =~-race); ~-*weight,* heavy-weight rider, also weight carried apart from weight for age as test, (boxing) see BOX[5]*ing-weights.* **2.** (colloq.). Heavy blow, big person or thing. [orig. unkn.]

wĕn[1], n. More or less permanent tumour of benign character on scalp or other part of body; goitre; (fig.) abnormally large or congested city (*the great* ~, London). [OE *wen*(n), *wæn*(n), of unkn. orig.; cf. Du. *wen,* MLG *wene,* LG *wehne* tumour, wart]

wĕn[2], n. The Old English and early Middle English letter ᵽ (w). [OE, var. of *wyn* joy (see WINSOME) used as beginning with the letter, cf. THORN]

wĕnch, n., & v.i. & t. **1.** Girl or young woman, lass, (esp. of rustics or servants, or joc. & colloq.: *a strapping, buxom,* etc., ~); || (arch.) strumpet. **2.** vb. Court (dial.); whore, whence ~'ER[1] n. (arch.). [shortened f. ME *wenchel,* f. OE *wencel* child (*wancol* weak, tottering)]

wĕnd[1], v.t. & i. Direct one's *way*; (arch.) go. [OE *wendan,* OS -*ian,* OHG *wentan,* ON *venda,* Goth. *wandjan,* causative of Gmc **wendan* WIND[3]]

Wĕnd[2], n. One of a Slavic people formerly spread over N. Germany, & now inhabiting E. Saxony. Hence ~'IC, ~'ISH, aa. [f. G *Wende, Winde*]

Wĕns'leydāle (-zlĭ-), n. Kind of cheese. [~ in Yorks.]

went. See GO[1], WEND[1] etym.

wĕn'tletrăp (-tel-), n. Shellfish with spiral shell of many whorls. [f. Du. *wenteltrap* winding stair, spiral shell]

wept. See WEEP.

were, weren't (wẽrnt). See BE.

were'wolf, wer'wolf, (wẽr'wo͝olf), n. (myth.; pl. -*ves*). Human being turned into wolf. [OE *werewulf,* = (M)Du. *weerwolf,* MHG *werwolf* (G *wer-, wehr-*); the first element is usu., but doubtfully, identified w. OE *wer* man]

wert. See BE.

Wer'therīsm (vārter-), n. Morbid sentimentality as of Werther in Goethe's *Sorrows of Werther* (1774). [-ISM(3)]

Wesleyan (wĕz'lĭan, wĕs², wĕzlē'an), a. & n. (hist.). (Member) of the denomination founded by John Wesley (d. 1791). Hence ∼ISM(3) n. [-AN]

wĕst, adv., n., & a. (abbr. W.). **1.** Towards or in the region in front of observer on equator at equinox who faces setting sun (∼ BY¹ *north* or *south*; ∼ *of*, farther ∼ than; DUE¹ ∼; *lies* etc. *east & ∼*, lengthwise along line between east & ∼; *go*, *gone*, ∼, sl., die, dead); ∼*-north-∼*, ∼*--south-∼*, advv., nn., & aa., (regions) midway between ∼ & north-∼, south-∼ (with uses & derivatives corresponding to those of ∼, as ∼*-north-∼erly*, ∼*-north-∼ern*, ∼*-north-∼wardly*; see WESTERLY etc.); hence ∼'WARD adv., n., & a., ∼*-*WARDS adv. & n. **2.** n. Cardinal point lying ∼; western part of England, Scotland, Ireland, or Europe, part of U.S. beyond earlier settled States or ∼ of Mississippi; = OCCIDENT (*Empire of the W∼*, WESTERN *Empire*); western part of any country; ∼ *wind*. **3.** adj. Situated, dwelling, in or more towards the ∼; ∼ *longitude*; ‖ ∼ *central*, abbr. W.C., London postal district; ‖ ∼ *country*, part of England ∼ of line from Southampton to mouth of Severn; *W∼* INDIES, whence *W∼-Indian* a.; *W∼ End*, richer & more fashionable district in ∼ of London; (of wind) coming from the ∼; ‖ ∼*-country*, of or from or characteristic of the∼ country; ‖ ∼*-countryman* (or *-woman*), native of it; *W∼-end*, in or characteristic of W∼ End. [OE, OS, OHG *west*, ON *vestr* f. Gmc *wes-t-*, cogn. w. L *vesper*, Gk *hesperos*]

wĕs'tering, a. & part. Tending towards the west (usu. of sun). [f. *wester* vb f. WEST adv. +-ER⁵]

wĕs'terlў, a. & adv. = foll. (rare); (of direction) towards the west; (of wind) blowing from the west or thereabouts. [f. WEST as EASTERLY]

wĕs'tern, a. & n. **1.** Living or situated in, coming from, the west (*W∼ Empire*, one of two parts, with Rome as capital, of. *Eastern Empire* with Constantinople, into which Theodosius divided Roman Empire 395; *W∼* or *Latin Church*, part of Christian church that continued to acknowledge the popes at the Greek schism, see GREEK); = OCCIDENTA*l*; (of wind) westerly (rare); hence ∼ER¹(4) n., ∼IZE(3) v.t., make (oriental people or country) ∼ in ideas, institutions, etc., ∼MOST a. **2.** n. ∼er; a film or novel dealing with American cowboys, rustlers, sheriffs, etc. [OE *westerne* (-ERN)]

wĕst'ing, n. Westward progress or deviation esp. in sailing (cf. NORTHING). [-ING¹]

Wĕst'minster, n.· City forming part of London (∼ *Abbey*, fig., glorious death such as would entitle one to place among celebrities there buried); (the Houses of)

Parliament, the political arena; member of ∼ School; STATUTE *of* ∼.

wĕt, a., v.t. (-tt-), & n. **1.** Soaked, covered, dabbled, moistened, or supplied, with or *with* water or other liquid (∼ *sponge*, *land*, *road*, *table*, *eyes*, *cheeks*, *clothes*, *feet*; *am* ∼ *to the skin*, with clothes soaked through); *not prohibiting or opposing use of alcohol; (sl.) crazy, futile; ∼ BLANKET¹; ∼ *bargain*, closed with drink; ∼ BOB⁵; ∼ *bulb*, see DRY¹*-bulb thermometer*; ∼ *dock*, in which ship can float; ∼ *pack*, wrapping of body in ∼ cloths enclosed in dry blankets etc.; ∼ *plate* in photog., sensitized collodion plate exposed while ∼; rainy (∼ *day*, *weather*); ∼*-nurse*, (n.) woman employed to suckle another's child, (v.t.) act as ∼-nurse to (child); hence ∼'NESS n., ∼t'ISH¹(2) a. **2.** v.t. Make ∼ (∼ *bargain*, close it with drink; ∼ one's *whistle*, drink); hence ∼t'ING¹(1) n. **3.** n. Moisture, liquid that ∼s something, rainy weather; (sl.) a drink; *opponent of prohibition. [OE *wǣt* adj. = ON *vátr*, superseded in ME (*wet*) by p.p. of the vb; n. (OE *wǣt*) & vb (OE *wǣtan*) f. adj.; rel. to WATER]

wĕth'er (-dh-), n. Castrated ram. [OE *wether*, OS *withar*, OHG *widar*, ON *vethr*, Goth. *withrus*]

wey (wā), n. Unit of weight varying from 2 cwt to 3 cwt with different kinds of goods. [orig. identical w. *weigh* n., OE *wǣg*(*e*), balance, weight, OS, OHG *wāga*, ON *vág* f. Gmc *wǣg-* WEIGH]

wh-. In a few of the words beginning thus the w is, as indicated in the pronunc. brackets, not sounded; in all others the h is silent in ordinary modern usage, but the earlier sound, = hw, is retained by the Scots, Irish, Welsh, & northern English, & by some purists in pronunciation, as well as for the nonce in unfamiliar wds or such as might be confused with commoner wds having no -h- (*whet*, *whey*).

whăck, v.t., & n. **1.** Strike heavily with stick etc., thwack, whence ∼'ING¹(1) n.; (sl.) go shares in, distribute. **2.** n. Heavy blow esp. with stick; (sl.) share (*have had my∼ of pleasure*). [imit., or alt. f. THWACK]

whăck'er, n. (sl.). Thing or person big of its kind. [-ER¹; cf. *thumper*, *whopper*, etc.]

whăck'ing, a. (sl.). Big of its kind. [-ING²; see prec.]

whale, n. & v.i. **1.** Kinds of large fishlike marine mammal some of which are hunted for their oil, spermaceti, ∼bone, ambergris, etc. (*right*, *arctic*, *Greenland*, or *bowhead* ∼, kind yielding best ∼bone; SPERM², *humpback*, *bottle-nosed*, etc., ∼; *bull*, *cow*, ∼, adult male, female, ∼; *very like a ∼*, ironical assent to absurd statement, see *Hamlet* III. ii. 399). **2.** *A* ∼ *of* (colloq.), no end of; *a* ∼ *on*, *at*, *for*, very good at or keen on (something); ∼*-boat*, (double-bowed like those) used in whaling; ~'*bone*, elastic horny substance growing in thin parallel plates in upper jaw of certain ~s, & used in many kinds of manufacture; ~-*calf*, young ~; ~-*fin*, commerc. name for ~bone; ~-*head*, African bird allied to herons & storks; ~-*line*, superior rope 2 in. round used in whaling; ~'*man*, seaman engaged in whaling; ~-*oil*, train oil or sperm oil got from ~s. **3.** v.i. Be engaged in ~-*fishing*; *whaling-gun*, for firing harpoon etc. at ~s; *whaling-master*, captain of a whaler. [OE *hwæl*, = OHG *wal*, ON *hvalr*]

whāl′er, n. Whaling ship or man; kind of clinker-built seaboat with pointed stern, carried by some warships. [-ER[1]]

whăng, v.t. & i:, & n. (colloq.). **1.** Strike heavily & loudly, whack; (of drum etc.) sound (as) under blow. **2.** n. ~ing sound or blow. [imit.]

whăngee′ (-ngg-), n. Cane made from a kind of Chinese bamboo. [Chin. *huang*]

wharf (wôrf), n. (pl. *-fs, -ves*) & v.t. **1.** Wooden or stone platform beside which ship may be moored for (un)loading etc.; hence ~'AGE(1, 4) n. **2.** v.t. Moor (ship) at, store (goods) on, ~. [OE *hwearf*, = MLG *warf, werf*]

whar′finger (wôrfinjer), n. Wharf-owner. [app. f. earlier **wharfager*, f. *wharfage* +-ER[1]; cf. *messenger*]

what (wŏt), a. & pron. interrog., excl., & rel. **1.** adj.: (*a*) interrog., asking for selection from indefinite number (cf. *which* from definite number; ~ *books have you read?*; *don't know ~ plan he will try*) or for specification of amount or number or kind (~ *money, men, abilities, has he?*; ~ *news?*; ~ *matter?*, ~ *does it matter?*; ~ *good, use, is it?*, ~ *purpose will it serve?*; ~ *manner of man is he?*; *I know ~ difficulties there are*, cf. *c*); (*b*) excl., ~ *how great or strange or otherwise remarkable for good or ill (~ a fool you are!*; ~ *impudence!*; ~ *an idea!*; ~ *genius he has!*) or, before adj. & n., = how (~ *partial judges we are!*); (*c*) rel., = the — that, any — that, as much *or* many — as, (*dispose of ~ difficulties there are*, cf. *a*; *lend me ~ money or men you can*; *will give you ~ help is possible*; ~ *time*, arch., when, while). **2.** pron.: (*a*) interrog., = ~ thing(s)?, with many modifications given by context, & often in ellipt. uses for sentence, some of which are here illustrated (*so ~?*, colloq.; freq. implying that one is at a loss ~ to do or think; ~ *will people say?*, is it respectable to do it?; *W~?*, i.e. did you say; ~ *ho!*, excl. of greeting or hailing; ~ *is he?*, i.e. in respect of occupation; ~, *do you really mean it?*, i.e. I must have heard wrongly; ~ *if we were to try?*, i.e. would result; ~ *for?*, for ~ reason or purpose?; ~-*for* n. (sl.), severe punishment, reprimand, etc., as *he gave him ~-for*; ~ *though we are*

poor?, i.e. does it matter; ~ *next?*, no absurdity can outdo this; ~ *of* or *about* —?, i.e. ~ news?, or how can you dispose of this point?; *well*, ~ *of it?*, formula admitting fact but not inference etc. from it; ~ *is he the better for it?*, in ~ way or to ~ extent; ~ *is your name?*; ~ *not* usu. without interrog. mark, many other things of the same kind, anything; ~-*not*, piece of furniture with shelves for knickknacks; ~ *like is he?*, provincial for ~ *is he like?* or *what sort of man is he?*, ~-*d'ye- -call-him, -her, -it, -'em*, ~*'s-his* (or *-her, -its)-name*, substitutes for name that has slipped memory; *I wonder ~ you are*; *don't know ~ he said*; ~ *followed is doubtful*, cf. *c*; *cannot guess~ he was attempting*, cf. *c*; **~ have you* (sl.), anything else of that sort; *I know* ~, have a new idea; *I'll tell you* ~, i.e. the truth or right course is; *know* ~*'s* ~, i.e. a good thing etc. from a bad etc.); (*b*) excl., = ~ thing(s)!, how much!, etc. (~ *he has suffered!*); (*c*) rel., = that or those which, the thing(s) that, anything that, a thing that, (~ *followed was unpleasant*, cf. *a*; *did ~ he was attempting*, cf. *a*; ~ *I have written I have written*; ~ *I know not is not knowledge*; *give me ~ you can*; ~ *is called* the general reader; *come ~ will or may*, in spite of any results etc.; *tell me ~ you remember of it*; *but*, ~ *even you must condemn, he was lying*; *will do ~ I can for you*; *use no arguments but ~ you believe in yourself*; so also various more or less incorrect colloq. uses of *but ~* for *but*, as *not a day comes but~ makes a change, not a man but~ likes her, not a day but~ it rains, I never see him but~ I think, I don't know but~ I will*, NOT *but ~*; ~ *with* —, between various causes etc., as ~ *with drink & ~ with fright, he did not know much about the facts*). [OE *hwæt*, OHG (*h*)*waz*, ON *hvat*, Goth. *hwa* f. Gmc **hwat* f. Aryan *q^wod* (cf. L *quod*) neut. sing. of *q^wos* WHO]

whatĕv′er (wŏt-),**whate′er**(poet.;wŏtār′), a. & pron. indef. rel. used (1) = prec. in rel. uses with addition of or emphasis on indefinite sense (~ *I have is yours*; ~ *measures are considered best*; *do ~ you like*); (2) in indef. concessive clauses where *what* is not possible, =though any- (thing), as ~ *results follow*, ~ *happens*, ~ *friends we may offend, we shall have done our duty*; (3) ellipt. for ~ *it, he*, etc., *may be*,=*at all* after noun in negative context (never *whate'er*), as *there is no doubt ~, is there any chance~?, no one ~ would accept, cannot see any one ~*; (4) colloq. for *what* EVER. [ME; WHAT+EVER]

What′man (-ŏt-), n. (attrib.). ~ (*paper*), brand of paper used for drawing, water- -colours, engraving, & photography. [maker's name]

what′sō (arch.; -ŏt-), **whatsoĕv′er** (em-

phatic), **whatsoe'er'** (poet.; wŏtsŏāt'),
aa. & pronn. = WHATEVER (1, 2), & *whatso-*
ever = also WHATEVER (3). [ME, reduced
f. OE *swā hwæt swā*]

‖ **whaup**, n. Curlew (chiefly Sc.). [imit. of
cry]

wheal[1], mis-spelling of WALE, WEAL.

‖ **wheal**[2], n. (Cornwall). Mine (esp. tin-
mine). [Cornish *huel*]

wheat, n. (Highly nutritious seeds of)
kinds of corn-plant bearing dense four-
-sided spike of grain (esp. *winter* or *un-*
bearded ~, *summer* or *bearded* ~, &
German ~ or *spelt*); ~-*grass*, couch-grass.
Hence ~'EN[5] a. [OE *hwǣte*, OS *hwēti*,
OHG *weizzi*, ON *hveiti*, Goth. *hwaiteis*
f. Gmc *hwaitjaz f. *hwīt- WHITE]

wheat'ear, n. Small bird with white belly
& rump. [earlier *wheatears* (WHITE, ARSE)]

Wheat'stone bridge, n. Apparatus for
measuring electrical resistances. [C.
Wheatstone, English physicist (d. 1875)]

whee'dl|e, v.t. Coax *into* doing or *into*
good temper etc., persuade by flattery or
endearments, cajole, humour for one's
own ends; get (thing) by ~*ing out of* person; cheat (person) *out of* thing by ~*ing*.
Hence ~ER[1] n., ~ING[2] a., ~ING LY[2] adv.
[orig. obsc.; perh. f. OE *wǣdlian* beg
(*wǣdl* poverty)]

wheel[1], n. 1. Circular frame or disc
arranged to revolve on axis & used to
facilitate motion of vehicle or for various
mechanical purposes, machine etc. of
which a ~ is an essential part, object
resembling a ~, (BALANCE, CATHERINE, COG[1],
FLY[3], MILL[1], OVERSHOT, PADDLE, POTTER'S,
RATCHET, SPIN*ning*, STEER*ing*, SUN-*&-planet*,
UNDERSHOT, ~; *eccentric* ~, turning on
axis not at its centre; *fifth* ~, apparatus
enabling front ~s etc. of four-wheeled
conveyance to be slewed, also see FIFTH
~; ~*s within* ~s, intricate machinery,
indirect or secret agencies; *the* ~*s of life*,
the vital processes etc.; ~ *of life* (obs.),
scientific toy converting series of pictures
of successive attitudes into semblance of
continuous motion; *Fortune's* ~, ~ with
which Fortune is depicted as symbol of
ups & downs, also fig. vicissitudes; *break*
on the ~, maim & kill on medieval instrument of torture that revolved with
victim bound on it; BREAK[1] *butterfly on*
~; *a* FLY[1] *on the* ~; *put* SPOKE[1] *in* one's
~, one's SHOULDER *to the* ~; ~ *& axle*,
utilization of leverage given by difference
in circumference between ~ & its axle,
called one of the MECHANICAL *powers*; *go*
on ~*s*, smoothly); Fortune's ~ (*we may*
be rich at the next turn of the ~); steering-
-~ (*don't speak to the man at the* ~).
2. Motion as of ~, circular motion, motion
of line as on pivoted end esp. as military
evolution, (*street arab turning* ~*s in the*
gutter; the ~*s & somersaults of the gulls*;
right, left, etc., ~, words of command to
company etc. in line to swing round on
right, left, flank as pivot). 3. ~'BARROW[2];

~ *base*, distance between front & rear
axles of vehicle; ~ *chair*, invalid's on
~s; ~*-horse*, wheeler; ~*-house*, steersman's shelter; ~*-lock*, (gun with) antiquated lock having steel ~ to rub against
flint etc.; ~*-seat*, part of axle fitting into
hub; ~*-tread*, part of carriage etc. ~ that
touches ground; ~ *window*, circular with
spokelike tracery; ~'*wright*, maker of ~s.
Hence (-)~ED[2] (-ld), ~'LESS, aa. [OE
hweogol, hwēol, MDu. *wiel*, MLG *wēl*, ON
hjól, hvél, f. Gmc **hwe(g)ula*, cogn. w. Gk
kuklos CYCLE]

wheel[2], v.t. & i. Swing (t. & i. of line of
men etc.) round in line on one flank as
pivot, (loosely) change direction lit. or
fig., face another way, (often *round*);
push or pull (wheeled thing esp. wheel-
barrow or Bath chair or its load or occupant, or furniture on castors) in some
direction; go in circles or curves; ride on
bicycle. [ME, f. prec.]

wheel'er, n. In vbl senses; also: rear
horse in four-in-hand, tandem, etc.
(cf. LEADER); FOUR-~; ‖ wheelwright.
[WHEEL[1, 2], -ER[1]]

wheez|e, v.i. & t., & n. 1. Breathe with
audible friction; ~*e out*, utter with ~ing.
2. n. Sound of ~ing, whence ~'Y[2] a.,
~'ILY[2] adv., ~'INESS n.; (theatr. sl.) joke,
anecdote, etc., interpolated by actor
during performance; (sl.) scheme, plan.
[prob. f. ON *hvæsa* to hiss]

whelk[1], n. Kinds of marine spiral-shelled
mollusc, some used as food. [ME *wilke*,
welke f. OE *wioloc, weoloc*, of unkn. orig.]

whelk[2], n. Pimple. Hence ~ED[2] (-kt) a.
[OE *hwylca* (*hwelian* suppurate), see
WALE]

whelm, v.t. (poet., rhet.). Engulf, submerge, overwhelm. [perh. f. OE **hwel-*
man = *hwylfan* overturn, whence dial.
whelve]

whelp, n., & v.i. & t. 1. Young dog, pup;
young lion, tiger, bear, wolf, etc., cub;
disagreeable or ill-bred child or youth.
2. vb. Produce pups or cubs or (derog.)
child, give birth to (esp. derog. of human
mother); originate (evil scheme etc.).
[OE, OS *hwelp*, OHG (*h)welf*, ON *hvelpr*]

when, adv. interrog. & rel., pron., & n.
1. adv. interrog. At what time?, on
what occasion?, how soon?, how long
ago?, (~ *did, shall, you see him?*; *don't*
know ~ *it was*; *say* ~, ellipt., i.e. process
is to begin or stop; in rhet. questions
equivalent to neg. statement, as ~ *shall*
we see his like again?, ~ *did I suggest such*
a thing?). 2. adv. rel. (With *time* etc. as
antecedent) at which (*the time* ~ *such*
things could happen is gone; *there are*
occasions, conjunctures, etc., ~); at the
or any time that, on the or any occasion
that, at whatever time, as soon as, (*he*
exclaimed ~ *he saw me*; ~ *Greek meets*
Greek; ~ *it rains he stays at home*; *shall*
have it ~ *you ask politely*; also ellipt. like
WHILE[2], *as he looked in* ~ *passing*, ~

found make a note of; also introducing exclamatory clause with ellipse of apodosis, as ~ *I think what I have done for that man!*); although, considering that, (*walks ~ he might ride; how could you, ~ you knew it might kill him?*); *how convince him ~ he will not listen?*); after or upon which, but just then, & then, (*the conflict began, ~ it soon appeared which was stronger; we were just coming to the point ~ the bell interrupted us*). **3.** pron. What (interrog.) or which (rel.) time (*till ~ can you stay?, from ~ does it date?; since ~ things have been better*). **4.** n. Time, date, occasion, (*told me the ~ & the how of it*). [OE *hwanne* etc., = OS *hwan*, OHG *wanne*, Goth. *hwan*, f. interrog. st. *hwa-* (WHO, WHAT), as *then* is of *tha-* (THE, THAT)]

whence, adv. interrog. & rel., pron., & n. (now poet., literary, etc.). **1.** From what place or source ? (being ousted by *where* — *from* in lit. sense & *how, why*, etc., in fig.; ~ *comes it that*, how is it that; *no one knows ~ she comes*); (with *place* etc. as antecedent) from which (*the source ~ these evils spring*; now usu. *from which*); to or rarely at or from the place from which (*return ~ you came; abides ~ he sent me; comes ~ he came*; now usu. *where — from, from where —*); ~*soev'er*, from whatever place or source. **2.** pron. What (interrog.) or which· (rel.) starting-place (*from~ is he? ; the source from~ it springs*). **3.** n. Source (*we know neither our ~ nor our whither*). [ME *whannes, whennes*, f. *whanne* (OE *hwanone* whence, f. st. *hwa-*, see prec.) + *-ES*; cf. THENCE]

whenev'er, whene'er' (poet.; -ār), **whensöev'er** (emphatic), adv. rel. indef. (cf. *when* EVER). At whatever time, on whatever occasion, as soon as, every time that. [SO, EVER]

where (wār), adv. interrog. & rel., pron., & n. **1.** adv. interrog. In or to what place or position lit. or fig., in what direction, at what part, in what respect, (~ *is Heaven? ; ~ did you read that?*, in what book; ~ *are you going?*, now usu. preferred to *whither; showed me ~ they were; ~ does it touch our interests? ; ~ are you looking?, ~ shall we be if prices fall now?*, how situated; *don't know ~ to have him*, said of person of elusive character; often in rhet. questions = neg. statements, as ~ *is the sense of it?, ~ is the use of trying?*). **2.** adv. rel. (see also WHERE-). (With *place* etc. as antecedent) in which (*places ~ they sing*; also with ellipse of noun, as ~ *he is weakest is in his facts*); in or to the or any place, in the direction or part or respect, in which (~ *your treasure is; go ~ you like; is, send him, ~ he will be taken care of; ~ the ancients knew nothing we know a little; that's ~ it is*, colloq., that is the real reason for it or point of it).

3. pron. What (interrog.) or which (rel.) place (~ *do you come from, are you going to? ;* vulg. in rel. use, as *the place ~ he comes from*). **4.** n. Place, scene of something, (*the ~s & whens are important*; cf. *any~, no~, every~*). [OE *hwǣr, hwār*, OS *hwār*, OHG (*h*)*wār, wā*, cf. also ON *hvar*, Goth. *hwar*; f. st. *hwa-* (see WHEN); cf. HERE, THERE]

where- (wār). **1.**~ is written in one word with appended prep. as substitute for the prep. preceding or following *what* interrog. pron. or *which* rel. pron. (~*by shall we know him? ; the signs ~by he shall be known; ~by I saw that he was angry*), cf. corresp. compounds of *there*; the use is becoming rare exc. either in formal or poet. or in joc. or uneducated writing or in special uses as noted : ~'**about'** (& see 2); ~**at'**; ~**by'**; ~'**fore** (for what reason?, why ?, on what account, on which account : also as n. pl. = reasons as *the whys & ~fores*); ~**from'**; ~**in'** (also ~**inso-ev'er**); ~**in'to**; ~**of'**; ~**on'**; ~**out'**; ~**through'**; ~**to'**; ~**un'der**; ~**un'to**; ~**upon'** (still common introducing new sentence in narrative); ~**with'** (or ~**withal'**; the longer form common as n. = money etc. needed for a purpose; *has not the ~withal to do it, or the ~withal*). **2.**~ in its proper local use is qualified in sense by additions : ~**abouts'** adv. interrog., where within considerable limits or vaguely (~*abouts is he? ; don't know even ~abouts to look*), (n., ~'*abouts*) person's or thing's locality roughly defined; ~**as'** conj., taking into consideration or having as premiss the fact that (esp. in legal preambles), in contrast or comparison with the fact that, but in contrast with what has been said; **wherev'er, where'er'** (poet.; -ār), ~**soev'er** (emphat.), advv. rel. indef., in or to whatever place etc.

whē'rrȳ, n. Light shallow rowing-boat usu. for carrying passengers. [orig. unkn.]

whet, v.t. (-tt-), & n. **1.** Sharpen by rubbing on or with stone etc.; stimulate (appetite, stomach, desire); ~'*stone*, shaped stone for tool-sharpening, thing that sharpens the wits. **2.** n. Sharpening; small quantity taken to create or creating appetite for more; dram. [OE *hwettan*, OHG *wezzan*, ON *hvetja*, f. *hwæt* bold, cf. OHG *hwaz* sharp]

wheth'er[1] (wĕdh-), a. & pron. interrog. & rel. (arch.). Which of the two. [OE *hwæther, hwe-*, = OS *hwethar*, OHG *hwedar*, ON *hvatharr*, Goth. *hvathar* f. Gmc **hwa-, *hwe-* (see WHEN) + -THER; cf. OTHER]

wheth'er[2] (wĕdh-), conj. **1.** Introducing indirect questions of which the direct form would be answerable with *yes* or *no* (*don't know ~ he will be here*); such questions involve an alternative, which may be unexpressed as above, expressed precisely

(~ *he is here or~ he is in London*, or more usu. ellipt. *or in London*), or expressed comprehensively by the negative (~ *he is here or~ he is not here*, or more usu. ellipt. *or not*); i.e., the alternative if expressed has always *or*, after which ~ is usu. repeated if subj. & vb are expressed; ~- -clauses may be appended directly to many adjj. & nn. as well as to vbs (*doubtful, uncertain, anxious*, etc., ~; *the question* etc. ~), though *as to* is often needlessly inserted; DOUBT[2] ~; ~ *or* NO[2]; formerly also with direct questions (~ *shall we live or die?*). 2. Used with following *or* or *or*~ (according as second alternative has its subj. & vb expressed, as in 1) to introduce the protasis having alternatives corresponding to a single conditional apodosis (~ *we stay or~ we go*, ~ *we go to him or he comes to us*, ~ *we go or not, the result will be bad*); ~ *or* NO[2]; formerly also when each alternative had apodosis (~ *we live, we live unto the Lord, &~ we die, we die* etc.). [f. prec.]

whew (hwū), int. expressing (usu. joc.) consternation.

whey (wā), n. Part of milk that remains liquid when the rest forms curds; ~-*faced* (arch.), pale esp. with fear. [OE *hwæg, hweg*, MDu. *wey*, f. Gmc **hwaja-*]

which, a. & pron. interrog. & rel. 1. adj. interrog. Asking for selection from alternatives conceived as limited in number or known (cf. WHAT; ~ *way shall we go?*; *say~ chapter you prefer*). 2. adj. rel. And, now, although, since, etc., this or these (now rare exc. with n. serving to sum up details of a compound or vague antecedent; *a smile & a shilling*, ~ *equipment is within most people's reach, will suffice*; ~ *things are an allegory*); *the* ~, arch. for~. 3. pron. interrog.~ person(s), ~ thing(s), (~ *of you am I to thank for this? ; say~ you would like best* ; ~ *is~?*, ~ of two etc. given persons etc. corresponds to one of given descriptions etc., & ~ to another ?). 4. pron. rel. (cf. THAT). Used to convert what would in the simplest grammar be an independent sentence into a subordinate clause by being substituted for a noun expressed in it after being expressed or implied in the sentence to which it is to be subordinated; = ~ person or persons (arch.), ~ thing(s) as modified by context, (*Our Father,~ art in heaven; the river* ~, or better *that, flows through London*; *the meeting*, ~ *was held in the Park, was a failure; he said he saw me there,~ was a lie*; occas. in clause preceding antecedent, as *moreover,~ you will hardly credit, he was not there himself; the* ~, arch. for ~; in the possessive case *whose* is occas. for convenience preferred to the usual *of* ~, as *the only place whose supply of baths is adequate*. [OE *hwelc, hwile*, = OS *hwilic*, OHG (*h*)*welih*, Goth. *hwaleiks* f. Gmc **hwa-, *hwi-* + **likobody* (LIKE[1], -LY[1]); cf. SUCH]

whichev'er, **whichsŏev'er** (emphat.), aa. & pronn. rel. indef. used correspondingly to WHATEVER, WHATSOEVER, but with the restricted area of choice that distinguishes WHICH from WHAT (cf. *which* EVER). [SO, EVER]

whid'ah-bīrd (-da-), n. Small W.-Afr. bird, male of which has tail-feathers of enormous length. [orig. WIDOW-*bird*, altered f. assoc. w. *Whidah* in Dahomey]

whiff[1], n., & v.i. & t. 1. Puff of air, smoke, odour, etc. (~ *of grape-shot*, a few discharges; *want a* ~ *of fresh air*); (commerc.) small cigar; ‖ light uncovered outrigged sculling-boat. 2. vb. Blow or puff (t. & i.) lightly. [imit.; perh. partly alt. of ME *weffe* foul smell]

whiff[2], n. Kind of flatfish. [perh.=prec.]

whiff[3], v.i. Fish with line towing bait near surface. [orig. unkn.]

whif'fle, v.i. & t., & n. 1. (Of wind) blow lightly, shift about, drive (ship) in varying directions; (of flame, leaves, & fig. of thought etc.) flicker, flutter, wander; make the sound of a light wind in breathing etc. 2. n. Slight movement of air. [f. WHIFF[1] + -LE(3)]

whig, n. & a. (Member) of the political party that, after the Revolution of 1688, aimed at subordinating the power of the crown to that of Parliament & the upper classes, passed the Reform Bill, & in the 19th c. was succeeded by the Liberals (opp. TORY; DISH[2] *the* ~s). Hence ~**g'ERY** (4), ~**g'ISM**(3), nn., ~**g'ISH**[1] a., ~**g'ishLY**[2] adv., ~**g'ishNESS** n., (-g-). [c. 1648 of Scottish Covenanters, prob. short for *whiggamer, -more*, of unascertained orig.]

while[1], n., & v.t. 1. Space of time, time occupied by or given to some action etc., (*have been waiting all this* ~; *go away for a* ~; *in a little* ~, soon; MEAN[2]~; *once in a* ~, occasionally, at long intervals; *have not seen him for a long* ~, *this long* ~ *past*; *happened a long* ~ *ago*; *that is enough for one* ~, for some time; *worth* ~ or *my* etc. ~, repaying the time spent in doing it etc.; *looked in her eyes the* ~ or *whilst*, during some other process; *the* ~ or *whilst*, poet., during the time that). 2. v.t. Pass (time, hour, etc.) *away* in leisurely manner. [OE *hwīl*, OS, OHG *hwīl*(*a*), ON *hvīla*, Goth. *hweila*, f. Gmc. **hwīlō*, cogn. w. L *quies* QUIET]

while[2], conj. 1. During the time that, for as long as, at the same time as, (*please write* ~ *I dictate; Jones got 98* ~ *his partner was making 15*; ~ *there is life there is hope*; also with ellipse of pronominal subject & *am, is, was*, etc., as ~ *reading I fell asleep, we are safe* ~ *in his care, he retained the consciousness of it* ~ *asleep*). 2. In contrast more or less marked with the fact that simultaneously, although, whereas, (chiefly journalistic) and, (*Nero fiddling* ~ *Rome burns*; ~ *I have no money to spend, you have nothing to spend money on*; ~ *I admit his good* *points I can see his bad*; also erron. ~ *admitting* etc., cf. the correct ellipses above; *Jones lost an arm, Brown a leg,* ~ *Robinson had both amputated*). [short for OE *thā hwīle the*, ME *the while that*]

whiles. See WHILST.

whil'om, adv. & a. **1.** (arch.). Once, formerly. **2.** adj. Quondam (*his* ~ *friend*). [OE *hwīlum*, dat. pl. of WHILE[1]; cf. OS, OHG *hwīlon*]

whilst, whiles (arch.; wīlz), conj. & n. — WHILE[2]; (n.) *the* ~, — *the* WHILE. [ME, orig. in comb., as *sumehwiles* etc., (WHILE[1] +-ES), +-*t* as in *amongst, amidst*]

whim, n. Sudden fancy, caprice, crotchet; kind of windlass for raising ore from mine; ~'*wham*, arch. [redupl. of ~], plaything, toy, ~. [orig. unkn.; perh. symbolic]

whim'brel, n. Kind of curlew. [perh. f. foll., f. the bird's cry]

whim'per, v.i. & t., & n. **1.** Make feeble querulous or frightened sounds, cry & whine softly; utter ~ingly; hence ~ER[1] n., ~ingLY[2] adv. **2.** n. Sound of ~ing. [imit., f. earlier dial. *whimp* +-ER[5]]

whim'sical (-z-), a. Capricious; odd-looking, fantastic. Hence ~ITY (-zīkăl[2]) n., ~LY[2] adv. [foll., -ICAL]

whim'sy (-zī), n. Crotchet, whim. [see WHIM[1]]

whin[1], n. Gorse, furze, (used in pl. also); ~'*chat*, kind of small bird. [prob. Scand., cf. Norw. *hvine, hvēn*, Sw. *hven*]

whin[2], whin'sill, whin'stone, nn. Kinds of basaltic rock or hard sandstone. [orig. unkn.]

whin|e, v.i. & t., & n. (Make) long-drawn complaining cry (as) of dog; (utter) querulous talk; utter ~ingly (often *out*). Hence ~'ER[1] n., ~'ingLY[2] adv. [OE *hwīnan*, ON *hvina*]

‖ **whing'er,** n. Short sword, dirk, or long knife. [app. rel. to 15th c. *whinyard*, of unkn. orig.]

whinn'y, v.i., & n. **1.** Neigh gently or joyfully. **2.** n. ~ing sound. [imit., cf. WHINE]

whip[1], v.t. & i. (-pp-). **1.** Move (t. & i.) with sudden motion, snatch, dart, (always with adv. or prep.; ~ *behind the cupboard*; ~*ped away to France*; ~*ped up her toy terrier*; ~ *out sword, knife*; ~ *off* one's *coat*). **2.** Bind (cord, stick) with close covering of twine, sew (seam) with overhand stitches. **3.** Flog, lash, (horse, boy, etc.; ~ *in, off, together,* of managing hounds with ~, & transf. followers esp. in Parliament; ~ *stream,* fish it with ~ping motion; ~ *horses on,* urge with whip; ~ *fault out of* person; ~ *eggs, cream,* beat into froth); (sl.) excel, defeat, (~ *creation,* beat all). **4.** Hoist (coal etc.) with rope passed through pulley. **5.** ~*ping-boy,* (hist.) boy educated with & chastised for young prince, (fig.) scapegoat; ~*ping--post,* to which persons were tied to be

~*ped*; ~*ping-top,* kept spinning by blows of lash. Hence ~p'ING[1](1, 4) n. [ME; early hist. uncert.; f. (M)Du., (M)LG *wippen* swing, leap, dance, = MHG *wipfen* dance]

whip[2], n. **1.** Instrument for urging on or punishing with lash attached to short or long stick; *good, poor,* etc., coachman (esp. of four-in-hand or tandem driver). **2.** (Also *whipper-in*) hunt official subordinate to huntsman charged with management of hounds; ‖ (transf.) official appointed to maintain discipline among, secure attendance of, & give necessary information to, members of his party in House of Parliament, also written notice (variously underscored with number of lines representing degrees of urgency, as *three-line* ~) requesting attendance on particular occasion. **3.** (Also ~*-&-derry*) rope-&-pulley hoisting apparatus. **4.** ~*cord,* tightly twisted cord such as is used for making ~-lashes (*his veins stood out like* ~*cord*); ~*-crane,* light derrick with tackle for hoisting; ~*-fish,* kind with dorsal fin produced into filament like ~*-lash*; ~*-gin,* tackle-block with hoisting rope with several ends each to be simultaneously hauled on; ~ *hand,* hand that holds ~ (esp. in *have the* ~ *hand of,* be in position to control); ~*-ray,* ray-fish with long slender tail; ~*-round,* appeal circulated among friends, members of a club or society, etc., for contributions (usu. for some charitable object); ~*-saw,* narrow saw-blade with ends held by frame; ~*-snake,* slender kinds. Hence ~p'Y[2] a., flexible, springy, ~p'INESS n. [ME; partly f. prec., partly f. (M)LG *wippe, wip,* quick movement, leap, etc.]

whipp'er, n. In vbl senses; esp.: ~*-in,* (now usu. shortened to) WHIP[2]; ~*-snapper,* small child, young & insignificant but presuming or intrusive person [perh. for *whipsnapper,* implying noise & unimportance]. [-ER[1]]

whipp'et, n. Cross-bred dog of modified greyhound type used for racing; (mil.) fast light tank. [perh. f. WHIP[1] +-ET]

whip'poorwill, n. American bird allied to goatsucker. [imit. of cry]

Whip'snāde, n. (Used for) ~ Park, in the Chilterns, a reserve for the breeding & exhibition of wild animals. [place]

whip'ster, n. Small child; ‖ trifling frivolous person such as should still be subject to the whip. [-STER]

whir(r), v.i. (part. *whir'ring*), & n. (Make) continuous buzzing or softly clicking sound as of bird's wings quickly flapped or cogwheels in rapid action. [ME, prob. Scand., cf. Da. *hvirre,* Norw. *kvirra*]

whirl, v.t. & i., & n. **1.** Swing (t. & i.) round & round, revolve (t. & i.) rapidly (~*ing* DERVISH); send (missile etc.), (of moving body) travel, swiftly in orbit or curve; convey or go rapidly *away* etc. in wheeled conveyance; (of brain, senses, etc.) be giddy, seem to spin round, (of thoughts etc.) follow each other in bewildering succession. **2.** n. ~*ing* movement (*my thoughts are in a* ~). **3.** ~*'pool*, circular eddy in sea etc.; ~*'wind*, mass of air ~ing rapidly round & round in cylindrical or funnel shape (*sow wind & reap* ~*wind*, suffer worse results of bad action). [ME; prob. f. ON *hvirfla* f. Gmc *hwerbh-* rotate]

whirl'igig (-g-), n. Kinds of spinning toy, (fig.) revolving motion (~ *of time*, changes of fortune); merry-go-round; kinds of water beetle that circle about on surface. [f. prec. + obs. *gig* whipping-top]

whisht. See WHIST[1].

whisk, n., & v.t. & i. **1.** Bunch of grass, hair, etc., to flap dust off, flies away, etc., with; instrument for beating up eggs or cream; quick movement (as) of ~ or of animal's tail. **2.** vb. Flap (dust, fly, etc.) *away* or *off*; beat up (eggs etc.); take *away* or *off* with sudden motion (*waiter* ~*ed my plate off*); convey or go lightly & quickly esp. out of sight (*was* ~*ed across channel in aeroplane*; *mouse* ~*s into its hole*); brandish lightly or flip or wave about (*went* ~*ing a cane, her tail*). [ME *wisk*, prob. Scand., cf. ON *visk* wisp, Sw. *viska* besom, Sw. *viska* to whisk]

whis'ker, n. Hair of man's cheek (cf. *moustache, beard*; usu. in pl.); bristle growing from upper lip of cat etc., set of such bristles on one side. Hence (-)~ED[2] (-*erd*) a. [f. WHISK vb + -ER[1]]

whis'ky[1], -key, n. Spirit distilled from malted barley, other grains, or sugar etc.; *whiskified* (joc.), affected by ~-drinking; ~-*liver*, liver-complaint from alcoholic poisoning. [short for *whiskybae*, var. of USQUEBAUGH]

whis'ky[2], n. Kind of light gig or chaise. [f. WHISK, w. ref. to lightness of motion]

whis'per, v.i. & t., & n. **1.** Speak without vibration of vocal cords; talk with intention of being audible only close at hand or to confidant; inform or bid (person) thus *that* or *to* do; converse privately, indulge in slander or plotting; put secretly in circulation (tale, *that*; esp. *it is* ~*ed that*); (of leaves, stream, etc.) rustle; ~*ing-gallery*, gallery, cave, etc., in which some acoustic peculiarity causes least sound made at a particular point to be audible at another far off; hence ~ER[1], ~ING[1] (1), nn., ~ingLY[2] adv. **2.** n. ~ing speech (*always talks in a* ~ or ~*s*); ~ed remark; STAGE[1] ~; rumour of unknown origin, mysterious hint; rustling sound. [O Northumb. *hwisprian*; cf. early Flem. *wisperen*, OHG (*h*)*wispalōn* (G *wispeln*)]

‖ **whist[1], whisht** (hw-), int. enjoining silence (now rare exc. in representations of Irish talk, -*sht*). [ME, cf. HIST, HUSH]

‖ **whist[2],** a. (arch.). Silent. [ME, f. prec.]

whist[3], n. Card game of mingled skill &

chance for four or exceptionally three or two persons (*long, short,* ~, with ten, five, points to game; DUMMY, *double* DUMMY, ~; RUBBER[2] *of* ~; ~ *drive*, PROGRESSIVE ~ party. [alt. f. (1621) *whisk* (perh. f. WHISK vb), w. ref. to the silence usual in the game]

whistl|e (wi'sl), v.i. & t., & n. **1.** Make with the lips or with instrument for the purpose, or (of birds etc.) with the voice, or (of missile, wind, etc.) by rapid motion, the shrill sound of breath forced through small orifice formed with lips (*boy, bird, steam-engine, driver, wind, bullet,* ~*es*; ~*e for a wind*, of becalmed sailors, whence *may* ~*e for it*, vainly wish; *let one go* ~*e*, disregard his wishes; ~*ing*, in names of kinds of bird & animal, as ~*ing eagle, marmot*); (obs.) act as informer, peach; summon or give signal to (dog, attendant) by ~ing (~*e down the wind* metaph. f. hawking, let go, abandon); give (tune etc.) by ~ing. **2.** n. ~ing sound or note; instrument for producing such sound (*penny* ~*e*, tin pipe with six holes giving notes; *steam* ~*e*, sounded by jet of steam; *pay for* one's ~*e* (of anecdotic orig.), pay high for some caprice); throat (WET one's ~*e*); *~e-stop*, small unimportant town on railway (~*e-stop speech*, electioneering speech made on tour at railway stations). [OE *hwis*(*t*)*lian*, *wistlian* (also *hwistle* n.), of imit. orig.; cf. ON *hvisla* whisper, MSw. *hvisla* whistle]

whistler (wis'ler), n. In vbl senses; esp.: kind of marmot; kinds of bird. [-ER[1]]

whit[1], n. Particle, least possible amount, (usu. in *no* ~, *not* or *never a* ~, not at all). [early mod. E *whyt, wyt*, app. alt. f. WIGHT in phr. *no wight* etc.]

Whit[2], a., **Whit'|sun,** a. & n. ~ *Sunday*, seventh Sunday after Easter, commemorating day of Pentecost; ~ *Monday, Tuesday*, those following; ~ *week*, that containing; ~ Sunday; ~*'suntide* (also ~*sun* as n.), ~ Sunday & following days; ~*'sun week*, ~ week. [late OE *Hwita Sunnandæg* White Sunday, app. w. ref. to white baptismal robes; from ME analysed as *Whit Sunday* or *Whitsun Day*, both used attrib. in same sense, & *Whitsun* as n. (ME *w*(*h*)*itsone*(*n*))]

white[1], a., & v.t. **1.** Resembling a surface reflecting sunlight without absorbing any of the visible rays, of the colour of fresh snow· or common salt or the common swan's plumage, having some approach to such colour, pale (~ *as a sheet*), less dark than other things of the same kind (*bleed* ~, fig., drain of wealth etc., w. ref. to hanging of calf to ~n veal), characterized by presence of some white, (~ in many -ED[2] compounds used esp. in naming animals etc., as ~-*backed, -beaked, -bearded, -bellied, -breasted, -crested, -crowned, -eyed, -faced, -footed, -fronted, -headed, -necked, -rumped, -tailed, -throated, -winged*). **2.** (Of water, air, light) transparent, colourless. **3.** (fig.). Innocent, unstained, of harmless kind. **4.** Of ~ men (see ~ *man* below; ~ *culture, civilization*, etc.). **5.** (pol.). Of royalist or counter-revolutionary or reactionary tendency (opp. RED, & cf. TERROR). **6.** ~ *alloy*, any of the cheap imitations of silver; ~ ANT; ~'*bait*, small fish prob. the fry of several kinds eaten fried in quantities when about 2 in. long; ~'*beam*, tree with silvery underleaf; ~ *bear*, polar bear; *W*~'*boy*, member of 18th-c. illegal agrarian association in Ireland wearing ~ frocks at nightly meetings & outrages; ~-*caps*, breakers out at sea; ~ *coal*, water power [F *houille blanche*]; ~ (snowy) *Christmas*; ~ *coffee* (with milk); ~-*collar worker*, one not engaged in manual labour; ~ *corpuscle*, = LEUCOcyte; ~ CROW[1], CURRANT; *W*~ *Czar* (hist.), (Asian phr. for) Czar of Russia; ~ ELEPHANT; ‖ ~ ENSIGN, flown by ships of British navy, cf. RED *ensign*; ~ FEATHER[1]; ~ *fish*, any kind of sea-fish except herring, salmon, and sea-trout; ~ FLAG[4], FRIAR, FROST; ‖ ~ *gloves* (presented to assize judge who finds no criminal cases to try); ~ GROUSE[1]; ~-*gum*, eruption on infant's neck & arms; ~ *hands*, (lit.) as sign of exemption from labour, (fig.) innocency or integrity; so ~-*handed*; ~ *heart-cherry*, pale heart-shaped kind; ~ HEAT[1] (lit., & fig. of passion etc.; so ~-*hot*); ~ *horses*, waves with ~ crests at sea; *W*~ *House*, official residence of U.S. president; ~ LEAD[1], LIE[1]; ~ *light*, colourless, e.g. ordinary daylight, also fig. of unprejudiced judgement; ~-*lipped*, esp. with fear; ~-*livered*, cowardly; ~ MAGIC; ~ *man*, member of one of the paler races chiefly inhabiting or having inhabited Europe, & characterized by a certain type of civilization (cf. *black, brown, red, yellow, man*; *the* ~ *man's burden*, task of leading the world forward), (colloq.) person of honourable character, good breeding, etc.; ~ *meat*, poultry, veal, rabbits, pork; ~ *metal*, = ~ *alloy*; ~ (sleepless) *night* [F *nuit blanche*]; ~-*out* n., atmospheric condition, esp. in polar regions, marked by dense snow-cloud & total obscuration of physical features [after BLACK[3]-*out*]; ‖ ~ *paper*, report issued by Government to give information; *W*~ (western) *Russia(n)*; ~ *sale* (of house- & body-linen); ~ SCOURGE; ~ *sheet*, penitent's garb (usu. *stand in a* ~ *sheet*, confess sin etc.); ~ *slave*, girl entrapped (& exported) for purpose of prostitution (*the* ~-*slave traffic*, ~ *slavery*); ~'*smith*, worker in tin, also polisher or galvanizer of iron; ~ *squall*, sudden tropical storm at sea announced only by line of ~ water approaching; ~'*thorn*, hawthorn (cf. BLACK[1]-*thorn*); ~ (counter-revolutionary) *terror*; ~-*throat*, kinds of small songbird; ~ *war*,

war without bloodshed, economic warfare; ~'*wash*, (n.) solution of quicklime or of whiting & size for brushing over walls, ceilings, etc., to give clean appearance, also fig. means employed to clear person or his memory of imputations, (v.t.) cover with ~wash, attempt to clear reputation of, (pass., of insolvent) get fresh start by passage through bankruptcy court; ~ *wine*, of amber or golden colour (opp. *red*); ~ *witch* (using power for beneficent purposes only); hence ~'LY[2] adv. (rare), whit'EN[6] v.t. & i., ~'NESS (-tn-) n., whit'ISH[1](2) a. **7.** v.t. (arch.). Make ~. [OE, (OS) *hwit*, OHG (*h*)*wiz*, ON *hvitr*, Goth. *hweits* f. Gmc *hwitaz]

white[2], n. White or nearly white colour; kinds of white pigment (*Chinese* etc. ~); white clothes or material (*dressed in* ~); albuminous part round yolk of egg; visible part round iris of eye; = *whiteman* (MEAN[3]~); kinds of butterfly; (med.; pl.) LEUCOrrhoea. [OE; f. prec.]

‖ **White'chapel** (-t-ch-), n., & v.i. **1.** ~ *cart*, light two-wheeled spring-cart used by shopkeepers for sending goods round. **2.** (whist). Lead from one-card suit with a view to subsequent trumping. [~ in London]

‖ **White'hall** (-t-hawl), n. (Used for) the Civil Service, the Government offices. [street in London]

white'ning (-tn-), n. = WHITING[1]. [*whiten* (WHITE[1]), -ING[1]]

whith'er (-dh-), adv. interrog. & rel. (chiefly arch.), & n. **1.** To what place or point? (now usu. *where?, where* — *to?, how far?*, etc., but cf. *I see* ~ *your question tends*), whence ~WARD adv.; (rel., with antecedent *place* etc.) to which (now usu. *to which, where*), (without antecedent) to the or (also ~*soever*) any place to which (now usu. *where*); = & thither. **2.** n. Destination (*our whence & our* ~; *no* ~, arch., to no place). [OE *hwider*, f. Gmc **hwi-*, cf. WHICH, + -THER (b)]

whit'ing[1], n. Chalk prepared by drying, grinding, etc., for use in whitewashing, plate-cleaning, etc. [WHITE[1] vb, -ING[1](4)]

whit'ing[2], n. Kind of sea-fish much used as food; ~-*pout*, fish with some resemblance to ~ & an inflatable membrane over part of head. [ME, f. (M)Du. *wijting*, app. f. WHITE[1] a. + -ING[3]]

whit'leather (-lĕdh-), n. White leather dressed with alum instead of being tanned. [WHITE[1]]

‖ **Whit'ley Coun'cil**, n. A council of representatives of employers & workers for discussion & settlement of industrial relations & conditions. Hence **Whit'ley**-ISM n., use of such methods for dealing with industrial problems. [J. H. *Whitley*, Speaker 1921–8]

whit'low (-ō), n. Inflammatory tumour on finger esp. about the nail. [ME *whitflaw, -flow*, app. = WHITE + FLAW[1], but perh. of LG orig.; cf. early mod. Du. *vijt, fijt*, LG *fit* whitlow]

Whitsun. See WHIT[2].

whit'tle[1], n. (arch.). Long knife, esp. such as is used by butchers. [var. of ME *thwitel* f. OE *thwitan* to cut + -LE(1)]

whit'tle[2], v.t. & i. Trim, carve, slice off pieces from, (wood) with knife; shape, thin down, cut repeatedly *at*, piece of wood with knife; reduce amount or effect of by repeated subtraction (usu. *down, away*). [f. prec.]

Whit'worth thread (-wê̂r-, -rĕd), n. Standard screw-thread for metal. [Sir Joseph *Whitworth*, English engineer (d. 1887)]

whit'y̆, a. Inclining to white (usu. in comb. with other colour-name, esp. ~- *-brown*). [-Y[2]]

whiz, whizz, v.i. (-zz-), & n. (Make) sound given by friction of body moving at great speed through air; ~*-bang* (army sl.), shell from a small-calibre high- -velocity gun. [imit.]

who (hoō), pron. pers. interrog. & rel. (obj. *whom* pr. hoōm; poss. WHOSE pr. hoōz). **1.** interrog. What person(s)?, which person(s)?, what sort of person(s) in re- gard to position or authority?, (~ *said so?*; ~*m* or colloq. ~ *do you mean?*, *told him* ~ *they were*, ~*m* or colloq. ~ *to look out for*; ~*se son is he?*; ~ *would have thought it?*, no one would; ~ *are the Joneses, I should like to know?*; ~ *am I that I should object?*; *know* ~ *'s* ~, ~ *or what each person is*; *a* ~ *'s* ~, list with description of notables; ~*-does-what dispute* or *strike*, one about which trade union is to do a particular job). **2.** rel. (Person or persons) that (*the man* ~*m you saw*; *those for* ~*se benefit it was done*; *any- one* ~ *chooses can apply*; *there is no one* ~ *we can believe is competent*, often incor- rectly ~*m*); (arch.) the or any person(s) that (~ *breaks pays*; ~*m the gods love die young*; *as* ~ *should say*, like a person ~ *said, as though one said*); and, but, though, since, if, etc., he, him, they, etc. (*sent it to Jones*, ~ *passed it on to Smith*; *is flirting with Dick*, ~*m she detests*). [OE *hwā*, OS *hwe*, OHG (*h*)*wer*, Goth. *hwas*, f. Gmc *hwaz, *hwez f. Aryan *qᵘᵒs*, *qᵘᵉs*, cogn. w. L *quis*, Gk *tis*; cf. WHAT]

whoa. See wo.

who'dŭ(n)nit (hoō-), n. (sl.). Detective or mystery story. [= *who done* (illiterate for *did*) *it?*]

whoëv'er, who'sō (arch.), **whosõëv'er** (emphat.), **whoe'er'** & **whosõe'er'** (poet.; -âr̂), (hoō-), pronn. pers. indef. rel. (cases as with WHO; *whomsoever* or the incorrect *whoever* is usu. substituted without special emphasis for *whomever*, & *whosesoever* occas. for *whose-ever*), used (1) as mod. equivalent of arch. *who* in indef. rel. sense (*whoever comes will be welcome*; *stopped whomsoever* or *whoever* or *whom-*

ever he saw; *return it to whose-ever* or *whosesoever address is on it*); (2) in indef. concessive clauses = though any one (*who- ever else objects, I do not*; *whose-ever it is, I mean to have it*; *whomsoever* or *who- ever* or *whomever I quote, you retain your opinion*); (3) vulg. for *who* EVER. [WHO, SO, EVER]

whole (hōl), a. & n. **1.** (arch.). In good health, well (*they that be* ~ *need not a physician*). **2.** In sound condition, unin- jured, not broken, intact, (*hope you will come back* ~; *got off with a* ~ *skin*; *there is not a plate left* ~; *has swallowed a raisin* ~). **3.** Integral, consisting of one or more units, without fractions, (~ *num- bers*, integers). **4.** Undiminished, without subtraction, (*bread made of* ~ *meal*, not deprived by bolting of some constitu- ents). **5.** (With *a* in sing.) not less than (*spent* ~ *years of misery*; *went up a* ~ *tone*; *lasted three* ~ *days*; ~ *regiments were cut down*; *talked a* ~ *lot of nonsense*); (with *the, his*, etc.) all that there is of (*the* ~ *truth, world, duty of man*; *do thing with one's* ~ *heart*, heartily, with concen- trated effort·etc., without doubts etc., whence ~**-heart**ED[2] a., ~**-heart'ed**LY[2] adv.,~**-heart'ed**NESS n.; *the* ~ *priesthood, city*, etc., all members or inhabitants of it; COMMITTEE *of the* ~ *House*; *go the* ~ HOG[1], whence ~**-hŏgg'ER**[1] (·g-) n.). **6.** ~- *-coloured*, all of one colour; ~*-hoofed*, with undivided hoofs; ~*-length'*, (portrait) re- presenting person from head to foot; *~ *note*, semibreve; ~*'sale*, (n., chiefly attrib.) selling of articles in large quanti- ties to be retailed by others (*a* ~*sale dealer*; *sells by* ~*sale*; ~*sale prices*), (adj. & adv.) on the ~sale plan, (transf.) on large scale, (*our business is* ~*sale only*; *sells* ~*sale*; *a* ~*sale slaughter took place*; *sends out begging letters* ~*sale*); ~*'saler*, ~sale dealer; hence ~*'*NESS (hōln-) n. **7.** n. Thing complete in itself; all that there is of something (often *of*; *the golden rule contains the* ~ *of morality*; *on* or *upon the* ~, taking into consideration every- thing that bears on the question, after weighing pros & cons etc.); organic unity, complete system, total made up of parts, (*nature is a* ~; *the* ~ *& the parts*). [OE *hāl*, OS *hēl*, OHG *heil*, ON *heill*, Goth *hails* f. Gmc *hailaz, cf. HALE; for *wh-* cf. WHORE]

whole'some (hōls-), a. Promoting physi- cal or moral health, salubrious, salutary, not morbid, (~ *food, air, exercise, advice, neglect, excitement*). Hence ~LY[2] adv., ~NESS n. [ME; prec., -SOME]

wholly (hōl·li), adv. Entirely, without abatement, (*I am* ~ *yours*); exclusively, without admixture, (*a* ~ *bad example*). [WHOLE, -LY[2]]

whom. See WHO. [formally repr. OE *hwām*, dat. of *hwā* WHO & *hwæt* WHAT]

whoop (hoōp). Var. of HOOP[2]; ~*ing cough*, infectious disease, esp. of children, with short violent cough followed by long sonorous inspiration. Hence ~'ER[1] n., in vbl senses; esp. (also ~er or ~ing swan) the wild or whistling swan.

*whoo'pee (wōō-), n. (colloq.). Make ~, rejoice noisily, have a roaring time. [f. prec.]

whŏp, v.t. (sl.; -pp-). Thrash, (fig.) defeat, overcome, whence ~p'ING[1](1) n.; (part.) very large of its kind (esp. a ~ping lie), whence ~p'ER[1] n. [orig. unkn.; var. of (dial.) wap]

whore (hōr), n., & v.i. 1. Prostitute, strumpet, (the SCARLET W~); ~-master, -monger, fornicator; hence ~'DOM (hōrd-) n. 2. v.i. (Of man) practise fornication; (fig., arch., esp. go a-whoring after strange gods etc.) practise idolatry or iniquity. [late OE hōre, OHG huora, ON hóra, f. Gmc *hōr- (whence ON hórr, Goth. hors) cogn. w. L carus dear; for wh- cf. WHOLE]

whŏrl, n. Ring of leaves or other organs round stem etc. of plant; one turn of a spiral; disc on spindle steadying its motion. Hence ~ED[2] (-ld) a. [ME wharwyl, whorwil, app. var. of WHIRL, infl. by wharve n., whorl of spindle]

whor'tleberry (wêrtelb-), n. = BILBERRY. [16th c., south-western dial. form of hurtleberry (c. 1450, of unkn. orig.); so whort, whortle for hurt, hurtle]

whose (hōōz). Possessive case of WHO, used also as case of WHICH 4; ~ever, ~soever, see WHOEVER. [ME hwǣs, later hwōs, whōs, alt. f. hwas, hwes, OE hwǣs, gen. of hwā WHO & hwæt WHAT, infl. by hwā, hwō WHO & hwām, hwōm WHOM]

whoso, whosoever. See WHOEVER.

why[1], adv. interrog. & rel., & n. (pl. ~s). 1. On what ground ?, for what reason ?, with what purpose ?, (~ did you do it?; cannot think ~ you came; often ellipt., as You are late; ~?, esp. in ~ so?, demand for grounds of statement or view); (rel.) on account of which (the reasons ~ he did it are obscure). 2. n. Reason, explanation, (cannot go into the ~s & wherefores now). [OE hwī, hwȳ instr. of hwæt WHAT, f. Gmc *hwī, Aryan q^wei, locative of q^wo-WHO]

why[2], int. expr. surprised discovery or recognition (~, it is surely Jones!; ~, what a bruise you have got!; ~, of course, that was it), protest at simplicity of question etc. ('What is twice two?' '~, four.' ~, a child could answer that), pause for reflection ('Is it true?' '~, yes, I think so'), objection (~, what is the harm?),introduction of apodosis (if silver will not do, ~, we must try gold), etc. [ellipt. uses of prec. interrog.]

wick[1], n. (Piece of) fibrous or spongy material by which lamp or candle flame is kept supplied with melted grease or oil; (surg.) gauze strip inserted in wound

to drain it. [OE wēoce, wēoc, = MDu. wiecke, MLG wēke, OHG wioh (G wieche)]

wick[2], n. Town, hamlet, district, (rare exc. in place-names as Hampton W~ or other compounds as baili-~). [OE wīc, OS wīk, OHG wich, app. f. L vicus, cogn. w. Gk oikos, Goth. weihs]

wick'ĕd, a. Sinful, iniquitous, vicious, given to or involving immorality, (~ Bible, edition of 1632 with not omitted in seventh commandment), offending intentionally against the right; spiteful, ill-tempered, intending or intended to give pain, playfully mischievous, roguish. Hence ~LY[2] adv., ~NESS n. [ME, f. obs. wick of same sense (perh. adj. use of OE wicca wizard)+-ED[1] as in WRETCHED]

wick'er, n. Plaited twigs or osiers as material of baskets, chairs, mats, protective covers, etc. (usu. attrib., as ~ chair), whence ~ED[2] (-erd) a.; ~-work, (things made of) ~. [ME, f. east Scand., cf. MSw. viker, early Da. vigger willow, f. root of Sw. vika bend]

wick'ĕt, n. 1. Small door or gate, esp. one beside or in the compass of a larger one for use when the latter is not open (also ~-door, -gate); turnstile entrance; aperture in door or wall usu. closed with sliding panel; door closing only lower half of doorway. 2. (crick.) One set of three stumps & two bails (keep ~, be ~-keeper, fieldsman stationed close behind batsman's ~; keep one's ~ up, succeed in not being put out); the ~s as defended by one batsman (5 ~s down, five men out; match won by 2 ~s, with three of winning side still not out); good etc. state of the pitch (play began on a perfect ~); be on a good, sticky, ~, (fig.) be in an advantageous, unfavourable, position. [ME, f. AF = ONF wiket, = OF guichet, of uncert. orig.]

widdershins. Var. of WITHERSHINS.

wide, a., adv., & n. 1. Measuring much or more than other things of same kind across or from side to side, broad, not narrow, (~ door, road, river, brim, margin, cloth, interval; ~ margin, fig., a good deal more allowed than is likely to be needed). 2. (appended to measurement) in width (a strip 3 ft ~). 3. Extending far, embracing much, of great extent, (has a ~ range; ~ fame, known to many; the ~ world, all the world great as it is; a ~ domain, large; is of ~ distribution, occurs in many places; a ~ generalization, covering many particulars; there is a ~ difference between; also adv., as the principle ranges ~, & esp. in far & ~), whence ~'LY[2] adv. 4. Not tight or close or restricted, loose, free, liberal, unprejudiced, general, (~ knickerbockers; ~ culture, not specialized; takes ~ views; hazard a ~ guess, one allowing margin for errors of detail; give ~ berth to, not go too near, keep

For pronunciation of words in wh- see WH-.

clear of, avoid). **5.** Open to full extent (*staring with ~ eyes*; also adv. or pred. a., as *yawned ~, open your mouth ~, window is ~ open, person is ~ awake*). **6.** At considerable distance from a point or mark, not within reasonable distance of, (*~ ball* in cricket, ball judged by umpire to pass wicket beyond batsman's reach & counting one to his side; *gave an answer quite ~ of the mark* or *purpose*; also adv. or pred. a., as *is bowling, shooting, ~*; *arrow fell ~ of target*). **7.** (sl.). Crafty (*a ~ boy*). **8.** n. A ~ ball; *the ~, the ~ world* (*broke to the ~*, sl., completely broke). **9.** ~ *awake* a. (colloq.), wary, knowing; *~-awake* n., soft *~*-brimmed felt hat; *~'spread', ~*ly disseminated (esp. of beliefs or impressions). Hence wid'en[6] v.t. & i., wid'ish[1] (2) a. [OE *wid*, OS *wid*, OHG *wit*, ON *vithr*, f. Gmc *widaz*]

wi(d)geon (wi'jn), n. Kinds of wild duck. [early 16th c., of F form, but unkn. orig.; cf. 17th c. F *vigeon, vingeon* kind of duck]

wid'ow (-ō), n., & v.t. **1.** Woman who has lost her husband by death & not married again (GRASS ~; *~'s* WEEDS; *~'s cruse*, supply that looks small, but proves inexhaustible, see 1 *Kings* xvii. 10–16; *~'s mite*, see *Mark* xii. 42; *~'s peak*, V-shaped growth of hair in centre of forehead; also attrib., as *~ lady, woman*); BLACK[1]*~; the ~* (sl.), champagne [f. the *Veuve* (F=~) Cliquot brand]; *~-bird*, black-plumaged African bird of genus *Vidua* (L = ~); hence *~*HOOD (-dōh-) n. **2.** v.t. Kill husband or mate of, deprive of husband or wife or mate, make into ~ or widower, (usu. in p.p.; *the ~ed father, mother*, etc.); (poet.) bereave of friend etc. [OE *widewe* etc., OS *widowa*, OHG *wituwa*, Goth. *widuwō*, cogn. w. L *vidua*, Skr. *vidhavā*]

wid'ower (-ōer), n. Man who has lost his wife by death & not married again. [ME, f. prec. + -ER[1]]

width, n. Distance or measurement from side to side; comprehensiveness or liberality of mind, views, etc.; piece of material of certain ~ (*shall want three ~s of it*). [17th c. (WIDE, -TH[1]), repl. *wideness*]

wield, v.t. Control, sway, hold & use, manage with the hands or otherwise, (*~ power, the sceptre, a kingdom* etc. chiefly poet., *weapon* lit. or fig.). [OE *wealdan* (-*wieldan*), OS, Goth. *waldan*, OHG *waltan*, ON *valda* f. Gmc *waldh-*]

wife, n. (pl. *-ves*). **1.** Woman, esp. one who is old & rustic or uneducated (now rare exc. in *old wives' tale*, foolish or superstitious tradition, & in comb. as FISH[1]*~*, HOUSEWIFE, MIDWIFE). **2.** Married woman esp. in relation to her husband (usu. *my* etc. *~, the ~ of*, or with epithet as-*will make a good ~; the ~*, joc or vulg., = my ~; *wedded, lawful, ~*, emphatic phrr. in contrast w. *mistress, concubine*, etc.; *all the* WORLD *& his ~*; *have, take, to ~*, = as

~). Hence *~*'HOOD (-fh-), wif'ie [-Y[3]], nn., *~*'LESS, *~*'LIKE, *~*'LY[1], (-fl-), aa. [OE *wif*, OS *wif*, OHG *wip*, ON *vif*; ult. orig. unkn.]

wig[1], n. Artificial head of hair formerly much worn as ornament, & still to conceal baldness or disguise appearance ‖ or as part of official dress esp. of judge or lawyer or of servant's livery (*there will be ~s on the green*, a free fight). Hence (-)*~*g̱ED[2] (-gd), *~*'LESS, aa. [short for PERIWIG; cf. WINKLE]

wig[2], v.t. (-gg-). Rebuke sharply, rate, (chiefly in the vbl n.). Hence *~*g̱'ING[1](1) (-g-) n. [app. f. *wig* n. rebuke (1804), in sl. or colloq. use]

wig'an, n. Stiff canvas-like material used for stiffening. [*Wigan* in Lancashire]

wigeon. See WI(D)GEON.

wig'gle, v.t. (colloq. or dial). Cause (something) to move from side to side; ‖ scull (a boat) with single oar over stern. [ME, cogn. w. or f. MDu., (M)LG *wiggelen*; cf. WAG[1] & WAGGLE]

wight (wit), n. (arch. or joc.). Person, being, (esp. *luckless, wretched*, etc., *~*). [OE (= OS, OHG) *wiht*, ON *vættr*, Goth. *waiht(s)*; ult. orig. unkn.]

wig'wăm (*or* -ŏm), n. N.-Amer. Indian's tent or hut of skins or mats or bark; *the W~*, Tammany Hall. [native]

wild, a., adv., & n. **1.** Not domesticated or cultivated (chiefly of animals & plants, & esp. of species allied to others that are not ~; in the commoner combinations ~ & the n. are hyphened, or treated as one wd with accent on ~; *~ beast, plant; ~ man*, savage; *~ ass; ~-boar; ~-duck; ~'fowl; ~ vine; ~'cat* lit., also fig. as a. or attrib. of finance or commercial speculations or strikes etc., reckless, unsound; *~-goose* lit., also in *~-goose chase*, absurdly impossible enterprise; *~ horse*, also in *be drawn by ~ horses*, form of torture & death; *~ hyacinth*, bluebell; *~* OATS; *~ scenery* etc., of conspicuously desolate appearance; *woodnotes ~*, spontaneous & artless poetry). **2.** (Of horses, game-birds, etc.) shy, given to shying, easily startled, hard to get near. **3.** Unrestrained, wayward, disorderly, irregular, out of control, unconventional, (*a ~ fellow*; *settled down after a ~ youth*; *~ work*, lawless doings; *hair hanging in ~ locks*; *living in ~ times*; *room is in ~ disorder*; *run ~*, grow unchecked or undisciplined or untrained). **4.** Tempestuous, violent, (*a ~ wind, night*, etc.). **5.** Intensely eager, excited, frantic, passionate, distracted, mad, (*is ~ with excitement, to try it*; *the ~ men*, extremists of a party etc.; *~ about* person or subject, enthusiastically devoted to; *~ delight, excitement, enthusiasm, grief, rage*; *~ looks, appearance*, etc., indicating distraction; *drive ~*, madden). **6.** Haphazard, rash, ill-considered, ill-aimed, disturbed by excitement, (*a ~ guess, shot, blow, venture*; *~ opinions,*

bowling; also as adv., as *shoot, talk,* ~).
7. ~*'fire,* = *Greek* FIRE[1] (*report spreads like* ~*fire,* very fast). Hence ~*'*ISH[1](2) a., ~*'*LY[2] adv., ~*'*NESS n. **8. n.** Desert, ~ tract. [OE *wilde,* OHG *wildi,* ON *villr,* Goth. *wiltheis,* also OE, OHG *wild* n., f. Gmc **willth-*]

wil'debëëst (v-), n. The gnu. [Afrikaans (now *wildebees,* pl. *wildebeeste*); (prec., BEAST)]

‖ **wil'der,** v.t. (poet.). Bewilder. [orig. obsc.; prob. extracted f. foll.]

wil'derness, n. Desert, uncultivated & uninhabited tract, (*voice in the* ~ etc., unregarded advocate of some reform, w. ref. to *Matt.* iii. 3 etc.; *wandering* etc. *in the* ~, of political party out of office, w. ref. to *Num.* xiv. 33 etc.); part of garden left wild; unlimited number or quantity *of.* [OE *wild(d)êornes,* f. *wil(d)dëor* WILD DEER, *see* -NESS]

wild'ing, n. Plant sown by natural agency, esp. wild crab-apple, or fruit of such plant (also attrib.). [-ING[3]]

wile, n., & v.t. **1.** Trick, cunning procedure, artifice, (usu. in pl.). **2.** v.t. Lure, entice, *away, into,* etc. (also incorrectly for WHILE[1] vb). [ME *wil,* perh. f. Scand. (ON *vél* craft)]

wil'ful, a. For which compulsion or ignorance or accident cannot be pleaded as excuse, intentional, deliberate, due to perversity or self-will, (~ *murder, waste, ignorance, disobedience*); obstinate, self-willed, headstrong, refractory. Hence ~LY[2] adv., ~NESS n. [ME; WILL[2], -FUL]

Wilhelmstrasse (vil'hĕlmshtrahse), n. (Used for) the German Foreign Office. [Berlin street]

will[1], v.t. & aux. (pres. *I, he, we, you, they,* ~ or *'ll, thou wilt* or *'lt*; past & condit. *I, he, we, you, they, would* pr. woŏd or *'d, thou wouldst* pr. woŏdst or *wouldest* or *'dst*; neg. forms ~ *not* or *wŏn't, would not* or *wouldn't,* or *'d not*; no other forms or parts used). **1.** (used irrespective of person with more or less of orig. sense of volition). Desire (thing; arch.; *what wilt thou?*; *what would they?*); want or desire or choose to (*the haven where I would be*; *come when you* ~); wish that, rarely *that* (usu. in condit. with optative effect; *I* often omitted; *it shall be as you* ~; *said it should be as we would*; *would* or *I would I were a bird!*; *would it were otherwise!*; *would God I had died!*, i.e. if only God had wished, or perh. ellipt. for *I would to God*; *I would to heaven I was dead*; *would-be,* prefixed as adj. or adv. to wd describing character that person vainly aspires to or that thing is meant to have, as *a would-be gentleman, smart saying*); consent or be prevailed on to (~ or *would not go any farther*; *wound would not heal*; *would you pass the salt?*; *would not do it for £100*); refuse to be prevailed on not to (*boys* ~ *be boys*; *accidents* ~ *happen*; *you* ~ *have your way*; *he* ~, *would,*

get in my light); be accustomed or observed from time to time to (~ *sit there for hours*; *now & then a blackbird would call*; ~ *succeed once in ten times*); be likely to turn out to (*this* ~ *be Waterloo, I suppose*; *I don't know who it would be*). **2.** As tense & mood auxiliaries ~ & *would* are used (a) in 2nd & 3rd person (1st having *shall, should*) to form a plain future or conditional statement or question (*you* ~ *hear soon enough*; *they would have been killed if they had let go*; ~ or *would you, they, be able to hear at such a distance?*, but cf. SHALL 5); (b) in 1st person (others having *shall, should*) to form a future or conditional statement expressing speaker's will or intention (*I* ~ *not be caught again*; *we would have come if you had given us longer notice*); (c) alternatively with *shall, should,* in sentences of type *a* changed in reporting to 1st from other person (*you say I* ~, *said I would, never manage it,* reporting ‘You ~ never’; now more usu. *shall, should*) or from first to other person (*he said he would never manage it,* reporting ‘I shall never’); (d) in reporting 1st pers. sentences of type *b* (*you promised you would not be caught again*). [OE **willan,* OS *-ian,* ON *vilja,* Goth *wiljan,* f. Gmc **wel(l)jan* f. **wel-, *wal-,* cogn. w. L *velle* wish]

will[2], n. **1.** Faculty by which person decides or conceives himself as deciding upon & initiating action (*mind consists of the understanding & the* ~; *freedom of the* ~, *free* ~, power of determining one's choice of action independently of causation). **2.** (Also ~*-power*) control exercised by deliberate purpose over impulse, self-control, (*has a strong, weak,* etc., ~). **3.** Deliberate or fixed intention (*the* ~ *to live in a patient is the surgeon's best ally*; *the* ~ *to power* etc., Germanisms for determination to win power etc.; *did it against my* ~, *of my own free* ~; *where there's a* ~ *there's a way*; *my poverty but not my* ~ *consents*). **4.** Energy of intention, power of effecting one's intentions or dominating other persons, (*do thing with a* ~, energetically; *has a* ~ *that overbears all opposition*). **5.** Contents of the ~, what is desired or ordained by person, (*thy* ~ *be done*; *what is your* ~?, what do you wish done ?*; *have* one's ~, getting thing desired; *worked his wicked* ~ *upon them*). **6.** Arbitrary discretion (esp. *at* ~, whenever one pleases; *tenant at* ~, who can be turned out without notice; ~*-worship,* arch., religion constructed to suit oneself). **7.** Disposition towards others, wishing of good or ill, (*good, ill,* ~, usu. as compd wds, & see GOODWILL). **8.** Directions written in legal form for disposition to be made of person's property & minor children after his death (often *last* ~ *& testament*; *nuncupative* ~, see NUNCUPATE; *make* one's ~). Hence (-)~ED[2] (-ld),

~ᴸLESS, aa. [OE *willa*, OS *willio*, OHG *willo*, Goth *vilja* f. Gmc *wel-* (prec.)]

will³, v.t. **1.** Have as contents of one's will, intend unconditionally, (*God ~s, ~eth, ~ed, that man should be happy*; *can we ~ what we are told to ~?*; *he who ~s success is half way to it*; (abs.) exercise will-power (*has no power to ~*; *~ing & wishing are not the same*). **2.** Instigate or impel or compel by exercise of will-power (*you can ~ yourself into contentment*; *mesmerist ~s patient to think himself well*; *~ed the genie into his presence*). **3.** Bequeath by will (*shall ~ my money to a hospital*). [OE *willian*, f. prec.]

will′ět, n. N.-Amer. snipe. [imit. of cry]

will′ing, a. Not reluctant, cheerfully ready, (*to do, or abs.*; *do not spur a ~ horse*); of, given etc. by, ~ person (~ *hands, help*, etc.). Hence ~LY² adv., ~NESS n. [WILL¹, -ING²]

will-o'-the-wisp′ (-dh-), n. = IGNIS FATUUS, JACK¹-o'-*lantern*; also, person of uncertain whereabouts or appearances. [orig. *Will with the wisp*; *wisp* = handful of (lighted) tow etc.]

will′ow¹ (-ō), n. **1.** Kinds of tree & shrub with pliant branches growing usu. near water in temperate climates, many of which yield osiers & some timber used for cricket bats & other purposes (*wear the ~*, mourn loss or absence of one's beloved, formerly indicated by garland of ~ leaves; *~-pattern*, conventional design of Chinese type done in blue on white china etc. introduced in England 1780). **2.** Cricket-bat (*handle the ~*, bat). **3.** ~*-herb*, kinds of plant, the commonest with leaves like ~ & pale purple flowers. [OE *welig*, OS *wilgia*, M Du. *wilghe*, MHG *wilge*, f. Gmc *walg-, *welg-*]

will′|ow² (-ō), v.t. & n., **will′|ў**, n. **1.** Clean (fibrous material) by beating, picking, etc., with machinery. **2.** n. (Also ~*ow*, ~*owing, -machine*) machine for ~owing. [*willow* for *willy* f. OE *wilige* wicker basket, rel. to *welig* (prec.)]

will′owy (-ōi), a. Abounding in willows; lithe & slender. [-Y²]

willў-nill′ў. See NILL.

wilt¹. See WILL¹.

wilt², v.t. & i. Wither (t. & i. of plant, leaf, flower), (make) droop. [of dial. orig., perh. alt. f. *wilk* WELK]

Wil′ton, n. (Also ~ *carpet*) kind of Brussels carpet with loops cut open into thick pile made at town of ~ in Wilts.

wil′|ў, a. Full of wiles, crafty, cunning. Hence ~iLY² adv., ~iNESS n. [ME; WILE, -Y²]

Wim′bledon (-bĕld-), n. (Used for) the lawn-tennis tournaments with championship matches etc. held at ~.

wim′ple, n., & v.t. & i. **1.** Covering of linen etc. worn by nuns & formerly by other women arranged in folds about head, cheeks, chin, & neck; (vb) put ~ upon, veil, arrange in folds. **2.** Winding,

twist, turn, ripple; (vb) fall in folds, (of stream) twist about, meander, ripple. [OE *wimpel*, OHG *-al* (G *-el* pennon), ON *vimpill*]

win, v.t. & i. (*won* pr. wŭn), & n. **1.** Secure as result of fighting or competition or (often *of* person, also colloq. *off* person) betting & gaming or of effort (~ *victory, fortress, prize, honour, fame, fortune,* one's BLUE², *wife*; ~ one's *spurs*, be knighted, (fig.) get recognition as expert at something; *won £5 of him at cards*, whence ~n′ings n. pl., see -ING¹(2); ~ one's *way*, progress by struggle etc.; ~ one's *bread*, earn livelihood, chiefly now in BREAD-*~ner*; ~ *ore* etc., get it from mine). **2.** Be victorious in (~ *battle, game, bet, race*; ~ *the field*, arch., be victorious in battle or fig.; ~ *the* TOSS); (abs.) ~ *race, contest, money*, etc. (~ *by a* HEAD¹, *in a* CANTER, HAND¹*s down, by two* etc. *lengths, easily*, etc.; ~*nING*¹-*post*, marking end of race; *the ~ning horse, side*, etc.; ~ *at cards*; *let those laugh who* ~); (part.) determining victory (*the ~ning hit, goal, card*, etc.). **3.** Make one's way to (~ *the shore, summit*, etc.). **4.** Make one's way, or (with compl.) become by successful effort, (~ *home*; ~ *through the day, through all difficulties*; ~ *free, clear*, etc.). **5.** Persuade, induce to do, gain over, (*you have won me*; *won him to consent*; *soon won his audience over*). **6.** Exercise increasing attraction *upon* (*a theory that ~s upon one by degrees*); (part. as adj.) charming, attractive, (*a ~ning smile, ~ning manners, personality*, etc.), whence ~n′ingLY² adv. **7.** ~*ning* HAZARD¹. Hence (-)~nER¹ n. **8.** n. A success or victory in a game (*has had three ~s & no defeats*). [OE, OS, OHG, Goth. *winnan*, ON *vinna*]

wince, v.i., & n. **1.** Show bodily or mental pain or distress by slight start or loss of composure, flinch, (often *under pain, the knife, at allusion*, etc.). **2.** n. Act of wincing. [f. AF *wencir* = OF *guencir, guenchir*, f. WG *wenkjan* (= OHG *wenken*); cf. WINCH, WINK]

win′cey, n. (pl. ~*s*). Strong material of wool & cotton or wool used for shirts etc. Hence ~ETTE′(2) (-sĭ-) n. [perh. corrupt. of LINSEY-WOOLSEY]

winch, n. Crank of wheel or axle; hoisting-machine, windlass. [OE *wince* f. Gmc *wenk-*, see WINCE]

Win′chèster¹, n. ~ (*rifle*), type of repeating rifle used esp. by big-game hunters. [O. F. ~, Amer. maker (d. 1880)]

Win′chèster², n. ~ (*quart*), (bottle holding) half a gallon. [~ in Hants, where standard measures were orig. deposited]

wind¹ (*poet. also* wī-), n. **1.** Air in more or less rapid natural motion, breeze or gale or blast, (*north* etc. ~, coming from N. etc.; *fair, contrary, ~*, helping, hindering, ship's course; *hot, cold, whistling, variable*, etc., ~*s*; *constant ~*, that always blows in same direction at same place; *periodical*

~, recurring at known periods; ~ *rises*, begins to blow or gets stronger; ~ *sound, scent, is carried by, comes on, the* ~; CAP-FUL, SLANT, *of* ~; ILL ~; *before, down, the* ~, helped by its force; WHISTLE *down the* ~; BETWEEN ~ *& water*; *sail, be, close to* or *near the* ~, as nearly against it as is consistent with using its force, (fig.) venture very near indecency or dishonesty; *in the* ~'*s eye, in the teeth of the* ~, directly against it; *on a* ~, naut., sailing against a ~ on either bow; *off the* ~, naut., sailing with the ~ on either quarter; *fling* or *cast prudence* etc. *to the* ~*s*, abandon, neglect, take no thought of; PUT[1] *the* ~ *up* one; *have* or *get the* ~ *up*, sl., be or become frightened; *go like the* ~, swiftly; *there is something in the* ~, there are signs that some step is being secretly prepared; *find out how the* ~ *blows* or *lies*, what developments are likely or what is the state of public opinion; *take the* ~ *out of* one's *sails*, frustrate him by anticipating his arguments, using his material, etc.; *sow* ~, *& reap* WHIRL~; *raise the* ~, fig., obtain money needed). **2.** ~ward position or *weather*-GAUGE[1] (*take* or *get the* ~ *of*). **3.** pl. The four cardinal points (*came from the four* ~*s*, from all directions; *scatter to the four* ~*s of heaven*). **4.** Mere empty words, unmeaning rhetoric. **5.** Artificially produced air-current, air stored for use or used as current, (collect.) part of band consisting of ~-instruments, (*organ stops when the* ~ *is exhausted*; *was knocked down by the* ~ *of the blow*; *the strings were drowned by the* ~, *the wood*-~, i.e. flutes etc., *by the brass*). **6.** Smell, conveyed on ~, indication of thing's whereabouts or existence, commencing publicity, (*get* ~ *of*, smell out, begin to suspect, hear rumour of; *take* or *get* ~, be rumoured). **7.** Gas generated in bowels etc. by indigestion, flatulence, (*break* ~, release it by anus; *baby* etc. *is troubled with* ~). **8.** Breath as needed in exertion, power of fetching breath without difficulty while running or making similar continuous effort, spot below centre of chest blow on which temporarily paralyses breathing, (*have lost, let me recover* or *get, my* ~; *has a good, bad,* ~; *broken* ~, see BROKEN--winded; *second* ~, recovery of ~ in course of exercise after initial breathlessness; *have* one's ~ *taken*, be paralysed by blow in the ~; *hit him in the* ~). **9.** ~'*bag*, wordy orator; ~-*bound*, unable to sail for contrary ~*s*; ~-*break*, fence, shrubs, etc., serving to break force of ~; ~-*cheater*, garment for protecting person from ~; ~-*chest*, box for compressed air in organ; ~-*colic*, pain caused by flatulence; ~--*cutter*, upper lip of mouth of flue-pipe in organ; ~-*egg*, unfertilized egg incapable of producing chicken; ~'*fall*, fruit blown down, (fig.) unexpected good fortune, esp. legacy; || ~ -*fanner*, = ~*hover*; ~-*flower* (poet.), the plant anemone; ~-*gall*, soft

tumour on horse's fetlock-joint; ~-*gauge*, anemometer, also instrument showing amount of ~ in organ, also apparatus attached to sights enabling allowance to be made for ~ in shooting; || ~'*hover*, kestrel; ~-*instrument*, musical instrument in which sound is produced by current of air, as organ, flute; ~-*jammer*, merchant sailing-ship; ~'*mill*, mill worked by action of ~ on sails (*fight* ~*mills*, tilt at imaginary foe or grievance, w. ref. to Don Quixote); ~'*pipe*, breathing-tube, trachea; ~-*row*, line of raked hay, corn--sheaves, peats, etc., made to allow of drying by ~; ~-*sail*, canvas funnel conveying air to lower parts of ship; || ~--*screen*, *~-shield*, (of glass in front of motor-car driver); ~-*sock*, canvas cylinder or cone flying from masthead to show direction of ~; ~-*spout*, waterspout, tornado, or whirl~; ~-*sucker*, *-sucking*, (horse with) the vice of noisily drawing in & swallowing breath; ~-*swept*, exposed; ~-TIGHT; ~-*tunnel*, tunnel-like apparatus for producing air-stream of known velocity past model aircraft etc. to investigate effect of ~ pressure on structure; ~'*ward* a. & n., (region) lying in the direction from which the ~ blows, exposed to the ~, (*look to* ~*ward*; *the* ~*ward side*; *get to* ~*ward of*, avoid smell of, also get weather GAUGE[1] of or fig. advantage over). Hence ~'*LESS* a. [OE, OS *wind*, OHG *wint*, ON *vindr*, Goth. *winds* f. Gmc **windaz* cogn. w. L *ventus*, f. root *wē-* blow, cf. WEATHER[1]]

wind[2], v.t. **1.** Sound (horn, bugle, blast, call) by blowing (wī-; *winded* or by confusion w. foll. *wound*). **2.** Detect presence of by scent (wī-; *winded*; *hounds, deer,* ~ *the fox, stalkers*; ~*ed his tobacco half a mile off*). **3.** Breathe, make breathe quick & deep by exercise, exhaust wind of, renew wind of by rest, (wī-; *winded*; *give horse a gallop to* ~ *him*; *am quite* ~*ed by the climb*; *rested to* ~ *the horses*). [f. prec.]

wind[3], v.i. & t. (*wound*), & n. **1.** Go in circular, spiral, curved, or crooked course, meander, (*path, river,* ~*s*; *herd* ~*s o'er the lea*; *creeper* ~*s round pole*; ~*ing staircase*, spiral; *in* ~*ing*, out of truth, askew); make one's or its *way* etc. circuitously, insinuate one*self into*, (*brook* ~*s its way*; *wound himself* or *his way into my affections*). **2.** Coil (t. & i.), wrap closely (t. & i.), surround with coil, embrace, (~ *cotton on reel, wool into ball*, etc.; also with *off* adv. or prep. = unwind; ~ person *round* one's *fingers*, exercise complete domination over; *wound the blanket round him, her arms round the child, the child in her arms*; ~ING[1]-*sheet*, in which corpse is wound; ~ *pegtop*, coil string round it; ~ *serpent* ~*s itself* or ~*s round victim*); hoist or draw by use of windlass etc. (~ *ship out of harbour, ore up from mine*). **3.** = ~ *up* (clock etc.). **4.** ~ *ship*, reverse positions of bow & stern. **5.** ~ *up*, coil the whole of (~ *up piece of string*), tighten coiling or coiled spring or fig. tension or intensity or efficiency of (~ *up strings of fiddle*; ~ *up clock* etc.; *is* ~*ing himself up for an effort or to do it*; *the administration needs* ~*ing up*, is slack; *person is wound up to fury*; *expectation was wound up to a high pitch*); bring to a conclusion, conclude t. & i., (*wound up his speech*, or *wound up, by declaring*; *shot his wife & child & wound up by stabbing himself*; ~ *up company*, arrange its affairs & dissolve it; *company* ~*s up*, ceases business, goes into liquidation, whence ~'ING¹-up n.); hence ~'ER¹(1, 2) n., ~'ingLY² adv. 6. n. Bend or turn in course; single turn in ~ing clock, string, etc.; ~-*up*, conclusion, finish. [OE, OS, OHG (-*tan*), Goth. *windan*, ON *vinda*, f. Gmc *wend-*, *wand-*, cf. WANDER, WEND¹]

win'dage, n. Difference between projectile's & gun-bore's diameter allowing escape of gas; (allowance for) influence of wind in deflecting missile. [-AGE]

wind'lass, n., & v.t. 1. Machine for hauling or hoisting on wheel-&-axle principle. 2. v.t. Hoist or haul with ~. [alt. (by assoc. w. dial. *windle* to wind) f. obs. (f. AF) *vindas*, = OF *guindas* f. ON *vindáss* (*vinde* wind +*áss* pole)]

‖ **win'dlestraw** (-del-), n. Old stalk of kinds of grass. [OE *windelstréaw* grass for plaiting (WIND³, STRAW)]

win'dow (-ō), n. 1. Opening in wall or roof of building, ship, carriage, etc., usu. filled with glass in fixed or sliding or hinged frames to admit light & sometimes air to room etc. (*look out of* ~ or *the* ~; *have all one's goods in the* ~, be superficial; *blank, blind, false*, ~, mouldings or recess as for ~ without aperture; BOW WINDOW; BAY³, CASEMENT, DORMER, FRENCH, ‖LATTICE, ORIEL, SASH², ~). 2. Opening in envelope to show address written on letter. 3. ~-*box*, slide for weights in sash-~, also box on ~-sill in which flowers are grown; ~-*dressing*, art of arranging goods attractively in shop-~, often fig. of adroit presentation of statistics etc.; ~ *envelope* (with opening or transparent part allowing address inside to show); ~-*shopping*, feasting one's eyes on the goods displayed in the shop-~s. Hence (-)~ED² (-ōd), ~LESS (-ōl-), aa. [ME, f. ON *vindauga* (WIND¹, EYE¹)]

Wind'sor (-z-), n. Town in Berks. (*House of* ~, style of British Royal Family assumed 1917; ~ *chair*, all of wood with curved support for back (& arms); *brown* ~ *soap*, brown scented kind; ‖ ~ *uniform*, blue coat with red collar & cuffs worn at ~ by the royal family, & by others having royal grant).

wind'|ȳ, a. Wind-swept (~*y hill-top, plain, situation*); in which wind is high (~*y night, weather, crossing*); wordy, verbose, empty, (~*y eloquence, logic, speaker*); generating or characterized by flatulence; (arch.)

windward (*on the* ~*y side of the law*, safely out of its reach); (sl.) frightened. Hence ~iLY² adv., ~iNESS n. [-Y²]

wine, n., & v.i. & t. 1. (Kinds of) fermented grape-juice (*is a sound* ~; DRY¹ or *sweet*, STILL¹ or *sparkling*, WHITE¹ or *red*, ~; *green* ~, in first year; *port* ~, port; COMET ~; *Adam's* ~, water; *good* ~ *needs no* BUSH¹; *new* ~ *in old bottles*, new principle too powerful to be restrained by ancient forms; *take* ~ *with*, pledge & be pledged by at table; SPIRIT *of* ~; TEAR²*s of strong* ~; *over the* WALNUTS *& the* ~; ~ *whey*, beverage of ~ & curdled milk; *in* ~, exhilarated or drunk with ~). 2. ‖ (At universities) party for ~-drinking after dinner (~*s have gone out of fashion*). 3. Fermented drink resembling ~ made from specified fruit etc. (*cowslip, currant, gooseberry, orange, palm*, ~). 4. Solution of drug in ~ (*quinine* ~; ~ *of opium*). 5. A dark-red tint. 6. ~'*bag*, ~skin, or ~bibber; ~'*bibber*, tippler, drunkard; so ~'*bibbing* a. & n.; ~'*bottle*, glass bottle for ~, also ~skin; ~'*bowl*, lit., also drinking habits etc.; ~-*carriage*, wheeled utensil for circulating ~ at table; ~-*cooler*, vessel in which ~bottles are cooled with ice; ~'*cup*, as ~bowl; ‖ ~'*fat*, arch., ~press; ~'*glass*, any glass for drinking ~ from, esp. of size used for sherry, often as measure (also ~'*glassful*) of medicine to be taken, = four tablespoons; ~-MARC; ~ *of Scotland*, whisky; ~-*palm*, kind from which ~ is made; ~'*press*, in which grapes are squeezed; ~'*sap*, large red American winter apple; ~'*skin*, whole skin of goat etc. sewn up & used to hold ~; ~-*stone*, tartaric deposit in ~-casks; ~-*vault*, cellar in which ~ is kept, also bar etc. where it is retailed; hence ~'LESS, win'Y², aa. 7. vb. Drink ~; entertain to ~; often *dine & ~*. [OE *win*, OS, OHG *win*, ON *vin*, Goth *wein* f. L *vinum*]

wing, n., & v.t. & i. 1. One of the limbs or organs by which the flight of a bird, bat, insect, angel, etc., is effected, part in non-flying bird or insect corresponding to ~, supporting part of flying-machine, (*clip one's* ~*s*, limit his movements or ambitions or expenditure; *come on the* ~*s of the wind*, swiftly; *lend, add*, ~*s to*, accelerate; *take under one's* ~, treat as protégé; *his* ~*s are sprouting* etc., his virtues are too great for a being below the degree of an angel; *money takes to itself* ~*s*, disappears); *high-, low-, mid-*~, aa., (of monoplane) having the ~s set near the top, near the bottom, in the middle, of the fuselage. 2. (joc.). (Esp. of wounding) arm. 3. More or less separate projecting part of something, esp. of building or battle array (*the north* ~ *was added in the 17th century*; *cavalry were massed on left* ~; ~*s* in theatre, sides of stage, pieces of side scenery); mudguard of motor vehicle. 4. (footb., hockey, etc.). Forward etc. whose place is either side of the centre

(also attrib., as ~ *three-quarter*). **5.**
‖ R.A.F. formation of two or more
squadrons. **6.** pl. Pilot's badge in R.A.F.
etc. **7.** ~ed flight, ~s, (*on the* ~, flying,
travelling, in motion ; *take*~, start flying).
8. ~-*beat*, one complete set of motions
with ~ in flying ; ~-*case*, horny cover,
a modified fore-~, protecting some insects' flying ~ ; ‖~ *commander*, officer
of AIR[1]-*force*; ~-*covert*, one of small
feathers covering insertion of bird's flying feathers; ~-*footed*, poet., swift; ~-
-*sheath*, = ~-*case*; ~-*spread*, measurement across~s when extended, surface or
area of aircraft's ~s ; ~-*stroke*, = ~-*beat*;
hence ~ED[2](winged, wing'id),~'LESS, aa.,
~'LET n. **9.** vb. Equip with ~s, enable to
fly or mount, send in flight, lend speed to,
(~ *arrow with eagle's feathers* or *at the*
mark; *vengeance* ~ed *the shaft*; ~ed *words*,
going like arrows to mark, significant;
ambition ~s *his spirit*; *fear* ~ed *his steps*;
~ed *horse*, Pegasus, poetry; ~ed *god*,
Mercury ; ~ed *Victory*, statue of goddess
of victory with ~s). **10.** Travel, traverse,
on ~s (*bird* ~s *its way*, ~s *to its mate*, ~s
the air). **11.** Wound (bird) in ~, (person)
in arm. [ME pl. *wenge*, -*en*, -*es* f. ON
vængir, pl. of *vængr*]

wink, v.i. & t., & n. **1.** Close & open eyes,
blink, close & open (eyes or eye), (of eye)
close & open, (*like* ~*ing*, sl., very quickly
or vigorously); momentarily close one
eye to awaken attention of or convey
private intimation to person (usu. *at*
person); (of light, star, etc.) twinkle,
shine intermittently; ~ *at*, shut one's
eyes to, purposely avoid seeing, affect not
to notice, connive at, (abuse, transgression, etc.). **2.** n. Act of ~ing, esp. as
signal etc. (*nod is as good as* ~ *to blind*
horse; *tip* one *the* ~, sl., give him signal
or intimation; *could not get a* ~ *of sleep*;
did not sleep a ~ *all night*; *forty* ~s, nap).
[OE *wincian*, OS *wincon*, f. Gmc *wenk*-,
cf. WINCE, WINCH]

winkle (wing'kl), n., & v.t. **1.** Edible sea
snail, periwinkle. **2.** v.t.~ *out*, extract or
eject (as a ~ from its shell with a pin).
[abbr. PERIWINKLE[2], cf. WIG[1]]

winn'ow (-ō), v.t. Fan (grain) free of chaff
etc., fan (chaff etc.) *away* or *out* or *from*;
sift, separate, clear of refuse or inferior
specimens or falsehood, clear (refuse etc.)
out or *away*, examine, sort, weed out;
(poet.) fan (air with wings), flap (wings),
stir (hair etc.). Hence ~ER[1](1, 2) (-ōer) n.
[OE *windwian* (WIND[1])]

win'some, a.: (Of person or his or her
appearance, manner, smile, etc.) charming, winning, attractive, engaging, bright.
Hence ~LY[2] adv., ~NESS n. [OE *wynsum*,
OS *wunsam*, OHG *wunnisam*, f. *wyn(n)*
joy +-SOME]

win'ter, n., & v.i. & t. **1.** Fourth season
of the year, Dec.–Feb. (astron., from
winter solstice to vernal equinox);
hard, *mild*, ~, with, without, much frost;

(attrib.) occurring, used, etc., in or lasting
for the ~ (~ *apple*, *cough*, *solstice*, etc.;
~ *sleep*, hibernation ; ~ *quarters*, esp. to
which troops retire for ~; ~ *garden*,
glass-covered space with plants etc. used
as lounge). **2.** (rhet., poet.). Year of life
(*a man of 50* ~s, 50 years old). **3.** ~-*cress*,
cruciferous plant formerly cultivated for
~ salad; ~-*green*, kinds of plant green
through ~; ~-*lodge* (bot.), bud or bulb
protecting plant's embryo through ~;
~-*tide* (poet.), ~; hence ~LESS, ~LY[2], aa.
4. vb. Spend the ~ *at*, *in*, etc.; keep or
feed (plants, cattle) during~. [OE *winter*,
OS, OHG *wintar*, ON *vetr*, Goth. *wintrus*
f. Gmc *went*-, prob. rel. to WET]

win'tr|y̆, a. Having the temperature,
storminess, or aspect appropriate to
winter, cold, windy, cheerless,(~*y weather*,
day, *sun*, *scene*); (of smile, greeting, etc.)
lacking warmth or interest or vivacity.
Hence ~ĪNESS n. [-Y[2]]

wipe, v.t. & i., & n. **1.** Clean or dry
surface of by rubbing with cloth, paper,
hand, etc. (~ *table*, *dish*, *face*, *hands*, etc.;
~ one's *eyes*, dry tears, cease weeping ; ~
one's *eye*, sl., steal march on him, get
advantage by anticipating him; ~ *out*
bath or other hollow utensil); get rid of,
clear *away* or *off*, take *up*, wash *out*, by
wiping (~ *away* or ~ *your tears*; ~ *up*
slops; ~ *out stain*, or fig. *disgrace*, *insult*,
etc., esp. by vengeance); ~ *out*, utterly
destroy, annihilate, (*their very name*, *the*
whole army, *was* ~d *out*); ~ *the floor with*
(sl.), inflict humiliating defeat or correction on (person); (sl.) take or aim sweeping
blow or stroke *at* (~d *at me with his stick*).
2. n. Act of wiping (*give this plate a* ~);
(sl.) sweeping blow (*fetched* or *took a* ~ *at*
him; *fetched him a* ~); (sl.) handkerchief.
[OE *wipian* (cf. OHG *wifan* wind round,
Goth. *weipan*), rel. to WHIP]

wire, n., & v.t. & i. **1.** (Piece of) metal
drawn out into form of thread or slender
round or square or tapelike flexible rod
(*platinum*, *silver*, *copper*, etc., ~; BARB[1]ed,
LIVE[1], ~; *telegraph* etc. ~s; *private* ~,
telegraph ~ reserved for person's exclusive use; *was sent for*, *sent congratula-*
tions, *by* ~, telegraph; *pull the* ~s,
control puppets by ~s or usu., fig.,
manage political party or movement by
secret influence). **2.** Telegraphic message
(*sent me a* ~). **3.** ~-*cloth*, ~ *gauze*, *netting*,
fabrics woven or twisted of ~ ; ~-*cutter*,
tool for cutting ~; ~-*dancer*, person
performing on stretched ~; ~'*draw*,
draw (metal) out into ~, (fig.) refine or
apply or press (argument, point, etc.)
with idle or excessive subtlety (esp. in
p.p.); ~-*edge*, false edge that turns back
when blade is over-sharpened; ~ *en-*
tanglement, arrangement of barbed or
other ~ set up to prevent rapid attack
of enemy; ~-*gun*, one made by coiling
flat ~ round tube; ~-*haired*, with stiff or
wiry hair (esp. of dogs); ~-*heel*, disease

of horse's foot; ~*'puller*, politician etc.
who pulls the ~s; ~ *rope*, made by twisting ~s together as strands; ~*-tapping*,
eavesdropping on telephone conversation; ~*-worm*, kinds of destructive larva;
~*-wove*, (of paper) = wove(WEAVE). **4. vb.**
Provide, fasten, etc., with ~(s); string
(beads) on ~ ; snare (bird) with ~ ; (electr.)
install circuits for lighting in (a house
etc.); (croquet) obstruct (ball, shot,
player) by ~ of hoop (chiefly pass.); telegraph (~ *me the result*; ~*d to him*; *was* ~*d
for*); ‖ (sl.) ~ *in*, operate vigorously, put
all one's force into some continuous effort..
[OE *wir*, MLG *wire*, ON *virr*]

wire'less (wīr̄l-), a., n., & v.i. & t. **1.**
Without wire(s), esp. in ~ TELEGRAPHY.
2. n. ~ telegraphy or telegram; ‖ ~
receiving set or broadcast or programme,
radio, (also attrib.). **3.** vb. Send ~, send
(message) or inform (person) by ~. [-LESS]

wir'‖ȳ, a. Made of wire (poet.); tough &
flexible as wire, (of persons) sinewy, untiring, whence ~ĬLY² adv., ~ĬNESS n. [-Y²]

wis, v.i. pres. 1st sing. (pseudo-arch.).
I know well (parenth.). [orig. in *I wis* =
obs. *iwis* certainly, erron. taken as ' I
know ' & as pres. tense of *wist* WIT¹]

wis'dom (-z-), n. Being wise, (possession
of) experience & knowledge together with
the power of applying them critically or
practically, sagacity, prudence, common
sense; wise sayings (*pour forth* ~ ; *W*~ *of
Solomon*, abbr. *Wisd.*, *W*~ *of Jesus the
Son of Sirach* or *Ecclesiasticus*, books of
Apocrypha); ~*-tooth*, molar usu. cut
after 20 years of age (*cut* one's ~*-teeth*,
gain discretion). [OE (OS) *wisdōm*, OHG
wistuom, ON *visdómr* (WISE¹, -DOM)]

wise¹ (-z), a., & v.t. & i. **1.** (Of persons)
having, (of action, course, speech, opinion,
etc.) dictated by or in harmony with
or showing, experience & knowledge
judiciously applied, sagacious, prudent,
sensible, discreet; having knowledge (~
after the event, of person who has failed to
foresee; *came away none the* ~*r* or *as* ~ *as
he went*, knowing no more than before;
where ignorance is bliss 'tis folly to be ~);
‖ (arch.) having occult power or knowledge of mysterious things (~ *man*,
wizard; ‖ ~ *woman*, witch, fortune-teller,
also midwife); suggestive of wisdom,
oracular, (*with a* ~ *shake of the head*; ~
saw, proverbial saying); *(sl.) *be* or *get* ~
to, be or become aware of; *(sl.) *put* one
~ (*to*), inform one (of), enlighten one
(concerning); *(sl.) ~ *crack*, smart pithy
remark (so ~*-crack* v.i.). **2.** vb. *~ *up*
(sl.), put or get ~. Hence ~'LY² (-zl-) adv.
[OE *wis*, OS, OHG *wis*, ON *viss*, Goth.
weis, f. Gmc *wisaz* f. *wittos* cogn. w.
WIT¹]

wise² (-z), n. Way, manner, guise, (*in
solemn* etc.~, arch.; esp. *in some*, *no*, *any*,
~, *on this* ~). [OE *wise*, OS, OHG *wisa*,
ON *visa* f. Gmc *wisōn*, *wisō* f. *wit-
WIT¹]

-wise (-z), suf. = prec., forming advv. of
manner as in *clock*~ with motion in direction of clock hands, *cross*~ with cross
arrangement, *length*~ with length arranged in given direction, with regard to
length, *no*~ in no way, not at all.

wise'acre (-zäker), n. Sententious dullard.
[16th c., f. MDu. *wijsseggher* soothsayer,
app. f. OHG *wizago*, w. assim. to *wijs*
WISE¹ & *seggher* sayer]

wish, v.t. & i., & n. **1.** Have as a desire
or aspiration (*that*-clause with *that* usu.
omitted, or obj. & compl. ; ~ *I had never
been born*, *were* or *was a bird*, *may live to
see it*; ~ *you would be quiet*; *it is to be
~ed that*, is desirable that; *I* ~ *it may
not prove*; fear it will; *could not* ~ *it
better*; ~ one*self dead*, *home*, *at home*, etc.;
~ person *happy*, *away*; ~ one *at the
devil* or *further*, ~ he were away). **2.** Want
with the kind of desire that tends to
affect result (*to* do, person or thing *to* do,
person or thing *-ed*, or rarely with simple
obj. esp. pronoun; *I* ~ *to go*, *you to do it*,
it finished or *to be finished*; *what do you
~?*; *they say they* ~ *peace*, *an interview*).
3. Be *well* or *ill* inclined to or *to* (~*es me
well*, *well to all men*, ~*es nobody ill*),
whence (-)~ER¹ n. **4.** Say one hopes for
(joy, luck, pleasant journey, sorrow, etc.)
in person's favour or against him (ind.
obj. or *to*; *I* ~ *you joy*, ~ *success to each
& all*); ~ person *joy of*, (iron.) hope he
will enjoy; express desire *for* (*has nothing
left to* ~ *for*; *would not* ~ *for anything
better*); (colloq.) foist (*up*)*on* person. **5.**
~(*ing*)-*bone*, merrythought (longer part
of it when broken between two persons
entitling holder to magic fulfilment of
any ~); ~*ing-cap*, magic cap securing to
wearer fulfilment of any ~. **6.** n. (Expression of) desire or aspiration, request,
implied command, (*the* ~ *is father to
the thought*, we believe thing because we ~
it true; *if* ~*es were horses beggars might
ride*; *has a great* ~ *to go to sea*, whence
~'FUL a., desirous (*to* do; ~*ful thinking*,
belief founded on ~es rather than facts);
good ~*es*, hopes felt or expressed for
another's happiness etc.; *cannot grant
your* ~; *he disregarded* or *disobeyed my
~es*); thing desired (*have got my* ~). [OE
wȳscan, OHG *wunsken*, ON *æskja*, f.
Gmc *wunskjan*, ult. cogn. w. WEEN]

wish'-wash (-ŏsh), n. Washy drink or
talk. [redupl. of WASH²]

wish'ȳ-washȳ (-wŏ-), a. Thin, sloppy,
(of soup, tea, talk, etc.). [redupl. of
WASHY]

wisp, n. **1.** Small bundle or twist of straw
etc. **2.** Flock (of snipe). [ME, of uncert.
orig.; cf. WFris. *wisp*]

wist. See WIT¹.

Wistar'ia, -tēr'-, n. Genus of pale-purple-
-flowered climbing plant. [C. *Wistar* (or
-ter), Amer. anatomist (d. 1818), -IA¹]

wist'ful, a. Affected with or betraying
vague yearnings or unsatisfied desire to

understand (of persons or usu. of eyes, look, voice, mood, etc.). Hence ~LY² adv., ~NESS n. [app. assim. of obs. *wistly* adv. intently (cf. WHIST¹˒ ²) to WISH*ful*, w. corresp. change of sense]

wit¹, v.t. & i. (arch.; pres. *I*, *he*, *wot*, *thou wottest*; past *wist*; inf. *wit*; part. ~*ting*; other parts not used). Know (*God wot*, knows; *I wot*, know well; *to ~*, that is to say, namely; ~*ting*, not unconscious or unintentional, whence ~t'ingLY² adv.). [OE, OS *witan*, OHG *wizzan*, ON *vita*, Goth. *witan*, f. Gmc *wait-*, *wit-*, cogn. w. L *vidēre*, Gk (*w*)*oida*, (*w*)*eidon*, Skr. VEDA]

wit², n. 1. (Sing. or pl.) intelligence, understanding, (*has not the ~, the ~s, ~ enough, to see*; *remedy is past the ~ of man to devise*; *out of* one's *~s*, mad, distracted; *has his ~s about him*, is observant or of lively intelligence; *has quick, slow*, etc., *~s, a nimble ~*, whence (-)~tED² a.; *at* one's *~'s end*, utterly at a loss; *live by* one's *~s*, by ingenious hand-to-mouth shifts; *the five ~s*, arch., the senses or the mind), whence ~'LESS a., ~'lèssLY² adv., ~'lèssNESS n. 2. (Power of giving sudden intellectual pleasure by) unexpected combining or contrasting of previously unconnected ideas or expressions (*possessed of both ~ & HUMOUR*; *pages sparkling with ~*), whence ~t'Y² a., ~t'iLY² adv., ~t'iNESS n. [OE *wit, gewit*(*t*), OS *wit*, OHG *wizzi*, ON *vit*, Goth. *-witi* f. *wit-* (prec.)]

wit³, n. Wise man (arch.); witty person (see prec.), person who talks wittily, whence ~'LING¹(2) n. [uses of prec.; 1st sense f. 15th, 2nd f. 17th, c.]

witch, n., & v.t. 1. Woman or (now rarely) man practising sorcery (*white ~*, using powers . for beneficent purposes only; *~es'* SABBATH), (fig.) fascinating or bewitching woman; ugly old woman, hag; (local) flat-fish resembling the lemon sole. 2. *~'craft*, sorcery, use of magic; *~-doctor*, = MEDICINE¹*-man*; *~-hunt*, (fig.) search for suspected Communists, spies, etc.; *~-meal*, pollen of CLUB¹*-moss*. 3. v.t. Bewitch (*the ~ing time of night*, Ham. III. ii. 406, time when ~es are active, midnight), esp. fig., fascinate, charm, whence ~'ERY(4, 5) n., ~'ING² a., ~'ingLY² adv. [OE *wicca* masc., *wicce* fem. f. *wiccian* vb, later prob. aphetic f. BEWITCH]

witch-. See WYCH-.

wit'enagĕmōt' (-g-), n. (hist.). Anglo-Saxon national council or parliament. [OE *witena* gen. pl. of *wita* wise man, *gemōt* meeting; cf. MOOT]

with (-dh, -th), prep. 1. In antagonism to, against, (*fight, quarrel, struggle, dispute, argue, compete, vie, ~*). 2. In or into company of or relation to, among, beside, (*come, go, walk, eat, live, spend the day, mix* t. & i., *meet, ~*; *king is expected ~* or *together ~ queen & court*; *numbered ~ the transgressors*; *compare ~*; *have nothing to do ~*; *deal ~*; *~ God*, dead & in heaven; *have ~ you*, arch., I accept your offer or challenge; so *done ~ you*). 3. Agreeably or in harmonious relations to (*I feel, think, sympathize, ~ you*; also with neg. wds in opp. sense, as *I disagree ~ you*; *he that is not ~ me is against me*; *vote ~ the Liberals*; *blue does not go ~ green*; *one ~*, part of same whole as). 4. Having, carrying, possessed of, characterized by, (*vase ~ handles, man ~ sinister expression*; *walking ~ a gun*; *went out ~ no hat on*; *~ child* or *young*, pregnant). 5. In the care or charge or possession of (*have no money ~ me*; *leave child, parcel, ~ nurse, porter*; *it rests ~ you to decide*; *the deal, decanter, next move, is ~ you*). 6. By use of as instrument or means (*cut it ~ a knife*; *have no pen to write ~*; *walks ~ a crutch*; *damn ~ faint praise*). 7. By addition or supply or acquisition or possession of as material (*fill it, overflowing, ~ water*; *laden ~ baggage*; *blessed ~ beauty*; *adorn ~ frescoes*). 8. In same way or direction or degree or at the same time as (*changes ~ the seasons*; *varies directly* or *inversely, increases, ~*; *rise ~ the sun*; *~ that*, thereupon, simultaneously; *begin ~*, take as starting-point). 9. Because or by operation of, owing to, (*trembles ~ fear*; *is down ~ fever*; *stiff, silent, ~ cold, shame*). 10. Displaying or so as to display, under favourable or unfavourable circumstances of, (*heard it ~ calmness*; *fought ~ courage*; *won ~ ease, difficulty, a good deal to spare*; *shot well ~ a good, wretched, light*). 11. In regard to, concerning, in the sphere of, in the mind or view of, (*be patient ~ him*; *bear, do*, or *put up, ~*, tolerate, be indulgent to; *my dealings ~ the natives*; *what do you want ~ me?*; *away, down, up, to the devil*, etc., *~ him*, take or send or put him, he may go, away etc.; *can do anything, nothing, ~ him*, influence or utilize him in any, no, direction; *~ God all things are possible*; *is it well ~ thee?*; *it is holiday time ~ us*; *the first object ~ him is*; *has great influence ~ theHouse*). 12. So as to be separated from (*part, break, dispense, ~*). 13. Despite, notwithstanding, the presence of (*~ all his learning, he is the simplest of men*; *~ many admirable qualities, the best of intentions, he failed completely*). [OE, OS *with*, ON *vith*, app. shortened f. Gmc *withrō* = OE *wither*, OHG *vidar* (G *wider*) against, ON *vithr*, Goth. *withra*]

withal' (-dhawl), adv. & prep. (arch.). 1. With it, in addition, moreover, as well, at the same time. 2. prep. (always after its expressed or omitted obj.). With (*what shall he fill his belly ~?*). [ME; prec., ALL]

withdraw' (-dh-), v.t. & i. Pull aside or back (*~ curtain*, one's *hand*); take away, remove, (boy from school, coins from circulation, horse from race, troops from position, favour etc. from person); retract (offer, statement, promise; *cries of ' ~ '*, demands that speaker shall unsay something as unparliamentary etc.); retire from presence or place, go aside or apart; ‖ *~ing-room* (arch.), DRAWING-ROOM. Hence *~AL*(2) n. [ME; WITH, DRAW¹]

with′e (-dhī, *or* widh), **with′y** (-dhī), n. (pl. *-thes* pr. -dhīz, *or* *-ths*). Tough flexible branch esp. of willow or osier used for binding bundles etc. [OE *withthe* (also *withig*, mod. *withy*), OHG *wida*, f. Gmc **withjōn*]

with′er (-dh-), v.t. & i. Make or become dry & shrivelled (often *up*), deprive of or lose vigour or vitality or freshness or importance (often *away*), decline, languish, decay, (*has a ~ed arm*; *flowers & beauty ~*; *age cannot ~ her*; *the individual ~s*, ceases to be important); blight with scorn etc. (*~ one with a look*, usu. joc.), whence *~ING²* a., *~ingLY²* adv. [ME, app. var. of WEATHER², different. for certain senses]

with′ers (-dherz), n. pl. Ridge between horse's shoulder-blades (*my ~ are unwrung*, imputation etc. does not touch me). [app. reduced f. (16th c.) *widersome* or *-sone*, f. *wither* (see WITH), as the part that resists strain of collar; second element obsc.]

‖ **with′ershins** (-dhershīnz), **widd′er-**, adv. (Sc.). In a direction contrary to apparent course of sun (considered as unlucky), counter-clockwise. [f. MLG *weddersins* f. MHG *widersinnes* (MHG *wider* against, *sin*, *sint* direction)]

withhōld′ (-dh-h-), v.t. (*-held*). Refrain from putting in action, refuse to grant, (*~ one's hand*, arch. for *hold*, not take action; *~ one's consent.* support, *the light of one's countenance*, etc.). [ME; WITH, HOLD¹]

within′ (-dh-), adv., n., & prep. **1.** Inside, to or at or on the inside, indoors, internally, (chiefly arch.; *clean ~ & without*; *go ~*, into house or room; *stay ~*, not go out of doors; *is Mr Jones ~?*, at home; *beauty without & foulness ~*; *make me pure ~*, in spirit; *Bishopsgate ~*, inside the walls). **2.** n. The inside (*as seen from ~*). **3.** prep. To or on or in the inside of, enclosed by, (*~ doors*, in or into house; *safe ~ the walls*; WHEEL¹s *~ wheels*); not beyond, not too far for, not transgressing, so as not to pass or exceed, subject to, (*live, keep, ~ one's income*; *~ the meaning of the Act* etc., covered by it; *immortality ~ the law*, not illegal; *keep it ~ bounds*; *a task well ~ his powers*; *running ~ himself*, without putting forth whole power; *is true ~ limits*; not too far for, near enough to affect or be affected by, not farther off than (*of* with sense *from*, or abs.), (*is ~ reach, sight, call*, near enough to reach or be reached etc.; often *of*, as *~ sight of port*; *is ~ three miles of a station*; *was ~ an ace of destruction*); in a time no longer than, before expiration

or since beginning of, (*of* with sense *from*, or abs.; *shall have it ~ an hour*; *~ a year of his death*, *~ a year, all was changed*; *have seen him ~ these three days*). [OE *withinnan* on the inside (WITH, *innan* adv., ME *inne* in)]

without′ (-dh-), adv., n., prep., & conj. **1.** Outside, to or at or on the outside, out-of-doors, externally, (chiefly arch.; *white within & ~*; *stands disconsolate ~*, outside the house etc.; *listening to the wind ~*). **2.** n. The outside, external sources, (*as seen from ~*; *the suggestion came from ~*). **3.** prep. Outside of (arch.; *met us ~ the gates*; *negotiations within & ~ the House*; *is ~ the pale of civilization*; *things ~ us*, all that is not ourselves); not having, not with, with no, devoid of, lacking, in want of, free from, with freedom from, not feeling or showing, in or with absence of, less, (*came ~ a hat*; *a rose ~ a thorn*; *am ~ friends* or *money*; *did it ~ difficulty* or *being discovered*; *act ~ hesitation*; *cannot live ~ her*, *go away ~ thanking you*; *is absolutely ~ fear, anxiety*; *cannot make an* OMELETTE *~ breaking eggs*; *~ health happiness is impossible*; *do, go, ~*, dispense with, also ellipt. dispense with something implied; COLD *~*; *~ doubt*, admittedly, certainly; *~* FAIL¹, PREJUDICE, RESERVE²; *~ end*, infinite, eternal; *goes ~ saying*, is too well known or obvious to need mention). **4.** conj. (arch., vulg.). Unless. [OE *withūtan* (WITH, *ūtan* adv., ME *ute(n)* out)]

withstănd′ (-dh-), v.t. & i. (*-stood*). Resist, oppose, (person, force, hardship, wear, etc.); make opposition (poet.). [OE *withstandan* (= ON *vithstanda*), see WITH, STAND]

withy. See WITHE.

wit′ness, n., & v.t. & i. **1.** Testimony, evidence, (*bear ~ to* or *of*, state one's belief in, state facts tending to establish), thing stated by way of evidence (*my ~ is not true*; arch.), confirmation (*stands there in ~ of the event*; *call to ~*, appeal to for confirmation); thing or person whose existence, position, state, etc., serves as testimony *to* or proof *of* (*is a living ~ to my clemency*); (also EYE-*~*) spectator *of* incident, bystander, person present at event; person giving sworn testimony in law-court or for legal purpose (*~ often used for the ~*); person attesting genuineness of signature to document by adding his signature; ‖ *~-box*, **~ stand*, enclosure in law-court reserved for *~es*. **2.** vb. State in evidence (noun, *that*, etc.; arch.); give evidence (*against, for*), serve as evidence (usu. *against, for, to*; *~* or *as ~ my poverty*, of which let my poverty be the proof); be a or the *~* (arch.; *~ Heaven!*, I call Heaven to *~*); indicate, serve as evidence of, (*a deathly pallor ~ed his agitation*); see, be spectator of; act as *~* of (document, signature, etc.). [OE *witnes* (WIT², -NESS)]

witt'icism, n. Witty remark, jest, (usu. in disparaging sense). [coined by Dryden f. WIT[1]*ly*, after *criticism*]

wittingly. See WIT[1].

‖ **witt'ol,** n. (arch.). Man who winks at wife's infidelity, acquiescent cuckold. [ME *wetewold*, app. formed by substitution of WIT[1] for first syllable of *cokewold* CUCKOLD]

wive, v.t. & i. (now rare). Provide with, take, wife. [OE *wīfian* (WIFE)]

wiv'ern, wȳv-, n. (her.). Winged two--legged dragon with barbed tail. [f. ME *wyver,* f. OF *wivre* (*guivre*), var. of *vivre* f. L VIPERA + *n*; cf. BITTERN]

wives. See WIFE.

wiz'ard, n. & a. **1.** Magician, sorcerer, male witch; person who effects seeming impossibilities; conjurer. **2.** adj. (sl.). Wonderful. Hence ~RY(4, 5) n. [ME *wysard* (WISE[1], -ARD)]

wiz'ened (-nd), **wiz'en, weaz'en,** a. Of shrivelled or dried-up appearance (chiefly of person or his face or look). [OE *wisnian,* OHG *wesanēn,* ON *visna*]

wizier. See VIZIR.

wō, whoa (wō'*a*), int. Stop (chiefly to horses); GEE-*wo*; *wo-back'*, int. used in backing horses.

woad, n., & v.t. **1.** (Plant yielding) kind of blue dye. **2.** v.t. Dye with ~. [OE *wād,* OHG *weit,* f. Gmc **waida-,* **waizda-*]

wob'ble, wa'bble (wŏ-), v.i., & n. **1.** (Of top or revolving body) revolve with changing inclinations, rock; (of person, missile, etc.) go unsteadily, vibrate from side to side, swerve, stagger; (fig.) vacillate, waver, act inconsistently, be inconstant, whence **wŏbb'lER[1]** n.; (of voice or sound) quaver, pulsate. **2.** n. Rocking movement, change of direction or policy, swerve, piece of vacillation. [corresp. to LG *wab(b)eln,* MHG *wabelen,* f. Gmc **wabh-,* cf. WAVER]

‖ **wŏdge,** n. (colloq.). Chunk. [alt. f. WEDGE]

wōe, n. (chiefly poet. or joc.). Affliction, bitter grief, distress, (*weal & ~,* prosperity & adversity; ~ *is me,* alas; ~ *be to,* a curse upon; ~ WORTH[2] *the day*); (pl.) calamities, troubles; ~*'begone* (-awn, -ŏn), dismal-looking [p.p. of OE *begān* (BY, GO) surround]. Hence~'FUL (wŏf-)a., ~'fulLY[2] adv., (often joc., as ~*ful ignorance,* ~*fully disappointed*). [OE *wā, wǣ,* OS, OHG *wē,* ON *vei, vǣ,* Goth. *wai,* f. Gmc *wai cogn. w. L *vae*]

wŏg, n. (sl.). Native of a Middle Eastern country, esp. Egypt. [orig. unkn.]

woke. See WAKE[1].

wōld, n. Piece of open uncultivated country, down or moor land. [OE (Anglian) *wald,* OS, OHG *vald,* ON *vǫllr* f. Gmc **walthuz;* see WEALD]

wolf (wŏŏ-), n. (pl. *-ves*), & v.t. **1.** Erect--eared straight-tailed harsh-furred tawny--grey wild gregarious carnivorous quadruped allied to dog, preying on sheep etc.

or combining in packs to hunt larger animals (*cry ~ too often,* raise false alarms till genuine ones are disregarded; *have, hold, ~ by the ears,* be in a precarious situation; *keep ~ from door,* avert starvation; ~ *in sheep's clothing,* hypocrite). **2.** Rapacious or greedy person, whence ~'ISH[1] a., ~'ishLY[2] adv., ~'ishNESS n., (wŏŏ-). **3.** (mus.). Jarring sound from some notes in a bowed instrument; out--of-tune effect when playing in extremer keys on old organs (before present 'equal temperament' was in use). **4.** ~-*cub,* young ~, ‖ junior boy scout; ~-*dog,* kinds of dog kept to guard sheep from wolves, also dog-&-~ hybrid; ~-*fish,* large voracious kind; ~-*hound,* Russian breed of dog, (also) Alsatian breed popular in U.K.; ~'s-*bane,* monk's-hood, aconite; ~'s--*claws, -foot,* club-moss; ‖ ~'s-*fist,* puff--ball [OE *fist* fart]; ~-*skin,* (mat, cloak, etc., made of) ~'s skin; ~'s-*milk,* kind of spurge; ~ *spider,* tarantula, also kinds that chase instead of netting prey; ~--*tooth,* supernumerary pre-molar in horse; ~-*whistle,* whistle of a male interested in and trying to attract the attention of a woman. **5.** v.t. Devour or swallow greedily (freq. *down*). [OE, OS *wulf,* OHG *wolf,* ON *ulfr,* Goth. *wulfs,* f. Gmc **wulfaz,* cogn. w. L *lupus,* Gk *lukos*]

wo'lfram (wŏŏ-), n. (Also ~*ite*) ore yielding tungsten, native tungstate of iron & manganese; (now usu. for) tungsten. [G, perh. f. WOLF + *rahm* cream, or MHG *rām* dirt, soot]

wo'lverēne (wŏŏ-), **-ine** (-ēn), n. American carnivorous mammal called also GLUTTON & *carcajou.* [obsc. f. *wolv-,* st. of WOLF]

wolves. See WOLF.

wo'man (wŏŏ-), n. (pl. *women* pr. wĭm'ĭn), & v.t. **1.** Adult human female (*every ~ is to him a lady;* ~*'s* or *women's rights,* position of legal equality with men demanded for women; *there's a ~ in it,* way of accounting for man's inexplicable conduct; ~ *with a past,* with some scandal attaching to her past life; ~ *of the world,* experienced in society, not raw & innocent; *play the ~,* weep or show fear; *make an honest ~ of,* marry after seducing; *tied to* ~*'s apron-strings,* controlled like child by her; *single ~,* spinster; *the* SCARLET ~; WISE[1] ~). **2.** (Without article) the average or typical ~, the female sex, any ~, (*how does ~ differ from man?; man born of ~, mortal man; is an excellent thing in ~; ~'s wit,* instinctive insight or resource; ~*'s* REASON[1]; *O W~,* in apostrophes). **3.** Queen's or great lady's female attendant, lady in waiting, (arch.; *sent one of her women to ask*). **4.** Man with feminine characteristics (*is a ~ in tenderness; the old women in the Cabinet; all the old women of both sexes*). **5.** *The* feminine emotions (*all the ~ in her rose in rebellion; stirred the ~ in him; has much of the ~ in his* *composition*). **6.** attrib. Female (~ *doctor, friend, counsellor, councillor*; ~ *suffrage,* extension or possession of political suffrage to or by women). **7.** (As suf.; chiefly in terms correl. to compounds in -*man*) ~ concerned or dealing or skilful with (*country~, shop~, horse~, church~, chair~, ferry~, apple~, needle~,* etc.; also by close comb. with adj., as *gentle~*). **8.** ~-*hater,* misogynist; ~*kind,* women (one's ~*kind,* wo'*menkind,* the women of one's family); *wo'menfolk,* women, one's ~kind; hence ~HOOD n. (=female maturity, womanly instincts, ~kind), ~LESS, ~LIKE, aa. **9.** v.t. Make behave like a ~, cause to weep etc.; address as ' ~ ', 'my good ~ ', etc., speak of as ' ~ ' (not 'lady'). [OE *wifmon(n), -man(n)* (WIFE, MAN), a formation peculiar to English, the ancient wd being WIFE]

wo'manish (wŏŏ-), a. (Of man or his feelings, conduct, looks, etc.) like women' or their ways etc. (usu. derog.), effeminate. Hence ~LY² adv., ~NESS n. [ME; -ISH¹]

wo'manize (wŏŏ-), -**ise** (-īz), v.t. & i. Make womanish; (of men) be licentious, frequent prostitutes. [-IZE]

wo'manl|y̆ (wŏŏ-), a. (Of woman or her feelings, conduct, etc.) having or showing the qualities befitting a woman, not masculine or girlish, (*a truly ~y woman*; ~*y modesty, compassion, tact,* etc.). Hence ~INESS n. [ME; -LY¹]

womb (wŏŏm), n. Organ in woman & other female mammals in which child or young is conceived & nourished till birth, uterus, (*falling of the ~,* PROLAPSUS; *fruit of the ~,* children; also fig., as *in the ~ of time,* of future events etc.). [OE *wamb, womb,* OHG *wamba,* ON *vǫmb,* Goth. *wamba*]

wŏm'băt, n. Australian marsupial mammal about size of badger. [f. native *womback, -at*]

women. See WOMAN.

won. See WIN.

wo'nder¹ (wŭ-), n. **1.** Miracle, prodigy, strange or remarkable thing or specimen or performance or event, (*signs & ~s,* miracles; *work ~s,* do miracles, succeed remarkably; whence ~-WORKER¹ n.; *the child is a ~,* marvellously precocious etc.; *did ~s,* had marvellous success; *seven ~s of the world,* sights, so called in antiquity; *a nine-days' ~,* event of passing interest; *for a ~,* esp. by way of welcome exception, as *you are punctual for a ~*; *what ~, it is no ~, no ~, that,* naturally, inevitably, of course, one cannot be surprised or might have guessed that, *that* usu. omitted; so *he refused, & no ~; is a ~ of delicate workmanship*). **2.** Emotion excited by what surpasses expectation or experience or seems inexplicable, surprise mingled with admiration or curiosity or bewilderment, (*were filled with ~; looked at him in silent* or *open-mouthed ~*). **3.**~*land,* fairyland,

a country of surprising fertility etc.; ~-*struck, -stricken,* filled or dumb with ~. [OE *wundor,* OS -*ar,* OHG *wuntar,* ON *undr,* of unkn. orig.]

wo'nder² (wŭ-), v.i. & t. Be filled with wonder, feel surprise, (usu. *at,* rarely *to* see etc., or abs.; *shall never cease to ~ at it; can you ~ at it?; I ~ at you* to child etc., am shocked by your conduct; ~*ed to hear your voice; the kind of person that never ~s*), whence ~ingLY² adv., ~MENT n., (wŭ-); be surprised to find *that* (*that* usu. omitted: *I ~ he didn't kill you*); be curious, desire, to know (~*why pain exists, who invented gas-lamps, what the time is, how to proceed,* etc.). [OE *wundrian* (prec.)]

wo'nderful (wŭ-), a. Marvellous, surprising, exceeding what was expected, remarkable, admirable. Hence ~LY² adv. [ME; -FUL]

wo'ndrous (wŭ-), a. & adv. (poet., rhet.). **1.** Wonderful; hence ~LY² adv., ~NESS n. **2.** adv. (qualifying adjj. only). Wonderfully (~ *kind* etc.). [alt. f. obs. *wonders* adv. (genit. of WONDER¹, cf. -ES), after *marvellous*]

|| wŏnk'y̆, a. (sl.). Shaky, groggy; unreliable. [fanciful]

wont¹ (wō-, wŭ-), pred. a. Accustomed *to* do (usu. after *is, was, are,* etc.; *as he was ~ to say*). [OE *gewunod* p.p. of *gewunian* (*wunian* dwell)]

wont² (wō-, wŭ-), v. aux. (poet.; pres. ind., ~, ~*est,* ~s or ~, pl. ~; past ind., ~, ~*est,* ~, pl. ~, or ~*ed* for ~). Be accustomed (usu. *to* do). [ME, f. prec., or back form. f. WONTED]

wont³ (wō-, wŭ-), n. What is customary in general or habitual to a person (*use & ~,* established custom; *according to his ~; it is my ~ to*). [16th c., of doubtful orig.]

won't. See WILL¹.

wont'ĕd (wō-, wŭ-), attrib. a. Habitual to person, (rarely) usual, (*heard me with his ~ courtesy*; *met with the ~ obstacles*). [either f. WONT³ + -ED, or an extension of WONT¹]

wŏŏ, v.t. (rhet.). Ask in marriage, pay amorous court to, ask the love of, whence ~'ER¹ n.; pursue, seek to win, (fame, fortune, etc.); (abs.) go courting, conduct oneself as ~er; coax, importune, try to persuade, (person usu. *to* do or *to* compliance etc.). Hence ~'ingLY² adv. [late OE *wōgian* intr., *āwōgian* trans., of unkn. orig.]

wŏŏ'but, ou'bĭt (ŏŏ-), n. = WOOLLY-*bear.* [ME *wolbode* (WOOL, +OE *budda* beetle)]

wŏŏd, n. **1.** Growing trees occupying considerable tract of ground, forest, (also pl. in same sense, as *came upon a clearing in the ~s; cannot see the ~ for trees,* details impede general view; *out of the ~,* out of danger etc.; *don't halloo till you are out of the ~,* assume too soon that difficulties are over), whence (-)~ED² a. **2.** Fibrous substance between pith & bark of tree, whether growing or cut for timber or fuel. **3.** *The* cask or unbottled storage of wine etc. (*in, from, the* ~). **4.** (mus.). (Also ~*-wind*) *the* wooden wind-instruments of a band etc. **5.** (Bowls) a BOWL² (first sense); (golf) a wooden club. **6.** ~*-agate*, showing grain of ~ ; ~ *anemone*, the wild flowering ANEMONE; ~*'bine* or *-bind*, honeysuckle; ~*-block*, die usu. of box-~ from which ~cuts are taken; ~*'cock*, kinds of game bird related to snipe; ~*'craft*, knowledge of forest conditions esp. as applied in hunting etc.; ~*'cut*, (print, usu. as illustration in book, taken from) engraving made on ~ ; ~*'cutter*, man who cuts ~, engraver of ~cuts; ~*-engraver*, maker of ~cuts, kinds of boring insect; ~*-fibre*, fibre got from ~ esp. as material for paper; ~*-gas*, carburetted hydrogen got from ~ ; ~ *ibis*, kind of N.-Amer. stork; ~*'land*, ~ed country, ~s, (often attrib., as ~*land scenery*; *the* ~*land choir*, birds); ~ *leopard*, kind of moth; ~*-louse*, kinds of small isopod land crustacean; || ~*'man*, forester, ~cutter; ~*-notes*, spontaneous poetry; ~*-nymph*, dryad, kinds of humming-bird & moth; ~*-opal*, silicified ~ ; ~ *paper*, made of ~-pulp; ~ *pavement*, wooden blocks used as paving of road; ~*'pecker*, kinds of bird that cling to tree-stems & tap them to discover insects; ~*-pie*, great spotted ~-pecker; ~*-pigeon*, ringdove; ~*-pulp*, ~-fibre reduced to pulp as material for paper; ~*'ruff*, kinds of white-flowered plant, *sweet* ~*ruff* grown esp. for fragrance of leaves when dried or crushed; ~*s'man*, dweller in or frequenter of ~s ; ~*.sorrel*, kinds of acid-juiced plant; ~ *spirit*, crude methyl alcohol got from ~ ; ~*-tar*, got from ~ ; ~*-warbler*, kind of bird; ~*-wasp*, kinds that hang nest in tree or burrow in rotten ~ ; ~*-wool*, fine pine shavings used as surgical dressing or for packing; ~*ᴸ work*, things made of ~, esp. the wooden part of a house etc. Hence ~*'LESS* a. [OE *widu, wiodu, wudu*, OHG *witu*, ON *vithr*, f. Gmc **widhuz*]

wōod'chŭck, n. Kind of N.-Amer. marmot. [f. Amer.-Ind. name, cf. Cree *wuchak, otchock*]

wōod'en, a. Made of wood (~ *head*, stupidity, whence ~-head**ED**² a., ~-head*-***ĕd**NESS (-hĕd-) n.; ~ *horse*, by use of which Troy was taken; ~ SPOON; ~ *walls*, warships); stiff, clumsy, without animation, inexpressive, (~ *motions, manners, stare, face*, etc.), whence ~LY² adv., ~NESS n. [-EN⁵]

wōod'ȳ, a. (Of region) abounding in woods, well-wooded; of the nature, consisting, of wood (*the* ~*y parts of a plant*; ~*y stem, tissue*); (rare) found in woods (~*y* NIGHTSHADE). Hence ~ἰNESS n. [ME; -Y²]

wōof, n. = WEFT¹. [ME *oof* f. OE *ōwef* (A- 1, *wef*=WEB)=that which is woven on

(to the warp); cf. ABB; *woof* by assoc. w. WARP² (in *warp and* (*w*)*oof*) or WEFT¹]

wŏol, n. **1.** Kind of hair distinguished by fineness & wavy structure & scaly surface forming fleece of sheep, goat, alpaca, etc., & occurring mixed with ordinary hair in coat of some other animals (*carding* or *short, combing* or *long*, ~, less, more, than 4 in. long & prepared by different processes for spinning; *dyed in the* ~, dyed before spinning or weaving, (fig.) thorough-going, out-&-out; *much cry & little* ~, disappointing result, fiasco; *go for* ~ *& come home shorn*, have tables turned on one), whence-~ED² (-ld) a. **2.** Woollen yarn, worsted, (*spent an hour matching* ~*s*; *Berlin* ~, fine dyed ~ for knitting etc.); woollen garments or cloth (*safest to wear*~). **3.** Soft short under-fur or down. **4.** Negro's hair, (joc.) any person's hair (*lose* one's ~, sl., show anger). **5.** Kinds of ~-like substance (COTTON¹ ~ ; LEAD¹ ~ ; *mineral* ~, made from molten slag subjected to strong blast & used for packing walls etc.). **6.** ~*-ball*, esp. lump of concreted ~ occas. formed in stomach of sheep etc.; ~*-carding, -combing*, processes by which short, long, ~ is prepared for spinning; ~*-dyed*, dyed in the ~, see above; ~*-fat, -oil*, lanolin; ~*-fell*, skin of sheep etc. with fleece still on; ~*-gathering*, absent-minded(ness), inattentive (mood); ||~*-hall*, ~-merchants' exchange or market; ~*-pack*, (formerly) 240-lb. bale of ~, also fleecy cloud; ||~*ᴸ sack*, ~-stuffed cushion on which Lord Chancellor sits in House of Lords (*reach* etc. *the* ~*sack*, become Lord Chancellor; *take seat on the* ~ *sack*, open proceedings in House of Lords); ~*-sorters' disease*, anthrax; ~*-stapler*, one who grades producer's ~ & sells to manufacturer; ~*-work*, embroidery with Berlin ~s imitating tapestry. [OE *wull*, OHG *wolla*, ON *ull*, Goth. *wulla* f. Gmc **wullō*]

wŏol'en, a. & n. **1.** Made of wool. **2.** n. ~ fabric, as blanket, flannel, cloth; ~*-draper*, retailer of ~s ; hence ~ETTE'(2) n. [-EN⁵]

wŏol'ȳ, a. & n. **1.** Bearing or naturally covered with wool or wool-like hair (*the* ~ *flock*); ~*-bear*, kinds of hairy caterpillar; *a* ~ *puppy, head*); resembling or suggesting wool (~ *hair, clouds*; ~ *voice*, husky); (paint.) lacking in definition or luminosity or incisiveness (~ *texture, style*, etc.); (fig., of the mind) confused & hazy; (bot.) downy, pubescent. **2.** n. Woollen garment, esp. sweater. Hence wŏol'ἰNESS n. [-Y²]

Wŏol'wich (-lĭj), n. (Used for) ~ Arsenal with magazines for naval & military stores; (formerly used for) the Royal Military Academy, ~, for cadets of Royal Engineers & Artillery. [~ in Kent]

woora'li (-ah-), **woorar'a.** = CURARE.

wop¹. See WHOP.

*Wŏp², n. (sl.). Mid- or South-European

(esp. Italian) immigrant in U.S. (cf. DAGO, SQUAREhead). [orig. unkn.]

word¹ (wêrd), n. **1.** Any sound or combination of sounds (or its written or printed symbol) recognized as a PART¹ of speech, conveying an idea or alternative ideas, & capable of serving as a member of, the whole of, or a substitute for, a sentence (*coin, play upon, torture, ~s; is not the ~ for it,* not an adequate description; *have no ~s to express my gratitude* etc.; *takes ~s for things; ~s are the wise man's counters & the fool's money; in a or one ~,* briefly, to sum up; *translate or repeat ~ for ~,* literally or verbatim). **2.** Speech (*honest in ~ & deed; bold in ~ only; by ~ of mouth,* orally). **3.** Thing said, saying, remark, conversation, (usu. in pl.; *take one at his~,* act on assumption that he means what he says; *fair or good ~s,* complimentary, conciliatory, flattering, etc.; *high, hard, warm, hot, sharp,* etc., *~s,* angry talk; *big ~s,* boasting, bluff; *burning ~s,* enthusiastic, inspiring, excited, etc.; *wild & whirling ~s,* not well weighed; *hard ~s break no bones, fine ~s butter no parsnips, ~s are but wind,* depreciations of talk as compared with action; *so ~s or things, ~s & deeds;* HOUSEHOLD ~; *in so many ~s,* bluntly, explicitly; *have ~s with,* quarrel with; *they had ~s,* quarrelled; *have a ~ with,* converse briefly with; *so a ~ with you* as demand for interview; *suit the action to the ~,* do at once what one has threatened etc.; *on or with the ~,* as soon as something has been said; *a ~ & a blow,* impetuous person's procedure; *proceed from ~s to blows; waste ~s,* talk vainly; *a ~ in, out of, season,* well, ill, timed advice or interference; *have the last ~,* not let opponent in altercation speak last; *the last ~ on a subject,* pronouncement including latest views & likely to be definitive; *a truer ~ was never spoken; have a ~ to say,* something worth hearing; *man of few ~s,* taciturn; *hasn't a ~ to throw at a dog,* is unsociably or superciliously taciturn; *say a good ~ for,* commend, defend; *give person one's good ~,* recommend him for post etc.; *eat one's ~s,* retract, apologize under compulsion; *~ of command, ~ or phrase giving direction* esp. to soldiers being drilled; *a ~ to the wise,* transl. of VERBUM SAPIENTI; *God's W~,* the scriptures; so *the W~ of God,* & see below). **4.** News, intelligence, a message, (*send ~ of; send ~; ~ came that* or *of*). **5.** One's promise, assurance, or responsible statement (*give person, give, pledge, pass,* one's ~, make promise or rarely statement; *keep, break,* one's ~; *I give you my ~ for it,* promise it shall be or state that it is so; so ellipt. *my ~ upon it; upon my ~,* on my honour, also as excl. at something that shocks; *~ of honour,* promise or statement made upon one's HONOUR¹; *a man of his ~,* a promise-

-keeper; *be as good as* one's ~, fulfil or exceed what one has promised; *his ~ is as good as his bond,* may be relied on). **6.** Command, order, password, motto, (*his ~ is law; give the ~ to do* or *for; act promptly at the ~; must give the ~ before you can pass; sharp's the ~,* exhortation to hurry). **7.** *The W~* (*of God*), Christ as mediator or manifestation of God to man. **8.** *~-blind, -deaf,* incapacitated by kinds of brain trouble from attaching meaning to ~s seen or heard; *~-book,* vocabulary; *~-painter, -painting,* graphic or picturesque writer, writing; *~-perfect,* knowing part, piece, etc., by heart; *~-picture,* piece of ~-painting; *~-play,* verbal fencing, also play on ~s, pun, etc.; *~-splitter, -splitting,* (maker of) oversubtle verbal distinctions; *~-square,* set of ~s so chosen that when they are written under each other the letters read downward in columns give same ~s, e.g. *rat, ado, too.* Hence *~'LESS* a. [OE, OS *word,* OHG *wort,* ON *orth,* Goth. *waurd,* f. Gmc *wordam]

word² (wêrd), v.t. Put into words, phrase, select words to express. Hence *~'ING*¹ n. [ME, f. prec.]

wor'd|y (wêr-), a. Verbose, given to or expressed in many words, diffuse; in, consisting of, words (*~y warfare*). Hence *~iLY*² adv., *~iNESS* n. [ME, -Y²]

wore. See WEAR¹˒³.

work¹ (wêrk), n. **1.** Expenditure of energy, striving, application of effort to some purpose, (*set to ~,* begin or make begin operations; *has got to, is at, ~ at last; all ~ & no play; never does a stroke of ~; never liked, will do no, ~*); (phys.) exertion of force in overcoming resistance or producing molecular change (*convert heat into ~; unit of ~,* lifting of 1 lb. for 1 ft; *internal ~,* exerted on molecules of a body). **2.** Task (to be) undertaken, materials (to be) used in task, (*the ~ of converting the heathen; have one's ~ cut out for one,* no light task, as much as one can do; *all in the day's ~,* normal; *bring your ~ downstairs,* i.e. sewing-materials, lesson-books, etc.). **3.** Thing done, achievement, thing made, book or piece of literary or musical composition, literary or other product *of,* specimen *of,* (theol., usu. in pl.) meritorious act as opposed to faith or grace, (*mighty ~s,* miracles; *a good day's ~,* much accomplished; *the ~s of God,* nature; *honest man the noblest ~ of God; the ~s of Cicero,* his writings; *a learned, historical, ~,* book; *a ~ of art,* fine picture, building, poem, etc.; *is the ~ of the devil; ~s of mercy,* charitable actions; *covenant of ~s,* O.-T. dispensation; *~s of* SUPERerogation). **4.** Doings or experiences of specified kind (*sharp, bloody, wild, ~; thirsty, dry, ~; make short ~ of,* quickly accomplish or get rid of or overcome). **5.** Employment, esp. the opportunity of earning money by labour, laborious occupation, (*is out of, is in regular, wants, is looking for, ~; many hands make light ~; do you want the ~ or the wages?; rich men's luxury makes ~ for the poor*). 6. (Usu. in pl., & in comb. or with adj.) piece of fortification, structure for defence, (*the ~s are impregnable; advanced, detached, defensive, ~s or ~; out~s, earth~*). 7. pl. Operations in building etc. (*public ~s*, such operations done by or for the State; RELIEF[1] *~s*; ‖ *Ministry of W~s*; CLERK *of the ~s*). 8. pl. Acting or operative part of machine (usu. *of; the ~s of a watch* etc.; *something must be wrong with the ~s*). 9. pl. (Often with sing. constr., usu. in comb. with attrib. n.) manufactory (*the owner of an iron, a glass, ~s; the ~s will be closed from 1st Oct.*). 10. (Articles having) ornamentation of kind specified by adj. or by usu. hyphened attrib. n., things or parts made of material or with tools etc. so specified, (*covered with elaborate ~; rustic, embossed, beaten, frosted*, etc., *~; wood~, iron~, stone~; fancy, needle, stucco, relief, poker, ~*; (naut.) UPPER *~s*. 11. *~'aday*, fit for or used or seen on *~*days, ordinary, practical, (now chiefly in *this ~aday world*); *~-bag, -basket, -box*, holding materials & implements for *~*. esp. for sewing; *~'day*, day other than Sunday or festival; *~* house, ‖ public institution for reception of paupers in parish or union of parishes (hist.), *house of correction for petty offenders; ~'man*, operative, man hired to do manual labour, person *good, bad, skilled, 'etc.*, at his job (*an ill ~man quarrels with his tools*); *~'manlike*, characteristic of a good *~man; ~'manship*, person's relative skill in doing task, relative finish or execution seen in manufactured article or *~* of art, one's making (*we are God's* or *of God's ~manship*); *~people, ~men* or *~women; ~'piece*, thing worked on with tool or machine; *~-room*, in which *~* is done; *~'shop*, room or building in which manufacture is carried on; *~-shy*, (adj.) disinclined to work, (n.) lazy wastrel; *~ study*, system of measuring jobs so that they can produce the best results for employees and employers; *~-table*,with drawers for sewing-materials etc.,; *~'woman*, female operative. Hence *~'LESS a.* [OE *weorc*, OS *werk*, OHG *werc*, ON *verk*, f. Gmc *werkam*, cogn. w. Gk (*w*)*ergon*]

work[2] (wḗrk), v.t. & i. (*~ed*; also *wrought* pr. rawt, arch. exc. as specified below). 1. Engage in or be engaged in bodily or mental work, carry on operations, make efforts, be a craftsman in some material, (*men must ~; ~ away* or *on*, continue to *~; ~ double* TIDES; *~ to rule*, make efficiency impossible by keeping every rule in & out of season, as substitute for open strike; *is ~ing at Greek, history, social reform; ~s, ~ed* or *wrought, in brass, leather, oils, distemper*; person is *hard to

~ with, impracticable; *is ~ing for, against, the cause*). 2. (Of machine, plan, etc.) operate, act, do its appointed work, (of person) put or keep (machine etc.) in operation, keep (person, horse, machine, etc.) going or at work, exact toil from, (*charm, drug, pump, scheme, ~s* or *will not ~; ~ ship, typewriter; ~s his men* etc. *too hard, to death*); (of wheel etc.) run, revolve, go through regular motions, (*strap, handle, wheel, ~s on a wheel, pivot, axle; ~ freely, stiffly*, etc.). 3. Carry on, manage, control, (*~ mine, scheme; ~s the coach from London to Brighton*, has charge of it; *my partner ~s the Liverpool district; is ~ed by wires, electricity*, etc.). 4. Have influence or effect, exercise influence on, (often *wrought; now let it ~*, leave it to produce its effect; *~ upon person* or his *mind* etc.; *all these things have ~ed together for good; the appeal wrought powerfully upon him; ~ the* ORACLE). 5. Bring about, effect, accomplish, produce as result, (often *wrought; ~ wonders, cures, mischief, a change; ~* one's *will*, accomplish one's purpose often *upon* person or thing; *will ~ it if I can*, sl., bring it about). 6. Be in motion, be agitated, cause agitation, ferment lit. & fig., (*face, features, ~ed violently; waves ~ to & fro; thoughts, conscience, ~ing within him; yeast began to ~; to be wroth with one we love doth ~ like madness in the brain*). 7. Make way or make (way etc.) or cause to make way slowly or with difficulty or by shifting motions (usu. with adv. or prep.), gradually become (loose, free, tight, etc.) by motion, (*stockings, shirt, ~ down, up; needle ~ed out eventually from her arm; ferrule has ~ed off, loose; ~ your knife through the card, your point in; grub ~s its way into* or *out of; wind has ~ed round; ship is ~ing eastwards; some influences ~ upwards, some downwards, in society; angler ~s up stream*). 8. Knead, hammer, fashion, into shape or desired consistence (*~ dough, clay*, etc.; *butter should be thoroughly ~ed; wrought iron*, forged or rolled, not cast). 9. Artificially & gradually excite *into* (*~ed his audience, himself, into enthusiasm, a rage*). 10. Do, make by, needlework or the like (*reads to them while they ~; ~ pattern, initials*, etc., on linen etc.; *is ~ing a shawl*). 11. Solve (sum) by mathematical processes. 12. Purchase (one's *passage*) with labour instead of money, also transf. 13. *~ in*, find place for (illustration, subject, etc.), admit of being introduced. 14. *~ off*, get rid of, get over, find customers etc. for, (*~s off his bad temper on his servants; has ~ed off his debauch; ~ off 3000 copies; ~s off old jokes on us*). 15. *~ out*, find (amount etc.) or solve (sum) by calculation, (of amount etc.) be calculated *at* (*~s out at £6 10s.*), (of sum) give definite result (*will not ~ out*), exhaust with work (*person, mine, etc.,*

is quite ~ed out), accomplish or attain with difficulty (~ out one's salvation), provide for or plan all details of (has ~ed out a scheme of invasion); ~-out n. (esp. boxing, sports, etc.), a practice or test. **16.** ~ up, bring gradually to efficient state, elaborate in description (often *wrought*), advance gradually *to* (climax), excite (persons, expectations, etc.) by degrees (often *wrought*; *his wrought-up nerves*; *is in a highly wrought-up state*, nervous, hysterical), mingle (materials) into whole, acquire familiarity with (subject) by study. [OE *wyrcan* (Gmc **wurkjan*), *wircan* (Gmc **werkjan*), *we(o)rcan* (f. *we(o)rc* n.); Gmc **werk-*, **wurk-*, see prec.]

wor′k|able (wêr-), a. That can be worked, that will work, that is worth working, practicable, feasible. Hence ~ABIL′ITY, ~ableNESS, nn., ~abLY[2] adv. [-ABLE]

wor′ker (wêr-), n. In vbl senses; esp., (also ~ *bee*, *ant*, etc.) undeveloped female of various social insects. [ME; -ER[1]]

wor′king[1] (wêr-), n. In vbl senses; also or esp.: way thing works or result of its ~ (*the* ~s *of his face, conscience, fancy*); mine, quarry, etc., or part of it in which work is being or has been done (*was found in a disused* ~); ~ *day*, = WORK[1]-*day*, also hours of the twenty-four devoted to work; ~ *capital, expenses*, those required by or devoted to actual carrying on of business; ~ *drawing, plan* (serving as guide for building or construction); ~ *lunch* etc., meal at which business, policy, etc. are discussed; ~-*out*, calculation of results, elaboration of details; ~ *party*, (esp.) committee etc. appointed to secure efficiency in an industry etc. or to investigate & report on some question. [ME; -ING[1]]

wor′king[2] (wêr-), a. In vbl senses; esp., engaged in manual labour (~ *man*; *the* ~ *class*). [-ING[2]]

world (wêr-), n. **1.** Time or state or scene of existence (*the* or *this* ~, mortal life; *the other* or *next* ~, *the* ~ *to come*, life after death; *the lower* ~, hell, Earth; *Prince of this* ~, the devil; *we bring nothing into the* ~, at birth; *bring child into the* ~, beget or bear it; *make the best of both* ~s, reconcile secular & spiritual interests; *the end of the* ~, cessation of all mortal life by destruction of universe or otherwise; ~ *without end*, for ever). **2.** Secular interests & occupations (*the* ~, *the flesh, & the devil*, kinds of temptation; *forsake the* ~). **3.** The universe, all creation, everything, (*the creation of the* ~; *the best of all possible* ~s; *in the* ~, at all, that exists, etc., as *who, how, what, in the* ~ *was it?, nothing in the* ~; *for all the* ~ *like*, precisely like; *carry the* ~ *before one*, have rapid & complete success). **4.** Everything that exists outside oneself (*the external* ~, all phenomena; *the* ~ *of dreams*, things as they seem in dreams; *would not do it for*

the, to gain the whole, ~; *she is all the* ~ *to me*; *would give the* ~ *to know*). **5.** The earth, heavenly body supposed to resemble it, its countries & their inhabitants, all people, the earth as known or in some respect limited, (*go round the* ~; *to the* ~'s *end*, to farthest attainable distance; *a universe of* ~s; *are there other* ~s *than ours?*; *citizen of the* ~, cosmopolitan; *all the* ~'s *a stage*; *make a noise in the* ~, be widely talked of; *all the* ~ *knows*, it is generally known; *makes the whole* ~ *kin*; *the wise old* ~, general experience & custom; ~ *politics, movement, tendency*, affecting or seen among many peoples; *the Old W*~, Europe, Asia, & Africa, part known by ancients to exist; *the New W*~, America; *the Roman* etc. ~, as much of the ~ as concerned Rome etc.; *the Anglo-Saxon, English-speaking*, etc., ~). **6.** Human affairs, their course & conditions, active life, (*so wags the* ~; *how goes the* ~ *with you?*; *know, see, the* ~, have, acquire, experience; *man of the* ~, experienced practical tolerant person; *begin the* ~, start one's career; *all 's right with the* ~, expression of optimism; *take the* ~ *as it is, as* one *finds it*, be adaptable; *let the* ~ *slide*, not try to influence events, also disregard convention & public opinion). **7.** Average or respectable or fashionable society or people or their customs or opinions (*the great* ~, fashionable society; *all the* ~ *& his wife*, all with pretensions to fashion; *what will the* ~ *say?*, dare we defy opinion?; *live out of the* ~, avoid society). **8.** All that concerns or all who belong to specified department or class, sphere, domain, (*the literary, scientific, sporting, animal, ancient,* ~; *the* ~ *of letters, art, sport*). **9.** A vast or infinite number or amount or extent (*a* ~ *of meaning, trouble, faults*; *a* ~ *of waters*, expanse of sea; *a* ~ *too wide* etc., by far). **10.** *To the* ~ (sl.), utterly (*tired, drunk*, etc., *to the* ~, perh. by misapplication of *dead to the* ~); ~ *language*, that was or will be or is meant to be universal, also spoken in more than one part of ~; ~-*old*, (usu. by exag.) old as creation; ~-*power*, powerful State whose policy etc. may affect the ~ at large; ~-*weary*, tired of existence; ~-*wide*, spread over the ~, known or found everywhere. [OE *w(e)orold, world*, OS *werold*, OHG *weralt*, ON *verǫld*, f. Gmc **wer-* man + **aldh-* age, ELD]

wor′ldling (wêr-), n. Worldly person. [-LING[1]]

wor′ldly (wêr-), a. Temporal, earthly, (~ *goods, property*); exclusively or preponderantly concerned with or devoted to the affairs of this life, esp. to pursuit of wealth or pleasure (~ *wisdom*, esp. prudence in advancing one's own interests; ~ *people, life*, etc.); OTHER-~; ~-*minded*, intent on ~ things, whence ~-**mind′ed**NESS n.; ~-*wise*, having ~

wisdom. Hence **wor′ldli**NESS (wêr-) n. [-LY¹]

worm¹ (wêrm), n. **1.** Kinds of invertebrate limbless or apparently limbless creeping animal, esp. such as are segmented in rings or are parasitic in the intestines or tissues (also in compd names of larvae, insects, lizards, etc., with some resemblance to ∼s, as *silk, glow, slow, ∼*; *dog, child, has* ∼s, internal parasites; *food for* ∼s, of person when dead; *a* ∼ *will turn*, the meekest will resist or retaliate if pushed too far; *the* ∼ *of conscience*, gnawing pain of remorse; so *where their* ∼ *dieth not*; *am a* ∼ *today*, out of sorts & spiritless, w. ref. to *Ps.* xxii. 6). **2.** Insignificant or contemptible person. **3.** Spiral part of screw, spiral cartridge-extractor, spiral pipe of still in which vapour is cooled & condensed. **4.** Ligament under dog's tongue. **5.** ∼-*cast*, tubular mass of earth voided by earth∼; ∼′*eaten*, gnawn by ∼s, full of ∼-holes, (fig.) antiquated; ∼-*fishing*, with ∼ for bait; ∼-*gear*, arrangement of toothed wheel worked by revolving spiral; ∼-*hole*, left in wood, fruit, etc., by passage of ∼; ∼-*holed*, ∼eaten (lit.); ∼-*seed*, (Levantine plant bearing) seed used to expel intestinal ∼s; ∼′*s-eye view* (joc.), as seen from below (opp. *bird's-eye view*); ∼-*wheel*, wheel of ∼-gear. Hence ∼′Y² a., ∼′INESS n. [OE *wyrm*, OS, OHG *wurm*, ON *ormr*, Goth. *waurms*, cogn. w. L *vermis*]

worm² (wêrm), v.t. & i. **1.** Insinuate one*self into* (*favour*, person's *confidence*, etc.); convey one*self*, progress, make one's *way*, with crawling motion (∼*ed himself* or *his way* or ∼*ed through the bushes*). **2.** Draw (secret etc.) by crafty persistence *out* (*of* person). **3.** Cut worm of (dog's tongue). **4.** Rid (garden-bed etc.) of worms. [f. prec.]

worm′wood (wêr-), n. Kinds of perennial herb with bitter, tonic, & stimulating qualities used in preparation of vermouth & absinth & in medicine; bitter mortification or its cause. [alt. f. obs. *wermod* (OE *wermod*, OS -*mōde*, OHG -*muot*, of unkn. orig.), after WORM, WOOD; cf. VERMOUTH]

wôrn. See WEAR¹.

wo′rrit (wŭ-), v.t. & i., & n. = foll. (vulg.).

wo′rr|y (wŭ-), v.t. & i., & n. **1.** (Of dogs) bite (rat, sheep, dog) repeatedly, shake or pull about with the teeth (∼*y problem* etc. *out*, assail it again & again till it is solved; ∼*y the sword* in fencing, try to fluster opponent by small movements in quick succession); tease, harass, importune, be continuously or intermittently troublesome to, allow no rest or peace of mind to (∼*y* one*self*, take needless trouble; *is much* ∼*ied*, full of uneasiness; *wears a* ∼*ied look*, looks anxious or troubled); give way to anxiety, let the mind dwell on troubles, fret; *I should* ∼*y* (colloq.), it doesn't trouble me at all; ∼*y along*, manage to advance in spite of obstacles;

hence ∼**iMENT** n., ∼**y̆ing**LY² adv. **2.** n. Hound's ∼ying of quarry; (usu. in pl.) care(s), thing(s) ∼ying person; cares, ∼ied state, over-anxiety; hence ∼ILESS a. [OE *wyrgan* kill, OHG *wurgan*, f. Gmc *wurgjan*]

worse (wêrs), a. & adv. comp., & n. **1.** More BAD or BADLY; (as pred. a.) in or into less good health (*is* ∼ *today*, *is getting* ∼), in less good condition or circumstances (*is none the* ∼ *for it*). **2.** n. ∼ thing(s) (*have* ∼ *to tell*; *but* ∼ *followed*, *remains*); *the* ∼, defeat in contest (*have*, *put to*, *the* ∼, be defeated, defeat), ∼ condition (*a change for the* ∼). Hence **wor′sen**⁶ (wêr-) v.t. & i. [OE *wyrsa, wiersa*, OS *wirsa*, OHG *wirsiro*, ON *verri*, Goth. *wairsiza* f. Gmc *wers-*, cf. WAR¹]

wor′ship (wêr-), n., & v.t. & i. (-pp-). **1.** (arch.). Worthiness, merit, recognition given or due to these, honour & respect, (*men of* ∼, worthies: *win*, *have*, ∼, reach, enjoy, high repute; ‖ so still in *your*, *his*, *W*∼, used to or of certain magistrates, or to show respect for person of higher station or ironical pretence of this), whence ∼FUL a., ∼fulLY² adv., ∼fulNESS n. **2.** Reverent homage or service paid to God (*public* ∼, *the hours of* ∼, *forms of* ∼, etc., church **services**; *place of* ∼, church); adoration or devotion comparable to this felt or shown towards person or principle (*an object of* ∼; *regarding her with* ∼ *in his eyes*; *the* ∼ *of rank*, *wealth*, *intellect*, *athletics*). **3.** vb. Adore as divine, pay religious homage to; idolize, regard with adoration, (∼*s the ground she treads on*); attend public ∼ (*where does he* ∼?), whence ∼PER¹ n.; be full of adoration. [OE *weorthscipe* (WORTH¹, -SHIP)]

worst (wêr-), a. & adv. sup., n., & v.t. **1.** Most BAD, BADLY. **2.** n. ∼ part, feature, state, possible assumption, event, possible issue, or action (*the* ∼ *of the storm is over*; *the* ∼ *of it is that* —; *saw him at his* ∼; *when things are at the* or *their* ∼; *at* ∼, *at the* ∼, *our lives are safe*; *get the* ∼ *of it*, be ∼ed; *have*, *put to*, *the* ∼, be defeated, defeat; *the* ∼ *has happened*; *be prepared for the* ∼; *if the* ∼ *comes to the* ∼, if the ∼ happens; *do your*, *let him* etc. *do his* etc., ∼, expression of defiance). **3.** v.t. Get the better of, defeat, outdo, best. [OE *wyrsta* etc., adj., *wyrst* adv., f. Gmc *wersista* (*wers-* WORSE +-EST)]

wor′stĕd (wŏŏs-), n. Woollen yarn (often attrib., as ∼ *sock*). [*Worste(a)d* in Norfolk]

wort (wêrt), n. **1.** Plant, herb, (rare exc. in comb., as *spleen*, *stitch*, -∼). **2.** Infusion of malt before it is fermented into beer. [sense 1 f. OE *wyrt* = OS *wurt*, OHG, G *wurz*, ON *urt*, Goth. *waurts*, cogn. w. ROOT, L *radix*; sense 2 f. OE *wyrt* = OS *wurtja*, MHG, G *würze*, derivative f. same st.]

worth¹ (wêrth), pred. a. (governing noun like trans. part.), & n. **1.** Of value equivalent to (is ~ much, little, nothing, about 2/6; is little ~, poet., ~ little; BIRD in the hand is ~ two in bush; what is the house ~?; the rarer it is the more it is ~). 2. Deserving, worthy of, bringing compensation for, (~ one's salt, earning one's keep by good service; ~ doing, hearing, notice, the trouble, WHILE[1], an effort, troubling oneself about, etc.; ~ it, colloq., ~ while; to reign is ~ ambition; game not ~ the CANDLE; I give you, you must take, this for what it is ~, I do not guarantee its truth, wisdom, etc.). 3. Possessed of, having property amounting to, (is, died, ~ a million; spent all he was ~ on it; for all one is ~, colloq., with one's utmost efforts, without reserve). 4. ~-while, that is ~ while (a ~-while experiment). 5. n. What a person or thing is ~, value, merit, high merit or excellence, (of great, little, no, ~; persons of ~; true ~ often goes unrecognized), whence ~'LESS a., ~'lèsSLY[2] adv., ~'lèsSNESS n. 6. Coin's equivalent of commodity (give me a shilling's, half a crown's, ~ of stamps; also in comb. as penny~, two-penny~ or -pennorth, three-ha'porth etc.). [OE weorth etc. a. & n., = OS werth, OHG werd, ON verth(r), Goth. wairth(s)]

worth[2] (wĕrth), v.t. 3rd sing. subjunct. (arch.). Befall (only in woe ~ the day = cursed be). [OE weorthan become, = OHG werdan, Goth. wairthan]

worthy (wĕr'dhĭ), a. & n. 1. Estimable, having some moral worth, of a fair degree of merit, respectable, (a ~ man; has lived a ~ life; often with patronizing effect, cf. HONEST, as I asked the ~ rustic whether); deserving of or deserving of or deserving to be or do (is ~ of or rarely ~ remembrance or being remembered; is ~ to be remembered, take the lead; also in comb. as praise~, blame~); corresponding to the worth of or of, adequate, appropriate, of sufficient worth or merit, (in words ~ of or ~ the occasion; is not ~ of or ~ my sword, steel; has found a ~ adversary, received a ~ reward); hence wor'thiLY[2] adv., wor'thiNESS n., (wĕr'dhĭ-). 2. n. ~ person, person of some distinction in his country, time, etc., (esp. in pl., as the Worthies of England; an Elizabethan etc. ~). [ME wurthi etc., f. WORTH[1] n. +-Y[2]]

wot. See WIT[1].

would. See WILL[1].

would-bē (wŏŏd-), a. & adv. prefixed to n. or adj. expressing a quality aspired to or intended (~ gentleman, facetious). [WILL[1], BE]

wound[1] (wōŏn-), n., & v.t. 1. Injury done by cut or stab or blow or tear to animal or vegetable tissues including & usu. going beyond the cutting or piercing or breaking or tearing of the skin or bark or other integument, (fig.) injury done to person's reputation etc. or pain inflicted on his feelings, (poet.) pangs of love, (receive, inflict, make, heal, a ~; incised, punctured, contused, lacerated, ~; open, incurable, festering, mortal, ~); ~-wort, kinds of plant supposed to have healing properties; hence ~'LESS a. 2. v.t. Inflict ~ on (often fig., esp. ~ed vanity, feelings; willing to ~, spiteful). [OE wund, OS -da, OHG -ta, ON und; vb f. OE wundian]

wound[2]. See WIND[2, 3].

woura'li. See CURARE.

wove(n). See WEAVE.

*wow, int. expr. astonishment & admiration; (n., sl.) a sensational success. [16th c., orig. Sc.]

wows'er (-z-), n. (Austral.). Puritanical fanatic. [orig. unkn.]

wr-. In all words beginning thus w is silent.

wräck, n. Wreckage; sea-weed cast up & used for manure etc. [ME wrak f. MDu. wrak or MLG wra(c)k, a parallel form. to OE wræc, rel. to wrecan WREAK; cf. WRECK, RACK[1]]

wraith, n. Person's double or apparition seen shortly before or after his death; ghost. [orig. Sc., of unkn. orig.]

wrangle (răng'gl), v.i., & n. Brawl, (engage in) loud or vulgar or confused argument or altercation or quarrel. [ME; cf. LG wrangelen, MHG rangelen, frequent. of rangen to struggle; cogn. w. WRING]

wräng'ler (-ngg-), n. In vbl senses; ‖ also, (Camb. Univ.) person placed in first class of mathematical tripos (person in 2nd, 3rd, class being called senior, junior, ŏp'tĭmē; senior ~, first in first class when it was arranged in order of merit), whence ~SHIP n. [-ER[1]; spec. sense f. obs. sense of vb dispute publicly on a thesis]

wräp, v.t. & i. (-pp-), & n. 1. Enfold, enclose or pack or conceal in folded or soft encircling material, (often up; ~ it in paper, cotton wool; ~ up parcel; mountain, affair, is ~ped in mist, mystery; ~s up his meaning in tortuous sentences, allegory); (p.p. with up) engrossed or confined (mother, country's prosperity, is ~ped up in her child, its shipping); ~ up, put on ~s (mind you ~ up well if you go out); arrange or draw (pliant covering) round or about person or thing (~ped her shawl closer about her), whence ~p'ING[1](3) n.; overlap (intr.; the edges should, do not, ~). 2. n. (Usu. in pl.) shawl(s), rug(s), cloak(s), neckerchief(s), etc., as addition to ordinary clothes. [ME, of unkn. orig.]

wräpp'age, n. Wrapping(s). [-AGE]

wräpp'er, n. In vbl senses: esp.: (garment resembling) dressing-gown; paper enclosing newspaper or similar packet for posting; (freq. detachable) paper cover of book, outer tobacco-leaf of superior quality enclosing cigar. [-ER[1]]

In words beginning with wr-, w is silent.

wrapt. = RAPT.

wrässe, n. Kinds of thick-lipped strong-toothed bright-coloured rock-haunting sea-fish. [f. Corn. *wrach*, mutated f. *gwrach*, = W *gwrach*]

wrath (raw-), n. Anger, indignation, (poet., rhet., or joc.; *vessels, children, of* ~, persons destined to divine chastisement; *slow to* ~, not irascible). Hence ~'FUL a., ~'fuLY² adv. [OE *wræththu* f. *wrāth* WROTH +-*thu* -TH¹]

wreak, v.t. Avenge (wrong, wronged person; arch.); give play or satisfaction to, put in operation, (*vengeance, rage,* etc., usu. *upon* enemy etc.; rarely *desire* etc., as ~ one's *thoughts upon expression,* find adequate words). [OE *wrecan* drive, avenge, etc., OS *wrekan,* OHG *rechan,* ON *reka,* Goth. *wrikan* f. Gmc **wrekan,* cogn. w. L *urgēre;* cf. WRACK, WRECK]

wreath, n. (*pl. pr.* -dhz). Flowers or leaves strung or woven or wound together into ring for wearing on head or for decorating statue, building, coffin, etc., carved imitation of such ~; similar ring of soft twisted material such as silk; curl *of* smoke, circular or curved band *of* cloud, (poet.) circle *of* dancers or spectators. [OE *writha* f. wk grade of *writhan* WRITHE]

wreathe (-dh), v.t. & i. Encircle as or with or as with a wreath (*face* ~*d in smiles*); form (flowers, silk, etc.) into wreath; wind one's *arms* etc. or (of snake etc.) it*self round* person etc.; make (garland); (of smoke etc.) move in shape of wreaths. [16th c., partly back form. f. *wrethen,* p.p. of WRITHE, partly f. prec.]

wreck, n., & v.t. & i. 1. Ruin, destruction, disablement, esp., of ship (*save ship,* one's *fortunes, from* ~; *gale caused many* ~*s; the* ~ *of the Hesperus, of his life*); ship that has suffered ~, greatly damaged or disabled building or person, disorganized remains or sorry remnant *of,* (*shores are strewn with* ~*s; person, building, is a* ~; *is but a* or *the* ~ *of his former self*); goods etc. cast up by the sea (~ *of the sea*'*belongs to the Crown*); ~-*master,* officer appointed to take charge of goods etc. cast up from ~*ed* ship. 2. vb. Cause ~ of (ship, train, hopes, undertaking, person or his fortunes), (p.p.) involved in ship-~ (~*ed* sailors, goods); ||~*ing* amendment (pol.), alteration designed to frustrate the whole purpose of a bill; suffer~ (rare; *this is the obstacle your hopes will* ~ *on*). [ME, f. AF *wrec, wrech* (cf. VAREC), f. ON **wrek,* f. Gmc **wrecan* to drive, see WREAK, WRACK; vb f. n.]

wreck'age, n. Wrecked material, remnants, fragments. [-AGE]

wreck'er, n. In vbl senses; also: man who tries from shore to bring about shipwreck with a view to profiting by wreckage or who steals such wreckage; person employed in recovering wrecked ship or its contents; man who demolishes buildings etc. [-ER¹]

wren¹, n. Kinds of very small cock-tailed short-winged European songbird (often *Jenny W*~). [OE *wrenna,* obsc. rel. to OHG *wrendo, -ilo,* Icel. *rindill*]

|| **Wren²,** n. Member of the Women's Royal Naval Service, organized in 1917.

wrench, n., & v.t. 1. Violent twist or oblique pull or tearing off, (fig.) pain caused by parting, (*gave a* ~ *to his ankle, at the door-handle; leaving home was a great* ~). 2. Implement made to grip & turn nuts, bolts, etc. 3. v.t. Twist or pull violently round or sideways, injure or pull *off* or *away* by twisting, (~*ed the door open, his horse's head round, his ankle, fowl's head off, opponent's sword from him*); pervert, wrest, (facts etc.). [OE *wrencan* twist, OHG *rencken*]

wrest, v.t., & n. 1. Twist, deflect, distort, pervert, (~*s the law to suit himself;* ~ *the facts, sense* or *words of a passage,* etc.); force or wrench away from person's grasp (~*ed his sword from him*). 2. n. Key for tuning harp etc.; ~-*block,* part of piano holding ~-*pins,* to which strings are attached. [OE *wræstan,* = ON *reista,* f. Gmc **wraistjan,* rel. to WRIST]

wre'stl|e (-sl), v.i. & t., & n. 1. Grapple with & try to throw adversary esp. in sporting contest under code of rules (*with,* or abs.); have ~ing-match with; contend, grapple, do one's utmost to deal, *with* evil, temptation, duty, task, problem, etc.; ~*e with God* or *in prayer,* pray fervently; hence ~ER¹, ~ING¹, nn., (rĕs'l-). 2. n. ~ing-match; hard struggle. [OE **wræstlian,* f. prec. +-LE(3)]

wretch, n. Very unfortunate or miserable person; despicable person, person without conscience or shame (often as term of playful abuse). [OE *wrecca* = OHG *reccho* exile, adventurer (G *recke*) f. Gmc **wrak-, *wrek-,* see WREAK]

wretch'ed, a. Miserable, unhappy, afflicted; inferior, of bad quality or no merit, contemptible, unsatisfactory, causing discontent or discomfort or nuisance, confounded, (~ *weather, health, horse, inn, accommodation, poetry, poet,* etc.); (with nn. of condemnation) great, severe, excessive, (~ *insufficiency, stupidity,* etc.). Hence ~LY² adv., ~NESS n. [irreg. f. prec. +-ED¹, cf. WICKED]

wrick, rick, v.t., & n. 1. Slightly sprain or strain (neck, back, joint). 2. n. Sprain or strain (*have a* ~ *in my neck; gave my back a*~). [earlier (18th c.) *rick;* cf. MLG *vorwricken* sprain; dial. *wrig* sprain, WRIGGLE]

wrig'gl|e, v.i. & t., & n. 1. (Of worm etc.) move body with short twistings, (of animals or persons) make wormlike motions, (fig.) be slippery, practise evasion; make way *along, through, out, in,* etc., by ~ing (often fig., as ~*e out of a difficulty*); move one*self,* one's *body, tail, hand,* etc., with ~ing motion; make one's *way* by~ing. **2.** n. ~ing movement. [f. (M)LG *wriggeln* frequent. of *wriggen,* whence E dial. *wrig* to twist]

wright (rīt), n. Workman, maker, (now rare exc. in comb. as *ship, wheel, play,* -~, or with help of context as *the wheel must go to the ~ for repair*). [OE *wryhta, wyrhta* f. *wurh-,* var. of *wurk-* WORK²]

wring, v.t. (*wrŭng*), & n. **1.** Squeeze, squeeze & twist, twist forcibly, break by twisting, pervert sense of, torture, (~ person's *hand,* press it with emotion; ~ one's *hands,* squeeze them together in sign of great distress; ~ *out* or ~ *clothes,* press water from them by twisting; ~*ing wet,* or colloq. ~*ing,* so wet as to need ~ing; ~ *neck* of, kill *chicken* etc.; *has wrung the words from their true meaning; soul was wrung with agony*); extract by squeezing, get *out* by pressure or importunity, extort, (~ *water, groan, consent, money, from* or *out of* or *out*); hence (-)~ER¹(2) n. **2.** n. Squeeze (*gave my hand, give those clothes, a* ~). [OE (OS) *wringan,* OHG *ringan,* rel. to WRANGLE, WRONG]

wrinkle (rǐng'kl), n., & v.t. & i. **1.** Furrow-like crease or depression or ridge in the skin (esp. of the kind produced by age) or other flexible surface; hence **wrink′ly²** a.; (colloq.) piece of serviceable information not generally known, tip, dodge, (*is full of* ~s; *gave me, put me up to, a* ~ *or two*). **2.** vb. Produce ~s in (often *up; he* ~*d his forehead;* ~*d with age*); assume ~s, show ~d appearance. [orig. obsc.; n. & vb app. back form. f. *wrinkled,* repr. OE *gewrinclod* sinuous]

wrist, n. Joint connecting hand with forearm; (effect got in fencing, ball-games, sleight-of-hand, etc., by) working of the hand from the ~ alone (*his wonderful* ~; *that was all* ~); (mech., also ~-*pin*) stud projecting from crank etc. as attachment for connecting-rod; ~'*bănd,* band usu. of folded & starched linen forming or concealing end of shirt-sleeve, cuff; ~-*drop,* paralysis of forearm muscles from lead- -poisoning; ~ *watch* (attached to ~). [OE *wrist* (= MHG, ON *rist*), prob. f. *writh-* wk grade of *writhan* WRITHE]

wrist′lèt, n. Band or ring worn on wrist to strengthen or guard it or as ornament, bracelet, handcuff, etc. (~ *watch,* attached to ~). [-LET]

writ¹, n. *Holy, sacred,* ~, the Bible; form of written command in name of sovereign, State, court, etc., issued to official or other person & directing him to act or abstain from acting in some way (~ *of attachment, habeas corpus, subpoena,* etc.; *serve* ~ *on* one, deliver it to him ; ~ *runs* in district etc., is theoretically valid or is actually respected). [OE *writ,* ON *rit,* Goth. *writs* f. wk grade of *writan* WRITE]

writ². See foll.

write, v.i. & t. (*wrōte,* arch. *writ; written,* arch. *writ*). **1.** Trace symbols representing word(s) esp. with pen or pencil or typewriter on paper or parchment, trace (such symbols), trace the symbols that represent or constitute (word, special script, etc.), (fig.) stamp marks indicating (quality or conditions) *on* or *in* or *over* person's face etc., (~ *well, legibly, disgracefully,* etc. ; ~ *in ink, in pencil;* ~*s a good, niggling,* etc., *hand,* produces good etc. writing; *cannot read or* ~ ; *can* ~ *his alphabet, the Greek letters, Greek;* ~ *your letters separate;* ~ one's *name; has honesty written in his face; a paper written all over,* covered with writing; *a notice is written up on the wall; what I have written I have written,* of refusal to correct, see *John* xix. 22 ; ~ *thing down,* record or take note of it in writing; ~ *off,* ~ & dispatch letter; ~ *out,* ~ the whole of, ~ in full; ~ *out fair,* make fair copy of; *name is written in book of life,* included in the list of the saved; *written in* or *on water,* transient; *writ large,* on a large scale, in a magnified form). **2.** Fill, draw up or fill in, with writing (*has written three sheets;* ~ *cheque, certificate, application,* etc.; ~ *up the books, reports,* etc., make entries bringing them up to date). **3.** Compose for written or printed reproduction or publication, put into literary form & set down in writing, be engaged temporarily or permanently in such composition, compose books etc. well etc., (*is writing a book, article, his life, poetry, a novel, report, letter,* etc. ; ~ *off,* compose with facility ; ~*s cleverly, like an angel;* ~*s a little, in* or *for the papers, for a living,* etc.). **4.** ~ & send letter (*to* person or abs., also commerc. or colloq. without *to;* ~*s home once a week; have written to him; we wrote you last week; will* ~ *off,* or ~, *for a fresh supply*). **5.** Send or convey (person or *to* person news, *that, how,* etc.) by letter (~ *me all the news, the result, how you got home; wrote to his mother that he was bullied*). **6.** State in writing or print (*Herodotus* ~*s, it is written, that*). **7.** Describe, put *down,* in writing as (~*s himself esquire;* ~ *me down an ass*). **8.** ~ *down,* disparage in writing, (also) reduce nominal value of (stock); ~ *off,* cancel, recognize in writing the non-existence or annulment of, (bad debts, sums absorbed by depreciation, etc.); ~ *out,* refl., exhaust by writing (*has written himself out,* has no ideas etc. left); ~ *up,* praise in writing, also elaborate account of (incident etc.), bring (diary etc.) up to date. [OE *writan* score, write, OS *writan* cut, write, OHG *rizan* tear, draw, ON *rīta* score, write]

writ′er, n. In vbl senses; esp.: ‖ clerk in certain offices, whence ~SHIP n.; author; manual teaching how to write specified language (*French* etc.~); ‖ ~ *to the signet,* abbr. *W.S.,* Scots solicitor conducting cases before Court of SESSION ; ~'*s cramp* or *palsy,* muscular affection incapacitating for writing. [OE; -ER¹]

writhe (rīdh), *v.i.* & *t.,* & *n.* **1.** Twist or roll oneself about (as) in acute pain, squirm; twist (one's body etc.) about; shrink mentally, be stung or bitterly annoyed, *(under, at,* insult etc.; *with* shame etc.). **2.** *n.* Act of writhing. [OE *writhan,* OHG *ridan,* ON *ritha,* rel. to WREATH(E), WREST, WRIST]

writ'ing, *n.* In vbl senses; also: written document; piece of literary work done, book, article, etc., *(the ~s of Plato);* put *thing* in ~, write it down; *~-case,* holding ~-materials; *~-desk,* ·desk; *~-ink,* opp. *printing-ink; the ~ on the wall,* ominously significant event etc. (see *Dan.* v); *~-paper,* paper for ~ on esp. cut to size usual for letters; *~-table,* KNEE¹-hole or other table kept for ~ at. [ME; -ING¹]

written. See WRITE.

wrŏng, *a. (more, most),* n., adv. (no comp.), & *v.t.* **1.** Out of order, in(to) bad condition, *(something is ~ with him; my liver is or has gone or has got ~; what's ~ with —?,* colloq., surely no substitute is wanted); contrary to law or morality, wicked, *(knows the right from the ~; lying is ~);* other than the right or the more or most desirable *(always does the ~ thing; took the ~ way; the ~ answer, move; in the ~ box,* awkwardly placed, in a difficulty, at a disadvantage; *is ~ side out,* inside out; *has hold of the ~ end of the stick,* has inverted a theory, position, etc.; *on the ~ side of 40* etc., older than; *~ side of the* BLANKET; *~'un,* crick., GOOGLY; *~ fount,* abbr. *w.f.,* notice to compositor that letter or word is not of right FOUNT²); mistaken, in error, *(a ~ opinion, guess, decision, hypothesis; I think you are, can prove you, ~);* *~-headed,* perverse & obstinate; hence *~'LY²* adv. **2.** *n.* What is morally *~,* ~ action, *(the difference between right & ~; can two ~s make a right? ; do ~,* sin, offend, transgress, whence *~'doER¹, ~'doING¹,* nn., (-dōo-); *king can do no ~,* maxim expressing principle of ministerial responsibility in constitutional monarchy); injustice, unjust action or treatment, *(do ~ to; suffer ~; has done me a great ~; you do me ~,* malign me; *complains of her ~s);* position of or responsibility for having caused quarrel, made the mistake, been the offender, etc. *(you were, they are both, in the ~; put one in the ~,* show or make it appear that he was the offender); hence (of actions) *~'FUL a., ~'fuLLY² adv., ~'ful-* NESS n. **3.** *adv.* (usu. placed last). Amiss, in ~ direction, with incorrect result, *(aim, guess, answer, do sum, sort things, ~; you told, led, me ~; go ~,* take ~ path, esp. fig.); *(colloq.) get in ~ with* person, incur his dislike, *get* person *in ~,* bring him into disfavour. **4.** *v.t.* Treat unjustly,

do ~ to, *(his deeply ~ed wife);* mistakenly attribute bad motives etc. to *(I assure you you~ me).* [late OE *wrang* f. ON **wrangr, rangr,* rel. to WRING]

‖ **wrŏng'ous,** *a.* (Sc. law). Illegal, unjust. [alt. f. ME *wrangwis* f. *wrang* WRONG + *-wis,* after *rihtwīs* RIGHTEOUS]

wrote. See WRITE.

wroth (rō-, rŏ-), pred. *a.* (rhet., poet., or joc.). Angry. [OE *wrāth,* f. var. st. of *writhan* WRITHE; cf. OS *wrēth,* OHG *reid,* ON *reithr*]

wrought. See WORK².

wrung. See WRING.

wry, *a. (-ier, -iest,* or *-yer, -yest).* Distorted, turned to one side, skew, *(~ face, mouth,* grimace expressing disgust; *has a ~ nose); ~'bill,* kind of plover; *~'mouth,* kinds of fish; *~-mouthed,* ironically flattering etc.; *~'neck,* bird allied to woodpeckers able to turn head over shoulder. Hence *~'NESS n.* [f. OE *wrigian* tend, incline, in ME deviate, swerve, contort]

wy'andŏtte, *n.* American breed of fowl. [name of Amer.-Ind. tribe]

wych-, wich-, witch-, preff. in names of trees, as *~-alder, -elm, -hazel.* [OE *wice, wic,* app. f. Gmc **wik-* bend., cogn. w. WEAK]

wye, *n.* Letter Y; thing so shaped.

Wy̆ke'hamist (-kam-), *a.* & *n.* (Past or present member) of Winchester college. [f. mod. L *Wykehamista* (16th c.), William of *Wykeham,* founder (d. 1404), -IST]

‖ **wy̆nd,** *n.* (Sc.). Alley in Scots town. [app. f. st. of WIND³ n.]

wyvern. See WIVERN.

X

X (ĕks), letter (pl. *Xs,* X's). (As Rom. numeral) 10, as IX 9, xv 15, lx 60, XC 90, MX 1010, DXL 540; (alg.; *x*) first unknown quantity (cf. A, Y), (transf.) incalculable or mysterious factor or influence *(X-RAY¹s).*

Xanthipp'e (zăntĭ-), *n.* Shrewish wife. [wife of Socrates]

xăn'th|(o)- (z-), comb. form of Gk *xanthos* yellow: *~ate,* a salt of *~ic* acid; *~ĕin(e),* soluble part of yellow colouring-matter in flowers; *~ic,* yellowish *(~ic acid,* ethyl--disulpho-carbonic acid with yellow salts; *~ic flowers,* typically yellow & never passing into blue but only into red or white, opp. *cyanic flowers* with blue as typical & red or white as alternative colours); *~ŏch'rŏi* (-k-) n. pl. (ethnol.), blonds or fair whites (cf. MELANOCHROI); *~omĕl'anous* (ethnol.), with black hair & yellow or brown or olive skin; *~ophyll,* yellow colouring-matter occurring with chlorophyll in plants; *~ous* (ethnol.), yellow or Mongoloid.

xĕb'ĕc (z-), *n.* Small three-masted Mediterranean vessel with some square & some lateen sails. [alt. f. F *chebec* after Sp. *xabeque*]

xĕn|(o)- (z-), comb. form of Gk *xenos* strange(r); ~'*ial*, of hospitality or relations between host & guest; ~*ŏg'amy* (bot.), cross-fertilization; ~'*olith* (geol.), stone or rock occurring in a system of rock to which it does not belong; ~*ophŏb'ia*, morbid dislike of foreigners, so ~'*o*PHOBE.

xĕn'ŏn (z-), n. (chem.). Heavy inert gaseous element. [Gk, neut. of *xenos* strange]

xēr|(o)- (z-), comb. form of Gk *xēros* dry: ~*ăn'sis* [Gk, f. *xērainō* dry up], desiccation, drying up; ~*ăn'themum*, kinds of annual with everlasting composite flowers; ~*ŏg'raphy*, process of electrostatic printing or dry photography in which negatively-charged powder is sprinkled on a positively-charged surface, so ~*ogrăph'ic* a.; ~*ŏph'ilous* (bot.), adapted to hot & dry climate; ~*ŏphthăl⌐ mia*, ophthalmia without discharge.

xī, n. Greek letter (*Ξ*, *ξ*) = x. [Gk]

xiph|(ĭ, -o)- (z-), comb. form of Gk *xiphos* sword; ~'*oid*, sword-shaped (~*oid appendage, cartilage,* or *process,* or ~*oid* as n., lower end of sternum); ~*ïstern'um*, ~oid appendage.

Xmas (krĭs'mas), n. Abbr. for CHRISTMAS.

xō'anŏn (z-), n. (Gk ant.; pl. *-ana*). Primitive usu. wooden image of deity supposed to have fallen from heaven. [Gk (*xuō* scrape)]

X⌐rays, n. pl. (Now usu. term for)*Röntgen* RAY's; attrib. in sing., as *X-ray examination, photograph.* Hence **X-ray'** v.t., examine or treat or photograph with ~. [see X]

xȳl'ĕm (z-), n. (bot.). Woody tissue (opp. PHLOEM). [f. Gk *xulon*, cf. PHLOEM]

xȳl|(o)- (z-), comb. form of Gk *xulon* wood; ~*obal'samum*, (decoction of) dried twigs of balm-of-Gilead tree; ~'*ocarp*, (tree with) hard woody fruit, so ~*ocarp'ous* a.; ~'*ograph*, a (esp. 15th-c.) wood-engraving, also a decorative pattern got by mechanical reproduction of wood-grain, so ~*ŏg'raphy*, ~*ŏg'rapher*, ~*ograph'ic*; ~'*onite*, = CELLULOID n.; ~*ŏph'agous*, (of insects) feeding on wood [-PHAGOUS]; ~'*ophone*, musical instrument of wooden bars graduated in length & vibrating when struck.

xȳs'ter (z-), n. (surg.). Instrument for scraping bones. [f. Gk *xustēr* (*xuō* scrape)]

xȳs'tus (z-), n. (pl. *-ti*). Covered portico used by athletes for exercise in classical antiquity; garden walk or terrace. [L, f. Gk *xustos* smooth (*xuō* scrape)]

Y

Y (wī), letter, (pl. *Ys*, *Y's*). (Alg.; *y*) second unknown quantity (cf. X, B); Y⌐ -shaped arrangement of lines, piping, roads, etc., forked clamp or support,

(often attrib., as *Y-branch, -cartilage, -joint, -ligament*); *Y-cross*, Y-shaped cross esp. on chasubles suggesting figure of crucified Christ; *Y-gun*, gun with two firing-arms for discharging depth-bombs (usu. mounted aft in destroyers); *Y-level*, surveying-level mounted on Ys; *Y-moth*, kind called also *gamma* with mark like Y or gamma on wings; *Y-track*, Y of railway-line with two branches running into main track enabling engine to reverse direction by running down one branch into stem & returning up the other.

ȳ-, pref. common in ME & still found in a few arch. forms (*yclad* clad, YCLEPT, *ywis* surely), repr. OE, Du., & G *ge-* as pref. of p.pp., collective nn., & other wds; the same element is seen under different forms in ALIKE, AMONG, AWARE, EITHER, ENOUGH, HANDIWORK.

-y[1], suf. (a) repr., thr. (O)F *-ie*, Rom. *-ia* (forming nn. of state or condition) = L *-ia* (Gk *-ia, -eia*). E wds in *-y* repr. (i) AF learned adoptives, f. L, in *-ie*, as *glory, victory* (AF *glorie*, OF *gloire*), (ii) similar forms in (O)F, as *fury* (OF *furie*, besides organic *fuire*), (iii) OF formations on OF adjj., as *courtesy* (OF *corteisie* f. *corteis* courteous), (iv) L wds dir., as *family, irony*; so (v) in names of countries, as *Brittany, Italy, Normandy*. The corresp. of adjj. in *-ic* & *-ous* to nn. in *-y* makes possible the form., after Gk types, of such wds as *brachycephaly, synchrony* f. *brachycephalic, synchronous.* Meanings: (1) state, condition, quality; (2) an activity or its result; (3) concrete meanings from these (*company, library*); cf. *-*IA[1]. (b) repr., first thr. AF *-ie*, later by dir. adaptation, L *-ium* appended to vbl roots to denote an act, as *remedy* (AF *-ie*, L *-ium*), *colloquy* (L *colloquium*).

-y[2], suf. forming adjj., repr. OE *-ig*; when the n. ends in *-y*, the suf. is spelt *-ey*, as in *skyey, clayey*; in nn. ending in vowel + *-e*, this is retained, as in *gluey*; occas. there is variation, as in *hom(e)y, nos(e)y.* The general sense is 'full of', 'having the qualities of', as in *bony, thorny, angry, slangy*, in later use freq. colloq. or trivial, as *mousy, hammy, messy, oniony*, &, w. sense 'addicted to', *booky, doggy, horsy.* From 15th c. appended to adjj., as *dusky, hugy, vasty, slippery*; so w. adjj. of colour, w. sense of -ISH[1](2), as *yellowy*, & esp. in comb., as *pinky-white.* Added to vb stems w. meaning 'inclined or apt to' (do something), as *blowy, drowsy, sticky, runny.*

-y[3], *-ie*, suf. w. dim. sense, earliest (1400) in Sc. proper names; of unkn. orig. Appears in proper names, as *Annie, Betty, Sally, Micky*; in names of tools etc., as *jemmy, jenny*; added to common nn., as *laddie, lassie, granny, doggie, slavey*; mod. colloq. uses are *bookie, nightie, undies, talkies, movies.*

-y[4], suf. repr. AF, OF *-e, -ee*, F *-é, -ée*, f.

L -*atu*-, -*ala*; see -ATE[1, 2], -ADE, -ADO, -EE.
(a) in nn. (= -ATE[1]), as *county, army*; this
suf. appears in other forms, as in *assignee,
journey, attorney, valley*; (b) in adjj. (=
-ATE[2]), as in *easy, tawny*, & chiefly in
heraldic terms, as *barry, lozengy*, occas.
w. var. in -*é*, as *tenny, tenné* (= *tawny*).

yacht (yŏt), n., & v.i. 1. Light sailing-
-vessel kept, & usu. specially built &
rigged, for racing; vessel propelled by
sails, steam, electricity, or motive power
other than oars, & used for private
pleasure excursions, cruising, travel,
etc.; ~-*club*, esp. for ~-*racing*; ~'*s'man*,
person who ~s. 2. v.i. Race or cruise in
~; hence ~'ING[1] (yŏt-) n. [f. early mod.
Du. *jaghi(e)* = *jaghtschip*, f. *jag(h)t* chase
+*jagen* to hunt]

‖ **yäf'fle**, **yäff'il**, n. The green woodpecker. [imit. of laughing cry]

yäg'er (-g-), n. Member of certain German
military corps esp. of riflemen. [f. G
jäger orig. = hunter (*jagen* hunt)]

yah, int. of derision.

yahoo' (-a-h-), n. Brute in human shape
(*Gulliver's Travels*); coarse person of bestial passions & habits. [made by Swift]

Yahveh' (-vä) n., **Yahweh'** (-wä) n.,
Yah'vist n., **Yahvis'tic** a. = JEHOVAH,
JEHOVIST(*ic*).

yäk, n. Long-haired humped grunting
wild or domesticated ox of Tibet; ~ *lace*,
heavy kind made from ~'s hair. [f.
Tibetan *gyak*]

Yäle löck, n. Cylinder lock for doors etc.
invented by L. Yale (d. 1868). [P]

yäm, n. (Edible tuber of) kinds of tropical
climbing plant. [f. Port. *inhame* or Sp.
igname, of unkn. orig.]

Ya'ma (yah-), n. Hindu god of departed
spirits & judge of the dead. [Skr.]

ya'men, -*un*, (yah-), n. Chinese mandarin's official residence (*the Tsung li* ~,
Chinese Foreign Office). [Chin. (*ya* general's marquee, *mun* gate)]

yämm'er, v.i., & n. (colloq. & dial.).
Lament, wail, grumble. [f. OE *geōmrian*
f. *geōmor* sorrowful]

yänk[1], v.t. & i., & n. (colloq.). 1. Pull
(lever etc., or abs.) with a jerk. 2. n.
Sudden hard pull. [orig. unkn.]

Yänk[2], n. (colloq.). Yankee. [abbr.]

Yänk'ee (-kI), n. Inhabitant of New
England; Federal soldier or inhabitant
of northern States in American civil war;
‖ inhabitant of U.S., American; (attrib.)
of or as of the ~s (~ *notions*, American
appliances etc.); ~ *Doodle*, American
tune & song regarded as a national air;
y~fied, of acquired ~ character [-FY].
Hence ~DOM, ~ISM(2, 4), nn. [source
unascert.; perh. f. Du. *Janke* dim. of *Jan*
John used derisively (1683); a widely
accepted conjecture derives *Jankees* pl.
f. *Jengees*, Ind. pronunc. of *English*]

yaourt (yah'oort), n. Curd-like food prepared from milk fermented by action of
certain cultures. [f. Turk. *yŏghurt*]

yäp, v.i. (-pp-), & n. 1. Bark shrilly or
fussily; (colloq.) chatter, talk idly. 2. n.
Shrill or fussy bark. [imit.]

yäp'öck, n. S.-American water-opossum,
with webbed hind feet. [f. *Oyapok*, S.-
-Amer. river]

yäpp, n. Kind of bookbinding with limp
leather cover projecting considerably.
[name of London bookseller (c. 1860)]

yärb'orough (-ru), n. Whist or bridge
hand with no card above a 9. [f. an Earl
of *Y*~ who betted against its occurrence]

yärd[1], n. 1. The unit of long measure,
= 3 ft, 36 in., or 1/1760 mile (abbr. *yd*;
100 ~s, esp. flat-race distance; *square,
cubic*, ~); ~-*length of* material (*5* ~*s, a
~ & a half, of cloth*). 2. Cylindrical spar
tapering to each end slung horizontally
(*square* ~) or slantwise (*lateen* ~) across
mast to support sail (*lower, topsail, topgallant, royal*, ~, according tc sail supported; *man the* ~*s*, place men, stand,
along ~s as form of salute). 3. ~-*arm*,
either end of sail ~; ~ *measure*, rod, tape,
etc., a ~ long' & usu. divided into feet,
inches, & quarters or fifths; ~'*stick,
-wand*, rigid ~-measure; ~*stick*, (fig.)
standard of comparison. [OE *gierd*,
gyrd, OS *gerdia*, OHG *gerta* f. Gmc
gazdjō; cf. GAD-FLY]

yärd[2], n., & v.t. 1. Piece of enclosed
ground, especially one surrounded by or
attached to building(s) or used for some
manufacturing or other purpose often
specified by combination with another
word (CHURCH[1], COURT[1], DOCK[4], FARM[1],
KALE, RICK[1], TIMBER, -~, VINEYARD; *brick*-
~, where bricks are made; *railway*-~,
space near station where rolling-stock is
kept, trains made up, etc.; *stock*-~, where
cattle are penned; *tan*-~, *tanning*-
-ground); ‖ the *Y*~, SCOTLAND YARD; ~-
man, -master, man working in, manager
of, railway-~. 2. v.t. Put (cattle) into
stock-~, so ~'AGE(4) n. [OE *geard*, OS
gard, OHG *gart*, ON *garthr* (GARTH), Goth.
gards; cf. GARDEN]

yärn, n., & v.i. 1. Any spun thread esp. of
kinds prepared for weaving, knitting, or
rope-making (~-*beam* or *roll*, on which
warp-threads are wound for weaving).
2. (colloq.). Story, traveller's tale, anecdote, rambling discourse, (*spin a* ~, ~*s*,
tell ~s). 3. v.i. (colloq.). Tell ~s. [OE
gearn, OHG, ON *garn*]

yä'rrow (-ō), n. Common perennial herb
with pungent smell & astringent taste,
milfoil. [OE *gearwe*, OHG *gar(a)wa* (G
garbe), of unkn. orig.]

yäsh'mäk, n. Veil worn by Moslem women in public. [Arab.]

yät'aghan (-gän), n. Mohammedan sword
without guard or cross-piece. [Turk.]

yaw, v.i., & n. (naut., aeron.). 1. (Of ship
or aircraft) fail to hold straight course,
fall off, go unsteadily. 2. n. Deviation of
ship etc. from course. [cf. ON *jaga*
swing]

‖ **yawl**[1], v.i. & n. (rare). Howl, yell. [ME, imit.]

yawl[2], n. Kinds of small boat, esp. ship's jolly-boat with four or six oars; two-masted fore-&-aft sailing-boat with mizzen-mast stepped abaft the rudder post; kind of fishing-boat. [17th c., app. f. MLG *jolle* or Du. *jol*, of unkn. orig.]

yawn, v.i. & i. & n. **1.** (Of chasm etc.) gape, be wide open, (*a~ing gulf*, *rent*, etc.; *hell ~s for him*), (of person or animal) open the mouth wide as effect of drowsiness, boredom, etc.; utter or say with a ~ (*~ed goodnight*; '*What is the use?*' *he ~ed*). **2.** n. Act of ~ing. Hence ~'**ingLY**[2] adv. [OE *ginian*, *geonian*, OHG *ginôn*; rel. to OE *gānian*, *gīnan*, ON *gina*]

yaws (-z), n. pl. Framboesia. [orig. unkn.]

ȳclēpt', a. (arch., joc.). Called (so-&-so). [Y-, obs. *clepe* call, OE *clipian*, -ED[1]]

ye (yē *or* yi *acc. to emphasis*), 2nd pers. pron. pl. (cf. THOU, YOU) now only poet., arch., religious, or joc. or colloq., & almost exclusively (after confusion in 15th-18th cc.) as subjective case (*blessed are ye when men shall hate you*; *ye zephyrs gay*; *ye gods!*, int.; *ye gods & little fishes!* joc.; *go it, ye cripples!*, joc. encouragement; also written or spoken for *you* in some familiar phrr., as *How d'ye do?*, *What d'ye think?*, *Thank ye, I tell ye*). [OE *ge*, *gē*, *gie*, = OS *gi*, *ge*, OHG *ir*, ON *ér*, ult. f. Gmc **jūs*, **juz* (= Goth, *jus*), cf. Skr. *yū-yám*]

yea (yā), particle & n. (arch.; pl. *~s*). Yes (*let your communication be ~*, *~ nay, nay*, yes & no without oaths; *~s & nays*, arch., ayes & noes, affirmative & negative votes; *~ &*, & moreover); indeed, nay, (*ready*, *~ eager*). [OE *gēa*, *gē*, OS, OHG, ON *já*, Goth. *ja*, *jai* f. Gmc **ja*, **je*]

yean, v.t. & i. Bring forth (lamb, kid), bring forth lamb or kid. [perh. OE *geēanian* (Y- *+ ēantan*, obs. *ean*)]

yean'ling, n. Young lamb or kid. [-LING[1]]

year, n. **1.** Time occupied by the earth in one revolution round the sun (also *astronomical*, *equinoctial*, *natural*, *solar*, *tropical*, *~*; 365d. 5h. 48′ 46″ in length) or (*astral* or *sidereal ~*, longer by 20′ 23″) by the sun in recovering its previous apparent relation to the fixed stars or (*Platonic* or *Great* or *Perfect ~*, estimated by ancient astronomers at about 26000 *~s*) by the celestial bodies in recovering their relative positions at the Creation. **2.** Period of days (esp. *common ~* of 365 or *leap-~* or *bissextile ~* of 366 reckoned from 1st Jan.) used by community for dating or other purposes commencing on a certain day & corresponding more or less exactly in length to the astronomical ~ (also *legal*, *civil*, *calendar*, *~*; *lunar ~*, of 12 lunar months; LUNI-SOLAR *~*; NEW[1], OLD, *~*; *Gregorian*, *Julian*, *~*, as fixed by GREGORIAN, JULIAN, calendars; SABBATICAL *~*; *~ of GRACE, of our* LORD; *in the~ 1963*; *in the ~ 1*, lit., & = very long ago; *from*

~ to ~, *~ by ~*, as *~s* go by, each *~*; *~ in ~ out*, right through the *~*, continuously). **3.** Period of the same length as a civil *~* commencing at any day (*Christian*, *Church*, *ecclesiastical*, *~*), round of sacred seasons reckoned from & to Advent; *the fiscal ~*, reckoned from 1st April for taxing purposes; *the school ~*, *~'s* school terms usu. reckoned from beginning of autumn term; *a ~ & a day*, period specified in some legal matters; *was away for two ~s*; *it is ~s since we met*). **4.** pl. Age, time of life, (*young for his ~s*, bearing age lightly; *in ~s*, old). **5.** *~-book*, annual publication bringing information on some subject up to date; *~-long*, lasting a *~*. [OE *gēar*, OS, OHG *jār*, ON *ār*, Goth. *jēr* f. Gmc **jæram*, cogn. w. Gk *hōros* year, *hōra* season]

year'ling, n. & a. **1.** Animal more than one & less than two years old; (racing) colt a year old dating from 1st Jan. of year of foaling. **2.** adj. A year old, having existed or been so-&-so for a year, (*~ heifer*, *bride*). [-LING[1]]

year'lȳ, a. & adv. (Occurring etc.) once a year or every year or by or for the year, annual(ly). [OE; -LY[1, 2]]

yearn (yẽrn), v.i. & (impers., arch.) t. Be filled with longing or compassion or tenderness (*for* or *after* rest, home, affection, etc.; *to do*; *towards* or *to* person etc.), whence *~*'ING[1] n., *~*'ING[2] a., *~*'ingLY[2] adv.; ‖ *it ~s me*, arch., I *~* or am troubled. [OE *giernan*, OS *girnean*, ON *girna*, Goth. *gairnjan*]

yeast, n. Yellowish frothy viscous substance consisting of fungous cells developed by germination in contact with saccharine liquids & producing alcoholic fermentation, used in brewing beer, making wine, distilling spirit, & raising bread etc.; *~-powder*, substitute for *~* used in bread-making. [OE *gist*, MDu. *ghist*, MHG *jest*, ON *jastr*, f. Gmc **jes-* boil, ferment, cogn. w. Gk *zeõ* boil]

yeast'lȳ, a. Frothy like yeast (*~y waves* etc.); in a ferment, working like yeast, (*a ~y conscience*, *turmoil*, *imaginings*); wordy, superficial, (*a ~y fellow*; *~y talk*, *professions*). Hence *~*INESS n. [-Y[2]]

*yĕgg, n. (sl.). (Also *~'man*) travelling burglar or safe-breaker. [said to be a surname]

yelk. See YOLK.

yĕll, v.i. & t., & n. (Make, utter with) shrill cry of pain or anger or fright, high-pitched shout, or uncontrollable burst of laughter (*~ed with pain*, *fury*, *delight*, *laughter*; *~ out an oath*, *orders*; *~ed curses*, *my name*, *a refusal*, *defiance*; *with ~s of horror* etc.); (U.S. Univv.) organized cry used by students e.g. in encouraging their representatives in athletic contests. [OE, OHG *gellan*, ON *gjalla*, rel. to *galan* (cf. NIGHTINGALE)]

yĕll'ow (-ō), a. (*~er*, *~est*) & n., & v.t. & i. **1.** Of the colour between green & orange in the spectrum, coloured like buttercup or primrose or lemon or sulphur or gold, (with many names of plants, animals, etc., as ~ *rattle*, *wagtail*, *ochre*, *jaundice*; often also in comb. with parts of body etc., as ~-*bill*, -*head*, -*legs*, -*root*, -*rump*, -*seed*, -*shank*, -*tail*, -*throat*, -*top*, -*wood*, forming animal & plant names; ‖ ~ *boy*, obs. sl., gold coin; ~ *cartilage*, elastic kind forming artery-walls etc.; ~ *fever*, or *Jack*, tropical fever with jaundice & black vomit; ~ *jacket*, state garment in China for royal persons & subjects selected for high honour; *the* SERE *&* ~ *leaf*; ~ *men*, *races*, etc., Chinese, Japanese, Mongols, etc.; ~ *metal*, brass of 60 parts copper & 40 parts zinc; *the* ~ *peril*, the danger that the ~ races may overwhelm the white or overrun the world; *the* ~ *press*, sensational newspapers esp. of chauvinistic tendencies, orig. of U.S. newspapers urging war with Spain 1898; ~ *spot*, point of acutest vision in retina. **2.** (fig.). (Of looks, mood, feelings, etc.) jealous, envious, suspicious; (colloq.) cowardly. **3.** ‖ ~*back*, cheap novel in ~ paper boards common in 19th c., also French novel in ~ paper cover; ~-*gum*, infants' black jaundice; ~-(*h*)*ammer*, bunting with ~ head & neck & breast [*hammer* prob. not a corruption, but of separate orig.]; hence ~ISH[1](2) (-ŏĭ-), ~Y[2] (-ŏĭ), aa., ~NESS (-ŏn-) n. **4.** n. ~ colour; kinds of ~ pigment; (colloq.) cowardice; kinds of moth & butterfly; *the*~s, jaundice, (arch.) jealousy, * a peach-disease. **5.** vb. Turn ~ (*paper* ~*ed with age*; *the* ~*ing leaves*). [OE *geolu*, OS, OHG *gelo*, f. Gmc **gelwaz*, cf. GOLD]

yelp, v.i., & n. (Utter) cry (as) of dog in pain or in eager anticipation. [f. OE *gielpan* = MDu. *gelfen* f. Gmc **galpjan*]

yen[1], n. (pl. *yen*). Japanese monetary unit. [Jap., f. Chin. *yüan* round, dollar]

yĕn[2], n., & v.i. (sl.). **1.** Longing, yearning. **2.** v.i. Yearn. [Chin., = craving as for opium]

yeo′man (yō-), n. (pl. *-men*). **1.** (hist.). Person qualified by possessing free land of 40/- annual value to serve on juries, vote for knight of shire, etc. **2.** ‖ Small landowner, farmer, person of middle class engaged in agriculture; ‖ member of the yeomanry force. **3.** (nav.). ‖ ~ *of signals*, petty officer in branch concerned with visual signalling; *petty officer performing clerical duties on board ship. **4.** ~('s) *service*, help in need; ~ *of the guard*, BEEFeater. Hence ~LY[1] a. [ME *yoman*, *yeman*, prob. = YOUNG+MAN]

yeo′manry̆ (yō-), n. Yeomen; ‖ volunteer cavalry force raised from farmers etc. [-RY]

-yer, suf. var. of -IER, esp. after *w*, as *bowyer*, *lawyer*, *sawyer*.

yĕr′cum. See MUDAR. [Tamil]

yĕs, particle equivalent to affirmative sentence, & n. (pl. ~*es*). **1.** The answer to

your question is affirmative, it is as you say or as I have said, your request or command will be complied with, the statement made or course intended is correct or satisfactory, (~ *&*, ~ *or*, forms for substituting stronger phr., as *I could endure*, ~, *& enjoy it*; *he would beat me*, ~, *and you too*; ~?, indeed?, is that so?); (in answer to summons or address) I am here, I hear or am attending to you, (~?, what more have you to say?). **2.** n. The word or answer ~ (*say* ~, consent; *confine yourself to* ~ *& no* or ~*es & noes*); ~-*man* (colloq.), characterless, obedient, weakly acquiescent person. [OE *gēse*, *gīse*, prob. f. *gēa* YEA+*sī* 3 sing. pres. subj. of *bēon* BE]

yĕs′ter- in comb. (1) in ~*day* n. & adv., (on) the day before today (*he arrived* ~*day*; *is but of* ~*day*, of recent origin; *the day before* ~*day*, n. & adv.; often attrib. as ~*day morning*); (2) chiefly poet. with sense of ~*day*, in compds serving as nn. & advv. for which ordinary usage prefers ~*day* — or *last* —; so ~-*morn*(*ing*) (usu. ~*day morning*), ~-*eve*, ~-*even*(*ing*), (Sc.) *yestreen′*, (usu. ~*day evening*), ~*night* (usu. *last night*); (3) poet. w. sense *last past* in ~-*year* n. & adv. (usu: *last year*). [OE *geostran*, *gystrandæg* (cf. Goth. *gistradagis*); cf. (without ' day ') MDu. *gisteren*, OHG *gestaron*]

yĕt, adv. & conj. **1.** As late as now or then, with continuance to this or to that time, still, (*there is* ~ *time*; *is he* ~ *alive*? *there is life in the old dog* ~; *much* ~ *remains to be done*; *there is one* ~ *missing*; *his hands were* ~ *red with blood*; *his* ~ *unfinished task*; *I seem to see him* ~; *while it was* ~ *morning*). **2.** (With neg. context) so soon as now or then, by this or by that time, so far, in the immediate future, (*it is not time* ~; *is he dead* ~?; *they have not* ~ *heard*; *I have never* ~ *lied*; *the largest* ~ *found*; *haven't you learnt* ~ *that fire burns*?; *need you go* ~?; *it will not happen just* ~; *these things are not* ~). **3.** Again, in addition, (~ *once more* or ~ *once*; *another & ~ another*; ~ *again*; *more & ~ more*); (with *nor*) either (*won't listen to me nor* ~ *to her*). **4.** Before the matter is done with, before all is over, in the time that still remains, (*he will win*, *I will be even with you*, ~). **5.** (With compar.) even (*a* ~ *more difficult*, *easier*, *task*). **6.** Nevertheless, *and* in spite of that, *but* for all that, (*though they curse*, ~ *bless thou*; *&*, *having nothing*, ~ *hath all*; *it is strange*, *& ~ it is true*; *strange & ~ true*; *the logic seems sound*, *but* ~ *it does not convince me*). **7.** *As* ~, up to now or then (esp. w. suggestion that the statement would not be true of later time; *it has worked well as* ~; *a conscience as* ~ *clear*). **8.** conj. But at the same time, & ~, (~ *what is the use of it all?*; *faint* ~ *pursuing*; *a rough* ~ *ready helper*). [OE *giet*(*a*), = OFris. *ieta*, of unkn. orig.]

yet′i (yă-), n. Native (Sherpa) name for the *Abominable* SNOWman.

yew, n. (Wood of) kinds of slow-growing dark-leaved evergreen tree (also ∼-*tree*) often planted in graveyards & used formerly for making bows & still in cabinet--making. [OE *īw, ēow*, OS *īh*, OHG *īw, īwa* (G *eibe*), f. Gmc *°ihw-, °igw-*]

Yg(g)′drasil (Ig-), n. (Scand. myth.). Tree whose roots & branches bind together heaven & earth & hell. [ON *yg(g)drasill* app. f. *Yggr* name of Odin + *drasill* horse]

Yid, n. (sl. contempt.). Jew. [back form. f. foll.]

Yidd′ish, a. & n. (In) a form of old German (with words borrowed from many modern languages) spoken by Jews in or. from central and eastern Europe. [f. G *jüdisch* Jewish]

yield, v.t. & i., & n. 1. Produce or give or bring as fruit or result (*earth ∼s her increase*; *land ∼s good crops*; *investment ∼s 5%*; *tax∼s a handsome revenue, little*; *sin ∼s bitter fruit*); (abs., of land etc.) repay cultivation etc. *well, poorly*, etc. 2. Give up, deliver over, surrender (trans.), resign (trans.), comply with demand for, concede, (∼ *fortress* etc.; ∼ *oneself prisoner*; ∼ *possession*, one's *pride of place*; ∼ *precedence to*; ∼ *the palm*, be surpassed; ∼ *submission, consent*, submit, consent; ∼ *up the ghost*, die; ∼ *the point*, concede it in argument); surrender (intr.), make submission *to*, give consent or change one's course in deference *to*, comply with demand (whence ∼′ING² a., ∼′ingLY² adv.), be inferior or confess inferiority *to*, (*town ∼ed without awaiting assault*; ∼ *to superior force, persuasion*; *courage never to submit or* ∼ ; *I* ∼ *to none in appreciation of his merits*). 3. n. Amount ∼ed or produced, output, return. [OE *gieldan*, OS *geldan*, OHG *geltan*, ON *gjalda*, Goth. *-gildan*, f. Gmc *°geldhan*]

-yl, suf. (chem.) used to form wds denoting a RADICAL, as *amyl, ethyl*, f. F *-yle* f. Gk *hulē* wood, substance.

yl′äng-yl′äng (ēl⸛, -ēl⸛), n. Malayan tree from the flowers of which a perfume is distilled; the perfume itself. [Tagalog *dlang-ilang*]

yōd′el, v.t. & i. (-ll-), & n. 1. Sing (t. & i.), make melodious inarticulate sounds, with frequent changes between falsetto & normal voice in the manner of Swiss & Tyrolese mountaineers. 2. n. ∼ling cry, match of∼ling. [f. G dial. *jodeln*]

yōg′a, n. Hindu system of philosophic meditation & asceticism designed to effect the reunion of the devotee's soul with the universal spirit. [Hind. f. Skr., = union]

yogh (yŏχ), n. The Middle-English letter 3 used for certain values of g & y. [prob. f. ME 3oc yoke, as beginning with the sound]

yog(h)urt (yōg′oort), n. Var. of YAOURT.

yōg′i (-gĭ), n. Devotee of yoga. Hence **yōg′ISM**(3) (-g-) n. [Hind. (YOGA)]

yŏ⸛heave-hō′, yohō′, intt. used by sailors in heaving together.

yoicks, int. & n., **yoick,** v.i. & t. Foxhunter's halloo; (vb) cry yoicks, urge (hounds) *on* etc. with it. [orig. unkn.; also *hoicks, hoik, hyke*]

yōke, n., & v.t. & i. 1. Wooden cross-piece fastened over necks of two oxen etc. & attached to the plough or waggon that they are to (help to) draw; (Rom. hist.) uplifted ∼ or arch of three spears symbolizing it under which defeated enemy was made to march (*send, pass* intr., *under the* ∼); (fig.) sway or dominion or servitude (*submitted to his* ∼ ; *the heavy* ∼ *of opinion*; *had never endured the* ∼); (fig.) bond of union esp. the marriage tie. 2. Pair *of* oxen etc. (‖∼ *of land*, arch., as much as one ∼ of oxen can plough in a day). 3. Piece of timber shaped to fit person's shoulders & support pail etc. at each end. 4. Separately made shoulder--piece of shirt or coat or blouse, or waist--piece of skirt, from which the rest is suspended. 5. Cross-bar on which bell swings; cross-bar of rudder to whose ends ropes are fastened; coupling-piece of two pipes discharging into one; kinds of coupling or controlling piece in machinery. 6. ∼-*bone*, cheek-bone connecting bones of head & face; ∼′*fellow*, ∼′*mate*, partner in marriage, work, etc.; ∼′*lines, -ropes*, with which rudder-∼ is worked. 7. vb. Put ∼ upon; couple or unite (esp. pair) in marriage or otherwise, link (one *to* another); (intr.) match or work together (*together, with*, or abs.; *do not ∼ well*). [OE *geoc*, OHG *joh*, OS, Goth. *juk*, ON *ok*, cogn. w. L *jugum*]

yōk′el, n. Rustic, country bumpkin. [orig. obsc.]

yolk (yōk), (now rare) **yĕlk,** n. Yellow part of egg; sebaceous secretion from skin of sheep, wool-oil; ∼-*bag, -sac*, membrane enclosing∼ of egg. Hence (-)∼ED² (yŏkt), ∼Y² (yōk′Ĭ), aa. [OE *geolca* (YELLOW)]

yön, a., adv., & pron. 1. Yonder (a. & adv.; arch. or poet. or provincial). 2. pron. (arch. etc.). Yonder person or thing. [OE *geon*, OHG *jener*, ON *enn*, Goth. *jains*]

yön′der, a. & adv. (Situated) over there, in the direction towards which I am looking or pointing, within or conceived as within view but distant. [ME, cf. OS *gendra*, Goth. *jaindrē*]

yōre, n. Old times (now only in *of* ∼, formerly, in or of old days). [OE *gēara*, of obsc. orig.]

York[1], n. ∼ *& Lancaster*, rival royal houses & parties in the Wars of the Roses (∼-*&-Lancaster rose*, parti-coloured kind); *House of* ∼, kings Edw. IV–Rich. III ; ∼ *stone*, kind used in building.

yörk[2], v.t. Bowl with yorker. [back form.]

yŏrk′er, n. Ball so bowled as to pitch immediately in front of batsman's block (also *tice*). [prob. f. *York*, as introduced in Yorkshire, -ER¹]

Yŏrk′ist, a. & n. (Adherent) of family descended from Edmund Duke of York son of Edward III, or of the White-rose party fighting for it in Wars of the Roses. [-IST]

Yŏrk′shire (-er), **n.** County (~ *flannel*, undyed; ~ *grit*, stone used in polishing marble; ~ *pudding*, batter baked under & eaten with meat esp. beef; ~ *stone*, kind used in building; ~ *terrier*, small shaggy toy kind).

you (ŭ or yŏŏ *acc. to emphasis*), 2nd pers. pron. sing. (w. pl. vb) & pl. (arch. etc. subj. pl. YE; arch. etc. sing. THOU, *thee*; possess. YOUR, YOURS). **1.** The person(s) or thing(s) addressed (~ *are mad, an angel, all fools; who sent ~?; I choose ~ three; the rest of ~ can stay here; ~ & I or me; ~'re another*, vulg., retort to one who calls names; occas. expressed w. imperat., as *don't ~ go away, begin ~* or *~ begin*; as voc. w. n. in apposition = exclamatory statement, as ~ *fool!*, ~ *darling!*, occas. w. ~ appended also, as ~ *idiot ~!*; as voc. calling attention, as ~ *there, what is your name?*). **2.** (arch.). Yourself (*get ~ gone, begone;* ~ *should find ~ a wife; sit ~ down*). **3.** (In general statements) one, any one, all concerned, every one, a person, (~ *never can tell; what are ~ to do with a child like this?; it is bad at first, but ~ soon get used to it; there's a shot for ~!*). [OE *ēow acc.* & *dat.* of *gē* YE; *ye* f. more frequent use of obj. case, & *thou* & *thee* (cf. similar substitutes in F, G, It.) as more courteous form]

young (yŭ-), **a.** (~*er*, ~*est*, pr. -ngg-), & **n.** (only in collect. sing). **1.** Not far advanced in life or growth or development, of recent birth or origin or formation, not yet old, still vigorous, immature, youthful, inexperienced, (*a ~ child, man, animal, plant, nation, institution; a ~ family,* of ~ *children; a ~ person,* servants' phr. for unknown ~ woman of lower classes; *the ~ person*, those whose innocence must be shielded from the indecent in talk & literature; ~ *people,* esp. the marriageable; *my etc.* ~ *man* or *woman*, sweetheart; *the night, year, century, is yet ~*, still near its beginning; OLD *head on ~ shoulders;* ~ *& OLD; you ~ rascal* etc., usu. in playful address to child; *a ~ man in a hurry*, esp. ardent reformer; ~ *for his* YEARS; *men are now ~ at fifty; an old man but a ~ convert;* ~ BLOOD¹; ~*er son,* esp. member of noble family poor owing to primogeniture; ~ *things,* often indulgently etc. of persons; *is ~ in crime,* unpractised; ~ *Jones,* esp. Jones the son; ~ *'un,* youngster, often as voc.; *in my ~ days,* while I was ~; ~ *love, ambition,* etc., felt in or characteristic of youth; *the* ~*er* before or after name of

person to be distinguished from another, as *the* ~*er Pitt, Teniers the* ~*er*; so *the* ~ PRETENDER; ~ *England, Ireland, Italy,* etc., especially as names of political parties claiming to speak for the rising generation; *Y~ Turks,* esp. the party that in 1908 forced the Sultan to restore the constitution; ~*ers occas.* as n. pl. opp. *elders,* as *is kind to his* ~*ers*). Hence ~′ISH¹(2) a., ~′LING¹ n. (poet.). **2. n.** Offspring esp. of animals before or soon after birth (*with* ~, pregnant; *cares for, deserts, its* ~). [OE *geong,* OS *jung,* OHG *junc,* ON *ungr,* Goth. *juggs,* f. Gmc **ju(wu)ngaz,* cogn. w. L *juvencus, juvenis*]

you′ngster (yŭ-), **n.** Child, esp. active or lively boy. [-STER]

you′nker (yŭ-), **n.** Youngster (arch. or colloq.); = JUNKER. [f. MDu. *jonckher* (*jonc* young, *hēre* lord)]

your (ŭr, yŏr, yer, *acc. to emphasis*), attrib. a. Of, belonging to, spoken of by, done to or by, you (~ *danger, hat, expectations; so this is* ~ *immaculate saint!;* ~ *dismissal of him, by him;* ~ *father & mine;* ~ *& my father, fathers;* cf. foll.); (colloq. & chiefly arch., now usu. w. depreciatory implication) much talked of, well known, familiar, (*no one so fallible as* ~ *expert in handwriting;* ~ *facetious bore is the worst of all*). [(1) OE *ēower* gen. pl. of *gē* YE; (2) OE *ēower, -ru, -er* possess. adj.]

yours (ŭrz, yŏrz), **pron. & pred. a. 1.** The one(s) belonging to or of you (*my father & ~;* ~ *& my father,* erron. for *your &; my father is not ~; I like ~ better;* ~ *is the only way; am no child of ~; that cough of ~; some friends of ~; you & ~,* you & *your family, property,* etc.; ~ *is to hand, your letter has come;* so ~ *of the 11th* etc.). **2. adj.** Belonging to you, at your service, (*it is ~ if you will accept it; ever ~,* ~ *truly,* FAITHFULLY, OBEDIENTLY, etc., epistolary formulae preceding signature; ~ *truly,* joc., I, as *but ~ truly was not taking any,* I refused etc.); *what 's ~?* (colloq.), what will you drink? [prec., -ES, see OURS]

yourself′ (ŭr- etc., as in YOUR), **pron.** (pl. -*ves*). (Emphat.) you in person, in particular, in your normal state, & not another or others, or alone (usu. in apposition w. *you* except in commands, & either next after it or later, rarely substituted for it; *please see to it* ~ or *yourselves; you* ~ *said so* or *you said so* ~; ~ *have said it,* arch., poet., etc.; *by* ~, alone, as *why are you sitting by* ~?, also unaided, as *you cannot do it by yourselves; it is* ~ *I want, not your money; how's* ~?, sl., how are you?, esp. after answering similar inquiry; *be~*, colloq., pull ~ together; *you are not quite* ~ *tonight,* are out of humour etc.); (refl.) the person(s) previously described as *you,* or to whom a command is addressed (*have you hurt* ~?; *you seemed pleased with yourselves; ask* ~ *whether it is not true*). [YOUR, SELF]

youth (ûth), n. (*pl. pr.* ûdhz). Being young, adolescence, (the vigour or enthusiasm or weakness or inexperience or other characteristic of) the period between childhood & full manhood or womanhood, (*has all the appearance of extreme* ~; *in my hot, raw, vigorous,* etc. ~; *from ~ onwards*; ~'*s a stuff will not endure*; *the secret of perpetual, of keeping one's,* ~; *the* ~ *of the world,* early times), whence ~'FUL (ûth-) a., ~'fuLLY² adv., ~'fulNESS n.; youLG man (*as a* ~ *of 20*; *promising, lanky,* etc., ~*s*); young men & women (*the* ~ *of the country*; *loves to be surrounded by* ~; *our* ~ *are infected with commerciality*); ~ *centre, club,* place or organization provided for leisure-time activities of young people; ~ *hostel,* place where hikers etc. can put up for the night. [OE *geoguth,* OS *juguth,* OHG *jugund,* f. WG **jugunthi-* f. **juwunthi-* (YOUNG, -TH¹)]

yowl. Var. of YAWL¹.

y̆tterb'|ium, n. (chem.). Rare-earth metallic element. Hence ~IC a. [*Ytterby* in Sweden, -IUM]

y̆tt'r|ium, n. (chem.). Rare-earth metallic element. Hence ~IC, ~ious, aa., ~o- comb. form. [as prec.]

yŭcc'a, n. Kinds of American white--flowered liliaceous plant. [Carib]

Yugoslav. See JUGOSLAV.

yule (ûl), n. The Christmas festival (also ~-*tide*; ~-*log,* burnt on Christmas Eve). [OE *gēol*(a), cf. ON *jól,* ult. orig. obsc.]

Z

Z (zĕd; *zē), letter (pl. *Zs, Z's, zeds*); (Alg.; *z*) third unknown quantity (cf. c, x).

Zăd'kiĕl, n. (Used for) a popular astrological almanac founded by R. J. Morrison (d. 1874), who adopted this pseudonym.

zăf'fre (-*er*), **zăff'er,** n. Impure oxide of cobalt used in making cobalt-blue & as blue pigment in enamelling & porcelain--painting. [f. It. *zaffera* or F *zafre,* f. Arab. *sofre*]

Zăm'bŏ. Var. of SAMBO (in first sense).

zăn'y̆, n. (Hist.) attendant clown awkwardly mimicking chief clown in shows, merry andrew; (mod.) person given to buffoonery, foolish jester, half-witted person. [f. F *zani,* or It. *zan*(*n*)*i,* Venetian form of *Gianni, Giovanni* John]

Zănzibār'i, n. & a. (Native) of Zanzibar.

zăp'tieh (-ă), n. Turkish policeman. [f. Turk. *ḍabtiyeh* f. Arab. *ḍabt* administration]

Zarathustr-. See ZOROASTRIAN.

zari'ba (-rē-), **-rēb'a,** n. Hedged or palisaded enclosure for protection of camp or village in the Sudan etc. [f. Arab. *zarība* pen]

zax. Var. of SAX.

zeal, n. Earnestness or fervour in advancing a cause or rendering service, hearty & persistent endeavour. So ~'ous (zĕl-)

a., ~'ousLY² adv. [ME *zele* f. LL f. Gk *zēlos*]

zeal'ot (zĕl-), n. Uncompromising or extreme partisan, fanatic, (Z~, one of a Jewish sect resisting the Romans A.D. 6--70). Hence ~RY(4) n. [f. eccl. L f. Gk *zēlōtēs* (prec., -OT²)]

zebec(k). Var. of XEBEC.

zĕb'ra, n. Kinds of striped quadruped (true or mountain ~, Burchell's ~, quagga) allied to ass or horse; (attrib., & in comb. w. names of animals etc.) striped like ~ (~ *markings,* ~ *caterpillar,* ~ *woodpecker,* ~*-wood,* etc.); ~ *crossing,* striped street-crossing where pedestrians have precedence over other traffic. Hence **zĕb'rINE¹** a. [It. or Pg., f. Congolese]

zĕb'ū, n. The E.-Ind. humped ox. [F (zé-)]

zĕd, n. Letter Z. [f. F *zède* f. L f. Gk *zēta*]

zĕd'oary̆, n. Kinds (*long, round,* ~) of aromatic gingerlike substance made from rootstock of E.-Ind. plants & used in medicine, perfumery, & dyeing. [f. med. L *zedoarium* f. Arab. *zedwār*]

xeit'geist (tsītgi-), n. Spirit of the times, drift of thought & feeling in a period. [G]

xelōs'ŏ, mus. direction. With fervour. [It.]

zĕmin'dăr, n. (Anglo-Ind.). (Hist.) district governor & revenue-farmer under Mogul empire; (later) Indian landed proprietor paying land-tax to British government. [Hind., f. Pers. *zamīndār* (*zamīn* earth, *dār* holder)]

zĕmst'vō, n. (hist.; pl. ~*s*). Local elective assembly regulating affairs of district in Russia. [Russ., f. *zemlya* land]

zena'na (-ah-), n. Part of house in which women of high-caste families are secluded in India (~ *mission,* of women visiting ~*s* to spread medical & other reform among inmates); ~ (*cloth*), a light fabric for women's dresses. [Hind., f. Pers. *zanāna* (*zan* woman)]

Zĕnd, n. Ancient language of the Iranian family, allied to Sanskrit, named from the Zend-Avesta (Avesta or text & Zend or commentary) or Zoroastrian scriptures.

zĕn'ith (*or* zēn-), n. Point of heavens directly above observer (opp. NADIR); (transf.) highest point, time or place of greatest power or prosperity or happiness, (*is at his, its, the,* ~); ~-*distance,* arc intercepted between any body & ~, complement of body's altitude. Hence ~AL a. [ME, f. OF *cenit*(*h*) or med. L *cenit* f. Arab. *samt* (*ar-rās*) way (over the head)]

zē'olite, n. Any one of a number of minerals consisting mainly of hydrous silicates of lime, soda, & alumina, commonly found in the cavities of igneous rocks. [f. Gk *zeō* boil + -LITE; from their characteristic swelling & fusing before the blowpipe]

zĕph'yr (-*er*), n. 1. The west wind personified (Z~); balmy breeze, light **wind.**

2. Athlete's thin gauzy jersey for running, rowing, boxing, etc. in; kinds of dress-material. [f. L *l*. Gk *zephuros* west wind]

Zĕpp′elin, n. (colloq. *Zĕpp*). Large dirigible airship of type built (*c.* 1900), orig. for military use in Germany. [Count ~, inventor]

zēr′ō, n. (pl. ~s). Figure 0, cipher; no quantity or number, nil; starting-point in scales from which positive & negative quantity is reckoned (~ in thermometers, freezing-point of water or other point selected to reckon from; *absolute* ~ in temperature, point at which the particles whose motion constitutes heat would be at rest, estimated at −273.16° C.); (mil.) point of time from which the start of each movement in a timed programme is at a specified interval; lowest point, bottom of scale, nullity, nadir; *fly at* ~ (under 1,000 ft). [f. F *zéro* or It. *zero* f. Arab. *çifr* CIPHER]

zĕst, n. Piquancy, stimulating flavour, (esp. fig.; *adds a* ~ *to*); keen enjoyment or interest, gusto, (*entered into it with* ~). [17th c., f. F *zeste* orange or lemon peel, of unkn. orig.]

zēt′a, n. Greek letter (*Z*, ζ) = z. [Gk (*zē*-)]

zĕtĕt′ic, a. (rare). Proceeding by inquiry. [f. Gk *zētētikos* (*zēleō* seek, -IC)]

zeug′ma, n. (gram.). Figure of speech in which a verb or adjective does duty with two nouns to one of which it is strictly applicable while the word appropriate to the other is not used (e.g. *kill the boys & sc.* destroy *the luggage, with weeping eyes & sc.* grieving *hearts*; cf. SYLLEPSIS). Hence **zeugmăt′ic** a. [L f. Gk (genit. *-atos*), f. *zeugnumi* yoke]

Zeus, n. (Gk ant.). King of the Olympian gods. [Gk]

zib′ĕt, n. The Asian or Indian civet. [f. med. L *zibethum* as CIVET]

zig′zăg, a., n., adv., & v.i. (-gg-). **1.** With abrupt alternate right & left turns, with alternating salient & re-entrant angles, with motion as of tacking ship, (*a* ~ *line, course, road, fence, trench, flash of lightning*). **2.** n. ~ line or (esp. for mounting steep hill) road' or (in sieges) set of trenches. **3.** adv. With ~ course. **4.** v.i. Go ~. [F, f. G *zickzack*]

zill′ah (-*a*), n. Administrative district in India. [Hind. *zilah* f. Arab. *ḍilah*]

zinc, n., & v.t. **1.** A white metallic element much used in the arts esp. as component of brass & German silver, as roofing material, as coating for sheet iron (cf. GALVANIZE), in electric batteries, & in relief-printing blocks (*flowers of* ~ or ~ *oxide,* powder used as white pigment & in kinds of ointment & cement); hence (spelt, before -i-, with -c- or -k- or -ck-) ~′IC, ~′IF′EROUS, ~′OID, aa., ~′IFY v.t.; ~′IFICA′TION n., ~′OUS (esp. of negative pole of voltaic battery), **zink′ʏ²,** aa.,

~o· comb. form. **2.** v.t. (-*k*· or -*ck*·). Coat with~. [f. G *zink*, of obsc. orig.]

zinc′ō, n. (pl. ~s), & vb. = ZINCOGRAPH. [abbr.]

zinc′|ograph (-ahf), n., & v.i. & t. **1.** Zinc plate with design etched in relief on it for printing from, picture taken from it. **2.** vb. Etch (t. & i.) on zinc, reproduce (design) thus. So ~ŌG′RAPHY, ~ŌG′RAPHER nn., ~OGRAPH′IC a. [ZINCO-, -GRAPH]

zinc′otȳpe, n. = prec. n. [as prec., TYPE]

Zĭng′arō (-ngg-), n. (pl. *-rī*). Gipsy. [It.]

zinn′ia, n. Kinds of composite plant with showy rayed flowers of deep red & other colours. [J. G. *Zinn* German botanist (d. 1759), -IA¹]

Zi′on, n. (Holy hill of) ancient Jerusalem; the Hebrew theocracy; the Christian Church; the Heavenly Jerusalem or kingdom of heaven, whence ~WARDS adv.; ‖ (name for) nonconformist chapel. [f. eccl. L *Sion* f. Heb. *Tsiyōn* orig. hill]

Zi′on|ism, n. A movement resulting in the re-establishment of a Jewish nation in Palestine. So ~IST. [-ISM(3)]

zip, n. Light sharp sound, as of bullet passing through air, the sudden tearing of cloth, etc.; (fig.) energy, ' pep '; ~· *-fastener,* (also *zipp′er*) fastening device consisting of two flexible stringers operated by means of the constriction of a sliding clip pulled between them. [imit.]

zĭrc′on, n. A silicate of zirconium of which some varieties (HYACINTH, JARGON²) are cut into gems. [f. F *zircone* f. Arab. *zarqūn*]

zĭrcōn′ium, n. A metallic element found chiefly in zircon & used to alloy iron. Hence **zĭrcōn′ic** a., **zĭrc′onATE¹**(3) n. [-IUM]

zith′er|(n), n. Simple flat many-stringed instrument placed on table or knees & played partly with fingers of left hand & partly with plectrum in right hand. Hence ~IST(1) n. [G (as CITHER)]

zlŏt′ȳ, n. Polish coin. [Pol.]

Zō′ar, n. Place of refuge, sanctuary. [*Gen.* xix]

zōd′iăc, n. A belt of the heavens limited by lines about 8° from the ecliptic on each side, including all apparent positions of the sun & planets as known to the ancients, & divided into 12 equal parts called *signs of the* ~ (Aries, Taurus, Gemini, Cancer, Leo, Virgo, Libra, Scorpio, Sagittarius, Capricorn(us), Aquarius, Pisces) each formerly containing the similarly named *zodiacal constellation* but now by precession of equinoxes coinciding with the constellation that bears the name of the preceding sign (e.g. the constellations Pisces, Aries, are now in the signs Aries, Taurus); (transf., now rare) complete course, circuit, or compass. [ME, f. OF *zodiaque* f. L *l*. late Gk *zōdiakos* f. *zō(i)dion* dim. of *zō(i)on* animal]

zodi′acal, a. Of, in, the zodiac (~ *light,* luminous tract of sky shaped like tall triangle occas. seen in east before sunrise or in west after sunset esp. in tropics). [f. LL *zodiacus* adj. (as prec.)+-AL]

zō'étrōpe, n. WHEEL¹ of life. [irreg. f. Gk *zōē* life, *tropos* turn]

zō'har, n. A cabalistic textbook prob. of 14th c. called Bible of the Mystics. [Heb., = brightness]

zō'ic, a. Of animals; (geol., of rocks etc.) containing fossils, with traces of animal or plant life. [f. Gk *zōikos* (*zōon* see ZODIAC, -IC)]

Zōl'a|ism, n. Absence of reserve, detailed realism, in describing the gross or immoral. So ~IST(2) n., ~ESQUE' (-ěsk), ~is'TIC, aa. [*Zola*, French novelist d. 1902, -ISM]

zollverein (tsŏl'ferīn), n. Union of States having a common customs-tariff against outsiders & usu. free trade with each other. [G]

zŏm'bĭ(e), n. A corpse said to be revived by witchcraft. [orig. unkn.]

zōne, n., & v.t. 1. Belt or girdle worn round the body (chiefly arch. & poet.; *maiden* or *virgin* ~, symbol of virginity; *loose the maiden* ~ *of*, deprive of virginity). 2. Encircling band or stripe distinguishable in colour or texture or character from the rest of the object encircled. 3. (Geog.) any of five divisions of the earth bounded by circles parallel to the equator (*frigid* ~s, N. of arctic, S. of antarctic, circle; *torrid* ~, between the tropics; *North, South, temperate* ~, between frigid & torrid ~s); area enclosed between two exact or approximate concentric circles; part of surface of sphere enclosed between two parallel planes, or of cone or cylinder between such planes cutting it perpendicularly to axis; any well-defined tract of more or less beltlike form; ~ *time*, local time for any longitude as opposed to Greenwich time; hence zōn'AL, zōn'ARY¹, zōn'ūlAR¹ [-UL-], zōn'ATE² (bot., zool.), aa., zōn'ALLY² adv. 4. v.t. Encircle as or with ~; arrange or distribute by ~s. [F, or f. L f. Gk *zōnē* girdle (*zōnnumi* gird)]

Zōō, n. (colloq.). Zoological garden, esp. that in London. [abbr.]

zōo-, comb. form of Gk *zōos* living, *zōon* an animal (see ZODIAC), = of animals, of animal life, (occas. as opp. vegetables & minerals, occas. excluding man also or especially); *zōōg'amy*, sexual reproduction; ~*geōg'raphy*, zoology dealing with local distribution of animals, so ~*geōg'rapher*, ~*geograph'ic(al)*; *zōōg'raphy*, descriptive zoology, so *zōōg'rapher*, ~*graph'ic(al)*, *zōōg'raphist*; *zōōl'atry*, religious worship of animals; *zō'olite*, fossil animal, fossilized animal substance; *zō'omancy*, divination from appearances or behaviour of animals; ~*morph'ic*, dealing with or represented under animal forms, having gods of beastlike form (cf. *anthropomorphic*), so ~*morph'ism*; *zō'o-*

phȳte, kinds of plantlike animal, esp. holothurians, starfishes, jelly-fishes, sea anemones, & sponges, so ~*phȳt'ic*, ~*phȳtŏl'ogy*, ~*phȳtolo'gical*, ~*phȳtŏl'ogist*; *zō'osperm*, spermatozoon, also ~spore; *zō'ospore*, spore capable of motion, so ~*spŏ'ric*; *zōŏt'omy*, dissection or anatomy of animals other than man.

zō'oid, a. & n. 1. Of incompletely animal nature. 2. n. Organic body or cell resembling but not being animal or plant; more or less independent organism given by gemmation or fission; member of compound organism. [prec., -OID]

zōŏl'og|ȳ, n. Natural history of animals, science of their structure, physiology, classification, habits, & distribution. So zōōlō'gICAL a. (~*ical garden*, public garden or park with collection of animals kept for exhibition), zōōlō'gICALLY² adv., ~IST(3) n. [f. mod. L *zoologia* (ZOO-, -LOGY)]

zōōm, v.i., & n. 1. Force aeroplane to mount at high speed & steep angle. 2. n. Aeroplane's steep climb; ~ *lens* (cinemat. etc.), lens which by variation of focal length enables quick transmission from long shot to close-up. [imit.]

zō'ril, n. Carnivorous quadruped of Africa & Asia Minor allied to skunk & weasel. [f. F *zorille* f. Sp. *zorrilla* (*zorra* fox)]

Zōrōās'trian, Zărathus'tr- (-thŏō-), nn. & aa. (Follower) of Zoroaster, Zarathustra, or Zerduscht, (adherent) of the religious system taught by him & his followers in the Zend-Avesta based on the conflict between Ormuzd god of light & good & Ahriman god of darkness & evil, the religion of the magi & ancient Persia still held by Parsees & occas. called *fire-worship*. Hence Zōrōās'trian-ISM(3), Zărathus'tr(ian)ism, nn. [f. L f. Gk *Zoroastrēs* f. Zend *Zarathustra*, -IAN]

zouave (zŏō'ahv), n. 1. Member of French light-infantry corps orig. formed of Algerians & retaining Oriental uniform. 2. Woman's short jacket like that of ~ uniform. [name of tribe]

‖ zounds (-z), int. (arch.) of indignation. [= (*God*)*'s wounds* (i.e. Christ's on the cross)]

zucchĕtt'a, -ĕtt'ō, (tsŏŏk-), n. R.-C. ecclesiastic's skull-cap, black for priest, purple for bishop, red for cardinal, & white for Pope. [It. (-*a*), dim. of *zucca* gourd]

Zulu (zōōl'ōō), n. Member, language, of a S.-Afr. Kaffir people. [native]

zwieback (tswēb'ahk), n. Kind of biscuit rusk or sweet cake toasted in slices. [G]

Zwing'lian (tswĭngg-), a. & n. (Follower) of the Swiss religious reformer Zwingli (1484-1531). [-IAN]

zȳg'al, a. H-shaped (esp. of brain-fissures). [as foll., -AL]

zȳg(o)-, comb. form of Gk *zugon* yoke: *zygapŏph'ysis*, one of the processes on a vertebra serving as articulation with another; *zygodac'tyl* a. & n., *-ylous* a., (bird) with toes disposed in pairs, two toes pointing forward & two backward; *zygomorph'ous*, (of flower) divisible into similar halves only in one plane; *zyg'o-spore*, spore formed by conjugation of two similar gametes.

zȳgōm'a, n. (pl. ~*ta*). Bony arch of cheek, yoke-bone. Hence **zȳgomät'ic** a. [f. Gk *zugōma* f. *zugon* yoke]

zȳgōs'is, n. (biol.). = CONJUGATION. [f. Gk *zugōsis* joining (prec.)]

zȳg'ōte, n. Product of the fusion of two gametes, e.g. zygospore. [f. Gk *zugoō* yoke (*zugon*)]

zȳmōs'is, n. Fermentation; zymotic disease in general or any form of it. [f. Gk *zumōsis* f. *zumoō* ferment f. *zumē* leaven, see -OSIS]

zȳmŏt'ic, a. Of fermentation (~ *diseases,* epidemic, endemic, contagious, or sporadic diseases regarded as caused by multiplication of germs introduced from without). [f. Gk *zumōtikos* (prec., -OTIC)]

ADDENDA

NOTE

THESE addenda consist of (1) words not recorded in the body of the dictionary, and (2) further senses and constructions of words already treated. Additions of the latter kind, being arranged as appendages to existing articles, are readily distinguished by the absence of pronunciation, grammatical description, and etymology from the independent articles dealing with new words. References are in SMALL CAPITALS.

age². Hence **ag(e)ING¹** (āj′ing) n., change of properties occurring in some metals after heat treatment or cold working.

ălmacăn′tar, -muc-, n. Line of constant altitude above the horizon. [f. F *almucantarat* f. Arab. (AL-², *qanṭarah* a bridge)]

anaemia. (Also) deficiency of red blood-corpuscles or their haemoglobin.

band¹. **~′width** (electr. etc.), range of frequencies.

beat³, n. (Also **~′nik**) one of the **~** *generation*, young people adopting unconventional dress, manners, habits, etc., as a means of self-expression and social protest. [**~nik** after *sputnik*]

bing′ō (-ngg-), n. Modern development of LOTTO. [orig. unkn.]

cāde, n. Pet lamb or foal. [orig. unkn.]

charis′m|a (k-; -z-), n. Divine gift or talent; capacity to inspire followers with devotion and enthusiasm. Hence **~-AT′IC** a. [f. Gk *kharisma*]

chromat|o-.~ŏg′raphy(chem.),separation of compounds by allowing a solution of them to trickle through a column of adsorbing material so that the different compounds are adsorbed in separate coloured layers constituting a *chrŏm′atogram* (k-).

coast¹. **~′guard,** (also) body of men formed orig. to prevent smuggling, now chiefly a life-saving service, member of this body.

commissioner. **C~** *for Oaths,* solicitor authorized to administer oaths to persons making affidavits.

deuterium. Cf. PROTIUM.

dipole. (Also, radio) type of aerial used at short wave-lengths.

electro-. **~*phorēs′is*,** movement of suspended colloidal particles under the influence of an electric field; **~***phorĕt′ic* a.**

eschatology. (Also, esp. *realized* **~**) the present realization of the last things in the Christian life.

ethic. **~al,** (also, of proprietary products) advertised only in the medical press and not to the general public.

fringe (n.). **~** *benefits*, perquisites, benefits of various kinds provided by employers to supplement money wages and salaries.

gro′schen (-ōshn), n. **1.** (hist.). Small silver German coin. **2.** (colloq.). German 10-pfennig piece. **3.** Smallest Austrian coin, 1|100 of schilling. [G]

hood (n.). Also: detachable capelike garment worn over academic gown etc. to indicate degree; (waterproof) folding top of motor-car, perambulator, etc.

Hŏpp′us (cŭb′ic) fŏŏt, n. Unit of volume measurement based on the square of the quarter-girth, still used in British Commonwealth forestry for the cubic content of round logs or trees. [E. *Hoppus* (d. 1758), surveyor and compiler of calculating tables]

implō′sion (-zhn), n. (phonet.). Closing the glottis simultaneously with the stop position, and then compressing the air between the glottis stoppage and the mouth one. So **implōs′IVE** a. & n. [f. L IM¹ (*plodere plos-* = *plaudere* clap), see -ION]

In′terpŏl (I-), n. International police organization, with headquarters in Paris, for tracking down criminals. [*International police*]

king¹. **~-*crab*,** * (also) large edible spider-crab.

landscape. (Also, v.t. & i.) improve by **~**-gardening etc., engage in **~**-gardening.

lās′er (-z-), n. = *optical* MASER. [*light amplification by stimulated emission of radiation*]

rand. (Also, *pr.* rahnt) unit of S.-Afr. decimal currency (= 100 cents), adopted 1961.

mark¹. (*God*) *save the* ~; (also, in literary usage) an expression of impatient scorn.

mās′er (-z-), n. Device for amplifying microwaves; *optical* ~ (for amplifying light waves). [*microwave amplification by stimulated emission of radiation*]

master¹. (Also, *M*~) courtesy title usu. given to eldest son of Scottish viscount or baron, as *the M*~ *of Falkland.*

micro-¹. ~*dot,* photograph reduced to the size of a dot or a very small spot.

mutation. So **mūt′**ANT a. & n. (biol.), (individual) differing from its parents as a result of ~.

semi-. ~*conduc′tor,* a solid, non-conducting in pure state or at low temperatures, which is a conductor when impure or at higher temperatures.

sērv′o-|mĕch′anism (-k-), n. Power--assisted device usu. for controlling movement (e.g. a brake). So ~*control* n. [f. L *servus* slave, MECHANISM]

standard. ~ *English,* the form of English used, with local variations, by most cultured English-speaking people, so ~ *pronunciation.*

statesman. *Elder* ~, distinguished retired ~ etc. whose advice is available to all.

ouch². ow, intt. expr. sudden pain.

•uh⸗huh′ (ŭhŭ), int. expr. affirmation.

pastel. (Also, attrib., of colour) soft, subdued.

pērm′afrost (-aws-, -ŏs-), n. Permanently frozen subsoil in arctic regions. [f. PERMA(NENT) FROST]

virus. (Also) ultramicroscopic organic particle existing only within cells of animal and plant bodies and capable of producing various diseases.

APPENDIX I

GENERAL ABBREVIATIONS

(For list of special abbreviations used in text see pp. xiv–xvi)

ABBREVIATIONS are made chiefly in two ways. (1) The beginning of the word is given, and at any point (after one letter, after all but one letter, or anywhere between) it is cut short with a full stop; so N. = North, Liv. = Livy, syn. = synonym; the full stop serves to announce that it is needless to go further with the word. (The mathematical abbreviations for cosecant, cosine, cotangent, secant, sine, and tangent, namely cosec, cos, cot, sec, sin, and tan, are used without the full stop. Sometimes, as in ENSA and SCAPA, the full stop is omitted between the letters.) (2) Some portion of the middle of the word is dropped out, the first and last letters being retained with or without others between; so wt = weight, hrs = hours, exrx = executrix, Abp = Archbishop; the writing of a full stop at the end of these on the analogy of that in (1), though now usual, is to be deprecated; it is not a natural device (as in (1)), but artificial; it has very rarely the merit of announcing that the letters printed are not a full word, since that is nearly always clear without it (*caps* for *capitals* is one of the few exceptions); and it has always the demerit of failing to let the reader know that in the riddle he is called upon to read the last as well as the first letter is given him. There is also a mixed class in which the full stop at the end does convey that the end of the word is missing, but without implying (as in (1)) that all the letters up to that point are present; such are cg. = c(enti)g(ram), cf. = c(on)f(er), avdp. = av(oir)d(u)p(ois); the first two of these consist of the initial letters of their words' etymological elements, the last gives the first letter followed by such of the consonants as may suggest the general sound.

The method adopted in the following list is to omit the otiose full stop in accordance with the view expressed above; it is, however, to be understood that all abbreviations here given without the full stop may also be, and more frequently are, used with it. The U.S. State names and those of British counties should be mentioned; in the former we give the full stop or omit it as explained above (Vt, Va, Ky, for Vermont, Virginia, Kentucky; Mass., O., Oreg., for Massachusetts, Ohio, Oregon); in the latter we write the full stop after the 's' (Yorks., Leics., Berks., etc.) as representing *shire*. Viz and oz are preferred to viz. and oz. on the ground that the z itself represents a written terminal flourish.

A., adult (i.e. for adults only, referring to cinema picture); air; alto; *avancer* (on timepiece regulator, = to accelerate).

A.A., anti-aircraft; Automobile Association.

A.A.A.,*Agricultural Adjustment Administration; Amateur Athletic Association.

A.A.F., Auxiliary Air Force.

A.A.G., Assistant Adjutant-General.

A.A.I., Associate of the Chartered Auctioneers' & Estate Agents' Institute.

A. and M., Ancient and Modern (Hymns).

A.A.Q.M.G., Assistant Adjutant and Quartermaster-General.

A.B., able-bodied seaman.

A.B.C., the alphabet; alphabetical train time-table; Aerated Bread Company('s Shop).

ab init., *ab initio* (= from the beginning).

Abp, Archbishop.

A.C., aircraftman; Alpine Club; alternating current; *ante Christum* (= before Christ).

a/c, account.

A.C.A., Associate of the Institute of Chartered Accountants.

acc., account.

A.C.F., Army Cadet Force.

A.C.G.B., Arts Council of Great Britain.

A.C.I., Army Council Instruction.

A.C.I.I., Associate of the Chartered Insurance Institute.

A.C.I.S., Associate of the Chartered Institute of Secretaries.

A.C.W., aircraftwoman.

A.C.W.A., Associate of the Institute of Cost & Works Accountants.

A.D., *anno Domini* (= in the year of our Lord).

A.D.C., aide-de-camp; Amateur Dramatic Club.

ad fin., *ad finem* (= towards the end).

ad init., *ad initium* (= at the beginning).

Adjt, Adjutant.

Adm., Admiral.

advt, advertisement.

Æ (see A in dictionary).

A.E.A., Atomic Energy Authority.

A.E.F., Amalgamated Union of Engineering & Foundry Workers.

A.F., Admiral of the Fleet.

A.F.A., Amateur Football Association.

A.F.A.S., Associate of the Faculty of Architects & Surveyors.

A.F.C., Air Force Cross.

A.F.L., American Federation of Labour.

A.F.M., Air Force Medal.

A.F.O., Admiralty Fleet Order.

A.F.S., Army Fire Service; Auxiliary Fire Service.

A.F.V., Armoured Fighting Vehicle.

A.G., Adjutant-General; air gunner.

A.H., *anno Hegirae* (= in the year of the Hegira).

A.I., Admiralty Instruction.

A.I.A., Associate of the Institute of Actuaries.

A.I.B., Associate of the Institute of Bankers.

A.I.D., A.I.H., artificial insemination by donor, by husband.

A.I.M.T.A., Associate of the Institute of Municipal Treasurers & Accountants.

A.Inst.P., Associate of the Institute of Physics.

a.l., autograph letter.

A.L.A., American Library Association.

Ala, Alabama.

Alas., Alaska.

Alban, (Bp) of St Albans (see Cantuar.).

Ald., Alderman.

a.l.s., autograph letter signed.

A.M., Air Ministry; Albert Medal; = M.A.

a.m., *anno mundi* (= in the year of the world); *ante meridiem* (= before noon).

A.M.D.G., *ad majorem Dei gloriam* (= to the greater glory of God).

A.M.G.(O.T.), Allied Military Government (of Occupied Territory).

A.M.I.C.E., A.M.I.E.E., A.M.I.Mech. E., A.M.I.Mun.E., Associate Member of Institution of Civil, Electrical, Mechanical, Municipal, Engineers.

A.M.S., Army Medical Staff (*or* Service).

A.M.S.E., Associate Member of the Society of Engineers.

A.M.T.P.I., Associate Member of the Town Planning Institute.

A.O., Army Order.

A.O.C.(-in-C.), Air Officer Commanding (-in-Chief).

A. of F., Admiral of the Fleet.

A.P., Associated Press.

A.P.M., Assistant Provost-Marshal.

Apocr., Apocrypha.

Apr., April.

A.Q.M.G., Assistant Quartermaster- -General.

A.R., advice of receipt; annual return.

A.R.A., Associate of the Royal Academy.

A.R.A.D., Associate of the Royal Academy of Dancing.

A.R.A.M., Associate of the Royal Academy of Music.

A.R.C.A.,A.R.C.M.,A.R.C.O.,A.R.C.S., Associate of the Royal College of Art, of Music, of Organists, of Science.

Argyl., Argyllshire.

A.R.I.B.A., Associate of the Royal Institute of British Architects.

A.R.I.C., Associate of the Royal Institute of Chemistry.

A.R.I.C.S., Associate of the Royal Institution of Chartered Surveyors.

Ariz., Arizona.

Ark., Arkansas.

A.R.P., air-raid precautions.

arr., arrives etc.

A.R.S.H., Associate of the Royal Society for the Promotion of Health.

A.R.W.S., Associate of the Royal Society of Painters in Water Colours.

A.S., Anglo-Saxon.

A/S, anti-submarine.

Asaph., (Bishop) of St Asaph (see Cantuar.).

A.S.C., American Society of Cinematographers.

A.S.E., Amalgamated Society (*or* Associate of the Society) of Engineers.

A.S.L.E.F., Associated Society of Locomotive Engineers & Firemen.

A.S.L.I.B., Association of Special Libraries & Information Bureaux.

A.S.R.S., Amalgamated Society of Railway Servants.

A.S.W., anti-submarine warfare.

Asst, Assistant.

A.T.A.(S.), Air Transport Auxiliary (Service).

A.T.C., Air Training Corps.

A.T.S., Auxiliary Territorial Service.

Å.U., Ångström unit.

A.U.C., *ab urbe condita* or *anno urbis conditae* (= from, in the year of, the founding of the city, i.e. Rome).

Aug., August.

a.u.n., *absque ulla nota* (= unmarked).

A.V., Authorized Version (of the Bible).

avdp., avoirdupois.

A.V.M., Air Vice-Marshal.

A.W.O.L., absent without leave.

B, black (of pencil-lead).

B., *Beatus, -a* (= Blessed).

b., born; (in cricket) bowled, bye.

B.A., Bachelor of Arts; British Academy.

B.Agr(ic)., Bachelor of Agriculture.

B.A.O.R., British Army of the Rhine.

Bart, Baronet.

Bart's, St Bartholomew's Hospital.

Bath: & Well:, (Bishop) of Bath & Wells (see Cantuar.).

B.B., Boys' Brigade.

BB, BBB, double-, treble-, black (of pencil-lead).

B.B.C., British Broadcasting Corporation.

B.C., Battery Commander; before Christ; British Columbia.

B.C.A., Bureau of Current Affairs.

B.Ch., = Ch.B.

B.C.L., Bachelor of Civil Law.

B.Com., Bachelor of Commerce.

B.D., Bacheler of Divinity.

Bdr, Bombardier.

B.D.S., Bachelor of Dental Surgery.

bds, boards (in bookbinding).

B.D.S.T., British double summer time.

B.E., (Order of the) British Empire.

B.E.A., British European Airways.

B.Ed., Bachelor of Education.

Beds., Bedfordshire.

B.E.F., British Expeditionary Force.

B.E.M., British Empire Medal.

B.Eng., Bachelor of Engineering.

Berks., Berkshire.

b.f., bloody fool; bold face (type); brought forward.

B.F.B.S., British & Foreign Bible Society.

b.h.p., brake horse-power.

B.I.F., British Industries Fair.

B.L., Bachelor of Law.

B.Litt., Bachelor of Letters.

B.M., Bachelor of Medicine.

B.M.A., British Medical Association.

B.Mus., Bachelor of Music.

B.N.C., Brasenose College, Oxford.

B.O., body odour.

B.O.A., British Optical Association.

B.O.A.C., British Overseas Airways Corporation.

B.O.T., Board of Trade.

bot, bought.

B.P., British Pharmacopoeia; British Public.

Bp, Bishop.

B.Q.M.S., Battery Quartermaster-Sergeant.

B.R., British Railways.

B.R.C.S., British Red Cross Society.

brev., brevet.

Brig.(-Gen.), Brigadier(-General).

Brit., Britain; British.

Britt., *Brit(t)an(n)iarum* (= of the Britains, on coins).

Bros, brothers.

B.S.A., Birmingham Small Arms (Co.); British South Africa.

B.S.A.A.C., British South American Airways Corporation.

B.Sc., Bachelor of Science.

b.s.g.d.g., *brevelé sans garantie du gou-*

vernement (= patented without government guarantee).

B.S.M., Battery Sergeant-Major.

B.S.I., British Standards Institution.

B.S.T., British summer time.

Bt, Baronet.

B.T.C., British Transport Commission.

B.Th.U., Btu, British thermal unit.

Bucks., Buckinghamshire.

B.U.P., British United Press.

B.V.M., *Beata Virgo Maria* (= the Blessed Virgin Mary).

B.W.I., British West Indies.

B.W.T.A., British Women's Temperance Association.

C, centum (= 100); coulomb.

C., Centigrade.

c., caught; cent(s); century; chapter; (c.) *circa*; *circiter*; colt; cubic.

C.A., Chartered Accountant (Sc.).

C.A.B., citizens' advice bureau; *Civil Aeronautics Board.

Cal(if)., California.

Cambs., Cambridgeshire.

Can., Canada.

c. & b., caught & bowled.

Cant., Canticles.

Cantab., Cantabrigian.

Cantuar., of Canterbury. (The signature of certain bishops consists of their Christian name(s) or initial(s) followed by an abbreviation of the Latin adj. of place; thus Dr Ramsey signs *Michael Cantuar.*).

cap., *caput* (= chapter).

caps, capital letters.

Capt., Captain.

Card., Cardinal.

Carliol, (Bishop) of Carlisle (see Cantuar.).

C.B., Companion of the Bath; confinement etc. to barracks; counter bombardment.

C.B.E., Commander of (the Order of) the British Empire.

C.C., Consular Corps; County Council(lor); cricket club.

c.c., cubic centimetre.

C.C.C., *Civilian Conservation Corps; || Corpus Christi College, Cambridge.

C.C.S., casualty clearing station; Ceylon Civil Service.

C.D., Civil Defence; Contagious Diseases (Acts).

c.d., c.div, cum dividend.

Cdr, Commander.

c.d.v, *carte de visite* (= visiting-card).

C.E, Church of England; Civil Engineer.

C.E.A., Central Electricity Authority.

Cels., Celsius.

C.E.M.A., Council for the Encouragement of Music & the Arts (now Arts Council of Great Britain).

C.E.M.S., Church of England Men's Society.

Cent., Centigrade.

cent., century.

Cestr., (Bishop) of Chester (see Cantuar.).

C.E.T.S., Church of England Temperance Society.

C.F., Chaplain to the Forces.

cf., *confer* (= compare).

cg., centigram.

C.G.M., Conspicuous Gallantry Medal.

C.G.S., centimetre, gram, second (as elements in a system of scientific measurement); Chief of the General Staff.

C.G.T., *Confédération Générale du Travail* (F, = General Confederation of Labour).

C.H., Companion of Honour.

ch., chap., chapter.

Chas, Charles.

Ch.B., *Chirurgiae Baccalaureus* (= Bachelor of Surgery).

Ch. Ch., Christ Church, Oxford.

C.H.E.L., Cambridge History of English Literature.

Ches., Cheshire.

Ch.M., *Chirurgiae Magister* (= Master of Surgery).

Chron., Chronicles (O.T.).

C.I., Channel Islands; (Order of the) Crown of India.

Cicestr., (Bishop) of Chichester (see Cantuar.).

C.I.D., Committee for Imperial Defence; Criminal Investigation Department.

C.I.E., Companion of (the Order of) the Indian Empire.

c.i.f., cost, insurance, freight.

C.I.G.S., Chief of the Imperial General Staff.

C.-in-C., Commander-in-Chief.

C.I.O., Congress of Industrial Organizations.

circ., *circa*; *circiter*.

C.J., Chief Justice.

cl., centilitre; class; classical.

Clar., Clarendon (type).

cm, cm., centimetre.

C.M.A.S., Clergy Mutual Assurance Society.

C.M.B., (certificated by) Central Midwives' Board; coastal motor-boat.

Cmd, command paper (with series number, as *Cmd 7957*).

Cmdre, Commodore.

C.M.G., Companion of (the Order of) St Michael & St George.

Cmnd, = **Cmd.**

C.M.S., Church Missionary Society.

C.N.D., CND, Campaign for Nuclear Disarmament.

C.O., Colonial Office; commanding officer; conscientious objector.

Co., company; county.

c/o, care of.

C.O.D., cash on delivery; Concise Oxford Dictionary.

C. of E., Church of England.

C.O.I., Central Office of Information.

Col, Colonel; Colossians (N.T.).

col., column.

Coll., College.

Colo., Colorado.

Col.-S(er)gt, Colour-Sergeant.

Conn., Connecticut.

Cons., Conservative; Consul.

Co-op., Co-operative Society.

C.O.P.E.C., COPEC, Conference on Politics, Economics, & Citizenship.

Cor., Corinthians (N.T.).

Corn., Cornwall.

Corp., Corporal.

cos, cosine.

cosec, cosecant.

cot, cotangent.

Coy, Company.

c.p., candle-power.

cp., compare.

Cpl, Corporal.

C.P.O., Chief Petty Officer.

C.P.R., Canadian Pacific Railway.

C.P.R.E., Council for the Preservation of Rural England.

C.Q.M.S., Company Quartermaster-Sergeant.

Cr, Creditor.

C.R.A., C.R.E., Commander, Royal Artillery, Royal Engineers.

cres., *crescendo.*

crim. con., criminal conversation.

C.R.O., Commonwealth Relations Office.

C.S.C., Conspicuous Service Cross.

C.S.C.S., Civil Service Co-operative Stores.

C.S.I., Companion of (the Order of) the Star of India.

C.S.M., Company Sergeant-Major.

C.T.C., Cyclists' Touring Club.

cu., cub., cubic.

C.U.A.C., C.U.A.F.C., Cambridge University Athletic Club, Association Football Club.

C.U.B.C., C.U.C.C., C.U.D.S., C.U.G.C., C.U.H.C., C.U.L.T.C., Cambridge University Boat Club, Cricket Club, Dramatic Society, Golf Club, Hockey Club, Lawn Tennis Club.

cum., cumulative.

Cumb., Cumberland.

cum d., cum div., cum dividend.

C.U.P., Cambridge University Press.

C.U.R.U.F.C., Cambridge University Rugby Union Football Club.

C.V.O., Commander of the Royal Victorian Order.

C.W.S., Co-operative Wholesale Society.

cwt, hundredweight.

d., date; daughter; *dele* (= expunge); *denarius* (= penny); departs etc.; died.

d—, damn.

D.A., District Attorney.

D.A.A.G., Deputy Assistant Adjutant-General.

D.A.B., Dictionary of American Biography.

D.A.D.M.S., D.A.D.O.S., Deputy Assistant Director of Medical, Ordnance, Services.

D.A.G., Deputy Adjutant-General.

dag., decagram.
Dak., Dakota.
dal., decalitre.
dam., decametre.
Dan., Daniel (also O.T.).
D.A.Q.M.G., Deputy Assistant Quarter-master-General.
D.B.E., Dame Commander of (the Order of) the British Empire.
D.C., *da capo* (= repeat from the beginning; also **d.c.**); direct current; District of Columbia.
D.C.L., Doctor of Civil Law.
D.C.L.I., Duke of Cornwall's Light Infantry.
D.C.M., Distinguished Conduct Medal; District Court Martial.
D.D., Doctor of Divinity; *dono dedit* (= gave as a gift; also **d.d.**).
d—d, damned.
D.D.D., *dat, dicat, dedicat* (= gives, devotes, & dedicates; also **d.d.d.**).
D.D.S., Doctor of Dental Surgery.
D.D.T., dichlor-diphenyl-trichlorethane (an insecticide).
Dec., December.
deg., degree.
Del., Delaware.
del., *delineavit* (= drew this).
dep., departs etc.
dept, department.
Des. R.C.A., Designer of the Royal College of Art.
Deut., Deuteronomy (O.T.).
D.F., direction-finder (*or* -finding).
D.F.C., D.F.M., Distinguished Flying Cross, Medal.
D.G., *Dei gratia* (= by the grace of God); Dragoon Guards.
dg., decigram.
dim., *diminuendo*; (dim.) diminutive etc.
dkg., dkl., dkm., decagram, decalitre, decametre.
D.L., Deputy Lieutenant.
dl., decilitre.
D.L.I., Durham Light Infantry.
D.Lit., Doctor of Literature.
D.Litt., Doctor of Letters.
D.M., Doctor of Medicine.
dm., decimetre.
D.M.I., Director of Military Intelligence.
D.Mus., Doctor of Music.
d—n, damn.
D.N.B., Dictionary of National Biography.
do, ditto.
dol., dollar(s).
D.O.M., *Deo optimo maximo* (= to God the best & greatest).
D.O.R.A., Defence of the Realm Act.
doz., dozen.
D.P., displaced person.
D.P.H., Diploma in Public Health.
D.Ph(il)., Doctor of Philosophy.
D.P.I., Director of Public Instruction.
D.R., dead reckoning; dispatch rider.
Dr, Debtor; Doctor.
dr., drachm.

dram. pers., *dramatis personae* (= characters of the play).
D.S., *dal segno* (= repeat from the mark).
D.S.C., Distinguished Service Cross.
D.Sc., Doctor of Science.
D.S.M., D.S.O., Distinguished Service Medal, Order.
d.t(s)., D.T., delirium tremens.
Dunelm., (Bishop) of Durham (see Cantuar.).
D.Th(eol)., Doctor of Theology.
D.V., *Deo volente* (= God willing).
dwt, pennyweight.
dyn(am)., dynamics.

E., East (as compass point, & as London postal district); Egyptian (in £E); Engineering.
E. & O. E., errors & omissions excepted.
E.B., Encyclopaedia Britannica.
E. by N., E by N, East by North.
Ebor., (Archbishop) of York (see Cantuar.).
E. by S., E by S, East by South.
E.C., East Central (London postal district).
E.C.A., Economic Co-operation Administration (now M.S.A.).
Eccles., Ecclesiastes (O.T.).
Ecclus, Ecclesiasticus (Apocr.).
E.C.U., English Church Union.
Ed., Edward.
ed., editor etc.
E.D.C., European Defence Community.
E.D.D., English Dialect Dictionary.
Edin., Edinburgh.
Edm., Edmund.
E.D.S., English Dialect Society.
Edw., Edward.
E.E.C., European Economic Community.
E.E.T.S., Early English Text Society.
E.F.T.A., Ef'ta, European Free Trade Association.
e.g., *exempli gratia* (= for example).
E.I.S., Educational Institute of Scotland.
E. long., East longitude.
E.M.F., electromotive force.
E.N.E., ENE, East-north-east.
ENSA, Entertainments National Service Association; also **En'sa.**
ent. Sta. Hall, entered at Stationers' Hall.
E.P., electroplate.
Eph., Ephesians (N.T.).
E.P.N.S., electroplated nickel silver.
E.P.T., excess profits tax.
E.R., *Elizabeth Regina* (= Queen Elizabeth); East Riding (of Yorkshire).
E.R.P., European Recovery Programme.
E.S.E., ESE, East-south-east.
Esq., Esquire.
Esth., Esther (O.T.).
E.T.A., estimated time of arrival.
etc., et cetera.
et seq., et seqq., et sq., et sqq., *et sequentia* (= and what follows).
E.T.U., Electrical Trades Union.
E.W.O., Essential Work Order.
exc., except; *excudit* (= engraved this).
ex div., ex dividend.

Exod., Exodus (O.T.).
Exon., (Bishop) of Exeter (see Cantuar.).
exor(s), executor(s).
exrx, executrix.
Ezek., Ezekiel (O.T.).

F, fine (of pencil-lead); French.
F., Fahrenheit.
f., feet; feminine; filly; folio; foot; franc(s); free; from.
f, *forte* (= loud).
F.A., Football Association.
F.A.A., Fleet Air Arm.
f.a.a., free of all average.
Fahr., Fahrenheit.
F.A.I., Fellow of the Chartered Auctioneers' & Estate Agents' Institute.
F.A.N.Y., First Air Nursing Yeomanry.
F.A.O., Food & Agriculture Organization.
f.a.s., free alongside ship.
F.B.A., Fellow of the British Academy.
F.B.I., *Federal Bureau of Investigation; || Federation of British Industries.
F.B.O.A., Fellow of the British Optical Association.
F.C., Football Club.
F.C.A., Fellow of the Institute of Chartered Accountants.
fcap, fcp, foolscap.
F.C.I.I., Fellow of the Chartered Insurance Institute.
F.C.I.S., Fellow of the Chartered Institute of Secretaries.
F.C.W.A., Fellow of the Institute of Cost & Works Accountants.
F.D., *Fidei Defensor* (= Defender of the Faith).
Feb., February.
fec., *fecit* or *fecerunt* (= made).
F.E.I.S., Fellow of the Educational Institute of Scotland.
***F.E.R.A.,** Federal Emergency Relief Administration.
ff, *fortissimo* (= very loud).
F.F.A.S., Fellow of the Faculty of Architects & Surveyors.
f.g.a., free of general average.
F.G.C.M., field general court-martial.
F.G.S., Fellow of the Geological Society.
F.H., fire hydrant.
F.I.A., Fellow of the Institute of Actuaries.
F.I.A.T., *Fabbrica Italiana Automobili Torino* (= Italian automobile factory, Turin).
F.I.B., Fellow of the Institute of Bankers.
Fid. Def., = F.D.
fi. fa., *fieri facias* (= see it is done).
fig., figure.
F.I.J., Fellow of the Institute of Journalists.
F.I.M.T.A., Fellow of the Institute of Municipal Treasurers & Accountants.
fin., *ad finem* (= towards the end).
F.Inst.P., Fellow of the Institute of Physics.
f.l., *falsa lectio* (= false reading).

fl., florin(s); *floruit* (= flourished).
Fla, Florida.
flor., *floruit* (= flourished).
F.L.S., Fellow of the Linnean Society.
Flt-Lt, -Sgt, Flight-Lieutenant, -Sergeant.
F.M., Field-Marshal.
F.O., Flying Officer; Foreign Office.
fo, folio.
f.o.b., free on board.
f.o.r., free on rail.
F.P., field punishment; fire plug; former pupil.
fp, *forte-piano* (= loud, then soft).
F.P.S., Fellow of the Pharmaceutical Society.
Fr, Father.
Fr., French.
fr., franc(s).
F.R.A.D., Fellow of the Royal Academy of Dancing.
F.R.A.M., Fellow of the Royal Academy of Music.
F.R.A.S., Fellow of the Royal Astronomical Society.
F.R.C.M., F.R.C.O., F.R.C.P.(E.), Fellow of the Royal College of Music, of Organists, of Physicians (of Edinburgh).
F.R.C.S.(E.), Fellow of the Royal College of Surgeons (of Edinburgh).
F.R.G.S., Fellow of the Royal Geographical Society.
Fri., Friday.
F.R.I.B.A., Fellow of the Royal Institute of British Architects.
F.R.I.C., Fellow of the Royal Institute of Chemistry.
F.R.I.C.S., Fellow of the Royal Institution of Chartered Surveyors.
Frl., *Fräulein* (= Miss).
F.R.P.S., Fellow of the Royal Photographic Society.
F.R.S., Fellow of the Royal Society.
F.R.S.A., F.R.S.E., Fellow of the Royal Society of Arts, of Edinburgh.
F.R.S.G.S., Fellow of the Royal Scottish Geographical Society.
F.R.S.H., Fellow of the Royal Society for the Promotion of Health.
F.R.S.L., F.R.S.S., Fellow of the Royal Society of Literature, of the Royal Statistical Society.
F.S., Fleet Surgeon.
F.S.A., Fellow of the Society of Antiquaries, of Arts.
F.S.E., Fellow of the Society of Engineers.
F.S.M.C., Freeman of the Spectacle Makers' Company.
F.S.R., Field Service Regulations.
F.S.S., Fellow of the Statistical Society.
F.S.S.U., Federated Superannuation System for Universities.
ft, feet; foot.
fur., furlong.
F.W.A., Family Welfare Association.
F.Z.S., Fellow of the Zoological Society.

G, gram(me).

Ga, Georgia.

Gal., Galatians (N.T.).

gal., gallon(s).

G.A.T.T., General Agreement on Tariffs & Trade.

G.B., Great Britain.

G.B.E., Knight (or Dame) Grand Cross (of the Order) of the British Empire.

G.B.S., George Bernard Shaw.

G.C., George Cross.

G.C.A., ground-control(led) approach (of aircraft).

G.C.B., Knight Grand Cross of the Bath.

G.C.E., General Certificate of Education.

G.C.F., greatest common factor.

G.C.I.E., Knight Grand Commander (of the Order) of the Indian Empire.

G.C.M., general court-martial; greatest common measure.

G.C.M.G., Knight Grand Cross (of the Order) of St Michael & St George.

G.C.S.I., Knight Grand Commander (of the Order) of the Star of India.

G.C.V.O., Knight Grand Cross of the (Royal) Victorian Order.

Gen., General; Genesis (O.T.).

Geo., George.

Ger., German.

G.G., Grenadier Guards.

G.H.Q., General Headquarters.

*G.I., government issue; (colloq.) enlisted man.

Gib., Gibraltar.

Glam., Glamorganshire.

Glos., Gloucestershire.

G.M., George Medal.

gm., gram(s).

G.M.C., General Medical Council.

G.M.T., Greenwich mean time.

G.O.C.(-in-C.), General Officer Commanding(-in-Chief).

G.O.M., grand old man.

G.P., general practitioner (doctor).

G.P.I., general paralysis of the insane.

G.P.O., General Post Office.

G.R., general reserve; Georgius Rex (= King George).

gr., grain(s); grammar.

Grad. Inst. P., Graduate of the Institute of Physics.

G.S., general service.

gs, guineas.

G.S.O., General Staff Officer.

gym., gymnasium; gymnastics.

H, hard (of pencil-lead).

h., hour(s).

H.A.A., heavy anti-aircraft.

Hab., Habakkuk (O.T.).

H.A.C., Honourable Artillery Company.

Hag., Haggai (O.T.).

h. & c., hot & cold (water).

Hants, Hampshire.

HB, hard black (of pencil-lead).

H.B.M., Her (or His) Britannic Majesty.

H.C. (B.), House of Commons (Bill).

H.C.F., highest common factor.

H.C.S., Home Civil Service.

H.E., high explosive; His Excellency.

Heb., Hebrew; Hebrews (N.T.).

hectog., hectol., hectom., hectogram, hectolitre, hectometre.

Herts., Hertfordshire.

hf bd, half-bound.

hf cf, half-calf.

H.G., High German (also HG); His (or Her) Grace; Holy Ghost; Home Guard; Horse Guards.

hg., hectogram.

H.H., His (or Her) Highness; His Holiness (the Pope).

HH, double-hard (of pencil-lead).

hhd, hogshead.

HHH, treble-hard (of pencil-lead).

H.I.H., H.I.M., His (or Her) Imperial Highness, Majesty.

H.K., House of Keys (Isle of Man).

H.L., House of Lords.

hl., hectolitre.

H.L.I., Highland Light Infantry.

H.M., Her (or His) Majesty.

hm., hectometre.

H.M.A.S., H.M.C.S., Her (or His) Majesty's Australian, Canadian, Ship.

H.M.I.(S.), Her (or His) Majesty's Inspector (of Schools).

H.M.S., H.M.T., Her (or His) Majesty's Ship, Trawler.

H.O., Home Office; hostilities only.

ho., house.

Hon., Honorary; Honourable.

Hon. Sec., Honorary Secretary.

Hos., Hosea (O.T.).

h.p., half-pay; high pressure; hire purchase; horse-power.

H.Q., Headquarters.

hr, hour.

H.R.H., His (or Her) Royal Highness.

hrs, hours.

H.S.E., hic sepultus est (= here is buried).

H.S.H., His (or Her) Serene Highness.

h.t., high tension.

ht wt, hit wicket.

Hunts., Huntingdonshire.

h.w., hit wicket.

H.W.M., high-water mark.

Hy, Henry.

I., Idaho; Island(s).

I.A., Indian Army.

Ia, Iowa.

I.A.T.A., International Air Transport Association.

ib., ibid., ibidem.

i/c, in charge.

I.C.B.M., inter-continental ballistic missile.

I.C.I., Imperial Chemical Industries.

I.C.S., Indian Civil Service.

id., idem.

I.D.B., illicit diamond-buying.

I.E., (Order of the) Indian Empire.

i.e., id est.

i.h.p., indicated horse-power.

IHS (see dictionary).

Ill., Illinois.

I.L.O., International Labour Organization.

I.L.P., Independent Labour Party.

I.M.S., Indian Medical Service.

in., inch(es).

Inc., Incorporated.

incog., incognito.

Ind., India(n); Indiana.

inf., infra.

init., initio.

I.N.R.I., *Iesus Nazarenus Rex Iudaeorum* (= Jesus of Nazareth, King of the Jews).

inst., instant (= of the current month).

int. comb., internal combustion.

internat., international.

inv., invenit, invenerunt.

I. of M., I. of W., Isle of Man, of Wight.

I.O.G.T., International Order of Good Templars.

I.O.M., Isle of Man.

IOU (see dictionary).

I.O.W., Isle of Wight.

I.Q., intelligence quotient.

i.q., idem quod.

I.R.A., I.R.B., Irish Republican Army, Brotherhood.

I.R.B.M., intermediate-range ballistic missile.

I.R.O., International Refugee Organization.

Is., Isaiah (also Isa.); Island.

I.S.O., Imperial Service Order.

I.T.A.,Independent Television Authority.

it(al)., italic (type).

I.W., Isle of Wight.

I.W.T.(D.), Inland Water Transport (Department).

I.W.W., Industrial Workers of the World.

J., Judge; Justice.

J.A., Judge Advocate.

J.A.G., Judge Advocate-General.

Jam., Jamaica; James (N.T.).

Jan., January.

Jas, James.

J.C., Justice Clerk.

Jer., Jeremiah.

jn, junction.

Jno., John.

Jon., Jonathan.

Jos., Joseph.

Josh., Joshua (also O.T.).

J.P., Justice of the Peace.

Jr, junior.

J.T.C., Junior Training Corps (in schools).

Jud., Judith (Apocr.).

Judg., Judges (O.T.).

jun., junior.

Kan., Kansas.

K.B., King's Bench.

K.B.E., Knight Commander (of the Order) of the British Empire.

K.C., King's College; King's Counsel; Knight(s) of Columbus.

kc., kilocycle(s).

K.C.B., K.C.I.E., K.C.M.G., K.C.S.I., K.C.V.O., Knight Commander of the Bath, (of the Order) of the Indian Empire, (of ¡the Order) of St Michael & St George, of the Star of India, of the (Royal) Victorian Order.

K.G., Knight (of the Order) of the Garter.

kg., kilogram.

K.H.C., K.H.P., K.H.S., Honorary Chaplain, Physician, Surgeon, to the King.

*K.K.K., Ku Klux Klan.

kl., kilolitre.

km., kilometre.

Knt, Knight.

K.O., knock-out.

K.O.S.B., K.O.Y.L.I., King's Own Scottish Borderers, Yorkshire Light Infantry.

K.P., Knight (of the Order) of St Patrick.

K.R., King's Regulations.

K.R.R.C., King's Royal Rifle Corps.

K.S., King's Scholar.

K.S.L.I., King's Shropshire Light Infantry.

K.T., Knight (of the Order) of the Thistle; Knight Templar.

Kt, Knight.

kv., kilovolt.

kw., kW., kilowatt.

Ky., Kentucky.

L, Latin; learner (on motor vehicle); Roman numeral = 50.

L., Liberal.

l., left; *libra(e)* = pound(s); line; lira; lire; litre(s).

La, Louisiana.

L.A.A., light anti-aircraft.

Lab., Labour; Labrador.

L.A.C., leading aircraftman; London Athletic Club.

Lam., Lamentations (O.T.).

Lancs., Lancashire.

Lat., Latin.

lat., latitude.

l.b., leg-bye.

lb., *libra(e)* = pound(s) in weight.

L.-Bdr, Lance-Bombardier.

l.b.w., leg before wicket.

L.C., left centre (of stage).

l.c., *loco citato*; lower case (of print).

L.C.C., London County Council.

L.C.J., Lord Chief Justice.

L.C.M., lowest common multiple.

L.C.P., Licentiate of the College of Preceptors.

L.-Cpl, Lance-Corporal.

Ld, limited; Lord.

L.D.S., Licentiate in Dental Surgery.

L.E.A., Local Education Authority.

Leics., Leicestershire.

Lev., Leviticus (O.T.).

L.F.A.S., Licentiate of the Faculty of Architects & Surveyors.

L.G., Life Guards.

L.G.U., Ladies' Golf Union.
Lib., Liberal.
Lieut., Lieutenant.
Lieut.-Col., -Gen., -Gov., Lieutenant-
-Colonel, -General, -Governor.
L.I.F.O., L.I.L.O., last in first out, last in
last out (stock valuation).
Lincs., Lincolnshire.
Linn., Linnaeus.
Lit. Hum., *literae humaniores.*
Litt.D., *literarum doctor.*
Liv., Livy.
L.J., Lord Justice.
L.JJ., Lords Justices.
ll., lines.
LL.B., *legum baccalaureus* (= Bachelor of
Laws).
LL.D., *legum doctor* (= Doctor of Laws).
L.M.S., London Missionary Society.
loc. cit., *loco citato.*
log., logarithm; logic.
Londin., London., (Bishop) of London
(see Cantuar.).
long., longitude.
loq., *loquitur.*
l.p., large paper; long-playing (record;
also L.P.); long primer; low pressure.
L.R.A.D., Licentiate of the Royal Aca-
demy of Dancing.
L.R.A.M., Licentiate of the Royal Aca-
demy of Music.
L.R.C., Leander, London, Rowing Club.
L.R.C.P., L.R.C.S., Licentiate of the
Royal College of Physicians, Surgeons.
l.s., *locus sigilli* (= the place of the
seal).
L.S.D., ~ £. s. d.; Lightermen, Stove-
dores, & Dockers; lysergic acid diethyla-
mide.
L.S.O., London Symphony Orchestra.
Lt, Lieutenant.
l.t., landed terms; low tension.
L.T.A., Lawn Tennis Association; Lon-
don Teachers' Association.
L.T.C., Lawn Tennis Club.
Lt-Col., Lt-Cdr, Lieutenant-Colonel,
-Commander.
Ltd, Limited.
Lt-Gen., Lt-Gov., Lieutenant-General,
-Governor.
L.W.M., low-water mark.
LXX, Septuagint.
£, *libra(e)* (= pounds sterling).
£E, pounds Egyptian.
£. s. d. (see dictionary).
£T, pounds Turkish.

M., Monsieur.
m., maiden (over); male; mark(s) (coin);
married; masculine; metre(s); mile(s);
million(s); minute(s).
M.A., Master of Arts; Military Aca-
demy.
M.A.B., Metropolitan Asylums Board.
Macc., Maccabees (Apocr.).
Maj., Major; Maj.-Gen., Major-General.
Mal., Malachi (O.T.).

Man., Manitoba (also Manit.).
Mancun., (Bishop) of Manchester (see
Cantuar.).
M. & B., initials of manufacturers (May
& Baker) used as name of therapeutic
drug (also M. & B. 693).
Mar., March.
Mass., Massachusetts.
matric., matriculation.
Matt., Matthew.
M.B., *medicinae baccalaureus* (= Bachelor
of Medicine).
M.B.E., Member (of the Order) of the
British Empire.
M.Brit.I.R.E., Member of the British
Institution of Radio Engineers.
M.C., Master of Ceremonies; Member of
Congress (or Council); Military Cross.
M.C.C., Marylebone Cricket Club.
M.Ch., *magister chirurgiae* (= Master of
Surgery).
M.D., *medicinae doctor* (= Doctor of
Medicine); mentally deficient.
Md, Maryland.
Me, Maine; *Maitre* (French advocate's
title).
mem., *memento* (= remember).
memo., memorandum.
Messrs (see MESSIEURS).
met., meteorology etc.
Met.R., Metropolitan Railway (London).
Metro., Metropolitan Railway (Paris).
mf, *mezzo forte* (= half loud).
M.F.H., Master of Foxhounds.
m.g., machine gun.
mg., milligram(s).
Mgr, Monseigneur; Monsignor (pl. Mgri).
M.I., Military Intelligence (*M.I.5*, branch
dealing with security & counter-espionage
in Britain); Mounted Infantry.
Mic., Micah (O.T.).
M.I.C.E., Member of the Institution of
Civil Engineers.
Mich., Michaelmas; Michigan.
Milt., Milton.
M.I.Mech.E., M.I.Mun.E., Member of
the Institution of Mechanical, Municipal,
Engineers.
Minn., Minnesota.
misc., miscellaneous; miscellany.
Miss., Mississippi.
M.I.T., Massachusetts Institute of Tech-
nology.
M.J.I., Member of the Institute of
Journalists.
mk, mark (coin).
ml., millilitre(s).
M.L.A., Member of the Legislative
Assembly; Modern Languages Associa-
tion.
M.L.F., multilateral (nuclear) force.
Mlle, Mademoiselle (pl. Mlles).
M.L.N.S., Ministry of Labour & National
Service.
M.M., Military Medal.
MM., Messieurs.
mm., millimetre(s).
Mme, Madame (pl. Mmes).

M.Mus., Master of Music.

M.N., Merchant Navy.

M.N.I., Ministry of National Insurance.

M.O., mass observation; Medical Officer; money order.

Mo., Missouri.

Mods, Moderations (Oxf. Univ.).

M.O.H., Medical Officer of Health; Ministry of Health.

Mon., Monday; Monmouthshire.

Mont., Montana.

M.P., Member of Parliament; military police.

mp, *mezzo piano* (= half soft).

M.P.B.W., Ministry of Public Building & Works.

m.p.g., m.p.h., miles per gallon, per hour.

M.P.N.I., MPNI, Ministry of Pensions and National Insurance.

M.P.S., Member of the Pharmaceutical (*or* Philological *or* Physical) Society.

M.R., Master of the Rolls; municipal reform(er).

Mr (see MISTER).

M.R.B.M., medium-range ballistic missile.

M.R.C.P. (E., I.), Member of the Royal College of Physicians (of Edinburgh, of Ireland).

M.R.C.S. (E., I.), Member of the Royal College of Surgeons (of Edinburgh, of Ireland).

M.R.C.V.S., Member of the Royal College of Veterinary Surgeons.

M.R.G.S., Member of the Royal Geographical Society.

Mrs (see dictionary).

M.R.S.H., Member of the Royal Society for the Promotion of Health.

MS., manuscript.

M.S.A., Mutual Security Agency (replacing E.C.A.).

M.Sc., Master of Science.

M.S.E., Member of the Society of Engineers.

M.S.L., mean sea-level.

M.S.M., Meritorious Service Medal.

MSS., manuscripts.

M.T., Mechanical (*or* Motor) Transport.

Mt, Mount.

M.T.B., motor torpedo-boat.

M.T.P.I., Member of the Town Planning Institute.

Mus.B(ac)., **Mus.D(oc).**, **Mus.M.**, *musicae baccalaureus, doctor, magister* (= Bachelor, Doctor, Master, of Music).

M.V., motor vessel; (also **m.v.**) muzzle velocity.

M.V.O., Member of the (Royal) Victorian Order.

M.W.B., Metropolitan Water Board.

Mx, Middlesex.

N., Nationalist; Navigator; New; North (as compass point, & as London postal district).

n., neuter; nominative; noon; noun.

N.A.A.F.I., Navy, Army, & Air Force Institute(s) (also **Naafi**, pr. năf'ĭ).

Nah., Nahum (O.T.).

N.A.L.G.O., National & Local Government Officers' Association (also **Năl'gō**).

N.A.S., National Association of Schoolmasters.

N.A.S.D., National Amalgamated Stevedores & Dockers.

Nat., Nathaniel; National(ist).

N.A.T.O., North Atlantic Treaty Organization (also **Nāt'ō**).

NATSOPA, National Association of Operative Printers & Assistants (now merged with others to form **S.O.G.A.T.**)

N.B., New Brunswick; North Britain; *nota bene*.

n.b., no ball (Cricket).

N. by E., N by E, North by East.

N.B.G., n.b.g., no bloody good.

N. by W., N by W, North by West.

N.C., North Carolina.

N.C.B., National Coal Board.

N.C.C.V.D., National Council for Combating Venereal Diseases.

N.C.O., non-commissioned officer.

n.d., no date; not dated.

N.Dak., North Dakota.

N.D.C., National Defence Contribution.

N.E., NE, North-east(ern).

N.E. by E., NE by E, N.E. by N., NE by N, North-east by East, by North.

Neb(r)., Nebraska.

N.E.D., New English Dictionary (=O.E.D.).

N.E.D.C., National Economic Development Council (colloq. **Nĕdd'y**).

Neh., Nehemiah (O.T.).

nem. con., nem. dis(s)., *nemine contradicente, dissentiente.*

Nev., Nevada.

N.F., Newfoundland; Norman French.

N.F.S., National Fire Service.

N.F.U., National Farmers' Union.

N.H., New Hampshire.

N.H.I., National Health Insurance.

n.h.p., nominal horse-power.

N.H.S., National Health Service.

N.I.C., National Incomes Commission (colloq. **Nick'y**).

N.J., New Jersey.

N.L., National Liberal; north latitude (also **N.lat.**).

N.L.C., N.L.F., National Liberal Club, Federation.

N.Mex., New Mexico.

N.N.E., NNE, North-north-east.

N.N.W., NNW, North-north-west.

N.O., natural order.

n.o., not out (Cricket).

Nº, *numero* (= in number); number.

N.O.D., Naval Ordnance Department.

N.O.I.C., Naval Officer in charge.

nom., nominal.

non-com., non-commissioned officer.

non-U, not upper-class.

Northants., Northamptonshire.

Northumb., Northumberland.

Norvic., (Bishop) of Norwich (see Cantuar.).

Nºˢ, nos, numbers.

Notts., Nottinghamshire.
Nov., November.
N.P., Notary Public.
n.p., net personalty; new paragraph.
n.p. or d., no place or date.
N.R., Northern Rhodesia; North Riding (of Yorkshire).
nr, near.
N.R.A., *National Recovery Administration; National Rifle Association.
N.S., new series; new style; Nova Scotia.
n.s., not sufficient (funds to meet cheque).
N.S.A., National Skating Association.
N.S.P.C.C., National Society for the Prevention of Cruelty to Children.
N.S.W., New South Wales.
N.T., New Testament; Northern Territory (Australia).
N.U.G.M.W., National Union of General & Municipal Workers.
N.U.M., National Union of Mineworkers.
Num., Numbers (O.T.).
N.U.R., N.U.S.E.C., N.U.T., National Union of Railwaymen, of Societies for Equal Citizenship, of Teachers.
N.W., NW, North-west; North-western (London postal district).
N.W. by N., NW by N, N.W. by W., NW by W, North-west by North, by West.
N.W. Prov., North-west Provinces (India).
N.W.T., North-west Territories (Canada).
N.Y.(C.), New York (City).
N.Z., New Zealand.

O., observer; Ohio.
O.A.S., on active service; Organization of American States.
ob., obiit.
Obad., Obadiah (O.T.).
obdt, obedient.
O.B.E., Officer of the (Order of the) British Empire.
ob.s.p., obiit sine prole (= died without issue).
O.C., Officer Commanding.
Oct., October.
oct., octavo.
O.C.T.U., Officer Cadets Training Unit (also **Oc'tu**).
O.E.C.D., Organization for European Co-operation & Development (formerly O.E.E.C.).
O.E.D., Oxford English Dictionary.
O.E.E.C., Organization for European Economic Co-operation.
O.F.C., Overseas Food Corporation.
O.F.M., Order of Friars Minor.
O.F.S., Orange Free State.
O.H.M.S., on Her (*or* His) Majesty's Service.
O.K., all correct.
Okla, Oklahoma.
Ol., Olympiad.
O.M., Order of Merit.
Ont., Ontario.
O.P., observation post; (also **o.p.**)

opposite prompt (side, in theatre);
Ordinis Praedicatorum (= of the Order of Preachers, i.e. Dominicans).
o.p., out of print; over proof.
op., opus.
op. cit., *opere citato* (= in the work quoted).
opp., opposite.
O.R., other ranks.
ord., ordained; order; ordinary.
Ore(g)., Oregon.
O.S., old series; old style; ordinary seaman; Ordnance Survey; outsize.
O.S.A., O.S.B., O.S.D., O.S.F., of the Order of St Augustine, Benedict, Dominic, Francis.
O.T., Old Testament.
O.T.C., Officers' Training Corps.
O.U.A.C., O.U.A.F.C., O.U.B.C., O.U.C.C., Oxford University Athletic, Association Football, Boat, Cricket, Club.
O.U.D.S., Oxford University Dramatic Society.
O.U.G.C., O.U.H.C., O.U.L.T.C., Oxford University Golf, Hockey, Lawn Tennis, Club.
O.U.P., Oxford University Press.
O.U.R.F.C., Oxford University Rugby Football Club.
Oxf., Oxford.
Oxon., (Bishop) of Oxford (see Cantuar.); Oxfordshire; Oxford University.
oz, ounce(s).

P., (car) park; pawn (Chess); pedestrian (crossing).
p., page; particle; past; perch.
p, piano.
P.A., Press Association.
p.a., per annum.
Pa, Pennsylvania.
P. & O., Peninsular & Oriental (Steamship Co.).
par., paragraph.
P.A.Y.E., pay as you earn.
Paym.(-Gen.), Paymaster(-General).
P.B., Prayer Book.
P.B.I., poor bloody infantry.
P.C., police constable; postcard; Privy Council(lor).
p.c., per cent; postcard.
pd, paid.
pdr, -pounder (of fish, gun, etc.).
P.D.S.A., People's Dispensary for Sick Animals.
p.e., personal estate.
P.E.N., (International Association of) Poets, Playwrights, Editors, Essayists, & Novelists.
pen(in)., peninsula.
Penn., Penna, Pennsylvania.
P.E.P., Political & Economic Planning.
per pro., per procurationem (= by proxy).
Pet., Peter (N.T.).
Petriburg., (Bishop) of Peterborough (see Cantuar.).
P.F., Procurator Fiscal.

pf, piano forte (= soft, then loud).
*p.f.c., private first class.
P.G., paying guest.
P.G.A., Professional Golfers' Association.
Ph.B., Ph.D., *philosophiae baccalaureus, doctor* (= Bachelor, Doctor, of Philosophy).
Phil., Philippians (N.T.).
phot., photograph.
pinx., pinxit.
pizz., pizzicato.
pl., place; plate; plural.
P.L.A., Port of London Authority.
P.M., Prime Minister; Provost-Marshal.
p.m., *post meridiem*; post mortem.
P.M.G., Paymaster-General; Postmaster-General.
p.m.h., production per man-hour.
P.M.O., Principal Medical Officer.
pnxt, pinxit.
P.O., Petty Officer; Pilot Officer; postal order; Post Office.
pop., population.
P.O.S.B., Post Office Savings Bank.
P.O.W., prisoner of war.
P.P., parcel post; Parish Priest.
p.p., past participle; = *per pro.*
pp., pages.
pp, pianissimo.
P.P.C., *pour prendre congé* (= to take leave).
P.P.S., Parliamentary Private Secretary; *post postscriptum* (= further postscript).
P.R., proportional representation.
pr, pair; -pounder.
P.R.A., President of the Royal Academy.
P.R.B., Pre-Raphaelite Brotherhood.
Preb., Prebendary.
Pref., Preface.
pref., preference etc.; prefix.
prep., preparation; preposition.
Pres., President.
P.R.O., Public Relations Officer.
Prof., Professor.
Prol., Prologue.
prop., proposition.
pro tem., pro tempore (= for the time).
Prov., Proverbs (O.T.).
prox., proximo.
prox. acc., proxime accessit.
P.S., police sergeant; postscript; (also **p.s.**) prompt side.
Ps., Psalms (O.T.).
P.S.A., Pleasant Sunday Afternoon.
P.T., physical training.
pt, part; pint; port.
Pte, Private (soldier).
P.T.O., please turn over.
pty, proprietary.
Pty Co., Proprietary Company.
P.W.D., Public Works Department.
pxt, pinxit.

Q., Queen.
q., query.
Q.A.I.M.N.S., Queen Alexandra's Imperial Military Nursing Service.
Q.B., Q.C., Queen's Bench, Counsel.

Q.E.D., Q.E.F., Q.E.I., see QUOD.
Q.F., quick-firing (gun).
q.l., quantum libet.
Q.M., Quartermaster.
Q.M.G., Q.M.S., Quartermaster-General, -Sergeant.
q.p., quantum placet.
qr, quarter.
Q.S., Quarter Sessions.
q.s., quantum sufficit.
q.t. (sl.), quiet (*on the strict q.t.*, privately, avoiding notice).
qt, quart(s).
qu., quasi; query.
quant. suff., quantum sufficit.
Que., Quebec.
quot., quotation etc.
q.v., *quantum vis* (= as much as you wish); QUOD[2] *vide.*
qy, query.

R., Réaumur; *Regina*; *retarder* (on timepiece regulator, = to retard); *Rex*; River.
R., railway; right; run(s); rupee.
R.A., Royal Academy (*or* Academician); Royal Artillery.
R.A.A.F., Royal Australian Air Force; Royal Auxiliary Air Force.
R.A.C., Royal Armoured Corps; Royal Automobile Club.
rad., radical.
R.A.D.A., Royal Academy of Dramatic Art.
R.A.D.C., R.A.E.C., Royal Army Dental, Educational, Corps.
R.A.F.(V.R.), Royal Air Force (Volunteer Reserve).
R.A.G.C., Royal & Ancient Golf Club, St Andrews; also **R. & A.**
rall., rallentando.
R.A.M., Royal Academy of Music.
R.A.M.C., Royal Army Medical Corps.
R.A.N., Royal Australian Navy.
R.A.O.C., R.A.P.C., R.A.S.C., R.A.V.C., Royal Army Ordnance, Pay, Service, Veterinary, Corps.
R.B., Rifle Brigade.
R.B.A., R.B.S., Royal (Society of) British Artists, Sculptors.
R.C., Red Cross; right centre (of stage); Roman Catholic.
R.C.A.F., Royal Canadian Air Force.
R.C.M., Royal College of Music.
R.C.M.P., Royal Canadian Mounted Police.
R.C.N., Royal Canadian Navy; Royal College of Nursing.
R.C.N.C., Royal Corps of Naval Constructors.
R.C.O., Royal College of Organists.
R.C. of Sig., Royal Corps of Signals.
R.C.P., R.C.S., Royal College of Physicians, of Surgeons.
R.D., refer to drawer; Royal (Naval Reserve) Decoration.
rd, road.
R.D.C., Rural District Council.

R.E., Royal Engineers.

recd, received.

regt, regiment.

R.E.M.E., Royal Electrical & Mechanical Engineers.

repr., represent etc.; reprinted.

R. (et) I., *Regina* (*et*) *Imperatrix* (= Queen & Empress); *Rex* (*et*) *Imperator* (= King & Emperor).

Rev., Revelation (N.T.); Reverend.

rev., revolution.

Revd, Reverend.

R.F., Royal Fusiliers.

R.F.C., *Reconstruction Finance Corporation; Rugby Football Club.

R.G.S., Royal Geographical Society.

R.H., Royal Highlanders; Royal Highness.

R.H.A., R.H.G., Royal Horse Artillery, Guards.

R.H.S., Royal Horticultural, Humane, Society.

R.I., = R. et I.; Rhode Island; Royal Institute (of Painters in Water Colours); Royal Institution.

R.I.A., Royal Irish Academy.

R.I.B.A., Royal Institute of British Architects.

R.I.C., Royal Irish Constabulary.

R.I.I.A., Royal Institute of International Affairs.

R.I.P., *requiesca(n)t in pace.*

R.M., Resident Magistrate; Royal Mail; Royal Marines.

R.M.A., Royal Military Academy (Sandhurst; formerly Woolwich).

R.M.C., Royal Military College (Sandhurst; now R.M.A.).

R.M.L., Royal Mail Lines Ltd.

R.M.S., Royal Mail Steamer.

R.N., Royal Navy.

R.N.C., R.N.D., Royal Naval College, Division.

R.N.L.I., Royal National Lifeboat Institution.

R.N.(V.)R., Royal Naval (Volunteer) Reserve.

R.N.Z.A.F., R.N.Z.N., Royal New Zealand Air Force, Navy.

Robt, Robert.

R.O.C., Royal Observer Corps.

Roffen., (Bishop) of Rochester (see Cantuar.).

Rom., Romans (N.T.).

rom., roman (type).

R.P.S., Royal Photographic Society.

R.Q.M.S., Regimental Quartermaster-Sergeant.

R.R.C., (Lady of the) Royal Red Cross.

R.S., Royal Scots; Royal Society.

Rs, rupees.

R.S.A., Royal Scottish Academy; Royal Society of Arts.

R.S.D., R.S.E., Royal Society of Dublin, of Edinburgh.

R.S.F., Royal Scots Fusiliers.

R.S.M., Regimental Sergeant-Major.

R.S.O., railway sub-office.

R.S.P.C.A., Royal Society for the Prevention of Cruelty to Animals.

R.S.V.P., *répondez s'il vous plaît.*

R.S.W., Royal Scottish Society of Painters in Water Colours.

R.T., R/T, radio-telegraphy, -telephony.

Rt Hon., Right Honourable.

R.T.O., Railway Transport Officer.

R.T.R., Royal Tank Regiment.

Rt Rev., Right Reverend.

R.T.S., Religious Tract Society.

R.U., Rugby Union.

R.U.R., Royal Ulster Rifles.

R.V., Revised Version (of Bible).

R.W.S., Royal Society of Painters in Water Colours.

Ry, railway.

R.Y.S., Royal Yacht Squadron.

℞, recipe.

R̶, rupee.

Rs, rupees.

Rx, tens of rupees.

S., Saint; Signor; soprano; South(ern); Submarines.

s., second; shilling; singular; *solidus*; son.

S.A., Salvation Army; South Africa; (also SA.) *Sturmabteilung* (= storm detachment; Nazi party army).

S.A.A., small arms ammunition.

Salop, Shropshire.

Sam., Samuel (O.T.).

S. & M., (Bishop) of Sodor & Man (see Cantuar.).

Sarum., (Bishop) of Salisbury (see Cantuar.).

Sask., Saskatchewan.

Sat., Saturday.

S.A.T.B., soprano, alto, tenor, bass.

S. by E., S by E, S. by W., S by W, South by East, by West.

S.C., South Carolina; Special Constable.

sc, scilicet; sculpsit.

SCAPA, Society for Checking the Abuses of Public Advertising.

s. caps, small capital letters.

S.C.C., Sea Cadet Corps.

sch., scholar; school.

scil., scilicet.

S.C.M., State Certified Midwife.

sculps., sculpsit.

s.d., several dates.

S.Dak., South Dakota.

S.E., SE, South-east; South-eastern (London postal district).

S.E.A.T.O., South-east Asia Treaty Organization (also Seat'ō).

S.E. by E., SE by E, S.E. by S., SE by S, South-east by East, by South.

Sec., Secretary.

sec., second.

sect., section.

Sen., Senate; Senator; Senior (also Senr).

S.E.N., State Enrolled Nurse.

Sept., September; Septuagint.

seq(q)., *sequentes, sequentia.*

Sergt, Sergeant.

s.f., sub finem.

sf, sforzando.

S.F.A., Scottish Football Association.

s.g., specific gravity.

s.g.d.g., sans garantie du gouvernement (= without government guarantee).

Sgt, Sergeant.

sh., shilling(s).

S.H.A.P.E., Supreme Headquarters Allied Powers in Europe (also **Shape**).

s.h.p., shaft horse-power.

S.I., (Order of the) Star of India.

S.J., Society of Jesus.

S.J.A., St. John Ambulance (Association & Brigade).

*S.J.C., Supreme Judicial Court.

S. lat., South latitude.

S.M., Sergeant-Major; short metre.

S.M.O., Senior Medical Officer.

s.m.p., sine mascula prole (= without male issue).

S.N.O., Senior Naval Officer.

S.O., Staff Officer; Stationery Office; sub-office.

Soc., Socialist; Society.

S.O.E.D., Shorter Oxford English Dictionary.

S.O.G.A.T., Society of Graphical & Allied Trades.

Sol.-Gen., Solicitor-General.

Som., Somerset.

Song of Sol., Song of Solomon (O.T.).

S.O.S. (see dictionary).

sov., sovs, sovereign(s) (coin).

S.P., starting price (Betting); stirrup pump.

s.p., sine prole (= without issue).

S.P.C.K., Society for Promoting Christian Knowledge.

S.P.E., Society for Pure English.

S.P.G., Society for the Propagation of the Gospel.

sp. gr., specific gravity.

S.P.Q.R., senatus populusque Romanus (= the senate & people of Rome); small profits & quick returns.

S.P.R., Society for Psychical Research.

s.p.s., sine prole superstite (= without surviving issue).

sq., square.

sq(q)., sequentes, sequentia.

Sqn. Ldr., Squadron Leader.

S.R., Scottish Rifles.

Sr, Senior.

S.R.N., State Registered Nurse.

S.R.O., Statutory Rules & Orders.

SS., Saints.

S.S., Schutzstaffel (= protection patrol; Nazi police force; also **SS.**); screw steamer; (also **s.s.**) steamship.

S.S.A.F.A., Soldiers', Sailors', & Airmen's Families Association.

S.S.C., Solicitor to the Supreme Court (Scotland).

S.S.E., SSE, South-south-east.

S.S.J.E., Society of St John the Evangelist.

S.S.W., SSW, South-south-west.

St, Saint; Strait; Street.

st., stem; stone (weight); stumped.

Staffs., Staffordshire.

S.T.C., Senior Training Corps (at universities).

S.T.D., subscriber trunk dialling (telephony).

St. Ex(ch)., Stock Exchange.

stg, sterling.

S.T.P., sanctae theologiae professor (= Professor of Sacred Theology).

str., stroke (oar).

S.T.S., Scottish Text Society.

Sts, Saints.

Sun., Sunday.

sup., superlative; supra (= above).

suppl., supplement.

Supt, Superintendent.

surg., surgeon; surgery.

sus. per coll. (see dictionary).

s.v., sub voce.

S.W., SW, South-west; South-western (London postal district).

S.W. by S., SW by S, S.W. by W., SW by W, South-west by South, by West.

S.Y., steam yacht.

T, tenor; Turkish (pounds).

t., taken (Betting); ton(s).

T.A., Territorial Army.

t. & o., taken & offered.

T.B., torpedo-boat; tubercle bacillus; tuberculosis.

T.B.D., torpedo-boat destroyer.

T.C., Town Council(lor).

T.C.D., Trinity College, Dublin.

T.D., Teachta Dála (= Deputy of Dail); Territorial (Officer's) Decoration.

t.e.g., top edge(s) gilt.

temp. (see dictionary).

Tenn., Tennessee.

Tex., Texas.

T.F., Territorial Force.

T.G.W.U., Transport & General Workers' Union.

Thess., Thessalonians (N.T.).

Thos, Thomas.

Thurs., Thursday.

T.H.W.M., Trinity high-water mark.

T.I.H., Their Imperial Highnesses.

Tim., Timothy (N.T.).

Tit., Titus (N.T.).

T.N.T., trinitrotoluene.

T.O., Transport Officer; turn over.

Toc H (see dictionary).

T.R.C., Thames Rowing Club.

Treas., Treasurer.

T.R.H., Their Royal Highnesses.

trs., transpose.

Truron., (Bishop) of Truro (see Cantuar.).

T.S.H., Their Serene Highnesses.

T.S.O., town sub-office.

T.S.S.A., Transport Salaried Staffs Association.

T.T., teetotaller; Tourist Trophy; tuberculin tested.

T.U., Trade Union.

T.U.C., Trades Union Congress.
Tues., Tuesday.
TV, T.V., television.
T.V.A., Tennessee Valley Authority.
T.W.A., Trans World Airlines.
12mo, duodecimo.
T.Y.C., Thames Yacht Club.

U., universal (i.e. for everyone, referring to cinema picture); upper-class.
U.A.R., United Arab Republic.
u.c., upper case (of print).
U.C.C.A., Universities Central Council on Admissions.
U.D.C., Urban District Council.
U.K.(A.), United Kingdom (Alliance).
ult., ultimo.
U.N., United Nations.
U.N.E.S.C.O., United Nations Educational, Scientific, & Cultural Organization (also **Unes'co**).
Univ., University.
U.N.O., United Nations Organization (also **Uno**).
U.N.R.R.A., United Nations Relief & Rehabilitation Administration (also **UNRRA, Unrra**, pr. ŭn'rah).
U.P., United Presbyterian; United Press.
u.p., under proof.
U.S., United States (of America).
U.S.A., United States of America; United States Army.
U.S.(A.)A.F., United States (Army) Air Force.
U.S.N., United States Navy.
U.S.S., United States Senate; United States Ship (*or* Steamer).
U.S.S.C., United States Supreme Court.
U.S.S.R., Union of Soviet Socialist Republics.
Ut., Utah.

V, *Vergeltungswaffe* (= reprisal weapon; **V 1**, flying bomb; **V 2**, long-range rocket projectile).
v., verse; versus; *vide*; volt.
V.A., Vice-Admiral; (Order of) Victoria & Albert.
Va, Virginia.
V.A.D., Voluntary Aid Detachment.
V.C., Vice-Chancellor; Victoria Cross.
V.D., venereal disease; Volunteer (Officer's) Decoration.
v.d., various dates.
V.D.H., valvular disease of the heart.
VE, victory in Europe (*VE day*, 8/5/45).
Ven., Venerable.
v.f., very fair.
V.G., Vicar-General.
v.g., very good.
V.H.F., VHF, very high frequency.
Vic., Victoria.
V.I.P., very important person.
Vis., Visct, Viscount.
viz, *videlicet.*
VJ, victory in Japan (*VJ day*, 15/8/45 or in U.S. 2/9/45).
v.l., varia lectio.

V.O., Victorian Order.
vol., volume.
V.R., *Victoria Regina* (= Queen Victoria); Volunteer Reserve.
V.S., Veterinary Surgeon.
Vt, Vermont.
V.T.O.L., VTOL, vertical take-off & landing.
Vulg., Vulgate.
vv., verses.

W., Welsh; West (as compass point, & as London postal district).
w., watt; wicket; wide; wife; with.
W.A.A.C., Women's Army Auxiliary Corps (in 1914–18 war.)
W.A.A.F., Women's Auxiliary Air Force.
w.a.f., with all faults.
War., Warwickshire.
Wash., Washington.
W. by N., W by N, **W. by S.**, W by S, West by North, by South.
W.C., West Central (London postal district).
w.c., water closet.
W.C.A., Women's Christian Association.
W.D., War Department.
W.D.A., W.D.C., War Damage Act, Contribution.
W.E.A., Workers' Educational Association.
Wed., Wednesday.
w.f., wrong fount.
W.F.T.U., World Federation of Trade Unions.
W.I., West Indies; Women's Institute.
Wigorn., (Bishop) of Worcester (see Cantuar.).
Wilts., Wiltshire.
Winton., (Bishop) of Winchester (see Cantuar.).
Wisc., Wisconsin.
Wisd., Wisdom (of Solomon; Apocr.).
W/L, wave-length.
W.L.A., Women's Land Army.
W. long., West longitude.
Wm, William.
W.N.W., WNW, West-north-west.
W.O., War Office; Warrant Officer.
Worcs., Worcestershire.
W.P., weather permitting.
W.P.B., waste-paper basket.
W.R., West Riding (of Yorkshire).
W.R.A.C., W.R.A.F., Women's Royal Army Corps, Air Force.
W.R.I., War Risk Insurance; Women's Rural Institute.
W.R.N.S., Women's Royal Naval Service.
W.S., Writer to the Signet.
W.S.P.U., Women's Social & Political Union.
W.S.W., WSW., West-south-west.
W/T, wireless telegraphy, telephony.
wt, weight.
W. Va, West Virginia.
W.V.S., Women's Voluntary Service(s).
Wyo., Wyoming.

x-cp., ex coupon.
xd, x-d., x-div., ex dividend.
x-i., ex interest.
Xmas, Christmas.
x-n., ex new shares.
Xt(ian), Christ(ian), (prop. χ = Gk letter chi, formed like English X).

Y., Yeomanry.
yᵉ (pr. as *the*), the (*y* a survival in corrupt form of obs. þ, symbol for th; still used as archaism).
Yeo(m)., Yeomanry.

Y.H.A., Youth Hostels Association.
Y.L.I., Yorkshire Light Infantry.
Y.M.C.A., Young Men's Christian Association.
Yorks., Yorkshire.
yr(s), year(s); your(s).
yᵗ (pr. as *that*), that (conj.; as *yᵉ*).
Y.W.C.A., Young Women's Christian Association.

Zech., Zechariah (O.T.).
Zeph., Zephaniah (O.T.).

APPENDIX II
PRONUNCIATION OF NON-ENGLISH WORDS

THE words in the following Appendix list are those containing sounds that (like the French nasals and the Scottish ch) are non-English and therefore not covered by our notation. In this appendix they are arranged in three lists: the words in their ordinary form; the anglicized pronunciation, denoted by the same symbols as those used throughout the dictionary, but with extra symbols to represent the unEnglish sounds; and the foreign pronunciation in the alphabet of the Société Phonétique Internationale.

CONSONANTS

In the anglicized pronunciation the new symbol to be noted is CH, which is used here to represent a soft guttural sound between sh and k, heard in Scottish words like *loch* and common in German.

In the International Phonetic alphabet the consonants have their usual values, except the following:

j	is the sound in Eng. *young*		ʒ	is the sound in Eng. *vision*	
ɲ	„	„	Fr. *digne*	χ	„	„	Scottish and German *loch.*
ʃ	„	„	Eng. *shout*			

VOWELS

The nasal vowels characteristic of French are pronounced 'through the nose', that is, with the soft palate at the back of the mouth lowered so that the breath passes through the nasal passages. The nasal vowels are four; and are approximately the nasalized forms of the vowels in English *at, art, all, earl.* In the anglicized pronunciation they are denoted by ăṅ, ahṅ, awṅ, e͞rṅ, in the phonetic alphabet by ɛ̃ ɑ̃ ɔ̃ œ̃. These vowels are all heard in the phrase 'un bon vin blanc' (œ̃ bɔ̃ vɛ̃ blɑ̃).

The vowels in the International Phonetic alphabet are as follows:

a as in Fr. patte			o as in Fr. note	
ɑ	„	pas	ɔ	„	bon (= nasalized aw)
ɑ̃	„	ban (= nasalized ah)	ø	„	peu
e	„	dé	œ	„	seul
ɛ	„	fait	œ̃	„	brun (= nasalized e͞r)
ɛ̃	„	fin (= nasalized ă)	u	„	tout
ə	„	de (obscure)	y	„	pu
i	„	ni	ɥ	„	buis
o	„	beau			

· denotes that the preceding syllable is long.

Ordinary Form	Anglicized Pronunciation	Foreign Pronunciation
abandon	ăbahṅ′dawṅ	abɑ̃dɔ̃
abattoir	ăbat′wahr	abatwa·r
accouchement	ăko͞o′shmahṅ	akuʃmɑ̃
accoucheur	ăko͞o′she͞r	akuʃœ·r
accoucheuse	ăko͞o′she͞rz	akuʃø·z
acharnement	ăsha͞rn′mahṅ	aʃarnəmɑ̃
à deux	ah de͞r′	a dø
affaire de cœur	ăfār′ de ke͞r′	afɛ·r də kœ·r

Ordinary Form	Anglicized Pronunciation	Foreign Pronunciation
à fond	ah fawṅ′	a fɔ̃
agent provocateur	ah'zhahṅ prŏvŏkahtēr′	aӡᾶ prɔvɔkatœ·r
aide-de-camp	ā′ de kahṅ′	ɛ·dəkᾶ
âme damnée	ahm dahn'ā	a·m da·ne
amende honorable	ămahṅd′ ŏnōrah'bl	amᾶ·d ɔnorabl
ancien régime	ahṅ'syaṅ rāzhēm′	ᾶsjẽ reӡim
à outrance	ah ōō′trahṅs	a utrᾶ·s
aperçu	ahp′ārsōō	apersy
aplomb	ah'plawṅ	aplɔ̃
arme blanche	aṙm blahṅ′sh	arm blᾶ·ʃ
arrière-pensée	a'rĭăr pahṅ′sā	arjɛ·r pᾶ·se
arrondissement	ărondēs'mahṅ	arɔ̃dismᾶ
atelier	ăt′elyā	atəlje
au fond	ō fawṅ′	o fɔ̃
au grand sérieux	ō grahṅ sĕrēēr′	o grᾶ serjø
au naturel	ō·nătūrĕl′	o natyrɛl
ausgleich	ows'glīċh	ausglaix
avion	ăv′yawṅ	avjɔ̃

B

ballon d'essai	băl′awṅ dĕsā′	balɔ̃ dese
bas bleu	bah blēr′	ba blø
battue	bătōō′	baty
beau monde	bō mawnd	bo mɔ̃·d
bêche-de-mer	băsh′ de maṙ	bɛ·ʃ də mɛ·r
bersaglieri	bărsahlyăr′ō	bersaljɛ·ri
bon	bawṅ	bɔ̃
bon-bon	bŏn'bŏn	bɔ̃bɔ̃
bonne bouche	bŏn bōō′sh	bɔn buʃ
bonnes fortunes	bŏn fōrtŭn′	bɔn fortyn
bon ton	bawṅ tawṅ	bɔ̃ tɔ̃
bon vivant	bawṅ vĕ′vahṅ	bɔ̃ vi·vᾶ
bouillon	bōōl′yawṅ	bujɔ̃

C

café chantant	kăf′ā shŏ′ntahṅ	kafe ʃᾶ·tᾶ
cancan	kahṅ'kahṅ	kᾶkᾶ
carte blanche	kărt blahṅsh	kart blᾶ·ʃ
char-à-bancs	shă′răbăng	ʃarabᾶ
charlotte russe	shăr′lŏt rōōs′	ʃarlot rys
chartreuse	shărtrērz′	ʃartrø·z
chassé-croisé	shăs′ā krwah′zā	ʃase krwaze
chevalier d'industrie	shĕvălēr′ dăṅ′dōōstrē	ʃ(ə)valje dẽdystri
chiffon	shĭf′ŏn	ʃifɔ̃
chignon	shĭnŏn′, shēn′yŏn	ʃiɲɔ̃
chose jugée	shŏz zhōō′zhā	ʃo·z ӡy·ӡe
chronique scandaleuse	krŏn′ēk skahṅdălērz′	kronik skᾶdalø·z
ci-devant	sē devahṅ′	sidvᾶ
coiffeur	kwah'fēr	kwafœ·r
coiffure	kwah'fūr	kwafy·r
communiqué	komū′nĭkā	kɔmynike
concierge	kawṅ'siărzh	kɔ̃sjɛrӡ
confrère	kŏn'frăr	kɔ̃frɛ·r
congé	kawṅ'zhā	kɔ̃ӡe
consommé	konsŏ'mā	kɔ̃some
contretemps	kawṅ'tretahṅ	kɔ̃·trətᾶ
convenances	kawṅ'venahṅs	kɔ̃vnᾶ·s
cordon bleu	kŏr'dawṅ blēr	kordɔ̃ blø
corps de ballet	kŏr de băl′ā	ko·r də bale
coup-de-main	kōō′ de măṅ	kudmẽ
cul-de-sac	kōōl′ de săk	kydsak
curé	kū'rā	kyre

Ordinary Form	Anglicized Pronunciation	Foreign Pronunciation

D

début	dā'boŏ	deby
débutant	dā'boŏtahṅ	debytā
débutante	dā'boŏtahṅt	debytā·t
dégagé	dāgah'zhā	degaʒe
de haut en bas	de ōtahṅ bah'	də ho tā ba
démenti	dāmahṅ'tĕ	demã·ti
dénouement	dānoŏ'mahṅ	denumā
déshabillé	dāzahbē'yā	dezabije
détente	dātŏ'nt	detã·t
deux-temps	dĕr̄ tahṅ	də tā
distingué	distă'nggā	distɛ̃·gə
double entendre	doŏbl ahṅtahŭ'dr	dubl ātã·dr
douceur	doŏ'sĕr	dusœ·r
doyen	doi'yen	dwajɛ̃
duvet	doŏ'vā	dyve

E

eau sucrée	ō soŏ'krā	o sykrə
éclaircissement	ĕklārsēs'mahṅ	eklɛrsismā
édition de luxe	edish'on de loŏks	edisjɔ d(ə)lyks
élan	ā'lahṅ	elã
embonpoint	ahṅbawṅpwăṅ'	ãbɔpwɛ̃
embouchure	ahṅboŏshoŏr'	ãbuʃy·r
émeute	ĭmŭ't	emə·t
empressement	ahṅprĕs'mahṅ	ãprɛsmā
enceinte	ahṅsăṅt'	ãsɛ̃·t
encore	ŏngkōr'	ãko·r
enfant terrible	ahṅ'fahṅ tĕrĕbl'	ãfã tɛri·bl
en garçon	ahṅ găr'sawṅ	ã garsɔ
ennui	ŏn'wē	ãnɥi
ennuyé	ŏnwē'yā	ãnɥijə
en passant	ahṅ păs'ahṅ	ã pasã
ensemble	ahṅsahṅbl'	ãsã·bl
entente cordiale	ŏntŏ'nt kŏrdĭahl'	ãtã·t kordjal
entourage	ŏntoŏrah'zh	ãtura·ʒ
entr'acte	ŏ'ntrăkt	ã·trakt
entrée	ŏ'ntrā	ã·tre
entremets	ŏ'ntremā	ã·trəmɛ
entre nous	ŏ'ntre noŏ	ã·trə nu
entrepôt	ŏ'ntrepō	ã·trəpo
entresol	ŏ'ntresŏl	ã·trəsol
espièglerie	ĕspĭā'glerē	ɛspjɛglərī

F

faience	fah'yahṅs	fajã·s
fainéant	fā'nāahṅ	fenɛã
fait accompli	făt ahkawṅ'plē	fɛtakɔpli
fanfare	făṅ'fār	fãfa·r
fauteuil	fōtĕr'ĕ ɩ	fotœ·j
femme de chambre	făm de shahṅ'br	fam də ʃã·br
fête champêtre	făt shahṅpātr'	fɛ̦t ʃãpɛ·tr
feuilleton	fĕr'yeťawṅ	fœjtɔ
fiancé(e)	fēahṅ'sā	fjã·se
fin-de-siècle	făṅ de syăkl'	fɛ̃ də sjɛkl
fine champagne	fēn shahṅpĭn'	fin' ʃãpaɲ
franc-tireur	frahṅ tĕrĕr'	frã tirœ·r

G

gamin	găm'ăṅ	gamɛ̃
garçon	găr'sawṅ	garsɔ
gendarme	zhŏn'dărm	ʒãdarm
gendarmerie	zhŏndărm'erē	ʒãdarmərī

Ordinary Form	Anglicized Pronunciation	Foreign Pronunciation
genre	zhahn̄r	ʒã·r
gourmand	gŏor′mahn̄	gurmã
gourmandise	gŏor′mahn̄dĕz	gurmãdiz
grande	grahn̄d	grã·d
grand seigneur	grahn̄ sĕnyêr′	grã sɛɲœ·r
gratin	grăt′ăn̄	gratɛ̃
grisaille	grēzĭl′	griza·j
guilloche	gēyŏsh′	gijoʃ
guipure	gē′pūr	gipy·r

H

hauteur	ōtêr′	ho·tœ·r
hors concours	ôrr kawn̄kŏor′	hor kõku·r
hors de combat	ôrdekawm′bah	hor d(ə)kõba
hors-d'œuvre	ôrdêr′vr	hordœ·vr

I–K

ingénue	ăn̄′zhănŏo	ɛ̃geny
insouciance	ăn̄sŏos′yahn̄s	ɛ̃susjã·s
insouciant	ăn̄sŏos′yahn̄	ɛ̃susjã
instantané	ăn̄stăntah′nā	ɛ̃stãtane
jeu	zhêr	ʒø
jeu d'esprit	zhêr dĕsprē′	ʒø dɛspri
jeunesse dorée	zhêr′nĕs dōr′ă̄	ʒœnɛs do·re
jongleur	zhawn̄′glêr	ʒõ·glœ·r
julienne	zhŏolyĕn′	ʒyljɛn
kümmel	kŏom′el	küməl

L

langue-d'oc	lahn̄ge dŏk′	lã·gdok
langue-d'oïl	lahn̄ge doil′	lã·gdoil
le roi le veult	le rwah le vêr	lə rwa lə vø
le roi s'avisera	le rwah sahvē′zerah	lə rwa savizəra
liaison	liă′zn	ljɛzõ
lingerie	lă′n̄zherē	lɛ̃·ʒri
littérateur	lētêrahtêr′	literatœ·r
loch	lŏCH	loχ
lough	lŏCH	loχ

M

mademoiselle	mădemwazĕ′l.	madmwazɛl, mamzɛl
manqué	mahn̄′kā	mã·ke
mariage de convenance	mă′riahzh de kawn̄′venahn̄s	marja·ʒ də kõvnã·s
marron glacé	mă′rŏn glah′sā	marõ glase
marseillaise	marselāz′	masɛjɛz
masseur	măsêr′	masœ·r
masseuse	măsêrz′	masø·z
mauvaise honte	mōvāz ŏn̄t′	movɛ·z hõ·t
mauvais quart d'heure	mō′vă kărdêr′	movɛ kardœ·r
mauvais sujet	mō′vă sŏo′zhă	movɛ syʒɛ
mélange	māl′ahn̄zh	melã·ʒ
menu	mĕnŏo′, mĕn′ŭ	m(ə)ny
mésalliance	măzăl′Iahn̄s	mezaljã·s
mignon	mē′nyawn̄	miɲõ
milieu	mē′lyêr	miljø
mise en scène	mēzahn̄sān′	mi·z ã sɛ·n
mitrailleuse	mētralyêrz′	mitrajø·z
moire antique	mwahr ŏntē′k	mwa·r ãtik
monseigneur	mawn̄sĕnyêr′	mõsɛɲœ·r
monsieur	mesyêr′	m(ə)sjø
morgue anglaise	môrg ahn̄glāz′	morg ãglɛ·z
mot juste	mō zhŏost′	mo ʒyst

Ordinary Form	Anglicized Pronunciation	Foreign Pronunciation

N–O

nom-de-guerre	nŏm de găr'	nɔ̃ də gɛ·r
nom-de-plume	nŏm de plōōm'	nɔ̃ də plym
nuance	nŭ'ahŋs	nyã·s
och	ŏCH	ɔχ
ombre	awŋ'br	ɔ̃·br
on dit	ŏn dē'	ɔ̃ di

P

par excellence	păr ĕ'kselahŋs	par ɛksɛlã·s
parvenu	păr'venōō	parvəny
pas-de-deux	pah de dĕr'	pa də də
passé	pă'sā	pase
passementerie	păs'mentrĭ	pasmã·tri
pas seul	pah sŭl'	pa sœl
pâté	pă'tā	pa·te
patois	pă'twah	patwa
peignoir	pă'nwăr	pɛɲwa·r
penchant	pahŋ'shahŋ	pã·ʃã
père	păr	pɛ·r
petits soins	pĕtē swăŋ'	p(ə)ti swɛ̃
pibroch	pē'brŏCH	pibroχ
pièce-de-résistance	pē'ăs de răzĕs'tahŋs	pjɛs də rezistã·s
pince-nez	păŋs'nā	pɛ̃·sne
pis aller	pēzăl'ā	pizale
planchette	plahŋshĕt'	plã·ʃɛt
poilu	pwah'lōō	pwaly
pompon	pŏm'pŏn	pɔ̃·pɔ̃
poseur	pōzĕr'	po·zœ·r
poste restante	pōst rĕ'stahŋt	post restã·t
prie-dieu	prēdyĕr'	pridjə
Provençal	prŏvahŋsah'l	provã·sal
purée	pŭr'ā	py·re
pur sang	pŭr sahŋ'	pyrsã

Q–R

quand même	kahŋ măm'	kã mɛ·m
raconteur	răkŏntĕr'	rakɔ̃tœ·r
raconteuse	răkŏntĕrz'	rakɔ̃tœ·z
raison d'être	ră'zawŋ dă'tr	rɛzɔ̃ dɛ·tr
ranz des vaches	rahŋs dă vahsh'	rã·s de vaʃ
rapprochement	răprŏsh'mahŋ	raprɔʃmã
Réaumur	ră'ōmūr	reomyr
réchauffé	răshō'fā	reʃo·fe
recherché	reshăr'shă	rəʃɛrʃe
réclame	ră'klahm	rekla·m
renaissance	rĕnă'sahŋs	rənɛsã·s
rencontre	rahŋkawŋ'tr	rãkɔ̃·tr
répondez s'il vous plaît	răpawŋ'dă sĭ vōō plă	repɔ̃de si vu plɛ
restaurant	rĕ'storahŋ	rɛstorã
résumé	ră'zōōmă	rezyme
robe-de-chambre	rŏb de shahŋ'br	rob də ʃã·br
roturier	rŏtū'rēă	rotyrje
ruche	rōōsh	ryʃ
ruse	rōōz	ryz
rusé	rōō'ză	ryze

S

salle-à-manger	săl a mahŋ'zhă	salamãʒe
salle d'attente	săl dătahŋ't	saldatã·t
salon	săl'awŋ	salɔ̃
sang-froid	sahŋfrwah'	sã frwa

Ordinary Form	Anglicized Pronunciation	Foreign Pronunciation
sans cérémonie	sahn̊ sĕ'rĕmŏnē	sᾱ seremoni
sansculotte	sahn̊'kŏōlŏt	sᾱ kylŏt
sans façon	sahn̊ fås'awn̊	sᾱ fasɔ̃
sans gêne	sahn̊ zhā'n	sᾱ ӡe·n
sans peur et sans reproche	sahn̊ pĕr' ᾱ sahn̊ rĕprŏsh'	sᾱ pœ·r e sᾱ rəprɔʃ
sans phrase	sahn̊ frahz'	sᾱ fra·z
sans souci	sahn̊ sŏō'sē	sᾱ susi
Sassenach	săs'enahcӊ	sasənaχ
savant	săv'ahn̊	savᾱ
séance	sā'ahn̊s	seᾱs
Sevres	sā'vr	sε·vr
soi-disant	swah dĕ'zahn̊	swadizᾱ
soixante-quinze	swah'zahn̊t kǎn̊z'	swasᾱ·t kε̃·z
soupçon	sŏō'psawn̊	supsɔ̃
succès d'estime	sŏŏksᾱ dĕstĕ'm	syksε dεstim
succès fou	sŏŏksᾱ fŏō'	syksε fu

T

tableau vivant	tăb'lō vĕ'vahn̊	tablo vivᾱ
tic douloureux	tĭk dŏlerŏō'	tik dulurə
timbre	tăm'ber	tε̃br
tirailleur	tĕrahyĕr'	tiraʃœ·r
torchon	tŏr'shŏn	torʃɔ̃
tout ensemble	tŏōt ahn̊sahn̊'bl	tutᾱsᾱ·bl
train de luxe	trăn̊ de lŏōks'	trε̃ dlyks
trente-et-quarante	trahn̊t ᾱ kă'rahn̊t	trᾱ·t e karᾱ·t
trois-temps	trwah tahn̊	trwa tᾱ
trouvaille	trŏō'vĭl	tru·vaʃ
tulle	tŏŏl, tūl	tyl

V

Valenciennes	vălensĕnz'	valᾱ·sjεn
ventre à terre	vahn̊'trahtār'	vᾱ·trate·r
vingt-et-un	vǎn̊t ᾱ ĕrn̊	vε̃te œ̃
vin ordinaire	vǎn̊ ŏrdĭnār'	vε̃ ordinε·r
vol-au-vent	vŏl'ōvahn̊	volovᾱ

APPENDIX III

PRONUNCIATION OF PROPER NAMES

THIS list is intended as a guide to the pronunciation of some difficult proper names frequently met with. It makes no claim to completeness, and many geographical names in particular have had to be omitted.

One or two general points may perhaps be noted here: Classical names ending in -es are usually pronounced (-ēz). In New Zealand and in many other overseas countries native names are normally pronounced with all vowels sounded (and pronounced as Italian vowels, i.e. *a* = ah, *e* = ā or ĕ, *i* = ē or ĭ, *u* = oo). The U.S. pronunciation of some American place-names differs from the usual English pronunciation; in the following list such specifically U.S. pronunciations are preceded by an asterisk. There are many proper names (e.g. Kerr, Smyth) the pronunciation of which varies according to the family or individual referred to; such names have usually been omitted.

The following symbols have been employed in indicating pronunciation, in addition to those in the body of the work:

χ = *ch* in the Scottish pronunciation of *loch*.
ğ = 'soft' *g* in *ginger*.
ñ indicates that the preceding vowel is nasalized.

Aar'on (ār-)
Abbeville (ăb'vĕl)
Abĕd'nĕgō
A'bel (ā-)
Ab'élărd (ă-)
Abī'jah (-*a*)
Aboukir (ahbōōkēr')
About (ah'bōō)
A'brahăm (ā-)
Abruz'zi (-brōōtsī)
Abȳd'ŏs
Accra (ăk'ra or akrah')
Acĕl'dama (-k- or -s-)
Ach'erŏn (ăk-)
Achĭt'ōphĕl (*ak*-)
Ad'élaide (ă-)
A'den (ā-)
Adīrŏn'dăck (ă-)
Adonā'īs (ă-)
Adriăt'ĭc (ā-)
Aeğē'an
Aeğī'na
Æl'frĭc (ă-)
Aenē'ăs
Aen'ĕīd
Ae'olus
Aes'chȳlus (-k-)
Aes'ŏp
Afghăn'īstăn (ăfg-; or -ahn; or ăfgănīstăn')
A'găg (ă-)
Agincourt (ăğ'ĭnkôrt)
Ag'ra (ah- or ă-)
Aī'da (ah-ē-)
Aix-la-Chapelle (ā'ks-lah-shăpĕl')
Aix-les-Bains (ā'ks-lā-băñ)
Ajmēr' (ah-)
Alabama (ălabah'ma; * -bă-)

Albani (ălbah'nī)
Al'banȳ (awl'-)
Alcan'tara (ălcahn-)
Alcĕs'tĭs (ă-)
Alcĭbī'adēs (ă-; -z)
Alḍĕb'aran (ă-)
Alğĕcīr'as (ă-)
Alğēr'īa (ă-)
Algiers (ălğēīz')
Allahabad (ăla-habăd')
Alleghany (ălĕgăn'ī; or -ănī)
Almerĭ'a (ă-)
Alsace (ăl'săs; or -ās)
Amiens [French city] (ăm'īăñ)
Amiens [in Shakespeare] (ăm'īens)
A'mŏs (ā-)
Anăc'rĕon
An'ăm (ă-)
Anani'as (ă•)
Anchises (ăngkī'sēz)
Anḍes (ăn'dēz)
An'droclēs (ă-; -z)
Andrŏm'ache (ă-; -ăkī)
Andrŏm'ĕda (ă-)
Anḍrŏn'īcus [in Shakespeare] (ă-)
Anğĕl'īcō (ă-)
An'ğĕvĭn (ă-)
Angōī'a (ăngg-; or ăng'gora)
Antæ'us (ă-)
Anthæa (ăn'thī*a*)
Antĭg'onĕ (ă-)
Antigua (ăntē'gwa)
Antĭn'ōus (ă-)
Antonĭn'us (ă-)
Apĕll'ēs (-z)
Aphrōdīt'ĕ (ă-)
Apŏllīnăr'īs

Appalăch'ian (ă-; or -ăch-)
Aquin'ăs
Arăch'nē (-kn-)
Aravalli (arah'vallī)
Archimedes (ärkĭmēd'ēz)
Areŏpagĭt'ica (ă-; or -g-)
Aréthūs'a (ă-; -za)
Ar'ğentīne (är-)
Argyll (ärgīl')
Ariăd'nē (ă-)
Ar'ĭel (är-)
Arĭstīd'ēs (ă-; -z)
Arĭstŏph'anēs (ă-; -z)
A'rĭstŏtle (ă-)
Arizōn'a (ă-)
Arkansas (är'kₐnsaw)
Artaxerxes (ärtagzₑr'ksēz)
Ar'tĕmĭs (är-)
Ar'un (är-)
A'rundel (ă-)
Asia (ā'sha)
Assi'sĭ (ăsē-)
Assouan (ăsŏŏăn')
Astär'tē (ă-)
Astrakhan (ăstrₐkăn')
Atalăn'ta (ă-)
A'tē (ă- or ah-)
Athēn'ē
Ath'ens (ă-; -z)
At'ropŏs (ă-)
Auch'inlĕck (awk⁻, Scottish ŏχ⁻)
Auğē'as
Augŭs'tĭne
Aurēl'ĭus
Autŏl'ÿcus
Av'alon (ă-)
Avignon (äv'ēnyawñ)
A'von (ā-)
Azores' (-ôrz)
Az'rāel (ă-)
Bach (bahχ)
Ba'den (bah-)
Bă'den-Pow'ell (-ŏel)
Bagehot (băğ'et)
Bahamas (bₐ-hah'mₐz)
Baiæ (bī'ē)
Băléă'rĭc (or balēr'ĭc)
Băll'ĭol
Bălmŏ'ral
Bălthazär' [in Shakespeare]
Balu'chistăn (-lŏŏk-; or balŏŏkĭstăn')
Bantu (bah'ntŏŏ; or băn-)
Barăbb'as
Bärbăd'os (-ŏz)
Bär'mēcīde
Barŏd'a
Bărŏt'sēland
Băs'ăn
Băsh'ăn
Băs'ra (-z-; or bŭs-)
Bassan'ĭō (-ahn-)
Băstille' (-tēl)
Basut'ŏlănd (-ŏŏ-)
Batăv'ĭa
Băt'on Rouge (rŏŏzh)
Bau'cĭs
Bayeux (bă-yŏŏ')
Bayreuth (bī'roit)

Bea'consfield (bĕ- or bē-)
Beauchamp (bē'chₐm)
Beaulieu (bū'lĭ)
Beaune (bōn)
Bĕchua'na (-kŭahnₐ; or bĕch-)
Bēĕl'zébŭb (or bĕĕl-)
Beethoven (bāt'ōven)
Behr'ĭng (bĕ-; or bär-)
Beira (bī'ra)
Beirut (bā'rōōt)
Bĕl'ğium (-ₐm)
Bĕl'ĭal
Bĕllăgg'ĭō (-j-)
Bellē'rophon
Bĕlli'nĭ (-lē-)
Belvoir (bĕv'er)
Bēnär'ēs (-z; or bĕ-)
Bĕn'tham (-tₐm)
Berkeley (bärk'lĭ)
Bĕrk'ley [America]
Berkshire (bärk'sher)
Berlioz (bär'lĭōs)
Bĕrmūd'as (-z)
Berwick (bĕ'rĭk)
Bethune [English surname] (bē'ten)
Bicester (bĭs'ter)
Bĭd'ēford
Bĭg'élow (-g-; -ō)
Bĭhär'
Bīkanir' (-ēr)
Bĭlbā'ō
Blanc (-ahñ)
Bleriot (blē'rĭō)
Bloem'fŏntein (-ōō-; -ăn)
Blücher (blŏŏk'er)
Bŏadĭcē'a
Bŏcca'cciō (-kahch-)
Bŏd'iham (-dĭₐm)
Bŏdleian (-lē'ₐn)
Bŏĕth'ĭus
Bohun (bŏŏn)
Boleyn (bŏŏl'ĭn)
Bom'pas (-ŭm-)
Boŏtes (bō-ō'tēz)
Bŏrdeaux' (-dō)
Bŏrdōn'ē
Bō'tha (-tₐ)
Bŏttĭcĕll'ĭ (-chĕl-)
Boulogne (bŏŏlōn')
Bourchier (bow'cher)
Bow (bō)
Bŏz (or -ō-)
Braemär' (brä-)
Brāse'nōse (-zn-; -z)
Breadal'bane (ĕdawl-)
Brougham (brŏŏm or brŏŏ'ₐm)
Bruges (brŏŏzh)
Buccleuch (bₐklŏŏ')
Bŭch'arĕst (-ker-)
Bŭd'apĕst'
Buenos Aires (bwĕn'ozär'ĭz; or bŏŏ'ĭn-)
Bulawayo (bŏŏlawī'ō)
Bŭr'leigh (-lĭ)
Bÿr'on
Bysshe (bĭsh)
Bÿzăn'tĭum
Căb'ot
Căd'ĭz

Cadog'an (-ŭg-)
Cæd'mon (kä-)
Caen (kahṅ)
Cagliostro (kälïŏs'trō)
Cai'aphäs (kī-)
Cairo (kīr'ō)
Caius [Roman name] (kī'us)
Caius [Cambridge college] (kēz)
Căl'ais (-ĭs or -ä or -ĭ)
Cälèdŏn'ïa
Callg'ūla
Callï'opė
Cämbȳs'ēs (-z)
Cämpa'gna (-ahnya)
Campbell (kăm'bl)
Căn'berra
Cändä'cè
Canōp'us
Carăc'tacus
Carew' (-ōō)
Carew [Thomas, 1589-1639] (kār'ï)
Cār'ey
Cär'lisle' (-lïl)
Carmär'then (-dh-)
Carnär'von
Cär'nĕg'ie (-gï; or -ägï)
Cärolin'a
Căsablän'ca
Cässïopei'a (-ĕa)
Cästile' (-ēl)
Căthay'
Catrï'ona (or kătrĭō'na)
Catŭll'us
Căv'ell
Cavour' (-oor)
Cecil (sĕsl or sĭsl)
Cècïl'ïa
Cellïui (chĕlĕ'nï)
Cenci (chĕn'chï)
Cēr'ēs (-z)
Cĕrvän'tēs (-z)
Ceylŏn' (sï-)
Cézänne' (sä-)
Chäl'kïs (k-)
Chamonix (shăm'onï)
Chapultĕpĕc' (chahpōōl-)
Chä'ring Cross (-aws; or chär-)
Charlemagne (shärl'emän)
Chär'teris (-terz)
Chăt'ham (-tam)
Chautau'qua (sha-; -kwa)
Cherbourg (shĕr'boorg)
Cher'wĕll (chär-)
Chicago (shïkah'gō, *shïkaw'gō)
Chïl'è
Chiswick (chïz'ïk)
Chloe (klō'ï)
Cholmondeley (chŭm'lï)
Chopin (shōp'äṅ or shō-)
Cicero (sïs'erō)
Cimabu'e (chē-; -ōō-ï)
Cimarŏs'a (chē-; -z-)
Cïncïnnät'ï (or -ah-)
Cïr'encĕster (or sïs'ïster)
Clăv'erhouse (or klăv'erz)
Clerk'enwell (klär-)
Clough (klŭf, klōō)
Clovĕll'ȳ

Cŏch'ïn-Chïn'a
Cŏckaigne' (-kän)
Cœur de Lion (kŭrdelĕ'awŭ)
Colbourne (kōb'en)
Cŏl'chïs (-k-)
Cologne' (-ōn)
Colom'bō (-ŭm-)
Colŏn'
Cŏlora'dō (-ah-; *-ä-)
Colquhoun (ko-hōōn')
Cŏm'ō
Comte (kauṅt)
Connect'ïcut (-nĕt-)
Con'stable (kŭn-)
Cophĕt'ūa
Cŏr'dïller'a (-lyära)
Cŏr'neille' (-nä)
Cŏr'rot (-rō)
Cŏrrĕgg'ïō (-j-)
Cŏr'tĕs (-z; or -ïz)
Cow'per (kōō-)
Creusa (krèōō'za)
Crichton (krït'on)
Crïmè'a
Crō'cè (-ch-)
Cullŏd'en
Cȳm'bēline (-lĕn)
Cȳn'ĕwulf (k-; -ōōlf)
Cȳrēn'è
Cȳthēr'a
Czech (chĕk)
Dæd'alus
Dahōm'ey (da-h-)
Dakŏt'a
Dän'äĕ (-ï)
Dän'tè
Dăph'nè
Dār'ēs (-z)
Darï'us
Daudet (dō'dä)
Däv'entrȳ (or dän'trï)
Da'vōs (dah-; or davōs')
Debŭss'y (-ū)
De Crespigny (dekrĕp'ïnï; or krĕs-)
De'gäs (dä-)
Dehra Dun (dä'ra-dōōn')
Dĕlagō'a
De la Mare (dĕlamär')
Delhi (dĕl'ï)
Dĕl'ïus
Dĕl'phï
Dĕmēt'er
Dĕmēt'rïus (or -mĕt-)
Dĕmŏc'rïtus
Dĕmŏs'thenēs (-z)
Dĕn'bigh (-bï)
De Reszke (derĕs'kï)
Dĕr'went
Descartes (dăk'ärt)
Desdémōn'a (dĕz-)
Des Moines (dïmoin')
Dĕtroit'
Deutsch'länd (doich-)
Diderot (dēd'erō)
Dïd'ō
Dieppe (dē-ĕp')
Dijon (dē'zhawṅ)
Dïōclē'tian (-shïan)

Dĭŏğ'énĕs (-z)
Diomĕd'ĕs (-z)
Dionў̆s'ĭus
Dionў̆s'us
Dĭsrael'Ĭ (-zrăl-)
Domĭ'tian (-shĭan)
Dŏn Giova'nnĭ (ğŏvah-)
Dŏn Ju'an (jŏōan)
Dŏnne
Donne [John, 1573–1631] (dŭn)
Dŏn Quĭx'ŏte (or kwĭk'set)
Do'theboys (dŏōdhe-)
Doug'las (dŭg-)
Drey'fus (drā-)
Dŭb'lĭn
Dŭl'wich (-lĭj)
Dŭ'mas (-mah)
Dŭ Maurier (mŏr'ĭā)
Dŭmfries' (-ēs)
Dŭnĕd'ĭn
Dŭr'ban
Durham (dŭ'ram)
Dvořák (dvŏr'zhăk)
Ebbw (ĕb'ŏō)
Ed'ĭnburgh (ĕ-; -bure)
Eiff'el tower (ĭf-)
Einstein (īn'stĭn)
Eire (ār'ĕ)
El'Ĭ (ē-)
El'ĭa (ē-)
El'ў̆ (ē-)
Empĕd'oclĕs (ĕ-; -z)
Endў̆m'ĭŏn (ĕ-)
Eng'land (ĭngg-)
Entŏbb'ĕ (ĕ-)
Eph'ĕsus (ĕf-)
Epĭcŭr'us (ĕ-)
E'rĕwhŏn (ĕ-)
Erie (ēr'ĭ)
Erin (ĕ'rĭn or ēr'-)
Es'tĕ (ĕ-)
Estŏn'ĭa (ĕ-)
Etherege (ĕth'erĭj)
Eubœa (ūbĭ'a)
Euphrāt'ĕs (-z)
Euph'ūĕs (-z)
Eurĭp'ĭdĕs (ūr-; -z)
Europe (ūr'op)
Eurў̆d'ĭcĕ (ūr-)
Evĕlin'a (ĕ-; -ēna)
Ev'elў̆n (ĕ- or ĕ-)
Eyck (īk)
Ezĕk'ĭel (Ĭ-)
Făg'ĭn (-g-)
Făll'odon
Făr'quhar (-kwer)
Făt'ĭma
Fa(u)lk'land (fawk-)
Faust (fowst)
Featherstonehaugh (făn'shaw)
Fĭde'lĭŏ (-dā-)
Fiennes (fĭnz)
Fie'solĕ (fĕ-āz-)
Fĭg'arŏ
Fiji (fĕ'jĕ)
Fĭnĭsterre' (-ār)
Flŏr'ĕs (-z)
Flŏ'rida

Foch (fŏsh)
Fŏlk'estone (fŏks-)
Fŏrtūnāt'us
Frăncĕs'ca (or -chĕs-)
Freud (froid)
Frŏ'bel (frĕr-)
Frŏb'ĭsher
Froude (frŏōd)
Frowde (-owd; or -ŏōd)
Gala'pagŏs (gahlah-)
Găl'ĕn
Găllĭe'o (-āŏ)
Galle (gawl)
Galsworthy (gaw'lzwerdhĬ)
Gamāl'ĭel
Găn'ğĕs (-z)
Gĕdd'ĕs (g-)
Gcoff'rey (ğĕf-)
Ghats (gawts)
Ghirlăndai'o (gĕr-; -dĭ'yŏ)
Giaour (ğowr)
Gĭbral'tar (ğ-; -awl-)
Gĭd'ĕa (g-)
Gĭl'ĕăd (g-)
Gillĕtte' (ğ-)
Giŏrgĭŏ'nĕ (ğ-; -ğ-)
Giŏtt'ŏ (ğ-)
Giovanni (ğŏvah'nĬ)
Glamis (glahmz)
Glăs'gow (-zgŏ)
Gloucester (glŏs'ter)
Gluck (-ŏŏk)
Gŏ'a
Gŏd'almĭng
Gŏda'varĭ (-dah-)
Godĭv'a
Goethe (gĕr'te)
Gounod (gŏōn'ŏ)
Gracchus (grăk'us)
Grătia'nŏ (-shĭah-)
Greuse (grĕrz)
Grieg (grēg)
Grĭn'delwald (-vahld)
Groote Schoor (grŏt'skoor)
Gros'venor (grŏv-)
Guadeloupe (gwahdĕlŏōp')
Guatemala (gwătĭmah'la)
Gudrun (gŏōd'rŏōn)
Guelph (gwĕlf)
Guiana (gĭ-ah'na)
Gŭsta'vus (-tah-)
Haar'lem (hăr-)
Hăg'ăr
Hăgg'āĭ
Hague (hăg)
Haifa (hĭf'a)
Hain'ault (-awt)
Hait'Ĭ (or hĭ-)
Hăk'luyt (-ŏŏt)
Hare'wŏŏd (hăr-; locally hăr-)
Hăr'lĕch (-χ)
Hă'run-ăl-Răsch'id (-rŏō-; -shĭd)
Harwich (hă'rĭj)
Hăr'wĭch [America]
Hausa (hou'za)
Havre (hah'vr)
Hawai'i (-wĭ-ĭ)
Haw'arden (-erd-; or hărd-)

Haw'orth (or how'erth)
Hay'dn (hī-)
Hĕb'rīdēs (-z)
Hĕc'atė
He'gel (hāg-)
Hei'delbĕrg (hī-)
Heine (hī'nė)
Hĕll'ĕspŏnt
Hĕm'ans
Hĕn'gĭst (-ngg-)
Hĕ'raclēs (-z)
Hĕraclit'us
Hĕrcūlān'ėum
Hĕ'rėford
Hĕ'rėward
Hĕrmī'onė
Hĕrŏd'ĭas
Hĕrŏd'otus
Hert'ford [England] (hárf-)
Hĕrt'ford [America]
Herts (hárts)
Hĕspĕ'rĭdēs (-z)
Hīawath'a (-wŏ-)
Hil'dėbrănd
Hĭmalay'a (or hĭmah'lĭa)
Hĭn'du-Kush (-dōō kōōsh)
Hĭppŏc'ratēs (-z)
Hĭppŏl'ȳta
Hŏbb'ėma
Hŏ'bōken
Hoh'enlĭn'den (hōen-)
Hŏl'bein (-bĭn)
Hŏl'born (hōben)
Hŏlŏfĕr'nēs (-z)
Hŏl'ȳrōōd
Hŏl'ȳwĕll
Hŏm'er
Hŏndū́r'ás
Hŏnolu'lu (-lōōlōō)
Hous'ton (hōōs-)
Hūd'Ibrás
Hun'yadĭ (hōōn-yah-)
Hū́r'on
Hȳd'erabăd
Hȳgei'a (-Ia)
Hȳmĕtt'us
Hȳpā'tia (-shĭa)
Hȳpĕr'ion
Iago (I-ah'gō)
Ián'thė (I-)
Ic'arus (I-)
Idaho (i'da-hō)
Id'ō (ē-)
Idūmē'a (I-)
Illinois' (I-; -noi)
Illȳ'ria (I-)
Indĭăn'a (I-)
Indĭanăp'olĭs (I-)
Inge (ing or ĭnḡ)
Ingelow (ĭn'ḡĭlō)
In'Igō (I-)
In'terlaken (I-; -lah-)
Iŏlăn'thė (I-)
Iŏl'chus (I-; -k-)
Iŏn'a (I-)
I'owa (I-)
Iphĭgénī'a (I-)
Iquique (Ikē'kĭ)

Irawad'ī (I-; -wŏd-)
I'roquois (I-; -kwoi or -kwah)
Isaac (iz'ac)
Isaiah (Izi'a)
Is'Is (I-)
Is'leworth (Izelw-)
Ismailia (Izmah-ē'lĭa)
Isŏc'ratēs (I-; -z)
Isolde (Izŏl'da)
Ispahan (Ispa-hahn')
Ith'aca (I-)
Ixī'on (I-)
Jä'ĕl
Jaipur (jīpoor')
Jáīr'us (or jīr'us)
Janeir'ō (-ēī'-)
Jăph'ĕt
Jä'ques [in Shakespeare] (-kwiz)
Ja'va (jah-)
Je'na (yä-)
Jĕ'rome (or Jĕrōm')
Jĕr'vaulx (-vō)
Jōhănn'ėsbūrg
Jŏl'ĭĕt
Jōsĕph'us
Jungfrau (yōŏng'frou)
Kaap'stadt (kah-; -t)
Kabul' (-ōŏl; or kaw'bōŏl)
Kalahár'ī (kah-; -ee)
Kălamazōō'
Kăndahár' (-da-h-)
Kăn'sas [state] (-nz-)
Kăn'sas [city] (-ns-)
Kara'chI (-rah-)
Kăttėgát'
Kĕ'ble
Kĕd'ár
Kĕntŭck'ȳ
Kĕ'nya
Kĕr'guelén (-gĭl-)
Keswick (kĕz'Ik)
Keynes (kānz)
Khártoum' (k-; -ōōm)
Khayyám (kI-ahm)
Khȳb'er (k-)
Kiel (kĕl)
Kiev (kĕĕf')
Kĭl'Imanjár'ō
Kirkcud'bright (kerkōō'brī)
Knollys (nōlz)
Kōb'ė
Kreisler (krIs'ler)
Kreutzer (kroit'ser)
Lăbouchère' (-bōōshár)
Lăch'ėsĭs (-k-)
Laér'tēs (-z)
Lafitte (lahfēt')
Lăg'ōs
La Junta (lah hōŏn'ta)
L'Alle'grō (lălä-)
Lancelot (lahn'slet)
Lăŏc'ōŏn
Lascelles (lăs'els)
Las Pal'mas (lahs pahl-)
Lausănne' (lōz-)
Lăv'ėngrō
Lăv'erȳ (or lä-)
Lăvoi'sier (-vwahzyä)

Leam'ington (lĕm-)
Leăn'der (or lĕ-)
Lĕd'a
Le Feuvre (fĕv'er)
Leicester (lĕs'ter)
Leigh (lē)
Lein'ster (lĕn-)
Leip'zig (līp-)
Leith (lē-)
Lĕl'and
Lĕl'ŷ
Lĕn'īn
Leominster (lĕm'ster)
Leonărd'ō (lă-on-)
Le Queux (lekŭ')
Leveson-Gower (lōō'sen-gōr')
Lhăs'a (lă-)
Liège (liāzh')
Li'ma (lē-)
Līmoges' (-ōzh)
Līszt (-st)
Llan- [as the first element in Welsh names]
   (hlăn-)
Llewĕll'ŷn (hlōō-)
Loh'ĕngrīn (lō-)
Lŏngīn'us (-nj-)
Lōr'ĕlei (-ī)
Lŏs An'gĕlĕs (-ăngg-, also -anğ-; -z)
Louisiăn'a (lōō-ēz-)
Lou'īsvīlle (lōō-)
Lourdes (loord)
Lourĕn'çŏ Mărques' (-sō; -ks)
Luga'nō (lōōgah-)
Lў'cīdăs
Lўcŭr'gus
Lў'lŷ
Lўm'ington
Lympne (līm)
Lўsăn'der
Mă'cĕdon
Mackay (makī')
Macleod (maklowd')
Madrăs' (or -ahs)
Madrīd'
Măd'ūra
Mae'terlīnck (mah- or mă-)
Măf'ĕkīng
Magĕll'an (-g-)
Măggīōr'ĕ (-j-)
Mahōn' (ma-h-; or -ōōn)
Mahony (mah'nī)
Mainwaring (măn'erīng)
Măl'achī (-k-)
Măl'herbe (-lărb)
Măl'orŷ
Mal'ta (mawl-)
Mal'vern (mawl-)
Măn'et (-ă)
Măr'īon (or mă-)
Marjoribănks (măr'chb-)
Mărque'săs (-kă-)
Măr'tīneau (-nō)
Mărtīnique' (-ĕk)
Măr'ŷlănd (*mĕ-)
Mă'rylebone (-eleben; or mă'rīben)
Masaï' (-sī; or mah'sī)
Măssachus'ĕtts (-ōō-)
Măss'enet (enă)

Mătabĕl'ŏ
Maurī'tius (-shyes)
Mazzini (mădzĕn'ī)
Mĕch'līn (-kl-)
Mĕdĕ'a
Mĕd'īcī (-chī)
Mĕdīn'a (-ē-)
Mĕdīn'a [America]
Meis'tersīnger (mī-)
Mĕn'ai (-nī)
Mĕn'delssohn (-son; or -sŏn)
Mĕnĕlă'us
Menzies (mĕn'zīz, mĕng'īs, mīng'īs)
Mĕrcĕd'ēs (-z)
Mĕrcŭ'tīō (-shī-)
Mĕ'rĕdīth (in Wales mĕrĕd'īth)
Mĕ'rope
Mĕssin'a (-sē-)
Mĕtt'ernīch (-k)
Mey'nell (mĕ- or mā-)
Miăm'ī
Mīch'igan (-shī-)
Mīd'ăs
Milăn' (or mīl'an)
Mill'ais (-ā)
Milngavie (mīlgī')
Minnĕăp'olīs
Minnĕsōt'a
Mīrăn'da
Mīssour'ī (-oor-; *mīz-)
Mīthrīdăt'ēs (-z)
Mītўlĕn'ĕ (or -ē)
Mōbile' (-ēl)
Moh'īcan (mō-; properly mō-hē'-)
Mohun (mōōn)
Mōl'ière (-liăr)
Mōna'cō (-ah-)
Mŏntaigne' (-ăn)
Mŏnta'na (-ah-; *-ă-)
Mŏntrĕal' (-awl)
Mŏrōn'ĕ
Mŏs'cow (-ō)
Moul'main
Mōzambique' (-bĕk)
Müller (mŭl'er)
Mŭn'ich (-īk)
Mūrīll'ō
Mўcē'næ
Mўtīlĕn'ĕ (or -ē)
Nairōb'ī (nīr-)
Nă'omī
Năp'īer (or napĕr')
Natăl'
Năv'ajo (-a-hō)
Nĕpal' (-awl)
Nĕva'da (-vah; *-ă-)
Newfoundland' (-fĕnd-)
Niăg'ara
Nibelung (nēb'elŏong)
Nietzsche (nē'che)
Nī'ğer
Niğēr'īa
Nil'ğīrī (-g-)
Nīn'ĕveh (-vī)
Norwich (nŏ'rīj)
Nўăs(s)'a
Ob'an (ō-)
Ober-ămm'ergau (ō-; -gow)

Ob'eron (ŏ-)
Odўss'eus (-ūs)
Oenŏn'ê (ē-)
Ohī'ō (ō-h-)
Oklahōm'a (ō-)
Omaha (ōma-hah'; •-aw)
Oman (ōmahn')
Ontār'ĭō (ŏ-)
Ophēl'ĭa (ō-)
Orĕs'tēs (ŏ-; -z)
Orī'on (ō-)
Orlê'ans (ôr-; -z)
Orleans [America] (ôrlēnz')
Orpheus (ôr'fūs)
Orsino (ôrsēn'ō)
Osīr'ĭs (ō-)
Os'ler (ō-)
Ota'gō (ōtah-)
Othĕll'ō (ō-)
Ottawa (ŏt'a-wa)
Ottŭm'wa (ŏ-)
Ouida (wē'da)
Ouse (ōōz)
Ov'ĭd (ŏ-)
Pach'mann (pahk-)
Păderew'skĭ (-ĕvskĭ)
Pāgani'nĭ (-ēn-)
Pagliacci (păliăch'ĭ)
Pălamĕd'ĕs (-z)
Păl'amon
Pălĕstri'na (-ēn-)
Păll'ăs
Pāll Măll' (or pĕl'mŏl')
Pănama' (-ah)
Pāph'ōs
Pă'raguay (-gwā or -gwĭ)
Pārnăss'us
Parŏll'ĕs
Pās'teur (-ĕr)
Patrŏc'lus
Pau (pō)
Pausān'ĭăs
Pavī'a
Pēkĭn'
Pēl'eus (-lŭs)
Pĕloponnēs'us
Pĕl'ŏps
Pĕnnsўlvān'ĭa
Pĕnthĕsĭlĕ'a
Pepys (pēps or pĕps or pĕp'ĭs)
Pêr'dĭta
Pêrgole'sĕ (-lāz-)
Pĕ'rĭclēs (-z)
Pĕ'rrault (-rō)
Pêrsĕph'onĕ
Pêrsĕp'olĭs
Pêr'seus (-ūs)
Peru' (-ōō)
Pĕrugĭ'nō (-ōōgĕ-)
Peshawar (peshôr')
Pĕstalŏzz'ĭ (-tsĭ)
Pĕsth (-st)
Pĕt'ra
Pĕt'rārch (-k)
Pĕtru'chĭo (-ōōk- or -ōōch-)
Phæd'ra
Phā'ĕthŏn
Phārsāl'ĭa

Phĭlĕm'ŏn
Phō'cĭs
Phœb'ê (fē-)
Phœnĭc'ĭa (fē-)
Phrўn'ê
Pie'dmont (pē- or pyĕ- or pyă-)
Pietermă'rĭtzbūrg (pē-; or -rĭtz'-)
Pīla'tus (-ah-)
Pĭnēr'ō
Pīræ'us
Plăt'ō
Plĭn'ў
Plotĭn'us
Plu'tārch (-ōō-; -k)
Pole Carew (pōōl' kăr'ĭ)
Pŏllaiuo'lō (-lĭ-ŏŏ-ō-)
Pŏlўb'ĭus
Pŏlўc'ratĕs (-z)
Pŏlўphēm'us
Pŏlўx'ĕna
Pom'frĕt (pŭm-)
Pŏmpei'ĭ (-ēĭ or -āĕ)
Pŏrt Said (sah'ĭd or sād)
Pŏsei'don (-sī-)
Potŏm'ăc
Poughkeep'sie (pokĭp-)
Poussin (pōō'săn)
Pō'wўs
Prăxĭt'elĕs (-z)
Prêtōr'ĭa
Prī'am
Promĕth'eus (-ūs)
Prŏs'erpīne
Proust (prōōst)
Ptŏl'emў (t-)
Puccini (pōōchē'nĭ)
Pŭnjab' (-ahb)
Pў'ramus
Pўtch'ley
Pўthăg'orăs
Quèbĕc'
Răb'elais (-elā)
Răc'ine (-sēn)
Rae'būrn (rā-)
Rajputana (rahjpōōtah'na)
Raleigh (raw'lĭ or rah- or ră-)
Răm'ĕsēs (-z)
Răn'ĕlagh (-le)
Răph'ăel
Ra'walpĭndĭ (rah-w-)
Read'ĭng (rĕd-)
Reger (rāg'er)
Reu'ter (roi-)
Reyk'javĭk (rĕkya-)
Rheims (rēms)
Rhŏdĕ'sĭa (rō-; -z- or -s-; also -zha, -sha)
Rī'ca (rē-)
Rĭch'elieu (-shelŭ)
Rio (rē'ō)
Rĭvĭer'a (-āra)
Robespierre (rōbz'pyăr)
Rŏcke'fĕller (-kf-, •-kĭf-)
Rŏm'ney (or rŭm-)
Röntgen (rĕrn'tyen)
Rōō'sevĕlt (-sv-, •-sĭv-)
Rossĕtt'ĭ (rōz-)
Rōtoru'a (-ōōa)
Rouen (rōō'ahn)

Rŏx'burgh (-brė)
Ruy Blas (rwē blahs)
Sachĕv'erell (-sh-)
Săg'ĭnaw
Sainte-Beuve (sănt bėrv)
Saint-Saens (săṅ sahṅs)
Salis'burў (sawlzb-)
Salŏm'ė
Salŏn'Ica (or sălŏnē')
Săn'chŏ (-ngk-)
Săn Diego (dē-ā'gō)
Săn Jacin'tŏ
Săn Joaquin (wahkēn')
Săn Jose (hōsā')
Săn Juan' (hwahn)
Săn Re'mō (rā-)
Săn'ta Fé (fä)
Săntĭa'gŏ (-ah-)
Sărasa'tė (-ah-)
Sara'wak (-rah-)
Săskătch'ėwan
Săskatōōn'
Sault Sainte Marie (sōō sănt mär'Ĭ; or sănt)
Săvonarŏl'a
Sca'fĕll' (scaw-)
Scăl'ĭger
Schėhēreza'dė (sh-; -ezah-)
Schĕnĕc'tadў (sk-)
Schu'bėrt (shōō-)
Schuy'ler (skĭ-)
Schuy'lkĭll (skōōl-)
Scĭll'ў (s-)
Scĭp'ĭŏ (s-)
Scrĭ'abĭn
Scone (skōōn)
Sėătt'le
Sėdăn'
Sĕd'bergh [school] (-ber; -bėrg)
Sĕd'bergh [town] (-ber)
Seine (sān)
Sĕm'ėlė
Sĕmĭ'ramĭs
Sĕn'ėca
Sĕnėgal' (-awl)
Sĕnnăch'erĭb (-k-)
Sĕt'ėbŏs
Shrews'burў (-ōōz- or -ōz-)
Sĭăm'
Sĭerr'a Lėone' (-är-; -ōn-)
Sĭm'ėon
Sĭm'on
Simplon (săṅ'plawṅ).
Sĭ'nai (-nĭī)
Sĭs'ўphus
Sĭ'va (shė-)
Skĭdd'aw (or skĭddaw')
Slough (slow)
Smĕth'wick (-dhĭk)
Sŏc'ratēs (-z)
Sŏfĭ'a
Sŏma'lĭ (-ah-)
Som'ersĕt (sŭm-)
Sŏph'oclēs (-z)
Southey (sow'dhĭ)
Southwark (sŭdh'ark)
Sou'za (-ōō-)
Srĭna'gar (-ah-)

St Al'bans (awl-)
Stendhal (stahṅ'dahl)
St John (sĭn'jon)
St Lou'Is (sănt lōō-)
St Ma'lŏ (-ah-)
Stŏke Pŏ'gĕs
Strachan (strawn or strah'χan)
Streath'am (strĕt-)
Stuy'vėsant (stĭ-)
Sudăn' (sōō- or sŏŏ-)
Su'ėz (-ōō-)
Suma'tra (sōōmah-)
Sumurun (sŏŏmŏŏrōŏn')
Surăt' (sōō-)
Sŭsquėhănn'a (-kw-)
Swa'zĭlănd (swah-)
Sўnge (-ng)
Sўr'acūse (-z)
Sў'racūse [America]
Tăg'us
Tahi'tĭ (tah-hē-)
Taj Mahal (tahj mahahl')
Tăngănyi'ka (-ngg-; -yė-)
Tăngier' (-jēr)
Tănnhäu'ser (-hoiz-)
Tărragŏn'a
Tchaikovsky (chĭkŏv'skĭ)
Tecŭm'seh (-sĕ)
Teh'răn (tācr-)
Teignmouth (tĭn'meth)
Tĕlĕm'achus (-kus)
Tĕnerif(f)e' (-ĕf)
Tĕrpsĭch'orė (-k-)
Tĭĕ'rra dĕl Fuego (fŏŏā'gō)
Tĕrtŭll'ian
Thame (tām)
Thames (tĕmz)
Thăn'ėt
Thēbes (-bz)
Thĕmĭst'oclēs (-z)
Thĕ'obald (-awld; or tĭb'ald)
Thĕŏd'orĭc
Thĕrmŏp'ўlæ
Thĕrsit'ēs (-z)
Thĕs'eus (-ūs)
Thĕs'pĭs
Thĕssalonĭ'ca
Thĕss'alў
Thĭs'bė (-z-)
Thom'as (tŏm-)
Thomas [Ambroise] (tŏ'mah)
Thŏĭ'eau (-ō)
Thŭcўd'ĭdēs (-z)
Tĭbēr'ĭus
Tĭbĕt'
Tĭbŭll'us
Tĭci'nŏ (-chē-)
Tĭf'lĭs
Tĭg'rĭs
Tim'ŏa
Tĭntăg'el
Tĭtăn'ĭa
Tĭt'ian (-shĭ-)
Tĭt'us
Tĭv'olĭ
Tōbi'as
Tŏ'kўŏ
Tŏlė'dŏ (or -ā'dō)

Tŏ'rrès
Tŏt'nès
Toulon (tōōlawǹ')
Toulouse (tōōlōōz')
Touraine' (tōō-)
Tours (toor)
Tow'cester (tŏ'ster)
Trafăl'gar (or trăfălgăr')
Trăj'an
Trăn'skei (-kī)
Transvaal (trah'nsvahl)
Trèvi'so (-vēz-)
Trĭchĭnŏp'olĭ
Trĭĕste'
Trĭnc'ŏmalee'
Trŏll'ope (-ep)
Trŏss'ăchs (-ks)
Trou'vĭlle (-ōō-)
Tucson (tōō'sawǹ; or -ăn)
Tuileries (twēl'erē)
Tūrĭn' (or tūr'ĭn)
Tŭrkĕstăn'
Tŭskĕ'gee
Tussaud's' (-sōz)
Tȳ'chō (-k-)
Tȳn'dale (-dl)
Tȳ'rol (or tĭrōl' or tĭrŏl')
Tȳ'rwhitt (-rĭt)
Ugăn'da (ū- or ōō-)
Uh'land (ōō-)
U'ĭst (ū-)
Ulŷss'ēs (ū-; -z)
Uphăr'sĭn (ū-)
Urī'ah (ūr-)
Ur'ĭel (ūr-)
Urquhart (ūr'kert)
Uruguay (ōō'rōōgway'; or -ǫ)
Ush'ant (ū-)
Utah (ū'tah, •ū'taw)
U Thant (ōō thŭnt)
Utrecht (ūtrĕkt')
Văl'kȳrie
Văl'ois (-wah)
Vălparais'ō (-z-)
Văn'burgh (-brè)
Văsăr'ĭ
Văs'cō da Ga'ma (gah·)
Văthĕk
Vaughan (vawn)
Vauxhall (vŏks'hawl')
Vèlăs'quez (-kwĭz or -kĭz)
Vĕn'ĕzŭĕ'la
Vĕr'de
Ver'dĭ (văr-)
Vĕr'dun (or văr-)
Vĕr'ğĭl
Verne (vărn)
Vĕrone'se (-ăzĭ)
Vĕ'rulam (-ōō-)
Vèsŭv'ĭus
Vichy (vē'shē)
Vĭĕnn'a

Vĭg'ō
Vill'iers (-lerz)
Vĭn'ci (-chĭ)
Vi'ola
Vĭr'ğĭl
Vosges (vōzh)
Wa'băsh (waw-)
Wadham (wŏd'am)
Wag'ner (vah-)
Waldegrāve (wawl'g-)
Wantage (wŏn'tĭj)
Wapp'ĭng (wŏ-)
Wăr'ĭng
Warwick (wŏ'rĭk)
Watteau (wŏt'ō)
Wazĭr'ĭstan (-ēr-; -ahn)
Wear [river] (wēr)
We'ber (vā-)
Wednes'bury (wĕnzb-)
Wei'mār (vī-)
Weiss'hŏrn (vīs-h-)
Welwyn (wĕl'ĭn)
Wemyss (wēmz)
We'ser (vāz- or wēz-)
Whewell (hūl)
Wies'baden (vēzbah-)
Wĭs'bĕch (-z-)
Wĭscŏn'sĭn
Wŏŏl'wich (-lĭj)
Wŏŏtt'on
Worcester (wŏŏs'ter)
Wŏrms (v-; -z)
Wrĕk'ĭn (r-)
Wȳch'erley
Wȳc'lĭf
Wȳc'ombe (-om)
Wȳk'eham (-kam)
Wymondham [Norfolk] (wĭnd'am)
Wȳŏ'mĭng
Xăv'ĭer (z-)
Xĕn'ophon (z-)
Xĕr'xĕs (z-; -z)
Xhosa (kaw'sa)
Yeats (yāts)
Ye'men (yā-)
Yeo'vil (yō-)
Yŏkōha'ma (-hah-)
Yŏsĕm'ĭtè
Ypres (ēpr, wĭ'perz)
Ysaye (ĭsī'ĭ)
Yucatan' (ū-; -ahn)
Zăcharī'ah (-a)
Zeiss (zīs)
Zĕlōt'ēs (-z)
Zĕn'ō
Zĭmba'bwè (-bah-)
Zŏ'è
Zŏl'a
Zŏrōăs'ter
Zürich (zūr'ĭk)
Zui'der Zee' (zī-)

APPENDIX IV

WEIGHTS AND MEASURES

(a) ENGLISH AND METRIC EQUIVALENTS

Linear Measure:	**English to Metric**
1 inch	= 25·3999 millimetres.
1 foot (12 inches)	= 0·30480 metre.
1 yard (3 feet)	= 0·9144 metre.
1 pole (5½ yards)	= 5·02919 metres.
1 chain (22 yards)	= 20·11678 metres.
1 furlong (220 yards)	= 201·16778 metres.
1 mile (1,760 yards)	= 1·60934 kilometres.

Square Measure:

1 square inch	= 6·45159 sq. centimetres.
1 square foot (144 sq. in.)	= 9·29028 sq. decimetres.
1 square yard (9 sq. ft.)	= 0·836126 sq. metre.
1 perch (30¼ sq. yards)	= 25·29280 sq. metres.
1 rood (40 perches)	= 10·11712 ares.
1 acre (4,840 sq. yards)	= 0·40468 hectare.
1 square mile (640 acres)	= 258·99824 hectares.

Cubic Measure:

1 cubic inch	= 16·3870 cubic centimetres.
1 cubic foot (1,728 cub. in.)	= 0·02832 cubic metre.
1 cubic yard (27 cub. ft.)	= 0·764553 cubic metre.

Measure of Capacity:

1 gill	= 1·42058 decilitres.
1 pint (4 gills)	= 0·56823 litre.
1 quart (2 pints)	= 1·13646 litres.
1 gallon (4 quarts)	= 4·5459631 litres.
1 peck (2 gallons)	= 9·0917 litres.
1 bushel (8 gallons)	= 3·6366 dekalitres.
1 quarter (8 bushels)	= 2·90935 hectolitres.

Apothecaries' Measure:

1 fluid drachm (60 minims)	= 3·55145 millilitres.
1 fluid ounce (8 drachms)	= 2·84123 centilitres.
1 gal. (8 pints or 160 fluid ounces)	= 4·54596 litres.

Avoirdupois Weight:

1 grain	= 0·0648 gram.
1 dram (27·34 grains)	= 1·77185 grams.
1 ounce (16 drams)	= 28·34953 grams.
1 pound (16 ounces)	= 0·45359237 kilogram.
1 stone (14 lb.)	= 6·35029 kilograms.
1 quarter (28 lb.)	= 12·70059 kilograms.
1 hundredweight (cwt. = 112 lb.)	= 50·80235 kilograms.
1 ton (20 cwt.)	= 1·01604 metric tons.

Troy Weight:

1 pennyweight (24 grains)	= 1·55517 grams.
1 ounce (480 grains avdp.)	= 31·10348 grams.

Apothecaries' Weight:

1 scruple (20 grains)	⇐	1·29598 grams.
1 drachm (3 scruples)	⇐	3·88794 grams.
1 ounce (8 drachms)	⇐	31·10348 grams.

The Apothecaries' ounce is the Troy ounce of 480 Avoirdupois grains.

(b) METRIC AND ENGLISH EQUIVALENTS

Linear Measure: **Metric to English**

1 millimetre (1/1000 m.)	⇐	0·03937 inch.
1 centimetre (1/100 m.)	⇐	0·39370 inch.
1 decimetre (1/10 m.)	⇐	3·93701 inches.
1 metre (m.)	⇐	1·0936143 yards.
1 decametre (10 m.)	⇐	10·93614 yards.
1 hectometre (100 m.)	⇐	109·3614 yards.
1 kilometre (1,000 m.)	⇐	0·62137 mile.
1 myriametre (10,000 m.)	⇐	6·21372 miles.

Square Measure:

1 sq. centimetre	⇐	0·15500 sq. inch.
1 sq. decimetre (100 sq. centimetres)	⇐	15·50006 sq. inches.
1 sq. metre or centiare (100 sq. decimetres)	} =	{ 10·76393 sq. feet. { 1·19599 sq. yards.
1 are (100 sq. metres)	⇐	119·59926 sq. yards.
1 hectare (100 ares or 10,000 sq. metres)	⇐	2·47106 acres.

Cubic Measurement:

1 cubic centimetre (1,000 cub. millimetres)	⇐	0·06102 cubic inch.
1 cubic decimetre (1,000 cub. centimetres)	⇐	61·02394 cubic inches.
1 cubic metre or stere (1,000 cub. decimetres)	} =	{ 35·31477 cubic feet. { 1·307954 cubic yards.

Measure of Capacity:

1 millilitre (1/1000 litre)	⇐	0·00704 gill.
1 centilitre (1/100 litre)	⇐	0·07039 gill.
1 decilitre (1/10 litre)	⇐	0·17598 pint.
1 litre	⇐	1·75985 pints.
1 decalitre (10 litres)	⇐	2·19981 gallons.
1 hectolitre (100 litres)	⇐	2·74976 bushels.
1 kilolitre (1,000 litres)	⇐	3·43720 quarters.

Weight:

1 milligram (1/1000 gm.)	⇐	0·01543 grain.
1 centigram (1/100 gm.)	⇐	0·15432 grain.
1 decigram (1/10 gm.)	⇐	1·54324 grains.
1 gram	⇐	15·43236 grains.
1 decagram (10 gm.)	⇐	5·64383 drams.
1 hectogram (100 gm.)	⇐	3·52740 ounces.
1 kilogram (1,000 gm.)	⇐	2·2046223 lb.
1 myriagram (10 kg.)	⇐	22·04622 lb.
1 quintal (100 kg.)	⇐	1·96841 cwt.
1 tonne (1,000 kg.)	⇐	0·98420 ton.

	Troy	0·03215 ounce.
	,,	15·43236 grains.
1 gram = {	Apothecaries'	0·25721 drachm.
	,,	0·77162 scruple.
	,,	15·43236 grains.

NOTES

NOTES

NOTES

NOTES

NOTES

NOTES

NOTES

NOTES